THE FIRST 100 YEARS OF THE
ACLU

A COMPENDIUM OF ADVOCACY BEFORE
THE UNITED STATES SUPREME COURT

VOLUME 3 OF 3

1920—2020

CONCEIVED AND COMPILED BY
STEVEN C. MARKOFF

CASE SUMMARY EDITOR
JESSICA PIERUCCI

FOREWORD BY
ERWIN CHEMERINSKY

A GENUINE RARE BIRD BOOK

Rare Bird Books
6044 North Figueroa Street
Los Angeles, California 90042
rarebirdbooks.com

FIRST HARDCOVER EDITION

ISBN-13: 978-1-64428-510-7 [THREE-VOLUME SLIPCASE SET]
ISBN-13: 978-1-64428-511-4 [VOLUME ONE]
ISBN-13: 978-1-64428-512-1 [VOLUME TWO]
ISBN-13: 978-1-64428-513-8 [VOLUME THREE]

For more information, address:
Rare Bird Books Subsidiary Rights Department
6044 North Figueroa Street
Los Angeles, California 90042

Printed in China

10 9 8 7 6 5 4 3 2 1

Library of Congress Cataloging-in-Publication Data available upon request

Appendix C

ACLU/U.S. Supreme Court Case Summaries

continued from Volume II

856. Buckley v. American Constitutional Law Foundation, Inc.

(Decided January 12, 1999; 525 U.S. 182)

I. ISSUE

A. Issues Discussed

First Amendment, freedom of speech, elections

B. Legal Question Presented

Whether "three conditions Colorado places on the ballot-initiative process: (1) the requirement that initiative-petition circulators be registered voters; (2) the requirement that they wear an identification badge bearing the circulator's name; and (3) the requirement that proponents of an initiative report the names and addresses of all paid circulators and the amount paid to each circulator," violate the First Amendment.

C. Supreme Court's Answer

The three conditions violate the First Amendment's guarantee of freedom of speech.

II. CASE SUMMARY

A. Background

"Colorado allows its citizens to make laws directly through initiatives placed on election ballots. We review in this case three conditions Colorado places on the ballot-initiative process: (1) the requirement that initiative-petition circulators be registered voters; (2) the requirement that they wear an identification badge bearing the circulator's name; and (3) the requirement that proponents of an initiative report the names and addresses of all paid circulators and the amount paid to each circulator. . . .

The complaint in this action was filed in 1993 in the United States District Court for the District of Colorado pursuant to 42 U.S.C. § 1983; it challenged six of Colorado's many controls on the initiative-petition process. Plaintiffs, now respondents, included American Constitutional Law Foundation, Inc., a nonprofit, public interest organization that supports direct democracy, and several individual participants in Colorado's initiative process. In this opinion we refer to plaintiffs-respondents, collectively, as ACLF. . . .

The District Court, after a bench trial, struck down the badge requirement and portions of the disclosure requirements, but upheld the age and affidavit requirements and the six-month limit on petition circulation. The District Court also found that the registration requirement 'limits the number of persons available to circulate . . . and, accordingly, restricts core political speech.' Nevertheless, that court upheld the registration requirement. In 1980, the District Court noted, the registration requirement had been adopted by Colorado's voters as a constitutional amendment. For that reason, the District Court believed, the restriction was 'not subject to any level of scrutiny.'

The Court of Appeals affirmed in part and reversed in part. That court properly sought guidance from our recent decisions on ballot access, and on handbill distribution. Initiative-petition circulators, the Tenth Circuit recognized, resemble handbill distributors, in that both seek to promote public support for a particular issue or position. Initiative- petition circulators also resemble candidate-petition signature gatherers, however, for both seek ballot access. In common with the District Court, the Tenth Circuit upheld, as reasonable regulations of the ballot-initiative process, the age restriction, the six-month limit on petition circulation, and the affidavit requirement. The Court of Appeals struck down the requirement that petition circulators be registered voters, and also held portions of the badge and disclosure requirements invalid as trenching unnecessarily and improperly on political expression."

The Supreme Court granted certiorari to review the case and affirmed.

B. Counsel of Record / ACLU Attorney

ACLU Side (Respondent / Appellee): Neil D. O'Toole argued the cause for appellees.

Opposing Side (Petitioner / Appellant): Gale A. Norton, Attorney General of Colorado, argued the cause for appellant.

III. AMICI CURIAE

ACLU Side (Respondent / Appellee)

Brief of amici curiae filed on behalf of the ACLU, et al., by David C. Warren, Steven R. Shapiro, L. Doris Freedman, and Mark Silverstein.

Brief of amici curiae filed on behalf of the Initiative & Referendum Institute by Stephen J. Safranek.

Brief of amici curiae filed on behalf of National Voter Outreach, Inc., by Barnaby W. Zall.

Opposing Side (Petitioner / Appellant)

Brief of amici curiae filed on behalf of the State of Washington, et al., by Christine O. Gregoire, Attorney General of Washington, and Jean M. Wilkinson and William Berggren Collins, Assistant Attorneys General, and by the Attorneys

General for their respective States as follows: Bruce M. Botelho of Alaska, Grant Woods of Arizona, Daniel E. Lungren of California, Alan G. Lance of Idaho, Thomas J. Miller of Iowa, Carla J. Stovall of Kansas, Andrew Ketterer of Maine, Mike Moore of Mississippi, W. A. Drew Edmondson of Oklahoma, Betty D. Montgomery of Ohio, Hardy Myers of Oregon, and Mark Barnett of South Dakota.

Brief of amici curiae filed on behalf of the Council of State Governments, et al., by Richard Ruda and Ronald D. Maines.

IV. THE SUPREME COURT'S DECISION

"As the Tenth Circuit recognized in upholding the age restriction, the six-month limit on circulation, and the affidavit requirement, States allowing ballot initiatives have considerable leeway to protect the integrity and reliability of the initiative process, as they have with respect to election processes generally. We have several times said 'no litmus-paper test' will separate valid ballot-access provisions from invalid interactive speech restrictions; we have come upon 'no substitute for the hard judgments that must be made.' But the First Amendment requires us to be vigilant in making those judgments, to guard against undue hindrances to political conversations and the exchange of ideas. . . .

In sum, assuming that a residence requirement would be upheld as a needful integrity-policing measure—a question we, like the Tenth Circuit, have no occasion to decide because the parties have not placed the matter of residence at issue—the added registration requirement is not warranted. That requirement cuts down the number of message carriers in the ballot-access arena without impelling cause. . . .

In sum, we conclude, as did the Court of Appeals, that Colorado's current badge requirement discourages participation in the petition circulation process by forcing name identification without sufficient cause. We reiterate this qualification: In its final observation, the Court of Appeals noted that ACLF's 'arguments and evidence focus[ed] entirely on [the circulator identification] requirement'; therefore, that court expressed no opinion whether the additional requirements—that the badge disclose the circulator's paid or volunteer status, and if paid, by whom —'would pass constitutional muster standing alone.' We similarly confine our decision. . . .

In sum, we agree with the Court of Appeals appraisal: Listing paid circulators and their income from circulation 'forc[es] paid circulators to surrender the anonymity enjoyed by their volunteer counterparts," no more than tenuously related to the substantial interests disclosure serves, Colorado's reporting requirements, to the extent that they target paid circulators, 'fai[l] exacting scrutiny.' . . .

For the reasons stated, we conclude that the Tenth Circuit correctly separated necessary or proper ballot-access controls from restrictions that unjustifiably inhibit the circulation of ballot-initiative petitions. Therefore, the judgment of the Court of Appeals is affirmed."

V. JUSTICE VOTE

6 Pro ACLU Side vs. 3 Con Opposing Side

ACLU Side (Respondent / Appellee)

1. Ginsburg, R. – Wrote majority opinion
2. Thomas, C. – Wrote concurring opinion
3. Stevens, J. – Joined majority opinion
4. Scalia, A. – Joined majority opinion
5. Kennedy, A. – Joined majority opinion
6. Souter, D. – Joined majority opinion

Opposing Side (Petitioner / Appellant)

1. Rehnquist, W. – Wrote dissenting opinion
2. O'Connor, S. – Wrote opinion concurring in part and dissenting in part
3. Breyer, S. – Joined O'Connor's opinion

VI. A WIN OR LOSS FOR THE ACLU?

The ACLU, as amicus curiae, urged affirmance of the judgment of the Court of Appeals for the Tenth Circuit; the Supreme Court affirmed in a 6-3 vote, giving the ACLU an apparent win.

857. Roberts v. Galen of Virginia, Inc.

(Decided January 13, 1999; 525 U.S. 249)

I. ISSUE

A. Issues Discussed

Civil rights, Emergency Medical Treatment and Active Labor Act, healthcare

B. Legal Question Presented

Whether "in order to state a claim in an [Emergency Medical Treatment and Active Labor Act] suit alleging a violation of § 1395dd(b)'s stabilization requirement, a plaintiff must show that the hospital's inappropriate stabilization resulted from an improper motive such as one involving the indigency, race, or sex of the patient."

C. Supreme Court's Answer

Section 1395dd(b) does not require an improper motive.

II. CASE SUMMARY

A. Background

"The Emergency Medical Treatment and Active Labor Act (EMTALA), as added by § 9121(b) of the Consolidated Omnibus Budget Reconciliation Act of 1985, 100 Stat. 164, and as amended, 42 U.S.C. § 1395dd, places obligations of screening and stabilization upon hospitals and emergency rooms that receive patients suffering from an 'emergency medical condition.' . . .

Wanda Johnson was run over by a truck in May 1992, and was rushed to respondent's hospital, the Humana Hospital–University of Louisville, in Louisville, Kentucky (Humana). Johnson had been severely injured and had suffered serious injuries to her brain, spine, right leg, and pelvis. After about six weeks' stay at Humana, during which time Johnson's health remained in a volatile state, respondent's agents arranged for her transfer to the Crestview Health Care Facility, across the river in Indiana.

Johnson was transferred to Crestview on July 24, 1992, but upon arrival at that facility, her condition deteriorated significantly. Johnson was taken to the Midwest Medical Center, also in Indiana, where she remained for many months and incurred substantial medical expenses as a result of her deterioration. Johnson applied for financial assistance under Indiana's Medicaid program, but her application was rejected on the ground that she had failed to satisfy Indiana's residency requirements. Petitioner Jane Roberts, Johnson's guardian, then filed this federal action under § 1395dd(d) as codified, alleging violations of § 1395dd(b).

The District Court granted summary judgment for respondents on the grounds that petitioner had failed to show that "either the medical opinion that Johnson was stable or the decision to authorize her transfer was caused by an improper motive." The Court of Appeals affirmed, holding that in order to state a claim in an EMTALA suit alleging a violation of § 1395dd(b)'s stabilization requirement, a plaintiff must show that the hospital's inappropriate stabilization resulted from an improper motive such as one involving the indigency, race, or sex of the patient."

The Supreme Court granted certiorari to review the case and reversed.

B. Counsel of Record / ACLU Attorney

ACLU Side (Petitioner / Appellant): Joseph H. Mattingly, III, argued the cause for appellant.

Opposing Side (Respondent / Appellee): Carter G. Phillips argued the cause for appellee.

III. AMICI CURIAE

ACLU Side (Petitioner / Appellant)

Brief of amici curiae filed on behalf of the NOW Legal Defense and Education Fund, the ACLU Women's Rights Project, et al., by M. Elaine Johnston and Martha F. Davis.

Brief of amici curiae filed on behalf of the United States by James A. Feldman, Solicitor General Waxman, Assistant Attorney General Hunger, Deputy Solicitor General Kneedler, Barbara C. Biddle, and Carl E. Goldfarb.

Opposing Side (Respondent / Appellee)

Brief of amici curiae filed on behalf of the American Hospital Association, et al., by Thomas W. Merrill, Fredric I. Entin, James A. Henderson, Leonard A. Nelson, Katherine O. Orrico, and Robert M. Portman.

IV. THE SUPREME COURT'S DECISION

"[T]here is no question that the text of § 1395dd(b) does not require an 'appropriate' stabilization, nor can it reasonably be read to require an improper motive. This fact is conceded by respondent, which notes in its brief that 'the 'motive' test adopted by the court below . . . lacks support in any of the traditional sources of statutory construction.' Although the concession of a point on appeal by respondent is by no means dispositive of a legal issue, we take it as further indication of the correctness of our decision today, and hold that §1395dd(b) contains no express or implied 'improper motive' requirement.

Although respondent presents two alternative grounds for . . . affirmance . . . , we decline to address these claims at this stage in the litigation. The Court granted certiorari on only the EMTALA issue, and these claims do not appear to have been sufficiently developed . . . .

Accordingly, we reverse the Court of Appeals' holding that the District Court's grant of summary judgment was proper and remand the case for further proceedings consistent with this opinion."

V. JUSTICE VOTE

9 Pro ACLU Side vs. 0 Con Opposing Side

ACLU Side (Petitioner / Appellant)

1. Rehnquist, W. – Per curiam decision
2. Stevens, J. – Per curiam decision
3. O'Connor, S. – Per curiam decision
4. Scalia, A. – Per curiam decision
5. Kennedy, A. – Per curiam decision
6. Thomas, C. – Per curiam decision
7. Souter, D. – Per curiam decision
8. Ginsburg, R. – Per curiam decision
9. Breyer, S. – Per curiam decision

VI. A WIN OR LOSS FOR THE ACLU?

The ACLU filed as amicus curiae urging reversal of the judgment of the Court of Appeals; the Supreme Court reversed in a per curiam decision with a 9-0 vote, giving the ACLU an apparent win.

858. Department of Commerce v. United States House of Representatives

(Decided January 25, 1999; 525 U.S. 316)

I. ISSUE

A. Issues Discussed

Governmental authority, census, Fourteenth Amendment

B. Legal Question Presented

Does the proposed use of statistical sampling to generate U.S. Census data violate the Census Act?

C. Supreme Court's Answer

The proposed use of statistical sampling violates the Census Act.

II. CASE SUMMARY

A. Background

"The Census Bureau (Bureau) has announced a plan to use two forms of statistical sampling in the 2000 Decennial Census to address a chronic and apparently growing problem of 'undercounting' certain identifiable groups of individuals. Two sets of plaintiffs filed separate suits challenging the legality and constitutionality of the Bureau's plan. . . .

The first suit, styled Clinton v. Glavin, was filed on February 12, 1998, in the District Court for the Eastern District of Virginia by four counties . . . and residents of 13 States . . . , who claimed that the Bureau's planned use of statistical sampling to apportion Representatives among the States violates the Census Act and the Census Clause of the Constitution. They sought a declaration that the Bureau's plan is unlawful and/or unconstitutional and an injunction barring use of the NRFU and ICM sampling procedures in the 2000 census.

The District Court held that the case was ripe for review, that the plaintiffs satisfied the requirements for Article III standing, and that the Census Act prohibited use of the challenged sampling procedures to apportion Representatives. The District Court concluded that, because the statute was clear on its face, the court did not need to reach the constitutional questions presented. It thus denied defendants' motion to dismiss, granted plaintiffs' motion for summary judgment, and permanently enjoined the use of the challenged sampling procedures to determine the population for purposes of congressional apportionment. . . .

The second challenge was filed by the United States House of Representatives on February 20, 1998, in the District Court for the District of Columbia. The House sought a declaration that the Bureau's proposed use of sampling to determine the population for purposes of apportioning Members of the House of Representatives among the several States violates the Census Act and the Constitution. The House also sought a permanent injunction barring use of the challenged sampling procedures in the apportionment aspect of the 2000 census.

The District Court held that the House had Article III standing, the suit was ripe for review, equitable concerns did not warrant dismissal, the suit did not violate separation of powers principles, and the Census Act does not permit the use of the challenged sampling procedures in counting the population for apportionment. Because it held that the Census Act does not allow for the challenged sampling procedures, it declined to reach the House's constitutional challenge under the Census Clause. The District Court denied the defendants' motion to dismiss, granted the plaintiffs' motion for summary judgment, and issued an injunction preventing defendants from using the challenged sampling methods in the apportionment aspect of the 2000 census."

The Supreme Court granted certiorari to review the consolidated cases and affirmed.

B. Counsel of Record / ACLU Attorney

ACLU Side (Petitioner / Appellant): Solicitor General Seth P. Waxman argued the cause for appellants.

Opposing Side (Respondent / Appellee): Maureen E. Mahoney argued the cause for appellee United States House of Representatives.

Michael A. Carvin argued the cause for appellees Matthew J. Glavin, et al.

III. AMICI CURIAE

ACLU Side (Petitioner / Appellant)

Brief of amici curiae filed on behalf of the Brennan Center for Justice at New York University School of Law, the ACLU, et al., by Steven R. Shapiro, Louis M. Bograd, Burt Neuborne, Deborah Goldberg, and Richard R. Buery, Jr.

Additional briefs of amici curiae were filed on behalf of the State of Texas, the County of Westchester, the American Federation of State, County, and Municipal Employees, et al., the Brennan Center for Justice, et al., the Japanese American Citizens League, the NAACP Legal Defense and Educational Fund, Inc., Jerome Gray, et al., and the District of Columbia State Democratic Committee.

Opposing Side (Respondent / Appellee)

Briefs of amici curiae were filed on behalf of the State of Wisconsin, et al., the Washington Legal Foundation, et al., the City of Omaha, the Landmark Legal Foundation, the National Citizens Legal Network, et al., the Foundation to Preserve the Integrity of the Census, and the National Republican Legislators Association, et al.

IV. THE SUPREME COURT'S DECISION

"There is undoubtedly a 'traceable' connection between the use of sampling in the decennial census and Indiana's expected loss of a Representative, and there is a substantial likelihood that the requested relief—a permanent injunction against the proposed uses of sampling in the census—will redress the alleged injury.

Appellees have also established standing on the basis of the expected effects of the use of sampling in the 2000 census on intrastate redistricting. . . . States use the population numbers generated by the federal decennial census for federal congressional redistricting. [T]he appellees . . . have a strong claim that they will be injured by the Bureau's plan because their votes will be diluted vis-à-vis residents of counties with larger 'undercount' rates. . . . For the reasons discussed above, this expected intrastate vote dilution satisfies the injury-in-fact, causation, and redressibility requirements. Accordingly, appellees have again carried their burden under Rule 56 and have established standing to pursue this case. . . .

We accordingly arrive at the dispute over the meaning of the relevant provisions of the Census Act. The District Court below examined the plain text and legislative history of the Act and concluded that the proposed use of statistical sampling to determine population for purposes of apportioning congressional seats among the States violates the Act. We agree.

[T]he Bureau itself concluded in 1980 that the Census Act, as amended, 'clearly' continued the 'historical precedent of using the 'actual Enumeration' for purposes of apportionment, while eschewing estimates based on sampling or other statistical procedures, no matter how sophisticated.' . . .

For the reasons stated, we conclude that the Census Act prohibits the proposed uses of statistical sampling in calculating the population for purposes of apportionment. Because we so conclude, we find it unnecessary to reach the constitutional question presented. Accordingly, we affirm the judgment of the District Court for the Eastern District of Virginia in Clinton v. Glavin, No. 98-564. As this decision also resolves the substantive issues presented by Department of Commerce v. United States House of Representatives, No. 98-404, that case no longer presents a substantial federal question. The appeal in that case is therefore dismissed."

V. JUSTICE VOTE

4 Pro ACLU Side vs. 5 Con Opposing Side

ACLU Side (Petitioner / Appellant)

1. Breyer, S. – Wrote opinion concurring in part and dissenting in part, joined Stevens' dissent in part
2. Stevens, J. – Wrote dissenting opinion
3. Ginsburg, R. – Wrote dissenting opinion, joined Stevens' dissent in part
4. Souter, D. – Joined Stevens' dissent in part, joined Ginsburg's dissent

Opposing Side (Respondent / Appellee)

1. O'Connor, S. – Wrote majority opinion
2. Rehnquist, W. – Joined Scalia's concurrence in part
3. Scalia, A. – Wrote concurring opinion
4. Kennedy, A. – Joined Scalia's concurrence in part
5. Thomas, C. – Joined Scalia's concurrence

VI. A WIN OR LOSS FOR THE ACLU?

The ACLU filed as amicus curiae urging reversal of the judgment of the District Court; the Supreme Court affirmed in a 5-4 vote, giving the ACLU an apparent loss.

859. National Collegiate Athletic Ass'n v. Smith

(Decided February 23, 1999; 525 U.S. 459)

I. ISSUE

A. Issues Discussed

Civil rights, gender, Fourteenth Amendment

B. Legal Question Presented

"[W]hether a private organization that does not receive federal financial assistance is subject to Title IX because it receives payments from entities that do."

C. Supreme Court's Answer

A private organization that does not receive federal financial assistance is not subject to Title IX solely because it receives payments from entities that receive federal funding.

II. CASE SUMMARY

A. Background

"This case concerns the amenability of the National Collegiate Athletic Association (NCAA or Association) to a private action under Title IX of the Education Amendments of 1972. The NCAA is an unincorporated association of approximately 1,200 members, including virtually all public and private universities and four-year colleges conducting major athletic programs in the United States; the Association serves to maintain intercollegiate athletics as an integral part of its members' educational programs. Title IX proscribes sex discrimination in 'any education program or activity receiving Federal financial assistance.'

The complainant in this case, Renee M. Smith, sued the NCAA under Title IX alleging that the Association discriminated against her on the basis of her sex by denying her permission to play intercollegiate volleyball at federally assisted institutions. Reversing the District Court's refusal to allow Smith to amend her pro se complaint, the Court of Appeals for the Third Circuit held that the NCAA's receipt of dues from federally funded member institutions would suffice to bring the Association within the scope of Title IX."

The Supreme Court granted certiorari to review the case, vacated, and remanded.

B. Counsel of Record / ACLU Attorney

ACLU Side (Respondent / Appellee): Carter G. Phillips argued the cause for appellee.

Deputy Solicitor General Edwin S. Kneedler argued the cause for the United States, as amicus curiae, by special leave of Court.

Opposing Side (Petitioner / Appellant): John G. Roberts, Jr., argued the cause for appellants.

III. AMICI CURIAE

ACLU Side (Respondent / Appellee)

Brief of amici curiae filed on behalf of the National Women's Law Center, the American Association of University Women, the ACLU, et al., by Marcia D. Greenberger, Leslie T. Annexstein, Lois G. Williams, Brad E. Biegon, Deborah L. Brake, Neena K. Chaudhry and Dina R. Lassow. Brief of amici curiae filed on behalf of the United States by Deputy Solicitor General Kneedler, Solicitor General Waxman, Acting Assistant Attorney General Lee, Deputy Solicitor General Underwood, Irving L. Gornstein, Dennis J. Dimsey, and Marie K. McElderry.

Brief of amici curiae filed on behalf of Michael Bowers, et al., by Barbara E. Ransom and Max Lapertosa.

Brief of amici curiae filed on behalf of Trial Lawyers for Public Justice, P. C., et al., by Adele P. Kimmel, Arthur H. Bryant, and J. Richard Cohen.

Opposing Side (Petitioner / Appellant)

Brief of amici curiae filed on behalf of the American Council on Education, et al., by Richard O. Duvall, Robin L. Rosenberg, David A. Vaughan, and Sheldon Elliot Steinbach.

IV. THE SUPREME COURT'S DECISION

"Section 106.2(h) defines 'recipient' to include any entity 'to whom Federal financial assistance is extended directly or through another recipient and which operates an education program or activity which receives or benefits from such assistance.' The first part of this definition makes clear that Title IX coverage is not triggered when an entity merely benefits from federal funding. Thus, the regulation accords with the teaching of Grove City and Paralyzed Veterans: Entities that receive federal assistance, whether directly or through an intermediary, are recipients within the meaning of Title IX; entities that only benefit economically from federal assistance are not.

The Third Circuit's conclusion that the NCAA would be subject to the requirements of Title IX if it received dues from its federally funded members is inconsistent with this precedent. Unlike the earmarked student aid in Grove City, there is no allegation that NCAA members paid their dues with federal funds earmarked for that purpose. At most, the Association's receipt of dues demonstrates that it indirectly benefits from the federal assistance afforded its members. This showing, without more, is insufficient to trigger Title IX coverage. . . .

For the reasons stated, we conclude that the Court of Appeals erroneously held that dues payments from recipients of federal funds suffice to subject the NCAA to suit under Title IX. Accordingly, we vacate the judgment of the Third Circuit and remand the case for further proceedings consistent with this opinion."

V. JUSTICE VOTE

0 Pro ACLU Side vs. 9 Con Opposing Side

Opposing Side (Petitioner / Appellant)

1. Ginsburg, R. – Wrote majority opinion
2. Rehnquist, W. – Joined majority opinion
3. Stevens, J. – Joined majority opinion
4. O'Connor, S. – Joined majority opinion
5. Scalia, A. – Joined majority opinion
6. Kennedy, A. – Joined majority opinion
7. Souter, D. – Joined majority opinion
8. Thomas, C. – Joined majority opinion
9. Breyer, S. – Joined majority opinion

VI. A WIN OR LOSS FOR THE ACLU?

The ACLU filed as amicus curiae urging affirmance of the judgment of the Court of Appeals for the Third Circuit; the Supreme Court vacated the judgment in a 9-0 vote, giving the ACLU an apparent loss.

860. Reno v. American-Arab Anti-Discrimination Committee

(Decided February 24, 1999; 525 U.S. 471)

I. ISSUE

A. Issues Discussed

Immigration/Citizenship

B. Legal Question Presented

"Respondents sued petitioners for allegedly targeting them for deportation because of their affiliation with a politically unpopular group. While their suit was pending, Congress passed the Illegal Immigration Reform and Immigrant Responsibility Act of 1996 (IIRIRA), which contains a provision restricting judicial review of the Attorney General's 'decision or action' to 'commence proceedings, adjudicate cases, or execute removal orders against any alien under this Act.' The issue before us is whether, as petitioners contend, this provision deprives the federal courts of jurisdiction over respondents' suit."

C. Supreme Court's Answer

"Respondents' challenge to the Attorney General's decision to 'commence proceedings' against them falls squarely within § 1252(g)—indeed, as we have discussed, the language seems to have been crafted with such a challenge precisely in mind—and nothing elsewhere in § 1252 provides for jurisdiction."

II. CASE SUMMARY

A. Background

"The Immigration and Naturalization Service (INS), a division of the Department of Justice, instituted deportation proceedings in 1987 against Bashar Amer, Aiad Barakat, Julie Mungai, Amjad Obeid, Ayman Obeid, Naim Sharif, Khader Hamide, and Michel Shehadeh, all of whom belong to the Popular Front for the Liberation of Palestine (PFLP), a group that the Government characterizes as an international terrorist and communist organization. . . .

Since this suit seeking to prevent the initiation of deportation proceedings was filed—in 1987, during the administration of Attorney General Edwin Meese—it has made four trips through the District Court for the Central District of California and the United States Court of Appeals for the Ninth Circuit. The first two concerned jurisdictional issues not now before us. Then, in 1994, the District Court preliminarily enjoined deportation proceedings against the six temporary residents, holding that they were likely to prove that the INS did not enforce routine status requirements against immigrants who were not members of disfavored terrorist groups and that the possibility of deportation, combined with the chill to their First Amendment rights while the proceedings were pending, constituted irreparable injury. With regard to Hamide and Shehadeh's claims, however, the District Court granted summary judgment to the federal parties for reasons not pertinent here. . . .

While the Attorney General's appeal of th[e] last decision was pending, Congress passed IIRIRA which, inter alia, repealed the old judicial-review scheme set forth in § 1105a and instituted a new (and significantly more restrictive) one in 8 U.S.C. § 1252. The Attorney General filed motions in both the District Court and Court of Appeals, arguing that § 1252(g) deprived them of jurisdiction over respondents' selective-enforcement claim. The District Court denied the motion, and the Attorney General's appeal from that denial was consolidated with the appeal already pending in the Ninth Circuit.

It is the judgment and opinion in that appeal which is before us here . . . . It affirmed the existence of jurisdiction under § 1252, and reaching the merits of the injunctions, again affirmed the District Court. The Attorney General's petition for rehearing en banc was denied over the dissent of three judges."

The Supreme Court granted certiorari to review the case.

B. Counsel of Record / ACLU Attorney

ACLU Side (Respondent / Appellee): David D. Cole argued the cause for appellees. With him on the briefs were Steven R. Shapiro, Lucas Guttentag, and Lee Gelernt of the American Civil Liberties Union Foundation, Paul L. Hoffman of the ACLU Foundation of Southern California, Marc Van Der Hout, Mark T. Hansen, and John Walker,

Opposing Side (Petitioner / Appellant): Malcolm L. Stewart argued the cause for appellants. With him on the briefs were Solicitor General Waxman, Assistant Attorney General Hunger, Deputy Solicitor General Kneedler, and Douglas N. Letter.

III. AMICI CURIAE

ACLU Side (Respondent / Appellee)

Brief of amici curiae filed on behalf of the American Bar Association by Philip S. Anderson, Jeffrey L. Bleich, and Carol Wolchok.
Brief of amici curiae filed on behalf of the American Immigration Law Foundation et al. by Ira J. Kurzban and Nadine K. Wettstein.
Brief of amici curiae filed on behalf of the Brennan Center for Justice at New York University School of Law by Burt Neuborne.
Brief of amici curiae filed on behalf of the National Immigration Law Center by Linton Joaquin and Gerald L. Neuman.

Opposing Side (Petitioner / Appellant)

Brief of amici curiae filed on behalf of the Criminal Justice Legal Foundation by Kent S. Scheidegger.
Brief of amici curiae filed on behalf of the Washington Legal Foundation et al. by Daniel J. Popeo and Richard A. Samp.

IV. THE SUPREME COURT'S DECISION

"Before enactment of IIRIRA, judicial review of most administrative action under the INA was governed by 8 U.S.C. § 1105a, a special statutory-review provision directing that 'the sole and exclusive procedure for . . . the judicial review of all final orders of deportation' shall be that set forth in the Hobbs Act, which gives exclusive jurisdiction to the courts of appeals. Much of the Court of Appeals' analysis in AADC I was devoted to the question whether this pre-IIRIRA provision applied to selective-enforcement claims. . . .

Whether we must delve further into the details of this issue depends upon whether, after the enactment of IIRIRA, § 1105a continues to apply to this case. On the surface of things, at least, it does not. Although the general rule set forth in § 309(c)(1) of IIRIRA is that the revised procedures for removing aliens, including the judicial-review procedures of § 1252, do not apply to aliens who were already in either exclusion or deportation proceedings on IIRIRA's effective date, . . . § 306(c)(1) of IIRIRA directs that a single provision, § 1252(g), shall apply 'without limitation to claims arising from all past, pending, or future exclusion, deportation, or removal proceedings.' . . .

This provision seemingly governs here, depriving the federal courts of jurisdiction '[e]xcept as provided in this section.' But whether it is as straightforward as that depends . . . . Here, and in the courts below, both petitioners and respondents have treated § 1252(g) as covering all or nearly all deportation claims. . . . This broad understanding of § 1252(g), combined with IIRIRA's effective-date provisions, creates an interpretive anomaly. . . .

We think the seeming anomaly that prompted the parties' strained readings of § 1252(g)—and that at least accompanied the Court of Appeals' strained reading—is a mirage. . . .

Our narrow reading of § 1252(g) makes sense of the statutory scheme as a whole, for it resolves the supposed tension between § 306(c)(1) and § 309(c)(1). In cases to which § 1252(g) applies, the rest of § 1252 is incorporated through the '[e]xcept as provided in this section' clause. This incorporation does not swallow § 309(c)(1)'s general rule that §§ 1252(a)-(f) do not apply to pending cases, for § 1252(g) applies to only a limited subset of deportation claims. Yet it is also faithful to § 306(c)(1)'s command that § 1252(g) be applied 'without limitation' (i.e., including the '[e]xcept as provided' clause) to 'claims arising from all past, pending, or future exclusion, deportation, or removal proceedings.'

Respondents' challenge to the Attorney General's decision to 'commence proceedings' against them falls squarely within § 1252(g)—indeed, as we have discussed, the language seems to have been crafted with such a challenge precisely in mind—and nothing elsewhere in § 1252 provides for jurisdiction. . . . § 1252(f) plainly serves as a limit on injunctive relief rather than a jurisdictional grant. . . .

Finally, we must address respondents' contention that, since the lack of prior factual development for their claim will render the § 1252(a)(1) exception to § 1252(g) unavailing; since habeas relief will also be unavailable; and since even if one or both were available they would come too late to prevent the 'chilling effect' upon their First Amendment rights; the doctrine of constitutional doubt requires us to interpret § 1252(g) in such fashion as to permit immediate review of their selective-enforcement claims. We do not believe that the doctrine of constitutional doubt has any application here. As a general matter-and assuredly in the context of claims such as those put forward in the present case-an alien unlawfully in this country has no constitutional right to assert selective enforcement as a defense against his deportation. . . .

To resolve the present controversy, we need not rule out the possibility of a rare case in which the alleged basis of discrimination is so outrageous that the foregoing considerations can be overcome. Whether or not there be such exceptions, the general rule certainly applies here. . . .

Because 8 U.S.C. § 1252(g) deprives the federal courts of jurisdiction over respondents' claims, we vacate the judgment of the Ninth Circuit and remand with instructions for it to vacate the judgment of the District Court."

V. JUSTICE VOTE

1 Pro ACLU Side vs. 8 Con Opposing Side

ACLU Side (Respondent / Appellee)

1. Souter, D. – Wrote dissenting opinion

Opposing Side (Petitioner / Appellant)

1. Scalia, A. – Wrote majority opinion
2. Thomas, C. – Joined majority opinion
3. Ginsburg, R. – Wrote concurring opinion
4. O'Connor, S. – Joined majority opinion
5. Stevens, J. – Wrote concurring opinion
6. Breyer, S. – Joined Ginsburg's concurrence in part
7. Kennedy, A. – Joined majority opinion
8. Rehnquist, W. – Joined majority opinion

VI. A WIN OR LOSS FOR THE ACLU?

The ACLU argued the case for appellee, urging affirmance; the Supreme Court vacated and remanded the Court of Appeals' decision by an 8-1 vote, giving the ACLU an apparent loss.

861. Saenz v. Roe

(Decided May 17, 1999; 526 U.S. 489)

I. ISSUE

A. Issues Discussed

Civil rights, residency requirements, welfare benefits, Fourteenth Amendment

B. Legal Question Presented

Whether a California "statute limiting the maximum welfare benefits available to newly arrived residents . . . was constitutional when it was enacted and, if not, whether an amendment to the Social Security Act enacted by Congress in 1996 affects that determination."

C. Supreme Court's Answer

The statute was unconstitutional when enacted and was not resuscitated by the 1996 amendment to the Social Security Act.

II. CASE SUMMARY

A. Background

"In 1992, in order to make a relatively modest reduction in its vast welfare budget, the California Legislature enacted § 11450.03 of the state Welfare and Institutions Code. That section sought to change the California AFDC program by limiting new residents, for the first year they live in California, to the benefits they would have received in the State of their prior residence. Because in 1992 a state program either had to conform to federal specifications or receive a waiver from the Secretary of Health and Human Services in order to qualify for federal reimbursement, § 11450.03 required approval by the Secretary to take effect. In October 1992, the Secretary issued a waiver purporting to grant such approval.

On December 21, 1992, three California residents who were eligible for AFDC benefits filed an action in the Eastern District of California challenging the constitutionality of the durational residency requirement in § 11450.03. Each plaintiff alleged that she had recently moved to California to live with relatives in order to escape abusive family circumstances. . . .

The District Court issued a temporary restraining order and, after a hearing, preliminarily enjoined implementation of the statute. District Judge Levi found that the statute 'produces substantial disparities in benefit levels and makes no accommodation for the different costs of living that exist in different states. [H]e concluded that the statute placed 'a penalty on the decision of new residents to migrate to the State and be treated on an equal basis with existing residents.' In his view, if the purpose of the measure was to deter migration by poor people into the State, it would be unconstitutional for that reason. And even if the purpose was only to conserve limited funds, the State had failed to explain why the entire burden of the saving should be imposed on new residents. The Court of Appeals summarily affirmed for the reasons stated by the District Judge."

The Supreme Court granted certiorari to review the case and affirmed.

B. Counsel of Record / ACLU Attorney

ACLU Side (Respondent / Appellee): Mark D. Rosenbaum argued the cause for appellees. With him on the brief were David S. Schwartz, Daniel P. Tokaji, Rocio L. Cordoba, Peter J. Eliasberg, Sherry Leiwant, Andrea D. Williams, Risa E. Kaufman, Evan H. Caminker, Laurence H. Tribe, Martha F. Davis, Karl Manheim, Steven R. Shapiro, Alan L. Schlosser, Richard Rothschild, Clare Pastore and Jordan C. Budd.

Opposing Side (Petitioner / Appellant): Theodore Garelis argued for appellants. With him on the briefs were Attorney General of California Daniel E. Lungren, Senior Assistant Attorney General Charlton G. Holland, III, Supervising Deputy Attorney General Frank S. Furtek, and Deputy Attorney General Janie L. Daigle.

Solicitor General Seth P. Waxman argued the cause for the United States, as amicus curiae, urging reversal in part and affirmance in part.

III. AMICI CURIAE

ACLU Side (Respondent / Appellee)

Brief of amici curiae filed on behalf of ACORN, et al., by Paul M. Dodyk, Victor F. Caldwell, and Henry A. Freedman.

Brief of amici curiae filed on behalf of the American Bar Association by Philip S. Anderson, Elena N. Broder, and Paul M. Smith.

Brief of amici curiae filed on behalf of the Brennan Center for Justice at New York University School of Law, et al., by Burt Neuborne, Elizabeth Daniel, Richard R. Buery, and Deborah Goldberg.

Brief of amici curiae filed on behalf of Catholic Charities USA, et al., by Louis R. Cohen, Christopher Davies, and Lydia Alix Fillingham.

Brief of amici curiae filed on behalf of the National Law Center on Homelessness and Poverty by Ann E. Bushmiller, Edward R. McNicholas, and Maria Foscarinis.

Brief of amici curiae filed on behalf of Sixty-six Organizations Serving Domestic Violence Survivors by Susan Frietsche.

Brief of amici curiae filed on behalf of Social Scientists by Lawrence S. Lustberg and Lori Outzs Borgen.

Brief of amici curiae filed on behalf of William Cohen, et al., by Roderick M. Hills, Jr., and Charles S. Sims.

Opposing Side (Petitioner / Appellant)

Brief of amici curiae filed on behalf of the United States by Solicitor General Waxman, Assistant Attorney General Hunger, Deputy Solicitor General Kneedler, Edward C. DuMont, Mark B. Stern, Kathleen Moriarty Mueller, and Peter J. Smith, urging reversal in part and affirmance in part.

Brief of amici curiae filed on behalf of the Commonwealth of Pennsylvania, et al., by Attorney General D. Michael Fisher, Chief Deputy Attorney General John G. Knorr III, Attorney

General of Ohio Betty D. Montgomery, and State Solicitor Jeffrey S. Sutton, and by the Attorneys General for their respective States as follows: Bill Pryor of Alabama, Robert A. Butterworth of Florida, Thurbert E. Baker of Georgia, Margery S. Bronster of Hawaii, J. Joseph Curran, Jr., of Maryland, Hubert H. Humphrey III of Minnesota, Joseph P. Mazurek of Montana, Frankie Sue Del Papa of Nevada, Philip T. McLaughlin of New Hampshire, Dennis C. Vacco of New York, Michael F. Easley of North Carolina, Heidi Heitkamp of North Dakota, Jeffrey B. Pine of Rhode Island, and Christine O. Gregoire of Washington.

Brief of amici curiae filed on behalf of the Institute for Justice by Douglas W. Kmiec, William H. Mellor, and Clint Bolick.

Brief of amici curiae filed on behalf of the National Governors' Association, et al., by Richard Ruda and James I. Crowley.

Brief of amici curiae filed on behalf of the Pacific Legal Foundation by Sharon L. Browne and Deborah J. La Fetra.

Brief of amici curiae filed on behalf of the Washington Legal Foundation, et al., by Daniel J. Popeo and Richard A. Samp.

IV. THE SUPREME COURT'S DECISION

"The 'right to travel' discussed in our cases embraces at least three different components. It protects the right of a citizen of one State to enter and to leave another State, the right to be treated as a welcome visitor rather than an unfriendly alien when temporarily present in the second State, and, for those travelers who elect to become permanent residents, the right to be treated like other citizens of that State. . . .

What is at issue in this case . . . is this third aspect of the right to travel—the right of the newly arrived citizen to the same privileges and immunities enjoyed by other citizens of the same State. That right is protected not only by the new arrival's status as a state citizen, but also by her status as a citizen of the United States. . . .

The classifications challenged in this case—and there are many—are defined entirely by (a) the period of residency in California and (b) the location of the prior residences of the disfavored class members. The favored class of beneficiaries includes all eligible California citizens who have resided there for at least one year, plus those new arrivals who last resided in another country or in a State that provides benefits at least as generous as California's. Thus, within the broad category of citizens who resided in California for less than a year, there are many who are treated like lifetime residents. And within the broad subcategory of new arrivals who are treated less favorably, there are many smaller classes whose benefit levels are determined by the law of the States from whence they came. To justify § 11450.03, California must therefore explain not only why it is sound fiscal policy to discriminate against those who have been citizens for less than a year, but also why it is permissible to apply such a variety of rules within that class.

These classifications may not be justified by a purpose to deter welfare applicants from migrating to California for three reasons. First, although it is reasonable to assume that some persons may be motivated to move for the purpose of obtaining higher benefits, the empirical evidence reviewed by the District Judge, which takes into account the high cost of living in California, indicates that the number of such persons is quite small—surely not large enough to justify a burden on those who had no such motive. Second, California has represented to the Court that the legislation was not enacted for any such reason. Third, even if it were, as we squarely held in Shapiro v. Thompson, 394 U.S. 618 (1969), such a purpose would be unequivocally impermissible. . . .

The question that remains is whether congressional approval of durational residency requirements in the 1996 amendment to the Social Security Act somehow resuscitates the constitutionality of § 11450.03. That question is readily answered, for we have consistently held that Congress may not authorize the States to violate the Fourteenth Amendment. Moreover, the protection afforded to the citizen by the Citizenship Clause of that Amendment is a limitation on the powers of the National Government as well as the States. . . .

Citizens of the United States, whether rich or poor, have the right to choose to be citizens 'of the State wherein they reside.' U.S. Const., Amdt. 14, § 1. The States, however, do not have any right to select their citizens. The Fourteenth Amendment, like the Constitution itself, was, as Justice Cardozo put it, 'framed upon the theory that the peoples of the several states must sink or swim together, and that in the long run prosperity and salvation are in union and not division.'

The judgment of the Court of Appeals is affirmed."

V. JUSTICE VOTE

7 Pro ACLU Side vs. 2 Con Opposing Side

ACLU Side (Respondent / Appellee)

1. Stevens, J. – Wrote majority opinion
2. O'Connor, S. – Joined majority opinion
3. Scalia, A. – Joined majority opinion
4. Kennedy, A. – Joined majority opinion
5. Souter, D. – Joined majority opinion
6. Ginsburg, R. – Joined majority opinion
7. Breyer, S. – Joined majority opinion

Opposing Side (Petitioner / Appellant)

1. Rehnquist, W. – Wrote dissenting opinion, joined Thomas' dissent
2. Thomas, C. – Wrote dissenting opinion, joined Rehnquist's dissent

VI. A WIN OR LOSS FOR THE ACLU?

The ACLU, as counsel for appellee, urged affirmance of the judgment of the Court of Appeals; the Supreme Court affirmed in a 7-2 vote, giving the ACLU an apparent win.

862. Hunt v. Cromartie

(Decided May 17, 1999; 526 U.S. 541)

I. ISSUE

A. Issues Discussed

Race, voting rights

B. Legal Question Presented

"[W]hether appellees were entitled to summary judgment on their claim that North Carolina's Twelfth Congressional District, as established by the State's 1997 congressional redistricting plan, constituted an unconstitutional racial gerrymander in violation of the Equal Protection Clause of the Fourteenth Amendment."

C. Supreme Court's Answer

"Perhaps, after trial, the evidence will support a finding that race was the State's predominant motive, but we express no position as to that question. We decide only that this case was not suited for summary disposition."

II. CASE SUMMARY

A. Background

"This is the third time in six years that litigation over North Carolina's Twelfth Congressional District has come before this Court. The first time around, we held that plaintiffs whose complaint alleged that the State had deliberately segregated voters into districts on the basis of race without compelling justification stated a claim for relief under the Equal Protection Clause of the Fourteenth Amendment. After remand, we affirmed the District Court's finding that North Carolina's District 12 classified voters by race and further held that the State's reapportionment scheme was not narrowly tailored to serve a compelling interest.

In response to our decision in Shaw II, the State enacted a new districting plan. . . .

Appellees believed the new District 12, like the old one, to be the product of an unconstitutional racial gerrymander. They filed suit . . . seeking to enjoin elections under the State's 1997 plan. The parties filed competing motions for summary judgment and supporting materials, and the three-judge District Court heard argument on the pending motions, but before either party had conducted discovery and without an evidentiary hearing. Over one judge's dissent, the District Court granted appellees' motion and entered the injunction they sought."

The Supreme Court granted certiorari to review the case.

B. Counsel of Record / ACLU Attorney

ACLU Side (Petitioner / Appellant): Walter E. Dellinger argued the cause for appellants. With him on the briefs were Michael F. Easley, Attorney General of North Carolina, Edwin M. Speas, Jr., Chief Deputy Attorney General, Tiare B. Smiley, Special Deputy Attorney General, and Melissa L. Saunders. Todd A. Cox, Adam Stein, Elaine R. Jones, Theodore M. Shaw, Norman J. Chachkin, Jacqueline A. Berrien, and Victor A. Bolden filed briefs for appellants-intervenors Smallwood et al.

James A. Feldman argued the cause for the United States as amici curiae.

Opposing Side (Respondent / Appellee): Robinson O. Everett argued the cause for appellees. With him on the brief was Martin G. McGee.

III. AMICI CURIAE

ACLU Side (Petitioner / Appellant)

Brief of amici curiae filed on behalf of the American Civil Liberties Union by Laughlin McDonald, Neil Bradley, Maha Zaki, Cristina Correia, and Steven R. Shapiro.

Brief of amici curiae filed on behalf of the United States by James A. Feldman, Solicitor General Waxman, Acting Assistant Attorney General Yeomans, Deputy Solicitor General Underwood, David K. Flynn, and Louis E. Peraertz.

Brief of amici curiae filed on behalf of Brennan Center for Justice at New York University School of Law et al. by Burt Neuborne and Deborah Goldberg.

Brief of amici curiae filed on behalf of Congresswoman Corrine Brown et al. by Paul M. Smith, Donald B. Verrilli, Jr., and J. Gerald Hebert.

Brief of amici curiae filed on behalf of the Lawyers' Committee for Civil Rights Under Law by Matthew J. Zinn, David A. Stein, James U. Blacksher, Jack W. Londen, Daniel F. Kolb, Norman Redlich, Barbara R. Arnwine, Thomas J. Henderson, and Edward Still.

Opposing Side (Respondent / Appellee)

No briefs of amici curiae were filed in support of appellee.

IV. THE SUPREME COURT'S DECISION

"Our decisions have established that all laws that classify citizens on the basis of race, including racially gerrymandered districting schemes, are constitutionally suspect and must be strictly scrutinized. When racial classifications are explicit, no inquiry into legislative purpose is necessary. A facially neutral law, on the other hand, warrants strict scrutiny only if it can be proved that the law was 'motivated by a racial purpose or object,' or if it is "unexplainable on grounds other than race." The task of assessing a jurisdiction's motivation, however, is not a simple matter; on the contrary, it is an inherently complex endeavor, one requiring the trial court to perform a 'sensitive inquiry into such circumstantial and direct evidence of intent as may be available.'

Districting legislation ordinarily, if not always, classifies tracts of land, precincts, or census blocks, and is race neutral on its face. North Carolina's 1997 plan was not atypical; appellees, therefore, were required to prove that District 12 was drawn with an impermissible racial motive—in this context, strict scrutiny applies if race was the 'predominant factor' motivating the legislature's districting decision. To carry their burden, appellees were obliged to show—using direct or circumstantial evidence, or a combination of both—that 'the legislature subordinated traditional race-neutral districting principles, including but not limited to compactness, contiguity, and respect for political subdivisions or communities defined by actual shared interests, to racial considerations.'

Appellees offered only circumstantial evidence in support of their claim. . . .

Viewed in toto, appellees' evidence tends to support an inference that the State drew its district lines with an impermissible racial motive—even though they presented no direct evidence of intent. Summary judgment, however, is appropriate only where there is no genuine issue of material fact and the moving party is entitled to judgment as a matter of law. . . .

The District Court nevertheless was only partially correct in stating that the material facts before it were uncontroverted. The legislature's motivation is itself a factual question. . . .

Accepting appellants' political motivation explanation as true, as the District Court was required to do in ruling on appellees' motion for summary judgment, appellees were not entitled to judgment as a matter of law. Our prior decisions have made clear that a jurisdiction may engage in constitutional political gerrymandering, even if it so happens that the most loyal Democrats happen to be black Democrats and even if the State were conscious of that fact. Evidence that blacks constitute even a supermajority in one congressional district while amounting to less than a plurality in a neighboring district will not, by itself, suffice to prove that a jurisdiction was motivated by race in drawing its district lines when the evidence also shows a high correlation between race and party preference.

Of course, neither appellees nor the District Court relied exclusively on appellees' boundary segment evidence, and appellees submitted other evidence tending to show that the General Assembly was motivated by racial considerations in drawing District 12—most notably, District 12's shape and its lack of compactness. But in ruling on a motion for summary judgment, the nonmoving party's evidence 'is to be believed, and all justifiable inferences are to be drawn in [that party's] favor.' While appellees' evidence might allow the District Court to find that the State acted with an impermissible racial motivation, despite the State's explanation as supported by the Peterson affidavit, it does not require that the court do so. All that can be said on the record before us is that motivation was in dispute. . . .

Outright admissions of impermissible racial motivation are infrequent and plaintiffs often must rely upon other evidence. Summary judgment in favor of the party with the burden of persuasion, however, is inappropriate when the evidence is susceptible of different interpretations or inferences by the trier of fact. . . .

In reaching our decision, we are fully aware that the District Court is more familiar with the evidence than this Court, and is likewise better suited to assess the General Assembly's motivations. Perhaps, after trial, the evidence will support a finding that race was the State's predominant motive, but we express no position as to that question. We decide only that this case was not suited for summary disposition. The judgment of the District Court is reversed."

V. JUSTICE VOTE

9 Pro ACLU Side vs. 0 Con Opposing Side

ACLU Side (Petitioner / Appellant)

1. Thomas, C. – Wrote majority opinion
2. O'Connor, S. – Joined majority opinion
3. Stevens, J. – Wrote concurring opinion
4. Souter, D. – Joined Stevens' concurrence
5. Ginsburg, R. – Joined Stevens' concurrence
6. Breyer, S. – Joined Stevens' concurrence
7. Scalia, A. – Joined majority opinion
8. Kennedy, A. – Joined majority opinion
9. Rehnquist, W. – Joined majority opinion

VI. A WIN OR LOSS FOR THE ACLU?

The ACLU filed as amicus curiae urging reversal of the judgment of the district court; the Supreme Court reversed in a 9-0 vote, giving the ACLU an apparent win.

863. Wilson v. Layne

(Decided May 24, 1999; 526 U.S. 603)

I. ISSUE

A. Issues Discussed

Criminal justice, Fourth Amendment, criminal procedure, search and seizure, right to privacy

B. Legal Question Presented

Whether a "media ride-along" when officers execute an arrest warrant violates the Fourth Amendment.

C. Supreme Court's Answer

A "media ride-along" when officers execute an arrest warrant violates the Fourth Amendment, however, the law was unclear when this incident occured so officers in this case are entitled to qualified immunity.

II. CASE SUMMARY

A. Background

"In early 1992, the Attorney General of the United States approved 'Operation Gunsmoke,' a special national fugitive apprehension program in which United States Marshals worked with state and local police to apprehend dangerous criminals. . . . One of the dangerous fugitives identified as a target of 'Operation Gunsmoke' was Dominic Wilson, the son of petitioners Charles and Geraldine Wilson. Dominic Wilson had violated his probation on previous felony charges of robbery, theft, and assault with intent to rob, and the police computer listed 'caution indicators' that he was likely to be armed, to resist arrest, and to 'assaul[t] police.' The computer also listed his address as 909 North StoneStreet Avenue in Rockville, Maryland. Unknown to the police, this was actually the home of petitioners, Dominic Wilson's parents. Thus, in April 1992, the Circuit Court for Montgomery County issued three arrest warrants for Dominic Wilson, one for each of his probation violations. The warrants were each addressed to 'any duly authorized peace officer,' and commanded such officers to arrest him and bring him 'immediately' before the Circuit Court to answer an indictment as to his probation violation. The warrants made no mention of media presence or assistance.

In the early morning hours of April 16, 1992, a Gunsmoke team of Deputy United States Marshals and Montgomery County Police officers assembled to execute the Dominic Wilson warrants. The team was accompanied by a reporter and a photographer from the Washington Post, who had been invited by the Marshals to accompany them on their mission as part of a Marshals Service ride-along policy.

At around 6:45 a.m., the officers, with media representatives in tow, entered the dwelling at 909 North StoneStreet Avenue in the Lincoln Park neighborhood of Rockville. Petitioners Charles and Geraldine Wilson were still in bed when they heard the officers enter the home. Petitioner Charles Wilson, dressed only in a pair of briefs, ran into the living room to investigate. Discovering at least five men in street clothes with guns in his living room, he angrily demanded that they state their business, and repeatedly cursed the officers. Believing him to be an angry Dominic Wilson, the officers quickly subdued him on the floor. Geraldine Wilson next entered the living room to investigate, wearing only a night-gown. She observed her husband being restrained by the armed officers.

When their protective sweep was completed, the officers learned that Dominic Wilson was not in the house, and they departed. During the time that the officers were in the home, the Washington Post photographer took numerous pictures. The print reporter was also apparently in the living room observing the confrontation between the police and Charles Wilson. At no time, however, were the reporters involved in the execution of the arrest warrant. The Washington Post never published its photographs of the incident.

Petitioners sued the law enforcement officials in their personal capacities for money damages under Bivens v. Six Unknown Fed. Narcotics Agents, 403 U.S. 388 (1971) (the U.S. Marshals Service respondents), and Rev. Stat. § 1979, 42 U.S.C. § 1983 (the Montgomery County Sheriff's Department respondents). They contended that the officers' actions in bringing members of the media to observe and record the attempted execution of the arrest warrant violated their Fourth Amendment rights. The District Court denied respondents' motion for summary judgment on the basis of qualified immunity.

On interlocutory appeal to the Court of Appeals, a divided panel reversed and held that respondents were entitled to qualified immunity. The case was twice reheard en banc, where a divided Court of Appeals again upheld the defense of qualified immunity. The Court of Appeals declined to decide whether the actions of the police violated the Fourth Amendment. It concluded instead that because no court had held (at the time of the search) that media presence during a police entry into a residence violated the Fourth Amendment, the right allegedly violated by respondents was not 'clearly established' and thus qualified immunity was proper."

The Supreme Court granted certiorari to review the case and affirmed.

B. Counsel of Record / ACLU Attorney

ACLU Side (Petitioner / Appellant): Richard K. Willard argued the cause for appellants. With him on the briefs were David H. Coburn, James S. Felt, Richard Seligman, Steven R. Shapiro, Arthur B. Spitzer and Dwight H. Sullivan.

Opposing Side (Respondent / Appellee): Richard A. Cordray argued the cause for federal appellees.

Assistant Attorney General of Maryland Lawrence P. Fletcher-Hill argued the cause for state appellees. With him on the briefs were Attorney General J. Joseph Curran, Jr., Deputy Attorney General Carmen M. Shephard, and Assistant Attorney Generals Andrew H. Baida and John B. Howard, Jr.

III. AMICI CURIAE

ACLU Side (Petitioner / Appellant)

No briefs of amici curiae were filed in support of appellant.

Opposing Side (Respondent / Appellee)

Brief of amici curiae filed on behalf of ABC Inc., et al., by Lee Levine, James E. Grossberg, Jay Ward Brown, Henry S. Hoberman, Richard M. Schmidt, Jr., Susanna M. Lowy, Harold W Fuson, Jr., Barbara Wartelle Wall, Ralph E. Goldberg, Karlene W Goller, Jerry S. Birenz, Slade R. Metcalf, Jack N. Goodman, David S. J. Brown, Rene P. Milam, George Freeman, and Jane E. Kirtley.

IV. THE SUPREME COURT'S DECISION

"A court evaluating a claim of qualified immunity 'must first determine whether the plaintiff has alleged the deprivation of an actual constitutional right at all, and if so, proceed to determine whether that right was clearly established at the time of the alleged violation.' . . .

Certainly the presence of reporters inside the home was not related to the objectives of the authorized intrusion. Respondents concede that the reporters did not engage in the execution of the warrant, and did not assist the police in their task. The reporters therefore were not present for any reason related to the justification for police entry into the home—the apprehension of Dominic Wilson.

This is not a case in which the presence of the third parties directly aided in the execution of the warrant. Where the police enter a home under the authority of a warrant to search for stolen property, the presence of third parties for the purpose of identifying the stolen property has long been approved by this Court and our common-law tradition. . . .

The reasons advanced by respondents, taken in their entirety, fall short of justifying the presence of media inside a home. We hold that it is a violation of the Fourth Amendment for police to bring members of the media or other third parties into a home during the execution of a warrant when the presence of the third parties in the home was not in aid of the execution of the warrant. . . .

Since the police action in this case violated petitioners' Fourth Amendment right, we now must decide whether this right was clearly established at the time of the search. . . .

We hold that it was not unreasonable for a police officer in April 1992 to have believed that bringing media observers along during the execution of an arrest warrant (even in a home) was lawful. . . .

Given such an undeveloped state of the law, the officers in this case cannot have been 'expected to predict the future course of constitutional law.' Between the time of the events of this case and today's decision, a split among the Federal Circuits in fact developed on the question whether media ride-alongs that enter homes subject the police to money damages. If judges thus disagree on a constitutional question, it is unfair to subject police to money damages for picking the losing side of the controversy.

For the foregoing reasons, the judgment of the Court of Appeals is affirmed."

V. JUSTICE VOTE

1 Pro ACLU Side vs. 8 Con Opposing Side

ACLU Side (Petitioner / Appellant)

1. Stevens, J. – Wrote opinion concurring in part and dissenting in part

Opposing Side (Respondent / Appellee)

1. Rehnquist, W. – Wrote majority opinion
2. O'Connor, S. – Joined majority opinion
3. Scalia, A. – Joined majority opinion
4. Kennedy, A. – Joined majority opinion
5. Souter, D. – Joined majority opinion
6. Thomas, C. – Joined majority opinion
7. Ginsburg, R. – Joined majority opinion
8. Breyer, S. – Joined majority opinion

VI. A WIN OR LOSS FOR THE ACLU?

The ACLU, as counsel for appellants, urged reversal of the judgment of the Court of Appeals; the Supreme Court affirmed in an 8-1 vote, giving the ACLU an apparent loss.

864. Davis v. Monroe County Board of Education

(Decided May 24, 1999; 526 U.S. 629)

I. ISSUE

A. Issues Discussed

Civil rights, harassment, discrimination, liability

B. Legal Question Presented

"[W]hether a private damages action may lie against the school board in cases of student-on-student harassment."

C. Supreme Court's Answer

"We conclude that it may, but only where the funding recipient acts with deliberate indifference to known acts of harassment in its programs or activities. Moreover, we conclude that such an action will lie only for harassment that is so severe, pervasive, and objectively offensive that it effectively bars the victim's access to an educational opportunity or benefit."

II. CASE SUMMARY

A. Background

"Petitioner brought suit against the Monroe County Board of Education and other defendants, alleging that her fifth-grade daughter had been the victim of sexual harassment by another student in her class. Among petitioner's claims was a claim for monetary and injunctive relief under Title IX of the Education Amendments of 1972 (Title IX), 86 Stat. 373, as amended, 20 U.S.C. § 1681 et seq. The District Court dismissed petitioner's Title IX claim on the ground that 'student-on-student,' or peer, harassment provides no ground for a private cause of action under the statute. The Court of Appeals for the Eleventh Circuit, sitting en banc, affirmed. . . .

Petitioner's minor daughter, LaShonda, was allegedly the victim of a prolonged pattern of sexual harassment by one of her fifth-grade classmates at Hubbard Elementary School, a public school in Monroe County, Georgia. According to petitioner's complaint, the harassment began in December 1992, when the classmate, G.F., attempted to touch LaShonda's breasts and genital area and made vulgar statements such as "I want to get in bed with you" and "I want to feel your boobs." . . . G.F.'s conduct allegedly continued for many months. . . .

Petitioner alleges that no disciplinary action was taken in response to G.F.'s behavior toward LaShonda. In addition to her conversations with [teachers] Fort and Pippen, petitioner alleges that she spoke with Principal Querry in mid-May 1993. When petitioner inquired as to what action the school intended to take against G.F., Querry simply stated, "I guess I'll have to threaten him a little bit harder." Yet, petitioner alleges, at no point during the many months of his reported misconduct was G.F. disciplined for harassment. Indeed, Querry allegedly asked petitioner why LaShonda "was the only one complaining."

Nor, according to the complaint, was any effort made to separate G.F. and LaShonda. On the contrary, notwithstanding LaShonda's frequent complaints, only after more than three months of reported harassment was she even permitted to change her classroom seat so that she was no longer seated next to G.F. Moreover, petitioner alleges that, at the time of the events in question, the Monroe County Board of Education (Board) had not instructed its personnel on how to respond to peer sexual harassment and had not established a policy on the issue."

The Supreme Court granted certiorari to review the case and reversed.

B. Counsel of Record / ACLU Attorney

ACLU Side (Petitioner / Appellant): Verna L. Williams argued the cause for appellant. With her on the briefs were Marcia D. Greenberger, Leslie T. Annexstein, Nancy Perkins, and Stevenson Munro.

Deputy Solicitor General Barbara D. Underwood argued the cause for the United States, as amicus curiae, by special leave of Court.

Opposing Side (Respondent / Appellee): W. Warren Plowden, Jr., argued the cause for appellees.

III. AMICI CURIAE

ACLU Side (Petitioner / Appellant)

Brief of amici curiae filed on behalf of the ACLU, et al., by Sara L. Mandelbaum, Karen R. Marks, and Steven R. Shapiro.

Brief of amici curiae filed on behalf of the United States by Deputy Solicitor General Barbara D. Underwood, Solicitor General Waxman, Acting Assistant Attorney General Lee, Beth S. Brinkmann, Dennis J. Dimsey, and Linda F. Thome.

Brief of amici curiae filed on behalf of the National Education Association, et al., by Judith L. Lichtman and Donna R. Lenhoff.

Brief of amici curiae filed on behalf of the NOW Legal Defense and Education Fund, et al., by Martha F. Davis, Julie Goldscheid, Yolanda S. Wu, David S. Ettinger, Lisa R. Jaskol, and Mary-Christine Sungaila.

Brief of amici curiae filed on behalf of the Rutherford Institute by John W. Whitehead and Steven H. Aden.

Opposing Side (Respondent / Appellee)

Brief of amici curiae filed on behalf of the National School Boards Association, et al., by Lisa A. Brown, Jennifer Jacobs, and Julie Underwood.

Brief of amici curiae filed on behalf of Students for Individual Liberty, et al., by James A. Moody.

Brief of amici curiae filed on behalf of the Independent Women's Forum by Richard P. Ward, Peter L. Ebb, Jennifer C. Braceras, and Anita K. Blair.

IV. THE SUPREME COURT'S DECISION

"We must determine whether a district's failure to respond to student-on-student harassment in its schools can support a private suit for money damages. This Court has indeed recognized an implied private right of action under Title IX, and we have held that money damages are available in such suits. Because we have repeatedly treated Title IX as legislation enacted pursuant to Congress' authority under the Spending Clause, however, private damages actions are available only where recipients of federal funding had adequate notice that they could be liable for the conduct at issue. When Congress acts pursuant to its spending power, it generates legislation 'much in the nature of a contract: in return for federal funds, the States agree to comply with federally imposed conditions.' In interpreting language in spending legislation, we thus 'insis[t] that Congress speak with a clear voice,' recognizing that '[t]here can, of course, be no knowing acceptance [of the terms of the putative contract] if a State is unaware of the conditions [imposed by the legislation] or is unable to ascertain what is expected of it.' . . .

While it remains to be seen whether petitioner can show that the Board's response to reports of G.F.'s misconduct was clearly unreasonable in light of the known circumstances, petitioner may be able to show that the Board 'subject[ed]' LaShonda to discrimination by failing to respond in any way over a period of five months to complaints of G.F.'s in-school misconduct from LaShonda and other female students. . . .

The relationship between the harasser and the victim necessarily affects the extent to which the misconduct can be said to breach Title IX's guarantee of equal access to educational benefits and to have a systemic effect on a program or activity. Peer harassment, in particular, is less likely to satisfy these requirements than is teacher-student harassment. . . .

Applying this standard to the facts at issue here, we conclude that the Eleventh Circuit erred in dismissing petitioner's complaint. Petitioner alleges that her daughter was the victim of repeated acts of sexual harassment by G.F. over a 5–month period, and there are allegations in support of the conclusion that G.F.'s misconduct was severe, pervasive, and objectively offensive. The harassment was not only verbal; it included numerous acts of objectively offensive touching, and, indeed, G.F. ultimately pleaded guilty to criminal sexual misconduct. Moreover, the complaint alleges that there were multiple victims who were sufficiently disturbed by G.F.'s misconduct to seek an audience with the school principal. Further, petitioner contends that the harassment had a concrete, negative effect on her daughter's ability to receive an education. The complaint also suggests that petitioner may be able to show both actual knowledge and deliberate indifference on the part of the Board, which made no effort whatsoever either to investigate or to put an end to the harassment.

On this complaint, we cannot say 'beyond doubt that [petitioner] can prove no set of facts in support of [her] claim which would entitle [her] to relief.' Accordingly, the judgment of the United States Court of Appeals for the Eleventh Circuit is reversed, and the case is remanded for further proceedings consistent with this opinion."

V. JUSTICE VOTE

5 Pro ACLU Side vs. 4 Con Opposing Side

ACLU Side (Petitioner / Appellant)

1. O'Connor, S. – Wrote majority opinion
2. Stevens, J. – Joined majority opinion
3. Souter, D. – Joined majority opinion
4. Ginsburg, R. – Joined majority opinion
5. Breyer, S. – Joined majority opinion

Opposing Side (Respondent / Appellee)

1. Kennedy, A. – Wrote dissenting opinion
2. Rehnquist, W. – Joined Kennedy's dissent
3. Scalia, A. – Joined Kennedy's dissent
4. Thomas, C. –Joined Kennedy's dissent

VI. A WIN OR LOSS FOR THE ACLU?

The ACLU filed as amicus curiae urging reversal of the judgment of the Court of Appeals for the Eleventh Circuit; the Supreme Court reversed in a 5-4 vote, giving the ACLU an apparent win.

865. City of Chicago v. Morales

(Decided June 10, 1999; 527 U.S. 41)

I. ISSUE

A. Issues Discussed

Fourteenth Amendment, due process, vagueness

B. Legal Question Presented

"[W]hether the Supreme Court of Illinois correctly held that the ordinance [prohibiting loitering by gang members] violates the Due Process Clause of the Fourteenth Amendment to the Federal Constitution."

C. Supreme Court's Answer

"[W]e conclude that the ordinance enacted by the city of Chicago is unconstitutionally vague."

II. CASE SUMMARY

A. Background

"In 1992, the Chicago City Council enacted the Gang Congregation Ordinance, which prohibits 'criminal street gang members' from 'loitering' with one another or with other persons in any public place. . . .

During the three years of its enforcement, the police issued over 89,000 dispersal orders and arrested over 42,000 people for violating the ordinance. In the ensuing enforcement proceedings, 2 trial judges upheld the constitutionality of the ordinance, but 11 others ruled that it was invalid. In respondent Youkhana's case, the trial judge held that the 'ordinance fails to notify individuals what conduct is prohibited, and it encourages arbitrary and capricious enforcement by police.'

The Illinois Appellate Court affirmed the trial Court's ruling in the Youkhana case, consolidated and affirmed other pending appeals in accordance with Youkhana, and reversed the convictions of respondents Gutierrez, Morales, and others. The Appellate Court was persuaded that the ordinance impaired the freedom of assembly of nongang members in violation of the First Amendment to the Federal Constitution and Article I of the Illinois Constitution, that it was unconstitutionally vague, that it improperly criminalized status rather than conduct, and that it jeopardized rights guaranteed under the Fourth Amendment.

The Illinois Supreme Court affirmed."

The Supreme Court granted certiorari to review the case and affirmed.

B. Counsel of Record / ACLU Attorney

ACLU Side (Respondent / Appellee): Harvey Grossman argued the cause for appellees. With him on the brief were Morris D. Lipson, Adam D. Schwartz, Rita Fry, James H. Redoy, Barbara O'Toole, and Steven R. Shapiro.

Opposing Side (Petitioner / Appellant): Lawrence Rosenthal argued the cause for appellant. With him on the briefs were Brian L. Crowe, Benna Ruth Solomon, Timothy W. Joranko, and Julian N. Henriques, Jr.

III. AMICI CURIAE

ACLU Side (Respondent / Appellee)

Brief of amici curiae filed on behalf of the Chicago Alliance for Neighborhood Safety, et al., by Stephen J. Schulhofer, Randall L. Kennedy, and Randolph N. Stone.

Brief of amici curiae filed on behalf of the Illinois Attorneys for Criminal Justice by Robert Hirschhorn and Steven A. Greenberg.

Brief of amici curiae filed on behalf of the National Association of Criminal Defense Lawyers by David M. Porter and Donald A. Dripps.

Brief of amici curiae filed on behalf of the National Black Police Association, et al., by Elaine R. Jones, Theodore M. Shaw, George H. Kendall, Laura E. Hankins, Marc O. Beem, Michael S. D'Orsi, and Diane F. Klotnia.

Brief of amici curiae filed on behalf of the National Law Center on Homelessness & Poverty, et al., by Robert M. Bruskin, Alexander B. Berger,, Maria Foscarinis, and Kelly A. Cunningham.

Brief of amici curiae filed on behalf of See Forever/the Maya Angelou Public Charter School, et al., by Louis R. Cohen, John Payton, Alex C. Lakatos, David Domenici, and James Forman, Jr.

Opposing Side (Petitioner / Appellant)

Brief of amici curiae filed on behalf of the United States by Solicitor General Waxman, Deputy Solicitor General Underwood, and James A. Feldman.

Brief of amici curiae filed on behalf of the State of Ohio, et al., by Betty D. Montgomery, Attorney General of Ohio, Jeffrey S. Sutton, State Solicitor, Robert C. Maier, and David M. Gormley, and by the Attorneys General for their respective jurisdictions as follows: William H. Pryor, Jr., of Alabama, Bruce M. Botelho of Alaska, Grant Woods of Arizona, Daniel E. Lungren of California, Gale A. Norton of Colorado, John M. Bailey of Connecticut, M. Jane Brady of Delaware, Robert A. Butterworth of Florida, Thurbert E. Baker of Georgia, James E. Ryan of Illinois, Jeffrey A. Modisett of Indiana, Carla J. Stovall of Kansas, A. B. Chandler III of Kentucky, Richard P. Ieyoub of Louisiana, J. Joseph Curran, Jr., of Maryland, Frank J. Kelley of Michigan, Hubert H. Humphrey III of Minnesota, Michael C. Moore of Mississippi, Jeremiah W. (Jay) Nixon of Missouri, Joseph P. Mazurek of Montana, Don Stenberg of Nebraska, Frankie Sue Del Papa of Nevada, Dennis C. Vacco of New York, Michael F. Easley of North Carolina, D. Michael Fisher of Pennsylvania, Carlos Lugo-Fiol of Puerto Rico, Jeffrey B. Pine of Rhode Island, Charles M. Condon of South Carolina, Mark Barnett of South Dakota, Jan Graham of Utah, Julio A. Brady of the Virgin Islands, and Mark O. Earley of Virginia.

Brief of amici curiae filed on behalf of the Center for the Community Interest by Richard K. Willard and Roger L. Conner.

Brief of amici curiae filed on behalf of the Chicago Neighborhood Organizations by Michele L. Odorizzi, Steffen N. Johnson, Dan M. Kahan, Tracey L. Meares, and Jeffrey W. Sarles.

Brief of amici curiae filed on behalf of the Los Angeles County District Attorney by Gil Garcetti, pro se, George M. Palmer, and Brent Dail Riggs.

Brief of amici curiae filed on behalf of the National District Attorneys Association, et al., by Kristin Linsley Myles, Daniel P. Collins, Stephen E. Morrissey, William L. Murphy, and Wayne W. Schmidt.

Brief of amici curiae filed on behalf of the Washington Legal Foundation, et al., by Daniel J. Popeo and Richard A. Samp.

Brief of amici curiae filed on behalf of the U. S. Conference of Mayors, et al., by Richard Ruda, Miguel A. Estrada, and Mark A. Perry.

IV. THE SUPREME COURT'S DECISION

"The city correctly points out that imprecise laws can be attacked on their face under two different doctrines. First, the overbreadth doctrine permits the facial invalidation of laws that inhibit the exercise of First Amendment rights if the impermissible applications of the law are substantial when 'judged in relation to the statute's plainly legitimate sweep.' Second, even if an enactment does not reach a substantial amount of constitutionally protected conduct, it may be impermissibly vague because it fails to establish standards for the police and public that are sufficient to guard against the arbitrary deprivation of liberty interests.

While we, like the Illinois courts, conclude that the ordinance is invalid on its face, we do not rely on the overbreadth doctrine. . . .

Vagueness may invalidate a criminal law for either of two independent reasons. First, it may fail to provide the kind of notice that will enable ordinary people to understand what conduct it prohibits; second, it may authorize and even encourage arbitrary and discriminatory enforcement. Accordingly, we first consider whether the ordinance provides fair notice to the citizen and then discuss its potential for arbitrary enforcement. . . .

This ordinance is . . . vague 'not in the sense that it requires a person to conform his conduct to an imprecise but comprehensible normative standard, but rather in the sense that no standard of conduct is specified at all.' . . .

The broad sweep of the ordinance also violates "the requirement that a legislature establish minimal guidelines to govern law enforcement." There are no such guidelines in the ordinance. . . .

In our judgment, the Illinois Supreme Court correctly concluded that the ordinance does not provide sufficiently specific limits on the enforcement discretion of the police 'to meet constitutional standards for definiteness and clarity.' We recognize the serious and difficult problems testified to by the citizens of Chicago that led to the enactment of this ordinance. 'We are mindful that the preservation of liberty depends in part on the maintenance of social order.' However, in this instance the city has enacted an ordinance that affords too much discretion to the police and too little notice to citizens who wish to use the public streets.

Accordingly, the judgment of the Supreme Court of Illinois is affirmed."

V. JUSTICE VOTE

6 Pro ACLU Side vs. 3 Con Opposing Side

ACLU Side (Respondent / Appellee)

1. Stevens, J. – Wrote majority opinion
2. O'Connor, S. – Wrote concurring opinion
3. Kennedy, A. – Wrote concurring opinion
4. Breyer, S. – Wrote concurring opinion, joined O'Connor's concurrence
5. Souter, D. – Joined majority opinion
6. Ginsburg, R. – Joined majority opinion

Opposing Side (Petitioner / Appellant)

1. Scalia, A. – Wrote dissenting opinion, joined Thomas' dissent
2. Thomas, C. – Wrote dissenting opinion
3. Rehnquist, W. – Joined Thomas' dissent

VI. A WIN OR LOSS FOR THE ACLU?

The ACLU, as counsel for respondent, urged affirmance of the judgment of the Supreme Court of Illinois; the U.S. Supreme Court affirmed in a 6-3 vote, giving the ACLU an apparent win.

866. Lilly v. Virginia

(Decided June 10, 1999; 527 U.S. 116)

I. ISSUE

A. Issues Discussed

Criminal procedure, Sixth Amendment, Confrontation Clause

B. Legal Question Presented

"[W]hether the accused's Sixth Amendment right 'to be confronted with the witnesses against him' was violated by admitting into evidence at his trial a nontestifying accomplice's entire confession that contained some statements against the accomplice's penal interest and others that inculpated the accused."

C. Supreme Court's Answer

Admission of the nontestifying accomplice's confession violated the accused's Sixth Amendment rights under the Confrontation Clause.

II. CASE SUMMARY

A. Background

"On December 4, 1995, three men—Benjamin Lee Lilly (petitioner), his brother Mark, and Mark's roommate, Gary Wayne Barker—broke into a home and stole nine bottles of liquor, three loaded guns, and a safe. The next day, the men drank the stolen liquor, robbed a small country store, and shot at geese with their stolen weapons. After their car broke down, they abducted Alex DeFilippis and used his vehicle to drive to a deserted location. One of them shot and killed DeFilippis. The three men then committed two more robberies before they were apprehended by the police late in the evening of December 5.

After taking them into custody, the police questioned each of the three men separately. Petitioner did not mention the murder to the police and stated that the other two men had forced him to participate in the robberies. Petitioner's brother Mark and Barker told the police somewhat different accounts of the crimes, but both maintained that petitioner masterminded the robberies and was the one who had killed DeFilippis.

A tape recording of Mark's initial oral statement indicates that he was questioned from 1:35 a.m. until 2:12 a.m. on December 6. The police interrogated him again from 2:30 a.m. until 2:53 a.m. During both interviews, Mark continually emphasized how drunk he had been during the entire spree. When asked about his participation in the string of crimes, Mark admitted that he stole liquor during the initial burglary and that he stole a 12–pack of beer during the robbery of the liquor store. Mark also conceded that he had handled a gun earlier that day and that he was present during the more serious thefts and the homicide.

The police told Mark that he would be charged with armed robbery and that, unless he broke 'family ties,' petitioner 'may be dragging you right in to a life sentence.' Mark acknowledged that he would be sent away to the penitentiary. He claimed, however, that while he had primarily been drinking, petitioner and Barker had 'got some guns or something' during the initial burglary. Mark said that Barker had pulled a gun in one of the robberies.

He further insisted that petitioner had instigated the carjacking and that he (Mark) 'didn't have nothing to do with the shooting' of DeFilippis. In a brief portion of one of his statements, Mark stated that petitioner was the one who shot DeFilippis.

The Commonwealth of Virginia charged petitioner with several offenses, including the murder of DeFilippis, and tried him separately. At trial, the Commonwealth called Mark as a witness, but he invoked his Fifth Amendment privilege against self-incrimination. The Commonwealth therefore offered to introduce into evidence the statements Mark made to the police after his arrest, arguing that they were admissible as declarations of an unavailable witness against penal interest. Petitioner objected on the ground that the statements were not actually against Mark's penal interest because they shifted responsibility for the crimes to Barker and to petitioner, and that their admission would violate the Sixth Amendment's Confrontation Clause. The trial judge overruled the objection and admitted the tape recordings and written transcripts of the statements in their entirety. The jury found petitioner guilty of robbery, abduction, carjacking, possession of a firearm by a felon, and four charges of illegal use of a firearm, for which offenses he received consecutive prison sentences of two life terms plus 27 years. The jury also convicted petitioner of capital murder and recommended a sentence of death, which the court imposed.

The Supreme Court of Virginia affirmed petitioner's convictions and sentences."

The U.S. Supreme Court granted certiorari to review the case and reversed.

B. Counsel of Record / ACLU Attorney

ACLU Side (Petitioner / Appellant): Ira S. Sacks argued the cause for appellant.

Opposing Side (Respondent / Appellee): Katherine P. Baldwin, Assistant Attorney General of Virginia, argued the cause for appellee.

III. AMICI CURIAE

ACLU Side (Petitioner / Appellant)

Brief of amici curiae filed on behalf of the ACLU Foundation by Margaret A. Berger, Richard D. Friedman, and Steven R. Shapiro.

Brief of amici curiae filed on behalf of the National Association of Criminal Defense Attorneys by William S. Geimer, Lisa Kemler, and Marvin Miller.

Opposing Side (Respondent / Appellee)

Brief of amici curiae filed on behalf of the State of Nebraska, et al., by Don Stenberg, Attorney General of Nebraska; J. Kirk Brown, Assistant Attorney General; and Michael C. Stern, Acting Attorney General of Guam; and by the Attorneys General for their respective States as follows: Janet Napolitano of Arizona, Carla J. Stovall of Kansas, Richard P. leyoub of Louisiana, J. Joseph Curran, Jr., of Maryland, Michael C. Moore of Mississippi, Joseph P. Mazurek of Montana, Frankie Sue Del Papa of Nevada, Michael F. Easley of North Carolina, Heidi Heitkamp of North Dakota, Betty D. Montgomery of Ohio, Hardy Myers of Oregon, D. Michael Fisher of Pennsylvania, Charles M. Condon of South Carolina, Mark Barnett of South Dakota, and Paul G. Summers of Tennessee.

Brief of amici curiae filed on behalf of the Criminal Justice Legal Foundation by Kent S. Scheidegger and Charles L. Hobson.

IV. THE SUPREME COURT'S DECISION

"The residual 'trustworthiness' test credits the axiom that a rigid application of the Clause's standard for admissibility might in an exceptional case exclude a statement of an unavailable witness that is incontestably probative, competent, and reliable, yet nonetheless outside of any firmly rooted hearsay exception. When a court can be confident . . . that 'the declarant's truthfulness is so clear from the surrounding circumstances that the test of cross-examination would be of marginal utility,' the Sixth Amendment's residual 'trustworthiness' test allows the admission of the declarant's statements.

[A]ny inherent unreliability that accompanies co-conspirator statements made during the course and in furtherance of the conspiracy is per se rebutted by the circumstances giving rise to the long history of admitting such statements. Nonetheless, the historical underpinnings of the Confrontation Clause and the sweep of our prior confrontation cases offer one cogent reminder: It is highly unlikely that the presumptive unreliability that attaches to accomplices' confessions that shift or spread blame can be effectively rebutted when the statements are given under conditions that implicate the core concerns of the old ex parte affidavit practice—that is, when the government is involved in the statements' production, and when the statements describe past events and have not been subjected to adversarial testing.

Applying these principles, the Commonwealth's asserted guarantees of trustworthiness fail to convince us that Mark's confession was sufficiently reliable as to be admissible without allowing petitioner to cross-examine him. That other evidence at trial corroborated portions of Mark's statements is irrelevant. We have squarely rejected the notion that 'evidence corroborating the truth of a hearsay statement may properly support a finding that the statement bears 'particularized guarantees of trustworthiness.'' . . .

The Commonwealth's next proffered basis for reliability—that Mark knew he was exposing himself to criminal liability—merely restates the fact that portions of his statements were technically against penal interest. And as we have explained, such statements are suspect insofar as they inculpate other persons. . . . Similarly, the absence of an express promise of leniency to Mark does not enhance his statements' reliability to the level necessary for their untested admission. The police need not tell a person who is in custody that his statements may gain him leniency in order for the suspect to surmise that speaking up, and particularly placing blame on his cohorts, may inure to his advantage.

It is abundantly clear that neither the words that Mark spoke nor the setting in which he was questioned provides any basis for concluding that his comments regarding petitioner's guilt were so reliable that there was no need to subject them to adversarial testing in a trial setting. Mark was in custody for his involvement in, and knowledge of, serious crimes and made his statements under the supervision of governmental authorities. He was primarily responding to the officers' leading questions, which were asked without any contemporaneous cross-examination by adverse parties. Thus, Mark had a natural motive to attempt to exculpate himself as much as possible. Mark also was obviously still under the influence of alcohol. Each of these factors militates against finding that his statements were so inherently reliable that cross-examination would have been superfluous. . . .

The admission of the untested confession of Mark Lilly violated petitioner's Confrontation Clause rights. Adhering to our general custom of allowing state courts initially to assess the effect of erroneously admitted evidence in light of substantive state criminal law, we leave it to the Virginia courts to consider in the first instance whether this Sixth Amendment error was 'harmless beyond a reasonable doubt.' Accordingly, the judgment of the Supreme Court of Virginia is reversed, and the case is remanded for further proceedings."

V. JUSTICE VOTE

9 Pro ACLU Side vs. 0 Con Opposing Side

ACLU Side (Petitioner / Appellant)

1. Stevens, J. – Wrote majority opinion
2. Ginsburg, R. – Joined majority opinion
3. Breyer, S. – Wrote concurring opinion
4. Souter, D. – Joined majority opinion
5. Rehnquist, W. – Wrote concurring opinion
6. Kennedy, A. – Joined Rehnquist's concurrence
7. O'Connor, S. – Joined Rehnquist's concurrence
8. Scalia, A. – Wrote concurring opinion
9. Thomas, C. – Wrote concurring opinion

VI. A WIN OR LOSS FOR THE ACLU?

The ACLU filed as amicus curiae urging reversal of the judgment of the Virginia Supreme Court; the U.S. Supreme Court reversed and remanded in a 9-0 vote, giving the ACLU an apparent win.

867. Greater New Orleans Broadcasting Ass'n, Inc. v. United States

(Decided June 14, 1999; 527 U.S. 173)

I. ISSUE

A. Issues Discussed

First Amendment, freedoms of press, speech, and association, commercial speech

B. Legal Question Presented

Whether 18 U.S.C. § 1304 which "prohibits some, but by no means all, broadcast advertising of lotteries and casino gambling" may be applied in Louisiana where private casino gambling is legal.

C. Supreme Court's Answer

"[W]e hold that § 1304 may not be applied to advertisements of private casino gambling that are broadcast by radio or television stations located in Louisiana, where such gambling is legal."

II. CASE SUMMARY

A. Background

"Federal law prohibits some, but by no means all, broadcast advertising of lotteries and casino gambling. In United States v. Edge Broadcasting Co., 509 U.S. 418 (1993), [the Supreme Court] upheld the constitutionality of 18 U.S.C. § 1304 as applied to broadcast advertising of Virginia's lottery by a radio station located in North Carolina, where no such lottery was authorized. . . .

Petitioners are an association of Louisiana broadcasters and its members who operate FCC-licensed radio and television stations in the New Orleans metropolitan area. But for the threat of sanctions pursuant to § 1304 and the FCC's companion regulation, petitioners would broadcast promotional advertisements for gaming available at private, for-profit casinos that are lawful and regulated in both Louisiana and neighboring Mississippi. . . .

Petitioners brought this action against the United States and the FCC in the District Court for the Eastern District of Louisiana, praying for a declaration that § 1304 and the FCC's regulation violate the First Amendment as applied to them, and for an injunction preventing enforcement of the statute and the rule against them. [T]he District Court ruled in favor of the Government. The court applied the standard for assessing commercial speech restrictions set out in Central Hudson Gas & Elec. Corp. v. Public Serv. Comm'n of N.Y., 447 U.S. 557, 566, (1980) . . . .

A divided panel of the Court of Appeals for the Fifth Circuit agreed with the District Court's application of Central Hudson, and affirmed the grant of summary judgment to the Government. . . .

While the broadcasters' petition for certiorari was pending [the Supreme Court] decided 44 Liquormart, Inc. v. Rhode Island, 517 U.S. 484 (1996). Because the opinions in that case concluded that our precedent both preceding and following Posadas had applied the Central Hudson test more strictly, [the Supreme Court] granted the broadcasters' petition, vacated the judgment of the Court of Appeals, and remanded the case for further consideration.

On remand, the Fifth Circuit majority adhered to its prior conclusion. The majority recognized that at least part of the Central Hudson inquiry had 'become a tougher standard for the state to satisfy,' but held that § 1304's restriction on speech sufficiently advanced the asserted governmental interests and was not 'broader than necessary to control participation in casino gambling.'"

The Supreme Court granted certiorari to review the case again and reversed.

B. Counsel of Record / ACLU Attorney

ACLU Side (Petitioner / Appellant): Bruce J. Ennis, Jr., argued the cause for appellants.

Opposing Side (Respondent / Appellee): Deputy Solicitor General Barbara Underwood argued the cause for appellees.

III. AMICI CURIAE

ACLU Side (Petitioner / Appellant)

Brief of amici curiae filed on behalf of the National Association of Broadcasters, American Association of Advertising Agencies, the ACLU, et al., by P. Cameron De Yore, Gregory J. Kopta, Eric M. Stahl, Davis Wright, Henry L. Baumann, Jack N. Goodman, Steven A. Bookshester, Steven R. Shapiro, Anne Nobel Ervine, Jerry S. Birenz, Slade R. Metcalf, Laurence H. Winer, Xenia M. Boone, David S. J. Brown, Rene P. Milam, and Eric Rubin.

Brief of amici curiae filed on behalf of the American Advertising Federation by Richard E. Wiley, Benjamin B. Reed, Wallace S. Snyder, Jeffrey L. Perlman, and Daniel E. Troy.

Brief of amici curiae filed on behalf of the American Gaming Association by John G. Roberts, Jr., David G. Leitch, Adam K. Levin, Judy L. Patterson, and Frank J. Fahrenkopf, Jr.

Brief of amici curiae filed on behalf of the Association of National Advertisers, Inc., by John J. Walsh, Steven G. Brody, and Gilbert H. Weil.

Brief of amici curiae filed on behalf of the Institute for Justice by William H. Mellor, Clint Bolick, Matthew B. Berry, and Scott G. Bullock.

Brief of amici curiae filed on behalf of the Washington Legal Foundation by David H. Remes, Patricia A. Barald, Faith D. Kasparian, Daniel J. Popeo, and Richard A. Samp.

Opposing Side (Respondent / Appellee)

No briefs of amici curiae were filed in support of appellee.

IV. THE SUPREME COURT'S DECISION

"The operation of § 1304 and its attendant regulatory regime is so pierced by exemptions and inconsistencies that the Government cannot hope to exonerate it. Under current law, a broadcaster may not carry advertising about privately operated commercial casino gambling, regardless of the location of the station or the casino. On the other hand, advertisements for tribal casino gambling authorized by state compacts—whether operated by the tribe or by a private party pursuant to a management contract—are subject to no such broadcast ban, even if the broadcaster is located in, or broadcasts to, a jurisdiction with the strictest of antigambling policies. . . .

The FCC's interpretation and application of §§ 1304 and 1307 underscore the statute's infirmity. Attempting to enforce the underlying purposes and policy of the statute, the FCC has permitted broadcasters to tempt viewers with claims of 'Vegas-style excitement' at a commercial 'casino,' if 'casino' is part of the establishment's proper name and the advertisement can be taken to refer to the casino's amenities . . . . While we can hardly fault the FCC in view of the statute's focus on the suppression of certain types of information, the agency's practice is squarely at odds with the governmental interests asserted in this case. . . .

From what we can gather, the Government is committed to prohibiting accurate product information, not commercial enticements of all kinds, and then only when conveyed over certain forms of media and for certain types of gambling—indeed, for only certain brands of casino gambling—and despite the fact that messages about the availability of such gambling are being conveyed over the airwaves by other speakers.

Even putting aside the broadcast exemptions for arguably distinguishable sorts of gambling that might also give rise to social costs about which the Federal Government is concerned—such as state lotteries and parimutuel betting on horse and dog races—the Government presents no convincing reason for pegging its speech ban to the identity of the owners or operators of the advertised casinos. . . .

The second interest asserted by the Government—the derivative goal of 'assisting' States with policies that disfavor private casinos—adds little to its case. We cannot see how this broadcast restraint, ambivalent as it is, might directly and adequately further any state interest in dampening consumer demand for casino gambling if it cannot achieve the same goal with respect to the similar federal interest.

Furthermore, even assuming that the state policies on which the Federal Government seeks to embellish are more coherent and pressing than their federal counterpart, §1304 sacrifices an intolerable amount of truthful speech about lawful conduct when compared to all of the policies at stake and the social ills that one could reasonably hope such a ban to eliminate. . . .

Accordingly, respondents cannot overcome the presumption that the speaker and the audience, not the Government, should be left to assess the value of accurate and nonmisleading information about lawful conduct. Had the Federal Government adopted a more coherent policy, or accommodated the rights of speakers in States that have legalized the underlying conduct, this might be a different case. But under current federal law, as applied to petitioners and the messages that they wish to convey, the broadcast prohibition in 18 U.S.C. § 1304 and 47 CFR § 73.1211 (1998) violates the First Amendment. The judgment of the Court of Appeals is therefore reversed."

V. JUSTICE VOTE

9 Pro ACLU Side vs. 0 Con Opposing Side

ACLU Side (Petitioner / Appellant)

1. Stevens, J. – Wrote majority opinion
2. Ginsburg, R. – Joined majority opinion
3. Breyer, S. – Joined majority opinion
4. Souter, D. – Joined majority opinion
5. Kennedy, A. – Joined majority opinion
6. O'Connor, S. – Joined majority opinion
7. Scalia, A. – Joined majority opinion
8. Rehnquist, W. – Wrote concurring opinion
9. Thomas, C. – Wrote concurring opinion

VI. A WIN OR LOSS FOR THE ACLU?

The ACLU filed as amicus curiae urging reversal of the judgment of the Court of Appeals; the Supreme Court reversed in a 9-0 vote, giving the ACLU an apparent win.

868. Martin v. Hadix

(Decided June 21, 1999; 527 U.S. 343)

I. ISSUE

A. Issues Discussed

Criminal justice, prisons, attorney's fees, prisoners' rights

B. Legal Question Presented

How § "803(d)(3) of the Prison Litigation Reform Act of 1995 [which] places limits on the fees that may be awarded to attorneys who litigate prisoner lawsuits . . . applies to cases that were pending when the PLRA became effective on April 26, 1996."

C. Supreme Court's Answer

"We conclude that § 803(d)(3) limits attorney's fees with respect to postjudgment monitoring services performed after the PLRA's effective date but it does not so limit fees for postjudgment monitoring performed before the effective date."

II. CASE SUMMARY

A. Background

"The fee disputes before us arose out of two class action lawsuits challenging the conditions of confinement in the Michigan prison system.

[B]y 1987, [the two cases] Glover and Hadix were on parallel paths. In both cases, the District Court had concluded that the plaintiffs were entitled to postjudgment monitoring fees under 42 U.S.C. § 1988, and the parties had established a system for awarding those fees on a semiannual basis. Moreover, in both cases, the District Court had established specific market rates for awarding fees. By the time the [Prison Litigaiton Reform Act (PLRA)] was enacted, the prevailing market rate in both cases had been set at $150 per hour.

The fee landscape changed with the passage of the PLRA on April 26, 1996. The PLRA, as its name suggests, contains numerous provisions governing the course of prison litigation in the federal courts. . . . The section of the PLRA at issue here, § 803(d)(3), places a cap on the size of attorney's fees that may be awarded in prison litigation suits . . . .

Questions involving the PLRA first arose in both Glover and Hadix with respect to fee requests for postjudgment monitoring performed before the PLRA was enacted. In both cases, in early 1996, the plaintiffs submitted fee requests for work performed during the last half of 1995. These requests were still pending when the PLRA became effective on April 26, 1996. In both cases, the District Court concluded that the PLRA fee cap did not limit attorney's fees for services performed in these cases prior to the effective date of the Act. The Sixth Circuit affirmed this interpretation of the PLRA on appeal.

Fee requests next were filed in both Glover and Hadix for services performed between January 1, 1996, and June 30, 1996, a time period encompassing work performed both before and after the effective date of the PLRA. As relevant to this case, the defendant state prison officials argued that these fee requests were subject to the fee cap found in § 803(d)(3) of the PLRA, and the District Court accepted this argument in part. In nearly identical orders issued in the two cases, the court reiterated its earlier conclusion that the PLRA does not limit fees for work performed before April 26, 1996, but concluded that the PLRA fee cap does limit fees for services performed after the effective date.

The Court of Appeals for the Sixth Circuit consolidated the appeals from these orders, and, as relevant here, affirmed in part and reversed in part. According to the Court of Appeals, the PLRA's fee limitation does not apply to fee requests such as those in Hadix and Glover that relate to cases that were pending on the date of enactment."

The Supreme Court granted certiorari to review the case, affirmed in part, and reversed in part.

B. Counsel of Record / ACLU Attorney

ACLU Side (Respondent / Appellee): Deborah LaBelle argued the cause for appellees.

Opposing Side (Petitioner / Appellant): Thomas L. Casey, Solicitor General of Michigan, argued the cause for appellants.

III. AMICI CURIAE

ACLU Side (Respondent / Appellee)

Brief of amici curaie filed on behalf of the ACLU, et al., by Elizabeth Alexander, Donna H. Lee, Eric Balaban, Steven R. Shapiro, Michael J. Steinberg, and Kary L. Moss.

Opposing Side (Petitioner / Appellant)

Brief of amici curiae filed on behalf of the State of Ohio, et al., by Betty D. Montgomery, Attorney General of Ohio; and Stuart W. Harris and Todd R. Marti, Assistant Attorneys General; by L. A. Prager, Corporation Counsel of the District of Columbia; and by the Attorneys General for their respective jurisdictions as follows: Bill Pryor of Alabama, Bruce M. Botelho of Alaska, Grant Woods of Arizona, Daniel E. Lungren of California, M. Jane Brady of Delaware, Robert A. Butterworth of Florida, Thurbert E. Baker of Georgia, Robert H. Kono of Guam, Margery S. Bronster of Hawaii, Alan G. Lance of Idaho, Jim Ryan of Illinois, Jeffrey A. Modisett of Indiana, Tom Miller of Iowa, Carla J. Stovall of Kansas, Richard P. Ieyoub of Louisiana, J. Joseph Curran, Jr., of Maryland, Scott Harshbarger of Massachusetts, Hubert H. Humphrey III of Minnesota, Mike Moore of Mississippi, Joseph P. Mazurek of Montana, Don Stenberg of Nebraska, Frankie Sue Del Papa of Nevada, Peter Verniero of New Jersey, Dennis C. Vacco of New York, Michael F. Easley of North Carolina, W. A. Drew Edmondson of Oklahoma, Hardy Myers of Oregon, D. Michael Fisher of Pennsylvania, Jeffrey B. Pine of Rhode Island, Charles M. Condon of South Carolina, Mark Barnett of South Dakota, John Knox Walkup of Tennessee, Jan Graham of Utah, William H. Sorrell of Vermont, Mark L. Earley of Virginia, Christine O. Gregoire of Washington, and Darrell V. McGraw of West Virginia.

IV. THE SUPREME COURT'S DECISION

"For postjudgment monitoring performed before the effective date of the PLRA, the PLRA's attorney's fees provisions . . .

would have a retroactive effect contrary to the usual assumption that congressional statutes are prospective in operation. . . . The District Court entered orders establishing that the fees were to be awarded at prevailing market rates, and specifically set those rates . . . . Thus, when the lawyers provided these post-judgment monitoring services before the enactment of the PLRA, they worked in reasonable reliance on this fee schedule. . . . To give effect to the PLRA's fees limitations, after the fact, would 'attac[h] new legal consequences' to completed conduct. . . .

With respect to postjudgment monitoring performed after the effective date of the PLRA, by contrast, there is no retroactivity problem. On April 26, 1996, through the PLRA, the plaintiffs' attorneys were on notice that their hourly rate had been adjusted. From that point forward, they would be paid at a rate consistent with the dictates of the law. After April 26, 1996, any expectation of compensation at the pre-PLRA rates was unreasonable. There is no manifest injustice in telling an attorney performing post-judgment monitoring services that, going forward, she will earn a lower hourly rate than she had earned in the past. If the attorney does not wish to perform services at this new, lower pay rate, she can choose not to work. In other words, as applied to work performed after the effective date of the PLRA, the PLRA has future effect on future work; this does not raise retroactivity concerns.

[W]e conclude that the PLRA contains no express command about its temporal scope. Because we find that the PLRA, if applied to post-judgment monitoring services performed before the effective date of the Act, would have a retroactive effect inconsistent with our assumption that statutes are prospective, in the absence of an express command by Congress to apply the Act retroactively, we decline to do so. With respect to post-judgment monitoring performed after the effective date, by contrast, there is no retroactive effect, and the PLRA fees cap applies to such work. Accordingly, the judgment of the Court of Appeals for the Sixth Circuit is affirmed in part and reversed in part."

V. JUSTICE VOTE

2 Pro ACLU Side vs. 7 Con Opposing Side

ACLU Side (Respondent / Appellee)

1. Ginsburg, R. – Wrote opinion, concurring in part and dissenting in part
2. Stevens, J. – Joined Ginsburg's opinion

Opposing Side (Petitioner / Appellant)

1. O'Connor, S. – Wrote majority opinion
2. Rehnquist, W. – Joined majority opinion
3. Kennedy, A. – Joined majority opinion
4. Souter, D. – Joined majority opinion
5. Thomas, C. – Joined majority opinion
6. Breyer, S. – Joined majority opinion
7. Scalia, A. – Wrote concurring opinion

VI. A WIN OR LOSS FOR THE ACLU?

The ACLU filed as amicus curiae urging affirmance of the judgment of the Court of Appeals for the Sixth Circuit; the Supreme Court affirmed in part and reversed in part in a 7-2 vote, giving the ACLU an apparent loss.

869. Sutton v. United Air Lines, Inc.

(Decided June 22, 1999; 527 U.S. 471)

I. ISSUE

A. Issues Discussed

Civil rights, disability discrimination

B. Legal Question Presented

Whether "the determination of whether an individual is disabled should be made with reference to measures that mitigate the individual's impairment, including, in this instance, eyeglasses and contact lenses."

C. Supreme Court's Answer

"[W]e hold that the determination of whether an individual is disabled should be made with reference to measures that mitigate the individual's impairment, including, in this instance, eyeglasses and contact lenses. In addition, we hold that petitioners failed to allege properly that respondent 'regarded' them as having a disability within the meaning of the ADA."

II. CASE SUMMARY

A. Background

"Petitioners are twin sisters, both of whom have severe myopia. Each petitioner's uncorrected visual acuity is 20/200 or worse in her right eye and 20/400 or worse in her left eye, but '[w]ith the use of corrective lenses, each . . . has vision that is 20/20 or better.' . . .

In 1992, petitioners applied to respondent for employment as commercial airline pilots. They met respondent's basic age, education, experience, and Federal Aviation Administration certification qualifications. After submitting their applications for employment, both petitioners were invited by respondent to an interview and to flight simulator tests. Both were told during their interviews, however, that a mistake had been made in inviting them to interview because petitioners did not meet respondent's minimum vision requirement, which was uncorrected visual acuity of 20/100 or better. Due to their failure to meet this requirement, petitioners' interviews were terminated, and neither was offered a pilot position.

In light of respondent's proffered reason for rejecting them, petitioners filed a charge of disability discrimination under the ADA with the Equal Employment Opportunity Commission (EEOC). After receiving a right to sue letter, petitioners filed suit in the United States District Court for the District of Colorado, alleging that respondent had discriminated against them 'on the basis of their disability, or because [respondent] regarded [petitioners] as having a disability' in violation of the ADA. Specifically, petitioners alleged that due to their severe myopia they actually have a substantially limiting impairment or are regarded as having such an impairment, and are thus disabled under the Act.

The District Court dismissed petitioners' complaint for failure to state a claim upon which relief could be granted. [T]he Court of Appeals for the Tenth Circuit affirmed the District Court's judgment."

The Supreme Court granted certiorari to review the case and affirmed.

B. Counsel of Record / ACLU Attorney

ACLU Side (Petitioner / Appellant): Van Aaron Hughes argued the cause for appellants.

Deputy Solicitor General Edward S. Kneedler argued the cause for the United States, as amicus curiae, by special leave of Court.

Opposing Side (Respondent / Appellee): Roy T. Englert argued the cause for the appellees.

III. AMICI CURIAE

ACLU Side (Petitioner / Appellant)

Brief of amici curiae filed on behalf of the ACLU Foundation by Louis M. Bograd, Chai R. Feldblum, Steven R. Shapiro, and Matthew A. Coles.

Brief of amici curiae filed on behalf of the United States by Deputy Solicitor General Edward S. Kneedler, Solicitor General Waxman, Acting Assistant Attorney General Lee, Deputy Solicitor General Underwood, James A. Feldman, Jessica Dunsay Silver, Seth M. Galanter, C. Gregory Stewart, Paula R. Bruner, Philip B. Sklover and Carolyn L. Wheeler.

Brief of amici curiae filed on behalf of AIDS Action, et al., by Claudia Center, Sarah Colby, and Guy Wallace

Brief of amici curiae filed on behalf of the American Federation of Labor and Congress of Industrial Organizations by Jonathan P. Hiatt, Marsha S. Berzon, and Laurence Gold.

Brief of amici curiae filed on behalf of the National Employment Lawyers Association by Gary Phelan and Paula A. Brantner.

Opposing Side (Respondent / Appellee)

Brief of amici curiae filed on behalf of the Air Transport Association of America, Inc., by John J. Gallagher, Robert P. Warren, David A. Berg, Kenneth M. Willner, Neal D. Mollen, and Margaret H. Spurlin.

Brief of amici curiae filed on behalf of the Equal Employment Advisory Council, et al., by Ann Elizabeth Reesman, Corrie L. Fischel, Stephen A. Bokat, Robin S. Conrad, Sussan Mahallati Kysela, and J. Walker Henry.

Brief of amici curiae filed on behalf of LPA, Inc., by Daniel V. Yager.

Brief of amici curiae filed on behalf of the Society for Human Resource Management by Peter J. Petesch, Thomas J. Walsh, Jr., Timothy S. Bland, and David S. Harvey, Jr.

Brief of amici curiae filed on behalf of Senator Tom Harkin, et al., by Arlene B. Mayerson and Chantal M. Sampogna.

IV. THE SUPREME COURT'S DECISION

"We conclude that the complaint was properly dismissed. In reaching that result, we hold that the determination of whether an individual is disabled should be made with reference to measures that mitigate the individual's impairment, including, in this instance, eyeglasses and contact lenses. In addition, we hold that petitioners failed to allege properly that respondent 'regarded' them as having a disability within the meaning of the ADA. . . .

We conclude that respondent is correct that the approach adopted by the agency guidelines—that persons are to be evaluated in their hypothetical uncorrected state—is an impermissible interpretation of the ADA. Looking at the Act as a whole, it is apparent that if a person is taking measures to correct for, or mitigate, a physical or mental impairment, the effects of those measures—both positive and negative—must be taken into account when judging whether that person is 'substantially limited' in a major life activity and thus 'disabled' under the Act. . . .

Because the phrase 'substantially limits' appears in the Act in the present indicative verb form, we think the language is properly read as requiring that a person be presently—not potentially or hypothetically—substantially limited in order to demonstrate a disability. A 'disability' exists only where an impairment 'substantially limits' a major life activity, not where it 'might,' 'could,' or 'would' be substantially limiting if mitigating measures were not taken. A person whose physical or mental impairment is corrected by medication or other measures does not have an impairment that presently 'substantially limits' a major life activity. . . .

The definition of disability also requires that disabilities be evaluated 'with respect to an individual' and be determined based on whether an impairment substantially limits the 'major life activities of such individual.' . . .

Assuming without deciding that working is a major life activity . . . petitioners have failed to allege adequately that their poor eyesight is regarded as an impairment that substantially limits them in the major life activity of working. They allege only that respondent regards their poor vision as precluding them from holding positions as a 'global airline pilot.' . . .

Because petitioners have not alleged, and cannot demonstrate, that respondent's vision requirement reflects a belief that petitioners' vision substantially limits them, we agree with the decision of the Court of Appeals affirming the dismissal of petitioners' claim that they are regarded as disabled.

For these reasons, the judgment of the Court of Appeals for the Tenth Circuit is affirmed."

V. JUSTICE VOTE

2 Pro ACLU Side vs. 7 Con Opposing Side

ACLU Side (Petitioner / Appellant)

1. Stevens, J. – Wrote dissenting opinion
2. Breyer, S. – Wrote dissenting opinion, joined Stevens' opinion

Opposing Side (Respondent / Appellee)

1. O'Connor, S. – Wrote majority opinion
2. Rehnquist, W. – Joined majority opinion
3. Scalia, A. – Joined majority opinion
4. Kennedy, A. – Joined majority opinion
5. Souter, D. – Joined majority opinion
6. Thomas, C. – Joined majority opinion
7. Ginsburg, R. – Wrote concurring opinion

VI. A WIN OR LOSS FOR THE ACLU?

The ACLU, as amicus curiae, urged reversal of the judgment of the Court of Appeals for the Tenth Circuit; the Supreme Court affirmed in a 7-2 vote, giving the ACLU an apparent loss.

870. Kolstad v. American Dental Ass'n

(Decided June 22, 1999; 527 U.S. 526)

I. ISSUE

A. Issues Discussed

Civil rights, gender discrimination, Title VII

B. Legal Question Presented

What are "the circumstances under which punitive damages may be awarded in an action under Title VII."

C. Supreme Court's Answer

"We have concluded that an employer's conduct need not be independently 'egregious' to satisfy § 1981a's requirements for a punitive damages award, although evidence of egregious misconduct may be used to meet the plaintiff's burden of proof."

II. CASE SUMMARY

A. Background

Petitioner, Carol Kolstad, sued respondent, the American Dental Association under Title VII of the Civil Rights Act of 1964, asserting gender discrimination occurred when respondent decided to promote Tom Spangler instead of Kolstad. Petitioner alleged, and introduced evidence to show, that "the entire selection process was a sham," the "stated reasons for selecting Spangler were pretext for gender discrimination, and that Spangler had been chosen for the position before the formal selection process began. . . .

The District Court denied petitioner's request for a jury instruction on punitive damages. . . . Petitioner appealed from the District Court's decisions denying her requested jury instruction on punitive damages and her request for reinstatement and attorney's fees. Respondent cross-appealed from the denial of its motion for judgment as a matter of law. In a split decision, a panel of the Court of Appeals for the District of Columbia reversed the District Court's decision denying petitioner's request for an instruction on punitive damages. . . .

The Court of Appeals subsequently agreed to rehear the case en banc, limited to the punitive damages question. In a divided opinion, the court affirmed the decision of the District Court."

The Supreme Court granted certiorari to review the case, vacated, and remanded.

B. Counsel of Record / ACLU Attorney

ACLU Side (Petitioner / Appellant): Eric Schnapper argued the cause for appellant.

Solicitor General Waxman argued the cause for the United States, et al., as amici curiae, by special leave of Court.

Opposing Side (Respondent / Appellee): Raymond C. Fay argued the cause for appellee.

III. AMICI CURIAE

ACLU Side (Petitioner / Appellant)

Brief of amici curiae filed on behalf of the Lawyers' Committee for Civil Rights Under Law, the NAACP, the Mexican American Legal Defense and Educational Fund, the National Partnership for Women & Families, the National Women's Law Center, the National Organization for Women Legal Defense and Education Fund, and the ACLU by James M. Finberg, Jonathan D. Selbin, Joshua P. Davis, Paulina Do Amaral, Jack W. Londen, Daniel F. Kolb, Barbara R. Arnwine, Thomas J. Henderson, Richard T. Seymour, Teresa A. Ferrante, Dennis C. Hayes, Willie Abrams, Antonia Hernandez, Patricia Mendoza, Judith L. Lichtman, Amalia Rioia, Donna R. Lenhoff, Judith C. Appelbaum, Martha F. Davis, Yolanda S. Wu, and Steven R. Shapiro.

Brief of amici curiae filed on behalf of the United States, et al., by Solicitor General Waxman, Acting Assistant Attorney General Lee, Deputy Solicitor General Underwood, Patricia A. Millett, Dennis J. Dimsey, Gregory B. Friel, C. Gregory Stewart, Philip B. Sklover, Vincent J. Blackwood, and Robert J. Gregory.

Additional briefs of amici curiae were filed on behalf of the Trial Lawyers of America, the National Employment Lawyers Association, et al., and the Rutherford Institute.

Opposing Side (Respondent / Appellee)

Brief of amici curiae filed on behalf of the Equal Employment Advisory Council by Robert E. Williams and Ann Elizabeth Reesman.

Brief of amici curiae filed on behalf of the National Retail Foundation by Robert P. Joy and Robert P. Morris.

Brief of amici curiae filed on behalf of the Society for Human Resource Management by D. Gregory Valenza, Michael J. Lotito, Nancy L. O'Neill, and Roger S. Kaplan.

Brief of amici curiae filed on behalf of the Washington Legal Foundation by Michael J. Connolly, David A. Lawrence, Clifford J. Scharman, Daniel J. Popeo, and Paul D. Kamenar.

Brief of amici curiae filed on behalf of the Chamber of Commerce of the United States by Timothy B. Dyk, Daniel H. Bromberg, John B. Kennedy, Stephen A. Bokat, Sussan M. Kysela, and Robin S. Conrad.

IV. THE SUPREME COURT'S DECISION

"With the passage of the 1991 Act, Congress provided for additional remedies, including punitive damages, for certain classes of Title VII and ADA violations.

The 1991 Act limits compensatory and punitive damages awards, however, to cases of 'intentional discrimination' . . . .

Congress plainly sought to impose two standards of liability—one for establishing a right to compensatory damages and another, higher standard that a plaintiff must satisfy to qualify for a punitive award. . . .

While egregious misconduct is evidence of the requisite mental state, §1981a does not limit plaintiffs to this form of evidence, and the section does not require a showing of egregious or outrageous discrimination independent of the employer's state of mind. . . .

The employer must act with 'malice or with reckless indifference to [the plaintiffs] federally protected rights.' The terms 'malice' or 'reckless indifference' pertain to the employers knowledge that it may be acting in violation of federal law, not its awareness that it is engaging in discrimination. . . .

We have concluded that an employer's conduct need not be independently 'egregious' to satisfy §1981a's requirements for a punitive damages award, although evidence of egregious misconduct may be used to meet the plaintiff's burden of proof. We leave for remand the question whether petitioner can identify facts sufficient to support an inference that the requisite mental state can be imputed to respondent. . . .

For the foregoing reasons, the decision of the Court of Appeals is vacated, and the case is remanded for proceedings consistent with this opinion."

V. JUSTICE VOTE

7 Pro ACLU Side vs. 2 Con Opposing Side

ACLU Side (Petitioner / Appellant)

1. O'Connor, S. – Wrote majority opinion
2. Stevens, J. – Wrote opinion concurring in part and dissenting in part
3. Souter, D. – Joined Stevens' opinion
4. Ginsburg, R. – Joined Stevens' opinion
5. Breyer, S. – Joined Stevens' opinion
6. Scalia, A. – Joined majority opinion
7. Kennedy, A. – Joined majority opinion

Opposing Side (Respondent / Appellee)

1. Rehnquist, W. – Wrote opinion concurring in part and dissenting in part
2. Thomas, C. – Joined Rehnquist's opinion

VI. A WIN OR LOSS FOR THE ACLU?

The ACLU filed as amicus curiae urging reversal of the judgment of the Court of Appeals for the District of Columbia Circuit; the Supreme Court vacated and remanded in a 9-0 vote, giving the ACLU an apparent win.

871. Olmstead v. L.C. ex rel. Zimring

(Decided June 22, 1999; 527 U.S. 581)

I. ISSUE

A. Issues Discussed

Civil rights, disability discrimination

B. Legal Question Presented

"[W]hether the proscription of discrimination [in Title II of the Americans with Disabilities Act] may require placement of persons with mental disabilities in community settings rather than in institutions."

C. Supreme Court's Answer

"The answer, we hold, is a qualified yes. Such action is in order when the State's treatment professionals have determined that community placement is appropriate, the transfer from institutional care to a less restrictive setting is not opposed by the affected individual, and the placement can be reasonably accommodated, taking into account the resources available to the State and the needs of others with mental disabilities."

II. CASE SUMMARY

A. Background

"Respondents L.C. and E.W. are mentally retarded women; L.C. has also been diagnosed with schizophrenia, and E.W. with a personality disorder. Both women have a history of treatment in institutional settings. In May 1992, L.C. was voluntarily admitted to Georgia Regional Hospital at Atlanta (GRH), where she was confined for treatment in a psychiatric unit. By May 1993, her psychiatric condition had stabilized, and L. C.'s treatment team at GRH agreed that her needs could be met appropriately in one of the community-based programs the State supported. Despite this evaluation, L.C. remained institutionalized until February 1996, when the State placed her in a community-based treatment program.

E.W. was voluntarily admitted to GRH in February 1995; like L.C., E.W. was confined for treatment in a psychiatric unit. In March 1995, GRH sought to discharge E.W. to a homeless shelter, but abandoned that plan after her attorney filed an administrative complaint. By 1996, E.W.'s treating psychiatrist concluded that she could be treated appropriately in a community-based setting. She nonetheless remained institutionalized until a few months after the District Court issued its judgment in this case in 1997.

In May 1995, when she was still institutionalized at GRH, L.C. filed suit in the United States District Court for the Northern District of Georgia, challenging her continued confinement in a segregated environment. Her complaint invoked 42 U.S.C. § 1983 and provisions of the ADA, §§ 12131–12134, and named as defendants, now petitioners, the Commissioner of the Georgia Department of Human Resources, the Superintendent of GRH, and the Executive Director of the Fulton County Regional Board (collectively, the State). L.C. alleged that the State's failure to place her in a community-based program, once her treating professionals determined that such placement was appropriate, violated, inter alia, Title II of the ADA. L. C.'s pleading requested, among other things, that the State place her in a community care residential program, and that she receive treatment with the ultimate goal of integrating her into the mainstream of society. E.W. intervened in the action, stating an identical claim.

The District Court granted partial summary judgment in favor of L.C. and E.W. The court held that the State's failure to place L.C. and E.W. in an appropriate community-based treatment program violated Title II of the ADA. . . .

The Court of Appeals for the Eleventh Circuit affirmed the judgment of the District Court, but remanded for reassessment of the State's cost-based defense."

The Supreme Court granted certiorari to review the case, affirmed in part, vacated in part, and remanded.

B. Counsel of Record / ACLU Attorney

ACLU Side (Respondent / Appellee): Michael H. Gottesman argued the cause for appellees.

Irving L. Gornstein argued the cause for the United States, as amicus curiae, by special leave of Court.

Opposing Side (Petitioner / Appellant): Beverly Patricia Downing, Senior Assistant Attorney General of Georgia, argued the cause for appellants.

III. AMICI CURIAE

ACLU Side (Respondent / Appellee)

Brief of amici curiae filed on behalf of the ACLU, et al., by Laurie Webb Daniel and Steven R. Shapiro.

Brief of amici curiae filed on behalf of the United States by Irving L. Gornstein, Solicitor General Waxman, Acting Assistant Attorney General Lee, Deputy Solicitor General Underwood, Jessica Dunsay Silver, and Gregory B. Friel.

Additional briefs of amici curiae were filed on behalf of the American Association on Mental Retardation, et al., the American Psychiatric Association, et al., 58 Former State Commissioners and Directors of Mental Health and Developmental Disabilities, et al., the National Council on Disability, the National Mental Health Consumers' Self-Help Clearinghouse, et al., Dick Thornburgh, et al., People First of Georgia, et al., ADAPT, et al., and the Voice of the Retarded, et al.

Opposing Side (Petitioner / Appellant)

Brief of amici curiae filed on behalf of the State of Nevada, et al., by Frankie Sue Del Papa, Attorney General of Nevada; Anne B. Cathcart, Special Assistant Attorney General; Mike Moore, Attorney General of Mississippi; Robert E. Sanders, Assistant Attorney General; John Cornyn, Attorney General of Texas; Andy Taylor, First Assistant Attorney General; Linda S. Eads, Deputy Attorney General; and Gregory S. Coleman, Solicitor General; and by the Attorneys General for their respective States as follows: Ken L. Salazar of Colorado, Jeffrey A. Modisett of Indiana, Margery S. Bronster of Hawaii, Richard P. leyoub of Louisiana, Thomas F. Reilly of Massachusetts, Joseph P. Mazurek of Montana, Charles M. Condon of South Carolina, Paul G. Summers of Tennessee, Christine O. Gregoire of Washington, and Gay Woodhouse of Wyoming.

Brief of amici curiae filed on behalf of the National Conference of State Legislatures, et al., by Richard Ruda and James I. Crowley.

IV. THE SUPREME COURT'S DECISION

"We affirm the Court of Appeals' decision in substantial part. Unjustified isolation, we hold, is properly regarded as discrimination based on disability. But we recognize, as well, the States' need to maintain a range of facilities for the care and treatment of persons with diverse mental disabilities, and the States' obligation to administer services with an even hand. Accordingly, we further hold that the Court of Appeals' remand instruction was unduly restrictive. In evaluating a State's fundamental-alteration defense, the District Court must consider, in view of the resources available to the State, not only the cost of providing community-based care to the litigants, but also the range of services the State provides others with mental disabilities, and the State's obligation to mete out those services equitably.

[T]he State generally may rely on the reasonable assessments of its own professionals in determining whether an individual 'meets the essential eligibility requirements' for habilitation in a community-based program. Absent such qualification, it would be inappropriate to remove a patient from the more restrictive setting. Nor is there any federal requirement that community-based treatment be imposed on patients who do not desire it. In this case, however, there is no genuine dispute concerning the status of L.C. and E.W. as individuals 'qualified' for noninstitutional care: The State's own professionals determined that community-based treatment would be appropriate for L.C. and E.W., and neither woman opposed such treatment. . . .

To maintain a range of facilities and to administer services with an even hand, the State must have more leeway than the courts below understood the fundamental-alteration defense to allow. If, for example, the State were to demonstrate that it had a comprehensive, effectively working plan for placing qualified persons with mental disabilities in less restrictive settings, and a waiting list that moved at a reasonable pace not controlled by the State's endeavors to keep its institutions fully populated, the reasonable-modifications standard would be met. In such circumstances, a court would have no warrant effectively to order displacement of persons at the top of the community-based treatment waiting list by individuals lower down who commenced civil actions.

For the reasons stated, we conclude that, under Title II of the ADA, States are required to provide community-based treatment for persons with mental disabilities when the State's treatment professionals determine that such placement is appropriate, the affected persons do not oppose such treatment, and the placement can be reasonably accommodated, taking into account the resources available to the State and the needs of others with mental disabilities. The judgment of the Eleventh Circuit is therefore affirmed in part and vacated in part, and the case is remanded for further proceedings."

V. JUSTICE VOTE

6 Pro ACLU Side vs. 3 Con Opposing Side

ACLU Side (Respondent / Appellee)

1. Ginsberg, R. – Wrote majority opinion
2. Stevens, J. – Wrote concurring opinion
3. O'Connor, S. – Joined majority opinion
4, Souter, D. – Joined majority opinion
5. Kennedy, A. – Wrote concurring opinion
6. Breyer, S. – Joined Kennedy's concurrence, in part

Opposing Side (Petitioner / Appellant)

1. Thomas, C. – Wrote dissenting opinion
2. Rehnquist, W. – Joined Thomas' dissent
3. Scalia, A. – Joined Thomas' dissent

VI. A WIN OR LOSS FOR THE ACLU?

The ACLU filed as amicus curiae urging affirmance of the judgment of the Court of Appeals for the Eleventh Circuit; the Supreme Court affirmed in part, vacated in part, and remanded, in a 6-3 vote, giving the ACLU an apparent win.

872. United States v. Weatherhead

(Decided December 3, 1999; 528 U.S. 1042)

I. ISSUE

A. Issues Discussed

Governmental authority, federalism, Freedom of Information Act, First Amendment, Fifth Amendment

B. Legal Question Presented

"Whether the court of appeals erred in holding that the Freedom of Information Act's national security exemption, 5 U.S.C. 552(b)(1), does not apply to a letter sent in confidence from the government of Great Britain to the Department of Justice concerning a sensitive extradition matter, where the State Department officials' uncontested affidavits explain that disclosure and the resultant breach of the British government's trust will damage the United States' foreign relations both by impairing the United States' ability to engage in and receive confidential diplomatic communications and by impeding international law enforcement cooperation."[1]

C. Supreme Court's Answer

The case is moot and the decision in this case below must be vacated on remand.

II. CASE SUMMARY

A. Background

"Appellant Leslie R. Weatherhead ("Weatherhead") appeals under the Freedom of Information Act ("FOIA"), 5 U.S.C. § 552. The request sought a letter from the British Foreign Office to the United States Department of Justice ("Justice") related to the extradition of Sally Croft and Susan Hagan. The United States Department of State ("State Department") withheld the letter under FOIA Exemption 1, which protects classified information from disclosure. 5 U.S.C. § 552(b)(1). The district court initially ordered the letter's disclosure. The government sought reconsideration of that decision, which the district court granted after conducting in camera review and concluding that the letter contained 'highly sensitive and injurious material.'"[2]

The Court of Appeals reversed. The Supreme Court granted certiorari to review the case, vacated and remanded.

B. Counsel of Record / ACLU Attorney

ACLU Side (Respondent / Appellee): Charles J. Cooper, Andrew G. McBride, David H. Thompson, and Margaret A. Ryan filed a brief of appellee.

Opposing Side (Petitioner / Appellant): David R. Andrews, Steven Garfinkel, Solicitor General Waxman, Acting Assistant Attorney General Ogden, Deputy Solicitor General Kneedler, Assistant to the Solicitor General Patricia A. Millett, Leonard Schaitman, John P. Schnitker, and August E. Flentje filed a brief for appellant.

III. AMICI CURIAE

ACLU Side (Respondent / Appellee)

Brief of amici curiae filed on behalf of the Center for National Security Studies, the National Security Archive, the Federation of American Scientists, and the ACLU, by Kate Martin, Mark H. Lynch, Jay T. Smith, Elizabeth Snodgrass, Gregory M. Williams, Gerald J. Russello, Louis M. Bograd, and Steven R. Shapiro,

Brief of amici curiae filed on behalf of the National Association of Criminal Defense Lawyers by Christine M. Lee, Eleanor H. Smith, and Lisa B. Kemler.

Brief of amici curiae filed on behalf of the Reporters Committee for Freedom of the Press, et al., by Gregg P. Leslie, Bruce W. Sanford, Robert D. Lystad, Bruce W. Brown, and Gregory H. Kahn.

Opposing Side (Petitioner / Appellant)

No briefs of amici curiae were filed in support of appellant.

IV. THE SUPREME COURT'S DECISION

"Judgment vacated, and case remanded to the United States Court of Appeals for the Ninth Circuit with directions to order the vacation of the judgment of the United States District Court for the Eastern District of Washington to dismiss the case as moot."

V. JUSTICE VOTE

1 Pro ACLU Side vs. 8 Con Opposing Side

ACLU Side (Respondent / Appellee)

1. Scalia, A. – Dissented without an opinion

Opposing Side (Petitioner / Appellant)

1. Ginsburg, R. – Per curiam decision
2. Stevens, J. – Per curiam decision
3. O'Connor, S. – Per curiam decision
4. Thomas, C. – Per curiam decision
5. Breyer, S. – Per curiam decision
6. Souter, D. – Per curiam decision
7. Kennedy, A. – Per curiam decision
8. Rehnquist, W. – Per curiam decision

VI. A WIN OR LOSS FOR THE ACLU?

The ACLU filed as amicus curiae urging affirmance of the judgment of the Court of Appeals for the Ninth Circuit; the Supreme Court vacated and remanded in an 8-1 vote, giving the ACLU an apparent loss.

1 Brief for the Petitioners at I., United States v. Weatherhead, 528 U.S. 1042 (1999) (No, 98-1904).

2 Weatherhead v. United States, 157 F.3d 735 (9th Cir. 1998).

873. Illinois v. Wardlow

(Decided January 12, 2000; 528 U.S. 119)

I. ISSUE

A. Issues Discussed

4th Amendment

B. Legal Question Presented

Whether the officers' stop of Wardlow violated the Fourth Amendment to the Constitution.

C. Supreme Court's Answer

"We hold that the officers' stop did not violate the Fourth Amendment to the United States Constitution."

II. CASE SUMMARY

A. Background

"On September 9, 1995, Officers Nolan and Harvey were working as uniformed officers in the special operations section of the Chicago Police Department. The officers were driving the last car of a four-car caravan converging on an area known for heavy narcotics trafficking in order to investigate drug transactions. The officers were traveling together because they expected to find a crowd of people in the area, including lookouts and customers.

As the caravan passed 4035 West Van Buren, Officer Nolan observed respondent Wardlow standing next to the building holding an opaque bag. Respondent looked in the direction of the officers and fled. Nolan and Harvey turned their car southbound, watched him as he ran through the gangway and an alley, and eventually cornered him on the street. Nolan then exited his car and stopped respondent. He immediately conducted a protective patdown search for weapons because in his experience it was common for there to be weapons in the near vicinity of narcotics transactions. During the frisk, Officer Nolan squeezed the bag respondent was carrying and felt a heavy, hard object similar to the shape of a gun. The officer then opened the bag and discovered a .38-caliber handgun with five live rounds of ammunition. The officers arrested Wardlow.

The Illinois trial court denied respondent's motion to suppress, finding the gun was recovered during a lawful stop and frisk. Following a stipulated bench trial, Wardlow was convicted of unlawful use of a weapon by a felon. The Illinois Appellate Court reversed Wardlow's conviction, concluding that the gun should have been suppressed because Officer Nolan did not have reasonable suspicion sufficient to justify an investigative stop pursuant to Terry v. Ohio, 392 U. S. 1 (1968).

The Illinois Supreme Court agreed. [T]he court held that the stop and subsequent arrest violated the Fourth Amendment."

The Supreme Court granted certiorari to review the case and reversed.

B. Counsel of Record / ACLU Attorney

ACLU Side (Respondent / Appellee): James B. Koch argued the cause for appellee.

Opposing Side (Petitioner / Appellant): Richard A. Devine argued the cause for appellant.

Malcolm L. Stewart argued the cause for the United States, as amicus curiae, by special leave of Court.

III. AMICI CURIAE

ACLU Side (Respondent / Appellee)

Brief of amici curiae filed on behalf of the ACLU, et al., by Tracey Maclin, Steven R. Shapiro, Harvey Grossman, and Barbara E. Bergman.

Brief of amici curiae filed on behalf of the NAACP Legal Defense & Educational Fund, Inc., by Elaine R. Jones, Theodore M. Shaw, George H. Kendall, and Laura E. Hankins.

Brief of amici curiae filed on behalf of the Rutherford Institute by John W. Whitehead and Steven H. Aden.

Opposing Side (Petitioner / Appellant)

Brief of amici curiae filed on behalf of the United States by Malcolm L. Stewart, Solicitor General Waxman, Assistant Attorney General Robinson, Deputy Solicitor General Dreeben, and Deborah Watson.

Brief of amici curiae filed on behalf of the State of Ohio, et al., by Betty D. Montgomery, Attorney General of Ohio, Edward B. Foley, State Solicitor, Robert C. Maier and Alejandro Almaguer, Assistant Solicitors, and Thomas R. Keller, Acting Attorney General of Hawaii, and by the Attorneys General for their respective States as follows: Bill Pryor of Alabama, Ken Salazar of Colorado, M. Jane Brady of Delaware, Alan G. Lance of Idaho, Carla J. Stovall of Kansas, Richard P. Ieyoub of Louisiana, Mike Hatch of Minnesota, Michael C. Moore of Mississippi, Don Stenberg of Nebraska, Frankie Sue Del Papa of Nevada, Michael P. Easley of North Carolina, W. A. Drew Edmondson of Oklahoma, Charles M. Condon of South Carolina, Mark L. Barnett of South Dakota, and Mark L. Earley of Virginia.

Brief of amici curiae filed on behalf of the Wayne County Prosecuting Attorney by John D. O'Hair, pro se, Timothy A. Baughman, and Jeffrey Caminsky.

Brief of amici curiae filed on behalf of Americans for Effective Law Enforcement, Inc., et al., by Wayne W. Schmidt, James P. Manak, and Richard Weintraub.

Brief of amici curiae filed on behalf of the Criminal Justice Legal Foundation by Kent S. Scheidegger and Charles L. Hobson.

Brief of amici curiae filed on behalf of the National Association of Police Organizations, et al., by Stephen R. McSpadden.

IV. THE SUPREME COURT'S DECISION

"This case, involving a brief encounter between a citizen and a police officer on a public street, is governed by the analysis we first applied in Terry. In Terry, we held that an officer may, consistent with the Fourth Amendment, conduct a brief, investigatory stop when the officer has a reasonable, articulable suspicion that criminal activity is afoot. While "reasonable suspicion" is a less demanding standard than probable cause and requires a showing considerably less than preponderance of the evidence, the Fourth Amendment requires at least a minimal level of objective justification for making the stop. The officer must be able to articulate more than an 'inchoate and unparticularized suspicion or 'hunch" of criminal activity. . . .

An individual's presence in an area of expected criminal activity, standing alone, is not enough to support a reasonable, particularized suspicion that the person is committing a crime. But officers are not required to ignore the relevant characteristics of a location . . . . Accordingly, we have previously noted the fact that the stop occurred in a 'high crime area' among the relevant contextual considerations in a Terry analysis.

In this case, moreover, it was not merely respondent's presence in an area of heavy narcotics trafficking that aroused the officers' suspicion, but his unprovoked flight upon noticing the police. Our cases have also recognized that nervous, evasive behavior is a pertinent factor in determining reasonable suspicion. [T]he determination of reasonable suspicion must be based on commonsense judgments and inferences about human behavior. We conclude Officer Nolan was justified in suspecting that Wardlow was involved in criminal activity, and, therefore, in investigating further. . . .

Flight, by its very nature, is not 'going about one's business'; in fact, it is just the opposite. Allowing officers confronted with such flight to stop the fugitive and investigate further is quite consistent with the individual's right to go about his business or to stay put and remain silent in the face of police questioning.

Respondent and amici also argue that there are innocent reasons for flight from police and that, therefore, flight is not necessarily indicative of ongoing criminal activity. This fact is undoubtedly true, but does not establish a violation of the Fourth Amendment. Even in Terry, the conduct justifying the stop was ambiguous and susceptible of an innocent explanation. The officer observed two individuals pacing back and forth in front of a store, peering into the window and periodically conferring. All of this conduct was by itself lawful, but it also suggested that the individuals were casing the store for a planned robbery. Terry recognized that the officers could detain the individuals to resolve the ambiguity.

In allowing such detentions, Terry accepts the risk that officers may stop innocent people. Indeed, the Fourth Amendment accepts that risk in connection with more drastic police action; persons arrested and detained on probable cause to believe they have committed a crime may turn out to be innocent. The Terry stop is a far more minimal intrusion, simply allowing the officer to briefly investigate further. If the officer does not learn facts rising to the level of probable cause, the individual must be allowed to go on his way. But in this case the officers found respondent in possession of a handgun, and arrested him for violation of an Illinois firearms statute. No question of the propriety of the arrest itself is before us.

The judgment of the Supreme Court of Illinois is reversed . . . ."

V. JUSTICE VOTE

4 Pro ACLU Side vs. 5 Con Opposing Side

ACLU Side (Respondent / Appellee)

1. Stevens, J. – Wrote dissenting opinion
2. Souter, D. – Joined Stevens' opinion
3. Ginsburg, R. – Joined Stevens' opinion
4. Breyer, S. – Joined Stevens' opinion

Opposing Side (Petitioner / Appellant)

1. Rehnquist, W. – Wrote majority opinion
2. O'Connor, S. – Joined majority opinion
3. Scalia, A. – Joined majority opinion
4. Kennedy, A. – Joined majority opinion
5. Thomas, C. – Joined majority opinion

VI. A WIN OR LOSS FOR THE ACLU?

The ACLU, as amicus curiae, urged affirmance of the judgment of the Illinois Supreme Court; the U.S. Supreme Court reversed in a 5-4 vote, giving the ACLU an apparent loss.

874. Reno v. Condon

(Decided January 12, 2000; 528 U.S. 141)

I. ISSUE

A. Issues Discussed

Federalism, Regulation

B. B. Legal Question Presented

Whether the Driver's Privacy Protection Act of 1994 violates constitutional federalism principles.

C. Supreme Court's Answer

"We hold that in enacting [the Driver's Privacy Protection Act of 1994] Congress did not run afoul of the federalism principles enunciated in New York v. United States, 505 U. S. 144 (1992), and Printz v. United States, 521 U. S. 898 (1997)."

II. CASE SUMMARY

A. Background

"The Driver's Privacy Protection Act of 1994 (DPPA or Act), 18 U. S. C. §§ 2721–2725 (1994 ed. and Supp. IV), regulates the disclosure of personal information contained in the records of state motor vehicle departments (DMVs). . . .

State DMVs require drivers and automobile owners to provide personal information, which may include a person's name, address, telephone number, vehicle description, Social Security number, medical information, and photograph, as a condition of obtaining a driver's license or registering an automobile. Congress found that many States, in turn, sell this personal information to individuals and businesses. . . .

The DPPA establishes a regulatory scheme that restricts the States' ability to disclose a driver's personal information without the driver's consent. . . . The DPPA's ban on disclosure of personal information does not apply if drivers have consented to the release of their data. . . . The DPPA's prohibition of nonconsensual disclosures is also subject to a number of statutory exceptions. . . .

South Carolina law conflicts with the DPPA's provisions. Under that law, the information contained in the State's DMV records is available to any person or entity that fills out a form listing the requester's name and address and stating that the information will not be used for telephone solicitation. S. C. Code Ann. §§56–3–510 to 56–3–540 (Supp. 1998). South Carolina's DMV retains a copy of all requests for information from the State's motor vehicle records, and it is required to release copies of all requests relating to a person upon that person's written petition. §56–3–520. State law authorizes the South Carolina DMV to charge a fee for releasing motor vehicle information, and it requires the DMV to allow drivers to prohibit the use of their motor vehicle information for certain commercial activities. §§ 56– 3–530, 56–3–540.

Following the DPPA's enactment, South Carolina and its Attorney General, respondent Condon, filed suit in the United States District Court for the District of South Carolina, alleging that the DPPA violates the Tenth and Eleventh Amendments to the United States Constitution. The District Court concluded that the Act is incompatible with the principles of federalism inherent in the Constitution's division of power between the States and the Federal Government. The court accordingly granted summary judgment for the State and permanently enjoined the Act's enforcement against the State and its officers. The Court of Appeals for the Fourth Circuit affirmed, concluding that the Act violates constitutional principles of federalism."

The Supreme Court granted certiorari to review the case and reversed.

B. Counsel of Record / ACLU Attorney

ACLU Side (Petitioner / Appellant): Solicitor General Waxman argued the cause for appellant.

Opposing Side (Respondent / Appellee): Charlie Condon, pro se, Attorney General of South Carolina, argued the cause for appellee.

III. AMICI CURIAE

ACLU Side (Petitioner / Appellant)

Brief of amici curiae filed on behalf of the Feminist Majority Foundation, ACLU, et al., by Erwin Chemerinsky and Sara N. Love.

Brief of amici curiae filed on behalf of the Electronic Privacy Information Center by Marc Rotenberg.

Brief of amici curiae filed on behalf of the Screen Actors Guild, et al.

Opposing Side (Respondent / Appellee)

Brief of amici curiae filed on behalf of the State of Alabama, et al., by Bill Pryor, Attorney General of Alabama, John J. Park, Jr., Assistant Attorney General, and Thomas H. Odom, and by the Attorneys General for their respective States as follows: Ken Salazar of Colorado, Joseph P. Mazurek of Montana, Don Stenberg of Nebraska, Philip T. McLaughlin of New Hampshire, Michael F. Easley of North Carolina, W. A. Drew Edmondson of Oklahoma, D. Michael Fisher of Pennsylvania, Sheldon Whitehouse of Rhode Island, Jan Graham of Utah, Mark L. Earley of Virginia, and James E. Doyle of Wisconsin.

Brief of amici curiae filed on behalf of the Home School Legal Defense Association by Michael P. Farris.

Brief of amici curiae filed on behalf of the National Conference of State Legislatures, et al., by Richard Ruda and Charles A. Rothfeld.

Brief of amici curiae filed on behalf of the Pacific Legal Foundation by Anne M. Hayes and Deborah J. La Fetra.

Brief of amici curiae filed on behalf of the Washington Legal Foundation by Daniel J. Popeo and R. Shawn Gunnarson.

Brief of amici curiae filed on behalf of the Reporters Committee for Freedom of the Press, et al., by Gregg P. Leslie.

IV. THE SUPREME COURT'S DECISION

"The United States asserts that the DPPA is a proper exercise of Congress' authority to regulate interstate commerce under the Commerce Clause, U. S. Const., Art. I, § 8, cl. 3.2 The United States bases its Commerce Clause argument on the fact that the personal, identifying information that the DPPA regulates is a 'thin[g] in interstate commerce,' and that the sale or release of that information in interstate commerce is therefore a proper subject of congressional regulation. We agree with the United States' contention. The motor vehicle information which the States have historically sold is used by insurers, manufacturers, direct marketers, and others engaged in interstate commerce to contact drivers with customized solicitations. The information is also used in the stream of interstate commerce by various public and private entities for matters related to interstate motoring. Because drivers' information is, in this context, an article of commerce, its sale or release into the interstate stream of business is sufficient to support congressional regulation. . . .

But the fact that drivers' personal information is, in the context of this case, an article in interstate commerce does not conclusively resolve the constitutionality of the DPPA. In New York and Printz, we held federal statutes invalid, not because Congress lacked legislative authority over the subject matter, but because those statutes violated the principles of federalism contained in the Tenth Amendment. . . .

We agree with South Carolina's assertion that the DPPA's provisions will require time and effort on the part of state employees, but reject the State's argument that the DPPA violates the principles laid down in either New York or Printz. We think, instead, that this case is governed by our decision in South Carolina v. Baker, 485 U.S. 505 (1988). In Baker, we upheld a statute that prohibited States from issuing unregistered bonds because the law 'regulate[d] state activities,' rather than 'seek[ing] to control or influence the manner in which States regulate private parties.' . . .

Like the statute at issue in Baker, the DPPA does not require the States in their sovereign capacity to regulate their own citizens. The DPPA regulates the States as the owners of data bases. It does not require the South Carolina Legislature to enact any laws or regulations, and it does not require state officials to assist in the enforcement of federal statutes regulating private individuals. We accordingly conclude that the DPPA is consistent with the constitutional principles enunciated in New York and Printz. . . .

The judgment of the Court of Appeals is therefore reversed."

V. JUSTICE VOTE

9 Pro ACLU Side vs. 0 Con Opposing Side

ACLU Side (Petitioner / Appellant)

1. Rehnquist, W. – Wrote majority opinion
2. Kennedy, A. – Joined majority opinion
3. Breyer, S. – Joined majority opinion
4. Ginsburg, R. – Joined majority opinion

5. Souter, D. – Joined majority opinion
6. Thomas, C. – Joined majority opinion
7. O'Connor, S. – Joined majority opinion
8. Stevens, J. – Joined majority opinion
9. Scalia, A. – Joined majority opinion

VI. A WIN OR LOSS FOR THE ACLU?

The ACLU, as amicus curiae, urged reversal of the judgment of the Court of Appeals; the Supreme Court reversed in a 9-0 vote, giving the ACLU an apparent win.

875. Friends of the Earth v. Laidlaw Environmental Services

(Decided January 12, 2000; 528 U.S. 167)

I. ISSUE

A. Issues Discussed

Regulation, Mootness

B. B. Legal Question Presented

Whether this citizen-suit alleging violation of the Clean Water Act was required to be dismissed as moot after the defendant came into compliance with the Act.

C. Supreme Court's Answer

"The appellate court erred in concluding that a citizen suitor's claim for civil penalties must be dismissed as moot when the defendant, albeit after commencement of the litigation, has come into compliance."

II. CASE SUMMARY

A. Background

"This case presents an important question concerning the operation of the citizen-suit provisions of the Clean Water Act. Congress authorized the federal district courts to entertain Clean Water Act suits initiated by 'a person or persons having an interest which is or may be adversely affected.' 33 U. S. C. §§ 1365(a), (g). To impel future compliance with the Act, a district court may prescribe injunctive relief in such a suit; additionally or alternatively, the court may impose civil penalties payable to the United States Treasury. §1365(a). In the Clean Water Act citizen suit now before us, the District Court determined that injunctive relief was inappropriate because the defendant, after the institution of the litigation, achieved substantial compliance with the terms of its discharge permit. The court did, however, assess a civil penalty of $405,800. The 'total deterrent effect' of the penalty would be adequate to forestall future violations, the court reasoned, taking into account that the defendant 'will be required to reimburse plaintiffs for a significant amount of legal fees and has, itself, incurred significant legal expenses.'

The Court of Appeals vacated the District Court's order. The case became moot, the appellate court declared, once the defendant fully complied with the terms of its permit and the plaintiff failed to appeal the denial of equitable relief. '[C]ivil penalties payable to the government,' the Court of Appeals stated, 'would not redress any injury Plaintiffs have suffered.' Nor were attorneys' fees in order, the Court of Appeals noted, because absent relief on the merits, plaintiffs could not qualify as prevailing parties."

The Supreme Court granted certiorari to review the case and reversed.

B. Counsel of Record / ACLU Attorney

ACLU Side (Petitioner / Appellant): Bruce J. Terris argued the cause for appellant.

Jeffrey P. Minear argued the cause for the United States as amicus curiae, by special leave of court.

Opposing Side (Respondent / Appellee): Donald A. Cockrill argued the cause for appellee.

III. AMICI CURIAE

ACLU Side (Petitioner / Appellant)

Brief of amici curiae filed on behalf of Public Citizen and the ACLU by Colette G. Matzzie, Brian Wolfman, and Steven R. Shapiro.

Brief of amici curiae filed on behalf of the United States by Jeffrey P. Minear,

Solicitor General Waxman, Assistant Attorney General Schiffer, Deputy Solicitor General Wallace, and David C. Shilton.

Brief of amici curiae filed on behalf of the State of California, et al., by Jeremiah W. (Jay) Nixon, Attorney General of Missouri, James R. Layton, State Solicitor, Joseph P. Bindbeutel and William J. Bryan, Assistant Attorneys General, Bill Lockyer, Attorney General of California, Roderick E. Walston, Chief Assistant Attorney General, Richard M. Frank, Assistant Attorney General, and Linus Masouredis, Deputy Attorney General, and by the Attorneys General for their respective States as follows: Mark Pryor of Arkansas, M. Jane Brady of Dela- ware, James E. Ryan of Illinois, Jennifer M. Granholm of Michigan, Mike Moore of Mississippi, Patricia A. Madrid of New Mexico, Eliot Spitzer of New York, Michael F. Easley of North Carolina, Sheldon Whitehouse of Rhode Island, Paul G. Summers of Tennessee, and Christine O. Gregoire of Washington.

Brief of amici curiae filed on behalf of Americans for the Environment by John D. Echeverria.

Brief of amici curiae filed on behalf of the Natural Resources Defense Council, Inc., et al., by Michael Axline and David A. Nicholas.

Opposing Side (Respondent / Appellee)

Brief of amici curiae filed on behalf of the State of South Carolina by Charles M. Condon, Attorney General, and Kenneth P. Woodington, Senior Assistant Attorney General.

Brief of amici curiae filed on behalf of the Alliance of Automobile Manufacturers, et al., by Scott M. DuBoff, Kenneth S. Kaufman, Robin S. Conrad, David R. Case, J. Walker Henry, Jan Amundson, and Deborah Ann Hottel.

Brief of amici curiae filed on behalf of the California Association of Sanitation Agencies by Louis F. Claiborne and John Briscoe.

Brief of amici curiae filed on behalf of Hercules Inc., by Joel

Schneider and Peter L. Frattarelli.

Brief of amici curiae filed on behalf of the Washington Legal Foundation, et al., by Daniel J. Popeo and Paul D. Kamenar.

Brief of amici curiae filed on behalf of 40 California Cities, et al., by Rick W. Jarvis.

Brief of amici curiae filed on behalf of the Pacific Legal Foundation, et al., by Robin L. Rivett and M. Reed Hopper.

IV. THE SUPREME COURT'S DECISION

"The appellate court erred in concluding that a citizen suitor's claim for civil penalties must be dismissed as moot when the defendant, albeit after commencement of the litigation, has come into compliance. . . . A defendant's voluntary cessation of allegedly unlawful conduct ordinarily does not suffice to moot a case. The Court of Appeals . . . misperceived the remedial potential of civil penalties. Such penalties may serve, as an alternative to an injunction, to deter future violations and thereby redress the injuries that prompted a citizen suitor to commence litigation. . . .

The Constitution's case-or-controversy limitation on federal judicial authority, Art. III, §2, underpins both our standing and our mootness jurisprudence, but the two inquiries differ in respects critical to the proper resolution of this case, so we address them separately. Because the Court of Appeals was persuaded that the case had become moot and so held, it simply assumed without deciding that FOE had initial standing. . . . But because we hold that the Court of Appeals erred in declaring the case moot, we have an obligation to assure ourselves that FOE had Article III standing at the outset of the litigation. We therefore address the question of standing before turning to mootness. . . .

We have held that environmental plaintiffs adequately allege injury in fact when they aver that they use the affected area and are persons 'for whom the aesthetic and recreational values of the area will be lessened' by the challenged activity.

[T]he affidavits and testimony presented by FOE in this case assert that Laidlaw's discharges, and the affiant members' reasonable concerns about the effects of those discharges, directly affected those affiants' recreational, aesthetic, and economic interests. These submissions present dispositively more than the mere 'general averments' and 'conclusory allegations' found inadequate in National Wildlife Federation. . . .

Laidlaw argues next that even if FOE had standing to seek injunctive relief, it lacked standing to seek civil penalties. Here the asserted defect is not injury but redressability. . . . Laidlaw is right to insist that a plaintiff must demonstrate standing separately for each form of relief sought. . . . But it is wrong to maintain that citizen plaintiffs facing ongoing violations never have standing to seek civil penalties. . . .

It can scarcely be doubted that, for a plaintiff who is injured or faces the threat of future injury due to illegal conduct ongoing at the time of suit, a sanction that effectively abates that conduct and prevents its recurrence provides a form of redress. Civil penalties can fit that description. To the extent that they encourage defendants to discontinue current violations and deter them from committing future ones, they afford redress to citizen plaintiffs who are injured or threatened with injury as a consequence of ongoing unlawful conduct. . . .

Here, the civil penalties sought by FOE carried with them a deterrent effect that made it likely, as opposed to merely speculative, that the penalties would redress FOE's injuries by abating current violations and preventing future ones—as the District Court reasonably found when it assessed a penalty of $405,800. . . .

Satisfied that FOE had standing under Article III to bring this action, we turn to the question of mootness.

The only conceivable basis for a finding of mootness in this case is Laidlaw's voluntary conduct—either its achievement by August 1992 of substantial compliance with its NPDES permit or its more recent shutdown of the Roebuck facility. It is well settled that 'a defendant's voluntary cessation of a challenged practice does not deprive a federal court of its power to determine the legality of the practice.' '[I]f it did, the courts would be compelled to leave '[t]he defendant . . . free to return to his old ways." In accordance with this principle, the standard we have announced for determining whether a case has been mooted by the defendant's voluntary conduct is stringent: 'A case might become moot if subsequent events made it absolutely clear that the allegedly wrongful behavior could not reasonably be expected to recur.' The 'heavy burden of persua[ding]' the court that the challenged conduct cannot reasonably be expected to start up again lies with the party asserting mootness. . . .

Laidlaw also asserts, in a supplemental suggestion of mootness, that the closure of its Roebuck facility, which took place after the Court of Appeals issued its decision, mooted the case. The facility closure, like Laidlaw's earlier achievement of substantial compliance with its permit requirements, might moot the case, but—we once more reiterate—only if one or the other of these events made it absolutely clear that Laidlaw's permit violations could not reasonably be expected to recur. The effect of both Laidlaw's compliance and the facility closure on the prospect of future violations is a disputed factual matter. FOE points out, for example—and Laidlaw does not appear to contest—that Laidlaw retains its NPDES permit. These issues have not been aired in the lower courts; they remain open for consideration on remand. . . .

It is for the District Court, not this Court, to address in the first instance any request for reimbursement of costs, including fees. . . .

For the reasons stated, the judgment of the United States Court of Appeals for the Fourth Circuit is reversed, and the case is remanded for further proceedings consistent with this opinion."

V. JUSTICE VOTE

7 Pro ACLU Side vs. 2 Con Opposing Side

ACLU Side (Petitioner / Appellant)

1. Ginsburg, R. – Wrote majority opinion
2. Rehnquist, W. – Joined majority opinion
3. Kennedy, A. – Wrote concurring opinion
4. Breyer, S. – Joined majority opinion
5. Souter, D. – Joined majority opinion
6. O'Connor, S. – Joined majority opinion
7. Stevens, J. – Wrote concurring opinion

Opposing Side (Respondent / Appellee)

1. Scalia, A. – Wrote dissenting opinion
2. Thomas, C. – Joined Scalia's dissent

VI. A WIN OR LOSS FOR THE ACLU?

The ACLU, as amicus curiae, urged reversal of the judgment of the Court of Appeals; the Supreme Court reversed in a 7-2 vote, giving the ACLU an apparent win.

876. Nixon v. Shrink Missouri Government PAC

(Decided January 24, 2000; 528 U.S. 377)

I. ISSUE

A. Issues Discussed

Voting Rights

B. Legal Question Presented

"[W]hether Buckley v. Valeo, 424 U. S. 1 (1976) (per curiam), is authority for state limits on contributions to state political candidates and whether the federal limits approved in Buckley, with or without adjustment for inflation, define the scope of permissible state limitations today."

C. Supreme Court's Answer

"We hold Buckley to be authority for comparable state regulation, which need not be pegged to Buckley's dollars."

II. CASE SUMMARY

A. Background

This case concerns Missouri's political contribution statute. The challenged portion reads "'[t]o elect an individual to the office of governor, lieutenant governor, secretary of state, state treasurer, state auditor or attorney general, [[t]he amount of contributions made by or accepted from any person other than the candidate in any one election shall not exceed] one thousand dollars.' Mo. Rev. Stat. §130.032.1(1) (1998 Cum. Supp.)."

"Respondents Shrink Missouri Government PAC, a political action committee, and Zev David Fredman, a candidate for the 1998 Republican nomination for state auditor, sought to enjoin enforcement of the contribution statute as violating their First and Fourteenth Amendment rights (presumably those of free speech, association, and equal protection, al- though the complaint did not so state). Shrink Missouri gave $1,025 to Fredman's candidate committee in 1997, and another $50 in 1998. Shrink Missouri represented that, without the limitation, it would contribute more to the Fredman campaign. Fredman alleged he could campaign effectively only with more generous contributions than §130.032.1 allowed.

On cross-motions for summary judgment, the District Court sustained the statute.

. . . The Court of Appeals for the Eighth Circuit nonetheless enjoined enforcement of the law pending appeal, and ultimately reversed the District Court. Finding that Buckley had 'articulated and applied a strict scrutiny standard of review,' the Court of Appeals held that Missouri was bound to demonstrate 'that it has a compelling interest and that the contribution limits at issue are narrowly drawn to serve that interest.'"

The Supreme Court granted certiorari to review the case and reversed.

B. Counsel of Record / ACLU Attorney

ACLU Side (Respondent / Appellee): D. Bruce La Pierre argued the cause for appellee. With him on the briefs for appellees Shrink Missouri Government PAC, et al., was Patric Lester.

Deborah Goldberg, Burt Neuborne, and Gerald P. Greiman filed briefs for Joan Bray as appellee under Supreme Court Rule 12.6.

Opposing Side (Petitioner / Appellant): Jeremiah W. Nixon, Attorney General of Missouri, pro se, argued the cause for appellant. With him on the briefs were James R. Layton, State Solicitor, Paul R. Maguffee, Assistant Attorney General, Carter G. Phillips, Virginia A. Seitz, and Joseph R. Guerra.

Solicitor General Waxman argued the cause for the United States, as amicus curiae, by special leave of Court.

III. AMICI CURIAE

ACLU Side (Respondent / Appellee)

Brief of amici curiae filed on behalf of the ACLU, et al., by Joel M. Gora and Steven R. Shapiro.

Brief of amici curiae filed on behalf of the First Amendment Project of the Americans Back in Charge Foundation, et al., by Cleta D. Mitchell and Paul E. Sullivan.

Brief of amici curiae filed on behalf of Gun Owners of America, et al., by William J. Olson and John S. Miles.

Brief of amici curiae filed on behalf of the James Madison Center for Free Speech by James Bopp, Jr.

Brief of amici curiae filed on behalf of the National Right to Life PAC State Fund, et al., by Mr. Bopp.

Brief of amici curiae filed on behalf of the Pacific Legal Foundation, et al., by Sharon L. Browne.

Brief of amici curiae filed on behalf of Senator Mitch McConnell, et al., by Bobby R. Burchfield.

Brief of amici curiae filed on behalf of U. S. Term Limits, Inc., by Stephen J. Safranek.

Opposing Side (Petitioner / Appellant)

Brief of amici curiae filed on behalf of the United States by Solicitor General Waxman, Acting Assistant Attorney General Ogden, Deputy Solicitor General Underwood, Malcolm L. Stewart, Douglas N. Letter, and Michael Jay Singer.

Brief of amici curiae filed on behalf of the State of Ohio, et al., by Betty D. Montgomery, Attorney General of Ohio, Edward B. Foley, State Solicitor, David M. Gormley, Iver A. Stridiron, Acting Attorney General of the U. S. Virgin Islands, and by the Attorneys General for their respective States as follows: Barbara Ritchie of Alaska, Janet Napolitano of Arizona, Mark Pryor of Arkansas, Ken Salazar of Colorado, Richard Blumenthal of Connecticut, M. Jane Brady of Delaware, Robert A. Butterworth of Florida, Margery S. Bronster of Hawaii, Alan G. Lance of Idaho, Jeffrey A. Modisett of

Indiana, Thomas J. Miller of Iowa, Carla J. Stovall of Kansas, Albert B. Chandler III of Kentucky, Richard P. Ieyoub of Louisiana, Andrew Ketterer of Maine, J. Joseph Curran, Jr., of Maryland, Thomas F. Reilly of Massachusetts, Mike Hatch of Minnesota, Joseph P. Mazurek of Montana, Patricia A. Madrid of New Mexico, Eliot Spitzer of New York, Michael F. Easley of North Carolina, W. A. Drew Edmondson of Oklahoma, Sheldon Whitehouse of Rhode Island, Paul G. Summers of Tennessee, Jan Graham of Utah, William H. Sorrell of Vermont, and Christine O. Gregoire of Washington.

Brief of amici curiae filed on behalf of Common Cause, et al., by Roger M. Witten, Daniel H. Squire, Donald J. Simon, and Fred Wertheimer.

Brief of amici curiae filed on behalf of Public Citizen by Alan B. Morrison and David C. Vladeck.

Brief of amici curiae filed on behalf of the Secretary of State of Arkansas, et al., by Gregory Luke, John C. Bonifaz, and Brenda Wright.

Brief of amici curiae filed on behalf of Senator John F. Reed, et al., by Donald B. Verrilli, Jr., Deanne E. Maynard, and Gregory P. Magarian.

Brief of amici curiae filed on behalf of Paul Allen Beck, et al., by Evan A. Davis.

Brief of amici curiae filed on behalf of Norman Dorsen, et al., by Charles S. Sims.

IV. THE SUPREME COURT'S DECISION

"In defending its own statute, Missouri espouses those same interests of preventing corruption and the appearance of it that flows from munificent campaign contributions. Even without the authority of Buckley, there would be no serious question about the legitimacy of the interests claimed, which, after all, underlie bribery and antigratuity statutes. While neither law nor morals equate all political contributions, without more, with bribes, we spoke in Buckley of the perception of corruption 'inherent in a regime of large individual financial contributions' to candidates for public office as a source of concern 'almost equal' to quid pro quo improbity. The public interest in countering that perception was, indeed, the entire answer to the overbreadth claim raised in the Buckley case. This made perfect sense. . . .

Nor do we see any support for respondents' various arguments that in spite of their striking resemblance to the limitations sustained in Buckley, those in Missouri are so different in kind as to raise essentially a new issue about the adequacy of the Missouri statute's tailoring to serve its purposes. Here, as in Buckley, '[t]here is no indication . . . that the contribution limitations imposed by the [law] would have any dramatic[ally] adverse effect on the funding of campaigns and political associations,' and thus no showing that 'the limitations prevented candidates and political commit- tees from amassing the resources necessary for effective advocacy.' . . .

Respondents seem to assume that Buckley set a minimum constitutional threshold for contribution limits, which in dollars adjusted for loss of purchasing power are now well above the lines drawn by Missouri. But this assumption is a fundamental misunderstanding of what we held.

In Buckley, we specifically rejected the contention that $1,000, or any other amount, was a constitutional minimum below which legislatures could not regulate. [W]e referred instead to the outer limits of contribution regulation by asking whether there was any showing that the limits were so low as to impede the ability of candidates to 'amas[s] the resources necessary for effective advocacy.' We asked, in other words, whether the contribution limitation was so radical in effect as to render political association ineffective, drive the sound of a candidate's voice below the level of notice, and render contributions pointless. Such being the test, the issue in later cases cannot be truncated to a narrow question about the power of the dollar, but must go to the power to mount a campaign with all the dollars likely to be forthcoming. As Judge Gibson put it, the dictates of the First Amendment are not mere functions of the Consumer Price Index. . . .

There is no reason in logic or evidence to doubt the sufficiency of Buckley to govern this case in support of the Missouri statute. The judgment of the Court of Appeals is, accordingly, reversed, and the case is remanded for proceedings consistent with this opinion."

V. JUSTICE VOTE

3 Pro ACLU Side vs. 6 Con Opposing Side

ACLU Side (Respondent / Appellee)

1. Kennedy, A. – Wrote dissenting opinion
2. Thomas, C. – Wrote dissenting opinion
3. Scalia, A. – Joined Thomas' dissent

Opposing Side (Petitioner / Appellant)

1. Souter, D. – Wrote majority opinion
2. Rehnquist, W. – Joined majority opinion
3. Stevens, J. – Wrote concurring opinion
4. O'Connor, S. – Joined majority opinion
5. Breyer, S. – Wrote concurring opinion
6. Ginsburg, R. – Joined Breyer's concurrence

VI. A WIN OR LOSS FOR THE ACLU?

The ACLU, as amicus curiae, urged affirmance of the judgment of the Court of Appeals; the Supreme Court reversed in a 6-3 vote, giving the ACLU an apparent loss.

877. Village of Willowbrook v. Olech

(Decided February 23, 2000; 528 U.S. 562)

I. ISSUE

A. Issues Discussed

Equal Protection, Class Action Suits

B. B. Legal Question Presented

"[W]hether the Equal Protection Clause gives rise to a cause of action on behalf of a 'class of one' where the plaintiff did not allege membership in a class or group."

C. Supreme Court's Answer

"Our cases have recognized successful equal protection claims brought by a 'class of one,' where the plaintiff alleges that she has been intentionally treated differently from others similarly situated and that there is no rational basis for the difference in treatment."

II. CASE SUMMARY

A. Background

"Respondent Grace Olech and her late husband Thaddeus asked petitioner Village of Willowbrook (Village) to connect their property to the municipal water supply. The Village at first conditioned the connection on the Olechs granting the Village a 33-foot easement. The Olechs objected, claiming that the Village only required a 15-foot easement from other property owners seeking access to the water supply. After a 3-month delay, the Village relented and agreed to provide water service with only a 15-foot easement.

Olech sued the Village, claiming that the Village's demand of an additional 18-foot easement violated the Equal Protection Clause of the Fourteenth Amendment. Olech asserted that the 33-foot easement demand was 'irrational and wholly arbitrary'; that the Village's demand was actually motivated by ill will resulting from the Olechs' previous filing of an unrelated, successful lawsuit against the Village; and that the Village acted either with the intent to deprive Olech of her rights or in reckless disregard of her rights.

The District Court dismissed the lawsuit pursuant to Federal Rule of Civil Procedure 12(b)(6) for failure to state a cognizable claim under the Equal Protection Clause. Relying on Circuit precedent, the Court of Appeals for the Seventh Circuit reversed, holding that a plaintiff can allege an equal protection violation by asserting that state action was motivated solely by a "spiteful effort to 'get' him for reasons wholly unrelated to any legitimate state objective." It determined that Olech's complaint sufficiently alleged such a claim."

The Supreme Court granted certiorari to review the case and affirmed the judgment of the Court of Appeals.

B. Counsel of Record / ACLU Attorney

ACLU Side (Respondent / Appellee): John R. Wimmer argued the cause for appellee.

Irving L. Gornstein argued the cause for the United States, as amicus curiae, by special leave of court.

Opposing Side (Petitioner / Appellant): James L. DeAno argued the cause for appellant.

III. AMICI CURIAE

ACLU Side (Respondent / Appellee)

Brief of amici curiae filed on behalf of the ACLU by Harvey Grossman, Steven R. Shapiro, and Richard J. O'Brien.

Brief of amici curiae filed on behalf of the United States by Irving L. Gornstein, Solicitor General Waxman, Acting Assistant Attorney General Ogden, Deputy Solicitor General Underwood, and Mark B. Stern.

Opposing Side (Petitioner / Appellant)

Brief of amici curiae filed on behalf of the International City/County Management Association, et al., Richard Ruda, James I. Crowley, and Donald B. Ayer.

IV. THE SUPREME COURT'S DECISION

"We granted certiorari to determine whether the Equal Protection Clause gives rise to a cause of action on behalf of a 'class of one' where the plaintiff did not allege membership in a class or group.

Our cases have recognized successful equal protection claims brought by a 'class of one,' where the plaintiff alleges that she has been intentionally treated differently from others similarly situated and that there is no rational basis for the difference in treatment. In so doing, we have explained that "[t]he purpose of the equal protection clause of the Fourteenth Amendment is to secure every person within the State's jurisdiction against intentional and arbitrary discrimination, whether occasioned by express terms of a statute or by its improper execution through duly constituted agents."

That reasoning is applicable to this case. Olech's complaint can fairly be construed as alleging that the Village intentionally demanded a 33-foot easement as a condition of connecting her property to the municipal water supply where the Village required only a 15-foot easement from other similarly situated property owners. The complaint also alleged that the Village's demand was 'irrational and wholly arbitrary' and that the Village ultimately connected her property after receiving a clearly adequate 15-foot easement. These allegations, quite apart from the Village's subjective motivation, are sufficient to state a claim for relief under traditional equal protection analysis. We therefore affirm the judgment of the Court of Appeals, but do not reach the alternative theory of 'subjective ill will' relied on by that court."

V. JUSTICE VOTE

9 Pro ACLU Side vs. 0 Con Opposing Side

ACLU Side (Respondent / Appellee)

1. Souter, D. – Per curiam decision
2. Kennedy, A. – Per curiam decision
3. Thomas, C. – Per curiam decision
4. Scalia, A. – Per curiam decision
5. Rehnquist, W. – Per curiam decision
6. Stevens, J. – Per curiam decision
7. O'Connor, S. – Per curiam decision
8. Ginsburg, R. – Per curiam decision
9. Breyer, S. – Wrote concurring opinion

VI. A WIN OR LOSS FOR THE ACLU?

The ACLU, as amicus curiae, urged affirmance of the judgment of the Court of Appeals; the Supreme Court affirmed in a per curiam decision, giving the ACLU an apparent win.

878. Board of Regents of the University of Wisconsin System v. Southworth

(Decided March 22, 2000; 529 U.S. 217)

I. ISSUE

A. Issues Discussed

First Amendment, Freedom of speech

B. B. Legal Question Presented

Whether the mandatory student activity fee at the University of Wisconsin violates the First Amendment.

C. Supreme Court's Answer

"The First Amendment permits a public university to charge its students an activity fee used to fund a program to facilitate extra-curricular student speech if the program is viewpoint neutral. We do not sustain, however, the student referendum mechanism of the University's program, which appears to permit the exaction of fees in violation of the viewpoint neutrality principle. As to that aspect of the program, we remand for further proceedings."

II. CASE SUMMARY

A. Background

"Respondents are a group of students at the University of Wisconsin (hereinafter University). They brought a First Amendment challenge to a mandatory student activity fee imposed by petitioner Board of Regents of the University of Wisconsin System and used in part by the University to support student organizations engaging in political or ideological speech. Respondents object to the speech and expression of some of the student organizations. Relying upon our precedents which protect members of unions and bar associations from being required to pay fees used for speech the members find objectionable, both the District Court and the Court of Appeals invalidated the University's student fee program. The University contends that its mandatory student activity fee and the speech which it supports are appropriate to further its educational mission."

The Supreme Court granted certiorari to review the case and reversed.

B. Counsel of Record / ACLU Attorney

ACLU Side (Petitioner / Appellant): Susan K. Ullman, Assistant Attorney General of Wisconsin, argued the cause for appellant.

Opposing Side (Respondent / Appellee): Jordan W. Lorence argued the cause for appellee.

III. AMICI CURIAE

ACLU Side (Petitioner / Appellant)

Brief of amici curiae filed on behalf of the ACLU, et al., by Jon G. Furlow, Steven R. Shapiro, Elliot M. Mincberg, and Judith E. Schaeffer.

Brief of amici curiae filed on behalf of the State of New York, et al., by Eliot Spitzer, Attorney General of New York, Preeta D. Bansal, Solicitor General, Peter H. Schiff, Deputy Solicitor General, Laura Etlinger, Assistant Attorney General, and Mark B. Rotenberg, and by the Attorneys General for their respective States as follows: Mark Pryor of Arkansas, Ken Salazar of Colorado, Thurbert E. Baker of Georgia, Thomas R. Keller of Hawaii, Thomas J. Miller of Iowa, Richard P. Ieyoub of Louisiana, J. Joseph Curran, Jr., of Maryland, Thomas F. Reilly of Massachusetts, Mike Hatch of Minnesota, Joseph P. Mazurek of Montana, Michael F. Easley of North Carolina, Betty D. Montgomery of Ohio, and Paul G. Summers of Tennessee.

Brief of amici curiae filed on behalf of the State of Oregon by Hardy Myers, Attorney General, David Schuman, Deputy Attorney General, and Michael D. Reynolds, Solicitor General.

Brief of amici curiae filed on behalf of the American Council on Education, et al., by Stephen S. Dunham, Leonard M. Niehoff, and Sheldon E. Steinbach.

Brief of amici curiae filed on behalf of the American Federation of Labor and Congress of Industrial Organizations by Jonathan P. Hiatt, James B. Coppess, and Laurence Gold.

Brief of amici curiae filed on behalf of the Brennan Center for Justice at New York University School of Law by Scott D. Makar, Robert Bergen, Michael J. Frevola, and Burt Neuborne.

Brief of amici curiae filed on behalf of the Lesbian, Gay, Bisexual, and Transgender Campus Center at UW- Madison, et al., by Patricia M. Logue and Ruth E. Harlow.

Brief of amici curiae filed on behalf of the National Legal Aid Defenders Association, Student Legal Services Section, by Ned R. Jaeckle and Kathleen A. Cushing.

Brief of amici curiae filed on behalf of the National Education Association by Robert H. Chanin, Andrew D. Roth, and Michael D. Simpson.

Brief of amici curiae filed on behalf of the New York Public Interest Research Group by Alexander R. Sussman.

Brief of amici curiae filed on behalf of the Student Press Law Center, et al., by Lucy A. Dalglish.

Brief of amici curiae filed on behalf of Student Rights Law Center, Inc., by Mitchel D. Grotch.

Brief of amici curiae filed on behalf of the United States Student Association, et al., by David C. Vladeck and Alan B. Morrison.

Brief of amici curiae filed on behalf of United Council of University of Wisconsin Students, Inc., by Mark B. Hazelbaker.

Brief of amici curiae filed on behalf of the University of California Student Association by Michael S. Sorgen and Amy R. Levine.

Brief of amici curiae filed on behalf of the Wisconsin Student Public Interest Research Group, et al., by Daniel H. Squire, Craig Goldblatt, and Francisco Medina.

Opposing Side (Respondent / Appellee)

Brief of amici curiae filed on behalf of the Atlantic Legal Foundation by Martin S. Kaufman and Edwin L. Lewis III.

Brief of amici curiae filed on behalf of the American Center for Law and Justice by Jay Alan Sekulow, Mark Nathan Troobnick, and James Matthew Henderson, Sr.

Brief of amici curiae filed on behalf of the Christian Legal Society by Steven T. McFarland, Samuel B. Casey, and Thomas C. Berg.

Brief of amici curiae filed on behalf of the Family Research

Institute by Roy H. Nelson.
Brief of amici curiae filed on behalf of Liberty Counsel by Mathew D. Staver.
Brief of amici curiae filed on behalf of the National Legal Foundation by Barry C. Hodge.
Brief of amici curiae filed on behalf of the National Right to Work Legal Defense Foundation, Inc., by Raymond J. LaJeunesse, Jr.
Brief of amici curiae filed on behalf of the National Smokers Alliance by Renee Giachino.
Brief of amici curiae filed on behalf of the Pacific Legal Foundation, et al., by Deborah J. La Fetra.
Brief of amici curiae filed on behalf of the Washington Legal Foundation, et al., by Daniel E. Troy, Daniel J. Popeo, and Paul D. Kamenar.
Brief of amici curiae filed on behalf of First Freedoms Foundation by Michael D. Dean.
Brief of amici curiae filed on behalf of the Rutherford Institute by John W. Whitehead and Steven H. Aden.
Brief of amici curiae filed on behalf of Owen Brennan Rounds, et al., by Thomas H. Nelson.
Brief of amici curiae filed on behalf of Americans United for Separation of Church and State, et al., by Steven K. Green, Steven M. Freeman, and Ayesha N. Khan, in support of neither party.

IV. THE SUPREME COURT'S DECISION

"The University of Wisconsin exacts the fee at issue for the sole purpose of facilitating the free and open exchange of ideas by, and among, its students. We conclude the objecting students may insist upon certain safeguards with respect to the expressive activities which they are required to support. Our public forum cases are instructive here by close analogy. This is true even though the student activities fund is not a public forum in the traditional sense of the term and despite the circumstance that those cases most often involve a demand for access, not a claim to be exempt from supporting speech. The standard of viewpoint neutrality found in the public forum cases provides the standard we find controlling. We decide that the viewpoint neutrality requirement of the University program is in general sufficient to protect the rights of the objecting students. The student referendum aspect of the program for funding speech and expressive activities, however, appears to be inconsistent with the viewpoint neutrality requirement. . . .

If the University conditions the opportunity to receive a college education, an opportunity comparable in importance to joining a labor union or bar association, on an agreement to support objectionable, extracurricular expression by other students, the rights acknowledged in Abood and Keller become implicated. It infringes on the speech and beliefs of the individual to be required, by this mandatory student activity fee program, to pay subsidies for the objectionable speech of others without any recognition of the State's corresponding duty to him or her. Yet recognition must be given as well to the important and substantial purposes of the University, which seeks to facilitate a wide range of speech. . . .

The University may determine that its mission is well served if students have the means to engage in dynamic discussions of philosophical, religious, scientific, social, and political subjects in their extracurricular campus life outside the lecture hall. If the University reaches this conclusion, it is entitled to impose a mandatory fee to sustain an open dialogue to these ends.

The University must provide some protection to its students' First Amendment interests, however. The proper measure, and the principal standard of protection for objecting students, we conclude, is the requirement of viewpoint neutrality in the allocation of funding support. . . .

When a university requires its students to pay fees to support the extracurricular speech of other students, all in the interest of open discussion, it may not prefer some viewpoints to others. There is symmetry then in our holding here and in Rosenberger: Viewpoint neutrality is the justification for requiring the student to pay the fee in the first instance and for ensuring the integrity of the program's operation once the funds have been collected. We conclude that the University of Wisconsin may sustain the extracurricular dimensions of its programs by using mandatory student fees with viewpoint neutrality as the operational principle.

The parties have stipulated that the program the University has developed to stimulate extracurricular student expression respects the principle of viewpoint neutrality. If the stipulation is to continue to control the case, the University's program in its basic structure must be found consistent with the First Amendment. . . .

It remains to discuss the referendum aspect of the University's program. . . . A remand is necessary and appropriate to resolve this point; and the case in all events must be reexamined in light of the principles we have discussed.

The judgment of the Court of Appeals is reversed, and the case is remanded for further proceedings consistent with this opinion."

V. JUSTICE VOTE

9 Pro ACLU Side vs. 0 Con Opposing Side

ACLU Side (Petitioner / Appellant)

1. Kennedy, A. – Wrote majority opinion
2. Rehnquist, W. – Joined majority opinion
3. Ginsburg, R. – Joined majority opinion
4. Thomas, C. – Joined majority opinion
5. O'Connor, S. – Joined majority opinion
6. Scalia, A. – Joined majority opinion
7. Souter, D. – Wrote concurring opinion
8. Breyer, S. – Joined Souter's concurrence
9. Stevens, J. – Joined Souter's concurrence

VI. A WIN OR LOSS FOR THE ACLU?

The ACLU, as amicus curiae, urged reversal of the judgment of the Court of Appeals; the Supreme Court reversed in a 9-0 vote, giving the ACLU an apparent win.

879. Garner v. Jones

(Decided March 28, 2000; 529 U.S. 244)

I. ISSUE

A. Issues Discussed: Prison

Ex Post Facto Clause

B. Legal Question Presented

"[W]hether the retroactive application of a Georgia law permitting the extension of intervals between parole considerations violates the Ex Post Facto Clause."

C. Supreme Court's Answer

The retroactive application of the Georgia law does not necessarily violate the Ex Post Facto Clause. The relevant consideration "is whether the amended Georgia Rule creates a significant risk of prolonging respondent's incarceration. . . .The Court of Appeals' analysis failed to reveal whether the amendment to Rule 475-3-.05(2), in its operation, created a significant risk of increased punishment for respondent. Respondent claims he has not been permitted sufficient discovery to make this showing. The matter of adequate discovery is one for the Court of Appeals or, as need be, for the District Court in the first instance."

II. CASE SUMMARY

A. Background

"In 1974 respondent Robert L. Jones began serving a life sentence after his conviction for murder in the State of Georgia. He escaped from prison some five years later and, after being a fugitive for over two years, committed another murder. He was apprehended, convicted, and in 1982 sentenced to a second life term.

Under Georgia law, at all times relevant here, the State's Board of Pardons and Paroles (Board or Parole Board) has been required to consider inmates serving life sentences for parole after seven years. Ga. Code Ann. §42-9-45(b) (1982). The issue in this case concerns the interval between proceedings to reconsider those inmates for parole after its initial denial. At the time respondent committed his second offense, the Board's Rules required reconsiderations to take place every three years. Ga. Rules & Regs., Rule 475-3- .05(2) (1979). In 1985, after respondent had begun serving his second life sentence, the Parole Board, acting under its authority to 'set forth . . . the times at which periodic reconsideration [for parole] shall take place,' Ga. Code Ann. §42- 9-45(a) (1982), amended its Rules to provide that '[r]econsideration of those inmates serving life sentences who have been denied parole shall take place at least every eight years,' Ga. Rules & Regs., Rule 475-3-.05(2) (1985).

The Parole Board considered respondent for parole in 1989, seven years after the 1982 conviction. It denied release and, consistent with the 1985 amendment to Rule 475- 3-.05(2), reconsideration was set for 1997, eight years later. In 1991, however, the United States Court of Appeals for the Eleventh Circuit held that retroactive application of the amended Rule violated the Ex Post Facto Clause. In compliance with that decision, in effect reinstating its earlier 3-year Rule, the Parole Board reconsidered respondent's case in 1992 and in 1995. Both times parole was denied, the Board citing for its action respondent's 'multiple offenses' and the 'circumstances and nature of' the second offense.

In 1995 the Parole Board determined that our decision in California Dept. of Corrections v. Morales, 514 U. S. 499 (1995), had rejected the rationale underlying the Eleventh Circuit's decision in Akins. The Board resumed scheduling parole reconsiderations at least every eight years, and so at respondent's 1995 review it set the next consideration for 2003. Had the Board wished to do so, it could have shortened the interval, but the 8-year period was selected based on respondent's 'multiple offenses' and the 'circumstances and nature of' his second offense. Respondent, acting pro se, brought this action under Rev. Stat. §1979, 42 U. S. C. § 1983, claiming, inter alia, the amendment to Rule 475-3-.05(2) violated the Ex Post Facto Clause. . . . Respondent requested leave to conduct discovery to support his claim, but the District Court denied the motion and entered summary judgment for petitioners. . . .

The Court of Appeals reversed, finding the amended Georgia Rule distinguishable in material respects from the California law sustained in Morales."

The Supreme Court granted certiorari to review the case and reversed.

B. Counsel of Record / ACLU Attorney

ACLU Side (Respondent / Appellee): Elizabeth Thompson Kertscher argued the cause for appellee.

Opposing Side (Petitioner / Appellant): Christopher S. Brasher, Senior Assistant Attorney General of Georgia, argued the cause for appellant.

III. AMICI CURIAE

ACLU Side (Respondent / Appellee)

Brief of amici curiae filed on behalf of the ACLU, et al., by Jill A. Pryor, Steven R. Shapiro, and Gerald Weber.

Opposing Side (Petitioner / Appellant)

No briefs of amici curiae were filed on behalf of appellant.

IV. THE SUPREME COURT'S DECISION

"The States are prohibited from enacting an ex post facto law. U. S. Const., Art. I, § 10, cl. 1. One function of the Ex Post Facto Clause is to bar enactments which, by retroactive operation, increase the punishment for a crime after its commission. Retroactive changes in laws governing parole of prisoners, in some instances, may be violative of this precept. . . .

The question is whether the amended Georgia Rule creates a significant risk of prolonging respondent's incarceration. The requisite risk is not inherent in the framework of amended Rule 475-3-.05(2), and it has not otherwise been demonstrated on the record. . . .

The law changing the frequency of parole reviews is qualified in two important respects. First, the law vests the Parole Board with discretion as to how often to set an inmate's date for reconsideration, with eight years for the maximum. See Ga. Rules & Regs., Rule 475-3-.05(2) (1985) ("Reconsideration . . . shall take place at least every eight years"). Second, the Board's policies permit 'expedited parole reviews in the event of a change in their circumstance or where the Board receives new information that would warrant a sooner review.' These qualifications permit a more careful and accurate exercise of the discretion the Board has had from the outset. Rather than being required to review cases pro forma, the Board may set reconsideration dates according to the likelihood that a review will result in meaningful considerations as to whether an inmate is suitable for release. The Board's stated policy is to provide for reconsideration at 8-year intervals 'when, in the Board's determination, it is not reasonable to expect that parole would be granted during the intervening years.' The policy enables the Board to put its resources to better use, to ensure that those prisoners who should receive parole come to its attention. By concentrating its efforts on those cases identified as having a good possibility of early release, the Board's Rules might result in the release of some prisoners earlier than would have been the case otherwise.

The particular case of respondent well illustrates that the Board's Rule changes are designed for the better exercise of the discretion it had from the outset. Given respondent's criminal history, including his escape from prison and the commission of a second murder, it is difficult to see how the Board increased the risk of his serving a longer time when it decided that its parole review should be exercised after an 8-year, not a 3-year, interval. Yet if such a risk develops, respondent may, upon a showing of either 'a change in [his] circumstance[s]' or the Board's receipt of 'new information,' seek an earlier review before the 8-year interval runs its course. . . .

When the rule does not by its own terms show a significant risk, the respondent must demonstrate, by evidence drawn from the rule's practical implementation by the agency charged with exercising discretion, that its retroactive application will result in a longer period of incarceration than under the earlier rule. . . . In the case before us, respondent must show that as applied to his own sentence the law created a significant risk of increasing his punishment. This remains the issue in the case, though the general operation of the Georgia parole system may produce relevant evidence and inform further analysis on the point. . . .

On the record in this case, we cannot conclude the change in Georgia law lengthened respondent's time of actual imprisonment. . . .

The Court of Appeals' analysis failed to reveal whether the amendment to Rule 475–3–.05(2), in its operation, created a significant risk of increased punishment for respondent. Respondent claims he has not been permitted sufficient discovery to make this showing. The matter of adequate discovery is one for the Court of Appeals or, as need be, for the District Court in the first instance. The judgment of the Court of Appeals is reversed, and the case is remanded for proceedings consistent with this opinion."

V. JUSTICE VOTE

3 Pro ACLU Side vs. 6 Con Opposing Side

ACLU Side (Respondent / Appellee)

1. Souter, D. – Wrote dissenting opinion
2. Stevens, J. – Joined Souter's dissent
3. Ginsburg, R. – Joined Souter's dissent

Opposing Side (Petitioner / Appellant)

1. Kennedy, A. – Wrote majority opinion
2. Rehnquist, W. – Wrote majority opinion
3. O'Connor, S. – Joined majority opinion
4. Thomas, C. – Joined majority opinion
5. Breyer, S. – Joined majority opinion
6. Scalia, A. – Wrote concurring opinion

VI. A WIN OR LOSS FOR THE ACLU?

The ACLU, as amicus curiae, urged affirmance of the judgment of the Court of Appeals; the Supreme Court reversed in a 6-3 vote, giving the ACLU an apparent loss.

880. Florida v. J. L.

(Decided March 28, 2000; 529 U.S. 266)

I. ISSUE

A. Issues Discussed

4th Amendment

B. B. Legal Question Presented

"[W]hether an anonymous tip that a person is carrying a gun is, without more, sufficient to justify a police officer's stop and frisk of that person."

C. Supreme Court's Answer

"[A]n anonymous tip that a person is carrying a gun is [not], without more, sufficient to justify a police officer's stop and frisk of that person."

II. CASE SUMMARY

A. Background

"On October 13, 1995, an anonymous caller reported to the Miami-Dade Police that a young black male standing at a particular bus stop and wearing a plaid shirt was carrying a gun. So far as the record reveals, there is no audio recording of the tip, and nothing is known about the informant. Sometime after the police received the tip—the record does not say how long— two officers were instructed to respond. They arrived at the bus stop about six minutes later and saw three black males 'just hanging out [there].' One of the three, respondent J. L., was wearing a plaid shirt. Apart from the tip, the officers had no reason to suspect any of the three of illegal conduct. The officers did not see a firearm, and J. L. made no threatening or otherwise unusual movements. One of the officers approached J. L., told him to put his hands up on the bus stop, frisked him, and seized a gun from J. L.'s pocket. The second officer frisked the other two individuals, against whom no allegations had been made, and found nothing.

J. L., who was at the time of the frisk '10 days shy of his 16th birth[day],' was charged under state law with carrying a concealed firearm without a license and possessing a firearm while under the age of 18. He moved to suppress the gun as the fruit of an unlawful search, and the trial court granted his motion. The intermediate appellate court reversed, but the Supreme Court of

Florida quashed that decision and held the search invalid under the Fourth Amendment."

The Supreme Court granted certiorari to review the case and affirmed.

B. Counsel of Record / ACLU Attorney

ACLU Side (Respondent / Appellee): Harvey J. Sepler argued the cause for appellee.

Opposing Side (Petitioner / Appellant): Michael J. Neimand, Assistant Attorney General of Florida, argued the cause for appellant.

Irving L. Gornstein argued the cause for the United States, as amicus curiae, by special leave of court.

III. AMICI CURIAE

ACLU Side (Respondent / Appellee)

Brief of amici curiae filed on behalf of the National Association of Criminal Defense Lawyers, the ACLU, et al., by James J. Tomkovicz and Barbara E. Bergman.

Briefs of amici curiae filed on behalf of the Congress of Racial Equality, Inc., by Stefan B. Tahmassebi.

Brief of amici curiae filed on behalf of the National Rifle Association of America, et al., by Robert Dowlut and David B. Kopel.

Brief of amici curiae filed on behalf of the Rutherford Institute by John W. Whitehead and Steven H. Aden.

Opposing Side (Petitioner / Appellant)

Brief of amici curiae filed on behalf of the United States by Irving L. Gornstein, Solicitor General Waxman, Assistant Attorney General Robinson, and Deputy Solicitor General Dreeben.

Brief of amici curiae filed on behalf of Americans for Effective Law Enforcement, Inc., et al., by Wayne W. Schmidt, James P. Manak, Richard Weintraub, and Bernard J. Farber.

Brief of amici curiae filed on behalf of the Justice Coalition by Scott D. Makar.

Brief of amici curiae filed on behalf of the National Association of Police Organizations by Stephen R. McSpadden.

Brief of amici curiae filed on behalf of the State of Illinois, et al., by James E. Ryan, Attorney General of Illinois, Joel D. Bertocchi, Solicitor General, William Browers and Michael M. Glick, Assistant Attorneys General, and Dan Schweitzer, joined by the Attorneys General for their respective jurisdictions as follows: Bill Pryor of Alabama, Janet Napolitano of Arizona, Mark Pryor of Arkansas, Bill Lockyer of California, Ken Salazar of Colorado, John M. Bailey of Connecticut, M. Jane Brady of Delaware, Earl I. Anzai of Hawaii, Jeffrey A. Modisett of Indiana, Thomas J. Miller of Iowa, Carla J. Stovall of Kansas, Richard P. Ieyoub of Louisiana, J. Joseph Curran of Maryland, Jennifer M. Granholm of Michigan, Mike Hatch of Minnesota, Jeremiah W. (Jay) Nixon of Missouri, Joseph P. Mazurek of Montana, Frankie Sue Del Papa of Nevada, Philip T. McLaughlin of New Hampshire, Patricia A. Madrid of New Mexico, Michael F. Easley of North Carolina, Betty D. Montgomery of Ohio, W. A. Drew Edmondson of Oklahoma, Hardy Myers of Oregon, D. Michael Fisher of Pennsylvania, Jose A. Fuentes Agostini of Puerto Rico, Sheldon Whitehouse of Rhode Island, Charles M. Condon of South Carolina, Paul G. Summers of Tennessee, John Cornyn of Texas, Jan Graham of Utah, Christine O. Gregoire of Washington, and Gay Woodhouse of Wyoming.

IV. THE SUPREME COURT'S DECISION

"Our 'stop and frisk' decisions begin with Terry v. Ohio, 392 U. S. 1 (1968). This Court held in Terry:

'[W]here a police officer observes unusual conduct which leads him reasonably to conclude in light of his experience that criminal activity may be afoot and that the persons with whom he is dealing may be armed and presently dangerous, where in the course of investigating this behavior he identifies himself as a policeman and makes reasonable inquiries, and where nothing in the initial stages of the encounter serves to dispel his reasonable fear for his own or others' safety, he is entitled for the protection of himself and others in the area to conduct a carefully limited search of the outer clothing of such persons in an attempt to discover weapons which might be used to assault him.'

In the instant case, the officers' suspicion that J. L. was carrying a weapon arose not from any observations of their own but solely from a call made from an unknown location by an unknown caller. Unlike a tip from a known informant whose reputation can be assessed and who can be held responsible if her allegations turn out to be fabricated, 'an anonymous tip alone seldom demonstrates the informant's basis of knowledge or veracity.' As we have recognized, however, there are situations in which an anonymous tip, suitably corroborated, exhibits 'sufficient indicia of reliability to provide reasonable suspicion to make the investigatory stop.' The question we here confront is whether the tip pointing to J. L. had those indicia of reliability. . . .

The anonymous call concerning J. L. provided no predictive information and therefore left the police without means to test the informant's knowledge or credibility. That the allegation about the gun turned out to be correct does not suggest that the officers, prior to the frisks, had a reasonable basis for suspecting J. L. of engaging in unlawful conduct: The reasonableness of official suspicion must be measured by what the officers knew before they conducted their search. All the police had to go on in this case was the bare report of an unknown, unaccountable informant who neither explained how he knew about the gun nor supplied any basis for believing he had inside information about J. L. . . .

An accurate description of a subject's readily observable location and appearance is of course reliable in this limited sense: It will help the police correctly identify the person whom the tipster means to accuse. Such a tip, however, does not show that the tipster has knowledge of concealed criminal activity. The reasonable suspicion here at issue requires that a tip be reliable in its assertion of illegality, not just in its tendency to identify a determinate person. . . .

A second major argument advanced by Florida and the United States as amicus is, in essence, that the standard Terry analysis should be modified to license a 'firearm exception.' Under such an exception, a tip alleging an illegal gun would justify a stop and frisk even if the accusation would fail standard pre-search reliability testing. We decline to adopt this position. . . .

The judgment of the Florida Supreme Court is affirmed."

V. JUSTICE VOTE

9 Pro ACLU Side vs. 0 Con Opposing Side

ACLU Side (Respondent / Appellee)

1. Ginsburg, R. – Wrote majority opinion
2. Souter, D. – Joined majority opinion
3. Stevens, J. – Joined majority opinion
4. O'Connor, S. – Joined majority opinion
5. Thomas, C. – Joined majority opinion
6. Breyer, S. – Joined majority opinion
7. Scalia, A. – Joined majority opinion
8. Kennedy, A. – Wrote concurring opinion
9. Rehnquist, W. – Joined Kennedy's concurrence

VI. A WIN OR LOSS FOR THE ACLU?

The ACLU, as amicus curiae, urged affirmance of the judgment of the Florida Supreme Court; the U.S. Supreme Court affirmed in a 9-0 vote, giving the ACLU an apparent win.

881. Erie v. Pap's A. M.

(Decided March 29, 2000; 529 U.S. 277)

I. ISSUE

A. Issues Discussed

1st Amendment, Freedom of Speech

B. Legal Question Presented

"[W]hether the Pennsylvania Supreme Court properly evaluated the . . . constitutionality under the First Amendment" of a city ordinance banning public nudity.

C. Supreme Court's Answer

"We hold that Erie's ordinance is a content-neutral regulation that satisfies the four-part test of United States v. O'Brien, 391 U. S. 367 (1968)."

II. CASE SUMMARY

A. Background

"On September 28, 1994, the city council for the city of Erie, Pennsylvania, enacted Ordinance 75–1994, a public indecency ordinance that makes it a summary offense to knowingly or intentionally appear in public in a 'state of nudity.' Respondent Pap's, a Pennsylvania corporation, operated an establishment in Erie known as 'Kandyland' that featured totally nude erotic dancing performed by women. To comply with the ordinance, these dancers must wear, at a minimum, 'pasties' and a 'G-string.' On October 14, 1994, two days after the ordinance went into effect, Pap's filed a complaint against the city of Erie, the mayor of the city, and members of the city council, seeking declaratory relief and a permanent injunction against the enforcement of the ordinance.

The Court of Common Pleas of Erie County granted the permanent injunction and struck down the ordinance as unconstitutional. On cross appeals, the Commonwealth Court reversed the trial court's order.

The Pennsylvania Supreme Court granted review and reversed, concluding that the public nudity provisions of the ordinance violated respondent's rights to freedom of expression as protected by the First and Fourteenth Amendments."

The Supreme Court granted certiorari to review the case and reversed.

B. Counsel of Record / ACLU Attorney

ACLU Side (Respondent / Appellee): John H. Weston argued the cause for appellee.

Opposing Side (Petitioner / Appellant): Gregory A. Karle argued the cause for appellant.

III. AMICI CURIAE

ACLU Side (Respondent / Appellee)

Brief of amici curiae filed on behalf of the ACLU, et al., by Steven R. Shapiro, Witold J. Walczak, Bruce J. Ennis, Jr., and Paul M. Smith.

Brief of amici curiae filed on behalf of the American Association for Nude Recreation by Robert T. Page.

Brief of amici curiae filed on behalf of Deja Vu Consulting, Inc., et al., by Bradley J. Shafer.

Brief of amici curiae filed on behalf of Feminists for Free Expression by Mary D. Dorman.

Brief of amici curiae filed on behalf of the First Amendment Lawyers Association by Randall D. B. Tigue, Steven H. Swander, and Richard L. Wilson.

Brief of amici curiae filed on behalf of the Thomas Jefferson Center for Protection of Free Expression, et al., by J. Joshua Wheeler.

Brief of amici curiae filed for Bill Conte, on behalf of The Dante Project: Inferno, et al., by Jack R. Burns.

Opposing Side (Petitioner / Appellant)

Brief of amici curiae filed on behalf of Brevard County, Florida, by Scott L. Knox.

Brief of amici curiae filed on behalf of the American Liberties Institute, et al., by Frederick H. Nelson, Lonnie N. Groot, and Anthony A. Garganese.

Brief of amici curiae filed on behalf of Erie County Citizen's Coalition Against Violent Pornography by Keith O. Barrows.

Brief of amici curiae filed on behalf of Morality in Media, Inc., et al., by Paul J. McGeady, Bruce A. Taylor, and Janet M. LaRue.

Brief of amici curiae filed on behalf of the National Family Legal Foundation by Len L. Munsil.

Brief of amici curiae filed on behalf of Orange County, Florida, by Joel D. Prinsell.

Brief of amici curiae filed on behalf of the State of Kansas, et al., by Carla J. Stovall, Attorney General of Kansas, Stephen R. McAllister, State Solicitor, Betty D. Montgomery, Attorney General of Ohio, Edward B. Foley, State Solicitor, and Elise Porter, Assistant Solicitor, and by the Attorneys General for their respective States as follows: Alan G. Lance of Idaho, Richard P. Ieyoub of Louisiana, Jennifer M. Granholm of

Michigan, Mike Moore of Mississippi, Joseph P. Mazurek of Montana, Don Stenberg of Nebraska, D. Michael Fisher of Pennsylvania, Charles M. Condon of South Carolina, Paul G. Summers of Tennessee, John Cornyn of Texas, Jan Graham of Utah, and Mark L. Earley of Virginia.

IV. THE SUPREME COURT'S DECISION

"As a preliminary matter, we must address the justiciability question. "[A] case is moot when the issues presented are no longer 'live' or the parties lack a legally cognizable interest in the outcome." . . .

Here, Pap's submitted an affidavit stating that it had 'ceased to operate a nude dancing establishment in Erie.' Pap's asserts that the case is therefore moot because '[t]he outcome of this case will have no effect upon Respondent.' Simply closing Kandyland is not sufficient to render this case moot, however. Pap's is still incorporated under Pennsylvania law, and it could again decide to operate a nude dancing establishment in Erie. . . .

Here it is the plaintiff who, having prevailed below, now seeks to have the case declared moot. And it is the city of Erie that seeks to invoke the federal judicial power to obtain this Court's review of the Pennsylvania Supreme Court decision. The city has an ongoing injury because it is barred from enforcing the public nudity provisions of its ordinance. If the challenged ordinance is found constitutional, then Erie can enforce it, and the availability of such relief is sufficient to prevent the case from being moot. And Pap's still has a concrete stake in the outcome of this case because, to the extent Pap's has an interest in resuming operations, it has an interest in preserving the judgment of the Pennsylvania Supreme Court. Our interest in preventing litigants from attempting to manipulate the Court's jurisdiction to insulate a favorable decision from review further counsels against a finding of mootness here. . . .

The ordinance here . . . is on its face a general prohibition on public nudity. By its terms, the ordinance regulates conduct alone. It does not target nudity that contains an erotic message; rather, it bans all public nudity, regardless of whether that nudity is accompanied by expressive activity.

[T]he ordinance prohibiting public nudity is aimed at combating crime and other negative secondary effects caused by the presence of adult entertainment establishments like Kandyland and not at suppressing the erotic message conveyed by this type of nude dancing. Put another way, the ordinance does not attempt to regulate the primary effects of the expression, i. e., the effect on the audience of watching nude erotic dancing, but rather the secondary effects, such as the impacts on public health, safety, and welfare, which we have previously recognized are 'caused by the presence of even one such' establishment. . . .

Even if we had not already rejected the view that a ban on public nudity is necessarily related to the suppression of the erotic message of nude dancing, we would do so now because the premise of such a view is flawed. The State's interest in preventing harmful secondary effects is not related to the suppression of expression. In trying to control the secondary effects of nude dancing, the ordinance seeks to deter crime and the other deleterious effects caused by the presence of such an establishment in the neighborhood. . . .

Here, Erie's ordinance is on its face a content-neutral restriction on conduct. Even if the city thought that nude dancing at clubs like Kandyland constituted a particularly problematic instance of public nudity, the regulation is still properly evaluated as a content-neutral restriction because the interest in combating the secondary effects associated with those clubs is unrelated to the suppression of the erotic message conveyed by nude dancing.

We conclude that Erie's asserted interest in combating the negative secondary effects associated with adult entertainment establishments like Kandyland is unrelated to the suppression of the erotic message conveyed by nude dancing. The ordinance prohibiting public nudity is therefore valid if it satisfies the four-factor test from O'Brien for evaluating restrictions on symbolic speech. . . .

Applying that standard here, we conclude that Erie's ordinance is justified under O'Brien. The first factor of the O'Brien test is whether the government regulation is within the constitutional power of the government to enact. Here, Erie's efforts to protect public health and safety are clearly within the city's police powers. The second factor is whether the regulation furthers an important or substantial government interest. The asserted interests of regulating conduct through a public nudity ban and of combating the harmful secondary effects associated with nude dancing are undeniably important. . . .

The ordinance also satisfies O'Brien's third factor, that the government interest is unrelated to the suppression of free expression . . . . The fourth and final O'Brien factor—that the restriction is no greater than is essential to the furtherance of the government interest— is satisfied as well. The ordinance regulates conduct, and any incidental impact on the expressive element of nude dancing is de minimis. The requirement that dancers wear pasties and G-strings is a minimal restriction in furtherance of the asserted government interests, and the restriction leaves ample capacity to convey the dancer's erotic message. . . .

We hold, therefore, that Erie's ordinance is a content-neutral regulation that is valid under O'Brien. Accordingly, the judgment of the Pennsylvania Supreme Court is reversed, and the case is remanded for further proceedings."

V. JUSTICE VOTE

3 Pro ACLU Side vs. 6 Con Opposing Side

ACLU Side (Respondent / Appellee)

1. Stevens, J. – Wrote dissenting opinion
2. Ginsburg, R. – Joined Stevens' dissent
3. Souter, D. – Joined parts I & II of the opinion, wrote opinion concurring in part and dissenting in part

Opposing Side (Petitioner / Appellant)

1. O'Connor, S. – Wrote majority opinion
2. Rehnquist, W. – Joined majority opinion
3. Kennedy, A. – Joined majority opinion
4. Breyer, S. – Joined majority opinion
5. Scalia, A. – Wrote concurring opinion
6. Thomas, C. – Joined Scalia's concurrence

VI. A WIN OR LOSS FOR THE ACLU?

The ACLU, as amicus curiae, urged affirmance of the judgment of the Pennsylvania Supreme Court; the U.S. Supreme Court reversed in a 6-3 vote, giving the ACLU an apparent loss.

882. Williams v. Taylor

(Decided April 18, 2000; 529 U.S. 362)

I. ISSUE

A. Issues Discussed

Criminal procedure, death penalty

B. Legal Question Presented

"[W]hether Terry Williams' constitutional right to the effective assistance of counsel as defined in Strickland v. Washington, 466 U. S. 668 (1984), was violated, and whether the judgment of the Virginia Supreme Court refusing to set aside his death sentence 'was contrary to, or involved an unreasonable application of, clearly established Federal law, as determined by the Supreme Court of the United States,' within the meaning of 28 U.S.C. § 2254(d)(1)."

C. Supreme Court's Answer

"[T]he Virginia Supreme Court rendered a 'decision that was contrary to, or involved an unreasonable application of, clearly established Federal law.' Williams' constitutional right to the effective assistance of counsel as defined in Strickland v. Washington, 466 U. S. 668 (1984), was violated."

II. CASE SUMMARY

A. Background

"In September 1986, Williams was convicted of robbery and capital murder. . . .

The jury found a probability of future dangerousness and unanimously fixed Williams' punishment at death. The trial judge concluded that such punishment was 'proper' and 'just' and imposed the death sentence. The Virginia Supreme Court affirmed the conviction and sentence. . . .

In 1988 Williams filed for state collateral relief in the Danville Circuit Court. The petition was subsequently amended, and the Circuit Court (the same judge who had presided over Williams' trial and sentencing) held an evidentiary hearing on Williams' claim that trial counsel had been ineffective. Based on the evidence adduced after two days of hearings, Judge Ingram found that Williams' conviction was valid, but that his trial attorneys had been ineffective during sentencing. Among the evidence reviewed that had not been presented at trial were documents prepared in connection with Williams' commitment when he was 11 years old that dramatically described mistreatment, abuse, and neglect during his early childhood, as well as testimony that he was 'borderline mentally retarded,' had suffered repeated head injuries, and might have mental impairments organic in origin. The habeas hearing also revealed that the same experts who had testified on the State's behalf at trial believed that Williams, if kept in a 'structured environment,' would not pose a future danger to society.

Counsel's failure to discover and present this and other significant mitigating evidence was 'below the range expected of reasonable, professional competent assistance of counsel.' Counsel's performance thus 'did not measure up to the standard required under the holding of Strickland v. Washington, 466 U. S. 668 (1984), and [if it had,] there is a reasonable probability that the result of the sentencing phase would have been different.' Judge Ingram therefore recommended that Williams be granted a rehearing on the sentencing phase of his trial.

The Virginia Supreme Court did not accept that recommendation. Although it assumed, without deciding, that trial counsel had been ineffective, it disagreed with the trial judge's conclusion that Williams had suffered sufficient prejudice to warrant relief. . . .

Having exhausted his state remedies, Williams sought a federal writ of habeas corpus pursuant to 28 U. S. C. § 2254. After reviewing the state habeas hearing transcript and the state courts' findings of fact and conclusions of law, the federal trial judge agreed with the Virginia trial judge: The death sentence was constitutionally infirm. . . .

The Federal Court of Appeals reversed. It construed §2254(d)(1) as prohibiting the grant of habeas corpus relief unless the state court "decided the question by interpreting or applying the relevant precedent in a manner that reasonable jurists would all agree is unreasonable." Applying that standard, it could not say that the Virginia Supreme Court's decision on the prejudice issue was an unreasonable application of the tests developed in either Strickland or Lockhart. It explained that the evidence that Williams presented a future danger to society was 'simply overwhelming,' it endorsed the Virginia Supreme Court's interpretation of Lockhart, and it characterized the state court's understanding of the facts in this case as 'reasonable.'"

The Supreme Court granted certiorari to review the case and reversed.

B. Counsel of Record / ACLU Attorney

ACLU Side (Petitioner / Appellant): John J. Gibbons argued the cause for appellant.

Opposing Side (Respondent / Appellee): Robert Q. Harris, Assistant Attorney General of Virginia, argued the cause for appellee.

III. AMICI CURIAE

ACLU Side (Petitioner / Appellant)

Brief of amici curiae filed on behalf of the ACLU by Larry W. Yackle and Steven R. Shapiro.

Brief of amici curiae filed on behalf of the American Bar Association by Philip S. Anderson, Abe Krash, Kathleen A. Behan, and John A. Freedman.

Brief of amici curiae filed on behalf of the National Association of Criminal Defense Lawyers by John D. Cline and Lisa B. Kemler.

Brief of amici curiae filed on behalf of the Virginia College of Criminal Defense Attorneys, et al., by Gerald T. Zerkin.

Brief of amici curiae filed on behalf of Professors Lance G. Banning, et al., by Barry Levenstam and Jeffrey T. Shaw.

Brief of amici curiae filed on behalf of Marvin E. Frankel, et al., by Abner J. Mikva.

Opposing Side (Respondent / Appellee)

Brief of amici curiae filed on behalf of the State of California, et al., by Bill Lockyer, Attorney General of California, David Druliner, Chief Assistant Attorney General, Dane R. Gillette, Senior Assistant Attorney General, and Donald E. De Nicola and Ward A. Campbell, Deputy Attorneys General, joined by the Attorneys General for their respective States as follows: Bill Pryor of Alabama, Bruce M. Botelho of Alaska, Mark Pryor of Arkansas, Ken Salazar of Colorado, John M. Bailey of Connecticut, M. Jane Brady of Delaware, Robert A. Butterworth of Florida, Thurbert E. Baker of Georgia, Alan G. Lance of Idaho, James E. Ryan of Illinois, Carla Stovall of Kansas, Richard P. Ieyoub of Louisiana, J. Joseph Curran, Jr., of Maryland, Thomas F. Reilly of Massachusetts, Michael C. Moore of Mississippi, Jeremiah W. (Jay) Nixon of Missouri, Joseph P. Mazurek of Montana, Don Stenberg of Nebraska, Frankie Sue Del Papa of Nevada, John J. Farmer, Jr., of New Jersey, Patricia A. Madrid of New Mexico, Michael E. Easley of North Carolina, Heidi Heitkamp of North Dakota, Betty D. Montgomery of Ohio, W. A. Drew Edmondson of Oklahoma, Hardy Myers of Oregon, D. Michael Fisher of Pennsylvania, Charles M. Condon of South Carolina, Mark Barnett of South Dakota, Paul G. Summers of Tennessee, John Cornyn of Texas, Jan Graham of Utah, Christine O. Gregoire of Washington, and Darrell McGraw, Jr., of West Virginia.

Brief of amici curiae filed on behalf of the Criminal Justice Legal Foundation by Kent S. Scheidegger.

IV. THE SUPREME COURT'S DECISION

"The warden here contends that federal habeas corpus relief is prohibited by the amendment to 28 U. S. C. § 2254, enacted as a part of the Antiterrorism and Effective Death Penalty Act of 1996 (AEDPA).

[T]he statute directs federal courts to attend to every state-court judgment with utmost care, but it does not require them to defer to the opinion of every reasonable state-court judge on the content of federal law. If, after carefully weighing all the reasons for accepting a state court's judgment, a federal court is convinced that a prisoner's custody—or, as in this case, his sentence of death—violates the Constitution, that independent judgment should prevail. Otherwise the federal 'law as determined by the Supreme Court of the United States' might be applied by the federal courts one way in Virginia and another way in California. In light of the well-recognized interest in ensuring that federal courts interpret federal law in a uniform way, we are convinced that Congress did not intend the statute to produce such a result. . . .

In this case, Williams contends that he was denied his constitutionally guaranteed right to the effective assistance of counsel when his trial lawyers failed to investigate and to present substantial mitigating evidence to the sentencing jury. The threshold question under AEDPA is whether Williams seeks to apply a rule of law that was clearly established at the time his state-court conviction became final. That question is easily answered because the merits of his claim are squarely governed by our holding in Strickland v. Washington, 466 U. S. 668 (1984). . . .

Williams is therefore entitled to relief if the Virginia Supreme Court's decision rejecting his ineffective-assistance claim was either 'contrary to, or involved an unreasonable application of,' that established law. It was both. . . .

In our judgment, the state trial judge was correct both in his recognition of the established legal standard for determining counsel's effectiveness, and in his conclusion that the entire post-conviction record, viewed as a whole and cumulative of mitigation evidence presented originally, raised 'a reasonable probability that the result of the sentencing proceeding would have been different' if competent counsel had presented and explained the significance of all the available evidence. It follows that the Virginia Supreme Court rendered a 'decision that was contrary to, or involved an unreasonable application of, clearly established Federal law.' Williams' constitutional right to the effective assistance of counsel as defined in Strickland v. Washington, 466 U. S. 668 (1984), was violated.

Accordingly, the judgment of the Court of Appeals is reversed, and the case is remanded for further proceedings."

V. JUSTICE VOTE

6 Pro ACLU Side vs. 3 Con Opposing Side

ACLU Side (Petitioner / Appellant)

1. Stevens, J. – Wrote majority opinion
2. O'Connor, S. – Delivered the majority opinion as to Part II
3. Kennedy, A. – Wrote concurring opinion
4. Souter, D. – Joined majority opinion
5. Ginsburg, R. – Joined majority opinion
6. Breyer, S. – Joined majority opinion

Opposing Side (Respondent / Appellee)

1. Rehnquist, W. – Wrote opinion concurring in part and dissenting in part
2. Scalia, A. – Joined Rehnquist's opinion
3. Thomas, C. – Joined Rehnquist's opinion

VI. A WIN OR LOSS FOR THE ACLU?

The ACLU, as amicus curiae, urged reversal of the judgment of the Court of Appeals; the Supreme Court reversed in a 6-3 vote, giving the ACLU an apparent win.

883. Troxel v. Granville

(Decided June 5, 2000; 530 U.S. 57)

I. ISSUE

A. Issues Discussed

14th Amendment, Due Process Clause

B. Legal Question Presented

"[W]e are asked to decide whether §26.10.160(3), as applied to Tommie Granville and her family, violates the Federal Constitution."

C. Supreme Court's Answer

"We . . . hold that the application of §26.10.160(3) to Granville and her family violated her due process right to make decisions concerning the care, custody, and control of her daughters."

II. CASE SUMMARY

A. Background

"Tommie Granville and Brad Troxel shared a relationship that ended in June 1991. The two never married, but they had two daughters, Isabelle and Natalie. Jenifer and Gary Troxel are Brad's parents, and thus the paternal grandparents of Isabelle and Natalie. After Tommie and Brad separated in 1991, Brad lived with his parents and regularly brought his daughters to his parents' home for weekend visitation. Brad committed suicide in May 1993. Although the Troxels at first continued to see Isabelle and Natalie on a regular basis after their son's death, Tommie Granville informed the Troxels in October 1993 that she wished to limit their visitation with her daughters to one short visit per month.

In December 1993, the Troxels commenced the present action by filing, in the Washington Superior Court for Skagit County, a petition to obtain visitation rights with Isabelle and Natalie. The Troxels filed their petition under two Washington statutes, Wash. Rev. Code §§ 26.09.240 and 26.10.160(3) (1994). Only the latter statute is at issue in this case. Section 26.10.160(3) provides: 'Any person may petition the court for visitation rights at any time including, but not limited to, custody proceedings. The court may order visitation rights for any person when visitation may serve the best interest of the child whether or not there has been any change of circumstances.' At trial, the Troxels requested two weekends of overnight visitation per month and two weeks of visitation each summer. Granville did not oppose visitation altogether, but instead asked the court to order one day of visitation per month with no overnight stay. In 1995, the Superior Court issued an oral ruling and entered a visitation decree ordering visitation one weekend per month, one week during the summer, and four hours on both of the petitioning grandparents' birthdays.

Granville appealed, during which time she married Kelly Wynn. Before addressing the merits of Granville's appeal, the Washington Court of Appeals remanded the case to the Superior Court for entry of written findings of fact and conclusions of law. On remand, the Superior Court found that visitation was in Isabelle's and Natalie's best interests . . . .

Approximately nine months after the Superior Court entered its order on remand, Granville's husband formally adopted Isabelle and Natalie.

The Washington Court of Appeals reversed the lower court's visitation order and dismissed the Troxels' petition for visitation, holding that nonparents lack standing to seek visitation under §26.10.160(3) unless a custody action is pending. . . .

The Washington Supreme Court granted the Troxels' petition for review and, after consolidating their case with two other visitation cases, affirmed. . . . The court rested its decision on the Federal Constitution, holding that §26.10.160(3) unconstitutionally infringes on the fundamental right of parents to rear their children."

The Supreme Court granted certiorari to review the case and affirmed.

B. Counsel of Record / ACLU Attorney

ACLU Side (Respondent / Appellee): Catherine W. Smith argued the cause for appellee.

Opposing Side (Petitioner / Appellant): Mark D. Olson argued the cause for appellant.

III. AMICI CURIAE

ACLU Side (Respondent / Appellee)

Brief of amici curiae filed on behalf of the ACLU, et al., by Matthew A. Coles, Michael P. Adams, Catherine Weiss, and Steven R. Shapiro.

Brief of amici curiae filed on behalf of the American Academy of Matrimonial Lawyers by Barbara Ellen Handschu and Sanford K. Ain.

Brief of amici curiae filed on behalf of the American Center for Law and Justice by Jay Alan Sekulow, Colby May, Vincent McCarthy, and John P. Tuskey.

Brief of amici curiae filed on behalf of the Coalition for the Restoration of Parental Rights by Karen A. Wyle.

Brief of amici curiae filed on behalf of the Institute for Justice, et al., by William H. Mellor, Clint Bolick, and Scott G. Bullock.

Brief of amici curiae filed on behalf of the Center for the Original Intent of the Constitution by Michael P. Farris.

Brief of amici curiae filed on behalf of the Christian Legal Society, et al., by Kimberlee Wood Colby, Gregory S. Baylor, and Carl H. Esbeck.

Brief of amici curiae filed on behalf of the Lambda Legal Defense and Education Fund, et al., by Patricia M. Logue, Ruth E. Harlow, and Beatrice Dohrn.

Brief of amici curiae filed on behalf of the Society of Catholic Social Scientists by Stephen M. Krason and Richard W. Garnett.

Brief of amici curiae filed on behalf of Debra Hein by Stuart M. Wilder.

Brief of amici curiae filed on behalf of the Domestic Violence Project, Inc. /Safe House (Michigan), et al., by Anne L. Argiroff and Ann L. Routt.

Brief of amici curiae filed on behalf of the Center for Children's Policy Practice & Research at the University of Pennsylvania by Barbara Bennett Woodhouse.

Brief of amici curiae filed on behalf of the Northwest Women's Law Center, et al., by Cathy J. Zavis.

Brief of amici curiae filed on behalf of the National Association of Counsel for Children by Robert C. Fellmeth and Joan Hollinger.

Opposing Side (Petitioner / Appellant)

Brief of amici curiae filed on behalf of the State of Washington, et al., by Christine O. Gregoire, Attorney General of Washington, and Maureen A. Hart, Senior Assistant Attorney General, and by the Attorneys General for their respective States as follows: Mark Pryor of Arkansas, Bill Lockyer of California, Ken

Salazar of Colorado, Earl I. Anzai of Hawaii, Carla J. Stovall of Kansas, Jeremiah W. (Jay) Nixon of Missouri, Joseph P. Mazurek of Montana, John J. Farmer, Jr., of New Jersey, Heidi Heitkamp of North Dakota, Betty D. Montgomery of Ohio, and Paul G. Summers of Tennessee;

Brief of amici curiae filed on behalf of AARP, et al., by Rochelle Bobroff, Bruce Vignery, and Michael Schuster.

Brief of amici curiae filed on behalf of Grandparents United for Children's Rights, Inc., by Judith Sperling Newton and Carol M. Gapen.

Brief of amici curiae filed on behalf of the National Conference of State Legislatures, et al., by Richard Ruda and James I. Crowley.

Brief of amici curiae filed on behalf of the Grandparent Caregiver Law Center of the Brookdale Center on Aging.

IV. THE SUPREME COURT'S DECISION

"The Fourteenth Amendment provides that no State shall 'deprive any person of life, liberty, or property, without due process of law.' We have long recognized that the Amendment's Due Process Clause, like its Fifth Amendment counterpart, 'guarantees more than fair process.' The Clause also includes a substantive component that 'provides heightened protection against government interference with certain fundamental rights and liberty interests.'

The liberty interest at issue in this case—the interest of parents in the care, custody, and control of their children— is perhaps the oldest of the fundamental liberty interests recognized by this Court. . . .

Section 26.10.160(3), as applied to Granville and her family in this case, unconstitutionally infringes on that fundamental parental right. The Washington nonparental visitation statute is breathtakingly broad. According to the statute's text, '[a]ny person may petition the court for visitation rights at any time,' and the court may grant such visitation rights whenever 'visitation may serve the best interest of the child.' § 26.10.160(3) (emphases added). That language effectively permits any third party seeking visitation to subject any decision by a parent concerning visitation of the parent's children to state-court review. Once the visitation petition has been filed in court and the matter is placed before a judge, a parent's decision that visitation would not be in the child's best interest is accorded no deference. . . .

The Superior Court's order was not founded on any special factors that might justify the State's interference with Granville's fundamental right to make decisions concerning the rearing of her two daughters. To be sure, this case involves a visitation petition filed by grandparents soon after the death of their son—the father of Isabelle and Natalie—but the combination of several factors here compels our conclusion that §26.10.160(3), as applied, exceeded the bounds of the Due Process Clause.

[T]he Troxels did not allege, and no court has found, that Granville was an unfit parent. That aspect of the case is important, for there is a presumption that fit parents act in the best interests of their children. . . .

The judge's comments suggest that he presumed the grandparents' request should be granted unless the children would be 'impact[ed] adversely.' In effect, the judge placed on Granville, the fit custodial parent, the burden of disproving that visitation would be in the best interest of her daughters. . . .

The decisional framework employed by the Superior Court directly contravened the traditional presumption that a fit parent will act in the best interest of his or her child. . . .

We therefore hold that the application of §26.10.160(3) to Granville and her family violated her due process right to make decisions concerning the care, custody, and control of her daughters.

Accordingly, the judgment of the Washington Supreme Court is affirmed."

V. JUSTICE VOTE

6 Pro ACLU Side vs. 3 Con Opposing Side

ACLU Side (Respondent / Appellee)

1. O'Connor, S. – Wrote majority opinion
2. Rehnquist, W. – Joined majority opinion
3. Ginsburg, R. – Joined majority opinion
4. Breyer, S. – Joined majority opinion
5. Souter, D. – Wrote concurring opinion
6. Thomas, C. – Wrote concurring opinion

Opposing Side (Petitioner / Appellant)

1. Stevens, J. – Wrote dissenting opinion
2. Scalia, A. – Wrote dissenting opinion
3. Kennedy, A. – Wrote dissenting opinion

VI. A WIN OR LOSS FOR THE ACLU?

The ACLU, as amicus curiae, urged affirmance of the judgment of the Washington Supreme Court; the U.S. Supreme Court affirmed in a 6-3 vote, giving the ACLU an apparent win.

884. Reeves v. Sanderson Plumbing Products, Inc.

(Decided June 12, 2000; 530 U.S. 133)

I. ISSUE

A. Issues Discussed

Civil procedure, Employment

B. Legal Question Presented

"[W]e must resolve whether a defendant is entitled to judgment as a matter of law when the plaintiff's case consists exclusively of a prima facie case of discrimination and sufficient evidence for the trier of fact to disbelieve the defendant's legitimate, nondiscriminatory explanation for its action. We must also decide whether the employer was entitled to judgment as a matter of law under the particular circumstances presented here."

C. Supreme Court's Answer

"[A] plaintiff's prima facie case of discrimination (as defined in McDonnell Douglas Corp. v. Green, 411 U. S. 792, 802 (1973)), combined with sufficient evidence for a reasonable factfinder to reject the employer's nondiscriminatory explanation for its decision, is adequate to sustain a finding of liability for intentional discrimination. Given that petitioner established a prima facie case of discrimination, introduced enough evidence for the jury to reject respondent's explanation, and produced additional evidence of age-based animus, there was sufficient evidence for the jury to find that respondent had intentionally discriminated."

II. CASE SUMMARY

A. Background

"In October 1995, petitioner Roger Reeves was 57 years old and had spent 40 years in the employ of respondent, Sanderson Plumbing Products, Inc., a manufacturer of toilet seats and covers. Petitioner worked in a department known as the 'Hinge Room,' where he supervised the 'regular line.' Joe Oswalt, in his mid-thirties, supervised the Hinge Room's 'special line,' and Russell Caldwell, the manager of the Hinge Room and age 45, supervised both petitioner and Oswalt. Petitioner's responsibilities included recording the attendance and hours of those under his supervision, and reviewing a weekly report that listed the hours worked by each employee.

In the summer of 1995, Caldwell informed Powe Chesnut, the director of manufacturing and the husband of company president Sandra Sanderson, that 'production was down' in the Hinge Room because employees were often absent and were 'coming in late and leaving early.' Because the monthly attendance reports did not indicate a problem, Chesnut ordered an audit of the Hinge Room's timesheets for July, August, and September of that year. According to Chesnut's testimony, that investigation revealed 'numerous timekeeping errors and misrepresentations on the part of Caldwell, Reeves, and Oswalt.' Following the audit, Chesnut, along with Dana Jester, vice president of human resources, and Tom Whitaker, vice president of operations, recommended to company president Sanderson that petitioner and Caldwell be fired. In October 1995, Sanderson followed the recommendation and discharged both petitioner and Caldwell.

In June 1996, petitioner filed suit in the United States District Court for the Northern District of Mississippi, contending that he had been fired because of his age in violation of the Age Discrimination in Employment Act of 1967 (ADEA), 81 Stat. 602, as amended, 29 U. S. C. § 621 et seq. At trial, respondent contended that it had fired petitioner due to his failure to maintain accurate attendance records, while petitioner attempted to demonstrate that respondent's explanation was pretext for age discrimination. Petitioner introduced evidence that he had accurately recorded the attendance and hours of the employees under his supervision, and that Chesnut, whom Oswalt described as wielding 'absolute power' within the company, had demonstrated age-based animus in his dealings with petitioner.

During the trial, the District Court twice denied oral motions by respondent for judgment as a matter of law under Rule 50 of the Federal Rules of Civil Procedure, and the case went to the jury. The court instructed the jury that '[i]f the plaintiff fails to prove age was a determinative or motivating factor in the decision to terminate him, then your verdict shall be for the defendant.' So charged, the jury returned a verdict in favor of petitioner, awarding him $35,000 in compensatory damages, and found that respondent's age discrimination had been 'willfu[l].' The District Court accordingly entered judgment for petitioner in the amount of $70,000, which included $35,000 in liquidated damages based on the jury's finding of willfulness. Respondent then renewed its motion for judgment as a matter of law and alternatively moved for a new trial, while petitioner moved for front pay. The District Court denied respondent's motions and granted petitioner's, awarding him $28,490.80 in front pay for two years' lost income.

The Court of Appeals for the Fifth Circuit reversed, holding that petitioner had not introduced sufficient evidence to sustain the jury's finding of unlawful discrimination. After noting respondent's proffered justification for petitioner's discharge, the court acknowledged that petitioner 'very well may' have offered sufficient evidence for 'a reasonable jury [to] have found that [respondent's] explanation for its employment decision was pretextual.' The court explained, however, that this was 'not dispositive' of the ultimate issue—namely, 'whether Reeves presented sufficient evidence that his age motivated [respondent's] employment decision.' Addressing this question, the court weighed petitioner's additional evidence of discrimination against other circumstances surrounding his discharge. Specifically, the court noted that Chesnut's age-based comments 'were not made in the direct context of Reeves's termination'; there was no allegation that the two other individuals who had recommended that petitioner be fired (Jester and Whitaker) were motivated by age; two of the decisionmakers involved in petitioner's discharge (Jester and Sanderson) were over the age of 50; all three of the Hinge Room supervisors were accused of inaccurate recordkeeping; and several of respondent's management positions were filled by persons over age 50 when petitioner was fired. On this basis, the court concluded that petitioner had not introduced sufficient evidence for a rational jury to conclude that he had been discharged because of his age."

The Supreme Court granted certiorari to review the case and reversed.

B. Counsel of Record / ACLU Attorney

ACLU Side (Petitioner / Appellant): Jim Waide argued the cause for appellant.

Patricia A. Millett argued the cause for the United States, et al., as amici curiae, by special leave of court.

Opposing Side (Respondent / Appellee): Taylor B. Smith argued the cause for the appellee.

III. AMICI CURIAE

ACLU Side (Petitioner / Appellant)

Brief of amici curiae filed on behalf of the Lawyers' Committee For Civil Rights under Law; NAACP Legal Defense & Educational Fund, Inc., National Association for the Advancement of Colored People; Mexican American Legal Defense and Educational Fund; National Partnership for Women & Families; National Women's Law Center; NOW Legal Defense and Education Fund; and ACLU, by Daniel F. Kolb, Norman Redlich, Barbara R. Arnwine, Thomas J. Henderson, Richard T. Seymour, Teresa A. Ferrante, Elainy

R. Jones, Theodore M. Shaw, Norman J. Chachkin, Charles Stephen Ralston, Dennis C. Hayes, Antonia Hernandez, Judith L. Lichtman, Donna R. Lenhoff, Marcia D. Greenberger, Judith C. Appelbaum, Martha F. Davis, Sara L. Mandelbaum, and Steven R. Shapiro.

Brief of amici curiae filed on behalf of the United States, et al., by Patricia A. Millett, Solicitor General Waxman, Deputy Solicitor General Underwood, Matthew D. Roberts, C. Gregory Stewart, and Philip B. Sklover.

Brief of amici curiae filed on behalf of the AARP by Thomas W. Osborne, Laurie A. McCann, Sally Dunaway, and Melvin Radowitz.

Brief of amici curiae filed on behalf of the Association of Trial Lawyers of America by Jeffrey Robert White.

Brief of amici curiae filed on behalf of the Hispanic National Bar Association by Seth J. Benezra, Luis Perez, and Gilbert M. Roman.

Brief of amici curiae filed on behalf of the National Employment Lawyers Association by Paul W. Mollica and Paula A. Brantner.

Opposing Side (Respondent / Appellee)

Brief of amici curiae filed on behalf of the Alabama Retail Association by John J. Coleman III and Marcel L. Debruge.

Brief of amici curiae filed on behalf of the Chamber of Commerce of the United States by Marshall B. Babson, Stanley Strauss, Stephen A. Bokat, and Robin S. Conrad.

Brief of amici curiae filed on behalf of the Equal Employment Advisory Council by Ann Elizabeth Reesman.

Brief of amici curiae filed on behalf of the Product Liability Advisory Council, Inc., by Andrew L. Frey, Charles Rothfeld, and Stephen M. Shapiro.

Brief of amici curiae filed on behalf of the Society for Human Resource Management by Peter J. Petesch, Thomas J. Walsh, Jr., Timothy S. Bland, and John E. Duvall.

Brief of amici curiae filed on behalf of the Texas Association of Business and Chamber of Commerce by Dean J. Schaner and Scott M. Nelson.

IV. THE SUPREME COURT'S DECISION

"Under the ADEA, it is 'unlawful for an employer . . . to fail or refuse to hire or to discharge any individual or otherwise discriminate against any individual with respect to his compensation, terms, conditions, or privileges of employment, because of such individual's age.' 29 U. S. C. § 623(a)(1). When a plaintiff alleges disparate treatment, 'liability depends on whether the protected trait (under the ADEA, age) actually motivated the employer's decision.' That is, the plaintiff's age must have 'actually played a role in [the employer's decisionmaking] process and had a determinative influence on the outcome.' Recognizing that 'the question facing triers of fact in discrimination cases is both sensitive and difficult,' and that '[t]here will seldom be 'eyewitness' testimony as to the employer's mental processes,' the Courts of Appeals, including the Fifth Circuit in this case, have employed some variant of the framework articulated in McDonnell Douglas to analyze ADEA claims that are based principally on circumstantial evidence. . . .

McDonnell Douglas and subsequent decisions have 'established an allocation of the burden of production and an order for the presentation of proof in . . . discriminatory- treatment cases.' First, the plaintiff must establish a prima facie case of discrimination. It is undisputed that petitioner satisfied this burden here: (i) at the time he was fired, he was a member of the class protected by the ADEA ('individuals who are at least 40 years of age,' 29 U. S. C. § 631(a)), (ii) he was otherwise qualified for the position of Hinge Room supervisor, (iii) he was discharged by respondent, and (iv) respondent successively hired three persons in their thirties to fill petitioner's position. The burden therefore shifted to respondent to 'produc[e] evidence that the plaintiff was rejected, or someone else was preferred, for a legitimate, nondiscriminatory reason.' This burden is one of production, not persuasion; it 'can involve no credibility assessment.' Respondent met this burden by offering admissible evidence sufficient for the trier of fact to conclude that petitioner was fired because of his failure to maintain accurate attendance records. Accordingly, 'the McDonnell Douglas framework—with its presumptions and burdens'—disappeared, and the sole remaining issue was 'discrimination vel non.'

[T]he Court of Appeals proceeded from the assumption that a prima facie case of discrimination, combined with sufficient evidence for the trier of fact to disbelieve the defendant's legitimate, nondiscriminatory reason for its decision, is insufficient as a matter of law to sustain a jury's finding of intentional discrimination.

In so reasoning, the Court of Appeals misconceived the evidentiary burden borne by plaintiffs who attempt to prove intentional discrimination through indirect evidence. . . . The ultimate question is whether the employer intentionally discriminated, and proof that 'the employer's proffered reason is unpersuasive, or even obviously contrived, does not necessarily establish that the plaintiff's proffered reason . . . is correct.' In other words, '[i]t is not enough . . . to disbelieve the employer; the factfinder must believe the plaintiff's explanation of intentional discrimination.'

[A] plaintiff's prima facie case, combined with sufficient evidence to find that the employer's asserted justification is false, may permit the trier of fact to conclude that the employer unlawfully discriminated.

This is not to say that such a showing by the plaintiff will always be adequate to sustain a jury's finding of liability. Certainly there will be instances where, although the plaintiff has established a prima facie case and set forth sufficient evidence to reject the defendant's explanation, no rational factfinder could conclude that the action was discriminatory. . . .

Whether judgment as a matter of law is appropriate in any particular case will depend on a number of factors. Those include the strength of the plaintiff's prima facie case, the probative value of the proof that the employer's explanation is false, and any other evidence that supports the employer's case and that properly may be considered on a motion for judgment as a matter of law. For purposes of this case, we need not—and could not—resolve all of the circumstances in which such factors would entitle an employer to judgment as a matter of law. It suffices to say that, because a prima facie case and sufficient evidence to reject the employer's explanation may permit a finding of liability, the Court of Appeals erred in proceeding from the premise that a plaintiff must always introduce additional, independent evidence of discrimination. . . .

The remaining question is whether, despite the Court of Appeals' misconception of petitioner's evidentiary burden, respondent was nonetheless entitled to judgment as a matter of law. Under Rule 50, a court should render judgment as a matter of law when 'a party has been fully heard on an issue and there is no legally sufficient evidentiary basis for a reasonable jury to find for that party on that issue.'

[I]t is apparent that respondent was not entitled to judgment as a matter of law. In this case, in addition to establishing a prima facie case of discrimination and creating a jury issue as to the falsity of the employer's explanation, petitioner introduced additional evidence that Chesnut was motivated by age-based animus and was principally responsible for petitioner's firing. . . .

In holding that the record contained insufficient evidence to sustain the jury's verdict, the Court of Appeals misapplied the standard of review dictated by Rule 50. Again, the court disregarded critical evidence favorable to petitioner— namely, the evidence supporting petitioner's prima facie case and undermining respondent's nondiscriminatory explanation. The court also failed to draw all reasonable inferences in favor of petitioner. . . .

The ultimate question in every employment discrimination case involving a claim of disparate treatment is whether the plaintiff was the victim of intentional discrimination. Given the evidence in the record supporting petitioner, we see no reason to subject the parties to an additional round of litigation before the Court of Appeals rather than to resolve the matter here. The District Court plainly informed the jury that petitioner was required to show 'by a preponderance of the evidence that his age was a determining and motivating factor in the decision of [respondent] to terminate him.' The court instructed the jury that, to show that respondent's explanation was a pretext for discrimination, petitioner had to demonstrate '1, that the stated reasons were not the real reasons for [petitioner's] discharge; and 2, that age discrimination was the real reason for [petitioner's] discharge.' (emphasis added). Given that petitioner established a prima facie case of discrimination, introduced enough evidence for the jury to reject respondent's explanation, and produced additional evidence of age-based animus, there was sufficient evidence for the jury to find that respondent had intentionally discriminated. The District Court was therefore correct to submit the case to the jury, and the Court of Appeals erred in overturning its verdict.

For these reasons, the judgment of the Court of Appeals is reversed."

V. JUSTICE VOTE

9 Pro ACLU Side vs. 0 Con Opposing Side

ACLU Side (Petitioner / Appellant)

1. O'Connor, S. – Wrote majority opinion
2. Rehnquist, W. – Joined majority opinion
3. Stevens, J. – Joined majority opinion
4. Kennedy, A. – Joined majority opinion
5. Souter, D. – Joined majority opinion
6. Ginsburg, R. – Wrote concurring opinion
7. Breyer, S. – Joined majority opinion
8. Scalia, A. – Joined majority opinion
9. Thomas, C. – Joined majority opinion

VI. A WIN OR LOSS FOR THE ACLU?

The ACLU, as amicus curiae, urged reversal of the judgment of the Court of Appeals; the Supreme Court reversed in a 9-0 vote, giving the ACLU an apparent win.

885. Santa Fe Independent School District v. Doe

(Decided June 19, 2000; 530 U.S. 290)

I. ISSUE

A. Issues Discussed

1st Amendment, Religion, Establishment Clause

B. Legal Question Presented

"'Whether petitioner's policy permitting student-led, student-initiated prayer at football games violates the Establishment Clause.'"

C. Supreme Court's Answer

The policy violates the Establishment Clause of the First Amendment.

II. CASE SUMMARY

A. Background

"Prior to 1995, the Santa Fe High School student who occupied the school's elective office of student council chaplain delivered a prayer over the public address system before each varsity football game for the entire season. This practice, along with others, was challenged in District Court as a violation of the Establishment Clause of the First Amendment. While these proceedings were pending in the District Court, the school district adopted a different policy that permits, but does not require, prayer initiated and led by a student at all home games. The District Court entered an order modifying that policy to permit only nonsectarian, non-proselytizing prayer. The Court of Appeals held that, even as modified by the District Court, the football prayer policy was invalid."

The Supreme Court granted certiorari to review the case and affirmed.

B. Counsel of Record / ACLU Attorney

ACLU Side (Respondent / Appellee): Anthony P. Griffin argued the cause for appellee. With him on the briefs were Douglas Laycock and Steven R. Shapiro, ACLU affiliated attorneys.

Opposing Side (Petitioner / Appellant): Jay Alan Sekulow argued the cause for appellant. With him on the briefs were Colby M. May, James M. Henderson, Sr., Mark N. Troobnick, Walter M. Weber, Paul D. Clement, John G. Stepanovich, Thomas P. Monaghan, Stuart J. Roth, John P. Tuskey, Joel H. Thornton, David A. Cortman, and Kelly Shackelford.

John Cornyn, Attorney General of Texas, argued the cause for the State of Texas, et al., as amici curiae, by special leave of court.

III. AMICI CURIAE

ACLU Side (Respondent / Appellee)

Brief of amici curiae filed on behalf of the American Jewish Congress, et al., by Walter E. Dellinger and Marc D. Stern;

Brief of amici curiae filed on behalf of the Baptist Joint Committee on Public Affairs, et al., by Derek H. Davis and Melissa Rogers.

Brief of amici curiae filed on behalf of the Student Press Law Center by Richard A. Simpson and S. Mark Goodman, in support of neither party.

Opposing Side (Petitioner / Appellant)

Brief of amici curiae filed on behalf of the State of Texas, et al., by John Cornyn, Attorney General of Texas, Andy Taylor, First Assistant Attorney General, Linda S. Eads, Deputy Attorney General, Gregory S. Coleman, Solicitor General, Julie Caruthers Parsley, Deputy Solicitor General, and Meredith B. Parenti, Assistant Solicitor General.

Brief of amici curiae filed on behalf of the Christian Legal Society by Steffen N. Johnson, Stephen M. Shapiro, Michael W. McConnell, and Kimberlee W. Colby.

Brief of amici curiae filed on behalf of Liberty Counsel, et al., by Mathew D. Staver and Jerry Falwell, Jr.

Brief of amici curiae filed on behalf of the Northstar Legal Center by Jordan W. Lorence.

Brief of amici curiae filed on behalf of Spearman Independent School District, et al., by Roger D. Hepworth.

Brief of amici curiae filed on behalf of the Texas Association of School Boards Legal Assistance Fund by David M. Feldman and Myra C. Schexnayder.

Brief of amici curiae filed on behalf of the Texas Justice Foundation, et al., by Linda L. Schlueter.

Brief of amici curiae filed on behalf of Senator James M. Inhofe, et al., by Barry C. Hodge.

Brief of amici curiae filed on behalf of Congressman Steve Largent, et al., by Brett M. Kavanaugh.

Brief of amici curiae filed on behalf of Marian Ward, et al., by Kelly J. Coghlan.

Brief of amici curiae filed on behalf of Texas Public School Students, et al., by John L. Carter.

Brief of amici curiae filed on behalf of the Rutherford Institute by John W. Whitehead, Steven H. Aden, and James A. Hayes, Jr.

IV. THE SUPREME COURT'S DECISION

"In cases involving state participation in a religious activity, one of the relevant questions is 'whether an objective observer, acquainted with the text, legislative history, and implementation of the statute, would perceive it as a state endorsement of prayer in public schools.' Regardless of the listener's support for, or objection to, the message, an objective Santa Fe High School student will unquestionably perceive the inevitable pregame prayer as stamped with her school's seal of approval.

The text and history of this policy, moreover, reinforce our objective student's perception that the prayer is, in actuality, encouraged by the school. When a governmental entity professes a secular purpose for an arguably religious policy, the government's characterization is, of course, entitled to some deference. But it is nonetheless the duty of the courts to 'distinguis[h] a sham secular purpose from a sincere one.'

According to the District, the secular purposes of the policy are to 'foste[r] free expression of private persons . . . as well [as to] solemniz[e] sporting events, promot[e] good sportsmanship and student safety, and establis[h] an appropriate environment for competition.' We note, however, that the District's approval of only one specific kind of message, an 'invocation,' is not necessary to further any of these purposes. Additionally, the fact that only one student is permitted to give a content-limited message suggests that this policy does little to 'foste[r] free expression." Furthermore, regardless of whether one considers a sporting event an appropriate occasion for solemnity, the use of an invocation to foster such solemnity is impermissible when, in actuality, it constitutes prayer sponsored by the school. And it is unclear what type of message would be both appropriately "solemnizing" under the District's policy and yet nonreligious. . . .

This case comes to us as the latest step in developing litigation brought as a challenge to institutional practices that unquestionably violated the Establishment Clause. One of those practices was the District's long-established tradition of sanctioning student-led prayer at varsity football games. The narrow question before us is whether implementation of the October policy insulates the continuation of such prayers from constitutional scrutiny. It does not. Our inquiry into this question not only can, but must, include an examination of the circumstances surrounding its enactment. Whether a government activity violates the Establishment Clause is 'in large part a legal question to be answered on the basis of judicial interpretation of social facts. . . . Every government practice must be judged in its unique circumstances . . . .' Our discussion in the previous sections demonstrates that in this case the District's direct involvement with school prayer exceeds constitutional limits. . . .

To properly examine this policy on its face, we 'must be deemed aware of the history and context of the community and forum.' Our examination of those circumstances above leads to the conclusion that this policy does not provide the District with the constitutional safe harbor it sought. The policy is invalid on its face because it establishes an improper majoritarian election on religion, and unquestionably has the purpose and creates the perception of encouraging the delivery of prayer at a series of important school events.

The judgment of the Court of Appeals is, accordingly, affirmed."

V. JUSTICE VOTE

6 Pro ACLU Side vs. 3 Con Opposing Side

ACLU Side (Respondent / Appellee)

1. Stevens, J. – Wrote majority opinion
2. O'Connor, S. – Joined majority opinion
3. Kennedy, A. – Joined majority opinion
4. Souter, D. – Joined majority opinion
5. Ginsburg, R. – Joined majority opinion
6. Breyer, S. – Joined majority opinion

Opposing Side (Petitioner / Appellant)

1. Rehnquist, W. – Wrote dissenting opinion
2. Scalia, A. – Joined Rehnquist's dissent
3. Thomas, C. – Joined Rehnquist's dissent

VI. A WIN OR LOSS FOR THE ACLU?

The ACLU, as counsel of record, urged affirmance of the judgment of the Court of Appeals; the Supreme Court affirmed in a 6-3 vote, giving the ACLU an apparent win.

886. Miller v. French

(Decided June 19, 2000; 530 U.S. 327)

I. ISSUE

A. Issues Discussed

Prison

B. Legal Question Presented

"[W]hether a district court may enjoin the operation of the PLRA's automatic stay provision and, if not, whether that provision violates separation of powers principles."

C. Supreme Court's Answer

"§3626(e)(2) precludes a district court from exercising its equitable powers to enjoin the automatic stay. [W]e conclude that this provision does not violate separation of powers principles."

II. CASE SUMMARY

A. Background

"The Prison Litigation Reform Act of 1995 (PLRA) establishes standards for the entry and termination of prospective relief in civil actions challenging prison conditions. §§801–810, 110 Stat. 1321–66 to 1321–77. If prospective relief under an existing injunction does not satisfy these standards, a defendant or intervenor is entitled to 'immediate termination' of that relief. 18 U. S. C. § 3626(b)(2) (1994 ed., Supp. IV). And under the PLRA's 'automatic stay' provision, a motion to terminate prospective relief 'shall operate as a stay' of that relief during the period beginning 30 days after the filing of the motion (extendable to up to 90 days for 'good cause') and ending when the court rules on the motion. §§ 3626(e)(2), (3). The superintendent of Indiana's Pendleton Correctional Facility, which is currently operating under an ongoing injunction to remedy violations of the Eighth Amendment regarding conditions of confinement, filed a motion to terminate prospective relief under the PLRA. Respondent prisoners moved to enjoin the operation of the automatic stay provision of §3626(e)(2), arguing that it is unconstitutional. The District Court enjoined the stay, and the Court of Appeals for the Seventh Circuit affirmed."

The Supreme Court granted certiorari to review the case and reversed.

B. Counsel of Record / ACLU Attorney

ACLU Side (Respondent / Appellee): Kenneth J. Falk argued the cause for appellees in both cases. With him on the brief were Jacquelyn E. Bowie, Hamid R. Kashani, Steven R. Shapiro, and Elizabeth Alexander, ACLU affiliated attorneys.

Opposing Side (Petitioner / Appellant): Jon Laramore, Deputy Attorney General of Indiana, argued the cause for appellants in No. 99–224. With him on the briefs were Karen M. Freeman-Wilson, Attorney General, Jeffrey A. Modisett, former Attorney General, and Wayne E. Uhl and Geoffrey G. Slaughter, Deputy Attorneys General.

Deputy Solicitor General Underwood argued the cause for the United States in No. 99–582. With her on the briefs were Solicitor General Waxman, Acting Assistant Attorney General Lee, Irving L. Gornstein, and Mark L. Gross.

III. AMICI CURIAE

ACLU Side (Respondent / Appellee)

Brief of amici curiae filed on behalf of Public Citizen by Alan B. Morrison and David C. Vladeck.

Brief of amici curiae filed on behalf of Arizona State Prison System Inmates by John P. Frank.

Brief of amici curiae filed on behalf of Erwin Chemerinsky, et al., by Mr. Chemerinsky, pro se.

Opposing Side (Petitioner / Appellant)

Brief of amici curiae filed on behalf of the State of Texas, et al., by John Cornyn, Attorney General of Texas, Andy Taylor, First Assistant Attorney General, Shane Phelps, Deputy Attorney General, Gregory S. Coleman, Solicitor General, Charles K. Eldred, Assistant Attorney General, and Robert Rigsby, Acting Corporation Counsel of the District of Columbia, and by the Attorneys General for their respective States as follows: Bill Pryor of Alabama, Bruce M. Botelho of Alaska, Robert A. Russell, Jr., of Arkansas, Bill Lockyer of California, M. Jane Brady of Delaware, Robert A. Butterworth of Florida, James E. Ryan of Illinois, Carla J. Stovall of Kansas, J. Joseph Curran, Jr., of Maryland, Jennifer M. Granholm of Michigan, Mike Moore of Mississippi, Jeremiah W. (Jay) Nixon of Missouri, Joseph P. Mazurek of Montana, Don Stenberg of Nebraska, Frankie Sue Del Papa of Nevada, Philip T. McLaughlin of New Hampshire, John J. Farmer, Jr., of New Jersey, Betty D. Montgomery of Ohio, W. A. Drew Edmondson of Oklahoma, D. Michael Fisher of Pennsylvania, Charlie Condon of South Carolina, Mark Barnett of South Dakota, Paul G. Summers of Tennessee, Jan Graham of Utah, Christine O. Gregoire of Washington, and Gay Woodhouse of Wyoming.

Brief of amici curiae filed on behalf of Americans for Effective Law Enforcement, Inc., et al., by Wayne W. Schmidt, Bernard J. Farber, James P. Manak, and Richard Weintraub.

Brief of amici curiae filed on behalf of the Criminal Justice Legal Foundation by Kent S. Scheidegger and Charles L. Hobson.

Brief of amici curiae filed on behalf of the National Governors' Association, et al., by Richard Ruda and James I. Crowley.

Brief of amici curiae filed on behalf of the Washington Legal Foundation, et al., by Paul D. Clement, Daniel J. Popeo, and R. Shawn Gunnarson.

Brief of amici curiae filed on behalf of the Association of State Correctional Administrators, et al., by Sarah B. Vandenbraak, Michael D. Hess, Leonard J. Koerner, and Lorna B. Goodman.

IV. THE SUPREME COURT'S DECISION

"We address the statutory question first. Both the State and the prisoner class agree, as did the majority and dissenting judges below, that §3626(e)(2) precludes a district court from exercising its equitable powers to enjoin the automatic stay. . . .

Like the Court of Appeals, we find that §3626(e)(2) is unambiguous, and accordingly, we cannot adopt Justice Breyer's 'more flexible interpretation' of the statute. Any construction that preserved courts' equitable discretion to enjoin the automatic stay would effectively convert the PLRA's mandatory stay into a discretionary one. Because this would be plainly contrary to Congress' intent in enacting the stay provision, we must confront the constitutional issue. . . .

The Constitution enumerates and separates the powers of the three branches of Government in Articles I, II, and III, and it is this 'very structure' of the Constitution that exemplifies the concept of separation of powers. While the boundaries between the three branches are not "hermetically' sealed,' the Constitution prohibits one branch from encroaching on the central prerogatives of another. . . .

Respondent prisoners contend that § 3626(e)(2) encroaches on the central prerogatives of the Judiciary and thereby violates the separation of powers doctrine.

[T]he automatic stay of §3626(e)(2) does not unconstitutionally 'suspend' or reopen a judgment of an Article III court. Section 3626(e)(2) does not by itself 'tell judges when, how, or what to do.' Instead, §3626(e)(2) merely reflects the change implemented by §3626(b), which does the 'heavy lifting' in the statutory scheme by establishing new standards for prospective relief. Section 3626 prohibits the continuation of prospective relief that was 'approved or granted in the absence of a finding by the court that the relief is narrowly drawn, extends no further than necessary to correct the violation of the Federal right, and is the least intrusive means to correct the violation,' §3626(b)(2), or in the absence of 'findings based on the record that prospective relief remains necessary to correct a current and ongoing violation of a Federal right, extends no further than necessary to correct the violation of the Federal right, and that the prospective relief is narrowly drawn and the least intrusive means to correct the violation,' §3626(b)(3). Accordingly, if prospective relief under an existing decree had been granted or approved absent such findings, then that prospective relief must cease, see §3626(b)(2), unless and until the court makes findings on the record that such relief remains necessary to correct an ongoing violation and is narrowly tailored, see §3626(b)(3). The PLRA's automatic stay provision assists in the enforcement of §§3626(b)(2) and (3) by requiring the court to stay any prospective relief that, due to the change in the underlying standard, is no longer enforceable, i. e., prospective relief that is not supported by the findings specified in §§ 3626(b)(2) and (3). . . .

In contrast to due process, which principally serves to protect the personal rights of litigants to a full and fair hearing, separation of powers principles are primarily addressed to the structural concerns of protecting the role of the independent Judiciary within the constitutional design. In this action, we have no occasion to decide whether there could be a time constraint on judicial action that was so severe that it implicated these structural separation of powers concerns. The PLRA does not deprive courts of their adjudicatory role, but merely provides a new legal standard for relief and encourages courts to apply that standard promptly.

Through the PLRA, Congress clearly intended to make operation of the automatic stay mandatory, precluding courts from exercising their equitable powers to enjoin the stay. And we conclude that this provision does not violate separation of powers principles. Accordingly, the judgment of the Court of Appeals for the Seventh Circuit is reversed, and the action is remanded for further proceedings consistent with this opinion."

V. JUSTICE VOTE

4 Pro ACLU Side vs. 5 Con Opposing Side

ACLU Side (Respondent / Appellee)

1. Souter, D. – Wrote opinion concurring in part and dissenting in part
2. Ginsburg, R. – Joined Souter's opinion
3. Breyer, S. – Wrote dissenting opinion
4. Stevens, J. – Joined Breyer's dissent

Opposing Side (Petitioner / Appellant)

1. O'Connor, S. – Wrote majority opinion
2. Rehnquist, W. – Joined majority opinion
3. Scalia, A. – Joined majority opinion
4. Kennedy, A. – Joined majority opinion
5. Thomas, C. – Joined majority opinion

VI. A WIN OR LOSS FOR THE ACLU?

The ACLU, as counsel of record, urged affirmance of the judgment of the Court of Appeals; the Supreme Court reversed in a 5-4 vote, giving the ACLU an apparent loss.

887. Dickerson v. United States

(Decided June 26, 2000; 530 U.S. 428)

I. ISSUE

A. Issues Discussed

Criminal procedure

B. Legal Question Presented

Whether Miranda may be overruled by an Act of Congress.

C. Supreme Court's Answer

"We hold that Miranda, being a constitutional decision of this Court, may not be in effect overruled by an Act of Congress, and we decline to overrule Miranda ourselves."

II. CASE SUMMARY

A. Background

"Petitioner Dickerson was indicted for bank robbery, conspiracy to commit bank robbery, and using a firearm in the course of committing a crime of violence, all in violation of the applicable provisions of Title 18 of the United States Code. Before trial, Dickerson moved to suppress a statement he had made at a Federal Bureau of Investigation field office, on the grounds that he had not received 'Miranda warnings' before being interrogated. The District Court granted his motion to suppress, and the Government took an interlocutory appeal to the United States Court of Appeals for the Fourth Circuit. That court, by a divided vote, reversed the District Court's suppression order. It agreed with the District Court's conclusion that petitioner had not received Miranda warnings before making his statement. But it went on to hold that §3501, which in effect makes the admissibility of statements such as Dickerson's turn solely on whether they were made voluntarily, was satisfied in this case. It then concluded that our decision in Miranda was not a constitutional holding, and that, therefore, Congress could by statute have the final say on the question of admissibility."

The Supreme Court granted certiorari to review the case and reversed.

B. Counsel of Record / ACLU Attorney

ACLU Side (Petitioner / Appellant): James W. Hundley argued the cause for appellant.

Opposing Side (Respondent / Appellee): Solicitor General Waxman argued the cause for the United States.

Paul G. Cassell argued the cause, as amicus curiae, by special leave of court.

III. AMICI CURIAE

ACLU Side (Petitioner / Appellant)

Brief of amici curiae filed on behalf of the ACLU by Jonathan L. Abram, Audrey J. Anderson, Steven R. Shapiro, Vivian Berger, Susan N. Herman, and Stephen Schulhofer.

Brief of amici curiae filed on behalf of the House Democratic Leadership by Charles Tiefer and Jonathan W. Cuneo.

Brief of amici curiae filed on behalf of the National Association of Criminal Defense Lawyers et al. by Paul M. Smith, Deanne E. Maynard, Lisa B. Kemler, and John T. Philipsborn.

Brief of amici curiae filed on behalf of the National Legal Aid and Defender Association by Charles D. Weisselberg and Michelle Falkoff.

Brief of amici curiae filed on behalf of the Rutherford Institute by James Joseph Lynch, Jr., and John W. Whitehead.

Brief of amici curiae filed on behalf of Griffin B. Bell by Robert S. Litt, John A. Freedman, and Daniel C. Richman.

Brief of amici curiae filed on behalf of Benjamin R. Civiletti by Mr. Civiletti, pro se, Kenneth C. Bass III, and John F. Cooney.

Opposing Side (Respondent / Appellee)

Brief of amici curiae filed by Paul G. Cassell, Daniel J. Popeo, and Paul D. Kamenar.

Brief of amici curiae filed on behalf of the State of South Carolina, et al., by Charles M. Condon, Attorney General of South Carolina, Treva Ashworth, Deputy Attorney General, Kenneth P. Woodington, Senior Assistant Attorney General, and Travey Colton Green, Assistant Attorney General.

Brief of amici curiae filed on behalf of the Maricopa County Attorney's Office by Theodore B. Olson, Douglas R. Cox, and Miguel A. Estrada.

Brief of amici curiae filed on behalf of Arizona Voices for Victims, et al., by Douglas Beloof.

Brief of amici curiae filed on behalf of the Bipartisan Legal Advisory Group of the United States House of Representatives by Geraldine R. Gennet, Kerry W. Kircher, and Michael L. Stern.

Brief of amici curiae filed on behalf of the Center for the Community Interest, et al., by Daniel P. Collins, Kristin Linsley Myles, and Kelly M. Klaus.

Brief of amici curiae filed on behalf of the Center for the Original Intent of the Constitution by Michael P. Farris.

Brief of amici curiae filed on behalf of Citizens for Law and Order, et al., by Theodore M. Cooperstein.

Brief of amici curiae filed on behalf of the Criminal Justice Legal Foundation by Kent S. Scheidegger, Charles L. Hobson, and Edwin Meese III.

Brief of amici curiae filed on behalf of the Federal Bureau of Investigation Agents Association by Robert F. Hoyt.

Brief of amici curiae filed on behalf of the Fraternal Order of Police by Patrick F. Philbin and Thomas T. Rutherford.

Brief of amici curiae filed on behalf of the National Association of Police Organizations, et al., by Stephen R. McSpadden, Robert J. Cynkar, and Margaret A. Ryan.

Brief of amici curiae filed on behalf of the National District Attorneys Association, et al., by Lynne Abraham, Ronald Eisenberg, Jeffrey C. Sullivan, John M. Tyson, Jr., Grover Trask, Christine A. Cooke, John B. Dangler, and Richard E. Trodden.

Brief of amici curiae filed on behalf of Former Attorneys General of the United States William P. Barr and Edwin Meese III by Andrew G. McBride.

Brief of amici curiae filed on behalf of Senator Orrin G. Hatch, et al., by Senator Hatch, pro se.

Brief of amici curiae filed on behalf of Manning & Marder, Kass, Ellrod, Ramirez by Davis J. Wilson.

Brief of amici curiae filed on behalf of Americans for Effective Law Enforcement, Inc., et al., by Wayne W. Schmidt, James P. Manak, and Bernard J. Farber, in support of neither party.

IV. THE SUPREME COURT'S DECISION

"In Miranda v. Arizona, 384 U. S. 436 (1966), we held that certain warnings must be given before a suspect's statement made during custodial interrogation could be admitted in evidence. In the wake of that decision, Congress enacted 18 U. S. C. § 3501, which in essence laid down a rule that the admissibility of such statements should turn only on whether or not they were voluntarily made. We hold that Miranda, being a constitutional decision of this Court, may not be in effect overruled by an Act of Congress, and we decline to overrule Miranda ourselves. We therefore hold that Miranda and its progeny in this Court govern the admissibility of statements made during custodial interrogation in both state and federal courts. . . .

Given §3501's express designation of voluntariness as the touchstone of admissibility, its omission of any warning requirement, and the instruction for trial courts to consider a nonexclusive list of factors relevant to the circumstances of a confession, we agree with the Court of Appeals that Congress intended by its enactment to overrule Miranda. Because of the obvious conflict between our decision in Miranda and §3501, we must address whether Congress has constitutional authority to thus supersede Miranda. If Congress has such authority, §3501's totality- of-the-circumstances approach must prevail over Miranda's requirement of warnings; if not, that section must yield to Miranda's more specific requirements.

The law in this area is clear. This Court has supervisory authority over the federal courts, and we may use that authority to prescribe rules of evidence and procedure that are binding in those tribunals. However, the power to judicially create and enforce nonconstitutional 'rules of procedure and evidence for the federal courts exists only in the absence of a relevant Act of Congress.' Congress retains the ultimate authority to modify or set aside any judicially created rules of evidence and procedure that are not required by the Constitution.

But Congress may not legislatively supersede our decisions interpreting and applying the Constitution. This case therefore turns on whether the Miranda Court announced a constitutional rule or merely exercised its supervisory authority to regulate evidence in the absence of congressional direction. . . .

The dissent argues that it is judicial overreaching for this Court to hold § 3501 unconstitutional unless we hold that the Miranda warnings are required by the Constitution, in the sense that nothing else will suffice to satisfy constitutional requirements. But we need not go further than Miranda to decide this case. In Miranda, the Court noted that reliance on the traditional totality-of-the-circumstances test raised a risk of overlooking an involuntary custodial confession, a risk that the Court found unacceptably great when the confession is offered in the case in chief to prove guilt. The Court therefore concluded that something more than the totality test was necessary. As discussed above, §3501 reinstates the totality test as sufficient. Section 3501 therefore cannot be sustained if Miranda is to remain the law. . . .

In sum, we conclude that Miranda announced a constitutional rule that Congress may not supersede legislatively. Following the rule of stare decisis, we decline to overrule Miranda ourselves. The judgment of the Court of Appeals is therefore reversed."

V. JUSTICE VOTE

7 Pro ACLU Side vs. 2 Con Opposing Side

ACLU Side (Petitioner / Appellant)

1. Rehnquist, W. – Wrote majority opinion
2. Stevens, J. – Joined majority opinion
3. O'Connor, S. – Joined majority opinion
4. Kennedy, A. – Joined majority opinion
5. Souter, D. – Joined majority opinion
6. Ginsburg, R. – Joined majority opinion
7. Breyer, S. – Joined majority opinion

Opposing Side (Respondent / Appellee)

1. Scalia, A. – Wrote dissenting opinion
2. Thomas, C. – Joined Scalia's dissent

VI. A WIN OR LOSS FOR THE ACLU?

The ACLU, as amicus curiae, urged reversal of the judgment of the Court of Appeals; the Supreme Court reversed in a 7-2 vote, giving the ACLU an apparent win.

888. Boy Scouts of America v. Dale

(Decided June 28, 2000; 530 U.S. 640)

I. ISSUE

A. Issues Discussed

1st Amendment

B. Legal Question Presented

"[W]hether applying New Jersey's public accommodations law [to require the Boy Scouts to accept a homosexual man as an assistant scoutmaster] violates the Boy Scouts' First Amendment right of expressive association."

C. Supreme Court's Answer

"[T]he application of New Jersey's public accommodations law to require that the Boy Scouts accept [a homosexual man] as an assistant scoutmaster runs afoul of the Scouts' freedom of expressive association."

II. CASE SUMMARY

A. Background

"Petitioners are the Boy Scouts of America and the Monmouth Council, a division of the Boy Scouts of America (collectively, Boy Scouts). The Boy Scouts is a private, not-for-profit organization engaged in instilling its system of values in young people. The Boy Scouts asserts that homosexual conduct is inconsistent with the values it seeks to instill. Respondent is James Dale, a former Eagle Scout whose adult membership in the Boy Scouts was revoked when the Boy Scouts learned that he is an avowed homosexual and gay rights activist. The New Jersey Supreme Court held that New Jersey's public accommodations law requires that the Boy Scouts readmit Dale."

The Supreme Court granted certiorari to review the case and reversed.

B. Counsel of Record / ACLU Attorney

ACLU Side (Respondent / Appellee): Evan Wolfson argued the cause for appellee.

Opposing Side (Petitioner / Appellant): George A. Davidson argued the cause for appellant.

III. AMICI CURIAE

ACLU Side (Respondent / Appellee)

Brief of amici curiae filed on behalf of the ACLU, et al., by Matthew A. Coles, Steven R. Shapiro, Sara L. Mandelbaum, and Lenora M. Lapidus.

Brief of amici curiae filed on behalf of the State of New Jersey by John J. Farmer, Jr., Attorney General, Jeffrey Burstein, Senior Deputy Attorney General, and Charles S. Cohen, Deputy Attorney General.

Brief of amici curiae filed on behalf of the State of New York, et al., by Eliot Spitzer, Attorney General of New York, Preeta D. Bansal, Solicitor General, and Adam L. Aronson, Assistant Solicitor General, and by the Attorneys General for their respective States as follows: Bill Lockyer of California, Earl I. Anzai of Hawaii, J. Joseph Curran, Jr., of Maryland, Thomas F. Reilly of Massachusetts, Philip T. McLaughlin of New Hampshire, W. A. Drew Edmondson of Oklahoma; Hardy Myers of Oregon, William H. Sorrell of Vermont, and Christine O. Gregoire of Washington.

Brief of amici curiae filed on behalf of the city of Atlanta, et al., by Peter T. Barbur, Sara M. Darehshori, James K. Hahn, David I. Schulman, Jeffrey L. Rogers, Madelyn F. Wessel, Thomas J. Berning, Lawrence E. Rosenthal, Benna Ruth Solomon, Michael D. Hess, Leonard J. Koerner, Florence A. Hutner, and Louise Renne.

Brief of amici curiae filed on behalf of the American Association of School Administrators, et al., by Mitchell A. Karlan.

Brief of amici curiae filed on behalf of the American Bar Association by William G. Paul and Robert H. Murphy.

Brief of amici curiae filed on behalf of the American Jewish Congress by Marc D. Stern.

Brief of amici curiae filed on behalf of the American Psychological Association by Paul M. Smith, Nory Miller, James L. McHugh, and Nathalie F. P. Gilfoyle.

Brief of amici curiae filed on behalf of the American Public Health Association, et al., by Marvin E. Frankel, Jeffrey S. Trachtman, and Kerri Ann Law.

Brief of amici curiae filed on behalf of Bay Area Lawyers for Individual Freedom, et al., by Edward W. Swanson and Paula A. Brantner.

Brief of amici curiae filed on behalf of Deans of Divinity Schools and Rabbinical Institutions by David A. Schulz.

Brief of amici curiae filed on behalf of the National Association for the Advancement of Colored People by Dennis C. Hayes and David T. Goldberg.

Brief of amici curiae filed on behalf of Parents, Families, and Friends of Lesbians and Gays, Inc., et al. by John H. Pickering, Daniel H. Squire, and Carol J. Banta.

Brief of amici curiae filed on behalf of the Society of American Law Teachers by Nan D. Hunter and David Cole; and for Roland Pool, et al., by David M. Gische and Merril Hirsh.

Brief of amici curiae filed on behalf of the General Board of Church and Society of the United Methodist Church, et al., by Michael D. Silverman.

Opposing Side (Petitioner / Appellant)

Brief of amici curiae filed on behalf of Agudath Israel of America by David Zwiebel.

Brief of amici curiae filed on behalf of the American Center for Law and Justice, et al., by Jay Alan Sekulow, Vincent McCarthy, John P. Tuskey, and Laura B. Hernandez.

Brief of amici curiae filed on behalf of the American Civil Rights Union by Peter J. Ferrara.

Brief of amici curiae filed on behalf of the Becket Fund for Religious Liberty by Kevin J. Hasson and Eric W. Treene.

Brief of amici curiae filed on behalf of the California State Club Association, et al., by William I. Edlund.

Brief of amici curiae filed on behalf of the Center for the Original Intent of the Constitution by Michael P. Farris.

Brief of amici curiae filed on behalf of the Christian Legal Society, et al., by Kimberlee Wood Colby and Carl H. Esbeck.

Brief of amici curiae filed on behalf of the Claremont Institute Center for Constitutional Jurisprudence by Edwin Meese III.

Brief of amici curiae filed on behalf of the Eagle Forum Education & Legal Defense Fund, et al., by Erik S. Jaffe.

Brief of amici curiae filed on behalf of the Family Defense Council, et al., by William E. Fay III.

Brief of amici curiae filed on behalf of the Family Research Council by Janet M. LaRue.

Brief of amici curiae filed on behalf of Gays and Lesbians for Individual Liberty by William H. Mellor, Clint Bolick, and Scott G. Bullock.

Brief of amici curiae filed on behalf of the Individual Rights Foundation by Paul A. Hoffman and Patrick J. Manshardt.

Brief of amici curiae filed on behalf of the Institute for Public Affairs of the Union of Orthodox Jewish Con- gregations of America by Nathan J. Diament.

Brief of amici curiae filed on behalf of the Liberty Legal Institute by Kelly Shackelford and George B. Flint.

Brief of amici curiae filed on behalf of the National Catholic Committee on Scouting, et al., by Von G. Keetch.

Brief of amici curiae filed on behalf of the National Legal Foundation by Barry C. Hodge.

Brief of amici curiae filed on behalf of the Pacific Legal Foundation by John H. Findley.

Brief of amici curiae filed on behalf of Public Advocate of the United States, et al., by William J. Olson and John S. Miles.

Brief of amici curiae filed on behalf of the United States Catholic Conference, et al., by Mark E. Chopko and Jeffrey Hunter Moon.

Brief of amici curiae filed on behalf of John J. Hurley, et al., by Chester Darling, Michael Williams, and Dwight G. Duncan.

IV. THE SUPREME COURT'S DECISION

"To determine whether a group is protected by the First Amendment's expressive associational right, we must determine whether the group engages in 'expressive association.' The First Amendment's protection of expressive association is not reserved for advocacy groups. But to come within its ambit, a group must engage in some form of expression, whether it be public or private. . . .

During the time spent with the youth members, the scoutmasters and assistant scoutmasters inculcate them with the Boy Scouts' values—both expressly and by example. It seems indisputable that an association that seeks to transmit such a system of values engages in expressive activity. . . .

Given that the Boy Scouts engages in expressive activity, we must determine whether the forced inclusion of Dale as an assistant scoutmaster would significantly affect the Boy Scouts' ability to advocate public or private viewpoints. This inquiry necessarily requires us first to explore, to a limited extent, the nature of the Boy Scouts' view of homosexuality. . . .

The Boy Scouts asserts that it 'teach[es] that homosexual conduct is not morally straight,' and that it does 'not want to promote homosexual conduct as a legitimate form of behavior.' We accept the Boy Scouts' assertion. We need not inquire further to determine the nature of the Boy Scouts' expression with respect to homosexuality. But because the record before us contains written evidence of the Boy Scouts' view- point, we look to it as instructive, if only on the question of the sincerity of the professed beliefs. . . .

We must then determine whether Dale's presence as an assistant scoutmaster would significantly burden the Boy Scouts' desire to not 'promote homosexual conduct as a legitimate form of behavior.' As we give deference to an association's assertions regarding the nature of its expression, we must also give deference to an association's view of what would impair its expression. . . .

Dale, by his own admission, is one of a group of gay Scouts who have 'become leaders in their community and are open and honest about their sexual orientation.' Dale was the copresident of a gay and lesbian organization at college and remains a gay rights activist. Dale's presence in the Boy Scouts would, at the very least, force the organization to send a message, both to the youth members and the world, that the Boy Scouts accepts homosexual conduct as a legitimate form of behavior. . . .

Here, we have found that the Boy Scouts believes that homosexual conduct is inconsistent with the values it seeks to instill in its youth members; it will not 'promote homosexual conduct as a legitimate form of behavior.' [T]he presence of Dale as an assistant scoutmaster would . . . interfere with the Boy Scout's choice not to propound a point of view contrary to its beliefs. . . .

Having determined that the Boy Scouts is an expressive association and that the forced inclusion of Dale would significantly affect its expression, we inquire whether the application of New Jersey's public accommodations law to require that the Boy Scouts accept Dale as an assistant scoutmaster runs afoul of the Scouts' freedom of expressive association. We conclude that it does. . . .

We have already concluded that a state requirement that the Boy Scouts retain Dale as an assistant scoutmaster would significantly burden the organization's right to oppose or disfavor homosexual conduct. The state interests embodied in New Jersey's public accommodations law do not justify such a severe intrusion on the Boy Scouts' rights to freedom of expressive association. That being the case, we hold that the First Amendment prohibits the State from imposing such a requirement through the application of its public accommodations law. . . .

We are not, as we must not be, guided by our views of whether the Boy Scouts' teachings with respect to homosexual conduct are right or wrong; public or judicial disapproval of a tenet of an organization's expression does not justify the State's effort to compel the organization to accept members where such acceptance would derogate from the organization's expressive message. . . .

The judgment of the New Jersey Supreme Court is reversed, and the case is remanded for further proceedings not inconsistent with this opinion."

V. JUSTICE VOTE

4 Pro ACLU Side vs. 5 Con Opposing Side

ACLU Side (Respondent / Appellee)

1. Stevens, J. – Wrote dissenting opinion
2. Souter, D. – Joined Stevens' opinion
3. Ginsburg, R. – Joined Stevens' opinion
4. Breyer, S. – Joined Stevens' opinion

Opposing Side (Petitioner / Appellant)

1. Rehnquist, W. – Wrote majority opinion
2. O'Connor, S. – Joined majority opinion
3. Scalia, A. – Joined majority opinion
4. Kennedy, A. – Joined majority opinion
5. Thomas, C. – Joined majority opinion

VI. A WIN OR LOSS FOR THE ACLU?

The ACLU, as amicus curiae, urged affirmance of the judgment of the New Jersey Supreme Court; the U.S. Supreme Court reversed in a 5-4 vote, giving the ACLU an apparent loss.

889. Hill v. Colorado

(Decided June 28, 2000; 530 U.S. 703)

I. ISSUE

A. Issues Discussed

1st Amendment, Freedom of Speech

B. Legal Question Presented

Whether "a 1993 Colorado statute that regulates speech-related conduct within 100 feet of the entrance to any health care facility" violates the speaker's First Amendment rights.

C. Supreme Court's Answer

The Colorado statute does not violate the speaker's First Amendment rights.

II. CASE SUMMARY

A. Background

"At issue is the constitutionality of a 1993 Colorado statute that regulates speech-related conduct within 100 feet of the entrance to any health care facility. The specific section of the statute that is challenged, Colo. Rev. Stat. §18–9–122(3) (1999), makes it unlawful within the regulated areas for any person to 'knowingly approach' within eight feet of another person, without that person's consent, 'for the purpose of passing a leaflet or handbill to, displaying a sign to, or engaging in oral protest, education, or counseling with such other person . . . .' Although the statute prohibits speakers from approaching unwilling listeners, it does not require a standing speaker to move away from anyone passing by. Nor does it place any restriction on the content of any message that anyone may wish to communicate to anyone else, either inside or outside the regulated areas. It does, however, make it more difficult to give unwanted advice, particularly in the form of a handbill or leaflet, to persons entering or leaving medical facilities. . . .

Five months after the statute was enacted, petitioners filed a complaint in the District Court for Jefferson County, Colorado, praying for a declaration that §18–9–122(3) was facially invalid and seeking an injunction against its enforcement. They stated that prior to the enactment of the statute, they had engaged in 'sidewalk counseling' on the public ways and sidewalks within 100 feet of the entrances to facilities where human abortion is practiced or where medical personnel refer women to other facilities for abortions."

After extensive litigation, "[t]he Colorado Supreme Court granted certiorari and affirmed the judgment of the Court of Appeals" upholding the statute.

The Supreme Court granted certiorari to review the case and affirmed.

B. Counsel of Record / ACLU Attorney

ACLU Side (Petitioner / Appellant): Jay Alan Sekulow argued the cause for appellant.

Opposing Side (Respondent / Appellee): Michael E. McLachlan, Solicitor General of Colorado, argued the cause for appellee.

Deputy Solicitor General Underwood argued the cause for the United States, as amicus curiae, by special leave of court.

III. AMICI CURIAE

ACLU Side (Petitioner / Appellant)

Brief of amici curiae filed on behalf of the ACLU by Steven R. Shapiro.

Brief of amici curiae filed on behalf of Liberty Counsel by Mathew D. Staver.

Brief of amici curiae filed on behalf of People for the Ethical Treatment of Animals by David N. Ventker.

Brief of amici curiae filed on behalf of the American Federation of Labor and Congress of Industrial Organizations by Jonathan P. Hiatt and Laurence Gold.

Brief of amici curiae filed on behalf of the Life Legal Defense Foundation by Andrew W. Zepeda.

Opposing Side (Respondent / Appellee)

Brief of amici curiae filed on behalf of the United States by Deputy Solicitor General Underwood, Solicitor General Waxman, Acting Assistant Attorney General Lee, Beth S. Brinkmann, David K. Flynn, and Louis E. Peraertz.

Brief of amici curiae filed on behalf of the State of New York, et al., by Eliot Spitzer, Attorney General of New York, Preeta D. Bansal, Solicitor General, Carol Fischer, Assistant Solicitor General, and Jennifer K. Brown, Assistant Attorney General, and by the Attorneys General for their respective States as follows: Janet Napolitano of Arizona, Bill Lockyer of California, Richard Blumenthal of Connecticut, Earl I. Anzai of Hawaii, Carla J. Stovall of Kansas, Andrew Ketterer of Maine, J. Joseph Curran, Jr., of Maryland, Thomas F. Reilly of Massachusetts, Jeremiah W. (Jay) Nixon of Missouri, Joseph P. Mazurek of Montana, Frankie Sue Del Papa of Nevada, Patricia A. Madrid of New Mexico, W. A. Drew Edmondson of Oklahoma, Hardy Myers of Oregon, Sheldon Whitehouse of Rhode Island, William H. Sorrell of Vermont, and Christine O. Gregoire of Washington.

Brief of amici curiae filed on behalf of the City of Boulder, et al., by Daniel E. Muse and James C. Thomas.

Brief of amici curiae filed on behalf of the American College of Obstetricians and Gynecologists, et al., by Carter G. Phillips, Mark E. Haddad, Ann E. Allen, Michael L. Ile, and Leonard A. Nelson.

Brief of amici curiae filed on behalf of the National Abortion and Reproductive Rights Action League, et al., by Lucinda M. Finley, Jennifer C. Jaff, Martha F. Davis, Roslyn Powell, and Yolanda S. Wu.

IV. THE SUPREME COURT'S DECISION

"Before confronting the question whether the Colorado statute reflects an acceptable balance between the constitutionally protected rights of law-abiding speakers and the interests of unwilling listeners, it is appropriate to examine the competing interests at stake. A brief review of both sides of the dispute reveals that each has legitimate and important concerns. . . .

The right to free speech, of course, includes the right to attempt to persuade others to change their views, and may not be curtailed simply because the speaker's message may be offensive to his audience. But the protection afforded to offensive messages does not always embrace offensive speech that is so intrusive that the unwilling audience cannot avoid it. . . .

The recognizable privacy interest in avoiding unwanted communication varies widely in different settings. It is far less important when 'strolling through Central Park' than when 'in the confines of one's own home,' or when persons are 'powerless to avoid' it. . . . More specific to the facts of this case, we have recognized that '[t]he First Amendment does not demand that patients at a medical facility undertake Herculean efforts to escape the cacophony of political protests.'

The unwilling listener's interest in avoiding unwanted communication has been repeatedly identified in our cases. It is an aspect of the broader 'right to be let alone' . . . .

All four of the state court opinions upholding the validity of this statute concluded that it is a content-neutral time, place, and manner regulation. . . . It is therefore appropriate to comment on the 'content neutrality' of the statute. . . .

The Colorado courts correctly concluded that §18–9– 122(3) is content neutral. . . .

We also agree with the state courts' conclusion that §18–9–122(3) is a valid time, place, and manner regulation under the test applied in Ward because it is 'narrowly tailored.' We already have noted that the statute serves governmental interests that are significant and legitimate and that the restrictions are content neutral. We are likewise persuaded that the statute is 'narrowly tailored' to serve those interests and that it leaves open ample alternative channels for communication. As we have emphasized on more than one occasion, when a content-neutral regulation does not entirely foreclose any means of communication, it may satisfy the tailoring requirement even though it is not the least restrictive or least intrusive means of serving the statutory goal.

The three types of communication regulated by §18–9– 122(3) are the display of signs, leafletting, and oral speech. The 8-foot separation between the speaker and the audience should not have any adverse impact on the readers' ability to read signs displayed by demonstrators. In fact, the separation might actually aid the pedestrians' ability to see the signs by preventing others from surrounding them and impeding their view. Furthermore, the statute places no limitations on the number, size, text, or images of the placards. And, as with all of the restrictions, the 8-foot zone does not affect demonstrators with signs who remain in place.

With respect to oral statements, the distance certainly can make it more difficult for a speaker to be heard, particularly if the level of background noise is high and other speakers are competing for the pedestrian's attention. Notably, the statute places no limitation on the number of speakers or the noise level, including the use of amplification equipment, although we have upheld such restrictions in past cases. More significantly, this statute does not suffer from the failings that compelled us to reject the 'floating buffer zone' in Schenck. Unlike the 15-foot zone in Schenck, this 8-foot zone allows the speaker to communicate at a 'normal conversational distance.' Additionally, the statute allows the speaker to remain in one place, and other individuals can pass within eight feet of the protester without causing the protester to violate the statute. Finally, here there is a 'knowing' requirement that protects speakers 'who thought they were keeping pace with the targeted individual' at the proscribed distance from inadvertently violating the statute.

It is also not clear that the statute's restrictions will necessarily impede, rather than assist, the speakers' efforts to communicate their messages. The statute might encourage the most aggressive and vociferous protesters to moderate their confrontational and harassing conduct, and thereby make it easier for thoughtful and law-abiding sidewalk counselors like petitioners to make themselves heard. But whether or not the 8-foot interval is the best possible accommodation of the competing interests at stake, we must accord a measure of deference to the judgment of the Colorado Legislature. Once again, it is worth reiterating that only attempts to address unwilling listeners are affected.

The burden on the ability to distribute handbills is more serious because it seems possible that an 8-foot interval could hinder the ability of a leafletter to deliver handbills to some unwilling recipients. The statute does not, however, prevent a leafletter from simply standing near the path of oncoming pedestrians and proffering his or her material, which the pedestrians can easily accept. And, as in all leafletting situations, pedestrians continue to be free to decline the tender. . . .

Finally, in determining whether a statute is narrowly tailored, we have noted that '[w]e must, of course, take account of the place to which the regulations apply in determining whether these restrictions burden more speech than necessary.' States and municipalities plainly have a substantial interest in controlling the activity around certain public and private places. . . .

Persons who are attempting to enter health care facilities—for any purpose—are often in particularly vulnerable physical and emotional conditions. The State of Colorado has responded to its substantial and legitimate interest in protecting these persons from unwanted encounters, confrontations, and even assaults by enacting an exceedingly modest restriction on the speakers' ability to approach. . . .

This restriction is thus reasonable and narrowly tailored. . . . The judgment of the Colorado Supreme Court is affirmed."

V. JUSTICE VOTE

3 Pro ACLU Side vs. 6 Con Opposing Side

ACLU Side (Petitioner / Appellant)

1. Scalia, A. – Wrote dissenting opinion
2. Thomas, C. – Joined Scalia's dissent
3. Kennedy, A. – Wrote dissenting opinion

Opposing Side (Respondent / Appellee)

1. Stevens, J. – Wrote majority opinion
2. Rehnquist, W. – Joined majority opinion
3. Souter, D. – Wrote concurring opinion
4. O'Connor, S. – Joined Souter's concurrence
5. Ginsburg, R. – Joined Souter's concurrence
6. Breyer, S. – Joined Souter's concurrence

VI. A WIN OR LOSS FOR THE ACLU?

The ACLU, as amicus curiae, urged reversal of the judgment of the Colorado Supreme Court; the U.S. Supreme Court affirmed in a 6-3 vote, giving the ACLU an apparent loss.

890. Mitchell v. Helms

(Decided June 28, 2000; 530 U.S. 793)

I. ISSUE

A. Issues Discussed

1st Amendment, Religion, Establishment Clause

B. Legal Question Presented

"The question is whether Chapter 2, as applied in Jefferson Parish, Lousiana, is a law respecting an establishment of religion, because many of the private schools receiving Chapter 2 aid in that parish are religiously affiliated."

C. Supreme Court's Answer

"[W]e hold that Chapter 2 is not a law respecting an establishment of religion. Jefferson Parish need not exclude religious schools from its Chapter 2 program."

II. CASE SUMMARY

A. Background

"As part of a longstanding school-aid program known as Chapter 2, the Federal Government distributes funds to state and local governmental agencies, which in turn lend educational materials and equipment to public and private schools, with the enrollment of each participating school determining the amount of aid that it receives. . . .

Chapter 2 channels federal funds to local educational agencies (LEA's), which are usually public school districts, via state educational agencies (SEA's), to implement programs to assist children in elementary and secondary schools. . . .

LEA's and SEA's must offer assistance to both public and private schools (although any private school must be non-profit). §§ 7312(a), 7372(a)(1). Participating private schools receive Chapter 2 aid based on the number of children enrolled in each school, see §7372(a)(1), and allocations of Chapter 2 funds for those schools must generally be 'equal (consistent with the number of children to be served) to expenditures for programs . . . for children enrolled in the public schools of the [LEA],' §7372(b). LEA's must in all cases 'assure equitable participation' of the children of private schools 'in the purposes and benefits' of Chapter 2. § 7372(a)(1); see § 7372(b). Further, Chapter 2 funds may only 'supplement and, to the extent practical, increase the level of funds that would . . . be made available from non-Federal sources.' § 7371(b). LEA's and SEA's may not operate their programs 'so as to supplant funds from non-Federal sources.'

Several restrictions apply to aid to private schools. Most significantly, the 'services, materials, and equipment' provided to private schools must be 'secular, neutral, and non- ideological.' §7372(a)(1). In addition, private schools may not acquire control of Chapter 2 funds or title to Chapter 2 materials, equipment, or property. §7372(c)(1). . . .

In Jefferson Parish (the Louisiana governmental unit at issue in this case), as in Louisiana as a whole, private schools have primarily used their allocations for nonrecurring expenses, usually materials and equipment. In the 1986–1987 fiscal year, for example, 44% of the money budgeted for private schools in Jefferson Parish was spent by LEA's for acquiring library and media materials, and 48% for instructional equipment. . . .

It appears that, in an average year, about 30% of Chapter 2 funds spent in Jefferson Parish are allocated for private schools. For the 1985–1986 fiscal year, 41 private schools participated in Chapter 2. For the following year, 46 participated, and the participation level has remained relatively constant since then. Of these 46, 34 were Roman Catholic; 7 were otherwise religiously affiliated; and 5 were not religiously affiliated. . . .

Respondents filed suit in December 1985, alleging, among other things, that Chapter 2, as applied in Jefferson Parish, violated the Establishment Clause of the First Amendment of the Federal Constitution. The case's tortuous history over the next 15 years indicates well the degree to which our Establishment Clause jurisprudence has shifted in recent times, while nevertheless retaining anomalies with which the lower courts have had to struggle."

After 15 years of litigation, ultimately the Fifth Circuit "held Chapter 2 unconstitutional."

The Supreme Court granted certiorari to review the case and reversed.

B. Counsel of Record / ACLU Attorney

ACLU Side (Respondent / Appellee): Deputy Solicitor General Underwood and Lee Boothby argued the cause for appellee.

Opposing Side (Petitioner / Appellant): Michael W. McConnell argued the cause for appellant.

III. AMICI CURIAE

ACLU Side (Respondent / Appellee)

Brief of amici curiae filed on behalf of the ACLU, et al., by Drew S. Days III, Anthony M. Radice, Lev L. Dassin, and Laura R. Taichman.

Brief of amici curiae filed on behalf of the Baptist Joint Committee on Public Affairs by Melissa Rogers and J. Brent Walker.

Brief of amici curiae filed on behalf of the Interfaith Religious Liberty Foundation, et al., by Derek Davis and Alan J. Reinach.

Brief of amici curiae filed on behalf of the National Committee for Public Education and Religious Liberty, et al., by Marshall Beil and Philip Goldstein.

Brief of amici curiae filed on behalf of the National Education Association by Robert H. Chanin, Jeremiah A. Collins, and Michael D. Simpson.

Brief of amici curiae filed on behalf of the National Jewish Commission on Law and Public Affairs by Dennis Rapps, David Zwiebel, Nathan Diament, and Nathan Lewin.

Brief of amici curiae filed on behalf of the National School Boards Association, et al., by Julie Underwood, Jay Worona, and Pilar Sokol.

Brief of amici curiae filed on behalf of the Institute for Justice, et al., by William H. Mellor and Clint Bolick, in support of neither party.

Opposing Side (Petitioner / Appellant)

Brief of amici curiae filed on behalf of the State of Ohio, et al., by Betty D. Montgomery, Attorney General of Ohio, Edward B. Foley, State Solicitor, Robert C. Maier, Assistant Solicitor, and by the Attorneys General for their respective States as follows: Ken Salazar of Colorado, Robert A. Butterworth of Florida, James E. Ryan of Illinois, Thomas J. Miller of Iowa, Carla J. Stovall of Kansas, Richard P. Ieyoub of Louisiana, Jennifer M. Granholm of Michigan, Mike Moore of Mississippi, Don Stenberg of Nebraska, John J. Farmer, Jr., of New Jersey, Charles M. Condon of South Carolina, and Mark L. Earley of Virginia.

Brief of amici curiae filed on behalf of the City of New York, et al., by Michael D. Hess, Leonard J. Koerner, and Edward F. X. Hart.

Brief of amici curiae filed on behalf of the American Center for Law and Justice by JayAlan Sekulow, John P. Tuskey, Walter W. Weber, Colby M. May, and Vincent P. McCarthy.

Brief of amici curiae filed on behalf of the Arizona Council for Academic Private Education, et al., by Edward McGlynn Gaffney, Jr., and David J. Hessler.

Brief of amici curiae filed on behalf of the AVI CHAI Foundation by Nathan Lewin, Julia E. Guttman, and Jody Manier Kris.
Brief of amici curiae filed on behalf of the Becket Fund for Religious Liberty by Kevin J. Hasson and Eric W. Treene.
Brief of amici curiae filed on behalf of the Catholic League for Religious and Civil Rights by Robert P. George.
Brief of amici curiae filed on behalf of the Knights of Columbus by Kevin T. Baine and Emmet T. Flood.
Brief of amici curiae filed on behalf of the United States Catholic Conference by Mark E. Chopko, John A. Liekweg, and Jeffrey Hunter Moon.
Brief of amici curiae filed on behalf of the Washington Legal Foundation by Daniel J. Popeo and R. Shawn Gunnarson.
Brief of amici curiae filed on behalf of the Rutherford Institute by John W. Whitehead and Steven H. Aden.
Brief of amici curiae filed on behalf of the Christian Legal Society, et al., by Steven T. McFarland, Samuel B. Casey, and Carl H. Esbeck.
Brief of amici curiae filed on behalf of the Pacific Legal Foundation by Sharon L. Browne and Deborah J. La Fetra.

IV. THE SUPREME COURT'S DECISION

"The Establishment Clause of the First Amendment dictates that 'Congress shall make no law respecting an establishment of religion.' . . .

In this case, our inquiry under Agostini's purpose and effect test is a narrow one. Because respondents do not challenge the District Court's holding that Chapter 2 has a secular purpose, and because the Fifth Circuit also did not question that holding, we will consider only Chapter 2's effect. Further, in determining that effect, we will consider only the first two Agostini criteria, since neither respondents nor the Fifth Circuit has questioned the District Court's holding that Chapter 2 does not create an excessive entanglement. Considering Chapter 2 in light of our more recent case law, we conclude that it neither results in religious indoctrination by the government nor defines its recipients by reference to religion. We therefore hold that Chapter 2 is not a 'law respecting an establishment of religion.' In so holding, we acknowledge what both the Ninth and Fifth Circuits saw was inescapable—Meek and Wolman are anomalies in our case law. We therefore conclude that they are no longer good law. . . .

As we indicated in Agostini, and have indicated elsewhere, the question whether governmental aid to religious schools results in governmental indoctrination is ultimately a question whether any religious indoctrination that occurs in those schools could reasonably be attributed to governmental action. . . . We have also indicated that the answer to the question of indoctrination will resolve the question whether a program of educational aid 'subsidizes' religion, as our religion cases use that term. . . .

Applying the two relevant Agostini criteria, we see no basis for concluding that Jefferson Parish's Chapter 2 program 'has the effect of advancing religion.' Chapter 2 does not result in governmental indoctrination, because it determines eligibility for aid neutrally, allocates that aid based on the private choices of the parents of schoolchildren, and does not provide aid that has an impermissible content. Nor does Chapter 2 define its recipients by reference to religion.

Taking the second criterion first, it is clear that Chapter 2 aid 'is allocated on the basis of neutral, secular criteria that neither favor nor disfavor religion, and is made available to both religious and secular beneficiaries on a nondiscriminatory basis.' Aid is allocated based on enrollment: 'Private schools receive Chapter 2 materials and equipment based on the per capita number of students at each school,' and allocations to private schools must 'be equal (consistent with the number of children to be served) to expenditures for programs under this subchapter for children enrolled in the public schools of the [LEA],' 20 U. S. C. § 7372(b). . . . The allocation criteria therefore create no improper incentive. . . .

Chapter 2 also satisfies the first Agostini criterion. The program makes a broad array of schools eligible for aid without regard to their religious affiliations or lack thereof. § 7372; see § 7353(a)(3). We therefore have no difficulty concluding that Chapter 2 is neutral with regard to religion. . . .

Finally, Chapter 2 satisfies the first Agostini criterion because it does not provide to religious schools aid that has an impermissible content. The statute explicitly bars anything of the sort, providing that all Chapter 2 aid for the benefit of children in private schools shall be 'secular, neutral, and nonideological,' § 7372(a)(1), and the record indicates that the Louisiana SEA and the Jefferson Parish LEA have faithfully enforced this requirement insofar as relevant to this case. . . .

There is evidence that equipment has been, or at least easily could be, diverted for use in religious classes. [T]he evidence of actual diversion and the weakness of the safeguards against actual diversion are not relevant to the constitutional inquiry, whatever relevance they may have under the statute and regulations. . . .

In short, Chapter 2 satisfies both the first and second primary criteria of Agostini. It therefore does not have the effect of advancing religion. For the same reason, Chapter 2 also 'cannot reasonably be viewed as an endorsement of religion.' Accordingly, we hold that Chapter 2 is not a law respecting an establishment of religion. Jefferson Parish need not exclude religious schools from its Chapter 2 program. To the extent that Meek and Wolman conflict with this holding, we overrule them.. . .

The judgment of the Fifth Circuit is reversed."

V. JUSTICE VOTE

3 Pro ACLU Side vs. 6 Con Opposing Side

ACLU Side (Respondent / Appellee)

1. Souter, D. – Wrote dissenting opinion
2. Stevens, J. – Joined Souter's dissent
3. Ginsburg, R. – Joined Souter's dissent

Opposing Side (Petitioner / Appellant)

1. Thomas, C. – Wrote majority opinion
2. Rehnquist, W. – Joined majority opinion
3. Scalia, A. – Joined majority opinion
4. Kennedy, A. – Joined majority opinion
5. O'Connor, S. – Wrote concurring opinion
6. Breyer, S. – Joined O'Connor's concurrence

VI. A WIN OR LOSS FOR THE ACLU?

The ACLU, as amicus curiae, urged affirmance of the judgment of the Fifth Circuit; the Supreme Court reversed in a 6-3 vote, giving the ACLU an apparent loss.

891. Stenberg v. Carhart

(Decided June 28, 2000; 530 U.S. 914)

I. ISSUE

A. Issues Discussed

Federal Rights, Abortion

B. Legal Question Presented

"[W]hether Nebraska's statute, making criminal the performance of a 'partial birth abortion,' violates the Federal Constitution, as interpreted in Planned Parenthood of Southeastern Pa. v. Casey, 505 U. S. 833 (1992), and Roe v. Wade, 410 U. S. 113 (1973)."

C. Supreme Court's Answer

"We conclude that it does for at least two independent reasons. First, the law lacks any exception "for the preservation of the . . . health of the mother." Second, it 'imposes an undue burden on a woman's ability' to choose a D&E abortion, thereby unduly burdening the right to choose abortion itself."

II. CASE SUMMARY

A. Background

Nebraska has a statute "banning 'partial birth abortion.' The statute reads as follows:

'No partial birth abortion shall be performed in this state, unless such procedure is necessary to save the life of the mother whose life is endangered by a physical disorder, physical illness, or physical injury, including a life-endangering physical condition caused by or arising from the pregnancy itself.' Neb. Rev. Stat. Ann. §28–328(1) (Supp. 1999).

The statute defines 'partial birth abortion' as: 'an abortion procedure in which the person performing the abortion partially delivers vaginally a living unborn child before killing the unborn child and completing the delivery." § 28–326(9).

It further defines 'partially delivers vaginally a living unborn child before killing the unborn child' to mean 'deliberately and intentionally delivering into the vagina a living unborn child, or a substantial portion thereof, for the purpose of performing a procedure that the person performing such procedure knows will kill the unborn child and does kill the unborn child.'

The law classifies violation of the statute as a 'Class III felony' carrying a prison term of up to 20 years, and a fine of up to $25,000. §§28–328(2), 28–105. It also provides for the automatic revocation of a doctor's license to practice medicine in Nebraska. §28–328(4). . . .

Dr. Leroy Carhart is a Nebraska physician who performs abortions in a clinical setting. He brought this lawsuit in Federal District Court seeking a declaration that the Nebraska statute violates the Federal Constitution, and asking for an injunction forbidding its enforcement. After a trial on the merits, during which both sides presented several expert witnesses, the District Court held the statute unconstitutional. On appeal, the Eighth Circuit affirmed."

The Supreme Court granted certiorari to review the case and affirmed.

B. Counsel of Record / ACLU Attorney

ACLU Side (Respondent / Appellee): Simon Heller argued the cause for appellee.

Opposing Side (Petitioner / Appellant): Don Stenberg, Attorney General of Nebraska, pro se, argued the cause for appellant.

III. AMICI CURIAE

ACLU Side (Respondent / Appellee)

Brief of amici curiae filed on behalf of the ACLU, et al., by Catherine Weiss, Steven R. Shapiro, and Colleen K. Connell.

Brief of amici curiae filed on behalf of the United States by Solicitor General Waxman, Deputy Solicitor General Underwood, Paul R. Q. Wolfson, Harriet S. Rabb, Marcy J. Wilder, and Kenneth Y. Choe.

Brief of amici curiae filed on behalf of the State of California by Bill Lockyer, Attorney General, Peter J. Siggins, Chief Deputy Attorney General, and Patricia A. Wynne, Special Assistant Attorney General.

Brief of amici curiae filed on behalf of the State of New York, et al., by Eliot Spitzer, Attorney General of New York, Preeta D. Bansal, Solicitor General, and Jennifer K. Brown, Assistant Attorney General, Andrew Ketterer, Attorney General of Maine, Hardy Myers, Attorney General of Oregon, and William H. Sorrell, Attorney General of Vermont.

Brief of amici curiae filed on behalf of the American College of Obstetricians and Gynecologists, et al., by Adam L. Frank, A. Stephen Hut, Jr., and Matthew A. Brill.

Brief of amici curiae filed on behalf of the Naral Foundation, et al., by James P. Joseph, Nancy L. Perkins, and Elizabeth Arndorfer.

Brief of amici curiae filed on behalf of Planned Parenthood of Wisconsin, et al., by Roger K. Evans, Eve C. Gartner, and Dara Klassel.

Brief of amici curiae filed on behalf of the Religious Coalition for Reproductive Choice, et al., by Carrie Y. Flaxman.

Brief of amici curiae filed on behalf of Seventy-five Organizations Committed to Women's Equality by Susan Frietsche, Carol E. Tracy, Martha F. Davis, Roslyn Powell, and Yolanda S. Wu.

Brief of amici curiae filed on behalf of Senator Barbara Boxer, et al., by Robert Lewin, Kevin J. Curnin, Claude G. Szyfer, and Robert Abrams.

Opposing Side (Petitioner / Appellant)

Brief of amici curiae filed on behalf of the State of Louisiana, et al., by Richard P. Ieyoub, Attorney General of Louisiana, Roy A. Mongrue, Jr., Assistant Attorney General, Dorinda C. Bordlee, Special Assistant Attorney General, Mike Moore, Attorney General of Mississippi, Nikolas T. Nikas, and Stephen M. Crampton.

Brief of amici curiae filed on behalf of the State of Texas by John Cornyn, Attorney General, Andy Taylor, First Assistant Attorney General, Linda S. Eads, Deputy Attorney General, Gregory S. Coleman, Solicitor General, and Julie Caruthers Parsley, Deputy Solicitor General.
Brief of amici curiae filed on behalf of the State of Wisconsin by James E. Doyle, Attorney General, and Susan K. Ullman, Assistant Attorney General.
Brief of amici curiae filed on behalf of Agudath Israel of America by David Zwiebel.
Brief of amici curiae filed on behalf of the American Center for Law and Justice, et al., by Jay Alan Sekulow, James M. Henderson, Sr., Walter M. Weber, Thomas P. Monaghan, Richard Thompson, and Edward L. White III.
Brief of amici curiae filed on behalf of the Association of American Physicians and Surgeons, et al., by Teresa Stanton Collett.
Brief of amici curiae filed on behalf of Family First by Paul Benjamin Linton.
Brief of amici curiae filed on behalf of Feminists for Life of America, et al., by Dwight G. Duncan.
Brief of amici curiae filed on behalf of the Knights of Columbus by Pat A. Cipollone and Carl A. Anderson.
Brief of amici curiae filed on behalf of the National Association of Prolife Nurses, Inc., by William C. Porth and Robert P. George.
Brief of amici curiae filed on behalf of the National Right to Life Committee by James Bopp, Jr., Richard E. Coleson, and Thomas J. Marzen.
Brief of amici curiae filed on behalf of the Rutherford Institute by Thomas W. Strahan, John W. Whitehead, and Steven H. Aden.
Brief of amici curiae filed on behalf of the United States Catholic Conference, et al., by Mark E. Chopko and Michael F. Moses.
Brief of amici curiae filed on behalf of Representative Charles T. Canady, et al., by James Bopp, Jr., Richard E. Coleson, and Thomas J. Marzen.
Brief of amici curiae filed on behalf of the Commonwealth of Virginia, et al., by Mark L. Earley, Attorney General of Virginia, William H. Hurd, Solicitor General, and Daniel J. Poynor, Alison P. Landry, and Anthony P. Meredith, Assistant Attorneys General, Claire J. V. Richards, James Bopp, Jr., Richard E. Coleson, Thomas J. Marzen, Richard F. Collier, Jr., and by the Attorneys General for their respective States as follows: Bill Pryor of Alabama, Alan G. Lance of Idaho, James E. Ryan of Illinois, Thomas J. Miller of Iowa, Jennifer M. Granholm of Michigan, Heidi Heitkamp of North Dakota, Betty D. Montgomery of Ohio, D. Michael Fisher of Pennsylvania, Charlie Condon of South Carolina, Mark Barnett of South Dakota, and Jan Graham of Utah.
Brief of amici curiae filed on behalf of the Family Research Council by Teresa R. Wagner.

IV. THE SUPREME COURT'S DECISION

"Three established principles determine the issue before us. We shall set them forth in the language of the joint opinion in Casey. First, before 'viability . . . the woman has a right to choose to terminate her pregnancy.'

Second, 'a law designed to further the State's interest in fetal life which imposes an undue burden on the woman's decision before fetal viability' is unconstitutional. An 'undue burden is . . . shorthand for the conclusion that a state regulation has the purpose or effect of placing a substantial obstacle in the path of a woman seeking an abortion of a nonviable fetus.'

Third, "subsequent to viability, the State in promoting its interest in the potentiality of human life may, if it chooses, regulate, and even proscribe, abortion except where it is necessary, in appropriate medical judgment, for the preservation of the life or health of the mother." . . .

The question before us is whether Nebraska's statute, making criminal the performance of a 'partial birth abortion,' violates the Federal Constitution, as interpreted in Planned Parenthood of Southeastern Pa. v. Casey, 505 U. S. 833 (1992), and Roe v. Wade, 410 U. S. 113 (1973). We conclude that it does for at least two independent reasons. First, the law lacks any exception "for the preservation of the . . . health of the mother." Second, it 'imposes an undue burden on a woman's ability' to choose a D&E abortion, thereby unduly burdening the right to choose abortion itself. We shall discuss each of these reasons in turn. . . .

The Casey plurality opinion reiterated what the Court held in Roe; that "subsequent to viability, the State in promoting its interest in the potentiality of human life may, if it chooses, regulate, and even proscribe, abortion except where it is necessary, in appropriate medical judgment, for the preservation of the life or health of the mother."

The fact that Nebraska's law applies both previability and postviability aggravates the constitutional problem presented. The State's interest in regulating abortion previability is considerably weaker than postviability. Since the law requires a health exception in order to validate even a postviability abortion regulation, it at a minimum requires the same in respect to previability regulation. . . .

Nebraska has not convinced us that a health exception is 'never necessary to preserve the health of women.' Rather, a statute that altogether forbids D&X creates a significant health risk. The statute consequently must contain a health exception. This is not to say, as Justice Thomas and Justice Kennedy claim, that a State is prohibited from proscribing an abortion procedure whenever a particular physician deems the procedure preferable. By no means must a State grant physicians 'unfettered discretion' in their selection of abortion methods. But where substantial medical authority supports the proposition that banning a particular abortion procedure could endanger women's health, Casey requires the statute to include a health exception when the procedure is "necessary, in appropriate medical judgment, for the preservation of the life or health of the mother." Requiring such an exception in this case is no departure from Casey, but simply a straightforward application of its holding. . . .

The Eighth Circuit found the Nebraska statute unconstitutional because, in Casey's words, it has the 'effect of placing a substantial obstacle in the path of a woman seeking an abortion of a nonviable fetus.' It thereby places an 'undue burden' upon a woman's right to terminate her pregnancy before viability. Nebraska does not deny that the statute imposes an 'undue burden' if it applies to the more commonly used D&E procedure as well as to D&X. And we agree with the Eighth Circuit that it does so apply. . . .

In sum, using this law some present prosecutors and future Attorneys General may choose to pursue physicians who use D&E procedures, the most commonly used method for performing previability second trimester abortions. All those who perform abortion procedures using that method must fear prosecution, conviction, and imprisonment. The result is an undue burden upon a woman's right to make an abortion decision. We must consequently find the statute unconstitutional.

The judgment of the Court of Appeals is affirmed."

V. JUSTICE VOTE

5 Pro ACLU Side vs. 4 Con Opposing Side

ACLU Side (Respondent / Appellee)

1. Breyer, S. – Wrote majority opinion
2. O'Connor, S. – Wrote concurring opinion
3. Souter, D. – Joined majority opinion
4. Ginsburg, R. – Wrote concurring opinion, joined Stevens' concurrence
5. Stevens, J. – Wrote concurring opinion, joined Ginsburg's concurrence

Opposing Side (Petitioner / Appellant)

1. Rehnquist, W. – Wrote dissenting opinion, joined Kennedy's and Thomas' dissents
2. Scalia, A. – Wrote dissenting opinion, joined Thomas' dissent
3. Kennedy, A. – Wrote dissenting opinion
4. Thomas, C. – Wrote dissenting opinion

VI. A WIN OR LOSS FOR THE ACLU?

The ACLU, as amicus curiae, urged affirmance of the judgment of the Court of Appeals; the Supreme Court affirmed in a 5-4 vote, giving the ACLU an apparent win.

892. City of Indianapolis v. Edmond

(Decided November 28, 2000; 531 U.S. 32)

I. ISSUE

A. Issues Discussed

4th Amendment, Drugs

B. Legal Question Presented

Whether a city of Indianapolis "highway checkpoint program whose primary purpose is the discovery and interdiction of illegal narcotics" violates the Fourth Amendment.

C. Supreme Court's Answer

"Because the primary purpose of the Indianapolis checkpoint program is ultimately indistinguishable from the general interest in crime control, the checkpoints violate the Fourth Amendment."

II. CASE SUMMARY

A. Background

"In August 1998, the city of Indianapolis began to operate vehicle checkpoints on Indianapolis roads in an effort to interdict unlawful drugs. The city conducted six such roadblocks between August and November that year, stopping 1,161 vehicles and arresting 104 motorists. Fifty-five arrests were for drug-related crimes, while 49 were for offenses unrelated to drugs. The overall 'hit rate' of the program was thus approximately nine percent.

The parties stipulated to the facts concerning the operation of the checkpoints by the Indianapolis Police Department (IPD) for purposes of the preliminary injunction proceedings instituted below. At each checkpoint location, the police stop a predetermined number of vehicles. Approximately 30 officers are stationed at the checkpoint. Pursuant to written directives issued by the chief of police, at least one officer approaches the vehicle, advises the driver that he or she is being stopped briefly at a drug checkpoint, and asks the driver to produce a license and registration. The officer also looks for signs of impairment and conducts an open-view examination of the vehicle from the outside. A narcotics- detection dog walks around the outside of each stopped vehicle.

The directives instruct the officers that they may conduct a search only by consent or based on the appropriate quantum of particularized suspicion. The officers must conduct each stop in the same manner until particularized suspicion develops, and the officers have no discretion to stop any vehicle out of sequence. The city agreed in the stipulation to operate the checkpoints in such a way as to ensure that the total duration of each stop, absent reasonable suspicion or probable cause, would be five minutes or less.

The affidavit of Indianapolis Police Sergeant Marshall DePew, although it is technically outside the parties' stipulation, provides further insight concerning the operation of the checkpoints. According to Sergeant DePew, checkpoint locations are selected weeks in advance based on such considerations as area crime statistics and traffic flow. The checkpoints are generally operated during daylight hours and are identified with lighted signs reading, "NARCOTICS CHECKPOINT ______ MILE AHEAD, NARCOTICS K-9 IN USE, BE PREPARED TO STOP. " Once a group of cars has been stopped, other traffic proceeds without interruption until all the stopped cars have been processed or diverted for further processing. Sergeant DePew also stated that the average stop for a vehicle not subject to further processing lasts two to three minutes or less.

Respondents James Edmond and Joell Palmer were each stopped at a narcotics checkpoint in late September 1998. Respondents then filed a lawsuit on behalf of themselves and the class of all motorists who had been stopped or were subject to being stopped in the future at the Indianapolis drug checkpoints. Respondents claimed that the roadblocks violated the Fourth Amendment of the United States Constitution and the search and seizure provision of the Indiana Constitution. Respondents requested declaratory and injunctive relief for the class, as well as damages and attorney's fees for themselves.

Respondents then moved for a preliminary injunction. Although respondents alleged that the officers who stopped them did not follow the written directives, they agreed to the stipulation concerning the operation of the checkpoints for purposes of the preliminary injunction proceedings. The parties also stipulated to certification of the plaintiff class. The United States District Court for the Southern District of Indiana agreed to class certification and denied the motion for a preliminary injunction, holding that the checkpoint program did not violate the Fourth Amendment. A divided panel of the United States Court of Appeals for the Seventh Circuit reversed, holding that the checkpoints contravened the Fourth Amendment. The panel denied rehearing."

The Supreme Court granted certiorari to review the case and affirmed.

B. Counsel of Record / ACLU Attorney

ACLU Side (Respondent / Appellee): Kenneth J. Falk argued the cause for appellee. With him on the brief were Jacquelyn E. Bowie, Sean C. Lemieux, and Steven R. Shapiro, ACLU affiliated attorneys.

Opposing Side (Petitioner / Appellant): A. Scott Chinn argued the cause for appellant. With him on the briefs were Anthony W. Overholt, Matthew R. Gutwein, and Thomas M. Fisher.

Patricia A. Millett argued the cause for the United States, as amicus curiae, by special leave of court.

III. AMICI CURIAE

ACLU Side (Respondent / Appellee)

Brief of amici curiae filed on behalf of the National Association of Criminal Defense Lawyers, et al., by Wesley MacNeil Oliver and Barbara Bergman.

Brief of amici curiae filed on behalf of the Rutherford Institute by John W. Whitehead and Steven H. Aden.

Brief of amici curiae filed on behalf of Americans for Effective Law Enforcement, Inc., et al., by Wayne W. Schmidt, James P. Manak, Richard Weintraub, and Bernard J. Farber, in support of neither party.

Opposing Side (Petitioner / Appellant)

Brief of amici curiae filed on behalf of the United States by Patricia A. Millett Solicitor General Waxman, Assistant Attorney General Robinson, and Deputy Solicitor General Dreeben.

Brief of amici curiae filed on behalf of the State of Kansas, et al., by Carla J. Stovall, Attorney General of Kansas, Stephen R. McAllister, State Solicitor, Jared S. Maag, Assistant Attorney General, and John M. Bailey, Chief State's Attorney of Connecticut, and by the Attorneys General for their respective States as follows: Bill Pryor of Alabama, Janet Napolitano of Arizona, Mark Pryor of Arkansas, Bill Lockyer of California, Robert A. Butterworth of Florida, James E. Ryan of Illinois, Karen M. Freeman-Wilson of Indiana, Thomas J. Miller of Iowa, Michael C. Moore of Mississippi, Don Stenberg of Nebraska, W. A. Drew Edmondson of Oklahoma, Jan Graham of Utah, and Mark L. Earley of Virginia.

Brief of amici curiae filed on behalf of the National League of Cities, et al., by Richard Ruda and James I. Crowley.

Brief of amici curiae filed on behalf of the Washington Legal Foundation, et al., by Daniel J. Popeo.

IV. THE SUPREME COURT'S DECISION

"The Fourth Amendment requires that searches and seizures be reasonable. A search or seizure is ordinarily unreasonable in the absence of individualized suspicion of wrongdoing. . . .

It is well established that a vehicle stop at a highway checkpoint effectuates a seizure within the meaning of the Fourth Amendment. The fact that officers walk a narcotics-detection dog around the exterior of each car at the Indianapolis checkpoints does not transform the seizure into a search. . . .

We have never approved a checkpoint program whose primary purpose was to detect evidence of ordinary criminal wrongdoing. Rather, our checkpoint cases have recognized only limited exceptions to the general rule that a seizure must be accompanied by some measure of individualized suspicion. We suggested in Prouse that we would not credit the 'general interest in crime control' as justification for a regime of suspicionless stops. Consistent with this suggestion, each of the checkpoint programs that we have approved was designed primarily to serve purposes closely related to the problems of policing the border or the necessity of ensuring roadway safety. Because the primary purpose of the Indianapolis narcotics checkpoint program is to uncover evidence of ordinary criminal wrongdoing, the program contravenes the Fourth Amendment. . . .

The primary purpose of the Indianapolis narcotics checkpoints is in the end to advance 'the general interest in crime control.' We decline to suspend the usual requirement of individualized suspicion where the police seek to employ a checkpoint primarily for the ordinary enterprise of investigating crimes. We cannot sanction stops justified only by the generalized and ever-present possibility that interrogation and inspection may reveal that any given motorist has committed some crime. . . .

Because the primary purpose of the Indianapolis checkpoint program is ultimately indistinguishable from the general interest in crime control, the checkpoints violate the Fourth Amendment. The judgment of the Court of Appeals is, accordingly, affirmed."

V. JUSTICE VOTE

6 Pro ACLU Side vs. 3 Con Opposing Side

ACLU Side (Respondent / Appellee)

1. O'Connor, S. – Wrote majority opinion
2. Stevens, J. – Joined majority opinion
3. Kennedy, A. – Joined majority opinion
4. Souter, D. – Joined majority opinion
5. Ginsburg, R. – Joined majority opinion
6. Breyer, S. – Joined majority opinion

Opposing Side (Petitioner / Appellant)

1. Rehnquist, W. – Wrote dissenting opinion
2. Thomas, C. – Wrote dissenting opinion, joined Rehnquist's dissent
3. Scalia, A. – Joined Rehnquist's dissent, in part

VI. A WIN OR LOSS FOR THE ACLU?

The ACLU, as counsel of record, urged affirmance of the judgment of the Court of Appeals; the Supreme Court affirmed in a 6-3 vote, giving the ACLU an apparent win.

893. Bush v. Palm Beach County Canvassing Board

(Decided December 1, 2000; 531 U.S. 70)

I. ISSUE

A. Issues Discussed

Voting

B. Legal Question Presented

"[W]hether the decision of the Florida Supreme Court, by effectively changing the State's elector appointment procedures after election day, violated the Due Process Clause or 3 U. S. C. § 5, and whether the decision of that court changed the manner in which the State's electors are to be selected, in violation of the legislature's power to designate the manner for selection under Art. II, § 1, cl. 2, of the United States Constitution."

C. Supreme Court's Answer

"After reviewing the opinion of the Florida Supreme Court, we find 'that there is considerable uncertainty as to the precise grounds for the decision.' This is sufficient reason for us to decline at this time to review the federal questions asserted to be present."

II. CASE SUMMARY

A. Background

"On November 8, 2000, the day following the Presidential election, the Florida Division of Elections reported that Governor Bush had received 2,909,135 votes, and respondent Democrat Vice President Albert Gore, Jr., had received 2,907,351, a margin of 1,784 in Governor Bush's favor. Under Fla. Stat. §102.141(4) (2000), because the margin of victory was equal to or less than one-half of one percent of the votes cast, an automatic machine recount occurred. The recount resulted in a much smaller margin of victory for Governor Bush. Vice President Gore then exercised his statutory right to submit written requests for manual recounts to the canvassing board of any county. He requested recounts in four counties: Volusia, Palm Beach, Broward, and Miami-Dade.

The parties urged conflicting interpretations of the Florida Election Code respecting the authority of the canvassing boards, the Secretary of State (hereinafter Secretary), and the Elections Canvassing Commission. On November 14, in an action brought by Volusia County, and joined by the Palm Beach County Canvassing Board, Vice President Gore, and the Florida Democratic Party, the Florida Circuit Court ruled that the statutory 7-day deadline was mandatory, but that the Volusia board could amend its returns at a later date. The court further ruled that the Secretary, after 'considering all attendant facts and circumstances,' could exercise her discretion in deciding whether to include the late amended returns in the statewide certification.

The Secretary responded by issuing a set of criteria by which she would decide whether to allow a late filing. The Secretary ordered that, by 2 p.m. the following day, November 15, any county desiring to forward late returns submit a written statement of the facts and circumstances justifying a later filing. Four counties submitted statements, and, after reviewing the submissions, the Secretary determined that none justified an extension of the filing deadline. On November 16, the Florida Democratic Party and Vice President Gore filed an emergency motion in the state court, arguing that the Secretary had acted arbitrarily and in contempt of the court's earlier ruling. The following day, the court denied the motion, ruling that the Secretary had not acted arbitrarily and had exercised her discretion in a reasonable manner consistent with the court's earlier ruling. The Democratic Party and Vice President Gore appealed to the First District Court of Appeal, which certified the matter to the Florida Supreme Court. That court accepted jurisdiction and sua sponte entered an order enjoining the Secretary and the Elections Canvassing Commission from finally certifying the results of the election and declaring a winner until further order of that court.

The Supreme Court, with the expedition requisite for the controversy, issued its decision on November 21. As the court saw the matter, there were two principal questions: whether a discrepancy between an original machine return and a sample manual recount resulting from the way a ballot has been marked or punched is an 'error in vote tabulation' justifying a full manual recount; and how to reconcile what it spoke of as two conflicts in Florida's election laws: (a) between the timeframe for conducting a manual recount under Fla. Stat. §102.166 (2000) and the timeframe for submitting county returns under §§102.111 and 102.112, and (b) between §102.111, which provides that the Secretary 'shall . . . ignor[e]' late election returns, and §102.112, which provides that she 'may . . . ignor[e]' such returns.

With regard to the first issue, the court held that, under the plain text of the statute, a discrepancy between a sample manual recount and machine returns due to the way in which a ballot was punched or marked did constitute an 'error in vote tabulation' sufficient to trigger the statutory provisions for a full manual recount.

With regard to the second issue, the court held that the 'shall . . . ignor[e]' provision of §102.111 conflicts with the 'may . . . ignor[e]' provision of §102.112, and that the 'may . . . ignor[e]' provision controlled. The court turned to the questions whether and when the Secretary may ignore late manual recounts. The court relied in part upon the right to vote set forth in the Declaration of Rights of the Florida Constitution in concluding that late manual recounts could be rejected only under limited circumstances. The court then stated: '[B]ecause of our reluctance to rewrite the Florida Election Code, we conclude that we must invoke the equitable powers of this Court to fashion a remedy . . . .' The court thus imposed a deadline of November 26, at 5 p.m., for a return of ballot counts. The 7-day deadline of §102.111, assuming it would have applied, was effectively extended by 12 days. The court further directed the Secretary to accept manual counts submitted prior to that deadline."

The Supreme Court granted certiorari to review the case, vacated the decision below, and remanded the case.

B. Counsel of Record / ACLU Attorney

ACLU Side (Respondent / Appellee): Paul F. Hancock, Deputy Attorney General of Florida, argued the cause for appellee Butterworth, Attorney General of Florida.

Laurence H. Tribe argued the cause for appellees Gore, et al.

Opposing Side (Petitioner / Appellant): Theodore B. Olson argued the cause for appellant.

Joseph P. Klock, Jr., argued the cause for Katherine Harris, et al., appellees under Supreme Court Rule 12.6, in support of appellant.

III. AMICI CURIAE

ACLU Side (Respondent / Appellee)

Brief of amici curiae filed on behalf of the ACLU by Steven R. Shapiro, Laughlin McDonald, and James K. Green.

Brief of amici curiae filed on behalf of the State of Iowa, et al., by Thomas J. Miller, Attorney General of Iowa, Dennis W. Johnson, Solicitor General, and Tam B. Ormiston, Deputy Attorney General, and by the Attorneys General for their respective States as follows: Bill Lockyer of California, Richard Blumenthal of Connecticut, Earl I. Anzai of Hawaii, Karen M. Freeman-Wilson of Indiana, Andrew Ketterer of Maine, J. Joseph Curran, Jr., of Maryland, Thomas F. Reilly of Massachusetts, Joseph P. Mazurek of Montana, Frankie Sue Del Papa of Nevada, Patricia A. Madrid of New Mexico, Drew Edmondson of Oklahoma, Hardy Myers of Oregon, and Sheldon Whitehouse of Rhode Island.

Brief of amici curiae filed on behalf of the Coalition for Local Sovereignty by Kenneth B. Clark, in support of neither party.

Brief of amici curiae filed on behalf of the Florida Senate, et al., by Charles Fried, Einer Elhauge, and Roger J. Magnuson, in support of neither party.

Brief of amici curiae filed on behalf of the Disenfranchised Voters in the USA, et al., by Ilise Levy Feitshans, in support of neither party.

Opposing Side (Petitioner / Appellant)

Brief of amici curiae filed on behalf of the State of Alabama, et al., by Bill Pryor, Attorney General of Alabama, and Margaret L. Fleming, John J. Park, Jr., Charles B. Campbell, Scott L. Rouse, A. Vernon Barnett IV, and Richard E. Trewhella, Jr., Assistant Attorneys General.

Brief of amici curiae filed on behalf of the Commonwealth of Virginia, et al., by Mark L. Earley, Attorney General of Virginia, Randolph A. Beales, Chief Deputy Attorney General, William Henry Hurd, Solicitor General, Judith Williams Jagdmann, Deputy Attorney General, Siran S. Faulders and Maureen Riley Matsen, Senior Assistant Attorneys General, Eleanor Anne Chesney, Anthony P. Meredith, and Valerie L. Myers, Assistant Attorneys General, Charlie Condon, Attorney General of South Carolina, and Don Stenberg, Attorney General of Nebraska.

Brief of amici curiae filed on behalf of William H. Haynes, et al., by Jay Alan Sekulow, Thomas P. Monaghan, Stuart J. Roth, Colby M. May, James M. Henderson, Sr., David A. Cortman, Griffin B. Bell, Paul D. Clement, and Jeffrey S. Bucholtz.

Brief of amici curiae filed on behalf of the American Civil Rights Union by John C. Armor and Peter Ferrara.

IV. THE SUPREME COURT'S DECISION

"As a general rule, this Court defers to a state court's interpretation of a state statute. But in the case of a law enacted by a state legislature applicable not only to elections to state offices, but also to the selection of Presidential electors, the legislature is not acting solely under the authority given it by the people of the State, but by virtue of a direct grant of authority made under Art. II, §1, cl. 2, of the United States Constitution. That provision reads:

'Each State shall appoint, in such Manner as the Legislature thereof may direct, a Number of Electors, equal to the whole Number of Senators and Representatives to which the State may be entitled in the Congress . . . .'

Although we did not address the same question petitioner raises here, in McPherson v. Blacker, 146 U. S. 1, 25 (1892), we said:

'[Art. II, §1, cl. 2,] does not read that the people or the citizens shall appoint, but that 'each State shall'; and if the words 'in such manner as the legislature thereof may direct,' had been omitted, it would seem that the legislative power of appointment could not have been successfully questioned in the absence of any provision in the state constitution in that regard. Hence the insertion of those words, while operating as a limitation upon the State in respect of any attempt to circumscribe the legislative power, cannot be held to operate as a limitation on that power itself.'

There are expressions in the opinion of the Supreme Court of Florida that may be read to indicate that it construed the Florida Election Code without regard to the extent to which the Florida Constitution could, consistent with Art. II, §1, cl. 2, 'circumscribe the legislative power.' The opinion states, for example, that '[t]o the extent that the Legislature may enact laws regulating the electoral process, those laws are valid only if they impose no 'unreasonable or unnecessary' restraints on the right of suffrage' guaranteed by the State Constitution. The opinion also states that '[b]ecause election laws are intended to facilitate the right of suffrage, such laws must be liberally construed in favor of the citizens' right to vote . . . .'

In addition, 3 U. S. C. § 5 provides in pertinent part:

'If any State shall have provided, by laws enacted prior to the day fixed for the appointment of the electors, for its final determination of any controversy or contest concerning the appointment of all or any of the electors of such State, by judicial or other methods or procedures, and such determination shall have been made at least six days before the time fixed for the meeting of the electors, such determination made pursuant to such law so existing on said day, and made at least six days prior to said time of meeting of the electors, shall be conclusive, and shall govern in the counting of the electoral votes as provided in the Constitution, and as hereinafter regulated, so far as the ascertainment of the electors appointed by such State is concerned.'

The parties before us agree that whatever else may be the effect of this section, it creates a 'safe harbor' for a State insofar as congressional consideration of its electoral votes is concerned. If the state legislature has provided for final determination of contests or controversies by a law made prior to election day, that determination shall be conclusive if made at least six days prior to said time of meeting of the electors. The Florida Supreme Court cited 3 U. S. C. §§ 1–10 in a footnote of its opinion, but did not discuss § 5. Since § 5 contains a principle of federal law that would assure finality of the State's determination if made pursuant to a state law in effect before the election, a legislative wish to take advantage of the 'safe harbor' would counsel against any construction of the Election Code that Congress might deem to be a change in the law.

After reviewing the opinion of the Florida Supreme Court, we find 'that there is considerable uncertainty as to the precise grounds for the decision.' This is sufficient reason for us to decline at this time to review the federal questions asserted to be present.

'It is fundamental that state courts be left free and unfettered by us in interpreting their state constitutions. But it is equally important that ambiguous or obscure adjudications by state courts do not stand as barriers to a determination by this Court of the validity under the federal constitution of state action. Intelligent exercise of our appellate powers compels us to ask for the elimination of the obscurities and ambiguities from the opinions in such cases.'

Specifically, we are unclear as to the extent to which the Florida Supreme Court saw the Florida Constitution as circumscribing the legislature's authority under Art. II, §1, cl. 2. We are also unclear as to the consideration the Florida Supreme Court accorded to 3 U. S. C. § 5. The judgment of the Supreme Court of Florida is therefore vacated, and the case is remanded for further proceedings not inconsistent with this opinion."

V. JUSTICE VOTE

0 Pro ACLU Side vs. 9 Con Opposing Side

Opposing Side (Petitioner / Appellant)

1. Stevens, J. – Per curiam decision
2. Souter, D. – Per curiam decision
3. Ginsburg, R. – Per curiam decision
4. Breyer, S. – Per curiam decision
5. Rehnquist, W. – Per curiam decision
6. O'Connor, S. – Per curiam decision
7. Scalia, A. – Per curiam decision
8. Kennedy, A. – Per curiam decision
9. Thomas, C. – Per curiam decision

VI. A WIN OR LOSS FOR THE ACLU?

The ACLU, as amicus curiae, urged affirmance of the judgment of the Florida Supreme Court; the U.S. Supreme Court vacated the judgment and remanded the case in a per curiam decision, giving the ACLU an apparent loss.

894. Legal Services Corp. v. Velazquez

(Decided February 28, 2001; 531 U.S. 533)

I. ISSUE

A. Issues Discussed

First Amendment, press, speech, association

A. Legal Question Presented:

Whether prohibiting "legal representation funded by recipients of LSC moneys if the representation involves an effort to amend or otherwise challenge existing welfare law" "violates the First Amendment rights of LSC grantees and their clients."

B. Supreme Court's Answer:

"We agree that the restriction violates the First Amendment, and we affirm the judgment of the Court of Appeals."

II. CASE SUMMARY

A. Background

"[T]he Legal Services Corporation Act . . . establishes the Legal Services Corporation (LSC) . . . . LSC's mission is to distribute funds appropriated by Congress to eligible local grantee organizations 'for the purpose of providing financial support for legal assistance in noncriminal proceedings or matters to persons financially unable to afford legal assistance.' . . .

Each year LSC appropriates funds to grantees or recipients that hire and supervise lawyers for various professional activities, including representation of indigent clients seeking welfare benefits.

This suit requires us to decide whether one of the conditions imposed by Congress on the use of LSC funds violates the First Amendment rights of LSC grantees and their clients. [T]he restriction . . . prohibits legal representation funded by recipients of LSC moneys if the representation involves an effort to amend or otherwise challenge existing welfare law. As interpreted by the LSC and by the Government, the restriction prevents an attorney from arguing to a court that a state statute conflicts with a federal statute or that either a state or federal statute by its terms or in its application is violative of the United States Constitution.

Lawyers employed by New York City LSC grantees, together with private LSC contributors, LSC indigent clients, and various state and local public officials whose governments contribute to LSC grantees, brought suit in the United States District Court for the Eastern District of New York to declare the restriction, among other provisions of the Act, invalid. The United States Court of Appeals for the Second Circuit approved an injunction against enforcement of the provision as an impermissible viewpoint-based discrimination in violation of the First Amendment. [The Supreme Court] granted certiorari" to review the case.

B. Counsel of Record

ACLU Side (Respondent / Appellee): Burt Neuborne argued the cause for appellees in both cases. With him on the brief were Laura K. Abel, Kimani, Paul-Emile, Paul K. Sonn, David S. Udell, Peter M. Fishbein, and Alan E. Rothman.

Opposing Side (Petitioner / Appellant): Alan Levine argued the cause for appellant. With him on the briefs was Stephen L. Ascher.

Deputy Solicitor General Kneedler argued the cause for appellant. With him on the briefs were Solicitor General Waxman, Acting Assistant Attorney General Ogden, Beth S. Brinkmann, Barbara L. Herwig, and Matthew M. Collette.

III. AMICI CURIAE

ACLU Side (Respondent / Appellee)

Brief of amici curiae filed on behalf of the American Civil Liberties Union, the New York Civil Liberties Union, the National Legal and Defender Association, the National Coalition Against Censorship, and the Center for Constitutional Rights by Arthur N. Eisenberg and Steven R. Shapiro.

Brief of amici curiae filed on behalf of the New York State Bar Association et al. by Bruce A. Green and Lawrence S. Lustberg.

Brief of amici curiae filed on behalf of the American Judicature Society by Frederick A. O. Schwarz, Jr.

Opposing Side (Petitioner / Appellant)

Brief of amici curiae filed on behalf of the Pacific Legal Foundation by John H. Findley.

Brief of amici curiae filed on behalf of the Washington Legal Foundation et al. by Daniel J. Popeo and R. Shawn Gunnarson.

IV. THE SUPREME COURT'S DECISION

"From the inception of the LSC, Congress has placed restrictions on its use of funds. . . .

We are concerned with the statutory provision which excludes LSC representation in cases which 'involve an effort to amend or otherwise challenge existing law in effect on the date of the initiation of the representation.'. . .

Interpretation of the law and the Constitution is the primary mission of the judiciary when it acts within the sphere of its authority to resolve a case or controversy. . . . An informed, independent judiciary presumes an informed, independent bar. Under § 504(a)(16), however, cases would be presented by LSC attorneys who could not advise the courts of serious questions of statutory validity. The disability is inconsistent with the proposition that attorneys should present all the reasonable and well-grounded arguments necessary for proper resolution of the case. By seeking to prohibit the analysis of certain legal issues and to truncate presentation to the courts, the enactment under review prohibits speech and expression upon which courts must depend for the proper exercise of the judicial power. . . .

The restriction imposed by the statute here threatens severe impairment of the judicial function. Section 504(a)(16) sifts out cases presenting constitutional challenges in order to insulate the Government's laws from judicial inquiry. If the restriction on speech and legal advice were to stand, the result would be two tiers of cases. In cases where LSC counsel were attorneys of record, there would be lingering doubt whether the truncated representation had resulted in complete analysis of the case, full advice to the client, and proper presentation to the court. The courts and the public would come to question the adequacy and fairness of professional representations when the attorney, either consciously to comply with this statute or unconsciously to continue the representation despite the statute, avoided all reference to questions of statutory validity and constitutional authority. A scheme so inconsistent with accepted separation-of-powers principles is an insufficient basis to sustain or uphold the restriction on speech.

It is no answer to say the restriction on speech is harmless because, under LSC's interpretation of the Act, its attorneys can withdraw. This misses the point. The statute is an attempt to draw lines around the LSC program to exclude from litigation those arguments and theories Congress finds unacceptable but which by their nature are within the province of the courts to consider.

The restriction on speech is even more problematic because in cases where the attorney withdraws from a representation, the client is unlikely to find other counsel. The explicit premise for providing LSC attorneys is the necessity to make available representation 'to persons financially unable to afford legal assistance.' There often will be no alternative source for the client to receive vital information respecting constitutional and statutory rights bearing upon claimed benefits. Thus, with respect to the litigation services Congress has funded, there is no alternative channel for expression of the advocacy Congress seeks to restrict. . . .

It is fundamental that the First Amendment "was fashioned to assure unfettered interchange of ideas for the bringing about of political and social changes desired by the people." There can be little doubt that the LSC Act funds constitutionally protected expression . . . .

Congress was not required to fund an LSC attorney to represent indigent clients; and when it did so, it was not required to fund the whole range of legal representations or relationships. The LSC and the United States, however, in effect ask us to permit Congress to define the scope of the litigation it funds to exclude certain vital theories and ideas. The attempted restriction is designed to insulate the Government's interpretation of the Constitution from judicial challenge. The Constitution does not permit the Government to confine litigants and their attorneys in this manner. We must be vigilant when Congress imposes rules and conditions which in effect insulate its own laws from legitimate judicial challenge. Where private speech is involved, even Congress' antecedent funding decision cannot be aimed at the suppression of ideas thought inimical to the Government's own interest.

For the reasons we have set forth, the funding condition is invalid. The Court of Appeals considered whether the language restricting LSC attorneys could be severed from the statute so that the remaining portions would remain operative. It reached the reasoned conclusion to invalidate the fragment of § 504(a)(16) found contrary to the First Amendment, leaving the balance of the statute operative and in place. That determination was not discussed in the briefs of either party or otherwise contested here, and in the exercise of our discretion and prudential judgment we decline to address it.

The judgment of the Court of Appeals is affirmed."

V. JUSTICE VOTE

5 Pro ACLU Side vs. 4 Con Opposing Side

ACLU Side (Respondent / Appellee)

1. Kennedy, A. – Wrote majority opinion
2. Ginsburg, R. – Joined majority opinion
3. Souter, D. – Joined majority opinion
4. Stevens, J. – Joined majority opinion
5. Breyer, S. – Joined majority opinion

Opposing Side (Petitioner / Appellant)

1. Scalia, A. – Wrote dissenting opinion
2. Rehnquist, W. – Joined Scalia's dissent
3. Thomas, C. – Joined Scalia's dissent
4. O'Connor, S. – Joined Scalia's dissent

VI. A WIN OR LOSS FOR THE ACLU?

The ACLU filed as amicus curiae, urging affirmance; the Supreme Court upheld the Court of Appeals' decision by a 5-4 vote, giving the ACLU an apparent win.

895. Ferguson v. City of Charleston

(Decided March 21, 2001; 532 U.S. 67)

I. ISSUE

A. Issues Discussed

4th Amendment, drugs

C. Legal Question Presented

"[W]hether a state hospital's performance of a diagnostic test to obtain evidence of a patient's criminal conduct for law enforcement purposes is an unreasonable search if the patient has not consented to the procedure. More narrowly, the question is whether the interest in using the threat of criminal sanctions to deter pregnant women from using cocaine can justify a departure from the general rule that an official nonconsensual search is unconstitutional if not authorized by a valid warrant."

D. Supreme Court's Answer:

"The Fourth Amendment's general prohibition against nonconsensual, warrantless, and suspicionless searches necessarily applies to such a policy."

II. CASE SUMMARY

A. Background

"In the fall of 1988, staff members at the public hospital operated in the city of Charleston by the Medical University of South Carolina (MUSC) became concerned about an apparent increase in the use of cocaine by patients who were receiving prenatal treatment. In response to this perceived increase, as of April 1989, MUSC began to order drug screens to be performed on urine samples from maternity patients who were suspected of using cocaine. If a patient tested positive, she was then referred by MUSC staff to the county substance abuse commission for counseling and treatment. However, despite the referrals, the incidence of cocaine use among the patients at MUSC did not appear to change.

Some four months later, Nurse Shirley Brown . . . heard a news broadcast reporting that the police in Greenville, South Carolina, were arresting pregnant users of cocaine on the theory that such use harmed the fetus and was therefore child abuse. Nurse Brown discussed the story with MUSC's general counsel, Joseph C. Good, Jr., who then contacted Charleston Solicitor Charles Condon in order to offer MUSC's cooperation in prosecuting mothers whose children tested positive for drugs at birth.

After receiving Good's letter, Solicitor Condon took . . . steps in developing the policy at issue in this case. . . . Their deliberations led to MUSC's adoption of . . . 'POLICY M-7,' dealing with the subject of 'Management of Drug Abuse During Pregnancy.'

The first three pages of Policy M-7 set forth the procedure to be followed by the hospital staff to 'identify/assist pregnant patients suspected of drug abuse.' . . . Most important, it added the threat of law enforcement intervention that 'provided the necessary 'leverage' to make the [p]olicy effective.' . . .

Petitioners are 10 women who received obstetrical care at MUSC and who were arrested after testing positive for cocaine. Four of them were arrested during the initial implementation of the policy; they were not offered the opportunity to receive drug treatment as an alternative to arrest. The others were arrested after the policy was modified in 1990; they either failed to comply with the terms of the drug treatment program or tested positive for a second time. . . .

Petitioners' complaint challenged the validity of the policy under various theories, including the claim that warrantless and nonconsensual drug tests conducted for criminal investigatory purposes were unconstitutional searches. . . . The jury found for respondents.

Petitioners appealed, arguing that the evidence was not sufficient to support the jury's consent finding. The Court of Appeals for the Fourth Circuit affirmed, but without reaching the question of consent."

The Supreme Court granted certiorari to review the case.

B. Counsel of Record

ACLU Side (Petitioner / Appellant): Priscilla J. Smith argued the cause for appellants. With her on the briefs were Simon Heller, Lynn Paltrow, Susan Frietsche, David S. Cohen, Susan Dunn, David Rudovsky, and Seth Kreimer

Opposing Side (Respondent / Appellee): Robert H. Hood argued the cause for appellees. With him on the brief were Barbara Wynne Showers and Mary Agnes Hood Craig.

III. AMICI CURIAE

ACLU Side (Petitioner / Appellant)

Brief of amici curiae filed on behalf of the American Civil Liberties Union; NOW Legal Defense and Education Fund; National Organization for Women Foundation, Inc.; African-American Women Evolving; Americans for Democratic Action, Inc.; Center for Constitutional Rights; Center for Women Policy Studies; Chicago Abortion Fund; Choice; Connecticut Women's Education and Legal Fund; Hawaii State Coalition Against Domestic Violence; Hawai'i Women Lawyers; Iowa Coalition Against Domestic Violence; Medical Students for Choice; National Association of Women Lawyers; National Center for Pro-Choice Majority; National Network of Abortion Funds; National Society of Genetic Counselors; Northwest Women's Law Center; South Carolina Coalition Against Domestic Violence and Sexual Assault; South Dakota Coalition Against Domestic Violence and Sexual Assault; Women's Law Center of Maryland, Inc.; and Wider Opportunities For Women by Julie E. Sternberg, Steven

R. Shapiro, Sara L. Mandelbaum, Catherine Weiss, Louise Melling, Louis M. Bograd, Martha F. Davis, Yolanda S. Wu, and Roslyn Powell.

Brief of amici curiae filed on behalf of the American Medical Association by Michael Ile, Anne Murphy, and Leonard Nelson.

Brief of amici curiae filed on behalf of the American Public Health Association et al. by Daniel N. Abrahamson and David T. Goldberg.

Brief of amici curiae filed on behalf of the NARAL Foundation et al. by Nancy L. Perkins and Jodi Michael.

Brief of amici curiae filed on behalf of the National Coalition for Child Protection Reform et al. by Carolyn A. Kubitschek.

Brief of amici curiae filed on behalf of the Rutherford Institute by John W. Whitehead and Steven H. Aden.

Opposing Side (Respondent / Appellee)

No briefs of amici curiae were filed in support of appellee.

IV. THE SUPREME COURT'S DECISION

"Because MUSC is a state hospital, the members of its staff are government actors, subject to the strictures of the Fourth Amendment. Moreover, the urine tests conducted by those staff members were indisputably searches within the meaning of the Fourth Amendment. Neither the District Court nor the Court of Appeals concluded that any of the nine criteria used to identify the women to be searched provided either probable cause to believe that they were using cocaine, or even the basis for a reasonable suspicion of such use. Rather, the District Court and the Court of Appeals viewed the case as one involving MUSC's right to conduct searches without warrants or probable cause. Furthermore, given the posture in which the case comes to us, we must assume for purposes of our decision that the tests were performed without the informed consent of the patients.

Because the hospital seeks to justify its authority to conduct drug tests and to turn the results over to law enforcement agents without the knowledge or consent of the patients, this case differs from the four previous cases in which we have considered whether comparable drug tests 'fit within the closely guarded category of constitutionally permissible suspicionless searches.' . . .

In each of those cases, we employed a balancing test that weighed the intrusion on the individual's interest in privacy against the 'special needs' that supported the program. As an initial matter, we note that the invasion of privacy in this case is far more substantial than in those cases. . . .

The critical difference between those four drug-testing cases and this one, however, lies in the nature of the 'special need' asserted as justification for the warrantless searches. In each of those earlier cases, the 'special need' that was advanced as a justification for the absence of a warrant or individualized suspicion was one divorced from the State's general interest in law enforcement. . . . In this case, however, the central and indispensable feature of the policy from its inception was the use of law enforcement to coerce the patients into substance abuse treatment. . . .

Respondents argue in essence that their ultimate purpose—namely, protecting the health of both mother and child—is a beneficent one. In Chandler, however, we did not simply accept the State's invocation of a 'special need.' Instead, we carried out a 'close review' of the scheme at issue before concluding that the need in question was not 'special,' as that term has been defined in our cases. In this case, a review of the M–7 policy plainly reveals that the purpose actually served by the MUSC searches 'is ultimately indistinguishable from the general interest in crime control.' . . .

While the ultimate goal of the program may well have been to get the women in question into substance abuse treatment and off of drugs, the immediate objective of the searches was to generate evidence for law enforcement purposes in order to reach that goal. The threat of law enforcement may ultimately have been intended as a means to an end, but the direct and primary purpose of MUSC's policy was to ensure the use of those means. In our opinion, this distinction is critical. Because law enforcement involvement always serves some broader social purpose or objective, under respondents' view, virtually any nonconsensual suspicionless search could be immunized under the special needs doctrine by defining the search solely in terms of its ultimate, rather than immediate, purpose. Such an approach is inconsistent with the Fourth Amendment. Given the primary purpose of the Charleston program, which was to use the threat of arrest and prosecution in order to force women into treatment, and given the extensive involvement of law enforcement officials at every stage of the policy, this case simply does not fit within the closely guarded category of 'special needs.'

. . .

The stark and unique fact that characterizes this case is that Policy M–7 was designed to obtain evidence of criminal conduct by the tested patients that would be turned over to the police and that could be admissible in subsequent criminal prosecutions. While respondents are correct that drug abuse both was and is a serious problem, 'the gravity of the threat alone cannot be dispositive of questions concerning what means law enforcement officers may employ to pursue a given purpose.' The Fourth Amendment's general prohibition against nonconsensual, warrantless, and suspicionless searches necessarily applies to such a policy.

Accordingly, the judgment of the Court of Appeals is reversed, and the case is remanded for further proceedings consistent with this opinion."

V. JUSTICE VOTE

6 Pro ACLU Side vs. 3 Con Opposing Side

ACLU Side (Petitioner / Appellant)

1. Stevens, J. – Wrote majority opinion
2. O'Connor, S. – Joined majority opinion
3. Souter, D. – Joined majority opinion
4. Ginsburg, R. – Joined majority opinion
5. Breyer, S. – Joined majority opinion
6. Kennedy, A. – Wrote concurring opinion

Opposing Side (Respondent / Appellee)

1. Scalia, A. – Wrote dissenting opinion
2. Rehnquist, W. – Joined Scalia's dissent in part
3. Thomas, C. – Joined Scalia's dissent in part

VI. A WIN OR LOSS FOR THE ACLU?

The ACLU filed as amicus curiae urging reversal of the judgment of the Court of Appeals; the Supreme Court reversed and remanded in a 6-3 vote, giving the ACLU an apparent win.

896. Shaw v. Murphy

(Decided April 18, 2001; 532 U.S. 223)

I. ISSUE

A. Issues Discussed

Prison, 1st Amendment, press, speech, association

B. Legal Question Presented

"[W]hether prisoners possess a First Amendment right to provide legal assistance that enhances the protections otherwise available under Turner." Turner provides that "restrictions on prisoners' communications to other inmates are constitutional if the restrictions are 'reasonably related to legitimate penological interests.'"

C. Supreme Court's Answer

"We . . . decline to cloak the provision of legal assistance with any First Amendment protection above and beyond the protection normally accorded prisoners' speech. Instead, the proper constitutional test is the one we set forth in Turner."

II. CASE SUMMARY

A. Background

"While respondent Kevin Murphy was incarcerated at the Montana State Prison, he served as an 'inmate law clerk,' providing legal assistance to fellow prisoners. Upon learning that inmate Pat Tracy had been charged with assaulting Correctional Officer Glen Galle, Murphy decided to assist Tracy with his defense. Prison rules prohibited Murphy's assignment to the case, but he nonetheless investigated the assault. After discovering that other inmates had complained about Officer Galle's conduct, Murphy sent Tracy a letter . . . .

In accordance with prison policy, prison officials intercepted the letter, and petitioner Robert Shaw, an officer in the maximum-security unit, reviewed it. Based on the accusations against Officer Galle, Shaw cited Murphy for violations of the prison's rules prohibiting insolence, interference with due process hearings, and conduct that disrupts or interferes with the security and orderly operation of the institution. After a hearing, Murphy was found guilty of violating the first two prohibitions. The hearings officer sanctioned him by imposing a suspended sentence of 10 days' detention and issuing demerits that could affect his custody level.

In response, Murphy brought this action, seeking declaratory and injunctive relief under Rev. Stat. § 1979, 42 U.S.C. § 1983. The case was styled as a class action, brought on behalf of himself, other inmate law clerks, and other prisoners. The complaint alleged that the disciplining of Murphy violated due process, the rights of inmates to access the courts, and, as relevant here, Murphy's First Amendment rights, including the right to provide legal assistance to other inmates.

After discovery, the District Court granted petitioners' motion for summary judgment on all of Murphy's claims. On the First Amendment claim, the court found that Murphy was not formally acting as an inmate law clerk when he wrote the letter, and that Murphy's claims should therefore 'be analyzed without consideration of any privilege that law clerk status might provide.' The District Court then applied our decision in Turner v. Safley, which held that a prison regulation impinging on inmates' constitutional rights is valid 'if it is reasonably related to legitimate penological interests.' Finding a 'valid, rational connection between the prison inmate correspondence policy and the objectives of prison order, security, and inmate rehabilitation,' the District Court rejected Murphy's First Amendment claim.

The Court of Appeals for the Ninth Circuit reversed. It premised its analysis on the proposition that 'inmates have a First Amendment right to assist other inmates with their legal claims.' Murphy enjoyed this right of association, the court concluded, because he was providing legal advice that potentially was relevant to Tracy's defense. The Court of Appeals then applied our decision in Turner, but it did so only against the backdrop of this First Amendment right, which, the court held, affected the balance of the prisoner's interests against the government's interests. Concluding that the balance tipped in favor of Murphy, the Court of Appeals upheld Murphy's First Amendment claim.

Other Courts of Appeals have rejected similar claims. . . . To resolve the conflict, [the Supreme Court] granted certiorari."

B. Counsel of Record

ACLU Side (Respondent / Appellee): Jeffrey T. Renz argued the cause for appellee.

Opposing Side (Petitioner / Appellant): David L. Ohler, Special Assistant Attorney General of Montana, argued the cause for appellants. With him on the briefs were Joseph P. Mazurek, Attorney General, and Diana Leibinger-Koch, Special Assistant Attorney General.

Patricia A. Millett argued the cause for the United States, as amicus curiae, by special leave of court.

III. AMICI CURIAE

ACLU Side (Respondent / Appellee)

Brief of amici curiae filed on behalf of the Legal Aid Society of the City of New York, American Civil Liberties Union, Human Rights Watch, and Southern Center for Human Rights by Daniel L. Greenberg, John Boston, Mary Lynne Werlwas, Elizabeth Alexander, Margaret Winter, David C. Fathi, Jamie Fellner, Stephen Bright, and Tamara Serwer.

Opposing Side (Petitioner / Appellant)

Brief of amici curiae filed on behalf of the United States by Patricia A. Millett, Solicitor General Waxman, Assistant Attorney General Ogden, Deputy Solicitor General Underwood, Gregory G. Garre, Barbara L. Herwig, and John Hoyle.

Brief of amici curiae filed on behalf of the State of Florida et al. by Robert A. Butterworth, Attorney General of Florida, Thomas E. Warner, Solicitor General, and Cecilia Bradley, Assistant Attorney General, and by the Attorneys General for their respective States as follows: Bill Pryor of Alabama, Mark Pryor of Arkansas, M. Jane Brady of Delaware, James E. Ryan of Illinois, Thomas J. Miller of Iowa, Carla J. Stovall of Kansas, Richard P. Ieyoub of Louisiana, Thomas F. Reilly of Massachusetts, Don Stenberg of Nebraska, Philip T. McLaughlin of New Hampshire, Heidi Heitkamp of North Dakota, Betty D. Montgomery of Ohio, W. A. Drew Edmondson of Oklahoma, Jan Graham of Utah, William H. Sorrell of Vermont, and Mark L. Earley of Virginia.

Brief of amici curiae filed on behalf of the Criminal Justice Legal Foundation by Kent S. Scheidegger and Charles L. Hobson.

IV. THE SUPREME COURT'S DECISION

"In this case, we are not asked to decide whether prisoners have any First Amendment rights when they send legal correspondence to one another. In Turner, we held that restrictions on inmate-to-inmate communications pass constitutional muster only if the restrictions are reasonably related to legitimate and neutral governmental objectives. We did not limit our holding to nonlegal correspondence, and petitioners do not ask us to construe it that way. Instead, the question presented here simply asks whether Murphy possesses a First Amendment right to provide legal advice that enhances the protections otherwise available under Turner. The effect of such a right, as the Court of Appeals described it, would be that inmate-to-inmate correspondence that includes legal assistance would receive more First Amendment protection than correspondence without any legal assistance. We conclude that there is no such special right. . . .

To increase the constitutional protection based upon the content of a communication first requires an assessment of the value of that content. But the Turner test, by its terms, simply does not accommodate valuations of content. On the contrary, the Turner factors concern only the relationship between the asserted penological interests and the prison regulation.

Moreover, under Turner and its predecessors, prison officials are to remain the primary arbiters of the problems that arise in prison management. . . . If courts were permitted to enhance constitutional protection based on their assessments of the content of the particular communications, courts would be in a position to assume a greater role in decisions affecting prison administration. . . .

Finally, even if we were to consider giving special protection to particular kinds of speech based upon content, we would not do so for speech that includes legal advice. Augmenting First Amendment protection for inmate legal advice would undermine prison officials' ability to address the 'complex and intractable' problems of prison administration. . . .

We thus decline to cloak the provision of legal assistance with any First Amendment protection above and beyond the protection normally accorded prisoners' speech. Instead, the proper constitutional test is the one we set forth in Turner. . . .

Under Turner, the question remains whether the prison regulations, as applied to Murphy, are 'reasonably related to legitimate penological interests.' To prevail, Murphy must overcome the presumption that the prison officials acted within their 'broad discretion.' Petitioners ask us to answer, rather than remand, the question whether Murphy has satisfied this heavy burden. We decline petitioners' request, however, because we granted certiorari only to decide whether inmates possess a special First Amendment right to provide legal assistance to fellow inmates. . . .

The judgment of the Court of Appeals is reversed, and the case is remanded for further proceedings consistent with this opinion."

V. JUSTICE VOTE

0 Pro ACLU Side vs. 9 Con Opposing Side

Opposing Side (Petitioner / Appellant)

1. Thomas, C. – Wrote majority opinion
2. Ginsburg, R. – Wrote concurring opinion
3. Souter, D. – Joined majority opinion
4. O'Connor, S. – Joined majority opinion
5. Stevens, J. – Joined majority opinion
6. Breyer, S. – Joined majority opinion
7. Scalia, A. – Joined majority opinion
8. Kennedy, A. – Joined majority opinion
9. Rehnquist, W. – Joined majority opinion

VI. A WIN OR LOSS FOR THE ACLU?

The ACLU filed as amicus curiae, urging affirmance; the Supreme Court reversed the Court of Appeals' decision by a 9-0 vote, giving the ACLU an apparent loss.

897. Easley v. Cromartie

(Decided April 18, 2001; 532 U.S. 234)

I. ISSUE

A. Issues Discussed

Civil rights, race, voting rights

B. Legal Question Presented

Whether the District Court erred in finding North Carolina violated the Equal Protection Clause by determining "that North Carolina's Legislature used race as the 'predominant factor' in drawing its 12th Congressional District's 1997 boundaries."

C. Supreme Court's Answer

The District Court's conclusion was "clearly erroneous."

II. CASE SUMMARY

A. Background

The U.S. Supreme Court previously determined in Shaw I and Shaw II that North Carolina's 12th Congressional District boundaries violated the U.S. Constitution because race was a "predominant factor" in drawing the district's boundaries. In response to these decisions, North Carolina's legislature redrew the district's boundaries in 1997.

The 1997 boundaries were the subject of the Court's third decision in this line of cases. "A three-judge District Court, with one judge dissenting, had granted summary judgment in favor of those challenging the district's boundaries. The court found that the legislature again had 'used criteria . . . that are facially race driven,' in violation of the Equal Protection Clause. It based this conclusion upon 'uncontroverted material facts' showing that the boundaries created an unusually shaped district, split counties and cities, and in particular placed almost all heavily Democratic-registered, predominantly African–American voting precincts, inside the district while locating some heavily Democratic-registered, predominantly white precincts, outside the district. This latter circumstance, said the court, showed that the legislature was trying to maximize new District 12's African–American voting strength, not the district's Democratic voting strength.

[The Supreme] Court reversed. [The Court] agreed with the District Court that the new district's shape, the way in which it split towns and counties, and its heavily African–American voting population all helped the plaintiffs' case. But neither that evidence by itself, nor when coupled with the evidence of Democratic registration, was sufficient to show, on summary judgment, the unconstitutional race-based objective that plaintiffs claimed. . . . .

On remand, the parties undertook additional discovery. The three-judge District Court held a 3–day trial. And the court again held (over a dissent) that the legislature had unconstitutionally drawn District 12's new 1997 boundaries."

The Supreme Court noted probable jurisdiction to review the case, and reversed in its fourth decision for this line of cases.

B. Counsel of Record

ACLU Side (Petitioner / Appellant): Walter E. Dellinger and Adam Stein argued the cause for appellants. With them on the briefs were Michael F. Easley, former Attorney General of North Carolina, Tiare B. Smiley and Norma S. Harrell, Special Deputy Attorneys General, Brian D. Boyle, Todd A. Cox, Norman J. Chachkin, and Jacqueline A. Berrien.

Opposing Side (Respondent / Appellee): Robinson O. Everett argued the cause for appellees. With him on the brief were Martin B. McGee and Douglas E. Markham.

III. AMICI CURIAE

ACLU Side (Petitioner / Appellant)

Brief of amici curiae filed on behalf of the American Civil Liberties Union by Laughlin McDonald, Neil Bradley, Cristina Correia, and Bryan Sells.

Brief of amici curiae filed on behalf of the United States by Solicitor General Waxman, Acting Assistant Attorney General Yeomans, Deputy Solicitor General Underwood, James A. Feldman, David K. Flynn, and Louis E. Peraertz.

Opposing Side (Respondent / Appellee)

No briefs of amici curiae were filed in support of appellee.

IV. THE SUPREME COURT'S DECISION

"The issue in this case is evidentiary. We must determine whether there is adequate support for the District Court's key findings, particularly the ultimate finding that the legislature's motive was predominantly racial, not political. In making this determination, we are aware that, under Shaw I and later cases, the burden of proof on the plaintiffs (who attack the district) is a 'demanding one.' The Court has specified that those who claim that a legislature has improperly used race as a criterion, in order, for example, to create a majority-minority district, must show at a minimum that the 'legislature subordinated traditional race-neutral districting principles . . . to racial considerations.' Race must not simply have been 'a motivation for the drawing of a majority-minority district, but 'the 'predominant factor' motivating the legislature's districting decision.' Plaintiffs must show that a facially neutral law 'is 'unexplainable on grounds other than race.'" . . .

The critical District Court determination—the matter for which we remanded this litigation—consists of the finding that race rather than politics predominantly explains District 12's 1997 boundaries. That determination rests upon three findings (the district's shape, its splitting of towns and counties, and its high African–American voting population) that we previously found insufficient to support summary judgment. Given the undisputed evidence that racial identification is highly correlated with political affiliation in North Carolina, these facts in and of themselves cannot, as a matter of law, support the District Court's judgment. . . . The District Court rested, however, upon five new subsidiary findings to conclude that District 12's lines are the product of no 'mer[e] correlat[ion],' but are instead a result of the predominance of race in the legislature's line-drawing process.

In considering each subsidiary finding, we have given weight to the fact that the District Court was familiar with this litigation, heard the testimony of each witness, and considered all the evidence with care. Nonetheless, we cannot accept the District Court's findings as adequate for reasons . . . which we can summarize as follows:

First, the primary evidence upon which the District Court relied for its 'race, not politics,' conclusion is evidence of voting registration, not voting behavior; and that is precisely the kind of evidence that we said was inadequate the last time this case was before us. Second, the additional evidence to which appellees' expert, Dr. Weber, pointed, and the statements made by Senator Cooper and Gerry Cohen, simply do not provide significant additional support for the District Court's conclusion. Third, the District Court, while not accepting the contrary conclusion of appellants' expert, Dr. Peterson, did not (and as far as the record reveals, could not) reject much of the significant supporting factual information he provided. Fourth, in any event, appellees themselves have provided us with charts summarizing evidence of voting behavior and those charts tend to refute the court's 'race, not politics,' conclusion. . . .

We concede the record contains a modicum of evidence offering support for the District Court's conclusion. That evidence includes the Cohen e-mail, Senator Cooper's reference to 'racial balance,' and to a minor degree, some aspects of Dr. Weber's testimony. The evidence taken together, however, does not show that racial considerations predominated in the drawing of District 12's boundaries. That is because race in this case correlates closely with political behavior. The basic question is whether the legislature drew District 12's boundaries because of race rather than because of political behavior (coupled with traditional, nonracial districting considerations). It is not, as the dissent contends, whether a legislature may defend its districting decisions based on a 'stereotype' about African–American voting behavior. And given the fact that the party attacking the legislature's decision bears the burden of proving that racial considerations are 'dominant and controlling,' given the 'demanding' nature of that burden of proof, and given the sensitivity, the 'extraordinary caution,' that district courts must show to avoid treading upon legislative prerogatives, the attacking party has not successfully shown that race, rather than politics, predominantly accounts for the result. The record leaves us with the 'definite and firm conviction,' that the District Court erred in finding to the contrary. And we do not believe that providing appellees a further opportunity to make their 'precinct swapping' arguments in the District Court could change this result.

We can put the matter more generally as follows: In a case such as this one where majority-minority districts (or the approximate equivalent) are at issue and where racial identification correlates highly with political affiliation, the party attacking the legislatively drawn boundaries must show at the least that the legislature could have achieved its legitimate political objectives in alternative ways that are comparably consistent with traditional districting principles. That party must also show that those districting alternatives would have brought about significantly greater racial balance. Appellees failed to make any such showing here. We conclude that the District Court's contrary findings are clearly erroneous. . . .

The judgment of the District Court is reversed."

V. JUSTICE VOTE

5 Pro ACLU Side vs. 4 Con Opposing Side

ACLU Side (Petitioner / Appellant)

1. Breyer, S. – Wrote majority opinion
2. Stevens, J. – Joined majority opinion
3. Souter, D. – Joined majority opinion
4. Ginsburg, R. – Joined majority opinion
5. O'Connor, S. – Joined majority opinion

Opposing Side (Respondent / Appellee)

1. Thomas, C. – Wrote dissenting opinion
2. Rehnquist, W. – Joined Thomas' dissent
3. Scalia, A. – Joined Thomas' dissent
4. Kennedy, A. – Joined Thomas' dissent

VI. A WIN OR LOSS FOR THE ACLU?

The ACLU filed as amicus curiae urging reversal of the judgment of the District Court; the Supreme Court reversed in a 5-4 vote, giving the ACLU an apparent win.

898. Alexander v. Sandoval

(Decided April 24, 2001; 532 U.S. 275)

I. ISSUE

A. Issues Discussed

Civil rights, race

B. Legal Question Presented

"[W]hether private individuals may sue to enforce disparate-impact regulations promulgated under Title VI of the Civil Rights Act of 1964."

C. Supreme Court's Answer

"Neither as originally enacted nor as later amended does Title VI display an intent to create a freestanding private right of action to enforce regulations promulgated under § 602. We therefore hold that no such right of action exists."

II. CASE SUMMARY

A. Background

"The Alabama Department of Public Safety (Department), of which petitioner James Alexander is the director, accepted grants of financial assistance from the United States Department of Justice (DOJ) and Department of Transportation (DOT) and so subjected itself to the restrictions of Title VI of the Civil Rights Act of 1964. Section 601 of that Title provides that no person shall, 'on the ground of race, color, or national origin, be excluded from participation in, be denied the benefits of, or be subjected to discrimination under any program or activity' covered by Title VI. Section 602 authorizes federal agencies 'to effectuate the provisions of [§ 601] . . . by issuing rules, regulations, or orders of general applicability,' and the DOJ in an exercise of this authority promulgated a regulation forbidding funding recipients to 'utilize criteria or methods of administration which have the effect of subjecting individuals to discrimination because of their race, color, or national origin . . . .' . . .

The State of Alabama amended its Constitution in 1990 to declare English 'the official language of the state of Alabama.' Pursuant to this provision and, petitioners have argued, to advance public safety, the Department decided to administer state driver's license examinations only in English. Respondent Sandoval, as representative of a class, brought suit in the United States District Court for the Middle District of Alabama to enjoin the English-only policy, arguing that it violated the DOJ regulation because it had the effect of subjecting non-English speakers to discrimination based on their national origin. The District Court agreed. It enjoined the policy and ordered the Department to accommodate non-English speakers. Petitioners appealed to the Court of Appeals for the Eleventh Circuit, which affirmed. Both courts rejected petitioners' argument that Title VI did not provide respondents a cause of action to enforce the regulation."

The Supreme Court granted certiorari to review the case.

B. Counsel of Record

ACLU Side (Respondent / Appellee): Eric Schnapper argued the cause for private appellees. With him on the brief were J. Richard Cohen, Rhonda

Brownstein, Elizabeth Kleinberg, Rohit Nepal, Eric Schnapper, Steven R. Shapiro of the American Civil Liberties Union Foundation, Edward Chen of the American Civil Liberties Union, and Christopher Ho.

Solicitor General Waxman argued the cause for the United States as appellee. With him on the brief were Assistant Attorney

General Lee, Deputy Solicitor General Underwood, Paul R. Q. Wolfson, Dennis J. Dimsey, and Seth M. Galanter.

Opposing Side (Petitioner / Appellant): Jeffrey S. Sutton argued the cause for appellants. With him on the briefs were Bill Pryor, Attorney General of Alabama, and John J. Park, Jr., Assistant Attorney General.

III. AMICI CURIAE

ACLU Side (Respondent / Appellee)

Brief of amici curiae filed on behalf of the NAACP Legal Defense & Educational Fund, Inc., et al. by Elaine R. Jones, Norman J. Chachkin, David T. Goldberg, Kenneth Kimerling, Barbara J. Olshansky, Robert Garcı´a, John Payton, Norman Redlich, Barbara R. Arnwine, and Thomas J. Henderson.

Brief of amici curiae filed on behalf of the National Women's Law Center et al. by George W. Jones, Jr., Jacqueline G. Cooper, Marcia D. Greenberger, Verna L. Williams, and Leslie T. Annexstein.

Brief of amici curiae filed on behalf of the Center on Race, Poverty and the Environment et al. by Luke W. Cole and Douglas Parker.

Opposing Side (Petitioner / Appellant)

Brief of amici curiae filed on behalf of Beauty Enterprises, Inc., by Joseph E. Schmitz and Richard C. Robinson.

Brief of amici curiae filed on behalf of the Eagle Forum Education & Legal Defense Fund by Karen Tripp and Phyllis Schlafly.

Brief of amici curiae filed on behalf of the National Association of Manufacturers by Michael W. Steinberg, Michael A. McCord, and Jan Amundson.

Brief of amici curiae filed on behalf of the National Collegiate Athletic Association by David P. Bruton, Michael W. McTigue, Jr., and Elsa Kircher Cole.

Brief of amici curiae filed on behalf of Pro-English et al. by Barnaby W. Zall.

Brief of amici curiae filed on behalf of U. S. English by Mr. Schmitz.

Brief of amici curiae filed on behalf of the Washington Legal Foundation et al. by Daniel J. Popeo and Richard A. Samp.

Brief of amici curiae filed on behalf of Robert C. Jubelirer et al. by John P. Krill, Jr., and David R. Fine.

Brief of amici curiae filed on behalf of the Pacific Legal Foundation et al. by John H. Findley.

Brief of amici curiae filed on behalf of the Central Puget Sound Regional Transit Authority by Paul J. Lawrence.

IV. THE SUPREME COURT'S DECISION

"Although Title VI has often come to this Court, it is fair to say (indeed, perhaps an understatement) that our opinions have not eliminated all uncertainty regarding its commands. For purposes of the present case, however, it is clear from our decisions, from Congress's amendments of Title VI, and from the parties' concessions that three aspects of Title VI must be taken as given. First, private individuals may sue to enforce § 601 of Title VI and obtain both injunctive relief and damages. . . .

Second, it is similarly beyond dispute—and no party disagrees—that § 601 prohibits only intentional discrimination. . . .

Third, we must assume for purposes of deciding this case that regulations promulgated under § 602 of Title VI may validly proscribe activities that have a disparate impact on racial groups, even though such activities are permissible under § 601. . . .

Respondents assert that the issue in this case, like the first two described above, has been resolved by our cases. To reject a private cause of action to enforce the disparate-impact regulations, they say, we would '[have] to ignore the actual language of Guardians and Cannon.' The language in Cannon to which respondents refer does not in fact support their position . . . . In Guardians, the Court held that private individuals could not recover compensatory damages under Title VI except for intentional discrimination. . . . Neither that case, nor any other in this Court, has held that the private right of action exists. . . .

We must face now the question avoided by Lau, because we have since rejected Lau's interpretation of § 601 as reaching beyond intentional discrimination. It is clear now that the disparate-impact regulations do not simply apply § 601—since they indeed forbid conduct that § 601 permits—and therefore clear that the private right of action to enforce § 601 does not include a private right to enforce these regulations. . . . That right must come, if at all, from the independent force of § 602. As stated earlier, we assume for purposes of this decision that § 602 confers the authority to promulgate disparate-impact regulations; the question remains whether it confers a private right of action to enforce them. If not, we must conclude that a failure to comply with regulations promulgated under § 602 that is not also a failure to comply with § 601 is not actionable. . . .

Respondents would have us revert in this case to the understanding of private causes of action that held sway 40 years ago when Title VI was enacted. . . . We abandoned that understanding in Cort v. Ash, 422 U.S. 66 (1975)—which itself interpreted a statute enacted under the ancien regime—and have not returned to it since. . . . Having sworn off the habit of venturing beyond Congress's intent, we will not accept respondents' invitation to have one last drink. . . .

We have never accorded dispositive weight to context shorn of text. In determining whether statutes create private rights of action, as in interpreting statutes generally, . . . legal context matters only to the extent it clarifies text.

We therefore begin (and find that we can end) our search for Congress's intent with the text and structure of Title VI. Section 602 authorizes federal agencies 'to effectuate the provisions of [§ 601] ... by issuing rules, regulations, or orders of general applicability.' It is immediately clear that the 'rights-creating' language so critical to the Court's analysis in Cannon of § 601 . . . is completely absent from § 602. . . . So far as we can tell, this authorizing portion of § 602 reveals no congressional intent to create a private right of action.

Nor do the methods that § 602 goes on to provide for enforcing its authorized regulations manifest an intent to create a private remedy; if anything, they suggest the opposite. . . .

Both the Government and respondents argue that the regulations contain rights-creating language and so must be privately enforceable, but that argument skips an analytical step. Language in a regulation may invoke a private right of action that Congress through statutory text created, but it may not create a right that Congress has not. . . . Thus, when a statute has provided a general authorization for private enforcement of regulations, it may perhaps be correct that the intent displayed in each regulation can determine whether or not it is privately enforceable. But it is most certainly incorrect to say that language in a regulation can conjure up a private cause of action that has not been authorized by Congress. Agencies may play the sorcerer's apprentice but not the sorcerer himself.

The last string to respondents' and the Government's bow is their argument that two amendments to Title VI 'ratified' this Court's decisions finding an implied private right of action to enforce the disparate-impact regulations. . . . One problem with this argument is that . . . none of our decisions establishes (or even assumes) the private right of action at issue here . . . . Another problem is that the incorporation claim itself is flawed. . . .

Neither as originally enacted nor as later amended does Title VI display an intent to create a freestanding private right of action to enforce regulations promulgated under § 602. We therefore hold that no such right of action exists. Since we reach this conclusion applying our standard test for discerning private causes of action, we do not address petitioners' additional argument that implied causes of action against States (and perhaps nonfederal state actors generally) are inconsistent with the clear statement rule of Pennhurst State School and Hospital v. Halderman, 451 U.S. 1 (1981).

The judgment of the Court of Appeals is reversed."

V. JUSTICE VOTE

4 Pro ACLU Side vs. 5 Con Opposing Side

ACLU Side (Respondent / Appellee)

1. Stevens, J. – Wrote dissenting opinion
2. Ginsburg, R. – Joined Stevens' dissent
3. Souter, D. – Joined Stevens' dissent
4. Breyer, S. – Joined Stevens' dissent

Opposing Side (Petitioner / Appellant)

1. Scalia, A. – Wrote majority opinion
2. Rehnquist, W. – Joined majority opinion
3. O'Connor, S. – Joined majority opinion
4. Thomas, C. – Joined majority opinion
5. Kennedy, A. – Joined majority opinion

VI. A WIN OR LOSS FOR THE ACLU?

The ACLU argued the case for appellee, urging affirmance; the Supreme Court reversed the Court of Appeals' decision by a 5-4 vote, giving the ACLU an apparent loss.

899. Atwater v. City of Lago Vista

(Decided April 24, 2001; 532 U.S. 318)

I. ISSUE

A. Issues Discussed

4th Amendment

B. Legal Question Presented

"[W]hether the Fourth Amendment forbids a warrantless arrest for a minor criminal offense, such as a misdemeanor seatbelt violation punishable only by a fine."

C. Supreme Court's Answer

"[T]he standard of probable cause 'applie[s] to all arrests, without the need to 'balance' the interests and circumstances involved in particular situations.' If an officer has probable cause to believe that an individual has committed even a very minor criminal offense in his presence, he may, without violating the Fourth Amendment, arrest the offender."

II. CASE SUMMARY

A. Background

"In Texas, if a car is equipped with safety belts, a front-seat passenger must wear one, and the driver must secure any small child riding in front. Violation of either provision is 'a misdemeanor punishable by a fine not less than $25 or more than $50.' Texas law expressly authorizes '[a]ny peace officer [to] arrest without warrant a person found committing a violation' of these seatbelt laws, although it permits police to issue citations in lieu of arrest.

In March 1997, petitioner Gail Atwater was driving her pickup truck in Lago Vista, Texas, with her 3-year-old son and 5-year-old daughter in the front seat. None of them was wearing a seatbelt. Respondent Bart Turek, a Lago Vista police officer at the time, observed the seatbelt violations and pulled Atwater over. According to Atwater's complaint . . . , Turek approached the truck and 'yell[ed]' something to the effect of '[w]e've met before' and '[y]ou're going to jail.' He then called for backup and asked to see Atwater's driver's license and insurance documentation, which state law required her to carry. When Atwater told Turek that she did not have the papers because her purse had been stolen the day before, Turek said that he had 'heard that story two-hundred times.'

Atwater asked to take her 'frightened, upset, and crying' children to a friend's house nearby, but Turek told her, '[y]ou're not going anywhere.' As it turned out, Atwater's friend learned what was going on and soon arrived to take charge of the children. Turek then handcuffed Atwater, placed her in his squad car, and drove her to the local police station, where booking officers had her remove her shoes, jewelry, and eyeglasses, and empty her pockets. Officers took Atwater's 'mug shot' and placed her, alone, in a jail cell for about one hour, after which she was taken before a magistrate and released on $310 bond.

Atwater was charged with driving without her seatbelt fastened, failing to secure her children in seatbelts, driving without a license, and failing to provide proof of insurance. She ultimately pleaded no contest to the misdemeanor seatbelt offenses and paid a $50 fine; the other charges were dismissed. . . .

Atwater and her husband, petitioner Michael Haas, filed suit in a Texas state court under 42 U.S.C. § 1983 against Turek and respondents City of Lago Vista and Chief of Police Frank Miller. So far as concerns us, petitioners (whom we will simply call Atwater) alleged that respondents (for simplicity, the City) had violated Atwater's Fourth Amendment 'right to be free from unreasonable seizure,' and sought compensatory and punitive damages.

The City removed the suit to the United States District Court for the Western District of Texas. [T]he District Court ruled the Fourth Amendment claim 'meritless' and granted the City's summary judgment motion. A panel of the United States Court of Appeals for the Fifth Circuit reversed. . . .

Sitting en banc, the Court of Appeals vacated the panel's decision and affirmed the District Court's summary judgment for the City."

The Supreme Court granted certiorari to review the case.

B. Counsel of Record

ACLU Side (Petitioner / Appellant): Robert C. DeCarli argued the cause for appellants. With him on the briefs were Debra Irwin, Pamela McGraw, and Michael F. Sturley.

Opposing Side (Respondent / Appellee): R. James George, Jr., argued the cause for appellees. With him on the brief were William W. Krueger III and Joanna R. Lippman.

Gregory S. Coleman, Solicitor General of Texas, argued the cause for the State of Texas et al. as amici curiae urging affirmance.

III. AMICI CURIAE

ACLU Side (Petitioner / Appellant)

Brief of amici curiae filed on behalf of the American Civil Liberties Union, the ACLU of Texas, The Mexican-American Legal Defense and Educational Fund, and the National Police Accountability Project of the National Lawyers Guild by Susan N. Herman, Steven R. Shapiro, William C. Harrell, and Joseph P. Berra.

Brief of amici curiae filed on behalf of Americans for Effective Law Enforcement, Inc., by Wayne W. Schmidt, James P. Manak, and Bernard J. Farber.

Brief of amici curiae filed on behalf of the Cato Institute by Timothy Lynch.

Brief of amici curiae filed on behalf of the Institute on Criminal Justice at the University of Minnesota Law School et al. by Richard S. Frase.

Brief of amici curiae filed on behalf of the National Association of Criminal Defense Lawyers et al. by Wesley MacNeil Oliver and Joshua Dratel.

Brief of amici curiae filed on behalf of the Texas Criminal Defense Lawyers Association by Greg Westfall and William S. Harris.

Opposing Side (Respondent / Appellee)

Brief of amici curiae filed on behalf of the State of Texas et al. by Gregory S. Coleman, Solicitor General of Texas, John Cornyn, Attorney General, Andy Taylor, First Assistant Attorney General, and Lisa R. Eskow, Assistant Attorney General, and the Attorneys General for their respective States as follows: Mark Pryor of Arkansas, Ken Salazar of Colorado, M. Jane Brady of Delaware, Carla J. Stovall of Kansas, J. Joseph Curran, Jr., of Maryland, Joseph P. Mazurek of Montana, W. A. Drew Edmondson of Oklahoma, Charles M. Condon of South Carolina, and Mark L. Earley of Virginia.

Brief of amici curiae filed on behalf of the United States by Solicitor General Waxman, Assistant Attorney General Robinson, Deputy Solicitor General Dreeben, and Patricia A. Millett.

Brief of amici curiae filed on behalf of the National League of Cities et al. by Richard Ruda and James I. Crowley.

Brief of amici curiae filed on behalf of the Texas Police Chiefs Association by James McLaughlin, Jr.

IV. THE SUPREME COURT'S DECISION

"The Fourth Amendment safeguards '[t]he right of the people to be secure in their persons, houses, papers, and effects, against unreasonable searches and seizures.' In reading the Amendment, we are guided by 'the traditional protections against unreasonable searches and seizures afforded by the common law at the time of the framing' . . . . Thus, the first step here is to assess Atwater's claim that peace officers' authority to make warrantless arrests for misdemeanors was restricted at common law . . . . Atwater's specific contention is that 'founding-era common-law rules' forbade peace officers to make warrantless misdemeanor arrests except in cases of 'breach of the peace,' a category she claims was then understood narrowly as covering only those nonfelony offenses 'involving or tending toward violence.' Although her historical argument is by no means insubstantial, it ultimately fails. . . .

We begin with the state of pre-founding English common law and find that, even after making some allowance for variations in the common-law usage of the term 'breach of the peace,' the 'founding-era common-law rules' were not nearly as clear as Atwater claims; on the contrary, the common-law commentators (as well as the sparsely reported cases) reached divergent conclusions with respect to officers' warrantless misdemeanor arrest power. Moreover, in the years leading up to American independence, Parliament repeatedly extended express warrantless arrest authority to cover misdemeanor-level offenses not amounting to or involving any violent breach of the peace. . . .

A second, and equally serious, problem for Atwater's historical argument is posed by the 'divers Statutes,' enacted by Parliament well before this Republic's founding that authorized warrantless misdemeanor arrests without reference to violence or turmoil. . . .

The significance of these early English statutes lies not in proving that any common-law rule barring warrantless misdemeanor arrests that might have existed would have been subject to statutory override; the sovereign Parliament could of course have wiped away any judge-made rule. The point is that the statutes riddle Atwater's supposed common-law rule with enough exceptions to unsettle any contention that the law of the mother country would have left the Fourth Amendment's Framers of a view that it would necessarily have been unreasonable to arrest without warrant for a misdemeanor unaccompanied by real or threatened violence. . . .

An examination of specifically American evidence is to the same effect. Neither the history of the framing era nor subsequent legal development indicates that the Fourth Amendment was originally understood, or has traditionally been read, to embrace Atwater's position. . . .

To begin with, Atwater has cited no particular evidence that those who framed and ratified the Fourth Amendment sought to limit peace officers' warrantless misdemeanor arrest authority to instances of actual breach of the peace, and our own review of the recent and respected compilations of framing-era documentary history has likewise failed to reveal any such design. . . .

Nor does Atwater's argument from tradition pick up any steam from the historical record as it has unfolded since the framing, there being no indication that her claimed rule has ever become 'woven ... into the fabric' of American law. . . . The story, on the contrary, is of two centuries of uninterrupted (and largely unchallenged) state and federal practice permitting warrantless arrests for misdemeanors not amounting to or involving breach of the peace. . . .

While it is true here that history, if not unequivocal, has expressed a decided, majority view that the police need not obtain an arrest warrant merely because a misdemeanor stopped short of violence or a threat of it, Atwater does not wager all on history. Instead, she asks us to mint a new rule of constitutional law on the understanding that when historical practice fails to speak conclusively to a claim grounded on the Fourth Amendment, courts are left to strike a current balance between individual and societal interests by subjecting particular contemporary circumstances to traditional standards of reasonableness. Atwater accordingly argues for a modern arrest rule, one not necessarily requiring violent breach of the peace, but nonetheless forbidding custodial arrest, even upon probable cause, when conviction could not ultimately carry any jail time and when the government shows no compelling need for immediate detention. . . .

But we have traditionally recognized that a responsible Fourth Amendment balance is not well served by standards requiring sensitive, case-by-case determinations of government need, lest every discretionary judgment in the field be converted into an occasion for constitutional review. . . .

Accordingly, we confirm today what our prior cases have intimated: the standard of probable cause 'applie[s] to all arrests, without the need to 'balance' the interests and circumstances involved in particular situations.' If an officer has probable cause to believe that an individual has committed even a very minor criminal offense in his presence, he may, without violating the Fourth Amendment, arrest the offender. . . .

Atwater's arrest satisfied constitutional requirements. There is no dispute that Officer Turek had probable cause to believe that Atwater had committed a crime in his presence. She admits that neither she nor her children were wearing seatbelts, as required by Tex. Transp.Code Ann. § 545.413 (1999). Turek was accordingly authorized (not required, but authorized) to make a custodial arrest without balancing costs and benefits or determining whether or not Atwater's arrest was in some sense necessary.

Nor was the arrest made in an 'extraordinary manner, unusually harmful to [her] privacy or . . . physical interests.' As our citations in Whren make clear, the question whether a search or seizure is 'extraordinary' turns, above all else, on the manner in which the search or seizure is executed. . . . Atwater's arrest was surely 'humiliating,' as she says in her brief, but it was no more 'harmful to . . . privacy or . . . physical interests' than the normal custodial arrest. She was handcuffed, placed in a squad car, and taken to the local police station, where officers asked her to remove her shoes, jewelry, and glasses, and to empty her pockets. They then took her photograph and placed her in a cell, alone, for about an hour, after which she was taken before a magistrate, and released on $310 bond. The arrest and booking were inconvenient and embarrassing to Atwater, but not so extraordinary as to violate the Fourth Amendment.

The Court of Appeals's en banc judgment is affirmed."

V. JUSTICE VOTE

4 Pro ACLU Side vs. 5 Con Opposing Side

ACLU Side (Petitioner / Appellant)

1. O'Connor, S. – Wrote dissenting opinion
2. Stevens, J. – Joined O'Connor's dissent
3. Ginsburg, R. – Joined O'Connor's dissent
4. Breyer, S. – Joined O'Connor's dissent

Opposing Side (Respondent / Appellee)

1. Souter, D. – Wrote majority opinion
2. Rehnquist, W. – Joined majority opinion
3. Scalia, A. – Joined majority opinion
4. Kennedy, A. – Joined majority opinion
5. Thomas, C. – Joined majority opinion

VI. A WIN OR LOSS FOR THE ACLU?

The ACLU filed as amicus curiae urging reversal of the judgment of the Court of Appeals; the Supreme Court affirmed in a 5-4 vote, giving the ACLU an apparent loss.

900. U.S. v. Oakland Cannabis Buyers' Coop.

(Decided May 14, 2001; 532 U.S. 483)

I. ISSUE

A. Issues Discussed

Drugs

B. Legal Question Presented

"[W]hether there is a medical necessity exception to" the "Controlled Substances Act, 84 Stat. 1242, 21 U.S.C. § 801 et seq., prohibit[ion of] the manufacture and distribution of various drugs, including marijuana."

C. Supreme Court's Answer

"[W]e hold that medical necessity is not a defense to manufacturing and distributing marijuana."

II. CASE SUMMARY

A. Background

"In November 1996, California voters enacted an initiative measure entitled the Compassionate Use Act of 1996. Attempting '[t]o ensure that seriously ill Californians have the right to obtain and use marijuana for medical purposes,' the statute creates an exception to California laws prohibiting the possession and cultivation of marijuana. . . . In the wake of this voter initiative, several groups organized 'medical cannabis dispensaries' . . . . Respondent Oakland Cannabis Buyers' Cooperative is one of these groups. . . .

In January 1998, the United States sued . . . in the United States District Court for the Northern District of California. Seeking to enjoin the Cooperative from distributing and manufacturing marijuana, the United States argued that, whether or not the Cooperative's activities are legal under California law, they violate federal law. Specifically, the Government argued that the Cooperative violated the Controlled Substances Act's prohibitions on distributing, manufacturing, and possessing with the intent to distribute or manufacture a controlled substance. [T]he District Court granted a preliminary injunction.

The Cooperative did not appeal the injunction but instead openly violated it by distributing marijuana to numerous persons. To terminate these violations, the Government initiated contempt proceedings. . . . The District Court found the Cooperative in contempt and, at the Government's request, modified the preliminary injunction to empower the United States Marshal to seize the Cooperative's premises. . . .

The Cooperative appealed both the contempt order and the denial of the Cooperative's motion to modify. Before the Court of Appeals for the Ninth Circuit decided the case, however, the Cooperative voluntarily purged its contempt by promising the District Court that it would comply with the initial preliminary injunction. Consequently, the Court of Appeals determined that the appeal of the contempt order was moot.

The denial of the Cooperative's motion to modify the injunction, however, presented a live controversy that was appealable under 28 U.S.C. § 1292(a)(1). Reaching the merits of this issue, the Court of Appeals reversed and remanded. . . . Remanding the case, the Court of Appeals instructed the District Court to consider 'the criteria for a medical necessity exemption, and, should it modify the injunction, to set forth those criteria in the modification order.' Following these instructions, the District Court granted the Cooperative's motion to modify the injunction to incorporate a medical necessity defense.

The United States petitioned for certiorari to review the Court of Appeals' decision that medical necessity is a legally cognizable defense to violations of the Controlled Substances Act. Because the decision raises significant questions as to the ability of the United States to enforce the Nation's drug laws, [the Supreme Court] granted certiorari."

B. Counsel of Record

ACLU Side (Respondent / Appellee): Gerald F. Uelmen argued the cause for appellees. With him on the brief were James J. Brosnahan, Annette P. Carnegie, Christina Kirk-Kazhe, Robert A. Raich, and Randy E. Barnett.

Opposing Side (Petitioner / Appellant): Acting Solicitor General Underwood argued the cause for the United States. With her on the briefs were former Solicitor General Waxman, Assistant Attorney General Ogden, Deputy Solicitor General Kneedler, and Lisa Schiavo Blatt.

III. AMICI CURIAE

ACLU Side (Respondent / Appellee)

Brief of amici curiae filed on behalf of the American Civil Liberties Union, the ACLU of Northern California, the ACLU of Southern California, and the ACLU of San Diego and Imperial Counties by Steven R. Shapiro, Graham Boyd, Nelson Tebbe, Ann Brick, Daniel P. Tokaji, and Jordan C. Budd.

Brief of amici curiae filed on behalf of the State of California by Bill Lockyer, Attorney General, and David De Alba, Special Assistant Attorney General.

Brief of amici curiae filed on behalf of the American Public Health Association et al. by Daniel N. Abrahamson.

Brief of amici curiae filed on behalf of the Marijuana Policy Project et al. by Cheryl Flax-Davidson.

Brief of amici curiae filed on behalf of the National Organization for the Reform of Marijuana Laws et al. by R. Keith Stroup, John Wesley Hall, Jr., and Lisa B. Kemler.

Brief of amici curiae filed on behalf of Edward Neil Brundridge et al. by Thomas V. Loran III.

Brief of amici curiae filed on behalf of Sheriff Mark N. Dion et al. by Julie M. Carpenter.

Briefs of amici curiae filed on behalf of the California Medical Association et al. by Catherine I. Hanson and Alice P. Mead.

Opposing Side (Petitioner / Appellant)

Brief of amici curiae filed on behalf of the Family Research Council by Janet M. LaRue.

Brief of amici curiae filed on behalf of the Institute on Global Drug Policy of the Drug Free America Foundation et al. by David G. Evans and John E. Lamp.

IV. THE SUPREME COURT'S DECISION

"The Controlled Substances Act provides that, '[e]xcept as authorized by this subchapter, it shall be unlawful for any person knowingly or intentionally . . . to manufacture, distribute, or dispense, or possess with intent to manufacture, distribute, or dispense, a controlled substance.' 21 U.S.C. § 841(a)(1). . . . For marijuana . . . , there is but one express exception, and it is available only for Government-approved research projects, § 823(f). Not conducting such a project, the Cooperative cannot, and indeed does not, claim this statutory exemption.

The Cooperative contends, however, that notwithstanding the apparently absolute language of § 841(a), the statute is subject to additional, implied exceptions, one of which is medical necessity. According to the Cooperative, because necessity was a defense at common law, medical necessity should be read into the Controlled Substances Act. We disagree.

As an initial matter, we note that it is an open question whether federal courts ever have authority to recognize a necessity defense not provided by statute. . . .

We need not decide, however, whether necessity can ever be a defense when the federal statute does not expressly provide for it. In this case, to resolve the question presented, we need only recognize that a medical necessity exception for marijuana is at odds with the terms of the Controlled Substances Act. . . .

Under any conception of legal necessity, one principle is clear:

The defense cannot succeed when the legislature itself has made a 'determination of values.' In the case of the Controlled Substances Act, the statute reflects a determination that marijuana has no medical benefits worthy of an exception (outside the confines of a Government-approved research project). . . .

For these reasons, we hold that medical necessity is not a defense to manufacturing and distributing marijuana. . . .

The Cooperative contends that, even if the Controlled Substances Act forecloses the medical necessity defense, there is an alternative ground for affirming the Court of Appeals. This case, the Cooperative reminds us, arises from a motion to modify an injunction to permit distributions that are medically necessary. According to the Cooperative, the Court of Appeals was correct that the District Court had 'broad equitable discretion' to tailor the injunctive relief to account for medical necessity, irrespective of whether there is a legal defense of necessity in the statute. To sustain the judgment below, the argument goes, we need only reaffirm that federal courts, in the exercise of their equity jurisdiction, have discretion to modify an injunction based upon a weighing of the public interest.

We disagree. Although district courts whose equity powers have been properly invoked indeed have discretion in fashioning injunctive relief (in the absence of a statutory restriction), the Court of Appeals erred concerning the factors that the district courts may consider in exercising such discretion. . . .

As an initial matter, the Cooperative is correct that, when district courts are properly acting as courts of equity, they have discretion unless a statute clearly provides otherwise. . . .

The Cooperative is also correct that the District Court in this case had discretion. . . .

But the mere fact that the District Court had discretion does not suggest that the District Court, when evaluating the motion to modify the injunction, could consider any and all factors that might relate to the public interest or the conveniences of the parties, including the medical needs of the Cooperative's patients. On the contrary, a court sitting in equity cannot 'ignore the judgment of Congress, deliberately expressed in legislation.' A district court cannot, for example, override Congress' policy choice, articulated in a statute, as to what behavior should be prohibited. 'Once Congress, exercising its delegated powers, has decided the order of priorities in a given area, it is . . . for the courts to enforce them when enforcement is sought.' Courts of equity cannot, in their discretion, reject the balance that Congress has struck in a statute. Their choice (unless there is statutory language to the contrary) is simply whether a particular means of enforcing the statute should be chosen over another permissible means; their choice is not whether enforcement is preferable to no enforcement at all. Consequently, when a court of equity exercises its discretion, it may not consider the advantages and disadvantages of nonenforcement of the statute, but only the advantages and disadvantages of 'employing the extraordinary remedy of injunction' over the other available methods of enforcement. . . . To the extent the district court considers the public interest and the conveniences of the parties, the court is limited to evaluating how such interest and conveniences are affected by the selection of an injunction over other enforcement mechanisms. . . .

In this case, the Court of Appeals erred by considering relevant the evidence that some people have 'serious medical conditions for whom the use of cannabis is necessary in order to treat or alleviate those conditions or their symptoms,' that these people 'will suffer serious harm if they are denied cannabis,' and that 'there is no legal alternative to cannabis for the effective treatment of their medical conditions.' As explained above, in the Controlled Substances Act, the balance already has been struck against a medical necessity exception. Because the statutory prohibitions cover even those who have what could be termed a medical necessity, the Act precludes consideration of this evidence. It was thus error for the Court of Appeals to instruct the District Court on remand to consider 'the criteria for a medical necessity exemption, and, should it modify the injunction, to set forth those criteria in the modification order.'

The judgment of the Court of Appeals is reversed, and the case is remanded for further proceedings consistent with this opinion."

V. JUSTICE VOTE

0 Pro ACLU Side vs. 8 Con Opposing Side

Opposing Side (Petitioner / Appellant)

1. Thomas, C. – Wrote majority opinion
2. Rehnquist, W. – Joined majority opinion
3. O'Connor, S. – Joined majority opinion
4. Scalia, A. – Joined majority opinion
5. Kennedy, A. – Joined majority opinion
6. Stevens, J. – Wrote concurring opinion
7. Ginsburg, R. – Joined Stevens' concurrence
8. Souter, D. – Joined Stevens' concurrence
9. Breyer, S – Took no part in the decision

VI. A WIN OR LOSS FOR THE ACLU?

The ACLU filed as amicus curiae urging affirmance of the judgment of the Court of Appeals; the Supreme Court reversed the Court of Appeals' decision by an 8-0 vote, giving the ACLU an apparent loss.

901. Bartnicki v. Vopper

(Decided May 21, 2001; 532 U.S. 514)

I. ISSUE

A. Issues Discussed

1st Amendment, press, speech, association

B. Legal Question Presented

"[W]hat degree of protection, if any, the First Amendment provides to speech that discloses the contents of an illegally intercepted communication."

C. Supreme Court's Answer

"[P]rivacy concerns give way when balanced against the interest in publishing matters of public importance." "[A] stranger's illegal conduct does not suffice to remove the First Amendment shield from speech about a matter of public concern."

II. CASE SUMMARY

A. Background

"During 1992 and most of 1993, the Pennsylvania State Education Association, a union representing the teachers at the Wyoming Valley West High School, engaged in collective-bargaining negotiations with the school board. Petitioner Kane, then the president of the local union, testified that the negotiations were "contentious" and received 'a lot of media attention.' In May 1993, petitioner Bartnicki, who was acting as the union's 'chief negotiator,' used the cellular phone in her car to call Kane and engage in a lengthy conversation about the status of the negotiations. An unidentified person intercepted and recorded that call. . . .

In the early fall of 1993, the parties accepted a nonbinding arbitration proposal that was generally favorable to the teachers. In connection with news reports about the settlement, respondent Vopper, a radio commentator who had been critical of the union in the past, played a tape of the intercepted conversation on his public affairs talk show. . . . After filing suit . . . , Bartnicki and Kane (hereinafter petitioners) learned through discovery that Vopper had obtained the tape from respondent Jack Yocum . . . . Yocum, who was added as a defendant, testified that he had found the tape in his mailbox shortly after the interception. . . .

In their amended complaint, petitioners alleged that their telephone conversation had been surreptitiously intercepted by an unknown person using an electronic device, that Yocum had obtained a tape of that conversation, and that he intentionally disclosed it to Vopper, as well as other individuals and media representatives. . . . The amended complaint alleged that each of the defendants 'knew or had reason to know' that the recording of the private telephone conversation had been obtained by means of an illegal interception. . . .

After the parties completed their discovery, they filed cross-motions for summary judgment. . . . The District Court rejected the first statutory argument . . . . With respect to the second statutory argument, the District Court agreed that petitioners had to prove that the interception in question was intentional, but concluded that the text of the interception raised a genuine issue of material fact with respect to intent. . . . Finally, the District Court rejected respondents' First Amendment defense . . . .

Thereafter, the District Court granted a motion for an interlocutory appeal, pursuant to 28 U.S.C. § 1292(b). . . . The Court of Appeals accepted the appeal, and the United States, also a petitioner, intervened pursuant to 28 U.S.C. § 2403 in order to defend the constitutionality of the federal statute.

All three members of the panel agreed with petitioners and the Government that the federal and Pennsylvania wiretapping statutes are 'content-neutral' and therefore subject to 'intermediate scrutiny.' Applying that standard, the majority concluded that the statutes were invalid because they deterred significantly more speech than necessary to protect the privacy interests at stake."

The Supreme Court granted certiorari to review the case.

B. Counsel of Record

ACLU Side (Respondent / Appellee): Lee Levine argued the cause for appellees Vopper et al. With him on the brief was Jay Ward Brown.

Thomas C. Goldstein argued the cause for appellee Yokum. With him on the brief were Erik S. Jaffe and Frank J. Aritz

Opposing Side (Petitioner / Appellant): Jeremiah A. Collins argued the cause for appellants. With him on the briefs were Raymond P. Wendolowski and Scott C. Gartley.

Solicitor General Waxman argued the cause for the United States. With him on the briefs were Assistant Attorney General Ogden, Deputy Solicitor General Dreeben, Jeffrey A. Lamken, and Douglas N. Letter

III. AMICI CURIAE

ACLU Side (Respondent / Appellee)

Brief of amici curiae filed on behalf of the American Civil Liberties Union and the ACLU of Pennsylvania by Steven R. Shapiro.

Brief of amici curiae filed on behalf of Dow Jones & Co., Inc., by Theodore B. Olson, Theodore J. Boutrous, Jr., and Jack M. Weiss.

Brief of amici curiae filed on behalf of the Liberty Project by Nory Miller and Julia M. Carpenter.

Brief of amici curiae filed on behalf of Media Entities and Organizations by Floyd Abrams, George Freeman, Adam Liptak, Richard A. Bernstein, Jerry S. Birenz, Henry S. Hoberman, David A. Schulz, Eve Burton, Susanna M. Lowy, Harold W. Fuson, Jr., Barbara W. Wall, Anne Noble, Kenneth Vittor, Rene´ P. Milam, Lucy Dalglish, Bruce W. Sanford, and Eric Lieberman.

Brief of amici curiae filed on behalf of WFAA–TV et al. by Laurence H. Tribe, Jonathan S. Massey, William D. Sims, Jr., Thomas S. Leatherbury, and Marie R. Yeates.

Brief of amici curiae filed on behalf of Representative James A. McDermott by Frank Cicero, Jr., Christopher Landau, and Daryl Joseffer.

Opposing Side (Petitioner / Appellant)

Brief of amici curiae filed on behalf of the Cellular Telecommunications Industry Association by Howard J. Symons and Michael F. Altschul.

Brief of amici curiae filed on behalf of Representative John A. Boehner by Michael A. Carvin and David H. Thompson.

IV. THE SUPREME COURT'S DECISION

"Simply put, the issue here is this: 'Where the punished publisher of information has obtained the information in question in a manner lawful in itself but from a source who has obtained it unlawfully, may the government punish the ensuing publication of that information based on the defect in a chain?'

Our refusal to construe the issue presented more broadly is consistent with this Court's repeated refusal to answer categorically whether truthful publication may ever be punished consistent with the First Amendment. . . .

Accordingly, we consider whether, given the facts of these cases, the interests served by § 2511(1)(c) can justify its restrictions on speech.

The Government identifies two interests served by the statute—first, the interest in removing an incentive for parties to intercept private conversations, and second, the interest in minimizing the harm to persons whose conversations have been illegally intercepted. . . .

Although this suit demonstrates that there may be an occasional situation in which an anonymous scanner will risk criminal prosecution by passing on information without any expectation of financial reward or public praise, surely this is the exceptional case. Moreover, there is no basis for assuming that imposing sanctions upon respondents will deter the unidentified scanner from continuing to engage in surreptitious interceptions. . . . Accordingly, the Government's first suggested justification for applying § 2511(1)(c) to an otherwise innocent disclosure of public information is plainly insufficient.

The Government's second argument, however, is considerably stronger. Privacy of communication is an important interest, and Title III's restrictions are intended to protect that interest . . . .

We need not decide whether that interest is strong enough to justify the application of § 2511(c) to disclosures of trade secrets or domestic gossip or other information of purely private concern. . . . In other words, the outcome of these cases does not turn on whether § 2511(1)(c) may be enforced with respect to most violations of the statute without offending the First Amendment. . . .

In these cases, privacy concerns give way when balanced against the interest in publishing matters of public importance. As Warren and Brandeis stated in their classic law review article: 'The right of privacy does not prohibit any publication of matter which is of public or general interest.' . . .

Our opinion in New York Times Co. v. Sullivan, 376 U.S. 254 (1964), reviewed many of the decisions that settled the 'general proposition that freedom of expression upon public questions is secured by the First Amendment.' Those cases all relied on our 'profound national commitment to the principle that debate on public issues should be uninhibited, robust, and wide-open,' . . . It was the overriding importance of that commitment that supported our holding that neither factual error nor defamatory content, nor a combination of the two, sufficed to remove the First Amendment shield from criticism of official conduct.

We think it clear that parallel reasoning requires the conclusion that a stranger's illegal conduct does not suffice to remove the First Amendment shield from speech about a matter of public concern. The months of negotiations over the proper level of compensation for teachers at the Wyoming Valley West High School were unquestionably a matter of public concern, and respondents were clearly engaged in debate about that concern. That debate may be more mundane than the Communist rhetoric that inspired Justice Brandeis' classic opinion in Whitney v. California, 274 U.S., at 372, but it is no less worthy of constitutional protection.

The judgment is affirmed."

V. JUSTICE VOTE

6 Pro ACLU Side vs. 3 Con Opposing Side

ACLU Side (Respondent / Appellee)

1. Stevens, J. – Wrote majority opinion
2. Ginsburg, R. – Joined majority opinion
3. Souter, D. – Joined majority opinion
4. O'Connor, S. – Joined Breyer's concurrence
5. Breyer, S. – Wrote concurring opinion
6. Kennedy, A. – Joined majority opinion

Opposing Side (Petitioner / Appellant)

1. Rehnquist, W. – Wrote dissenting opinion
2. Thomas, C. – Joined Rehnquist's dissent
3. Scalia, A. – Joined Rehnquist's dissent

V.A WIN OR LOSS FOR THE ACLU?

The ACLU filed as amicus curiae urging affirmance of the judgment of the Court of Appeals; the Supreme Court affirmed the Court of Appeals' decision by a 6-3 vote, giving the ACLU an apparent win.

902. Buckhannon Board & Care Home, Inc. v. West Virginia Department of Health & Human Resources

(Decided May 29, 2001; 532 U.S. 598)

I. ISSUE

A. Issues Discussed

Civil rights

B. Legal Question Presented

Whether "prevailing party" "includes a party that has failed to secure a judgment on the merits or a court-ordered consent decree, but has nonetheless achieved the desired result because the lawsuit brought about a voluntary change in the defendant's conduct."

C. Supreme Court's Answer

No, "we hold that the 'catalyst theory' is not a permissible basis for the award of attorney's fees under the FHAA and ADA."

II. CASE SUMMARY

A. Background

"Buckhannon Board and Care Home, Inc., which operates care homes that provide assisted living to their residents, failed an inspection by the West Virginia Office of the State Fire Marshal because some of the residents were incapable of 'self-preservation' as defined under state law. . . . On October 28, 1997, after receiving cease and desist orders requiring the closure of its residential care facilities within 30 days, Buckhannon Board and Care Home, Inc., on behalf of itself and other similarly situated homes and residents (hereinafter petitioners), brought suit in the United States District Court for the Northern District of West Virginia against the State of West Virginia, two of its agencies, and 18 individuals (hereinafter respondents), seeking declaratory and injunctive relief that the 'self-preservation' requirement violated the Fair Housing Amendments Act of 1988 (FHAA), and the Americans with Disabilities Act of 1990 (ADA).

Respondents agreed to stay enforcement of the cease-and-desist orders pending resolution of the case and the parties began discovery. In 1998, the West Virginia Legislature enacted two bills eliminating the 'self-preservation' requirement, . . . and respondents moved to dismiss the case as moot. The District Court granted the motion, finding that the 1998 legislation had eliminated the allegedly offensive provisions and that there was no indication that the West Virginia Legislature would repeal the amendments.

Petitioners requested attorney's fees as the 'prevailing party' under the FHAA, . . . and ADA . . . . Petitioners argued that they were entitled to attorney's fees under the 'catalyst theory,' which posits that a plaintiff is a 'prevailing party' if it achieves the desired result because the lawsuit brought about a voluntary change in the defendant's conduct. Although most Courts of Appeals recognize the 'catalyst theory,' the Court of Appeals for the Fourth Circuit rejected it . . . . The District Court accordingly denied the motion and, for the same reason, the Court of Appeals affirmed in an unpublished, per curiam opinion"

The Supreme Court granted certiorari to review the case, and affirmed.

B. Counsel of Record

ACLU Side (Petitioner / Appellant): Webster J. Arceneaux III argued the cause for appellant. With him on the briefs was Brian A. Glasser.

Beth S. Brinkmann argued the cause for the United States as amicus curiae, by special leave of the Court.

Opposing Side (Respondent / Appellee): David P. Cleek, Senior Deputy Attorney General of West Virginia, argued the cause for appellee. With him on the briefs was Darrell V. McGraw, Jr., Attorney General.

III. AMICI CURIAE

ACLU Side (Petitioner / Appellant)

Brief of amici curiae filed on behalf of Public Citizen and the American Civil Liberties Union by Steven R. Shapiro, Harvey Grossman, Brian Wolfman, Arthur B. Spitzer, and Adam Schwartz.

Brief of amici curiae filed on behalf of the United States by Beth S. Brinkmann, former Solicitor General Waxman, Acting Solicitor General Underwood, Assistant Attorney General Lee, Jeffrey P. Minear, Jessica Dunsay Silver, and Kevin K. Russell.

Brief of amici curiae filed on behalf of the Friends of the Earth et al. by Bruce J. Terris, Carolyn Smith Pravlik, and Sarah A. Adams.

Opposing Side (Respondent / Appellee)

Brief of amici curiae filed on behalf of the State of Maryland et al. by J. Joseph Curran, Jr., Attorney General of Maryland, and Maureen M. Dove and Andrew H. Baida, Assistant Attorneys General, and by the Attorneys General for their respective States as follows: Bill Pryor of Alabama, Bill Lockyer of California, Ken Salazar of Colorado, M. Jane Brady of Delaware, Robert A. Butterworth of Florida, James E. Ryan of Illinois, Carla J. Stovall of Kansas, Richard P. Ieyoub of Louisiana, Thomas F. Reilly of Massachusetts, Jeremiah W (Jay) Nixon of Missouri, Joseph P. Mazurek of Montana, Don Stenberg of Nebraska, Philip T. McLaughlin of New Hampshire, Michael F. Easley of North Carolina, Heidi Heitkamp of North Dakota, Betty D. Montgomery of Ohio, W. A. Drew Edmondson of Oklahoma, Hardy Myers of Oregon, D. Michael Fisher of Pennsylvania, Sheldon Whitehouse of Rhode Island, Charles M. Condon of South Carolina, Mark Barnett of South Dakota, Paul G. Summers of Tennessee, John Cornyn of Texas, Jan Graham of Utah, and Mark L. Earley of Virginia.

Brief of amici curiae filed on behalf of the Alliance of Automobile Manufacturers, Inc., by Charles A. Newman and Jerome H. Block.

Brief of amici curiae filed on behalf of Los Angeles County et al. by Elwood Lui and Jeffrey S. Sutton.

Brief of amici curiae filed on behalf of the National Conference of State Legislatures et al. by Richard Ruda, James I. Crowley, Jacqueline G. Cooper, and Paul J. Watford;

Brief of amici curiae filed on behalf of the Pacific Legal Foundation by M. Reed Hopper.

IV. THE SUPREME COURT'S DECISION

"In the United States, parties are ordinarily required to bear their own attorney's fees—the prevailing party is not entitled to collect from the loser. Under this 'American Rule,' we follow 'a general practice of not awarding fees to a prevailing party absent explicit statutory authority.' Congress, however, has authorized the award of attorney's fees to the 'prevailing party' in numerous statutes in addition to those at issue here, such as the Civil Rights Act of 1964, the Voting Rights Act Amendments of 1975, and the Civil Rights Attorney's Fees Awards Act of 1976 . . . .

In designating those parties eligible for an award of litigation costs, Congress employed the term 'prevailing party,' a legal term of art. Black's Law Dictionary defines 'prevailing party' as '[a] party in whose favor a judgment is rendered, regardless of the amount of damages awarded <in certain cases, the court will award attorney's fees to the prevailing party>.—Also termed successful party.' This view that a 'prevailing party' is one who has been awarded some relief by the court can be distilled from our prior cases. . . .

These decisions, taken together, establish that enforceable judgments on the merits and court-ordered consent decrees create the 'material alteration of the legal relationship of the parties' necessary to permit an award of attorney's fees. . . .

We think, however, the 'catalyst theory' falls on the other side of the line from these examples. It allows an award where there is no judicially sanctioned change in the legal relationship of the parties. Even under a limited form of the 'catalyst theory,' a plaintiff could recover attorney's fees if it established that the 'complaint had sufficient merit to withstand a motion to dismiss for lack of jurisdiction or failure to state a claim on which relief may be granted.' This is not the type of legal merit that our prior decisions, based upon plain language and congressional intent, have found necessary. . . . A defendant's voluntary change in conduct, although perhaps accomplishing what the plaintiff sought to achieve by the lawsuit, lacks the necessary judicial imprimatur on the change. Our precedents thus counsel against holding that the term 'prevailing party' authorizes an award of attorney's fees without a corresponding alteration in the legal relationship of the parties. . . .

Given the clear meaning of "prevailing party" in the fee-shifting statutes, we need not determine which way these various policy arguments cut. In Alyeska, we said that Congress had not 'extended any roving authority to the Judiciary to allow counsel fees as costs or otherwise whenever the courts might deem them warranted.' To disregard the clear legislative language and the holdings of our prior cases on the basis of such policy arguments would be a similar assumption of a 'roving authority.' For the reasons stated above, we hold that the 'catalyst theory' is not a permissible basis for the award of attorney's fees under the FHAA and ADA.

The judgment of the Court of Appeals is affirmed."

V. JUSTICE VOTE

4 Pro ACLU Side vs. 5 Con Opposing Side

ACLU Side (Petitioner / Appellant)

1. Ginsburg, R. – Wrote dissenting opinion
2. Stevens, J. – Joined Ginsburg's dissent
3. Souter, D. – Joined Ginsburg's dissent
4. Breyer, S. – Joined Ginsburg's dissent

Opposing Side (Respondent / Appellee)

1. Rehnquist, W. – Wrote majority opinion
2. O'Connor, S. – Joined majority opinion
3. Kennedy, A. – Joined majority opinion
4. Scalia, A. – Wrote concurring opinion
5. Thomas, C. – Joined Scalia's concurrence

VI. A WIN OR LOSS FOR THE ACLU?

The ACLU filed as amicus curiae urging reversal of the judgment of the Court of Appeals; the Supreme Court affirmed in a 5-4 vote, giving the ACLU an apparent loss.

903. Booth v. Churner

(Decided May 29, 2001; 532 U.S. 731)

I. ISSUE

A. Issues Discussed

Prison, 8th Amendment

B. Legal Question Presented

"[W]hether an inmate seeking only money damages must complete a prison administrative process that could provide some sort of relief on the complaint stated, but no money."

C. Supreme Court's Answer

Exhaustion is required. "Congress has mandated exhaustion clearly enough, regardless of the relief offered through administrative procedures."

II. CASE SUMMARY

A. Background

"Petitioner, Timothy Booth, was an inmate at the State Correctional Institution at Smithfield, Pennsylvania, when he began this action under Rev. Stat. § 1979, 42 U.S.C. § 1983, in the United States District Court for the Middle District of Pennsylvania. He claimed that respondent corrections officers at Smithfield violated his Eighth Amendment right to be free from cruel and unusual punishment by assaulting him, bruising his wrists in tightening and twisting handcuffs placed upon him, throwing cleaning material in his face, and denying him medical attention to treat ensuing injuries. Booth sought various forms of injunctive relief, including transfer to another prison, as well as several hundred thousand dollars in money damages.

The Pennsylvania Department of Corrections provided an administrative grievance system at the time. . . . While the grievance system addressed complaints of the abuse and excessive force Booth alleged, it had no provision for recovery of money damages.

Before resorting to federal court, Booth filed an administrative grievance charging at least some of the acts of abuse he later alleged in his action. He did not, however, go beyond the first step, and never sought intermediate or final administrative review after the prison authority denied relief.

Booth's failure to avail himself of the later stages of the administrative process led the District Court to dismiss the complaint without prejudice for failure to exhaust 'administrative remedies ... available' within the meaning of 42 U.S.C. § 1997e(a). The Court of Appeals for the Third Circuit affirmed, rejecting Booth's argument that the statutory exhaustion requirement is inapposite to his case simply because the Commonwealth's administrative process could not award him the monetary relief he sought (money then being the only relief still requested, since Booth's transfer to another institution had mooted his claims for injunctive orders). Although the Third Circuit acknowledged that several other Courts of Appeals had held the exhaustion requirement subject to exception when the internal grievance procedure could not provide an inmate-plaintiff with the purely monetary relief requested in his federal action, . . . the court found no such exception in the statute . . . ."

The Supreme Court granted certiorari to review the case, and affirmed.

B. Counsel of Record

ACLU Side (Petitioner / Appellant): Nancy Winkelman argued the cause for appellant. With her on the briefs were Joseph T. Lukens and Ralph N. Sianni.

Irving L. Gornstein argued the cause for the United States, as amicus curiae, by special leave of Court.

Opposing Side (Respondent / Appellee): Gerald J. Pappert, First Deputy Attorney General of Pennsylvania, argued the cause for appellees. With him on the briefs were D. Michael Fisher, Attorney General, John G. Knorr III, Chief Deputy Attorney General, and Gwendolyn T. Mosley and Calvin R. Koons, Senior Deputy Attorneys General.

III. AMICI CURIAE

ACLU Side (Petitioner / Appellant)

Brief of amici curiae filed on behalf of the American Civil Liberties Union, the Legal Aid Society of the City of New

York, and the Prison Reform Advocacy Center by David C. Fathi, Elizabeth Alexander, Margaret Winter, Daniel L. Greenberg, John Boston, Milton Zelermyer, and Alphonse A. Gerhardstein.

Brief of amici curiae filed on behalf of the United States by Irving L. Gornstein, Acting Solicitor General Underwood, former Solicitor General Waxman, former Assistant Attorney General Ogden, Barbara L. Herwig, and Peter R. Maier.

Brief of amici curiae filed on behalf of the Association of the Bar of the City of New York by Michael B. Mushlin and William J. Rold.

Brief of amici curiae filed on behalf of the Brennan Center for Justice et al. by Robert J. Lukens, Richard P. Weishaupt, and Jonathan M. Stein.

Opposing Side (Respondent / Appellee)

Brief of amici curiae filed on behalf of the State of Ohio et al. by Betty D. Montgomery, Attorney General of Ohio, Stephen P. Carney, Associate Solicitor, and Todd R. Marti, Assistant Attorney General, and by the Attorneys General for their respective jurisdictions as follows: Bill Pryor of Alabama, Bruce M. Botelho of Alaska, Janet Napolitano of Arizona, Mark Pryor of Arkansas, Bill Lockyer of California, Ken Salazar of Colorado, Richard Blumenthal of Connecticut, M. Jane Brady of Delaware, Robert R. Rigsby of the District of Columbia, Robert A. Butterworth of Florida, Thurbert E. Baker of Georgia, John F. Tarantino of Guam, Earl I. Anzai of Hawaii, Alan Lance of Idaho, James E. Ryan of Illinois, Karen Freeman-Wilson of Indiana, Thomas J. Miller of Iowa, Carla J. Stovall of Kansas, Albert B. Chandler III of Kentucky, Richard P. Ieyoub of Louisiana, G. Steven Rowe of Maine, J. Joseph Curran, Jr., of Maryland, Thomas F. Reilly of Massachusetts, Jennifer M. Granholm of Michigan, Mike Hatch of Minnesota, Mike Moore of Mississippi, Jeremiah W. (Jay) Nixon of Missouri, Mike McGrath of Montana, Don Stenberg of Nebraska, Frankie Sue Del Papa of Nevada, Philip T. McLaughlin of New Hampshire, John J. Farmer, Jr., of New Jersey, Patricia A. Madrid of New Mexico, Eliot Spitzer of New York, Roy Cooper of North Carolina, Wayne Stenehjem of North Dakota, W. A. Drew Edmondson of Oklahoma, Hardy Myers of Oregon, Sheldon Whitehouse of Rhode Island, Charles M. Condon of South Carolina, Mark Barnett of South Dakota, Paul G. Summers of Tennessee, John Cornyn of Texas, Mark L. Shurtleff of Utah, William H. Sorrell of Vermont, Mark L. Earley of Virginia, Iver A. Stridiron of the Virgin Islands, Christine O. Gregoire of Washington, and Gay Woodhouse of Wyoming.

IV. THE SUPREME COURT'S DECISION

"In the aftermath of the Prison Litigation Reform Act of 1995, 42 U.S.C. § 1997e(a) provides that

'[n]o action shall be brought with respect to prison conditions under section 1983 of this title, or any other Federal law, by a prisoner confined in any jail, prison, or other correctional facility until such administrative remedies as are available are exhausted.'

The meaning of the phrase 'administrative remedies ... available' is the crux of the case . . . . The dispute here . . . comes down to whether or not a remedial scheme is 'available' where, as in Pennsylvania, the administrative process has authority to take some action in response to a complaint, but not the remedial action an inmate demands to the exclusion of all other forms of redress.

In seeking the congressional intent, the parties urge us to give weight to practical considerations, among others . . . .

Each of the parties also says that the plain meaning of the words 'remedies' and 'available' in the phrase 'such administrative remedies ... available' is controlling. But as it turns out both of them quote some of the same dictionary definitions of 'available' 'remedies,' and neither comes up with anything conclusive. . . .

We find clearer pointers toward the congressional objective in two considerations, the first being the broader statutory context in which 'available' 'remedies' are mentioned. The entire modifying clause in which the words occur is this: 'until such administrative remedies as are available are exhausted.' The 'available' 'remed[y]' must be 'exhausted' before a complaint under § 1983 may be entertained. While the modifier 'available' requires the possibility of some relief for the action complained of (as the parties agree), the word 'exhausted' has a decidedly procedural emphasis. It makes sense only in referring to the procedural means, not the particular relief ordered. It would, for example, be very strange usage to say that a prisoner must 'exhaust' an administrative order reassigning an abusive guard before a prisoner could go to court and ask for something else; or to say (in States that award money damages administratively) that a prisoner must 'exhaust' his damages award before going to court for more. How would he 'exhaust' a transfer of personnel? Would he have to spend the money to 'exhaust' the monetary relief given him? It makes no sense to demand that someone exhaust 'such administrative [redress]' as is available; one 'exhausts' processes, not forms of relief, and the statute provides that one must.

A second consideration, statutory history, confirms the suggestion that Congress meant to require procedural exhaustion regardless of the fit between a prisoner's prayer for relief and the administrative remedies possible. Before § 1997e(a) was amended by the Act of 1995, a court had discretion (though no obligation) to require a state inmate to exhaust 'such ... remedies as are available,' but only if those remedies were 'plain, speedy, and effective.' That scheme, however, is now a thing of the past, for the amendments eliminated both the discretion to dispense with administrative exhaustion and the condition that the remedy be 'plain, speedy, and effective' before exhaustion could be required.

The significance of deleting that condition is apparent in light of our decision two years earlier in McCarthy v. Madigan. . . . In holding that exhaustion was not required, we reasoned in part from the language of § 1997e(a) that required an 'effective' administrative remedy as a precondition to exhaustion. When a prisoner sought only money damages, we indicated, only a procedure able to provide money damages would be 'effective' within the meaning of the statute. . . .

When Congress replaced the text of the statute as construed in McCarthy with the exhaustion requirement at issue today, it presumably understood that under McCarthy the term 'effective' in the former § 1997e(a) eliminated the possibility of requiring exhaustion of administrative remedies when an inmate sought only monetary relief and the administrative process offered none.

It has to be significant that Congress removed the very term we had previously emphasized in reaching the result Booth now seeks, and the fair inference to be drawn is that Congress meant to preclude the McCarthy result. Congress's imposition of an obviously broader exhaustion requirement makes it highly implausible that it meant to give prisoners a strong inducement to skip the administrative process simply by limiting prayers for relief to money damages not offered through administrative grievance mechanisms.

Thus, we think that Congress has mandated exhaustion clearly enough, regardless of the relief offered through administrative procedures. Cf. McCarthy, 503 U.S., at 144, 112 S.Ct. 1081 ('Where Congress specifically mandates, exhaustion is required'). We accordingly affirm the judgment of the Third Circuit."

V. JUSTICE VOTE

0 Pro ACLU Side vs. 9 Con Opposing Side

Opposing Side (Respondent / Appellee)

1. Souter, D. – Wrote majority opinion
2. O'Connor, S. – Joined majority opinion
3. Stevens, J. – Joined majority opinion
4. Thomas, C. – Joined majority opinion
5. Ginsburg, R. – Joined majority opinion
6. Breyer, S. – Joined majority opinion
7. Scalia, A. – Joined majority opinion
8. Kennedy, A. – Joined majority opinion
9. Rehnquist, W. – Joined majority opinion

VI. A WIN OR LOSS FOR THE ACLU?

The ACLU filed as amicus curiae urging reversal of the judgment of the Court of Appeals; the Supreme Court affirmed in a 9-0 vote, giving the ACLU an apparent loss.

904. Pollard v. E. I. du Pont de Nemours & Co.

(Decided June 4, 2001; 532 U.S. 843)

I. ISSUE

A. Issues Discussed

Civil rights, gender, federal

B. Legal Question Presented

"[W]hether a front pay award is an element of compensatory damages under the Civil Rights Act of 1991."

C. Supreme Court's Answer

"[W]e conclude that front pay is not an element of compensatory damages within the meaning of § 1981a, and, therefore, we hold that the statutory cap of § 1981a(b)(3) is inapplicable to front pay."

II. CASE SUMMARY

A. Background

"Petitioner Sharon Pollard sued her former employer, E.I. du Pont de Nemours and Company (DuPont), alleging that she had been subjected to a hostile work environment based on her sex, in violation of Title VII of the Civil Rights Act of 1964. After a trial, the District Court found that Pollard was subjected to co-worker sexual harassment of which her supervisors were aware. The District Court further found that the harassment resulted in a medical leave of absence from her job for psychological assistance and her eventual dismissal for refusing to return to the same hostile work environment. The court awarded Pollard $107,364 in backpay and benefits, $252,997 in attorney's fees, and, as relevant here, $300,000 in compensatory damages—the maximum permitted under the statutory cap for such damages in 42 U.S.C. § 1981a(b)(3). The Court of Appeals affirmed, concluding that the record demonstrated that DuPont employees engaged in flagrant discrimination based on sex and that DuPont managers and supervisors did not take adequate steps to stop it.

The issue presented for review here is whether front pay constitutes an element of 'compensatory damages' under 42 U.S.C. § 1981a and thus is subject to the statutory damages cap imposed by that section. Although courts have defined 'front pay' in numerous ways, front pay is simply money awarded for lost compensation during the period between judgment and reinstatement or in lieu of reinstatement. . . . For the purposes of this opinion, it is not necessary for us to explain when front pay is an appropriate remedy. The question before us is only whether front pay, if found to be appropriate, is an element of compensatory damages under the Civil Rights Act of 1991 and thus subject to the Act's statutory cap on such damages.

Here, the District Court observed that 'the $300,000.00 award is, in fact, insufficient to compensate plaintiff,' but it stated that it was bound by the Sixth Circuit's decision in Hudson v. Reno, which held that front pay was subject to the cap. On appeal, Pollard argued that Hudson was wrongly decided because front pay is not an element of compensatory damages, but rather a replacement for the remedy of reinstatement in situations in which reinstatement would be inappropriate. She also argued that § 1981a, by its very terms, explicitly excludes from the statutory cap remedies that traditionally were available under Title VII, which she argued included front pay. The Court of Appeals agreed with Pollard's arguments but considered itself bound by Hudson. The Sixth Circuit declined to rehear the case en banc.

The Sixth Circuit's decision in Hudson was one of the first appellate opinions to decide whether front pay is an element of compensatory damages subject to the statutory cap set forth in § 1981a(b)(3). Contrary to the Sixth Circuit's resolution of this question, the other Courts of Appeals to address it have concluded that front pay is a remedy that is not subject to the limitations of § 1981a(b)(3). [The Supreme Court] granted certiorari to resolve this conflict."

B. Counsel of Record

ACLU Side (Petitioner / Appellant): Kathleen L. Caldwell argued the cause for petitioner. With her on the briefs was Eric Schnapper.

Matthew D. Roberts argued the cause for the United States, as amicus curiae, by special leave of Court.

Opposing Side (Respondent / Appellee): Raymond Michael Ripple argued the cause for appellee. With him on the briefs was Donna L. Goodman

III. AMICI CURIAE

ACLU Side (Petitioner / Appellant)

Briefs of amici curiae filed on behalf of the Lawyers' Committee for Civil Rights Under Law, the American Civil Liberties Union, the National Women's Law Center, the National Partnership for Women & Families, the NOW Legal Defense and Education Fund,

the National Asian Pacific American Legal Consortium, the American Federation of Government Employees, and AARP by Richard M. Wyner, Matthew M. Hoffman, Michele Lee Svonkin, Rebecca E. Rapp, Charles T. Lester, Jr., John Payton, Norman Redlich, Barbara R. Arnwine, Thomas J. Henderson, Brenda Ford Harding, Steven R. Shapiro, Lenora M. Lapidus, Sara L. Mandelbaum, Marcia D. Greenberger, Judith C. Appelbaum, Judith L. Lichtman, Donna R. Lenhoff, Martha F. Davis, Karen K. Narasaki, Vincent A. Eng, Mark D. Roth, and Laurie A. McCann.

Brief of amici curiae filed on behalf of the United States by Matthew D. Roberts, Acting Solicitor General Underwood, Acting Assistant Attorney General Yeomans, Austin C. Schlick, Dennis J. Dimsey, Jennifer Levin, Gwendolyn Young Reams, Phillip B. Sklover, Carolyn L. Wheeler, and Caren I. Friedman.

Brief of amici curiae filed on behalf of the National Employment Lawyers Association et al. by Woodley B. Osborne, H. Candace Gorman, and Paula A. Brantner.

Opposing Side (Respondent / Appellee)

Brief of amici curiae filed on behalf of the Equal Employment Advisory Council et al. by Robert E. Williams, Ann Elizabeth Reesman, Stephen A. Bokat, and Robin S. Conrad.

Brief of amici curiae filed on behalf of the Society for Human Resource Management by Paul Salvatore.

IV. THE SUPREME COURT'S DECISION

"Plaintiffs who allege employment discrimination on the basis of sex traditionally have been entitled to such remedies as injunctions, reinstatement, backpay, lost benefits, and attorney's fees under § 706(g) of the Civil Rights Act of 1964. In the Civil Rights Act of 1991, Congress expanded the remedies available to these plaintiffs by permitting, for the first time, the recovery of compensatory and punitive damages. 42 U.S.C. § 1981a(a)(1) ('[T]he complaining party may recover compensatory and punitive damages as allowed in subsection (b) of this section, in addition to any relief authorized by section 706(g) of the Civil Rights Act of 1964'). The amount of compensatory damages awarded under § 1981a for 'future pecuniary losses, emotional pain, suffering, inconvenience, mental anguish, loss of enjoyment of life, and other nonpecuniary losses,' and the amount of punitive damages awarded under § 1981a, however, may not exceed the statutory cap set forth in § 1981a(b)(3). The statutory cap is based on the number of people employed by the respondent. In this case, the cap is $300,000 because DuPont has more than 500 employees.

The Sixth Circuit has concluded that front pay constitutes compensatory damages awarded for future pecuniary losses and thus is subject to the statutory cap of § 1981a(b)(3). For the reasons discussed below, we conclude that front pay is not an element of compensatory damages within the meaning of § 1981a, and, therefore, we hold that the statutory cap of § 1981a(b)(3) is inapplicable to front pay. . . .

In 1972, Congress expanded § 706(g) to specify that a court could, in addition to awarding those remedies previously listed in the provision, award any other equitable relief as the court deems appropriate.' After this amendment to § 706(g), courts endorsed a broad view of front pay. . . . By 1991, virtually all of the courts of appeals had recognized that "front pay" was a remedy authorized under § 706(g). In fact, no court of appeals appears to have ever held to the contrary. . . .

In the abstract, front pay could be considered compensation for 'future pecuniary losses,' in which case it would be subject to the statutory cap. § 1981a(b)(3). The term 'compensatory damages ... for future pecuniary losses' is not defined in the statute, and, out of context, its ordinary meaning could include all payments for monetary losses after the date of judgment. However, we must not analyze one term of § 1981a in isolation. . . . When § 1981a is read as a whole, the better interpretation is that front pay is not within the meaning of compensatory damages in § 1981a(b)(3), and thus front pay is excluded from the statutory cap.

In the Civil Rights Act of 1991, Congress determined that victims of employment discrimination were entitled to additional remedies. Congress expressly found that 'additional remedies under Federal law are needed to deter unlawful harassment and intentional discrimination in the workplace,' without giving any indication that it wished to curtail previously available remedies. Congress therefore made clear through the plain language of the statute that the remedies newly authorized under § 1981a were in addition to the relief authorized by § 706(g). Section 1981a(a)(1) provides that, in intentional discrimination cases brought under Title VII, 'the complaining party may recover compensatory and punitive damages as allowed in subjection (b) of [§ 1981a], in addition to any relief authorized by section 706(g) of the Civil Rights Act of 1964, from the respondent.' (Emphasis added.) And § 1981a(b)(2) states that '[c]ompensatory damages awarded under [§ 1981a] shall not include backpay, interest on backpay, or any other type of relief authorized under section 706(g) of the Civil Rights Act of 1964.' Emphasis added.) According to these statutory provisions, if front pay was a type of relief authorized under § 706(g), it is excluded from the meaning of compensatory damages under § 1981a. . . .

As to front pay awards that are made in lieu of reinstatement, we construe § 706(g) as authorizing these awards as well. We see no logical difference between front pay awards made when there eventually is reinstatement and those made when there is not. . . .

Because front pay is a remedy authorized under § 706(g), Congress did not limit the availability of such awards in § 1981a. Instead, Congress sought to expand the available remedies by permitting the recovery of compensatory and punitive damages in addition to previously available remedies, such as front pay. . . .

The judgment of the Court of Appeals is reversed, and the case is remanded for further proceedings consistent with this opinion."

V. JUSTICE VOTE

8 Pro ACLU Side vs. 0 Con Opposing Side

ACLU Side (Petitioner / Appellant)

1. Thomas, C. – Wrote majority opinion
2. Souter, D. – Joined majority opinion
3. Stevens, J. – Joined majority opinion
4. Ginsburg, R. – Joined majority opinion
5. Breyer, S. – Joined majority opinion
6. Scalia, A. – Joined majority opinion
7. Kennedy, A. – Joined majority opinion
8. Rehnquist, W. – Joined majority opinion

O'Connor, S – Took no part in the decision

VI. A WIN OR LOSS FOR THE ACLU?

The ACLU filed as amicus curiae urging reversal of the judgment of the Court of Appeals; the Supreme Court reversed and remanded in an 8-0 vote, giving the ACLU an apparent win.

905. Kyllo v. United States

(Decided June 11, 2001; 533 U.S. 27)

I. ISSUE

A. Issues Discussed

4th Amendment, drugs

B. Legal Question Presented

"This case presents the question whether the use of a thermal-imaging device aimed at a private home from a public street to detect relative amounts of heat within the home constitutes a 'search' within the meaning of the Fourth Amendment."

C. Supreme Court's Answer

"Where, as here, the Government uses a device that is not in general public use, to explore details of the home that would previously have been unknowable without physical intrusion, the surveillance is a 'search' and is presumptively unreasonable without a warrant."

II. CASE SUMMARY

A. Background

"In 1991 Agent William Elliott of the United States Department of the Interior came to suspect that marijuana was being grown in the home belonging to petitioner Danny Kyllo, part of a triplex on Rhododendron Drive in Florence, Oregon. Indoor marijuana growth typically requires high-intensity lamps. In order to determine whether an amount of heat was emanating from petitioner's home consistent with the use of such lamps, at 3:20 a.m. on January 16, 1992, Agent Elliott and Dan Haas used an Agema Thermovision 210 thermal imager to scan the triplex. Thermal imagers detect infrared radiation, which virtually all objects emit but which is not visible to the naked eye. The imager converts radiation into images based on relative warmth—black is cool, white is hot, shades of gray connote relative differences; in that respect, it operates somewhat like a video camera showing heat images. The scan of Kyllo's home took only a few minutes and was performed from the passenger seat of Agent Elliott's vehicle across the street from the front of the house and also from the street in back of the house. The scan showed that the roof over the garage and a side wall of petitioner's home were relatively hot compared to the rest of the home and substantially warmer than neighboring homes in the triplex. Agent Elliott concluded that petitioner was using halide lights to grow marijuana in his house, which indeed he was. Based on tips from informants, utility bills, and the thermal imaging, a Federal Magistrate Judge issued a warrant authorizing a search of petitioner's home, and the agents found an indoor growing operation involving more than 100 plants. Petitioner was indicted on one count of manufacturing marijuana, in violation of 21 U.S.C. § 841(a)(1). He unsuccessfully moved to suppress the evidence seized from his home and then entered a conditional guilty plea.

The Court of Appeals for the Ninth Circuit remanded the case for an evidentiary hearing regarding the intrusiveness of thermal imaging. On remand the District Court found that the Agema 210 'is a non-intrusive device which emits no rays or beams and shows a crude visual image of the heat being radiated from the outside of the house'; it 'did not show any people or activity within the walls of the structure'; '[t]he device used cannot penetrate walls or windows to reveal conversations or human activities'; and '[n]o intimate details of the home were observed.' Based on these findings, the District Court upheld the validity of the warrant that relied in part upon the thermal imaging, and reaffirmed its denial of the motion to suppress. A divided Court of Appeals initially reversed, but that opinion was withdrawn and the panel (after a change in composition) affirmed, with Judge Noonan dissenting. The court held that petitioner had shown no subjective expectation of privacy because he had made no attempt to conceal the heat escaping from his home, and even if he had, there was no objectively reasonable expectation of privacy because the imager 'did not expose any intimate details of Kyllo's life,' only 'amorphous 'hot spots' on the roof and exterior wall.'"

The Supreme Court granted certiorari to review the case, and reversed.

B. Counsel of Record

ACLU Side (Petitioner / Appellant): Kenneth Lerner argued the cause for appellant.

Opposing Side (Respondent / Appellee): Deputy Solicitor General Dreeben argued the cause for the United States. With him on the briefs were former Solicitor General Waxman, Assistant Attorney General Robinson, Irving L. Gornstein, and Deborah Watson.

III. AMICI CURIAE

ACLU Side (Petitioner / Appellant)

Brief of amici curiae filed on behalf of the National Association of Criminal Defense Lawyers and the American Civil Liberties Union by James J. Tomkovicz, Lisa B. Kemler, and Steven R. Shapiro.

Brief of amici curiae filed on behalf of the Liberty Project by Julie M. Carpenter.

Opposing Side (Respondent / Appellee)

No briefs of amici curiae were filed in support of appellee.

IV. THE SUPREME COURT'S DECISION

"The Fourth Amendment provides that '[t]he right of the people to be secure in their persons, houses, papers, and effects, against unreasonable searches and seizures, shall not be violated.' 'At the very core' of the Fourth Amendment 'stands the right of a man to retreat into his own home and there be free from unreasonable governmental intrusion.' With few exceptions, the question whether a warrantless search of a home is reasonable and hence constitutional must be answered no.

On the other hand, the antecedent question whether or not a Fourth Amendment 'search' has occurred is not so simple under our precedent. The permissibility of ordinary visual surveillance of a home used to be clear because, well into the 20th century, our Fourth Amendment jurisprudence was tied to common-law trespass. . . . Visual surveillance was unquestionably lawful because "the eye cannot by the laws of England be guilty of a trespass." We have since decoupled violation of a person's Fourth Amendment rights from trespassory violation of his property, but the lawfulness of warrantless visual surveillance of a home has still been preserved. As we observed in California v. Ciraolo, '[t]he Fourth Amendment protection of the home has never been extended to require law enforcement officers to shield their eyes when passing by a home on public thoroughfares.' . . .

In assessing when a search is not a search, we have applied somewhat in reverse the principle first enunciated in Katz v. United States. Katz involved eavesdropping by means of an electronic listening device placed on the outside of a telephone booth—a location not within the catalog ('persons, houses, papers, and effects') that the Fourth Amendment protects against unreasonable searches. We held that the Fourth Amendment nonetheless protected Katz from the warrantless eavesdropping because he 'justifiably relied' upon the privacy of the telephone booth. As Justice Harlan's oft-quoted concurrence described it, a Fourth Amendment search occurs when the government violates a subjective expectation of privacy that society recognizes as reasonable. We have subsequently applied this principle to hold that a Fourth Amendment search does not occur—even when the explicitly protected location of a house is concerned—unless 'the individual manifested a subjective expectation of privacy in the object of the challenged search,' and 'society [is] willing to recognize that expectation as reasonable. . . .

The present case involves officers on a public street engaged in more than naked-eye surveillance of a home. We have previously reserved judgment as to how much technological enhancement of ordinary perception from such a vantage point, if any, is too much. While we upheld enhanced aerial photography of an industrial complex in Dow Chemical, we noted that we found 'it important that this is not an area immediately adjacent to a private home, where privacy expectations are most heightened,' (emphasis in original). . . .

The question we confront today is what limits there are upon this power of technology to shrink the realm of guaranteed privacy. . . .

We think that obtaining by sense-enhancing technology any information regarding the interior of the home that could not otherwise have been obtained without physical 'intrusion into a constitutionally protected area,' constitutes a search—at least where (as here) the technology in question is not in general public use. This assures preservation of that degree of privacy against government that existed when the Fourth Amendment was adopted. On the basis of this criterion, the information obtained by the thermal imager in this case was the product of a search. . . .

The Government also contends that the thermal imaging was constitutional because it did not 'detect private activities occurring in private areas.' . . . In the home, our cases show, all details are intimate details, because the entire area is held safe from prying government eyes. . . .

We have said that the Fourth Amendment draws 'a firm line at the entrance to the house.' That line, we think, must be not only firm but also bright—which requires clear specification of those methods of surveillance that require a warrant. While it is certainly possible to conclude from the videotape of the thermal imaging that occurred in this case that no 'significant' compromise of the homeowner's privacy has occurred, we must take the long view, from the original meaning of the Fourth Amendment forward.

'The Fourth Amendment is to be construed in the light of what was deemed an unreasonable search and seizure when it was adopted, and in a manner which will conserve public interests as well as the interests and rights of individual citizens.'

Where, as here, the Government uses a device that is not in general public use, to explore details of the home that would previously have been unknowable without physical intrusion, the surveillance is a 'search' and is presumptively unreasonable without a warrant.

Since we hold the Thermovision imaging to have been an unlawful search, it will remain for the District Court to determine whether, without the evidence it provided, the search warrant issued in this case was supported by probable cause—and if not, whether there is any other basis for supporting admission of the evidence that the search pursuant to the warrant produced.

The judgment of the Court of Appeals is reversed; the case is remanded for further proceedings consistent with this opinion."

V. JUSTICE VOTE

5 Pro ACLU Side vs. 4 Con Opposing Side

ACLU Side (Petitioner / Appellant)

1. Scalia, A. – Wrote majority opinion
2. Thomas, C. – Joined majority opinion

3. Souter, D. – Joined majority opinion
4. Ginsburg, R. – Joined majority opinion
5. Breyer, S. – Joined majority opinion

Opposing Side (Respondent / Appellee)

1. Stevens, J. – Wrote dissenting opinion
2. Kennedy, A. – Joined Stevens' dissent
3. O'Connor, S. – Joined Stevens' dissent
4. Rehnquist, W. – Joined Stevens' dissent

VI. A WIN OR LOSS FOR THE ACLU?

The ACLU filed as amicus curiae urging reversal of the judgment of the Court of Appeals; the Supreme Court reversed and remanded in a 5-4 vote, giving the ACLU an apparent win.

906. Nguyen v. INS

(Decided June 11, 2001; 533 U.S. 53)

I. ISSUE

A. Issues Discussed

Gender, immigration/citizenship

B. Legal Question Presented

"Title 8 U.S.C. § 1409 governs the acquisition of United States citizenship by persons born to one United States citizen parent and one noncitizen parent when the parents are unmarried and the child is born outside of the United States or its possessions. The statute imposes different requirements for the child's acquisition of citizenship depending upon whether the citizen parent is the mother or the father. The question before us is whether the statutory distinction is consistent with the equal protection guarantee embedded in the Due Process Clause of the Fifth Amendment."

C. Supreme Court's Answer

"We hold that § 1409(a) is consistent with the constitutional guarantee of equal protection."

II. CASE SUMMARY

A. Background

"Petitioner Tuan Anh Nguyen was born in Saigon, Vietnam, on September 11, 1969, to copetitioner Joseph Boulais and a Vietnamese citizen. Boulais and Nguyen's mother were not married. Boulais always has been a citizen of the United States, and he was in Vietnam under the employ of a corporation. . . . In June 1975, Nguyen, then almost six years of age, came to the United States. He became a lawful permanent resident and was raised in Texas by Boulais.

In 1992, when Nguyen was 22, he pleaded guilty in a Texas state court to two counts of sexual assault on a child. . . . Three years later, the United States Immigration and Naturalization Service (INS) initiated deportation proceedings against Nguyen as an alien who had been convicted of two crimes involving moral turpitude, as well as an aggravated felony. . . . The Immigration Judge found him deportable.

Nguyen appealed to the Board of Immigration Appeals and, in 1998, while the matter was pending, his father obtained an order of parentage from a state court, based on DNA testing. . . . The Board dismissed Nguyen's appeal, rejecting his claim to United States citizenship because he had failed to establish compliance with 8 U.S.C. § 1409(a), which sets forth the requirements for one who was born out of wedlock and abroad to a citizen father and a noncitizen mother.

Nguyen and Boulais appealed to the Court of Appeals for the Fifth Circuit, arguing that § 1409 violates equal protection by providing different rules for attainment of citizenship by children born abroad and out of wedlock depending upon whether the one parent with American citizenship is the mother or the father. The court rejected the constitutional challenge to § 1409(a)."

The Supreme Court granted certiorari to review the case.

B. Counsel of Record

ACLU Side (Petitioner / Appellant): Martha F. Davis argued the cause for appellants. With her on the briefs were Nancy A. Falgout, Steven R. Shapiro and Lucas Guttentag of the American Civil Liberties Union Foundation, Julie Goldscheid, Sherry J. Leiwant, and Marcellene E. Hearn.

Opposing Side (Respondent / Appellee): Deputy Solicitor General Kneedler argued the cause for appellee. With him on the brief were Solicitor General Waxman, Assistant Attorney General Ogden, Austin C. Schlick, Michael Jay Singer, and John S. Koppel.

III. AMICI CURIAE

ACLU Side (Petitioner / Appellant)

Brief of amici curiae filed on behalf of Equality Now et al. by Ogden Northrup Lewis and Jessica Neuwirth.

Brief of amici curiae filed on behalf of the National Women's Law Center et al. by Nancy Duff Campbell, Joan Entmacher, Dina R. Lassow, and Nancy L. Perkins.

Brief of amici curiae filed on behalf of the Asian American Legal Defense and Education Fund, Inc., by Moses Silverman and Kenneth Kimerling.

Opposing Side (Respondent / Appellee)

No briefs of amici curiae were filed in support of appellee.

IV. THE SUPREME COURT'S DECISION

"Title 8 U.S.C. § 1409 governs the acquisition of United States citizenship by persons born to one United States citizen parent and one noncitizen parent when the parents are unmarried and the child is born outside of the United States or its possessions. The statute imposes different requirements for the child's acquisition of citizenship depending upon whether the citizen parent is the mother or the father. The question before us is whether the statutory distinction is consistent with the equal protection guarantee embedded in the Due Process Clause of the Fifth Amendment. . . .

For a gender-based classification to withstand equal protection scrutiny, it must be established "at least that the [challenged] classification serves 'important governmental objectives and that the discriminatory means employed' are 'substantially related to the achievement of those objectives.'" For reasons to follow, we conclude § 1409 satisfies this standard. . . .

The statutory distinction relevant in this case . . . is that § 1409(a)(4) requires one of three affirmative steps to be taken if the citizen parent is the father, but not if the citizen parent is the mother: legitimation; a declaration of paternity under oath by the father; or a court order of paternity. [T]he imposition of the requirement for a paternal relationship, but not a maternal one, is justified by two important governmental objectives. We discuss each in turn. . . .

The first governmental interest to be served is the importance of assuring that a biological parent-child relationship exists. . . .

The second important governmental interest furthered in a substantial manner by § 1409(a)(4) is the determination to ensure that the child and the citizen parent have some demonstrated opportunity or potential to develop not just a relationship that is recognized, as a formal matter, by the law, but one that consists of the real, everyday ties that provide a connection between child and citizen parent and, in turn, the United States. . . .

Petitioners and their amici argue in addition that, rather than fulfilling an important governmental interest, § 1409 merely embodies a gender-based stereotype. [C]ontrary to petitioners' assertions, § 1409 addresses an undeniable difference in the circumstance of the parents at the time a child is born . . . . There is nothing irrational or improper in the recognition that at the moment of birth—a critical event in the statutory scheme and in the whole tradition of citizenship law—the mother's knowledge of the child and the fact of parenthood have been established in a way not guaranteed in the case of the unwed father. This is not a stereotype. . . .

Having concluded that facilitation of a relationship between parent and child is an important governmental interest, the question remains whether the means Congress chose to further its objective—the imposition of certain additional requirements upon an unwed father—substantially relate to that end. Under this test, the means Congress adopted must be sustained.

First, it should be unsurprising that Congress decided to require that an opportunity for a parent-child relationship occur during the formative years of the child's minority. . . .

Second, petitioners argue that § 1409(a)(4) is not effective. In particular, petitioners assert that, although a mother will know of her child's birth, 'knowledge that one is a parent, no matter how it is acquired, does not guarantee a relationship with one's child.' They thus maintain that the imposition of the additional requirements of § 1409(a)(4) only on the children of citizen fathers must reflect a stereotype that women are more likely than men to actually establish a relationship with their children. . . .

In this difficult context of conferring citizenship on vast numbers of persons, the means adopted by Congress are in substantial furtherance of important governmental objectives. The fit between the means and the important end is 'exceedingly persuasive.' We have explained that an 'exceedingly persuasive justification' is established 'by showing at least that the classification serves 'important governmental objectives and that the discriminatory means employed' are 'substantially related to the achievement of those objectives." Section 1409 meets this standard. . . .

In analyzing § 1409(a)(4), we are mindful that the obligation it imposes with respect to the acquisition of citizenship by the child of a citizen father is minimal. . . . In this case, the unfortunate, even tragic, circumstance is that Boulais did not pursue, or perhaps did not know of, these simple steps and alternatives. Any omission, however, does not nullify the statutory scheme.

Section 1409(a), moreover, is not the sole means by which the child of a citizen father can attain citizenship. An individual who fails to comply with § 1409(a), but who has substantial ties to the United States, can seek citizenship in his or her own right, rather than via reliance on ties to a citizen parent. This option now may be foreclosed to Nguyen, but any bar is due to the serious nature of his criminal offenses, not to an equal protection denial or to any supposed rigidity or harshness in the citizenship laws. . . .

The statutory scheme's satisfaction of the equal protection scrutiny we apply to gender-based classifications constitutes a sufficient basis for upholding it. It should be noted, however, that, even were we to conclude that the statute did not meet this standard of review, petitioners would face additional obstacles before they could prevail. . . .

To fail to acknowledge even our most basic biological differences—such as the fact that a mother must be present at birth but the father need not be—risks making the guarantee of equal protection superficial, and so disserving it. Mechanistic classification of all our differences as stereotypes would operate to obscure those misconceptions and prejudices that are real. The distinction embodied in the statutory scheme here at issue is not marked by misconception and prejudice, nor does it show disrespect for either class. The difference between men and women in relation to the birth process is a real one, and the principle of equal protection does not forbid Congress to address the problem at hand in a manner specific to each gender.

The judgment of the Court of Appeals is affirmed."

V. JUSTICE VOTE

4 Pro ACLU Side vs. 5 Con Opposing Side

ACLU Side (Petitioner / Appellant)

1. O'Connor, S. – Wrote dissenting opinion
2. Souter, D. – Joined O'Connor's dissent
3. Ginsburg, R. – Joined O'Connor's dissent
4. Breyer, S. – Joined O'Connor's dissent

Opposing Side (Respondent / Appellee)

1. Kennedy, A. – Wrote majority opinion
2. Rehnquist, W. – Joined majority opinion
3. Stevens, J. – Joined majority opinion
4. Scalia, A. – Wrote concurring opinion
5. Thomas, C. – Joined Scalia's concurrence

VI. A WIN OR LOSS FOR THE ACLU?

The ACLU argued the case for petitioner, urging reversal; the Supreme Court affirmed in a 5-4 vote, giving the ACLU an apparent loss.

907. Good News Club v. Milford Central School

(Decided June 11, 2001; 533 U.S. 98)

I. ISSUE

A. Issues Discussed

1st Amendment, religion

B. Legal Question Presented

"The first question is whether Milford Central School violated the free speech rights of the Good News Club when it excluded the Club from meeting after hours at the school. The second question is whether any such violation is justified by Milford's concern that permitting the Club's activities would violate the Establishment Clause."

C. Supreme Court's Answer

"We conclude that Milford's restriction violates the Club's free speech rights and that no Establishment Clause concern justifies that violation."

II. CASE SUMMARY

A. Background

"N.Y. Educ. Law § 414 enumerates several purposes for which local boards may open their schools to public use. In 1992, respondent Milford Central School (Milford) enacted a community use policy adopting seven of § 414's purposes . . . . Two of the stated purposes are relevant here. First, district residents may use the school for 'instruction in any branch of education, learning or the arts.' Second, the school is available for 'social, civic and recreational meetings and entertainment events, and other uses pertaining to the welfare of the community, provided that such uses shall be nonexclusive and shall be opened to the general public.'

Stephen and Darleen Fournier . . . are sponsors of the local Good News Club, a private Christian organization for children ages 6 to 12. [I]n September 1996 the Fourniers submitted a request to Dr. Robert McGruder, interim superintendent of the district, in which they sought permission to hold the Club's weekly afterschool meetings in the school cafeteria. . . . McGruder formally denied the Fourniers' request on the ground that the proposed use—to have 'a fun time of singing songs, hearing a Bible lesson and memorizing scripture,'—was 'the equivalent of religious worship.' According to McGruder, the community use policy, which prohibits use 'by any individual or organization for religious purposes,' foreclosed the Club's activities.

In response to a letter submitted by the Club's counsel, Milford's attorney requested information to clarify the nature of the Club's activities. . . .

McGruder and Milford's attorney reviewed the materials and concluded that 'the kinds of activities proposed to be engaged in by the Good News Club were not a discussion of secular subjects such as child rearing, development of character and development of morals from a religious perspective, but were in fact the equivalent of religious instruction itself.' In February 1997, the Milford Board of Education adopted a resolution rejecting the Club's request to use Milford's facilities 'for the purpose of conducting religious instruction and Bible study.'

In March 1997, petitioners . . . filed an action under Rev.Stat. § 1979, 42 U.S.C. § 1983, against Milford in the United States District Court for the Northern District of New York. The Club alleged that Milford's denial of its application violated its free speech rights under the First and Fourteenth Amendments, its right to equal protection under the Fourteenth Amendment, and its right to religious freedom under the Religious Freedom Restoration Act of 1993

The Club moved for a preliminary injunction . . . . [T]he District Court granted the injunction. . . .

In August 1998, the District Court vacated the preliminary injunction and granted Milford's motion for summary judgment. . . .

The Club appealed, and a divided panel of the United States Court of Appeals for the Second Circuit affirmed."

The Supreme Court granted certiorari to review the case.

B. Counsel of Record

ACLU Side (Respondent / Appellee): Frank W. Miller argued the cause for appellee. With him on the brief were Benjamin J. Ferrara and Norman H. Gross.

Opposing Side (Petitioner / Appellant): Thomas Marcelle argued the cause for appellants. With him on the briefs were John W. Whitehead and Steven H. Aden.

III. AMICI CURIAE

ACLU Side (Respondent / Appellee)

Brief of amici curiae filed on behalf of Americans United for Separation of Church and State, the American Civil Liberties Union, the American Jewish Committee, the New York Civil Liberties Union, and People for the American Way Foundation by Ayesha N. Khan, Steven K. Green, Steven R. Shapiro, Jerome J. Shestack, Jeffrey P. Sinensky, Kara Stein, Eddie Tabash, Arthur N. Eisenberg, Elliot M. Mincberg, and Judith E. Schaeffer.

Brief of amici curiae filed on behalf of the American Jewish Congress by Mark D. Stern.

Brief of amici curiae filed on behalf of the Anti-Defamation League et al. by Jeffrey R. Babbin, David B. Isbell, Martin E. Karlinsky, and Steven M. Freeman.

Brief of amici curiae filed on behalf of the National School Boards Association et al. by Julie K. Underwood.

Brief of amici curiae filed on behalf of the New York State School Boards Association, Inc., by Jay Worona, Pilar Sokol, and John A. Miller.

Opposing Side (Petitioner / Appellant)

Brief of amici curiae filed on behalf of the State of Alabama et al. by Bill Pryor, Attorney General of Alabama, Margaret L. Fleming, John J. Park, Jr., and Charles B. Campbell, Assistant Attorneys General, and by the Attorneys General for their respective States as follows: Thomas J. Miller of Iowa, Richard P. Ieyoub of Louisiana, Mike Moore of Mississippi, Don Stenberg of Nebraska, Betty D. Montgomery of Ohio, Charles M. Condon of South Carolina, Paul G. Summers of Tennessee,

John Cornyn of Texas, Jan Graham of Utah, and Mark L. Earley of Virginia.

Brief of amici curiae filed on behalf of the American Center for Law & Justice et al. by Jay Alan Sekulow, Colby M. May, James M. Henderson, Sr., Walter M. Weber, Paul D. Clement, and Jeffrey S. Bucholtz.

Brief of amici curiae filed on behalf of Child Evangelism Fellowship, Inc., et al. by Herbert G. Grey, Darren C. Walker, Gregory S. Baylor, andKimberlee Wood Colby.

Brief of amici curiae filed on behalf of the Christian Legal Society et al. by Carl H. Esbeck and Nathan J. Diament.

Brief of amici curiae filed on behalf of the Liberty Legal Institute by Viet D. Dinh, John L. Carter, and Kelly Shackelford.

Brief of amici curiae filed on behalf of the National Council of Churches et al. by Carter G. Phillips, Gene C. Schaerr, and Nicholas P. Miller.

Brief of amici curiae filed on behalf of the National Jewish Commission on Law and Public Affairs by Nathan Lewin, Dennis Rapps, and David Zwiebel.

Brief of amici curiae filed on behalf of the Northstar Legal Center et al. by Jordan W. Lorence and Joseph Infranco.

Brief of amici curiae filed on behalf of the Solidarity Center for Law and Justice, P. C., by James P. Kelly III.

Brief of amici curiae filed on behalf of Wallbuilders, Inc., by Barry C. Hodge.

Brief of amici curiae filed on behalf of Sally Campbell by Brett M. Kavanaugh and Stuart J. Roth.

Brief of amici curiae filed on behalf of Carol Hood by Kevin J. Hasson, Eric W. Treene, Roman P. Storzer, and Anthony R. Picarello, Jr.

Brief of amici curiae filed on behalf of Douglas Laycock by Mr. Laycock, pro se.

Brief of amici curiae filed on behalf of 20 Theologians and Scholars of Religion by Michael W. McConnell and Steffen N. Johnson.

IV. THE SUPREME COURT'S DECISION

"When the State establishes a limited public forum, the State is not required to and does not allow persons to engage in every type of speech. The State may be justified 'in reserving [its forum] for certain groups or for the discussion of certain topics.' The State's power to restrict speech, however, is not without limits. The restriction must not discriminate against speech on the basis of viewpoint, and the restriction must be 'reasonable in light of the purpose served by the forum.' . . .

Applying this test, we first address whether the exclusion constituted viewpoint discrimination. We are guided in our analysis by two of our prior opinions, Lamb's Chapel and Rosenberger. . . . Concluding that Milford's exclusion of the Good News Club based on its religious nature is indistinguishable from the exclusions in these cases, we hold that the exclusion constitutes viewpoint discrimination. Because the restriction is viewpoint discriminatory, we need not decide whether it is unreasonable in light of the purposes served by the forum.

Milford has opened its limited public forum to activities that serve a variety of purposes, including events 'pertaining to the welfare of the community.' Milford interprets its policy to permit discussions of subjects such as child rearing, and of 'the development of character and morals from a religious perspective.' . . .

Just as there is no question that teaching morals and character development to children is a permissible purpose under Milford's policy, it is clear that the Club teaches morals and character development to children. . . .

Like the church in Lamb's Chapel, the Club seeks to address a subject otherwise permitted under the rule, the teaching of morals and character, from a religious standpoint. . . . Thus, the exclusion of the Good News Club's activities, like the exclusion of Lamb's Chapel's films, constitutes unconstitutional viewpoint discrimination.

Our opinion in Rosenberger also is dispositive. . . .

Despite our holdings in Lamb's Chapel and Rosenberger, the Court of Appeals, like Milford, believed that its characterization of the Club's activities as religious in nature warranted treating the Club's activities as different in kind from the other activities permitted by the school. . . .

We disagree that something that is 'quintessentially religious' or 'decidedly religious in nature' cannot also be characterized properly as the teaching of morals and character development from a particular viewpoint. . . . What matters for purposes of the Free Speech Clause is that we can see no logical difference in kind between the invocation of Christianity by the Club and the invocation of teamwork, loyalty, or patriotism by other associations to provide a foundation for their lessons. It is apparent that the unstated principle of the Court of Appeals' reasoning is its conclusion that any time religious instruction and prayer are used to discuss morals and character, the discussion is simply not a 'pure' discussion of those issues. According to the Court of Appeals, reliance on Christian principles taints moral and character instruction in a way that other foundations for thought or viewpoints do not. We, however, have never reached such a conclusion. Instead, we reaffirm our holdings in Lamb's Chapel and Rosenberger that speech discussing otherwise permissible subjects cannot be excluded from a limited public forum on the ground that the subject is discussed from a religious viewpoint. Thus, we conclude that Milford's exclusion of the Club from use of the school, pursuant to its community use policy, constitutes impermissible viewpoint discrimination.

[A]ccording to Milford, its restriction was required to avoid violating the Establishment Clause. We disagree. . . .

First, we have held that 'a significant factor in upholding governmental programs in the face of Establishment Clause attack is their neutrality towards religion.' . . . Because allowing the Club to speak on school grounds would ensure neutrality, not threaten it, Milford faces an uphill battle . . . .

Second, to the extent we consider whether the community would feel coercive pressure to engage in the Club's activities, the relevant community would be the parents, not the elementary school children. . . . Milford does not suggest that the parents of elementary school children would be confused about whether the school was endorsing religion. . . .

Third, whatever significance we may have assigned in the Establishment Clause context to the suggestion that elementary school children are more impressionable than adults, . . . we have never extended our Establishment Clause jurisprudence to foreclose private religious conduct during nonschool hours merely because it takes place on school premises . . . .

Fourth, even if we were to consider the possible misperceptions by schoolchildren in deciding whether Milford's permitting the Club's activities would violate the Establishment Clause, the facts of this case simply do not support Milford's conclusion. . . .

Finally, even if we were to inquire into the minds of schoolchildren in this case, we cannot say the danger that children would misperceive the endorsement of religion is any greater than the danger that they would perceive a hostility toward the religious viewpoint if the Club were excluded from the public forum. . . .

We cannot operate, as Milford would have us do, under the assumption that any risk that small children would perceive endorsement should counsel in favor of excluding the Club's religious activity. . . . There are countervailing constitutional concerns related to rights of other individuals in the community. In this case, those countervailing concerns are the free speech rights of the Club and its members. . . . And, we have already found that those rights have been violated, not merely perceived to have been violated, by the school's actions toward the Club.

We are not convinced that there is any significance in this case to the possibility that elementary school children may witness the Good News Club's activities on school premises, and therefore we can find no reason to depart from our holdings in Lamb's Chapel and Widmar. Accordingly, we conclude that permitting the Club to meet on the school's premises would not have violated the Establishment Clause. . . .

When Milford denied the Good News Club access to the school's limited public forum on the ground that the Club was religious in nature, it discriminated against the Club because of its religious viewpoint in violation of the Free Speech Clause of the First Amendment. Because Milford has not raised a valid Establishment Clause claim, we do not address the question whether such a claim could excuse Milford's viewpoint discrimination. . . .

The judgment of the Court of Appeals is reversed, and the case is remanded for further proceedings consistent with this opinion."

V. JUSTICE VOTE

3 Pro ACLU Side vs. 6 Con Opposing Side

ACLU Side (Respondent / Appellee)

1. Stevens, J. – Wrote dissenting opinion
2. Souter, D. – Wrote dissenting opinion
3. Ginsburg, R. – Joined Souter's dissent

Opposing Side (Petitioner / Appellant)

1. Thomas, C. – Wrote majority opinion
2. O'Connor, S. – Joined majority opinion
3. Kennedy, A. – Joined majority opinion
4. Rehnquist, W. – Joined majority opinion
5. Scalia, A. – Wrote concurring opinion
6. Breyer, S. – Wrote concurring opinion

VI. A WIN OR LOSS FOR THE ACLU?

The ACLU filed as amicus curiae urging affirmance of the judgment of the Court of Appeals; the Supreme Court reversed the Court of Appeals' decision by a 6-3 vote, giving the ACLU an apparent loss.

908. Saucier v. Katz

(Decided June 18, 2001; 533 U.S. 194)

I. ISSUE

A. Issues Discussed

4th Amendment, military

B. Legal Question Presented

"[W]hether the requisite analysis to determine qualified immunity is so intertwined with the question whether the officer used excessive force in making the arrest that qualified immunity and constitutional violation issues should be treated as one question, to be decided by the trier of fact."

C. Supreme Court's Answer

"[T]he ruling on qualified immunity requires an analysis not susceptible of fusion with the question whether unreasonable force was used in making the arrest."

II. CASE SUMMARY

A. Background

"In autumn of 1994, the Presidio Army Base in San Francisco was the site of an event to celebrate conversion of the base to a national park. . . . Respondent Elliot Katz was concerned that the Army's Letterman Hospital would be used for conducting experiments on animals. . . . To voice opposition to the possibility that the hospital might be used for experiments, respondent brought with him a cloth banner, approximately 4 by 3 feet, that read 'Please Keep Animal Torture Out of Our National Parks.' . . .

Respondent sat in the front row of the public seating area. At about the time Vice President Gore began speaking, respondent removed the banner from his jacket, started to unfold it, and walked toward the fence and speakers' platform.

Petitioner Donald Saucier is a military police officer who was on duty that day. He had been warned by his superiors of the possibility of demonstrations, and respondent had been identified as a potential protester. Petitioner and Sergeant Steven Parker . . . recognized respondent and moved to intercept him as he walked toward the fence. As he reached the barrier and began placing the banner on the other side, the officers grabbed respondent from behind, took the banner, and rushed him out of the area. Each officer had one of respondent's arms, half-walking, half-dragging him, with his feet 'barely touching the ground.' Respondent was wearing a visible, knee-high leg brace, although petitioner later testified he did not remember noticing it at the time. Saucier and Parker took respondent to a nearby military van, where, respondent claims, he was shoved or thrown inside. The reason for the shove remains unclear. It seems agreed that respondent placed his feet somewhere on the outside of the van, perhaps the bumper, but there is a dispute whether he did so to resist. As a result of the shove, respondent claims, he fell to the floor of the van, where he caught himself just in time to avoid any injury. The officers drove respondent to a military police station, held him for a brief time, and then released him. . . .

Respondent brought this action in the United States District Court for the Northern District of California against petitioner and other officials pursuant to Bivens v. Six Unknown Fed. Narcotics Agents, alleging, inter alia, that defendants had violated respondent's Fourth Amendment rights by using excessive force to arrest him. The District Court granted the defendants' motions for summary judgment on the grounds of qualified immunity on all claims other than the excessive force claim against Saucier. . . .

In the United States Court of Appeals for the Ninth Circuit petitioner filed an interlocutory appeal from the denial of qualified immunity. The Court of Appeals affirmed, noting at the outset its two-part analysis for qualified immunity questions. . . .

Saucier, represented by the Government of the United States, sought review here. [The Supreme Court] granted certiorari."

B. Counsel of Record

ACLU Side (Respondent / Appellee): J. Kirk Boyd argued the cause for appellee. With him on the brief was David H. Williams.

Opposing Side (Petitioner / Appellant): Deputy Solicitor General Clement argued the cause for appellant. With him on the briefs were former Solicitor General Waxman, Acting Solicitor General Underwood, Assistant Attorney General Ogden, Jeffrey A. Lamken, Barbara L. Herwig, and Edward Himmelfarb.

III. AMICI CURIAE

ACLU Side (Respondent / Appellee)

Brief of amici curiae filed on behalf of the American Civil Liberties Union the ACLU of Northern California, the National Lawyers Guild, the Center for Constitutional Rights, and Lambda Legal Defense and Education Fund by David Rudovsky, Michael Avery, Ruth E. Harlow, Steven R. Shapiro, William Goodman, and Alan L. Schlosser

Brief of amici curiae filed on behalf of the Association of the Bar of the City of New York by Leon Friedman and Ronald J. Tabak.

Opposing Side (Petitioner / Appellant)

Brief of amici curiae filed on behalf of the State of Texas et al. by John Cornyn, Attorney General of Texas, Andy Taylor, First Assistant Attorney General, Gregory S. Coleman, Solicitor General, and Lisa R. Eskow, Assistant Solicitor General, joined by the Attorneys General for their respective States as follows: Bill Pryor of Alabama, Bruce M. Botelho of Alaska, Mark Pryor of Arkansas, Bill Lockyer of California, Ken Salazar of Colorado, Richard Blumenthal of Connecticut, M. Jane Brady of Delaware, James E. Ryan of Illinois, Richard P. Ieyoub of Louisiana, J. Joseph Curran, Jr., of Maryland, Thomas F. Reilly of Massachusetts, Mike Moore of Mississippi, Joseph P. Mazurek of Montana, Don Stenberg of Nebraska, Eliot Spitzer of New York, Heidi Heitkamp of North Dakota, Betty D. Montgomery of Ohio, W. A. Drew Edmondson of Oklahoma, Hardy Myers of Oregon, D. Michael Fisher of Pennsylvania, Charles M. Condon of South Carolina, Mark Barnett of South Dakota, Paul G. Summers of Tennessee, Jan Graham of Utah, William H. Sorrell of Vermont, and Christine O. Gregoire of Washington.

Brief of amici curiae filed on behalf of the Grand Lodge of the Fraternal Order of Police by Tom Rutherford.

Brief of amici curiae filed on behalf of the National Association of Police Organizations et al. by Stephen R. McSpadden.

IV. THE SUPREME COURT'S DECISION

"The Court of Appeals ruled first that the right was clearly established; and second that the reasonableness inquiry into excessive force meant that it need not consider aspects of qualified immunity, leaving the whole matter to the jury. This approach cannot be reconciled with Anderson v. Creighton, however, and was in error in two respects. As we shall explain, the first inquiry must be whether a constitutional right would have been violated on the facts alleged; second, assuming the violation is established, the question whether the right was clearly established must be considered on a more specific level than recognized by the Court of Appeals.

In a suit against an officer for an alleged violation of a constitutional right, the requisites of a qualified immunity defense must be considered in proper sequence. Where the defendant seeks qualified immunity, a ruling on that issue should be made early in the proceedings so that the costs and expenses of trial are avoided where the defense is dispositive. Qualified immunity is 'an entitlement not to stand trial or face the other burdens of litigation.' The privilege is 'an immunity from suit rather than a mere defense to liability; and like an absolute immunity, it is effectively lost if a case is erroneously permitted to go to trial.' As a result, 'we repeatedly have stressed the importance of resolving immunity questions at the earliest possible stage in litigation.'

A court required to rule upon the qualified immunity issue must consider, then, this threshold question: Taken in the light most favorable to the party asserting the injury, do the facts alleged show the officer's conduct violated a constitutional right? This must be the initial inquiry. . . .

The case was presented to the Court of Appeals on the assumption that respondent's seizure and brief detention did not violate clearly established First Amendment privileges and did not violate the Fourth Amendment right to be free from arrest without probable cause, as distinct from the force used to detain. The sole question, then, is whether the force used violated a clearly established Fourth Amendment protection so that petitioner was not entitled to immunity.

Our instruction to the district courts and courts of appeals to concentrate at the outset on the definition of the constitutional right and to determine whether, on the facts alleged, a constitutional violation could be found is important. As we have said, the procedure permits courts in appropriate cases to elaborate the constitutional right with greater degrees of specificity. Because we granted certiorari only to determine whether qualified immunity was appropriate, however, and because of the limits imposed upon us by the questions on which we granted review, we will assume a constitutional violation could have occurred under the facts alleged based simply on the general rule prohibiting excessive force, then proceed to the question whether this general prohibition against excessive force was the source for clearly established law that was contravened in the circumstances this officer faced. There was no contravention under this standard. Though it is doubtful that the force used was excessive, we need not rest our conclusion on that determination. The question is what the officer reasonably understood his powers and responsibilities to be, when he acted, under clearly established standards.

Respondent's excessive force claim for the most part depends upon the 'gratuitously violent shove' allegedly received when he was placed into the van, although respondent notes as well that the alleged violation resulted from the 'totality of the circumstances,' including the way he was removed from the speaking area.

These circumstances, however, disclose substantial grounds for the officer to have concluded he had legitimate justification under the law for acting as he did. In Graham we noted that '[o]ur Fourth Amendment jurisprudence has long recognized that the right to make an arrest or investigatory stop necessarily carries with it the right to use some degree of physical coercion or threat thereof to effect it.' A reasonable officer in petitioner's position could have believed that hurrying respondent away from the scene, where the Vice President was speaking and respondent had just approached the fence designed to separate the public from the speakers, was within the bounds of appropriate police responses. . . .

As for the shove respondent received when he was placed into the van, those same circumstances show some degree of urgency. We have approved the observation that '[n]ot every push or shove, even if it may later seem unnecessary in the peace of a judge's chambers, violates the Fourth Amendment.' Pushes and shoves, like other police conduct, must be judged under the Fourth Amendment standard of reasonableness.

In the circumstances presented to this officer, which included the duty to protect the safety and security of the Vice President of the United States from persons unknown in number, neither respondent nor the Court of Appeals has identified any case demonstrating a clearly established rule prohibiting the officer from acting as he did, nor are we aware of any such rule. Our conclusion is confirmed by the uncontested fact that the force was not so excessive that respondent suffered hurt or injury. On these premises, petitioner was entitled to qualified immunity, and the suit should have been dismissed at an early stage in the proceedings.

The judgment of the Court of Appeals is reversed, and the case is remanded for further proceedings consistent with this opinion."

V. JUSTICE VOTE

0 Pro ACLU Side vs. 9 Con Opposing Side

Opposing Side (Petitioner / Appellant)

1. Kennedy, A. – Wrote majority opinion
2. Thomas, C. – Joined majority opinion
3. Ginsburg, R. – Wrote concurring opinion
4. Souter, D. – Wrote opinion concurring in part and dissenting in part
5. O'Connor, S. – Joined majority opinion
6. Stevens, J. – Joined Ginsburg's concurrence
7. Breyer, S. – Joined Ginsburg's concurrence
8. Scalia, A. – Joined majority opinion
9. Rehnquist, W. – Joined majority opinion

VI. A WIN OR LOSS FOR THE ACLU?

The ACLU filed as amicus curiae urging affirmance of the judgment of the Court of Appeals; the Supreme Court reversed by a 9-0 vote, giving the ACLU an apparent loss.

909. INS v. St. Cyr

(Decided June 25, 2001; 533 U.S. 289)

I. ISSUE

A. Issues Discussed

Immigration/citizenship

B. Legal Question Presented

"Both the Antiterrorism and Effective Death Penalty Act of 1996 (AEDPA) . . . and the Illegal Immigration Reform and Immigrant Responsibility Act of 1996 (IIRIRA) . . . contain comprehensive amendments to the Immigration and Nationality Act (INA) . . . . This case raises two important questions about the impact of those amendments. The first question is a procedural one, concerning the effect of those amendments on the availability of habeas corpus jurisdiction under 28 U.S.C. § 2241. The second question is a substantive one, concerning the impact of the amendments on conduct that occurred before their enactment and on the availability of discretionary relief from deportation."

C. Supreme Court's Answer

"[W]e conclude that habeas jurisdiction under § 2241 was not repealed by AEDPA and IIRIRA. . . .

We . . . hold that § 212(c) relief remains available for aliens, like respondent, whose convictions were obtained through plea agreements and who, notwithstanding those convictions, would have been eligible for § 212(c) relief at the time of their plea under the law then in effect."

II. CASE SUMMARY

A. Background

"Respondent, Enrico St. Cyr, is a citizen of Haiti who was admitted to the United States as a lawful permanent resident in 1986. Ten years later, on March 8, 1996, he pleaded guilty in a state court to a charge of selling a controlled substance in violation of Connecticut law. That conviction made him deportable. Under pre-AEDPA law applicable at the time of his conviction, St. Cyr would have been eligible for a waiver of deportation at the discretion of the Attorney General. However, removal proceedings against him were not commenced until April 10, 1997, after both AEDPA and IIRIRA became effective, and, as the Attorney General interprets those statutes, he no longer has discretion to grant such a waiver.

In his habeas corpus petition, respondent has alleged that the restrictions on discretionary relief from deportation contained in the 1996 statutes do not apply to removal proceedings brought against an alien who pleaded guilty to a deportable crime before their enactment. The District Court accepted jurisdiction of his application and agreed with his submission. In accord with the decisions of four other Circuits, the Court of Appeals for the Second Circuit affirmed."

The Supreme Court granted certiorari to review the case.

B. Counsel of Record

ACLU Side (Respondent / Appellee): Lucas Guttentag of the ACLU Foundation argued the cause for appellee. With him on the brief were Lee Gelernt, Ahilan Arulanantham, Judy Rabinovitz, Steven R. Shapiro, Jayashri Srikantiah, and Liliana M. Garces of the ACLU Foundation, Michael G. Moore, Paul A. Engelmayer, and Christopher J. Meade.

Opposing Side (Petitioner / Appellant): Deputy Solicitor General Kneedler argued the cause for appellant. With him on the briefs were Acting Solicitor General Underwood, Acting Assistant Attorney General Schiffer, Paul R. Q. Wolfson, Stephen C. Robinson, Donald E. Keener, Alison R. Drucker, Ernesto H. Molina, and James K. Filan, Jr

III. AMICI CURIAE

ACLU Side (Respondent / Appellee)

Brief of amici curiae filed on behalf of the Florida Immigrant Advocacy Center et al. by Rebecca Sharpless.

Brief of amici curiae filed on behalf of the National Association of Criminal Defense Lawyers et al. by Manuel D. Vargas and Joshua L. Dratel.

Brief of amici curiae filed on behalf of Legal Historians by James Oldham, Michael J. Wishnie, and Douglas W. Baruch.

Opposing Side (Petitioner / Appellant)

Brief of amici curiae filed on behalf of the Washington Legal Foundation by Daniel J. Popeo and R. Shawn Gunnarson.

IV. THE SUPREME COURT'S DECISION

"Three statutes enacted in recent years have reduced the size of the class of aliens eligible for . . . discretionary relief. In 1990, Congress amended § 212(c) to preclude from discretionary relief anyone convicted of an aggravated felony who had served a term of imprisonment of at least five years. In 1996, in § 440(d) of AEDPA, Congress identified a broad set of offenses for which convictions would preclude such relief. And finally, that same year, Congress passed IIRIRA. That statute . . . repealed § 212(c) . . . and replaced it with a new section that gives the Attorney General the authority to cancel removal for a narrow class of inadmissible or deportable aliens . . . . So narrowed, that class does not include anyone previously 'convicted of any aggravated felony.'

In the Attorney General's opinion, these amendments have entirely withdrawn his § 212(c) authority to waive deportation for aliens previously convicted of aggravated felonies. Moreover, as a result of other amendments adopted in AEDPA and IIRIRA, the Attorney General also maintains that there is no judicial forum available to decide whether these statutes did, in fact, deprive him of the power to grant such relief. [W]e disagree on both points. In our view, a federal court does have jurisdiction to decide the merits of the legal question, and the District Court and the Court of Appeals decided that question correctly in this case. . . .

The first question we must consider is whether the District Court retains jurisdiction under the general habeas corpus statute, 28 U.S.C. § 2241, to entertain St. Cyr's challenge. . . .

The District Court held, and the Court of Appeals agreed, that it had jurisdiction to answer that question in a habeas corpus proceeding. The INS argues, however, that four sections of the 1996 statutes . . . stripped the courts of jurisdiction to decide the question of law presented by respondent's habeas corpus application.

For the INS to prevail it must overcome both the strong presumption in favor of judicial review of administrative action and the longstanding rule requiring a clear statement of congressional intent to repeal habeas jurisdiction. . . . Implications from statutory text or legislative history are not sufficient to repeal habeas jurisdiction; instead, Congress must articulate specific and unambiguous statutory directives to effect a repeal. . . .

If it were clear that the question of law could be answered in another judicial forum, it might be permissible to accept the INS' reading of § 1252. But the absence of such a forum, coupled with the lack of a clear, unambiguous, and express statement of congressional intent to preclude judicial consideration on habeas of such an important question of law, strongly counsels against adopting a construction that would raise serious constitutional questions. Accordingly, we conclude that habeas jurisdiction under § 2241 was not repealed by AEDPA and IIRIRA. . . .

The absence of a clearly expressed statement of congressional intent also pervades our review of the merits of St. Cyr's claim. Two important legal consequences ensued from respondent's entry of a guilty plea in March 1996: (1) He became subject to deportation, and (2) he became eligible for a discretionary waiver of that deportation under the prevailing interpretation of § 212(c). When IIRIRA went into effect in April 1997, the first consequence was unchanged except for the fact that the term 'removal' was substituted for 'deportation.' The issue that remains to be resolved is whether IIRIRA § 304(b) changed the second consequence by eliminating respondent's eligibility for a waiver. . . .

'The inquiry into whether a statute operates retroactively demands a commonsense, functional judgment about 'whether the new provision attaches new legal consequences to events completed before its enactment." A statute has retroactive effect when it "takes away or impairs vested rights acquired under existing laws, or creates a new obligation, imposes a new duty, or attaches a new disability, in respect to transactions or considerations already past . . . ." As we have repeatedly counseled, the judgment whether a particular statute acts retroactively 'should be informed and guided by 'familiar considerations of fair notice, reasonable reliance, and settled expectations." . . .

We find nothing in IIRIRA unmistakably indicating that Congress considered the question whether to apply its repeal of § 212(c) retroactively to such aliens. We therefore hold that

§ 212(c) relief remains available for aliens, like respondent, whose convictions were obtained through plea agreements and who, notwithstanding those convictions, would have been eligible for § 212(c) relief at the time of their plea under the law then in effect.
The judgment is affirmed."

V. JUSTICE VOTE

5 Pro ACLU Side vs. 4 Con Opposing Side

ACLU Side (Respondent / Appellee)

1. Stevens, J. – Wrote majority opinion
2. Kennedy, A. – Joined majority opinion
3. Souter, D. – Joined majority opinion
4. Ginsburg, R. – Joined majority opinion
5. Breyer, S. – Joined majority opinion

Opposing Side (Petitioner / Appellant)

1. O'Connor – Wrote dissenting opinion, joined Scalia's dissent in part
2. Scalia, A. – Wrote dissenting opinion
3. Thomas, C. – Joined Scalia's dissent
4. Rehnquist, W. – Joined Scalia's dissent

VI. A WIN OR LOSS FOR THE ACLU?

The ACLU argued the case for appellee, urging affirmance; the Supreme Court affirmed the Court of Appeals' decision by a 5-4 vote, giving the ACLU an apparent win.

910. Calcano-Martinez v. INS

(Decided June 25, 2001; 533 U.S. 348)

I. ISSUE

A. Issues Discussed

Immigration/citizenship

B. Legal Question Presented

Whether a lawful permanent resident subject to final orders of removal may seek relief through direct review at the Court of Appeals, petition for habeas corpus at the district court, or not at all.

C. Supreme Court's Answer

"[W]e agree with the Court of Appeals that it lacks jurisdiction to hear the petitions for direct review at issue in this case and that petitioners must, therefore, proceed with their petitions for habeas corpus if they wish to obtain relief."

II. CASE SUMMARY

A. Background

"Deboris Calcano-Martinez, Sergio Madrid, and Fazila Khan are all lawful permanent residents of the United States subject to administratively final orders of removal. They conceded that they are deportable based upon their past criminal convictions, but each filed both a petition for review in the Second Circuit pursuant to 8 U.S.C. § 1252(a)(1) and a habeas corpus petition in the District Court pursuant to 28 U.S.C. § 2241 in order to challenge the Board of Immigration Appeals' determination that, as a matter of law, petitioners were ineligible to apply for a discretionary waiver of deportation under former § 212(c) of the Immigration and Nationality Act. Their petitions for review were consolidated in the Court of Appeals, which subsequently dismissed the petitions for lack of jurisdiction, holding that petitioners could nevertheless pursue their constitutional and statutory claims in a district court habeas action brought pursuant to 28 U.S.C. § 2241. [The Supreme Court] granted certiorari in this case and in INS v. St. Cyr, 531 U.S. 1107 (2001), in order to comprehensively consider whether aliens in the petitioners' position may seek relief in the Court of Appeals (pursuant to 8 U.S.C. § 1252(a)(1)); in the district court (pursuant to 28 U.S.C. § 2241); or not at all."

B. Counsel of Record

ACLU Side (Petitioner / Appellant): Lucas Guttentag of the ACLU Foundation argued the cause for appellants. With him on the briefs were Lee Gelernt, Steven R. Shapiro, Jayashri Srikantiah, and Liliana M. Garces of the ACLU Foundation, Kerry W. Bretz, Jules E. Coven, Alan Michael Strauss, Paul A. Engelmayer, and Christopher J. Meade.

Opposing Side (Respondent / Appellee): Deputy Solicitor General Kneedler argued the cause for appellee. With him on the brief were Acting Solicitor General Underwood, Acting Assistant Attorney General Schiffer, Paul R. Q. Wolfson, Donald E. Keener, William J. Howard, Ernesto H. Molina, and James A. O'Brien III.

III. AMICI CURIAE

ACLU Side (Petitioner / Appellant)

Brief of amici curiae filed on behalf of the American Bar Association by Martha W. Barnett, Jeffrey L. Bleich, Gerald Neuman, and Kelly M. Klaus.

Opposing Side (Respondent / Appellee)

No briefs of amici curiae were filed in support of appellee.

IV. THE SUPREME COURT'S DECISION

"For the reasons stated below and in our opinion in INS v. St. Cyr, 533 U.S. 289, we agree with the Court of Appeals that it lacks jurisdiction to hear the petitions for direct review at issue in this case and that petitioners must, therefore, proceed with their petitions for habeas corpus if they wish to obtain relief.

As part of the Illegal Immigration Reform and Immigrant Responsibility Act of 1996 (IIRIRA), Congress adopted new provisions governing the judicial review of immigration orders. . . . Like the prior statute, the new provision vests the courts of appeals with the authority to consider petitions challenging 'final orders' commanding the 'removal' of aliens from the United States. § 1252(a)(1). However, unlike the previous provisions, the new statute expressly precludes the courts of appeals from exercising 'jurisdiction to review any final order of removal against any alien who is removable by reason of' a conviction for certain criminal offenses, including any aggravated felony.

As petitioners in this case were convicted of 'aggravated felonies' within the meaning of the relevant statutes, the plain language of § 1252(a)(2)(C) fairly explicitly strips the courts of appeals of jurisdiction to hear their claims on petitions for direct review. Without much discussion, the Court of Appeals so held.

Before this Court, petitioners primarily argue that constitutional considerations and background principles of statutory interpretation require that they be afforded some forum for the adjudication of the merits of their claims. They devote the bulk of their briefs to arguing that the Court of Appeals—motivated by these concerns—properly interpreted IIRIRA's jurisdiction-stripping provision not to preclude aliens such as petitioners from pursuing habeas relief pursuant to 28 U.S.C. § 2241. In the alternative, they argue that we might construe the same provisions as stripping jurisdiction from the courts of appeals over only some matters, leaving in place their jurisdiction to directly review petitions raising claims previously cognizable under § 2241.

We agree with petitioners that leaving aliens without a forum for adjudicating claims such as those raised in this case would raise serious constitutional questions. We also agree with petitioners—and the Court of Appeals—that these concerns can best be alleviated by construing the jurisdiction-stripping provisions of that statute not to preclude aliens such as petitioners from pursuing habeas relief pursuant to § 2241.

Finding no support in the text or history of § 1252 for concluding that the courts of appeals retain jurisdiction to hear petitions such as those brought in this case, but concluding that Congress has not spoken with sufficient clarity to strip the district courts of jurisdiction to hear habeas petitions raising identical claims, we affirm the judgment of the Court of Appeals in all particulars."

V. JUSTICE VOTE

5 Pro ACLU Side vs. 4 Con Opposing Side

ACLU Side (Petitioner / Appellant)

1. Stevens, J. – Wrote majority opinion
2. Souter, D. – Joined majority opinion
3. Ginsburg, R. – Joined majority opinion
4. Breyer, S. – Joined majority opinion
5. Kennedy, A. – Joined majority opinion

Opposing Side (Respondent / Appellee)

1. O'Connor, S. – Wrote dissenting opinion
2. Scalia, A. – Wrote dissenting opinion
3. Rehnquist, W. – Joined Scalia's dissent
4. Thomas, C. – Joined Scalia's dissent

VI. A WIN OR LOSS FOR THE ACLU?

The ACLU argued the cause for appellant urging the Supreme Court to allow their clients to seek relief at the Court of Appeals or district court; the Supreme Court decided to allow them to seek relief at the district court in a 5-4 vote, giving the ACLU an apparent win.

911. FEC v. Colo. Republican Fed. Campaign Comm.

(Decided June 25, 2001; 533 U.S. 431)

I. ISSUE

A. Issues Discussed

1st Amendment, press, speech, association

B. Legal Question Presented

"The issue in this case is . . . whether a party is . . . in a different position from other political speakers, giving it a claim to demand a generally higher standard of scrutiny before its coordinated spending can be limited."

C. Supreme Court's Answer

"We hold that a party's coordinated expenditures, unlike expenditures truly independent, may be restricted to minimize circumvention of contribution limits. We therefore reject the Party's facial challenge . . . ."

II. CASE SUMMARY

A. Background

"In [Colorado I, the Supreme Court] held that spending limits set by the Federal Election Campaign Act were unconstitutional as applied to the Colorado Republican Party's independent expenditures in connection with a senatorial campaign. We remanded for consideration of the party's claim that all limits on expenditures by a political party in connection with congressional campaigns are facially unconstitutional and thus unenforceable even as to spending coordinated with a candidate. . . .

The Federal Election Commission (FEC or Commission) originally took the position that any expenditure by a political party in connection with a particular election for federal office was presumed to be coordinated with the party's candidate. The Commission thus operated on the assumption that all expenditure limits imposed on political parties were, in essence, contribution limits and therefore constitutional. . . .

Colorado I was an as-applied challenge to § 441a(d)(3) (which we spoke of as the Party Expenditure Provision), occasioned by the Commission's enforcement action against the Colorado Republican Federal Campaign Committee (Party) for exceeding the campaign spending limit through its payments for radio advertisements attacking Democratic Congressman and senatorial candidate Timothy Wirth. [T]he principal opinion in Colorado I agreed that the limitations were unconstitutional as applied to the advertising expenditures at issue. [T]he Members of the Court who joined the principal opinion thought the payments were 'independent expenditures'. . . owing to the facts that the Party spent the money before selecting its own senatorial candidate and without any arrangement with potential nominees.

The Party's broader claim remained: that although prior decisions of this Court had upheld the constitutionality of limits on coordinated expenditures by political speakers other than parties, the congressional campaign expenditure limitations on parties themselves are facially unconstitutional, and so are incapable of reaching party spending even when coordinated with a candidate. We remanded that facial challenge, which had not been fully briefed or considered below. On remand the District Court held for the Party, and a divided panel of the Court of Appeals for the Tenth Circuit affirmed. [The Supreme Court] granted certiorari to resolve the question left open by Colorado I, and we now reverse."

B. Counsel of Record

ACLU Side (Respondent / Appellee): Jan Witold Baran argued the cause for appellee. With him on the brief were Thomas W. Kirby and Carol A. Laham.

Opposing Side (Petitioner / Appellant): Acting Solicitor General Underwood argued the cause for appellant. With her on the briefs were former Solicitor General Waxman, Malcolm L. Stewart, Lawrence M. Noble, Richard B. Bader, and David Kolker.

III. AMICI CURIAE

ACLU Side (Respondent / Appellee)

Brief of amici curiae filed on behalf of the American Civil Liberties Union and the ACLU of Colorado by Mark J. Lopez, Steven R. Shapiro, and Joel M. Gora.

Brief of amici curiae filed on behalf of the California Republican Party by Charles H. Bell, Jr.

Brief of amici curiae filed on behalf of the Missouri Republican Party by D. Bruce La Pierre and W. Bevis Schock.

Brief of amici curiae filed on behalf of the National Republican Congressional Committee by Benjamin L. Ginsberg.

Opposing Side (Petitioner / Appellant)

Brief of amici curiae filed on behalf of the State of Missouri et al. by Jeremiah W. (Jay) Nixon, Attorney General of Missouri, and James R. Layton, State Solicitor, joined by the Attorneys General for their respective States as follows: Ken Salazar of Colorado, Earl I. Anzai of Hawaii, Joseph P. Mazurek of Montana, Eliot Spitzer of New York, W. A. Drew Edmondson of Oklahoma, and William H. Sorrell of Vermont.

Brief of amici curiae filed on behalf of Common Cause et al. by Roger M. Witten, Daniel H. Squire, Donald J. Simon, and Fred Wertheimer.

Brief of amici curiae filed on behalf of the National Voting Rights Institute by David A. Wilson, John C. Bonifaz, Brenda Wright, and Gregory G. Luke.Senator John F. Reed et al. by Donald B. Verrilli, Jr., and Deanne E. Maynard.

Brief of amici curiae filed on behalf of Paul Allen Beck et al. by Burt Neuborne.

IV. THE SUPREME COURT'S DECISION

"Spending for political ends and contributing to political candidates both fall within the First Amendment's protection of speech and political association. But ever since we first reviewed the 1971 Act, we have understood that limits on political expenditures deserve closer scrutiny than restrictions on political contributions. Restraints on expenditures generally curb more expressive and associational activity than limits on contributions do. . . .

Given these differences, we have routinely struck down limitations on independent expenditures by candidates, other individuals, and groups, . . . while repeatedly upholding contribution limits . . . .

Colorado I addressed the FEC's effort to stretch the functional treatment of coordinated expenditures further than the plain application of the statutory definition. . . . The principal opinion observed that '[t]he independent expression of a political party's views is 'core' First Amendment activity no less than is the independent expression of individuals, candidates, or other political committees.' Since the FEC did not advance any other convincing reason for refusing to draw the independent-coordinated line accepted since Buckley, that was the end of the case so far as it concerned independent spending.

But that still left the question whether the First Amendment allows coordinated election expenditures by parties to be treated functionally as contributions, the way coordinated expenditures by other entities are treated. . . . The issue in this case is, accordingly, whether a party is otherwise in a different position from other political speakers, giving it a claim to demand a generally higher standard of scrutiny before its coordinated spending can be limited. The issue is posed by two questions: does limiting coordinated spending impose a unique burden on parties, and is there reason to think that coordinated spending by a party would raise the risk of corruption posed when others spend in coordination with a candidate? The issue is best viewed through the positions developed by the Party and the Government in this case. . . .

The Party's argument that its coordinated spending, like its independent spending, should be left free from restriction under the Buckley line of cases boils down to this: because a party's most important speech is aimed at electing candidates and is itself expressed through those candidates, any limit on party support for a candidate imposes a unique First Amendment burden. . . .

The Government argues that if coordinated spending were unlimited, circumvention would increase: because coordinated spending is as effective as direct contributions in supporting a candidate, an increased opportunity for coordinated spending would aggravate the use of a party to funnel money to a candidate from individuals and nonparty groups, who would thus bypass the contribution limits that Buckley upheld. . . .

Each of the competing positions is plausible at first blush. Our evaluation of the arguments, however, leads us to reject the Party's claim to suffer a burden unique in any way that should make a categorical difference under the First Amendment. On the other side, the Government's contentions are ultimately borne out by evidence, entitling it to prevail in its characterization of party coordinated spending as the functional equivalent of contributions. . . .

There are two basic arguments here. The first turns on the relationship of a party to a candidate: a coordinated relationship between them so defines a party that it cannot function as such without coordinated spending, the object of which is a candidate's election. We think political history and political reality belie this argument. The second argument turns on the nature of a party as uniquely able to spend in ways that promote candidate success. We think that this argument is a double-edged sword, and one hardly limited to political parties. . . .

We . . . apply to a party's coordinated spending limitation the same scrutiny we have applied to the other political actors, that is, scrutiny appropriate for a contribution limit, enquiring whether the restriction is 'closely drawn' to match what we have recognized as the 'sufficiently important' government interest in combating political corruption With the standard thus settled, the issue remains whether adequate evidentiary grounds exist to sustain the limit under that standard, on the theory that unlimited coordinated spending by a party raises the risk of corruption (and its appearance) through circumvention of valid contribution limits. Indeed, all Members of the Court agree that circumvention is a valid theory of corruption; the remaining bone of contention is evidentiary. . . .

Since there is no recent experience with unlimited coordinated spending, the question is whether experience under the present law confirms a serious threat of abuse from the unlimited coordinated party spending as the Government contends. . . . It clearly does. Despite years of enforcement of the challenged limits, substantial evidence demonstrates how candidates, donors, and parties test the limits of the current law, and it shows beyond serious doubt how contribution limits would be eroded if inducement to circumvent them were enhanced by declaring parties' coordinated spending wide open. . . .

There is no significant functional difference between a party's coordinated expenditure and a direct party contribution to the candidate, and there is good reason to expect that a party's right of unlimited coordinated spending would attract increased contributions to parties to finance exactly that kind of spending. Coordinated expenditures of money donated to a party are tailor-made to undermine contribution limits. Therefore the choice here is not, as in Buckley and Colorado I, between a limit on pure contributions and pure expenditures. The choice is between limiting contributions and limiting expenditures whose special value as expenditures is also the source of their power to corrupt. Congress is entitled to its choice. . . .

We hold that a party's coordinated expenditures, unlike expenditures truly independent, may be restricted to minimize circumvention of contribution limits. We therefore reject the Party's facial challenge and, accordingly, reverse the judgment of the United States Court of Appeals for the Tenth Circuit."

V. JUSTICE VOTE

4 Pro ACLU Side vs. 5 Con Opposing Side

ACLU Side (Respondent / Appellee)

1. Thomas, C. – Wrote dissenting opinion
2. Scalia, A. – Joined Thomas' dissent
3. Kennedy, A. – Joined Thomas' dissent
4. Rehnquist, W. – Joined Thomas' dissent, in part

Opposing Side (Petitioner / Appellant)

1. Souter, D. – Wrote majority opinion
2. Ginsburg, R. – Joined majority opinion
3. O'Connor, S. – Joined majority opinion
4. Stevens, J. – Joined majority opinion
5. Breyer, S. – Joined majority opinion

VI. A WIN OR LOSS FOR THE ACLU?

The ACLU filed as amicus curiae urging affirmance; the Supreme Court reversed the Court of Appeals' decision by a 5-4 vote, giving the ACLU an apparent loss.

912. Lorillard Tobacco Co. v. Reilly

(Decided June 28, 2001; 533 U.S. 525)

I. ISSUE

A. Issues Discussed

1st Amendment, press, speech, association

B. Legal Question Presented

"The first question presented . . . is whether certain cigarette advertising regulations are pre-empted by the Federal Cigarette Labeling and Advertising Act . . . . The second question presented is whether certain regulations governing the advertising and sale of tobacco products violate the First Amendment."

C. Supreme Court's Answer

"[W]e hold that the Attorney General's outdoor and point-of-sale advertising regulations targeting cigarettes are pre-empted by the FCLAA."

"We conclude that the sales practices regulations withstand First Amendment scrutiny."

II. CASE SUMMARY

A. Background

"In January 1999, the Attorney General of Massachusetts promulgated comprehensive regulations governing the advertising and sale of cigarettes, smokeless tobacco, and cigars. Petitioners, a group of cigarette, smokeless tobacco, and cigar manufacturers and retailers, filed suit in Federal District Court claiming that the regulations violate federal law and the United States Constitution. In large measure, the District Court determined that the regulations are valid and enforceable. The United States Court of Appeals for the First Circuit affirmed in part and reversed in part, concluding that the regulations are not pre-empted by federal law and do not violate the First Amendment. The first question presented . . . is whether certain cigarette advertising regulations are pre-empted by the Federal Cigarette Labeling and Advertising Act . . . . The second question presented is whether certain regulations governing the advertising and sale of tobacco products violate the First Amendment."

The Supreme Court granted certiorari to review the case.

B. Counsel of Record

ACLU Side (Petitioner / Appellant): Jeffrey S. Sutton argued the cause for appellants. With him on the briefs were Daniel P. Collins, Michael R. Doyen, Fred A. Rowley, Jr., Kenneth S. Geller, Andrew L. Frey, Richard M. Zielinski, John L. Strauch, Gregory G. Katsas, John B. Connarton, Jr., Patricia A. Barald, and David H. Remes. James V. Kearney filed a brief for appellants. With Mr. Kearney on the brief were Christopher Harris and Richard P. Bress. Peter J. McKenna and Eric S. Sarner filed a brief for appellants.

Opposing Side (Respondent / Appellee): William W. Porter, Assistant Attorney General of the Commonwealth of Massachusetts, argued the cause for respondents in both cases. With him on the brief were Thomas F. Reilly, Attorney General, and Susan Paulson, Assistant Attorney General.

Acting Solicitor General Underwood argued the cause for the United States, as amicus curiae, by special leave of court.

III. AMICI CURIAE

ACLU Side (Petitioner / Appellant)

Brief of amici curiae filed on behalf of the Newspaper Association of America, American Civil Liberties Union, American Civil Liberties Union of Massachusetts, Dow Jones & Company, Inc., Magazine Publishers of America, Inc., and the Reporters Committee for Freedom of the Press by Bruce E.H. Johnson, P. Cameron DeVore, Eric M. Stahl, René P. Milam, Steven R. Shapiro, Stuart D. Karle, Robin Bierstedt, Lucy Dalglish, Gregg Leslie, and Ashley Gauthier.

Brief of amici curiae filed on behalf of the American Advertising Federation et al. by Daniel E. Troy and Robin S. Conrad.

Brief of amici curiae filed on behalf of the American Association of Advertising Agencies et al. by Penelope S. Farthing.

Brief of amici curiae filed on behalf of the Association of National Advertisers, Inc., by Steven G. Brody, John J. Walsh, and Gilbert H. Weil.

Brief of amici curiae filed on behalf of Infinity Outdoor, Inc., et al. by Floyd Abrams and Joel Kurtzberg.

Brief of amici curiae filed on behalf of the National Association of Convenience Stores by Scott A. Sinder and John B. Williams.

Brief of amici curiae filed on behalf of the Product Liability Advisory Council, Inc., by Leslie G. Landau.

Brief of amici curiae filed on behalf of the Washington Legal Foundation by Daniel J. Popeo and Richard A. Samp.

Opposing Side (Respondent / Appellee)

Brief of amici curiae filed on behalf of the United States by Acting Solicitor General Underwood, Acting Assistant Attorney General Schiffer, Deputy Solicitor General Kneedler, Irving L. Gornstein, and Douglas N. Letter.

Brief of amici curiae filed on behalf of the State of California et al. by Seth E. Mermin and Corinne Lee Murphy, Deputy Attorneys General of California, Bill Lockyer, Attorney General, Richard M. Frank, Chief Assistant Attorney General, Herschel T. Elkins and Dennis Eckhart, Senior Assistant Attorneys General, Ronald A. Reiter, Supervising Deputy Attorney General, and Robert R. Rigsby, Corporation Counsel of the District of Columbia, and by the Attorneys General for their respective jurisdictions as follows: Bruce M. Botelho of Alaska, Janet Napolitano of Arizona, Mark Pryor of Arkansas, Ken Salazar of Colorado, Richard Blumenthal of Connecticut, Robert A. Butterworth of Florida, Earl I. Anzai of Hawaii, Alan G. Lance of Idaho, Jim Ryan of Illinois, Steve Carter of Indiana, Tom Miller of Iowa, Carla J. Stovall of Kansas, Richard P. Ieyoub of Louisiana, Steve Rowe of Maine, J. Joseph Curran, Jr., of Maryland, Mike Hatch of Minnesota, Mike Moore of Mississippi, Jeremiah W. Nixon of Missouri, Mike McGrath of Montana, Frankie Sue Del Papa of Nevada, Philip T. McLaughlin of New Hampshire, John Farmer of New Jersey, Patricia Madrid of New Mexico, Eliot Spitzer of New York, Wayne Stenehjem of North Dakota, Herbert D. Soll of the Northern Mariana Islands, Betty D. Montgomery of Ohio, W. A. Drew Edmondson of Oklahoma, Hardy Myers of Oregon, Mike Fisher of Pennsylvania, Sheldon Whitehouse of Rhode Island, Mark Barnett of South Dakota, Paul Summers of Tennessee, John Cornyn of Texas, Mark Shurtleff of Utah, William H. Sorrell of Vermont, Christine O. Gregoire of Washington, Darrel V. McGraw, Jr., of West Virginia, and James E. Doyle of Wisconsin.

Brief of amici curiae filed on behalf of the Cities of Oakland, California, et al. by Stephen P. Berzon, Michael E. Wall, Lawrence Rosenthal, and Benna Ruth Solomon.

Brief of amici curiae filed on behalf of the City of Los Angeles et al. by Mark E. Haddad, James M. Harris, Joseph R. Guerra, and James K. Hahn.

Brief of amici curiae filed on behalf of the City of New York et al. by Michael D. Hess, Leonard J. Koerner, Elizabeth Susan Natrella, Richard M. Weinberg, and Sandra R. Gutman.

Brief of amici curiae filed on behalf of the American Legacy Foundation by A. Stephen Hut, Jr., John Payton, Patrick J. Carome, and Matthew A. Brill.

Brief of amici curiae filed on behalf of the American Medical Association et al. by Donald W. Garner.

Brief of amici curiae filed on behalf of the National Center for Tobacco-Free Kids et al. by David Vladeck, Allison M. Zieve, Alan B. Morrison, and Matthew L. Myers.

Brief of amici curiae filed on behalf of the National Conference of State Legislatures et al. by Richard Ruda, James I. Crowley, and D. Bruce La Pierre.

Brief of amici curiae filed on behalf of the Tobacco Control Resource Center, Inc., by Richard A. Daynard.

Brief of amici curiae were filed on behalf of the State's Attorney of Dupage County, Illinois, et al. by Richard Hodyl, Jr., Joseph E. Birkett, and Nancy J. Wolfe.

Brief of amici curiae filed on behalf of the American Planning Association by Randal R. Morrison.

IV. THE SUPREME COURT'S DECISION

"Before reaching the First Amendment issues, we must decide to what extent federal law pre-empts the Attorney General's regulations. . . .

Article VI, cl. 2, of the United States Constitution commands that the laws of the United States 'shall be the supreme Law of the Land; . . . any Thing in the Constitution or Laws of any State to the Contrary notwithstanding.' . . . This relatively clear and simple mandate has generated considerable discussion in cases where we have had to discern whether Congress has pre-empted state action in a particular area. State action may be foreclosed by express language in a congressional enactment, by implication from the depth and breadth of a congressional scheme that occupies the legislative field, or by implication because of a conflict with a congressional enactment. . . .

The FCLAA's pre-emption provision does not cover smokeless tobacco or cigars.

In these cases, our task is to identify the domain expressly pre-empted . . . .

In sum, we fail to see how the FCLAA and its pre-emption provision permit a distinction between the specific concern about minors and cigarette advertising and the more general concern about smoking and health in cigarette advertising, especially in light of the fact that Congress crafted a legislative solution for those very concerns. We also conclude that a distinction between state regulation of the location as opposed to the content of cigarette advertising has no foundation in the text of the pre-emption provision. . . . Accordingly, we hold that the Attorney General's outdoor and point-of-sale advertising regulations targeting cigarettes are pre-empted by the FCLAA. . . .

By its terms, the FCLAA's pre-emption provision only applies to cigarettes. Accordingly, we must evaluate the smokeless tobacco and cigar petitioners' First Amendment challenges to the State's outdoor and point-of-sale advertising regulations. . . .

For over 25 years, the Court has recognized that commercial speech does not fall outside the purview of the First Amendment. Instead, the Court has afforded commercial speech a measure of First Amendment protection "commensurate" with its position in relation to other constitutionally guaranteed expression. In recognition of the 'distinction between speech proposing a commercial transaction, which occurs in an area traditionally subject to government regulation, and other varieties of speech,' Central Hudson, we developed a framework for analyzing regulations of commercial speech . . . . The analysis contains four elements . . .

Petitioners urge us to reject the Central Hudson analysis and apply strict scrutiny. . . . But here . . . we see 'no need to break new ground. Central Hudson . . . provides an adequate basis for decision.'

Only the last two steps of Central Hudson's four-part analysis are at issue here. . . .

The third step of Central Hudson concerns the relationship between the harm that underlies the State's interest and the means identified by the State to advance that interest. . . .

The last step of the Central Hudson analysis 'complements' the third step, 'asking whether the speech restriction is not more extensive than necessary to serve the interests that support it.' . . . Focusing on the third and fourth steps of the Central Hudson analysis, we first address the outdoor advertising and point-of-sale advertising regulations for smokeless tobacco and cigars. We then address the sales practices regulations for all tobacco products. . . .

The outdoor advertising regulations prohibit smokeless tobacco or cigar advertising within a 1,000–foot radius of a school or playground. . . .

Our review of the record reveals that the Attorney General has provided ample documentation of the problem with underage use of smokeless tobacco and cigars. In addition, we disagree with petitioners' claim that there is no evidence that preventing targeted campaigns and limiting youth exposure to advertising will decrease underage use of smokeless tobacco and cigars. On this record and in the posture of summary judgment, we are unable to conclude that the Attorney General's decision to regulate advertising of smokeless tobacco and cigars in an effort to combat the use of tobacco products by minors was based on mere 'speculation [and] conjecture.' . . .

Whatever the strength of the Attorney General's evidence to justify the outdoor advertising regulations, however, we conclude that the regulations do not satisfy the fourth step of the Central Hudson analysis. . . . The broad sweep of the regulations indicates that the Attorney General did not 'carefully calculat[e] the costs and benefits associated with the burden on speech imposed' by the regulations. . . .

We conclude that the Attorney General has failed to show that the outdoor advertising regulations for smokeless tobacco and cigars are not more extensive than necessary to advance the State's substantial interest in preventing underage tobacco use. . . .

A careful calculation of the costs of a speech regulation does not mean that a State must demonstrate that there is no incursion on legitimate speech interests, but a speech regulation cannot unduly impinge on the speaker's ability to propose a commercial transaction and the adult listener's opportunity to obtain information about products. After reviewing the outdoor advertising regulations, we find the calculation in these cases insufficient for purposes of the First Amendment. . . .

Massachusetts has also restricted indoor, point-of-sale advertising for smokeless tobacco and cigars. . . .

We conclude that the point-of-sale advertising regulations fail both the third and fourth steps of the Central Hudson analysis. . . .

We conclude that the restriction on the height of indoor advertising is invalid under Central Hudson's third and fourth prongs. . . .

The Attorney General also promulgated a number of regulations that restrict sales practices by cigarette, smokeless tobacco, and cigar manufacturers and retailers. . . .

As we read the regulations, they basically require tobacco retailers to place tobacco products behind counters and require customers to have contact with a salesperson before they are able to handle a tobacco product. . . .

We conclude that the sales practices regulations withstand First Amendment scrutiny. The means chosen by the State are narrowly tailored to prevent access to tobacco products by minors, are unrelated to expression, and leave open alternative avenues for vendors to convey information about products and for would-be customers to inspect products before purchase. . . .

Congress enacted a comprehensive scheme to address cigarette smoking and health in advertising and pre-empted state regulation of cigarette advertising that attempts to address that same concern, even with respect to youth. The First Amendment also constrains state efforts to limit advertising of tobacco products, because so long as the sale and use of tobacco is lawful for adults, the tobacco industry has a protected interest in communicating information about its products and adult customers have an interest in receiving that information.

To the extent that federal law and the First Amendment do not prohibit state action, States and localities remain free to combat the problem of underage tobacco use by appropriate means. The judgment of the United States Court of Appeals for the First Circuit is therefore affirmed in part and reversed in part, and the cases are remanded for further proceedings consistent with this opinion."

V. JUSTICE VOTE

5 Pro ACLU Side vs. 4 Con Opposing Side

ACLU Side (Petitioner / Appellant)

1. O'Connor, S. – Wrote majority opinion
2. Rehnquist, W. – Joined Stevens' opinion
3. Thomas, C. – Joined majority opinion in part, wrote concurring opinion
4. Scalia, A. – Joined majority opinion in part, joined Kennedy's concurrence
5. Kennedy, A. – Joined majority opinion in part, wrote concurring opinion

Opposing Side (Respondent / Appellee)

1. Stevens, J. – Wrote opinion concurring in part and dissenting in part
2. Souter, D. – Wrote opinion concurring in part and dissenting in part, joined Stevens' opinion in part
3. Ginsburg, R. – Joined Stevens' opinion
4. Breyer, S. – Joined Stevens' opinion

VI. A WIN OR LOSS FOR THE ACLU?

The ACLU filed as amicus curiae urging reversal of the judgment of the Court of Appeals; the Supreme Court affirmed in part, reversed in part, and remanded in a 5-4 vote, giving the ACLU an apparent win.

913. Zadvydas v. Davis

(Decided June 28, 2001; 533 U.S. 678)

I. ISSUE

A. Issues Discussed

Immigration/citizenship

B. Legal Question Presented

"[W]hether [the] post-removal-period statute authorizes the Attorney General to detain a removable alien indefinitely beyond the removal period or only for a period reasonably necessary to secure the alien's removal."

C. Supreme Court's Answer

"In our view, the statute, read in light of the Constitution's demands, limits an alien's post-removal-period detention to a period reasonably necessary to bring about that alien's removal from the United States. It does not permit indefinite detention."

II. CASE SUMMARY

A. Background

"When an alien has been found to be unlawfully present in the United States and a final order of removal has been entered, the Government ordinarily secures the alien's removal during a subsequent 90–day statutory 'removal period,' during which time the alien normally is held in custody.

A special statute authorizes further detention if the Government fails to remove the alien during those 90 days. . . .

In these cases, we must decide whether this post-removal-period statute authorizes the Attorney General to detain a removable alien indefinitely beyond the removal period or only for a period reasonably necessary to secure the alien's removal. . . .

We consider two separate instances of detention. The first concerns Kestutis Zadvydas, a resident alien who was born, apparently of Lithuanian parents, in a displaced persons camp in Germany in 1948. . . .

Zadvydas has a long criminal record, . . . and, in 1994, [was] ordered deported to Germany.

In 1994, Germany told the INS that it would not accept Zadvydas . . . . Shortly thereafter, Lithuania refused to accept Zadvydas . . . . In 1996, the INS asked the Dominican Republic (Zadvydas' wife's country) to accept him, but this effort proved unsuccessful. In 1998, Lithuania rejected, as inadequately documented, Zadvydas' effort to obtain Lithuanian citizenship based on his parents' citizenship; Zadvydas' reapplication is apparently still pending.

The INS kept Zadvydas in custody after expiration of the removal period. In September 1995, Zadvydas filed a petition for a writ of habeas corpus under 28 U.S.C. § 2241 challenging his continued detention. In October 1997, a Federal District Court granted that writ and ordered him released under supervision. . . .

The Fifth Circuit reversed this decision. It concluded that Zadvydas' detention did not violate the Constitution because eventual deportation was not 'impossible,' good-faith efforts to remove him from the United States continued, and his detention was subject to periodic administrative review. . . .

The second case is that of Kim Ho Ma. Ma was born in Cambodia in 1977. When he was two, his family fled, . . . he has lived [in the United States] as a resident alien since the age of seven. In 1995, at age 17, Ma was involved in a gang-related shooting, convicted of manslaughter, and sentenced to 38 months' imprisonment. He served two years, after which he was released into INS custody.

In light of his conviction of an 'aggravated felony,' Ma was ordered removed. . . . The 90–day removal period expired in early 1999, but the INS continued to keep Ma in custody, because . . . it was 'unable to conclude that Mr. Ma would remain nonviolent and not violate the conditions of release.'

In 1999, Ma filed a petition for a writ of habeas corpus under 28 U.S.C. § 2241. [T]he Federal District Court for the Western District of Washington . . . issued a joint order holding that the Constitution forbids post-removal-period detention unless there is 'a realistic chance that [the] alien will be deported' . . . .The District Court then held an evidentiary hearing, decided that there was no 'realistic chance' that Cambodia (which has no repatriation treaty with the United States) would accept Ma, and ordered Ma released.

The Ninth Circuit affirmed Ma's release. . . .

Zadvydas asked us to review the decision of the Fifth Circuit authorizing his continued detention. The Government asked us to review the decision of the Ninth Circuit forbidding Ma's continued detention. [The Supreme Court] granted writs in both cases, agreeing to consider both statutory and related constitutional questions."

B. Counsel of Record

ACLU Side (Respondent / Appellee): Jay W. Stansell argued the cause for appellee in No. 00–38. With him on the brief were Thomas W. Hillier

II and Jennifer E. Wellman.

Robert F. Barnard argued the cause for appellant in No. 99–7791. With him on the briefs was Virginia Laughlin Schlueter.

Opposing Side (Petitioner / Appellant): Deputy Solicitor General Kneedler argued the cause for appellees in No. 99–7791 and appellants in No. 00–38. With him on the briefs were Acting Solicitor General Underwood, former Solicitor General Waxman, Assistant Attorney General Ogden, Beth S. Brinkmann, Donald Keener, and Quynh Vu.

III. AMICI CURIAE

ACLU Side (Respondent / Appellee)

Brief of amici curiae filed on behalf of the American Civil Liberties Union and the American Civil Liberties Union of Washington by Judy Rabinovitz, Lucas Guttentag, Steven R. Shapiro, Wanyong Lai Austin, Jayashri Srikantiah, and Aaron H. Caplan.

Brief of amici curiae filed on behalf of the Catholic Legal Immigration Network, Inc., et al. by Laurie Joyce and Josh Dratel.

Brief of amici curiae filed on behalf of the American Association of Jews from the Former USSR et al. by Nancy Morawetz.

Brief of amici curiae filed on behalf of the Lawyers Committee for Human Rights by Seth M. M. Stodder.

Brief of amici curiae filed on behalf of Human Rights Watch et al. by William J. Aceves and Paul L. Hoffman.

Brief of amici curiae filed on behalf of Carolyn Patty Blum et al. by George A. Cumming, Jr., and Charles D. Weisselberg.

Opposing Side (Petitioner / Appellant)

Brief of amici curiae filed on behalf of the Washington Legal Foundation et al. by Daniel J. Popeo and Richard A. Samp.

IV. THE SUPREME COURT'S DECISION

"The Government argues that the statute means what it literally says. It sets no 'limit on the length of time beyond the removal period that an alien who falls within one of the Section 1231(a)(6) categories may be detained.' Hence, 'whether to continue to detain such an alien and, if so, in what circumstances and for how long' is up to the Attorney General, not up to the courts.

'[I]t is a cardinal principle' of statutory interpretation, however, that when an Act of Congress raises 'a serious doubt' as to its constitutionality, 'this Court will first ascertain whether a construction of the statute is fairly possible by which the question may be avoided.' We have read significant limitations into other immigration statutes in order to avoid their constitutional invalidation. . . . For similar reasons, we read an implicit limitation into the statute before us. In our view, the statute, read in light of the Constitution's demands, limits an alien's post-removal-period detention to a period reasonably necessary to bring about that alien's removal from the United States. It does not permit indefinite detention. . . .

A statute permitting indefinite detention of an alien would raise a serious constitutional problem. The Fifth Amendment's Due Process Clause forbids the Government to 'depriv[e]' any 'person . . . of . . . liberty . . . without due process of law.' Freedom from imprisonment—from government custody, detention, or other forms of physical restraint—lies at the heart of the liberty that Clause protects. And this Court has said that government detention violates that Clause unless the detention is ordered in a criminal proceeding with adequate procedural protections, or, in certain special and 'narrow' nonpunitive 'circumstances,' where a special justification, such as harm-threatening mental illness, outweighs the 'individual's constitutionally protected interest in avoiding physical restraint.' . . .

We have found nothing in the history of these statutes that clearly demonstrates a congressional intent to authorize indefinite, perhaps permanent, detention. Consequently, interpreting the statute to avoid a serious constitutional threat, we conclude that, once removal is no longer reasonably foreseeable, continued detention is no longer authorized by statute. . . .

We realize that recognizing . . . necessary Executive leeway will often call for difficult judgments. In order to limit the occasions when courts will need to make them, we think it practically necessary to recognize some presumptively reasonable period of detention. . . .

While an argument can be made for confining any presumption to 90 days, we doubt that when Congress shortened the removal period to 90 days in 1996 it believed that all reasonably foreseeable removals could be accomplished in that time. We do have reason to believe, however, that Congress previously doubted the constitutionality of detention for more than six months. Consequently, for the sake of uniform administration in the federal courts, we recognize that period. After this 6-month period, once the alien provides good reason to believe that there is no significant likelihood of removal in the reasonably foreseeable future, the Government must respond with evidence sufficient to rebut that showing. And for detention to remain reasonable, as the period of prior post-removal confinement grows, what counts as the 'reasonably foreseeable future' conversely would have to shrink. This 6-month presumption, of course, does not mean that every alien not removed must be released after six months. To the contrary, an alien may be held in confinement until it has been determined that there is no significant likelihood of removal in the reasonably foreseeable future. . . .

The Fifth Circuit held Zadvydas' continued detention lawful as long as 'good faith efforts to effectuate . . . deportation continue' and Zadvydas failed to show that deportation will prove 'impossible.' But this standard would seem to require an alien seeking release to show the absence of any prospect of removal—no matter how unlikely or unforeseeable—which demands more than our reading of the statute can bear. The Ninth Circuit held that the Government was required to release Ma from detention because there was no reasonable likelihood of his removal in the foreseeable future. But its conclusion may have rested solely upon the 'absence' of an 'extant or pending' repatriation agreement without giving due weight to the likelihood of successful future negotiations. Consequently, we vacate the judgments below and remand both cases for further proceedings consistent with this opinion."

V. JUSTICE VOTE

5 Pro ACLU Side vs. 4 Con Opposing Side

ACLU Side (Respondent / Appellee)

1. Breyer, S. – Wrote majority opinion
2. Stevens, J. – Joined majority opinion
3. O'Connor, S. – Joined majority opinion
4. Souter, D. – Joined majority opinion
5. Ginsburg, R. – Joined majority opinion

Opposing Side (Petitioner / Appellant)

1. Scalia, A. – Wrote dissenting opinion, joined Kennedy's dissent in part
2. Thomas, C. – Joined Scalia's dissent, joined Kennedy's dissent in part
3. Kennedy, A. – Wrote dissenting opinion
4. Rehnquist, W. – Joined Kennedy's dissent

VI. A WIN OR LOSS FOR THE ACLU?

The ACLU filed as amicus curiae urging affirmance in 00-38; the Supreme Court vacated the Court of Appeals' decisions in both cases and remanded for further proceedings consistent with its opinion by a 5-4 vote, giving the ACLU an apparent win.

914. Correctional Services Corp. v. Malesko

(Decided November 27, 2001; 534 U.S. 61)

I. ISSUE

A. Issues Discussed

Prison

B. Legal Question Presented

"[W]hether the implied damages action first recognized in Bivens v. Six Unknown Fed. Narcotics Agents, 403 U.S. 388, 91 S.Ct. 1999, 29 L.Ed.2d 619 (1971), should be extended to allow recovery against a private corporation operating a halfway house under contract with the Bureau of Prisons."

C. Supreme Court's Answer

The implied damages action recognized in Bivens will not be extended to a private corporation operating a halfway house under contract with the federal government.

II. CASE SUMMARY

A. Background

"Petitioner Correctional Services Corporation (CSC), under contract with the federal Bureau of Prisons (BOP), operates Community Corrections Centers and other facilities that house federal prisoners and detainees. Since the late 1980's, CSC has operated Le Marquis Community Correctional Center (Le Marquis), a halfway house located in New York City. Respondent John E. Malesko is a former federal inmate . . . . During his imprisonment, respondent was diagnosed with a heart condition and treated with prescription medication. Respondent's condition limited his ability to engage in physical activity, such as climbing stairs.

In February 1993, the BOP transferred respondent to Le Marquis . . . . Respondent was assigned to living quarters on the fifth floor. On or about March 1, 1994, CSC instituted a policy at Le Marquis requiring inmates residing below the sixth floor to use the staircase rather than the elevator to travel from the first-floor lobby to their rooms. There is no dispute that respondent was exempted from this policy on account of his heart condition. Respondent alleges that on March 28, 1994, however, Jorge Urena, an employee of CSC, forbade him to use the elevator to reach his fifth-floor bedroom. Respondent protested that he was specially permitted elevator access, but Urena was adamant. Respondent then climbed the stairs, suffered a heart attack, and fell, injuring his left ear.

Three years after this incident occurred, respondent filed a pro se action against CSC . . . in the United States District Court for the Southern District of New York. Two years later, now acting with counsel, respondent filed an amended complaint . . . . The amended complaint alleged that CSC, Urena, and unnamed defendants were 'negligent in failing to obtain requisite medication for [respondent's] condition and were further negligent by refusing [respondent] the use of the elevator.' It further alleged that respondent injured his left ear and aggravated a pre-existing condition '[a]s a result of the negligence of the Defendants.' Respondent demanded judgment in the sum of $1 million in compensatory damages, $3 million in anticipated future damages, and punitive damages 'for such sum as the Court and/or [j]ury may determine.'

The District Court treated the amended complaint as raising claims under Bivens v. Six Unknown Fed. Narcotics Agents, and dismissed respondent's cause of action in its entirety. . . .

The Court of Appeals for the Second Circuit affirmed in part, reversed in part, and remanded. That court affirmed dismissal of respondent's claims against individual defendants as barred by the statute of limitations. Respondent has not challenged that ruling . . . . With respect to CSC, the Court of Appeals remarked that Meyer expressly declined "to expand the category of defendants against whom Bivens-type actions may be brought to include not only federal agents, but federal agencies as well." But the court reasoned that private entities like CSC should be held liable under Bivens to 'accomplish the . . . important Bivens goal of providing a remedy for constitutional violations.'"

The Supreme Court granted certiorari to review the case.

B. Counsel of Record

ACLU Side (Respondent / Appellee): Steven Pasternak argued the cause for appellee. With him on the brief was David C. Vladeck.

Opposing Side (Petitioner / Appellant): Carter G. Phillips argued the cause for appellant. With him on the briefs were Frank R. Volpe, George P. Stasiuk, and Karen M. Morinelli.

Jeffrey A. Lamken argued the cause for the United States as

amicus curiae, by special leave of court.

III. AMICI CURIAE

ACLU Side (Respondent / Appellee)

Brief of amici curiae filed on behalf of the American Civil Liberties Union by Elizabeth Alexander, Margaret Winter, David Fathi, and Steven R. Shapiro.

Brief of amici curiae filed on behalf of the Legal Aid Society of the City of New York by Daniel L. Greenberg and John Boston.

Opposing Side (Petitioner / Appellant)

Brief of amici curiae filed on behalf of the United States by Jeffrey A. Lamken, Acting Solicitor General Underwood, Deputy Solicitor General Clement, Barbara L. Herwig, and Thomas M. Bondy.

IV. THE SUPREME COURT'S DECISION

"In Bivens v. Six Unknown Fed. Narcotics Agents, 403 U.S. 388, 91 S.Ct. 1999, 29 L.Ed.2d 619 (1971), we recognized for the first time an implied private action for damages against federal officers alleged to have violated a citizen's constitutional rights. Respondent now asks that we extend this limited holding to confer a right of action for damages against private entities acting under color of federal law. . . . We have heretofore refused to imply new substantive liabilities under such circumstances, and we decline to do so here. . . .

[I]t is clear that the claim urged by respondent is fundamentally different from anything recognized in Bivens or subsequent cases. In 30 years of Bivens jurisprudence we have extended its holding only twice, to provide an otherwise nonexistent cause of action against individual officers alleged to have acted unconstitutionally, or to provide a cause of action for a plaintiff who lacked any alternative remedy for harms caused by an individual officer's unconstitutional conduct. Where such circumstances are not present, we have consistently rejected invitations to extend Bivens, often for reasons that foreclose its extension here.

The purpose of Bivens is to deter individual federal officers from committing constitutional violations. Meyer made clear that the threat of litigation and liability will adequately deter federal officers for Bivens purposes no matter that they may enjoy qualified immunity, are indemnified by the employing agency or entity, or are acting pursuant to an entity's policy. Meyer also made clear that the threat of suit against an individual's employer was not the kind of deterrence contemplated by Bivens. . . . This case is, in every meaningful sense, the same. . . .

Respondent claims that even under Meyer's deterrence rationale, implying a suit against private corporations acting under color of federal law is still necessary to advance the core deterrence purpose of Bivens. . . .

There is no reason for us to consider extending Bivens beyond this core premise here. . . .

Nor are we confronted with a situation in which claimants in respondent's shoes lack effective remedies. It was conceded at oral argument that alternative remedies are at least as great, and in many respects greater, than anything that could be had under Bivens. . . .

In sum, respondent is not a plaintiff in search of a remedy as in Bivens and Davis. Nor does he seek a cause of action against an individual officer, otherwise lacking, as in Carlson. Respondent instead seeks a marked extension of Bivens, to contexts that would not advance Bivens' core purpose of deterring individual officers from engaging in unconstitutional wrongdoing. The caution toward extending Bivens remedies into any new context, a caution consistently and repeatedly recognized for three decades, forecloses such an extension here.

The judgment of the Court of Appeals is reversed."

V. JUSTICE VOTE

4 Pro ACLU Side vs. 5 Con Opposing Side

ACLU Side (Respondent / Appellee)

1. Stevens, J. – Wrote dissenting opinion
2. Souter, D. – Joined Stevens' dissent
3. Ginsburg, R. – Joined Stevens' dissent
4. Breyer, S. – Joined Stevens' dissent

Opposing Side (Petitioner / Appellant)

1. Rehnquist, W. – Wrote majority opinion
2. Thomas, C. – Joined Scalia's concurrence
3. O'Connor, S. – Joined majority opinion
4. Scalia, A. – Wrote concurring opinion
5. Kennedy, A. – Joined majority opinion

VI. A WIN OR LOSS FOR THE ACLU?

The ACLU filed as amici curiae urging affirmance; the Supreme Court reversed the Court of Appeals' decision by a 5-4 vote, giving the ACLU an apparent loss.

915. Adarand Constructors, Inc. v. Mineta

(Decided November 27, 2001; 534 U.S. 103)

I. ISSUE

A. Issues Discussed

Civil rights, race

B. Legal Question Presented

"[W]hether the Court of Appeals was correct when it concluded that the Department of Transportation's (DOT's) Disadvantaged Business Enterprise (DBE) program is consistent with the constitutional guaranty of equal protection."

C. Supreme Court's Answer

Declining to address the question presented, the Court dismissed the writ of certiorari as improvidently granted.

II. CASE SUMMARY

A. Background

This is the third time this case appeared before the U.S. Supreme Court. In Adarand I, the Supreme Court "held that strict scrutiny governs whether race-based classifications violate the equal protection component of the Fifth Amendment's Due Process Clause." The court then "remanded for a determination whether the race-based components of the DOT's DBE program could survive this standard of review."

"On remand, the District Court for the District of Colorado found that no such race-based component then in operation could so survive. The Court of Appeals vacated the District Court's judgment, reasoning that petitioner's cause of action had been mooted because the Colorado Department of Transportation had recently certified petitioner as a DBE. Finding it not at all clear that petitioner's certification was valid under DOT regulations, [the Supreme Court] again granted certiorari, reversed the Court of Appeals, and remanded for a determination on the merits consistent with Adarand I."

"[T]he Court of Appeals affirmed in part and reversed in part. The Court of Appeals agreed with the District Court that the DOT's DBE program was unconstitutional as it was administered in 1997. It further agreed that the automatic use of financial incentives to encourage the award of subcontracts to DBEs, as originally contemplated by the DOT's Subcontractor Compensation Clause (SCC) program, was 'unconstitutional under Adarand [I's] strict standard of scrutiny.' The Secretary of Transportation never challenged these rulings and has since discontinued any and all use of the SCC program."

"The Court of Appeals next turned its attention to new regulations issued by the Secretary of Transportation under the Transportation Equity Act for the 21st Century. These regulations pertain almost exclusively to use of federal funds for highway projects let by States and localities, which the Court of Appeals found to be the only 'relevant' aspect of the DBE program under review. The Court of Appeals further noted that petitioner either lacked standing or had waived its right to challenge any other race-conscious program. Finally, the Court of Appeals held that, by virtue of the new regulatory framework under which the DOT's state and local DBE program now operates, that program passed constitutional muster under Adarand I.

[The Supreme Court] again granted certiorari to decide whether the Court of Appeals misapplied the strict scrutiny standard announced in Adarand I."

B. Counsel of Record

ACLU Side (Respondent / Appellee): Theodore B. Olson argued the cause for appellee. With him on the brief were Assistant Attorney General Boyd, Deputy Solicitor General Clement, Jeffrey A. Lamken, Mark L. Gross, Teresa Kwong, Paul M. Geier, Peter J. Plocki, Peter S. Smith, and Edward V. A. Kussy.

Opposing Side (Petitioner / Appellant): William Perry Pendley argued the cause for appellant.

III. AMICI CURIAE

ACLU Side (Respondent / Appellee)

Brief of amici curiae filed on behalf of the Lawyers' Committee for Civil Rights Under Law, American Civil Liberties Union, Mexican American Legal Defense and Educational Fund, National Association for the Advancement of Colored People, and People for the American Way Foundation by John A. Payton, Charles T. Lester, Jr., Norman Redlich, Barbara R. Arnwine, Thomas J. Henderson, Steven R. Shapiro, Christopher A. Hansen, E. Vincent Warren, Antonia Hernandez, Dennis C. Hayes, and Elliot M. Mincberg.

Brief of amici curiae filed on behalf of the City and County of Denver by Eileen Penner and J. Wallace Wortham, Jr.

Brief of amici curiae filed on behalf of the NOW Legal Defense and Education Fund et al. by Martha F. Davis and Mitchell A. Lowenthal.

Brief of amici curiae filed on behalf of the Minority Business Enterprise Legal Defense and Education Fund, Inc., et al. by Bradley S. Phillips, Paul J. Watford, and Fred A. Rowley, Jr.

Brief of amici curiae filed on behalf of the NAACP Legal Defense and Educational Fund, Inc., by Elaine R. Jones, Theodore M. Shaw, Norman J. Chachkin, James L. Cott, and Robert H. Stroup.

Brief of amici curiae filed on behalf of the National League of Cities et al. by Richard Ruda, James I. Crowley, and Robert Brauneis.

Brief of amici curiae filed on behalf of the Office of Communication of the United Church of Christ et al. by David Honig and Shelby D. Green.

Brief of amici curiae filed on behalf of the Women First National Legislative Committee et al. by Edward W. Correia.

Brief of amici curiae filed on behalf of Senator Max Baucus et al. by Mr. Correia

Brief of amici curiae filed on behalf of the National Asian Pacific American Legal Consortium et al. by Mark A. Packman, Jonathan M. Cohen, and Vincent A. Eng.

Opposing Side (Petitioner / Appellant)

Brief of amici curiae filed on behalf of the Associated General Contractors of America, Inc., by John G. Roberts, Jr., and Michael E. Kennedy.

Brief of amici curiae filed on behalf of the Center for Individual Rights by Michael E. Rosman.

Brief of amici curiae filed on behalf of the Claremont Institute Center for Constitutional Jurisprudence by Edwin Meese III.

Brief of amici curiae filed on behalf of GEOD Corp. et al. by Martin S. Kaufman and Briscoe R. Smith.

Brief of amici curiae filed on behalf of the Pacific Legal Foundation et al. by John H. Findley and Sharon L. Browne.

Brief of amici curiae filed on behalf of the Southeastern Legal Foundation, Inc., by Walter H. Ryland and Valle Simms Dutcher.

Brief of amici curiae filed on behalf of L. S. Lee, Inc., by Mr. Ryland.

Brief of amici curiae filed on behalf of Social Science and Comparative Law Scholars by Clark D. Cunningham, in support of neither party.

IV. THE SUPREME COURT'S DECISION

"We again granted certiorari to decide whether the Court of Appeals misapplied the strict scrutiny standard announced in Adarand I. We anticipated that we would be able to review the same 'relevant program' that was addressed by the Court of Appeals. But since certiorari was granted there has been a shift in the posture of the case that precludes such review.

Both parties agree that the Court of Appeals confined its opinion to the constitutionality of the DOT's DBE program as it pertains to the use of federal funds for highway projects let by States and localities. … These regulations clearly permit the award of contracts based on race-conscious measures in jurisdictions where petitioner operates, and, as the Government concedes, provide petitioner with a potential basis for prospective relief, at least to the extent petitioner challenges them . . . .

Petitioner now asserts, however, that it is not challenging any part of DOT's state and local procurement program. Instead, it claims to be challenging only the statutes and regulations that pertain to DOT's direct procurement of highway construction on federal lands. But the statutes and regulations relating to direct procurement are quite different from the statutes and regulations reviewed by the Court of Appeals. . . .

This shift in posture requires dismissal of the writ for two reasons. First, the Court of Appeals has not considered whether the various race-based programs applicable to direct federal contracting could satisfy strict scrutiny. . . .

Second, to reach the merits of any challenge to statutes and regulations relating to direct federal procurement would require a threshold examination of whether petitioner has standing to challenge such statutes and regulations. . . .

We are obliged to examine standing sua sponte where standing has erroneously been assumed below. . . . But we do not examine standing sua sponte simply to reach an issue for which standing has been denied below—exactly what petitioner asks that we do here. . . .

'Mindful that this is a court of final review and not first view,' . . . we thus decline to reach the merits of petitioner's present challenge. Petitioner points out that this case presents questions of fundamental national importance calling for final resolution by this Court. But the importance of an issue should not distort the principles that control the exercise of our jurisdiction. To the contrary, 'by adhering scrupulously to the customary limitations on our discretion regardless of the significance of the underlying issue, we promote respect ... for the Court's adjudicatory process.' We also 'ensure that we are not tempted to engage in ill-considered decisions of questions not presented in the petition.'

For the foregoing reasons, the writ of certiorari is dismissed as improvidently granted."

V. JUSTICE VOTE

9 Pro ACLU Side vs. 0 Con Opposing Side

ACLU Side (Respondent / Appellee)

1. Rehnquist, W. – Per curiam decision
2. Stevens, J. – Per curiam decision
3. O'Connor, S. – Per curiam decision
4. Scalia, A. – Per curiam decision
5. Kennedy, A. – Per curiam decision
6. Thomas, C. – Per curiam decision
7. Souter, D. – Per curiam decision
8. Ginsburg, R. – Per curiam decision
9. Breyer, S. – Per curiam decision

VI. A WIN OR LOSS FOR THE ACLU?

The ACLU filed as amicus curiae urging affirmance of the judgment of the Court of Appeals. In a per curiam decision, the Court dismissed the writ of certiorari as improvidently granted, thus allowing the decision below to stand and giving the ACLU an apparent win.

916. EEOC v. Waffle House, Inc.

(Decided January 15, 2002; 534 U.S. 279)

I. ISSUE

A. Issues Discussed

Federal, regulation

B. Legal Question Presented

"[W]hether an agreement between an employer and an employee to arbitrate employment-related disputes bars the Equal Employment Opportunity Commission (EEOC) from pursuing victim-specific judicial relief, such as backpay, reinstatement, and damages, in an enforcement action alleging that the employer has violated Title I of the Americans with Disabilities Act of 1990."

C. Supreme Court's Answer

An agreement to arbitrate between employer and employee does not bar the EEOC from pursuing victim-specific judicial relief.

II. CASE SUMMARY

A. Background

"In his application for employment with respondent, Eric Baker agreed that 'any dispute or claim' concerning his employment would be 'settled by binding arbitration.' As a condition of employment, all prospective Waffle House employees are required to sign an application containing a similar mandatory arbitration agreement. Baker began working as a grill operator at one of respondent's restaurants on August 10, 1994. Sixteen days later he suffered a seizure at work and soon thereafter was discharged. Baker did not initiate arbitration proceedings, nor has he in the seven years since his termination, but he did file a timely charge of discrimination with the EEOC alleging that his discharge violated the ADA.

After an investigation and an unsuccessful attempt to conciliate, the EEOC filed an enforcement action against respondent in the Federal District Court for the District of South Carolina, pursuant to § 107(a) of the ADA . . . and § 102 of the Civil Rights Act of 1991 . . . . The EEOC's complaint alleged that respondent engaged in employment practices that violated the ADA, including its discharge of Baker 'because of his disability,' and that its violation was intentional, and 'done with malice or with reckless indifference to [his] federally protected rights.' The complaint requested the court to grant injunctive relief to 'eradicate the effects of [respondent's] past and present unlawful employment practices,' to order specific relief designed to make Baker whole, including backpay, reinstatement, and compensatory damages, and to award punitive damages for malicious and reckless conduct.

Respondent filed a petition under the Federal Arbitration Act (FAA) to stay the EEOC's suit and compel arbitration, or to dismiss the action. Based on a factual determination that Baker's actual employment contract had not included the arbitration provision, the District Court denied the motion. The Court of Appeals granted an interlocutory appeal and held that a valid, enforceable arbitration agreement between Baker and respondent did exist. The court then proceeded to consider 'what effect, if any, the binding arbitration agreement between Baker and Waffle House has on the EEOC . . . . [T]he court concluded that the agreement did not foreclose the enforcement action because the EEOC was not a party to the contract, and it has independent statutory authority to bring suit in any federal district court where venue is proper. Nevertheless, the court held that the EEOC was precluded from seeking victim-specific relief in court because the policy goals expressed in the FAA required giving some effect to Baker's arbitration agreement. . . .

Therefore, according to the Court of Appeals, when an employee has signed a mandatory arbitration agreement, the EEOC's remedies in an enforcement action are limited to injunctive relief.

Several Courts of Appeals have considered this issue and reached conflicting conclusions."

The Supreme Court granted certiorari to review the case.

B. Counsel of Record

ACLU Side (Petitioner / Appellant): Paul D. Clement argued the cause for appellant. With him on the briefs were Solicitor General Olson, Acting Solicitor General Underwood, Acting Assistant Attorney General Yeomans, James A. Feldman, Gwendolyn Young Reams, Philip B. Sklover, Lorraine C. Davis, and Robert J. Gregory.

Opposing Side (Respondent / Appellee): David L. Gordon argued the cause for appellee. With him on the brief were D. Gregory Valenza, Stephen F. Fisher, and Thomas C. Goldstein.

III. AMICI CURIAE

ACLU Side (Petitioner / Appellant)

Brief of amici curiae filed on behalf of the National Employment Lawyers Association, the American Civil Liberties Union, and Trial Lawyers for Public Justice by Michael Rubin, Scott A. Kronland, Cliff Palefsky, Steven R. Shapiro, Lenora M. Lapidus, F. Paul Bland, Jr., Arthur H. Bryant, and Paula A. Brantner.

Brief of amici curiae filed on behalf of the State of Missouri et al. by Jeremiah W. (Jay) Nixon, Attorney General of Missouri, James R. Layton, State Solicitor, and Alana M. Barragan-Scott, Deputy Solicitor, and by the Attorneys General for their respective jurisdictions as follows: Bruce M. Botelho of Alaska, Janet Napolitano of Arizona, Mark Pryor of Arkansas, Bill Lockyer of California, Ken Salazar of Colorado, Robert A. Butterworth of Florida, Earl I. Anzai of Hawaii, James E. Ryan of Illinois, Steve Carter of Indiana, Thomas J. Miller of Iowa, Carla J. Stovall of Kansas, Richard P. Ieyoub of Louisiana, J. Joseph Curran, Jr., of Maryland, Thomas F. Reilly of Massachusetts, Mike Hatch of Minnesota, Mike McGrath of Montana, Don Stenberg of Nebraska, Frankie Sue Del Papa of Nevada, John J. Farmer, Jr., of New Jersey, Patricia A. Madrid of New Mexico, Eliot Spitzer of New York, Betty D. Montgomery of Ohio, Sheldon Whitehouse of Rhode Island, Mark Barnett of South Dakota, Mark Shurtleff of Utah, William H. Sorrell of Vermont, Darrell V. McGraw, Jr., of West Virginia, and Herbert D. Soll of the Northern Mariana Islands.

Brief of amici curiae filed on behalf of the Maryland Commission on Human Relations et al. by Lee D. Hoshall and Elizabeth Colette.

Brief of amici curiae filed on behalf of AARP by Thomas W. Osborne, Laurie A. McCann, and Melvin Radowitz.

Brief of amici curiae filed on behalf of the American Federation of Labor and Congress of Industrial Organizations by Jonathan P. Hiatt, James B. Coppess, and Laurence Gold.

Brief of amici curiae filed on behalf of the Lawyers' Committee for Civil Rights Under Law et al. by Paul W. Mollica, John Payton, Norman Redlich, Barbara R. Arnwine, Thomas J. Henderson, Karen K. Narasaki, Vincent A. Eng, Judith L. Lichtman, Martha F. Davis, Yolanda S. Wu, Marcia D. Greenberger, and Judith Appelbaum.

Brief of amici curiae filed on behalf of the National Whistleblower Center by Stephen M. Kohn, Michael D. John, and David K. Colapinto.

Opposing Side (Respondent / Appellee)

Brief of amici curiae filed on behalf of Associated Industries of Massachusetts et al. by Michael E. Malamut.

Brief of amici curiae filed on behalf of the Council for Employment Law Equity by Walter Dellinger, Samuel Estreicher, and Mark A. de Bernardo.

Brief of amici curiae filed on behalf of the Equal Employment Advisory Council by Ann Elizabeth Reesman and Rae T. Vann.

IV. THE SUPREME COURT'S DECISION

"The FAA provides for stays of proceedings in federal district courts when an issue in the proceeding is referable to arbitration, and for orders compelling arbitration when one party has failed or refused to comply with an arbitration agreement. We have read these provisions to 'manifest a 'liberal federal policy favoring arbitration agreements.'' Absent some ambiguity in the agreement, however, it is the language of the contract that defines the scope of disputes subject to arbitration. . . .

The Court of Appeals wisely did not adopt respondent's reading of § 706(g). Instead, it simply sought to balance the policy goals of the FAA against the clear language of Title VII and the agreement.

While this may be a more coherent approach, it is inconsistent with our recent arbitration cases. The FAA directs courts to place arbitration agreements on equal footing with other contracts, but it 'does not require parties to arbitrate when they have not agreed to do so.' . . . Because the FAA is 'at bottom a policy guaranteeing the enforcement of private contractual arrangements,' we look first to whether the parties agreed to arbitrate a dispute, not to general policy goals, to determine the scope of the agreement. While ambiguities in the language of the agreement should be resolved in favor of arbitration, we do not override the clear intent of the parties, or reach a result inconsistent with the plain text of the contract, simply because the policy favoring arbitration is implicated. 'Arbitration under the [FAA] is a matter of consent, not coercion.' Here there is no ambiguity. No one asserts that the EEOC is a party to the contract, or that it agreed to arbitrate its claims. It goes without saying that a contract cannot bind a nonparty. Accordingly, the proarbitration policy goals of the FAA do not require the agency to relinquish its statutory authority if it has not agreed to do so. . . .

It is true, as respondent and its amici have argued, that Baker's conduct may have the effect of limiting the relief that the EEOC may obtain in court. If, for example, he had failed to mitigate his damages, or had accepted a monetary settlement, any recovery by the EEOC would be limited accordingly. . . . As we have noted, it 'goes without saying that the courts can and should preclude double recovery by an individual.'

But no question concerning the validity of his claim or the character of the relief that could be appropriately awarded in either a judicial or an arbitral forum is presented by this record. Baker has not sought arbitration of his claim, nor is there any indication that he has entered into settlement negotiations with respondent. It is an open question whether a settlement or arbitration judgment would affect the validity of the EEOC's claim or the character of relief the EEOC may seek. The only issue before this Court is whether the fact that Baker has signed a mandatory arbitration agreement limits the remedies available to the EEOC. The text of the relevant statutes provides a clear answer to that question. They do not authorize the courts to balance the competing policies of the ADA and the FAA or to second-guess the agency's judgment concerning which of the remedies authorized by law that it shall seek in any given case.

Moreover, it simply does not follow from the cases holding that the employee's conduct may affect the EEOC's recovery that the EEOC's claim is merely derivative. We have recognized several situations in which the EEOC does not stand in the employee's shoes. . . . And, in this context, the statute specifically grants the EEOC exclusive authority over the choice of forum and the prayer for relief once a charge has been filed. The fact that ordinary principles of res judicata, mootness, or mitigation may apply to EEOC claims does not contradict these decisions, nor does it render the EEOC a proxy for the employee.

The judgment of the Court of Appeals is reversed, and the case is remanded for further proceedings consistent with this opinion."

V. JUSTICE VOTE

6 Pro ACLU Side vs. 3 Con Opposing Side

ACLU Side (Petitioner / Appellant)

1. Stevens, J. – Wrote majority opinion
2. O'Connor, S. – Joined majority opinion
3. Souter, D. – Joined majority opinion
4. Ginsburg, R. – Joined majority opinion
5. Breyer, S. – Joined majority opinion
6. Kennedy, A. – Joined majority opinion

Opposing Side (Respondent / Appellee)

1. Thomas, C. – Wrote dissenting opinion
2. Rehnquist, W. – Joined Thomas' dissent
3. Scalia, A. – Joined Thomas' dissent

VI. A WIN OR LOSS FOR THE ACLU?

The ACLU filed as amicus curiae urging reversal of the judgment of the Court of Appeals; the Supreme Court reversed and remanded in a 6-3 vote, giving the ACLU an apparent win.

917. Kansas v. Crane

(Decided January 22, 2002; 534 U.S. 407)

I. ISSUE

A. Issues Discussed

Civil rights, state

B. Legal Question Presented

Whether the Kansas Supreme Court interpreted the U.S. Supreme Court's decision in Kansas v. Hendricks in an overly restrictive manner. Hendricks upheld the Kansas Sexually Violent Predator Act as constitutional.

C. Supreme Court's Answer

The Kansas Supreme Court did interpret Hendricks in an overly restrictive manner. The constitution requires a lack of control determination under the Kansas Sexually Violent Predator Act, but there does not need to be a determination of total or complete lack of control.

II. CASE SUMMARY

A. Background

"In Hendricks, [the U.S. Supreme] Court upheld the Kansas Sexually Violent Predator Act against constitutional challenge. In doing so, the Court characterized the confinement at issue as civil, not criminal, confinement. And it held that the statutory criterion for confinement embodied in the statute's words 'mental abnormality or personality disorder' satisfied "substantive' due process requirements.' . . .

In the present case the State of Kansas asks [the U.S. Supreme Court] to review the Kansas Supreme Court's application of Hendricks. The State here seeks the civil commitment of Michael Crane, a previously convicted sexual offender who, according to at least one of the State's psychiatric witnesses, suffers from both exhibitionism and antisocial personality disorder. After a jury trial, the Kansas District Court ordered Crane's civil commitment. But the Kansas Supreme Court reversed. In that court's view, the Federal Constitution as interpreted in Hendricks insists upon 'a finding that the defendant cannot control his dangerous behavior'—even if (as provided by Kansas law) problems of 'emotional capacity' and not 'volitional capacity' prove the 'source of bad behavior' warranting commitment. And the trial court had made no such finding.

Kansas now argues that the Kansas Supreme Court wrongly read Hendricks as requiring the State always to prove that a dangerous individual is completely unable to control his behavior. That reading, says Kansas, is far too rigid."

The Supreme Court granted certiorari to review the case.

B. Counsel of Record

ACLU Side (Respondent / Appellee): John C. Donham argued the cause for appellee.

Opposing Side (Petitioner / Appellant): Carla J. Stovall, Attorney General of Kansas, argued the cause for appellant. With her on the briefs was Stephen R. McAllister, State Solicitor

III. AMICI CURIAE

ACLU Side (Respondent / Appellee)

Brief of amici curiae filed on behalf of the National Association of Criminal Defense Lawyers, the National Legal Aid and Defender Association, the American Civil Liberties Union, and the Committee for Public Counsel Services by Jody Manier Kris, Lisa Kemler, and Steven R. Shapiro.

Brief of amici curiae filed on behalf of the American Psychiatric Association et al. by Richard G. Taranto.

Opposing Side (Petitioner / Appellant)

Brief of amici curiae filed on behalf of the State of Illinois et al. by James E. Ryan, Attorney General of Illinois, Joel D. Bertocchi, Solicitor General, and William L. Browers, Lisa Anne Hoffman, and Margaret M. O'Connell, Assistant Attorneys General, and by the Attorneys General for their respective States as follows: Bill Pryor of Alabama, Janet Napolitano of Arizona, Bill Lockyer of California, M. Jane Brady of Delaware, Robert A. Butterworth of Florida, Thomas J. Miller of Iowa, J. Joseph Curran, Jr., of Maryland, Thomas F. Reilly of Massachusetts, Mike Moore of Mississippi, Jeremiah W. (Jay) Nixon of Missouri, Don Stenberg of Nebraska, John J. Farmer, Jr., of New Jersey, Wayne Stenehjem of North Dakota, W. A. Drew Edmondson of Oklahoma, D. Michael Fisher of Pennsylvania, Charles M. Condon of South Carolina, Christine O. Gregoire of Washington, and James E. Doyle of Wisconsin.

Brief of amici curiae filed on behalf of the Association for the Treatment of Sexual Abusers by John J. Sullivan and Michael E. Lackey, Jr.

Brief of amici curiae filed on behalf of the Washington Legal Foundation et al. by Daniel J. Popeo and Richard A. Samp.

IV. THE SUPREME COURT'S DECISION

"We agree with Kansas insofar as it argues that Hendricks set forth no requirement of total or complete lack of control. Hendricks referred to the Kansas Act as requiring a "mental abnormality" or "personality disorder" that makes it 'difficult, if not impossible, for the [dangerous] person to control his dangerous behavior.' The word 'difficult' indicates that the lack of control to which this Court referred was not absolute. Indeed, as different amici on opposite sides of this case agree, an absolutist approach is unworkable. . . .

We do not agree with the State, however, insofar as it seeks to claim that the Constitution permits commitment of the type of dangerous sexual offender considered in Hendricks without any lack-of-control determination. Hendricks underscored the constitutional importance of distinguishing a dangerous sexual offender subject to civil commitment 'from other dangerous persons who are perhaps more properly dealt with exclusively through criminal proceedings.' That distinction is necessary lest 'civil commitment' become a 'mechanism for retribution or general deterrence'—functions properly those of criminal law, not civil commitment. The presence of what the 'psychiatric profession itself classifie[d] . . . as a serious mental disorder' helped to make that distinction in Hendricks. And a critical distinguishing feature of that 'serious . . . disorder' there consisted of a special and serious lack of ability to control behavior. . . .

We recognize that Hendricks as so read provides a less precise constitutional standard than would those more definite rules for which the parties have argued. But the Constitution's safeguards of human liberty in the area of mental illness and the law are not always best enforced through precise bright-line rules. For one thing, the States retain considerable leeway in defining the mental abnormalities and personality disorders that make an individual eligible for commitment. For another, the science of psychiatry, which informs but does not control ultimate legal determinations, is an ever-advancing science, whose distinctions do not seek precisely to mirror those of the law. . . . Consequently, we have sought to provide constitutional guidance in this area by proceeding deliberately and contextually, elaborating generally stated constitutional standards and objectives as specific circumstances require. Hendricks embodied that approach. . . .

For these reasons, the judgment of the Kansas Supreme Court is vacated, and the case is remanded for further proceedings not inconsistent with this opinion."

V. JUSTICE VOTE

2 Pro ACLU Side vs. 7 Con Opposing Side

ACLU Side (Respondent / Appellee)

1. Scalia, A. – Wrote dissenting opinion
2. Thomas, C. – Joined Scalia's dissent

Opposing Side (Petitioner / Appellant)

1. Breyer, S. – Wrote majority opinion
2. Ginsburg, R. – Joined majority opinion
3. Rehnquist, W. – Joined majority opinion
4. Stevens, J. – Joined majority opinion
5. O'Connor, S. – Joined majority opinion
6. Kennedy, A. – Joined majority opinion
7. Souter, D. – Joined majority opinion

VI. A WIN OR LOSS FOR THE ACLU?

The ACLU filed as amicus curiae urging affirmance of the judgment of the Kansas Supreme Court. The Court vacated the Kansas Supreme Court's decision by a 7-2 vote, giving the ACLU an apparent loss.[1]

918. Swierkiewicz v. Sorema N. A.

(Decided February 26, 2002; 534 U.S. 506)

I. ISSUE

A. Issues Discussed

Federal, civil rights

B. Legal Question Presented

"[W]hether a complaint in an employment discrimination lawsuit must contain specific facts establishing a prima facie case of discrimination under the framework set forth by this Court in McDonnell Douglas Corp. v. Green, 411 U.S. 792, 93 S.Ct. 1817, 36 L.Ed.2d 668 (1973)."

C. Supreme Court's Answer

"We hold that an employment discrimination complaint need not include such facts and instead must contain only 'a short and plain statement of the claim showing that the pleader is entitled to relief.' Fed. Rule Civ. Proc. 8(a)(2)."

II. CASE SUMMARY

A. Background

"Petitioner Akos Swierkiewicz is a native of Hungary, who at the time of his complaint was 53 years old. In April 1989, petitioner began working for respondent Sorema N. A., a reinsurance company headquartered in New York and principally owned and controlled by a French parent corporation. Petitioner was initially employed in the position of senior vice president and chief underwriting officer (CUO). Nearly six years later, François M. Chavel, respondent's Chief Executive Officer, demoted petitioner to a marketing and services position and transferred the bulk of his underwriting responsibilities to Nicholas Papadopoulo, a 32-year-old who, like Mr. Chavel, is a French national. About a year later, Mr. Chavel stated that he wanted to 'energize' the underwriting department and appointed Mr. Papadopoulo as CUO. Petitioner claims that Mr. Papadopoulo had only one year of underwriting experience at the time he was promoted, and therefore was less experienced and less qualified to be CUO than he, since at that point he had 26 years of experience in the insurance industry.

Following his demotion, petitioner contends that he 'was isolated by Mr. Chavel . . . excluded from business decisions and meetings and denied the opportunity to reach his true potential at SOREMA.' Petitioner unsuccessfully attempted to meet with Mr. Chavel to discuss his discontent. Finally, in April 1997, petitioner sent a memo to Mr. Chavel outlining his grievances and requesting a severance package. Two weeks later, respondent's general counsel presented petitioner with two options: He could either resign without a severance package or be dismissed. Mr. Chavel fired petitioner after he refused to resign.

Petitioner filed a lawsuit alleging that he had been terminated on account of his national origin in violation of Title VII of the Civil Rights Act of 1964 and on account of his age in violation of the Age Discrimination in Employment Act of 1967 (ADEA). The United States District Court for the Southern District of New York dismissed petitioner's complaint because it found that he 'ha[d] not adequately alleged a prima facie case, in that he ha[d] not adequately alleged circumstances that support an inference of discrimination.' The United States Court of Appeals for the Second Circuit affirmed the dismissal . . . ."

The Supreme Court granted certiorari to review the case.

B. Counsel of Record

ACLU Side (Petitioner / Appellant): Harold I. Goodman argued the cause and filed briefs for appellant.

Jeffrey P. Minear argued the cause for the United States et al. as amici curiae.

Opposing Side (Respondent / Appellee): Lauren Reiter Brody argued the cause for appellee. With her on the brief was Frances Kulka Browne.

III. AMICI CURIAE

ACLU Side (Petitioner / Appellant)

Brief of amici curiae filed on behalf of National Employment Lawyers Association, AARP, American Civil Liberties Union, the National Partnership for Women and Families, the National Women's Law Center, and NOW Legal Defense and Education Fund by Paul W. Mollica, Paula A. Brantner, Daniel B. Kohrman, Thomas W. Osborne, Melvin Radowitz, Steven R. Shapiro, Lenora M. Lapidus, James D. Esseks, Judith L. Lichtman, Jocelyn C. Frye, Marcia D.Greenberger, Deborah Chalfie, and Martha F. Davis.

Brief of amici curiae filed on behalf of the United States et al. by Jeffrey P. Minear, Solicitor General Olson, Assistant Attorney General Boyd, Deputy Solicitor General Clement, Patricia A. Millett, and Philip B. Sklover.

Brief of amici curiae filed on behalf of the Lawyers' Committee for Civil Rights Under Law by John A. Payton, Gary T. Johnson, Norman Redlich, Barbara R. Arnwine, Thomas J. Henderson, and Nancy L. Perkins.

Opposing Side (Respondent / Appellee)

Brief of amici curiae filed on behalf of the Center for Individual Freedom by Linda Van Winkle Deacon and Julie Arias Young.

Brief of amici curiae filed on behalf of the Equal Employment Advisory Council by Ann Elizabeth Reesman and Katherine Y. K. Cheung.

IV. THE SUPREME COURT'S DECISION

Applying Circuit precedent, the Court of Appeals required petitioner to plead a prima facie case of discrimination in order to survive respondent's motion to dismiss. In the Court of Appeals'

1 The dissenters, Justices Scalia and Thomas, would reverse instead of vacate the Kansas Supreme Court's decision. They are dissenting by not technically on the ACLU's side.

view, petitioner was thus required to allege in his complaint: (1) membership in a protected group; (2) qualification for the job in question; (3) an adverse employment action; and (4) circumstances that support an inference of discrimination.

The prima facie case under McDonnell Douglas, however, is an evidentiary standard, not a pleading requirement. In McDonnell Douglas, this Court made clear that '[t]he critical issue before us concern[ed] the order and allocation of proof in a private, non-class action challenging employment discrimination.' (emphasis added). . . .

This Court has never indicated that the requirements for establishing a prima facie case under McDonnell Douglas also apply to the pleading standard that plaintiffs must satisfy in order to survive a motion to dismiss. . . .

In addition, under a notice pleading system, it is not appropriate to require a plaintiff to plead facts establishing a prima facie case because the McDonnell Douglas framework does not apply in every employment discrimination case. . . .

Moreover, the precise requirements of a prima facie case can vary depending on the context and were 'never intended to be rigid, mechanized, or ritualistic.' . . .

Furthermore, imposing the Court of Appeals' heightened pleading standard in employment discrimination cases conflicts with Federal Rule of Civil Procedure 8(a)(2), which provides that a complaint must include only 'a short and plain statement of the claim showing that the pleader is entitled to relief.' . . .

Rule 8(a)'s simplified pleading standard applies to all civil actions, with limited exceptions. . . .

Other provisions of the Federal Rules of Civil Procedure are inextricably linked to Rule 8(a)'s simplified notice pleading standard. . . . Given the Federal Rules' simplified standard for pleading, '[a] court may dismiss a complaint only if it is clear that no relief could be granted under any set of facts that could be proved consistent with the allegations.' . . .

Applying the relevant standard, petitioner's complaint easily satisfies the requirements of Rule 8(a) because it gives respondent fair notice of the basis for petitioner's claims. . . .

Respondent argues that allowing lawsuits based on conclusory allegations of discrimination to go forward will burden the courts and encourage disgruntled employees to bring unsubstantiated suits. Whatever the practical merits of this argument, the Federal Rules do not contain a heightened pleading standard for employment discrimination suits. A requirement of greater specificity for particular claims is a result that 'must be obtained by the process of amending the Federal Rules, and not by judicial interpretation.' . . .

For the foregoing reasons, we hold that an employment discrimination plaintiff need not plead a prima facie case of discrimination and that petitioner's complaint is sufficient to survive respondent's motion to dismiss. Accordingly, the judgment of the Court of Appeals is reversed, and the case is remanded for further proceedings consistent with this opinion."

V. JUSTICE VOTE

9 Pro ACLU Side vs. 0 Con Opposing Side

ACLU Side (Petitioner / Appellant)

1. Thomas, C. – Wrote majority opinion
2. O'Connor, S. – Joined majority opinion
3. Stevens, J. – Joined majority opinion
4. Souter, D. – Joined majority opinion
5. Ginsburg, R. – Joined majority opinion
6. Breyer, S. – Joined majority opinion
7. Scalia, A. – Joined majority opinion
8. Kennedy, A. – Joined majority opinion
9. Rehnquist, W. – Joined majority opinion

VI. A WIN OR LOSS FOR THE ACLU?

The ACLU filed as amicus curiae urging reversal of the judgment of the Court of Appeals; the Supreme Court reversed and remanded in a 9-0 vote, giving the ACLU an apparent win.

919. Dep't of Hous. & Urban Dev. v. Rucker

(Decided March 26, 2002; 535 U.S. 125)

I. ISSUE

A. Issues Discussed

Drugs

B. Legal Question Presented

Whether "42 U.S.C. § 1437d(l)(6) unambiguously requires lease terms that vest local public housing authorities with the discretion to evict tenants for the drug-related activity of household members and guests whether or not the tenant knew, or should have known, about the activity."

C. Supreme Court's Answer

"Section 1437d(l)(6) requires lease terms that give local public housing authorities the discretion to terminate the lease of a tenant when a member of the household or a guest engages in drug-related activity, regardless of whether the tenant knew, or should have known, of the drug-related activity."

II. CASE SUMMARY

A. Background

"[T]he Anti–Drug Abuse Act of 1988 . . . provides that each 'public housing agency shall utilize leases which . . . provide that any criminal activity that threatens the health, safety, or right to peaceful enjoyment of the premises by other tenants or any drug-related criminal activity on or off such premises, engaged in by a public housing tenant, any member of the tenant's household, or any guest or other person under the tenant's control, shall be cause for termination of tenancy.' 42 U.S.C. § 1437d(l)(6). Petitioners say that this statute requires lease terms that allow a local public housing authority to evict a tenant when a member of the tenant's household or a guest engages in drug-related criminal activity, regardless of whether the tenant knew, or had reason to know, of that activity. Respondents say it does not. We agree with petitioners.

Respondents are four public housing tenants of the Oakland Housing Authority (OHA). Paragraph 9(m) of respondents' leases, track[s] the language of § 1437d(l)(6) . . . .

In late 1997 and early 1998, OHA instituted eviction proceedings in state court against respondents, alleging violations of this lease provision. . . .

United States Department of Housing and Urban Development (HUD) regulations administering § 1437d(l)(6) require lease terms authorizing evictions in these circumstances. The HUD regulations closely track the statutory language, and provide that '[i]n deciding to evict for criminal activity, the [public housing authority] shall have discretion to consider all of the circumstances of the case . . . .' . . .

After OHA initiated the eviction proceedings in state court, respondents commenced actions against HUD, OHA, and OHA's director in United States District Court. . . . The District Court issued a preliminary injunction, enjoining OHA from 'terminating the leases of tenants pursuant to paragraph 9(m) of the 'Tenant Lease' for drug-related criminal activity that does not occur within the tenant's apartment unit when the tenant did not know of and had no reason to know of, the drug-related criminal activity.'

A panel of the Court of Appeals reversed . . . . An en banc panel of the Court of Appeals reversed and affirmed the District Court's grant of the preliminary injunction."

The Supreme Court granted certiorari to review the case.

B. Counsel of Record

ACLU Side (Respondent / Appellee): Paul Renne argued the cause for appellees in both cases. With him on the brief were James Donato, Whitty Somvichian, and John Murcko.

Opposing Side (Petitioner / Appellant): James A. Feldman argued the cause for the federal appellant. With him on the briefs were Solicitor General Olson, Assistant Attorney General McCallum, Deputy Solicitor General Kneedler, Barbara C. Biddle, Howard S. Scher, Richard A. Hauser, Carole W. Wilson, Howard M. Schmeltzer, and Harold J. Rennett. Gary T. Lafayette argued the cause for the private appellants. With him on the briefs was Susan T. Kumagai.

III. AMICI CURIAE

ACLU Side (Respondent / Appellee)

Brief of amici curiae filed on behalf of the American Civil Liberties Union and the ACLU of Northern California by Mark J. Lopez, Steven R. Shapiro, and Alan L. Schlosser.

Brief of amici curiae filed on behalf of AARP et al. by Catherine M. Bishop and Julie E. Levin.

Brief of amici curiae filed on behalf of the National Network to End Domestic Violence et al. by Bruce D. Sokler and Fernando R. Laguarda.

Brief of amici curiae filed on behalf of the Pennsylvania Association of Resident Councils et al. by Eileen D. Yacknin and Richard S. Matesic.

Brief of amici curiae filed on behalf of Lawrence Lessig et al. by David T. Goldberg and Daniel N. Abrahamson.

Brief of amici curiae filed on behalf of the Coalition to Protect Public Housing et al. by Kirsten D. Levingston, Michael S. Feldberg, and Martha F. Davis.

Opposing Side (Petitioner / Appellant)

Brief of amici curiae filed on behalf of the Council of Large Public Housing Authorities et al. by William F. Maher and Robert A. Graham.

Brief of amici curiae filed on behalf of the International City-County Management Association et al. by Richard Ruda and James I. Crowley.

Brief of amici curiae filed on behalf of the Washington Legal Foundation et al. by Daniel J. Popeo and Richard A. Samp.

IV. THE SUPREME COURT'S DECISION

"We . . . reverse, holding that 42 U.S.C. § 1437d(l)(6) unambiguously requires lease terms that vest local public housing authorities with the discretion to evict tenants for the drug-related activity of household members and guests whether or not the tenant knew, or should have known, about the activity.

That this is so seems evident from the plain language of the statute. . . . The en banc Court of Appeals thought the statute did not address 'the level of personal knowledge or fault that is required for eviction.' Yet Congress' decision not to impose any qualification in the statute, combined with its use of the term 'any' to modify 'drug-related criminal activity,' precludes any knowledge requirement. . . .

The en banc Court of Appeals also thought it possible that 'under the tenant's control' modifies not just 'other person,' but also 'member of the tenant's household' and 'guest.' . . . But this interpretation runs counter to basic rules of grammar. . . . Thus, the plain language of § 1437d(l)(6) requires leases that grant public housing authorities the discretion to terminate tenancy without regard to the tenant's knowledge of the drug-related criminal activity.

Comparing § 1437d(l)(6) to a related statutory provision reinforces the unambiguous text. . . .

The en banc Court of Appeals next resorted to legislative history. The Court of Appeals correctly recognized that reference to legislative history is inappropriate when the text of the statute is unambiguous. . . .

Nor was the en banc Court of Appeals correct in concluding that this plain reading of the statute leads to absurd results. The statute does not require the eviction of any tenant who violated the lease provision. Instead, it entrusts that decision to the local public housing authorities . . . .

In another effort to avoid the plain meaning of the statute, the en banc Court of Appeals invoked the canon of constitutional avoidance. But that canon 'has no application in the absence of statutory ambiguity.' . . .

The en banc Court of Appeals held that HUD's interpretation 'raise[s] serious questions under the Due Process Clause of the Fourteenth Amendment,' because it permits 'tenants to be deprived of their property interest without any relationship to individual wrongdoing.' . . . The government is not attempting to criminally punish or civilly regulate respondents as members of the general populace. It is instead acting as a landlord of property that it owns, invoking a clause in a lease to which respondents have agreed and which Congress has expressly required. . . .

We hold that 'Congress has directly spoken to the precise question at issue.' Section 1437d(l)(6) requires lease terms that give local public housing authorities the discretion to terminate the lease of a tenant when a member of the household or a guest engages in drug-related activity, regardless of whether the tenant knew, or should have known, of the drug-related activity.

Accordingly, the judgment of the Court of Appeals is reversed, and the cases are remanded for further proceedings consistent with this opinion."

V. JUSTICE VOTE

0 Pro ACLU Side vs. 8 Con Opposing Side

Opposing Side (Petitioner / Appellant)

1. Rehnquist, W. – Wrote majority opinion
2. Thomas, C. – Joined majority opinion
3. Ginsburg, R. – Joined majority opinion
4. Souter, D. – Joined majority opinion
5. O'Connor, S. – Joined majority opinion
6. Stevens, J. – Joined majority opinion
7. Scalia, A. – Joined majority opinion
8. Kennedy, A. – Joined majority opinion
9. Breyer, S – Took no part in the decision

VI. A WIN OR LOSS FOR THE ACLU?

The ACLU filed as amicus curiae urging affirmance; the Supreme Court reversed the Court of Appeals' decision by an 8-0 vote, giving the ACLU an apparent loss.

920. Hoffman Plastic Compounds, Inc. v. NLRB

(Decided March 27, 2002; 535 U.S. 137)

I. ISSUE

A. Issues Discussed

Immigration/citizenship, regulation

B. Legal Question Presented

Whether the National Labor Relations Board can award backpay to an undocumented immigrant lacking authorization to work in the United States.

C. Supreme Court's Answer

"We hold that such relief is foreclosed by federal immigration policy, as expressed by Congress in the Immigration Reform and Control Act of 1986 (IRCA)."

II. CASE SUMMARY

A. Background

"In May 1988, petitioner hired Jose Castro . . . . Before being hired . . . , Castro presented documents that appeared to verify his authorization to work in the United States. In December 1988, the United Rubber, Cork, Linoleum, and Plastic Workers of America, AFL–CIO, began a union-organizing campaign at petitioner's production plant. Castro and several other employees supported the organizing campaign and distributed authorization cards to co-workers. In January 1989, Hoffman laid off Castro and other employees engaged in these organizing activities.

Three years later, in January 1992, respondent Board found that Hoffman unlawfully selected four employees, including Castro, for layoff 'in order to rid itself of known union supporters' in violation of § 8(a)(3) of the National Labor Relations Act (NLRA). To remedy this violation, the Board ordered that Hoffman (1) cease and desist from further violations of the NLRA, (2) post a detailed notice to its employees regarding the remedial order, and (3) offer reinstatement and backpay to the four affected employees. . . .

In June 1993, the parties proceeded to a compliance hearing before an Administrative Law Judge (ALJ) to determine the amount of backpay owed to each discriminatee. On the final day of the hearing, Castro testified that he was born in Mexico and that he had never been legally admitted to, or authorized to work in, the United States. He admitted gaining employment with Hoffman only after tendering a birth certificate belonging to a friend who was born in Texas. . . . Based on this testimony, the ALJ found the Board precluded from awarding Castro backpay or reinstatement as such relief would be contrary to Sure–Tan, Inc. v. NLRB, 467 U.S. 883 (1984), and in conflict with IRCA, which makes it unlawful for employers knowingly to hire undocumented workers or for employees to use fraudulent documents to establish employment eligibility.

In September 1998, four years after the ALJ's decision, and nine years after Castro was fired, the Board reversed with respect to backpay. Citing its earlier decision in A.P.R.A. Fuel Oil Buyers Group, Inc., 320 N.L.R.B. 408 (1995), the Board determined that 'the most effective way to accommodate and further the immigration policies embodied in [IRCA] is to provide the protections and remedies of the [NLRA] to undocumented workers in the same manner as to other employees.' . . .

Hoffman filed a petition for review of the Board's order in the Court of Appeals. A panel of the Court of Appeals denied the petition for review. After rehearing the case en banc, the court again denied the petition for review and enforced the Board's order."

The Supreme Court granted certiorari to review the case.

B. Counsel of Record

ACLU Side (Respondent / Appellee): Paul R. Q. Wolfson argued the cause for appellee. With him on the brief were Solicitor General Olson, Deputy Solicitor General Wallace, Arthur F. Rosenfeld, John H. Ferguson, Norton J. Come, and John Emad Arbab.

Opposing Side (Petitioner / Appellant): Ryan D. McCortney argued the cause for appellant. With him on the briefs was Maurice Baskin.

III. AMICI CURIAE

ACLU Side (Respondent / Appellee)

Brief of amici curiae filed on behalf of the American Civil Liberties Union Foundation and Make the Road by Walking, Inc., by Benjamin I. Sachs, Steven R. Shapiro, Craig Goldblatt, Trevor W. Morrison, Adam B. Cox, and Lucas Guttentag.

Brief of amici curiae filed on behalf of the State of New York et al. by Eliot Spitzer, Attorney General of New York, Caitlin J. Halligan, Solicitor General, Daniel Smirlock, Deputy Solicitor General, and M. Patricia Smith and Seth Kupperberg,

Assistant Attorneys General, and by the Attorneys General for their respective jurisdictions as follows: Janet Napolitano of Arizona, Bill Lockyer of California, Earl I. Anzai of Hawaii, Thomas F. Reilly of Massachusetts, Darrell V. McGraw, Jr., of West Virginia, and Anabelle Rodriguez of Puerto Rico.

Brief of amici curiae filed on behalf of the American Federation of Labor and Congress of Industrial Organizations by Jonathan P. Hiatt, James B. Coppess, and Michael Rubin.

Brief of amici curiae filed on behalf of Employers and Employer Organizations by David A. Schulz, Jeffrey H. Drichta, and Michael J. Wishnie.

Brief of amici curiae filed on behalf of the National Employment Law Project et al. by Rebecca Smith, James Reif, and James Williams.

Opposing Side (Petitioner / Appellant)

Brief of amici curiae filed on behalf of the Equal Employment Advisory Council et al. by Ann Elizabeth Reesman and Daniel V. Yager.

IV. THE SUPREME COURT'S DECISION

"This case exemplifies the principle that the Board's discretion to select and fashion remedies for violations of the NLRA, though generally broad, is not unlimited. Since the Board's inception, we have consistently set aside awards of reinstatement or backpay to employees found guilty of serious illegal conduct in connection with their employment. . . .

Our decision in Sure–Tan followed this line of cases and set aside an award closely analogous to the award challenged here. . . .

It is against this decisional background that we turn to the question presented here. The parties and the lower courts focus much of their attention on Sure–Tan, particularly its express limitation of backpay to aliens 'lawfully entitled to be present and employed in the United States.' All agree that as a matter of plain language, this limitation forecloses the award of backpay to Castro. Castro was never lawfully entitled to be present or employed in the United States, and thus, under the plain language of Sure–Tan, he has no right to claim backpay. The Board takes the view, however, that read in context, this limitation applies only to aliens who left the United States and thus cannot claim backpay without lawful reentry. The Court of Appeals agreed with this view. Another Court of Appeals, however, agrees with Hoffman, and concludes that Sure–Tan simply meant what it said, i.e., that any alien who is 'not lawfully entitled to be present and employed in the United States' cannot claim backpay. We need not resolve this controversy. For whether isolated sentences from Sure–Tan definitively control, or count merely as persuasive dicta in support of petitioner, we think the question presented here better analyzed through a wider lens, focused as it must be on a legal landscape now significantly changed.

The Southern S.S. Co. line of cases established that where the Board's chosen remedy trenches upon a federal statute or policy outside the Board's competence to administer, the Board's remedy may be required to yield. . . .

Under the IRCA regime, it is impossible for an undocumented alien to obtain employment in the United States without some party directly contravening explicit congressional policies. . . . The Board asks that we overlook this fact and allow it to award backpay to an illegal alien for years of work not performed, for wages that could not lawfully have been earned, and for a job obtained in the first instance by a criminal fraud. We find, however, that awarding backpay to illegal aliens runs counter to policies underlying IRCA . . . . Therefore, as we have consistently held in like circumstances, the award lies beyond the bounds of the Board's remedial discretion. . . .

Lack of authority to award backpay does not mean that the employer gets off scot-free. The Board here has already imposed other significant sanctions against Hoffman—sanctions Hoffman does not challenge. These include orders that Hoffman cease and desist its violations of the NLRA, and that it conspicuously post a notice to employees setting forth their rights under the NLRA and detailing its prior unfair practices. . . . We have deemed such 'traditional remedies' sufficient to effectuate national labor policy regardless of whether the 'spur and catalyst' of backpay accompanies them. . . . As we concluded in Sure–Tan, 'in light of the practical workings of the immigration laws,' any 'perceived deficienc[y] in the NLRA's existing remedial arsenal' must be 'addressed by congressional action,' not the courts. In light of IRCA, this statement is even truer today.

The judgment of the Court of Appeals is reversed."

V. JUSTICE VOTE

4 Pro ACLU Side vs. 5 Con Opposing Side

ACLU Side (Respondent / Appellee)

1. Breyer, S. – Wrote dissenting opinion
2. Stevens, J. – Joined Breyer's dissent
3. Souter, D. – Joined Breyer's dissent
4. Ginsburg, R. – Joined Breyer's dissent

Opposing Side (Petitioner / Appellant)

1. Rehnquist, W. – Wrote majority opinion
2. Thomas, C. – Joined majority opinion
3. O'Connor, S. – Joined majority opinion
4. Scalia, A. – Joined majority opinion
5. Kennedy, A. – Joined majority opinion

VI. A WIN OR LOSS FOR THE ACLU?

The ACLU filed as amicus curiae urging affirmance; the Supreme Court reversed the Court of Appeals' decision by a 5-4 vote, giving the ACLU an apparent loss.

921. Ashcroft v. Free Speech Coalition

(Decided April 16, 2002; 535 U.S. 234)

I. ISSUE

A. Issues Discussed

1st Amendment, obscenity, press, speech, association

B. Legal Question Presented

"We consider in this case whether the Child Pornography Prevention Act of 1996 (CPPA) abridges the freedom of speech. . . . The principal question to be resolved . . . is whether the CPPA is constitutional where it proscribes a significant universe of speech that is neither obscene under Miller nor child pornography under Ferber."

C. Supreme Court's Answer

"[T]he prohibitions of §§ 2256(8)(B) and 2256(8)(D) are overbroad and unconstitutional."

II. CASE SUMMARY

A. Background

"We consider in this case whether the Child Pornography Prevention Act of 1996 (CPPA) abridges the freedom of speech. The CPPA extends the federal prohibition against child pornography to sexually explicit images that appear to depict minors but were produced without using any real children. The statute prohibits, in specific circumstances, possessing or distributing these images, which may be created by using adults who look like minors or by using computer imaging. The new technology, according to Congress, makes it possible to create realistic images of children who do not exist. . . .

Respondents . . . challenge § 2256(8)(D). . . . Section 2256(8)(D) defines child pornography to include any sexually explicit image that was 'advertised, promoted, presented, described, or distributed in such a manner that conveys the impression' it depicts 'a minor engaging in sexually explicit conduct.' . . .

Fearing that the CPPA threatened the activities of its members, respondent Free Speech Coalition and others challenged the statute in the United States District Court for the Northern District of California. The Coalition, a California trade association for the adult-entertainment industry, alleged that its members did not use minors in their sexually explicit works, but they believed some of these materials might fall within the CPPA's expanded definition of child pornography. The other respondents are Bold Type, Inc., the publisher of a book advocating the nudist lifestyle; Jim Gingerich, a painter of nudes; and Ron Raffaelli, a photographer specializing in erotic images. Respondents alleged that the 'appears to be' and 'conveys the impression' provisions are overbroad and vague, chilling them from producing works protected by the First Amendment. The District Court disagreed and granted summary judgment to the Government. The court dismissed the overbreadth claim because it was 'highly unlikely' that any 'adaptations of sexual works like 'Romeo and Juliet,' . . . will be treated as 'criminal contraband."

The Court of Appeals for the Ninth Circuit reversed. . . . The Court of Appeals voted to deny the petition for rehearing en banc, over the dissent of three judges."

The Supreme Court granted certiorari to review the case.

B. Counsel of Record

ACLU Side (Respondent / Appellee): H. Louis Sirkin argued the cause for appellees. With him on the brief were Laura A. Abrams and John P. Feldmeier.

Opposing Side (Petitioner / Appellant): Deputy Solicitor General Clement argued the cause for appellants. With him on the briefs were Solicitor General Olson, Acting Solicitor General Underwood, Acting Assistant Attorney General Schiffer, Deputy Solicitor General Kneedler, Irving L. Gornstein, Barbara L. Herwig, and Jacob M. Lewis.

III. AMICI CURIAE

ACLU Side (Respondent / Appellee)

Brief of amici curiae filed on behalf of the American Civil Liberties Union, Institute for the Advanced Study of Human Sexuality, National Association of Criminal Defense Lawyers, Reporters Committee for Freedom of the Press, Feminists for Free Expression, Society of Professional Journalists, and Radio-Television News Directors Association by Ann Brick, William Bennett Turner, Ann E. Beeson, and Steven R. Shapiro.

Brief of amici curiae filed on behalf of the Association of American Publishers, Inc., et al. by R. Bruce Rich, Jonathan Bloom, and Michael A. Bamberger.

Brief of amici curiae filed on behalf of the Liberty Project by Jodie L. Kelley and Daniel Mach.

Opposing Side (Petitioner / Appellant)

Brief of amici curiae filed on behalf of the State of New Jersey et al. by John J. Farmer, Jr., Attorney General of New Jersey, and Patrick DeAlmeida and Carol Johnston, Deputy Attorneys General, and Patrick DeAlmeida and Carol Johnston, Deputy Attorneys General, and by the Attorneys General for their respective jurisdictions as follows: Bill Pryor of Alabama, Bruce M. Botelho of Alaska, Janet Napolitano of Arizona, Mark Pryor of Arkansas, Ken Salazar of Colorado, Richard Blumenthal of Connecticut, M. Jane Brady of Delaware, Robert A. Butterworth of Florida, Earl I. Anzai of Hawaii, James E. Ryan of Illinois, Steve Carter of Indiana, Thomas J. Miller of Iowa, Carla J. Stovall of Kansas, J. Joseph Curran, Jr., of Maryland, Thomas F. Reilly of Massachusetts, Jennifer M. Granholm of Michigan, Mike Hatch of Minnesota, Mike Moore of Mississippi, Don Stenberg of Nebraska, Frankie Sue Del Papa of Nevada, Patricia A. Madrid of New Mexico, Roy Cooper of North Carolina, Wayne Stenehjem of North Dakota, Herbert D. Soll of the Northern Mariana Islands, Betty D. Montgomery of Ohio, W. A. Drew Edmondson of Oklahoma, Hardy Myers of Oregon, D. Michael Fisher of Pennsylvania, Sheldon Whitehouse of Rhode Island, Charles M. Condon of South Carolina, John Cornyn of Texas, Mark L. Shurtleff of Utah, Mark L. Earley of Virginia, Christine O. Gregoire of Washington, and James E. Doyle of Wisconsin.

Brief of amici curiae filed on behalf of the National Center for Missing & Exploited Children by Dennis DeConcini and Susan M. Kalp.

Brief of amici curiae filed on behalf of the National Law Center for Children and Families et al. by J. Robert Flores, Bruce A. Taylor, and Janet M. LaRue.

Brief of amici curiae filed on behalf of the National Legal Foundation by Barry C. Hodge.

Brief of amici curiae filed on behalf of Morality in Media, Inc., by Robin S. Whitehead.
Brief of amici curiae filed on behalf of Senator Sam Brownback et al. by Jay Alan Sekulow, Stuart J. Roth, James M. Henderson, Sr., David A. Cortman, Colby M. May, Walter M. Weber, and Benjamin W. Bull.

IV. THE SUPREME COURT'S DECISION

"As a general principle, the First Amendment bars the government from dictating what we see or read or speak or hear. The freedom of speech has its limits; it does not embrace certain categories of speech, including defamation, incitement, obscenity, and pornography produced with real children. While these categories may be prohibited without violating the First Amendment, none of them includes the speech prohibited by the CPPA. . . .

As we have noted, the CPPA is much more than a supplement to the existing federal prohibition on obscenity. Under Miller v. California, 413 U.S. 15 (1973), the Government must prove that the work, taken as a whole, appeals to the prurient interest, is patently offensive in light of community standards, and lacks serious literary, artistic, political, or scientific value. The CPPA, however, extends to images that appear to depict a minor engaging in sexually explicit activity without regard to the Miller requirements. . . .

Ferber upheld a prohibition on the distribution and sale of child pornography, as well as its production, because these acts were 'intrinsically related' to the sexual abuse of children in two ways. . . .

In contrast to the speech in Ferber, speech that itself is the record of sexual abuse, the CPPA prohibits speech that records no crime and creates no victims by its production. . . .

The second flaw in the Government's position is that Ferber did not hold that child pornography is by definition without value. On the contrary, the Court recognized some works in this category might have significant value, but relied on virtual images—the very images prohibited by the CPPA—as an alternative and permissible means of expression . . . . Ferber, then, not only referred to the distinction between actual and virtual child pornography, it relied on it as a reason supporting its holding. Ferber provides no support for a statute that eliminates the distinction and makes the alternative mode criminal as well.

The CPPA, for reasons we have explored, is inconsistent with Miller and finds no support in Ferber. The Government seeks to justify its prohibitions in other ways. . . .

In sum, § 2256(8)(B) covers materials beyond the categories recognized in Ferber and Miller, and the reasons the Government offers in support of limiting the freedom of speech have no justification in our precedents or in the law of the First Amendment. The provision abridges the freedom to engage in a substantial amount of lawful speech. For this reason, it is overbroad and unconstitutional.

Respondents challenge § 2256(8)(D) as well. This provision bans depictions of sexually explicit conduct that are 'advertised, promoted, presented, described, or distributed in such a manner that conveys the impression that the material is or contains a visual depiction of a minor engaging in sexually explicit conduct.' The parties treat the section as nearly identical to the provision prohibiting materials that appear to be child pornography. . . .

We disagree with this view. The CPPA prohibits sexually explicit materials that 'conve[y] the impression' they depict minors. While that phrase may sound like the 'appears to be' prohibition in § 2256(8)(B), it requires little judgment about the content of the image. . . .

The Government does not offer a serious defense of this provision, and the other arguments it makes in support of the CPPA do not bear on § 2256(8)(D). . . .

§ 2256(8)(D) is substantially overbroad and in violation of the First Amendment. . . .

For the reasons we have set forth, the prohibitions of §§ 2256(8)(B) and 2256(8)(D) are overbroad and unconstitutional. Having reached this conclusion, we need not address respondents' further contention that the provisions are unconstitutional because of vague statutory language.

The judgment of the Court of Appeals is affirmed."

V. JUSTICE VOTE

6 Pro ACLU Side vs. 3 Con Opposing Side

ACLU Side (Respondent / Appellee)

1. Kennedy, A. – Wrote majority opinion
2. Ginsburg, R. – Joined majority opinion
3. Souter, D. – Joined majority opinion
4. Stevens, J. – Joined majority opinion
5. Breyer, S. – Joined majority opinion
6. Thomas, C. – Wrote concurring opinion

Opposing Side (Petitioner / Appellant)

1. O'Connor, S. – Wrote opinion concurring in part and dissenting in part
2. Rehnquist, W. – Wrote dissenting opinion, joined O'Connor's opinion in part
3. Scalia, A. – Joined Rehnquist's dissent in part, Joined O'Connor's opinion in part

VI. A WIN OR LOSS FOR THE ACLU?

The ACLU filed as amicus curiae urging affirmance; the Supreme Court affirmed the Court of Appeals' decision by a 6-3 vote, giving the ACLU an apparent win.

922. Ashcroft v. American Civil Liberties Union

(Decided May 13, 2002; 535 U.S. 564)

I. ISSUE

A. Issues Discussed

1st Amendment, obscenity, press, speech, association

B. Legal Question Presented

"This case presents the narrow question whether the Child Online Protection Act's (COPA or Act) use of 'community standards' to identify 'material that is harmful to minors' violates the First Amendment."

C. Supreme Court's Answer

"We hold . . . that COPA's reliance on community standards to identify 'material that is harmful to minors' does not by itself render the statute substantially overbroad for purposes of the First Amendment."

II. CASE SUMMARY

A. Background

"Congress first attempted to protect children from exposure to pornographic material on the Internet by enacting the Communications Decency Act of 1996 (CDA). The CDA prohibited the knowing transmission over the Internet of obscene or indecent messages to any recipient under 18 years of age. It also forbade any individual from knowingly sending over or displaying on the Internet certain 'patently offensive' material in a manner available to persons under 18 years of age. . . .

The CDA provided two affirmative defenses to those prosecuted under the statute. The first protected individuals who took 'good faith, reasonable, effective, and appropriate actions' to restrict minors from accessing obscene, indecent, and patently offensive material over the Internet. The second shielded those who restricted minors from accessing such material 'by requiring use of a verified credit card, debit account, adult access code, or adult personal identification number.'

Notwithstanding these affirmative defenses, in Reno v. American Civil Liberties Union, we held that the CDA's regulation of indecent transmissions and the display of patently offensive material ran afoul of the First Amendment. . . .

After our decision in Reno v. American Civil Liberties Union, Congress explored other avenues for restricting minors' access to pornographic material on the Internet. In particular, Congress passed and the President signed into law the Child Online Protection Act. COPA prohibits any person from 'knowingly and with knowledge of the character of the material, in interstate or foreign commerce by means of the World Wide Web, mak[ing] any communication for commercial purposes that is available to any minor and that includes any material that is harmful to minors.'

Apparently responding to our objections to the breadth of the CDA's coverage, Congress limited the scope of COPA's coverage in at least three ways. First, while the CDA applied to communications over the Internet as a whole, including, for example, e-mail messages, COPA applies only to material displayed on the World Wide Web. Second, unlike the CDA, COPA covers only communications made for commercial purposes.' And third, while the CDA prohibited 'indecent' and 'patently offensive' communications, COPA restricts only the narrower category of 'material that is harmful to minors.' . . .

Like the CDA, COPA also provides affirmative defenses to those subject to prosecution under the statute. An individual may qualify for a defense if he, 'in good faith, has restricted access by minors to material that is harmful to minors—(A) by requiring the use of a credit card, debit account, adult access code, or adult personal identification number; (B) by accepting a digital certificate that verifies age; or (C) by any other reasonable measures that are feasible under available technology.' . . .

One month before COPA was scheduled to go into effect, respondents filed a lawsuit challenging the constitutionality of the statute in the United States District Court for the Eastern District of Pennsylvania. Respondents are a diverse group of organizations, most of which maintain their own Web sites. . . . Respondents' Web sites contain 'resources on obstetrics, gynecology, and sexual health; visual art and poetry; resources designed for gays and lesbians; information about books and stock photographic images offered for sale; and online magazines.'

In their complaint, respondents alleged that, although they believed that the material on their Web sites was valuable for adults, they feared that they would be prosecuted under COPA because some of that material 'could be construed as 'harmful to minors' in some communities.' Respondents' facial challenge claimed, that COPA violated adults' rights under the First and Fifth Amendments because it (1) 'create[d] an effective ban on constitutionally protected speech by and to adults'; (2) '[was] not the least restrictive means of accomplishing any compelling governmental purpose'; and (3) '[was] substantially overbroad.'

The District Court granted respondents' motion for a preliminary injunction, barring the Government from enforcing the Act until the merits of respondents' claims could be adjudicated. . . .

The Attorney General of the United States appealed the District Court's ruling. The United States Court of Appeals for the Third Circuit affirmed.

[The Supreme Court] granted the Attorney General's petition for certiorari to review the Court of Appeals' determination that COPA likely violates the First Amendment because it relies, in part, on community standards to identify material that is harmful to minors, and now vacate the Court of Appeals' judgment."

B. Counsel of Record

ACLU Side (Respondent / Appellee): Ann E. Beeson, of the American Civil Liberties Union Foundation, argued the cause for appellees. With her on the briefs were Christopher A. Hansen and Steven R. Shapiro of the American Civil Liberties Union Foundation, Stefan Presser of the American Civil Liberties Union of Pennsylvania, David L. Sobel, Alexandra A. E. Shapiro, Christopher R. Harris, Michele M. Pyle, Mark H. Goldberg, and Lee Tien.

Opposing Side (Petitioner / Appellant): Solicitor General Olson argued the cause for appellant. With him on the briefs were Acting Assistant Attorney General Schiffer, Deputy Solicitor General Kneedler, Irving L. Gornstein, Barbara L. Herwig, Jacob M. Lewis, and Charles Scarborough.

III. AMICI CURIAE

ACLU Side (Respondent / Appellee)

Brief of amici curiae filed on behalf of the American Society of Journalists and Authors et al. by Carl A. Solano, Theresa E. Loscalzo, Jennifer DuFault James, Joseph T. Lukens, and Dionna K. Litvin.

Brief of amici curiae filed on behalf of the Association of National Advertisers, Inc., by Steven G. Brody and Gilbert H. Weil.

Brief of amici curiae filed on behalf of the Association of American Publishers, Inc., et al. by R. Bruce Rich and Jonathan Bloom.

Brief of amici curiae filed on behalf of the Chamber of Commerce of the United States by Jodie L. Kelley, Paul M. Smith, and Robert Corn-Revere.

Brief of amici curiae filed on behalf of the Society for the Scientific Study of Sexuality et al. by Marjorie Heins and Joan E. Bertin.

Brief of amici curiae filed on behalf of Volunteer Lawyers for the Arts et al. by Charles L. Kerr, Elliot M. Mincberg, and Lawrence S. Ottinger.

Opposing Side (Petitioner / Appellant)

Brief of amici curiae filed on behalf of the County of DuPage by Richard Hodyl, Jr., Joseph E. Birkett, and Nancy J. Wolfe.

Brief of amici curiae filed on behalf of the American Center for Law and Justice by Jay Alan Sekulow, James M. Henderson, Sr., Colby M. May, and Walter M. Weber.

Brief of amici curiae filed on behalf of Morality in Media, Inc., et al. by Paul J. McGeady, Robin S. Whitehead, and Janet M. LaRue.

Brief of amici curiae filed on behalf of Wallbuilders, Inc., by Barry C. Hodge.

Brief of amici curiae filed on behalf of Senator John S. McCain et al. by Bruce A. Taylor.

Brief of amici curiae filed on behalf of Senator Raymond N. Haynes et al. by Richard D. Ackerman and Gary G. Kreep.

IV. THE SUPREME COURT'S DECISION

"The First Amendment states that 'Congress shall make no law ... abridging the freedom of speech.' . . . However, this principle, like other First Amendment principles, is not absolute. . . .

Miller set forth the governing three-part test for assessing whether material is obscene and thus unprotected by the First Amendment: '(a) [W]hether 'the average person, applying contemporary community standards ' would find that the work, taken as a whole, appeals to the prurient interest; (b) whether the work depicts or describes, in a patently offensive way, sexual conduct specifically defined by the applicable state law; and (c) whether the work, taken as a whole, lacks serious literary, artistic, political, or scientific value.'. . .

The Court of Appeals, however, concluded that this Court's prior community standards jurisprudence 'has no applicability to the Internet and the Web' because 'Web publishers are currently without the ability to control the geographic scope of the recipients of their communications.' We therefore must decide whether this technological limitation renders COPA's reliance on community standards constitutionally infirm. . . .

Because juries would apply different standards across the country, and Web publishers currently lack the ability to limit access to their sites on a geographic basis, the Court of Appeals feared that COPA's 'community standards' component would effectively force all speakers on the Web to abide by the 'most puritan' community's standards. And such a requirement, the Court of Appeals concluded, 'imposes an overreaching burden and restriction on constitutionally protected speech.' . . .

The CDA's use of community standards to identify patently offensive material, however, was particularly problematic in light of that statute's unprecedented breadth and vagueness. . . .

COPA, by contrast, does not appear to suffer from the same flaw because it applies to significantly less material than did the CDA and defines the harmful-to-minors material restricted by the statute in a manner parallel to the Miller definition of obscenity. To fall within the scope of COPA, works must not only 'depic[t], describ[e], or represen[t], in a manner patently offensive with respect to minors,' particular sexual acts or parts of the anatomy, they must also be designed to appeal to the prurient interest of minors and, 'taken as a whole, lac[k] serious literary, artistic, political, or scientific value for minors.'

These additional two restrictions substantially limit the amount of material covered by the statute. . . .

When the scope of an obscenity statute's coverage is sufficiently narrowed by a 'serious value' prong and a 'prurient interest' prong, we have held that requiring a speaker disseminating material to a national audience to observe varying community standards does not violate the First Amendment. . . .

If a publisher chooses to send its material into a particular community, this Court's jurisprudence teaches that it is the publisher's responsibility to abide by that community's standards. The publisher's burden does not change simply because it decides to distribute its material to every community in the Nation. . . . If a publisher wishes for its material to be judged only by the standards of particular communities, then it need only take the simple step of utilizing a medium that enables it to target the release of its material into those communities. . . .

Respondents argue that COPA is 'unconstitutionally overbroad' because it will require Web publishers to shield some material behind age verification screens that could be displayed openly in many communities across the Nation if Web speakers were able to limit access to their sites on a geographic basis. '[T]o prevail in a facial challenge,' however, 'it is not enough for a plaintiff to show 'some' overbreadth.' Rather, 'the overbreadth of a statute must not only be real, but substantial as well.' At this stage of the litigation, respondents have failed to satisfy this burden, at least solely as a result of COPA's reliance on community standards. Because Congress has narrowed the range of content restricted by COPA in a manner analogous to Miller's definition of obscenity, we conclude, consistent with our holdings in Hamling and Sable, that any variance caused by the statute's reliance on community standards is not substantial enough to violate the First Amendment. . . .

The scope of our decision today is quite limited. We hold only that COPA's reliance on community standards to identify 'material that is harmful to minors' does not by itself render the statute substantially overbroad for purposes of the First Amendment. . . .

For the foregoing reasons, we vacate the judgment of the Court of Appeals and remand the case for further proceedings."

V. JUSTICE VOTE

1 Pro ACLU Side vs. 8 Con Opposing Side

ACLU Side (Respondent / Appellee)

1. Stevens, J. – Wrote dissenting opinion

Opposing Side (Petitioner / Appellant)

1. Thomas, C. – Wrote majority opinion
2. Ginsburg, R. – Joined Kennedy's concurrence

3. Souter, D. – Joined Kennedy's concurrence
4. O'Connor, S. – Wrote concurring opinion
5. Breyer, S. – Wrote concurring opinion
6. Scalia, A. – Joined majority opinion
7. Kennedy, A. – Wrote concurring opinion
8. Rehnquist, W. – Joined majority opinion

VI. A WIN OR LOSS FOR THE ACLU?

The ACLU, as a party of record and counsel of record, argued the case for appellee, urging affirmance; the Supreme Court vacated and remanded the Court of Appeals' decision by an 8-1 vote, giving the ACLU an apparent loss.

923. Verizon Maryland, Inc. v. Pub. Serv. Comm'n of Maryland

(Decided May 20, 2002; 535 U.S. 635)

I. ISSUE

A. Issues Discussed

Immunity

B. Legal Question Presented

"[W]hether federal district courts have jurisdiction over a telecommunication carrier's claim that the order of a state utility commission requiring reciprocal compensation for telephone calls to Internet Service Providers violates federal law."

C. Supreme Court's Answer

"We conclude that 28 U.S.C. § 1331 provides a basis for jurisdiction over Verizon's claim that the Commission's order requiring reciprocal compensation for ISP-bound calls is pre-empted by federal law. We also conclude that the doctrine of Ex parte Young permits Verizon's suit to go forward against the state commissioners in their official capacities."

II. CASE SUMMARY

A. Background

"The Telecommunications Act of 1996 . . . created a new telecommunications regime designed to foster competition in local telephone markets. Toward that end, the Act imposed various obligations on incumbent local-exchange carriers (LECs), including a duty to share their networks with competitors. . . .

As required by the Act, the incumbent LEC in Maryland, petitioner Verizon Maryland Inc., formerly known as Bell Atlantic Maryland, Inc., negotiated an interconnection agreement with competitors, including MFS Intelenet of Maryland, later acquired by respondent MCI WorldCom, Inc. The Maryland Public Service Commission (Commission) approved the agreement. Six months later, Verizon informed WorldCom that it would no longer pay reciprocal compensation for telephone calls made by Verizon's customers to the local access numbers of Internet Service Providers (ISPs), claiming that ISP traffic was not 'local traffic' subject to the reciprocal compensation agreement because ISPs connect customers to distant Web sites. WorldCom disputed Verizon's claim and filed a complaint with the Commission. The Commission found in favor of WorldCom, ordering Verizon 'to timely forward all future interconnection payments owed [WorldCom] for telephone calls placed to an ISP' and to pay WorldCom any reciprocal compensation that it had withheld pending resolution of the dispute. Verizon appealed to a Maryland state court, which affirmed the order.

Subsequently, the Federal Communications Commission (FCC) issued a ruling—later vacated by the Court of Appeals for the District of Columbia Circuit . . . which categorized ISP-bound calls as nonlocal for purposes of reciprocal compensation but concluded that, absent a federal compensation mechanism for those calls, state commissions could construe interconnection agreements as requiring reciprocal compensation. Verizon filed a new complaint with the Commission, arguing that the FCC ruling established that Verizon was no longer required to provide reciprocal compensation for ISP traffic. In a 3–to–2 decision, the Commission rejected this contention, concluding that, as a matter of state contract law, WorldCom and Verizon had agreed to treat ISP-bound calls as local traffic subject to reciprocal compensation.

Verizon filed an action in the United States District Court for the District of Maryland . . . . In its complaint, Verizon sought declaratory and injunctive relief from the Commission's order, alleging that the determination that Verizon must pay reciprocal compensation to WorldCom for ISP traffic violated the 1996 Act and the FCC ruling.

The District Court dismissed the action, and a divided panel of the Court of Appeals for the Fourth Circuit affirmed."

The Supreme Court granted certiorari to review the case.

B. Counsel of Record

ACLU Side (Petitioner / Appellant): Mark L. Evans argued the cause for appellant Verizon Maryland Inc. With him on the briefs were Michael K. Kellogg, Sean A. Lev, Aaron M. Panner, William P. Barr, Mark J. Mathis, Michael D. Lowe, and David A. Hill. Barbara McDowell argued the cause for the United States. With her on the briefs were Solicitor General Olson, Acting Assistant Attorney General Katsas, Deputy Solicitor General Wallace, Mark B. Stern, Charles W. Scarborough, and John A. Rogovin

Opposing Side (Respondent / Appellee): Susan Stevens Miller argued the cause for appellee Public Service Commission of Maryland. Paul
M. Smith, William M. Hohengarten, Michael B. DeSanctis, Darryl M. Bradford, John J. Hamill, Thomas F. O'Neil III, William Single IV, and Brian J. Leske filed briefs for appellee MCI WorldCom, Inc., et al.

III. AMICI CURIAE

ACLU Side (Petitioner / Appellant)

Brief of amici curiae filed on behalf of the NOW Legal Defense and Education Fund, American Civil Liberties Union Foundation, National Asian Pacific American Legal Consortium, National Senior Citizens Law Center, National Women's Law Center, and People for the American Way Foundation by Lesley Szanto Friedman, Aidan Synnott,

Patricia E. Ronan, Martha F. Davis, Isabelle Katz Pinzler, Wendy R. Weiser, Steven R. Shapiro, Karen K. Narasaki, Vincent A. Eng, Herbert Semmel, Marcia D. Greenberger, Dina R. Lassow, and Elliot M. Mincberg.

Opposing Side (Respondent / Appellee)

Brief of amici curiae filed on behalf of the State of Illinois by James E. Ryan, Attorney General, Joel D. Bertocchi, Solicitor General, A. Benjamin Goldgar and Michael P. Doyle, Assistant Attorneys General, Myra L. Karegianes, John P. Kelliher, and Thomas R. Stanton.

Brief of amici curiae filed on behalf of the Virginia State Corporation Commission by William H. Chambliss.

Brief of amici curiae filed on behalf of the Pennsylvania Public Utility Commission by Maryanne Reynolds Martin, Bohdan R. Pankiw, and Robert J. Longwell.

IV. THE SUPREME COURT'S DECISION

"WorldCom, Verizon, and the United States contend that 47 U.S.C. § 252(e)(6) and 28 U.S.C. § 1331 independently grant federal courts subject-matter jurisdiction to determine whether the Commission's order requiring that Verizon pay WorldCom reciprocal compensation for ISP-bound calls violates the 1996 Act. . . .

Verizon alleged in its complaint that the Commission violated the Act and the FCC ruling when it ordered payment of reciprocal compensation for ISP-bound calls. . . . We have no doubt that federal courts have jurisdiction under § 1331 to entertain such a suit. . . .

Here, resolution of Verizon's claim turns on whether the Act, or an FCC ruling issued thereunder, precludes the Commission from ordering payment of reciprocal compensation, and there is no suggestion that Verizon's claim is "immaterial" or "wholly insubstantial and frivolous."

Verizon's claim thus falls within 28 U.S.C. § 1331's general grant of jurisdiction, and contrary to the Fourth Circuit's conclusion, nothing in 47 U.S.C. § 252(e)(6) purports to strip this jurisdiction. . . .

And finally, none of the other provisions of the Act evince any intent to preclude federal review of a commission determination. If anything, they reinforce the conclusion that § 252(e)(6)'s silence on the subject leaves the jurisdictional grant of § 1331 untouched. . . .

Whether the Commission waived its immunity is another question we need not decide, because—as the same parties also argue—even absent waiver, Verizon may proceed against the individual commissioners in their official capacities, pursuant to the doctrine of Ex parte Young, 209 U.S. 123 (1908).

In determining whether the doctrine of Ex parte Young avoids an Eleventh Amendment bar to suit, a court need only conduct a 'straightforward inquiry into whether [the] complaint alleges an ongoing violation of federal law and seeks relief properly characterized as prospective.' . . . As for Verizon's prayer for declaratory relief: That, to be sure, seeks a declaration of the past, as well as the future, ineffectiveness of the Commission's action, so that the past financial liability of private parties may be affected. But no past liability of the State, or of any of its commissioners, is at issue. It does not impose upon the State 'a monetary loss resulting from a past breach of a legal duty on the part of the defendant state officials.' Insofar as the exposure of the State is concerned, the prayer for declaratory relief adds nothing to the prayer for injunction. . . .

Nor does the 1996 Act display any intent to foreclose jurisdiction under Ex parte Young . . . .

We conclude that 28 U.S.C. § 1331 provides a basis for jurisdiction over Verizon's claim that the Commission's order requiring reciprocal compensation for ISP-bound calls is pre-empted by federal law. We also conclude that the doctrine of Ex parte Young permits Verizon's suit to go forward against the state commissioners in their official capacities. We vacate the judgment of the Court of Appeals and remand these cases for further proceedings consistent with this opinion."

V. JUSTICE VOTE

8 Pro ACLU Side vs. 0 Con Opposing Side

ACLU Side (Petitioner / Appellant)

1. Scalia, A. – Wrote majority opinion
2. Stevens, J. – Joined majority opinion
3. Rehnquist, W. – Joined majority opinion
4. Thomas, C. – Joined majority opinion
5. Kennedy, A. – Wrote concurring opinion
6. Souter, D. – Wrote concurring opinion
7. Ginsburg, R. – Joined Souter's concurrence
8. Breyer, S. – Joined Souter's concurrence
9. O'Connor, S – Took no part in the decision

VI. A WIN OR LOSS FOR THE ACLU?

The ACLU filed as amicus curiae urging reversal of the judgment of the Court of Appeals; the Supreme Court vacated and remanded in an 8-0 vote, giving the ACLU an apparent win.

924. Bell v. Cone

(Decided May 28, 2002; 535 U.S. 685)

I. ISSUE

A. Issues Discussed

Criminal procedure, death penalty

B. Legal Question Presented

Whether respondent presented a valid claim for ineffective assistance of counsel during his sentencing hearing.

C. Supreme Court's Answer

"We hold that respondent's claim was governed by Strickland, and that the state court's decision neither was 'contrary to,' nor involved 'an unreasonable application of, clearly established Federal law' under the provisions of 28 U.S.C. § 2254(d)(1)."

II. CASE SUMMARY

A. Background

"In 1982, respondent was convicted of, and sentenced to death for, the murder of an elderly couple, [the Todds,] in Memphis,

Tennessee. The killings culminated a 2-day crime rampage . . . .

The defense conceded that respondent committed most of the acts in question, but sought to prove that he was not guilty by reason of insanity. . . . Rejecting his insanity defense, the jury found him guilty on all charges.

Punishment for the first-degree murder counts was fixed in a separate sentencing hearing that took place the next day and lasted about three hours. Under then-applicable Tennessee law, a death sentence was required if the jury found unanimously that the State proved beyond a reasonable doubt the existence of at least one statutory aggravating circumstance that was not outweighed by any mitigating circumstance. . . .

The jury found in both murder cases four aggravating factors and no mitigating circumstances substantial enough to outweigh them. The Tennessee Supreme Court affirmed respondent's convictions and sentence on appeal, and [the U.S. Supreme Court] denied certiorari.

Respondent then petitioned for state postconviction relief, contending that his counsel rendered ineffective assistance during the sentencing phase by failing to present mitigating evidence and by waiving final argument. [T]he Tennessee Criminal Court rejected this contention. The Tennessee Court of Criminal Appeals affirmed. . . . Describing counsel's representation as 'very conscientious,' the court concluded that his performance was within the permissible range of competency, citing Baxter v. Rose, 523 S.W.2d 930 (Tenn.1975), a decision the Tennessee Supreme Court deems to have announced the same attorney performance standard as Strickland v. Washington, 466 U.S. 668 (1984). . . . The Tennessee Supreme Court denied respondent permission to appeal, and [the U.S. Supreme Court] denied further review.

In 1997, after his second application for state postconviction relief was dismissed, respondent sought a federal writ of habeas corpus under 28 U.S.C. § 2254 . . . . His petition alleged numerous grounds for relief including ineffective assistance at the sentencing phase. The District Court ruled that respondent did not meet § 2254(d)'s requirements and denied the petition.

The Court of Appeals affirmed the refusal to issue a writ with respect to respondent's conviction, but reversed with respect to his sentence."

The Supreme Court granted certiorari to review the case.

B. Counsel of Record

ACLU Side (Respondent / Appellee): Robert L. Hutton, by appointment of the Court, argued the cause for appellee.

Opposing Side (Petitioner / Appellant): Michael E. Moore, Solicitor General of Tennessee, argued the cause for appellant. With him on the briefs were Gordon W. Smith, Associate Solicitor General, and Jennifer L. Smith, Assistant Attorney General.

Lisa Schiavo Blatt argued the cause for the United States as amicus curiae.

III. AMICI CURIAE

ACLU Side (Respondent / Appellee)

Brief of amici curiae filed on behalf of the American Civil Liberties Union and the ACLU of Tennessee by Larry W. Yackle and Steven R. Shapiro.

Brief of amici curiae filed on behalf of the National Association of Criminal Defense Lawyers by Walter Dellinger, Pamela Harris, and David M. Porter.

Opposing Side (Petitioner / Appellant)

Brief of amici curiae filed on behalf of the United States by Lisa Schiavo Blatt, Solicitor General Olson, Assistant Attorney General Chertoff, and Deputy Solicitor General Dreeben.

Brief of amici curiae filed on behalf of the State of Ohio et al. by Betty D. Montgomery, Attorney General of Ohio, David M. Gormley, State Solicitor, and Matthew Hellman, Assistant Attorney General, and by the Attorneys General for their respective jurisdictions as follows: Bill Pryor of Alabama, Janet Napolitano of Arizona, Bill Lockyer of California, M. Jane Brady of Delaware, Robert A. Butterworth of Florida, Steve Carter of Indiana, Richard P. Ieyoub of Louisiana, J. Joseph Curran, Jr., of Maryland, Jeremiah W. (Jay) Nixon of Missouri, Mike McGrath of Montana, Don Stenberg of Nebraska, Frankie Sue Del Papa of Nevada, David Samson of New Jersey, W. A. Drew Edmondson of Oklahoma, Hardy Myers of Oregon, Mark Barnett of South Dakota, John Cornyn of Texas, Mark L. Shurtleff of Utah, Iver A. Stridiron of the Virgin Islands, Jerry Kilgore of Virginia, Christine O. Gregoire of Washington, and Hoke MacMillan of Wyoming.

Brief of amici curiae filed on behalf of the Criminal Justice Legal Foundation by Kent S. Scheidegger.

IV. THE SUPREME COURT'S DECISION

"The Antiterrorism and Effective Death Penalty Act of 1996 modified a federal habeas court's role in reviewing state prisoner applications in order to prevent federal habeas 'retrials' and to ensure that state-court convictions are given effect to the extent possible under law. . . .

Petitioner contends that the Court of Appeals exceeded its statutory authority to grant relief under § 2254(d)(1) because the decision of the Tennessee courts was neither contrary to nor an unreasonable application of the clearly established law of Strickland. Respondent counters that he is entitled to relief under § 2254(d)(1)'s 'contrary to' clause because the state court applied the wrong legal rule. In his view, Cronic, not Strickland, governs the analysis of his claim that his counsel rendered ineffective assistance at the sentencing hearing. We address this issue first.

In Strickland, which was decided the same day as Cronic, we announced a two-part test for evaluating claims that a defendant's counsel performed so incompetently in his or her representation of a defendant that the defendant's sentence or conviction should be reversed. We reasoned that there would be a sufficient indication that counsel's assistance was defective . . . if the defendant proved two things: first, that counsel's 'representation fell below an objective standard of reasonableness,' and second, that 'there is a reasonable probability that, but for counsel's unprofessional errors, the result of the proceeding would have been different.' . . .

In Cronic, we . . . determined that the court had erred and remanded to allow the claim to be considered under Strickland's test. In the course of deciding this question, we identified three situations implicating the right to counsel that involved circumstances 'so likely to prejudice the accused that the cost of litigating their effect in a particular case is unjustified.' . . .

Second, we posited that a . . . presumption [of an unfair trial] was warranted if 'counsel entirely fails to subject the prosecution's case to meaningful adversarial testing.' . . .

Respondent argues that his claim fits within the second exception identified in Cronic . . . . We disagree. . . .

The aspects of counsel's performance challenged by respondent—the failure to adduce mitigating evidence and the waiver of closing argument—are plainly of the same ilk as other specific attorney errors we have held subject to Strickland's performance and prejudice components. . . .

We hold, therefore, that the state court correctly identified the principles announced in Strickland as those governing the analysis of respondent's claim. Consequently, we find no merit in respondent's contention that the state court's adjudication was contrary to our clearly established law. . . .

The remaining issue, then, is whether respondent can obtain relief on the ground that the state court's adjudication of his claim involved an 'unreasonable application' of Strickland.. . .

For respondent to succeed, however, he must do more than show that he would have satisfied Strickland's test if his claim were being analyzed in the first instance, because under § 2254(d)(1), it is not enough to convince a federal habeas court that, in its independent judgment, the state-court decision applied Strickland incorrectly. Rather, he must show that the Tennessee Court of Appeals applied Strickland to the facts of his case in an objectively unreasonable manner. This, we conclude, he cannot do. . . .

We cautioned in Strickland that a court must indulge a 'strong presumption' that counsel's conduct falls within the wide range of reasonable professional assistance because it is all too easy to conclude that a particular act or omission of counsel was unreasonable in the harsh light of hindsight. Given the choices available to respondent's counsel and the reasons we have identified, we cannot say that the state court's application of Strickland's attorney-performance standard was objectively unreasonable. The judgment of the Court of Appeals is therefore reversed, and the case is remanded for further proceedings consistent with this opinion."

V. JUSTICE VOTE

1 Pro ACLU Side vs. 8 Con Opposing Side

ACLU Side (Respondent / Appellee)

1. Stevens, J. – Wrote dissenting opinion

Opposing Side (Petitioner / Appellant)

1. Rehnquist, W. – Wrote majority opinion
2. Thomas, C. – Joined majority opinion
3. Ginsburg, R. – Joined majority opinion
4. Souter, D. – Joined majority opinion
5. O'Connor, S. – Joined majority opinion
6. Breyer, S. – Joined majority opinion
7. Scalia, A. – Joined majority opinion
8. Kennedy, A. – Joined majority opinion

VI. A WIN OR LOSS FOR THE ACLU?

The ACLU filed as amicus curiae, urging affirmance; the Supreme Court reversed the Court of Appeals' decision by an 8-1 vote, giving the ACLU an apparent loss.

925. Chevron U.S.A., Inc. v. Echazabal

(Decided June 10, 2002; 536 U.S. 73)

I. ISSUE

A. Issues Discussed

Regulation

B. Legal Question Presented

"A regulation of the Equal Employment Opportunity Commission authorizes refusal to hire an individual because his performance on the job would endanger his own health, owing to a disability. The question in this case is whether the Americans with Disabilities Act of 1990 permits the regulation."

C. Supreme Court's Answer

The Americans with Disabilities Act of 1990 permits this Equal Employment Opportunity Commission regulation authorizing "refusal to hire an individual because his performance on the job would endanger his own health, owing to a disability."

II. CASE SUMMARY

A. Background

"Beginning in 1972, respondent Mario Echazabal worked for independent contractors at an oil refinery owned by petitioner Chevron U.S.A. Inc. Twice he applied for a job directly with Chevron, which offered to hire him if he could pass the company's physical examination. Each time, the exam showed liver abnormality or damage, the cause eventually being identified as Hepatitis C, which Chevron's doctors said would be aggravated by continued exposure to toxins at Chevron's refinery. In each instance, the company withdrew the offer, and the second time it asked the contractor employing Echazabal either to reassign him to a job without exposure to harmful chemicals or to remove him from the refinery altogether. The contractor laid him off in early 1996.

Echazabal filed suit, ultimately removed to federal court, claiming, among other things, that Chevron violated the Americans with Disabilities Act (ADA or Act) in refusing to hire him, or even to let him continue working in the plant, because of a disability, his liver condition. [T]he District Court granted summary judgment for Chevron. . . .

On appeal, the Ninth Circuit asked for briefs on a threshold question not raised before, whether the EEOC's regulation recognizing a threat-to-self defense, exceeded the scope of permissible rulemaking under the ADA. The Circuit held that it did and reversed the summary judgment."

The Supreme Court granted certiorari to review the case.

B. Counsel of Record

ACLU Side (Respondent / Appellee): Samuel R. Bagenstos argued the cause for appellee. With him on the brief were Larry Minsky and Chai R. Feldblum.

Opposing Side (Petitioner / Appellant): Stephen M. Shapiro argued the cause for appellant. With him on the briefs were James D. Holzhauer, Robert P. Davis, and Evan M. Tager.

Lisa Schiavo Blatt argued the cause for the United States et al. as amici curiae.

III. AMICI CURIAE

ACLU Side (Respondent / Appellee)

Brief of amici curiae filed on behalf of the American Civil Liberties Union, Equal Rights Advocates, the National Women's Law Center, the Northwest Women's Law Center, NOW Legal Defense and Education Fund, the Puerto Rican Legal Defense and Education Fund, Women Employed, and the Women's Law Project by Matthew A. Coles, James D. Esseks, Steven R. Shapiro, Lenora M. Lapidus, Emily J. Martin, and Romana Mancini.

Brief of amici curiae filed on behalf of the American Association of People with Disabilities et al. by John Townsend Rich, Arlene Mayerson, Daniel B. Kohrman, Ira A. Burnim, and Jennifer Mathis.

Brief of amici curiae filed on behalf of the American Public Health Association et al. by Catherine A. Hanssens and Jon W. Davidson.

Brief of amici curiae filed on behalf of the National Council on Disability by Peter Blanck, Diane Kutzko, Mark L. Zaiger, Douglas R. Oelschlaeger, and Sarah J. Gayer.

Brief of amici curiae filed on behalf of the National Employment Lawyers Association by Gary Phelan.

Opposing Side (Petitioner / Appellant)

Brief of amici curiae filed on behalf of the United States et al., by Lisa Schiavo Blatt, Solicitor General Olson, Deputy Solicitor General Clement, Assistant Attorney General McCallum, Marleigh D. Dover, Matthew Collette, Phillip B. Sklover, Carolyn L. Wheeler, and Robert J. Gregory.

Brief of amici curiae filed on behalf of the American College of Occupational and Environmental Medicine et al. by Craig E. Stewart.

Brief of amici curiae filed on behalf of the Chamber of Commerce of the United States et al. by Roy T. Englert, Jr., Kathryn S. Zecca, Stephen A. Bokat, and Robin S. Conrad.

Brief of amici curiae filed on behalf of the Employers Group by Fred W. Alvarez and Christine A. Kendrick.

Brief of amici curiae filed on behalf of the Equal Employment Advisory Council et al. by Ann Elizabeth Reesman, Jan S. Amundson, and Quentin Riegel.

Brief of amici curiae filed on behalf of the Pacific Legal Foundation et al. by Anne M. Hayes and M. Reed Hopper.

Brief of amici curiae filed on behalf of the Society for Human Resource Management by Peter J. Petesch and John E. Duvall.

IV. THE SUPREME COURT'S DECISION

"Section 102 of the ADA prohibits 'discriminat[ion] against a qualified individual with a disability because of the disability . . . in regard to' a number of actions by an employer, including 'hiring.' The statutory definition of 'discriminat[ion]' covers a number of things an employer might do to block a disabled person from advancing in the workplace, such as 'using qualification standards . . . that screen out or tend to screen out an individual with a disability.' By that same definition, as well as by separate provision, the Act creates an affirmative defense for action under a qualification standard 'shown to be job-related for the position in question and . . . consistent with business necessity.' Such a standard may include 'a requirement that an individual shall not pose a direct threat to the health or safety of other individuals in the workplace,' if the individual cannot perform the job safely with reasonable accommodation. By regulation, the EEOC carries the defense one step further, in allowing an employer to screen out a potential worker with a disability not only for risks that he would pose to others in the workplace but for risks on the job to his own health or safety as well . . . .

Chevron relies on the regulation here, since it says a job in the refinery would pose a 'direct threat' to Echazabal's health. . . .

As for the textual bar to any agency action as a matter of law, Echazabal says that Chevron loses on the threshold question whether the statute leaves a gap for the EEOC to fill. . . .

The argument follows . . . the interpretive canon, expressio unius est exclusio alterius, 'expressing one item of [an] associated group or series excludes another left unmentioned.' The rule is fine when it applies, but this case joins some others in showing when it does not. . . .

Expressio unius just fails to work here.

Since Congress has not spoken exhaustively on threats to a worker's own health, the agency regulation can claim adherence under the rule in Chevron, 467 U.S., at 843, so long as it makes sense of the statutory defense for qualification standards that are 'job-related and consistent with business necessity.' Chevron's reasons for calling the regulation reasonable are unsurprising: moral concerns aside, it wishes to avoid time lost to sickness, excessive turnover from medical retirement or death, litigation under state tort law, and the risk of violating the national Occupational Safety and Health Act of 1970. Although Echazabal claims that none of these reasons is legitimate, focusing on the concern with OSHA will be enough to show that the regulation is entitled to survive.

Echazabal points out that there is no known instance of OSHA enforcement, or even threatened enforcement, against an employer who relied on the ADA to hire a worker willing to accept a risk to himself from his disability on the job. In Echazabal's mind, this shows that invoking OSHA policy and possible OSHA liability is just a red herring to excuse covert discrimination. But there is another side to this. The text of OSHA itself says its point is 'to assure so far as possible every working man and woman in the Nation safe and healthful working conditions' . . . .

Nor can the EEOC's resolution be fairly called unreasonable as allowing the kind of workplace paternalism the ADA was meant to outlaw. . . .

Finally, our conclusions that some regulation is permissible and this one is reasonable are not open to Echazabal's objection that they reduce the direct threat provision to 'surplusage.' The mere fact that a threat-to-self defense reasonably falls within the general 'job related' and 'business necessity' standard does not mean that Congress accomplished nothing with its explicit provision for a defense based on threats to others. . . .

Accordingly, we reverse the judgment of the Court of Appeals and remand the case for proceedings consistent with this opinion."

V. JUSTICE VOTE

0 Pro ACLU Side vs. 9 Con Opposing Side

ACLU Side (Respondent / Appellee)

1. Souter, D. – Wrote majority opinion
2. Thomas, C. – Joined majority opinion
3. Ginsburg, R. – Joined majority opinion
4. O'Connor, S. – Joined majority opinion
5. Stevens, J. – Joined majority opinion
6. Breyer, S. – Joined majority opinion
7. Scalia, A. – Joined majority opinion
8. Kennedy, A. – Joined majority opinion
9. Rehnquist, W. – Joined majority opinion

VI. A WIN OR LOSS FOR THE ACLU?

The ACLU filed as amicus curiae, urging affirmance; the Supreme Court reversed the Court of Appeals' decision by a 9-0 vote, giving the ACLU an apparent loss.

926. Watchtower Bible & Tract Soc'y of New York, Inc. v. Village of Stratton

(Decided June 17, 2002; 536 U.S. 150)

I. ISSUE

A. Issues Discussed

1st Amendment, press, speech, association, religion

B. Legal Question Presented

"'Does a municipal ordinance that requires one to obtain a permit prior to engaging in the door-to-door advocacy of a political cause and to display upon demand the permit, which contains one's name, violate the First Amendment protection accorded to anonymous pamphleteering or discourse?'"

C. Supreme Court's Answer

The challenged ordinance violates the First Amendment and is invalid.

II. CASE SUMMARY

A. Background

"Petitioners contend that a village ordinance making it a misdemeanor to engage in door-to-door advocacy without first registering with the mayor and receiving a permit violates the First Amendment. . . .

Petitioners brought this action against the Village and its mayor in the United States District Court for the Southern District of Ohio, seeking an injunction against the enforcement of several sections of Ordinance No. 1998-5 regulating uninvited peddling and solicitation on private property in the Village. Petitioners' complaint alleged that the ordinance violated several constitutional rights, including the free exercise of religion, free speech, and the freedom of the press. . . .

Section 116.01 prohibits 'canvassers' and others from 'going in and upon' private residential property for the purpose of promoting any 'cause' without first having obtained a permit pursuant to § 116.03. . . . The ordinance sets forth grounds for the denial or revocation of a permit, but the record before us does not show that any application has been denied or that any permit has been revoked. Petitioners did not apply for a permit. . . .

Although Jehovah's Witnesses do not consider themselves to be 'solicitors' because they make no charge for their literature or their teaching, leaders of the church testified at trial that they would honor 'no solicitation' signs in the Village. They also explained at trial that they did not apply for a permit because they derive their authority to preach from Scripture. 'For us to seek a permit from a municipality to preach we feel would almost be an insult to God.' . . .

The District Court upheld most provisions of the ordinance as valid, content-neutral regulations that did not infringe on petitioners' First Amendment rights. The court did, however, require the Village to accept narrowing constructions of three provisions. . . .

The Court of Appeals for the Sixth Circuit affirmed."

The Supreme Court granted certiorari to review the case.

B. Counsel of Record:

ACLU Side (Petitioner / Appellant): Paul D. Polidoro argued the cause for appellants. With him on the briefs were Philip Brumley, Richard D. Moake, and Donald T. Ridley.

Opposing Side (Respondent / Appellee): Abraham Cantor argued the cause and filed a brief for appellees.

David M. Gormley, State Solicitor of Ohio, argued the cause for the State of Ohio et al. as amici curiae in support of appellees.

III. AMICI CURIAE

ACLU Side (Petitioner / Appellant)

Brief of amici curiae filed on behalf of Commonwealth of the Northern Mariana Islands by Herbert D. Soll, Attorney General, David Collins, and Karen M. Klaver.

Brief of amici curiae filed on behalf of the Center for Individual Freedom by Eric S. Jaffe.

Brief of amici curiae filed on behalf of the Church of Jesus Christ of Latter-day Saints by Von G. Keetch.

Brief of amici curiae filed on behalf of the Electronic Privacy Information Center et al. by Marc Rotenberg, Steven R. Shapiro, and Raymond Vasvari.

Brief of amici curiae filed on behalf of RealCampaignReform.org, Inc., et al. by William J. Olson, John S. Miles, and Herbert W. Titus.

Brief of amici curiae filed on behalf of Independent Baptist Churches of America by Thomas W. King III.

Brief of amici curiae filed on behalf of the Brennan Center for Justice by Burt Neuborne, Deborah Goldberg, and Richard L. Hasen in support of neither party.

Opposing Side (Respondent / Appellee)

Brief of amici curiae filed on behalf of the State of Ohio et al. by David M. Gormley, State Solicitor of Ohio, Betty D. Montgomery, Attorney General of Ohio, Elise W. Porter and Kirk A. Lindsey, Assistant Solicitors, and the Attorneys General for their respective States as follows: Richard Blumenthal of Connecticut, Steve Carter of Indiana, Thomas J. Miller of Iowa, Richard P. Ieyoub of Louisiana, J. Joseph Curran, Jr., of Maryland, Thomas Reilly of Massachusetts, Frankie Sue Del Papa of Nevada, W. A. Drew Edmondson of Oklahoma, and Hoke MacMillan of Wyoming.

Brief of amici curiae filed on behalf of the Ohio Municipal League by Barry M. Byron and John E. Gotherman.

Brief of amici curiae filed on behalf of the International Municipal Lawyers Association et al. by Richard Ruda and James I. Crowley.

IV. THE SUPREME COURT'S DECISION

"For over 50 years, the Court has invalidated restrictions on door-to-door canvassing and pamphleteering. It is more than historical accident that most of these cases involved First Amendment challenges brought by Jehovah's Witnesses, because door-to-door canvassing is mandated by their religion. . . .

The Village argues that three interests are served by its ordinance: the prevention of fraud, the prevention of crime, and the protection of residents' privacy. We have no difficulty concluding, in light of our precedent, that these are important interests that the Village may seek to safeguard through some form of regulation of solicitation activity. We must also look, however, to the amount of speech covered by the ordinance and whether there is an appropriate balance between the affected speech and the governmental interests that the ordinance purports to serve.

The text of the Village's ordinance prohibits 'canvassers' from going on private property for the purpose of explaining or promoting any 'cause,' unless they receive a permit and the residents visited have not opted for a 'no solicitation' sign. Had this provision been construed to apply only to commercial activities and the solicitation of funds, arguably the ordinance would have been tailored to the Village's interest in protecting the privacy of its residents and preventing fraud. Yet, even though the Village has explained that the ordinance was adopted to serve those interests, it has never contended that it should be so narrowly interpreted. . . .

The mere fact that the ordinance covers so much speech raises constitutional concerns. It is offensive-not only to the values protected by the First Amendment, but to the very notion of a free society-that in the context of everyday public discourse a citizen must first inform the government of her desire to speak to her neighbors and then obtain a permit to do so. Even if the issuance of permits by the mayor's office is a ministerial task that is performed promptly and at no cost to the applicant, a law requiring a permit to engage in such speech constitutes a dramatic departure from our national heritage and constitutional tradition. Three obvious examples illustrate the pernicious effect of such a permit requirement.

First, as our cases involving distribution of unsigned handbills demonstrate, there are a significant number of persons who support causes anonymously. . . . The requirement that a canvasser must be identified in a permit application filed in the mayor's office and available for public inspection necessarily results in a surrender of that anonymity. . . .

Second, requiring a permit as a prior condition on the exercise of the right to speak imposes an objective burden on some speech of citizens holding religious or patriotic views. As our World War II-era cases dramatically demonstrate, there are a significant number of persons whose religious scruples will prevent them from applying for such a license. . . .

Third, there is a significant amount of spontaneous speech that is effectively banned by the ordinance. . . .

The breadth and unprecedented nature of this regulation does not alone render the ordinance invalid. Also central to our conclusion that the ordinance does not pass First Amendment scrutiny is that it is not tailored to the Village's stated interests. Even if the interest in preventing fraud could adequately support the ordinance insofar as it applies to commercial transactions and the solicitation of funds, that interest provides no support for its application to petitioners, to political campaigns, or to enlisting support for unpopular causes. The Village, however, argues that the ordinance is nonetheless valid because it serves the two additional interests of protecting the privacy of the resident and the prevention of crime.

With respect to the former, it seems clear that § 107 of the ordinance, which provides for the posting of 'No Solicitation' signs and which is not challenged in this case, coupled with the resident's unquestioned right to refuse to engage in conversation with unwelcome visitors, provides ample protection for the unwilling listener. . . .

With respect to the latter, it seems unlikely that the absence of a permit would preclude criminals from knocking on doors and engaging in conversations not covered by the ordinance. . . .

The rhetoric used in the World War II-era opinions that repeatedly saved petitioners' coreligionists from petty prosecutions reflected the Court's evaluation of the First Amendment freedoms that are implicated in this case. The value judgment that then motivated a united democratic people fighting to defend those very freedoms from totalitarian attack is unchanged. It motivates our decision today.

The judgment of the Court of Appeals is reversed, and the case is remanded for further proceedings consistent with this opinion."

V. JUSTICE VOTE

8 Pro ACLU Side vs. 1 Con Opposing Side

ACLU Side (Petitioner / Appellant)

1. Stevens, J. – Wrote majority opinion
2. O'Connor, S. – Joined majority opinion
3. Souter, D. – Joined Breyer's concurrence
4. Ginsburg, R. – Joined Breyer's concurrence
5. Breyer, S. – Wrote concurring opinion

6. Scalia, A. – Wrote concurring opinion
7. Kennedy, A. – Joined majority opinion
8. Thomas, C. – Joined Scalia's concurrence

Opposing Side (Respondent / Appellee)

1. Rehnquist, W. – Wrote dissenting opinion

VI. A WIN OR LOSS FOR THE ACLU?

The ACLU filed as amicus curiae urging reversal of the judgment of the Court of Appeals; the Supreme Court vacated and remanded in an 8-1 vote, giving the ACLU an apparent win.

927. Gonzaga Univ. v. Doe

(Decided June 20, 2002; 536 U.S. 273)

I. ISSUE

A. Issues Discussed

Federal, civil rights

B. Legal Question Presented

"[W]hether a student may sue a private university for damages under . . . 42 U.S.C. § 1983, to enforce provisions of the Family Educational Rights and Privacy Act of 1974 . . . which prohibit the federal funding of educational institutions that have a policy or practice of releasing education records to unauthorized persons."

C. Supreme Court's Answer

"We hold such an action foreclosed because the relevant provisions of FERPA create no personal rights to enforce under 42 U.S.C. § 1983."

II. CASE SUMMARY

A. Background

"Respondent John Doe is a former undergraduate in the School of Education at Gonzaga University, a private university in Spokane, Washington. He planned to graduate and teach at a Washington public elementary school. Washington at the time required all of its new teachers to obtain an affidavit of good moral character from a dean of their graduating college or university. In October 1993, Roberta League, Gonzaga's 'teacher certification specialist,' overheard one student tell another that respondent engaged in acts of sexual misconduct against Jane Doe, a female undergraduate. League launched an investigation and contacted the state agency responsible for teacher certification, identifying respondent by name and discussing the allegations against him. Respondent did not learn of the investigation, or that information about him had been disclosed, until March 1994, when he was told by League and others that he would not receive the affidavit required for certification as a Washington schoolteacher.

Respondent then sued Gonzaga and League (petitioners) in state court. He alleged violations of Washington tort and contract law, as well as a pendent violation of § 1983 for the release of personal information to an 'unauthorized person' in violation of FERPA. A jury found for respondent on all counts, awarding him $1,155,000, including $150,000 in compensatory damages and $300,000 in punitive damages on the FERPA claim.

The Washington Court of Appeals reversed in relevant part, concluding that FERPA does not create individual rights and thus cannot be enforced under § 1983. The Washington Supreme Court reversed that decision, and ordered the FERPA damages reinstated"

The Supreme Court granted certiorari to review the case.

B. Counsel of Record:

ACLU Side (Respondent / Appellee): Beth S. Brinkmann argued the cause for appellee. With her on the brief were Drew S. Days III and Lois K. Perrin.

Opposing Side (Petitioner / Appellant): John G. Roberts, Jr., argued the cause for appellants. With him on the briefs were Martin Michaelson, Charles K. Wiggins, and Kenneth W. Masters.

Patricia A. Millett argued the cause for the United States as amicus curiae.

III. AMICI CURIAE

ACLU Side (Respondent / Appellee)

Brief of amici curiae filed on behalf of the American Civil Liberties Union and the ACLU of Washington by Aaron H. Caplan, Jordan Gross, and Steven R. Shapiro.

Opposing Side (Petitioner / Appellant)

Brief of amici curiae filed on behalf of the United States by Patricia A. Millett, Solicitor General Olson, Assistant Attorney General McCallum, Deputy Solicitor General Kneedler, Mark B. Stern, Alisa B. Klein, and Anne Murphy.

Brief of amici curiae filed on behalf of the State of Illinois et al. by James E. Ryan, Attorney General of Illinois, Joel D. Bertocchi, Solicitor General, Michael P. Doyle, Assistant Attorney General, and Dan Schweitzer, and by the Attorneys General for their respective States as follows: Bill Pryor of Alabama, M. Jane Brady of Delaware, Robert A. Butterworth of Florida, Earl I. Anzai of Hawaii, J. Joseph Curran, Jr., of Maryland, Mike Moore of Mississippi, Don Stenberg of Nebraska, Frankie Sue Del Papa of Nevada, David Samson of New Jersey, Betty D. Montgomery of Ohio, Hardy Myers of Oregon, Mark L. Shurtleff of Utah, Christine O. Gregoire of Washington, and Hoke MacMillan of Wyoming.

Brief of amici curiae filed on behalf of the American Association of Community Colleges et al. by Philip Burling, John M. Stevens, and Sheldon E. Steinbach.

Brief of amici curiae filed on behalf of the Reporters Committee for Freedom of the Press et al. by Gregg P. Leslie, Lucy A. Dalglish, Bruce W. Sanford, and S. Mark Goodman.

IV. THE SUPREME COURT'S DECISION

"Congress enacted FERPA under its spending power to condition the receipt of federal funds on certain requirements relating to the access and disclosure of student educational records. . . .

Respondent contends that this statutory regime confers upon any student enrolled at a covered school or institution a federal right, enforceable in suits for damages under § 1983, not to have 'education records' disclosed to unauthorized persons without the student's express written consent. But we have never before held, and decline to do so here, that spending legislation drafted in terms resembling those of FERPA can confer enforceable rights. . . .

We now reject the notion that our cases permit anything short of an unambiguously conferred right to support a cause of action brought under § 1983. Section 1983 provides a remedy only for the deprivation of 'rights, privileges, or immunities secured by the Constitution and laws' of the United States. Accordingly, it is rights, not the broader or vaguer 'benefits' or 'interests,' that may be enforced under the authority of that section. . . .

We have recognized that whether a statutory violation may be enforced through § 1983 'is a different inquiry than that involved in determining whether a private right of action can be implied from a particular statute.' But the inquiries overlap in one meaningful respect—in either case we must first determine whether Congress intended to create a federal right. . . .

Plaintiffs suing under § 1983 do not have the burden of showing an intent to create a private remedy because § 1983 generally supplies a remedy for the vindication of rights secured by federal statutes. . . . But the initial inquiry—determining whether a statute confers any right at all—is no different from the initial inquiry in an implied right of action case, the express purpose of which is to determine whether or not a statute 'confer[s] rights on a particular class of persons.' . . .

A court's role in discerning whether personal rights exist in the § 1983 context should therefore not differ from its role in discerning whether personal rights exist in the implied right of action context. . . .

With this principle in mind, there is no question that FERPA's nondisclosure provisions fail to confer enforceable rights. To begin with, the provisions entirely lack the sort of 'rights-creating' language critical to showing the requisite congressional intent to create new rights. . . .

FERPA's nondisclosure provisions further speak only in terms of institutional policy and practice, not individual instances of disclosure. . . .

Our conclusion that FERPA's nondisclosure provisions fail to confer enforceable rights is buttressed by the mechanism that Congress chose to provide for enforcing those provisions. . . . Pursuant to these provisions, the Secretary created the Family Policy Compliance Office (FPCO) 'to act as the Review Board required under the Act [and] to enforce the Act with respect to all applicable programs.' The FPCO permits students and parents who suspect a violation of the Act to file individual written complaints. . . .

In sum, if Congress wishes to create new rights enforceable under § 1983, it must do so in clear and unambiguous terms—no less and no more than what is required for Congress to create new rights enforceable under an implied private right of action. FERPA's nondisclosure provisions contain no rights-creating language, they have an aggregate, not individual, focus, and they serve primarily to direct the Secretary of Education's distribution of public funds to educational institutions. They therefore create no rights enforceable under § 1983. Accordingly, the judgment of the Supreme Court of Washington is reversed, and the case is remanded for further proceedings not inconsistent with this opinion."

V. JUSTICE VOTE

2 Pro ACLU Side vs. 7 Con Opposing Side

ACLU Side (Respondent / Appellee)

1. Stevens, J. – Wrote dissenting opinion
2. Ginsburg, R. – Joined Stevens' dissent

Opposing Side (Petitioner / Appellant)

1. Rehnquist, W. – Wrote majority opinion
2. Thomas, C. – Joined majority opinion
3. Scalia, A. – Joined majority opinion
4. O'Connor, S. – Joined majority opinion
5. Kennedy, A. – Joined majority opinion
6. Breyer, S. – Wrote concurring opinion
7. Souter, D. – Joined Breyer's concurrence

VI. A WIN OR LOSS FOR THE ACLU?

The ACLU filed as amicus curiae urging affirmance; the Supreme Court reversed the Washington Supreme Court's decision by a 7-2 vote, giving the ACLU an apparent loss.

928. Atkins v. Virginia

(Decided June 20, 2002; 536 U.S. 304)

I. ISSUE

A. Issues Discussed

8th Amendment, death penalty

B. Legal Question Presented

Whether the death penalty for "mentally retarded persons" is "cruel and unusual punishment" that is "prohibited by the Eighth Amendment to the Federal Constitution."

C. Supreme Court's Answer

"Construing and applying the Eighth Amendment in the light of our 'evolving standards of decency,' we . . . conclude that [the death penalty] is excessive and that the Constitution 'places a substantive restriction on the State's power to take the life' of a mentally retarded offender."

II. CASE SUMMARY

A. Background

"Petitioner, Daryl Renard Atkins, was convicted of abduction, armed robbery, and capital murder, and sentenced to death. . . .

In the penalty phase, the defense relied on one witness, Dr. Evan Nelson, a forensic psychologist who had evaluated Atkins before trial and concluded that he was 'mildly mentally retarded.' . . .

The jury sentenced Atkins to death, but the Virginia Supreme Court ordered a second sentencing hearing because the trial court had used a misleading verdict form. At the resentencing, Dr. Nelson again testified. The State presented an expert rebuttal witness, Dr. Stanton Samenow, who expressed the opinion that Atkins was not mentally retarded, but rather was of 'average intelligence, at least,' and diagnosable as having antisocial personality disorder. The jury again sentenced Atkins to death.

The Supreme Court of Virginia affirmed the imposition of the death penalty. . . .

Justice Hassell and Justice Koontz dissented. They rejected Dr. Samenow's opinion that Atkins possesses average intelligence as 'incredulous as a matter of law,' and concluded that 'the imposition of the sentence of death upon a criminal defendant who has the mental age of a child between the ages of 9 and 12 is excessive.' In their opinion, 'it is indefensible to conclude that individuals who are mentally retarded are not to some degree less culpable for their criminal acts. By definition, such individuals have substantial limitations not shared by the general population. A moral and civilized society diminishes itself if its system of justice does not afford recognition and consideration of those limitations in a meaningful way.'

Because of the gravity of the concerns expressed by the dissenters, and in light of the dramatic shift in the state legislative landscape that has occurred in the past 13 years, [the Supreme Court] granted certiorari to revisit the issue that [they] first addressed in the Penry case."

B. Counsel of Record

ACLU Side (Petitioner / Appellant) James W. Ellis argued the cause for appellant. With him on the briefs were Robert E. Lee, Mark E. Olive, and Charles E. Haden

Opposing Side (Respondent / Appellee)

Pamela A. Rumpz, Assistant Attorney General of Virginia, argued the cause for appellee. With her on the brief was Randolph A. Beales, Attorney General.

III. AMICI CURIAE

ACLU Side (Petitioner / Appellant)

Brief of amici curiae filed on behalf of the American Civil Liberties Union, the ACLU of North Carolina, and the Equal Justice Initiative of Alabama by Larry W. Yackle, Bryan A. Stevenson, Steven R. Shapiro, and Diann Y. Rust-Tierney.

Brief of amici curiae filed on behalf of the American Association on Mental Retardation et al. by James W. Ellis, April Land, Christian G. Fritz, Michael B. Browde, and Stanley S. Herr. the American Bar Association by Martha W. Barnett and David M. Gossett.

Brief of amici curiae filed on behalf of the American Psychological Association et al. by Paul M. Smith, William M. Hohengarten, Nathalie F. P. Gilfoyle, James L. McHugh, and Richard G. Taranto.

Brief of amici curiae filed on behalf of the European Union by Richard J. Wilson.

Brief of amici curiae filed on behalf of the United States Catholic Conference et al. by Mark E. Chopko, Jeffrey Hunter Moon, and Michael R. Moses.

Brief of amici curiae filed on behalf of Morton Abramowitz et al. by Harold Hongju Koh and Stanley S. Herr.

Opposing Side (Respondent / Appellee)

Brief of amici curiae filed on behalf of the State of Alabama et al. by Bill Pryor, Attorney General of Alabama, and J. Clayton Crenshaw, Henry M. Johnson, James R. Houts, A. Vernon Barnett IV, Michael B. Billingsley, and David R. Clark, Assistant Attorneys General, Michael C. Moore, Attorney General of Mississippi, Frankie Sue Del Papa, Attorney General of Nevada, Charles M. Condon, Attorney General of South Carolina, and Mark L. Shurtleff, Attorney General of Utah.

Brief of amici curiae filed on behalf of the Criminal Justice Legal Foundation by Kent S. Scheidegger and Charles L. Hobson.

IV. THE SUPREME COURT'S DECISION

"The Eighth Amendment succinctly prohibits '[e]xcessive' sanctions. It provides: 'Excessive bail shall not be required, nor excessive fines imposed, nor cruel and unusual punishments inflicted.' . . .

Proportionality review under . . . evolving standards should be informed by "objective factors to the maximum possible extent." We have pinpointed that the 'clearest and most reliable objective evidence of contemporary values is the legislation enacted by the country's legislatures.' . . .

Guided by our approach in [prior] cases, we shall first review the judgment of legislatures that have addressed the suitability of imposing the death penalty on the mentally retarded and then consider reasons for agreeing or disagreeing with their judgment. . . .

In [1986], the public reaction to the execution of a mentally retarded murderer in Georgia apparently led to the enactment of the first state statute prohibiting such executions. In 1988, when Congress enacted legislation reinstating the federal death penalty, it expressly provided that a 'sentence of death shall not be carried out upon a person who is mentally retarded.' In 1989, Maryland enacted a similar prohibition. It was in that year that we decided Penry, and concluded that those two state enactments, 'even when added to the 14 States that have rejected capital punishment completely, do not provide sufficient evidence at present of a national consensus.'

Much has changed since then. Responding to the national attention received by the Bowden execution and our decision in Penry, state legislatures across the country began to address the issue. In 1990, Kentucky and Tennessee enacted statutes . . . , as did New Mexico in 1991, and Arkansas, Colorado, Washington, Indiana, and Kansas in 1993 and 1994. In 1995, when New York reinstated its death penalty, it emulated the Federal Government by expressly exempting the mentally retarded. Nebraska followed suit in 1998. [I]n 2000 and 2001 six more States—South Dakota, Arizona, Connecticut, Florida, Missouri, and North Carolina—joined the procession. The Texas Legislature unanimously adopted a similar bill, and bills have passed at least one house in other States, including Virginia and Nevada.

It is not so much the number of these States that is significant, but the consistency of the direction of change. . . . The practice, therefore, has become truly unusual, and it is fair to say that a national consensus has developed against it.

To the extent there is serious disagreement about the execution of mentally retarded offenders, it is in determining which offenders are in fact retarded. . . .

Mentally retarded persons frequently know the difference between right and wrong and are competent to stand trial. Because of their impairments, however, by definition they have diminished capacities . . . .

Gregg v. Georgia . . . identified 'retribution and deterrence of capital crimes by prospective offenders' as the social purposes served by the death penalty. Unless the imposition of the death penalty on a mentally retarded person 'measurably contributes to one or both of these goals, it 'is nothing more than the purposeless and needless imposition of pain and suffering,' and hence an unconstitutional punishment.'

With respect to retribution—the interest in seeing that the offender gets his 'just deserts'—the severity of the appropriate punishment necessarily depends on the culpability of the offender. Since Gregg, our jurisprudence has consistently confined the imposition of the death penalty to a narrow category of the most serious crimes. . . . Thus, pursuant to our narrowing jurisprudence, which seeks to ensure that only the most deserving of execution are put to death, an exclusion for the mentally retarded is appropriate.

With respect to deterrence—the interest in preventing capital crimes by prospective offenders—'it seems likely that 'capital punishment can serve as a deterrent only when murder is the result of premeditation and deliberation.'' . . . Thus, executing the mentally retarded will not measurably further the goal of deterrence. . . .

Our independent evaluation of the issue reveals no reason to disagree with the judgment of 'the legislatures that have recently addressed the matter' and concluded that death is not a suitable punishment for a mentally retarded criminal. We are not persuaded that the execution of mentally retarded criminals will measurably advance the deterrent or the retributive purpose of the death penalty. Construing and applying the Eighth Amendment in the light of our 'evolving standards of decency,' we therefore conclude that such punishment is excessive and that the Constitution 'places a substantive restriction on the State's power to take the life' of a mentally retarded offender.

The judgment of the Virginia Supreme Court is reversed and the case is remanded for further proceedings not inconsistent with this opinion."

V. JUSTICE VOTE

6 Pro ACLU Side vs. 3 Con Opposing Side

ACLU Side (Petitioner / Appellant)

1. Stevens, J. – Wrote majority opinion
2. O'Connor, S. – Joined majority opinion
3. Souter, D. – Joined majority opinion
4. Ginsburg, R. – Joined majority opinion
5. Breyer, S. – Joined majority opinion
6. Kennedy, A. – Joined majority opinion

Opposing Side (Respondent / Appellee)

1. Rehnquist, W. – Wrote dissenting opinion, joined Scalia's dissent
2. Thomas, C. – Joined Rehnquist's dissent, joined Scalia's dissent
3. Scalia, A. – Wrote dissenting opinion, joined Rehnquist's dissent

VI. A WIN OR LOSS FOR THE ACLU?

The ACLU filed as amicus curiae urging reversal of the judgment of the court below; the Supreme Court reversed and remanded in a 6-3 vote, giving the ACLU an apparent win.

929. Christopher v. Harbury

(Decided June 20, 2002; 536 U.S. 403)

I. ISSUE

A. Issues Discussed

Federal, civil rights, civil procedure

B. Legal Question Presented

Whether one count of a complaint alleging denial of "access to the courts . . . states an actionable claim."

C. Supreme Court's Answer

"We hold that it does not, for two reasons. As stated in the complaint, it fails to identify an underlying cause of action for relief that the plaintiff would have raised had it not been for the deception alleged. And even after a subsequent, informal amendment accepted by the Court of Appeals, respondent fails to seek any relief presently available for denial of access to courts that would be unavailable otherwise."

II. CASE SUMMARY

A. Background

"Respondent-plaintiff in this case alleges that Government officials intentionally deceived her in concealing information that her husband, a foreign dissident, was being detained and tortured in his own country by military officers of his government, who were paid by the Central Intelligence Agency (CIA). One count of the complaint, brought after the husband's death, charges that the official deception denied respondent access to the courts by leaving her without information, or reason to seek information, with which she could have brought a lawsuit that might have saved her husband's life. The issue is whether this count states an actionable claim. . . .

Harbury filed suit in the District Court for the District of Columbia . . . . The complaint, as amended, listed 28 causes of action under federal, state, and international law. . . .

For failure to state a claim, the District Court dismissed all counts for declaratory and injunctive relief (counts 1–3, 6–9, 14, 16). It also dismissed all the Bivens counts: those on behalf of Bamaca's estate for his torture and execution said to have violated his Fifth Amendment due process rights (counts 4–5), and those brought on Harbury's own behalf based on the claimed violation of her constitutional rights of familial association (counts 10–13), access to courts (count 15), and free speech and access to

Government (count 17). But the District Court denied the defendants' motion to dismiss the tort claims at common law (counts 18–27) and international law (count 28). . . .

Harbury did not pursue her claims for declaratory or injunctive relief, and appealed only the dismissal of the Bivens causes of action. The Court of Appeals for the District of Columbia Circuit affirmed the dismissal of the Bivens claims of violations of Bamaca's due process rights, Harbury's rights of familial association, and her free speech and petition rights. It reversed the dismissal, however, of Harbury's Bivens claim against the State Department and NSC defendants for denial of access to courts. . . .

Three categories of claims were left in the case after the Court of Appeals's decision: the various common law tort claims including intentional infliction of emotional distress, the international law claim against the CIA defendants (neither of which the District Court had dismissed), and Harbury's Bivens claims against the State Department and NSC defendants for preventing access to courts (which the Court of Appeals reinstated). The defendant officials petitioned for review of the court's holding as to the claim of denial of access to courts, but Harbury did not cross-petition on the other Bivens claims, leaving the Bivens access claim the sole matter before" the Supreme Court.

The Supreme Court granted certiorari to review the case.

B. Counsel of Record:

ACLU Side (Respondent / Appellee): Jennifer K. Harbury, appellee, argued the cause and filed a brief pro se.

Opposing Side (Petitioner / Appellant): Richard A. Cordray argued the cause for appellants. With him on the briefs was Harry Litman.

Solicitor General Olson argued the cause for the United States as amicus curiae.

III. AMICI CURIAE

ACLU Side (Respondent / Appellee)

Brief of amici curiae filed on behalf of the Lawyers' Committee for Civil Rights of the San Francisco Bay Area and the American Civil Liberties Union by Robert E. Borton, Scott D. Wiener, Robert Rubin, Steven R. Shapiro, and Lucas Guttentag.

Brief of amici curiae filed on behalf of the Association of Trial Lawyers of America by Jeffrey R. White and Laura C. Tharney.

Brief of amici curiae filed on behalf of the Brennan Center for Justice by Jodie L. Kelley.

Opposing Side (Petitioner / Appellant)

Brief of amici curiae filed on behalf of the United States by Solicitor General Olson, Assistant Attorney General McCallum, Deputy Solicitor General Clement, Patricia A. Millett, Barbara L. Herwig, and Robert M. Loeb.

IV. THE SUPREME COURT'S DECISION

"This Court's prior cases on denial of access to courts have not extended over the entire range of claims that have been brought under that general rubric elsewhere, but if we consider examples in the Courts of Appeals as well as our own, two categories emerge. . . .

While the circumstances thus vary, the ultimate justification for recognizing each kind of claim is the same. Whether an access claim turns on a litigating opportunity yet to be gained or an opportunity already lost, the very point of recognizing any access claim is to provide some effective vindication for a separate and distinct right to seek judicial relief for some wrong. However unsettled the basis of the constitutional right of access to courts, our cases rest on the recognition that the right is ancillary to the underlying claim, without which a plaintiff cannot have suffered injury by being shut out of court. . . . It follows that the underlying cause of action, whether anticipated or lost, is an element that must be described in the complaint, just as much as allegations must describe the official acts frustrating the litigation. It follows, too, that when the access claim (like this one) looks backward, the complaint must identify a remedy that may be awarded as recompense but not otherwise available in some suit that may yet be brought. There is, after all, no point in spending time and money to establish the facts constituting denial of access when a plaintiff would end up just as well off after litigating a simpler case without the denial-of-access element. . . .

In sum, the right of a defendant in a backward-looking access suit to obtain early dismissal of a hopelessly incomplete claim for relief coincides in this case with the obligation of the Judicial Branch to avoid deciding constitutional issues needlessly. For the sake of each, the complaint should state the underlying claim in accordance with Federal Rule of Civil Procedure 8(a), just as if it were being independently pursued, and a like plain statement should describe any remedy available under the access claim and presently unique to it. . . .

Under these standards, Harbury's complaint did not come even close to stating a constitutional claim for denial of access upon which relief could be granted. While we cannot read the complaint without appreciating Harbury's anguish, neither can we read it without appreciating the position of the District Judge who described Harbury's various requests for relief as 'nearly unintelligible.' . . .

Nothing happened in the Court of Appeals to improve Harbury's position. That court, too, was frustrated by the failure to identify the predicate claim and the need for relief otherwise unattainable, but it gave Harbury's counsel an opportunity at oral argument to supply the missing allegations. Counsel responded that Harbury would have brought an action for intentional infliction of emotional distress as one wrong for which she could have sought the injunctive relief that might have saved her husband's life . . . .

We think, however, that treating the amendment as an adequate statement was error. For even on the assumption that Harbury could surmount all difficulties raised by treating the underlying claim as one for intentional infliction of emotional distress, she could not satisfy the requirement that a backward-looking denial-of-access claim provide a remedy that could not be obtained on an existing claim. . . .

The judgment of the Court of Appeals is reversed, and the case is remanded for further proceedings consistent with this opinion."

V. JUSTICE VOTE

0 Pro ACLU Side vs. 9 Con Opposing Side

Opposing Side (Petitioner / Appellant)

1. Souter, D. – Wrote majority opinion
2. Ginsburg, R. – Joined majority opinion
3. O'Connor, S. – Joined majority opinion
4. Stevens, J. – Joined majority opinion
5. Breyer, S. – Joined majority opinion
6. Scalia, A. – Joined majority opinion
7. Kennedy, A. – Joined majority opinion
8. Rehnquist, W. – Joined majority opinion
9. Thomas, C. – Wrote concurring opinion

VI. A WIN OR LOSS FOR THE ACLU?

The ACLU filed as amicus curiae, urging affirmance; the Supreme Court reversed the Court of Appeals' decision by a 9-0 vote, giving the ACLU an apparent loss.

930. Zelman v. Simmons-Harris

(Decided June 27, 2002; 536 U.S. 639)

I. ISSUE

A. Issues Discussed

1st Amendment, religion

B. Legal Question Presented

"The State of Ohio has established a pilot program designed to provide educational choices to families with children who reside in the Cleveland City School District. The question presented is whether this program offends the Establishment Clause of the United States Constitution."

C. Supreme Court's Answer

"In keeping with an unbroken line of decisions rejecting challenges to similar programs, we hold that the program does not offend the Establishment Clause."

II. CASE SUMMARY

A. Background

"For more than a generation, . . . Cleveland's public schools have been among the worst performing public schools in the Nation. . . .

It is against this backdrop that Ohio enacted . . . its Pilot Project Scholarship Program. The program provides financial assistance to families in any Ohio school district that is or has been 'under federal court order requiring supervision and operational management of the district by the state superintendent.' Cleveland is the only Ohio school district to fall within that category.

The program provides two basic kinds of assistance to parents of children in a covered district. First, the program provides tuition aid for students . . . to attend a participating public or private school of their parent's choosing. Second, the program provides tutorial aid for students who choose to remain enrolled in public school.

The tuition aid portion of the program is designed to provide educational choices to parents who reside in a covered district. Any private school, whether religious or nonreligious, may participate in the program and accept program students so long as the school is located within the boundaries of a covered district and meets statewide educational standards. . . .

In the 1999–2000 school year, [m]ore than 3,700 students participated in the scholarship program, most of whom (96%) enrolled in religiously affiliated schools. . . .

In July 1999, respondents filed this action in United States District Court, seeking to enjoin the reenacted program on the ground that it violated the Establishment Clause of the United States Constitution. [T]he District Court granted summary judgment for respondents. In December 2000, a divided panel of the Court of Appeals affirmed the judgment of the District Court . . . ."

The Supreme Court granted certiorari to review the case.

B. Counsel of Record:

ACLU Side (Respondent / Appellee): Robert H. Chanin argued the cause for appellees Simmons-Harris et al. in all cases. With him on the brief were Andrew D. Roth, Laurence Gold, Steven R. Shapiro of the ACLU Foundation, Raymond Vasvari of the ACLU of Ohio Foundation, Inc., Elliot M. Mincberg, and Judith E. Schaeffer. Marvin E. Frankel argued the cause for appellees Gatton et al. in all cases. With him on the brief were David J. Strom, Donald J. Mooney, Jr., and Marc D. Stern.

Opposing Side (Petitioner / Appellant): Judith L. French, Assistant Attorney General of Ohio, argued the cause for appellants in No. 00–1751. With her on the briefs were Betty D. Montgomery, Attorney General, David M. Gormley, State Solicitor, Karen L. Lazorishak, James G. Tassie, and Robert L. Strayer, Assistant Attorneys General, Kenneth W. Starr, and Robert R. Gasaway. David J. Young argued the cause for appellants in No. 00–1777. With him on the briefs were Michael R. Reed and David J. Hessler. Clint Bolick, William H. Mellor, Richard D. Komer, Robert Freedman, David Tryon, and Charles Fried filed briefs for appellants in No. 00–1779.

Solicitor General Olson argued the cause for the United States as amicus curiae.

III. AMICI CURIAE

ACLU Side (Respondent / Appellee)

Brief of amici curiae filed on behalf of the American Jewish Committee et al. by Howard G. Kristol, Erwin Chemerinsky, Jeffrey P. Sinensky, Kara H. Stein, Arthur H. Bryant, and Victoria W. Ni.

Brief of amici curiae filed on behalf of the Anti-Defamation League by Martin E. Karlinsky, Daniel J. Beller, Steven M. Freeman, and Frederick M. Lawrence.

Brief of amici curiae filed on behalf of the Council on Religious Freedom et al. by Lee Boothby and Alan J. Reinach.

Brief of amici curiae filed on behalf of the NAACP Legal Defense and Educational Fund, Inc., et al. by Norman J. Chachkin, Elaine R. Jones, Theodore M. Shaw, James L. Cott, Dennis D. Parker, and Dennis Courtland Hayes.

Brief of amici curiae filed on behalf of the National Committee for Public Education and Religious Liberty by Geoffrey F. Aronow and Stanley Geller.

Brief of amici curiae filed on behalf of the National School Boards Association et al. by Julie K. Underwood, Scott Bales, and James Martin.

Brief of amici curiae filed on behalf of the Ohio Association for Public Education and Religious Liberty by Patrick Farrell Timmins, Jr.

Brief of amici curiae filed on behalf of the Ohio School Boards Association et al. by Kimball H. Carey and Susan B. Greenberger.

Brief of amici curiae filed on behalf of the California Alliance for Public Schools by Robin B. Johansen and Joseph Remcho.

Opposing Side (Petitioner / Appellant)

Brief of amici curiae filed on behalf of the United States by Solicitor General Olson, Assistant Attorney General McCallum, Deputy Solicitor General Kneedler, Gregory G. Garre, Robert M. Loeb, and Lowell V. Sturgill, Jr.

Brief of amici curiae filed on behalf of the State of Florida et al. by Robert A. Butterworth, Attorney General of Florida, Thomas E. Warner, Solicitor General, and Matthew J. Conigliaro, Deputy Solicitor General, and by the Attorneys General for their respective States as follows: Bill Pryor of Alabama, M. Jane Brady of Delaware, Don Stenberg of Nebraska, D. Michael Fisher of Pennsylvania, Charles M. Condon of South Carolina, and Randolph A. Beales of Virginia.

Brief of amici curiae filed on behalf of the State of Wisconsin by Stephen P. Hurley, Gordon P. Giampietro, and Donald A. Daugherty, Jr.

Brief of amici curiae filed on behalf of Gary E. Johnson, Governor of New Mexico, by Jeffrey S. Bucholtz.

Brief of amici curiae filed on behalf of Mayor Rudolph W. Giuliani et al. by Michael D. Hess, Corporation Counsel of the City of New York, Leonard J. Koerner, and Edward F. X. Hart.

Brief of amici curiae filed on behalf of Councilwoman Fannie Lewis by Steffen N. Johnson, Stephen M. Shapiro, Robert M. Dow, Jr., and Richard P. Hutchison.

Brief of amici curiae filed on behalf of the American Education Reform Council by Louis R. Cohen, C. Boyden Gray, and Todd Zubler.

Brief of amici curiae filed on behalf of the American Civil Rights Union by Peter J. Ferrara.

Brief of amici curiae filed on behalf of the American Center for Law and Justice, Inc., et al. by Jay Alan Sekulow, James M. Henderson, Sr., Colby M. May, Vincent McCarthy, and Walter M. Weber.

Brief of amici curiae filed on behalf of the Association of Christian Schools International et al. by Edward McGlynn Gaffney, Jr., and Richard A. Epstein.

Brief of amici curiae filed on behalf of the Becket Fund for Religious Liberty by Kevin J. Hasson, Eric W. Treene, Roman P. Storzer, Anthony R. Picarello, Jr., and Richard Garnett.

Brief of amici curiae filed on behalf of the Black Alliance for Educational Options by Samuel Estreicher.

Brief of amici curiae filed on behalf of the Catholic League for Religious and Civil Rights by Robert P. George.

Brief of amici curiae filed on behalf of the Center for Education Reform et al. by Robert A. Destro and Joseph E. Schmitz.

Brief of amici curiae filed on behalf of the Center for Individual Freedom et al. by Erik S. Jaffe.

Brief of amici curiae filed on behalf of Children First America et al. by Harold J. (Tex) Lezar, Jr., and Stephen G. Gilles.

Brief of amici curiae filed on behalf of the Christian Legal Society et al. by Stuart J. Lark and Gregory S. Baylor.

Brief of amici curiae filed on behalf of the Claremont Institute Center for Constitutional Jurisprudence by Edwin Meese III.

Brief of amici curiae filed on behalf of the Coalition for Local Sovereignty by Kenneth B. Clark.

Brief of amici curiae filed on behalf of the National Association of Independent Schools by Allen G. Siegel.

Brief of amici curiae filed on behalf of the National Jewish Commission on Law and Public Affairs by Nathan Lewin, Dennis Rapps, Nathan Diament, and David Zwiebel.

Brief of amici curiae filed on behalf of the REACH Alliance by Philip J. Murren.

Brief of amici curiae filed on behalf of the Rutherford Institute by John W. Whitehead, Steven H. Aden, Robert R. Melnick, and James J. Knicely.

Brief of amici curiae filed on behalf of the Solidarity Center for Law and Justice, P. C., by James P. Kelly III.

Brief of amici curiae filed on behalf of the United States Conference of Catholic Bishops by Mark E. Chopko, John Liekweg, and Jeffrey Hunter Moon.

Brief of amici curiae filed on behalf of Hugh Calkins, pro se.

Brief of amici curiae filed on behalf of Vermonters for Better Education by Michael D. Dean.

Brief of amici curiae filed on behalf of John E. Coons et al. by Mr. Coons, pro se, and Stephen D. Sugarman, pro se.

Brief of amici curiae filed on behalf of Jesse H. Choper et al. by Mr. Choper, pro se, William Bassett, Teresa Collett, David Forte, Richard Garnett, Lino Graglia, Michael Heise, Gail Heriot, Roderick Hills, Grant Nelson, Michael Perry, David Post, Charles Rice, Rosemary Salomone, Gregory Sisk, Steve Smith, and Harry Tepker.

Brief of amici curiae filed on behalf of Ira J. Paul et al. by Sharon L. Browne.

IV. THE SUPREME COURT'S DECISION

"The Establishment Clause of the First Amendment, applied to the States through the Fourteenth Amendment, prevents a State from enacting laws that have the 'purpose' or 'effect' of advancing or inhibiting religion. . . . There is no dispute that the program challenged here was enacted for the valid secular purpose of providing educational assistance to poor children in a demonstrably failing public school system. Thus, the question presented is whether the Ohio program nonetheless has the forbidden 'effect' of advancing or inhibiting religion.

To answer that question, our decisions have drawn a consistent distinction between government programs that provide aid directly to religious schools, . . . and programs of true private choice, in which government aid reaches religious schools only as a result of the genuine and independent choices of private individuals. . . . Three times we have confronted Establishment Clause challenges to neutral government programs that provide aid directly to a broad class of individuals, who, in turn, direct the aid to religious schools or institutions of their own choosing. Three times we have rejected such challenges. . . .

Mueller, Witters, and Zobrest thus make clear that where a government aid program is neutral with respect to religion, and provides assistance directly to a broad class of citizens who, in turn, direct government aid to religious schools wholly as a result of their own genuine and independent private choice, the program is not readily subject to challenge under the Establishment Clause. . . .

We believe that the program challenged here is a program of true private choice, consistent with Mueller, Witters, and Zobrest, and thus constitutional. As was true in those cases, the Ohio program is neutral in all respects toward religion. It is part of a general and multifaceted undertaking by the State of Ohio to provide educational opportunities to the children of a failed school district. It confers educational assistance directly to a broad class of individuals defined without reference to religion . . . . The program permits the participation of all schools within the district, religious or nonreligious. Adjacent public schools also may participate and have a financial incentive to do so. Program benefits are available to participating families on neutral terms, with no reference to religion. . . .

Respondents suggest that even without a financial incentive for parents to choose a religious school, the program creates a 'public perception that the State is endorsing religious practices and beliefs.' But we have repeatedly recognized that no reasonable observer would think a neutral program of private choice, where state aid reaches religious schools solely as a result of the numerous independent decisions of private individuals, carries with it the imprimatur of government endorsement. . . .

There also is no evidence that the program fails to provide genuine opportunities for Cleveland parents to select secular educational options for their school-age children. . . .

In sum, the Ohio program is entirely neutral with respect to religion. It provides benefits directly to a wide spectrum of individuals, defined only by financial need and residence in a particular school district. It permits such individuals to exercise genuine choice among options public and private, secular and religious. The program is therefore a program of true private choice. In keeping with an unbroken line of decisions rejecting challenges to similar programs, we hold that the program does not offend the Establishment Clause.

The judgment of the Court of Appeals is reversed."

V. JUSTICE VOTE

4 Pro ACLU Side vs. 5 Con Opposing Side

ACLU Side (Respondent / Appellee)

1. Souter, D. – Wrote dissenting opinion, joined Breyer's dissent
2. Stevens, J. – Wrote dissenting opinion, joined Souter's and Breyer's dissents
3. Ginsburg, R. – Joined Souter's dissent
4. Breyer, S. – Wrote dissenting opinion, joined Souter's dissent

Opposing Side (Petitioner / Appellant)

1. Rehnquist, W. – Wrote majority opinion
2. Thomas, C. – Wrote concurring opinion
3. O'Connor, S. – Wrote concurring opinion
4. Scalia, A. – Joined majority opinion
5. Kennedy, A. – Joined majority opinion

VI. A WIN OR LOSS FOR THE ACLU?

The ACLU argued the case for appellee, urging affirmance; the Supreme Court reversed the Court of Appeals' decision by a 5-4 vote, giving the ACLU an apparent loss.

931. Hope v. Pelzer

1(Decided June 27, 2002; 536 U.S. 730)

I. ISSUE

A. Issues Discussed

8th Amendment, prison

B. Legal Question Presented

"[W]hether the Court of Appeals' qualified immunity holding comports with [the U.S. Supreme Court] decision in United States v. Lanier, 520 U.S. 259 (1997)."

C. Supreme Court's Answer

"The 'fair and clear warning,' Lanier, 520 U.S., at 271, that [prior] cases provided was sufficient to preclude the defense of qualified immunity at the summary judgment stage."

II. CASE SUMMARY

A. Background

"In 1995, Alabama was the only State that followed the practice of chaining inmates to one another in work squads. It was also the only State that handcuffed prisoners to 'hitching posts' if they either refused to work or otherwise disrupted work squads. Hope was handcuffed to a hitching post on two occasions. . . .

Hope filed suit under Rev. Stat. § 1979, 42 U.S.C. § 1983, in the United States District Court for the Northern District of Alabama against three guards involved in the May incident, one of whom also handcuffed him to the hitching post in June. The case was referred to a Magistrate Judge who treated the responsive affidavits filed by the defendants as a motion for summary judgment. Without deciding whether 'the very act of placing him on a restraining bar for a period of hours as a form of punishment' had violated the Eighth Amendment, the Magistrate concluded that the guards were entitled to qualified immunity. The District Court agreed, and entered judgment for respondents.

The United States Court of Appeals for the Eleventh Circuit affirmed."

The Supreme Court granted certiorari to review the case.

B. Counsel of Record

ACLU Side (Petitioner / Appellant): Craig T. Jones argued the cause for appellant. With him on the brief were James Mendelsohn, J. Richard Cohen, and Rhonda Brownstein.

Austin C. Schlick argued the cause for the United States as amicus curiae.

Opposing Side (Respondent / Appellee): Nathan A. Forrester, Solicitor General of Alabama, argued the cause for appellees. With him on the brief were Bill Pryor, Attorney General, Alyce S. Robertson, Deputy Solicitor General, and Margaret Fleming and Ellen Leonard-Thomas, Assistant Attorneys General.

Gene C. Schaerr argued the cause for the State of Missouri et al. as amici curiae.

III. AMICI CURIAE

ACLU Side (Petitioner / Appellant)

Brief of amici curiae filed on behalf of the American Civil Liberties Union, the ACLU of Alabama, the ACLU of Florida, and the ACLU of Georgia by Mark R. Brown, James K. Green, and Steven R. Shapiro.

Brief of amici curiae filed on behalf of the United States by Austin C. Schlick, Solicitor General Olson, Assistant Attorneys General McCallum and Boyd, Deputy Solicitor General Clement, Barbara L. Herwig, and Richard A. Olderman.

Opposing Side (Respondent / Appellee)

Brief of amici curiae filed on behalf of the State of Missouri et al., by Gene C. Schaerr, Jeremiah W. Nixon, Attorney General of Missouri, and James R. Layton, State Solicitor, Robert H. Kono, Acting Attorney General of Guam, and Carter G. Phillips, joined by the Attorneys General for their respective States as follows: Richard Blumenthal of Connecticut, Earl I. Anzai of Hawaii, Steve Carter of Indiana, Richard P. Ieyoub of Louisiana, Mike Moore of Mississippi, Don Stenberg of Nebraska, Frankie Sue Del Papa of Nevada, W. A. Drew Edmondson of Oklahoma, Hardy Myers of Oregon, D. Michael Fisher of Pennsylvania, Sheldon Whitehouse of Rhode Island, Mark L. Shurtleff of Utah, and Darrell V. McGraw, Jr., of West Virginia.

IV. THE SUPREME COURT'S DECISION

"The threshold inquiry a court must undertake in a qualified immunity analysis is whether plaintiff's allegations, if true, establish a constitutional violation. The Court of Appeals held that 'the policy and practice of cuffing an inmate to a hitching post or similar stationary object for a period of time that surpasses that necessary to quell a threat or restore order is a violation of the Eighth Amendment.' . . . We agree with the Court of Appeals that the attachment of Hope to the hitching post under the circumstances alleged in this case violated the Eighth Amendment.

Despite their participation in this constitutionally impermissible conduct, respondents may nevertheless be shielded from liability for civil damages if their actions did not violate 'clearly established statutory or constitutional rights of which a reasonable person would have known.' In assessing whether the Eighth Amendment violation here met the Harlow test, the Court of Appeals required that the facts of previous cases be "materially similar' to Hope's situation.' This rigid gloss on the qualified immunity standard, though supported by Circuit precedent, is not consistent with our cases.

As we have explained, qualified immunity operates 'to ensure that before they are subjected to suit, officers are on notice their conduct is unlawful.' . . .

Officers sued in a civil action for damages under 42 U.S.C. § 1983 have the same right to fair notice as do defendants charged with the criminal offense defined in 18 U.S.C. § 242. Section 242 makes it a crime for a state official to act 'willfully' and under color of law to deprive a person of rights protected by the Constitution. In United States v. Lanier, 520 U.S. 259 (1997), we held that the defendant was entitled to 'fair warning' that his conduct deprived his victim of a constitutional right, and that the standard for determining the adequacy of that warning was the same as the standard for determining whether a constitutional right was 'clearly established' in civil litigation under § 1983. . . .

Accordingly, pursuant to Lanier, the salient question that the Court of Appeals ought to have asked is whether the state of the law in 1995 gave respondents fair warning that their alleged treatment of Hope was unconstitutional. It is to this question that we now turn.

The use of the hitching post as alleged by Hope 'unnecessar[ily] and wanton[ly] inflicted pain,' and thus was a clear violation of the Eighth Amendment. Arguably, the violation was so obvious that our own Eighth Amendment cases gave respondents fair warning that their conduct violated the Constitution. . . .

Even if there might once have been a question regarding the constitutionality of this practice, the Eleventh Circuit precedent of Gates and Ort, as well as the DOJ report condemning the practice, put a reasonable officer on notice that the use of the hitching post under the circumstances alleged by Hope was unlawful. The 'fair and clear warning,' Lanier, 520 U.S., at 271, that these cases provided was sufficient to preclude the defense of qualified immunity at the summary judgment stage. . . .

The judgment of the Court of Appeals is reversed."

V. JUSTICE VOTE

6 Pro ACLU Side vs. 3 Con Opposing Side

ACLU Side (Petitioner / Appellant)

1. Stevens, J. – Wrote majority opinion
2. O'Connor, S. – Joined majority opinion
3. Souter, D. – Joined majority opinion
4. Ginsburg, R. – Joined majority opinion
5. Breyer, S. – Joined majority opinion
6. Kenedy, A. – Joined majority opinion

Opposing Side (Respondent / Appellee)

1. Thomas, C. – Wrote dissenting opinion
2. Rehnquist, W. – Joined Thomas' dissent
3. Scalia, A. – Joined Thomas' dissent

VI. A WIN OR LOSS FOR THE ACLU?

The ACLU filed as amicus curiae urging reversal of the judgment of the Court of Appeals; the Supreme Court reversed in a 6-3 vote, giving the ACLU an apparent win.

932. Republican Party of Minnesota v. White

(Decided June 27, 2002; 536 U.S. 765)

I. ISSUE

A. Issues Discussed

1st Amendment, press, speech, association

B. Legal Question Presented

"[W]hether the First Amendment permits the Minnesota Supreme Court to prohibit candidates for judicial election in that State from announcing their views on disputed legal and political issues."

C. Supreme Court's Answer

"The Minnesota Supreme Court's canon of judicial conduct prohibiting candidates for judicial election from announcing their views on disputed legal and political issues violates the First Amendment."

II. CASE SUMMARY

A. Background

"Since Minnesota's admission to the Union in 1858, the State's Constitution has provided for the selection of all state judges by popular election. Since 1912, those elections have been nonpartisan. Since 1974, they have been subject to a legal restriction which states that a 'candidate for a judicial office, including an incumbent judge,' shall not 'announce his or her views on disputed legal or political issues.' This prohibition, promulgated by the Minnesota Supreme Court and based on Canon 7(B) of the 1972 American Bar Association (ABA) Model Code of Judicial Conduct, is known as the 'announce clause.' Incumbent judges who violate it are subject to discipline, including removal, censure, civil penalties, and suspension without pay. Lawyers who run for judicial office also must comply with the announce clause. . . . Those who violate it are subject to disbarment, suspension, and probation.

In 1996, one of the petitioners, Gregory Wersal, ran for associate justice of the Minnesota Supreme Court. In the course of the campaign, he distributed literature criticizing several Minnesota Supreme Court decisions on issues such as crime, welfare, and abortion. A complaint against Wersal challenging, among other things, the propriety of this literature was filed with the Office of Lawyers Professional Responsibility . . . . The Lawyers Board dismissed the complaint; with regard to the charges that his campaign materials violated the announce clause, it expressed doubt whether the clause could constitutionally be enforced. Nonetheless, fearing that further ethical complaints would jeopardize his ability to practice law, Wersal withdrew from the election. In 1998, Wersal ran again for the same office. Early in that race, he sought an advisory opinion from the Lawyers Board with regard to whether it planned to enforce the announce clause. The Lawyers Board responded equivocally, stating that, although it had significant doubts about the constitutionality of the provision, it was unable to answer his question because he had not submitted a list of the announcements he wished to make.

Shortly thereafter, Wersal filed this lawsuit in Federal District Court against respondents, seeking a declaration that the announce clause violates the First Amendment and an injunction against its enforcement. [T]he District Court found in favor of respondents, holding that the announce clause did not violate the First Amendment. Over a dissent by Judge Beam, the United States Court of Appeals for the Eighth Circuit affirmed."

The Supreme Court granted certiorari to review the case.

B. Counsel of Record:

ACLU Side (Petitioner / Appellant): James Bopp, Jr., argued the cause for appellants Republican Party of Minnesota et al. With him on the briefs were Thomas J. Marzen, Richard E. Coleson, and Ronald D. Rotunda. William F. Mohrman and Erick G. Kaardal filed briefs for appellants Wersal et al.

Opposing Side (Respondent / Appellee): Alan I. Gilbert, Chief Deputy and Solicitor General of Minnesota, argued the cause for appellees. With him on the brief were Mike Hatch, Attorney General, Kristine L. Eiden, Deputy Attorney General, and Julie Ralston Aoki, Mark B. Levinger, and Thomas C. Vasaly, Assistant Attorneys General.

III. AMICI CURIAE

ACLU Side (Petitioner / Appellant)

Brief of amici curiae filed on behalf of the American Civil Liberties Union and the Minnesota Civil Liberties Union by David B. Isbell, David H. Remes, M. Stacey Bach, and Steven R. Shapiro.

Brief of amici curiae filed on behalf of the American Center for Law and Justice by Jay Alan Sekulow, James H. Henderson, Sr., Colby M. May, and Walter M. Weber.

Brief of amici curiae filed on behalf of the Chamber of Commerce of the United States by Jan Witold Baran and Stephen A. Bokat.

Brief of amici curiae filed on behalf of Minnesota State Representative Philip Krinkie et al. by Raymond C. Ortman, Jr.

Brief of amici curiae filed on behalf of Public Citizen by Allison M. Zieve, David C. Vladeck, and Scott L. Nelson.

Brief of amici curiae filed on behalf of State Supreme Court Justices by Erik S. Jaffe.

Brief of amici curiae filed on behalf of the Idaho Conservation League et al. by John D. Echeverria, in support of neither side.

Opposing Side (Respondent / Appellee)

Brief of amici curiae filed on behalf of the State of California et al. by Bill Lockyer, Attorney General of California, and Manuel M. Medeiros, State Solicitor, and by the Attorneys General for their respective States as follows: Janet Napolitano of Arizona, Jeremiah W. (Jay) Nixon of Missouri, Mike McGrath of Montana, W. A. Drew Edmondson of Oklahoma,

Hardy Myers of Oregon, John Cornyn of Texas, and Christine O. Gregoire of Washington.
Brief of amici curiae filed on behalf of the Ad hoc Committee of Former Justices and Friends Dedicated to an Independent Judiciary by S. Shawn Stephens and Andy Taylor.
Brief of amici curiae filed on behalf of the American Bar Association by Robert E. Hirshon, Reagan Wm. Simpson, and Warren S. Huang.
Brief of amici curiae filed on behalf of the Minnesota State Bar Association by Wayne D. Struble.
Brief of amici curiae filed on behalf of the Brennan Center for Justice at NYU School of Law et al. by Scott Bales and Deborah Goldberg.
Brief of amici curiae filed on behalf of the Conference of Chief Justices by Roy A. Schotland, George T. Patton, Jr., Sarah Steele Riordan, and Robert F. Bauer.
Brief of amici curiae filed on behalf of the Missouri Bar by Joseph C. Blanton, Jr.
Brief of amici curiae filed on behalf of Pennsylvanians for Modern Courts by Edmund B. Spaeth, Jr., and Brett G. Sweitzer.
Brief of amici curiae filed on behalf of the National Association of Criminal Defense Lawyers by David W. Ogden, Jonathan J. Frankel, Neil M. Richards, and Lisa Kemler.

IV. THE SUPREME COURT'S DECISION

"Before considering the constitutionality of the announce clause, we must be clear about its meaning. Its text says that a candidate for judicial office shall not 'announce his or her views on disputed legal or political issues.' . . .

There are, however, some limitations that the Minnesota Supreme Court has placed upon the scope of the announce clause that are not (to put it politely) immediately apparent from its text. The statements that formed the basis of the complaint against Wersal in 1996 included criticism of past decisions of the Minnesota Supreme Court. . . . Although one would think that all of these statements touched on disputed legal or political issues, they did not (or at least do not now) fall within the scope of the announce clause. . . .

There are yet further limitations upon the apparent plain meaning of the announce clause: In light of the constitutional concerns, the District Court construed the clause to reach only disputed issues that are likely to come before the candidate if he is elected judge. . . .

It seems to us, however, that—like the text of the announce clause itself—these limitations upon the text of the announce clause are not all that they appear to be. First, respondents acknowledged at oral argument that statements critical of past judicial decisions are not permissible if the candidate also states that he is against stare decisis. . . . Second, limiting the scope of the clause to issues likely to come before a court is not much of a limitation at all. . . . Third, construing the clause to allow 'general' discussions of case law and judicial philosophy turns out to be of little help in an election campaign. . . .

Respondents contend that this still leaves plenty of topics for discussion on the campaign trail. . . . Indeed, the Judicial Board has printed a list of preapproved questions which judicial candidates are allowed to answer. . . . Whether this list of preapproved subjects, and other topics not prohibited by the announce clause, adequately fulfill the First Amendment's guarantee of freedom of speech is the question to which we now turn.

As the Court of Appeals recognized, the announce clause both prohibits speech on the basis of its content and burdens a category of speech that is 'at the core of our First Amendment freedoms'—speech about the qualifications of candidates for public office. The Court of Appeals concluded that the proper test to be applied to determine the constitutionality of such a restriction is what our cases have called strict scrutiny; the parties do not dispute that this is correct. Under the strict-scrutiny test, respondents have the burden to prove that the announce clause is (1) narrowly tailored, to serve (2) a compelling state interest. . . .

The Court of Appeals concluded that respondents had established two interests as sufficiently compelling to justify the announce clause: preserving the impartiality of the state judiciary and preserving the appearance of the impartiality of the state judiciary. . . .

The short of the matter is this: In Minnesota, a candidate for judicial office may not say 'I think it is constitutional for the legislature to prohibit same-sex marriages.' He may say the very same thing, however, up until the very day before he declares himself a candidate, and may say it repeatedly (until litigation is pending) after he is elected. As a means of pursuing the objective of open-mindedness that respondents now articulate, the announce clause is so woefully underinclusive as to render belief in that purpose a challenge to the credulous. . . .

Moreover, the notion that the special context of electioneering justifies an abridgment of the right to speak out on disputed issues sets our First Amendment jurisprudence on its head. '[D]ebate on the qualifications of candidates' is 'at the core of our electoral process and of the First Amendment freedoms,' not at the edges. 'The role that elected officials play in our society makes it all the more imperative that they be allowed freely to express themselves on matters of current public importance.' 'It is simply not the function of government to select which issues are worth discussing or debating in the course of a political campaign.' We have never allowed the government to prohibit candidates from communicating relevant information to voters during an election. . . .

To sustain the announce clause, the Eighth Circuit relied heavily on the fact that a pervasive practice of prohibiting judicial candidates from discussing disputed legal and political issues developed during the last half of the 20th century. . . . The practice of prohibiting speech by judicial candidates on disputed issues, however, is neither long nor universal. . . .

There is an obvious tension between the article of Minnesota's popularly approved Constitution which provides that judges shall be elected, and the Minnesota Supreme Court's announce clause which places most subjects of interest to the voters off limits. . . . If the State chooses to tap the energy and the legitimizing power of the democratic process, it must accord the participants in that process . . . the First Amendment rights that attach to their roles.'

The Minnesota Supreme Court's canon of judicial conduct prohibiting candidates for judicial election from announcing their views on disputed legal and political issues violates the First Amendment. Accordingly, we reverse the grant of summary judgment to respondents and remand the case for proceedings consistent with this opinion."

V. JUSTICE VOTE

5 Pro ACLU Side vs. 4 Con Opposing Side

ACLU Side (Petitioner / Appellant)

1. Scalia, A. – Wrote majority opinion
2. O'Connor, S. – Wrote concurring opinion
3. Kennedy, A. – Wrote concurring opinion
4. Rehnquist, W. – Joined majority opinion
5. Thomas, C. – Joined majority opinion

Opposing Side (Respondent / Appellee)

1. Stevens, J. – Wrote dissenting opinion, joined Ginsburg's dissent
2. Ginsburg, R. – Wrote dissenting opinion, joined Stevens' dissent
3. Souter, D. – Joined Stevens' and Ginsburg's dissents
4. Breyer, S. – Joined Stevens' and Ginsburg's dissents

VI. A WIN OR LOSS FOR THE ACLU?

The ACLU filed as amicus curiae urging reversal of the judgment of the Court of Appeals; the Supreme Court reversed in a 5-4 vote, giving the ACLU an apparent win.

933. Bd. of Ed. of Indep. Sch. Dist. No. 92 of Pottawatomie Cty. v. Earls

(Decided June 27, 2002; 536 U.S. 822)

I. ISSUE

A. Issues Discussed

Drugs, 4th Amendment

B. Legal Question Presented

Whether "[t]he Student Activities Drug Testing Policy implemented by the Board of Education of Independent School District No. 92 of Pottawatomie County [which] requires all students who participate in competitive extracurricular activities to submit to drug testing" is constitutional.

C. Supreme Court's Answer

"Because this Policy reasonably serves the School District's important interest in detecting and preventing drug use among its students, we hold that it is constitutional."

II. CASE SUMMARY

A. Background

"In the fall of 1998, the School District adopted the Student Activities Drug Testing Policy (Policy), which requires all middle and high school students to consent to drug testing in order to participate in any extracurricular activity. . . . Under the Policy, students are required to take a drug test before participating in an extracurricular activity, must submit to random drug testing while participating in that activity, and must agree to be tested at any time upon reasonable suspicion. The urinalysis tests are designed to detect only the use of illegal drugs . . . .

At the time of their suit, both respondents attended Tecumseh High School. Respondent Lindsay Earls was a member of the show choir, the marching band, the Academic Team, and the National Honor Society. Respondent Daniel James sought to participate in the Academic Team. Together with their parents, Earls and James brought a Rev. Stat. § 1979, 42 U.S.C. § 1983, action against the School District, challenging the Policy both on its face and as applied to their participation in extracurricular activities. They alleged that the Policy violates the Fourth Amendment as incorporated by the Fourteenth Amendment and requested injunctive and declarative relief. They also argued that the School District failed to identify a special need for testing students who participate in extracurricular activities, and that the 'Drug Testing Policy neither addresses a proven problem nor promises to bring any benefit to students or the school.'

[T]he United States District Court for the Western District of Oklahoma rejected respondents' claim that the Policy was unconstitutional and granted summary judgment to the School District. . . .

The United States Court of Appeals for the Tenth Circuit reversed, holding that the Policy violated the Fourth Amendment."

The Supreme Court granted certiorari to review the case.

B. Counsel of Record

ACLU Side (Respondent / Appellee): Graham A. Boyd, of the ACLU Foundation, argued the cause for respondents. With him on the brief was Steven R. Shapiro, also of the ACLU Foundation.

Opposing Side (Petitioner / Appellant): Linda Maria Meoli argued the cause for appellants. With her on the briefs were Stephanie J. Mather and William P. Bleakley.

Deputy Solicitor General Clement argued the cause for the United States as amicus curiae.

III. AMICI CURIAE

ACLU Side (Respondent / Appellee)

Brief of amici curiae filed on behalf of the American Academy of Pediatrics et al. by David T. Goldberg and Daniel N. Abrahamson.

Brief of amici curiae filed on behalf of Jean Burkett et al. by Craig Goldblatt.

Brief of amici curiae filed on behalf of the Juvenile Law Center et al. by Marsha L. Levick.

Brief of amici curiae filed on behalf of the National Association of Criminal Defense Lawyers et al. by John Wesley Hall, Jr., Lisa B. Kemler, Timothy Lynch, and Kevin B. Zeese.

Brief of amici curiae filed on behalf of the Rutherford Institute by John W. Whitehead, Steven H. Aden, and Jamin B. Raskin.

Brief of amici curiae filed on behalf of Professor Akhil Reed Amar et al. by Julia M. Carpenter.

Opposing Side (Petitioner / Appellant)

Brief of amici curiae filed on behalf of the United States by Deputy Solicitor General Clement, Solicitor General Olson,

Assistant Attorney General McCallum, Gregory G. Garre, Leonard Schaitman, and Lowell V. Sturgill, Jr.
Brief of amici curiae filed on behalf of the Washington Legal Foundation et al. by Richard Willard, Daniel J. Popeo, and Richard A. Samp.
Brief of amici curiae filed on behalf of the National School Boards Association et al. by Julie K. Underwood, Christopher B. Gilbert, and Thomas E. Wheeler.
Brief of amici curiae filed on behalf of the Drug-Free Schools Coalition et al. by David G. Evans.

IV. THE SUPREME COURT'S DECISION

"The Fourth Amendment to the United States Constitution protects '[t]he right of the people to be secure in their persons, houses, papers, and effects, against unreasonable searches and seizures.' Searches by public school officials, such as the collection of urine samples, implicate Fourth Amendment interests. We must therefore review the School District's Policy for 'reasonableness,' which is the touchstone of the constitutionality of a governmental search. . . .

In Vernonia, this Court held that the suspicionless drug testing of athletes was constitutional. The Court, however, did not simply authorize all school drug testing, but rather conducted a fact-specific balancing of the intrusion on the children's Fourth Amendment rights against the promotion of legitimate governmental interests. Applying the principles of Vernonia to the somewhat different facts of this case, we conclude that Tecumseh's Policy is also constitutional.

We first consider the nature of the privacy interest allegedly compromised by the drug testing. As in Vernonia, the context of the public school environment serves as the backdrop for the analysis of the privacy interest at stake and the reasonableness of the drug testing policy in general. . . .

A student's privacy interest is limited in a public school environment where the State is responsible for maintaining discipline, health, and safety. . . .

We therefore conclude that the students affected by this Policy have a limited expectation of privacy.

Next, we consider the character of the intrusion imposed by the Policy. . . .

Under the Policy, a faculty monitor waits outside the closed restroom stall for the student to produce a sample and must 'listen for the normal sounds of urination in order to guard against tampered specimens and to insure an accurate chain of custody.' . . . This procedure is virtually identical to that reviewed in Vernonia, except that it additionally protects privacy by allowing male students to produce their samples behind a closed stall. Given that we considered the method of collection in Vernonia a 'negligible' intrusion, the method here is even less problematic.

In addition, the Policy clearly requires that the test results be kept in confidential files separate from a student's other educational records and released to school personnel only on a 'need to know' basis. . . .

Moreover, the test results are not turned over to any law enforcement authority. Nor do the test results here lead to the imposition of discipline or have any academic consequences. Rather, the only consequence of a failed drug test is to limit the student's privilege of participating in extracurricular activities. . . .

Given the minimally intrusive nature of the sample collection and the limited uses to which the test results are put, we conclude that the invasion of students' privacy is not significant.

Finally, this Court must consider the nature and immediacy of the government's concerns and the efficacy of the Policy in meeting them. . . . The drug abuse problem among our Nation's youth has hardly abated since Vernonia was decided in 1995. In fact, evidence suggests that it has only grown worse. . . .

Additionally, the School District in this case has presented specific evidence of drug use at Tecumseh schools. . . .

Given the nationwide epidemic of drug use, and the evidence of increased drug use in Tecumseh schools, it was entirely reasonable for the School District to enact this particular drug testing policy. . . .

Finally, we find that testing students who participate in extracurricular activities is a reasonably effective means of addressing the School District's legitimate concerns in preventing, deterring, and detecting drug use. . . . Evaluating the Policy in this context, we conclude that the drug testing of Tecumseh students who participate in extracurricular activities effectively serves the School District's interest in protecting the safety and health of its students.

Within the limits of the Fourth Amendment, local school boards must assess the desirability of drug testing schoolchildren. In upholding the constitutionality of the Policy, we express no opinion as to its wisdom. Rather, we hold only that Tecumseh's Policy is a reasonable means of furthering the School District's important interest in preventing and deterring drug use among its schoolchildren. Accordingly, we reverse the judgment of the Court of Appeals."

V. JUSTICE VOTE

4 Pro ACLU Side vs. 5 Con Opposing Side

ACLU Side (Respondent / Appellee)

1. O'Connor, S. – Wrote dissenting opinion, joined Ginsburg's dissent
2. Souter, D. – Joined O'Connor's and Ginsburg's dissents
3. Ginsburg, R. – Wrote dissenting opinion
4. Stevens, J. – Joined Ginsburg's dissent

Opposing Side (Petitioner / Appellant)

1. Thomas, C. – Wrote majority opinion
2. Breyer, S. – Wrote concurring opinion
3. Scalia, A. – Joined majority opinion
4. Kennedy, A. – Joined majority opinion
5. Rehnquist, W. – Joined majority opinion

VI. A WIN OR LOSS FOR THE ACLU?

The ACLU argued the case for appellee, urging affirmance; the Supreme Court reversed the Court of Appeals' decision by a 5-4 vote, giving the ACLU an apparent loss.

934. Connecticut Dep't of Pub. Safety v. Doe

(Decided March 5, 2003; 538 U.S. 1)

I. ISSUE

A. Issues Discussed

State, civil rights

B. Legal Question Presented

"[W]hether the United States Court of Appeals for the Second Circuit properly enjoined the public disclosure of Connecticut's sex offender registry."

C. Supreme Court's Answer

"We . . . reverse the judgment of the Court of Appeals because due process does not require the opportunity to prove a fact that is not material to the State's statutory scheme."

II. CASE SUMMARY

A. Background

"'Sex offenders are a serious threat in this Nation.' '[T]he victims of sex assault are most often juveniles,' and '[w]hen convicted sex offenders reenter society, they are much more likely than any other type of offender to be re-arrested for a new rape or sexual assault.' Connecticut, like every other State, has responded to these facts by enacting a statute designed to protect its communities from sex offenders and to help apprehend repeat sex offenders. Connecticut's 'Megan's Law' applies to all persons convicted of criminal offenses against a minor, violent and nonviolent sexual offenses, and felonies committed for a sexual purpose. Covered offenders must register with the Connecticut Department of Public Safety (DPS) upon their release into the community. . . .

The statute requires DPS to compile the information gathered from registrants and publicize it. In particular, the law requires DPS to post a sex offender registry on an Internet Website and to make the registry available to the public in certain state offices. Whether made available in an office or via the Internet, the registry must be accompanied by the following warning: "Any person who uses information in this registry to injure, harass or commit a criminal act against any person included in the registry or any other person is subject to criminal prosecution." . . .

Petitioners include the state agencies and officials charged with compiling the sex offender registry and posting it on the Internet. Respondent Doe (hereinafter respondent) is a convicted sex offender who is subject to Connecticut's Megan's Law. He filed this action pursuant to Rev. Stat. § 1979, 42 U.S.C. § 1983, on behalf of himself and similarly situated sex offenders, claiming that the law violates, inter alia, the Due Process Clause of the Fourteenth Amendment. Specifically, respondent alleged that he is not a "dangerous sexual offender," and that the Connecticut law 'deprives him of a liberty interest—his reputation combined with the alteration of his status under state law—without notice or a meaningful opportunity to be heard.' The District Court granted summary judgment for respondent on his due process claim. The court then certified a class of individuals subject to the Connecticut law, and permanently enjoined the law's public disclosure provisions.

The Court of Appeals affirmed . . . ."

The Supreme Court granted certiorari to review the case.

B. Counsel of Record:

ACLU Side (Respondent / Appellee): Shelley R. Sadin argued the cause for appellees. With her on the brief were Drew S. Days III, Beth S. Brinkmann, Seth M. Galanter, Philip Tegeler of the Connecticut Civil Liberties Union Foundation, and Steven R. Shapiro of the ACLU Foundation.

Opposing Side (Petitioner / Appellant): Richard Blumenthal, Attorney General of Connecticut, argued the cause for appellants. With him on the briefs were Gregory T. D'Auria, Associate Attorney General, and Lynn D. Wittenbrink, Perry Zinn Rowthorn, and Mark F. Kohler, Assistant Attorneys General.

Solicitor General Olson argued the cause for the United States as amicus curiae.

III. AMICI CURIAE

ACLU Side (Respondent / Appellee)

Brief of amici curiae filed on behalf of the Association for the Treatment of Sexual Abusers by David A. Reiser.

Brief of amici curiae filed on behalf of the Office of the Public Defender for the State of New Jersey by Peter A. Garcia, Michael Z. Buncher, and Brian J. Neff.

Brief of amici curiae filed on behalf of the Public Defender Service for the District of Columbia et al. by James W. Klein, Samia A. Fam, and Corinne A. Beckwith.

Opposing Side (Petitioner / Appellant)

Brief of amici curiae filed on behalf of the United States by Solicitor General Olson, Assistant Attorney General McCallum, Deputy Solicitor General Clement, Gregory G. Garre, Leonard Schaitman, and Mark W. Pennak.

Brief of amici curiae filed on behalf of the District of Columbia et al. by Robert R. Rigsby, Corporation Counsel of the District of Columbia, Charles L. Reischel, Deputy Corporation Counsel, and Edward E. Schwab, Senior Assistant Corporation Counsel, and by the Attorneys General for their respective jurisdictions as follows: Bill Pryor of Alabama, Bruce M. Botelho of Alaska, Janet Napolitano of Arizona, Bill Lockyer of California, Ken Salazar of Colorado, M. Jane Brady of Delaware, Robert A. Butterworth of Florida, Thurbert E. Baker of Georgia, Earl I. Anzai of Hawaii, James E. Ryan of Illinois, Steve Carter of Indiana, Carla J. Stovall of Kansas, Albert B. Chandler III of Kentucky, Richard P. Ieyoub of Louisiana, J. Joseph Curran, Jr., of Maryland, Jennifer M. Granholm of Michigan, Mike Moore of Mississippi, Jeremiah W. (Jay) Nixon of Missouri, Don Stenberg of Nebraska, Frankie Sue Del Papa of Nevada, Patricia A. Madrid of New Mexico, Eliot Spitzer of New York, Robert Torres of the Northern Mariana Islands, W. A. Drew Edmondson of Oklahoma, Hardy Myers of Oregon, Anabelle Rodríguez of Puerto Rico, Charles M. Condon of South Carolina, Mark Barnett of South Dakota, Paul G. Summers of Tennessee, John Cornyn of Texas, Mark L. Shurtleff of Utah, Jerry W. Kilgore of Virginia, Christine

O. Gregoire of Washington, Darrell V. McGraw, Jr., of West Virginia, and James E. Doyle of Wisconsin.

Brief of amici curiae filed on behalf of the National Governors Association et al. by Richard Ruda and James I. Crowley.

Brief of amici curiae filed on behalf of the Center for the Community Interest by Robert J. Del Tufo.

Brief of amici curiae filed on behalf of the Criminal Justice Legal Foundation by Kent S. Scheidegger.

Brief of amici curiae filed on behalf of the Reporters Committee for Freedom of the Press by Lucy A. Dalglish and Gregg P. Leslie.

IV. THE SUPREME COURT'S DECISION

"In Paul v. Davis, 424 U.S. 693 (1976), we held that mere injury to reputation, even if defamatory, does not constitute the deprivation of a liberty interest. Petitioners urge us to reverse the Court of Appeals on the ground that, under Paul v. Davis, respondent has failed to establish that petitioners have deprived him of a liberty interest. We find it unnecessary to reach this question, however, because even assuming, arguendo, that respondent has been deprived of a liberty interest, due process does not entitle him to a hearing to establish a fact that is not material under the Connecticut statute.

In cases such as Wisconsin v. Constantineau, 400 U.S. 433 (1971), and Goss v. Lopez, 419 U.S. 565 (1975), we held that due process required the government to accord the plaintiff a hearing to prove or disprove a particular fact or set of facts. But in each of these cases, the fact in question was concededly relevant to the inquiry at hand. Here, however, the fact that respondent seeks to prove—that he is not currently dangerous—is of no consequence under Connecticut's Megan's Law. As the DPS Website explains, the law's requirements turn on an offender's conviction alone—a fact that a convicted offender has already had a procedurally safeguarded opportunity to contest. . . . No other fact is relevant to the disclosure of registrants' information. Indeed, the disclaimer on the Website explicitly states that respondent's alleged nondangerousness simply does not matter. . . .

In short, even if respondent could prove that he is not likely to be currently dangerous, Connecticut has decided that the registry information of all sex offenders—currently dangerous or not—must be publicly disclosed. Unless respondent can show that that substantive rule of law is defective (by conflicting with a provision of the Constitution), any hearing on current dangerousness is a bootless exercise. It may be that respondent's claim is actually a substantive challenge to Connecticut's statute 'recast in 'procedural due process' terms.' Nonetheless, respondent expressly disavows any reliance on the substantive component of the Fourteenth Amendment's protections, and maintains, as he did below, that his challenge is strictly a procedural one. But States are not barred by principles of 'procedural due process' from drawing such classifications. Such claims 'must ultimately be analyzed' in terms of substantive, not procedural, due process. Because the question is not properly before us, we express no opinion as to whether Connecticut's Megan's Law violates principles of substantive due process.

Plaintiffs who assert a right to a hearing under the Due Process Clause must show that the facts they seek to establish in that hearing are relevant under the statutory scheme. Respondent cannot make that showing here. The judgment of the Court of Appeals is therefore reversed."

V. JUSTICE VOTE

0 Pro ACLU Side vs. 9 Con Opposing Side

Opposing Side (Petitioner / Appellant)

1. Rehnquist, W. – Wrote majority opinion
2. Thomas, C. – Joined majority opinion
3. Ginsburg, R. – Joined Souter's concurrence
4. Souter, D. – Wrote concurring opinion
5. O'Connor, S. – Joined majority opinion
6. Stevens, J. – Wrote concurring opinion
7. Breyer, S. – Joined majority opinion
8. Scalia, A. – Wrote concurring opinion
9. Kennedy, A. – Joined majority opinion

VI. A WIN OR LOSS FOR THE ACLU?

The ACLU argued the case for appellee, urging affirmance; the Supreme Court reversed the Court of Appeals' decision by a 9-0 vote, giving the ACLU an apparent loss.

935. Lockyer v. Andrade

(Decided March 5, 2003; 538 U.S. 63)

I. ISSUE

A. Issues Discussed

8th Amendment

B. Legal Question Presented

"[W]hether the United States Court of Appeals for the Ninth Circuit erred in ruling that the California Court of Appeal's decision affirming Leandro Andrade's two consecutive terms of 25 years to life in prison for a 'third strike' conviction is contrary to, or an unreasonable application of, clearly established federal law as determined by this Court within the meaning of 28 U.S.C. § 2254(d)(1)."

C. Supreme Court's Answer

"The gross disproportionality principle reserves a constitutional violation for only the extraordinary case. In applying this principle for § 2254(d)(1) purposes, it was not an unreasonable application of our clearly established law for the California Court of Appeal to affirm Andrade's sentence of two consecutive terms of 25 years to life in prison."

II. CASE SUMMARY

A. Background

"Because of his 1990 misdemeanor conviction, the State charged Andrade in this case with two counts of petty theft with a prior conviction, in violation of Cal. Penal Code Ann. § 666. Under California law, petty theft with a prior conviction is a so-called 'wobbler' offense because it is punishable either as a misdemeanor or as a felony. The decision to prosecute petty theft with a prior conviction as a misdemeanor or as a felony is in the discretion of the prosecutor. The trial court also has discretion to reduce the charge to a misdemeanor at the time of sentencing.

Under California's three strikes law, any felony can constitute the third strike, and thus can subject a defendant to a term of 25 years to life in prison. In this case, the prosecutor decided to charge the two counts of theft as felonies rather than misdemeanors. The trial court denied Andrade's motion to reduce the offenses to misdemeanors, both before the jury verdict and again in state habeas proceedings.

A jury found Andrade guilty of two counts of petty theft with a prior conviction. According to California law, a jury must also find that a defendant has been convicted of at least two serious or violent felonies that serve as qualifying offenses under the three strikes regime. In this case, the jury made a special finding that Andrade was convicted of three counts of first-degree residential burglary. A conviction for first-degree residential burglary qualifies as a serious or violent felony for the purposes of the three strikes law. As a consequence, each of Andrade's convictions for theft . . . triggered a separate application of the three strikes law. Pursuant to California law, the judge sentenced Andrade to two consecutive terms of 25 years to life in prison. . . .

On direct appeal in 1997, the California Court of Appeal affirmed Andrade's sentence of two consecutive terms of 25 years to life in prison. . . .

After the Supreme Court of California denied discretionary review, Andrade filed a petition for a writ of habeas corpus in Federal District Court. The District Court denied his petition. The Ninth Circuit granted Andrade a certificate of appealability as to his claim that his sentence violated the Eighth Amendment, and subsequently reversed the judgment of the District Court."

The Supreme Court granted certiorari to review the case.

B. Counsel of Record

ACLU Side (Respondent / Appellee):

Erwin Chemerinsky argued the cause for appellee. With him on the brief were Paul Hoffman, Jordan C. Budd of the ACLU of San Diego and Imperial Counties, Steven R. Shapiro of the ACLU Foundation, Mark D. Rosenbaum and Daniel P. Tokaji of the ACLU Foundation of Southern California, and Alan L. Schlosser of the ACLU Foundation of Northern California.

Opposing Side (Petitioner / Appellant): Douglas P. Danzig, Deputy Attorney General of California, argued the cause for appellant. With him on the briefs were Bill Lockyer, Attorney General, pro se, Robert R. Anderson, Chief Assistant Attorney General, Gary W. Schons, Senior Assistant Attorney General, and Carl H. Horst, Supervising Deputy Attorney General.

III. AMICI CURIAE

ACLU Side (Respondent / Appellee)

Brief of amici curiae filed on behalf of the California Public Defenders Association by Kenneth I. Clayman.

Brief of amici curiae filed on behalf of Families to Amend California's Three Strikes et al. by Gerald F. Uelmen.

Brief of amici curiae filed on behalf of the National Association of Criminal Defense Lawyers by Sheryl Gordon McCloud.

Brief of amici curiae filed on behalf of Donald Ray Hill by Susan S. Azad and Kathryn M. Davis.

Brief of amici curiae filed on behalf of Michael P. Judge by Albert J. Menaster and Alex Ricciardulli.

Opposing Side (Petitioner / Appellant)

Brief of amici curiae filed on behalf of the Criminal Justice Legal Foundation et al. by Kent S. Scheidegger and Charles L. Hobson.

Brief of amici curiae filed on behalf of the California District Attorneys Association by Dennis L. Stout and Grover D. Merritt.

IV. THE SUPREME COURT'S DECISION

"Andrade's argument in this Court is that two consecutive terms of 25 years to life for stealing approximately $150 in videotapes is grossly disproportionate in violation of the Eighth Amendment. Andrade similarly maintains that the state court decision affirming his sentence is 'contrary to, or involved an unreasonable application of, clearly established Federal law, as determined by the Supreme Court of the United States.' . . .

As a threshold matter here, we first decide what constitutes 'clearly established Federal law, as determined by the Supreme Court of the United States.' . . .

Through this thicket of Eighth Amendment jurisprudence, one governing legal principle emerges as 'clearly established' under § 2254(d)(1): A gross disproportionality principle is applicable to sentences for terms of years.

Our cases exhibit a lack of clarity regarding what factors may indicate gross disproportionality. . . .

Thus, in this case, the only relevant clearly established law amenable to the 'contrary to' or 'unreasonable application of' framework is the gross disproportionality principle, the precise contours of which are unclear, applicable only in the 'exceedingly rare' and 'extreme' case. . . .

The final question is whether the California Court of Appeal's decision affirming Andrade's sentence is 'contrary to, or involved an unreasonable application of,' this clearly established gross disproportionality principle.

First, a state court decision is 'contrary to our clearly established precedent if the state court applies a rule that contradicts the governing law set forth in our cases' or 'if the state court confronts a set of facts that are materially indistinguishable from a decision of this Court and nevertheless arrives at a result different from our precedent.' In terms of length of sentence and availability of parole, severity of the underlying offense, and the impact of recidivism, Andrade's sentence implicates factors relevant in both Rummel and Solem. . . . Harmelin allows a state court to reasonably rely on Rummel in determining whether a sentence is grossly disproportionate. The California Court of Appeal's decision was therefore not 'contrary to' the governing legal principles set forth in our cases.

Andrade's sentence also was not materially indistinguishable from the facts in Solem. The facts here fall in between the facts in Rummel and the facts in Solem. . . . Consequently, the state court did not 'confron[t] a set of facts that are materially indistinguishable from a decision of this Court and nevertheless arriv[e] at a result different from our precedent.'

Second, '[u]nder the 'unreasonable application' clause, a federal habeas court may grant the writ if the state court identifies the correct governing legal principle from this Court's decisions but unreasonably applies that principle to the facts of the prisoner's case.' The 'unreasonable application' clause requires the state court decision to be more than incorrect or erroneous. The state court's application of clearly established law must be objectively unreasonable. . . .

It is not enough that a federal habeas court, in its 'independent review of the legal question,' is left with a "firm conviction" that the state court was "erroneous." We have held precisely the opposite: 'Under § 2254(d)(1)'s 'unreasonable application' clause, then, a federal habeas court may not issue the writ simply because that court concludes in its independent judgment that the relevant state-court decision applied clearly established federal law erroneously or incorrectly.' Rather, that application must be objectively unreasonable. . . .

The gross disproportionality principle reserves a constitutional violation for only the extraordinary case. In applying this principle for § 2254(d)(1) purposes, it was not an unreasonable application of our clearly established law for the California Court of Appeal to affirm Andrade's sentence of two consecutive terms of 25 years to life in prison.

The judgment of the United States Court of Appeals for the Ninth Circuit, accordingly, is reversed."

V. JUSTICE VOTE

4 Pro ACLU Side vs. 5 Con Opposing Side

ACLU Side (Respondent / Appellee)

1. Souter, D. – Wrote dissenting opinion
2. Stevens, J. – Joined Souter's dissent
3. Ginsburg, R. – Joined Souter's dissent
4. Breyer, S. – Joined Souter's dissent

Opposing Side (Petitioner / Appellant)

1. O'Connor, S. – Wrote majority opinion
2. Thomas, C. – Joined majority opinion
3. Scalia, A. – Joined majority opinion
4. Kennedy, A. – Joined majority opinion
5. Rehnquist, W. – Joined majority opinion

VI. A WIN OR LOSS FOR THE ACLU?

The ACLU argued the case for appellee, urging affirmance; the Supreme Court reversed the Court of Appeals' decision by a 5-4 vote, giving the ACLU an apparent loss.

936. Smith v. Doe

(Decided March 5, 2003; 538 U.S. 84)

I. ISSUE

A. Issues Discussed

Federal, civil rights

B. Legal Question Presented

"The Alaska Sex Offender Registration Act requires convicted sex offenders to register with law enforcement authorities, and much of the information is made public. We must decide whether the registration requirement is a retroactive punishment prohibited by the Ex Post Facto Clause."

C. Supreme Court's Answer

"Our examination of the Act's effects leads to the determination that respondents cannot show, much less by the clearest proof, that the effects of the law negate Alaska's intention to establish a civil regulatory scheme. The Act is nonpunitive, and its retroactive application does not violate the Ex Post Facto Clause."

II. CASE SUMMARY

A. Background

"The State of Alaska enacted the Alaska Sex Offender Registration Act (Act) on May 12, 1994. Like its counterparts in other States, the Act is termed a 'Megan's Law.' . . .

The Alaska law, which is our concern in this case, contains two components: a registration requirement and a notification system. Both are retroactive. . . .

The information is forwarded to the Alaska Department of Public Safety, which maintains a central registry of sex offenders. § 18.65.087(a). Some of the data . . . are kept confidential. The following information is made available to the public: 'the sex offender's or child kidnapper's name, aliases, address, photograph, physical description, description[,] license [and] identification numbers of motor vehicles, place of employment, date of birth, crime for which convicted, date of conviction, place and court of conviction, length and conditions of sentence, and a statement as to whether the offender or kidnapper is in compliance with [the update] requirements . . . or cannot be located.' . . . Alaska has chosen to make most of the nonconfidential information available on the Internet. . . .

Respondents John Doe I and John Doe II were convicted of sexual abuse of a minor, an aggravated sex offense. . . . Although convicted before the passage of the Act, respondents are covered by it. . . . Both respondents, along with respondent Jane Doe, wife of John Doe I, brought an action under Rev. Stat. § 1979, 42 U.S.C. § 1983, seeking to declare the Act void as to them under the Ex Post Facto Clause of Article I, § 10, cl. 1, of the Constitution and the Due Process Clause of § 1 of the Fourteenth Amendment. The United States District Court for the District of Alaska granted summary judgment for petitioners. In agreement with the District Court, the Court of Appeals for the Ninth Circuit determined the state legislature had intended the Act to be a nonpunitive, civil regulatory scheme; but, in disagreement with the District Court, it held the effects of the Act were punitive despite the legislature's intent. In consequence, it held the Act violates the Ex Post Facto Clause. "

The Supreme Court granted certiorari to review the case.

B. Counsel of Record:

ACLU Side (Respondent / Appellee): Darryl L. Thompson argued the cause for appellees. With him on the brief was Verne E. Rupright.

Opposing Side (Petitioner / Appellant): John G. Roberts, Jr., argued the cause for appellants. With him on the briefs were Jonathan S. Franklin, Catherine E. Stetson, Cynthia M. Cooper, and Bruce M. Botelho, Attorney General of Alaska.

Solicitor General Olson argued the cause for the United States as amicus curiae urging reversal. With him on the brief were Assistant Attorney General McCallum, Deputy Solicitor General Dreeben, Patricia A. Millett, Leonard Schaitman, Mark W. Pennak, and Wendy M. Keats. III.

AMICI CURIAE

ACLU Side (Respondent / Appellee)

Brief of amici curiae filed on behalf of the American Civil Liberties Union, the Alaska Civil Liberties Union, and the National Association of Criminal Defense Lawyers by Lawrence S. Lustberg, Steven R. Shapiro, Jessica A. Roth, and Joshua L. Dratel.

Brief of amici curiae filed on behalf of the Office of the Public Defender for the State of New Jersey, the Association of Criminal Defense Lawyers of New Jersey, and the American Civil Liberties Union of New Jersey by Peter A. Garcia, Michael Z. Buncher, Brian J. Neff, Richard S. Lehrich, and Edward Barocas.

Brief of amici curiae filed on behalf of Citizens for Penal Reform, Inc., by W. Andrew McCullough.

Brief of amici curiae filed on behalf of the Electronic Privacy Information Center by Marc Rotenberg.

Brief of amici curiae filed on behalf of the Massachusetts Committee for Public Counsel Services by Carol A. Donovan.

Brief of amici curiae filed on behalf of the Public Defender Service for the District of Columbia by James W. Klein, Samia A. Fam, and Corinne A. Beckwith.

Opposing Side (Petitioner / Appellant)

Brief of amici curiae filed on behalf of the State of California ex rel. Bill Lockyer by Mr. Lockyer, Attorney General of California, Robert R. Anderson, Chief Assistant Attorney General, Jo Graves, Senior Assistant Attorney General, Stan Cross, Supervising Deputy Attorney General, Janet E. Neeley, Deputy Attorney General, Ken Salazar, Attorney General of Colorado, Alan Gilbert, Solicitor General, Donald S. Quick, Deputy Attorney General, Matthew S. Holman, Assistant Attorney General, and Robert R. Rigsby, Corporation Counsel of the District of Columbia, and by the Attorneys General for their respective jurisdictions as follows: Bill Pryor of Alabama, Janet Napolitano of Arizona, Richard Blumenthal of Connecticut, M. Jane Brady of Delaware, Robert A. Butterworth of Florida, Thurbert E. Baker of Georgia, Earl I. Anzai of Hawaii, James E. Ryan of Illinois, Steve Carter of Indiana, Carla J. Stovall of Kansas, Albert B. Chandler III of Kentucky, Richard P. Ieyoub of Louisiana, J. Joseph Curran, Jr., of Maryland, Thomas F. Reilly of Massachusetts, Mike Moore of Mississippi, Jeremiah W. (Jay) Nixon of Missouri, Mike McGrath of Montana, Don Stenberg of Nebraska, Frankie Sue Del Papa of Nevada, Philip T. McLaughlin of New Hampshire, David Samson of New Jersey, Patricia A. Madrid of New Mexico, Eliot Spitzer of New York, Wayne Stenehjem of North Dakota, Betty D. Montgomery of Ohio, W. A. Drew Edmondson of Oklahoma, Hardy Myers of Oregon, D. Michael Fisher of Pennsylvania, Anabelle Rodríguez of Puerto Rico, Charles M. Condon of South Carolina, Mark Barnett of South Dakota, Paul G. Summers of Tennessee, John Cornyn of Texas, Mark L. Shurtleff of Utah, William H. Sorrell of Vermont, Iver A. Stridiron of the Virgin Islands, Christine O. Gregoire of Washington, Darrell V. McGraw, Jr., of West Virginia, and James E. Doyle of Wisconsin.

Brief of amici curiae filed on behalf of the Council of State Governments et al. by Richard Ruda and James I. Crowley.

Brief of amici curiae filed on behalf of the Reporters Committee for Freedom of the Press Lucy A. Dalglish and Gregg P. Leslie.

IV. THE SUPREME COURT'S DECISION

"This is the first time we have considered a claim that a sex offender registration and notification law constitutes retroactive punishment forbidden by the Ex Post Facto Clause. The framework for our inquiry, however, is well established. We must 'ascertain whether the legislature meant the statute to establish 'civil' proceedings.' If the intention of the legislature was to impose punishment, that ends the inquiry. If, however, the intention was to enact a regulatory scheme that is civil and nonpunitive, we must further examine whether the statutory scheme is "so punitive either in purpose or effect as to negate [the State's] intention' to deem it 'civil." . . .

Whether a statutory scheme is civil or criminal 'is first of all a question of statutory construction.' . . .

We conclude, as did the District Court and the Court of Appeals, that the intent of the Alaska Legislature was to create a civil, nonpunitive regime. . . .

In analyzing the effects of the Act we refer to the seven factors noted in Kennedy v. Mendoza-Martinez, 372 U.S. 144 (1963), as a useful framework. . . . The factors most relevant to our analysis are whether, in its necessary operation, the regulatory scheme: has been regarded in our history and traditions as a punishment; imposes an affirmative disability or restraint; promotes the traditional aims of punishment; has a rational connection to a nonpunitive purpose; or is excessive with respect to this purpose. . . .

It must be acknowledged that notice of a criminal conviction subjects the offender to public shame, the humiliation increasing in proportion to the extent of the publicity. . . . These facts do not render Internet notification punitive. The purpose and the principal effect of notification are to inform the public for its own safety, not to humiliate the offender. . . .

We next consider whether the Act subjects respondents to an 'affirmative disability or restraint.' . . .

The Act imposes no physical restraint, and so does not resemble the punishment of imprisonment, which is the paradigmatic affirmative disability or restraint. . . . The Act does not restrain activities sex offenders may pursue but leaves them free to change jobs or residences. . . .

The State concedes that the statute might deter future crimes. Respondents seize on this proposition to argue that the law is punitive, because deterrence is one purpose of punishment. This proves too much. Any number of governmental programs might deter crime without imposing punishment. . . .

The Act's rational connection to a nonpunitive purpose is a '[m]ost significant' factor in our determination that the statute's effects are not punitive. . . .

In concluding the Act was excessive in relation to its regulatory purpose, the Court of Appeals relied in large part on two propositions: first, that the statute applies to all convicted sex offenders without regard to their future dangerousness; and, second, that it places no limits on the number of persons who have access to the information. Neither argument is persuasive. . . .

The excessiveness inquiry of our ex post facto jurisprudence is not an exercise in determining whether the legislature has made the best choice possible to address the problem it seeks to remedy. The question is whether the regulatory means chosen are reasonable in light of the nonpunitive objective. The Act meets this standard.

The two remaining Mendoza-Martinez factors—whether the regulation comes into play only on a finding of scienter and whether the behavior to which it applies is already a crime—are of little weight in this case. . . .

Our examination of the Act's effects leads to the determination that respondents cannot show, much less by the clearest proof, that the effects of the law negate Alaska's intention to establish a civil regulatory scheme. The Act is nonpunitive, and its retroactive application does not violate the Ex Post Facto Clause. The judgment of the Court of Appeals for the Ninth Circuit is reversed, and the case is remanded for further proceedings consistent with this opinion."

V. JUSTICE VOTE

3 Pro ACLU Side vs. 6 Con Opposing Side

ACLU Side (Respondent / Appellee)

1. Stevens, J. – Wrote dissenting opinion
2. Ginsburg, R. – Wrote dissenting opinion
3. Breyer, S. – Joined Ginsburg's dissent

Opposing Side (Petitioner / Appellant)

1. Kennedy, A. – Wrote majority opinion
2. Thomas, C. – Joined majority opinion
3. Souter, D. – Wrote concurring opinion
4. O'Connor, S. – Joined majority opinion
5. Scalia, A. – Joined majority opinion
6. Rehnquist, W. – Joined majority opinion

VI. A WIN OR LOSS FOR THE ACLU?

The ACLU filed as amicus curiae, urging affirmance; the Supreme Court reversed the Court of Appeals' decision by a 6-3 vote, giving the ACLU an apparent loss.

937. Virginia v. Black

(Decided April 7, 2003; 538 U.S. 343)

I. ISSUE

A. Issues Discussed

1st Amendment, press, speech, association, race

B. Legal Question Presented

"[W]hether the Commonwealth of Virginia's statute banning cross burning with 'an intent to intimidate a person or group of persons' violates the First Amendment."

C. Supreme Court's Answer

"We conclude that while a State, consistent with the First Amendment, may ban cross burning carried out with the intent to intimidate, the provision in the Virginia statute treating any cross burning as prima facie evidence of intent to intimidate renders the statute unconstitutional in its current form."

II. CASE SUMMARY

A. Background

"Respondents Barry Black, Richard Elliott, and Jonathan O'Mara were convicted separately of violating Virginia's cross-burning statute . . . .

On August 22, 1998, Barry Black led a Ku Klux Klan rally in Carroll County, Virginia. . . .

At the conclusion of the rally, the crowd circled around a 25- to 30-foot cross. [T]he cross 'then all of a sudden . . . went up in a flame.' . . .

Black was charged with burning a cross with the intent of intimidating a person or group of persons, in violation of § 18.2-423. . . . The jury found Black guilty, and fined him $2,500. The Court of Appeals of Virginia affirmed Black's conviction.

On May 2, 1998, respondents Richard Elliott and Jonathan O'Mara, as well as a third individual, attempted to burn a cross on the yard of James Jubilee. . . .

Elliott and O'Mara were charged with attempted cross burning and conspiracy to commit cross burning. O'Mara pleaded guilty . . . , reserving the right to challenge the constitutionality of the cross-burning statute. The judge sentenced O'Mara to 90 days in jail and fined him $2,500. The judge also suspended 45 days of the sentence and $1,000 of the fine. . . .

The jury found Elliott guilty of attempted cross burning and acquitted him of conspiracy to commit cross burning. It sentenced Elliott to 90 days in jail and a $2,500 fine. The Court of Appeals of Virginia affirmed the convictions of both Elliott and O'Mara.

Each respondent appealed to the Supreme Court of Virginia, arguing that § 18.2-423 is facially unconstitutional. The Supreme

Court of Virginia consolidated all three cases, and held that the statute is unconstitutional on its face."

The Supreme Court granted certiorari to review the case.

B. Counsel of Record

ACLU Side (Respondent / Appellee): Rodney A. Smolla argued the cause for appellee. With him on the briefs were Rebecca K. Glenberg of the American Civil Liberties Union of Virginia, James O. Broccoletti, David P. Baugh, Sara G. Davis, and Kevin E. Martingayle.

Opposing Side (Petitioner / Appellant): William H. Hurd, State Solicitor of Virginia, argued the cause for appellant. With him on the brief were Jerry W. Kilgore, Attorney General, Maureen Riley Matsen and William E. Thro, Deputy State Solicitors, and Alison P. Landry, Assistant Attorney General. Deputy Solicitor General Dreeben argued the cause for the United States as amicus curiae.

III. AMICI CURIAE

ACLU Side (Respondent / Appellee)

Brief of amici curiae filed on behalf of the Council of Conservative Citizens by Edgar J. Steele.

Brief of amici curiae filed on behalf of the Rutherford Institute by John W. Whitehead and Steven H. Aden.

Brief of amici curiae filed on behalf of the Thomas Jefferson Center for the Protection of Free Expression by Robert M. O'Neil and J. Joshua Wheeler.

Brief of amici curiae filed on behalf of the Anti-Defamation League et al. by Martin E. Karlinsky, Howard W Goldstein, Steven M. Freeman, Frederick M. Lawrence, and Elliot M. Mincberg in support of neither party.

Opposing Side (Petitioner / Appellant)

Brief of amici curiae filed on behalf of the United States by Deputy Solicitor General Dreeben, Solicitor General Olson, Assistant Attorney General Boyd, Barbara McDowell, Jessica Dunsay Silver, and Linda F. Thome.

Brief of amici curiae filed on behalf of the State of California by Bill Lockyer, Attorney General, Manuel M. Medeiros, State Solicitor General, Richard M. Frank, Chief Assistant Attorney General, and Angela Sierra, Deputy Attorney General.

Brief of amici curiae filed on behalf of the State of New Jersey et al. by David Samson, Attorney General of New Jersey, and Carol Johnston, Deputy Attorney General, and by the Attorneys General for their respective States as follows: Janet Napolitano of Arizona, Richard Blumenthal of Connecticut, Thomas J. Miller of Iowa, J. Joseph Curran, Jr., of Maryland, Thomas F. Reilly of Massachusetts, Jennifer M. Granholm of Michigan, Don Stenberg of Nebraska, Frankie Sue Del Papa of Nevada, Roy Cooper of North Carolina, W. A. Drew Edmondson of Oklahoma, Hardy Myers of Oregon, Mark L. Shurtleff of Utah, and William H. Sorrell of Vermont.

Brief of amici curiae filed on behalf of the Criminal Justice Legal Foundation by Kent S. Scheidegger.

IV. THE SUPREME COURT'S DECISION

"The First Amendment, applicable to the States through the Fourteenth Amendment, provides that 'Congress shall make no law . . . abridging the freedom of speech.' . . .

The protections afforded by the First Amendment, however, are not absolute, and we have long recognized that the government may regulate certain categories of expression . . . .

Respondents do not contest that some cross burnings fit within th[e] meaning of intimidating speech, and rightly so. [T]he history of cross burning in this country shows that cross burning is often intimidating, intended to create a pervasive fear in victims that they are a target of violence. . . .

It is true . . . that the burning of a cross is symbolic expression. . . .

The fact that cross burning is symbolic expression, however, does not resolve the constitutional question. The Supreme Court of Virginia relied upon R.A.V. v. City of St. Paul to conclude that once a statute discriminates on the basis of this type of content, the law is unconstitutional. We disagree. . . .

We did not hold in R.A.V. that the First Amendment prohibits all forms of content-based discrimination within a proscribable area of speech. Rather, we specifically stated that some types of content discrimination did not violate the First Amendment . . . .

The First Amendment permits Virginia to outlaw cross burnings done with the intent to intimidate because burning a cross is a particularly virulent form of intimidation. . . . A ban on cross burning carried out with the intent to intimidate is fully consistent with our holding in R.A.V. . . . .

The Supreme Court of Virginia ruled in the alternative that Virginia's cross-burning statute was unconstitutionally overbroad due to its provision stating that '[a]ny such burning of a cross shall be prima facie evidence of an intent to intimidate a person or group of persons.' . . .

[T]he prima facie evidence provision, as interpreted through the jury instruction and as applied in Barry Black's case, is unconstitutional on its face. [A]ll we hold is that because of the interpretation of the prima facie evidence provision given by the jury instruction, the provision makes the statute facially invalid at this point. We also recognize the theoretical possibility that the court, on remand, could interpret the provision in a manner different from that so far set forth in order to avoid the constitutional objections we have described. We leave open that possibility. We also leave open the possibility that the provision is severable . . . .

With respect to Barry Black, we agree with the Supreme Court of Virginia that his conviction cannot stand, and we affirm the judgment of the Supreme Court of Virginia. With respect to Elliott and O'Mara, we vacate the judgment of the Supreme Court of Virginia, and remand the case . . . ."

V. JUSTICE VOTE

7 Pro ACLU Side vs. 2 Con Opposing Side

ACLU Side (Respondent / Appellee)

1. O'Connor, S. – Wrote majority opinion
2. Rehnquist, W. – Joined majority opinion
3. Stevens, J. – Wrote concurring opinion

4. Breyer, S. – Joined majority opinion
5. Ginsburg, R. – Joined Souter's opinion
6. Souter, D. – Wrote opinion concurring in part and dissenting in part
7. Kennedy, A. – Joined Souter's opinion

Opposing Side (Petitioner / Appellant)

1. Scalia, A. – Wrote opinion concurring in part and dissenting in part
2. Thomas, C. – Wrote dissenting opinion, joined Scalia's opinion in part

VI. A WIN OR LOSS FOR THE ACLU?

The ACLU served as counsel for appellee urging affirmance; the Supreme Court affirmed in part and vacated in part the Court of Appeals' decision by a 7-2 vote, giving the ACLU an apparent win.

938. Medical Board of California v. Hason

(Decided April 7, 2003; 538 U.S. 958)

I. ISSUE

A. Issues Discussed

Civil rights, federal

B. Legal Question Presented

"May state governments be sued for violating Title II of the Americans with Disabilities Act, which prohibits discrimination against individuals with disabilities in government 'services, programs, or activities'? More specifically, is Title II of the Americans with Disabilities Act a proportionate and congruent means to prevent and remedy pervasive violations of the constitutional rights of people with disabilities that deny equal access to the basic functions of state governments?"[1]

C. Supreme Court's Answer

"Writ of certiorari to the United States Court of Appeals for the Ninth Circuit dismissed without award of damages and costs."

II. CASE SUMMARY

A. Background

"In March of 1995, Michael J. Hason, M.D., applied for a license to practice medicine in the state of California. In April of 1998, the California Medical Board denied, for reasons of mental illness, Dr. Hason's application for a medical license. Dr. Hason subsequently filed a pro se complaint in federal district court alleging violations of his rights under the United States Constitution (brought pursuant to 42 U.S.C. § 1983) and Title II of the ADA, 42 U.S.C. § 12132. The complaint also alleged state law tort claims which are not at issue on this appeal.

Dr. Hason's complaint named as defendants The Medical Board of the State of California ['The Medical Board'], the Department of Consumer Affairs of the State of California and its director, and various other individuals that were either members of or otherwise affiliated with the Medical Board (in both their official and personal capacities). Dr. Hason sought both damages and injunctive relief.

On April 25, 2000, the District Court dismissed Dr. Hason's complaint without prejudice as to the individual defendants in their personal capacities, and with prejudice as to the two named state agencies and the individual defendants in their official capacities. The Report and Recommendation of the United States Magistrate Judge, which was affirmed in its entirety by the District Court, stated three reasons for dismissing Dr. Hason's complaint. First, the Report concluded that Dr. Hason's claims were barred by the Eleventh Amendment. Second, the Report concluded that Dr. Hason failed to state a claim upon which relief could be granted under Title II of the ADA. Third, the Report concluded that Dr. Hason's claims against the individual defendants in their personal capacities should be dismissed for failure to prosecute."[2]

The Ninth Circuit Court of Appeals reversed. The Supreme Court granted certiorari to review the case.

B. Counsel of Record

ACLU Side (Respondent / Appellee): Brief for appellee filed by Mark D. Rosenbaum of the ACLU Foundation of Southern California, Steven R. Shapiro of the American Civil Liberties

Union Foundation, Paul M. Smith, Erwin Chemerinsky, and Paul Hoffman.

Brief filed on behalf of the United States by Theodore B. Olson, Solicitor General, Ralph F. Boyd, Jr., Assistant Attorney General, Paul D. Clement, Deputy Solicitor General, Patricia A. Millett, Assistant to the Solicitor General, and Jessica Dunsay Silver and Kevin Russell, Attorneys for the Department of Justice.

Opposing Side (Petitioner / Appellant): Brief for appellant filed by Bill Lockyer, Attorney General of California, Manuel M. Medeiros, State Solicitor General

Andrea Lynn Hoch, Chief Assistant Attorney General, Civil Division, and Paul H. Dobson, Senior Assistant Attorney General.

III. AMICI CURIAE

ACLU Side (Respondent / Appellee)

Brief of amici curiae filed on behalf of Matthew Kiman and Joseph Popovich by Douglas M. Pravda, Michael H. Gottesman, Samuel R. Bagenstos, Seth P. Waxman, Nancy Sternberg Tierney, Richard C. Haber, and Brian D. Sullivan.

Brief of amici curiae filed on behalf of the States of Minnesota, Connecticut, Illinois, Kentucky, Massachusetts, Missouri, New Mexico, Vermont, Washington, West Virginia, and Wisconsin by Mike Hatch, Attorney General of Minnesota, Gary R. Cunningham and Kristyn M. Anderson, Assistant Attorneys General, and by the Attorneys General for their respective jurisdictions as follows: Richard Blumenthal of Connecticut, Lisa Madigan of Illinois, Albert B. Chandler III of Kentucky, Thomas F. Reilly of Massachusetts, Jeremiah W. (Jay) Nixon

1 Brief of Respondent at 2, Med. Bd. of California v. Hason, 538 U.S. 958 (2003) (No. 02-479).

2 *Hason v. Med. Bd. of California*, 279 F.3d 1167, 1169–70 (9th Cir. 2002).

of Missouri, Patricia A. Madrid of New Mexico, William H. Sorrell of Vermont, Christine O. Gregoire of Washington, Darrel V. McGraw, Jr. of West Virginia, and Peggy A. Lautenschlager of Wisconsin.

Brief of amici curiae filed on behalf of the American Association of People with Disabilities, et al. by Elizabeth B. McCallum, Andrew P. Tower, Kristien Carbonez, Thomas Dillickrath, Richard Groseclose, Kristen McAhren, Ira A. Burnim, Mary Giliberti, Jennifer Mathis, and Judge David L. Bazelon.

Brief of amici curiae filed on behalf of the National Association of Protection and Advocacy Systems by Sharon Masling, John Townsend Rich, James Chad Oppenheimer, and David M. Booth.

Brief of amici curiae filed on behalf of the Lawyers' Committee for Civil Rights Under Law, the National Asian Pacific American Legal Consortium, the National Association for the Advancement of Colored People, and the Puerto Rican Legal Defense and Education Fund by Barbara R. Arnwine, Thomas J. Henderson, Michael Foreman, Kristin M. Dadey, Charles Lester, Jr., Teresa Wynn Roseborough, Deborah M. Danzig, Jennifer N. Ide, Neeru Gupta, Andrew Broy, Nicole Lawson, Vincent A. Eng, Dennis C. Hayes, Foster Maer, and Mayra Peters-Quintero.

Brief of amici curiae filed on behalf of Former Senator Dole, Senators Kennedy and Harkin, and Representative Hoyer by Arlene B. Mayerson, Silvia Yee, and Claudia Center.

Opposing Side (Petitioner / Appellant)

Brief of amici curiae filed on behalf of the Commonwealth of Virginia, the States of Alabama, Delaware, Hawaii, Nebraska, Tennessee, Texas and Utah by Jerry W. Kilgore, Attorney General of Virginia, William H. Hurd, State Solicitor, Maureen Riley Matsen, William E. Thro, Deputy State Solicitors, and by the Attorneys General for their respective jurisdictions as follows: William H. Pryor Jr. of Alabama, M. Jane Brady of Delaware, Mark J. Bennett of Hawaii, Jon Bruning of Nebraska, Paul G. Summers of Tennessee, Greg Abbott of Texas, and Mark L. Shurtleff of Utah.

IV. THE SUPREME COURT'S DECISION

"Writ of certiorari to the United States Court of Appeals for the Ninth Circuit dismissed without award of damages and costs."

V. JUSTICE VOTE

9 Pro ACLU Side vs. 0 Con Opposing Side

ACLU Side (Respondent / Appellee)

1. Thomas, C. – Memorandum decision to dismiss
2. Ginsburg, R. – Memorandum decision to dismiss
3. Souter, D. – Memorandum decision to dismiss
4. O'Connor, S. – Memorandum decision to dismiss
5. Stevens, J. – Memorandum decision to dismiss
6. Breyer, S. – Memorandum decision to dismiss
7. Scalia, A. – Memorandum decision to dismiss
8. Kennedy, A. – Memorandum decision to dismiss
9. Rehnquist, W. – Memorandum decision to dismiss

VI. A WIN OR LOSS FOR THE ACLU?

The ACLU filed as counsel for appellee, urging affirmance; the Supreme Court dismissed the writ of certiorari in response to appellant's motion to dismiss, thus upholding the Court of Appeals' decision by default, giving the ACLU an apparent win.[1]

939. Demore v. Kim

(Decided April 29, 2003; 538 U.S. 510)

I. ISSUE

A. Issues Discussed

Immigration/Citizenship

B. Legal Question Presented

Whether immigrants subject to pending removal proceedings may be lawfully detained while the proceedings are pending.

C. Supreme Court's Answer

"We hold that Congress, justifiably concerned that deportable criminal aliens who are not detained continue to engage in crime and fail to appear for their removal hearings in large numbers, may require that persons such as respondent be detained for the brief period necessary for their removal proceedings."

II. CASE SUMMARY

A. Background

"Section 236(c) of the Immigration and Nationality Act . . . provides that '[t]he Attorney General shall take into custody any alien who' is removable from this country because he has been convicted of one of a specified set of crimes. Respondent is a citizen of the Republic of South Korea. He entered the United States in 1984, at the age of six, and became a lawful permanent resident of the United States two years later. In July 1996, he was convicted of first-degree burglary in state court in California and, in April 1997, he was convicted of a second crime, 'petty theft with priors.' The Immigration and Naturalization Service (INS) charged respondent with being deportable from the United States in light of these convictions, and detained him pending his removal hearing. . . .

In conceding that he was deportable, respondent forwent a hearing at which he would have been entitled to raise any nonfrivolous argument available to demonstrate that he was not properly included in a mandatory detention category. Respondent instead filed a habeas corpus action pursuant to 28 U.S.C. § 2241 in the United States District Court for the Northern District of California challenging the constitutionality of § 1226(c) itself. He argued that his detention under § 1226(c) violated due process because the INS had made no determination that he posed either a danger to society or a flight risk.

---

1 Appellant filed a motion to dismiss the case before oral argument. As a result, the case was never argued before the U.S. Supreme Court for a decision on the merits. The decision by the Ninth Circuit was thus upheld by default given that the U.S. Supreme Court did not ultimately make a decision in the case. Individual votes of justices as to the motion to dismiss are not known.

The District Court agreed with respondent that § 1226(c)'s requirement of mandatory detention for certain criminal aliens was unconstitutional. The District Court therefore granted respondent's petition subject to the INS' prompt undertaking of an individualized bond hearing to determine whether respondent posed either a flight risk or a danger to the community. Following that decision, the District Director of the INS released respondent on $5,000 bond.

The Court of Appeals for the Ninth Circuit affirmed."

The Supreme Court granted certiorari to review the case.

B. Counsel of Record

ACLU Side (Respondent / Appellee): Judy Rabinovitz of the American Civil Liberties Union Foundation argued the cause for appellee. With her on the brief were Lucas Guttentag, Lee Gelernt, Steven R. Shapiro, and Liliana M. Garces of the ACLU Foundation, A. Stephen Hut, Jr., Christopher J. Meade, Gregory S. Chernack, Katherine A. Fleet, Brian Condon, and Jayashri Srikantiah of the ACLU Foundation of Northern California.

Opposing Side (Petitioner / Appellant): Solicitor General Olson argued the cause for appellants. With him on the briefs were Assistant Attorney General McCallum, Deputy Solicitor General Kneedler, Austin C. Schlick, Donald E. Keener, and Mark C. Walters.

III. AMICI CURIAE

ACLU Side (Respondent / Appellee)

Brief of amici curiae filed on behalf of the American Bar Association by Alfred P. Carlton, Jr., and Jeffrey L. Bleich.

Brief of amici curiae filed on behalf of Citizens and Immigrants for Equal Justice et al. by Nancy Morawetz.

Brief of amici curiae filed on behalf of International Human Rights Organizations by William J. Aceves and Paul L. Hoffman.

Brief of amici curiae filed on behalf of Law Professors by Daniel Kanstroom.

Brief of amici curiae filed on behalf of the National Asian Pacific American Legal Consortium et al. by Richard A. Cordray, Eugene F. Chay, Vincent A. Eng, and William L. Taylor.

Brief of amici curiae filed on behalf of T. Alexander Aleinikoff et al. by Anthony J. Orler.

Opposing Side (Petitioner / Appellant)

Brief of amici curiae filed on behalf of the Washington Legal Foundation et al. by Daniel J. Popeo and Richard A. Samp.

IV. THE SUPREME COURT'S DECISION

"We address first the argument that 8 U.S.C. § 1226(e) deprives us of jurisdiction to hear this case. . . .

This Court has held that 'where Congress intends to preclude judicial review of constitutional claims its intent to do so must be clear.' . . . And, where a provision precluding review is claimed to bar habeas review, the Court has required a particularly clear statement that such is Congress' intent. . . .

Section 1226(e) contains no explicit provision barring habeas review, and we think that its clear text does not bar respondent's constitutional challenge to the legislation authorizing his detention without bail. . . .

Having determined that the federal courts have jurisdiction to review a constitutional challenge to § 1226(c), we proceed to review respondent's claim. Section 1226(c) mandates detention during removal proceedings for a limited class of deportable aliens—including those convicted of an aggravated felony. Congress adopted this provision against a backdrop of wholesale failure by the INS to deal with increasing rates of criminal activity by aliens. . . .

Congress . . . had before it evidence that one of the major causes of the INS' failure to remove deportable criminal aliens was the agency's failure to detain those aliens during their deportation proceedings. . . .

In his habeas corpus challenge, respondent did not contest Congress' general authority to remove criminal aliens from the United States. Nor did he argue that he himself was not 'deportable' within the meaning of § 1226(c). Rather, respondent argued that the Government may not, consistent with the Due Process Clause of the Fifth Amendment, detain him for the brief period necessary for his removal proceedings. . . .

'It is well established that the Fifth Amendment entitles aliens to due process of law in deportation proceedings.' At the same time, however, this Court has recognized detention during deportation proceedings as a constitutionally valid aspect of the deportation process. . . .

In the present case, the statutory provision at issue governs detention of deportable criminal aliens pending their removal proceedings. Such detention necessarily serves the purpose of preventing deportable criminal aliens from fleeing prior to or during their removal proceedings, thus increasing the chance that, if ordered removed, the aliens will be successfully removed. . . .

In sum, the detention at stake under § 1226(c) lasts roughly a month and a half in the vast majority of cases in which it is invoked, and about five months in the minority of cases in which the alien chooses to appeal. Respondent was detained for somewhat longer than the average—spending six months in INS custody prior to the District Court's order granting habeas relief, but respondent himself had requested a continuance of his removal hearing.

For the reasons set forth above, respondent's claim must fail. Detention during removal proceedings is a constitutionally permissible part of that process. . . . The INS detention of respondent, a criminal alien who has conceded that he is deportable, for the limited period of his removal proceedings, is governed by these cases. The judgment of the Court of Appeals is reversed."

V. JUSTICE VOTE

4 Pro ACLU Side vs. 5 Con Opposing Side

ACLU Side (Respondent / Appellee)

1. Souter, D. – Wrote opinion concurring in part and dissenting in part
2. Stevens, J. – Joined Souter's opinion
3. Ginsburg, R. – Joined Souter's opinion
4. Breyer, S. – Wrote opinion concurring in part and dissenting in part

Opposing Side (Petitioner / Appellant)

1. Rehnquist, W. – Wrote majority opinion
2. Thomas, C. – Joined majority opinion, joined O'Connor's concurrence
3. O'Connor, S. – Wrote concurring opinion
4. Scalia, A. – Joined majority opinion, joined O'Connor's concurrence
5. Kennedy, A. – Wrote concurring opinion

VI. A WIN OR LOSS FOR THE ACLU?

The ACLU argued the case for appellee, urging affirmance; the Supreme Court reversed the Court of Appeals' decision by a 5-4 vote, giving the ACLU an apparent loss.

940. Nevada Dep't of Human Res. v. Hibbs

(Decided May 27, 2003; 538 U.S. 721)

I. ISSUE

A. Issues Discussed

Civil rights, gender, federal, state

B. Legal Question Presented

"[W]hether an individual may sue a State for money damages in federal court for violation of § 2612(a)(1)(C)," the family-care provision of the Family and Medical Leave Act.

C. Supreme Court's Answer

"We hold that employees of the State of Nevada may recover money damages in the event of the State's failure to comply with the family-care provision of the Act."

II. CASE SUMMARY

A. Background

"Petitioners include the Nevada Department of Human Resources (Department) and two of its officers. Respondent William Hibbs (hereinafter respondent) worked for the Department's Welfare Division. In April and May 1997, he sought leave under the [Family and Medical Leave Act (FMLA)] to care for his ailing wife, who was recovering from a car accident and neck surgery. The Department granted his request for the full 12 weeks of FMLA leave and authorized him to use the leave intermittently as needed between May and December 1997. Respondent did so until August 5, 1997, after which he did not return to work. In October 1997, the Department informed respondent that he had exhausted his FMLA leave, that no further leave would be granted, and that he must report to work by November 12, 1997. Respondent failed to do so and was terminated.

Respondent sued petitioners in the United States District Court seeking damages and injunctive and declaratory relief for, inter alia, violations of 29 U.S.C. § 2612(a)(1)(C). The District Court awarded petitioners summary judgment on the grounds that the FMLA claim was barred by the Eleventh Amendment and that respondent's Fourteenth Amendment rights had not been violated. Respondent appealed, and the United States intervened under 28 U.S.C. § 2403 to defend the validity of the FMLA's application to the States. The Ninth Circuit reversed."

The Supreme Court granted certiorari to review the case.

B. Counsel of Record

ACLU Side (Respondent / Appellee): Cornelia T. L. Pillard argued the cause for appellee Hibbs. With her on the brief were Jonathan J. Frankel, Judith L. Lichtman, and Treva J. Hearne.

Assistant Attorney General Dinh argued the cause for the United States.

Opposing Side (Petitioner / Appellant): Paul G. Taggart, Deputy Attorney General of Nevada, argued the cause for appellants. With him on the briefs were Frankie Sue Del Papa, Attorney General, and Traci L. Lovitt.

III. AMICI CURIAE

ACLU Side (Respondent / Appellee)

Brief of amici curiae filed on behalf of the United States by Assistant Attorney General Dinh, Solicitor General Olson, Assistant Attorneys General Boyd and McCallum, Deputy Solicitor General Clement, Patricia A. Millett, Mark B. Stern, and Kathleen Kane.

Brief of amici curiae filed on behalf of the National Women's Law Center, American Civil Liberties Union, et al. by Walter Dellinger, Pamela Harris, Pamela Quinn, Shannon Pazur, Marcia D. Greenberger, Judith C. Appelbaum, Dina R. Lassow, and Deborah Chalfie.

Brief of amici curiae filed on behalf of the State of New York et al. by Eliot Spitzer, Attorney General of New York, Caitlin J. Halligan, Solicitor General, Michelle Aronowitz, Deputy Solicitor General, Denise A. Hartman, Robert H. Easton, and David Axinn, Assistant Solicitors General, and Hilary Klein, Assistant Attorney General, and by the Attorneys General for their respective States as follows: Richard Blumenthal of Connecticut, James Ryan of Illinois, Michael Hatch of Minnesota, Patricia A. Madrid of New Mexico, and Christine O. Gregoire of Washington.

Brief of amici curiae filed on behalf of the American Federation of Labor and Congress of Industrial Organizations by Jonathan P. Hiatt, James B. Coppess, Laurence Gold, and Michael H. Gottesman.

Brief of amici curiae filed on behalf of the Lawyers' Committee for Civil Rights Under Law et al. by Sidney S. Rosdeitcher, Barbara R. Arnwine, Thomas J. Henderson, Michael Foreman, Vincent A. Eng, Dennis Courtland Hayes, and Angela Ciccolo.

Brief of amici curiae filed on behalf of Senator Christopher Dodd et al. by Mark E. Haddad and Carter G. Phillips.

Brief of amici curiae filed on behalf of Alice Kessler-Harris et al. by Isabelle Katz Pinzler, Conrad K. Harper, and William T. Russell, Jr.

Opposing Side (Petitioner / Appellant)

Brief of amici curiae filed on behalf of the State of Alabama et al. by Bill Pryor, Attorney General of Alabama, Nathan A. Forrester, Solicitor General, and Charles B. Campbell, Deputy Solicitor General, and by the Attorneys General for their respective States as follows: Bruce M. Botelho of Alaska, M.

Jane Brady of Delaware, Earl I. Anzai of Hawaii, Steve Carter of Indiana, Don Stenberg of Nebraska, Betty D. Montgomery of Ohio, W. A. Drew Edmondson of Oklahoma, Charles M. Condon of South Carolina, Paul G. Summers of Tennessee, John Cornyn of Texas, Mark Shurtleff of Utah, and Jerry W. Kilgore of Virginia.

Brief of amici curiae filed on behalf of the Coalition for Local Sovereignty by Kenneth B. Clark.

Brief of amici curiae filed on behalf of the Pacific Legal Foundation by Deborah J. La Fetra.

IV. THE SUPREME COURT'S DECISION

"The Family and Medical Leave Act of 1993 (FMLA or Act) entitles eligible employees to take up to 12 work weeks of unpaid leave annually for any of several reasons, including the onset of a 'serious health condition' in an employee's spouse, child, or parent. The Act creates a private right of action to seek both equitable relief and money damages 'against any employer (including a public agency) in any Federal or State court of competent jurisdiction,' should that employer 'interfere with, restrain, or deny the exercise of' FMLA rights. We hold that employees of the State of Nevada may recover money damages in the event of the State's failure to comply with the family-care provision of the Act. . . .

For over a century now, we have made clear that the Constitution does not provide for federal jurisdiction over suits against nonconsenting States.

Congress may, however, abrogate such immunity in federal court if it makes its intention to abrogate unmistakably clear in the language of the statute and acts pursuant to a valid exercise of its power under § 5 of the Fourteenth Amendment. . . . The clarity of Congress' intent here is not fairly debatable. . . . This case turns, then, on whether Congress acted within its constitutional authority when it sought to abrogate the States' immunity for purposes of the FMLA's family-leave provision.

In enacting the FMLA, Congress relied on two of the powers vested in it by the Constitution: its Article I commerce power and its power under § 5 of the Fourteenth Amendment to enforce that Amendment's guarantees. . . .

Two provisions of the Fourteenth Amendment are relevant here: Section 5 grants Congress the power 'to enforce' the substantive guarantees of § 1—among them, equal protection of the laws—by enacting 'appropriate legislation.' Congress may, in the exercise of its § 5 power, do more than simply proscribe conduct that we have held unconstitutional. "Congress' power 'to enforce' the Amendment includes the authority both to remedy and to deter violation of rights guaranteed thereunder by prohibiting a somewhat broader swath of conduct, including that which is not itself forbidden by the Amendment's text." In other words, Congress may enact so-called prophylactic legislation that proscribes facially constitutional conduct, in order to prevent and deter unconstitutional conduct. . . .

The FMLA aims to protect the right to be free from gender-based discrimination in the workplace. We have held that statutory classifications that distinguish between males and females are subject to heightened scrutiny. For a gender-based classification to withstand such scrutiny, it must 'serv[e] important governmental objectives,' and 'the discriminatory means employed [must be] substantially related to the achievement of those objectives.' The State's justification for such a classification 'must not rely on overbroad generalizations about the different talents, capacities, or preferences of males and females.' We now inquire whether Congress had evidence of a pattern of constitutional violations on the part of the States in this area.

The history of the many state laws limiting women's employment opportunities is chronicled in—and, until relatively recently, was sanctioned by—this Court's own opinions. . . .

Congress responded to this history of discrimination by abrogating States' sovereign immunity in Title VII of the Civil Rights Act of 1964, and we sustained this abrogation in Fitzpatrick. But state gender discrimination did not cease. . . .

In sum, the States' record of unconstitutional participation in, and fostering of, gender-based discrimination in the administration of leave benefits is weighty enough to justify the enactment of prophylactic § 5 legislation. . . .

We believe that Congress' chosen remedy, the family-care leave provision of the FMLA, is 'congruent and proportional to the targeted violation.' . . .

By creating an across-the-board, routine employment benefit for all eligible employees, Congress sought to ensure that family-care leave would no longer be stigmatized as an inordinate drain on the workplace caused by female employees, and that employers could not evade leave obligations simply by hiring men. By setting a minimum standard of family leave for all eligible employees, irrespective of gender, the FMLA attacks the formerly state-sanctioned stereotype that only women are responsible for family caregiving, thereby reducing employers' incentives to engage in discrimination by basing hiring and promotion decisions on stereotypes. . . .

For the above reasons, we conclude that § 2612(a)(1)(C) is congruent and proportional to its remedial object, and can 'be understood as responsive to, or designed to prevent, unconstitutional behavior.'

The judgment of the Court of Appeals is therefore affirmed."

V. JUSTICE VOTE

6 Pro ACLU Side vs. 3 Con Opposing Side

ACLU Side (Respondent / Appellee)

1. Rehnquist, W. – Wrote majority opinion
2. O'Connor, S. – Joined majority opinion
3. Souter, D. – Wrote concurring opinion
4. Ginsburg, R. – Joined Souter's concurrence
5. Breyer, S. – Joined Souter's concurrence
6. Stevens, J. – Wrote concurring opinion

Opposing Side (Petitioner / Appellant)

1. Thomas, C. – Joined Kennedy's dissent
2. Scalia, A. – Wrote dissenting opinion, joined Kennedy's dissent
3. Kennedy, A. – Wrote dissenting opinion

VI. A WIN OR LOSS FOR THE ACLU?

The ACLU filed as amicus curiae urging affirmance; the Supreme Court affirmed the Court of Appeals' decision by a 6-3 vote, giving the ACLU an apparent win.

941. Chavez v. Martinez

(Decided May 27, 2003; 538 U.S. 760)

I. ISSUE

A. Issues Discussed

Criminal procedure

B. Legal Question Presented

Whether "Chavez was . . . entitled to a defense of qualified immunity because he violated Martinez's clearly established constitutional rights."

C. Supreme Court's Answer

"We conclude that Martinez's allegations fail to state a violation of his constitutional rights."

II. CASE SUMMARY

A. Background

"On November 28, 1997, police officers Maria Peã and Andrew Salinas were near a vacant lot in a residential area of Oxnard, California, investigating suspected narcotics activity. While Peã and Salinas were questioning an individual, they heard a bicycle approaching on a darkened path that crossed the lot. They ordered the rider, respondent Martinez, to dismount, spread his legs, and place his hands behind his head. Martinez complied. Salinas then conducted a patdown frisk and discovered a knife in Martinez's waistband. An altercation ensued.

There is some dispute about what occurred during the altercation. The officers claim that Martinez drew Salinas' gun from its holster and pointed it at them; Martinez denies this. Both sides agree, however, that Salinas yelled, "He's got my gun!" Peã then drew her gun and shot Martinez several times, causing severe injuries that left Martinez permanently blinded and paralyzed from the waist down. The officers then placed Martinez under arrest.

Petitioner Chavez, a patrol supervisor, arrived on the scene minutes later with paramedics. Chavez accompanied Martinez to the hospital and then questioned Martinez there while he was receiving treatment from medical personnel. The interview lasted a total of about 10 minutes, over a 45-minute period, with Chavez leaving the emergency room for periods of time to permit medical personnel to attend to Martinez.

At first, most of Martinez's answers consisted of 'I don't know,' 'I am dying,' and 'I am choking.' Later in the interview, Martinez admitted that he took the gun from the officer's holster and pointed it at the police. He also admitted that he used heroin regularly. At one point, Martinez said 'I am not telling you anything until they treat me,' yet Chavez continued the interview. At no point during the interview was Martinez given warnings under Miranda v. Arizona, 384 U.S. 436 (1966).

Martinez was never charged with a crime, and his answers were never used against him in any criminal prosecution. Nevertheless, Martinez filed suit under Rev. Stat. § 1979, 42 U.S.C. § 1983, maintaining that Chavez's actions violated his Fifth Amendment right not to be 'compelled in any criminal case to be a witness against himself,' as well as his Fourteenth Amendment substantive due process right to be free from coercive questioning. The District Court granted summary judgment to Martinez as to Chavez's qualified immunity defense on both the Fifth and Fourteenth Amendment claims. Chavez took an interlocutory appeal to the Ninth Circuit, which affirmed the District Court's denial of qualified immunity."

The Supreme Court granted certiorari to review the case.

B. Counsel of Record

ACLU Side (Respondent / Appellee): Richard S. Paz argued the cause for appellee. With him on the brief was Sonia Mercado.

Opposing Side (Petitioner / Appellant): Lawrence S. Robbins argued the cause for appellant. With him on the briefs were Roy T. Englert, Jr., Kathryn S. Zecca, Alan E. Wisotsky, Jeffrey Held, and Gary L. Gillig.

Deputy Solicitor General Clement argued the cause for the United States as amicus curiae.

III. AMICI CURIAE

ACLU Side (Respondent / Appellee)

Brief of amici curiae filed on behalf of the American Civil Liberties Union Foundation et al. by Mark D. Rosenbaum, Ben Wizner, Steven R. Shapiro, Susan N. Herman, John T. Philipsborn, and Erwin Chemerinsky.

Brief of amici curiae filed on behalf of the Association of Trial Lawyers of America by Jeffrey L. Needle.

Brief of amici curiae filed on behalf of the National Police Accountability Project et al. by Susan R. Klein and Michael Avery.

Opposing Side (Petitioner / Appellant)

Brief of amici curiae filed on behalf of the United States by Deputy Solicitor General Clement, Solicitor General Olson, Assistant Attorney General Chertoff, Assistant Attorney General McCallum, John P. Elwood, Barbara L. Herwig, and Peter R. Maier.

Brief of amici curiae filed on behalf of the State of California ex rel. Bill Lockyer by Mr. Lockyer, Attorney General, pro se, Robert R. Anderson, Chief Assistant Attorney General, Jo Graves, Senior Assistant Attorney General, Stan Cross, Supervising Deputy Attorney General, and Lee E. Seale and Patrick J. Whalen, Deputy Attorneys General.

Brief of amici curiae filed on behalf of the City of Escondido by Jeffrey R. Epp and Richard J. Schneider.

Brief of amici curiae filed on behalf of 50 California Cities et al. by Girard Fisher.

Brief of amici curiae filed on behalf of the Criminal Justice Legal Foundation by Kent S. Scheidegger and Charles L. Hobson.

Brief of amici curiae filed on behalf of the National Association of Police Organizations by Devallis Rutledge and William J. Johnson.

IV. THE SUPREME COURT'S DECISION

"In deciding whether an officer is entitled to qualified immunity, we must first determine whether the officer's alleged conduct violated a constitutional right. If not, the officer is entitled to qualified immunity, and we need not consider whether the asserted right was 'clearly established.' We conclude that Martinez's allegations fail to state a violation of his constitutional rights. . . .

The Fifth Amendment, made applicable to the States by the Fourteenth Amendment, requires that '[n]o person . . . shall be compelled in any criminal case to be a witness against himself.' We fail to see how, based on the text of the Fifth Amendment, Martinez can allege a violation of this right, since Martinez was never prosecuted for a crime, let alone compelled to be a witness against himself in a criminal case.

Although Martinez contends that the meaning of 'criminal case' should encompass the entire criminal investigatory process, including police interrogations, we disagree. In our view, a 'criminal case' at the very least requires the initiation of legal proceedings. . . .

Here, Martinez was never made to be a 'witness' against himself in violation of the Fifth Amendment's Self-Incrimination Clause . . . . The text of the Self-Incrimination Clause simply cannot support the Ninth Circuit's view that the mere use of compulsive questioning, without more, violates the Constitution. . . .

Nor can the Ninth Circuit's approach be reconciled with our case law. It is well established that the government may compel witnesses to testify at trial or before a grand jury, on pain of contempt, so long as the witness is not the target of the criminal case in which he testifies. Even for persons who have a legitimate fear that their statements may subject them to criminal prosecution, we have long permitted the compulsion of incriminating testimony so long as those statements (or evidence derived from those statements) cannot be used against the speaker in any criminal case. We have also recognized that governments may penalize public employees and government contractors (with the loss of their jobs or government contracts) to induce them to respond to inquiries, so long as the answers elicited (and their fruits) are immunized from use in any criminal case against the speaker. . . . By contrast, no 'penalty' may ever be imposed on someone who exercises his core Fifth Amendment right not to be a 'witness' against himself in a 'criminal case.' . . . Our holdings in these cases demonstrate that, contrary to the Ninth Circuit's view, mere coercion does not violate the text of the Self-Incrimination Clause absent use of the compelled statements in a criminal case against the witness. . . .

Although our cases have permitted the Fifth Amendment's self-incrimination privilege to be asserted in noncriminal cases, . . . that does not alter our conclusion that a violation of the constitutional right against self-incrimination occurs only if one has been compelled to be a witness against himself in a criminal case.

In the Fifth Amendment context, we have created prophylactic rules designed to safeguard the core constitutional right protected by the Self-Incrimination Clause. . . .

Rules designed to safeguard a constitutional right, however, do not extend the scope of the constitutional right itself . . . . Because we find that Chavez's alleged conduct did not violate the Self-Incrimination Clause, we reverse the Ninth Circuit's denial of qualified immunity as to Martinez's Fifth Amendment claim.

Our views on the proper scope of the Fifth Amendment's Self-Incrimination Clause do not mean that police torture or other abuse that results in a confession is constitutionally permissible so long as the statements are not used at trial; it simply means that the Fourteenth Amendment's Due Process Clause, rather than the Fifth Amendment's Self-Incrimination Clause, would govern the inquiry in those cases and provide relief in appropriate circumstances. . . .

We are satisfied that Chavez's questioning did not violate Martinez's due process rights. . . .

The Court has held that the Due Process Clause also protects certain 'fundamental liberty interest[s]' from deprivation by the government, regardless of the procedures provided, unless the infringement is narrowly tailored to serve a compelling state interest. . . .

The lack of any 'guideposts for responsible decisionmaking' in this area, and our oft-stated reluctance to expand the doctrine of substantive due process, . . . counsel against recognizing a new 'fundamental liberty interest' in this case.

We conclude that Martinez has failed to allege a violation of the Fourteenth Amendment, and it is therefore unnecessary to inquire whether the right asserted by Martinez was clearly established. . . .

Because Chavez did not violate Martinez's Fifth and Fourteenth Amendment rights, he was entitled to qualified immunity. The judgment of the Court of Appeals for the Ninth Circuit is therefore reversed, and the case is remanded for further proceedings."

V. JUSTICE VOTE

3 Pro ACLU Side vs. 6 Con Opposing Side

ACLU Side (Respondent / Appellee)

1. Stevens, J. – Wrote opinion concurring in part and dissenting in part, joined Kennedy's opinion, joined Souter's opinion in part
2. Kennedy, A. – Wrote opinion concurring in part and dissenting in part, joined Souter's opinion in part
3. Ginsburg, R. – Wrote opinion concurring in part and dissenting in part, joined Kennedy's opinion in part, joined Souter's opinion in part

Opposing Side (Petitioner / Appellant)

1. Thomas, C. – Wrote plurality opinion
2. Rehnquist, W. – Joined Thomas' opinion
3. Souter, D. – Wrote concurring opinion, part II of which was for the Court
4. O'Connor, S. – Joined Thomas' opinion in part
5. Breyer, S. – Joined Souter's opinion
6. Scalia, A. – Joined Thomas' opinion in part, wrote opinion concurring in part

VI. A WIN OR LOSS FOR THE ACLU?

The ACLU filed as amicus curiae urging affirmance; the Supreme Court reversed and remanded the Court of Appeals' decision by a 6-3 vote, giving the ACLU an apparent loss.[1]

---

1 This plurality decision had a 6-3 vote as to Justice Thomas' opinion and a 5-4 vote as to part of Justice Souter's opinion.

942. Desert Palace, Inc. v. Costa

(Decided June 9, 2003; 539 U.S. 90)

I. ISSUE

A. Issues Discussed

Civil rights, gender, federal

B. Legal Question Presented

"[W]hether a plaintiff must present direct evidence of discrimination in order to obtain a mixed-motive instruction under Title VII of the Civil Rights Act of 1964, as amended by the Civil Rights Act of 1991 (1991 Act)."

C. Supreme Court's Answer

"We hold that direct evidence is not required."

II. CASE SUMMARY

A. Background

"Since 1964, Title VII has made it an 'unlawful employment practice for an employer . . . to discriminate against any individual . . . , because of such individual's race, color, religion, sex, or national origin." . . . In Price Waterhouse v. Hopkins, 490 U.S. 228 (1989), the Court considered whether an employment decision is made 'because of' sex in a 'mixed-motive' case, i.e., where both legitimate and illegitimate reasons motivated the decision. The Court concluded that, under § 2000e–2(a)(1), an employer could 'avoid a finding of liability . . . by proving that it would have made the same decision even if it had not allowed gender to play such a role.' . . . The Court was divided, however, over the predicate question of when the burden of proof may be shifted to an employer to prove the affirmative defense. . . .

Two years after Price Waterhouse, Congress passed the 1991 Act 'in large part [as] a response to a series of decisions of this Court interpreting the Civil Rights Acts of 1866 and 1964.' In particular, § 107 of the 1991 Act, which is at issue in this case, 'respond[ed]' to Price Waterhouse by 'setting forth standards applicable in 'mixed motive' cases' in two new statutory provisions. The first establishes an alternative for proving that an 'unlawful employment practice' has occurred . . . .

The second provides that, with respect to 'a claim in which an individual proves a violation under section 2000e–2(m),' the employer has a limited affirmative defense that does not absolve it of liability, but restricts the remedies available to a plaintiff. . . .

Since the passage of the 1991 Act, the Courts of Appeals have divided over whether a plaintiff must prove by direct evidence that an impermissible consideration was a 'motivating factor' in an adverse employment action. . . .

Petitioner Desert Palace, Inc., dba Caesar's Palace Hotel & Casino of Las Vegas, Nevada, employed respondent Catharina Costa as a warehouse worker and heavy equipment operator. Respondent was the only woman in this job and in her local Teamsters bargaining unit.

Respondent experienced a number of problems with management and her co-workers that led to an escalating series of disciplinary sanctions, including informal rebukes, a denial of privileges, and suspension. Petitioner finally terminated respondent after she was involved in a physical altercation in a warehouse elevator with fellow Teamsters member Herbert Gerber. Petitioner disciplined both employees because the facts surrounding the incident were in dispute, but Gerber, who had a clean disciplinary record, received only a 5–day suspension.

Respondent subsequently filed this lawsuit against petitioner in the United States District Court for the District of Nevada, asserting claims of sex discrimination and sexual harassment under Title VII. . . .

Based on . . . evidence, the District Court denied petitioner's motion for judgment as a matter of law, and submitted the case to the jury with instructions, two of which are relevant here. . . .

The Court of Appeals initially vacated and remanded, holding that the District Court had erred in giving the mixed-motive instruction because respondent had failed to present 'substantial evidence of conduct or statements by the employer directly reflecting discriminatory animus.' In addition, the panel concluded that petitioner was entitled to judgment as a matter of law on the termination claim because the evidence was insufficient to prove that respondent was 'terminated because she was a woman.'

The Court of Appeals reinstated the District Court's judgment after rehearing the case en banc."

The Supreme Court granted certiorari to review the case.

B. Counsel of Record

ACLU Side (Respondent / Appellee): Robert N. Peccole argued the cause for appellee. With him on the brief was Eric Schnapper.

Opposing Side (Petitioner / Appellant): Mark J. Ricciardi argued the cause for appellant. With him on the brief were Roger K. Quillen, Paul A. Ades, and Corbett N. Gordon.

Irving L. Gornstein argued the cause for the United States as amicus curiae.

III. AMICI CURIAE

ACLU Side (Respondent / Appellee)

Brief of amici curiae filed on behalf of the Lawyers' Committee for Civil Rights Under Law, American Civil Liberties Union, AARP, American Association of People with Disabilities, National Association for the Advancement of Colored People, National Asian Pacific American Legal Consortium, National Partnership for Women & Families, and Women Employed by Michael C. Subit, Barbara R. Arnwine, Thomas J. Henderson, Michael L. Foreman, Kristin M. Dadey, Thomas W. Osborne, Laurie A. McCann, Daniel B. Kohrman, Melvin Radowitz, Andy Imparato, Stephen R. Shapiro, Lenora M. Lapidus, Jennifer Arnett Lee, Vincent A. Eng, Judith L. Lichtman, Jocelyn C. Frye, Dennis C. Hayes, and Yolanda Y. Riley.

Brief of amici curiae filed on behalf of the American Federation of Labor and Congress of Industrial Organizations by Jonathan P. Hiatt, James B. Coppess, and Laurence Gold.

Brief of amici curiae filed on behalf of the Association of Trial Lawyers of America by Jeffrey L. Needle.

Brief of amici curiae filed on behalf of Ann B. Hopkins by Douglas B. Huron.

Brief of amici curiae filed on behalf of the National Employment Lawyers Association by Ronald B. Schwartz and Jenifer Bosco.

Opposing Side (Petitioner / Appellant)

Brief of amici curiae filed on behalf of the United States by Irving L. Gornstein, Solicitor General Olson, Assistant Attorneys General McCallum and Boyd, Deputy Solicitor General Clement, Dennis J. Dimsey, and Teresa Kwong.

Brief of amici curiae filed on behalf of the Equal Employment Advisory Council et al.by Ann Elizabeth Reesman, Katherine Y. K. Cheung, Stephen A. Bokat, and Ellen D. Bryant.

IV. THE SUPREME COURT'S DECISION

"This case provides us with the first opportunity to consider the effects of the 1991 Act on jury instructions in mixed-motive cases. Specifically, we must decide whether a plaintiff must present direct evidence of discrimination in order to obtain a mixed-motive instruction under 42 U.S.C. § 2000e–2(m). . . .

Our precedents make clear that the starting point for our analysis is the statutory text. And where, as here, the words of the statute are unambiguous, the "judicial inquiry is complete." . . .

In addition, Title VII's silence with respect to the type of evidence required in mixed-motive cases also suggests that we should not depart from the '[c]onventional rul[e] of civil litigation [that] generally appl[ies] in Title VII cases.' That rule requires a plaintiff to prove his case 'by a preponderance of the evidence,' using 'direct or circumstantial evidence.' . . .

Finally, the use of the term 'demonstrates' in other provisions of Title VII tends to show further that § 2000e2(m) does not incorporate a direct evidence requirement. . . .

For the reasons stated above, we agree with the Court of Appeals that no heightened showing is required under § 2000e–2(m). . . .

In order to obtain an instruction under § 2000e–2(m), a plaintiff need only present sufficient evidence for a reasonable jury to conclude, by a preponderance of the evidence, that 'race, color, religion, sex, or national origin was a motivating factor for any employment practice.' Because direct evidence of discrimination is not required in mixed-motive cases, the Court of Appeals correctly concluded that the District Court did not abuse its discretion in giving a mixed-motive instruction to the jury. Accordingly, the judgment of the Court of Appeals is affirmed."

V. JUSTICE VOTE

9 Pro ACLU Side vs. 0 Con Opposing Side

ACLU Side (Respondent / Appellee)

1. Thomas, C. – Wrote majority opinion
2. Ginsburg, R. – Wrote concurring opinion
3. Souter, D. – Joined majority opinion
4. O'Connor, S. – Wrote concurring opinion
5. Stevens, J. – Joined majority opinion
6. Breyer, S. – Joined majority opinion
7. Scalia, A. – Joined majority opinion
8. Kennedy, A. – Joined majority opinion
9. Rehnquist, W. – Joined majority opinion

VI. A WIN OR LOSS FOR THE ACLU?

The ACLU filed as amicus curiae urging affirmance; the Supreme Court affirmed the Court of Appeals' decision by a 9-0 vote, giving the ACLU an apparent win.

943. Virginia v. Hicks

(Decided June 16, 2003; 539 U.S. 113)

I. ISSUE

A. Issues Discussed

1st Amendment, press, speech, association

B. Legal Question Presented

"The issue presented in this case is whether the Richmond Redevelopment and Housing Authority's trespass policy is facially invalid under the First Amendment's overbreadth doctrine."

C. Supreme Court's Answer

The policy is not facially invalid under the overbreadth doctrine of the First Amendment.

II. CASE SUMMARY

A. Background

"The Richmond Redevelopment and Housing Authority (RRHA) owns and operates a housing development for low-income residents called Whitcomb Court. Until June 23, 1997, the city of Richmond owned the streets within Whitcomb Court. The city council decided, however, to 'privatize' these streets in an effort to combat rampant crime and drug dealing in Whitcomb Court—much of it committed and conducted by nonresidents. The council enacted Ordinance No. 97–181–197 . . . .

The city then conveyed these streets by a recorded deed to the RRHA . . . . This deed required the RRHA to "give the appearance that the closed street, particularly at the entrances, are no longer public streets and that they are in fact private streets." To this end, the RRHA posted red-and-white signs on each apartment building—and every 100 feet along the streets—of Whitcomb Court, which state: "NO TRESPASSING[.] PRIVATE PROPERTY[.] YOU ARE NOW ENTERING PRIVATE PROPERTY AND STREETS OWNED BY RRHA. UNAUTHORIZED PERSONS WILL BE SUBJECT TO ARREST AND PROSECUTION. UNAUTHORIZED VEHICLES WILL BE TOWED AT OWNERS EXPENSE." The RRHA also enacted a policy authorizing the Richmond police [to give trespassers notice forbidding them from returning to the property.]

Persons who trespass after being notified not to return are subject to prosecution under Va.Code Ann. § 18.2–119 (1996) . . . .

Respondent Kevin Hicks, a nonresident of Whitcomb Court, has been convicted on two prior occasions of trespassing there and once of damaging property there. Those convictions are not at issue in this case. While the property-damage charge was pending, the RRHA gave Hicks written notice barring him from Whitcomb Court, and Hicks signed this notice in the presence of a police officer. Twice after receiving this notice Hicks asked for permission to return; twice the Whitcomb Court housing manager said 'no.' That did not stop Hicks; in January 1999 he again trespassed at Whitcomb Court and was arrested and convicted under § 18.2–119.

At trial, Hicks maintained that the RRHA's policy limiting access to Whitcomb Court was both unconstitutionally overbroad and void for vagueness. On appeal of his conviction, a three-judge panel of the Court of Appeals of Virginia initially rejected Hicks' contentions, but the en banc Court of Appeals reversed. . . . The Virginia Supreme Court affirmed the en banc Court of Appeals, but for different reasons."

The Supreme Court granted certiorari to review the case.

B. Counsel of Record

ACLU Side (Respondent / Appellee): Steven D. Benjamin argued the cause for appellee. With him on the brief were Amanda Frost, Brian Wolfman, and Alan B. Morrison.

Opposing Side (Petitioner / Appellant): William H. Hurd, State Solicitor of Virginia, argued the cause for appellant. With him on the briefs were Jerry W. Kilgore, Attorney General, Maureen Riley Matsen and William E. Thro, Deputy State Solicitors, and Christy A. McCormick and A. Cameron O'Brion, Assistant Attorneys General.

Deputy Solicitor General Dreeben argued the cause for the United States as amicus curiae.

III. AMICI CURIAE

ACLU Side (Respondent / Appellee)

Brief of amici curiae filed on behalf of the American Civil Liberties Union, the ACLU of Virginia, and the National Association of Criminal Defense by Mark J. Lopez, Steven R. Shapiro, Rebecca Glenberg, and David M. Porter.

Brief of amici curiae filed on behalf of the DKT Liberty Project by Julia M. Carpenter.

Brief of amici curiae filed on behalf of the Richmond Tenants Organization et al. by Catherine M. Bishop.

Brief of amici curiae filed on behalf of the Thomas Jefferson Center for the Protection of Free Expression by J. Joshua Wheeler and Robert M. O'Neil.

Brief of amici curiae filed on behalf of Watchtower Bible and Tract Society of New York, Inc., by Paul D. Polidoro and Philip Brumley.

Opposing Side (Petitioner / Appellant)

Brief of amici curiae filed on behalf of the United States by Deputy Solicitor General Dreeben, Solicitor General Olson, Assistant Attorneys General Chertoff and McCallum, James A. Feldman, Michael Jay Singer, and Stephanie R. Marcus.

Brief of amici curiae filed on behalf of the City of Richmond et al. by William G. Broaddus, Jonathan T. Blank, William H. Baxter II, Godfrey T. Pinn, Jr., and John A. Rupp.

Brief of amici curiae filed on behalf of the Council of Large Public Housing Authorities et al. by Robert A. Graham, William F. Maher, and Carl A. S. Coan III.

Brief of amici curiae filed on behalf of the Criminal Justice Legal Foundation by Kent S. Scheidegger.

Brief of amici curiae filed on behalf of the National League of Cities et al. by Richard Ruda and James I. Crowley.

Brief of amici curiae filed on behalf of the State of Alabama et al. by Jeremiah W. (Jay) Nixon, Attorney General of Missouri, James R. Layton, State Solicitor, Erwin O. Switzer III, and Michele L. Jackson, Assistant Attorney General of Alabama, and by the Attorneys General for their respective jurisdictions as follows: Gregg D. Renkes of Alaska, M. Jane Brady of Delaware, Mark J. Bennett of Hawaii, Steve Carter of Indiana, Charlie J. Crist, Jr., of Florida, Mike Moore of Mississippi, Jim Petro of Ohio, W. A. Drew Edmondson of Oklahoma, Hardy Myers of Oregon, Anabelle Rodríguez of Puerto Rico, Lawrence E. Long of South Dakota, Paul G. Summers of Tennessee, Greg Abbott of Texas, and Mark L. Shurtleff of Utah.

IV. THE SUPREME COURT'S DECISION

"Hicks does not contend that he was engaged in constitutionally protected conduct when arrested; nor does he challenge the validity of the trespass statute under which he was convicted. Instead he claims that the RRHA policy barring him from Whitcomb Court is overbroad under the First Amendment, and cannot be applied to him—or anyone else. . . .

We have provided this expansive remedy out of concern that the threat of enforcement of an overbroad law may deter or 'chill' constitutionally protected speech—especially when the overbroad statute imposes criminal sanctions. . . .

As we noted in Broadrick, however, there comes a point at which the chilling effect of an overbroad law, significant though it may be, cannot justify prohibiting all enforcement of that law—particularly a law that reflects 'legitimate state interests in maintaining comprehensive controls over harmful, constitutionally unprotected conduct.' . . .

Petitioner asks this Court to impose restrictions on 'the use of overbreadth standing,' limiting the availability of facial overbreadth challenges to those whose own conduct involved some sort of expressive activity. . . . Whether Virginia's courts should have entertained this overbreadth challenge is entirely a matter of state law.

This Court may, however, review the Virginia Supreme Court's holding that the RRHA policy violates the First Amendment. We may examine, in particular, whether the claimed overbreadth in the RRHA policy is sufficiently 'substantial' to produce facial invalidity. . . . We accordingly proceed to that merits inquiry . . . .

Hicks, of course, was not arrested for leafleting or demonstrating without permission. He violated the RRHA's written rule that persons who receive a barment notice must not return to RRHA property. The Virginia Supreme Court, based on its objection to the 'unwritten' requirement that demonstrators and leafleters obtain advance permission, declared the entire RRHA trespass policy overbroad and void—including the written rule that those who return after receiving a barment notice are subject to arrest. Whether these provisions are severable is of course a matter of state law, and the Virginia Supreme Court has implicitly decided that they are not—that all components of the RRHA trespass policy must stand or fall together. It could not properly decree that they fall by reason of the overbreadth doctrine, however, unless the trespass policy, taken as a whole, is substantially overbroad judged in relation to its plainly legitimate sweep. The overbreadth claimant bears the burden of demonstrating, 'from the text of [the law] and from actual fact,' that substantial overbreadth exists.

Hicks has not made such a showing with regard to the RRHA policy taken as a whole . . . .

As for the written provision authorizing the police to arrest those who return to Whitcomb Court after receiving a barment notice: That certainly does not violate the First Amendment as applied to persons whose postnotice entry is not for the purpose of engaging in constitutionally protected speech. . . . Here, . . . it is Hicks' nonexpressive conduct—his entry in violation of the notice-barment rule—not his speech, for which he is punished as a trespasser.

Most importantly, both the notice-barment rule and the 'legitimate business or social purpose' rule apply to all persons who enter the streets of Whitcomb Court, not just to those who seek to engage in expression. . . . Rarely, if ever, will an overbreadth challenge succeed against a law or regulation that is not specifically addressed to speech or to conduct necessarily associated with speech (such as picketing or demonstrating). Applications of the RRHA policy that violate the First Amendment can still be remedied through as-applied litigation, but the Virginia Supreme Court should not have used the 'strong medicine' of overbreadth to invalidate the entire RRHA trespass policy. Whether respondent may challenge his conviction on other grounds—and whether those claims have been properly preserved—are issues we leave open on remand. . . .

For these reasons, we reverse the judgment of the Virginia Supreme Court and remand the case for further proceedings not inconsistent with this opinion."

V. JUSTICE VOTE

0 Pro ACLU Side vs. 9 Con Opposing Side

Opposing Side (Petitioner / Appellant)

1. Scalia, A. – Wrote majority opinion
2. Thomas, C. – Wrote majority opinion
3. Ginsburg, R. – Wrote concurring opinion
4. Souter, D. – Wrote concurring opinion
5. O'Connor, S. – Joined majority opinion
6. Stevens, J. – Joined majority opinion
7. Breyer, S. – Joined Souter's concurrence
8. Kennedy, A. – Joined majority opinion
9. Rehnquist, W. – Joined majority opinion

VI. A WIN OR LOSS FOR THE ACLU?

The ACLU filed as amicus curiae urging affirmance; the U.S. Supreme Court reversed the Virginia Supreme Court's decision by a 9-0 vote, giving the ACLU an apparent loss.

944. Overton v. Bazzetta

(Decided June 16, 2003; 539 U.S. 126)

I. ISSUE

A. Issues Discussed

Prison, civil rights, state

B. Legal Question Presented

"The State of Michigan, by regulation, places certain restrictions on visits with prison inmates. The question before the Court is whether the regulations violate the substantive due process mandate of the Fourteenth Amendment, or the First or Eighth Amendments as applicable to the States through the Fourteenth Amendment."

C. Supreme Court's Answer

"[E]ach of the challenged regulations bears a rational relationship to a legitimate penological interest" and is valid.

II. CASE SUMMARY

A. Background

"The population of Michigan's prisons increased in the early 1990's. More inmates brought more visitors, straining the resources available for prison supervision and control. . . .

The incidence of substance abuse in the State's prisons also increased in this period. . . .

In response to these concerns, the Michigan Department of Corrections (MDOC or Department) revised its prison visitation policies in 1995, promulgating the regulations here at issue. One aspect of the Department's approach was to limit the visitors a prisoner is eligible to receive, in order to decrease the total number of visitors.

Under MDOC's regulations, an inmate may receive visits only from individuals placed on an approved visitor list, except that qualified members of the clergy and attorneys on official business may visit without being listed. The list may include an unlimited number of members of the prisoner's immediate family and 10 other individuals the prisoner designates, subject to some restrictions. Minors under the age of 18 may not be placed on the list unless they are the children, stepchildren, grandchildren, or siblings of the inmate. If an inmate's parental rights have been terminated, the child may not be a visitor. A child authorized to visit must be accompanied by an adult who is an immediate family member of the child or of the inmate or who is the legal guardian of the child. An inmate may not place a former prisoner on the visitor list unless the former prisoner is a member of the inmate's immediate family and the warden has given prior approval.

The Department's revised policy also sought to control the widespread use of drugs and alcohol among prisoners. Prisoners who commit multiple substance-abuse violations are not permitted to receive any visitors except attorneys and members of the clergy. An inmate subject to this restriction may apply for reinstatement of visitation privileges after two years. Reinstatement is within the warden's discretion.

Respondents are prisoners, their friends, and their family members. They brought this action under Rev. Stat. § 1979, 42 U.S.C. § 1983, alleging that the restrictions upon visitation violate the First, Eighth, and Fourteenth Amendments. It was certified as a class action under Federal Rule of Criminal Procedure 23. . . .

The case before us concerns the regulations as they pertain to noncontact visits.

The United States District Court for the Eastern District of Michigan agreed with the prisoners that the regulations pertaining to noncontact visits were invalid. The Sixth Circuit affirmed . . . ."

The Supreme Court granted certiorari to review the case.

B. Counsel of Record

ACLU Side (Respondent / Appellee): Deborah LaBelle argued the cause for appellees. With her on the brief were Barbara R. Levine and Patricia A. Streeter.

Opposing Side (Petitioner / Appellant): Thomas L. Casey, Solicitor General of Michigan, argued the cause for appellants. With him on the briefs were Mike Cox, Attorney General, and Leo H. Friedman, Mark Matus, and Lisa C. Ward, Assistant Attorneys General.

Jeffrey A. Lamken argued the cause for the United States as amicus curiae.

III. AMICI CURIAE

ACLU Side (Respondent / Appellee)

Brief of amici curiae filed on behalf of the American Civil Liberties Union et al. by Elizabeth Alexander, David C. Fathi, Steven R. Shapiro, Lenora M. Lapidus, Daniel L. Greenberg, John Boston, Michael J. Steinberg, and Kary L. Moss.

Brief of amici curiae filed on behalf of the National Council on Crime and Delinquency et al. by Jill M. Wheaton.

Brief of amici curiae filed on behalf of the Public Defender Service for the District of Columbia et al. by Paul Denenfeld and Giovanna Shay.

Brief of amici curiae filed on behalf of the National Council of Law Raza et al. by Roderick M. Hills, Jr.

Opposing Side (Petitioner / Appellant)

Brief of amici curiae filed on behalf of the United States by Jeffrey A. Lamken, Solicitor General Olson, Assistant Attorney General McCallum, Deputy Solicitor General Clement, and Robert M. Loeb.

Brief of amici curiae filed on behalf of the State of Colorado et al. by Ken Salazar, Attorney General of Colorado, Alan J. Gilbert, Solicitor General, and Juliana M. Zolynas, Assistant Attorney General, and by the Attorneys General for their respective States as follows: William H. Pryor, Jr., of Alabama, Charlie Crist of Florida, Thurbert E. Baker of Georgia, Alan G. Lance of Idaho, Steve Carter of Indiana, J. Joseph Curran, Jr., of Maryland, Mike Moore of Mississippi, Jeremiah W. (Jay) Nixon of Missouri, Don Stenberg of Nebraska, Frankie Sue Del Papa of Nevada, Wayne Stenehjem of North Dakota, W. A. Drew Edmondson of Oklahoma, Hardy Myers of Oregon, D. Michael Fisher of Pennsylvania, Mark Barnett of South Dakota, Paul G. Summers of Tennessee, Greg Abbott of Texas, Mark L. Shurtleff of Utah, and Patrick J. Crank of Wyoming.

Brief of amici curiae filed on behalf of the Criminal Justice Legal Foundation by Kent S. Scheidegger and Charles L. Hobson.

IV. THE SUPREME COURT'S DECISION

"The Court of Appeals agreed with the District Court that the restrictions on noncontact visits are invalid. This was error. . . .

We do not hold, and we do not imply, that any right to intimate association is altogether terminated by incarceration or is always irrelevant to claims made by prisoners. We need not attempt to explore or define the asserted right of association at any length or determine the extent to which it survives incarceration because the challenged regulations bear a rational relation to legitimate penological interests. This suffices to sustain the regulation in question. . . . We must accord substantial deference to the professional judgment of prison administrators . . . . The burden, moreover, is not on the State to prove the validity of prison regulations but on the prisoner to disprove it. Respondents have failed to do so here.

In Turner we held that four factors are relevant in deciding whether a prison regulation affecting a constitutional right that survives incarceration withstands constitutional challenge: whether the regulation has a "valid, rational connection" to a legitimate governmental interest; whether alternative means are open to inmates to exercise the asserted right; what impact an accommodation of the right would have on guards and inmates and prison resources; and whether there are 'ready alternatives' to the regulation.

Turning to the restrictions on visitation by children, we conclude that the regulations bear a rational relation to MDOC's valid interests in maintaining internal security and protecting child visitors from exposure to sexual or other misconduct or from accidental injury. The regulations promote internal security, perhaps the most legitimate of penological goals, by reducing the total number of visitors and by limiting the disruption caused by children in particular. Protecting children from harm is also a legitimate goal. . . .

As for the regulation requiring children to be accompanied by a family member or legal guardian, it is reasonable to ensure that the visiting child is accompanied and supervised by those adults charged with protecting the child's best interests.

Respondents argue that excluding minor nieces and nephews and children as to whom parental rights have been terminated bears no rational relationship to these penological interests. We reject this contention, and in all events it would not suffice to invalidate the regulations as to all noncontact visits. To reduce the number of child visitors, a line must be drawn, and the categories set out by these regulations are reasonable. . . .

MDOC's regulation prohibiting visitation by former inmates bears a self-evident connection to the State's interest in maintaining prison security and preventing future crimes. . . .

Finally, the restriction on visitation for inmates with two substance-abuse violations, a bar which may be removed after two years, serves the legitimate goal of deterring the use of drugs and alcohol within the prisons. . . . Withdrawing visitation privileges is a proper and even necessary management technique to induce compliance with the rules of inmate behavior, especially for high-security prisoners who have few other privileges to lose. . . .

Having determined that each of the challenged regulations bears a rational relationship to a legitimate penological interest, we consider whether inmates have alternative means of exercising the constitutional right they seek to assert. Were it shown that no alternative means of communication existed, though it would not be conclusive, it would be some evidence that the regulations were unreasonable. That showing, however, cannot be made. . .

Another relevant consideration is the impact that accommodation of the asserted associational right would have on guards, other inmates, the allocation of prison resources, and the safety of visitors. Accommodating respondents' demands would cause a significant reallocation of the prison system's financial resources and would impair the ability of corrections officers to protect all who are inside a prison's walls. When such consequences are present, we are 'particularly deferential' to prison administrators' regulatory judgments.

Finally, we consider whether the presence of ready alternatives undermines the reasonableness of the regulations. Turner does not impose a least-restrictive-alternative test, but asks instead whether the prisoner has pointed to some obvious regulatory alternative that fully accommodates the asserted right while not imposing more than a de minimis cost to the valid penological goal. Respondents have not suggested alternatives meeting this high standard for any of the regulations at issue. . . .

Respondents also claim that the restriction on visitation for inmates with two substance-abuse violations is a cruel and unusual condition of confinement in violation of the Eighth Amendment. The restriction undoubtedly makes the prisoner's confinement more difficult to bear. But it does not, in the circumstances of this case, fall below the standards mandated by the Eighth Amendment. . . .

The judgment of the Court of Appeals is reversed."

V. JUSTICE VOTE

0 Pro ACLU Side vs. 9 Con Opposing Side

Opposing Side (Petitioner / Appellant)

1. Kennedy, A. – Wrote majority opinion
2. Thomas, C. – Wrote concurring opinion
3. Ginsburg, R. – Joined Stevens' concurrence
4. Souter, D. – Joined Stevens' concurrence
5. O'Connor, S. – Joined majority opinion
6. Stevens, J. – Wrote concurring opinion
7. Breyer, S. – Joined Stevens' concurrence
8. Scalia, A. – Joined Thomas' concurrence
9. Rehnquist, W. – Joined majority opinion

VI. A WIN OR LOSS FOR THE ACLU?

The ACLU filed as amicus curiae urging affirmance; the Supreme Court reversed the Court of Appeals' decision by a 9-0 vote, giving the ACLU an apparent loss.

945. Sell v. United States

(Decided June 16, 2003; 539 U.S. 166)

I. ISSUE

A. Issues Discussed

Criminal procedure

B. Legal Question Presented

"The question presented is whether the Constitution permits the Government to administer antipsychotic drugs involuntarily to a mentally ill criminal defendant—in order to render that defendant competent to stand trial for serious, but nonviolent, crimes."

C. Supreme Court's Answer

"We conclude that the Constitution allows the Government to administer those drugs, even against the defendant's will, in limited circumstances, i.e., upon satisfaction of conditions that we shall describe."

II. CASE SUMMARY

A. Background

"Petitioner Charles Sell, once a practicing dentist, has a long and unfortunate history of mental illness. . . .

In May 1997, the Government charged Sell with submitting fictitious insurance claims for payment. A Federal Magistrate Judge (Magistrate), after ordering a psychiatric examination, found Sell 'currently competent,' but noted that Sell might experience 'a psychotic episode' in the future. The Magistrate released Sell on bail. A grand jury later produced a superseding indictment charging Sell and his wife with 56 counts of mail fraud, 6 counts of Medicaid fraud, and 1 count of money laundering.

In early 1998, the Government claimed that Sell had sought to intimidate a witness. The Magistrate held a bail revocation hearing. Sell's behavior at his initial appearance was, in the judge's words, "totally out of control" . . . . A psychiatrist reported that Sell could not sleep because he expected the Federal Bureau of Investigation (FBI) to "come busting through the door," and concluded that Sell's condition had worsened. After considering that report and other testimony, the Magistrate revoked Sell's bail.

In April 1998, the grand jury issued a new indictment charging Sell with attempting to murder the FBI agent who had arrested him and a former employee who planned to testify against him in the fraud case. The attempted murder and fraud cases were joined for trial.

In early 1999, Sell asked the Magistrate to reconsider his competence to stand trial. [T]he Magistrate found that Sell was 'mentally incompetent to stand trial.' . . .

Two months later, Medical Center staff recommended that Sell take antipsychotic medication. Sell refused to do so. The staff sought permission to administer the medication against Sell's will. That effort is the subject of the present proceedings."

The Supreme Court granted certiorari to review the case.

B. Counsel of Record

ACLU Side (Petitioner / Appellant): Barry A. Short argued the cause for appellant. With him on the briefs were Neal F. Perryman, Mark N. Light, Norman S. London, and Lee T. Lawless

Opposing Side (Respondent / Appellee): Deputy Solicitor General Dreeben argued the cause for the United States. With him on the briefs were Solicitor General Olson, Assistant Attorney General Chertoff, Lisa Schiavo Blatt, and Joseph C. Wyderko.

III. AMICI CURIAE

ACLU Side (Petitioner / Appellant)

Brief of amici curiae filed on behalf of the American Civil Liberties Union of Eastern Missouri by Peter A. Joy.

Brief of amici curiae filed on behalf of the Center for Cognitive Liberty & Ethics by Richard Glen Boire.

Brief of amici curiae filed on behalf of the Drug Policy Alliance by David T. Goldberg and Daniel N. Abrahamson.

Brief of amici curiae filed on behalf of the National Association of Criminal Defense Lawyers by Burton H. Shostak.

Brief of amici curiae filed on behalf of the New York State Association of Criminal Defense Lawyers by Joshua L. Dratel.

Brief of amici curiae filed on behalf of the Rutherford Institute by John W. Whitehead and Steven H. Aden.

Opposing Side (Respondent / Appellee)

Brief of amici curiae filed on behalf of the American Psychological Association by David W. Ogden, Paul R. Q. Wolfson, and Nathalie F. P. Gilfoyle.

Brief of amici curiae filed on behalf of the American Psychiatric Association et al. by Richard G. Taranto.

IV. THE SUPREME COURT'S DECISION

"We first examine whether the Eighth Circuit had jurisdiction to decide Sell's appeal. The District Court's judgment, from which Sell had appealed, was a pretrial order. That judgment affirmed a Magistrate's order requiring Sell involuntarily to receive medication. . . .

How was it possible for Sell to appeal from such an order? The law normally requires a defendant to wait until the end of the trial to obtain appellate review of a pretrial order. . . .

Nonetheless, there are exceptions to this rule. . . . And this District Court order does appear to fall within the 'collateral order' exception. . . .

We conclude that the District Court order from which Sell appealed was an appealable 'collateral order.' The Eighth Circuit had jurisdiction to hear the appeal. And we consequently have jurisdiction to decide the question presented, whether involuntary medication violates Sell's constitutional rights. . . .

We turn now to the basic question presented: Does forced administration of antipsychotic drugs to render Sell competent to stand trial unconstitutionally deprive him of his 'liberty' to reject medical treatment? . . . Two prior precedents . . . set forth the framework for determining the legal answer. . . .

These two cases, Harper and Riggins, indicate that the Constitution permits the Government involuntarily to administer antipsychotic drugs to a mentally ill defendant facing serious criminal charges in order to render that defendant competent to stand trial, but only if the treatment is medically appropriate, is substantially unlikely to have side effects that may undermine the fairness of the trial, and, taking account of less intrusive alternatives, is necessary significantly to further important governmental trial-related interests.

This standard will permit involuntary administration of drugs solely for trial competence purposes in certain instances. But those instances may be rare. That is because the standard says or fairly implies the following:

First, a court must find that important governmental interests are at stake. . . .

Second, the court must conclude that involuntary medication will significantly further those concomitant state interests. . . .

Third, the court must conclude that involuntary medication is necessary to further those interests. . . .

Fourth, as we have said, the court must conclude that administration of the drugs is medically appropriate, i.e., in the patient's best medical interest in light of his medical condition. . . .

The Medical Center and the Magistrate in this case, applying standards roughly comparable to those set forth here and in Harper, approved forced medication substantially, if not primarily, upon grounds of Sell's dangerousness to others. But the District Court and the Eighth Circuit took a different approach. The District Court found 'clearly erroneous' the Magistrate's conclusion regarding dangerousness, and the Court of Appeals agreed. Both courts approved forced medication solely in order to render Sell competent to stand trial. . . .

For these reasons, we believe that the present orders authorizing forced administration of antipsychotic drugs cannot stand. The Government may pursue its request for forced medication on the grounds discussed in this opinion, including grounds related to the danger Sell poses to himself or others. Since Sell's medical condition may have changed over time, the Government should do so on the basis of current circumstances.

The judgment of the Eighth Circuit is vacated, and the case is remanded for further proceedings consistent with this opinion."

V. JUSTICE VOTE

3 Pro ACLU Side vs. 6 Con Opposing Side

ACLU Side (Petitioner / Appellant)

1. Scalia, A. – Wrote dissenting opinion
2. O'Connor, S. – Joined Scalia's dissent
3. Thomas, C. – Joined Scalia's dissent

Opposing Side (Respondent / Appellee)

1. Breyer, S. – Wrote majority opinion
2. Stevens, J. – Joined majority opinion
3. Souter, D. – Joined majority opinion
4. Ginsburg, R. – Joined majority opinion
5. Kennedy, A. – Joined majority opinion
6. Rehnquist, W. – Joined majority opinion

VI. A WIN OR LOSS FOR THE ACLU?

The ACLU filed as amicus curiae urging reversal of the judgment of the Court of Appeals; the Supreme Court vacated and remanded in a 6-3 vote, giving the ACLU an apparent loss.

946. U.S. v. American Library Ass'n, Inc.

(Decided June 23, 2003; 539 U.S. 194)

I. ISSUE

A. Issues Discussed

1st Amendment, press, speech, association

B. Legal Question Presented

Whether the Children's Internet Protection Act requirement for public libraries to install pornography blocking software to receive federal funding for Internet access violates the First Amendment.

C.Supreme Court's Answer

"Because public libraries' use of Internet filtering software does not violate their patrons' First Amendment rights, CIPA does not induce libraries to violate the Constitution, and is a valid exercise of Congress' spending power. Nor does CIPA impose an unconstitutional condition on public libraries."

II. CASE SUMMARY

A. Background

"To address the problems associated with the availability of Internet pornography in public libraries, Congress enacted the Children's Internet Protection Act (CIPA). Under CIPA, a public library may not receive federal assistance to provide Internet access unless it installs software to block images that constitute obscenity or child pornography, and to prevent minors from obtaining access to material that is harmful to them. The District Court held these provisions facially invalid on the ground that they induce public libraries to violate patrons' First Amendment rights."

The Supreme Court granted certiorari to review the case.

B. Counsel of Record

ACLU Side (Respondent / Appellee): Paul M. Smith argued the cause for appellees. With him on the brief for appellees American Library Association, Inc., et al. were Theresa A. Chmara, Daniel Mach, Elliot M. Mincberg, and Lawrence S. Ottinger. Christopher A. Hansen, Ann Beeson, and Steven R. Shapiro of the American Civil Liberties Union Foundation, Stefan Presser of the ACLU of Pennsylvania, Charles S. Sims, Lee Tien, Thomas Sponsler, and David L. Sobel filed a brief for appellees Multnomah County Public Library et al.

Opposing Side (Petitioner / Appellant): Solicitor General Olson argued the cause for appellants. With him on the briefs were Assistant Attorney General McCallum, Deputy Solicitor General Kneedler, Irving L. Gornstein, Barbara L. Herwig, and Jacob M. Lewis.

III. AMICI CURIAE

ACLU Side (Respondent / Appellee)

Brief of amici curiae filed on behalf of the Association of American Publishers, Inc., et al. by R. Bruce Rich, Jonathan Bloom, and John B. Morris, Jr.

Brief of amici curiae filed on behalf of the Brennan Center for Justice by Burt Neuborne, Laura K. Abel, and David S. Udell.

Brief of amici curiae filed on behalf of the Cleveland Public Library et al. by David W. Ogden.

Brief of amici curiae filed on behalf of Partnership for Progress on the Digital Divide et al. by Marjorie Heins.

Brief of amici curiae filed on behalf of the Online Policy Group, Inc., et al. by Daniel H. Bromberg and Charles R. A. Morse.

Brief of amici curiae filed on behalf of Jonathan Wallace d/b/a The Ethical Spectacle by Michael B. Green and Jonathan D. Wallace.

Brief of amici curiae filed on behalf of the National School Boards Association et al. by Julie Underwood, Naomi Gittins, and Stuart L. Knade, in support of neither party.

Opposing Side (Petitioner / Appellant)

Brief of amici curiae filed on behalf of the State of Texas by Greg Abbott, Attorney General, Barry R. McBee, First Assistant Attorney General, Jeffrey S. Boyd, Deputy Attorney General, Philip A. Lionberger, Solicitor General, and Amy Warr and Ryan D. Clinton, Assistant Solicitors General.

Brief of amici curiae filed on behalf of the American Center for Law and Justice et al. by Jay Alan Sekulow, Colby M. May, Ben Bull, James M. Henderson, Joel H. Thornton, John P. Tuskey, and Laura B. Hernandez.

Brief of amici curiae filed on behalf of the American Civil Rights Union by Peter Ferrara.

Brief of amici curiae filed on behalf of Cities, Mayors, and County Commissioners by Kelly Shackelford.

Brief of amici curiae filed on behalf of the Greenville, South Carolina, Public Library et al. by Kenneth C. Bass III.

Brief of amici curiae filed on behalf of the National Law Center for Children and Families et al. by Kristina A. Bullock, Bruce A. Taylor, and Janet M. LaRue.

Brief of amici curiae filed on behalf of Sen. Trent Lott et al. by Brian Fahling, Stephen M. Crampton, and Michael J. DePrimo.

IV. THE SUPREME COURT'S DECISION

"Congress has wide latitude to attach conditions to the receipt of federal assistance in order to further its policy objectives. But Congress may not 'induce' the recipient 'to engage in activities that would themselves be unconstitutional.' To determine whether libraries would violate the First Amendment by employing the filtering software that CIPA requires, we must first examine the role of libraries in our society.

Public libraries pursue the worthy missions of facilitating learning and cultural enrichment. . . . To fulfill their traditional missions, public libraries must have broad discretion to decide what material to provide to their patrons. Although they seek to provide a wide array of information, their goal has never been to provide 'universal coverage.' . . .

We have held in two analogous contexts that the government has broad discretion to make content-based judgments in deciding what private speech to make available to the public. . . .

The principles underlying Forbes and Finley also apply to a public library's exercise of judgment in selecting the material it provides to its patrons. Just as forum analysis and heightened judicial scrutiny are incompatible with the role of public television stations and the role of the NEA, they are also incompatible with the discretion that public libraries must have to fulfill their traditional missions. Public library staffs necessarily consider content in making collection decisions and enjoy broad discretion in making them.

The public forum principles on which the District Court relied are out of place in the context of this case. . . .

Nor does Internet access in a public library satisfy our definition of a 'designated public forum.' . . .

The District Court disagreed because, whereas a library reviews and affirmatively chooses to acquire every book in its collection, it does not review every Web site that it makes available. Based on this distinction, the court reasoned that a public library enjoys less discretion in deciding which Internet materials to make available than in making book selections. We do not find this distinction constitutionally relevant. A library's failure to make quality-based judgments about all the material it furnishes from the Web does not somehow taint the judgments it does make. . . .

Moreover, because of the vast quantity of material on the Internet and the rapid pace at which it changes, libraries cannot possibly segregate, item by item, all the Internet material that is appropriate for inclusion from all that is not. . . .

Like the District Court, the dissents fault the tendency of filtering software to 'overblock'—that is, to erroneously block access to constitutionally protected speech that falls outside the categories that software users intend to block. . . . Assuming that such erroneous blocking presents constitutional difficulties, any such concerns are dispelled by the ease with which patrons may have the filtering software disabled. . . .

Appellees urge us to affirm the District Court's judgment on the alternative ground that CIPA imposes an unconstitutional condition on the receipt of federal assistance. . . .

We need not decide this question because, even assuming that appellees may assert an 'unconstitutional conditions' claim, this claim would fail on the merits. . . .

Because public libraries' use of Internet filtering software does not violate their patrons' First Amendment rights, CIPA does not induce libraries to violate the Constitution, and is a valid exercise of Congress' spending power. Nor does CIPA impose an unconstitutional condition on public libraries. Therefore, the judgment of the District Court for the Eastern District of Pennsylvania is reversed."

V. JUSTICE VOTE

3 Pro ACLU Side vs. 6 Con Opposing Side

ACLU Side (Respondent / Appellee)

1. Stevens, J. – Wrote dissenting opinion
2. Souter, D. – Wrote dissenting opinion
3. Ginsburg, R. – Joined Souter's dissent

Opposing Side (Petitioner / Appellant)

1. Rehnquist, W. – Wrote plurality opinion
2. Thomas, C. – Joined plurality opinion
3. O'Connor, S. – Joined plurality opinion
4. Breyer, S. – Wrote concurring opinion
5. Scalia, A. – Joined plurality opinion
6. Kennedy, A. – Wrote concurring opinion

VI. A WIN OR LOSS FOR THE ACLU?

The ACLU argued the case for appellee, urging affirmance; the Supreme Court reversed the district court's decision by a 6-3 vote, giving the ACLU an apparent loss.

947. Gratz v. Bollinger

(Decided June 23, 2003; 539 U.S. 244)

I. ISSUE

A. Issues Discussed

Race, civil rights

B. Legal Question Presented

"[W]hether 'the University of Michigan's use of racial preferences in undergraduate admissions violate[s] the Equal Protection Clause of the Fourteenth Amendment, Title VI of the Civil Rights Act of 1964 (42 U.S.C. § 2000d), or 42 U.S.C. § 1981.'"

C. Supreme Court's Answer

"[B]ecause the University's use of race in its current freshman admissions policy is not narrowly tailored to achieve respondents' asserted compelling interest in diversity, the admissions policy violates the Equal Protection Clause of the Fourteenth Amendment. We further find that the admissions policy also violates Title VI and 42 U.S.C. § 1981."

II. CASE SUMMARY

A. Background

"Petitioners Jennifer Gratz and Patrick Hamacher both applied for admission to the University of Michigan's (University) College of Literature, Science, and the Arts (LSA) as residents of the State of Michigan. Both petitioners are Caucasian. . . . Gratz was notified in April that the LSA was unable to offer her admission. She enrolled in the University of Michigan at Dearborn, from which she graduated in the spring of 1999.

Hamacher applied for admission to the LSA for the fall of 1997. . . .Hamacher's application was . . . denied in April 1997, and he enrolled at Michigan State University.

In October 1997, Gratz and Hamacher filed a lawsuit in the United States District Court for the Eastern District of Michigan against the University, the LSA, James Duderstadt, and Lee Bollinger. Petitioners' complaint was a class-action suit alleging 'violations and threatened violations of the rights of the plaintiffs and the class they represent to equal protection of the laws under the Fourteenth Amendment . . . , and for racial discrimination in violation of 42 U.S.C. §§ 1981, 1983 and 2000d et seq." . . .

The District Court granted petitioners' motion for class certification . . . .

The University has changed its admissions guidelines a number of times during the period relevant to this litigation . . . .

OUA considers a number of factors in making admissions decisions, including high school grades, standardized test scores, high school quality, curriculum strength, geography, alumni relationships, and leadership. OUA also considers race. During all periods relevant to this litigation, the University has considered African-Americans, Hispanics, and Native Americans to be 'underrepresented minorities,' and it is undisputed that the University admits 'virtually every qualified . . . applicant' from these groups. . . .

The District Court found the admissions guidelines the LSA used from 1995 through 1998 to be more problematic. In the court's view, the University's prior practice of 'protecting' or 'reserving' seats for underrepresented minority applicants effectively kept nonprotected applicants from competing for those slots. This system, the court concluded, operated as the functional equivalent of a quota and ran afoul of Justice Powell's opinion in Bakke.

Based on these findings, the court granted petitioners' motion for summary judgment with respect to the LSA's admissions programs in existence from 1995 through 1998, and respondents' motion with respect to the LSA's admissions programs for 1999 and 2000. Accordingly, the District Court denied petitioners' request for injunctive relief.

The District Court issued an order consistent with its rulings and certified two questions for interlocutory appeal to the Sixth Circuit pursuant to 28 U.S.C. § 1292(b). Both parties appealed aspects of the District Court's rulings, and the Court of Appeals heard the case en banc on the same day as Grutter v. Bollinger. The Sixth Circuit later issued an opinion in Grutter, upholding the admissions program used by the University of Michigan Law School, and the petitioner in that case sought a writ of certiorari from this Court. Petitioners asked this Court to grant certiorari in this case as well, despite the fact that the Court of Appeals had not yet rendered a judgment, so that this Court could address the constitutionality of the consideration of race in university admissions in a wider range of circumstances."

The Supreme Court granted certiorari to review the case.

B. Counsel of Record

ACLU Side (Respondent / Appellee): John Payton argued the cause for appellees. With him on the brief for appellee Bollinger et al. were John H. Pickering, Brigida Benitez, Craig Goldblatt, Terry A. Maroney, Maureen E. Mahoney, Marvin Krislov, Jonathan Alger, Jeffrey Lehman, Evan Caminker, Philip J. Kessler, and Leonard M. Niehoff. Christopher A. Hansen and E. Vincent Warren of the American Civil Liberties Union Foundation, Elaine R. Jones, Theodore M. Shaw, Norman J. Chachkin, James L. Cott, Melissa S. Woods, Brent E. Simmons and Michael J. Steinberg of the ACLU Fund of Michigan, Antonia Hernandez, Thomas Saenz, Patricia Mendoza, Victor Viramontes, Godfrey J. Dillard, Milton R. Henry, and Reginald M. Turner filed a brief for appellee Patterson et al.

Opposing Side (Petitioner / Appellant): Kirk O. Kolbo argued the cause for appellants. With him on the briefs were David F. Herr, R. Lawrence Purdy, Michael C. McCarthy, Michael E. Rosman, Hans Bader, and Kerry L. Morgan.

Solicitor General Olson argued the cause for the United States as amicus curiae.

III. AMICI CURIAE

ACLU Side (Respondent / Appellee)

Brief of amici curiae filed on behalf of Members of the United States Congress by Leslie T. Thornton and Steven M. Schneebaum.

Brief of amici curiae filed on behalf of the State of Maryland et al. by J. Joseph Curran, Jr., Attorney General of Maryland, Andrew H. Baida, Solicitor General, Mark J. Davis and William F. Brockman, Assistant Attorneys General, Eliot Spitzer, Attorney General of New York, Caitlin J. Halligan, Solicitor General, Michelle Aronowitz, Deputy Solicitor General, and Julie Mathy Sheridan and Sachin S. Pandya, Assistant Solicitors General, and by the Attorneys General for their respective jurisdictions as follows: Terry Goddard of Arizona, Bill Lockyer of California, Ken Salazar of Colorado, Richard Blumenthal of Connecticut, Lisa Madigan of Illinois, Thomas J. Miller of Iowa, G. Steven Rowe of Maine, Thomas F. Reilly of Massachusetts, Mike Hatch of Minnesota, Mike McGrath of Montana, Patricia A. Madrid of New Mexico, Roy Cooper of North Carolina, W. A. Drew Edmondson of Oklahoma, Hardy Myers of Oregon, Patrick Lynch of Rhode Island, William H. Sorrell of Vermont, Iver A. Stridiron of the Virgin Islands, Christine O. Gregoire of Washington, Darrell V. McGraw, Jr., of West Virginia, and Peggy A. Lautenschlager of Wisconsin.

Brief of amici curiae filed on behalf of the State of New Jersey by David Samson, Attorney General, Jeffrey Burstein, Assistant Attorney General, and Donna Arons and Anne Marie Kelly, Deputy Attorneys General.

Brief of amici curiae filed on behalf of New York City Council Speaker A. Gifford Miller et al. by Jack Greenberg and Saul B. Shapiro.

Brief of amici curiae filed on behalf of the City of Philadelphia, Pennsylvania, et al. by Victor A. Bolden and Nelson A. Diaz.

Brief of amici curiae filed on behalf of the American Educational Research Association et al. by Angelo N. Ancheta.

Brief of amici curiae filed on behalf of the American Jewish Committee et al. by Stewart D. Aaron, Thomas M. Jancik, Jeffrey P. Sinensky, Kara H. Stein, and Richard T. Foltin.

Brief of amici curiae filed on behalf of the American Psychological Association by Paul R. Friedman, William F. Sheehan, and Nathalie F. P. Gilfoyle.

Brief of amici curiae filed on behalf of Amherst College et al. by Charles S. Sims.

Brief of amici curiae filed on behalf of the Authors of the Texas Ten Percent Plan by Rolando L. Rios.

Brief of amici curiae filed on behalf of the Bay Mills Indian Community et al. by Vanya S. Hogen.

Brief of amici curiae filed on behalf of the College Board by Janet Pitterle Holt.

Brief of amici curiae filed on behalf of Columbia University et al. by Floyd Abrams, Susan Buckley, and James J. Mingle.
Brief of amici curiae filed on behalf of Harvard University et al. by Laurence H. Tribe, Jonathan S. Massey, Beverly Ledbetter, Robert B. Donin, and Wendy S. White.
Brief of amici curiae filed on behalf of Howard University by Janell M. Byrd.
Brief of amici curiae filed on behalf of the Lawyers' Committee for Civil Rights Under Law et al. by John S. Skilton, Barbara R. Arnwine, Thomas J. Henderson, Dennis C. Hayes, Marcia D. Greenberger, Judith L. Lichtman, and Jocelyn C. Frye.
Brief of amici curiae filed on behalf of the Leadership Conference on Civil Rights et al. by Robert N. Weiner and William L. Taylor.
Brief of amici curiae filed on behalf of the National Coalition of Blacks for Reparations in America et al. by Kevin Outterson.
Brief of amici curiae filed on behalf of the National Education Association et al. by Robert H. Chanin, John M. West, Elliot Mincberg, Larry P. Weinberg, and John C. Dempsey.
Brief of amici curiae filed on behalf of the National Urban League et al. by William A. Norris and Michael C. Small.
Brief of amici curiae filed on behalf of the New America Alliance by Thomas R. Julin and D. Patricia Wallace.
Brief of amici curiae filed on behalf of Northeastern University by Daryl J. Lapp and Lisa A. Sinclair.
Brief of amici curiae filed on behalf of the NOW Legal Defense and Education Fund et al. by Wendy R. Weiser and Martha F. Davis.
Brief of amici curiae filed on behalf of the United Negro College Fund et al. by Drew S. Days III and Beth S. Brinkmann.
Brief of amici curiae filed on behalf of the University of Pittsburgh et al. by David C. Frederick and Sean A. Lev.
Brief of amici curiae filed on behalf of Lieutenant General Julius W. Becton, Jr., et al. by Virginia A. Seitz, Joseph R. Reeder, Robert P. Charrow, and Kevin E. Stern.
Brief of amici curiae filed on behalf of Senator Thomas A. Daschle et al. by David T. Goldberg and Penny Shane.
Brief of amici curiae filed on behalf of the Hayden Family by Roy C. Howell.
Brief of amici curiae filed on behalf of Glenn C. Loury et al. by Jeffrey F. Liss and James J. Halpert.
Brief of amici curiae filed on behalf of Michigan Governor Jennifer M. Granholm by John D. Pirich and Mark A. Goldsmith.
Brief of amici curiae filed on behalf of the American Federation of Labor and Congress of Industrial Organizations by Harold Craig Becker, David J. Strom, Jonathan P. Hiatt, and Daniel W. Sherrick.
Brief of amici curiae filed on behalf of the Black Women Lawyers Association of Greater Chicago, Inc., by Sharon E. Jones.
Brief of amici curiae filed on behalf of Carnegie Mellon University et al. by W. Thomas McGough, Jr., Kathy M. Banke, Gary L. Kaplan, and Edward N. Stoner II.
Brief of amici curiae filed on behalf of General Motors Corp. by Kenneth S. Geller, Eileen Penner, and Thomas A. Gottschalk.
Brief of amici curiae filed on behalf of Human Rights Advocates et al. by Constance de la Vega.
Brief of amici curiae filed on behalf of the Massachusetts Institute of Technology et al. by Donald B. Ayer, Elizabeth Rees, Debra L. Zumwalt, and Stacey J. Mobley.
Brief of amici curiae filed on behalf of the National Asian Pacific American Legal Consortium et al. by Mark A. Packman, Jonathan M. Cohen, Karen K. Narasaki, Vincent A. Eng, and Trang Q. Tran.
Brief of amici curiae filed on behalf of the National Council of La Raza et al. by Vilma S. Martinez and Jeffrey L. Bleich.
Brief of amici curiae filed on behalf of Banks Broadcasting, Inc., by Elizabeth G. Taylor.
Brief of amici curiae filed on behalf of the National School Boards Association et al. by Julie Underwood and Naomi Gittins.
Brief of amici curiae filed on behalf of Representative John Conyers, Jr., et al. by Paul J. Lawrence and Anthony R. Miles.
Brief of amici curiae filed on behalf of Representative Richard A. Gephardt et al. by Andrew L. Sandler and Mary L. Smith.

Opposing Side (Petitioner / Appellant)

Brief of amici curiae filed on behalf of the United States by Solicitor General Olson, Assistant Attorney General Boyd, and Deputy Solicitor General Clement.
Brief of amici curiae filed on behalf of the State of Florida et al. by Charlie Crist, Attorney General of Florida, Christopher M. Kise, Solicitor General, Louis F. Hubener, Deputy Solicitor General, and Daniel Woodring.
Brief of amici curiae filed on behalf of the Cato Institute by Robert A. Levy, Timothy Lynch, James L. Swanson, and Samuel Estreicher.
Brief of amici curiae filed on behalf of the Center for Equal Opportunity et al. by Roger Clegg and C. Mark Pickrell.
Brief of amici curiae filed on behalf of the Center for Individual Freedom by Renee L. Giachino.
Brief of amici curiae filed on behalf of the Center for New Black Leadership by Clint Bolick, William H. Mellor, and Richard D. Komer.
Brief of amici curiae filed on behalf of the Center for the Advancement of Capitalism by David Reed Burton.
Brief of amici curiae filed on behalf of the Claremont Institute Center for Constitutional Jurisprudence by Edwin Meese III.
Brief of amici curiae filed on behalf of the Michigan Association of Scholars by William F. Mohrman.
Brief of amici curiae filed on behalf of the National Association of Scholars by William H. Allen, Oscar M. Garibaldi, and Keith A. Noreika.
Brief of amici curiae filed on behalf of the Pacific Legal Foundation by John H. Findley.
Brief of amici curiae filed on behalf of the Reason Foundation by Martin S. Kaufman.
Brief of amici curiae filed on behalf of the Asian American Legal Foundation by Daniel C. Girard and Gordon M. Fauth, Jr.
Brief of amici curiae filed on behalf of Duane C. Ellison, by Mr. Ellison, pro se, and Carl V. Angelis.
Brief of amici curiae filed on behalf of the Anti-Defamation League by Martin E. Karlinsky and Steven M. Freeman, in support of neither party.

Brief of amici curiae filed on behalf of the Equal Employment Advisory Council by Jeffrey A. Norris and Ann Elizabeth Reesman, in support of neither party.

Brief of amici curiae filed on behalf of Exxon Mobil Corp. by Richard R. Brann, in support of neither party.

Brief of amici curiae filed on behalf of 3M et al. by David W. DeBruin, Deanne E. Maynard, Daniel Mach, Russell W. Porter, Jr., Charles R. Wall, Martin J. Barrington, Deval L. Patrick, John R. Parker, Jr., William J. O'Brien, Gary P. Van Graafeiland, Kathryn A. Oberly, Randall E. Mehrberg, Donald M. Remy, Ben W. Heineman, Jr., Brackett B. Denniston III, Elpidio Villarreal, Wayne A. Budd, J. Richard Smith, Stewart S. Hudnut, John A. Shutkin, Theodore L. Banks, Kenneth C. Frazier, David R. Andrews, Jeffrey B. Kindler, Teresa M. Holland, Charles W. Gerdts III, John L. Sander, Mark P. Klein, and Stephen P. Sawyer.

IV. THE SUPREME COURT'S DECISION

"As they have throughout the course of this litigation, petitioners contend that the University's consideration of race in its undergraduate admissions decisions violates § 1 of the Equal Protection Clause of the Fourteenth Amendment, Title VI, and 42 U.S.C. § 1981. We consider first whether petitioners have standing to seek declaratory and injunctive relief, and, finding that they do, we next consider the merits of their claims. . . .

Petitioners argue, first and foremost, that the University's use of race in undergraduate admissions violates the Fourteenth Amendment. . . . But for the reasons set forth today in Grutter v. Bollinger, the Court has rejected these arguments of petitioners.

Petitioners alternatively argue that even if the University's interest in diversity can constitute a compelling state interest, the District Court erroneously concluded that the University's use of race in its current freshman admissions policy is narrowly tailored to achieve such an interest. . .

It is by now well established that 'all racial classifications reviewable under the Equal Protection Clause must be strictly scrutinized.' . . .

To withstand our strict scrutiny analysis, respondents must demonstrate that the University's use of race in its current admissions program employs 'narrowly tailored measures that further compelling governmental interests.' . . . We find that the University's policy, which automatically distributes 20 points, or one-fifth of the points needed to guarantee admission, to every single 'underrepresented minority' applicant solely because of race, is not narrowly tailored to achieve the interest in educational diversity that respondents claim justifies their program.

In Bakke, Justice Powell reiterated that '[p]referring members of any one group for no reason other than race or ethnic origin is discrimination for its own sake.' He then explained, however, that in his view it would be permissible for a university to employ an admissions program in which 'race or ethnic background may be deemed a 'plus' in a particular applicant's file.' . . . Such a system, in Justice Powell's view, would be 'flexible enough to consider all pertinent elements of diversity in light of the particular qualifications of each applicant.' . . .

The current LSA policy does not provide such individualized consideration. . . . Moreover, . . . the LSA's automatic distribution of 20 points has the effect of making 'the factor of race . . . decisive' for virtually every minimally qualified underrepresented minority applicant. . . .

Respondents contend that '[t]he volume of applications and the presentation of applicant information make it impractical for [LSA] to use the . . . admissions system' upheld by the Court today in Grutter. But the fact that the implementation of a program capable of providing individualized consideration might present administrative challenges does not render constitutional an otherwise problematic system. . . .

We conclude, therefore, that because the University's use of race in its current freshman admissions policy is not narrowly tailored to achieve respondents' asserted compelling interest in diversity, the admissions policy violates the Equal Protection Clause of the Fourteenth Amendment. We further find that the admissions policy also violates Title VI and 42 U.S.C. § 1981. Accordingly, we reverse that portion of the District Court's decision granting respondents summary judgment with respect to liability and remand the case for proceedings consistent with this opinion."

V. JUSTICE VOTE

3 Pro ACLU Side vs. 6 Con Opposing Side

ACLU Side (Respondent / Appellee)

1. Stevens, J. – Wrote dissenting opinion
2. Souter, D. – Wrote dissenting opinion, joined Stevens' and Ginsburg's dissents
3. Ginsburg, R. – Wrote dissenting opinion, joined Souter's dissent in part

Opposing Side (Petitioner / Appellant)

1. Rehnquist, W. – Wrote majority opinion
2. O'Connor, S. – Wrote concurring opinion
3. Breyer, S. – Wrote concurring opinion, joined O'Connor's concurrence in part, joined Ginsburg's dissent in part
4. Thomas, C. – Wrote concurring opinion
5. Scalia, A. – Joined majority opinion
6. Kennedy, A. – Joined majority opinion

VI. A WIN OR LOSS FOR THE ACLU?

The ACLU argued the case for appellee, urging affirmance; the Supreme Court reversed in part and remanded the District Court's decision by a 6-3 vote, giving the ACLU an apparent loss.

948. Grutter v. Bollinger

(Decided June 23, 2003; 539 U.S. 306)

I. ISSUE

A. Issues Discussed

Race, civil rights

B. Legal Question Presented

"[W]hether the use of race as a factor in student admissions by the University of Michigan Law School (Law School) is unlawful."

C. Supreme Court's Answer

"[T]he Equal Protection Clause does not prohibit the Law School's narrowly tailored use of race in admissions decisions to further a compelling interest in obtaining the educational benefits that flow from a diverse student body."

II. CASE SUMMARY

A. Background

"The Law School ranks among the Nation's top law schools. It receives more than 3,500 applications each year for a class of around 350 students. Seeking to 'admit a group of students who individually and collectively are among the most capable,' the Law School looks for individuals with 'substantial promise for success in law school' and 'a strong likelihood of succeeding in the practice of law and contributing in diverse ways to the well-being of others.' More broadly, the Law School seeks 'a mix of students with varying backgrounds and experiences who will respect and learn from each other.' In 1992, the dean of the Law School charged a faculty committee with crafting a written admissions policy to implement these goals. In particular, the Law School sought to ensure that its efforts to achieve student body diversity complied with this Court's most recent ruling on the use of race in university admissions. Upon the unanimous adoption of the committee's report by the Law School faculty, it became the Law School's official admissions policy. . . .

The policy aspires to 'achieve that diversity which has the potential to enrich everyone's education and thus make a law school class stronger than the sum of its parts.' The policy does not restrict the types of diversity contributions eligible for 'substantial weight' in the admissions process, but instead recognizes 'many possible bases for diversity admissions.' The policy does, however, reaffirm the Law School's longstanding commitment to 'one particular type of diversity,' that is, 'racial and ethnic diversity with special reference to the inclusion of students from groups which have been historically discriminated against, like African–Americans, Hispanics and Native Americans, who without this commitment might not be represented in our student body in meaningful numbers.' . . .

Petitioner Barbara Grutter is a white Michigan resident who applied to the Law School in 1996 with a 3.8 GPA and 161 LSAT score. The Law School initially placed petitioner on a waiting list, but subsequently rejected her application. In December 1997, petitioner filed suit in the United States District Court for the Eastern District of Michigan . . . . Petitioner alleged that respondents discriminated against her on the basis of race in violation of the Fourteenth Amendment; Title VI of the Civil Rights Act of 1964; and Rev. Stat. § 1977, as amended. . . .

During the 15–day bench trial, the parties introduced extensive evidence concerning the Law School's use of race in the admissions process. . . .

In the end, the District Court concluded that the Law School's use of race as a factor in admissions decisions was unlawful. . . .

Sitting en banc, the Court of Appeals reversed the District Court's judgment and vacated the injunction."

The Supreme Court granted certiorari to review the case.

B. Counsel of Record

ACLU Side (Respondent / Appellee): Maureen E. Mahoney argued the cause for appellee Bollinger et al. With her on the brief were John H. Pickering, John Payton, Brigida Benitez, Craig Goldblatt, Terry A. Maroney, Marvin Krislov, Jonathan Alger, Evan Caminker, Philip J. Kessler, and Leonard M. Niehoff.

Miranda K. S. Massie and George B. Washington filed a brief for appellee James et al.

Opposing Side (Petitioner / Appellant): Kirk O. Kolbo argued the cause for appellant. With him on the briefs were David F. Herr, R. Lawrence Purdy, Michael C. McCarthy, Michael E. Rosman, Hans Bader, and Kerry L. Morgan.

Solicitor General Olson argued the cause for the United States as amicus curiae.

III. AMICI CURIAE

ACLU Side (Respondent / Appellee)

Brief of amici curiae filed on behalf of the NAACP Legal Defense and Educational Fund, Inc. and the American Civil Liberties Union by Elaine R. Jones, Theodore M. Shaw, Norman J. Chachkin, Robert H. Stroup, Elise C. Boddie, Damon T. Hewitt, Chinh Q. Le, Lia B. Epperson, Stephen R. Shapiro, Christopher A. Hansen, and E. Vincent Warren.

Brief of amici curiae filed on behalf of the State of Maryland et al. by J. Joseph Curran, Jr., Attorney General of Maryland, Andrew H. Baida, Solicitor General, Mark J. Davis and William F. Brockman, Assistant Attorneys General, Eliot Spitzer, Attorney General of New York, Caitlin J. Halligan, Solicitor General, Michelle Aronowitz, Deputy Solicitor General, and Julie Mathy Sheridan and Sachin S. Pandya, Assistant Solicitors General, and by the Attorneys General for their respective jurisdictions as follows: Terry Goddard of Arizona, Bill Lockyer of California, Ken Salazar of Colorado, Richard Blumenthal of Connecticut, Lisa Madigan of Illinois, Thomas J. Miller of Iowa, G. Steven Rowe of Maine, Thomas F. Reilly of Massachusetts, Mike Hatch of Minnesota, Mike McGrath of Montana, Patricia A. Madrid of New Mexico, Roy Cooper of North Carolina, W. A. Drew Edmondson of Oklahoma, Hardy Myers of Oregon, Patrick Lynch of Rhode Island, William H. Sorrell of Vermont, Iver A. Stridiron of the Virgin Islands, Christine O. Gregoire of Washington, Darrell V. McGraw, Jr., of West Virginia, and Peggy A. Lautenschlager of Wisconsin.

Brief of amici curiae filed on behalf of the State of New Jersey by David Samson, Attorney General, Jeffrey Burstein, Assistant Attorney General, and Donna Arons and Anne Marie Kelly, Deputy Attorneys General.

Brief of amici curiae filed on behalf of New York City Council Speaker A. Gifford Miller et al. by Jack Greenberg and Saul B. Shapiro.

Brief of amici curiae filed on behalf of the City of Philadelphia, Pennsylvania, et al. by Victor A. Bolden and Nelson A. Diaz.

Brief of amici curiae filed on behalf of the American Bar Association by Paul M. Dodyk and Rowan D. Wilson.
Brief of amici curiae filed on behalf of the American Educational Research Association et al. by Angelo N. Ancheta.
Brief of amici curiae filed on behalf of the American Jewish Committee et al. by Stewart D. Aaron, Thomas M. Jancik, Jeffrey P. Sinensky, Kara H. Stein, and Richard T. Foltin.
Brief of amici curiae filed on behalf of the American Law Deans Association by Samuel Issacharoff.
Brief of amici curiae filed on behalf of the American Psychological Association by Paul R. Friedman, William F. Sheehan, and Nathalie F. P. Gilfoyle.
Brief of amici curiae filed on behalf of the American Sociological Association et al. by Bill Lann Lee and Deborah J. Merritt.
Brief of amici curiae filed on behalf of Amherst College et al. by Charles S. Sims.
Brief of amici curiae filed on behalf of the Arizona State University College of Law by Ralph S. Spritzer and Paul Bender.
Brief of amici curiae filed on behalf of the Association of American Law Schools by Pamela S. Karlan.
Brief of amici curiae filed on behalf of the Association of American Medical Colleges et al. by Robert A. Burgoyne and Joseph A. Keyes, Jr.
Brief of amici curiae filed on behalf of the Bay Mills Indian Community et al. by Vanya S. Hogen.
Brief of amici curiae filed on behalf of the Clinical Legal Education Association by Timothy A. Nelsen, Frances P. Kao, and Eric J. Gorman.
Brief of amici curiae filed on behalf of Columbia University et al. by Floyd Abrams and Susan Buckley.
Brief of amici curiae filed on behalf of the Graduate Management Admission Council et al. by Stephen M. McNabb.
Brief of amici curiae filed on behalf of the Harvard Black Law Students Association et al. by George W. Jones, Jr., William J. Jefferson, Theodore V. Wells, Jr., and David W. Brown.
Brief of amici curiae filed on behalf of Harvard University et al. by Laurence H. Tribe, Jonathan S. Massey, Beverly Ledbetter, Robert B. Donin, and Wendy S. White.
Brief of amici curiae filed on behalf of the Hispanic National Bar Association et al. by Gilbert Paul Carrasco.
Brief of amici curiae filed on behalf of Howard University by Janell M. Byrd.
Brief of amici curiae filed on behalf of Indiana University by James Fitzpatrick, Lauren K. Robel, and Jeffrey Evans Stake.
Brief of amici curiae filed on behalf of the King County Bar Association by John Warner Widell, John H. Chun, and Melissa O'Loughlin White.
Brief of amici curiae filed on behalf of the Law School Admission Council by Walter Dellinger, Pamela Harris, and Jonathan D. Hacker.
Brief of amici curiae filed on behalf of the Lawyers' Committee for Civil Rights Under Law et al. by John S. Skilton, David E. Jones, Barbara R. Arnwine, Thomas J. Henderson, Dennis C. Hayes, Marcia D. Greenberger, and Judith L. Lichtman.
Brief of amici curiae filed on behalf of the Leadership Conference on Civil Rights et al. by Robert N. Weiner and William L. Taylor.
Brief of amici curiae filed on behalf of the Mexican American Legal Defense and Educational Fund et al. by Antonia Hernandez.
Brief of amici curiae filed on behalf of the Michigan Black Law Alumni Society by Christopher J. Wright, Timothy J. Simeone, and Kathleen McCree Lewis.
Brief of amici curiae filed on behalf of the National Center for Fair & Open Testing by John T. Affeldt and Mark Savage.
Brief of amici curiae filed on behalf of the National Coalition of Blacks for Reparations in America et al. by Kevin Outterson.
Brief of amici curiae filed on behalf of the National Education Association et al. by Robert H. Chanin, John M. West, Elliot Mincberg, Larry P. Weinberg, and John C. Dempsey.
Brief of amici curiae filed on behalf of the National Urban League et al. by William A. Norris and Michael C. Small.
Brief of amici curiae filed on behalf of the New America Alliance by Thomas R. Julin and D. Patricia Wallace.
Brief of amici curiae filed on behalf of the New Mexico Hispanic Bar Association et al. by Edward Benavidez.
Brief of amici curiae filed on behalf of the NOW Legal Defense and Educational Fund et al. by Wendy R. Weiser and Martha F. Davis.
Brief of amici curiae filed on behalf of the School of Law of the University of North Carolina by John Charles Boger, Julius L. Chambers, and Charles E. Daye.
Brief of amici curiae filed on behalf of the Society of American Law Teachers by Michael Selmi and Gabriel J. Chin.
Brief of amici curiae filed on behalf of the UCLA School of Law Students of Color by Sonia Mercado.
Brief of amici curiae filed on behalf of the United Negro College Fund et al. by Drew S. Days III and Beth S. Brinkmann.
Brief of amici curiae filed on behalf of the University of Michigan Asian Pacific American Law Students Association et al. by Jerome S. Hirsch.
Brief of amici curiae filed on behalf of the University of Pittsburgh et al. by David C. Frederick and Sean A. Lev.
Brief of amici curiae filed on behalf of Judith Areen et al. by Neal Katyal and Kumiki Gibson.
Brief of amici curiae filed on behalf of Lieutenant General Julius W. Becton, Jr., et al. by Virginia A. Seitz, Joseph R. Reeder, Robert P. Charrow, and Kevin E. Stern.
Brief of amici curiae filed on behalf of Hillary Browne et al. by Gregory Alan Berry.
Brief of amici curiae filed on behalf of Senator Thomas A. Daschle et al. by David T. Goldberg and Penny Shane.
Brief of amici curiae filed on behalf of the Hayden Family by Roy C. Howell.
Brief of amici curiae filed on behalf of Glenn C. Loury by Jeffrey F. Liss and James J. Halpert.
Brief of amici curiae filed on behalf of 13,922 Current Law Students at Accredited American Law Schools by Julie R. O'Sullivan and Peter J. Rubin.
Brief of amici curiae filed on behalf of Michigan Governor Jennifer M. Granholm by John D. Pirich and Mark A. Goldsmith.
Brief of amici curiae filed on behalf of Members and Former Members of the Pennsylvania General Assembly et al. by Mark B. Cohen and Eric S. Fillman.

Brief of amici curiae filed on behalf of the American Council on Education et al. by Martin Michaelson, Alexander E. Dreier, and Sheldon E. Steinbach.

Brief of amici curiae filed on behalf of the American Federation of Labor and Congress of Industrial Organizations by Harold Craig Becker, David J. Strom, Jonathan P. Hiatt, and Daniel W. Sherrick.

Brief of amici curiae filed on behalf of the National Asian Pacific American Legal Consortium et al. by Mark A. Packman, Karen K. Narasaki, Vincent A. Eng, and Trang Q. Tran.

Brief of amici curiae filed on behalf of the Massachusetts Institute of Technology et al. by Donald B. Ayer, Elizabeth Rees, Debra L. Zumwalt, and Stacey J. Mobley.

Brief of amici curiae filed on behalf of Human Rights Advocates et al. by Constance de la Vega.

Brief of amici curiae filed on behalf of General Motors Corp. by Kenneth S. Geller, Eileen Penner, and Thomas A. Gottschalk.

Brief of amici curiae filed on behalf of the Committee of Concerned Black Graduates of ABA Accredited Law Schools et al. by Mary Mack Adu.

Brief of amici curiae filed on behalf of the Coalition for Economic Equity et al. by Eva J. Paterson and Eric K. Yamamoto.

Brief of amici curiae filed on behalf of the Carnegie Mellon University et al. by W. Thomas McGough, Jr., Kathy M. Banke, Gary L. Kaplan, and Edward N. Stoner II.

Brief of amici curiae filed on behalf of the Black Women Lawyers Association of Greater Chicago, Inc., by Sharon E. Jones.

Brief of amici curiae filed on behalf of the National School Boards Association et al. by Julie Underwood and Naomi Gittins.

Brief of amici curiae filed on behalf of Representative Richard A. Gephardt et al. by Andrew L. Sandler and Mary L. Smith.

Brief of amici curiae filed on behalf of Representative John Conyers, Jr., et al. by Paul J. Lawrence and Anthony R. Miles.

Brief of amici curiae filed on behalf of Veterans of the Southern Civil Rights Movement et al. by Mitchell Zimmerman.

Brief of amici curiae filed on behalf of the New York State Black and Puerto Rican Legislative Caucus by Victor Goode.

Brief of amici curiae filed on behalf of the Boston Bar Association et al. by Thomas E. Dwyer, Jr., and Joseph L. Kociubes.

Brief of amici curiae filed on behalf of Media Companies by Elizabeth G. Taylor.

Opposing Side (Petitioner / Appellant)

Brief of amici curiae filed on behalf of the United States by Solicitor General Olson, Assistant Attorney General Boyd, and Deputy Solicitor General Clement.

Brief of amici curiae filed on behalf of the State of Florida et al. by Charlie Crist, Attorney General of Florida, Christopher M. Kise, Solicitor General, Louis F. Hubener, Deputy Solicitor General, and Daniel Woodring.

Brief of amici curiae filed on behalf of the Cato Institute by Robert A. Levy, Timothy Lynch, James L. Swanson, and Samuel Estreicher.

Brief of amici curiae filed on behalf of the Center for Equal Opportunity et al. by Roger Clegg and C. Mark Pickrell.

Brief of amici curiae filed on behalf of the Center for Individual Freedom by Renee L. Giachino.

Brief of amici curiae filed on behalf of the Center for New Black Leadership by Clint Bolick, William H. Mellor, and Richard D. Komer.

Brief of amici curiae filed on behalf of the Center for the Advancement of Capitalism by David Reed Burton.

Brief of amici curiae filed on behalf of the Claremont Institute Center for Constitutional Jurisprudence by Edwin Meese III.

Brief of amici curiae filed on behalf of the Michigan Association of Scholars by William F. Mohrman.

Brief of amici curiae filed on behalf of the National Association of Scholars by William H. Allen, Oscar M. Garibaldi, and Keith A. Noreika.

Brief of amici curiae filed on behalf of the Pacific Legal Foundation by John H. Findley.

Brief of amici curiae filed on behalf of Law Professor Larry Alexander et al. by Erik S. Jaffe.

Brief of amici curiae filed on behalf of the Reason Foundation by Martin S. Kaufman.

Brief of amici curiae filed on behalf of the Asian American Legal Foundation by Daniel C. Girard and Gordon M. Fauth, Jr.

Brief of amici curiae filed on behalf of Ward Connerly by Manuel S. Klausner and Patrick J. Manshardt.

Brief of amici curiae filed on behalf of 3M et al. by David W. DeBruin, Deanne E. Maynard, Daniel Mach, Russell W. Porter, Jr., Charles R. Wall, Martin J. Barrington, Deval L. Patrick, William J. O'Brien, Gary P. Van Graafeiland, Kathryn A. Oberly, Randall E. Mehrberg, Donald M. Remy, Ben W. Heineman, Jr., Brackett B. Denniston III, Elpidio Villarreal, Wayne A. Budd, J. Richard Smith, Stewart S. Hudnut, John A. Shutkin, Theodore L. Banks, Kenneth C. Frazier, David R. Andrews, Jeffrey B. Kinder, Teresa M. Holland, Charles W. Gerdts III, John L. Sander, Mark P. Klein, and Stephen P. Sawyer.

Brief of amici curiae filed on behalf of the Anti-Defamation League by Martin E. Karlinsky and Steven M. Freeman in support of neither party.

Brief of amici curiae filed on behalf of Exxon Mobil Corp. by Richard R. Brann in support of neither party.

Brief of amici curiae filed on behalf of the Criminal Justice Legal Foundation by Kent S. Scheidegger in support of neither party.

Brief of amici curiae filed on behalf of the Equal Employment Advisory Council by Jeffrey A. Norris and Ann Elizabeth Reesman in support of neither party.

Brief of amici curiae filed on behalf of the Massachusetts School of Law by Lawrence R. Velvel in support of neither party.

IV. THE SUPREME COURT'S DECISION

"We last addressed the use of race in public higher education over 25 years ago. In the landmark Bakke case, we reviewed a racial set-aside program that reserved 16 out of 100 seats in a medical school class for members of certain minority groups. The decision produced six separate opinions, none of which commanded a majority of the Court. . . . The only holding for the Court in Bakke was that a 'State has a substantial interest that legitimately may be served by a properly devised admissions program involving the competitive consideration of race and ethnic origin.' Thus, we reversed that part of the lower court's judgment that enjoined the university 'from any consideration of the race of any applicant.'

Since this Court's splintered decision in Bakke, Justice Powell's opinion announcing the judgment of the Court has served as the touchstone for constitutional analysis of race-conscious admissions policies. Public and private universities across the Nation have modeled their own admissions programs on Justice Powell's views on permissible race-conscious policies.

[T]oday we endorse Justice Powell's view that student body diversity is a compelling state interest that can justify the use of race in university admissions. . . .

We have held that all racial classifications imposed by government 'must be analyzed by a reviewing court under strict scrutiny.' . . .

Context matters when reviewing race-based governmental action under the Equal Protection Clause. . . .

With these principles in mind, we turn to the question whether the Law School's use of race is justified by a compelling state interest. Before this Court, as they have throughout this litigation, respondents assert only one justification for their use of race in the admissions process: obtaining 'the educational benefits that flow from a diverse student body.' In other words, the Law School asks us to recognize, in the context of higher education, a compelling state interest in student body diversity. . . .

Today, we hold that the Law School has a compelling interest in attaining a diverse student body.

The Law School's educational judgment that such diversity is essential to its educational mission is one to which we defer.. . .

We have long recognized that, given the important purpose of public education and the expansive freedoms of speech and thought associated with the university environment, universities occupy a special niche in our constitutional tradition. . . .

Even in the limited circumstance when drawing racial distinctions is permissible to further a compelling state interest, government is still 'constrained in how it may pursue that end: [T]he means chosen to accomplish the [government's] asserted purpose must be specifically and narrowly framed to accomplish that purpose.' . . .

To be narrowly tailored, a race-conscious admissions program cannot use a quota system—it cannot 'insulat[e] each category of applicants with certain desired qualifications from competition with all other applicants.' Instead, a university may consider race or ethnicity only as a "plus' in a particular applicant's file,' without 'insulat[ing] the individual from comparison with all other candidates for the available seats.' . . .

We find that the Law School's admissions program bears the hallmarks of a narrowly tailored plan. . . .

Here, the Law School engages in a highly individualized, holistic review of each applicant's file, giving serious consideration to all the ways an applicant might contribute to a diverse educational environment. The Law School affords this individualized consideration to applicants of all races. . . .

We acknowledge that 'there are serious problems of justice connected with the idea of preference itself.' Narrow tailoring, therefore, requires that a race-conscious admissions program not unduly harm members of any racial group. . . .

We are satisfied that the Law School's admissions program does not. Because the Law School considers 'all pertinent elements of diversity,' it can (and does) select nonminority applicants who have greater potential to enhance student body diversity over underrepresented minority applicants. . . .

We agree that, in the context of its individualized inquiry into the possible diversity contributions of all applicants, the Law School's race-conscious admissions program does not unduly harm nonminority applicants.

We are mindful, however, that '[a] core purpose of the Fourteenth Amendment was to do away with all governmentally imposed discrimination based on race.' Accordingly, race-conscious admissions policies must be limited in time. . . .

In the context of higher education, the durational requirement can be met by sunset provisions in race-conscious admissions policies and periodic reviews to determine whether racial preferences are still necessary to achieve student body diversity. . . .

We take the Law School at its word that it would 'like nothing better than to find a race-neutral admissions formula' and will terminate its race-conscious admissions program as soon as practicable. . . . It has been 25 years since Justice Powell first approved the use of race to further an interest in student body diversity in the context of public higher education. Since that time, the number of minority applicants with high grades and test scores has indeed increased. We expect that 25 years from now, the use of racial preferences will no longer be necessary to further the interest approved today. . . .

In summary, the Equal Protection Clause does not prohibit the Law School's narrowly tailored use of race in admissions decisions to further a compelling interest in obtaining the educational benefits that flow from a diverse student body. Consequently, petitioner's statutory claims based on Title VI and 42 U.S.C. § 1981 also fail. . . . The judgment of the Court of Appeals for the Sixth Circuit, accordingly, is affirmed."

V. JUSTICE VOTE

5 Pro ACLU Side vs. 4 Con Opposing Side

ACLU Side (Respondent / Appellee)

1. O'Connor, S. – Wrote majority opinion
2. Stevens, J. – Joined majority opinion
3. Souter, D. – Joined majority opinion
4. Ginsburg, R. – Wrote concurring opinion
5. Breyer, S. – Joined Ginsburg's concurrence

Opposing Side (Petitioner / Appellant)

1. Thomas, C. – Wrote opinion concurring in part and dissenting in part, joined Scalia's opinion, joined Rehnquist's dissent, joined the majority opinion in part
2. Scalia, A. – Wrote opinion concurring in part and dissenting in part, joined Thomas' opinion in part, joined Rehnquist's dissent, joined the majority opinion in part
3. Kennedy, A. – Wrote dissenting opinion, joined Rehnquist's dissent
4. Rehnquist, W. – Wrote dissenting opinion

VI. A WIN OR LOSS FOR THE ACLU?

The ACLU filed as amicus curiae urging affirmance; the Supreme Court affirmed the Court of Appeals' decision by a 5-4 vote, giving the ACLU an apparent win.

949. Georgia v. Ashcroft

(Decided June 26, 2003; 539 U.S. 461)

A. Issues Discussed

Voting rights

B. Legal Question Presented

"[W]hether Georgia's State Senate redistricting plan should have been precleared under § 5 of the Voting Rights Act of 1965 . . . ."

C. Supreme Court's Answer

"The District Court failed to consider all the relevant factors when it examined whether Georgia's Senate plan resulted in a retrogression of black voters' effective exercise of the electoral franchise. . . . Given the evidence submitted in this case, we find that Georgia likely met its burden of showing nonretrogression."

I. ISSUE

II. CASE SUMMARY

A. Background

"Over the past decade, the propriety of Georgia's state and congressional districts has been the subject of repeated litigation. . . .

All parties here concede that the 1997 plan is the benchmark plan for this litigation because it was in effect at the time of the 2001 redistricting effort. . . .

After the 2000 census, the Georgia General Assembly began the process of redistricting the Senate once again. . . .

The plan as designed by Senator Brown's committee kept true to the dual goals of maintaining at least as many majority-minority districts while also attempting to increase Democratic strength in the Senate. . . .

The Governor signed the Senate plan into law on August 24, 2001, and Georgia subsequently sought to obtain preclearance. . . .

Pursuant to § 5 of the Voting Rights Act, a covered jurisdiction like Georgia has the option of either seeking administrative preclearance through the Attorney General of the United States or seeking judicial preclearance by instituting an action in the United States District Court for the District of Columbia for a declaratory judgment that the voting change comports with § 5. Georgia chose the latter method, filing suit seeking a declaratory judgment that the State Senate plan does not violate § 5. . . .

A three-judge panel of the District Court held that Georgia's State Senate apportionment violated § 5, and was therefore not entitled to preclearance. . . .

After the District Court refused to preclear the plan, Georgia enacted another plan, largely similar to the one at issue here, except that it added black voters to Districts 2, 12, and 26. The District Court precleared this plan. No party has contested the propriety of the District Court's preclearance of the Senate plan as amended. Georgia asserts that it will use the plan as originally enacted if it receives preclearance.

[The Supreme Court] noted probable jurisdiction to consider whether the District Court should have precleared the plan as originally enacted by Georgia in 2001 . . . ."

The Supreme Court granted certiorari to review the case.

B. Counsel of Record

ACLU Side (Respondent / Appellee): Malcolm L. Stewart argued the cause for the federal appellees. With him on the brief were Solicitor General Olson, Assistant Attorney General Boyd, Deputy Solicitor General Clement, and Mark L. Gross.

E. Marshall Braden argued the cause for appellee intervenors. With him on the brief were Amy M. Henson, Frank B. Strickland, and Anne W. Lewis.

Opposing Side (Petitioner / Appellant): David F. Walbert argued the cause for appellant. With him on the briefs were Thurbert E. Baker, Attorney General of Georgia, Dennis R. Dunn, Deputy Attorney General, and Mark H. Cohen

III. AMICI CURIAE

ACLU Side (Respondent / Appellee)

Brief of amici curiae filed on behalf of the Georgia Coalition for the Peoples' Agenda by Laughlin McDonald, Neil Bradley, Bryan Sells, and Meredith E.B. Bell of the American Civil Liberties Union Foundation, and Barbara R. Arnwine, Thomas J. Henderson, Anita Hodgkiss, Elaine R. Jones, Norman J. Chachkin, Debo B. Adegbile, and Todd A. Cox.

Opposing Side (Petitioner / Appellant)

No briefs of amici curiae were filed in support of appellant.

IV. THE SUPREME COURT'S DECISION

"Section 5 of the Voting Rights Act 'has a limited substantive goal: "to insure that no voting-procedure changes would be made that would lead to a retrogression in the position of racial minorities with respect to their effective exercise of the electoral franchise." Thus, a plan that merely preserves 'current minority voting strength' is entitled to § 5 preclearance. Indeed, a voting change with a discriminatory but nonretrogressive purpose or effect does not violate § 5. And 'no matter how unconstitutional it may be,' a plan that is not retrogressive should be precleared under § 5. . . .

Georgia argues that a plan should be precleared under § 5 if the plan would satisfy § 2 of the Voting Rights Act of 1965, 42 U.S.C. § 1973. We have, however, 'consistently understood' § 2 to 'combat different evils and, accordingly, to impose very different duties upon the States.' . . .

Georgia argues that even if compliance with § 2 does not automatically result in preclearance under § 5, its State Senate plan should be precleared because it does not lead to 'a retrogression in the position of racial minorities with respect to their effective exercise of the electoral franchise.'

While we have never determined the meaning of 'effective exercise of the electoral franchise,' this case requires us to do so in some detail. . . .

Section 5 gives States the flexibility to choose one theory of effective representation over the other. . . .

The District Court failed to consider all the relevant factors when it examined whether Georgia's Senate plan resulted in a retrogression of black voters' effective exercise of the electoral franchise. . . .

Given the evidence submitted in this case, we find that Georgia likely met its burden of showing nonretrogression. . . .

The purpose of the Voting Rights Act is to prevent discrimination in the exercise of the electoral franchise and to foster our transformation to a society that is no longer fixated on race. . . . While courts and the Department of Justice should be vigilant in ensuring that States neither reduce the effective exercise of the electoral franchise nor discriminate against minority voters, the Voting Rights Act, as properly interpreted, should encourage the transition to a society where race no longer matters: a society where integration and color-blindness are not just qualities to be proud of, but are simple facts of life.

The District Court is in a better position to reweigh all the facts in the record in the first instance in light of our explication of retrogression. The judgment of the District Court for the District of Columbia, accordingly, is vacated, and the case is remanded for further proceedings consistent with this opinion."

V. JUSTICE VOTE

4 Pro ACLU Side vs. 5 Con Opposing Side

ACLU Side (Respondent / Appellee)

1. Souter, D. – Wrote dissenting opinion
2. Stevens, J. – Joined Souter's dissent
3. Ginsburg, R. – Joined Souter's dissent
4. Breyer, S. – Joined Souter's dissent

Opposing Side (Petitioner / Appellant)

1. O'Connor, S. – Wrote majority opinion
2. Thomas, C. – Wrote concurring opinion
3. Scalia, A. – Joined majority opinion
4. Kennedy, A. – Wrote concurring opinion
5. Rehnquist, W. – Joined majority opinion

VI. A WIN OR LOSS FOR THE ACLU?

The ACLU filed as amicus curiae urging affirmance; the Supreme Court vacated and remanded the district court's decision by a 5-4 vote, giving the ACLU an apparent loss.

950. Lawrence v. Texas

(Decided June 26, 2003; 539 U.S. 558)

I. ISSUE

A. Issues Discussed

Privacy

B. Legal Question Presented

"Whether petitioners' criminal convictions under the Texas 'Homosexual Conduct' law—which criminalizes sexual intimacy by same-sex couples, but not identical behavior by different-sex couples—violate the Fourteenth Amendment guarantee of equal protection of the laws. . . . Whether petitioners' criminal convictions for adult consensual sexual intimacy in the home violate their vital interests in liberty and privacy protected by the Due Process Clause of the Fourteenth Amendment. . . . Whether Bowers v. Hardwick . . . should be overruled."

C. Supreme Court's Answer

"Bowers was not correct when it was decided, and it is not correct today. It ought not to remain binding precedent. Bowers v. Hardwick should be and now is overruled. . . . The Texas statute furthers no legitimate state interest which can justify its intrusion into the personal and private life of the individual."

II. CASE SUMMARY

A. Background

"The question before the Court is the validity of a Texas statute making it a crime for two persons of the same sex to engage in certain intimate sexual conduct.

In Houston, Texas, officers of the Harris County Police Department were dispatched to a private residence in response to a reported weapons disturbance. They entered an apartment where one of the petitioners, John Geddes Lawrence, resided. The right of the police to enter does not seem to have been questioned. The officers observed Lawrence and another man, Tyron Garner, engaging in a sexual act. The two petitioners were arrested, held in custody overnight, and charged and convicted before a Justice of the Peace.

The complaints described their crime as 'deviate sexual intercourse, namely anal sex, with a member of the same sex (man).' The applicable state law is Tex. Penal Code Ann. § 21.06(a) (2003). It provides: 'A person commits an offense if he engages in deviate sexual intercourse with another individual of the same sex.' . . .

The petitioners exercised their right to a trial de novo in Harris County Criminal Court. They challenged the statute as a violation of the Equal Protection Clause of the Fourteenth Amendment and of a like provision of the Texas Constitution. Those contentions were rejected. The petitioners, having entered a plea of nolo contendere, were each fined $200 and assessed court costs of $141.25.

The Court of Appeals for the Texas Fourteenth District considered the petitioners' federal constitutional arguments under both the Equal Protection and Due Process Clauses of the Fourteenth Amendment. After hearing the case en banc the court, in a divided opinion, rejected the constitutional arguments and affirmed the convictions. The majority opinion indicates that the Court of Appeals considered our decision in Bowers v. Hardwick, 478 U.S. 186 (1986), to be controlling on the federal due process aspect of the case. Bowers then being authoritative, this was proper."

The Supreme Court granted certiorari to review the case.

B. Counsel of Record

ACLU Side (Petitioner / Appellant): Paul M. Smith argued the cause for appellants. With him on the briefs were William M. Hohengarten, Daniel Mach, Mitchell Katine, Ruth E. Harlow, Patricia M. Logue, and Susan L. Sommer.

Opposing Side (Respondent / Appellee): Charles A. Rosenthal, Jr., argued the cause for appellee. With him on the brief were William J. Delmore III and Scott A. Durfee.

III. AMICI CURIAE

ACLU Side (Petitioner / Appellant)

Brief of amici curiae filed on behalf of the American Civil Liberties Union and the ACLU of Texas by Laurence H. Tribe, William Clark Harrell, James D. Esseks, Steven R. Shapiro, and Matthew A. Coles.

Brief of amici curiae filed on behalf of the Alliance of Baptists et al. by Robert A. Long, Jr., and Thomas L. Cubbage III.

Brief of amici curiae filed on behalf of the American Psychological Association et al. by David W. Ogden, Paul R. Q. Wolfson, Richard G. Taranto, Nathalie F. P. Gilfoyle, and Carolyn I. Polowy.

Brief of amici curiae filed on behalf of the American Public Health Association et al. by Jeffrey S. Trachtman and Norman C. Simon.

Brief of amici curiae filed on behalf of the Cato Institute by Robert A. Levy.

Brief of amici curiae filed on behalf of Constitutional Law Professors by Pamela S. Karlan and William B. Rubenstein.

Brief of amici curiae filed on behalf of the Human Rights Campaign et al. by Walter Dellinger, Pamela Harris, and Jonathan D. Hacker.

Brief of amici curiae filed on behalf of the Log Cabin Republicans et al. by C. Martin Meekins.

Brief of amici curiae filed on behalf of the NOW Legal Defense and Education Fund by David C. Codell, Laura W. Brill, and Wendy R. Weiser.

Brief of amici curiae filed on behalf of Professors of History by Roy T. Englert, Jr., Alan Untereiner, and Sherri Lynn Wolson.

Brief of amici curiae filed on behalf of the Republican Unity Coalition et al. by Erik S. Jaffe.

Brief of amici curiae filed on behalf of Mary Robinson et al. by Harold Hongju Koh and Joseph F. Tringali.

Brief of amici curiae filed on behalf of the American Bar Association by Alfred P. Carlton, Jr., Ruth N. Borenstein, and Beth S. Brinkmann.

Brief of amici curiae filed on behalf of the Institute for Justice by William H. Mellor, Clint Bolick, Dana Berliner, and Randy E. Barnett.

Brief of amici curiae filed on behalf of the National Lesbian and Gay Law Association et al. by Chai R. Feldblum, J. Paul Oetken, and Scott Ruskay-Kidd.

Opposing Side (Respondent / Appellee)

Brief of amici curiae filed on behalf of the State of Alabama et al. by William H. Pryor, Jr., Attorney General of Alabama, Nathan A. Forrester, Solicitor General, and George M. Weaver, and by the Attorneys General for their respective States as follows: Henry D. McMaster of South Carolina and Mark L. Shurtleff of Utah.

Brief of amici curiae filed on behalf of Agudath Israel of America by David Zwiebel.

Brief of amici curiae filed on behalf of the American Center for Law and Justice by Jay Alan Sekulow, Stuart J. Roth, Colby M. May, James M. Henderson, Sr., Joel H. Thornton, and Walter M. Weber.

Brief of amici curiae filed on behalf of the American Family Association, Inc., et al. by Stephen M. Crampton, Brian Fahling, and Michael J. DePrimo.

Brief of amici curiae filed on behalf of the Center for Arizona Policy et al. by Len L. Munsil.

Brief of amici curiae filed on behalf of the Center for Law and Justice International by Thomas Patrick Monaghan and John P. Tuskey.

Brief of amici curiae filed on behalf of the Center for Marriage Law by Vincent P. McCarthy and Lynn D. Wardle.

Brief of amici curiae filed on behalf of the Center for the Original Intent of the Constitution by Michael P. Farris and Jordan W. Lorence.

Brief of amici curiae filed on behalf of Concerned Women for America by Janet M. LaRue.

Brief of amici curiae filed on behalf of the Family Research Council, Inc., by Robert P. George.

Brief of amici curiae filed on behalf of First Principles, Inc., by Ronald D. Ray.

Brief of amici curiae filed on behalf of Liberty Counsel by Mathew D. Staver and Rena M. Lindevaldsen.

Brief of amici curiae filed on behalf of the Pro Family Law Center et al. by Richard D. Ackerman and Gary G. Kreep.

Brief of amici curiae filed on behalf of Public Advocate of the United States et al. by Herbert W. Titus and William J. Olson.

Brief of amici curiae filed on behalf of the Texas Eagle Forum et al. by Teresa Stanton Collett.

Brief of amici curiae filed on behalf of Texas Legislator Warren Chisum et al. by Kelly Shackelford and Scott Roberts.

Brief of amici curiae filed on behalf of the Texas Physicians Resource Council et al. by Glen Lavy.

Brief of amici curiae filed on behalf of United Families International by Paul Benjamin Linton.

IV. THE SUPREME COURT'S DECISION

"We conclude the case should be resolved by determining whether the petitioners were free as adults to engage in the private conduct in the exercise of their liberty under the Due Process Clause of the Fourteenth Amendment to the Constitution. For this inquiry we deem it necessary to reconsider the Court's holding in Bowers.

There are broad statements of the substantive reach of liberty under the Due Process Clause in earlier cases, . . . but the most pertinent beginning point is our decision in Griswold v. Connecticut, 381 U.S. 479 (1965). . . .

After Griswold it was established that the right to make certain decisions regarding sexual conduct extends beyond the marital relationship. In Eisenstadt v. Baird, 405 U.S. 438 (1972), the Court invalidated a law prohibiting the distribution of contraceptives to unmarried persons. . . .

The opinions in Griswold and Eisenstadt were part of the background for the decision in Roe v. Wade, 410 U.S. 113 (1973). . . . Roe recognized the right of a woman to make certain fundamental decisions affecting her destiny and confirmed once more that the protection of liberty under the Due Process Clause has a substantive dimension of fundamental significance in defining the rights of the person.

In Carey v. Population Services Int'l, 431 U.S. 678 (1977), the Court confronted a New York law forbidding sale or distribution of contraceptive devices to persons under 16 years of age. Although there was no single opinion for the Court, the law was invalidated. . . . This was the state of the law with respect to some of the most relevant cases when the Court considered Bowers v. Hardwick.

The facts in Bowers had some similarities to the instant case. . . .

In summary, the historical grounds relied upon in Bowers are more complex than the majority opinion and the concurring opinion by Chief Justice Burger indicate. Their historical premises are not without doubt and, at the very least, are overstated. . . .

The sweeping references by Chief Justice Burger to the history of Western civilization and to Judeo-Christian moral and ethical standards did not take account of other authorities pointing in an opposite direction. . . .

Two principal cases decided after Bowers cast its holding into even more doubt. . . .

The foundations of Bowers have sustained serious erosion from our recent decisions in Casey and Romer. When our precedent has been thus weakened, criticism from other sources is of greater significance. In the United States criticism of Bowers has been substantial and continuing, disapproving of its reasoning in all respects, not just as to its historical assumptions. . . .

The doctrine of stare decisis is essential to the respect accorded to the judgments of the Court and to the stability of the law. It is not, however, an inexorable command. . . .

Bowers was not correct when it was decided, and it is not correct today. It ought not to remain binding precedent. Bowers v. Hardwick should be and now is overruled. . . .

The Texas statute furthers no legitimate state interest which can justify its intrusion into the personal and private life of the individual. . . .

The judgment of the Court of Appeals for the Texas Fourteenth District is reversed, and the case is remanded for further proceedings not inconsistent with this opinion."

V. JUSTICE VOTE

6 Pro ACLU Side vs. 3 Con Opposing Side

ACLU Side (Petitioner / Appellant)

1. Kennedy, A. – Wrote majority opinion
2. O'Connor, S. – Wrote concurring opinion
3. Stevens, J. – Joined majority opinion
4. Souter, D. – Joined majority opinion
5. Ginsburg, R. – Joined majority opinion
6. Breyer, S. – Joined majority opinion

Opposing Side (Respondent / Appellee)

1. Scalia, A. – Wrote dissenting opinion
2. Rehnquist, W. – Joined Scalia's dissent
3. Thomas, C. – Wrote dissenting opinion, joined Scalia's dissent

V. WIN OR LOSS FOR THE ACLU?

The ACLU filed as amicus curiae urging reversal of the judgment of the Court of Appeals; the Supreme Court reversed in a 6-3 vote, giving the ACLU an apparent win.

951. Nike, Inc. v. Kasky

(Decided June 26, 2003; 539 U.S. 654)

I. ISSUE

A. Issues Discussed

1st Amendment, press, speech, association

B. Legal Question Presented

"[T]wo questions: (1) whether a corporation participating in a public debate may 'be subjected to liability for factual inaccuracies on the theory that its statements are 'commercial speech' because they might affect consumers' opinions about the business as a good corporate citizen and thereby affect their purchasing decisions'; and (2) even assuming the California Supreme Court properly characterized such statements as commercial speech, whether the 'First Amendment, as applied to the states through the Fourteenth Amendment, permit[s] subjecting speakers to the legal regime approved by that court in the decision below.'"

C. Supreme Court's Answer

"The writ of certiorari is dismissed as improvidently granted."

II. CASE SUMMARY

A. Background

"Justice STEVENS, with whom Justice GINSBURG joins, and with whom justice SOUTER joins as to Part III, concurring.

Beginning in 1996, Nike was besieged with a series of allegations that it was mistreating and underpaying workers at foreign facilities. Nike responded to these charges in numerous ways, such as by sending out press releases, writing letters to the editors of various newspapers around the country, and mailing letters to university presidents and athletic directors. In addition, in 1997, Nike commissioned a report by former Ambassador to the United Nations Andrew Young on the labor conditions at Nike production facilities. After visiting 12 factories, 'Young issued a report that commented favorably on working conditions in the factories and found no evidence of widespread abuse or mistreatment of workers.'

In April 1998, respondent Marc Kasky, a California resident, sued Nike for unfair and deceptive practices under California's Unfair Competition Law and False Advertising Law. Respondent asserted that 'in order to maintain and/or increase its sales,' Nike made a number of 'false statements and/or material omissions of fact' concerning the working conditions under which Nike products are manufactured. Respondent alleged 'no harm or damages whatsoever regarding himself individually,' but rather brought the suit 'on behalf of the General Public of the State of California and on information and belief.'

Nike filed a demurrer to the complaint, contending that respondent's suit was absolutely barred by the First Amendment. The trial court sustained the demurrer without leave to amend and entered a judgment of dismissal. Respondent appealed, and the California Court of Appeal affirmed, holding that Nike's statements 'form[ed] part of a public dialogue on a matter of public concern within the core area of expression protected by the First Amendment.' The California Court of Appeal also rejected respondent's argument that it was error for the trial court to deny him leave to amend, reasoning that there was 'no reasonable possibility' that the complaint could be amended to allege facts that would justify any restrictions on what was—in the court's view—Nike's 'noncommercial speech.'

On appeal, the California Supreme Court reversed and remanded for further proceedings. The court held that '[b]ecause the messages in question were directed by a commercial speaker to a commercial audience, and because they made representations of fact about the speaker's own business operations for the purpose of promoting sales of its products, . . . [the] messages are commercial speech.' However, the court emphasized that the suit 'is still at a preliminary stage, and that whether any false representations were made is a disputed issue that has yet to be resolved.'"

The Supreme Court initially granted certiorari to review the case.

B. Counsel of Record

ACLU Side (Petitioner / Appellant): Laurence H. Tribe argued the cause for appellants. With him on the briefs were Thomas C. Goldstein, Amy Howe, Walter Dellinger, David J. Brown, and James N. Penrod.

Solicitor General Olson argued the cause for the United States as amicus curiae urging reversal. With him on the brief were Assistant Attorney General McCallum, Deputy Solicitor General Clement, Jeffrey P. Minear, and Jeffrey A. Lamken.

Opposing Side (Respondent / Appellee): Paul R. Hoeber argued the cause for appellee. With him on the brief were Alan M. Caplan, Roderick P. Bushnell, Patrick J. Coughlin, Randi Dawn Bandman, Albert H. Meyerhoff, and Sylvia Sum.

III. AMICI CURIAE

ACLU Side (Petitioner / Appellant)

Brief of amici curiae filed on behalf of the American Civil Liberties Union and the ACLU of Northern California by Mark J. Lopez, Steven R. Shapiro, and Ann Brick.

Brief of amici curiae filed on behalf of ABC Inc. et al. by Bruce E. H. Johnson, P. Cameron DeVore, Kelli L. Sager, Henry S. Hoberman, Theresa A. Chmara, Richard M. Schmidt, Jr., David A. Schulz, R. Bruce Rich, Jonathan Bloom, Susanna M. Lowy, Anthony M. Bongiorno, Harold W. Fuson, Jr., Jonathan R. Donnellan, Stuart D. Karle, Barbara W. Wall, Jack N. Goodman, James M. Lichtman, Neal A. Jackson, George Freeman, René P. Milam, Henry Z. Horbaczewski, Lucy A. Dalglish, Jane E. Kirtley, Bruce W. Sanford, Robin Bierstedt, Karlene W. Goller, and Eric N. Lieberman.

Brief of amici curiae filed on behalf of the American Federation of Labor and Congress of Industrial Organizations by Jonathan P. Hiatt, James B. Coppess, and Laurence Gold.

Brief of amici curiae filed on behalf of the Arthur W. Page Society et al. by Bruce P. Keller and Michael R. Potenza.

Brief of amici curiae filed on behalf of the Association of National Advertising, Inc., et al. by Howard J. Rubin and Cory Greenberg.

Brief of amici curiae filed on behalf of the Business Roundtable by Carter G. Phillips, Alan Charles Raul, and Joseph R. Guerra.

Brief of amici curiae filed on behalf of the Center for Individual Freedom by Erik S. Jaffe and Renee L. Giachino.

Brief of amici curiae filed on behalf of the Center for the Advancement of Capitalism by Thomas A. Bowden.

Brief of amici curiae filed on behalf of the Chamber of Commerce of the United States of America by Kenneth W. Starr, Richard A. Cordray, and Robin S. Conrad.

Brief of amici curiae filed on behalf of the Civil Justice Association of California by Fred J. Hiestand.

Brief of amici curiae filed on behalf of Defenders of Property Rights et al. by Nancie G. Marzulla and Roger J. Marzulla.

Brief of amici curiae filed on behalf of ExxonMobil et al. by David H. Remes.

Brief of amici curiae filed on behalf of the National Association of Manufacturers by Andrew L. Frey, Andrew H. Schapiro, Kenneth S. Geller, David M. Gossett, Martin H. Redish, Jan S. Amundson, and Quentin Riegel.

Brief of amici curiae filed on behalf of the Pacific Legal Foundation et al. by Deborah J. La Fetra.

Brief of amici curiae filed on behalf of Pfizer Inc. by Bert W. Rein, Jeffrey B. Kindler, and Steven C. Kany.

Brief of amici curiae filed on behalf of the Product Liability Advisory Council, Inc., by Steven G. Brody.

Brief of amici curiae filed on behalf of SRiMedia et al. by Thomas H. Clarke, Jr.

Brief of amici curiae filed on behalf of the Thomas Jefferson Center for the Protection of Free Expression et al. by Robert M. O'Neil and J. Joshua Wheeler.

Brief of amici curiae filed on behalf of the Washington Legal Foundation et al. by Daniel J. Popeo and Richard A. Samp.

William Perry Pendley and Joseph F. Becker filed a brief for the Mountain States Legal Foundation as amicus curiae.

Opposing Side (Respondent / Appellee)

Brief of amici curiae filed on behalf of the State of California et al. by Bill Lockyer, Attorney General of California, Manuel Medeiros, State Solicitor General, Richard M. Frank, Chief Assistant Attorney General, Herschel T. Elkins, Senior Assistant Attorney General, and Ronald A. Reiter, Supervising Deputy Attorney General, and by the Attorneys General for their respective jurisdictions as follows: Gregg D. Renkes of Alaska, Terry Goddard of Arizona, Richard Blumenthal of Connecticut, Charles J. Crist, Jr., of Florida, Lisa Madigan of Illinois, Richard Ieyoub of Louisiana, G. Steven Rowe of Maine, J. Joseph Curran, Jr., of Maryland, Mike Hatch of Minnesota, Patricia A. Madrid of New Mexico, Eliot Spitzer of New York, Wayne Stenehjem of North Dakota, Jim Petro of Ohio, W. A. Drew Edmondson of Oklahoma, Anabelle Rodríguez of Puerto Rico, Lawrence E. Long of South Dakota, William H. Sorrell of Vermont, and Darrell V. McGraw, Jr., of West Virginia.

Brief of amici curiae filed on behalf of the Campaign Legal Center by Trevor Potter.
Brief of amici curiae filed on behalf of the Consumer Attorneys of California by Sharon J. Arkin.
Brief of amici curiae filed on behalf of Domini Social Investments LLC et al. by James E. Pfander.
Brief of amici curiae filed on behalf of Global Exchange by William Aceves.
Brief of amici curiae filed on behalf of the National Association of Consumer Advocates by Robert M. Bramson.
Brief of amici curiae filed on behalf of Public Citizen by Alan B. Morrison, Allison M. Zieve, Scott L. Nelson, and David C. Vladeck.
Brief of amici curiae filed on behalf of ReclaimDemocracy.org by Brenda Wright, Lisa J. Danetz, John C. Bonifaz, and Bonita Tenneriello.
Brief of amici curiae filed on behalf of the Sierra Club et al. by Patrick Gallagher and Thomas McGarity.
Brief of amici curiae filed on behalf of Representative Dennis J. Kucinich et al. by Erwin Chemerinsky and Catherine Fisk.

IV. THE SUPREME COURT'S DECISION

"The writ of certiorari is dismissed as improvidently granted."

V. JUSTICE VOTE

3 Pro ACLU Side vs. 6 Con Opposing Side

ACLU Side (Petitioner / Appellant)

1. Breyer, S. – Wrote dissenting opinion
2. O'Connor, S. – Joined Breyer's dissent
3. Kennedy, A. – Wrote dissenting opinion

Opposing Side (Respondent / Appellee)

1. Rehnquist, W. – Per curiam decision
2. Thomas, C. – Per curiam decision
3. Scalia, A. – Per curiam decision
4. Stevens, J. – Wrote concurring opinion
5. Souter, D. – Joined Stevens' concurrence in part
6. Ginsburg, R. – Joined Stevens' concurrence

VI. A WIN OR LOSS FOR THE ACLU?

The ACLU filed as amicus curiae urging reversal of the judgment of the California Supreme Court; the Supreme Court dismissed the writ of certiorari as improvidently granted, thus allowing the decision below to stand, in a 6-3 per curiam decision, giving the ACLU an apparent loss.

952. Arizona v. Gant

(Decided October 20, 2003; 540 U.S. 963)

I. ISSUE

A. Issues Discussed

4th Amendment

B. Legal Question Presented

"Whether the court below properly concluded that the State failed to satisfy its burden of proving that the warrantless, suspicionless search of the interior of respondent's automobile was justified as a search incident to arrest, when the arrest took place after respondent had voluntarily exited and walked away from his automobile, the State presented no evidence that the interior of the automobile was arguably within respondent's 'area of immediate control' at the time of the arrest, and the search took place after the police had handcuffed him and secured him in the back of a police vehicle?"[1]

C. Supreme Court's Answer

"On writ of certiorari to the Court of Appeals of Arizona, Division Two. Judgment vacated, and case remanded to the Court of Appeals of Arizona, Division Two, for reconsideration in light of State v. Dean, 206 Ariz. 158, 76 P.3d 429 (Ariz.2003)."

II. CASE SUMMARY

A. Background

"After a jury trial, appellant Rodney Gant was found guilty of unlawful possession of cocaine for sale and unlawful possession of drug paraphernalia. The trial court sentenced him to concurrent, mitigated prison terms, the longest of which was three years. . . .

Gant argues that the trial court erred in denying his motion to suppress a handgun and a plastic bag of cocaine found when his vehicle was searched after his arrest, asserting that the warrantless search violated his Fourth Amendment rights. . . .

In his motion to suppress the evidence found in his vehicle, Gant did not contest the lawfulness of his arrest but, rather, argued only that the ensuing warrantless search of his vehicle was illegal because no exceptions to the Fourth Amendment's warrant requirement applied. The state argued that the search was lawful because it had been conducted incident to Gant's arrest or, alternatively, that, because the police had probable cause to search his vehicle, a warrantless search was permissible under the automobile exception to the Fourth Amendment's warrant requirement. The trial court denied Gant's motion, finding that the search of the car was lawful because it was a search incident to his arrest. [The Court of Appeals of Arizona] disagree[d]."[2]

The Supreme Court granted certiorari to review the case.

B. Counsel of Record

ACLU Side (Respondent / Appellee): Briefs filed on behalf of appellee by Jeffrey T. Green, Isaac Adams, and Thomas F. Jacobs.

Opposing Side (Petitioner / Appellant): Briefs filed on behalf of appellant by Walter Dellinger, Terry Goddard, Attorney General, Mary R. O'Grady, Solicitor General, Randall M. Howe, Chief Counsel Criminal Appeals Section, Kathleen P. Sweeney, Assistant Attorney General, and Eric J. Olsson, Assistant Attorney General.

---

1 Brief of Respondent at i, Arizona v. Gant, 540 U.S. 963 (2003) (No. 02-1019) 2003 WL 22087477, at *i.

2 *State v. Gant*, 43 P.3d 188 (Ariz. Ct. App. 2002).

III. AMICI CURIAE

ACLU Side (Respondent / Appellee)

Brief of amici curiae filed on behalf of the American Civil Liberties Union, and the National Association of Criminal Defense Lawyers by Tracey Maclin, Steven R. Shapiro, and Lisa Kemler.

Brief of amici curiae filed on behalf of the American Civil Liberties Union and ACLU of Arizona by Graham A. Boyd, Dan Pachoda, James J. Tomkovicz, and Steven R. Shapiro.

Brief of amici curiae filed on behalf of the National Association of Federal Defenders by Frances H. Pratt, Philip J. Lynch, Judith H. Mizner, Stephen C. Moss, Beth S. Brinkmann, Seth M. Galanter, Ketanji Brown Jackson, and Lila M. Bateman.

Brief of amici curiae filed on behalf of National Association of Criminal Defense Lawyers by Amy Howe, Kevin K. Russell, Thomas C. Goldstein, Jeffrey L. Fisher, and Pamela S. Karlan.

Opposing Side (Petitioner / Appellant)

Brief of amici curiae filed on behalf of the United States by Paul D. Clement, Solicitor General, Alice S. Fisher, Assistant Attorney General, Michael R. Dreeben, Deputy Solicitor General, Anthony A. Yang, Assistant to the Solicitor General, and Joseph F. Palmer.

Brief of amici curiae filed on behalf of Los Angeles County by Steve Cooley, District Attorney of Los Angeles County, Lael R. Rubin, Head Deputy, Appellate Division, Brentford J. Ferreira, Deputy District Attorney, and Phyllis C. Asayama, Deputy District Attorney.

Brief of amici curiae filed on behalf of National Association of Police Organizations, Inc. by William J. Johnson and Devallis Rutledge.

Brief of amici curiae filed on behalf of Americans for Effective Law Enforcement, Inc., The International Association of Chiefs of Police, The National Sheriffs' Association, The Arizona Law Enforcement Legal Advisors' Association and The Arizona Association of Chiefs of Police by Gene Voegtlin, Richard Weintraub, Michael E. McNeff, Eric B. Edwards, Bernard J. Farber, Wayne W. Schmidt, and James P. Manak.

IV. THE SUPREME COURT'S DECISION

"On writ of certiorari to the Court of Appeals of Arizona, Division Two. Judgment vacated, and case remanded to the Court of Appeals of Arizona, Division Two, for reconsideration in light of State v. Dean, 206 Ariz. 158, 76 P.3d 429 (Ariz.2003)."

V. JUSTICE VOTE

0 Pro ACLU Side vs. 9 Con Opposing Side

Opposing Side (Petitioner / Appellant)

1. Thomas, C. – Per curiam decision
2. Ginsburg, R. – Per curiam decision
3. Souter, D. – Per curiam decision
4. O'Connor, S. – Per curiam decision
5. Stevens, J. – Per curiam decision
6. Breyer, S. – Per curiam decision
7. Scalia, A. – Per curiam decision
8. Kennedy, A. – Per curiam decision
9. Rehnquist, W. – Per curiam decision

VI. A WIN OR LOSS FOR THE ACLU?

The ACLU filed as amicus curiae urging affirmance; the Supreme Court vacated and remanded the Court of Appeals of Arizona's decision by a per curiam 9-0 vote, giving the ACLU an apparent loss.

953. McConnell v. Federal Election Comm'n

(Decided December 10, 2003; 540 U.S. 93)

I. ISSUE

A. Issues Discussed

1st Amendment, press, speech, association

B. Legal Question Presented

Whether the numerous challenged provisions of the Bipartisan Campaign Reform Act of 2002 are constitutional, in particular under the First Amendment.

C. Supreme Court's Answer

Most of the challenged provisions of the Bipartisan Campaign Reform Act of 2002 are constitutional and comply with the First Amendment.

II. CASE SUMMARY

A. Background

"The Bipartisan Campaign Reform Act of 2002 (BCRA), 116 Stat. 81, contains a series of amendments to the Federal Election Campaign Act of 1971, . . . the Communications Act of 1934, . . . and other portions of the United States Code . . . that are challenged in these cases. . . .

BCRA is the most recent federal enactment designed 'to purge national politics of what was conceived to be the pernicious influence of 'big money' campaign contributions.' . . .

Three important developments in the years after our decision in Buckley persuaded Congress that further legislation was necessary to regulate the role that corporations, unions, and wealthy contributors play in the electoral process . . . the increased importance of 'soft money,' the proliferation of 'issue ads,' and the disturbing findings of a Senate investigation into campaign practices related to the 1996 federal elections. . . .

In BCRA, Congress enacted many of the committee's proposed reforms. BCRA's central provisions are designed to address Congress' concerns about the increasing use of soft money and issue advertising to influence federal elections. Title I regulates the use of soft money by political parties, officeholders, and candidates. Title II primarily prohibits corporations and labor unions from using general treasury funds for communications that are intended to, or have the effect of, influencing the outcome of federal elections.

Section 403 of BCRA provides special rules for actions challenging the constitutionality of any of the Act's provisions. Eleven such actions were filed promptly after the statute went into effect in March 2002. As required by § 403, those actions were filed in the District Court for the District of Columbia and heard by a three-judge court. Section 403 directed the District Court to advance the cases on the docket and to expedite their disposition 'to the greatest possible extent.' The court received a voluminous record compiled by the parties and ultimately delivered a decision embodied in a two-judge per curiam opinion and three separate, lengthy opinions, each of which contained extensive commentary on the facts and a careful analysis of the legal issues. The three judges reached unanimity on certain issues but differed on many. Their judgment, entered on May 1, 2003, held some parts of BCRA unconstitutional and upheld others.

As authorized by § 403, all of the losing parties filed direct appeals to this Court within 10 days. On June 5, 2003, [the Supreme Court] noted probable jurisdiction" to review the case.

B. Counsel of Record

ACLU Side (Petitioner / Appellant): Briefs in No. 02–1734 were filed for appellant American Civil Liberties Union by Mark J. Lopez, Steven R. Shapiro, and Joel M. Gora.

Kenneth W. Starr and Floyd Abrams argued the cause for plaintiffs below, Senator Mitch McConnell et al., appellants in No. 02–1674 and cross-appellees in Nos. 02–1676 and 02–1702. With them on the briefs were Edward W. Warren, Susan Buckley, Brian Markley, Kathleen M. Sullivan, Valle Simms Dutcher, L. Lynn Hogue, Jan Witold Baran, Lee E. Goodman, G. Hunter Bates, Jack N. Goodman, and Jerianne Timmerman.

Bobby R. Burchfield argued the cause for the political party plaintiffs below. With him on the briefs for the Republican National Committee et al., appellants in No. 02–1727, the California Democratic Party et al., appellants in No. 02–1753, and the Libertarian National Committee, Inc., one of the appellants in No. 02–1733, were Thomas O. Barnett, Robert K. Kelner, Richard W. Smith, Lance H. Olson, Deborah B. Caplan, Joseph E. Sandler, John Hardin Young, Charles H. Bell, Jr., Jan Witold Baran, Lee E. Goodman, Thomas J. Josefiak, Benjamin L. Ginsberg, Eric A. Kuwana, Michael A. Carvin, James Bopp, Jr., Richard E. Coleson, and Thomas J. Marzen.

Laurence E. Gold argued the cause for plaintiffs below, the American Federation of Labor and Congress of Industrial Organizations et al., appellants in No. 02–1755 and appellees in Nos. 02–1676 and 02–1702. With him on the briefs were Jona than P. Hiatt, Michael B. Trister, and Larry P. Weinberg.

Jay Alan Sekulow argued the cause for plaintiffs below, Emily Echols et al. With him on the brief were James M. Henderson, Sr., Stuart J. Roth, Colby M. May, Joel H. Thornton, Walter M. Weber, James Bopp, Jr., Richard E. Coleson, and Thomas J. Marzen.

Briefs in No. 02–1675 were filed for appellants National Rifle Association et al. by Charles J. Cooper, David H. Thompson, Hamish P. M. Hume, Brian S. Koukoutchos, and Cleta Mitchell.

Briefs in No. 02–1733 were filed for plaintiffs-appellants/ cross-appellees National Right to Life Committee, Inc., et al. by James Bopp, Jr., Richard E. Coleson, and Thomas J. Marzen.

Briefs in No. 02–1740 were filed for appellants Victoria Jackson Gray Adams et al. by John C. Bonifaz, Bonita P. Tenneriello, Lisa J. Danetz, Brenda Wright, and David A. Wilson.

Briefs in No. 02–1747 were filed for appellants Congressman Ron Paul et al. by William J. Olson, John S. Miles, Herbert W. Titus, and Gary G. Kreep.

Briefs in No. 02–1756 were filed for appellants Chamber of Commerce of the United States et al. by Jan Witold Baran, Lee E. Goodman, Stephen A. Bokat, and Jan Amundson.

Opposing Side (Respondent / Appellee): Solicitor General Olson and Deputy Solicitor General Clement argued the cause for federal defendants below, the Federal Election Commission et al. With them on the briefs were Assistant Attorney General Keisler, Malcolm L. Stewart, Gregory G. Garre, Douglas N. Letter, Dana J. Martin, Terry M. Henry, Lawrence H. Norton, Richard B. Bader, and David Kolker.

Seth P. Waxman argued the cause for the intervenor-defendants below, Senator John McCain et al. With him on the briefs were Randolph D. Moss, Edward C. DuMont, Paul R. Q. Wolfson, Roger M. Witten, Burt Neuborne, Frederick A. O. Schwarz, Jr., Charles G. Curtis, Jr., David J. Harth, Bradley S. Phillips, E. Joshua Rosenkranz, Alan B. Morrison, Scott L. Nelson, Eric J. Mogilnicki, Michael D. Leffel, Fred Wertheimer, Alexandra Edsall, and Trevor Potter.

III. AMICI CURIAE

ACLU Side (Petitioner / Appellant)

Brief of amici curiae filed on behalf of the Commonwealth of Virginia et al. by Jerry Kilgore, Attorney General of Virginia, and Craig Engle, and by the Attorneys General for their respective States as follows: Lawrence Wasden of Idaho, Steve Carter of Indiana, Phill Kline of Kansas, Jon Bruning of Nebraska, Wayne Stenehjem of North Dakota, Jim Petro of Ohio, Henry McMaster of South Carolina, Larry Long of South Dakota, and Mark Shurtleff of Utah.

Brief of amici curiae filed on behalf of the Cato Institute et al. by Erik S. Jaffe.

Brief of amici curiae filed on behalf of the Honorable J. Dennis Hastert by J. Randolph Evans and Stefan C. Passantino.

Brief of amici curiae filed on behalf of Rodney A. Smith by Clark Bensen.

Brief of amici curiae filed on behalf of Public Campaign by Gregory Luke.

Brief of amici curiae filed on behalf of the American Civil Rights Union by John C. Armor and Peter Ferrara.

Opposing Side (Respondent / Appellee)

Brief of amici curiae filed on behalf of Former Leaders of the American Civil Liberties Union by Norman Dorsen, Roger Bearden, Gregory Silbert, and Eric M. Lieberman.

Brief of amici curiae filed on behalf of the Center for Governmental Studies by Richard L. Hasen.

Brief of amici curiae filed on behalf of Thomas D. Grant et al. by Christopher J. Wright and Timothy J. Simeone.

Brief of amici curiae filed on behalf of Bipartisan Former Members of the United States Congress by Randy L. Dryer and J. Michael Bailey.
Brief of amici curiae filed on behalf of the California Student Public Interest Research Group, Inc., et al. by Bonita Tenneriello, John C. Bonifaz, Brenda Wright, Lisa J. Danetz, and David A. Wilson.
Brief of amici curiae filed on behalf of the Center for Responsive Politics by Lawrence M. Noble and Paul Sanford.
Brief of amici curiae filed on behalf of the Committee for Economic Development et al. by Steven Alan Reiss, R. Bruce Rich, and Jonathan Bloom.
Brief of amici curiae filed on behalf of Common Cause et al. by Donald J. Simon, Daniel B. Kohrman, and Michael Schuster.
Brief of amici curiae filed on behalf of the Allen Temple Baptist Church et al. by Martin R. Glick.
Brief of amici curiae filed on behalf of the Interfaith Alliance Foundation et al. by Evan A. Davis.
Brief of amici curiae filed on behalf of the League of Women Voters by Daniel R. Ortiz.
Brief of amici curiae filed on behalf of Norman J. Ornstein et al. by Teresa W. Roseborough and Judith A. O'Brien.
Brief of amici curiae filed on behalf of Delaware State Representative Michael Castle et al. by Richard Briffault, Charles Tiefer, and Jonathan W. Cuneo.
Brief of amici curiae filed on behalf of the State of Iowa et al. by Thomas J. Miller, Attorney General of Iowa, and Thomas Andrews, Assistant Attorney General, William H. Sorrell, Attorney General of Vermont, and Bridget C. Asay, Assistant Attorney General, and Richard Blumenthal, Attorney General of Connecticut, and by the Attorneys General for their respective jurisdictions as follows: Terry Goddard of Arizona, Ken Salazar of Colorado, Albert B. Chandler III of Kentucky, Richard P. Ieyoub of Louisiana, G. Steven Rowe of Maine, Thomas F. Reilly of Massachusetts, Mike Hatch of Minnesota, Mike Moore of Mississippi, Jeremiah (Jay) Nixon of Missouri, Mike McGrath of Montana, Eliot Spitzer of New York, W. A. Drew Edmondson of Oklahoma, Anabelle Rodríguez of Puerto Rico, Patrick Lynch of Rhode Island, Christine O. Gregoire of Washington, Peggy Lautenschlager of Wisconsin, and Iver A. Stridiron of the Virgin Islands.
Brief of amici curiae filed on behalf of the Honorable Fred Thompson by David C. Frederick.
Brief of amici curiae filed on behalf of Dr. David Moshman by Kevin H. Theriot.

IV. THE SUPREME COURT'S DECISION

"Justice STEVENS and Justice O'CONNOR delivered the opinion of the Court with respect to BCRA Titles I and II.

The Bipartisan Campaign Reform Act of 2002 (BCRA), 116 Stat. 81, contains a series of amendments to the Federal Election Campaign Act of 1971, . . . the Communications Act of 1934, . . . and other portions of the United States Code . . . that are challenged in these cases. In this opinion [Justices STEVENS and O'CONNOR] discuss Titles I and II of BCRA. The opinion of the Court delivered by THE CHIEF JUSTICE discusses Titles III and IV, and the opinion of the Court delivered by Justice BREYER discusses Title V. . . .

Title I is Congress' effort to plug the soft-money loophole. The cornerstone of Title I is new FECA § 323(a), which prohibits national party committees and their agents from soliciting, receiving, directing, or spending any soft money. In short, § 323(a) takes national parties out of the soft-money business. . . .

Plaintiffs mount a facial First Amendment challenge to new FECA § 323, as well as challenges based on the Elections Clause, U.S. Const., Art. I, § 4, principles of federalism, and the equal protection component of the Due Process Clause. . . .

In sum, there is substantial evidence to support Congress' determination that large soft-money contributions to national political parties give rise to corruption and the appearance of corruption.

Accordingly, we reject the plaintiffs' First Amendment challenge to new FECA § 323(a). . . .

We . . . conclude that § 323(b), on its face, is closely drawn to match the important governmental interests of preventing corruption and the appearance of corruption. . . .

We reverse and uphold § 323(d), narrowly construing the section's ban on donations to apply only to the donation of funds not raised in compliance with FECA. . . .

We . . . uphold § 323(e) [and] § 323(f) against plaintiffs' First Amendment challenge. . . .

Several plaintiffs contend that Title I exceeds Congress' Election Clause authority to 'make or alter' rules governing federal elections, U.S. Const., Art. I, § 4, and, by impairing the authority of the States to regulate their own elections, violates constitutional principles of federalism. . . . Title I of BCRA only regulates the conduct of private parties. . . .

Given that finding, we cannot conclude that those interests are insufficient to ground Congress' exercise of its Elections Clause power. . . .

Finally, plaintiffs argue that Title I violates the equal protection component of the Due Process Clause of the Fifth Amendment because it discriminates against political parties in favor of special interest groups . . . . We conclude that this disparate treatment does not offend the Constitution. . . .

Accordingly, we affirm the judgment of the District Court insofar as it upheld §§ 323(e) and 323(f). We reverse the judgment of the District Court insofar as it invalidated §§ 323(a), 323(b), and 323(d). . . .

We affirm the District Court's judgment to the extent that it upheld the constitutionality of FECA § 316(b)(2); to the extent that it invalidated any part of § 316(b)(2), we reverse the judgment. . . .

Accordingly, the judgment of the District Court upholding § 316(c)(6) as so limited is affirmed. . . .

The portion of the judgment of the District Court invalidating BCRA § 213 is affirmed. . . .

The portions of the District Court judgment rejecting plaintiffs' challenges to BCRA § 214 are affirmed. . . .

Accordingly, we affirm in part and reverse in part the District Court's judgment with respect to Titles I and II."

V. JUSTICE VOTE

4 Pro ACLU Side vs. 5 Con Opposing Side[1]

ACLU Side (Petitioner / Appellant)

1. Scalia, A. – Wrote opinion dissenting with respect to BCRA Title I and concurring in part and dissenting in part with respect to BCRA Title II
2. Thomas, C. – Wrote opinion dissenting with respect to BCRA Title I and concurring in part and dissenting in part with respect to BCRA Title II
3. Kennedy, A. – Wrote opinion concurring and dissenting in part with respect to BCRA Titles I and II
4. Rehnquist, W. – Wrote opinion dissenting with respect to BCRA Title I

Opposing Side (Respondent / Appellee)

1. Stevens, J. – Co-wrote majority opinion for BCRA Titles I and II
2. O'Connor, S. – Co-wrote majority opinion for BCRA Titles I and II
3. Souter, D. – Joined Stevens and O'Connor's opinion
4. Ginsburg, R. – Joined Stevens and O'Connor's opinion
5. Breyer, S. – Joined Stevens and O'Connor's opinion

VI. A WIN OR LOSS FOR THE ACLU?

The ACLU filed as appellants urging reversal of the judgment of the district court; the Supreme Court affirmed in part and reversed in part in a 5-4 vote, giving the ACLU an apparent loss.

954. Maryland v. Pringle

(Decided December 15, 2003; 540 U.S. 366)

I. ISSUE

A. Issues Discussed

4th Amendment, criminal justice

B. Legal Question Presented

"It is uncontested in the present case that the officer, upon recovering the five plastic glassine baggies containing suspected cocaine, had probable cause to believe a felony had been committed. . . . The sole question is whether the officer had probable cause to believe that Pringle committed that crime."

C. Supreme Court's Answer

"We hold that the officer had probable cause to believe that Pringle had committed the crime of possession of a controlled substance. Pringle's arrest therefore did not contravene the Fourth and Fourteenth Amendments."

1 The justices authored separate opinions of the Court for BCRA Titles I and II, BCRA Titles III and IV, and BCRA Title V and various concurrences and dissents. This represents the opinion for BCRA Titles I and II and dissents and concurrences with respect to these titles. ACLU appellants challenged the constitutionality of BCRA Title II. Consult the full court opinion for complete information about the various opinions and their nuances.

II. CASE SUMMARY

A. Background

"In the early morning hours a passenger car occupied by three men was stopped for speeding by a police officer. The officer, upon searching the car, seized $763 of rolled-up cash from the glove compartment and five glassine baggies of cocaine from between the back-seat armrest and the back seat. After all three men denied ownership of the cocaine and money, the officer arrested each of them. . . .

Later that morning, [one of the arrestees,] Pringle waived his rights under Miranda v. Arizona, 384 U.S. 436 (1966), and gave an oral and written confession in which he acknowledged that the cocaine belonged to him, that he and his friends were going to a party, and that he intended to sell the cocaine or '[u]se it for sex.' Pringle maintained that the other occupants of the car did not know about the drugs, and they were released.

The trial court denied Pringle's motion to suppress his confession as the fruit of an illegal arrest, holding that the officer had probable cause to arrest Pringle. A jury convicted Pringle of possession with intent to distribute cocaine and possession of cocaine. He was sentenced to 10 years' incarceration without the possibility of parole. The Court of Special Appeals of Maryland affirmed.

The Court of Appeals of Maryland, by divided vote, reversed . . . ."
The Supreme Court granted certiorari to review the case.

B. Counsel of Record

ACLU Side (Respondent / Appellee): Nancy S. Forster argued the cause for appellee. With her on the brief were Stephen E. Harris and Sherrie Glasser.

Opposing Side (Petitioner / Appellant): Gary E. Bair, Solicitor General of Maryland, argued the cause for appellant. With him on the briefs were J. Joseph Curran, Jr., Attorney General, and Kathryn Grill Graeff and Shannon E. Avery, Assistant Attorneys General.

Sri Srinivasan argued the cause for the United States as amicus curiae.

III. AMICI CURIAE

ACLU Side (Respondent / Appellee)

Brief of amici curiae filed on behalf of the American Civil Liberties Union, the ACLU of Maryland, and the National Association of Criminal Defense Lawyers by Tracey Maclin, Steven R. Shapiro, and Lisa Kemler.

Opposing Side (Petitioner / Appellant)

Brief of amici curiae filed on behalf of the United States by Sri Srinivasan, Solicitor General Olson, Assistant Attorney General Chertoff, Deputy Solicitor General Dreeben, and Deborah Watson.

Brief of amici curiae filed on behalf of the State of Ohio et al. by Jim Petro, Attorney General of Ohio, Douglas R. Cole, State Solicitor, Stephen P. Carney, Senior Deputy Solicitor, and Diane Richards Brey, Deputy Solicitor, and by the Attorneys General for their respective jurisdictions as follows: William H. Pryor, Jr., of Alabama, Gregg Renkes of Alaska,

Christopher L. Morano of Connecticut, M. Jane Brady of Delaware, Mark J. Bennett of Hawaii, Lisa Madigan of Illinois, Richard P. Ieyoub of Louisiana, Michael A. Cox of Michigan, Jeremiah W. (Jay) Nixon of Missouri, Mike McGrath of Montana, Brian Sandoval of Nevada, Patricia A. Madrid of New Mexico, W. A. Drew Edmondson of Oklahoma, Anabelle Rodríguez of Puerto Rico, Henry Dargan McMaster of South Carolina, Larry Long of South Dakota, Greg Abbott of Texas, Mark L. Shurtleff of Utah, Jerry W. Kilgore of Virginia, and Darrell V. McGraw, Jr., of West Virginia.

Brief of amici curiae filed on behalf of the Criminal Justice Legal Foundation by Kent S. Scheidegger and Charles L. Hobson

IV. THE SUPREME COURT'S DECISION

"Under the Fourth Amendment, made applicable to the States by the Fourteenth Amendment, Mapp v. Ohio, 367 U.S. 643 (1961), the people are 'to be secure in their persons, houses, papers, and effects, against unreasonable searches and seizures, . . . and no Warrants shall issue, but upon probable cause . . . .' Maryland law authorizes police officers to execute warrantless arrests, inter alia, for felonies committed in an officer's presence or where an officer has probable cause to believe that a felony has been committed or is being committed in the officer's presence. A warrantless arrest of an individual in a public place for a felony, or a misdemeanor committed in the officer's presence, is consistent with the Fourth Amendment if the arrest is supported by probable cause. . . .

It is uncontested in the present case that the officer, upon recovering the five plastic glassine baggies containing suspected cocaine, had probable cause to believe a felony had been committed. . . . The sole question is whether the officer had probable cause to believe that Pringle committed that crime.

The long-prevailing standard of probable cause protects 'citizens from rash and unreasonable interferences with privacy and from unfounded charges of crime,' while giving 'fair leeway for enforcing the law in the community's protection.' . . .

The probable-cause standard is incapable of precise definition or quantification into percentages because it deals with probabilities and depends on the totality of the circumstances. . . .

To determine whether an officer had probable cause to arrest an individual, we examine the events leading up to the arrest, and then decide 'whether these historical facts, viewed from the standpoint of an objectively reasonable police officer, amount to' probable cause.

In this case, Pringle was one of three men riding in a Nissan Maxima at 3:16 a.m. There was $763 of rolled-up cash in the glove compartment directly in front of Pringle. Five plastic glassine baggies of cocaine were behind the back-seat armrest and accessible to all three men. Upon questioning, the three men failed to offer any information with respect to the ownership of the cocaine or the money.

We think it an entirely reasonable inference from these facts that any or all three of the occupants had knowledge of, and exercised dominion and control over, the cocaine. Thus, a reasonable officer could conclude that there was probable cause to believe Pringle committed the crime of possession of cocaine, either solely or jointly. . . .

We hold that the officer had probable cause to believe that Pringle had committed the crime of possession of a controlled substance. Pringle's arrest therefore did not contravene the Fourth and Fourteenth Amendments. Accordingly, the judgment of the Court of Appeals of Maryland is reversed, and the case is remanded for further proceedings not inconsistent with this opinion."

V. JUSTICE VOTE

0 Pro ACLU Side vs. 9 Con Opposing Side

Opposing Side (Petitioner / Appellant)

1. Rehnquist, W. – Wrote unanimous opinion
2. Thomas, C. – Joined unanimous opinion
3. Ginsburg, R. – Joined unanimous opinion
4. Souter, D. – Joined unanimous opinion
5. O'Connor, S. – Joined unanimous opinion
6. Stevens, J. – Joined unanimous opinion
7. Breyer, S. – Joined unanimous opinion
8. Scalia, A. – Joined unanimous opinion
9. Kennedy, A. – Joined unanimous opinion

VI. A WIN OR LOSS FOR THE ACLU?

The ACLU filed as amicus curiae urging affirmance; the Supreme Court reversed the Court of Appeals of Maryland's decision by a 9-0 vote, giving the ACLU an apparent loss.

955. Illinois v. Lidster

(Decided January 13, 2004; 540 U.S. 419)

I. ISSUE

A. Issues Discussed

4th Amendment

B. Legal Question Presented

Whether police stops at "a highway checkpoint where police stopped motorists to ask them for information about a recent hit-and-run accident" violated the Fourth Amendment.

C. Supreme Court's Answer

"We hold that the police stops were reasonable, hence, constitutional."

II. CASE SUMMARY

A. Background

"On Saturday, August 23, 1997, just after midnight, an unknown motorist traveling eastbound on a highway in Lombard, Illinois, struck and killed a 70-year-old bicyclist. The motorist drove off without identifying himself. About one week later at about the same time of night and at about the same place, local police set up a highway checkpoint designed to obtain more information about the accident from the motoring public.

Police cars with flashing lights partially blocked the eastbound lanes of the highway. The blockage forced traffic to slow down, leading to lines of up to 15 cars in each lane. As each vehicle drew up to the checkpoint, an officer would stop it for 10 to 15 seconds, ask the occupants whether they had seen anything happen there the previous weekend, and hand each driver a flyer. The flyer said 'ALERT ... FATAL HIT & RUN ACCIDENT' and requested 'ASSISTANCE IN IDENTIFYING THE VEHICLE AND DRIVER INVOLVED IN THIS ACCIDENT WHICH KILLED A 70 YEAR OLD BICYCLIST.'

Robert Lidster, the respondent, drove a minivan toward the checkpoint. As he approached the checkpoint, his van swerved, nearly hitting one of the officers. The officer smelled alcohol on Lidster's breath. He directed Lidster to a side street where another officer administered a sobriety test and then arrested Lidster. Lidster was tried and convicted in Illinois state court of driving under the influence of alcohol.

Lidster challenged the lawfulness of his arrest and conviction on the ground that the government had obtained much of the relevant evidence through use of a checkpoint stop that violated the Fourth Amendment. The trial court rejected that challenge. But an Illinois appellate court reached the opposite conclusion. The Illinois Supreme Court agreed with the appellate court."

The Supreme Court granted certiorari to review the case.

B. Counsel of Record

ACLU Side (Respondent / Appellee): Donald John Ramsell argued the cause and filed a brief for appellee.

Opposing Side (Petitioner / Appellant): Gary Feinerman, Solicitor General of Illinois, argued the cause for appellant. With him on the briefs were Lisa Madigan, Attorney General, and Linda D. Woloshin, Lisa Anne Hoffman, and Karen Kaplan, Assistant Attorneys General.

Patricia A. Millett argued the cause for the United States as amicus curiae.

III. AMICI CURIAE

ACLU Side (Respondent / Appellee)

Brief of amici curiae filed on behalf of the National Association of Criminal Defense Lawyers, the American Civil Liberties Union, and the ACLU of Illinois by Lawrence S. Lustberg, Shavar D. Jeffries, Joshua L. Dratel, Steven R. Shapiro, and Harvey Grossman.

Brief of amici curiae filed on behalf of the National College for DUI Defense by Barry T. Simons and W. Troy McKinney.

Opposing Side (Petitioner / Appellant)

Brief of amici curiae filed on behalf of the United States by Patricia A. Millett, Solicitor General Olson, Acting Assistant Attorney General Wray, Deputy Solicitor General Dreeben, and Patty Merkamp Stemler.

Brief of amici curiae filed on behalf of the State of Ohio et al. by Jim Petro, Attorney General of Ohio, Douglas R. Cole, State Solicitor, and Robert C. Maier, Assistant Solicitor, Robert J. Spagnoletti, Acting Corporation Counsel of the District of Columbia, and by the Attorneys General for their respective jurisdictions as follows: William H. Pryor, Jr., of Alabama, Terry Goddard of Arizona, M. Jane Brady of Delaware, Steve Carter of Indiana, Thomas J. Miller of Iowa, G. Steven Rowe of Maine, J. Joseph Curran, Jr., of Maryland, Mike Hatch of Minnesota, Mike McGrath of Montana, Brian Sandoval of Nevada, Peter Heed of New Hampshire, W. A. Drew Edmondson of Oklahoma, Hardy Myers of Oregon, D. Michael Fisher of Pennsylvania, Henry Dargan McMaster of South Carolina, Lawrence E. Long of South Dakota, Greg Abbott of Texas, Mark L. Shurtleff of Utah, William H. Sorrell of Vermont, Jerry W. Kilgore of Virginia, and Iver A. Stridiron of the Virgin Islands.

Brief of amici curiae filed on behalf of the Criminal Justice Legal Foundation by Kent S. Scheidegger and Charles L. Hobson.

Brief of amici curiae filed on behalf of the Illinois Association of Chiefs of Police et al. by James G. Sotos.

IV. THE SUPREME COURT'S DECISION

"The Illinois Supreme Court basically held that our decision in Edmond governs the outcome of this case. We do not agree. Edmond involved a checkpoint at which police stopped vehicles to look for evidence of drug crimes committed by occupants of those vehicles. After stopping a vehicle at the checkpoint, police would examine (from outside the vehicle) the vehicle's interior; they would walk a drug-sniffing dog around the exterior; and, if they found sufficient evidence of drug (or other) crimes, they would arrest the vehicle's occupants. We found that police had set up this checkpoint primarily for general 'crime control' purposes . . . . We noted that the stop was made without individualized suspicion. And we held that the Fourth Amendment forbids such a stop, in the absence of special circumstances.

The checkpoint stop here differs significantly from that in Edmond. The stop's primary law enforcement purpose was not to determine whether a vehicle's occupants were committing a crime, but to ask vehicle occupants, as members of the public, for their help in providing information about a crime in all likelihood committed by others. The police expected the information elicited to help them apprehend, not the vehicle's occupants, but other individuals.

Edmond's language, as well as its context, makes clear that the constitutionality of this latter, information-seeking kind of stop was not then before the Court. . . .

Neither do we believe, Edmond aside, that the Fourth Amendment would have us apply an Edmond-type rule of automatic unconstitutionality to brief, information-seeking highway stops of the kind now before us. . . .

Further, the law ordinarily permits police to seek the voluntary cooperation of members of the public in the investigation of a crime. . . .

Finally, we do not believe that an Edmond-type rule is needed to prevent an unreasonable proliferation of police checkpoints. . . .

These considerations, taken together, convince us that an Edmond-type presumptive rule of unconstitutionality does not apply here. That does not mean the stop is automatically, or even presumptively, constitutional. It simply means that we must judge its reasonableness, hence, its constitutionality, on the basis of the individual circumstances. And as this Court said in Brown v. Texas, 443 U.S. 47 (1979), in judging reasonableness, we look to 'the gravity of the public concerns served by the seizure, the degree to which the seizure advances the public interest, and the severity of the interference with individual liberty.' . . .

We now consider the reasonableness of the checkpoint stop before us in light of the factors just mentioned, an issue that, in our view, has been fully argued here. We hold that the stop was constitutional.

The relevant public concern was grave. Police were investigating a crime that had resulted in a human death. . . .

The stop advanced this grave public concern to a significant degree. The police appropriately tailored their checkpoint stops to fit important criminal investigatory needs. . . .

Most importantly, the stops interfered only minimally with liberty of the sort the Fourth Amendment seeks to protect. Viewed objectively, each stop required only a brief wait in line—a very few minutes at most. Contact with the police lasted only a few seconds. . . . Police contact consisted simply of a request for information and the distribution of a flyer. . . . Viewed subjectively, the contact provided little reason for anxiety or alarm. The police stopped all vehicles systematically. . . . And there is no allegation here that the police acted in a discriminatory or otherwise unlawful manner while questioning motorists during stops.

For these reasons we conclude that the checkpoint stop was constitutional.

The judgment of the Illinois Supreme Court is reversed."

V. JUSTICE VOTE

3 Pro ACLU Side vs. 6 Con Opposing Side

ACLU Side (Respondent / Appellee)

1. Stevens, J. – Wrote opinion concurring in part and dissenting in part
2. Ginsburg, R. – Joined Stevens' opinion
3. Souter, D. – Joined Stevens' opinion

Opposing Side (Petitioner / Appellant)

1. Breyer, S. – Wrote majority opinion
2. Thomas, C. – Joined majority opinion
3. O'Connor, S. – Joined majority opinion
4. Scalia, A. – Joined majority opinion
5. Kennedy, A. – Joined majority opinion
6. Rehnquist, W. – Joined majority opinion

VI. A WIN OR LOSS FOR THE ACLU?

The ACLU argued filed as amicus curiae urging affirmance; the Supreme Court reversed the Supreme Court of Illinois' decision by a 6-3 vote, giving the ACLU an apparent loss.

956. Frew v. Hawkins

(Decided January 14, 2004; 540 U.S. 431)

I. ISSUE

A. Issues Discussed

Immunity, federalism

B. Legal Question Presented

"[W]hether the Eleventh Amendment bars enforcement of a federal consent decree entered into by state officials."

C. Supreme Court's Answer

Enforcement of the federal consent decree does not violate the Eleventh Amendment.

II. CASE SUMMARY

A. Background

"Medicaid is a cooperative federal-state program that provides federal funding for state medical services to the poor. State participation is voluntary; but once a State elects to join the program, it must administer a state plan that meets federal requirements. One requirement is that every participating State must have an Early and Periodic Screening, Diagnosis, and Treatment (EPSDT) program. EPSDT programs provide health care services to children to reduce lifelong vulnerability to illness or disease. The EPSDT provisions of the Medicaid statute require participating States to provide various medical services to eligible children, and to provide notice of the services.

Petitioners here are mothers of children eligible for EPSDT services in Texas. In 1993 they filed a civil action pursuant to Rev. Stat. § 1979, 42 U.S.C. § 1983, seeking injunctive relief . . . .

Petitioners alleged that the Texas program did not satisfy the requirements of federal law. They asserted that the Texas program did not ensure eligible children would receive health, dental, vision, and hearing screens; failed to meet annual participation goals; and gave eligible recipients inadequate notice of available services. Petitioners also claimed the program lacked proper case management and corrective procedures and did not provide uniform services throughout Texas. . . .

Following extensive settlement negotiations, petitioners and the state officials agreed to resolve the suit by entering into a consent decree. The District Court conducted a fairness hearing, approved the consent decree, and entered it in 1996.

Judicial enforcement of the 1996 consent decree is the subject of the present dispute. The decree is a detailed document about 80 pages long that orders a comprehensive plan for implementing the federal statute. In contrast with the brief and general mandate in the statute itself, the consent decree requires the state officials to implement many specific procedures. . . .

Two years after the consent decree was entered, petitioners filed a motion to enforce it in the District Court. The state officials, it was alleged, had not complied with the decree in various respects. The officials denied the allegations and maintained that the Eleventh Amendment rendered the decree unenforceable even if they were in noncompliance. After an evidentiary hearing, the District Court issued a detailed opinion concluding that certain provisions of the consent decree had been violated. The District Court rejected the Eleventh Amendment argument, and directed the parties to submit proposals outlining possible remedies for the violations.

The state officials filed an interlocutory appeal, and the Court of Appeals for the Fifth Circuit reversed."

The Supreme Court granted certiorari to review the case.

B. Counsel of Record

ACLU Side (Petitioner / Appellant): Susan Finkelstein Zinn argued the cause for appellants. With her on the briefs were Edward B. Cloutman III and Jane Kathryn Swanson.

Irving L. Gornstein argued the cause for the United States as amicus curiae.

Opposing Side (Respondent / Appellee): Rafael Edward Cruz, Solicitor General of Texas, argued the cause for appellees. With him on the briefs were Greg Abbott, Attorney General, Barry R. McBee, First Assistant Attorney General, Jeffrey S. Boyd, Deputy Attorney General, and Melanie P. Sarwal, Assistant Solicitor General.

III. AMICI CURIAE

ACLU Side (Petitioner / Appellant)

Brief of amici curiae filed on behalf of the United States by Irving L. Gornstein, Solicitor General Olson, Assistant Attorney General McCallum, Deputy Solicitor General Kneedler, Mark B. Stern, and Alisa B. Klein.

Brief of amici curiae filed on behalf of the AARP, the American Association of People with Disabilities, the American Civil Liberties Union, the Anti-Defamation League, the Judge David L. Bazelon Center for Mental Health Law, Children's Rights, the National Association of Protection and Advocacy Systems, The National Health Law Program, and NOW Legal Defense and Education Fund by David T. Goldberg.

Opposing Side (Respondent / Appellee)

Brief of amici curiae filed on behalf of the State of Utah et al. by Mark L. Shurtleff, Attorney General of Utah, and Alain C. Balmanno and Joni J. Jones, Assistant Attorneys General, and by the Attorneys General for their respective States as follows: Ken Salazar of Colorado, M. Jane Brady of Delaware, Mark J. Bennett of Hawaii, Lawrence Wasden of Idaho, Richard P. Ieyoub of Louisiana, J. Joseph Curran, Jr., of Maryland, Michael A. Cox of Michigan, Mike Moore of Mississippi, Brian Sandoval of Nevada, Peter W. Heed of New Hampshire, Wayne Stenehjem of North Dakota, W. A. Drew Edmondson of Oklahoma, D. Michael Fisher of Pennsylvania, Lawrence E. Long of South Dakota, Jerry Kilgore of Virginia, William H. Sorrell of Vermont, Peg Lautenschlager of Wisconsin, and Pat Crank of Wyoming.

Brief of amici curiae filed on behalf of the National Conference of State Legislatures et al. by Richard Ruda and James I. Crowley.

IV. THE SUPREME COURT'S DECISION

"Petitioners advance two reasons why the consent decree can be enforced without violating the Eleventh Amendment. First, they argue the State waived its Eleventh Amendment immunity in the course of litigation. Second, they contend that enforcement is permitted under the principles of Ex parte Young, 209 U.S. 123 (1908). We agree that the decree is enforceable under Ex parte Young, and so we do not address the waiver argument.

This case involves the intersection of two areas of federal law: the reach of the Eleventh Amendment and the rules governing consent decrees. The Eleventh Amendment confirms the sovereign status of the States by shielding them from suits by individuals absent their consent. To ensure the enforcement of federal law, however, the Eleventh Amendment permits suits for prospective injunctive relief against state officials acting in violation of federal law. . . .

Consent decrees have elements of both contracts and judicial decrees. . . .

This brings us to the intersection of the principles governing consent decrees and the Eleventh Amendment. As we understand their argument, the state officials do not contend that the terms of the decree were impermissible under Ex parte Young. Nor do they contend that the consent decree failed to comply with Firefighters. The officials challenge only the enforcement of the decree, not its entry. They argue that the Eleventh Amendment narrows the circumstances in which courts can enforce federal consent decrees involving state officials. . . .

We disagree with this view of the Eleventh Amendment. The decree is a federal-court order that springs from a federal dispute and furthers the objectives of federal law. . . .

The state officials warn that enforcement of consent decrees can undermine the sovereign interests and accountability of state governments. . . . The concerns they express are legitimate ones. If not limited to reasonable and necessary implementations of federal law, remedies outlined in consent decrees involving state officeholders may improperly deprive future officials of their designated legislative and executive powers. They may also lead to federal-court oversight of state programs for long periods of time even absent an ongoing violation of federal law.

When a federal court has entered a consent decree under Ex parte Young, the law's primary response to these concerns has its source not in the Eleventh Amendment but in the court's equitable powers and the direction given by the Federal Rules of Civil Procedure. . . .

The federal court must exercise its equitable powers to ensure that when the objects of the decree have been attained, responsibility for discharging the State's obligations is returned promptly to the State and its officials. As public servants, the officials of the State must be presumed to have a high degree of competence in deciding how best to discharge their governmental responsibilities. A State, in the ordinary course, depends upon successor officials, both appointed and elected, to bring new insights and solutions to problems of allocating revenues and resources. The basic obligations of federal law may remain the same, but the precise manner of their discharge may not. If the State establishes reason to modify the decree, the court should make the necessary changes; where it has not done so, however, the decree should be enforced according to its terms.

The judgment of the Court of Appeals is reversed, and the case is remanded for further proceedings consistent with this opinion."

V. JUSTICE VOTE

9 Pro ACLU Side vs. 0 Con Opposing Side

ACLU Side (Petitioner / Appellant)

1. Kennedy, A. – Wrote majority opinion
2. O'Connor, S. – Joined majority opinion

3. Stevens, J. – Joined majority opinion
4. Souter, D. – Joined majority opinion
5. Ginsburg, R. – Joined majority opinion
6. Breyer, S. – Joined majority opinion
7. Scalia, A. – Joined majority opinion
8. Rehnquist, W. – Joined majority opinion
9. Thomas, C. – Joined majority opinion

VI. A WIN OR LOSS FOR THE ACLU?

The ACLU filed as amicus curiae urging reversal of the judgment of the Court of Appeals; the Supreme Court reversed in a 9-0 vote, giving the ACLU an apparent win.

957. Doe v. Chao

(Decided February 24, 2004; 540 U.S. 614)

I. ISSUE

A. Issues Discussed

Regulation

B. Legal Question Presented

"The question before us is whether plaintiffs must prove some actual damages to qualify for a minimum statutory award of $1,000."

C. Supreme Court's Answer

"The statute guarantees $1,000 only to plaintiffs who have suffered some actual damages."

II. CASE SUMMARY

A. Background

"Petitioner Buck Doe filed for benefits under the Black Lung Benefits Act with the Office of Workers' Compensation Programs, the division of the Department of Labor responsible for adjudicating it. The application form called for a Social Security number, which the agency then used to identify the applicant's claim, as on documents like 'multicaptioned' notices of hearing dates, sent to groups of claimants, their employers, and the lawyers involved in their cases. The Government concedes that following this practice led to disclosing Doe's Social Security number beyond the limits set by the Privacy Act.

Doe joined with six other black lung claimants to sue the Department of Labor, alleging repeated violations of the Act and seeking certification of a class of "all claimants for Black Lung Benefits since the passage of the Privacy Act." Early on, the United States stipulated to an order prohibiting future publication of applicants' Social Security numbers on multicaptioned hearing notices, and the parties then filed cross-motions for summary judgment. The District Court denied class certification and entered judgment against all individual plaintiffs except Doe, finding that their submissions had raised no issues of cognizable harm. As to Doe, the court accepted his uncontroverted evidence of distress on learning of the improper disclosure, granted summary judgment, and awarded $1,000 in statutory damages under 5 U.S.C. § 552a(g)(4).

A divided panel of the Fourth Circuit affirmed in part but reversed on Doe's claim, holding the United States entitled to summary judgment across the board."

The Supreme Court granted certiorari to review the case.

B. Counsel of Record

ACLU Side (Petitioner / Appellant): Jack W. Campbell IV argued the cause for appellant. With him on the briefs were Donald B. Ayer, Dominick V. Freda, and Joseph E. Wolfe.

Opposing Side (Respondent / Appellee): Malcolm L. Stewart argued the cause for appellee. With him on the brief were Solicitor General Olson, Assistant Attorney General Keisler, Deputy Solicitor General Kneedler, Patricia A. Millett, Leonard Schaitman, Anthony A. Yang, Howard M. Radzely, Allen H. Feldman, Nathaniel I. Spiller, and Michael P. Doyle.

III. AMICI CURIAE

ACLU Side (Petitioner / Appellant)

Brief of amici curiae filed on behalf of the Electronic Privacy Information Center, American Civil Liberties Union, American Library Association, Asian American Legal Defense and Education Fund, Center for Democracy and Technology, Consumer Project on Technology, Electronic Frontier Foundation, National Consumers League, Privacy Rights Clearinghouse, Privacy Activism, U.S. Public Interest Research Group, and 16 Legal Scholars and Technical Experts by Marc Rotenberg and David L. Sobel. Chris Jay Hoofnagle, and Marcia Hofmann.

Brief of amici curiae filed on behalf of Linda R. Tripp et al. by David K. Colapinto, Stephen M. Kohn, and Michael D. Kohn.

Opposing Side (Respondent / Appellee)

Brief of amici curiae filed on behalf of the Reporters Committee for Freedom of the Press by Lucy A. Dalglish.

IV. THE SUPREME COURT'S DECISION

"'[I]n order to protect the privacy of individuals identified in information systems maintained by Federal agencies, it is necessary . . . to regulate the collection, maintenance, use, and dissemination of information by such agencies.' Privacy Act of 1974. The Act gives agencies detailed instructions for managing their records and provides for various sorts of civil relief to individuals aggrieved by failures on the Government's part to comply with the requirements.

Subsection (g)(1) recognizes a civil action for agency misconduct fitting within any of four categories (the fourth, in issue here, being a catchall), and then makes separate provision for the redress of each. . . .

Doe argues that subsection (g)(4)(A) entitles any plaintiff adversely affected by an intentional or willful violation to the $1,000 minimum on proof of nothing more than a statutory violation: anyone suffering an adverse consequence of intentional or willful disclosure is entitled to recovery. The Government claims the minimum guarantee goes only to victims who prove some actual damages. We think the Government has the better side of the argument.

To begin with, the Government's position is supported by a straightforward textual analysis. . . .

There are three loose ends. Doe's argument suggests it would have been illogical for Congress to create a cause of action for anyone who suffers an adverse effect from intentional or willful agency action, then deny recovery without actual damages. But this objection assumes that the language in subsection (g)(1)(D) recognizing a federal 'civil action' on the part of someone adversely affected was meant, without more, to provide a complete cause of action, and of course this is not so. . . .

Next, Doe also suggests there is something peculiar in offering some guaranteed damages, as a form of presumed damages not requiring proof of amount, only to those plaintiffs who can demonstrate actual damages. But this approach parallels another remedial scheme that the drafters of the Privacy Act would probably have known about. . . .

In a final effort to save his claim, Doe points to a pair of statutes with remedial provisions that are worded similarly to § 552a(g)(4). . . . He contends that legislative history of these subsequent enactments shows that Congress sometimes used language similar to 5 U.S.C. § 552a(g)(4) with the object of authorizing true liquidated damages remedies. . . . There are two problems with this argument. . . .

The 'entitle[ment] to recovery' necessary to qualify for the $1,000 minimum is not shown merely by an intentional or willful violation of the Act producing some adverse effect. The statute guarantees $1,000 only to plaintiffs who have suffered some actual damages. The judgment of the Fourth Circuit is affirmed."

V. JUSTICE VOTE

3 Pro ACLU Side vs. 6 Con Opposing Side

ACLU Side (Petitioner / Appellant)

1. Stevens, J. – Joined Ginsburg's dissent
2. Ginsburg, R. – Wrote dissenting opinion
3. Breyer, S. – Wrote dissenting opinion, joined Ginsburg's dissent

Opposing Side (Respondent / Appellee)

1. Souter, D. – Wrote majority opinion
2. Rehnquist, W. – Joined majority opinion
3. Thomas, C. – Joined majority opinion
4. Scalia, A. – Joined majority opinion in part
5. Kennedy, A. – Joined majority opinion
6. O'Connor, S. – Joined majority opinion

VI. A WIN OR LOSS FOR THE ACLU?

The ACLU filed as amicus curiae urging reversal of the judgment of the Court of Appeals; the Supreme Court affirmed in a 6-3 vote, giving the ACLU an apparent loss.

958. Locke v. Davey

(Decided February 25, 2004; 540 U.S. 712)

I. ISSUE

A. Issues Discussed

1st Amendment, religion

B. Legal Question Presented

"[W]hether Washington, pursuant to its own constitution, which has been authoritatively interpreted as prohibiting even indirectly funding religious instruction that will prepare students for the ministry, . . . can deny [Promise Scholars scholarship] funding [for a degree in devotional theology] without violating the Free Exercise Clause."

C. Supreme Court's Answer

"We hold that such an exclusion from an otherwise inclusive aid program does not violate the Free Exercise Clause of the First Amendment."

II. CASE SUMMARY

A. Background

"The State of Washington established the Promise Scholarship Program to assist academically gifted students with postsecondary education expenses. In accordance with the State Constitution, students may not use the scholarship at an institution where they are pursuing a degree in devotional theology. . . .

A student who applies for the scholarship and meets the academic and income requirements is notified that he is eligible for the scholarship if he meets the enrollment requirements. Once the student enrolls at an eligible institution, the institution must certify that the student is enrolled at least half time and that the student is not pursuing a degree in devotional theology. The institution, rather than the State, determines whether the student's major is devotional. . . .

Respondent, Joshua Davey, was awarded a Promise Scholarship, and chose to attend Northwest College. Northwest is a private, Christian college affiliated with the Assemblies of God denomination, and is an eligible institution under the Promise Scholarship Program. Davey had 'planned for many years to attend a Bible college and to prepare [himself] through that college training for a lifetime of ministry, specifically as a church pastor.' To that end, when he enrolled in Northwest College, he decided to pursue a double major in pastoral ministries and business management/administration. There is no dispute that the pastoral ministries degree is devotional and therefore excluded under the Promise Scholarship Program.

At the beginning of the 1999–2000 academic year, Davey met with Northwest's director of financial aid. He learned for the first time at this meeting that he could not use his scholarship to pursue a devotional theology degree. He was informed that to receive the funds appropriated for his use, he must certify in writing that he was not pursuing such a degree at Northwest. He refused to sign the form and did not receive any scholarship funds.

Davey then brought an action under Rev.Stat. § 1979, 42 U.S.C. § 1983, against various state officials (hereinafter State) in the District Court for the Western District of Washington to enjoin the State from refusing to award the scholarship solely because a student is pursuing a devotional theology degree, and for damages. He argued the denial of his scholarship based on his decision to pursue a theology degree violated, inter alia, the Free Exercise, Establishment, and Free Speech Clauses of the First Amendment, as incorporated by the Fourteenth Amendment, and the Equal Protection Clause of the Fourteenth Amendment. After the District Court denied Davey's request for a preliminary injunction, the parties filed cross-motions for summary judgment. The District Court rejected Davey's constitutional claims and granted summary judgment in favor of the State.

A divided panel of the United States Court of Appeals for the Ninth Circuit reversed."

The Supreme Court granted certiorari to review the case.

B. Counsel of Record

ACLU Side (Petitioner / Appellant): Narda Pierce, Solicitor General of Washington, argued the cause for appellants. With her on the briefs were Christine O. Gregoire, Attorney General, William Berggren Collins, Senior Assistant Attorney General, and Michael J. Shinn, Assistant Attorney General.

Opposing Side (Respondent / Appellee): Jay Alan Sekulow argued the cause for appellee. With him on the brief were Stuart J. Roth, Colby M. May, James M. Henderson, Sr., Walter M. Weber, David A. Cortman, Alan E. Sears, and Benjamin W. Bull.

Solicitor General Olson argued the cause for the United States as amicus curiae.

III. AMICI CURIAE

ACLU Side (Petitioner / Appellant)

Brief of amici curiae filed on behalf of the American Civil Liberties Union, American Civil Liberties Union of Washington, Americans United for Separation of Church and State, People for the American Way Foundation and Lambda Legal Defense & Education Fund by Aaron H. Caplan, Steven R. Shapiro, Julie E. Sternberg, Ayesha N. Khan, Elliot M. Mincberg, and Susan L. Sommer.

Brief of amici curiae filed on behalf of the State of Vermont et al. by William H. Sorrell, Attorney General of Vermont, and Timothy B. Tomasi, Chief Assistant Attorney General, by Anabelle Rodríguez, Secretary of Justice of Puerto Rico, and by the Attorneys General for their respective jurisdictions as follows: Thomas F. Reilly of Massachusetts, Jeremiah W. (Jay) Nixon of Missouri, Hardy Myers of Oregon, Lawrence E. Long of South Dakota, and Clyde Lemons, Jr., of the Northern Mariana Islands.

Brief of amici curiae filed on behalf of the American Jewish Congress et al. by Marc D. Stern, K. Hollyn Hollman, Jeffrey Sinensky, Kara Stein, and David Strom.

Brief of amici curiae filed on behalf of the Anti-Defamation League et al. by David Lash, Steven M. Freeman, Steven C. Sheinberg, Martin E. Karlinsky, Erwin Chemerinsky, and Frederick M. Lawrence.

Brief of amici curiae filed on behalf of the National Education Association by Robert H. Chanin, Andrew D. Roth, and Laurence Gold.

Brief of amici curiae filed on behalf of the National School Boards Association et al. by David H. Remes and Julie Underwood.

Brief of amici curiae filed on behalf of Robert S. Alley et al. by Steven K. Green.

Opposing Side (Respondent / Appellee)

Brief of amici curiae filed on behalf of the United States by Solicitor General Olson, Assistant Attorney General Acosta, Deputy Solicitor General Clement, Gregory G. Garre, David K. Flynn, and Eric W. Treene.

Brief of amici curiae filed on behalf of the State of Alabama by William H. Pryor, Jr., Attorney General of Alabama, Nathan A. Forrester, Solicitor General, and Margaret L. Fleming, Assistant Attorney General.

Brief of amici curiae filed on behalf of the State of Florida et al. by Charles J. Crist, Jr., Attorney General of Florida, Christopher M. Kise, Solicitor General, Raquel A. Rodriguez, and Daniel Woodring.

Brief of amici curiae filed on behalf of the State of Texas et al. by Greg Abbott, Attorney General of Texas, Barry R. McBee, First Assistant Attorney General, Edward D. Burbach, Deputy Attorney General, Rafael Edward Cruz, Solicitor General, Joseph D. Hughes and Cassandra Robertson, Assistant Solicitors General, Mike Moore, Attorney General of Mississippi, and Mark L. Shurtleff, Attorney General of Utah.

Brief of amici curiae filed on behalf of the Association of Southern Baptist Colleges and Schools et al. by Carter G. Phillips, Gene C. Schaerr, and Nicholas P. Miller.

Brief of amici curiae filed on behalf of the Becket Fund for Religious Liberty et al. by Kevin J. Hasson, Roman P. Storzer, and Anthony R. Picarello, Jr.

Brief of amici curiae filed on behalf of the Black Alliance for Educational Options by Samuel Estreicher and Brett M. Schuman.

Brief of amici curiae filed on behalf of the Council for Christian Colleges & Universities et al. by Gregory S. Baylor and Thomas C. Berg.

Brief of amici curiae filed on behalf of the Fairness Foundation by Kenneth W. Starr, Robert R. Gasaway, and Ashley C. Parrish.

Brief of amici curiae filed on behalf of the Institute for Justice et al. by Richard D. Komer, Clint Bolick, and William H. Mellor.

Brief of amici curiae filed on behalf of the Landmark Legal Foundation by Richard P. Hutchison and Michael J. O'Neill.

Brief of amici curiae filed on behalf of Liberty Counsel by Mathew D. Staver and Rena M. Lindevaldsen.

Brief of amici curiae filed on behalf of the National Jewish Commission on Law and Public Affairs by Nathan Lewin, Dennis Rapps, David Zwiebel, Richard B. Stone, and Nathan J. Diament.

Brief of amici curiae filed on behalf of the National Legal

Foundation by Barry C. Hodge.
Brief of amici curiae filed on behalf of the Solidarity Center for Law and Justice, P. C., by James P. Kelly III.
Brief of amici curiae filed on behalf of Teresa M. Becker by Richard Thompson.
Brief of amici curiae filed on behalf of the Common Good Legal Defense Fund et al. by John G. Stepanovich and Keith A. Fournier.
Brief of amici curiae filed on behalf of the United States Conference of Catholic Bishops et al. by Mark E. Chopko and Jeffrey Hunter Moon.

IV. THE SUPREME COURT'S DECISION

"The Religion Clauses of the First Amendment provide: 'Congress shall make no law respecting an establishment of religion, or prohibiting the free exercise thereof.' These two Clauses, the Establishment Clause and the Free Exercise Clause, are frequently in tension. Yet we have long said that 'there is room for play in the joints' between them. . . .

This case involves that 'play in the joints' described above. Under our Establishment Clause precedent, the link between government funds and religious training is broken by the independent and private choice of recipients. As such, there is no doubt that the State could, consistent with the Federal Constitution, permit Promise Scholars to pursue a degree in devotional theology, and the State does not contend otherwise. The question before us, however, is whether Washington, pursuant to its own constitution, which has been authoritatively interpreted as prohibiting even indirectly funding religious instruction that will prepare students for the ministry, . . . can deny them such funding without violating the Free Exercise Clause. . . .

Far from evincing the hostility toward religion which was manifest in Lukumi, we believe that the entirety of the Promise Scholarship Program goes a long way toward including religion in its benefits. The program permits students to attend pervasively religious schools, so long as they are accredited. . . . And under the Promise Scholarship Program's current guidelines, students are still eligible to take devotional theology courses. . . .

In short, we find neither in the history or text of Article I, § 11, of the Washington Constitution, nor in the operation of the Promise Scholarship Program, anything that suggests animus toward religion. Given the historic and substantial state interest at issue, we therefore cannot conclude that the denial of funding for vocational religious instruction alone is inherently constitutionally suspect.

Without a presumption of unconstitutionality, Davey's claim must fail. The State's interest in not funding the pursuit of devotional degrees is substantial and the exclusion of such funding places a relatively minor burden on Promise Scholars. If any room exists between the two Religion Clauses, it must be here. We need not venture further into this difficult area in order to uphold the Promise Scholarship Program as currently operated by the State of Washington.

The judgment of the Court of Appeals is therefore reversed."

V. JUSTICE VOTE

7 Pro ACLU Side vs. 2 Con Opposing Side

ACLU Side (Petitioner / Appellant)

1. Rehnquist, W. – Wrote majority opinion
2. O'Connor, S. – Joined majority opinion
3. Stevens, J. – Joined majority opinion
4. Souter, D. – Joined majority opinion
5. Ginsburg, R. – Joined majority opinion
6. Breyer, S. – Joined majority opinion
7. Kennedy, A. – Joined majority opinion

Opposing Side (Respondent / Appellee)

1. Scalia, A. – Wrote dissenting opinion
2. Thomas, C. – Wrote dissenting opinion, joined Scalia's dissent

VI. A WIN OR LOSS FOR THE ACLU?

The ACLU filed as amicus curiae urging reversal of the judgment of the Court of Appeals; the Supreme Court reversed in a 7-2 vote, giving the ACLU an apparent win.

959. Crawford v. Washington

(Decided March 8, 2004; 541 U.S. 36)

I. ISSUE

A. Issues Discussed

Criminal procedure

B. Legal Question Presented

Whether playing a tape recorded statement by a witness without the opportunity for cross examination of the witness "complied with the Sixth Amendment's guarantee that, '[i]n all criminal prosecutions, the accused shall enjoy the right . . . to be confronted with the witnesses against him.'"

C. Supreme Court's Answer

"In this case, the State admitted Sylvia's [recorded] testimonial statement against petitioner, despite the fact that he had no opportunity to cross-examine her. That alone is sufficient to make out a violation of the Sixth Amendment. . . . Where testimonial statements are at issue, the only indicium of reliability sufficient to satisfy constitutional demands is the one the Constitution actually prescribes: confrontation."

II. CASE SUMMARY

A. Background

"On August 5, 1999, Kenneth Lee was stabbed at his apartment. Police arrested petitioner later that night. After giving petitioner and his wife Miranda warnings, detectives interrogated each of them twice. Petitioner eventually confessed that he and Sylvia had gone in search of Lee because he was upset over an earlier incident in which Lee had tried to rape her. The two had found Lee at his apartment, and a fight ensued in which Lee was stabbed in the torso and petitioner's hand was cut. . . .

Sylvia generally corroborated petitioner's story about the events leading up to the fight, but her account of the fight itself was arguably different—particularly with respect to whether Lee had drawn a weapon before petitioner assaulted him . . . .

The State charged petitioner with assault and attempted murder. At trial, he claimed self-defense. Sylvia did not testify because of the state marital privilege, which generally bars a spouse from testifying without the other spouse's consent. In Washington, this privilege does not extend to a spouse's out-of-court statements admissible under a hearsay exception . . . so the State sought to introduce Sylvia's tape-recorded statements to the police as evidence that the stabbing was not in self-defense. Noting that Sylvia had admitted she led petitioner to Lee's apartment and thus had facilitated the assault, the State invoked the hearsay exception for statements against penal interest.

Petitioner countered that, state law notwithstanding, admitting the evidence would violate his federal constitutional right to be 'confronted with the witnesses against him.' . . . The trial court here admitted the statement . . . . The jury convicted petitioner of assault.

The Washington Court of Appeals reversed. . . .

The Washington Supreme Court reinstated the conviction, unanimously concluding that, although Sylvia's statement did not fall under a firmly rooted hearsay exception, it bore guarantees of trustworthiness . . . ."

The Supreme Court granted certiorari to review the case.

B. Counsel of Record

ACLU Side (Petitioner / Appellant): Jeffrey L. Fisher, by appointment of the Court, argued the cause for appellant. With him on the briefs was Bruce E. H. Johnson.

Opposing Side (Respondent / Appellee): Steven C. Sherman argued the cause for respondent. With him on the brief was John Michael Jones.

Deputy Solicitor General Dreeben argued the cause for the United States as amicus curiae.

III. AMICI CURIAE

ACLU Side (Petitioner / Appellant)

Brief of amici curiae filed on behalf of the National Association of Criminal Defense Lawyers the American Civil Liberties Union and the ACLU of Washington by Jeffrey T. Green, David M. Porter, Steven R. Shapiro, Robert N. Hochman, and Matthew J. Press.

Brief of amici curiae filed on behalf of Sherman J. Clark et al. by Richard D. Friedman and David A. Moran.

Opposing Side (Respondent / Appellee)

Brief of amici curiae filed on behalf of the United States by Deputy Solicitor General Dreeben, Solicitor General Olson, Acting Assistant Attorney General Wray, Sri Srinivasan, and Joel M. Gershowitz.

IV. THE SUPREME COURT'S DECISION

"The Sixth Amendment's Confrontation Clause provides that, '[i]n all criminal prosecutions, the accused shall enjoy the right ... to be confronted with the witnesses against him.' . . . Roberts says that an unavailable witness's out-of-court statement may be admitted so long as it has adequate indicia of reliability—i.e., falls within a 'firmly rooted hearsay exception' or bears 'particularized guarantees of trustworthiness.' Petitioner argues that this test strays from the original meaning of the Confrontation Clause and urges us to reconsider it. . . .

The Constitution's text does not alone resolve this case. . . . We must therefore turn to the historical background of the Clause to understand its meaning. . . .

This history supports two inferences about the meaning of the Sixth Amendment. . . .

First, the principal evil at which the Confrontation Clause was directed was the civil-law mode of criminal procedure, and particularly its use of ex parte examinations as evidence against the accused. . . .

In sum, even if the Sixth Amendment is not solely concerned with testimonial hearsay, that is its primary object, and interrogations by law enforcement officers fall squarely within that class. . . .

The historical record also supports a second proposition: that the Framers would not have allowed admission of testimonial statements of a witness who did not appear at trial unless he was unavailable to testify, and the defendant had had a prior opportunity for cross-examination. . . .

Our case law has been largely consistent with these two principles. . . .

Our cases have thus remained faithful to the Framers' understanding: Testimonial statements of witnesses absent from trial have been admitted only where the declarant is unavailable, and only where the defendant has had a prior opportunity to cross-examine. . . .

Although the results of our decisions have generally been faithful to the original meaning of the Confrontation Clause, the same cannot be said of our rationales. . . .

Members of this Court and academics have suggested that we revise our doctrine to reflect more accurately the original understanding of the Clause. . . . They offer two proposals: First, that we apply the Confrontation Clause only to testimonial statements, leaving the remainder to regulation by hearsay law—thus eliminating the overbreadth referred to above. Second, that we impose an absolute bar to statements that are testimonial, absent a prior opportunity to cross-examine—thus eliminating the excessive narrowness referred to above.

In White, we considered the first proposal and rejected it. . . . This case does, however, squarely implicate the second proposal. . . .

Where testimonial statements are involved, we do not think the Framers meant to leave the Sixth Amendment's protection to the vagaries of the rules of evidence, much less to amorphous notions of 'reliability.' . . .

Dispensing with confrontation because testimony is obviously reliable is akin to dispensing with jury trial because a defendant is obviously guilty. This is not what the Sixth Amendment prescribes. . . .

Where nontestimonial hearsay is at issue, it is wholly consistent with the Framers' design to afford the States flexibility in their development of hearsay law—as does Roberts, and as would an approach that exempted such statements from Confrontation Clause scrutiny altogether. Where testimonial evidence is at issue, however, the Sixth Amendment demands what the common law required: unavailability and a prior opportunity for cross-examination. . . .

In this case, the State admitted Sylvia's testimonial statement against petitioner, despite the fact that he had no opportunity to cross-examine her. That alone is sufficient to make out a violation of the Sixth Amendment. Roberts notwithstanding, we decline to mine the record in search of indicia of reliability. Where testimonial statements are at issue, the only indicium of reliability sufficient to satisfy constitutional demands is the one the Constitution actually prescribes: confrontation.

The judgment of the Washington Supreme Court is reversed, and the case is remanded for further proceedings not inconsistent with this opinion."

V. JUSTICE VOTE

9 Pro ACLU Side vs. 0 Con Opposing Side

ACLU Side (Petitioner / Appellant)

1. Scalia, A. – Wrote majority opinion
2. Stevens, J. – Joined majority opinion
3. Souter, D. – Joined majority opinion
4. Ginsburg, R. – Joined majority opinion
5. Breyer, S. – Joined majority opinion
6. Kennedy, A. – Joined majority opinion
7. Thomas, C. – Joined majority opinion
8. Rehnquist, W. – Wrote concurring opinion
9. O'Connor, S. – Joined Rehnquist's concurrence

VI. A WIN OR LOSS FOR THE ACLU?

The ACLU filed as amicus curiae urging reversal of the judgment of the Washington Supreme Court; the U.S. Supreme Court reversed in a 9-0 vote, giving the ACLU an apparent win.

960. Vieth v. Jubelirer

(Decided April 28, 2004; 541 U.S. 267)

I. ISSUE

A. Issues Discussed

Voting rights

B. Legal Question Presented

"[W]hether our decision in Bandemer was in error, and, if not, what the standard should be."

C. Supreme Court's Answer

"Eighteen years of essentially pointless litigation have persuaded us that Bandemer is incapable of principled application. We would therefore overrule that case, and decline to adjudicate these political gerrymandering claims."

II. CASE SUMMARY

A. Background

"The population figures derived from the 2000 census showed that Pennsylvania was entitled to only 19 Representatives in Congress, a decrease in 2 from the Commonwealth's previous delegation. Pennsylvania's General Assembly took up the task of drawing a new districting map. At the time, the Republican Party controlled a majority of both state Houses and held the Governor's office. Prominent national figures in the Republican Party pressured the General Assembly to adopt a partisan redistricting plan as a punitive measure against Democrats for having enacted pro-Democrat redistricting plans elsewhere. The Republican members of Pennsylvania's House and Senate worked together on such a plan. On January 3, 2002, the General Assembly passed its plan, which was signed into law by Governor Schweiker as Act 1.

Plaintiffs, registered Democrats who vote in Pennsylvania, brought suit in the United States District Court for the Middle District of Pennsylvania, seeking to enjoin implementation of Act 1 under Rev. Stat. § 1979, 42 U.S.C. § 1983. . . . The complaint alleged . . . that the legislation created malapportioned districts, in violation of the one-person, one-vote requirement of Article I, § 2, of the United States Constitution, and that it constituted a political gerrymander, in violation of Article I and the Equal Protection Clause of the Fourteenth Amendment. With regard to the latter contention, the complaint alleged that the districts created by Act 1 were 'meandering and irregular,' and 'ignor[ed] all traditional redistricting criteria, including the preservation of local government boundaries, solely for the sake of partisan advantage.' . . .

The defendants moved to dismiss. The District Court granted the motion with respect to the political gerrymandering claim, and (on Eleventh Amendment grounds) all claims against the Commonwealth; but it declined to dismiss the apportionment claim as to other defendants. On trial of the apportionment claim, the District Court ruled in favor of plaintiffs. It retained jurisdiction over the case pending the court's review and approval of a remedial redistricting plan. On April 18, 2002, Governor Schweiker signed into law Act No. 2002–34, . . . a remedial plan that the Pennsylvania General Assembly had enacted to cure the apportionment problem of Act 1.

Plaintiffs moved to impose remedial districts, arguing that the District Court should not consider Act 34 to be a proper remedial scheme, both because it was malapportioned, and because it constituted an unconstitutional political gerrymander like its predecessor. The District Court denied this motion, concluding that the new districts were not malapportioned, and rejecting the political gerrymandering claim for the reasons previously assigned in Vieth I. The plaintiffs appealed the dismissal of their Act 34 political gerrymandering claim."

The Supreme Court granted certiorari to review the case.

B. Counsel of Record

ACLU Side (Petitioner / Appellant): Paul M. Smith argued the cause for appellants. With him on the briefs were Thomas J. Perrelli, Bruce V. Spiva, Sam Hirsch, Daniel Mach, and Robert B. Hoffman.

Opposing Side (Respondent / Appellee): John P. Krill, Jr., argued the cause for appellee Jubelirer et al. With him on the brief were Linda J. Shorey and Julia M. Glencer.

J. Bart DeLone, Senior Deputy Attorney General of Pennsylvania, argued the cause for appellee Cortés et al. With him on the brief were D. Michael Fisher, Attorney General, and John G. Knorr III, Chief Deputy Attorney General.

III. AMICI CURIAE

ACLU Side (Petitioner / Appellant)

Brief of amici curiae filed on behalf of the American Civil Liberties Union and the Brennan Center for Justice at NYU School of Law by Burt Neuborne, Deborah Goldberg, J. J. Gass, Adam H. Morse, Steven R. Shapiro, Arthur N. Eisenberg, Laughlin McDonald, Neil Bradley, Ronald A. Klain, and Charles E. Borden.

Brief of amici curiae filed on behalf of the Texas House Democratic Caucus et al. by J. Gerald Hebert and Pamela S. Karlan.

Brief of amici curiae filed on behalf of Public Citizen et al. by Alan B. Morrison, Amanda Frost, and Scott Nelson; for the Reform Institute et al. by Daniel R. Ortiz and Trevor Potter.

Brief of amici curiae filed on behalf of JoAnn Erfer et al. by Einer Elhauge.

Brief of amici curiae filed on behalf of Pennsylvania State Senator Robert J. Mellow by Gladys M. Brown.

Opposing Side (Respondent / Appellee)

Brief of amici curiae filed on behalf of Alabama State Senator Lowell Barron et al. by James U. Blacksher and Robert D. Segall.

Brief of amici curiae filed on behalf of the Center for Research into Governmental Processes, Inc., by Jamin B. Raskin.

Brief of amici curiae filed on behalf of the DKT Liberty Project by Scott A. Sinder.

Brief of amici curiae filed on behalf of Bernard Grofman et al. by H. Reed Witherby.

Brief of amici curiae filed on behalf of Jack N. Rakove et al. by Joseph R. Guerra and Stephen B. Kinnaird.

IV. THE SUPREME COURT'S DECISION

"Political gerrymanders are not new to the American scene. . . .

It is significant that the Framers provided a remedy for such practices in the Constitution. Article I, § 4, while leaving in state legislatures the initial power to draw districts for federal elections, permitted Congress to 'make or alter' those districts if it wished. . . .

Eighteen years ago, we held that the Equal Protection Clause grants judges the power—and duty—to control political gerrymandering, see Davis v. Bandemer, 478 U.S. 109 (1986). It is to consideration of this precedent that we now turn. . . .

Over the dissent of three Justices, the Court held in Davis v. Bandemer that, since it was 'not persuaded that there are no judicially discernible and manageable standards by which political gerrymander cases are to be decided,' such cases were justiciable. . . .

Eighteen years of judicial effort with virtually nothing to show for it justify us in revisiting the question whether the standard promised by Bandemer exists. [N]o judicially discernible and manageable standards for adjudicating political gerrymandering claims have emerged. Lacking them, we must conclude that political gerrymandering claims are nonjusticiable and that Bandemer was wrongly decided. . . .

We turn next to consideration of the standards proposed by today's dissenters. [T]he mere fact that these four dissenters come up with three different standards—all of them different from the two proposed in Bandemer and the one proposed here by appellants—goes a long way to establishing that there is no constitutionally discernible standard. . . .

We conclude that neither Article I, § 2, nor the Equal Protection Clause, nor (what appellants only fleetingly invoke) Article I, § 4, provides a judicially enforceable limit on the political considerations that the States and Congress may take into account when districting.

Considerations of stare decisis do not compel us to allow Bandemer to stand. That case involved an interpretation of the Constitution, and the claims of stare decisis are at their weakest in that field, where our mistakes cannot be corrected by Congress. They are doubly weak in Bandemer because the majority's inability to enunciate the judicially discernible and manageable standard that it thought existed (or did not think did not exist) presaged the need for reconsideration in light of subsequent experience. And they are triply weak because it is hard to imagine how any action taken in reliance upon Bandemer could conceivably be frustrated—except the bringing of lawsuits, which is not the sort of primary conduct that is relevant.

While we do not lightly overturn one of our own holdings, 'when governing decisions are unworkable or are badly reasoned, 'this Court has never felt constrained to follow precedent." Eighteen years of essentially pointless litigation have persuaded us that Bandemer is incapable of principled application. We would therefore overrule that case, and decline to adjudicate these political gerrymandering claims.

The judgment of the District Court is affirmed."

V. JUSTICE VOTE

4 Pro ACLU Side vs. 5 Con Opposing Side

ACLU Side (Petitioner / Appellant)

1. Stevens, J. – Wrote dissenting opinion
2. Souter, D. – Wrote dissenting opinion
3. Ginsburg, R. – Joined Souter's dissent
4. Breyer, S. – Wrote dissenting opinion

Opposing Side (Respondent / Appellee)

1. Scalia, A. – Wrote plurality opinion
2. Rehnquist, W. – Joined Scalia's opinion
3. O'Connor, S. – Joined Scalia's opinion
4. Thomas, C. – Joined Scalia's opinion
5. Kennedy, A. – Wrote concurring opinion

VI. A WIN OR LOSS FOR THE ACLU?

The ACLU filed as amicus curiae urging reversal of the judgment of the District Court; the Supreme Court affirmed in a 5-4 vote, giving the ACLU an apparent loss.

961. Thornton v. United States

(Decided May 24, 2004; 541 U.S. 615)

I. ISSUE

A. Issues Discussed

4th Amendment

B. Legal Question Presented

"[W]hether Belton's rule is limited to situations where the officer makes contact with the occupant while the occupant is inside the vehicle, or whether it applies as well when the officer first makes contact with the arrestee after the latter has stepped out of his vehicle."

C. Supreme Court's Answer

"We . . . conclude that Belton governs even when an officer does not make contact until the person arrested has left the vehicle."

II. CASE SUMMARY

A. Background

"Officer Deion Nichols of the Norfolk, Virginia, Police Department, who was in uniform but driving an unmarked police car, first noticed petitioner Marcus Thornton when petitioner slowed down so as to avoid driving next to him. Nichols suspected that petitioner knew he was a police officer and for some reason did not want to pull next to him. His suspicions aroused, Nichols pulled off onto a side street and petitioner passed him. After petitioner passed him, Nichols ran a check on petitioner's license tags, which revealed that the tags had been issued to a 1982 Chevy two-door and not to a Lincoln Town Car, the model of car petitioner was driving. Before Nichols had an opportunity to pull him over, petitioner drove into a parking lot, parked, and got out of the vehicle. Nichols saw petitioner leave his vehicle as he pulled in behind him. He parked the patrol car, accosted petitioner, and asked him for his driver's license. He also told him that his license tags did not match the vehicle that he was driving.

Petitioner appeared nervous. He began rambling and licking his lips; he was sweating. Concerned for his safety, Nichols asked petitioner if he had any narcotics or weapons on him or in his vehicle. Petitioner said no. Nichols then asked petitioner if he could pat him down, to which petitioner agreed. Nichols felt a bulge in petitioner's left front pocket and again asked him if he had any illegal narcotics on him. This time petitioner stated that he did, and he reached into his pocket and pulled out two individual bags, one containing three bags of marijuana and the other containing a large amount of crack cocaine. Nichols handcuffed petitioner, informed him that he was under arrest, and placed him in the back seat of the patrol car. He then searched petitioner's vehicle and found a BryCo 9–millimeter handgun under the driver's seat.

A grand jury charged petitioner with possession with intent to distribute cocaine base, possession of a firearm after having been previously convicted of a crime punishable by a term of imprisonment exceeding one year, and possession of a firearm in furtherance of a drug trafficking crime. Petitioner sought to suppress, inter alia, the firearm as the fruit of an unconstitutional search. After a hearing, the District Court denied petitioner's motion to suppress . . . . A jury convicted petitioner on all three counts; he was sentenced to 180 months' imprisonment and 8 years of supervised release.

Petitioner appealed, challenging only the District Court's denial of the suppression motion. . . . The United States Court of Appeals for the Fourth Circuit affirmed."

The Supreme Court granted certiorari to review the case.

B. Counsel of Record

ACLU Side (Petitioner / Appellant): Frank W. Dunham, Jr., argued the cause for appellant. With him on the briefs were Walter B. Dalton, Frances H. Pratt, and Kenneth P. Troccoli.

Opposing Side (Respondent / Appellee): Gregory G. Garre argued the cause for the United States. With him on the brief were Solicitor General Olson, Assistant Attorney General Wray, and Deputy Solicitor General Dreeben.

III. AMICI CURIAE

ACLU Side (Petitioner / Appellant)

Brief of amici curiae filed on behalf of the American Civil Liberties Union, the ACLU of Virginia, and the National Association of Criminal Defense Lawyers by Tracey Maclin, Steven R. Shapiro, and Lisa Kemler.

Opposing Side (Respondent / Appellee)

Brief of amici curiae filed on behalf of the State of Arizona et al. by Terry Goddard, Attorney General of Arizona, Mary R. O'Grady, Solicitor General, Randall M. Howe, Chief Counsel, and Kathleen P. Sweeney and Eric J. Olsson, Assistant Attorneys General, and by the Attorneys General for their respective States as follows: William H. Pryor, Jr., of Alabama, M. Jane Brady of Delaware, Charles J. Crist, Jr., of Florida, Mark J. Bennett of Hawaii, Lisa Madigan of Illinois, Steve Carter of Indiana, Phill Kline of Kansas, J. Joseph Curran, Jr., of Maryland, Michael A. Cox of Michigan, Jeremiah W. (Jay) Nixon of Missouri, Mike McGrath of Montana, Wayne Stenehjem of North Dakota, W. A. Drew Edmondson of Oklahoma, Hardy Myers of Oregon, Henry D. McMaster of South Carolina, Greg Abbott of Texas, Mark L. Shurtleff of Utah, William H. Sorrell of Vermont, Jerry W. Kilgore of Virginia, and Patrick J. Crank of Wyoming.

Brief of amici curiae filed on behalf of Shashank S. Upadhye by Shashank S. Upadhye, pro se, in support of neither party.

IV. THE SUPREME COURT'S DECISION

"In Belton, an officer overtook a speeding vehicle on the New York Thruway and ordered its driver to pull over. Suspecting that the occupants possessed marijuana, the officer directed them to get out of the car and arrested them for unlawful possession. He searched them and then searched the passenger compartment of the car. We considered the constitutionally permissible scope of a search in these circumstances and sought to lay down a workable rule governing that situation. . . .

We therefore held that 'when a policeman has made a lawful

custodial arrest of the occupant of an automobile, he may, as a contemporaneous incident of that arrest, search the passenger compartment of that automobile.' . . .

In all relevant aspects, the arrest of a suspect who is next to a vehicle presents identical concerns regarding officer safety and the destruction of evidence as the arrest of one who is inside the vehicle. An officer may search a suspect's vehicle under Belton only if the suspect is arrested. A custodial arrest is fluid and '[t]he danger to the police officer flows from the fact of the arrest, and its attendant proximity, stress, and uncertainty.' . . . The stress is no less merely because the arrestee exited his car before the officer initiated contact, nor is an arrestee less likely to attempt to lunge for a weapon or to destroy evidence if he is outside of, but still in control of, the vehicle. In either case, the officer faces a highly volatile situation. It would make little sense to apply two different rules to what is, at bottom, the same situation. . . .

So long as an arrestee is the sort of 'recent occupant' of a vehicle such as petitioner was here, officers may search that vehicle incident to the arrest.

The judgment of the Court of Appeals is affirmed."

V. JUSTICE VOTE

2 Pro ACLU Side vs. 7 Con Opposing Side

ACLU Side (Petitioner / Appellant)

1. Stevens, J. – Wrote dissenting opinion
2. Souter, D. – Joined Stevens' dissent

Opposing Side (Respondent / Appellee)

1. Rehnquist, W. – Wrote majority opinion
2. Thomas, C. – Joined majority opinion
3. Kennedy, A. – Joined majority opinion
4. Breyer, S. – Joined majority opinion
5. O'Connor, S. – Wrote opinion concurring in part
6. Ginsburg, R. – Joined Scalia's concurrence
7. Scalia, A. – Wrote concurring opinion

VI. A WIN OR LOSS FOR THE ACLU?

The ACLU filed as amicus curiae urging reversal of the judgment of the Court of Appeals; the Supreme Court affirmed in a 7-2 vote, giving the ACLU an apparent loss.

962. Elk Grove United School District v. Newdow

(Decided June 14, 2004; 542 U.S. 1)

I. ISSUE

A. Issues Discussed

1st Amendment, religion

B. Legal Question Presented

"[W]hether Newdow has standing to invoke the jurisdiction of the federal courts" on a First Amendment challenge to daily recitation of the Pledge of Allegiance in a public school classroom, including the phrase "under God."

C. Supreme Court's Answer

"We conclude that Newdow lacks standing and therefore reverse the Court of Appeals' decision."

II. CASE SUMMARY

A. Background

"Each day elementary school teachers in the Elk Grove Unified School District (School District) lead their classes in a group recitation of the Pledge of Allegiance. Respondent, Michael A. Newdow, is an atheist whose daughter participates in that daily exercise. Because the Pledge contains the words 'under God,' he views the School District's policy as a religious indoctrination of his child that violates the First Amendment. A divided panel of the Court of Appeals for the Ninth Circuit agreed with Newdow."

The Supreme Court granted certiorari to review the case.

B. Counsel of Record

ACLU Side (Respondent / Appellee): Michael A. Newdow, pro se, argued the cause and filed a brief as appellee.

Opposing Side (Petitioner / Appellant): Terence J. Cassidy argued the cause for appellants. With him on the briefs was Michael W. Pott.

Solicitor General Olson argued the cause for the United States as appellee under this Court's Rule 12.6 in support of appellants. With him on the briefs were Assistant Attorney General Keisler, Deputy Solicitor General Clement, Deputy Assistant Attorney General Katsas, Patricia A. Millett, Robert M. Loeb, Lowell V. Sturgill, and Sushma Soni.

III. AMICI CURIAE

ACLU Side (Respondent / Appellee)

Brief of amici curiae filed on behalf of Americans United for Separation of Church and State, American Civil Liberties Union, and Americans for Religious Liberty by David H. Remes, Ayesha Khan, Steven R. Shapiro, Karin L. Kizer, Vijay Shanker, Ruth K. Miller, Matthew K. Handley, Noah B. Monick, Jason M. Knott, Fuad Rana, and Jenny R. Silverman.

Brief of amici curiae filed on behalf of American Atheists by Paul Sanford.

Brief of amici curiae filed on behalf of the American Humanist Association et al. by Elizabeth L. Hileman.

Brief of amici curiae filed on behalf of the Anti-Defamation League by Martin E. Karlinsky, Martin S. Lederman, Steven M. Freeman, Michael Lieberman, Frederick M. Lawrence, Howard W. Goldstein, and Erwin Chemerinsky.

Brief of amici curiae filed on behalf of Associated Pantheist Groups by Michael C. Worsham and Dov M. Szego.

Brief of amici curiae filed on behalf of Atheists for Human Rights by Jerold M. Gorski.

Brief of amici curiae filed on behalf of Buddhist Temples et al. by Kenneth R. Pierce.

Brief of amici curiae filed on behalf of the Church of Freethought by Keith Alan.

Brief of amici curiae filed on behalf of the Council for Secular Humanism by Edward Tabash.

Brief of amici curiae filed on behalf of the Freedom from Religion Foundation, Inc., by Robert Reitano Tiernan.
Brief of amici curiae filed on behalf of Historians and Law Scholars by Steven K. Green and Steven G. Gey.
Brief of amici curiae filed on behalf of Religious Scholars and Theologians by Peter Irons.
Brief of amici curiae filed on behalf of Rob Sherman Advocacy by Richard D. Grossman.
Brief of amici curiae filed on behalf of Seattle Atheists et al. by Gary D. Borek.
Brief of amici curiae filed on behalf of United Fathers of America et al. by Mr. Gorski.
Brief of amici curiae filed on behalf of Rev. Dr. Betty Jane Bailey et al. by Douglas Laycock.
Brief of amici curiae filed on behalf of Christopher L. Eisgruber et al. by Lawrence G. Sager.
Brief of amici curiae filed on behalf of Barbara A. McGraw by Ms. McGraw, pro se.
Brief of amici curiae filed on behalf of Atheists and other Freethinkers by Dean Robert Johansson.
Brief of amici curiae filed on behalf of Mister Thorne by Ronald K. Losch.
Brief of amici curiae filed on behalf of the Atheist Law Center by Pamela L. Sumners and Larry Darby.
Brief of amici curiae filed on behalf of Joseph R. Grodin by Neal Katyal and Richard A. Epstein in support of neither party.

Opposing Side (Petitioner / Appellant)

Brief of amici curiae filed on behalf of the State of Texas et al. by Greg Abbott, Attorney General of Texas, R. Ted Cruz, Solicitor General, Barry R. McBee, First Assistant Attorney General, Edward D. Burbach and Don R. Willett, Deputy Attorneys General, Peter C. Harvey, Acting Attorney General of New Jersey, and Gerald J. Pappert, Acting Attorney General of Pennsylvania, and by the Attorneys General for their respective States as follows: William H. Pryor, Jr., of Alabama, Gregg D. Renkes of Alaska, Terry Goddard of Arizona, Mike Beebe of Arkansas, Bill Lockyer of California, Ken Salazar of Colorado, Richard Blumenthal of Connecticut, M. Jane Brady of Delaware, Charles J. Crist, Jr., of Florida, Thurbert E. Baker of Georgia, Mark J. Bennett of Hawaii, Lawrence G. Wasden of Idaho, Lisa Madigan of Illinois, Steve Carter of Indiana, Thomas J. Miller of Iowa, Phill Kline of Kansas, A. B. "Ben" Chandler of Kentucky, Richard P. Ieyoub of Louisiana, G. Steven Rowe of Maine, J. Joseph Curran, Jr., of Maryland, Thomas F. Reilly of Massachusetts, Michael A. Cox of Michigan, Mike Hatch of Minnesota, Mike Moore of Mississippi, Jeremiah W. "Jay" Nixon of Missouri, Mike McGrath of Montana, Jon Bruning of Nebraska, Brian Sandoval of Nevada, Peter W. Heed of New Hampshire, Patricia A. Madrid of New Mexico, Eliot Spitzer of New York, Roy Cooper of North Carolina, Wayne Stenehjem of North Dakota, Jim Petro of Ohio, W. A. Drew Edmondson of Oklahoma, Hardy Myers of Oregon, Patrick C. Lynch of Rhode Island, Henry McMaster of South Carolina, Lawrence E. Long of South Dakota, Paul G. Summers of Tennessee, Mark L. Shurtleff of Utah, William H. Sorrell of Vermont, Jerry W. Kilgore of Virginia, Christine O. Gregoire of Washington, Darrell V. McGraw, Jr., of West Virginia, Peg Lautenschlager of Wisconsin, and Patrick J. Crank of Wyoming.
Brief of amici curiae filed on behalf of the American Civil Rights Union by John C. Armor and Peter Ferrara.
Brief of amici curiae filed on behalf of the American Jewish Congress by Marc D. Stern and Norman Redlich.
Brief of amici curiae filed on behalf of the American Legion by Eric L. Hirschhorn and Philip B. Onderdonk, Jr.
Brief of amici curiae filed on behalf of the Bipartisan Legal Advisory Group of the United States House of Representatives by Geraldine R. Gennet, Kerry W. Kircher, and Michael L. Stern.
Brief of amici curiae filed on behalf of the Catholic League for Religious and Civil Rights et al. by Edward L. White III and Charles S. LiMandri.
Brief of amici curiae filed on behalf of the Center for Individual Freedom by Renee L. Giachino.
Brief of amici curiae filed on behalf of the Christian Legal Society et al. by Gregory S. Baylor, Kimberlee Wood Colby, and Stuart J. Lark.
Brief of amici curiae filed on behalf of Citizens United Foundation by William J. Olson and John S. Miles.
Brief of amici curiae filed on behalf of the Claremont Institute Center for Constitutional Jurisprudence by John C. Eastman, Edwin Meese III, and Phillip J. Griego.
Brief of amici curiae filed on behalf of Focus on the Family et al. by Benjamin W. Bull, Jordan W. Lorence, Kevin H. Theriot, Robert H. Tyler, and Patrick A. Trueman.
Brief of amici curiae filed on behalf of Grassfire.net by John G. Stepanovich.
Brief of amici curiae filed on behalf of the Institute in Basic Life Principles et al. by Bernard P. Reese, Jr.
Brief of amici curiae filed on behalf of the Knights of Columbus by Kevin J. Hasson, Anthony R. Picarello, Jr., Roman P. Storzer, Carl A. Anderson, Paul R. Devin, and Robert A. Destro.
Brief of amici curiae filed on behalf of Liberty Counsel et al. by Mathew D. Staver and Rena M. Lindevaldsen.
Brief of amici curiae filed on behalf of the National Education Association by Robert H. Chanin and Jeremiah A. Collins.
Brief of amici curiae filed on behalf of the National Jewish Commission on Law and Public Affairs by Nathan Lewin, Alyza D. Lewin, Dennis Rapps, David Zwiebel, and Richard B. Stone.
Brief of amici curiae filed on behalf of the National Lawyers Association Foundation by Dennis Owens and Robert C. Cannada.
Brief of amici curiae filed on behalf of the National School Boards Association by Lisa A. Brown, Erin Glenn Busby, Julie Underwood, and Naomi Gittins.
Brief of amici curiae filed on behalf of the Pacific Justice Institute by Peter D. Lepiscopo.
Brief of amici curiae filed on behalf of the Pacific Research Institute et al. by Sharon L. Browne and Russell C. Brooks.

Brief of amici curiae filed on behalf of the Rutherford Institute by John W. Whitehead and Steven H. Aden.
Brief of amici curiae filed on behalf of the United States Senate by Patricia Mack Bryan, Morgan J. Frankel, Grant R. Vinik, and Thomas E. Caballero.
Brief of amici curiae filed on behalf of Wallbuilders, Inc., by Barry C. Hodge.
Brief of amici curiae filed on behalf of Senator George Allen et al. by Jay Alan Sekulow, Stuart J. Roth, Colby M. May, James M. Henderson, Walter M. Weber, Joel H. Thornton, John P. Tuskey, and Laura B. Hernandez.
Brief of amici curiae filed on behalf of Sandra L. Banning by Kenneth W. Starr, Robert R. Gasaway, Ashley C. Parrish, Stephen W. Parrish, and Paul E. Sullivan.
Brief of amici curiae filed on behalf of Senator John Cornyn et al. by Mr. Cornyn, pro se.
Brief of amici curiae filed on behalf of Idaho Governor Dirk Kempthorne et al. by L. Michael Bogert and David F. Hensley.
Brief of amici curiae filed on behalf of Congressman Ron Paul et al. by Richard D. Ackerman and Gary G. Kreep.
Brief of amici curiae filed on behalf of the Common Good Foundation et al. by Keith A. Fournier and John G. Stepanovich.
Brief of amici curiae filed on behalf of Thurston Greene by Mr. Greene, pro se.

IV. THE SUPREME COURT'S DECISION

"The Pledge of Allegiance was initially conceived more than a century ago. . . .

In 1942, in the midst of World War II, Congress adopted, and the President signed, a Joint Resolution . . . .

This resolution, which marked the first appearance of the Pledge of Allegiance in positive law, confirmed the importance of the flag as a symbol of our Nation's indivisibility and commitment to the concept of liberty.

Congress revisited the Pledge of Allegiance 12 years later when it amended the text to add the words 'under God.' The House Report that accompanied the legislation observed that, '[f]rom the time of our earliest history our peoples and our institutions have reflected the traditional concept that our Nation was founded on a fundamental belief in God.' The resulting text is the Pledge as we know it today: 'I pledge allegiance to the Flag of the United States of America, and to the Republic for which it stands, one Nation under God, indivisible, with liberty and justice for all.' . . .

Under California law, 'every public elementary school' must begin each day with 'appropriate patriotic exercises.' The statute provides that '[t]he giving of the Pledge of Allegiance to the Flag of the United States of America shall satisfy' this requirement. The Elk Grove Unified School District has implemented the state law by requiring that '[e]ach elementary school class recite the pledge of allegiance to the flag once each day.' Consistent with our case law, the School District permits students who object on religious grounds to abstain from the recitation. . . .

The complaint seeks a declaration that the 1954 Act's addition of the words 'under God' violated the Establishment and Free Exercise Clauses of the United States Constitution, as well as an injunction against the School District's policy requiring daily recitation of the Pledge. It alleges that Newdow has standing to sue on his own behalf and on behalf of his daughter as 'next friend.' . . .

After the Court of Appeals' initial opinion was announced, Sandra Banning, the mother of Newdow's daughter, filed a motion for leave to intervene, or alternatively to dismiss the complaint. She declared that although she and Newdow shared 'physical custody' of their daughter, a state-court order granted her 'exclusive legal custody' of the child, 'including the sole right to represent [the daughter's] legal interests and make all decision[s] about her education' and welfare. Banning further stated that her daughter is a Christian who believes in God and has no objection either to reciting or hearing others recite the Pledge of Allegiance, or to its reference to God. Banning expressed the belief that her daughter would be harmed if the litigation were permitted to proceed, because others might incorrectly perceive the child as sharing her father's atheist views. Banning accordingly concluded, as her daughter's sole legal custodian, that it was not in the child's interest to be a party to Newdow's lawsuit. On September 25, 2002, the California Superior Court entered an order enjoining Newdow from including his daughter as an unnamed party or suing as her 'next friend.' That order did not purport to answer the question of Newdow's Article III standing.

In a second published opinion, the Court of Appeals reconsidered Newdow's standing in light of Banning's motion. The court noted that Newdow no longer claimed to represent his daughter, but unanimously concluded that 'the grant of sole legal custody to Banning' did not deprive Newdow, 'as a noncustodial parent, of Article III standing to object to unconstitutional government action affecting his child.' . . .

On February 28, 2003, the Court of Appeals issued an order amending its first opinion and denying rehearing en banc. . . .

In every federal case, the party bringing the suit must establish standing to prosecute the action. . . .

The command to guard jealously and exercise rarely our power to make constitutional pronouncements requires strictest adherence when matters of great national significance are at stake. . . .

Consistent with these principles, our standing jurisprudence contains two strands: Article III standing, which enforces the Constitution's case-or-controversy requirement, and prudential standing, which embodies 'judicially self-imposed limits on the exercise of federal jurisdiction.' . . .

One of the principal areas in which this Court has customarily declined to intervene is the realm of domestic relations. . . .

[T]he extent of the standing problem raised by the domestic relations issues in this case was not apparent until August 5, 2002, when Banning filed her motion for leave to intervene or dismiss the complaint following the Court of Appeals' initial decision. . . .

Newdow's parental status is defined by California's domestic relations law. Our custom on questions of state law ordinarily is to defer to the interpretation of the Court of Appeals for the Circuit in which the State is located. In this case, the Court of Appeals, which possesses greater familiarity with California law, concluded that state law vests in Newdow a cognizable right to influence his daughter's religious upbringing. . . .

Nothing that either Banning or the School Board has done, however, impairs Newdow's right to instruct his daughter in his religious views. Instead, Newdow requests relief that is more ambitious . . . . The California cases simply do not stand for the proposition that Newdow has a right to dictate to others what they may and may not say to his child respecting religion. . . .

In our view, it is improper for the federal courts to entertain a claim by a plaintiff whose standing to sue is founded on family law rights that are in dispute when prosecution of the lawsuit may have an adverse effect on the person who is the source of the plaintiff's claimed standing. When hard questions of domestic relations are sure to affect the outcome, the prudent course is for the federal court to stay its hand rather than reach out to resolve a weighty question of federal constitutional law. . . . We conclude that, having been deprived under California law of the right to sue as next friend, Newdow lacks prudential standing to bring this suit in federal court.

The judgment of the Court of Appeals is reversed."

V. JUSTICE VOTE

0 Pro ACLU Side vs. 8 Con Opposing Side

Opposing Side (Petitioner / Appellant)

1. Stevens, J. – Wrote majority opinion
2. Thomas, C. – Joined Rehnquist's opinion in part, wrote concurring opinion
3. Ginsburg, R. – Joined majority opinion
4. Souter, D. – Joined majority opinion
5. O'Connor, S. – Joined Rehnquist's opinion, wrote concurring opinion
6. Breyer, S. – Joined majority opinion
7. Kennedy, A. – Joined majority opinion
8. Rehnquist, W. – Wrote concurring opinion
9. Scalia A – Took no part in the decision.

V. A WIASHCRON OR LOSS FOR THE ACLU?

The ACLU filed as amicus curiae urging affirmance; the Supreme Court reversed the Court of Appeals' decision by an 8-0 vote, giving the ACLU an apparent loss.

963. Hibbs v. Winn

(Decided June 14, 2004; 542 U.S. 88)

I. ISSUE

A. Issues Discussed

1st Amendment, religion

B. Legal Question Presented

"[W]hether the Tax Injunction Act (TIA or Act), 28 U.S.C. § 1341, which prohibits a lower federal court from restraining 'the assessment, levy or collection of any tax under State law,' bars the suit."

C. Supreme Court's Answer

"Their suit, we hold, is not the kind § 1341 proscribes."

II. CASE SUMMARY

A. Background

"Plaintiffs-respondents, Arizona taxpayers, filed suit in the United States District Court for the District of Arizona, challenging Ariz.Rev.Stat. Ann. § 43–1089 as incompatible with the Establishment Clause. Section 43–1089 provides a credit to taxpayers who contribute money to 'school tuition organizations' (STOs). An STO is a nonprofit organization that directs moneys, in the form of scholarship grants, to students enrolled in private elementary or secondary schools. . . . When taxpayers donate money to a qualified STO, § 43–1089 allows them, in calculating their Arizona tax liability, to credit up to $500 of their donation (or $625 for a married couple filing jointly, § 43–1089(A)(2)).

In effect, § 43–1089 gives Arizona taxpayers an election. They may direct $500 (or, for joint-return filers, $625) to an STO, or to the Arizona Department of Revenue. As long as donors do not give STOs more than their total tax liability, their $500 or $625 contributions are costless.

The Arizona Supreme Court, by a 3–to–2 vote, rejected a facial challenge to § 43–1089 before the statute went into effect. . . .

Respondents' federal-court complaint . . . alleged that § 43–1089 'authorizes the formation of agencies that have as their sole purpose the distribution of State funds to children of a particular religious denomination or to children attending schools of a particular religious denomination.' Respondents sought injunctive and declaratory relief, and an order requiring STOs to pay funds still in their possession 'into the state general fund.'

[T]he District Court held that the TIA required dismissal of the suit.

The Court of Appeals for the Ninth Circuit reversed . . . ."

The Supreme Court granted certiorari to review the case.

B. Counsel of Record

ACLU Side (Respondent / Appellee): Marvin S. Cohen argued the cause for appellees. With him on the brief were Paul Bender, Isabel Humphrey, and Steven R. Shapiro of the American Civil Liberties Union Foundation.

Opposing Side (Petitioner / Appellant): Terry Goddard, Attorney General of Arizona, argued the cause for appellant. With him on the briefs were Mary O'Grady, Solicitor General, Paula S. Bickett, and Joseph Kanefield, Special Assistant Attorney General.

Deputy Solicitor General Hungar argued the cause for the United States as amicus curiae.

III. AMICI CURIAE

ACLU Side (Respondent / Appellee)

Brief of amici curiae filed on behalf of the NAACP Legal Defense & Educational Fund, Inc., by Elaine R. Jones, Theodore M. Shaw, and Norman J. Chachkin.

Brief of amici curiae filed on behalf of Americans United for Separation of Church and State et al. by Ayesha N. Khan, Elliot M. Mincberg, and Judith E. Schaeffer.

Opposing Side (Petitioner / Appellant)

Brief of amici curiae filed on behalf of the United States by Deputy Solicitor General Hungar, Solicitor General Olson,

Assistant Attorney General O'Connor, Kent L. Jones, and Kenneth L. Greene.

Brief of amici curiae filed on behalf of the State of California et al. by Bill Lockyer, Attorney General of California, Manuel M. Mederios, State Solicitor General, Andrea Lynn Hoch, Chief Assistant Attorney General, David S. Chaney, Senior Assistant Attorney General, Randall P. Borcherding, Supervising Deputy Attorney General, Kristian D. Whitten, Deputy Attorney General, and Anabelle Rodríguez, Secretary of Justice of Puerto Rico, and by the Attorneys General for their respective jurisdictions as follows: William H. Pryor, Jr., of Alabama, Gregg D. Renkes of Alaska, Mike Beebe of Arkansas, Ken Salazar of Colorado, M. Jane Brady of Delaware, Charles J. Crist, Jr., of Florida, Thurbert E. Baker of Georgia, Douglas B. Moylan of Guam, Mark J. Bennett of Hawaii, Lawrence G. Wasden of Idaho, Lisa Madigan of Illinois, Steve Carter of Indiana, Thomas J. Miller of Iowa, Richard P. Ieyoub of Louisiana, Steven Rowe of Maine, J. Joseph Curran, Jr., of Maryland, Thomas F. Reilly of Massachusetts, Michael A. Cox of Michigan, Mike Moore of Mississippi, Jeremiah W. (Jay) Nixon of Missouri, Mike McGrath of Montana, Brian Sandoval of Nevada, Peter W. Heed of New Hampshire, Peter C. Harvey of New Jersey, Patricia A. Madrid of New Mexico, Eliot Spitzer of New York, Wayne Stenehjem of North Dakota, Jim Petro of Ohio, Hardy Myers of Oregon, D. Michael Fisher of Pennsylvania, Patrick C. Lynch of Rhode Island, Henry McMaster of South Carolina, Lawrence E. Long of South Dakota, Paul G. Summers of Tennessee, Greg Abbott of Texas, Mark L. Shurtleff of Utah, Jerry W. Kilgore of Virginia, Christine O. Gregoire of Washington, Darrell V. McGraw, Jr., of West Virginia, and Peggy A. Lautenschlager of Wisconsin.

Brief of amici curiae filed on behalf of the Council of State Governments et al. by Richard Ruda and James I. Crowley.

Brief of amici curiae filed on behalf of the Honorable Trent Franks et al. by Benjamin W. Bull.

IV. THE SUPREME COURT'S DECISION

"Arizona law authorizes income-tax credits for payments to organizations that award educational scholarships and tuition grants to children attending private schools. Plaintiffs below, respondents here, brought an action in federal court challenging § 43–1089, and seeking to enjoin its operation, on Establishment Clause grounds. . . .

In decisions spanning a near half century, courts in the federal system, including this Court, have entertained challenges to tax credits authorized by state law, without conceiving of § 1341 as a jurisdictional barrier. On this first occasion squarely to confront the issue, we confirm the authority federal courts exercised in those cases. . . .

We examine in this opinion both the scope of the term 'assessment' as used in the TIA, and the question whether the Act was intended to insulate state tax laws from constitutional challenge in lower federal courts even when the suit would have no negative impact on tax collection. Concluding that this suit implicates neither § 1341's conception of assessment nor any of the statute's underlying purposes, we affirm the judgment of the Court of Appeals. . . .

To determine whether this litigation falls within the TIA's prohibition, it is appropriate, first, to identify the relief sought. Respondents seek prospective relief only. . . . Taking account of the prospective nature of the relief requested, does respondents' suit, in 28 U.S.C. § 1341's words, seek to 'enjoin, suspend or restrain the assessment, levy or collection of any tax under State law'? The answer to that question turns on the meaning of the term 'assessment' as employed in the TIA. . . .

The Government did not describe the term as synonymous with the entire plan of taxation. Nor did it disassociate the word 'assessment' from the company ('levy or collection') that word keeps. Instead, and in accord with our understanding, the Government related 'assessment' to the term's collection-propelling function. . . .

In sum, this Court has interpreted and applied the TIA only in cases Congress wrote the Act to address, i.e., cases in which state taxpayers seek federal-court orders enabling them to avoid paying state taxes. We have read harmoniously the § 1341 instruction conditioning the jurisdictional bar on the availability of 'a plain, speedy and efficient remedy in state court. The remedy inspected in our decisions was not one designed for the universe of plaintiffs who sue the State. Rather, it was a remedy tailormade for taxpayers. . . .

In other federal courts as well, § 1341 has been read to restrain state taxpayers from instituting federal actions to contest their liability for state taxes, but not to stop third parties from pursuing constitutional challenges to tax benefits in a federal forum. . . .

Further, numerous federal-court decisions—including decisions of this Court reviewing lower federal-court judgments—have reached the merits of third-party constitutional challenges to tax benefits without mentioning the TIA. . . .

In a procession of cases not rationally distinguishable from this one, no Justice or member of the bar of this Court ever raised a § 1341 objection that, according to the petitioner in this case, should have caused us to order dismissal of the action for want of jurisdiction. . . . Consistent with the decades-long understanding prevailing on this issue, respondents' suit may proceed without any TIA impediment.

For the reasons stated, the judgment of the United States Court of Appeals for the Ninth Circuit is affirmed."

V. JUSTICE VOTE

5 Pro ACLU Side vs. 4 Con Opposing Side

ACLU Side (Respondent / Appellee)

1. Ginsburg, R. – Wrote majority opinion
2. Stevens, J. – Wrote concurring opinion
3. O'Connor, R. – Joined majority opinion
4. Breyer, S. – Joined majority opinion
6. Souter, D. – Joined majority opinion

Opposing Side (Petitioner / Appellant)

1. Kennedy, A. – Wrote dissenting opinion
2. Thomas, C. – Joined Kennedy's dissent
3. Scalia, A. – Joined Kennedy's dissent
4. Rehnquist, W. – Joined Kennedy's dissent

VI. A WIN OR LOSS FOR THE ACLU?

The ACLU argued the case for appellee, urging affirmance; the Supreme Court affirmed the Court of Appeals' decision by a 5-4 vote, giving the ACLU an apparent win.

964. Pennsylvania State Police v. Suders

(Decided June 14, 2004; 542 U.S. 129)

I. ISSUE

A. Issues Discussed

Civil rights, gender

B. Legal Question Presented

"[W]hether a constructive discharge brought about by supervisor harassment ranks as a tangible employment action and therefore precludes assertion of the affirmative defense articulated in Ellerth and Faragher."

C. Supreme Court's Answer

"We conclude that an employer does not have recourse to the Ellerth/Faragher affirmative defense when a supervisor's official act precipitates the constructive discharge; absent such a 'tangible employment action,' however, the defense is available to the employer whose supervisors are charged with harassment."

II. CASE SUMMARY

A. Background

"In March 1998, the PSP hired Suders as a police communications operator for the McConnellsburg barracks. Suders' supervisors were Sergeant Eric D. Easton, Station Commander at the McConnellsburg barracks, Patrol Corporal William D. Baker, and Corporal Eric B. Prendergast. Those three supervisors subjected Suders to a continuous barrage of sexual harassment that ceased only when she resigned from the force. . . .

In September 2000, Suders sued the PSP in Federal District Court, alleging, inter alia, that she had been subjected to sexual harassment and constructively discharged, in violation of Title VII of the Civil Rights Act of 1964. At the close of discovery, the District Court granted the PSP's motion for summary judgment. Suders' testimony, the District Court recognized, sufficed to permit a trier of fact to conclude that the supervisors had created a hostile work environment. The court nevertheless held that the PSP was not vicariously liable for the supervisors' conduct. . . .

The Court of Appeals for the Third Circuit reversed and remanded the case for disposition on the merits."

The Supreme Court granted certiorari to review the case.

B. Counsel of Record

ACLU Side (Respondent / Appellee): Donald A. Bailey argued the cause and filed a brief for appellee.

Opposing Side (Petitioner / Appellant): John G. Knorr III, Chief Deputy Attorney General of Pennsylvania, argued the cause for appellant. With him on the briefs were Gerald J. Pappert, Acting Attorney General, and Howard G. Hopkirk and Sarah C. Yerger, Deputy Attorneys General.

Irving L. Gornstein argued the cause for the United States as amicus curiae.

III. AMICI CURIAE

ACLU Side (Respondent / Appellee)

Brief of amici curiae filed on behalf of the Lawyers' Committee for Civil Rights Under Law, AARP, the American Civil Liberties Union Foundation, the Legal Aid Society — Employment Law Center, the National Asian Pacific American Legal Consortium, the National Association for the Advancement of Colored People, the National Employment Lawyers Association, the National Partnership for Women and Families, the National Women's Law Center, and NOW Legal Defense and Education Fund by Barbara R. Arnwine, Thomas J. Henderson, Michael L. Foreman, Sarah C. Crawford, Audrey Wiggins, Susan Grover, Patricia Roberts, Daniel B. Kohrman, Laurie A. McCann, Thomas Osborne, Melvin Radowitz, Steven R. Shapiro, Lenora M. Lapidus, Jennifer Arnett, Patricia A. Shiu, Claudia Center, Dennis C. Hayes, Janette Wipper, Angela Dalfen, Vincent A. Eng, Judith L. Lichtman, Jocelyn C. Frye, Queyen L. Ta, Jocelyn Samuels, Dina R. Lassow, and Jennifer K. Brown.

Brief of amici curiae filed on behalf of the American Federation of Labor and Congress of Industrial Organizations by Jonathan P. Hiatt, James B. Coppess, and Laurence Gold.

Opposing Side (Petitioner / Appellant)

Brief of amici curiae filed on behalf of the United States by Irving L. Gornstein, Solicitor General Olson, Assistant Attorney General Acosta, Deputy Solicitor General Clement, Eric S. Dreiband, and Lorraine C. Davis.

Brief of amici curiae filed on behalf of the Chamber of Commerce of the United States by Peter Buscemi, Harry A. Rissetto, Stephen A. Bokat, and Robin S. Conrad.

Brief of amici curiae filed on behalf of the Equal Employment Advisory Council by Ann Elizabeth Reesman and Katherine Y. K. Cheung.

Brief of amici curiae filed on behalf of the Society for Human Resource Management by Allan H. Weitzman, Sarah A. Mindes, Edward Cerasia II, Lawrence Z. Lorber, and Paul Salvatore

IV. THE SUPREME COURT'S DECISION

"Under the constructive discharge doctrine, an employee's reasonable decision to resign because of unendurable working conditions is assimilated to a formal discharge for remedial purposes. . . . The inquiry is objective: Did working conditions become so intolerable that a reasonable person in the employee's position would have felt compelled to resign? . . .

We agree with the lower courts and the EEOC that Title VII encompasses employer liability for a constructive discharge. . . .

This case concerns an employer's liability for one subset of Title VII constructive discharge claims: constructive discharge resulting from sexual harassment, or 'hostile work environment,' attributable to a supervisor. Our starting point is the framework Ellerth and Faragher established to govern employer liability for sexual harassment by supervisors. [T]hose decisions delineate two categories of hostile work environment claims: (1) harassment that 'culminates in a tangible employment action,' for which employers are strictly liable, and (2) harassment that takes place in the absence of a tangible employment action, to which employers may assert an affirmative defense. With the background set out above in mind, we turn to the key issues here at stake: Into which Ellerth/Faragher category do hostile-environment constructive discharge claims fall-and what proof burdens do the parties bear in such cases. . . .

The constructive discharge here at issue stems from, and can be regarded as an aggravated case of, sexual harassment or hostile work environment. . . .

In its summation, the Third Circuit qualified its holding that a constructive discharge itself 'constitutes a tangible employment action within the meaning of Ellerth and Faragher.' The affirmative defense Ellerth and Faragher delineated, the court said, might be imported into the anterior issue whether 'the employee's decision to resign was reasonable under the circumstances.' . . .

The Third Circuit left open when and how the Ellerth/Faragher considerations would be brought home to the fact trier. . . .

We see no cause for leaving the district courts thus unguided. Following Ellerth and Faragher, the plaintiff who alleges no tangible employment action has the duty to mitigate harm, but the defendant bears the burden to allege and prove that the plaintiff failed in that regard. The plaintiff might elect to allege facts relevant to mitigation in her pleading or to present those facts in her case in chief, but she would do so in anticipation of the employer's affirmative defense, not as a legal requirement. . . .

We agree with the Third Circuit that the case, in its current posture, presents genuine issues of material fact concerning Suders' hostile work environment and constructive discharge claims. We hold, however, that the Court of Appeals erred in declaring the affirmative defense described in Ellerth and Faragher never available in constructive discharge cases. Accordingly, we vacate the Third Circuit's judgment and remand the case for further proceedings consistent with this opinion."

V. JUSTICE VOTE

1 Pro ACLU Side vs. 8 Con Opposing Side

ACLU Side (Respondent / Appellee)

1. Thomas, C. – Wrote dissenting opinion

Opposing Side (Petitioner / Appellant)

1. Ginsburg, R. – Wrote majority opinion
2. Souter, D. – Joined majority opinion
3. O'Connor, S. – Joined majority opinion
4. Stevens, J. – Joined majority opinion
5. Breyer, S. – Joined majority opinion
6. Scalia, A. – Joined majority opinion
7. Kennedy, A. – Joined majority opinion
8. Rehnquist, W. – Joined majority opinion

VI. A WIN OR LOSS FOR THE ACLU?

The ACLU filed as amicus curiae urging affirmance; the Supreme Court vacated the Court of Appeals' decision by an 8-1 vote, giving the ACLU an apparent loss.

965. Hiibel v. Sixth Judicial District Court of Nevada, Humboldt County

(Decided June 21, 2004; 542 U.S. 177)

I. ISSUE

A. Issues Discussed

4th Amendment, criminal procedure

B. Legal Question Presented

Whether Nevada's "stop and identify" statute violates "the Fourth and Fifth Amendments to the United States Constitution, applicable to the States through the Fourteenth Amendment" as applied to petitioner.

C. Supreme Court's Answer

The statute complies with the Fourth and Fifth Amendments as applied to petitioner.

II. CASE SUMMARY

A. Background

"The sheriff's department in Humboldt County, Nevada, received an afternoon telephone call reporting an assault. The caller reported seeing a man assault a woman in a red and silver GMC truck on Grass Valley Road. Deputy Sheriff Lee Dove was dispatched to investigate. When the officer arrived at the scene, he found the truck parked on the side of the road. A man was standing by the truck, and a young woman was sitting inside it. The officer observed skid marks in the gravel behind the vehicle, leading him to believe it had come to a sudden stop.

The officer approached the man and explained that he was investigating a report of a fight. The man appeared to be intoxicated. The officer asked him if he had 'any identification on [him]' . . . . After continued refusals to comply with the officer's request for identification, the man began to taunt the officer by placing his hands behind his back and telling the officer to arrest him and take him to jail. . . . After warning the man that he would be arrested if he continued to refuse to comply, the officer placed him under arrest.

We now know that the man arrested on Grass Valley Road is Larry Dudley Hiibel. Hiibel was charged with 'willfully resist[ing], delay[ing] or obstruct [ing] a public officer in discharging or attempting to discharge any legal duty of his office' in violation of Nev.Rev.Stat. (NRS) § 199.280 (2003). . . .

Hiibel was tried in the Justice Court of Union Township. The court agreed that Hiibel's refusal to identify himself as required by § 171.123 'obstructed and delayed Dove as a public officer in attempting to discharge his duty' in violation of § 199.280. Hiibel was convicted and fined $250. The Sixth Judicial District Court affirmed, rejecting Hiibel's argument that the application of

§ 171.123 to his case violated the Fourth and Fifth Amendments. On review the Supreme Court of Nevada rejected the Fourth Amendment challenge in a divided opinion. Hiibel petitioned for rehearing, seeking explicit resolution of his Fifth Amendment challenge. The petition was denied without opinion."

The Supreme Court granted certiorari to review the case.

B. Counsel of Record

ACLU Side (Petitioner / Appellant): Robert E. Dolan argued the cause for appellant. With him on the briefs were James P. Logan, Jr., and Harriet E. Cummings.

Opposing Side (Respondent / Appellee): Conrad Hafen, Senior Deputy Attorney General of Nevada, argued the cause for appellees. With him on the brief were Brian Sandoval, Attorney General, and David Allison.

Sri Srinivasan argued the cause for the United States as amicus curiae.

III. AMICI CURIAE

ACLU Side (Petitioner / Appellant)

Brief of amici curiae filed on behalf of the American Civil Liberties Union by Steven R. Shapiro, Lawrence S. Lustberg, Jennifer Ching, and Mark A. Berman.

Brief of amici curiae filed on behalf of the Cato Institute by Timothy Lynch and M. Christine Klein.

Brief of amici curiae filed on behalf of the National Law Center on Homelessness & Poverty et al. by Carter G. Phillips, Edward R. McNicholas, and Rebecca K. Troth.

Brief of amici curiae filed on behalf of John Gilmore by James P. Harrison.

Brief of amici curiae filed on behalf of the Electronic Frontier Foundation by Robert Weisberg.

Brief of amici curiae filed on behalf of PrivacyActivism et al. by William M. Simpich.

Opposing Side (Respondent / Appellee)

Brief of amici curiae filed on behalf of the United States by Sri Srinivasan, Solicitor General Olson, Assistant Attorney General Wray, Deputy Solicitor General Dreeben, and Joel M. Gershowitz.

Brief of amici curiae filed on behalf of the Criminal Justice Legal Foundation by Kent S. Scheidegger and Charles L. Hobson.

Brief of amici curiae filed on behalf of the National Association of Police Organizations by Joel D. Bertocchi and Philip Allen Lacovara.

Brief of amici curiae filed on behalf of the Electronic Privacy Information Center et al. by Marc Rotenberg and David L. Sobel in support of neither party.

IV. THE SUPREME COURT'S DECISION

"NRS § 171.123(3) is an enactment sometimes referred to as a 'stop and identify' statute. . . .

Hiibel argues that his conviction cannot stand because the officer's conduct violated his Fourth Amendment rights. We disagree.

The principles of Terry permit a State to require a suspect to disclose his name in the course of a Terry stop. The reasonableness of a seizure under the Fourth Amendment is determined 'by balancing its intrusion on the individual's Fourth Amendment interests against its promotion of legitimate government interests.' The Nevada statute satisfies that standard. . . .

The stop, the request, and the State's requirement of a response did not contravene the guarantees of the Fourth Amendment. . . .

Petitioner further contends that his conviction violates the Fifth Amendment's prohibition on compelled self-incrimination. . . .

In this case petitioner's refusal to disclose his name was not based on any articulated real and appreciable fear that his name would be used to incriminate him, or that it 'would furnish a link in the chain of evidence needed to prosecute' him. . . . While we recognize petitioner's strong belief that he should not have to disclose his identity, the Fifth Amendment does not override the Nevada Legislature's judgment to the contrary absent a reasonable belief that the disclosure would tend to incriminate him.

The narrow scope of the disclosure requirement is also important. . . . Still, a case may arise where there is a substantial allegation that furnishing identity at the time of a stop would have given the police a link in the chain of evidence needed to convict the individual of a separate offense. In that case, the court can then consider whether the privilege applies, and, if the Fifth Amendment has been violated, what remedy must follow. We need not resolve those questions here.

The judgment of the Nevada Supreme Court is affirmed."

V. JUSTICE VOTE

4 Pro ACLU Side vs. 5 Con Opposing Side

ACLU Side (Petitioner / Appellant)

1. Stevens, J. – Wrote dissenting opinion
2. Souter, D. – Joined Breyer's dissent
3. Ginsburg, R. – Joined Breyer's dissent
4. Breyer, S. – Wrote dissenting opinion

Opposing Side (Respondent / Appellee)

1. Kennedy, A. – Wrote majority opinion
2. O'Connor, S. – Joined majority opinion
3. Rehnquist, W. – Joined majority opinion
4. Thomas, C. – Joined majority opinion
5. Scalia, A. – Joined majority opinion

VI. A WIN OR LOSS FOR THE ACLU?

The ACLU filed as amicus curiae urging reversal of the judgment of the Nevada Supreme Court; the U.S. Supreme Court affirmed in a 5-4 vote, giving the ACLU an apparent loss.

966. Blakely v. Washington

(Decided June 24, 2004; 542 U.S. 296)

I. ISSUE

A. Issues Discussed

Criminal procedure

B. Legal Question Presented

"Petitioner Ralph Howard Blakely, Jr., pleaded guilty to the kidnaping of his estranged wife. The facts admitted in his plea, standing alone, supported a maximum sentence of 53 months. Pursuant to state law, the court imposed an 'exceptional' sentence of 90 months after making a judicial determination that he had acted with 'deliberate cruelty.' We consider whether this violated petitioner's Sixth Amendment right to trial by jury."

C. Supreme Court's Answer

"Because the State's sentencing procedure did not comply with the Sixth Amendment, petitioner's sentence is invalid."

II. CASE SUMMARY

A. Background

"Petitioner married his wife Yolanda in 1973. He was evidently a difficult man to live with, having been diagnosed at various times with psychological and personality disorders including paranoid schizophrenia. His wife ultimately filed for divorce. In 1998, he abducted her from their orchard home . . . binding her with duct tape and forcing her at knifepoint into a wooden box in the bed of his pickup truck. In the process, he implored her to dismiss the divorce suit and related trust proceedings.

When the couple's 13-year-old son Ralphy returned home from school, petitioner ordered him to follow in another car, threatening to harm Yolanda with a shotgun if he did not do so. Ralphy escaped and sought help when they stopped at a gas station, but petitioner continued on with Yolanda to a friend's house in Montana. He was finally arrested after the friend called the police.

The State charged petitioner with first-degree kidnaping. Upon reaching a plea agreement, however, it reduced the charge to second-degree kidnaping involving domestic violence and use of a firearm. Petitioner entered a guilty plea admitting the elements of second-degree kidnaping and the domestic-violence and firearm allegations, but no other relevant facts.

The case then proceeded to sentencing. In Washington, second-degree kidnaping is a class B felony. State law provides that '[n]o person convicted of a [class B] felony shall be punished by confinement . . . exceeding . . . a term of ten years.' Other provisions of state law, however, further limit the range of sentences a judge may impose. . . . A judge may impose a sentence above the standard range if he finds 'substantial and compelling reasons justifying an exceptional sentence.' . . . When a judge imposes an exceptional sentence, he must set forth findings of fact and conclusions of law supporting it. A reviewing court will reverse the sentence if it finds that 'under a clearly erroneous standard there is insufficient evidence in the record to support the reasons for imposing an exceptional sentence.'

Pursuant to the plea agreement, the State recommended a sentence within the standard range of 49 to 53 months. After hearing Yolanda's description of the kidnaping, however, the judge rejected the State's recommendation and imposed an exceptional sentence of 90 months—37 months beyond the standard maximum. He justified the sentence on the ground that petitioner had acted with 'deliberate cruelty,' a statutorily enumerated ground for departure in domestic-violence cases.

Faced with an unexpected increase of more than three years in his sentence, petitioner objected. The judge accordingly conducted a 3-day bench hearing featuring testimony from petitioner, Yolanda, Ralphy, a police officer, and medical experts. . . .

The judge adhered to his initial determination of deliberate cruelty.

Petitioner appealed, arguing that this sentencing procedure deprived him of his federal constitutional right to have a jury determine beyond a reasonable doubt all facts legally essential to his sentence. The State Court of Appeals affirmed . . . . The Washington Supreme Court denied discretionary review."

The Supreme Court granted certiorari to review the case.

B. Counsel of Record

ACLU Side (Petitioner / Appellant): Jeffrey L. Fisher argued the cause and filed briefs for appellant.

Opposing Side (Respondent / Appellee): John D. Knodell III argued the cause and filed a brief for appellee.

Deputy Solicitor General Dreeben argued the cause for the United States as amicus curiae.

III. AMICI CURIAE

ACLU Side (Petitioner / Appellant)

Brief of amici curiae filed on behalf of the American Civil Liberties Union and the American Civil Liberties Union of Washington by James E. Lobsenz, Nancy L. Talner, Aaron H. Caplan, and Steven R. Shapiro.

Brief of amici curiae filed on behalf of the Kansas Appellate Defender Office by Randall L. Hodgkinson.

Brief of amici curiae filed on behalf of the National Association of Criminal Defense Lawyers et al. by David M. Porter and Sheryl Gordon McCloud.

Opposing Side (Respondent / Appellee)

Brief of amici curiae filed on behalf of the United States by John D. Knodell III, Deputy Solicitor General Dreeben, Solicitor General Olson, Assistant Attorney General Wray, Matthew D. Roberts, and Nina Goodman.

Brief of amici curiae filed on behalf of the State of Alabama et al. by William H. Pryor, Jr., Attorney General of Alabama, Kevin C. Newsom, Solicitor General, Michael B. Billingsley, Deputy Solicitor General, and Nathan A. Forrester, and by the Attorneys General for their respective States as follows: M. Jane Brady of Delaware, Charles J. Crist, Jr., of Florida, Mark J. Bennett of Hawaii, Lisa Madigan of Illinois, Jon Bruning of Nebraska, Hardy Myers of Oregon, Greg Abbott of Texas, Mark L. Shurtleff of Utah, and Jerry W. Kilgore of Virginia.

Brief of amici curiae filed on behalf of the Criminal Justice Legal Foundation by Kent S. Scheidegger.

IV. THE SUPREME COURT'S DECISION

"This case requires us to apply the rule we expressed in Apprendi v. New Jersey, 530 U.S. 466 (2000): 'Other than the fact of a prior conviction, any fact that increases the penalty for a crime beyond the prescribed statutory maximum must be submitted to a jury, and proved beyond a reasonable doubt.' . . .

In this case, petitioner was sentenced to more than three years above the 53–month statutory maximum of the standard range because he had acted with 'deliberate cruelty.' The facts supporting that finding were neither admitted by petitioner nor found by a jury. The State nevertheless contends that there was no Apprendi violation because the relevant 'statutory maximum' is not 53 months, but the 10–year maximum for class B felonies in § 9A.20.021(1)(b). It observes that no exceptional sentence may exceed that limit. Our precedents make clear, however, that the 'statutory maximum' for Apprendi purposes is the maximum sentence a judge may impose solely on the basis of the facts reflected in the jury verdict or admitted by the defendant. . . . In other words, the relevant 'statutory maximum' is not the maximum sentence a judge may impose after finding additional facts, but the maximum he may impose without any additional findings. When a judge inflicts punishment that the jury's verdict alone does not allow, the jury has not found all the facts 'which the law makes essential to the punishment,' and the judge exceeds his proper authority.

The judge in this case could not have imposed the exceptional 90–month sentence solely on the basis of the facts admitted in the guilty plea. . . .

Because the State's sentencing procedure did not comply with the Sixth Amendment, petitioner's sentence is invalid. . . .

Petitioner was sentenced to prison for more than three years beyond what the law allowed for the crime to which he confessed, on the basis of a disputed finding that he had acted with 'deliberate cruelty.' The Framers would not have thought it too much to demand that, before depriving a man of three more years of his liberty, the State should suffer the modest inconvenience of submitting its accusation to 'the unanimous suffrage of twelve of his equals and neighbours,' rather than a lone employee of the State.

The judgment of the Washington Court of Appeals is reversed, and the case is remanded for further proceedings not inconsistent with this opinion."

V. JUSTICE VOTE

5 Pro ACLU Side vs. 4 Con Opposing Side

ACLU Side (Petitioner / Appellant)

1. Scalia, A. – Wrote majority opinion
2. Stevens, J. – Joined majority opinion
3. Souter, D. – Joined majority opinion
4. Ginsburg, R. – Joined majority opinion
5. Thomas, C. – Joined majority opinion

Opposing Side (Respondent / Appellee)

1. O'Connor, S. – Wrote dissenting opinion, joined Breyer's dissent
2. Breyer, S. – Joined O'Connor's dissent, joined Kennedy's dissent, wrote dissenting opinion
3. Rehnquist, W. – Joined O'Connor's dissent in part
4. Kennedy, A. – Joined O'Connor's dissent in part, wrote dissenting opinion

VI. A WIN OR LOSS FOR THE ACLU?

The ACLU filed as amicus curiae urging reversal of the judgment of the Washington Court of Appeals; the Supreme Court reversed in a 5-4 vote, giving the ACLU an apparent win.

967. Beard v. Banks

(Decided June 24, 2004; 542 U.S. 406)

I. ISSUE

A. Issues Discussed

Criminal procedure

B. Legal Question Presented

"In Mills v. Maryland, 486 U.S. 367 (1988), and McKoy v. North Carolina, 494 U.S. 433 (1990), this Court held invalid capital sentencing schemes that require juries to disregard mitigating factors not found unanimously. In this case, we must determine whether the rule announced in Mills and McKoy can be applied on federal habeas corpus review to a defendant whose conviction became final in 1987."

C. Supreme Court's Answer

"Under our retroactivity analysis as set forth in Teague v. Lane, 489 U.S. 288 (1989), federal habeas corpus petitioners may not avail themselves of new rules of criminal procedure outside two narrow exceptions. We conclude that Mills announced a new rule that does not fall within either of Teague's exceptions."

II. CASE SUMMARY

A. Background

"More than 20 years ago, a jury convicted respondent, George Banks, of 12 counts of first-degree murder, and the trial court sentenced him to death. . . . Direct review ended when this Court denied certiorari on October 5, 1987. Approximately eight months later, this Court handed down its decision in Mills, supra, which announced that the Constitution forbids States from imposing a requirement that the jury find a potential mitigating factor unanimously before that factor may be considered in the sentencing decision.

Respondent pursued state postconviction relief on the theory that the instructions and verdict form given to the jury in his case violated the Mills principle, but the Pennsylvania Supreme Court rejected this claim on the merits. Respondent then turned to the federal courts. Although the District Court denied relief, the Court of Appeals for the Third Circuit reversed respondent's death sentence. In reaching its decision, the Court of Appeals declined to apply the retroactivity analysis set forth in Teague v. Lane, supra, to the question whether Mills applied retroactively to respondent. . . . We summarily reversed . . . .

On remand, the Court of Appeals considered the retroactive application of Mills. [T]he court held that Mills applied retroactively to respondent and reinstated the remainder of its previous opinion, again granting respondent relief from his death sentence."

The Supreme Court granted certiorari to review the case.

B. Counsel of Record

ACLU Side (Respondent / Appellee): Albert J. Flora, Jr., argued the cause for appellee. With him on the brief were Basil G. Russin, Joseph Cosgrove, Matthew C. Lawry, and Maureen Kearney Rowley.

Opposing Side (Petitioner / Appellant): Ronald Eisenberg argued the cause for appellants. With him on the briefs were Scott C. Gartley, Thomas W. Dolgenos, and Lynne Abraham.

III. AMICI CURIAE

ACLU Side (Respondent / Appellee)

Brief of amici curiae filed on behalf of the American Civil Liberties Union, the ACLU of Pennsylvania, and the National Association of Criminal Defense Lawyers by Larry Yackle, Joshua Dratel, Steven R. Shapiro, and Stefan Presser.

Brief of amici curiae filed on behalf of the Pennsylvania Association of Criminal Defense Lawyers by Louis M. Natali, Jr., and Peter Goldberger.

Opposing Side (Petitioner / Appellant)

Brief of amici curiae filed on behalf of the Criminal Justice Legal Foundation by Kent S. Scheidegger.

IV. THE SUPREME COURT'S DECISION

"Under Teague, the determination whether a constitutional rule of criminal procedure applies to a case on collateral review involves a three-step process. First, the court must determine when the defendant's conviction became final. Second, it must ascertain the 'legal landscape as it then existed,' and ask whether the Constitution, as interpreted by the precedent then existing, compels the rule. That is, the court must decide whether the rule is actually 'new.' Finally, if the rule is new, the court must consider whether it falls within either of the two exceptions to nonretroactivity....

Ordinarily, ascertaining the date on which a defendant's conviction becomes final poses no difficulties: State convictions are final 'for purposes of retroactivity analysis when the availability of direct appeal to the state courts has been exhausted and the time for filing a petition for a writ of certiorari has elapsed or a timely filed petition has been finally denied.' ... Respondent, however, urges a different rule....

In short, our rule for determining when a state conviction becomes final applies to this case without modification, and we agree with the Court of Appeals that respondent's conviction became final in 1987....

We must therefore assay the legal landscape as of 1987 and ask 'whether the rule later announced in [Mills] was dictated by then-existing precedent-whether, that is, the unlawfulness of [respondent's] conviction was apparent to all reasonable jurists.' ...

In reaching its conclusion, the Court in Mills and McKoy relied on a line of cases beginning with Lockett v. Ohio, 438 U.S. 586 (1978) (plurality opinion), and Eddings v. Oklahoma, 455 U.S. 104 (1982)....

The generalized Lockett rule (that the sentencer must be allowed to consider any mitigating evidence) could be thought to support the Court's conclusion in Mills and McKoy. But what is essential here is that it does not mandate the Mills rule....

Given the brand new attention Mills paid to individual jurors and the relevance of the what/how distinction drawn in Saffle (which again distinguishes Mills from the Lockett line), we must conclude that the Mills rule 'br[o]k[e] new ground.' Accordingly, Mills announced a new rule, which does not apply to respondent on collateral review, unless, of course, it falls under one of Teague's exceptions....

Teague's bar on retroactive application of new rules of constitutional criminal procedure has two exceptions. First, the bar does not apply to rules forbidding punishment 'of certain primary conduct [or to] rules prohibiting a certain category of punishment for a class of defendants because of their status or offense.' There is no argument that this exception applies here. The second exception is for "watershed rules of criminal procedure implicating the fundamental fairness and accuracy of the criminal proceeding." ...

However laudable the Mills rule might be, 'it has none of the primacy and centrality of the rule adopted in Gideon.' The Mills rule applies fairly narrowly and works no fundamental shift in 'our understanding of the bedrock procedural elements' essential to fundamental fairness. We therefore conclude that the Mills rule does not fall within the second Teague exception....

We hold that Mills announced a new rule of constitutional criminal procedure that falls within neither Teague exception. Accordingly, that rule cannot be applied retroactively to respondent. The judgment of the Court of Appeals is reversed, and the case is remanded for further proceedings consistent with this opinion."

V. JUSTICE VOTE

4 Pro ACLU Side vs. 5 Con Opposing Side

ACLU Side (Respondent / Appellee)

1. Stevens, J. – Wrote dissenting opinion
2. Souter, D – Wrote dissenting opinion, joined Stevens' dissent
3. Ginsburg, R. – Joined Stevens' and Souter's dissents
4. Breyer, S. – Joined Stevens' dissent

Opposing Side (Petitioner / Appellant)

1. Thomas, C. – Wrote majority opinion
2. O'Connor, S. – Joined majority opinion
3. Scalia, A. – Joined majority opinion
4. Kennedy, A. – Joined majority opinion
5. Rehnquist, W. – Joined majority opinion

VI. A WIN OR LOSS FOR THE ACLU?

The ACLU filed as amicus curiae urging affirmance; the Supreme Court reversed the Court of Appeals' decision by a 5-4 vote, giving the ACLU an apparent loss.

968. Rumsfeld v. Padilla

(Decided June 28, 2004; 542 U.S. 426)

I. ISSUE

A. Issues Discussed

Military, criminal procedure

B. Legal Question Presented

"We confront two questions: First, did Padilla properly file his habeas petition in the Southern District of New York; and second, did the President possess authority to detain Padilla militarily."

C. Supreme Court's Answer

"We answer the threshold question in the negative and thus do not reach the second question presented."

II. CASE SUMMARY

A. Background

"Respondent Jose Padilla is a United States citizen detained by the Department of Defense pursuant to the President's determination that he is an 'enemy combatant' who conspired with al Qaeda to carry out terrorist attacks in the United States. . . .

On May 8, 2002, Padilla flew from Pakistan to Chicago's O'Hare International Airport. As he stepped off the plane, Padilla was apprehended by federal agents executing a material witness warrant issued by the United States District Court for the Southern District of New York (Southern District) in connection with its grand jury investigation into the September 11th terrorist attacks. Padilla was then transported to New York, where he was held in federal criminal custody. On May 22, acting through appointed counsel, Padilla moved to vacate the material witness warrant.

Padilla's motion was still pending when, on June 9, the President issued an order to Secretary of Defense Donald H. Rumsfeld designating Padilla an 'enemy combatant' and directing the Secretary to detain him in military custody. . . .

That same day, Padilla was taken into custody by Department of Defense officials and transported to the Consolidated Naval Brig in Charleston, South Carolina. He has been held there ever since.

On June 11, Padilla's counsel, claiming to act as his next friend, filed in the Southern District a habeas corpus petition under 28 U.S.C. § 2241. The petition, as amended, alleged that Padilla's military detention violates the Fourth, Fifth, and Sixth Amendments and the Suspension Clause, Art. I, § 9, cl. 2, of the United States Constitution. The amended petition named as respondents President Bush, Secretary Rumsfeld, and Melanie A. Marr, Commander of the Consolidated Naval Brig. . . .

The Government moved to dismiss, arguing that Commander Marr, as Padilla's immediate custodian, is the only proper respondent to his habeas petition, and that the District Court lacks jurisdiction over Commander Marr because she is located outside the Southern District. On the merits, the Government contended that the President has authority to detain Padilla militarily pursuant to the Commander in Chief Clause of the Constitution, Art. II, § 2, cl. 1, the congressional AUMF, and this Court's decision in Ex parte Quirin, 317 U.S. 1 (1942).

The District Court issued its decision in December 2002. The court held that the Secretary's 'personal involvement' in Padilla's military custody renders him a proper respondent to Padilla's habeas petition, and that it can assert jurisdiction over the Secretary under New York's long-arm statute, notwithstanding his absence from the Southern District.' On the merits, however, the court accepted the Government's contention that the President has authority to detain as enemy combatants citizens captured on American soil during a time of war.

The Court of Appeals for the Second Circuit reversed. . . .

Reaching the merits, the Court of Appeals held that the President lacks authority to detain Padilla militarily."

The Supreme Court granted certiorari to review the case.

B. Counsel of Record

ACLU Side (Respondent / Appellee): Jennifer S. Martinez argued the cause for respondents. With her on the brief were Donna R. Newman, Andrew G. Patel, Jonathan M. Freiman, David W. DeBruin, William M. Hohengarten, and Matthew Hersh.

Opposing Side (Petitioner / Appellant): Deputy Solicitor General Clement argued the cause for appellant. With him on the briefs were Solicitor General Olson, Sri Srinivasan, and Jonathan L. Marcus.

III. AMICI CURIAE

ACLU Side (Respondent / Appellee)

Brief of amici curiae filed on behalf of the American Civil Liberties Union, New York Civil Liberties Union, and Trial Lawyers for Public Justice by Arthur N. Eisenberg, Arthur H. Bryant, Rebecca E. Epstein, Richard H. Frankel, Steven R. Shapiro, Sharon M. McGowan, Lucas Guttentag, and Robin L. Goldfaden.

Brief of amici curiae filed on behalf of the Association of the Bar of the City of New York et al. by Joseph Gerard Davis.

Brief of amici curiae filed on behalf of the Beverly Hills Bar Association et al. by Bridget Arimond, Stephen F. Rohde, and Marc J. Poster.

Brief of amici curiae filed on behalf of the Center for National Security Studies et al. by John Payton, Seth P. Waxman, Paul R. Q. Wolfson, Kate Martin, and Joseph Onek.

Brief of amici curiae filed on behalf of Global Rights by James F. Fitzpatrick, Kathleen A. Behan, and Gay J. McDougall.

Brief of amici curiae filed on behalf of Others Are Us et al. by Jonathan D. Wallace.

Brief of amici curiae filed on behalf of the Rutherford Institute et al. by Carter G. Phillips, Mark E. Haddad, Joseph R. Guerra, and Elliot M. Mincberg.

Brief of amici curiae filed on behalf of the Spartacist League et al. by Rachel H. Wolkenstein.

Brief of amici curiae filed on behalf of Bruce A. Ackerman et al. by Jules Lobel, Bar bara Olshansky, Nancy Chang, and Shayana Kadidal.

Brief of amici curiae filed on behalf of Susan Akram et al. by Daniel Kanstroom.

Brief of amici curiae filed on behalf of Philip Alston et al. by David N. Rosen, Homer E. Moyer, Jr., and Michael T. Brady.
Brief of amici curiae filed on behalf of the Honorable John Conyers, Jr., et al. by Brian S. Koukoutchos.
Brief of amici curiae filed on behalf of Samuel R. Gross et al. by Jonathan L. Hafetz, Lawrence S. Lustberg, and Michael J. Wishnie.
Brief of amici curiae filed on behalf of Louis Henkin et al. by Donald Francis Donovan, Carl Micarelli, and J. Paul Oetken.
Brief of amici curiae filed on behalf of Fred Korematsu et al. by Arturo J. González and Jon B. Streeter.
Brief of amici curiae filed on behalf of Janet Reno et al. by Robert S. Litt and Theodore D. Frank.
Brief of amici curiae filed on behalf of the National Association of Criminal Defense Lawyers et al. by Donald G. Rehkopf, Jr., and Lisa B. Kemler.
Brief of amici curiae filed on behalf of the Public Defender Service for the District of Columbia by Catharine F. Easterly, Giovanna Shay, and Timothy P. O'Toole.
Brief of amici curiae filed on behalf of the Honorable Shirley M. Hufstedler et al. by Robert P. LoBue.
Brief of amici curiae filed on behalf of William J. Aceves et al. by Linda A. Malone and Jordan J. Paust.
Brief of amici curiae filed on behalf of Payam Akhavan et al. by Allison Marston Danner.
Brief of amici curiae filed on behalf of David J. Scheffer et al. by Mr. Scheffer, pro se.

Opposing Side (Petitioner / Appellant)

Brief of amici curiae filed on behalf of the Commonwealth of Virginia by Jerry W. Kilgore, Attorney General of Virginia, William H. Hurd, State Solicitor, Maureen Riley Matsen and William E. Thro, Deputy State Solicitors, Alison P. Landry, Senior Assistant Attorney General, and Courtney M. Malveaux and Russell E. McGuire, Assistant Attorneys General.
Brief of amici curiae filed on behalf of the American Center for Law & Justice by Jay Alan Sekulow, Thomas P. Monaghan, Stuart J. Roth, Colby M. May, James M. Henderson, Sr., Joel H. Thornton, and Robert W. Ash.
Brief of amici curiae filed on behalf of the Cato Institute by Timothy Lynch.
Brief of amici curiae filed on behalf of the Criminal Justice Legal Foundation by Kent S. Scheidegger.
Brief of amici curiae filed on behalf of the Washington Legal Foundation et al. by Daniel J. Popeo and Richard A. Samp.
Brief of amici curiae filed on behalf of Senator John Cornyn et al. by Senator Cornyn, pro se.

IV. THE SUPREME COURT'S DECISION

"The question whether the Southern District has jurisdiction over Padilla's habeas petition breaks down into two related subquestions. First, who is the proper respondent to that petition? And second, does the Southern District have jurisdiction over him or her? We address these questions in turn. . . .

The federal habeas statute straightforwardly provides that the proper respondent to a habeas petition is 'the person who has custody over [the petitioner].' . . .

In accord with the statutory language and Wales' immediate custodian rule, longstanding practice confirms that in habeas challenges to present physical confinement—'core challenges'—the default rule is that the proper respondent is the warden of the facility where the prisoner is being held, not the Attorney General or some other remote supervisory official. . . .

Padilla's argument reduces to a request for a new exception to the immediate custodian rule based upon the 'unique facts' of this case. While Padilla's detention is undeniably unique in many respects, it is at bottom a simple challenge to physical custody imposed by the Executive—the traditional core of the Great Writ. There is no indication that there was any attempt to manipulate behind Padilla's transfer—he was taken to the same facility where other al Qaeda members were already being held, and the Government did not attempt to hide from Padilla's lawyer where it had taken him. His detention is thus not unique in any way that would provide arguable basis for a departure from the immediate custodian rule. Accordingly, we hold that Commander Marr, not Secretary Rumsfeld, is Padilla's custodian and the proper respondent to his habeas petition. . . .

We turn now to the second subquestion. District courts are limited to granting habeas relief 'within their respective jurisdictions.' We have interpreted this language to require 'nothing more than that the court issuing the writ have jurisdiction over the custodian.' Thus, jurisdiction over Padilla's habeas petition lies in the Southern District only if it has jurisdiction over Commander Marr. We conclude it does not.

Congress added the limiting clause—'within their respective jurisdictions'—to the habeas statute in 1867 to avert the 'inconvenient [and] potentially embarrassing'" possibility that 'every judge anywhere [could] issue the Great Writ on behalf of applicants far distantly removed from the courts whereon they sat.' Accordingly, with respect to habeas petitions 'designed to relieve an individual from oppressive confinement,' the traditional rule has always been that the Great Writ is 'issuable only in the district of confinement.' . . .

The proviso that district courts may issue the writ only 'within their respective jurisdictions' forms an important corollary to the immediate custodian rule in challenges to present physical custody under § 2241. Together they compose a simple rule that has been consistently applied in the lower courts, including in the context of military detentions: Whenever a § 2241 habeas petitioner seeks to challenge his present physical custody within the United States, he should name his warden as respondent and file the petition in the district of confinement. . . .

This rule, derived from the terms of the habeas statute, serves the important purpose of preventing forum shopping by habeas petitioners. Without it, a prisoner could name a high-level supervisory official as respondent and then sue that person wherever he is amenable to long-arm jurisdiction. The result would be rampant forum shopping, district courts with overlapping jurisdiction, and the very inconvenience, expense, and embarrassment Congress sought to avoid when it added the jurisdictional limitation 137 years ago. . . .

The District of South Carolina, not the Southern District of New York, was the district court in which Padilla should have brought his habeas petition. We therefore reverse the judgment of the Court of Appeals and remand the case for entry of an order of dismissal without prejudice."

V. JUSTICE VOTE

4 Pro ACLU Side vs. 5 Con Opposing Side

ACLU Side (Respondent / Appellee)

1. Stevens, J. – Wrote dissenting opinion
2. Souter, D. – Joined Stevens' dissent
3. Ginsburg, R. – Joined Stevens' dissent
4. Breyer, S. – Joined Stevens' dissent

Opposing Side (Petitioner / Appellant)

1. Rehnquist, W. – Wrote majority opinion
2. Thomas, C. – Joined majority opinion
3. O'Connor, S. – Joined Kennedy's concurrence
4. Scalia, A. – Joined majority opinion
5. Kennedy, A. – Wrote concurring opinion

VI. A WIN OR LOSS FOR THE ACLU?

The ACLU filed as amicus curiae urging affirmance; the Supreme Court reversed the Court of Appeals' decision by a 5-4 vote, giving the ACLU an apparent loss.

969. Rasul v. Bush

(Decided June 28, 2004; 542 U.S. 466)

I. ISSUE

A. Issues Discussed

Prison, criminal justice

B. Legal Question Presented

"[W]hether United States courts lack jurisdiction to consider challenges to the legality of the detention of foreign nationals captured abroad in connection with hostilities and incarcerated at the Guantanamo Bay Naval Base, Cuba."

C. Supreme Court's Answer

"What is presently at stake is only whether the federal courts have jurisdiction to determine the legality of the Executive's potentially indefinite detention of individuals who claim to be wholly innocent of wrongdoing. Answering that question in the affirmative, we reverse the judgment of the Court of Appeals . . . ."

II. CASE SUMMARY

A. Background

"On September 11, 2001, agents of the al Qaeda terrorist network hijacked four commercial airliners and used them as missiles to attack American targets. . . . In response to the attacks, Congress passed a joint resolution authorizing the President to use 'all necessary and appropriate force against those nations, organizations, or persons he determines planned, authorized, committed, or aided the terrorist attacks . . . or harbored such organizations or persons.' Acting pursuant to that authorization, the President sent U.S. Armed Forces into Afghanistan to wage a military campaign against al Qaeda and the Taliban regime that had supported it.

Petitioners in these cases are 2 Australian citizens and 12 Kuwaiti citizens who were captured abroad during hostilities between the United States and the Taliban. Since early 2002, the U.S. military has held them—along with, according to the Government's estimate, approximately 640 other non-Americans captured abroad—at the naval base at Guantanamo Bay. . . .

In 2002, petitioners, through relatives acting as their next friends, filed various actions in the U.S. District Court for the District of Columbia challenging the legality of their detention at the base. All alleged that none of the petitioners has ever been a combatant against the United States or has ever engaged in any terrorist acts. They also alleged that none has been charged with any wrongdoing, permitted to consult with counsel, or provided access to the courts or any other tribunal.

The two Australians, Mamdouh Habib and David Hicks, each filed a petition for writ of habeas corpus, seeking release from custody, access to counsel, freedom from interrogations, and other relief. Fawzi Khalid Abdullah Fahad Al Odah and the 11 other Kuwaiti detainees filed a complaint seeking to be informed of the charges against them, to be allowed to meet with their families and with counsel, and to have access to the courts or some other impartial tribunal. . . .

Construing all three actions as petitions for writs of habeas corpus, the District Court dismissed them for want of jurisdiction. . . . The Court of Appeals affirmed."

The Supreme Court granted certiorari to review the case.

B. Counsel of Record

ACLU Side (Petitioner / Appellant): John J. Gibbons argued the cause for appellants in both cases. With him on the briefs for appellant Rasul et al. in No. 03-334 were Joseph Margulies, Barbara J. Olshansky, and Michael Ratner. Thomas B. Wilner, Neil H. Koslowe, and Kristine A. Huskey filed briefs for appellant Al Odah et al. in both cases.

Opposing Side (Respondent / Appellee): Solicitor General Olson argued the cause for appellees in both cases. With him on the brief were Assistant Attorney General Keisler, Deputy Solicitor General Clement, Deputy Assistant Attorney General Katsas, Gregory G. Garre, Douglas N. Letter, Robert M. Loeb, Sharon Swingle, and William H. Taft IV.

III. AMICI CURIAE

ACLU Side (Petitioner / Appellant)

Brief of amici curiae filed on behalf of the Bipartisan Coalition of National and International Non-Governmental Organizations by Jonathan M. Freiman, Michael H. Posner, Deborah Pearlstein, Fiona Doherty. (The American Civil Liberties Union is one of the organizations included in the bipartisan coalition.)

Brief of amici curiae filed on behalf of Hungarian Jews et al. by Steve W. Berman, R. Brent Walton, Jonathan W. Cuneo, David W. Stanley, Michael Waldman, and Samuel J. Dubbin.

Brief of amici curiae filed on behalf of the International Commission of Jurists et al. by William J. Butler and A. Hays Butler.

Brief of amici curiae filed on behalf of the National Institute of Military Justice by Ronald W. Meister.
Brief of amici curiae filed on behalf of Abdullah Al-Joaid by Mary Patricia Michel.
Brief of amici curiae filed on behalf of Diego C. Asencio et al. by William M. Hannay.
Brief of amici curiae filed on behalf of David M. Brahms et al. by James C. Schroeder.
Brief of amici curiae filed on behalf of the Honorable John H. Dalton et al. by Harold Hongju Koh, Gerald L. Neuman, Phillip H. Rudolph, and Daniel Feldman.
Brief of amici curiae filed on behalf of Leslie H. Jackson et al. by Thomas F. Cullen, Jr., and Christian G. Vergonis.
Brief of amici curiae filed on behalf of the Honorable Nathaniel R. Jones et al. by David J. Bradford.
Brief of amici curiae filed on behalf of Omar Ahmed Khadr by John A. E. Pottow.
Brief of amici curiae filed on behalf of Fred Korematsu by Stephen J. Schulhofer, Evan R. Chesler, Dale Minami, and Eric K. Yamamoto.
Brief of amici curiae filed on behalf of the Center for Justice and Accountability et al. by Nicholas W. Van Aelstyn, Warrington S. Parker III, Thomas P. Brown, Christian E. Mammen, and Elizabeth A. Brown.
Brief of amici curiae filed on behalf of the Commonwealth Lawyers Association by Stephen J. Pollak and John Townsend Rich.
Brief of amici curiae filed on behalf of the Human Rights Institute of the International Bar Association by Pamela Rogers Chepiga.
Brief of amici curiae filed on behalf of International Law Expert by James R. Klimaski.
Brief of amici curiae filed on behalf of 175 Members of Both Houses of the Parliament of the United Kingdom of Great Britain and Northern Ireland by Edwin S. Matthews, Jr., and Edward H. Tillinghast III.
Brief of amici curiae filed on behalf of Sir J. H. Baker et al. by James Oldham and Michael J. Wishnie.
Brief of amici curiae filed on behalf of Professor John H. Barton et al. by Mr. Barton, pro se, and Barry E. Carter.

Opposing Side (Respondent / Appellee)

Brief of amici curiae filed on behalf of the State of Alabama et al. by John J. Park, Jr., Assistant Attorney General of Alabama, Richard F. Allen, Acting Attorney General of Alabama, and Kevin Newsom, Solicitor General, and by the Attorneys General for their respective States as follows: Jim Petro of Ohio, Greg Abbott of Texas, and Jerry W. Kilgore of Virginia.
Brief of amici curiae filed on behalf of the Honorable Bill Owens, Governor of Colorado, et al. by Richard A. Westfall and Allan L. Hale.
Brief of amici curiae filed on behalf of the American Center for Law & Justice et al. by Jay Alan Sekulow, Thomas P. Monaghan, Stuart J. Roth, Colby M. May, James M. Henderson, Sr., Joel H. Thornton, and Robert W. Ash.
Brief of amici curiae filed on behalf of Citizens for the Common Defence by Carter G. Phillips.
Brief of amici curiae filed on behalf of the Washington Legal Foundation et al. by Daniel J. Popeo and Richard A. Samp.
Brief of amici curiae filed on behalf of Professor Kenneth Anderson et al. by David B. Rivkin, Jr., Lee A. Casey, Darin R. Bartram, Ruth Wedgwood, Charles Fried, and Max Kampelman.
Brief of amici curiae filed on behalf of the Honorable William P. Barr et al. by Andrew G. McBride.
Brief of amici curiae filed on behalf of Military Attorneys Assigned to the Defense in the Office of Military Commissions by Neal Katyal, Sharon A. Shaffer, Philip Sundel, Mark A. Bridges, and Michael D. Mori in support of neither party.

IV. THE SUPREME COURT'S DECISION

"Congress has granted federal district courts, 'within their respective jurisdictions,' the authority to hear applications for habeas corpus by any person who claims to be held 'in custody in violation of the Constitution or laws or treaties of the United States.' . . .

The question now before us is whether the habeas statute confers a right to judicial review of the legality of executive detention of aliens in a territory over which the United States exercises plenary and exclusive jurisdiction, but not 'ultimate sovereignty.' . . .

Respondents' primary submission is that the answer to the jurisdictional question is controlled by our decision in Eisentrager. In that case, we held that a Federal District Court lacked authority to issue a writ of habeas corpus to 21 German citizens who had been captured by U.S. forces in China, tried and convicted of war crimes by an American military commission headquartered in Nanking, and incarcerated in the Landsberg Prison in occupied Germany. . . .

Because subsequent decisions of this Court have filled the statutory gap that had occasioned Eisentrager's resort to 'fundamentals,' persons detained outside the territorial jurisdiction of any federal district court no longer need rely on the Constitution as the source of their right to federal habeas review. In Braden v. 30th Judicial Circuit Court of Ky., 410 U.S. 484 (1973), this Court held, contrary to Ahrens, that the prisoner's presence within the territorial jurisdiction of the district court is not 'an invariable prerequisite' to the exercise of district court jurisdiction under the federal habeas statute. . . . Braden thus established that Ahrens can no longer be viewed as establishing 'an inflexible jurisdictional rule,' and is strictly relevant only to the question of the appropriate forum, not to whether the claim can be heard at all.

Because Braden overruled the statutory predicate to Eisentrager's holding, Eisentrager plainly does not preclude the exercise of § 2241 jurisdiction over petitioners' claims. . . .

Putting Eisentrager and Ahrens to one side, respondents contend that we can discern a limit on § 2241 through application of the 'longstanding principle of American law' that congressional legislation is presumed not to have extraterritorial application unless such intent is clearly manifested. Whatever traction the presumption against extraterritoriality might have in other contexts, it certainly has no application to the operation of the habeas statute with respect to persons detained within 'the territorial jurisdiction' of the United States. By the express terms of its agreements with Cuba, the United States exercises 'complete jurisdiction and control' over the Guantanamo Bay Naval Base, and may continue to exercise such control permanently if it so chooses. . . . Aliens held at the base, no less than American citizens, are entitled to invoke the federal courts' authority under § 2241. . . .

In the end, the answer to the question presented is clear. Petitioners contend that they are being held in federal custody in violation of the laws of the United States. No party questions the District Court's jurisdiction over petitioners' custodians. Section 2241, by its terms, requires nothing more. We therefore hold that § 2241 confers on the District Court jurisdiction to hear petitioners' habeas corpus challenges to the legality of their detention at the Guantanamo Bay Naval Base. . . .

In addition to invoking the District Court's jurisdiction under § 2241, the Al Odah petitioners' complaint invoked the court's jurisdiction under 28 U.S.C. § 1331, the federal-question statute, as well as § 1350, the Alien Tort Statute. . . .

As explained above, Eisentrager itself erects no bar to the exercise of federal-court jurisdiction over the petitioners' habeas corpus claims. It therefore certainly does not bar the exercise of federal-court jurisdiction over claims that merely implicate the 'same category of laws listed in the habeas corpus statute.' . . . The fact that petitioners in these cases are being held in military custody is immaterial to the question of the District Court's jurisdiction over their nonhabeas statutory claims. . . .

Whether and what further proceedings may become necessary after respondents make their response to the merits of petitioners' claims are matters that we need not address now. What is presently at stake is only whether the federal courts have jurisdiction to determine the legality of the Executive's potentially indefinite detention of individuals who claim to be wholly innocent of wrongdoing. Answering that question in the affirmative, we reverse the judgment of the Court of Appeals and remand these cases for the District Court to consider in the first instance the merits of petitioners' claims."

V. JUSTICE VOTE

6 Pro ACLU Side vs. 3 Con Opposing Side

ACLU Side (Petitioner / Appellant)

1. Stevens, J. – Wrote majority opinion
2. O'Connor, S. – Joined majority opinion
3. Souter, D. – Joined majority opinion
4. Ginsburg, R. – Joined majority opinion
5. Breyer, S. – Joined majority opinion
6. Kennedy, A. – Wrote concurring opinion

Opposing Side (Respondent / Appellee)

1. Scalia, A. – Wrote dissenting opinion
2. Rehnquist, W. – Joined Scalia's dissent
3. Thomas, C. – Joined Scalia's dissent

VI. A WIN OR LOSS FOR THE ACLU?

The ACLU filed as amicus curiae urging reversal of the judgment of the Court of Appeals; the Supreme Court reversed in a 6-3 vote, giving the ACLU an apparent win.

970. Hamdi v. Rumsfeld

(Decided June 28, 2004; 542 U.S. 507)

I. ISSUE

A. Issues Discussed

Criminal procedure, military

B. Legal Question Presented

"[W]hether the Executive has the authority to detain citizens who qualify as 'enemy combatants.'"

C. Supreme Court's Answer

"We hold that although Congress authorized the detention of combatants in the narrow circumstances alleged here, due process demands that a citizen held in the United States as an enemy combatant be given a meaningful opportunity to contest the factual basis for that detention before a neutral decisionmaker."

II. CASE SUMMARY

A. Background

"On September 11, 2001, the al Qaeda terrorist network used hijacked commercial airliners to attack prominent targets in the United States. . . . One week later, . . . Congress passed a resolution authorizing the President to 'use all necessary and appropriate force against those nations, organizations, or persons he determines planned, authorized, committed, or aided the terrorist attacks' or 'harbored such organizations or persons, in order to prevent any future acts of international terrorism against the United States by such nations, organizations or persons.' Soon thereafter, the President ordered United States Armed Forces to Afghanistan, with a mission to subdue al Qaeda and quell the Taliban regime that was known to support it.

This case arises out of the detention of a man whom the Government alleges took up arms with the Taliban during this conflict. His name is Yaser Esam Hamdi. Born in Louisiana in 1980, Hamdi moved with his family to Saudi Arabia as a child. By 2001, the parties agree, he resided in Afghanistan. At some point that year, he was seized by members of the Northern Alliance, a coalition of military groups opposed to the Taliban government, and eventually was turned over to the United States military. . . . The Government contends that Hamdi is an 'enemy combatant,' and that this status justifies holding him in the United States indefinitely—without formal charges or proceedings—unless and until it makes the determination that access to counsel or further process is warranted.

In June 2002, Hamdi's father, Esam Fouad Hamdi, filed the present petition for a writ of habeas corpus . . . .

The District Court found that Hamdi's father was a proper next friend, appointed the federal public defender as counsel for the petitioners, and ordered that counsel be given access to Hamdi. The United States Court of Appeals for the Fourth Circuit reversed that order . . . .

On remand, the Government filed a response and a motion to dismiss the petition. It attached to its response a declaration from one Michael Mobbs . . . .

Mobbs . . . set forth what remains the sole evidentiary support that the Government has provided to the courts for Hamdi's detention. . . .

After the Government submitted this declaration, the Fourth Circuit directed the District Court to proceed in accordance with its earlier ruling and, specifically, to "consider the sufficiency of the Mobbs declaration as an independent matter before proceeding further." The District Court found that the Mobbs Declaration fell 'far short' of supporting Hamdi's detention. . . . It ordered the Government to turn over numerous materials for in camera review . . . . The court indicated that all of these materials were necessary for 'meaningful judicial review' of whether Hamdi's detention was legally authorized and whether Hamdi had received sufficient process to satisfy the Due Process Clause of the Constitution and relevant treaties or military regulations.

The Government sought to appeal the production order . . . . The Fourth Circuit reversed . . . .

The Fourth Circuit denied rehearing en banc . . . ."

The Supreme Court granted certiorari to review the case.

B. Counsel of Record

ACLU Side (Petitioner / Appellant): Frank W. Dunham, Jr., argued the cause for appellants. With him on the briefs were Geremy C. Kamens, Kenneth P. Troccoli, and Frances H. Pratt.

Opposing Side (Respondent / Appellee): Deputy Solicitor General Clement argued the cause for appellees. With him on the brief were Solicitor General Olson, Gregory G. Garre, and John A. Drennan.

III. AMICI CURIAE

ACLU Side (Petitioner / Appellant)

Brief of amici curiae filed on behalf of the American Civil Liberties Union, the American Jewish Committee, Trial Lawyers for Public Justice, and Union for Reform Judaism by Steven R. Shapiro, Sharon M. McGowan, David Saperstein, Jeffrey Sinensky, Kara Stein, and Arthur Bryant.

Brief of amici curiae filed on behalf of the American Bar Association by Dennis W. Archer and Barry Sullivan.

Brief of amici curiae filed on behalf of AmeriCares et al. by Steven M. Pesner, Michael Small, and Jeffrey P. Kehne.

Brief of amici curiae filed on behalf of the Cato Institute by Timothy Lynch; for Global Rights by James F. Fitzpatrick, Kathleen A. Behan, and Gay J. McDougall.

Brief of amici curiae filed on behalf of William J. Aceves et al. by Douglas W. Baruch.

Brief of amici curiae filed on behalf of Charles B. Gittings, Jr., by Donald G. Rehkopf, Jr.

Brief of amici curiae filed on behalf of the Honorable Nathaniel R. Jones et al. by Robert P. LoBue.

Brief of amici curiae filed on behalf of Douglas Peterson et al. by Philip Allen Lacovara and Andrew J. Pincus.

Brief of amici curiae filed on behalf of Mary Robinson et al. by Harold Hongju Koh and Jonathan M. Freiman.

Opposing Side (Respondent / Appellee)

Brief of amici curiae filed on behalf of the American Center for Law & Justice by Jay Alan Sekulow, Thomas P. Monaghan, Stuart J. Roth, Colby M. May, James M. Henderson, Sr., Joel H. Thornton, John P. Tuskey, and Shannon D. Woodruff.

Brief of amici curiae filed on behalf of the Center for American Unity et al. by Barnaby W. Zall.

Brief of amici curiae filed on behalf of the Claremont Institute Center for Constitutional Jurisprudence by John C. Eastman and Edwin Meese III.

Brief of amici curiae filed on behalf of Citizens for the Common Defence by Adam H. Charnes.

Brief of amici curiae filed on behalf of the Washington Legal Foundation et al. by Thomas V. Loran, William T. DeVinney, Daniel J. Popeo, and Richard A. Samp.

Brief of amici curiae filed on behalf of Senator John Cornyn et al. by Senator Cornyn, pro se.

Brief of amici curiae filed on behalf of the Eagle Forum Education & Legal Defense Fund by Karen B. Tripp.

IV. THE SUPREME COURT'S DECISION

"The threshold question before us is whether the Executive has the authority to detain citizens who qualify as 'enemy combatants.' There is some debate as to the proper scope of this term, and the Government has never provided any court with the full criteria that it uses in classifying individuals as such. It has made clear, however, that, for purposes of this case, the 'enemy combatant' that it is seeking to detain is an individual who, it alleges, was "part of or supporting forces hostile to the United States or coalition partners" in Afghanistan and who "engaged in an armed conflict against the United States" there. We therefore answer only the narrow question before us: whether the detention of citizens falling within that definition is authorized. . . .

The AUMF authorizes the President to use 'all necessary and appropriate force' against 'nations, organizations, or persons' associated with the September 11, 2001, terrorist attacks. . . . We conclude that detention of individuals falling into the limited category we are considering . . . is so fundamental and accepted an incident to war as to be an exercise of the 'necessary and appropriate force' Congress has authorized the President to use. . . .

There is no bar to this Nation's holding one of its own citizens as an enemy combatant. . . .

In light of these principles, it is of no moment that the AUMF does not use specific language of detention. Because detention to prevent a combatant's return to the battlefield is a fundamental incident of waging war, in permitting the use of 'necessary and appropriate force,' Congress has clearly and unmistakably authorized detention in the narrow circumstances considered here. . . .

Hamdi contends that the AUMF does not authorize indefinite or perpetual detention. Certainly, we agree that indefinite detention for the purpose of interrogation is not authorized. . . . The United States may detain, for the duration of these hostilities, individuals legitimately determined to be Taliban combatants who 'engaged in an armed conflict against the United States.' If the record establishes that United States troops are still involved in active combat in Afghanistan, those detentions are part of the exercise of 'necessary and appropriate force,' and therefore are authorized by the AUMF. . . .

Even in cases in which the detention of enemy combatants is legally authorized, there remains the question of what process is constitutionally due to a citizen who disputes his enemy-combatant status. . . .

In sum, while the full protections that accompany challenges to detentions in other settings may prove unworkable and inappropriate in the enemy-combatant setting, the threats to military operations posed by a basic system of independent review are not so weighty as to trump a citizen's core rights to challenge meaningfully the Government's case and to be heard by an impartial adjudicator. . . .

Hamdi asks us to hold that the Fourth Circuit also erred by denying him immediate access to counsel upon his detention and by disposing of the case without permitting him to meet with an attorney. Since our grant of certiorari in this case, Hamdi has been appointed counsel, with whom he has met for consultation purposes on several occasions, and with whom he is now being granted unmonitored meetings. He unquestionably has the right to access to counsel in connection with the proceedings on remand. No further consideration of this issue is necessary at this stage of the case. . . .

The judgment of the United States Court of Appeals for the Fourth Circuit is vacated, and the case is remanded for further proceedings."

V. JUSTICE VOTE

6 Pro ACLU Side vs. 3 Con Opposing Side

ACLU Side (Petitioner / Appellant)

1. O'Connor, S. – Wrote plurality opinion
2. Souter, D. – Wrote opinion concurring in part and dissenting in part and concurring in the judgment
3. Ginsburg, R. – Joined Souter's opinion
4. Breyer, S. – Joined plurality opinion
5. Kennedy, A. – Joined plurality opinion
6. Rehnquist, W. – Joined plurality opinion

Opposing Side (Respondent / Appellee)

1. Thomas, C. – Wrote dissenting opinion
2. Scalia, A. – Wrote dissenting opinion
3. Stevens, J. – Joined Scalia's dissent

VI. A WIN OR LOSS FOR THE ACLU?

The ACLU filed as amicus curiae urging reversal of the judgment of the Court of Appeals; the Supreme Court vacated and remanded in a 6-3 vote, giving the ACLU an apparent win.

971. Missouri v. Seibert

(Decided June 28, 2004; 542 U.S. 600)

I. ISSUE

A. Issues Discussed

Criminal procedure

B. Legal Question Presented

"This case tests a police protocol for custodial interrogation that calls for giving no warnings of the rights to silence and counsel until interrogation has produced a confession. Although such a statement is generally inadmissible, since taken in violation of Miranda v. Arizona, 384 U.S. 436 (1966), the interrogating officer follows it with Miranda warnings and then leads the suspect to cover the same ground a second time. The question here is the admissibility of the repeated statement."

C. Supreme Court's Answer

"Because this midstream recitation of warnings after interrogation and unwarned confession could not effectively comply with Miranda's constitutional requirement, we hold that a statement repeated after a warning in such circumstances is inadmissible."

II. CASE SUMMARY

A. Background

"Respondent Patrice Seibert's 12–year–old son Jonathan had cerebral palsy, and when he died in his sleep she feared charges of neglect because of bedsores on his body. In her presence, two of her teenage sons and two of their friends devised a plan to conceal the facts surrounding Jonathan's death by incinerating his body in the course of burning the family's mobile home, in which they planned to leave Donald Rector, a mentally ill teenager living with the family, to avoid any appearance that Jonathan had been unattended. Seibert's son Darian and a friend set the fire, and Donald died.

Five days later, the police awakened Seibert at 3 a.m. at a hospital where Darian was being treated for burns. In arresting her, Officer Kevin Clinton followed instructions from Rolla, Missouri, Officer Richard Hanrahan that he refrain from giving Miranda warnings. After Seibert had been taken to the police station and left alone in an interview room for 15 to 20 minutes, Officer Hanrahan questioned her without Miranda warnings for 30 to 40 minutes, squeezing her arm and repeating 'Donald was also to die in his sleep.' After Seibert finally admitted she knew Donald was meant to die in the fire, she was given a 20–minute coffee and cigarette break. Officer Hanrahan then turned on a tape recorder, gave Seibert the Miranda warnings, and obtained a signed waiver of rights from her. He resumed the questioning with 'Ok, 'trice, we've been talking for a little while about what happened on Wednesday the twelfth, haven't we?' and confronted her with her prewarning statements . . . .

After being charged with first-degree murder for her role in Donald's death, Seibert sought to exclude both her prewarning and postwarning statements. At the suppression hearing, Officer Hanrahan testified that he made a 'conscious decision' to withhold Miranda warnings . . . .

The trial court suppressed the prewarning statement but admitted the responses given after the Miranda recitation. A jury convicted Seibert of second-degree murder. On appeal, the Missouri Court of Appeals affirmed . . . .

The Supreme Court of Missouri reversed . . . ."

The U.S. Supreme Court granted certiorari to review the case.

B. Counsel of Record

ACLU Side (Respondent / Appellee): Amy M. Bartholow argued the cause and filed a brief for appellee.

Opposing Side (Petitioner / Appellant): Karen K. Mitchell, Chief Deputy Attorney General of Missouri, argued the cause for appellant.

With her on the briefs were Jeremiah W. (Jay) Nixon, Attorney General, James R. Layton, State Solicitor, and Shaun J. Mackelprang and Karen P. Hess, Assistant Attorneys General.

Irving L. Gornstein argued the cause for the United States as amicus curiae.

III. AMICI CURIAE

ACLU Side (Respondent / Appellee)

Brief of amici curiae filed on behalf of the American Civil Liberties Union, the ACLU of Eastern Missouri, and the National Association of Criminal Defense Lawyers by Jonathan L. Abram, E. Desmond Hogan, Christopher T. Handman, William H. Johnson, Kristin K. Cohen, Steven R. Shapiro, Ben Wizner, and Lisa Kemler.

Brief of amici curiae filed on behalf of Michael R. Bromwich et al. by George A. Cumming, Jr., Charles D. Weisselberg, Stephen J. Schulhofer, Kirsten D. Levingston, Frederick A. O. Schwarz, Jr., and Tom Gerety.

Opposing Side (Petitioner / Appellant)

Brief of amici curiae filed on behalf of the United States by Irving L. Gornstein, Solicitor General Olson, Acting Assistant Attorney General Wray, Deputy Solicitor General Dreeben, and Jonathan L. Marcus.

IV. THE SUPREME COURT'S DECISION

"'In criminal trials, in the courts of the United States, wherever a question arises whether a confession is incompetent because not voluntary, the issue is controlled by that portion of the Fifth Amendment . . . commanding that no person 'shall be compelled in any criminal case to be a witness against himself.'" . . .

In Miranda, we explained that the 'voluntariness doctrine in the state cases . . . encompasses all interrogation practices which are likely to exert such pressure upon an individual as to disable him from making a free and rational choice.' . . .

Accordingly, 'to reduce the risk of a coerced confession and to implement the Self–Incrimination Clause,' . . . this Court in Miranda concluded that 'the accused must be adequately and effectively apprised of his rights and the exercise of those rights must be fully honored.' Miranda conditioned the admissibility at trial of any custodial confession on warning a suspect of his rights: failure to give the prescribed warnings and obtain a waiver of rights before custodial questioning generally requires exclusion of any statements obtained. Conversely, giving the warnings and getting a waiver has generally produced a virtual ticket of admissibility . . . . To point out the obvious, this common consequence would not be common at all were it not that Miranda warnings are customarily given under circumstances allowing for a real choice between talking and remaining silent. . . .

The technique of interrogating in successive, unwarned and warned phases raises a new challenge to Miranda. Although we have no statistics on the frequency of this practice, it is not confined to Rolla, Missouri. . . .

By any objective measure, applied to circumstances exemplified here, it is likely that if the interrogators employ the technique of withholding warnings until after interrogation succeeds in eliciting a confession, the warnings will be ineffective in preparing the suspect for successive interrogation, close in time and similar in content. After all, the reason that question-first is catching on is as obvious as its manifest purpose, which is to get a confession the suspect would not make if he understood his rights at the outset; the sensible underlying assumption is that with one confession in hand before the warnings, the interrogator can count on getting its duplicate, with trifling additional trouble. Upon hearing warnings only in the aftermath of interrogation and just after making a confession, a suspect would hardly think he had a genuine right to remain silent, let alone persist in so believing once the police began to lead him over the same ground again. A more likely reaction on a suspect's part would be perplexity about the reason for discussing rights at that point, bewilderment being an unpromising frame of mind for knowledgeable decision. What is worse, telling a suspect that 'anything you say can and will be used against you,' without expressly excepting the statement just given, could lead to an entirely reasonable inference that what he has just said will be used, with subsequent silence being of no avail. Thus, when Miranda warnings are inserted in the midst of coordinated and continuing interrogation, they are likely to mislead and 'depriv[e] a defendant of knowledge essential to his ability to understand the nature of his rights and the consequences of abandoning them.' By the same token, it would ordinarily be unrealistic to treat two spates of integrated and proximately conducted questioning as independent interrogations subject to independent evaluation simply because Miranda warnings formally punctuate them in the middle. . . .

Strategists dedicated to draining the substance out of Miranda cannot accomplish by training instructions what Dickerson held Congress could not do by statute. Because the question-first tactic effectively threatens to thwart Miranda's purpose of reducing the risk that a coerced confession would be admitted, and because the facts here do not reasonably support a conclusion that the warnings given could have served their purpose, Seibert's postwarning statements are inadmissible. The judgment of the Supreme Court of Missouri is affirmed."

V. JUSTICE VOTE

5 Pro ACLU Side vs. 4 Con Opposing Side

ACLU Side (Respondent / Appellee)

1. Souter, D. – Wrote majority opinion
2. Stevens, J. – Joined majority opinion
3. Ginsburg, R. – Joined majority opinion
4. Breyer, S. – Wrote concurring opinion
5. Kennedy, A. – Wrote concurring opinion

Opposing Side (Petitioner / Appellant)

1. Thomas, C. – Joined O'Connor's dissent
2. O'Connor, S. – Wrote dissenting opinion
3. Scalia, A. – Joined O'Connor's dissent
4. Rehnquist, W. – Joined O'Connor's dissent

VI. A WIN OR LOSS FOR THE ACLU?

The ACLU filed as amicus curiae urging affirmance; the Supreme Court affirmed the Missouri Supreme Court's decision by a 5-4 vote, giving the ACLU an apparent win.

972. United States v. Patane

(Decided June 28, 2004; 542 U.S. 630)

I. ISSUE

A. Issues Discussed

4th Amendment, criminal procedure

B. Legal Question Presented

"In this case we must decide whether a failure to give a suspect the warnings prescribed by Miranda v. Arizona, 384 U.S. 436 (1966), requires suppression of the physical fruits of the suspect's unwarned but voluntary statements."

C. Supreme Court's Answer

"Because the Miranda rule protects against violations of the Self-Incrimination Clause, which, in turn, is not implicated by the introduction at trial of physical evidence resulting from voluntary statements, we answer the question presented in the negative."

II. CASE SUMMARY

A. Background

"In June 2001, respondent, Samuel Francis Patane, was arrested for harassing his ex-girlfriend, Linda O'Donnell. He was released on bond, subject to a temporary restraining order that prohibited him from contacting O'Donnell. Respondent apparently violated the restraining order by attempting to telephone O'Donnell. On June 6, 2001, Officer Tracy Fox of the Colorado Springs Police Department began to investigate the matter. On the same day, a county probation officer informed an agent of the Bureau of Alcohol, Tobacco and Firearms (ATF), that respondent, a convicted felon, illegally possessed a .40 Glock pistol. The ATF relayed this information to Detective Josh Benner, who worked closely with the ATF. Together, Detective Benner and Officer Fox proceeded to respondent's residence.

After reaching the residence and inquiring into respondent's attempts to contact O'Donnell, Officer Fox arrested respondent for violating the restraining order. Detective Benner attempted to advise respondent of his Miranda rights but got no further than the right to remain silent. At that point, respondent interrupted, asserting that he knew his rights, and neither officer attempted to complete the warning.

Detective Benner then asked respondent about the Glock. Respondent was initially reluctant to discuss the matter, stating: 'I am not sure I should tell you anything about the Glock because I don't want you to take it away from me.' Detective Benner persisted, and respondent told him that the pistol was in his bedroom. Respondent then gave Detective Benner permission to retrieve the pistol. Detective Benner found the pistol and seized it.

A grand jury indicted respondent for possession of a firearm by a convicted felon, in violation of 18 U.S.C. § 922(g)(1). The District Court granted respondent's motion to suppress the firearm, reasoning that the officers lacked probable cause to arrest respondent for violating the restraining order. It therefore declined to rule on respondent's alternative argument that the gun should be suppressed as the fruit of an unwarned statement.

The Court of Appeals reversed the District Court's ruling with respect to probable cause but affirmed the suppression order on respondent's alternative theory."

The Supreme Court granted certiorari to review the case.

B. Counsel of Record

ACLU Side (Respondent / Appellee): Jill M. Wichlens argued the cause for appellee. With her on the brief were Michael G. Katz and Virginia L. Grady.

Opposing Side (Petitioner / Appellant): Deputy Solicitor General Dreeben argued the cause for appellent. With him on the briefs were Solicitor General Olson, Acting Assistant Attorney General Wray, James A. Feldman, and Joseph C. Wyderko.

III. AMICI CURIAE

ACLU Side (Respondent / Appellee)

Brief of amici curiae filed on behalf of the National Association of Criminal Defense Lawyers, the American Civil Liberties Union, and the California Attorneys for Criminal Justice by James J. Tomkovicz, David M. Porter, and Steven R. Shapiro.

Brief of amici curiae filed on behalf of the Brennan Center for Justice by Stephen J. Schulhofer, Frederick A. O. Schwarz, Jr., Tom Gerety, and E. Joshua Rosenkranz.

Opposing Side (Petitioner / Appellant)

Brief of amici curiae filed on behalf of the State of Alabama et al. by William H. Pryor, Jr., Attorney General of Alabama, Nathan A. Forrester, Solicitor General, Michael B. Billingsley, Deputy Solicitor General, Marc A. Starrett, Assistant Attorney General, and by the Attorneys General for their respective States as follows: M. Jane Brady of Delaware, Charles J. Crist, Jr., of Florida, Mark J. Bennett of Hawaii, Lisa Madigan of Illinois, Steve Carter of Indiana, Mike McGrath of Montana, Jim Petro of Ohio, D. Michael Fisher of Pennsylvania, Lawrence E. Long of South Dakota, Paul G. Summers of Tennessee, Greg Abbott of Texas, Mark L. Shurtleff of Utah, William H. Sorrell of Vermont, Jerry W. Kilgore of Virginia, Peggy A. Lautenschlager of Wisconsin, and Patrick J. Crank of Wyoming.

Brief of amici curiae filed on behalf of the Criminal Justice Legal Foundation by Kent S. Scheidegger.

IV. THE SUPREME COURT'S DECISION

"As we explain below, the Miranda rule is a prophylactic employed to protect against violations of the Self-Incrimination Clause. The Self-Incrimination Clause, however, is not implicated by the admission into evidence of the physical fruit of a voluntary statement. Accordingly, there is no justification for extending the Miranda rule to this context. And just as the Self-Incrimination Clause primarily focuses on the criminal trial, so too does the

Miranda rule. The Miranda rule is not a code of police conduct, and police do not violate the Constitution (or even the Miranda rule, for that matter) by mere failures to warn. For this reason, the exclusionary rule articulated in cases such as Wong Sun does not apply. Accordingly, we reverse the judgment of the Court of Appeals and remand the case for further proceedings. . . .

In the present case, the Court of Appeals, relying on Dickerson, wholly adopted the position that the taking of unwarned statements violates a suspect's constitutional rights. And, of course, if this were so, a strong deterrence-based argument could be made for suppression of the fruits.

But Dickerson's characterization of Miranda as a constitutional rule does not lessen the need to maintain the closest possible fit between the Self-Incrimination Clause and any judge-made rule designed to protect it. And there is no such fit here. Introduction of the nontestimonial fruit of a voluntary statement, such as respondent's Glock, does not implicate the Self-Incrimination Clause. The admission of such fruit presents no risk that a defendant's coerced statements (however defined) will be used against him at a criminal trial. In any case, '[t]he exclusion of unwarned statements . . . is a complete and sufficient remedy' for any perceived Miranda violation. There is simply no need to extend (and therefore no justification for extending) the prophylactic rule of Miranda to this context.

Similarly, because police cannot violate the Self-Incrimination Clause by taking unwarned though voluntary statements, an exclusionary rule cannot be justified by reference to a deterrence effect on law enforcement, as the Court of Appeals believed. Our decision not to apply Wong Sun to mere failures to give Miranda warnings was sound at the time Tucker and Elstad were decided, and we decline to apply Wong Sun to such failures now.

The Court of Appeals ascribed significance to the fact that, in this case, there might be 'little [practical] difference between [respondent's] confessional statement' and the actual physical evidence. The distinction, the court said, 'appears to make little sense as a matter of policy.' But, putting policy aside, we have held that '[t]he word 'witness' in the constitutional text limits the' scope of the Self-Incrimination Clause to testimonial evidence. The Constitution itself makes the distinction. And although it is true that the Court requires the exclusion of the physical fruit of actually coerced statements, it must be remembered that statements taken without sufficient Miranda warnings are presumed to have been coerced only for certain purposes and then only when necessary to protect the privilege against self-incrimination. . . . For the reasons discussed above, we decline to extend that presumption further.

Accordingly, we reverse the judgment of the Court of Appeals and remand the case for further proceedings."

V. JUSTICE VOTE

4 Pro ACLU Side vs. 5 Con Opposing Side

ACLU Side (Respondent / Appellee)

1. Souter, D. – Wrote dissenting opinion
2. Stevens, J. – Joined Souter's dissent
3. Ginsburg, R. – Joined Souter's dissent
4. Breyer, S. – Wrote dissenting opinion

Opposing Side (Petitioner / Appellant)

1. Thomas, C. – Wrote plurality opinion
2. O'Connor, S. – Joined Kennedy's concurrence
3. Scalia, A. – Joined plurality opinion
4. Kennedy, A. – Wrote concurring opinion
5. Rehnquist, W. – Joined plurality opinion

VI. A WIN OR LOSS FOR THE ACLU?

The ACLU filed as amicus curiae urging affirmance; the Supreme Court reversed the Court of Appeals' decision by a 5-4 vote, giving the ACLU an apparent loss.

973. Ashcroft v. American Civil Liberties Union

(Decided June 29, 2004; 542 U.S. 656)

I. ISSUE

A. Issues Discussed

1st Amendment, press, speech, association, obscenity

B. Legal Question Presented

"This case presents a challenge to a statute enacted by Congress to protect minors from exposure to sexually explicit materials on the Internet, the Child Online Protection Act (COPA). We must decide whether the Court of Appeals was correct to affirm a ruling by the District Court that enforcement of COPA should be enjoined because the statute likely violates the First Amendment."

C. Supreme Court's Answer

"On this record, the Government has not shown that the less restrictive alternatives proposed by respondents should be disregarded. Those alternatives, indeed, may be more effective than the provisions of COPA. The District Court did not abuse its discretion when it entered the preliminary injunction."

II. CASE SUMMARY

A. Background

"COPA is the second attempt by Congress to make the Internet safe for minors by criminalizing certain Internet speech. The first attempt was the Communications Decency Act of 1996 . . . . The Court held the CDA unconstitutional because it was not narrowly tailored to serve a compelling governmental interest and because less restrictive alternatives were available. . . .

COPA imposes criminal penalties of a $50,000 fine and six months in prison for the knowing posting, for 'commercial purposes,' of World Wide Web content that is 'harmful to minors.' . . .

Respondents, Internet content providers and others concerned with protecting the freedom of speech, filed suit in the United States District Court for the Eastern District of Pennsylvania. They sought a preliminary injunction against enforcement of the statute. After considering testimony from witnesses presented by both respondents and the Government, the District Court issued an order granting the preliminary injunction. . . .

The Government appealed the District Court's decision to the United States Court of Appeals for the Third Circuit. The Court of Appeals affirmed the preliminary injunction, but on a different ground. . . . We granted certiorari and reversed, holding that the community-standards language did not, standing alone, make the statute unconstitutionally overbroad. We emphasized, however, that our decision was limited to that narrow issue. We remanded the case to the Court of Appeals to reconsider whether the District Court had been correct to grant the preliminary injunction. On remand, the Court of Appeals again affirmed the District Court. The Court of Appeals concluded that the statute was not narrowly tailored to serve a compelling Government interest, was overbroad, and was not the least restrictive means available for the Government to serve the interest of preventing minors from using the Internet to gain access to materials that are harmful to them."

The Supreme Court granted certiorari to review the case.

B. Counsel of Record

ACLU Side (Respondent / Appellee): Ann E. Beeson of the American Civil Liberties Union Foundation argued the cause for appellees. With her on the brief were Christopher R. Harris, Michele M. Pyle, Mark H. Goldberg, Nia Cross, David L. Sobel, Lee Tien, and Christopher A. Hansen, Sharon M. McGowan, and Steven R. Shapiro of the American Civil Liberties Union Foundation, and Stefan Presser of the American Civil Liberties Union of Pennsylvania.

Opposing Side (Petitioner / Appellant): Solicitor General Olson argued the cause for appellant. With him on the briefs were Assistant Attorney General Keisler, Deputy Solicitor General Kneedler, Irving L. Gornstein, Barbara L. Herwig, Charles W. Scarborough, and August E. Flentje.

III. AMICI CURIAE

ACLU Side (Respondent / Appellee)

Brief of amici curiae filed on behalf of the American Society of Journalists and Authors et al. by Carl A. Solano, Theresa E. Loscalzo, Jennifer DuFault James, and Stephen J. Shapiro.

Brief of amici curiae filed on behalf of the Association of American Publishers, Inc., et al. by R. Bruce Rich, Jonathan Bloom, Jerry Berman, John B. Morris, Jr., and Robert Corn-Revere.

Brief of amici curiae filed on behalf of Volunteer Lawyers for the Arts et al. by Seth M. Galanter, Charles H. Kennedy, Lois K. Perrin, and Elliot M. Mincberg.

Opposing Side (Petitioner / Appellant)

Brief of amici curiae filed on behalf of DuPage County, Illinois, by Richard Hodyl, Jr., and Joseph E. Birkett.

Brief of amici curiae filed on behalf of the American Center for Law and Justice et al. by Jay Alan Sekulow, Stuart J. Roth, Colby M. May, Joel H. Thornton, John P. Tuskey, and Shannon D. Woodruff.

Brief of amici curiae filed on behalf of Focus on the Family et al. by William Wagner, Steve Reed, and Pat Trueman.

Brief of amici curiae filed on behalf of Morality in Media, Inc., by Paul J. McGeady.

Brief of amici curiae filed on behalf of WallBuilders, Inc., by Barry C. Hodge.

Brief of amici curiae filed on behalf of Senator John S. McCain et al. by Carol A. Clancy and Bruce A. Taylor.

IV. THE SUPREME COURT'S DECISION

"'This Court, like other appellate courts, has always applied the abuse of discretion standard on review of a preliminary injunction.' . . . If the underlying constitutional question is close, therefore, we should uphold the injunction and remand for trial on the merits. Applying this mode of inquiry, we agree with the Court of Appeals that the District Court did not abuse its discretion in entering the preliminary injunction. Our reasoning in support of this conclusion, however, is based on narrower, more specific grounds than the rationale the Court of Appeals adopted. . . . Because we affirm the District Court's decision to grant the preliminary injunction for the reasons relied on by the District Court, we decline to consider the correctness of the other arguments relied on by the Court of Appeals.

In deciding whether to grant a preliminary injunction, a district court must consider whether the plaintiffs have demonstrated that they are likely to prevail on the merits. . . . As the Government bears the burden of proof on the ultimate question of COPA's constitutionality, respondents must be deemed likely to prevail unless the Government has shown that respondents' proposed less restrictive alternatives are less effective than COPA. Applying that analysis, the District Court concluded that respondents were likely to prevail. That conclusion was not an abuse of discretion, because on this record there are a number of plausible, less restrictive alternatives to the statute.

The primary alternative considered by the District Court was blocking and filtering software. . . .

There are also important practical reasons to let the injunction stand pending a full trial on the merits. First, the potential harms from reversing the injunction outweigh those of leaving it in place by mistake. . . .

Second, there are substantial factual disputes remaining in the case. . . .

Third, and on a related point, the factual record does not reflect current technological reality—a serious flaw in any case involving the Internet. . . .

On a final point, it is important to note that this opinion does not hold that Congress is incapable of enacting any regulation of the Internet designed to prevent minors from gaining access to harmful materials. . . . This opinion does not foreclose the District Court from concluding, upon a proper showing by the Government that meets the Government's constitutional burden as defined in this opinion, that COPA is the least restrictive alternative available to accomplish Congress' goal. . . .

On this record, the Government has not shown that the less restrictive alternatives proposed by respondents should be disregarded. Those alternatives, indeed, may be more effective than the provisions of COPA. The District Court did not abuse its discretion when it entered the preliminary injunction. The judgment of the Court of Appeals is affirmed, and the case is remanded for further proceedings consistent with this opinion."

V. JUSTICE VOTE

5 Pro ACLU Side vs. 4 Con Opposing Side

ACLU Side (Respondent / Appellee)

1. Kennedy, A. – Wrote majority opinion
2. Thomas, C. – Joined majority opinion
3. Ginsburg, R. – Joined Stevens' concurrence
4. Souter, D. – Joined majority opinion
5. Stevens, J. – Wrote concurring opinion

Opposing Side (Petitioner / Appellant)

1. Scalia, A. – Wrote dissenting opinion
2. Breyer, S. – Wrote dissenting opinion
3. Rehnquist, W. – Joined Breyer's dissent
4. O'Connor, S. – Joined Breyer's dissent

VI. A WIN OR LOSS FOR THE ACLU?

The ACLU, as a party of record and counsel of record, argued the case for appellee, urging affirmance; the Supreme Court affirmed the Court of Appeals' decision by a 5-4 vote, giving the ACLU an apparent win.

974. Sosa v. Alvarez-Machain

Decided June 29, 2004; 542 U.S. 692)

I. ISSUE

A. Issues Discussed

Federal, civil rights, immunity

B. Legal Question Presented

"The two issues are whether respondent Alvarez–Machain's allegation that the Drug Enforcement Administration instigated his abduction from Mexico for criminal trial in the United States supports a claim against the Government under the Federal Tort Claims Act (FTCA or Act), 28 U.S.C. §§ 1346(b)(1), 2671–2680, and whether he may recover under the Alien Tort Statute (ATS), 28 U.S.C. § 1350."

C. Supreme Court's Answer

"We hold that he is not entitled to a remedy under either statute."

II. CASE SUMMARY

A. Background

"In 1985, an agent of the Drug Enforcement Administration (DEA), Enrique Camarena–Salazar, was captured on assignment in Mexico and taken to a house in Guadalajara, where he was tortured over the course of a 2–day interrogation, then murdered. Based in part on eyewitness testimony, DEA officials in the United States came to believe that respondent Humberto Alvarez–Machain (Alvarez), a Mexican physician, was present at the house and acted to prolong the agent's life in order to extend the interrogation and torture.

In 1990, a federal grand jury indicted Alvarez for the torture and murder of Camarena–Salazar, and the United States District Court for the Central District of California issued a warrant for his arrest. The DEA asked the Mexican Government for help in getting Alvarez into the United States, but when the requests and negotiations proved fruitless, the DEA approved a plan to hire Mexican nationals to seize Alvarez and bring him to the United States for trial. As so planned, a group of Mexicans, including petitioner Jose Francisco Sosa, abducted Alvarez from his house, held him overnight in a motel, and brought him by private plane to El Paso, Texas, where he was arrested by federal officers.

Once in American custody, Alvarez moved to dismiss the indictment on the ground that his seizure was 'outrageous governmental conduct,' and violated the extradition treaty between the United States and Mexico. The District Court agreed, the Ninth Circuit affirmed, and we reversed, holding that the fact of Alvarez's forcible seizure did not affect the jurisdiction of a federal court. The case was tried in 1992, and ended at the close of the Government's case, when the District Court granted Alvarez's motion for a judgment of acquittal.

In 1993, after returning to Mexico, Alvarez began the civil action before us here. He sued Sosa, Mexican citizen and DEA operative Antonio Garate–Bustamante, five unnamed Mexican civilians, the United States, and four DEA agents. So far as it matters here, Alvarez sought damages from the United States under the FTCA, alleging false arrest, and from Sosa under the ATS, for a violation of the law of nations. The former statute authorizes suit 'for ... personal injury ... caused by the negligent or wrongful act or omission of any employee of the Government while acting within the scope of his office or employment.' The latter provides in its entirety that '[t]he district courts shall have original jurisdiction of any civil action by an alien for a tort only, committed in violation of the law of nations or a treaty of the United States.'

The District Court granted the Government's motion to dismiss the FTCA claim, but awarded summary judgment and $25,000 in damages to Alvarez on the ATS claim. A three-judge panel of the Ninth Circuit then affirmed the ATS judgment, but reversed the dismissal of the FTCA claim.

A divided en banc court came to the same conclusion."

The Supreme Court granted certiorari to review the case.

B. Counsel of Record

ACLU Side (Respondent / Appellee): Paul L. Hoffman argued the cause for appellee Alvarez-Machain in both cases. With him on the brief were Erwin Chemerinsky, Michael Morrison, Ralph G. Steinhardt, W. Allan Edmiston, Douglas E. Mirell, Steven R. Shapiro of the American Civil Liberties Union, Mark D. Rosenbaum, Ranjana Natarajan, Dilan Esper, and Alan Castillo of the ACLU Foundation of Southern California.

Opposing Side (Petitioner / Appellant): Deputy Solicitor General Clement argued the cause for the United States, as appellant in No. 03–485, and respondent under this Court's Rule 12.6 in support of petitioner in No. 03–339. With him on the briefs were Solicitor General Olson, Acting Assistant Attorney General Schiffer, Deputy Solicitor General Kneedler, Deputy Assistant Attorney General Katsas, Gregory G. Garre, Jeffrey A. Lamken, Douglas N. Letter, Barbara L. Herwig, Robert M. Loeb, and William H. Taft IV.

Carter G. Phillips argued the cause for appellant in No. 03–339. With him on the briefs were Joseph R. Guerra, Marinn F. Carlson, Maria T. DiGiulian, Ryan D. Nelson, and Charles S. Leeper.

III. AMICI CURIAE

ACLU Side (Respondent / Appellee)

Brief of amici curiae filed on behalf of Alien Friends Representing Hungarian Jews and Bougainvilleans Interests by Steve W. Berman, R. Brent Walton, Jonathan W. Cuneo, David W. Stanley, Michael Waldman, and Samuel J. Dubbin.

Brief of amici curiae filed on behalf of Amnesty International et al. by Beth Stephens.

Brief of amici curiae filed on behalf of the Center for Justice and Accountability et al. by Laurel E. Fletcher, Peter Weiss, and Jennifer Green.

Brief of amici curiae filed on behalf of the Center for Women Policy Studies et al. by Rhonda Copelon.

Brief of amici curiae filed on behalf of the Presbyterian Church of Sudan et al. by Carey R. D'Avino, Stephen A. Whinston, and Lawrence Kill.

Brief of amici curiae filed on behalf of the World Jewish Congress et al. by Bill Lann Lee, Stanley M. Chesley, Paul De Marco, Burt Neuborne, and Michael D. Hausfeld.

Brief of amici curiae filed on behalf of Wendy A. Adams et al. by William J. Aceves and David S. Weissbrodt.

Brief of amici curiae filed on behalf of Mary Robinson et al. by Harold Hongju Koh, John M. Townsend, and William R. Stein.

Brief of amici curiae filed on behalf of Barry Amundsen et al. by Penny M. Venetis.

Brief of amici curiae filed on behalf of the International Labor Rights Fund et al. by Terrence P. Collingsworth and Natacha Thys.

Brief of amici curiae filed on behalf of Vikram Amar et al. by Nicholas W. van Aelstyn.

Brief of amici curiae filed on behalf of James Akins et al. by Thomas E. Bishop.

Brief of amici curiae filed on behalf of the Government of the Commonwealth of Australia et al. by Donald I. Baker and W. Todd Miller.

Brief of amici curiae filed on behalf of the European Commission by Jeffrey P. Cunard in support of neither party.

Opposing Side (Petitioner / Appellant)

Brief of amici curiae filed on behalf of the National Association of Manufacturers by Paul R. Friedman, John Townsend Rich, William F. Sheehan, Jan S. Amundson, and Quentin Riegel.

Brief of amici curiae filed on behalf of the National Foreign Trade Council et al. by Daniel M. Petrocelli, M. Randall Oppenheimer, Walter E. Dellinger III, Pamela A. Harris, and Robin S. Conrad.

Brief of amici curiae filed on behalf of the Pacific Legal Foundation by Anthony T. Caso.

Brief of amici curiae filed on behalf of the Washington Legal Foundation et al. by Donald B. Ayer, Christian G. Vergonis, Daniel J. Popeo, and Richard A. Samp.

Brief of amici curiae filed on behalf of Samuel Estreicher et al. by Paul B. Stephan and Mr. Estreicher, pro se.

IV. THE SUPREME COURT'S DECISION

"The Government seeks reversal of the judgment of liability under the FTCA on two principal grounds. It argues that the arrest could not have been tortious, because it was authorized by 21 U.S.C. § 878, setting out the arrest authority of the DEA, and it says that in any event the liability asserted here falls within the FTCA exception to waiver of sovereign immunity for claims 'arising in a foreign country.' We think the exception applies and decide on that ground. . . .

The FTCA 'was designed primarily to remove the sovereign immunity of the United States from suits in tort and, with certain specific exceptions, to render the Government liable in tort as a private individual would be under like circumstances.' . . . But the Act also limits its waiver of sovereign immunity in a number of ways. . . .

Here the significant limitation on the waiver of immunity is the Act's exception for '[a]ny claim arising in a foreign country,' a provision that on its face seems plainly applicable to the facts of this action. . . .

Notwithstanding the straightforward language of the foreign country exception, the Ninth Circuit allowed the action to proceed under what has come to be known as the 'headquarters doctrine.' . . . Headquarters claims 'typically involve allegations of negligent guidance in an office within the United States of employees who cause damage while in a foreign country, or of activities which take place within a foreign country.' In such instances, these courts have concluded that § 2680(k) does not bar suit.

The reasoning of the Ninth Circuit here was that, since Alvarez's abduction in Mexico was the direct result of wrongful acts of planning and direction by DEA agents located in California, 'Alvarez's abduction fits the headquarters doctrine like a glove.' . . .

Thus, the Ninth Circuit held that Alvarez's claim did not 'aris[e] in' a foreign country.

The potential effect of this sort of headquarters analysis flashes the yellow caution light. . . . The headquarters doctrine threatens to swallow the foreign country exception whole, certainly at the pleadings stage.

The need for skepticism is borne out by two considerations. One of them is pertinent to cases like this one, where harm was arguably caused both by individual action in a foreign country as well as by planning in the United States; the other is suggested simply because the harm occurred on foreign soil. . . .

We . . . hold that the FTCA's foreign country exception bars all claims based on any injury suffered in a foreign country, regardless of where the tortious act or omission occurred. . . .

Alvarez has also brought an action under the ATS against petitioner Sosa, who argues (as does the United States supporting him) that there is no relief under the ATS because the statute does no more than vest federal courts with jurisdiction, neither creating nor authorizing the courts to recognize any particular right of action without further congressional action. . . . .

In sum, although the ATS is a jurisdictional statute creating no new causes of action, the reasonable inference from the historical materials is that the statute was intended to have practical effect the moment it became law. The jurisdictional grant is best read as having been enacted on the understanding that the common law would provide a cause of action for the modest number of international law violations with a potential for personal liability at the time. . . .

We think it is correct, then, to assume that the First Congress understood that the district courts would recognize private causes of action for certain torts in violation of the law of nations . . . . We assume, too, that no development in the two centuries from the enactment of § 1350 to the birth of the modern line of cases beginning with Filartiga v. Pena–Irala, 630 F.2d 876 (C.A.2 1980), has categorically precluded federal courts from recognizing a claim under the law of nations as an element of common law . . . . Accordingly, we think courts should require any claim based on the present-day law of nations to rest on a norm of international character accepted by the civilized world and defined with a specificity comparable to the features of the 18th-century paradigms we have recognized. This requirement is fatal to Alvarez's claim. . . .

Whatever may be said for the broad principle Alvarez advances, in the present, imperfect world, it expresses an aspiration that exceeds any binding customary rule having the specificity we require. Creating a private cause of action to further that aspiration would go beyond any residual common law discretion we think it appropriate to exercise. It is enough to hold that a single illegal detention of less than a day, followed by the transfer of custody to lawful authorities and a prompt arraignment, violates no norm of customary international law so well defined as to support the creation of a federal remedy. . . .

The judgment of the Court of Appeals is reversed."

V. JUSTICE VOTE

0 Pro ACLU Side vs. 9 Con Opposing Side

Opposing Side (Petitioner / Appellant)

1. Souter, D. – Wrote majority opinion
2. Thomas, C. – Joined majority opinion in part, joined Scalia's opinion
3. Ginsburg, R. – Joined majority opinion in part, wrote opinion concurring in part and concurring in the judgment
4. O'Connor, S. – Joined majority opinion in
5. Stevens, J. – Joined majority opinion
6. Breyer, S. – Joined majority opinion in part, joined Ginsburg's opinion, wrote opinion concurring in part and concurring in the judgment
7. Scalia, A. – Joined majority opinion in part, wrote opinion concurring in part and concurring in the judgment
8. Kennedy, A. – Joined majority opinion
9. Rehnquist, W. – Joined majority opinion in part, joined Scalia's opinion

VI. A WIN OR LOSS FOR THE ACLU?

The ACLU argued the case for appellee, urging affirmance; the Supreme Court reversed the Court of Appeals' decision by a 9-0 vote, giving the ACLU an apparent loss.

975. Leocal v. Ashcroft

(Decided November 9, 2004; 543 U.S. 1)

I. ISSUE

A. Issues Discussed

Immigration/Citizenship

B. Legal Question Presented

Whether a conviction for "driving under the influence of alcohol (DUI) and causing serious bodily injury" is "a 'crime of violence' under 18 U.S.C. § 16, and therefore an 'aggravated felony' under the Immigration and Nationality Act (INA)," making petitioner deportable.

C. Supreme Court's Answer

This DUI conviction is not a "crime of violence" and, therefore, does not make petitioner eligible for deportation.

II. CASE SUMMARY

A. Background

"Petitioner Josue Leocal, a Haitian citizen who is a lawful permanent resident of the United States, was convicted in 2000 of driving under the influence of alcohol (DUI) and causing serious bodily injury, in violation of Florida law. Classifying this conviction as a 'crime of violence' under 18 U.S.C. § 16, and therefore an 'aggravated felony' under the Immigration and Nationality Act (INA), an Immigration Judge and the Board of Immigration Appeals (BIA) ordered that petitioner be deported pursuant to § 237(a) of the INA. The Court of Appeals for the Eleventh Circuit agreed, dismissing petitioner's petition for review."

The Supreme Court granted certiorari to review the case.

B. Counsel of Record

ACLU Side (Petitioner / Appellant): J. Sedwick Sollers III argued the cause for appellant. With him on the briefs were Patricia L. Maher and Michael J. Ciatti.

Opposing Side (Respondent / Appellee): Dan Himmelfarb argued the cause for appellees. With him on the brief were Acting Solicitor General Clement, Assistant Attorney General Keisler, Deputy Solicitors General Dreeben and Kneedler, Donald E. Keener, and Greg D. Mack.

III. AMICI CURIAE

ACLU Side (Petitioner / Appellant)

Brief of amici curiae filed on behalf of the National Association of Criminal Defense Lawyers, American Civil Liberties Union, American Immigration Lawyers Association, Defending Immigrants Parternships, and New York State Defenders Association by Paul A. Engelmayer, Douglas F. Curtis, Jon Connolly, Joshua L. Dratel, Richard Willstatter, Lucas Guttentag, Steven R. Shapiro, Robin L. Goldfaden, Lory Diana Rosenberg, Jeanne A. Butterfield, Marianne Yang, and Manuel D. Vargas.

Brief of amici curiae filed on behalf of Citizens and Immigrants for Equal Justice et al. by Carmine D. Boccuzzi, Jr.

Brief of amici curiae filed on behalf of the Midwest Immigrant & Human Rights Center by Shashank S. Upadhye.

Opposing Side (Respondent / Appellee)

No briefs of amici curiae were filed on behalf of appellee.

IV. THE SUPREME COURT'S DECISION

"Title 18 U.S.C. § 16 was enacted as part of the Comprehensive Crime Control Act of 1984, which broadly reformed the federal criminal code in such areas as sentencing, bail, and drug enforcement, and which added a variety of new violent and nonviolent offenses. Congress employed the term 'crime of violence' in numerous places in the Act, such as for defining the elements of particular offenses, . . . or for directing when a hearing is required before a charged individual can be released on bail, see § 3142(f) . . . . Congress therefore provided in § 16 a general definition of the term 'crime of violence' to be used throughout the Act. Section 16 has since been incorporated into a variety of statutory provisions, both criminal and noncriminal.

Here, pursuant to § 237(a) of the INA, the Court of Appeals applied § 16 to find that petitioner's DUI conviction rendered him deportable. In determining whether petitioner's conviction falls within the ambit of § 16, the statute directs our focus to the 'offense' of conviction. . . . This language requires us to look to the elements and the nature of the offense of conviction, rather than to the particular facts relating to petitioner's crime.

Florida Stat. § 316.193(3)(c)(2) makes it a third-degree felony for a person to operate a vehicle while under the influence and, 'by reason of such operation, caus[e] . . . [s]erious bodily injury to another.' The Florida statute, while it requires proof of causation of injury, does not require proof of any particular mental state. . . . The question here is whether § 16 can be interpreted to include such offenses.

Our analysis begins with the language of the statute. . . .

Whether or not the word 'use' alone supplies a mens rea element, the parties' primary focus on that word is too narrow. . . . The key phrase in § 16(a)—the 'use . . . of physical force against the person or property of another'—most naturally suggests a higher degree of intent than negligent or merely accidental conduct. Petitioner's DUI offense therefore is not a crime of violence under § 16(a).

Neither is petitioner's DUI conviction a crime of violence under § 16(b). . . .

In construing both parts of § 16, we cannot forget that we ultimately are determining the meaning of the term 'crime of violence.' The ordinary meaning of this term, combined with § 16's emphasis on the use of physical force against another person (or the risk of having to use such force in committing a crime), suggests a category of violent, active crimes that cannot be said naturally to include DUI offenses. . . .

Section 16 therefore cannot be read to include petitioner's conviction for DUI causing serious bodily injury under Florida law. . . .

Drunk driving is a nationwide problem, as evidenced by the efforts of legislatures to prohibit such conduct and impose appropriate penalties. But this fact does not warrant our shoehorning it into statutory sections where it does not fit. The judgment of the United States Court of Appeals for the Eleventh Circuit is therefore reversed, and the case is remanded for further proceedings consistent with this opinion."

V. JUSTICE VOTE

9 Pro ACLU Side vs. 0 Con Opposing Side

ACLU Side (Petitioner / Appellant)

1. Rehnquist, W. – Wrote unanimous opinion
2. Thomas, C. – Joined unanimous opinion
3. O'Connor, S. – Joined unanimous opinion
4. Stevens, J. – Joined unanimous opinion
5. Souter, D. – Joined unanimous opinion
6. Ginsburg, R. – Joined unanimous opinion
7. Breyer, S. – Joined unanimous opinion
8. Scalia, A. – Joined unanimous opinion
9. Kennedy, A. – Joined unanimous opinion

VI. A WIN OR LOSS FOR THE ACLU?

The ACLU filed as amicus curiae urging reversal of the judgment of the Court of Appeals; the Supreme Court reversed in a 9-0 vote, giving the ACLU an apparent win.

976. Kowalski v. Tesmer

(Decided December 13, 2004; 543 U.S. 125)

I. ISSUE

A. Issues Discussed

Criminal procedure

B. Legal Question Presented

"[W]hether [the attorneys who brought this case] have standing to raise the rights of others."

C. Supreme Court's Answer

"[W]e hold that the attorneys do not have third-party standing to assert the rights of Michigan indigent defendants denied appellate counsel."

II. CASE SUMMARY

A. Background

"In 1994, Michigan amended its Constitution to provide that 'an appeal by an accused who pleads guilty or nolo contendere shall be by leave of the court' and not as of right. Following this amendment, several Michigan state judges began to deny appointed appellate counsel to indigents who pleaded guilty, and the Michigan Legislature subsequently codified this practice. Under the statute, which was scheduled to go into effect on April 1, 2000, appointment of appellate counsel for indigents who plead guilty is prohibited, with certain mandatory and permissive exceptions.

A challenge to the Michigan practice was filed in the United States District Court for the Eastern District of Michigan. The named plaintiffs included the two attorney respondents and three indigents who were denied appellate counsel after pleading guilty. Pursuant to Rev. Stat. § 1979, 42 U.S.C. § 1983, they alleged that the Michigan practice and statute denied indigents their federal constitutional rights to due process and equal protection. They sought declaratory and injunctive relief against the practice and the statute.

A day before the statute was to take effect, the District Court issued an order holding the practice and statute unconstitutional. It ultimately issued an injunction that bound all Michigan state judges, requiring them not to deny appellate counsel to any indigent who pleaded guilty. A panel of the Court of Appeals for the Sixth Circuit reversed. The panel held that Younger v. Harris, 401 U.S. 37 (1971), abstention barred the suit by the indigents but that the attorneys had third-party standing to assert the rights of indigents. It then held that the statute was constitutional. The Court of Appeals granted rehearing en banc and reversed. The en banc majority agreed with the panel on standing but found that the statute was unconstitutional."

The Supreme Court granted certiorari to review the case.

B. Counsel of Record

ACLU Side (Respondent / Appellee): David A. Moran argued the cause for appellees. With him on the briefs were Mark Granzotto, Michael J. Steinberg and Kary L. Moss of the American Civil Liberties Union Foundation of Michigan, and Steven R. Shapiro of the American Civil Liberties Union Foundation.

Opposing Side (Petitioner / Appellant): Thomas L. Casey, Solicitor General of Michigan, argued the cause for petitioners. With him on the briefs was Michael A. Cox, Attorney General.

Judy E. Bregman filed briefs for respondent Kolenda in support of petitioners.

III. AMICI CURIAE

ACLU Side (Respondent / Appellee)

Brief of amici curiae filed on behalf of the American Bar Association by Dennis W. Archer, Seth P. Waxman, and Paul R. Q. Wolfson.

Brief of amici curiae filed on behalf of the National Association of Criminal Defense Lawyers et al. by Anthony J. Franze, Sheila B. Scheuerman, Steven D. Benjamin, and Paul M. Rashkind.

Brief of amici curiae filed on behalf of the National Legal Aid and Defender Association by Elliot H. Scherker and Karen M. Gottlieb.

Opposing Side (Petitioner / Appellant)

Brief of amici curiae filed on behalf of the State of Iowa et al. by Thomas J. Miller, Attorney General of Iowa, Douglas R. Marek, Deputy Attorney General, Darrel Mullins, Assistant Attorney General, and Gene C. Schaerr, and by the Attorneys General for their respective States as follows: Troy King of Alabama, Charles J. Crist of Florida, Mark J. Bennett of Hawaii, Lisa Madigan of Illinois, Steve Carter of Indiana, Gregory D. Stumbo of Kentucky, Charles C. Foti, Jr., of Louisiana, J. Joseph Curran, Jr., of Maryland, Mike McGrath of Montana, Jon Bruning of Nebraska, Brian Sandoval of Nevada, Jim Petro of Ohio, W. A. Drew Edmondson of Oklahoma, Hardy Myers of Oregon, Henry D. McMaster of South Carolina, Paul G. Summers of Tennessee, Greg Abbott of Texas, Mark L. Shurtleff of Utah, Jerry W. Kilgore of Virginia, and Christine O. Gregoire of Washington.

Brief of amici curiae filed on behalf of Wayne County, Michigan, by Timothy A. Baughman.

IV. THE SUPREME COURT'S DECISION

"The doctrine of standing asks whether a litigant is entitled to have a federal court resolve his grievance. This inquiry involves 'both constitutional limitations on federal-court jurisdiction and prudential limitations on its exercise.' In this case, we do not focus on the constitutional minimum of standing, which flows from Article III's case-or-controversy requirement. Instead, we shall assume the attorneys have satisfied Article III and address the alternative threshold question whether they have standing to raise the rights of others.

We have adhered to the rule that a party 'generally must assert his own legal rights and interests, and cannot rest his claim to relief on the legal rights or interests of third parties.' This rule assumes that the party with the right has the appropriate incentive to challenge (or not challenge) governmental action and to do so with the necessary zeal and appropriate presentation. . . .

We have not treated this rule as absolute, however, recognizing that there may be circumstances where it is necessary to grant a third party standing to assert the rights of another. But we have limited this exception by requiring that a party seeking third-party standing make two additional showings. First, we have asked whether the party asserting the right has a 'close' relationship with the person who possesses the right. Second, we have considered whether there is a 'hindrance' to the possessor's ability to protect his own interests.

We have been quite forgiving with these criteria in certain circumstances. . . .

The attorneys in this case invoke the attorney-client relationship to demonstrate the requisite closeness. Specifically, they rely on a future attorney-client relationship with as yet unascertained Michigan criminal defendants 'who will request, but be denied, the appointment of appellate counsel, based on the operation' of the statute. . . .

The attorneys before us do not have a 'close relationship' with their alleged 'clients;' indeed, they have no relationship at all.

We next consider whether the attorneys have demonstrated that there is a 'hindrance' to the indigents' advancing their own constitutional rights against the Michigan scheme. . . .

While we agree that an attorney would be valuable to a criminal defendant challenging the constitutionality of the scheme, we do not think that the lack of an attorney here is the type of hindrance necessary to allow another to assert the indigent defendants' rights. . . .

In this case, the three indigent criminal defendants who were originally plaintiffs in this § 1983 action were appropriately dismissed under Younger. As the Court of Appeals unanimously recognized, they had ongoing state criminal proceedings and ample avenues to raise their constitutional challenge in those proceedings. There also was no extraordinary circumstance requiring federal intervention. An unwillingness to allow the Younger principle to be thus circumvented is an additional reason to deny the attorneys third-party standing.

In sum, we hold that the attorneys do not have third-party standing to assert the rights of Michigan indigent defendants denied appellate counsel. We agree with the dissenting opinion in the Court of Appeals that 'it would be a short step from the . . . grant of third-party standing in this case to a holding that lawyers generally have third-party standing to bring in court the claims of future unascertained clients.'

The judgment of the Court of Appeals is therefore reversed, and the case is remanded for further proceedings consistent with this opinion."

V. JUSTICE VOTE

3 PRO ACLU SIDE VS. 6 CON OPPOSING SIDE

ACLU Side (Respondent / Appellee)

1. Stevens, J. – Joined Ginsburg's dissent
2. Ginsburg, R. – Wrote dissenting opinion
3. Souter, D. – Joined Ginsburg's dissent

Opposing Side (Petitioner / Appellant)

1. Rehnquist, W. – Wrote majority opinion
2. Thomas, C. – Wrote concurring opinion
3. O'Connor, S. – Joined majority opinion
4. Breyer, S. – Joined majority opinion
5. Scalia, A. – Joined majority opinion
6. Kennedy, A. – Joined majority opinion

VI. A WIN OR LOSS FOR THE ACLU?

The ACLU argued the cause for respondent urging affirmance; the Supreme Court reversed the Court of Appeals' decision by a 6-3 vote, giving the ACLU an apparent loss.

977. Clark v. Martinez

(Decided January 12, 2005; 543 U.S. 371)

I. ISSUE

A. Issues Discussed

Immigration/Citizenship

B. Legal Question Presented

"[W]hether th[e] construction of § 1231(a)(6) that we applied to the second category of aliens covered by the statute [in deciding Zadvydas v. Davis] applies as well to the first—that is, to the category of aliens 'ordered removed who [are] inadmissible under [§]1182.'"

C. Supreme Court's Answer

"Since the Government has suggested no reason why the period of time reasonably necessary to effect removal is longer for an inadmissible alien, the 6-month presumptive detention period we prescribed in Zadvydas applies."

II. CASE SUMMARY

A. Background

"Sergio Suarez Martinez (respondent in No. 03-878) and Daniel Benitez (petitioner in No. 03-7434) arrived in the United States from Cuba in June 1980 as part of the Mariel boatlift, . . . and were paroled into the country pursuant to the Attorney General's authority under 8 U.S.C. § 1182(d)(5). Until 1996, federal law permitted Cubans who were paroled into the United States to adjust their status to that of lawful permanent resident after one year. Neither Martinez nor Benitez qualified for this adjustment, however, because, by the time they applied, both men had become inadmissible because of prior criminal convictions in the United States. . . . Both men were convicted of additional felonies after their adjustment applications were denied . . . .

The Attorney General revoked Martinez's parole in December 2000. Martinez was taken into custody by the INS, and removal proceedings were commenced against him. An Immigration Judge found him inadmissible by reason of his prior convictions, and lack of sufficient documentation, and ordered him removed to Cuba. Martinez did not appeal. The INS continued to detain him after expiration of the 90-day removal period, and he remained in custody until he was released pursuant to the District Court order that was affirmed by the Court of Appeals' decision on review here.

Benitez's parole was revoked in 1993 (shortly after he was imprisoned for his convictions of that year), and the INS immediately initiated removal proceedings against him. In December 1994, an Immigration Judge determined Benitez to be excludable and ordered him deported . . . . Benitez did not seek further review. At the completion of his state prison term, the INS took him into custody for removal, and he continued in custody after expiration of the 90-day removal period. In September 2003, Benitez received notification that he was eligible for parole, contingent on his completion of a drug-abuse treatment program. Benitez completed the program while his case was pending before this Court, and shortly after completion was paroled for a period of one year. On October 15, 2004, two days after argument in this Court, Benitez was released from custody to sponsoring family members.

Both aliens filed a petition for a writ of habeas corpus under 28 U.S.C. § 2241 to challenge their detention beyond the 90-day removal period. In Martinez's case, the District Court for the District of Oregon accepted that removal was not reasonably foreseeable, and ordered the INS to release Martinez under conditions that the INS believed appropriate. The Court of Appeals for the Ninth Circuit summarily affirmed . . . . In Benitez's case, the District Court for the Northern District of Florida also concluded that removal would not occur in the 'foreseeable future,' but nonetheless denied the petition. The Court of Appeals for the Eleventh Circuit affirmed . . . ."

The Supreme Court granted certiorari to review both cases.

B. Counsel of Record

ACLU Side (Respondent / Appellee): Christine Stebbins Dahl, by appointment of the Court, argued the cause for appellee in No. 03-878. With her on the brief was Stephen R. Sady.

John S. Mills, by appointment of the Court, argued the cause for appellant in No. 03–7434. With him on the briefs were Tracy S. Carlin and Rebecca B. Creed.

Opposing Side (Petitioner / Appellant): Deputy Solicitor General Kneedler argued the cause for appellants in No. 03–878 and appellee in No. 03–7434. With him on the briefs were Acting Solicitor General Clement, former Solicitor General Olson, Assistant Attorney General Keisler, Patricia A. Millett, and Donald E. Keener.

III. AMICI CURIAE

ACLU Side (Respondent / Appellee)

Brief of amici curiae filed on behalf of the American Bar Association by Dennis W. Archer, John J. Gibbons, Lawrence S. Lustberg, Jonathan L. Hafetz, and Philip G. Gallagher.

Brief of amici curiae filed on behalf of the American Civil Liberties Union by Judy Rabinovitz, Lucas Guttentag, Steven R. Shapiro, Paul A. Engelmayer, and David Sapir Lesser.

Brief of amici curiae filed on behalf of the American Immigration Law Foundation Legal Action Center et al. by George E. Quillin, G. Michael Halfenger, and Michael D. Leffel.

Brief of amici curiae filed on behalf of the Florida Immigrant Advocacy Center et al. by Stephen F. Hanlon.

Brief of amici curiae filed on behalf of the Lawyers Committee for Human Rights et al. by Steven E. Fineman, Bill Lann Lee, and Deborah Pearlstein.

Brief of amici curiae filed on behalf of Legal and Service Organizations by Joseph F. Tringali.

Brief of amici curiae filed on behalf of the North Carolina Justice and Community Development Center by James E. Coleman, Jr.

Brief of amici curiae filed on behalf of Regina Germain et al. by David J. Bodney.

Brief of amici curiae filed on behalf of the Cuban American Bar Association et al. by Catherine E. Stetson, William H. Johnson, and Gilbert Paul Carrasco.

Brief of amici curiae filed on behalf of National Refugee Resettlement and Advocacy Organizations by Peter M. Friedman.

Brief of amici curiae filed on behalf of Religious Organizations by Isabelle M. Carrillo.

Brief of amici curiae filed on behalf of Stuart E. Eizenstat et al. by David H. Remes.

Brief of amici curiae filed on behalf of Law Professors by Jonathan J. Ross and Melford O. Cleveland.

Opposing Side (Petitioner / Appellant)

Brief of amici curiae filed on behalf of the Washington Legal Foundation et al. by Daniel J. Popeo and Richard A. Samp.

IV. THE SUPREME COURT'S DECISION

"Title 8 U.S.C. § 1231(a)(6) provides, in relevant part, as follows: 'An alien ordered removed who is inadmissible under section 1182 of this title, removable under section 1227(a)(1)(C), 1227(a)(2), or 1227(a)(4) of this title or who has been determined by the [Secretary] to be a risk to the community or unlikely to comply with the order of removal, may be detained beyond the removal period and, if released, shall be subject to the terms of supervision in paragraph (3).'

By its terms, this provision applies to three categories of aliens: (1) those ordered removed who are inadmissible under § 1182, (2) those ordered removed who are removable under § 1227(a)(1)(C), § 1227(a)(2), or § 1227(a)(4), and (3) those ordered removed whom the Secretary determines to be either a risk to the community or a flight risk. In Zadvydas v. Davis, 533 U.S. 678 (2001), the Court interpreted this provision to authorize the Attorney General (now the Secretary) to detain aliens in the second category only as long as 'reasonably necessary' to remove them from the country. . . . The Court further held that the presumptive period during which the detention of an alien is reasonably necessary to effectuate his removal is six months; after that, the alien is eligible for conditional release if he can demonstrate that there is 'no significant likelihood of removal in the reasonably foreseeable future.'

The question presented by these cases, and the question that evoked contradictory answers from the Ninth and Eleventh Circuits, is whether this construction of § 1231(a)(6) that we applied to the second category of aliens covered by the statute applies as well to the first—that is, to the category of aliens 'ordered removed who [are] inadmissible under [§]1182.' We think the answer must be yes. The operative language of § 1231(a)(6), 'may be detained beyond the removal period,' applies without differentiation to all three categories of aliens that are its subject. To give these same words a different meaning for each category would be to invent a statute rather than interpret one. . . .

The Government fears that the security of our borders will be compromised if it must release into the country inadmissible aliens who cannot be removed. If that is so, Congress can attend to it. But for this Court to sanction indefinite detention in the face of Zadvydas would establish within our jurisprudence, beyond the power of Congress to remedy, the dangerous principle that judges can give the same statutory text different meanings in different cases.

Since the Government has suggested no reason why the period of time reasonably necessary to effect removal is longer for an inadmissible alien, the 6-month presumptive detention period we prescribed in Zadvydas applies. Both Martinez and Benitez were detained well beyond six months after their removal orders became final. The Government having brought forward nothing to indicate that a substantial likelihood of removal subsists despite the passage of six months (indeed, it concedes that it is no longer even involved in repatriation negotiations with Cuba); and the District Court in each case having determined that removal to Cuba is not reasonably foreseeable; the petitions for habeas corpus should have been granted. Accordingly, we affirm the judgment of the Ninth Circuit, reverse the judgment of the Eleventh Circuit, and remand both cases for proceedings consistent with this opinion."

V. JUSTICE VOTE

7 Pro ACLU Side vs. 2 Con Opposing Side

ACLU Side (Respondent / Appellee)

1. Scalia, A. – Wrote majority opinion
2. Ginsburg, R. – Joined majority opinion
3. Souter, D. – Joined majority opinion
4. O'Connor, S. – Wrote concurring opinion
5. Stevens, J. – Joined majority opinion
6. Breyer, S. – Joined majority opinion
7. Kennedy, A. – Joined majority opinion

Opposing Side (Petitioner / Appellant)

1. Thomas, C. – Wrote dissenting opinion
2. Rehnquist, W. – Joined Thomas' dissent in part

VI. A WIN OR LOSS FOR THE ACLU?

The ACLU filed as amicus curiae urging reversal in the Eleventh Circuit case; the Supreme Court reversed the Eleventh Circuit Court of Appeals' decision by a 7-2 vote, giving the ACLU an apparent win.

978. Illinois v. Caballes

(Decided January 24, 2005; 543 U.S. 405)

I. ISSUE

A. Issues Discussed

4th Amendment, drugs

B. Legal Question Presented

"'Whether the Fourth Amendment requires reasonable, articulable suspicion to justify using a drug-detection dog to sniff a vehicle during a legitimate traffic stop.'"

C. Supreme Court's Answer

"A dog sniff conducted during a concededly lawful traffic stop that reveals no information other than the location of a substance that no individual has any right to possess does not violate the Fourth Amendment."

II. CASE SUMMARY

A. Background

"Illinois State Trooper Daniel Gillette stopped respondent for speeding on an interstate highway. When Gillette radioed the police dispatcher to report the stop, a second trooper, Craig Graham, a member of the Illinois State Police Drug Interdiction Team, overheard the transmission and immediately headed for the scene with his narcotics-detection dog. When they arrived, respondent's car was on the shoulder of the road and respondent was in Gillette's vehicle. While Gillette was in the process of writing a warning ticket, Graham walked his dog around respondent's car. The dog alerted at the trunk. Based on that alert, the officers searched the trunk, found marijuana, and arrested respondent. The entire incident lasted less than 10 minutes.

Respondent was convicted of a narcotics offense and sentenced to 12 years' imprisonment and a $256,136 fine. The trial judge denied his motion to suppress the seized evidence and to quash his arrest. He held that the officers had not unnecessarily prolonged the stop and that the dog alert was sufficiently reliable to provide probable cause to conduct the search. Although the Appellate Court affirmed, the Illinois Supreme Court reversed, concluding that because the canine sniff was performed without any "specific and articulable facts" to suggest drug activity, the use of the dog 'unjustifiably enlarg[ed] the scope of a routine traffic stop into a drug investigation.'"

The Supreme Court granted certiorari to review the case.

B. Counsel of Record

ACLU Side (Respondent / Appellee): Ralph E. Meczyk argued the cause for appellee. With him on the brief was Lawrence H. Hyman.

Opposing Side (Petitioner / Appellant): Lisa Madigan, Attorney General of Illinois, argued the cause for appellant. With her on the briefs were Gary Feinerman, Solicitor General, and Linda D. Woloshin and Mary Fleming, Assistant Attorneys General.

Assistant Attorney General Wray argued the cause for the United States as amicus curiae.

III. AMICI CURIAE

ACLU Side (Respondent / Appellee)

Brief of amici curiae filed on behalf of the American Civil Liberties Union and the ACLU of Illinois by Barry Sullivan, Jacob I. Corré, Lisa D. Johnson, Steven R. Shapiro, Shannon P. Bartlett, and Harvey Grossman.

Brief of amici curiae filed on behalf of the National Association of Criminal Defense Lawyers by Jeffrey T. Green, John Wesley Hall, Jr., and David M. Siegel.

Opposing Side (Petitioner / Appellant)

Brief of amici curiae filed on behalf of the United States by Assistant Attorney General Wray, former Solicitor General Olson, Deputy Solicitor General Dreeben, James A. Feldman, and John A. Drennan.

Brief of amici curiae filed on behalf of the State of Arkansas et al. by Mike Beebe, Attorney General of Arkansas, Lauren Elizabeth Heil, Assistant Attorney General, and Dan Schweitzer, and by the Attorneys General for their respective States as follows: Troy King of Alabama, Terry Goddard of Arizona, Christopher L. Morano of Connecticut, M. Jane Brady of Delaware, Thurbert E. Baker of Georgia, Mark J. Bennett of Hawaii, Lawrence G. Wasden of Idaho, Steve Carter of Indiana, Phill Kline of Kansas, Charles C. Foti of Louisiana, G. Steven Rowe of Maine, J. Joseph Curran, Jr., of Maryland, Michael A. Cox of Michigan, Jon Bruning of Nebraska, Peter C. Harvey of New Jersey, Patricia A. Madrid of New Mexico, Roy Cooper of North Carolina, Wayne Stenehjem of North Dakota, Jim Petro of Ohio, Hardy Myers of Oregon, Henry D. McMaster of South Carolina, Lawrence E. Long of South Dakota, Greg Abbott of Texas, Mark L. Shurtleff of Utah, William H. Sorrell of Vermont, Jerry Kilgore of Virginia, and Patrick J. Crank of Wyoming.

Brief of amici curiae filed on behalf of the Illinois Association of

Chiefs of Police et al. by James G. Sotos.

IV. THE SUPREME COURT'S DECISION

"Here, the initial seizure of respondent when he was stopped on the highway was based on probable cause and was concededly lawful. It is nevertheless clear that a seizure that is lawful at its inception can violate the Fourth Amendment if its manner of execution unreasonably infringes interests protected by the Constitution. A seizure that is justified solely by the interest in issuing a warning ticket to the driver can become unlawful if it is prolonged beyond the time reasonably required to complete that mission. In an earlier case involving a dog sniff that occurred during an unreasonably prolonged traffic stop, the Illinois Supreme Court held that use of the dog and the subsequent discovery of contraband were the product of an unconstitutional seizure. We may assume that a similar result would be warranted in this case if the dog sniff had been conducted while respondent was being unlawfully detained.

In the state-court proceedings, however, the judges carefully reviewed the details of Officer Gillette's conversations with respondent and the precise timing of his radio transmissions to the dispatcher to determine whether he had improperly extended the duration of the stop to enable the dog sniff to occur. We . . . accept the state court's conclusion that the duration of the stop in this case was entirely justified by the traffic offense and the ordinary inquiries incident to such a stop. . . .

In our view, conducting a dog sniff would not change the character of a traffic stop that is lawful at its inception and otherwise executed in a reasonable manner, unless the dog sniff itself infringed respondent's constitutionally protected interest in privacy. Our cases hold that it did not.

Official conduct that does not 'compromise any legitimate interest in privacy' is not a search subject to the Fourth Amendment. We have held that any interest in possessing contraband cannot be deemed 'legitimate,' and thus, governmental conduct that only reveals the possession of contraband 'compromises no legitimate privacy interest.' . . .

Accordingly, the use of a well-trained narcotics-detection dog—one that 'does not expose noncontraband items that otherwise would remain hidden from public view,'—during a lawful traffic stop, generally does not implicate legitimate privacy interests. In this case, the dog sniff was performed on the exterior of respondent's car while he was lawfully seized for a traffic violation. Any intrusion on respondent's privacy expectations does not rise to the level of a constitutionally cognizable infringement. . . .

A dog sniff conducted during a concededly lawful traffic stop that reveals no information other than the location of a substance that no individual has any right to possess does not violate the Fourth Amendment.

The judgment of the Illinois Supreme Court is vacated, and the case is remanded for further proceedings not inconsistent with this opinion."

V. JUSTICE VOTE

2 Pro ACLU Side vs. 6 Con Opposing Side

ACLU Side (Respondent / Appellee)

1. Ginsburg, R. – Wrote dissenting opinion
2. Souter, D. – Joined Ginsburg's dissent

Opposing Side (Petitioner / Appellant)

1. Stevens, J. – Wrote majority opinion
2. Thomas, C. – Joined majority opinion
3. O'Connor, S. – Joined majority opinion
4. Breyer, S. – Joined majority opinion
5. Scalia, A. – Joined majority opinion
6. Kennedy, A. – Joined majority opinion

Rehnquist, W. – Took no part in the decision.

VI. A WIN OR LOSS FOR THE ACLU?

The ACLU filed as amicus curiae urging affirmance; the Supreme Court vacated the Illinois Supreme Court's decision by a 6-2 vote, giving the ACLU an apparent loss.

979. Johnson v. California

(Decided February 23, 2005; 543 U.S. 499)

I. ISSUE

A. Issues Discussed

Prison

B. Legal Question Presented

"The California Department of Corrections (CDC) has an unwritten policy of racially segregating prisoners in double cells in reception centers for up to 60 days each time they enter a new correctional facility. We consider whether strict scrutiny is the proper standard of review for an equal protection challenge to that policy."

C. Supreme Court's Answer

"We hold only that strict scrutiny is the proper standard of review and remand the case to allow the Court of Appeals for the Ninth Circuit, or the District Court, to apply it in the first instance."

II. CASE SUMMARY

A. Background

"CDC institutions house all new male inmates and all male inmates transferred from other state facilities in reception centers for up to 60 days upon their arrival. . . . Double-cell assignments in the reception centers are based on a number of factors, predominantly race. In fact, the CDC has admitted that the chances of an inmate being assigned a cellmate of another race are "[p]retty close" to zero percent. . . .

The CDC's asserted rationale for this practice is that it is necessary to prevent violence caused by racial gangs. . . . The CDC claims that it must therefore segregate all inmates while it determines whether they pose a danger to others.

With the exception of the double cells in reception areas, the rest of the state prison facilities—dining areas, yards, and cells—are fully integrated. After the initial 60-day period, prisoners are allowed to choose their own cellmates. The CDC usually grants inmate requests to be housed together, unless there are security reasons for denying them. . . .

Garrison Johnson is an African-American inmate in the custody of the CDC. He has been incarcerated since 1987 and, during that time, has been housed at a number of California prison facilities. Upon his arrival at Folsom prison in 1987, and each time he was transferred to a new facility thereafter, Johnson was double-celled with another African-American inmate.

Johnson filed a complaint pro se in the United States District Court for the Central District of California on February 24, 1995, alleging that the CDC's reception-center housing policy violated his right to equal protection under the Fourteenth Amendment by assigning him cellmates on the basis of his race. . . . The District Court dismissed his complaint for failure to state a claim. The Court of Appeals for the Ninth Circuit reversed and remanded, holding that Johnson had stated a claim for racial discrimination in violation of the Equal Protection Clause of the Fourteenth Amendment.

On remand, Johnson was appointed counsel and granted leave to amend his complaint. . . .

After discovery, the parties moved for summary judgment. The District Court granted summary judgment to the defendants on grounds that they were entitled to qualified immunity because their conduct was not clearly unconstitutional. The Court of Appeals for the Ninth Circuit affirmed. . . .

The Court of Appeals denied Johnson's petition for rehearing en banc."

The Supreme Court granted certiorari to review the case.

B. Counsel of Record

ACLU Side (Petitioner / Appellant): Bert H. Deixler argued the cause for appellant. With him on the briefs were Charles S. Sims, Lois D. Thompson, and Tanya L. Forsheit.

Acting Solicitor General Clement argued the cause for the United States as amicus curiae.

Opposing Side (Respondent / Appellee): Frances T. Grunder, Senior Assistant Attorney General of California, argued the cause for appellees. With her on the brief were Bill Lockyer, Attorney General, Manuel M. Medeiros, Solicitor General, Robert R. Anderson, Chief Assistant Attorney General, and Sara Turner, Supervising Deputy Attorney General.

III. AMICI CURIAE

ACLU Side (Petitioner / Appellant)

Brief of amici curiae filed on behalf of the United States by Acting Solicitor General Clement, former Solicitor General Olson, Assistant Attorney General Acosta, David B. Salmons, David K. Flynn, and Tovah R. Calderon.

Brief of amici curiae filed on behalf of the American Civil Liberties Union and its Three California Affiliates by Elizabeth Alexander, Craig A. Cowie, David C. Fathi, Steven R. Shapiro, Jordan C. Budd, Alan Schlosser, Ben Wizner, Peter J. Eliasberg, and Mark D. Rosenbaum.

Brief of amici curiae filed on behalf of Former State Corrections Officials by Michael C. Small.

Brief of amici curiae filed on behalf of the Pacific Legal Foundation by John H. Findley in support of neither party.

Opposing Side (Respondent / Appellee)

Brief of amici curiae filed on behalf of the State of Utah et al. by Mark L. Shurtleff, Attorney General of Utah, and Gene C. Schaerr, and by the Attorneys General for their respective States as follows: Troy King of Alabama, Gregg D. Renkes of Alaska, M. Jane Brady of Delaware, Lawrence G. Wasden of Idaho, Brian Sandoval of Nevada, Kelly A. Ayotte of New Hampshire, and Wayne Stenehjem of North Dakota.

Brief of amici curiae filed on behalf of the National Association of Black Law Enforcement Officers, Inc., by David T. Goldberg.

IV. THE SUPREME COURT'S DECISION

"We have held that 'all racial classifications [imposed by government] . . . must be analyzed by a reviewing court under strict scrutiny.' Under strict scrutiny, the government has the burden of proving that racial classifications 'are narrowly tailored measures that further compelling governmental interests.' . . .

The CDC claims that its policy should be exempt from our categorical rule because it is 'neutral'—that is, it 'neither benefits nor burdens one group or individual more than any other group or individual.' In other words, strict scrutiny should not apply because all prisoners are 'equally' segregated. The CDC's argument ignores our repeated command that 'racial classifications receive close scrutiny even when they may be said to burden or benefit the races equally.' . . .

We have previously applied a heightened standard of review in evaluating racial segregation in prisons. . . .

The need for strict scrutiny is no less important here, where prison officials cite racial violence as the reason for their policy. As we have recognized in the past, racial classifications 'threaten to stigmatize individuals by reason of their membership in a racial group and to incite racial hostility.' Indeed, by insisting that inmates be housed only with other inmates of the same race, it is possible that prison officials will breed further hostility among prisoners and reinforce racial and ethnic divisions. . . .

Because the CDC's policy is an express racial classification, it is 'immediately suspect.' We therefore hold that the Court of Appeals erred when it failed to apply strict scrutiny to the CDC's policy and to require the CDC to demonstrate that its policy is narrowly tailored to serve a compelling state interest. . . .

The CDC invites us to make an exception to the rule that strict scrutiny applies to all racial classifications, and instead to apply the deferential standard of review articulated in Turner v. Safley, 482 U.S. 78 (1987), because its segregation policy applies only in the prison context. We decline the invitation. . . .

The right not to be discriminated against based on one's race is not susceptible to the logic of Turner. It is not a right that need necessarily be compromised for the sake of proper prison administration. On the contrary, compliance with the Fourteenth Amendment's ban on racial discrimination is not only consistent with proper prison administration, but also bolsters the legitimacy of the entire criminal justice system. . . .

We did not relax the standard of review for racial classifications in prison in Lee, and we refuse to do so today. Rather, we explicitly reaffirm what we implicitly held in Lee: The 'necessities of prison security and discipline,' are a compelling government interest justifying only those uses of race that are narrowly tailored to address those necessities. . . .

The fact that strict scrutiny applies 'says nothing about the ultimate validity of any particular law; that determination is the job of the court applying strict scrutiny.' At this juncture, no such determination has been made. On remand, the CDC will have the burden of demonstrating that its policy is narrowly tailored with regard to new inmates as well as transferees. Prisons are dangerous places, and the special circumstances they present may justify racial classifications in some contexts. Such circumstances can be considered in applying strict scrutiny, which is designed to take relevant differences into account. . . .

We do not decide whether the CDC's policy violates the Equal Protection Clause. We hold only that strict scrutiny is the proper standard of review and remand the case to allow the Court of Appeals for the Ninth Circuit, or the District Court, to apply it in the first instance. . . . The judgment of the Court of Appeals is reversed, and the case is remanded for further proceedings consistent with this opinion."

V. JUSTICE VOTE

5 Pro ACLU Side vs. 3 Con Opposing Side

ACLU Side (Petitioner / Appellant)

1. O'Connor, S. – Wrote majority opinion
2. Ginsburg, R. – Wrote concurring opinion
3. Souter, D. – Joined Ginsburg's concurrence
4. Breyer, S. – Joined Ginsburg's concurrence
5. Kennedy, A. – Joined majority opinion

Opposing Side (Respondent / Appellee)

1. Thomas, C. – Wrote dissenting opinion
2. Scalia, A. – Joined Thomas' dissent
3. Stevens, J. – Wrote dissenting opinion

Rehnquist, W. – Took no part in the decision.

VI. A WIN OR LOSS FOR THE ACLU?

The ACLU filed as amicus curiae urging reversal of the judgment of the Court of Appeals; the Supreme Court reversed in a 5-3 vote, giving the ACLU an apparent win.

980. Roper v. Simmons

(Decided March 1, 2005; 543 U.S. 551)

I. ISSUE

A. Issues Discussed

8th Amendment, death penalty

B. Legal Question Presented

"This case requires us to address, for the second time in a decade and a half, whether it is permissible under the Eighth and Fourteenth Amendments to the Constitution of the United States to execute a juvenile offender who was older than 15 but younger than 18 when he committed a capital crime."

C. Supreme Court's Answer

"The Eighth and Fourteenth Amendments forbid imposition of the death penalty on offenders who were under the age of 18 when their crimes were committed."

II. CASE SUMMARY

A. Background

"At the age of 17, when he was still a junior in high school, Christopher Simmons, the respondent here, committed murder. About nine months later, after he had turned 18, he was tried and sentenced to death. There is little doubt that Simmons was the instigator of the crime. . . .

The State charged Simmons with burglary, kidnaping, stealing, and murder in the first degree. As Simmons was 17 at the time of the crime, he was outside the criminal jurisdiction of Missouri's juvenile court system. He was tried as an adult. . . . The jury having returned a verdict of murder, the trial proceeded to the penalty phase.

The State sought the death penalty. . . .

During closing arguments, both the prosecutor and defense counsel addressed Simmons' age, which the trial judge had instructed the jurors they could consider as a mitigating factor. . . .

The jury recommended the death penalty after finding the State had proved each of the three aggravating factors submitted to it. Accepting the jury's recommendation, the trial judge imposed the death penalty.

Simmons obtained new counsel, who moved in the trial court to set aside the conviction and sentence. One argument was that Simmons had received ineffective assistance at trial. . . .

The trial court found no constitutional violation by reason of ineffective assistance of counsel and denied the motion for post-conviction relief. In a consolidated appeal from Simmons' conviction and sentence, and from the denial of postconviction relief, the Missouri Supreme Court affirmed. The federal courts denied Simmons' petition for a writ of habeas corpus.

After these proceedings in Simmons' case had run their course, this Court held that the Eighth and Fourteenth Amendments prohibit the execution of a mentally retarded person. Simmons filed a new petition for state postconviction relief, arguing that the reasoning of Atkins established that the Constitution prohibits the execution of a juvenile who was under 18 when the crime was committed.

The Missouri Supreme Court agreed. . . .

[I]t set aside Simmons' death sentence and resentenced him to 'life imprisonment without eligibility for probation, parole, or release except by act of the Governor.'"

The Supreme Court granted certiorari to review the case.

B. Counsel of Record

ACLU Side (Respondent / Appellee): Seth P. Waxman argued the cause for appellee. With him on the brief were David W. Ogden and Jennifer Herndon.

Opposing Side (Petitioner / Appellant): James R. Layton, State Solicitor of Missouri, argued the cause for appellant. With him on the briefs were Jeremiah W. (Jay) Nixon, Attorney General, and Stephen D. Hawke and Evan J. Buchheim, Assistant Attorneys General.

III. AMICI CURIAE

ACLU Side (Respondent / Appellee)

Brief of amici curiae filed on behalf of the NAACP Legal Defense and Educational Fund, Inc., the American Civil Liberties Union, the National Association of Criminal Defense Lawyers, the National Bar Association, the National Urban League Institute for Opportunity and Equality, the National Black Police Association, the National Conference of Black Lawyers, and the National Black Law Students Association by Theodore M. Shaw, Norman J. Chachkin, Miriam Gohara, Christina A. Swarns, Steven R. Shapiro, Barry C. Scheck, Clyde E. Bailey, Sr., Charles J. Hamilton, Jr., Gilda Sherrod-Ali, and Diann Y. Rust-Tierney.

Brief of amici curiae filed on behalf of the State of New York et al. by Eliot Spitzer, Attorney General of New York, Caitlin J. Halligan, Solicitor General, Daniel Smirlock, Deputy Solicitor General, and Jean Lin and Julie Loughran, Assistant Solicitors General, and by the Attorneys General for their respective States as follows: Thomas J. Miller of Iowa, Phill Kline of Kansas, J. Joseph Curran, Jr., of Maryland, Mike Hatch of Minnesota, Patricia A. Madrid of New Mexico, Hardy Myers of Oregon, and Darrell V. McGraw, Jr., of West Virginia; for the American Bar Association by Dennis W. Archer, Amy R. Sabrin, and Matthew W. S. Estes.

Brief of amici curiae filed on behalf of the American Psychological Association et al. by Drew S. Days III, Beth S. Brinkmann, Sherri N. Blount, Timothy C. Lambert, Nathalie F. P. Gilfoyle, and Lindsay Childress-Beatty.

Brief of amici curiae filed on behalf of the Coalition for Juvenile Justice by Joseph D. Tydings.

Brief of amici curiae filed on behalf of the Constitution Project by Laurie Webb Daniel and Virginia E. Sloan.

Brief of amici curiae filed on behalf of the Human Rights Committee of the Bar of England and Wales et al. by Michael Bochenek, Audrey J. Anderson, William H. Johnson, and Thomas H. Speedy Rice.

Brief of amici curiae filed on behalf of the Juvenile Law Center et al. by Marsha L. Levick, Lourdes M. Rosado, Steven A. Drizin, Barbara Bennett Woodhouse, Michael C. Small, and Jeffrey P. Kehne.

Brief of amici curiae filed on behalf of the Missouri Ban Youth Executions Coalition by Joseph W. Luby.

Brief of amici curiae filed on behalf of the United States Conference of Catholic Bishops et al. by Mark E. Chopko and Michael F. Moses.

Brief of amici curiae filed on behalf of Former U. S. Diplomats Morton Abramowitz et al. by Harold Hongju Koh, Donald Francis Donovan, and Stephen B. Bright.

Brief of amici curiae filed on behalf of the European Union et al. by Richard J. Wilson.

Brief of amici curiae filed on behalf of the American Medical Association et al. by Joseph T. McLaughlin, E. Joshua Rosenkranz, and Stephane M. Clare.

Brief of amici curiae filed on behalf of Murder Victims' Families for Reconciliation by Kate Lowenstein.

Brief of amici curiae filed on behalf of the National Legal Aid and Defender Association by Michael Mello.

Brief of amici curiae filed on behalf of President James Earl Carter, Jr., et al. by Thomas F. Geraghty.

Opposing Side (Petitioner / Appellant)

Brief of amici curiae filed on behalf of the State of Alabama et al. by Troy King, Attorney General of Alabama, Kevin C. Newsom, Solicitor General, and A. Vernon Barnett IV, Deputy Solicitor General, and by the Attorneys General for their respective States as follows: M. Jane Brady of Delaware, W. A. Drew Edmondson of Oklahoma, Greg Abbott of Texas, Mark L. Shurtleff of Utah, and Jerry W. Kilgore of Virginia.

Brief of amici curiae filed on behalf of the Justice for All Alliance by Dan Cutrer.

IV. THE SUPREME COURT'S DECISION

"The Eighth Amendment provides: 'Excessive bail shall not be required, nor excessive fines imposed, nor cruel and unusual punishments inflicted.' The provision is applicable to the States through the Fourteenth Amendment. . . .

The prohibition against 'cruel and unusual punishments,' like other expansive language in the Constitution, must be interpreted according to its text, by considering history, tradition, and precedent, and with due regard for its purpose and function in the constitutional design. To implement this framework we have established the propriety and affirmed the necessity of referring to 'the evolving standards of decency that mark the progress of a maturing society' to determine which punishments are so disproportionate as to be cruel and unusual. . . .

Just as the Atkins Court reconsidered the issue decided in Penry, we now reconsider the issue decided in Stanford. The beginning point is a review of objective indicia of consensus, as expressed in particular by the enactments of legislatures that have addressed the question. These data give us essential instruction. We then must determine, in the exercise of our own independent judgment, whether the death penalty is a disproportionate punishment for juveniles. . . .

As in Atkins, the objective indicia of consensus in this case—the rejection of the juvenile death penalty in the majority of States; the infrequency of its use even where it remains on the books; and the consistency in the trend toward abolition of the practice—provide sufficient evidence that today our society views juveniles, in the words Atkins used respecting the mentally retarded, as 'categorically less culpable than the average criminal.' . . .

A majority of States have rejected the imposition of the death penalty on juvenile offenders under 18, and we now hold this is required by the Eighth Amendment.

Because the death penalty is the most severe punishment, the Eighth Amendment applies to it with special force. Capital punishment must be limited to those offenders who commit 'a narrow category of the most serious crimes' and whose extreme culpability makes them 'the most deserving of execution.' . . .

Three general differences between juveniles under 18 and adults demonstrate that juvenile offenders cannot with reliability be classified among the worst offenders. First, as any parent knows and as the scientific and sociological studies respondent and his amici cite tend to confirm, '[a] lack of maturity and an underdeveloped sense of responsibility are found in youth more often than in adults and are more understandable among the young. These qualities often result in impetuous and ill-considered actions and decisions.' . . .

The second area of difference is that juveniles are more vulnerable or susceptible to negative influences and outside pressures, including peer pressure. . . .

The third broad difference is that the character of a juvenile is not as well formed as that of an adult. The personality traits of juveniles are more transitory, less fixed.

These differences render suspect any conclusion that a juvenile falls among the worst offenders. . . .

These considerations mean Stanford v. Kentucky should be deemed no longer controlling on this issue. . . .

In holding that the death penalty cannot be imposed upon juvenile offenders, we take into account the circumstance that some States have relied on Stanford in seeking the death penalty against juvenile offenders. This consideration, however, does not outweigh our conclusion that Stanford should no longer control in those few pending cases or in those yet to arise. . . .

The Eighth and Fourteenth Amendments forbid imposition of the death penalty on offenders who were under the age of 18 when their crimes were committed. The judgment of the Missouri Supreme Court setting aside the sentence of death imposed upon Christopher Simmons is affirmed."

V. JUSTICE VOTE

5 Pro ACLU Side vs. 4 Con Opposing Side

ACLU Side (Respondent / Appellee)

1. Kennedy, A. – Wrote majority opinion
2. Stevens, J. – Wrote concurring opinion
3. Souter, D. – Joined majority opinion
4. Breyer, S. – Joined majority opinion
5. Ginsburg, R. – Joined Stevens' concurrence

Opposing Side (Petitioner / Appellant)

1. O'Connor, S. – Wrote dissenting opinion
2. Scalia, A. – Wrote dissenting opinion
3. Rehnquist, W. – Joined Scalia's dissent
4. Thomas, C. – Joined Scalia's dissent

VI. A WIN OR LOSS FOR THE ACLU?

The ACLU filed as amicus curiae urging affirmance; the Supreme Court affirmed the Missouri Supreme Court's decision by a 5-4 vote, giving the ACLU an apparent win.

981. Ballard v. Commissioner of Internal Revenue

(Decided March 7, 2005; 544 U.S. 40)

I. ISSUE

A. Issues Discussed

Civil procedure, regulation

B. Legal Question Presented

"[W]hether the Tax Court may exclude from the record on appeal Rule 183(b) reports submitted by special trial judges."

C. Supreme Court's Answer

"[N]o statute authorizes, and the current text of Rule 183 does not warrant, the concealment at issue."

II. CASE SUMMARY

A. Background

"After repeated Internal Revenue Service audits spanning several years, taxpayers Claude Ballard, Burton W. Kanter, and Robert Lisle received multiple notices of deficiency from the Commissioner of Internal Revenue (Commissioner). . . . As to each asserted deficiency, Ballard, Kanter, and Lisle filed petitions for redetermination in the Tax Court. . . .

Tax Court Rule 183 governs the Tax Court's review of the special trial judge's findings and opinion.

After Ballard, Kanter, and Lisle sought review in the Tax Court, the Chief Judge assigned the consolidated case to Special Trial Judge D. Irvin Couvillion for trial. Judge Couvillion presided over a five-week trial during the summer of 1994, and the parties' briefing was completed in May 1995. . . . On or before September 2, 1998, Judge Couvillion submitted to the Chief Judge a report containing his findings of fact and opinion, 'as required by [Tax Court] Rule 183(b).' On September 2, 1998, the Chief Judge assigned the case to Tax Court Judge Howard A. Dawson, Jr., 'for review [of the special trial judge's report] and, if approved, for adoption.' Fifteen months later, on December 15, 1999, the Chief Judge 'reassigned' the case 'from [Judge] Couvillion to [Judge] Dawson.' That same day, Judge Dawson issued the decision of the Tax Court.

Judge Dawson found that Ballard, Kanter, and Lisle had acted with intent to deceive the Commissioner, and held them liable for underpaid taxes and substantial fraud penalties. In so ruling, Judge Dawson purported to adopt the findings contained in the report submitted by Judge Couvillion: 'The Court agrees with and adopts the opinion of the Special Trial Judge, which is set forth below.' Judge Dawson's decision consists in its entirety of a document, over 600 pages in length, labeled 'Opinion of the Special Trial Judge.'

The taxpayers came to believe that the document titled 'Opinion of the Special Trial Judge' was not in fact a reproduction of Judge Couvillion's Rule 183(b) report. A declaration, dated August 21, 2000, submitted by Kanter's attorney, Randall G. Dick, accounts for this belief. Dick attested to conversations with two Tax Court judges regarding the Tax Court's decision. According to the declaration, the judges told Dick that in the Rule 183(b) report submitted to the Chief Judge, Judge Couvillion had concluded that Ballard, Kanter, and Lisle did not owe taxes with respect to payments made by certain individuals seeking to do business with Prudential, and that the fraud penalty was not applicable. . . .

Concerned that Judge Dawson had modified or rejected special trial judge findings tending in their favor, the taxpayers filed three successive motions in the Tax Court; each motion sought access to the report Special Trial Judge Couvillion had submitted to the Chief Judge or, in the alternative, permission to place the special trial judge's report under seal in the record on appeal. The Tax Court denied the motions. . . .

Ballard therefore appealed to the Eleventh Circuit, Kanter to the Seventh Circuit, and Lisle to the Fifth Circuit. All three Courts of Appeals accepted the Commissioner's argument that the special trial judge's signature on the Tax Court's final decision rendered that decision in fact Special Trial Judge Couvillion's report. . . . The appeals courts further agreed with the Commissioner that the special trial judge's original report, submitted to the Chief Judge pursuant to Rule 183(b), qualified as a confidential document, shielded as part of the Tax Court's internal deliberative process.

[T]he Seventh and Eleventh Circuits proceeded to the merits of the Tax Court's final decision and affirmed that decision in principal part. The Fifth Circuit's judgment, which is not before this Court, reversed the fraud penalties assessed against Lisle for evidentiary insufficiency but upheld the Tax Court's determination of tax deficiencies for certain years. . . ."

The Supreme Court granted certiorari to review the case.

B. Counsel of Record

ACLU Side (Petitioner / Appellant): Stephen M. Shapiro argued the cause for appellants in both cases. On the briefs in No. 03–184 were Vester T. Hughes, Jr., Robert E. Davis, David J. Schenck, Christopher D. Kratovil, Steven S. Brown, Royal B. Martin, and William G. Sullivan. With Mr. Shapiro on the briefs in No. 03–1034 were Richard H. Pildes, Peter J. Rubin, N. Jerold Cohen, Teresa Wynn Roseborough, Philip Allen Lacovara, and Randall G. Dick.

Opposing Side (Respondent / Appellee): Deputy Solicitor General Hungar argued the cause for appellee in both cases. With him on the brief were Acting Solicitor General Clement, Assistant Attorney General O'Connor, Deputy Assistant Attorney General Morrison, Traci L. Lovitt, Kenneth L. Greene, and Steven W. Parks.

III. AMICI CURIAE

ACLU Side (Petitioner / Appellant)

Brief of amici curiae filed on behalf of Public Citizen, Inc. and the American Civil Liberties Union by Scott L. Nelson, Alan B. Morrison, and Steven R. Shapiro.

Brief of amici curiae filed on behalf of the National Federation of Independent Business Legal Foundation by H. Christopher Bartolomucci; and for Senator David Pryor et al. by Roderick M. Hills, Jr.

Brief of amici curiae filed on behalf of Leandra Lederman by Leandra Lederman, pro se.

Opposing Side (Respondent / Appellee)

No briefs of amici curiae were filed in support of appellee.

IV. THE SUPREME COURT'S DECISION

"These cases concern the Tax Court's employment of special trial judges, auxiliary officers appointed by the Chief Judge of the Tax Court to assist in the work of the court. Unlike Tax Court judges, who are appointed by the President for 15-year terms, special trial judges have no fixed term of office. Any case before the Tax Court may be assigned to a special trial judge for hearing. Ultimate decision in cases involving tax deficiencies that exceed $50,000, however, is reserved for the Tax Court.

Tax Court Rule 183 governs the two-tiered proceedings in which a special trial judge hears the case, but the Tax Court itself renders the final decision. The Rule directs that, after trial and submission of briefs, the special trial judge 'shall submit a report, including findings of fact and opinion, to the Chief Judge, and the Chief Judge will assign the case to a Judge . . . of the Court.' In acting on the report, the Tax Court judge to whom the case is assigned must give '[d]ue regard . . . to the circumstance that the [s]pecial [t]rial [j]udge had the opportunity to evaluate the credibility of the witnesses.' Further, factfindings contained in the report 'shall be presumed to be correct.' The final Tax Court decision 'may adopt the [s]pecial [t]rial [j]udge's report or may modify it or may reject it in whole or in part.'

Until 1983, special trial judge reports, as submitted to the Chief Judge, were made public and were included in the record on appeal. . . . Since the January 16, 1984 effective date of the rule revision, the post-trial report submitted to the Chief Judge, then transmitted to the Tax Court judge assigned to make the final decision, has been both withheld from the public and excluded from the record on appeal. Further, since that time, Tax Court judges have refrained from disclosing, in any case, whether the final decision in fact 'modi[fies]' or 'reject[s] [the special trial judge's initial report] in whole or in part.' Instead, the final decision invariably begins with a stock statement that the Tax Court judge 'agrees with and adopts the opinion of the [s]pecial [t]rial [j]udge.' Whether and how the opinion thus adopted deviates from the special trial judge's original report is never made public.

Petitioners are taxpayers who were unsuccessful in the Tax Court and on appeal. They object to the concealment of the special trial judge's initial report and, in particular, exclusion of the report from the record on appeal. They urge that, under the Tax Court's current practice, the parties and the Court of Appeals lack essential information: One cannot tell whether, as Rule 183(c) requires, the final decision reflects '[d]ue regard' for the special trial judge's 'opportunity to evaluate the credibility of [the] witnesses,' and presumes the correctness of that judge's initial factfindings. We agree that no statute authorizes, and the current text of Rule 183 does not warrant, the concealment at issue. We so hold, mindful that it is routine in federal judicial and administrative decisionmaking both to disclose the initial report of a hearing officer, and to make that report part of the record available to an appellate forum. A departure of the bold character practiced by the Tax Court—the creation and attribution solely to the special trial judge of a superseding report composed in unrevealed collaboration with a regular Tax Court judge—demands, at the very least, full and fair statement in the Tax Court's own Rules. . . .

The idiosyncratic procedure the Commissioner describes and defends, although not the system of adjudication that Rule 183 currently creates, is one the Tax Court might someday adopt. Were the Tax Court to amend its Rules to express the changed character of the Tax Court judge's review of special trial judge reports, that change would, of course, be subject to appellate review for consistency with the relevant federal statutes and due process. . . .

For the reasons stated, the judgments of the Courts of Appeals for the Seventh and Eleventh Circuits are reversed, and the cases are remanded for further proceedings consistent with this opinion."

V. JUSTICE VOTE

7 Pro ACLU Side vs. 2 Con Opposing Side

ACLU Side (Petitioner / Appellant)

1. Ginsburg, R. – Wrote majority opinion
2. O'Connor, S. – Joined majority opinion
3. Stevens, J. – Joined majority opinion
4. Souter, D. – Joined majority opinion
5. Breyer, S. – Joined majority opinion
6. Scalia, A. – Joined Kennedy's concurrence
7. Kennedy, A. – Wrote concurring opinion

Opposing Side (Respondent / Appellee)

1. Rehnquist, W. – Wrote dissenting opinion
2. Thomas, C. – Joined Rehnquist's dissent

VI. A WIN OR LOSS FOR THE ACLU?

The ACLU filed as amicus curiae urging reversal of the judgments of the Courts of Appeals; the Supreme Court reversed in a 7-2 vote, giving the ACLU an apparent win.

982. Muehler v. Mena

(Decided March 22, 2005; 544 U.S. 93)

I. ISSUE

A. Issues Discussed

4th Amendment

B. Legal Question Presented

Whether Mena's detention in handcuffs during a search to execute a warrant violated her Fourth Amendment rights.

C. Supreme Court's Answer

"We hold that Mena's detention in handcuffs for the length of the search was consistent with our opinion in Michigan v. Summers, 452 U.S. 692 (1981), and that the officers' questioning during that detention did not violate her Fourth Amendment rights."

II. CASE SUMMARY

A. Background

"Based on information gleaned from the investigation of a gang-related, driveby shooting, petitioners Muehler and Brill had reason to believe at least one member of a gang—the West Side Locos—lived at 1363 Patricia Avenue. They also suspected that the individual was armed and dangerous, since he had recently been involved in the driveby shooting. As a result, Muehler obtained a search warrant for 1363 Patricia Avenue that authorized a broad search of the house and premises . . . .

At 7 a.m. on February 3, 1998, petitioners, along with the SWAT team and other officers, executed the warrant. Mena was asleep in her bed when the SWAT team, clad in helmets and black vests adorned with badges and the word 'POLICE,' entered her bedroom and placed her in handcuffs at gunpoint. The SWAT team also handcuffed three other individuals found on the property. The SWAT team then took those individuals and Mena into a converted garage . . . .

Aware that the West Side Locos gang was composed primarily of illegal immigrants, the officers had notified the Immigration and Naturalization Service (INS) that they would be conducting the search, and an INS officer accompanied the officers executing the warrant. During their detention in the garage, an officer asked for each detainee's name, date of birth, place of birth, and immigration status. The INS officer later asked the detainees for their immigration documentation. Mena's status as a permanent resident was confirmed by her papers.

The search of the premises yielded a .22 caliber handgun with .22 caliber ammunition, a box of .25 caliber ammunition, several baseball bats with gang writing, various additional gang paraphernalia, and a bag of marijuana. Before the officers left the area, Mena was released.

In her § 1983 suit against the officers she alleged that she was detained 'for an unreasonable time and in an unreasonable manner' in violation of the Fourth Amendment. In addition, she claimed that the warrant and its execution were overbroad, that the officers failed to comply with the 'knock and announce' rule, and that the officers had needlessly destroyed property during the search. The officers moved for summary judgment, asserting that they were entitled to qualified immunity, but the District Court denied their motion. The Court of Appeals affirmed that denial, except for Mena's claim that the warrant was overbroad; on this claim the Court of Appeals held that the officers were entitled to qualified immunity. After a trial, a jury, pursuant to a special verdict form, found that Officers Muehler and Brill violated Mena's Fourth Amendment right to be free from unreasonable seizures by detaining her both with force greater than that which was reasonable and for a longer period than that which was reasonable. The jury awarded Mena $10,000 in actual damages and $20,000 in punitive damages against each petitioner for a total of $60,000.

The Court of Appeals affirmed the judgment . . . ."

The Supreme Court granted certiorari to review the case.

B. Counsel of Record

ACLU Side (Respondent / Appellee): Paul L. Hoffman argued the cause for appellee. With him on the brief were Benjamin Schonbrun, Michael S. Morrison, and Erwin Chemerinsky.

Opposing Side (Petitioner / Appellant): Carter G. Phillips argued the cause for appellants. With him on the briefs were Joseph R. Guerra and David H. Hirsch.

Kannon K. Shanmugam argued the cause for the United States as amicus curiae.

III. AMICI CURIAE

ACLU Side (Respondent / Appellee)

Brief of amici curiae filed on behalf of the American Civil Liberties Union and ACLU Foundation of Southern California by Mark D. Rosenbaum, Ahilan T. Arulanantham, Anil Kalhan, Steven R. Shapiro, Lucas Guttentag, and Lee Gelernt.

Brief of amici curiae filed on behalf of the National Association of Criminal Defense Lawyers by Henk Brands and Pamela Harris.

Brief of amici curiae filed on behalf of the National Latino Officers Association et al. by Baher Azmy, Lawrence S. Lustberg, and Jonathan L. Hafetz.

Opposing Side (Petitioner / Appellant)

Brief of amici curiae filed on behalf of the United States by Kannon K. Shanmugam, Acting Solicitor General Clement, Assistant Attorney General Wray, and Deputy Solicitor General Dreeben.

Brief of amici curiae filed on behalf of the National League of Cities et al. by Richard Ruda and James I. Crowley.

Brief of amici curiae filed on behalf of the Police Officers Research Association of California Legal Defense Fund et al. by Michael J. Hansen in support of petition for writ of certiorari.

IV. THE SUPREME COURT'S DECISION

"In Michigan v. Summers, 452 U.S. 692 (1981), we held that officers executing a search warrant for contraband have the authority 'to detain the occupants of the premises while a proper search is conducted.' . . .

Mena's detention was, under Summers, plainly permissible. An officer's authority to detain incident to a search is categorical; it does not depend on the 'quantum of proof justifying detention or the extent of the intrusion to be imposed by the seizure.' Thus, Mena's detention for the duration of the search was reasonable under Summers because a warrant existed to search 1363 Patricia Avenue and she was an occupant of that address at the time of the search.

Inherent in Summers' authorization to detain an occupant of the place to be searched is the authority to use reasonable force to effectuate the detention. . . .

The officers' use of force in the form of handcuffs to effectuate Mena's detention in the garage, as well as the detention of the three other occupants, was reasonable because the governmental interests outweigh the marginal intrusion. The imposition of correctly applied handcuffs on Mena, who was already being lawfully detained during a search of the house, was undoubtedly a separate intrusion in addition to detention in the converted garage. The detention was thus more intrusive than that which we upheld in Summers. . . .

But this was no ordinary search. The governmental interests in not only detaining, but using handcuffs, are at their maximum when, as here, a warrant authorizes a search for weapons and a wanted gang member resides on the premises. In such inherently dangerous situations, the use of handcuffs minimizes the risk of harm to both officers and occupants. . . .

Mena argues that, even if the use of handcuffs to detain her in the garage was reasonable as an initial matter, the duration of the use of handcuffs made the detention unreasonable. The duration of a detention can, of course, affect the balance of interests under Graham. However, the 2– to 3–hour detention in handcuffs in this case does not outweigh the government's continuing safety interests. As we have noted, this case involved the detention of four detainees by two officers during a search of a gang house for dangerous weapons. We conclude that the detention of Mena in handcuffs during the search was reasonable.

The Court of Appeals also determined that the officers violated Mena's Fourth Amendment rights by questioning her about her immigration status during the detention. This holding, it appears, was premised on the assumption that the officers were required to have independent reasonable suspicion in order to question Mena concerning her immigration status because the questioning constituted a discrete Fourth Amendment event. But the premise is faulty. We have 'held repeatedly that mere police questioning does not constitute a seizure.' . . .

In summary, the officers' detention of Mena in handcuffs during the execution of the search warrant was reasonable and did not violate the Fourth Amendment. Additionally, the officers' questioning of Mena did not constitute an independent Fourth Amendment violation. Mena has advanced in this Court, as she did before the Court of Appeals, an alternative argument for affirming the judgment below. She asserts that her detention extended beyond the time the police completed the tasks incident to the search. Because the Court of Appeals did not address this contention, we too decline to address it.

The judgment of the Court of Appeals is therefore vacated, and the case is remanded for further proceedings consistent with this opinion."

V. JUSTICE VOTE

0 Pro ACLU Side vs. 9 Con Opposing Side

Opposing Side (Petitioner / Appellant)

1. Rehnquist, W. – Wrote majority opinion
2. Ginsburg, R. – Joined Stevens' concurrence
3. Souter, D. – Joined Stevens' concurrence
4. Stevens, J. – Wrote concurring opinion
5. Thomas, C. – Joined majority opinion
6. O'Connor, S. – Joined majority opinion
7. Breyer, S. – Joined Stevens' concurrence
8. Scalia, A. – Joined majority opinion
9. Kennedy, A. – Wrote concurring opinion

VI. A WIN OR LOSS FOR THE ACLU?

The ACLU filed as amicus curiae urging affirmance; the Supreme Court vacated the Court of Appeals' decision by a 9-0 vote, giving the ACLU an apparent loss.

983. Jackson v. Birmingham Bd. of Educ.

(Decided March 29, 2005; 544 U.S. 167)

I. ISSUE

A. Issues Discussed

Gender, civil rights

B. Legal Question Presented

"[W]hether the private right of action implied by Title IX encompasses claims of retaliation."

C. Supreme Court's Answer

"We hold that it does where the funding recipient retaliates against an individual because he has complained about sex discrimination."

II. CASE SUMMARY

A. Background

"According to the complaint, Jackson has been an employee of the Birmingham school district for over 10 years. In 1993, the Board hired Jackson to serve as a physical education teacher and girls' basketball coach. Jackson was transferred to Ensley High School in August 1999. At Ensley, he discovered that the girls' team was not receiving equal funding and equal access to athletic equipment and facilities. The lack of adequate funding, equipment, and facilities made it difficult for Jackson to do his job as the team's coach.

In December 2000, Jackson began complaining to his supervisors about the unequal treatment of the girls' basketball team, but to no avail. Jackson's complaints went unanswered, and the school failed to remedy the situation. Instead, Jackson began to receive negative work evaluations and ultimately was removed as the girls' coach in May 2001. Jackson is still employed by the Board as a teacher, but he no longer receives supplemental pay for coaching.

After the Board terminated Jackson's coaching duties, he filed suit in the United States District Court for the Northern District of Alabama. He alleged, among other things, that the Board violated Title IX by retaliating against him for protesting the discrimination against the girls' basketball team. The Board moved to dismiss on the ground that Title IX's private cause of action does not include claims of retaliation. The District Court granted the motion to dismiss.

The Court of Appeals for the Eleventh Circuit affirmed."

The Supreme Court granted certiorari to review the case.

B. Counsel of Record

ACLU Side (Petitioner / Appellant): Walter Dellinger argued the cause for appellant. With him on the briefs were Marcia D. Greenberger, Jocelyn Samuels, Dina R. Lassow, Matthew D. Roberts, and Pamela A. Harris.

Irving L. Gornstein argued the cause for the United States as amicus curiae.

Opposing Side (Respondent / Appellee): Kenneth L. Thomas argued the cause for appellee. With him on the brief was Valerie L. Acoff.

Kevin C. Newsom, Solicitor General of Alabama, argued the cause for the State of Alabama et al. as amici curiae.

III. AMICI CURIAE

ACLU Side (Petitioner / Appellant)

Brief of amici curiae filed on behalf of the United States by Irving L. Gornstein, Acting Solicitor General Clement, Assistant Attorney General Acosta, Dennis J. Dimsey, and Linda F. Thome.

Brief of amici curiae filed on behalf of the American Bar Association by Robert J. Grey, Jr., Nancy L. Perkins, and Kristen Galles.

Brief of amici curiae filed on behalf of the Leadership Conference on Civil Rights by Virginia A. Seitz, Steven Shapiro, and Lenora M. Lapidus.

Brief of amici curiae filed on behalf of the National Education Association et al. by Jeremiah A. Collins, Alice O'Brien, David M. Rabban, Donna R. Euben, and Ann D. Springer.

Brief of amici curiae filed on behalf of the National Partnership for Women & Families et al. by Caroline M. Brown.

Brief of amici curiae filed on behalf of New York Lawyers for the Public Interest et al. by Jeffrey A. Lamken, Macey Reasoner Stokes, J. Richard Cohen, and Rhonda Brownstein.

Brief of amici curiae filed on behalf of Birch Bayh by John F. Cooney, Margaret N. Strand, and Kevin O. Faley.

Brief of amici curiae filed on behalf of the Women's Sports Foundation et al. by Nancy Hogshead-Makar and Howard R. Rubin.

Opposing Side (Respondent / Appellee)

Brief of amici curiae filed on behalf of the State of Alabama et al. by Kevin C. Newsom, Solicitor General of Alabama, Troy King, Attorney General, and the Attorneys General for their respective States as follows: M. Jane Brady of Delaware, Mark J. Bennett of Hawaii, Brian Sandoval of Nevada, Hardy Myers of Oregon, Lawrence E. Long of South Dakota, Paul G. Summers of Tennessee, Mark L. Shurtleff of Utah, and Jerry W. Kilgore of Virginia.

Brief of amici curiae filed on behalf of the Eagle Forum Education & Legal Defense Fund by Andrew L. Schlafly.

Brief of amici curiae filed on behalf of the National School Boards Association et al. by Julie Underwood and Naomi Gittins.

Brief of amici curiae filed on behalf of the National Wrestling Coaches Association by Lawrence J. Joseph.

Brief of amici curiae filed on behalf of the Pacific Legal Foundation by John H. Findley.

Brief of amici curiae filed on behalf of the College Sports Council by Mr. Joseph in support of neither party.

IV. THE SUPREME COURT'S DECISION

"Title IX prohibits sex discrimination by recipients of federal education funding. . . . More than 25 years ago, in Cannon v. University of Chicago, 441 U.S. 677 (1979), we held that Title IX implies a private right of action to enforce its prohibition on intentional sex discrimination. In subsequent cases, we have defined the contours of that right of action. . . .

In all of these cases, we relied on the text of Title IX, which, subject to a list of narrow exceptions not at issue here, broadly prohibits a funding recipient from subjecting any person to 'discrimination' 'on the basis of sex.' Retaliation against a person because that person has complained of sex discrimination is another form of intentional sex discrimination encompassed by Title IX's private cause of action. . . . We conclude that when a funding recipient retaliates against a person because he complains of sex discrimination, this constitutes intentional 'discrimination' 'on the basis of sex,' in violation of Title IX.

The Court of Appeals' conclusion that Title IX does not prohibit retaliation because the 'statute makes no mention of retaliation,' ignores the import of our repeated holdings construing 'discrimination' under Title IX broadly. Though the statute does not mention sexual harassment, we have held that sexual harassment is intentional discrimination encompassed by Title IX's private right of action. . . .

Nor are we convinced by the Board's argument that, even if Title IX's private right of action encompasses discrimination, Jackson is not entitled to invoke it because he is an 'indirect victi[m]' of sex discrimination. The statute is broadly worded; it does not require that the victim of the retaliation must also be the victim of the discrimination that is the subject of the original complaint. . . .

The Board is correct in pointing out that, because Title IX was enacted as an exercise of Congress' powers under the Spending Clause, 'private damages actions are available only where recipients of federal funding had adequate notice that they could be liable for the conduct at issue.' . . .

The Board insists that we should not interpret Title IX to prohibit retaliation because it was not on notice that it could be held liable for retaliating against those who complain of Title IX violations. We disagree. Funding recipients have been on notice that they could be subjected to private suits for intentional sex discrimination under Title IX since 1979, when we decided Cannon. . . .

We therefore conclude that retaliation against individuals because they complain of sex discrimination is 'intentional conduct that violates the clear terms of the statute,' and that Title IX itself therefore supplied sufficient notice to the Board that it could not retaliate against Jackson after he complained of discrimination against the girls' basketball team. . . .

To prevail on the merits, Jackson will have to prove that the Board retaliated against him because he complained of sex discrimination. The amended complaint alleges that the Board retaliated against Jackson for complaining to his supervisor, Ms. Evelyn Baugh, about sex discrimination at Ensley High School. At this stage of the proceedings, '[t]he issue is not whether a plaintiff will ultimately prevail but whether the claimant is entitled to offer evidence to support the claims.' Accordingly, the judgment of the Court of Appeals for the Eleventh Circuit is reversed, and the case is remanded for further proceedings consistent with this opinion."

V. JUSTICE VOTE

5 Pro ACLU Side vs. 4 Con Opposing Side

ACLU Side (Petitioner / Appellant)

1. O'Connor, S. – Wrote majority opinion
2. Ginsburg, R. – Joined majority opinion
3. Stevens, J. – Joined majority opinion
4. Souter, D. – Joined majority opinion
5. Breyer, S. – Joined majority opinion

Opposing Side (Respondent / Appellee)

1. Rehnquist, W. – Joined Thomas' dissent
2. Thomas, C. – Wrote dissenting opinion
3. Scalia, A. – Joined Thomas' dissent
4. Kennedy, A. – Joined Thomas' dissent

VI. A WIN OR LOSS FOR THE ACLU?

The ACLU filed as amicus curiae urging reversal of the judgment of the Court of Appeals; the Supreme Court reversed in a 5-4 vote, giving the ACLU an apparent win.

984. Cutter v. Wilkinson

(Decided May 31, 2005; 544 U.S. 709)

I. ISSUE

A. Issues Discussed

Prison, 1st Amendment, religion

B. Legal Question Presented

"[W]hether RLUIPA's institutionalized-persons provision, § 3 of the Act, is consistent with the Establishment Clause of the First Amendment."

C. Supreme Court's Answer

"§ 3 of RLUIPA, we hold, does not, on its face, exceed the limits of permissible government accommodation of religious practices."

II. CASE SUMMARY

A. Background

"Section 3 of the Religious Land Use and Institutionalized Persons Act of 2000 (RLUIPA or Act) provides in part: 'No government shall impose a substantial burden on the religious exercise of a person residing in or confined to an institution,' unless the burden furthers 'a compelling governmental interest,' and does so by 'the least restrictive means.' Plaintiffs below, petitioners here, are current and former inmates of institutions operated by the Ohio Department of Rehabilitation and Correction and assert that they are adherents of 'nonmainstream' religions: the Satanist, Wicca, and Asatru religions, and the Church of Jesus Christ Christian. They complain that Ohio prison officials (respondents here), in violation of RLUIPA, have failed to accommodate their religious exercise . . . .

In response to petitioners' complaints, respondent prison officials have mounted a facial challenge to the institutionalized-persons provision of RLUIPA; respondents contend, inter alia, that the Act improperly advances religion in violation of the First Amendment's Establishment Clause. The District Court denied respondents' motion to dismiss petitioners' complaints, but the Court of Appeals reversed that determination."

The Supreme Court granted certiorari to review the case.

B. Counsel of Record

ACLU Side (Petitioner / Appellant): David Goldberger argued the cause for appellants. With him on the briefs were Marc D. Stern and Benson A. Wolman.

Acting Solicitor General Clement argued the cause for the United States as appellee under this Court's Rule 12.6 in support of appellants. With him on the briefs were Assistant Attorney General Keisler, Patricia A. Millett, Mark B. Stern, and Michael S. Raab.

Opposing Side (Respondent / Appellee): Douglas R. Cole, State Solicitor of Ohio, argued the cause for appellees. With him on the brief were Jim Petro, Attorney General, Stephen P. Carney, Senior Deputy Solicitor, and Todd R. Marti and Franklin E. Crawford, Assistant Solicitors.

III. AMICI CURIAE

ACLU Side (Petitioner / Appellant)

Brief of amici curiae filed on behalf of Americans United for Separation of Church and State and the American Civil Liberties Union by David M. Gossett, Kristina Silja Bennard, David C. Fathi, Ayesha N. Khan, Richard B. Katskee, Alex J. Luchenitser, and Steven R. Shapiro.

Brief of amici curiae filed on behalf of the State of New York et al. by Eliot Spitzer, Attorney General of New York, Caitlin J. Halligan, Solicitor General, Daniel Smirlock, Deputy Solicitor General, and Jean Lin and Benjamin N. Gutman, Assistant Solicitors General, and by Christine O. Gregoire, Attorney General of Washington.

Brief of amici curiae filed on behalf of the American Correctional Chaplains Association et al. by Gene C. Schaerr.

Brief of amici curiae filed on behalf of the National Association of Evangelicals et al. by Douglas Laycock and Nathan J. Diament.

Brief of amici curiae filed on behalf of Sen. Orrin G. Hatch et al. by Martin S. Lederman.

Brief of amici curiae filed on behalf of the Coalition for the Free Exercise of Religion by Anthony R. Picarello, Jr., and K. Hollyn Hollman.

Brief of amici curiae filed on behalf of the Rutherford Institute by James J. Knicely and John W. Whitehead.

Opposing Side (Respondent / Appellee)

Brief of amici curiae filed on behalf of the Commonwealth of Virginia et al. by Judith Williams Jagdmann, Attorney General of Virginia, William E. Thro, State Solicitor General, Maureen Riley Matsen, Deputy Attorney General, and Matthew M. Cobb, Carla R. Collins, Eric A. Gregory, Joel C. Hoppe, Courtney M. Malveaux, Valerie L. Myers, A. Cameron O'Brion, Ronald N. Regnery, D. Mathias Roussy, Jr., and William R. Sievers, Associate State Solicitors General, by Alva A. Swan, Acting Attorney General of the Virgin Islands, and by the Attorneys General for their respective States as follows: Gregg D. Renkes of Alaska, Lawrence G. Wasden of Idaho, Thomas J. Miller of Iowa, Jon Bruning of Nebraska, Wayne Stenehjem of North Dakota, W. A. Drew Edmondson of Oklahoma, and Darrell V. McGraw, Jr., of West Virginia.

Brief of amici curiae filed on behalf of the American Jail Association et al. by Michael N. Beekhuizen and Michael H. Carpenter.

Brief of amici curiae filed on behalf of the Claremont Institute Center for Constitutional Jurisprudence by John C. Eastman and Edwin Meese III.

Brief of amici curiae filed on behalf of the International Municipal Lawyers Association et al. by Marci A. Hamilton.

IV. THE SUPREME COURT'S DECISION

"The Religion Clauses of the First Amendment provide: 'Congress shall make no law respecting an establishment of religion, or prohibiting the free exercise thereof.' The first of the two Clauses, commonly called the Establishment Clause, commands a separation of church and state. The second, the Free Exercise Clause, requires government respect for, and noninterference with, the religious beliefs and practices of our Nation's people. While the two Clauses express complementary values, they often exert conflicting pressures. . . .

Our decisions recognize that 'there is room for play in the joints' between the Clauses, some space for legislative action neither compelled by the Free Exercise Clause nor prohibited by the Establishment Clause. . . . In accord with the majority of Courts of Appeals that have ruled on the question, we hold that § 3 of RLUIPA fits within the corridor between the Religion Clauses: On its face, the Act qualifies as a permissible legislative accommodation of religion that is not barred by the Establishment Clause.

Foremost, we find RLUIPA's institutionalized-persons provision compatible with the Establishment Clause because it alleviates exceptional government-created burdens on private religious exercise. . . . Furthermore, the Act on its face does not founder on shoals our prior decisions have identified: Properly applying RLUIPA, courts must take adequate account of the burdens a requested accommodation may impose on nonbeneficiaries, and they must be satisfied that the Act's prescriptions are and will be administered neutrally among different faiths. . . .

Section 3 covers state-run institutions—mental hospitals, prisons, and the like—in which the government exerts a degree of control unparalleled in civilian society and severely disabling to private religious exercise. . . . RLUIPA thus protects institutionalized persons who are unable freely to attend to their religious needs and are therefore dependent on the government's permission and accommodation for exercise of their religion. . . .

We do not read RLUIPA to elevate accommodation of religious observances over an institution's need to maintain order and safety. Our decisions indicate that an accommodation must be measured so that it does not override other significant interests. . . .

We have no cause to believe that RLUIPA would not be applied in an appropriately balanced way, with particular sensitivity to security concerns. . . . Lawmakers . . . anticipated that courts would apply the Act's standard with 'due deference to the experience and expertise of prison and jail administrators in establishing necessary regulations and procedures to maintain good order, security and discipline, consistent with consideration of costs and limited resources.'

Finally, RLUIPA does not differentiate among bona fide faiths. . . . It confers no privileged status on any particular religious sect, and singles out no bona fide faith for disadvantageous treatment. . . .

In upholding RLUIPA's institutionalized-persons provision, we emphasize that respondents 'have raised a facial challenge to [the Act's] constitutionality, and have not contended that under the facts of any of [petitioners'] specific cases . . . [that] applying RLUIPA would produce unconstitutional results.' The District Court, noting the underdeveloped state of the record, concluded: A finding 'that it is factually impossible to provide the kind of accommodations that RLUIPA will require without significantly compromising prison security or the levels of service provided to other inmates' cannot be made at this juncture. We agree. . . .

Should inmate requests for religious accommodations become excessive, impose unjustified burdens on other institutionalized persons, or jeopardize the effective functioning of an institution, the facility would be free to resist the imposition. In that event, adjudication in as-applied challenges would be in order. . . .

For the reasons stated, the judgment of the United States Court of Appeals for the Sixth Circuit is reversed, and the case is remanded for further proceedings consistent with this opinion."

V. JUSTICE VOTE

9 Pro ACLU Side vs. 0 Con Opposing Side

ACLU Side (Petitioner / Appellant)

1. O'Connor, S. – Wrote majority opinion
2. Stevens, J. – Joined majority opinion
3. Souter, D. – Joined majority opinion
4. Ginsburg, R. – Joined majority opinion
5. Breyer, S. – Joined majority opinion
6. Scalia, A. – Joined majority opinion
7. Kennedy, A. – Joined majority opinion
8. Rehnquist, W. – Joined majority opinion
9. Thomas, C. – Wrote concurring opinion

VI. A WIN OR LOSS FOR THE ACLU?

The ACLU filed as amicus curiae urging reversal of the judgment of the Court of Appeals; the Supreme Court reversed in a 9-0 vote, giving the ACLU an apparent win.

985. Johnson v. California

(Decided June 13, 2005; 545 U.S. 162)

I. ISSUE

A. Issues Discussed

Criminal procedure, race

B. Legal Question Presented

"The Supreme Court of California and the United States Court of Appeals for the Ninth Circuit have provided conflicting answers to the following question: 'Whether to establish a prima facie case under Batson v. Kentucky, 476 U.S. 79 (1986), the objector must show that it is more likely than not that the other party's peremptory challenges, if unexplained, were based on impermissible group bias?'"

C. Supreme Court's Answer

"We agree with the Ninth Circuit that the question presented must be answered in the negative, and accordingly reverse the judgment of the California Supreme Court."

II. CASE SUMMARY

A. Background

"Petitioner Jay Shawn Johnson, a black male, was convicted in a California trial court of second-degree murder and assault on a white 19-month-old child, resulting in death. During jury selection, a number of prospective jurors were removed for cause until 43 eligible jurors remained, 3 of whom were black. The prosecutor used 3 of his 12 peremptory challenges to remove the black prospective jurors. The resulting jury, including alternates, was all white.

After the prosecutor exercised the second of his three peremptory challenges against the prospective black jurors, defense counsel objected on the ground that the challenge was unconstitutionally based on race under both the California and United States Constitutions. . . . The trial judge did not ask the prosecutor to explain the rationale for his strikes. Instead, the judge simply found that petitioner had failed to establish a prima facie case under the governing state precedent, People v. Wheeler, 22 Cal.3d 258 (1978), reasoning "that there's not been shown a strong likelihood that the exercise of the peremptory challenges were based upon a group rather than an individual basis." The judge did, however, warn the prosecutor that "we are very close."

Defense counsel made an additional motion the next day when the prosecutor struck the final remaining prospective black juror. Counsel argued that the prosecutor's decision to challenge all of the prospective black jurors constituted a 'systematic attempt to exclude African-Americans from the jury panel.' The trial judge still did not seek an explanation from the prosecutor. Instead, she explained that her own examination of the record had convinced her that the prosecutor's strikes could be justified by race-neutral reasons. . . .

The California Court of Appeal set aside the conviction. Over the dissent of one judge, the majority ruled that the trial judge had erred by requiring petitioner to establish a 'strong likelihood' that the peremptory strikes had been impermissibly based on race. . . .

Respondent appealed, and the California Supreme Court reinstated petitioner's conviction over the dissent of two justices."

The Supreme Court granted certiorari to review the case.

B. Counsel of Record

ACLU Side (Petitioner / Appellant): Stephen B. Bedrick argued the cause for appellant. With him on the briefs was Eric Schnapper.

Opposing Side (Respondent / Appellee): Seth K. Schalit, Supervising Deputy Attorney General of California, argued the cause for appellee. With him on the brief were Bill Lockyer, Attorney General, Robert R. Anderson, Chief Assistant Attorney General, Gerald A. Engler, Senior Assistant Attorney General, and Laurence K. Sullivan, Supervising Deputy Attorney General.

III. AMICI CURIAE

ACLU Side (Petitioner / Appellant)

Brief of amici curiae filed on behalf of the NAACP Legal Defense and Educational Fund, Inc., the American Civil Liberties Union, the American Civil Liberties Union of Northern California, the Lawyers' Committee for Civil Rights Under Law, and the National Association of Criminal Defense Lawyers by Theodore M. Shaw, Norman J. Chachkin, Miriam Gohara, Christina A. Swarns, Steven R. Shapiro, Alan L. Schlosser, Pamela Harris, Barbara R. Arnwine, Michael L. Foreman, Audrey Wiggins, Sarah Crawford, Barry Sullivan, Margaret J. Simpson, and Duane Pozza.

Opposing Side (Respondent / Appellee)

Brief of amici curiae filed on behalf of the Criminal Justice Legal Foundation by Kent S. Scheidegger and Charles L. Hobson.

IV. THE SUPREME COURT'S DECISION

"The issue in this case is narrow but important. It concerns the scope of the first of three steps this Court enumerated in Batson, which together guide trial courts' constitutional review of peremptory strikes. . . . First, the defendant must make out a prima facie case 'by showing that the totality of the relevant facts gives rise to an inference of discriminatory purpose.' Second, once the defendant has made out a prima facie case, the 'burden shifts to the State to explain adequately the racial exclusion' by offering permissible race-neutral justifications for the strikes. Third, '[i]f a race-neutral explanation is tendered, the trial court must then decide . . . whether the opponent of the strike has proved purposeful racial discrimination.'

The question before us is whether Batson permits California to require at step one that 'the objector must show that it is more likely than not the other party's peremptory challenges, if unexplained, were based on impermissible group bias.' Although we recognize that States do have flexibility in formulating appropriate procedures to comply with Batson, we conclude that California's 'more likely than not' standard is an inappropriate yardstick by which to measure the sufficiency of a prima facie case.

We begin with Batson itself, which on its own terms provides no support for California's rule. . . .

We did not intend the first step to be so onerous that a defendant would have to persuade the judge—on the basis of all the facts, some of which are impossible for the defendant to know with certainty—that the challenge was more likely than not the product of purposeful discrimination. Instead, a defendant satisfies the requirements of Batson's first step by producing evidence sufficient to permit the trial judge to draw an inference that discrimination has occurred. . . .

In this case the inference of discrimination was sufficient to invoke a comment by the trial judge 'that 'we are very close,'' and on review, the California Supreme Court acknowledged that 'it certainly looks suspicious that all three African-American prospective jurors were removed from the jury.' Those inferences that discrimination may have occurred were sufficient to establish a prima facie case under Batson.

The facts of this case well illustrate that California's 'more likely than not' standard is at odds with the prima facie inquiry mandated by Batson. The judgment of the California Supreme Court is therefore reversed, and the case is remanded for further proceedings not inconsistent with this opinion."

V. JUSTICE VOTE

8 Pro ACLU Side vs. 1 Con Opposing Side

ACLU Side (Petitioner / Appellant)

1. Stevens, J. – Wrote majority opinion
2. Ginsburg, R. – Joined majority opinion
3. O'Connor, S. – Joined majority opinion
4. Souter, D. – Joined majority opinion
5. Breyer, S. – Wrote concurring opinion
6. Scalia, A. – Joined concurring opinion
7. Kennedy, A. – Joined majority opinion
8. Rehnquist, W. – Joined majority opinion

Opposing Side (Respondent / Appellee)

1. Thomas, C. – Wrote dissenting opinion

VI. A WIN OR LOSS FOR THE ACLU?

The ACLU filed as amicus curiae urging reversal of the judgment of the California Supreme Court; the U.S. Supreme Court reversed in an 8-1 vote, giving the ACLU an apparent win.

986. Wilkinson v. Austin

(Decided June 13, 2005; 545 U.S. 209)

I. ISSUE

A. Issues Discussed

Prison

B. Legal Question Presented

"This case involves the process by which Ohio classifies prisoners for placement at its highest security prison, known as a 'Supermax' facility. . . . We must consider what process the Fourteenth Amendment to the United States Constitution requires Ohio to afford to inmates before assigning them to Supermax."

C. Supreme Court's Answer

"We hold that the procedures Ohio has adopted provide sufficient procedural protection to comply with due process requirements."

II. CASE SUMMARY

A. Background

"In 1998, Ohio opened its only Supermax facility, the Ohio State Penitentiary (OSP), after a riot in one of its maximum-security prisons. . . .

Conditions at OSP are more restrictive than any other form of incarceration in Ohio . . . . In OSP almost every aspect of an inmate's life is controlled and monitored. Inmates must remain in their cells, which measure 7 by 14 feet, for 23 hours per day. . . .

It is fair to say OSP inmates are deprived of almost any environmental or sensory stimuli and of almost all human contact.

Aside from the severity of the conditions, placement at OSP is for an indefinite period of time, limited only by an inmate's sentence. . . . Inmates otherwise eligible for parole lose their eligibility while incarcerated at OSP.

Placement at OSP is determined in the following manner: Upon entering the prison system, all Ohio inmates are assigned a numerical security classification from level 1 through level 5, with 1 the lowest security risk and 5 the highest. The initial security classification . . . is subject to modification at any time . . . . Level 5 inmates are placed in OSP, and levels 1 through 4 inmates are placed at lower security facilities throughout the State.

Ohio concedes that when OSP first became operational, the procedures used to assign inmates to the facility were inconsistent and undefined. . . . In an effort to establish guidelines for the selection and classification of inmates suitable for OSP, Ohio issued Department of Rehabilitation and Correction Policy 111-07 (Aug. 31, 1998). This policy has been revised at various points but relevant here are two versions: the 'Old Policy' and the 'New Policy.' The Old Policy took effect on January 28, 1999, but problems with assignment appear to have persisted even under this written set of standards. After forming a committee to study the matter and retaining a national expert in prison security, Ohio promulgated the New Policy in early 2002. The New Policy provided more guidance regarding the factors to be considered in placement decisions and afforded inmates more procedural protection against erroneous placement at OSP. . . .

This action began when a class of current and former OSP inmates brought suit under Rev. Stat. § 1979, 42 U.S.C. § 1983, in the United States District Court for the Northern District of Ohio against various Ohio prison officials. . . .

The inmates' complaint alleged that Ohio's Old Policy, which was in effect at the time the suit was brought, violated due process. In addition the inmates brought a claim that certain conditions at OSP violated the Eighth Amendment's ban on cruel and unusual punishments, but that claim was settled in the District Court. . . . On the eve of trial Ohio promulgated its New Policy and represented that it contained the procedures to be followed in the future. The District Court and Court of Appeals evaluated the adequacy of the New Policy, and it therefore forms the basis for our determination here.

[T]he District Court made findings and conclusions and issued a detailed remedial order. . . .

Ohio appealed. . . . The Court of Appeals for the Sixth Circuit affirmed the District Court's conclusion that the inmates had a liberty interest in avoiding placement at OSP. The Court of Appeals also affirmed the District Court's procedural modifications in their entirety. Finally, it set aside the District Court's far-reaching substantive modifications, concluding they exceeded the scope of the District Court's authority. This last aspect of the Court of Appeals' ruling is not the subject of review in this Court."

The Supreme Court granted certiorari to review the case.

B. Counsel of Record

ACLU Side (Respondent / Appellee): Jules Lobel argued the cause for appellees. With him on the brief was Staughton Lynd of the American Civil Liberties Union of Ohio Foundation.

Opposing Side (Petitioner / Appellant): Jim Petro, Attorney General of Ohio, argued the cause for appellants. With him on the briefs were Douglas R. Cole, State Solicitor, Stephen P. Carney, Senior Deputy Solicitor, and Todd R. Marti and Franklin E. Crawford, Assistant Solicitors.

Deanne E. Maynard argued the cause for the United States as amicus curiae.

III. AMICI CURIAE

ACLU Side (Respondent / Appellee)

Brief of amici curiae filed on behalf of Corrections Professionals by Walter J. Dickey.

Brief of amici curiae filed on behalf of Human Rights Watch et al. by Geoffrey F. Aronow, Molly Wieser, Thomas F. Geraghty, and Andrea D. Lyon.

Brief of amici curiae filed on behalf of Professors and Practitioners of Psychology and Psychiatry by Michael E. Deutsch.

Brief of amici curiae filed on behalf of Percy Pitzer by Joseph Margulies.

Opposing Side (Petitioner / Appellant)

Brief of amici curiae filed on behalf of the United States by Deanne E. Maynard, Acting Solicitor General Clement, Assistant Attorney General Wray, Deputy Solicitor General Dreeben, Jonathan L. Marcus, and Steven L. Lane.

Brief of amici curiae filed on behalf of the State of California et al. by Bill Lockyer, Attorney General of California, Manuel M. Medeiros, State Solicitor General, Robert R. Anderson, Chief Assistant Attorney General, Frances T. Grunder, Senior Assistant Attorney General, and Thomas S. Patterson, Supervising Deputy Attorney General, by John W. Suthers, Interim Attorney General of Colorado, and by the Attorneys General for their respective States as follows: Gregg D. Renkes of Alaska, Terry Goddard of Arizona, M. Jane Brady of Delaware, Mark J. Bennett of Hawaii, Lisa Madigan of Illinois, G. Steven Rowe of Maine, Thomas F. Reilly of Massachusetts, Jeremiah W. (Jay) Nixon of Missouri, Jon Bruning of Nebraska, Brian Sandoval of

Nevada, W. A. Drew Edmondson of Oklahoma, Hardy Myers of Oregon, Thomas W. Corbett, Jr., of Pennsylvania, Henry D. McMaster of South Carolina, Greg Abbott of Texas, Jerry W. Kilgore of Virginia, and Rob McKenna of Washington.

IV. THE SUPREME COURT'S DECISION

"We need reach the question of what process is due only if the inmates establish a constitutionally protected liberty interest, so it is appropriate to address this threshold question at the outset.

The Fourteenth Amendment's Due Process Clause protects persons against deprivations of life, liberty, or property . . . .

We have held that the Constitution itself does not give rise to a liberty interest in avoiding transfer to more adverse conditions of confinement. . . . We have also held, however, that a liberty interest in avoiding particular conditions of confinement may arise from state policies or regulations, subject to the important limitations set forth in Sandin v. Conner, 515 U.S. 472 (1995). . . .

The Sandin standard requires us to determine if assignment to OSP 'imposes atypical and significant hardship on the inmate in relation to the ordinary incidents of prison life.' In Sandin's wake the Courts of Appeals have not reached consistent conclusions . . . . We need not resolve the issue here, however, for we are satisfied that assignment to OSP imposes an atypical and significant hardship under any plausible baseline. . . .

It follows that respondents have a liberty interest in avoiding assignment to OSP. . . .

A liberty interest having been established, we turn to the question of what process is due an inmate whom Ohio seeks to place in OSP. . . .

Applying the three factors set forth in Mathews, we find Ohio's New Policy provides a sufficient level of process. We first consider the significance of the inmate's interest in avoiding erroneous placement at OSP. Prisoners held in lawful confinement have their liberty curtailed by definition, so the procedural protections to which they are entitled are more limited than in cases where the right at stake is the right to be free from confinement at all. . . .

The second factor addresses the risk of an erroneous placement under the procedures in place, and the probable value, if any, of additional or alternative procedural safeguards. . . .

Ohio provides multiple levels of review for any decision recommending OSP placement, with power to overturn the recommendation at each level. . . .

The third Mathews factor addresses the State's interest. . . .

Prison security, imperiled by the brutal reality of prison gangs, provides the backdrop of the State's interest. . . .

The problem of scarce resources is another component of the State's interest. . . .

We now hold that the New Policy as described in this opinion strikes a constitutionally permissible balance between the factors of the Mathews framework. . . . On remand, the Court of Appeals, or the District Court, may consider in the first instance what, if any, prospective relief is still a necessary and appropriate remedy for due process violations under Ohio's previous policies. . . .

The Court of Appeals was correct to find the inmates possess a liberty interest in avoiding assignment at OSP. The Court of Appeals was incorrect, however, to sustain the procedural modifications ordered by the District Court. . . .

The judgment of the Court of Appeals is affirmed in part and reversed in part, and the case is remanded for further proceedings consistent with this opinion."

V. JUSTICE VOTE

0 Pro ACLU Side vs. 9 Con Opposing Side

Opposing Side (Petitioner / Appellant)

1. Kennedy, A. – Wrote majority opinion
2. Ginsburg, R. – Joined majority opinion
3. Souter, D. – Joined majority opinion
4. Stevens, J. – Joined majority opinion
5. Thomas, C. – Joined majority opinion
6. O'Connor, S. – Joined majority opinion
7. Breyer, S. – Joined majority opinion
8. Scalia, A. – Joined majority opinion
9. Rehnquist, W. – Joined majority opinion

VI. A WIN OR LOSS FOR THE ACLU?

The ACLU served as counsel for respondents urging affirmance; the Supreme Court affirmed in part, reversed in part, and remanded the Court of Appeals' decision in favor of Wilkinson by a 9-0 vote, giving the ACLU an apparent loss.[1]

987. Halbert v. Michigan

(Decided June 23, 2005; 545 U.S. 605)

I. ISSUE

A. Issues Discussed

Criminal procedure

B. Legal Question Presented

Whether "the Due Process and Equal Protection Clauses require the appointment of counsel for defendants, convicted on their pleas, who seek access to first-tier review in the Michigan Court of Appeals."

C. Supreme Court's Answer

"[W]e hold that the Due Process and Equal Protection Clauses require the appointment of counsel for defendants, convicted on their pleas, who seek access to first-tier review in the Michigan Court of Appeals."

---

1 This decision is a technical loss for the ACLU because the court upheld due process rights for prisoners in a Supermax detention facility, an outcome favorable to the ACLU's position, but at the same time rejected more extensive protections, a loss for the ACLU. https://www.aclu.org/news/supreme-courts-decision-upholds-prisoners-due-process-protections-limits-their-reach

II. CASE SUMMARY

A. Background

"In 1994, Michigan voters approved a proposal amending the State Constitution to provide that 'an appeal by an accused who pleads guilty or nolo contendere shall be by leave of the court.' Thereafter, 'several Michigan state judges began to deny appointed appellate counsel to indigents' convicted by plea. Rejecting challenges based on the Equal Protection and Due Process Clauses of the Fourteenth Amendment to the Federal Constitution, the Michigan Supreme Court upheld this practice, and its codification in Mich. Comp. Laws Ann. § 770.3a.

Petitioner Antonio Dwayne Halbert, convicted on his plea of nolo contendere, sought the appointment of counsel to assist him in applying for leave to appeal to the Michigan Court of Appeals. The state trial court and the Court of Appeals denied Halbert's requests for appointed counsel, and the Michigan Supreme Court declined review."

The Supreme Court granted certiorari to review the case.

B. Counsel of Record

ACLU Side (Petitioner / Appellant): David A. Moran argued the cause for appellant. On the briefs were Mark Granzotto, Terence R. Flanagan, Michael J. Steinberg and Kary L. Moss of the American Civil Liberties Union Foundation of Michigan, and Steven R. Shapiro of the American Civil Liberties Union Foundation.

Opposing Side (Respondent / Appellee): Bernard Eric Restuccia, Assistant Attorney General of Michigan, argued the cause for appellee. With him on the brief were Michael A. Cox, Attorney General, and Thomas L. Casey, Solicitor General.

Gene C. Schaerr argued the cause for the State of Louisiana et al. as amici curiae.

III. AMICI CURIAE

ACLU Side (Petitioner / Appellant)

Brief of amici curiae filed on behalf of the American Bar Association by Robert J. Grey, Jr., Seth P. Waxman, Paul R. Q. Wolfson, and Noah A. Levine.

Brief of amici curiae filed on behalf of the National Association of Criminal Defense Lawyers et al. by Anthony J. Franze, Sheila B. Scheuerman, and Paul M. Rashkind.

Brief of amici curiae filed on behalf of the National Legal Aid & Defender Association by Elliot H. Scherker and Karen M. Gottlieb.

Opposing Side (Respondent / Appellee)

Brief of amici curiae filed on behalf of the State of Louisiana et al. by Gene C. Schaerr, Charles C. Foti, Attorney General of Louisiana, Mimi Hunley, Assistant Attorney General, Julie E. Cullen, Linda T. Coberly, and Charles B. Klein, and by the Attorneys General for their respective States as follows: Troy King of Alabama, John W. Suthers of Colorado, Mark J. Bennett of Hawaii, Steve Carter of Indiana, J. Joseph Curran, Jr., of Maryland, Jim Hood of Mississippi, Mike McGrath of Montana, Brian Sandoval of Nevada, Jim Petro of Ohio, W. A. Drew Edmondson of Oklahoma, Henry D. McMaster of South Carolina, Lawrence E. Long of South Dakota, Paul G. Summers of Tennessee, Greg Abbott of Texas, Mark L. Shurtleff of Utah, and Rob McKenna of Washington.

Brief of amici curiae filed on behalf of Wayne County, Michigan by Timothy A. Baughman.

IV. THE SUPREME COURT'S DECISION

"The Federal Constitution imposes on the States no obligation to provide appellate review of criminal convictions. Having provided such an avenue, however, a State may not 'bolt the door to equal justice' to indigent defendants. . . . Griffin held that, when a State conditions an appeal from a conviction on the provision of a trial transcript, the State must furnish free transcripts to indigent defendants who seek to appeal. Douglas relied on Griffin's reasoning to hold that, in first appeals as of right, States must appoint counsel to represent indigent defendants. Ross held, however, that a State need not appoint counsel to aid a poor person in discretionary appeals to the State's highest court, or in petitioning for review in this Court. . . .

Petitioner Halbert's case is framed by two prior decisions of this Court concerning state-funded appellate counsel, Douglas and Ross. The question before us is essentially one of classification: With which of those decisions should the instant case be aligned? We hold that Douglas provides the controlling instruction. Two aspects of the Michigan Court of Appeals' process following plea-based convictions lead us to that conclusion. First, in determining how to dispose of an application for leave to appeal, Michigan's intermediate appellate court looks to the merits of the claims made in the application. Second, indigent defendants pursuing first-tier review in the Court of Appeals are generally ill equipped to represent themselves. . . .

Whether formally categorized as the decision of an appeal or the disposal of a leave application, the Court of Appeals' ruling on a plea-convicted defendant's claims provides the first, and likely the only, direct review the defendant's conviction and sentence will receive. Parties like Halbert, however, are disarmed in their endeavor to gain first-tier review. . . .

Navigating the appellate process without a lawyer's assistance is a perilous endeavor for a layperson, and well beyond the competence of individuals, like Halbert, who have little education, learning disabilities, and mental impairments. . . .

While the State has a legitimate interest in reducing the workload of its judiciary, providing indigents with appellate counsel will yield applications easier to comprehend. Michigan's Court of Appeals would still have recourse to summary denials of leave applications in cases not warranting further review. And when a defendant's case presents no genuinely arguable issue, appointed counsel may so inform the court. . . .

Michigan contends that, even if Halbert had a constitutionally guaranteed right to appointed counsel for first-level appellate review, he waived that right by entering a plea of nolo contendere. We disagree. At the time he entered his plea, Halbert, in common with other defendants convicted on their pleas, had no recognized right to appointed appellate counsel he could elect to forgo. Moreover, . . . the trial court did not tell Halbert, simply and directly, that in his case, there would be no access to appointed counsel. . . .

For the reasons stated, we vacate the judgment of the Michigan Court of Appeals and remand the case for further proceedings not inconsistent with this opinion."

V. JUSTICE VOTE

6 Pro ACLU Side vs. 3 Con Opposing Side

ACLU Side (Petitioner / Appellant)

1. Ginsburg, R. – Wrote majority opinion
2. O'Connor, S. – Joined majority opinion
3. Stevens, J. – Joined majority opinion
4. Souter, D. – Joined majority opinion
5. Breyer, S. – Joined majority opinion
6. Kennedy, A. – Joined majority opinion

Opposing Side (Respondent / Appellee)

1. Rehnquist, W. – Joined Thomas' dissent in part
2. Thomas, C. – Wrote dissenting opinion
3. Scalia, A – Joined Thomas' dissent

VI. A WIN OR LOSS FOR THE ACLU?

The ACLU argued the cause for appellant urging reversal of the judgment of the Court of Appeals; the Supreme Court vacated and remanded in a 6-3 vote, giving the ACLU an apparent win.

988. Town of Castle Rock v. Gonzales

(Decided June 27, 2005; 545 U.S. 748)

I. ISSUE

A. Issues Discussed

Civil rights

B. Legal Question Presented

"[W]hether an individual who has obtained a state-law restraining order has a constitutionally protected property interest in having the police enforce the restraining order when they have probable cause to believe it has been violated."

C. Supreme Court's Answer

"We conclude . . . that respondent did not, for purposes of the Due Process Clause, have a property interest in police enforcement of the restraining order against her husband."

II. CASE SUMMARY

A. Background

"The horrible facts of this case are contained in the complaint that respondent Jessica Gonzales filed in Federal District Court. . . . Respondent alleges that petitioner, the town of Castle Rock, Colorado, violated the Due Process Clause of the Fourteenth Amendment to the United States Constitution when its police officers, acting pursuant to official policy or custom, failed to respond properly to her repeated reports that her estranged husband was violating the terms of a restraining order. . . .

According to the complaint, at about 5 or 5:30 p.m. on Tuesday, June 22, 1999, respondent's husband took the three daughters while they were playing outside the family home. . . . At about 7:30 p.m., she called the Castle Rock Police Department, which dispatched two officers. . . . 'When [the officers] arrived . . . , she showed them a copy of the TRO and requested that it be enforced and the three children be returned to her immediately. [The officers] stated that there was nothing they could do about the TRO and suggested that [respondent] call the Police Department again if the three children did not return home by 10:00 p.m.'

At approximately 8:30 p.m., respondent talked to her husband on his cellular telephone. He told her 'he had the three children [at an] amusement park in Denver.' She called the police again and asked them to 'have someone check for' her husband or his vehicle at the amusement park and 'put out an [all points bulletin]' for her husband, but the officer with whom she spoke 'refused to do so,' again telling her to 'wait until 10:00 p.m. and see if' her husband returned the girls.

At approximately 10:10 p.m., respondent called the police and said her children were still missing, but she was now told to wait until midnight. She called at midnight and told the dispatcher her children were still missing. She went to her husband's apartment and, finding nobody there, called the police at 12:10 a.m.; she was told to wait for an officer to arrive. When none came, she went to the police station at 12:50 a.m. and submitted an incident report. The officer who took the report 'made no reasonable effort to enforce the TRO or locate the three children. Instead, he went to dinner.'

At approximately 3:20 a.m., respondent's husband arrived at the police station and opened fire with a semiautomatic handgun he had purchased earlier that evening. Police shot back, killing him. Inside the cab of his pickup truck, they found the bodies of all three daughters, whom he had already murdered.

On the basis of the foregoing factual allegations, respondent brought an action under Rev. Stat. § 1979, 42 U.S.C. § 1983, claiming that the town violated the Due Process Clause . . . .

Before answering the complaint, the defendants filed a motion to dismiss under Federal Rule of Civil Procedure 12(b)(6). The District Court granted the motion . . . .

A panel of the Court of Appeals affirmed the rejection of a substantive due process claim, but found that respondent had alleged a cognizable procedural due process claim. On rehearing en banc, a divided court reached the same disposition . . . . "

The Supreme Court granted certiorari to review the case.

B. Counsel of Record

ACLU Side (Respondent / Appellee): Brian J. Reichel argued the cause and filed a brief for appellee.

Opposing Side (Petitioner / Appellant): John C. Eastman argued the cause for appellant. With him on the briefs were Thomas S. Rice, Eric M. Ziporin, and Erik S. Jaffe.

John P. Elwood argued the cause for the United States as amicus curiae.

III. AMICI CURIAE

ACLU Side (Respondent / Appellee)

Brief of amici curiae filed on behalf of the American Civil Liberties Union et al. by Caroline M. Brown, Steven R. Shapiro, and Lenora M. Lapidus.

Brief of amici curiae filed on behalf of AARP by Stuart R. Cohen, Susan Ann Silverstein, and Michael Schuster.

Brief of amici curiae filed on behalf of International Law Scholars et al. by Jennifer K. Brown and Rhonda Copelon.

Brief of amici curiae filed on behalf of the National Association of Women Lawyers et al. by Lorelie S. Masters.

Brief of amici curiae filed on behalf of the National Black Police Association et al. by Richard W. Smith and Joan S. Meier.

Brief of amici curiae filed on behalf of the National Coalition Against Domestic Violence et al. by Naomi G. Beer, Libby Y. Mote, and Michele E. Stone.

Brief of amici curiae filed on behalf of the National Network to End Domestic Violence et al. by Fernando R. Laguarda.

Brief of amici curiae filed on behalf of Peggy Kerns et al. by David G. Hall and James C. Harrington.

Brief of amici curiae filed on behalf of the Family Violence Prevention Fund et al. by Deanne M. Ottaviano and Janine A. Carlan.

Opposing Side (Petitioner / Appellant)

Brief of amici curiae filed on behalf of the United States by John P. Elwood, Acting Solicitor General Clement, Assistant Attorney General Keisler, Michael Jay Singer, and Howard S. Scher.

Brief of amici curiae filed on behalf of the Denver Police Protective Association et al. by David J. Bruno and Michael T. Lowe.

Brief of amici curiae filed on behalf of the International Municipal Lawyers Association et al. by Brad D. Bailey and Kathryn L. Schroeder.

IV. THE SUPREME COURT'S DECISION

"The Fourteenth Amendment to the United States Constitution provides that a State shall not 'deprive any person of life, liberty, or property, without due process of law.' In 42 U.S.C. § 1983, Congress has created a federal cause of action for 'the deprivation of any rights, privileges, or immunities secured by the Constitution and laws.' Respondent claims the benefit of this provision on the ground that she had a property interest in police enforcement of the restraining order against her husband; and that the town deprived her of this property without due process by having a policy that tolerated nonenforcement of restraining orders.

As the Court of Appeals recognized, we left a similar question unanswered in DeShaney v. Winnebago County Dept. of Social Servs., 489 U.S. 189 (1989), another case with 'undeniably tragic' facts . . . .

The procedural component of the Due Process Clause does not protect everything that might be described as a 'benefit': 'To have a property interest in a benefit, a person clearly must have more than an abstract need or desire' and 'more than a unilateral expectation of it. He must, instead, have a legitimate claim of entitlement to it.' Such entitlements are, "of course, . . . not created by the Constitution. Rather, they are created and their dimensions are defined by existing rules or understandings that stem from an independent source such as state law." . . .

Our cases recognize that a benefit is not a protected entitlement if government officials may grant or deny it in their discretion. . . .

We do not believe that . . . provisions of Colorado law truly made enforcement of restraining orders mandatory. A well established tradition of police discretion has long coexisted with apparently mandatory arrest statutes. . . .

We conclude, therefore, that respondent did not, for purposes of the Due Process Clause, have a property interest in police enforcement of the restraining order against her husband. It is accordingly unnecessary to address the Court of Appeals' determination that the town's custom or policy prevented the police from giving her due process when they deprived her of that alleged interest.

In light of today's decision and that in DeShaney, the benefit that a third party may receive from having someone else arrested for a crime generally does not trigger protections under the Due Process Clause, neither in its procedural nor in its 'substantive' manifestations. This result reflects our continuing reluctance to treat the Fourteenth Amendment as "a font of tort law," but it does not mean States are powerless to provide victims with personally enforceable remedies. Although the framers of the Fourteenth Amendment and the Civil Rights Act of 1871, 17 Stat. 13 (the original source of § 1983), did not create a system by which police departments are generally held financially accountable for crimes that better policing might have prevented, the people of Colorado are free to craft such a system under state law.

The judgment of the Court of Appeals is reversed."

V. JUSTICE VOTE

2 Pro ACLU Side vs. 7 Con Opposing Side

ACLU Side (Respondent / Appellee)

1. Ginsburg, R. – Joined Stevens' dissent
2. Stevens, J. – Wrote dissenting opinion

Opposing Side (Petitioner / Appellant)

1. Scalia, A. – Wrote majority opinion
2. Souter, D. – Wrote concurring opinion
3. Thomas, C. – Joined majority opinion
4. O'Connor, S. – Joined majority opinion
5. Breyer, S. – Joined Souter's concurrence
6. Kennedy, A. – Joined majority opinion
7. Rehnquist, W. – Joined majority opinion

VI. A WIN OR LOSS FOR THE ACLU?

The ACLU filed as amicus curiae urging affirmance; the Supreme Court reversed the Court of Appeals' decision by a 7-2 vote, giving the ACLU an apparent loss.

989. McCreary County v. American Civil Liberties Union of Kentucky

(Decided June 27, 2005; 545 U.S. 844)

I. ISSUE

A. Issues Discussed

1st Amendment, religion

B. Legal Question Presented

"[W]hether a determination of the counties' purpose is a sound basis for ruling on the Establishment Clause complaints, and whether evaluation of the counties' claim of secular purpose for the ultimate displays may take their evolution into account."

C. Supreme Court's Answer

"We hold that the counties' manifest objective may be dispositive of the constitutional enquiry, and that the development of the presentation should be considered when determining its purpose."

II. CASE SUMMARY

A. Background

"Executives of two counties posted a version of the Ten Commandments on the walls of their courthouses. After suits were filed charging violations of the Establishment Clause, the legislative body of each county adopted a resolution calling for a more extensive exhibit meant to show that the Commandments are Kentucky's 'precedent legal code.' The result in each instance was a modified display of the Commandments surrounded by texts containing religious references as their sole common element. After changing counsel, the counties revised the exhibits again by eliminating some documents, expanding the text set out in another, and adding some new ones. . . .

In the summer of 1999, petitioners McCreary County and Pulaski County, Kentucky (hereinafter Counties), put up in their respective courthouses large, gold-framed copies of an abridged text of the King James version of the Ten Commandments, including a citation to the Book of Exodus. . . .

In November 1999, respondents American Civil Liberties Union of Kentucky et al. sued the Counties in Federal District Court under Rev. Stat. § 1979, 42 U.S.C. § 1983, and sought a preliminary injunction against maintaining the displays, which the ACLU charged were violations of the prohibition of religious establishment included in the First Amendment of the Constitution. Within a month, and before the District Court had responded to the request for injunction, the legislative body of each County authorized a second, expanded display . . . .

As directed by the resolutions, the Counties expanded the displays of the Ten Commandments in their locations. . . .

After argument, the District Court entered a preliminary injunction on May 5, 2000, ordering that the 'display . . . be removed from [each] County Courthouse IMMEDIATELY' and that no county official 'erect or cause to be erected similar displays.' . . .

The Counties filed a notice of appeal from the preliminary injunction but voluntarily dismissed it after hiring new lawyers. They then installed another display in each courthouse, the third within a year. No new resolution authorized this one, nor did the Counties repeal the resolutions that preceded the second. . . .

The ACLU moved to supplement the preliminary injunction to enjoin the Counties' third display, and the Counties responded with several explanations for the new version . . . .

As requested, the trial court supplemented the injunction, and a divided panel of the Court of Appeals for the Sixth Circuit affirmed."

The Supreme Court granted certiorari to review the case.

B. Counsel of Record

ACLU Side (Respondent / Appellee): David A. Friedman of the American Civil Liberties Union of Kentucky argued the cause for appellees. With him on the brief were Lili R. Lutgens of the American Civil Liberties Union of Kentucky and Steven R. Shapiro of the ACLU Foundation.

Opposing Side (Petitioner / Appellant): Mathew D. Staver argued the cause for appellants. With him on the briefs were Erik W. Stanley, Rena M. Lindevaldsen, Bruce W. Green, and Mary E. McAlister.

Acting Solicitor General Clement argued the cause for the United States as amicus curiae.

III. AMICI CURIAE

ACLU Side (Respondent / Appellee)

Brief of amici curiae filed on behalf of American Atheists by Robert J. Bruno.

Brief of amici curiae filed on behalf of the American Humanist Association et al. by Elizabeth L. Hileman.

Brief of amici curiae filed on behalf of Americans United for Separation of Church and State et al. by William M. Hohengarten, Ian Heath Gershengorn, Ayesha Khan, Richard B. Katskee, and Judith E. Schaeffer.

Brief of amici curiae filed on behalf of the AntiDefamation League et al. by Jeffrey R. Babbin, Aaron S. Bayer, Kenneth D. Heath, Frederick M. Lawrence, Daniel S. Alter, and Steven M. Freeman.

Brief of amici curiae filed on behalf of the Atheist Law Center et al. by Pamela L. Sumners and Larry Darby.

Brief of amici curiae filed on behalf of the Baptist Joint Committee et al. by Douglas Laycock, Jeffrey P. Sinensky, K. Hollyn Hollman, and Marc D. Stern.

Brief of amici curiae filed on behalf of the Council for Secular Humanism et al. by Ronald A. Lindsay.

Brief of amici curiae filed on behalf of the Freedom from Religion Foundation by James A. Friedman and James D. Peterson.

Brief of amici curiae filed on behalf of Legal Historians and Law Scholars by Steven K. Green.

Brief of amici curiae filed on behalf of the National School Boards Association et al. by Julie Underwood in support of neither party.

Opposing Side (Petitioner / Appellant)

Brief of amici curiae filed on behalf of the United States by Acting Solicitor General Clement, Assistant Attorney General Keisler, Deputy Assistant Attorney General Katsas, Patricia A. Millett, Robert M. Loeb, and Lowell V. Sturgill, Jr.

Brief of amici curiae filed on behalf of the State of Alabama et al. by Troy King, Attorney General of Alabama, Kevin C. Newsom, Solicitor General, and Charles B. Campbell, Assistant Attorney General, and by the Attorneys General for their respective States as follows: Charles J. Crist, Jr., of Florida, Lawrence G. Wasden of Idaho, Steve Carter of Indiana, Phill Kline of Kansas, Gregory D. Stumbo of Kentucky, Charles C. Foti, Jr., of Louisiana, Jim Hood of Mississippi, Jim Petro of Ohio, Gerald J. Pappert of Pennsylvania, Henry McMaster of South Carolina, Greg Abbott of Texas, Mark L. Shurtleff of Utah, Jerry W. Kilgore of Virginia, and Patrick J. Crank of Wyoming.

Brief of amici curiae filed on behalf of the State of Minnesota et al. by Mike Hatch, Attorney General of Minnesota, and John S. Garry, Assistant Attorney General, and by the Attorneys General for their respective States as follows: Lisa Madigan of Illinois, Thomas J. Miller of Iowa, Jeremiah W. (Jay) Nixon of Missouri, Patricia A. Madrid of New Mexico, W. A. Drew Edmondson of Oklahoma, and Peggy A. Lautenschlager of Wisconsin.

Brief of amici curiae filed on behalf of the American Center for Law and Justice by Jay Alan Sekulow, Stuart J. Roth, Francis J. Manion, and Walter M. Weber.

Brief of amici curiae filed on behalf of the American Legion by Kelly Shackelford and Philip B. Onderdonk, Jr.

Brief of amici curiae filed on behalf of the American Liberties Institute et al. by Frederick H. Nelson.

Brief of amici curiae filed on behalf of the Ashbrook Center for Public Affairs et al. by Steven C. Seeger.

Brief of amici curiae filed on behalf of the Becket Fund for Religious Liberty by Anthony R. Picarello, Jr.

Brief of amici curiae filed on behalf of the Conservative Legal Defense and Education Fund et al. by Herbert W. Titus and William J. Olson.

Brief of amici curiae filed on behalf of the Eagle Forum Education & Legal Defense Fund by Douglas G. Smith and Phyllis Schlafly.

Brief of amici curiae filed on behalf of Faith and Action et al. by Bernard P. Reese, Jr.

Brief of amici curiae filed on behalf of the Family Research Council, Inc., et al. by Robert P. George.

Brief of amici curiae filed on behalf of the Foundation for Moral Law, Inc., by Benjamin D. DuPré and Gregory M. Jones.

Brief of amici curiae filed on behalf of Judicial Watch, Inc., by Paul J. Orfanedes and Meredith L. Cavallo.

Brief of amici curiae filed on behalf of the Pacific Justice Institute by Peter D. Lepiscopo.

Brief of amici curiae filed on behalf of the Rutherford Institute by John W. Whitehead.

Brief of amici curiae filed on behalf of the Thomas More Law Center by Edward L. White III.

Brief of amici curiae filed on behalf of Wallbuilders, Inc., by Barry C. Hodge.

IV. THE SUPREME COURT'S DECISION

"Twenty-five years ago in a case prompted by posting the Ten Commandments in Kentucky's public schools, this Court recognized that the Commandments 'are undeniably a sacred text in the Jewish and Christian faiths' and held that their display in public classrooms violated the First Amendment's bar against establishment of religion. Stone found a predominantly religious purpose in the government's posting of the Commandments, given their prominence as "an instrument of religion." The Counties ask for a different approach here by arguing that official purpose is unknowable and the search for it inherently vain. In the alternative, the Counties would avoid the District Court's conclusion by having us limit the scope of the purpose enquiry so severely that any trivial rationalization would suffice, under a standard oblivious to the history of religious government action like the progression of exhibits in this case. . . .

Ever since Lemon v. Kurtzman summarized the three familiar considerations for evaluating Establishment Clause claims, looking to whether government action has 'a secular legislative purpose' has been a common, albeit seldom dispositive, element of our cases. . . .

The touchstone for our analysis is the principle that the 'First Amendment mandates governmental neutrality between religion and religion, and between religion and nonreligion.' When the government acts with the ostensible and predominant purpose of advancing religion, it violates that central Establishment Clause value of official religious neutrality, there being no neutrality when the government's ostensible object is to take sides. . . .

Despite the intuitive importance of official purpose to the realization of Establishment Clause values, the Counties ask us to abandon Lemon's purpose test, or at least to truncate any enquiry into purpose here. Their first argument is that the very consideration of purpose is deceptive: according to them, true 'purpose' is unknowable, and its search merely an excuse for courts to act selectively and unpredictably in picking out evidence of subjective intent. The assertions are as seismic as they are unconvincing. . . .

After declining the invitation to abandon concern with purpose wholesale, we also have to avoid the Counties' alternative tack of trivializing the enquiry into it. The Counties would read the cases as if the purpose enquiry were so naive that any transparent claim to secularity would satisfy it, and they would cut context out of the enquiry, to the point of ignoring history, no matter what bearing it actually had on the significance of current circumstances. There is no precedent for the Counties' arguments, or reason supporting them. . . .

This case comes to us on appeal from a preliminary injunction. We accordingly review the District Court's legal rulings de novo, and its ultimate conclusion for abuse of discretion. . . .

In holding the preliminary injunction adequately supported by evidence that the Counties' purpose had not changed at the third stage, we do not decide that the Counties' past actions forever taint any effort on their part to deal with the subject matter. We hold only that purpose needs to be taken seriously under the Establishment Clause and needs to be understood in light of context; an implausible claim that governmental purpose has changed should not carry the day in a court of law any more than in a head with common sense. It is enough to say here that district courts are fully capable of adjusting preliminary relief to take account of genuine changes in constitutionally significant conditions.

Nor do we have occasion here to hold that a sacred text can never be integrated constitutionally into a governmental display on the subject of law, or American history. . . .

Given the ample support for the District Court's finding of a predominantly religious purpose behind the Counties' third display, we affirm the Sixth Circuit in upholding the preliminary injunction."

V. JUSTICE VOTE

5 Pro ACLU Side vs. 4 Con Opposing Side

ACLU Side (Respondent / Appellee)

1. Souter, D. – Wrote majority opinion
2. Ginsburg, R. – Joined majority opinion
3. Stevens, J. – Joined majority opinion
4. O'Connor, S. – Wrote concurring opinion
5. Breyer, S. – Joined majority opinion

Opposing Side (Petitioner / Appellant)

1. Rehnquist, W. – Joined Scalia's dissent
2. Thomas, C. – Joined Scalia's dissent
3. Scalia, A. – Wrote dissenting opinion
4. Kennedy, A. – Joined Scalia's dissent in part

VI. A WIN OR LOSS FOR THE ACLU?

The ACLU argued the case for respondents urging affirmance; the Supreme Court affirmed the Court of Appeals' decision by a 5-4 vote, giving the ACLU an apparent win.

990. Metro-Goldwyn-Mayer Studios, Inc. v. Grokster, Ltd.

(Decided June 27, 2005; 545 U.S. 913)

I. ISSUE

A. Issues Discussed

Government authority

B. Legal Question Presented

"The question is under what circumstances the distributor of a product capable of both lawful and unlawful use is liable for acts of copyright infringement by third parties using the product."

C. Supreme Court's Answer

"We hold that one who distributes a device with the object of promoting its use to infringe copyright, as shown by clear expression or other affirmative steps taken to foster infringement, is liable for the resulting acts of infringement by third parties."

II. CASE SUMMARY

A. Background

"Respondents, Grokster, Ltd., and StreamCast Networks, Inc., defendants in the trial court, distribute free software products that allow computer users to share electronic files through peer-to-peer networks, so called because users' computers communicate directly with each other, not through central servers. [P]eer-to-peer networks are employed to store and distribute electronic files by universities, government agencies, corporations, and libraries, among others.

Other users of peer-to-peer networks include individual recipients of Grokster's and StreamCast's software, and although the networks that they enjoy through using the software can be used to share any type of digital file, they have prominently employed those networks in sharing copyrighted music and video files without authorization. A group of copyright holders (MGM for short, but including motion picture studios, recording companies, songwriters, and music publishers) sued Grokster and StreamCast for their users' copyright infringements, alleging that they knowingly and intentionally distributed their software to enable users to reproduce and distribute the copyrighted works in violation of the Copyright Act. MGM sought damages and an injunction. . . .

After discovery, the parties on each side of the case cross-moved for summary judgment. The District Court limited its consideration to the asserted liability of Grokster and StreamCast for distributing the current versions of their software, leaving aside whether either was liable 'for damages arising from past versions of their software, or from other past activities.' The District Court held that those who used the Grokster and Morpheus software to download copyrighted media files directly infringed MGM's copyrights, a conclusion not contested on appeal, but the court nonetheless granted summary judgment in favor of Grokster and StreamCast as to any liability arising from distribution of the then-current versions of their software. Distributing that software gave rise to no liability in the court's view, because its use did not provide the distributors with actual knowledge of specific acts of infringement.

The Court of Appeals affirmed."

The Supreme Court granted certiorari to review the case.

B. Counsel of Record

ACLU Side (Respondent / Appellee): Richard G. Taranto argued the cause for appellees. With him on the brief were H. Bartow Farr III, Cindy A. Cohn, Fred Von Lohmann, Michael H. Page, Mark A. Lemley, Charles S. Baker, and Matthew A. Neco

Opposing Side (Petitioner / Appellant): Donald B. Verrilli, Jr., argued the cause for appellants. With him on the briefs for the motion picture studio and recording company appellants were Ian Heath Gershengorn, William M. Hohengarten, Steven B. Fabrizio, Thomas J. Perrelli, Matthew J. Oppenheim, David E. Kendall, Thomas G. Hentoff, Kenneth W. Starr, Russell J. Frackman, George M. Borkowski, Robert M. Schwartz, Gregory P. Goeckner, Dean C. Garfield, Elaine J. Goldenberg, Matthew Hersh, Steven M. Marks, and Stanley Pierre-Louis. Carey R. Ramos, Peter L. Felcher, Aidan Synnott, Theodore

K. Cheng, Kelli L. Sager, Andrew J. Thomas, Jeffrey H. Blum, and Jeffrey L. Fisher filed briefs for the songwriter and music publisher appellants.

Acting Solicitor General Clement argued the cause for the United States as amicus curiae.

III. AMICI CURIAE

ACLU Side (Respondent / Appellee)

Brief of amici curiae filed on behalf of the American Civil Liberties Union, the American Civil Liberties Union of Northern California, the American Civil Liberties Union Foundation of San Diego and Imperial Counties, the American Library Association, the Association of Research Libraries, the American Association of Law Libraries, the Medical Library Association, the Special Libraries Association, the Internet Archive, and Project Gutenberg by Ann Brick, Christopher A. Hansen, Steven R. Shapiro, Aden J. Fine, Sharon M. Mcgowan, Gabrielle Prisco, Jordan C. Budd, and Elvira Cacciavillani.

Brief of amici curiae filed on behalf of Altnet, Inc., by Roderick G. Dorman.

Brief of amici curiae filed on behalf of the American Conservative Union et al. by David Post.

Brief of amici curiae filed on behalf of the Cellular Telecommunications & Internet Association et al. by Andrew G. McBride, Joshua S. Turner, Michael Altschul, James W. Olson, Frank L. Politano, Laura Kaster, Jeffrey A. Rackow, Grier C. Raclin, Michael Standard, John Thorne, Sarah B. Deutsch, and Paul J. Larkin, Jr.

Brief of amici curiae filed on behalf of the Consumer Electronics Association et al. by Bruce G. Joseph and Scott E. Bain.

Brief of amici curiae filed on behalf of the Consumer Federation of America et al. by Peter Jaszi.

Brief of amici curiae filed on behalf of the Distributed Computing Industry Association by Mr. Dorman.

Brief of amici curiae filed on behalf of the Eagle Forum Education & Legal Defense Fund by Andrew L. Schlafly and Karen B. Tripp.

Brief of amici curiae filed on behalf of the Free Software Foundation et al. by Eben Moglen.

Brief of amici curiae filed on behalf of Intel Corp. by James M. Burger and Jonathan D. Hart.

Brief of amici curiae filed on behalf of Internet Law Faculty by William W. Fisher III and Jonathan Zittrain.

Brief of amici curiae filed on behalf of Law Professors by J. Glynn Lunney, Jr.

Brief of amici curiae filed on behalf of the National Association of Shareholder and Consumer Attorneys by Kevin P. Roddy and Matthew E. Van Tine.

Brief of amici curiae filed on behalf of Sixty Intellectual Property and Technology Law Professors et al. by Deirdre K. Mulligan and Pamela Samuelson.

Brief of amici curiae filed on behalf of Sovereign Artists et al. by James R. Wheaton.

Brief of amici curiae filed on behalf of Computer Science Professor Harold Abelson et al. by James S. Tyre.

Brief of amici curiae filed on behalf of Professor Edward Lee et al. by Mr. Lee, pro se.

Brief of amici curiae filed on behalf of Charles Nesson by Mr. Nesson, pro se.

Brief of amici curiae filed on behalf of Malla Pollack et al. by Ms. Pollack, pro se.

Brief of amici curiae filed on behalf of Creative Commons by Lawrence Lessig.

Brief of amici curiae filed on behalf of Emerging Technology Companies by Michael Traynor and Matthew D. Brown.

Brief of amici curiae filed on behalf of Media Studies Professors by Roy I. Liebman.

Brief of amici curiae filed on behalf of the National Venture Capital Association by Michael K. Kellogg, Mark L. Evans, and David L. Schwarz.

Brief of amici curiae filed on behalf of Sharman Networks Limited by Mr. Dorman.

Brief of amici curiae filed on behalf of Felix Oberholzer-Gee et al. by Carl H. Settlemyer III and Arnold P. Lutzker.

Brief of amici curiae filed on behalf of Innovation Scholars and Economists by Laurence F. Pulgram in support of affirmance.

Brief of amici curiae filed on behalf of Audible Magic Corp. et al. by Bruce V. Spiva and Jeremy H. Stern in support of neither party.

Brief of amici curiae filed on behalf of Bridgemar Services, Ltd. d/b/a iMesh.com by Jeffrey A. Kimmel in support of neither party.

Brief of amici curiae filed on behalf of the Digital Media Association et al. by Lawrence Robbins, Alan Untereiner, Markham C. Erickson, and Jerry Berman in support of neither party.

Brief of amici curiae filed on behalf of IEEE-USA by Matthew J. Conigliaro, Andrew C. Greenberg, Joseph H. Lang, Jr., and Daniel E. Fisher in support of neither party.

Brief of amici curiae filed on behalf of the Intellectual Property Owners Association by James H. Pooley in support of neither party.

Brief of amici curiae filed on behalf of SNOCAP, Inc., by Joel W. Nomkin in support of neither party.

Brief of amici curiae filed on behalf of Lee A. Hollaar by Lloyd W. Sadler in support of neither party.

Brief of amici curiae filed on behalf of U.S. Senator Patrick Leahy et al. by Mr. Leahy, pro se, and Senator Orrin G. Hatch, pro se in support of neither party.

Opposing Side (Petitioner / Appellant)

Brief of amici curiae filed on behalf of the United States by Acting Solicitor General Clement, Assistant Attorney General Keisler, Deputy Solicitor General Hungar, Douglas H. Hallward-Driemeier, Anthony A. Yang, David O. Carson, and John M. Whealan.

Brief of amici curiae filed on behalf of the State of Utah et al. by Mark Shurtleff, Attorney General of Utah, and by the Attorneys General for their respective jurisdictions as follows: Troy King of Alabama, Gregg Renkes of Alaska, Terry Goddard of Arizona, Mike Beebe of Arkansas, M. Jane Brady of Delaware, Charles J. Crist, Jr., of Florida, Thurbert E. Baker of Georgia, Douglas B. Moylan of Guam, Mark J. Bennett of Hawaii, Lawrence G. Wasden of Idaho, Lisa Madigan of Illinois, Steve Carter of Indiana, Phill Kline of Kansas, Gregory D. Stumbo of Kentucky, Charles C. Foti, Jr., of Louisiana, Thomas F. Reilly of Massachusetts, Michael A. Cox of Michigan, Mike Hatch of Minnesota, Jim Hood of Mississippi, Jeremiah W. (Jay) Nixon of Missouri, Mike McGrath of Montana, Jon Bruning of Nebraska, Brian Sandoval of Nevada, Peter C. Harvey of New Jersey, Patricia A. Madrid of New Mexico, Roy Cooper of North Carolina, Wayne Stenehjem of North Dakota, Jim Petro of Ohio, W. A. Drew Edmondson of Oklahoma, Thomas W. Corbett, Jr., of Pennsylvania, Patrick Lynch of Rhode Island, Henry McMaster of South Carolina, Lawrence E. Long of South Dakota, Paul G. Summers of Tennessee, Greg Abbott of Texas, William H. Sorrell of Vermont, Jerry Kilgore of Virginia, Darrell V. McGraw, Jr., of West Virginia, and Peg Lautenschlager of Wisconsin.

Brief of amici curiae filed on behalf of the American Federation of Musicians of the United States and Canada et al. by George H. Cohen, Patricia Polach, and Laurence Gold.

Brief of amici curiae filed on behalf of the American Society of Composers, Authors and Publishers et al. by I. Fred Koenigsberg, Michael E. Salzman, and Marvin L. Berenson.

Brief of amici curiae filed on behalf of Americans for Tax Reform by Carter G. Phillips, Alan Charles Raul, Jay T. Jorgensen, and Eric A. Shumsky.

Brief of amici curiae filed on behalf of the Commissioner of Baseball et al. by Robert Alan Garrett and Hadrian R. Katz.

Brief of amici curiae filed on behalf of Defenders of Property Rights by Theodore B. Olson, Thomas H. Dupree, Jr., Matthew D. McGill, Nancie G. Marzulla, and Roger Marzulla.

Brief of amici curiae filed on behalf of International Rights Owners by Christopher Wolf.

Brief of amici curiae filed on behalf of Kids First Coalition et al. by Viet D. Dinh.

Brief of amici curiae filed on behalf of Law Professors et al. by James Gibson.

Brief of amici curiae filed on behalf of Macrovision Corp. by Geoffrey L. Beauchamp, Kelly G. Huller, and James H. Salter.

Brief of amici curiae filed on behalf of Napster, LLC, et al. by Barry I. Slotnick.

Brief of amici curiae filed on behalf of the National Academy of Recording Arts & Sciences, Inc., et al. by Jon A. Baumgarten and Jay L. Cooper.

Brief of amici curiae filed on behalf of the National Association of Broadcasters by Marsha J. MacBride, Jane E. Mago, Benjamin F. P. Ivins, and Jerianne Timmerman.

Brief of amici curiae filed on behalf of the National Association of Recording Merchandisers by Alan R. Malasky and Melanie Martin-Jones.

Brief of amici curiae filed on behalf of the Progress & Freedom Foundation by James V. DeLong.

Brief of amici curiae filed on behalf of the Video Software Dealers Association by John T. Mitchell.

Brief of amici curiae filed on behalf of Professor Peter S. Menell et al. by Mr. Menell, pro se.

Brief of amici curiae filed on behalf of the Business Software Alliance by E. Edward Bruce and Robert A. Long, Jr.

Brief of amici curiae filed on behalf of Kenneth J. Arrow et al. by David A. Strauss.

Brief of amici curiae filed on behalf of the American Intellectual Property Law Association by Rick D. Nydegger and Melvin C. Garner in support of vacatur and remand.

IV. THE SUPREME COURT'S DECISION

"MGM and many of the amici fault the Court of Appeals's holding for upsetting a sound balance between the respective values of supporting creative pursuits through copyright protection and promoting innovation in new communication technologies by limiting the incidence of liability for copyright infringement. The more artistic protection is favored, the more technological innovation may be discouraged; the administration of copyright law is an exercise in managing the tradeoff.

The tension between the two values is the subject of this case, with its claim that digital distribution of copyrighted material threatens copyright holders as never before, because every copy is identical to the original, copying is easy, and many people (especially the young) use file-sharing software to download copyrighted works. . . .

The argument for imposing indirect liability in this case is . . . a powerful one, given the number of infringing downloads that occur every day using StreamCast's and Grokster's software. When a widely shared service or product is used to commit infringement, it may be impossible to enforce rights in the protected work effectively against all direct infringers, the only practical alternative being to go against the distributor of the copying device for secondary liability on a theory of contributory or vicarious infringement. . . .

Despite the currency of these principles of secondary liability, this Court has dealt with secondary copyright infringement in only one recent case, and because MGM has tailored its principal claim to our opinion there, a look at our earlier holding is in order. . . .

In sum, this case is significantly different from Sony and reliance on that case to rule in favor of StreamCast and Grokster was error. Sony dealt with a claim of liability based solely on distributing a product with alternative lawful and unlawful uses, with knowledge that some users would follow the unlawful course. The case struck a balance between the interests of protection and innovation by holding that the product's capability of substantial lawful employment should bar the imputation of fault and consequent secondary liability for the unlawful acts of others.

MGM's evidence in this case most obviously addresses a different basis of liability for distributing a product open to alternative uses. Here, evidence of the distributors' words and deeds going beyond distribution as such shows a purpose to cause and profit from third-party acts of copyright infringement. If liability for inducing infringement is ultimately found, it will not be on the basis of presuming or imputing fault, but from inferring a patently illegal objective from statements and actions showing what that objective was.

There is substantial evidence in MGM's favor on all elements of inducement, and summary judgment in favor of Grokster and

StreamCast was error. On remand, reconsideration of MGM's motion for summary judgment will be in order.

The judgment of the Court of Appeals is vacated, and the case is remanded for further proceedings consistent with this opinion."

V. JUSTICE VOTE

0 Pro ACLU Side vs. 9 Con Opposing Side

Opposing Side (Petitioner / Appellant)

1. Souter, D. – Wrote majority opinion
2. Ginsburg, R. – Wrote concurring opinion
3. Stevens, J. – Joined Breyer's concurrence
4. Thomas, C. – Joined majority opinion
5. O'Connor, S. – Joined Breyer's concurrence
6. Breyer, S. – Wrote concurring opinion
7. Scalia, A. – Joined majority opinion
8. Kennedy, A. – Joined Ginsburg's concurrence
9. Rehnquist, W. – Joined Ginsburg's concurrence

VI. A WIN OR LOSS FOR THE ACLU?

The ACLU filed as amicus curiae urging affirmance; the Supreme Court vacated the Court of Appeals' decision by a 9-0 vote, giving the ACLU an apparent loss.

991. National Cable and Television Communications Ass'n v. Brand X Internet Services

(Decided June 27, 2005; 545 U.S. 967)

I. ISSUE

A. Issues Discussed

Regulation

B. Legal Question Presented

"In the order under review, the Federal Communications Commission concluded that cable companies that sell broadband Internet service do not provide 'telecommunications servic[e]' as the Communications Act defines that term, and hence are exempt from mandatory common-carrier regulation under Title II. We must decide whether that conclusion is a lawful construction of the Communications Act under Chevron U.S.Inc. v. Natural Resources Defense Council, Inc., 467 U.S. 837 (1984), and the Administrative Procedure Act, 5 U.S.C. § 551 et seq."

C. Supreme Court's Answer

"We hold that it is."

II. CASE SUMMARY

A. Background

"At issue in these cases is the proper regulatory classification under the Communications Act of broadband cable Internet service. The Act, as amended by the Telecommunications Act of 1996, defines two categories of regulated entities relevant to these cases: telecommunications carriers and information-service providers. The Act regulates telecommunications carriers, but not information-service providers, as common carriers. . . .

These two statutory classifications originated in the late 1970's, as the Commission developed rules to regulate data-processing services offered over telephone wires. . . .

In September 2000, the Commission initiated a rulemaking proceeding to, among other things, apply these classifications to cable companies that offer broadband Internet service directly to consumers. In March 2002, that rulemaking culminated in the Declaratory Ruling under review in these cases. In the Declaratory Ruling, the Commission concluded that broadband Internet service provided by cable companies is an 'information service' but not a 'telecommunications service' under the Act, and therefore not subject to mandatory Title II common-carrier regulation. In support of this conclusion, the Commission relied heavily on its Universal Service Report. . . .

The integrated nature of Internet access and the high-speed wire used to provide Internet access led the Commission to conclude that cable companies providing Internet access are not telecommunications providers. This conclusion, the Commission reasoned, followed from the logic of the Universal Service Report. The Report had concluded that, though Internet service 'involves data transport elements' because 'an Internet access provider must enable the movement of information between customers' own computers and distant computers with which those customers seek to interact,' it also 'offers end users information-service capabilities inextricably intertwined with data transport.' . . .

The Commission applied this same reasoning to cable companies offering broadband Internet access. Its logic was that, like non-facilities-based ISPs, cable companies do not 'offe[r] telecommunications service to the end user, but rather . . . merely us[e] telecommunications to provide end users with cable modem service.' Though the Commission declined to apply mandatory Title II common-carrier regulation to cable companies, it invited comment on whether under its Title I jurisdiction it should require cable companies to offer other ISPs access to their facilities on common-carrier terms. Numerous parties petitioned for judicial review, challenging the Commission's conclusion that cable modem service was not telecommunications service. By judicial lottery, the Court of Appeals for the Ninth Circuit was selected as the venue for the challenge.

The Court of Appeals granted the petitions in part, vacated the Declaratory Ruling in part, and remanded to the Commission for further proceedings."

The Supreme Court granted certiorari to review the case.

B. Counsel of Record

ACLU Side (Respondent / Appellee): Thomas C. Goldstein argued the cause for appellees in both cases. With him on the brief were Amy Howe, John W. Butler, Earl W. Comstock, Alison B. Macdonald, Harvey L. Reiter, Matthew J. Verschelden, and Andrew Jay Schwartzman.

William H. Sorrell, Attorney General of Vermont, David Borsykowsky, Assistant Attorney General, and Ellen S. LeVine filed a brief in both cases for appellees State of Vermont et al.

Michael K. Kellogg, Sean A. Lev, and James G. Harralson filed a brief in both cases for appellees BellSouth et al.

Andrew G. McBride, Eve Klindera Reed, William P. Barr, Michael E. Glover, Edward Shakin, and John P. Frantz filed a brief in both cases for appellees Verizon Telephone Companies et al.

Mark D. Schneider, Marc A. Goldman, and Jeffrey A. Rackow filed a brief in both cases for appellee MCI, Inc.

Opposing Side (Petitioner / Appellant): Paul T. Cappuccio argued the cause for appellants in No. 04–277. With him on the briefs were Howard J. Symons, Tara M. Corvo, Paul Glist, John D. Seiver, David E. Mills, Daniel L. Brenner, Neal M. Goldberg, Michael S. Schooler, Edward J. Weiss, and Henk Brands.

Deputy Solicitor General Hungar argued the cause for federal appellants in No. 04–281. With him on the briefs were Acting Solicitor General Clement, Assistant Attorney General Pate, Deputy Assistant Attorney General Delrahim, James A. Feldman, Catherine G. O'Sullivan, Nancy C. Garrison, John A. Rogovin, Austin C. Schlick, Daniel M. Armstrong, Jacob M. Lewis, and Nandan M. Joshi.

III. AMICI CURIAE

ACLU Side (Respondent / Appellee)

Brief of amici curiae filed on behalf of the American Civil Liberties Union and the Brennan Center for Justice at NYU School of Law by Steven R. Shapiro, Christopher A. Hansen, Jennifer Stisa Granick, Barry Steinhardt, Adam H. Morse, and Marjorie Heins.

Brief of amici curiae filed on behalf of the State of New Jersey, Board of Public Utilities, by Peter C. Harvey, Attorney General of New Jersey, Andrea M. Silkowitz, Assistant Attorney General, and Kenneth J. Sheehan, Deputy Attorney General.

Brief of amici curiae filed on behalf of AARP et al. by Stacy Canan and Michael Schuster.

Brief of amici curiae filed on behalf of the National Association of Regulatory Utility Commissioners by James Bradford Ramsay.

Opposing Side (Petitioner / Appellant)

Brief of amici curiae filed on behalf of the Telecommunications Industry Association by Colleen L. Boothby and Andrew M. Brown.

Brief of amici curiae filed on behalf of the Washington Legal Foundation by Daniel J. Popeo and David Price.

IV. THE SUPREME COURT'S DECISION

"We first consider whether we should apply Chevron's framework to the Commission's interpretation of the term 'telecommunications service.' We conclude that we should. We also conclude that the Court of Appeals should have done the same, instead of following the contrary construction it adopted in Portland. . . .

We next address whether the Commission's construction of the definition of 'telecommunications service' is a permissible reading of the Communications Act under the Chevron framework. Chevron established a familiar two-step procedure for evaluating whether an agency's interpretation of a statute is lawful. At the first step, we ask whether the statute's plain terms 'directly addres[s] the precise question at issue.' If the statute is ambiguous on the point, we defer at step two to the agency's interpretation so long as the construction is 'a reasonable policy choice for the agency to make.' The Commission's interpretation is permissible at both steps. . . .

We first set forth our understanding of the interpretation of the Communications Act that the Commission embraced. The issue before the Commission was whether cable companies providing cable modem service are providing a 'telecommunications service' in addition to an 'information service.'

The Commission first concluded that cable modem service is an 'information service,' a conclusion unchallenged here. . . .

At the same time, the Commission concluded that cable modem service was not 'telecommunications service.' . . .

In sum, if the Act fails unambiguously to classify non-facilities-based information-service providers that use telecommunications inputs to provide an information service as 'offer[ors]' of 'telecommunications,' then it also fails unambiguously to classify facilities-based information-service providers as telecommunications-service offerors; the relevant definitions do not distinguish facilities-based and non-facilities-based carriers. That silence suggests, instead, that the Commission has the discretion to fill the consequent statutory gap. . . .

We also conclude that the Commission's construction was 'a reasonable policy choice for the [Commission] to make' at Chevron's second step. . . .

Respondent MCI, Inc., urges that the Commission's treatment of cable modem service is inconsistent with its treatment of DSL service, . . . and therefore is an arbitrary and capricious deviation from agency policy. . . .

We conclude, however, that the Commission provided a reasoned explanation for treating cable modem service differently from DSL service. . . .

The questions the Commission resolved in the order under review involve a 'subject matter [that] is technical, complex, and dynamic.' The Commission is in a far better position to address these questions than we are. Nothing in the Communications Act or the Administrative Procedure Act makes unlawful the Commission's use of its expert policy judgment to resolve these difficult questions. The judgment of the Court of Appeals is reversed, and the cases are remanded for further proceedings consistent with this opinion."

V. JUSTICE VOTE

3 Pro ACLU Side vs. 6 Con Opposing Side

ACLU Side (Respondent / Appellee)

1. Scalia, A. – Wrote dissenting opinion
2. Ginsburg, R. – Joined Scalia's dissent
3. Souter, D. – Joined Scalia's dissent

Opposing Side (Petitioner / Appellant)

1. Thomas, C. – Wrote majoriy opinion
2. Stevens, J. – Wrote concurring opinion
3. O'Connor, S. – Joined majority opinion
4. Breyer, S. – Wrote concurring opinion
5. Rehnquist, W. – Joined majority opinion
6. Kennedy, A. – Joined majority opinion

VI. A WIN OR LOSS FOR THE ACLU?

The ACLU filed as amicus curiae urging affirmance; the Supreme Court reversed the Court of Appeals' decision by a 6-3 vote, giving the ACLU an apparent loss.

992. U.S. v. Georgia

(Decided January 10, 2006; 546 U.S. 151)

I. ISSUE

A. Issues Discussed

Civil rights, federal, state

B. Legal Question Presented

"[W]hether a disabled inmate in a state prison may sue the State for money damages under Title II of the Americans with Disabilities Act of 1990 . . . ."

C. Supreme Court's Answer

"[I]nsofar as Title II creates a private cause of action for damages against the States for conduct that actually violates the Fourteenth Amendment, Title II validly abrogates state sovereign immunity."

II. CASE SUMMARY

A. Background

"Petitioner in No. 04–1236, Tony Goodman, is a paraplegic inmate in the Georgia prison system who, at all relevant times, was housed at the Georgia State Prison in Reidsville. After filing numerous administrative grievances in the state prison system, Goodman filed a pro se complaint in the United States District Court for the Southern District of Georgia challenging the conditions of his confinement. He named as defendants the State of Georgia and the Georgia Department of Corrections (state defendants) and several individual prison officials. He brought claims under Rev. Stat. § 1979, 42 U.S.C. § 1983, Title II of the ADA, and other provisions not relevant here, seeking both injunctive relief and money damages against all defendants.

Goodman's pro se complaint and subsequent filings in the District Court included many allegations, both grave and trivial, regarding the conditions of his confinement in the Reidsville prison. . . .

The District Court adopted the Magistrate Judge's recommendation that the allegations in the complaint were vague and constituted insufficient notice pleading as to Goodman's § 1983 claims. It therefore dismissed the § 1983 claims against all defendants without providing Goodman an opportunity to amend his complaint. The District Court also dismissed his Title II claims against all individual defendants. Later, after [the U.S. Supreme Court's] decision in Garrett, the District Court granted summary judgment to the state defendants on Goodman's Title II claims for money damages, holding that those claims were barred by state sovereign immunity.

Goodman appealed to the United States Court of Appeals for the Eleventh Circuit. The United States, petitioner in No. 04–1203, intervened to defend the constitutionality of Title II's abrogation of state sovereign immunity. The Eleventh Circuit determined that the District Court had erred in dismissing all of Goodman's § 1983 claims, because Goodman's multiple pro se filings in the District Court alleged facts sufficient to support 'a limited number of Eighth–Amendment claims under § 1983' against certain individual defendants. The Court of Appeals held that the District Court should have given Goodman leave to amend his complaint to develop three Eighth Amendment claims relating to his conditions of confinement . . . .

The court remanded the suit to the District Court to permit Goodman to amend his complaint, while cautioning Goodman not to reassert all the § 1983 claims included in his initial complaint, 'some of which [we]re obviously frivolous.'

The Eleventh Circuit did not address the sufficiency of Goodman's allegations under Title II. Instead, relying on its prior decision in Miller v. King, 384 F.3d 1248 (2004), the Court of Appeals affirmed the District Court's holding that Goodman's Title II claims for money damages against the State were barred by sovereign immunity."

The Supreme Court granted certiorari to review the case.

B. Counsel of Record

ACLU Side (Petitioner / Appellant): Solicitor General Clement argued the cause for the United States in No. 04–1203. With him on the brief were Acting Assistant Attorney General Schlozman, Patricia A. Millett, David K. Flynn, and Sarah E. Harrington.

Samuel R. Bagenstos argued the cause for appellant in No. 04–1236. With him on the briefs were Drew S. Days III, Beth S. Brinkmann, and Seth M. Galanter.

Opposing Side (Respondent / Appellee): Gregory A. Castanias argued the cause for appellees in both cases. With him on the brief were Thurbert E. Baker, Attorney General of Georgia, Kathleen M. Pacious, Deputy Attorney General, John C. Jones, Senior Assistant Attorney General, and David E. Langford, Assistant Attorney General.

Gene C. Schaerr argued the cause and filed a brief for the State of Tennessee et al. as amici curiae.

III. AMICI CURIAE

ACLU Side (Petitioner / Appellant)

Brief of amici curiae filed on behalf of ADAPT; American Academy of Psychiatry and the Law; American Civil Liberties Union; American Civil Liberties Union of Georgia; American Council of the Blind; American Diabetes Association; American Psychiatric Association; Center for HIV Law and Policy; Citizens United for Rehabilitation of Errants; Human Rights Watch; Lambda Legal Defense and Education Fund, Inc.; The Legal Aid Society of New York City; National Association for Rights Protection and Advocacy; National Association of the Deaf; National Health Law Program; National Multiple Sclerosis Society; National Spinal Cord Injury Association; Prison Legal News; Southern Poverty Law Center by Paul M. Smith, Mark R. Heilbrun, Heather M. Trew, Stephen F. Gold, Elizabeth Alexander, David C. Fathi, Brian Dimmick, James Ross, Jonathan Givner, Jennifer Sinton, Richard Taranto, Gerald Weber, Catherine Hanssens,

Steve Banks, John Boston, Betsy Ginsberg, Kelby Brick, Jane Perkins, Sarah Sommers, Rhonda Brownstein, Susan Stefan, and Leonard Zandrow.

Brief of amici curiae filed on behalf of the American Association on Mental Retardation et al. by James W. Ellis, Michael B. Browde, and April Land.

Brief of amici curiae filed on behalf of the American Bar Association by Robert J. Grey, Jr.

Brief of amici curiae filed on behalf of former President George H. W. Bush by C. Boyden Gray and A. Stephen Hut, Jr.

Brief of amici curiae filed on behalf of the Lawyers' Committee for Civil Rights Under Law et al. by Charles Lester, Jr., Barbara R. Arnwine, Michael L. Foreman, Ossai Miazad, Vincent A. Eng, Elliot M. Mincberg, and Angela Ciccolo.

Brief of amici curiae filed on behalf of the National Disability Rights Network by Kathleen Behan and Joan A. Magagna.

Brief of amici curiae filed on behalf of Paralyzed Veterans of America et al. by Jerrold J. Ganzfried and Elizabeth B. McCallum.

Brief of amici curiae filed on behalf of Dick Thornburgh et al. by Charles D. Siegal, Bradley S. Phillips, Daniel P. Collins, Peter Blanck, Arlene Mayerson, and Eve Hill.

Opposing Side (Respondent / Appellee)

Brief of amici curiae filed on behalf of the State of Tennessee et al. by Gene C. Schaerr, Paul G. Summers, Attorney General of Tennessee, Michael E. Moore, Solicitor General, Linda T. Coberly, E. King Poor, Roberto J. Sánchez Ramos, Secretary of Justice of Puerto Rico, and the Attorneys General for their respective States as follows: Troy King of Alabama, John W. Suthers of Colorado, M. Jane Brady of Delaware, Lawrence G. Wasden of Idaho, Mike Cox of Michigan, Brian Sandoval of Nevada, Kelly A. Ayotte of New Hampshire, W. A. Drew Edmondson of Oklahoma, Hardy Myers of Oregon, Rob McKenna of Washington, and Patrick J. Crank of Wyoming.

IV. THE SUPREME COURT'S DECISION

"In reversing the dismissal of Goodman's § 1983 claims, the Eleventh Circuit held that Goodman had alleged actual violations of the Eighth Amendment by state agents on the grounds set forth above. The State does not contest this holding, and we did not grant certiorari to consider the merits of Goodman's Eighth Amendment claims; we assume without deciding, therefore, that the Eleventh Circuit's treatment of these claims was correct. Moreover, Goodman urges, and the State does not dispute, that this same conduct that violated the Eighth Amendment also violated Title II of the ADA. In fact, it is quite plausible that the alleged deliberate refusal of prison officials to accommodate Goodman's disability-related needs in such fundamentals as mobility, hygiene, medical care, and virtually all other prison programs constituted 'exclu[sion] from participation in or . . . deni[al of] the benefits of' the prison's 'services, programs, or activities.' . . . Therefore, Goodman's claims for money damages against the State under Title II were evidently based, at least in large part, on conduct that independently violated the provisions of § 1 of the Fourteenth Amendment. . . . In this respect, Goodman differs from the claimants in our other cases addressing Congress's ability to abrogate sovereign immunity pursuant to its § 5 powers. . . .

While the Members of this Court have disagreed regarding the scope of Congress's 'prophylactic' enforcement powers under § 5 of the Fourteenth Amendment, . . . no one doubts that § 5 grants Congress the power to 'enforce . . . the provisions' of the Amendment by creating private remedies against the States for actual violations of those provisions. . . . This enforcement power includes the power to abrogate state sovereign immunity by authorizing private suits for damages against the States. Thus, insofar as Title II creates a private cause of action for damages against the States for conduct that actually violates the Fourteenth Amendment, Title II validly abrogates state sovereign immunity. The Eleventh Circuit erred in dismissing those of Goodman's Title II claims that were based on such unconstitutional conduct.

From the many allegations in Goodman's pro se complaint and his subsequent filings in the District Court, it is not clear precisely what conduct he intended to allege in support of his Title II claims. Because the Eleventh Circuit did not address the issue, it is likewise unclear to what extent the conduct underlying Goodman's constitutional claims also violated Title II. Moreover, the Eleventh Circuit ordered that the suit be remanded to the District Court to permit Goodman to amend his complaint, but instructed him to revise his factual allegations to exclude his 'frivolous' claims—some of which are quite far afield from actual constitutional violations (under either the Eighth Amendment or some other constitutional provision), or even from Title II violations. . . . It is therefore unclear whether Goodman's amended complaint will assert Title II claims premised on conduct that does not independently violate the Fourteenth Amendment. Once Goodman's complaint is amended, the lower courts will be best situated to determine in the first instance, on a claim-by-claim basis, (1) which aspects of the State's alleged conduct violated Title II; (2) to what extent such misconduct also violated the Fourteenth Amendment; and (3) insofar as such misconduct violated Title II but did not violate the Fourteenth Amendment, whether Congress's purported abrogation of sovereign immunity as to that class of conduct is nevertheless valid. . . .

The judgment of the Eleventh Circuit is reversed, and the suit is remanded for further proceedings consistent with this opinion."

V. JUSTICE VOTE

9 Pro ACLU Side vs. 0 Con Opposing Side

ACLU Side (Petitioner / Appellant)

1. Scalia, A. – Wrote majority opinion
2. O'Connor, S. – Joined majority opinion
3. Stevens, J. – Wrote concurring opinion
4. Thomas, C. – Joined majority opinion
5. Breyer, S. – Joined majority opinion
6. Kennedy, A. – Joined majority opinion
7. Ginsburg, R. – Joined Stevens' concurrence
8. Souter, D. – Joined majority opinion
9. Roberts, J. – Joined majority opinion

VI. A WIN OR LOSS FOR THE ACLU?

The ACLU filed as amicus curiae urging reversal of the judgment of the Court of Appeals; the Supreme Court reversed in a 9-0 vote, giving the ACLU an apparent win.

993. Gonzales v. Oregon

(Decided January 17, 2006; 546 U.S. 243)

I. ISSUE

A. Issues Discussed

Drugs, federal, state, regulation

B. Legal Question Presented

"[W]hether the Controlled Substances Act allows the United States Attorney General to prohibit doctors from prescribing regulated drugs for use in physician-assisted suicide, notwithstanding a state law permitting the procedure."

C. Supreme Court's Answer

"[W]e conclude the CSA's prescription requirement does not authorize the Attorney General to bar dispensing controlled substances for assisted suicide in the face of a state medical regime permitting such conduct."

II. CASE SUMMARY

A. Background

"In 1994, Oregon became the first State to legalize assisted suicide when voters approved a ballot measure enacting the Oregon Death With Dignity Act (ODWDA). . . .

The drugs Oregon physicians prescribe under ODWDA are regulated under a federal statute, the Controlled Substances Act (CSA or Act). The CSA allows these particular drugs to be available only by a written prescription from a registered physician. In the ordinary course the same drugs are prescribed in smaller doses for pain alleviation.

A November 9, 2001, Interpretive Rule issued by the Attorney General addresses the implementation and enforcement of the CSA with respect to ODWDA. It determines that using controlled substances to assist suicide is not a legitimate medical practice and that dispensing or prescribing them for this purpose is unlawful under the CSA. The Interpretive Rule's validity under the CSA is the issue before us. . . .

In response the State of Oregon, joined by a physician, a pharmacist, and some terminally ill patients, all from Oregon, challenged the Interpretive Rule in federal court. The United States District Court for the District of Oregon entered a permanent injunction against the Interpretive Rule's enforcement.

A divided panel of the Court of Appeals for the Ninth Circuit granted the petitions for review and held the Interpretive Rule invalid."

The Supreme Court granted certiorari to review the case.

B. Counsel of Record

ACLU Side (Respondent / Appellee): Robert M. Atkinson, Senior Assistant Attorney General of Oregon, argued the cause for appellees. With him on the brief for appellee State of Oregon were Hardy Myers, Attorney General, Peter Shepherd, Deputy Attorney General, and Mary H. Williams, Solicitor General. Nicholas W. van Aelstyn, Aaron S. Jacobs, and Kathryn L. Tucker filed a brief for Patient-Appellees. Eli D. Stutsman filed a brief for appellees Peter A. Rasmussen, M. D., et al.

Opposing Side (Petitioner / Appellant): Solicitor General Clement argued the cause for appellants. With him on the briefs were Assistant Attorney General Keisler, Deputy Solicitor General Kneedler, Deputy Assistant Attorney General Katsas, Douglas Hallward-Driemeier, Mark B. Stern, and Jonathan H. Levy.

III. AMICI CURIAE

ACLU Side (Respondent / Appellee)

Brief of amici curiae filed on behalf of the American Civil Liberties Union and the ACLU of Oregon by Andrew L. Frey, David M. Gossett, Kristina Silja Bennard, Steven R. Shapiro, and Charles F. Hinkle.

Brief of amici curiae filed on behalf of the State of California et al. by Bill Lockyer, Attorney General of California, and Taylor S. Carey, Special Assistant Attorney General, and by the Attorneys General for their respective jurisdictions as follows: Robert J. Spagnoletti of the District of Columbia, Jim Hood of Mississippi, Jeremiah W. (Jay) Nixon of Missouri, and Mike McGrath of Montana.

Brief of amici curiae filed on behalf of the American College of Legal Medicine by Miles J. Zaremski.

Brief of amici curiae filed on behalf of the American Public Health Association by David T. Goldberg, Sean H. Donahue, and Daniel N. Abrahamson.

Brief of amici curiae filed on behalf of Autonomy, Inc., et al. by Amy R. Sabrin.

Brief of amici curiae filed on behalf of the Cato Institute by Pamela Harris.

Brief of amici curiae filed on behalf of the Coalition of Medical Associations and Societies et al. by Geoffrey J. Michael.

Brief of amici curiae filed on behalf of the Coalition of Mental Health Professionals by Steven Alan Reiss.

Brief of amici curiae filed on behalf of Healthlaw Professors by Arthur B. LaFrance.

Brief of amici curiae filed on behalf of Members of the Oregon Congressional Delegation by William R. Stein.

Brief of amici curiae filed on behalf of Margaret P. Battin et al. by Rebecca P. Dick and Ronald A. Lindsay.

Brief of amici curiae filed on behalf of Richard Briffault et al. by David W. Ogden and Paul R. Q. Wolfson.

Brief of amici curiae filed on behalf of 52 Religious and Religious Freedom Organizations and Leaders by Gregory A. Castanias and Lawrence D. Rosenberg.

Brief of amici curiae filed on behalf of Surviving Family Members by Robert A. Free and Katrin E. Frank.

Opposing Side (Petitioner / Appellant)

Brief of amici curiae filed on behalf of the American Center for Law and Justice by Jay Alan Sekulow, Colby M. May, James M. Henderson, Sr., Walter M. Weber, Thomas P. Monaghan, and Charles E. Rice.

Brief of amici curiae filed on behalf of Americans United for Life by Nikolas T. Nikas.

Brief of amici curiae filed on behalf of the Catholic Medical Association by Teresa Stanton Collett.

Brief of amici curiae filed on behalf of the Christian Medical Association et al. by Steven H. Aden, Gregory S. Baylor, and Kimberlee W. Colby.

Brief of amici curiae filed on behalf of Focus on the Family et al. by William Wagner, Nelson P. Miller, Stephen W. Reed, and Patrick A. Trueman.

Brief of amici curiae filed on behalf of the International Task Force on Euthanasia and Assisted Suicide by Rita L. Marker.

Brief of amici curiae filed on behalf of Liberty Counsel by Mathew D. Staver, Erik W. Stanley, Rena M. Lindevaldsen, and Mary E. McAlister.

Brief of amici curiae filed on behalf of the National Association of Pro-Life Nurses by Daniel Avila.

Brief of amici curiae filed on behalf of the National Legal Center for the Medically Dependent & Disabled, Inc., by James Bopp, Jr., Thomas J. Marzen, and Richard E. Coleson.

Brief of amici curiae filed on behalf of Not Dead Yet et al. by Max Lapertosa.

Brief of amici curiae filed on behalf of the Pro-Life Legal Defense Fund et al. by Dwight G. Duncan, Thomas M. Harvey, and Richard F. Collier, Jr.

Brief of amici curiae filed on behalf of the Thomas More Society by Paul Benjamin Linton and Thomas Brejcha.

Brief of amici curiae filed on behalf of the United States Conference of Catholic Bishops et al. by Mark E. Chopko and Michael F. Moses.

Brief of amici curiae filed on behalf of Senator Rick Santorum et al. by Donald A. Daugherty, Jr.

Brief of amici curiae filed on behalf of Physicians for Compassionate Care Educational Foundation by Gregory P. Lynch.

IV. THE SUPREME COURT'S DECISION

"Executive actors often must interpret the enactments Congress has charged them with enforcing and implementing. The parties before us are in sharp disagreement both as to the degree of deference we must accord the Interpretive Rule's substantive conclusions and whether the Rule is authorized by the statutory text at all. Although balancing the necessary respect for an agency's knowledge, expertise, and constitutional office with the courts' role as interpreter of laws can be a delicate matter, familiar principles guide us. An administrative rule may receive substantial deference if it interprets the issuing agency's own ambiguous regulation. An interpretation of an ambiguous statute may also receive substantial deference. Deference in accordance with Chevron, however, is warranted only 'when it appears that Congress delegated authority to the agency generally to make rules carrying the force of law, and that the agency interpretation claiming deference was promulgated in the exercise of that authority.' Otherwise, the interpretation is 'entitled to respect' only to the extent it has the 'power to persuade.' . . .

If, in the course of exercising his authority, the Attorney General uses his analysis in the Interpretive Rule only for guidance in deciding when to prosecute or deregister, then the question remains whether his substantive interpretation is correct. Since the Interpretive Rule was not promulgated pursuant to the Attorney General's authority, its interpretation of 'legitimate medical purpose' does not receive Chevron deference. Instead, it receives deference only in accordance with Skidmore. . . . The deference here is tempered by the Attorney General's lack of expertise in this area and the apparent absence of any consultation with anyone outside the Department of Justice who might aid in a reasoned judgment. In any event, under Skidmore, we follow an agency's rule only to the extent it is persuasive, and for the reasons given and for further reasons set out below, we do not find the Attorney General's opinion persuasive. . . .

In deciding whether the CSA can be read as prohibiting physician-assisted suicide, we look to the statute's text and design. The statute and our case law amply support the conclusion that Congress regulates medical practice insofar as it bars doctors from using their prescription-writing powers as a means to engage in illicit drug dealing and trafficking as conventionally understood. Beyond this, however, the statute manifests no intent to regulate the practice of medicine generally. . . .

In the face of the CSA's silence on the practice of medicine generally and its recognition of state regulation of the medical profession it is difficult to defend the Attorney General's declaration that the statute impliedly criminalizes physician-assisted suicide. . . .

For all these reasons, we conclude the CSA's prescription requirement does not authorize the Attorney General to bar dispensing controlled substances for assisted suicide in the face of a state medical regime permitting such conduct. . . .

The Government, in the end, maintains that the prescription requirement delegates to a single executive officer the power to effect a radical shift of authority from the States to the Federal Government to define general standards of medical practice in every locality. The text and structure of the CSA show that Congress did not have this far-reaching intent to alter the federal-state balance and the congressional role in maintaining it.

The judgment of the Court of Appeals is affirmed."

V. JUSTICE VOTE

6 Pro ACLU Side vs. 3 Con Opposing Side

ACLU Side (Respondent / Appellee)

1. Kennedy, A. – Wrote majority opinion
2. O'Connor, S. – Joined majority opinion
3. Stevens, J. – Joined majority opinion
4. Breyer, S. – Joined majority opinion
5. Ginsburg, R. – Joined majority opinion
6. Souter, D. – Joined majority opinion

Opposing Side (Petitioner / Appellant)

1. Thomas, C. – Wrote dissenting opinion, joined Scalia's dissent
2. Scalia, A. – Wrote dissenting opinion
3. Roberts, J. – Joined Scalia's dissent

VI. A WIN OR LOSS FOR THE ACLU?

The ACLU filed as amicus curiae urging affirmance; the Supreme Court affirmed the Court of Appeals' decision by a 6-3 vote, giving the ACLU an apparent win.

994. Ayotte v. Planned Parenthood of Northern New England

(Decided January 18, 2006; 546 U.S. 320)

I. ISSUE

A. Issues Discussed

Privacy, civil rights

B. Legal Question Presented

"If enforcing a statute that regulates access to abortion would be unconstitutional in medical emergencies, what is the appropriate judicial response?"

C. Supreme Court's Answer

"We hold that invalidating the statute entirely is not always necessary or justified, for lower courts may be able to render narrower declaratory and injunctive relief."

II. CASE SUMMARY

A. Background

"In 2003, New Hampshire enacted the Parental Notification Prior to Abortion Act. The Act prohibits physicians from performing an abortion on a pregnant minor (or a woman for whom a guardian or conservator has been appointed) until 48 hours after written notice of the pending abortion is delivered to her parent or guardian. Notice may be delivered personally or by certified mail. Violations of the Act are subject to criminal and civil penalties.

The Act allows for three circumstances in which a physician may perform an abortion without notifying the minor's parent. First, notice is not required if '[t]he attending abortion provider certifies in the pregnant minor's record that the abortion is necessary to prevent the minor's death and there is insufficient time to provide the required notice.' Second, a person entitled to receive notice may certify that he or she has already been notified. Finally, a minor may petition a judge to authorize her physician to perform an abortion without parental notification. The judge must so authorize if he or she finds that the minor is mature and capable of giving informed consent, or that an abortion without notification is in the minor's best interests. These judicial bypass proceedings 'shall be confidential and shall be given precedence over other pending matters so that the court may reach a decision promptly and without delay,' and access to the courts 'shall be afforded [to the] pregnant minor 24 hours a day, 7 days a week.' The trial and appellate courts must each rule on bypass petitions within seven days.

The Act does not explicitly permit a physician to perform an abortion in a medical emergency without parental notification. . . .

Respondents are Dr. Wayne Goldner, an obstetrician and gynecologist who has a private practice in Manchester, and three clinics that offer reproductive health services. . . . Before the Act took effect, respondents brought suit under 42 U.S.C. § 1983, alleging that the Act is unconstitutional because it fails 'to allow a physician to provide a prompt abortion to a minor whose health would be endangered' by delays inherent in the Act. Respondents also challenged the adequacy of the Act's life exception and of the judicial bypass' confidentiality provision.

The District Court declared the Act unconstitutional and permanently enjoined its enforcement. . . .

The Court of Appeals for the First Circuit affirmed."

The Supreme Court granted certiorari to review the case.

B. Counsel of Record

ACLU Side (Respondent / Appellee): Jennifer Dalven of the American Civil Liberties Union Foundation argued the cause for appellees. With her on the briefs were Dara Klassel and Martin P. Honigberg, and Steven R. Shapiro, Louise Melling, Talcott Camp, Corinne Schiff, Brigitte Amiri, Diana Kasdan of the American Civil Liberties Union Foundation, and Lawrence A. Vogelman of the New Hampshire Civil Liberties Union.

Opposing Side (Petitioner / Appellant): Kelly A. Ayotte, Attorney General of New Hampshire, appellant, argued the cause pro se. With her on the briefs were Michael A. Delaney, Deputy Attorney General, Daniel J. Mullen, Associate Attorney General, and Laura E. B. Lombardi and Anthony I. Blenkinsop, Assistant Attorneys General.

Solicitor General Clement argued the cause for the United States as amicus curiae.

III. AMICI CURIAE

ACLU Side (Respondent / Appellee)

Brief of amici curiae filed on behalf of the American College of Obstetricians and Gynecologists et al. by A. Stephen Hut, Jr., and Kimberly A. Parker.

Brief of amici curiae filed on behalf of the Center for Adolescent Health & the Law et al. by Elizabeth B. McCallum, Susan Frietsche, and David S. Cohen.

Brief of amici curiae filed on behalf of the Center for Reproductive Rights et al. by Sanford M. Cohen, Simon Heller, and Priscilla Smith.

Brief of amici curiae filed on behalf of the National Coalition Against Domestic Violence et al. by Maria T. Vullo and Julie Goldscheid.

Brief of amici curiae filed on behalf of Organizations Committed to Women's Equality by Jennifer K. Brown.

Brief of amici curiae filed on behalf of the Religious Coalition for Reproductive Choice et al. by Caroline M. Brown.

Brief of amici curiae filed on behalf of New Hampshire Governor John H. Lynch by Katherine M. Hanna.

Brief of amici curiae filed on behalf of New Hampshire State

Representative Terie Norelli et al. by Kenneth J. Barnes.

Brief of amici curiae filed on behalf of the Legal Defense for Unborn Children by Alan Ernest in support of neither party.

Brief of amici curiae filed on behalf of NARAL Pro-Choice America Foundation et al. by Elizabeth A. Cavendish, James P. Joseph, and Leslie M. Hill.

Brief of amici curiae filed on behalf of the Legal Defense for Unborn Children by Alan Ernest in support of neither party.

Opposing Side (Petitioner / Appellant)

Brief of amici curiae filed on behalf of the United States by Solicitor General Clement, Assistant Attorney General Keisler, Kannon K. Shanmugam, and Marleigh D. Dover.

Brief of amici curiae filed on behalf of the State of Texas et al. by Greg Abbott, Attorney General of Texas, Barry R. McBee, First Assistant Attorney General, Edward D. Burbach, Deputy Attorney General, R. Ted Cruz, Solicitor General, and Joel L. Thollander, Assistant Solicitor General, and by the Attorneys General for their respective States as follows: Troy King of Alabama, Mike Beebe of Arkansas, John W. Suthers of Colorado, M. Jane Brady of Delaware, Charles J. Crist, Jr., of Florida, Lawrence G. Wasden of Idaho, Phill Kline of Kansas, Michael A. Cox of Michigan, Jim Hood of Mississippi, Wayne Stenehjem of North Dakota, Jim Petro of Ohio, Thomas W. Corbett, Jr., of Pennsylvania, Lawrence E. Long of South Dakota, Paul G. Summers of Tennessee, Mark L. Shurtleff of Utah, Judith Williams Jagdmann of Virginia, and Patrick J. Crank of Wyoming.

Brief of amici curiae filed on behalf of the American Association of Pro Life Obstetricians and Gynecologists et al. by Steven H. Aden.

Brief of amici curiae filed on behalf of the American Center for Law and Justice by Jay Alan Sekulow, Thomas P. Monaghan, Stuart J. Roth, and Walter M. Weber.

Brief of amici curiae filed on behalf of the Association of American Physicians & Surgeons et al. by Dorinda C. Bordlee, Nikolas T. Nikas, and James L. Hirsen.

Brief of amici curiae filed on behalf of the Eagle Forum Education & Legal Defense Fund by Andrew L. Schlafly.

Brief of amici curiae filed on behalf of the Family Research Council, Inc., et al. by Robert P. George.

Brief of amici curiae filed on behalf of the National Legal Foundation by Barry C. Hodge.

Brief of amici curiae filed on behalf of New Hampshire Legislators by Teresa Stanton Collett.

Brief of amici curiae filed on behalf of the Rutherford Institute by John W. Whitehead and James J. Knicely.

Brief of amici curiae filed on behalf of the Thomas More Society by Paul Benjamin Linton and Thomas Brejcha.

Brief of amici curiae filed on behalf of the United States Conference of Catholic Bishops et al. by Mark E. Chopko and Michael F. Moses.

Brief of amici curiae filed on behalf of University Faculty for Life by Richard G. Wilkins.

Brief of amici curiae filed on behalf of Alaska Lieutenant Governor Loren Leman et al. by Kevin Gilbert Clarkson.

Brief of amici curiae filed on behalf of Minnesota Governor Tim Pawlenty et al. by Ms. Collett; for Harlon Reeves by Kelly Shackelford.

Brief of amici curiae filed on behalf of Margie Riley et al. by James Joseph Lynch, Jr.

Brief of amici curiae filed on behalf of New Hampshire State Representative Kathleen Souza et al. by Clarke D. Forsythe and Denise M. Burke.

Brief of amici curiae filed on behalf of James P. Weiers et al. by Len L. Munsil.

Brief of amici curiae filed on behalf of the Horatio R. Storer Foundation, Inc., by James Bopp, Jr., and Thomas J. Marzen.

Brief of amici curiae filed on behalf of Liberty Counsel by Mathew D. Staver, Erik W. Stanley, Rena M. Lindevaldsen, and Mary E. McAlister.

Brief of amici curiae filed on behalf of Maureen L. Curley et al. by Philip D. Moran.

IV. THE SUPREME COURT'S DECISION

"As the case comes to us, three propositions—two legal and one factual—are established. First, States unquestionably have the right to require parental involvement when a minor considers terminating her pregnancy, because of their 'strong and legitimate interest in the welfare of [their] young citizens, whose immaturity, inexperience, and lack of judgment may sometimes impair their ability to exercise their rights wisely.' Accordingly, we have long upheld state parental involvement statutes like the Act before us, and we cast no doubt on those holdings today. . . .

Second, New Hampshire does not dispute, and our precedents hold, that a State may not restrict access to abortions that are "necessary, in appropriate medical judgment, for the preservation of the life or health of the mother." . . .

Third, New Hampshire has not taken real issue with the factual basis of this litigation: In some very small percentage of cases, pregnant minors, like adult women, need immediate abortions to avert serious and often irreversible damage to their health. . . .

We turn to the question of remedy: When a statute restricting access to abortion may be applied in a manner that harms women's health, what is the appropriate relief? Generally speaking, when confronting a constitutional flaw in a statute, we try to limit the solution to the problem. . . .

Three interrelated principles inform our approach to remedies. First, we try not to nullify more of a legislature's work than is necessary . . . .

Second, mindful that our constitutional mandate and institutional competence are limited, we restrain ourselves from 'rewrit[ing] state law to conform it to constitutional requirements' even as we strive to salvage it. . . .

Third, the touchstone for any decision about remedy is legislative intent, for a court cannot 'use its remedial powers to circumvent the intent of the legislature.' . . . After finding an application or portion of a statute unconstitutional, we must next ask: Would the legislature have preferred what is left of its statute to no statute at all? . . .

In this case, the courts below chose the most blunt remedy—permanently enjoining the enforcement of New Hampshire's parental notification law and thereby invalidating it entirely. . . .

In the case that is before us, however, we agree with New Hampshire that the lower courts need not have invalidated the law wholesale. . . . Only a few applications of New Hampshire's parental notification statute would present a constitutional problem. So long as they are faithful to legislative intent, then, in this case the lower courts can issue a declaratory judgment and an injunction prohibiting the statute's unconstitutional application.

There is some dispute as to whether New Hampshire's legislature intended the statute to be susceptible to such a remedy. . . . Because this is an open question, we remand for the lower courts to determine legislative intent in the first instance. . . .

Either an injunction prohibiting unconstitutional applications or a holding that consistency with legislative intent requires invalidating the statute in toto should obviate any concern about the Act's life exception. We therefore need not pass on the lower courts' alternative holding. Finally, if the Act does survive in part on remand, the Court of Appeals should address respondents' separate objection to the judicial bypass' confidentiality provision. The judgment of the Court of Appeals is vacated, and the case is remanded for further proceedings consistent with this opinion."

V. JUSTICE VOTE

0 Pro ACLU Side vs. 9 Con Opposing Side

Opposing Side (Petitioner / Appellant)

1. O'Connor, S. – Wrote majority opinion
2. Stevens, J. – Joined majority opinion
3. Thomas, C. – Joined majority opinion
4. Breyer, S. – Joined majority opinion
5. Scalia, A. – Joined majority opinion
6. Kennedy, A. – Joined majority opinion
7. Ginsburg, R. – Joined majority opinion
8. Souter, D. – Joined majority opinion
9. Roberts, J. – Joined majority opinion

VI. A WIN OR LOSS FOR THE ACLU?

The ACLU served as counsel for respondent urging affirmance; the Supreme Court vacated and remanded the Court of Appeals' decision by a 9-0 vote, giving the ACLU an apparent loss.

995. Wisconsin Right to Life, Inc. v. Federal Election Commission

(Decided January 23, 2006; 546 U.S. 410)

I. ISSUE

A. Issues Discussed

Voting rights

B. Legal Question Presented

Whether the Bipartisan Campaign Reform Act of 2002's prohibition on "electioneering communications" can be constitutionally applied to Wisconsin Right to Life, Inc.

C. Supreme Court's Answer

This as-applied challenge to the prohibition can proceed.

II. CASE SUMMARY

A. Background

"The Bipartisan Campaign Reform Act of 2002 (BCRA) prohibits corporations from using their general treasury funds to pay for any 'electioneering communications.' . . . Appellant Wisconsin Right to Life, Inc. (WRTL), brought this action against the Federal Election Commission (FEC), seeking a judgment declaring BCRA unconstitutional as applied to several broadcast advertisements that it intended to run during the 2004 election. WRTL also sought a preliminary injunction barring the FEC from enforcing BCRA against those advertisements. WRTL does not dispute that its advertisements are covered by BCRA's definition of prohibited electioneering communications. Instead, it contends that BCRA cannot be constitutionally applied to its particular communications because they constitute 'grassroots lobbying advertisements.' Although the FEC has statutory authority to exempt by regulation certain communications from BCRA's prohibition on electioneering communications, at this point, it has not done so for the types of advertisements at issue here.

The three-judge District Court denied the motion for a preliminary injunction and subsequently dismissed WRTL's complaint in an unpublished opinion."

The Supreme Court noted probable jurisdiction to review the case.

B. Counsel of Record

ACLU Side (Petitioner / Appellant): James Bopp, Jr., argued the cause for appellant. With him on the briefs were Richard E. Coleson and M. Miller Baker.

Opposing Side (Respondent / Appellee): Solicitor General Clement argued the cause for appellee. With him on the brief were Deputy Solicitor General Garre, Malcolm L. Stewart, Lawrence H. Norton, Richard B. Bader, David Kolker, and Harry J. Summers.

III. AMICI CURIAE

ACLU Side (Petitioner / Appellant)

Brief of amici curiae filed on behalf of the American Civil Liberties Union by Steven R. Shapiro, Mark J. Lopez, and Joel M. Gora.

Brief of amici curiae filed on behalf of the American Federation of Labor and Congress of Industrial Organizations by Jonathan P. Hiatt, Laurence E. Gold, and Michael B. Trister.

Brief of amici curiae filed on behalf of the Center for Competitive Politics et al. by Erik S. Jaffe.

Brief of amici curiae filed on behalf of the Chamber of Commerce of the United States of America by Jan Witold Baran, Thomas W. Kirby, Caleb P. Burns, Stephen A. Bokat, and Amar D. Sarwal.

Brief of amici curiae filed on behalf of Citizens United et al. by Herbert W. Titus, William J. Olson, and John S. Miles.

Brief of amici curiae filed on behalf of Senator Mitch McConnell by Theodore B. Olson and Douglas R. Cox.
Brief of amici curiae filed on behalf of the Alliance for Justice by Ruth Eisenberg.
Brief of amici curiae filed on behalf of the Coalition of Public Charities by Robert F. Bauer.

Opposing Side (Respondent / Appellee)

Brief of amici curiae filed on behalf of AARP et al. by Daniel R. Ortiz.
Brief of amici curiae filed on behalf of Douglas L. Bailey by Randy L. Dryer.
Brief of amici curiae filed on behalf of Frances R. Hill by J. Gerald Hebert.
Brief of amici curiae filed on behalf of Senator John McCain et al. by Bradley S. Phillips, Seth P. Waxman, Randolph D. Moss, Roger M. Witten, Fred Wertheimer, Donald J. Simon, Alan Morrison, Charles G. Curtis, Jr., Trevor Potter, Paul Ryan, and Scott L. Nelson.
Brief of amici curiae filed on behalf of Norman Ornstein et al. by H. Christopher Bartolomucci.

IV. THE SUPREME COURT'S DECISION

"Appellant asks us to reverse the judgment of the District Court because that court incorrectly read a footnote in our opinion in McConnell v. Federal Election Comm'n, 540 U.S. 93 (2003), as foreclosing any 'as-applied' challenges to the prohibition on electioneering communications. We agree with WRTL that the District Court misinterpreted the relevance of our 'uphold[ing] all applications of the primary definition' of electioneering communications. Contrary to the understanding of the District Court, that footnote merely notes that because we found BCRA's primary definition of 'electioneering communication' facially valid when used with regard to BCRA's disclosure and funding requirements, it was unnecessary to consider the constitutionality of the backup definition Congress provided. In upholding § 203 against a facial challenge, we did not purport to resolve future as-applied challenges.

The FEC argues that the District Court also rested its decision on the alternative ground that the facts of this case 'suggest that WRTL's advertisements may fit the very type of activity McConnell found Congress had a compelling interest in regulating.' It is not clear to us, however, that the District Court intended its opinion to rest on this ground. For one thing, the court used the word 'may.' For another, its separate opinion dismissing WRTL's challenge with prejudice characterized its previous opinion as holding that 'WRTL's 'as-applied' challenge to BCRA is foreclosed by the Supreme Court's decision in McConnell.' Given this ambiguity, we cannot say with certainty that the District Court's dismissal was based on this alternative ground.

We therefore vacate the judgment and remand the case for the District Court to consider the merits of WRTL's as-applied challenge in the first instance."

V. JUSTICE VOTE

9 Pro ACLU Side vs. 0 Con Opposing Side

ACLU Side (Petitioner / Appellant)

1. O'Connor, S. – Per curiam decision
2. Stevens, J. – Per curiam decision
3. Thomas, C. – Per curiam decision
4. Breyer, S. – Per curiam decision
5. Scalia, A. – Per curiam decision
6. Kennedy, A. – Per curiam decision
7. Ginsburg, R. – Per curiam decision
8. Souter, D. – Per curiam decision
9. Roberts, J. – Per curiam decision

VI. A WIN OR LOSS FOR THE ACLU?

The ACLU filed as amicus curiae urging reversal of the judgment of the District Court; the Supreme Court vacated and remanded in a 9-0 per curiam vote, giving the ACLU an apparent win.

996. Gonzales v. O Centro Espírita Beneficente União do Vegetal

(Decided February 21, 2006; 546 U.S. 418)

I. ISSUE

A. Issues Discussed

Religion, drugs

B. Legal Question Presented

Whether the Government "has a compelling interest in the uniform application of the Controlled Substances Act, such that no exception to the ban on use of the hallucinogen can be made to accommodate [a] sect's sincere religious practice."

C. Supreme Court's Answer

"We conclude that the Government has not carried the burden expressly placed on it by Congress in the Religious Freedom Restoration Act, and affirm the grant of the preliminary injunction."

II. CASE SUMMARY

A. Background

"A religious sect with origins in the Amazon Rainforest receives communion by drinking a sacramental tea, brewed from plants unique to the region, that contains a hallucinogen regulated under the Controlled Substances Act by the Federal Government. The Government concedes that this practice is a sincere exercise of religion, but nonetheless sought to prohibit the small American branch of the sect from engaging in the practice, on the ground that the Controlled Substances Act bars all use of the hallucinogen. The sect sued to block enforcement against it of the ban on the sacramental tea, and moved for a preliminary injunction.

It relied on the Religious Freedom Restoration Act of 1993, which prohibits the Federal Government from substantially burdening a person's exercise of religion, unless the Government 'demonstrates that application of the burden to the person' represents the least restrictive means of advancing a compelling interest. The District Court granted the preliminary injunction, and the Court of Appeals affirmed."

The Supreme Court granted certiorari to review the case.

B. Counsel of Record

ACLU Side (Respondent / Appellee): Nancy Hollander argued the cause for appellees. With her on the brief were John W. Boyd and Zachary A. Ives.

Opposing Side (Petitioner / Appellant): Deputy Solicitor General Kneedler argued the cause for appellants. With him on the brief were Solicitor General Clement, Assistant Attorney General Keisler, Deputy Assistant Attorney General Katsas, Patricia A. Millett, Michael Jay Singer, and Matthew M. Collette.

III. AMICI CURIAE

ACLU Side (Respondent / Appellee)

Brief of amici curiae filed on behalf of the Baptist Joint Committee, the National Association of Evangelicals and other Religious and Public Policy Organizations, including the American Civil Liberties Union, by Gene C. Schaerr, Andrew C. Nichols, Linda T. Coberly, Thomas C. Berg, and Gregory S. Baylor.

Brief of amici curiae filed on behalf of the Council on Spiritual Practices et al. by David T. Goldberg.

Brief of amici curiae filed on behalf of the United States Conference of Catholic Bishops by Mark E. Chopko and Jeffrey Hunter Moon.

Brief of amici curiae filed on behalf of Dr. John H. Halpern et al. by Roy S. Haber.

Brief of amici curiae filed on behalf of Douglas Laycock by Mr. Laycock, pro se.

Brief of amici curiae filed on behalf of the International Academy for Freedom of Religion and Belief et al. by Lee Boothby, Derek Davis, Robert A. Destro, and W. Cole Durham, Jr.

Brief of amici curiae filed on behalf of the Liberty Legal Institute by Kelly Shackelford.

Brief of amici curiae filed on behalf of Various Religious and Civil Rights Organizations by Anthony R. Picarello, Jr.

Brief of amici curiae filed on behalf of Robert Gable et al. by Peter D.

Kennedy.

Opposing Side (Petitioner / Appellant)

Brief of amici curiae filed on behalf of the Tort Claimants' Committee et al. by Marci A. Hamilton.

IV. THE SUPREME COURT'S DECISION

"In Employment Div., Dept. of Human Resources of Ore. v. Smith, 494 U.S. 872 (1990), this Court held that the Free Exercise Clause of the First Amendment does not prohibit governments from burdening religious practices through generally applicable laws. In Smith, we rejected a challenge to an Oregon statute that denied unemployment benefits to drug users, including Native Americans engaged in the sacramental use of peyote. . . .

Congress responded by enacting the Religious Freedom Restoration Act of 1993 (RFRA), which adopts a statutory rule comparable to the constitutional rule rejected in Smith. Under RFRA, the Federal Government may not, as a statutory matter, substantially burden a person's exercise of religion, 'even if the burden results from a rule of general applicability.' The only exception recognized by the statute requires the Government to satisfy the compelling interest test—to 'demonstrat[e] that application of the burden to the person—(1) is in furtherance of a compelling governmental interest; and (2) is the least restrictive means of furthering that compelling governmental interest.' A person whose religious practices are burdened in violation of RFRA 'may assert that violation as a claim or defense in a judicial proceeding and obtain appropriate relief.' . . .

The Government begins by invoking the well-established principle that the party seeking pretrial relief bears the burden of demonstrating a likelihood of success on the merits. The Government argues that the District Court lost sight of this principle in issuing the injunction based on a mere tie in the evidentiary record.

A majority of the en banc Court of Appeals rejected this argument, and so do we. . . .

The Government's second line of argument rests on the Controlled Substances Act itself. . . . Under the Government's view, there is no need to assess the particulars of the UDV's use or weigh the impact of an exemption for that specific use, because the Controlled Substances Act serves a compelling purpose and simply admits of no exceptions. . . .

RFRA, and the strict scrutiny test it adopted, contemplate an inquiry more focused than the Government's categorical approach. . . .

Under the more focused inquiry required by RFRA and the compelling interest test, the Government's mere invocation of the general characteristics of Schedule I substances, as set forth in the Controlled Substances Act, cannot carry the day. . . .

The well-established peyote exception also fatally undermines the Government's broader contention that the Controlled Substances Act establishes a closed regulatory system that admits of no exceptions under RFRA. . . .

We have no cause to pretend that the task assigned by Congress to the courts under RFRA is an easy one. . . . But Congress has determined that courts should strike sensible balances, pursuant to a compelling interest test that requires the Government to address the particular practice at issue. Applying that test, we conclude that the courts below did not err in determining that the Government failed to demonstrate, at the preliminary injunction stage, a compelling interest in barring the UDV's sacramental use of hoasca.

The judgment of the United States Court of Appeals for the Tenth Circuit is affirmed, and the case is remanded for further proceedings consistent with this opinion."

V. JUSTICE VOTE

8 Pro ACLU Side vs. 0 Con Opposing Side

ACLU Side (Respondent / Appellee)

1. Roberts, J. – Wrote majority opinion
2. Stevens, J. – Joined majority opinion
3. Thomas, C. – Joined majority opinion

4. Breyer, S. – Joined majority opinion
5. Scalia, A. – Joined majority opinion
6. Kennedy, A. – Joined majority opinion
7. Ginsburg, R. – Joined majority opinion
8. Souter, D. – Joined majority opinion

Alito, S – Took no part in the decision

VI. A WIN OR LOSS FOR THE ACLU?

The ACLU filed as amicus curiae urging affirmance; the Supreme Court affirmed the Court of Appeals' decision by an 8-0 vote, giving the ACLU an apparent win.

997. Rumsfeld v. Forum for Academic & Institutional Rights, Inc.

(Decided March 6, 2006; 547 U.S. 47)

I. ISSUE

A. Issues Discussed

1st Amendment, press, speech, association

B. Legal Question Presented

Whether the Solomon Amendment, which "specifies that if any part of an institution of higher education denies military recruiters access equal to that provided other recruiters, the entire institution would lose certain federal funds," violates law schools' First Amendment freedoms of speech or association.

C. Supreme Court's Answer

"Congress could require law schools to provide equal access to military recruiters without violating the schools' freedoms of speech or association . . . ."

II. CASE SUMMARY

A. Background

"When law schools began restricting the access of military recruiters to their students because of disagreement with the Government's policy on homosexuals in the military, Congress responded by enacting the Solomon Amendment. That provision specifies that if any part of an institution of higher education denies military recruiters access equal to that provided other recruiters, the entire institution would lose certain federal funds. The law schools responded by suing, alleging that the Solomon Amendment infringed their First Amendment freedoms of speech and association. The District Court disagreed but was reversed by a divided panel of the Court of Appeals for the Third Circuit, which ordered the District Court to enter a preliminary injunction against enforcement of the Solomon Amendment."

The Supreme Court granted certiorari to review the case.

B. Counsel of Record

ACLU Side (Respondent / Appellee): E. Joshua Rosenkranz argued the cause for appellees. With him on the brief were Sharon E. Frase and Warrington S. Parker III.

Opposing Side (Petitioner / Appellant): Solicitor General Clement argued the cause for appellants. With him on the brief were Assistant Attorney General Keisler, Deputy Solicitor General Kneedler, Deputy Assistant Attorney General Katsas, Irving L. Gornstein, and Douglas N. Letter.

III. AMICI CURIAE

ACLU Side (Respondent / Appellee)

Brief of amici curiae filed on behalf of the American Civil Liberties Union et al. by Kenneth Y. Choe, Steven R. Shapiro, Matthew A. Coles, and James D. Esseks.

Brief of amici curiae filed on behalf of the American Association of University Professors by Kathleen M. Sullivan, Donna R. Euben, Ann D. Springer, and David M. Rabban.

Brief of amici curiae filed on behalf of the Association of American Law Schools by Paul M. Smith, William M. Hohengarten, and Daniel Mach.

Brief of amici curiae filed on behalf of Bay Area Lawyers for Individual Freedom et al. by Beth S. Brinkmann, Seth M. Galanter, and Ruth N. Borenstein.

Brief of amici curiae filed on behalf of the Cato Institute by Gregory S. Coleman.

Brief of amici curiae filed on behalf of Columbia University et al. by Seth P. Waxman, Randolph D. Moss, James J. Mingle, Ada Meloy, and Wendy S. White.

Brief of amici curiae filed on behalf of NALP (the National Association for Law Placement) et al. by Sam Heldman and Hilary E. Ball.

Brief of amici curiae filed on behalf of the National Lawyers Guild by Zachary Wolfe.

Brief of amici curiae filed on behalf of the National Lesbian and Gay Law Association et al. by Jonathan L. Hafetz and Lawrence S. Lustberg.

Brief of amici curiae filed on behalf of the Servicemembers Legal Defense Network by Linda T. Coberly, Tyler M. Paetkau, Sharra E. Greer, Kathi S. Westcott, and Gene C. Schaerr.

Brief of amici curiae filed on behalf of the Student/Faculty Alliance for Military Equality by Carmine D. Boccuzzi, Jr.

Brief of amici curiae filed on behalf of William Alford et al. by Walter Dellinger and Pamela Harris.

Brief of amici curiae filed on behalf of Robert A. Burt et al. by Paul M. Dodyk and David N. Rosen.

Brief of amici curiae filed on behalf of 56 Columbia Law School Faculty Members by Jonathan D. Schiller and David A. Barrett.

Brief of amici curiae filed on behalf of the Pacific Legal Foundation by John H. Findley and Harold E. Johnson in support of neither party.

Opposing Side (Petitioner / Appellant)

Brief of amici curiae filed on behalf of the State of Texas et al. by Greg Abbott, Attorney General of Texas, R. Ted Cruz, Solicitor General, Barry R. McBee, First Assistant Attorney General, Edward D. Burbach, Deputy Attorney General, and Joel L. Thollander and Adam W. Aston, Assistant Solicitors General, and by the Attorneys General for their respective States as follows: Troy King of Alabama, John W. Suthers of Colorado,

M. Jane Brady of Delaware, Charles J. Crist, Jr., of Florida, Steve Carter of Indiana, Phill Kline of Kansas, Michael A. Cox of Michigan, Lawrence E. Long of South Dakota, Mark L. Shurtleff of Utah, and Darrell V. McGraw, Jr., of West Virginia.

Brief of amici curiae filed on behalf of the American Civil Rights Union by Peter Ferrara.

Brief of amici curiae filed on behalf of the American Legion by Robert P. Parker and Philip B. Onderdonk, Jr.

Brief of amici curiae filed on behalf of the Boy Scouts of America by George A. Davidson, Carla A. Kerr, Scott H. Christensen, and David K. Park.

Brief of amici curiae filed on behalf of the Center for Individual Rights et al. by Gerald Walpin.

Brief of amici curiae filed on behalf of the Christian Legal Society et al. by Gregory S. Baylor and Steven H. Aden.

Brief of amici curiae filed on behalf of the Claremont Institute Center for Constitutional Jurisprudence by John C. Eastman and Edwin Meese III.

Brief of amici curiae filed on behalf of the Eagle Forum Education & Legal Defense Fund by Andrew L. Schlafly.

Brief of amici curiae filed on behalf of the Judge Advocates Association by Gregory M. Huckabee and Brett D. Barkey.

Brief of amici curiae filed on behalf of Law Professors et al. by Andrew G. McBride, William S. Consovoy, Daniel Polsby, and Joseph Zengerle.

Brief of amici curiae filed on behalf of the National Legal Foundation by Barry C. Hodge.

Brief of amici curiae filed on behalf of Charles S. Abbot et al. by Martin S. Kaufman, Joe R. Reeder, Philip R. Sellinger, and John P. Einwechter.

Brief of amici curiae filed on behalf of Congressman Richard Pombo et al. by William Perry Pendley and Joseph F. Becker.

IV. THE SUPREME COURT'S DECISION

"The Solomon Amendment denies federal funding to an institution of higher education that 'has a policy or practice . . . that either prohibits, or in effect prevents' the military 'from gaining access to campuses, or access to students . . . on campuses, for purposes of military recruiting in a manner that is at least equal in quality and scope to the access to campuses and to students that is provided to any other employer.' The statute provides an exception for an institution with 'a longstanding policy of pacifism based on historical religious affiliation.' The Government and FAIR agree on what this statute requires: In order for a law school and its university to receive federal funding, the law school must offer military recruiters the same access to its campus and students that it provides to the nonmilitary recruiter receiving the most favorable access. . . .

We think it appropriate in the present case to consider whether institutions can comply with the Solomon Amendment by applying a general nondiscrimination policy to exclude military recruiters.

We conclude that they cannot and that the Government and FAIR correctly interpret the Solomon Amendment. . . .

We therefore read the Solomon Amendment the way both the Government and FAIR interpret it. It is insufficient for a law school to treat the military as it treats all other employers who violate its nondiscrimination policy. Under the statute, military recruiters must be given the same access as recruiters who comply with the policy. . . .

This case does not require us to determine when a condition placed on university funding goes beyond the 'reasonable' choice offered in Grove City and becomes an unconstitutional condition. It is clear that a funding condition cannot be unconstitutional if it could be constitutionally imposed directly. Because the First Amendment would not prevent Congress from directly imposing the Solomon Amendment's access requirement, the statute does not place an unconstitutional condition on the receipt of federal funds. . . .

The Solomon Amendment neither limits what law schools may say nor requires them to say anything. Law schools remain free under the statute to express whatever views they may have on the military's congressionally mandated employment policy, all the while retaining eligibility for federal funds. . . . As a general matter, the Solomon Amendment regulates conduct, not speech. It affects what law schools must do—afford equal access to military recruiters—not what they may or may not say. . . .

In this case, FAIR has attempted to stretch a number of First Amendment doctrines well beyond the sort of activities these doctrines protect. The law schools object to having to treat military recruiters like other recruiters, but that regulation of conduct does not violate the First Amendment. To the extent that the Solomon Amendment incidentally affects expression, the law schools' effort to cast themselves as just like the schoolchildren in Barnette, the parade organizers in Hurley, and the Boy Scouts in Dale plainly overstates the expressive nature of their activity and the impact of the Solomon Amendment on it, while exaggerating the reach of our First Amendment precedents.

Because Congress could require law schools to provide equal access to military recruiters without violating the schools' freedoms of speech or association, the Court of Appeals erred in holding that the Solomon Amendment likely violates the First Amendment. We therefore reverse the judgment of the Third Circuit and remand the case for further proceedings consistent with this opinion."

V. JUSTICE VOTE

0 Pro ACLU Side vs. 8 Con Opposing Side

Opposing Side (Petitioner / Appellant)

1. Roberts, J. – Wrote majority opinion
2. Stevens, J. – Joined majority opinion
3. Thomas, C. – Joined majority opinion
4. Breyer, S. – Joined majority opinion
5. Scalia, A. – Joined majority opinion
6. Kennedy, A. – Joined majority opinion
7. Ginsburg, R. – Joined majority opinion
8. Souter, D. – Joined majority opinion

Alito, S. – Took no part in the decision.

VI. A WIN OR LOSS FOR THE ACLU?

The ACLU filed as amicus curiae urging affirmance; the Supreme Court reversed the Court of Appeals' decision by an 8-0 vote, giving the ACLU an apparent loss.

998. Garcetti v. Ceballos

(Decided May 30, 2006; 547 U.S. 410)

I. ISSUE

A. Issues Discussed

1st Amendment, press, speech, association

B. Legal Question Presented

"The question presented by the instant case is whether the First Amendment protects a government employee from discipline based on speech made pursuant to the employee's official duties."

C. Supreme Court's Answer

"We hold that when public employees make statements pursuant to their official duties, the employees are not speaking as citizens for First Amendment purposes, and the Constitution does not insulate their communications from employer discipline."

II. CASE SUMMARY

A. Background

"Respondent Richard Ceballos has been employed since 1989 as a deputy district attorney for the Los Angeles County District Attorney's Office. . . . In February 2000, a defense attorney contacted Ceballos about a pending criminal case. The defense attorney said there were inaccuracies in an affidavit used to obtain a critical search warrant. The attorney informed Ceballos that he had filed a motion to traverse, or challenge, the warrant, but he also wanted Ceballos to review the case. According to Ceballos, it was not unusual for defense attorneys to ask calendar deputies to investigate aspects of pending cases.

After examining the affidavit and visiting the location it described, Ceballos determined the affidavit contained serious misrepresentations. . . .

Ceballos spoke on the telephone to the warrant affiant, a deputy sheriff from the Los Angeles County Sheriff's Department, but he did not receive a satisfactory explanation for the perceived inaccuracies. He relayed his findings to his supervisors, petitioners Carol Najera and Frank Sundstedt, and followed up by preparing a disposition memorandum. The memo explained Ceballos' concerns and recommended dismissal of the case. On March 2, 2000, Ceballos submitted the memo to Sundstedt for his review. A few days later, Ceballos presented Sundstedt with another memo, this one describing a second telephone conversation between Ceballos and the warrant affiant.

Based on Ceballos' statements, a meeting was held to discuss the affidavit. Attendees included Ceballos, Sundstedt, and Najera, as well as the warrant affiant and other employees from the sheriff's department. The meeting allegedly became heated, with one lieutenant sharply criticizing Ceballos for his handling of the case.

Despite Ceballos' concerns, Sundstedt decided to proceed with the prosecution, pending disposition of the defense motion to traverse. The trial court held a hearing on the motion. Ceballos was called by the defense and recounted his observations about the affidavit, but the trial court rejected the challenge to the warrant.

Ceballos claims that in the aftermath of these events he was subjected to a series of retaliatory employment actions. The actions included reassignment from his calendar deputy position to a trial deputy position, transfer to another courthouse, and denial of a promotion. Ceballos initiated an employment grievance, but the grievance was denied based on a finding that he had not suffered any retaliation. Unsatisfied, Ceballos sued in the United States District Court for the Central District of California, asserting, as relevant here, a claim under Rev. Stat. § 1979, 42 U.S.C. § 1983. He alleged petitioners violated the First and Fourteenth Amendments by retaliating against him based on his memo of March 2. . . .

Petitioners moved for summary judgment, and the District Court granted their motion. . . .

The Court of Appeals for the Ninth Circuit reversed . . . ."

The Supreme Court granted certiorari to review the case.

B. Counsel of Record

ACLU Side (Respondent / Appellee): Bonnie I. Robin-Vergeer argued and reargued the cause for appellee. With her on the brief were Scott L. Nelson and Brian Wolfman

Opposing Side (Petitioner / Appellant): Cindy S. Lee argued and reargued the cause for appellants. With her on the briefs were Jin S. Choi and Doraine F. Meyer.

Dan Himmelfarb argued, and Deputy Solicitor General Kneedler reargued, the cause for the United States as amicus curiae.

III. AMICI CURIAE

ACLU Side (Respondent / Appellee)

Brief of amici curiae filed on behalf of the National Association of Criminal Defense Lawyers, the American Civil Liberties Union, and the American Civil Liberties Union of Southern California by Michael C. Small, Jeffrey L. Fisher, Peter Eliasberg, and Steven R. Shapiro.

Brief of amici curiae filed on behalf of the American Federation of Labor and Congress of Industrial Organizations by Jonathan P. Hiatt, James B. Coppess, and Laurence Gold.

Brief of amici curiae filed on behalf of the Association of Deputy District Attorneys et al. by Jody Manier Kris.

Brief of amici curiae filed on behalf of the Government Accountability Project et al. by Joanne Royce.

Brief of amici curiae filed on behalf of the National Treasury Employees Union by Gregory O'Duden, Elaine D. Kaplan, Barbara A. Atkin, and Julie Sarah Lehrman.

Brief of amici curiae filed on behalf of the Thomas Jefferson Center for the Protection of Free Expression et al. by J. Joshua Wheeler, Robert M. O'Neil, Donna R. Euben, and David M. Rabban.

Brief of amici curiae filed on behalf of the National Education Association by Robert H. Chanin and Jeremiah A. Collins.

Opposing Side (Petitioner / Appellant)

Brief of amici curiae filed on behalf of the United States by Dan Himmelfarb, Deputy Solicitor General Kneedler, Solicitor General Clement, Assistant Attorney General Keisler, Mr. Himmelfarb, William Kanter, Michael E. Robinson, Mark A. Robbins, Steven E. Abow, and Robin M. Richardson.

Brief of amici curiae filed on behalf of the International Municipal Lawyers Association by Gene C. Schaerr, Linda T. Coberly, Peter Kryn Dykema, and Henry W. Underhill, Jr.

Brief of amici curiae filed on behalf of the National Association of Counties et al. by Richard Ruda and James I. Crowley.

Brief of amici curiae filed on behalf of the National School Boards Association by Naomi Gittins, Julie Underwood, Lisa Soronen, and Thomas E. Wheeler II.

IV. THE SUPREME COURT'S DECISION

A. "As the Court's decisions have noted, for many years 'the unchallenged dogma was that a public employee had no right to object to conditions placed upon the terms of employment—including those which restricted the exercise of constitutional rights.' That dogma has been qualified in important respects. The Court has made clear that public employees do not surrender all their First Amendment rights by reason of their employment. Rather, the First Amendment protects a public employee's right, in certain circumstances, to speak as a citizen addressing matters of public concern. . . .

Pickering and the cases decided in its wake identify two inquiries to guide interpretation of the constitutional protections accorded to public employee speech. The first requires determining whether the employee spoke as a citizen on a matter of public concern. If the answer is no, the employee has no First Amendment cause of action based on his or her employer's reaction to the speech. If the answer is yes, then the possibility of a First Amendment claim arises. The question becomes whether the relevant government entity had an adequate justification for treating the employee differently from any other member of the general public. . . .

The Court's decisions, then, have sought both to promote the individual and societal interests that are served when employees speak as citizens on matters of public concern and to respect the needs of government employers attempting to perform their important public functions. . . . Underlying our cases has been the premise that while the First Amendment invests public employees with certain rights, it does not empower them to 'constitutionalize the employee grievance.' . . .

With these principles in mind we turn to the instant case. Respondent Ceballos believed the affidavit used to obtain a search warrant contained serious misrepresentations. He conveyed his opinion and recommendation in a memo to his supervisor. That Ceballos expressed his views inside his office, rather than publicly, is not dispositive. Employees in some cases may receive First Amendment protection for expressions made at work. . . .

The memo concerned the subject matter of Ceballos' employment, but this, too, is nondispositive. . . .

The controlling factor in Ceballos' case is that his expressions were made pursuant to his duties as a calendar deputy. . . . That consideration—the fact that Ceballos spoke as a prosecutor fulfilling a responsibility to advise his supervisor about how best to proceed with a pending case—distinguishes Ceballos' case from those in which the First Amendment provides protection against discipline. We hold that when public employees make statements pursuant to their official duties, the employees are not speaking as citizens for First Amendment purposes, and the Constitution does not insulate their communications from employer discipline. . . .

Proper application of our precedents thus leads to the conclusion that the First Amendment does not prohibit managerial discipline based on an employee's expressions made pursuant to official responsibilities. Because Ceballos' memo falls into this category, his allegation of unconstitutional retaliation must fail. . . .

The judgment of the Court of Appeals is reversed, and the case is remanded for proceedings consistent with this opinion."

V. JUSTICE VOTE

4 Pro ACLU Side vs. 5 Con Opposing Side

ACLU Side (Respondent / Appellee)

1. Souter, D. – Wrote dissenting opinion
2. Stevens, J. – Wrote dissenting opinion, joined Souter's dissent
3. Ginsburg, R. – Joined Souter's dissent
4. Breyer, S. – Wrote dissenting opinion

Opposing Side (Petitioner / Appellant)

1. Kennedy, A. – Wrote majority opinion
2. Alito, S. – Joined majority opinion
3. Thomas, C. – Joined majority opinion
4. Scalia, A. – Joined majority opinion
5. Roberts, J. – Joined majority opinion

VI. A WIN OR LOSS FOR THE ACLU?

The ACLU filed as amicus curiae urging affirmance; the Supreme Court reversed the Court of Appeals' decision by a 5-4 vote, giving the ACLU an apparent loss.

999. Hudson v. Michigan

(Decided June 15, 2006; 547 U.S. 586)

I. ISSUE

A. Issues Discussed

4th Amendment, drugs

B. Legal Question Presented

"[W]hether violation of the 'knock-and-announce' rule requires the suppression of all evidence found in the search."

C. Supreme Court's Answer

"Resort to the massive remedy of suppressing evidence of guilt is unjustified."

II. CASE SUMMARY

A. Background

"Police obtained a warrant authorizing a search for drugs and firearms at the home of petitioner Booker Hudson. They discovered both. Large quantities of drugs were found, including cocaine rocks in Hudson's pocket. A loaded gun was lodged between the cushion and armrest of the chair in which he was sitting. Hudson was charged under Michigan law with unlawful drug and firearm possession.

This case is before us only because of the method of entry into the house. When the police arrived to execute the warrant, they announced their presence, but waited only a short time—perhaps 'three to five seconds'—before turning the knob of the unlocked front door and entering Hudson's home. Hudson moved to suppress all the inculpatory evidence, arguing that the premature entry violated his Fourth Amendment rights.

The Michigan trial court granted his motion. On interlocutory review, the Michigan Court of Appeals reversed . . . . The Michigan Supreme Court denied leave to appeal. Hudson was convicted of drug possession. He renewed his Fourth Amendment claim on appeal, but the Court of Appeals rejected it and affirmed the conviction. The Michigan Supreme Court again declined review."

The Supreme Court granted certiorari to review the case.

B. Counsel of Record

ACLU Side (Petitioner / Appellant): David A. Moran argued and reargued the cause for appellant. With him on the briefs were Timothy O'Toole, Richard D. Korn, Steven R. Shapiro of the American Civil Liberties Union Foundation, and Michael J. Steinberg and Kary L. Moss of the American Civil Liberties Union Fund of Michigan.

Opposing Side (Respondent / Appellee): Timothy A. Baughman argued and reargued the cause and filed a brief for appellee.

David B. Salmons argued and reargued the cause for the United States as amicus curiae.

III. AMICI CURIAE

ACLU Side (Petitioner / Appellant)

Brief of amici curiae filed on behalf of the Cato Institute et al. by Tracey Maclin, Timothy Lynch, and Joshua L. Dratel.

Opposing Side (Respondent / Appellee)

Brief of amici curiae filed on behalf of the United States by David B. Salmons, Solicitor General Clement, Assistant Attorney General Fisher, Deputy Solicitor General Dreeben, and Deborah Watson.

Brief of amici curiae filed on behalf of the Criminal Justice Legal Foundation by Kent S. Scheidegger and Charles L. Hobson.

IV. THE SUPREME COURT'S DECISION

"The common-law principle that law enforcement officers must announce their presence and provide residents an opportunity to open the door is an ancient one. [I]n Wilson, we were asked whether the rule was also a command of the Fourth Amendment. [W]e concluded that it was.

We recognized that the new constitutional rule we had announced is not easily applied. Wilson and cases following it have noted the many situations in which it is not necessary to knock and announce. . . .

Happily, these issues do not confront us here. From the trial level onward, Michigan has conceded that the entry was a knock-and-announce violation. The issue here is remedy. Wilson specifically declined to decide whether the exclusionary rule is appropriate for violation of the knock-and-announce requirement. That question is squarely before us now. . . .

In Weeks v. United States, we adopted the federal exclusionary rule for evidence that was unlawfully seized from a home without a warrant in violation of the Fourth Amendment. . . .

Suppression of evidence, however, has always been our last resort, not our first impulse. . . .

What the knock-and-announce rule has never protected . . . is one's interest in preventing the government from seeing or taking evidence described in a warrant. Since the interests that were violated in this case have nothing to do with the seizure of the evidence, the exclusionary rule is inapplicable. . . .

In sum, the social costs of applying the exclusionary rule to knock-and-announce violations are considerable; the incentive to such violations is minimal to begin with, and the extant deterrences against them are substantial—incomparably greater than the factors deterring warrantless entries when Mapp was decided. Resort to the massive remedy of suppressing evidence of guilt is unjustified. . . .

For the foregoing reasons we affirm the judgment of the Michigan Court of Appeals."

V. JUSTICE VOTE

4 Pro ACLU Side vs. 5 Con Opposing Side

ACLU Side (Petitioner / Appellant)

1. Stevens, J. – Joined Breyer's dissent
2. Breyer, S. – Wrote dissenting opinion
3. Ginsburg, R. – Joined Breyer's dissent
4. Souter, D. – Joined Breyer's dissent

Opposing Side (Respondent / Appellee)

1. Scalia, A. – Wrote majority opinion
2. Alito, S. – Wrote majority opinion
3. Thomas, C. – Joined majority opinion
4. Kennedy, A. – Wrote concurring opinion
5. Roberts, J. – Joined majority opinion

VI. A WIN OR LOSS FOR THE ACLU?

The ACLU argued the cause on behalf of appellant urging reversal of the judgment of the Michigan Court of Appeals; the Supreme Court affirmed in a 5-4 vote, giving the ACLU an apparent loss.

1000. Davis v. Washington

(Decided June 19, 2006; 547 U.S. 813)

I. ISSUE

A. Issues Discussed

Criminal procedure

B. Legal Question Presented

"These cases require us to determine when statements made to law enforcement personnel during a 911 call or at a crime scene are 'testimonial' and thus subject to the requirements of the Sixth Amendment's Confrontation Clause."

C. Supreme Court's Answer

"Statements are nontestimonial when made in the course of police interrogation under circumstances objectively indicating that the primary purpose of the interrogation is to enable police assistance to meet an ongoing emergency. They are testimonial when the circumstances objectively indicate that there is no such ongoing emergency, and that the primary purpose of the interrogation is to establish or prove past events potentially relevant to later criminal prosecution."

II. CASE SUMMARY

A. Background

"The relevant statements in Davis v. Washington, No. 05–5224, were made to a 911 emergency operator . . . . [T]he operator ascertained that McCottry was involved in a domestic disturbance with her former boyfriend Adrian Davis . . . .

The State charged Davis with felony violation of a domestic no-contact order. 'The State's only witnesses were the two police officers who responded to the 911 call. Both officers testified that McCottry exhibited injuries . . . , but neither officer could testify as to the cause . . . .' McCottry . . . did not appear. Over Davis's objection, based on the Confrontation Clause of the Sixth Amendment, the trial court admitted the recording of her exchange with the 911 operator, and the jury convicted him. The Washington Court of Appeals affirmed. The Supreme Court of Washington . . . affirmed . . . .

In Hammon v. Indiana, No. 05–5705, police responded . . . to a 'reported domestic disturbance' at the home of Hershel and Amy Hammon. . . .

After hearing Amy's account, the officer 'had her fill out and sign a battery affidavit.' . . .

The State charged Hershel with domestic battery and with violating his probation. Amy . . . did not appear . . . . The State called the officer who had questioned Amy, and asked him to recount what Amy told him and to authenticate the affidavit. Hershel's counsel repeatedly objected . . . . Nonetheless, the trial court admitted the affidavit . . . .

The trial judge found Hershel guilty on both charges, and the Indiana Court of Appeals affirmed in relevant part. The Indiana Supreme Court also affirmed . . . ."

The Supreme Court granted certiorari to review the case.

B. Counsel of Record / ACLU Attorney

ACLU Side (Petitioner / Appellant): Jeffrey L. Fisher argued the cause for appellant in No. 05–5224. With him on the briefs was Nancy Collins.

Richard D. Friedman argued the cause for appellant in No. 05–5705. With him on the briefs was Kimberly A. Jackson.

Opposing Side (Respondent / Appellee): James M. Whisman argued the cause for appellee in No. 05–5224. With him on the brief were Norm Maleng, Deborah A. Dwyer, and Lee D. Yates.

Thomas M. Fisher, Solicitor General of Indiana, argued the cause for appellee in No. 05–5705. With him on the brief were Steve Carter, Attorney General, and Nicole M. Schuster and Julie A. Hoffman, Deputy Attorneys General.

Deputy Solicitor General Dreeben argued the cause for the United States as amicus curiae in No. 05-5224.

Irving L. Gornstein argued the cause for the United States as amicus curiae in No. 05-5705.

III. AMICI CURIAE

ACLU Side (Petitioner / Appellant)

Brief of amici curiae filed on behalf of the American Civil Liberties Union et al. by Jordan Gross, Steven R. Shapiro, Lenora Lapidus, Ken Falk, and Aaron Caplan.

Brief of amici curiae filed on behalf of the National Association of Criminal Defense Lawyers et al. by Timothy P. O'Toole, Catharine F. Easterly, Andrea Roth, Corinne Beckwith, Pamela Harris, and Sheryl McCloud.

Opposing Side (Respondent / Appellee)

Brief of amici curiae filed on behalf of the United States in No. 05-5224 by Deputy Solicitor General Dreeben, Solicitor General Clement, Assistant Attorney General Fisher, Irving L. Gornstein, and Joel M. Gershowitz.

Brief of amici curiae filed on behalf of the United States in No. 05-5705 by Irving L. Gornstein, Solicitor General Clement, Assistant Attorney General Fisher, and Deputy Solicitor General Dreeben.

Brief of amici curiae filed on behalf of the State of Illinois et al. by Lisa Madigan, Attorney General of Illinois, Gary Feinerman, Solicitor General, Michael Scodro, Deputy Solicitor General, and Linda D. Woloshin and Anderson M. Gansner, Assistant Attorneys General, by Christopher L. Morano, Chief State's Attorney of Connecticut, and by the Attorneys General for their respective States as follows: Troy King of Alabama, Terry Goddard of Arizona, Mike Beebe of Arkansas, Bill Lockyer of California, John W. Suthers of Colorado, Carl C. Danberg of Delaware, Charles J. Crist, Jr., of Florida, Mark J. Bennett of Hawaii, Lawrence G. Wasden of Idaho, Phill Kline of Kansas, J. Joseph Curran, Jr., of Maryland, Thomas F. Reilly of Massachusetts, Michael A. Cox of Michigan, Jeremiah W. (Jay) Nixon of Missouri, Jon Bruning of Nebraska, George J. Chanos of Nevada, Patricia A. Madrid of New Mexico, Jim Petro of Ohio, W. A. Drew Edmondson of Oklahoma, Lawrence E. Long of South Dakota, Greg Abbott of Texas, Mark L. Shurtleff of Utah, William

Sorrell of Vermont, Darrell V. McGraw, Jr., of West Virginia, and Patrick J. Crank of Wyoming.

Brief of amici curiae filed on behalf of Cook County, Illinois, by Richard A. Devine and Veronica Calderon Malavia.

Brief of amici curiae filed on behalf of the National Association of Counsel for Children by Anthony J. Franze.

Brief of amici curiae filed on behalf of the National District Attorneys Association by Mark Ryan Dwyer, David M. Cohn, Susan Axelrod, and Joshua A. Engel.

Brief of amici curiae filed on behalf of the National Network to End Domestic Violence et al. by Antonia B. Ianniello, Michael D. Rips, Jennifer K. Brown, Lynn Hecht Schafran, Joan S. Meier, and Fernando R. Laguarda.

Brief of amici curiae filed on behalf of Wayne County, Michigan by Kym L. Worthy and Timothy A. Baughman.

IV. THE SUPREME COURT'S DECISION

"The Confrontation Clause of the Sixth Amendment provides: 'In all criminal prosecutions, the accused shall enjoy the right . . . to be confronted with the witnesses against him.' In Crawford v. Washington, 541 U.S. 36 (2004), we held that this provision bars 'admission of testimonial statements of a witness who did not appear at trial unless he was unavailable to testify, and the defendant had had a prior opportunity for cross-examination.' A critical portion of this holding, and the portion central to resolution of the two cases now before us, is the phrase 'testimonial statements.' . . .

Without attempting to produce an exhaustive classification of all conceivable statements . . . as either testimonial or nontestimonial, it suffices to decide the present cases to hold as follows: Statements are nontestimonial when made in the course of police interrogation under circumstances objectively indicating that the primary purpose of the interrogation is to enable police assistance to meet an ongoing emergency. They are testimonial when the circumstances objectively indicate that there is no such ongoing emergency, and that the primary purpose of the interrogation is to establish or prove past events potentially relevant to later criminal prosecution. . . .

The question before us in Davis . . . is whether, objectively considered, the interrogation that took place in the course of the 911 call produced testimonial statements. . . .

We conclude . . . that the circumstances of McCottry's interrogation objectively indicate its primary purpose was to enable police assistance to meet an ongoing emergency. She simply was not acting as a witness; she was not testifying. . . .

[W]e agree with the Washington Supreme Court that they were not testimonial. . . .

Determining the testimonial or nontestimonial character of the statements that were the product of the interrogation in Hammon is a much easier task, since they were not much different from the statements we found to be testimonial in Crawford. . . .

We have determined that, absent a finding of forfeiture by wrongdoing, the Sixth Amendment operates to exclude Amy Hammon's affidavit. . . .

We affirm the judgment of the Supreme Court of Washington in No. 05-5224. We reverse the judgment of the Supreme Court of Indiana in No. 05-5705, and remand . . . ."

V. JUSTICE VOTE

0 Pro ACLU Side vs. 9 Con Opposing Side

Opposing Side (Respondent / Appellee)

1. Scalia, A. – Wrote majority opinion
2. Alito, S. – Joined majority opinion
3. Stevens, J. – Joined majority opinion
4. Thomas, C. – Wrote opinion concurring in part and dissenting in part
5. Breyer, S. – Joined majority opinion
6. Kennedy, A. – Joined majority opinion
7. Ginsburg, R. – Joined majority opinion
8. Souter, D. – Joined majority opinion
9. Roberts, J. – Joined majority opinion

VI. A WIN OR LOSS FOR THE ACLU?

The ACLU filed as amicus curiae urging reversal of the judgments in the lower courts; the Supreme Court affirmed No. 05-5224 in a 9-0 vote, giving the ACLU an apparent loss.

1001. Samson v. California

(Decided June 19, 2006; 547 U.S. 843)

I. ISSUE

A. Issues Discussed

4th Amendment

B. Legal Question Presented

"California law provides that every prisoner eligible for release on state parole 'shall agree in writing to be subject to search or seizure by a parole officer or other peace officer at any time of th day or night, with or without a search warrant and with or without cause.' [This case considers] whether a suspicionless search, conducted under the authority of this statute, violates the Constitution."

C. Supreme Court's Answer

"We hold that it does not."

II. CASE SUMMARY

A. Background

"Donald Curtis Samson was on state parole in California, following a conviction for being a felon in possession of a firearm. . . . Officer Alex Rohleder . . . observed petitioner walking down a street with a woman and a child. Based on a prior contact with petitioner, Officer Rohleder was aware that petitioner was on parole and believed that he was facing an at-large warrant. Accordingly, Officer Rohleder stopped petitioner and asked him whether he had an outstanding parole warrant. Petitioner responded that there was no outstanding warrant and that he 'was in good standing with his parole agent.' Officer Rohleder confirmed, by radio dispatch, that petitioner was on parole and that he did not have an outstanding warrant. Nevertheless, pursuant to Cal.Penal Code Ann. § 3067(a) and based solely on petitioner's status as a parolee, Officer Rohleder searched petitioner. During the search, Officer Rohleder found a cigarette box in petitioner's left breast pocket. Inside the box he found a plastic baggie containing methamphetamine.

The State charged petitioner with possession of methamphetamine . . . . The trial court denied petitioner's motion to suppress the methamphetamine evidence, finding that Cal.Penal Code Ann. § 3067(a) authorized the search and that the search was not 'arbitrary or capricious.' A jury convicted petitioner of the possession charge, and the trial court sentenced him to seven years' imprisonment.

The California Court of Appeal affirmed."

The Supreme Court granted certiorari to review the case.

B. Counsel of Record / ACLU Attorney

ACLU Side (Petitioner / Appellant): Robert A. Long argued the cause for appellant. With him on the briefs was Martin Kassman.

Opposing Side (Respondent / Appellee): Ronald E. Niver, Deputy Attorney General of California, argued the cause for appellee. With him on the brief were Bill Lockyer, Attorney General, Robert R. Anderson, Chief Assistant Attorney General, Manuel M. Medeiros, State Solicitor General, Donald E. De Nicola, Deputy Solicitor General, Gerald A. Engler, Senior Assistant Attorney General, Martin S. Kaye, Supervising Deputy Attorney General, and Doris A. Calandra, Deputy Attorney General.

Jonathan L. Marcus argued the cause for the United States as amicus curiae.

III. AMICI CURIAE

ACLU Side (Petitioner / Appellant)

Brief of amici curiae filed on behalf of the American Civil Liberties Union and the ACLU of Northern California by Graham A. Boyd, Steven R. Shapiro, and Alan Schlosser.

Brief of amici curiae filed on behalf of the California Public Defenders Association et al. by Michael C. McMahon and Kenneth I. Clayman.

Brief of amici curiae filed on behalf of Citizens United for Rehabilitation of Errants by Robert Weisberg.

Brief of amici curiae filed on behalf of the National Association of Criminal Defense Lawyers by Carter G. Phillips, Jeffrey T. Green, and Pamela Harris.

Opposing Side (Respondent / Appellee)

Brief of amici curiae filed on behalf of the United States by Jonathan L. Marcus, Solicitor General Clement, Assistant Attorney General Fisher, Deputy Solicitor General Dreeben, and Deborah Watson.

Brief of amici curiae filed on behalf of the State of Pennsylvania et al. by Thomas W. Corbett, Jr., Attorney General of Pennsylvania, Howard G. Hopkirk, Senior Deputy Attorney General, and John G. Knorr III, Chief Deputy Attorney General, and by the Attorneys General for their respective States as follows: Mike Beebe of Arkansas, John W. Suthers of Colorado, Mark J. Bennett of Hawaii, Lawrence G. Wasden of Idaho, Lisa Madigan of Illinois, Gregory D. Stumbo of Kentucky, J. Joseph Curran, Jr., of Maryland, Michael A. Cox of Michigan, Jim Hood of Mississippi, Jeremiah W. (Jay) Nixon of Missouri, George J. Chanos of Nevada, Wayne Stenehjem of North Dakota, Hardy Myers of Oregon, Lawrence E. Long of South Dakota, Paul G. Summers of Tennessee, Greg Abbott of Texas, Mark L. Shurtleff of Utah, Rob McKenna of Washington, Darrell V. McGraw, Jr., of West Virginia, and Patrick J. Crank of Wyoming.

Brief of amici curiae filed on behalf of Americans for Effective Law Enforcement, Inc., et al. by Wayne W. Schmidt, James P. Manak, Richard Weintraub, and Bernard J. Farber.

Brief of amici curiae filed on behalf of the Criminal Justice Legal Foundation by Kent S. Scheidegger and Charles L. Hobson.

Brief of amici curiae filed on behalf of Los Angeles County by Scott Wm. Davenport.

Brief of amici curiae filed on behalf of Los Angeles County District Attorney Steve Cooley by Mr. Cooley, pro se, Lael R. Rubin, Brentford J. Ferreira, and Phyllis C. Asayama.

IV. THE SUPREME COURT'S DECISION

"'[U]nder our general Fourth Amendment approach' we 'examin[e] the totality of the circumstances' to determine whether a search is reasonable within the meaning of the Fourth Amendment. Whether a search is reasonable 'is determined by assessing, on the one hand, the degree to which it intrudes upon an individual's privacy and, on the other, the degree to which it is needed for the promotion of legitimate governmental interests.'

We recently applied this approach in United States v. Knights. . . . Balancing . . . interests, we held that '[w]hen an officer has reasonable suspicion that a probationer subject to a search condition is engaged in criminal activity, there is enough likelihood that criminal conduct is occurring that an intrusion on the probationer's significantly diminished privacy interests is reasonable.' . . .

As we noted in Knights, parolees are on the 'continuum' of state-imposed punishments. On this continuum, parolees have fewer expectations of privacy than probationers, because parole is more akin to imprisonment than probation is to imprisonment. . . .

The extent and reach of these conditions clearly demonstrate that parolees like petitioner have severely diminished expectations of privacy by virtue of their status alone.

Additionally, as we found 'salient' in Knights with respect to the probation search condition, the parole search condition under California law—requiring inmates who opt for parole to submit to suspicionless searches by a parole officer or other peace officer 'at any time,' Cal.Penal Code Ann. § 3067(a)—was 'clearly expressed' to petitioner. . . . Examining the totality of the circumstances pertaining to petitioner's status as a parolee, 'an established variation on imprisonment,' including the plain terms of the parole search condition, we conclude that petitioner did not have an expectation of privacy that society would recognize as legitimate.

The State's interests, by contrast, are substantial. . . .

Contrary to petitioner's contention, California's ability to conduct suspicionless searches of parolees serves its interest in reducing recidivism, in a manner that aids, rather than hinders, the reintegration of parolees into productive society. . . .

Thus, we conclude that the Fourth Amendment does not

prohibit a police officer from conducting a suspicionless search of a parolee. Accordingly, we affirm the judgment of the California Court of Appeal."

V. JUSTICE VOTE

3 Pro ACLU Side vs. 6 Con Opposing Side

ACLU Side (Petitioner / Appellant)

1. Stevens, J. – Wrote dissenting opinion
2. Breyer, S. – Joined Stevens' dissent
3. Souter, D. – Joined Stevens' dissent

Opposing Side (Respondent / Appellee)

1. Thomas, C. – Wrote majority opinion
2. Roberts, J. – Joined majority opinion
3. Scalia, A. – Joined majority opinion
4. Kennedy, A. – Joined majority opinion
5. Ginsburg, R. – Joined majority opinion
6. Alito, S. – Joined majority opinion

VI. A WIN OR LOSS FOR THE ACLU?

The ACLU filed as amicus curiae urging reversal of the judgment of the California Court of Appeal; the Supreme Court reversed in a 6-3 vote, giving the ACLU an apparent loss.

1002. Fernandez-Vargas v. Gonzales

(Decided June 22, 2006; 548 U.S. 30)

I. ISSUE

A. Issues Discussed

Immigration/Citizenship

B. Legal Question Presented

"For some time, the law has provided that an order for removing an alien present unlawfully may be reinstated if he leaves and unlawfully enters again. The Illegal Immigration Reform and Immigrant Responsibility Act of 1996 (IIRIRA) enlarged the class of illegal reentrants whose orders may be reinstated and limited the possible relief from a removal order available to them. The questions here are whether the new version of the reinstatement provision is correctly read to apply to individuals who reentered the United States before IIRIRA's effective date, and whether such a reading may be rejected as impermissibly retroactive."

C. Supreme Court's Answer

"We hold the statute applies to those who entered before IIRIRA and does not retroactively affect any right of, or impose any burden on, the continuing violator of the INA now before us."

II. CASE SUMMARY

A. Background

"In 1950, Congress provided that deportation orders issued against some aliens who later reentered the United States illegally could be reinstated. . . .

In IIRIRA, Congress replaced this reinstatement provision with one that toed a harder line, as the old § 242(f) was displaced by the new § 241(a)(5) . . . .

Unlike its predecessor, § 241(a)(5) applies to all illegal reentrants, explicitly insulates the removal orders from review, and generally forecloses discretionary relief . . . .

Humberto Fernandez–Vargas is a citizen of Mexico, who first came to the United States . . . only to be deported for immigration violations, and to reenter, several times . . . . Then . . . for over 20 years he remained undetected in Utah, where he . . . fathered a son, who is a United States citizen. . . . Fernandez–Vargas married the boy's mother, . . . a United States citizen. She soon filed a relative-visa petition on behalf of her husband . . . . The filings apparently tipped off the authorities . . . , and . . . the Government began proceedings under § 241(a)(5) that eventuated in reinstating Fernandez–Vargas's 1981 deportation order . . . . He was detained for 10 months before being removed . . . .

Fernandez–Vargas petitioned . . . to review the reinstatement order. He took the position that because he illegally reentered the country before IIRIRA's effective date, the controlling reinstatement provision was the old § 242(f), which meant he was eligible to apply for adjustment . . . , and he said that the new § 241(a)(5) would be impermissibly retroactive if it barred his application for adjustment. The Court of Appeals held that § 241(a)(5) did bar Fernandez–Vargas's application . . . ."

The Supreme Court granted certiorari to review the case.

B. Counsel of Record / ACLU Attorney

ACLU Side (Petitioner / Appellant): David M. Gossett argued the cause for appellant. With him on the briefs was Andrew Tauber.

Opposing Side (Respondent / Appellee): Sri Srinivasan argued the cause for appellee. With him on the brief were Solicitor General Clement, Assistant Attorney General Keisler, Deputy Solicitor General Kneedler, Donald E. Keener, and Alison Marie Igoe.

III. AMICI CURIAE

ACLU Side (Petitioner / Appellant)

Brief of amici curiae filed on behalf of the American Immigration Law Foundation, American Immigration Lawyers Association, Capital Area Immigrants' Rights Coalition, Immigrants' Rights Project of The American Civil Liberties Union, Midwest Immigrant and Human Rights Center, National Immigration Law Center, National Immigration Project of the National Lawyers Guild, Northwest Immigrant Rights Project, and The Texas Lawyers' Committee for Civil Rights Under Law by Trina A. Realmuto, Matt Adams, Marc Van Der Hout, and Stacy Tolchin.

Opposing Side (Respondent / Appellee)

No briefs of amici curiae were filed in support of appellee.

IV. THE SUPREME COURT'S DECISION

"Statutes are disfavored as retroactive when their application 'would impair rights a party possessed when he acted, increase a party's liability for past conduct, or impose new duties with respect to transactions already completed.' . . . Accordingly, it has become 'a rule of general application' that 'a statute shall not be given retroactive effect unless such construction is required by explicit language or by necessary implication.' . . .

Fernandez-Vargas fights at each step of the way, arguing that Congress intended that INA § 241(a)(5) would not apply to illegal reentrants like him who returned to this country before the provision's effective date; and in any event, that application of the provision to such illegal reentrants would have an impermissibly retroactive effect, to be avoided by applying the presumption against it. We are not persuaded by either contention. . . .

Needless to say, Congress did not complement the new version of § 241(a)(5) with any clause expressly dealing with individuals who illegally reentered the country before IIRIRA's April 1, 1997, effective date . . . .

One conclusion can be stated, however. Common principles of statutory interpretation fail to unsettle the apparent application of § 241(a)(5) to any reentrant present in the country . . . .

This facial reading is confirmed by two features of IIRIRA . . . . One is in the text of that provision itself, showing that it applies to Fernandez-Vargas today not because he reentered in 1982 or at any other particular time, but because he chose to remain after the new statute became effective. The second is the provision setting IIRIRA's effective date, which shows that Fernandez-Vargas had an ample warning of the coming change in the law, but chose to remain until the old regime expired and § 241(a)(5) took its place. . . .

What Fernandez-Vargas complains of is the application of new law to continuously illegal action within his control both before and after the new law took effect. He claims a right to continue illegal conduct indefinitely under the terms on which it began, an entitlement of legal stasis for those whose lawbreaking is continuous. But '[i]f every time a man relied on existing law in arranging his affairs, he were made secure against any change in legal rules, the whole body of our law would be ossified forever.'

Because we conclude that § 241(a)(5) has no retroactive effect when applied to aliens like Fernandez-Vargas, we affirm the judgment of the Court of Appeals."

V. JUSTICE VOTE

1 Pro ACLU Side vs. 8 Con Opposing Side

ACLU Side (Petitioner / Appellant)

1. Stevens, J. – Wrote dissenting opinion

Opposing Side (Respondent / Appellee)

1. Souter, D. – Wrote majority opinion
2. Alito, S. – Joined majority opinion
3. Thomas, C. – Joined majority opinion
4. Breyer, S. – Joined majority opinion
5. Scalia, A. – Joined majority opinion
6. Kennedy, A. – Joined majority opinion
7. Ginsburg, R. – Joined majority opinion
8. Roberts, J. – Joined majority opinion

VI. A WIN OR LOSS FOR THE ACLU?

The ACLU filed as amicus curiae urging reversal of the judgment of the Court of Appeals; the Supreme Court affirmed in an 8-1 vote, giving the ACLU an apparent loss.

1003. Burlington Northern & Santa Fe Ry. Co. v. White

(Decided June 22, 2006; 548 U.S. 53)

I. ISSUE

A. Issues Discussed

Civil rights, federal

B. Legal Question Presented

One component of "Title VII of the Civil Rights Act of 1964 . . . —its antiretaliation provision—prohibits an employer from 'discriminat[ing] against' an employee or job applicant because that individual 'opposed any practice' made unlawful by Title VII or 'made a charge, testified, assisted, or participated in' a Title VII proceeding or investigation. . . .

Does that provision confine actionable retaliation to activity that affects the terms and conditions of employment? And how harmful must the adverse actions be to fall within its scope?"

C. Supreme Court's Answer

"We conclude that the antiretaliation provision does not confine the actions and harms it forbids to those that are related to employment or occur at the workplace. We also conclude that the provision covers those (and only those) employer actions that would have been materially adverse to a reasonable employee or job applicant. In the present context that means that the employer's actions must be harmful to the point that they could well dissuade a reasonable worker from making or supporting a charge of discrimination."

II. CASE SUMMARY

A. Background

"This case arises out of actions that supervisors at . . . Burlington . . . took against . . . Sheila White, the only woman working in the Maintenance of Way department . . . .

White complained . . . that her immediate supervisor, Bill Joiner, had repeatedly told her that women should not be working in the Maintenance of Way department. Joiner . . . also made insulting and inappropriate remarks to her in front of her male colleagues. . . . Burlington suspended Joiner for 10 days and ordered . . . a sexual-harassment training . . . .

Brown . . . told White that he was removing her from forklift duty . . . . [T]he reassignment reflected co-workers' complaints that, in fairness, a "more senior man" should have the 'less arduous and cleaner job' of forklift operator. . . .

White filed a complaint with the Equal Employment Opportunity Commission . . . . White filed a second retaliation charge . . . claiming that Brown had placed her under surveillance and was monitoring her daily activities. . . .

White and her immediate supervisor, Percy Sharkey [had a disagreement.] Brown immediately suspended White without pay. White invoked internal grievance procedures. Those procedures led Burlington to conclude that White had not been insubordinate. Burlington reinstated White to her position and awarded her backpay . . . . White filed an additional retaliation charge with the EEOC based on the suspension. . . .

After exhausting administrative remedies, White filed this Title VII action against Burlington in federal court. . . . A jury found in White's favor . . . .

[The] Sixth Circuit . . . affirmed the District Court's judgment in White's favor . . . ."

The Supreme Court granted certiorari to review the case.

B. Counsel of Record / ACLU Attorney

ACLU Side (Respondent / Appellee): Donald A. Donati argued the cause for appellee. With him on the briefs were William B. Ryan and Eric Schnapper.

Opposing Side (Petitioner / Appellant): Carter G. Phillips argued the cause for appellant. With him on the briefs were Stephen B. Kinnaird, Eric A. Shumsky, James H. Gallegos, Lawrence M. Stroik, David M. Pryor, and Bryan P. Neal.

Deputy Solicitor General Garre argued the cause for the United States as amicus curiae.

III. AMICI CURIAE

ACLU Side (Respondent / Appellee)

Brief of amici curiae filed on behalf of the National Women's Law Center, American Association of University Women, American Civil Liberties Union, Association for Gender Equity Leadership in Education, Association of Trial Lawyers of America, Business and Professional Women/USA, California Women's Law Center, Connecticut Women's Education and Legal Fund, Dads and Daughters, Equal Rights Advocates, Feminist Majority, Legal Aid Society - Employment Law Center, Legal Momentum, Myra Sadker Advocates for Gender Equity, National Alliance for Partnerships in Equity, National Association of Collegiate Women Athletics Administrators, National Association of Women Lawyers, National Council of Jewish Women, National Council of Women's Organizations, National Education Association, National Partnership for Women and Families, National Women's History Project, Northwest Women's Law Center, Pick Up the Pace, United Church of Christ, Women Employed, Women Work! The National Network for Women's Employment, Women's Law Center of Maryland, Womens Law Project, and Women's Sports Foundation by Thomas C. Goldstein, Amy Howe, Kevin K. Russell, Pamela S. Karlan, Marcia D. Greenberger, Jocelyn Samuels, Dina R. Lassow, and Charlotte Fishman.

Brief of amici curiae filed on behalf of the American Federation of Labor and Congress of Industrial Organizations et al. by Jonathan P. Hiatt, James B. Coppess, William A. Bon, Laurence Gold, and Mitchell M. Kraus.

Brief of amici curiae filed on behalf of the National Employment Lawyers Association et al. by Douglas B. Huron, Stephen Z. Chertkof, Andrew S. Golub, and Marissa M. Tirona.

Brief of amici curiae filed on behalf of the Lawyers' Committee for Civil Rights Under Law et al. by Michael Foreman, Sarah Crawford, and Dennis Courtland Hayes.

Opposing Side (Petitioner / Appellant)

Brief of amici curiae filed on behalf of the United States by Deputy Solicitor General Garre, Solicitor General Clement, Assistant Attorney General Kim, Acting Assistant Attorney General Katsas, Irving L. Gornstein, Marleigh D. Dover, and Stephanie R. Marcus.

Brief of amici curiae filed on behalf of the Association of American Railroads by Maureen E. Mahoney, Jonathan C. Su, and Daniel Saphire.

Brief of amici curiae filed on behalf of the Equal Employment Advisory Council et al. by Ann Elizabeth Reesman, Laura Anne Giantris, Stephen A. Bokat, Robin S. Conrad, and Ellen Dunham Bryant.

Brief of amici curiae filed on behalf of the International Municipal Lawyers Association by Frank Waite and Elizabeth Lutton

Brief of amici curiae filed on behalf of the Pacific Legal Foundation by Deborah J. La Fetra.

Brief of amici curiae filed on behalf of the Society for Human Resource Management et al. by Allan H. Weitzman, Paul Salvatore, and Edward Cerasia II.

IV. THE SUPREME COURT'S DECISION

"Title VII's antiretaliation provision forbids employer actions that 'discriminate against' an employee . . . because he has 'opposed' a practice that Title VII forbids or has 'made a charge, testified, assisted, or participated in' a Title VII 'investigation, proceeding, or hearing.' [D]ifferent Circuits have come to different conclusions about whether the challenged action has to be employment or workplace related and . . . how harmful . . . .

We granted certiorari to resolve this disagreement. To do so requires us to decide whether Title VII's antiretaliation provision forbids only those employer actions and resulting harms that are related to employment or the workplace. And we must characterize how harmful an act of retaliatory discrimination must be in order to fall within the provision's scope. . . .

[W]e conclude . . . the antiretaliation provision extends beyond workplace-related or employment-related retaliatory acts and harm. . . .

The antiretaliation provision protects an individual . . . from retaliation that produces an injury or harm. [A] plaintiff must show that a reasonable employee would have found the challenged action materially adverse, 'which in this context means it well might have 'dissuaded a reasonable worker from making or supporting a charge of discrimination.'' . . .

Applying this standard . . . , we believe that there was a sufficient evidentiary basis to support the jury's verdict on White's retaliation claim. The jury found that two . . . actions amounted to retaliation: the reassignment . . . from forklift duty . . . and the 37–day suspension without pay. . . .

Our holding today makes clear that the jury was not required to find that the challenged actions were related to the terms or conditions of employment. And insofar as the jury also found that the actions were 'materially adverse,' its findings are adequately supported. . . .

We do not find Burlington's . . . reference to the nature of Title VII's remedies convincing. After all, throughout its history, Title VII has provided for injunctions to 'bar like discrimination in the future,' an important form of relief. . . .

Neither do we find convincing any claim of insufficient evidence. . . . Many reasonable employees would find a month without a paycheck to be a serious hardship. And White described to the jury the . . . hardship that 37 days of having 'no income, no money' in fact caused. . . . Thus, the jury's conclusion that the 37–day suspension without pay was materially adverse was a reasonable one. . . .

For these reasons, the judgment of the Court of Appeals is affirmed."

V. JUSTICE VOTE

9 Pro ACLU Side vs. 0 Con Opposing Side

ACLU Side (Respondent / Appellee)

1. Breyer, S. – Wrote majority opinion
2. Ginsburg, R. – Joined majority opinion
3. Souter, D. – Joined majority opinion
4. Stevens, J. – Joined majority opinion
5. Thomas, C. – Joined majority opinion
6. Alito, S. – Wrote concurring opinion
7. Scalia, A. – Joined majority opinion
8. Kennedy, A. – Joined majority opinion
9. Roberts, J. – Joined majority opinion

VI. A WIN OR LOSS FOR THE ACLU?

The ACLU filed as amicus curiae urging affirmance; the Supreme Court affirmed the Court of Appeals' decision by a 9-0 vote, giving the ACLU an apparent win.

1004. Woodford v. Ngo

(Decided June 22, 2006; 548 U.S. 81)

I. ISSUE

A. Issues Discussed

Prison, civil rights, federal, state

B. Legal Question Presented

"[W]hether a prisoner can satisfy the Prison Litigation Reform Act's exhaustion requirement, 42 U.S.C. § 1997e(a), by filing an untimely or otherwise procedurally defective administrative grievance or appeal."

C. Supreme Court's Answer

"We hold that proper exhaustion of administrative remedies is necessary."

II. CASE SUMMARY

A. Background

"Congress enacted the Prison Litigation Reform Act of 1995 (PLRA) in 1996 in the wake of a sharp rise in prisoner litigation in the federal courts. . . .

A centerpiece of the PLRA's effort 'to reduce the quantity . . . of prisoner suits' is an 'invigorated' exhaustion provision, § 1997e(a). . . .

Exhaustion is no longer left to the discretion of the district court, but is mandatory. . . . Indeed, . . . a prisoner must now exhaust administrative remedies even where the relief sought—monetary damages—cannot be granted by the administrative process. . . .

California has a grievance system for prisoners who seek to challenge their conditions of confinement. . . .

Respondent is a prisoner . . . . [R]espondent was placed in administrative segregation for allegedly engaging in 'inappropriate activity' in the prison chapel. Two months later, respondent was returned to the general population, but . . . prohibited from participating in 'special programs,' including a variety of religious activities. Approximately six months after that restriction was imposed, respondent filed a grievance . . . . That grievance was rejected as untimely because it was not filed within 15 working days of the action . . . .

Respondent appealed that decision internally without success, and subsequently sued petitioners . . . under 42 U.S.C. § 1983 . . . . The District Court granted petitioners' motion to dismiss because respondent had not fully exhausted his administrative remedies . . . .

The Court of Appeals for the Ninth Circuit reversed and held that respondent had exhausted administrative remedies . . . because no such remedies remained available . . . ."

The Supreme Court granted certiorari to review the case.

B. Counsel of Record / ACLU Attorney

ACLU Side (Respondent / Appellee): Meir Feder argued the cause for appellee. With him on the brief were Charles R. A. Morse and Donald B. Ayer.

Opposing Side (Petitioner / Appellant): Jennifer G. Perkell, Deputy Attorney General of California, argued the cause for appellants. With her on the briefs were Bill Lockyer, Attorney General, Manuel M. Madeiros, State Solicitor General, James M. Humes, Chief Assistant Attorney General, Frances T. Grunder, Senior Assistant Attorney General, and Thomas S. Patterson, Supervising Deputy Attorney General.

Dan Himmelfarb argued the cause for the United States as amicus curiae.

III. AMICI CURIAE

ACLU Side (Respondent / Appellee)

Brief of amici curiae filed on behalf of the American Civil Liberties Union, American Civil Liberties Union of Northern California, Legal Aid Society of the City of New York, Ohio Justice and Policy Center, Prison Law Office, Prisoners' Legal Services of New York, and the Uptown People's Law Center by Margo Schlanger, David C. Fathi, Elizabeth Alexander, Steven R. Shapiro, Steven Banks, and John Boston.

Brief of amici curiae filed on behalf of the American Bar Association by Michael S. Greco.

Brief of amici curiae filed on behalf of the Jerome N. Frank Legal Services Organization of the Yale Law School by Giovanna Shay.

Brief of amici curiae filed on behalf of Law Professors by Kermit Roosevelt III, Erwin Chemerinsky, David L. Franklin, Amanda Frost, Seth Kreimer, Daniel Manville, John Oakley, Malla Pollack, and David Rudovsky, all pro se.

Opposing Side (Petitioner / Appellant)

Brief of amici curiae filed on behalf of Dan Himmelfarb, Solicitor General Clement, Assistant Attorney General Keisler, Deputy Solicitor General Garre, and Barbara L. Herwig.

Brief of amici curiae filed on behalf of the State of New York et al. by Eliot Spitzer, Attorney General of New York, Caitlin J. Halligan, Solicitor General, Robert H. Easton, Deputy Solicitor General, and Richard Dearing, Assistant Solicitor General, and by the Attorneys General for their respective jurisdictions as follows: Troy King of Alabama, Terry Goddard of Arizona, Mike Beebe of Arkansas, John W. Suthers of Colorado, Carl C. Danberg of Delaware, Robert J. Spagnoletti of the District of Columbia, Thurbert E. Baker of Georgia, Mark J. Bennett of Hawaii, Lawrence G. Wasden of Idaho, Lisa Madigan of Illinois, Thomas J. Miller of Iowa, Phill Kline of Kansas, Thomas F. Reilly of Massachusetts, Michael A. Cox of Michigan, Jeremiah W. (Jay) Nixon of Missouri, Mike McGrath of Montana, Jon Bruning of Nebraska, George J. Chanos of Nevada, Wayne Stenehjem of North Dakota, Jim Petro of Ohio, W. A. Drew Edmondson of Oklahoma, Hardy Myers of Oregon, Thomas W. Corbett, Jr., of Pennsylvania, Henry McMaster of South Carolina, Greg Abbott of Texas, Mark L. Shurtleff of Utah, William H. Sorrell of Vermont, Judith Williams Jagdmann of Virginia, Kerry E. Drue of the Virgin Islands, and Rob McKenna of Washington.

IV. THE SUPREME COURT'S DECISION

"The PLRA provides as follows:

'No action shall be brought with respect to prison conditions under section 1983 of this title, or any other Federal law, by a prisoner confined in any jail, prison, or other correctional facility until such administrative remedies as are available are exhausted.' § 1997e(a) (2000 ed.) (emphasis added).

There is no dispute that this language requires a prisoner to 'exhaust' administrative remedies, but the parties differ sharply in their understanding of the meaning of this requirement. Petitioners argue that this provision requires proper exhaustion. This means, according to petitioners, that a prisoner must complete the administrative review process in accordance with the applicable procedural rules, including deadlines, as a precondition to bringing suit in federal court. Respondent, on the other hand, argues that this provision demands what he terms 'exhaustion simpliciter.' In his view, § 1997e(a) simply means that a prisoner may not bring suit in federal court until administrative remedies are no longer available. Under this interpretation, the reason why administrative remedies are no longer available is irrelevant. . . .

The key for determining which of these interpretations of § 1997e(a) is correct lies in the term of art 'exhausted.' . . .

Proper exhaustion demands compliance with an agency's deadlines and other critical procedural rules because no adjudicative system can function effectively without imposing some orderly structure on the course of its proceedings. . . .

The habeas statute generally requires a state prisoner to exhaust state remedies before filing a habeas petition in federal court. . . .

With this background in mind, we are persuaded that the PLRA exhaustion requirement requires proper exhaustion. . . .

Respondent's remaining arguments regarding the interpretation of 42 U.S.C. § 1997e(a) are unconvincing. . . .

[W]e reverse the judgment of the Court of Appeals for the Ninth Circuit and remand . . . ."

V. JUSTICE VOTE

3 Pro ACLU Side vs. 6 Con Opposing Side

ACLU Side (Respondent / Appellee)

1. Stevens, J. – Wrote dissenting opinion
2. Ginsburg, R. – Joined Stevens' dissent
3. Souter, D. – Joined Stevens' dissent

Opposing Side (Petitioner / Appellant)

1. Alito, S. – Wrote majority opinion
2. Thomas, C. – Joined majority opinion
3. Breyer, S. – Wrote concurring opinion
4. Scalia, A. – Joined majority opinion
5. Kennedy, A. – Joined majority opinion
6. Roberts, J. – Joined majority opinion

VI. A WIN OR LOSS FOR THE ACLU?

The ACLU filed as amicus curiae urging affirmance; the Supreme Court reversed the Court of Appeals' decision by a 6-3 vote, giving the ACLU an apparent loss.

1005. Randall v. Sorrell

(Decided June 26, 2006; 548 U.S. 230)

I. ISSUE

A. Issues Discussed

1st Amendment, press, speech, association, voting rights

B. Legal Question Presented

Whether "a Vermont campaign finance statute that limits both (1) the amounts that candidates for state office may spend on their campaigns (expenditure limitations) and (2) the amounts that individuals, organizations, and political parties may contribute to those campaigns (contribution limitations)" violates the First Amendment.

C. Supreme Court's Answer

"We hold that both sets of limitations are inconsistent with the First Amendment."

II. CASE SUMMARY

A. Background

"In 1997, Vermont enacted a . . . stringent campaign finance law . . . . Act 64 . . . imposes mandatory expenditure limits on the total amount a candidate for state office can spend during a 'two-year general election cycle,' i.e., the primary plus the general election . . . .

Act 64 also imposes strict contribution limits. . . .

A political committee is subject to these same limits. So is a political party, defined broadly . . . . Thus, for example, the statute treats the local, state, and national affiliates of the Democratic Party as if they were a single entity . . . .

The Act also imposes a limit . . . upon the amount any individual can give to a political party during a 2-year general election cycle.

The petitioners are individuals who have run for state office . . . , citizens who vote in . . . and contribute to . . . campaigns, and political parties and committees that participate in Vermont politics. Soon after Act 64 became law, they brought this lawsuit . . . .

The District Court agreed with the petitioners that the Act's expenditure limits violate the First Amendment. The court also held unconstitutional the Act's limits on the contributions of political parties to candidates. At the same time, the court found the Act's other contribution limits constitutional.

Both sides appealed. A divided panel of the Court of Appeals for the Second Circuit held that all of the Act's contribution limits are constitutional. It also held that the Act's expenditure limits may be constitutional."

The Supreme Court granted certiorari to review the case.

B. Counsel of Record / ACLU Attorney

ACLU Side (Petitioner / Appellant): James Bopp, Jr., argued the cause for appellants in Nos. 04–1528 and 04–1530. On the briefs for appellants in No. 04–1528 were Peter F. Langrock, Mitchell L. Pearl, and Mark J. Lopez, Steven R. Shapiro, and Joel M. Gora of the American Civil Liberties Union Foundation. Mr. Bopp filed briefs for the Vermont Republican State Committee et al., appellants in No. 04–1530.

Opposing Side (Respondent / Appellee): William H. Sorrell, Attorney General of Vermont, pro se, argued the cause for appellees in Nos. 04–1528 and 04– 1530 and cross-petitioners in No. 04–1697. With him on the brief were Timothy B. Tomasi, Eve Jacobs-Carnahan, and Bridget C. Asay, Assistant Attorneys General, and Carter G. Phillips.

Brenda Wright argued the cause for appellees/cross-petitioners Vermont Public Interest Research Group et al. With her on the brief were Lisa J. Danetz, John C. Bonifaz, Thomas C. Goldstein, and Scott P. Lewis.

III. AMICI CURIAE

ACLU Side (Petitioner / Appellant)

Brief of amici curiae filed on behalf of the American Federation of Labor and Congress of Industrial Organizations by Jonathan P. Hiatt, Laurence E. Gold, and Michael B. Trister.

Brief of amici curiae filed on behalf of Senator Mitch McConnell by Theodore B. Olson and Douglas R. Cox.

Brief of amici curiae filed on behalf of the Republican National Committee by Bobby R. Burchfield, M. Miller Baker, and Thomas J. Josefiak.

Opposing Side (Respondent / Appellee)

Brief of amici curiae filed on behalf of Heidi Behrens-Benedict by Scott N. Auby.

Brief of amici curiae filed on behalf of Senator John F. Reed by Donald B. Verrilli, Jr.

Brief of amici curiae filed on behalf of the State of Connecticut et al. by Richard Blumenthal, Attorney General of Connecticut, and Jane R. Rosenberg, Assistant Attorney General, and by the Attorneys General for their respective States as follows: Terry Goddard of Arizona, Mike Beebe of Arkansas, Bill Lockyer of California, Lisa Madigan of Illinois, Tom Miller of Iowa, Gregory D. Stumbo of Kentucky, J. Joseph Curran, Jr., of Maryland, Mike Hatch of Minnesota, Jim Hood of Mississippi, Jeremiah W. (Jay) Nixon of Missouri, Mike McGrath of Montana, Patricia A. Madrid of New Mexico, Eliot Spitzer of New York, W. A. Drew Edmondson of Oklahoma, Patrick Lynch of Rhode Island, Peggy A. Lautenschlager of Wisconsin, and Patrick J. Crank of Wyoming.

Brief of amici curiae filed on behalf of the Secretary of State of New Hampshire et al. by Philip Allen Lacovara, Charles A. Rothfeld, and Daniel T. Brown.

Brief of amici curiae filed on behalf of the Democratic National Committee by Joseph E. Sandler.

Brief of amici curiae filed on behalf of the Center for Democracy and Election Management at American University by Ilann M. Maazel.

Brief of amici curiae filed on behalf of ReclaimDemocracy.org by Daniel J. H. Greenwood.

Brief of amici curiae filed on behalf of the Equal Justice Society et al. by Martin R. Glick.

Brief of amici curiae filed on behalf of TheRestofUs.org et al. by Douglas R. M. Nazarian, Patricia A. Brannan, and Martha M. Tierney.

Brief of amici curiae filed on behalf of Current and Former State Court Justices and Judges by Deborah Goldberg.

Brief of amici curiae filed on behalf of Bill Bradley et al. by Mark C. Alexander, John J. Gibbons, and Lawrence S. Lustberg.

Brief of amici curiae filed on behalf of Norman Dorsen et al. by Burt Neuborne and Mr. Dorsen, pro se.

Brief of amici curiae filed on behalf of Senator John McCain et al. by Seth P. Waxman, Roger M. Witten, Randolph D. Moss, Bradley S. Phillips, Donald J. Simon, Alan Morrison, J. Gerald Hebert, Trevor Potter, Paul Ryan, Charles G. Curtis, Jr., Fred Wertheimer, and Scott L. Nelson.

Brief of amici curiae filed on behalf of the Center for Competitive Politics et al. by Erik S. Jaffe.

IV. THE SUPREME COURT'S DECISION

"We turn first to the Act's expenditure limits. Do those limits violate the First Amendment's free speech guarantees? . . .

The respondents recognize that, in respect to expenditure limits, Buckley appears to be a controlling—and unfavorable—precedent. They seek to overcome that precedent in two ways. First, they ask us in effect to overrule Buckley. . . .

We can find here no such special justification that would require us to overrule Buckley. . . .

The respondents also ask us to distinguish these cases from Buckley. But we can find no significant basis for that distinction. . . .

And, given Buckley's continued authority, we must conclude that Act 64's expenditure limits violate the First Amendment. . . .

We turn now to . . . the constitutionality of Act 64's contribution limits. . . .

In sum, Act 64's contribution limits are substantially lower than both the limits we have previously upheld and comparable limits in other States. . . . We consequently must examine the record independently and carefully to determine whether Act 64's contribution limits are 'closely drawn' to match the State's interests. . . .

Our examination . . . convinces us that, from a constitutional perspective, Act 64's contribution limits are too restrictive. . . .

[F]ive sets of considerations, taken together, lead us to conclude that Act 64's contribution limits are not narrowly tailored. Rather, the Act burdens First Amendment interests by threatening to inhibit effective advocacy by those who seek election, particularly challengers; its contribution limits mute the voice of political parties; they hamper participation in campaigns through volunteer activities; and they are not indexed for inflation. . . . It disproportionately burdens numerous First Amendment interests, and consequently, in our view, violates the First Amendment. . . .

We conclude that Act 64's expenditure limits violate the First Amendment as interpreted in Buckley v. Valeo. We also conclude that the specific details of Act 64's contribution limits require us to hold that those limits violate the First Amendment, for they burden First Amendment interests in a manner that is disproportionate to the public purposes they were enacted to advance. . . . Accordingly, the judgment of the Court of Appeals is reversed, and the cases are remanded . . . ."

V. JUSTICE VOTE

6 Pro ACLU Side vs. 3 Con Opposing Side

ACLU Side (Petitioner / Appellant)

1. Breyer, S. – Wrote majority opinion
2. Alito, S. – Wrote concurring opinion
3. Thomas, C. – Wrote concurring opinion
4. Scalia, A. – Joined Thomas' concurrence
5. Kennedy, A. – Wrote concurring opinion
6. Roberts, J. – Joined majority opinion

Opposing Side (Respondent / Appellee)

1. Stevens, J. – Wrote dissenting opinion, joined Souter's dissent in part
2. Souter, D. – Wrote dissenting opinion
3. Ginsburg, R. – Joined Souter's dissent

VI. A WIN OR LOSS FOR THE ACLU?

The ACLU argued the cause for appellants urging reversal of the judgment of the Court of Appeals; the Supreme Court reversed in a 6-3 vote, giving the ACLU an apparent win.

1006. Beard v. Banks

(Decided June 28, 2006; 548 U.S. 521)

I. ISSUE

A. Issues Discussed

Prison

B. Legal Question Presented

"[W]hether a Pennsylvania prison policy that 'denies newspapers, magazines, and photographs' to a group of specially dangerous and recalcitrant inmates 'violate[s] the First Amendment.'"

C. Supreme Court's Answer

"While we do not deny the constitutional importance of the interests in question, we find, on the basis of the record now before us, that prison officials have set forth adequate legal support for the policy. And the plaintiff, a prisoner who attacks the policy, has failed to set forth 'specific facts' that, in light of the deference that courts must show to the prison officials, could warrant a determination in his favor."

II. CASE SUMMARY

A. Background

"The prison regulation at issue applies to certain prisoners housed in Pennsylvania's Long Term Segregation Unit. The LTSU is the most restrictive of the three special units . . . reserved for the Commonwealth's 'most incorrigible, recalcitrant inmates.' . . .

At all three units, residents are typically confined to cells for 23 hours a day, have limited . . . the commissary or . . . visitors, and . . . may not watch television or listen to the radio.

Prisoners at level 2 of the LTSU face the most severe form of the restrictions listed above. They have no access to the commissary, they may have only one visitor per month (an immediate family member), and they are not allowed phone calls except in emergencies. In addition they (unlike all other prisoners in the Commonwealth) are restricted in the manner at issue here: They have no access to newspapers, magazines, or personal photographs. They are nonetheless permitted legal and personal correspondence, religious and legal materials, two library books, and writing paper. . . .

Ronald Banks, . . . then a prisoner confined to LTSU level 2, filed this federal-court action . . . . Banks claimed that the level 2 policy (Policy) forbidding inmates all access to newspapers, magazines, and photographs bears no reasonable relation to any legitimate penological objective and consequently violates the First Amendment. . . .

On the basis of the record . . . , the Magistrate recommended that the District Court grant the Secretary's motion for summary judgment and deny that of Banks. The District Court accepted the Magistrate's recommendation.

On appeal, a divided Third Circuit panel reversed . . . ."

The Supreme Court granted certiorari to review the case.

B. Counsel of Record / ACLU Attorney

ACLU Side (Respondent / Appellee): Jere Krakoff argued the cause for appellee. With him on the brief was Andrew Shubin.

Opposing Side (Petitioner / Appellant): Louis J. Rovelli, Executive Deputy Attorney General of Pennsylvania, argued the cause for appellant. With him on the briefs were Thomas W. Corbett, Jr., Attorney General, Calvin R. Koons and Kemal A. Mericli, Senior Deputy Attorneys General, and John G. Knorr III, Chief Deputy Attorney General.

Jonathan L. Marcus argued the cause for the United States as amicus curiae.

III. AMICI CURIAE

ACLU Side (Respondent / Appellee)

Brief of amici curiae filed on behalf of the American Civil Liberties Union, ACLU of Pennsylvania, The Legal Aid Society, People for the American Way Foundation, American Friends Service Committee, and California Prison Focus by David C. Fathi, Jeffrey M. Monks, Elizabeth Alexander, Steven R. Shapiro, Witold J. Walczak, Steven Banks, John Boston, Deborah Liu, Charles F.A. Carbone, and Elliot M. Mincberg.

Brief of amici curiae filed on behalf of the Becket Fund for Religious Liberty by Anthony R. Picarello, Jr.

Brief of amici curiae filed on behalf of Prison Legal News et al. by Sanford Jay Rosen, Lucy A. Dalglish, Gregg P. Leslie, and Michael A. Bamberger.

Brief of amici curiae filed on behalf of Lumumba Kenyatta Incumaa by Justin S. Antonipillai.

Opposing Side (Petitioner / Appellant)

Brief of amici curiae filed on behalf of the United States by Jonathan L. Marcus, Solicitor General Clement, Assistant Attorney General Keisler, Deputy Solicitor General Garre, Sri Srinivasan, Barbara L. Herwig, and Edward Himmelfarb.

Brief of amici curiae filed on behalf of the Council of State Governments et al. by Richard Ruda and James I. Crowley.

IV. THE SUPREME COURT'S DECISION

"Turner v. Safley, 482 U.S. 78 (1987), and Overton v. Bazzetta, 539 U.S. 126 (2003), contain the basic substantive legal standards governing this case. . . . Turner reconciled these principles by holding that restrictive prison regulations are permissible if they are "reasonably related' to legitimate penological interests,' and are not an "exaggerated response" to such objectives.

The Secretary . . . set forth several justifications for the prison's policy . . . . We need go no further than the first justification, that of providing increased incentives for better prison behavior. Applying the well-established substantive and procedural standards set forth . . . , we find . . . that the Secretary's justification is adequate. And that finding here warrants summary judgment in the Secretary's favor. . . .

[T]he LTSU's 40 inmates, about 0.01 percent of the total prison population, constitute the "worst of the worst," those who 'have proven by the history of their behavior in prison, the necessity of holding them in the rigorous regime of confinement' of the LTSU. . . .

[W]e believe that the first rationale itself satisfies Turner's requirements. First, the statement and deposition set forth a "valid, rational connection" between the Policy and "legitimate penological objectives." . . .

As to the second factor, the statement and deposition make clear that, as long as the inmate remains at level 2, no 'alternative means of exercising the right' remain open to him. . . .

As to the third factor, the statement and deposition indicate that, were prison authorities to seek to 'accommodat[e] . . . the asserted constitutional right,' the resulting 'impact' would be negative. . . . Similarly, as to the fourth factor, neither the statement nor the deposition describes, points to, or calls to mind any 'alternative method of accommodating the claimant's constitutional complaint . . . that fully accommodates the prisoner's rights at de minimis cost to valid penological interests.' . . .

Here prison authorities responded adequately through their statement and deposition to the allegations in the complaint. And the plaintiff failed to point to "specific facts" in the record that could 'lead a rational trier of fact to find' in his favor.

The judgment of the Court of Appeals for the Third Circuit is reversed, and the case is remanded . . . ."

V. JUSTICE VOTE

2 Pro ACLU Side vs. 6 Con Opposing Side

ACLU Side (Respondent / Appellee)

1. Ginsburg, R. – Wrote dissenting opinion, joined Stevens' dissent
2. Stevens, J. – Wrote dissenting opinion

Opposing Side (Petitioner / Appellant)

1. Breyer, S. – Wrote majority opinion
2. Thomas, C. – Wrote concurring opinion
3. Scalia, A. – Joined Thomas' concurrence
4. Kennedy, A. – Joined majority opinion
5. Souter, D. – Joined majority opinion
6. Roberts, J. – Joined majority opinion

Alito, S. – Took no part in the decision.

VI. A WIN OR LOSS FOR THE ACLU?

The ACLU filed as amicus curiae urging affirmance; the Supreme Court reversed the Court of Appeals' decision by a 6-2 vote, giving the ACLU an apparent loss.

1007. Hamdan v. Rumsfeld

(Decided June 29, 2006; 548 U.S. 557)

I. ISSUE

A. Issues Discussed

Military

B. Legal Question Presented

"[W]hether the military commission convened to try Hamdan has authority to do so, and whether Hamdan may rely on the Geneva Conventions in these proceedings."

C. Supreme Court's Answer

"[W]e conclude that the military commission convened to try Hamdan lacks power to proceed because its structure and procedures violate both the UCMJ and the Geneva Conventions. Four of us also conclude . . . that the offense with which Hamdan has been charged is not an 'offens[e] that by . . . the law of war may be tried by military commissions.'"

II. CASE SUMMARY

A. Background

"Petitioner Salim Ahmed Hamdan, a Yemeni national, is in custody at an American prison in Guantanamo Bay, Cuba. In November 2001, . . . Hamdan was captured . . . . In June 2002, he was transported to Guantanamo Bay. Over a year later, the President deemed him eligible for trial by military commission for then-unspecified crimes. After another year had passed, Hamdan was charged with one count of conspiracy 'to commit . . . offenses triable by military commission.'

Hamdan filed petitions for writs of habeas corpus and mandamus to challenge the Executive Branch's intended means of prosecuting this charge. He concedes that a court-martial constituted in accordance with the Uniform Code of Military Justice (UCMJ) would have authority to try him. His objection is that the military commission the President has convened lacks such authority, for two principal reasons: First, neither congressional Act nor the common law of war supports trial by this commission for the crime of conspiracy—an offense that, Hamdan says, is not a violation of the law of war. Second, Hamdan contends, the procedures that the President has adopted to try him violate the most basic tenets of military and international law, including the principle that a defendant must be permitted to see and hear the evidence against him.

The District Court granted Hamdan's request for a writ of habeas corpus. The Court of Appeals for the District of Columbia Circuit reversed."

The Supreme Court granted certiorari to review the case.

B. Counsel of Record / ACLU Attorney

ACLU Side (Petitioner / Appellant): Neal Katyal argued the cause for appellant. With him on the briefs were Harry H. Schneider, Jr., Joseph M. McMillan, Charles C. Sipos, Charles Swift, Thomas C. Goldstein, Amy Howe, and Kevin K. Russell.

Opposing Side (Respondent / Appellee): Solicitor General Clement argued the cause for appellees. With him on the brief were Assistant Attorney General Keisler, Deputy Solicitor General Garre, Deputy Assistant Attorney General Katsas, Jonathan L. Marcus, Kannon K. Shanmugam, Douglas N. Letter, and Robert M. Loeb.

III. AMICI CURIAE

ACLU Side (Petitioner / Appellant)

Brief of amici curiae filed on behalf of the American Civil Liberties Union by Steven R. Shapiro, Ben Wizner, Omar C. Jadwat, and Lee Gelernt.

Brief of amici curiae filed on behalf of the American Jewish Committee et al. by Marvin L. Gray, Jr., Jeffrey L. Fisher, Jeffrey P. Sinensky, Kara H. Stein, John W. Whitehead, Elliot M. Mincberg, Arthur H. Bryant, and Victoria W. Ni.

Brief of amici curiae filed on behalf of the Association of the Bar of the City of New York et al. by James J. Benjamin, Jr., and Steven M. Pesner.

Brief of amici curiae filed on behalf of the Brennan Center for Justice et al. by Sidney S. Rosdeitcher and Jonathan Hafetz.

Brief of amici curiae filed on behalf of the Cato Institute by Timothy Lynch.

Brief of amici curiae filed on behalf of the Center for Constitutional Rights et al. by Barbara J. Olshansky and William H. Goodman.

Brief of amici curiae filed on behalf of International Law Professors by Linda A. Malone and Jordan J. Paust.

Brief of amici curiae filed on behalf of Law Professors by Claudia Callaway.

Brief of amici curiae filed on behalf of Military Law Historians, Scholars, and Practitioners by Teresa Wynn Roseborough, Charles Lester, Jr., John A. Chandler, and Elizabeth V. Tanis.

Brief of amici curiae filed on behalf of the National Association of Criminal Defense Lawyers by Donald G. Rehkopf, Jr.

Brief of amici curiae filed on behalf of the National Institute of Military Justice et al. by Eugene R. Fidell, Stephen A. Saltzburg, Kathleen A. Duignan, and Diane Marie Amann.

Brief of amici curiae filed on behalf of Specialists in Conspiracy and International Law by George P. Fletcher, pro se.

Brief of amici curiae filed on behalf of the Yemeni National Organization for Defending Rights and Freedoms by Lawrence D. Rosenberg.

Brief of amici curiae filed on behalf of Madeleine K. Albright et al. by Harold Hongju Koh and Jonathan M. Freiman.

Brief of amici curiae filed on behalf of David Brahms et al. by Andrew J. Pincus, Jay C. Johnson, and Andrew Tauber.

Brief of amici curiae filed on behalf of Norman Dorsen et al. by Burt Neuborne.

Brief of amici curiae filed on behalf of Louise Doswald-Beck et al. by Bridget Arimond, David J. Scheffer, and Steven A. Kaufman.

Brief of amici curiae filed on behalf of Richard A. Epstein et al. by Aaron M. Panner, Joseph S. Hall, and Mr. Epstein, pro se.

Brief of amici curiae filed on behalf of Louis Fisher by Lawrence S. Lustberg.

Brief of amici curiae filed on behalf of Ibrahim Ahmed Mahmoud al Qosi by Paul S. Reichler and Sharon A. Shaffer.

Brief of amici curiae filed on behalf of Binyam Mohamed by Clive A. Stafford Smith and Joseph Margulies.

Brief of amici curiae filed on behalf of Jack N. Rakove et al. by Pamela S. Karlan.

Brief of amici curiae filed on behalf of the Human Rights Committee of the Bar of England and Wales et al. by Stephen J. Pollak and John Townsend Rich.

Brief of amici curiae filed on behalf of the Center for National Security Studies et al. by John Payton, Seth P. Waxman, Paul R. Q. Wolfson, Kate Martin, and Joseph Onek.

Brief of amici curiae filed on behalf of Certain Former Federal Judges by Paul C. Saunders.

Brief of amici curiae filed on behalf of Legal Scholars and Historians by Daniel C. Tepstein.

Brief of amici curiae filed on behalf of the Office of Chief Defense Counsel, Office of Military Commissions, by Dwight H. Sullivan and Michael D. Mori.

Brief of amici curiae filed on behalf of Retired Generals and Admirals et al. by David H. Remes.

Brief of amici curiae filed on behalf of the Urban Morgan Institute for Human Rights by Christopher J. Wright and Timothy J. Simeone.
Brief of amici curiae filed on behalf of Lawrence M. Friedman et al. by William F. Alderman.
Brief of amici curiae filed on behalf of Ryan Goodman et al. by Mark A. Packman.
Brief of amici curiae filed on behalf of Louis Henkin et al. by Carlos M. Vázquez, pro se.
Brief of amici curiae filed on behalf of David Hicks by Joshua L. Dratel, Mr. Mori, Marc A. Goldman, and Michael B. DeSanctis.
Brief of amici curiae filed on behalf of Arthur R. Miller by Mr. Remes.
Brief of amici curiae filed on behalf of Richard D. Rosen et al. by Steven H. Goldblatt.
Brief of amici curiae filed on behalf of More Than 300 Detainees Incarcerated at U. S. Naval Station, Guantanamo Bay, Cuba, et al. by Thomas B. Wilner, Neil H. Koslowe, and Kristine A. Huskey.
Brief of amici curiae filed on behalf of 422 Current and Former Members of the United Kingdom and European Union Parliaments by Claude B. Stansbury.
Brief of amici curiae filed on behalf of Human Rights First et al. by Robert P. LoBue and Deborah Pearlstein.

Opposing Side (Respondent / Appellee)

Brief of amici curiae filed on behalf of the American Center for Law and Justice et al. by Jay Alan Sekulow, Stuart J. Roth, James M. Henderson, Sr., Colby M. May, and Robert W. Ash.
Brief of amici curiae filed on behalf of Common Defence by Daniel P. Collins.
Brief of amici curiae filed on behalf of Former Attorneys General of the United States et al. by Andrew G. McBride and Kathryn Comerford Todd.
Brief of amici curiae filed on behalf of the Washington Legal Foundation et al. by Daniel J. Popeo and Richard A. Samp.
Brief of amici curiae filed on behalf of the Criminal Justice Legal Foundation by Kent S. Scheidegger.
Brief of amici curiae filed on behalf of Senator Lindsey Graham et al. by Jeffrey A. Lamken.

IV. THE SUPREME COURT'S DECISION

"The military commission, a tribunal neither mentioned in the Constitution nor created by statute, was born of military necessity. . . .

Together, the UCMJ, the AUMF, and the DTA at most acknowledge a general Presidential authority to convene military commissions in circumstances where justified under the 'Constitution and laws,' including the law of war. Absent a more specific congressional authorization, the task of this Court is, as it was in Quirin, to decide whether Hamdan's military commission is so justified. It is to that inquiry we now turn. . . .

The common law governing military commissions may be gleaned from past practice . . . .

Quirin is the model the Government invokes most frequently to defend the commission convened to try Hamdan. . . . Quirin represents the high-water mark of military power to try enemy combatants for war crimes. . . .

Far from making the requisite substantial showing, the Government has failed even to offer a 'merely colorable' case for inclusion of conspiracy among those offenses cognizable by law-of-war military commission. . . .

Whether or not the Government has charged Hamdan with an offense against the law of war cognizable by military commission, the commission lacks power to proceed. The UCMJ conditions the President's use of military commissions on compliance not only with the American common law of war, but also with the rest of the UCMJ itself, insofar as applicable, and with the 'rules and precepts of the law of nations,' Quirin—including . . . the four Geneva Conventions signed in 1949. The procedures that the Government has decreed will govern Hamdan's trial by commission violate these laws. . . .

We have assumed, as we must, that the allegations made in the Government's charge against Hamdan are true. We have assumed, moreover, the truth of the message implicit in that charge . . . . It bears emphasizing that Hamdan does not challenge, and we do not today address, the Government's power to detain him for the duration of active hostilities in order to prevent . . . harm. But in undertaking to try Hamdan and subject him to criminal punishment, the Executive is bound to comply with the rule of law . . . .

The judgment of the Court of Appeals is reversed, and the case is remanded . . . ."

V. JUSTICE VOTE

5 Pro ACLU Side vs. 3 Con Opposing Side

ACLU Side (Petitioner / Appellant)

1. Stevens, J. – Wrote majority opinion
2. Breyer, S. – Wrote concurring opinion, joined Kennedy's concurrence in part
3. Kennedy, A. – Wrote concurring opinion, joined Breyer's concurrence
4. Ginsburg, R. – Joined Breyer's concurrence, joined Kennedy's concurrence in part
5. Souter, D. – Joined Breyer's concurrence, joined Kennedy's concurrence in part

Opposing Side (Respondent / Appellee)

1. Alito, S. – Wrote dissenting opinion, joined Scalia's dissent, joined Thomas' dissent in part
2. Thomas, C. – Wrote dissenting opinion, Joined Scalia's dissent, joined Alito's dissent in part
3. Scalia, A. – Wrote dissenting opinion, joined Thomas' dissent, joined Alito's dissent in part

Roberts, J – Took no part in the decision

VI. A WIN OR LOSS FOR THE ACLU?

The ACLU filed as amicus curiae urging reversal of the judgment of the Court of Appeals; the Supreme Court reversed in a 5-3 vote, giving the ACLU an apparent win.

1008. Lopez v. Gonzales

(Decided December 5, 2006; 549 U.S. 47)

I. ISSUE

A. Issues Discussed

Immigration/citizenship

B. Legal Question Presented

"[W]hether conduct made a felony under state law but a misdemeanor under the Controlled Substances Act is a 'felony punishable under the Controlled Substances Act.'"

C. Supreme Court's Answer

"[W]e hold that a state offense constitutes a 'felony punishable under the Controlled Substances Act' only if it proscribes conduct punishable as a felony under that federal law."

II. CASE SUMMARY

A. Background

"The Immigration and Nationality Act . . . defines . . . 'aggravated felony' by a list that mentions 'illicit trafficking in a controlled substance . . . .' . . .

Under the immigration statutes . . . the Attorney General's discretion to cancel the removal of a person otherwise deportable does not reach a convict of an aggravated felony. Nor is an aggravated felon eligible for asylum. And under the sentencing law, the Federal Guidelines attach special significance to the 'aggravated felony' designation . . . .

Although petitioner Jose Antonio Lopez entered the United States illegally in 1986, in 1990 he became a legal permanent resident. In 1997, he was arrested . . . , pleaded guilty to aiding and abetting another person's possession of cocaine, and was sentenced to five years' imprisonment. He was released for good conduct after 15 months.

After his release, the Immigration and Naturalization Service (INS) began removal proceedings against Lopez, on two grounds: that his state conviction was a controlled substance violation, and was also for an aggravated felony. Lopez conceded the controlled substance violation but contested the aggravated felony determination . . . . At first, the Immigration Judge agreed with Lopez. . . . But after the Board of Immigration Appeals (BIA) switched its position on the issue, the same judge ruled that Lopez's drug crime was an aggravated felony . . . . That left Lopez ineligible for cancellation of removal, and the judge ordered him removed. The BIA affirmed, and the Court of Appeals affirmed . . . ."

The Supreme Court granted certiorari to review the case.

B. Counsel of Record / ACLU Attorney

ACLU Side (Petitioner / Appellant): Robert A. Long, Jr., argued the cause for appellant. With him on the briefs was Theodore P. Metzler.

Opposing Side (Respondent / Appellee): Deputy Solicitor General Kneedler argued the cause for appellee. With him on the brief were Solicitor General Clement, Assistant Attorneys General Keisler and Fisher, Deputy Solicitor General Dreeben, Patricia A. Millett, and Donald E. Keener.

III. AMICI CURIAE

ACLU Side (Petitioner / Appellant)

Brief of amici curiae filed on behalf of the NYSDA Immigrant Defense Project, American Civil Liberties Union, American Immigration Lawyers Association, Immigrant Legal Resource Center, National Association of Criminal Defense Lawyers, and National Legal Aid and Defender Association by Christopher J. Meade, Nora Freeman Engstrom, Steven R. Shapiro, Lucas Guttentag, Cecillia D. Wang, Marianne C. Yang, Benita Jain, and Manuel D. Vargas.

Brief of amici curiae filed on behalf of the American Bar Association by Michael S. Greco and David W. DeBruin.

Brief of amici curiae filed on behalf of the Asian American Justice Center et al. by Jayashri Srikantiah.

Brief of amici curiae filed on behalf of the Center for Court Innovation et al. by Nancy Morawetz.

Brief of amici curiae filed on behalf of Former General Counsels of the Immigration and Naturalization Service by Neal Mollen.

Brief of amici curiae filed on behalf of Human Rights First by Linda T. Coberly and Gene C. Schaerr.

Opposing Side (Respondent / Appellee)

Brief of amici curiae filed on behalf of the State of Texas et al. by Greg Abbott, Attorney General of Texas, R. Ted Cruz, Solicitor General, Kent C. Sullivan, First Assistant Attorney General, Don Clemmer, Deputy Attorney General, and Amy Warr, Assistant Solicitor General, and by the Attorneys General for their respective States as follows: Mike Beebe of Arkansas, John W. Suthers of Colorado, Carl C. Danberg of Delaware, Lawrence Wasden of Idaho, Phill Kline of Kansas, Kelly A. Ayotte of New Hampshire, Thomas W. Corbett, Jr., of Pennsylvania, Mark L. Shurtleff of Utah, and Robert F. McDonnell of Virginia.

Brief of amici curiae filed on behalf of the Washington Legal Foundation et al. by Daniel J. Popeo and Richard A. Samp.

IV. THE SUPREME COURT'S DECISION

"The INA makes Lopez guilty of an aggravated felony if he has been convicted of 'illicit trafficking in a controlled substance . . . including,' but not limited to, 'a drug trafficking crime . . . .' Lopez's state conviction was for helping someone else possess cocaine in South Dakota, which state law treated as the equivalent of possessing the drug, a state felony. Mere possession is not, however, a felony under the federal CSA, although possessing more than what one person would have for himself will support conviction for the federal felony of possession with intent to distribute . . . .

Despite this federal misdemeanor treatment, the Government argues that possession's felonious character as a state crime can turn it into an aggravated felony under the INA. . . .

There are a few things wrong with this argument, the first being its incoherence with any commonsense conception of 'illicit trafficking,' the term ultimately being defined. . . .

First, an offense that necessarily counts as 'illicit trafficking' under the INA is a 'drug trafficking crime' under § 924(c), that is, a 'felony punishable under the [CSA].' And if we want to know what felonies might qualify, the place to go is to the definitions of crimes punishable as felonies under the CSA; where else would one naturally look? . . .

The Government stresses that the text does not read 'punishable as a felony,' and that by saying simply 'punishable' Congress left the door open to counting state felonies . . . . But we do not normally speak or write the Government's way. . . .

The Government tries to justify its unusual reading of a defined term in the criminal code on the basis of a single sentence in the INA. But nothing in the penultimate sentence of § 1101(a)(43) suggests that Congress changed the meaning of 'felony punishable under the [CSA]' when it took that phrase from Title 18 and incorporated it into Title 8's definition of 'aggravated felony.' . . .

Finally, the Government's reading would render the law of alien removal and the law of sentencing for illegal entry into the country dependent on varying state criminal classifications . . . . We cannot imagine that Congress took the trouble to incorporate its own statutory scheme of felonies and misdemeanors if it meant courts to ignore it whenever a State chose to punish a given act more heavily. . . .

In sum, we hold that a state offense constitutes a 'felony punishable under the Controlled Substances Act' only if it proscribes conduct punishable as a felony under that federal law. The judgment of the Court of Appeals is reversed, and the case is remanded . . . ."

V. JUSTICE VOTE

8 Pro ACLU Side vs. 1 Con Opposing Side

ACLU Side (Petitioner / Appellant)

1. Souter, D. – Wrote majority opinion
2. Alito, S. – Joined majority opinion
3. Stevens, J. – Joined majority opinion
4. Breyer, S. – Joined majority opinion
5. Scalia, A. – Joined majority opinion
6. Kennedy, A. – Joined majority opinion
7. Ginsburg, R. – Joined majority opinion
8. Roberts, J. – Joined majority opinion

Opposing Side (Respondent / Appellee)

1. Thomas, C. – Wrote dissenting opinion

VI. A WIN OR LOSS FOR THE ACLU?

The ACLU filed as amicus curiae urging reversal of the judgment of the Court of Appeals; the Supreme Court reversed in a 8-1 vote, giving the ACLU an apparent win.

1009. Jones v. Bock

(Decided January 22, 2007; 549 U.S. 199)

I. ISSUE

A. Issues Discussed

Prison

B. Legal Question Presented

Whether "rules requir[ing] a prisoner to allege and demonstrate exhaustion in his complaint, permit[ting] suit only against defendants who were identified by the prisoner in his grievance, and requir[ing] courts to dismiss the entire action if the prisoner fails to satisfy the exhaustion requirement as to any single claim in his complaint" are required by the Prison Litigation Reform Act of 1995.

C. Supreme Court's Answer

The U.S. Supreme Court "conclude[s] that these rules are not required by the PLRA, and that crafting and imposing them exceeds the proper limits on the judicial role."

II. CASE SUMMARY

A. Background

"In an effort to address the large number of prisoner complaints filed in federal court, Congress enacted the Prison Litigation Reform Act of 1995 (PLRA). Among other reforms, the PLRA mandates early judicial screening of prisoner complaints and requires prisoners to exhaust prison grievance procedures before filing suit. The Sixth Circuit . . . adopted several procedural rules designed to implement this exhaustion requirement and facilitate early judicial screening. These rules require a prisoner to allege and demonstrate exhaustion in his complaint, permit suit only against defendants who were identified by the prisoner in his grievance, and require courts to dismiss the entire action if the prisoner fails to satisfy the exhaustion requirement as to any single claim in his complaint. . . .

Petitioners are [three] inmates in the custody of the Michigan Department of Corrections (MDOC). At the time petitioners filed their grievances, MDOC Policy Directive 03.02.130 (Nov. 1, 2000) set forth the applicable grievance procedures. The policy directive describes what issues are grievable and contains instructions for . . . grievances. . . .

Jones sought review in a petition for certiorari, arguing that the Sixth Circuit's heightened pleading requirement and total exhaustion rule contravene the clear language of the Federal Rules of Civil Procedure and the PLRA. Williams and Walton filed a joint petition under this Court's Rule 12.4, contending that the rule requiring every defendant to be named during the grievance process is not required by the PLRA, and also challenging the total exhaustion rule. [The U.S. Supreme Court] granted both petitions for certiorari, and consolidated the cases for . . . review."

B. Counsel of Record / ACLU Attorney

ACLU Side (Petitioner / Appellant): Jean-Claude André argued the cause and filed briefs for appellants.

Opposing Side (Respondent / Appellee): Linda M. Olivieri, Assistant Attorney General of Michigan, argued the cause for appellees. With her on the brief were Michael A. Cox, Attorney General, Thomas L. Casey, Solicitor General, and John L. Thurber, Assistant Attorney General.

III. AMICI CURIAE

ACLU Side (Petitioner / Appellant)

Brief of amici curiae filed on behalf of the American Civil Liberties Union, ACLU of Michigan, The Legal Aid Society, Jerome N. Frank Legal Services Organization, Prison Legal News, Prison Legal Services, Prison and Corrections Section of the Michigan State Bar, Ohio Justice & Policy Center and the Uptown People's Law Center by Jeffrey Monks, Margaret Winter, Elizabeth Alexander, Steven R. Shapiro, Michael J. Steinberg, Kary L. Moss, John Boston, Giovanna Shay, Jerome N. Frank, Paul D. Reingold, Alan Mills, Anthony Pogorzelski, Stephen Hanlon, Sandra Girard, and David A. Singleton.

Opposing Side (Respondent / Appellee)

Brief of amici curiae filed on behalf of the State of New York et al. by Eliot Spitzer, former Attorney General of New York, Caitlin J. Halligan, Solicitor General, Daniel Smirlock, Deputy Solicitor General, Peter H. Schiff, Senior Counsel, and Robert M. Goldfarb and Martin A. Hotvet, Assistant Solicitors General, and by the Attorneys General and former Attorneys General for their respective jurisdictions as follows: Troy King of Alabama, David Ma´ rquez of Alaska, Mike Beebe of Arkansas, Bill Lockyer of California, John W. Suthers of Colorado, Carl C. Danberg of Delaware, Robert J. Spagnoletti of the District of Columbia, Charles J. Crist, Jr., of Florida, Mark J. Bennett of Hawaii, Lawrence G. Wasden of Idaho, Lisa Madigan of Illinois, J. Joseph Curran, Jr., of Maryland, Jeremiah W. (Jay) Nixon of Missouri, Mike McGrath of Montana, Jon Bruning of Nebraska, George J. Chanos of Nevada, Wayne Stenehjem of North Dakota, Jim Petro of Ohio, W. A. Drew Edmondson of Oklahoma, Hardy Myers of Oregon, Thomas W. Corbett, Jr., of Pennsylvania, Patrick Lynch of Rhode Island, Henry McMaster of South Carolina, Lawrence E. Long of South Dakota, Paul G. Summers of Tennessee, Greg Abbott of Texas, Mark L. Shurtleff of Utah, Robert F. McDonnell of Virginia, Rob McKenna of Washington, Darrell V. McGraw, Jr., of West Virginia, Peggy A. Lautenschlager of Wisconsin, and Patrick J. Crank of Wyoming.

IV. THE SUPREME COURT'S DECISION

"There is no question that exhaustion is mandatory under the PLRA and that unexhausted claims cannot be brought in court. What is less clear is whether it falls to the prisoner to plead and demonstrate exhaustion in the complaint, or to the defendant to raise lack of exhaustion as an affirmative defense. . . .

We conclude that failure to exhaust is an affirmative defense . . . , and that inmates are not required to specially plead or demonstrate exhaustion in their complaints. . . .

We do not determine whether the grievances filed by petitioners satisfied the requirement of 'proper exhaustion,' but simply conclude that exhaustion is not per se inadequate simply because an individual later sued was not named in the grievances. We leave it to the court below in the first instance to determine the sufficiency of the exhaustion in these cases. . . .

The final issue concerns how courts should address complaints in which the prisoner has failed to exhaust some, but not all, of the claims asserted in the complaint. All agree that no unexhausted claim may be considered. The issue is whether the court should proceed with the exhausted claims, or instead. . . dismiss the entire action . . . .

[T]he effect of a total exhaustion rule could be that inmates will file various claims in separate suits, to avoid the possibility of an unexhausted claim tainting the others. That would certainly not comport with the purpose of the PLRA to reduce the quantity of inmate suits. Additionally, district judges who delve into a prisoner complaint only to realize it contains an unexhausted claim, requiring dismissal of the entire complaint under the total exhaustion rule, will often have to begin the process all over again when the prisoner refiles. In light of typically short prison grievance time limits, prisoners' refiled complaints will often be identical to what the district court would have considered had it simply dismissed unexhausted claims as it encountered them and proceeded with the exhausted ones. . . .

We are not insensitive to the challenges faced by the lower federal courts in managing their dockets . . . . We once again reiterate, however—as we did unanimously in Leatherman, Swierkiewicz, and Hill—that adopting different and more onerous pleading rules to deal with particular categories of cases should be done through established rulemaking procedures, and not on a case-by-case basis by the courts.

The judgments of the United States Court of Appeals for the Sixth Circuit are reversed, and the cases are remanded . . . ."

V. JUSTICE VOTE

9 Pro ACLU Side vs. 0 Con Opposing Side

ACLU Side (Petitioner / Appellant)

1. Roberts, J. – Wrote majority opinion
2. Alito, S. – Joined majority opinion
3. Stevens, J. – Joined majority opinion
4. Thomas, C. – Joined majority opinion
5. Breyer, S. – Joined majority opinion
6. Scalia, A. – Joined majority opinion
7. Kennedy, A. – Joined majority opinion
8. Ginsburg, R. – Joined majority opinion
9. Souter, D. – Joined majority opinion

VI. A WIN OR LOSS FOR THE ACLU?

The ACLU filed as amicus curiae urging reversal of the judgment of the Court of Appeals; the Supreme Court reversed in a 9-0 vote, giving the ACLU an apparent win.

1010. Lawrence v. Florida

(Decided February 20, 2007; 549 U.S. 327)

I. ISSUE

A. Issues Discussed

Criminal procedure

B. Legal Question Presented

"[W]hether a state application is still 'pending' when the state courts have entered a final judgment on the matter but a petition for certiorari has been filed in [the U.S. Supreme] Court."

C. Supreme Court's Answer

"We hold that it is not."

II. CASE SUMMARY

A. Background

"The trial court sentenced Lawrence to death. The Florida Supreme Court affirmed . . . , and [the U.S. Supreme] Court denied certiorari on January 20, 1998.

On January 19, 1999, 364 days later, Lawrence filed an application for state postconviction relief in a Florida trial court. The court denied relief, and the Florida Supreme Court affirmed . . . . Lawrence sought review of the denial of state postconviction relief . . . . [The U.S. Supreme Court] denied certiorari on March 24, 2003.

While Lawrence's petition for certiorari was pending, he filed the present federal habeas application. The Federal District Court dismissed it as untimely under § 2244(d)'s 1-year limitations period. All but one day of the limitations period had lapsed during the 364 days between the time Lawrence's conviction became final and when he filed for state postconviction relief. The limitations period was then tolled while the Florida courts entertained his state application. After the Florida Supreme Court issued its mandate, Lawrence waited another 113 days—well beyond the 1 day that remained in the limitations period—to file his federal habeas application. As a consequence, his federal application could be considered timely only if the limitations period continued to be tolled during this Court's consideration of his petition for certiorari. [T]he District Court concluded that Lawrence had only one day to file a federal habeas application after the Florida Supreme Court issued its mandate. The Eleventh Circuit affirmed."

The Supreme Court granted certiorari to review the case.

B. Counsel of Record / ACLU Attorney

ACLU Side (Petitioner / Appellant): Mary Catherine Bonner argued the cause for appellant. With her on the briefs were Wanda Raiford, Jeffrey T. Green, William M. Norris, and Diane E. Courselle.

Opposing Side (Respondent / Appellee): Christopher M. Kise argued the cause for appellee. With him on the brief were Charles J. Crist, Jr., Attorney General of Florida, and James A. McKee, Deputy Solicitor General.

III. AMICI CURIAE

ACLU Side (Petitioner / Appellant)

Brief of amici curiae filed on behalf of the American Civil Liberties Union and the ACLU of Florida by John Holdridge, Brian W. Stull, Steven R. Shapiro, and Larry W. Yackle.

Brief of amici curiae filed on behalf of the National Association of Criminal Defense Lawyers by Matthew M. Shors and Pamela Harris.

Opposing Side (Respondent / Appellee)

Brief of amici curiae filed on behalf of the State of Alabama et al. by Troy King, Attorney General of Alabama, Kevin C. Newsom, Solicitor General, and James R. Houts, Assistant Attorney General, and by the Attorneys General for their respective States as follows: Mike Beebe of Arkansas, Bill Lockyer of California, John W. Suthers of Colorado, Carl C. Danberg of Delaware, Thurbert E. Baker of Georgia, Mark J. Bennett of Hawaii, Lawrence G. Wasden of Idaho, Lisa Madigan of Illinois, Steve Carter of Indiana, Tom Miller of Iowa, Phill Kline of Kansas, Gregory D. Stumbo of Kentucky, Jim Hood of Mississippi, Jeremiah W. (Jay) Nixon of Missouri, Jon Bruning of Nebraska, George J. Chanos of Nevada, Kelly A. Ayotte of New Hampshire, Wayne Stenehjem of North Dakota, Jim Petro of Ohio, W. A. Drew Edmondson of Oklahoma, Thomas W. Corbett, Jr., of Pennsylvania, Henry D. McMaster of South Carolina, Lawrence E. Long of South Dakota, Paul G. Summers of Tennessee, Greg Abbott of Texas, Mark L. Shurtleff of Utah, Robert F. McDonnell of Virginia, Rob McKenna of Washington, and Darrell V. McGraw, Jr., of West Virginia.

IV. THE SUPREME COURT'S DECISION

"The Antiterrorism and Effective Death Penalty Act of 1996 . . . sets a 1-year statute of limitations for . . . federal habeas corpus relief from a state-court judgment. This limitations period is tolled while a state prisoner seeks postconviction relief in state court . . . .

AEDPA's limitations period was tolled from the filing of Lawrence's petition for state postconviction relief until the Florida Supreme Court issued its mandate affirming the denial of that petition. At issue here is whether the limitations period was also tolled during the pendency of Lawrence's petition for certiorari to this Court seeking review of the denial of state postconviction relief. If it was tolled, Lawrence's federal habeas application was timely. So we must decide whether, according to § 2244(d)(2), an 'application for State post-conviction or other collateral review' 'is pending' while this Court considers a certiorari petition. . . .

This tolling rule would provide an incentive for prisoners to file certiorari petitions—regardless of the merit of the claims asserted—so that they receive additional time to file their habeas applications. . . .

We have not decided whether § 2244(d) allows for equitable tolling. Because the parties agree that equitable tolling is available, we assume . . . that it is. To be entitled to equitable tolling, Lawrence must show '(1) that he has been pursuing his rights diligently, and (2) that some extraordinary circumstance stood in his way' and prevented timely filing.

Lawrence makes several arguments . . . that equitable tolling applies to his case. . . .

In sum, Lawrence has fallen far short of showing 'extraordinary circumstances' necessary to support equitable tolling. . . .

The Court of Appeals correctly determined that the filing of a petition for certiorari before this Court does not toll the statute of limitations under § 2244(d)(2). It also correctly declined to equitably toll the limitations period in the factual circumstances of Lawrence's case. For these reasons, the judgment of the Court of Appeals is affirmed."

V. JUSTICE VOTE

4 Pro ACLU Side vs. 5 Con Opposing Side

ACLU Side (Petitioner / Appellant)

1. Ginsburg, R. – Wrote dissenting opinion
2. Stevens, J. – Joined Ginsburg's dissent
3. reyer, S. – Joined Ginsburg's dissent
4. Souter, D. – Joined Ginsburg's dissent

Opposing Side (Respondent / Appellee)

1. Thomas, C. – Wrote majority opinion
2. Alito, S. – Joined majority opinion
3. Scalia, A. – Joined majority opinion
4. Kennedy, A. – Joined majority opinion
5. Roberts, J. – Joined majority opinion

VI. A WIN OR LOSS FOR THE ACLU?

The ACLU filed as amicus curiae urging reversal of the judgment of the Court of Appeals; the Supreme Court affirmed in a 5-4 vote, giving the ACLU an apparent loss.

1011. Gonzales v. Carhart

(Decided April 18, 2007; 550 U.S. 124)

I. ISSUE

A. Issues Discussed

Privacy

B. Legal Question Presented

Whether "the Partial-Birth Abortion Ban Act of 2003 (Act), a federal statute regulating abortion procedures" is a facially valid law.

C. Supreme Court's Answer

"We conclude the Act should be sustained against the objections lodged by the broad, facial attack brought against it."

II. CASE SUMMARY

A. Background

"In No. 05–380 (Carhart) respondents are . . . doctors who perform second-trimester abortions. . . . They challenged the constitutionality of the [Partial-Birth Abortion Ban] Act and sought a permanent injunction against its enforcement. In 2004, after a 2–week trial, the District Court granted a permanent injunction that prohibited the Attorney General from enforcing the Act in all cases but those in which there was no dispute the fetus was viable. The Court of Appeals for the Eighth Circuit affirmed. . . .

In No. 05–1382 (Planned Parenthood) . . . Planned Parenthood entities sought to enjoin enforcement of the Act . . . . The City and County of San Francisco intervened as a plaintiff. In 2004, the District Court held a trial . . . and it, too, enjoined the Attorney General from enforcing the Act. The Court of Appeals for the Ninth Circuit affirmed. . . .

The abortion procedure that was the impetus for the numerous bans on 'partial-birth abortion,' including the Act, is a variation of th[e] standard D & E [(dilation & evacuation)]. . . .

D & E and intact D & E are not the only second-trimester abortion methods. Doctors also may abort a fetus through medical induction."

The Supreme Court granted certiorari to review the case.

B. Counsel of Record / ACLU Attorney

ACLU Side (Respondent / Appellee): Priscilla J. Smith argued the cause for appellees in No. 05–380. With her on the brief were Janet Crepps, Nan E. Strauss, Sanford M. Cohen, and Jerry M. Hug. Eve C. Gartner argued the cause for Planned Parenthood appellees in No. 05–1382. With her on the brief were Roger K. Evans, Helene T. Krasnoff, and Beth H. Parker. Dennis J. Herrera, Therese M. Stewart, and Kathleen S. Morris filed a brief for appellee City and County of San Francisco in No. 05–1382.

Opposing Side (Petitioner / Appellant): Solicitor General Clement argued the cause for appellant in both cases. With him on the briefs were Assistant Attorney General Keisler, Deputy Solicitor General Garre, Deputy Assistant Attorney General Katsas, Kannon K. Shanmugam, Marleigh D. Dover, and Catherine Y. Hancock.

III. AMICI CURIAE

ACLU Side (Respondent / Appellee)

Brief of amici curiae filed on behalf of the American Civil Liberties Union, New York Civil Liberties Union, and National Abortion Federation by Elisabeth Ryden Benjamin, Galen Leigh Sherwin, Talcott Camp, Steven R. Shapiro, Louise Melling, and Brigitte Amiri.

Brief of amici curiae filed on behalf of the American College of Obstetricians and Gynecologists by Caroline M. Brown.

Brief of amici curiae filed on behalf of the Institute for Reproductive Health Access et al. by J. Peter Coll, Jr., and Linda A. Rosenthal.

Brief of amici curiae filed on behalf of the National Women's Law Center et al. by Elizabeth B. McCallum, Marcia D. Greenberger, Dina R. Lassow, and Gretchen Borchelt.

Brief of amici curiae filed on behalf of the Religious Coalition for Reproductive Choice et al. by Karen L. Hagberg.

Brief of amici curiae filed on behalf of 52 Members of Congress by Claude G. Szyfer.

Brief of amici curiae filed on behalf of Former Federal Prosecutors by Maria T. Vullo.

Brief of amici curiae filed on behalf of the Cato Institute by Jonathan D. Hacker.

Brief of amici curiae filed on behalf of Stephen Chasen, M. D., et al. by Talcott Camp, Brigitte Amiri, Elisabeth Ryden Benjamin, A. Stephen Hut, Kimberly Parker, and Lorie A. Chaiten.

Brief of amici curiae filed on behalf of the American Medical Women's Association et al. by Ms. Chaiten, Carter G. Phillips, Eamon P. Joyce, and Robert N. Hochman.

Brief of amici curiae filed on behalf of the California Medical Association by Alan B. Morrison, Pamela S. Karlan, Jeffrey L. Fisher, Amy Howe, and Kevin K. Russell.

Brief of amici curiae filed on behalf of the NARAL Pro-Choice America Foundation et al. by Andrew T. Karron and Cathleen M. Mahoney.

Brief of amici curiae filed on behalf of Constitutional Law Professors by Kathryn M. Davis.

Brief of amici curiae filed on behalf of Statisticians by Molly S. Boast and Christian R. Everdell.

Opposing Side (Petitioner / Appellant)

Brief of amici curiae filed on behalf of the American Association of Pro Life Obstetricians and Gynecologists et al. by Clarke D. Forsythe and Denise M. Burke.

Brief of amici curiae filed on behalf of the American Center for Law and Justice et al. by Jay Alan Sekulow, Stuart J. Roth, Walter M. Weber, Thomas P. Monaghan, John P. Tuskey, Laura B. Hernandez, and Shannon D. Woodruff.

Brief of amici curiae filed on behalf of the National Legal Foundation by Barry C. Hodge.

Brief of amici curiae filed on behalf of the Right to Life Advocates, Inc., by Richard W. Schmude.

Brief of amici curiae filed on behalf of the Thomas More Society, Inc., by Paul Benjamin Linton and Thomas Brejcha.

Brief of amici curiae filed on behalf of Jill Stanek et al. by Mathew D. Staver, Anita L. Staver, Erik W. Stanley, Rena M. Lindevaldsen, and Mary E. McAlister.

Brief of amici curiae filed on behalf of the State of Texas et al. by Greg Abbott, Attorney General of Texas, Barry R. McBee, First Assistant Attorney General, Edward D. Burbach, Deputy Attorney General, R. Ted Cruz, Solicitor General, and Joel L. Thollander, Assistant Solicitor General, and by the Attorneys General for their respective States as follows: Troy King of Alabama, Mike Beebe of Arkansas, Charles J. Crist, Jr., of Florida, Steve Carter of Indiana, Jeremiah W. (Jay) Nixon of Missouri, Wayne Stenehjem of North Dakota, Jim Petro of Ohio, Thomas W. Corbett, Jr., of Pennsylvania, Henry McMaster of South Carolina, Lawrence E. Long of South Dakota, Mark L. Shurtleff of Utah, and Robert F. McDonnell of Virginia; for the Family Research Council et al. by William L. Saunders; for the Foundation for Moral Law, Inc., by Benjamin D. DuPré and Gregory M. Jones.

Brief of amici curiae filed on behalf of the Horatio R. Storer Foundation, Inc., by James Bopp, Jr., Thomas J. Marzen, and Richard E. Coleson.

Brief of amici curiae filed on behalf of Judicial Watch, Inc., by Meredith L. Di Liberto.

Brief of amici curiae filed on behalf of the Pro-Life Legal Defense Fund et al. by Dwight G. Duncan, Philip D. Moran, Gregory S. Baylor, and Steven H. Aden.

Brief of amici curiae filed on behalf of the Thomas More Law Center et al. by Edward L. White III.

Brief of amici curiae filed on behalf of the United States Conference of Catholic Bishops et al. by Mark E. Chopko and Michael F. Moses.

Brief of amici curiae filed on behalf of the United States Justice Foundation et al. by D. Colette Wilson and Gary G. Kreep.

Brief of amici curiae filed on behalf of Gianna Jessen et al. by Kelly Shackelford.

Brief of amici curiae filed on behalf of Congressman Ron Paul et al. by Teresa Stanton Collett.

Brief of amici curiae filed on behalf of Margie Riley et al. by James Joseph Lynch, Jr.

Brief of amici curiae filed on behalf of John M. Thorp, Jr., M. D., et al. by Nikolas T. Nikas and James L. Hirsen.

Brief of amici curiae filed on behalf of the Christian Legal Society et al. by Richard W. Garnett, Gregory S. Baylor, and Steven H. Aden.

Brief of amici curiae filed on behalf of the Christian Medical and Dental Associations et al. by Ms. Collett.

Brief of amici curiae filed on behalf of Matercare International et al. by Mr. Nikas, Dorinda C. Bordlee, and Mr. Hirsen.

Brief of amici curiae filed on behalf of Professor Hadley Arkes et al. by John C. Eastman and Edwin Meese III.

Brief of amici curiae filed on behalf of the Eagle Forum Education & Legal Defense Fund by Andrew L. Schlafly.

Brief of amici curiae filed on behalf of the Rutherford Institute by John W. Whitehead.

Brief of amici curiae filed on behalf of Sandra Cano et al. by Linda Boston Schlueter, Allan E. Parker, Jr., and Richard Clayton Trotter.

Brief of amici curiae filed on behalf of Faith and Action et al. by Bernard P. Reese, Jr.

Brief of amici curiae filed on behalf of Legal Defense for Unborn Children by Alan Ernest in support of neither party.

IV. THE SUPREME COURT'S DECISION

"Whatever one's views concerning the Casey joint opinion, it is evident a premise central to its conclusion—that the government has a legitimate and substantial interest in preserving and promoting fetal life—would be repudiated were the Court now to affirm the judgments of the Courts of Appeals. . . .

We begin with a determination of the Act's operation and effect. A straightforward reading of the Act's text demonstrates its purpose and the scope of its provisions: It regulates and proscribes, with exceptions or qualifications to be discussed, performing the intact D & E procedure. . . .

We conclude that the Act is not void for vagueness, does not impose an undue burden from any overbreadth, and is not invalid on its face. . . .

Under the principles accepted as controlling here, the Act, as we have interpreted it, would be unconstitutional 'if its purpose or effect is to place a substantial obstacle in the path of a woman seeking an abortion before the fetus attains viability.' The abortions affected by the Act's regulations take place both previability and postviability; so the quoted language and the undue burden analysis it relies upon are applicable. The question is whether the Act, measured by its text in this facial attack, imposes a substantial obstacle to late-term, but previability, abortions. The Act does not on its face impose a substantial obstacle, and we reject this further facial challenge to its validity. . . .

The considerations we have discussed support our further determination that these facial attacks should not have been entertained in the first instance. In these circumstances the proper means to consider exceptions is by as-applied challenge. . . . In an as-applied challenge the nature of the medical risk can be better quantified and balanced . . . .

The Act is open to a proper as-applied challenge in a discrete case. No as-applied challenge need be brought if the prohibition in the Act threatens a woman's life because the Act already contains a life exception. . . .

Respondents have not demonstrated that the Act, as a facial matter, is void for vagueness, or that it imposes an undue burden on a woman's right to abortion based on its overbreadth or lack of a health exception. For these reasons the judgments of the Courts of Appeals for the Eighth and Ninth Circuits are reversed."

V. JUSTICE VOTE

4 Pro ACLU Side vs. 5 Con Opposing Side

ACLU Side (Respondent / Appellee)

1. Ginsburg, R. – Wrote dissenting opinion
2. Stevens, J. – Joined Ginsburg's dissent
3. Souter, D. – Joined Ginsburg's dissent
4. Breyer, S. – Joined Ginsburg's dissent

Opposing Side (Petitioner / Appellant)

1. Kennedy, A. – Wrote majority opinion
2. Alito, S. – Joined majority opinion
3. Thomas, C. – Wrote concurring opinion
4. Scalia, A. – Joined Thomas' concurrence
5. Roberts, J. – Joined majority opinion

VI. A WIN OR LOSS FOR THE ACLU?

The ACLU filed as amicus curiae urging affirmance; the Supreme Court reversed the Court of Appeals' decisions by a 5-4 vote, giving the ACLU an apparent loss.

1012. Scott v. Harris

(Decided April 30, 2007; 550 U.S. 372)

I. ISSUE

A. Issues Discussed

4th Amendment

B. Legal Question Presented

"[W]hether a law enforcement official can, consistent with the Fourth Amendment, attempt to stop a fleeing motorist from continuing his public-endangering flight by ramming the motorist's car from behind. Put another way: Can an officer take actions that place a fleeing motorist at risk of serious injury or death in order to stop the motorist's flight from endangering the lives of innocent bystanders?"

C. Supreme Court's Answer

"A police officer's attempt to terminate a dangerous high-speed car chase that threatens the lives of innocent bystanders does not violate the Fourth Amendment, even when it places the fleeing motorist at risk of serious injury or death."

II. CASE SUMMARY

A. Background

"In March 2001, a Georgia county deputy clocked respondent's vehicle traveling at 73 miles per hour on a road with a 55–mile–per–hour speed limit. The deputy activated his blue flashing lights indicating that respondent should pull over. Instead, respondent sped away, initiating a chase . . . . The deputy radioed his dispatch to report that he was pursuing a fleeing vehicle, and broadcast its license plate number. Petitioner, Deputy Timothy Scott, heard the radio communication and joined the pursuit . . . . In the midst of the chase, respondent pulled into the parking lot of a shopping center and was nearly boxed in by the various police vehicles. Respondent evaded the trap by making a sharp turn, colliding with Scott's police car, exiting the parking lot, and speeding off . . . .

Scott took over as the lead pursuit vehicle. Six minutes and nearly 10 miles after the chase had begun, Scott decided to attempt . . . a 'Precision Intervention Technique ('PIT') maneuver, which causes the fleeing vehicle to spin to a stop.' Having radioed his supervisor for permission, Scott was told to "[g]o ahead and take him out." Instead, Scott applied his push bumper to the rear of respondent's vehicle. As a result, respondent lost control of his vehicle, which left the roadway, ran down an embankment, overturned, and crashed. Respondent was badly injured and was rendered a quadriplegic.

Respondent filed suit against Deputy Scott . . . alleging . . . use of excessive force resulting in an unreasonable seizure under the Fourth Amendment. In response, Scott filed a motion for summary judgment based on . . . qualified immunity. The District Court denied the motion . . . . [T]he United States Court of Appeals for the Eleventh Circuit affirmed . . . ."

The Supreme Court granted certiorari to review the case.

B. Counsel of Record / ACLU Attorney

ACLU Side (Respondent / Appellee): Craig T. Jones argued the cause for appellee. With him on the brief was Andrew C. Clarke.

Opposing Side (Petitioner / Appellant): Philip W. Savrin argued the cause for appellant. With him on the briefs were Sun S. Choy and Orin S. Kerr.

Deputy Solicitor General Garre argued the cause for the United States as amicus curiae.

III. AMICI CURIAE

ACLU Side (Respondent / Appellee)

Brief of amici curiae filed on behalf of the American Civil Liberties Union and ACLU of Georgia by Hamilton P. Fox III, Brian C. Spahn, Steven R. Shapiro, and Gerald R. Weber.

Brief of amici curiae filed on behalf of the National Association of Criminal Defense Lawyers by Jonathan D. Hacker, Nicole A. Saharsky, and Pamela Harris.

Brief of amici curiae filed on behalf of the National Police Accountability Project by Karen Blum, Howard Friedman, and Myong J. Joun.

Brief of amici curiae filed on behalf of the Georgia Association of Chiefs of Police, Inc., by Michael A. Caldwell in support of neither party.

Opposing Side (Petitioner / Appellant)

Brief of amici curiae filed on behalf of the United States by Deputy Solicitor General Garre, Solicitor General Clement, Assistant Attorney General Keisler, Jonathan L. Marcus, and Barbara L. Herwig.

Brief of amici curiae filed on behalf of the State of Illinois et al. by Lisa Madigan, Attorney General of Illinois, Gary Feinerman, Solicitor General, and Michael Scodro, Deputy Solicitor General, by Craig J. Tillery, Acting Attorney General of Alaska, by Roberto J. Sánchez-Ramos, Secretary of Justice of Puerto Rico, and by the Attorneys General for their respective States as follows: Troy King of Alabama, Terry Goddard of Arizona, Mike Beebe of Arkansas, Bill Lockyer of California, John W. Suthers of Colorado, Thurbert E. Baker of Georgia, Mark J. Bennett of Hawaii, Lawrence G. Wasden of Idaho, Steve Carter of Indiana, Thomas F. Reilly of Massachusetts, Michael A. Cox of Michigan, Jim Hood of Mississippi, Mike McGrath of Montana, Kelly A. Ayotte of New Hampshire, Wayne Stenehjem of North Dakota, W. A. Drew Edmondson of Oklahoma, Hardy Myers of Oregon, Thomas W. Corbett, Jr., of Pennsylvania, Patrick Lynch of Rhode Island, Henry McMaster of South Carolina, Robert E. Cooper, Jr., of Tennessee, Greg Abbott of Texas, Mark L. Shurtleff of Utah, William H. Sorrell of Vermont, Robert F. McDonnell of Virginia, and Patrick J. Crank of Wyoming.

Brief of amici curiae filed on behalf of the National Association of Counties et al. by Richard Ruda, Charles A. Rothfeld, Andrew J. Pincus, and Dan Kahan.

IV. THE SUPREME COURT'S DECISION

"In resolving questions of qualified immunity, courts are required to resolve a 'threshold question: Taken in the light most favorable to the party asserting the injury, do the facts alleged show the officer's conduct violated a constitutional right? . . . If . . . the court finds a violation of a constitutional right, 'the next, sequential step is to ask whether the right was clearly established . . . .' . . . We therefore turn to the threshold inquiry: whether Deputy Scott's actions violated the Fourth Amendment. . . .

The first step . . . is to determine the relevant facts. . . . In qualified immunity cases, this usually means adopting . . . the plaintiff's version . . . .

There is, however, an added wrinkle in this case: . . . a videotape . . . . The videotape quite clearly contradicts the version of the story told by respondent . . . .

At the summary judgment stage, facts must be viewed in the light most favorable to the nonmoving party only if there is a 'genuine' dispute . . . . When . . . blatantly contradicted by the record, . . . a court should not adopt that version of the facts . . . .

That was the case here with regard to the factual issue whether respondent was driving in such fashion as to endanger human life. . . .

[W]e think it is quite clear that Deputy Scott did not violate the Fourth Amendment. . . . The question . . . is whether Scott's actions were objectively reasonable. . . .

[I]t is clear from the videotape that respondent posed an actual and imminent threat . . . . It is equally clear that Scott's actions posed a high likelihood of serious injury or death to respondent . . . . We think it appropriate in this process to take into account not only the number of lives at risk, but also their relative culpability. . . . We have little difficulty in concluding it was reasonable for Scott to take the action that he did.

But wait, says respondent: Couldn't the innocent public . . . have been protected . . . if the police had simply ceased their pursuit? [T]he police need not have taken that chance . . . .

Instead, we lay down a . . . rule: A police officer's attempt to terminate a dangerous high-speed car chase that threatens the lives of innocent bystanders does not violate the Fourth Amendment, even when it places the fleeing motorist at risk of serious injury or death. . . .

The car chase that respondent initiated in this case posed a substantial and immediate risk of serious physical injury to others . . . . Scott's attempt to terminate the chase by forcing respondent off the road was reasonable, and Scott is entitled to summary judgment. The Court of Appeals' judgment to the contrary is reversed."

V. JUSTICE VOTE

1 Pro ACLU Side vs. 8 Con Opposing Side

ACLU Side (Respondent / Appellee)

1. Stevens, J. – Wrote dissenting opinion

Opposing Side (Petitioner / Appellant)

1. Scalia, A. – Wrote majority opinion
2. Alito, S. – Joined majority opinion
3. Thomas, C. – Joined majority opinion
4. Breyer, S. – Wrote concurring opinion
5. Kennedy, A. – Joined majority opinion
6. Ginsburg, R. – Wrote concurring opinion
7. Souter, D. – Joined majority opinion
8. Roberts, J. – Joined majority opinion

VI. A WIN OR LOSS FOR THE ACLU?

The ACLU filed as amicus curiae urging affirmance; the Supreme Court reversed the Court of Appeals' decision by an 8-1 vote, giving the ACLU an apparent loss.

1013. Ledbetter v. Goodyear Tire & Rubber Co.

(Decided May 29, 2007; 550 U.S. 618)

I. ISSUE

A. Issues Discussed

Gender, civil rights

B. Legal Question Presented

"'Whether and under what circumstances a plaintiff may bring an action under Title VII of the Civil Rights Act of 1964 alleging illegal pay discrimination when the disparate pay is received during the statutory limitations period, but is the result of intentionally discriminatory pay decisions that occurred outside the limitations period.'"

C. Supreme Court's Answer

"Ultimately, 'experience teaches that strict adherence to the procedural requirements specified by the legislature is the best guarantee of evenhanded administration of the law.' By operation of §§ 2000e–5(e)(1) and 2000e–5(f)(1), a Title VII 'claim is time barred if it is not filed within these time limits.' We therefore reject the suggestion that an employment practice committed with no improper purpose and no discriminatory intent is rendered unlawful nonetheless because it gives some effect to an intentional discriminatory act that occurred outside the charging period."

II. CASE SUMMARY

A. Background

"Lilly Ledbetter . . . worked for . . . Goodyear Tire & Rubber Company . . . from 1979 until 1998. [S]alaried employees at the plant were given or denied raises based on their supervisors' evaluation of their performance. In March 1998, Ledbetter submitted a questionnaire to the EEOC alleging certain acts of sex discrimination, and in July of that year she filed a formal EEOC charge. After taking early retirement in November 1998, Ledbetter commenced this action, in which she asserted, among other claims, a Title VII pay discrimination claim and a claim under the Equal Pay Act of 1963 (EPA).

The District Court granted summary judgment in favor of Goodyear on several of Ledbetter's claims, . . . but allowed others . . . to proceed to trial. . . . Ledbetter introduced evidence that . . . several supervisors had given her poor evaluations because of her sex, that as a result . . . her pay was not increased as much as it would have been if she had been evaluated fairly, and that these past pay decisions continued to affect the amount of her pay throughout her employment. [S]he was being paid significantly less than . . . male colleagues. [T]he jury found for Ledbetter and awarded her backpay and damages.

On appeal, Goodyear contended that Ledbetter's pay discrimination claim was time barred with respect to all pay decisions made prior to September 26, 1997—that is, 180 days before the filing of her EEOC questionnaire. And Goodyear argued that no discriminatory act relating to Ledbetter's pay occurred after that date.

The Court of Appeals for the Eleventh Circuit reversed . . . ."

The Supreme Court granted certiorari to review the case.

B. Counsel of Record / ACLU Attorney

ACLU Side (Petitioner / Appellant): Kevin K. Russell argued the cause for appellant. With him on the briefs were Amy Howe, Pamela S. Karlan, Jeffrey L. Fisher, Robert L. Wiggins, Jr., and Jon C. Goldfarb.

Opposing Side (Respondent / Appellee): Glen D. Nager argued the cause for appellee. With him on the brief were Michael A. Carvin, Shay Dvoretzky, and Jay St. Clair.

Irving L. Gornstein argued the cause for the United States as amicus curiae.

III. AMICI CURIAE

ACLU Side (Petitioner / Appellant)

Brief of amici curiae filed on behalf of the National Partnership for Women & Families, 9to5, National Association of Working Women, American Association of University Women, American Civil Liberties Union, Coalition of Labor Union Women, Connecticut Women's Education & Legal Fund, Equal Rights Advocates, Feminist Majority Foundation, HADASSAH, Legal Momentum, MANA National Latina Organization, National Asian Pacific American Women's Forum, National Association of Social Workers, National Council of Women's Organizations, National Organization for Women Foundation, National Women's Law Center, Northwest Women's Law Center, Pick Up the Pace, the Women's Law Center of Maryland, Wider Opportunities for Women, Women Employed, Women's Advocacy Project, Inc., Women's Bar Association of the District of Columbia, Women's Law Project by Deborah L. Brake, Judith L. Lichtman, Jocelyn C. Frye, Marcia D. Greenberger, Jocelyn Samuels, Dina R. Lassow, and Joanna L. Grossman.

Brief of amici curiae filed on behalf of the National Employment Lawyers Association et al. by Joseph M. Sellers, Christine E. Webber, James M. Finberg, Eve H. Cervantez, Michael Foreman, Sarah Crawford, Terisa E. Chaw, Dennis Courtland Hayes, Thomas W. Osborne, Daniel B. Kohrman, Laurie A. McCann, Melvin Radowitz, Patricia A. Shiu, and Shelley A. Gregory.

Opposing Side (Respondent / Appellee)

Brief of amici curiae filed on behalf of the United States by Irving L. Gornstein, Solicitor General Clement, Assistant Attorney General Kim, Deputy Solicitor General Garre, and Dennis J. Dimsey.

Brief of amici curiae filed on behalf of the Chamber of Commerce of the United States of America et al. by Neal D. Mollen, Carson H. Sullivan, Robin S. Conrad, Shane Brennan, and Karen R. Harned.

Brief of amici curiae filed on behalf of the Equal Employment Advisory Council et al. by Ann Elizabeth Reesman and Laura A. Giantris.

IV. THE SUPREME COURT'S DECISION

"Title VII of the Civil Rights Act of 1964 makes it an 'unlawful employment practice' to discriminate 'against any individual with respect to his compensation . . . because of such individual's . . . sex.' An individual wishing to challenge an employment practice under this provision must first file a charge with the EEOC. Such a charge must be filed within a specified period (either 180 or 300 days, depending on the State) 'after the alleged unlawful employment practice occurred' . . . .

In addressing the issue whether an EEOC charge was filed on time, we have stressed the need to identify with care the specific employment practice that is at issue. Ledbetter points to two different employment practices as possible candidates. Primarily, she urges us to focus on the paychecks that were issued to her during the EEOC charging period (the 180–day period preceding the filing of her EEOC questionnaire), each of which, she contends, was a separate act of discrimination. Alternatively, Ledbetter directs us to the 1998 decision denying her a raise, and she argues that this decision was 'unlawful because it carried forward intentionally discriminatory disparities from prior years.' Both of these arguments fail because they would require us in effect to jettison the defining element of the legal claim on which her Title VII recovery was based. . . .

Ultimately, 'experience teaches that strict adherence to the procedural requirements specified by the legislature is the best guarantee of evenhanded administration of the law.' [A] Title VII 'claim is time barred if it is not filed within these time limits.' We therefore reject the suggestion that an employment practice committed with no improper purpose and no discriminatory intent is rendered unlawful nonetheless because it gives some effect to an intentional discriminatory act that occurred outside the charging period. Ledbetter's claim is, for this reason, untimely. . . .

Because Ledbetter did not file timely EEOC charges relating to . . . discriminatory pay decisions in the past, she cannot maintain a suit based on that past discrimination . . . .

Ledbetter's policy arguments for giving special treatment to pay claims find no support in the statute and are inconsistent with our precedents. We apply the statute as written, and this means that any unlawful employment practice, including those involving compensation, must be presented to the EEOC within the period prescribed by statute. . . .

[T]he judgment of the Court of Appeals for the Eleventh Circuit is affirmed."

V. JUSTICE VOTE

4 Pro ACLU Side vs. 5 Con Opposing Side

ACLU Side (Petitioner / Appellant)

1. Ginsburg, R. – Wrote dissenting opinion
2. Stevens, J. – Joined Ginsburg's dissent
3. Breyer, S. – Joined Ginsburg's dissent
4. Souter, D. – Joined Ginsburg's dissent

Opposing Side (Respondent / Appellee)

1. Alito, S. – Wrote majority opinion
2. Roberts, J. – Joined majority opinion
3. Scalia, A. – Joined majority opinion
4. Kennedy, A. – Joined majority opinion
5. Thomas, C. – Joined majority opinion

VI. A WIN OR LOSS FOR THE ACLU?

The ACLU filed as amicus curiae urging reversal of the judgment of the Court of Appeals; the Supreme Court affirmed in a 5-4 vote, giving the ACLU an apparent loss.

1014. Uttecht v. Brown

(Decided June 4, 2007; 551 U.S. 1)

I. ISSUE

A. Issues Discussed

Death penalty, criminal procedure

B. Legal Question Presented

Whether the Court of Appeals erred in not deferring to the trial court's determination to dismiss Juror Z.

C. Supreme Court's Answer

"Courts reviewing claims of Witherspoon–Witt error . . . owe deference to the trial court, which is in a superior position to determine the demeanor and qualifications of a potential juror. The Court of Appeals neglected to accord this deference. And on this record it was error to find that Juror Z was not substantially impaired."

II. CASE SUMMARY

A. Background

"Respondent Cal Coburn Brown robbed, raped, tortured, and murdered one woman in Washington. Two days later, he robbed, raped, tortured, and attempted to murder a second woman in California. Apprehended, Brown confessed to these crimes and pleaded guilty to the California offenses, for which he received a sentence of life imprisonment. The State of Washington, however, sought the death penalty and brought Brown to trial. Based on the jury's verdicts . . . , Brown was sentenced to death. His conviction and sentence were affirmed by the Supreme Court of the State of Washington.

Brown filed a petition for writ of habeas corpus in the United States District Court for the Western District of Washington. The District Court denied the petition, but the United States Court of Appeals for the Ninth Circuit reversed. The Court of Appeals considered, among other arguments for setting aside the capital sentence, the contention that under Witherspoon v. Illinois, 391 U.S. 510 (1968), and its progeny, the state trial court had violated Brown's Sixth and Fourteenth Amendment rights by excusing three potential jurors—whom we refer to as Jurors X, Y, and Z—for cause. The State moved to excuse these jurors due to the concern that they could not be impartial in deciding whether to impose a death sentence. The Court of Appeals held it was proper to excuse Jurors X and Y, but agreed with the defense that it was unconstitutional to excuse Juror Z for cause. On this premise the court held that Brown's death sentence could not stand, requiring that Brown receive a new sentencing trial more than a decade after his conviction."

The Supreme Court granted certiorari to review the case.

B. Counsel of Record / ACLU Attorney

ACLU Side (Respondent / Appellee): Suzanne Lee Elliott, by appointment of the Court, argued the cause for appellee. With her on the brief was Gilbert H. Levy.

Opposing Side (Petitioner / Appellant): John J. Samson, Assistant Attorney General of Washington, argued the cause for appellant.

With him on the briefs were Robert M. McKenna, Attorney General, Paul D. Weisser, Senior Counsel, and William Berggren Collins and Jay D. Geck, Deputy Solicitors General.

Deputy Solicitor General Dreeben argued the cause for the United States as amicus curiae.

III. AMICI CURIAE

ACLU Side (Respondent / Appellee)

Brief of amici curiae filed on behalf of the American Civil Liberties Union and the ACLU of Washington by John Holdridge, Brian W. Stull, Sarah A. Dunne, Nancy L. Talner, Steven R. Shapiro, and Larry Yackle.

Brief of amici curiae filed on behalf of the National Association of Criminal Defense Lawyers by Amy Howe, Kevin K. Russell, Thomas C. Goldstein, Jeffrey L. Fisher, Pamela S. Karlan, and Susan Rozelle.

Opposing Side (Petitioner / Appellant)

Brief of amici curiae filed on behalf of the United States by Deputy Solicitor General Dreeben, Solicitor General Clement, Assistant Attorney General Fisher, and Sri Srinivasan.

Brief of amici curiae filed on behalf of the State of Oregon et al. by Hardy Myers, Attorney General of Oregon, Mary Williams, Solicitor General, Rolf Moan, Assistant Attorney General, and Dan Schweitzer, and by the Attorneys General for their respective States as follows: Dustin McDaniel of Arkansas, Edmund G. Brown, Jr., of California, John W. Suthers of Colorado, Joseph R. Biden III of Delaware, Lawrence G. Wasden of Idaho, Lisa Madigan of Illinois, Steve Carter of Indiana, Jeremiah W. (Jay) Nixon of Missouri, Mike McGrath of Montana, Jon Bruning of Nebraska, Catherine Cortez Masto of Nevada, Kelly A. Ayotte of New Hampshire, Gary G. King of New Mexico, Marc Dann of Ohio, W. A. Drew Edmondson of Oklahoma, Thomas W. Corbett, Jr., of Pennsylvania, Henry D. McMaster of South Carolina, Lawrence E. Long of South Dakota, Greg Abbott of Texas, Mark L. Shurtleff of Utah, Robert F. McDonnell of Virginia, and Patrick J. Crank of Wyoming.

IV. THE SUPREME COURT'S DECISION

"The . . . precedents establish at least four principles of relevance here. First, a criminal defendant has the right to an impartial jury drawn from a venire that has not been tilted in favor of capital punishment . . . . Second, the State has a strong interest in having jurors who are able to apply capital punishment within the framework state law prescribes. Third, to balance these interests, a juror who is substantially impaired in his or her ability to impose the death penalty . . . can be excused for cause; but if the juror is not substantially impaired, removal for cause is impermissible. Fourth, in determining whether the removal . . . would vindicate the State's interest without violating the defendant's right, the trial court makes a judgment based in part on . . . demeanor . . . , a judgment owed deference . . . .

By not according the required deference, the Court of Appeals failed to respect the limited role of federal habeas relief in this area prescribed by Congress and by our cases. . . .

The State challenged Juror Z, explaining that he was confused about the conditions under which death could be imposed . . . . Before the trial court could ask Brown for a response, the defense volunteered, 'We have no objection.' The court then excused Juror Z. . . .

From our own review of the state trial court's ruling, we conclude the trial court acted well within its discretion in granting the State's motion to excuse Juror Z. . . .

We reject the conclusion of the Court of Appeals that the excusal of Juror Z entitles Brown to federal habeas relief. The need to defer to the trial court's ability to perceive jurors' demeanor does not foreclose the possibility that a reviewing court may reverse the trial court's decision . . . . But where, as here, there is lengthy questioning of a prospective juror and the trial court has supervised a diligent and thoughtful voir dire, the trial court has broad discretion. The record does not show the trial court exceeded this discretion in excusing Juror Z; indeed the transcript shows considerable confusion on the part of the juror, amounting to substantial impairment. . . .

Capital defendants have the right to be sentenced by an impartial jury. The State may not infringe this right by eliminating from the venire those whose scruples against the death penalty would not substantially impair the performance of their duties. Courts . . . , however, . . . owe deference to the trial court, which is in a superior position to determine the demeanor and qualifications of a potential juror. The Court of Appeals neglected to accord this deference. And . . . it was error to find that Juror Z was not substantially impaired. The judgment of the Court of Appeals is reversed, and . . . remanded . . . ."

V. JUSTICE VOTE

4 Pro ACLU Side vs. 5 Con Opposing Side

ACLU Side (Respondent / Appellee)

1. Stevens, J. – Wrote dissenting opinion
2. Souter, D. – Joined Stevens' dissent, joined Breyer's dissent
3. Ginsburg, R. – Joined Stevens' dissent
4. Breyer, S. – Wrote dissenting opinion, Joined Stevens' dissent

Opposing Side (Petitioner / Appellant)

1. Kennedy, A. – Wrote majority opinion
2. Alito, S. – Joined majority opinion
3. Thomas, C. – Joined majority opinion
4. Scalia, A. – Joined majority opinion
5. Roberts, J. – Joined majority opinion

VI. A WIN OR LOSS FOR THE ACLU?

The ACLU filed as amicus curiae urging affirmance; the Supreme Court reversed the Court of Appeals' decision by a 5-4 vote, giving the ACLU an apparent loss.

1015. Sole v. Wyner

(Decided June 4, 2007; 551 U.S. 74)

I. ISSUE

A. Issues Discussed

Civil procedure

B. Legal Question Presented

"Does a plaintiff who gains a preliminary injunction after an abbreviated hearing, but is denied a permanent injunction after a dispositive adjudication on the merits, qualify as a 'prevailing party' within the compass of § 1988(b)?"

C. Supreme Court's Answer

"[A] final decision on the merits denying permanent injunctive relief ordinarily determines who prevails in the action for purposes of § 1988(b)."

II. CASE SUMMARY

A. Background

"In mid-January 2003, . . . T.A. Wyner notified the Florida Department of Environmental Protection (DEP) of her intention to create on Valentine's Day . . . an antiwar artwork. The work would consist of nude individuals assembled into a peace sign. By letter dated February 6, DEP informed Wyner that her peace sign display would be lawful only if the participants complied with the 'Bathing Suit Rule' . . . . That rule required patrons, in all areas of Florida's state parks, to wear, at a minimum, a thong and, if female, a bikini top.

To safeguard the . . . display . . . Wyner filed suit . . . on February 12, 2003. . . .

The day after the complaint was filed . . . the District Court heard Wyner's emergency motion for a preliminary injunction. [T]he court granted the preliminary injunction. . . .

The peace symbol display took place at MacArthur Beach the next day. . . .

Thereafter, Wyner pursued her demand for a permanent injunction. . . .

A week later, . . . the court denied plaintiff's motion for summary judgment and granted defendants' motion for summary final judgment. [T]he court awarded plaintiff counsel fees covering the first phase of the litigation.

The Florida officials appealed, challenging both the order granting a preliminary injunction and the award of counsel fees. Wyner, however, pursued no appeal from the final order denying a permanent injunction. The Court of Appeals for the Eleventh Circuit held first that defendants' challenges to the preliminary injunction were moot . . . . The court then affirmed the counsel fees award . . . ."

The Supreme Court granted certiorari to review the case.

B. Counsel of Record / ACLU Attorney

ACLU Side (Respondent / Appellee): Seth M. Galanter argued the cause for appellees. With him on the brief were Beth S. Brinkmann, Brian R. Matsui, James K. Green, Randall C. Marshall of the ACLU Foundation of Florida, Inc., and Steven R. Shapiro of the American Civil Liberties Union Foundation.

Opposing Side (Petitioner / Appellant): Virginia A. Seitz argued the cause for appellants. With her on the briefs were Carri S. Leininger and James O. Williams, Jr.

Patricia A. Millett argued the cause for the United States as amicus curiae.

III. AMICI CURIAE

ACLU Side (Respondent / Appellee)

Brief of amici curiae filed on behalf of Americans United for Separation of Church and State et al. by Andrew J. Pincus, Charles A. Rothfeld, Dana Berliner, John W. Whitehead, Giovanna Shay, Ayesha N. Khan, Richard B. Katskee, Alex J. Luchenitser, Ronald A. Lindsay, Brian Wolfman, Steven Schwartz, and Judith E. Schaeffer.

Brief of amici curiae filed on behalf of the Brennan Center for Justice by Laura W. Brill and Wendy R. Weiser.

Brief of amici curiae filed on behalf of the Center for Individual Rights by Michael E. Rosman.

Brief of amici curiae filed on behalf of the Chief Justice Earl Warren Institute on Race, Ethnicity and Diversity et al. by Catherine R. Albiston.

Opposing Side (Petitioner / Appellant)

Brief of amici curiae filed on behalf of the United States by Patricia A. Millett, Solicitor General Clement, Deputy Solicitor General Garre, Michael Jay Singer, and Michael E. Robinson.

Brief of amici curiae filed on behalf of the Commonwealth of Virginia et al. by Robert F. McDonnell, Attorney General of Virginia, William C. Mims, Chief Deputy Attorney General, William E. Thro, State Solicitor General, Stephen R. McCullough, Deputy State Solicitor General, and Dan Schweitzer, by Roberto J. Sánchez-Ramos, Secretary of Justice of Puerto Rico, and by the Attorneys General for their respective States as follows: Troy King of Alabama, Talis J. Colberg of Alaska, Terry Goddard of Arizona, Dustin McDaniel of Arkansas, John W. Suthers of Colorado, Thurbert E. Baker of Georgia, Mark J. Bennett of Hawaii, Lisa Madigan of Illinois, Steve Carter of Indiana, Mike Cox of Michigan, Jeremiah W. (Jay) Nixon of Missouri, George J. Chanos of Nevada, Kelly A. Ayotte of New Hampshire, Wayne Stenehjem of North Dakota, Thomas W. Corbett, Jr., of Pennsylvania, Henry McMaster of South Carolina, Larry Long of South Dakota, Robert E. Cooper, Jr., of Tennessee, Mark L. Shurtleff of Utah, Robert M. McKenna of Washington, Darrell V. McGraw, Jr., of West Virginia, J. B. Van Hollen of Wisconsin, and Patrick J. Crank of Wyoming.

Brief of amici curiae filed on behalf of the National League of Cities et al. by Richard Ruda and Lawrence Rosenthal.

IV. THE SUPREME COURT'S DECISION

"'The touchstone of the prevailing party inquiry,' . . . is 'the material alteration of the legal relationship of the parties in a manner which Congress sought to promote in the fee statute.' . . .

At the preliminary injunction stage, the court is called upon to assess the probability of the plaintiff's ultimate success on the merits. . . .

In this case, the preliminary injunction hearing was necessarily hasty and abbreviated. . . . Its tentative character . . . would have made a fee request at the initial stage premature.

Of controlling importance to our decision, the eventual ruling on the merits for defendants, after both sides considered the case fit for final adjudication, superseded the preliminary ruling. . . . At the summary judgment stage, with the benefit of a fuller record, the District Court recognized that its initial assessment was incorrect. . . .

Wyner contends that the preliminary injunction was not undermined by the subsequent adjudication on the merits because the decision to grant preliminary relief was an 'as applied' ruling. In developing this argument, she asserts that the officials engaged in impermissible content-based administration of the Bathing Suit Rule. But the District Court assumed, 'for the purposes of [its initial] order,' the content neutrality of the state officials' conduct. . . . That specification is controlling. . . .

The final decision in Wyner's case rejected the same claim she advanced in her preliminary injunction motion: that the state law banning nudity in parks was unconstitutional as applied to expressive, nonerotic nudity. At the end of the fray, Florida's Bathing Suit Rule remained intact, and Wyner had gained no enduring 'chang[e] . . .' . . . .

Wyner is not a prevailing party, we conclude, for her initial victory was ephemeral. A plaintiff who 'secur[es] a preliminary injunction, then loses on the merits as the case plays out and judgment is entered against [her],' has '[won] a battle but los[t] the war.' . . .

We decide only that a plaintiff who gains a preliminary injunction does not qualify for an award of counsel fees under § 1988(b) if the merits of the case are ultimately decided against her. . . .

[T]he judgment of the Court of Appeals is reversed, and the case is remanded . . . ."

V. JUSTICE VOTE

0 Pro ACLU Side vs. 9 Con Opposing Side

Opposing Side (Petitioner / Appellant)

1. Ginsburg, R. – Wrote majority opinion
2. Alito, S. – Joined majority opinion
3. Stevens, J. – Joined majority opinion
4. Thomas, C. – Joined majority opinion
5. Breyer, S. – Joined majority opinion
6. Scalia, A. – Joined majority opinion
7. Kennedy, A. – Joined majority opinion
8. Souter, D. – Joined majority opinion
9. Roberts, J. – Joined majority opinion

VI. A WIN OR LOSS FOR THE ACLU?

The ACLU argue the cause for appellees urging affirmance; the Supreme Court reversed the Court of Appeals' decision by a 9-0 vote, giving the ACLU an apparent loss.

1016. Long Island Care at Home, Ltd. v. Coke

(Decided June 11, 2007; 551 U.S. 158)

I. ISSUE

A. Issues Discussed

Regulation

B. Legal Question Presented

"[W]hether, in light of the statute's text and history, and a different (apparently conflicting) regulation, the Department's regulation is valid and binding."

C. Supreme Court's Answer

"We conclude that it is."

II. CASE SUMMARY

A. Background

"Congress amended the Fair Labor Standards Act . . . to include many 'domestic service' employees not previously subject to its minimum wage and maximum hour requirements. . . . Congress simultaneously created an exemption that excluded . . . certain . . . employees 'employed in domestic service employment,' including . . . companionship workers . . . .

The Department of Labor . . . then promulgated a set of regulations that included two regulations at issue here. The first . . . defines . . . 'domestic service employment' . . . .

The second . . . says that exempt companionship workers include those

'who are employed by an employer or agency other than the family or household using their services . . . [whether or not] such an employee [is assigned] to more than one household or family in the same workweek . . . .'

Evelyn Coke . . . , a domestic worker who provides 'companionship services' . . . , brought this lawsuit against her former employer . . . . She alleged that petitioners failed to pay her the minimum wages and overtime wages to which she was entitled . . . . All parties assume . . . that the FLSA entitles Coke to the payments if, but only if, the statutory exemption for 'companionship services' does not apply to companionship workers paid by third-party agencies . . . . The District Court . . . dismissed . . . .

[T]he Second Circuit found the Department's third-party regulation 'unenforceable' . . . . [The U.S. Supreme Court] vacated the Second Circuit's decision and remanded . . . so that the Circuit could consider a recent DOL 'Advisory Memorandum' explaining . . . the regulation. [T]he Second Circuit . . . again held the regulation unenforceable."

The Supreme Court granted certiorari to review the case a second time.

B. Counsel of Record / ACLU Attorney

ACLU Side (Respondent / Appellee): Harold Craig Becker argued the cause for appellee. With him on the brief was Michael Shen.

Opposing Side (Petitioner / Appellant): H. Bartow Farr III argued the cause for appellants. With him on the briefs were Richard G.

Taranto and Daniel S. Alter.
David B. Salmons argued the cause for the United States as amicus curiae.

III. AMICI CURIAE

ACLU Side (Respondent / Appellee)

Brief of amici curiae filed on behalf of the Urban Justice Center, Brennan Center for Justice, Asian American Legal Defense and Education Fund, Mexican American Legal Defense and Educational Fund, Puerto Rican Legal Defense and Education Fund, National Women's Law Center, National Partnership for Women and Families, Legal Momentum, Washington Lawyers' Committee for Civil Rights and Urban Affairs and American Civil Liberties Union by Molly K. Biklen, Raymond H. Brescia, Paul K. Sonn, Rajesh D. Nayak, and David T. Goldberg.
Brief of amici curiae filed on behalf of AARP et al. by Stacy Canan, Bruce Vignery, and Michael Schuster.
Brief of amici curiae filed on behalf of the Alliance for Retired Americans et al. by Jonathan P. Hiatt, James B. Coppess, Patrick J. Szymanski, and Carol R. Golubock.
Brief of amici curiae filed on behalf of Law Professors et al. by James Reif.

Opposing Side (Petitioner / Appellant)

Brief of amici curiae filed on behalf of the United States by David B. Salmons, Solicitor General Clement, Deputy Solicitor General Kneedler, Jonathan L. Snare, Steven J. Mandel, and Edward D. Sieger.
Brief of amici curiae filed on behalf of the City of New York et al. by Michael A. Cardozo, Stephen J. A. Acquario, Leonard J. Koerner, and Susan Choi-Hausman.
Brief of amici curiae filed on behalf of the Continuing Care Leadership Coaltion, Inc., et al. by Peter G. Bergmann, Kathy H. Chin, Aaron J. Schindel, John Longstreth, Joel L. Hodes, and Ellen M. Bach.
Brief of amici curiae filed on behalf of the National Association for Home Care & Hospice, Inc., by William A. Dombi.
Brief of amici curiae filed on behalf of the National Private Duty Association by Trenten P. Bausch.

IV. THE SUPREME COURT'S DECISION

"We have previously pointed out that the "power of an administrative agency to administer a congressionally created . . . program necessarily requires the formulation of policy and the making of rules to fill any gap left, implicitly or explicitly, by Congress." When an agency fills such a 'gap' reasonably, and in accordance with other applicable (e.g., procedural) requirements, the courts accept the result as legally binding. . . .

[T]he FLSA explicitly leaves gaps . . . as to the scope and definition of statutory terms such as 'domestic service employment' and 'companionship services.' It provides the Department with the power to fill these gaps through rules and regulations. . . . The subject matter of the regulation in question concerns a matter in respect to which the agency is expert . . . .

Respondent argues . . . that a thorough examination of the regulation's content, its method of promulgation, and its context reveals serious legal problems . . . . In particular, respondent claims that the regulation falls outside the scope of Congress' delegation; that it is inconsistent with another, legally governing regulation; that it is an 'interpretive' regulation not warranting judicial deference; and that it was improperly promulgated. We shall examine each of these claims in turn. . . .

[W]e conclude that the Department's interpretation of the two regulations falls well within the principle that an agency's interpretation of its own regulations is 'controlling' unless '"plainly erroneous or inconsistent with"' the regulations being interpreted. . . .

Respondent also argues that, even if the third-party regulation is within the scope of the statute's delegation, is perfectly reasonable, and otherwise complies with the law, courts still should not treat the regulation as legally binding. . . .

Like respondent, the Court of Appeals concluded that the third-party regulation did not fill a statutory gap and hence was not legally binding. . . .

The three contrary considerations to which the Court of Appeals points are insufficient . . . to overcome the other factors . . . , all of which suggest that courts should defer to the Department's rule. . . .

Respondent's final claim is that the 1974 agency notice-and-comment procedure, leading to the promulgation of the third-party regulation, was legally 'defective' because notice was inadequate and the Department's explanation also inadequate. We do not agree. . . .

For these reasons the Court of Appeals' judgment is reversed, and we remand . . . ."

V. JUSTICE VOTE

0 Pro ACLU Side vs. 9 Con Opposing Side

Opposing Side (Petitioner / Appellant)

1. Breyer, S. – Wrote majority opinion
2. Alito, S. – Joined majority opinion
3. Stevens, J. – Joined majority opinion
4. Thomas, C. – Joined majority opinion
5. Scalia, A. – Joined majority opinion
6. Kennedy, A. – Joined majority opinion
7. Ginsburg, R. – Joined majority opinion
8. Souter, D. – Joined majority opinion
9. Roberts, J. – Joined majority opinion

VI. A WIN OR LOSS FOR THE ACLU?

The ACLU filed as amicus curiae urging affirmance; the Supreme Court reversed the Court of Appeals' decision by a 9-0 vote, giving the ACLU an apparent loss.

1017. Brendlin v. California

(Decided June 18, 2007; 551 U.S. 249)

I. ISSUE

A. Issues Discussed

4th Amendment, drugs

B. Legal Question Presented

"When a police officer makes a traffic stop, the driver of the car is seized within the meaning of the Fourth Amendment. The question in this case is whether the same is true of a passenger."

C. Supreme Court's Answer

"We hold that a passenger is seized as well and so may challenge the constitutionality of the stop."

II. CASE SUMMARY

A. Background

"Deputy Sheriff Robert Brokenbrough and his partner saw a parked Buick with expired registration tags. . . . Brokenbrough learned that an application for renewal of registration was being processed. The officers saw the car again on the road, and . . . noticed its display of a temporary operating permit . . . . The officers decided to pull the Buick over to verify that the permit matched the vehicle . . . . Brokenbrough asked the driver, Karen Simeroth, for her license and saw a passenger . . . Bruce Brendlin . . . . He recalled that either Scott or Bruce Brendlin had dropped out of parole supervision and asked Brendlin to identify himself. Brokenbrough . . . verified that Brendlin was a parole violator with an outstanding no-bail warrant for his arrest. . . . Brokenbrough went to the passenger side of the Buick, ordered him out of the car at gunpoint, and declared him under arrest. When the police searched Brendlin incident to arrest, they found an orange syringe cap . . . . A patdown search of Simeroth revealed syringes and a plastic bag of a green leafy substance, and she was also formally arrested. Officers then searched the car and found tubing, a scale, and other things used to produce methamphetamine.

Brendlin . . . moved to suppress the evidence obtained in the searches . . . as fruits of an unconstitutional seizure . . . . The trial court denied the suppression motion . . . . Brendlin pleaded guilty, . . . and was sentenced to four years in prison. . . .

California Court of Appeal reversed . . . . [T]he Supreme Court of California reversed."

The Supreme Court granted certiorari to review the case.

B. Counsel of Record / ACLU Attorney

ACLU Side (Petitioner / Appellant): Elizabeth M. Campbell argued the cause for appellant. With her on the briefs were Jeffrey T. Green, Richard A. Kaplan, and Sarah O'Rourke Schrup.

Opposing Side (Respondent / Appellee): Clifford E. Zall, Deputy Attorney General of California, argued the cause for appellee. With him on the brief were Edmund G. Brown, Jr., Attorney General, Manuel M. Medeiros, State Solicitor General, Dane R. Gillette, Chief Assistant Attorney General, Michael P. Farrell, Senior Assistant Attorney General, Donald E. de Nicola, Deputy State Solicitor, Michael A. Canzoneri, Supervising Deputy Attorney General, and Doris A. Calandra, Deputy Attorney General.

III. AMICI CURIAE

ACLU Side (Petitioner / Appellant)

Brief of amici curiae filed on behalf of the American Civil Liberties Union, the ACLU of Northern California, the Asian American Legal Defense and Education Fund, and the National Association for the Advancement of Colored People by Michael T. Risher, Steven R. Shapiro, Emily Chiang, Reginald T. Shuford, Alexis Agathocleous, Dennis D. Parker, Susan N. Herman, Dennis Courtland Hayes, Victor L. Goode, and Kenneth Kimerling.

Brief of amici curiae filed on behalf of the National Association of Criminal Defense Lawyers et al. by Jonathan E. Nuechterlein, Sambhav Sankar, Pamela Harris, and Frances H. Pratt.

Opposing Side (Respondent / Appellee)

Brief of amici curiae filed on behalf of Wayne County, Michigan by Kym L. Worthy and Timothy A. Baughman.

IV. THE SUPREME COURT'S DECISION

"A person is seized by the police and thus entitled to challenge the government's action under the Fourth Amendment when the officer, "by means of physical force or show of authority," terminates or restrains his freedom of movement, . . . 'through means intentionally applied,' . . . . A police officer may make a seizure by a show of authority and without the use of physical force, but there is no seizure without actual submission . . . .

When the actions of the police do not show an unambiguous intent to restrain or when an individual's submission . . . takes the form of passive acquiescence, there needs to be some test . . . . The test was devised by Justice Stewart . . . who wrote that a seizure occurs if 'in view of all of the circumstances surrounding the incident, a reasonable person would have believed that he was not free to leave.' . . .

The law is settled that in Fourth Amendment terms a traffic stop entails a seizure of the driver . . . . And although we have not, until today, squarely answered the question whether a passenger is also seized, we have said over and over in dicta that during a traffic stop an officer seizes everyone in the vehicle . . . .

The State concedes that the police had no adequate justification to pull the car over, but argues that the passenger was not seized and thus cannot claim that the evidence was tainted by an unconstitutional stop. We resolve this question by asking whether a reasonable person in Brendlin's position . . . would have believed himself free to 'terminate the encounter' between the police and himself. We think that in these circumstances any reasonable passenger would have understood the police officers to be exercising control to the point that no one in the car was free to depart without police permission. . . .

Brendlin was seized from the moment Simeroth's car came to a halt on the side of the road, and it was error to deny his suppression motion on the ground that seizure occurred only at the formal arrest. It will be for the state courts to consider in the first instance whether suppression turns on any other issue. The judgment of the Supreme Court of California is vacated, and the case is remanded . . . ."

V. JUSTICE VOTE

9 Pro ACLU Side vs. 0 Con Opposing Side

ACLU Side (Petitioner / Appellant)

1. Souter, D. – Wrote majority opinion
2. Alito, S. – Joined majority opinion

3. Stevens, J. – Joined majority opinion
4. Thomas, C. – Joined majority opinion
5. Breyer, S. – Joined majority opinion
6. Scalia, A. – Joined majority opinion
7. Kennedy, A. – Joined majority opinion
8. Ginsburg, R. – Joined majority opinion
9. Roberts, J. – Joined majority opinion

VI. A WIN OR LOSS FOR THE ACLU?

The ACLU filed as amicus curiae urging reversal of the judgment of the Supreme Court of California; the Supreme Court vacated in a 9-0 vote, giving the ACLU an apparent win.

1018. Morse v. Frederick

(Decided June 25, 2007; 551 U.S. 393)

I. ISSUE

A. Issues Discussed

1st Amendment, press, speech, association

B. Legal Question Presented

"[W]hether Frederick had a First Amendment right to wield his banner, and, if so, whether that right was so clearly established that the principal may be held liable for damages."

C. Supreme Court's Answer

"We conclude that the school officials in this case did not violate the First Amendment by confiscating the pro-drug banner and suspending the student responsible for it. . . .

We resolve the first question against Frederick, and therefore have no occasion to reach the second."

II. CASE SUMMARY

A. Background

"[T]he Olympic Torch Relay passed through Juneau, Alaska . . . . The torchbearers were to proceed along a street in front of Juneau–Douglas High School (JDHS) . . . . Deborah Morse, the school principal, decided to permit staff and students to participate . . . . Students were allowed to leave class to observe the relay from either side of the street. Teachers and administrative officials monitored the students' actions.

Respondent Joseph Frederick . . . joined his friends . . . across the street from the school to watch the event. . . . As the torchbearers and camera crews passed by, Frederick and his friends unfurled a 14–foot banner bearing the phrase: 'BONG HiTS 4 JESUS.' . . .

Principal Morse immediately . . . demanded that the banner be taken down. Everyone but Frederick complied. Morse confiscated the banner and . . . suspended him for 10 days. Morse later explained that she told Frederick to take the banner down because she thought it encouraged illegal drug use, in violation of established school policy. . . .

Frederick administratively appealed his suspension, but the Juneau School District Superintendent upheld it, limiting it to time served (eight days). . . .

The Juneau School District Board of Education upheld the suspension.

Frederick then filed suit under 42 U.S.C. § 1983, alleging that the school board and Morse had violated his First Amendment rights. . . . The District Court granted summary judgment for the school board and Morse . . . .

The Ninth Circuit reversed."

The Supreme Court granted certiorari to review the case.

B. Counsel of Record / ACLU Attorney

ACLU Side (Respondent / Appellee): Douglas K. Mertz argued the cause for appellee. With him on the brief were Jason Brandeis of the ACLU of Alaska Foundation, and Steven R. Shapiro, Catherine N. Crump, and Jonathan B. Miller of the ACLU Foundation.

Opposing Side (Petitioner / Appellant): Kenneth W. Starr argued the cause for appellants. With him on the briefs were Rick Richmond and Eric W. Hagen.

Deputy Solicitor General Kneedler argued the cause for the United States as amicus curiae.

III. AMICI CURIAE

ACLU Side (Respondent / Appellee)

Brief of amici curiae filed on behalf of the American Center for Law and Justice by Jay Alan Sekulow, Colby M. May, Stuart J. Roth, James M. Henderson, Sr., and Walter M. Weber.

Brief of amici curiae filed on behalf of the Center for Individual Rights by Michael E. Rosman; for the Christian Legal Society by Gregory S. Baylor, Kimberlee Wood Colby, and Steven H. Aden.

Brief of amici curiae filed on behalf of the Drug Policy Alliance et al. by David T. Goldberg and Daniel N. Abrahamson.

Brief of amici curiae filed on behalf ofthe Lambda Legal Defense and Education Fund, Inc., by Jon W. Davidson, Gregory R. Nevins, F. Brian Chase, and James P. Madigan.

Brief of amici curiae filed on behalf of the National Coalition Against Censorship et al. by Preeta D. Bansal, Joan E. Bertin, and Marjorie Heins.

Brief of amici curiae filed on behalf of the Rutherford Institute by James J. Knicely and John W. Whitehead.

Brief of amici curiae filed on behalf of Students for Sensible Drug Policy by Brooks M. Beard.

Brief of amici curiae filed on behalf of the Student Press Law Center et al. by Sonja R. West, Michele L. Earl-Hubbard, S. Mark Goodman, and Michael C. Hiestand.

Brief of amici curiae filed on behalf of the Alliance Defense Fund by Kevin H. Theriot, Benjamin W. Bull, and Jordan W. Lorence.

Brief of amici curiae filed on behalf of Liberty Counsel by Mathew D. Staver, Anita L. Staver, Erik W. Stanley, and Mary E. McAlister.

Brief of amici curiae filed on behalf of the Liberty Legal Institute by Kelly J. Shackelford, Douglas Laycock, and Robert A. Destro.

Opposing Side (Petitioner / Appellant)

Brief of amici curiae filed on behalf of the United States by Deputy Solicitor General Kneedler, Solicitor General Clement, Assistant Attorney General Keisler, Deputy Solicitor General Garre, Daryl Joseffer, Robert D. Kamenshine, Kent D. Talbert, Stephen H. Freid, Edward H. Jurith, and Linda V. Priebe.

Brief of amici curiae filed on behalf of D. A. R. E. America et al. by Gene C. Schaerr, Steffen N. Johnson, and Linda T. Coberly.

Brief of amici curiae filed on behalf of the National School Boards Association et al. by Michael E. Smith, Francisco M. Negrón, Jr., Naomi E. Gittins, Thomas E. M. Hutton, and Lisa E. Soronen.

IV. THE SUPREME COURT'S DECISION

"Our cases make clear that students do not 'shed their constitutional rights to freedom of speech or expression at the schoolhouse gate.' At the same time, we have held that 'the constitutional rights of students in public school are not automatically coextensive with the rights of adults in other settings,' and that the rights of students 'must be 'applied in light of the special characteristics of the school environment.'' Consistent with these principles, we hold that schools may take steps to safeguard those entrusted to their care from speech that can reasonably be regarded as encouraging illegal drug use. We conclude that the school officials in this case did not violate the First Amendment by confiscating the pro-drug banner and suspending the student responsible for it. . . .

At the outset, we reject Frederick's argument that this is not a school speech case . . . .

The message on Frederick's banner is cryptic. . . . But Principal Morse thought the banner would be interpreted by those viewing it as promoting illegal drug use, and that interpretation is plainly a reasonable one. . . .

The question thus becomes whether a principal may, consistent with the First Amendment, restrict student speech at a school event, when that speech is reasonably viewed as promoting illegal drug use. We hold that she may. . . .

[W]e have held in the Fourth Amendment context that 'while children assuredly do not 'shed their constitutional rights . . . at the schoolhouse gate,' . . . the nature of those rights is what is appropriate for children in school.' . . .

Even more to the point, these cases also recognize that deterring drug use by schoolchildren is an 'important—indeed, perhaps compelling' interest. . . .

School principals have a difficult job, and a vitally important one. When Frederick suddenly and unexpectedly unfurled his banner, Morse had to decide to act—or not act—on the spot. It was reasonable for her to conclude that the banner promoted illegal drug use—in violation of established school policy—and that failing to act would send a powerful message to the students in her charge, including Frederick, about how serious the school was about the dangers of illegal drug use. The First Amendment does not require schools to tolerate at school events student expression that contributes to those dangers.

The judgment of the United States Court of Appeals for the Ninth Circuit is reversed, and the case is remanded . . . ."

V. JUSTICE VOTE

4 Pro ACLU Side vs. 5 Con Opposing Side

ACLU Side (Respondent / Appellee)

1. Stevens, J. – Wrote dissenting opinion
2. Souter, D. – Joined Stevens' dissent
3. Ginsburg, R. – Joined Stevens' dissent
4. Breyer, S. – Wrote opinion concurring in part and dissenting in part

Opposing Side (Petitioner / Appellant)

1. Roberts, J. – Wrote majority opinion
2. Alito, S. – Wrote concurring opinion
3. Thomas, C. – Wrote concurring opinion
4. Scalia, A. – Joined majority opinion
5. Kennedy, A. – Joined Alito's concurrence

VI. A WIN OR LOSS FOR THE ACLU?

The ACLU argued the cause for appellee urging affirmance; the Supreme Court reversed the Court of Appeals' decision by a 5-4 vote, giving the ACLU an apparent loss.

1019. Federal Election Commission v. Wisconsin Right to Life, Inc.

(Decided June 25, 2007; 551 U.S. 449)

I. ISSUE

A. Issues Discussed

Voting rights, 1st Amendment, press, speech, association

B. Legal Question Presented

"[W]hether it is consistent with the First Amendment for BCRA § 203 to prohibit WRTL from running these three ads."

C. Supreme Court's Answer

"We conclude that the speech at issue in this as-applied challenge is not the 'functional equivalent' of express campaign speech. We further conclude that the interests held to justify restricting corporate campaign speech or its functional equivalent do not justify restricting issue advocacy, and accordingly we hold that BCRA § 203 is unconstitutional as applied to the advertisements at issue in these cases."

II. CASE SUMMARY

A. Background

"Section 203 of the Bipartisan Campaign Reform Act of 2002 (BCRA) makes it a federal crime for any corporation to broadcast . . . any communication that names a federal candidate for elected office and is targeted to the electorate. In McConnell v. Federal Election Comm'n, 540 U.S. 93 (2003), this Court considered whether § 203 was facially overbroad . . . . The Court concluded that there was no overbreadth concern to the extent the speech in question was the 'functional equivalent' of express campaign speech. On the other hand, the Court 'assume[d]' that the interests it had found to 'justify the regulation of campaign speech might not apply to the regulation of genuine issue ads.' The Court nonetheless determined that § 203 was not facially overbroad. . . .

Last Term, we reversed a lower court ruling . . . that our decision in McConnell left 'no room' for as-applied challenges to § 203. We held on the contrary that '[i]n upholding § 203 against a facial challenge, we did not purport to resolve future as-applied challenges.'

We now confront such an as-applied challenge. Resolving it requires us first to determine whether the speech at issue is the 'functional equivalent' of speech expressly advocating the election or defeat of a candidate for federal office, or instead a 'genuine issue a[d].'"

The Supreme Court granted certiorari to review the case.

B. Counsel of Record / ACLU Attorney

ACLU Side (Respondent / Appellee): James Bopp, Jr., argued the cause for appellee in both cases. With him on the brief were Richard E. Coleson, Jeffrey P. Gallant, Raeanna S. Moore, and M. Miller Baker.

Opposing Side (Petitioner / Appellant): Solicitor General Clement argued the cause for appellant in No. 06–969. With him on the briefs were Deputy Solicitor General Garre, Malcolm L. Stewart, Richard B. Bader, David Kolker, Harry J. Summers, and Kevin Deeley. Seth P. Waxman argued the cause for appellants in No. 06–970. With him on the briefs were Randolph D. Moss, Danielle Spinelli, Roger M. Witten, Donald J. Simon, Scott L. Nelson, Trevor Potter, J. Gerald Hebert, Paul S. Ryan, Charles G. Curtis, Jr., Fred Wertheimer, Alan B. Morrison, and Bradley S. Phillips.

III. AMICI CURIAE

ACLU Side (Respondent / Appellee)

Brief of amici curiae filed on behalf of the American Civil Liberties Union by Steven R. Shapiro, Mark J. Lopez, and Joel M. Gora.

Brief of amici curiae filed on behalf of the Alliance for Justice by Michael B. Trister and B. Holly Schadler.

Brief of amici curiae filed on behalf of the American Federation of Labor and Congress of Industrial Organizations by Jonathan P. Hiatt and Laurence E. Gold.

Brief of amici curiae filed on behalf of the Center for Competitive Politics et al. by Erik S. Jaffe.

Brief of amici curiae filed on behalf of the Chamber of Commerce of the United States of America by Jan Witold Baran, Thomas W. Kirby, Caleb P. Burns, Steven J. Law, Robin S. Conrad, Amar D. Sarwal, and Judith K. Richmond.

Brief of amici curiae filed on behalf of Citizens United et al. by Herbert W. Titus, William J. Olson, John S. Miles, and Mark B. Weinberg.

Brief of amici curiae filed on behalf of the Family Research Council et al. by Kathleen M. Sullivan and Stephen W. Reed.

Brief of amici curiae filed on behalf of the National Association of Realtors by David C. Frederick, Brendan J. Crimmins, Laurene K. Janik, and Ralph W. Holmen.

Brief of amici curiae filed on behalf of the Republican National Committee by Thomas J. Josefiak.

Brief of amici curiae filed on behalf of United States Senator Mitch McConnell by Theodore B. Olson, Douglas R. Cox, and Amir C. Tayrani.

Brief of amici curiae filed on behalf of the American Center for Law and Justice et al. by Jay Alan Sekulow, Stuart J. Roth, James M. Henderson, Sr., and Stephen W. Reed.

Brief of amici curiae filed on behalf of a Coalition of Public Charities by Robert F. Bauer.

Brief of amici curiae filed on behalf of the National Rifle Association by Charles J. Cooper, Brian S. Koukoutchos, and David H. Thompson.

Opposing Side (Petitioner / Appellant)

Brief of amici curiae filed on behalf of the Committee for Economic Development et al. by H. Christopher Bartolomucci.

Brief of amici curiae filed on behalf of the League of Women Voters of the United States et al. by Daniel R. Ortiz.

Brief of amici curiae filed on behalf of Richard Briffault et al. by Richard L. Hasen, Martin S. Lederman, Mr. Briffault, and David S. Ettinger.

Brief of amici curiae filed on behalf of Norman Dorsen et al. by Burt Neuborne and Deborah Goldberg.

IV. THE SUPREME COURT'S DECISION

"WRTL rightly concedes that its ads are prohibited by BCRA § 203. . . . WRTL further concedes that its ads do not fit under any of BCRA's exceptions to the term 'electioneering communication.' The only question, then, is whether it is consistent with the First Amendment for BCRA § 203 to prohibit WRTL from running these three ads. . . .

Because WRTL's ads may reasonably be interpreted as something other than as an appeal to vote for or against a specific candidate, we hold they are not the functional equivalent of express advocacy, and therefore fall outside the scope of McConnell's holding. . . .

BCRA § 203 can be constitutionally applied to WRTL's ads only if it is narrowly tailored to further a compelling interest. This Court has never recognized a compelling interest in regulating ads . . . that are neither express advocacy nor its functional equivalent. The District Court below considered interests that might justify regulating WRTL's ads here, and found none sufficiently compelling. We reach the same conclusion. . . .

Because WRTL's ads are not express advocacy or its functional equivalent, and because appellants identify no interest sufficiently compelling to justify burdening WRTL's speech, we hold that BCRA § 203 is unconstitutional as applied to WRTL's 'Wedding,' 'Loan,' and 'Waiting' ads. . . .

McConnell held that express advocacy of a candidate or his opponent by a corporation shortly before an election may be prohibited, along with the functional equivalent of such express advocacy. We have no occasion to revisit that determination today. But when it comes to defining what speech qualifies as the functional equivalent of express advocacy subject to such a ban—the issue we do have to decide—we give the benefit of the doubt to speech, not censorship. The First Amendment's command that 'Congress shall make no law . . . abridging the freedom of speech' demands at least that.

The judgment of the United States District Court for the District of Columbia is affirmed."

V. JUSTICE VOTE

5 Pro ACLU Side vs. 4 Con Opposing Side

ACLU Side (Respondent / Appellee)

1. Roberts, J. – Wrote majority opinion
2. Alito, S. – Wrote concurring opinion
3. Kennedy, A. – Joined majority opinion
4. Scalia, A. – Joined majority opinion
5. Thomas, C. – Joined majority opinion

Opposing Side (Petitioner / Appellant)

1. Souter, D. – Wrote dissenting opinion
2. Stevens, J. – Joined Souter's dissent
3. Breyer, S. – Joined Souter's dissent
4. Ginsburg, R. – Joined Souter's dissent

VI. A WIN OR LOSS FOR THE ACLU?

The ACLU filed as amicus curiae urging affirmance; the Supreme Court affirmed the District Court's decision by a 5-4 vote, giving the ACLU an apparent win.

1020. Hein v. Freedom From Religion Foundation, Inc.

(Decided June 25, 2007; 551 U.S. 587)

I. ISSUE

A. Issues Discussed

1st Amendment, religion

B. Legal Question Presented

"In Flast v. Cohen, 392 U.S. 83 (1968), [the U.S. Supreme Court] recognized a narrow exception to the general rule against federal taxpayer standing. Under Flast, a plaintiff asserting an Establishment Clause claim has standing to challenge a law authorizing the use of federal funds in a way that allegedly violates the Establishment Clause. In the present case, Congress did not specifically authorize the use of federal funds to pay for the conferences or speeches that the plaintiffs challenged. . . .

The question that is presented here is whether this broad reading of Flast is correct."

C. Supreme Court's Answer

"We hold that it is not."

II. CASE SUMMARY

A. Background

"This is a lawsuit in which it was claimed that conferences held as part of the President's Faith-Based and Community Initiatives program violated the Establishment Clause of the First Amendment . . . . The plaintiffs contend that they meet the standing requirements of Article III of the Constitution because they pay federal taxes.

It has long been established, however, that the payment of taxes is generally not enough to establish standing to challenge an action taken by the Federal Government. . . .

In Flast v. Cohen, 392 U.S. 83 (1968), we recognized a narrow exception to the general rule against federal taxpayer standing. . . .

The respondents are Freedom From Religion Foundation, Inc., a nonstock corporation 'opposed to government endorsement of religion,' and three of its members. Respondents brought suit . . . alleging that petitioners violated the Establishment Clause by organizing conferences at which faith-based organizations allegedly 'are singled out as being particularly worthy of federal funding . . .' . . . .

The only asserted basis for standing was that . . . respondents are federal taxpayers . . . .

The District Court dismissed the claims . . . for lack of standing. . . .

United States Court of Appeals for the Seventh Circuit reversed. . . .

The Court of Appeals denied en banc review by a vote of 7 to 4."

The Supreme Court granted certiorari to review the case.

B. Counsel of Record / ACLU Attorney

ACLU Side (Respondent / Appellee): Andrew J. Pincus argued the cause for appellees. With him on the brief were Charles A. Rothfeld, Richard L. Bolton, and Giovanna Shay.

Opposing Side (Petitioner / Appellant): Solicitor General Clement argued the cause for appellants. With him on the briefs were Assistant Attorney General Keisler, Deputy Solicitor General Garre, Patricia A. Millett, Robert M. Loeb, and Lowell V. Sturgill, Jr.

III. AMICI CURIAE

ACLU Side (Respondent / Appellee)

Brief of amici curiae filed on behalf of the American Civil Liberties Union, Americans United for Separation of Church and State, Baptist Joint Committee for Religious Liberty, People for the American Way Foundation, and Anti-Defamation League by Anne Harkavy, Kelly Brooke Snyder, Caroline Rogus, Judith E. Schaeffer, Howard W. Goldstein, Steven M. Freeman, Steven C. Sheinberg, Steven R. Shapiro, Daniel Mach, Ayesha N. Khan, Richard B. Katskee, and K. Hollyn Hollman.

Brief of amici curiae filed on behalf of American Atheists, Inc., by Robert Corn-Revere, Ronald G. London, David M. Shapiro, and Edwin F. Kagin.

Brief of amici curiae filed on behalf of the American Jewish Congress et al. by Marc D. Stern and Jeffrey Sinensky.

Brief of amici curiae filed on behalf of the Center for Inquiry et al. by Irvin B. Nathan, Daniel S. Pariser, and Ronald A. Lindsay.

Brief of amici curiae filed on behalf of Legal and Religious Historians and Law Scholars by Matthew M. Shors and Steven K. Green.

Opposing Side (Petitioner / Appellant)

Brief of amici curiae filed on behalf of the State of Indiana et al. by Steve Carter, Attorney General of Indiana, Thomas M. Fisher, Solicitor General, and Julie A. Hoffman, Deputy Attorney General, and by the Attorneys General for their respective States as follows: Troy King of Alabama, John Suthers of Colorado, Bill McCollum of Florida, Michael A. Cox of Michigan, George J. Chanos of Nevada, Wayne Stenehjem of North Dakota, W. A. Drew Edmondson of Oklahoma, Henry McMaster of South Carolina, Greg Abbott of Texas, Robert F. McDonnell of Virginia, and Rob McKenna of Washington.

Brief of amici curiae filed on behalf of the American Center for Law and Justice by Jay Alan Sekulow, Walter M. Weber, Colby M. May, Stuart J. Roth, John P. Tuskey, and Laura B. Hernandez.

Brief of amici curiae filed on behalf of the Christian Legal Society by Gregory S. Baylor and Steven H. Aden.

Brief of amici curiae filed on behalf of the Foundation for Moral Law, Inc., by Roy S. Moore, Gregory M. Jones, and Benjamin D. DuPré.

Brief of amici curiae filed on behalf of We Care America by Benjamin W. Bull and Jordan Lorence.

IV. THE SUPREME COURT'S DECISION

"Article III of the Constitution limits the judicial power of the United States to the resolution of 'Cases' and 'Controversies,' and "Article III standing . . . enforces the Constitution's case-or-controversy requirement." . . .

'[O]ne of the controlling elements in the definition of a case or controversy under Article III' is standing. The requisite elements of Article III standing are well established: 'A plaintiff must allege personal injury fairly traceable to the defendant's allegedly unlawful conduct and likely to be redressed by the requested relief.' . . .

As a general matter, the interest of a federal taxpayer in seeing that Treasury funds are spent in accordance with the Constitution does not give rise to the kind of redressable 'personal injury' required for Article III standing. . . .

In Flast, the Court carved out a narrow exception to the general constitutional prohibition against taxpayer standing. . . . The Court set out a two-part test for determining whether a federal taxpayer has standing to challenge an allegedly unconstitutional expenditure . . . .

The Court held that the taxpayer-plaintiffs in Flast had satisfied both prongs of this test: The plaintiff's 'constitutional challenge [was] made to an exercise by Congress of its power under Art. I, § 8, to spend for the general welfare,' and she alleged a violation of the Establishment Clause, which 'operates as a specific constitutional limitation upon the exercise by Congress of the taxing and spending power conferred by Art. I, § 8.' . . .

Respondents argue that this case falls within the Flast exception, which they read to cover any 'expenditure of government funds in violation of the Establishment Clause.' But this broad reading fails to observe 'the rigor with which the Flast exception to the Frothingham principle ought to be applied.' . . .

In short, this case falls outside 'the narrow exception' that Flast 'created to the general rule against taxpayer standing established in Frothingham.' Because the expenditures that respondents challenge were not expressly authorized or mandated by any specific congressional enactment, respondents' lawsuit is not directed at an exercise of congressional power and thus lacks the requisite 'logical nexus' between taxpayer status 'and the type of legislative enactment attacked.' . . .

[T]he judgment of the Court of Appeals for the Seventh Circuit is reversed."

V. JUSTICE VOTE

4 Pro ACLU Side vs. 5 Con Opposing Side

ACLU Side (Respondent / Appellee)

1. Souter, D. – Wrote dissenting opinion
2. Ginsburg, R. – Joined Souter's dissent
3. Breyer, S. – Joined Souter's dissent
4. Stevens, J. – Joined Souter's dissent

Opposing Side (Petitioner / Appellant)

1. Alito, S. – Wrote majority opinion
2. Thomas, C. – Wrote concurring opinion
3. Scalia, A. – Joined Thomas' concurrence
4. Kennedy, A. – Joined majority opinion
5. Roberts, J. – Joined majority opinion

VI. A WIN OR LOSS FOR THE ACLU?

The ACLU filed as amicus curiae urging affirmance; the Supreme Court reversed the Court of Appeals' decision by a 5-4 vote, giving the ACLU an apparent loss.

1021. Parents Involved in Community Schools v. Seattle School Dist. No. 1

(Decided June 28, 2007; 551 U.S. 701)

I. ISSUE

A. Issues Discussed

Race

B. Legal Question Presented

"[W]hether a public school that had not operated legally segregated schools or has been found to be unitary may choose to classify students by race and rely upon that classification in making school assignments."

C. Supreme Court's Answer

"The school districts in these cases have not carried the heavy burden of demonstrating that we should allow [classifications based on race] once again—even for very different reasons. For schools that never segregated on the basis of race, such as Seattle, or that have removed the vestiges of past segregation, such as Jefferson County, the way 'to achieve a system of determining admission to the public schools on a nonracial basis,' is to stop assigning students on a racial basis."

II. CASE SUMMARY

A. Background

"The school districts in these cases voluntarily adopted student assignment plans that rely upon race to determine which public schools certain children may attend. The Seattle school district classifies children as white or nonwhite; the Jefferson County school district as black or 'other.' In Seattle, this racial classification is used to allocate slots in oversubscribed high schools. In Jefferson County, it is used to make certain elementary school assignments and to rule on transfer requests. In each case, the school district relies upon an individual student's race in assigning that student to a particular school, so that the racial balance at the school falls within a predetermined range based on the racial composition of the school district as a whole. Parents of students denied assignment to particular schools under these plans solely because of their race brought suit, contending that allocating children to different public schools on the basis of race violated the Fourteenth Amendment guarantee of equal protection. The Courts of Appeals below upheld the plans."

The Supreme Court granted certiorari to review the case.

B. Counsel of Record / ACLU Attorney

ACLU Side (Respondent / Appellee): Michael Madden argued the cause for appellees in No. 05–908. With him on the brief were Carol Sue Janes, Maree F. Sneed, John W. Borkowski, Audrey J. Anderson, Gary L. Ikeda, Shannon McMinimee, and Eric Schnapper. Francis J. Mellen, Jr., argued the cause for appellees in No. 05–915. With him on the brief were Byron E. Leet and Rosemary Miller

Opposing Side (Petitioner / Appellant): Harry J. F. Korrell argued the cause for appellant in No. 05–908. With him on the briefs were Daniel B. Ritter and Eric B. Martin. Teddy B. Gordon argued the cause and filed briefs for appellant in No. 05–915.

Solicitor General Clement argued the cause for the United States as amicus curiae urging reversal in both cases.

III. AMICI CURIAE

ACLU Side (Respondent / Appellee)

Brief of amici curiae filed on behalf of the American Civil Liberties Union, the ACLU of Kentucky, and the ACLU of Washington by Dennis D. Parker, Katherine Y. Kim, Elora Mukherjee, Reginald T. Shuford, Christopher A. Hansen, and Steven R. Shapiro.

Brief of amici curiae filed on behalf of the Commonwealth of Massachusetts by Thomas F. Reilly, Attorney General of Massachusetts, and Richard W. Cole and John R. Hitt, Assistant Attorneys General.

Brief of amici curiae filed on behalf of the State of New York et al. by Eliot Spitzer, Attorney General of New York, Caitlin J. Halligan, Solicitor General, Michelle Aronowitz, Deputy Solicitor General, and Laura R. Johnson and Diana R. H. Winters, Assistant Solicitors General, by Roberto J. Sánchez Ramos, Secretary of Justice of Puerto Rico, and by the Attorneys General for their respective jurisdictions as follows: Richard Blumenthal of Connecticut, Robert J. Spagnoletti of the District of Columbia, Lisa Madigan of Illinois, Thomas Miller of Iowa, Greg Stumbo of Kentucky, G. Steven Rowe of Maine, J. Joseph Curran, Jr., of Maryland, Jeremiah W. (Jay) Nixon of Missouri, Stuart Rabner of New Jersey, Patricia A. Madrid of New Mexico, Roy Cooper of North Carolina, Hardy Myers of Oregon, Patrick Lynch of Rhode Island, Mark L. Shurtleff of Utah, William H. Sorrell of Vermont, Rob McKenna of Washington, and Peggy A. Lautenschlager of Wisconsin.

Brief of amici curiae filed on behalf of the American Council on Education et al. by Michael P. Boudett, Dean Richlin, and Robert E. Toone.

Brief of amici curiae filed on behalf of the American Educational Research Association by Angelo N. Ancheta.

Brief of amici curiae filed on behalf of the American Psychological Association et al. by John Payton, David W. Ogden, Nathalie F. P. Gilfoyle, and Lindsay Childress-Beatty.

Brief of amici curiae filed on behalf of the Anti-Defamation League by Martin E. Karlinsky, Erwin Chemerinsky, Frederick M. Lawrence, Jonathan K. Baum, Steven M. Freeman, Howard W. Goldstein, and Steven C. Sheinberg.

Brief of amici curiae filed on behalf of the Asian American Justice Center et al. by Mark A. Packman, Jonathan M. Cohen, Karen Narasaki, and Vincent Eng.

Brief of amici curiae filed on behalf of the Asian American Legal Defense and Education Fund et al. by Marc Wolinsky and Kenneth Kimerling.

Brief of amici curiae filed on behalf of the Association of the Bar of the City of New York by Jonathan I. Blackman and David Rush.

Brief of amici curiae filed on behalf of the Black Women Lawyers' Association of Greater Chicago, Inc., by Sharon E. Jones.

Brief of amici curiae filed on behalf of the Brennan Center for Justice et al. by Warrington S. Parker III, Deborah Goldberg, and David J. Harth.

Brief of amici curiae filed on behalf of the Caucus for Structural Equity by Daniel R. Shulman.

Brief of amici curiae filed on behalf of the Civil Rights Clinic at Howard University School of Law by Aderson Bellegarde François.

Brief of amici curiae filed on behalf of the Coalition to Defend Affirmative Action, Integration, & Immigrant Rights and Fight for Equality By Any Means Necessary (BAMN) et al. by George B. Washington.

Brief of amici curiae filed on behalf of the Collaborative of Catholic Leaders et al. by Terrence J. Fleming.

Brief of amici curiae filed on behalf of the Council of the Great City Schools et al. by Julie Wright Halbert and Pamela Harris.

Brief of amici curiae filed on behalf of Historians by Jack Greenberg.

Brief of amici curiae filed on behalf of Historians of the Civil Rights Era by Theodore V. Wells, Jr., and David W. Brown.

Brief of amici curiae filed on behalf of Housing Scholars et al. by Michael B. de Leeuw.

Brief of amici curiae filed on behalf of Interested Human Rights Clinics et al. by Cynthia J. Larsen and Martha F. Davis.

Brief of amici curiae filed on behalf of Latino Organizations by John D. Trasviña and Diana S. Sen.

Brief of amici curiae filed on behalf of the Lawyers' Committee for Civil Rights of the San Francisco Bay Area by Steven A. Hirsch and Robert Rubin.
Brief of amici curiae filed on behalf of the Leadership Conference on Civil Rights et al. by Andrew J. Pincus, Carolyn P. Osolinik, and William L. Taylor.
Brief of amici curiae filed on behalf of the Massachusetts Association of School Superintendents et al. by Joseph Leghorn.
Brief of amici curiae filed on behalf of the NAACP by Dennis Courtland Hayes and Preeta D. Bansal.
Brief of amici curiae filed on behalf of the NAACP Legal Defense & Educational Fund, Inc., by Theodore M. Shaw, Jacqueline A. Berrien, Norman J. Chachkin, Victor A. Bolden, Chinh Q. Le, and David T. Goldberg.
Brief of amici curiae filed on behalf of the National Collegiate Athletic Association et al. by Margaret A. Keane.
Brief of amici curiae filed on behalf of the National Education Association et al. by Robert H. Chanin, Jonathan P. Hiatt, Harold Craig Becker, David Strom, Elliot Mincberg, Alice O'Brien, and Larry Weinberg.
Brief of amici curiae filed on behalf of the National Parent Teacher Association by Rachel D. Godsil and Michelle Adams.
Brief of amici curiae filed on behalf of the National School Boards Association et al. by Thomas C. Goldstein, Francisco M. Negrón, and Michael C. Small.
Brief of amici curiae filed on behalf of the National Women's Law Center et al. by Walter Dellinger, Mark S. Davies, Nicole A. Saharsky, Marcia D. Greenberger, Jocelyn Samuels, Dina R. Lassow, and Judith L. Lichtman.
Brief of amici curiae filed on behalf of Religious Organizations et al. by William T. Russell, Jr.
Brief of amici curiae filed on behalf of the Swann Fellowship et al. by Anita S. Earls, Julius L. Chambers, Charles E. Daye, and John Charles Boger.
Brief of amici curiae filed on behalf of Former United States Secretaries of Education et al. by Drew S. Days III, Beth S. Brinkmann, and Seth M. Galanter.
Brief of amici curiae filed on behalf of the Urban League of Metropolitan Seattle et al. by Rebecca J. Roe.
Brief of amici curiae filed on behalf of the Honorable Clifford L. Alexander, Jr., et al. by Jonathan S. Franklin.
Brief of amici curiae filed on behalf of Senator Edward M. Kennedy et al. by Andy Liu, David L. Haga, Laurel Pyke Malson, and Beth Nolan.
Brief of amici curiae filed on behalf of Representative Jim McDermott et al. by William R. Weissman.
Brief of amici curiae filed on behalf of Amy Stuart Wells et al. by Kenneth D. Heath.
Brief of amici curiae filed on behalf of 19 Former Chancellors of the University of California by Goodwin Liu.
Brief of amici curiae filed on behalf of 553 Social Scientists by Liliana M. Garces.
Brief of amici curiae filed on behalf of Walt Sherlin by Martha Melinda Lawrence.
Brief of amici curiae filed on behalf of the Alliance for Education et al. by David J. Burman, Michael W. Hoge, and J. Shan Mullin.
Brief of amici curiae filed on behalf of the Los Angeles Unified School District by Peter W. James.
Brief of amici curiae filed on behalf of the National Lawyers Guild by David Gespass and Zachary Wolfe.
Brief of amici curiae filed on behalf of Human Rights Advocacy Groups et al. by David Weissbrodt.
Brief of amici curiae filed on behalf of the Louisville Area Chamber of Commerce, Inc. (d/b/a Greater Louisville Inc.), et al. by John K. Bush.
Brief of amici curiae filed on behalf of the Prichard Committee for Academic Excellence by Sheryl G. Snyder, Amy D. Cubbage, and Phillip J. Shepherd.
Brief of amici curiae filed on behalf of Media & Telecommunication Cos. by Elizabeth G. Taylor.
Brief of amici curiae filed on behalf of Joseph E. Brann et al. by Robert N. Weiner and Richard Jerome.

Opposing Side (Petitioner / Appellant)

Brief of amici curiae filed on behalf of the United States by Solicitor General Clement, Assistant Attorney General Kim, Deputy Solicitor General Garre, David B. Salmons, David K. Flynn, Angela M. Miller, and Kent D. Talbert.
Brief of amici curiae filed on behalf of the Pacific Legal Foundation et al. by Sharon L. Browne and Paul J. Beard II.
Brief of amici curiae filed on behalf of the Project on Fair Representation et al. by Bert W. Rein.
Brief of amici curiae filed on behalf of Various School Children from Lynn, Massachusetts, by Michael Williams and Chester Darling.
Brief of amici curiae filed on behalf of David J. Armor et al. by Robert N. Driscoll.
Brief of amici curiae filed on behalf of Governor John Ellis "Jeb" Bush et al. by Daniel J. Woodring, Raquel A. Rodriguez, and Nathan A. Adams IV.
Brief of amici curiae filed on behalf of the Center for Individual Rights by Michael E. Rosman and Erik S. Jaffe.
Brief of amici curiae filed on behalf of the Competitive Enterprise Institute by Hans Bader.
Brief of amici curiae filed on behalf of the Mountain States Legal Foundation by William Perry Pendley.
Brief of amici curiae filed on behalf of Dr. John Murphy et al. by John R. Munich.
Brief of amici curiae filed on behalf of the Asian American Legal Foundation by Gordon M. Fauth, Jr.

IV. THE SUPREME COURT'S DECISION

"It is well established that when the government distributes burdens or benefits on the basis of individual racial classifications, that action is reviewed under strict scrutiny. . . . In order to satisfy this searching standard of review, the school districts must demonstrate that the use of individual racial classifications in the assignment plans here under review is 'narrowly tailored' to achieve a 'compelling' government interest. . . .

[I]t suffices to note that our prior cases, in evaluating the use of racial classifications in the school context, have recognized two interests that qualify as compelling. The first is the compelling interest of remedying the effects of past intentional discrimination. . . .

The second . . . is the interest in diversity in higher education upheld in Grutter . . . .

The present cases are not governed by Grutter. . . .

Perhaps recognizing that reliance on Grutter cannot sustain their plans, both school districts assert additional interests . . . to justify their race-based assignments. . . .

The en banc Ninth Circuit declared that 'when a racially diverse school system is the goal . . . , there is no more effective means than a consideration of race to achieve the solution.' [T]his conclusory argument cannot sustain the plans. . . .

The districts assert . . . that the way in which they have employed individual racial classifications is necessary . . . . The minimal effect these classifications have on student assignments, however, suggests that other means would be effective. . . .

If the need for the racial classifications embraced by the school districts is unclear, even on the districts' own terms, the costs are undeniable. . . .

Before Brown, schoolchildren were told where they could and could not go to school based on the color of their skin. The school districts in these cases have not carried the heavy burden of demonstrating that we should allow this once again—even for very different reasons. For schools that never segregated on the basis of race, such as Seattle, or that have removed the vestiges of past segregation, such as Jefferson County, the way 'to achieve a system of determining admission to the public schools on a nonracial basis,' is to stop assigning students on a racial basis. The way to stop discrimination on the basis of race is to stop discriminating on the basis of race.

The judgments of the Courts of Appeals for the Sixth and Ninth Circuits are reversed, and the cases are remanded . . . ."

V. JUSTICE VOTE

4 PRO ACLU SIDE VS. 5 CON OPPOSING SIDE

ACLU Side (Respondent / Appellee)

1. Stevens, J. – Wrote dissenting opinion, joined Breyer's dissent
2. Breyer, S. – Wrote dissenting opinion
3. Ginsburg, R. – Joined Breyer's dissent
4. Souter, D. – Joined Breyer's dissent

Opposing Side (Petitioner / Appellant)

1. Roberts, J. – Wrote plurality opinion
2. Alito, S. – Joined plurality opinion
3. Thomas, C. – Wrote concurring opinion
4. Scalia, A. – Joined plurality opinion
5. Kennedy, A. – Wrote concurring opinion

VI. A WIN OR LOSS FOR THE ACLU?

The ACLU filed as amicus curiae urging affirmance; the Supreme Court reversed the Courts of Appeals' decisions by a 5-4 vote, giving the ACLU an apparent loss.

1022. Kimbrough v. U.S.

(Decided December 10, 2007; 552 U.S. 85)

I. ISSUE

A. Issues Discussed

Drugs, criminal procedure

B. Legal Question Presented

"Under the statute criminalizing the manufacture and distribution of crack cocaine, 21 U.S.C. § 841, and the relevant Guidelines prescription, § 2D1.1, a drug trafficker dealing in crack cocaine is subject to the same sentence as one dealing in 100 times more powder cocaine. The question here presented is whether . . . 'a sentence . . . outside the guidelines range is per se unreasonable when it is based on a disagreement with the sentencing disparity for crack and powder cocaine offenses.'"

C. Supreme Court's Answer

"We hold that, under Booker, the cocaine Guidelines, like all other Guidelines, are advisory only, and that the Court of Appeals erred in holding the crack/powder disparity effectively mandatory. A district judge must include the Guidelines range in the array of factors warranting consideration. The judge may determine, however, that, in the particular case, a within-Guidelines sentence is 'greater than necessary to serve the objectives of sentencing. In making that determination, the judge may consider the disparity between the Guidelines' treatment of crack and powder cocaine offenses."

II. CASE SUMMARY

A. Background

"This Court's remedial opinion in United States v. Booker, 543 U.S. 220 (2005), instructed district courts to read the United States Sentencing Guidelines as 'effectively advisory.' In accord with 18 U.S.C. § 3553(a), the Guidelines, formerly mandatory, now serve as one factor among several courts must consider in determining an appropriate sentence. . . .

Under the statute criminalizing the manufacture and distribution of crack cocaine and the relevant Guidelines prescription, a drug trafficker dealing in crack cocaine is subject to the same sentence as one dealing in 100 times more powder cocaine. . . .

In September 2004, petitioner Derrick Kimbrough was . . . charged with four offenses . . . . Kimbrough pleaded guilty to all four charges. . . .

Kimbrough's plea subjected him to an aggregate sentence of 15 years to life in prison: 10 years to life for the three drug offenses, plus a consecutive term of 5 years to life for the firearm offense. In order to determine the appropriate sentence within this statutory range, the District Court first calculated Kimbrough's sentence under the advisory Sentencing Guidelines. . . . An offense level of 34 and a criminal history category of II yielded a Guidelines range of 168 to 210 months for the three drug charges. The Guidelines sentence for the firearm offense was the statutory minimum, 60 months. Kimbrough's final advisory Guidelines range was thus 228 to 270 months, or 19 to 22.5 years.

A sentence in this range, in the District Court's judgment, would have been 'greater than necessary' to accomplish the purposes of sentencing set forth in 18 U.S.C. § 3553(a). . . .

In an unpublished per curiam opinion, the Fourth Circuit vacated the sentence."

The Supreme Court granted certiorari to review the case.

B. Counsel of Record / ACLU Attorney

ACLU Side (Petitioner / Appellant): Michael S. Nachmanoff argued the cause for appellant. With him on the briefs were Frances H. Pratt, Geremy C. Kamens, and Kenneth P. Troccoli.

Opposing Side (Respondent / Appellee): Deputy Solicitor General Dreeben argued the cause for the United States. With him on the brief were Solicitor General Clement, Assistant Attorney General Fisher, Kannon K. Shanmugam, Nina Goodman, and Jeffrey P. Singdahlsen.

III. AMICI CURIAE

ACLU Side (Petitioner / Appellant)

Brief of amici curiae filed on behalf of the American Civil Liberties Union by Adam B. Wolf, Graham A. Boyd, and Steven R. Shapiro.

Brief of amici curiae filed on behalf of Federal Public and Community Defenders et al. by Mark Osler, Carlos A. Williams, Henry J. Bemporad, Brett G. Sweitzer, and David L. McColgin.

Brief of amici curiae filed on behalf of the NAACP Legal Defense and Educational Fund, Inc., by Ian Heath Gershengorn, Theodore M. Shaw, Jacqueline A. Berrien, Christina Swarns, and Johanna Steinberg.

Brief of amici curiae filed on behalf of the National Association of Criminal Defense Lawyers by Miguel A. Estrada, David Debold, and Peter Goldberger.

Brief of amici curiae filed on behalf of the Sentencing Project et al. by Matthew M. Shors and Pammela Quinn.

Opposing Side (Respondent / Appellee)

No briefs of amici curiae filed in support of appellee.

IV. THE SUPREME COURT'S DECISION

"Although chemically similar, crack and powder cocaine are handled very differently for sentencing purposes. The 100—to—1 ratio yields sentences for crack offenses three to six times longer than those for powder offenses involving equal amounts of drugs. . . .

With this history of the crack/powder sentencing ratio in mind, we next consider the status of the Guidelines tied to the ratio after our decision in United States v. Booker, 543 U.S. 220 (2005). In Booker, the Court held that the mandatory Sentencing Guidelines system violated the Sixth Amendment. The Booker remedial opinion determined that the appropriate cure was to sever and excise the provision of the statute that rendered the Guidelines mandatory. This modification of the federal sentencing statute, we explained, 'makes the Guidelines effectively advisory.' . . .

We have accordingly recognized that, in the ordinary case, the Commission's recommendation of a sentencing range will 'reflect a rough approximation of sentences that might achieve § 3553(a)'s objectives.' . . .

The crack cocaine Guidelines, however, present no occasion for elaborative discussion of this matter because those Guidelines do not exemplify the Commission's exercise of its characteristic institutional role. . . . Indeed, the Commission itself has reported that the crack/powder disparity produces disproportionately harsh sanctions . . . .

The ultimate question in Kimbrough's case is 'whether the sentence was reasonable—i.e., whether the District Judge abused his discretion in determining that the § 3553(a) factors supported a sentence of [15 years] and justified a substantial deviation from the Guidelines range.' The sentence the District Court imposed on Kimbrough was 4.5 years below the bottom of the Guidelines range. But in determining that 15 years was the appropriate prison term, the District Court properly homed in on the particular circumstances of Kimbrough's case and accorded weight to the Sentencing Commission's consistent and emphatic position that the crack/powder disparity is at odds with § 3553(a). Indeed, aside from its claim that the 100—to—1 ratio is mandatory, the Government did not attack the District Court's downward variance as unsupported by § 3553(a). Giving due respect to the District Court's reasoned appraisal, a reviewing court could not rationally conclude that the 4.5–year sentence reduction Kimbrough received qualified as an abuse of discretion. . . .

[T]he judgment of the United States Court of Appeals for the Fourth Circuit is reversed, and the case is remanded . . . ."

V. JUSTICE VOTE

7 Pro ACLU Side vs. 2 Con Opposing Side

ACLU Side (Petitioner / Appellant)

1. Ginsburg, R. – Wrote majority opinion
2. Stevens, J. – Joined majority opinion
3. Breyer, S. – Joined majority opinion
4. Scalia, A. – Wrote concurring opinion
5. Kennedy, A. – Joined majority opinion
6. Souter, D. – Joined majority opinion
7. Roberts, J. – Joined majority opinion

Opposing Side (Respondent / Appellee)

1. Alito, S. – Wrote dissenting opinion
2. Thomas, C. – Wrote dissenting opinion

VI. A WIN OR LOSS FOR THE ACLU?

The ACLU filed as amicus curiae urging reversal of the judgment of the Court of Appeals; the Sureme Court reversed in a 7-2 vote, giving the ACLU an apparent win.

1023. New York State Bd. of Elections v. Lopez Torres

(Decided January 16, 2008; 552 U.S. 196)

I. ISSUE

A. Issues Discussed

Voting rights

B. Legal Question Presented

"The State of New York requires that political parties select their nominees for Supreme Court Justice at a convention of delegates chosen by party members in a primary election. We consider whether this electoral system violates the First Amendment rights of prospective party candidates."

C. Supreme Court's Answer

"New York State has thrice (in 1846, 1911, and 1921) displayed a willingness to reconsider its method of selecting Supreme Court Justices. If it wishes to return to the primary system that it discarded in 1921, it is free to do so; but the First Amendment does not compel that."

II. CASE SUMMARY

A. Background

"The Supreme Court of New York is the State's trial court of general jurisdiction . . . .

Over the years, New York has changed the method by which Supreme Court Justices are selected several times. . . .

A law enacted in 1921 required parties to select their candidates for the Supreme Court by a convention composed of delegates elected by party members. . . .

Respondent López Torres was elected in 1992 to the civil court for Kings County . . . . She claims that soon after her election, party leaders began to demand that she make patronage hires, and that her consistent refusal to do so caused the local party to oppose her unsuccessful candidacy at the Supreme Court nominating conventions in 1997, 2002, and 2003. The following year, López Torres [and others] . . . brought suit . . . against the New York Board of Elections . . . . They contended that New York's election law burdened the rights of challengers seeking to run against candidates favored by the party leadership . . . . [T]hey sought a declaration that New York's convention system for selecting Supreme Court Justices violates their First Amendment rights, and an injunction mandating . . . a direct primary election to select party nominees for Supreme Court Justice.

The District Court issued a preliminary injunction granting the relief requested, pending the New York Legislature's enactment of a new statutory scheme. A unanimous panel of the United States Court of Appeals for the Second Circuit affirmed."

The Supreme Court granted certiorari to review the case.

B. Counsel of Record / ACLU Attorney

ACLU Side (Respondent / Appellee): Frederick A. O. Schwarz, Jr., argued the cause for appellees. With him on the brief were Burt Neuborne, Deborah Goldberg, Kent A. Yalowitz, and Paul M. Smith.

Opposing Side (Petitioner / Appellant): Theodore B. Olson argued the cause for appellants New York State Board of Elections et al. With him on the briefs were Matthew D. McGill, Michael S. Diamant, Todd D. Valentine, Randy M. Mastro, and Jennifer L. Conn. Andrew J. Rossman argued the cause for appellants New York County Democratic Committee et al. With him on the briefs were Steven M. Pesner, James P. Chou, James E. d'Auguste, Vincenzo A. DeLeo, Edward P. Lazarus, Carter G. Phillips, Thomas C. Goldstein, Joseph L. Forstadt, Ernst H. Rosenberger, Burton N. Lipshie, David A. Sifre, and Arthur W. Greig. Andrew M. Cuomo, Attorney General of New York, Barbara D. Underwood, Solicitor General, Benjamin N. Gutman, Deputy Solicitor General, and Denise A. Hartman, Assistant Solicitor General, filed briefs for appellant the State of New York.

III. AMICI CURIAE

ACLU Side (Respondent / Appellee)

Brief of amici curiae filed on behalf of the American Civil Liberties Union and New York Civil Liberties Union by Arthur N. Eisenberg, Laughlin McDonald, and Steven R. Shapiro.

Brief of amici curiae filed on behalf of the City of New York et al. by Preeta D. Bansal, Barry Kamins, Michael A. Cardozo, Victor A. Kovner, and Kathryn Grant Madigan.

Brief of amici curiae filed on behalf of the Asian American Legal Defense and Education Fund et al. by Mariann Meier Wang.

Brief of amici curiae filed on behalf of the Cato Institute et al. by Erik S. Jaffe.

Brief of amici curiae filed on behalf of Guy-Uriel E. Charles et al. by Ellen D. Katz, pro se.

Brief of amici curiae filed on behalf of the New York County Lawyers' Association by Stephanie G. Wheeler and Bradley P. Smith.

Brief of amici curiae filed on behalf of the Washington Legal Foundation by Daniel J. Popeo and Richard A. Samp.

Brief of amici curiae filed on behalf of John Dunne by Andrew H. Schapiro.

Brief of amici curiae filed on behalf of Charles J. Hynes by Paul A. Engelmayer.

Brief of amici curiae filed on behalf of Edward I. Koch by Mr. Koch, pro se, and Bruce S. Kaplan.

Brief of amici curiae filed on behalf of Thomas Mann et al. by Daniel R. Ortiz, J. Gerald Hebert, and Paul S. Ryan.

Brief of amici curiae filed on behalf of Former New York State Judges et al. by Holly K. Kulka and Jonathan R. Dowell.

Opposing Side (Petitioner / Appellant)

Brief of amici curiae filed on behalf of the Asian American Bar Association of New York by Steven B. Shapiro and Vincent T. Chang.

Brief of amici curiae filed on behalf of the Mid-Manhattan Branch of the NAACP et al. by Gene C. Schaerr, Steffen N. Johnson, Linda T. Coberly, and Michael J. Friedman.

Brief of amici curiae filed on behalf of the Republican National Committee by H. Christopher Bartolomucci.

IV. THE SUPREME COURT'S DECISION

"A political party has a First Amendment right to limit its membership as it wishes, and to choose a candidate-selection process that will in its view produce the nominee who best represents its political platform. These rights are circumscribed, however, when the State gives the party a role in the election process—as New York has done here . . . . Then . . . the party's racially discriminatory action may become state action that violates the Fifteenth Amendment. And then also the State acquires a legitimate governmental interest in ensuring the fairness of the party's nominating process . . . .

In the present case, however, the party's associational rights are at issue (if at all) only as a shield and not as a sword. Respondents are in no position to rely on the right that the First Amendment confers on political parties to structure their internal party processes and to select the candidate of the party's choosing. Indeed, both the Republican and Democratic state parties have intervened from the very early stages of this litigation to defend New York's electoral law. The weapon wielded by these plaintiffs is their own claimed associational right not only to join, but to have a certain degree of influence in, the party. They contend that New York's electoral system does not go far enough—does not go as far as the Constitution demands—in ensuring that they will have a fair chance of prevailing in their parties' candidate-selection process.

This contention finds no support in our precedents. . . .

Respondents' real complaint is . . . that the convention process that follows the delegate election does not give them a realistic chance to secure the party's nomination. . . .

Selection by convention has been a traditional means of choosing party nominees. While a State may determine it is not desirable and replace it, it is not unconstitutional. . . .

Respondents put forward . . . the assertion that party loyalty in New York's judicial districts renders the general-election ballot 'uncompetitive.' They argue that the existence of entrenched 'one-party rule' demands that the First Amendment be used to impose additional competition in the nominee-selection process of the parties. . . . This is a novel and implausible reading of the First Amendment. . . .

New York State has thrice (in 1846, 1911, and 1921) displayed a willingness to reconsider its method of selecting Supreme Court Justices. If it wishes to return to the primary system that it discarded in 1921, it is free to do so; but the First Amendment does not compel that. We reverse the Second Circuit's contrary judgment."

V. JUSTICE VOTE

0 Pro ACLU Side vs. 9 Con Opposing Side

Opposing Side (Petitioner / Appellant)

1. Scalia, A. – Wrote majority opinion
2. Alito, S. – Joined majority opinion
3. Stevens, J. – Wrote concurring opinion
4. Thomas, C. – Joined majority opinion
5. Breyer, S. – Joined Kennedy's concurrence in part
6. Kennedy, A. – Wrote concurring opinion
7. Ginsburg, R. – Joined majority opinion
8. Souter, D. – Joined Stevens' concurrence
9. Roberts, J. – Joined majority opinion

VI. A WIN OR LOSS FOR THE ACLU?

The ACLU filed as amicus curiae urging affirmance; the Supreme Court reversed the Court of Appeals' decision by a 9-0 vote, giving the ACLU an apparent loss.

1024. Danforth v. Minnesota

(Decided February 20, 2008; 552 U.S. 264)

I. ISSUE

A. Issues Discussed

Criminal procedure

B. Legal Question Presented

"[W]hether Teague constrains the authority of state courts to give broader effect to new rules of criminal procedure than is required by that opinion."

C. Supreme Court's Answer

"We have never suggested that it does, and now hold that it does not."

II. CASE SUMMARY

A. Background

"In 1996, a Minnesota jury found petitioner Stephen Danforth guilty of first-degree criminal sexual conduct with a minor. The 6–year–old victim did not testify at trial, but the jury saw and heard a videotaped interview of the child. On appeal from his conviction, Danforth argued that the tape's admission violated the Sixth Amendment's guarantee that '[i]n all criminal prosecutions, the accused shall enjoy the right . . . to be confronted with the witnesses against him.' [T]he Minnesota Court of Appeals concluded that the tape 'was sufficiently reliable to be admitted into evidence,' and affirmed the conviction. The conviction became final in 1998 . . . .

[The U.S. Supreme Court then] announced a 'new rule' . . . . In Crawford v. Washington, 541 U.S. 36 (2004), we held that where testimonial statements are at issue, 'the only indicium of reliability sufficient to satisfy constitutional demands is . . . confrontation.'

Shortly thereafter, petitioner filed a state postconviction petition, in which he argued that he was entitled to a new trial because . . . the taped interview violated . . . Crawford. [T]he Minnesota trial court and the Minnesota Court of Appeals concluded that Crawford did not apply . . . . The State Supreme Court granted review to consider two arguments: (1) that the lower courts erred in holding that Crawford did not apply retroactively under Teague; and (2) that the state court was 'free to apply a broader retroactivity standard than that of Teague,' and should apply the Crawford rule to petitioner's case even if federal law did not require it to do so. The court rejected both . . . ."

The Supreme Court granted certiorari to review the case.

B. Counsel of Record / ACLU Attorney

ACLU Side (Petitioner / Appellant): Benjamin J. Butler argued the cause for appellant. With him on the briefs was Roy G. Spurbeck.

Opposing Side (Respondent / Appellee): Patrick C. Diamond argued the cause for appellee. With him on the brief were Lori Swanson, Attorney General of Minnesota, Michael O. Freeman, and Jean Burdorf.

III. AMICI CURIAE

ACLU Side (Petitioner / Appellant)

Brief of amici curiae filed on behalf of the American Civil Liberties Union and the ACLU of Minnesota by Larry Yackle, Steven R. Shapiro, and John Holdridge.

Brief of amici curiae filed on behalf of the National Association of Criminal Defense Lawyers by Jeffrey A. Lamken and Pamela Harris.

Opposing Side (Respondent / Appellee)

Brief of amici curiae filed on behalf of the State of Alaska et al. by Talis J. Colberg, Attorney General of Alaska, and Timothy W. Terrell, Assistant Attorney General.

Brief of amici curiae filed on behalf of the State of Kansas et al. by Paul J. Morrison, Attorney General of Kansas, Stephen R. McAllister, Solicitor General, and Jared S. Maag, Deputy Solicitor General, and by the Attorneys General for their respective States as follows: Troy King of Alabama, Tom Miller of Iowa, Michael A. Cox of Michigan, W. A. Drew Edmondson of Oklahoma, Greg Abbott of Texas, Mark L. Shurtleff of Utah, and Robert F. McDonnell of Virginia in support of neither party.

IV. THE SUPREME COURT'S DECISION

"For much of our Nation's history, federal constitutional rights—such as the Sixth Amendment confrontation right at issue in Crawford—were not binding on the States. . . .

The ratification of the Fourteenth Amendment radically changed the federal courts' relationship with state courts. That Amendment . . . is the source of this Court's power to decide whether a defendant in a state proceeding received a fair trial . . . .

In Crawford we accepted the petitioner's argument that the interpretation of the Sixth Amendment right to confrontation that we had previously endorsed in Roberts, 448 U.S. 56, needed reconsideration because it 'stray[ed] from the original meaning of the Confrontation Clause.' . . . We held that the 'Constitution prescribes a procedure for determining the reliability of testimony in criminal trials, and we, no less than the state courts, lack authority to replace it with one of our own devising.'

Thus, our opinion in Crawford announced a 'new rule'—as that term is defined in Teague—because the result in that case 'was not dictated by precedent existing at the time the defendant's conviction became final.' It was not, however, a rule 'of our own devising' or the product of our own views about sound policy. . . .

Our decision today must also be understood against the backdrop of our somewhat confused and confusing 'retroactivity' cases . . . .

In sum, the Teague decision limits the kinds of constitutional violations that will entitle an individual to relief on federal habeas, but does not in any way limit the authority of a state court, when reviewing its own state criminal convictions, to provide a remedy for a violation that is deemed 'nonretroactive' under Teague. . . .

The State contends that two of our prior decisions—Michigan v. Payne and American Trucking Assns., Inc. v. Smith—cast doubt on state courts' authority to provide broader remedies for federal constitutional violations than mandated by Teague. We disagree. . . .

A decision by this Court that a new rule does not apply retroactively under Teague does not imply that there was no right and thus no violation of that right at the time of trial—only that no remedy will be provided in federal habeas courts. It is fully consistent with a government of laws to recognize that the finality of a judgment may bar relief. . .

Accordingly, the judgment of the Supreme Court of Minnesota is reversed, and the case is remanded . . . . As was true in Michigan v. Payne, the Minnesota court is free to reinstate its judgment disposing of the petition for state postconviction relief."

V. JUSTICE VOTE

7 Pro ACLU Side vs. 2 Con Opposing Side

ACLU Side (Petitioner / Appellant)

1. Stevens, J. – Wrote majority opinion
2. Alito, S. – Joined majority opinion
3. Thomas, C. – Joined majority opinion
4. Breyer, S. – Joined majority opinion
5. Scalia, A. – Joined majority opinion
6. Ginsburg, R. – Joined majority opinion
7. Souter, D. – Joined majority opinion

Opposing Side (Respondent / Appellee)

1. Roberts, J. – Wrote dissenting opinion
2. Kennedy, A. – Joined Roberts' dissent

VI. A WIN OR LOSS FOR THE ACLU?

The ACLU filed as amicus curiae urging vacating the judgment of the Minnesota Supreme Court; the U.S. Supreme Court reversed in a 7-2 vote, giving the ACLU an apparent win.

1025. Baze v. Rees

(Decided April 16, 2008; 553 U.S. 35)

I. ISSUE

A. Issues Discussed

Death penalty, 8th Amendment

B. Legal Question Presented

"[W]hether Kentucky's lethal injection protocol satisfies the Eighth Amendment."

C. Supreme Court's Answer

"We hold that it does."

II. CASE SUMMARY

A. Background

"Like 35 other States and the Federal Government, Kentucky has chosen to impose capital punishment for certain crimes. . . . Kentucky has altered its method of execution over time to more humane means . . . . That progress has led to the use of lethal injection . . . .

Petitioners in this case—each convicted of double homicide—acknowledge that the lethal injection procedure, if applied as intended, will result in a humane death. They nevertheless contend that the lethal injection protocol is unconstitutional under the Eighth Amendment's ban on 'cruel and unusual punishments,' because of the risk that the protocol's terms might not be properly followed, resulting in significant pain. They propose an alternative protocol, one that they concede has not been adopted by any State and has never been tried.

The trial court held extensive hearings and entered detailed findings of fact and conclusions of law. It recognized that '[t] here are no methods of legal execution that are satisfactory to those who oppose the death penalty on moral, religious, or societal grounds,' but concluded that Kentucky's procedure 'complies with the constitutional requirements against cruel and unusual punishment.' The State Supreme Court affirmed."

The Supreme Court granted certiorari to review the case.

B. Counsel of Record / ACLU Attorney

ACLU Side (Petitioner / Appellant): Donald B. Verrilli, Jr., argued the cause for appellants. With him on the briefs were David M. Barron, Ginger D. Anders, and John Anthony Palombi.

Opposing Side (Respondent / Appellee): Roy T. Englert, Jr., argued the cause for appellees. On the brief were Gregory D. Stumbo, Attorney General of Kentucky, David A. Smith, Assistant Attorney General, Jeffrey T. Middendorf, and John C. Cummings.

Deputy Solicitor General Garre argued the cause for the United States as amicus curiae.

III. AMICI CURIAE

ACLU Side (Petitioner / Appellant)

Brief of amici curiae filed on behalf of the American Civil Liberties Union, the ACLU of Kentucky, and the Rutherford Institute by John Holdridge, John W. Whitehead, and Steven R. Shapiro.

Brief of amici curiae filed on behalf of the Fordham University School of Law, Louis Stein Center for Law and Ethics, by Alison J. Nathan, Bruce A. Green, and Bruce V. Spiva.

Brief of amici curiae filed on behalf ofHuman Rights Watch by Andrew J. Pincus and Charles A. Rothfeld.

Brief of amici curiae filed on behalf of Michael Morales et al. by Elisabeth Semel and Ty Alper.

Brief of amici curiae filed on behalf of the American Association of Jewish Lawyers and Jurists by Nathan Lewin, Alyza D. Lewin, Stephen R. Greenwald, and Robert L. Weinberg.

Brief of amici curiae filed on behalf of Critical Care Providers et al. by Bradley S. Phillips, Paul Watford, and Julie D. Cantor.

Brief of amici curiae filed on behalf of Dr. Kevin Concannon et al. by Simona G. Strauss.

Brief of amici curiae filed on behalf of the American Society of Anesthesiologists by Lawrence J. Fox and Lisa S. McCalmont in support of neither party.

Brief of amici curiae filed on behalf of the Anesthesia Awareness Campaign, Inc., by Richard M. Wyner in support of neither party.

Opposing Side (Respondent / Appellee)

Brief of amici curiae filed on behalf of the United States by Deputy Solicitor General Garre, Solicitor General Clement, Assistant Attorney General Fisher, Kannon K. Shanmugam, and Robert J. Erickson.

Brief of amici curiae filed on behalf of the State of Texas et al. by Greg Abbott, Attorney General of Texas, Kent C. Sullivan, First Assistant Attorney General, Eric J. R. Nichols, Deputy Attorney General for Criminal Justice, R. Ted Cruz, Solicitor General, and Sean D. Jordan, Deputy Solicitor General, by Kevin T. Kane, Chief State's Attorney of Connecticut, and by the Attorneys General for their respective States as follows: Troy King of Alabama, Dustin McDaniel of Arkansas, John W. Suthers of Colorado, Joseph R. Biden III of Delaware, Bill McCollum of Florida, Thurbert E. Baker of Georgia, Lawrence G. Wasden of Idaho, Paul J. Morrison of Kansas, Jim Hood of Mississippi, Jeremiah W. (Jay) Nixon of Missouri, Mike McGrath of Montana, Catherine Cortez Masto of Nevada, W. A. Drew Edmondson of Oklahoma, Henry D. McMaster of South Carolina, Lawrence E. Long of South Dakota, Robert E. Cooper, Jr., of Tennessee, Mark L. Shurtleff of Utah, and Bruce A. Salzburg of Wyoming.

Brief of amici curiae filed on behalf of the Criminal Justice Legal Foundation by Kent S. Scheidegger.

IV. THE SUPREME COURT'S DECISION

"We begin with the principle . . . that capital punishment is constitutional. [T]he Constitution does not demand the avoidance of all risk of pain in carrying out executions.

Petitioners do not claim that it does. Rather, they contend that the Eighth Amendment prohibits procedures that create an 'unnecessary risk' of pain. . . .

Kentucky responds that this 'unnecessary risk' standard is tantamount to a requirement that States adopt the "least risk" alternative in carrying out an execution . . . . Instead, Kentucky urges the Court to approve the "substantial risk" test . . . .

Petitioners do not claim that lethal injection . . . constitute[s] the cruel or wanton infliction of pain. . . .

Instead, petitioners claim that there is a significant risk that the procedures will not be properly followed . . . resulting in severe pain . . . . We have explained that to prevail on such a claim there must be a 'substantial risk of serious harm,' an 'objectively intolerable risk of harm' that prevents prison officials from pleading that they were 'subjectively blameless for purposes of the Eighth Amendment.'

Simply because an execution method may result in pain . . . does not establish the sort of 'objectively intolerable risk of harm' that qualifies as cruel and unusual. . . .

Accordingly, we reject petitioners' proposed 'unnecessary risk' standard, as well as the dissent's 'untoward' risk variation.

Instead, the proffered alternatives must effectively address a 'substantial risk of serious harm.' To qualify, the alternative procedure must be feasible, readily implemented, and in fact significantly reduce a substantial risk of severe pain. . . .

In applying these standards to the facts of this case, we note at the outset that it is difficult to regard a practice as 'objectively intolerable' when it is in fact widely tolerated. . . .

Kentucky has adopted a method of execution believed to be the most humane available, one it shares with 35 other States. . . . The risks of maladministration . . . cannot remotely be characterized as 'objectively intolerable.' Kentucky's decision to adhere to its protocol . . . cannot be viewed as probative of the wanton infliction of pain under the Eighth Amendment. Finally, the alternative that petitioners belatedly propose has problems of its own, and has never been tried by a single State. . . .

The judgment below concluding that Kentucky's procedure is consistent with the Eighth Amendment is, accordingly, affirmed."

V. JUSTICE VOTE

2 Pro ACLU Side vs. 7 Con Opposing Side

ACLU Side (Petitioner / Appellant)

1. Ginsburg, R. – Wrote dissenting opinion
2. Souter, D. – Joined Ginsburg's dissent

Opposing Side (Respondent / Appellee)

1. Roberts, J. – Wrote majority opinion
2. Alito, S. – Wrote concurring opinion
3. Stevens, J. – Wrote concurring opinion
4. Thomas, C. – Wrote concurring opinion, joined Scalia's concurrence
5. Breyer, S. – Wrote concurring opinion
6. Scalia, A. – Wrote concurring opinion, joined Thomas' concurrence
7. Kennedy, A. – Joined majority opinion

VI. A WIN OR LOSS FOR THE ACLU?

The ACLU filed as amicus curiae urging reversal of the judgment of the state supreme court; the U.S. Supreme Court affirmed in a 7-2 vote, giving the ACLU an apparent loss.

1026. Virginia v. Moore

(Decided April 23, 2008; 553 U.S. 164)

I. ISSUE

A. Issues Discussed

4th Amendment

B. Legal Question Presented

"[W]hether a police officer violates the Fourth Amendment by making an arrest based on probable cause but prohibited by state law."

C. Supreme Court's Answer

"When officers have probable cause to believe that a person has committed a crime in their presence, the Fourth Amendment permits them to make an arrest, and to search the suspect in order to safeguard evidence and ensure their own safety."

II. CASE SUMMARY

A. Background

"On February 20, 2003, two city of Portsmouth police officers stopped a car driven by David Lee Moore. They had heard over the police radio that a person known as 'Chubs' was driving with a suspended license, and one of the officers knew Moore by that nickname. The officers determined that Moore's license was in fact suspended, and arrested him for the misdemeanor of driving on a suspended license, which is punishable under Virginia law by a year in jail and a $2,500 fine. The officers subsequently searched Moore and found that he was carrying 16 grams of crack cocaine and $516 in cash.

Under state law, the officers should have issued Moore a summons instead of arresting him. . . .

Moore was charged with possessing cocaine with the intent to distribute . . . . He filed a pretrial motion to suppress the evidence from the arrest search. Virginia law does not . . . require suppression of evidence obtained in violation of state law. Moore argued, however, that suppression was required by the Fourth Amendment. The trial court denied the motion, and after a bench trial found Moore guilty of the drug charge and sentenced him to a 5-year prison term . . . . The conviction was reversed by a panel of Virginia's intermediate court on Fourth Amendment grounds, reinstated by the intermediate court sitting en banc, and finally reversed again by the Virginia Supreme Court."

The Supreme Court granted certiorari to review the case.

B. Counsel of Record / ACLU Attorney

ACLU Side (Respondent / Appellee): Thomas C. Goldstein argued the cause for appellee. With him on the brief were S. Jane Chittom, Pamela S. Karlan, Jeffrey L. Fisher, Amy Howe, and Kevin K. Russell.

Opposing Side (Petitioner / Appellant): Stephen R. McCullough, Deputy State Solicitor General of Virginia, argued the cause for appellant. With him on the briefs were Robert F. McDonnell, Attorney General, William E. Thro, State Solicitor General, William C. Mims, Chief Deputy Attorney General, Marla Graff Decker, Deputy Attorney General, and Leah A. Darron, Senior Assistant Attorney General.

Deputy Solicitor General Dreeben argued the cause for the United States as amicus curiae.

III. AMICI CURIAE

ACLU Side (Respondent / Appellee)

Brief of amici curiae filed on behalf of the American Civil Liberties Union and the ACLU of Virginia by Susan N. Herman, Steven R. Shapiro, Emily Chiang, and Rebecca Glenberg.

Brief of amici curiae filed on behalf of the American Bar Association by William H. Neukom and Rory K. Little.

Brief of amici curiae filed on behalf of the Virginia Trial Lawyers Association by David B. Hargett.
Brief of amici curiae filed on behalf of the National Association of Criminal Defense Lawyers by E. Joshua Rosenkranz, Warrington S. Parker III, and Pamela Harris.

Opposing Side (Petitioner / Appellant)

Brief of amici curiae filed on behalf of the United States by Deputy Solicitor General Dreeben, Solicitor General Clement, Assistant Attorney General Fisher, and Matthew D. Roberts.
Brief of amici curiae filed on behalf of the State of Texas et al. by Greg Abbott, Attorney General of Texas, Kent C. Sullivan, First Assistant Attorney General, Eric J. R. Nichols, Deputy Attorney General for Criminal Justice, R. Ted Cruz, Solicitor General, and Susanna Dokupil and Adam W. Aston, Assistant Solicitors General, by Roberto J. Sa´nchez-Ramos, Secretary of Justice of Puerto Rico, and by the Attorneys General for their respective States as follows: Troy King of Alabama, Terry Goddard of Arizona, Dustin McDaniel of Arkansas, John W. Suthers of Colorado, Bill McCollum of Florida, Lawrence G. Wasden of Idaho, Michael A. Cox of Michigan, Jim Hood of Mississippi, Catherine Cortez Masto of Nevada, Kelly A. Ayotte of New Hampshire, W. A. Drew Edmondson of Oklahoma, Hardy Myers of Oregon, Thomas W. Corbett, Jr., of Pennsylvania, Henry D. McMaster of South Carolina, Lawrence E. Long of South Dakota, Mark L. Shurtleff of Utah, and Bruce A. Salzburg of Wyoming.
Brief of amici curiae filed on behalf of Wayne County, Michigan, by Kym L. Worthy and Timothy A. Baughman.

IV. THE SUPREME COURT'S DECISION

"The Fourth Amendment protects 'against unreasonable searches and seizures' of (among other things) the person. . . .

When history has not provided a conclusive answer, we have analyzed a search or seizure in light of traditional standards of reasonableness 'by assessing, on the one hand, the degree to which it intrudes upon an individual's privacy and, on the other, the degree to which it is needed for the promotion of legitimate governmental interests.' That methodology provides no support for Moore's Fourth Amendment claim. In a long line of cases, we have said that when an officer has probable cause to believe a person committed even a minor crime in his presence, the balancing of private and public interests is not in doubt. The arrest is constitutionally reasonable. . . .

Our decisions counsel against changing this calculus when a State chooses to protect privacy beyond the level that the Fourth Amendment requires. . . .

We conclude that warrantless arrests for crimes committed in the presence of an arresting officer are reasonable under the Constitution, and that while States are free to regulate such arrests . . . , state restrictions do not alter the Fourth Amendment's protections. . . .

Moore argues that even if the Constitution allowed his arrest, it did not allow the arresting officers to search him. We have recognized . . . that officers may perform searches incident to constitutionally permissible arrests . . . to ensure their safety and safeguard evidence. . . .

The Virginia Supreme Court may have concluded that Knowles required the exclusion . . . because, under state law, the officers . . . should have issued him a citation instead. This argument might have force if the Constitution forbade Moore's arrest . . . . But the arrest rules that the officers violated were those of state law alone, and . . . it is not the province of the Fourth Amendment to enforce state law. That Amendment does not require the exclusion of evidence obtained from a constitutionally permissible arrest. . . .

We reaffirm against a novel challenge what we have signaled for more than half a century. When officers have probable cause to believe that a person has committed a crime in their presence, the Fourth Amendment permits them to make an arrest, and to search the suspect in order to safeguard evidence and ensure their own safety. The judgment of the Supreme Court of Virginia is reversed, and the case is remanded . . . ."

V. JUSTICE VOTE

0 Pro ACLU Side vs. 9 Con Opposing Side

Opposing Side (Petitioner / Appellant)

1. Scalia, A. – Wrote majority opinion
2. Alito, S. – Joined majority opinion
3. Stevens, J. – Joined majority opinion
4. Thomas, C. – Joined majority opinion
5. Breyer, S. – Joined majority opinion
6. Kennedy, A. – Joined majority opinion
7. Ginsburg, R. – Wrote concurring opinion
8. Souter, D. – Joined majority opinion
9. Roberts, J. – Joined majority opinion

VI. A WIN OR LOSS FOR THE ACLU?

The ACLU filed as amicus curiae urging affirmance; the U.S. Supreme Court reversed the Supreme Court of Virginia's decision by a 9-0 vote, giving the ACLU an apparent loss.

1027. Crawford v. Marion County Election Bd.

(Decided April 28, 2008; 553 U.S. 181)

I. ISSUE

A. Issues Discussed

Voting rights

B. Legal Question Presented

"At issue in these cases is the constitutionality of an Indiana statute requiring citizens voting in person on election day, or casting a ballot in person at the office of the circuit court clerk prior to election day, to present photo identification issued by the government."

C. Supreme Court's Answer

"The state interests identified as justifications for SEA 483 [the voter identification law] are both neutral and sufficiently strong to require us to reject petitioners' facial attack on the statute."

II. CASE SUMMARY

A. Background

"Referred to as either the 'Voter ID Law' or 'SEA 483,' the statute [requiring government issued photo identification to vote] applies to in-person voting . . . . The requirement does not apply to absentee ballots . . . , and . . . contains an exception for persons . . . in a state-licensed facility . . . . A voter who is indigent or has a religious objection to being photographed may cast a provisional ballot . . . . A voter who has photo identification but is unable to present that identification on election day may file a provisional ballot that will be counted if she brings her photo identification . . . within 10 days. No photo identification is required in order to register to vote, and the State offers free photo identification to qualified voters able to establish their residence and identity.

[T]he Indiana Democratic Party and the Marion County Democratic Central Committee (Democrats) filed suit . . . . A second suit . . . was brought on behalf of two elected officials and several nonprofit organizations . . . .

The complaints in the consolidated cases allege that the new law substantially burdens the right to vote in violation of the Fourteenth Amendment; that it is neither a necessary nor appropriate method of avoiding election fraud; and that it will arbitrarily disfranchise qualified voters who do not possess the required identification and will place an unjustified burden on those who cannot readily obtain such identification. . . .

District Judge Barker . . . grant[ed] defendants' motion for summary judgment. . . .

A divided panel of the Court of Appeals affirmed. . . ."

The Supreme Court granted certiorari to review the case.

B. Counsel of Record / ACLU Attorney

ACLU Side (Petitioner / Appellant): Paul M. Smith argued the cause for appellants in both cases. With him on the briefs for appellants in No. 07–25 were Sam Hirsch, William R. Groth, and Joseph E. Sandler. Kenneth J. Falk, Jacquelyn Bowie Suess, and Gavin M. Rose of the ACLU of Indiana, Laughlin McDonald, Neil T. Bradley, and Steven R. Shapiro of the American Civil Liberties Union Foundation, Pamela S. Karlan, Jeffrey L. Fisher, Angela Ciccolo, and Victor L. Goode filed briefs for appellants in No. 07–21.

Opposing Side (Respondent / Appellee): Thomas M. Fisher, Solicitor General of Indiana, argued the cause for appellees in both cases. With him on the brief for the state appellees were Steve Carter, Attorney General, and Julie A. Brubaker and Heather L. Hagan, Deputy Attorneys General. Jon Laramore and James B. Osborn filed a brief for appellee Marion County Election Board.

Solicitor General Clement argued the cause for the United States as amicus curiae.

III. AMICI CURIAE

ACLU Side (Petitioner / Appellant)

Brief of amici curiae filed on behalf of the Asian American Legal Defense and Education Fund et al. by Jonathan P. Guy and Kenneth Kimerling.

Brief of amici curiae filed on behalf of the Brennan Center for Justice et al. by Sidney S. Rosdeitcher and Wendy R. Weiser.

Brief of amici curiae filed on behalf of Current and Former State Secretaries of State by Daniel F. Kolb.

Brief of amici curiae filed on behalf of the Cyber Privacy Project et al. by Jonathan Albano.

Brief of amici curiae filed on behalf of the Electronic Privacy Information Center et al. by Marc Rotenberg.

Brief of amici curiae filed on behalf of Historians et al. by J. Gerald Hebert, Paul S. Ryan, and Charles J. Ogletree, Jr.

Brief of amici curiae filed on behalf of the Lawyers' Committee for Civil Rights Under Law et al. by Walter E. Dellinger, Sri Srinivasan, Jon M. Greenbaum, and Michael L. Murphy.

Brief of amici curiae filed on behalf of the Mexican American Legal Defense and Educational Fund by Matthew M. Shors, Michael C. Camunéz, John Trasviná, and Nina Perales.

Brief of amici curiae filed on behalf of the NAACP Legal Defense and Educational Fund, Inc., by Theodore M. Shaw, Jacqueline A. Berrien, Debo P. Adegbile, Ryan P. Haygood, and Kristen M. Clarke.

Brief of amici curiae filed on behalf of the National Congress of American Indians et al. by Vernle C. Durocher, Jr., and Glenn M. Salvo.

Brief of amici curiae filed on behalf of the National Law Center on Homelessness & Poverty et al. by Carter G. Phillips and Edward R. McNicholas.

Brief of amici curiae filed on behalf of Rock the Vote et al. by Charles S. Sims and Emily Stern.

Brief of amici curiae filed on behalf of the Rutherford Institute by John W. Whitehead.

Brief of amici curiae filed on behalf of R. Michael Alvarez et al. by Samuel R. Bagenstos and Milton Sherman.

Brief of amici curiae filed on behalf of Richard L. Hasen by Mr. Hasen, pro se.

Brief of amici curiae filed on behalf of Congressman Keith Ellison by Gerard Treanor.

Brief of amici curiae filed on behalf of Senator Dianne Feinstein et al. by Robert F. Bauer.

Brief of amici curiae filed on behalf of AARP et al. by Patricia A. Brannan, Daniel B. Kohrman, and Michael R. Schuster.

Brief of amici curiae filed on behalf of the Asian American Justice Center et al. by Mark A. Packman, Jonathan M. Cohen, Karen Narasaki, Vincent Eng, and Myron Quon.

Brief of amici curiae filed on behalf of the Association of Community Organizations for Reform Now by David Overlock Stewart.

Brief of amici curiae filed on behalf of the League of Women Voters of Indiana, Inc., et al. by Karen Celestino-Horseman, Thomas N. Austin, Bruce G. Jones, Lewis J. Liman, Nelson A. Nettles, and Raymond L. Faust.

Brief of amici curiae filed on behalf of Christopher S. Elmendorf et al. by Daniel P. Tokaji.

Brief of amici curiae filed on behalf of Dr. Frederic C. Schaffer et al. by Bradley S. Phillips.

Opposing Side (Respondent / Appellee)

Brief of amici curiae filed on behalf of the United States by Solicitor General Clement, Acting Assistant Attorney General Becker, Deputy Solicitor General Garre, Douglas Hallward-Driemeier, Diana K. Flynn, and Christy A. McCormick.

Brief of amici curiae filed on behalf of the State of Texas et al. by Greg Abbott, Attorney General of Texas, R. Ted Cruz, Solicitor General, Kent C. Sullivan, First Assistant Attorney General, David S. Morales, Deputy Attorney General for Civil Litigation, and Philip A. Lionberger, Assistant Solicitor General, by Roberto J. Sánchez-Ramos, Secretary of Justice of Puerto Rico, and by the Attorneys General for their respective States as follows: Troy King of Alabama, John W. Suthers of Colorado; Bill McCollum of Florida; Mark J. Bennett of Hawaii, Michael A. Cox of Michigan, Jon Bruning of Nebraska, and Lawrence E. Long of South Dakota.

Brief of amici curiae filed on behalf of Georgia Secretary of State Karen C. Handel by Thurbert E. Baker, Attorney General of Georgia, Dennis R. Dunn, Deputy Attorney General, Stefan E. Ritter, Senior Assistant Attorney General, Mark H. Cohen, and Anne W. Lewis.

Brief of amici curiae filed on behalf of the American Civil Rights Union by Peter J. Ferrara.

Brief of amici curiae filed on behalf of the American Unity Legal Defense Fund by Barnaby W. Zall.

Brief of amici curiae filed on behalf of the Center for Equal Opportunity et al. by John B. Nalbandian and Geoffrey Slaughter.

Brief of amici curiae filed on behalf of the Conservative Party of New York State by Martin S. Kaufman.

Brief of amici curiae filed on behalf of Democrat and Republican Election Professionals by Mark F. Hearne II.

Brief of amici curiae filed on behalf of the Evergreen Freedom Foundation by Michael J. Reitz.

Brief of amici curiae filed on behalf of the Lawyers Democracy Fund by Charles H. Bell, Jr., Harvey M. Tettlebaum, and Mark G. Arnold.

Brief of amici curiae filed on behalf of the Mountain States Legal Foundation by William Perry Pendley.

Brief of amici curiae filed on behalf of the Republican National Committee by Thomas J. Josefiak.

Brief of amici curiae filed on behalf of the Washington Legal Foundation by Bert W. Rein, Daniel J. Popeo, and Richard A. Samp.

Brief of amici curiae filed on behalf of Doris Anne Sadler by Wayne C. Turner and Michael R. Limrick.

Brief of amici curiae filed on behalf of the Pacific Legal Foundation by John H. Findley, Sharon L. Browne, and Steven Geoffrey Gieseler.

Brief of amici curiae filed on behalf of Senator Mitch McConnell et al. by Mr. Hearne.

Brief of amici curiae filed on behalf of Erwin Chemerinsky by Richard W. Clary in support of neither party.

IV. THE SUPREME COURT'S DECISION

"[U]nder the standard applied in Harper, even rational restrictions on the right to vote are invidious if they are unrelated to voter qualifications. In Anderson v. Celebrezze, 460 U.S. 780 (1983), however, we confirmed the general rule that 'evenhanded restrictions that protect the integrity and reliability of the electoral process itself' are not invidious and satisfy the standard set forth in Harper. . . .

We therefore begin our analysis of the constitutionality of Indiana's statute by focusing on those interests. . . .

The State has identified several state interests that arguably justify the burdens that SEA 483 imposes on voters and potential voters. . . .

Given the fact that petitioners have advanced a broad attack . . . , seeking relief that would invalidate the statute . . . , they bear a heavy burden of persuasion. . . .

Petitioners ask this Court . . . to perform a unique balancing analysis that looks specifically at a small number of voters who may experience a special burden under the statute and weighs their burdens against the State's broad interests in protecting election integrity. . . .

In sum, on the basis of the record that has been made in this litigation, we cannot conclude that the statute imposes 'excessively burdensome requirements' on any class of voters. A facial challenge must fail where the statute has a '"plainly legitimate sweep."' When we consider only the statute's broad application to all Indiana voters we conclude that it 'imposes only a limited burden on voters' rights.' The "precise interests" advanced by the State are therefore sufficient to defeat petitioners' facial challenge to SEA 483.

In their briefs, petitioners stress the fact that all of the Republicans in the General Assembly voted in favor of SEA 483 and the Democrats were unanimous in opposing it. . . . It is fair to infer that partisan considerations may have played a significant role . . . .

But if a nondiscriminatory law is supported by valid neutral justifications, those justifications should not be disregarded simply because partisan interests may have provided one motivation for the votes of individual legislators. The state interests identified as justifications for SEA 483 are both neutral and sufficiently strong to require us to reject petitioners' facial attack on the statute. The application of the statute to the vast majority of Indiana voters is amply justified by the valid interest in protecting 'the integrity and reliability of the electoral process.'

The judgment of the Court of Appeals is affirmed."

V. JUSTICE VOTE

3 Pro ACLU Side vs. 6 Con Opposing Side

ACLU Side (Petitioner / Appellant)

1. Souter, D. – Wrote dissenting opinion
2. Ginsburg, R. – Joined Souter's dissent
3. Breyer, S. – Wrote dissenting opinion

Opposing Side (Respondent / Appellee)

1. Stevens, J. – Wrote majority opinion
2. Alito, S. – Joined Scalia's concurrence
3. Thomas, C. – Joined Scalia's concurrence
4. Scalia, A. – Wrote concurring opinion
5. Kennedy, A. – Joined majority opinion

6. Roberts, J. – Joined majority opinion

VI. A WIN OR LOSS FOR THE ACLU?

The ACLU argued the cause for appellant urging reversal of the judgment of the Court of Appeals; the Supreme Court affirmed in a 6-3 vote, giving the ACLU an apparent loss.

1028. Riley v. Kennedy

(Decided May 27, 2008; 553 U.S. 406)

I. ISSUE

A. Issues Discussed

Voting rights

B. Legal Question Presented

"Must the State obtain fresh preclearance in order to reinstate the election practice prevailing before enactment of the law struck down by the State's Supreme Court?"

C. Supreme Court's Answer

"We hold that, for § 5 purposes, the invalidated law never gained 'force or effect.' Therefore, the State's reversion to its prior practice did not rank as a 'change' requiring preclearance."

II. CASE SUMMARY

A. Background

"This case presents a novel question concerning § 5 of the Voting Rights Act of 1965. The setting, in a nutshell: A covered State passed a law adopting a new election practice, obtained the preclearance required by § 5, and held an election. Soon thereafter, the law under which the election took place was invalidated by the State's highest court on the ground that it violated a controlling provision of the State's Constitution. . . .

The voting practice at issue . . . is the method used to fill midterm vacancies . . . .

When [a] 2005 vacancy arose, three Mobile County voters and Alabama state legislators . . . filed suit . . . . The . . . state trial court ordered Governor Riley to call a special election.

While the Governor's appeal to the Alabama Supreme Court was pending, Mobile County's election officials obtained preclearance . . . . In November 2005, however, the Alabama Supreme Court reversed the trial court's order. . . .

Kennedy commenced the instant suit . . . . Invoking § 5, she sought declaratory relief and an injunction barring Governor Riley from filling the Commission vacancy by appointment unless and until Alabama gained preclearance . . . .

In August 2006, the three-judge court . . . granted the requested declaration. . . .

In November 2007, we postponed a determination of jurisdiction . . . .

In the meantime, a special election was held . . . to fill the vacancy resulting from the District Court's order vacating Chastang's appointment. Chastang ran . . . but was defeated by Merceria Ludgood, who garnered nearly 80% of the vote. . . . Ludgood continues to occupy the District One seat on the Commission."

The Supreme Court granted certiorari to review the case.

B. Counsel of Record / ACLU Attorney

ACLU Side (Respondent / Appellee): Pamela S. Karlan argued the cause for appellees. With her on the brief were Edward Still, Amy Howe, Kevin Russell, Sam Heldman, Jeffrey L. Fisher, and Thomas C. Goldstein.

Kannon K. Shanmugam argued the cause for the United States as amicus curiae supporting appellees in part.

Opposing Side (Petitioner / Appellant): Kevin C. Newsom argued the cause for appellant. With him on the briefs were Troy King, Attorney General of Alabama, and Margaret L. Fleming, James W. Davis, and Misty S. Fairbanks, Assistant Attorneys General, Matthew H. Lembke, John C. Neiman, Jr., and Scott Burnett Smith.

III. AMICI CURIAE

ACLU Side (Respondent / Appellee)

Brief of amici curiae filed on behalf of the American Civil Liberties Union and ACLU of Alabama by Laughlin McDonald, Neil Bradley, Bryan Sells, Meredith E.B. Bell-Platts, Nancy Abudu, Brian Sutherland, and Steven R. Shapiro.

Brief of amici curiae filed on behalf of the United States by Kannon K. Shanmugam, Solicitor General Clement, Acting Assistant Attorney General Becker, Deputy Solicitor General Garre, Eric D. Miller, Diana K. Flynn, Gregory B. Friel, and Sarah E. Harrington.

Brief of amici curiae filed on behalf of the Lawyers' Committee for Civil Rights Under Law by Jonathan E. Nuechterlein, Daniel S. Volchok, and Jon M. Greenbaum.

Brief of amici curiae filed on behalf of the NAACP Legal Defense and Educational Fund, Inc., by Kristen Clarke, Theodore M. Shaw, Jacqueline A. Berrien, Debo P. Adegbile, and Ryan P. Haygood.

Opposing Side (Petitioner / Appellant)

Brief of amici curiae filed on behalf of the State of Florida et al. by Bill McCollum, Attorney General of Florida, Gene C. Schaerr, and Steffen N. Johnson, and by the Attorneys General for their respective States as follows: Talis J. Colberg of Alaska, James D. Caldwell of Louisiana, Kelly A. Ayotte of New Hampshire, Gary K. King of New Mexico, Henry D. McMaster of South Carolina, Lawrence E. Long of South Dakota, and Bob McDonnell of Virginia.

Brief of amici curiae filed on behalf of the Project on Fair Representation by Bert W. Rein.

Brief of amici curiae filed on behalf of Former State Court Justice Charles Fried et al. by H. Christopher Bartolomucci.

Brief of amici curiae filed on behalf of Abigail Thernstrom et al. by Keith A. Noreika.

IV. THE SUPREME COURT'S DECISION

"Properly framed, the issue before us is whether § 5 required Alabama to obtain preclearance before reinstating the practice of gubernatorial appointment in the wake of the decision by its highest court invalidating the special-election law. . . .

For the reasons that follow, we conclude that the 1985 Act was never 'in force or effect' within the meaning of § 5. At all relevant times, therefore, the baseline practice for filling midterm vacancies on the Commission was the pre–1985 practice of gubernatorial appointment. The State's reinstatement of that practice thus did not constitute a change requiring preclearance. . . .

We have directly addressed the § 5 term of art 'in force or effect' on three prior occasions. [T]hese precedents do not control this case because they differ in a critical respect. . . .

We decline to adopt a rigid interpretation of 'in force or effect' that would deny state supreme courts the opportunity to correct similar errors in the future. . . .

Although our reasoning and the particular facts of this case should make the narrow scope of our holding apparent, we conclude with some cautionary observations. First, the presence of a judgment by Alabama's highest court declaring the 1985 Act invalid under the State Constitution is critical to our decision. . . . Second, the 1985 Act was challenged the first time it was invoked and struck down shortly thereafter. The same result would not necessarily follow if a practice were invalidated only after enforcement without challenge in several previous elections. . . . Finally, the consequence of the Alabama Supreme Court's decision in Stokes was to reinstate a practice—gubernatorial appointment—identical to the State's § 5 baseline. . . .

For the reasons stated, the judgment of the United States District Court for the Middle District of Alabama is reversed, and the case is remanded . . . ."

V. JUSTICE VOTE

2 Pro ACLU Side vs. 7 Con Opposing Side

ACLU Side (Respondent / Appellee)

1. Stevens, J. – Wrote dissenting opinion
2. Souter, D. – Joined Stevens' dissent

Opposing Side (Petitioner / Appellant)

1. Ginsburg, R. – Wrote majority opinion
2. Alito, S. – Joined majority opinion
3. Thomas, C. – Joined majority opinion
4. Breyer, S. – Joined majority opinion
5. Scalia, A. – Joined majority opinion
6. Kennedy, A. – Joined majority opinion
7. Roberts, J. – Joined majority opinion

VI. A WIN OR LOSS FOR THE ACLU?

The ACLU filed as amicus curiae urging affirmance; the Supreme Court reversed the district court's decision by a 7-2 vote, giving the ACLU an apparent loss.

1029. CBOCS West, Inc. v. Humphries

(Decided May 27, 2008; 553 U.S. 442)

I. ISSUE

A. Issues Discussed

Race, civil rights

B. Legal Question Presented

"A longstanding civil rights law, first enacted just after the Civil War, provides that '[a]ll persons within the jurisdiction of the United States shall have the same right in every State and Territory to make and enforce contracts . . . as is enjoyed by white citizens.' The basic question before us is whether the provision encompasses a complaint of retaliation against a person who has complained about a violation of another person's contract-related 'right.'"

C. Supreme Court's Answer

"We conclude that it does."

II. CASE SUMMARY

A. Background

"The case before us arises out of a claim by respondent, Hedrick G. Humphries, a former assistant manager of a Cracker Barrel restaurant, that CBOCS West, Inc. (Cracker Barrel's owner), dismissed him (1) because of racial bias (Humphries is a black man) and (2) because he had complained to managers that a fellow assistant manager had dismissed another black employee, Venus Green, for race-based reasons. Humphries timely filed a charge with the Equal Employment Opportunity Commission (EEOC) . . . and received a 'right to sue' letter. He then filed a complaint . . . charging that CBOCS' actions violated both Title VII of the Civil Rights Act of 1964 and the older 'equal contract rights' provision here at issue, § 1981. The District Court dismissed Humphries' Title VII claims for failure to pay necessary filing fees on a timely basis. It then granted CBOCS' motion for summary judgment on Humphries' two § 1981 claims. Humphries appealed.

The U.S. Court of Appeals for the Seventh Circuit ruled against Humphries and upheld the District Court's grant of summary judgment in respect to his direct discrimination claim. But it ruled in Humphries' favor and remanded for a trial in respect to his § 1981 retaliation claim. In doing so, the Court of Appeals rejected CBOCS' argument that § 1981 did not encompass a claim of retaliation."

The Supreme Court granted certiorari to review the case.

B. Counsel of Record / ACLU Attorney

ACLU Side (Respondent / Appellee): Cynthia H. Hyndman argued the cause for appellee. With her on the brief were Aleeza M. Strubel and Eric Schnapper.

Solicitor General Clement argued the cause for the United States as amicus curiae.

Opposing Side (Petitioner / Appellant): Michael W. Hawkins argued the cause for appellant. With him on the briefs were Michael J. Newman and Michael Zylstra.

III. AMICI CURIAE

ACLU Side (Respondent / Appellee)

Brief of amici curiae filed on behalf of the Leadership Conference on Civil Rights (of which the ACLU is a member) and Leadership Conference on Civil Rights Education Fund by Paul R. Q. Wolfson, Anne Harkavy, Juliana Mirabilio, Susan S. Friedman, Megan Moran-Gates, Andrea Loveless, and Michael Foreman.

Brief of amici curiae filed on behalf of the United States by Solicitor General Clement, Acting Assistant Attorney General Becker, Deputy Solicitor General Garre, Curtis E. Gannon, and Dennis J. Dimsey.

Brief of amici curiae filed on behalf of the State of New York et al. by Andrew M. Cuomo, Attorney General of New York, Barbara D. Underwood, Solicitor General, and Benjamin N. Gutman, Deputy Solicitor General, and by the Attorneys General for their respective States as follows: Terry Goddard of Arizona, Richard Blumenthal of Connecticut, Lisa Madigan of Illinois, Thomas Miller of Iowa, Douglas F. Gansler of Maryland, Martha Coakley of Massachusetts, Jeremiah W. (Jay) Nixon of Missouri, Catherine Cortez Masto of Nevada, Anne Milgram of New Jersey, Marc Dann of Ohio, Hardy Myers of Oregon, William H. Sorrell of Vermont, and Darrell V. McGraw, Jr., of West Virginia.

Brief of amici curiae filed on behalf of Historian Mary Frances Berry et al. by Melissa Hart and Charles J. Ogletree, Jr.

Brief of amici curiae filed on behalf of Members of Congress by Aaron M. Panner and Priya R. Aiyar.

Brief of amici curiae filed on behalf of the National Employment Lawyers Association by Douglas B. Huron, Stephen Z. Chertkof, and Tammany M. Kramer.

Opposing Side (Petitioner / Appellant)

Brief of amici curiae filed on behalf of the Chamber of Commerce of the United States of America by Catherine E. Stetson, Robin S. Conrad, and Shane Brennan.

Brief of amici curiae filed on behalf of the Equal Employment Advisory Council et al. by Rae T. Vann, Karen R. Harned, and Elizabeth Milito.

IV. THE SUPREME COURT'S DECISION

"The question before us is whether § 1981 encompasses retaliation claims. We conclude that it does. And because our conclusion rests in significant part upon principles of stare decisis, we begin by examining the pertinent interpretive history. . . .

The upshot is this: (1) In 1969, Sullivan . . . recognized that § 1982 encompasses a retaliation action; (2) this Court has long interpreted §§ 1981 and 1982 alike; (3) in 1989, Patterson . . . narrowed § 1981 by excluding from its scope conduct . . . where retaliation would most likely be found; but in 1991, Congress enacted legislation that superseded Patterson and explicitly defined the scope of § 1981 to include post-contract-formation conduct; and (4) since 1991, the lower courts have uniformly interpreted § 1981 as encompassing retaliation actions. . . .

Sullivan, as interpreted and relied upon by Jackson, as well as the long line of related cases where we construe §§ 1981 and 1982 similarly, lead us to conclude that the view that § 1981 encompasses retaliation claims is indeed well embedded in the law. That being so, considerations of stare decisis strongly support our adherence to that view. . . .

CBOCS' several arguments . . . cannot justify a departure from what we have just described as the well-embedded interpretation of § 1981. . . .

We conclude that considerations of stare decisis strongly support our adherence to Sullivan and the long line of related cases where we interpret §§ 1981 and 1982 similarly. CBOCS' arguments do not convince us to the contrary. We consequently hold that 42 U.S.C. § 1981 encompasses claims of retaliation. The judgment of the Court of Appeals is affirmed."

V. JUSTICE VOTE

7 Pro ACLU Side vs. 2 Con Opposing Side

ACLU Side (Respondent / Appellee)

1. Breyer, S. – Wrote majority opinion
2. Alito, S. – Joined majority opinion
3. Stevens, J. – Joined majority opinion
4. Kennedy, A. – Joined majority opinion
5. Ginsburg, R. – Joined majority opinion
6. Souter, D. – Joined majority opinion
7. Roberts, J. – Joined majority opinion

Opposing Side (Petitioner / Appellant)

1. Thomas, C. – Wrote dissenting opinion
2. Scalia, A. – Joined Thomas' dissent

VI. A WIN OR LOSS FOR THE ACLU?

The ACLU filed as amicus curiae urging affirmance; the Supreme Court affirmed the Court of Appeals' decision by a 7-2 vote, giving the ACLU an apparent win.

1030. Engquist v. Oregon Department of Agriculture

(Decided June 9, 2008; 553 U.S. 591)

I. ISSUE

A. Issues Discussed

Federal, civil rights

B. Legal Question Presented

"[W]hether a public employee can state a claim under the Equal Protection Clause by alleging that she was arbitrarily treated differently from other similarly situated employees, with no assertion that the different treatment was based on the employee's membership in any particular class."

C. Supreme Court's Answer

"We hold that such a 'class-of-one' theory of equal protection has no place in the public employment context."

II. CASE SUMMARY

A. Background

"Anup Engquist . . . was hired . . . by Norma Corristan to . . . a laboratory within the Oregon Department of Agriculture (ODA). . . . Engquist experienced repeated problems with Joseph Hyatt . . . . Corristan responded by directing Hyatt to attend diversity and anger management training. . . .

John Szczepanski [began] supervising Corristan, Hyatt, and Engquist. Szczepanski told a client that he could not 'control' Engquist, and that Engquist and Corristan 'would be gotten rid of.' When Engquist and Hyatt both applied for a . . . managerial post . . . , Szczepanski chose Hyatt despite Engquist's greater experience . . . . [D]uring . . . budget cuts . . . , Szczepanski eliminated Corristan's position. . . . Engquist was informed that her position was being eliminated . . . . Engquist's collective-bargaining agreement gave her the opportunity either to 'bump' to another position at her level, or to take a demotion. She was . . . unqualified for the only other position at her level and declined a demotion . . . .

Engquist subsequently brought suit . . . alleging violations of federal antidiscrimination statutes, the Equal Protection and Due Process Clauses . . . , and state law. . . .

The District Court granted the respondents' motion for summary judgment as to some of Engquist's claims, but allowed others to go forward, including . . . equal protection . . . .

The jury rejected Engquist's claims of discrimination . . . but found in her favor on the class-of-one claim. . . . The jury also found for Engquist on several of her other claims, and awarded her $175,000 in compensatory damages and $250,000 in punitive damages.

The Court of Appeals reversed in relevant part."

The Supreme Court granted certiorari to review the case.

B. Counsel of Record / ACLU Attorney

ACLU Side (Petitioner / Appellant): Neal Katyal argued the cause for appellant. With him on the briefs were David H. Remes, Jeffrey C. Wu, Virginia A. Seitz, Jeffrey T. Green, Quin M. Sorenson, Craig A. Crispin, and Sarah O'Rourke Schrup.

Opposing Side (Respondent / Appellee): Janet A. Metcalf, Assistant Attorney General of Oregon, argued the cause for appellees. With her on the brief were Hardy Myers, Attorney General, Peter Shepherd, Deputy Attorney General, and Mary H. Williams, Solicitor General.

Lisa S. Blatt argued the cause for the United States as amicus curiae.

III. AMICI CURIAE

ACLU Side (Petitioner / Appellant)

Brief of amici curiae filed on behalf of the Lambda Legal Defense and Education Fund, Disability Rights Education and Defense Fund, American Association of People with Disabilities, American Civil Liberties Union, Gay & Lesbian Advocates & Defenders, National Center for Lesbian Rights, Human Rights Campaign, and National Gay and Lesbian Task Force by William M. Hohengarten, Jon W. Davidson, Susan L. Sommer, Steven R. Shapiro, Gary D. Buseck, Joshua A. Block, Kara Suffredini, and Shannon Price Minter.

Brief of amici curiae filed on behalf of the National Association of Police Organizations, Inc., et al. by William John Johnson and J. Michael McGuinness.

Brief of amici curiae filed on behalf of the National Education Association et al. by John M. West, Michael D. Simpson, Harold Craig Becker, and Jonathan P. Hiatt.

Brief of amici curiae filed on behalf of the National Employment Lawyers Association by Kathleen Eldergill.

Brief of amici curiae filed on behalf of the National Fraternal Order of Police by Larry H. James and Christina L. Corl.

Brief of amici curiae filed on behalf of Richard Epstein et al. by Aaron M. Panner.

Brief of amici curiae filed on behalf of Meir J. Westreich by Mr. Westreich, pro se.

Opposing Side (Respondent / Appellee)

Brief of amici curiae filed on behalf of the United States by Lisa S. Blatt, former Solicitor General Clement, Acting Solicitor General Garre, Acting Assistant Attorney General Bucholtz, and Irene M. Solet.

Brief of amici curiae filed on behalf of the Commonwealth of Pennsylvania et al. by Thomas W. Corbett, Jr., Attorney General of Pennsylvania, John G. Knorr III, Chief Deputy Attorney General, and Calvin R. Koons, Senior Deputy Attorney General, by Roberto J. Sánchez-Ramos, Secretary of Justice of Puerto Rico, and by the Attorneys General for their respective States as follows: Bill McCollum of Florida, Mark J. Bennett of Hawaii, Lisa Madigan of Illinois, Tom Miller of Iowa, Mike McGrath of Montana, Catherine Cortez Masto of Nevada, Marc Dann of Ohio, W. A. Drew Edmondson of Oklahoma, Lawrence E. Long of South Dakota, Robert E. Cooper, Jr., of Tennessee, Mark Shurtleff of Utah, Robert M. McKenna of Washington, and Bruce A. Salzburg of Wyoming.

Brief of amici curiae filed on behalf of the League of California Cities et al. by Brian P. Walter.

Brief of amici curiae filed on behalf of the National Conference of State Legislatures et al. by Richard Ruda.

Brief of amici curiae filed on behalf of the National School Boards Association by Francisco M. Negrón, Jr., Naomi Gittins, Lisa E. Soronen, Elizabeth Eynon-Kokrda, and Kenneth W. Hartman.

IV. THE SUPREME COURT'S DECISION

"Engquist argues that the Equal Protection Clause forbids public employers from irrationally treating one employee differently . . . , regardless of whether the different treatment is based on the employee's membership in a particular class. . . .

We do not quarrel with the premises of Engquist's argument. It is well settled that the Equal Protection Clause 'protect[s] persons, not groups,' and that the Clause's protections apply to administrative as well as legislative acts. It is equally well settled that States do not escape the strictures of the Equal Protection Clause in their role as employers. We do not, however, agree that Engquist's conclusion follows from these premises. Our traditional view of the core concern of the Equal Protection Clause as a shield against arbitrary classifications, combined with unique considerations applicable when the government acts as employer as opposed to sovereign, lead us to conclude that the class-of-one theory of equal protection does not apply in the public employment context. . . .

Our precedent in the public employee context therefore establishes two main principles: First, although government employees do not lose their constitutional rights when they accept their positions, those rights must be balanced against the realities of the employment context. Second, in striking the appropriate balance, we consider whether the asserted employee right implicates the basic concerns of the relevant constitutional provision, or whether the claimed right can more readily give way to the requirements of the government as employer. With these principles in mind, we come to the question whether a class of one theory of equal protection is cognizable in the public employment context. . . .

In concluding that the class-of-one theory of equal protection has no application in the public employment context . . . we are guided . . . by the 'common-sense realization that government offices could not function if every employment decision became a constitutional matter.' . . .

In short, ratifying a class-of-one theory of equal protection in the context of public employment would impermissibly 'constitutionalize the employee grievance.' 'The federal court is not the appropriate forum in which to review the multitude of personnel decisions that are made daily by public agencies.' Public employees typically have a variety of protections from just the sort of personnel actions about which Engquist complains, but the Equal Protection Clause is not one of them.

The judgment of the Court of Appeals is affirmed."

V. JUSTICE VOTE

3 Pro ACLU Side vs. 6 Con Opposing Side

ACLU Side (Petitioner / Appellant)

1. Stevens, J. – Wrote dissenting opinion
2. Ginsburg, R. – Joined Stevens' dissent
3. Souter, D. – Joined Stevens' dissent

Opposing Side (Respondent / Appellee)

1. Roberts, J. – Wrote majority opinion
2. Alito, S. – Joined majority opinion
3. Thomas, C. – Joined majority opinion
4. Breyer, S. – Joined majority opinion
5. Scalia, A. – Joined majority opinion
6. Kennedy, A. – Joined majority opinion

VI. A WIN OR LOSS FOR THE ACLU?

The ACLU filed as amicus curiae urging reversal of the judgment of the Court of Appeals; the Supreme Court affirmed in a 6-3 vote, giving the ACLU an apparent loss.

1031. Boumediene v. Bush

(Decided June 12, 2008; 553 U.S. 723)

I. ISSUE

A. Issues Discussed

Military, criminal procedure

B. Legal Question Presented

Whether the Guantanamo detainees party to the case "have the constitutional privilege of habeas corpus."

C. Supreme Court's Answer

"We hold these petitioners do have the habeas corpus privilege."

II. CASE SUMMARY

A. Background

"Under the Authorization for Use of Military Force (AUMF), the President is authorized 'to use all necessary and appropriate force against those nations, organizations, or persons he determines planned, authorized, committed, or aided the terrorist attacks that occurred on September 11, 2001, or harbored such organizations or persons, in order to prevent any future acts of international terrorism against the United States . . . .' . . .

Interpreting the AUMF, the Department of Defense ordered the detention of these petitioners, and they were transferred to Guantanamo. . . . All are foreign nationals, but none is a citizen of a nation now at war with the United States. Each denies he is a member of the al Qaeda terrorist network . . . or of the Taliban regime . . . . Each petitioner appeared before a separate CSRT; was determined to be an enemy combatant; and has sought a writ of habeas corpus . . . .

[After passage of the Military Commissions Act of 2006 (MCA) and extensive litigation throughout the court system, t]he Court of Appeals concluded that MCA § 7 must be read to strip from it, and all federal courts, jurisdiction to consider petitioners' habeas corpus applications, that petitioners are not entitled to the privilege of the writ or the protections of the Suspension Clause, and, as a result, that it was unnecessary to consider whether Congress provided an adequate and effective substitute for habeas corpus in the DTA."

The Supreme Court granted certiorari to review the case.

B. Counsel of Record / ACLU Attorney

ACLU Side (Petitioner / Appellant): Seth P. Waxman argued the cause for appellants in both cases. With him on the briefs for appellant Lakhdar Boumediene et al. in No. 06–1195 were Paul R. Q. Wolfson, Jonathan G. Cedarbaum, Douglas F. Curtis, Paul M. Winke, Stephen H. Oleskey, Robert C. Kirsch, Mark C. Fleming, and Pratik A. Shah. David J. Cynamon, Matthew J. MacLean, David H. Remes, and Marc D. Falkoff filed briefs for appellant Khaled A. F. Al Odah et al. in No. 06–1196. Thomas B. Wilner, Neil H. Koslowe, George Brent Mickum IV, John J. Gibbons, Lawrence S. Lustberg, Michael Ratner, J. Wells Dixon, Shayana Kadidal, Mark S. Sullivan, Pamela Rogers Chepiga, Joseph Margulies, Erwin Chemerinsky, Baher Azmy,

Kristine Huskey, Douglas J. Behr, and Clive Stafford Smith filed briefs for appellant Jamil El-Banna et al. in No. 06–1196. William C. Kuebler, Rebecca Snyder, and Walter Dellinger filed a brief for Omar Khadr as appellee in No. 06–1196 under this Court's Rule 12.6 in support of appellants.

Opposing Side (Respondent / Appellee): Former Solicitor General Clement argued the cause for appellees in both cases. With him on the brief were Acting Solicitor General Garre, Assistant Attorney General Keisler, Principal Deputy Associate Attorney General Katsas, Eric D. Miller, Douglas N. Letter, Robert M. Loeb, August E. Flentje, Pamela M. Stahl, and Jennifer Paisner.

III. AMICI CURIAE

ACLU Side (Petitioner / Appellant)

Brief of amici curiae filed on behalf of the American Civil Liberties Union and Public Justice by Cecillia D. Wang, Lucas Guttentag, Steven R. Shapiro, Arthur H. Bryant, and Victoria W. Ni.

Brief of amici curiae filed on behalf of the American Bar Association by William H. Neukom and Sidney S. Rosdeitcher.

Brief of amici curiae filed on behalf of the Association of the Bar of the City of New York by Arthur F. Fergenson and David E. Nachman.

Brief of amici curiae filed on behalf of Canadian Parliamentarians and Professors of Law by William R. Stein and Scott H. Christensen.

Brief of amici curiae filed on behalf of the Cato Institute by Timothy Lynch.

Brief of amici curiae filed on behalf of the Coalition of Non-Governmental Organizations by Jonathan S. Franklin, Stephen M. McNabb, Sharon Bradford Franklin, and John W. Whitehead.

Brief of amici curiae filed on behalf of the Federal Public Defender for the Southern District of Florida by Paul M. Rashkind.

Brief of amici curiae filed on behalf of Former Federal Judges by Beth S. Brinkmann, Seth M. Galanter, Ketanji Brown Jackson, and Agnieszka M. Fryszman.

Brief of amici curiae filed on behalf of Former United States Diplomat Diego C. Asencio et al. by Douglass Cassel.

Brief of amici curiae filed on behalf of International Humanitarian Law Experts by Harrison J. Frahn IV and Beth Van Schaack.

Brief of amici curiae filed on behalf of Professors of Constitutional Law and Federal Jurisdiction by Margaret L. Sanner, Gerald L. Neuman, pro se, and Harold Hongju Koh, pro se.

Brief of amici curiae filed on behalf of Retired Military Officers by James C. Schroeder, Gary A. Isaac, and Philip Allen Lacovara.

Brief of amici curiae filed on behalf of Specialists in Israeli Military Law and Constitutional Law by Stephen J. Schulhofer, Charles T. Lester, Jr., John A. Chandler, and Avital Stadler.

Brief of amici curiae filed on behalf of the United Nations High Commissioner for Human Rights by Donald Francis Donovan, Catherine M. Amirfar, and William H. Taft V.

Brief of amici curiae filed on behalf of Salim Hamdan by Neal K. Katyal, Harry H. Schneider, Jr., Joseph M. McMillan, Laurence H. Tribe, Kevin K. Russell, and Charles Swift.

Brief of amici curiae filed on behalf of United States Senator Arlen Specter, by Sen. Specter, pro se.

Brief of amici curiae filed on behalf of 383 United Kingdom and European Parliamentarians by Claude B. Stansbury.

Brief of amici curiae filed on behalf of Amnesty International et al. by Paul L. Hoffman and William J. Aceves.

Brief of amici curiae filed on behalf of the Commonwealth Lawyers Association by John Townsend Rich and Stephen J. Pollak.

Brief of amici curiae filed on behalf of Federal Courts and International Law Professors by David C. Vladeck.

Brief of amici curiae filed on behalf of Legal Historians by James Oldham, Michael J. Wishnie, and Jonathan Hafetz.

Brief of amici curiae filed on behalf of the National Institute of Military Justice by Jennifer S. Martinez, Ronald W. Meister, Stephen A. Saltzburg, and Arnon D. Siegel.

Brief of amici curiae filed on behalf of International Law Scholars by Sarah H. Paoletti.

Brief of amici curiae filed on behalf of the Juvenile Law Center et al. by Marsha L. Levick.

Brief of amici curiae filed on behalf of Scholar Paul Finkelman et al. by David Overlock Stewart.

Opposing Side (Respondent / Appellee)

Brief of amici curiae filed on behalf of the Criminal Justice Legal Foundation by Kent S. Scheidegger.

Brief of amici curiae filed on behalf of for Retired Generals and Admirals et al. by Daniel J. Popeo and Richard A. Samp.

Brief of amici curiae filed on behalf of the Foundation for Defence of Democracies et al. by Andrew G. McBride.

Brief of amici curiae filed on behalf of the American Center for Law and Justice by Jay Alan Sekulow, Stuart J. Roth, and Robert W. Ash.

IV. THE SUPREME COURT'S DECISION

"As a threshold matter, we must decide whether MCA § 7 denies . . . jurisdiction to hear habeas corpus actions pending at the time of its enactment. We hold the statute does deny that jurisdiction, so that, if the statute is valid, petitioners' cases must be dismissed. . . .

The Court of Appeals was correct to take note of the legislative history when construing the statute, and we agree with its conclusion that the MCA deprives the federal courts of jurisdiction to entertain the habeas corpus actions now before us. . . .

In deciding the constitutional questions . . . we must determine whether petitioners [cases] are barred . . . either because of their status . . . or their physical location . . . .

We hold that Art. I, § 9, cl. 2, of the Constitution has full effect at Guantanamo Bay. . . . Petitioners . . . are entitled to . . . habeas corpus to challenge . . . their detention. . . .

In light of this holding the question becomes whether the statute stripping jurisdiction to issue the writ avoids the Suspension Clause mandate because Congress has provided adequate substitute procedures for habeas corpus. . . .

Petitioners have met their burden of establishing that the DTA review process is, on its face, an inadequate substitute for habeas corpus. . . .

The detainees in these cases are entitled to a prompt habeas corpus hearing.

Our decision today holds only that petitioners before us are entitled to seek the writ; that the DTA review procedures are an inadequate substitute for habeas corpus; and that petitioners in these cases need not exhaust the review procedures . . . before proceeding with their habeas actions in the District Court. The only law we identify as unconstitutional is MCA § 7. Accordingly, both the DTA and the CSRT process remain intact. . . .

It bears repeating that our opinion does not address the content of the law that governs petitioners' detention. . . . We hold that petitioners may invoke . . . habeas corpus. The laws and Constitution are designed to survive, and remain in force, in extraordinary times. Liberty and security can be reconciled; and in our system they are reconciled within the framework of the law. The Framers decided that habeas corpus, a right of first importance, must be a part of that framework, a part of that law.

The determination by the Court of Appeals that the Suspension Clause and its protections are inapplicable to petitioners was in error. The judgment of the Court of Appeals is reversed. The cases are remanded to the Court of Appeals with instructions that it remand the cases to the District Court for proceedings consistent with this opinion."

V. JUSTICE VOTE

5 Pro ACLU Side vs. 4 Con Opposing Side

ACLU Side (Petitioner / Appellant)

1. Kennedy, A. – Wrote majority opinion
2. Stevens, J. – Joined majority opinion
3. Breyer, S. – Joined Souter's concurrence
4. Ginsburg, R. – Joined Souter's concurrence
5. Souter, D. – Wrote concurring opinion

Opposing Side (Respondent / Appellee)

1. Roberts, J. – Wrote dissenting opinion, joined Scalia's dissent
2. Scalia, A. – Wrote dissenting opinion, joined Roberts' dissent
3. Thomas, C. – Joined Roberts' dissent, joined Scalia's dissent
4. Alito, S. – Joined Roberts' dissent, joined Scalia's dissent

VI. A WIN OR LOSS FOR THE ACLU?

The ACLU filed as amicus curiae urging reversal of the judgment of the Court of Appeals; the Supreme Court reversed in a 5-4 vote, giving the ACLU an apparent win.

1032. Kennedy v. Louisiana

(Decided June 25, 2008; 554 U.S. 407)

I. ISSUE

A. Issues Discussed

8th Amendment, death penalty

B. Legal Question Presented

"[W]hether the Constitution bars respondent from imposing the death penalty for the rape of a child where the crime did not result, and was not intended to result, in death of the victim."

C. Supreme Court's Answer

"We hold the Eighth Amendment prohibits the death penalty for this offense. The Louisiana statute is unconstitutional."

II. CASE SUMMARY

A. Background

"Patrick Kennedy . . . seeks to set aside his death sentence under the Eighth Amendment. He was charged by . . . with the aggravated rape of his then–8–year–old stepdaughter. After a jury trial petitioner was convicted and sentenced to death under a state statute authorizing capital punishment for the rape of a child under 12 years of age. . . .

Petitioner's crime was one that cannot be recounted in these pages in a way sufficient to capture in full the hurt and horror inflicted . . . or to convey the revulsion society, and the jury that represents it, sought to express by sentencing petitioner to death. . . .

The State charged petitioner with aggravated rape of a child under La. Stat. Ann. § 14:42 and sought the death penalty. . . .

The jury unanimously determined that petitioner should be sentenced to death. The Supreme Court of Louisiana affirmed. . . .

The court acknowledged that petitioner would be the first person executed for committing child rape since La. Stat. Ann. § 14:42 was amended in 1995 and that Louisiana is in the minority of jurisdictions that authorize the death penalty for the crime of child rape."

The Supreme Court granted certiorari to review the case.

B. Counsel of Record / ACLU Attorney

ACLU Side (Petitioner / Appellant): Jeffrey L. Fisher argued the cause for appellant. With him on the briefs were Pamela S. Karlan, Jelpi P. Picou, G. Ben Cohen, and Martin A. Stern.

Opposing Side (Respondent / Appellee): Juliet L. Clark argued the cause for appellee. With her on the brief were Paul D. Connick, Jr., and Terry M. Boudreaux.

R. Ted Cruz, Solicitor General of Texas, argued the cause for the State of Texas et al. as amici curiae.

III. AMICI CURIAE

ACLU Side (Petitioner / Appellant)

Brief of amici curiae filed on behalf of the American Civil Liberties Union, the ACLU of Louisiana, and the NAACP Legal Defense and Educational Fund, Inc. by John Holdridge,

Theodore M. Shaw, Jacqueline A. Berrien, Christina Swarns, Steven R. Shapiro, and Dennis D. Parker.

Brief of amici curiae filed on behalf of the Louisiana Association of Criminal Defense Lawyers et al. by Paul R. Baier.

Brief of amici curiae filed on behalf of the National Association of Criminal Defense Lawyers et al. by Stuart F. Delery and Barbara E. Bergman.

Brief of amici curiae filed on behalf of the National Association of Social Workers et al. by David M. Gossett, Carolyn I. Polowy, and Joseph Thai.

Brief of amici curiae filed on behalf of Leading British Law Associations et al. by Sandra L. Babcock.

Opposing Side (Respondent / Appellee)

Brief of amici curiae filed on behalf of the State of Texas et al. by R. Ted Cruz, Solicitor General of Texas, Greg Abbott, Attorney General of Texas, Kent C. Sullivan, First Assistant Attorney General, Eric J. R. Nichols, Deputy Attorney General for Criminal Justice, Philip A. Lionberger, Assistant Solicitor General, Troy King, Attorney General of Alabama, Jim Davis and Will Parker, Assistant Attorneys General, and by the Attorneys General for their respective States as follows: John W. Suthers of Colorado, Lawrence G. Wasden of Idaho, Jim Hood of Mississippi, Jeremiah W. (Jay) Nixon of Missouri, W. A. Drew Edmondson of Oklahoma, Henry D. McMaster of South Carolina, and Robert M. McKenna of Washington.

Brief of amici curiae filed on behalf of Missouri Govenor Matt Blunt et al. by Christopher Landau and Nathan Mammen.

IV. THE SUPREME COURT'S DECISION

"The Court explained in Atkins, and Roper, that the Eighth Amendment's protection against excessive or cruel and unusual punishments flows from the basic 'precept of justice that punishment for [a] crime should be graduated and proportioned to [the] offense.' . . .

Evolving standards of decency must embrace and express respect for the dignity of the person, and the punishment of criminals must conform to that rule. [P]unishment is justified under one or more of three principal rationales: rehabilitation, deterrence, and retribution. It is the last of these, retribution, that most often can contradict the law's own ends. This is of particular concern when the Court interprets the meaning of the Eighth Amendment in capital cases. When the law punishes by death, it risks its own sudden descent into brutality, transgressing the constitutional commitment to decency and restraint.

For these reasons we have explained that capital punishment must 'be limited to those offenders who commit 'a narrow category of the most serious crimes' . . . .

Applying this principle, we held in Roper and Atkins that the execution of juveniles and mentally retarded persons are punishments violative of the Eighth Amendment . . . . The Court further has held that the death penalty can be disproportionate to the crime itself where the crime did not result, or was not intended to result, in death of the victim. . . .

Based both on consensus and our own independent judgment, our holding is that a death sentence for one who raped but did not kill a child, and who did not intend to assist another in killing the child, is unconstitutional under the Eighth and Fourteenth Amendments. . . .

As we have said in other Eighth Amendment cases, objective evidence of contemporary values as it relates to punishment for child rape is entitled to great weight, but it does not end our inquiry. . . . We turn, then, to the resolution of the question before us, which is informed by our precedents and our own understanding of the Constitution . . . .

Each of these propositions, standing alone, might not establish the unconstitutionality of the death penalty for the crime of child rape. Taken in sum, however, they demonstrate the serious negative consequences of making child rape a capital offense. These considerations lead us to conclude, in our independent judgment, that the death penalty is not a proportional punishment for the rape of a child. . . .

The judgment of the Supreme Court of Louisiana upholding the capital sentence is reversed. This case is remanded . . . ."

V. JUSTICE VOTE

5 Pro ACLU Side vs. 4 Con Opposing Side

ACLU Side (Petitioner / Appellant)

1. Kennedy, A. – Wrote majority opinion
2. Stevens, J. – Joined majority opinion
3. Breyer, S. – Joined majority opinion
4. Ginsburg, R. – Joined majority opinion
5. Souter, D. – Joined majority opinion

Opposing Side (Respondent / Appellee)

1. Alito, S. – Wrote dissenting opinion
2. Thomas, C. – Joined Alito's dissent
3. Scalia, A. – Joined Alito's dissent
4. Roberts, J. – Joined Alito's dissent

VI. A WIN OR LOSS FOR THE ACLU?

The ACLU filed as amicus curiae urging reversal of the judgment of the Supreme Court of Louisiana; the U.S. Supreme Court reversed in a 5-4 vote, giving the ACLU an apparent win.

1033. Herring v. U.S.

(Decided January 14, 2009; 555 U.S. 135)

I. ISSUE

A. Issues Discussed

4th Amendment

B. Legal Question Presented

"The Fourth Amendment forbids 'unreasonable searches and seizures,' and this usually requires the police to have probable cause or a warrant before making an arrest. What if an officer reasonably believes there is an outstanding arrest warrant, but that belief turns out to be wrong because of a negligent bookkeeping error by another police employee?"

C. Supreme Court's Answer

"We hold that in these circumstances the jury should not be barred from considering all the evidence."

II. CASE SUMMARY

A. Background

"Anderson learned that . . . Herring had driven to the . . . Sheriff's Department to retrieve something from his impounded truck. Herring was no stranger to law enforcement, and Anderson asked the county's warrant clerk, Sandy Pope, to check for any outstanding warrants . . . . When she found none, Anderson asked Pope to check with Sharon Morgan . . . in neighboring Dale County. After checking Dale County's computer database, Morgan replied that there was an active arrest warrant . . . . Pope relayed the information to Anderson and asked Morgan to fax over a copy . . . . Anderson . . . followed Herring . . . and arrested him. A search incident to the arrest revealed methamphetamine . . . and a pistol (which as a felon he could not possess) . . . .

There had, however, been a mistake . . . . [W]hen Morgan went . . . to retrieve the actual warrant . . . , Morgan was unable to find it. She called a court clerk and learned that the warrant had been recalled . . . . Morgan immediately called Pope . . . and Pope contacted Anderson . . . . This all unfolded in 10 to 15 minutes, but Herring had already been arrested and found with the gun and drugs . . . .

Herring was indicted . . . for illegally possessing the gun and drugs . . . . He moved to suppress the evidence on the ground that his initial arrest had been illegal because the warrant had been rescinded. The Magistrate Judge recommended denying the motion because the arresting officers had acted in a good-faith belief that the warrant was still outstanding. . . . The District Court adopted the Magistrate Judge's recommendation, and the Court of Appeals for the Eleventh Circuit affirmed."

The Supreme Court granted certiorari to review the case.

B. Counsel of Record / ACLU Attorney

ACLU Side (Petitioner / Appellant): Pamela S. Karlan argued the cause for appellant. With her on the briefs were Jeffrey L. Fisher, Amy Howe, Kevin K. Russell, Ronald W. Wise, and Thomas C. Goldstein.

Opposing Side (Respondent / Appellee): Deputy Solicitor General Dreeben argued the cause for the United States. With him on the brief were Solicitor General Garre, Acting Assistant Attorney General Friedrich, Toby J. Heytens, and Deborah Watson.

III. AMICI CURIAE

ACLU Side (Petitioner / Appellant)

Brief of amici curiae filed on behalf of the American Civil Liberties Union and the ACLU of Alabama by Geoffrey F. Aronow, William H. Forman, Eric G. Barber, and Steven R. Shapiro.

Brief of amici curiae filed on behalf of the Electronic Privacy Information Center et al. by Marc Rotenberg.

Brief of amici curiae filed on behalf of the National Association of Criminal Defense Lawyers by Pamela Harris and Walter Dellinger.

Opposing Side (Respondent / Appellee)

No briefs of amici curiae were filed in support of appellee.

IV. THE SUPREME COURT'S DECISION

"When a probable-cause determination was based on reasonable but mistaken assumptions, the person subjected to a search or seizure has not necessarily been the victim of a constitutional violation. The very phrase 'probable cause' confirms that the Fourth Amendment does not demand all possible precision. And whether the error can be traced to a mistake by a state actor or some other source may bear on the analysis. For purposes of deciding this case, however, we accept the parties' assumption that there was a Fourth Amendment violation. The issue is whether the exclusionary rule should be applied. . . .

1. The fact that a Fourth Amendment violation occurred—i.e., that a search or arrest was unreasonable—does not necessarily mean that the exclusionary rule applies. . . .

2. The extent to which the exclusionary rule is justified by these deterrence principles varies with the culpability of the law enforcement conduct. . . .

3. To trigger the exclusionary rule, police conduct must be sufficiently deliberate that exclusion can meaningfully deter it, and sufficiently culpable that such deterrence is worth the price paid by the justice system. As laid out in our cases, the exclusionary rule serves to deter deliberate, reckless, or grossly negligent conduct, or in some circumstances recurring or systemic negligence. The error in this case does not rise to that level. . . .

4. We do not suggest that all recordkeeping errors by the police are immune from the exclusionary rule. In this case, however, the conduct at issue was not so objectively culpable as to require exclusion. . . .

Petitioner's claim that police negligence automatically triggers suppression cannot be squared with the principles underlying the exclusionary rule . . . . In light of our repeated holdings that the deterrent effect of suppression must be substantial and outweigh any harm to the justice system, we conclude that when police mistakes are the result of negligence such as that described here, rather than systemic error or reckless disregard of constitutional requirements, any marginal deterrence does not 'pay its way.' In such a case, the criminal should not 'go free because the constable has blundered.'

The judgment of the Court of Appeals for the Eleventh Circuit is affirmed."

V. JUSTICE VOTE

4 Pro ACLU Side vs. 5 Con Opposing Side

ACLU Side (Petitioner / Appellant)

1. Stevens, J. – Joined Ginsburg's dissent
2. Breyer, S. – Wrote dissenting opinion, joined Ginsburg's dissent
3. Ginsburg, R. – Wrote dissenting opinion
4. Souter, D. – Joined Ginsburg's dissent and Breyer's dissent

Opposing Side (Respondent / Appellee)

1. Roberts, J. – Wrote majority opinion
2. Alito, S. – Joined majority opinion
3. Thomas, C. – Joined majority opinion
4. Scalia, A. – Joined majority opinion
5. Kennedy, A. – Joined majority opinion

VI. A WIN OR LOSS FOR THE ACLU?

The ACLU filed as amicus curiae urging reversal of the judgment of the Court of Appeals; the Supreme Court affirmed in a 5-4 vote, giving the ACLU an apparent loss.

1034. Pearson v. Callahan

(Decided January 21, 2009; 555 U.S. 223)

I. ISSUE

A. Issues Discussed

4th Amendment, drugs

B. Legal Question Presented

"[W]hether the mandatory procedure set out in Saucier should be retained."

C. Supreme Court's Answer

"We now hold that the Saucier procedure should not be regarded as an inflexible requirement and that petitioners are entitled to qualified immunity on the ground that it was not clearly established at the time of the search that their conduct was unconstitutional."

II. CASE SUMMARY

A. Background

"This is an action brought by respondent under Rev. Stat. § 1979, 42 U.S.C. § 1983, against state law enforcement officers who conducted a warrantless search of his house incident to his arrest for the sale of methamphetamine to an undercover informant whom he had voluntarily admitted to the premises. The Court of Appeals held that petitioners were not entitled to summary judgment on qualified immunity grounds. Following the procedure we mandated in Saucier v. Katz, 533 U.S. 194 (2001), the Court of Appeals held, first, that respondent adduced facts sufficient to make out a violation of the Fourth Amendment and, second, that the unconstitutionality of the officers' conduct was clearly established. In granting review, [the Supreme Court] required the parties to address the additional question whether the mandatory procedure set out in Saucier should be retained."

The Supreme Court granted certiorari to review the case.

B. Counsel of Record / ACLU Attorney

ACLU Side (Respondent / Appellee): Theodore P. Metzler, Jr., argued the cause for appellee. With him on the brief were Robert A. Long, Jr., and James K. Slavens.

Opposing Side (Petitioner / Appellant): Peter Stirba argued the cause for appellants. With him on the briefs were Meb W. Anderson and Orin S. Kerr.

Malcolm L. Stewart argued the cause for the United States as amicus curiae.

III. AMICI CURIAE

ACLU Side (Respondent / Appellee)

Brief of amici curiae filed on behalf of the ACLU by Steven R. Shapiro, Catherine Crump, Allen M. Hopper, and Adam B. Wolf.

Brief of amici curiae filed on behalf of the National Association of Criminal Defense Lawyers by Jeffrey A. Lamken and Barbara Bergman.

Brief of amici curiae filed on behalf of the National Campaign to Restore Civil Rights by Beth S. Brinkmann, Seth M. Galanter, and Michael Gerard.

Brief of amici curiae filed on behalf of the National Police Accountability Project et al. by Michael Avery, John Burton, Stephen M. Latimer, David Rudovsky, and Jeffrey L. Needle.

Brief of amici curiae filed on behalf of the Liberty Legal Institute by Kelly J. Shackelford.

Brief of amici curiae filed on behalf of the Texas Association of School Boards by Ramón G. Viada III in support of neither party.

Opposing Side (Petitioner / Appellant)

Brief of amici curiae filed on behalf of the United States by Malcolm L. Stewart, former Solicitor General Garre, Acting Assistant Attorneys General Friedrich and Katsas, Deputy Solicitor General Dreeben, Ann Wallace, Barbara L. Herwig, and Edward Himmelfarb.

Brief of amici curiae filed on behalf of the State of Illinois et al. by Lisa Madigan, Attorney General of Illinois, Michael A. Scodro, Solicitor General, and Jane Elinor Notz, Deputy Solicitor General, by Roberto J. Sánchez-Ramos, Secretary of Justice of Puerto Rico, and by the Attorneys General for their respective States as follows: Troy King of Alabama, Talis J. Colberg of Alaska, Dustin McDaniel of Arkansas, Edmund G. Brown, Jr., of California, John W. Suthers of Colorado, Bill McCollum of Florida, Thurbert E. Baker of Georgia, Mark J. Bennett of Hawaii, Lawrence G. Wasden of Idaho, Steve Carter of Indiana, Martha Coakley of Massachusetts, Michael A. Cox of Michigan, Jim Hood of Mississippi, Mike McGrath of Montana, Catherine Cortez Masto of Nevada, Kelly A. Ayotte of New Hampshire, Anne Milgram of New Jersey, W. A. Drew Edmondson of Oklahoma, Thomas W. Corbett, Jr., of Pennsylvania, Patrick C. Lynch of Rhode Island, Henry D. McMaster of South Carolina, Lawrence E. Long of South Dakota, Robert E. Cooper, Jr., of Tennessee, Greg Abbott of Texas, Mark L. Shurtleff of Utah, William H. Sorrell of Vermont, Robert M. McKenna of Washington, Darrell V. McGraw, Jr., of West Virginia, J. B. Van Hollen of Wisconsin, and Bruce A. Salzburg of Wyoming.

Brief of amici curiae filed on behalf of the National Association of Counties et al. by Richard Ruda and Lawrence Rosenthal.

IV. THE SUPREME COURT'S DECISION

"The doctrine of qualified immunity protects government officials 'from liability for civil damages insofar as their conduct does not violate clearly established statutory or constitutional rights of which a reasonable person would have known.' . . .

In Saucier, this Court mandated a two-step sequence for resolving government officials' qualified immunity claims. First, a court must decide whether the facts that a plaintiff has alleged . . . make out a violation of a constitutional right. Second, if the plaintiff has satisfied this first step, the court must decide whether the right at issue was 'clearly established' at the time of defendant's alleged misconduct. Qualified immunity is applicable unless the official's conduct violated a clearly established constitutional right. . . .

In considering whether the Saucier procedure should be modified or abandoned, we must begin with the doctrine of stare decisis. . . .

Where a decision has 'been questioned by Members of the Court in later decisions and [has] defied consistent application by the lower courts,' these factors weigh in favor of reconsideration. Collectively, the factors we have noted make our present reevaluation of the Saucier two-step protocol appropriate. . . .

On reconsidering the procedure required in Saucier, we conclude that, while the sequence set forth there is often appropriate, it should no longer be regarded as mandatory. The judges of the district courts and the courts of appeals should be permitted to exercise their sound discretion in deciding which of the two prongs of the qualified immunity analysis should be addressed first in light of the circumstances . . . .

Turning to the conduct of the officers here, we hold that petitioners are entitled to qualified immunity because the entry did not violate clearly established law. An officer conducting a search is entitled to qualified immunity where clearly established law does not show that the search violated the Fourth Amendment. . .

Because the unlawfulness of the officers' conduct in this case was not clearly established, petitioners are entitled to qualified immunity. We therefore reverse the judgment of the Court of Appeals."

V. JUSTICE VOTE

0 Pro ACLU Side vs. 9 Con Opposing Side

Opposing Side (Petitioner / Appellant)

1. Alito, S. – Wrote majority opinion
2. Stevens, J. – Joined majority opinion
3. Thomas, C. – Joined majority opinion
4. Breyer, S. – Joined majority opinion
5. Scalia, A. – Joined majority opinion
6. Kennedy, A. – Joined majority opinion
7. Ginsburg, R. – Joined majority opinion
8. Souter, D. – Joined majority opinion
9. Roberts, J. – Joined majority opinion

VI. A WIN OR LOSS FOR THE ACLU?

The ACLU filed as amicus curiae urging affirmance; the Supreme Court reversed the Court of Appeals' decision by a 9-0 vote, giving the ACLU an apparent loss.

1035. Fitzgerald v. Barnstable School Comm.

(Decided January 21, 2009; 555 U.S. 246)

I. ISSUE

A. Issues Discussed

Gender, civil rights

B. Legal Question Presented

"The issue in this case of peer-on-peer sexual harassment is whether Title IX of the Education Amendments of 1972, 86 Stat. 373, 20 U.S.C. § 1681(a), precludes an action under Rev. Stat. § 1979, 42 U.S.C. § 1983, alleging unconstitutional gender discrimination in schools."

C. Supreme Court's Answer

"[W]e conclude that Title IX was not meant to be an exclusive mechanism for addressing gender discrimination in schools, or a substitute for § 1983 suits as a means of enforcing constitutional rights. Accordingly, we hold that § 1983 suits based on the Equal Protection Clause remain available to plaintiffs alleging unconstitutional gender discrimination in schools."

II. CASE SUMMARY

A. Background

"[T]he daughter of . . . Lisa and Robert Fitzgerald was a kindergarten student . . . . [S]he told her parents that . . . a third-grade boy on the school bus would bully her into lifting her skirt. Lisa Fitzgerald immediately called the school principal, Frederick Scully, who arranged a meeting . . . with the Fitzgeralds, their daughter, and another school official, Lynda Day. Scully and Day then questioned the alleged bully . . . . the bus driver and several students . . . . She concluded that she could not corroborate . . . .

The Fitzgeralds' daughter . . . provided new details . . . . [T]he boy coerced her into pulling down her underpants and spreading her legs. Scully scheduled a second meeting . . .

[T]he local police department . . . concluded there was insufficient evidence . . . . Scully . . . concluded there was insufficient evidence . . . . Scully did propose remedial measures to the Fitzgeralds. He suggested transferring their daughter to a different bus or leaving rows of empty seats between the kindergarteners and older students . . . . The Fitzgeralds felt that these proposals punished their daughter . . . and countered with alternative proposals. . . .

The Fitzgeralds began driving their daughter to school . . . , but she continued to report unsettling incidents at school. The Fitzgeralds reported each incident to Scully. . . .

[T]he Fitzgeralds filed suit . . . alleging that the school system's response . . . had been inadequate . . . . The school committee . . . filed a motion to dismiss, which the District Court granted as to the § 1983 claims and the state-law claims. On the Title IX claim, the school committee filed a motion for summary judgment, which the District Court also granted.

The Court of Appeals for the First Circuit affirmed.

The Supreme Court granted certiorari to review the case.

B. Counsel of Record / ACLU Attorney

ACLU Side (Petitioner / Appellant): Charles A. Rothfeld argued the cause for appellants. With him on the briefs were Andrew J. Pincus, Dan M. Kahan, and Anne Glennon.

Opposing Side (Respondent / Appellee): Kay H. Hodge argued the cause for appellees. With her on the brief were Joan L. Stein and John M. Simon.

III. AMICI CURIAE

ACLU Side (Petitioner / Appellant)

Brief of amici curiae filed on behalf of the American Civil Liberties Union and the National Women's Law Center et al. by Steven R. Shapiro, Lenora M. Lapidus, Marcia D. Greenberger, Jocelyn Samuels, and Dina R. Lassow.

Brief of amici curiae filed on behalf of the American Bar Association by H. Thomas Wells, Jr., Richard M. Zuckerman, and Kristen Galles.

Brief of amici curiae filed on behalf of the National Association of Women Lawyers by Margaret Drew, Beth L. Kaufman, Mary Therese Nagel, and Joanne Simboli Hodge.

Brief of amici curiae filed on behalf of the Pacific Legal Foundation by John H. Findley and Steven Geoffrey Gieseler.

Opposing Side (Respondent / Appellee)

Brief of amici curiae filed on behalf of the National School Boards Association et al. by Lisa A. Brown, Ada Meloy, Francisco M. Negrón, Jr., Naomi Gittins, Thomas Hutton, and Lisa Soronen.

IV. THE SUPREME COURT'S DECISION

"In three cases, this Court has found that statutory enactments precluded claims . . . . These cases establish that '[t]he crucial consideration is what Congress intended.' . . .

In all three cases, the statutes . . . required plaintiffs to comply with particular procedures and/or to exhaust particular administrative remedies prior to filing suit. Offering plaintiffs a direct route to court via § 1983 would have circumvented these procedures and given plaintiffs access to tangible benefits—such as damages, attorney's fees, and costs—that were unavailable under the statutes. 'Allowing a plaintiff to circumvent' the statutes' provisions in this way would have been 'inconsistent with Congress' carefully tailored scheme.' . . .

Section 901(a) of Title IX provides:

'No person in the United States shall, on the basis of sex, be excluded from participation in, be denied the benefits of, or be subjected to discrimination under any education program or activity receiving Federal financial assistance.' 20 U.S.C. § 1681(a).

The statute's only express enforcement mechanism, § 1682, is an administrative procedure resulting in the withdrawal of federal funding from institutions that are not in compliance. In addition, this Court has recognized an implied private right of action. In a suit brought pursuant to this private right, both injunctive relief and damages are available.

These remedies—withdrawal of federal funds and an implied cause of action—stand in stark contrast to the 'unusually elaborate,' 'carefully tailored,' and 'restrictive' enforcement schemes of the statutes . . . in Sea Clammers, Smith, and Rancho Palos Verdes. Unlike those statutes, Title IX has no administrative exhaustion requirement and no notice provisions. . . .

In light of the divergent coverage of Title IX and the Equal Protection Clause, as well as the absence of a comprehensive remedial scheme comparable to those at issue in Sea Clammers, Smith, and Rancho Palos Verdes, we conclude that Title IX was not meant to be an exclusive mechanism for addressing gender discrimination in schools, or a substitute for § 1983 suits as a means of enforcing constitutional rights. Accordingly, we hold that § 1983 suits based on the Equal Protection Clause remain available to plaintiffs alleging unconstitutional gender discrimination in schools. . . .

This conclusion is consistent with Title IX's context and history. . . .

Accordingly, we reverse the Court of Appeals' judgment that the District Court's dismissal of the § 1983 claims was proper and remand . . . ."

V. JUSTICE VOTE

9 Pro ACLU Side vs. 0 Con Opposing Side

ACLU Side (Petitioner / Appellant)

1. Alito, S. – Wrote majority opinion
2. Stevens, J. – Joined majority opinion
3. Thomas, C. – Joined majority opinion
4. Breyer, S. – Joined majority opinion
5. Scalia, A. – Joined majority opinion
6. Kennedy, A. – Joined majority opinion
7. Ginsburg, R. – Joined majority opinion
8. Souter, D. – Joined majority opinion
9. Roberts, J. – Joined majority opinion

VI. A WIN OR LOSS FOR THE ACLU?

The ACLU filed as amicus curiae urging reversal of the judgment of the Court of Appeals; the Supreme Court reversed in a 9-0 vote, giving the ACLU an apparent win.

1036. Crawford v. Metropolitan Government of Nashville & Davidson County, Tennessee

(Decided January 26, 2009; 555 U.S. 271)

I. ISSUE

A. Issues Discussed

Civil rights, gender

B. Legal Question Presented

"Title VII of the Civil Rights Act of 1964 . . . forbids retaliation by employers against employees who report workplace race or gender discrimination. The question here is whether this protection extends to an employee who speaks out about discrimination not on her own initiative, but in answering questions during an employer's internal investigation."

C. Supreme Court's Answer

"We hold that it does."

II. CASE SUMMARY

A. Background

"In 2002, respondent Metropolitan Government of Nashville and Davidson County, Tennessee (Metro), began looking into rumors of sexual harassment by the Metro School District's employee relations director, Gene Hughes. When Veronica Frazier, a Metro human resources officer, asked petitioner Vicky Crawford, a 30-year Metro employee, whether she had witnessed 'inappropriate behavior' on the part of Hughes, Crawford described several instances of sexually harassing behavior: once, Hughes had answered her greeting, "Hey Dr. Hughes, [w]hat's up?," by grabbing his crotch and saying "[Y]ou know what's up"; he had repeatedly "put his crotch up to [her] window"; and on one occasion he had entered her office and "grabbed her head and pulled it to his crotch." Two other employees also reported being sexually harassed by Hughes. Although Metro took no action against Hughes, it did fire Crawford and the two other accusers soon after finishing the investigation, saying in Crawford's case that it was for embezzlement. Crawford claimed Metro was retaliating for her report of Hughes's behavior and filed a charge of a Title VII violation with the Equal Employment Opportunity Commission (EEOC), followed by this suit . . . .

The District Court granted summary judgment for Metro. . . . The Court of Appeals affirmed . . . ."

The Supreme Court granted certiorari to review the case.

B. Counsel of Record / ACLU Attorney

ACLU Side (Petitioner / Appellant): Eric Schnapper argued the cause for appellant. With him on the briefs was Ann Buntin Steiner.

Lisa S. Blatt argued the cause for the United States as amicus curiae.

Opposing Side (Respondent / Appellee): Francis H. Young argued the cause for appellee. With him on the brief was James L. Charles.

III. AMICI CURIAE

ACLU Side (Petitioner / Appellant)

Brief of amici curiae filed on behalf of the National Women's Law Center and 31 organizations, including the American Civil Liberties Union, by Melissa Hart, Marcia D. Greenberger, Jocelyn F. Samuels, and Dina R. Lassow.

Brief of amici curiae filed on behalf of the United States by Lisa S. Blatt, former Solicitor General Clement, Solicitor General Garre, Acting Assistant Attorney General Becker, Dennis J. Dimsey, Angela M. Miller, Ronald S. Cooper, Carolyn L. Wheeler, and Jennifer S. Goldstein.

Brief of amici curiae filed on behalf of the State of Ohio et al. by Marc Dann, Attorney General of Ohio, William P. Marshall, Solicitor General, Benjamin C. Mizer and Kimberly A. Olson, Deputy Solicitors, and Susan A. Choe, Patrick M. Dull, and Duffy W. Jamieson, Assistant Attorneys General, by Roberto J. Sánchez-Ramos, Secretary of Justice of Puerto Rico, and by the Attorneys General for their respective States as follows: Talis J. Colberg of Alaska, Terry Goddard of Arizona, Richard Blumenthal of Connecticut, Beau Biden of Delaware, Bill McCollum of Florida, Mark J. Bennett of Hawaii, Lisa Madigan of Illinois, Tom Miller of Iowa, Jack Conway of Kentucky, Martha Coakley of Massachusetts, Michael A. Cox of Michigan, Mike McGrath of Montana, Anne Milgram of New Jersey, Gary K. King of New Mexico, Andrew M. Cuomo of New York, Mark L. Shurtleff of Utah, William H. Sorrell of Vermont, and Darrell V. McGraw, Jr., of West Virginia.

Brief of amici curiae filed on behalf of the Leadership Conference on Civil Rights et al. by Michael L. Foreman and Michael B. de Leeuw.

Brief of amici curiae filed on behalf of the National Employment Lawyers Association et al. by Bruce B. Elfvin, Christina M. Royer, Mary L. Heen, Adele P. Kimmel, and Catherine K. Ruckelshaus.

Brief of amici curiae filed on behalf of the Tennessee Education Association et al. by Richard L. Colbert and Courtney L. Wilbert.

Opposing Side (Respondent / Appellee)

Brief of amici curiae filed on behalf of the Chamber of Commerce of the United States of America by Catherine E. Stetson, Jessica L. Ellsworth, Robin S. Conrad, and Shane Brennan.

Brief of amici curiae filed on behalf of the Equal Employment Advisory Council et al. by Rae T. Vann, Alexandra Tsiros, Karen R. Harned, and Elizabeth G. Milito.

Brief of amici curiae filed on behalf of the National School Boards Association by Francisco M. Negrón, Jr., Lisa E. Soronen, F. Damon Kitchen, Jack R. Wallace, and Robert J. Sniffen.

IV. THE SUPREME COURT'S DECISION

"The opposition clause makes it 'unlawful . . . for an employer to discriminate against any . . . employe[e] . . . because he has opposed any practice made . . . unlawful . . . by this subchapter.' The term 'oppose' . . . carries its ordinary meaning . . . .

The statement Crawford . . . gave to Frazier is thus covered by the opposition clause, as an ostensibly disapproving account of sexually obnoxious behavior toward her by a fellow employee, an answer she says antagonized her employer to the point of sacking her on a false pretense. . . .

The Sixth Circuit thought answering questions fell short of opposition, taking the view that the clause "demands active, consistent 'opposing' activities to warrant . . . protection against retaliation," . . . and that an employee must 'instigat[e] or initiat[e]' a complaint to be covered. But though these requirements obviously exemplify opposition as commonly understood, they are not limits of it.

'Oppose' goes beyond 'active, consistent' behavior in ordinary discourse, where we would naturally use the word to speak of someone who has taken no action at all to advance a position beyond disclosing it. . . . There is, then, no reason to doubt that a person can 'oppose' by responding to someone else's question just as surely as by provoking the discussion, and nothing in the statute requires a freakish rule protecting an employee who reports discrimination on her own initiative but not one who reports the same discrimination in the same words when her boss asks a question. . . .

Because Crawford's conduct is covered by the opposition clause, we do not reach her argument that the Sixth Circuit misread the participation clause as well. . . .

The judgment of the Court of Appeals for the Sixth Circuit is reversed, and the case is remanded . . . ."

V. JUSTICE VOTE

9 Pro ACLU Side vs. 0 Con Opposing Side

ACLU Side (Petitioner / Appellant)

1. Souter, D. – Wrote majority opinion
2. Alito, S. – Wrote concurring opinion
3. Stevens, J. – Joined majority opinion
4. Thomas, C. – Joined Alito's concurrence
5. Breyer, S. – Joined majority opinion
6. Scalia, A. – Joined majority opinion
7. Kennedy, A. – Joined majority opinion
8. Ginsburg, R. – Joined majority opinion
9. Roberts, J. – Joined majority opinion

VI. A WIN OR LOSS FOR THE ACLU?

The ACLU filed as amicus curiae urging reversal of the judgment of the Court of Appeals; the Supreme Court reversed in a 9-0 vote, giving the ACLU an apparent win.

1037. Van de Kamp v. Goldstein

(Decided January 26, 2009; 555 U.S. 335)

I. ISSUE

A. Issues Discussed

Federal, civil rights

B. Legal Question Presented

"We here consider the scope of a prosecutor's absolute immunity from claims asserted under Rev. Stat. § 1979, 42 U.S.C. § 1983. We ask whether that immunity extends to claims that the prosecution failed to disclose impeachment material due to: (1) a failure properly to train prosecutors, (2) a failure properly to supervise prosecutors, or (3) a failure to establish an information system containing potential impeachment material about informants."

C. Supreme Court's Answer

"We conclude that a prosecutor's absolute immunity extends to all these claims."

II. CASE SUMMARY

A. Background

"Thomas Goldstein . . . filed a habeas corpus action . . . . He claimed that . . . his conviction [for murder] depended in critical part upon the testimony of Edward Floyd Fink, a jailhouse informant; that Fink's testimony was unreliable, indeed false; that Fink had previously received reduced sentences for providing prosecutors with favorable testimony in other cases; that at least some prosecutors in the Los Angeles County District Attorney's Office knew about the favorable treatment; that the office had not provided Goldstein's attorney with that information; and that . . . the prosecution's failure to provide Goldstein's attorney with this potential impeachment information had led to his erroneous conviction.

After an evidentiary hearing the District Court agreed with Goldstein that Fink had not been truthful and that if the prosecution had told Goldstein's lawyer that Fink had received prior rewards in return for favorable testimony it might have made a difference. The court ordered the State either to grant Goldstein a new trial or to release him. The Court of Appeals affirmed the District Court's determination. And the State decided that, rather than retry Goldstein (who had already served 24 years of his sentence), it would release him.

Upon his release Goldstein filed this § 1983 action . . . .

Petitioners, claiming absolute immunity from such a § 1983 action, asked the District Court to dismiss the complaint. The District Court denied the motion to dismiss . . . . The Ninth Circuit . . . affirmed the District Court's 'no immunity' determination."

The Supreme Court granted certiorari to review the case.

B. Counsel of Record / ACLU Attorney

ACLU Side (Respondent / Appellee): E. Joshua Rosenkranz argued the cause for appellee. With him on the brief were Timothy S. Mehok, William H. Forman, Ronald O. Kaye, David S. McLane, Marilyn E. Bednarski, and David A. Thomas.

Opposing Side (Petitioner / Appellant): Timothy T. Coates argued the cause for appellants. With him on the briefs was Steven J. Renick.

Deputy Solicitor General Dreeben argued the cause for the United States as amicus curiae.

III. AMICI CURIAE

ACLU Side (Respondent / Appellee)

Brief of amici curiae filed on behalf of the American Civil Liberties Union, the ACLU of Southern California, the ACLU of Northern California, and the National Association of Criminal Defense Lawyers by Alexandra Natapoff, M. Allen Hopper, Steven R. Shapiro, Scott M. Michelman, Benjamin B. Gould, Michael T. Risher, Peter J. Eliasberg, and Jeffrey L. Fisher.

Brief of amici curiae filed on behalf of the Constitutional Accountability Center by Elizabeth B. Wydra, Sean H. Donahue, and David T. Goldberg.

Brief of amici curiae filed on behalf of the Innocence Network et al. by Peter D. Isakoff, Peter J. Neufeld, and Barry Scheck.

Brief of amici curiae filed on behalf of Law Professors by John R. Cuti and Margaret Z. Johns.

Opposing Side (Petitioner / Appellant)

Brief of amici curiae filed on behalf of the United States by Deputy Solicitor General Dreeben, former Solicitor General

Garre, Assistant Attorney General Katsas, Lisa S. Blatt, Barbara L. Herwig, and Mark W. Pennak.

Brief of amici curiae filed on behalf of the State of Kansas et al. by Stephen N. Six, Attorney General of Kansas, Stephen R. McAllister, Solicitor General, and Jared S. Maag, Deputy Solicitor General, by Kevin T. Kane, Chief State's Attorney of Connecticut, by Peter J. Nickles, Acting Attorney General of the District of Columbia, and by the Attorneys General for their respective States as follows: Troy King of Alabama, Talis J. Colberg of Alaska, Terry Goddard of Arizona, Dustin McDaniel of Arkansas, Edmund G. Brown, Jr., of California, John W. Suthers of Colorado, Joseph R. Biden III of Delaware, Bill McCollum of Florida, Thurbert E. Baker of Georgia, Mark J. Bennett of Hawaii, Lawrence G. Wasden of Idaho, Lisa Madigan of Illinois, Steve Carter of Indiana, Tom Miller of Iowa, Jack Conway of Kentucky, James D. Caldwell of Louisiana, G. Steven Rowe of Maine, Douglas F. Gansler of Maryland, Martha Coakley of Massachusetts, Michael A. Cox of Michigan, Lori Swanson of Minnesota, Jim Hood of Mississippi, Jeremiah W. (Jay) Nixon of Missouri, Mike McGrath of Montana, Jon Bruning of Nebraska, Catherine Cortez Masto of Nevada, Kelly A. Ayotte of New Hampshire, Gary K. King of New Mexico, Andrew Cuomo of New York, Roy Cooper of North Carolina, Wayne Stenehjem of North Dakota, Nancy H. Rogers of Ohio, W. A. Drew Edmondson of Oklahoma, Hardy Myers of Oregon, Thomas W. Corbett, Jr., of Pennsylvania, Patrick C. Lynch of Rhode Island, Henry McMaster of South Carolina, Lawrence E. Long of South Dakota, Robert E. Cooper, Jr., of Tennessee, Greg Abbott of Texas, Mark L. Shurtleff of Utah, William H. Sorrell of Vermont, Robert F. McDonnell of Virginia, Robert M. McKenna of Washington, Darrell V. McGraw, Jr., of West Virginia, J. B. Van Hollen of Wisconsin, and Bruce A. Salzburg of Wyoming.

Brief of amici curiae filed on behalf of Cook County, Illinois, by Richard A. Devine, Patrick T. Driscoll, Jr., and Paul A. Castiglione.

Brief of amici curiae filed on behalf of Los Angeles County, California, by Steve Cooley, Lael R. Rubin, Brentford Ferreira, and Roberta Schwartz.

Brief of amici curiae filed on behalf of the City of New York by Michael A. Cardozo, Leonard J. Koerner, and Elizabeth Susan Natrella.

Brief of amici curiae filed on behalf of the National Association of Counties et al. by Richard Ruda.

Brief of amici curiae filed on behalf of the National District Attorneys Association et al. by W. Scott Thorpe.

Brief of amici curiae filed on behalf of the New York State District Attorneys Association by Anthony J. Servino, James A. Murphy III, Anthony J. Girese, and Mark Dwyer.

IV. THE SUPREME COURT'S DECISION

"In Imbler, this Court considered prosecutorial actions that are 'intimately associated with the judicial phase of the criminal process.' And . . . held that prosecutors are absolutely immune from liability in § 1983 lawsuits brought under such circumstances. . . .

In concluding that the prosecutor was absolutely immune, the Court pointed out that legislators have long 'enjoyed absolute immunity for their official actions' . . . .

In the years since Imbler, we have held that absolute immunity applies when a prosecutor prepares to initiate a judicial proceeding, or appears in court to present evidence in support of a search warrant application. We have held that absolute immunity does not apply when a prosecutor gives advice to police during a criminal investigation, when the prosecutor makes statements to the press, or when a prosecutor acts as a complaining witness in support of a warrant application. This case . . . requires us to consider how immunity applies where a prosecutor is engaged in certain administrative activities. . . .

[W]e conclude that prosecutors involved in such supervision or training or information-system management enjoy absolute immunity from the kind of legal claims at issue here. . . .

We recognize . . . that sometimes such immunity deprives a plaintiff of compensation that he undoubtedly merits; but the impediments to the fair, efficient functioning of a prosecutorial office that liability could create lead us to find that Imbler must apply here. . . .

We treat separately Goldstein's claim that the Los Angeles County District Attorney's Office should have established a system that would have permitted prosecutors 'handling criminal cases to access information pertaining to the benefits provided to jailhouse informants and other impeachment information.' . . .

[W]here a § 1983 plaintiff claims that a prosecutor's management of a trial-related information system is responsible for a constitutional error . . . , the prosecutor responsible for the system enjoys absolute immunity just as would the prosecutor who handled the . . . trial . . . .

[W]e conclude that petitioners are entitled to absolute immunity in respect to Goldstein's claims that their supervision, training, or information-system management was constitutionally inadequate. Accordingly, the judgment of the Court of Appeals is reversed, and the case is remanded . . . ."

V. JUSTICE VOTE

0 Pro ACLU Side vs. 9 Con Opposing Side

Opposing Side (Petitioner / Appellant)

1. Breyer, S. – Wrote majority opinion
2. Alito, S. – Joined majority opinion
3. Stevens, J. – Joined majority opinion
4. Thomas, C. – Joined majority opinion
5. Scalia, A. – Joined majority opinion
6. Kennedy, A. – Joined majority opinion
7. Ginsburg, R. – Joined majority opinion
8. Souter, D. – Joined majority opinion
9. Roberts, J. – Joined majority opinion

VI. A WIN OR LOSS FOR THE ACLU?

The ACLU filed as amicus curiae urging affirmance; the Supreme Court reversed the Court of Appeals' decision by a 9-0 vote, giving the ACLU an apparent loss.

1038. Bartlett v. Strickland

(Decided March 9, 2009; 556 U.S. 1)

I. ISSUE

A. Issues Discussed

Voting rights

B. Legal Question Presented

"This case requires us to interpret § 2 of the Voting Rights Act of 1965, 79 Stat. 437, as amended, 42 U.S.C. § 1973 (2000 ed.). The question is whether the statute can be invoked to require state officials to draw election-district lines to allow a racial minority to join with other voters to elect the minority's candidate of choice, even where the racial minority is less than 50 percent of the voting-age population in the district to be drawn."

C. Supreme Court's Answer

"We decline now to expand the reaches of § 2 to require, by force of law, the voluntary cooperation our society has achieved. Only when a geographically compact group of minority voters could form a majority in a single-member district has the first Gingles requirement been met."

II. CASE SUMMARY

A. Background

"It is common ground that state election-law requirements . . . may be superseded by federal law . . . . Here the question is whether § 2 of the Voting Rights Act requires district lines to be drawn that otherwise would violate the Whole County Provision. . . .

District 18 . . . emerged from the General Assembly's third redistricting attempt . . . . [T]he African-American voting-age population had fallen below 50 percent . . . and the General Assembly no longer could draw a geographically compact majority-minority district. Rather than draw District 18 to keep Pender County whole, however, the General Assembly drew it by splitting portions of Pender and New Hanover counties. District 18 has an African-American voting-age population of 39.36 percent. Had it left Pender County whole, the General Assembly could have drawn District 18 with an African-American voting-age population of 35.33 percent. The General Assembly's reason for splitting Pender County was to give African-American voters the potential to join with majority voters to elect the minority group's candidate of its choice. Failure to do so, state officials now submit, would have diluted the minority group's voting strength in violation of § 2. . . .

Pender County . . . filed the instant suit . . . . The plaintiffs alleged that the 2003 plan violated the Whole County Provision by splitting Pender County into two House districts. The state-official defendants answered that dividing Pender County was required by § 2. . . .

The court . . . determined . . . that § 2 required the General Assembly to split Pender County. The court sustained the lines for District 18 on that rationale. . . .

The Supreme Court of North Carolina reversed."

The Supreme Court granted certiorari to review the case.

B. Counsel of Record / ACLU Attorney

ACLU Side (Petitioner / Appellant): Christopher G. Browning, Jr., argued the cause for appellants. With him on the briefs were Roy Cooper, Attorney General of North Carolina, Grayson G. Kelley, Tiare B. Smiley, Alexander McC. Peters, Susan K. Nichols, Walter Dellinger, Sri Srinivasan, and Irving L. Gornstein.

Opposing Side (Respondent / Appellee): Carl W. Thurman III argued the cause and filed a brief for appellees.

Daryl Joseffer argued the cause for the United States as amicus curiae.

III. AMICI CURIAE

ACLU Side (Petitioner / Appellant)

Brief of amici curiae filed on behalf of the National Association for the Advancement of Colored People, Cindy Moore, Milford Farrior, Mary Jordan, and the American Civil Liberties Union by Anita S. Earls, Laughlin McDonald, Steven R. Shapiro, Pamela S. Karlan, Jeffrey L. Fisher, and Thomas C. Goldstein.

Brief of amici curiae filed on behalf of the State of Illinois et al. by Lisa Madigan, Attorney General of Illinois, Michael A. Scodro, Solicitor General, and Jane Elinor Notz, Deputy Solicitor General, and by the Attorneys General for their respective States as follows: Terry Goddard of Arizona, Edmund G. Brown, Jr., of California, Richard Blumenthal of Connecticut, Thurbert E. Baker of Georgia, Stephen N. Six of Kansas, Jack Conway of Kentucky, Douglas F. Gansler of Maryland, Martha Coakley of Massachusetts, Jim Hood of Mississippi, Jeremiah W. (Jay) Nixon of Missouri, Anne Milgram of New Jersey, Gary K. King of New Mexico, and Nancy H. Rogers of Ohio.

Brief of amici curiae filed on behalf of the Campaign Legal Center by J. Gerald Hebert, Paul S. Ryan, and Tara Malloy.

Brief of amici curiae filed on behalf of the Lawyers' Committee for Civil Rights Under Law et al. by Matthew M. Hoffman, Stephen J. Pollak, William F. Sheehan, John Townsend Rich, Jon M. Greenbaum, John Payton, Jacqueline A. Berrien, Debo P. Adegbile, Ryan P. Haygood, and Brenda Wright.

Brief of amici curiae filed on behalf of the League of Women Voters of the United States by Sam Hirsch and Lloyd Leonard.

Brief of amici curiae filed on behalf of Sanford D. Bishop, Jr., et al. by Jeh Charles Johnson.

Brief of amici curiae filed on behalf of the Mexican American Legal Defense and Educational Fund et al. by Lois D. Thompson and Nina Perales.

Opposing Side (Respondent / Appellee)

Brief of amici curiae filed on behalf of the United States by Daryl Joseffer, former Solicitor General Garre, Acting Assistant Attorney General Becker, Kannon K. Shanmugam, Diana K. Flynn, and Angela M. Miller.

Brief of amici curiae filed on behalf of the Florida House of Representatives by Bill McCollum, Attorney General of Florida, Scott D. Makar, Solicitor General, and Craig D. Feiser, Deputy Solicitor General.

Brief of amici curiae filed on behalf of the American Legislative Exchange Council et al. by E. Marshall Braden and Clark H. Bensen.
Brief of amici curiae filed on behalf of the Pacific Legal Foundation et al. by Sharon L. Browne.
Brief of amici curiae filed on behalf of Nathaniel Persily et al. by Mr. Persily, pro se, and Michael B. de Leeuw in support of neither party.

IV. THE SUPREME COURT'S DECISION

"Passage of the Voting Rights Act of 1965 was an important step in the struggle to end discriminatory treatment of minorities who seek to . . . vote. Though the Act as a whole was the subject of debate and controversy, § 2 prompted little criticism. The likely explanation . . . is that, as first enacted, § 2 tracked, in part, the text of the Fifteenth Amendment. . . .

In 1982, . . . Congress amended § 2, giving the statute its current form. . . .

This Court first construed the amended version of § 2 in Thornburg v. Gingles, 478 U.S. 30 (1986). . . . The Court identified three 'necessary preconditions' for a claim that the use of multimember districts constituted actionable vote dilution under § 2 . . . .

This case turns on whether the first Gingles requirement can be satisfied when the minority group makes up less than 50 percent of the voting-age population in the . . . district. The parties agree on all other parts of the Gingles analysis, so the dispositive question is: What size minority group is sufficient to satisfy the first Gingles requirement? . . .

The present case involves an intermediate type of district—a so-called crossover district. . . .

Unlike any of the standards proposed . . . , the majority-minority rule relies on an objective, numerical test: Do minorities make up more than 50 percent of the voting-age population in the relevant geographic area? That rule provides straightforward guidance . . . .

[N]o federal court of appeals has held that § 2 requires creation of coalition districts. Instead, all to consider the question have interpreted the first Gingles factor to require a majority-minority standard. . . . We decline to depart from the uniform interpretation . . . .

Our holding that § 2 does not require crossover districts does not consider the permissibility of such districts as a matter of legislative choice or discretion. . . .

Our holding also should not be interpreted to entrench majority-minority districts by statutory command, for that, too, could pose constitutional concerns. . . .

Some commentators suggest that racially polarized voting is waning . . . . Still, racial discrimination and racially polarized voting are not ancient history. Much remains to be done to ensure that citizens of all races have equal opportunity to share and participate in our democratic processes . . . ; and § 2 must be interpreted to ensure that continued progress. . . .

We decline now to expand the reaches of § 2 to require . . . the voluntary cooperation our society has achieved. Only when a geographically compact group of minority voters could form a majority in a single-member district has the first Gingles requirement been met.

The judgment of the Supreme Court of North Carolina is affirmed."

V. JUSTICE VOTE

4 Pro ACLU Side vs. 5 Con Opposing Side

ACLU Side (Petitioner / Appellant)

1. Stevens, J. – Joined Souter's dissent
2. Breyer, S. – Wrote dissenting opinion, joined Souter's dissent
3. Ginsburg, R. – Wrote dissenting opinion, joined Souter's dissent
4. Souter, D. – Wrote dissenting opinion

Opposing Side (Respondent / Appellee)

1. Kennedy, A. – Wrote majority opinion
2. Roberts, J. – Joined majority opinion
3. Alito, S. – Joined majority opinion
4. Thomas, C. – Wrote concurring opinion
5. Scalia, A. – Joined Thomas' concurrence

VI. A WIN OR LOSS FOR THE ACLU?

The ACLU filed as amicus curiae urging reversal of the judgment of the Supreme Court of North Carolina; the Supreme Court reversed in a 5-4 vote, giving the ACLU an apparent loss.

1039. Vermont v. Brillon

(Decided March 9, 2009; 556 U.S. 81)

I. ISSUE

A. Issues Discussed

Criminal procedure

B. Legal Question Presented

Whether delays sought by assigned counsel are attributable to the defendant when considering a Sixth Amendment claim concerning the "right to a speedy trial."

C. Supreme Court's Answer

"We hold that the Vermont Supreme Court erred in ranking assigned counsel essentially as state actors in the criminal justice system. Assigned counsel, just as retained counsel, act on behalf of their clients, and delays sought by counsel are ordinarily attributable to the defendants they represent."

II. CASE SUMMARY

A. Background

"This case concerns the Sixth Amendment guarantee that '[i]n all criminal prosecutions, the accused shall enjoy the right to a speedy . . . trial.' Michael Brillon . . . was arrested in July 2001 on felony domestic assault and habitual offender charges. Nearly three years later, in June 2004, he was tried by jury, found guilty as charged, and sentenced to 12 to 20 years in prison. The Vermont Supreme Court vacated Brillon's conviction and held that the charges against him must be dismissed because he had been denied his right to a speedy trial.

During the time between Brillon's arrest and his trial, at least six different attorneys were appointed to represent him. Brillon 'fired' the first, who served from July 2001 to February 2002. His third lawyer, who served from March 2002 until June 2002, was allowed to withdraw when he reported that Brillon had threatened his life. The Vermont Supreme Court charged against Brillon the delays associated with those periods, but charged against the State periods in which assigned counsel failed 'to move his case forward.'"

The Supreme Court granted certiorari to review the case.

B. Counsel of Record / ACLU Attorney

ACLU Side (Respondent / Appellee): William A. Nelson argued the cause for appellee. With him on the brief was Donald B. Verrilli, Jr.

Opposing Side (Petitioner / Appellant): Christina Rainville argued the cause for appellant. With her on the briefs was Erica A. Marthage.

Leondra R. Kruger argued the cause for the United States as amicus curiae.

III. AMICI CURIAE

ACLU Side (Respondent / Appellee)

Opposing Side (Petitioner / Appellant)

Brief of amici curiae filed on behalf of the American Civil Liberties Union, the ACLU of Vermont, and the National Association of Criminal Defense Lawyers by Anthony J. Franze, Joel D. Rohlf, Steven R. Shapiro, Robin L. Dahlberg, Dan Barrett, and Maureen Dimino.

Brief of amici curiae filed on behalf of Retired State Court Justices by Samuel Spital and Alan D. Reitzfeld.

Brief of amici curiae filed on behalf of the Vermont Network Against Domestic and Sexual Violence et al. by Cheryl Hanna. Brief of amici curiae filed on behalf of the United States by Leondra R. Kruger, former Solicitor General Garre, Acting Assistant Attorney General Friedrich, then-Deputy Solicitor General Dreeben, and Joseph C. Wyderko.

Brief of amici curiae filed on behalf of the State of Utah et al. by Mark L. Shurtleff, Attorney General of Utah, J. Frederic Voros, Jr., Chief, Criminal Appeals Division, and Christine F. Soltis and Ryan D. Tenney, Assistant Attorneys General, by Richard S. Gebelein, Chief Deputy Attorney General of Delaware, and by the Attorneys General for their respective States as follows: Troy King of Alabama, Talis J. Colberg of Alaska, Terry Goddard of Arizona, Dustin McDaniel of Arkansas, John W. Suthers of Colorado, Bill McCollum of Florida, Mark J. Bennett of Hawaii, Lawrence G. Wasden of Idaho, Lisa Madigan of Illinois, Steve Carter of Indiana, Thomas J. Miller of Iowa, Steve Six of Kansas, Jack Conway of Kentucky, G. Steven Rowe of Maine, Martha Coakley of Massachusetts, Michael A. Cox of Michigan, Lori Swanson of Minnesota, Mike McGrath of Montana, Jon Bruning of Nebraska, Catherine Cortez Masto of Nevada, Kelly A. Ayotte of New Hampshire, Anne Milgram of New Jersey, Gary K. King of New Mexico, Roy Cooper of North Carolina, Wayne Stenehjem of North Dakota, Nancy H. Rogers of Ohio, W. A. Drew Edmondson of Oklahoma, Hardy Myers of Oregon, Thomas W. Corbett, Jr., of Pennsylvania, Patrick C. Lynch of Rhode Island, Henry D. McMaster of South Carolina, Lawrence E. Long of South Dakota, Robert E. Cooper, Jr., of Tennessee, Greg Abbott of Texas, Robert F. McDonnell of Virginia, Robert M. McKenna of Washington, and Bruce A. Salzburg of Wyoming.

Brief of amici curiae filed on behalf of the National Governors Association et al. by Richard Ruda.

IV. THE SUPREME COURT'S DECISION

"The Sixth Amendment guarantees that '[i]n all criminal prosecutions, the accused shall enjoy the right to a speedy . . . trial.' . . .

Primarily at issue here is the reason for the delay in Brillon's trial. . . . Deliberate delay 'to hamper the defense' weighs heavily against the prosecution. '[M]ore neutral reason[s] such as negligence or overcrowded courts' weigh less heavily 'but nevertheless should be considered since the ultimate responsibility for such circumstances must rest with the government rather than with the defendant.'

In contrast, delay caused by the defense weighs against the defendant . . . .

Because 'the attorney is the [defendant's] agent when acting, or failing to act, in furtherance of the litigation,' delay caused by the defendant's counsel is also charged against the defendant. . . . [A] ssigned counsel ordinarily is not considered a state actor. . . .

Barker 's formulation 'necessarily compels courts to approach speedy trial cases on an ad hoc basis,' and the balance arrived at in close cases ordinarily would not prompt this Court's review. But the Vermont Supreme Court made a fundamental error in its application of Barker that calls for this Court's correction. The Vermont Supreme Court erred in attributing to the State delays caused by 'the failure of several assigned counsel . . . to move his case forward,' and in failing adequately to take into account the role of Brillon's disruptive behavior in the overall balance. . . .

In sum, delays caused by defense counsel are properly attributed to the defendant, even where counsel is assigned. '[A]ny inquiry into a speedy trial claim necessitates a functional analysis of the right in the particular context of the case,' and the record in this case does not show that Brillon was denied his constitutional right to a speedy trial. . . .

[T]he judgment of the Vermont Supreme Court is reversed, and the case is remanded . . . ."

V. JUSTICE VOTE

2 Pro ACLU Side vs. 7 Con Opposing Side

ACLU Side (Respondent / Appellee)

1. Breyer, S. – Wrote dissenting opinion
2. Stevens, J. – Joined Breyer's dissent

Opposing Side (Petitioner / Appellant)

1. Ginsburg, R. – Wrote majority opinion

2. Alito, S. – Wrote majority opinion
3. Thomas, C. – Joined majority opinion
4. Scalia, A. – Joined majority opinion
5. Kennedy, A. – Joined majority opinion
6. Souter, D. – Joined majority opinion
7. Roberts, J. – Joined majority opinion

VI. A WIN OR LOSS FOR THE ACLU?

The ACLU filed as amicus curiae urging affirmance; the Supreme Court reversed the Vermont Supreme Court's decision by a 7-2 vote, giving the ACLU an apparent loss.

1040. Arizona v. Gant

(Decided April 21, 2009; 556 U.S. 332)

I. ISSUE

A. Issues Discussed

4th Amendment, drugs

B. Legal Question Presented

Whether "the search-incident-to-arrest exception to the Fourth Amendment's warrant requirement" applies when the arrestee is not "within reaching distance of the passenger compartment at the time of the search [and] it is [not] reasonable to believe the vehicle contains evidence of the offense of arrest."

C. Supreme Court's Answer

"Police may search a vehicle incident to a recent occupant's arrest only if the arrestee is within reaching distance of the passenger compartment at the time of the search or it is reasonable to believe the vehicle contains evidence of the offense of arrest. When these justifications are absent, a search of an arrestee's vehicle will be unreasonable unless police obtain a warrant or show that another exception to the warrant requirement applies."

II. CASE SUMMARY

A. Background

"After Rodney Gant was arrested for driving with a suspended license, handcuffed, and locked in the back of a patrol car, police officers searched his car and discovered cocaine in the pocket of a jacket on the backseat. Because Gant could not have accessed his car to retrieve weapons or evidence at the time of the search, the Arizona Supreme Court held that the search-incident-to-arrest exception to the Fourth Amendment's warrant requirement, as defined in Chimel v. California, 395 U.S. 752 (1969), and applied to vehicle searches in New York v. Belton, 453 U.S. 454 (1981), did not justify the search in this case."

The Supreme Court granted certiorari to review the case.

B. Counsel of Record / ACLU Attorney

ACLU Side (Respondent / Appellee): Thomas F. Jacobs argued the cause for appellee. With him on the brief was Jeffrey T. Green.

Opposing Side (Petitioner / Appellant): Joseph T. Maziarz, Assistant Attorney General of Arizona, argued the cause for appellant. With him on the briefs were Terry Goddard, Attorney General, Mary R. O'Grady, Solicitor General, Kent E. Cattani, Chief Counsel, Randall M. Howe, Former Chief Counsel, and Nicholas D. Acedo, Assistant Attorney General.

Anthony A. Yang argued the cause for the United States as amicus curiae.

III. AMICI CURIAE

ACLU Side (Respondent / Appellee)

Brief of amici curiae filed on behalf of the American Civil Liberties Union and ACLU of Arizona by James J. Tomkovicz, Steven R. Shapiro, Dan Pachoda, and Graham A. Boyd.

Brief of amici curiae filed on behalf of the National Association of Criminal Defense Lawyers by Jeffrey L. Fisher, Pamela S. Karlan, Amy Howe, Kevin K. Russell, and Thomas C. Goldstein.

Brief of amici curiae filed on behalf of the National Association of Federal Defenders by Beth S. Brinkmann, Seth M. Galanter, Ketanji Brown Jackson, Lila M. Bateman, Frances H. Pratt, Philip J. Lynch, Judith H. Mizner, and Stephen C. Moss.

Opposing Side (Petitioner / Appellant)

Brief of amici curiae filed on behalf of the United States by Anthony A. Yang, former Solicitor General Clement, former Assistant Attorney General Fisher, and Deputy Solicitor General Dreeben.

Brief of amici curiae filed on behalf of the State of Florida et al. by Bill McCollum, Attorney General of Florida, Scott D. Makar, Solicitor General, and Craig D. Feiser and Courtney Brewer, Deputy Solicitors General, and by the Attorneys General for their respective States as follows: Troy King of Alabama, Talis J. Colberg of Alaska, Edmund G. Brown, Jr., of California, John W. Suthers of Colorado, Mark J. Bennett of Hawaii, Lawrence G. Wasden of Idaho, Lisa Madigan of Illinois, Steve Carter of Indiana, Steven N. Six of Kansas, Douglas F. Gansler of Maryland, Michael A. Cox of Michigan, Lori Swanson of Minnesota, Jeremiah W. (Jay) Nixon of Missouri, Kelly A. Ayotte of New Hampshire, Gary K. King of New Mexico, Wayne Stenehjem of North Dakota, W. A. Drew Edmondson of Oklahoma, Hardy Myers of Oregon, Thomas W. Corbett, Jr., of Pennsylvania, Lawrence E. Long of South Dakota, Robert E. Cooper, Jr., of Tennessee, Robert M. McKenna of Washington, J. B. Van Hollen of Wisconsin, and Bruce A. Salzburg of Wyoming.

Brief of amici curiae filed on behalf of Americans for Effective Law Enforcement, Inc., et al. by Wayne W. Schmidt, James P. Manak, Richard Weintraub, Michael E. McNeff, Eric B. Edwards, and Bernard J. Farber.

Brief of amici curiae filed on behalf of the National Association of Police Organizations, Inc., by William J. Johnson and Devallis Rutledge.

Brief of amici curiae filed on behalf of Los Angeles County District Attorney Steve Cooley et al. by Mr. Cooley, pro se, Lael R. Rubin, Brentford J. Ferreira, and Phyllis C. Asayama.

IV. THE SUPREME COURT'S DECISION

"[O]ur analysis begins . . . with the basic rule that 'searches . . . without prior approval . . . are . . . unreasonable under the Fourth Amendment—subject only to a few . . . exceptions.' Among the exceptions to the warrant requirement is a search incident to a lawful arrest. . . .

In Chimel, we held that a search incident to arrest may only include 'the arrestee's person and the area 'within his immediate control' . . . .

In Belton, we considered Chimel's application to the automobile context. . . .

[W]e held that when an officer lawfully arrests 'the occupant of an automobile, he may . . . search the passenger compartment . . . ' and any containers therein. That holding was based in large part on our assumption 'that articles inside . . . the passenger compartment of an automobile are in fact generally . . . within 'the area into which an arrestee might reach."

The Arizona Supreme Court read our decision in Belton as merely delineating 'the proper scope of a search of the interior of an automobile' incident to an arrest. That is, when the passenger compartment is within an arrestee's reaching distance, Belton supplies the generalization that the entire compartment and any containers therein may be reached. On that view of Belton, the state court concluded that the search of Gant's car was unreasonable because Gant clearly could not have accessed his car at the time of the search. . . .

Gant . . . urges us to adopt the reading of Belton followed by the Arizona Supreme Court. . . .

The State argues that Belton searches are reasonable regardless of the possibility of access . . . because that expansive rule correctly balances law enforcement interests, including the interest in a bright-line rule, with an arrestee's limited privacy interest in his vehicle.

For several reasons, we reject the State's argument. . . .

Construing Belton broadly to allow vehicle searches incident to any arrest would serve no purpose except to provide a police entitlement, and it is anathema to the Fourth Amendment to permit a warrantless search on that basis. . . .

Police may search a vehicle incident to a recent occupant's arrest only if the arrestee is within reaching distance of the passenger compartment at the time of the search or it is reasonable to believe the vehicle contains evidence of the offense of arrest. When these justifications are absent, a search of an arrestee's vehicle will be unreasonable unless police obtain a warrant or show that another exception to the warrant requirement applies. The Arizona Supreme Court correctly held that this case involved an unreasonable search. Accordingly, the judgment of the State Supreme Court is affirmed."

V. JUSTICE VOTE

5 Pro ACLU Side vs. 4 Con Opposing Side

ACLU Side (Respondent / Appellee)

1. Stevens, J. – Wrote majority opinion
2. Scalia, A. – Wrote concurring opinion
3. Souter, D. – Joined majority opinion
4. Thomas, C. – Joined majority opinion
5. Ginsburg, R. – Joined majority opinion

Opposing Side (Petitioner / Appellant)

1. Alito, S. – Wrote dissenting opinion
2. Breyer, S. – Wrote dissenting opinion, joined Alito's dissent in part
3. Kennedy, A. – Joined Alito's dissent
4. Roberts, J. – Joined Alito's dissent

VI. A WIN OR LOSS FOR THE ACLU?

The ACLU filed as amicus curiae urging affirmance; the Supreme Court affirmed the Arizona Supreme Court's decision by a 5-4 vote, giving the ACLU an apparent win.

1041. Nken v. Holder

(Decided April 22, 2009; 556 U.S. 418)

I. ISSUE

A. Issues Discussed

Immigration/Citizenship

B. Legal Question Presented

Whether "a statutory provision that sharply restricts the circumstances under which a court may issue an injunction blocking the removal of an alien from this country . . . applies to the granting of a stay by a court of appeals while it considers the legality of a removal order."

C. Supreme Court's Answer

"[T]he authority of a court of appeals to stay an order of removal under the traditional criteria governing stays remains fully intact, and is not affected by the statutory provision governing injunctions."

II. CASE SUMMARY

A. Background

"Jean Marc Nken, a citizen of Cameroon, entered the United States on a transit visa . . . . [H]e applied for asylum . . . , withholding of removal . . ., and deferral of removal . . . . Nken claimed he had been persecuted . . . for participation in protests against the Cameroonian Government, and would be subject to further persecution if he returns to Cameroon.

An Immigration Judge denied Nken relief after concluding that he was not credible. The Board of Immigration Appeals (BIA) affirmed, and also declined to remand for consideration of Nken's application for adjustment of status based on his marriage to an American citizen. After the BIA denied a motion to reopen, Nken filed a petition for review of the BIA's removal order in the Court of Appeals for the Fourth Circuit. His petition was denied. Nken then filed a second motion to reopen, which was also denied, followed by a second petition for review, which was denied as well.

Nken filed a third motion to reopen, this time alleging that changed circumstances in Cameroon made his persecution more likely. The BIA denied the motion . . . . Nken again sought review in the Court of Appeals, and also moved to stay his deportation pending resolution of his appeal. . . . The Court of Appeals denied Nken's motion without comment.

Nken then applied to th[e U.S Supreme] Court for a stay of removal pending adjudication of his petition for review, and asked in the alternative that [the court] grant certiorari to resolve a split among the Courts of Appeals on what standard governs a request for such a stay. [The court] granted certiorari, and stayed petitioner's removal pending further order . . . ."

B. Counsel of Record / ACLU Attorney

ACLU Side (Petitioner / Appellant): Lindsay C. Harrison argued the cause for appellant. With her on the briefs were Donald B. Verrilli, Jr., Ian Heath Gershengorn, and Jared O. Freedman.

Opposing Side (Respondent / Appellee): Then-Acting Solicitor General Kneedler argued the cause for appellee. With him on the brief were former Solicitor General Garre, Assistant Attorney General Katsas, Principal Deputy Assistant Attorney General Dupree, Nicole A. Saharsky, Donald Keener, Melissa Neiman-Kelting, Song E. Park, and Andrew C. MacLachlan.

III. AMICI CURIAE

ACLU Side (Petitioner / Appellant)

Opposing Side (Respondent / Appellee)

Brief of amici curiae filed on behalf of Law Professor Sarah H. Cleveland et al. by Cecillia D. Wang, Lucas Guttentag, Gerald L. Neuman, pro se, Steven R. Shapiro, and Lee Gelernt, all of the American Civil Liberties Union Foundation.

Brief of amici curiae filed on behalf of the American Immigration Lawyers Association et al. by Paul R. Q. Wolfson and Adam Raviv. Brief of amici curiae filed on behalf of the Washington Legal Foundation et al. by Daniel J. Popeo and Richard A. Samp.

IV. THE SUPREME COURT'S DECISION

"The question . . . stems from changes in judicial review of immigration procedures brought on by the Illegal Immigration Reform and Immigrant Responsibility Act of 1996 (IIRIRA) which substantially amended the Immigration and Nationality Act (INA). . . .

Before IIRIRA, courts of appeals lacked jurisdiction to review the deportation order of an alien who had already left . . . . Accordingly, an alien who appealed a decision of the BIA was typically entitled to remain . . . for the duration of judicial review. . . .

IIRIRA inverted these provisions to allow for more prompt removal. . . .

IIRIRA [also] restricted the availability of injunctive relief . . . .

This provision, particularly subsection (f)(2), is the source of the parties' disagreement. . . .

The parties agree that courts of appeals considering a petition for review of a removal order may . . . block removal while adjudicating . . . . They disagree over the standard . . . .

Mindful that statutory interpretation turns on 'the language itself, the specific context . . . , and the broader context of the statute . . . ,' we conclude that the traditional stay factors—not § 1252(f)(2)—govern a request for a stay pending judicial review. . . .

[A]pplying the subsection (f)(2) standard in the stay context results in something that does not remotely look like a stay. . . . [A]n alien need not satisfy the demanding standard of § 1252(f)(2) when asking a court of appeals to stay removal pending judicial review. . . .

So what standard does govern? The question presented . . . offers the alternative of "the traditional test for stays," but the parties dispute what that test is. . . .

[T]hose legal principles have been distilled into . . . four factors: '(1) whether the stay applicant has made a strong showing that he is likely to succeed on the merits; (2) whether the applicant will be irreparably injured . . . ; (3) whether issuance of the stay will substantially injure . . . parties interested . . . ; and (4) where the public interest lies.' . . .

Once an applicant satisfies the first two factors, the traditional stay inquiry calls for assessing the harm to the opposing party and weighing the public interest. . . .

Of course there is a public interest in preventing aliens from being wrongfully removed, . . . where they are likely to face substantial harm. But that is no basis for the blithe assertion of an 'absence of any injury to the public interest' when a stay is granted. . . .

The Court of Appeals did not indicate what standard it applied . . . , but Circuit precedent required the application of § 1252(f)(2). Because we have concluded that § 1252(f)(2) does not govern, we vacate the judgment of the Court of Appeals and remand . . . ."

V. JUSTICE VOTE

7 Pro ACLU Side vs. 2 Con Opposing Side

ACLU Side (Petitioner / Appellant)

1. Roberts, J. – Wrote majority opinion
2. Stevens, J. – Joined majority opinion
3. Breyer, S. – Joined majority opinion
4. Scalia, A. – Joined Kennedy's concurrence
5. Kennedy, A. – Wrote concurring opinion
6. Ginsburg, R. – Joined majority opinion
7. Souter, D. – Joined majority opinion

Opposing Side (Respondent / Appellee)

1. Alito, S. – Wrote dissenting opinion
2. Thomas, C. – Joined Alito's dissent

VI. A WIN OR LOSS FOR THE ACLU?

The ACLU filed as amicus curiae urging reversal of the judgment of the Court of Appeals; the Supreme Court vacated and remanded in a 7-2 vote, giving the ACLU an apparent win.

1042. F.C.C. v. Fox Television Stations, Inc.

(Decided April 28, 2009; 556 U.S. 502)

I. ISSUE

A. Issues Discussed

Regulation

B. Legal Question Presented

"Federal law prohibits the broadcasting of 'any . . . indecent . . . language,' 18 U.S.C. § 1464, which includes expletives referring to sexual or excretory activity or organs. This case concerns the adequacy of the Federal Communications Commission's explanation of its decision that this sometimes forbids the broadcasting of indecent expletives even when the offensive words are not repeated."

C. Supreme Court's Answer

"We decline to 'substitute [our] judgment for that of the agency,' and we find the Commission's orders neither arbitrary nor capricious."

II. CASE SUMMARY

A. Background

"The Communications Act of 1934 . . . established a system of limited-term broadcast licenses subject to various 'conditions' . . . .

One of the burdens that licensees shoulder is the indecency ban—the statutory proscription against 'utter[ing] any obscene, indecent, or profane language . . . ,' which Congress has instructed the Commission to enforce between the hours of 6 a.m. and 10 p.m. . . .

This case concerns utterances in two live broadcasts aired by Fox Television Stations, Inc., and its affiliates prior to the Commission's Golden Globes Order. . . .

[T]he Commission released 'Notices of Apparent Liability' for a number of broadcasts that the Commission deemed actionably indecent . . . . Multiple parties petitioned the Court of Appeals for the Second Circuit for judicial review of the order, asserting a variety of constitutional and statutory challenges. . . .

The order asserted that both broadcasts under review would have been actionably indecent under the staff rulings and Commission dicta in effect prior to the Golden Globes Order . . . .

Although the Commission determined that Fox encouraged the offensive language by using suggestive scripting in the 2003 broadcast, and unreasonably failed to take adequate precautions in both broadcasts, the order again declined to impose any forfeiture or other sanction for either of the broadcasts.

Fox returned to the Second Circuit for review of the Remand Order, and various intervenors . . . joined the action. The Court of Appeals reversed the agency's orders . . . ."

The Supreme Court granted certiorari to review the case.

B. Counsel of Record / ACLU Attorney

ACLU Side (Respondent / Appellee): Carter G. Phillips argued the cause for appellees. With him on the brief for appellee Fox Television Stations, Inc., were R. Clark Wadlow, Jennifer Tatel, David S. Petron, and Quin M. Sorenson. Miguel A. Estrada, Andrew S. Tulumello, Matthew D. McGill, Richard Cotton, Susan Weiner, Robert Corn-Revere, Jonathan H. Anschell, Susanna M. Lowy, and Seth P. Waxman filed a brief for appellee NBC Universal, Inc., et al. Andrew Jay Schwartzman and Parul Desai filed a brief for appellee Center for Creative Voices in Media, Inc.

Opposing Side (Petitioner / Appellant): Former Solicitor General Garre argued the cause for appellants. With him on the briefs were former Solicitor General Clement, Assistant Attorney General Katsas, Eric D. Miller, Thomas M. Bondy, Anne Murphy, Matthew B. Berry, Joseph R. Palmore, Jacob M. Lewis, and Nandan M. Joshi.

III. AMICI CURIAE

ACLU Side (Respondent / Appellee)

Brief of amici curiae filed on behalf of the American Civil Liberties Union, the New York Civil Liberties Union, the American Booksellers Foundation for Free Expression, the American Federation of Television and Radio Artists, AFL-CIO, Directors Guild of America, Minnesota Public Radio/American Public Media, the National Alliance for Media Arts and Culture, the National Coalition against Censorship, the National Federation of Community Broadcasters, Pen American Center, Screen Actors Guild, Southern California Public Radio, the Tully Center for Free Speech, Washington Area Lawyers for the Arts, the Woodhull Freedom Foundation, and Writers Guild of America, West by Marjorie Heins, Steven R. Shapiro, and Christopher A. Hansen.

Brief of amici curiae filed on behalf of the ABC Television Affiliates Association by Wade H. Hargrove, Mark J. Prak, and David Kushner.

Brief of amici curiae filed on behalf of the California Broadcasters Association et al. by Kathleen M. Sullivan and Gregg P. Skall.

Brief of amici curiae filed on behalf of the Center for Democracy & Technology et al. by John B. Morris, Jr., and Sophia S. Cope.

Brief of amici curiae filed on behalf of Former FCC Commissioners and Officials by Timothy K. Lewis, Carl A. Solano, and Nancy Winkelman, and by Henry Geller, Newton N. Minow, and Glen O. Robinson, all pro se.

Brief of amici curiae filed on behalf of the National Association of Broadcasters et al. by Paul M. Smith, Marsha J. MacBride, Jane E. Mago, and Jerianne Timmerman.

Brief of amici curiae filed on behalf of Public Broadcasters by Robert A. Long, Jr., Jonathan D. Blake, and Jonathan L. Marcus; for Time Warner Inc. by Christopher Landau.

Brief of amici curiae filed on behalf of the Thomas Jefferson Center for the Protection of Free Expression et al. by Robert M. O'Neil and J. Joshua Wheeler.

Brief of amici curiae filed on behalf of the American Academy of Pediatrics et al. by Angela J. Campbell, James N. Horwood, and Tillman L. Lay.

Opposing Side (Petitioner / Appellant)

Brief of amici curiae filed on behalf of the Alliance Defense Fund et al. by Benjamin W. Bull and Glen Lavy.

Brief of amici curiae filed on behalf of the American Center for Law and Justice et al. by Jay Alan Sekulow, Stuart J. Roth, Colby M. May, John Tuskey, and Shannon D. Woodruff.

Brief of amici curiae filed on behalf of the Center for Constitutional Jurisprudence by John C. Eastman, David L. Llewellyn, Jr., and Edwin Meese III.

Brief of amici curiae filed on behalf of the Decency Enforcement Center for Television by Thomas B. North.
Brief of amici curiae filed on behalf of Morality in Media, Inc., by Robin S. Whitehead.
Brief of amici curiae filed on behalf of National Religious Broadcasters by Craig L. Parshall, Joseph C. Chautin III, Elise M. Stubbe, and Mark A. Balkin.
Brief of amici curiae filed on behalf of the Parents Television Council by Robert R. Sparks, Jr.
Brief of amici curiae filed on behalf of Free Press et al. by Marvin Ammori in support of neither party.

IV. THE SUPREME COURT'S DECISION

"We find no basis in the Administrative Procedure Act or in our opinions for a requirement that all agency change be subjected to more searching review. . . .

[T]he requirement that an agency provide reasoned explanation . . . would ordinarily demand that it display awareness that it is changing position. . . . And of course the agency must show that there are good reasons for the new policy. But it need not demonstrate . . . that the reasons for the new policy are better . . . ; it suffices that the new policy is permissible . . . , that there are good reasons for it, and that the agency believes it to be better . . . .

In this appeal . . . , the broadcasters' arguments have repeatedly referred to the First Amendment. If they mean to invite us to apply a more stringent arbitrary-and-capricious review to agency actions that implicate constitutional liberties, we reject the invitation. . . .

[T]he Commission's new enforcement policy and its order finding the broadcasts actionably indecent were neither arbitrary nor capricious. . . .

The Second Circuit did not definitively rule on the constitutionality of the Commission's orders, but respondents nonetheless ask us to decide their validity under the First Amendment. This Court, however, is one of final review, 'not of first view.' . . . We see no reason to abandon our usual procedures in a rush to judgment without a lower court opinion. We decline to address the constitutional questions at this time. . . .

The Second Circuit believed that children today 'likely hear this language far more often from other sources than they did in the 1970s when the Commission first began sanctioning indecent speech,' and that this cuts against more stringent regulation of broadcasts. Assuming the premise is true . . . the conclusion does not necessarily follow. The Commission could reasonably conclude that the pervasiveness of foul language, and the coarsening of public entertainment in other media such as cable, justify more stringent regulation of broadcast programs so as to give conscientious parents a relatively safe haven for their children. In the end, the Second Circuit and the broadcasters quibble with the Commission's policy choices and not with the explanation it has given. We decline to 'substitute [our] judgment for that of the agency,' and we find the Commission's orders neither arbitrary nor capricious.

The judgment of the United States Court of Appeals for the Second Circuit is reversed, and the case is remanded . . . ."

V. JUSTICE VOTE

4 Pro ACLU Side vs. 5 Con Opposing Side

ACLU Side (Respondent / Appellee)

1. Stevens, J. – Wrote dissenting opinion, joined Breyer's dissent
2. Ginsburg, R. – Wrote dissenting opinion, joined Breyer's dissent
3. Breyer, S. – Wrote dissenting opinion
4. Souter, D. – Joined Breyer's dissent

Opposing Side (Petitioner / Appellant)

1. Scalia, A. – Wrote majority opinion
2. Alito, S. – Joined majority opinion
3. Thomas, C. – Wrote concurring opinion
4. Kennedy, A. – Wrote concurring opinion
5. Roberts, J. – Joined majority opinion

VI. A WIN OR LOSS FOR THE ACLU?

The ACLU filed as amicus curiae urging affirmance; the Supreme Court reversed the Court of Appeals' decision by a 5-4 vote, giving the ACLU an apparent loss.

1043. Montejo v. Louisiana

(Decided May 26, 2009; 556 U.S. 778)

I. ISSUE

A. Issues Discussed

Criminal procedure

B. Legal Question Presented

"We consider in this case the scope and continued viability of the rule announced by this Court in Michigan v. Jackson, 475 U.S. 625 (1986), forbidding police to initiate interrogation of a criminal defendant once he has requested counsel at an arraignment or similar proceeding."

C. Supreme Court's Answer

"In sum, when the marginal benefits of the Jackson rule are weighed against its substantial costs to the truth-seeking process and the criminal justice system, we readily conclude that the rule does not 'pay its way.' Michigan v. Jackson should be and now is overruled."

II. CASE SUMMARY

A. Background

"Montejo was arrested . . . in connection with the robbery and murder of Lewis Ferrari . . . .

Montejo waived his rights under Miranda v. Arizona, 384 U.S. 436 (1966), and was interrogated at the sheriff's office . . . . Montejo repeatedly changed his account of the crime, at first claiming that he had only driven Moore to the victim's home, and ultimately admitting that he had shot and killed Ferrari in the course of a botched burglary. These police interrogations were videotaped. . . .

Montejo was brought before a judge for . . . a '72-hour hearing'—a preliminary hearing required under state law. [T]he minute record indicates what transpired: 'The defendant being charged with First Degree Murder, Court ordered N[o] Bond . . . . Further, Court ordered the Office of Indigent Defender be appointed to represent the defendant.' . . .

[T]wo police detectives visited Montejo back at the prison and requested that he accompany them on an excursion to locate the murder weapon . . . . Montejo was again read his Miranda rights and agreed to go along; during the excursion, he wrote an inculpatory letter of apology to the victim's widow. Only upon their return did Montejo finally meet his court-appointed attorney, who was quite upset that the detectives had interrogated his client in his absence.

At trial, the letter of apology was admitted over defense objection. The jury convicted Montejo of first-degree murder, and he was sentenced to death.

The Louisiana Supreme Court affirmed the conviction and sentence."

The Supreme Court granted certiorari to review the case.

B. Counsel of Record / ACLU Attorney

ACLU Side (Petitioner / Appellant): Donald B. Verrilli, Jr., argued the cause for appellant. With him on the briefs were Ian Heath Gershengorn, Katherine A. Fallow, Matthew S. Hellman, William M. Hohengarten, Jelpi P. Picou, and G. Ben Cohen.

Opposing Side (Respondent / Appellee): Kathryn Landry argued the cause for appellee. With her on the briefs were James D. "Buddy" Caldwell, S. Kyle Duncan, Walter P. Reed, Houston C. Gascon III, and Scott C. Gardner.

III. AMICI CURIAE

ACLU Side (Petitioner / Appellant)

Brief of amici curiae filed on behalf of the National Association of Criminal Defense Lawyers, the American Civil Liberties Union, the American Civil Liberties Union of Louisiana, the Brennan Center for Justice at New York University School of Law, and the Southern Center for Human Rights by Jonathan L. Marcus, Barbara Bergman, Steven Shapiro, Robin Dahlberg, David S. Udell, Anna E. Lumelsky, Gary Feldon, Katie Schwartzmann, Stephen B. Bright, William R. Montross, Jr., Melanca Clark, and Sidney S. Rosdeitcher.

Brief of amici curiae filed on behalf of the Louisiana Public Defenders Association by G. Paul Marx.

Brief of amici curiae filed on behalf of the National Legal Aid and Defender Association et al. by Catharine F. Easterly and Sandra K. Levick.

Brief of amici curiae filed on behalf of Larry D. Thompson et al. by Robert N. Weiner, Andrew T. Karron, and John A. Freedman.

Brief of amici curiae filed on behalf of the Criminal Justice Institute of Harvard Law School by Stephen Singer.

Brief of amici curiae filed on behalf of the Public Defender Service for the District of Columbia et al. by Sandra K. Levick, Catharine F. Easterly, and David L. McColgin.

Opposing Side (Respondent / Appellee)

Brief of amici curiae filed on behalf of the United States by Solicitor General Kagan, then-Acting Assistant Attorney General Glavin, Deputy Solicitor General Dreeben, Nicole A. Saharsky, and Joel M. Gershowitz.

Brief of amici curiae filed on behalf of the State of New Mexico et al. by Gary K. King, Attorney General of New Mexico, and M. Victoria Wilson, Assistant Attorney General, by Richard S. Gebelein, Chief Deputy Attorney General of Delaware, and by the Attorneys General for their respective States as follows: Troy King of Alabama, Terry Goddard of Arizona, John W. Suthers of Colorado, Bill McCollum of Florida, Lawrence G. Wasden of Idaho, Steve Six of Kansas, Douglas F. Gansler of Maryland, Kelly A. Ayotte of New Hampshire, W. A. Drew Edmondson of Oklahoma, Hardy Myers of Oregon, Thomas W. Corbett, Jr., of Pennsylvania, Mark L. Shurtleff of Utah, Robert F. McDonnell of Virginia, Robert M. McKenna of Washington, and Bruce A. Salzburg of Wyoming.

IV. THE SUPREME COURT'S DECISION

"Under the rule adopted by the Louisiana Supreme Court, a criminal defendant must . . . 'assert' his Sixth Amendment right at the preliminary hearing, before the Jackson protections are triggered. If he does so, the police may not initiate further interrogation in the absence of counsel. But if the court on its own appoints counsel, with the defendant taking no affirmative action to invoke his right to counsel, then police are free to initiate further interrogations provided that they first obtain an otherwise valid waiver by the defendant of his right to have counsel present.

This rule would apply well enough in States that require the indigent defendant formally to request counsel before any appointment is made . . . .

But many States follow other practices. . . .

The only question raised by this case, and the only one addressed by the Jackson rule, is whether courts must presume that such a waiver is invalid under certain circumstances. . . . Edwards v. Arizona, 451 U.S. 477 (1981), decided that once 'an accused has invoked his right to have counsel present during custodial interrogation . . . [he] is not subject to further interrogation . . . until counsel has been made available,' unless he initiates the contact. . . .

Jackson represented a 'wholesale importation of the Edwards rule into the Sixth Amendment.' . . .

With this understanding of what Jackson stands for and whence it came, it should be clear that Montejo's interpretation of that decision—that no represented defendant can ever be approached by the State and asked to consent to interrogation—is off the mark. . . .

We do not think that stare decisis requires us to expand significantly the holding of a prior decision . . . in order to cure its practical deficiencies. To the contrary, the fact that a decision has proved 'unworkable' is a traditional ground for overruling it. . . .

What does the Jackson rule . . . achieve by way of preventing unconstitutional conduct? . . .

In sum, when the marginal benefits of the Jackson rule are weighed against its substantial costs to the truth-seeking process and the criminal justice system, we readily conclude that the rule does not 'pay its way.' Michigan v. Jackson should be and now is overruled. . . .

Although our holding means that the Louisiana Supreme Court correctly rejected Montejo's claim under Jackson, we think that Montejo should be given an opportunity to contend that his letter of apology should still have been suppressed under the rule of Edwards. . . .

The judgment of the Louisiana Supreme Court is vacated, and the case is remanded . . . ."

V. JUSTICE VOTE

4 Pro ACLU Side vs. 5 Con Opposing Side

ACLU Side (Petitioner / Appellant)

1. Stevens, J. – Wrote dissenting opinion
2. Breyer, S. – Wrote dissenting opinion, joined Stevens' dissent in part
3. Ginsburg, R. – Joined Stevens' dissent
4. Souter, D. – Joined Stevens' dissent

Opposing Side (Respondent / Appellee)

1. Scalia, A. – Wrote majority opinion
2. Roberts, J. – Joined majority opinion
3. Kennedy, A. – Joined Alito's concurrence
4. Thomas, C. – Joined majority opinion
5. Alito, S. – Wrote concurring opinion

VI. A WIN OR LOSS FOR THE ACLU?

The ACLU filed as amicus curiae urging reversal of the judgment of the Louisiana Supreme Court; the Supreme Court vacated while overruling a case the ACLU urged upholding in a 5-4 vote, giving the ACLU an apparent loss.

1044. Nijhawan v. Holder

(Decided June 15, 2009; 557 U.S. 29)

I. ISSUE

A. Issues Discussed

Immigration/Citizenship

B. Legal Question Presented

"Federal immigration law provides that any 'alien who is convicted of an aggravated felony at any time after admission is deportable.' 8 U.S.C. § 1227(a)(2)(A)(iii) (emphasis added). A related statute defines 'aggravated felony' in terms of a set of listed offenses that includes 'an offense that . . . involves fraud or deceit in which the loss to the victim or victims exceeds $10,000.' § 1101(a)(43)(M)(i) (emphasis added). The question before us is whether the italicized language refers to an element of the fraud or deceit 'offense' as set forth in the particular fraud or deceit statute defining the offense of which the alien was previously convicted."

C. Supreme Court's Answer

"We conclude . . . that the italicized language does not refer to an element of the fraud or deceit crime. Rather it refers to the particular circumstances in which an offender committed a (more broadly defined) fraud or deceit crime on a particular occasion."

II. CASE SUMMARY

A. Background

"Petitioner, an alien, immigrated to the United States in 1985. In 2002 he was indicted for conspiring to commit mail fraud, wire fraud, bank fraud, and money laundering. A jury found him guilty. But because none of these statutes requires a finding of any particular amount of victim loss, the jury made no finding about the amount of the loss. At sentencing petitioner stipulated that the loss exceeded $100 million. The court then imposed a sentence of 41 months in prison and required restitution of $683 million.

In 2005 the Government, claiming that petitioner had been convicted of an 'aggravated felony,' sought to remove him from the United States. The Immigration Judge found that petitioner's conviction was for crimes of fraud and deceit; that the sentencing stipulation and restitution order showed that the victims' loss exceeded $10,000; and that petitioner's conviction consequently fell within the immigration statute's 'aggravated felony' definition. . . . The Board of Immigration Appeals agreed. So did the Third Circuit."

The Supreme Court granted certiorari to review the case.

B. Counsel of Record / ACLU Attorney

ACLU Side (Petitioner / Appellant): Thomas E. Moseley argued the cause for appellant. With him on the briefs was Peter C. Salerno.

Opposing Side (Respondent / Appellee): Curtis E. Gannon argued the cause for appellee. With him on the brief were Solicitor General Kagan, Acting Assistant Attorney General Hertz, Deputy Solicitor General Kneedler, Donald E. Keener, Jennifer J. Keeney, W. Manning Evans, Holly M. Smith, Andrew C. MacLachlan, Saul Greenstein, and Erica B. Miles.

III. AMICI CURIAE

ACLU Side (Petitioner / Appellant)

Brief of amici curiae filed on behalf of the American Civil Liberties Union, American Immigration Lawyers Association, Asian Law Caucus, Florence Immigrant and Refugee Rights Project, Florida Immigrant Advocacy Center, Immigrant Defense Project, National Immigration Law Center, National Immigration Project of the National Lawyers Guild and Northwest Immigrant Rights Project by Jayashri Srikantiah, Cecillia D. Wang, Lucas Guttentag, Caroline P. Cincotta, Alina Das, and Steven R. Shapiro.

Brief of amici curiae filed on behalf of the Asian American Justice Center et al. by Vincent A. Eng, Karen K. Narasaki, David A. Kettel, and Donald W. Yoo.

Brief of amici curiae filed on behalf of the National Association of Criminal Defense Lawyers by Iris E. Bennett, Michael A. Hoffman, and Joshua L. Dratel.

Brief of amici curiae filed on behalf of Akio Kawashima et al. by Jenny Lin-Alva, Edward O. C. Ord, and Thomas J. Whalen.

Opposing Side (Respondent / Appellee)

No briefs of amici curiae were filed in support of appellee.

IV. THE SUPREME COURT'S DECISION

"The question here . . . is whether the italicized statutory words 'offense that involves fraud or deceit in which the loss to the . . . victims exceeds $10,000' should be interpreted in the first sense (. . . 'categorical'), . . . or in the second sense (. . . 'circumstance-specific') . . . . If the first, we must look to the statute . . . to determine whether it has an appropriate monetary threshold; if the second, we must look to the facts and circumstances . . . .

Petitioner argues that we should interpret the subsection of the 'aggravated felony' statute before us as requiring use of th[e] 'categorical' approach. He says that the statute's language . . . refers to a generic kind of crime, not a crime as committed on a particular occasion. . . .

[W]e conclude that the 'fraud and deceit' provision before us calls for a 'circumstance-specific,' not a 'categorical,' interpretation. The 'aggravated felony' statute of which it is a part differs in general from ACCA . . . . And the 'fraud and deceit' provision differs specifically from ACCA's provisions. . . .

The upshot is that the 'aggravated felony' statute, unlike ACCA, contains some language that refers to generic crimes and some language that almost certainly refers to the specific circumstances in which a crime was committed. The question before us then is to which category subparagraph (M)(i) belongs. . . .

We conclude that Congress did not intend subparagraph (M)(i)'s monetary threshold to be applied categorically, i.e., to only those fraud and deceit crimes generically defined to include that threshold. Rather, the monetary threshold applies to the specific circumstances surrounding an offender's commission of a fraud and deceit crime on a specific occasion. . . .

Petitioner, as an alternative argument, says that we should nonetheless borrow from Taylor what that case called a 'modified categorical approach.' . . .

We agree with petitioner that the statute foresees the use of fundamentally fair procedures . . . . But we do not agree that fairness requires the evidentiary limitations he proposes. . . .

We can find nothing unfair about the immigration judge's having here relied upon earlier sentencing-related material. The defendant's own stipulation . . . shows that the conviction involved losses considerably greater than $10,000. The court's restitution order shows the same. In the absence of any conflicting evidence . . . this evidence is clear and convincing.

The Court of Appeals concluded that petitioner's prior federal conviction consequently falls within the scope of subparagraph (M)(i). And we affirm its judgment."

V. JUSTICE VOTE

0 Pro ACLU Side vs. 9 Con Opposing Side

Opposing Side (Respondent / Appellee)

1. Breyer, S. – Wrote majority opinion
2. Alito, S. – Joined majority opinion
3. Stevens, J. – Joined majority opinion
4. Thomas, C. – Joined majority opinion
5. Scalia, A. – Joined majority opinion
6. Kennedy, A. – Joined majority opinion
7. Ginsburg, R. – Joined majority opinion
8. Souter, D. – Joined majority opinion
9. Roberts, J. – Joined majority opinion

VI. A WIN OR LOSS FOR THE ACLU?

The ACLU filed as amicus curiae urging reversal of the judgment of the Court of Appeals; the Supreme Court affirmed in a 9-0 vote, giving the ACLU an apparent loss.

1045. District Attorney's Office for the Third Judicial Dist. v. Osborne

(Decided June 18, 2009; 557 U.S. 52)

I. ISSUE

A. Issues Discussed

Criminal procedure

B. Legal Question Presented

"[W]hether Osborne's claims could be pursued using § 1983, and whether he has a right under the Due Process Clause to obtain postconviction access to the State's evidence for DNA testing."

C. Supreme Court's Answer

"We see nothing inadequate about the procedures Alaska has provided to vindicate its state right to postconviction relief in general, and nothing inadequate about how those procedures apply to those who seek access to DNA evidence."

II. CASE SUMMARY

A. Background

"Osborne and Jackson were convicted by an Alaska jury of kidnaping, assault, and sexual assault. [T]he trial judge sentenced Osborne to 26 years . . . . His conviction and sentence were affirmed on appeal.

Osborne then sought postconviction relief . . . . He claimed that he had asked his attorney, Sidney Billingslea, to seek more discriminating restriction-fragment-length-polymorphism (RFLP) DNA testing . . . and argued that she was constitutionally ineffective for not doing so. Billingslea testified that . . . she had concluded that further testing would do more harm than good. . . . Because she believed Osborne was guilty, "insisting on a more advanced . . . DNA test would have served to prove that Osborne committed the alleged crimes." The Alaska Court of Appeals . . . rejected Osborne's claim. . . .

Osborne also sought the DNA testing that Billingslea had failed to perform . . . . [T]he Alaska Court of Appeals concluded that Osborne had no right to the RFLP test. . . .

Osborne had also been active in federal court . . . . He claimed . . . a constitutional right to access the DNA evidence for . . . short-tandem-repeat (STR) testing . . . . The District Court first dismissed the claim . . . . The . . . Court of Appeals for the Ninth Circuit reversed . . . .

On cross-motions for summary judgment after remand, the District Court concluded that 'there does exist, under the unique and specific facts presented, a very limited constitutional right to the testing sought.' . . . It therefore granted summary judgment in favor of Osborne.

The Court of Appeals affirmed . . . ."

The Supreme Court granted certiorari to review the case.

B. Counsel of Record / ACLU Attorney

ACLU Side (Respondent / Appellee): Peter J. Neufeld argued the cause for appellee. With him on the brief were Barry C. Scheck, Nina R. Morrison, David T. Goldberg, Kannon K. Shanmugam, Anna-Rose Mathieson, Robert C. Bundy, and Randall S. Cavanaugh.

Opposing Side (Petitioner / Appellant): Kenneth M. Rosenstein, Assistant Attorney General of Alaska, argued the cause for appellants. With him on the briefs were Richard A. Svobodny, Acting Attorney General, Talis J. Colberg, former Attorney General, Diane L. Wendlandt, Assistant Attorney General, Roy T. Englert, Jr., and Alan E. Untereiner.

Deputy Solicitor General Katyal argued the cause for the United States as amicus curiae.

III. AMICI CURIAE

ACLU Side (Respondent / Appellee)

Brief of amici curiae filed on behalf of the American Civil Liberties Union, Rutherford Institute, and National Associaiton of Criminal Defense Lawyers by Walter Dellinger, Irving L. Gornstein, Shannon M. Pazur, Steven R. Shapiro, John W. Whitehead, and Barbara E. Bergman.

Brief of amici curiae filed on behalf of Current and Former Prosecutors by Donald B. Ayer.

Brief of amici curiae filed on behalf of Eleven Individuals Who Have Received Clemency Through DNA Testing by Jeffrey L. Fisher, Pamela S. Karlan, Lawrence C. Marshall, Amy Howe, Kevin K. Russell, and Thomas C. Goldstein.

Brief of amici curiae filed on behalf of Individuals Exonerated by Post-Conviction DNA Testing by Paul A. Engelmayer.

Brief of amici curiae filed on behalf of Jeanette Popp et al. by Kenneth W. Starr and Mark T. Cramer.

Opposing Side (Petitioner / Appellant)

Brief of amici curiae filed on behalf of the United States by Deputy Solicitor General Katyal, former Solicitor General Garre, Acting Assistant Attorney General Friedrich, former Deputy Solicitor General Joseffer, and Curtis E. Gannon.

Brief of amici curiae filed on behalf of the State of California et al. by Edmund G. Brown, Jr., Attorney General of California, Dane R. Gillette, Chief Assistant Attorney General, Donald E. de Nicola, Deputy Solicitor General, Gerald A. Engler, Senior Assistant Attorney General, and Enid A. Camps and Michael Chamberlain, Deputy Attorneys General, by John D. Seidel, Senior Assistant Attorney General of Colorado, and by the Attorneys General for their respective States as follows: Terry Goddard of Arizona, Dustin McDaniel of Arkansas, John W. Suthers of Colorado, Joseph R. "Beau" Biden III of Delaware, Bill McCollum of Florida, Lawrence G. Wasden of Idaho, Thomas J. Miller of Iowa, Steve Six of Kansas, Jack Conway of Kentucky, James D. "Buddy" Caldwell of Louisiana, G. Steven Rowe of Maine, Douglas F. Gansler of Maryland, Martha Coakley of Massachusetts, Michael A. Cox of Michigan, Lori Swanson of Minnesota, Jon Bruning of Nebraska, Kelly A. Ayotte of New Hampshire, Gary K. King of New Mexico, Wayne Stenehjem of North Dakota, W. A. Drew Edmondson of Oklahoma, Hardy Myers of Oregon, Thomas W. Corbett, Jr., of Pennsylvania, Patrick C. Lynch of Rhode Island, Lawrence E. Long of South Dakota, Robert E. Cooper, Jr., of Tennessee, Mark L. Shurtleff of Utah, Robert F. McDonnell of Virginia, Robert M. McKenna of Washington, J. B. Van Hollen of Wisconsin, and Bruce A. Salzburg of Wyoming. Brief of amici curiae filed on behalf of the City of New York by Michael A. Cardozo, Leonard J. Koerner, Edward F. X. Hart, and Drake A. Colley.

Brief of amici curiae filed on behalf of the Council of State Governments et al. by Richard Ruda.

Brief of amici curiae filed on behalf of K. G. et al. by Paul G. Cassell.

IV. THE SUPREME COURT'S DECISION

"Modern DNA testing can provide . . . new evidence unlike anything known before. . . .

[However, t]he availability of technologies not available at trial cannot mean that every criminal conviction . . . is . . . in doubt. . . .

'No State shall . . . deprive any person of life, liberty, or property, without due process of law.' This Clause imposes procedural limitations on a State's power . . . . We must first examine this asserted liberty interest to determine what process (if any) is due. . . .

Osborne does . . . have a liberty interest in demonstrating his innocence with new evidence under state law. . . .

The Court of Appeals went too far, however, in concluding that the Due Process Clause requires that certain familiar preconviction trial rights be extended to protect Osborne's postconviction liberty interest. . . .

Instead, the question is whether consideration of Osborne's claim within the framework of the State's procedures for postconviction relief 'offends some principle of justice . . . ranked as fundamental' . . . . Federal courts may upset a State's postconviction relief procedures only if they are fundamentally inadequate to vindicate the substantive rights provided.

We see nothing inadequate about the procedures Alaska has provided [or] how those procedures apply to those who seek access to DNA evidence. . . .

The Court of Appeals below relied only on procedural due process, but Osborne seeks to defend the judgment on the basis of substantive due process . . . . We reject the invitation and conclude . . . that there is no such substantive due process right. . . .

DNA evidence will undoubtedly lead to changes in the criminal justice system. . . . The question is whether further change will primarily be made by legislative revision and judicial interpretation of the existing system, or whether the Federal Judiciary must leap ahead . . . .

Federal courts should not presume that state criminal procedures will be inadequate to deal with technological change. The criminal justice system . . . cannot be perfect. DNA evidence shows that it has not been. But there is no basis for Osborne's approach of assuming that because DNA has shown that these procedures are not flawless, DNA evidence must be treated as categorically outside the process, rather than within it. . . .

The judgment of the Court of Appeals is reversed, and the case is remanded . . . ."

V. JUSTICE VOTE

4 Pro ACLU Side vs. 5 Con Opposing Side

ACLU Side (Respondent / Appellee)

1. Stevens, J. – Wrote dissenting opinion
2. Ginsburg, R. – Joined Stevens' dissent
3. Breyer, S. – Joined Stevens' dissent
4. Souter, D. – Wrote dissenting opinion, joined Stevens' dissent in part

Opposing Side (Petitioner / Appellant)

1. Roberts, J. – Wrote majority opinion
2. Alito, S. – Wrote concurring opinion
3. Thomas, C. – Joined Alito's concurrence in part
4. Scalia, A. – Joined majority opinion
5. Kennedy, A. – Joined Alito's concurrence

VI. A WIN OR LOSS FOR THE ACLU?

The ACLU filed as amicus curiae urging affirmance; the Supreme Court reversed the Court of Appeals' decision by a 5-4 vote, giving the ACLU an apparent loss.

1046. Northwest Austin Mun. Utility Dist. No. One v. Holder

(Decided June 22, 2009; 557 U.S. 193)

I. ISSUE

A. Issues Discussed

Voting rights, race

B. Legal Question Presented

Whether "§ 5 of the Voting Rights Act" is constitutional.

C. Supreme Court's Answer

"We agree that the district is eligible under the Act to seek bailout. We therefore reverse, and do not reach the constitutionality of § 5."

II. CASE SUMMARY

A. Background

"The plaintiff in this case is a small utility district raising a big question—the constitutionality of § 5 of the Voting Rights Act. . . .

Northwest Austin Municipal Utility District Number One was created in 1987 to deliver city services to residents of a portion of Travis County, Texas. It is governed by a board of five members, elected to staggered terms of four years. The district does not register voters but is responsible for its own elections; for administrative reasons, those elections are run by Travis County. Because the district is located in Texas, it is subject to the obligations of § 5, although there is no evidence that it has ever discriminated on the basis of race.

The district filed suit . . . seeking relief under the statute's bailout provisions and arguing in the alternative that, if interpreted to render the district ineligible for bailout, § 5 was unconstitutional. The three-judge District Court rejected both claims. Under the statute, only a 'State or political subdivision' is permitted to seek bailout, and the court concluded that the district was not a political subdivision because that term includes only 'counties, parishes, and voter-registering subunits.' Turning to the district's constitutional challenge, the court concluded that the 25-year extension of § 5 was constitutional both because 'Congress . . . rationally concluded that extending [§]5 was necessary to protect minorities from continued racial discrimination in voting' and because 'the 2006 Amendment qualifies as a congruent and proportional response to the continuing problem of racial discrimination in voting.'"

The Supreme Court granted certiorari to review the case.

B. Counsel of Record / ACLU Attorney

ACLU Side (Respondent / Appellee): Deputy Solicitor General Katyal argued the cause for the federal appellee. With him on the brief were then-Acting Solicitor General Kneedler, Acting Assistant Attorney General King, Douglas Hallward-Driemeier, Steven H. Rosenbaum, Diana K. Flynn, Sarah E. Harrington, and T. Christian Herren, Jr.

Debo P. Adegbile argued the cause for the intervenor-appellees. With him on the brief for intervenor-appellee Rodney Louis et al. were John Payton, Jacqueline A. Berrien, Ryan P. Haygood, Kristen M. Clarke, Joshua Civin, Samuel Spital, Kathryn Kolbert, Nina Perales, Jose Garza, George Korbel, and Judith A. Sanders-Castro.

Seth P. Waxman, Paul R. Q. Wolfson, Jonathan E. Nuechterlein, Ariel B. Waldman, Rebecca G. Deutsch, Micah S. Myers, Joshua M. Salzman, Nathan A. Bruggeman, Jon M. Greenbaum, Robert A. Kengle, Marcia Johnson-Blanco, Mark A. Posner, Laughlin McDonald of the American Civil Liberties Union, Steven R. Shapiro of the American Civil Liberties Union, Michael Kator, Jeremy Wright, Arthur B. Spitzer of the ACLU of the National Capital Area, Lisa Graybill of the ACLU Foundation of Texas, Anson Asaka, and Angela Ciccolo filed a brief for intervenor-appellee Texas State Conference of NAACP Branches et al.

Renea Hicks filed a brief for appellee Travis County.

Opposing Side (Petitioner / Appellant): Gregory S. Coleman argued the cause for appellant. With him on the briefs was Christian J. Ward.

III. AMICI CURIAE

ACLU Side (Respondent / Appellee)

Brief of amici curiae filed on behalf of the State of North Carolina et al. by Roy Cooper, Attorney General of North Carolina, Christopher G. Browning, Jr., Tiare B. Smiley, Alexander McC. Peters, and Susan K. Nichols, and by the Attorneys General for their respective States as follows: Terry Goddard of Arizona, Edmund G. Brown, Jr., of California, James D. Caldwell of Louisiana, Jim Hood of Mississippi, and Andrew Cuomo of New York.

Brief of amici curiae filed on behalf of Alaska Native Voters et al. by James Thomas Tucker.

Brief of amici curiae filed on behalf of the American Bar Association by H. Thomas Wells, Jr., and Christopher T. Handman.

Brief of amici curiae filed on behalf of the Asian American Legal Defense and Education Fund et al. by Theodore K. Cheng.

Brief of amici curiae filed on behalf of the Brennan Center for Justice at New York University School of Law by Paul M. Smith, Marc A. Goldman, Wendy Weiser, and Sidney S. Rosdeitcher.

Brief of amici curiae filed on behalf of the Civil Rights Clinic at Howard University School of Law by Aderson Bellegarde François.

Brief of amici curiae filed on behalf of the Constitutional Accountability Center by Clifford M. Sloan, Douglas T. Kendall, and Elizabeth B. Wydra.

Brief of amici curiae filed on behalf of Former Republican Officeholders by Trevor Potter, Tara Malloy, and Paul S. Ryan.

Brief of amici curiae filed on behalf of Jurisdictions That Have Bailed Out Under the Voting Rights Act by J. Gerald Hebert and George Warren Shanks.

Brief of amici curiae filed on behalf of the Leadership Conference on Civil Rights et al. by Matthew M. Hoffman, Stephen J. Pollak, John Townsend Rich, and William L. Taylor.

Brief of amici curiae filed on behalf of Members of the Texas House of Representatives by Lynn E. Blais, Michael F. Sturley, and David C. Frederick.

Brief of amici curiae filed on behalf of the Navajo Nation et al. by Marvin S. Cohen and Louis Denetsosie.

Brief of amici curiae filed on behalf of Julius Chambers et al. by William D. Kissinger; for Congressman John Conyers, Jr., et al. by Pamela S. Karlan, Jeffrey L. Fisher, Amy Howe, Kevin K. Russell, and Thomas C. Goldstein.

Brief of amici curiae filed on behalf of Nicholas deB. Katzenbach et al. by Samuel R. Bagenstos.

Brief of amici curiae filed on behalf of Congresswoman Barbara Lee et al. by Juan Cartagena.

Brief of amici curiae filed on behalf of Congressman John Lewis by Mr. François.

Brief of amici curiae filed on behalf of the Asian American Justice Center et al. by Allegra R. Rich, David M. Burns, Taron K. Murakami, Karen K. Narasaki, and Vincent A. Eng.

Opposing Side (Petitioner / Appellant)

Brief of amici curiae filed on behalf of the Mountain States Legal Foundation by J. Scott Detamore.

Brief of amici curiae filed on behalf of the Southeastern Legal Foundation by Shannon Lee Goessling and Bert W. Rein.

Brief of amici curiae filed on behalf of Georgia Governor Sonny Perdue by Anne W. Lewis, Special Attorney General of Georgia.

Brief of amici curiae filed on behalf of Dr. Abigail Thernstrom et al. by Michael A. Carvin.

Brief of amici curiae filed on behalf of the Pacific Legal Foundation et al. by Sharon L. Browne.

Brief of amici curiae filed on behalf of the Scharf-Norton Center for Constitutional Litigation, Goldwater Institute, by Clint Bolick and Nicholas C. Dranias.

Brief of amici curiae filed on behalf of Nathaniel Persily et al. by Mr. Persily, pro se in support of neither party.

Brief of amici curiae filed on behalf of Bob Riley, Governor of Alabama, by Corey L. Maze, Solicitor General of Alabama, and Misty S. Fairbanks, Assistant Attorney General in support of neither party.

IV. THE SUPREME COURT'S DECISION

"Our usual practice is to avoid the unnecessary resolution of constitutional questions. We agree that the district is eligible under the Act to seek bailout. We therefore reverse, and do not reach the constitutionality of § 5. . . .

The Fifteenth Amendment promises that the 'right of citizens . . . to vote shall not be denied or abridged . . . on account of race, color, or previous condition of servitude.' . . . The first century of congressional enforcement . . . , however, can only be regarded as a failure. . . .

Congress responded with the Voting Rights Act. . . .

§ 5 . . . suspended all changes in state election procedure until they were . . . approved by a three-judge Federal District Court in Washington, D.C., or the Attorney General. . . .

Congress reauthorized the Act [multiple times] . . . . We upheld each of these reauthorizations . . . . It is that latest extension that is now before us. . . .

The historic accomplishments of the Voting Rights Act are undeniable. . . .

At the same time, § 5 . . . imposes substantial 'federalism costs.' . . .

The parties do not agree on the standard to apply in deciding whether . . . Congress exceeded its Fifteenth Amendment enforcement power in extending the preclearance requirements. . . .

In assessing those questions, we . . . fully appreciate that judging the constitutionality of an Act of Congress is 'the . . . most delicate duty that this Court is called on to perform.' . . .

'[I]t is a well-established principle governing the prudent exercise of this Court's jurisdiction that normally the Court will not decide a constitutional question if there is some other ground . . . to dispose of the case.' Here, the district also raises a statutory claim . . . .

Section 4(b) of the Voting Rights Act authorizes a bailout suit by a 'State or political subdivision.' There is no dispute that the district is a political subdivision of the State of Texas in the ordinary sense of the term. . . .

We therefore hold that all political subdivisions . . . are eligible to file a bailout suit. . . .

More than 40 years ago, this Court concluded that 'exceptional conditions' . . . justified extraordinary legislation . . . . In part due to the success of that legislation, we are now a very different Nation. Whether conditions continue to justify such legislation is a difficult constitutional question we do not answer today. We conclude instead that the Voting Rights Act permits all political subdivisions . . . to seek relief from its preclearance requirements.

The judgment of the District Court is reversed, and the case is remanded . . . ."

V. JUSTICE VOTE

1 Pro ACLU Side vs. 8 Con Opposing Side

ACLU Side (Respondent / Appellee)

1. Thomas, C. – Wrote opinion concurring in part and dissenting in part

Opposing Side (Petitioner / Appellant)

1. Roberts, J. – Wrote majority opinion
2. Alito, S. – Wrote majority opinion
3. Stevens, J. – Joined majority opinion
4. Breyer, S. – Joined majority opinion
5. Scalia, A. – Joined majority opinion
6. Kennedy, A. – Joined majority opinion
7. Ginsburg, R. – Joined majority opinion
8. Souter, D. – Joined majority opinion

VI. A WIN OR LOSS FOR THE ACLU?

The ACLU argued the cause for intervenor-appellees urging affirmance; the Supreme Court reversed the Court of Appeals' decision by an 8-1 vote, giving the ACLU an apparent loss.

1047. Safford Unified School Dist. No. 1 v. Redding

(Decided June 25, 2009; 557 U.S. 364)

I. ISSUE

A. Issues Discussed

4th Amendment, drugs

B. Legal Question Presented

"The issue here is whether a 13–year–old student's Fourth Amendment right was violated when she was subjected to a search of her bra and underpants by school officials acting on reasonable suspicion that she had brought forbidden prescription and over-the-counter drugs to school."

C. Supreme Court's Answer

"Because there were no reasons to suspect the drugs presented a danger or were concealed in her underwear, we hold that the search did violate the Constitution, but because there is reason to question the clarity with which the right was established, the official who ordered the unconstitutional search is entitled to qualified immunity from liability."

II. CASE SUMMARY

A. Background

"The events . . . began in 13–year–old Savana Redding's math class . . . . The assistant principal . . . , Kerry Wilson, . . . asked Savana to go to his office. There, he showed her a day planner . . . in which there were several knives, lighters, a permanent marker, and a cigarette. Wilson asked Savana whether the planner was hers; she said it was, but that . . . she had lent it to her friend . . . . Savana stated that none of the items . . . belonged to her.

Wilson then showed Savana . . . ibuprofen 400–mg pills, and one . . . naproxen 200–mg pill . . . banned under school rules without advance permission. He asked Savana if she knew anything about the pills. Savana answered that she did not. Wilson then told Savana that he had received a report that she was giving these pills to fellow students; Savana denied it and agreed to let Wilson search her belongings. Helen Romero, an administrative assistant, came into the office, and together with Wilson they searched Savana's backpack, finding nothing.

At that point, Wilson instructed Romero to take Savana to the school nurse's office to search her clothes for pills. Romero and the nurse, Peggy Schwallier, asked Savana to remove her jacket, socks, and shoes, [then] stretch pants and a T-shirt . . . . Finally, Savana was told to pull her bra out and to the side and shake it, and to pull out the elastic on her underpants, thus exposing her breasts and pelvic area to some degree. No pills were found.

Savana's mother filed suit . . . . The individuals . . . moved for summary judgment . . . . The District Court for the District of Arizona granted the motion on the ground that there was no Fourth Amendment violation, and . . . the Ninth Circuit affirmed. A closely divided Circuit sitting en banc, however, reversed."

The Supreme Court granted certiorari to review the case.

B. Counsel of Record / ACLU Attorney

ACLU Side (Respondent / Appellee): Adam B. Wolf of the American Civil Liberties Union Foundation argued the cause for appellee. With him on the brief were Graham A. Boyd, M. Allen Hopper, and Steven R. Shapiro of the American Civil Liberties Union Foundation, Daniel Joseph Pochoda of the ACLU of Arizona, Bruce G. Macdonald, and Andrew J. Petersen.

Opposing Side (Petitioner / Appellant): Matthew W. Wright argued the cause for appellants. With him on the briefs was David K. Pauole.

David A. O'Neil argued the cause for the United States as amicus curiae.

III. AMICI CURIAE

ACLU Side (Respondent / Appellee)

Brief of amici curiae filed on behalf of the Juvenile Law Center et al. by Marsha L. Levick.

Brief of amici curiae filed on behalf of the National Association of Social Workers et al. by Julia M. Carpenter, Carolyn I. Polowy, and Michael D. Simpson.

Brief of amici curiae filed on behalf of the Rutherford Institute et al. by John W. Whitehead, Clint Bolick, Nicholas C. Dranias, Timothy Lynch, and Ilya Shapiro.

Brief of amici curiae filed on behalf of the Urban Justice Center et al. by Raymond H. Brescia.

Opposing Side (Petitioner / Appellant)

Brief of amici curiae filed on behalf of the United States by David A. O'Neil, then-Acting Solicitor General Kneedler, Acting Assistant Attorney General Hertz, Deputy Solicitor General Katyal, Leonard Schaitman, Robert Kamenshine, Mark Pennak, Edward H. Jurith, Linda V. Priebe, Philip H. Rosenfelt, Stephen H. Freid, Daniel J. Dell'Orto, and Karen L. Lambert.

Brief of amici curiae filed on behalf of the National School Boards Association et al. by David R. Day, Francisco M. Negrón, Jr., and Thomas E. M. Hutton.

IV. THE SUPREME COURT'S DECISION

"The Fourth Amendment . . . generally requires a law enforcement officer to have probable cause for conducting a search. . . .

In T.L.O., we . . . held that for searches by school officials '. . . the public interest is best served by a Fourth Amendment standard of reasonableness that stops short of probable cause.' We have thus applied a standard of reasonable suspicion . . . and have held that a school search 'will be permissible in its scope when the measures adopted are reasonably related to the objectives of the search and not excessively intrusive in light of the age and sex of the student and the nature of the infraction.' . . .

[W]hat was missing . . . was any indication of danger to the students from . . . the drugs . . . and any reason to suppose that Savana was carrying pills in her underwear. We think that the combination of these deficiencies was fatal to finding the search reasonable. . . .

We do mean, though, to make it clear that the T.L.O. concern to limit a school search to reasonable scope requires the support of reasonable suspicion of danger or of resort to underwear for hiding evidence of wrongdoing before a search can reasonably make the quantum leap from outer clothes and backpacks to exposure of intimate parts. . . .

A school official searching a student is 'entitled to qualified immunity where clearly established law does not show that the search violated the Fourth Amendment.' . . .

T.L.O. directed school officials to limit the intrusiveness of a search, 'in light of the age and sex of the student and the nature of the infraction,' and as we have just said at some length, the intrusiveness of the strip search here cannot be seen as justifiably related to the circumstances. But we realize that the lower courts have reached divergent conclusions regarding how the T.L.O. standard applies to such searches. . . .

We think these differences of opinion from our own are substantial enough to require immunity for the school officials in this case. . . .

The strip search of Savana Redding was unreasonable and a violation of the Fourth Amendment, but petitioners Wilson, Romero, and Schwallier are nevertheless protected from liability through qualified immunity. Our conclusions here do not resolve, however, the question of the liability of petitioner Safford Unified School District # 1 under Monell v. New York City Dept. of Social Servs., 436 U.S. 658 (1978), a claim the Ninth Circuit did not address. The judgment of the Ninth Circuit is therefore affirmed in part and reversed in part, and this case is remanded for consideration of the Monell claim."

V. JUSTICE VOTE

8 Pro ACLU Side vs. 1 Con Opposing Side

ACLU Side (Respondent / Appellee)

1. Souter, D. – Wrote majority opinion
2. Roberts, J. – Joined majority opinion
3. Scalia, A. – Joined majority opinion
4. Kennedy, A. – Joined majority opinion
5. Breyer, S. – Joined majority opinion
6. Alito, S. – Joined majority opinion
7. Ginsburg, R. – Wrote opinion concurring in part and dissenting in part, joined Stevens' opinion
8. Stevens, J. – Wrote opinion concurring in part and dissenting in part

Opposing Side (Petitioner / Appellant)

1. Thomas, C. – Wrote opinion concurring in part and dissenting in part

VI. A WIN OR LOSS FOR THE ACLU?

The ACLU argued the cause for appellee urging affirmance; the Supreme Court affirmed in part and reversed in part the Court of Appeals' decision by an 8-1 vote, giving the ACLU an apparent win.

1048. Ricci v. DeStefano

(Decided June 29, 2009; 557 U.S. 557)

I. ISSUE

A. Issues Discussed

Civil rights, race, federal

B. Legal Question Presented

"This action presents two provisions of Title VII to be interpreted and reconciled, with few, if any, precedents in the courts of appeals discussing the issue. Depending on the resolution of the statutory claim, a fundamental constitutional question could also arise."

C. Supreme Court's Answer

"We conclude that race-based action like the City's in this case is impermissible under Title VII unless the employer can demonstrate a strong basis in evidence that, had it not taken the action, it would have been liable under the disparate-impact statute. The respondents, we further determine, cannot meet that threshold standard. As a result, the City's action in discarding the tests was a violation of Title VII. In light of our ruling under the statutes, we need not reach the question whether respondents' actions may have violated the Equal Protection Clause."

II. CASE SUMMARY

A. Background

"118 New Haven firefighters took examinations to qualify for promotion to the rank of lieutenant or captain. . . . The results would determine which firefighters would be considered for promotions during the next two years, and the order . . . . Many firefighters studied for months, at considerable personal and financial cost.

When the examination results showed that white candidates had outperformed minority candidates, . . . politicians opened a public debate . . . . Some firefighters argued the tests should be discarded because the results showed the tests to be discriminatory. They threatened a discrimination lawsuit if the City made promotions based on the tests. Other firefighters said the exams were neutral and fair. And they, in turn, threatened a discrimination lawsuit if the City . . . ignored the test results and denied promotions to the candidates who had performed well. In the end the City . . . threw out the examinations.

Certain white and Hispanic firefighters who likely would have been promoted based on their good test performance sued . . . . The suit alleges that, by discarding the test results, the City . . . discriminated against the plaintiffs based on their race, in violation of both Title VII of the Civil Rights Act of 1964 and the Equal Protection Clause of the Fourteenth Amendment. The City and the officials defended their actions, arguing that if they had certified the results, they could have faced liability under Title VII for adopting a practice that had a disparate impact on the minority firefighters. The District Court granted summary judgment for the defendants, and the Court of Appeals affirmed."

The Supreme Court granted certiorari to review the case.

B. Counsel of Record / ACLU Attorney

ACLU Side (Respondent / Appellee): Christopher J. Meade argued the cause for appellees in both cases. With him on the brief were Seth P. Waxman, Anne K. Small, Victor A. Bolden, Kathleen M. Foster, David T. Goldberg, and Richard A. Roberts.

Opposing Side (Petitioner / Appellant): Gregory S. Coleman argued the cause for petitioners in both cases. With him on the briefs were Edward C. Dawson, Dori K. Goldman, and Karen Lee Torre.

Deputy Solicitor General Kneedler argued the cause for the United States as amicus curiae.

III. AMICI CURIAE

ACLU Side (Respondent / Appellee)

Brief of amici curiae filed on behalf of the American Civil Liberties Union et al. by Kevin K. Russell, Amy Howe, Pamela S. Karlan, Jeffrey L. Fisher, Steven R. Shapiro, Emily J. Martin, and Dennis D. Parker.

Brief of amici curiae filed on behalf of the State of Maryland et al. by Douglas F. Gansler, Attorney General of Maryland, Austin C. Schlick, Steven M. Sullivan, and Michele J. McDonald, by Richard A. Svobodny, Acting Attorney General of Alaska, and by the Attorneys General for their respective States as follows: Dustin McDaniel of Arkansas, Tom Miller of Iowa, Catherine Cortez Masto of Nevada, and Mark L. Shurtleff of Utah.

Brief of amici curiae filed on behalf of the Asian American Justice Center et al. by Vincent A. Eng and Karen K. Narasaki.

Brief of amici curiae filed on behalf of the Equal Employment Advisory Council by Rae T. Vann, Jeffrey A. Norris, and Lorence L. Kessler.

Brief of amici curiae filed on behalf of Industrial-Organizational Psychologists by David C. Frederick and Derek T. Ho.

Brief of amici curiae filed on behalf of the International Association of Black Professional Fire Fighters et al. by Christy B. Bishop and Dennis R. Thompson.

Brief of amici curiae filed on behalf of the International Association of Hispanic Firefighters et al. by Marcia L. McCormick.

Brief of amici curiae filed on behalf of the International Municipal Lawyers Association et al. by Andrew J. Pincus and Charles Rothfeld.

Brief of amici curiae filed on behalf of the Lawyers' Committee for Civil Rights Under Law et al. by Michael L. Foreman, Sarah Crawford, Catherine Sun Wood, Marc H. Morial, Angela Ciccolo, and Eva Paterson.

Brief of amici curiae filed on behalf of the NAACP Legal Defense & Educational Fund, Inc., by John Payton, Jacqueline A. Berrien, Debo P. Adegbile, Matthew Colangelo, and Joshua Civin.

Brief of amici curiae filed on behalf of the National Partnership for Women & Families et al. by Helen Norton, Judith L. Lichtman, Marcia D. Greenberger, and Jocelyn Samuels.

Brief of amici curiae filed on behalf of the New York Law School Racial Justice Project by Elise C. Boddie.

Brief of amici curiae filed on behalf of the Opportunity Agenda by Ankur J. Goel and Alan Jenkins.

Brief of amici curiae filed on behalf of the Society for Human Resource Management by Samuel Estreicher, Meir Feder, Donald B. Ayer, and Lawrence D. Rosenberg.

Opposing Side (Petitioner / Appellant)

Brief of amici curiae filed on behalf of the United States by Deputy Solicitor General Kneedler, Acting Assistant Attorney General King, Deputy Solicitor General Katyal, Lisa S. Blatt, Leondra R. Kruger, Steven H. Rosenbaum, Jessica Dunsay Silver, Gregory B. Friel, Lisa J. Stark, Carol A. DeDeo, Edward D. Sieger, Carolyn L. Wheeler, and Gail S. Coleman.

Brief of amici curiae filed on behalf of the American Civil Rights Union by Peter J. Ferrara.

Brief of amici curiae filed on behalf of Bridgeport Firefighters for Merit Employment, Inc., by Stewart I. Edelstein.

Brief of amici curiae filed on behalf of the Cato Institute et al. by Ilya Shapiro and Manuel S. Klausner.

Brief of amici curiae filed on behalf of the Center for Individual Rights et al. by Michael E. Rosman.

Brief of amici curiae filed on behalf of the Concerned American Firefighters Association, Philadelphia Chapter, by Gregory J. Sullivan.

Brief of amici curiae filed on behalf of the Eagle Forum Education and Legal Defense Fund by Douglas G. Smith.

Brief of amici curiae filed on behalf of Law Professors et al. by Martin S. Kaufman.

Brief of amici curiae filed on behalf of the Mountain States Legal Foundation by J. Scott Detamore.

Brief of amici curiae filed on behalf of the National Association of Police Organizations by Scott M. Abeles.

Brief of amici curiae filed on behalf of the Pacific Legal Foundation et al. by Sharon L. Browne, Alan W. Foutz, and Steven G. Gieseler.

Brief of amici curiae filed on behalf of Joe Oakley et al. by Henry C. Shelton III, Brian S. Faughnan, and Emily C. Taube.

Brief of amici curiae filed on behalf of the Claremont Institute Center for Constitutional Jurisprudence by John C. Eastman and Edwin Meese III.

Brief of amici curiae filed on behalf of Kedar Bhatia by Alan Sager.

Brief of amici curiae filed on behalf of the Anti-Defamation League by Michael F. Smith, Martin E. Karlinsky, Howard W. Goldstein, Steven M. Freeman, and Steven C. Sheinberg in support of neither party.

IV. THE SUPREME COURT'S DECISION

"Petitioners raise a statutory claim, under the disparate-treatment prohibition of Title VII, and a constitutional claim . . . . A decision for petitioners on their statutory claim would provide the relief sought, so we consider it first. . . .

Title VII prohibits both intentional discrimination (known as 'disparate treatment') as well as, in some cases, practices that are not intended to discriminate but in fact have a disproportionately adverse effect on minorities (known as 'disparate impact'). . . .

Our analysis begins with this premise: The City's actions would violate the disparate-treatment prohibition . . . absent some valid defense. [T]he City chose not to certify the examination results because of the statistical disparity based on race . . . .

Applying the strong-basis-in-evidence standard to Title VII gives effect to both the disparate-treatment and disparate-impact provisions, allowing violations of one in the name of compliance with the other only in certain, narrow circumstances. The standard leaves ample room for employers' voluntary compliance efforts . . . and to Congress's efforts to eradicate workplace discrimination. And the standard appropriately constrains employers' discretion in making race-based decisions: It limits that discretion to cases in which there is a strong basis in evidence of disparate-impact liability, but it is not so restrictive that it allows employers to act only when there is a provable, actual violation. . . .

If an employer cannot rescore a test based on the candidates' race, then . . . it may not take the greater step of discarding the test altogether to achieve a more desirable racial distribution . . .—absent a strong basis in evidence that the test was deficient and that discarding the results is necessary to avoid violating the disparate-impact provision. . . .

For the foregoing reasons, we adopt the strong-basis-in-evidence standard as a matter of statutory construction to resolve any conflict between the disparate-treatment and disparate-impact provisions of Title VII. . . .

We hold only that, under Title VII, before an employer can engage in intentional discrimination for the asserted purpose of avoiding or remedying an unintentional disparate impact, the employer must have a strong basis in evidence to believe it will be subject to disparate-impact liability if it fails to take the race-conscious, discriminatory action. . . .

Petitioners are entitled to summary judgment on their Title VII claim, and we therefore need not decide the underlying constitutional question. The judgment of the Court of Appeals is reversed, and the cases are remanded . . . ."

V. JUSTICE VOTE

4 Pro ACLU Side vs. 5 Con Opposing Side

ACLU Side (Respondent / Appellee)

1. Ginsburg, R. – Wrote dissenting opinion
2. Stevens, J. – Joined Ginsburg's dissent
3. Souter, D. – Joined Ginsburg's dissent
4. Breyer, S. – Joined Ginsburg's dissent

Opposing Side (Petitioner / Appellant)

1. Kennedy, A. – Wrote majority opinion
2. Thomas, C. – Joined Alito's concurrence
3. Scalia, A. – Wrote concurring opinion, joined Alito's concurrence
4. Roberts, J. – Joined majority opinion
5. Alito, S. – Wrote concurring opinion

VI. A WIN OR LOSS FOR THE ACLU?

The ACLU filed as amicus curiae urging affirmance; the Supreme Court reversed the Court of Appeals' decision by a 5-4 vote, giving the ACLU an apparent loss.

1049. Alvarez v. Smith

(Decided December 8, 2009; 558 U.S. 87)

I. ISSUE

A. Issues Discussed

State, civil rights

B. Legal Question Presented

"[W]hether Illinois law provides a sufficiently speedy opportunity for an individual, whose car or cash police have seized without a warrant, to contest the lawfulness of the seizure."

C. Supreme Court's Answer

"At the time of oral argument . . . we learned that the underlying property disputes have all ended. The State has returned all the cars that it seized, and the individual property owners have either forfeited any relevant cash or have accepted as final the State's return of some of it. We consequently find the case moot, and we therefore vacate the judgment of the Court of Appeals and remand the case to that court with instructions to dismiss."

II. CASE SUMMARY

A. Background

"Illinois law provides for forfeiture of movable personal property (including cars and cash) used 'to facilitate' a drug crime. [T]he statute gives the State up to 142 days . . . to begin judicial forfeiture proceedings—during which time the statute permits the State to keep the car or cash within its possession.

On November 22, 2006, six individuals . . . brought this federal civil rights action against . . . . They claimed that the failure of the State to provide a speedy postseizure hearing violated the federal Due Process Clause. . . .

The defendants moved to dismiss the complaint on the ground that Seventh Circuit precedent made clear that 'the Constitution does not require any procedure prior to the actual forfeiture proceeding.' On February 22, 2007, the District Court granted the motion to dismiss. It also denied the plaintiffs' motion for class certification. The plaintiffs appealed.

On May 2, 2008, the Seventh Circuit decided the appeal in the plaintiffs' favor. . . .

On February 23, 2009, [the U.S. Supreme Court] granted certiorari to review the Seventh Circuit's 'due process' determination. . . . We then recognized that the case might be moot, and we asked the parties to address the question of mootness at the forthcoming oral argument.

At oral argument counsel for both sides confirmed that there was no longer any dispute about ownership or possession of the relevant property."

B. Counsel of Record / ACLU Attorney

ACLU Side (Respondent / Appellee): Thomas Peters argued the cause for appellees. With him on the brief were Craig B. Futterman and Richard Epstein.

Opposing Side (Petitioner / Appellant): Paul A. Castiglione argued the cause for appellant. With him on the briefs were Anita Alvarez, pro se, Patrick T. Driscoll, Jr., and Alan J. Spellberg.

William M. Jay argued the cause for the United States as amicus curiae.

III. AMICI CURIAE

ACLU Side (Respondent / Appellee)

Brief of amici curiae filed on behalf of the American Civil Liberties Union and the ACLU of Illinois by Graham Boyd, Scott Michelman, Steven R. Shapiro, Emma Andersson, and Harvey Grossman.

Brief of amici curiae filed on behalf of the Cato Institute et al. by David B. Smith, Clint Bolick, Nicholas C. Dranias, Ilya Shapiro, and Manuel S. Klausner.

Brief of amici curiae filed on behalf of the Institute for Justice by William H. Mellor, Scott G. Bullock, and Robert P. Frommer.

Brief of amici curiae filed on behalf of the Legal Aid Society by Thomas M. O'Brien.

Brief of amici curiae filed on behalf of the National Police Accountability Project by Andrew B. Reid.

Brief of amici curiae filed on behalf of the Women's Criminal Defense Bar Association by Harold J. Krent.

Opposing Side (Petitioner / Appellant)

Brief of amici curiae filed on behalf of the United States by William M. Jay, Solicitor General Kagan, Assistant Attorneys General Breuer and West, Deputy Solicitor General Katyal, Harry Harbin, Michael S. Raab, David A. Martin, and Alfonso Robles.

Brief of amici curiae filed on behalf of the State of Illinois et al. by Lisa Madigan, Attorney General of Illinois, Michael A. Scodro, Solicitor General, Jane Elinor Notz, Deputy Solicitor General, Eldad Malamuth, Assistant Attorney General, and by the Attorneys General for their respective States as follows: Troy King of Alabama, Terry Goddard of Arizona, John W. Suthers of Colorado, Thurbert E. Baker of Georgia, Mark J. Bennett of Hawaii, Lawrence G. Wasden of Idaho, Gregory F. Zoeller of Indiana, Thomas J. Miller of Iowa, Martha Coakley of Massachusetts, Michael A. Cox of Michigan, Catherine Cortez Masto of Nevada, Richard Cordray of Ohio, Thomas W. Corbett, Jr., of Pennsylvania, Henry McMaster of South Carolina, Greg Abbott of Texas, Mark L. Shurtleff of Utah, Robert M. McKenna of Washington, J. B. Van Hollen of Wisconsin, and Bruce A. Salzburg of Wyoming.

Brief of amici curiae filed on behalf of the National Association of Counties et al. by Richard Ruda.

IV. THE SUPREME COURT'S DECISION

"The Constitution permits this Court to decide legal questions only in the context of actual 'Cases' or 'Controversies.' . . . In this case there is no longer any actual controversy between the parties about ownership or possession of the underlying property.

The State's Attorney argues that there is a continuing controversy over damages. We concede that the plaintiffs filed a motion in the District Court seeking damages. But the plaintiffs filed their motion after the Seventh Circuit issued its opinion. And, after this Court granted certiorari, the Court of Appeals recalled its mandate, taking the case away from the District Court before the District Court could respond to the motion. Thus, we have before us a complaint that seeks only declaratory and injunctive relief, not damages. . . .

The parties, of course, continue to dispute the lawfulness of the State's hearing procedures. But that dispute is no longer embedded in any actual controversy about the plaintiffs' particular legal rights. Rather, it is an abstract dispute about the law . . . .

We can find no special circumstance here that might warrant our continuing to hear the case. . . . Consequently, the case is moot. . . .

It is less easy to say whether we should order the judgment below vacated. The statute that enables us to vacate a lower court judgment when a case becomes moot is flexible . . . .

[W]e conclude that the terminations here fall on the 'happenstance' side of the line. . . . To our knowledge . . . , no one in those cases raised the procedural question at issue here. Rather, the issues in those six cases were issues solely of state substantive law: Were the cars and the cash forfeitable or not? And court docket sheets suggest that the six state cases terminated on substantive grounds in the ordinary course of such state proceedings. . . .

For these reasons, we believe that the presence of this federal case played no significant role in the termination of the separate state-court proceedings. . . .

We consequently conclude that we should follow our ordinary practice, thereby 'clear[ing] the path for future relitigation of the issues.' Thus, nothing in this opinion prevents the plaintiffs from bringing a claim for damages based on the conduct alleged in their complaint.

We therefore vacate the judgment of the Court of Appeals and remand the case to that court with instructions to dismiss."

V. JUSTICE VOTE

0 Pro ACLU Side vs. 9 Con Opposing Side

Opposing Side (Petitioner / Appellant)

1. Breyer, S. – Wrote majority opinion
2. Alito, S. – Joined majority opinion

3. Stevens, J. – Wrote opinion concurring in part and dissenting in part
4. Thomas, C. – Joined majority opinion
5. Scalia, A. – Joined majority opinion
6. Kennedy, A. – Joined majority opinion
7. Ginsburg, R. – Joined majority opinion
8. Sotomayor, S. – Joined majority opinion
9. Roberts, J. – Joined majority opinion

1050. Kucana v. Holder

(Decided January 20, 2010; 558 U.S. 233)

I. ISSUE

A. Issues Discussed

Federal, civil rights

B. Legal Question Presented

"[W]hether the proscription of judicial review stated in § 1252(a)(2)(B) applies not only to Attorney General determinations made discretionary by statute, but also to determinations declared discretionary by the Attorney General himself through regulation."

C. Supreme Court's Answer

"We hold that the key words 'specified under this subchapter' refer to statutory, but not to regulatory, specifications."

II. CASE SUMMARY

A. Background

"Petitioner Agron Kucana moved to reopen his removal proceedings, asserting new evidence in support of his plea for asylum. An Immigration Judge (IJ) denied the motion, the Board of Immigration Appeals (BIA or Board) sustained the IJ's ruling, and the U.S. Court of Appeals for the Seventh Circuit concluded that it lacked jurisdiction to review the administrative determination. For that conclusion, the court relied on a provision added to the Immigration and Nationality Act . . . by the Illegal Immigration Reform and Immigrant Responsibility Act of 1996 (IIRIRA). The provision found dispositive by the Seventh Circuit states that no court shall have jurisdiction to review any action of the Attorney General 'the authority for which is specified under this subchapter to be in the discretion of the Attorney General.'"

The Supreme Court granted certiorari to review the case.

B. Counsel of Record / ACLU Attorney

ACLU Side (Petitioner / Appellant): Rick M. Schoenfield argued the cause for appellant. With him on the briefs were Michael R. Lang, Elaine J. Goldenberg, and Lindsay C. Harrison.

Opposing Side (Respondent / Appellee): Nicole A. Saharsky argued the cause for appellee in support of appellant. With her on the briefs were Solicitor General Kagan, Assistant Attorney General West, Deputy Solicitor General Kneedler, Deputy Assistant Attorney General Osuna, Donald E. Keener, Jennifer P. Levings, and Melissa Neiman-Kelting.

Amanda C. Leiter, by invitation of the Court, argued the cause and filed a brief as amicus curiae in support of the judgment below. With her on the brief was RonNell Andersen Jones.

III. AMICI CURIAE

ACLU Side (Petitioner / Appellant)

Brief of amici curiae filed on behalf of the American Civil Liberties Union by Lee Gelernt, Caroline Cincotta, Steven R. Shapiro, and Lucas Guttentag.

Brief of amici curiae filed on behalf of Law Professors by Anne Harkavy, Catherine M. A. Carroll, and Stephen I. Vladeck, pro se.

Brief of amici curiae filed on behalf of the National Immigrant Justice Center et al. by Jeffrey T. Green, Quin M. Sorenson, and Charles Roth.

Opposing Side (Respondent / Appellee)

Brief of amici curiae filed on behalf of the Washington Legal Foundation et al. by Daniel J. Popeo and Richard A. Samp.

IV. THE SUPREME COURT'S DECISION

"In IIRIRA, Congress for the first time codified certain rules, earlier prescribed by the Attorney General, governing the reopening process. . . .

The motion to reopen is an 'important safeguard' intended 'to ensure a proper and lawful disposition' of immigration proceedings. . . .

The Board's discretionary authority to act on a motion to reopen . . . is 'specified' not in a statute, but only in the Attorney General's regulation, which instructs: 'The decision to grant or deny a motion to reopen . . . is within the discretion of the Board, subject to the restrictions of this section. The Board has discretion to deny a motion to reopen even if the party moving has made out a prima facie case for relief.' . . .

On the reading amicus advances, § 1252(a)(2)(B)(ii) would bar judicial review of any decision that an executive regulation places within the BIA's discretion . . . . On the parties' reading, however, § 1252(a)(2)(B)(ii) precludes judicial review only when the statute itself specifies the discretionary character of the Attorney General's authority. . . .

As the parties and amicus recognize, their diverse renderings of 'under' . . . do not equip us to resolve this case. The word 'under' is chameleon; it 'has many dictionary definitions and must draw its meaning from its context.' Examining, in statutory context, the provision in which the word 'under' is embedded, we conclude that the parties' position stands on firmer ground. . . .

The history of the relevant statutory provisions corroborates our determination that § 1252(a)(2)(B)(ii) does not proscribe judicial review of denials of motions to reopen. . . .

Any lingering doubt about the proper interpretation of 8 U.S.C. § 1252(a)(2)(B)(ii) would be dispelled by a familiar principle of statutory construction: the presumption favoring judicial review of administrative action. . . .

Finally, we stress a paramount factor in the decision we render today. By defining the various jurisdictional bars by reference to other provisions in the INA itself, Congress ensured that it, and only it, would limit the federal courts' jurisdiction. . . .

[T]he judgment of the United States Court of Appeals for the Seventh Circuit is reversed, and the case is remanded . . . ."

V. JUSTICE VOTE

9 Pro ACLU Side vs. 0 Con Opposing Side

ACLU Side (Petitioner / Appellant)

1. Ginsburg, R. – Wrote majority opinion
2. Alito, S. – Wrote concurring opinion
3. Stevens, J. – Joined majority opinion
4. Thomas, C. – Joined majority opinion
5. Breyer, S. – Joined majority opinion
6. Scalia, A. – Joined majority opinion
7. Kennedy, A. – Joined majority opinion
8. Sotomayor, S. – Joined majority opinion
9. Roberts, J. – Joined majority opinion

VI. A WIN OR LOSS FOR THE ACLU?

The ACLU filed as amicus curiae urging reversal of the judgment of the Court of Appeals; the Supreme Court reversed in a 9-0 vote, giving the ACLU an apparent win.

1051. Wood v. Allen

(Decided January 20, 2010; 558 U.S. 290)

I. ISSUE

A. Issues Discussed

Criminal procedure

B. Legal Question Presented

"First, [the Supreme Court] granted review of a question that has divided the Courts of Appeals: whether, in order to satisfy § 2254(d)(2), a petitioner must establish only that the state-court factual determination on which the decision was based was 'unreasonable,' or whether § 2254(e)(1) additionally requires a petitioner to rebut a presumption that the determination was correct with clear and convincing evidence. [The court] also granted review of the question whether the state court reasonably determined that Wood's counsel made a 'strategic decision' not to pursue or present evidence of his mental deficiencies."

C. Supreme Court's Answer

"We conclude . . . that the state court's factual determination was reasonable even under petitioner's reading of § 2254(d)(2), and therefore we need not address that provision's relationship to § 2254(e)(1)."

II. CASE SUMMARY

A. Background

"The Antiterrorism and Effective Death Penalty Act of 1996 contains two provisions governing federal-court review of state-court factual findings. Under 28 U.S.C. § 2254(d)(2), a federal court may not grant a state prisoner's application for a writ of habeas corpus based on a claim already adjudicated on the merits in state court unless that adjudication 'resulted in a decision that was based on an unreasonable determination of the facts in light of the evidence presented in the State court proceeding.' Under § 2254(e)(1), 'a determination of a factual issue made by a State court shall be presumed to be correct,' and the petitioner 'shall have the burden of rebutting the presumption of correctness by clear and convincing evidence.' In this case, petitioner, a capital defendant, challenges the key factual finding made by the Alabama state court that denied his application for postconviction relief: that his attorneys' failure to pursue and present mitigating evidence of his borderline mental retardation was a strategic decision rather than a negligent omission. Petitioner argues that the state court's finding was unreasonable under § 2254(d)(2) and that, in denying his federal habeas petition, the Court of Appeals for the Eleventh Circuit erroneously conflated this standard with that of § 2254(e)(1), which petitioner contends is not applicable in cases, such as this one, not involving a separate federal habeas evidentiary hearing."

The Supreme Court granted certiorari to review the case.

B. Counsel of Record / ACLU Attorney

ACLU Side (Petitioner / Appellant): Kerry Alan Scanlon argued the cause for appellant. With him on the briefs were David O. Bickart, Robert M. Grass, Karen R. Robinson, Dionne A. Fraser, and Brady W. Mills.

Opposing Side (Respondent / Appellee): Corey L. Maze, Solicitor General of Alabama, argued the cause for appellees. With him on the brief were Troy King, Attorney General, and Henry M. Johnson, Assistant Attorney General.

III. AMICI CURIAE

ACLU Side (Petitioner / Appellant)

Brief of amici curiae filed on behalf of the American Civil Liberties Union and the American Civil Liberties Union of Alabama by Larry W. Yackle, Steven R. Shapiro, John Holdridge, Allison Neal, and Brian W. Stull.

Brief of amici curiae filed on behalf of the National Association of Criminal Defense Lawyers by Jonathan L. Marcus and Barbara E. Bergman.

Opposing Side (Respondent / Appellee)

Brief of amici curiae filed on behalf of the State of Indiana et al. by Gregory F. Zoeller, Attorney General of Indiana, Thomas M. Fisher, Solicitor General, and Stephen R. Creason, Section Chief, by Richard S. Gebelein, Chief Deputy Attorney General of Delaware, and by the Attorneys General for their respective States as follows: John W. Suthers of Colorado, Bill McCollum of Florida, Thurbert E. Baker of Georgia, Tom Miller of Iowa, Steve Six of Kansas, James D. "Buddy" Caldwell of Louisiana, Martha Coakley of Massachusetts, Jim Hood of Mississippi, Steve Bullock of Montana, Gary K. King of New Mexico, Richard Cordray of Ohio, Henry D. McMaster of South Carolina, Robert E. Cooper, Jr., of Tennessee, Greg Abbott of Texas, Mark L. Shurtleff of Utah, William C. Mims of Virginia, and Bruce A. Salzburg of Wyoming.

Brief of amici curiae filed on behalf of the Criminal Justice Legal Foundation by Kent S. Scheidegger.

IV. THE SUPREME COURT'S DECISION

"Notwithstanding statements we have made about the relationship between §§ 2254(d)(2) and (e)(1) in cases that did not squarely present the issue, we have explicitly left open the question whether § 2254(e)(1) applies in every case presenting a challenge under § 2254(d)(2).... Although we granted certiorari to resolve the question of how §§ 2254(d)(2) and (e)(1) fit together, we find once more that we need not reach this question, because our view of the reasonableness of the state court's factual determination in this case does not turn on any interpretive difference regarding the relationship between these provisions. For present purposes, we assume for the sake of argument that the factual determination at issue should be reviewed, as Wood urges, only under § 2254(d)(2) and not under § 2254(e)(1). We conclude that, under § 2254(d)(2), the state court's finding that Wood's counsel made a strategic decision not to pursue or present evidence of Wood's mental deficiencies was not an unreasonable determination of the facts in light of the evidence presented in the state-court proceedings. We therefore do not need to decide whether that determination should be reviewed under the arguably more deferential standard set out in § 2254(e)(1)....

Reviewing all of the evidence, we agree with the State that even if it is debatable, it is not unreasonable to conclude that, after reviewing the Kirkland report, counsel made a strategic decision not to inquire further into the information contained in the report about Wood's mental deficiencies and not to present to the jury such information .... For that reason, we agree with the Court of Appeals that the District Court erred in holding to the contrary....

Wood also argues that the state-court decision involved an unreasonable application of Strickland under § 2254(d)(1) because counsel failed to make a reasonable investigation of Wood's mental deficiencies before deciding not to pursue or present such evidence....

It is true that Wood's petition discussed the Eleventh Circuit's misapplication of § 2254(d)(1) and Strickland. But 'the fact that [petitioner] discussed this issue ... does not bring it before us.... We therefore do not address Wood's argument that the state court unreasonably applied Strickland in rejecting his ineffective-assistance-of-counsel claim on the merits....

We hold simply that, even under petitioner's reading of § 2254(d)(2), the state court's conclusion that Wood's counsel made a strategic decision not to pursue or present evidence of his mental deficiencies was not an unreasonable determination of the facts. Accordingly, we affirm the judgment of the Court of Appeals for the Eleventh Circuit."

V. JUSTICE VOTE

2 Pro ACLU Side vs. 7 Con Opposing Side

ACLU Side (Petitioner / Appellant)

1. Stevens, J. – Wrote dissenting opinion
2. Kennedy, A. – Joined Stevens' dissent

Opposing Side (Respondent / Appellee)

1. Sotomayor, S. – Wrote majority opinion
2. Alito, S. – Joined majority opinion
3. Thomas, C. – Joined majority opinion
4. Breyer, S. – Joined majority opinion
5. Scalia, A. – Joined majority opinion
6. Ginsburg, R. – Joined majority opinion
7. Roberts, J. – Joined majority opinion

VI. A WIN OR LOSS FOR THE ACLU?

The ACLU filed as amicus curiae urging reversal of the judgment of the Court of Appeals; the Supreme Court affirmed in a 7-2 vote, giving the ACLU an apparent loss.

1052. Citizens United v. Federal Election Com'n

(Decided January 21, 2010; 558 U.S. 310)

I. ISSUE

A. Issues Discussed

1st Amendment, press, speech, association

B. Legal Question Presented

As relvant to the ACLU's amicus brief in the case, whether BCRA § 203 is unconstitutional.

C. Supreme Court's Answer

"Austin is overruled, so it provides no basis for allowing the Government to limit corporate independent expenditures. As the Government appears to concede, overruling Austin 'effectively invalidate[s] not only BCRA Section 203, but also 2 U.S.C. 441b's prohibition on the use of corporate treasury funds for express advocacy.' Section 441b's restrictions on corporate independent expenditures are therefore invalid and cannot be applied to Hillary."

II. CASE SUMMARY

A. Background

"Citizens United is a nonprofit corporation....

Citizens United has an annual budget of about $12 million. Most of its funds are from donations by individuals; but, in addition, it accepts a small portion of its funds from for-profit corporations.

In January 2008, Citizens United released a film entitled Hillary: The Movie.... It is a 90-minute documentary about then-Senator Hillary Clinton, who was a candidate in the Democratic Party's 2008 Presidential primary elections....

Before the Bipartisan Campaign Reform Act of 2002 (BCRA), federal law prohibited—and still does prohibit—corporations and unions from using general treasury funds to make direct contributions to candidates or independent expenditures that expressly advocate the election or defeat of a candidate, through any form of media .... BCRA § 203 amended § 441b to prohibit any 'electioneering communication' as well....

Citizens United wanted to make Hillary available through video-on-demand .... It feared, however, that both the film and the ads would be covered by § 441b's ban on corporate-funded independent expenditures, thus subjecting the corporation to civil and criminal penalties under § 437g. . . . Citizens United sought declaratory and injunctive relief against the FEC. It argued that (1) § 441b is unconstitutional as applied to Hillary; and (2) BCRA's disclaimer and disclosure requirements, BCRA §§ 201 and 311, are unconstitutional as applied to Hillary and to the three ads for the movie.

The District Court denied Citizens United's motion for a preliminary injunction, . . . and then granted the FEC's motion for summary judgment . . . ."

The Supreme Court granted certiorari to review the case.

B. Counsel of Record / ACLU Attorney

ACLU Side (Petitioner / Appellant): Theodore B. Olson argued and reargued the cause for appellant. With him on the briefs were Matthew D. McGill, Amir C. Tayrani, and Michael Boos.

Floyd Abrams argued the cause for Senator Mitch McConnell as amicus curiae. With him on the brief was Susan Buckley.

Opposing Side (Respondent / Appellee): Solicitor General Kagan reargued the cause for appellee. Deputy Solicitor General Stewart argued the cause for appellee on the original argument. With them on the briefs were then-Acting Solicitor General Kneedler, William M. Jay, Thomasenia P. Duncan, David Kolker, Kevin Deeley, and Adav Noti.

Seth P. Waxman argued the cause for Senator John McCain et al. as amici curiae urging affirmance. With him on the briefs were Randolph D. Moss, Roger M. Witten, Scott L. Nelson, Alan B. Morrison, Brian Wolfman, Trevor Potter, J. Gerald Hebert, Paul S. Ryan, Tara Malloy, Fred Wertheimer, and Donald J. Simon.

III. AMICI CURIAE

ACLU Side (Petitioner / Appellant)

Brief of amici curiae filed on behalf of the American Civil Liberties Union by Steven R. Shapiro, Joel M. Gora, and Mark J. Lopez.

Brief of amici curiae filed on behalf of the Alliance Defense Fund by Benjamin W. Bull, Erik W. Stanley, and Robert J. McCully.

Brief of amici curiae filed on behalf of the American Civil Rights Union by Peter Ferrara.

Brief of amici curiae filed on behalf of the American Federation of Labor and Congress of Industrial Organizations by Jonathan P. Hiatt and Laurence E. Gold.

Brief of amici curiae filed on behalf of the Cato Institute by Benjamin D. Wood, Glenn M. Willard, William J. McGinley, and Ilya Shapiro.

Brief of amici curiae filed on behalf of the Center for Competitive Politics by Stephen M. Hoersting and Reid Alan Cox.

Brief of amici curiae filed on behalf of the Chamber of Commerce of the United States of America by Jan Witold Baran, Thomas W. Kirby, Caleb P. Burns, Robin S. Conrad, Amar D. Sarwal, Steven J. Law, and Judith K. Richmond.

Brief of amici curiae filed on behalf of the Committee for Truth in Politics, Inc., by James Bopp, Jr., and Richard E. Coleson.

Brief of amici curiae filed on behalf of the Foundation for Free Expression by Deborah J. Dewart and James L. Hirsen.

Brief of amici curiae filed on behalf of the National Rifle Association by Charles J. Cooper, David H. Thompson, and David Lehn.

Brief of amici curiae filed on behalf of the Reporters Committee for Freedom of the Press by Lucy A. Dalglish and Gregg P. Leslie.

Brief of amici curiae filed on behalf of the Wyoming Liberty Group et al. by Benjamin Barr.

Brief of amici curiae filed on behalf of the American Justice Partnership et al. by Cleta Mitchell and Michael J. Lockerby.

Brief of amici curiae filed on behalf of the California Broadcasters Association et al. by Lawrence H. Norton, James A. Kahl, and Gregg P. Skall.

Brief of amici curiae filed on behalf of the California First Amendment Coalition by Gary L. Bostwick and Jean-Paul Jassy.

Brief of amici curiae filed on behalf of Campaign Finance Scholars by Allison R. Hayward, pro se.

Brief of amici curiae filed on behalf of the Center for Constitutional Jurisprudence by Anthony T. Caso, Edwin Meese III, and John C. Eastman.

Brief of amici curiae filed on behalf of the Fidelis Center for Law and Policy et al. by Patrick T. Gillen.

Brief of amici curiae filed on behalf of the Free Speech Defense and Education Fund, Inc., et al. by William J. Olson, Herbert W. Titus, John S. Miles, and Mark B. Weinberg.

Brief of amici curiae filed on behalf of the Institute for Justice by William R. Maurer, William H. Mellor, Steven M. Simpson, and Robert W. Gall.

Brief of amici curiae filed on behalf of Judicial Watch, Inc., by Paul J. Orfanedes and Dale L. Wilcox.

Brief of amici curiae filed on behalf of the Michigan Chamber of Commerce by Richard D. McLellan, Gary P. Gordon, John D. Pirich, and Andrea L. Hansen.

Brief of amici curiae filed on behalf of the Pacific Legal Foundation by Deborah J. La Fetra and Damien M. Schiff.

Brief of amici curiae filed on behalf of Seven Former Chairmen of the Federal Election Commission et al. by Messrs. Bopp and Coleson.

Opposing Side (Respondent / Appellee)

Brief of amici curiae filed on behalf of the American Independent Business Alliance by Brenda Wright, Lisa J. Danetz, and Daniel J. H. Greenwood.

Brief of amici curiae filed on behalf of the Campaign Legal Center et al. by Messrs. Potter and Hebert, Ms. Malloy, and Messrs. Ryan, Simon, and Wertheimer.

Brief of amici curiae filed on behalf of the Center for Political Accountability et al. by Karl J. Sandstrom.

Brief of amici curiae filed on behalf of the League of Women Voters of the United States et al. by Douglas T. Kendall, Elizabeth B. Wydra, David H. Gans, and Lloyd J. Leonard.

Brief of amici curiae filed on behalf of the Program on Corporations, Law and Democracy et al. by Jeffrey D. Clements.

Brief of amici curiae filed on behalf of the Sunlight Foundation et al. by Gary S. Stein.

Brief of amici curiae filed on behalf of Norman Ornstein et al. by H. Christopher Bartolomucci.

Brief of amici curiae filed on behalf of the Center for Independent Media et al. by Monica Youn.

Brief of amici curiae filed on behalf of the Center for Political Accountability et al. by Mr. Sandstrom.

Brief of amici curiae filed on behalf of the Committee for Economic Development by Paul M. Smith.

Brief of amici curiae filed on behalf of the Democratic National Committee by Robert F. Bauer and David J. Burman.

Brief of amici curiae filed on behalf of Justice at Stake et al. by James E. Scarboro.

Brief of amici curiae filed on behalf of Public Good by Seth E. Mermin.

Brief of amici curiae filed on behalf of Representative Chris Van Hollen et al. by Bradley S. Phillips and Aaron S. Lowenstein.

Brief of amici curiae filed on behalf of the State of Montana et al. by Steve Bullock, Attorney General of Montana, and Anthony Johnstone, Solicitor, by Terry Goddard, Attorney General of Arizona, Mary R. O'Grady, Solicitor General, and Orville B. Fitch II, Acting Attorney General of New Hampshire, and by the Attorneys General for their respective States as follows: Richard Blumenthal of Connecticut, Bill McCollum of Florida, Mark J. Bennett of Hawaii, Lisa Madigan of Illinois, Tom Miller of Iowa, Steve Six of Kansas, Douglas F. Gansler of Maryland, Martha Coakley of Massachusetts, Michael A. Cox of Michigan, Lori Swanson of Minnesota, Jim Hood of Mississippi, Anne Milgram of New Jersey, Gary K. King of New Mexico, Roy Cooper of North Carolina, Wayne Stenehjem of North Dakota, Richard Cordray of Ohio, W. A. Drew Edmondson of Oklahoma, Thomas W. Corbett, Jr., of Pennsylvania, Patrick C. Lynch of Rhode Island, Lawrence E. Long of South Dakota, Robert E. Cooper, Jr., of Tennessee, William H. Sorrell of Vermont, and Darrell V. McGraw, Jr., of West Virginia in support of neither party.

Brief of amici curiae filed on behalf of Former Officials of the American Civil Liberties Union by Norman Dorsen and Burt Neuborne, both pro se, in support of neither party.

Brief of amici curiae filed on behalf of the Hachette Book Group, Inc., et al. by Michael J. Chepiga in support of neither party.

Brief of amici curiae filed on behalf of the Independent Sector by M. Devereux Chatillon in support of neither party.

IV. THE SUPREME COURT'S DECISION

"The ongoing chill upon speech that is beyond all doubt protected makes it necessary in this case to invoke the earlier precedents that a statute which chills speech can and must be invalidated where its facial invalidity has been demonstrated. For these reasons we find it necessary to reconsider Austin. . . .

The law before us is an outright ban, backed by criminal sanctions. . . .

Section 441b is a ban on corporate speech notwithstanding the fact that a PAC created by a corporation can still speak. . . .

Section 441b's prohibition on corporate independent expenditures is thus a ban on speech. . . .Our precedent is to be respected unless the most convincing of reasons demonstrates that adherence to it puts us on a course that is sure error. . . .

For the reasons above, it must be concluded that Austin was not well reasoned. . . .

Due consideration leads to this conclusion: Austin should be and now is overruled. . . .

Austin is overruled, so it provides no basis for allowing the Government to limit corporate independent expenditures. As the Government appears to concede, overruling Austin 'effectively invalidate[s] not only BCRA Section 203, but also 2 U.S.C. 441b's prohibition on the use of corporate treasury funds for express advocacy.' Section 441b's restrictions on corporate independent expenditures are therefore invalid and cannot be applied to Hillary.

Given our conclusion we are further required to overrule the part of McConnell that upheld BCRA § 203's extension of § 441b's restrictions on corporate independent expenditures. . . . This part of McConnell is now overruled. . . .

Citizens United next challenges BCRA's disclaimer and disclosure provisions as applied to Hillary and the three advertisements for the movie. . . .

[W]e find the statute valid as applied to the ads for the movie and to the movie itself. . . .

We find no constitutional impediment to the application of BCRA's disclaimer and disclosure requirements to a movie broadcast via video-on-demand. And there has been no showing that, as applied in this case, these requirements would impose a chill on speech or expression. . . .

The judgment of the District Court is reversed with respect to the constitutionality of 2 U.S.C. § 441b's restrictions on corporate independent expenditures. The judgment is affirmed with respect to BCRA's disclaimer and disclosure requirements. The case is remanded . . . ."

V. JUSTICE VOTE

5 Pro ACLU Side vs. 4 Con Opposing Side

ACLU Side (Petitioner / Appellant)

1. Kennedy, A. – Wrote majority opinion
2. Alito, S. – Joined Roberts' concurrence, joined Scalia's concurrence
3. Thomas, C. – Wrote opinion concurring in part and dissenting in part, joined Scalia's concurrence in part
4. Scalia, A. – Wrote concurring opinion
5. Roberts, J. – Wrote concurring opinion

Opposing Side (Respondent / Appellee)

1. Breyer, S. – Joined Stevens' opinion
2. Stevens, J. – Wrote opinion concurring in part and dissenting in part
3. Ginsburg, R. – Joined Stevens' opinion
4. Sotomayor, S. – Joined Stevens' opinion

VI. A WIN OR LOSS FOR THE ACLU?

The ACLU filed as amicus curiae urging the court to declare § 203 of BCRA unconstitutional; the Supreme Court reversed in part and affirmed in part, including declaring § 203 of BCRA unconstitutional, in a 5-4 vote as to § 203, giving the ACLU an apparent win.

VI. A WIN OR LOSS FOR THE ACLU?

The ACLU filed as amicus curiae urging affirmance; the Supreme Court vacated and remanded the Court of Appeals' decision by a 9-0 vote, giving the ACLU an apparent loss.

1053. Kiyemba v. Obama

(Decided March 1, 2010; 559 U.S. 131)

I. ISSUE

A. Issues Discussed

Prison

B. Legal Question Presented

"[W]hether a federal court exercising habeas jurisdiction has the power to order the release of prisoners held at Guantanamo Bay 'where the Executive detention is indefinite and without authorization in law, and release into the continental United States is the only possible effective remedy.'"

C. Supreme Court's Answer

"No court has yet ruled in this case in light of the new facts, and we decline to be the first to do so."

II. CASE SUMMARY

A. Background

The Supreme Court "granted certiorari, on the question whether a federal court exercising habeas jurisdiction has the power to order the release of prisoners held at Guantanamo Bay 'where the Executive detention is indefinite and without authorization in law, and release into the continental United States is the only possible effective remedy.' By now, however, each of the detainees at issue in this case has received at least one offer of resettlement in another country. Most of the detainees have accepted an offer of resettlement; five detainees, however, have rejected two such offers and are still being held at Guantanamo Bay."

B. Counsel of Record / ACLU Attorney

ACLU Side (Petitioner / Appellant): Brief for appellants filed by Eric A. Tirschwell, Michael J. Sternhell, Darren LaVerne, Seema Saifee, Elizabeth P. Gilson, J. Wells Dixon, Angela C. Vigil, Sabin Willett, Rheba Rutkowski, Neil McGaraghan, Jason S. Pinney, Susan Baker Manning, George Clarke, and Clive Stafford Smith.

Opposing Side (Respondent / Appellee): Brief for appellees filed by Solicitor General Elena Kagan, Assistant Attorney General Tony West, Deputy Solicitor General Edwin S. Kneedler, Nicole A. Saharsky and Leondra R. Kruger, Assistants to the Solicitor General, Douglas N. Letter, Thomas M. Bondy, Robert M. Loeb, and Sharon Swingle.

III. AMICI CURIAE

ACLU Side (Petitioner / Appellant)

Brief of amici curiae filed on behalf of the American Civil Liberties Union by Lucas Guttentag, Cecillia D. Wang, Jennifer Chang Newell, Omar C. Jadwat, Steven R. Shapiro, Jonathan Hafetz, and Judy Rabinovitz.

Brief of amici curiae filed on behalf of the National Immigrant Justice Center et al. by Bernard Taylor, Christina McClain, Jeffrey Freeman, Angela Marston, Karen Carroll, Charles Roth, and Stephen W. Manning.

Brief of amici curiae filed on behalf of Uyghur American Association by Robert Abrahams, Daniel L. Greenberg, Mark S. Mandel, and John G. Mateus.

Brief of amici curiae filed on behalf of Scholars of Nineteenth-Century American Legal History by David Overlock Stewart, Stacy A. Tromble, and Amy E. Craig.

Brief of amici curiae filed on behalf of Public International Law & Policy Group by Michael P. Scharf, Paul R. Williams, Melissa Waters, and Meghan Stewart.

Brief of amici curiae filed on behalf of Charles B. Gittings, Jr. by Howard N. Meyer.

Brief of amici curiae filed on behalf of Right Honourable Lord Goldsmith QC et al. by Jennifer R. Cowan.

Brief of amici curiae filed on behalf of the Federal Public Defender for the District Court of Oregon by Steven T. Wax, and Stephen R. Sady.

Brief of amici curiae filed on behalf of International Law Experts by Hope R. Metcalf and Oona A. Hathaway.

Brief of amici curiae filed on behalf of the Association of the Bar of the City of New York et al. by Sidney S. Rosdeitcher, Alex Young K. Oh, Philip G. Barber, David G. Clunie, Elizabeth Goitein, Emily Berman, Aziz Huq, Sharon Bradford Franklin, Margery F. Baker, Deborah Liu, John W. Whitehead, and Malia N. Brink.

Brief of amici curiae filed on behalf of Amnesty International et al. by Widney Brown, Ian D. Seiderman, Paul L. Hoffman, and Adrienne J. Quarry.

Brief of amici curiae filed on behalf of Retired Federal Judges by James C. Schroeder, Gary A. Isaac, Stephen J. Kane, Stephen S. Sanders, Chad M. Clamage, and Joshua M. Grenard.

Brief of amici curiae filed on behalf of Law Professors by Daniel Kanstroom and Theodore D. Frank.

Brief of amici curiae filed on behalf of Legal and Historical Scholars by David Overlock Stewart and Amy E. Craig.

Brief of amici curiae filed on behalf of Law Professors by Charles D. Weisselberg, Lucas Guttentag, and Theodore D. Frank.

Opposing Side (Respondent / Appellee)

Brief of amici curiae filed on behalf of Brief of amici curiae filed on behalf of Immigration Reform Law Institute by Michael M. Hethmon.

Brief of amici curiae filed on behalf of Scott C. Black, Lt. Gen. US Army (Ret.) et al. by Daniel J. Popeo, Richard A. Samp, and Michael Rybak.

Brief of amici curiae filed on behalf of Defense of Democracies by Adam J. White, Chad N. Boudreaux, Aaron M. Streett, William L. Thompson III, and Kathryn M. Kelley.

IV. THE SUPREME COURT'S DECISION

"This change in the underlying facts may affect the legal issues presented. No court has yet ruled in this case in light of the new facts, and we decline to be the first to do so. . . .

Under these circumstances, we vacate the judgment and remand the case to the United States Court of Appeals for the District of Columbia Circuit. It should determine, in the first instance, what further proceedings in that court or in the District Court are necessary and appropriate for the full and prompt disposition of the case in light of the new developments."

V. JUSTICE VOTE

9 Pro ACLU Side vs. 0 Con Opposing Side

ACLU Side (Petitioner / Appellant)

1. Alito, S. – Per curiam opinion
2. Stevens, J. – Per curiam opinion
3. Thomas, C. – Per curiam opinion
4. Breyer, S. – Per curiam opinion
5. Scalia, A. – Per curiam opinion
6. Kennedy, A. – Per curiam opinion
7. Ginsburg, R. – Per curiam opinion
8. Sotomayor, S. – Per curiam opinion
9. Roberts, J. – Per curiam opinion

VI. A WIN OR LOSS FOR THE ACLU?

The ACLU filed as amicus curiae urging reversal of the judgment of the Court of Appeals; the Supreme Court vacated and remanded in a 9-0 per curiam decision, giving the ACLU an apparent win.

1054. Berghuis v. Smith

(Decided March 30, 2010; 559 U.S. 314)

I. ISSUE

A. Issues Discussed

Criminal procedure

B. Legal Question Presented

"The Sixth Amendment secures to criminal defendants the right to be tried by an impartial jury drawn from sources reflecting a fair cross section of the community. The question presented in this case is whether that right was accorded to respondent Diapolis Smith, an African-American convicted of second-degree murder by an all-white jury in Kent County, Michigan in 1993."

C. Supreme Court's Answer

"[O]ur Duren decision hardly establishes—no less 'clearly' so—that Smith was denied his Sixth Amendment right to an impartial jury drawn from a fair cross section of the community."

II. CASE SUMMARY

A. Background

"Christopher Rumbley was shot and killed during a bar brawl . . . . The bar was crowded at the time of the brawl, with 200-to-300 people on the premises. All patrons of the bar were African-American. The State charged Smith with the murder in Kent County Circuit Court.

Voir dire for Smith's trial took place . . . . The venire panel included between 60 and 100 individuals. The parties agree that, at most, three venire members were African-American. Smith unsuccessfully objected to the composition of the venire panel.

Smith's case proceeded to trial before an all-white jury. The case for the prosecution turned on the identity of the man who shot Rumbley. Thirty-seven witnesses from the bar, including Smith, testified at the trial. Of those, two testified that Smith fired the gun. Five testified that the shooter was not Smith, and the remainder made no identifications of the shooter. The jury convicted Smith of second-degree murder and possession of a firearm during a felony, and the court sentenced him to life imprisonment with the possibility of parole. . . .

On first appeal, the Michigan Court of Appeals ordered the trial court to conduct an evidentiary hearing on Smith's fair-cross-section claim. . . .

The court . . . rejected Smith's fair-cross-section claim. . . .

The Michigan Supreme Court, in turn, reversed the Court of Appeals' judgment . . . .

Smith filed a habeas corpus petition . . . reasserting his fair-cross-section claim. . . .

[T]he District Court dismissed Smith's habeas petition.

The Court of Appeals reversed."

The Supreme Court granted certiorari to review the case.

B. Counsel of Record / ACLU Attorney

ACLU Side (Respondent / Appellee): James Sterling Lawrence argued the cause and filed a brief for appellee.

Opposing Side (Petitioner / Appellant): B. Eric Restuccia, Solicitor General of Michigan, argued the cause for appellant. With him on the briefs were Michael A. Cox, Attorney General, Joel D. McGormley, Division Chief, and Timothy K. McMorrow, Special Assistant Attorney General.

III. AMICI CURIAE

ACLU Side (Respondent / Appellee)

Brief of amici curiae filed on behalf of the National Association of Criminal Defense Lawyers, the American Civil Liberties Union, and the National Jury Project by Clifford M. Sloan, Thomas M. Meyer, Joshua Dratel, Neil Lombardo, Ray D. McKenzie, Patrick Haggerty, and Steven R. Shapiro.

Brief of amici curiae filed on behalf of the Charles Hamilton Houston Institute for Race & Justice et al. by Michael B. de Leeuw.

Brief of amici curiae filed on behalf of the NAACP Legal Defense & Educational Fund, Inc., by John Payton, Debo P. Adegbile, Christina Swarns, Johanna B. Steinberg, Jin Hee Lee, Vincent M. Southerland, Virginia A. Seitz, Gary Feinerman, Jeffrey T. Green, Rebecca K. Troth, and Sarah O'Rourke Schrup.

Brief of amici curiae filed on behalf of Social Scientists et al. by Erik Levin, David Kairys, and Jack C. Auspitz.

Opposing Side (Petitioner / Appellant)

Brief of amici curiae filed on behalf of the State of Connecticut et al. by Kevin T. Kane, Chief State's Attorney of Connecticut, Harry Weller, Senior Assistant State's Attorney, and Michael E. O'Hare, Supervisory Assistant State's Attorney, and by the Attorneys General for their respective States as follows: Terry Goddard of Arizona, John W. Suthers of Colorado, Lawrence G. Wasden of Idaho, Douglas F. Gansler of Maryland, Gary K. King of New Mexico, Wayne Stenehjem of North Dakota, Richard Cordray of Ohio, Thomas W. Corbett, Jr., of Pennsylvania, Henry D. McMaster of South Carolina, Marty J. Jackley of South Dakota, Robert E. Cooper, Jr., of Tennessee, Mark L. Shurtleff of Utah, and J. B. Van Hollen of Wisconsin.

Brief of amici curiae filed on behalf of the Criminal Justice Legal Foundation by Kent S. Scheidegger.

IV. THE SUPREME COURT'S DECISION

"The Sixth Amendment secures to criminal defendants the right to be tried by an impartial jury drawn from sources reflecting a fair cross section of the community. . . .

In Duren v. Missouri, 439 U.S. 357 (1979), this Court described three showings a criminal defendant must make to establish a prima facie violation of the Sixth Amendment's fair-cross-section requirement. He or she must show: '(1) that the group alleged to be excluded is a 'distinctive' group in the community; (2) that the representation of this group in venires from which juries are selected is not fair and reasonable in relation to the number of such persons in the community; and (3) that this underrepresentation is due to systematic exclusion of the group in the jury-selection process.' . . .

[N]either Duren nor any other decision of this Court specifies the . . . test courts must use to measure the representation of distinctive groups in jury pools. The courts below . . . noted three methods . . . in lower federal court decisions: absolute disparity, comparative disparity, and standard deviation.

Each test is imperfect. . . .

No 'clearly established' precedent of this Court supports Smith's claim that he can make out a prima facie case merely by pointing to a host of factors that, individually or in combination, might contribute to a group's underrepresentation. . . .

This Court, furthermore, has never 'clearly established' that jury-selection-process features of the kind on Smith's list can give rise to a fair-cross-section claim. In Taylor, we 'recognized broad discretion in the States' to 'prescribe relevant qualifications for their jurors and to provide reasonable exemptions. And in Duren, the Court understood that hardship exemptions resembling those Smith assails might well 'survive a fair-cross-section challenge.' In sum, the Michigan Supreme Court's decision rejecting Smith's fair-cross-section claim is consistent with Duren and 'involved [no] unreasonable application o[f] clearly established Federal law.' . . .

[T]he judgment of the Court of Appeals for the Sixth Circuit is reversed, and the case is remanded . . . ."

V. JUSTICE VOTE

0 Pro ACLU Side vs. 9 Con Opposing Side

Opposing Side (Petitioner / Appellant)

1. Ginsburg, R. – Wrote majority opinion
2. Alito, S. – Joined majority opinion
3. Stevens, J. – Joined majority opinion
4. Thomas, C. – Wrote concurring opinion
5. Breyer, S. – Joined majority opinion
6. Scalia, A. – Joined majority opinion
7. Kennedy, A. – Joined majority opinion
8. Sotomayor, S. – Joined majority opinion
9. Roberts, J. – Joined majority opinion

VI. A WIN OR LOSS FOR THE ACLU?

The ACLU filed as amicus curiae urging affirmance; the Supreme Court reversed the Court of Appeals' decision by a 9-0 vote, giving the ACLU an apparent loss.

1055. U.S. v. Stevens

(Decided April 20, 2010; 559 U.S. 460)

I. ISSUE

A. Issues Discussed

1st Amendment, press, speech, association

B. Legal Question Presented

"Congress enacted 18 U.S.C. § 48 to criminalize the commercial creation, sale, or possession of certain depictions of animal cruelty. The statute does not address underlying acts harmful to animals, but only portrayals of such conduct. The question presented is whether the prohibition in the statute is consistent with the freedom of speech guaranteed by the First Amendment."

C. Supreme Court's Answer

"We . . . need not and do not decide whether a statute limited to crush videos or other depictions of extreme animal cruelty would be constitutional. We hold only that § 48 is not so limited but is instead substantially overbroad, and therefore invalid under the First Amendment."

II. CASE SUMMARY

A. Background

"Section 48 establishes a criminal penalty of up to five years in prison for anyone who knowingly 'creates, sells, or possesses a depiction of animal cruelty,' if done 'for commercial gain' in interstate or foreign commerce. . . .

The legislative background of § 48 focused primarily on . . . 'crush videos.' . . .

This case, however, involves an application of § 48 to depictions of animal fighting. . . . Respondent Robert J. Stevens ran a business, 'Dogs of Velvet and Steel,' and an associated Web site, through which he sold videos of pit bulls engaging in dogfights and attacking other animals. . . . On the basis of these videos, Stevens was indicted on three counts of violating § 48.

Stevens moved to dismiss the indictment, arguing that § 48 is facially invalid under the First Amendment. The District Court denied the motion. . . . It went on to hold that § 48 is not substantially overbroad, because the exceptions clause sufficiently narrows the statute to constitutional applications. The jury convicted Stevens on all counts, and the District Court sentenced him to three concurrent sentences of 37 months' imprisonment, followed by three years of supervised release.

The en banc Third Circuit, over a three-judge dissent, declared § 48 facially unconstitutional and vacated Stevens's conviction." The Supreme Court granted certiorari to review the case.

B. Counsel of Record / ACLU Attorney

ACLU Side (Respondent / Appellee): Patricia A. Millett argued the cause for appellee. With her on the brief were Thomas C. Goldstein, Kevin R. Amer, Jeffrey L. Fisher, Lisa B. Freeland, Michael J. Novara, Karen Sirianni Gerlach, and Robert Corn-Revere.

Opposing Side (Petitioner / Appellant): Deputy Solicitor General Katyal argued the cause for the United States. On the briefs were Solicitor General Kagan, Assistant Attorney General Breuer, Deputy Solicitor General Dreeben, Nicole A. Saharsky, and Vicki S. Marani.

III. AMICI CURIAE

ACLU Side (Respondent / Appellee)

Brief of amici curiae filed on behalf of the DKT Liberty Project, the American Civil Liberties Union, and the Center for Democracy and Technology by Paul M. Smith, Katherine A. Fallow, Steven R. Shapiro, Jessica Ring Amunson, Joshua A. Block, and John B. Morris, Jr.

Brief of amici curiae filed on behalf of the Association of American Publishers, Inc., et al. by R. Bruce Rich, Jonathan Bloom, and Michael A. Bamberger.

Brief of amici curiae filed on behalf of the Cato Institute by Gene C. Schaerr, Geoffrey P. Eaton, Ilya Shapiro, and Linda T. Coberly.

Brief of amici curiae filed on behalf of Bruce Ackerman et al. by Craig Green, pro se.

Brief of amici curiae filed on behalf of the Endangered Breed Association et al. by Judith A. Brecka.

Brief of amici curiae filed on behalf of the First Amendment Lawyers Association by Cathy E. Crosson, Clyde F. DeWitt III, and Lawrence G. Walters.

Brief of amici curiae filed on behalf of the National Coalition Against Censorship et al. by Andrew E. Tauber, Jeffrey P. Cunard, and Joan E. Bertin.

Brief of amici curiae filed on behalf of the National Rifle Association of America, Inc., by R. Hewitt Pate III, Ryan A. Shores, and Lewis F. Powell III.

Brief of amici curiae filed on behalf of the National Shooting Sports Foundation, Inc., by Lawrence G. Keane and Christopher P. Johnson.

Brief of amici curiae filed on behalf of the Professional Outdoor Media Association et al. by Beth Heifetz.

Brief of amici curiae filed on behalf of the Reporters Committee for Freedom of the Press et al. by Lucy A. Dalglish, Gregg P. Leslie, Kevin M. Goldberg, David Ardia, Marshall W. Anstandig, Mickey H. Osterreicher, George Freeman, René P. Milam, Barbara L. Camens, William Jay Powell, and Bruce W. Sanford.

Brief of amici curiae filed on behalf of the Safari Club International et al. by Douglas S. Burdin and William J. McGrath.

Brief of amici curiae filed on behalf of the Thomas Jefferson Center for the Protection of Free Expression by J. Joshua Wheeler.

Opposing Side (Petitioner / Appellant)

Brief of amici curiae filed on behalf of the State of Florida et al. by Bill McCollum, Attorney General of Florida, Scott D. Makar, Solicitor General, and Timothy D. Osterhaus and Craig D. Feiser, Deputy Solicitors General, and by the Attorneys General for their respective States as follows: Troy King of Alabama, Terry Goddard of Arizona, Dustin McDaniel of Arkansas, Edmund G. Brown, Jr., of California, John Suthers of Colorado, Richard Blumenthal of Connecticut, Mark J. Bennett of Hawaii, Lisa Madigan of Illinois, Gregory F. Zoeller of Indiana, Jack Conway of Kentucky, James D. "Buddy" Caldwell of Louisiana, Douglas F. Gansler of Maryland, Michael A. Cox of Michigan, Jim Hood of Mississippi, Steve Bullock of Montana, Kelly A. Ayotte of New Hampshire, Gary K. King of New Mexico, Roy Cooper of North Carolina, Richard Cordray of Ohio, Patrick C. Lynch of Rhode Island, Henry D. McMaster of South Carolina, Greg Abbott of Texas, Mark L. Shurtleff of Utah, William C. Mims of Virginia, and Darrell V. McGraw, Jr., of West Virginia.

Brief of amici curiae filed on behalf of the American Society for the Prevention of Cruelty to Animals by Ian C. Schaefer.

Brief of amici curiae filed on behalf of the Animal Legal Defense Fund by Karen JohnsonMcKewan and Warrington S. Parker III.

Brief of amici curiae filed on behalf of the Center on the Administration of Criminal Law by Paul D. Clement, Anthony S. Barkow, and Rachel E. Barkow.

Brief of amici curiae filed on behalf of a Group of American Law Professors by Megan A. Senatori and Pamela D. Frasch, both pro se.

Brief of amici curiae filed on behalf of the Humane Society of the United States by J. Scott Ballenger, Claudia M. O'Brien, Melissa B. Arbus, Jonathan R. Lovvorn, and Kimberly D. Ockene.

Brief of amici curiae filed on behalf of the Northwest Animal Rights Network by James H. Jones, Jr.

Brief of amici curiae filed on behalf of the Washington Legal Foundation et al. by Daniel J. Popeo and Richard A. Samp.

Brief of amici curiae filed on behalf of the International Society for Animal Rights by Henry Mark Holzer and Lance J. Gotko.

IV. THE SUPREME COURT'S DECISION

"The Government's primary submission is that § 48 necessarily complies with the Constitution because the banned depictions of animal cruelty, as a class, are categorically unprotected by the First Amendment. We disagree. . . .

Section 48 explicitly regulates expression based on content: The statute restricts 'visual [and] auditory depiction[s],' such as photographs, videos, or sound recordings, depending on whether they depict conduct in which a living animal is intentionally harmed. As such, § 48 is "presumptively invalid,' and the Government bears the burden to rebut that presumption.' . . .

Stevens challenged § 48 on its face, arguing that any conviction secured under the statute would be unconstitutional. The court below decided the case on that basis, and we granted the Solicitor General's petition for certiorari to determine 'whether 18 U.S.C. 48 is facially invalid under the Free Speech Clause of the First Amendment.' . . .

In the First Amendment context . . . this Court recognizes 'a second type of facial challenge,' whereby a law may be invalidated as overbroad if 'a substantial number of its applications are unconstitutional, judged in relation to the statute's plainly legitimate sweep.' . . . As the parties have presented the issue, . . . the constitutionality of § 48 hinges on how broadly it is construed. It is to that question that we now turn. . . .

We read § 48 to create a criminal prohibition of alarming breadth. . . .

The Government's attempt to narrow the statutory ban, however, requires an unrealistically broad reading of the exceptions clause. . . .

Not to worry, the Government says: The Executive Branch construes § 48 to reach only 'extreme' cruelty, and it 'neither has brought nor will bring a prosecution for anything less' . . .

To read § 48 as the Government desires requires rewriting, not just reinterpretation. . . .

Our construction of § 48 decides the constitutional question; the Government makes no effort to defend the constitutionality of § 48 as applied beyond crush videos and . . . animal fighting. . . .

Nor does the Government seriously contest that the presumptively impermissible applications of § 48 (properly construed) far outnumber any permissible ones. . . . We therefore need not and do not decide whether a statute limited to crush videos or other depictions of extreme animal cruelty would be constitutional. We hold only that § 48 is not so limited but is instead substantially overbroad, and therefore invalid under the First Amendment.

The judgment of the United States Court of Appeals for the Third Circuit is affirmed."

V. JUSTICE VOTE

8 Pro ACLU Side vs. 1 Con Opposing Side

ACLU Side (Respondent / Appellee)

1. Roberts, J. – Wrote majority opinion
2. Stevens, J. – Joined majority opinion
3. Thomas, C. – Joined majority opinion
4. Breyer, S. – Joined majority opinion
5. Scalia, A. – Joined majority opinion
6. Kennedy, A. – Joined majority opinion
7. Ginsburg, R. – Joined majority opinion
8. Sotomayor, S. – Joined majority opinion

Opposing Side (Petitioner / Appellant)

1. Alito, S. – Wrote dissenting opinion

VI. A WIN OR LOSS FOR THE ACLU?

The ACLU filed as amicus curiae urging affirmance; the Supreme Court affirmed the Court of Appeals' decision by an 8-1 vote, giving the ACLU an apparent win.

1056. Perdue v. Kenny A.

(Decided April 21, 2010; 559 U.S. 542)

I. ISSUE

A. Issues Discussed

Civil rights, federal

B. Legal Question Presented

"[W]hether the calculation of an attorney's fee, under federal fee-shifting statutes, based on the 'lodestar,' i.e., the number of hours worked multiplied by the prevailing hourly rates, may be increased due to superior performance and results."

C. Supreme Court's Answer

"We have stated in previous cases that such an increase is permitted in extraordinary circumstances, and we reaffirm that rule. But as we have also said in prior cases, there is a strong presumption that the lodestar is sufficient; factors subsumed in the lodestar calculation cannot be used as a ground for increasing an award above the lodestar; and a party seeking fees has the burden of identifying a factor that the lodestar does not adequately take into account and proving with specificity that an enhanced fee is justified."

II. CASE SUMMARY

A. Background

"Respondents . . . are children in the Georgia foster-care system and their next friends. They filed this class action . . . . Claiming that deficiencies in the foster-care system in two counties near Atlanta violated their federal and state constitutional and statutory rights, respondents sought injunctive and declaratory relief, as well as attorney's fees and expenses.

The United States District Court for the Northern District of Georgia eventually referred the case to mediation, where the parties entered into a consent decree, which the District Court approved. The consent decree resolved all pending issues other than the fees that respondents' attorneys were entitled to receive under 42 U.S.C. § 1988. . . .

Respondents submitted a request for more than $14 million in attorney's fees. Half of that amount was based on their calculation of the lodestar—roughly 30,000 hours multiplied by hourly rates of $200 to $495 for attorneys and $75 to $150 for non attorneys. In support of their fee request, respondents submitted affidavits asserting that these rates were within the range of prevailing market rates for legal services in the relevant market.

The other half of the amount that respondents sought represented a fee enhancement for superior work and results. . . . Petitioners objected to the fee request, contending that some of the proposed hourly rates were too high, that the hours claimed were excessive, and that the enhancement would duplicate factors that were reflected in the lodestar amount.

The District Court awarded fees of approximately $10.5 million. . . .

Relying on prior Circuit precedent, a panel of the Eleventh Circuit affirmed. . . .

The Eleventh Circuit denied rehearing en banc over the dissent of three judges."

The Supreme Court granted certiorari to review the case.

B. Counsel of Record / ACLU Attorney

ACLU Side (Respondent / Appellee): Paul D. Clement argued the cause for appellees. With him on the brief were Marcia Robinson Lowry, Ira P. Lustbader, and Jeffrey O. Bramlett.

Opposing Side (Petitioner / Appellant): Mark H. Cohen argued the cause for appellants. With him on the briefs were Thurbert E. Baker, Attorney General of Georgia, Dennis R. Dunn, Deputy Attorney General, Shalen S. Nelson, Senior Assistant Attorney General, and Elizabeth M. Williamson, Assistant Attorney General.

Pratik A. Shah argued the cause for the United States as amicus curiae.

III. AMICI CURIAE

ACLU Side (Respondent / Appellee)

Brief of amici curiae filed on behalf of the Lawyers' Committee for Civil Rights Under Law, AARP, Alliance for Justice, American Civil Liberties Union, Mexican American Legal Defense and Education Fund, National Disability Rights Network, National Partnership for Women and Families, National Urban League, National Women's Law Center, and Public Citizen by Michael B. de Leeuw, Sarah Crawford, Jordan Barry, Jan Sysel, Joanna Kazakova, Benjamin Whetsell, Susan Silverstein, Kenneth W. Zeller, Michael Schuster, Nan Aron, Steven R. Shapiro, Cynthia Valenzuela, Judith G. Storandt, Judith L. Lichtman, Sharyn A. Tejani, Marc H. Morial, Patrick Gusman, Fatima Goss Graves, Dina Lassow, and Allison M. Zieve.

Brief of amici curiae filed on behalf of the American Association for Justice et al. by Jeffrey Robert White.

Brief of amici curiae filed on behalf of the Civil Rights Clinic at Howard University School of Law by Aderson Bellegarde François.

Brief of amici curiae filed on behalf of Lucian A. Bebchuk et al. by Deanne E. Maynard and W. Stephen Smith.

Brief of amici curiae filed on behalf of the Liberty Legal Institute et al. by Kelly J. Shackelford, Hiram S. Sasser III, Ilya Shapiro, William H. Mellor, Scott Bullock, Jay Alan Sekulow, Mathew Staver, and James Bopp, Jr.

Brief of amici curiae filed on behalf of the NAACP Legal Defense & Educational Fund, Inc., by John Payton, Debo P. Adegbile, Matthew Colangelo, Joshua Civin, and Kristen Clarke.

Brief of amici curiae filed on behalf of the New York State Bar Association et al. by Lisa E. Cleary.

Brief of amici curiae filed on behalf of Small Private Law Firms That Rely on Statutory Fee Awards in Public Interest Litigation by Sanford Jay Rosen.

Opposing Side (Petitioner / Appellant)

Brief of amici curiae filed on behalf of the United States by Pratik A. Shah, Solicitor General Kagan, Assistant Attorney General West, Deputy Solicitor General Katyal, Michael Jay Singer, and Jeffrica Jenkins Lee.

Brief of amici curiae filed on behalf of the State of Alabama et al. by Troy King, Attorney General of Alabama, and Corey L. Maze, Solicitor General, and by the Attorneys General for their respective jurisdictions as follows: Daniel S. Sullivan of Alaska, Dustin McDaniel of Arkansas, John W. Suthers of Colorado, Peter J. Nickles of the District of Columbia, Bill McCollum of Florida, Mark J. Bennett of Hawaii, Lawrence G. Wasden of Idaho, Greg Zoeller of Indiana, Janet T. Mills of Maine, Douglas F. Gansler of Maryland, Martha Coakley of Massachusetts, Michael A. Cox of Michigan, Jon Bruning of Nebraska, Catherine C. Masto of Nevada, Kelly A. Ayotte of New Hampshire, Anne Milgram of New Jersey, Wayne Stenehjem of North Dakota, Richard Cordray of Ohio, W. A. Drew Edmondson of Oklahoma, Thomas W. Corbett, Jr., of Pennsylvania, Patrick C. Lynch of Rhode Island, Henry D. McMaster of South Carolina, Lawrence E. Long of South Dakota, Robert E. Cooper, Jr., of Tennessee, Mark L. Shurtleff of Utah, William H. Sorrell of Vermont, William C. Mims of Virginia, Robert M. McKenna of Washington, J. B. Van Hollen of Wisconsin, and Bruce A. Salzburg of Wyoming.

Brief of amici curiae filed on behalf of the Association County Commissioners of Georgia by James F. Grubiak.

Brief of amici curiae filed on behalf of the National Governors Association et al. by Richard Ruda.

Brief of amici curiae filed on behalf of the National Sheriffs' Association et al. by Travis Wisdom and Robert Spence.

Brief of amici curiae filed on behalf of the Old Republic Insurance Co. et al. by Mark E. Solomons, Laura Metcoff Klaus, and Francis Edwin Froelich.

Brief of amici curiae filed on behalf of the Washington Legal Foundation by Daniel J. Popeo and Richard A. Samp.

Brief of amici curiae filed on behalf of the National School Boards Association by Thomas E. Wheeler II, Francisco M. Negrón, Jr., Naomi E. Gittins, Thomas E. M. Hutton, and Lisa E. Soronen.

IV. THE SUPREME COURT'S DECISION

"The general rule in our legal system is that each party must pay its own attorney's fees and expenses, but Congress enacted 42 U.S.C. § 1988 in order to ensure that federal rights are adequately enforced. Section 1988 provides that a prevailing party in certain civil rights actions may recover 'a reasonable attorney's fee as part of the costs.' Unfortunately, the statute does not explain what Congress meant by a 'reasonable' fee, and therefore the task of identifying an appropriate methodology for determining a 'reasonable' fee was left for the courts.

One possible method was set out in Johnson v. Georgia Highway Express, Inc. . . . .

An alternative, the lodestar approach, . . . 'achieved dominance in the federal courts' . . . .

Although the lodestar method is not perfect, it has several important virtues. First, . . . the lodestar looks to 'the prevailing market rates in the relevant community.' . . . Second, the lodestar method is readily administrable, . . . and . . . 'objective,' and thus cabins the discretion of trial judges, permits meaningful judicial review, and produces reasonably predictable results. . . .

In light of what we have said in prior cases, we reject any contention that a fee determined by the lodestar method may not be enhanced in any situation. . . .

In this case, we are asked to decide whether either the quality of an attorney's performance or the results obtained are factors that may properly provide a basis for an enhancement. . . . When a plaintiff's attorney achieves results that are more favorable than would have been predicted . . . , the outcome may be attributable to superior performance and commitment of resources by plaintiff's counsel. Or the outcome may result from inferior performance by defense counsel, unanticipated defense concessions, unexpectedly favorable rulings by the court, an unexpectedly sympathetic jury, or simple luck. [S]uperior results are relevant only to the extent it can be shown that they are the result of superior attorney performance. . . . We conclude that there are a few such circumstances but that these circumstances are indeed 'rare' . . . and require specific evidence that the lodestar fee would not have been 'adequate to attract competent counsel' . . . .

[T]he District Court did not provide proper justification . . . . The court increased the lodestar award by 75% but . . . this figure appears to have been essentially arbitrary. . . .

Section 1988 serves an important public purpose by making it possible for persons without means to bring suit to vindicate their rights. But unjustified enhancements that serve only to enrich attorneys are not consistent with the statute's aim. . . .

[T]he judgment of the Court of Appeals is reversed, and the case is remanded . . . ."

V. JUSTICE VOTE

4 Pro ACLU Side vs. 5 Con Opposing Side

ACLU Side (Respondent / Appellee)

1. Breyer, S. – Wrote opinion concurring in part and dissenting in part
2. Stevens, J. – Joined Breyer's opinion
3. Ginsburg, R. – Joined Breyer's opinion
4. Sotomayor, S. – Joined Breyer's opinion

Opposing Side (Petitioner / Appellant)

1. Alito, S. – Wrote majority opinion
2. Thomas, C. – Wrote concurring opinion
3. Scalia, A. – Joined majority opinion
4. Kennedy, A. – Wrote concurring opinion
5. Roberts, J. – Joined majority opinion

VI. A WIN OR LOSS FOR THE ACLU?

The ACLU filed as amicus curiae urging affirmance; the Supreme Court reversed the Court of Appeals' decision by a 5-4 vote, giving the ACLU an apparent loss.

1057. Salazar v. Buono

(Decided April 28, 2010; 559 U.S. 700)

I. ISSUE

A. Issues Discussed

Federalism

B. Legal Question Presented

"[W]hether the District Court properly enjoined the Government from implementing the land-transfer statute."

C. Supreme Court's Answer

"Even assuming that the land-transfer statute was an attempt to prevent removal of the cross, it does not follow that an injunction against its implementation was appropriate."

II. CASE SUMMARY

A. Background

"In 1934, private citizens placed a Latin cross on a rock outcropping in a remote section of the Mojave Desert. Their purpose and intent was to honor American soldiers who fell in World War I. The original cross deteriorated over time, but a reconstructed one now stands at the same place. It is on federal land.

The Court is asked to consider a challenge, not to the first placement of the cross or its continued presence on federal land, but to a statute that would transfer the cross and the land on which it stands to a private party. . . . The District Court permanently enjoined the Government from implementing the statute. The Court of Appeals affirmed."

The Supreme Court granted certiorari to review the case.

B. Counsel of Record / ACLU Attorney

ACLU Side (Respondent / Appellee): Peter J. Eliasberg of the ACLU Foundation of Southern California argued the cause for appellee. With him on the brief were Steven R. Shapiro and Daniel Mach of the American Civil Liberties Union Foundation, Michael C. Small, and William B. Rubenstein.

Opposing Side (Petitioner / Appellant): Solicitor General Kagan argued the cause for appellants. With her on the briefs were Acting Assistant Attorney General Cruden, Deputy Solicitor General Katyal, Jeffrey B. Wall, Andrew C. Mergen, Charles R. Shockey, and Kathryn E. Kovacs.

III. AMICI CURIAE

ACLU Side (Respondent / Appellee)

Brief of amici curiae filed on behalf of the American Humanist Association et al. by Robert V. Ritter and Elizabeth L. Hileman.

Brief of amici curiae filed on behalf of the American Jewish Congress et al. by Andrew J. Pincus, Marc D. Stern, and Kara H. Stein.

Brief of amici curiae filed on behalf of the American Muslim Armed Forces and Veterans Affairs Council et al. by Douglas Laycock.

Brief of amici curiae filed on behalf of Americans United for Separation of Church and State et al. by Ayesha N. Khan, Richard B. Katskee, Steven M. Freeman, Steven C. Sheinberg, Pedro L. Irigonegaray, Margery F. Baker, and Mark J. Pelavin.
Brief of amici curiae filed on behalf of the Baptist Joint Committee for Religious Liberty et al. by Stephen B. Kinnaird, James W. Gilliam, and K. Hollyn Hollman.
Brief of amici curiae filed on behalf of the Center for Inquiry by Daniel S. Pariser, Ronald A. Lindsay, and Derek C. Araujo.
Brief of amici curiae filed on behalf of David Antoon et al. by Elaine J. Goldenberg.
Brief of amici curiae filed on behalf of the Freedom from Religion Foundation by Richard L. Bolton.
Brief of amici curiae filed on behalf of Jewish War Veterans of the United States of America, Inc., by A. Stephen Hut, Jr.
Brief of amici curiae filed on behalf of the Jewish Social Policy Action Network by Theodore R. Mann, Judah I. Labovitz, and Jeffrey I. Pasek.
Brief of amici curiae filed on behalf of Public Employees for Environmental Responsibility et al. by Sri Srinivasan and Irving L. Gornstein.

Opposing Side (Petitioner / Appellant)

Brief of amici curiae filed on behalf of the State of Indiana et al. by Gregory F. Zoeller, Attorney General of Indiana, Thomas M. Fisher, Solicitor General, and Heather L. Hagan and Ashley E. Tatman, Deputy Attorneys General, by Richard A. Svobodny, Acting Attorney General of Alaska, and by the Attorneys General for their respective States as follows: Troy King of Alabama, John W. Suthers of Colorado, Bill McCollum of Florida, Lawrence G. Wasden of Idaho, James D. "Buddy" Caldwell of Louisiana, Michael A. Cox of Michigan, Henry McMaster of South Carolina, Greg Abbott of Texas, and Mark L. Shurtleff of Utah.
Brief of amici curiae filed on behalf of the American Center for Law and Justice et al. by Jay Alan Sekulow, Stuart J. Roth, Colby M. May, James M. Henderson, Sr., Walter M. Weber, John P. Tuskey, and Laura B. Hernandez.
Brief of amici curiae filed on behalf of the American Legion Department of California by Benjamin W. Bull, Joseph P. Infranco, and Robert H. Tyler.
Brief of amici curiae filed on behalf of the Becket Fund for Religious Liberty by Kevin J. Hasson, Eric C. Rassbach, and Hannah C. Smith.
Brief of amici curiae filed on behalf of the Boy Scouts of America by George A. Davidson, Carla A. Kerr, Scott H. Christensen, and David K. Park.
Brief of amici curiae filed on behalf of the Christian Legal Society et al. by Carl H. Esbeck.
Brief of amici curiae filed on behalf of Citizens United et al. by Darrin R. Toney, John N. Childs, and Michael Boos.
Brief of amici curiae filed on behalf of the Eagle Forum Education and Legal Defense Fund by Douglas G. Smith.
Brief of amici curiae filed on behalf of Faith and Action et al. by Bernard P. Reese, Jr.
Brief of amici curiae filed on behalf of the Foundation for Free Expression by James L. Hirsen and Deborah J. Dewart.
Brief of amici curiae filed on behalf of the Foundation for Moral Law by John A. Eidsmoe and Benjamin D. DuPré.
Brief of amici curiae filed on behalf of the International Municipal Lawyers Association by Robert N. Driscoll.
Brief of amici curiae filed on behalf of the National Legal Foundation by Steven W. Fitschen.
Brief of amici curiae filed on behalf of the Thomas More Law Center et al. by Robert Joseph Muise, Charles S. LiMandri, and Manuel S. Klausner.
Brief of amici curiae filed on behalf of the Utah Highway Patrol Association et al. by Michael A. Sink and Frank D. Mylar, Jr.
Brief of amici curiae filed on behalf of Veterans of Foreign Wars of the United States et al. by Kelly J. Shackelford, Hiram S. Sasser III, R. Ted Cruz, Allyson N. Ho, Aaron Streett, Samuel Burk, Philip B. Onderdonk, Jr., Daniel J. Murphy, Chad M. Pinson, and James A. Clark.
Brief of amici curiae filed on behalf of the American Civil Rights Union by Peter J. Ferrara.
Brief of amici curiae filed on behalf of the Fidelis Center for Law & Policy et al. by Patrick T. Gillen.
Brief of amici curiae filed on behalf of Liberty Counsel by Mathew D. Staver, Anita L. Staver, Stephen M. Crampton, and Mary E. McAlister.

IV. THE SUPREME COURT'S DECISION

"The question now before the Court is whether the District Court properly enjoined the Government from implementing the land-transfer statute. The District Court did not consider whether the statute, in isolation, would have violated the Establishment Clause, and it did not forbid the land transfer as an independent constitutional violation. Rather, the court enjoined compliance with the statute on the premise that the relief was necessary to protect the rights Buono had secured through the 2002 injunction.

An injunction is an exercise of a court's equitable authority, to be ordered only after taking into account all of the circumstances that bear on the need for prospective relief. . . .

Here, the District Court did not engage in the appropriate inquiry. The land-transfer statute was a substantial change in circumstances bearing on the propriety of the requested relief. The court, however, did not acknowledge the statute's significance. . . .

A court must find prospective relief that fits the remedy to the wrong or injury that has been established. . . . The relevant question is whether an ongoing exercise of the court's equitable authority is supported by the prior showing of illegality, judged against the claim that changed circumstances have rendered prospective relief inappropriate.

The District Court granted the 2002 injunction based solely on its conclusion that presence of the cross on federal land conveyed an impression of governmental endorsement of religion. . . .

The District Court failed to consider whether, in light of the change in law and circumstances effected by the land-transfer statute, the 'reasonable observer' standard continued to be the appropriate framework through which to consider the Establishment Clause concerns . . . .

The land-transfer statute's bearing on this dispute must first be determined. To date, this Court's jurisprudence in this area has refrained from making sweeping pronouncements, and this case is ill suited for announcing categorical rules. In light of the finding of unconstitutionality in Buono I, and the highly fact-specific nature of the inquiry, it is best left to the District Court to undertake the analysis in the first instance. On remand, if Buono continues to challenge implementation of the statute, the District Court should conduct a proper inquiry as described above. . . .

The judgment of the Court of Appeals is reversed, and the case is remanded . . . ."

V. JUSTICE VOTE

4 Pro ACLU Side vs. 5 Con Opposing Side

ACLU Side (Respondent / Appellee)

1. Stevens, J. – Wrote dissenting opinion
2. Ginsburg, R. – Joined Stevens' dissent
3. Breyer, S. – Wrote dissenting opinion
4. Sotomayor, S. – Joined Stevens' dissent

Opposing Side (Petitioner / Appellant)

1. Kennedy, A. – Wrote majority opinion
2. Alito, S. – Wrote concurring opinion
3. Thomas, C. – Joined Scalia's concurrence
4. Scalia, A. – Wrote concurring opinion
5. Roberts, J. – Wrote concurring opinion

VI. A WIN OR LOSS FOR THE ACLU?

The ACLU argued the cause for appellee urging affirmance; the Supreme Court reversed the Court of Appeals' decision by a 5-4 vote, giving the ACLU an apparent loss.

1058. Hui v. Castaneda

(Decided May 3, 2010; 559 U.S. 799)

I. ISSUE

A. Issues Discussed

Prison

B. Legal Question Presented

"[W]hether 42 U.S.C. § 233(a) precludes an action under Bivens v. Six Unknown Fed. Narcotics Agents, 403 U.S. 388 (1971), against U.S. Public Health Service (PHS) personnel for constitutional violations arising out of their official duties."

C. Supreme Court's Answer

"Based on the plain language of § 233(a), we conclude that PHS officers and employees are not personally subject to Bivens actions for harms arising out of such conduct."

II. CASE SUMMARY

A. Background

"Francisco Castaneda was detained by U.S. Immigration and Customs Enforcement (ICE) . . . beginning in March 2006. [W]hen Castaneda arrived . . . he had on his penis an irregular, raised lesion that measured roughly two centimeters square. Castaneda promptly brought his condition to the attention of medical personnel . . . .

Between March 2006 and January 2007, Castaneda persistently sought treatment . . . . [T]he lesion became increasingly painful and interfered with his urination, defecation, and sleep. In December 2006, Castaneda additionally reported a lump in his groin. A PHS physician's assistant and three outside specialists repeatedly advised that Castaneda needed a biopsy to ascertain whether he had cancer. Petitioners denied requests . . . as 'elective.' Instead, Castaneda was treated with ibuprofen and antibiotics and was given an additional ration of boxer shorts.

After a fourth specialist recommended a biopsy in January 2007, the procedure was finally authorized. [H]owever, ICE released Castaneda from custody on February 5. A week later, biopsy results confirmed that Castaneda was suffering from penile cancer. The next day, Castaneda had his penis amputated, and he began chemotherapy . . . . The treatment was unsuccessful, and Castaneda died in February 2008.

Three months before his death, Castaneda filed suit . . . . Castaneda raised medical negligence claims . . . under the FTCA and Bivens claims . . . deliberate indifference to his serious medical needs in violation of his Fifth, Eighth, and Fourteenth Amendment rights. . . .

Petitioners moved to dismiss . . . . The District Court denied the motion . . . .

The Court of Appeals for the Ninth Circuit affirmed . . . ."

The Supreme Court granted certiorari to review the case.

B. Counsel of Record / ACLU Attorney

ACLU Side (Respondent / Appellee): Conal Doyle argued the cause for appellees. With him on the brief were Adele P. Kimmel, Amy Radon, Arthur H. Bryant, Leslie A. Brueckner, and Thomas M. Dempsey

Opposing Side (Petitioner / Appellant): Elaine J. Goldenberg argued the cause for appellants. With her on the briefs for appellant Stephen Gonsalves were Paul M. Smith, William M. Hohengarten, Matthew S. Hellman, and David P. Sheldon. Steven J. Renick and Patrick L. Hurley filed briefs for appellant Esther Hui.

Pratik A. Shah argued the cause for the United States as amicus curiae.

III. AMICI CURIAE

ACLU Side (Respondent / Appellee)

Brief of amici curiae filed on behalf of the American Civil Liberties Union by Jeffrey W. Sarles, Stephen S. Sanders, Gabriel B. Eber, and Steven R. Shapiro.

Brief of amici curiae filed on behalf of National Experts on Health Services for Detained Persons by Jonathan S. Franklin

and Tillman J. Breckenridge.
Brief of amici curiae filed on behalf of the National Immigrant Justice Center by Suzanne Sahakian and Charles Roth.
Brief of amici curiae filed on behalf of Representative John Conyers, Jr., et al. by Jonathan S. Massey.

Opposing Side (Petitioner / Appellant)

Brief of amici curiae filed on behalf of the United States by Pratik A. Shah, Solicitor General Kagan, Assistant Attorney General West, Deputy Solicitor General Kneedler, Barbara L. Herwig, Howard S. Scher, and David S. Cade.
Brief of amici curiae filed on behalf of the Commissioned Officers Association of the United States Public Health Service, Inc., et al. by Timothy B. Hyland.

IV. THE SUPREME COURT'S DECISION

"Our inquiry in this case begins and ends with the text of § 233(a). . . .

Section 233(a) grants absolute immunity to PHS officers and employees for actions arising out of the performance of medical or related functions within the scope of their employment by barring all actions against them for such conduct. . . .

In advocating a contrary reading of § 233(a), respondents rely heavily on our opinion in Carlson, as did the Court of Appeals. Carlson, however, is inapposite to the issue in this case. . . .

Because petitioners in Carlson invoked no official immunity, the Court did not address that question. Instead, it considered whether a remedy was available under the Eighth Amendment for alleged violations of the Cruel and Unusual Punishments Clause notwithstanding that a federal remedy was also available under the FTCA. . . .

This case presents the separate question whether petitioners are immune from suit for the alleged violations. . . . Because petitioners invoke only the immunity provided by § 233(a), the question in this case is answered solely by reference to whether that provision gives petitioners the immunity they claim. . . .

[T]he text of § 233(a) plainly indicates that it precludes a Bivens action against petitioners for the harm alleged in this case. Respondents offer three arguments in support of their claim that it does not. None persuades us that § 233(a) means something other than what it says. . . .

[R]espondents' arguments do not undermine our conclusion that the immunity provided by § 233(a) precludes Bivens actions . . . .

In construing § 233(a) in petitioners' favor, we are mindful of the confines of our judicial role. Respondents' amici caution that providing special immunity for PHS personnel is contrary to the public interest. Respondents likewise contend that allowing Bivens claims against PHS personnel is necessary to ensure an adequate standard of care in federal detention facilities, and they further urge that permitting such actions would not endanger PHS' institutional interests as it would simply place PHS personnel in the same position as other federal employees who perform similar functions. We are required, however, to read the statute according to its text. Because § 233(a) plainly precludes a Bivens action against petitioners for the harms alleged in this case, we reverse the judgment of the Ninth Circuit and remand . . . ."

V. JUSTICE VOTE

0 Pro ACLU Side vs. 9 Con Opposing Side

Opposing Side (Petitioner / Appellant)

1. Sotomayor, S. – Wrote majority opinion
2. Alito, S. – Joined majority opinion
3. Stevens, J. – Joined majority opinion
4. Thomas, C. – Joined majority opinion
5. Breyer, S. – Joined majority opinion
6. Scalia, A. – Joined majority opinion
7. Kennedy, A. – Joined majority opinion
8. Ginsburg, R. – Joined majority opinion
9. Roberts, J. – Joined majority opinion

VI. A WIN OR LOSS FOR THE ACLU?

The ACLU filed as amicus curiae urging affirmance; the Supreme Court reversed the Court of Appeals' decision by a 9-0 vote, giving the ACLU an apparent loss.

1059. Lewis v. City of Chicago

(Decided May 24, 2010; 560 U.S. 205)

I. ISSUE

A. Issues Discussed

Race, regulation

B. Legal Question Presented

"[W]hether a plaintiff who does not file a timely charge challenging the adoption of a practice—here, an employer's decision to exclude employment applicants who did not achieve a certain score on an examination—may assert a disparate-impact claim in a timely charge challenging the employer's later application of that practice."

C. Supreme Court's Answer

"[A] plaintiff establishes a prima facie disparate-impact claim by showing that the employer 'uses a particular employment practice that causes a disparate impact' on one of the prohibited bases. Petitioners' claim satisfies that requirement."

II. CASE SUMMARY

A. Background

"In July 1995, the city of Chicago (City) administered a written examination to over 26,000 applicants seeking to serve in the Chicago Fire Department. . . . It announced . . . that it would begin drawing randomly from the top tier of scorers, i.e., those who scored 89 or above . . . 'well qualified.' Those drawn from this group would proceed to the next phase . . . . Those who scored below 65 . . . learned by letters . . . that they had failed the test. . . .

[T]hose who scored between 65 and 88, . . . 'qualified'—were notified that they had passed . . . but that, based on the City's projected hiring needs and the number of 'well-qualified' applicants, it was not likely they would be called for further processing. . . .

On May 16, 1996, the City selected its first class . . . and repeated the process nine more times over the next six years. . . . In the last round it exhausted th[e well-qualified] pool, so it filled the remaining slots with 'qualified' candidates instead.

On March 31, 1997, Crawford M. Smith, an African-American applicant who scored in the 'qualified' range and had not been hired . . . , filed a charge of discrimination with the EEOC. Five others followed suit, and . . . the EEOC issued all six of them right-to-sue letters. [T]hey filed this civil action against the City, alleging . . . that its practice . . . caused a disparate impact on African-Americans . . . . The District Court certified a class . . . .

The City sought summary judgment on the ground that petitioners had failed to file EEOC charges within 300 days after their claims accrued. The District Court denied the motion . . . . [T]he District Court ruled for petitioners . . . .

The Seventh Circuit reversed."

The Supreme Court granted certiorari to review the case.

B. Counsel of Record / ACLU Attorney

ACLU Side (Petitioner / Appellant): John Payton argued the cause for appellants. With him on the briefs were Debo P. Adegbile, Matthew Colangelo, Joshua Civin, Clyde E. Murphy, Judson H. Miner, George F. Galland, Jr., Matthew J. Piers, Patrick O. Patterson, Jr., Fay Clayton, Cynthia H. Hyndman, and Bridget Arimond.

Deputy Solicitor General Katyal argued the cause for the United States as amicus curiae.

Opposing Side (Respondent / Appellee): Benna Ruth Solomon argued the cause for appellee. With her on the brief were Myriam Zreczny Kasper and Nadine Jean Wichern.

III. AMICI CURIAE

ACLU Side (Petitioner / Appellant)

Brief of amici curiae filed on behalf of the National Partnership for Women & Families and the National Women's Law Center et al., including the American Civil Liberties Union, by Helen Norton, Judith L. Lichtman, Marcia D. Greenberger, Audrey Wiggins, Sarah Crawford, Michael L. Foreman, Sharyn Tejani, Sandra Pullma, Fatima Goss Graves, and Helen Norton.

Brief of amici curiae filed on behalf of the United States by Deputy Solicitor General Katyal, Solicitor General Kagan, Assistant Attorney General Perez, Deputy Assistant Attorney General Bagenstos, Leondra R. Kruger, Dennis J. Dimsey, Teresa Kwong, Lorraine C. Davis, and Anne Noel Occhialino.

Brief of amici curiae filed on behalf of the International Association of Official Human Rights Agencies by Kevin K. Russell, Amy Howe, Pamela S. Karlan, and Jeffrey L. Fisher.

Opposing Side (Respondent / Appellee)

Brief of amici curiae filed on behalf of the City of New York et al. by Michael A. Cardozo, Leonard J. Koerner, and Elizabeth Susan Natrella.

Brief of amici curiae filed on behalf of the Equal Employment Advisory Council et al. by Rae T. Vann, Karen R. Harned, and Elizabeth Milito.

Brief of amici curiae filed on behalf of the Pacific Legal Foundation by Sharon L. Browne.

IV. THE SUPREME COURT'S DECISION

"Before beginning a Title VII suit, a plaintiff must first file a timely EEOC charge. In this case, petitioners' charges were due within 300 days 'after the alleged unlawful employment practice occurred.' Determining whether a plaintiff's charge is timely thus requires 'identify[ing] precisely the 'unlawful employment practice' of which he complains.' Petitioners here challenge the City's practice of picking only those who had scored 89 or above on the 1995 examination when it later chose applicants to advance. Setting aside the first round of selection in May 1996, which all agree is beyond the cutoff, no one disputes that the conduct petitioners challenge occurred within the charging period. The real question, then, is not whether a claim predicated on that conduct is timely, but whether the practice thus defined can be the basis for a disparate-impact claim at all.

We conclude that it can. . . .

[A] plaintiff establishes a prima facie disparate-impact claim by showing that the employer 'uses a particular employment practice that causes a disparate impact' . . . .

Title VII does not define 'employment practice,' but . . . the term encompasses the conduct of which petitioners complain: the exclusion of passing applicants who scored below 89 . . . .

The City and its amici warn that our reading will result in a host of practical problems . . . . Employers may face new disparate-impact suits for practices they have used . . . for years. . . .

Truth to tell, however, both readings of the statute produce puzzling results. Under the City's reading, if an employer adopts an unlawful practice and no timely charge is brought, it can continue using the practice indefinitely, with impunity, despite ongoing disparate impact. . . .

[I]t is not our task to assess the consequences of each approach . . . . Our charge is to give effect to the law Congress enacted. By enacting § 2000e-2(k)(1)(A)(i), Congress allowed claims to be brought against an employer who uses a practice that causes disparate impact, whatever the employer's motives and whether or not he has employed the same practice in the past. . . .

The City asserts that one aspect of the District Court's judgment still must be changed. The first round of hiring firefighters occurred outside the charging period even for the earliest EEOC charge. Yet the District Court, applying the continuing-violation theory, awarded relief based on those acts. Petitioners do not disagree, and they do not oppose the City's request for a remand to resolve this issue. We therefore leave it to the Seventh Circuit to determine, to the extent that point was properly preserved, whether the judgment must be modified in light of our decision. . . .

The judgment of the Court of Appeals is reversed, and the case is remanded . . . ."

V. JUSTICE VOTE

9 Pro ACLU Side vs. 0 Con Opposing Side

ACLU Side (Petitioner / Appellant)

1. Scalia, A. – Wrote majority opinion
2. Alito, S. – Joined majority opinion
3. Stevens, J. – Joined majority opinion

4. Thomas, C. – Joined majority opinion
5. Breyer, S. – Joined majority opinion
6. Kennedy, A. – Joined majority opinion
7. Ginsburg, R. – Joined majority opinion
8. Sotomayor, S. – Joined majority opinion
9. Roberts, J. – Joined majority opinion

VI. A WIN OR LOSS FOR THE ACLU?

The ACLU filed as amicus curiae urging reversal of the judgment of the Court of Appeals; the Supreme Court reversed in a 9-0 vote, giving the ACLU an apparent win.

1060. Berghuis v. Thompkins

(Decided June 1, 2010; 560 U.S. 370)

I. ISSUE

A. Issues Discussed

Criminal procedure

B. Legal Question Presented

Whether Thompkins was subject to a violation of his Miranda rights, and "whether Thompkins' counsel provided ineffective assistance by failing to request a limiting instruction regarding how the jury could consider the outcome of Purifoy's trial."

C. Supreme Court's Answer

"[A] suspect who has received and understood the Miranda warnings, and has not invoked his Miranda rights, waives the right to remain silent by making an uncoerced statement to the police. Thompkins did not invoke his right to remain silent and stop the questioning." In addition, Thompkins is not able to demonstrate the failure to request a limiting instruction constitutes ineffective assistance of counsel in his case

II. CASE SUMMARY

A. Background

"The United States Court of Appeals for the Sixth Circuit, in a habeas corpus proceeding challenging a Michigan conviction for first-degree murder and certain other offenses, ruled that there had been two separate constitutional errors in the trial that led to the jury's guilty verdict. First, the Court of Appeals determined that a statement by the accused, relied on at trial by the prosecution, had been elicited in violation of Miranda v. Arizona, 384 U.S. 436 (1966). Second, it found that failure to ask for an instruction relating to testimony from an accomplice was ineffective assistance by defense counsel. Both of these contentions had been rejected in Michigan courts and in the habeas corpus proceedings before the United States District Court. Certiorari was granted to review the decision by the Court of Appeals on both points. The warden of a Michigan correctional facility is the petitioner here, and Van Chester Thompkins, who was convicted, is the respondent."

B. Counsel of Record / ACLU Attorney

ACLU Side (Respondent / Appellee): Elizabeth L. Jacobs argued the cause and filed a brief for appellee.

Opposing Side (Petitioner / Appellant): B. Eric Restuccia, Solicitor General of Michigan, argued the cause for appellant. With him on the briefs were Michael A. Cox, Attorney General, and Brad H. Beaver and William E. Molner, Assistant Attorneys General.

Nicole A. Saharsky argued the cause for the United States as amicus curiae.

III. AMICI CURIAE

ACLU Side (Respondent / Appellee)

Opposing Side (Petitioner / Appellant)

Brief of amici curiae filed on behalf of the National Association of Criminal Defense Lawyers and the American Civil Liberties Union by Jonathan L. Abram, Catherine E. Stetson, Christopher T. Handman, Dominic F. Perella, M. Veronica Yepez, Jonathan D. Hacker, and Steven R. Shapiro. Brief of amici curiae filed on behalf of the United States by Nicole A. Saharsky. Solicitor General Kagan, Assistant Attorney General Breuer, Deputy Solicitor General Dreeben, and Deborah Watson.

Brief of amici curiae filed on behalf of the Criminal Justice Legal Foundation by Kent S. Scheidegger.

Brief of amici curiae filed on behalf of Wayne County, Michigan, by Kym L. Worthy and Timothy A. Baughman.

IV. THE SUPREME COURT'S DECISION

"Under AEDPA, a federal court may not grant a habeas corpus application . . . unless the state court's decision 'was contrary to, or involved an unreasonable application of, clearly established Federal law . . . ,' or 'was based on an unreasonable determination of the facts . . . .' . . .

All concede that the warning given in this case was in full compliance with [Miranda] requirements. The dispute centers on the response—or nonresponse—from the suspect. . . .

Thompkins makes various arguments that his answers to questions from the detectives were inadmissible. He first contends that he 'invoke[d] his privilege' to remain silent by not saying anything for a sufficient period of time . . . .

This argument is unpersuasive. . . .

We next consider whether Thompkins waived his right to remain silent. . . . The . . . waiver must be 'voluntary . . . ,' and 'made with a full awareness of both . . . the right being abandoned and the consequences of the decision to abandon it.' . . .

Thompkins waived his right to remain silent. There is no basis . . . to conclude that he did not understand his rights; and . . . it follows that he chose not to invoke or rely on those rights . . . .

Third, there is no evidence that Thompkins' statement was coerced. . . . Thompkins knowingly and voluntarily made a statement to police, so he waived his right to remain silent. . . .

Thompkins next argues that, even if his answer . . . could constitute a waiver of his right to remain silent, the police were not allowed to question him until they obtained a waiver first. Butler forecloses this argument. . . .

In sum, a suspect who has received and understood the Miranda warnings, and has not invoked his Miranda rights, waives the right to remain silent by making an uncoerced statement to the police. Thompkins did not invoke his right to remain silent and stop the questioning. Understanding his rights in full, he waived his right to remain silent by making a voluntary statement to the police. The police, moreover, were not required to obtain a waiver of Thompkins' right to remain silent before interrogating him. . . .

The second issue in this case is whether Thompkins' counsel provided ineffective assistance . . . .

It seems doubtful that failure to request the instruction about the earlier acquittal or conviction was deficient . . . ; but on the assumption that it was, . . . Thompkins cannot show prejudice. . . .

The judgment of the Court of Appeals is reversed, and the case is remanded with instructions to deny the petition."

V. JUSTICE VOTE

4 Pro ACLU Side vs. 5 Con Opposing Side

ACLU Side (Respondent / Appellee)

1. Stevens, J. – Joined Sotomayor's dissent
2. Breyer, S. – Joined Sotomayor's dissent
3. Ginsburg, R. – Joined Sotomayor's dissent
4. Sotomayor, S. – Wrote dissenting opinion

Opposing Side (Petitioner / Appellant)

1. Kennedy, A. – Wrote majority opinion
2. Alito, S. – Joined majority opinion
3. Thomas, C. – Joined majority opinion
4. Scalia, A. – Joined majority opinion
5. Roberts, J. – Joined majority opinion

VI. A WIN OR LOSS FOR THE ACLU?

The ACLU filed as amicus curiae urging affirmance; the Supreme Court reversed the Court of Appeals' decision by a 5-4 vote, giving the ACLU an apparent loss.

1061. Barber v. Thomas

(Decided June 7, 2010; 560 U.S. 474)

I. ISSUE

A. Issues Discussed

Prison

B. Legal Question Presented

Whether the Federal Bureau of Prisons' calculation method "to award prisoners credit against prison time as a reward for good behavior" is proper.

C. Supreme Court's Answer

"We conclude that the Bureau's method reflects the most natural reading of the statute, and we reject petitioners' legal challenge."

II. CASE SUMMARY

A. Background

"A federal sentencing statute provides:

'[A] prisoner who is serving a term of imprisonment of more than 1 year . . . may receive credit toward the service of the prisoner's sentence, beyond the time served, of up to 54 days at the end of each year of the prisoner's . . . imprisonment, beginning at the end of the first year . . . . [C]redit for the last year or portion of a year of the . . . imprisonment shall be prorated and credited within the last six weeks of the sentence.' . . .

The Bureau of Prisons (BOP) applies this statute using a methodology that petitioners in this case challenge as unlawful. . . .

They say . . . § 3624(b)(1) requires a . . . calculation based upon the length of . . . imprisonment that the sentencing judge imposes, not the length . . . the prisoner actually serves. . . .

The District Court in each of these cases rejected the prisoner's challenge. And in each instance the Court of Appeals affirmed the District Court."

The Supreme Court granted certiorari to review the case.

B. Counsel of Record / ACLU Attorney

ACLU Side (Petitioner / Appellant): Stephen R. Sady argued the cause for appellants. him on the briefs was Lynn Deffebach.

Opposing Side (Respondent / Appellee): Jeffrey B. Wall argued the cause for appellee. With him on the brief were Solicitor General Kagan, Assistant Attorney General Breuer, Deputy Solicitor General Dreeben, and Kevin R. Gingras.

III. AMICI CURIAE

ACLU Side (Petitioner / Appellant)

Brief of amici curiae filed on behalf of the National Association of Criminal Defense Lawyers, the National Association of Federal Defenders, the Federal Public and Community Defenders in the United States, Families Against Mandatory Minimums, the American Civil Liberties Union, and Law Deans and Faculty by Jeffrey T. Green, Peter C. Pfaffenroth, Matthew D. Krueger, Lowell J. Schiller, Steven R. Shapiro, Paul M. Rashkind, Frances H. Pratt, Brett G. Sweitzer, Jonathan Hacker, Mary Price, Amy Fettig, and Peter Goldberger.

Brief of amici curiae filed on behalf of Pierce O'Donnell by George J. Terwilliger III and Daniel B. Levin.

Opposing Side (Respondent / Appellee)

No briefs of amici curiae filed in support of appellee.

IV. THE SUPREME COURT'S DECISION

"Having now considered petitioners' arguments, we conclude that that we must reject their legal challenge. The statute's language and its purpose . . . convince us that the BOP's calculation method is lawful. For one thing, that method tracks the language of § 3624(b). . . .

We are unable similarly to reconcile petitioners' approach with the statute. . . .

The BOP's approach furthers the objective of § 3624. It ties . . . good time credits directly to good behavior during the preceding year of imprisonment. By contrast, petitioners' approach, insofar as it would award up to 54 days per year of time sentenced as opposed to time served, allows a prisoner to earn credit for both the portion of his sentence that he serves and the portion of his sentence that he offsets with earned good time credit. In other words, petitioners argue that the BOP should award good time credit not only for the days a prisoner spends in prison and behaves appropriately, but also for days that he will not spend in prison at all, such as Year 10 in our example. By doing so, it loosens the statute's connection between good behavior and the award of good time and transforms the nature of the exception to the basic sentence-imposed-is-sentence-served rule. And to that extent, it is inconsistent with the statute's basic purpose. . . .

[W]e conclude that the BOP's methodology is lawful. The Ninth Circuit's judgment is affirmed."

V. JUSTICE VOTE

3 Pro ACLU Side vs. 6 Con Opposing Side

ACLU Side (Petitioner / Appellant)

1. Stevens, J. – Joined Kennedy's dissent
2. Kennedy, A. – Wrote dissenting opinion
3. Ginsburg, R. – Joined Kennedy's dissent

Opposing Side (Respondent / Appellee)

1. Breyer, S. – Wrote majority opinion
2. Alito, S. – Joined majority opinion
3. Thomas, C. – Joined majority opinion
4. Scalia, A. – Joined majority opinion
5. Sotomayor, S. – Joined majority opinion
6. Roberts, J. – Joined majority opinion

VI. A WIN OR LOSS FOR THE ACLU?

The ACLU filed as amicus curiae urging reversal of the judgment of the Court of Appeals; the Supreme Court affirmed in a 6-3 vote, giving the ACLU an apparent loss.

1062. Holland v. Florida

(Decided June 14, 2010; 560 U.S. 631)

I. ISSUE

A. Issues Discussed

Criminal procedure

B. Legal Question Presented

What is the appropriate standard for equitable tolling of a missed habeas corpus petition deadline?

C. Supreme Court's Answer

"[A] 'petitioner' is 'entitled to equitable tolling' only if he shows '(1) that he has been pursuing his rights diligently, and (2) that some extraordinary circumstance stood in his way' and prevented timely filing. In this case, the 'extraordinary circumstances' at issue involve an attorney's failure to satisfy professional standards of care."

II. CASE SUMMARY

A. Background

"AEDPA states that '[a] 1-year period of limitation shall apply to an application for a writ of habeas corpus by a person in custody pursuant to the judgment of a State court.' It also says that '[t]he time during which a properly filed application for State post-conviction . . . review' is 'pending shall not be counted' against the 1-year period.

On January 19, 2006, Albert Holland filed a pro se habeas corpus petition . . . . Both Holland . . . and the State of Florida . . . agree that, unless equitably tolled, the statutory limitations period applicable to Holland's petition expired approximately five weeks before the petition was filed. Holland asked the District Court to toll the limitations period for equitable reasons. . . .

[T]he Federal District Court held that the facts did not warrant equitable tolling and that consequently Holland's petition was untimely. The court, noting that Collins had prepared numerous filings on Holland's behalf in the state courts, and suggesting that Holland was a difficult client, intimated, but did not hold, that Collins' professional conduct in the case was at worst merely 'negligent.' But the court rested its holding on an alternative rationale: It wrote that, even if Collins' 'behavior could be characterized as an 'extraordinary circumstance,'' Holland 'did not seek any help from the court system to find out the date [the] mandate issued denying his state habeas petition, nor did he seek aid from 'outside supporters.'' Hence, the court held, Holland did not 'demonstrate' the 'due diligence' necessary to invoke 'equitable tolling.'

On appeal, the Eleventh Circuit agreed . . . that Holland's habeas petition was untimely. . . .

Holland petitioned for certiorari. Because the Court of Appeals' application of the equitable tolling doctrine to instances of professional misconduct conflicts with the approach taken by other Circuits, [the U.S. Supreme Court] granted the petition."

B. Counsel of Record / ACLU Attorney

ACLU Side (Petitioner / Appellant): Todd G. Scher, by appointment of the Court, argued the cause and filed briefs for appellant.

Opposing Side (Respondent / Appellee): Scott D. Makar, Solicitor General of Florida, argued the cause for appellee. With him on the brief were Bill McCollum, Attorney General, Louis F. Hubener, Chief Deputy Solicitor General, Craig D. Feiser, Timothy D. Osterhaus, Courtney Brewer, and Ronald A. Lathan, Deputy Solicitors General, Carolyn M. Snurkowski, Assistant Deputy Attorney General, Candance M. Sabella, Chief Assistant Attorney General, and Sandra S. Jaggard and Lisa-Marie Lerner, Assistant Attorneys General.

III. AMICI CURIAE

ACLU Side (Petitioner / Appellant)

Brief of amici curiae filed on behalf of the American Civil Liberties Union and the American Civil Liberties Union of Florida by Larry Yackle, Steven R. Shapiro, John Holdridge, Brian Stull, Randall C. Marshall, and Maria Kayanan.

Brief of amici curiae filed on behalf of Eleven Legal Historians by William F. Sheehan.

Brief of amici curiae filed on behalf of Legal Ethics Professors et al. by Lawrence J. Fox, pro se, William L. Carr, and Susan D. Reece Martyn, pro se.

Opposing Side (Respondent / Appellee)

Brief of amici curiae filed on behalf of the State of Texas et al. by James C. Ho, Solicitor General of Texas, Greg Abbott, Attorney General, C. Andrew Weber, First Assistant Attorney General, Eric J. R. Nichols, Deputy Attorney General, Edward L. Marshall, Assistant Attorney General, and James P. Sullivan, Assistant Solicitor General, and by the Attorneys General for their respective States as follows: Troy King of Alabama, John W. Suthers of Colorado, Joseph R. Biden III of Delaware, Mark J. Bennett of Hawaii, Lawrence G. Wasden of Idaho, Lisa Madigan of Illinois, Gregory F. Zoeller of Indiana, Tom Miller of Iowa, Steve Six of Kansas, Jack Conway of Kentucky, James D. "Buddy" Caldwell of Louisiana, Chris Koster of Missouri, Jon Bruning of Nebraska, Catherine Cortez Masto of Nevada, Gary K. King of New Mexico, Thomas W. Corbett, Jr., of Pennsylvania, Marty J. Jackley of South Dakota, Robert E. Cooper, Jr., of Tennessee, Mark L. Shurtleff of Utah, Robert M. McKenna of Washington, and Bruce A. Salzburg of Wyoming.

Brief of amici curiae filed on behalf of the Criminal Justice Legal Foundation by Kent S. Scheidegger.

IV. THE SUPREME COURT'S DECISION

"We have not decided whether AEDPA's statutory limitations period may be tolled . . . . Now, . . . we hold that § 2244(d) is subject to equitable tolling in appropriate cases. . . .

We have previously made clear that a 'petitioner' is 'entitled to equitable tolling' only if he shows '(1) that he has been pursuing his rights diligently, and (2) that some extraordinary circumstance stood in his way' and prevented timely filing. In this case, the 'extraordinary circumstances' at issue involve an attorney's failure to satisfy professional standards of care. . . .

We have said that courts of equity 'must be governed by rules and precedents no less than the courts of law.' But we have also made clear that often the 'exercise of a court's equity powers . . . must be made on a case-by-case basis.' . . .

We have previously held that 'a garden variety claim of excusable neglect,' such as a simple 'miscalculation' that leads a lawyer to miss a filing deadline, does not warrant equitable tolling. But the case before us does not involve, and we are not considering, a 'garden variety claim' of attorney negligence. Rather, the facts of this case present far more serious instances of attorney misconduct. And, as we have said, although the circumstances of a case must be 'extraordinary' before equitable tolling can be applied, we hold that such circumstances are not limited to those that satisfy the test that the Court of Appeals used in this case. . . .

The record facts . . . suggest that this case may well be an 'extraordinary' instance in which petitioner's attorney's conduct constituted far more than 'garden variety' or 'excusable neglect.' . . . Here, Collins failed to file Holland's federal petition on time despite Holland's many letters that repeatedly emphasized the importance of his doing so. Collins apparently did not do the research necessary to find out the proper filing date, despite Holland's letters that went so far as to identify the applicable legal rules. Collins failed to inform Holland in a timely manner about the crucial fact that the Florida Supreme Court had decided his case, again despite Holland's many pleas for that information. And Collins failed to communicate with his client over a period of years, despite various pleas from Holland that Collins respond to his letters. . . .

[B]ecause we conclude that the District Court's determination must be set aside, we leave it to the Court of Appeals to determine whether the facts in this record entitle Holland to equitable tolling, or whether further proceedings . . . might indicate that respondent should prevail.

The judgment below is reversed, and the case is remanded . . . ."

V. JUSTICE VOTE

7 Pro ACLU Side vs. 2 Con Opposing Side

ACLU Side (Petitioner / Appellant)

1. Breyer, S. – Wrote majority opinion
2. Alito, S. – Wrote concurring opinion
3. Stevens, J. – Joined majority opinion
4. Kennedy, A. – Joined majority opinion
5. Ginsburg, R. – Joined majority opinion
6. Sotomayor, S. – Joined majority opinion
7. Roberts, J. – Joined majority opinion

Opposing Side (Respondent / Appellee)

1. Scalia, A. – Wrote dissenting opinion
2. Thomas, C. – Joined Scalia's dissent in part

VI. A WIN OR LOSS FOR THE ACLU?

The ACLU filed as amicus curiae urging reversal of the judgment of the Court of Appeals; the Supreme Court reversed in a 7-2 vote, giving the ACLU an apparent win.

1063. City of Ontario v. Quon

(Decided June 17, 2010; 560 U.S. 746)

I. ISSUE

A. Issues Discussed

4th Amendment

B. Legal Question Presented

Whether the "privacy of [text] messages [on an employer owned pager] is protected by the ban on 'unreasonable searches and seizures' found in the Fourth Amendment to the United States Constitution, made applicable to the States by the Due Process Clause of the Fourteenth Amendment."

C. Supreme Court's Answer

"Because the search was reasonable, petitioners did not violate respondents' Fourth Amendment rights . . . ."

II. CASE SUMMARY

A. Background

"Jeff Quon was employed by the Ontario Police Department (OPD). . . .

[T]he City . . . 'Computer Usage, Internet and E-Mail Policy' . . . specified that the City 'reserves the right to monitor . . . network activity . . . . Users should have no expectation of privacy . . . .' Quon signed a statement acknowledging . . . the Computer Policy. . . .

[T]he City made clear . . . that the[y] would treat text messages the same way as . . . e-mails. . . .

Quon exceeded his monthly text message character allotment. . . . Duke suggested that Quon could reimburse . . . rather than . . . audit . . . . Quon wrote a check to the City for the overage. . . .

Quon [then] exceeded his character limit three or four times. . . . Scharf decided to determine . . . if the overages were for personal messages. Scharf told Duke to request transcripts . . . .

Duke . . . discovered that many of the messages . . . were not work related, and some . . . sexually explicit. . . . Scharf referred the matter to OPD's internal affairs division for an investigation . . . .

McMahon used Quon's work schedule to . . . eliminate any messages Quon sent while off duty. . . . Quon sent or received 456 messages during work hours . . . of which . . . 57 were work related . . . . The report concluded that Quon had violated OPD rules. Quon was allegedly disciplined. . . .

Raising claims under . . . the Stored Communications Act (SCA); and California law, Quon filed suit . . . . [claiming] petitioners violated respondents' Fourth Amendment rights and the SCA by obtaining and reviewing the transcript . . . .

The jury concluded that Scharf ordered the audit to determine the efficacy of the character limits. The District Court accordingly held that petitioners did not violate the Fourth Amendment. . . .

The United States Court of Appeals for the Ninth Circuit reversed in part."

The Supreme Court granted certiorari to review the case.

B. Counsel of Record / ACLU Attorney

ACLU Side (Respondent / Appellee): Dieter C. Dammeier argued the cause for appellees. With him on the brief was Michael A. McGill.

Opposing Side (Petitioner / Appellant): Kent L. Richland argued the cause for appellants. With him on the briefs were Kent J. Bullard and Dimitrios C. Rinos.

Deputy Solicitor General Katyal argued the cause for the United States as amicus curiae.

III. AMICI CURIAE

ACLU Side (Respondent / Appellee)

Brief of amici curiae filed on behalf of the Electronic Frontier Foundation, Center for Democracy & Technology, American Civil Liberties Union, and Public Citizen by Andrew J. Pincus, Charles Rothfeld, Dan M. Kahan, Scott L. Shuchart, Gregory A. Beck, and Steven R. Shapiro.

Brief of amici curiae filed on behalf of the American Federation of Labor and Congress of Industrial Organizations by Lynn K. Rhinehart, James B. Coppess, and Laurence Stephen Gold.

Brief of amici curiae filed on behalf of the Electronic Privacy Information Center et al. by Marc Rotenberg.

Brief of amici curiae filed on behalf of the New York Intellectual Property Law Association by Jonathan E. Moskin and Mark J. Abate.

Brief of amici curiae filed on behalf of The Rutherford Institute by John W. Whitehead.

Opposing Side (Petitioner / Appellant)

Brief of amici curiae filed on behalf of the United States by Deputy Solicitor General Katyal, Solicitor General Kagan, Assistant Attorney General Breuer, William M. Jay, Josh Goldfoot, and Vijay Shanker.

Brief of amici curiae filed on behalf of the League of California Cities et al. by Nancy B. Thorington and Joseph M. Quinn.

Brief of amici curiae filed on behalf of Los Angeles Times Communications LLC et al. by Kelli L. Sager and Jeffrey L. Fisher.

Brief of amici curiae filed on behalf of the National League of Cities et al. by Richard Ruda, Robert A. Long, Jr., and Joshua H. Whitman.

Brief of amici curiae filed on behalf of the National School Boards Association et al. by Francisco M. Negrón, Jr., Naomi E. Gittins, Lisa E. Soronen, and Sonja H. Trainor.

IV. THE SUPREME COURT'S DECISION

"[T]he Fourth Amendment's protection extends beyond the sphere of criminal investigations. . . . The Fourth Amendment applies as well when the Government acts . . . as an employer.

The Court discussed this principle in O'Connor. [T]hat '[i] ndividuals do not lose Fourth Amendment rights merely because they work for the government . . . .' . . .

The O'Connor Court did disagree on the proper analytical framework for Fourth Amendment claims against government employers. . . .

The case can be decided by determining that the search was reasonable even assuming Quon had a reasonable expectation of privacy. The two O'Connor approaches—the plurality's and Justice SCALIA's—therefore lead to the same result here. . . .

Even if Quon had a reasonable expectation of privacy in his text messages, petitioners did not necessarily violate the Fourth Amendment by obtaining and reviewing the transcripts. Although as a general matter, warrantless searches 'are per se unreasonable under the Fourth Amendment,' . . . the "special needs" of the workplace justify [an] exception.

Under the approach of the O'Connor plurality, when conducted for a 'noninvestigatory, work-related purpos[e]' or for the 'investigatio[n] of work-related misconduct,' a government employer's warrantless search is reasonable if it is "justified at its inception" and if "the measures adopted are reasonably related to the objectives of the search and not excessively intrusive in light of" the circumstances giving rise to the search. The search here satisfied the standard of the O'Connor plurality and was reasonable under that approach. . . .

Because the search was motivated by a legitimate work-related purpose, and because it was not excessive in scope, the search was reasonable under the approach of the O'Connor plurality. . . . The search was reasonable, and the Court of Appeals erred by holding to the contrary. Petitioners did not violate Quon's Fourth Amendment rights. . . .

Because the search was reasonable, petitioners did not violate respondents' Fourth Amendment rights, and the court below erred by concluding otherwise. The judgment of the Court of Appeals for the Ninth Circuit is reversed, and the case is remanded . . . ."

V. JUSTICE VOTE

0 Pro ACLU Side vs. 9 Con Opposing Side

Opposing Side (Petitioner / Appellant)

1. Kennedy, A. – Wrote majority opinion
2. Alito, S. – Joined majority opinion
3. Stevens, J. – Wrote concurring opinion
4. Thomas, C. – Joined majority opinion
5. Breyer, S. – Joined majority opinion
6. Scalia, A. – Wrote concurring opinion
7. Ginsburg, R. – Joined majority opinion
8. Sotomayor, S. – Joined majority opinion
9. Roberts, J. – Joined majority opinion

VI. A WIN OR LOSS FOR THE ACLU?

The ACLU filed as amicus curiae urging affirmance; the Supreme Court reversed the Court of Appeals' decision by a 9-0 vote, giving the ACLU an apparent loss.

1064. Holder v. Humanitarian Law Project

(Decided June 21, 2010; 561 U.S. 1)

I. ISSUE

A. Issues Discussed

1st Amendment, press, speech, association

B. Legal Question Presented

Whether the material-support "statute is too vague, in violation of the Fifth Amendment, and" whether "it infringes [plaintiffs'] rights to freedom of speech and association, in violation of the First Amendment."

C. Supreme Court's Answer

"We conclude that the material-support statute is constitutional as applied to the particular activities plaintiffs have told us they wish to pursue. We do not, however, address the resolution of more difficult cases that may arise under the statute in the future."

II. CASE SUMMARY

A. Background

"Congress has prohibited . . . 'material support or resources' to certain foreign organizations that engage in terrorist activity. . . . The plaintiffs . . . seek to provide support to two such organizations. Plaintiffs claim that they seek to facilitate only the lawful, nonviolent purposes of those groups, and that applying the material-support law . . . violates the Constitution. . . .

The District Court entered a permanent injunction against applying to plaintiffs the bans on 'personnel' and 'training' support. The Court of Appeals affirmed.

Meanwhile . . . Congress amended the definition of 'material support or resources' to add the term 'expert advice or assistance.' [P]laintiffs filed a second action challenging the constitutionality of that term as applied to them. . . .

[T]he District Court held that the term 'expert advice or assistance' was impermissibly vague. The District Court rejected, however, plaintiffs' First Amendment claims . . . .

The parties cross-appealed. . . . Congress again amended § 2339B . . . .

The en banc [Court of Appeals] affirmed the rejection of plaintiffs' First Amendment claims . . . . In light of IRTPA, however, the en banc court vacated the panel's 2003 judgment with respect to vagueness, and remanded . . . . The Ninth Circuit panel assigned to the cross-appeals in plaintiffs' second action (relating to 'expert advice or assistance') also remanded in light of IRTPA.

The District Court consolidated the two actions on remand. . . . The parties moved for summary judgment, and the District Court granted partial relief to plaintiffs on vagueness grounds.

The Court of Appeals affirmed once more. . . .

The Government petitioned for certiorari, and plaintiffs filed a conditional cross-petition. [The U.S. Supreme Court] granted both petitions."

B. Counsel of Record / ACLU Attorney

ACLU Side (Respondent / Appellee): David D. Cole argued the cause for appellants in No. 09–89 and appellees in No. 08–1498. With him on the briefs were Shayana Kadidal, Jules Lobel, Richard G. Taranto, Carol Sobel, Paul Hoffman, and Visuvanathan Rudrakumaran.

Opposing Side (Petitioner / Appellant): Solicitor General Kagan argued the cause for appellees in No. 09–89 and appellants in No. 08–1498. With her on the briefs were Assistant Attorney General West, Deputy Solicitor General Katyal, Jeffrey B. Wall, and Douglas N. Letter.

III. AMICI CURIAE

ACLU Side (Respondent / Appellee)

Brief of amici curiae filed on behalf of the Carter Center, Christian Peacemaker Teams, Grassroots International, Human Rights Watch, International Crisis Group, The Institute for Conflict Analysis and Resolution at George Mason University, The Kroc Institute for International Peace Studies at Notre Dame University, Operation USA, and Peace Appeal Foundation by Melissa Goodman, Steven R. Shapiro, Jameel Jaffer, and Laurence I. Schwartztol, all of the American Civil Liberties Union Foundation.

Brief of amici curiae filed on behalf of Victims of the McCarthy Era by John A. Freedman, Sara K. Pildis, and Stephen F. Rohde.

Brief of amici curiae filed on behalf of Academic Researchers et al. by Burt Neuborne, Elizabeth Goitein, David Udell, and Sidney S. Rosdeitcher.

Brief of amici curiae filed on behalf of the Constitution Project et al. by David M. Gossett, Sharon Bradford Franklin, and John W. Whitehead.

Opposing Side (Petitioner / Appellant)

Brief of amici curiae filed on behalf of the Anti-Defamation League by David M. Raim, Steven M. Freeman, Michael Lieberman, and Steven C. Sheinberg.

Brief of amici curiae filed on behalf of the Center on the Administration of Criminal Law by Michael Y. Scudder, Jr., and Anthony S. Barkow.

Brief of amici curiae filed on behalf of the Center for Constitutional Jurisprudence et al. by John C. Eastman, Edwin Meese III, and David B. Rivkin, Jr.

Brief of amici curiae filed on behalf of Scholars, Attorneys, and Former Public Officials with Experience in Terrorism-Related Issues by Bradford A. Berenson and Peter Margulies.

Brief of amici curiae filed on behalf of Major General John D. Altenburg, U. S. Army (Ret.) et al. by Daniel J. Popeo and Richard A. Samp.

IV. THE SUPREME COURT'S DECISION

"Plaintiffs challenge § 2339B's prohibition on . . . material support . . . . They raise three constitutional claims. First, plaintiffs claim that § 2339B violates the Due Process Clause of the Fifth Amendment because these four statutory terms are impermissibly vague. Second, plaintiffs claim that § 2339B violates their freedom of speech under the First Amendment. Third, plaintiffs claim that § 2339B violates their First Amendment freedom of association. . . .

Plaintiffs . . . contend that we should interpret the material-support statute . . . to require proof that a defendant intended to further a foreign terrorist organization's illegal activities. . . .

We reject plaintiffs' interpretation of § 2339B because it is inconsistent with the text . . . .

Plaintiffs' interpretation is also untenable in light of the sections immediately surrounding § 2339B, both of which do refer to intent to further terrorist activity. . . .

Finally, plaintiffs . . . argue that a specific intent requirement should apply only when the material-support statute applies to speech. . . . It is therefore clear that plaintiffs are asking us not to interpret § 2339B, but to revise it. . . .

We turn to the question whether the material-support statute, as applied to plaintiffs, is impermissibly vague under the Due Process Clause of the Fifth Amendment. . . .

Under a proper analysis, plaintiffs' claims of vagueness lack merit. . . .

We next consider whether the material-support statute, as applied to plaintiffs, violates the freedom of speech guaranteed by the First Amendment. . . .

We simply hold that, in prohibiting the particular forms of support that plaintiffs seek to provide to foreign terrorist groups, § 2339B does not violate the freedom of speech. . . .

Plaintiffs' final claim is that the material-support statute violates their freedom of association under the First Amendment. . . .

The Court of Appeals correctly rejected this claim because the statute does not penalize mere association with a foreign terrorist organization. . . .

Plaintiffs also argue that the material-support statute burdens their freedom of association because it prevents them from providing support to . . . foreign terrorist organizations, but not to other groups. . . . Congress is not required to ban material support to every group or none at all. . . .

The judgment of the United States Court of Appeals for the Ninth Circuit is affirmed in part and reversed in part, and the cases are remanded . . . ."

V. JUSTICE VOTE

3 Pro ACLU Side vs. 6 Con Opposing Side

ACLU Side (Respondent / Appellee)

1. Breyer, S. – Wrote dissenting opinion
2. Ginsburg, R. – Joined Breyer's dissent
3. Sotomayor, S. – Joined Breyer's dissent

Opposing Side (Petitioner / Appellant)

1. Roberts, J. – Wrote majority opinion
2. Alito, S. – Joined majority opinion
3. Stevens, J. – Joined majority opinion
4. Thomas, C. – Joined majority opinion
5. Scalia, A. – Joined majority opinion
6. Kennedy, A. – Joined majority opinion

VI. A WIN OR LOSS FOR THE ACLU?

The ACLU filed as amicus curiae urging affirmance in part and reversal in part; the Supreme Court affirmed in part and reversed in part the Court of Appeals' decision, in a decision opposed to the ACLU's urgings, by a 6-3 vote, giving the ACLU an apparent loss.

1065. Christian Legal Society v. Martinez

(Decided June 28, 2010; 561 U.S. 661)

I. ISSUE

A. Issues Discussed

1st Amendment, religion

B. Legal Question Presented

"May a public law school [consistent with the First Amendment,] condition its official recognition of a student group—and the attendant use of school funds and facilities—on the organization's agreement to open eligibility for membership and leadership to all students?"

C. Supreme Court's Answer

"[W]e reject [Christian Legal Society]'s First Amendment challenge. Compliance with Hastings' all-comers policy, we conclude, is a reasonable, viewpoint-neutral condition on access to the student-organization forum."

II. CASE SUMMARY

A. Background

"Through its 'Registered Student Organization' (RSO) program, Hastings extends official recognition to student groups. Several benefits attend this school-approved status. . . .

RSOs must . . . comply with Hastings' 'Policies and Regulations Applying to College Activities, Organizations and Students.' . . .

Hastings interprets the Nondiscrimination Policy . . . to mandate acceptance of all comers . . . .

In 2004, CLS became the first student group to [seek an exemption]. . . . CLS chapters must adopt bylaws that . . . require members and officers to sign a 'Statement of Faith' and to conduct their lives in accord with prescribed principles. Among those tenets is the belief that sexual activity should not occur outside of marriage between a man and a woman; CLS thus interprets its bylaws to exclude from affiliation anyone who engages in 'unrepentant homosexual conduct.' CLS also excludes students who hold religious convictions different from . . . the Statement of Faith. . . .

CLS submitted . . . an application for RSO . . . [T]he Law School rejected the application . . . .

CLS formally requested an exemption . . . , but Hastings declined to grant one. . . .

CLS did not obtain RSO status. It did, however, operate independently . . . .

CLS filed suit . . . . Its complaint alleged that Hastings' refusal to grant . . . RSO status violated CLS's First and Fourteenth Amendment rights to free speech, expressive association, and free exercise of religion. The suit sought injunctive and declaratory relief. . . .

[T]he U.S. District Court for the Northern District of California ruled in favor of Hastings. . . .

On appeal, the Ninth Circuit affirmed . . . ."

The Supreme Court granted certiorari to review the case.

B. Counsel of Record / ACLU Attorney

ACLU Side (Respondent / Appellee): Gregory G. Garre argued the cause for appellees. With him on the brief for appellees Hastings College of the Law were Maureen E. Mahoney, J. Scott Ballenger, Lori Alvino McGill, and Ethan P. Schulman. Paul M. Smith, Duane C. Pozza, Shannon P. Minter, and Christopher F. Stoll filed a brief for appellee-intervenor Hastings Outlaw.

Opposing Side (Petitioner / Appellant): Michael W. McConnell argued the cause for appellant. With him on the briefs were Kimberlee Wood Colby, Gregory S. Baylor, Timothy J. Tracey, and M. Casey Mattox.

III. AMICI CURIAE

ACLU Side (Respondent / Appellee)

Brief of amici curiae filed on behalf of the American Civil Liberties Union, American Civil Liberties Union of Northern California, and the National Education Association by Steven R. Shapiro, Matthew A. Coles, James D. Esseks, Rose A. Saxe, Daniel Mach, and Heather L. Weaver.

Brief of amici curiae filed on behalf of the American Bar Association by Carolyn B. Lamm, A. Stephen Hut, Jr., and Paul R. Q. Wolfson.

Brief of amici curiae filed on behalf of the American Council on Education et al. by H. Christopher Bartolomucci and Ada Meloy.

Brief of amici curiae filed on behalf of the American Humanist Association et al. by Robert V. Ritter.

Brief of amici curiae filed on behalf of the American Jewish Committee et al. by Samuel Estreicher, D. Theodore Rave, Jr., Kara H. Stein, Ayesha N. Khan, and David Saperstein.

Brief of amici curiae filed on behalf of the Anti-Defamation League et al. by Robert G. Sugarman, Steven M. Freeman, and Steven C. Sheinberg.

Brief of amici curiae filed on behalf of Associated Students of the University of California, Hastings College of Law, by Simon J. Frankel and Kelly P. Finley.

Brief of amici curiae filed on behalf of the Association of American Law Schools by Sherry F. Colb.

Brief of amici curiae filed on behalf of the Center for Inquiry by Carmine D. Boccuzzi, Jorge G. Tenreiro, Ronald A. Lindsay, and Derek C. Araujo.

Brief of amici curiae filed on behalf of the International Municipal Lawyers Association et al. by Deanne E. Maynard, Seth M. Galanter, Charles W. Thompson, Jr., and John Daniel Reaves.

Brief of amici curiae filed on behalf of the Lambda Legal Defense and Education Fund, Inc., et al. by Clifford M. Sloan, Bradley A. Klein, Jon W. Davidson, Susan L. Sommer, Gary D. Buseck, and Mary L. Bonauto.

Brief of amici curiae filed on behalf of the National LGBT Bar Association et al. by Michael T. Reynolds.

Brief of amici curiae filed on behalf of the National School Boards Association et al. by Lisa S. Blatt, Trenton H. Norris, Francisco M. Negrón, Jr., and Naomi E. Gittins.

Brief of amici curiae filed on behalf of State Universities et al. by Andrew J. Pincus, Charles Rothfeld, and Scott L. Shuchart.

Brief of amici curiae filed on behalf of the Commonwealth of Massachusetts et al. by Martha Coakley, Attorney General of Massachusetts, Irving L. Gornstein, Kathryn E. Tarbert, and Walter Dellinger, and by the Attorneys General for their respective States as follows: Douglas F. Gansler of Maryland and William H. Sorrell of Vermont.

Brief of amici curiae filed on behalf of the Society of American Law Teachers by Robert M. Abrahams and Daniel L. Greenberg.

Brief of amici curiae filed on behalf of the Baptist Joint Committee for Religious Liberty et al. by J. Brent Walker, K. Hollyn Hollman, and James T. Gibson in support of neither party.

Opposing Side (Petitioner / Appellant)

Brief of amici curiae filed on behalf of the State of Michigan et al. by Michael A. Cox, Attorney General of Michigan, B. Eric Restuccia, Solicitor General, Joel D. McGormley, and Laura L. Moody, Assistant Attorney General, and by the Attorneys

General for their respective States as follows: Troy King of Alabama, John W. Suthers of Colorado, Bill McCollum of Florida, Lawrence G. Wasden of Idaho, James D. "Buddy" Caldwell of Louisiana, Jon Bruning of Nebraska, Gary K. King of New Mexico, Thomas W. Corbett, Jr., of Pennsylvania, Henry D. McMaster of South Carolina, Marty J. Jackley of South Dakota, Mark L. Shurtleff of Utah, Kenneth T. Cuccinelli II of Virginia, and Darrell V. McGraw, Jr., of West Virginia.

Brief of amici curiae filed on behalf of Advocates International by Samuel E. Ericsson and Samuel B. Casey.

Brief of amici curiae filed on behalf of Agudath Israel of America by Jeffrey Ira Zuckerman and David Zwiebel.

Brief of amici curiae filed on behalf of the American Center for Law and Justice et al. by Jay Alan Sekulow, Stuart J. Roth, Walter M. Weber, Paul D. Clement, and Adam M. Conrad.

Brief of amici curiae filed on behalf of the American Islamic Congress et al. by Douglas Laycock, Kevin J. Hasson, Eric C. Rassbach, and Hannah C. Smith.

Brief of amici curiae filed on behalf of the Boy Scouts of America by George A. Davidson, Carla A. Kerr, Scott H. Christensen, and David K. Park.

Brief of amici curiae filed on behalf of the Cato Institute by Richard A. Epstein and Ilya Shapiro.

Brief of amici curiae filed on behalf of the Center for Constitutional Jurisprudence by Anthony T. Caso and Edwin Meese III.

Brief of amici curiae filed on behalf of Christian Medical and Dental Associations et al. by Thomas C. Berg, Richard W. Garnett IV, Kelly J. Shackelford, and Hiram S. Sasser III.

Brief of amici curiae filed on behalf of Commissioned II Love Outreach Ministries et al. by Steven W. Fitschen.

Brief of amici curiae filed on behalf of Eugene H. Merrill et al. by Timothy Belz and Carl H. Esbeck.

Brief of amici curiae filed on behalf of the Foundation for Individual Rights in Education et al. by Harvey A. Silverglate and Greg Lukianoff.

Brief of amici curiae filed on behalf of the Justice and Freedom Fund by James L. Hirsen and Deborah J. Dewart.

Brief of amici curiae filed on behalf of Liberty Counsel et al. by Mathew D. Staver, Anita L. Staver, Stephen M. Crampton, and Mary E. McAlister.

Brief of amici curiae filed on behalf of the Pacific Justice Institute et al. by Peter D. Lepiscopo.

Brief of amici curiae filed on behalf of The Rutherford Institute by John W. Whitehead and James J. Knicely.

Brief of amici curiae filed on behalf of the Union of Orthodox Jewish Congregations of America by Nathan J. Diament, Michael S. Lazaroff, and Mark D. Harris.

Brief of amici curiae filed on behalf of the United States Conference of Catholic Bishops by Anthony R. Picarello, Jr., and Jeffrey Hunter Moon.

Brief of amici curiae filed on behalf of the Association of Christian Schools International et al. by Stuart J. Lark.

Brief of amici curiae filed on behalf of the Eagle Forum Education & Legal Defense Fund by Andrew L. Schlafly.

Brief of amici curiae filed on behalf of Gays and Lesbians for Individual Liberty by Thomas G. Hungar.

Brief of amici curiae filed on behalf of Students for Life America et al. by James Bopp, Jr.

IV. THE SUPREME COURT'S DECISION

"In support of the argument that Hastings' all-comers policy treads on its First Amendment rights . . . , CLS draws on two lines of decisions. First, . . . this Court has employed forum analysis to determine when a governmental entity . . . may place limitations on speech. . . .

Second, . . . this Court has rigorously reviewed laws . . . that constrain associational freedom. . . .

CLS would have us engage each line of cases independently, but its expressive-association and free-speech arguments merge: Who speaks on its behalf, CLS reasons, colors what concept is conveyed. [T]hree observations lead us to conclude that our limited-public-forum precedents supply the appropriate framework for assessing both CLS's speech and association rights. . . .

In sum, we are persuaded that our limited-public-forum precedents adequately respect both CLS's speech and expressive-association rights, and fairly balance those rights against Hastings' interests as property owner and educational institution. We turn to the merits of the instant dispute, therefore, with the limited-public-forum decisions as our guide. . . .

[W]e do not write on a blank slate; we have three times before considered clashes between public universities and student groups seeking official recognition or its attendant benefits. . . .

In all three cases, we ruled that student groups had been unconstitutionally singled out because of their points of view. 'Once it has opened a limited [public] forum,' we emphasized, 'the State must respect the lawful boundaries it has itself set.' . . . 'The State may not exclude speech where its distinction is not reasonable in light of the purpose served by the forum, . . . nor may it discriminate against speech on the basis of . . . viewpoint.' . . .

Finding Hastings' open-access condition on RSO status reasonable and viewpoint neutral, we reject CLS's free-speech and expressive-association claims. . . .

On remand, the Ninth Circuit may consider CLS's pretext argument if . . . it is preserved. . . .

[W]e affirm the Court of Appeals' ruling that the all-comers policy is constitutional and remand . . ."

V. JUSTICE VOTE

5 Pro ACLU Side vs. 4 Con Opposing Side

ACLU Side (Respondent / Appellee)

1. Ginsburg, R. – Wrote majority opinion
2. Stevens, J. – Wrote concurring opinion
3. Breyer, S. – Joined majority opinion
4. Kennedy, A. – Wrote concurring opinion
5. Sotomayor, S. – Joined majority opinion

Opposing Side (Petitioner / Appellant)

1. Alito, S. – Wrote dissenting opinion
2. Thomas, C. – Joined Alito's dissent
3. Scalia, A. – Joined Alito's dissent

4. Roberts, J. – Joined Alito's dissent

VI. A WIN OR LOSS FOR THE ACLU?

The ACLU filed as amicus curiae urging affirmance; the Supreme Court affirmed the Court of Appeals' decision by a 5-4 vote, giving the ACLU an apparent win.

1066. National Aeronautics and Space Administration v. Nelson

(Decided January 19, 2011; 562 U.S. 134)

I. ISSUE

A. Issues Discussed

Privacy

B. Legal Question Presented

Whether "the background-check process violates a constitutional right to informational privacy" for Jet Propulsion Laboratory employees serving as government contractors.

C. Supreme Court's Answer

"We assume, without deciding, that the Constitution protects a privacy right of the sort mentioned in Whalen and Nixon. We hold, however, that the challenged portions of the Government's background check do not violate this right in the present case."

II. CASE SUMMARY

A. Background

"The National Aeronautics and Space Administration (NASA) is an independent federal agency charged with planning and conducting the Government's 'space activities.' . . .

One NASA facility, the Jet Propulsion Laboratory (JPL) in Pasadena, California, is staffed exclusively by contract employees. . . .

Twenty-eight JPL employees are respondents here. [N]one has ever been the subject of a Government background investigation. . . . In some instances, individual contracts required background checks . . . , but no blanket policy was in place.

The Government has recently taken steps to eliminate this two-track approach . . . . The Department of Commerce implemented this directive by mandating that contract employees with long-term access to federal facilities complete a standard background check, typically the National Agency Check with Inquiries (NACI). . . .

JPL management informed employees that anyone failing to complete the NACI process by October 2007 would be denied access to JPL and would face termination by Cal Tech. . . .

[R]espondents brought this suit, claiming . . . that the background-check process violates a constitutional right to informational privacy. . . . The District Court denied respondents' motion for a preliminary injunction, but the Ninth Circuit granted an injunction pending appeal, and later reversed . . . .

Over the dissents of five judges, the Ninth Circuit denied rehearing en banc."

The Supreme Court granted certiorari to review the case.

B. Counsel of Record / ACLU Attorney

ACLU Side (Respondent / Appellee): Dan Stormer argued the cause for appellees. With him on the brief were Virginia Keeny, Paul R. Q. Wolfson, and Shirley Cassin Woodward.

Opposing Side (Petitioner / Appellant): Acting Solicitor General Katyal argued the cause for appellants. With him on the briefs were Assistant Attorney General West, Deputy Solicitor General Kneedler, Nicole A. Saharsky, Mark B. Stern, and Benjamin M. Shultz.

III. AMICI CURIAE

ACLU Side (Respondent / Appellee)

Brief of amici curiae filed on behalf of the American Civil Liberties Union et al. by Aden J. Fine, Steven R. Shapiro, Jameel Jaffer, David Blair-Loy, Peter J. Eliasberg, Alan L. Schlosser, Peter Bibring, Michael Risher, and Sean Riordan.

Brief of amici curiae filed on behalf of the American Astronomical Society by Jeffrey F. Pryce and Alice E. Loughran.

Brief of amici curiae filed on behalf of the California Employment Lawyers Association by Marc A. Coleman.

Brief of amici curiae filed on behalf of the Drug Policy Alliance by David T. Goldberg, Sean H. Donahue, and Daniel N. Abrahamson.

Brief of amici curiae filed on behalf of the Electronic Frontier Foundation by Jennifer Stisa Granick.

Brief of amici curiae filed on behalf of the Electronic Privacy Information Center et al. by Marc Rotenberg.

Brief of amici curiae filed on behalf of the Union of Concerned Scientists by Diane J. Curran.

Opposing Side (Petitioner / Appellant)

Brief of amici curiae filed on behalf of the Consumer Data Industry Association et al. by Christopher A. Mohr and Michael R. Klipper.

IV. THE SUPREME COURT'S DECISION

"As noted, respondents contend that portions of SF–85 and Form 42 violate their 'right to informational privacy.' This Court considered a similar claim in Whalen, 429 U.S. 589, which concerned New York's practice of collecting 'the names and addresses of all persons' prescribed dangerous drugs with both 'legitimate and illegitimate uses.' . . .

As was our approach in Whalen, we will assume for present purposes that the Government's challenged inquiries implicate a privacy interest of constitutional significance. We hold, however, that, whatever the scope of this interest, it does not prevent the Government from asking reasonable questions of the sort included on SF–85 and Form 42 in an employment background investigation that is subject to the Privacy Act's safeguards against public disclosure. . . .

Not only are SF–85 and Form 42 reasonable in light of the

Government interests at stake, they are also subject to substantial protections against disclosure to the public. Both Whalen and Nixon recognized that government 'accumulation' of 'personal information' for 'public purposes' may pose a threat to privacy. But both decisions also stated that a 'statutory or regulatory duty to avoid unwarranted disclosures' generally allays these privacy concerns. . . .

Respondents in this case, like the patients in Whalen and former President Nixon, attack only the Government's collection of information on SF-85 and Form 42. And here, no less than in Whalen and Nixon, the information collected is shielded by statute from 'unwarranted disclosur[e].' . . .

Notwithstanding these safeguards, respondents argue that statutory exceptions to the Privacy Act's disclosure bar leave its protections too porous to supply a meaningful check against 'unwarranted disclosures.' . . .

In light of the protection provided by the Privacy Act's nondisclosure requirement, and because the challenged portions of the forms consist of reasonable inquiries in an employment background check, we conclude that the Government's inquiries do not violate a constitutional right to informational privacy. . . .

[T]he judgment of the Court of Appeals is reversed, and the case is remanded . . . ."

V. JUSTICE VOTE

0 Pro ACLU Side vs. 8 Con Opposing Side

Opposing Side (Petitioner / Appellant)

1. Alito, S. – Wrote majority opinion
2. Thomas, C. – Wrote concurring opinion, joined Scalia's concurrence
3. Breyer, S. – Joined majority opinion
4. Scalia, A. – Wrote concurring opinion
5. Kennedy, A. – Joined majority opinion
6. Ginsburg, R. – Joined majority opinion
7. Sotomayor, S. – Joined majority opinion
8. Roberts, J. – Joined majority opinion

Kagan, E. – Took no part in the decision.

VI. A WIN OR LOSS FOR THE ACLU?

The ACLU filed as amicus curiae urging affirmance; the Supreme Court reversed the Court of Appeals' decision by an 8-0 vote, giving the ACLU an apparent loss.

1067. Thompson v. North American Stainless, LP

(Decided January 24, 2011; 562 U.S. 170)

I. ISSUE

A. Issues Discussed

Civil rights, federal

B. Legal Question Presented

"First, did NAS's firing of Thompson constitute unlawful retaliation? And second, if it did, does Title VII grant Thompson a cause of action?"

C. Supreme Court's Answer

"With regard to the first question, we have little difficulty concluding that if the facts alleged by Thompson are true, then NAS's firing of Thompson violated Title VII. . . . [W]e think Thompson well within the zone of interests sought to be protected by Title VII. He is a person aggrieved with standing to sue."

II. CASE SUMMARY

A. Background

"Until 2003, both petitioner Eric Thompson and his fiance, Miriam Regalado, were employees of respondent North American Stainless (NAS). In February 2003, the Equal Employment Opportunity Commission (EEOC) notified NAS that Regalado had filed a charge alleging sex discrimination. Three weeks later, NAS fired Thompson.

Thompson then filed a charge with the EEOC. After conciliation efforts proved unsuccessful, he sued NAS in the United States District Court for the Eastern District of Kentucky under Title VII of the Civil Rights Act of 1964, claiming that NAS had fired him in order to retaliate against Regalado for filing her charge with the EEOC. The District Court granted summary judgment to NAS, concluding that Title VII 'does not permit third party retaliation claims.' After a panel of the Sixth Circuit reversed the District Court, the Sixth Circuit granted rehearing en banc and affirmed by a 10–to–6 vote. The court reasoned that because Thompson did not 'engag[e] in any statutorily protected activity, either on his own behalf or on behalf of Miriam Regalado,' he 'is not included in the class of persons for whom Congress created a retaliation cause of action.'"

The Supreme Court granted certiorari to review the case.

B. Counsel of Record / ACLU Attorney

ACLU Side (Petitioner / Appellant): Eric Schnapper argued the cause for appellant. With him on the briefs were David O'Brien Suetholz, Lisa S. Blatt, and Anthony Franze.

Acting Principal Deputy Solicitor General Kruger argued the cause for the United States as amicus curiae.

Opposing Side (Respondent / Appellee): Leigh Gross Latherow argued the cause for appellee. With her on the brief were William H. Jones, Jr., Gregory L. Monge, and Nathaniel K. Adams.

III. AMICI CURIAE

ACLU Side (Petitioner / Appellant)

Brief of amici curiae filed on behalf of the National Women's Law Center et al., including the American Civil Liberties Union, by Helen Norton, Marcia D. Greenberger, Dina R. Lassow, and Emily J. Martin.

Brief of amici curiae filed on behalf of the National Employment Lawyers Association et al. by Michael L. Foreman, Rebecca M. Hamburg, Jeffrey R. White, Daniel B. Kohrman, Linda D. Kilb,

Sarah C. Crawford, and Claudia Center.

Brief of amici curiae filed on behalf of the United States by Acting Principal Deputy Solicitor General Kruger, Acting Solicitor General Katyal, Assistant Attorney General Perez, Deputy Assistant Attorney General Bagenstos, Joseph R. Palmore, P. David Lopez, Carolyn L. Wheeler, and Gail S. Coleman.

Opposing Side (Respondent / Appellee)

Brief of amici curiae filed on behalf of the Chamber of Commerce of the United States of America by Patricia A. Millett, Robin S. Conrad, and Shane B. Kawka.

Brief of amici curiae filed on behalf of the Equal Employment Advisory Council et al. by Rae T. Vann, Quentin Riegel, Karen R. Harned, and Elizabeth Milito.

IV. THE SUPREME COURT'S DECISION

"Title VII provides that '[i]t shall be an unlawful employment practice for an employer to discriminate against any of his employees . . . because he has made a charge' under Title VII. . . .

It is undisputed that Regalado's filing of a charge with the EEOC was protected conduct under Title VII. In the procedural posture of this case, we are also required to assume that NAS fired Thompson in order to retaliate against Regalado for filing a charge of discrimination. This case therefore presents two questions: First, did NAS's firing of Thompson constitute unlawful retaliation? And second, if it did, does Title VII grant Thompson a cause of action? . . .

With regard to the first question, we have little difficulty concluding that if the facts alleged by Thompson are true, then NAS's firing of Thompson violated Title VII. . . .

We think it obvious that a reasonable worker might be dissuaded from engaging in protected activity if she knew that her fiance would be fired. . . .

Although we acknowledge the force of this point, we do not think it justifies a categorical rule that third-party reprisals do not violate Title VII. . . .

The more difficult question in this case is whether Thompson may sue NAS for its alleged violation of Title VII. The statute provides that 'a civil action may be brought . . . by the person claiming to be aggrieved.' . . . The provision unquestionably permits a person 'claiming to be aggrieved' to bring 'a civil action.' It is arguable that the aggrievement referred to is nothing more than the minimal Article III standing, which consists of injury in fact caused by the defendant and remediable by the court. But Thompson's claim undoubtedly meets those requirements, so . . . he may sue. . . .

[T]here is a common usage of the term 'person aggrieved' that avoids the extremity of equating it with Article III and yet is fully consistent with our application of the term in Trafficante. . . .

Applying that test here, we conclude that Thompson falls within the zone of interests protected by Title VII. Thompson was an employee of NAS, and the purpose of Title VII is to protect employees from their employers' unlawful actions. Moreover, . . . Thompson is not an accidental victim of the retaliation—collateral damage, so to speak, of the employer's unlawful act. To the contrary, injuring him was the employer's intended means of harming Regalado. Hurting him was the unlawful act by which the employer punished her. In those circumstances, we think Thompson well within the zone of interests sought to be protected by Title VII. He is a person aggrieved with standing to sue. . . .

The judgment of the Sixth Circuit is reversed, and the case is remanded . . . ."

V. JUSTICE VOTE

8 Pro ACLU Side vs. 0 Con Opposing Side

ACLU Side (Petitioner / Appellant)

1. Scalia, A. – Wrote majority opinion
2. Alito, S. – Joined majority opinion
3. Thomas, C. – Joined majority opinion
4. Breyer, S. – Joined Ginsburg's concurrence
5. Kennedy, A. – Joined majority opinion
6. Ginsburg, R. – Wrote concurring opinion
7. Sotomayor, S. – Joined majority opinion
8. Roberts, J. – Joined majority opinion

Kagan, E. – Took no part in the decision.

VI. A WIN OR LOSS FOR THE ACLU?

The ACLU filed as amicus curiae urging reversal of the judgment of the Court of Appeals; the Supreme Court reversed in an 8-0 vote, giving the ACLU an apparent win.

1068. FCC v. AT&T Inc.

(Decided March 1, 2011; 562 U.S. 397)

I. ISSUE

A. Issues Discussed

Privacy

B. Legal Question Presented

"The Freedom of Information Act requires federal agencies to make records and documents publicly available upon request, unless they fall within one of several statutory exemptions. One of those exemptions covers law enforcement records, the disclosure of which 'could reasonably be expected to constitute an unwarranted invasion of personal privacy.' 5 U.S.C. § 552(b)(7)(C). The question presented is whether corporations have 'personal privacy' for the purposes of this exemption."

C. Supreme Court's Answer

"We reject the argument that because 'person' is defined for purposes of FOIA to include a corporation, the phrase 'personal privacy' in Exemption 7(C) reaches corporations as well. The protection in FOIA against disclosure of law enforcement information on the ground that it would constitute an unwarranted invasion of personal privacy does not extend to corporations."

II. CASE SUMMARY

A. Background

"The Freedom of Information Act request at issue in this case relates to an investigation of respondent AT & T Inc., conducted by the Federal Communications Commission. AT & T participated in an FCC-administered program—the E-Rate (or Education-Rate) program—that was created to enhance access for schools and libraries to advanced telecommunications and information services. In August 2004, AT & T voluntarily reported to the FCC that it might have overcharged the Government for services it provided as part of the program.

The FCC's Enforcement Bureau launched an investigation. As part of that investigation, AT & T provided the Bureau various documents . . . . The FCC and AT & T resolved the matter in December 2004 through a consent decree . . . .

Several months later, CompTel—'a trade association representing some of AT & T's competitors'—submitted a FOIA request seeking "[a]ll pleadings and correspondence" in the Bureau's file on the AT & T investigation. AT & T opposed CompTel's request . . . .

The Bureau concluded that some of the information AT & T had provided . . . should be protected from disclosure under FOIA Exemption 4 . . . . The Bureau concluded that 'individuals identified in [AT & T's] submissions' have 'privacy rights' . . . . The Bureau did not, however, apply that exemption to the corporation itself . . . .

On review the FCC agreed with the Bureau. . . .

AT & T sought review in the Court of Appeals for the Third Circuit, and that court rejected the FCC's reasoning. . . . The court accordingly ruled 'that FOIA's text unambiguously indicates that a corporation may have a 'personal privacy' interest . . . .'"

The Supreme Court granted certiorari to review the case.

B. Counsel of Record / ACLU Attorney

ACLU Side (Petitioner / Appellant): Anthony A. Yang argued the cause for appellants. With him on the briefs were Acting Solicitor General Katyal, Assistant Attorney General West, Deputy Solicitor General Kneedler, Leonard Schaitman, Henry C. Whitaker, Austin C. Schlick, Daniel M. Armstrong, and Michael A. Krasnow. Mary C. Albert, Adina H. Rosenbaum, and Michael H. Page filed briefs for appellee CompTel in support of appellants.

Opposing Side (Respondent / Appellee): Geoffrey M. Klineberg argued the cause for appellee AT&T Inc. With him on the brief was Brendan J. Crimmins.

III. AMICI CURIAE

ACLU Side (Petitioner / Appellant)

Brief of amici curiae filed on behalf of Citizens for Responsibility and Ethics in Washington, The Electronic Frontier Foundation, The American Civil Liberties Union, The American Library Association, The Association of Research Libraries, The National Security Archive, and OpenTheGovernment.org by Anne L. Weismann and David L. Sobel.

Brief of amici curiae filed on behalf of the Collaboration on Government Secrecy by Daniel J. Metcalfe.

Brief of amici curiae filed on behalf of the Constitutional Accountability Center by Douglas T. Kendall, Elizabeth B. Wydra, and David H. Gans.

Brief of amici curiae filed on behalf of Free Press by Aparna Sridhar and Coriell S. Wright.

Brief of amici curiae filed on behalf of the Project on Government Oversight et al. by Neal Goldfarb, Sandra Chance, and Cornish Hitchcock.

Brief of amici curiae filed on behalf of the Reporters Committee for Freedom of the Press et al. by Lucy A. Dalglish, Kevin M. Goldberg, Jonathan Bloom, David Ardia, David M. Giles, Peter Scheer, Mickey H. Osterreicher, René P. Milam, George Freeman, Bruce W. Sanford, Bruce D. Brown, Laurie A. Babinski, David S. Bralow, and Eric N. Lieberman.

Brief of amici curiae filed on behalf of the Electronic Privacy Information Center et al. by Marc Rotenberg.

Opposing Side (Respondent / Appellee)

Brief of amici curiae filed on behalf of the Business Roundtable by Alan Charles Raul and Gordon D. Todd.

Brief of amici curiae filed on behalf of the Chamber of Commerce of the United States of America by Patricia A. Millett and Robin S. Conrad.

Brief of amici curiae filed on behalf of the National Association of Manufacturers by Ethan P. Schulman, Clifton S. Elgarten, Jennifer N. Waters, and Quentin Riegel.

IV. THE SUPREME COURT'S DECISION

"Like the Court of Appeals below, AT & T relies on the argument that the word 'personal' in Exemption 7(C) incorporates the statutory definition of the word 'person.' . . .

We disagree. . . .

AT & T concludes that the FCC has simply failed to demonstrate that the phrase 'personal privacy' 'necessarily excludes the privacy of corporations.' But construing statutory language is not merely an exercise in ascertaining 'the outer limits of [a word's] definitional possibilities.' AT & T has given us no sound reason in the statutory text or context to disregard the ordinary meaning of the phrase 'personal privacy.' . . .

The meaning of "personal privacy" in Exemption 7(C) is further clarified by the rest of the statute. Congress enacted Exemption 7(C) against the backdrop of pre-existing FOIA exemptions, and the purpose and scope of Exemption 7(C) becomes even more apparent when viewed in this context. . . .

So at the time Congress enacted Exemption 7(C), it had in place an exemption that plainly covered a corporation's commercial and financial information, and another that we have described as relating to 'individuals.' The language of Exemption 7(C) tracks the latter.

The Government has long interpreted . . . 'personal privacy' in Exemption 7(C) accordingly. . . .

We reject the argument that because 'person' is defined for purposes of FOIA to include a corporation, the phrase 'personal privacy' in Exemption 7(C) reaches corporations as well. The protection in FOIA against disclosure of law enforcement information on the ground that it would constitute an unwarranted invasion of personal privacy does not extend to corporations. We trust that AT & T will not take it personally.

The judgment of the Court of Appeals is reversed."

V. JUSTICE VOTE

8 Pro ACLU Side vs. 0 Con Opposing Side

ACLU Side (Petitioner / Appellant)

1. Roberts, J. – Wrote majority opinion
2. Alito, S. – Joined majority opinion
3. Thomas, C. – Joined majority opinion
4. Breyer, S. – Joined majority opinion
5. Scalia, A. – Joined majority opinion
6. Kennedy, A. – Joined majority opinion
7. Ginsburg, R. – Joined majority opinion
8. Sotomayor, S. – Joined majority opinion

Kagan, E. – Took no part in the decision.

VI. A WIN OR LOSS FOR THE ACLU?

The ACLU filed as amicus curiae urging reversal of the judgment of the Court of Appeals; the Supreme Court reversed in an 8-0 vote, giving the ACLU an apparent win.

1069. Snyder v. Phelps

(Decided March 2, 2011; 562 U.S. 443)

I. ISSUE

A. Issues Discussed

1st Amendment, press, speech, association

B. Legal Question Presented

"A jury held members of the Westboro Baptist Church liable for millions of dollars in damages for picketing near a soldier's funeral service. The picket signs reflected the church's view that the United States is overly tolerant of sin and that God kills American soldiers as punishment. The question presented is whether the First Amendment shields the church members from tort liability for their speech in this case."

C. Supreme Court's Answer

"Given that Westboro's speech was at a public place on a matter of public concern, that speech is entitled to 'special protection' under the First Amendment. . . .For all these reasons, the jury verdict imposing tort liability on Westboro for intentional infliction of emotional distress must be set aside."

II. CASE SUMMARY

A. Background

"Fred Phelps founded the Westboro Baptist Church . . . . The church's congregation believes that God hates and punishes the United States for its tolerance of homosexuality . . . . The church frequently communicates its views by picketing, often at military funerals. . . .

Marine Lance Corporal Matthew Snyder was killed in Iraq in the line of duty. . . .

On the day of the memorial service, the Westboro congregation members picketed on public land adjacent to public streets near the Maryland State House, the United States Naval Academy, and Matthew Snyder's funeral. . . .

The church had notified the authorities in advance of its intent to picket at the time of the funeral, and the picketers complied with police instructions . . . .

Snyder alleged five state tort law claims: defamation, publicity given to private life, intentional infliction of emotional distress, intrusion upon seclusion, and civil conspiracy. . . .

The District Court awarded Westboro summary judgment on Snyder's claims for defamation and publicity . . . . A trial was held on the remaining claims. . . .

A jury found for Snyder on the intentional infliction of emotional distress, intrusion upon seclusion, and civil conspiracy claims, and held Westboro liable for $2.9 million in compensatory damages and $8 million in punitive damages. Westboro filed several post-trial motions . . . . The District Court remitted the punitive damages award to $2.1 million, but left the jury verdict otherwise intact.

In the Court of Appeals, Westboro's primary argument was that the church was entitled to judgment as a matter of law . . . . The Court of Appeals agreed."

The Supreme Court granted certiorari to review the case.

B. Counsel of Record / ACLU Attorney

ACLU Side (Respondent / Appellee): Margie J. Phelps argued the cause and filed a brief for appellees.

Opposing Side (Petitioner / Appellant): Sean E. Summers argued the cause for appellant. With him on the briefs were Alex E. Snyder and Craig T. Trebilcock.

III. AMICI CURIAE

ACLU Side (Respondent / Appellee)

Brief of amici curiae filed on behalf of the American Civil Liberties Union and the American Civil Liberties Union of Maryland by Joel Kleinman, David Schur, David Rocah, Steven R. Shapiro, and Deborah A. Jeon.

Brief of amici curiae filed on behalf of the Foundation for Individual Rights in Education et al. by Greg Lukianoff and Eugene Volokh, pro se.

Brief of amici curiae filed on behalf of the Reporters Committee for Freedom of the Press et al. by Robert CornRevere, John R. Eastburg, Thomas R. Burke, Bruce E. H. Johnson, Lucy A. Dalglish, Gregg P. Leslie, Kevin M. Goldberg, Jonathan Bloom, David Ardia, David M. Giles, Peter Scheer, Eve Burton, Jonathan R. Donnellan, Mickey H. Osterreicher, George Freeman, René P. Milam, Barbara L. Camens, Bruce W. Sanford, Bruce D. Brown, Laurie A. Babinski, and David S. Bralow.

Brief of amici curiae filed on behalf of the Rutherford Institute by John W. Whitehead and James J. Knicely.

Brief of amici curiae filed on behalf of the Thomas Jefferson Center for the Protection of Free Expression et al. by J. Joshua

Wheeler, Clay Calvert, Joan E. Bertin, and Robert D. Richards.

Brief of amici curiae filed on behalf of Liberty Counsel by Mathew D. Staver, Anita L. Staver, Stephen M. Crampton, and Mary E. McAlister.

Brief of amici curiae filed on behalf of Scholars of First Amendment Law by Charles F. Smith.

Brief of amici curiae filed on behalf of the Anti-Defamation League by Leonard M. Niehoff, Martin E. Karlinsky, Mark S. Finkelstein, Steven M. Freeman, and Steven C. Sheinberg in support of neither party.

Opposing Side (Petitioner / Appellant)

Brief of amici curiae filed on behalf of the State of Kansas et al. by Steve Six, Attorney General of Kansas, Stephen R. McAllister, Solicitor General, and Kristafer R. Ailslieger, Deputy Solicitor General, and by the Attorneys General for their respective jurisdictions as follows: Troy King of Alabama, Daniel S. Sullivan of Alaska, Terry Goddard of Arizona, Dustin McDaniel of Arkansas, Edmund G. Brown, Jr., of California, John W. Suthers of Colorado, Richard Blumenthal of Connecticut, Joseph R. Biden III of Delaware, Peter J. Nickles of the District of Columbia, Bill McCollum of Florida, Thurbert E. Baker of Georgia, Mark J. Bennett of Hawaii, Lawrence G. Wasden of Idaho, Lisa Madigan of Illinois, Gregory F. Zoeller of Indiana, Tom Miller of Iowa, Jack Conway of Kentucky, James D. "Buddy" Caldwell of Louisiana, Douglas F. Gansler of Maryland, Martha Coakley of Massachusetts, Michael A. Cox of Michigan, Lori Swanson of Minnesota, Jim Hood of Mississippi, Chris Koster of Missouri, Steve Bullock of Montana, Jon Bruning of Nebraska, Catherine Cortez Masto of Nevada, Michael A. Delaney of New Hampshire, Paula T. Dow of New Jersey, Gary K. King of New Mexico, Andrew Cuomo of New York, Roy A. Cooper of North Carolina, Wayne Stenehjem of North Dakota, Richard Cordray of Ohio, W. A. Drew Edmondson of Oklahoma, John R. Kroger of Oregon, Thomas W. Corbett, Jr., of Pennsylvania, Patrick C. Lynch of Rhode Island, Henry D. McMaster of South Carolina, Marty J. Jackley of South Dakota, Robert E. Cooper, Jr., of Tennessee, Greg Abbott of Texas, Mark L. Shurtleff of Utah, William H. Sorrell of Vermont, Robert M. McKenna of Washington, Darrell V. McGraw, Jr., of West Virginia, J. B. Van Hollen of Wisconsin, and Bruce A. Salzburg of Wyoming.

Brief of amici curiae filed on behalf of the American Legion by Gene C. Schaerr, Steffen N. Johnson, Linda T. Coberly, and Phil Onderdonk.

Brief of amici curiae filed on behalf of the Center for Constitutional Jurisprudence by David L. Llewellyn, Jr.

Brief of amici curiae filed on behalf of the Veterans of Foreign Wars of the United States by Timothy J. Nieman and Lawrence M. Maher.

Brief of amici curiae filed on behalf of Senator Harry Reid et al. by Walter Dellinger and Jonathan D. Hacker.

Brief of amici curiae filed on behalf of the American Center for Law and Justice by Jay Alan Sekulow, Stuart J. Roth, Colby M. May, and Walter M. Weber.

Brief of amici curiae filed on behalf of John Marshall Law School Veterans Legal Support Center & Clinic et al. by Michael Seng.

IV. THE SUPREME COURT'S DECISION

"Whether the First Amendment prohibits holding Westboro liable for its speech in this case turns largely on whether that speech is of public or private concern, as determined by all the circumstances of the case. . . .

The 'content' of Westboro's signs plainly relates to broad issues of interest to society at large, rather than matters of 'purely private concern.' . . .

Given that Westboro's speech was at a public place on a matter of public concern, that speech is entitled to 'special protection' under the First Amendment. Such speech cannot be restricted simply because it is upsetting or arouses contempt. . . .

For all these reasons, the jury verdict imposing tort liability on Westboro for intentional infliction of emotional distress must be set aside. . . .

The jury also found Westboro liable for the state law torts of intrusion upon seclusion and civil conspiracy. . . .

Snyder argues that even assuming Westboro's speech is entitled to First Amendment protection generally, the church is not immunized from liability for intrusion upon seclusion because Snyder was a member of a captive audience at his son's funeral. We do not agree. . . .

Here, Westboro stayed well away from the memorial service. [T]here is no indication that the picketing in any way interfered with the funeral service itself. . . .

Because we find that the First Amendment bars Snyder from recovery for intentional infliction of emotional distress or intrusion upon seclusion . . . we must likewise hold that Snyder cannot recover for civil conspiracy based on those torts. . . .

Our holding today is narrow. We are required in First Amendment cases to carefully review the record, and the reach of our opinion here is limited by the particular facts before us. . . .

Westboro believes that America is morally flawed; many Americans might feel the same about Westboro. Westboro's funeral picketing is certainly hurtful and its contribution to public discourse may be negligible. But Westboro addressed matters of public import on public property, in a peaceful manner, in full compliance with the guidance of local officials. . . .

Speech is powerful. It can stir people to action, move them to tears of both joy and sorrow, and—as it did here—inflict great pain. On the facts before us, we cannot react to that pain by punishing the speaker. . . .

The judgment of the United States Court of Appeals for the Fourth Circuit is affirmed."

V. JUSTICE VOTE

8 Pro ACLU Side vs. 1 Con Opposing Side

ACLU Side (Respondent / Appellee)

1. Roberts, J. – Wrote majority opinion
2. Kagan, E. – Joined majority opinion
3. Thomas, C. – Joined majority opinion
4. Breyer, S. – Wrote concurring opinion
5. Scalia, A. – Joined majority opinion
6. Kennedy, A. – Joined majority opinion
7. Ginsburg, R. – Joined majority opinion

8. Sotomayor, S. – Joined majority opinion

Opposing Side (Petitioner / Appellant)

1. Alito, S. – Wrote dissenting opinion

VI. A WIN OR LOSS FOR THE ACLU?

The ACLU filed as amicus curiae urging affirmance; the Supreme Court affirmed the Court of Appeals' decision by an 8-1 vote, giving the ACLU an apparent win.

1070. Milner v. Dep't of Navy

(Decided March 7, 2011; 562 U.S. 562)

I. ISSUE

A. Issues Discussed

Regulation, miltary

B. Legal Question Presented

What is "the scope of Exemption 2, which protects from disclosure material that is 'related solely to the internal personnel rules and practices of an agency.'"

C. Supreme Court's Answer

"Exemption 2, consistent with the plain meaning of the term 'personnel rules and practices,' encompasses only records relating to issues of employee relations and human resources. The explosives maps and data requested here do not qualify for withholding under that exemption."

II. CASE SUMMARY

A. Background

"Congress enacted FOIA to overhaul the public-disclosure section of the Administrative Procedure Act (APA), 5 U.S.C. § 1002 (1964 ed.). . . .

At issue here is Exemption 2, which shields from compelled disclosure documents 'related solely to the internal personnel rules and practices of an agency.' . . .

The FOIA request at issue here arises from the Navy's operations at Naval Magazine Indian Island, a base in Puget Sound, Washington. The Navy keeps weapons, ammunition, and explosives on the island. To aid in the storage and transport of these munitions, the Navy uses data known as Explosive Safety Quantity Distance (ESQD) information. ESQD information prescribes 'minimum separation distances' for explosives and helps the Navy design and construct storage facilities to prevent chain reactions in case of detonation. . . .

In 2003 and 2004, petitioner Glen Milner, a Puget Sound resident, submitted FOIA requests for all ESQD information relating to Indian Island. The Navy refused to release the data, stating that disclosure would threaten the security of the base and surrounding community. In support of its decision to withhold the records, the Navy invoked Exemption 2.

The District Court granted summary judgment to the Navy, and the Court of Appeals affirmed . . . ."

The Supreme Court granted certiorari to review the case.

B. Counsel of Record / ACLU Attorney

ACLU Side (Petitioner / Appellant): David S. Mann argued the cause for appellant. With him on the briefs were Michael W. Gendler and Brendan W. Donckers.

Opposing Side (Respondent / Appellee): Anthony A. Yang argued the cause for appellee. With him on the brief were Acting Solicitor General Katyal, Assistant Attorney General West, Deputy Solicitor General Kneedler, Leonard Schaitman, Howard S. Scher, Peter A. Winn, J. Page Turney, and Judy A. Conlow.

III. AMICI CURIAE

ACLU Side (Petitioner / Appellant)

Brief of amici curiae filed on behalf of Public Citizen, the American Civil Liberties Union, the American Civil Liberties Union of Washington, Citizens for Responsibility and Ethics in Washington, the Electronic Frontier Foundation, the National Security Archive, and OpenTheGovernment.org by Adina H. Rosenbaum and Allison M. Zieve.

Brief of amici curiae filed on behalf of Allied Daily Newspapers of Washington et al. by Katherine A. George.

Brief of amici curiae filed on behalf of the Reporters Committee for Freedom of the Press et al. by Lucy A. Dalglish, Kevin M. Goldberg, David Ardia, David M. Giles, Peter Scheer, Charles D. Tobin, Mickey H. Osterreicher, René P. Milam, Barbara L. Camens, Bruce W. Sanford, Bruce D. Brown, Laurie A. Babinski, David S. Bralow, and Eric N. Lieberman.

Opposing Side (Respondent / Appellee)

No briefs of amici curiae were filed in support of appellee.

IV. THE SUPREME COURT'S DECISION

"Our consideration of Exemption 2's scope starts with its text. . . . Judicial decisions since FOIA's enactment have analyzed and reanalyzed the meaning of the exemption. But . . . little attention has . . . 'related solely to the internal personnel rules and practices of an agency.'

The key word . . . is 'personnel.' When used as an adjective, as it is here to modify 'rules and practices,' that term refers to human resources matters. . . .

Exemption 2 . . . does not reach the ESQD information at issue here. . . . By no stretch of imagination do they relate to 'personnel rules and practices,' as that term is most naturally understood. They concern the physical rules governing explosives, not the workplace rules governing sailors . . . . The Navy therefore may not use Exemption 2 . . . to prevent disclosure . . . .

The Government offers two alternative readings of Exemption 2 to support withholding the ESQD information. We cannot square either with the statute. . . .

Although we cannot interpret Exemption 2 as the Government proposes, we recognize the strength of the Navy's interest in protecting the ESQD data and maps and other similar information. . . .

We also note, however, that the Government has other tools at hand to shield national security information and other sensitive materials. Most notably, Exemption 1 of FOIA prevents access to classified documents. . . . The Government generally may classify material even after receiving a FOIA request . . . . Exemption 3 . . . applies to records that any other statute exempts from disclosure, thus offering Congress an established, streamlined method to authorize the withholding of specific records that FOIA would not otherwise protect. And Exemption 7 . . . protects 'information compiled for law enforcement purposes' that meets one of six criteria, including if its release 'could reasonably be expected to endanger the life or physical safety of any individual.' . . .

If these or other exemptions do not cover records whose release would threaten the Nation's vital interests, the Government may of course seek relief from Congress. All we hold today is that Congress has not enacted the FOIA exemption the Government desires. We leave to Congress, as is appropriate, the question whether it should do so. . . .

Exemption 2, consistent with the plain meaning of the term 'personnel rules and practices,' encompasses only records relating to issues of employee relations and human resources. The explosives maps and data requested here do not qualify for withholding under that exemption. We therefore reverse the judgment of the Court of Appeals and remand the case . . . ."

V. JUSTICE VOTE

8 Pro ACLU Side vs. 1 Con Opposing Side

ACLU Side (Petitioner / Appellant)

1. Kagan, E. – Wrote majority opinion
2. Alito, S. – Wrote concurring opinion
3. Thomas, C. – Joined majority opinion
4. Scalia, A. – Joined majority opinion
5. Kennedy, A. – Joined majority opinion
6. Ginsburg, R. – Joined majority opinion
7. Sotomayor, S. – Joined majority opinion
8. Roberts, J. – Joined majority opinion

Opposing Side (Respondent / Appellee)

1. Breyer, S. – Wrote dissenting opinion

VI. A WIN OR LOSS FOR THE ACLU?

The ACLU filed as amicus curiae urging reversal of the judgment of the Court of Appeals; the Supreme Court reversed in an 8-1 vote, giving the ACLU an apparent win.

1071. Connick v. Thompson

(Decided March 29, 2011; 563 U.S. 51)

I. ISSUE

A. Issues Discussed

Criminal procedure

B. Legal Question Presented

"[W]hether a district attorney's office may be held liable under § 1983 for failure to train based on a single Brady violation."

C. Supreme Court's Answer

"We hold that it cannot."

II. CASE SUMMARY

A. Background

"The Orleans Parish District Attorney's Office now concedes that, in prosecuting respondent John Thompson for attempted armed robbery, prosecutors failed to disclose evidence that should have been turned over to the defense under Brady v. Maryland, 373 U.S. 83 (1963). Thompson was convicted. Because of that conviction Thompson elected not to testify in his own defense in his later trial for murder, and he was again convicted. Thompson spent 18 years in prison, including 14 years on death row. One month before Thompson's scheduled execution, his investigator discovered the undisclosed evidence from his armed robbery trial. The reviewing court determined that the evidence was exculpatory, and both of Thompson's convictions were vacated.

After his release from prison, Thompson sued petitioner Harry Connick, in his official capacity as the Orleans Parish district attorney, for damages under Rev. Stat. § 1979, 42 U.S.C. § 1983. Thompson alleged that Connick had failed to train his prosecutors adequately about their duty to produce exculpatory evidence and that the lack of training had caused the nondisclosure in Thompson's robbery case. The jury awarded Thompson $14 million, and the Court of Appeals for the Fifth Circuit affirmed by an evenly divided en banc court."

The Supreme Court granted certiorari to review the case.

B. Counsel of Record / ACLU Attorney

ACLU Side (Respondent / Appellee): J. Gordon Cooney, Jr., argued the cause for appellee. With him on the brief were Michael L. Banks, R. Ted Cruz, and Allyson N. Ho.

Opposing Side (Petitioner / Appellant): Stuart Kyle Duncan, Appellate Chief, Louisiana Attorney General's Office, argued the cause for appellants. With him on the briefs were James D. "Buddy" Caldwell, Attorney General, Ross W. Bergethon and Robert Abendroth, Assistant Attorneys General, Graymond F. Martin, and Donna R. Andrieu.

III. AMICI CURIAE

ACLU Side (Respondent / Appellee)

Brief of amici curiae filed on behalf of the American Civil Liberties Union, the American Civil Liberties Union of Louisiana, and the Southern Poverty Law Center by Lisa S. Blatt, John A. Freedman, Joshua P. Wilson, Steven R. Shapiro, Joseph M. Meadows, Eric J. McKeown, Mary Bauer, and Katie Schwartzmann.

Brief of amici curiae filed on behalf of the Center on the Administration of Criminal Law, New York University School of Law, et al. by Martin J. Siegel, Anthony S. Barkow, and David B. Edwards.

Brief of amici curiae filed on behalf of Former Federal Civil Rights Officials et al. by Paul D. Clement, Jeffrey S. Bucholtz, Adam Conrad, Kelly Shackelford, Hiram S. Sasser III, and Pamela S. Karlan.

Brief of amici curiae filed on behalf of the Innocence Network by Peter D. Isakoff, Keith A. Findley, Peter J. Neufeld, and Barry Scheck.

Brief of amici curiae filed on behalf of the National Association of Criminal Defense Lawyers by Joel B. Rudin and Joshua L. Dratel.

Brief of amici curiae filed on behalf of the Alliance Defense Fund et al. by Glen Lavy, Thomas Marcelle, and Ilya Shapiro.

Opposing Side (Petitioner / Appellant)

Brief of amici curiae filed on behalf of the National District Attorneys Association et al. by Edward C. Dawson and Richard B. Farrer.

Brief of amici curiae filed on behalf of the National League of Cities et al. by Richard Ruda, Stephen B. Kinnaird, Alexander M. R. Lyon, and Stephanos Bibas.

Brief of amici curiae filed on behalf of the Orleans Parish Assistant District Attorneys by Valentin M. Solino.

Brief of amici curiae filed on behalf of the District Attorneys Association of the State of New York by Anthony J. Servino and Steven A. Bender.

IV. THE SUPREME COURT'S DECISION

"The Brady violation conceded in this case occurred when . . . prosecutors involved with Thompson's armed robbery prosecution failed to disclose the crime lab report to Thompson's counsel. Under Thompson's failure-to-train theory, he bore the burden of proving both (1) that Connick, the policymaker for the district attorney's office, was deliberately indifferent to the need to train the prosecutors about their Brady disclosure obligation with respect to evidence of this type and (2) that the lack of training actually caused the Brady violation in this case. Connick argues that he was entitled to judgment as a matter of law because Thompson did not prove that he was on actual or constructive notice of, and therefore deliberately indifferent to, a need for more or different Brady training. We agree. . . .

A pattern of similar constitutional violations by untrained employees is 'ordinarily necessary' to demonstrate deliberate indifference for purposes of failure to train. . . .

Instead of relying on a pattern of similar Brady violations, Thompson relies on the 'single-incident' liability that this Court hypothesized in Canton. . . .

Failure to train prosecutors in their Brady obligations does not fall within the narrow range of Canton's hypothesized single-incident liability. . . .

We do not assume that prosecutors will always make correct Brady decisions or that guidance . . . would not assist prosecutors. But showing merely that additional training would have been helpful in making difficult decisions does not establish municipal liability. . . .

The role of a prosecutor is to see that justice is done. . . . But the only issue before us is whether Connick, as the policymaker for the district attorney's office, was deliberately indifferent to the need to train the attorneys under his authority.

We conclude that this case does not fall within the narrow range of 'single-incident' liability hypothesized in Canton as a possible exception to the pattern of violations necessary to prove deliberate indifference in § 1983 actions alleging failure to train. The District Court should have granted Connick judgment as a matter of law on the failure-to-train claim because Thompson did not prove a pattern of similar violations that would 'establish that the 'policy of inaction' [was] the functional equivalent of a decision by the city itself to violate the Constitution.'

The judgment of the United States Court of Appeals for the Fifth Circuit is reversed."

V. JUSTICE VOTE

4 Pro ACLU Side vs. 5 Con Opposing Side

ACLU Side (Respondent / Appellee)

1. Kagan, E. – Joined Ginsburg's dissent
2. Breyer, S. – Joined Ginsburg's dissent
3. Ginsburg, R. – Wrote dissenting opinion
4. Sotomayor, S. – Joined Ginsburg's dissent

Opposing Side (Petitioner / Appellant)

1. Thomas, C. – Wrote majority opinion
2. Alito, S. – Joined Scalia's concurrence
3. Scalia, A. – Wrote concurring opinion
4. Kennedy, A. – Joined majority opinion
5. Roberts, J. – Joined majority opinion

VI. A WIN OR LOSS FOR THE ACLU?

The ACLU filed as amicus curiae urging affirmance; the Supreme Court reversed the Court of Appeals' decision by a 5-4 vote, giving the ACLU an apparent loss.

1072. Arizona Christian School Tuition Organization v. Winn

(Decided April 4, 2011; 563 U.S. 125)

I. ISSUE

A. Issues Discussed

Civil procedure, 1st Amendment, religion

B. Legal Question Presented

"[W]hether respondents, the plaintiffs in the trial court, satisfy the requisite elements of standing."

C. Supreme Court's Answer

"[R]espondents cannot take advantage of Flast's narrow exception to the general rule against taxpayer standing. As a consequence, respondents lacked standing to commence this action, and their suit must be dismissed for want of jurisdiction."

II. CASE SUMMARY

A. Background

"Respondents challenged § 43–1089, a provision of the Arizona Tax Code. Section 43–1089 allows Arizona taxpayers to obtain dollar-for-dollar tax credits . . . for contributions to STOs. . . . Under a version of § 43–1089 in effect during the pendency of this lawsuit, a charitable organization could be deemed an STO only upon certain conditions. . . .

In an earlier lawsuit filed in state court, Arizona taxpayers challenged § 43–1089, invoking both the United States Constitution and the Arizona Constitution. The Arizona Supreme Court rejected the taxpayers' claims on the merits. Th[e U.S. Supreme] Court denied certiorari.

The present action was filed in the United States District Court for the District of Arizona. . . . The Arizona taxpayers who brought the suit claimed that § 43–1089 violates the Establishment Clause of the First Amendment, as incorporated against the States by the Fourteenth Amendment. Respondents alleged that § 43–1089 allows STOs 'to use State income-tax revenues to pay tuition for students at religious schools,' some of which 'discriminate on the basis of religion in selecting students.' Respondents requested, among other forms of relief, an injunction against the issuance of § 43–1089 tax credits for contributions to religious STOs. The District Court dismissed . . . . The Court of Appeals reversed. Th[e U.S. Supreme] Court agreed with the Court of Appeals and affirmed.

On remand, the Arizona Christian School Tuition Organization and other interested parties intervened. The District Court once more dismissed . . . . Once again, the Court of Appeals reversed. . . . The full Court of Appeals denied en banc review, with eight judges dissenting."

The Supreme Court granted certiorari to review the case.

B. Counsel of Record / ACLU Attorney

ACLU Side (Respondent / Appellee): Paul Bender argued the cause for appellees in both cases. With him on the briefs were Isabel M. Humphrey, Paul Bender, Steven R. Shapiro and Daniel Mach of the American Civil Liberties Union Foundation, and Daniel Pochoda of the American Civil Liberties Union Foundation of Arizona.

Opposing Side (Petitioner / Appellant): Paula S. Bickett, Chief Counsel, Civil Appeals, argued the cause for appellants in both cases. With her on the briefs for appellant in No. 09–991 were Terry Goddard, Attorney General of Arizona, Mary O'Grady, Solicitor General, and Kathleen P. Sweeney and Barbara A. Bailey, Assistant Attorneys General. David A. Cortman, Benjamin W. Bull, and Jeremy D. Tedesco filed briefs for appellant in No. 09–987. Timothy D. Keller, William H. Mellor, Richard D. Komer, and Clark M. Neily III filed briefs for Glenn Dennard et al. as appellees under this Court's Rule 12.6 in support of appellants.

Acting Solicitor General Katyal argued the cause for the United States as amicus curiae.

III. AMICI CURIAE

ACLU Side (Respondent / Appellee)

Brief of amici curiae filed on behalf of the American Humanist Association et al. by Robert V. Ritter.

Brief of amici curiae filed on behalf of the National School Boards Association et al. by John W. Borkowski, Maree F. Sneed, Francisco M. Negrón, Jr., and Naomi Gittins.

Brief of amici curiae filed on behalf of Americans United for Separation of Church and State et al. by Gregory M. Lipper and Ayesha N. Khan.

Opposing Side (Petitioner / Appellant)

Brief of amici curiae filed on behalf of the United States by Acting Solicitor General Katyal, Assistant Attorney General West, Joseph R. Palmore, Robert M. Loeb, and Lowell Sturgill.

Brief of amici curiae filed on behalf of the State of Indiana et al. by Gregory F. Zoeller, Attorney General of Indiana, Thomas M. Fisher, Solicitor General, Heather L. Hagan and Ashley E. Tatman, Deputy Attorneys General, Michael A. Cox, Attorney General of Michigan, B. Eric Restuccia, Solicitor General, Joel D. McGormley, Appellate Division Chief, and by the Attorneys General for their respective States as follows: Troy King of Alabama, John Suthers of Colorado, Bill McCollum of Florida, Thurbert E. Baker of Georgia, James D. "Buddy" Caldwell of Louisiana, Jim Hood of Mississippi, Thomas W. Corbett, Jr., of Pennsylvania, Henry D. McMaster of South Carolina, Greg Abbott of Texas, Mark L. Shurtleff of Utah, and Robert M. McKenna of Washington.

Brief of amici curiae filed on behalf of the American Center for Law and Justice by Jay Alan Sekulow, Stuart J. Roth, Colby M. May, James M. Henderson, Sr., and Walter M. Weber.

Brief of amici curiae filed on behalf of the American Center for School Choice by Richard W. Garnett and John E. Coons.

Brief of amici curiae filed on behalf of the Becket Fund for Religious Liberty by Kevin J. Hasson, Eric C. Rassbach, Hannah C. Smith, and Luke W. Goodrich.

Brief of amici curiae filed on behalf of the Cato Institute et al. by Ilya Shapiro.

Brief of amici curiae filed on behalf of the Center for Constitutional Jurisprudence by John Eastman, Anthony T. Caso, and Edwin Meese III.

Brief of amici curiae filed on behalf of the Ethics and Religious Liberty Commission of the Southern Baptist Convention et al. by Kelly J. Shackleford and Hiram S. Sasser III.

Brief of amici curiae filed on behalf of the Florida School Choice Fund et al. by Nathan A. Adams IV.

Brief of amici curiae filed on behalf of the Jewish Tuition Organization et al. by Bennett Evan Cooper and Robert A. Destro.

Brief of amici curiae filed on behalf of the Pacific Legal Foundation by James S. Burling and Sharon L. Browne.

Brief of amici curiae filed on behalf of the United States Conference of Catholic Bishops et al. by Thomas C. Berg, Anthony R. Picarello, Jr., Jeffrey Hunter Moon, Douglas Laycock, Nathan J. Diament, and Kimberlee Wood Colby.

Brief of amici curiae filed on behalf of the Christian Educators Association International et al. by Robert H. Tyler and Jennifer L. Monk.

Brief of amici curiae filed on behalf of the Goldwater Institute et al. by Clint Bolick and Nicholas C. Dranias.

Brief of amici curiae filed on behalf of the Justice and Freedom Fund by James L. Hirsen and Deborah J. Dewart.

Brief of amici curiae filed on behalf of the Rutherford Institute by John W. Whitehead and Jason P. Gosselin.

Brief of amici curiae filed on behalf of Liberty Counsel et al. by Mathew D. Staver, Anita L. Staver, Stephen M. Crampton, and Mary E. McAlister.

IV. THE SUPREME COURT'S DECISION

"The concept and operation of the separation of powers in our National Government have their principal foundation in the first three Articles of the Constitution. Under Article III, the Federal Judiciary is vested with the 'Power' to resolve . . . 'Cases' or 'Controversies.' . . .

To state a case or controversy under Article III, a plaintiff must establish standing. . . .

Respondents suggest that their status as Arizona taxpayers provides them with standing to challenge the STO tax credit. [H]owever, standing cannot be based on a plaintiff's mere status as a taxpayer. . . .

The primary contention of respondents, of course, is that, despite the general rule that taxpayers lack standing to object to expenditures alleged to be unconstitutional, their suit falls within the exception established by Flast v. Cohen, 392 U.S. 83. . . .

Flast held that taxpayers have standing when two conditions are met.

The first condition is that there must be a 'logical link' between the plaintiff's taxpayer status 'and the type of legislative enactment attacked.' . . .

The second condition for standing under Flast is that there must be 'a nexus' between the plaintiff's taxpayer status and 'the precise nature of the constitutional infringement alleged.' . . .

Respondents contend that these principles demonstrate their standing to challenge the STO tax credit. In their view the tax credit is, for Flast purposes, . . . a governmental expenditure. That is incorrect.

The distinction between governmental expenditures and tax credits refutes respondents' assertion of standing. When Arizona taxpayers choose to contribute to STOs, they spend their own money, not money the State has collected from respondents or from other taxpayers. . . .

Furthermore, respondents cannot satisfy the requirements of causation and redressability. . . . Here . . . contributions result from the decisions of private taxpayers . . . . As a result, any injury suffered by respondents would not be remedied by an injunction limiting the tax credit's operation. . . .

Few exercises of the judicial power are more likely to undermine public confidence in the neutrality and integrity of the Judiciary than one which casts the Court in the role of a Council of Revision, conferring on itself the power to invalidate laws at the behest of anyone who disagrees with them. . . .

The present suit serves as an illustration of these principles. The fact that respondents are state taxpayers does not give them standing to challenge the subsidies that § 43-1089 allegedly provides to religious STOs. To alter the rules of standing or weaken their requisite elements would be inconsistent with the case-or-controversy limitation on federal jurisdiction imposed by Article III.

The judgment of the Court of Appeals is reversed."

V. JUSTICE VOTE

4 Pro ACLU Side vs. 5 Con Opposing Side

ACLU Side (Respondent / Appellee)

1. Kagan, E. – Wrote dissenting opinion
2. Ginsburg, R. – Joined Kagan's dissent
3. Breyer, S. – Joined Kagan's dissent
4. Sotomayor, S. – Joined Kagan's dissent

Opposing Side (Petitioner / Appellant)

1. Kennedy, A. – Wrote majority opinion
2. Alito, S. – Joined majority opinion
3. Thomas, C. – Joined Scalia's concurrence
4. Scalia, A. – Wrote concurring opinion
5. Roberts, J. – Joined majority opinion

VI. A WIN OR LOSS FOR THE ACLU?

The ACLU served as counsel for appellees urging affirmance; the Supreme Court reversed the Court of Appeals' decision by a 5-4 vote, giving the ACLU an apparent loss.

1073. Cullen v. Pinholster

(Decided April 4, 2011; 563 U.S. 170)

I. ISSUE

A. Issues Discussed

Criminal procedure

B. Legal Question Presented

"First, whether review under § 2254(d)(1) permits consideration of evidence introduced in an evidentiary hearing before the federal habeas court. Second, whether the Court of Appeals properly granted Pinholster habeas relief on his claim of penalty-phase ineffective assistance of counsel."

C. Supreme Court's Answer

"[W]e conclude that the Court of Appeals erred in considering the District Court evidence in its review under § 2254(d)(1). . . . The Court of Appeals' alternative holding was also erroneous. Pinholster has failed to demonstrate that the California Supreme Court unreasonably applied clearly established federal law to his penalty-phase ineffective-assistance claim on the state-court record. Section 2254(d) prohibits habeas relief."

II. CASE SUMMARY

A. Background

"Scott Lynn Pinholster and two accomplices broke into a house in the middle of the night and brutally beat and stabbed to death two men who happened to interrupt the burglary. A jury convicted Pinholster of first-degree murder, and he was sentenced to death.

After the California Supreme Court twice unanimously denied Pinholster habeas relief, a Federal District Court held an evidentiary hearing and granted Pinholster habeas relief under 28 U.S.C. § 2254 The District Court concluded that Pinholster's trial counsel had been constitutionally ineffective at the penalty phase of trial. Sitting en banc, the Court of Appeals for the Ninth Circuit affirmed. Considering the new evidence adduced in the District Court hearing, the Court of Appeals held that the California Supreme Court's decision 'was contrary to, or involved an unreasonable application of, clearly established Federal law.'"

The Supreme Court granted certiorari to review the case.

B. Counsel of Record / ACLU Attorney

ACLU Side (Respondent / Appellee): Sean K. Kennedy argued the cause for appellee. With him on the brief was Mark R. Drozdowski.

Opposing Side (Petitioner / Appellant): James William Bilderback II, Supervising Deputy Attorney General of California, argued the cause for appellant. With him on the briefs were Edmund G. Brown, Jr., Attorney General, Dane R. Gillette, Chief Assistant Attorney General, Pamela C. Hamanaka, Senior Assistant Attorney General, Donald E. de Nicola, Deputy State Solicitor General, and Lawrence M. Daniels and Keith H. Borjon, Supervising Deputy Attorneys General.

III. AMICI CURIAE

ACLU Side (Respondent / Appellee)

Brief of amici curiae filed on behalf of the American Civil Liberties Union by Larry Yackle, Steven R. Shapiro, and John Holdridge.

Brief of amici curiae filed on behalf of the Disability Rights Legal Center by Neil M. Soltman and Donald M. Falk.

Opposing Side (Petitioner / Appellant)

Brief of amici curiae filed on behalf of the State of Pennsylvania et al. by Thomas W. Corbett, Jr., Attorney General of Pennsylvania, and Amy Zapp, Chief Deputy Attorney General, and by the Attorneys General for their respective States as follows: Troy King of Alabama, Joseph R. Biden III of Delaware, Bill McCollum of Florida, Thurbert E. Baker of Georgia, Mark J. Bennett of Hawaii, Lawrence G. Wasden of Idaho, Gregory F. Zoeller of Indiana, Steve Bullock of Montana, Catherine Cortez Masto of Nevada, Gary K. King of New Mexico, Richard Cordray of Ohio, W. A. Drew Edmondson of Oklahoma, Henry D. McMaster of South Carolina, Marty J. Jackley of South Dakota, Greg Abbott of Texas, Mark L. Shurtleff of Utah, and Bruce A. Salzburg of Wyoming.

Brief of amici curiae filed on behalf of the Criminal Justice Legal Foundation by Kent S. Scheidegger.

IV. THE SUPREME COURT'S DECISION

"We first consider the scope of the record for a § 2254(d)(1) inquiry. The State argues that review is limited to the record that was before the state court that adjudicated the claim on the merits. Pinholster contends that evidence presented to the federal habeas court may also be considered. We agree with the State. . . .

As amended by AEDPA, 28 U.S.C. § 2254 sets several limits on the power of a federal court to grant an application for a writ of habeas corpus on behalf of a state prisoner. . . .

We now hold that review under § 2254(d)(1) is limited to the record that was before the state court that adjudicated the claim on the merits. . . .

Pinholster's contention that our holding renders § 2254(e)(2) superfluous is incorrect. Section 2254(e)(2) imposes a limitation on the discretion of federal habeas courts to take new evidence . . . .

Accordingly, we conclude that the Court of Appeals erred in considering the District Court evidence in its review under § 2254(d)(1). Although we might ordinarily remand for a properly limited review, the Court of Appeals also ruled . . . that Pinholster merited habeas relief even on the state-court record alone. Remand is therefore inappropriate, and we turn next to a review of the state-court record. . . .

The Court of Appeals' alternative holding was also erroneous. Pinholster has failed to demonstrate that the California Supreme Court unreasonably applied clearly established federal law to his penalty-phase ineffective-assistance claim . . . . Section 2254(d) prohibits habeas relief. . . .

'[A] habeas court must determine what arguments or theories . . . could have supporte[d] the state court's decision; and then it must ask whether it is possible fairminded jurists could disagree that those arguments or theories are inconsistent with the holding in a prior decision of this Court.' [W]e conclude that Pinholster has failed to meet that high threshold. . . .

Even if his trial counsel had performed deficiently, Pinholster also has failed to show that the California Supreme Court must have unreasonably concluded that Pinholster was not prejudiced. . . . We therefore 'reweigh the evidence in aggravation against the totality of available mitigating evidence.' . . .

Given what little additional mitigating evidence Pinholster presented in state habeas, we cannot say that the California Supreme Court's determination was unreasonable. . . .

Even if the Court of Appeals might have reached a different conclusion as an initial matter, it was not an unreasonable application of our precedent for the California Supreme Court to conclude that Pinholster did not establish prejudice. . . .

The judgment of the United States Court of Appeals for the Ninth Circuit is reversed."

V. JUSTICE VOTE

4 Pro ACLU Side vs. 5 Con Opposing Side

ACLU Side (Respondent / Appellee)

1. Kagan, E. – Joined Sotomayor's dissent in part
2. Ginsburg, R. – Joined Sotomayor's dissent in part
3. Sotomayor, S. – Wrote dissenting opinion
4. Breyer, S. – Wrote opinion concurring in part and dissenting in part

Opposing Side (Petitioner / Appellant)

1. Thomas, C. – Wrote majority opinion
2. Alito, S. – Wrote concurring opinion
3. Scalia, A. – Joined majority opinion
4. Kennedy, A. – Joined majority opinion
5. Roberts, J. – Joined majority opinion

VI. A WIN OR LOSS FOR THE ACLU?

The ACLU filed as amicus curiae urging affirmance; the Supreme Court reversed the Court of Appeals' decision by a 5-4 vote, giving the ACLU an apparent loss.

1074. Sossamon v. Texas

(Decided April 20, 2011; 563 U.S. 277)

I. ISSUE

A. Issues Discussed

Immunity

B. Legal Question Presented

"This case presents the question whether the States, by accepting federal funds, consent to waive their sovereign immunity to suits for money damages under the Religious Land Use and Institutionalized Persons Act of 2000 (RLUIPA)."

C. Supreme Court's Answer

"We hold that they do not. Sovereign immunity therefore bars this suit for damages against the State of Texas."

II. CASE SUMMARY

A. Background

"RLUIPA is Congress' second attempt to accord heightened statutory protection to religious exercise in the wake of this Court's decision in Employment Div., Dept. of Human Resources of Ore. v. Smith, 494 U.S. 872 (1990). Congress first enacted the Religious Freedom Restoration Act of 1993 (RFRA) . . . . We held RFRA unconstitutional as applied to state and local governments because it exceeded Congress' power . . . .

Congress responded by enacting RLUIPA pursuant to its Spending Clause and Commerce Clause authority. RLUIPA borrows important elements from RFRA . . . but RLUIPA is less sweeping in scope. It targets two areas of state and local action: land-use regulation, and restrictions on the religious exercise of institutionalized persons. . . .

Harvey Leroy Sossamon III is an inmate in the Robertson Unit of the Texas Department of Criminal Justice, Correctional Institutions Division. In 2006, Sossamon sued the State of Texas and various prison officials in their official capacities under RLUIPA's private cause of action, seeking injunctive and monetary relief. Sossamon alleged that two prison policies violated RLUIPA: (1) a policy preventing inmates from attending religious services while on cell restriction for disciplinary infractions; and (2) a policy barring use of the prison chapel for religious worship. The District Court granted summary judgment in favor of respondents and held, as relevant here, that sovereign immunity barred Sossamon's claims for monetary relief.

The Court of Appeals for the Fifth Circuit affirmed."

The Supreme Court granted certiorari to review the case.

B. Counsel of Record / ACLU Attorney

ACLU Side (Petitioner / Appellant): Kevin K. Russell argued the cause for appellant. With him on the briefs were Amy Howe, Patricia A. Millett, Thomas C. Goldstein, Pamela S. Karlan, and Jeffrey L. Fisher.

Sarah E. Harrington argued the cause for the United States as amicus curiae.

Opposing Side (Respondent / Appellee): James C. Ho, Solicitor General of Texas, argued the cause for appellees. With him on the brief were Greg Abbott, Attorney General, Daniel T. Hodge, First Assistant Attorney General, David S. Morales, Deputy First Assistant Attorney General, Bill Cobb, Deputy Attorney General, and Daniel L. Geyser and James P. Sullivan, Assistant Solicitors General.

III. AMICI CURIAE

ACLU Side (Petitioner / Appellant)

Brief of amici curiae filed on behalf of the American Civil Liberties Union, ACLU of Texas, Uptown People's Law Center, Washington Lawyer's Committee for Civil Rights and Urban Affairs, Americans United for Separation of Church and State, American Jewish Committee, Baptist Joint Committee for Religious Liberty, and the Interfaith Alliance Foundation by Gene C. Schaerr, Steffen N. Johnson, Adele Auxier, Linda T. Coberly, Daniel Mach, David C. Fathi, David M. Shapiro, Ayesha N. Khan, K. Hollyn Hollman, James T. Gibson, Marc Stern, Lisa Graybill, Alan Mills, Deborah M. Golden, Marc Stern, Richard Foltin, and Richard Foltin.

Brief of amici curiae filed on behalf of the United States by Sarah E. Harrington, Acting Solicitor General Katyal, Assistant Attorney General Perez, Deputy Assistant Attorney General Bagenstos, and Jessica Dunsay Silver.

Brief of amici curiae filed on behalf of the Becket Fund for Religious Liberty by Kevin J. Hasson, Eric C. Rassbach, Hannah C. Smith, and Luke W. Goodrich.

Brief of amici curiae filed on behalf of the National Association of Evangelicals by Kelly J. Shackelford and Hiram S. Sasser III.

Brief of amici curiae filed on behalf of Charles E. Sisney by Kathryn M. Davis, Peter R. Afrasiabi, and Richard L. Johnson.

Brief of amici curiae filed on behalf of the Christian Legal Society et al. by James K. Lehman, William C. Wood, Jr., Jay T. Thompson, and Kimberlee Wood Colby.

Brief of amici curiae filed on behalf of the Rutherford Institute by John W. Whitehead and Mitchell A. Karlan.

Opposing Side (Respondent / Appellee)

Brief of amici curiae filed on behalf of the State of Florida et al. by Bill McCollum, Attorney General of Florida, Scott D. Makar, Solicitor General, and Courtney Brewer, Deputy Solicitor General, and by the Attorneys General for their respective States as follows: Troy King of Alabama, Daniel S. Sullivan of Alaska, Terry Goddard of Arizona, Edmund G. Brown, Jr., of California, John W. Suthers of Colorado, Thurbert E. Baker of Georgia, Mark J. Bennett of Hawaii, Lawrence G. Wasden of Idaho, Lisa Madigan of Illinois, Gregory F. Zoeller of Indiana, Janet T. Mills of Maine, Douglas F. Gansler of Maryland, Michael A. Cox of Michigan, Jim Hood of Mississippi, Steve Bullock of Montana, Jon Bruning of Nebraska, Catherine Cortez Masto of Nevada, Michael A. Delaney of New Hampshire, Wayne Stenehjem of North Dakota, Richard Cordray of Ohio, W. A. Drew Edmondson of Oklahoma, Thomas W. Corbett, Jr., of Pennsylvania, Patrick C. Lynch of Rhode Island, Henry D. McMaster of South Carolina, Marty J. Jackley of South Dakota, Mark Shurtleff of

Utah, Kenneth T. Cuccinelli II of Virginia, J. B. Van Hollen of Wisconsin, and Bruce A. Salzburg of Wyoming.

IV. THE SUPREME COURT'S DECISION

"Sovereign immunity principles enforce an important constitutional limitation on the power of the federal courts. . . .

Accordingly, 'our test for determining whether a State has waived its immunity from federal-court jurisdiction is a stringent one.' . . .

For these reasons, a waiver of sovereign immunity 'will be strictly construed, in terms of its scope, in favor of the sovereign.' . . .

RLUIPA's authorization of 'appropriate relief against a government,' is not the unequivocal expression of state consent that our precedents require. '[A]ppropriate relief' does not so clearly and unambiguously waive sovereign immunity to private suits for damages that we can 'be certain that the State in fact consents' to such a suit. . . .

[T]he phrase 'appropriate relief' in RLUIPA is not so free from ambiguity that we may conclude that the States, by receiving federal funds, have unequivocally expressed intent to waive their sovereign immunity to suits for damages. Strictly construing that phrase in favor of the sovereign—as we must . . .—we conclude that it does not include suits for damages against a State. . . .

Sossamon contends that, because Congress enacted § 3 of RLUIPA pursuant to the Spending Clause, the States were necessarily on notice that they would be liable for damages. . . .

Sossamon's implied-contract-remedies proposal cannot be squared with our longstanding rule that a waiver of sovereign immunity must be expressly and unequivocally stated . . . .

Sossamon also argues that § 1003 of the Rehabilitation Act Amendments of 1986 independently put the State on notice that it could be sued for damages under RLUIPA. . . .

Even assuming that a residual clause like the one in § 1003 could constitute an unequivocal textual waiver, § 3 is not unequivocally a 'statute prohibiting discrimination' . . . .

We conclude that States, in accepting federal funding, do not consent to waive their sovereign immunity to private suits for money damages under RLUIPA because no statute expressly and unequivocally includes such a waiver. The judgment of the United States Court of Appeals for the Fifth Circuit is affirmed."

V. JUSTICE VOTE

2 Pro ACLU Side vs. 6 Con Opposing Side

ACLU Side (Petitioner / Appellant)

1. Breyer, S. – Joined Sotomayor's dissent
2. Sotomayor, S. – Wrote dissenting opinion

Opposing Side (Respondent / Appellee)

1. Thomas, A. – Wrote majority opinion
2. Alito, S. – Joined majority opinion
3. Scalia, A. – Joined majority opinion
4. Kennedy, A. – Joined majority opinion
5. Ginsburg, R. – Joined majority opinion
6. Roberts, J. – Joined majority opinion

Kagan, E. – Took no part in the decision.

VI. A WIN OR LOSS FOR THE ACLU?

The ACLU filed as amicus curiae urging reversal of the judgment of the Court of Appeals; the Supreme Court affirmed in a 6-2 vote, giving the ACLU an apparent loss.

1075. Brown v. Plata

(Decided May 23, 2011; 563 U.S. 493)

I. ISSUE

A. Issues Discussed

Prison

B. Legal Question Presented

"[W]hether [a] remedial order issued by the three-judge court [to cure cruel and unusual punishment clause violations in the California prisons] is consistent with requirements and procedures set forth in a congressional statute, the Prison Litigation Reform Act of 1995 (PLRA)."

C. Supreme Court's Answer

"This Court now holds that the PLRA does authorize the relief afforded in this case and that the court-mandated population limit is necessary to remedy the violation of prisoners' constitutional rights. The order of the three-judge court, subject to the right of the State to seek its modification in appropriate circumstances, must be affirmed."

II. CASE SUMMARY

A. Background

"This case arises from serious constitutional violations in California's prison system. The violations have persisted for years. They remain uncorrected. . . .

After years of litigation, it became apparent that a remedy for the constitutional violations would not be effective absent a reduction in the prison system population. The authority to order release of prisoners as a remedy to cure a systemic violation of the Eighth Amendment is a power reserved to a three-judge district court, not a single-judge district court. In accordance with that rule, the Coleman and Plata District Judges independently requested that a three-judge court be convened. The Chief Judge of the Court of Appeals for the Ninth Circuit convened a three-judge court composed of the Coleman and Plata District Judges and a third, Ninth Circuit Judge. . . .

The appeal presents the question whether the remedial order issued by the three-judge court is consistent with requirements and procedures set forth in a congressional statute, the Prison Litigation Reform Act of 1995 (PLRA)."

The Supreme Court granted certiorari to review the case.

B. Counsel of Record / ACLU Attorney

ACLU Side (Respondent / Appellee): Donald Specter argued the cause for appellees. With him on the briefs for Plata appellees was Rebekah Evenson. Paul D. Clement, Ashley C. Parrish,

Michael W. Bien, Jane E. Kahn, Ernest Galvan, Amy Whelan, Lisa Ells, Mr. Specter, and Ms. Evenson filed a brief for Coleman appellees. Laurie J. Hepler, Gregg McLean Adam, Gonzalo C. Martinez, Jeffrey L. Fisher, Pamela S. Karlan, Daniel M. Lindsay, and David A. Sanders filed a brief for California Correctional Peace Officers' Association, appellee under this Court's Rule 18.2, urging affirmance.

Opposing Side (Petitioner / Appellant): Carter G. Phillips argued the cause for appellants. With him on the briefs were Edmund G. Brown, Jr., Attorney General of California, James M. Humes, Chief Deputy Attorney General, Manuel M. Medeiros, State Solicitor General, Gordon Burns, Deputy Solicitor General, Jonathan L. Wolff and Rochelle C. East, Senior Assistant Attorneys General, Kyle A. Lewis and Danielle F. O'Bannon, Deputy Attorneys General, Eamon P. Joyce, Jerrold C. Schaefer, Paul B. Mello, S. Anne Johnson, Samantha D. Wolff, and Renju P. Jacob. Steven S. Kaufhold, Chad A. Stegeman, Thomas C. Goldstein, Troy D. Cahill, Gary S. Olson, Charles V. Fennessey, Rod Pacheco, William E. Mitchell, Alan D. Tate, and Martin J. Mayer filed briefs for California State Republican Legislators et al., appellees under this Court's Rule 18.2, urging reversal.

III. AMICI CURIAE

ACLU Side (Respondent / Appellee)

Brief of amici curiae filed on behalf of the American Civil Liberties Union et al. by David C. Fathi, David M. Shapiro, Steven R. Shapiro, Carl Takei, Steven M. Watt, Wade Henderson, Alvin J. Bronstein, Alan Schlosser, Peter J. Eliasberg, and David Blair-Loy.

Brief of amici curiae filed on behalf of the American Bar Association by Stephen N. Zack, Pierre H. Bergeron, George H. Kendall, and Margaret Colgate Love.

Brief of amici curiae filed on behalf of the American Psychiatric Association et al. by Aaron M. Panner, Nathalie F. P. Gilfoyle, and Ira A. Burnim.

Brief of amici curiae filed on behalf of the American Public Health Association et al. by Lisa S. Blatt and Beth H. Parker.

Brief of amici curiae filed on behalf of the Center on the Administration of Criminal Law et al. by J. C. Rozendaal and Anthony S. Barkow.

Brief of amici curiae filed on behalf of Corrections and Law Enforcement Personnel by William A. Burck.

Brief of amici curiae filed on behalf of Prison Fellowship et al. by James Stewart, Catherine Weiss, and Kenneth H. Zimmerman.

Opposing Side (Petitioner / Appellant)

Brief of amici curiae filed on behalf of the State of Louisiana et al. by James D. "Buddy" Caldwell, Attorney General of Louisiana, James Trey Phillips, First Assistant Attorney General, S. Kyle Duncan, Appellate Chief, Sarah Vandenbraak Hart, and Ronald Eisenberg, and by the Attorneys General for their respective States as follows: Troy King of Alabama, Daniel S. Sullivan of Alaska, Dustin McDaniel of Arkansas, John W. Suthers of Colorado, Joseph R. Biden III of Delaware, Lisa Madigan of Illinois, Martha Coakley of Massachusetts, Michael A. Cox of Michigan, Jim Hood of Mississippi, Gary King of New Mexico, Richard Cordray of Ohio, W. A. Drew Edmondson of Oklahoma, Thomas W. Corbett, Jr., of Pennsylvania, Henry D. McMaster of South Carolina, Robert E. Cooper, Jr., of Tennessee, Greg Abbott of Texas, and Kenneth T. Cuccinelli II of Virginia.

Brief of amici curiae filed on behalf of the Criminal Justice Legal Foundation by Kent S. Scheidegger.

Brief of amici curiae filed on behalf of the Greater Stockton Chamber of Commerce by Steven A. Herum and Brett S. Jolley.

Brief of amici curiae filed on behalf of J. Clark Kelso by George C. Harris, Deanne E. Maynard, and Brian R. Matsui in support of neither party.

IV. THE SUPREME COURT'S DECISION

"Before a three-judge court may be convened to consider whether to enter a population limit, the PLRA requires that the court have 'previously entered an order for less intrusive relief that has failed to remedy the deprivation of the Federal right sought to be remedied.' . . .

Having engaged in remedial efforts for 5 years in Plata and 12 in Coleman, the District Courts were not required to wait to see whether their more recent efforts would yield equal disappointment. . . .

Once a three-judge court has been convened, the court must find additional requirements satisfied . . . . The first of these requirements is that 'crowding is the primary cause of the violation . . . .' . . .

The three-judge court found the primary cause requirement satisfied by the evidence at trial. . . .

The three-judge court acknowledged that the violations were caused by factors in addition to overcrowding . . . . The . . . court nevertheless found that overcrowding was the primary cause . . . .

This understanding of the primary cause requirement is consistent with the text of the PLRA. . . .

The three-judge court was also required to find by clear and convincing evidence that 'no other relief will remedy the violation of the Federal right.' . . .

The Court cannot ignore the political and fiscal reality . . . . California's Legislature has not been willing or able to allocate the resources necessary . . . absent a reduction in overcrowding. . . .

The PLRA states that no prospective relief shall issue with respect to prison conditions unless it is narrowly drawn, extends no further than necessary to correct the violation of a federal right, and is the least intrusive means necessary to correct the violation. . .

Establishing the population at which the State could begin to provide constitutionally adequate medical and mental health care, and the appropriate time frame within which to achieve the necessary reduction, requires a degree of judgment. . . .

The three-judge court concluded that the population of California's prisons should be capped at 137.5% of design capacity. This conclusion is supported by the record. . . .

[T]he three-judge court did not err when it established a 2-year deadline for relief. . . .

These observations reflect the fact that the three-judge court's order . . . must remain open to appropriate modification. . . . The medical and mental health care provided by California's prisons falls below the standard of decency that inheres in the Eighth Amendment. This extensive and ongoing constitutional violation requires a remedy, and a remedy will not be achieved without a reduction in overcrowding. The relief ordered . . . is required by the Constitution and was authorized by Congress in the PLRA. The State shall implement the order without further delay.

The judgment of the three-judge court is affirmed."

V. JUSTICE VOTE

5 Pro ACLU Side vs. 4 Con Opposing Side

ACLU Side (Respondent / Appellee)

1. Kennedy, A. – Wrote majority opinion
2. Kagan, E. – Joined majority opinion
3. Breyer, S. – Joined majority opinion
4. Ginsburg, R. – Joined majority opinion
5. Sotomayor, S. – Joined majority opinion

Opposing Side (Petitioner / Appellant)

1. Alito, S. – Wrote dissenting opinion
2. Thomas, C. – Joined Scalia's dissent
3. Scalia, A. – Wrote dissenting opinion
4. Roberts, J. – Joined Alito's dissent

VI. A WIN OR LOSS FOR THE ACLU?

The ACLU filed as amicus curiae urging affirmance; the Supreme Court affirmed the three-judge court's decision by a 5-4 vote, giving the ACLU an apparent win.

1076. Chamber of Commerce of U.S. v. Whiting

(Decided May 26, 2011; 563 U.S. 582)

I. ISSUE

A. Issues Discussed

Immigration/Citizenship

B. Legal Question Presented

"A recently enacted Arizona statute—the Legal Arizona Workers Act—provides that the licenses of state employers that knowingly or intentionally employ unauthorized aliens may be, and in certain circumstances must be, suspended or revoked. The law also requires that all Arizona employers use a federal electronic verification system to confirm that the workers they employ are legally authorized workers. The question presented is whether federal immigration law preempts those provisions of Arizona law."

C. Supreme Court's Answer

"Because we conclude that the State's licensing provisions fall squarely within the federal statute's savings clause and that the Arizona regulation does not otherwise conflict with federal law, we hold that the Arizona law is not preempted."

II. CASE SUMMARY

A. Background

"Federal immigration law expressly preempts 'any State or local law imposing civil or criminal sanctions (other than through licensing and similar laws) upon those who employ . . . unauthorized aliens.' A recently enacted Arizona statute—the Legal Arizona Workers Act—provides that the licenses of state employers that knowingly or intentionally employ unauthorized aliens may be, and in certain circumstances must be, suspended or revoked. The law also requires that all Arizona employers use a federal electronic verification system to confirm that the workers they employ are legally authorized workers. The question presented is whether federal immigration law preempts those provisions of Arizona law. . . .

The District Court held that Arizona's law was not preempted. . . . The Court of Appeals affirmed . . . ."

The Supreme Court granted certiorari to review the case.

B. Counsel of Record / ACLU Attorney

ACLU Side (Petitioner / Appellant): Carter G. Phillips argued the cause for appellants. With him on the briefs were Eric A. Shumsky, Quin M. Sorenson, Matthew D. Krueger, Robin S. Conrad, Shane B. Kawka, David A. Selden, Julie A. Pace, Heidi Nunn-Gilman, Burt M. Rublin, Stephen P. Berzon, Jonathan Weissglass, Cynthia Valenzuela Dixon, Linton Joaquin, Karen C. Tumlin, Paul F. Eckstein, Joel W. Nomkin, Daniel Pochoda of the ACLU Foundation of Arizona, and Lucas Guttentag, Jennifer Chang Newell, Steven R. Shapiro, and Omar C. Jadwat of the American Civil Liberties Union Foundation.

Acting Solicitor General Katyal argued the cause for the United States as amicus curiae.

Opposing Side (Respondent / Appellee): Mary R. O'Grady, Solicitor General of Arizona, argued the cause for appellees. With her on the brief were Terry Goddard, Attorney General, Kathleen P. Sweeney and Christopher A. Munns, Assistant Attorneys General, Roger W. Hall, Eileen Gilbride, and Daniel S. Jurkowitz.

III. AMICI CURIAE

ACLU Side (Petitioner / Appellant)

Brief of amici curiae filed on behalf of the United States by Acting Solicitor General Katyal, Assistant Attorneys General West and Perez, Deputy Assistant Attorney General Bagenstos, William M. Jay, Mark L. Gross, and Nathaniel S. Pollock.

Brief of amici curiae filed on behalf of the Asian American Justice Center et al. by Kevin M. Fong, Pamela S. Karlan, Karen K. Narasaki, Steven M. Freeman, Steven C. Sheinberg, Kenneth Kimerling, Cesar A. Perales, Sarah C. Crawford, Audrey Wiggins, Christopher Ho, Araceli Martínez-Olguín, Rebecca Smith, and Mary Bauer.

Brief of amici curiae filed on behalf of Business Organizations by Walter Dellinger and Sri Srinivasan.

Brief of amici curiae filed on behalf of the Equal Employment Advisory Council by Rae T. Vann and Judith A. Lampley.

Brief of amici curiae filed on behalf of the National Immigrant

Justice Center et al. by Linda T. Coberly, Gene C. Schaerr, and Steffen N. Johnson.

Brief of amici curiae filed on behalf of the Service Employees International Union by Leon Dayan and Laurence Gold.

Brief of amici curiae filed on behalf of Representative Romano L. Mazzoli et al. by Paul M. Smith and Lindsay C. Harrison.

Opposing Side (Respondent / Appellee)

Brief of amici curiae filed on behalf of the State of Missouri et al. by Chris Koster, Attorney General of Missouri, James R. Layton, Solicitor General, Jeremiah J. Morgan, Deputy Solicitor General, and Arax R. Corn, Assistant Attorney General, and by the Attorneys General for their respective States as follows: Troy King of Alabama, Dustin McDaniel of Arkansas, Steve Six of Kansas, James D. Caldwell of Louisiana, Michael A. Cox of Michigan, Jim Hood of Mississippi, Jon Bruning of Nebraska, Wayne Stenehjem of North Dakota, Henry D. McMaster of South Carolina, Robert E. Cooper, Jr., of Tennessee, Mark L. Shurtleff of Utah, and Kenneth T. Cuccinelli II of Virginia.

Brief of amici curiae filed on behalf of the American Center for Law and Justice by Jay Alan Sekulow, Stuart J. Roth, Colby M. May, John P. Tuskey, and Laura B. Hernandez.

Brief of amici curiae filed on behalf of the American Unity Legal Defense Fund by Barnaby W. Zall.

Brief of amici curiae filed on behalf of the Eagle Forum Education & Legal Defense Fund by Lawrence J. Joseph.

Brief of amici curiae filed on behalf of the Immigration Reform Law Institute by Michael M. Hethmon.

Brief of amici curiae filed on behalf of NumbersUSA Education & Research Foundation by J. E. McNeil.

Brief of amici curiae filed on behalf of State Senator Russell Pearce by Paul J. Orfanedes and James F. Peterson.

IV. THE SUPREME COURT'S DECISION

"The Chamber of Commerce argues that Arizona's law is expressly preempted by IRCA's text and impliedly preempted because it conflicts with federal law. . . .

IRCA expressly preempts States from imposing 'civil or criminal sanctions' on those who employ unauthorized aliens, 'other than through licensing and similar laws.' The Arizona law, on its face, purports to impose sanctions through licensing laws. . . .

IRCA expressly preempts some state powers dealing with the employment of unauthorized aliens and it expressly preserves others. We hold that Arizona's licensing law falls well within the confines of the authority Congress chose to leave to the States and therefore is not expressly preempted. . . .

As an alternative to its express preemption argument, the Chamber contends that Arizona's law is impliedly preempted because it conflicts with federal law. . . .

We begin again with the relevant text. The provision of IIRIRA setting up . . . E-Verify contains no language circumscribing state action. It does, however, constrain federal action . . . .

Arizona's use of E-Verify does not conflict with the federal scheme. . . . And the consequences of not using E-Verify under the Arizona law are the same as the consequences of not using the system under federal law. In both instances, the only result is that the employer forfeits the otherwise available rebuttable presumption that it complied with the law. . . .

IRCA expressly reserves to the States the authority to impose sanctions on employers hiring unauthorized workers, through licensing and similar laws. In exercising that authority, Arizona has taken the route least likely to cause tension with federal law. It uses the Federal Government's own definition of 'unauthorized alien,' it relies solely on the Federal Government's own determination of who is an unauthorized alien, and it requires Arizona employers to use the Federal Government's own system for checking employee status. If even this gives rise to impermissible conflicts with federal law, then there really is no way for the State to implement licensing sanctions, contrary to the express terms of the savings clause.

Because Arizona's unauthorized alien employment law fits within the confines of IRCA's savings clause and does not conflict with federal immigration law, the judgment of the United States Court of Appeals for the Ninth Circuit is affirmed."

V. JUSTICE VOTE

3 Pro ACLU Side vs. 5 Con Opposing Side

ACLU Side (Petitioner / Appellant)

1. Breyer, S. – Wrote dissenting opinion
2. Ginsburg, R. – Joined Breyer's dissent
3. Sotomayor, S. – Wrote dissenting opinion

Opposing Side (Respondent / Appellee)

1. Roberts, J. – Wrote majority opinion
2. Alito, S. – Joined majority opinion
3. Thomas, C. – Wrote concurring opinion
4. Scalia, A. – Joined majority opinion
5. Kennedy, A. – Joined majority opinion

Kagan, E. – Took no part in the decision.

VI. A WIN OR LOSS FOR THE ACLU?

The ACLU served as counsel for appellant urging reversal of the judgment of the Court of Appeals; the Supreme Court affirmed in a 5-3 vote, giving the ACLU an apparent loss.

1077. Ashcroft v. al-Kidd

(Decided May 31, 2011; 563 U.S. 731)

I. ISSUE

A. Issues Discussed

4th Amendment, immunity

B. Legal Question Presented

"[W]hether a former Attorney General enjoys immunity from suit for allegedly authorizing federal prosecutors to obtain valid material-witness warrants for detention of terrorism suspects whom they would otherwise lack probable cause to arrest."

C. Supreme Court's Answer

"We hold that an objectively reasonable arrest and detention of a material witness pursuant to a validly obtained warrant cannot be challenged as unconstitutional on the basis of allegations that the arresting authority had an improper motive. Because Ashcroft did not violate clearly established law, we need not address the more difficult question whether he enjoys absolute immunity."

II. CASE SUMMARY

A. Background

"The federal material-witness statute authorizes judges to 'order the arrest of [a] person' whose testimony 'is material in a criminal proceeding . . . if it is shown that it may become impracticable to secure the presence of the person by subpoena.' . . .

[I]n the aftermath of the September 11th terrorist attacks, then-Attorney General John Ashcroft authorized federal prosecutors and law enforcement officials to use the material-witness statute to detain individuals with suspected ties to terrorist organizations. . . .

It is alleged that this pretextual detention policy led to the material-witness arrest of al-Kidd, a native-born United States citizen. . . . Al–Kidd remained in federal custody for 16 days and on supervised release until al-Hussayen's trial concluded 14 months later. Prosecutors never called him as a witness.

In March 2005, al-Kidd filed this Bivens action to challenge the constitutionality of Ashcroft's alleged policy . . . . Ashcroft filed a motion to dismiss based on absolute and qualified immunity, which the District Court denied. A divided panel of the United States Court of Appeals for the Ninth Circuit affirmed . . . .

Judge Bea dissented, and eight judges dissented from the denial of rehearing en banc."

The Supreme Court granted certiorari to review the case.

B. Counsel of Record / ACLU Attorney

ACLU Side (Respondent / Appellee): Lee Gelernt of the American Civil Liberties Union Foundation argued the cause for appellee. With him on the brief were Michael J. Wishnie, cooperating counsel for the ACLU, Cynthia J. Woolley, R. Keith Roark, Lea Cooper of the American Civil Liberties Union Foundation of Idaho, and Katherine Desormeau, Steven K. Shapiro, Lucas Guttentag, Tanaz Moghadam, and Michael K.T. Tan of the American Civil Liberties Union Foundation.

Opposing Side (Petitioner / Appellant): Acting Solicitor General Katyal argued the cause for appellant. With him on the briefs were Assistant Attorney General West, Acting Deputy Solicitor General Kruger, Eric D. Miller, and Matthew M. Collette.

III. AMICI CURIAE

ACLU Side (Respondent / Appellee)

Brief of amici curiae filed on behalf of the Center for Justice and Accountability by Jonathan C. Drimmer and Kathryn J. Gainey.

Brief of amici curiae filed on behalf of Former Federal Prosecutors by Aaron R. Marcu.

Brief of amici curiae filed on behalf of Human Rights Watch et al. by Joseph F. Tringali and Jeffrey L. Fisher.

Brief of amici curiae filed on behalf of Legal History and Criminal Procedure Law Professors by Stephanos Bibas and Peter C. Meier.

Brief of amici curiae filed on behalf of Legal Scholars by Kevin K. Russell and Amy Howe.

Brief of amici curiae filed on behalf of the Constitution Project by Christopher T. Handman and Sharon Bradford Franklin.

Opposing Side (Petitioner / Appellant)

Brief of amici curiae filed on behalf of William P. Barr et al. by Daniel J. Popeo and Richard A. Samp.

Brief of amici curiae filed on behalf of Wesley MacNeil Oliver by Mr. Oliver, pro se.

IV. THE SUPREME COURT'S DECISION

"Qualified immunity shields federal and state officials from money damages unless a plaintiff pleads facts showing (1) that the official violated a statutory or constitutional right, and (2) that the right was 'clearly established' at the time of the challenged conduct. . . .

In this case, the Court of Appeals' analysis at both steps . . . needs correction. . . .

The Fourth Amendment protects '[t]he right of the people to be secure in their persons, houses, papers, and effects, against unreasonable searches and seizures.' . . . Al–Kidd does not assert that Government officials would have acted unreasonably if they had used a material-witness warrant to arrest him for the purpose of securing his testimony for trial. He contests, however . . . the reasonableness of using the warrant to detain him as a suspected criminal.

Fourth Amendment reasonableness 'is predominantly an objective inquiry.' . . .

Two 'limited exception[s]' to this rule are our special-needs and administrative-search cases . . . .

Apart from those cases, we have almost uniformly rejected invitations to probe subjective intent. . . .

Because al-Kidd concedes that individualized suspicion supported the issuance of the material-witness arrest warrant; and does not assert that his arrest would have been unconstitutional absent the alleged pretextual use of the warrant; we find no Fourth Amendment violation. . . .

A Government official's conduct violates clearly established law when, at the time of the challenged conduct, '[t]he contours of [a] right [are] sufficiently clear' that every 'reasonable official would have understood that what he is doing violates that right.' . . . The constitutional question in this case falls far short of that threshold.

At the time of al-Kidd's arrest, not a single judicial opinion had held that pretext could render an objectively reasonable arrest pursuant to a material-witness warrant unconstitutional. . . .

Qualified immunity gives government officials breathing room to make reasonable but mistaken judgments about open legal questions. When properly applied, it protects 'all but the plainly incompetent or those who knowingly violate the law.' Ashcroft . . . deserves qualified immunity even assuming—contrafactually—that his alleged detention policy violated the Fourth Amendment. . . .

We hold that an objectively reasonable arrest and detention of a material witness pursuant to a validly obtained warrant cannot be challenged as unconstitutional on the basis of allegations that the arresting authority had an improper motive. Because Ashcroft did not violate clearly established law, we need not address the more difficult question whether he enjoys absolute immunity. The judgment of the Court of Appeals is reversed, and the case is remanded . . . ."

V. JUSTICE VOTE

0 Pro ACLU Side vs. 8 Con Opposing Side

Opposing Side (Petitioner / Appellant)

1. Scalia, A. – Wrote majority opinion
2. Alito, S. – Joined majority opinion
3. Thomas, C. – Joined majority opinion
4. Breyer, S. – Joined Kennedy's concurrence and Ginsburg's concurrence
5. Kennedy, A. – Wrote concurring opinion
6. Ginsburg, R. – Wrote concurring opinion, joined Kennedy's concurrence
7. Sotomayor, S. – Joined Kennedy's concurrence and Ginsburg's concurrence
8. Roberts, J. – Joined majority opinion

Kagan, E. – Took no part in the decision.

VI. A WIN OR LOSS FOR THE ACLU?

The ACLU served as counsel for appellee urging affirmance of the judgment of the Court of Appeals; the Supreme Court reversed in an 8-0 vote, giving the ACLU an apparent loss.

1078. Fox v. Vice

(Decided June 6, 2011; 563 U.S. 826)

I. ISSUE

A. Issues Discussed

Civil rights, civil procedure

B. Legal Question Presented

Whether "[i]n a suit of this kind, involving both frivolous and non-frivolous claims, a defendant may recover the reasonable attorney's fees he expended solely because of the frivolous allegations."

C. Supreme Court's Answer

"In this case, the plaintiff asserted both frivolous and non-frivolous claims [for attorney's fees]. We hold today that a court may grant reasonable fees to the defendant in this circumstance, but only for costs that the defendant would not have incurred but for the frivolous claims. A trial court has wide discretion in applying this standard. But here we must vacate the judgment below because the court used a different and incorrect standard in awarding fees."

II. CASE SUMMARY

A. Background

"This case arises out of an election for chief of police . . . . The candidates were petitioner Ricky Fox (the challenger) and respondent Billy Ray Vice (the incumbent). By Fox's account, Vice resorted to an assortment of dirty tricks to try to force Fox out of the race. . . . Yet all of these machinations failed; Fox won the election. And Vice got an even greater comeuppance: He was subsequently convicted of criminal extortion for his election-related conduct.

Fox, however, chose not to let the matter rest; he filed this suit . . . . Fox's complaint asserted both state-law claims, including defamation, and federal civil rights claims under 42 U.S.C. § 1983, including interference with his right to seek public office. . . .

At the end of discovery in the suit, Vice moved for summary judgment on Fox's federal claims. Fox conceded that the claims were 'no[t] valid,' and the District Court accordingly dismissed them with prejudice. In the same ruling, the court declined to exercise supplemental jurisdiction over the remaining state-law claims. The court instead remanded the now slimmed-down case to state court . . . .

Vice then asked the federal court for an award of attorney's fees under § 1988, arguing that Fox's federal claims were 'baseless and without merit.' . . .

The District Court granted the motion for attorney's fees on the ground that Fox's federal claims were frivolous. . . .

A divided Court of Appeals affirmed."

The Supreme Court granted certiorari to review the case.

B. Counsel of Record / ACLU Attorney

ACLU Side (Petitioner / Appellant): E. Joshua Rosenkranz argued the cause for appellant. With him on the briefs were Jessica S. Pers, Michael K. Gottlieb, J. Steven Broussard, and Randall E. Hart.

Opposing Side (Respondent / Appellee): Mark T. Stancil argued the cause for appellees. With him on the brief were Christopher P. Ieyoub, Kendrick J. Guidry, Toby J. Heytens, Daniel R. Ortiz, J. Mark Miller, Joseph B. Stamey, and John P. Elwood.

III. AMICI CURIAE

ACLU Side (Petitioner / Appellant)

Brief of amici curiae filed on behalf of the American Civil Liberties Union, Americans United for Separation of Church and State, Impact Fund, Lawyers' Committee for Civil Rights Under Law, The Legal Aid Society of New York City, National Employment Lawyers Association, New York, National Fair Housing Alliance, People for the American Way Foundation, and Public Justice by Andrew G. Celli, Jr., Debra L. Greenberger, and O. Andrew F. Wilson.

Brief of amici curiae filed on behalf of the Liberty Institute et al. by Mark C. Fleming, Sydenham B. Alexander III, Hiram S. Sasser III, Ilya Shapiro, Randall L. Wenger, Matthew R. Miller, James Bopp, Jr., and Jeffrey Gallant.

Opposing Side (Respondent / Appellee)

Brief of amici curiae filed on behalf of the State of Arkansas et al. by Dustin McDaniel, Attorney General of Arkansas, and Ali M. Brady, Assistant Attorney General, and by the Attorneys General for their respective States as follows: Luther Strange of Alabama, John Suthers of Colorado, Joseph R. Biden III of Delaware, Samuel S. Olens of Georgia, David M. Louie of Hawaii, Lawrence G. Wasden of Idaho, James D. "Buddy" Caldwell of Louisiana, William J. Schneider of Maine, Jim Hood of Mississippi, E. Scott Pruitt of Oklahoma, Alan Wilson of South Carolina, Greg Abbott of Texas, Mark L. Shurtleff of Utah, Kenneth T. Cuccinelli II of Virginia, Robert M. McKenna of Washington, and Bruce A. Salzburg of Wyoming.

Brief of amici curiae filed on behalf of the National Conference of State Legislatures et al. by Pierre H. Bergeron.

IV. THE SUPREME COURT'S DECISION

"Our legal system generally requires each party to bear his own litigation expenses, including attorney's fees, regardless whether he wins or loses.... But Congress has authorized courts to deviate from this background rule in certain types of cases by shifting fees from one party to another....

The statute involved here, 42 U.S.C. § 1988, allows the award of 'a reasonable attorney's fee' to 'the prevailing party' in various kinds of civil rights cases, including suits brought under § 1983....

In Christiansburg, we held that § 1988 also authorizes a fee award to a prevailing defendant, but under a different standard reflecting the 'quite different equitable considerations' at stake....

[P]laintiffs may receive fees under § 1988 even if they are not victorious on every claim....

Analogous principles indicate that a defendant may deserve fees even if not all the plaintiff's claims were frivolous....

Fee-shifting to recompense a defendant (as to recompense a plaintiff) is not all-or-nothing: A defendant need not show that every claim in a complaint is frivolous to qualify for fees.

The question then becomes one of allocation: In a lawsuit involving a mix of frivolous and non-frivolous claims, what work may the defendant receive fees for? ...

That congressional policy points to a ... meaningful standard: Section 1988 allows a defendant to recover reasonable attorney's fees incurred because of, but only because of, a frivolous claim....

The task remains of applying these principles to the fee award Vice received....

On this record, we must return the case to the lower courts. In a suit of this kind, involving both frivolous and non-frivolous claims, a defendant may recover the reasonable attorney's fees he expended solely because of the frivolous allegations. And that is all. Consistent with the policy underlying § 1988, the defendant may not receive compensation for any fees that he would have paid in the absence of the frivolous claims. We therefore vacate the judgment of the Court of Appeals and remand the case ...."

V. JUSTICE VOTE

9 Pro ACLU Side vs. 0 Con Opposing Side

ACLU Side (Petitioner / Appellant)

1. Kagan, E. – Wrote majority opinion
2. Alito, S. – Joined majority opinion
3. Thomas, C. – Joined majority opinion
4. Breyer, S. – Joined majority opinion
5. Scalia, A. – Joined majority opinion
6. Kennedy, A. – Joined majority opinion
7. Ginsburg, R. – Joined majority opinion
8. Sotomayor, S. – Joined majority opinion
9. Roberts, J. – Joined majority opinion

VI. A WIN OR LOSS FOR THE ACLU?

The ACLU filed as amicus curiae urging reversal of the judgment of the Court of Appeals; the Supreme Court vacated in a 9-0 vote, giving the ACLU an apparent win.

1079. J.D.B. v. North Carolina

(Decided June 16, 2011; 564 U.S. 261)

I. ISSUE

A. Issues Discussed

Criminal procedure

B. Legal Question Presented

"This case presents the question whether the age of a child subjected to police questioning is relevant to the custody analysis of Miranda v. Arizona, 384 U.S. 436 (1966)."

C. Supreme Court's Answer

"It is beyond dispute that children will often feel bound to submit to police questioning when an adult in the same circumstances would feel free to leave. Seeing no reason for police officers or courts to blind themselves to that commonsense reality, we hold that a child's age properly informs the Miranda custody analysis."

II. CASE SUMMARY

A. Background

"Petitioner J.D.B. was a 13-year-old, seventh-grade student ... when he was removed from his classroom by a uniformed police officer ... and questioned by police ....

J.D.B. was given neither Miranda warnings nor the opportunity to speak to his grandmother. Nor was he informed that he was free to leave ....

J.D.B. explained that he had been in the neighborhood where the crimes occurred because he was seeking work mowing lawns. ... The assistant principal urged J.D.B. to 'do the right thing' ....

Eventually, J.D.B. asked whether he would 'still be in trouble' if he returned the 'stuff.' In response, DiCostanzo explained that return of the stolen items would be helpful, but 'this thing is going to court' regardless. ... DiCostanzo then warned that he may need to seek a secure custody order .... When J.D.B. asked what a secure custody order was, DiCostanzo explained that 'it's where you get sent to juvenile detention before court.'

After learning of the prospect of juvenile detention, J.D.B.

confessed that he and a friend were responsible for the break-ins. DiCostanzo only then informed J.D.B. that he could refuse to answer the investigator's questions and that he was free to leave. . . . When the bell rang indicating the end of the schoolday, J.D.B. was allowed to leave to catch the bus home. . . .

Two juvenile petitions were filed against J.D.B. . . . . J.D.B.'s public defender moved to suppress his statements and the evidence derived . . . . [T]he trial court denied the motion . . . .

A divided panel of the North Carolina Court of Appeals affirmed. The North Carolina Supreme Court held . . . that J.D.B. was not in custody when he confessed . . . ."

The Supreme Court granted certiorari to review the case.

B. Counsel of Record / ACLU Attorney

ACLU Side (Petitioner / Appellant): Barbara S. Blackman argued the cause for appellant. With her on the briefs were S. Hannah Demeritt, Benjamin Dowling-Sendor, and Staples S. Hughes.

Opposing Side (Respondent / Appellee): Roy Cooper, Attorney General of North Carolina, argued the cause for appellee. With him on the brief were Christopher G. Browning, Jr., Solicitor General, Robert C. Montgomery, Special Deputy Attorney General, and LaToya B. Powell, Assistant Attorney General.

Eric J. Feigin argued the cause for the United States as amicus curiae.

III. AMICI CURIAE

ACLU Side (Petitioner / Appellant)

Brief of amici curiae filed on behalf of the American Civil Liberties Union by Catherine Y. Kim, Dennis D. Parker, Courtney A. Browie, and Steven R. Shapiro.

Brief of amici curiae filed on behalf of the American Bar Association by Stephen N. Zack.

Brief of amici curiae filed on behalf of the Center on Wrongful Convictions of Youth et al. by Angela C. Vigil and Steven A. Drizin.

Brief of amici curiae filed on behalf of the Juvenile Law Center et al. by Marsha L. Levick and Jessica R. Feierman.

Brief of amici curiae filed on behalf of the National Association of Criminal Defense Lawyers by Jeffrey T. Green, Mark D. Hopson, and Jonathan Hacker.

Opposing Side (Respondent / Appellee)

Brief of amici curiae filed on behalf of the United States by Eric J. Feigin, Acting Solicitor General Katyal, Assistant Attorney General Breuer, Deputy Solicitor General Dreeben, and William C. Brown.

Brief of amici curiae filed on behalf of the State of Indiana et al. by Gregory F. Zoeller, Attorney General of Indiana, Thomas M. Fisher, Solicitor General, Stephen R. Creason, Andrew A. Kobe, and Ellen H. Meilaender, Deputy Attorney General, by Kevin T. Kane, Chief State's Attorney of Connecticut, and William H. Ryan, Jr., Acting Attorney General of Pennsylvania, and by the Attorneys General for their respective jurisdictions as follows: Luther Strange of Alabama, Dustin McDaniel of Arkansas, Joseph R. Biden III of Delaware, Pamela Jo Bondi of Florida, Samuel S. Olens of Georgia, Leonardo M. Rapadas of Guam, David M. Louie of Hawaii, Lawrence G. Wasden of Idaho, Lisa Madigan of Illinois, Tom Miller of Iowa, Jack Conway of Kentucky, James D. Caldwell of Louisiana, William J. Schneider of Maine, Bill Schuette of Michigan, Steve Bullock of Montana, Jon Bruning of Nebraska, Catherine Cortez Masto of Nevada, Guillermo A. Somoza-Colombani of Puerto Rico, E. Scott Pruitt of Oklahoma, Michael DeWine of Ohio, Peter F. Kilmartin of Rhode Island, Alan Wilson of South Carolina, Marty J. Jackley of South Dakota, Robert E. Cooper, Jr., of Tennessee, Greg Abbott of Texas, Mark L. Shurtleff of Utah, Kenneth T. Cuccinelli II of Virginia, Robert M. McKenna of Washington, and Bruce A. Salzburg of Wyoming.

Brief of amici curiae filed on behalf of the National District Attorneys Association by John Charles Thomas and Megan Miller.

IV. THE SUPREME COURT'S DECISION

"Recognizing that the inherently coercive nature of custodial interrogation 'blurs the line between voluntary and involuntary statements,' this Court in Miranda adopted a set of prophylactic measures designed to safeguard the constitutional guarantee against self-incrimination. . . .

Because these measures protect the individual against the coercive nature of custodial interrogation, they are required "only where there has been such a restriction on a person's freedom as to render him 'in custody.'" As we have repeatedly emphasized, whether a suspect is 'in custody' is an objective inquiry. . . .

The State and its amici contend that a child's age has no place in the custody analysis . . . . We cannot agree. In some circumstances, a child's age 'would have affected how a reasonable person' in the suspect's position 'would perceive his or her freedom to leave.' That is, a reasonable child subjected to police questioning will sometimes feel pressured to submit when a reasonable adult would feel free to go. . . .

Reviewing the question de novo today, we hold that so long as the child's age was known to the officer at the time of police questioning, or would have been objectively apparent to a reasonable officer, its inclusion in the custody analysis is consistent with the objective nature of that test. . . .

The State and its amici offer numerous reasons that courts must blind themselves to a juvenile defendant's age. None is persuasive. . . .

The question remains whether J.D.B. was in custody when police interrogated him. We remand for the state courts to address that question, this time taking account of all of the relevant circumstances of the interrogation, including J.D.B.'s age at the time. The judgment of the North Carolina Supreme Court is reversed, and the case is remanded for proceedings not inconsistent with this opinion."

V. JUSTICE VOTE

5 Pro ACLU Side vs. 4 Con Opposing Side

ACLU Side (Petitioner / Appellant)

1. Sotomayor, S. – Wrote majority opinion

2. Kagan, E. – Joined majority opinion
3. Breyer, S. – Joined majority opinion
4. Kennedy, A. – Joined majority opinion
5. Ginsburg, R. – Joined majority opinion

Opposing Side (Respondent / Appellee)

1. Alito, S. – Wrote dissenting opinion
2. Thomas, C. – Joined Alito's dissent
3. Scalia, A. – Joined Alito's dissent
4. Roberts, J. – Joined Alito's dissent

VI. A WIN OR LOSS FOR THE ACLU?

The ACLU filed as amicus curiae urging reversal of the judgment of the North Carolina Supreme Court; the U.S. Supreme Court reversed in a 5-4 vote, giving the ACLU an apparent win.

1080. Wal-Mart Stores, Inc. v. Dukes

(Decided June 20, 2011; 564 U.S. 338)

I. ISSUE

A. Issues Discussed

Civil procedure, gender

B. Legal Question Presented

"The District Court and the Court of Appeals approved the certification of a class comprising about one and a half million plaintiffs, current and former female employees of petitioner Wal-Mart who allege that the discretion exercised by their local supervisors over pay and promotion matters violates Title VII by discriminating against women.... We consider whether the certification of the plaintiff class was consistent with Federal Rules of Civil Procedure 23(a) and (b)(2)."

C. Supreme Court's Answer

The certification of the plaintiff class was improper under Federal Rules of Civil Procedure 23(a) and (b)(2).

II. CASE SUMMARY

A. Background

"The named plaintiffs in this lawsuit, representing the 1.5 million members of the certified class, are three current or former Wal-Mart employees who allege that the company discriminated against them on the basis of their sex....

These plaintiffs, respondents here, ... claim that their local managers' discretion over pay and promotions is exercised disproportionately in favor of men....

Importantly for our purposes, respondents claim that the discrimination to which they have been subjected is common to all Wal-Mart's female employees.... Respondents therefore wish to litigate the Title VII claims ... in a nationwide class action....

[R]espondents moved the District Court to certify a plaintiff class consisting of "[a]ll women employed at any Wal-Mart domestic retail store at any time since December 26, 1998, who have been or may be subjected to Wal-Mart's challenged pay and management track promotions policies and practices." ... As evidence that there were indeed 'questions of law or fact common to' all the women of Wal-Mart, as Rule 23(a)(2) requires, respondents relied chiefly on three forms of proof: statistical evidence about pay and promotion disparities between men and women at the company, anecdotal reports of discrimination from about 120 of Wal-Mart's female employees, and the testimony of a sociologist, Dr. William Bielby, who conducted a 'social framework analysis' of Wal-Mart's 'culture' and personnel practices, and concluded that the company was 'vulnerable' to gender discrimination.

Wal-Mart unsuccessfully moved to strike much of this evidence. [T]he District Court granted respondents' motion and certified their proposed class....

A divided en banc Court of Appeals ... affirmed the District Court's certification order."

The Supreme Court granted certiorari to review the case.

B. Counsel of Record / ACLU Attorney

ACLU Side (Respondent / Appellee): Joseph M. Sellers argued the cause for appellees. With him on the brief were Brad Seligman, Jocelyn D. Larkin, Christine E. Webber, Jenny R. Yang, Kalpana Kotagal, Steven Stemerman, Elizabeth A. Lawrence, Arcelia Hurtado, Sheila Y. Thomas, Stephen Tinkler, and Merit Bennett.

Opposing Side (Petitioner / Appellant): Theodore J. Boutrous, Jr., argued the cause for appellant. With him on the briefs were Rachel S. Brass, Theane Evangelis Kapur, Theodore B. Olson, Mark A. Perry, and Amir C. Tayrani.

III. AMICI CURIAE

ACLU Side (Respondent / Appellee)

Brief of amici curiae filed on behalf of the American Civil Liberties Union and National Women's Law Center, et al. by Marcia D. Greenberger, Emily J. Martin

Fatima Goss Graves, Dina R. Lassow, Anne King, Lenora M. Lapidus, Steven R. Shapiro, Ariela M. Migdal, and Linda Lye.

Brief of amici curiae filed on behalf of the American Association for Justice by John Vail.

Brief of amici curiae filed on behalf of the American Sociological Association et al. by Michael B. Trister.

Brief of amici curiae filed on behalf of Civil Procedure Professors by Melissa Hart, Arthur R. Miller, and Paul M. Secunda, all pro se.

Brief of amici curiae filed on behalf of the Consumers Union of United States, Inc., et al. by Kevin K. Green and Mark R. Savage.

Brief of amici curiae filed on behalf of the Institute for Women's Policy Research by Linda M. Dardarian.

Brief of amici curiae filed on behalf of Law and Economics Professors by Robert S. Libman and Benjamin Blustein.

Brief of amici curiae filed on behalf of the NAACP Legal Defense and Educational Fund, Inc., et al. by John Payton and Debo P. Adegbile.

Brief of amici curiae filed on behalf of the National Employment Lawyers Association et al. by Cyrus Mehri, Pamela Coukos,

Janelle M. Carter, Rebecca M. Hamburg, Michael L. Foreman, James M. Finberg, Paul W. Mollica, Reginald T. Shuford, and William C. McNeil III.

Brief of amici curiae filed on behalf of Public Citizen, Inc., by Scott L. Nelson, Allison M. Zieve, and Brian Wolfman.

Brief of amici curiae filed on behalf of Public Justice, P. C., et al. by Monique Olivier, James C. Sturdevant, Arthur H. Bryant, F. Paul Bland, Jr., Victoria W. Ni, and Tracy D. Rezvani.

Brief of amici curiae filed on behalf of the United Food and Commercial Workers International Union et al. by Robert M. Weinberg, Andrew D. Roth, Laurence Gold, Patrick J. Szymanski, Edward P. Wendel, and Lynn K. Rhinehart.

Brief of amici curiae filed on behalf of the U. S. Women's Chamber of Commerce et al. by Judith L. Lichtman and Sarah Crawford.

Brief of amici curiae filed on behalf of Labor Economists and Statisticians by Daniel B. Edelman filed a brief for Labor Economists and Statisticians.

Opposing Side (Petitioner / Appellant)

Brief of amici curiae filed on behalf of Altria Group, Inc., et al. by Jeffrey A. Lamken, Robert K. Kry, and Martin V. Totaro.

Brief of amici curiae filed on behalf of the Association of Global Automakers, Inc., by Donald M. Falk, Dan Himmelfarb, Archis A. Parasharami, and Kevin Ranlett.

Brief of amici curiae filed on behalf of the Atlantic Legal Foundation et al. by Martin S. Kaufman, Martin J. Newhouse, and John Pagliaro.

Brief of amici curiae filed on behalf of the California Employment Law Council by Paul Grossman.

Brief of amici curiae filed on behalf of the Chamber of Commerce of the United States of America by John H. Beisner, Geoffrey M. Wyatt, Robin S. Conrad, and Shane B. Kawka.

Brief of amici curiae filed on behalf of Costco Wholesale Corp. by David B. Ross, Kenwood C. Youmans, David D. Kadue, Thomas J. Wybenga, and Gerald L. Maatman, Jr.

Brief of amici curiae filed on behalf of DRI–The Voice of the Defense Bar by R. Matthew Cairns, Carter G. Phillips, Jonathan F. Cohn, and Matthew D. Krueger.

Brief of amici curiae filed on behalf of the Equal Employment Advisory Council by Rae T. Vann.

Brief of amici curiae filed on behalf of Intel Corp. by Roy T. Englert, Jr., Mark T. Stancil, and A. Douglas Melamed.

Brief of amici curiae filed on behalf of the International Association of Defense Counsel by Mary-Christine Sungaila and Troy L. Booher.

Brief of amici curiae filed on behalf of the Pacific Legal Foundation by Timothy Sandefur.

Brief of amici curiae filed on behalf of the Retail Litigation Center, Inc., by Lisa S. Blatt.

Brief of amici curiae filed on behalf of the Securities Industry and Financial Markets Association by E. Joshua Rosenkranz, Michael Delikat, Jill L. Rosenberg, John D. Giansello, Gary R. Siniscalco, and Patricia K. Gillette.

Brief of amici curiae filed on behalf of the Society for Human Resource Management et al. by Camille A. Olson and James M. Harris.

Brief of amici curiae filed on behalf of the Washington Legal Foundation by Daniel J. Popeo and Richard A. Samp.

IV. THE SUPREME COURT'S DECISION

"Rule 23(a) ensures that . . . named plaintiffs are appropriate representatives of the class . . . . The Rule's four requirements—numerosity, commonality, typicality, and adequate representation—'effectively 'limit the class claims to those fairly encompassed by the named plaintiff's claims." . . .

The crux of this case is commonality—the rule requiring a plaintiff to show that 'there are questions of law or fact common to the class.' . . .

In this case, proof of commonality necessarily overlaps with respondents' merits contention that Wal-Mart engages in a pattern or practice of discrimination . . . . Here respondents wish to sue about literally millions of employment decisions at once. Without some glue holding the alleged reasons for all those decisions together, it will be impossible to say that examination of all the class members' claims for relief will produce a common answer to the crucial question why was I disfavored. . . .

In sum, . . . the members of the class: . . .

[H]ave little in common but their sex and this lawsuit.' . . .

We also conclude that respondents' claims for backpay were improperly certified under Federal Rule of Civil Procedure 23(b)(2). . . . We now hold that they may not [be certified], at least where (as here) the monetary relief is not incidental to the injunctive or declaratory relief. . . .

Given that structure, we think it clear . . . individualized monetary claims belong in Rule 23(b)(3). . . .

Contrary to the Ninth Circuit's view, Wal-Mart is entitled to individualized determinations of each employee's eligibility for backpay. . . .

We have established a procedure for trying pattern-or-practice cases that gives effect to these statutory requirements. When the plaintiff seeks individual relief such as reinstatement or backpay after establishing a pattern or practice of discrimination, 'a district court must usually conduct additional proceedings . . . to determine the scope of individual relief.' . . .

The Court of Appeals believed that it was possible to replace such proceedings with Trial by Formula. . . . We disapprove that novel project. . . .

The judgment of the Court of Appeals is reversed."

V. JUSTICE VOTE

4 Pro ACLU Side vs. 5 Con Opposing Side

ACLU Side (Respondent / Appellee)

1. Kagan, E. – Joined Ginsburg's opinion
2. Breyer, S. – Joined Ginsburg's opinion
3. Ginsburg, R. – Wrote opinion concurring in part and dissenting in part
4. Sotomayor, S. – Joined Ginsburg's opinion

Opposing Side (Petitioner / Appellant)

1. Scalia, A. – Wrote majority opinion

2. Alito, S. – Joined majority opinion
3. Thomas, C. – Joined majority opinion
4. Kennedy, A. – Joined majority opinion
5. Roberts, J. – Joined majority opinion

VI. A WIN OR LOSS FOR THE ACLU?

The ACLU filed as amicus curiae urging affirmance; the Supreme Court reversed the Court of Appeals' decision by a 5-4 vote, giving the ACLU an apparent loss.

1081. Borough of Duryea v. Guarnieri

(Decided June 20, 2011; 564 U.S. 379)

I. ISSUE

A. Issues Discussed

Union, 1st Amendment, press, speech, association

B. Legal Question Presented

"To show that an employer interfered with rights under the Speech Clause, the employee, as a general rule, must show that his speech was on a matter of public concern, as that term is defined in the precedents of this and other courts. Here the issue is whether that test applies when the employee invokes the Petition Clause."

C. Supreme Court's Answer

The public concern test applies under the Petition Clause.

II. CASE SUMMARY

A. Background

"Charles Guarnieri filed a union grievance challenging his termination as chief of police for the borough of Duryea . . . . His grievance proceeded to arbitration pursuant to the police union collective-bargaining agreement. The arbitrator found that the borough council . . . committed procedural errors . . . ; and . . . also found that Guarnieri engaged in misconduct, including 'attempting to intimidate Council members.' The arbitrator ordered Guarnieri reinstated after a disciplinary suspension.

Upon Guarnieri's return . . . , the council issued 11 directives instructing Guarnieri in the performance of his duties. . . . Guarnieri filed a second union grievance challenging the directives. The arbitrator instructed the council to modify or withdraw some of the[m] . . . .

Guarnieri filed this lawsuit . . . under 42 U.S.C. § 1983. Guarnieri claimed that his first union grievance was a petition protected by the Petition Clause of the First Amendment, and he alleged that the directives issued upon his reinstatement were retaliation . . . .

After this suit was filed, the council denied a request by Guarnieri for $338 in overtime. The United States Department of Labor investigated and concluded that Guarnieri was entitled to be paid. The council offered Guarnieri a check for the amount, but Guarnieri refused to accept it. Instead, Guarnieri amended his complaint to encompass the denial of overtime . . . .

The case proceeded to a jury. . . . The jury found in favor of Guarnieri. . . .

[T]he Court of Appeals . . . affirmed the award of compensatory damages, although it found insufficient evidence to sustain the award of punitive damages."

The Supreme Court granted certiorari to review the case.

B. Counsel of Record / ACLU Attorney

ACLU Side (Respondent / Appellee): Opposing Side (Petitioner / Appellant): Eric Schnapper argued the cause for respondent. With him on the brief was Cynthia L. Pollick. Daniel R. Ortiz argued the cause for appellants. With him on the briefs were James E. Ryan, Toby J. Heytens, David T. Goldberg, John P. Elwood, Karoline Mehalchick, and Mark T. Stancil.

Joseph R. Palmore argued the cause for the United States as amicus curiae.

III. AMICI CURIAE

ACLU Side (Respondent / Appellee)

Brief of amici curiae filed on behalf of the American Civil Liberties Union and the ACLU of Pennsylvania by Carter G. Phillips, Rebecca K. Troth, Witold J. Walczak, Steven R. Shapiro, Seth F. Kreimer, and Kenneth W. Gemmill.

Brief of amici curiae filed on behalf of the American Federation of Labor and Congress of Industrial Organizations by Lynn K. Rhinehart, James B. Coppess, Angelia D. Wade, and Laurence Gold.

Brief of amici curiae filed on behalf of the Justice and Freedom Fund by James L. Hirsen and Deborah J. Dewart.

Brief of amici curiae filed on behalf of the National Fraternal Order of Police et al. by Larry H. James and Christina L. Corl.

Opposing Side (Petitioner / Appellant)

Brief of amici curiae filed on behalf of the United States by Joseph R. Palmore, Acting Solicitor General Katyal, Assistant Attorney General West, Acting Deputy Solicitor General Kruger, Ann O'Connell, William Kanter, and Michael E. Robinson.

Brief of amici curiae filed on behalf of the State of Florida et al. by Bill McCollum, Attorney General of Florida, Scott D. Makar, Solicitor General, and Ronald A. Lathan, Deputy Solicitor General, by Russell A. Suzuki, Acting Attorney General of Hawaii, and by the Attorneys General for their respective States as follows: Troy King of Alabama, John Suthers of Colorado, Joseph R. Biden III of Delaware, Lisa Madigan of Illinois, Gregory F. Zoeller of Indiana, James D. "Buddy" Caldwell of Louisiana, Janet T. Mills of Maine, Michael A. Cox of Michigan, Jim Hood of Mississippi, Paula T. Dow of New Jersey, Richard Cordray of Ohio, W. A. Drew Edmondson of Oklahoma, Thomas W. Corbett, Jr., of Pennsylvania, Marty J. Jackley of South Dakota, Robert E. Cooper, Jr., of Tennessee, Greg Abbott of Texas, Mark L. Shurtleff of Utah, Darrell V. McGraw, Jr., of West Virginia, and Bruce A. Salzburg of Wyoming.

Brief of amici curiae filed on behalf of the National Conference of State Legislatures et al. by L. Rachel Helyar.

Brief of amici curiae filed on behalf of the National School Boards Association by Francisco M. Negrón, Jr., Naomi E.

Gittins, and Sonja H. Trainor.

IV. THE SUPREME COURT'S DECISION

"The question presented by this case is whether the history and purpose of the Petition Clause justify the imposition of broader liability when an employee invokes its protection instead of the protection afforded by the Speech Clause. . . .

Unrestrained application of the Petition Clause in the context of government employment would subject a wide range of government operations to invasive judicial superintendence. . . . This would raise serious federalism and separation-of-powers concerns. . . .

This case illustrates these risks and costs. . . .

If the Petition Clause were to apply even where matters of public concern are not involved, that would be unnecessary, or even disruptive, when there is already protection for the rights of public employees to file grievances and to litigate. . . .

In light of the government's interests in the public employment context, it would be surprising if Petition Clause claims by public employees were not limited . . . .

The public concern test was developed to protect these substantial government interests. . . .

The framework used to govern Speech Clause claims by public employees, when applied to the Petition Clause, will protect both the interests of the government and the First Amendment right. . . .

As under the Speech Clause, whether an employee's petition relates to a matter of public concern will depend on 'the content, form, and context of [the petition], as revealed by the whole record.' . . .

Of course in one sense the public may always be interested in how government officers are performing their duties. But as the Connick and Pickering test has evolved, that will not always suffice to show a matter of public concern. . . .

Because the Third Circuit did not find it necessary to apply this framework, there has been no determination as to how it would apply in the context of this case. . . . This Court need not consider this issue without the benefit of full briefs by the parties.

The judgment of the Court of Appeals is vacated, and the case is remanded . . . ."

V. JUSTICE VOTE

0 Pro ACLU Side vs. 9 Con Opposing Side

Opposing Side (Petitioner / Appellant)

1. Alito, S. – Wrote majority opinion
2. Kagan, E. – Joined majority opinion
3. Thomas, C. – Wrote concurring opinion
4. Breyer, S. – Joined majority opinion
5. Scalia, A. – Wrote opinion concurring in part and dissenting in part
6. Kennedy, A. – Joined majority opinion
7. Ginsburg, R. – Joined majority opinion
8. Sotomayor, S. – Joined majority opinion
9. Roberts, J. – Joined majority opinion

VI. A WIN OR LOSS FOR THE ACLU?

The ACLU filed as amicus curiae urging affirmance; the Supreme Court vacated the Court of Appeals' decision by a 9-0 vote, giving the ACLU an apparent loss.

1082. Turner v. Rogers

(Decided June 20, 2011; 564 U.S. 431)

I. ISSUE

A. Issues Discussed

Civil procedure

B. Legal Question Presented

"South Carolina's Family Court enforces its child support orders by threatening with incarceration for civil contempt those who are (1) subject to a child support order, (2) able to comply with that order, but (3) fail to do so. We must decide whether the Fourteenth Amendment's Due Process Clause requires the State to provide counsel (at a civil contempt hearing) to an indigent person potentially faced with such incarceration."

C. Supreme Court's Answer

"We conclude that where as here the custodial parent (entitled to receive the support) is unrepresented by counsel, the State need not provide counsel to the noncustodial parent (required to provide the support). But we attach an important caveat, namely, that the State must nonetheless have in place alternative procedures that assure a fundamentally fair determination of the critical incarceration-related question, whether the supporting parent is able to comply with the support order."

II. CASE SUMMARY

A. Background

"In June 2003 a South Carolina family court entered an order, which . . . required petitioner, Michael Turner, to pay [child support] . . . . Turner repeatedly failed to pay . . . and was held in contempt . . . . The fifth time he did not pay but completed a 6-month sentence.

After his release in 2006 Turner remained in arrears. On March 27, 2006, the clerk issued a new 'show cause' order. And . . . Turner's civil contempt hearing took place on January 3, 2008. Turner and Rogers were present, each without representation by counsel. . . .

[T]he judge stated,

'. . . I find the Defendant in willful contempt. I'm [going to] sentence him to twelve months in the Oconee County Detention Center. He may purge himself of the contempt and avoid the sentence by having a zero balance on or before his release. I've also placed a lien on any SSI or other benefits.'

The judge added . . . '[i]f you've got a job, I'll make you eligible for work release.' When Turner asked why he could not receive good-time or work credits, the judge said, '[b]ecause that's my ruling.'

The court made no express finding concerning Turner's ability to pay his arrearage . . . . Nor did the judge ask any followup questions or otherwise address the ability-to-pay issue. . . .

While serving his 12-month sentence, Turner, with the help of pro bono counsel, appealed. He claimed that the Federal Constitution entitled him to counsel at his contempt hearing. The South Carolina Supreme Court . . . rejected his 'right to counsel' claim."

The Supreme Court granted certiorari to review the case.

B. Counsel of Record / ACLU Attorney

ACLU Side (Petitioner / Appellant): Seth P. Waxman argued the cause for appellant. With him on the briefs were Paul R. Q. Wolfson, Catherine M. A. Carroll, Derek J. Enderlin, and Kathrine Haggard Hudgins.

Acting Principal Deputy Solicitor General Kruger argued the cause for the United States as amicus curiae.

Opposing Side (Respondent / Appellee): Stephanos Bibas argued the cause for appellees. With him on the brief were James A. Feldman, Amy Wax, Stephen B. Kinnaird, and Panteha Abdollahi.

III. AMICI CURIAE

ACLU Side (Petitioner / Appellant)

Brief of amici curiae filed on behalf of the National Association of Criminal Defense Lawyers, the Brennan Center for Justice, the National Legal Aid & Defender Association, the Southern Center for Human Rights, and the American Civil Liberties Union by Stephen J. McConnell, Malia N. Brink, Jeffrey T. Green, Edwin A. Burnette, Sarah Geraghty, Steven R. Shapiro. Meghan Rohling Kelly, Christina S. Keddie, David S. Caroline. Rebekah Diller, and Laura Abel.

Brief of amici curiae filed on behalf of the United States by Acting Principal Deputy Solicitor General Kruger, Acting Solicitor General Katyal, Assistant Attorney General West, Joseph R. Palmore, Leonard Schaitman, Edward Himmelfarb, and Robert E. Keith.

Brief of amici curiae filed on behalf of the American Bar Association by Stephen N. Zack and Nicholas P. Gellert.

Brief of amici curiae filed on behalf of the Center for Family Policy and Practice by Michael D. Leffel.

Brief of amici curiae filed on behalf of the Constitution Project by David M. Raim, Kate McSweeny, and Virginia E. Sloan.

Brief of amici curiae filed on behalf of the Legal Aid Society of the District of Columbia et al. by Peter D. Keisler, Edward R. McNicholas, Rebecca K. Troth, and David A. Reiser.

Brief of amici curiae filed on behalf of Elizabeth G. Patterson et al. by Lisa S. Blatt, Anthony J. Franze, and Sheila B. Scheuerman.

Opposing Side (Respondent / Appellee)

Brief of amici curiae filed on behalf of the State of Texas et al. by Greg Abbott, Attorney General of Texas, Jonathan F. Mitchell, Solicitor General, Daniel T. Hodge, First Assistant Attorney General, Bill Cobb, Deputy Attorney General, and David C. Mattax, and by the Attorneys General for their respective States as follows: Luther Strange of Alabama, Thomas C. Horne of Arizona, John W. Suthers of Colorado, Pamela Jo Bondi of Florida, David M. Louie of Hawaii, William J. Schneider of Maine, Jim Hood of Mississippi, Michael A. Delaney of New Hampshire, Alan Wilson of South Carolina, Mark L. Shurtleff of Utah, Kenneth T. Cuccinelli II of Virginia, and Bruce A. Salzburg of Wyoming.

Brief of amici curiae filed on behalf of Benjamin Barton et al. by Adam K. Mortara and Mr. Barton, pro se.

Brief of amici curiae filed on behalf of Senator Jim DeMint et al. by Noel J. Francisco.

IV. THE SUPREME COURT'S DECISION

"We must decide whether the Due Process Clause grants an indigent defendant, such as Turner, a right to state-appointed counsel at a civil contempt proceeding, which may lead to his incarceration. This Court's precedents provide no definitive answer . . . . This Court has long held that the Sixth Amendment grants an indigent defendant the right to state-appointed counsel in a criminal case. . . .

But the Sixth Amendment does not govern civil cases. Civil contempt differs from criminal contempt in that it seeks only to 'coerc[e] the defendant to do' what a court had previously ordered him to do. A court may not impose punishment 'in a civil contempt proceeding when it is clearly established that the alleged contemnor is unable to comply with the terms of the order.' . . .

Consequently, the Court has made clear . . . that, where civil contempt is at issue, the Fourteenth Amendment's Due Process Clause allows a State to provide fewer procedural protections . . . .

Given the importance of the interest at stake, it is obviously important to assure accurate decisionmaking in respect to the key 'ability to pay' question. . . .

On the other hand, the Due Process Clause does not always require the provision of counsel in civil proceedings where incarceration is threatened. And in determining whether the Clause requires a right to counsel here, we must . . . consider the . . . value of 'additional or substitute procedural safeguards.'

Doing so, we find three related considerations that, when taken together, argue strongly against the Due Process Clause requiring the State to provide indigents with counsel . . . .

First, the critical question . . . concerns, as we have said, the defendant's ability to pay. . . .

Second, sometimes, as here, the person opposing the defendant at the hearing is not the government represented by counsel but the custodial parent un represented by counsel. . . .

Third, . . . there is available a set of 'substitute procedural safeguards,' which, if employed together, can significantly reduce the risk of an erroneous deprivation of liberty. . . .

While recognizing the strength of Turner's arguments, we ultimately believe that the three considerations . . . must carry the day. . . . We consequently hold that the Due Process Clause does not automatically require the provision of counsel at civil contempt proceedings to an indigent individual . . . subject to a child support order, even if that individual faces incarceration (for up to a year). . . .

The record indicates that Turner received neither counsel nor the benefit of alternative procedures like those we have described. . . . The court nonetheless found Turner in contempt and ordered him incarcerated. Under these circumstances Turner's incarceration violated the Due Process Clause.

We vacate the judgment of the South Carolina Supreme Court and remand the case . . . ."

V. JUSTICE VOTE

5 Pro ACLU Side vs. 4 Con Opposing Side

ACLU Side (Petitioner / Appellant)

1. Breyer, S. – Wrote majority opinion
2. Kagan, E. – Joined majority opinion
3. Kennedy, A. – Joined majority opinion
4. Ginsburg, R. – Joined majority opinion
5. Sotomayor, S. – Joined majority opinion

Opposing Side (Respondent / Appellee)

1. Alito, S. – Joined Thomas' dissent in part
2. Thomas, C. – Wrote dissenting opinion
3. Scalia, A. – Joined Thomas' dissent
4. Roberts, J. – Joined Thomas' dissent in part

VI. A WIN OR LOSS FOR THE ACLU?

The ACLU filed as amicus curiae urging reversal of the judgment of the Court of Appeals; the Supreme Court vacated and remanded in a 5-4 vote, giving the ACLU an apparent win.

1083. Brown v. Entertainment Merchants Ass'n

(Decided June 27, 2011; 564 U.S. 786)

I. ISSUE

A. Issues Discussed

1st Amendment, obscenity

B. Legal Question Presented

"We consider whether a California law imposing restrictions on violent video games comports with the First Amendment."

C. Supreme Court's Answer

"Because the Act imposes a restriction on the content of protected speech, it is invalid unless California can demonstrate that it passes strict scrutiny—that is, unless it is justified by a compelling government interest and is narrowly drawn to serve that interest. . . .California cannot meet that standard."

II. CASE SUMMARY

A. Background

"California Assembly Bill 1179 (2005) prohibits the sale or rental of 'violent video games' to minors, and requires their packaging to be labeled '18.' The Act covers games 'in which the range of options available to a player includes killing, maiming, dismembering, or sexually assaulting an image of a human being, if those acts are depicted' in a manner that '[a] reasonable person, considering the game as a whole, would find appeals to a deviant or morbid interest of minors,' that is 'patently offensive to prevailing standards in the community as to what is suitable for minors,' and that 'causes the game, as a whole, to lack serious literary, artistic, political, or scientific value for minors.' Violation of the Act is punishable by a civil fine of up to $1,000.

Respondents, representing the video-game and software industries, brought a preenforcement challenge to the Act in the United States District Court for the Northern District of California. That court concluded that the Act violated the First Amendment and permanently enjoined its enforcement. The Court of Appeals affirmed . . . ."

The Supreme Court granted certiorari to review the case.

B. Counsel of Record / ACLU Attorney

ACLU Side (Respondent / Appellee): Paul M. Smith argued the cause for appellees. With him on the brief were Katherine A. Fallow, Matthew S. Hellman, Duane C. Pozza, William M. Hohengarten, and Kenneth L. Doroshow.

Opposing Side (Petitioner / Appellant): Zackery P. Morazzini, Supervising Deputy Attorney General of California, argued the cause for appellants. With him on the briefs were Edmund G. Brown, Jr., Attorney General, David S. Chaney, Chief Assistant Attorney General, Manuel M. Medeiros, State Solicitor General, Gordon Burns, Deputy Solicitor General, Jonathan K. Renner, Senior Assistant Attorney General, and Daniel J. Powell, Deputy Attorney General.

III. AMICI CURIAE

ACLU Side (Respondent / Appellee)

Brief of amici curiae filed on behalf of the American Civil Liberties Union, the National Coalition Against Censorship, and the National Youth Rights Association by Christopher A. Hansen, Steven R. Shapiro, David Blair-Loy, Joan E. Bertin, Peter J. Eliasberg, and Alan Schlosser.

Brief of amici curiae filed on behalf of the State of Rhode Island et al. by Patrick C. Lynch, Attorney General of Rhode Island, Joseph M. Lipner, and Elliot Brown, and by the Attorneys General for their respective jurisdictions as follows: Dustin McDaniel of Arkansas, Thurbert E. Baker of Georgia, Jon C. Bruning of Nebraska, Wayne Stenehjem of North Dakota, W. A. Drew Edmondson of Oklahoma, Guillermo A. Somoza-Colombani of Puerto Rico, Henry McMaster of South Carolina, Mark L. Shurtleff of Utah, and Robert M. McKenna of Washington.

Brief of amici curiae filed on behalf of Activision Blizzard, Inc., by Paul J. Watford.

Brief of amici curiae filed on behalf of the American Booksellers Foundation for Free Expression et al. by Michael A. Bamberger and Richard M. Zuckerman.

Brief of amici curiae filed on behalf of the Chamber of Commerce of the United States of America by Lisa S. Blatt, Christopher S. Rhee, Robin S. Conrad, and Amar Sarwal.

Brief of amici curiae filed on behalf of the Computer &

Communications Industry Association et al. by John B. Morris, Jr.

Brief of amici curiae filed on behalf of the Consumer Electronic Retailers Coalition et al. by Seth D. Greenstein.

Brief of amici curiae filed on behalf of the Entertainment Consumers Association et al. by William R. Stein, Daniel H. Weiner, Daniel C. Doeschner, and Jennifer Mercurio.

Brief of amici curiae filed on behalf of the First Amendment Lawyers Association by Lawrence G. Walters and Jennifer S. Kinsley.

Brief of amici curiae filed on behalf of First Amendment Scholars by Donald M. Falk and Eugene Volokh.

Brief of amici curiae filed on behalf of the Future of Music Coalition et al. by Andrew Jay Schwartzman.

Brief of amici curiae filed on behalf of Id Software LLC by James T. Drakeley, Kevin J. Keith, Paul E. Salamanca, and J. Griffin Lesher.

Brief of amici curiae filed on behalf of the International Game Developers Association et al. by Christopher J. Wright, Timothy J. Simeone, and Mark D. Davis.

Brief of amici curiae filed on behalf of the Marion B. Brechner First Amendment Project et al. by Clay Calvert and Robert D. Richards.

Brief of amici curiae filed on behalf of Microsoft Corp. by Theodore B. Olson and Matthew D. McGill.

Brief of amici curiae filed on behalf of the Motion Picture Association of America, Inc., et al. by Kannon K. Shanmugam, David E. Kendall, and Thomas G. Hentoff.

Brief of amici curiae filed on behalf of the National Association of Broadcasters by Robert A. Long, Jr., Stephen A. Weiswasser, Mark W. Mosier, Jane E. Mago, and Jerianne Timmerman.

Brief of amici curiae filed on behalf of the National Cable & Telecommunications Association by H. Bartow Farr III, Rick Chessen, Neal M. Goldberg, Michael S. Schooler, and Diane B. Burstein.

Brief of amici curiae filed on behalf of the Progress & Freedom Foundation et al. by Cindy Cohn.

Brief of amici curiae filed on behalf of Social Scientists et al. by Patricia A. Millett and Michael C. Small.

Brief of amici curiae filed on behalf of the Thomas Jefferson Center for the Protection of Free Expression et al. by Robert M. O'Neil and J. Joshua Wheeler.

Brief of amici curiae filed on behalf of Vindicia, Inc., by Alan Gura and Laura Possessky.

Brief of amici curiae filed on behalf of the Cato Institute by John P. Elwood, Ilya Shapiro, and Thomas S. Leatherbury.

Brief of amici curiae filed on behalf of the Comic Book Legal Defense Fund by Robert Corn-Revere and Ronald G. London.

Brief of amici curiae filed on behalf of the First Amendment Coalition by Gary L. Bostwick and Jean-Paul Jassy.

Brief of amici curiae filed on behalf of the Reporters Committee for Freedom of the Press et al. by Lucy Dalglish, Gregg P. Leslie, Kevin M. Goldberg, David Greene, Mickey H. Osterreicher, Bruce W. Sanford, Bruce D. Brown, and Laurie A. Babinski.

Brief of amici curiae filed on behalf of the Rutherford Institute by John W. Whitehead.

Opposing Side (Petitioner / Appellant)

Brief of amici curiae filed on behalf of the State of Louisiana et al. by James D. "Buddy" Caldwell, Attorney General of Louisiana, James Trey Phillips, First Assistant Attorney General, and S. Kyle Duncan, Appellate Chief, and by the Attorneys General for their respective States as follows: Richard Blumenthal of Connecticut, Bill McCollum of Florida, Mark J. Bennett of Hawaii, Lisa Madigan of Illinois, Douglas F. Gansler of Maryland, Michael A. Cox of Michigan, Lori Swanson of Minnesota, Jim Hood of Mississippi, Greg Abbott of Texas, and Kenneth T. Cuccinelli II of Virginia; for the Eagle Forum Education & Legal Defense Fund by Andrew L. Schlafly; and for California State Senator Leland Y. Yee et al. by Steven F. Gruel.

Brief of amici curiae filed on behalf of Common Sense Media by Theodore M. Shaw and Kevin W. Saunders.

IV. THE SUPREME COURT'S DECISION

"California correctly acknowledges that video games qualify for First Amendment protection. The Free Speech Clause exists principally to protect discourse on public matters, but we have long recognized that it is difficult to distinguish politics from entertainment, and dangerous to try. . . .

The most basic of those principles is this: '[A]s a general matter, . . . government has no power to restrict expression because of its message, its ideas, its subject matter, or its content.' There are of course exceptions. . . .

Last Term, in Stevens, we held that new categories of unprotected speech may not be added to the list by a legislature that concludes certain speech is too harmful to be tolerated. . . .

That holding controls this case. As in Stevens, California has tried to make violent-speech regulation look like obscenity regulation by appending a saving clause required for the latter. That does not suffice. . . .

Because the Act imposes a restriction on the content of protected speech, it is invalid unless California can demonstrate that it passes strict scrutiny—that is, unless it is justified by a compelling government interest and is narrowly drawn to serve that interest. . . .

California cannot meet that standard. . . .

California's legislation straddles the fence between (1) addressing a serious social problem and (2) helping concerned parents control their children. Both ends are legitimate, but when they affect First Amendment rights they must be pursued by means that are neither seriously underinclusive nor seriously overinclusive. As a means of protecting children from portrayals of violence, the legislation is seriously underinclusive, not only because it excludes portrayals other than video games, but also because it permits a parental or avuncular veto. And as a means of assisting concerned parents it is seriously overinclusive because it abridges the First Amendment rights of young people whose parents (and aunts and uncles) think violent video games are a harmless pastime. And the overbreadth in achieving one goal is not cured by the underbreadth in achieving the other. Legislation such as this, which is neither fish nor fowl, cannot survive strict scrutiny.

We affirm the judgment below."

V. JUSTICE VOTE

7 Pro ACLU Side vs. 2 Con Opposing Side

ACLU Side (Respondent / Appellee)

1. Scalia, A. – Wrote majority opinion
2. Alito, S. – Wrote concurring opinion
3. Kagan, E. – Joined majority opinion
4. Kennedy, A. – Joined majority opinion
5. Ginsburg, R. – Joined majority opinion
6. Sotomayor, S. – Joined majority opinion
7. Roberts, J. – Joined Alito's concurrence

Opposing Side (Petitioner / Appellant)

1. Thomas, C. – Wrote dissenting opinion
2. Breyer, S. – Wrote dissenting opinion

VI. A WIN OR LOSS FOR THE ACLU?

The ACLU filed as amicus curiae urging affirmance; the Supreme Court affirmed the Court of Appeals' decision by a 7-2 vote, giving the ACLU an apparent win.

1084. Hosanna-Tabor Evangelical Lutheran Church and School v. EEOC

(Decided January 11, 2012; 565 U.S. 171)

I. ISSUE

A. Issues Discussed

1st Amendment, religion

B. Legal Question Presented

"Certain employment discrimination laws authorize employees who have been wrongfully terminated to sue their employers for reinstatement and damages. The question presented is whether the Establishment and Free Exercise Clauses of the First Amendment bar such an action when the employer is a religious group and the employee is one of the group's ministers."

C. Supreme Court's Answer

"When a minister who has been fired sues her church alleging that her termination was discriminatory, the First Amendment has struck the balance for us. The church must be free to choose those who will guide it on its way."

II. CASE SUMMARY

A. Background

"Petitioner Hosanna–Tabor Evangelical Lutheran Church and School . . . operated a small school . . . offering a 'Christ-centered education' . . . .

The Synod classifies teachers into two categories: 'called' and 'lay.' . . . To be eligible to receive a call . . . a teacher must satisfy certain academic requirements. [A] call could be rescinded only for cause and by a supermajority vote of the congregation. . . .

Respondent Cheryl Perich was first employed . . . as a lay teacher . . . . After Perich completed her colloquy . . . , Hosanna–Tabor asked her to become a called teacher. Perich accepted . . . .

Perich became ill [and] began the . . . school year on disability leave. On January 27, 2005 . . . Perich notified the school principal, Stacey Hoeft, that she would be able to . . . work the following month. Hoeft responded that the school had already contracted . . . a lay teacher . . . .

[T]he congregation voted to offer Perich a 'peaceful release' . . . . Perich . . . produced a note from her doctor stating that she would be able to return to work on February 22. . . .

On . . . February 22 . . . Perich presented herself at the school. Hoeft asked her to leave but she would not do so until she obtained written documentation that she had reported to work. . . . Hoeft called Perich at home and told her that she would likely be fired. . . .

Following a school board meeting that evening, board chairman Scott Salo sent Perich a letter stating that Hosanna–Tabor was reviewing the process for rescinding her call in light of her 'regrettable' actions. . . . The congregation voted to rescind Perich's call on April 10 . . . .

The EEOC brought suit . . . , alleging that Perich had been fired in retaliation . . . .

The District Court . . . granted summary judgment in Hosanna–Tabor's favor. . . .

The Court of Appeals for the Sixth Circuit vacated and remanded . . . ."

The Supreme Court granted certiorari to review the case.

B. Counsel of Record / ACLU Attorney

ACLU Side (Respondent / Appellee): Leondra R. Kruger argued the cause for the federal appellee. With her on the brief were Solicitor General Verrilli, Assistant Attorney General Perez, Joseph R. Palmore, Dennis J. Dimsey, Sharon M. McGowan, P. David Lopez, Lorraine C. Davis, and Carolyn L. Wheeler. Walter Dellinger argued the cause for appellee Perich. With him on the brief were Sri Srinivasan, Anton Metlitsky, Loren L. Alikhan, James E. Roach, and Robert M. Vercruysse.

Opposing Side (Petitioner / Appellant): Douglas Laycock argued the cause for appellant. With him on the briefs were Kevin J. Hasson, Eric C. Rassbach, Hannah C. Smith, Luke W. Goodrich, Lori H. Windham, and James W. Erwin.

III. AMICI CURIAE

ACLU Side (Respondent / Appellee)

Brief of amici curiae filed on behalf of Americans United for Separation of Church and State, American Civil Liberties Union, ACLU of Michigan, National Council of Jewish Women, Sikh Council on Religion and Education, and Unitarian Universalist Association by Ayesha N. Khan, Gregory M. Lipper, Steven R. Shapiro, Daniel Mach, Michael J. Steinberg, and Robert S.H. Shapiro.

Brief of amici curiae filed on behalf of the American Humanist Association et al. by Elizabeth L. Hileman.

Brief of amici curiae filed on behalf of the NAACP Legal Defense Fund et al. by Kevin K. Russell, John Payton, Debo P. Adegbile, ReNika C. Moore, Ray P. McClain, Linda D. Kilb, Fatima Goss Graves, Dina Lassow, Judith L. Lichtman, and Sarah C.

Crawford.

Brief of amici curiae filed on behalf of the National Employment Lawyers Association by Eric Schnapper and Rebecca M. Hamburg.

Brief of amici curiae filed on behalf of the People for the American Way Foundation by David J. Bederman and Margery F. Baker.

Brief of amici curiae filed on behalf of Neil H. Cogan by Mr. Cogan, pro se.

Brief of amici curiae filed on behalf of the AntiDefamation League by Ian Scharfman, Steven M. Freeman, and Steven C. Sheinberg.

Brief of amici curiae filed on behalf of Antitrust Professors and Scholars by Harry First, pro se.

Brief of amici curiae filed on behalf of BishopAccountability.org et al. by Marci A. Hamilton.

Brief of amici curiae filed on behalf of Law and Religion Professors by Leslie C. Griffin.

Opposing Side (Petitioner / Appellant)

Brief of amici curiae filed on behalf of the American Association of Christian Schools by Robert J. McCully.

Brief of amici curiae filed on behalf of the American Bible Society et al. by Stuart J. Lark.

Brief of amici curiae filed on behalf of the American Center for Law and Justice et al. by Jay Alan Sekulow, Stuart J. Roth, Colby M. May, James M. Henderson, Sr., David French, Walter M. Weber, and Michael S. Anderson.

Brief of amici curiae filed on behalf of the American Jewish Committee et al. by David Dunn and Marc Stern.

Brief of amici curiae filed on behalf of the Council for Christian Colleges and Universities by Aaron D. Lindstrom and Matthew T. Nelson.

Brief of amici curiae filed on behalf of the Evangelical Covenant Church et al. by Michael W. McConnell.

Brief of amici curiae filed on behalf of the International Mission Board of the Southern Baptist Convention et al. by Gene C. Schaerr, Steffen N. Johnson, Michael T. Morley, Linda T. Coberly, and William P. Ferranti.

Brief of amici curiae filed on behalf of the Jewish Educational Center et al. by Kelly J. Shackelford and Hiram S. Sasser III.

Brief of amici curiae filed on behalf of the Justice and Freedom Fund by James L. Hirsen and Deborah J. Dewart.

Brief of amici curiae filed on behalf of the Lutheran Church—Missouri Synod by Christopher C. Lund and T. Michael Ward.

Brief of amici curiae filed on behalf of the Muslim-American Public Affairs Council et al. by Douglas R. Bush and Eric S. Baxter.

Brief of amici curiae filed on behalf of the National Jewish Commission on Law and Public Affairs by Nathan Lewin and Alyza D. Lewin.

Brief of amici curiae filed on behalf of Religious Organizations and Institutions by Carter G. Phillips, Edward R. McNicholas, David S. Petron, and Gordon D. Todd.

Brief of amici curiae filed on behalf of Religious Tribunal Experts by Megan L. Brown.

Brief of amici curiae filed on behalf of Trinity Baptist Church of Jacksonville, Inc., by Edward H. Trent and Joseph W. Hatchett.

Brief of amici curiae filed on behalf of the United States Conference of Catholic Bishops et al. by Kevin T. Baine, Anthony R. Picarello, Jr., Jeffrey Hunter Moon, Michael F. Moses, Von G. Keetch, and R. Shawn Gunnarson.

Brief of amici curiae filed on behalf of WallBuilders, Inc. by Steven W. Fitschen.

Brief of amici curiae filed on behalf of the International Center for Law and Religion Studies at Brigham Young University by W. Cole Durham, Jr., and Robert T. Smith.

Brief of amici curiae filed on behalf of The Rutherford Institute by John W. Whitehead, Bradley J. Andreozzi, and Jason P. Gosselin.

Brief of amici curiae filed on behalf of Eugene Volokh et al. by Thomas C. Berg, Carl H. Esbeck, Richard W. Garnett, K. Hollyn Hollman, Melissa Rogers, and Kimberlee Wood Colby.

Brief of amici curiae filed on behalf of the State of Michigan et al. by Bill Schuette, Attorney General of Michigan, John J. Bursch, Solicitor General, and B. Eric Restuccia, Deputy Solicitor General, and by the Attorneys General for their respective States as follows: Luther Strange of Alabama, Pamela Jo Bondi of Florida, Gregory F. Zoeller of Indiana, James D. "Buddy" Caldwell of Louisiana, Wayne Stenehjem of North Dakota, E. Scott Pruitt of Oklahoma, and Greg Abbott of Texas.

IV. THE SUPREME COURT'S DECISION

"The First Amendment provides, in part, that 'Congress shall make no law respecting an establishment of religion, or prohibiting the free exercise thereof.' . . . Both Religion Clauses bar the government from interfering with the decision of a religious group to fire one of its ministers. . . .

Until today, we have not had occasion to consider whether this freedom of a religious organization to select its ministers is implicated by a suit alleging discrimination in employment. The Courts of Appeals, in contrast, have had extensive experience with this issue. Since the passage of Title VII of the Civil Rights Act of 1964, and other employment discrimination laws, the Courts of Appeals have uniformly recognized the existence of a 'ministerial exception,' grounded in the First Amendment, that precludes application of such legislation to claims concerning the employment relationship between a religious institution and its ministers.

We agree that there is such a ministerial exception. . . .

Having concluded that there is a ministerial exception grounded in the Religion Clauses of the First Amendment, we consider whether the exception applies in this case. We hold that it does.

Every Court of Appeals to have considered the question has concluded that the ministerial exception is not limited to the head of a religious congregation, and we agree. . . . It is enough for us to conclude, in this our first case involving the ministerial exception, that the exception covers Perich, given all the circumstances of her employment. . . .

Because Perich was a minister within the meaning of the exception, the First Amendment requires dismissal of this employment discrimination suit against her religious employer. . . .

Today we hold only that the ministerial exception bars such

a suit. We express no view on whether the exception bars other types of suits . . . .

The interest of society in the enforcement of employment discrimination statutes is undoubtedly important. But so too is the interest of religious groups in choosing who will preach their beliefs, teach their faith, and carry out their mission. When a minister who has been fired sues her church alleging that her termination was discriminatory, the First Amendment has struck the balance for us. The church must be free to choose those who will guide it on its way.

The judgment of the Court of Appeals for the Sixth Circuit is reversed."

V. JUSTICE VOTE

0 Pro ACLU Side vs. 9 Con Opposing Side

Opposing Side (Petitioner / Appellant)

1. Roberts, J. – Wrote majority opinion
2. Alito, S. – Wrote concurring opinion
3. Kagan, E. – Joined Alito's concurrence
4. Thomas, C. – Wrote concurring opinion
5. Breyer, S. – Joined majority opinion
6. Scalia, A. – Joined majority opinion
7. Kennedy, A. – Joined majority opinion
8. Ginsburg, R. – Joined majority opinion
9. Sotomayor, S. – Joined majority opinion

VI. A WIN OR LOSS FOR THE ACLU?

The ACLU filed as amicus curiae urging affirmance; the Supreme Court reversed the Court of Appeals' decision by a 9-0 vote, giving the ACLU an apparent loss.

1085. Maples v. Thomas

(Decided January 18, 2012; 565 U.S. 266)

I. ISSUE

A. Issues Discussed

Criminal procedure, death penalty

B. Legal Question Presented

"The sole question this Court has taken up for review is whether, on the extraordinary facts of Maples' case, there is 'cause' to excuse [procedural] default" for failure to timely appeal.

C. Supreme Court's Answer

"Maples maintains that there is, for the lawyers he believed to be vigilantly representing him had abandoned the case without leave of court, without informing Maples they could no longer represent him, and without securing any recorded substitution of counsel. We agree."

II. CASE SUMMARY

A. Background

"Cory R. Maples is an Alabama capital prisoner sentenced to death . . . . At trial, he was represented by two appointed lawyers, minimally paid and with scant experience in capital cases. Maples sought postconviction relief in state court, alleging ineffective assistance of counsel . . . . His petition, filed in August 2001, was written by two New York attorneys serving pro bono, both associated with the same New York-based large law firm. . . .

In the summer of 2002, while Maples' postconviction petition remained pending in the Alabama trial court, his New York attorneys left the law firm; their new employment disabled them from continuing to represent Maples. They did not inform Maples of their departure . . . . Nor did they seek the Alabama trial court's leave to withdraw. . . .

In May 2003, the Alabama trial court denied Maples' petition. Notices of the court's order were posted to the New York attorneys at the address of the law firm . . . . Those postings were returned, unopened, to the trial court clerk, who attempted no further mailing. With no attorney of record in fact acting on Maples' behalf, the time to appeal ran out.

Thereafter, Maples petitioned for a writ of habeas corpus in federal court. The District Court and, in turn, the Eleventh Circuit, rejected his petition, pointing to . . . Maples' failure timely to appeal the Alabama trial court's order denying him postconviction relief. . . .

[The U.S. Supreme Court] granted certiorari to decide whether the uncommon facts presented here establish cause adequate to excuse Maples' procedural default."

B. Counsel of Record / ACLU Attorney

ACLU Side (Petitioner / Appellant): Gregory G. Garre argued the cause for appellant. With him on the briefs were J. Scott Ballenger and Derek D. Smith.

Opposing Side (Respondent / Appellee): John C. Neiman, Jr., Solicitor General of Alabama, argued the cause for appellee. With him on the brief were Luther Strange, Attorney General, William G. Parker, Jr., Assistant Attorney General, and Nicholas Q. Rosenkranz, Deputy Attorney General.

III. AMICI CURIAE

ACLU Side (Petitioner / Appellant)

Brief of amici curiae filed on behalf of the National Association of Criminal Defense Lawyers, the American Civil Liberties Union, and the ACLU of Alabama by Lisa S. Blatt, Anthony J. Franze, Steven R. Shapiro, Jonathan Hacker, R. Stanton Jones, Arpan A. Sura, and Matthew C. Phillips.

Brief of amici curiae filed on behalf of The Constitution Project et al. by Jonathan S. Franklin, Mark Emery, Virginia E. Sloan, Timothy Lynch, and Ilya Shapiro.

Brief of amici curiae filed on behalf of Former Alabama Appellate Court Justices et al. by Lisa W. Borden.

Brief of amici curiae filed on behalf of the NAACP Legal Defense & Educational Fund, Inc., by John Payton, Debo P. Adegbile, Christina Swarns, Joshua Civin, and Samuel Spital.

Brief of amici curiae filed on behalf of Deborah A. DeMott by Walter Dellinger, Anton Metlitsky, and Ms. DeMott, pro se.
Brief of amici curiae filed on behalf of the Alabama Criminal Defense Lawyers Association by Wayne Morse, Jr., and Susan J. Walker.
Brief of amici curiae filed on behalf of Legal Ethics Professors et al. by Lawrence J. Fox and Susan D. Reece Martyn, both pro se.

Opposing Side (Respondent / Appellee)

Brief of amici curiae filed on behalf of the State of Texas et al. by Greg Abbott, Attorney General of Texas, Daniel T. Hodge, First Assistant Attorney General, Don Clemmer, Deputy Attorney General, Jonathan F. Mitchell, Solicitor General, and Adam W. Aston, Assistant Solicitor General, and by the Attorneys General for their respective States as follows: Tom Horne of Arizona, Joseph R. Biden III of Delaware, Pamela Jo Bondi of Florida, Samuel S. Olens of Georgia, Lawrence G. Wasden of Idaho, James D. "Buddy" Caldwell of Louisiana, Jim Hood of Mississippi, Jon Bruning of Nebraska, Gary K. King of New Mexico, E. Scott Pruitt of Oklahoma, Linda L. Kelly of Pennsylvania, Alan Wilson of South Carolina, Marty J. Jackley of South Dakota, Robert E. Cooper, Jr., of Tennessee, Mark L. Shurtleff of Utah, Kenneth T. Cuccinelli II of Virginia, Robert M. McKenna of Washington, J. B. Van Hollen of Wisconsin, and Gregory A. Phillips of Wyoming.
Brief of amici curiae filed on behalf of the Criminal Justice Legal Foundation by Kent S. Scheidegger.

IV. THE SUPREME COURT'S DECISION

"As a rule, a state prisoner's habeas claims may not be entertained by a federal court 'when (1) 'a state court [has] declined to address [those] claims because the prisoner had failed to meet a state procedural requirement,' and (2) 'the state judgment rests on independent and adequate state procedural grounds.'' The bar to federal review may be lifted, however, if 'the prisoner can demonstrate cause for the [procedural] default [in state court] and actual prejudice as a result of the alleged violation of federal law.' . . .

Cause for a procedural default exists where 'something external to the petitioner, something that cannot fairly be attributed to him[,] . . . 'impeded [his] efforts to comply with the State's procedural rule.'' . . . Negligence on the part of a prisoner's postconviction attorney does not qualify . . . .

A markedly different situation is presented, however, when an attorney abandons his client without notice, and thereby occasions the default. . . .

We agree that, under agency principles, a client cannot be charged with the acts or omissions of an attorney who has abandoned him. Nor can a client be faulted for failing to act on his own behalf when he lacks reason to believe his attorneys of record, in fact, are not representing him. We therefore inquire whether Maples has shown that his attorneys of record abandoned him, thereby supplying the 'extraordinary circumstances beyond his control' . . . .

Unknown to Maples, not one of [his] lawyers was in fact serving as his attorney during the 42 days permitted for an appeal from the trial court's order. . . .

[In addition,] the very listing of [the attorneys] as his representatives meant that he had no right personally to receive notice. He in fact received none . . . . Given no reason to suspect that he lacked counsel . . . , Maples surely was blocked from complying with the State's procedural rule. . . .

In the unusual circumstances of this case, principles of agency law and fundamental fairness point to the . . . conclusion: There was indeed cause to excuse Maples' procedural default. [H]e had no reason to suspect that . . . he had been reduced to pro se status. . . . He has shown ample cause, we hold, to excuse the procedural default . . . .

For the reasons stated, the judgment of the Court of Appeals for the Eleventh Circuit is reversed, and the case is remanded . . . ."

V. JUSTICE VOTE

7 Pro ACLU Side vs. 2 Con Opposing Side

ACLU Side (Petitioner / Appellant)

1. Ginsburg, R. – Wrote majority opinion
2. Alito, S. – Wrote concurring opinion
3. Kagan, E. – Joined majority opinion
4. Breyer, S. – Joined majority opinion
5. Kennedy, A. – Joined majority opinion
6. Sotomayor, S. – Joined majority opinion
7. Roberts, J. – Joined majority opinion

Opposing Side (Respondent / Appellee)

1. Thomas, C. – Joined Scalia's dissent
2. Scalia, A. – Wrote dissenting opinion

VI. A WIN OR LOSS FOR THE ACLU?

The ACLU filed as amicus curiae urging reversal of the judgment of the Court of Appeals; the Supreme Court reversed in a 7-2 vote, giving the ACLU an apparent win.

1086. Golan v. Holder

(Decided January 18, 2012; 565 U.S. 302)

I. ISSUE

A. Issues Discussed

1st Amendment, press, speech, association

B. Legal Question Presented

Whether § 514 of the Uruguay Round Agreements Act (URAA) was a constitutional enactment by Congress.

C. Supreme Court's Answer

"[W]e conclude that § 514 does not transgress constitutional limitations on Congress' authority. Neither the Copyright and Patent Clause nor the First Amendment, we hold, makes the public domain, in any and all cases, a territory that works may never exit."

II. CASE SUMMARY

A. Background

"The Berne Convention for the Protection of Literary and Artistic Works . . . is the principal accord governing international copyright relations. [T]he United States joined . . . in 1989. . . . Congress, in 1994, gave works enjoying copyright protection abroad the same . . . protection available to U.S. works . . . in § 514 of the Uruguay Round Agreements Act (URAA) . . . .

Works encompassed by § 514 are granted the protection they would have enjoyed had the United States maintained copyright relations with the author's country or removed formalities incompatible with Berne. Foreign authors, however, gain no credit for the protection they lacked in years prior to § 514's enactment. . . .

Petitioners include [music professionals] who formerly enjoyed free access to works § 514 removed from the public domain. They maintain that the Constitution's Copyright and Patent Clause, Art. I, § 8, cl. 8, and First Amendment both decree the invalidity of § 514. . . .

In 2001, petitioners filed this lawsuit challenging § 514. . . . The District Court granted the Attorney General's motion for summary judgment. . . .

The Court of Appeals for the Tenth Circuit affirmed in part. . . . The case was remanded . . . .

On remand, the District Court's starting premise was uncontested: Section 514 does not regulate speech on the basis of its content; therefore the law would be upheld if 'narrowly tailored to serve a significant government interest.' Summary judgment was due petitioners, the court concluded . . . .

The Tenth Circuit reversed."

The Supreme Court granted certiorari to review the case.

B. Counsel of Record / ACLU Attorney

ACLU Side (Petitioner / Appellant): Anthony T. Falzone argued the cause for appellants. With him on the briefs were Julie A. Ahrens, Daniel K. Nazer, Hugh Q. Gottschalk, Carolyn J. Fairless, Thomas C. Goldstein, Amy Howe, Kevin K. Russell, and Pamela S. Karlan.

Opposing Side (Respondent / Appellee): Solicitor General Verrilli argued the cause for appellees. With him on the brief were Assistant Attorney General West, Deputy Solicitor General Stewart, Melissa Arbus Sherry, William Kanter, and John S. Koppel.

III. AMICI CURIAE

ACLU Side (Petitioner / Appellant)

Brief of amici curiae filed on behalf of the American Civil Liberties Union by Aden J. Fine, Steven R. Shapiro, and Ben Siracusa Hillman.

Brief of amici curiae filed on behalf of the American Library Association et al. by Corynne McSherry, Michael Barclay, Jonathan Band, and Geoffrey Brigham.

Brief of amici curiae filed on behalf of the Cato Institute by Nicholas Quinn Rosenkranz and Ilya Shapiro.

Brief of amici curiae filed on behalf of the Conductors Guild et al. by Steven A. Hirsch; for Creative Commons Corp. by Lawrence Lessig.

Brief of amici curiae filed on behalf of the Eagle Forum Education & Legal Defense Fund by Andrew L. Schlafly.

Brief of amici curiae filed on behalf of Google, Inc., by David T. Goldberg and Sean H. Donahue.

Brief of amici curiae filed on behalf of Heartland Angels, Inc., by Michael W. Carroll.

Brief of amici curiae filed on behalf of the Information Society Project at Yale Law School Professors and Fellows by Priscilla J. Smith.

Brief of amici curiae filed on behalf of the Justice and Freedom Fund by James L. Hirsen and Deborah J. Dewart.

Brief of amici curiae filed on behalf of Project Petrucci, LLC, by Charles Nesson.

Brief of amici curiae filed on behalf of Public Domain Interests by Jennifer M. Urban, Jeffrey P. Cunard, Peter Jaszi, and Pamela Samuelson.

Brief of amici curiae filed on behalf of Public Knowledge by Gigi B. Sohn.

Brief of amici curiae filed on behalf of Peter Decherney by Messrs. Carroll and Jaszi.

Brief of amici curiae filed on behalf of Daniel J. Gervais by Alan C. Friedberg.

Brief of amici curiae filed on behalf of H. Tomas Gomez-Arostegui et al. by Tyler T. Ochoa and Mr. GomezArostegui, both pro se.

Opposing Side (Respondent / Appellee)

Brief of amici curiae filed on behalf of the American Bar Association by William T. Robinson III, Steven M. Lieberman, and June M. Besek.

Brief of amici curiae filed on behalf of the American Intellectual Property Law Association by Edward R. Reines and David W. Hill.

Brief of amici curiae filed on behalf of the American Society of Composers, Authors and Publishers et al. by Christopher A. Mohr, Paul Bender, and Michael R. Klipper.

Brief of amici curiae filed on behalf of the International Coalition for Copyright Protection by Eric M. Lieberman and David B. Goldstein.

Brief of amici curiae filed on behalf of the International Publishers Association et al. by Gloria C. Phares.

Brief of amici curiae filed on behalf of the Intellectual Property Owners Association by J. Michael Jakes, Robert D. Litowitz, Margaret A. Esquenet, Mary Beth Walker, Douglas K. Norman, and Kevin H. Rhodes.

Brief of amici curiae filed on behalf of the Motion Picture Association of America by Seth P. Waxman and Randolph D. Moss.

Brief of amici curiae filed on behalf of the Franklin Pierce Center for Intellectual Property by Ann McCrackin.

IV. THE SUPREME COURT'S DECISION

"We first address petitioners' argument that Congress lacked authority, under the Copyright Clause, to enact § 514. The Constitution states that 'Congress shall have Power . . . [t]o promote the Progress of Science . . . by securing for limited Times to Authors . . . the exclusive Right to their . . . Writings.' Petitioners find in this grant of authority an impenetrable barrier to the extension of copyright protection to authors whose writings, for whatever reason, are in the public domain. We see no such barrier in the text of the Copyright Clause, historical practice, or our precedents. . . .

The text . . . does not exclude application of copyright protection to works in the public domain. . . .

Historical practice corroborates our reading . . . to permit full U.S. compliance with Berne. . . .

Petitioners' ultimate argument as to the Copyright and Patent Clause concerns its initial words. Congress is empowered to 'promote the Progress of Science and useful Arts' by enacting systems of copyright and patent protection. . . . Congress' copyright authority is tied to the progress of science; its patent authority, to the progress of the useful arts. . . .

Considered against this backdrop, § 514 falls comfortably within Congress' authority . . . .

Congress determined that exemplary adherence to Berne would serve the objectives of the Copyright Clause. We have no warrant to reject the rational judgment Congress made. . . .

We next explain why the First Amendment does not inhibit the restoration authorized by § 514. . . .

Congress determined that U.S. interests were best served by our full participation in the dominant system of international copyright protection. Those interests include ensuring exemplary compliance with our international obligations, securing greater protection for U.S. authors abroad, and remedying unequal treatment of foreign authors. The judgment § 514 expresses lies well within the ken of the political branches. It is our obligation, of course, to determine whether the action Congress took, wise or not, encounters any constitutional shoal. For the reasons stated, we are satisfied it does not. The judgment of the Court of Appeals for the Tenth Circuit is therefore affirmed."

V. JUSTICE VOTE

2 Pro ACLU Side vs. 6 Con Opposing Side

ACLU Side (Petitioner / Appellant)

1. Alito, S. – Joined Breyer's dissent
2. Breyer, S. – Wrote dissenting opinion

Opposing Side (Respondent / Appellee)

1. Ginsburg, R. – Wrote majority opinion
2. Thomas, C. – Joined majority opinion
3. Scalia, A. – Joined majority opinion
4. Kennedy, A. – Joined majority opinion
5. Sotomayor, S. – Joined majority opinion
6. Roberts, J. – Joined majority opinion

Kagan E. – Took no part in the decision.

VI. A WIN OR LOSS FOR THE ACLU?

The ACLU filed as amicus curiae urging reversal of the judgment of the Court of Appeals; the Supreme Court affirmed in a 6-2 vote, giving the ACLU an apparent loss.

1087. U.S. v. Jones

(Decided January 23, 2012; 565 U.S. 400)

I. ISSUE

A. Issues Discussed

4th Amendment

B. Legal Question Presented

"[W]hether the attachment of a Global-Positioning-System (GPS) tracking device to an individual's vehicle, and subsequent use of that device to monitor the vehicle's movements on public streets, constitutes a search or seizure within the meaning of the Fourth Amendment."

C. Supreme Court's Answer

"We hold that the Government's installation of a GPS device on a target's vehicle, and its use of that device to monitor the vehicle's movements, constitutes a 'search.'"

II. CASE SUMMARY

A. Background

"In 2004 respondent Antoine Jones, owner and operator of a nightclub in the District of Columbia, came under suspicion of trafficking in narcotics and was made the target of an investigation by a joint FBI and Metropolitan Police Department task force. . . .

[I]n 2005 the Government applied . . . for a warrant authorizing the use of an electronic tracking device on the Jeep Grand Cherokee registered to Jones's wife. A warrant issued, authorizing installation of the device in the District of Columbia and within 10 days.

On the 11th day, and not in the District of Columbia but in Maryland, agents installed a GPS tracking device on the undercarriage of the Jeep while it was parked in a public parking lot. Over the next 28 days, the Government used the device to track the vehicle's movements . . . .

The Government ultimately obtained a multiple-count indictment charging Jones and several alleged co-conspirators with . . . conspiracy to distribute and possess with intent to distribute five kilograms or more of cocaine and 50 grams or more of cocaine base . . . . Before trial, Jones filed a motion to suppress evidence obtained through the GPS device. The District Court granted the motion only in part, suppressing the data obtained while the vehicle was parked in the garage adjoining Jones's residence. . . .

In March 2007, a grand jury returned another indictment, charging Jones and others with the same conspiracy. The Government introduced at trial the same GPS-derived locational data admitted in the first trial. . . . The jury returned a guilty verdict, and the District Court sentenced Jones to life imprisonment.

The United States Court of Appeals for the District of Columbia Circuit reversed . . . . The D.C. Circuit denied the Government's petition for rehearing en banc . . . ."

The Supreme Court granted certiorari to review the case.

B. Counsel of Record / ACLU Attorney

ACLU Side (Respondent / Appellee): Stephen C. Leckar argued the cause for appellee. With him on the brief were Walter Dellinger and Jonathan D. Hacker.

Opposing Side (Petitioner / Appellant): Deputy Solicitor General Dreeben argued the cause for the United States. With him on the briefs were Solicitor General Verrilli, Assistant Attorney General Breuer, Ann O'Connell, and J. Campbell Barker.

III. AMICI CURIAE

ACLU Side (Respondent / Appellee)

Brief of amici curiae filed on behalf of the American Civil Liberties Union and ACLU of the Nation's Capital by Catherine Crump, Steven R. Shapiro, Jameel Jaffer, Arthur B. Spitzer, and Daniel I. Prywes.

Brief of amici curiae filed on behalf of the Cato Institute by Ilya Shapiro, James W. Harper, and Timothy Lynch.

Brief of amici curiae filed on behalf of the Center for Democracy & Technology et al. by Andrew J. Pincus, Charles A. Rothfeld, and Jeffrey A. Meyer.

Brief of amici curiae filed on behalf of The Constitution Project by Douglas Hallward-Driemeier, Michael Li-Ming Wong, and Sharon Bradford Franklin.

Brief of amici curiae filed on behalf of the Council on American-Islamic Relations by Nadhira Al Khalili.

Brief of amici curiae filed on behalf of the Electronic Privacy Information Center et al. by Marc Rotenberg.

Brief of amici curiae filed on behalf of Fourth Amendment Historians by Wesley M. Oliver and Fabio Arcila, Jr.

Brief of amici curiae filed on behalf of Gun Owners of America, Inc., et al. by Herbert W. Titus, William J. Olson, John S. Miles, Jeremiah L. Morgan, Mark B. Weinberg, Joseph W. Miller, and Gary G. Kreep.

Brief of amici curiae filed on behalf of the National Association of Criminal Defense Lawyers et al. by Jeffrey T. Green, Norman L. Reimer, Patricia Cresta-Savage, Rich Gilbert, Stephen P. Hardwick, Sarah O'Rourke Shrup, H. Louis Sirkin, Jennifer M. Kinsley, and Richard D. Willstatter.

Brief of amici curiae filed on behalf of the Owner-Operator Independent Drivers Association, Inc., by Paul D. Cullen, Sr., and Daniel E. Cohen.

Brief of amici curiae filed on behalf of the Yale Law School Information Society Project Scholars et al. by Priscilla J. Smith.

Brief of amici curiae filed on behalf of The Rutherford Institute et al. by John W. Whitehead and Rita M. Dunaway.

Opposing Side (Petitioner / Appellant)

Brief of amici curiae filed on behalf of the Center on the Administration of Criminal Law, New York University School of Law by Michael Y. Scudder, Jr., Lara A. Riley, and Anthony S. Barkow.

IV. THE SUPREME COURT'S DECISION

"The Fourth Amendment provides in relevant part that '[t]he right of the people to be secure in their persons, houses, papers, and effects, against unreasonable searches and seizures, shall not be violated.' It is beyond dispute that a vehicle is an 'effect' as that term is used in the Amendment. We hold that the Government's installation of a GPS device on a target's vehicle, and its use of that device to monitor the vehicle's movements, constitutes a 'search.'

It is important to be clear about what occurred in this case: The Government physically occupied private property for the purpose of obtaining information. We have no doubt that such a physical intrusion would have been considered a 'search' . . . .

The Government contends that several . . . cases foreclose the conclusion that [this] constituted a search. It relies principally on two cases in which we rejected Fourth Amendment challenges to 'beepers,' electronic tracking devices that represent another form of electronic monitoring. . . .

The Government also points to our exposition in New York v. Class, 475 U.S. 106 (1986), that '[t]he exterior of a car . . . is thrust into the public eye, and thus to examine it does not constitute a 'search.'' That statement is of marginal relevance here . . . .

Finally, the Government's position gains little support from our conclusion in Oliver v. United States, 466 U.S. 170 (1984), that officers' information-gathering intrusion on an 'open field' did not constitute a Fourth Amendment search even though it was a trespass at common law. Quite simply, an open field, unlike the curtilage of a home, is not one of those protected areas enumerated in the Fourth Amendment. The Government's physical intrusion on such an area—unlike its intrusion on the 'effect' at issue here—is of no Fourth Amendment significance. . . .

The judgment of the Court of Appeals for the D.C. Circuit is affirmed."

V. JUSTICE VOTE

9 Pro ACLU Side vs. 0 Con Opposing Side

ACLU Side (Respondent / Appellee)

1. Scalia, A. – Wrote majority opinion
2. Alito, S. – Joined majority opinion
3. Kagan, E. – Joined majority opinion
4. Thomas, C. – Joined majority opinion
5. Breyer, S. – Joined majority opinion
6. Kennedy, A. – Joined majority opinion
7. Ginsburg, R. – Joined majority opinion
8. Sotomayor, S. – Joined majority opinion
9. Roberts, J. – Joined majority opinion

VI. A WIN OR LOSS FOR THE ACLU?

The ACLU filed as amicus curiae urging affirmance; the Supreme Court affirmed the Court of Appeals' decision by a 9-0 vote, giving the ACLU an apparent win.

1088. Messerschmidt v. Millender

(Decided February 22, 2012; 565 U.S. 535)

I. ISSUE

A. Issues Discussed

Immunity

B. Legal Question Presented

"[W]hether Messerschmidt and Lawrence are entitled to immunity from damages, even assuming that the warrant should not have been issued."

C. Supreme Court's Answer

"Even if the warrant in this case were invalid, it was not so obviously lacking in probable cause that the officers can be considered 'plainly incompetent' for concluding otherwise." Therefore, Messerschmidt and Lawrence are entitled to qualified immunity.

II. CASE SUMMARY

A. Background

"Petitioner police officers conducted a search of respondents' home pursuant to a warrant issued by a neutral magistrate. The warrant authorized a search for all guns and gang-related material, in connection with the investigation of a known gang member for shooting at his ex-girlfriend with a pistol-gripped sawed-off shotgun, because she had 'call [ed] the cops' on him. Respondents brought an action seeking to hold the officers personally liable under 42 U.S.C. § 1983, alleging that the search violated their Fourth Amendment rights because there was not sufficient probable cause to believe the items sought were evidence of a crime. In particular, respondents argued that there was no basis to search for all guns simply because the suspect owned and had used a sawed-off shotgun, and no reason to search for gang material because the shooting at the ex-girlfriend for 'call[ing] the cops' was solely a domestic dispute. The Court of Appeals for the Ninth Circuit held that the warrant was invalid, and that the officers were not entitled to immunity from personal liability because this invalidity was so obvious that any reasonable officer would have recognized it, despite the magistrate's approval."

The Supreme Court granted certiorari to review the case.

B. Counsel of Record / ACLU Attorney

ACLU Side (Respondent / Appellee): Paul R. Q. Wolfson argued the cause for appellees. With him on the brief were Robert Mann, Olu K. Orange, and Shirley Cassin Woodward.

Opposing Side (Petitioner / Appellant): Timothy T. Coates argued the cause for appellants. With him on the briefs was Lillie Hsu.

Principal Deputy Solicitor General Srinivasan argued the cause for the United States as amicus curiae.

III. AMICI CURIAE

ACLU Side (Respondent / Appellee)

Brief of amici curiae filed on behalf of the American Civil Liberties Union by Steven R. Shapiro, Ezekiel R. Edwards, Jason D. Williamson, and Hayley E. Horowitz.

Brief of amici curiae filed on behalf of the National Rifle Association of America, Inc., et al. by Stephen P. Halbrook and C. D. Michel.

Opposing Side (Petitioner / Appellant)

Brief of amici curiae filed on behalf of the United States by Principal Deputy Solicitor General Srinivasan, Solicitor General Verrilli, Assistant Attorneys General Breuer and West, Deputy Solicitor General Dreeben, Acting Deputy Solicitor General Kruger, Sarah E. Harrington, John M. Pellettieri, Barbara L. Herwig, and August Flentje.

Brief of amici curiae filed on behalf of the State of Texas et al. by Greg Abbott, Attorney General of Texas, Jonathan F. Mitchell, Solicitor General, Daniel T. Hodge, First Assistant Attorney General, David C. Mattax, and David A. Talbot, Jr., and by the Attorneys General for their respective States as follows: Luther Strange of Alabama, John J. Burns of Alaska, Dustin McDaniel of Arkansas, John Suthers of Colorado, Joseph R. Biden III of Delaware, Pamela Jo Bondi of Florida, Samuel S. Olens of Georgia, David M. Louie of Hawaii, Lawrence G. Wasden of Idaho, Greg Zoeller of Indiana, Derek Schmidt of Kansas, James D. "Buddy" Caldwell of Louisiana, William J. Schneider of Maine, Bill Schuette of Michigan, Jim Hood of Mississippi, Steve Bullock of Montana, Jon Bruning of Nebraska, Gary King of New Mexico, Wayne Stenehjem of North Dakota, Linda L. Kelly of Pennsylvania, Peter F. Kilmartin of Rhode Island, Marty J. Jackley of South Dakota, Mark L. Shurtleff of Utah, J. B. Van Hollen of Wisconsin, and Gregory A. Phillips of Wyoming.

IV. THE SUPREME COURT'S DECISION

"'The doctrine of qualified immunity protects government officials 'from liability for civil damages insofar as their conduct does not violate clearly established statutory or constitutional rights of which a reasonable person would have known.'" . . .

Where the alleged Fourth Amendment violation involves a search or seizure pursuant to a warrant, the fact that a neutral magistrate has issued a warrant is the clearest indication that the officers acted in an objectively reasonable manner or, as we have sometimes put it, in 'objective good faith.' Nonetheless, under our precedents, the fact that a neutral magistrate has issued a warrant authorizing the allegedly unconstitutional search or seizure does not end the inquiry into objective reasonableness. Rather, we have recognized an exception allowing suit when 'it is obvious that no reasonably competent officer would have concluded that a warrant should issue.' . . .

Our precedents make clear, however, that the threshold for establishing this exception is a high one, and it should be. . . .

The Millenders contend, and the Court of Appeals held, that their case falls into this narrow exception. According to the Millenders, the officers 'failed to provide any facts or circumstances from which a magistrate could properly conclude that there was probable cause to seize the broad classes of items being sought,' and '[n]o reasonable officer would have presumed that such a warrant was valid.' We disagree. . . .

Whatever the use to which evidence of Bowen's gang involvement might ultimately have been put, it would not have been 'entirely unreasonable' for an officer to believe that the facts set out in the affidavit established a fair probability that such evidence would aid the prosecution of Bowen . . . .

Whether any of these facts, standing alone or taken together, actually establish probable cause is a question we need not decide. . . .

The question in this case is not whether the magistrate erred in believing there was sufficient probable cause to support the scope of the warrant he issued. It is instead whether the magistrate so obviously erred that any reasonable officer would have recognized the error. The occasions on which this standard will be met may be rare, but so too are the circumstances in which it will be appropriate to impose personal liability on a lay officer in the face of judicial approval of his actions. Even if the warrant in this case were invalid, it was not so obviously lacking in probable cause that the officers can be considered 'plainly incompetent' for concluding otherwise. The judgment of the Court of Appeals denying the officers qualified immunity must therefore be reversed."

V. JUSTICE VOTE

3 Pro ACLU Side vs. 6 Con Opposing Side

ACLU Side (Respondent / Appellee)

1. Kagan, E. – Wrote opinion concurring in part and dissenting in part
2. Ginsburg, R. – Joined Sotomayor's dissent
3. Sotomayor, S. – Wrote dissenting opinion

Opposing Side (Petitioner / Appellant)

1. Roberts, J. – Wrote majority opinion
2. Alito, S. – Joined majority opinion
3. Thomas, C. – Joined majority opinion
4. Breyer, S. – Wrote concurring opinion
5. Scalia, A. – Joined majority opinion
6. Kennedy, A. – Joined majority opinion

VI. A WIN OR LOSS FOR THE ACLU?

The ACLU filed as amicus curiae urging affirmance; the Supreme Court reversed the Court of Appeals' decision by a 6-3 vote, giving the ACLU an apparent loss.

1089. Douglas v. Independent Living Center of Southern California, Inc.

(Decided February 22, 2012; 565 U.S. 606)

I. ISSUE

A. Issues Discussed

Regulation

B. Legal Question Presented

"[W]hether, once the [Centers for Medicare & Medicaid Services (CMS)] has approved . . . state statutes, groups of Medicaid providers and beneficiaries may still maintain a Supremacy Clause action asserting that the state statutes are inconsistent with the federal Medicaid law."

C. Supreme Court's Answer

"In the present posture of these cases, we do not address whether the Ninth Circuit properly recognized a Supremacy Clause action to enforce this federal statute before the agency took final action. . . . Given the complexity of these cases, rather than ordering reargument, we vacate the Ninth Circuit's judgments and remand the cases, thereby permitting the parties to argue the matter before that Circuit in the first instance."

II. CASE SUMMARY

A. Background

"To qualify for federal [Medicaid] funds, States must submit to a federal agency . . . a state Medicaid plan that details the nature and scope of the State's Medicaid program. It must also submit any amendments . . . . And it must receive the agency's approval of the plan and any amendments. Before granting approval, the agency reviews the State's plan and amendments to determine whether they comply with the statutory and regulatory requirements . . . .

In 2008 and 2009, the California Legislature passed three statutes changing that State's Medicaid plan. . . .

The consolidated cases before us encompass five lawsuits brought by Medicaid providers and beneficiaries against state officials. Those cases produced seven decisions of the Court of Appeals for the Ninth Circuit. The decisions ultimately affirmed or ordered preliminary injunctions that prevented the State from implementing its statutes. . . .

In the meantime, the federal agency was also reviewing the same state statutes to determine whether they satisfied the same federal statutory conditions. In November 2010, agency officials concluded that they did not satisfy those conditions . . . . California then exercised its right to further administrative review . . . . The cases were in this posture when [the U.S. Supreme Court] granted certiorari to decide whether respondents could mount a Supremacy Clause challenge to the state statutes . . . .

About a month after . . . oral argument, the federal agency reversed course and approved several of California's statutory amendments to its plan."

B. Counsel of Record / ACLU Attorney

ACLU Side (Respondent / Appellee): Carter G. Phillips argued the cause for appellees in all cases. With him on the brief in No. 10–283 were Eric A. Shumsky, Quin M. Sorenson, Lowell J. Schiller, Michael S. Sorgen, and Dean L. Johnson. Lynn S. Carman and Stanley L. Friedman filed a brief for Independent Living Center of Southern California, Inc., et al., appellees in Nos. 09– 958 and 09–1158. Deanne E. Maynard, Seth M. Galanter, Craig J. Cannizzo, and Lloyd A. Bookman filed a brief for intervenor appelles in No. 09–958 and for California Pharmacists, appellees in No. 09–1158. Stephen P. Berzon,

Scott A. Kronland, and Stacey M. Leyton filed a brief for the Dominguez appellees in No. 09–1158.

Opposing Side (Petitioner / Appellant): Karin S. Schwartz, Supervising Deputy Attorney General of California, argued the cause for appellant in all cases. With her on the briefs were Kamala D. Harris, Attorney General, Manuel M. Medeiros, State Solicitor General, David S. Chaney, Chief Assistant Attorney General, Douglas M. Press and Julie Weng-Gutierrez, Senior Assistant Attorneys General, Richard T. Waldow, Susan M. Carson, and Jennifer M. Kim, Supervising Deputy Attorneys General, Gregory D. Brown and Carmen Snuggs, Deputy Attorneys General, and Dan Schweitzer.

Deputy Solicitor General Kneedler argued the cause for the United States as amicus curiae.

III. AMICI CURIAE

ACLU Side (Respondent / Appellee)

Brief of amici curiae filed on behalf of the American Civil Liberties Union et al. by Michael D. Gottesman, Paul R.Q. Wolfson, Shirley Cassin Woodward, Madhu Chugh, Steven R. Shapiro, Victor Viramontes, John Payton, Joshua Civin.

Brief of amici curiae filed on behalf of AARP et al. by Martha Jane Perkins, Stacy J. Canan, Michael R. Schuster, Barbara A. Jones, and Byron J. Gross.

Brief of amici curiae filed on behalf of the American Health Care Association et al. by Douglas Hallward-Driemeier, Charles A. Luband, Roger A. Schwartz, Tamara L. Seltzer, and Donna D. Fraiche.

Brief of amici curiae filed on behalf of the Chamber of Commerce of the United States of America by Alan Untereiner, Mark T. Stancil, Robin S. Conrad, Kate Comerford Todd, and Sheldon Gilbert.

Brief of amici curiae filed on behalf of former HHS Officials by Stephen I. Vladeck and Charles S. Sims.

Brief of amici curiae filed on behalf of Members of Congress by Paul M. Smith and Matthew S. Hellman.

Brief of amici curiae filed on behalf of the National Association of Chain Drug Stores et al. by Frederick R. Ball, Nicholas Lynn, Erin M. Duffy, Donald L. Bell II, and Mary Ellen Kleiman.

Brief of amici curiae filed on behalf of the American Medical Association et al. by Louis W. Bullock, Robert M. Blakemore, and James Eiseman, Jr.

Opposing Side (Petitioner / Appellant)

Brief of amici curiae filed on behalf of the United States by Deputy Solicitor General Kneedler, Acting Solicitor General Katyal, Acting Deputy Solicitor General Kruger, Deputy Assistant Attorney General Gershengorn, Melissa Arbus Sherry, and Mark B. Stern.

Brief of amici curiae filed on behalf of the State of Michigan et al. by Bill Schuette, Attorney General of Michigan, John J. Bursch, Solicitor General, Raymond O. Howd, and William R. Morris and Joshua S. Smith, Assistant Attorneys General, by William H. Ryan, Jr., former Acting Attorney General of Pennsylvania, and by the Attorneys General for their respective States as follows: Luther Strange of Alabama, John J. Burns of Alaska, Thomas C. Horne of Arizona, Dustin McDaniel of Arkansas, John W. Suthers of Colorado, George Jepsen of Connecticut, Joseph R. Biden III of Delaware, Pamela Jo Bondi of Florida, David M. Louie of Hawaii, Lawrence G. Wasden of Idaho, Gregory F. Zoeller of Indiana, James D. "Buddy" Caldwell of Louisiana, William J. Schneider of Maine, Douglas F. Gansler of Maryland, Jim Hood of Mississippi, Catherine Cortez Masto of Nevada, Roy Cooper of North Carolina, E. Scott Pruitt of Oklahoma, John R. Kroger of Oregon, Peter Kilmartin of Rhode Island, Marty J. Jackley of South Dakota, Robert E. Cooper, Jr., of Tennessee, Greg Abbott of Texas, Mark L. Shurtleff of Utah, William H. Sorrell of Vermont, Robert M. McKenna of Washington, Darrell V. McGraw, Jr., of West Virginia, J. B. Van Hollen of Wisconsin, and Gregory A. Phillips of Wyoming.

Brief of amici curiae filed on behalf of the National Governors Association et al. by Michael W. McConnell.

Brief of amici curiae filed on behalf of APA Watch by Lawrence J. Joseph.

IV. THE SUPREME COURT'S DECISION

"All parties agree that the agency's approval of the enjoined rate reductions does not make these cases moot. For one thing, the providers and beneficiaries continue to believe that the reductions violate the federal provision . . . . For another, federal-court injunctions remain in place . . . .

While the cases are not moot, they are now in a different posture. The federal agency charged with administering the Medicaid program has determined that the challenged rate reductions comply with federal law. That agency decision does not change the underlying substantive question, namely whether California's statutes are consistent with a specific federal statutory provision . . . . But it may change the answer. And it may require respondents now to proceed by seeking review of the agency determination . . . rather than in an action against California under the Supremacy Clause.

For one thing, the APA would likely permit respondents to obtain an authoritative judicial determination of the merits . . . . The Act provides for judicial review of final agency action. . . .

For another thing, respondents' basic challenge now presents the kind of legal question that ordinarily calls for APA review. . . .

Finally, to allow a Supremacy Clause action to proceed once the agency has reached a decision threatens potential inconsistency or confusion. . . .

But ordinarily review of agency action requires courts to apply certain standards of deference to agency decisionmaking. And the parties have not suggested reasons why courts should not now . . . apply those ordinary standards of deference.

Nor have the parties suggested reasons why, once the agency has taken final action, a court should reach a different result in a case like this one, depending upon whether the case proceeds in a Supremacy Clause action rather than under the APA for review of an agency decision. . . . If the two kinds of actions should reach the same result, the Supremacy Clause challenge is at best redundant. And to permit the continuation of the action in that form would seem to be inefficient . . . .

In the present posture of these cases, we do not address whether the Ninth Circuit properly recognized a Supremacy Clause action to enforce this federal statute before the agency took final action. To decide whether these cases may proceed directly under the Supremacy Clause now that the agency has acted, it will be necessary to take account, in light of the proceedings that have already taken place, of at least the matters we have set forth above. . . . Given the complexity of these cases, rather than ordering reargument, we vacate the Ninth Circuit's judgments and remand the cases, thereby permitting the parties to argue the matter before that Circuit in the first instance."

V. JUSTICE VOTE

4 Pro ACLU Side vs. 5 Con Opposing Side

ACLU Side (Respondent / Appellee)

1. Alito, S. – Joined Roberts' dissent
2. Thomas, C. – Joined Roberts' dissent
3. Scalia, A. – Joined Roberts' dissent
4. Roberts, J. – Wrote dissenting opinion

Opposing Side (Petitioner / Appellant)

1. Breyer, S. – Wrote majority opinion
2. Kagan, E. – Joined majority opinion
3. Kennedy, A. – Joined majority opinion
4. Ginsburg, R. – Joined majority opinion
5. Sotomayor, S. – Joined majority opinion

VI. A WIN OR LOSS FOR THE ACLU?

The ACLU filed as amicus curiae urging affirmance; the Supreme Court vacated the Court of Appeals' decision by a 5-4 vote, giving the ACLU an apparent loss.

1090. Coleman v. Court of Appeals of Maryland

(Decided March 20, 2012; 566 U.S. 30)

I. ISSUE

A. Issues Discussed

Immunity, gender

B. Legal Question Presented

"[W]hether a state employee is allowed to recover damages from the state entity that employs him by invoking one of the provisions of a federal statute that, in express terms, seeks to abrogate the States' immunity from suits for damages. The statute in question is the Family and Medical Leave Act of 1993."

C. Supreme Court's Answer

"In agreement with every Court of Appeals to have addressed this question, this Court now holds that suits against States under this provision are barred by the States' immunity as sovereigns in our federal system."

II. CASE SUMMARY

A. Background

"Petitioner Daniel Coleman was employed by the Court of Appeals of the State of Maryland. When Coleman requested sick leave, he was informed he would be terminated if he did not resign. Coleman then sued the state court in the United States District Court for the District of Maryland, alleging, inter alia, that his employer violated the FMLA by failing to provide him with self-care leave.

The District Court dismissed the suit on the basis that the Maryland Court of Appeals, as an entity of a sovereign State, was immune from the suit for damages. The parties do not dispute the District Court's ruling that the Maryland Court of Appeals is an entity or instrumentality of the State for purposes of sovereign immunity. The District Court concluded the FMLA's self-care provision did not validly abrogate the State's immunity from suit. The Court of Appeals for the Fourth Circuit affirmed, reasoning that, unlike the family-care provision at issue in Hibbs, the self-care provision was not directed at an identified pattern of gender-based discrimination and was not congruent and proportional to any pattern of sex-based discrimination on the part of States."

The Supreme Court granted certiorari to review the case.

B. Counsel of Record

ACLU Side (Petitioner / Appellant): Michael L. Foreman argued the cause for appellants. With him on the brief was Edward Smith, Jr.

Opposing Side (Respondent / Appellee): John B. Howard Jr., Deputy Attorney General of Maryland, argued the cause for appellee. With him on the brief were Douglas F. Gansler, Attorney General and William F. Brockman, Acting Solicitor General.

III. AMICI CURIAE

ACLU Side (Petitioner / Appellant)

Brief of amici curiae filed on behalf of the National Partnership for Women & Families, AARP, AFSCME International, American Civil Liberties Union, A Better Balance, National Employment Lawyers Association, National Senior Citizens Law Center, National Women's Law Center, 9to5, National Association of Working Women, and Service Employees International Union by Jonathan J. Frankel, Phillip Douglass, Steven D. Tibbets, Judith L. Lichtman, and Sarah Crawford.

Brief of amici curiae filed on behalf of Lawyers' Committee for Civil Rights Under Law by Jon Greenbaum, Jane Dolkart, Yosef J. Reimer, Maura M. Klugman, and Melody Wells.

Brief of amici curiae filed on behalf of Senator Tom Harkin et al. by Carter G. Phillips, Daron Watts, Peter Goodloe, Mark E. Haddad, Brent W. Wilner, Patrick Kennell, and Lillian Park.

Brief of amici curiae filed on behalf of the Constitutional Accountability Center by Douglas T. Kendall, Elizabeth B. Wydra, David H. Gans, Clifford M. Sloan, David E. Carney, Ray D. McKenzie, and Marques P. Richeson.

Opposing Side (Respondent / Appellee)

Brief of amici curiae filed on behalf of the State of Texas et al. by Greg Abbott, Attorney General of Texas, Daniel T. Hodge, First Assistant Attorney General, Bill Cobb, Deputy

Attorney General for Civil Litigation, Jonathan F. Mitchell, Solicitor General, Sean D. Jordan, Deputy Solicitor General, and by the Attorneys General for their respective States as follows: Luther Strange of Alabama, John J. Burns of Alaska, Thomas C. Horne of Arizona, Dustin McDaniel of Arkansas, John W. Suthers of Colorado, Samuel S. Olens of Georgia, Lawrence G. Wasden of Idaho, Gregory F. Zoeller of Indiana, Derek Schmidt of Kansas, Jack Conway of Kentucky, James D. "Buddy" Caldwell of Louisiana, William J. Schneider of Maine, Bill Schuette of Michigan, Jon Bruning of Nebraska, Michael A. Delaney of New Hampshire, Wayne Stenehjem of North Dakota, E. Scott Pruitt of Oklahoma, Linda L. Kelly of Pennsylvania, Alan Wilson of South Carolina, Robert E. Cooper, Jr., of Tennessee, Mark L. Shurtleff of Utah, Kenneth T. Cuccinelli II of Virginia, Darrell V. McGraw, Jr., of West Virginia, J. B. Van Hollen of Wisconsin, and Gregory A. Phillips of Wyoming.

IV. THE SUPREME COURT'S DECISION

"A foundational premise of the federal system is that States, as sovereigns, are immune from suits for damages, save as they elect to waive that defense. As an exception to this principle, Congress may abrogate the States' immunity from suit pursuant to its powers under § 5 of the Fourteenth Amendment.

Congress must 'mak[e] its intention to abrogate unmistakably clear in the language of the statute.' On this point the Act does express the clear purpose to abrogate the States' immunity. . . .

The question then becomes whether the self-care provision and its attempt to abrogate the States' immunity are a valid exercise of congressional power under § 5 of the Fourteenth Amendment. . . .

Whether a congressional Act passed under § 5 can impose monetary liability upon States requires an assessment of both the "evil' or 'wrong' that Congress intended to remedy,' and the means Congress adopted to address that evil. . . .

Faced with 'the States' record of unconstitutional participation in, and fostering of, gender-based discrimination in the administration of leave benefits,' Hibbs concluded that requiring state employers to give all employees the opportunity to take family-care leave was 'narrowly targeted at the faultline between work and family—precisely where sex-based overgeneralization has been and remains strongest.' . . .

The same cannot be said for requiring the States to give all employees the opportunity to take self-care leave. . . .

Standing alone, the self-care provision is not a valid abrogation of the States' immunity from suit. . . .

As a consequence of our constitutional design, money damages are the exception when sovereigns are defendants. Subjecting States to suits for damages pursuant to § 5 requires more than a theory for why abrogating the States' immunity aids in, or advances, a stated congressional purpose. To abrogate the States' immunity from suits for damages under § 5, Congress must identify a pattern of constitutional violations and tailor a remedy congruent and proportional to the documented violations. It failed to do so when it allowed employees to sue States for violations of the FMLA's self-care provision. The judgment of the Court of Appeals is affirmed."

V. JUSTICE VOTE

4 Pro ACLU Side vs. 5 Con Opposing Side

ACLU Side (Petitioner / Appellant)

1. Ginsburg, R. – Wrote dissenting opinion
2. Kagan, E. – Joined Ginsburg's dissent in part
3. Breyer, S. – Joined Ginsburg's dissent
4. Sotomayor, S. – Joined Ginsburg's dissent in part

Opposing Side (Respondent / Appellee)

1. Kennedy, A. – Wrote majority opinion
2. Roberts, J. – Joined majority opinion
3. Scalia, A. – Wrote concurring opinion
4. Thomas, C. – Wrote concurring opinion
5. Alito, S. – Joined majority opinion

VI. A WIN OR LOSS FOR THE ACLU?

The ACLU filed as amicus curiae urging reversal of the judgment of the Court of Appeals; the Supreme Court affirmed in a 5-4 vote, giving the ACLU an apparent loss.

1091. Mayo Collaborative Services v. Prometheus Laboratories, Inc.

(Decided March 20, 2012; 566 U.S. 66)

I. ISSUE

A. Issues Discussed

Regulation

B. Legal Question Presented

"The question before us is whether the [patent] claims do significantly more than simply describe . . . natural relations. To put the matter more precisely, do the patent claims add enough to their statements of the correlations to allow the processes they describe to qualify as patent-eligible processes that apply natural laws?"

C. Supreme Court's Answer

"We believe that the answer to this question is no."

II. CASE SUMMARY

A. Background

"The patents before us concern the use of thiopurine drugs in the treatment of autoimmune diseases . . . . When a patient ingests a thiopurine compound, his body metabolizes the drug, causing metabolites to form in his bloodstream. . . .

[T]he patents—U.S. Patent No. 6,355,623 ('623 patent) and U.S. Patent No. 6,680,302 ('302 patent)—embody findings that concentrations in a patient's blood of 6–TG or of 6–MMP metabolite beyond a certain level (400 and 7000 picomoles per 8x10 8 red blood cells, respectively) indicate that the dosage is likely too high for the patient, while concentrations in the blood of 6–TG metabolite lower than a certain level (about 230 picomoles per 8x10 8 red blood cells) indicate that the dosage is likely too low to be effective.

The patent claims seek to embody this research in a set of processes. . . .

Respondent, Prometheus Laboratories, Inc. . . . sells diagnostic tests that embody the processes the patents describe. . . . Mayo Clinic . . . bought and used those tests. But in 2004 Mayo announced that it intended to begin using and selling its own test . . . . Prometheus then brought this action claiming patent infringement.

The District Court found that Mayo's test infringed claim 7 of the '623 patent. . . .

Nonetheless the District Court ultimately granted summary judgment in Mayo's favor. . . .

On appeal, the Federal Circuit reversed. . . .

Mayo filed a petition for certiorari. [The U.S. Supreme Court] granted the petition, vacated the judgment, and remanded the case for reconsideration . . . . On remand the Federal Circuit reaffirmed its earlier conclusion. . . . Mayo again filed a petition for certiorari, which [the U.S. Supreme Court] granted."

B. Counsel of Record / ACLU Attorney

ACLU Side (Petitioner / Appellant): Stephen M. Shapiro argued the cause for appellants. With him on the briefs were Timothy S. Bishop, Jeffrey W. Sarles, Charles Rothfeld, Jonathan Singer, John Dragseth, Deanna Reichel, and Eugene Volokh.

Solicitor General Verrilli argued the cause for the United States as amicus curiae.

Opposing Side (Respondent / Appellee): Richard P. Bress argued the cause for appellee. With him on the brief were J. Scott Ballenger, Maximilian A. Grant, Matthew J. Moore, and Gabriel K. Bell.

III. AMICI CURIAE

ACLU Side (Petitioner / Appellant)

Brief of amici curiae filed on behalf of the American Civil Liberties Union by Sandra S. Park, Christopher A. Hansen, Lenora M. Lapidus, and Steven R. Shapiro.

Brief of amici curiae filed on behalf of the United States by Solicitor General Verrilli, Assistant Attorney General West, Deputy Solicitor General Stewart, Mark R. Freeman, Scott R. McIntosh, Kelsi Brown Corkran, Raymond T. Chen, Thomas W. Krause, and Scott C. Weidenfeller.

Brief of amici curiae filed on behalf of AARP et al. by Daniel B. Ravicher, Stacy Canan, and Michael Schuster.

Brief of amici curiae filed on behalf of the American College of Medical Genetics et al. by Katherine J. Strandburg.

Brief of amici curiae filed on behalf of ARUP Laboratories, Inc., et al. by Kathleen M. Sullivan and Brian Cannon.

Brief of amici curiae filed on behalf of the Cato Institute et al. by Ilya Shapiro, James W. Harper, Sam Kazman, and Manuel S. Klausner.

Brief of amici curiae filed on behalf of Nine Law Professors by Joshua D. Sarnoff.

Brief of amici curiae filed on behalf of Verizon Communications, Inc., et al. by Michael K. Kellogg, John Thorne, and Paul H. Roeder.

Brief of amici curiae filed on behalf of Microsoft Corp. et al. by Matthew D. McGill and William G. Jenks in support of neither party.

Brief of amici curiae filed on behalf of the New York Intellectual Property Law Association by Ronald M. Daignault, Matthew B. McFarlane, Anthony F. LoCicero, and Charles R. Macedo in support of neither party.

Brief of amici curiae filed on behalf of Roche Molecular Systems, Inc., et al. by Seth P. Waxman, Mark C. Fleming, Kevin A. Marks, Blair Elizabeth Taylor, Jeffrey A. Lamken, and Sonali S. Srivastava in support of neither party.

Briefs of amici curiae were filed for the Association Internationale pour la Protection de la Propriété Intellectuelle et al. by Peter C. Schechter and Richard P. Beem in support of neither party.

Opposing Side (Respondent / Appellee)

Brief of amici curiae filed on behalf of the American Intellectual Property Law Association by Denise W. DeFranco, David S. Forman, and William G. Barber.

Brief of amici curiae filed on behalf of the Association of University Technology Managers by Donald R. Ware and Barbara A. Fiacco.

Brief of amici curiae filed on behalf of the Biotechnology Industry Organization by Jeffrey P. Kushan and Eric A. Shumsky.

Brief of amici curiae filed on behalf of Genomic Health, Inc., et al. by Edward R. Reines.

Brief of amici curiae filed on behalf of the Intellectual Property Amicus Brief Clinic of the University of New Hampshire School of Law by Ann M. McCrackin.

Brief of amici curiae filed on behalf of the Intellectual Property Law Association of Chicago by Meredith Martin Addy and Charles Shifley.

Brief of amici curiae filed on behalf of the Intellectual Property Owners Association by Gary M. Hoffman, Kenneth W. Brothers, Douglas K. Norman, and Kevin H. Rhodes.

Brief of amici curiae filed on behalf of the Juhasz Law Firm, P. C., by Paul R. Juhasz.

Brief of amici curiae filed on behalf of Myriad Genetics, Inc., by Gregory A. Castanias and Jay Z. Zhang.

Brief of amici curiae filed on behalf of the National Venture Capital Association by Lynn H. Pasahow, Michael J. Shuster, and Carolyn Chang.

Brief of amici curiae filed on behalf of Novartis Corp. by Evan A. Young.

Brief of amici curiae filed on behalf of the Pharmaceutical Research and Manufacturers of America by Harry J. Roper, Paul M. Smith, and Elaine J. Goldenberg.

Brief of amici curiae filed on behalf of SAP America, Inc., by Erika H. Arner and Jeffrey A. Berkowitz.

Brief of amici curiae filed on behalf of CONNECT et al. by Douglas E. Olson, Ned Israelsen, and Timothy N. Tardibono.

Brief of amici curiae filed on behalf of Health Law, Policy, and Ethics Scholars by Mark S. Davies and Michael K. Gottlieb.

IV. THE SUPREME COURT'S DECISION

"Prometheus' patents set forth laws of nature—namely, relationships between concentrations of certain metabolites in the blood and the likelihood that a dosage of a thiopurine drug will prove ineffective or cause harm. . . . While it takes . . . the administration of a thiopurine drug . . . to trigger a manifestation of this relation . . . , the relation itself exists . . . apart from any human action. . . .

The question before us is whether the claims do significantly more than simply describe these natural relations. To put the matter more precisely, do the patent claims add enough to their statements of the correlations to allow the processes they describe to qualify as patent-eligible processes that apply natural laws? We believe that the answer to this question is no. . . .

If a law of nature is not patentable, then neither is a process reciting a law of nature, unless that process has additional features that provide practical assurance that the process is more than a drafting effort designed to monopolize the law of nature itself. . . .

What else is there in the claims before us? The process that each claim recites tells doctors interested in the subject about the correlations that the researchers discovered. In doing so, it recites an 'administering' step, a 'determining' step, and a 'wherein' step. These additional steps are not themselves natural laws but neither are they sufficient to transform the nature of the claim. . . .

The upshot is that the three steps simply tell doctors to gather data from which they may draw an inference . . . . For these reasons we believe that the steps are not sufficient to transform unpatentable natural correlations into patentable applications of those regularities. . . .

A more detailed consideration of the controlling precedents reinforces our conclusion. . . .

The claim before us presents a case for patentability that is weaker than the (patent-eligible) claim in Diehr and no stronger than the (unpatentable) claim in Flook. . . .

We need not, and do not, now decide whether were the steps at issue here less conventional, these features of the claims would prove sufficient to invalidate them. For here, as we have said, the steps add nothing of significance to the natural laws themselves. . . .

For these reasons, we conclude that the patent claims at issue here effectively claim the underlying laws of nature themselves. The claims are consequently invalid. And the Federal Circuit's judgment is reversed."

V. JUSTICE VOTE

9 Pro ACLU Side vs. 0 Con Opposing Side

ACLU Side (Petitioner / Appellant)

1. Breyer, S. – Wrote majority opinion
2. Alito, S. – Joined majority opinion
3. Kagan, E. – Joined majority opinion
4. Thomas, C. – Joined majority opinion
5. Scalia, A. – Joined majority opinion
6. Kennedy, A. – Joined majority opinion
7. Ginsburg, R. – Joined majority opinion
8. Sotomayor, S. – Joined majority opinion
9. Roberts, J. – Joined majority opinion

VI. A WIN OR LOSS FOR THE ACLU?

The ACLU filed as amicus curiae urging reversal of the judgment of the Court of Appeals; the Supreme Court reversed in a 9-0 vote, giving the ACLU an apparent win.

1092. Missouri v. Frye

(Decided March 21, 2012; 566 U.S. 134)

I. ISSUE

A. Issues Discussed

Criminal procedure

B. Legal Question Presented

"The initial question is whether the constitutional right to counsel extends to the negotiation and consideration of plea offers that lapse or are rejected. If there is a right to effective assistance with respect to those offers, a further question is what a defendant must demonstrate in order to show that prejudice resulted from counsel's deficient performance."

C. Supreme Court's Answer

"This Court now holds that, as a general rule, defense counsel has the duty to communicate formal offers from the prosecution to accept a plea on terms and conditions that may be favorable to the accused. . . . Under Strickland, the question then becomes what, if any, prejudice resulted from the breach of duty. . . . It is appropriate to allow the Missouri Court of Appeals to address this question in the first instance."

II. CASE SUMMARY

A. Background

"Galin Frye was charged with driving with a revoked license. Frye had been convicted for that offense on three other occasions, so the State of Missouri charged him with a class D felony, which carries a maximum term of imprisonment of four years.

On November 15, the prosecutor sent a letter to Frye's counsel offering a choice of two plea bargains. . . . The letter stated both offers would expire on December 28. Frye's attorney did not advise Frye that the offers had been made. The offers expired.

Frye's preliminary hearing was scheduled for January 4, 2008. On December 30, 2007, less than a week before the hearing, Frye was again arrested for driving with a revoked license. At the January 4 hearing, Frye waived his right to a preliminary hearing on the charge arising from the August 2007 arrest. He pleaded not guilty . . . but then changed his plea to guilty. . . . The state trial court accepted Frye's guilty plea. The prosecutor recommended a 3-year sentence, made no recommendation regarding probation, and requested 10 days shock time in jail. The trial judge sentenced Frye to three years in prison.

Frye filed for postconviction relief in state court. He alleged his counsel's failure to inform him of the prosecution's plea offer denied him the effective assistance of counsel. . . .

A state court denied the postconviction motion, but the Missouri Court of Appeals reversed . . . ."

The Supreme Court granted certiorari to review the case.

B. Counsel of Record / ACLU Attorney

ACLU Side (Respondent / Appellee): Emmett D. Queener argued the cause for appellee. With him on the brief was Craig A. Johnston.

Opposing Side (Petitioner / Appellant): Chris Koster, Attorney General of Missouri, argued the cause for appellant. With him on the briefs were James R. Layton, Solicitor General, and Shaun J. Mackelprang, Chief Counsel.

Anthony A. Yang argued the cause for the United States as amicus curiae.

III. AMICI CURIAE

ACLU Side (Respondent / Appellee)

Brief of amici curiae filed on behalf of the National Association of Criminal Defense Lawyers, Connecticut Criminal Defense Lawyers Association, and the American Civil Liberties Union Foundation by Jonathan D. Hacker, Loren L. Alikhan, Norman L. Reimer, Malia Brink, Steven R. Shapiro, Vanita Gupta, Ezekiel Edwards, and Conrad O. Seifert.

Brief of amici curiae filed on behalf of the American Bar Association by Stephen N. Zack, Margaret Colgate Love, Peter Goldberger, and Jill Wheaton.

Brief of amici curiae filed on behalf of the Constitution Project by John F. Cooney and Virginia Sloan.

Brief of amici curiae filed on behalf of the Center on the Administration of Criminal Law, New York University School of Law, by Daniel Meron, Lori Alvino McGill, and Anthony S. Barkow.

Opposing Side (Petitioner / Appellant)

Brief of amici curiae filed on behalf of the United States by Anthony A. Yang, former Acting Solicitor General Katyal, Assistant Attorney General Breuer, Deputy Solicitor General Dreeben, and Deborah Watson.

Brief of amici curiae filed on behalf of the State of Connecticut et al. by Kevin T. Kane, Chief State's Attorney of Connecticut, Michael E. O'Hare, Supervisory Assistant State's Attorney, and Michael J. Proto, Assistant State's Attorney, by William H. Ryan, Jr., former Acting Attorney General of Pennsylvania, and by the Attorneys General for their respective States as follows: John J. Burns of Alaska, Tom Horne of Arizona, John W. Suthers of Colorado, Joseph R. Biden III of Delaware, Pamela Jo Bondi of Florida, Samuel S. Olens of Georgia, David M. Louie of Hawaii, Lawrence G. Wasden of Idaho, Gregory F. Zoeller of Indiana, Derek Schmidt of Kansas, Jack Conway of Kentucky, Douglas F. Gansler of Maryland, Bill Schuette of Michigan, Steve Bullock of Montana, Jon Bruning of Nebraska, Paula T. Dow of New Jersey, Gary K. King of New Mexico, E. Scott Pruitt of Oklahoma, Alan Wilson of South Carolina, Marty J. Jackley of South Dakota, Robert E. Cooper, Jr., of Tennessee, Greg Abbott of Texas, Mark L. Shurtleff of Utah, Kenneth T. Cuccinelli II of Virginia, Robert M. McKenna of Washington, J. B. Van Hollen of Wisconsin, and Gregory A. Phillips of Wyoming.

Brief of amici curiae filed on behalf of the Criminal Justice Legal Foundation et al. by Kent S. Scheidegger.

IV. THE SUPREME COURT'S DECISION

"With respect to the right to effective counsel in plea negotiations, a proper beginning point is . . . two cases . . . considering the role of counsel in advising a client about a plea offer . . . .

In the case now before the Court the State, as petitioner, points out that the legal question presented is different from that in Hill and Padilla. In those cases the claim was that the prisoner's plea of guilty was invalid because counsel had provided incorrect advice pertinent to the plea. In the instant case, [t]he challenge is not to the advice pertaining to the plea that was accepted but rather to the course of legal representation that preceded it with respect to other potential pleas and plea offers. . . .

The inquiry then becomes how to define the duty and responsibilities of defense counsel in the plea bargain process. This is a difficult question. . . .

This Court now holds that, as a general rule, defense counsel has the duty to communicate formal offers from the prosecution to accept a plea on terms and conditions that may be favorable to the accused. . . . When defense counsel allowed the offer to expire without advising the defendant . . . , defense counsel did not render the effective assistance the Constitution requires. . . .

Here defense counsel did not communicate the formal offers to the defendant. As a result of that deficient performance, the offers lapsed. Under Strickland, the question then becomes what, if any, prejudice resulted from the breach of duty. . . .

To show prejudice from ineffective assistance of counsel where a plea offer has lapsed or been rejected because of counsel's deficient performance, defendants must demonstrate a reasonable probability they would have accepted the earlier plea offer had they been afforded effective assistance of counsel. Defendants must also demonstrate a reasonable probability the plea would have been entered without the prosecution canceling it or the trial court refusing to accept it . . . . To establish prejudice in this instance, it is necessary to show a reasonable probability that the end result of the criminal process would have been more favorable by reason of a plea . . . .

These standards must be applied to the instant case. . . . The Missouri Court of Appeals was correct that 'counsel's representation fell below an objective standard of reasonableness.'

The Court of Appeals erred, however, in articulating the precise standard for prejudice . . . .

We remand for the Missouri Court of Appeals to consider these state-law questions, because they bear on the federal question of Strickland prejudice. . . .

It is appropriate to allow the Missouri Court of Appeals to address this question in the first instance. The judgment of the Missouri Court of Appeals is vacated, and the case is remanded . . . ."

V. JUSTICE VOTE

5 Pro ACLU Side vs. 4 Con Opposing Side

ACLU Side (Respondent / Appellee)

1. Kennedy, A. – Wrote majority opinion
2. Kagan, E. – Joined majority opinion
3. Breyer, S. – Joined majority opinion

4. Ginsburg, R. – Joined majority opinion
5. Sotomayor, S. – Joined majority opinion

Opposing Side (Petitioner / Appellant)

1. Alito, S. – Joined Scalia's dissent
2. Thomas, C. – Joined Scalia's dissent
3. Scalia, A. – Wrote dissenting opinion
4. Roberts, J. – Joined Scalia's dissent

VI. A WIN OR LOSS FOR THE ACLU?

The ACLU filed as amicus curiae urging affirmance; the Supreme Court vacated the Missouri Court of Appeals' decision by a 5-4 vote, giving the ACLU an apparent win.

1093. Lafler v. Cooper

(Decided March 21, 2012; 566 U.S. 156)

I. ISSUE

A. Issues Discussed

Criminal procedure

B. Legal Question Presented

"The question for this Court is how to apply Strickland 's prejudice test where ineffective assistance results in a rejection of the plea offer and the defendant is convicted at the ensuing trial."

C. Supreme Court's Answer

"As to prejudice, respondent has shown that but for counsel's deficient performance there is a reasonable probability he and the trial court would have accepted the guilty plea. In addition, as a result of not accepting the plea and being convicted at trial, respondent received a minimum sentence 3½ times greater than he would have received under the plea. The standard for ineffective assistance under Strickland has thus been satisfied."

II. CASE SUMMARY

A. Background

"On the evening of March 25, 2003, respondent pointed a gun toward Kali Mundy's head and fired. [I]t is unclear why respondent did this . . . . In any event the shot missed and Mundy fled. Respondent followed in pursuit, firing repeatedly. Mundy was shot . . . but survived . . . .

Respondent was charged . . . with assault with intent to murder, possession of a firearm by a felon, possession of a firearm in the commission of a felony, misdemeanor possession of marijuana, and for being a habitual offender. On two occasions, the prosecution offered to dismiss two of the charges and to recommend a sentence of 51 to 85 months for the other two, in exchange for a guilty plea. In a communication with the court respondent . . . expressed a willingness to accept . . . . Respondent, however, later rejected the offer[s], allegedly after his attorney convinced him that the prosecution would be unable to establish his intent to murder Mundy . . . . On the first day of trial the prosecution offered a significantly less favorable plea deal, which respondent again rejected. After trial, respondent was convicted on all counts and received a mandatory minimum sentence of 185 to 360 months' imprisonment.

In a . . . hearing before the state trial court, respondent argued his attorney's advice to reject the plea constituted ineffective assistance. The trial judge rejected the claim, and the Michigan Court of Appeals affirmed. . . . The Michigan Supreme Court denied respondent's application for leave to file an appeal.

Respondent then filed a petition for federal habeas relief under 28 U.S.C. § 2254, renewing his ineffective-assistance-of-counsel claim. . . . [T]he District Court granted a conditional writ. . . .

The United States Court of Appeals for the Sixth Circuit affirmed . . . ."

The Supreme Court granted certiorari to review the case.

B. Counsel of Record / ACLU Attorney

ACLU Side (Respondent / Appellee): Valerie R. Newman, by appointment of the Court, argued the cause for appellee. With her on the brief were Jacqueline J. McCann, Jeffrey T. Green, and Sarah O'Rourke Schrup.

Opposing Side (Petitioner / Appellant): John J. Bursch, Solicitor General of Michigan, argued the cause for petitioner. With him on the briefs were Bill Schuette, Attorney General, B. Eric Restuccia, Deputy Solicitor General, and Joel D. McGormley.

William M. Jay argued the cause for the United States as amicus curiae.

III. AMICI CURIAE

ACLU Side (Respondent / Appellee)

Brief of amici curiae filed on behalf of the National Association of Criminal Defense Lawyers, Connecticut Criminal Defense Lawyers Association, and the American Civil Liberties Union Foundation by Jonathan D. Hacker, Loren L. Alikhan, Norman L. Reimer, Malia Brink, Steven R. Shapiro, Conrad O. Seifert, Vanita Gupta, and Ezekiel Edwards.

Brief of amici curiae filed on behalf of the American Bar Association by Stephen N. Zack, Margaret Colgate Love, Peter Goldberger, and Jill Wheaton.

Brief of amici curiae filed on behalf of the Constitution Project by John F. Cooney and Virginia Sloan.

Brief of amici curiae filed on behalf of the Center on the Administration of Criminal Law, New York University School of Law by Daniel Meron, Lori Alvino McGill, and Anthony S. Barkow.

Opposing Side (Petitioner / Appellant)

Brief of amici curiae filed on behalf of the United States by William M. Jay, former Acting Solicitor General Katyal, Assistant Attorney General Breuer, Deputy Solicitor General Dreeben, and Joel M. Gershowitz.

Brief of amici curiae filed on behalf of the State of Connecticut et al. by Kevin T. Kane, Chief State's Attorney of Connecticut, Michael E. O'Hare, Supervisory Assistant State's Attorney, and Michael J. Proto, Assistant State's Attorney, and by the Attorneys General for their respective States as follows: Luther Strange of Alabama, Tom Horne of Arizona, John W. Suthers of Colorado, Joseph R. Biden III of Delaware, Pamela Jo Bondi of Florida, Samuel S. Olens of Georgia, David M. Louie of Hawaii, Gregory F. Zoeller of Indiana, Derek

Schmidt of Kansas, Jack Conway of Kentucky, Douglas F. Gansler of Maryland, Steve Bullock of Montana, Jon Bruning of Nebraska, Paula T. Dow of New Jersey, Gary K. King of New Mexico, E. Scott Pruitt of Oklahoma, William H. Ryan, Jr., of Pennsylvania, Alan Wilson of South Carolina, Marty J. Jackley of South Dakota, Robert E. Cooper, Jr., of Tennessee, Greg Abbott of Texas, Mark L. Shurtleff of Utah, Kenneth T. Cuccinelli II of Virginia, Robert M. McKenna of Washington, J. B. Van Hollen of Wisconsin, and Gregory A. Phillips of Wyoming.

Brief of amici curiae filed on behalf of Wayne County, Michigan, by Kym L. Worthy and Timothy A. Baughman.

Brief of amici curiae filed on behalf of the Criminal Justice Legal Foundation et al. by Kent S. Scheidegger.

IV. THE SUPREME COURT'S DECISION

"[A] Sixth Amendment right to counsel . . . extends to the plea-bargaining process. . . .

The question for this Court is how to apply Strickland 's prejudice test where ineffective assistance results in a rejection of the plea offer and the defendant is convicted at the ensuing trial. . . .

To establish Strickland prejudice a defendant must 'show that there is a reasonable probability that, but for counsel's unprofessional errors, the result of the proceeding would have been different.' . . .

Petitioner and the Solicitor General propose a different, far more narrow, view of the Sixth Amendment. . . . The three reasons . . . offer[ed] for their approach are unpersuasive. . . .

In the end, petitioner's three arguments amount to one general contention: A fair trial wipes clean any deficient performance by defense counsel during plea bargaining. That position ignores the reality that criminal justice today is for the most part a system of pleas, not a system of trials. . . .

Even if a defendant shows ineffective assistance of counsel has caused the rejection of a plea leading to . . . a more severe sentence, there is the question of what constitutes an appropriate remedy. . . .

Sixth Amendment remedies should be 'tailored to the injury suffered from the constitutional violation and should not unnecessarily infringe on competing interests.' . . .

At this point . . . it suffices to note two considerations that are of relevance.

First, a court may take account of a defendant's earlier expressed willingness, or unwillingness, to accept responsibility for his or her actions. Second, it is not necessary here to decide as a constitutional rule that a judge is required to prescind . . . any information concerning the crime that was discovered after the plea offer was made. . . .

The standards for ineffective assistance of counsel when a defendant rejects a plea offer and goes to trial must now be applied to this case. . . .

Respondent has satisfied Strickland 's two-part test. [T]he fact of deficient performance has been conceded by all parties. . . .

As to prejudice, respondent has shown that but for counsel's deficient performance there is a reasonable probability he and the trial court would have accepted the guilty plea. . . .

As a remedy, the District Court ordered specific performance of the original plea agreement. The correct remedy . . . , however, is to order the State to reoffer the plea agreement. . . .

The judgment of the Court of Appeals for the Sixth Circuit is vacated, and the case is remanded . . . ."

V. JUSTICE VOTE

5 Pro ACLU Side vs. 4 Con Opposing Side

ACLU Side (Respondent / Appellee)

1. Kennedy, A. – Wrote majority opinion
2. Kagan, E. – Joined majority opinion
3. Breyer, S. – Joined majority opinion
4. Ginsburg, R. – Joined majority opinion
5. Sotomayor, S. – Joined majority opinion

Opposing Side (Petitioner / Appellant)

1. Alito, S. – Wrote dissenting opinion
2. Thomas, C. – Joined Scalia's dissent
3. Scalia, A. – Wrote dissenting opinion
4. Roberts, J. – Joined Scalia's dissent in part

VI. A WIN OR LOSS FOR THE ACLU?

The ACLU filed as amicus curiae urging affirmance; the Supreme Court vacated the Court of Appeals' decision by a 5-4 vote, giving the ACLU an apparent win.

1094. Florence v. Board of Chosen Freeholders of County of Burlington

(Decided April 2, 2012; 566 U.S. 318)

I. ISSUE

A. Issues Discussed

4th Amendment, prison

B. Legal Question Presented

"This case presents the question of what rules, or limitations, the Constitution imposes on searches of arrested persons who are to be held in jail while their cases are being processed. . . . [W] hether every detainee who will be admitted to the general population may be required to undergo a close visual inspection while undressed."

C. Supreme Court's Answer

"In addressing this type of constitutional claim courts must defer to the judgment of correctional officials unless the record contains substantial evidence showing their policies are an unnecessary or unjustified response to problems of jail security. That necessary showing has not been made in this case."

II. CASE SUMMARY

A. Background

"In 1998, . . . petitioner Albert Florence was arrested . . . . Petitioner entered a plea of guilty . . . and was sentenced to pay a fine in monthly installments. In 2003, after he fell behind on his payments and failed to appear at an enforcement hearing, a bench warrant was issued for his arrest. He paid the outstanding balance . . . ; but . . . the warrant remained . . . .

Two years later, in Burlington County, New Jersey, petitioner and his wife were stopped in their automobile by a state trooper. Based on the outstanding warrant in the computer system, the officer arrested petitioner and took him to the Burlington County Detention Center. . . .

[J]ail procedures required [o]fficers [to] check arrestees . . . as they disrobed. . . .

[At t]he Essex County Correctional Facility, where petitioner was taken after six days, [a]ll arriving detainees . . . were instructed to remove their clothing while an officer looked for body markings, wounds, and contraband. [A]n officer looked at their . . . body openings. . . . Petitioner . . . was required to lift his genitals, turn around, and cough in a squatting position . . . . He was released the next day, when the charges . . . were dismissed. . .

Seeking relief under 42 U.S.C. § 1983 for violations of his Fourth and Fourteenth Amendment rights, petitioner maintained that persons arrested for a minor offense could not be required to . . . expose . . . their bodies to close visual inspection as a routine part of the intake process. . . .

After discovery, the court granted petitioner's motion for summary judgment . . . . A divided panel of the United States Court of Appeals for the Third Circuit reversed . . . ."

The Supreme Court granted certiorari to review the case.

B. Counsel of Record / ACLU Attorney

ACLU Side (Petitioner / Appellant): Thomas C. Goldstein argued the cause for appellant. With him on the briefs were Susan Chana Lask, Amy Howe, Kevin K. Russell, Jeffrey L. Fisher, and Pamela S. Karlan.

Opposing Side (Respondent / Appellee): Carter G. Phillips argued the cause for appellees. With him on the brief for appellee Essex County Correctional Facility et al. were Eamon P. Joyce, Ryan C. Morris, and Alan Ruddy. Alfred W. Putnam, Jr., D. Alicia Hickok, and J. Brooks DiDonato filed a brief for appellee Board of Chosen Freeholders of the County of Burlington et al.

Nicole A. Saharsky argued the cause for the United States as amicus curiae.

III. AMICI CURIAE

ACLU Side (Petitioner / Appellant)

Brief of amici curiae filed on behalf of Former Attorney General of New Jersey Robert J. Del Tufo et al. by Steven R. Shapiro, David C. Fathi, and David M. Shapiro of the American Civil Liberties Union Foundation, and Edward Barocas, Jeanne LoCicero, and Alexander Shalom of the American Civil Liberties Union of New Jersey.

Brief of amici curiae filed on behalf of Academics on Gang Behavior by Evan P. Schultz.

Brief of amici curiae filed on behalf of the American Bar Association by Stephen N. Zack, Elaine J. Goldenberg, and Iris E. Bennett.

Brief of amici curiae filed on behalf of Current and Former Jail and Corrections Professionals by Craig A. Stewart, Lisa S. Blatt, Anthony J. Franze, and Dirk C. Phillips.

Brief of amici curiae filed on behalf of the Domestic Violence Legal Empowerment and Appeals Project et al. by Catherine E. Stetson and Jessica L. Ellsworth.

Brief of amici curiae filed on behalf of the Medical Society of New Jersey et al. by David J. Bederman.

Brief of amici curiae filed on behalf of the National Police Accountability Project by Kenneth N. Flaxman and Robert L. Herbst.

Brief of amici curiae filed on behalf of Psychiatrists by Seth P. Waxman and Daniel S. Volchok.

Brief of amici curiae filed on behalf of Sister Bernie Galvin et al. by Barrett S. Litt, Paul J. Estuar, Mark E. Merin, J. Christopher Mills, and Charles J. LaDuca.

Brief of amici curiae filed on behalf of the National Association of Criminal Defense Lawyers by Meir Feder and David Porter.

Opposing Side (Respondent / Appellee)

Brief of amici curiae filed on behalf of the United States by Nicole A. Saharsky, Solicitor General Verrilli, Assistant Attorney General West, Leondra R. Kruger, Barbara L. Herwig, and Edward Himmelfarb.

Brief of amici curiae filed on behalf of the State of Michigan et al. by Bill Schuette, Attorney General of Michigan, John J. Bursch, Solicitor General, and B. Eric Restuccia, Deputy Solicitor General, and by the Attorneys General for their respective States as follows: Luther Strange of Alabama, John W. Suthers of Colorado, Lawrence G. Wasden of Idaho, Jack Conway of Kentucky, James D. "Buddy" Caldwell of Louisiana, William J. Schneider of Maine, Roy Cooper of North Carolina, Mike DeWine of Ohio, E. Scott Pruitt of Oklahoma, Linda L. Kelly of Pennsylvania, and Mark L. Shurtleff of Utah.

Brief of amici curiae filed on behalf of Atlantic County et al. by Sean X. Kelly and Sean Robins.

Brief of amici curiae filed on behalf of Cook County by Anita Alvarez, Patrick T. Driscoll, Jr., and Paul A. Castiglione.

Brief of amici curiae filed on behalf of the City and County of San Francisco et al. by Dennis J. Herrera, Danny Chou, Vince Chhabria, and Christine Van Aken.

Brief of amici curiae filed on behalf of the County Commissioners Association of Pennsylvania by Robert L. Knupp and Anthony T. McBeth.

Brief of amici curiae filed on behalf of DRI– The Voice of the Defense Bar by R. Matthew Cairns and Mary Massaron Ross.

Brief of amici curiae filed on behalf of the Maine County Commissioners Association by Peter T. Marchesi.

Brief of amici curiae filed on behalf of the National Sheriffs' Association et al. by Robert Spence and Travis Wisdom.

Brief of amici curiae filed on behalf of the New Jersey County Jail Wardens Association by Stephen B. Kinnaird.

Brief of amici curiae filed on behalf of the Policemen's Benevolent Association, Local 249, et al. by James M. Mets.

Brief of amici curiae filed on behalf of the Texas Association of Counties et al. by David Iglesias and Robert Davis.

IV. THE SUPREME COURT'S DECISION

"The difficulties of operating a detention center must not be underestimated by the courts. . . . Maintaining safety and order at these institutions requires the expertise of correctional officials, who must have substantial discretion to devise reasonable solutions to the problems they face. The Court has . . . explained that a regulation impinging on an inmate's constitutional rights must be upheld 'if it is reasonably related to legitimate penological interests.'

The Court's opinion in Bell v. Wolfish, 441 U.S. 520 (1979), is the starting point for understanding how this framework applies to Fourth Amendment challenges. . . .

Policies designed to keep contraband out of . . . prisons have been upheld in cases . . . since Bell. . . .

These cases establish that correctional officials must be permitted to devise reasonable search policies to detect and deter the possession of contraband in their facilities. . . .

In many jails officials seek to improve security by requiring some kind of strip search . . . .

Persons arrested for minor offenses may be among the detainees processed at these facilities. . . .

The question here is whether undoubted security imperatives involved in jail supervision override the assertion that some detainees must be exempt from the more invasive search procedures at issue absent reasonable suspicion of a concealed weapon or other contraband. The Court has held that deference must be given to the officials in charge of the jail unless there is 'substantial evidence' demonstrating their response to the situation is exaggerated. Petitioner has not met this standard . . . .

Even assuming all the facts in favor of petitioner, the search procedures at the Burlington County Detention Center and the Essex County Correctional Facility struck a reasonable balance between inmate privacy and the needs of the institutions. The Fourth and Fourteenth Amendments do not require adoption of the framework of rules petitioner proposes.

The judgment of the Court of Appeals for the Third Circuit is affirmed."

V. JUSTICE VOTE

4 Pro ACLU Side vs. 5 Con Opposing Side

ACLU Side (Petitioner / Appellant)

1. Kagan, E. – Joined Breyer's dissent
2. Breyer, S. – Wrote dissenting opinion
3. Ginsburg, R. – Joined Breyer's dissent
4. Sotomayor, S. – Joined Breyer's dissent

Opposing Side (Respondent / Appellee)

1. Kennedy, A. – Wrote majority opinion
2. Alito, S. – Wrote concurring opinion
3. Thomas, C. – Joined majority opinion in part
4. Scalia, A. – Joined majority opinion
5. Roberts, J. – Wrote concurring opinion

VI. A WIN OR LOSS FOR THE ACLU?

The ACLU filed as amicus curiae urging reversal of the judgment of the Court of Appeals; the Supreme Court affirmed in a 5-4 vote, giving the ACLU an apparent loss.

1095. Reichle v. Howards

(Decided June 4, 2012; 566 U.S. 658)

I. ISSUE

A. Issues Discussed

1st Amendment, press, speech, association, immunity

B. Legal Question Presented

"[W]hether two federal law enforcement agents are immune from suit for allegedly arresting a suspect in retaliation for his political speech, when the agents had probable cause to arrest the suspect for committing a federal crime."

C. Supreme Court's Answer

"We conclude that, at the time of Howards' arrest, it was not clearly established that an arrest supported by probable cause could violate the First Amendment. We, therefore, reverse the judgment of the Court of Appeals denying petitioners qualified immunity."

II. CASE SUMMARY

A. Background

"On June 16, 2006, Vice President Richard Cheney visited a shopping mall . . . . A Secret Service protective detail accompanied the Vice President. . . .

Respondent Steven Howards . . . was engaged in a cell phone conversation when he noticed the Vice President greeting members of the public. Agent Doyle overheard Howards say, . . . "I'm going to ask [the Vice President] how many kids he's killed today." . . .

When Howards approached the Vice President, he told him that his "policies in Iraq are disgusting." The Vice President simply thanked Howards and moved along, but Howards touched the Vice President's shoulder as the Vice President departed. . . .

The agents determined that Agent Reichle, who coordinated the . . . team responsible for interviewing individuals suspected of violating the law, should question Howards. . . .

Agent Reichle approached Howards . . . and asked to speak with him. Howards refused and attempted to walk away. At that point, Agent Reichle stepped in front of Howards and asked if he had assaulted the Vice President. . . . Howards denied . . . . Agent Reichle also asked Howards whether he had touched the Vice President. Howards falsely denied . . . . After confirming . . . Doyle had . . . seen Howards touch the Vice President, [he] arrested Howards.

The Secret Service transferred Howards to the custody of the local sheriff's department. H[e] was charged by local officials with harassment . . . . The charge was eventually dismissed. . . .

Howards brought this action . . . alleg[ing] he was arrested and searched without probable cause [and] arrested in retaliation for criticizing the Vice President . . . .

Petitioners . . . moved for summary judgment . . . . The District

Court denied the motion. [T]he United States Court of Appeals for the Tenth Circuit affirmed in part and reversed in part."

The Supreme Court granted certiorari to review the case.

B. Counsel of Record / ACLU Attorney

ACLU Side (Respondent / Appellee): David A. Lane argued the cause for appellee. With him on the brief was Lauren L. Fontana.

Opposing Side (Petitioner / Appellant): Sean R. Gallagher argued the cause for appellants. With him on the briefs were Bennett L. Cohen, William E. Quirk, H. Christopher Bartolomucci, Viet D. Dinh, and Brian J. Field.

Deputy Solicitor General Srinivasan argued the cause for the United States as amicus curiae.

III. AMICI CURIAE

ACLU Side (Respondent / Appellee)

Brief of amici curiae filed on behalf of the American Civil Liberties Union and the ACLU of Colorado by Christopher A. Hansen and Steven R. Shapiro.

Brief of amici curiae filed on behalf of The Rutherford Institute by John W. Whitehead.

Brief of amici curiae filed on behalf of William G. Moore, Jr., by Paul M. Pohl and Christian G. Vergonis in support of neither party.

Opposing Side (Petitioner / Appellant)

Brief of amici curiae filed on behalf of the United States by Deputy Solicitor General Srinivasan, Solicitor General Verrilli, Assistant Attorney General West, Deputy Assistant Attorney General Brinkmann, Eric J. Feigin, Barbara L. Herwig, and Teal Luthy Miller.

Brief of amici curiae filed on behalf of the FBI Agents Association et al. by J. Brett Busby, E. Dee Martin, and Joshua C. Zive.

Brief of amici curiae filed on behalf of the International City/County Management Association et al. by Lisa E. Soronen.

IV. THE SUPREME COURT'S DECISION

"Qualified immunity shields government officials from civil damages liability unless the official violated a statutory or constitutional right that was clearly established at the time . . . .

To be clearly established, a right must be sufficiently clear 'that every 'reasonable official would [have understood] that what he is doing violates that right." . .

The 'clearly established' standard is not satisfied here. This Court has never recognized a First Amendment right to be free from a retaliatory arrest that is supported by probable cause; nor was such a right otherwise clearly established at the time of Howards' arrest. . . .

Here, the right in question is not the general right to be free from retaliation for one's speech, but the more specific right to be free from a retaliatory arrest that is otherwise supported by probable cause. This Court has never held that there is such a right. . . .

We next consider Tenth Circuit precedent. Assuming arguendo that controlling Court of Appeals' authority could be a dispositive source of clearly established law in the circumstances of this case, the Tenth Circuit's cases do not satisfy the 'clearly established' standard here. . . .

At the time of Howards' arrest, Hartman's impact on the Tenth Circuit's precedent governing retaliatory arrests was far from clear. Although the facts of Hartman involved only a retaliatory prosecution, reasonable officers could have questioned whether the rule of Hartman also applied to arrests. . . .

Hartman injected uncertainty into the law governing retaliatory arrests, particularly in light of Hartman's rationale and the close relationship between retaliatory arrest and prosecution claims. This uncertainty was only confirmed by subsequent appellate decisions that disagreed over whether the reasoning in Hartman applied similarly to retaliatory arrests. Accordingly, when Howards was arrested it was not clearly established that an arrest supported by probable cause could give rise to a First Amendment violation. Petitioners Reichle and Doyle are thus entitled to qualified immunity.

The judgment of the Court of Appeals is reversed, and the case is remanded . . . ."

V. JUSTICE VOTE

0 Pro ACLU Side vs. 8 Con Opposing Side

Opposing Side (Petitioner / Appellant)

1. Thomas, C. – Wrote majority opinion
2. Alito, S. – Joined majority opinion
3. Breyer, S. – Joined Ginsburg's concurrence
4. Scalia, A. – Joined majority opinion
5. Kennedy, A. – Joined majority opinion
6. Ginsburg, R. – Wrote concurring opinion
7. Sotomayor, S. – Joined majority opinion
8. Roberts, J. – Joined majority opinion

Kagan, E. – Took no part in the decision.

VI. A WIN OR LOSS FOR THE ACLU?

The ACLU filed as amicus curiae urging affirmance; the Supreme Court reversed the Court of Appeals' decision by an 8-0 vote, giving the ACLU an apparent loss.

1096. FCC v. Fox Television Stations

(Decided June 21, 2012; 567 U.S. 239)

I. ISSUE

A. Issues Discussed

1st Amendment, press, speech, association

B. Legal Question Presented

Whether the Federal Communication Commission's indecency enforcement regime is unconstitutionally vague.

C. Supreme Court's Answer

"The Commission failed to give Fox or ABC fair notice prior to the broadcasts in question that fleeting expletives and momentary nudity could be found actionably indecent. Therefore, the

Commission's standards as applied to these broadcasts were vague, and the Commission's orders must be set aside."

II. CASE SUMMARY

A. Background

"In FCC v. Fox Television Stations, Inc., 556 U.S. 502, 529 (2009) (Fox I), the Court held that the Federal Communication Commission's decision to modify its indecency enforcement regime to regulate so-called fleeting expletives was neither arbitrary nor capricious. . . . On remand, the Court of Appeals found the policy was vague and, as a result, unconstitutional. The case now returns to this Court for decision upon the constitutional question. . . .

Even though the incidents at issue in these cases took place before the Golden Globes Order, the Commission applied its new policy regarding fleeting expletives and fleeting nudity. It found the broadcasts by respondents Fox and ABC to be in violation of this standard. . . .

As to Fox, the Commission found the two Billboard Awards broadcasts indecent . . . .

Fox and various intervenors returned to the United States Court of Appeals for the Second Circuit, raising administrative, statutory, and constitutional challenges to the Commission's indecency regulations. In a 2–to–1 decision, with Judge Leval dissenting, the Court of Appeals found the Remand Order arbitrary and capricious because 'the FCC has made a 180–degree turn regarding its treatment of 'fleeting expletives' without providing a reasoned explanation justifying the about-face.' . . .

The procedural history regarding ABC is more brief. . . . The scene was deemed patently offensive as measured by contemporary community standards, and the Commission determined that '[t]he female actor's nudity is presented in a manner that clearly panders to and titillates the audience.' . . . In a summary order the United States Court of Appeals for the Second Circuit vacated the forfeiture order . . . ." The Supreme Court granted certiorari to review the case.

B. Counsel of Record / ACLU Attorney

ACLU Side (Respondent / Appellee): Carter G. Phillips argued the cause for appellees Fox Television Stations, Inc., et al. With him on the brief were Mark D. Schneider, David S. Petron, Ryan C. Morris, Miguel A. Estrada, Susan Weiner, Robert Corn-Revere, Ronald G. London, Jonathan H. Anschell, and Susanna M. Lowy. Seth P. Waxman argued the cause for appellees ABC, Inc., et al. With him on the brief were Paul R. Q. Wolfson, Daniel S. Volchok, and John W. Zucker. Wade H. Hargrove, Mark J. Prak, and David Kushner filed a brief for appellees ABC Television Affiliates Association et al. Robert A. Long, Jr., Jonathan D. Blake, and Jennifer A. Johnson filed a brief for appellees CBS Television Network Affiliates Association et al. Andrew Jay Schwartzman filed a brief for appellees Center for Creative Voices in Media et al.

Opposing Side (Petitioner / Appellant): Solicitor General Verrilli argued the cause for appellants. With him on the briefs were Assistant Attorney General West, Deputy Solicitor General Stewart, Joseph R. Palmore, Thomas M. Bondy, Anne Murphy, Austin C. Schlick, Peter Karanjia, Jacob M. Lewis, and Nandan M. Joshi.

III. AMICI CURIAE

ACLU Side (Respondent / Appellee)

Brief of amici curiae filed on behalf of the American Civil Liberties Union, the New York Civil Liberties Union, et al. by Steven R. Shapiro and Christopher A. Hansen.

Brief of amici curiae filed on behalf of the American Academy of Pediatrics et al. by Angela J. Campbell.

Brief of amici curiae filed on behalf of the Cato Institute et al. by John P. Elwood, Ilya Shapiro, Thomas S. Leatherbury, and Harold Feld.

Brief of amici curiae filed on behalf of the National Association of Broadcasters et al. by Paul M. Smith, Elaine J. Goldenberg, Jessica Ring Amunson, Jane E. Mago, and Jerianne Timmerman.

Brief of amici curiae filed on behalf of the Pennsylvania Center for the First Amendment et al. by Robert D. Richards and Clay Calvert.

Brief of amici curiae filed on behalf of the Public Broadcasting Service by Ryan M. Christian and Daniel B. Levin.

Brief of amici curiae filed on behalf of the Reporters Committee for Freedom of the Press et al. by Lucy A. Dalglish, Gregg P. Leslie, and David M. Giles.

Brief of amici curiae filed on behalf of the Student Press Law Center et al. by Gregory Stuart Smith.

Brief of amici curiae filed on behalf of the Thomas Jefferson Center for the Protection of Free Expression et al. by J. Joshua Wheeler.

Brief of amici curiae filed on behalf of Former FCC Officials by Henry Geller, Glen O. Robinson, and Newton N. Minow, all pro se, and by Timothy K. Lewis and Carl A. Solano.

Opposing Side (Petitioner / Appellant)

Brief of amici curiae filed on behalf of the American College of Pediatricians et al. by Bryan H. Beauman.

Brief of amici curiae filed on behalf of the Decency Enforcement Center for Television by Thomas B. North.

Brief of amici curiae filed on behalf of Focus on the Family et al. by J. Robert Flores.

Brief of amici curiae filed on behalf of Morality in Media, Inc., by Patrick A. Trueman and Robert W. Peters.

Brief of amici curiae filed on behalf of National Religious Broadcasters by Craig L. Parshall, Joseph C. Chautin III, and Elise M. Stubbe.

Brief of amici curiae filed on behalf of the Parents Television Council by Robert R. Sparks, Jr.

Brief of amici curiae filed on behalf of Judith A. Reisman et al. by Mathew D. Staver, Anita L. Staver, Stephen M. Crampton, and Mary E. McAlister.

Brief of amici curiae filed on behalf of the American Center for Law and Justice by Jay Alan Sekulow, Stuart J. Roth, Colby M. May, and Walter M. Weber in support of neither party.

Brief of amici curiae filed on behalf of the Yale Law School Information Society Project Scholars et al. by Priscilla J. Smith in support of neither party.

IV. THE SUPREME COURT'S DECISION

"A fundamental principle in our legal system is that laws which regulate persons or entities must give fair notice of conduct that is forbidden or required. . . .

Even when speech is not at issue, the void for vagueness doctrine addresses at least two connected but discrete due process concerns: first, that regulated parties should know what is required of them so they may act accordingly; second, precision and guidance are necessary so that those enforcing the law do not act in an arbitrary or discriminatory way. When speech is involved, rigorous adherence to those requirements is necessary to ensure that ambiguity does not chill protected speech.

These concerns are implicated here because, at the outset, the broadcasters claim they did not have, and do not have, sufficient notice of what is proscribed. . . .

The Government raises two arguments in response, but neither is persuasive. . . .

The Commission failed to give Fox or ABC fair notice . . . that fleeting expletives and momentary nudity could be found actionably indecent. Therefore, the Commission's standards as applied to these broadcasts were vague, and the Commission's orders must be set aside. . . .

It is necessary to make three observations about the scope of this decision. First, because the Court resolves these cases on fair notice grounds under the Due Process Clause, it need not address the First Amendment implications of the Commission's indecency policy. . . .

This leads to a second observation. Here, the Court rules that Fox and ABC lacked notice at the time of their broadcasts that the material they were broadcasting could be found actionably indecent under then-existing policies. Given this disposition, it is unnecessary for the Court to address the constitutionality of the current indecency policy as expressed in the Golden Globes Order and subsequent adjudications. . . .

Third, this opinion leaves the Commission free to modify its current indecency policy in light of its determination of the public interest and applicable legal requirements. And it leaves the courts free to review the current policy or any modified policy in light of its content and application. . . .

The judgments of the United States Court of Appeals for the Second Circuit are vacated, and the cases are remanded . . . ."

V. JUSTICE VOTE

0 Pro ACLU Side vs. 8 Con Opposing Side

Opposing Side (Petitioner / Appellant)

1. Kennedy, A. – Wrote majority opinion
2. Alito, S. – Joined majority opinion
3. Kagan, E. – Joined majority opinion
4. Thomas, C. – Joined majority opinion
5. Breyer, S. – Joined majority opinion
6. Scalia, A. – Joined majority opinion
7. Ginsburg, R. – Wrote concurring opinion
8. Roberts, J. – Joined majority opinion

Sotomayor, S. – Took no part in the decision.

VI. A WIN OR LOSS FOR THE ACLU?

The ACLU filed as amicus curiae urging affirmance; the Supreme Court vacated the Court of Appeals' decision by an 8-0 vote, giving the ACLU an apparent loss.

1097. Dorsey v. U.S.

I. ISSUE

A. Issues Discussed

Criminal procedure, drugs

B. Legal Question Presented

"In 2010, Congress enacted a new statute reducing the crack-to-powder cocaine disparity from 100–to–1 to 18–to–1. Fair Sentencing Act, 124 Stat. 2372. The new statute took effect on August 3, 2010. The question here is whether the Act's more lenient penalty provisions apply to offenders who committed a crack cocaine crime before August 3, 2010, but were not sentenced until after August 3."

C. Supreme Court's Answer

"We hold that the new, more lenient mandatory minimum provisions do apply to those pre-Act offenders."

II. CASE SUMMARY

A. Background

"Federal statutes impose mandatory minimum prison sentences upon those convicted of federal drug crimes. . . . Until 2010, the relevant statute imposed upon an offender who dealt in powder cocaine the same sentence it imposed upon an offender who dealt in one one-hundredth that amount of crack cocaine. . . .

In 2010, Congress enacted a new statute reducing the crack-to-powder cocaine disparity from 100–to–1 to 18–to–1. Fair Sentencing Act, 124 Stat. 2372. The new statute took effect on August 3, 2010. The question here is whether the Act's more lenient penalty provisions apply to offenders who committed a crack cocaine crime before August 3, 2010, but were not sentenced until after August 3. . . .

Corey Hill . . . unlawfully sold 53 grams of crack in March 2007, before the Fair Sentencing Act became law. . . . Hill was not sentenced, however, until December 2010 . . . . But [the judge] concluded that the Fair Sentencing Act's lower minimums apply only to those who committed a drug crime after August 3, 2010 . . . . Hence, the judge sentenced Hill to 10 years . . . . The Court of Appeals for the Seventh Circuit affirmed.

Edward Dorsey . . . sold 5.5 grams of crack in August 2008, before the Fair Sentencing Act took effect. . . . Dorsey was not sentenced . . . until September 2010 . . . . Under the Fair Sentencing Act, such an offender . . . was not subject to a mandatory minimum . . . .

The judge . . . concluded that the 1986 Drug Act's old minimums, not the new Fair Sentencing Act, applied . . . . The Court of Appeals for the Seventh Circuit affirmed, and denied rehearing en banc . . . ."

The Supreme Court granted certiorari to review the cases.

B. Counsel of Record / ACLU Attorney

ACLU Side (Petitioner / Appellant): Stephen E. Eberhardt, by appointment of the Court, argued the cause for appellants in both cases. With him on the briefs for appellant Hill in No. 11–5721 were William H. Theis, Mark D. Harris, Richard L. Spinogatti, Anna G. Kaminska, and Douglas A. Berman. Jonathan E. Hawley and Daniel T. Hansmeier filed briefs for appellant Dorsey in No. 11–5683.

Opposing Side (Respondent / Appellee): Deputy Solicitor General Dreeben argued the cause for the United States in both cases. With him on the briefs were Solicitor General Verrilli, Assistant Attorney General Breuer, and Mark R. Freeman.

Miguel A. Estrada, by invitation of the Court, argued the cause and filed a brief as amicus curiae in support of the judgments below.

III. AMICI CURIAE

ACLU Side (Petitioner / Appellant)

Brief of amici curiae filed on behalf of the American Civil Liberties Union, the ACLU of Illinois, et al. by Steven R. Shapiro, Dennis D. Parker, Lisa M. Bornstein, Kim M. Keenan, Daniel N. Abrahamson, Mary Price, Ezekiel R. Edwards, Nkechi Taifa, Anson Asaka, Theshia Naidoo, Tamar Todd, David Borden, Marc Mauer, and Kara Gotsch.

Brief of amici curiae filed on behalf of the Center on the Administration of Criminal Law, New York University School of Law, by Alexandra A. E. Shapiro and Rachel E. Barkow.

Brief of amici curiae filed on behalf of the National Association of Criminal Defense Lawyers et al. by Jeffrey T. Green, Peter Goldberger, Sarah O'Rourke Schrup, and Brett G. Sweitzer.

Brief of amici curiae filed on behalf of Former United States District Court Judge Paul G. Cassell et al. by Nancy Gertner and Mr. Cassell, both pro se.

Opposing Side (Respondent / Appellee)

Brief of amici curiae filed by Miguel A. Estrada, by invitation of the Court. With him on the brief were Scott P. Martin and Daniel L. Geyser.

IV. THE SUPREME COURT'S DECISION

"The timing issue before us is difficult in part because relevant language in different statutes argues in opposite directions. . . .

First, the 1871 saving statute permits Congress to apply a new Act's more lenient penalties to pre-Act offenders without expressly saying so in the new Act. . . .

Second, the Sentencing Reform Act sets forth a special and different background principle. That statute says that when 'determining the particular sentence to be imposed' in an initial sentencing, the sentencing court 'shall consider,' among other things, the 'sentencing range' established by the Guidelines that are 'in effect on the date the defendant is sentenced.' . . .

Third, language in the Fair Sentencing Act implies that Congress intended to follow the Sentencing Reform Act background principle here. . . .

Fourth, applying the 1986 Drug Act's old mandatory minimums to the post-August 3 sentencing of pre-August 3 offenders would create disparities of a kind that Congress enacted the Sentencing Reform Act and the Fair Sentencing Act to prevent. . . .

Fifth, not to apply the Fair Sentencing Act would do more than preserve a disproportionate status quo; it would make matters worse. . . .

Sixth, we have found no strong countervailing consideration. . . .

For these reasons considered as a whole, we conclude that Congress intended the Fair Sentencing Act's new, lower mandatory minimums to apply to the post-Act sentencing of pre-Act offenders. That is the Act's 'plain import' or 'fair implication.' . . .

We add one final point. Several arguments we have discussed involve the language of statutes that determine how new Guidelines take effect. What about those who committed an offense prior to August 3 and were sentenced after August 3 but before November 1, 2010—a period after the new Act's effective date but before the new Guidelines first took effect? Do the Fair Sentencing Act's new mandatory minimums apply to them?

In our view, the new Act's lower minimums apply to them as well. . . .

We vacate the Court of Appeals' judgments and remand these cases . . . ."

V. JUSTICE VOTE

5 Pro ACLU Side vs. 4 Con Opposing Side

ACLU Side (Petitioner / Appellant)

1. Breyer, S. – Wrote majority opinion
2. Kagan, E. – Joined majority opinion
3. Kennedy, A. – Joined majority opinion
4. Ginsburg, R. – Joined majority opinion
5. Sotomayor, S. – Joined majority opinion

Opposing Side (Respondent / Appellee)

1. Alito, S. – Joined Scalia's dissent
2. Thomas, C. – Joined Scalia's dissent
3. Scalia, A. – Wrote dissenting opinion
4. Roberts, J. – Joined Scalia's dissent

VI. A WIN OR LOSS FOR THE ACLU?

The ACLU filed as amicus curiae urging reversal of the judgment of the Court of Appeals; the Supreme Court vacated in a 5-4 vote, giving the ACLU an apparent win.

1098. Arizona v. U.S.

(Decided June 25, 2012; 567 U.S. 387)

I. ISSUE

A. Issues Discussed

Immigration/Citizenship

B. Legal Question Presented

"[W]hether federal law preempts and renders invalid four separate provisions of the state law," S.B. 1070, Arizona's Support Our Law Enforcement and Safe Neighborhoods Act.

C. Supreme Court's Answer

"The United States has established that §§ 3, 5(C), and 6 of S.B. 1070 are preempted. It was improper, however, to enjoin § 2(B) before the state courts had an opportunity to construe it and without some showing that enforcement of the provision in fact conflicts with federal immigration law and its objectives."

II. CASE SUMMARY

A. Background

"[T]he State of Arizona in 2010 enacted a statute called the Support Our Law Enforcement and Safe Neighborhoods Act. The law is often referred to as S.B. 1070 . . . . Its stated purpose is to 'discourage and deter the unlawful entry and presence of aliens and economic activity by persons unlawfully present in the United States.' . . . The question before the Court is whether federal law preempts and renders invalid four separate provisions of the state law. . . .

The United States filed this suit against Arizona, seeking to enjoin S.B. 1070 as preempted. Four provisions of the law are at issue here. Two create new state offenses. Section 3 makes failure to comply with federal alien-registration requirements a state misdemeanor. Section 5 . . . makes it a misdemeanor for an unauthorized alien to seek or engage in work in the State; . . . referred to as § 5(C). Two other provisions give specific arrest authority and investigative duties . . . . Section 6 authorizes officers to arrest without a warrant a person 'the officer has probable cause to believe . . . has committed any public offense that makes the person removable from the United States.' Section 2(B) provides that officers who conduct a stop, detention, or arrest must in some circumstances make efforts to verify the person's immigration status with the Federal Government.

The United States District Court for the District of Arizona issued a preliminary injunction preventing the four provisions at issue from taking effect. The Court of Appeals for the Ninth Circuit affirmed."

The Supreme Court granted certiorari to review the case.

B. Counsel of Record / ACLU Attorney

ACLU Side (Respondent / Appellee): Solicitor General Verrilli argued the cause for the United States. With him on the brief were Acting Assistant Attorney General Delery, Deputy Solicitor General Kneedler, Deputy Assistant Attorney General Brinkmann, William M. Jay, Mark B. Stern, Michael P. Abate, Benjamin M. Shultz, Daniel Tenny, Ivan K. Fong, and Harold Hongju Koh.

Opposing Side (Petitioner / Appellant): Paul D. Clement argued the cause for appellants. With him on the briefs were Viet D. Dinh, H. Christopher Bartolomucci, Joseph Sciarrotta, Jr., John J. Bouma, Robert A. Henry, and Kelly Kszywienski.

III. AMICI CURIAE

ACLU Side (Respondent / Appellee)

Brief of amici curiae filed on behalf of the American Civil Liberties Union et al. by Jennifer Chang Newell, Cecillia D. Wang, Thomas A. Saenz, Linton Joaquin, Karen C. Tumlin, Nora A. Preciado, Nina Perales, Daniel J. Pochoda, Steven R. Shapiro, Lee Gelernt, Omar C. Jadwat, Andre I. Segura, Nicholás Espíritu, Chris Newman, Bradley S. Phillips, Paul J. Watford, Victor Viramontes, Melissa S. Keaney, James Duff Lyall, Mee Mona, Jessica S. Chia, Aaron G. Leiderman, Jessica Karp, Laboni Hoq, Yungsuhn Park, Connie Choi, Carmina Ocampo, Joseph J. Ybarra, Lika C. Miyake, Benjamin J. Maro, and Margaret G. Ziegler.

Brief of amici curiae filed on behalf of the State of New York et al. by Eric T. Schneiderman, Attorney General of New York, Barbara D. Underwood, Solicitor General, Kristen Clarke, Cecelia C. Chang, Deputy Solicitor General, and Steven C. Wu, Assistant Solicitor General, by Kamala D. Harris, Attorney General of California, Manuel M. Medeiros, Solicitor General, Louis Verdugo, Senior Assistant Attorney General, and Antonette Cordero and Jose Zelidon-Zepeda, Deputy Attorneys General, and by the Attorneys General for their respective States as follows: George Jepsen of Connecticut, David M. Louie of Hawaii, Lisa Madigan of Illinois, Tom Miller of Iowa, Douglas F. Gansler of Maryland, Martha Coakley of Massachusetts, John R. Kroger of Oregon, Peter F. Kilmartin of Rhode Island, and William H. Sorrell of Vermont

Brief of amici curiae filed on behalf of the American Bar Association by William T. Robinson III and Douglas W. Baruch.

Brief of amici curiae filed on behalf of the American Federation of Labor and Congress of Industrial Organizations by Lynn K. Rhinehart, James B. Coppess, and Matthew J. Ginsburg.

Brief of amici curiae filed on behalf of the Anti-Defamation League by David J. Bodney, Steven M. Freeman, and Steven C. Sheinberg.

Brief of amici curiae filed on behalf of the Government of Argentina et al. by Henry L. Solano.

Brief of amici curiae filed on behalf of Arizona Attorneys for Criminal Justice et al. by David J. Euchner.

Brief of amici curiae filed on behalf of Arizona Employers for Immigration Reform et al. by Daryl M. Williams and Craig M. LaChance.

Brief of amici curiae filed on behalf of the Constitutional Accountability Center by Douglas T. Kendall, Elizabeth B. Wydra, and David H. Gans.

Brief of amici curiae filed on behalf of the County of Santa Clara, California, et al. by Greta S. Hansen, George A. Nilson, William R. Phelan, Jr., Zach Cowan, Michael B. Brough, Charlton deSaussure, Jr., Kenneth E. Gaines, Dana M. Thye, Craig Watkins, Irvin B. Nathan, Attorney General of the District of Columbia, Patrick W. Baker, Marion Joseph Radson, V. Lynn Whitfield, Gerald Masahiro Sato, Michael P. May, Jenny M. Morf, Victor A. Bolden, Michael A. Cardozo, Leonard J. Koerner, Harry Auerbach, Sara Grewing, Gerald T. Hendrickson, Edwin P. Rutan II, Martha S. Stonebrook, Dennis J. Herrera, Jayne W. Williams, Peter S. Holmes, Jean M. Boler, John B. Schochet, Michael W. L. McCrory, and John Daniel Reaves.

Brief of amici curiae filed on behalf of Terry Goddard et al. by Carmine D. Boccuzzi and Jorge G. Tenreiro.

Brief of amici curiae filed on behalf of Former Commissioners of the United States Immigration and Naturalization Service by

E. Joshua Rosenkranz, Jessica S. Pers, and Michael K. Gottlieb.
Brief of amici curiae filed on behalf of the Greater Houston Partnership by John P. Elwood and Alberto P. Cardenas, Jr.
Brief of amici curiae filed on behalf of the Leadership Conference on Civil and Human Rights et al. by Nancy Morawetz, Wade Henderson, and Lisa Bornstein.
Brief of amici curiae filed on behalf of Members of Congress by Michael B. de Leeuw and Jennifer L. Colyer.
Brief of amici curiae filed on behalf of the National Council of La Raza et al. by Clifford M. Sloan, Charles F. Walker, and Juan Cartagena.
Brief of amici curiae filed on behalf of the National Immigrant Justice Center et al. by Lindsay C. Harrison, Julie M. Carpenter, Charles Roth, Vikram K. Badrinath, and Stephen W. Manning.
Brief of amici curiae filed on behalf of the Republic of Haiti by Mr. Solano.
Brief of amici curiae filed on behalf of The Rutherford Institute by John W. Whitehead and Rita Dunaway.
Brief of amici curiae filed on behalf of the Service Employees International Union et al. by Stephen P. Berzon, Jonathan Weissglass, Judith A. Scott, Orrin Baird, Nicholas W. Clark, Bradley T. Raymond, and Patrick J. Szymanski.
Brief of amici curiae filed on behalf of State and Local Law Enforcement Officials by Andrew J. Pincus, Charles A. Rothfeld, and Jeffrey A. Meyer.
Brief of amici curiae filed on behalf of the United Mexican States by Mr. Solano.
Brief of amici curiae filed on behalf of the United States Conference of Catholic Bishops et al. by Brian J. Murray, Anthony R. Picarello, Jr., and Jeffrey Hunter Moon.
Brief of amici curiae filed on behalf of Madeleine K. Albright et al. by Seth P. Waxman, Paul R. Q. Wolfson, Shirley Cassin Woodward, and Michael D. Gottesman.
Brief of amici curiae filed on behalf of the Association of the Bar of the City of New York by Mark R. von Sternberg.

Opposing Side (Petitioner / Appellant)

Brief of amici curiae filed on behalf of the State of Michigan et al. by Bill Schuette, Attorney General of Michigan, John J. Bursch, Solicitor General, B. Eric Restuccia, Deputy Solicitor General, and Mark G. Sands, Assistant Attorney General, and by the Attorneys General for their respective States as follows: Luther Strange of Alabama, Pamela Jo Bondi of Florida, Samuel S. Olens of Georgia, Lawrence G. Wasden of Idaho, Gregory F. Zoeller of Indiana, Derek Schmidt of Kansas, James D. "Buddy" Caldwell of Louisiana, Jon Bruning of Nebraska, E. Scott Pruitt of Oklahoma, Linda L. Kelly of Pennsylvania, Alan Wilson of South Carolina, Marty J. Jackley of South Dakota, Kenneth T. Cuccinelli II of Virginia, Darrell V. McGraw, Jr., of West Virginia, and Gregory A. Phillips of Wyoming.
Brief of amici curiae filed on behalf of the American Civil Rights Union by Peter Ferrara.
Brief of amici curiae filed on behalf of the American Unity Legal Defense Fund by Barnaby W. Zall and John J. Park, Jr.
Brief of amici curiae filed on behalf of the Arizona Legislature by Peter A. Gentala and Gregrey G. Jernigan.
Brief of amici curiae filed on behalf of the Center for Constitutional Jurisprudence et al. by John C. Eastman, Anthony T. Caso, Edwin Meese III, and Manuel S. Klausner.
Brief of amici curiae filed on behalf of the Eagle Forum Education & Legal Defense Fund by Lawrence J. Joseph.
Brief of amici curiae filed on behalf of the Landmark Legal Foundation by Richard P. Hutchison.
Brief of amici curiae filed on behalf of the Liberty Legal Foundation by Van R. Irion.
Brief of amici curiae filed on behalf of Members of Congress et al. by Jay Alan Sekulow, Stuart J. Roth, Colby M. May, Laura B. Hernandez, and Michael M. Hethmon.
Brief of amici curiae filed on behalf of the Minuteman Civil Defense Corps et al. by Gary G. Kreep.
Brief of amici curiae filed on behalf of the Mountain States Legal Foundation by J. Scott Detamore.
Brief of amici curiae filed on behalf of the Secure States Initiative by Kris W. Kobach.
Brief of amici curiae filed on behalf of State Legislators for Legal Immigration et al. by Paul J. Orfanedes.
Brief of amici curiae filed on behalf of the Thomas More Law Center et al. by Robert J. Muise, David Yerushalmi, and Richard Thompson.
Brief of amici curiae filed on behalf of Joseph M. Arpaio by Thomas P. Liddy and Peter Muthig.
Brief of amici curiae filed on behalf of Lawrence J. Joyce by Mr. Joyce, pro se.
Brief of amici curiae filed on behalf of State Senator Russell Pearce by James F. Peterson and Geoffrey S. Kercsmar.
Brief of amici curiae filed on behalf of United States Representative Lamar Smith et al. by Daniel J. Popeo and Richard A. Samp.
Brief of amici curiae filed on behalf of Larry A. Dever by Brian Bergin and Kenneth Frakes.
Brief of amici curiae filed on behalf of Freedom Watch by Larry Klayman; and for U. S. Border Control et al. by Herbert W. Titus, William J. Olson, and John S. Miles.
Brief of amici curiae filed on behalf of EarthRights International by Richard L. Herz and Marco B. Simons in support of neither party.

IV. THE SUPREME COURT'S DECISION

"The issue is whether, under preemption principles, federal law permits Arizona to implement the state-law provisions in dispute. . . .

Section 3 of S.B. 1070 creates a new state misdemeanor. It forbids the 'willful failure to complete or carry an alien registration document . . . .' . . .

[W]ith respect to the subject of alien registration, Congress intended to preclude States from 'complement[ing] the federal law, or enforc[ing] additional or auxiliary regulations.' Section 3 is preempted by federal law. . . .

§ 5(C) enacts a state criminal prohibition where no federal counterpart exists. The provision makes it a state misdemeanor for 'an unauthorized alien to knowingly apply for work, solicit work in a public place or perform work as an employee or independent contractor' in Arizona. . . .

Congress decided it would be inappropriate to impose criminal penalties on aliens who . . . engage in unauthorized employment. It follows that a state law to the contrary is an obstacle . . . . Section 5(C) is preempted by federal law. . . .

Section 6 of S.B. 1070 provides that a state officer, 'without a warrant, may arrest a person if the officer has probable cause to believe . . . [the person] has committed any public offense that makes [him] removable from the United States.' . . .

Congress has put in place a system in which state officers may not make warrantless arrests . . . based on possible removability . . . . § 6 creates an obstacle . . . . Section 6 is preempted by federal law. . . .

Section 2(B) of S.B. 1070 requires state officers to make a 'reasonable attempt . . . to determine . . . immigration status.' . . if 'reasonable suspicion exists that the person . . . is unlawfully present . . . .' The law also provides that '[a]ny person who is arrested shall have [their] immigration status determined before . . . release . . . .' . . . .

The nature and timing of this case counsel caution in evaluating the validity of § 2(B). The Federal Government has brought suit . . . before the law has gone into effect. . . . As a result, the United States cannot prevail in its current challenge. . . . This opinion does not foreclose other preemption and constitutional challenges to the law as interpreted and applied after it goes into effect. . . .

The United States has established that §§ 3, 5(C), and 6 of S.B. 1070 are preempted. It was improper, however, to enjoin § 2(B) before the state courts had an opportunity to construe it and without some showing that enforcement of the provision in fact conflicts with federal immigration law . . . .

The judgment of the Court of Appeals for the Ninth Circuit is affirmed in part and reversed in part. The case is remanded . . . ."

V. JUSTICE VOTE

5 Pro ACLU Side vs. 3 Con Opposing Side

ACLU Side (Respondent / Appellee)

1. Kennedy, A. – Wrote majority opinion
2. Breyer, S. – Joined majority opinion
3. Ginsburg, R. – Joined majority opinion
4. Sotomayor, S. – Joined majority opinion
5. Roberts, J. – Joined majority opinion

Opposing Side (Petitioner / Appellant)

1. Alito, S. – Wrote opinion concurring in part and dissenting in part
2. Thomas, C. – Wrote opinion concurring in part and dissenting in part
3. Scalia, A. – Wrote opinion concurring in part and dissenting in part

Kagan, E. – Took no part in the decision.

VI. A WIN OR LOSS FOR THE ACLU?

The ACLU filed as amicus curiae urging affirmance; the Supreme Court affirmed in part and reversed in part the Court of Appeals' decision by a 5-3 vote, giving the ACLU an apparent win.

1099. National Fed'n of Indep. Business v. Sebelius

(Decided June 28, 2012; 567 U.S. 519)

I. ISSUE

A. Issues Discussed

Federalism

B. Legal Question Presented

"Today we resolve constitutional challenges to two provisions of the Patient Protection and Affordable Care Act of 2010: the individual mandate, . . . and the Medicaid expansion . . . . We ask only whether Congress has the power under the Constitution to enact the challenged provisions."

C. Supreme Court's Answer

"The Affordable Care Act is constitutional in part and unconstitutional in part. The individual mandate cannot be upheld as an exercise of Congress's power under the Commerce Clause. . . . As for the Medicaid expansion, that portion of the Affordable Care Act violates the Constitution by threatening existing Medicaid funding."

II. CASE SUMMARY

A. Background

"In 2010, Congress enacted the Patient Protection and Affordable Care Act . . . . This case concerns constitutional challenges to two key provisions, commonly referred to as the individual mandate and the Medicaid expansion.

The individual mandate requires most Americans to maintain 'minimum essential' health insurance coverage. . . .

On the day the President signed the Act into law, Florida and 12 other States filed a complaint in the Federal District Court for the Northern District of Florida. Those plaintiffs—who are both respondents and petitioners here, depending on the issue—were subsequently joined by 13 more States, several individuals, and the National Federation of Independent Business. The plaintiffs alleged . . . that the individual mandate provisions of the Act exceeded Congress's powers under Article I of the Constitution. The District Court agreed . . . .

The Court of Appeals for the Eleventh Circuit affirmed in part and reversed in part. . . .

Other Courts of Appeals have also heard challenges to the individual mandate. . . .

The second provision . . . directly challenged here is the Medicaid expansion. . . .

The Affordable Care Act expands the scope of the Medicaid program and increases the number of individuals the States must cover. . . .

The Court of Appeals unanimously held that the Medicaid expansion is a valid exercise of Congress's power under the Spending Clause. U.S. Const., Art. I, § 8, cl. 1. And the court rejected the States' claim that the threatened loss of all federal Medicaid funding violates the Tenth Amendment by coercing them into complying with the Medicaid expansion."

The Supreme Court granted certiorari to review the case.

B. Counsel of Record / ACLU Attorney

ACLU Side (Petitioner / Appellant): Solicitor General Verrilli argued the cause for appellants in No. 11–398 (Anti-Injunction Act). With him on the briefs were Assistant Attorney General West, Deputy Solicitor General Kneedler, Principal Deputy Assistant Attorney General DiCicco, Deputy Assistant Attorney General Brinkmann, Leondra R. Kruger, Mark B. Stern, Alisa B. Klein, Joel McElvain, M. Patricia Smith, William B. Schultz, and Kenneth Y. Choe.

Solicitor General Verrilli argued the cause for appellants in No. 11–398 (Minimum Coverage Provision). With him on the briefs were Assistant Attorney General West, Deputy Solicitor General Kneedler, Deputy Assistant Attorney General Brinkmann, Joseph R. Palmore, Mr. Stern, Ms. Klein, Ms. Smith, Mr. Schultz, and Mr. Choe.

Mr. Clement argued the cause and filed briefs for appellants in Nos. 11–393 and 11–400 (Severability). With him on the briefs for state appellants were Ms. Murphy, Ms. Bondi, Attorney General of Florida, Mr. Makar, Solicitor General, and Mr. Hubener, Mr. Osterhaus, and Mr. Winship, Mr. Strange, Attorney General of Alabama, Mr. Geraghty, Attorney General of Alaska, and Richard Svobodny, Acting Attorney General, Ms. Brewer, Governor of Arizona, and Mr. Horne, Attorney General, Mr. Suthers, Attorney General of Colorado, Mr. Olens, Attorney General of Georgia, Mr. Wasden, Attorney General of Idaho, Mr. Zoeller, Attorney General of Indiana, Mr. Branstad, Governor of Iowa, Mr. Schmidt, Attorney General of Kansas, Mr. Caldwell, Attorney General of Louisiana, Mr. Schneider, Attorney General of Maine, Mr. Schuette, Attorney General of Michigan, Mr. Wallace, by and through Mr. Bryant, Governor of Mississippi, Mr. Bruning, Attorney General of Nebraska, and Ms. Spohn, Mr. Sandoval, Governor of Nevada, Mr. Stenehjem, Attorney General of North Dakota, Mr. DeWine, Attorney General of Ohio, and Mr. Rivkin and Mr. Casey, Mr. Corbett, Governor of Pennsylvania, and Ms. Kelly, Attorney General, Mr. Wilson, Attorney General of South Carolina, Mr. Jackley, Attorney General of South Dakota, Mr. Abbott, Attorney General of Texas, and Mr. Cobb, Deputy Attorney General, Mr. Shurtleff, Attorney General of Utah, Mr. McKenna, Attorney General of Washington, Mr. Van Hollen, Attorney General of Wisconsin, and Mr. Mead, Governor of Wyoming. Mr. Carvin, Mr. Katsas, Mr. Marshall, Mr. Mooppan, Ms. Harned, and Mr. Barnett filed briefs for private appellants.

Mr. Clement argued the cause for appellants in No. 11–400 (Medicaid). With him on the briefs were Ms. Murphy, Ms. Bondi, Attorney General of Florida, and Mr. Makar, Solicitor General, and Mr. Hubener, Mr. Osterhaus, and Mr. Winship, Mr. Strange, Attorney General of Alabama, Mr. Svobodny, Acting Attorney General of Alaska, Ms. Brewer, Governor of Arizona, and Mr. Horne, Attorney General, Mr. Suthers, Attorney General of Colorado, Mr. Olens, Attorney General of Georgia, Mr. Wasden, Attorney General of Idaho, Mr. Zoeller, Attorney General of Indiana, Mr. Branstad, Governor of Iowa, Mr. Schmidt, Attorney General of Kansas, Mr. Caldwell, Attorney General of Louisiana, Mr. Schneider, Attorney General of Maine, Mr. Schuette, Attorney General of Michigan, Mr. Bruning, Attorney General of Nebraska, and Ms. Spohn, Mr. Sandoval, Governor of Nevada, Mr. Stenehjem, Attorney General of North Dakota, Mr. DeWine, Attorney General of Ohio, and Mr. Rivkin and Mr. Casey, Mr. Corbett, Governor of Pennsylvania, and Ms. Kelly, Attorney General, Mr. Wilson, Attorney General of South Carolina, Mr. Jackley, Attorney General of South Dakota, Mr. Abbott, Attorney General of Texas, and Mr. Cobb, Deputy Attorney General, Mr. Shurtleff, Attorney General of Utah, Mr. McKenna, Attorney General of Washington, Mr. Van Hollen, Attorney General of Wisconsin, and Mr. Mead, Governor of Wyoming.

Robert A. Long, Jr., by invitation of the Court, 565 U. S. 1048, argued the cause in No. 11–398 (Anti-Injunction Act) as amicus curiae in support of vacatur.

Opposing Side (Respondent / Appellee): Gregory G. Katsas argued the cause for appellees in No. 11–398 (Anti-Injunction Act). With him on the briefs for private appellees were Michael A. Carvin, C. Kevin Marshall, Hashim M. Mooppan, Karen R. Harned, and Randy E. Barnett. On the briefs for state appellees were Paul D. Clement, Erin E. Murphy, Conor B. Dugan, Erin M. Hawley, Pamela Jo Bondi, Attorney General of Florida, Scott D. Makar, Solicitor General, and Louis F. Hubener, Timothy D. Osterhaus, and Blaine H. Winship, Luther Strange, Attorney General of Alabama, Michael C. Geraghty, Attorney General of Alaska, Janice K. Brewer, Governor of Arizona, and Tom Horne, Attorney General, John W. Suthers, Attorney General of Colorado, Samuel S. Olens, Attorney General of Georgia, Lawrence G. Wasden, Attorney General of Idaho, Gregory F. Zoeller, Attorney General of Indiana, Terry Branstad, Governor of Iowa, Derek Schmidt, Attorney General of Kansas, James D. "Buddy" Caldwell, Attorney General of Louisiana, William J. Schneider, Attorney General of Maine, Bill Schuette, Attorney General of Michigan, Michael B. Wallace, by and through Phil Bryant, Governor of Mississippi, Jon Bruning, Attorney General of Nebraska, and Katherine J. Spohn, Brian Sandoval, Governor of Nevada, Wayne Stenehjem, Attorney General of North Dakota, Michael DeWine, Attorney General of Ohio, and David B. Rivkin and Lee A. Casey, Thomas W. Corbett, Jr., Governor of Pennsylvania, and Linda L. Kelly, Attorney General, Alan Wilson, Attorney General of South Carolina, Marty J. Jackley, Attorney General of South Dakota, Greg Abbott, Attorney General of Texas, and Bill Cobb, Deputy Attorney General, Mark L. Shurtleff, Attorney General of Utah, Robert M. McKenna, Attorney General of Washington, J. B. Van Hollen, Attorney General of Wisconsin, and Matthew Mead, Governor of Wyoming.

Mr. Clement argued the cause for state appellees in No. 11–398 (Minimum Coverage Provision). With him on the brief for appellees Florida et al. were Ms. Murphy, Ms. Bondi, Attorney General of Florida, Mr. Makar, Solicitor General, and Mr.

Hubener, Mr. Osterhaus, and Mr. Winship, Mr. Strange, Attorney General of Alabama, Mr. Geraghty, Attorney General of Alaska, Ms. Brewer, Governor of Arizona, and Mr. Horne, Attorney General, Mr. Suthers, Attorney General of Colorado, Mr. Olens, Attorney General of Georgia, Mr. Wasden, Attorney General of Idaho, Mr. Zoeller, Attorney General of Indiana, Mr. Branstad, Governor of Iowa, Mr. Schmidt, Attorney General of Kansas, Mr. Caldwell, Attorney General of Louisiana, Mr. Schneider, Attorney General of Maine, Mr. Schuette, Attorney General of Michigan, Mr. Wallace, by and through Mr. Bryant, Governor of Mississippi, Mr. Bruning, Attorney General of Nebraska, and Ms. Spohn, Mr. Sandoval, Governor of Nevada, Mr. Stenehjem, Attorney General of North Dakota, Mr. DeWine, Attorney General of Ohio, and Mr. Rivkin and Mr. Casey, Mr. Corbett, Governor of Pennsylvania, and Ms. Kelly, Attorney General, Mr. Wilson, Attorney General of South Carolina, Mr. Jackley, Attorney General of South Dakota, Mr. Abbott, Attorney General of Texas, and Mr. Cobb, Deputy Attorney General, Mr. Shurtleff, Attorney General of Utah, Mr. McKenna, Attorney General of Washington, Mr. Van Hollen, Attorney General of Wisconsin, and Mr. Mead, Governor of Wyoming. Mr. Carvin argued the cause for private respondents in No. 11–398 (Minimum Coverage Provision). With him on the brief were Mr. Katsas, Mr. Marshall, Mr. Mooppan, Ms. Harned, and Mr. Barnett.

Deputy Solicitor General Kneedler argued the cause for appellees in Nos. 11–393 and 11–400 (Severability). With him on the briefs were Solicitor General Verrilli, Assistant Attorney General West, Deputy Assistant Attorney General Brinkmann, Mr. Palmore, Mr. Stern, Ms. Klein, Ms. Smith, Mr. Schultz, and Mr. Choe.

Solicitor General Verrilli argued the cause for appellees in No. 11–400 (Medicaid). With him on the brief were Assistant Attorney General West, Deputy Solicitor General Kneedler, Deputy Assistant Attorney General Brinkmann, Ms. Kruger, Mr. Stern, Ms. Klein, Ms. Smith, Mr. Schultz, and Mr. Choe.

H. Bartow Farr III, by invitation of the Court, 565 U. S. 1048, argued the cause in Nos. 11–393 and 11–400 (Severability) and filed a brief as amicus curiae in support of the judgment below.

III. AMICI CURIAE

ACLU Side (Petitioner / Appellant)

Brief of amici curiae filed on behalf of the NAACP Legal Defense & Educational Fund, Inc., American Civil Liberties Union, and the Leadership Conference on Civil and Human Rights by John Payton, Debo P. Adegbile, Elise C. Boddie, ReNika C. Moore, Ria A. Tabacco, Joshua Civin, Steven R. Shapiro, and Lisa M. Bornstein.

Brief of amici curiae filed on behalf of Economists by Mr. Bradbury, Mr. Engel, and Mr. Park.

Brief of amici curiae filed on behalf of the Independence Institute by Mr. Kopel.

Brief of amici curiae filed on behalf of the Texas Public Policy Foundation et al. by Mr. Loyola and Mr. Epstein.

Brief of amici curiae filed on behalf of James F. Blumstein by Mr. Blumstein, pro se.

Brief of amici curiae filed by Robert A. Long, Jr., Emin Toro, Mark W. Mosier, and Henry B. Liu.

Brief of amici curiae filed on behalf of the State of Maryland et al. by Douglas F. Gansler, Attorney General of Maryland, John B. Howard, Jr., Deputy Attorney General, William F. Brockman, Acting Solicitor General, and Joshua N. Auerbach, Stephen M. Ruckman, and Sarah W. Rice, Assistant Attorneys General, and by the Attorneys General for their respective jurisdictions as follows: Kamala D. Harris of California, George Jepsen of Connecticut, Joseph R. Biden III of Delaware, Irvin B. Nathan of the District of Columbia, David M. Louie of Hawaii, Lisa Madigan of Illinois, Tom Miller of Iowa, Gary K. King of New Mexico, Eric T. Schneiderman of New York, John R. Kroger of Oregon, William H. Sorrell of Vermont, and Vincent F. Frazer of the Virgin Islands.

Brief of amici curiae filed on behalf of AARP by Thomas C. Goldstein, Kevin K. Russell, Stuart R. Cohen, Stacy Canan, and Michael Schuster.

Brief of amici curiae filed on behalf of Advocacy for Patients with Chronic Illness, Inc., by Jennifer C. Jaff.

Brief of amici curiae filed on behalf of the American Association of People with Disabilities et al. by Rochelle Bobroff and Simon Lazarus.

Brief of amici curiae filed on behalf of the American Cancer Society et al. by Mary P. Rouvelas and F. Sheffield Hale.

Brief of amici curiae filed on behalf of the American Federation of Labor and Congress of Industrial Organizations by Lynn K. Rhinehart, James B. Coppess, and Laurence Stephen Gold.

Brief of amici curiae filed on behalf of the American Nurses Association et al. by Ian Millhiser.

Brief of amici curiae filed on behalf of the California Endowment by Kathleen M. Sullivan, William B. Adams, and Crystal Nix Hines.

Brief of amici curiae filed on behalf of the California Public Employees' Retirement System by Peter H. Mixon.

Brief of amici curiae filed on behalf of Constitutional Law Scholars by Andrew J. Pincus, Gillian E. Metzger, and Trevor W. Morrison.

Brief of amici curiae filed on behalf of Health Care for All, Inc., et al. by Wendy E. Parmet and Lorianne M. Sainsbury-Wong.

Brief of amici curiae filed on behalf of Health Care Policy History Scholars by Geoffrey F. Aronow.

Brief of amici curiae filed on behalf of the Jewish Alliance for Law & Social Action et al. by Andrew M. Fischer.

Brief of amici curiae filed on behalf of the Lambda Legal Defense and Education Fund, Inc., et al. by Douglas HallwardDriemeier, Susan L. Sommer, Hayley J. Gorenberg, and Jon W. Davidson.

Brief of amici curiae filed on behalf of the National Women's Law Center et al. by Melissa Hart, Marcia D. Greenberger, and Judith G. Waxman.

Brief of amici curiae filed on behalf of Prescription Policy Choices et al. by Michael Kevin Outterson.

Brief of amici curiae filed on behalf of the Service Employees International Union et al. by Scott A. Kronland, Jonathan Weissglass, P. Casey Pitts, Judith A. Scott, Walter Kamiat,

Mark Schneider, and Patrick J. Szymanski.

Brief of amici curiae filed on behalf of the Small Business Majority Foundation, Inc., et al. by Douglas L. McSwain.

Brief of amici curiae filed on behalf of State Legislators from all Fifty States et al. by Douglas T. Kendall and Elizabeth B. Wydra.

Brief of amici curiae filed on behalf of Senate Majority Leader Harry Reid et al. by Walter Dellinger, Christopher J. Wright, and Timothy J. Simeone.

Brief of amici curiae filed on behalf of the American Center for Law & Justice et al. by Mr. Sekulow, Mr. Roth, Mr. May, Mr. Henderson, Mr. Weber, Mr. White, and Mr. Zimmerman.

Brief of amici curiae filed on behalf of the American Civil Rights Union by Mr. Ferrara.

Brief of amici curiae filed on behalf of America's Health Insurance Plans et al. by Patricia A. Millett, Orly Degani, James E. Tysse, and Roger G. Wilson.

Brief of amici curiae filed on behalf of the Chamber of Commerce of the United States of America by K. Lee Blalack II, Brian D. Boyle, Anton Metlitsky, Robin S. Conrad, Shane B. Kawka, and Kathryn Comerford Todd.

Brief of amici curiae filed on behalf of Economists by Mr. Bradbury, Mr. Engel, and Mr. Park.

Brief of amici curiae filed on behalf of the Family Research Council et al. by Nelson Lund.

Brief of amici curiae filed on behalf of the National Restaurant Association by Leon R. Sequeira, David M. Weiner, and Jennifer A. Kraft.

Brief of amici curiae filed on behalf of Indiana State Legislators et al. by Asheesh Agarwal and Mr. Christina.

Brief of amici curiae filed on behalf of the American Medical Student Association et al. by Mr. Millhiser.

Brief of amici curiae filed on behalf of the American Benefits Council by James R. Napoli, Mark D. Harris, Charles S. Sims, and Kathryn M. Wilber.

Brief of amici curiae filed on behalf of Tax Law Professors by Michael B. de Leeuw.

Brief of amici curiae filed on behalf of the Commonwealth of Massachusetts by Martha Coakley, Attorney General, and Thomas M. O'Brien, Daniel J. Hammond, and Emiliano Mazlen, Assistant Attorneys General.

Brief of amici curiae filed on behalf of the Governor of Washington Christine Gregoire by Kristin Houser, Adam J. Berger, Rebecca J. Roe, and William Rutzick.

Brief of amici curiae filed on behalf of Child Advocacy Organizations by Jeffrey O. Bramlett, Emmet J. Bondurant, and Barbara B. Woodhouse.

Brief of amici curiae filed on behalf of Economic Scholars by Richard L. Rosen and Michael D. Thorpe.

Brief of amici curiae filed on behalf of Young Invincibles by Paolo Annino.

Brief of amici curiae filed on behalf of Barry Friedman et al. by Jeffrey A. Lamken, Robert K. Kry, Martin V. Totaro, and Mr. Friedman, pro se.

Brief of amici curiae filed on behalf of the Competitive Enterprise Institute et al. by Thomas M. Christina, Jeffrey P. Dunlaevy, Sam Kazman, and Hans Bader.

Brief of amici curiae filed on behalf of the Justice and Freedom Fund by Deborah J. Dewart and James L. Hirsen.

Brief of amici curiae filed on behalf of the Western Center for Journalism by Mr. Kreep.

Brief of amici curiae filed on behalf of Mortimer Caplin et al. by Alan B. Morrison and Brian Wolfman in support of neither party.

Brief of amici curiae filed on behalf of Freedom Watch by Larry Klayman in support of neither party.

Brief of amici curiae filed on behalf of the Health Foundation of Greater Cincinnati by James A. Feldman in support of neither party.

Opposing Side (Respondent / Appellee)

Brief of amici curiae filed on behalf of the State of Oklahoma by E. Scott Pruitt, Attorney General of Oklahoma, and Patrick R. Wyrick, Solicitor General.

Brief of amici curiae filed on behalf of the Commonwealth of Virginia ex rel. Kenneth T. Cuccinelli II by Mr. Cuccinelli, Attorney General of Virginia, pro se, E. Duncan Getchell, Jr., Solicitor General, Charles E. James, Jr., Chief Deputy Attorney General, and Wesley G. Russell, Jr., Deputy Attorney General.

Brief of amici curiae filed on behalf of Missouri Attorney General Chris Koster by Mr. Koster, pro se, and Jeremiah J. Morgan, Deputy Solicitor General.

Brief of amici curiae filed on behalf of the American Catholic Lawyers Association, Inc., by Bertram P. Goltz, Jr.

Brief of amici curiae filed on behalf of the American Center for Law & Justice et al. by Mr. Sekulow, Mr. Roth, Mr. May, Mr. Henderson, Mr. Weber, Mr. White, and Mr. Zimmerman.

Brief of amici curiae filed on behalf of the American College of Pediatricians et al. by Nikolas T. Nikas, Dorinda C. Bordlee, Mark L. Rienzi, Mailee R. Smith, Denise M. Burke, Steven H. Aden, Matthew S. Bowman, and Catherine W. Short.

Brief of amici curiae filed on behalf of the American Legislative Exchange Council by John P. Elwood and Seth L. Cooper.

Brief of amici curiae filed by H. Bartow Farr III.

Brief of amici curiae filed on behalf of the Association of American Physicians and Surgeons, Inc., et al. by David P. Felsher and Andrew L. Schlafly.

Brief of amici curiae filed on behalf of the Authors of The Origins of the Necessary and Proper Clause et al. by David B. Kopel.

Brief of amici curiae filed on behalf of Blue Cross and Blue Shield of Massachusetts, Inc., by Dean Richlin, Robert E. Toone, and Joseph Halpern.

Brief of amici curiae filed on behalf of the Catholic Vote et al. by Patrick T. Gillen.

Brief of amici curiae filed on behalf of the Cato Institute et al. by Robert A. Levy, Ilya Shapiro, and Timothy Sandefur.

Brief of amici curiae filed on behalf of the Caesar Rodney Institute by Grant M. Lally.

Brief of amici curiae filed on behalf of the Center for Constitutional Jurisprudence et al. by Christopher R. J. Pace, John C. Eastman, Anthony T. Caso, Edwin Meese III, Todd F. Gaziano, Brian C. Baker, Carrie Severino, and Manuel S. Klausner.

Brief of amici curiae filed on behalf of Docs4PatientCare by Erik

S. Jaffe and John Hoff.
Brief of amici curiae filed on behalf of Economists by Steven G. Bradbury, Steven A. Engel, and Michael H. Park.
Brief of amici curiae filed on behalf of the Employer Solutions Staffing Group LLC by Rebecca J. Levine.
Brief of amici curiae filed on behalf of the HSA Coalition, Inc., et al. by Ed R. Haden.
Brief of amici curiae filed on behalf of the Independent Women's Forum by Kevin J. Hasson.
Brief of amici curiae filed on behalf of Judicial Watch, Inc., by Paul J. Orfanedes.
Brief of amici curiae filed on behalf of Members of the United States Senate by Ms. Severino.
Brief of amici curiae filed on behalf of the Mountain States Legal Foundation by James M. Manley and Steven J. Lechner.
Brief of amici curiae filed on behalf of the Montana Shooting Sports Association, Inc., by Quentin M. Rhoades; for Single Payer Action et al. by Oliver B. Hall.
Brief of amici curiae filed on behalf of the Tax Foundation by Joseph D. Henchman.
Brief of amici curiae filed on behalf of the Washington Legal Foundation et al. by Ilya Somin, Daniel J. Popeo, and Cory L. Andrews.
Brief of amici curiae filed on behalf of the 1851 Center for Constitutional Law by Christopher P. Finney and Curt C. Hartman.
Brief of amici curiae filed on behalf of Speaker of the House John Boehner by Ms. Severino.
Brief of amici curiae filed on behalf of Virginia Delegate Bob Marshall et al. by William J. Olson, Herbert W. Titus, John S. Miles, and Gary G. Kreep.
Brief of amici curiae filed on behalf of Sen. Rand Paul by Bridget Maloney Bush.
Brief of amici curiae filed on behalf of Stephen M. Trattner by Mr. Trattner, pro se.
Brief of amici curiae filed on behalf of Missouri Attorney General Chris Koster by Mr. Koster, pro se, and Mr. Morgan, Deputy Solicitor General.
Brief of amici curiae filed on behalf of Michigan Legal Services, Inc., by Gary A. Benjamin.
Brief of amici curiae filed on behalf of the Washington and Lee University School of Law Black Lung Clinic by Timothy C. MacDonnell.
Brief of amici curiae filed on behalf of the State of Oregon et al. by Mr. Kroger, Attorney General of Oregon, Anna M. Joyce, Solicitor General, and Keith Dubanevich, by Mr. Sorrell, Attorney General of Vermont, and Bridget C. Asay, Assistant Attorney General, by Ms. Gregoire, Governor of Washington, and Mr. Berger, Special Assistant Attorney General, and by the Attorneys General for their respective States as follows: Ms. Harris of California, Mr. Jepsen of Connecticut, Mr. Biden of Delaware, Mr. Louie of Hawaii, Ms. Madigan of Illinois, Mr. Miller of Iowa, Mr. Gansler of Maryland, Ms. Coakley of Massachusetts, Mr. King of New Mexico, and Mr. Schneiderman of New York.
Brief of amici curiae filed on behalf of the American Hospital Association et al. by Ms. Kanner, Ms. Stetson, Mr. Perella, Mr. Trinity, and Ms. Gilden.
Brief of amici curiae filed on behalf of Catholic Sisters by David J. Burman.
Brief of amici curiae filed on behalf of the Disability Rights Legal Center by Chris M. Amantea.
Brief of amici curiae filed on behalf of Faithful Reform in Health Care et al. by Thomas W. Coons, Charles M. English, and Wendy M. Yoviene.
Brief of amici curiae filed on behalf of Health Law & Policy Scholars et al. by Mr. Outterson.
Brief of amici curiae filed on behalf of the Leadership Conference on Civil and Human Rights et al. by Martha F. Davis and Risa E. Kaufman.
Brief of amici curiae filed on behalf of the National Health Law Program et al. by Ms. Perkins.
Brief of amici curiae filed on behalf of the National Minority AIDS Council et al. by Deanne E. Maynard and Marc A. Hearron; for the Service Employees International Union et al. by Stephen P. Berzon, Mr. Kronland, Ms. Scott, Mr. Kamiat, Mr. Schneider, and Mr. Szymanski.
Brief of amici curiae filed on behalf of State Legislators from the Fifty States et al. by Mr. Kendall and Ms. Wydra.
Brief of amici curiae filed on behalf of Senate Majority Leader Harry Reid et al. by Mr. Wright, Mr. Simeone, Mark D. Davis, and Mr. Dellinger.
Brief of amici curiae filed on behalf of David R. Riemer et al. by Mr. Strang.
Brief of amici curiae filed on behalf of David Satcher, M. D., et al. by Samuel R. Bagenstos, Ira A. Burnim, and Jennifer Mathis.
Brief of amici curiae filed on behalf of the American Center for Law & Justice by Jay Alan Sekulow, Stuart J. Roth, Colby M. May, James M. Henderson, Sr., Walter M. Weber, Edward L. White III, and Erik M. Zimmerman.
Brief of amici curiae filed on behalf of the Cato Institute by Ilya Shapiro.
Brief of amici curiae filed on behalf of Michigan Legal Services, Inc., by Mr. Benjamin.
Brief of amici curiae filed on behalf of the Center for Constitutional Jurisprudence et al. by Mr. Eastman, Mr. Caso, Mr. Meese, Mr. Sandefur, and Ilya Shapiro.
Brief of amici curiae filed on behalf of the Association of American Physicians and Surgeons et al. by Mr. Felsher and Mr. Schlafly.
Brief of amici curiae filed on behalf of Joella Swan et al. by Thomas E. Johnson and Grant Crandall.
Brief of amici curiae filed on behalf of David R. Riemer et al. by Mr. Strang.
Brief of amici curiae filed on behalf of the Texas Public Policy Foundation et al. by Mario Loyola, Richard Epstein, and Ilya Shapiro.
Brief of amici curiae filed on behalf of the National Indian Health Board et al. by Geoffrey D. Strommer, Carol L. Barbero, Elliott Milhollin, and William R. Norman.
Brief of amici curiae filed on behalf of Members of the United States Senate by James F. Bennett and Ms. Severino.
Brief of amici curiae filed on behalf of the Association of American Physicians and Surgeons et al. by Mr. Felsher and Mr. Schlafly.

Brief of amici curiae filed on behalf of the Asian & Pacific Islander American Health Forum et al. by Mark A. Packman, Jonathan M. Cohen, and Priscilla Huang.

Brief of amici curiae filed on behalf of the American Public Health Association et al. by Martha Jane Perkins and Corey S. Davis.

Brief of amici curiae filed on behalf of the American Hospital Association et al. by Ms. Kanner, Ms. Stetson, Mr. Perella, and Mr. Trinity.

Brief of amici curiae filed on behalf of the American Academy of Actuaries by Kannon K. Shanmugam and Mary E. Downs.

Brief of amici curiae filed on behalf of AARP et al. by Ms. Bobroff, Mr. Cohen, Ms. Canan, Bruce Vignery, and Mr. Schuster.

Brief of amici curiae filed on behalf of the State of California et al. by Ms. Harris, Attorney General of California, Travis LeBlanc, Special Assistant Attorney General, Manuel M. Medeiros, State Solicitor General, and Daniel J. Powell, Deputy Attorney General, by Christine O. Gregoire, Governor of Washington, and by the Attorneys General for their respective jurisdictions as follows: Mr. Jepsen of Connecticut, Mr. Biden of Delaware, Mr. Nathan of the District of Columbia, Mr. Louie of Hawaii, Ms. Madigan of Illinois, Mr. Miller of Iowa, Mr. Gansler of Maryland, Mr. King of New Mexico, Mr. Schneiderman of New York, Mr. Kroger of Oregon, and Mr. Sorrell of Vermont.

Brief of amici curiae filed on behalf of David R. Riemer et al. by Dean A. Strang.

Brief of amici curiae filed on behalf of Egon Mittelmann by Mr. Mittelmann, pro se.

Brief of amici curiae filed on behalf of the Thomas More Law Center et al. by Robert J. Muise, David Yerushalmi, and Richard Thompson.

Brief of amici curiae filed on behalf of The Rutherford Institute by Alfred W. Putnam, Jr., Jason P. Gosselin, D. Alicia Hickok, and John W. Whitehead.

Brief of amici curiae filed on behalf of Project Liberty by Allan E. Parker, R. Clayton Trotter, Kathleen Cassidy Goodman, and Steven W. Fitschen.

Brief of amici curiae filed on behalf of the Partnership for America by Charles J. Cooper, David H. Thompson, Howard C. Nielson, Jr., and Brian S. Koukoutchos.

Brief of amici curiae filed on behalf of Liberty University, Inc., et al. by Mr. Staver, Ms. Staver, Mr. Crampton, and Mr. McAlister in support of petitioners and respondents on the Anti-Injunction Act.

Brief of amici curiae filed on behalf of the Liberty Legal Foundation by Van R. Irion.

Brief of amici curiae filed on behalf of the Landmark Legal Foundation by Richard P. Hutchison.

Brief of amici curiae filed on behalf of the Institute for Justice by William H. Mellor, Dana Berliner, Steven M. Simpson, and Elizabeth Price Foley.

Brief of amici curiae filed on behalf of the Foundation for Moral Law, Inc., by John A. Eidsmoe and Benjamin D. DuPré.

Brief of amici curiae filed on behalf of Former United States Department of Justice Officials by Theodore B. Olson, Amir C. Tayrani, Joshua S. Lipshutz, Terence J. Pell, and Michael E. Rosman.

Brief of amici curiae filed on behalf of Constitutional Law and Economics Professors by Wilson R. Huhn.

Brief of amici curiae filed on behalf of the Citizens' Council for Health Freedom by John Remington Graham.

Brief of amici curiae filed on behalf of Citizens and Legislators in the Fourteen Health Care Freedom States by Nicholas C. Dranias, Clint D. Bolick, and Linda W. Knight.

Brief of amici curiae filed on behalf of the American Life League by Robert L. Sassone.

Brief of amici curiae filed on behalf of the American Hospital Association et al. by Sheree R. Kanner, Catherine E. Stetson, Dominic F. Perella, Lisa Gilden, and Frank R. Trinity.

Brief of amici curiae filed on behalf of the American Civil Rights Union et al. by Peter Ferrara.

Brief of amici curiae filed on behalf of the State Chambers of Commerce et al. by William V. Custer.

Brief of amici curiae filed on behalf of Liberty University, Inc., et al. by Mathew D. Staver, Anita L. Staver, Stephen M. Crampton, and Mary E. McAlister in support of petitioners and respondents on the Anti-Injunction Act.

Brief of amici curiae filed on behalf of the Center for the Fair Administration of Taxes by A. Lavar Taylor.

IV. THE SUPREME COURT'S DECISION

"The Affordable Care Act does not require that the penalty for failing to comply with the individual mandate be treated as a tax for purposes of the Anti–Injunction Act. The Anti–Injunction Act therefore does not apply to this suit, and we may proceed to the merits. . . .

The Government advances two theories for the proposition that Congress had constitutional authority to enact the individual mandate. First, the Government argues that Congress had the power to enact the mandate under the Commerce Clause. . . . Second, the Government argues that if the commerce power does not support the mandate, we should nonetheless uphold it as an exercise of Congress's power to tax. . . .

The individual mandate forces individuals into commerce precisely because they elected to refrain . . . . Such a law cannot be sustained under a clause authorizing Congress to 'regulate Commerce.' . . .

[N]either can it be upheld as a 'necessary and proper' component of the insurance reforms. The commerce power thus does not authorize the mandate. . . .

The Affordable Care Act's requirement that certain individuals pay a financial penalty for not obtaining health insurance may reasonably be characterized as a tax. Because the Constitution permits such a tax, it is not our role to forbid it, or to pass upon its wisdom or fairness. . . .

The Federal Government does not have the power to order people to buy health insurance. . . . The Federal Government does have the power to impose a tax on those without health insurance. Section 5000A is therefore constitutional, because it can reasonably be read as a tax. . . .

The States also contend that the Medicaid expansion exceeds

Congress's authority under the Spending Clause. . . .

Nothing in our opinion precludes Congress from offering funds under the Affordable Care Act to expand the availability of health care, and requiring that States accepting such funds comply with the conditions on their use. What Congress is not free to do is to penalize States that choose not to participate in that new program by taking away their existing Medicaid funding. . . . In light of the Court's holding, the Secretary cannot apply § 1396c to withdraw existing Medicaid funds for failure to comply with the requirements set out in the expansion. . . .

The Affordable Care Act is constitutional in part and unconstitutional in part. . . .

The Framers created a Federal Government of limited powers, and assigned to this Court the duty of enforcing those limits. The Court does so today. But the Court does not express any opinion on the wisdom of the Affordable Care Act. Under the Constitution, that judgment is reserved to the people.

The judgment of the Court of Appeals for the Eleventh Circuit is affirmed in part and reversed in part."

V. JUSTICE VOTE

5 Pro ACLU Side vs. 4 Con Opposing Side

ACLU Side (Petitioner / Appellant)

1. Roberts, J. – Wrote majority opinion
2. Kagan, E. – Joined majority opinion
3. Breyer, S. – Joined majority opinion
4. Ginsburg, R. – Joined majority opinion
5. Sotomayor, S. – Joined majority opinion

Opposing Side (Respondent / Appellee)

1. Alito, S. – Wrote a joint dissenting opinion
2. Thomas, C. – Wrote a joint dissenting opinion
3. Scalia, A. – Wrote a joint dissenting opinion
4. Kennedy, A. – Wrote a joint dissenting opinion

VI. A WIN OR LOSS FOR THE ACLU?

The ACLU filed as amicus curiae urging reversal of the judgment of the Court of Appeals on the minimum coverage provision; the Supreme Court reversed in a 5-4 vote as to the minimum coverage provision as a tax (the votes differed on other aspects of the case), giving the ACLU an apparent win.

1100. U.S. v. Alvarez

(Decided June 28, 2012; 567 U.S. 709)

I. ISSUE

A. Issues Discussed

1st Amendment, press, speech, association

B. Legal Question Presented

Whether the Stolen Valor Act violates the First Amendment's protection for freedom of speech.

C. Supreme Court's Answer

"The Stolen Valor Act infringes upon speech protected by the First Amendment."

II. CASE SUMMARY

A. Background

"In 2007, respondent attended his first public meeting as a board member of the Three Valley Water District Board. . . . He introduced himself as follows: "I'm a retired marine of 25 years. I retired in the year 2001. Back in 1987, I was awarded the Congressional Medal of Honor. I got wounded many times by the same guy." None of this was true. For all the record shows, respondent's statements were but a pathetic attempt to gain respect that eluded him. The statements do not seem to have been made to secure employment or financial benefits or admission to privileges reserved for those who had earned the Medal.

Respondent was indicted under the Stolen Valor Act for lying about the Congressional Medal of Honor at the meeting. The United States District Court for the Central District of California rejected his claim that the statute is invalid under the First Amendment. Respondent pleaded guilty to one count, reserving the right to appeal on his First Amendment claim. The United States Court of Appeals for the Ninth Circuit, in a decision by a divided panel, found the Act invalid under the First Amendment and reversed the conviction. With further opinions on the issue, and over a dissent by seven judges, rehearing en banc was denied."

The Supreme Court granted certiorari to review the case.

B. Counsel of Record / ACLU Attorney

ACLU Side (Respondent / Appellee): Jonathan D. Libby argued the cause for appellee. With him on the brief were Sean K. Kennedy and Brianna J. Fuller.

Opposing Side (Petitioner / Appellant): Solicitor General Verrilli argued the cause for the United States. With him on the briefs were Assistant Attorney General Breuer, Deputy Solicitor General Dreeben, and Ginger D. Anders.

III. AMICI CURIAE

ACLU Side (Respondent / Appellee)

Brief of amici curiae filed on behalf of the American Civil Liberties Union et al. by Jameel Jaffer, Steven R. Shapiro, and Peter J. Eliasberg.

Brief of amici curiae filed on behalf of the American Booksellers Foundation for Free Expression et al. by Michael A. Bamberger, Richard M. Zuckerman, and Jonathan Bloom.

Brief of amici curiae filed on behalf of the National Association of Criminal Defense Lawyers by Michael V Schafler and Jeffrey L. Fisher.

Brief of amici curiae filed on behalf of the Reporters Committee for Freedom of the Press et al. by Robert Corn-Revere, Ronald G. London, John R. Eastburg, Lucy A. Dalglish, Gregg P. Leslie, Richard A. Bernstein, Kevin M. Goldberg, David M. Giles, James Cregan, Charles D. Tobin, Mickey H. Osterreicher, George Freeman, Barbara L. Camens, Jonathan D. Hart, Richard J. Tofel, Bruce W. Sanford, Bruce D. Brown,

Laurie A. Babinski, Karlene W. Goller, and Eric N. Lieberman.
Brief of amici curiae filed on behalf of the Thomas Jefferson Center for the Protection of Free Expression by J. Joshua Wheeler, Bruce D. Brown, and Katayoun A. Donnelly.
Brief of amici curiae filed on behalf of Jonathan D. Varat by Mr. Varat, pro se, and Cary B. Lerman.
Brief of amici curiae filed on behalf of the First Amendment Coalition by Gary L. Bostwick and Jean-Paul Jassy.
Brief of amici curiae filed on behalf of the First Amendment Lawyers Association by Reed Lee and Allen Lichtenstein.
Brief of amici curiae filed on behalf of the Intellectual Property Amicus Brief Clinic of the University of New Hampshire School of Law by John M. Greabe and Keith M. Harrison in support of neither party.

Opposing Side (Petitioner / Appellant)

Brief of amici curiae filed on behalf of the State of Texas et al. by Greg Abbott, Attorney General of Texas, Arthur C. D'Andrea, Assistant Solicitor General, Daniel T. Hodge, First Assistant Attorney General, Bill Cobb, Deputy Attorney General, and Jonathan F. Mitchell, Solicitor General, and by the Attorneys General for their respective States as follows: Luther Strange of Alabama, John J. Burns of Alaska, John W. Suthers of Colorado, Pamela Jo Bondi of Florida, David M. Louie of Hawaii, Lawrence G. Wasden of Idaho, Gregory F. Zoeller of Indiana, Derek Schmidt of Kansas, James D. "Buddy" Caldwell of Louisiana, William J. Schneider of Maine, Bill Schuette of Michigan, Lori Swanson of Minnesota, Gary K. King of New Mexico, E. Scott Pruitt of Oklahoma, Linda L. Kelly of Pennsylvania, Peter F. Kilmartin of Rhode Island, Robert E. Cooper of Tennessee, Mark L. Shurtleff of Utah, and Darrell V. McGraw, Jr., of West Virginia.
Brief of amici curiae filed on behalf of the Legion of Valor of the United States et al. by Kent S. Scheidegger.
Brief of amici curiae filed on behalf of Veterans of Foreign Wars of the United States et al. by Gene C. Schaerr, Geoffrey P. Eaton, Michael T. Morley, and Linda T. Coberly.
Brief of amici curiae filed on behalf of the Congressional Medal of Honor Foundation by Kevin N. Ainsworth.
Brief of amici curiae filed on behalf of the American Legion by Aaron M. Streett and Philip B. Onderdonk.
Brief of amici curiae filed on behalf of Eugene Volokh et al. by Mr. Volokh, pro se.

IV. THE SUPREME COURT'S DECISION

"The Government contends the criminal prohibition is a proper means to further its purpose in creating and awarding the Medal. When content-based speech regulation is in question, however, exacting scrutiny is required. Statutes suppressing or restricting speech must be judged by the sometimes inconvenient principles of the First Amendment. By this measure, the statutory provisions under which respondent was convicted must be held invalid, and his conviction must be set aside. . . .

Respondent's claim to hold the Congressional Medal of Honor was false. . . . On this premise, respondent violated § 704(b); and, because the lie concerned the Congressional Medal of Honor, he was subject to an enhanced penalty under subsection (c). . . .

Although the First Amendment stands against any 'freewheeling authority to declare new categories of speech outside the scope of the First Amendment,' the Court has acknowledged that perhaps there exist 'some categories of speech that have been historically unprotected . . . but have not yet been specifically identified or discussed . . . in our case law.' Before exempting a category of speech from the normal prohibition on content-based restrictions, however, the Court must be presented with 'persuasive evidence that a novel restriction on content is part of a long (if heretofore unrecognized) tradition of proscription.' The Government has not demonstrated that false statements generally should constitute a new category of unprotected speech on this basis. . . .

Permitting the government to decree this speech to be a criminal offense . . . would endorse government authority to compile a list of subjects about which false statements are punishable. That governmental power has no clear limiting principle. . . .

In assessing content-based restrictions on protected speech, the Court has not adopted a free-wheeling approach, . . . but rather has applied the 'most exacting scrutiny.' Although the objectives the Government seeks to further by the statute are not without significance, the Court must, and now does, find the Act does not satisfy exacting scrutiny. . . .

Though few might find respondent's statements anything but contemptible, his right to make those statements is protected by the Constitution's guarantee of freedom of speech and expression. The Stolen Valor Act infringes upon speech protected by the First Amendment.

The judgment of the Court of Appeals is affirmed."

V. JUSTICE VOTE

6 Pro ACLU Side vs. 3 Con Opposing Side

ACLU Side (Respondent / Appellee)

1. Kennedy, A. – Wrote majority opinion
2. Kagan, E. – Joined Breyer's concurrence
3. Breyer, S. – Wrote concurring opinion
4. Ginsburg, R. – Joined majority opinion
5. Sotomayor, S. – Joined majority opinion
6. Roberts, J. – Joined majority opinion

Opposing Side (Petitioner / Appellant)

1. Alito, S. – Wrote dissenting opinion
2. Thomas, C. – Joined Alito's dissent
3. Scalia, A. – Joined Alito's dissent

VI. A WIN OR LOSS FOR THE ACLU?

The ACLU filed as amicus curiae urging affirmance; the Supreme Court affirmed the Court of Appeals' decision by a 6-3 vote, giving the ACLU an apparent win.

1101. Ryan v. Gonzales

(Decided January 8, 2013; 568 U.S. 57)

I. ISSUE

A. Issues Discussed

Criminal procedure, death penalty

B. Legal Question Presented

"These two cases present the question whether the incompetence of a state prisoner requires suspension of the prisoner's federal habeas corpus proceedings."

C. Supreme Court's Answer

"We hold that neither 18 U.S.C. § 3599 nor 18 U.S.C. § 4241 provides such a right and that the Courts of Appeals for the Ninth and Sixth Circuits both erred in holding that district courts must stay federal habeas proceedings when petitioners are adjudged incompetent."

II. CASE SUMMARY

A. Background

"Ernest Valencia Gonzales was convicted by an Arizona jury of felony murder, armed robbery, aggravated assault, first-degree burglary, and theft. . . . The trial court sentenced Gonzales to death on the murder charge and to various prison terms for the other crimes.

After exhausting state remedies, Gonzales filed a petition for a writ of habeas corpus . . . . While the petition was pending, Gonzales' appointed counsel moved to stay the proceedings, contending that Gonzales was no longer capable of rationally communicating with or assisting counsel. He argued that mental incompetence entitled Gonzales to a stay . . . .

[T]he District Court denied a stay after concluding that the claims . . . were record based or resolvable as a matter of law and thus would not benefit from Gonzales' input. . . .

Gonzales thereafter filed an emergency petition for a writ of mandamus in the Ninth Circuit. . . . Applying Nash and Rohan, the court granted the writ of mandamus . . . .

Sean Carter was convicted by an Ohio jury of aggravated murder, aggravated robbery, and rape, and sentenced to death for anally raping his adoptive grandmother, Veader Prince, and stabbing her to death. After exhausting his state-court appeals, Carter initiated federal habeas proceedings . . . . Carter eventually filed . . . a motion requesting a competency determination and a stay of the proceedings. The District Court granted the motion. . . .

The [Sixth Circuit] court . . . amended the District Court's judgment and ordered that Carter's petition be stayed indefinitely with respect to any claims that required his assistance."

The Supreme Court granted certiorari to review the cases.

B. Counsel of Record / ACLU Attorney

ACLU Side (Respondent / Appellee): Leticia Marquez argued the cause for appellee in No. 10–930. With her on the brief were Jon M. Sands, Dale A. Baich, Jeffrey T. Green, and Quin M. Sorenson. Scott Michelman, by appointment of the Court, 566 U. S. 1020, argued the cause for appellee in No. 11–218. With him on the brief were Scott L. Nelson, Allison M. Zieve, Linda Prucha, and Rachel Troutman.

Opposing Side (Petitioner / Appellant): Thomas C. Horne, Attorney General of Arizona, argued the cause for appellant in No. 10–930. With him on the briefs were David R. Cole, Solicitor General, Kent E. Cattani, Jeffrey A. Zick, and John Pressley Todd, Assistant Attorney General. Alexandra T. Schimmer, Solicitor General of Ohio, argued the cause for appellant in No. 11–218. With her on the briefs were Michael DeWine, Attorney General, David M. Lieberman, Deputy Solicitor, and Holly LeClair Welch, Assistant Attorney General.

Ann O'Connell argued the cause for the United States as amicus curiae.

III. AMICI CURIAE

ACLU Side (Respondent / Appellee)

Brief of amici curiae filed on behalf of the American Civil Liberties Union and the National Association of Federal Defenders by Brian W. Stull, Denise LeBoeuf, Steven R. Shapiro, and Sarah S. Gannett.

Brief of amici curiae filed on behalf of the American Bar Association by William T. Robinson III, Kevin M. Bolan, and Katherine A. H. Dyson.

Brief of amici curiae filed on behalf of the American Psychiatric Association et al. by Aaron M. Panner and Gregory G. Rapawy.

Brief of amici curiae filed on behalf of Retired Federal Judges by Elaine J. Goldenberg and Matthew S. Hellman.

Opposing Side (Petitioner / Appellant)

Brief of amici curiae filed on behalf of the United States by Ann O'Connell, Solicitor General Verrilli, Assistant Attorney General Breuer, Deputy Solicitor General Dreeben, and Deborah Watson.

Brief of amici curiae filed on behalf of the State of Utah by Mark L. Shurtleff, Attorney General of Utah, and Thomas B. Brunker, Assistant Attorney General, by Daniel Domenico, Solicitor General of Colorado, and by the Attorneys General for their respective States as follows: Luther Strange of Alabama, Dustin McDaniel of Arkansas, Joseph R. Biden III of Delaware, Samuel S. Olens of Georgia, Catherine Cortez Masto of Nevada, Gary King of New Mexico, E. Scott Pruitt of Oklahoma, Alan Wilson of South Carolina, Marty J. Jackley of South Dakota, Robert E. Cooper, Jr., of Tennessee, Robert M. McKenna of Washington, and Gregory A. Phillips of Wyoming.

Brief of amici curiae filed on behalf of Arizona Voice for Crime Victims Inc. by Todd Feltus, William T. Luzader III, and Steven J. Twist.

IV. THE SUPREME COURT'S DECISION

"Both the Ninth and Sixth Circuits have concluded that death row inmates pursuing federal habeas are entitled to a suspension of proceedings when found incompetent. The Ninth Circuit located this right in § 3599, while the Sixth Circuit located it in § 4241.

Neither section provides such a right. . . .

Section 3599(a)(2) guarantees . . . federally funded counsel. . . . But § 3599 does not direct district courts to stay proceedings when habeas petitioners are found incompetent. . . .

[W]e hold that § 3599 does not provide federal habeas petitioners with a 'statutory right' to competence. . . .

The Sixth Circuit . . . located the statutory right to competence during habeas proceedings in 18 U.S.C. § 4241. . . . § 4241 does not even apply to such proceedings. . . .

Both Gonzales and Carter argued . . . that district courts have the equitable power to stay proceedings when they determine that habeas petitioners are mentally incompetent. . . . For purposes of resolving these cases, it is unnecessary to determine the precise contours of the district court's discretion to issue stays. We address only its outer limits. . . .

In Gonzales' case, the District Court correctly found that all of Gonzales' properly exhausted claims were record based or resolvable as a matter of law, irrespective of Gonzales' competence. . . .

In Carter's case, the District Court concluded that four of Carter's claims could potentially benefit from Carter's assistance. However, three of these claims . . . do not warrant a stay.

It is unclear from the record whether Carter exhausted the fourth claim. If that claim was exhausted, it too would be record based. But even if Carter could show that the claim was both unexhausted and not procedurally defaulted, an indefinite stay would be inappropriate. . . .

If a district court concludes that the petitioner's claim could substantially benefit from the petitioner's assistance, the district court should take into account the likelihood that the petitioner will regain competence in the foreseeable future. Where there is no reasonable hope of competence, a stay is inappropriate . . . .

The judgment of the Ninth Circuit is reversed. We vacate the judgment of the Sixth Circuit and remand the case for proceedings consistent with this opinion."

V. JUSTICE VOTE

0 Pro ACLU Side vs. 9 Con Opposing Side

Opposing Side (Petitioner / Appellant)

1. Thomas, C. – Wrote majority opinion
2. Alito, S. – Joined majority opinion
3. Kagan, E. – Joined majority opinion
4. Breyer, S. – Joined majority opinion
5. Scalia, A. – Joined majority opinion
6. Kennedy, A. – Joined majority opinion
7. Ginsburg, R. – Joined majority opinion
8. Sotomayor, S. – Joined majority opinion
9. Roberts, J. – Joined majority opinion

VI. A WIN OR LOSS FOR THE ACLU?

The ACLU filed as amicus curiae urging affirmance; the Supreme Court reversed and vacated the Courts of Appeals' decisions by a 9-0 vote, giving the ACLU an apparent loss.

1102. Bailey v. U.S.

(Decided February 19, 2013; 568 U.S. 186)

I. ISSUE

A. Issues Discussed

4th Amendment

B. Legal Question Presented

"[W]hether the seizure of the person was reasonable when he was stopped and detained at some distance away from the premises to be searched when the only justification for the detention was to ensure the safety and efficacy of the search."

C. Supreme Court's Answer

"Detentions incident to the execution of a search warrant are reasonable under the Fourth Amendment because the limited intrusion on personal liberty is outweighed by the special law enforcement interests at stake. Once an individual has left the immediate vicinity of a premises to be searched, however, detentions must be justified by some other rationale."

II. CASE SUMMARY

A. Background

"[L]ocal police obtained a warrant to search a residence for a .380-caliber handgun. . . . Sneider and Gorbecki observed two men—later identified as petitioner Chunon Bailey and Bryant Middleton—leave . . . and enter a car parked in the driveway. . . . The detectives informed the search team of their intent to follow and detain the departing occupants. The search team then executed the search warrant at the apartment.

Detectives Sneider and Gorbecki tailed Bailey's car for about a mile . . . before pulling the vehicle over . . . . They ordered Bailey and Middleton out of the car and did a patdown search of both men. The officers . . . discovered a ring of keys in Bailey's pocket. . . . The officers put both men in handcuffs. When Bailey asked why, Gorbecki stated that they were being detained incident to the execution of a search warrant . . . . Bailey responded: 'I don't live there. Anything you find there ain't mine, and I'm not cooperating with your investigation.' . . .

By the time the group returned . . . , the search team had discovered a gun and drugs in plain view inside the apartment. Bailey and Middleton were placed under arrest, and Bailey's keys were seized incident to the arrest. . . . [O]ne of Bailey's keys opened the . . . apartment. . . .

Bailey was charged with three federal offenses . . . . At trial Bailey moved to suppress the apartment key and the statements he made when stopped by Detectives Sneider and Gorbecki. That evidence, Bailey argued, derived from an unreasonable seizure. After an evidentiary hearing the United States District Court for the Eastern District of New York denied the motion to suppress. . . . After a trial the jury found Bailey guilty on all three counts.

The Court of Appeals for the Second Circuit ruled that Bailey's detention was proper . . . ."

The Supreme Court granted certiorari to review the case.

B. Counsel of Record / ACLU Attorney

ACLU Side (Petitioner / Appellant): Kannon K. Shanmugam argued the cause for appellant. With him on the briefs were John S. Williams, C. J. Mahoney and Susan V. Tipograph.

Opposing Side (Respondent / Appellee): Jeffrey B. Wall argued the cause for the United States. With him on the brief were Solicitor General Verrilli, Assistant Attorney General Breuer, Deputy Solicitor General Dreeben, and Deborah Watson.

III. AMICI CURIAE

ACLU Side (Petitioner / Appellant)

Brief of amici curiae filed on behalf of the American Civil Liberties Union, the Cato Institute, and the New York Civil Liberties Union by Catherine M. A. Carroll, Madhu Chugh, Steven R. Shapiro, Ezekiel R. Edwards, Ilya Shapiro, and Timothy Lynch.

Brief of amici curiae filed on behalf of the National Association of Criminal Defense Lawyers by Jonathan D. Hacker and Anna-Rose Mathieson.

Brief of amici curiae filed on behalf of the National Association of Federal Defenders by Michael Y. Scudder and Sarah Gannett.

Opposing Side (Respondent / Appellee)

Brief of amici curiae filed on behalf of the State of Michigan et al. by Bill Schuette, Attorney General of Michigan, John J. Bursch, Solicitor General, Matthew T. Nelson, and Gaëtan Gerville-Réache, and by the Attorneys General for their respective jurisdictions as follows: Luther Strange of Alabama, Michael Geraghty of Alaska, Tom Horne of Arizona, Dustin McDaniel of Arkansas, John W. Suthers of Colorado, George Jepsen of Connecticut, Joseph R. Biden III of Delaware, Pamela Jo Bondi of Florida, Leonardo M. Rapadas of Guam, David M. Louie of Hawaii, Lawrence G. Wasden of Idaho, Gregory F. Zoeller of Indiana, Derek Schmidt of Kansas, Jack Conway of Kentucky, Catherine Cortez Masto of Nevada, Michael A. Delaney of New Hampshire, E. Scott Pruitt of Oklahoma, Linda L. Kelly of Pennsylvania, Marty J. Jackley of South Dakota, Robert E. Cooper, Jr., of Tennessee, Greg Abbott of Texas, Mark L. Shurtleff of Utah, Robert M. McKenna of Washington, and J. B. Van Hollen of Wisconsin.

IV. THE SUPREME COURT'S DECISION

"The Fourth Amendment . . . provides: 'The right of the people to be secure in their persons . . . against unreasonable searches and seizures, shall not be violated, and no Warrants shall issue, but upon probable cause . . . particularly describing the place to be searched, and the persons or things to be seized.' This Court has stated 'the general rule that Fourth Amendment seizures are 'reasonable' only if based on probable cause' to believe that the individual has committed a crime. . . .

In Summers, the Court . . . permitted officers executing a search warrant 'to detain the occupants of the premises while a proper search is conducted.' . . .

It is necessary, then, to discuss the reasons for the rule explained in Summers to determine if its rationale extends to a detention like the one here. . . .

In Summers, the Court recognized three important law enforcement interests that, taken together, justify the detention of an occupant who is on the premises during the execution of a search warrant: officer safety, facilitating the completion of the search, and preventing flight. . . .

In sum, of the three law enforcement interests identified . . . , none applies with . . . similar force to the detention of recent occupants beyond the immediate vicinity of the premises to be searched. . . . The categorical authority to detain incident to the execution of a search warrant must be limited to the immediate vicinity of the premises to be searched. . . .

Summers recognized that a rule permitting the detention of occupants on the premises during the execution of a search warrant, even absent individualized suspicion, was reasonable and necessary in light of the law enforcement interests in conducting a safe and efficient search. Because this exception grants substantial authority to police officers to detain outside of the traditional rules of the Fourth Amendment, it must be circumscribed.

A spatial constraint defined by the immediate vicinity of the premises to be searched is therefore required for detentions incident to the execution of a search warrant. . . .

Here, petitioner was detained at a point beyond any reasonable understanding of the immediate vicinity of the premises in question . . . .

Detentions incident to the execution of a search warrant are reasonable under the Fourth Amendment because the limited intrusion on personal liberty is outweighed by the special law enforcement interests at stake. Once an individual has left the immediate vicinity of a premises to be searched, however, detentions must be justified by some other rationale. . . .

The judgment of the Court of Appeals is reversed, and the case is remanded . . . ."

V. JUSTICE VOTE

6 Pro ACLU Side vs. 3 Con Opposing Side

ACLU Side (Petitioner / Appellant)

1. Kennedy, A. – Wrote majority opinion
2. Kagan, E. – Joined Scalia's concurrence
3. Scalia, A. – Wrote concurring opinion
4. Ginsburg, R. – Joined Scalia's concurrence
5. Sotomayor, S. – Joined majority opinion
6. Roberts, J. – Joined majority opinion

Opposing Side (Respondent / Appellee)

1. Alito, S. – Joined Breyer's dissent
2. Thomas, C. – Joined Breyer's dissent
3. Breyer, S. – Wrote dissenting opinion

VI. A WIN OR LOSS FOR THE ACLU?

The ACLU filed as amicus curiae urging reversal of the judgment of the Court of Appeals; the Supreme Court reversed in a 6-3 vote, giving the ACLU an apparent win.

1103. Florida v. Harris

(Decided February 19, 2013; 568 U.S. 237)

I. ISSUE

A. Issues Discussed

4th Amendment

B. Legal Question Presented

"In this case, we consider how a court should determine if the 'alert' of a drug-detection dog during a traffic stop provides probable cause to search a vehicle."

C. Supreme Court's Answer

"In short, a probable-cause hearing focusing on a dog's alert should proceed much like any other. The court should allow the parties to make their best case, consistent with the usual rules of criminal procedure. And the court should then evaluate the proffered evidence to decide what all the circumstances demonstrate."

II. CASE SUMMARY

A. Background

"William Wheetley is a K–9 Officer . . . . On June 24, 2006, he was on a routine patrol with Aldo, a German shepherd trained to detect certain narcotics . . . . Wheetley pulled over respondent Clayton Harris's truck because it had an expired license plate. On approaching the driver's-side door, Wheetley saw that Harris was 'visibly nervous,' unable to sit still, shaking, and breathing rapidly. Wheetley also noticed an open can of beer in the truck's cup holder. Wheetley asked Harris for consent to search the truck, but Harris refused. At that point, Wheetley retrieved Aldo from the patrol car and walked him around Harris's truck for a 'free air sniff.' Aldo alerted at the driver's-side door handle . . . .

Wheetley concluded, based principally on Aldo's alert, that he had probable cause to search the truck. His search did not turn up any of the drugs Aldo was trained to detect. But it did reveal . . . ingredients for making methamphetamine. Wheetley accordingly arrested Harris, who admitted after proper Miranda warnings that he routinely 'cooked' methamphetamine . . . and could not go 'more than a few days without using' it. The State charged Harris with possessing pseudoephedrine for use in manufacturing methamphetamine. . . .

Harris moved to suppress the evidence found in his truck on the ground that Aldo's alert had not given Wheetley probable cause for a search. . . .

The trial court concluded that Wheetley had probable cause to search Harris's truck and so denied the motion to suppress. . . . An intermediate state court summarily affirmed.

The Florida Supreme Court reversed . . . ."

The Supreme Court granted certiorari to review the case.

B. Counsel of Record / ACLU Attorney

ACLU Side (Respondent / Appellee): Glen P. Gifford argued the cause and filed a brief for appellee.

Opposing Side (Petitioner / Appellant): Gregory G. Garre argued the cause for appellant. With him on the briefs were Pamela Jo Bondi, Attorney General of Florida, Carolyn M. Snurkowski, Associate Deputy Attorney General, Robert J. Krauss, Chief-Assistant Attorney General, and Susan M. Shanahan, Assistant Attorney General.

Joseph R. Palmore argued the cause for the United States as amicus curiae.

III. AMICI CURIAE

ACLU Side (Respondent / Appellee)

Brief of amici curiae filed on behalf of the National Association of Criminal Defense Lawyers, the Florida Association of Criminal Defense Lawyers, the American Civil Liberties Union, and the American Civil Liberties Union of Florida by Danielle Spinelli, Annie L. Owens, Madhu Chugh, Weili J. Shaw, Jonathan D. Hacker, Mason C. Clutter, Steven R. Shapiro, Ezekiel R. Edwards, Michael Ufferman, Sonya Rudenstine, Randall C. Marshall, and Maria Kayanan.

Brief of amici curiae filed on behalf of the Electronic Privacy Information Center by Marc Rotenberg.

Brief of amici curiae filed on behalf of the Institute for Justice by William H. Mellor, Scott G. Bullock, Darpana M. Sheth, and Robert P. Frommer.

Brief of amici curiae filed on behalf of The Rutherford Institute by Anand Agneshwar, Lisa S. Blatt, Carl Nadler, John W. Whitehead, Rita M. Dunaway, and Charles I. Lugosi.

Brief of amici curiae filed on behalf of Fourth Amendment Scholars by Leslie A. Shoebotham.

Opposing Side (Petitioner / Appellant)

Brief of amici curiae filed on behalf of the United States by Joseph R. Palmore, Solicitor General Verrilli, Assistant Attorney General Breuer, and Deputy Solicitor General Dreeben.

Brief of amici curiae filed on behalf of the Commonwealth of Virginia et al. by Kenneth T. Cuccinelli II, Attorney General of Virginia, E. Duncan Getchell, Jr., Solicitor General, Charles E. James, Jr., Chief Deputy Attorney General, Wesley G. Russell, Jr., Deputy Attorney General, and Michael H. Brady, Assistant Attorney General, and by officials for their respective jurisdictions as follows: Luther Strange, Attorney General of Alabama, Tom Horne, Attorney General of Arizona, John W. Suthers, Attorney General of Colorado, Joseph R. Biden III, Attorney General of Delaware, Leonardo M. Rapadas, Attorney General of Guam, Lawrence G. Wasden, Attorney General of Idaho, Lisa Madigan, Attorney General of Illinois, Gregory F. Zoeller, Attorney General of Indiana, Derek Schmidt, Attorney General of Kansas, and John Campbell, Chief Deputy Attorney General, William J. Schneider, Attorney General of Maine, Bill Schuette, Attorney General of Michigan, Chris Koster, Attorney General of Missouri, Jon Bruning, Attorney General of Nebraska, Jeffrey S. Chiesa, Attorney General of New Jersey, Gary K. King, Attorney General of New Mexico, Wayne Stenehjem, Attorney General of North Dakota, E. Scott Pruitt, Attorney General of Oklahoma, John R. Kroger, Attorney General of Oregon, Linda L. Kelly, Attorney General of Pennsylvania, Guillermo Somoza-Colombani, Attorney General of Puerto Rico, and Luis R. Román Negrón, Solicitor

General, Greg Abbott, Attorney General of Texas, Mark L. Shurtleff, Attorney General of Utah, William H. Sorrell, Attorney General of Vermont, Robert M. McKenna, Attorney General of Washington, J. B. Van Hollen, Attorney General of Wisconsin, and Gregory A. Phillips, Attorney General of Wyoming.

Brief of amici curiae filed on behalf of the National Police Canine Association et al. by Arthur T. Daus III.

IV. THE SUPREME COURT'S DECISION

"A police officer has probable cause to conduct a search when 'the facts available . . . 'warrant a [person] of reasonable caution in the belief" that contraband or evidence of a crime is present. . . .

In evaluating whether the State has met this practical and common-sensical standard, we have consistently looked to the totality of the circumstances. . . .

The Florida Supreme Court flouted this established approach to . . . probable cause. To assess the reliability of a drug-detection dog, the court created a strict evidentiary checklist, whose every item the State must tick off. . . . That is the antithesis of a totality-of-the-circumstances analysis. . . .

In short, a probable-cause hearing focusing on a dog's alert should proceed much like any other. The court should allow the parties to make their best case, consistent with the usual rules of criminal procedure. And the court should then evaluate the proffered evidence to decide what all the circumstances demonstrate. If the State has produced proof from controlled settings that a dog performs reliably in detecting drugs, and the defendant has not contested that showing, then the court should find probable cause. If, in contrast, the defendant has challenged the State's case (by disputing the reliability of the dog overall or of a particular alert), then the court should weigh the competing evidence. In all events, the court should not prescribe, as the Florida Supreme Court did, an inflexible set of evidentiary requirements. The question—similar to every inquiry into probable cause—is whether all the facts surrounding a dog's alert, viewed through the lens of common sense, would make a reasonably prudent person think that a search would reveal contraband or evidence of a crime. A sniff is up to snuff when it meets that test. . . .

And here, Aldo's did. The record in this case amply supported the trial court's determination that Aldo's alert gave Wheetley probable cause to search Harris's truck. . . .

Because training records established Aldo's reliability in detecting drugs and Harris failed to undermine that showing, we agree with the trial court that Wheetley had probable cause to search Harris's truck. We accordingly reverse the judgment of the Florida Supreme Court."

V. JUSTICE VOTE

0 Pro ACLU Side vs. 9 Con Opposing Side

Opposing Side (Petitioner / Appellant)

1. Kagan, E. – Wrote majority opinion
2. Alito, S. – Joined majority opinion
3. Thomas, C. – Joined majority opinion
4. Breyer, S. – Joined majority opinion
5. Scalia, A. – Joined majority opinion
6. Kennedy, A. – Joined majority opinion
7. Ginsburg, R. – Joined majority opinion
8. Sotomayor, S. – Joined majority opinion
9. Roberts, J. – Joined majority opinion

VI. A WIN OR LOSS FOR THE ACLU?

The ACLU filed as amicus curiae urging affirmance; the Supreme Court reversed the Florida Supreme Court's decision by a 9-0 vote, giving the ACLU an apparent loss.

1104. Clapper v. Amnesty Int'l USA

(Decided February 26, 2013; 568 U.S. 398)

I. ISSUE

A. Issues Discussed

4th Amendment

B. Legal Question Presented

"Respondents are United States persons whose work, they allege, requires them to engage in sensitive international communications with individuals who they believe are likely targets of surveillance under § 1881Respondents seek a declaration that § 1881a is unconstitutional, as well as an injunction against § 1881a-authorized surveillance. The question before us is whether respondents have Article III standing to seek this prospective relief."

C. Supreme Court's Answer

"[R]espondents cannot manufacture standing by choosing to make expenditures based on hypothetical future harm that is not certainly impending. We therefore hold that respondents lack Article III standing."

II. CASE SUMMARY

A. Background

"In 1978, . . . Congress enacted the Foreign Intelligence Surveillance Act (FISA) to authorize . . . electronic surveillance of communications for foreign intelligence purposes. . . .

The present case involves a constitutional challenge to § 1881a. . . . Section 1881a provides that, upon the issuance of an order . . . , 'the Attorney General and the Director of National Intelligence may authorize jointly, . . . , the targeting of persons reasonably believed to be located outside the United States to acquire foreign intelligence information.' . . .

Respondents are attorneys and human rights, labor, legal, and media organizations whose work allegedly requires them to engage in sensitive and sometimes privileged . . . communications with colleagues, clients, sources, and other individuals located abroad. . . .

Respondents claim that § 1881a compromises their ability to locate witnesses, cultivate sources, obtain information, and communicate confidential information to their clients. . . . According to respondents, the threat of surveillance will compel them to travel abroad . . . to have in-person conversations. In addition, respondents declare that they have undertaken 'costly and burdensome measures' to protect . . . confidentiality . . . .

[R]espondents filed this action seeking (1) a declaration that § 1881a, on its face, violates the Fourth Amendment, the First Amendment, Article III, and separation-of-powers principles and (2) a permanent injunction against the use of § 1881a. . . .

After both parties moved for summary judgment, the District Court held that respondents do not have standing. On appeal, however, a panel of the Second Circuit reversed. . . . The Second Circuit denied rehearing en banc by an equally divided vote."

The Supreme Court granted certiorari to review the case.

B. Counsel of Record / ACLU Attorney

ACLU Side (Respondent / Appellee): Jameel Jaffer of the American Civil Liberties Union Foundation argued the cause for appellees. With him on the brief were Charles S. Sims and Matthew J. Morris, and Steven R. Shapiro, Alexander A. Abdo, and Mitra Ebadolahi of the American Civil Liberties Union Foundation, and Arthur N. Eisenburg and Christopher T. Dunn of the New York Civil Liberties Union Foundation.

Opposing Side (Petitioner / Appellant): Solicitor General Verrilli argued the cause for appellants. With him on the briefs were Acting Assistant Attorney General Delery, Deputy Solicitor General Kneedler, Anthony A. Yang, Douglas N. Letter, Thomas M. Bondy, Henry C. Whitaker, Robert S. Litt, Tricia S. Wellman, and Bradley A. Brooker.

III. AMICI CURIAE

ACLU Side (Respondent / Appellee)

Brief of amici curiae filed on behalf of the Canadian Civil Liberties Association et al. by Carmine D. Boccuzzi and Michael R. Lazerwitz.

Brief of amici curiae filed on behalf of the Center for Constitutional Rights et al. by Shayana Kadidal.

Brief of amici curiae filed on behalf of the Constitutional Accountability Center by Douglas T. Kendall, Elizabeth B. Wydra, and Rochelle Bobroff.

Brief of amici curiae filed on behalf of the Electronic Privacy Information Center et al. by Marc Rotenberg.

Brief of amici curiae filed on behalf of Former Church Committee Members and Staff by Sidney S. Rosdeitcher, Jonathan Hafetz, and Barbara Moses.

Brief of amici curiae filed on behalf of the Gun Owners Foundation et al. by William J. Olson, Herbert W. Titus, John S. Miles, Jeremiah L. Morgan, and Gary G. Kreep.

Brief of amici curiae filed on behalf of the National Association of Criminal Defense Lawyers by John D. Cline and Joshua L. Dratel.

Brief of amici curiae filed on behalf of the Reporters Committee for Freedom of the Press by Bruce D. Brown and Gregg P. Leslie.

Briefs of amici curiae were filed for the Committee on Civil Rights of the Association of the Bar of the City of New York by Peter T. Barbur and James G. Felakos.

Brief of amici curiae filed on behalf of the New York State Bar Association by Seymour W. James, Jr., and Gregory L. Diskant.

Opposing Side (Petitioner / Appellant)

Brief of amici curiae filed on behalf of John D. Ashcroft et al. by Richard A. Samp, Megan L. Brown, and Claire J. Evans.

IV. THE SUPREME COURT'S DECISION

"Article III of the Constitution limits federal courts' jurisdiction to certain 'Cases' and 'Controversies.' . . .

To establish Article III standing, an injury must be 'concrete, particularized, and actual or imminent; fairly traceable to the challenged action; and redressable by a favorable ruling.' . . .

Respondents assert that they can establish injury in fact that is fairly traceable to § 1881a because there is an objectively reasonable likelihood that their communications with their foreign contacts will be intercepted under § 1881a at some point in the future. This argument fails. . . .

First, it is speculative . . . .

Second, even if respondents could demonstrate that the targeting of their foreign contacts is imminent, respondents can only speculate as to whether the Government will seek to use § 1881a-authorized surveillance (rather than other methods) to do so. . . .

Third, even if respondents could show that the Government will seek . . . authorization to acquire the communications of respondents' foreign contacts under § 1881a, respondents can only speculate as to whether that court will authorize such surveillance. . . .

Fourth, even if the Government were to obtain . . . approval . . . it is unclear whether the Government would succeed in acquiring the communications of respondents' foreign contacts. And fifth, even if the Government were to conduct surveillance of respondents' foreign contacts, respondents can only speculate as to whether their own communications . . . would be incidentally acquired.

In sum, respondents' speculative chain of possibilities does not establish that injury based on potential future surveillance is certainly impending or is fairly traceable to § 1881a. . .

Respondents' alternative argument—namely, that they can establish standing based on the measures that they have undertaken to avoid § 1881a-authorized surveillance—fares no better. . . .

[R]espondents' self-inflicted injuries are not fairly traceable to the Government's purported activities under § 1881a, and their subjective fear of surveillance does not give rise to standing. . . .

We hold that respondents lack Article III standing because they cannot demonstrate that the future injury they purportedly fear is certainly impending and because they cannot manufacture standing by incurring costs in anticipation of non-imminent harm. We therefore reverse the judgment of the Second Circuit and remand . . . ."

V. JUSTICE VOTE

4 Pro ACLU Side vs. 5 Con Opposing Side

ACLU Side (Respondent / Appellee)

1. Kagan, E. – Joined Breyer's dissent
2. Breyer, S. – Wrote dissenting opinion
3. Ginsburg, R. – Joined Breyer's dissent

4. Sotomayor, S. – Joined Breyer's dissent

Opposing Side (Petitioner / Appellant)

1. Alito, S. – Wrote majority opinion
2. Thomas, C. – Joined majority opinion
3. Scalia, A. – Joined majority opinion
4. Kennedy, A. – Joined majority opinion
5. Roberts, J. – Joined majority opinion

VI. A WIN OR LOSS FOR THE ACLU?

The ACLU served as counsel for appellee urging affirmance; the Supreme Court reversed the Court of Appeals' decision by a 5-4 vote, giving the ACLU an apparent loss.

1105. Kiobel v. Royal Dutch Petroleum Co.

(Decided April 17, 2013; 569 U.S. 108)

I. ISSUE

A. Issues Discussed

Civil rights

B. Legal Question Presented

"[W]hether and under what circumstances courts may recognize a cause of action under the Alien Tort Statute, for violations of the law of nations occurring within the territory of a sovereign other than the United States."

C. Supreme Court's Answer

"We . . . conclude that the presumption against extraterritoriality applies to claims under the ATS, and that nothing in the statute rebuts that presumption. '[T]here is no clear indication of extraterritoriality here,' and petitioners' case seeking relief for violations of the law of nations occurring outside the United States is barred."

II. CASE SUMMARY

A. Background

"Petitioners were residents of Ogoniland, . . . Nigeria . . . . [R]espondents Royal Dutch Petroleum Company and Shell Transport and Trading Company, p.l.c., were holding companies incorporated in the Netherlands and England, respectively. Their joint subsidiary, respondent Shell Petroleum Development Company of Nigeria, Ltd. (SPDC), was incorporated in Nigeria, and engaged in oil exploration and production in Ogoniland. [A]fter concerned residents of Ogoniland began protesting the environmental effects of SPDC's practices, respondents enlisted the Nigerian Government to violently suppress the burgeoning demonstrations. . . . Nigerian military and police forces attacked Ogoni villages, beating, raping, killing, and arresting residents and destroying or looting property. . . .

Following the alleged atrocities, petitioners moved to the United States where they have been granted political asylum and now reside as legal residents. They filed suit . . . alleging jurisdiction under the Alien Tort Statute and requesting relief under customary international law. . . . According to petitioners, respondents violated the law of nations by aiding and abetting the Nigerian Government in committing (1) extrajudicial killings; (2) crimes against humanity; (3) torture and cruel treatment; (4) arbitrary arrest and detention; (5) violations of the rights to life, liberty, security, and association; (6) forced exile; and (7) property destruction. The District Court dismissed the first, fifth, sixth, and seventh claims . . . .

The Second Circuit dismissed the entire complaint, reasoning that the law of nations does not recognize corporate liability."

The Supreme Court granted certiorari to review the case.

B. Counsel of Record / ACLU Attorney

ACLU Side (Petitioner / Appellant): Paul L. Hoffman argued and reargued the cause for appellants. With him on the briefs were Erwin Chemerinsky and Carey R. D'Avino.

Opposing Side (Respondent / Appellee): Kathleen M. Sullivan argued and reargued the cause for appellees. With her on the briefs were Faith E. Gay, Sanford I. Weisburst, Isaac Nesser, and Todd S. Anten.

Solicitor General Verrilli reargued the cause for the United States as amicus curiae.

Deputy Solicitor General Kneedler argued the cause for the United States as amicus curiae.

III. AMICI CURIAE

ACLU Side (Petitioner / Appellant)

Brief of amici curiae filed on behalf of the American Civil Liberties Union by Steven R. Shapiro, Steven M. Watt, and Mitra Ebadolahi.

Brief of amici curiae filed on behalf of the American Federation of Labor and Congress of Industrial Organizations by Lynn K. Rhinehart, James B. Coppess, and Matthew J. Ginsburg.

Brief of amici curiae filed on behalf of the Association of the Bar of the City of New York by Stephen L. Kass.

Brief of amici curiae filed on behalf of Australian International Law Scholars by Donald Kris Anton, pro se.

Brief of amici curiae filed on behalf of Former United States Government Counterterrorism and Human Rights Officials by Ruth Wedgwood, Ronald L. Motley, Michael E. Elsner, Vincent I. Parrett, John M. Eubanks, and Brian T. Frutig.

Brief of amici curiae filed on behalf of the German Institute for Human Rights et al. by Richard R. Wiebe.

Brief of amici curiae filed on behalf of International Law Scholars by Ralph G. Steinhardt; for Law Professors of Civil Liberties and 42 U. S. C. § 1983 by Penny M. Venetis.

Brief of amici curiae filed on behalf of The Rutherford Institute by John W. Whitehead and Charles I. Lugosi.

Brief of amici curiae filed on behalf of the Yale Law School Center for Global Legal Challenges by Oona A. Hathaway and Jeffrey A. Meyer.

Brief of amici curiae filed on behalf of Abukar Hassan Ahmed et al. by Pamela S. Karlan, Jeffrey L. Fisher, Pamela Merchant, Andrea Evans, Natasha E. Fain, L. Kathleen Roberts, Thomas C. Goldstein, and Kevin K. Russell.

Brief of amici curiae filed on behalf of Volker Beck et al. by

Judith Brown Chomsky.

Brief of amici curiae filed on behalf of Barbara Aronstein Black et al. by Susan H. Farbstein and Tyler R. Giannini.

Brief of amici curiae filed on behalf of David J. Scheffer, by Mr. Scheffer, pro se.

Brief of amici curiae filed on behalf of Thomas J. Schoenbaum, by Mr. Schoenbaum, pro se.

Brief of amici curiae filed on behalf of Former Senator Arlen Specter et al. by William J. Aceves and Anthony DiCaprio.

Brief of amici curiae filed on behalf of Joseph E. Stiglitz by Michael D. Hausfeld.

Brief of amici curiae filed on behalf of the American Bar Association by William T. Robinson III, Robert P. LoBue, and Matthew Funk.

Brief of amici curiae filed on behalf of the Brennan Center for Justice at NYU School of Law by Burt Neuborne.

Brief of amici curiae filed on behalf of Civil Procedure Professors by Agnieszka M. Fryszman and Maureen E. McOwen.

Brief of amici curiae filed on behalf of Comparative Law Scholars et al. by Vivian Grosswald Curran and Anne Richardson.

Brief of amici curiae filed on behalf of EarthRights International by Richard L. Herz and Marco B. Simons.

Brief of amici curiae filed on behalf of Eleven Jewish Former Residents of Iran Whose Family Members "Disappeared" by Robert J. Tolchin.

Brief of amici curiae filed on behalf of Genocide Victims of Krajina, Croatia, by Robert J. Pavich, Ian Levin, John J. Pavich, and Anthony A. D'Amato.

Brief of amici curiae filed on behalf of the Government of the Argentine Republic by Jonathan M. Miller.

Brief of amici curiae filed on behalf of Human Rights First et al. by Mr. Aceves.

Brief of amici curiae filed on behalf of International Human Rights Organizations et al. by Katherine Gallagher and Peter Weiss.

Brief of amici curiae filed on behalf of Professors of Civil Procedure and Federal Courts by Allan Ides, pro se, Theresa M. Traber, and Bert Voorhees.

Brief of amici curiae filed on behalf of the Rutgers Law School Constitutional Litigation Clinic by Ms. Venetis.

Brief of amici curiae filed on behalf of Victims of the Hungarian Holocaust by Messrs. Pavich, Levin, and Pavich.

Brief of amici curiae filed on behalf of Juan Romagoza Arce et al. by Mses. Evans, Merchant, Fain, and Roberts.

Brief of amici curiae filed on behalf of Diego Asencio et al. by Douglass Cassel.

Brief of amici curiae filed on behalf of Omer Bartov et al. by Mses. Green and Chomsky and Beth Stephens.

Brief of amici curiae filed on behalf of Alex-Geert Castermans et al. by Gary L. Bostwick, and Mses. Fryszman and McOwen.

Brief of amici curiae filed on behalf of William R. Casto et al. by Mr. Giannini and Ms. Farbstein.

Brief of amici curiae filed on behalf of Martyn Day et al. by Michael D. Hausfeld.

Brief of amici curiae filed on behalf of Martin S. Flaherty et al. by Frederick W. Morris.

Brief of amici curiae filed on behalf of Anton Katz et al. by Carol A. Sobel.

Brief of amici curiae filed on behalf of Juan E. Méndez by Deena R. Hurwitz and Eric Alan Isaacson.

Brief of amici curiae filed on behalf of Navi Pillay by David Sloss.

Opposing Side (Respondent / Appellee)

Brief of amici curiae filed on behalf of the United States by Solicitor General Verrilli, Acting Assistant Attorney General Delery, Deputy Solicitor General Kneedler, Melissa Arbus Sherry, Robert M. Loeb, Assistant Attorney General West, Ms. Sherry, Douglas N. Letter, Mr. Loeb, Harold Hongju Koh, and Cameron F. Kerry.

Brief of amici curiae filed on behalf of the Association of German Chambers of Industry and Commerce et al. by Alan E. Untereiner and Mark T. Stancil.

Brief of amici curiae filed on behalf of BP America et al. by Paul D. Clement, Jeffrey M. Harris, John B. Bellinger III, Lisa S. Blatt, Ramon P. Marks, and R. Reeves Anderson.

Brief of amici curiae filed on behalf of the Cato Institute by Owen C. Pell and Ilya Shapiro.

Brief of amici curiae filed on behalf of the Chamber of Commerce of the United States of America by Neal Kumar Katyal, Christopher T. Handman, Dominic F. Perella, Robin S. Conrad, and Kate Comerford Todd.

Brief of amici curiae filed on behalf of the Clearing House Association L. L. C. by Andrew J. Pincus, Alex C. Lakatos, and Carl J. Summers.

Brief of amici curiae filed on behalf of Coca-Cola Co. et al. by Kristin Linsley Myles.

Brief of amici curiae filed on behalf of Engility Corp. by Ari S. Zymelman.

Brief of amici curiae filed on behalf of International Law Professors by Matthew J. Kemner, David M. Rice, Troy M. Yoshino, and Timothy C. Smith.

Brief of amici curiae filed on behalf of the National Foreign Trade Council et al. by Seth P. Waxman and Jonathan G. Cedarbaum.

Brief of amici curiae filed on behalf of the Product Liability Advisory Counsel, Inc., by Anne E. Cohen and David W. Rivkin.

Brief of amici curiae filed on behalf of Professors of International Law, Foreign Relations Law and Federal Jurisdiction by Meir Feder and Samuel Estreicher, pro se.

Brief of amici curiae filed on behalf of the Rio Tinto Group et al. by Jonathan D. Hacker, Anton Metlitsky, and Matthew T. Kline.

Brief of amici curiae filed on behalf of the US-China Law Society by Sienho Yee.

Brief of amici curiae filed on behalf of the Washington Legal Foundation et al. by Richard A. Samp.

Brief of amici curiae filed on behalf of Anthony J. Bellia, Jr., et al. by Christopher J. Paolella.

Brief of amici curiae filed on behalf of Chevron Corp. et al. by Jack Goldsmith.

Brief of amici curiae filed on behalf of the Federal Republic of Germany by Jeffrey Harris, Max Riederer von Paar, and Walter E. Diercks.

Brief of amici curiae filed on behalf of Former State Department

Legal Advisers by Kristin Linsley Myles and Daniel P. Collins.
Brief of amici curiae filed on behalf of the Government of the United Kingdom of Great Britain and Northern Ireland et al. by Messrs. Baker and W. Miller.
Brief of amici curiae filed on behalf of KBR, Inc., by David B. Rivkin, Jr., and Lee A. Casey.
Brief of amici curiae filed on behalf of OTP Bank by Thomas G. Corcoran, Jr., and Michael D. Ramsey.
Brief of amici curiae filed on behalf of Professors of Constitutional and Federal Civil Procedure Law by Richard A. Edlin.
Brief of amici curiae filed on behalf of Certain Plaintiffs in In re: Terrorist Attacks on September 11, 2001, by Carter G. Phillips, Richard D. Klinger, Jacqueline G. Cooper, Stephen A. Cozen, Elliott R. Feldman, Sean P. Carter, James P. Kreindler, Justin T. Green, Andrew J. Maloney III, Messrs. Motley and Elsner, Jerry S. Goldman, and Chris Leonardo in support of neither party.
Brief of amici curiae filed on behalf of Law of Nations Scholars by Mr. D'Amato in support of neither party.
Brief of amici curiae filed on behalf of the European Commission by Steven Alan Reiss and Gregory Silbert in support of neither party.
Brief of amici curiae filed on behalf of the Government of the Kingdom of the Netherlands et al. by Donald I. Baker and W. Todd Miller in support of neither party.
Brief of amici curiae filed on behalf of the Institute for Human Rights and Business et al. by Jennifer Green in support of neither party.
Brief of amici curiae filed on behalf of Nuremberg Historians et al. by Jonathan S. Massey in support of neither party.
Brief of amici curiae filed on behalf of John Ruggie et al. by Vincent F. O'Rourke, Jr in support of neither party.

IV. THE SUPREME COURT'S DECISION

"The question here is not whether petitioners have stated a proper claim under the ATS, but whether a claim may reach conduct occurring in the territory of a foreign sovereign. Respondents contend that claims under the ATS do not, relying primarily on a canon of statutory interpretation known as the presumption against extraterritorial application. . . .

We typically apply the presumption to discern whether an Act of Congress regulating conduct applies abroad. . . . The ATS, on the other hand, is 'strictly jurisdictional.' . . . But we think the principles underlying the canon of interpretation similarly constrain courts considering causes of action that may be brought under the ATS. . . .

The principles underlying the presumption against extraterritoriality thus constrain courts exercising their power under the ATS. . . .

Petitioners contend that even if the presumption applies, the text, history, and purposes of the ATS rebut it for causes of action brought under that statute. It is true that Congress . . . can indicate that it intends federal law to apply to conduct occurring abroad. . . . But to rebut the presumption, the ATS would need to evince a 'clear indication of extraterritoriality.' It does not. . . .

We therefore conclude that the presumption against extraterritoriality applies to claims under the ATS, and that nothing in the statute rebuts that presumption. '[T]here is no clear indication of extraterritoriality here,' and petitioners' case seeking relief for violations of the law of nations occurring outside the United States is barred. . . .

On these facts, all the relevant conduct took place outside the United States. And even where the claims touch and concern the territory of the United States, they must do so with sufficient force to displace the presumption against extraterritorial application. . . .

The judgment of the Court of Appeals is affirmed."

V. JUSTICE VOTE

0 Pro ACLU Side vs. 9 Con Opposing Side

Opposing Side (Respondent / Appellee)

1.Roberts, J. – Wrote majority opinion
2. Alito, S. – Wrote concurring opinion
3. Kagan, E. – Joined Breyer's concurrence
4. Thomas, C. – Joined Alito's concurrence
5. Breyer, S. – Wrote concurring opinion
6. Scalia, A. – Joined majority opinion
7. Kennedy, A. – Wrote concurring opinion
8. Ginsburg, R. – Joined Breyer's concurrence
9. Sotomayor, S. – Joined Breyer's concurrence

VI. A WIN OR LOSS FOR THE ACLU?

The ACLU filed as amicus curiae urging reversal of the judgment of the Court of Appeals; the Supreme Court affirmed in a 9-0 vote, giving the ACLU an apparent loss.

1106. Missouri v. McNeely

(Decided April 17, 2013; 569 U.S. 141)

I. ISSUE

A. Issues Discussed

4th Amendment

B. Legal Question Presented

"[W]hether the natural metabolization of alcohol in the bloodstream presents a per se exigency that justifies an exception to the Fourth Amendment's warrant requirement for nonconsensual blood testing in all drunk-driving cases."

C. Supreme Court's Answer

"We hold that in drunk-driving investigations, the natural dissipation of alcohol in the bloodstream does not constitute an exigency in every case sufficient to justify conducting a blood test without a warrant."

II. CASE SUMMARY

A. Background

"[A] Missouri police officer stopped Tyler McNeely's truck after observing it exceed the posted speed limit and repeatedly cross the centerline. The officer noticed several signs that McNeely was intoxicated . . . . McNeely acknowledged to the officer that he had consumed 'a couple of beers' at a bar . . . . After McNeely performed poorly on . . . field-sobriety tests and declined to use a portable breath-test device to measure his blood alcohol concentration (BAC), the officer placed him under arrest. . . .

[W]hen McNeely indicated that he would . . . refuse to provide a breath sample, the officer . . . took McNeely to a nearby hospital for blood testing. The officer did not attempt to secure a warrant. Upon arrival at the hospital, the officer asked McNeely whether he would consent to a blood test. Reading from a standard implied consent form, the officer explained to McNeely that under state law refusal to submit voluntarily to the test would lead to the immediate revocation of his driver's license for one year and could be used against him in a future prosecution. McNeely nonetheless refused. The officer then directed a hospital lab technician to take a blood sample . . . . Subsequent laboratory testing measured McNeely's BAC at 0.154 percent, which was well above the legal limit of 0.08 percent.

McNeely was charged with driving while intoxicated (DWI) . . . . He moved to suppress the results of the blood test, arguing in relevant part that, under the circumstances, taking his blood for chemical testing without first obtaining a search warrant violated his rights under the Fourth Amendment. The trial court agreed. . . . The Missouri Supreme Court affirmed."

The Supreme Court granted certiorari to review the case.

B. Counsel of Record / ACLU Attorney

ACLU Side (Respondent / Appellee): Steven R. Shapiro of the American Civil Liberties Union Foundation argued the cause for appellee. With him on the brief were Ezekiel R. Edwards and Brandon J. Buskey of the ACLU Foundation, Stephen C. Wilson, Stephen Douglas Bonney of the ACLU Foundation of Kansas & Western Missouri, and Anthony E. Rothert, and Grant R. Doty of the ACLU of Eastern Missouri.

Opposing Side (Petitioner / Appellant): John N. Koester, Jr., argued the cause and filed briefs for appellant.

Nicole A. Saharsky argued the cause for the United States as amicus curiae.

III. AMICI CURIAE

ACLU Side (Respondent / Appellee)

Brief of amici curiae filed on behalf of Law Professors by David C. Frederick, Michael F. Sturley, Lynn E. Blais, and Erin Glenn Busby.

Brief of amici curiae filed on behalf of the National College for DUI Defense et al. by Jeffrey T. Green, Sarah O'Rourke Schrup, Leonard R. Stamm, and Norman L. Reimer.

Brief of amici curiae filed on behalf of The Rutherford Institute by John W. Whitehead, Rita M. Dunaway, and Douglas R. McKusick.

Opposing Side (Petitioner / Appellant)

Brief of amici curiae filed on behalf of the United States by Nicole A. Saharsky, Solicitor General Verrilli, Assistant Attorney General Breuer, Deputy Solicitor General Dreeben, and Deborah Watson.

Brief of amici curiae filed on behalf of the State of Delaware et al. by Joseph R. Biden III, Attorney General of Delaware, Paul R. Wallace, and Sean P. Lugg and Karen V. Sullivan, Deputy Attorneys General, by Kevin T. Kane, Chief State's Attorney of Connecticut, and by the Attorneys General for their respective jurisdictions as follows: Luther Strange of Alabama, Dustin McDaniel of Arkansas, John W. Suthers of Colorado, Irvin B. Nathan of the District of Columbia, Pamela Jo Bondi of Florida, Leonardo M. Rapadas of Guam, Lawrence G. Wasden of Idaho, Lisa Madigan of Illinois, Gregory F. Zoeller of Indiana, Thomas H. Miller of Iowa, James D. "Buddy" Caldwell of Louisiana, William J. Schneider of Maine, Douglas F. Gansler of Maryland, Bill Schuette of Michigan, Lori Swanson of Minnesota, Jim Hood of Mississippi, Steve Bullock of Montana, Jon Bruning of Nebraska, Catherine Cortez Masto of Nevada, Jeffrey S. Chiesa of New Jersey, Gary King of New Mexico, Wayne Stenehjem of North Dakota, E. Scott Pruitt of Oklahoma, Ellen F. Rosenblum of Oregon, Peter F. Kilmartin of Rhode Island, Alan Wilson of South Carolina, Marty J. Jackley of South Dakota, Robert E. Cooper, Jr., of Tennessee, Mark Shurtleff of Utah, Robert M. McKenna of Washington, J. B. Van Hollen of Wisconsin, and Gregory A. Phillips of Wyoming.

Brief of amici curiae filed on behalf of Mothers Against Drunk Driving by James C. Ho.

Brief of amici curiae filed on behalf ofthe National District Attorneys Association et al. by Michael S. Wright, Scott Burns, and Albert C. Locher.

IV. THE SUPREME COURT'S DECISION

"The Fourth Amendment provides in relevant part that '[t]he right of the people to be secure in their persons, houses, papers, and effects, against unreasonable searches and seizures, shall not be violated, and no Warrants shall issue, but upon probable cause.' Our cases have held that a warrantless search of the person is reasonable only if it falls within a recognized exception. . . .

'One well-recognized exception,' and the one at issue in this case, 'applies when the exigencies of the situation make the needs of law enforcement so compelling that a warrantless search is objectively reasonable under the Fourth Amendment.' . . .

To determine whether a law enforcement officer faced an emergency that justified acting without a warrant, this Court looks to the totality of circumstances. . . .

The State properly recognizes that the reasonableness of a warrantless search under the exigency exception to the warrant requirement must be evaluated based on the totality of the circumstances. But the State nevertheless seeks a per se rule for blood testing in drunk-driving cases. . . .

But it does not follow that we should depart from careful case-by-case assessment of exigency and adopt the categorical rule proposed . . . . In those drunk-driving investigations where police officers can reasonably obtain a warrant before a blood sample can be drawn without significantly undermining the efficacy of the search, the Fourth Amendment mandates that they do so. . . .

The State argued before this Court that the fact that alcohol is naturally metabolized by the human body creates an exigent circumstance in every case. The State did not argue that there were exigent circumstances in this particular case . . . .

Having rejected the sole argument presented to us challenging the Missouri Supreme Court's decision, we affirm its judgment. . . .

We hold that in drunk-driving investigations, the natural dissipation of alcohol in the bloodstream does not constitute an exigency in every case sufficient to justify conducting a blood test without a warrant.

The judgment of the Missouri Supreme Court is affirmed."

V. JUSTICE VOTE

5 Pro ACLU Side vs. 4 Con Opposing Side

ACLU Side (Respondent / Appellee)

1. Sotomayor, S. – Wrote plurality opinion
2. Kagan, E. – Joined plurality opinion
3. Scalia, A. – Joined plurality opinion
4. Kennedy, A. – Wrote concurring opinion
5. Ginsburg, R. – Joined plurality opinion

Opposing Side (Petitioner / Appellant)

1. Alito, S. – Joined Roberts' opinion
2. Thomas, C. – Wrote dissenting opinion
3. Breyer, S. – Joined Roberts' opinion
4. Roberts, J. – Wrote opinion concurring in part and dissenting in part

VI. A WIN OR LOSS FOR THE ACLU?

The ACLU served as counsel for appellee urging affirmance; the Supreme Court affirmed the Missouri Supreme Court's decision by a 5-4 vote, giving the ACLU an apparent win.

1107. McBurney v. Young

(Decided April 29, 2013; 569 U.S. 221)

I. ISSUE

A. Issues Discussed

State, civil rights

B. Legal Question Presented

"[W]hether the Virginia Freedom of Information Act violates either the Privileges and Immunities Clause of Article IV of the Constitution or the dormant Commerce Clause. The Virginia Freedom of Information Act (FOIA), provides that 'all public records shall be open to inspection and copying by any citizens of the Commonwealth,' but it grants no such right to non-Virginians."

C. Supreme Court's Answer

"Petitioners, who are citizens of other States, unsuccessfully sought information under the Act and then brought this constitutional challenge. We hold, however, that petitioners' constitutional rights were not violated. By means other than the state FOIA, Virginia made available to petitioners most of the information that they sought, and the Commonwealth's refusal to furnish the additional information did not abridge any constitutionally protected privilege or immunity. Nor did Virginia violate the dormant Commerce Clause. The state Freedom of Information Act does not regulate commerce in any meaningful sense, but instead provides a service that is related to state citizenship."

II. CASE SUMMARY

A. Background

"Petitioners Mark J. McBurney and Roger W. Hurlbert are citizens of Rhode Island and California respectively. McBurney and Hurlbert each requested documents under the Virginia FOIA, but their requests were denied because of their citizenship. . . .

After [McBurney's] his ex-wife defaulted on her child support obligations, McBurney asked the Commonwealth's Division of Child Support Enforcement to file a petition for child support on his behalf. The agency complied, but only after a 9–month delay. . . . To ascertain the reason for the agency's delay, McBurney filed a Virginia FOIA request. . . . The agency denied McBurney's request on the ground that he was not a Virginia citizen. McBurney later requested the same documents under Virginia's Government Data Collection and Dissemination Practices Act, and through that request he received most of the information he had sought that pertained specifically to his own case. He did not, however, receive any general policy information about how the agency handled claims like his.

Hurlbert is the sole proprietor of Sage Information Services, a business that requests real estate tax records on clients' behalf from state and local governments across the United States. In 2008, Hurlbert was hired . . . to obtain real estate tax records for properties in Henrico County, Virginia. He filed a Virginia FOIA request . . . but his request was denied because he was not a Virginia citizen.

Petitioners filed suit under 42 U.S.C. § 1983, seeking declaratory and injunctive relief for violations of the Privileges and Immunities Clause and, in Hurlbert's case, the dormant Commerce Clause. The District Court granted Virginia's motion for summary judgment, and the Court of Appeals affirmed."

The Supreme Court granted certiorari to review the case.

B. Counsel of Record / ACLU Attorney

ACLU Side (Petitioner / Appellant): Deepak Gupta argued the cause for appellants. With him on the briefs were Gregory A. Beck, Jonathan E. Taylor, and Brian Wolfman.

Opposing Side (Respondent / Appellee): E. Duncan Getchell, Jr., Solicitor General of Virginia, argued the cause for appellees. With him on the brief were Kenneth T. Cuccinelli II, Attorney General, Patricia L. West, Chief Deputy Attorney General, Michael H. Brady, Assistant Attorney General, Joseph P. Rapisarda, Jr., and Benjamin A. Thorp IV.

III. AMICI CURIAE

ACLU Side (Petitioner / Appellant)

Brief of amici curiae filed on behalf of the American Civil Liberties Union et al. by Patrick J. Carome and Samir Jain.

Brief of amici curiae filed on behalf of the Coalition for Sensible Public Records Access et al. by Paul Bender, Christopher A.

Mohr, and Michael R. Klipper.
Brief of amici curiae filed on behalf of the Institute for Justice by William R. Maurer and William H. Mellor III.
Brief of amici curiae filed on behalf of Judicial Watch, Inc., et al. by James F. Peterson.
Brief of amici curiae filed on behalf of Public Justice, P. C., by Leah M. Nicholls, Arthur H. Bryant, and Leslie A. Bailey.
Brief of amici curiae filed on behalf of the Reporters Committee for Freedom of the Press et al. by Bruce D. Brown.

Opposing Side (Respondent / Appellee)

Brief of amici curiae filed on behalf of Local Government Attorneys of Virginia, Inc., et al. by R. Lucas Hobbs.
Brief of amici curiae filed on behalf of the National Conference of State Legislatures et al. by Stuart A. Raphael and Lisa E. Soronen.

IV. THE SUPREME COURT'S DECISION

"Under the Privileges and Immunities Clause, '[t]he Citizens of each State [are] entitled to all Privileges and Immunities of Citizens in the several States.' . . .

Petitioners allege that Virginia's citizens-only FOIA provision violates four different 'fundamental' privileges or immunities: the opportunity to pursue a common calling, the ability to own and transfer property, access to the Virginia courts, and access to public information. The first three items on that list, however, are not abridged by the Virginia FOIA, and the fourth—framed broadly—is not protected by the Privileges and Immunities Clause. . . .

While the Clause forbids a State from intentionally giving its own citizens a competitive advantage . . . the Clause does not require that a State tailor its every action to avoid any incidental effect on out-of-state tradesmen. . . .

Virginia . . . does not prevent citizens of other States from obtaining [necessary] documents [for property ownership and transfer]. Under Virginia law, 'any records and papers of every circuit court that are maintained by the clerk of the circuit court shall be open to inspection by any person and the clerk shall, when requested, furnish copies thereof.' . . .

A similar flaw undermines Hurlbert's claim that Virginia violates the Privileges and Immunities Clause by preventing citizens of other States from accessing real estate tax assessment records. . . . These records are considered nonconfidential under Virginia law and, accordingly, they may be posted online. Henrico County . . . follows this practice, as does almost every other county in the Commonwealth. . . .

Virginia law gives citizens and noncitizens alike access to judicial records. . . .

Finally, we reject petitioners' sweeping claim that the challenged provision of the Virginia FOIA violates the Privileges and Immunities Clause because it denies them the right to access public information on equal terms with citizens of the Commonwealth. We cannot agree that the Privileges and Immunities Clause covers this broad right. . . .

Because Virginia's citizens-only FOIA provision neither abridges any of petitioners' fundamental privileges and immunities nor impermissibly regulates commerce, petitioners' constitutional claims fail. The judgment below is affirmed."

V. JUSTICE VOTE

0 Pro ACLU Side vs. 9 Con Opposing Side

Opposing Side (Respondent / Appellee)

1. Alito, S. – Wrote majority opinion
2. Kagan, E. – Joined majority opinion
3. Thomas, C. – Wrote concurring opinion
4. Breyer, S. – Joined majority opinion
5. Scalia, A. – Joined majority opinion
6. Kennedy, A. – Joined majority opinion
7. Ginsburg, R. – Joined majority opinion
8. Sotomayor, S. – Joined majority opinion
9. Roberts, J. – Joined majority opinion

VI. A WIN OR LOSS FOR THE ACLU?

The ACLU filed as amicus curiae urging reversal of the judgment of the Court of Appeals; the Supreme Court affirmed in a 9-0 vote, giving the ACLU an apparent loss.

1108. Maryland v. King

(Decided June 3, 2013; 569 U.S. 435)

I. ISSUE

A. Issues Discussed

4th Amendment

B. Legal Question Presented

"[W]hether the Fourth Amendment prohibits the collection and analysis of a DNA sample from persons arrested, but not yet convicted, on felony charges."

C. Supreme Court's Answer

"[T]he Court concludes that DNA identification of arrestees is a reasonable search that can be considered part of a routine booking procedure. When officers make an arrest supported by probable cause to hold for a serious offense and they bring the suspect to the station to be detained in custody, taking and analyzing a cheek swab of the arrestee's DNA is, like fingerprinting and photographing, a legitimate police booking procedure that is reasonable under the Fourth Amendment."

II. CASE SUMMARY

A. Background

"In 2003 a man concealing his face and armed with a gun broke into a woman's home in Salisbury, Maryland. He raped her. The police were unable to identify or apprehend the assailant . . . but they did obtain from the victim a sample of the perpetrator's DNA.

In 2009 Alonzo King was arrested . . . and charged with first- and second-degree assault for menacing a group of people with a shotgun. As part of a routine booking procedure for serious offenses, his DNA sample was taken by applying a cotton swab or filter paper—known as a buccal swab—to the inside of his cheeks. The DNA was found to match the DNA taken from the Salisbury rape victim. King was tried and convicted for the rape. . . .

The Court of Appeals of Maryland, on review . . . , ruled that the DNA taken when King was booked for the 2009 charge was an unlawful seizure because obtaining and using the cheek swab was an unreasonable search of the person. It set the rape conviction aside."

The Supreme Court granted certiorari to review the case.

B. Counsel of Record / ACLU Attorney

ACLU Side (Respondent / Appellee): Kannon K. Shanmugam argued the cause for appellee. With him on the brief were James M. McDonald, David M. Horniak, Paul B. DeWolfe, and Stephen B. Mercer.

Opposing Side (Petitioner / Appellant): Katherine Winfree, Chief Deputy Attorney General of Maryland, argued the cause for appellant. With her on the briefs were Douglas F. Gansler, Attorney General, and Brian S. Kleinbord, Robert Taylor, Jr., Mary Ann Rapp Ince, Daniel J. Jawor, and Carrie J. Williams, Assistant Attorneys General.

Deputy Solicitor General Dreeben argued the cause for the United States as amicus curiae.

III. AMICI CURIAE

ACLU Side (Respondent / Appellee)

Brief of amici curiae filed on behalf of the American Civil Liberties Union, ACLU of Maryland, and ACLU of Northern California by Michael T. Risher, Peter C. Meier, Steven R. Shapiro, Ezekiel R. Edwards, Brandon J. Buskey, Eric A. long, Jamie L. Williams, and David R. Rocah.

Brief of amici curiae filed on behalf of the Council for Responsible Genetics by Matthew S. Hellman.

Brief of amici curiae filed on behalf of the Electronic Frontier Foundation by Jennifer Lynch, Lee Tien, and Hanni Fakhoury.

Brief of amici curiae filed on behalf of the Electronic Privacy Information Center et al. by Marc Rotenberg.

Brief of amici curiae filed on behalf of the National Association of Criminal Defense Lawyers by Lisa S. Blatt, Anthony J. Franze, and Jonathan Hacker.

Brief of amici curiae filed on behalf of the National Association of Federal Defenders by William M. Jay and Sarah S. Gannett.

Brief of amici curiae filed on behalf of the Public Defender Service for the District of Columbia by Sandra K. Levick.

Brief of amici curiae filed on behalf of Veterans for Common Sense by Eric D. Miller.

Brief of amici curiae filed on behalf of Robert Nussbaum et al. by Danielle Spinelli, Annie L. Owens, and Nicole Ries Fox.

Brief of amici curiae filed on behalf of the Howard University School of Law Civil Rights Clinic by Aderson B. François.

Brief of amici curiae filed on behalf of 14 Scholars of Forensic Evidence by Erin Murphy, pro se.

Brief of amici curiae filed on behalf of Genetics, Genomics and Forensic Science Researchers by Michael L. Foreman in support of neither party.

Opposing Side (Petitioner / Appellant)

Brief of amici curiae filed on behalf of the United States by Deputy Solicitor General Dreeben, Solicitor General Verrilli, Assistant Attorney General Breuer, Elaine J. Goldenberg, Robert A. Parker, and Christopher J. Smith.

Brief of amici curiae filed on behalf of the State of California et al. by Kamala D. Harris, Attorney General of California, Enid A. Camps, Deputy Attorney General, Dane R. Gillette, Chief Assistant Attorney General, Gerald A. Engler, Senior Assistant Attorney General, and Susan Duncan Lee, Acting State Solicitor General, by Kevin T. Kane, Chief State's Attorney of Connecticut, and by the Attorneys General and former Attorneys General for their respective jurisdictions as follows: Luther Strange of Alabama, Michael C. Geraghty of Alaska, Tom Horne of Arizona, Dustin McDaniel of Arkansas, John W. Suthers of Colorado, Joseph R. Biden III of Delaware, Irvin B. Nathan of the District of Columbia, Pamela Jo Bondi of Florida, Samuel S. Olens of Georgia, David M. Louie of Hawaii, Lawrence G. Wasden of Idaho, Lisa Madigan of Illinois, Gregory F. Zoeller of Indiana, Thomas J. Miller of Iowa, Derek Schmidt of Kansas, Jack Conway of Kentucky, James D. "Buddy" Caldwell of Louisiana, William J. Schneider of Maine, Martha Coakley of Massachusetts, Bill Schuette of Michigan, Lori Swanson of Minnesota, Jim Hood of Mississippi, Chris Koster of Missouri, Steve Bullock of Montana, Jon Bruning of Nebraska, Catherine Cortez Masto of Nevada, Michael A. Delaney of New Hampshire, Jeffrey S. Chiesa of New Jersey, Gary K. King of New Mexico, Eric T. Schneiderman of New York, Roy Cooper of North Carolina, Wayne Stenehjem of North Dakota, Michael DeWine of Ohio, E. Scott Pruitt of Oklahoma, Ellen F. Rosenblum of Oregon, Linda L. Kelly of Pennsylvania, Guillermo Somoza-Colombani of Puerto Rico, Peter F. Kilmartin of Rhode Island, Alan Wilson of South Carolina, Marty J. Jackley of South Dakota, Robert E. Cooper, Jr., of Tennessee, Greg Abbott of Texas, Mark L. Shurtleff of Utah, William H. Sorrell of Vermont, Kenneth T. Cuccinelli II of Virginia, Robert M. McKenna of Washington, Darrell V. McGraw, Jr., of West Virginia, J. B. Van Hollen of Wisconsin, and Gregory A. Phillips of Wyoming.

Brief of amici curiae filed on behalf of Susana Martinez, Governor of New Mexico, by Jeffrey S. Bucholtz.

Brief of amici curiae filed on behalf of DNA Saves et al. by Jonathan S. Franklin and Mark Emery.

Brief of amici curiae filed on behalf of the Global Alliance for Rapid DNA Testing by Theodore B. Olson, Amir C. Tayrani, and John W. Wolfe.

Brief of amici curiae filed on behalf of the Maryland Chiefs of Police Association, Inc., et al. by Karen J. Kruger, George Nilson, Suzanne Sangree, and Marc P. Hansen.

Brief of amici curiae filed on behalf of the Maryland Coalition Against Sexual Assault et al. by William C. Sammons.

Brief of amici curiae filed on behalf of the Maryland Crime Victims' Resource Center, Inc., et al. by Neal Kumar Katyal, Dominic F. Perella, Julie A. Grohovsky, and Russell P. Butler.

Brief of amici curiae filed on behalf of the National District Attorneys Association by Albert C. Locher.

Brief of amici curiae filed on behalf of the National Governors

Association et al. by Prashant K. Khetan, Lisa E. Soronen, and Richard Weintraub.

Brief of amici curiae filed on behalf of the Los Angeles County District Attorney by Irene Wakabayashi, Phyllis Asayama, and Roberta Schwartz.

IV. THE SUPREME COURT'S DECISION

"Although the DNA swab procedure used here presents a question the Court has not yet addressed, the framework for deciding the issue is well established. The Fourth Amendment, binding on the States by the Fourteenth Amendment, provides that '[t]he right of the people to be secure in their persons, houses, papers, and effects, against unreasonable searches and seizures, shall not be violated.' It can be agreed that using a buccal swab on the inner tissues of a person's cheek in order to obtain DNA samples is a search. . . .

'As the text of the Fourth Amendment indicates, the ultimate measure of the constitutionality of a governmental search is 'reasonableness.'' . . .

An assessment of reasonableness to determine the lawfulness of requiring this class of arrestees to provide a DNA sample is central to the instant case. . . .

The legitimate government interest served by the Maryland DNA Collection Act is one that is well established: the need for law enforcement officers in a safe and accurate way to process and identify the persons and possessions they must take into custody. . . .

In sum, there can be little reason to question 'the legitimate interest of the government in knowing for an absolute certainty the identity of the person arrested, in knowing whether he is wanted elsewhere, and in ensuring his identification in the event he flees prosecution.' . . .

The reasonableness of any search must be considered in the context of the person's legitimate expectations of privacy. . . .

The expectations of privacy of an individual taken into police custody 'necessarily [are] of a diminished scope.' . . .

In light of the context of a valid arrest supported by probable cause respondent's expectations of privacy were not offended by the minor intrusion of a brief swab . . . . Upon these considerations the Court concludes that DNA identification of arrestees is a reasonable search that can be considered part of a routine booking procedure. When officers make an arrest supported by probable cause to hold for a serious offense and they bring the suspect to the station to be detained in custody, taking and analyzing a cheek swab of the arrestee's DNA is, like fingerprinting and photographing, a legitimate police booking procedure that is reasonable under the Fourth Amendment.

The judgment of the Court of Appeals of Maryland is reversed."

V. JUSTICE VOTE

4 Pro ACLU Side vs. 5 Con Opposing Side

ACLU Side (Respondent / Appellee)

1. Kagan, E. – Joined Scalia's dissent
2. Scalia, A. – Wrote dissenting opinion
3. Ginsburg, R. – Joined Scalia's dissent
4. Sotomayor, S. – Joined Scalia's dissent

Opposing Side (Petitioner / Appellant)

1. Kennedy, A. – Wrote majority opinion
2. Alito, S. – Joined majority opinion
3. Thomas, C. – Joined majority opinion
4. Breyer, S. – Joined majority opinion
5. Roberts, J. – Joined majority opinion

VI. A WIN OR LOSS FOR THE ACLU?

The ACLU filed as amicus curiae urging affirmance; the Supreme Court reversed the Court of Appeals' decision by a 5-4 vote, giving the ACLU an apparent loss.

1109. Ass'n for Molecular Pathology v. Myriad Genetics

(Decided June 13, 2013; 569 U.S. 576)

I. ISSUE

A. Issues Discussed

Governmental authority

B. Legal Question Presented

"[W]hether a naturally occurring segment of deoxyribonucleic acid (DNA) is patent eligible under 35 U.S.C. § 101 by virtue of its isolation from the rest of the human genome. We also address the patent eligibility of synthetically created DNA known as complementary DNA (cDNA), which contains the same protein-coding information found in a segment of natural DNA but omits portions within the DNA segment that do not code for proteins."

C. Supreme Court's Answer

"[W]e hold that a naturally occurring DNA segment is a product of nature and not patent eligible merely because it has been isolated, but that cDNA is patent eligible because it is not naturally occurring."

II. CASE SUMMARY

A. Background

"This case involves patents filed by Myriad after it made [a] medical breakthrough. Myriad discovered the precise location and sequence of what are now known as the BRCA1 and BRCA2 genes. Mutations in these genes can dramatically increase an individual's risk of developing breast and ovarian cancer. . . .

Myriad's patents would, if valid, give it the exclusive right to isolate an individual's BRCA1 and BRCA2 genes . . . . The patents would also give Myriad the exclusive right to synthetically create BRCA cDNA. . . .

But isolation is necessary to conduct genetic testing, and Myriad was not the only entity to offer BRCA testing after it discovered the genes. The University of Pennsylvania's Genetic Diagnostic Laboratory (GDL) and others provided genetic testing services to women. Petitioner Dr. Harry Ostrer . . . routinely sent his patients' DNA samples to GDL for testing. After learning of GDL's testing and Ostrer's activities, Myriad sent letters to them asserting that the genetic testing infringed Myriad's patents. In response, GDL agreed to stop testing and informed Ostrer that it would no longer accept patient samples. . . .

Some years later, petitioner Ostrer, along with medical patients, advocacy groups, and other doctors, filed this lawsuit seeking a declaration that Myriad's patents are invalid under 35 U.S.C. § 101. . . . The District Court then granted summary judgment to petitioners . . . . The Federal Circuit reversed, and th[e U.S. Supreme] Court granted the petition for certiorari, vacated the judgment, and remanded the case . . . .

On remand, the Federal Circuit affirmed the District Court in part and reversed in part . . . ."

The Supreme Court granted certiorari to review the case.

B. Counsel of Record / ACLU Attorney

ACLU Side (Petitioner / Appellant): Christopher A. Hansen argued the cause for appellants. With him on the briefs were Daniel B. Ravicher, Aden J. Fine, Sabrina Y. Hassan, and Sandra S. Park, Christopher A. Hansen, Steven R. Shapiro, and Lenora M. Lapidus of the American Civil Liberties Union Foundation.

Solicitor General Verrilli argued the cause for the United States as amicus curiae urging affirmance in part and reversal in part, in support of neither party.

Opposing Side (Respondent / Appellee): Gregory A. Castanias argued the cause for appellees. With him on the brief were Jennifer L. Swize, Brian M. Poissant, Laura A. Coruzzi, Israel Sasha Mayergoyz, Dennis Murashko, Benjamin G. Jackson, and Matthew S. Gordon.

III. AMICI CURIAE

ACLU Side (Petitioner / Appellant)

Brief of amici curiae filed on behalf of the Canavan Foundation et al. by John L. Hendricks, Megan M. O'Laughlin, and John T. Tower.

Brief of amici curiae filed on behalf of GeneDx et al. by Aaron X. Fellmeth.

Brief of amici curiae filed on behalf of Genformatic LLC by Earl Landers Vickery and Daniel Binford Weaver.

Brief of amici curiae filed on behalf of Knowledge Ecology International by Krista L. Cox.

Brief of amici curiae filed on behalf of the International Center for Technology Assessment et al. by George A. Kimbrell.

Brief of amici curiae filed on behalf of the National Women's Health Network et al. by Debra Greenfield.

Brief of amici curiae filed on behalf of Eileen M. Kane, by Ms. Kane, pro se.

Brief of amici curiae filed on behalf of Kali N. Murray et al. by Ms. Murray, pro se.

Brief of amici curiae filed on behalf of AARP by Barbara Jones and Michael Schuster.

Brief of amici curiae filed on behalf of the American Medical Association et al. by Lori B. Andrews.

Brief of amici curiae filed on behalf of Fifteen Law Professors by Joshua D. Sarnoff, pro se.

Brief of amici curiae filed on behalf of InVitae Corp. by William P. Atkins; for the Juhasz Law Firm, P. C., by Paul R. Juhasz.

Brief of amici curiae filed on behalf of the Ethics & Religious Liberty Commission of the Southern Baptist Convention et al. by Sarah M. Shalf urging vacatur.

Brief of amici curiae filed on behalf of the United States by Solicitor General Verrilli, Principal Deputy Assistant Attorney General Delery, Deputy Solicitor General Stewart, Deputy Assistant Attorney General Brinkmann, Ginger D. Anders, Scott R. McIntosh, and Mark R. Freeman in support of neither party.

Brief of amici curiae filed on behalf of Academics in Law et al. by Roy I. Liebman in support of neither party.

Brief of amici curiae filed on behalf of CLS Bank International by Mark A. Perry and Brian M. Buroker in support of neither party.

Brief of amici curiae filed on behalf of Fédération Internationale des Conseils en Propriété Intellectuelle by Maxim H. Waldbaum and Robert D. Katz in support of neither party.

Brief of amici curiae filed on behalf of the Institute of Professional Representatives Before the European Patent Office by Mr. Liebman in support of neither party.

Brief of amici curiae filed on behalf of Sigram Schindler Beteiligungsgesellschaft mbH by Chidambaram S. Iyer in support of neither party.

Brief of amici curiae filed on behalf of Eric S. Lander by Gideon A. Schor in support of neither party.

Brief of amici curiae filed on behalf of James D. Watson by Matthew J. Dowd and James Wallace in support of neither party.

Opposing Side (Respondent / Appellee)

Brief of amici curiae filed on behalf of the American Bar Association by Laurel G. Bellows, John P. Elwood, and Stephen C. Stout.

Brief of amici curiae filed on behalf of the American Intellectual Property Law Association by Barbara R. Rudolph, Robert D. Litowitz, Erika Harmon Arner, Robert C. Stanley, and Jeffrey I. D. Lewis.

Brief of amici curiae filed on behalf of the Animal Health Institute et al. by Judy Jarecki-Black, Frank G. Smith, and Matthew W. Howell.

Brief of amici curiae filed on behalf of the Association of American Physicians & Surgeons, Inc., et al. by David P. Felsher and Andrew L. Schlafly.

Brief of amici curiae filed on behalf of the Biotechnology Industry Organization by Seth P. Waxman and Nicole Ries Fox.

Brief of amici curiae filed on behalf of the Coalition for 21st Century Medicine by Jeffrey A. Lamken and Michael G. Pattillo, Jr.

Brief of amici curiae filed on behalf of CropLife International by Evan A. Young.

Brief of amici curiae filed on behalf of the Federal Circuit Bar Association by Claire Laporte and Terence P. Stewart.

Brief of amici curiae filed on behalf of Genentech, Inc., et al. by Mr. Waxman, Ms. Fox, Kevin A. Marks, Blair Elizabeth Taylor, and D. Michael Young.

Brief of amici curiae filed on behalf of Gilead Sciences, Inc., et al.

by J. Timothy Keane and Rudolph A. Telscher.

Brief of amici curiae filed on behalf of Immatics Biotechnologies, GmbH, by Kristine L. Roberts.

Brief of amici curiae filed on behalf of InHouse Patent Counsel, LLC, by Rochelle K. Seide.

Brief of amici curiae filed on behalf of the Intellectual Property Owners Association by Paul H. Berghoff, Richard F. Phillips, and Kevin H. Rhodes.

Brief of amici curiae filed on behalf of the NanoBusiness Commercialization Association by Andrew S. Baluch, Harold C. Wegner, and Stephen B. Maebius.

Brief of amici curiae filed on behalf of the National Venture Capital Association by Lynn H. Pasahow, Michael J. Shuster, and Carolyn Chang.

Brief of amici curiae filed on behalf of the New York Intellectual Property Law Association by Matthew B. McFarlane, Ronald M. Daignault, Charles R. Macedo, Thomas J. Kowalski, Robert M. Isackson, and David F. Ryan.

Brief of amici curiae filed on behalf of the Pharmaceutical Research and Manufacturers of America by Kurt G. Calia, Alexa R. Hansen, Robert A. Long, Jr., and Natalie M. Derzko.

Brief of amici curiae filed on behalf of the University of Baltimore/Johns Hopkins University Center for Medicine & Law et al. by Bruce D. Abramson and Miles J. Zaremski.

Brief of amici curiae filed on behalf of Larry Geier et al. by Matthew S. Hellman and Joshua M. Segal.

Brief of amici curiae filed on behalf of Jeffrey A. Lefstin by Kevin B. Laurence.

Brief of amici curiae filed on behalf of the Boston Patent Law Association by Erik Paul Belt and Frank Porcelli.

Brief of amici curiae filed on behalf of the Intellectual Property Amicus Brief Clinic of the Franklin Pierce Center for Intellectual Property, University of New Hampshire School of Law, by Ann M. McCrackin.

Brief of amici curiae filed on behalf of Lynch Syndrome International by Gideon A. Schor.

Brief of amici curiae filed on behalf of MPEG LA, LLC, by Daryl L. Joseffer, Kenneth H. Sonnenfeld, and Lawrence A. Horn.

Brief of amici curiae filed on behalf of the Philadelphia Intellectual Property Law Association by Paul F. Prestia and Brian S. Seal.

Brief of amici curiae filed on behalf of Ananda Mohan Chakrabarty by Jonathan E. Singer and Craig E. Countryman.

Brief of amici curiae filed on behalf of Target Discovery, Inc., by David S. Forman, Courtney B. Casp, Victoria S. Lee, and Amelia F. Baur.

IV. THE SUPREME COURT'S DECISION

"Section 101 of the Patent Act provides:

'Whoever invents or discovers any new and useful . . . composition of matter, or any new and useful improvement thereof, may obtain a patent therefor, subject to the conditions and requirements of this title.'

We have 'long held that this provision contains an important implicit exception[:] Laws of nature, natural phenomena, and abstract ideas are not patentable.' . . .

The rule against patents on naturally occurring things is not without limits, however, for 'all inventions at some level embody, use, reflect, rest upon, or apply laws of nature, natural phenomena, or abstract ideas,' and 'too broad an interpretation of this exclusionary principle could eviscerate patent law.' . . . We must apply this well-established standard to determine whether Myriad's patents claim any 'new and useful . . . composition of matter,' or instead claim naturally occurring phenomena. . . .

It is undisputed that Myriad did not create or alter any of the genetic information encoded in the BRCA1 and BRCA2 genes. . . . Nor did Myriad create or alter the genetic structure of DNA. Instead, Myriad's principal contribution was uncovering the precise location and genetic sequence of the BRCA1 and BRCA2 genes within chromosomes 17 and 13. The question is whether this renders the genes patentable. . . .

Groundbreaking . . . discovery does not by itself satisfy the § 101 inquiry. . . .

These concessions weigh against deferring to the PTO's determination. . . .

cDNA does not present the same obstacles to patentability as naturally occurring, isolated DNA segments. . . .

It is important to note what is not implicated by this decision. First, there are no method claims before this Court. . . .

Similarly, this case does not involve patents on new applications of knowledge about the BRCA1 and BRCA2 genes. . . .

Nor do we consider the patentability of DNA in which the order of the naturally occurring nucleotides has been altered. . . . We merely hold that genes . . . are not patent eligible under § 101 simply because they have been isolated from the surrounding genetic material. . . .

[T]he judgment of the Federal Circuit is affirmed in part and reversed in part."

V. JUSTICE VOTE

9 Pro ACLU Side vs. 0 Con Opposing Side

ACLU Side (Petitioner / Appellant)

1. Thomas, C. – Wrote majority opinion
2. Alito, S. – Joined majority opinion
3. Kagan, E. – Joined majority opinion
4. Breyer, S. – Joined majority opinion
5. Scalia, A. – Wrote concurring opinion
6. Kennedy, A. – Joined majority opinion
7. Ginsburg, R. – Joined majority opinion
8. Sotomayor, S. – Joined majority opinion
9. Roberts, J. – Joined majority opinion

VI. A WIN OR LOSS FOR THE ACLU?

The ACLU served as counsel for appellant urging reversal of the judgment of the Court of Appeals; the Supreme Court affirmed in part and reversed in part in a 9-0 vote, giving the ACLU an apparent win.

1110. Arizona v. Inter Tribal Council of Arizona

(Decided June 17, 2013; 570 U.S. 1)

I. ISSUE

A. Issues Discussed

Immigration/Citizenship

B. Legal Question Presented

"[W]hether Arizona's evidence-of-citizenship requirement, as applied to Federal Form applicants, is pre-empted by the Act's mandate that States 'accept and use' the Federal Form."

C. Supreme Court's Answer

"We hold that 42 U.S.C. § 1973gg–4 precludes Arizona from requiring a Federal Form applicant to submit information beyond that required by the form itself. Arizona may, however, request anew that the EAC include such a requirement among the Federal Form's state-specific instructions, and may seek judicial review of the EAC's decision under the Administrative Procedure Act."

II. CASE SUMMARY

A. Background

"The National Voter Registration Act requires States to 'accept and use' a uniform federal form to register voters for federal elections. The contents . . . are prescribed by . . . the Election Assistance Commission. The Federal Form . . . does not require documentary evidence of citizenship; rather, it requires only that an applicant aver, under penalty of perjury, that he is a citizen. Arizona law requires voter-registration officials to 'reject' any application for registration, including a Federal Form, that is not accompanied by concrete evidence of citizenship. The question is whether Arizona's evidence-of-citizenship requirement . . . is pre-empted by the Act's mandate that States 'accept and use' the Federal Form. . . .

The two groups of plaintiffs . . . filed separate suits seeking to enjoin the voting provisions of Proposition 200. The District Court consolidated the cases and denied the plaintiffs' motions for a preliminary injunction. A two-judge motions panel of the Court of Appeals for the Ninth Circuit then enjoined Proposition 200 pending appeal. [The U.S. Supreme Court] vacated that order and allowed the impending 2006 election to proceed with the new rules in place. On remand, the Court of Appeals affirmed the District Court's initial denial of a preliminary injunction as to respondents' claim that the NVRA pre-empts Proposition 200's registration rules. The District Court then granted Arizona's motion for summary judgment . . . . A panel of the Ninth Circuit affirmed in part but reversed as relevant here, holding that 'Proposition 200's documentary proof of citizenship requirement conflicts with the NVRA's text, structure, and purpose.' The en banc Court of Appeals agreed."

The Supreme Court granted certiorari to review the case.

B. Counsel of Record / ACLU Attorney

ACLU Side (Respondent / Appellee): Patricia A. Millett argued the cause for appellees. With her on the brief for appellees Inter Tribal Council of Arizona, Inc., et al. were Laughlin McDonald of the American Civil Liberties Union Foundation, Jon M. Greenbaum, Mark A. Posner, Michael C. Small, Christopher M. Egleson, David J Bodney, David B. Rosenbaum, Thomas L. Hudson, Joe R Sparks, and Daniel B. Kohrman. Thomas A. Saenz, Nina Perales, and Karl J Sandstrom filed a brief for appellees Gonzalez et al.

Deputy Solicitor General Srinivasan argued the cause for the United States as amicus curiae.

Opposing Side (Petitioner / Appellant): Thomas C. Horne, Attorney General of Arizona, argued the cause for appellants. With him on the briefs for state appellants were David R. Cole, Solicitor General, Paula S. Bickett, Thomas M. Collins, Assistant Attorney General, Melissa G. Iyer, and M. Miller Baker. M. Colleen Connor filed a brief for appellants Twenty-six County Recorders and Election Directors.

III. AMICI CURIAE

ACLU Side (Respondent / Appellee)

Brief of amici curiae filed on behalf of the United States by Deputy Solicitor General Srinivasan, Solicitor General Verrilli, Assistant Attorney General Perez, John F Bash, Diana K. Flynn, and Holly A. Thomas.

Brief of amici curiae filed on behalf of the Asian American Legal Defense and Education Fund et al. by Michael D. Nolan.

Brief of amici curiae filed on behalf of Community Voter Registration Organizations by Walter Dellinger, Jonathan D. Hacker, Loren L. Alikhan, Brenda Wright, and Lisa J Danetz.

Brief of amici curiae filed on behalf of Constitutional Law Professors by Douglas T Kendall, Elizabeth B. Wydra, David H. Gans, Wendy R. Weiser, and Myrna Pérez.

Brief of amici curiae filed on behalf of Election Administrators by David W Ogden and Daniel S. Volchok.

Brief of amici curiae filed on behalf of LatinoJustice PRLDEF et al. by Michael Dore, Catherine Weiss, Natalie J Kraner, Lawrence Bluestone, and Juan Cartagena.

Brief of amici curiae filed on behalf of the League of Women Voters by Paul M. Smith, Michael B. DeSanctis, Jessica Ring Amunson, and Lloyd Leonard.

Brief of amici curiae filed on behalf of Members of Congress by Charles A. Rothfeld and Brian J Wong.

Brief of amici curiae filed on behalf of the NAACP Legal Defense & Educational Fund, Inc., et al. by Debo P Adegbile, Elise C. Boddie, Ryan P. Haygood, Joshua Civin, Michael B. de Leeuw, Wade Henderson, Lisa M. Bornstein, Steven M. Freeman, Jerome Gotkin, and Michael Arnold.

Brief of amici curiae filed on behalf of the National Education Association et al. by Alice O'Brien, Jason Walta, Judith A. Scott, Walter Kamiat, Mark Schneider, John J Sullivan, and William Lurye.

Brief of amici curiae filed on behalf of the Overseas Vote Foundation et al. by Pamela S. Karlan, Jeffrey L. Fisher, and Kevin K. Russell.

Opposing Side (Petitioner / Appellant)

Brief of amici curiae filed on behalf of the State of Alabama et al. by Luther Strange, Attorney General of Alabama, John C Neiman, Jr., Solicitor General, and Andrew L. Brasher, Deputy Solicitor General, and by the Attorneys General for their respective States as follows: Samuel S. Olens of Georgia, Derek Schmidt of Kansas, Bill Schuette of Michigan, E. Scott Pruitt of Oklahoma, and Greg Abbott of Texas.

Brief of amici curiae filed on behalf of the American Civil Rights Union et al. by Peter J Ferrara.

Brief of amici curiae filed on behalf of the American Unity Legal Defense Fund by Barnaby W Zall.

Brief of amici curiae filed on behalf of the Eagle Forum Education & Legal Defense Fund, Inc., by Lawrence J Joseph.

Brief of amici curiae filed on behalf of the Landmark Legal Foundation by Richard R Hutchison.

Brief of amici curiae filed on behalf of Members of Congress by Daniel E. Lungren.

Brief of amici curiae filed on behalf of the Mountain States Legal Foundation by Steven J Lechner.

Brief of amici curiae filed on behalf of Kris W. Kobach, Kansas Secretary of State, by Mr. Kobach, pro se, and Ryan A. Kriegshauser.

Brief of amici curiae filed on behalf of Arizona State Senator Russell Pearce by James F Peterson.

Brief of amici curiae filed on behalf of the Center for Constitutional Jurisprudence by John Eastman, Anthony T Caso, and Edwin Meese III.

IV. THE SUPREME COURT'S DECISION

"The [Elections] Clause empowers Congress to pre-empt state regulations governing the 'Times, Places and Manner' of holding congressional elections. . . .

The straightforward textual question here is whether Ariz.Rev. Stat. Ann. § 16–166(F), which requires state officials to 'reject' a Federal Form unaccompanied by documentary evidence of citizenship, conflicts with the NVRA's mandate that Arizona 'accept and use' the Federal Form. . . .

We conclude that the fairest reading of the statute is that a state-imposed requirement of evidence of citizenship not required by the Federal Form is 'inconsistent with' the NVRA's mandate that States 'accept and use' the Federal Form. If this reading prevails, the Elections Clause requires that Arizona's rule give way. . . .

Arizona contends, however, that its construction of the phrase 'accept and use' is necessary to avoid a conflict between the NVRA and Arizona's constitutional authority to establish qualifications (such as citizenship) for voting. Arizona is correct that the Elections Clause empowers Congress to regulate how federal elections are held, but not who may vote in them. . . .

Prescribing voting qualifications, therefore, 'forms no part of the power to be conferred upon the national government' by the Elections Clause, which is 'expressly restricted to the regulation of the times, the places, and the manner of elections.' . . .

Since, pursuant to the Government's concession, a State may request that the EAC alter the Federal Form to include information the State deems necessary to determine eligibility, and may challenge the EAC's rejection of that request in a suit under the Administrative Procedure Act, no constitutional doubt is raised by giving the 'accept and use' provision of the NVRA its fairest reading. That alternative means of enforcing its constitutional power to determine voting qualifications remains open to Arizona here. . . .

We hold that 42 U.S.C. § 1973gg–4 precludes Arizona from requiring a Federal Form applicant to submit information beyond that required by the form itself. Arizona may, however, request anew that the EAC include such a requirement among the Federal Form's state-specific instructions, and may seek judicial review of the EAC's decision under the Administrative Procedure Act.

The judgment of the Court of Appeals is affirmed."

V. JUSTICE VOTE

7 Pro ACLU Side vs. 2 Con Opposing Side

ACLU Side (Respondent / Appellee)

1. Scalia, A. – Wrote majority opinion
2. Kagan, E. – Joined majority opinion
3. Breyer, S. – Joined majority opinion
4. Kennedy, A. – Wrote concurring opinion
5. Ginsburg, R. – Joined majority opinion
6. Sotomayor, S. – Joined majority opinion
7. Roberts, J. – Joined majority opinion

Opposing Side (Petitioner / Appellant)

1. Alito, S. – Wrote dissenting opinion
2. Thomas, C. – Wrote dissenting opinion

VI. A WIN OR LOSS FOR THE ACLU?

The ACLU served as counsel for appellee urging affirmance; the Supreme Court affirmed the Court of Appeals' decision by a 7-2 vote, giving the ACLU an apparent win.

1111. Alleyne v. U.S.

(Decided June 17, 2013; 570 U.S. 99)

I. ISSUE

A. Issues Discussed

Criminal procedure

B. Legal Question Presented

"In Harris v. United States, 536 U.S. 545 (2002), this Court held that judicial factfinding that increases the mandatory minimum sentence for a crime is permissible under the Sixth Amendment. [This case concerns] whether that decision should be overruled."

C. Supreme Court's Answer

"Mandatory minimum sentences increase the penalty for a crime. It follows, then, that any fact that increases the mandatory minimum is an 'element' that must be submitted to the jury. Accordingly, Harris is overruled."

II. CASE SUMMARY

A. Background

"Petitioner Allen Ryan Alleyne and an accomplice devised a plan to rob a store manager as he drove the store's daily deposits to a local bank. By feigning car trouble, they tricked the manager to stop. Alleyne's accomplice approached the manager with a gun and demanded the store's deposits, which the manager surrendered. Alleyne was later charged with multiple federal offenses, including robbery affecting interstate commerce, 18 U.S.C. § 1951(a), and using or carrying a firearm in relation to a crime of violence, § 924(c)(1)(A). . . .

The jury convicted Alleyne. The jury indicated on the verdict form that Alleyne had '[u]sed or carried a firearm during and in relation to a crime of violence,' but did not indicate a finding that the firearm was '[b]randished.'

The presentence report recommended a 7-year sentence on the § 924(c) count, which reflected the mandatory minimum sentence for cases in which a firearm has been 'brandished,' § 924(c)(1)(A)(ii). Alleyne objected to this recommendation. . . . Alleyne contended that raising his mandatory minimum sentence based on a sentencing judge's finding that he brandished a firearm would violate his Sixth Amendment right to a jury trial.

The District Court overruled Alleyne's objection. . . . The Court of Appeals affirmed . . . ."

The Supreme Court granted certiorari to review the case.

B. Counsel of Record / ACLU Attorney

ACLU Side (Petitioner / Appellant): Mary E. Maguire argued the cause for appellant. With her on the briefs were Patrick L. Bryant, Frances H. Pratt, and Michael S. Nachmanof.

Opposing Side (Respondent / Appellee): Deputy Solicitor General Dreeben argued the cause for the United States. With him on the brief were Solicitor General Verrilli, Assistant Attorney General Breuer, and Eric J Feigin.

III. AMICI CURIAE

ACLU Side (Petitioner / Appellant)

Brief of amici curiae filed on behalf of the Sentencing Project and the American Civil Liberties Union by Frank M. Dickerson III, Charles M. Woodworth, Alison Siegler, Steven R. Shapiro, and Ezekiel R. Edwards.

Brief of amici curiae filed on behalf of the Center on the Administration of Criminal Law by Anthony S. Barkow, Rachel E. Barkow, Samuel L. Feder, and Matthew S. Hellman.

Brief of amici curiae filed on behalf of Families Against Mandatory Minimums by Gregory G. Rapawy, Mary Price, and Peter Goldberger.

Brief of amici curiae filed on behalf of the National Association of Criminal Defense Lawyers et al. by John B. Owens, Daniel B. Levin, Jonathan D Hacker, and Sarah S. Gannett.

Brief of amici curiae filed on behalf of the New York Council of Defense Lawyers by Marc L. Greenwald, Douglas A Berman, and Alexandra A. E. Shapiro.

Opposing Side (Respondent / Appellee)

Brief of amici curiae filed on behalf of the State of Texas et al. by Greg Abbott, Attorney General of Texas, Jonathan F Mitchell, Solicitor General, and Daniel T. Hodge, First Assistant Attorney General, and by the Attorneys General for their respective States as follows: Luther Strange of Alabama, Ton Horne of Arizona, John W Suthers of Colorado, Joseph R. Biden III of Delaware, Sam Olens of Georgia, David M. Louie of Hawaii, Derek Schmidt of Kansas, William J Schneider of Maine, Bill Schuette of Michigan, Chris Koster of Missouri, Jeffrey S. Chiesa of New Jersey, Gary K. King of New Mexico, Wayne Stenehiem of North Dakota, and Robert M. McKenna of Washington.

IV. THE SUPREME COURT'S DECISION

"Alleyne contends that Harris was wrongly decided and that it cannot be reconciled with our reasoning in Apprendi. We agree. . . .

Because there is no basis in principle or logic to distinguish facts that raise the maximum [sentence] from those that increase the minimum, Harris was inconsistent with Apprendi. It is, accordingly, overruled. . . .

In holding that facts that increase mandatory minimum sentences must be submitted to the jury, we take care to note what our holding does not entail. Our ruling today does not mean that any fact that influences judicial discretion must be found by a jury. We have long recognized that broad sentencing discretion, informed by judicial factfinding, does not violate the Sixth Amendment. . . .

Here, the sentencing range supported by the jury's verdict was five years' imprisonment to life. The District Court imposed the 7-year mandatory minimum sentence based on its finding by a preponderance of evidence that the firearm was 'brandished.' Because the finding of brandishing increased the penalty to which the defendant was subjected, it was an element, which had to be found by the jury beyond a reasonable doubt. The judge, rather than the jury, found brandishing, thus violating petitioner's Sixth Amendment rights.

Accordingly, we vacate the Fourth Circuit's judgment with respect to Alleyne's sentence on the § 924(c)(1)(A) conviction and remand the case for resentencing consistent with the jury's verdict."

V. JUSTICE VOTE

5 Pro ACLU Side vs. 4 Con Opposing Side

ACLU Side (Petitioner / Appellant)

1. Thomas, C. – Wrote majority opinion
2. Kagan, E. – Joined Sotomayor's concurrence
3. Breyer, S. – Wrote concurring opinion
4. Ginsburg, R. – Joined Sotomayor's concurrence
5. Sotomayor, S. – Wrote concurring opinion

Opposing Side (Respondent / Appellee)

1. Alito, S. – Wrote dissenting opinion
2. Scalia, A. – Joined Roberts' dissent

3. Kennedy, A. – Joined Roberts' dissent
4. Roberts, J. – Wrote dissenting opinion

VI. A WIN OR LOSS FOR THE ACLU?

The ACLU filed as amicus curiae urging reversal of the judgment of the Court of Appeals; the Supreme Court vacated in a 5-4 vote, giving the ACLU an apparent win.

1112. Salinas v. Texas

(Decided June 17, 2013; 570 U.S. 178)

I. ISSUE

A. Issues Discussed

Criminal procedure

B. Legal Question Presented

"[W]hether the prosecution may use a defendant's assertion of the privilege against self-incrimination during a noncustodial police interview as part of its case in chief."

C. Supreme Court's Answer

"Petitioner's Fifth Amendment claim fails because he did not expressly invoke the privilege against self-incrimination in response to the officer's question. It has long been settled that the privilege 'generally is not self-executing' and that a witness who desires its protection "must claim it.""

II. CASE SUMMARY

A. Background

"Without being placed in custody or receiving Miranda warnings, petitioner voluntarily answered the questions of a police officer who was investigating a murder. But petitioner balked when the officer asked whether a ballistics test would show that the shell casings found at the crime scene would match petitioner's shotgun. Petitioner was subsequently charged with murder . . . .

Petitioner did not testify at trial. Over his objection, prosecutors used his reaction to the officer's question during the 1993 interview as evidence of his guilt. The jury found petitioner guilty, and he received a 20–year sentence. On direct appeal to the Court of Appeals of Texas, petitioner argued that prosecutors' use of his silence as part of their case in chief violated the Fifth Amendment. The Court of Appeals rejected that argument, reasoning that petitioner's prearrest, pre-Miranda silence was not 'compelled' within the meaning of the Fifth Amendment. The Texas Court of Criminal Appeals . . . affirmed on the same ground."

The Supreme Court granted certiorari to review the case.

B. Counsel of Record / ACLU Attorney

ACLU Side (Petitioner / Appellant): Jeffrey L. Fisher argued the cause for appellant. With him on the briefs were Pamela S. Karlan, Dick DeGuerin, Neal Davis, and Kevin K. Russell.

Opposing Side (Respondent / Appellee): Alan Keith Curry argued the cause for appellee. With him on the brief were Carol M. Cameron, Eric Kugler, David C. Newell, and Mike Anderson.

Ginger D. Anders argued the cause for the United States as amicus curiae.

III. AMICI CURIAE

ACLU Side (Petitioner / Appellant)

Brief of amici curiae filed on behalf of the American Civil Liberties Union by Aaron D. Van Oort, Steven R. Shapiro, Trina K. Taylor, Erin L. Hoffman, and Jeffrey P. Justman.

Brief of amici curiae filed on behalf of the American Board of Criminal Lawyers by Henry W. Asbill and Brian J. Murray.

Brief of amici curiae filed on behalf of the National Association of Criminal Defense Lawyers et al. by Craig D. Singer, Jeffrey T. Green, and Angela Moore.

Brief of amici curiae filed on behalf of The Rutherford Institute et al. by John W. Whitehead, Rita M. Dunaway, and Timothy Lynch.

Opposing Side (Respondent / Appellee)

Brief of amici curiae filed on behalf of the United States by Ginger D. Anders, Solicitor General Verrilli, Assistant Attorney General Raman, Deputy Solicitor General Dreeben, and Deborah Watson.

Brief of amici curiae filed on behalf of the State of Illinois et al. by Lisa Madigan, Attorney General of Illinois, Michael A. Scodro, Solicitor General, and Jane Elinor Notz, Deputy Solicitor General, and by the Attorneys General for their respective States as follows: Luther Strange of Alabama, Tom Horne of Arizona, John W. Suthers of Colorado, Joseph R. Biden III of Delaware, Pamela Jo Bondi of Florida, David M. Louie of Hawaii, Lawrence G. Wasden of Idaho, Gregory F. Zoeller of Indiana, Derek Schmidt of Kansas, Jack Conway of Kentucky, Janet T. Mills of Maine, Bill Schuette of Michigan, Timothy C. Fox of Montana, Jon Bruning of Nebraska, Gary K. King of New Mexico, Wayne Stenehjem of North Dakota, E. Scott Pruitt of Oklahoma, Ellen F. Rosenblum. of Oregon, Kathleen G. Kane of Pennsylvania, Alan Wilson of South Carolina, Marty J. Jackley of South Dakota, Robert E. Cooper, Jr., of Tennessee, John E. Swallow of Utah, J. B. Van Hollen of Wisconsin, and Gregory A. Phillips of Wyoming.

Brief of amici curiae filed on behalf of Wayne County, Michigan, by Kym L. Worthy and Timothy A. Banghman.

Brief of amici curiae filed on behalf of the Criminal Justice Legal Foundation by Kent S. Scheidegger.

IV. THE SUPREME COURT'S DECISION

"The privilege against self-incrimination 'is an exception to the general principle that the Government has the right to everyone's testimony.' . . . [W]e have long held that a witness who "desires the protection of the privilege . . . must claim it" at the time he relies on it.

That requirement ensures that the Government is put on notice when a witness intends to rely on the privilege . . . .

We have previously recognized two exceptions to the requirement that witnesses invoke the privilege, but neither applies here. . . .

Petitioner urges us to adopt a third exception to the invocation requirement for cases in which a witness stands mute . . . . Our cases all but foreclose such an exception . . . . We therefore decline petitioner's invitation to craft a new exception . . . .

Our cases establish that a defendant normally does not invoke the privilege by remaining silent. . . .

We have also repeatedly held that the express invocation requirement applies even when an official has reason to suspect that the answer to his question would incriminate the witness. . . .

Petitioner does not dispute the vitality of either of those lines of precedent but instead argues that we should adopt an exception for cases at their intersection. Thus, petitioner would have us hold that although neither a witness' silence nor official suspicions are enough to excuse the express invocation requirement, the invocation requirement does not apply where a witness is silent in the face of official suspicions. For the same reasons that neither of those factors is sufficient by itself to relieve a witness of the obligation to expressly invoke the privilege, we conclude that they do not do so together. . . .

Finally, we are not persuaded by petitioner's arguments that applying the usual express invocation requirement . . . will prove unworkable in practice. . . .

Before petitioner could rely on the privilege against self-incrimination, he was required to invoke it. Because he failed to do so, the judgment of the Texas Court of Criminal Appeals is affirmed."

V. JUSTICE VOTE

4 Pro ACLU Side vs. 5 Con Opposing Side

ACLU Side (Petitioner / Appellant)

1. Kagan, E. – Joined Breyer's dissent
2. Breyer, S. – Wrote dissenting opinion
3. Ginsburg, R. – Joined Breyer's dissent
4. Sotomayor, S. – Joined Breyer's dissent

Opposing Side (Respondent / Appellee)

1. Alito, S. – Wrote majority opinion
2. Thomas, C. – Wrote concurring opinion
3. Scalia, A. – Joined Thomas' concurrence
4. Kennedy, A. – Joined majority opinion
5. Roberts, J. – Joined majority opinion

VI. A WIN OR LOSS FOR THE ACLU?

The ACLU filed as amicus curiae urging reversal of the judgment of the Texas Court of Criminal Appeals; the Supreme Court affirmed in a 5-4 vote, giving the ACLU an apparent loss.

1113. Agency for Int'l Dev. v. Alliance for Open Society Int'l

(Decided June 20, 2013; 570 U.S. 205)

I. ISSUE

A. Issues Discussed

1st Amendment, press, speech, association

B. Legal Question Presented

"The United States Leadership Against HIV/AIDS, Tuberculosis, and Malaria Act of 2003 . . . outlined a comprehensive strategy to combat the spread of HIV/AIDS around the world. As part of that strategy, . . . no funds may be used by an organization 'that does not have a policy explicitly opposing prostitution and sex trafficking.' . . . The question is whether that funding condition violates a recipient's First Amendment rights."

C. Supreme Court's Answer

"The Policy Requirement compels as a condition of federal funding the affirmation of a belief that by its nature cannot be confined within the scope of the Government program. In so doing, it violates the First Amendment and cannot be sustained."

II. CASE SUMMARY

A. Background

"Congress passed the Leadership Act in 2003 after finding that HIV/AIDS had 'assumed pandemic proportions . . . .' . . .

[Leadership Act] funds, however, come with two conditions: . . . Second, no funds made available may 'provide assistance to any group or organization that does not have a policy explicitly opposing prostitution and sex trafficking . . . .' . . .

Respondents are a group of domestic organizations engaged in combating HIV/AIDS overseas. . . . Respondents fear that adopting a policy explicitly opposing prostitution may alienate certain host governments, and may diminish the effectiveness of some of their programs by making it more difficult to work with prostitutes . . . .

In 2005, respondents Alliance for Open Society International and Pathfinder International commenced this litigation, seeking a declaratory judgment that the Government's implementation of the Policy Requirement violated their First Amendment rights. Respondents sought a preliminary injunction barring the Government from cutting off their funding . . . . The District Court granted such a preliminary injunction, and the Government appealed.

While the appeal was pending, HHS and USAID issued guidelines . . . .

The Court of Appeals summarily remanded the case . . . to consider whether the preliminary injunction was still appropriate in light of the new guidelines. On remand, the District Court issued a new preliminary injunction . . . , and the Government renewed its appeal.

The Court of Appeals affirmed."

The Supreme Court granted certiorari to review the case.

B. Counsel of Record / ACLU Attorney

ACLU Side (Respondent / Appellee): David W Bowker argued the cause for appellees. With him on the brief were Catherine M. A. Carroll, Rebekah Diller, Laura Abel, Mark C. Fleming, Jason D. Hirsch, Michael D. Gottesman, and Shalev Roisman.

Opposing Side (Petitioner / Appellant): Deputy Solicitor General Srinivasan argued the cause for appellants. With him on the briefs were Solicitor General Verrilli, Principal Deputy Assistant Attorney General Delery, Deputy Solicitor General

Kneedler, Jeffrey B. Wall, Michael S. Raab, and Sharon Swingle.

III. AMICI CURIAE

ACLU Side (Respondent / Appellee)

Brief of amici curiae filed on behalf of the American Civil Liberties Union and New York Civil Liberties Union by Arthur N. Eisenberg, Mariko Hirose, Steven R. Shapiro, Mie Lewis, and Lenora M. Lapidus.

Brief of amici curiae filed on behalf of the Becket Fund for Religious Liberty et al. by Eugene Volokh and Andrew L. Frey.

Brief of amici curiae filed on behalf of the Cato Institute by Steven A. Engel and Ilya Shapiro.

Brief of amici curiae filed on behalf of the Deans and Professors of Public Health et al. by Julie Carpenter and Jessica Ring Amunson.

Brief of amici curiae filed on behalf of Heartbeat International, Inc., by Brian J. Murray.

Brief of amici curiae filed on behalf of Independent Sector by Lawrence S. Lustberg.

Brief of amici curiae filed on behalf of the Thomas Jefferson Center for the Protection of Free Expression by J. Joshua Wheeler.

Brief of amici curiae filed on behalf of Certain Current and Former Members of Congress by Mark E. Haddad, Carter G. Phillips, Daron Watts, and Tacy F. Flint.

Brief of amici curiae filed on behalf of the Rutherford Institute by Megan L. Brown and John W. Whitehead.

Brief of amici curiae filed on behalf of the Secretariat of the Joint United Nations Programme on HIV/AIDS (UNAIDS Secretariat) by Igor V. Tinofeyev.

Opposing Side (Petitioner / Appellant)

Brief of amici curiae filed on behalf of the American Center for Law and Justice by Jay Alan Sekulow, Stuart J. Roth, Colby M. May, and Walter M. Weber.

Brief of amici curiae filed on behalf of the Coalition Against Trafficking in Women et al. by Alexander A. Yanos.

IV. THE SUPREME COURT'S DECISION

"The Policy Requirement mandates that recipients of Leadership Act funds explicitly agree with the Government's policy to oppose prostitution and sex trafficking. It is, however, a basic First Amendment principle that 'freedom of speech prohibits the government from telling people what they must say.' . . .

The Spending Clause of the Federal Constitution grants Congress the power '[t]o lay and collect Taxes, Duties, Imposts and Excises, to pay the Debts and provide for the common Defence and general Welfare of the United States.' . . . That power includes the authority to impose limits on the use of such funds to ensure they are used in the manner Congress intends. . . .

As a general matter, if a party objects to a condition on the receipt of federal funding, its recourse is to decline the funds. This remains true when the objection is that a condition may affect the recipient's exercise of its First Amendment rights. . . .

At the same time, however, we have held that the Government "may not deny a benefit to a person on a basis that infringes his constitutionally protected . . . freedom of speech even if he has no entitlement to that benefit." . . .

To begin, it is important to recall that the Leadership Act has two conditions relevant here. The first—unchallenged in this litigation—prohibits Leadership Act funds from being used 'to promote or advocate the legalization or practice of prostitution or sex trafficking.' The Government concedes that § 7631(e) by itself ensures that federal funds will not be used for the prohibited purposes.

The Policy Requirement therefore must be doing something more—and it is. . . . The Policy Requirement is an ongoing condition on recipients' speech and activities, a ground for terminating a grant after selection is complete. . . . This case is not about the Government's ability to enlist the assistance of those with whom it already agrees. It is about compelling a grant recipient to adopt a particular belief as a condition of funding.

By demanding that funding recipients adopt—as their own—the Government's view on an issue of public concern, the condition by its very nature affects 'protected conduct outside the scope of the federally funded program.' . . .

The Policy Requirement compels as a condition of federal funding the affirmation of a belief that by its nature cannot be confined within the scope of the Government program. In so doing, it violates the First Amendment and cannot be sustained. The judgment of the Court of Appeals is affirmed."

V. JUSTICE VOTE

6 Pro ACLU Side vs. 2 Con Opposing Side

ACLU Side (Respondent / Appellee)

1. Roberts, J. – Wrote majority opinion
2. Alito, S. – Joined majority opinion
3. Breyer, S. – Joined majority opinion
4. Kennedy, A. – Joined majority opinion
5. Ginsburg, R. – Joined majority opinion
6. Sotomayor, S. – Joined majority opinion

Opposing Side (Petitioner / Appellant)

1. Thomas, C. – Joined Scalia's dissent
2. Scalia, A. – Wrote dissenting opinion

Kagan, E. – Took no part in the decision.

VI. A WIN OR LOSS FOR THE ACLU?

The ACLU filed as amicus curiae urging affirmance; the Supreme Court affirmed the Court of Appeals decision by a 6-2 vote, giving the ACLU an apparent win.

1114. Shelby County v. Holder

(Decided June 25, 2013; 570 U.S. 529)

I. ISSUE

A. Issues Discussed

Voting rights

B. Legal Question Presented

"[W]hether the [Voting Rights] Act's extraordinary measures, including its disparate treatment of the States, continue to satisfy constitutional requirements."

C. Supreme Court's Answer

"Congress could have updated the coverage formula . . . , but did not do so. Its failure to act leaves us today with no choice but to declare § 4(b) unconstitutional. The formula in that section can no longer be used as a basis for subjecting jurisdictions to preclearance."

II. CASE SUMMARY

A. Background

"The Voting Rights Act of 1965 employed extraordinary measures to address an extraordinary problem. Section 5 of the Act required States to obtain federal permission before enacting any law related to voting—a drastic departure from basic principles of federalism. And § 4 of the Act applied that requirement only to some States—an equally dramatic departure from the principle that all States enjoy equal sovereignty. This was strong medicine, but Congress determined it was needed to address entrenched racial discrimination in voting . . . . Reflecting the unprecedented nature of these measures, they were scheduled to expire after five years.

Nearly 50 years later, they are still in effect . . . . There is no denying, however, that the conditions that originally justified these measures no longer characterize voting in the covered jurisdictions. . . .

At the same time, voting discrimination still exists; no one doubts that. The question is whether the Act's extraordinary measures, including its disparate treatment of the States, continue to satisfy constitutional requirements. . . .

Shelby County is located in Alabama, a covered jurisdiction. [I]n 2010, the county sued the Attorney General in Federal District Court in Washington, D.C., seeking a declaratory judgment that sections 4(b) and 5 of the Voting Rights Act are facially unconstitutional . . . . The District Court ruled against the county and upheld the Act. . . .

The Court of Appeals for the D.C. Circuit affirmed."

The Supreme Court granted certiorari to review the case.

B. Counsel of Record / ACLU Attorney

ACLU Side (Respondent / Appellee): Solicitor General Verrilli argued the cause for the federal appellee. With him on the brief were Assistant Attorney General Perez, Deputy Solicitor General Srinivasan, Sarah E. Harrington, and Diana K. Flynn.

Debo P. Adegbile argued the cause for appellees Bobby Pierson et al. M. Laughlin McDonald, Nancy G. Abudu, and Steven R. Shapiro of the American Civil Liberties Union Foundation, Arthur B. Spitzer of the American Civil Liberties Union of the Nation's Capital, and David I. Schoen of the ACLU of Alabama Foundation, and Kim Keenan filed a brief for appellee-intervenor Bobby Pierson et al. Mr. Adegbile, Elise C. Boddie, Ryan P. Haygood, Dale E. Ho, Natasha M. Korgaonkar, Leah C. Aden, Joshua Civin, Samuel Spital, William J Honan, Harold Barry Vasios, Marisa Marinelli, and Robert J. Burns filed a brief for appellee-intervenor Earl Cunningham et al. Jon M. Greenbaum, Mark A. Posner, Maura Eileen O'Connor, and John M. Nonna filed a brief for appellee-intervenor Bobby Lee Harris.

Opposing Side (Petitioner / Appellant): Bert W Rein argued the cause for appellant. With him on the briefs were William S. Consovoy, Thomas R. McCarthy, Brendan J. Morrissey, and Frank C. Ellis, Jr.

III. AMICI CURIAE

ACLU Side (Respondent / Appellee)

Brief of amici curiae filed on behalf of the State of New York et al. by Eric T. Schneiderman, Attorney General of New York, Barbara D. Underwood, Solicitor General, and Cecelia C. Chang, Deputy Solicitor General, and by the Attorneys General for their respective States as follows: Kamala D. Harris of California, Jim Hood of Mississippi, and Roy Cooper of North Carolina.

Brief of amici curiae filed on behalf of the City of New York et al. by Michael A. Cardozo and Leonard J. Koerner.

Brief of amici curiae filed on behalf of the Alabama Legislative Black Caucus et al. by James U. Blacksher.

Brief of amici curiae filed on behalf of the American Bar Association by Laurel G. Bellows and Jessica L. Ellsworth.

Brief of amici curiae filed on behalf of Asian American Public Interest Groups by Monte Cooper.

Brief of amici curiae filed on behalf of the Brennan Center for Justice at NYU School of Law by Paul M. Smith, Michael B. DeSanctis, Jessica Ring Amunson, Wendy Weiser, and Sidney S. Rosdeitcher.

Brief of amici curiae filed on behalf of Constitutional Law Scholars et al. by Douglas T. Kendall, Elizabeth B. Wydra, and David H. Gans.

Brief of amici curiae filed on behalf of Historians et al. by Derek T. Ho and David L. Schwarz.

Brief of amici curiae filed on behalf of Jurisdictions That Have Bailed Out by J. Gerald Hebert, Paul S. Ryan, and Tara Malloy.

Brief of amici curiae filed on behalf of the Leadership Conference on Civil and Human Rights et al. by Matthew M. Hoffman, Lisa M. Bornstein, Stephen J. Pollak, John Townsend Rich, and Sirisha V. Kalicheti.

Brief of amici curiae filed on behalf of National Latino Organizations by Mark E. Haddad, Juan Cartagena, Carter G. Phillips, Thomas A. Saenz, and Nina Perales.

Brief of amici curiae filed on behalf of the National Lawyers Guild by David Gespass.

Brief of amici curiae filed on behalf of the Navajo Nation et al. by Judith M. Dworkin and Patricia A. Ferguson-Bohnee.

Brief of amici curiae filed on behalf of Political Science and Law Professors by Anita Earls and Allison Riggs.

Brief of amici curiae filed on behalf of Section 5 Litigation Intervenors by Michael B. de Leeuw, Ezra D. Rosenberg, Gary Bledsoe, Jose Garza, David Honig, Robert S. Notzon, and Luis R. Vera, Jr.

Brief of amici curiae filed on behalf of Joaquin Avila et al. by Kieran P Ringgenberg and Perry M. Grossman.

Brief of amici curiae filed on behalf of Patricia A. Broussard et al. by Ms. Broussard, pro se.

Brief of amici curiae filed on behalf of Gabriel Chin et al. by Jeffrey T Green, Robert N Hochman, and Sarah O'Rourke Schrup.

Brief of amici curiae filed on behalf of Richard L. Engstrom et al. by Peter Buscemi.

Brief of amici curiae filed on behalf of Marcia L. Fudge et al. by Danielle Spinelli and Danielle Conley.

Brief of amici curiae filed on behalf of Senator C. Bradley Hutto et al. by Garrard R. Beeney, Michael A. Cooper, and Peter A. Steciuk.

Brief of amici curiae filed on behalf of Ellen D. Katz et al. by Lisa S. Blatt, Charles G. Curtis, Jr., and Anthony J. Franze.

Brief of amici curiae filed on behalf of Congressman John Lewis by Deborah N. Archer and Aderson B. Frangois.

Brief of amici curiae filed on behalf of Representative F. James Sensenbrenner, Jr., et al. by Pamela S. Karlan, Jeffrey L. Fisher, and Kevin K. Russell.

Brief of amici curiae filed on behalf of Dick Thornburgh et al. by Douglas Hallward-Driemeier and Elizabeth N. Dewar.

Brief of amici curiae filed on behalf of the Alaska Federation of Natives et al. by James T. Tucker and Natalie A. Landreth.

Brief of amici curiae filed on behalf of the National Bar Association by Jonathan M. Cohen, Mark A. Packman, and John Page.

Brief of amici curiae filed on behalf of Veterans of the Mississippi Civil Rights Movement by Mr. Frangois and Peggy Cooper Davis.

Opposing Side (Petitioner / Appellant)

Brief of amici curiae filed on behalf of the State of Alabama by Luther Strange, Attorney General, John C. Neiman, Jr., Solicitor General, Andrew L. Brasher, Deputy Solicitor General, and Kasdin E. Miller, Assistant Solicitor General.

Brief of amici curiae filed on behalf of the State of Alaska by Michael C Geraghty, Attorney General, Margaret Paton Walsh, Joanne M. Grace, and Ruth Botstein.

Brief of amici curiae filed on behalf of the State of Arizona et al. by Thomas C. Horne, Attorney General of Arizona, David R. Cole, Solicitor General, and Michele L. Forney, Assistant Attorney General, and by the Attorneys General for their respective States as follows: Sam Olens of Georgia, Alan Wilson of South Carolina, and Marty J. Jackley of South Dakota.

Brief of amici curiae filed on behalf of the State of Texas by Greg Abbott, Attorney General, Jonathan F. Mitchell, Solicitor General, Daniel T. Hodge, First Assistant Attorney General, Andrew S. Oldham, Deputy Solicitor General, and Matthew H. Frederick, Assistant Solicitor General.

Brief of amici curiae filed on behalf of the Abraham Lincoln Foundation for Public Policy Research, Inc., et al. by Herbert W. Titus, William J. Olson, John S. Miles, Jeremiah L. Morgan, and Gary G. Kreep.

Brief of amici curiae filed on behalf of the American Unity Legal Defense Fund by John J. Park, Jr., and Frank B. Strickland.

Brief of amici curiae filed on behalf of the Center for Constitutional Jurisprudence by Christian J. Ward, Scott A. Keller, April Farris, John C. Eastman, and Anthony T. Caso.

Brief of amici curiae filed on behalf of the Justice and Freedom Fund by James L. Hirsen and Deborah J. Dewart.

Brief of amici curiae filed on behalf of the National Black Chamber of Commerce by David B. Rivkin, Jr., Andrew M. Grossman, and Lee A. Casey.

Brief of amici curiae filed on behalf of Project 21 by Erik S. Jaffe.

Brief of amici curiae filed on behalf of the Reason Foundation by Douglas R. Cox, Tyler R. Green, and Manuel S. Klausner.

Brief of amici curiae filed on behalf of the Southeastern Legal Foundation by Aaron M. Streett and Shannon Lee Goessling.

Brief of amici curiae filed on behalf of John Nix et al. by Michael A. Carvin, Hashim M. Mooppan, and Michael E. Rosman.

Brief of amici curiae filed on behalf of the Cato Institute by Ilya Shapiro.

Brief of amici curiae filed on behalf of the Judicial Education Project by Richard K. Willard, Shannen W Coffin, and Carrie Severino.

Brief of amici curiae filed on behalf of the Landmark Legal Foundation by Richard P. Hutchison.

Brief of amici curiae filed on behalf of the Mountain States Legal Foundation by Steven J. Lechner.

Brief of amici curiae filed on behalf of the Pacific Legal Foundation et al. by Meriem L. Hubbard, Deborah J. La Fetra, Joshua P. Thompson, and Ralph W. Kasarda.

Brief of amici curiae filed on behalf of Former Government Officials by Jeffrey M. Harris and Mario Loyola.

Brief of amici curiae filed on behalf of Senate Majority Leader Harry M. Reid by Marc E. Elias, John M. Devaney, and Noah Guzzo Purcell.

Brief of amici curiae filed on behalf of Merced County, California, by James N. Fincher, Marguerite Mary Leoni, and Christopher E. Skinnell in support of neither party.

IV. THE SUPREME COURT'S DECISION

"In Northwest Austin, we stated that 'the Act imposes current burdens and must be justified by current needs.' And we concluded that 'a departure from the fundamental principle of equal sovereignty requires a showing that a statute's disparate geographic coverage is sufficiently related to the problem that it targets.' These basic principles guide our review of the question before us. . . .

Outside the strictures of the Supremacy Clause, States retain broad autonomy . . . .

Not only do States retain sovereignty under the Constitution, there is also a 'fundamental principle of equal sovereignty' among the States. . . .

The Voting Rights Act sharply departs from these basic principles. It suspends 'all changes to state election law—however innocuous—until they have been precleared by federal authorities . . . .' . . .

And despite the tradition of equal sovereignty, the Act applies to only nine States (and several additional counties). . . .

In 1966, we found these departures from the basic features of our system of government justified. . . .

Nearly 50 years later, things have changed dramatically. . . .

There is no doubt that these improvements are in large part

because of the Voting Rights Act. . . .

Yet the Act has not eased the restrictions in § 5 or narrowed the scope of . . . § 4(b) along the way. . . .

The provisions of § 5 apply only to those jurisdictions singled out by § 4. We now consider whether that coverage formula is constitutional in light of current conditions. . . .

Coverage today is based on decades-old data and eradicated practices. . . .

There is no valid reason to insulate the coverage formula from review merely because it was previously enacted 40 years ago. . . .

Striking down an Act of Congress 'is the gravest and most delicate duty that this Court is called on to perform.' We do not do so lightly. That is why, in 2009, we took care to avoid ruling on the constitutionality of the Voting Rights Act . . . . Congress could have updated the coverage formula at that time, but did not do so. Its failure to act leaves us today with no choice but to declare § 4(b) unconstitutional. The formula in that section can no longer be used as a basis for subjecting jurisdictions to preclearance.

Our decision in no way affects the permanent, nationwide ban on racial discrimination in voting found in § 2. We issue no holding on § 5 itself, only on the coverage formula. Congress may draft another formula based on current conditions. . . .

The judgment of the Court of Appeals is reversed."

V. JUSTICE VOTE

4 Pro ACLU Side vs. 5 Con Opposing Side

ACLU Side (Respondent / Appellee)

1. Kagan, E. – Joined Ginsburg's dissent
2. Breyer, S. – Joined Ginsburg's dissent
3. Ginsburg, R. – Wrote dissenting opinion
4. Sotomayor, S. – Joined Ginsburg's dissent

Opposing Side (Petitioner / Appellant)

1. Roberts, J. – Wrote majority opinion
2. Alito, S. – Joined majority opinion
3. Thomas, C. – Wrote concurring opinion
4. Scalia, A. – Joined majority opinion
5. Kennedy, A. – Joined majority opinion

VI. A WIN OR LOSS FOR THE ACLU?

The ACLU served as counsel for appellees urging affirmance; the Supreme Court reversed the Court of Appeals' decision by a 5-4 vote, giving the ACLU an apparent loss.

1115. Adoptive Couple v. Baby Girl

(Decided June 25, 2013; 570 U.S. 637)

I. ISSUE

A. Issues Discussed

Federal, civil rights

B. Legal Question Presented

Whether 25 U.S.C. § 1912(f) and § 1912(d) apply where a Cherokee Indian parent abandoned and never had custody of a Cherokee Indian child.

C. Supreme Court's Answer

"[W]e hold that 25 U.S.C. § 1912(f)—which bars involuntary termination of a parent's rights in the absence of a heightened showing that serious harm to the Indian child is likely to result from the parent's 'continued custody' of the child—does not apply when, as here, the relevant parent never had custody of the child. We further hold that § 1912(d)—which conditions involuntary termination of parental rights with respect to an Indian child on a showing that remedial efforts have been made to prevent the 'breakup of the Indian family'—is inapplicable when, as here, the parent abandoned the Indian child before birth and never had custody of the child."

II. CASE SUMMARY

A. Background

"Birth Mother (who is . . . Hispanic) and Biological Father (who is a member of the Cherokee Nation) became engaged . . . . The couple's relationship deteriorated . . . . Birth Mother sent Biological Father a text message asking if he would rather pay child support or relinquish his parental rights. Biological Father responded via text message that he relinquished his rights.

Birth Mother . . . put Baby Girl up for adoption. Because Birth Mother believed that Biological Father had Cherokee Indian heritage, her attorney contacted the Cherokee Nation to determine whether Biological Father was formally enrolled. The inquiry letter misspelled Biological Father's first name and incorrectly stated his birthday, and the Cherokee Nation responded that . . . it could not verify Biological Father's membership . . . .

Birth Mother selected Adoptive Couple, non-Indians . . . , to adopt Baby Girl. . . .

Approximately four months after Baby Girl's birth, Adoptive Couple served Biological Father with notice of the pending adoption. . . .

Biological Father sought custody and stated that he did not consent to . . . adoption. . . .

A trial took place in the South Carolina Family Court in September 2011 . . . . The Family Court concluded that Adoptive Couple had not carried the heightened burden under § 1912(f) of proving that Baby Girl would suffer serious emotional or physical damage if Biological Father had custody. The Family Court therefore denied Adoptive Couple's petition for adoption and awarded custody to Biological Father. On December 31, 2011, at the age of 27 months, Baby Girl was handed over to Biological Father, whom she had never met.

The South Carolina Supreme Court affirmed the Family Court's denial of the adoption and the award of custody to Biological Father."

The Supreme Court granted certiorari to review the case.

B. Counsel of Record / ACLU Attorney

ACLU Side (Respondent / Appellee): Paul D. Clement argued the cause for appellees Guardian ad Litem. With him on the briefs were Kelsi Brown Corkran and Thomas P. Lowndes.

Charles A. Rothfeld argued the cause for appellee Birth Father et al. With him on the brief for Birth Father were Andrew J. Pincus, Paul W Hughes, Michael B. Kimberly, Jeffrey A. Meyer, and John S. Nichols.

Todd Hembree, Chrissi Ross Nimmo, Lloyd B. Miller, William R. Perry, Anne D. Noto, Colin Cloud Hampson, and Carter G. Phillips filed a brief for appellee Cherokee Nation.

Deputy Solicitor General Kneedler argued the cause for the United States as amicus curiae.

Opposing Side (Petitioner / Appellant): Lisa S. Blatt argued the cause for appellants. With her on the briefs were Christopher S. Rhee, R. Reeves Anderson, Bob Wood, and Mark Fiddler.

III. AMICI CURIAE

ACLU Side (Respondent / Appellee)

Brief of amici curiae filed on behalf of the American Civil Liberties Union and the ACLU of South Carolina by Stephen L. Pevar, Steven R. Shapiro, Barbara A. Atwood, and Susan Dunn.

Brief of amici curiae filed on behalf of Deputy Solicitor General Kneedler, Solicitor General Verrilli, Assistant Attorney General Moreno, Deputy Assistant Attorney General Shenkman, Joseph R. Palmore, Amber Blaha, and Hilary C. Tompkins.

Brief of amici curiae filed on behalf of the State of Arizona et al. by Thomas C. Horne, Attorney General of Arizona, Dawn R. Williams, Assistant Attorney General, and Paula S. Bickett and Michael F Valenzuela, Assistant Attorneys General, and by the Attorneys General for their respective States as follows: Michael C. Geraghty of Alaska, Kamala D. Harris of California, John W Suthers of Colorado, George Jepsen of Connecticut, Samuel S. Olens of Georgia, Lawrence G. Wasden of Idaho, Lisa Madigan of Illinois, Janet T Mills of Maine, Bill Schuette of Michigan, Jim Hood of Mississippi, Timothy C. Fox of Montana, Gary K. King of New Mexico, Eric T Schneiderman of New York, Wayne Stenehjem of North Dakota, Ellen F Rosenblum of Oregon, Robert W Ferguson of Washington, and J B. Van Hollen of Wisconsin.

Brief of amici curiae filed on behalf of Adult Pre-ICWA Indian Adoptees by Edward C. DuMont and Alan E. Schoenfeld.

Brief of amici curiae filed on behalf of the Association of American Indian Affairs et al. by Jack F Trope.

Brief of amici curiae filed on behalf of Casey Family Programs et al. by Patricia A. Millett, Hyland Hunt, Martin Guggenheim, Alexandra Kim McKay, Diane L. Redleaf, Matthew D. Slater, and Faith R. Roessel.

Brief of amici curiae filed on behalf of Current and Former Members of Congress by Kathleen M. Sullivan.

Brief of amici curiae filed on behalf of Family Law Professors by Vernle C. Durocher, Jr.

Brief of amici curiae filed on behalf of the Friends Committee on National Legislation et al. by Philip M. Baker-Shenk.

Brief of amici curiae filed on behalf of Hamline University School of Law Child Advocacy Clinic by Mary Jo Brooks Hunter.

Brief of amici curiae filed on behalf of the Inter Tribal Council of Arizona et al. by Joe P Sparks, Samuel F Daughety, and Amanda Sampson Lomayesva.

Brief of amici curiae filed on behalf of the Lower Sioux Indian Community et al. by Jennifer Yatskis Dukart, Bruce Jones, Richard A. Duncan, Joseph Halloran, Jessica Intermill, Andrew Small, and Dennis Peterson.

Brief of amici curiae filed on behalf of the National Latina/o Psychological Association et al. by David M. Gische.

Brief of amici curiae filed on behalf of the National Native American Bar Association by Robert N. Clinton and Patricia Ferguson-Bohnee.

Brief of amici curiae filed on behalf of the Navajo Nation by Marcelino R. Gomez and K. Andrew Fitzgerald.

Brief of amici curiae filed on behalf of the Oklahoma Indian Child Welfare Association by Kelly Gaines Stoner.

Brief of amici curiae filed on behalf of Professors of Indian Law by Stuart Banner and Angela Riley.

Brief of amici curiae filed on behalf of the Seminole Nation of Oklahoma by Eugene K. Bertman and Jennifer Henshaw McBee.

Brief of amici curiae filed on behalf of the Seminole Tribe of Florida et al. by Jerry C. Straus, Geoffrey D. Strommer, Gregory A Smith, and Joseph H. Webster.

Brief of amici curiae filed on behalf of the Tanana Chiefs Conference, Inc., et al. by Heather Kendall, Paul M. Smith, Thomas J Perrelli, and Jessica Ring Amunson.

Brief of amici curiae filed on behalf of Wisconsin Tribes by Colette Routel, Sheila Corbine, Howard J Bichler, Kris M. Goodwill, and Robert W Orcutt.

Brief of amici curiae filed on behalf of the Minnesota Department of Human Services et al. by Scott H. Ikeda.

Brief of amici curiae filed on behalf of 63 California Indian Tribes by Dorothy Alther, Mark Radoff Delia Parr, and Maureen H. Geary.

Brief of amici curiae filed on behalf of Abby Abinanti by Ms. Abinanti, pro se.

Opposing Side (Petitioner / Appellant)

Brief of amici curiae filed on behalf of the Adoptive Parents Committee, Inc., by Frederick J Magovern.

Brief of amici curiae filed on behalf of the American Academy of Adoption Attorneys by Philip J McCarthy, Jr., and Mary Beck.

Brief of amici curiae filed on behalf of Birth Mother by Gregory G. Garre and Lori Alvino McGill.

Brief of amici curiae filed on behalf of Child Advocacy Organizations by Theane Evangelis Kapur, Joshua S. Lipshutz, and Barbara B. Woodhouse.

Brief of amici curiae filed on behalf of the Christian Alliance for Indian Child Welfare by Jon Metropoulos.

Brief of amici curiae filed on behalf of the Citizens Equal Rights Foundation by James J Devine, Jr.

Brief of amici curiae filed on behalf of the National Council for Adoption by John Jerabek.

Brief of amici curiae filed on behalf of Joan Heifetz Hollinger et al. by Mark W Mosier.

Brief of amici curiae filed on behalf of Bonnie Hofer et al. by Randall Tietjen and Thomas L. Hamlin.

IV. THE SUPREME COURT'S DECISION

"It is undisputed that, had Baby Girl not been 3/256 Cherokee, Biological Father would have had no right to object to her adoption under South Carolina law. . . . [W]e hold that neither § 1912(f) nor § 1912(d) bars the termination of his parental rights. . . .

Section 1912(f) conditions the involuntary termination of parental rights on a showing regarding the merits of 'continued custody of the child by the parent.' (Emphasis added.) . . . As a result, § 1912(f) does not apply in cases where the Indian parent never had custody of the Indian child. . . .

Our reading of § 1912(f) comports with the statutory text demonstrating that the primary mischief the ICWA was designed to counteract was the unwarranted removal of Indian children from Indian families due to the cultural insensitivity and biases of social workers and state courts. . . . In sum, when, as here, the adoption of an Indian child is voluntarily and lawfully initiated by a non-Indian parent with sole custodial rights, the ICWA's primary goal of preventing the unwarranted removal of Indian children and the dissolution of Indian families is not implicated. . . .

In sum, the South Carolina Supreme Court erred in finding that § 1912(f) barred termination of Biological Father's parental rights. . . .

Section 1912(d) provides that '[a]ny party' seeking to terminate parental rights to an Indian child under state law 'shall satisfy the court that active efforts have been made to provide remedial services and rehabilitative programs designed to prevent the breakup of the Indian family and that these efforts have proved unsuccessful.' (Emphasis added.) . . .

Consistent with the statutory text, we hold that § 1912(d) applies only in cases where an Indian family's 'breakup' would be precipitated by the termination of the parent's rights. . . . But when an Indian parent abandons an Indian child prior to birth . . . there is no 'relationship' that would be 'discontinu[ed]'—and no 'effective entity' that would be 'end[ed]'—by the termination of the Indian parent's rights. In such a situation, the 'breakup of the Indian family' has long since occurred, and § 1912(d) is inapplicable. . . .

We therefore reverse the judgment of the South Carolina Supreme Court and remand . . . ."

V. JUSTICE VOTE

4 Pro ACLU Side vs. 5 Con Opposing Side

ACLU Side (Respondent / Appellee)

1. Kagan, E. – Joined Sotomayor's dissent
2. Scalia, A. – Wrote dissenting opinion, joined Sotomayor's dissent in part
3. Ginsburg, R. – Joined Sotomayor's dissent
4. Sotomayor, S. – Wrote dissenting opinion

Opposing Side (Petitioner / Appellant)

1. Alito, S. – Wrote majority opinion
2. Thomas, C. – Wrote concurring opinion
3. Breyer, S. – Wrote concurring opinion
4. Kennedy, A. – Joined majority opinion
5. Roberts, J. – Joined majority opinion

VI. A WIN OR LOSS FOR THE ACLU?

The ACLU filed as amicus curiae urging affirmance; the Supreme Court reversed the South Carolina Supreme Court's decision by a 5-4 vote, giving the ACLU an apparent loss.

1116. Hollingsworth v. Perry

(Decided June 26, 2013; 570 U.S. 693)

I. ISSUE

A. Issues Discussed

Civil rights, state

B. Legal Question Presented

"In this case, petitioners, who oppose same-sex marriage, ask us to decide whether the Equal Protection Clause 'prohibits the State of California from defining marriage as the union of a man and a woman.'"

C. Supreme Court's Answer

"Because we find that petitioners do not have standing, we have no authority to decide this case on the merits, and neither did the Ninth Circuit."

II. CASE SUMMARY

A. Background

"In 2008, . . . California voters passed the ballot initiative at the center of this dispute, known as Proposition 8. That proposition amended the California Constitution to provide that '[o] nly marriage between a man and a woman is valid or recognized in California.' Shortly thereafter, the California Supreme Court rejected a procedural challenge to the amendment, and held that the Proposition was properly enacted under California law. . . .

Respondents, two same-sex couples who wish to marry, filed suit in federal court, challenging Proposition 8 . . . . [O]fficials refused to defend the law . . . . The District Court allowed petitioners—the official proponents of the initiative—to intervene to defend it. After a 12-day bench trial, the District Court declared Proposition 8 unconstitutional . . . .

[O]fficials elected not to appeal the District Court order. When petitioners did, the Ninth Circuit asked them to address 'why this appeal should not be dismissed for lack of Article III standing.' [T]he Ninth Circuit certified a question to the California Supreme Court . . . .

The California Supreme Court agreed to decide the certified question, and answered in the affirmative. . . .

Relying on that answer, the Ninth Circuit concluded that petitioners had standing under federal law to defend the constitutionality of Proposition 8. . . .

On the merits, the Ninth Circuit affirmed [and] held the Proposition unconstitutional . . . .

[The U.S. Supreme Court] granted certiorari to review that determination, and directed that the parties also brief and argue

'Whether petitioners have standing under Article III, § 2, of the Constitution . . . .'"

B. Counsel of Record / ACLU Attorney

ACLU Side (Respondent / Appellee): Theodore B. Olson argued the cause for appellees. With him on the brief for appellee Perry et al. were Matthew D. McGill, Amir C. Tayrani, Jeremy M. Goldman, David Boies, Theodore J. Boutrous, Jr., Christopher D. Dusseault, Theane Evangelis Kapur, Enrique A. Monagas, and Joshua S. Lipshutz. Dennis J. Herrera, Therese M. Stewart, Christine Van Aken, Vince Chhabria, and Mollie M. Lee filed a brief for appellee City and County of San Francisco.

Solicitor General Verrilli argued the cause for the United States as amicus curiae.

Opposing Side (Petitioner / Appellant): Charles J Cooper argued the cause for appellants. With him on the briefs were David H. Thompson, Howard C. Nielson, Jr., Peter A. Patterson, Andrew R Pugno, David Austin R. Nimocks, and James A. Campbell.

III. AMICI CURIAE

ACLU Side (Respondent / Appellee)

Brief of amici curiae filed on behalf of the Leadership Conference on Civil and Human Rights, Bar Associations and Public Interest and Legal Service Organizations, including the following organizations: the Leadership Conference on Civil and Human Rights, 9to5, American Association of University Women, American Civil Liberties Union, API Equality-Northern California, Asian American Institute, Asian American Justice Center, Asian & Pacific Islander American Health Forum, the Asian Law Caucus, the Boston Bar Association, the Center for American Progress, the Charles Houston Bar Association, Chinese for Affirmative Action, the Connecticut Women's Education and Legal Fund, the Courage Campaign, Empire Justice Center, Empire State Pride Agenda, Equal Rights Washington, EqualityMaine, Equality Maryland, Hispanic National Bar Association, Human Rights Campaign, Japanese American Citizens League, League of United Latin American Citizens, Legal Aid Society, the Lesbian, Gay, Bisexual & Transgender Community Center in New York City, LGBT Bar Association of Greater New York, Massachusetts LGBTQ Bar Association, MassEquality, Mattachine Society of Washington, D.C., Mexican American Legal Defense and Educational Fund, National Association for the Advancement of Colored People, NAACP Legal Defense and Educational Fund, National Action Network, National Black Justice Coalition, National Council of La Raza, National Gay and Lesbian Task Force Foundation, National LGBT Bar Association, National Organization for Women Foundation, New York Legal Assistance Group, New York State Bar Association, OCA - Asian Pacific American Advocates, One Iowa, Out & Equal Workplace Advocates, Permanent Commission on the Status of Women, Public Advocates Inc., Rainbow PUSH Coalition, Secular Woman, South Asian Bar Association of Connecticut, Vermont Freedom to Marry Task Force, and the Women's Bar Association of the State of New York by Anne M. Rodgers, Lauren Miller Etlinger, Travis A. Torrence, Tara Tune, Eliot Fielding Turner, Jamie Whitney, Geraldine W. Young, Jonathan S. Franklin, and Lisa Bornstein.

Brief of amici curiae filed on behalf of the United States by Solicitor General Verrilli. Principal Deputy Assistant Attorney General Delery, Deputy Solicitor General Srinivasan, Pratik A. Shah, Michael Jay Singer, and Jeffrey E. Sandberg.

Brief of amici curiae filed on behalf of the State of California by Kamala D. Harris, Attorney General, Daniel J. Powell, Deputy Attorney General, Rochelle C. East, Chief Deputy Attorney General, Kathleen A. Kenealy, Chief Assistant Attorney General, and Tamar Pachter, Supervising Deputy Attorney General.

Brief of amici curiae filed on behalf of the Commonwealth of Massachusetts et al. by Martha Coakley, Attorney General of Massachusetts, and Jonathan B. Miller, Maura T. Healey, Gabrielle Viator, and Genevieve C. Nadeau, Assistant Attorneys General, and by the Attorneys General for their respective jurisdictions as follows: George Jepsen of Connecticut, Joseph R. Biden III of Delaware, Irvin B. Nathan of the District of Columbia, Lisa Madigan of Illinois, Tom Miller of Iowa, Janet T. Mills of Maine, Douglas F. Gansler of Maryland, Michael A. Delaney of New Hampshire, Gary K. King of New Mexico, Eric T. Schneiderman of New York, Ellen F. Rosenblum of Oregon, William H. Sorrell of Vermont, and Robert W. Ferguson of Washington.

Brief of amici curiae filed on behalf of Adoption and Child Welfare Advocates by Michael F. Sturley and Lynn E. Blais.

Brief of amici curiae filed on behalf of the American Anthropological Association et al. by Sonya D. Winner.

Brief of amici curiae filed on behalf of American Companies by E. Joshua Rosenkranz, Karen G. Johnson-McKewan, Andrew D. Silverman, Michael K. Gottlieb, and Andrew G. Celli, Jr.

Brief of amici curiae filed on behalf of the American Federation of Labor and Congress of Industrial Organizations et al. by Nicole G. Berner, Patrick J. Szymanski, and Lynn K. Rhinehart.

Brief of amici curiae filed on behalf of the American Humanist Association et al. by Elizabeth L. Hileman.

Brief of amici curiae filed on behalf of the American Jewish Committee by Douglas Laycock, Marc D. Stern, and Thomas C. Berg.

Brief of amici curiae filed on behalf of the American Psychological Association et al. by Paul M. Smith, Nathalie F. P. Gilfoyle, and William F. Sheehan.

Brief of amici curiae filed on behalf of the American Sociological Association by Carmine D. Boccuzzi, Jr., and Scott Thompson.

Brief of amici curiae filed on behalf of the Anti-Defamation League et al. by Christopher T. Handman, Dominic F. Perella, and Steven M. Freeman.

Brief of amici curiae filed on behalf of the Beverly Hills Bar Association et al. by Irving H. Greines and Cynthia E. Tobisman.

Brief of amici curiae filed on behalf of the Bishops of the Episcopal Church in the State of California et al. by Jeffrey S. Trachtman, Norman C. Simon, Joshua D. Glick, and Jason M. Moff.

Brief of amici curiae filed on behalf of the California Council of Churches et al. by Eric Alan Isaacson and Stacey Marie Kaplan.

Brief of amici curiae filed on behalf of the California Teachers Association et al. by Christopher L. Lebsock and Arthur N. Bailey, Jr.

Brief of amici curiae filed on behalf of the Cato Institute et al. by Robert A. Levy, Ilya Shapiro, Douglas T. Kendall, Elizabeth B. Wydra, David H. Gans, and Judith E. Schaeffer.

Brief of amici curiae filed on behalf of Erwin Chemerinsky et al. by Elizabeth J. Cabraser, Kelly M. Dermody, Brendan P. Glackin, Anne B. Shaver, Alison M. Stocking, Lisa J. Cisneros, and Rachel J. Geman.

Brief of amici curiae filed on behalf of the Family Equality Council et al. by William J. Hibsher, K. Lee Marshall, David Greene, Katherine Keating, and Barbara Bennett Woodhouse.

Brief of amici curiae filed on behalf of Harold Hongju Koh et al. by Ruth N. Borenstein and Marc A. Hearron.

Brief of amici curiae filed on behalf of GLMA: Health Professionals Advancing LGBT Equality by Nicholas M. O'Donnell and Hector Vargas.

Brief of amici curiae filed on behalf of Garden State Equality by Lawrence S. Lustberg.

Brief of amici curiae filed on behalf of International Human Rights Advocates by Tejinder Singh.

Brief of amici curiae filed on behalf of the Lambda Legal Defense and Education Fund, Inc., et al. by Jon W Davidson, Jennifer C. Pizer, Camilla B. Taylor, Gary D. Buseck, Mary L. Bonauto, Hayley Gorenberg, and Susan L. Sommer.

Brief of amici curiae filed on behalf of Marriage Equality USA by Martin N. Buchanan.

Brief of amici curiae filed on behalf of the National Center for Lesbian Rights by Shannon P. Minter and Christopher F. Stoll.

Brief of amici curiae filed on behalf of the National Organization for Women Foundation et al. by Rebecca Edelson and Michael D. Rips.

Brief of amici curiae filed on behalf of the National Women's Law Center et al. by David C. Codell, Marcia D. Greenberger, Emily J. Martin, Barbara B. Brown, Stephen B. Kinnaird, and Jennifer S. Baldocchi.

Brief of amici curiae filed on behalf of Parents, Families and Friends of Lesbians and Gays, Inc., by Andrew J. Davis and Jiyun Cameron Lee.

Brief of amici curiae filed on behalf of the Southern Poverty Law Center by Jon B. Streeter.

Brief of amici curiae filed on behalf of Survivors of Sexual Orientation Change Therapies by Sanford Jay Rosen.

Brief of amici curiae filed on behalf of the Utah Pride Center et al. by Paul C. Burke, John W. Mackay, Brett L. Tolman, Jacquelyn D. Rogers, Mica McKinney, and Adam D. Wentz.

Brief of amici curiae filed on behalf of the Women's Equal Rights Legal Defense and Education Fund by Gloria R. Allred.

Brief of amici curiae filed on behalf of William N. Eskridge, Jr., et al. by Kathleen M. O'Sullivan.

Brief of amici curiae filed on behalf of Gary J. Gates by Marjorie Press Lindblom and Sarah E. Piepmeier.

Brief of amici curiae filed on behalf of Chris Kluwe et al. by John A. Dragseth and Timothy R. Holbrook.

Brief of amici curiae filed on behalf of Kenneth B. Mehlman et al. by Seth R. Waxman, Paul R. Q. Wolfson, Alan E. Schoenfeld, Mark C. Fleming, and Felicia H. Ellsworth.

Brief of amici curiae filed on behalf of Maria Nieto by David A. Kettel.

Brief of amici curiae filed on behalf of California Assembly Speaker John A. Pérez et al. by Laura W. Brill.

Brief of amici curiae filed on behalf of Edward D. Stein et al. by Frederick A. Brodie, Michael J Kass, and Kevin M. Fong.

Brief of amici curiae filed on behalf of Jonathan D. Wallace et al. by Mr. Wallace, pro se.

Brief of amici curiae filed on behalf of the American Academy of Matrimonial Lawyers et al. by Diana E. Richmond, Louis P. Feuchtbaum, and Richard B. Rosenthal.

Brief of amici curiae filed on behalf of Bay Area Lawyers for Individual Freedom et al. by Jerome C. Roth and Michelle T. Friedland.

Brief of amici curiae filed on behalf of California Professors of Family Law by Herma Hill Kay, Joan Heifetz Hollinger, Sean M. SeLegue, and John S. Throckmorton.

Brief of amici curiae filed on behalf of the Columbia Law School Sexuality & Gender Law Clinic et al. by Suzanne B. Goldberg.

Brief of amici curiae filed on behalf of Bruce Ackerman et al. by Lori Alvino McGill and Jessica E. Phillips.

Brief of amici curiae filed on behalf of Equality California by Christopher G. Caldwell and Albert Giang.

Brief of amici curiae filed on behalf of the Howard University School of Law Civil Rights Clinic by Aderson Bellegarde Frangois and Benjamin G. Shatz.

Brief of amici curiae filed on behalf of the Organization of American Historians et al. by Catherine E. Stetson and Mary Helen Wimberly.

Brief of amici curiae filed on behalf of Political Science Professors by Robert A. Long, Jr., and Mark W. Mosier.

Brief of amici curiae filed on behalf of the Honorable Judith S. Kaye (Retired) et al. by Ethan P. Schulman, Scott L. Winkelman, and Chiemi D. Suzuki.

Brief of amici curiae filed on behalf of Rev. Rick Yramategui et al. by William K. Rentz.

Opposing Side (Petitioner / Appellant)

Brief of amici curiae filed on behalf of the State of Indiana et al. by Gregory F. Zoeller, Attorney General of Indiana, and Thomas M. Fisher, Solicitor General, by Kenneth Cuccinelli, Attorney General of Virginia, and E. Duncan Getchell, Solicitor General, and by the Attorneys General for their respective States as follows: Luther Strange of Alabama, Michael C. Geraghty of Alaska, Tom C. Horne of Arizona, John W. Suthers of Colorado, Sam Olens of Georgia, Lawrence G. Wasden of Idaho, Derek Schmidt of Kansas, Timothy C. Fox of Montana, Jon Bruning of Nebraska, Wayne Stenehjem of North Dakota, Scott Pruitt of Oklahoma, Alan Wilson of South Carolina, Marty Jackley of South Dakota, Greg Abbott of Texas, John E. Swallow of Utah, Patrick Morrisey of West Virginia, and J. B. Van Hollen of Wisconsin.

Brief of amici curiae filed on behalf of the State of Michigan by Bill Schuette, Attorney General, John J. Bursch, Solicitor

General, B. Eric Restuccia, Deputy Solicitor General, Aaron D. Lindstrom, Assistant Solicitor General, and Joseph E. Potchen and Tonya C. Jeter, Assistant Attorneys General.

Brief of amici curiae filed on behalf of the American Civil Rights Union by Peter J. Ferrara.

Brief of amici curiae filed on behalf of the Becket Fund for Religious Liberty by Eric Rassbach, Lori Halstead Windham, and Addle Auxier Keim.

Brief of amici curiae filed on behalf of Catholic Answers et al. by Charles S. Limandri, Kimberlee Wood Colby, and Patrick T. Gillen.

Brief of amici curiae filed on behalf of Catholics for the Common Good et al. by Robert A. Destro.

Brief of amici curiae filed on behalf of the Center for Constitutional Jurisprudence by John C. Eastman, Anthony T. Caso, and Edwin Meese III.

Brief of amici curiae filed on behalf of Citizens United et al. by William J. Olson, Michael Boos, Herbert W. Titus, John S. Miles, and Jeremiah L. Morgan.

Brief of amici curiae filed on behalf of the Coalition of African American Pastors USA et al. by Lynn D. Wardle.

Brief of amici curiae filed on behalf of the Eagle Forum Education & Legal Defense Fund, Inc., by Lawrence J. Joseph.

Brief of amici curiae filed on behalf of the Ethics and Public Policy Center by M. Edward Whelan III.

Brief of amici curiae filed on behalf of the Family Research Council by Paul Benjamin Linton, Christopher M. Gacek, and Thomas L. Brejcha, Jr.

Brief of amici curiae filed on behalf of the Foundation for Moral Law by John A. Eidsmoe.

Brief of amici curiae filed on behalf of the High Impact Leadership Coalition by Cleta Mitchell.

Brief of amici curiae filed on behalf of International Jurists et al. by W. Cole Durham, Jr., and Robert Theron Smith.

Brief of amici curiae filed on behalf of Judicial Watch, Inc., et al. by Paul J. Orfanedes, Chris Fedeli, and Julie Axelrod.

Brief of amici curiae filed on behalf of Liberty Counsel, Inc., et al. by Mathew D. Staver, Anita L. Staver, Stephen M. Crampton, Mary E. McAlister, and Rena M. Lindevaldsen.

Brief of amici curiae filed on behalf of the Liberty, Life and Law Foundation et al. by Deborah J. Dewart.

Brief of amici curiae filed on behalf of the Lighted Candle Society by George M. Weaver and John L. Harmer.

Brief of amici curiae filed on behalf of the Marriage Anti-Defamation Alliance by Michael D. Dean.

Brief of amici curiae filed on behalf of Minnesota for Marriage by Teresa Stanton Collett.

Brief of amici curiae filed on behalf of the National Association of Evangelicals et al. by Von G. Keetch, Alexander Dushku, and R. Shawn Gunnarson.

Brief of amici curiae filed on behalf of Parents and Friends of Ex-Gays & Gays by Dean R. Broyles.

Brief of amici curiae filed on behalf of Patrick Henry College by Michael P. Farris and John Warwick Montgomery.

Brief of amici curiae filed on behalf of Scholars of History et al. by William C. Duncan.

Brief of amici curiae filed on behalf of Social Science Professors by Abram J. Pafford.

Brief of amici curiae filed on behalf of Thirty-Seven Scholars of Federalism and Judicial Restraint by Robert F. Nagel, pro se.

Brief of amici curiae filed on behalf of the Thomas More Law Center et al. by Richard Thompson and Robert H. Tyler.

Brief of amici curiae filed on behalf of the United States Conference of Catholic Bishops by Anthony R. Picarello, Jr., Jeffrey Hunter Moon, and Michael F. Moses.

Brief of amici curiae filed on behalf of the Westboro Baptist Church by Margie J. Phelps.

Brief of amici curiae filed on behalf of Helen M. Alvard by Ms. Alvard, pro se.

Brief of amici curiae filed on behalf of David Benkof et al. by Herbert G. Grey.

Brief of amici curiae filed on behalf of David Boyle by Mr. Boyle, pro se.

Brief of amici curiae filed on behalf of Paul McHugh by Gerard V. Bradley.

Brief of amici curiae filed on behalf of Matthew B. O'Brien by Kristen K. Waggoner.

Brief of amici curiae filed on behalf of Robert P. George et al. by Mr. George, pro se.

Brief of amici curiae filed on behalf of Leon R. Kass et al. by Nelson Lund and Kenneth A. Klukowski.

Brief of amici curiae filed on behalf of Daniel N. Robinson by Kevin T. Snider.

Brief of amici curiae filed on behalf of Walter Dellinger by Irving L. Gornstein, Jonathan D. Hacker, and Anton Metlitsky urging vacatur.

Brief of amici curiae filed on behalf of the Pacific Legal Foundation et al. by Meriem L. Hubbard and Harold E. Johnson in support of neither party.

IV. THE SUPREME COURT'S DECISION

"Article III of the Constitution confines the judicial power of federal courts to deciding actual 'Cases' or 'Controversies.' One essential aspect of this requirement is that any person invoking the power of a federal court must demonstrate standing to do so. . . .

Most standing cases consider whether a plaintiff has satisfied the requirement when filing suit, but Article III demands that an 'actual controversy' persist throughout all stages of litigation. . . . We therefore must decide whether petitioners had standing to appeal the District Court's order. . . .

After the District Court declared Proposition 8 unconstitutional . . . the inquiry under Article III changed. Respondents no longer had any injury to redress—they had won—and the state officials chose not to appeal.

The only individuals who sought to appeal that order were petitioners . . . . Here, however, petitioners had no 'direct stake' in the outcome of their appeal. . . .

Without a judicially cognizable interest of their own, petitioners attempt to invoke that of someone else. They assert that even if they have no cognizable interest in appealing the District Court's judgment, the State of California does, and they may assert that interest on the State's behalf. It is, however, a 'fundamental restriction on our authority' that '[i]n the ordinary course, a litigant must assert his or her own legal rights and interests, and cannot rest a claim to relief on the legal rights or interests of third parties.' . . .

We have never before upheld the standing of a private party to defend the constitutionality of a state statute when state officials have chosen not to. We decline to do so for the first time here.

Because petitioners have not satisfied their burden to demonstrate standing to appeal the judgment of the District Court, the Ninth Circuit was without jurisdiction to consider the appeal. The judgment of the Ninth Circuit is vacated, and the case is remanded with instructions to dismiss the appeal for lack of jurisdiction."

V. JUSTICE VOTE

5 Pro ACLU Side vs. 4 Con Opposing Side

ACLU Side (Respondent / Appellee)

1. Roberts, J. – Wrote majority opinion
2. Kagan, E. – Joined majority opinion
3. Breyer, S. – Joined majority opinion
4. Scalia, A. – Joined majority opinion
5. Ginsburg, R. – Joined majority opinion

Opposing Side (Petitioner / Appellant)

1. Alito, S. – Joined Kennedy's dissent
2. Thomas, C. – Joined Kennedy's dissent
3. Kennedy, A. – Wrote dissenting opinion
4. Sotomayor, S. – Joined Kennedy's dissent

VI. A WIN OR LOSS FOR THE ACLU?

The ACLU filed as amicus curiae urging affirmance; the Supreme Court vacated the Court of Appeals' decision by a 5-4 vote, giving the ACLU an apparent win.

1117. U.S. v. Windsor

(Decided June 26, 2013; 570 U.S. 744)

I. ISSUE

A. Issues Discussed

Federal, civil rights

B. Legal Question Presented

Whether § 3 of the Defense of Marriage Act is constitutional.

C. Supreme Court's Answer

"The federal statute is invalid, for no legitimate purpose overcomes the purpose and effect to disparage and to injure those whom the State, by its marriage laws, sought to protect in personhood and dignity. By seeking to displace this protection and treating those persons as living in marriages less respected than others, the federal statute is in violation of the Fifth Amendment."

II. CASE SUMMARY

A. Background

"Two women then resident in New York were married in a lawful ceremony in Ontario, Canada, in 2007. Edith Windsor and Thea Spyer returned to their home in New York City. When Spyer died in 2009, she left her entire estate to Windsor. Windsor sought to claim the estate tax exemption for surviving spouses. She was barred from doing so, however, by a federal law, the Defense of Marriage Act, which excludes a same-sex partner from the definition of 'spouse' as that term is used in federal statutes. Windsor paid the taxes but filed suit to challenge the constitutionality of this provision. The United States District Court and the Court of Appeals ruled that this portion of the statute is unconstitutional and ordered the United States to pay Windsor a refund."

The Supreme Court granted certiorari to review the case.

B. Counsel of Record / ACLU Attorney

ACLU Side (Respondent / Appellee): Roberta A. Kaplan argued the cause for appellee Windsor (merits). With her on the brief were Pamela S. Karlan, Jeffrey L. Fisher, Walter Rieman, Jaren Janghorbani, Colin S. Kelly, Julie E. Fink, Joshua D. Kaye, and James D. Esseks, Joshua A. Block, Leslie Cooper, Rose A. Saxe, and Steven R. Shapiro of the American Civil Liberties Union Foundation, and Arthur Eisenberg and Mariko Hirose of the New York Civil Liberties Union Foundation.

Paul D. Clement argued the cause for appellee Bipartisan Legal Advisory Group of the United States House of Representatives (jurisdiction). With him on the briefs were H. Christopher Bartolomucci, Nicholas J Nelson, Kerry W Kircher, Mary Beth Walker, and Eleni M. Roumel. Roberta A. Kaplan, Walter Rieman, Jaren Janghorbani, Colin S. Kelly, Arthur Eisenberg, Mariko Hirose, Pamela S. Karlan, Jeffrey L. Fisher, James D. Esseks, Joshua A. Block, Leslie Cooper, and Steven R. Shapiro filed briefs for appellee Windsor.

Mr. Clement argued the cause for appellee Bipartisan Legal Advisory Group of the United States House of Representatives (merits). With him on the briefs were Messrs. Bartolomucci, Nelson, Kircher, and Mses. Walker and Roumel.

Solicitor General Verrilli argued the cause for the United States (merits). With him on the brief were Principal Deputy Assistant Attorney General Delery, Deputy Solicitor General Srinivasan, Pratik A. Shah, and Messrs. Singer and Flentje.

Opposing Side (Petitioner / Appellant): Deputy Solicitor General Srinivasan argued the cause for the United States (jurisdiction). With him on the briefs were Solicitor General Verrilli, Principal Deputy Assistant Attorney General Delery, Eric J Feigin, Michael Jay Singer, and August E. Flentje.

Vicki C. Jackson, by appointment of the Court, 568 U. S. 1078, argued the cause as amicus curiae (jurisdiction).

III. AMICI CURIAE

ACLU Side (Respondent / Appellee)

Brief of amici curiae filed on behalf of the Honorable John K. Olson by G. Eric Brunstad, Jr., Collin O'Connor Udell, Matthew J. Delude, Constance Beverley, Alicia M. Farley, and

Amy Thayer.

Brief of amici curiae filed on behalf of 172 Members of the United States House of Representatives et al. by Miriam R. Nemetz, Richard B. Katskee, Michael B. Kimberly, and Heather C. Sawyer.

Brief of amici curiae filed on behalf of the State of New York et al. by Eric T. Schneiderman, Attorney General of New York, Barbara D. Underwood, Solicitor General, Cecelia C. Chang, Deputy Solicitor General, and Andrew W. Amend and Mark H. Shawhan, Assistant Solicitors General, Martha Coakley, Attorney General of Massachusetts, and Maura T. Healey, Jonathan B. Miller, and Joshua D. Jacobson, Assistant Attorneys General, and by the Attorneys General for their respective jurisdictions as follows: Kamala D. Harris of California, George Jepsen of Connecticut, Joseph R. Biden III of Delaware, Irvin B. Nathan of the District of Columbia, Lisa Madigan of Illinois, Thomas J. Miller of Iowa, Janet T. Mills of Maine, Douglas F. Gansler of Maryland, Michael A. Delaney of New Hampshire, Gary K. King of New Mexico, Ellen F. Rosenblum of Oregon, Peter F. Kilmartin of Rhode Island, William H. Sorrell of Vermont, and Robert W. Ferguson of Washington.

Brief of amici curiae filed on behalf of the American Bar Association by Laurel G. Bellows and Travis J. Tu.

Brief of amici curiae filed on behalf of the American Federation of Labor and Congress of Industrial Organizations et al. by Nicole G. Berner, Lynn K. Rhinehart, Patrick J. Szymanski, Alice O'Brien, and Jason Walta.

Brief of amici curiae filed on behalf of the American Humanist Association et al. by Elizabeth L. Hileman.

Brief of amici curiae filed on behalf of the American Jewish Committee by Douglas Laycock, Marc D. Stern, and Thomas C. Berg.

Brief of amici curiae filed on behalf of the American Psychological Association et al. by William F. Sheehan, Paul M. Smith, and Nathalie F. P. Gilfoyle.

Brief of amici curiae filed on behalf of the American Sociological Association by Carmine D. Boccuzzi, Jr.

Brief of amici curiae filed on behalf of the Anti-Defamation League et al. by Douglas Hallward-Driemeier and Steven M. Freeman.

Brief of amici curiae filed on behalf of Bishops of the Episcopal Church et al. by Jeffrey S. Trachtman, Norman C. Simon, Joshua D. Glick, and Jason M. Moff.

Brief of amici curiae filed on behalf of the Cato Institute et al. by Douglas T. Kendall, Elizabeth B. Wydra, David H. Gans, Judith E. Schaeffer, Robert A. Levy, and Ilya Shapiro.

Brief of amici curiae filed on behalf of Citizens for Responsibility and Ethics in Washington by Alan B. Morrison, Anne L. Weismann, and Melanie Sloan.

Brief of amici curiae filed on behalf of Family and Child Welfare Law Professors by H. Rodgin Cohen, Sharon L. Nelles, Garrard R. Beeney, Laura W. Brill, and Joan Heifetz Hollinger, pro se.

Brief of amici curiae filed on behalf of the Family Equality Council et al. by William J. Hibsher, K. Lee Marshall, Katherine Keating, and Barbara Bennett Woodhouse.

Brief of amici curiae filed on behalf of Federalism Scholars by Roy T. Englert, Jr., and Ernest A. Young, pro se.

Brief of amici curiae filed on behalf of Former Federal Election Commission Officials by Trevor Potter, pro se.

Brief of amici curiae filed on behalf of Former Federal Intelligence Officer by James F. Segroves.

Brief of amici curiae filed on behalf of Gay & Lesbian Advocates & Defenders et al. by Gary D. Buseck, Mary L. Bonauto, Susan L. Sommer, Jon W. Davidson, Tara L. Borelli, Paul M. Smith, Luke C. Platzer, and Melissa A. Cox.

Brief of amici curiae filed on behalf of GLMA: Health Professionals Advancing LGBT Equality by Nicholas M. O'Donnell and Hector Vargas.

Brief of amici curiae filed on behalf of Historians et al. by Catherine R. Connors.

Brief of amici curiae filed on behalf of the Institute for Justice by William H. Mellor, Robert J. McNamara, and Paul M. Sherman.

Brief of amici curiae filed on behalf of the Leadership Conference on Civil and Human Rights et al. by Jonathan S. Franklin, Lisa Bornstein, Anne M. Rodgers, Shannon P. Minter, Christopher F. Stoll, and Timothy S. Fisher.

Brief of amici curiae filed on behalf of the NAACP Legal Defense and Educational Fund, Inc., by Elise C. Boddie, Rachel M. Kleinman, Ria Tabacco Mar, and Joshua Civin.

Brief of amici curiae filed on behalf of the National Women's Law Center et al. by David C. Codell, Marcia D. Greenberger, Emily J. Martin, Barbara B. Brown, Stephen B. Kinnaird, and Jennifer S. Baldocchi.

Brief of amici curiae filed on behalf of the Partnership for New York City by Marc Wolinsky and Kevin S. Schwartz.

Brief of amici curiae filed on behalf of Political Science Professors by Robert A. Long, Jr., and Mark W. Mosier.

Brief of amici curiae filed on behalf of Scholars of the Constitutional Rights of Children by J. Robert Brown, Catherine E. Smith, and Kyle C. Velte.

Brief of amici curiae filed on behalf of Services and Advocacy for Gay, Lesbian, Bisexual and Transgender Elders et al. by Joseph F. Tringali and Robert E. Rains.

Brief of amici curiae filed on behalf of Survivors of Sexual Orientation Change Therapies by Sanford Jay Rosen.

Brief of amici curiae filed on behalf of 278 Employers and Organizations Representing Employers by Sabin Willett, Mary T. Huser, Susan Baker Manning, and John A. Polito.

Brief of amici curiae filed on behalf of the Utah Pride Center et al. by Paul C. Burke, John W. Mackay, Brett L. Tolman, Jacquelyn D. Rogers, Mica McKinney, and Adam D. Wentz.

Brief of amici curiae filed on behalf of Bruce Ackerman et al. by Lori Alvino McGill and Jessica E. Phillips.

Brief of amici curiae filed on behalf of Former Senator Bill Bradley et al. by Kevin K. Russell.

Brief of amici curiae filed on behalf of Gary J. Gates by Marjorie Press Lindblom and Sarah E. Piepmeier.

Brief of amici curiae filed on behalf of Nan D. Hunter et al. by Ms. Hunter and Suzanne B. Goldberg, both pro se.

Brief of amici curiae filed on behalf of the Honorable Lawrence J. Korb et al. by Carter G. Phillips and Eamon R. Joyce.

Brief of amici curiae filed on behalf of the Honorable John K. Olson by Messrs. Brunstad, Udell, and Delude, and Mses. Beverley, Farley, and Thayer.
Brief of amici curiae filed on behalf of Donna E. Shalala et al. by Lisa S. Blatt, Christopher S. Rhee, and Ara Beth Gershengorn.
Brief of amici curiae filed on behalf of Citizens United's National Committee for Family, Faith and Prayer et al. by Messrs. Titus, Olson, Miles, Morgan, and Boos.
Brief of amici curiae filed on behalf of Constitutional Jurisprudence by John C. Eastman, Anthony T. Caso, and Edwin Meese III.
Brief of amici curiae filed on behalf of Constitutional Law Scholars by Andrew J. Pincus, Charles A. Rothfeld, and Jeffrey A. Meyer.
Brief of amici curiae filed on behalf of the Empire State Pride Agenda et al. by Peter T. Barbur.
Brief of amici curiae filed on behalf of the Center for Fair Administration of Taxes by A. Lavar Taylor, for Family Law Professors et al. by Walter Dellinger, Dawn Sestito, and Amy R. Lucas.
Brief of amici curiae filed on behalf of Liberty Counsel by Mathew D. Staver, Anita L. Staver, Stephen M. Crampton, and Mary E. McAlister.
Brief of amici curiae filed on behalf of the Los Angeles County Bar Association et al. by Anita Susan Brenner.
Brief of amici curiae filed on behalf of the Organization of American Historians et al. by Catherine E. Stetson and Mary Helen Wimberly.
Brief of amici curiae filed on behalf of OutServe-SLDN Inc. by Abbe David Lowell and Christopher D. Man.

Opposing Side (Petitioner / Appellant)

Brief of amici curiae filed by Vicki C. Jackson, Patricia A. Millett, Ruthanne M. Deutsch, Michael C. Small, and Beth Heifetz.
Brief of amici curiae filed on behalf of the State of Indiana et al. by Gregory F. Zoeller, Attorney General of Indiana, and Thomas M. Fisher, Solicitor General, and by the Attorneys General for their respective States as follows: Luther Strange of Alabama, Michael C. Geraghty of Alaska, Tom C. Horne of Arizona, Sam Olens of Georgia, Lawrence G. Wasden of Idaho, Derek Schmidt of Kansas, Bill Schuette of Michigan, Timothy C. Fox of Montana, Wayne Stenehjem of North Dakota, Scott Pruitt of Oklahoma, Alan Wilson of South Carolina, Greg Abbott of Texas, John E. Swallow of Utah, Kenneth T. Cuccinelli II of Virginia, Patrick Morrisey of West Virginia, and J. B. Van Hollen of Wisconsin.
Brief of amici curiae filed on behalf of the American Civil Rights Union by Peter J. Ferrara.
Brief of amici curiae filed on behalf of the Becket Fund for Religious Liberty by Eric Rassbach, Lori Halstead Windham, and Addle Auxier Keim.
Brief of amici curiae filed on behalf of the Beverly LaHaye Institute et al. by Steven W. Fitschen.
Brief of amici curiae filed on behalf of Catholic Answers et al. by Charles S. Limandri, Kimberlee Wood Colby, and Patrick T. Gillen.
Brief of amici curiae filed on behalf of the Chaplain Alliance for Religious Liberty et al. by R. Bradley Lewis.
Brief of amici curiae filed on behalf of Citizens United's National Committee for Family, Faith and Prayer et al. by Herbert W. Titus, William J. Olson, John S. Miles, Jeremiah L. Morgan, and Michael Boos.
Brief of amici curiae filed on behalf of the Coalition for the Protection of Marriage by Monte Neil Stewart.
Brief of amici curiae filed on behalf of Concerned Women for America by Holly L. Carmichael.
Brief of amici curiae filed on behalf of the Eagle Forum Education & Legal Defense Fund, Inc., by Lawrence J. Joseph.
Brief of amici curiae filed on behalf of the Family Research Council by Paul Benjamin Linton, Thomas Brejcka, and Christopher M. Gacek.
Brief of amici curiae filed on behalf of the Foundation for Moral Law by John A. Eidsmoe.
Brief of amici curiae filed on behalf of International Jurists and Academics by W. Cole Durham, Jr., pro se, and Robert T. Smith.
Brief of amici curiae filed on behalf of Law Professors by Lynn D. Wardle, pro se.
Brief of amici curiae filed on behalf of the Liberty, Life and Law Foundation et al. by Deborah J. Dewart.
Brief of amici curiae filed on behalf of Manhattan Declaration Inc. by John Mauck.
Brief of amici curiae filed on behalf of the National Association of Evangelicals et al. by Von G. Keetch, Alexander Dushku, and R. Shawn Gunnarson.
Brief of amici curiae filed on behalf of the National Organization for Marriage by William C. Duncan.
Brief of amici curiae filed on behalf of Parents and Friends of Ex-Gays & Gays by Dean R. Broyles.
Brief of amici curiae filed on behalf of Social Science Professors by Abram J. Pafford.
Brief of amici curiae filed on behalf of the United States Conference of Catholic Bishops by Anthony R. Picarello, Jr., Jeffrey Hunter Moon, and Michael F. Moses.
Brief of amici curiae filed on behalf of the Westboro Baptist Church by Margie J Phelps.
Brief of amici curiae filed on behalf of Helen M. Alvard by Ms. Alvard, pro se.
Brief of amici curiae filed on behalf of David Boyle by Mr. Boyle, pro se.
Brief of amici curiae filed on behalf of Robert P. George et al. by Mr. George, pro se.
Brief of amici curiae filed on behalf of United States Senator Orrin G. Hatch et al. by Michael L. Stern.
Brief of amici curiae filed on behalf of Paul McHugh by Gerard V. Bradley.
Brief of amici curiae filed on behalf of Matthew B. O'Brien by Kristen K. Waggoner.
Brief of amici curiae filed on behalf of Dovid Z. Schwartz by Mr. Schwartz, pro se.
Brief of amici curiae filed on behalf of Former Senior Justice Department Officials et al. by Paul R. Q. Wolfson, Alan E. Schoenfeld, Mark C. Fleming, and Felicia H. Ellsworth.
Brief of amici curiae filed on behalf of Former Attorney General Edwin Meese III et al. by Jay Alan Sekulow, Stuart J. Roth,

Cecilia Noland-Heil, Laura Hernandez, and Erik Zimmerman in support of neither party.

IV. THE SUPREME COURT'S DECISION

"It is appropriate to begin by addressing whether either the Government or BLAG, or both of them, were entitled to appeal . . . and later to seek certiorari and appear as parties here.

There is no dispute that when this case was in the District Court it presented a concrete disagreement between opposing parties . . . .

In this case the United States retains a stake sufficient to support Article III jurisdiction . . . before this Court. The judgment in question orders the United States to pay Windsor the refund she seeks. An order directing the Treasury to pay money is 'a real and immediate economic injury' . . . .

These circumstances support the Court's decision to proceed to the merits. . . .

Against th[e] background of lawful same-sex marriage in some States, . . . DOMA should be considered as the beginning point in deciding whether it is valid under the Constitution. . . .

DOMA seeks to injure the very class New York seeks to protect. By doing so it violates basic due process and equal protection principles applicable to the Federal Government. . . .

And though Congress has great authority to design laws to fit its own conception of sound national policy, it cannot deny the liberty protected by the Due Process Clause of the Fifth Amendment.

What has been explained . . . should . . . establish that the principal purpose and the necessary effect of this law are to demean those persons who are in a lawful same-sex marriage. This requires the Court to hold, as it now does, that DOMA is unconstitutional as a deprivation of the liberty of the person protected by the Fifth Amendment of the Constitution. . . .

The class to which DOMA directs its restrictions and restraints are those persons who are joined in same-sex marriages made lawful by the State. . . . It imposes a disability on the class by refusing to acknowledge a status the State finds to be dignified and proper. DOMA instructs all federal officials, and indeed all persons with whom same-sex couples interact, including their own children, that their marriage is less worthy than the marriages of others. The federal statute is invalid, for no legitimate purpose overcomes the purpose and effect to disparage and to injure those whom the State, by its marriage laws, sought to protect in personhood and dignity. By seeking to displace this protection and treating those persons as living in marriages less respected than others, the federal statute is in violation of the Fifth Amendment. . . .

The judgment of the Court of Appeals for the Second Circuit is affirmed."

V. JUSTICE VOTE

5 Pro ACLU Side vs. 4 Con Opposing Side

ACLU Side (Respondent / Appellee)

1. Kennedy, A. – Wrote majority opinion
2. Kagan, E. – Joined majority opinion
3. Breyer, S. – Joined majority opinion
4. Ginsburg, R. – Joined majority opinion
5. Sotomayor, S. – Joined majority opinion

Opposing Side (Petitioner / Appellant)

1. Alito, S. – Wrote dissenting opinion
2. Thomas, C. – Joined Scalia's dissent and Alito's dissent in part
3. Scalia, A. – Wrote dissenting opinion
4. Roberts, J. – Wrote dissenting opinion, joined Scalia's dissent in part

VI. A WIN OR LOSS FOR THE ACLU?

The ACLU served as counsel for respondent urging affirmance; the Supreme Court affirmed the Court of Appeals' decision by a 5-4 vote, giving the ACLU an apparent win.

1118. Kansas v. Cheever

(Decided December 11, 2013; 571 U.S. 87)

I. ISSUE

A. Issues Discussed

Criminal procedure, drugs

B. Legal Question Presented

"The question here is whether the Fifth Amendment prohibits the government from introducing evidence from a court-ordered mental evaluation of a criminal defendant to rebut that defendant's presentation of expert testimony in support of a defense of voluntary intoxication."

C. Supreme Court's Answer

"We hold that where a defense expert who has examined the defendant testifies that the defendant lacked the requisite mental state to commit a crime, the prosecution may offer evidence from a court-ordered psychological examination for the limited purpose of rebutting the defendant's evidence."

II. CASE SUMMARY

A. Background

"On the morning of January 19, 2005, Scott Cheever shot and killed . . . law enforcement officers. . . . Cheever and his friends had cooked and smoked methamphetamine . . . .

The State charged Cheever with capital murder. But shortly thereafter . . . the Kansas Supreme Court found the State's death penalty scheme unconstitutional. [S]tate prosecutors dismissed their charges and allowed federal authorities to prosecute Cheever . . . .

In the federal case, Cheever filed notice that he 'intend[ed] to introduce expert evidence relating to his intoxication by methamphetamine . . . . [T]he District Court ordered Cheever to submit to a psychiatric evaluation by Michael Welner, a forensic psychiatrist, to assess how methamphetamine use had affected him when he shot Samuels. . . .

The federal case proceeded to trial. [But the court ultimately] dismissed the case . . . . Meanwhile, this Court . . . held that the

Kansas death penalty statute was constitutional. . . .

Kansas then brought a second state prosecution. . . . Cheever presented a voluntary-intoxication defense . . . .

After the defense rested, the State sought to present rebuttal testimony from Welner . . . . Defense counsel objected, arguing that . . . his testimony would violate the Fifth Amendment proscription against compelling an accused to testify against himself. The State countered that the testimony was necessary to rebut Cheever's voluntary-intoxication defense.

The trial court agreed with the State. . . .

The jury found Cheever guilty of murder and attempted murder. At the penalty phase, it unanimously voted to impose a sentence of death, and the trial court accepted that verdict.

On appeal to the Kansas Supreme Court, . . . vacated Cheever's conviction and sentence . . . ."

The Supreme Court granted certiorari to review the case.

B. Counsel of Record / ACLU Attorney

ACLU Side (Respondent / Appellee): Neal Kumar Katyal argued the cause for appellee. With him on the brief were Dominic F. Perella, Mary Helen Wimberly, and Debra J. Wilson.

Opposing Side (Petitioner / Appellant): Derek Schmidt, Attorney General of Kansas, argued the cause for appellant. With him on the briefs were Stephen R. McAllister, Solicitor General, Kristafer R. Ailslieger, Deputy Solicitor General, and Natalie Chalmers, Assistant Solicitor General.

Nicole A. Saharsky argued the cause for the United States as amicus curiae.

III. AMICI CURIAE

ACLU Side (Respondent / Appellee)

Brief of amici curiae filed on behalf of the American Civil Liberties Union and the American Civil Liberties Union of Kansas and Western Missouri by Catherine M. A. Carroll, Annie L. Owens, and Albinas J. Prizgintas.

Brief of amici curiae filed on behalf of the Judge David L. Bazelon Center for Mental Health Law by Mark D. Harris, Chantel L. Febus, Ira A. Burnim, and Jennifer Mathis.

Brief of amici curiae filed on behalf of the National Association of Criminal Defense Lawyers by Jeffrey T. Green and Barbara E. Bergman.

Opposing Side (Petitioner / Appellant)

Brief of amici curiae filed on behalf of the United States by Nicole A. Saharsky, Solicitor General Verrilli, Acting Assistant Attorney General Raman, Deputy Solicitor General Dreeben, and David M. Lieberman.

Brief of amici curiae filed on behalf of the State of California et al. by Kamala D. Harris, Attorney General of California, John Michael Chamberlain, Deputy Attorney General, Dane R. Gillette, Chief Assistant Attorney General, Donald E. de Nicola, Deputy State Solicitor General, and Gerald A. Engler, Senior Assistant Attorney General, and by the Attorneys General for their respective States as follows: Luther Strange of Alabama, Tom Horne of Arizona, Dustin McDaniel of Arkansas, Joseph R. Biden III of Delaware, Pamela Jo Bondi of Florida, Samuel S. Olens of Georgia, David M. Louie of Hawaii, Jack Conway of Kentucky, Chris Koster of Missouri, Jon Bruning of Nebraska, Catherine Cortez Masto of Nevada, Joseph A. Foster of New Hampshire, Jeffrey S. Chiesa of New Jersey, Gary K. King of New Mexico, Wayne Stenehjem of North Dakota, Michael DeWine of Ohio, E. Scott Pruitt of Oklahoma, Ellen F. Rosenblum of Oregon, Kathleen G. Kane of Pennsylvania, Alan Wilson of South Carolina, Marty J. Jackley of South Dakota, Robert E. Cooper, Jr., of Tennessee, John E. Swallow of Utah, Robert W. Ferguson of Washington, J. B. Van Hollen of Wisconsin, and Gregory A. Phillips of Wyoming.

Brief of amici curiae filed on behalf of the Criminal Justice Legal Foundation by Kent S. Scheidegger.

Brief of amici curiae filed on behalf of the National District Attorneys Association et al. by Albert C. Locher.

IV. THE SUPREME COURT'S DECISION

"The Fifth Amendment guarantees that '[n]o person . . . shall be compelled in any criminal case to be a witness against himself . . . .' We held in Estelle that under the Fifth Amendment, when a criminal defendant 'neither initiates a psychiatric evaluation nor attempts to introduce any psychiatric evidence,' his compelled statements to a psychiatrist cannot be used against him. . . .

In Buchanan, we addressed the admissibility of evidence from a court-ordered evaluation where—unlike in Estelle—a defendant had introduced psychiatric evidence related to his mental-status defense. We held that the Fifth Amendment allowed the prosecution to present evidence from the evaluation to rebut the defendant's affirmative defense of extreme emotional disturbance. . . .

The admission of this rebuttal testimony harmonizes with the principle that when a defendant chooses to testify in a criminal case, the Fifth Amendment does not allow him to refuse to answer related questions on cross-examination. . . .

The prosecution here elicited testimony from its expert only after Cheever offered expert testimony about his inability to form the requisite mens rea. The testimony of the government expert rebutted that of Cheever's expert. . . .

We hold that where a defense expert who has examined the defendant testifies that the defendant lacked the requisite mental state to commit a crime, the prosecution may offer evidence from a court-ordered psychological examination for the limited purpose of rebutting the defendant's evidence.

The judgment of the Kansas Supreme Court is therefore vacated, and the case is remanded . . . ."

V. JUSTICE VOTE

0 Pro ACLU Side vs. 9 Con Opposing Side

Opposing Side (Petitioner / Appellant)

1. Sotomayor, S. – Wrote majority opinion
2. Alito, S. – Joined majority opinion
3. Kagan, E. – Joined majority opinion
4. Thomas, C. – Joined majority opinion
5. Breyer, S. – Joined majority opinion
6. Scalia, A. – Joined majority opinion
7. Kennedy, A. – Joined majority opinion

8. Ginsburg, R. – Joined majority opinion
9. Roberts, J. – Joined majority opinion

VI. A WIN OR LOSS FOR THE ACLU?

The ACLU filed as amicus curiae urging affirmance; the Supreme Court vacated the Kansas Supreme Court's decision by a 9-0 vote, giving the ACLU an apparent loss.

1119. U.S. v. Apel

(Decided February 26, 2014; 571 U.S. 359)

I. ISSUE

A. Issues Discussed

Military

B. Legal Question Presented

"Federal law makes it a crime to reenter a 'military . . . installation' after having been ordered not to do so 'by any officer or person in command.' 18 U.S.C. § 1382. The question presented is whether a portion of an Air Force base that contains a designated protest area and an easement for a public road qualifies as part of a 'military installation.'"

C. Supreme Court's Answer

"Where a place with a defined boundary is under the administration of a military department, the limits of the 'military installation' for purposes of § 1382 are coterminous with the commanding officer's area of responsibility. Those limits do not change when the commander invites the public to use a portion of the base for a road, a school, a bus stop, or a protest area, especially when the commander reserves authority to protect military property by, among other things, excluding vandals and trespassers."

II. CASE SUMMARY

A. Background

"Vandenberg Air Force Base . . . sits on land owned by the United States and administered by the Department of the Air Force. It is the site of sensitive missile and space launch facilities. The commander of Vandenberg has designated it a 'closed base,' meaning that civilians may not enter without express permission. . . .

In the south corner of [an] intersection is an area that has been designated by the Federal Government for peaceful protests. . . .

Apel is an antiwar activist who demonstrates at Vandenberg. In March 2003, Apel trespassed beyond the designated protest area and threw blood on a sign . . . . He was convicted . . . , was sentenced to two months' imprisonment, and was barred from the Base for three years. In May 2007, Apel returned to Vandenberg to protest. When he trespassed again and was convicted, he received another order barring him from Vandenberg, this time permanently . . . .

Apel ignored the commander's order and reentered Vandenberg several times during 2008 and 2009. That led the Base commander to serve Apel with an updated order . . . .

Apel ignored this barment order too, and on three occasions in 2010 he reentered Vandenberg to protest in the designated area. Each time Vandenberg security personnel . . . instructed him to leave. . . . Apel refused. He was cited for violating § 1382 and escorted off Base property.

A Magistrate Judge convicted Apel and ordered him to pay . . . $355 in fines and fees. Apel appealed . . . . The District Court rejected Apel's defense . . . .

The United States Court of Appeals for the Ninth Circuit reversed . . . ."

The Supreme Court granted certiorari to review the case.

B. Counsel of Record / ACLU Attorney

ACLU Side (Respondent / Appellee): Erwin Chemerinsky argued the cause for appellee. With him on the brief were Kathryn M. Davis, Peter R. Afrasiabi, Paul L. Hoffman, Selwyn Chu, Peter J. Eliasberg of the ACLU Foundation of Southern California, and Steven R. Shapiro, Ben Wizner, and Brian M. Hauss of the American Civil Liberties Union Foundation.

Opposing Side (Petitioner / Appellant): Benjamin J Horwich argued the cause for the United States. With him on the briefs were Solicitor General Verrilli, Acting Assistant Attorney General Raman, Deputy Solicitor General Dreeben, and David M. Lieberman.

III. AMICI CURIAE

ACLU Side (Respondent / Appellee)

Brief of amici curiae filed on behalf of the Ground Zero Center for Nonviolent Action by Christine M. Salmi and John R. Tyler.

Brief of amici curiae filed on behalf of the National Association of Criminal Defense Lawyers by Michael V Schafler, Jeffrey L. Fisher, and Albert Giang.

Brief of amici curiae filed on behalf of the Nuclear Age Peace Foundation by Matthew D. Umhofer and Kevin J Minnick.

Brief of amici curiae filed on behalf of the Reporters Committee for Freedom of the Press et al. by Robert CornRevere, Ronald G. London, Bruce D. Brown, Gregg R Leslie, Kelli L. Sager, Richard A. Bernstein, Charles D. Tobin, Mickey H. Osterreicher, Barbara L. Camens, Jonathan D. Hart, Bruce W Sanford, and Laurie A. Babinski.

Brief of amici curiae filed on behalf of The Rutherford Institute by John W Whitehead.

Opposing Side (Petitioner / Appellant)

No briefs of amici curiae were filed in support of appellant.

IV. THE SUPREME COURT'S DECISION

"Apel does not dispute that he was 'found within' the lawful boundaries of Vandenberg . . . after having been 'ordered not to reenter' by the Base commander. § 1382. . . .

Against this straightforward interpretation, Apel insists that § 1382 applies only where the military exercises exclusive possession and control, which, he contends, does not include land subject to a roadway easement. . . .

Apel asserts that the Ninth Circuit's exclusive possession and control requirement 'derives directly from the text of § 1382.' It does not. . . .

Section 1382 is most naturally read to apply to places with a defined boundary under the command of a military officer. Apel argues, however, that Vandenberg's commander has no authority on the highways running through the Base or, apparently, in the designated protest area. His arguments more or less reduce to two contentions: that the highways and protest area lie 'outside the entrance to [a] closed military installation[ ],' and that they are 'uncontrolled' spaces where 'no military operations are performed.' Neither contention is sound. . . .

In sum, we decline Apel's invitation to require civilian judges to examine U.S. military sites . . . to determine which have roads, which have fences, and which have a sufficiently important, persistent military purpose. The use-it-or-lose-it rule . . . would frustrate the administration of military facilities and raise difficult questions for judges . . . . And it would discourage commanders from opening portions of their bases for the convenience of the public. We think a much better reading of § 1382 is that it reaches all property within the defined boundaries of a military place . . . .

Much of the rest of Apel's brief is devoted to arguing that § 1382 would be unconstitutional as applied to him on this Base. But the Court of Appeals never reached Apel's constitutional arguments, and we decline to do so in the first instance. . . .

Where a place with a defined boundary is under the administration of a military department, the limits of the 'military installation' for purposes of § 1382 are coterminous with the commanding officer's area of responsibility. Those limits do not change when the commander invites the public to use a portion of the base for a road, a school, a bus stop, or a protest area, especially when the commander reserves authority to protect military property by . . . excluding vandals and trespassers.

The judgment of the Court of Appeals is vacated, and the case is remanded . . . ."

V. JUSTICE VOTE

0 Pro ACLU Side vs. 9 Con Opposing Side

Opposing Side (Petitioner / Appellant)

1. Roberts, J. – Wrote majority opinion
2. Alito, S. – Wrote concurring opinion
3. Kagan, E. – Joined majority opinion
4. Thomas, C. – Joined majority opinion
5. Breyer, S. – Joined majority opinion
6. Scalia, A. – Joined majority opinion
7. Kennedy, A. – Joined majority opinion
8. Ginsburg, R. – Wrote concurring opinion
9. Sotomayor, S. – Joined Ginsburg's concurrence

VI. A WIN OR LOSS FOR THE ACLU?

The ACLU served as counsel for appellee urging affirmance; the Supreme Court vacated the Court of Appeals' decision by a 9-0 vote, giving the ACLU an apparent loss.

1120. Schuette v. Coalition to Defend Affirmative Action

(Decided April 22, 2014; 572 U.S. 291)

I. ISSUE

A. Issues Discussed

Race

B. Legal Question Presented

"[W]hether, and in what manner, voters in the States may choose to prohibit the consideration of racial preferences in governmental decisions, in particular with respect to school admissions."

C. Supreme Court's Answer

"There is no authority in the Constitution of the United States or in this Court's precedents for the Judiciary to set aside Michigan laws that commit this policy determination to the voters."

II. CASE SUMMARY

A. Background

"In response to the Court's decision in Gratz, the university revised its undergraduate admissions process, but the revision still allowed limited use of race-based preferences. After a statewide debate on the question of racial preferences in the context of governmental decisionmaking, the voters, in 2006, adopted an amendment to the State Constitution prohibiting state and other governmental entities in Michigan from granting certain preferences, including race-based preferences, in a wide range of actions and decisions. Under the terms of the amendment, race-based preferences cannot be part of the admissions process for state universities. That particular prohibition is central to the instant case.

The ballot proposal was called Proposal 2 and, after it passed by a margin of 58 percent to 42 percent, the resulting enactment became Article I, § 26, of the Michigan Constitution. . . .

Section 26 was challenged in two cases. . . . The United States District Court for the Eastern District of Michigan consolidated the cases.

In 2008, the District Court granted summary judgment to Michigan, thus upholding Proposal 2. The District Court denied a motion to reconsider . . . . A panel of the United States Court of Appeals for the Sixth Circuit reversed the grant of summary judgment. . . .

The Court of Appeals, sitting en banc, agreed with the panel decision."

The Supreme Court granted certiorari to review the case.

B. Counsel of Record / ACLU Attorney

ACLU Side (Respondent / Appellee): Mark D. Rosenbaum of the ACLU Foundation of Southern California argued the cause for appellees Cantrell et al. With him on the brief were Laurence H. Tribe, Joshua I. Civin, Karin A. DeMasi, Nicole M. Peles, Erwin Chemerinsky, Sherrilyn Ifill, Damon T. Hewitt, Melvin Butch Hollowell, Jr., Jerome R. Watson, Daniel P. Tokaji, David B. Sapp of the ACLU Foundation of Southern California,

Steven R. Shapiro and Dennis D. Parker of the ACLU Foundation, and Kary L. Moss, Michael J. Steinberg, and Mark P. Fancher of the ACLU Fund of Michigan.

Shanta Driver argued the cause for appellees Coalition to Defend Affirmative Action, Integration and Immigrant Rights and Fight for Equality by Any Means Necessary (BAMN) et al. With her on the brief were George B. Washington, Eileen R. Scheff Winifred Kao, and Doyle G. O'Connor. Stephanie R. Setterington filed a brief for appellees Board of Governors of Wayne State University et al. Leonard M. Niehoff filed a brief for appellees Regents of the University of Michigan et al.

Opposing Side (Petitioner / Appellant): John J Bursch, Solicitor General of Michigan, argued the cause for appellant. With him on the briefs were Bill Schuette, Attorney General, pro se, B. Eric Restuccia, Deputy Solicitor General, and Aaron D. Lindstrom, Assistant Solicitor General. Charles J. Cooper, David H. Thompson, Howard C. Nielson, Jr., Michael E. Rosman, and Alan K. Palmer filed a brief for appelle Russell in support of appellant.

III. AMICI CURIAE

ACLU Side (Respondent / Appellee)

Brief of amici curiae filed on behalf of the State of California et al. by Kamala D. Harris, Attorney General of .California, Antonette Benita Cordero, Deputy Attorney General, Susan Duncan Lee, Acting State Solicitor General, and Mark Breckler, Chief Assistant Attorney General, and by the Attorneys General for their respective jurisdictions as follows: Irvin B. Nathan of the District of Columbia, David M. Louie of Hawaii, Lisa Madigan of Illinois, Thomas J. Miller of Iowa, Gary K. King of New Mexico, and Ellen F. Rosenblum of Oregon.

Brief of amici curiae filed on behalf of the American Council on Education et al. by Martin Michaelson, Ada Meloy, and Alexander E. Dreier.

Brief of amici curiae filed on behalf of the Anti-Defamation League by Howard W. Goldstein, Samuel P. Groner, and Steven M. Freeman.

Brief of amici curiae filed on behalf of the Civil Rights Project/ Proyecto Derechos Civiles by Liliana M. Garces.

Brief of amici curiae filed on behalf of the Committee of Law Professors by Wilson R. Huhn.

Brief of amici curiae filed on behalf of Constitutional and Local Government Law Scholars by Pamela S. Karlan, Jeffrey L. Fisher, and Kevin K. Russell.

Brief of amici curiae filed on behalf of the Leadership Conference on Civil and Human Rights et al. by Mark E. Haddad, Quin M. Sorenson, Wade Henderson, and Lisa M. Bornstein.

Brief of amici curiae filed on behalf of the National Education Association et al. by Alice O'Brien, Jason Walta, and Judith A. Scott.

Brief of amici curiae filed on behalf of the National School Boards Association et al. by Francisco M. Negrdn, Jr., and Patricia J. Whitten.

Brief of amici curiae filed on behalf of the President and Chancellors of the University of California by Bradley S. Phillips, Michael J. Mongan, and Christopher M. Patti.

Brief of amici curiae filed on behalf of the San Francisco Bay Area Rapid Transit District by Matthew H. Burrows, Thomas C. Lee, and Joseph A. Hearst.

Brief of amici curiae filed on behalf of the San Francisco Unified School District et al. by G. Scott Emblidge.

Brief of amici curiae filed on behalf of the Society of American Law Teachers by David D. Cross.

Brief of amici curiae filed on behalf of Donald R. Kinder et al. by Catherine M. A. Carroll, Joshua M. Salzman, and Stuart D. Allen.

Brief of amici curiae filed on behalf of Paul Finkleman et al. by Andrew J.I. Pincus.

Brief of amici curiae filed on behalf of Gary Segura et al. by Derek T. Ho and Alexander S. Edelson.

Brief of amici curiae filed on behalf of California Social Science Researchers et al. by Elizabeth Ann Lawrence.

Brief of amici curiae filed on behalf of the Michigan Civil Rights Commission by Daniel M. Levy.

Opposing Side (Petitioner / Appellant)

Brief of amici curiae filed on behalf of the State of Arizona et al. by Thomas C. Horne, Attorney General of Arizona, Robert L. Ellman, Solicitor General, and Paula S. Bickett, and by the Attorneys General for their respective States as follows: Luther Strange of Alabama, Sam Olens of Georgia, E. Scott Pruitt of Oklahoma, and Patrick Morrisey of West Virginia.

Brief of amici curiae filed on behalf of the American Civil Rights Union et al. by Peter J. Ferrara and D. John Sauer.

Brief of amici curiae filed on behalf of the Asian Amerian Legal Foundation by Gordon M. Fauth, Jr.

Brief of amici curiae filed on behalf of the California Association of Scholars et al. by John C. Eastman, Anthony T. Caso, Edwin Meese III, Gail Heriot, and Manuel S. Klausner.

Brief of amici curiae filed on behalf of Former Attorneys of the Department of Justice Civil Rights Division by Michael F. Smith.

Brief of amici curiae filed on behalf of the Judicial Education Project by Carrie Severino.

Brief of amici curiae filed on behalf of Judicial Watch, Inc., et al. by Chris Fedeli and Julie Axelrod.

Brief of amici curiae filed on behalf of the Mountain States Legal Foundation by Steven J. Lechner.

Brief of amici curiae filed on behalf of the Pacific Legal Foundation et al. by Meriem L. Hubbard, Ralph W. Kasarda, and Joshua P. Thompson.

Brief of amici curiae filed on behalf of the XIV Foundation et al. by Robert N. Driscoll.

Brief of amici curiae filed on behalf of David Boyle by Mr. Boyle, pro se.

Brief of amici curiae filed on behalf of Carl Cohen et al. by Joel C. Mandelman.

Brief of amici curiae filed on behalf of Richard Sander by Stuart Taylor, Jr.

IV. THE SUPREME COURT'S DECISION

"Before the Court addresses the question presented, it is important to note what this case is not about. . . . The question here concerns not the permissibility of race-conscious admissions policies under the Constitution but whether, and in what manner, voters in the States may choose to prohibit the consideration of racial preferences in governmental decisions, in particular with respect to school admissions. . . .

In holding § 26 invalid in the context of student admissions at state universities, the Court of Appeals relied . . . on Seattle, . . . which it deemed to control the case. But that determination extends Seattle's holding in a case presenting quite different issues to reach a conclusion that is mistaken here. . . .

The broad rationale that the Court of Appeals adopted goes beyond the necessary holding and the meaning of the precedents said to support it; and in the instant case neither the formulation of the general rule . . . nor the precedents cited to authenticate it suffice to invalidate Proposal 2. The expansive reading of Seattle has no principled limitation and raises serious questions of compatibility with the Court's settled equal protection jurisprudence. . . . The rule that . . . respondents seek to establish here would contradict central equal protection principles. . . .

By approving Proposal 2 and thereby adding § 26 to their State Constitution, the Michigan voters exercised their privilege to enact laws as a basic exercise of their democratic power. . . .

For reasons already discussed, Mulkey, Hunter, and Seattle are not precedents that stand for the conclusion that Michigan's voters must be disempowered from acting. . . .

This case is not about how the debate about racial preferences should be resolved. It is about who may resolve it. There is no authority in the Constitution . . . or in this Court's precedents for the Judiciary to set aside Michigan laws that commit this policy determination to the voters. . . . Deliberative debate on sensitive issues such as racial preferences all too often may shade into rancor. But that does not justify removing certain court-determined issues from the voters' reach. Democracy does not presume that some subjects are either too divisive or too profound for public debate.

The judgment of the Court of Appeals for the Sixth Circuit is reversed."

V. JUSTICE VOTE

2 Pro ACLU Side vs. 6 Con Opposing Side

ACLU Side (Respondent / Appellee)

1. Ginsburg, R. – Joined Sotomayor's dissent
2. Sotomayor, S. – Wrote dissenting opinion

Opposing Side (Petitioner / Appellant)

1. Kennedy, A. – Wrote plurality opinion
2. Alito, S. – Joined concurring opinion
3. Thomas, C. – Joined Scalia's concurrence
4. Breyer, S. – Wrote concurring opinion
5. Scalia, A. – Wrote concurring opinion
6. Roberts, J. – Wrote concurring opinion

Kagan. E. – Took no part in the decision.

VI. A WIN OR LOSS FOR THE ACLU?

The ACLU served as counsel for appellee urging affirmance; the Supreme Court reversed the Court of Appeals' decision by a 6-2 vote, giving the ACLU an apparent loss.

1121. Town of Greece v. Galloway

(Decided May 5, 2014; 572 U.S. 565)

I. ISSUE

A. Issues Discussed

1st Amendment, religion

B. Legal Question Presented

"The Court must decide whether the town of Greece, New York, imposes an impermissible establishment of religion by opening its monthly board meetings with a prayer."

C. Supreme Court's Answer

"It must be concluded, consistent with the Court's opinion in Marsh v. Chambers, 463 U.S. 783 (1983), that no violation of the Constitution has been shown."

II. CASE SUMMARY

A. Background

"Greece . . . is in upstate New York. . . . In 1999, the newly elected town supervisor, John Auberger, decided to replicate the prayer practice he had found meaningful while serving in the county legislature. Following the roll call and recitation of the Pledge of Allegiance, Auberger would invite a local clergyman to the front of the room to deliver an invocation. . . .

The town followed an informal method for selecting prayer givers, all of whom were unpaid volunteers. . . . Its leaders maintained that a minister or layperson of any persuasion, including an atheist, could give the invocation. But nearly all of the congregations in town were Christian; and from 1999 to 2007, all of the participating ministers were too. . . .

Some of the ministers spoke in a distinctly Christian idiom . . . .

Respondents Susan Galloway and Linda Stephens attended town board meetings . . . . After respondents complained that Christian themes pervaded the prayers, . . . the town invited a Jewish layman and the chairman of the local Baha'i temple . . . . A Wiccan priestess . . . requested, and was granted, an opportunity to give the invocation.

Galloway and Stephens brought suit . . . . They alleged that the town violated the First Amendment's Establishment Clause by preferring Christians over other prayer givers . . . . They did not seek an end to the prayer practice, but rather requested an injunction that would limit the town to 'inclusive and ecumenical' prayers that referred only to a 'generic God' and would not associate the government with any one faith or belief.

The District Court . . . upheld the prayer practice as consistent with the First Amendment. . . .

The Court of Appeals for the Second Circuit reversed."

The Supreme Court granted certiorari to review the case.

B. Counsel of Record / ACLU Attorney

ACLU Side (Respondent / Appellee): Douglas Laycock argued the cause for appellees. With him on the brief were Ayesha N. Khan, Gregory M. Lipper, Charles A. Rothfeld, and Richard B. Katskee.

Opposing Side (Petitioner / Appellant): Thomas G. Hungar argued the cause for appellant. With him on the briefs were David A. Cortman, Brett B. Harvey, and Kevin Theriot.

Deputy Solicitor General Gershengorn argued the cause for the United States as amicus curiae.

III. AMICI CURIAE

ACLU Side (Respondent / Appellee)

Brief of amici curiae filed on behalf of the American Civil Liberties Union, the New York Civil Liberties Union, The Anti-Defamation League, and Interfaith Alliance Foundation by Daniel Mach, Heather L. Weaver, Steven R. Shapiro, Arthur N. Eisenberg, and Deborah H. Karpatkin.

Brief of amici curiae filed on behalf of the American Jewish Committee et al. by Eric A. Tirschwell, Marc D. Stern, and Craig L. Siegel.

Brief of amici curiae filed on behalf of the Center for Inquiry et al. by Lisa S. Blatt and Daniel S. Pariser.

Brief of amici curiae filed on behalf of the Freedom From Religion Foundation by Richard L. Bolton.

Brief of amici curiae filed on behalf of Law Professors by Christopher C. Lund.

Brief of amici curiae filed on behalf of 12 Members of Congress by John S. Moot and Kathryn Kavanagh Baran.

Brief of amici curiae filed on behalf of Political Scientists by Paul M. Smith and Marc A. Goldman.

Brief of amici curiae filed on behalf of the Unitarian Universalist Association of Congregations et al. by Deanne E. Maynard and Marc A. Hearron.

Brief of amici curiae filed on behalf of Erwin Chemerinsky et al. by Beth Heifetz.

Brief of amici curiae filed on behalf of Paul Finkelman et al. by Seth P. Waxman.

Brief of amici curiae filed on behalf of the Baptist Joint Committee for Religious Liberty et al. by Mark W. Mosier and K. Hollyn Hollman.

Brief of amici curiae filed on behalf of the Jewish Social Policy Action Network by Jeffrey Ivan Pasek, Theodore R. Mann, and Seth F. Kreimer.

Brief of amici curiae filed on behalf of the National Conference for Community and Justice by Stephen G. Harvey.

Opposing Side (Petitioner / Appellant)

Brief of amici curiae filed on behalf of the United States by Deputy Solicitor General Gershengorn, Solicitor General Verrilli, Acting Assistant Attorney General Delery, Deputy Solicitor General Kneedler, Sarah E. Harrington, Matthew M. Collette, and Lowell V. Sturgill, Jr.

Brief of amici curiae filed on behalf of the State of Indiana et al. by Gregory F. Zoeller, Attorney General of Indiana, Thomas M. Fisher, Solicitor General, Heather Hagan McVeigh, Deputy Attorney General, Greg Abbott, Attorney General of Texas, Daniel T. Hodge, First Assistant Attorney General, Jonathan F Mitchell, Solicitor General, and Adam W Aston, Deputy Solicitor General, and by the Attorneys General for their respective States as follows: Luther Strange of Alabama, Michael C. Geraghty of Alaska, Dustin McDaniel of Arkansas, John W. Suthers of Colorado, Pamela Jo Bondi of Florida, Samuel S. Olens of Georgia, Lawrence G. Wasden of Idaho, Derek Schmidt of Kansas, Jack Conway of Kentucky, James D. "Buddy" Caldwell of Louisiana, Bill Schuette of Michigan, Jim Hood of Mississippi, Timothy C. Fox of Montana, Jon Bruning of Nebraska, Michael DeWine of Ohio, E. Scott Pruitt of Oklahoma, Marty J. Jackley of South Dakota, Robert E. Cooper, Jr., of Tennessee, John E. Swallow of Utah, Kenneth T. Cuccinelli II of Virginia, and Patrick Morrisey of West Virginia.

Brief of amici curiae filed on behalf of the State of South Carolina by Alan Wilson, Attorney General, Robert D. Cook, Solicitor General, J. Emory Smith, Jr., Deputy Solicitor General, Brendan McDonald, Assistant Attorney General, and Tracey C. Green.

Brief of amici curiae filed on behalf of the American Center for Law and Justice by Jay Alan Sekulow, Stuart J. Roth, Colby M. May, and Walter M. Weber.

Brief of amici curiae filed on behalf of the American Civil Rights Union by Peter J. Ferrara.

Brief of amici curiae filed on behalf of the Center for Constitutional Jurisprudence by John Eastman, Anthony T. Caso, and Edwin Meese III.

Brief of amici curiae filed on behalf of the Chaplain Alliance for Religious Liberty by William C. Wood, Jr., Jay T. Thompson, and Miles E. Coleman.

Brief of amici curiae filed on behalf of the Foundation for Moral Law by John A. Eidsmoe.

Brief of amici curiae filed on behalf of the Justice and Freedom Fund by James L. Hirsen and Deborah J. Dewart.

Brief of amici curiae filed on behalf of the League of California Cities by Allison E. Burns and Joseph M. Adams.

Brief of amici curiae filed on behalf of Liberty Counsel by Mathew D. Staver, Anita L. Staver, Horatio G. Mihet, Stephen M. Crampton, and Mary E. McAlister.

Brief of amici curiae filed on behalf of Seven PrayerGivers by Barry A. Bostrom.

Brief of amici curiae filed on behalf of the Southeastern Legal Foundation by Shannon Lee Goessling.

Brief of amici curiae filed on behalf of the Southern Baptist Convention Ethics Religious Liberty Commission by Michael K. Whitehead and Jonathan R. Whitehead.

Brief of amici curiae filed on behalf of the Virginia Christian Alliance et al. by Rita M. Dunaway.

Brief of amici curiae filed on behalf of WallBuilders, Inc., by Steven W. Fitschen; for Daniel L. Akin et al. by Kelly J. Shackelford, Jeffrey C. Mateer, and Hiram S. Sasser III.

Brief of amici curiae filed on behalf of Nathan Lewin by Mr. Lewin, pro se, Alyza D. Lewin, and Dennis Rapps.

Brief of amici curiae filed on behalf of Robert E. Palmer by Evan A. Young, Aaron M. Streett, and Julie Marie Blake.

Brief of amici curiae filed on behalf of Senator Marco Rubio et al. by Steffen N. Johnson, Gene C. Schaerr, Elizabeth P. Papez, Andrew C. Nichols, Linda T. Coberly, and William P. Ferranti.
Brief of amici curiae filed on behalf of 85 Members of Congress by Kenneth A. Klukowski.
Brief of amici curiae filed on behalf of the Becket Fund for Religious Liberty by Eric C. Rassbach, Luke W. Goodrich, Diana M. Verm, and Daniel Blomberg.
Brief of amici curiae filed on behalf of the Board of Commissioners for Carroll County, Maryland, et al. by David C. Gibbs III, Barbara J. Weller, and Scott W. Gaylord.
Brief of amici curiae filed on behalf of the Faith and Action Networks by Bernard P. Reese.
Brief of amici curiae filed on behalf of the Rutherford Institute by John W. Whitehead and James J. Knicely.
Brief of amici curiae filed on behalf of Gerard V. Bradley et al. by Stephen B. Kinnaird and Christopher H. McGrath.
Brief of amici curiae filed on behalf of Brevard County, Florida, by Scott L. Knox.

IV. THE SUPREME COURT'S DECISION

"In Marsh v. Chambers, 463 U.S. 783, the Court found no First Amendment violation in the Nebraska Legislature's practice of opening its sessions with a prayer delivered by a chaplain paid from state funds. The decision concluded that legislative prayer, while religious in nature, has long been understood as compatible with the Establishment Clause. . . .

The Court's inquiry, then, must be to determine whether the prayer practice in the town of Greece fits within the tradition long followed in Congress and the state legislatures. Respondents assert that the town's prayer exercise falls outside that tradition and transgresses the Establishment Clause for two independent but mutually reinforcing reasons. First, they argue that Marsh did not approve prayers containing sectarian language or themes . . . . Second, they argue that the setting and conduct of the town board meetings create social pressures that force nonadherents to remain in the room or even feign participation in order to avoid offending the representatives who sponsor the prayer and will vote on matters citizens bring before the board. . . .

An insistence on nonsectarian or ecumenical prayer as a single, fixed standard is not consistent with the tradition of legislative prayer outlined in the Court's cases. . . .

To hold that invocations must be nonsectarian would force the legislatures that sponsor prayers and the courts that are asked to decide these cases to act as supervisors and censors of religious speech, a rule that would involve government in religious matters to a far greater degree than is the case under the town's current practice of neither editing or approving prayers in advance nor criticizing their content after the fact. . . .

Respondents further seek to distinguish the town's prayer practice from the tradition upheld in Marsh on the ground that it coerces participation by nonadherents. . . .

The inclusion of a brief, ceremonial prayer as part of a larger exercise in civic recognition suggests that its purpose and effect are to acknowledge religious leaders and the institutions they represent rather than to exclude or coerce nonbelievers. . . .

The prayer in this case has a permissible ceremonial purpose. It is not an unconstitutional establishment of religion. . . .

The town of Greece does not violate the First Amendment by opening its meetings with prayer that comports with our tradition and does not coerce participation by nonadherents. The judgment of the U.S. Court of Appeals for the Second Circuit is reversed."

V. JUSTICE VOTE

4 Pro ACLU Side vs. 5 Con Opposing Side

ACLU Side (Respondent / Appellee)

1. Kagan, E. – Wrote dissenting opinion
2. Breyer, S. – Wrote dissenting opinion, joined Kagan's dissent
3. Ginsburg, R. – Joined Kagan's dissent
4. Sotomayor, S. – Joined Kagan's dissent

Opposing Side (Petitioner / Appellant)

1. Kennedy, A. – Wrote majority opinion
2. Alito, S. – Wrote concurring opinion
3. Thomas, C. – Wrote concurring opinion
4. Scalia, A. – Joined Alito's concurrence and Thomas' concurrence in part
5. Roberts, J. – Joined majority opinion

VI. A WIN OR LOSS FOR THE ACLU?

The ACLU filed as amicus curiae urging affirmance; the Supreme Court reversed the Court of Appeals' decision by a 5-4 vote, giving the ACLU an apparent loss.

1122. Wood v. Moss

(Decided May 27, 2014; 572 U.S. 744)

I. ISSUE

A. Issues Discussed

Immunity

B. Legal Question Presented

"[W]hether the protesters have alleged violation of a clearly established First Amendment right based on the agents' decision to order the protesters moved from their original location in front of the Inn, first to the block just east of the Inn, and then another block farther."

C. Supreme Court's Answer

"Limiting our decision to th[e qualified immunity] question, we hold . . . that the agents are entitled to qualified immunity."

II. CASE SUMMARY

A. Background

"This case concerns a charge that two Secret Service agents, in carrying out their responsibility to protect the President, engaged in unconstitutional viewpoint-based discrimination. The episode in suit occurred in Jacksonville, Oregon . . . . President George

W. Bush, . . . was scheduled to spend the evening at a cottage in Jacksonville. With permission from local law enforcement officials, two groups assembled on opposite sides of the street on which the President's motorcade was to travel to reach the cottage. One group supported the President, the other opposed him.

The President made a last-minute decision to stop in town for dinner . . . . His motorcade therefore turned from the planned route and proceeded to the outdoor patio dining area of the Jacksonville Inn's restaurant. Learning of the route change, the protesters moved down the sidewalk to the area in front of the Inn. The President's supporters remained across the street and about a half block away from the Inn. At the direction of the Secret Service agents, state and local police cleared the block on which the Inn was located and moved the protesters some two blocks away to a street beyond handgun or explosive reach of the President. The move placed the protesters a block farther away from the Inn than the supporters. . . .

No decision of this Court so much as hinted that the [agents] on-the-spot action was unlawful because they failed to keep the protesters and supporters, throughout the episode, equidistant from the President.

The United States Court of Appeals for the Ninth Circuit ruled otherwise."

The Supreme Court granted certiorari to review the case.

B. Counsel of Record / ACLU Attorney

ACLU Side (Respondent / Appellee): Steven M. Wilker, on behalf of the ACLU Foundation of Oregon, Inc., argued the cause for appellees. With him on the brief were Arthur B. Spitzer of the American Civil Liberties Union of the Nation's Capital, Kevin Díaz of the ACLU Foundation of Oregon, Inc., and Steven R. Shapiro, and Ben Wizner of the American Civil Liberties Union Foundation.

Opposing Side (Petitioner / Appellant): Ian Heath Gershengorn argued the cause for appellants. With him on the briefs were Solicitor General Verrilli, Assistant Attorney General Delery, Barbara L. Herwig, Edward Himmelfarb, and Jeremy S. Brumbelow.

III. AMICI CURIAE

ACLU Side (Respondent / Appellee)

Brief of amici curiae filed on behalf of the NAACP Legal Defense & Educational Fund, Inc., by Rachel D. Godsil, Christina Swarns, ReNika C. Moore, Joshua Civin, and Johnathan Smith.

Brief of amici curiae filed on behalf of Professors of Civil Procedure by Allan Ides.

Opposing Side (Petitioner / Appellant)

Brief of amici curiae filed on behalf of the National Conference of State Legislatures et al. by Sean R. Gallagher, Bennett L. Cohen, and Lisa E. Soronen.

Brief of amici curiae filed on behalf of Public Justice P. C. by Alexander A Reinert, Claire Prestel, and Arthur Bryant in support of neither party.

IV. THE SUPREME COURT'S DECISION

"It is uncontested and uncontestable that government officials may not exclude from public places persons engaged in peaceful expressive activity solely because the government actor fears, dislikes, or disagrees with the views those persons express. It is equally plain that the fundamental right to speak secured by the First Amendment does not leave people at liberty to publicize their views "whenever and however and wherever they please." Our decision in this case starts from those premises.

The particular question before us is whether the protesters have alleged violation of a clearly established First Amendment right based on the agents' decision to order the protesters moved from their original location in front of the Inn, first to the block just east of the Inn, and then another block farther. . . .

The doctrine of qualified immunity protects government officials from liability for civil damages 'unless a plaintiff pleads facts showing (1) that the official violated a statutory or constitutional right, and (2) that the right was 'clearly established' at the time of the challenged conduct.' . . .

At the time of the Jacksonville incident, this Court had addressed a constitutional challenge to Secret Service actions on only one occasion. . . . We held that qualified immunity shielded the agents from claims that the arrest violated the plaintiff's rights . . . .

No decision of which we are aware . . . would alert Secret Service agents engaged in crowd control that they bear a First Amendment obligation 'to ensure that groups with different viewpoints are at comparable locations at all times.' Nor would the maintenance of equal access make sense in the situation the agents confronted. . . .

We note, moreover, that individual government officials 'cannot be held liable' in a Bivens suit 'unless they themselves acted [unconstitutionally].' We therefore decline to infer from alleged instances of misconduct on the part of particular agents an unwritten policy of the Secret Service to suppress disfavored expression . . . .

This case comes to us on the agents' petition to review the Ninth Circuit's denial of their qualified immunity defense. . . . Limiting our decision to that question, we hold, for the reasons stated, that the agents are entitled to qualified immunity. Accordingly, we reverse . . . the Court of Appeals."

V. JUSTICE VOTE

0 Pro ACLU Side vs. 9 Con Opposing Side

Opposing Side (Petitioner / Appellant)

1. Ginsburg, R. – Wrote majority opinion
2. Alito, S. – Joined majority opinion
3. Kagan, E. – Joined majority opinion
4. Thomas, C. – Joined majority opinion
5. Breyer, S. – Joined majority opinion
6. Scalia, A. – Joined majority opinion
7. Kennedy, A. – Joined majority opinion
8. Sotomayor, S. – Joined majority opinion
9. Roberts, J. – Joined majority opinion

VI. A WIN OR LOSS FOR THE ACLU?

The ACLU argued the cause for appellees urging affirmance; the Supreme Court reversed the Court of Appeals' decision by a 9-0 vote, giving the ACLU an apparent loss.

1123. Susan B. Anthony List v. Driehaus

(Decided June 16, 2014; 573 U.S. 149)

I. ISSUE

A. Issues Discussed

Voting rights

B. Legal Question Presented

"Petitioners in this case seek to challenge an Ohio statute that prohibits certain 'false statements' during the course of a political campaign. The question in this case is whether their preenforcement challenge to that law is justiciable—and in particular, whether they have alleged a sufficiently imminent injury for the purposes of Article III."

C. Supreme Court's Answer

"Petitioners in this case have demonstrated an injury in fact sufficient for Article III standing."

II. CASE SUMMARY

A. Background

"The Ohio statute at issue prohibits certain 'false statement[s]' 'during the course of any campaign for nomination or election to public office or office of a political party.' . . .

Petitioner Susan B. Anthony List (SBA) is a 'pro-life advocacy organization.' During the 2010 election cycle, . . . it issued a press release announcing its plan to 'educat[e] voters that their representative voted for a health care bill that includes taxpayer-funded abortion.' The press release listed then-Congressman Steve Driehaus, a respondent here, who voted for the ACA. SBA also sought to display a billboard in Driehaus' district condemning that vote. . . .

On October 4, 2010, Driehaus filed a complaint with the Ohio Elections Commission alleging, as relevant here, that SBA had violated §§ 3517.21(B)(9) and (10) by falsely stating that he had voted for 'taxpayer-funded abortion.' . . .

On October 18, 2010—after the panel's probable-cause determination, but before the scheduled Commission hearing—SBA filed suit in Federal District Court, seeking declaratory and injunctive relief . . . . The District Court stayed the action . . . . The Sixth Circuit denied SBA's motion for an injunction pending appeal. . . .

When Driehaus lost the election in November 2010, he moved to withdraw his complaint . . . . The Commission granted the motion with SBA's consent. Once the Commission proceedings were terminated, the District Court lifted the stay and SBA amended its complaint. . . .

The District Court dismissed both suits as non-justiciable, concluding that neither suit presented a sufficiently concrete injury for purposes of standing or ripeness. The Sixth Circuit affirmed on ripeness grounds."

The Supreme Court granted certiorari to review the case.

B. Counsel of Record / ACLU Attorney

ACLU Side (Petitioner / Appellant): Michael A. Carvin argued the cause for appellants. With him on the briefs were David R. Langdon, Christopher P. Finney, Curt C Hartman, and Robert A. Destro.

Eric J. Feigin argued the cause for the United States as amicus curiae in support of partial reversal.

Opposing Side (Respondent / Appellee): Eric E. Murphy, State Solicitor of Ohio, argued the cause for appellees. With him on the brief were Michael DeWine, Attorney General, and Samuel C. Peterson and Peter K. Glenn-Applegate, Deputy Solicitors.

III. AMICI CURIAE

ACLU Side (Petitioner / Appellant)

Brief of amici curiae filed on behalf of the American Civil Liberties Union and the American Civil Liberties Union of Ohio by Steven R. Shapiro, Lee Rowland, Brian M. Hauss, Freda J. Levenson, and Drew S. Dennis.

Brief of amici curiae filed on behalf of the Alliance Defending Freedom by David A. Cortman, Kevin H. Theriot, Heather Gebelin Hacker, and David J. Hacker.

Brief of amici curiae filed on behalf of the American Booksellers Association et al. by Michael A. Bamberger and Richard M. Zuckerman.

Brief of amici curiae filed on behalf of the Bioethics Defense Fund by Nikolas T. Nikas and Dorinda C. Bordlee.

Brief of amici curiae filed on behalf of the Cato Institute et al. by Ilya Shapiro.

Brief of amici curiae filed on behalf of the Center for Constitutional Jurisprudence by John C. Eastman, Anthony T. Caso, and Edwin Meese III.

Brief of amici curiae filed on behalf of the Christian Legal Society et al. by Frederick W. Claybrook, Jr., David D. Johnson, and Kimberlee Wood Colby.

Brief of amici curiae filed on behalf of the Center for Competitive Politics by Allen Dickerson and Tyler Martinez.

Brief of amici curiae filed on behalf of Citizens United et al. by Herbert W. Titus, William J. Olson, John S. Miles, Jeremiah L. Morgan, and Michael Connelly.

Brief of amici curiae filed on behalf of the First Amendment Lawyers Association by Jennifer M. Kinsley.

Brief of amici curiae filed on behalf of the Foundation for Individual Rights in Education by Jeffrey A. Rosen, John K. Crisham, Michael A. Fragoso, and Greg Lukianoff.

Brief of amici curiae filed on behalf of the General Conference of Seventh-Day Adventists et al. by Gene C. Schaerr, Todd R. McFarland, and Charles M. Kester.

Brief of amici curiae filed on behalf of the Government Integrity Fund by William M. Todd.

Brief of amici curiae filed on behalf of the Institute for Justice et al. by William H. Mellor, Dana Berlinger, Paul M. Sherman, and Manuel S. Klausner.

Brief of amici curiae filed on behalf of the Justice and Freedom

Fund by James L. Hirsen and Deborah J. Dewart.
Brief of amici curiae filed on behalf of the Republican National Committee by Michael T. Morley and John Phillippe.
Brief of amici curiae filed on behalf of the Southeastern Legal Foundation by Shannon Lee Goessling.
Brief of amici curiae filed on behalf of the Student Press Law Center by Adam H. Charnes and Richard D. Dietz.
Brief of amici curiae filed on behalf of the 1851 Center for Constitutional Law by Gregory A. Keyser.
Brief of amici curiae filed on behalf of the United States by Eric J. Feigin, Solicitor General Verrilli, Assistant Attorney General Delery, Deputy Solicitor General Kneedler, Michael S. Raab, and Jaynie Lilley supporting partial reversal.
Brief of amici curiae filed on behalf of Michael DeWine, Attorney General of Ohio by Erik S. Jaffe and Bradley A. Smith in support of neither party.

Opposing Side (Respondent / Appellee)

No briefs of amici curiae were filed in support of appellee.

IV. THE SUPREME COURT'S DECISION

"Article III of the Constitution limits the jurisdiction of federal courts to 'Cases' and 'Controversies.' . . . To establish Article III standing, a plaintiff must show (1) an 'injury in fact,' (2) a sufficient 'causal connection between the injury and the conduct complained of,' and (3) a 'likel[ihood]' that the injury 'will be redressed by a favorable decision.'

This case concerns the injury-in-fact requirement, which helps to ensure that the plaintiff has a 'personal stake in the outcome of the controversy.' . . .

One recurring issue in our cases is determining when the threatened enforcement of a law creates an Article III injury. . . .

Here, SBA and COAST contend that the threat of enforcement of the false statement statute amounts to an Article III injury in fact. We agree: Petitioners have alleged a credible threat of enforcement. . . .

First, petitioners have alleged 'an intention to engage in a course of conduct arguably affected with a constitutional interest.' . . .

Next, petitioners' intended future conduct is 'arguably . . . proscribed by [the] statute' they wish to challenge. The Ohio false statement law sweeps broadly, and covers the subject matter of petitioners' intended speech. . . .

Finally, the threat of future enforcement of the false statement statute is substantial. Most obviously, there is a history of past enforcement here: SBA was the subject of a complaint in a recent election cycle. . . . Here, the threat is even more substantial given that the Commission panel actually found probable cause to believe that SBA's speech violated the false statement statute. . . .

In sum, we find that both SBA and COAST have alleged a credible threat of enforcement. . . .

Petitioners in this case have demonstrated an injury in fact sufficient for Article III standing. We accordingly reverse the judgment of the United States Court of Appeals for the Sixth Circuit and remand the case for further proceedings consistent with this opinion, including a determination whether the remaining Article III standing requirements are met."

V. JUSTICE VOTE

9 Pro ACLU Side vs. 0 Con Opposing Side

ACLU Side (Petitioner / Appellant)

1. Thomas, C. – Wrote majority opinion
2. Alito, S. – Joined majority opinion
3. Kagan, E. – Joined majority opinion
4. Breyer, S. – Joined majority opinion
5. Scalia, A. – Joined majority opinion
6. Kennedy, A. – Joined majority opinion
7. Ginsburg, R. – Joined majority opinion
8. Sotomayor, S. – Joined majority opinion
9. Roberts, J. – Joined majority opinion

VI. A WIN OR LOSS FOR THE ACLU?

The ACLU filed as amicus curiae urging reversal of the judgment of the Court of Appeals; the Supreme Court reversed in a 9-0 vote, giving the ACLU an apparent win.

1124. Alice Corp. v. CLS Bank Int'l

(Decided June 19, 2014; 573 U.S. 208)

I. ISSUE

A. Issues Discussed

Governmental authority

B. Legal Question Presented

"The patents at issue in this case disclose a computer-implemented scheme for mitigating 'settlement risk' (i.e., the risk that only one party to a financial transaction will pay what it owes) by using a third-party intermediary. The question presented is whether these claims are patent eligible under 35 U.S.C. § 101, or are instead drawn to a patent-ineligible abstract idea."

C. Supreme Court's Answer

"We hold that the claims at issue are drawn to the abstract idea of intermediated settlement, and that merely requiring generic computer implementation fails to transform that abstract idea into a patent-eligible invention."

II. CASE SUMMARY

A. Background

"Petitioner Alice Corporation is the assignee of several patents that disclose schemes to manage certain forms of financial risk. . . .

In sum, the patents in suit claim (1) the foregoing method for exchanging obligations (the method claims), (2) a computer system configured to carry out the method for exchanging obligations (the system claims), and (3) a computer-readable medium containing program code for performing the method of exchanging obligations (the media claims). . . .

Respondents CLS Bank International and CLS Services Ltd. (together, CLS Bank) operate a global network that facilitates currency transactions. In 2007, CLS Bank filed suit against petitioner, seeking a declaratory judgment that the claims at issue are invalid, unenforceable, or not infringed. Petitioner counterclaimed, alleging infringement. Following this Court's decision in Bilski v. Kappos, 561 U.S. 593 (2010), the parties filed cross-motions for summary judgment on whether the asserted claims are eligible for patent protection under 35 U.S.C. § 101. The District Court held that all of the claims are patent ineligible because they are directed to the abstract idea of 'employing a neutral intermediary to facilitate simultaneous exchange of obligations in order to minimize risk.'

A divided panel of the United States Court of Appeals for the Federal Circuit reversed . . . . The Federal Circuit granted rehearing en banc, vacated the panel opinion, and affirmed the judgment of the District Court . . . ."

The Supreme Court granted certiorari to review the case.

B. Counsel of Record / ACLU Attorney

ACLU Side (Respondent / Appellee): Mark A. Perry argued the cause for appellees. With him on the brief were Helgi C. Walker and Brian M. Buroker.

Solicitor General Verrilli argued the cause for the United States as amicus curiae.

Opposing Side (Petitioner / Appellant): Carter G. Phillips argued the cause for appellant. With him on the briefs were Jeffrey P. Kushan, Constantine L. Trela, Jr., Tacy F. Flint, Adam L. Perlman, and Robert E. Sokohl.

III. AMICI CURIAE

ACLU Side (Respondent / Appellee)

Brief of amici curiae filed on behalf of the American Civil Liberties Union by Sandra S. Park, Steven R. Shapiro, Brian M. Hauss, and Lenora M. Lapidus.

Brief of amici curiae filed on behalf of the United States by Solicitor General Verrilli, Assistant Attorney General Delery, Deputy Solicitor General Stewart, Ginger D. Anders, Mark R. Freeman, and Scott C. Weidenfeller.

Brief of amici curiae filed on behalf of BSAIThe Software Alliance by Andrew J. Pincus and Paul W. Hughes.

Brief of amici curiae filed on behalf of the Clearing House Association L. L. C. et al. by William H. Burgess.

Brief of amici curiae filed on behalf of the Computer & Communications Industry Association by Matthew Levy.

Brief of amici curiae filed on behalf of the Electronic Frontier Foundation by Julie P. Samuels, Michael Barclay, Daniel K. Nazer, and Pamela Samuelson.

Brief of amici curiae filed on behalf of Google Inc. et al. by Daryl L. Joseffer, Karen F. Grohman, and Adam M. Conrad.

Brief of amici curiae filed on behalf of Juhasz Law Firm, P. C., by Paul R. Juhasz.

Brief of amici curiae filed on behalf of Law, Business, and Economics Scholars by Jason M. Schultz and Brian J. Love, both pro se.

Brief of amici curiae filed on behalf of Microsoft Corp. et al. by Jeffrey A. Lamken, John M. Whealan, Horacio E. Gutidrrez, Julie L. Sigall, and David W. Jones.

Brief of amici curiae filed on behalf of Public Knowledge et al. by Charles Duan and Jack Lerner.

Brief of amici curiae filed on behalf of Red Hat, Inc., by Robert H. Tiller.

Brief of amici curiae filed on behalf of RichRelevance, Inc., et al. by William M. Jay and Douglas J. Kline.

Brief of amici curiae filed on behalf of Software Freedom Law Center et al. by Eben Moglen.

Brief of amici curiae filed on behalf of Peter S. Menell et al. by Mr. Menell, pro se.

Brief of amici curiae filed on behalf of Tony Dutra by Mr. Dutra, pro se.

Brief of amici curiae filed on behalf of the American Antitrust Institute by Albert A. Foer, Richard M. Brunell, Randy M. Stutz, and Shubha Ghosh.

Brief of amici curiae filed on behalf of Checkpoint Software, Inc., et al. by Mark A. Lemley and Stefani E. Shanberg.

Opposing Side (Petitioner / Appellant)

Brief of amici curiae filed on behalf of Advanced Biological Laboratories, SA, by Robert R. Sachs and Daniel R. Brownstone.

Brief of amici curiae filed on behalf of Trading Technologies International, Inc., et al. by Charles J. Cooper, Vincent J. Colatriano, Steven F. Borsand, and Jay Q. Knobloch.

Brief of amici curiae filed on behalf of Margo Livesay by Ms. Livesay, pro se.

Brief of amici curiae filed on behalf of Dale R. Cook by Mr. Cook, pro se.

Brief of amici curiae filed on behalf of the American Intellectual Property Law Association by Jerry R. Selinger and Gero McClellan in support of neither party.

Brief of amici curiae filed on behalf of the Association of the Bar of the City of New York by Charles E. Miller and John Gladstone Mills III in support of neither party.

Brief of amici curiae filed on behalf of the Conejo Valley Bar Association by Steven C. Sereboff, Mark A Goldstein, Michael D. Harris, and M. Kala Sarvaiya in support of neither party.

Brief of amici curiae filed on behalf of IEEE-USA by Chris J Katopis in support of neither party.

Brief of amici curiae filed on behalf of the International Association for the Protection of Intellectual Property by Philip C. Swain and R. Mark Halligan in support of neither party.

Brief of amici curiae filed on behalf of International Business Machines Corp. by Paul D. Clement, Marian Underweiser, and Kenneth R. Corsello in support of neither party.

Brief of amici curiae filed on behalf of the Intellectual Property Law Association of Chicago by Margaret M. Duncan, Rita J Yoon, and Charles W Shifley in support of neither party.

Brief of amici curiae filed on behalf of the Intellectual Property Owners Association by D. Bartley Eppenauer, Andrew C. Cooper, Philip S. Johnson, and Kevin H. Rhodes in support of neither party.

Brief of amici curiae filed on behalf of the New York Intellectual Property Law Association by Anthony F. Lo Cicero, Charles R. Macedo, Joseph M. Casino, Michael J. Kasdan, and Bruce D.

Abramson in support of neither party.

Brief of amici curiae filed on behalf of Proove Biosciences, Inc., by Catherine Meshkin and Patrick R. Delaney in support of neither party.

Brief of amici curiae filed on behalf of Retailers by Peter J. Brann and Stacy O. Stitham in support of neither party.

Brief of amici curiae filed on behalf of SHFL Entertainment, Inc., by Adrian M. Pruetz, Erica J. Van Loon, Rex Hwang, and Charles C. Koole in support of neither party.

Brief of amici curiae filed on behalf of Sigram Schindler Beteiligungsgesellschaft mbH by Chidambaram S. Iyer in support of neither party.

Brief of amici curiae filed on behalf of Ronald M. Benrey by Robert R. Sachs and Daniel R. Brownstone in support of neither party.

Brief of amici curiae filed on behalf of Robin Feldman et al. by Mr. Feldman, pro se in support of neither party.

Brief of amici curiae filed on behalf of Brian R. Galvin by Roy Rainey in support of neither party.

Brief of amici curiae filed on behalf of Lee Hollaar et al. by Peter K. Trzyna, pro se in support of neither party.

Brief of amici curiae filed on behalf of James B. Lampert et al. by Mr. Lampert, pro se in support of neither party.

Brief of amici curiae filed on behalf of Paul R. Michel by Charles Hieken and John A. Dragseth in support of neither party.

IV. THE SUPREME COURT'S DECISION

"Section 101 of the Patent Act defines the subject matter eligible for patent protection. . . .

'We have long held that this provision contains an important implicit exception: Laws of nature, natural phenomena, and abstract ideas are not patentable.' . . .

We have described the concern that drives this exclusionary principle as one of pre-emption. . . .

At the same time, we tread carefully in construing this exclusionary principle lest it swallow all of patent law. . . .

Accordingly, in applying the § 101 exception, we must distinguish between patents that claim the "buildin[g] block[s]" of human ingenuity and those that integrate the building blocks into something more, thereby 'transform[ing]' them into a patent-eligible invention. . . .

We must first determine whether the claims at issue are directed to a patent-ineligible concept. We conclude that they are: These claims are drawn to the abstract idea of intermediated settlement. . . .

Because the claims at issue are directed to the abstract idea of intermediated settlement, we turn to the second step in Mayo's framework. We conclude that the method claims, which merely require generic computer implementation, fail to transform that abstract idea into a patent-eligible invention. . . .

Petitioner's claims to a computer system and a computer-readable medium fail for substantially the same reasons. Petitioner conceded below that its media claims rise or fall with its method claims. . . .

Because petitioner's system and media claims add nothing of substance to the underlying abstract idea, we hold that they too are patent ineligible under § 101. . . .

For the foregoing reasons, the judgment of the Court of Appeals for the Federal Circuit is affirmed."

V. JUSTICE VOTE

9 Pro ACLU Side vs. 0 Con Opposing Side

ACLU Side (Respondent / Appellee)

1. Thomas, C. – Wrote majority opinion
2. Alito, S. – Joined majority opinion
3. Kagan, E. – Joined majority opinion
4. Breyer, S. – Joined Sotomayor's concurrence
5. Scalia, A. – Joined majority opinion
6. Kennedy, A. – Joined majority opinion
7. Ginsburg, R. – Joined Sotomayor's concurrence
8. Sotomayor, S. – Wrote concurring opinion
9. Roberts, J. – Joined majority opinion

VI. A WIN OR LOSS FOR THE ACLU?

The ACLU filed as amicus curiae urging affirmance; the Supreme Court affirmed the Court of Appeals' decision by a 9-0 vote, giving the ACLU an apparent win.

1125. Lane v. Franks

(Decided June 19, 2014; 573 U.S. 228)

I. ISSUE

A. Issues Discussed

Immunity, 1st Amendment, press, speech, association

B. Legal Question Presented

"In Pickering, the Court struck the balance in favor of the public employee, extending First Amendment protection to a teacher who was fired after writing a letter to the editor of a local newspaper criticizing the school board that employed him. Today, we consider whether the First Amendment similarly protects a public employee who provided truthful sworn testimony, compelled by subpoena, outside the course of his ordinary job responsibilities."

C. Supreme Court's Answer

"We hold that it does."

II. CASE SUMMARY

A. Background

"Edward Lane [was] the Director of Community Intensive Training for Youth (CITY) . . . .

CITY faced significant financial difficulties. That prompted Lane to conduct a comprehensive audit . . . . The audit revealed that Suzanne Schmitz . . . had not been reporting to her CITY office. . . . Lane shared his finding with CACC's president and its attorney. They warned him that firing Schmitz could have negative repercussions . . . .

Lane nonetheless . . . fired her shortly thereafter. . . .

Schmitz' termination drew the attention of many, including

agents of the Federal Bureau of Investigation, which initiated an investigation into Schmitz' employment with CITY. . . .

Lane testified [at Schmitz' trial] . . . . The jury failed to reach a verdict. [F]ederal prosecutors retried Schmitz, and Lane testified once again. This time, the jury convicted Schmitz on three counts of mail fraud and four counts of theft . . . .

Lane began reporting to . . . Steve Franks, who had become president of CACC . . . . Lane recommended . . . layoffs to address the financial difficulties. . . . Franks decided to terminate 29 probationary CITY employees, including Lane. Shortly thereafter, however, Franks rescinded all but 2 of the 29 terminations—those of Lane and one other employee . . . . [Later,] CACC eliminated the CITY program and terminated the program's remaining employees. . . .

Lane sued Franks in his individual and official capacities . . . alleging that Franks had violated the First Amendment by firing him in retaliation for his testimony against Schmitz. . . .

The District Court granted Franks' motion for summary judgment. . . .

The Eleventh Circuit affirmed."

The Supreme Court granted certiorari to review the case.

B. Counsel of Record / ACLU Attorney

ACLU Side (Petitioner / Appellant): Tejinder Singh argued the cause for appellant. With him on the briefs were Thomas C. Goldstein and Kevin K. Russell.

Deputy Solicitor General Gershengorn argued the cause for the United States.

Opposing Side (Respondent / Appellee): Luther Strange, Attorney General of Alabama, argued the cause for appellee Burrow. With him on the briefs were Andrew L. Brasher, Solicitor General, and Megan A. Kirkpatrick, Assistant Solicitor General. Mark T. Waggoner argued the cause for appellee Franks. With him on the brief were Jennifer Morgan and Collin O'Connor Udell.

III. AMICI CURIAE

ACLU Side (Petitioner / Appellant)

Brief of amici curiae filed on behalf of the American Civil Liberties Union et al. by Lisa S. Blatt, Steven R. Shapiro, and Randall C. Marshall.

Brief of amici curiae filed on behalf of the United States by Deputy Solicitor General Gershengorn, Solicitor General Verrilli, Assistant Attorney General Delery, Rachel P. Kovner, Douglas N. Letter, Matthew M. Collette, and Robert D. Kamenshine.

Brief of amici curiae filed on behalf of the American Federation of Labor and Congress of Industrial Organizations by Lynn K. Rhinehart, Harold C. Becker, James B. Coppess, and Matthew J. Ginsburg.

Brief of amici curiae filed on behalf of the First Amendment Coalition by Floyd Abrams, Sogol D. Somekh, and Peter Scheer.

Brief of amici curiae filed on behalf of the Government Accountability Project by Andrew J. Pincus, Charles A. Rothfeld, Michael B. Kimberly, Paul W. Hughes, and Eugene R. Fidell.

Brief of amici curiae filed on behalf of Law Professors by Paul M. Secunda and Sheldon H. Nahmod.

Brief of amici curiae filed on behalf of the National Association of Police Organizations by J. Michael McGuinness.

Brief of amici curiae filed on behalf of the National Education Association et al. by Alice O'Brien, Jason Walta, Jeremiah A. Collins, Judith A. Scott, and William Lurye.

Brief of amici curiae filed on behalf of the Alliance Defending Freedom by David A. Cortman, Kevin H. Theriot, and David J. Hacker.

Brief of amici curiae filed on behalf of the National Whistleblower Center by Stephen M. Kohn, Michael D. Kohn, and David K. Colapinto.

Opposing Side (Respondent / Appellee)

Brief of amici curiae filed on behalf of International Municipal Lawyers Association, Inc., et al., by Matthew J. Delude and Charles W. Thompson, Jr.

IV. THE SUPREME COURT'S DECISION

"Speech by citizens on matters of public concern lies at the heart of the First Amendment . . . . This remains true when speech concerns information related to . . . public employment. . . .

Pickering provides the framework for analyzing whether the employee's interest or the government's interest should prevail in cases where the government seeks to curtail the speech of its employees. . . .

Against this backdrop, we turn to the question presented: whether the First Amendment protects a public employee who provides truthful sworn testimony, compelled by subpoena, outside the scope of his ordinary job responsibilities. We hold that it does. . . .

The first inquiry is whether the speech in question—Lane's testimony at Schmitz' trials—is speech as a citizen on a matter of public concern. It clearly is. . . .

The content of Lane's testimony—corruption in a public program and misuse of state funds—obviously involves a matter of significant public concern. . . .

We hold, then, that Lane's truthful sworn testimony at Schmitz' criminal trials is speech as a citizen on a matter of public concern. . . .

This does not settle the matter, however. . . . Under Pickering, if an employee speaks as a citizen on a matter of public concern, the next question is whether the government had 'an adequate justification for treating the employee differently from any other member of the public' . . . .

Here, the employer's side of the Pickering scale is entirely empty . . . . In these circumstances, we conclude that Lane's speech is entitled to protection under the First Amendment. . . .

Franks argues that even if Lane's testimony is protected under the First Amendment, the claims against him . . . should be dismissed on the basis of qualified immunity. We agree. . . .

Lane's speech is entitled to First Amendment protection, but because respondent Franks is entitled to qualified immunity, we affirm the judgment of the Eleventh Circuit as to the claims against Franks in his individual capacity. Our decision does not resolve, however, the claims against Burrow . . . . We therefore reverse the judgment of the Eleventh Circuit as to those claims and remand . . . .

[T]he judgment of the United States Court of Appeals for the Eleventh Circuit is affirmed in part and reversed in part, and the case is remanded . . . ."

V. JUSTICE VOTE

9 Pro ACLU Side vs. 0 Con Opposing Side

ACLU Side (Petitioner / Appellant)

1. Sotomayor, S. – Wrote majority opinion
2. Alito, S. – Joined Thomas' concurrence
3. Kagan, E. – Joined majority opinion
4. Thomas, C. – Wrote concurring opinion
5. Breyer, S. – Joined majority opinion
6. Scalia, A. – Joined Thomas' concurrence
7. Kennedy, A. – Joined majority opinion
8. Ginsburg, R. – Joined majority opinion
9. Roberts, J. – Joined majority opinion

VI. A WIN OR LOSS FOR THE ACLU?

The ACLU filed as amicus curiae urging reversal of the judgment of the Court of Appeals; the Supreme Court affirmed in part and reversed in part, but ruled on the side of the ACLU amici as to First Amendment protection, in a 9-0 vote, giving the ACLU an apparent win.

1126. Riley v. California

(Decided June 25, 2014; 573 U.S. 373)

I. ISSUE

A. Issues Discussed

4th Amendment

B. Legal Question Presented

"These two cases raise a common question: whether the police may, without a warrant, search digital information on a cell phone seized from an individual who has been arrested."

C. Supreme Court's Answer

"Our answer to the question of what police must do before searching a cell phone seized incident to an arrest is . . . simple—get a warrant."

II. CASE SUMMARY

A. Background

"In the first case, . . . David Riley was stopped . . . for . . . expired registration tags. . . . Riley was [ultimately] arrested for possession of concealed and loaded firearms when [a] search turned up two handguns under the car's hood.

An officer searched Riley incident to the arrest and . . . seized [and accessed] a cell phone . . . .

Riley was ultimately charged, in connection with [an] earlier shooting . . . . Riley moved to suppress all evidence . . . from his cell phone. . . . The trial court rejected that argument. . . . Riley was convicted . . . and received an enhanced sentence of 15 years to life in prison.

The California Court of Appeal affirmed. . . .

In the second case, a police officer . . . observed respondent Brima Wurie make an apparent drug sale . . . . [T]he officers seized two cell phones from Wurie's person. . . . [One] phone was repeatedly receiving calls from . . . 'my house' . . . . They . . . used an online phone directory to trace that phone number to an apartment building. . . .

They secured the apartment while obtaining a search warrant and . . . found and seized 215 grams of crack cocaine, marijuana, drug paraphernalia, a firearm and ammunition, and cash.

Wurie was charged . . . . He moved to suppress the evidence obtained from the search of the apartment, arguing that it was the fruit of an unconstitutional search of his cell phone. The District Court denied the motion. Wurie was convicted . . . and sentenced to 262 months . . . .

[T]he First Circuit . . . vacated Wurie's convictions . . . "

The Supreme Court granted certiorari to review the cases.

B. Counsel of Record / ACLU Attorney

ACLU Side (Petitioner / Appellant): Jeffrey L. Fisher argued the cause for appellant in No. 13-132. With him on the briefs were Patrick Morgan Ford and Donald B. Ayer.

Deputy Solicitor General Dreeben argued the cause for the United States in No. 13-212. With him on the briefs were Solicitor General Verrilli, Acting Assistant Attorney General Raman, John F. Bash, and Robert A. Parker.

Opposing Side (Respondent / Appellee): Edward C. DuMont, Solicitor General of California, argued the cause for appellee in No. 13-132. With him on the brief were Kamala D. Harris, Attorney General, Dane R. Gillette, Chief Assistant Attorney General, Julie L. Garland, Senior Assistant Attorney General, Steven T. Oetting and Craig J. Konnoth, Deputy Solicitors General, and Christine M. Levingston Bergman, Deputy Attorney General. Judith H. Mizner argued the cause and filed a brief for appellee in No. 13-212.

Deputy Solicitor General Dreeben argued the cause for the United States as amicus curiae urging affirmance in No. 13-132.

III. AMICI CURIAE

ACLU Side (Petitioner / Appellant)

Brief of amici curiae filed on behalf of the American Civil Liberties Union, the American Civil Liberties Union of Northern California, the American Civil Liberties Union of Southern California, and the American Civil Liberties Union of San Diego and Imperial Counties by Susan N. Herman, Steven R. Shapiro, Ezekiel R. Edwards, Catherine Crump, and Linda Lye.

Brief of amici curiae filed on behalf of the American Library Association et al. by William M. Jay, Grant R. Fondo, and Gerald G. Chacon, Jr.

Brief of amici curiae filed on behalf of the Center for Democracy & Technology et al. by Andrew J Pincus, Charles A. Rothfeld, Michael B. Kimberly, Paul W. Hughes, and Eugene R. Fidell.

Brief of amici curiae filed on behalf of the Constitutional Accountability Center by Douglas T. Kendall, Elizabeth B. Wydra, and Brianne J. Gorod.

Brief of amici curiae filed on behalf of Criminal Law Professors by Tillman J. Breckenridge and Patricia E. Roberts.

Brief of amici curiae filed on behalf of the National Press Photographers Association et al. by Robert Corn-Revere, Ronald G. London, Lisa B. Zycherman, and Thomas R. Burke.

Brief of amici curiae filed on behalf of the Cato Institute by Jim Harper and Ilya Shapiro.

Brief of amici curiae filed on behalf of the Electronic Privacy Information Center et al. by Marc Rotenberg.

Brief of amici curiae filed on behalf of the National Association of Criminal Defense Lawyers et al. by Bronson D. James, Jeffrey T. Green, and Michael W. Price.

Brief of amici curiae filed on behalf of the Cato Institute by Messrs. Harper and Shapiro.

Brief of amici curiae filed on behalf of Downsize DC Foundation et al. by Herbert W. Titus, William J. Olson, John S. Miles, Jeremiah L. Morgan, and Michael Connelly.

Brief of amici curiae filed on behalf of the National Association of Federal Defenders et al. by Jeffrey T. Green, Jacqueline G. Cooper, Sara S. Gannett, Daniel Kaplan, Keith M. Donoghue, Mason C. Clutter, and Sarah O. Schrup.

Brief of amici curiae filed on behalf of The Rutherford Institute by Anand Agneshwar, Carl S. Nadler, and John W. Whitehead.

Brief of amici curiae filed on behalf of Anna Aran et al. by Norman M. Garland and Michael M. Epstein, both pro se.

Brief of amici curiae filed on behalf of the DKT Liberty Project by Donald B. Mitchell, Jr., and James H. Hulme.

Opposing Side (Respondent / Appellee)

Brief of amici curiae filed on behalf of the United States by Deputy Solicitor General Dreeben, Solicitor General Verrilli, Acting Assistant Attorney General O'Neil, John F. Bash, and Robert A. Parker.

Brief of amici curiae filed on behalf of the State of Arizona et al. by Thomas C. Horne, Attorney General of Arizona, Robert L. Ellman, Solicitor General, Joseph T. Maziarz, Chief Counsel, and Michael T. O'Toole, Assistant Attorney General, and by the Attorneys General for their respective States as follows: John W. Suthers of Colorado, Joseph R. Biden III of Delaware, David M. Louie of Hawaii, Lawrence G. Wasden of Idaho, James D. Caldwell of Louisiana, Jim Hood of Mississippi, Catherine Cortez Masto of Nevada, Gary K. King of New Mexico, Wayne Stenehjem of North Dakota, Alan Wilson of South Carolina, Marty J. Jackley of South Dakota, Robert E. Cooper, Jr., of Tennessee, J. B. Van Hollen of Wisconsin, and Peter K. Michael of Wyoming.

Brief of amici curiae filed on behalf of the Association of State Criminal Investigative Agencies et al. by Gaëtan Gerville-Rdache, John J. Bursch, and Matthew T. Nelson.

Brief of amici curiae filed on behalf of Charles E. MacLean et al. by James J. Berles in support of neither party.

IV. THE SUPREME COURT'S DECISION

"As the text makes clear, 'the ultimate touchstone of the Fourth Amendment is 'reasonableness.'' . . . In the absence of a warrant, a search is reasonable only if it falls within a specific exception . . . .

The two cases . . . concern the reasonableness of a warrantless search incident to a lawful arrest. . . .

Although the existence of the exception for such searches has been recognized . . . , its scope has been debated . . . . That debate has focused on the extent to which officers may search property found on or near the arrestee. Three related precedents set forth the rules governing such searches . . . .

These cases require us to decide how the . . . doctrine applies to modern cell phones

[W]e generally determine whether to exempt a given type of search from the warrant requirement 'by assessing, on the one hand, the degree to which it intrudes upon an individual's privacy and, on the other, the degree to which it is needed for the promotion of legitimate governmental interests.' . . .

We . . . decline to extend Robinson to searches of data on cell phones, and hold instead that officers must generally secure a warrant before conducting such a search. . . .

Our holding . . . is not that the information on a cell phone is immune from search; it is instead that a warrant is generally required before such a search . . . .

Moreover, even though the search incident to arrest exception does not apply to cell phones, other case-specific exceptions may still justify a warrantless search of a particular phone. . . .

In light of the availability of the exigent circumstances exception, there is no reason to believe that law enforcement officers will not be able to address some of the more extreme hypotheticals . . . .

Modern cell phones are not just another technological convenience. With all they contain and all they may reveal, they hold for many Americans 'the privacies of life.' The fact that technology now allows an individual to carry such information in his hand does not make the information any less worthy of the protection for which the Founders fought. Our answer to the question of what police must do before searching a cell phone seized incident to an arrest is accordingly simple—get a warrant.

We reverse the judgment of the California Court of Appeal . . . and remand the case . . . . We affirm the judgment of the First Circuit . . . ."

V. JUSTICE VOTE

9 Pro ACLU Side vs. 0 Con Opposing Side

ACLU Side (Petitioner / Appellant)

1. Roberts, J. – Wrote majority opinion
2. Alito, S. – Wrote concurring opinion
3. Kagan, E. – Joined majority opinion
4. Thomas, C. – Joined majority opinion
5. Breyer, S. – Joined majority opinion
6. Scalia, A. – Joined majority opinion
7. Kennedy, A. – Joined majority opinion
8. Ginsburg, R. – Joined majority opinion
9. Sotomayor, S. – Joined majority opinion

VI. A WIN OR LOSS FOR THE ACLU?

The ACLU filed as amicus curiae urging reversal of the judgment of the California Court of Appeal; the Supreme Court reversed in a 9-0 vote, giving the ACLU an apparent win.

1127. McCullen v. Coakley

(Decided June 26, 2014; 573 U.S. 464)

I. ISSUE

A. Issues Discussed

1st Amendment, press, speech, association

B. Legal Question Presented

"A Massachusetts statute makes it a crime to knowingly stand on a 'public way or sidewalk' within 35 feet of an entrance or driveway to any place, other than a hospital, where abortions are performed. . . . The question presented is whether the statute violates the First Amendment."

C. Supreme Court's Answer

"The Commonwealth may not do that consistent with the First Amendment."

II. CASE SUMMARY

A. Background

"In 2000, the Massachusetts Legislature enacted the Massachusetts Reproductive Health Care Facilities Act. . . . The Act established a defined area with an 18-foot radius around the entrances and driveways of [abortion] facilities. . . .

The statute was modeled on a similar Colorado law that this Court had upheld . . . .

By 2007, some Massachusetts legislators and law enforcement officials had come to regard the 2000 statute as inadequate. . . .

To address these concerns, the Massachusetts Legislature amended the statute in 2007, replacing the six-foot no-approach zones . . . with a 35-foot fixed buffer zone . . . .

Some of the individuals who stand outside Massachusetts abortion clinics are fairly described as protestors . . . . Petitioners take a different tack. They attempt to engage women approaching the clinics in what they call 'sidewalk counseling' . . . .

Petitioners . . . claim . . . buffer zones . . . considerably hampered their counseling efforts. . . .

In January 2008, petitioners sued . . . . They sought to enjoin enforcement of the Act, alleging that it violates the First and Fourteenth Amendments, both on its face and as applied to them. The District Court denied petitioners' facial challenge after a bench trial . . . .

The Court of Appeals for the First Circuit affirmed. . . .

The case then returned to the District Court, which held that the First Circuit's decision foreclosed all but one of petitioners' as-applied challenges. After another bench trial, it denied the remaining as-applied challenge, finding that the Act left petitioners ample alternative channels of communication. The Court of Appeals once again affirmed."

The Supreme Court granted certiorari to review the case.

B. Counsel of Record / ACLU Attorney

ACLU Side (Respondent / Appellee): Jennifer Grace Miller, Assistant Attorney General of Massachusetts, argued the cause for appellees. With her on the brief were Martha Coakley, Attorney General, and Jonathan B. Miller and Sookyoung Shin, Assistant Attorneys General.

Deputy Solicitor General Gershengorn argued the cause for the United States as amicus curiae.

Opposing Side (Petitioner / Appellant): Mark L. Rienzi argued the cause for appellants. With him on the briefs were Edward C. DuMont, Todd C. Zubler, Jason D. Hirsch, Michael J DePrimo, and Philip D. Moran.

III. AMICI CURIAE

ACLU Side (Respondent / Appellee)

Brief of amici curiae filed on behalf of the American Civil Liberties Union and the American Civil Liberties Union Foundation of Massachusetts by Steven R. Shapiro, Ben Wizner, Nathan Freed Wessler, and Matthew R. Segal in support of neither party, and urging that the statute should be upheld as constitutional but the as applied challenge decision from the lower court should be vacated and remanded.

Brief of amici curiae filed on behalf of the United States by Deputy Solicitor General Gershengorn, Solicitor General Verrilli, Acting Assistant Attorney General Samuels, Elaine J. Goldenberg, Diana K. Flynn, and Sasha Samberg-Champion.

Brief of amici curiae filed on behalf of the State of New York et al. by Eric T. Schneiderman, Attorney General of New York, Barbara D. Underwood, Solicitor General, Andrea Oser, Deputy Solicitor General, and Zainab A. Chaudhry, Assistant Solicitor General, and by the Attorneys General for their respective jurisdictions as follows: Kamala D. Harris of California, George Jepsen of Connecticut, David M. Louie of Hawaii, Lisa Madigan of Illinois, Thomas J. Miller of Iowa, Janet T. Mills of Maine, Douglas F. Gansler of Maryland, Catherine Cortez Masto of Nevada, Gary K. King of New Mexico, Ellen F. Rosenblum of Oregon, William H. Sorrell of Vermont, Vincent F. Frazer of the Virgin Islands, and Robert W. Ferguson of Washington.

Brief of amici curiae filed on behalf of the American College of Obstetricians and Gynecologists et al. by Jack R. Bierig.

Brief of amici curiae filed on behalf of the AntiDefamation League et al. by Jeffrey S. Robbins, A. W. Phinney III, and Steven M. Freeman.

Brief of amici curiae filed on behalf of Civil Rights Organizations by Stephanie Toti.

Brief of amici curiae filed on behalf of the City and County of San Francisco, California, et al. by Abigail K. Hemani, Paul E. Nemser, Dennis J. Herrera, Christine Van Aken, George Nilson, Suzanne Sangree, Edward M. Pikula, Benna Ruth Solomon, Meghan L. Riley, Sara Grewing, Claudia M. McKenna, Susan L. Segal, Lara N. Baker-Morrish, and David M. Feldman.

Brief of amici curiae filed on behalf of Law Professors by Jonathan M. Albano.

Brief of amici curiae filed on behalf of the National Abortion Federation et al. by Maria T. Vullo.
Brief of amici curiae filed on behalf of the National League of Cities et al. by Mary Jean Dolan, Charles W. Thompson, Jr., and Lisa Soronen.
Brief of amici curiae filed on behalf of the Planned Parenthood League of Massachusetts et al. by Walter Dellinger and Claire Laporte.
Brief of amici curiae filed on behalf of the Victim Rights Law Center et al. by Lisa S. Blatt, Jonathan S. Martel, and Robert N. Weiner.
Brief of amici curiae filed on behalf of the Institute for Justice by William H. Mellor and Robert P. Frommer in support of neither party.

Opposing Side (Petitioner / Appellant)

Brief of amici curiae filed on behalf of the State of Michigan et al. by Bill Schuette, Attorney General of Michigan, John J. Bursch, Solicitor General, Aaron D. Lindstrom, Assistant Solicitor General, and Nicole Grimm, Assistant Attorney General, and by the Attorneys General for their respective States as follows: Luther Strange of Alabama, John W. Suthers of Colorado, Pamela Jo Bondi of Florida, Samuel S. Olens of Georgia, Derek Schmidt of Kansas, Timothy C. Fox of Montana, Jon Bruning of Nebraska, Michael DeWine of Ohio, E. Scott Pruitt of Oklahoma, Alan Wilson of South Carolina, and Patrick Morrisey of West Virginia.
Brief of amici curiae filed on behalf of the American Center for Law and Justice by Jay Alan Sekulow, Stuart J. Roth, Colby M. May, and Walter M. Weber.
Brief of amici curiae filed on behalf of the American Federation of Labor and Congress of Industrial Organizations by Lynn K. Rhinehart, Matthew J. Ginsburg, Harold C. Becker, and James B. Coppess.
Brief of amici curiae filed on behalf of Bioethics Defense Fund et al. by Nikolas T. Nikas and Dorinda C. Bordlee.
Brief of amici curiae filed on behalf of the Cato Institute by Ilya Shapiro.
Brief of amici curiae filed on behalf of Democrats for Life of America et al. by Thomas Berg.
Brief of amici curiae filed on behalf of Eagle Forum Education & Legal Defense Fund by Lawrence J. Joseph.
Brief of amici curiae filed on behalf of Justice and Freedom Fund by James L. Hirsen and Deborah J. Dewart.
Brief of amici curiae filed on behalf of Liberty Counsel by Mathew D. Staver, Anita L. Staver, Stephen M. Crampton, and Mary E. McAlister.
Brief of amici curiae filed on behalf of Life Legal Defense Foundation et al. by Catherine W. Short.
Brief of amici curiae filed on behalf of the National Hispanic Christian Leadership Conference et al. by John D. Inazu, Michael W. McConnell, and Kimberlee Wood Colby.
Brief of amici curiae filed on behalf of The Rutherford Institute by John W. Whitehead.
Brief of amici curiae filed on behalf of 12 Women Who Attest to the Importance of Free Speech in their Abortion Decisions by Carrie Severino.
Brief of amici curiae filed on behalf of 40 Days for Life by William L. Saunders.
Brief of amici curiae filed on behalf of Eugene Volokh et al. by Matthew A. Fitzgerald.
Brief of amici curiae filed on behalf of the Center for Constitutional Jurisprudence by John C. Eastman and Anthony T. Caso.

IV. THE SUPREME COURT'S DECISION

"By its very terms, the Massachusetts Act regulates access to 'public way[s]' and 'sidewalk[s].' Such areas occupy a 'special position in terms of First Amendment protection' because of their historic role as sites for discussion and debate. . . .

Consistent with the traditionally open character of public streets and sidewalks, we have held that the government's ability to restrict speech in such locations is 'very limited.' . . .

We have, however, afforded the government somewhat wider leeway to regulate features of speech unrelated to its content. . . .

While the parties agree that this test supplies the proper framework for assessing the constitutionality of the Massachusetts Act, they disagree about whether the Act satisfies the . . . three requirements. . . .

We . . . conclude that the Act is neither content nor viewpoint based and therefore need not be analyzed under strict scrutiny. . . .

Even though the Act is content neutral, it still must be 'narrowly tailored to serve a significant governmental interest.' . . .

The buffer zones burden substantially more speech than necessary . . . .

Respondents have but one reply: 'We have tried other approaches, but they do not work.' . . .

We cannot accept that contention. . . .

Given the vital First Amendment interests at stake, it is not enough for Massachusetts simply to say that other approaches have not worked.

Petitioners wish to converse with their fellow citizens about an important subject on the public streets and sidewalks—sites that have hosted discussions about the issues of the day throughout history. Respondents assert undeniably significant interests in maintaining public safety on those same streets and sidewalks . . . . But here the Commonwealth has pursued those interests by the extreme step of closing a substantial portion of a traditional public forum to all speakers. . . . The Commonwealth may not do that consistent with the First Amendment.

The judgment of the Court of Appeals for the First Circuit is reversed, and the case is remanded . . . ."

V. JUSTICE VOTE

0 Pro ACLU Side vs. 9 Con Opposing Side

Opposing Side (Petitioner / Appellant)

1. Roberts, J. – Wrote majority opinion
2. Alito, S. – Wrote concurring opinion
3. Kagan, E. – Joined majority opinion
4. Thomas, C. – Joined Scalia's concurrence
5. Breyer, S. – Joined majority opinion
6. Scalia, A. – Wrote concurring opinion
7. Kennedy, A. – Joined Scalia's concurrence

8. Ginsburg, R. – Joined majority opinion
9. Sotomayor, S. – Joined majority opinion

VI. A WIN OR LOSS FOR THE ACLU?

The ACLU filed as amicus curiae urging the court to uphold the statute; the Supreme Court reversed the Court of Appeals' decision and struck down the statute by a 9-0 vote, giving the ACLU an apparent loss.

1128. Burwell v. Hobby Lobby Stores, Inc.

(Decided June 30, 2014; 573 U.S. 682)

I. ISSUE

A. Issues Discussed

Religion, 1st Amendment

B. Legal Question Presented

"We must decide in these cases whether the Religious Freedom Restoration Act of 1993 (RFRA), 107 Stat. 1488, 42 U.S.C. § 2000bb et seq., permits the United States Department of Health and Human Services (HHS) to demand that three closely held corporations provide health-insurance coverage for methods of contraception that violate the sincerely held religious beliefs of the companies' owners."

C. Supreme Court's Answer

"We hold that the regulations that impose this obligation violate RFRA, which prohibits the Federal Government from taking any action that substantially burdens the exercise of religion unless that action constitutes the least restrictive means of serving a compelling government interest."

II. CASE SUMMARY

A. Background

"At issue in these cases are HHS regulations promulgated under the Patient Protection and Affordable Care Act of 2010 (ACA), 124 Stat. 119. . . .

Unless an exception applies, ACA requires an employer's group health plan or group-health-insurance coverage to furnish 'preventive care and screenings' for women . . . .

Norman and Elizabeth Hahn and their three sons are devout members of the Mennonite Church, a Christian denomination. The Mennonite Church opposes abortion and believes that '[t]he fetus in its earliest stages . . . shares humanity with those who conceived it.' . . .

Norman Hahn started a wood-working business . . . , Conestoga Wood Specialties . . . .

The Hahns and Conestoga sued . . . seeking to enjoin application of ACA's contraceptive mandate insofar as it requires them to provide health-insurance coverage for four FDA-approved contraceptives that may operate after the fertilization of an egg. . . .

The District Court denied a preliminary injunction, and the Third Circuit affirmed . . . .

David and Barbara Green . . . are Christians who own and operate . . . Hobby Lobby. . . .

One of David's sons started . . . , Mardel, which operates 35 Christian bookstores . . . .

Like the Hahns, the Greens believe that life begins at conception and that it would violate their religion to facilitate access to contraceptive drugs or devices that operate after that point. . . .

The Greens, Hobby Lobby, and Mardel sued HHS and other federal agencies and officials to challenge the contraceptive mandate under RFRA and the Free Exercise Clause. The District Court denied a preliminary injunction, and the plaintiffs appealed, moving for initial en banc consideration. The Tenth Circuit granted that motion and reversed in a divided opinion."

The Supreme Court granted certiorari to review the cases.

B. Counsel of Record / ACLU Attorney

ACLU Side (Petitioner / Appellant): Solicitor General Verrilli argued the cause for the federal parties in both cases. With him on the briefs were Assistant Attorney General Delery, Deputy Solicitor General Gershengorn, Deputy Solicitor General Kneedler, Joseph R. Palmore, Mark B. Stern, and Alisa B. Klein.

Opposing Side (Respondent / Appellee): Paul D. Clement argued the cause for appellants in No. 13-356 and for appellees in No. 13-354. With him on the brief in No. 13-354 were S. Kyle Duncan, Eric C. Rassbach, Luke W. Goodrich, Hannah C. Smith, Mark L. Rienzi, Lori H. Windham, and Adele Auxier Keim. On the brief in No. 13-356 were David A. Cortman, Kevin H. Theriot, Rory T. Gray, Jordan W. Lorence, Steven H. Aden, Gregory S. Baylor, Matthew S. Bowman, Charles W. Proctor III, and Randall L. Wenger.

III. AMICI CURIAE

ACLU Side (Petitioner / Appellant)

Brief of amici curiae filed on behalf of Julian Bond, the American Civil Liberties Union, the ACLU of Pennsylvania, the ACLU of Oklahoma, the NAACP Legal Defense & Educational Fund, Inc., and the National Coalition on Black Civic Participation by Brigitte Amiri, Louise Melling, Jennifer Lee, Steven R. Shapiro, Daniel Mach, Heather L. Weaver, Ryan D. Kiesel, Brady R. Henderson, and Witold J. Walczak.

Brief of amici curiae filed on behalf of the State of California et al. by Kamala D. Harris, Attorney General of California, Edward C. DuMont, Solicitor General, Kathleen A. Kenealy, Chief Assistant Attorney General, Julie Weng-Gutierrez, Senior Assistant Attorney General, Joshua N. Sondheimer, Deputy Attorney General, and Craig J. Konnoth, Deputy Solicitor General, Martha Coakley, Attorney General of Massachusetts, and Jonathan B. Miller, Joshua D. Jacobson, and Michelle L. Leung, Assistant Attorneys General, and by the Attorneys General for their respective jurisdictions as follows: George Jepsen of Connecticut, Joseph R. Biden III of Delaware, Irvin B. Nathan of the District of Columbia, David M. Louie of Hawaii, Lisa Madigan of Illinois, Tom Miller of Iowa, Janet T. Mills of Maine, Douglas F Gansler of Maryland, Gary K. King of New Mexico, Eric T. Schneiderman of New

York, Peter F. Kilmartin of Rhode Island, Ellen F. Rosenblum of Oregon, William H. Sorrell of Vermont, and Robert W. Ferguson of Washington.

Brief of amici curiae filed on behalf of the American College of Obstetricians and Gynecologists et al. by Bruce H. Schneider and Jennifer Blasdell.

Brief of amici curiae filed on behalf of the American Jewish Committee et al. by Marc D. Stern.

Brief of amici curiae filed on behalf of the Brennan Center for Justice at N. Y. U. School of Law by Wendy R. Weiser, Burt Neuborne, Norman Dorsen, and Helen Hershkoff.

Brief of amici curiae filed on behalf of the Center for Inquiry et al. by Edward Tabash and Ronald A. Lindsay.

Brief of amici curiae filed on behalf of the Constitutional Accountability Center by Douglas T. Kendall, Elizabeth B. Wydra, David H. Gans, and Brianne J. Gorod.

Brief of amici curiae filed on behalf of Corporate and Criminal Law Professors by Ryan M. Malone.

Brief of amici curiae filed on behalf of the Guttmacher Institute et al. by Walter Dellinger, Anton Metlitsky, Anna-Rose Mathieron, and Dawn Johnsen.

Brief of amici curiae filed on behalf of the Jewish Social Policy Action Network by Hope S. Freiwald, Seth Kreimer, Judah Labovitz, and Jeffrey Ivan Pasek.

Brief of amici curiae filed on behalf of Lambda Legal Defense and Education Fund, Inc., et al. by Thomas W. Ude, Jr., Camilla B. Taylor, and Jennifer C. Pizer.

Brief of amici curiae filed on behalf of the National Health Law Program et al. by Martha Jane Perkins.

Brief of amici curiae filed on behalf of the National League of Cities et al. by Dennis J. Herrera, Therese M. Stewart, Christine Van Aken, Mollie M. Lee, and Lisa Soronen.

Brief of amici curiae filed on behalf of the National Women's Law Center et al. by Charles E. Davidow, Marcia D. Greenberger, Judith G. Waxman, Emily J. Martin, and Gretchen Borchelt.

Brief of amici curiae filed on behalf of the Ovarian Cancer National Alliance et al. by Jessica L. Ellsworth.

Brief of amici curiae filed on behalf of Religious Organizations by Ayesha N. Khan and Gregory M. Lipper.

Brief of amici curiae filed on behalf of the U. S. Women's Chamber of Commerce et al. by Michael J. Gottlieb.

Brief of amici curiae filed on behalf of Frederick Mark Gedicks et al. by Mr. Gedicks, pro se, Catherine Weiss, and Natalie J Kraner.

Brief of amici curiae filed on behalf of Lawrence O. Gostin et al. by Ruth N. Borenstein, Marc A. Hearron, Julie Rikelman, Julianna S. Gonen, and Aram Schvey.

Brief of amici curiae filed on behalf of Sen. Patty Murray et al. by Catherine E. Stetson.

Brief of amici curiae filed on behalf of 91 Members of the United States House of Representatives by Carl Micarelli.

Brief of amici curiae filed on behalf of the Freedom from Religion Foundation et al. by Marci A. Hamilton.

Brief of amici curiae filed on behalf of Free Speech for People et al. by Ronald A. Fein, John C. Bonifaz, Ben T. Clements, and Jeffrey D. Clements.

Brief of amici curiae filed on behalf of Azusa Pacific University et al. by Stuart J. Lark in support of neither party.

Brief of amici curiae filed on behalf of Historians et al. by Jonathan Massey in support of neither party.

Opposing Side (Respondent / Appellee)

Brief of amici curiae filed on behalf of the State of Michigan et al. by Bill Schuette, Attorney General of Michigan, Aaron D. Lindstrom, Solicitor General, and B. Eric Restuccia, Deputy Solicitor General, Michael De Wine, Attorney General of Ohio, and Eric E. Murphy, State Solicitor, and by the Attorneys General for their respective States as follows: Luther Strange of Alabama, Michael C. Geraghty of Alaska, Thomas C. Horne of Arizona, John W. Suthers of Colorado, Pamela Jo Bondi of Florida, Samuel S. Olens of Georgia, Lawrence G. Wasden of Idaho, Derek Schmidt of Kansas, James D. "Buddy" Caldwell of Louisiana, Timothy C. Fox of Montana, Jon Bruning of Nebraska, Wayne Stenehjem of North Dakota, Alan Wilson of South Carolina, Marty J. Jackley of South Dakota, Greg Abbott of Texas, Sean D. Reyes of Utah, Patrick Morrisey of West Virginia, and J. B. Van Hollen of Wisconsin.

Brief of amici curiae filed on behalf of the American Freedom Law Center by Robert Joseph Muise and David Eliezer Yerushalmi.

Brief of amici curiae filed on behalf of the Association of American Physicians and Surgeons, Inc., et al. by David P. Felsher and Andrew L. Schlafly.

Brief of amici curiae filed on behalf of the Beverly Lahaye Institute et al. by Catherine W. Short.

Brief of amici curiae filed on behalf of the Breast Cancer Prevention Institute et al. by Nikolas T. Nikas, Dorinda C. Bordlee, and Patrick T. Gillen.

Brief of amici curiae filed on behalf of the Center for Constitutional Jurisprudence et al. by John Eastman, Anthony T. Caso, and Edwin Meese III.

Brief of amici curiae filed on behalf of the Christian Booksellers Association et al. by Michael W. McConnell.

Brief of amici curiae filed on behalf of the Christian Legal Society et al. by Douglas Laycock and Kimberlee Wood Colby.

Brief of amici curiae filed on behalf of the Church of the Lukumi Babalu Aye, Inc., et al. by Alexander Dushku.

Brief of amici curiae filed on behalf of the Council for Christian Colleges & Universities et al. by Matthew T. Nelson and John J. Bursch.

Brief of amici curiae filed on behalf of the C12 Group, LLC, by Mark D. Davis.

Brief of amici curiae filed on behalf of Democrats for Life of America et al. by Thomas C. Berg and Sandra P. Hagood.

Brief of amici curiae filed on behalf of Drury Development Corp. et al. by Denise M. Burke and Mailee R. Smith.

Brief of amici curiae filed on behalf of Electric Mirror, LLC, et al. by Scott J. Ward, Grerorge R. Grange II, Timothy R. Obitts, and Patrick D. Purtill.

Brief of amici curiae filed on behalf of the Ethics and Public Policy Center by Daniel P. Collins and Enrique Schaerer.

Brief of amici curiae filed on behalf of the Family Research Council by Erik S. Jaffee.

Brief of amici curiae filed on behalf of the Judicial Education Project by Carrie Severino and Jonathan Keim.

Brief of amici curiae filed on behalf of the Knights of Columbus

by Kevin P. Martin, William M. Jay, and John A. Marrella.
Brief of amici curiae filed on behalf of the Liberty Institute by Kelly J. Shackelford, Jeffrey C. Mateer, and Hiram S. Sasser III.
Brief of amici curiae filed on behalf of Liberty, Life, and Law Foundation et al. by Deborah J. Dewart and Thomas Brejcka.
Brief of amici curiae filed on behalf of the National Association of Evangelicals by Timothy Belz and Carl H. Esbeck.
Brief of amici curiae filed on behalf of the National Jewish Commission on Law and Public Affairs et al. by Nathan Lewin, Alyza D. Lewin, and Dennis Rapps.
Brief of amici curiae filed on behalf of Pacific Legal Foundation et al. by Timothy Sandefur and Manuel S. Klausner.
Brief of amici curiae filed on behalf of The Rutherford Institute by D. Alicia Hickok and John W. Whitehead.
Brief of amici curiae filed on behalf of Texas Black Americans for Life et al. by Lawrence J. Joyce.
Brief of amici curiae filed on behalf of the Thomas More Law Center by Richard Thompson and Erin Elizabeth Mersino.
Brief of amici curiae filed on behalf of Women's Public Policy Groups et al. by David R. Langdon and Rita M. Dunaway.
Brief of amici curiae filed on behalf of Women Speak for Themselves by Helen M. Alvard.
Brief of amici curiae filed on behalf of David Boyle by Mr. Boyle, pro se.
Brief of amici curiae filed on behalf of Daniel H. Branch by Mr. Branch, pro se.
Brief of amici curiae filed on behalf of Sen. Ted Cruz et al. by Sen. Cruz, pro se.
Brief of amici curiae filed on behalf of Joseph B. Scarnati III et al. by Jason P. Gosselin.
Brief of amici curiae filed on behalf of 9 Academic Institutions et al. by W. Cole Durham, Jr.
Brief of amici curiae filed on behalf of the State of Oklahoma by E. Scott Pruitt, Attorney General, and Patrick R. Wyrick, Solicitor General.
Brief of amici curiae filed on behalf of the American Civil Rights Union by Peter J. Ferrara.
Brief of amici curiae filed on behalf of the Catholic Medical Association by James E. Zucker and April L. Farris.
Brief of amici curiae filed on behalf of Judicial Watch, Inc., by Paul J. Orfanedes and Meredith L. Di Liberto.
Brief of amici curiae filed on behalf of National Religious Broadcasters by Craig L. Parshall.
Brief of amici curiae filed on behalf of 88 Members of Congress by Robert K. Kelner.
Brief of amici curiae filed on behalf of Eberle Communications Group, Inc., et al. by Herbert W. Titus, William J. Olson, John S. Miles, Jeremiah L. Morgan, and Michael Connelly.
Brief of amici curiae filed on behalf of the American Center for Law & Justice et al. by Jay Alan Sekulow, Stuart J. Roth, Jordan A. Sekulow, Colby M. May, Walter M. Weber, Francis J Manion, Geoffrey R. Surtees, Edward L. White III, and Erik M. Zimmerman.
Brief of amici curiae filed on behalf of the Cato Institute by Kevin T. Baine, Emmet T. Flood, C. J. Mahoney, and Ilya Shapiro.
Brief of amici curiae filed on behalf of Constitutional Law Scholars by Nathan S. Chapman.
Brief of amici curiae filed on behalf of Eagle Forum Education & Legal Defense Fund, Inc., by Lawrence J. Joseph.
Brief of amici curiae filed on behalf of the Foundation for Moral Law by John Eidsmoe.
Brief of amici curiae filed on behalf of Freedom X et al. by William J. Becker, Jr.
Brief of amici curiae filed on behalf of the Independent Women's Forum by Erin Morrow Hawley.
Brief of amici curiae filed on behalf of the International Conference of Evangelical Chaplain Endorsers by Arthur A. Schulcz, Sr.
Brief of amici curiae filed on behalf of J.E. Dunn Construction Group, Inc., et al. by Scott W. Gaylord.
Brief of amici curiae filed on behalf of John A. Ryan Institute for Catholic Social Thought by Teresa Stanton Collett.
Brief of amici curiae filed on behalf of Liberty University et al. by Mathew D. Staver, Anita L. Staver, Stephen M. Crampton, and Mary E. McAlister.
Brief of amici curiae filed on behalf of Massachusetts Citizens for Life, Inc., et al. by Dwight G. Duncan.
Brief of amici curiae filed on behalf of Reproductive Research Audit by Edward H. Trent.
Brief of amici curiae filed on behalf of the United States Conference of Catholic Bishops et al. by Noel J. Francisco, Anthony R. Picarello, Jr., Jeffrey Hunter Moon, and Michael F. Moses.
Brief of amici curiae filed on behalf of Westminster Theological Seminary by Kenneth R. Wynne and David E. Wynne.
Brief of amici curiae filed on behalf of Sen. Orrin G. Hatch et al. by Brendan M. Walsh, John D. Adams, and Matthew A. Fitzgerald.
Brief of amici curiae filed on behalf of 38 Protestant Theologians et al. by Jay T. Thompson and Miles Coleman.
Brief of amici curiae filed on behalf of 67 Catholic Theologians et al. by D. John Sauer.
Brief of amici curiae filed on behalf of Tri Valley Law, PC., by Marc A. Greendorfer.

IV. THE SUPREME COURT'S DECISION

"RFRA prohibits the 'Government [from] substantially burden[ing] a person's exercise of religion even if the burden results from a rule of general applicability' unless the Government 'demonstrates that application of the burden to the person—(1) is in furtherance of a compelling governmental interest; and (2) is the least restrictive means of furthering that compelling governmental interest.' The first question that we must address is whether this provision applies to regulations that govern the activities of for-profit corporations like Hobby Lobby, Conestoga, and Mardel. . . .

RFRA applies to 'a person's' exercise of religion, and RFRA itself does not define the term 'person.' We therefore look to the Dictionary Act . . . .

Under the Dictionary Act, 'the wor[d] 'person' . . . include[s] corporations, companies, associations, firms, partnerships, societies, and joint stock companies, as well as individuals.' . . .

We see nothing in RFRA that suggests a congressional intent to depart from the Dictionary Act definition, and HHS makes little effort to argue otherwise. . . .

This concession effectively dispatches any argument that the term 'person' as used in RFRA does not reach the closely held corporations involved in these cases. . . .

The principal argument advanced by HHS and the principal dissent regarding RFRA protection for Hobby Lobby, Conestoga, and Mardel focuses not on the statutory term 'person,' but on the phrase 'exercise of religion.' According to HHS and the dissent, these corporations are not protected by RFRA because they cannot exercise religion. Neither HHS nor the dissent, however, provides any persuasive explanation for this conclusion. . . .

For all these reasons, we hold that a federal regulation's restriction on the activities of a for-profit closely held corporation must comply with RFRA. . . .

Because RFRA applies in these cases, we must next ask whether the HHS contraceptive mandate 'substantially burden[s]' the exercise of religion. We have little trouble concluding that it does. . . .

Since the HHS contraceptive mandate imposes a substantial burden on the exercise of religion, we must . . . decide whether HHS has shown that the mandate both '(1) is in furtherance of a compelling governmental interest; and (2) is the least restrictive means of furthering that compelling governmental interest.' . . .

The contraceptive mandate, as applied to closely held corporations, violates RFRA. Our decision on that statutory question makes it unnecessary to reach the First Amendment claim . . . .

The judgment of the Tenth Circuit in No. 13–354 is affirmed; the judgment of the Third Circuit in No. 13–356 is reversed, and that case is remanded . . . ."

V. JUSTICE VOTE

4 Pro ACLU Side vs. 5 Con Opposing Side

ACLU Side (Petitioner / Appellant)

1. Kagan, E. – Joined Ginsburg's dissent in part, wrote a dissenting opinion with Breyer
2. Breyer, S. – Joined Ginsburg's dissent in part, wrote a dissenting opinion with Kagan
3. Ginsburg, R. – Wrote dissenting opinion
4. Sotomayor, S. – Joined Ginsburg's dissent

Opposing Side (Respondent / Appellee)

1. Alito, S. – Wrote majority opinion
2. Thomas, C. – Joined majority opinion
3. Scalia, A. – Joined majority opinion
4. Kennedy, A. – Wrote concurring opinion
5. Roberts, J. – Joined majority opinion

VI. A WIN OR LOSS FOR THE ACLU?

The ACLU filed as amicus curiae urging reversal of the judgment of the Tenth Circuit Court of Appeals and affirmance of the judgment of the Third Circuit Court of Appeals; the Supreme Court affirmed and reversed in a 5-4 vote, giving the ACLU an apparent loss.

1129. Heien v. North Carolina

(Decided December 15, 2014; 574 U.S. 54)

I. ISSUE

A. Issues Discussed

4th Amendment

B. Legal Question Presented

"In this case, an officer stopped a vehicle because one of its two brake lights was out, but a court later determined that a single working brake light was all the law required. The question presented is whether such a mistake of law can nonetheless give rise to the reasonable suspicion necessary to uphold the seizure under the Fourth Amendment."

C. Supreme Court's Answer

"We hold that it can. Because the officer's mistake about the brake-light law was reasonable, the stop in this case was lawful under the Fourth Amendment."

II. CASE SUMMARY

A. Background

"Sergeant Matt Darisse . . . sat in his patrol car . . . observing northbound traffic . . . . [A] Ford Escort passed by. Darisse thought the driver looked 'very stiff and nervous,' so he . . . began following the Escort. [T]he Escort braked as it approached a slower vehicle, but only the left brake light came on. Noting the faulty right brake light, Darisse . . . pulled the Escort over.

Two men were in the car: Maynor Javier Vasquez sat behind the wheel, and petitioner Nicholas Brady Heien lay across the rear seat. . . . Darisse . . . bec[a]me suspicious during the course of the stop—Vasquez appeared nervous, Heien remained lying down . . . , and the two gave inconsistent answers about their destination. . . . Darisse asked whether the men were transporting various types of contraband. Told no, Darisse asked whether he could search the Escort. Vasquez said he had no objection, but told Darisse he should ask Heien, because Heien owned the car. Heien gave his consent . . . . In the side compartment of a duffle bag, Darisse found a sandwich bag containing cocaine. . . .

The State charged Heien with attempted trafficking in cocaine. Heien moved to suppress the evidence seized from the car . . . . [T]he trial court denied the suppression motion, concluding that the faulty brake light had given Sergeant Darisse reasonable suspicion . . . , and that Heien's subsequent consent to the search was valid. Heien pleaded guilty . . . .

The North Carolina Court of Appeals reversed. The initial stop was not valid . . . because driving with only one working brake light was not . . . a violation of North Carolina law. . . .

The State appealed, and the North Carolina Supreme Court reversed."

The Supreme Court granted certiorari to review the case.

B. Counsel of Record / ACLU Attorney

ACLU Side (Petitioner / Appellant): Jeffrey L. Fisher argued the cause for appellants. With him on the brief were Michele Goldman and

Donald B. Ayer.

Opposing Side (Respondent / Appellee): Senior Deputy Attorney General Robert C. Montgomery argued the cause for appellee. With him on the brief were Roy Cooper, Attorney General of North Carolina, John F. Maddrey, Solicitor General of North Carolina, and Derrick C. Mertz, Assistant Attorney General.

Rachel P. Kovner argued the cause for the United States as amicus curiae.

III. AMICI CURIAE

ACLU Side (Petitioner / Appellant)

Brief of amici curiae filed on behalf of the National Association of Criminal Defense Lawyers, the Cato Institute, the American Civil Liberties Union, and the ACLU of North Carolina by Jonathan D. Hacker, Noah A. Levine, Jamie S. Dycus, Ari J. Savitzky, Carleen M. Zubrzycki, Steven R. Shapiro, Ezekiel R. Edwards, Christopher A. Brook, Joshua M. Salzman, and Ilya Shapiro.

Brief of amici curiae filed on behalf of Gun Owners Foundation et al. by Michael Connelly, William J. Olson, Herbert W. Titus, Robert J. Olson, John S. Miles, Jeremiah L. Morgan, and Mark B. Weinberg.

Brief of amici curiae filed on behalf of Professors Charles E. Maclean and Adam Lamparello by James J. Berles, Charles E. MacLean, and Adam Lamparello.

Brief of amici curiae filed on behalf of the Rutherford Institute by John W. Whitehead, Douglas R. McKusick, and Christopher F. Moriarty.

Opposing Side (Respondent / Appellee)

Brief of amici curiae filed on behalf of the United States by Solicitor General Verrilli, Assistant Attorney General Caldwell, Deputy Solicitor General Dreeben, Assistant Solicitor General Kovner, and John P. Taddei.

Brief of amici curiae filed on behalf of the Association of Prosecuting Attorneys by Gaëtan Gerville-Réache, John J. Bursch, and Matthew T. Nelson.

Brief of amici curiae filed on behalf of the State of Wisconsin et al. by J.B. Van Hollen, Attorney General of Wisconsin and Maura Fj Whelan, Assistant Attorney General, by John J. Hoffman Acting Attorney General of New Jersey, and by the Attorneys General for their respective jurisdictions as follows: Michael C. Geraghty of Alaska, Tom Horne of Arizona, Dustin McDaniel of Arkansas, Joseph R. Biden, III of Delaware, Irvin B. Nathan of the District of Columbia, David M. Louie of Hawaii, Gregory F. Zoeller of Indiana, Lawrence G. Wasden of Idaho, Thomas Miller of Iowa, Derek Schmidt of Kansas, Jack Conway of Kentucky, Janet T. Mills of Maine, Jim Hood of Mississippi, Gary K. King of New Mexico, Michael DeWine of Ohio, Peter F. Kilmartin of Rhode Island, William H. Sorrell of Vermont, and Peter K. Michael of Wyoming.

IV. THE SUPREME COURT'S DECISION

"A traffic stop for a suspected violation of law is a 'seizure' of the occupants of the vehicle and therefore must be conducted in accordance with the Fourth Amendment. All parties agree that to justify this type of seizure, officers need only 'reasonable suspicion' . . . . The question here is whether reasonable suspicion can rest on a mistaken understanding of the scope of a legal prohibition. We hold that it can. . . .

To be reasonable is not to be perfect, and so the Fourth Amendment allows for some mistakes on the part of government officials . . . . We have recognized that searches and seizures based on mistakes of fact can be reasonable. . . .

But reasonable men make mistakes of law, too, and such mistakes are no less compatible with the concept of reasonable suspicion. Reasonable suspicion arises from the combination of an officer's understanding of the facts and his understanding of the relevant law. The officer may be reasonably mistaken on either ground. Whether the facts turn out to be not what was thought, or the law turns out to be not what was thought, the result is the same: The facts are outside the scope of the law. There is no reason, under the text of the Fourth Amendment or our precedents, why this same result should be acceptable when reached by way of a reasonable mistake of fact, but not when reached by way of a similarly reasonable mistake of law. . . .

Here we have little difficulty concluding that the officer's error of law was reasonable. Although the North Carolina statute at issue refers to 'a stop lamp,' suggesting the need for only a single working brake light, it also provides that '[t]he stop lamp may be incorporated into a unit with one or more other rear lamps.' . . .

This 'stop lamp' provision, moreover, had never been previously construed by North Carolina's appellate courts. It was thus objectively reasonable for an officer in Sergeant Darisse's position to think that Heien's faulty right brake light was a violation of North Carolina law. And because the mistake of law was reasonable, there was reasonable suspicion justifying the stop.

The judgment of the Supreme Court of North Carolina is affirmed."

V. JUSTICE VOTE

1 Pro ACLU Side vs. 8 Con Opposing Side

ACLU Side (Petitioner / Appellant)

1. Sotomayor, S. – Wrote dissenting opinion

Opposing Side (Respondent / Appellee)

1. Roberts, J. – Wrote majority opinion
2. Alito, S. – Joined majority opinion
3. Kagan, E. – Wrote concurring opinion
4. Thomas, C. – Joined majority opinion
5. Breyer, S. – Joined majority opinion
6. Scalia, A. – Joined majority opinion
7. Kennedy, A. – Joined majority opinion
8. Ginsburg, R. – Joined Kagan's concurrence

VI. A WIN OR LOSS FOR THE ACLU?

The ACLU filed as amicus curiae urging reversal of the judgment of the North Carolina Supreme Court; the Supreme Court affirmed in an 8-1 vote, giving the ACLU an apparent loss.

1130. Holt v. Hobbs

(Decided January 20, 2015; 574 U.S. 352)

I. ISSUE

A. Issues Discussed

Prison

B. Legal Question Presented

Whether a prison grooming policy prohibiting a prisoner from growing a ½-inch beard in accordance with religious beliefs violates the Religious Land Use and Institutionalized Persons Act (RLUIPA).

C. Supreme Court's Answer

"In sum, we hold that the Department's grooming policy violates RLUIPA insofar as it prevents petitioner from growing a ½-inch beard in accordance with his religious beliefs."

II. CASE SUMMARY

A. Background

"Petitioner Gregory Holt, also known as Abdul Maalik Muhammad, is an Arkansas inmate and a devout Muslim who wishes to grow a ½-inch beard in accordance with his religious beliefs. Petitioner's objection to shaving his beard clashes with the Arkansas Department of Correction's grooming policy, which prohibits inmates from growing beards unless they have a particular dermatological condition. . . .

Petitioner filed a pro se complaint in Federal District Court challenging the grooming policy under RLUIPA. . . . In October 2011, the District Court granted petitioner a preliminary injunction and remanded to a Magistrate Judge for an evidentiary hearing. . . .

As a result of the preliminary injunction, petitioner had a short beard at the time of the hearing, and the Magistrate Judge commented: 'I look at your particular circumstance and I say, you know, it's almost preposterous to think that you could hide contraband in your beard.' Nevertheless, the Magistrate Judge recommended that the preliminary injunction be vacated and that petitioner's complaint be dismissed for failure to state a claim on which relief can be granted. . . .

The District Court adopted the Magistrate Judge's recommendation in full, and the Court of Appeals for the Eighth Circuit affirmed in a brief per curiam opinion, holding that the Department had satisfied its burden of showing that the grooming policy was the least restrictive means of furthering its compelling security interests."

The Supreme Court granted certiorari to review the case.

B. Counsel of Record / ACLU Attorney

ACLU Side (Petitioner / Appellant): Douglas Laycock argued the cause for appellants. With him on the brief were Eric C. Rassbach, Luke W. Goodrich, Mark L. Rienzi, Hannah C. Smith, and Joshua D. Hawley.

Assistant Solicitor General Yang argued the cause for the United States as amicus curiae.

Opposing Side (Respondent / Appellee): David A. Curran, Deputy Attorney General of Arkansas argued the cause for appellee. With him on the brief were Dustin Mcdaniel, Attorney General and Christine A. Cryer, Senior Assistant Attorney General.

III. AMICI CURIAE

ACLU Side (Petitioner / Appellant)

Brief of amici curiae filed on behalf of Former Corrections Officials John Clark et al. by Steven R. Shapiro, David Fath, and Daniel Mach of the American Civil Liberties Union Foundation, Randall C. Marshall of the American Civil Liberties Union of Alabama, and by Andrea W. Trento, Jonathan L. Abram, and Elizabeth Hagerty.

Brief of amici curiae filed on behalf of the United States by Solicitor General Verrilli, Acting Assistant Attorney General Samuels, Deputy Solicitor General Gershengorn, Assistant Solicitor General Harrington, Mark L. Gross, and April J. Anderson.

Brief of amici curiae filed on behalf of the Anti-Defamation League et al. by Derek L. Shaffer, Carolyn H. Thomas, and Archith Ramkumar.

Brief of amici curiae filed on behalf of the American Jewish Committee et al. by Adam S. Lurie, Samantha A. Dreilinger, Katherine A. Preston, and Marc D. Stern.

Brief of amici curiae filed on behalf of Former Prison Wardens by Carolyn F. Corwin and Stephanie Hall Barclay.

Brief of amici curiae filed on behalf of
Americans United for Separation of Church and State by Ayesha N. Khan, Gregory M. Lipper, Evan M. Tager, Richard B. Katskee, and James F. Tierney.

Brief of amici curiae filed on behalf of Alliance Defending Freedom by Kevin H. Theriot, Erik W. Stanley, Christiana M. Holcomb, and David A. Cortman.

Brief of amici curiae filed on behalf of the National Congress of American Indians and Huy by Joel West Williams, Richard A. Guest, Steven C. Moore, John Dossett, and Gabriel S. Galanda.

Brief of amici curiae filed on behalf of the National Jewish Commission on Law and Public Affairs ("Colpa"), et al. by Dennis Rapps, Nathan Lewin, and Alyza D. Lewin.

Brief of amici curiae filed on behalf of the Sikh Coalition and Muslim Public Affairs Council by Eric G. Osborne, Mark E. Haddad, and Collin P. Wedel.

Brief of amici curiae filed on behalf of Prison Fellowship Ministries et al. by Roger G. Brooks, Stefan H. Atkinson, and Amber L. Jordan.

Brief of amici curiae filed on behalf of Dr. Ronald L. Akers et al. by Kelly J. Shackelford, Jeffrey C. Mateer, Matthew J. Kacsmaryk, and Justin E. Butterfield.

Brief of amici curiae filed on behalf of International Mission Board of the Southern Baptist Convention et al. by Joel C. Haims, Tiffani B. Figueroa, Jeffrey M. David, Brian R. Matsui, Laura B. Heiman, and Derek Gaubatz.

Brief of amici curiae filed on behalf of Islamic Law Scholars by Christopher C. Lund.

Brief of amici curiae filed on behalf of Women's Prison Association by James A. Sonne.

Brief of amici curiae filed on behalf of the Rutherford Institute by Anand Agneshwar, Anna K. Thompson, Carl S. Nadler, John W. Whitehead, and Douglas R. McKusick.

Brief of amici curiae filed on behalf of Reformed Prisoners Jesse Wiese et al. by Matthew A. Fitzgerald and Providence E. Napoleon.

Opposing Side (Respondent / Appellee)

Brief of amici curiae filed on behalf of the State of Alabama et al. by Luther Strange, Attorney General of Alabama, Andrew L. Brasher, Solicitor General, Megan A. Kirkpatrick, Assistant Solicitor General, and by the Attorneys General for their respective jurisdictions as follows: Michael C. Geraghty of Alaska, Tom Horne of Arizona, Sam Olens of Georgia, David Louie of Hawaii, Greg Zoeller of Indiana, Derek Schmidt of Kansas, Jim Hood of Mississippi, Tim Fox of Montana, Jon Bruning of Nebraska, Wayne Stenehjem of North Dakota, Scott Pruitt of Oklahoma, Kathleen G. Kane of Pennsylvania, Alan Wilson of South Carolina, Marty J. Jackley of South Dakota, Greg Abbott of Texas, Patrick Morrisey of West Virginia, and Peter K. Michael of Wyoming.

IV. THE SUPREME COURT'S DECISION

"Under RLUIPA, petitioner bore the initial burden of proving that the Department's grooming policy implicates his religious exercise. . . . Here, the religious exercise at issue is the growing of a beard, which petitioner believes is a dictate of his religious faith . . . .

In addition to showing that the relevant exercise of religion is grounded in a sincerely held religious belief, petitioner also bore the burden of proving that the Department's grooming policy substantially burdened that exercise of religion. Petitioner easily satisfied that obligation. . . .

The District Court reached the opposite conclusion, but . . . misunderstood the analysis . . . .

Since petitioner met his burden of showing that the . . . grooming policy substantially burdened his exercise of religion, the burden shifted to the Department to show that its refusal to allow petitioner to grow a ½-inch beard '(1) [was] in furtherance of a compelling governmental interest; and (2) [was] the least restrictive means of furthering that compelling governmental interest.' . . .

The Department contends that enforcing this prohibition is the least restrictive means of furthering prison safety and security in two specific ways. . . .

The Department first claims that the no-beard policy prevents prisoners from hiding contraband. . . .

[T]he Department's interest in eliminating contraband cannot sustain its refusal . . . .

The Department contends that its grooming policy is necessary to further an additional compelling interest, i.e., preventing prisoners from disguising their identities. . . .

We are unpersuaded . . . for at least two reasons. First, the Department failed to show . . . that the dual-photo method cannot be employed at its institutions. Second, the Department failed to establish why the risk that a prisoner will shave . . . to disguise himself is so great . . . even though prisoners are allowed to grow mustaches, head hair, or ¼-inch beards for medical reasons. . . .

We emphasize that although RLUIPA provides substantial protection for the religious exercise of institutionalized persons, it also affords prison officials ample ability to maintain security. . . . First, . . . courts should not blind themselves to the fact that the analysis is conducted in the prison setting. Second, if an institution suspects that an inmate is using religious activity to cloak illicit conduct, 'prison officials may appropriately question . . . .' Third, even if a claimant's religious belief is sincere, an institution might be entitled to withdraw an accommodation if the claimant abuses the exemption in a manner that undermines the prison's compelling interests. . . .

In sum, we hold that the Department's grooming policy violates RLUIPA insofar as it prevents petitioner from growing a ½-inch beard in accordance with his religious beliefs. The judgment of the United States Court of Appeals for the Eighth Circuit is reversed, and the case is remanded . . . ."

V. JUSTICE VOTE

9 Pro ACLU Side vs. 0 Con Opposing Side

ACLU Side (Petitioner / Appellant)

1. Alito, S. – Wrote majority opinion
2. Kagan, E. – Joined majority opinion
3. Thomas, C. – Joined majority opinion
4. Breyer, S. – Joined majority opinion
5. Scalia, A. – Joined majority opinion
6. Kennedy, A. – Joined majority opinion
7. Ginsburg, R. – Wrote concurring opinion
8. Sotomayor, S. – Wrote concurring opinion, joined Ginsburg's concurrence
9. Roberts, J. – Joined majority opinion

VI. A WIN OR LOSS FOR THE ACLU?

The ACLU filed as amicus curiae urging reversal of the judgment of the Court of Appeals; the Supreme Court reversed in a 9-0 vote, giving the ACLU an apparent win.

1131. Young v. United Parcel Service, Inc.

(Decided March 25, 2015; 135 S.Ct. 1338; 575 U.S. _)

I. ISSUE

A. Issues Discussed

Gender

B. Legal Question Presented

"The Pregnancy Discrimination Act makes clear that Title VII's prohibition against sex discrimination applies to discrimination based on pregnancy. It also says that employers must treat 'women affected by pregnancy . . . the same for all employment-related purposes . . . as other persons not so affected but similar in their ability or inability to work.' 42 U.S.C. § 2000e(k). We must decide how this latter provision applies in the context of an employer's policy that accommodates many, but not all, workers with nonpregnancy-related disabilities."

C. Supreme Court's Answer

"In our view, the Act requires courts to consider the extent to which an employer's policy treats pregnant workers less favorably than it treats nonpregnant workers similar in their ability or inability to work. And here—as in all cases in which an individual plaintiff seeks to show disparate treatment through indirect evidence—it requires courts to consider any legitimate, nondiscriminatory, nonpretextual justification for these differences in treatment. Ultimately the court must determine whether the nature of the employer's policy and the way in which it burdens pregnant women shows that the employer has engaged in intentional discrimination."

II. CASE SUMMARY

A. Background

"Peggy Young, worked as a part-time driver for . . . United Parcel Service (UPS). . . . [A]fter suffering several miscarriages, she became pregnant. Her doctor told her that she should not lift more than 20 pounds . . . . UPS required drivers . . . to lift parcels weighing up to 70 pounds . . . . UPS told Young she could not work . . . . Young . . . stayed home without pay during most of the . . . pregnan[cy] and . . . lost her employee medical coverage.

Young subsequently brought this federal lawsuit. . . . Young said that her co-workers were willing to help her with heavy packages. She also said that UPS accommodated other drivers who were 'similar in their . . . inability to work.' . . .

UPS responded that the 'other persons' whom it had accommodated were (1) drivers who had become disabled on the job, (2) those who had lost their Department of Transportation (DOT) certifications, and (3) those who suffered from a disability covered by the Americans with Disabilities Act of 1990 (ADA). UPS said that, since Young did not fall within any of those categories, it had not discriminated against Young on the basis of pregnancy but had treated her just as it treated all 'other' relevant 'persons.' . . .

In July 2007, Young filed a pregnancy discrimination charge with the Equal Employment Opportunity Commission (EEOC). In September 2008, the EEOC provided her with a right-to-sue letter. Young then filed this complaint in Federal District Court. . . .

After discovery, UPS filed a motion for summary judgment. . . .

The District Court granted UPS' motion for summary judgment. . . .

On appeal, the Fourth Circuit affirmed."

The Supreme Court granted certiorari to review the case.

B. Counsel of Record / ACLU Attorney

ACLU Side (Petitioner / Appellant): Samuel R. Bagenstos argued the cause for appellants. With him on the brief was Sharon Fast Gustafson.

Solicitor General Verrilli argued the cause for the United States as amicus curiae.

Opposing Side (Respondent / Appellee): Caitlin J. Halligan argued the cause for appellee. With her on the brief were Rachel S. Brass, Mark A. Perry, Marisa C. Maleck, Kellam M. Conover, Emmett F. Mcgee, Jr., and Jill S. Distler.

III. AMICI CURIAE

ACLU Side (Petitioner / Appellant)

Brief of amici curiae filed on behalf of the American Civil Liberties Union and a Better Balance et al. by Deborah A. Jeon, Lenora M. Lapidus, Steven R. Shapiro, Ariela M. Migdal, Dina Bakst, Phoebe Taubman, and Elizabeth Gedmark.

Brief of amici curiae filed on behalf of the United States by Solicitor General Verrilli, Acting Assistant Attorney General Moran, Deputy Solicitor General Gershengorn, Assistant Solicitor General Harrington, Dennis J. Dimsey, Holly A. Thomas, and Bonnie I. Robin-Vergeer, P. David Lopez, Carolyn L. Wheeler, and Julie L. Gantz.

Brief of amici curiae filed on behalf of the United States by Solicitor General Verrilli, Acting Assistant Attorney General Samuels, Deputy Solicitor General Gershengorn, Assistant Solicitor General Harrington, Dennis J. Dimsey, Holly A. Thomas, and Bonnie I. Robin-Vergeer.

Brief of amici curiae filed on behalf of Law Professors and Women's and Civil Rights Organizations by Jelena Kolic, Joanna L. Grossman, and Deborah L. Brake.

Brief of amici curiae filed on behalf of Black Women's Health Imperative et al. by Jonathan M. Cohen, Kami E. Quinn, Jenna A. Hudson, Kristiné Hansen, and James Liddell.

Brief of amici curiae filed on behalf of U.S. Women's Chamber of Commerce et al. by David C. Frederick.

Brief of amici curiae filed on behalf of Members of Congress by Emily Martin, Andrew H. Bart, and Anne Cortina Perry.

Brief of amici curiae filed on behalf of 23 Pro-Life Organizations et al. by Thomas C. Berg, Teresa S. Collett, Ovide M. Lamontagne, Clarke D. Forsythe, Carrie Severino, and Jonathan Keim.

Brief of amici curiae filed on behalf of the National Education Association et al. by Judith A. Scott, Nicole G. Berner, Jennifer L. Hunter, Alice O'Brien, Jason Walta, Chaka Donaldson, William Lurye, Paula J. Caira, David Strom, and Nicholas W. Clark.

Brief of amici curiae filed on behalf of Bipartisan State and Local Legislators by Ellen Eardley.

Brief of amici curiae filed on behalf of Health Care Providers et al. by Judith L. Lichtman, Victoria S. Shabo, Sarah Lipton-Lubet, Sarah Fleisch Fink, Vasanthi Reddy, Stephanie D. Yost, Katherine M. Kimpel, Maya Sequeira, and Kate Mueting.

Brief of amici curiae filed on behalf of the Leadership Conference on Civil and Human Rights by Wade J. Henderson, Lisa M. Bornstein, and Maria T. Vullo.

Opposing Side (Respondent / Appellee)

Brief of amici curiae filed on behalf of the Equal Employment Advisory Council et al. by Karen Harned, Elizabeth Milito, and Rae T. Vann.

Brief of amici curiae filed on behalf of American Trucking Associations, Inc. by Prasad Sharma, Richard Pianka, Thomas R. Mccarthy, and William S. Consovoy.

Brief of amici curiae filed on behalf of Eagle Forum Education & Legal Defense Fund, Inc. by Lawrence J. Joseph.

Brief of amici curiae filed on behalf of U.S. Chamber of Commerce by Kathleen M. Sullivan, Quinn Emanuel, Lily Fu

Claffee, Kate Comerford Todd, Steven P. Lehotsky, Warren Postman, and Lori Alvino Mcgill.

IV. THE SUPREME COURT'S DECISION

"This case requires us to consider the application of the second clause [of the Pregnancy Discrimination Act] to a 'disparate-treatment' claim—a claim that an employer intentionally treated a complainant less favorably than employees with the 'complainant's qualifications' but outside the complainant's protected class. . . . .

The parties disagree about the interpretation of the Pregnancy Discrimination Act's second clause. . . . Does this clause mean that courts must compare workers only in respect to the work limitations that they suffer? Does it mean that courts must ignore all other similarities or differences between pregnant and nonpregnant workers? Or does it mean that courts, when deciding who the relevant 'other persons' are, may consider other similarities and differences as well? If so, which ones?

The differences between these possible interpretations come to the fore when a court, as here, must consider a workplace policy that distinguishes between pregnant and nonpregnant workers in light of characteristics not related to pregnancy. . . .

In our view, an individual pregnant worker who seeks to show disparate treatment through indirect evidence may do so through application of the McDonnell Douglas framework. That framework requires a plaintiff to make out a prima facie case of discrimination. But it is 'not intended to be an inflexible rule.' Rather, an individual plaintiff may establish a prima facie case by 'showing actions taken by the employer from which one can infer, if such actions remain unexplained, that it is more likely than not that such actions were based on a discriminatory criterion illegal under' Title VII. The burden of making this showing is 'not onerous.' In particular, making this showing is not as burdensome as succeeding on 'an ultimate finding of fact as to' a discriminatory employment action. Neither does it require the plaintiff to show that those whom the employer favored and those whom the employer disfavored were similar in all but the protected ways. . . .

We do not determine whether Young created a genuine issue of material fact as to whether UPS' reasons for having treated Young less favorably than it treated these other nonpregnant employees were pretextual. We leave a final determination . . . for the Fourth Circuit to make on remand . . . .

For the reasons above, we vacate the judgment of the Fourth Circuit and remand the case . . . ."

V. JUSTICE VOTE

6 Pro ACLU Side vs. 3 Con Opposing Side

ACLU Side (Petitioner / Appellant)

1. Breyer, S. – Wrote majority opinion
2. Alito, S. – Wrote concurring opinion
3. Kagan, E. – Joined majority opinion
4. Ginsburg, R. – Joined majority opinion
5. Sotomayor, S. – Joined majority opinion
6. Roberts, J. – Joined majority opinion

Opposing Side (Respondent / Appellee)

1. Thomas, C. – Joined Scalia's dissent
2. Scalia, A. – Wrote dissenting opinion
3. Kennedy, A. – Wrote dissenting opinion, joined Scalia's dissent

VI. A WIN OR LOSS FOR THE ACLU?

The ACLU filed as amicus curiae urging reversal of the judgment of the Court of Appeals; the Supreme Court vacated in a 6-3 vote, giving the ACLU an apparent win.

1132. Armstrong v. Exceptional Child Center, Inc.

(Decided March 31, 2015; 135 S.Ct. 1378; 575 U.S. _)

I. ISSUE

A. Issues Discussed

Federalism

B. Legal Question Presented

"We consider whether Medicaid providers can sue to enforce § (30)(A) of the Medicaid Act."

C. Supreme Court's Answer

"The sheer complexity associated with enforcing § 30(A), coupled with the express provision of an administrative remedy, § 1396c, shows that the Medicaid Act precludes private enforcement of § 30(A) in the courts."

II. CASE SUMMARY

A. Background

"Medicaid is a federal program that subsidizes the States' provision of medical services to 'families with dependent children and of aged, blind, or disabled individuals, whose income and resources are insufficient to meet the costs of necessary medical services.' . . .

In order to qualify for Medicaid funding, the State of Idaho adopted, and the Federal Government approved, a Medicaid 'plan,' § 1396a(a), which Idaho administers through its Department of Health and Welfare. . . .

Respondents are providers of habilitation services to persons covered by Idaho's Medicaid plan. They sued petitioners—two officials in Idaho's Department of Health and Welfare—in the United States District Court for the District of Idaho, claiming that Idaho violates § 30(A) by reimbursing providers of habilitation services at rates lower than § 30(A) permits. They asked the court to enjoin petitioners to increase these rates.

The District Court entered summary judgment for the providers, holding that Idaho had not set rates in a manner consistent with § 30(A). The Ninth Circuit affirmed."

The Supreme Court granted certiorari to review the case.

B. Counsel of Record / ACLU Attorney

ACLU Side (Respondent / Appellee): James M. Piotrowski argued the cause for appellee. With him on the briefs were Stephen P.

Berzon, Stacey M. Leyton, and Matthew J. Murray.
Deputy Solicitor General Kneedler argued the cause for the United States as amicus curiae.
Opposing Side (Petitioner / Appellant): Carl J. Withroe argued the cause for appellant. With him on the briefs were Lawrence G. Wasden, Steven L. Olsen, and Peg M. Dougherty.

III. AMICI CURIAE

ACLU Side (Respondent / Appellee)

Brief of amici curiae filed on behalf of the American Civil Liberties Union, the NAACP Legal Defense & Educational Fund, the Mexican American Legal Defense & Educational Fund, and the Lawyers' Committee for Civil Rights Under Law by Sherrilyn Ifill, Janai S. Nelson, Christina A. Swarns, Jin Hee Lee, Nina Perales, Steven R. Shapiro, Omar C. Jadwat, and Jon Greenbaum.

Brief of amici curiae filed on behalf of Medicaid Defense Fund by Lynn S. Carman.

Brief of amici curiae filed on behalf of National Health Law Program et al. by Kelly Bagby and Jane Perkins.

Brief of amici curiae filed on behalf of the American Network of Community Options and Resources et al. by Joel M. Hamme.

Brief of amici curiae filed on behalf of the American Hospital Association and the Federation of American Hospitals by Melinda Reid Hatton, Maureen D. Mudron, Dominic F. Perella, and Eugene A. Sokoloff.

Brief of amici curiae filed on behalf of Former HHS Officials by Matthew M. Hoffman, Andrew Kim, and Stephen I. Vladeck.

Brief of amici curiae filed on behalf of the American Medical Association et al. by Stuart H. Singer, Carl E. Goldfarb, Andrew L. Adler, Benjamin D. Geffen, and Joshua P. Riley.

Brief of amici curiae filed on behalf of Constitutional Accountability Center by Douglas T. Kendall, Elizabeth B. Wydra, David H. Gans, and Brianne J. Gorod.

Brief of amici curiae filed on behalf of Members of Congress by Paul M. Smith, Matthew S. Hellman, Leah J. Tulin, and Emily A. Bruemmer.

Brief of amici curiae filed on behalf of the American Association of People with Disabilities et al. by Samuel R. Bagenstos, Elizabeth B. Mccallum, and Erik Raven-Hansen.

Brief of amici curiae filed on behalf of the Chamber of Commerce of the United States of America by Kate Comerford Todd, Carter G. Phillips, Tyler R. Green, Peter D. Keisler, Quin M. Sorenson, and Lowell J. Schiller.

Opposing Side (Petitioner / Appellant)

Brief of amici curiae filed on behalf of the State of Texas et al. by Greg Abbott, Attorney General of Texas, Daniel T. Hodge, First Assistant Attorney General, Jonathan F. Mitchell, Solicitor General, and by the Attorneys General for their respective jurisdictions as follows: Luther Strange of Alabama, Michael C. Geraghty of Alaska, Thomas C. Horne of Arizona, Dustin Mcdaniel of Arkansas, George Jepsen of Connecticut, Joseph R. Biden III of Delaware, Sam Olens of Georgia, David M. Louie of Hawaii, Gregory F. Zoeller of Indiana, Derek Schmidt of Kansas, Douglas F. Gansler of Maryland, Bill Schuette of Michigan, Jim Hood of Mississippi, Jon Bruning of Nebraska, Catherine Cortez Masto of Nevada, Wayne Stenehjem of North Dakota, Michael Dewine of Ohio, E. Scott Pruitt of Oklahoma, Ellen F. Rosenblum of Oregon, Kathleen G. Kane of Pennsylvania, Alan Wilson of South Carolina, Marty J. Jackley of South Dakota, Robert E. Cooper, Jr. of Tennessee, Sean D. Reyes of Utah, J.B. Van Hollen of Wisconsin, and Peter K. Michael of Wyoming.

Brief of amici curiae filed on behalf of National Governors Association and Council of State Governments by Michael W. McConnell and Stephen S. Schwartz.

Brief of amici curiae filed on behalf of the California Health and Human Services Agency by Kamala D. Harris, Attorney General of California, Edward C. Dumont, Solicitor General, Kathleen A. Kenealy, Chief Assistant Attorney General, Julie Weng-Gutierrez, Senior Assistant Attorney General Gregory D. Brown, Deputy Solicitor General, Susan M. Carson, Supervising Deputy Attorney General, and Joshua N. Sondheimer, Deputy Attorney General.

IV. THE SUPREME COURT'S DECISION

"Respondents contend that our preemption jurisprudence—specifically, the fact that we have regularly considered whether to enjoin the enforcement of state laws that are alleged to violate federal law—demonstrates that the Supremacy Clause creates a cause of action for its violation. They are incorrect. . . .

The ability to sue to enjoin unconstitutional actions by state and federal officers is the creation of courts of equity, and reflects a long history of judicial review of illegal executive action, tracing back to England. . . .

We turn next to respondents' contention that, quite apart from any cause of action conferred by the Supremacy Clause, this suit can proceed against Idaho in equity.

The power of federal courts of equity to enjoin unlawful executive action is subject to express and implied statutory limitations. . . . In our view the Medicaid Act implicitly precludes private enforcement of § 30(A), and respondents cannot, by invoking our equitable powers, circumvent Congress's exclusion of private enforcement. . . .

The sheer complexity associated with enforcing § 30(A), coupled with the express provision of an administrative remedy, § 1396c, shows that the Medicaid Act precludes private enforcement of § 30(A) in the courts.

The dissent agrees with us that the Supremacy Clause does not provide an implied right of action, and that Congress may displace the equitable relief that is traditionally available to enforce federal law. It disagrees only with our conclusion that such displacement has occurred here. . . .

The last possible source of a cause of action for respondents is the Medicaid Act itself. They do not claim that, and rightly so. Section 30(A) lacks the sort of rights-creating language needed to imply a private right of action. . . .

Our precedents establish that a private right of action under federal law is not created by mere implication, but must be 'unambiguously conferred.' Nothing in the Medicaid Act suggests that Congress meant to change that for the commitments made under § 30(A). . . .

The judgment of the Ninth Circuit Court of Appeals is reversed."

V. JUSTICE VOTE

4 Pro ACLU Side vs. 5 Con Opposing Side

ACLU Side (Respondent / Appellee)

1. Kagan, E. – Joined Sotomayor's dissent
2. Kennedy, A. – Joined Sotomayor's dissent
3. Ginsburg, R. – Joined Sotomayor's dissent
4. Sotomayor, S. – Wrote dissenting opinion

Opposing Side (Petitioner / Appellant)

1. Scalia, A. – Wrote majority opinion
2. Alito, S. – Joined majority opinion
3. Thomas, C. – Joined majority opinion
4. Breyer, S. – Wrote concurring opinion
5. Roberts, J. – Joined majority opinion

VI. A WIN OR LOSS FOR THE ACLU?

The ACLU filed as amicus curiae urging affirmance; the Supreme Court reversed the Court of Appeals' decision by a 5-4 vote, giving the ACLU an apparent loss.

1133. Williams-Yulee v. Florida Bar

(Decided April 29, 2015; 135 S.Ct. 1656; 575 U.S. _)

I. ISSUE

A. Issues Discussed

1st Amendment, press, speech, association

B. Legal Question Presented

"[M]any . . . States prohibit judges and judicial candidates from personally soliciting funds for their campaigns. We must decide whether the First Amendment permits such restrictions on speech."

C. Supreme Court's Answer

"We hold that it does. Judges are not politicians, even when they come to the bench by way of the ballot. And a State's decision to elect its judiciary does not compel it to treat judicial candidates like campaigners for political office. A State may assure its people that judges will apply the law without fear or favor—and without having personally asked anyone for money."

II. CASE SUMMARY

A. Background

"Like Florida, most . . . States prohibit judicial candidates from soliciting campaign funds personally, but allow them to raise money through committees. According to the American Bar Association, 30 of the 39 States that elect trial or appellate judges have adopted restrictions similar to [Florida's] Canon 7C(1). . . .

Lanell Williams–Yulee . . . decided to run for a seat on the county court for Hillsborough County . . . . Shortly after filing paperwork to enter the race, Yulee drafted a letter announcing her candidacy [and soliciting campaign contributions]. . . .

Yulee signed the letter and mailed it to local voters [and] posted [it] on her campaign Web site.

Yulee's bid for the bench did not unfold as she had hoped. She lost the primary to the incumbent judge. Then the Florida Bar filed a complaint against her. [T]he Bar charged her with violating Rule 4–8.2(b) of the Rules Regulating the Florida Bar. That Rule requires judicial candidates to comply with applicable provisions of Florida's Code of Judicial Conduct, including the ban on personal solicitation of campaign funds in Canon 7C(1).

Yulee admitted that she had signed and sent the fundraising letter. But she argued that the Bar could not discipline her . . . because the First Amendment protects a judicial candidate's right to solicit campaign funds in an election. The Florida Supreme Court appointed a referee, who . . . recommended a finding of guilt. As a sanction, the referee recommended that Yulee be publicly reprimanded and . . . pay the costs of the proceeding ($1,860).

The Florida Supreme Court adopted the referee's recommendations."

The Supreme Court granted certiorari to review the case.

B. Counsel of Record / ACLU Attorney

ACLU Side (Petitioner / Appellant): Andrew J. Pincus argued the cause for appellants. With him on the brief were Ernest J. Myers, Lee W. Marcus, Eugene R. Fidell, Andrew J. Pincus, Charles A. Rothfeld, Michael B. Kimberly, and Paul W. Hughes.

Opposing Side (Respondent / Appellee): Barry Richard argued the cause for appellee. With him on the brief were Barry Richard and M. Hope Keating.

III. AMICI CURIAE

ACLU Side (Petitioner / Appellant)

Brief of amici curiae filed on behalf of the American Civil Liberties Union and American Civil Liberties Union of Florida by Steven R. Shapiro, Nancy G. Abudu, Robert Corn-Revere, Peter Karanjia, Ronald G. London, and Micah J. Ratner.

Brief of amici curiae filed on behalf of Randolph Wolfson et al. by James Bopp, Jr. and Anita Y. Milanovich.

Brief of amici curiae filed on behalf of the Thomas Jefferson Center for the Protection of Free Expression by Thomas E. Hogan and J. Joshua Wheeler.

Brief of amici curiae filed on behalf of Cameron A. Blau, Esq. by Christopher Wiest and Jack Gatlin.

Opposing Side (Respondent / Appellee)

Brief of amici curiae filed on behalf of Norman Dorsen, Aryeh Neier, Burt Neuborne, and John Shattuck as Past Leaders of the American Civil Liberties Union by Burt Neuborne and Norman Dorsen.

Brief of amici curiae filed on behalf of Free Speech for People and the Honorable James C. Nelson by Ronald A. Fein.

Brief of amici curiae filed on behalf of Professor Jed Shugerman by Jed Shugerman, Donald B. Ayer, Sarah A. Hunger, and Bryan J. Leitch.

Brief of amici curiae filed on behalf of Professors of Law,

Economics, and Polticial Science by Jessica Ring Amunson and Alex Trepp.

Brief of amici curiae filed on behalf of Public Citizen, Inc., et al. by Seth P. Waxman, Scott L. Nelson, Catherine M.A. Carroll, Allison M. Zieve, Rachel M. Clattenburg, Donald J. Simon, and Fred Wertheimer.

Brief of amici curiae filed on behalf of the State of Arizona et al. by Thomas C. Horne, Attorney General of Arizona, Robert L. Ellman, Solicitor General, and Paula S. Bickett, and by the Attorneys General for their respective jurisdictions as follows: Dustin McDaniel of Arkansas, Lawrence G. Wasden of Idaho, Gregory F. Zoeller of Indiana, Jim Hood of Mississippi, Wayne Stenehjem of North Dakota, Ellen F. Rosenbaum of Oregon, Kathleen G. Kane of Pennsylvania, Marty J. Jackley of South Dakota, William H. Sorrell of Vermont, and Robert W. Ferguson of Washington.

Brief of amici curiae filed on behalf of State and Local Judicial Reform Groups by Roger A. Cooper, Peter Fox, Paul Titus, Nancy Winkelman, and Shannon L.C. Ammon.

Brief of amici curiae filed on behalf of Brennan Center for Justice at NYU School of Law et al. by Wendy Weiser, Alicia L. Bannon, Matthew Menendez, Randolph S. Sherman, Robert M. Grass, Elizabeth Kennedy, Brenda Wright, Hayley Gorenberg, Eric Lesh, J. Gerald Hebert, Megan P. Mcallen, and Catherine Hinckley Kelley.

Brief of amici curiae filed on behalf of the Carter Center by Martha F. Davis, Boris Bershteyn, Román J. Rodriguez, and Benjamin S. Goldberg.

Brief of amici curiae filed on behalf of Conference of Chief Justices by George T. Patton, Jr., Karl J. Sandstrom, Joshua L. Kaul, Igor V. Timofeyev, and Danielle R.A. Susanj.

Brief of amici curiae filed on behalf of Thomas R. Phillips et al. by Scott E. Gant and Joshua Riley.

Brief of amici curiae filed on behalf of Major B. Harding et al. by Daniel L. Wallach.

Brief of amici curiae filed on behalf of the American Bar Association by Thomas P. Mcgarry, Joshua G. Vincent, Steven M. Puiszis, Matthew R. Henderson, Adam R. Vaught, and William C. Hubbard.

IV. THE SUPREME COURT'S DECISION

"The parties agree that Canon 7C(1) restricts Yulee's speech on the basis of its content by prohibiting her from soliciting contributions to her election campaign. The parties disagree, however, about the level of scrutiny that should govern our review. . . .

In sum, we hold today what we assumed in White: A State may restrict the speech of a judicial candidate only if the restriction is narrowly tailored to serve a compelling interest. . . .

We have emphasized that 'it is the rare case' in which a State demonstrates that a speech restriction is narrowly tailored to serve a compelling interest. But those cases do arise. . . . Here, Canon 7C(1) advances the State's compelling interest in preserving public confidence in the integrity of the judiciary, and it does so through means narrowly tailored to avoid unnecessarily abridging speech. This is therefore one of the rare cases in which a speech restriction withstands strict scrutiny. . . .

Yulee acknowledges the State's compelling interest in judicial integrity. She argues, however, that the Canon's failure to restrict other speech equally damaging to judicial integrity and its appearance undercuts the Bar's position. . . .

Canon 7C(1) raises no fatal underinclusivity concerns. The solicitation ban aims squarely at the conduct most likely to undermine public confidence in the integrity of the judiciary . . . .

Taken to its logical conclusion, the position advanced by Yulee . . . is that Florida may ban the solicitation of funds by judicial candidates only if the State bans all solicitation of funds in judicial elections. The First Amendment does not put a State to that all-or-nothing choice. . . .

Yulee argues that the Canon violates the First Amendment because it restricts too much [speech]. . . .

We decline to wade into this swamp. The First Amendment requires that Canon 7C(1) be narrowly tailored, not that it be 'perfectly tailored.' . . .

In sum, because Canon 7C(1) is narrowly tailored to serve a compelling government interest, the First Amendment poses no obstacle to its enforcement in this case. As a result of our decision, Florida may continue to prohibit judicial candidates from personally soliciting campaign funds . . . .

The desirability of judicial elections . . . has sparked disagreement for more than 200 years. . . .

It is not our place to resolve this enduring debate. Our limited task is to apply the Constitution to the question presented . . . . Judicial candidates have a First Amendment right to speak in support of their campaigns. States have a compelling interest in preserving public confidence in their judiciaries. When the State adopts a narrowly tailored restriction . . . , those principles do not conflict. . . .

The judgment of the Florida Supreme Court is affirmed."

V. JUSTICE VOTE

4 Pro ACLU Side vs. 5 Con Opposing Side

ACLU Side (Petitioner / Appellant)

1. Alito, S. – Wrote dissenting opinion
2. Thomas, C. – Joined Scalia's dissent
3. Scalia, A. – Wrote dissenting opinion
4. Kennedy, A. – Wrote dissenting opinion

Opposing Side (Respondent / Appellee)

1. Roberts, J. – Wrote majority opinion
2. Kagan, E. – Joined majority opinion
3. Breyer, S. – Wrote concurring opinion
4. Ginsburg, R. – Wrote concurring opinion
5. Sotomayor, S. – Joined majority opinion

VI. A WIN OR LOSS FOR THE ACLU?

The ACLU filed as amicus curiae urging reversal of the judgment of the Florida Supreme Court; the U.S. Supreme Court affirmed in a 5-4 vote, giving the ACLU an apparent loss.

1134. City and County of San Francisco v. Sheehan

(Decided May 18, 2015; 135 S.Ct. 1765; 575 U.S. _)

I. ISSUE

A. Issues Discussed

4th Amendment, immunity

B. Legal Question Presented

"The first question . . . asks whether [Title II of the ADA] 'requires law enforcement officers to provide accommodations to an armed, violent, and mentally ill suspect in the course of bringing the suspect into custody.' . . .

The second question presented is whether Reynolds and Holder can be held personally liable for the injuries that Sheehan suffered."

C. Supreme Court's Answer

"After reviewing the parties' submissions, we dismiss the first question as improvidently granted. We decide the second question and hold that the officers are entitled to qualified immunity because they did not violate any clearly established Fourth Amendment rights."

II. CASE SUMMARY

A. Background

"Respondent is Teresa Sheehan, a woman who suffers from a schizoaffective disorder. . . .

Sheehan lived in a group home . . . .

[Social worker] Hodge knocked on Sheehan's door . . . . He then used a key to enter . . . . Initially, she would not respond . . . . But she then sprang up, reportedly yelling, 'Get out of here! You don't have a warrant! I have a knife, and I'll kill you if I have to.' . . .

Officer Holder responded to police dispatch and headed toward the group home. . . .

[T]he officers went to Sheehan's room . . . . [T]he officers used Hodge's key to enter . . . . Sheehan reacted violently. She grabbed a kitchen knife . . . and began approaching the officers, yelling . . . . The officers . . . retreated and Sheehan closed the door . . . .'

Reynolds and Holder . . . could wait for backup . . . . Or they could . . . try to subdue Sheehan . . . . [T]hey did not . . . consider whether Sheehan's disability should be accommodated. . . .

With pistols drawn, the officers moved in. When Sheehan, knife in hand, saw them, she again yelled . . . . Reynolds began pepper-spraying Sheehan in the face, but Sheehan would not drop the knife. . . . Holder shot her twice, but she did not collapse. Reynolds then fired multiple shots. . . . Sheehan finally fell . . . . Sheehan survived. . . .

Sheehan . . . brought suit, alleging . . . that San Francisco violated the Americans with Disabilities Act . . . by subduing her in a manner that did not reasonably accommodate her disability. She also sued Reynolds and Holder in their personal capacities . . . .

The District Court granted summary judgment for petitioners. . . .

On appeal, the Ninth Circuit vacated in part."

The Supreme Court granted certiorari to review the case.

B. Counsel of Record / ACLU Attorney

ACLU Side (Respondent / Appellee): Leonard Feldman argued the cause for appellee. With him on the briefs were Ben Nisenbaum, Jill D. Bowman, and Hunter O. Ferguson.

Opposing Side (Petitioner / Appellant): Christine Van Aken and Ian H. Gershengorn argued the cause for appellant. With them on the briefs were Dennis J. Herrera, Christine Van Aken, Blake P. Loebs, and Peter J. Keith.

III. AMICI CURIAE

ACLU Side (Respondent / Appellee)

Brief of amici curiae filed on behalf of the American Civil Liberties Union, the American Diabetes Association, the Epilepsy Foundation, Mental Health America, the National Disability Rights Network, and the Arc, et al. by Steven R. Shapiro, Alan L. Schlosser, Claudia Center, Matthew Coles, and Susan P. Mizner.

Brief of amici curiae filed on behalf of American Psychiatric Association et al. by David W. Ogden, Daniel S. Volchok, Aron M. Panner, Thomas B. Bennett, Ira A. Burnim, and Alison N. Barkoff.

Brief of amici curiae filed on behalf of the Policy Council on Law Enforcement and the Mentally Ill by Anita S. Earls, William Harry Ehlies II, and Ian A. Mance.

Brief of amici curiae filed on behalf of National Police Accountability Project by Julia Sherwin and Michael J. Haddad.

Brief of amici curiae filed on behalf Eugene De Boise, Sr. by John Burton and W. Bevis Schock.

Opposing Side (Petitioner / Appellant)

Brief of amici curiae filed on behalf of National League of Cities et al. by Orry Korb, County Counsel of Santa Clara County, Danny Chou, Assistant County Counsel, Greta S. Hansen, Lead Deputy County Counsel, Melissa R. Kiniyalocts, Deputy County Counsel, and Daniel G. Lloyd.

Brief of amici curiae filed on behalf of the International Municipal Lawyers Association et al. by Sarah M. Shalf and Charles W. Thompson, Jr.

Brief of amici curiae filed on behalf of the United States by Solicitor General Verrilli, Acting Assistant Attorneys General Branda and Gupta, Deputy Solicitor General Gershengorn, Assistant Solicitor General Prelogar, Barbara L. Herwig, Sharon M. Mcgowan, Dana Kaersvang, and Holly A. Thomas supporting vacatur in part
and reversal in part.

IV. THE SUPREME COURT'S DECISION

"The first question . . . asks whether [Title II of the ADA] 'requires law enforcement officers to provide accommodations to an armed, violent, and mentally ill suspect in the course of bringing the suspect into custody.' . . .

Whether the statutory language . . . applies to arrests is an important question . . . . But San Francisco, the United States . . .

, and Sheehan all argue . . . that § 12132 applies to arrests. . . . As a result, we do not think that it would be prudent to decide the question . . . .

Because certiorari jurisdiction exists to clarify the law, its exercise 'is not a matter of right, but of judicial discretion.' [W]e dismiss the first question presented as improvidently granted. . . .

The second question presented is whether Reynolds and Holder can be held personally liable for the injuries that Sheehan suffered. We conclude they are entitled to qualified immunity. . . .

In this case, although we disagree with the Ninth Circuit's ultimate conclusion on the question of qualified immunity, we agree with its analysis in many respects. For instance, there is no doubt that the officers did not violate any federal right when they opened Sheehan's door the first time. . . .

Nor is there any doubt that had Sheehan not been disabled, the officers could have opened her door the second time without violating any constitutional rights. . . .

We also agree with the Ninth Circuit that after the officers opened Sheehan's door the second time, their use of force was reasonable. . . .

The real question, then, is whether, despite these dangerous circumstances, the officers violated the Fourth Amendment when they decided to reopen Sheehan's door rather than attempting to accommodate her disability. Here we come to another problem. . . . [B]ecause this question has not been adequately briefed, we decline to do so. Rather, we simply decide whether the officers' failure to accommodate Sheehan's illness violated clearly established law. It did not. . . .

In sum, we hold that qualified immunity applies because these officers had no 'fair and clear warning of what the Constitution requires.' Because the qualified immunity analysis is straightforward, we need not decide whether the Constitution was violated . . . .

For these reasons, the first question presented is dismissed as improvidently granted. On the second question, we reverse the judgment of the Ninth Circuit. The case is remanded for further proceedings consistent with this opinion."

V. JUSTICE VOTE

2 Pro ACLU Side vs. 6 Con Opposing Side

ACLU Side (Respondent / Appellee)

1. Kagan, E. – Joined Scalia's opinion
2. Scalia, A. – Wrote opinion concurring in part and dissenting in part

Opposing Side (Petitioner / Appellant)

1. Alito, S. – Wrote majority opinion
2. Thomas, C. – Joined majority opinion
3. Kennedy, A. – Joined majority opinion
4. Ginsburg, R. – Joined majority opinion
5. Sotomayor, S. – Joined majority opinion
6. Roberts, J. – Joined majority opinion

Breyer, S. – Took no part in the decision.

VI. A WIN OR LOSS FOR THE ACLU?

The ACLU filed as amicus curiae urging affirmance; the Supreme Court reversed in part the Court of Appeals' decision by a 6-2 vote, giving the ACLU an apparent loss.

1135. Elonis v. United States

(Decided June 1, 2015; 135 S.Ct. 2001; 575 U.S. _)

I. ISSUE

A. Issues Discussed

1st Amendment, press, speech, association, criminal procedure

B. Legal Question Presented

"Federal law makes it a crime to transmit in interstate commerce 'any communication containing any threat . . . to injure the person of another.' . . . The question is whether the statute also requires that the defendant be aware of the threatening nature of the communication, and—if not—whether the First Amendment requires such a showing."

C. Supreme Court's Answer

"The jury was instructed that the Government need prove only that a reasonable person would regard Elonis's communications as threats, and that was error. Federal criminal liability generally does not turn solely on the results of an act without considering the defendant's mental state. . . .

There is no dispute that the mental state requirement in Section 875(c) is satisfied if the defendant transmits a communication for the purpose of issuing a threat, or with knowledge that the communication will be viewed as a threat. . . . Given our disposition, it is not necessary to consider any First Amendment issues."

II. CASE SUMMARY

A. Background

"Anthony Douglas Elonis was an active user of the social networking Web site Facebook. . . . In May 2010, Elonis's wife of nearly seven years left him, taking with her their two young children. Elonis began 'listening to more violent music' and posting self-styled 'rap' lyrics inspired by the music. . . . This material was often interspersed with disclaimers that the lyrics were 'fictitious,' with no intentional 'resemblance to real persons.' . . .

A grand jury indicted Elonis for making threats to injure patrons and employees of the park [where he previously worked], his estranged wife, police officers, a kindergarten class, and an FBI agent, [who were all the subjects of violent posts] all in violation of 18 U.S.C. § 875(c). In the District Court, Elonis moved to dismiss the indictment for failing to allege that he had intended to threaten anyone. The District Court denied the motion . . . .

Elonis requested a jury instruction that 'the government must prove that he intended to communicate a true threat.' The District Court denied that request. . . .

The Government's closing argument emphasized that it was irrelevant whether Elonis intended the postings to be threats .

. . . A jury convicted Elonis . . . , acquitting only on the charge of threatening park patrons and employees. Elonis was sentenced to three years, eight months' imprisonment and three years' supervised release. . . .

The Court of Appeals [held] that the intent required by Section 875(c) is only the intent to communicate words that the defendant understands, and that a reasonable person would view as a threat."

The Supreme Court granted certiorari to review the case.

B. Counsel of Record / ACLU Attorney

ACLU Side (Petitioner / Appellant): John P. Elwood argued the cause for appellants.

With him on the brief were Ronald H. Levine, Abraham J. Rein, John P. Elwood, Ralph C. Mayrell, and Dmitry Slavin.

Opposing Side (Respondent / Appellee): Deputy Solicitor General Dreeben argued the cause for the United States. With him on the brief were Solicitor General Verrilli, Assistant Attorney General Caldwell, Assistant Solicitor General Feigin, and Sangita K. Rao.

III. AMICI CURIAE

ACLU Side (Petitioner / Appellant)

Brief of amici curiae filed on behalf of the American Civil Liberties Union, the Abrams Institute for Freedom of Expression, the Cato Institute, the Center for Democracy & Technology, and the National Coalition Against Censorship by Jack M. Balkin, David A. Schulz, Jonathan M. Manes, Joan E. Bertin, Steven R. Shapiro, Brian M. Hauss, Lee Rowland, Emma J. Llansó, and Ilya Shapiro.

Brief of amici curiae filed on behalf of the Marion B. Brechner First Amendment Project et al. by Clay Calvert and Marion B. Brechner.

Brief of amici curiae filed on behalf of People for Ethical Treatment of Animals, Inc. (PETA) et al. by Thomas Brejcha, Peter Breen, Brian J. Murray, and Meghan E. Sweeney.

Brief of amici curiae filed on behalf of the Center for Individual Rights by Michael E. Rosman and Christopher J. Hajec.

Brief of amici curiae filed on behalf of the Student Press Law Center et al. by Frank D. Lomonte, David Greene, Sean D. Jordan, Kent C. Sullivan, Peter Ligh, Travis Mock, and Katherine Glenn Bass.

Brief of amici curiae filed on behalf of the Reporters Committee for Freedom of the Press et al. by Bruce D. Brown, Gregg P. Leslie, and Emily R. Grannis.

Brief of amici curiae filed on behalf of the Rutherford Institute by John W. Whitehead, Douglas R. McKusick, and Jesse H. Baker IV.

Brief of amici curiae filed on behalf of the Thomas Jefferson Center for the Protection of Free Expression et al. by Robert D. Richards, J. Joshua Wheeler, and Clayton N. Hansen.

Opposing Side (Respondent / Appellee)

Brief of amici curiae filed on behalf of National Center for Victims of Crime by Rebecca J. Roe.

Brief of amici curiae filed on behalf of the State of Wisconsin et al. by J.B. Van Hollen Attorney General of Wisconsin and Thomas C. Bellavia, Assistant Attorney General, and by the Attorneys General for their respective jurisdictions as follows: Michael Geraghty of Alaska, Tom Horne of Arizona, John W. Suthers of Colorado, Irvin B. Nathan of the District of Columbia, Leonardo M. Rapadas of Guam, David M. Louie of Hawaii, Lawrence G. Wasden of Idaho, Lisa Madigan of Illinois, Thomas J. Miller of Iowa, Jack Conway of Kentucky, Janet T. Mills of Maine, Bill Schuette of Michigan, Jim Hood of Mississippi, Gary K. King of New Mexico, Kathleen G. Kane of Pennsylvania, Peter F. Kilmartin of Rhode Island, Alan Wilson of South Carolina, Sean D. Reyes of Utah, Kay Chopard Cohen of Virginia, and Robert W. Ferguson of Washington.

Brief of amici curiae filed on behalf of the National Network to End Domestic Violence et al. by Paulette Sullivan Moore, Helen Gerostathos Guyton, Sandra J. Badin, and Timothy J. Slattery.

Brief of amici curiae filed on behalf of the Anti-Defamation League by Steve M. Freeman, Lauren A. Jones, Seth M. Marnin, Christopher Wolf, Keith O'Doherty, and Arthur Kim.

Brief of amici curiae filed on behalf of the Domestic Violence Legal Empowerment and Appeals Project et al. by Joan S. Meier, David B. Salmons, Jonathan M. Albano, and Stephanie Schuster.

Brief of amici curiae filed on behalf of the Criminal Justice Legal Foundation by Kent S. Scheidegger.

IV. THE SUPREME COURT'S DECISION

"An individual who 'transmits in interstate or foreign commerce any communication containing any threat to kidnap any person or any threat to injure the person of another' is guilty of a felony and faces up to five years' imprisonment. 18 U.S.C. § 875(c). This statute requires that a communication be transmitted and that the communication contain a threat. It does not specify that the defendant must have any mental state with respect to these elements. In particular, it does not indicate whether the defendant must intend that his communication contain a threat. . . .

The most we can conclude from the language of Section 875(c) and its neighboring provisions is that Congress meant to proscribe a broad class of threats in Section 875(c), but did not identify what mental state, if any, a defendant must have to be convicted. . . .

The fact that the statute does not specify any required mental state, however, does not mean that none exists. We have repeatedly held that 'mere omission from a criminal enactment of any mention of criminal intent' should not be read 'as dispensing with it.' . . .

When interpreting federal criminal statutes that are silent on the required mental state, we read into the statute 'only that mens rea which is necessary to separate wrongful conduct from 'otherwise innocent conduct." . . .

Here 'the crucial element separating legal innocence from wrongful conduct' is the threatening nature of the communication. The mental state requirement must therefore apply to the fact that the communication contains a threat. . . .

In light of the foregoing, Elonis's conviction cannot stand. The jury was instructed that the Government need prove only that a reasonable person would regard Elonis's communications as threats, and that was error. Federal criminal liability generally does not turn solely on the results of an act without considering the defendant's mental state. . . .

There is no dispute that the mental state requirement in Section 875(c) is satisfied if the defendant transmits a communication for the purpose of issuing a threat, or with knowledge that the communication will be viewed as a threat. . . . Given our disposition, it is not necessary to consider any First Amendment issues. . . .

The judgment of the United States Court of Appeals for the Third Circuit is reversed, and the case is remanded for further proceedings consistent with this opinion."

V. JUSTICE VOTE

8 Pro ACLU Side vs. 1 Con Opposing Side

ACLU Side (Petitioner / Appellant)

1. Roberts, J. – Wrote majority opinion
2. Alito, S. – Wrote opinion concurring in part and dissenting in part
3. Kagan, E. – Joined majority opinion
4. Breyer, S. – Joined majority opinion
5. Scalia, A. – Joined majority opinion
6. Kennedy, A. – Joined majority opinion
7. Ginsburg, R. – Joined majority opinion
8. Sotomayor, S. – Joined majority opinion

Opposing Side (Respondent / Appellee)

1. Thomas, C. – Wrote dissenting opinion

VI. A WIN OR LOSS FOR THE ACLU?

The ACLU filed as amicus curiae urging reversal of the judgment of the Court of Appeals; the Supreme Court reversed in a 8-1 vote, giving the ACLU an apparent win.

1136. E.E.O.C. v. Abercrombie & Fitch Stores

(Decided June 1, 2015; 135 S.Ct. 2028; 575 U.S. _)

I. ISSUE

A. Issues Discussed

Civil rights, federal

B. Legal Question Presented

"Title VII of the Civil Rights Act of 1964 prohibits a prospective employer from refusing to hire an applicant in order to avoid accommodating a religious practice that it could accommodate without undue hardship. The question presented is whether this prohibition applies only where an applicant has informed the employer of his need for an accommodation."

C. Supreme Court's Answer

"We construe Title VII's silence as exactly that: silence. Its disparate-treatment provision prohibits actions taken with the motive of avoiding the need for accommodating a religious practice. A request for accommodation, or the employer's certainty that the practice exists, may make it easier to infer motive, but is not a necessary condition of liability."

II. CASE SUMMARY

A. Background

"Respondent Abercrombie & Fitch Stores, Inc., operates . . . clothing stores . . . . Consistent with the image Abercrombie seeks to project . . . , the company imposes a Look Policy that governs its employees' dress. The Look Policy prohibits 'caps'—a term the Policy does not define—as too informal for Abercrombie's desired image.

Samantha Elauf is a practicing Muslim who . . . wears a headscarf. She applied for a position in an Abercrombie store, and was interviewed by Heather Cooke, the store's assistant manager. Using Abercrombie's ordinary system for evaluating applicants, Cooke gave Elauf a rating that qualified her to be hired; Cooke was concerned, however, that Elauf's headscarf would conflict with the store's Look Policy.

Cooke sought the store manager's guidance . . . . When this yielded no answer, Cooke turned to Randall Johnson, the district manager. . . . Johnson told Cooke that Elauf's headscarf would violate the Look Policy, as would all other headwear, religious or otherwise, and directed Cooke not to hire Elauf.

The EEOC sued Abercrombie on Elauf's behalf, claiming that its refusal to hire Elauf violated Title VII. The District Court granted the EEOC summary judgment on the issue of liability, held a trial on damages, and awarded $20,000. The Tenth Circuit reversed . . . ."

The Supreme Court granted certiorari to review the case.

B. Counsel of Record / ACLU Attorney

ACLU Side (Petitioner / Appellant): Deputy Solicitor General Gershengorn argued the cause for appellants. With him on the brief were Solicitor General Verrilli,

Assistant Solicitor General Kovner, P. David Lopez, Carolyn L. Wheeler, Jennifer S. Goldstein, and James M. Tucker.

Opposing Side (Respondent / Appellee): Shay Dvoretzky argued the cause for appellee. With him on the brief were Mark A. Knueve, Daniel J. Clark, Eric S. Dreiband, Yaakov M. Roth, and Jeffrey R. Johnson.

III. AMICI CURIAE

ACLU Side (Petitioner / Appellant)

Brief of amici curiae filed on behalf of Fifteen Religious and Civil Rights Organizations by Daniel Mach of the American Civil Liberties Union Foundation and by Todd R. Mcfarland, Gene C. Schaerr, Dwayne Leslie, Zainab Al-Suwaij, Gurjot Kaur, Aisha Rahman, Stephen F. Rohde, Kimberlee Wood Colby, Carl H. Esbeck, Holly Hollman, Uleses C. Henderson, Jr., E. R. Lanier, and Roberta L. Steele.

Brief of amici curiae filed on behalf of Umme-Hani Khan by Zahra Billoo, Fatima Iqbal, Christopher Ho, and Marsha J. Chien.

Brief of amici curiae filed on behalf of the Becket Fund for

Religious Liberty by Eric S. Baxter, Eric C. Rassbach, Asma T. Uddin, and Diana M. Verm.

Brief of amici curiae filed on behalf of the American Jewish Committee et al. by Marc D. Stern, Douglas Laycock, David T. Goldberg, Toby J. Heytens, and Daniel R. Ortiz.

Brief of amici curiae filed on behalf of the American-Arab Anti-Discrimination Committee et al. by Abed A. Ayoub, Yolanda C. Rondon, and Andrew W. Cox.

Brief of amici curiae filed on behalf of the National Jewish Commission on Law and Public Affairs ("Colpa") et al. by Dennis Rapps, Nathan Lewin, and Alyza D. Lewin.

Brief of amici curiae filed on behalf of Lambda Legal Defense and Education Fund, Inc. by Gregory R. Nevins and Jennifer C. Pizer.

Brief of amici curiae filed on behalf of the State of Arizona et al. by Thomas C. Horne, Attorney General of Arizona, Robert L. Ellman, Solicitor General, Rose Daly-Rooney and Chris Carlsen, Assistant Attorneys General, and by the Attorneys General for their respective States as follows: Russell A. Suzuki of Hawaii, Lisa Madigan of Illinois, Douglas F. Gansler of Maryland, Dale Schowengerdt of Montana, Joseph A. Foster of New Hampshire, Eric T. Schneiderman of New York, Ellen F. Rosenblum of Oregon, and Robert W. Ferguson of Washington.

Brief of amici curiae filed on behalf of the Council on American-Islamic Relations by Jenifer Wicks and Munia Jabbar.

Opposing Side (Respondent / Appellee)

Brief of amici curiae filed on behalf of the Equal Employment Advisory Council by Rae T. Vann.

Brief of amici curiae filed on behalf of the Chamber of Commerce of the United States of America et al. by Kate Comerford Todd, Warren Postman, Melissa Arbus Sherry, Elana Nightingale Dawson, Karen R. Harned, and Elizabeth Milito.

Brief of amici curiae filed on behalf of the National Conference of State Legislatures et al. by Lisa Soronen, Charles W. Thompson, Jr., and Amanda Keller.

Brief of amici curiae filed on behalf of Cato Institute by Ilya Shapiro, Julio Colomba, and Brendan J. Morrissey.

IV. THE SUPREME COURT'S DECISION

"Title VII of the Civil Rights Act of 1964 prohibits two categories of employment practices. . . .

These two proscriptions, often referred to as the 'disparate treatment' (or 'intentional discrimination') provision and the 'disparate impact' provision, are the only causes of action under Title VII. . . .

Abercrombie's primary argument is that an applicant cannot show disparate treatment without first showing that an employer has 'actual knowledge' of the applicant's need for an accommodation. We disagree. Instead, an applicant need only show that his need for an accommodation was a motivating factor in the employer's decision. . . .

Thus, the rule for disparate-treatment claims based on a failure to accommodate a religious practice is straightforward: An employer may not make an applicant's religious practice, confirmed or otherwise, a factor in employment decisions. For example, suppose that an employer thinks (though he does not know for certain) that a job applicant may be an orthodox Jew who will observe the Sabbath, and thus be unable to work on Saturdays. If the applicant actually requires an accommodation of that religious practice, and the employer's desire to avoid the prospective accommodation is a motivating factor in his decision, the employer violates Title VII. . . .

We construe Title VII's silence as exactly that: silence. Its disparate-treatment provision prohibits actions taken with the motive of avoiding the need for accommodating a religious practice. A request for accommodation, or the employer's certainty that the practice exists, may make it easier to infer motive, but is not a necessary condition of liability.

Abercrombie argues in the alternative that a claim based on a failure to accommodate an applicant's religious practice must be raised as a disparate-impact claim, not a disparate-treatment claim. We think not. . . .

Nor does the statute limit disparate-treatment claims to only those employer policies that treat religious practices less favorably than similar secular practices. . . . An employer is surely entitled to have, for example, a no-headwear policy as an ordinary matter. But when an applicant requires an accommodation as an 'aspec[t] of religious . . . practice,' it is no response that the subsequent 'fail[ure] . . . to hire' was due to an otherwise-neutral policy. Title VII requires otherwise-neutral policies to give way to the need for an accommodation. . . .

The Tenth Circuit misinterpreted Title VII's requirements in granting summary judgment. We reverse its judgment and remand the case for further consideration consistent with this opinion."

V. JUSTICE VOTE

8 Pro ACLU Side vs. 1 Con Opposing Side

ACLU Side (Petitioner / Appellant)

1. Scalia, A. – Wrote majority opinion
2. Alito, S. – Wrote concurring opinion
3. Kagan, E. – Joined majority opinion
4. Breyer, S. – Joined majority opinion
5. Kennedy, A. – Joined majority opinion
6. Ginsburg, R. – Joined majority opinion
7. Sotomayor, S. – Joined majority opinion
8. Roberts, J. – Joined majority opinion

Opposing Side (Respondent / Appellee)

1. Thomas, C. – Wrote opinion concurring in part and dissenting in part

VI. A WIN OR LOSS FOR THE ACLU?

The ACLU filed as amicus curiae urging reversal of the judgment of the Court of Appeals; the Supreme Court reversed in an 8-1 vote, giving the ACLU an apparent win.

1137. Kerry v. Din

(Decided June 15, 2015; 135 S.Ct. 2128; 576 U.S. _)

I. ISSUE

A. Issues Discussed

Immigration/citizenship

B. Legal Question Presented

Whether Fauzia Din suffered a violation of her constitutional rights when her spouse was denied admission to the United States under the terrorism bar.

C. Supreme Court's Answer

"Because Fauzia Din was not deprived of 'life, liberty, or property' when the Government denied Kanishka Berashk admission to the United States, there is no process due to her under the Constitution. To the extent that she received any explanation for the Government's decision, this was more than the Due Process Clause required."

II. CASE SUMMARY

A. Background

"Fauzia Din came to the United States as a refugee in 2000, and became a naturalized citizen in 2007. She filed a petition to have Kanishka Berashk, whom she married in 2006, classified as her immediate relative. The petition was granted, and Berashk filed a visa application. The U.S. Embassy in Islamabad, Pakistan, interviewed Berashk and denied his application. A consular officer informed Berashk that he was inadmissible under § 1182(a)(3)(B) but provided no further explanation.

Din then brought suit in Federal District Court seeking a writ of mandamus directing the United States to properly adjudicate Berashk's visa application; a declaratory judgment that 8 U.S.C. § 1182(b)(2)-(3), which exempts the Government from providing notice to an alien found inadmissible under the terrorism bar, is unconstitutional as applied; and a declaratory judgment that the denial violated the Administrative Procedure Act. The District Court granted the Government's motion to dismiss, but the Ninth Circuit reversed."

The Supreme Court granted certiorari to review the case.

B. Counsel of Record / ACLU Attorney

ACLU Side (Respondent / Appellee): Mark E. Haddad argued the cause for appellee. With him on the briefs were Anoop Prasad, Jenny Zhao, Nasrina Bargzie, Yaman Salahi Winifred Kao, Geoffrey D. Deboskey, David R. Carpenter, Heidi Larson Howell Amanda Farfel, and Kathleen M. Mueller.

Opposing Side (Petitioner / Appellant): Deputy Solicitor General Kneedler argued the cause for appellant. With him on the briefs were Solicitor General Verrilli, Acting Assistant Attorney General Branda, Assistant Solicitor General Goldenberg, Colin A. Kisor, Stacey I. Young, Mary E. Mcleod, and Stevan E. Bunnell.

III. AMICI CURIAE

ACLU Side (Respondent / Appellee)

Brief of amici curiae filed on behalf of the American Civil Liberties Union by Steven R. Shapiro, Dror Ladin, Jameel Jaffer, and Hina Shamsi.

Brief of amici curiae filed on behalf of Law School Professors by Robert Pauw and Gibbs Houston Pauw.

Brief of amici curiae filed on behalf of the National Immigrant Justice Center et al. by Charles Roth, Charles A. Rothfeld, Andrew J. Pincus, Michael B. Kimberly, and Paul W. Hughes.

Brief of amici curiae filed on behalf of Former Consular Officers by Ira J. Kurzban, Edward F. Ramos, Jeffrey D. Kahn, and Trina Realmuto.

Brief of amici curiae filed on behalf of the California Women's Law Center by Jesenka Mrdjenovic, Jillian Stonecipher, and Theane Evangelis.

Brief of amici curiae filed on behalf of National Justice for our Neighbors et al. by John M. Gore and Brian J. Murray.

Opposing Side (Petitioner / Appellant)

No briefs of amici curiae were filed in support of appellant.

IV. THE SUPREME COURT'S DECISION

"The Fifth Amendment provides that '[n]o person shall be . . . deprived of life, liberty, or property, without due process of law.' . . . [I]t remains the case that no process is due if one is not deprived of 'life, liberty, or property.' The first question that we must ask, then, is whether the denial of Berashk's visa application deprived Din of any of these interests. Only if we answer in the affirmative must we proceed to consider whether the Government's explanation afforded sufficient process. . . .

Din, of course, could not conceivably claim that the denial of Berashk's visa application deprived her—or for that matter even Berashk—of life or property; and under the above described historical understanding, a claim that it deprived her of liberty is equally absurd. . . .

Here, a long practice of regulating spousal immigration precludes Din's claim that the denial of Berashk's visa application has deprived her of a fundamental liberty interest. Although immigration was effectively unregulated prior to 1875, as soon as Congress began legislating in this area it enacted a complicated web of regulations that erected serious impediments to a person's ability to bring a spouse into the United States. . . .

Only by diluting the meaning of a fundamental liberty interest and jettisoning our established jurisprudence could we conclude that the denial of Berashk's visa application implicates any of Din's fundamental liberty interests. . . .

Neither Din's right to live with her spouse nor her right to live within this country is implicated here. There is a 'simple distinction between government action that directly affects a citizen's legal rights, or imposes a direct restraint on his liberty, and action that is directed against a third party and affects the citizen only indirectly or incidentally.' . . .

Because Fauzia Din was not deprived of 'life, liberty, or property' when the Government denied Kanishka Berashk admission to the United States, there is no process due to her under the Constitution. To the extent that she received any explanation for the Government's decision, this was more than the Due Process Clause required. The judgment of the Ninth Circuit is vacated, and the case is remanded for further proceedings."

V. JUSTICE VOTE

4 Pro ACLU Side vs. 5 Con Opposing Side

ACLU Side (Respondent / Appellee)

1. Kagan, E. – Joined Breyer's dissent
2. Breyer, S. – Wrote dissenting opinion
3. Ginsburg, R. – Joined Breyer's dissent
4. Sotomayor, S. – Joined Breyer's dissent

Opposing Side (Petitioner / Appellant)

1. Scalia, A. – Wrote majority opinion
2. Alito, S. – Joined Kennedy's concurrence
3. Thomas, C. – Joined majority opinion
4. Kennedy, A. – Wrote concurring opinion
5. Roberts, J. – Joined majority opinion

VI. A WIN OR LOSS FOR THE ACLU?

The ACLU filed as amicus curiae urging affirmance; the Supreme Court vacated the Court of Appeals' decision by a 5-4 vote, giving the ACLU an apparent loss.

1138. Walker v. Texas Div., Sons of Confederate Veterans, Inc.

(Decided June 18, 2015; 135 S.Ct. 2239; 576 U.S. _)

I. ISSUE

A. Issues Discussed

1st Amendment, press, speech, association

B. Legal Question Presented

"In this case, the Texas Division of the Sons of Confederate Veterans proposed a specialty license plate design featuring a Confederate battle flag. The [Texas Department of Motor Vehicles] Board rejected the proposal. We must decide whether that rejection violated the Constitution's free speech guarantees."

C. Supreme Court's Answer

"We conclude that it did not."

II. CASE SUMMARY

A. Background

"Texas offers automobile owners a choice between ordinary and specialty license plates. Those who want the State to issue a particular specialty plate may propose a plate design . . . . If the Texas Department of Motor Vehicles Board approves the design, the State will make it available for display on vehicles registered in Texas.

In 2009, the Sons of Confederate Veterans, Texas Division (a nonprofit entity), applied to sponsor a specialty license plate . . . . At the bottom of the proposed plate were the words 'SONS OF CONFEDERATE VETERANS.' At the side was the organization's logo, a square Confederate battle flag framed by the words 'Sons of Confederate Veterans 1896.' A faint Confederate battle flag appeared in the background on the lower portion of the plate. Additionally, in the middle of the plate was the license plate number, and at the top was the State's name and silhouette. The Board's predecessor denied this application.

In 2010, SCV renewed its application before the Board. The Board invited public comment on its website and at an open meeting. After considering the responses, including a number of letters sent by elected officials who opposed the proposal, the Board voted unanimously against issuing the plate. . . .

In 2012, SCV and two of its officers (collectively SCV) brought this lawsuit against the chairman and members of the Board (collectively Board). SCV argued that the Board's decision violated the Free Speech Clause of the First Amendment, and it sought an injunction requiring the Board to approve the proposed plate design. The District Court entered judgment for the Board. A divided panel of the Court of Appeals for the Fifth Circuit reversed."

The Supreme Court granted certiorari to review the case.

B. Counsel of Record / ACLU Attorney

ACLU Side (Respondent / Appellee): Roger James George, Jr., argued the cause for appellee. With him on the briefs was John R. Mcconnell.

Opposing Side (Petitioner / Appellant): Scott A. Keller argued the cause for appellant. With him on the briefs were Greg Abbott, Attorney General of Texas, Daniel T. Hodge, First Assistant Attorney General, Jonathan F. Mitchell, Solicitor General, and Bill Davis, Arthur C. D'Andrea, Evan S. Greene, and Alex Potapov, Assistant Solicitors General, and Erika M. Kane, Assistant Attorney General.

III. AMICI CURIAE

ACLU Side (Respondent / Appellee)

Brief of amici curiae filed on behalf of the American Civil Liberties Union, the ACLU of North Carolina, and the ACLU of Texas by Christopher A. Brook, Rebecca L. Robertson, Steven R. Shapiro, and Lee Rowland.

Brief of amici curiae filed on behalf of Children First Foundation, Inc., by Jonathan D. Christman and Randall L. Wenger.

Brief of amici curiae filed on behalf of the Rutherford Institute by John W. Whitehead, Douglas R. Mckusick, D. Alicia Hickok, and Todd N. Hutchison.

Brief of amici curiae filed on behalf of Cato Institute et al. by Robert Corn-Revere and Ilya Shapiro.

Brief of amici curiae filed on behalf of Americans United for Separation of Church and State by Ayesha N. Khan and Gregory M. Lipper.

Brief of amici curiae filed on behalf of Foundation for Individual Rights in Education by Greg Lukianoff.

Brief of amici curiae filed on behalf of Choose Life, Wisconsin,

Inc., et al. by Thomas L. Brejcha, Jocelyn Floyd, Michael D. Dean, and Stephen M. Crampton.

Brief of amici curiae filed on behalf of the Becket Fund for Religious Liberty by Mark, Rienzi Eric Rassbach, and Eugene Volokh.

Opposing Side (Petitioner / Appellant)

Brief of amici curiae filed on behalf of Justice and Freedom Fund by Deborah J. Dewart and James L. Hirsen.

Brief of amici curiae filed on behalf of the State of Ohio et al. by Michael Dewine, Attorney General of Ohio, and Eric E. Murphy, Solicitor General, and by the Attorneys General for their respective States as follows: Dustin Mcdaniel of Arkansas, Bill Schuette of Michigan, John W. Suthers of Colorado, Chris Koster of Missouri, Russell A. Suzuki of Hawaii, Joseph A. Foster of New Hampshire, Lisa Madigan of Illinois, Hector E. Balderas of New Mexico, Gregory F. Zoeller of Indiana, and Robert W. Ferguson of Washington.

Brief of amici curiae filed on behalf of the American Center for Law and Justice et al. by Kimberlee Wood Colby, Jay Alan Sekulow, Stuart J. Roth, Colby M. May, Walter M. Weber, and Jordan A. Sekulow in support of neither party.

Brief of amici curiae filed on behalf of Phil Berger, President Pro Tempore of the North Carolina Senate by Scott W. Gaylord in support of neither party.

IV. THE SUPREME COURT'S DECISION

"When government speaks, it is not barred by the Free Speech Clause from determining the content of what it says. . . . Instead, the Free Speech Clause helps produce informed opinions among members of the public, who are then able to influence the choices of a government that, through words and deeds, will reflect its electoral mandate. . . .

Were the Free Speech Clause interpreted otherwise, government would not work. . . .

We have therefore refused '[t]o hold that the Government unconstitutionally discriminates on the basis of viewpoint when it chooses to fund a program dedicated to advance certain permissible goals, because the program in advancing those goals necessarily discourages alternative goals.' . . .

That is not to say that a government's ability to express itself is without restriction. . . . But, . . . when the government speaks it is entitled to promote a program, to espouse a policy, or to take a position. In doing so, it represents its citizens and it carries out its duties on their behalf. . . .

In our view, specialty license plates issued pursuant to Texas's statutory scheme convey government speech. Our reasoning rests primarily on . . . Summum . . . . We conclude here, as we did there, that our precedents regarding government speech (and not our precedents regarding forums for private speech) provide the appropriate framework through which to approach the case. . . .

Our analysis in Summum leads us to the conclusion that here, too, government speech is at issue. . . .

These considerations, taken together, convince us that the specialty plates here in question are similar enough to the monuments in Summum to call for the same result. . . .

The fact that private parties take part in the design and propagation of a message does not extinguish the governmental nature of the message or transform the government's role . . . .

Our determination that Texas's specialty license plate designs are government speech does not mean that the designs do not also implicate the free speech rights of private persons. We have acknowledged that drivers who display a State's selected license plate designs convey the messages communicated through those designs. . . . And we have recognized that the First Amendment stringently limits a State's authority to compel a private party to express a view with which the private party disagrees. But here, compelled private speech is not at issue. And just as Texas cannot require SCV to convey 'the State's ideological message,' SCV cannot force Texas to include a Confederate battle flag on its specialty license plates. . . .

[W]e hold that Texas's specialty license plate designs constitute government speech and that Texas was consequently entitled to refuse to issue plates featuring SCV's proposed design. Accordingly, the judgment of the United States Court of Appeals for the Fifth Circuit is reversed."

V. JUSTICE VOTE

4 Pro ACLU Side vs. 5 Con Opposing Side

ACLU Side (Respondent / Appellee)

1. Alito, S. – Wrote dissenting opinion
2. Scalia, A. – Joined Alito's dissent
3. Kennedy, A. – Joined Alito's dissent
4. Roberts, J. – Joined Alito's dissent

Opposing Side (Petitioner / Appellant)

1. Breyer, S. – Wrote majority opinion
2. Kagan, E. – Joined majority opinion
3. Thomas, C. – Joined majority opinion
4. Ginsburg, R. – Joined majority opinion
5. Sotomayor, S. – Joined majority opinion

VI. A WIN OR LOSS FOR THE ACLU?

The ACLU filed as amicus curiae urging affirmance; the Supreme Court reversed the Court of Appeals' decision by a 5-4 vote, giving the ACLU an apparent loss.

1139. Kingsley v. Hendrickson

(Decided June 22, 2015; 135 S.Ct. 2466; 576 U.S. _)

I. ISSUE

A. Issues Discussed

Prison

B. Legal Question Presented

"[W]hether, to prove an excessive force claim, a pretrial detainee must show that the officers were subjectively aware that their use of force was unreasonable, or only that the officers' use of that force was objectively unreasonable."

C. Supreme Court's Answer

"We conclude that the latter standard is the correct one."

II. CASE SUMMARY

A. Background

"Michael Kingsley . . . was . . . detained . . . . [A]n officer . . . noticed . . . paper covering the light fixture above Kingsley's bed. The officer told Kingsley to remove it; Kingsley refused . . . . The next morning, the jail administrator, Lieutenant Robert Conroy, ordered Kingsley to remove the paper. Kingsley once again refused. Conroy then told Kingsley that officers would remove the paper and that he would be moved to a receiving cell in the interim.

Shortly thereafter, four officers . . . ordered Kingsley to stand, back up to the door, and keep his hands behind him. When Kingsley refused to comply, the officers handcuffed him, forcibly removed him from the cell, carried him to a receiving cell, and placed him face down . . . .

Sergeant Hendrickson placed his knee in Kingsley's back and Kingsley told him in impolite language to get off. Kingsley testified that Hendrickson and Degner then slammed his head into the concrete bunk—an allegation the officers deny.

The parties agree, however, . . . Hendrickson directed Degner to stun Kingsley with a Taser; Degner applied a Taser to Kingsley's back for approximately five seconds; the officers then left the handcuffed Kingsley alone in the receiving cell; and officers returned to the cell 15 minutes later and removed Kingsley's handcuffs. . . .

Kingsley filed a § 1983 complaint . . . . The officers moved for summary judgment, which the District Court denied . . . . Kingsley's excessive force claim accordingly proceeded to trial. . . . The jury found in the officers' favor.

On appeal, Kingsley argued that the correct standard for judging a pretrial detainee's excessive force claim is objective unreasonableness. . . . A panel of the Court of Appeals disagreed . . . ."

The Supreme Court granted certiorari to review the case.

B. Counsel of Record / ACLU Attorney

ACLU Side (Petitioner / Appellant): Wendy M. Ward argued the cause for appellants. With her on the brief were Jeffrey T. Green, Jeffrey S. Ward, Adam N. Hallowell, Edward J. Pardon, Sarah O'Rourke Schrup, and Steven J. Horowitz.

Opposing Side (Respondent / Appellee): Paul D. Clement argued the cause for appellee. With him on the brief were D. Zachary Hudson, William R. Levi, Charles H. Bohl, Andrew A. Jones, Timothy H. Posnanski, Mpoli N. Simwanza-Johnson, and James C. Remington.

Assistant Solicitor General Bash argued the cause for the United States as amicus curiae.

III. AMICI CURIAE

ACLU Side (Petitioner / Appellant)

Brief of amici curiae filed on behalf of American Civil Liberties Union and American Civil Liberties Union of Wisconsin by Steven R. Shapiro, David C. Fathi, Laurence J. Dupuis, Catherine M.A. Carroll, Jacquelyn L. Stanley, and Wilmer Cutler Pickering.

Brief of amici curiae filed on behalf of Former Corrections Administrators and Experts by Arthur Loevy, Jon Loevy, Roshna Bala Keen, Steven Art, David B. Owens, and Sarah Grady.

Brief of amici curiae filed on behalf of the National Association of Criminal Defense Lawyers by Barbara E. Bergman, Mitchell F. Dolin, Jeff Kosseff, and David Metcalf.

Opposing Side (Respondent / Appellee)

Brief of amici curiae filed on behalf of the Rutherford Institute by John W. Whitehead, Stephen J. Neuberger, and Douglas R. McKusick.

Brief of amici curiae filed on behalf of National Association of Counties et al. by Lisa Soronen, Aaron M. Streett, Joshua Davis, J. Mark Little, and Shane Pennington.

Brief of amici curiae filed on behalf of the State of Indiana et al. by Gregory F. Zoeller, Attorney General of Indiana, Thomas M. Fisher, Solicitor General, and Heather Hagan Mcveigh and Lara Langeneckert, Deputy Attorneys General, and by the Attorneys General for their respective jurisdictions as follows: Mark Brnovich of Arizona, Matthew P. Denn of Delaware, Douglas S. Chin of Hawaii, Lisa Madigan of Illinois, Bill Schuette of Michigan, Joseph A. Foster of New Hampshire, Kathleen G. Kane of Pennsylvania, Alan Wilson of South Carolina, and Brad D. Schimel of Wisconsin.

Brief of amici curiae filed on of the United States by Assistant Solicitor General Bash, Solicitor General Verrilli, Acting Assistant Attorneys General Mizer and Gupta, Deputy Solicitor General Gershengorn, Barbara L. Herwig, Mark L. Gross, and Erin Aslan.

Brief of amici curiae filed on behalf of the National Sheriffs' Association et al. by Gregory C. Champagne, Maurice E. Bostick, Robert P. Faigin, Richard Hodsdon, Richard M. Weintraub, Carrie L. Hill, and Robert Spence urging a unified standard for use of force.

IV. THE SUPREME COURT'S DECISION

"In a case like this one, there are, in a sense, two separate state-of-mind questions. The first concerns the defendant's state of mind with respect to his physical acts . . . . The second question concerns the defendant's state of mind with respect to whether his use of force was 'excessive.' Here, as to the first question, there is no dispute. As to the second, . . . there is a dispute. We conclude with respect to that question that the relevant standard is objective not subjective. Thus, the defendant's state of mind is not a matter that a plaintiff is required to prove. . . .

We now consider the question before us here—the defendant's state of mind with respect to the proper interpretation of the force (a series of events in the world) that the defendant deliberately (not accidentally or negligently) used. In deciding whether the force deliberately used is, constitutionally speaking, 'excessive,' should courts use an objective standard only, or instead a subjective standard that takes into account a defendant's state of mind? It is with respect to this question that we hold that courts must use an objective standard. In short, we agree with the dissenting appeals court judge, the Seventh Circuit's jury instruction committee, and Kingsley, that a pretrial detainee must show only that the force purposely or knowingly used against him was objectively unreasonable.

A court (judge or jury) cannot apply this standard mechanically. Rather, objective reasonableness turns on the 'facts and circumstances of each particular case.' A court must make this determination from the perspective of a reasonable officer on the scene, including what the officer knew at the time, not with the 20/20 vision of hindsight. . . .

Considerations . . . may bear on the reasonableness . . . of the force used: the relationship between the need for the use of force and the amount of force used; the extent of the plaintiff's injury; any effort made by the officer to temper . . . the amount of force; the severity of the security problem at issue; the threat reasonably perceived by the officer; and whether the plaintiff was actively resisting. . . .

Several considerations have led us to conclude that the appropriate standard for a pretrial detainee's excessive force claim is solely an objective one. For one thing, it is consistent with our precedent. . . .

For another thing, experience suggests that an objective standard is workable. . . .

Finally, the use of an objective standard adequately protects an officer who acts in good faith. . . .

We now consider the lawfulness of the jury instruction given in this case in light of our adoption of an objective standard for pretrial detainees' excessive force claims. . . .

We agree with Kingsley that the instructions were erroneous. . . . [The instructions] suggested the jury should weigh respondents' subjective reasons for using force and subjective views about the excessiveness of the force. As we have just held, that was error. . . .

The decision of the Court of Appeals is vacated, and the case is remanded . . . ."

V. JUSTICE VOTE

5 Pro ACLU Side vs. 4 Con Opposing Side

ACLU Side (Petitioner / Appellant)

1. Breyer, S. – Wrote majority opinion
2. Kagan, E. – Joined majority opinion
3. Kennedy, A. – Joined majority opinion
4. Ginsburg, R. – Joined majority opinion
5. Sotomayor, S. – Joined majority opinion

Opposing Side (Respondent / Appellee)

1. Alito, S. – Wrote dissenting opinion
2. Thomas, C. – Joined Scalia's dissent
3. Scalia, A. – Wrote dissenting opinion
4. Roberts, J. – Joined Scalia's dissent

VI. A WIN OR LOSS FOR THE ACLU?

The ACLU filed as amicus curiae urging reversal of the judgment of the Court of Appeals; the Supreme Court vacated in a 5-4 vote, giving the ACLU an apparent win.

1140. Texas Dept. of Housing and Community Affairs v. Inclusive Communities Project, Inc.

(Decided June 25, 2015; 135 S.Ct. 2507; 576 U.S. _)

I. ISSUE

A. Issues Discussed

Race, regulation

B. Legal Question Presented

"[W]hether disparate-impact claims are cognizable under the Fair Housing Act . . . ."

C. Supreme Court's Answer

"The Court holds that disparate-impact claims are cognizable under the Fair Housing Act upon considering its results-oriented language, the Court's interpretation of similar language in Title VII and the ADEA, Congress' ratification of disparate-impact claims in 1988 against the backdrop of the unanimous view of nine Courts of Appeals, and the statutory purpose."

II. CASE SUMMARY

A. Background

"The Inclusive Communities Project, Inc. (ICP), is a Texas-based nonprofit corporation that assists low-income families in obtaining affordable housing. In 2008, the ICP brought this suit against the Department [of Housing and Community Affairs] and its officers in the United States District Court for the Northern District of Texas. As relevant here, it brought a disparate-impact claim under §§ 804(a) and 805(a) of the FHA. The ICP alleged the Department has caused continued segregated housing patterns by its disproportionate allocation of the tax credits, granting too many credits for housing in predominantly black inner-city areas and too few in predominantly white suburban neighborhoods. . . .

The District Court concluded that the ICP had established a prima facie case of disparate impact. It relied on two pieces of statistical evidence. . . .

The District Court then placed the burden on the Department to rebut the ICP's prima facie showing of disparate impact. [T]he District Court held that a defendant . . . must prove 'that there are no other less discriminatory alternatives to advancing their proffered interests.' Because, in its view, the Department 'failed to meet [its] burden of proving that there are no less discriminatory alternatives,' the District Court ruled for the ICP. . . .

While the . . . appeal was pending, the Secretary of Housing and Urban Development . . . issued a regulation interpreting the FHA to encompass disparate-impact liability. . . .

The Court of Appeals for the Fifth Circuit held . . . that disparate-impact claims are cognizable under the FHA. On the merits, however, the Court of Appeals reversed and remanded."

The Supreme Court granted certiorari to review the case.

B. Counsel of Record / ACLU Attorney

ACLU Side (Respondent / Appellee): Michael M. Daniel argued the cause for appellee. With him on the briefs was Laura B. Beshara.

Solicitor General Verrilli argued the cause for the United States as amicus curiae.

Opposing Side (Petitioner / Appellant): Scott A. Keller argued the cause for appellant. With him on the briefs were Greg Abbott, Attorney General of Texas, Daniel T. Hodge, First Assistant Attorney General, Jonathan F. Mitchell, Solicitor General, Andrew S. Oldham, Deputy Solicitor General, and Beth Klusmann and Alex Potapov, Assistant Solicitors General. Brent M. Rosenthal filed briefs for appellee Frazier Revitalization Inc.

III. AMICI CURIAE

ACLU Side (Respondent / Appellee)

Brief of amici curiae filed on behalf of the American Civil Liberties Union, the National Consumer Law Center, and Legal Momentum, et al. by Stuart T. Rossman, Jelena Kolic, Steven R. Shapiro, Laurence M. Schwartztol, Sandra S. Park, Rachel E. Goodman, Lenora M. Lapidus, and Michaela L. Wallin.

Brief of amici curiae filed on behalf of National Community Land Trust Network by Joseph M. Sellers and Peter Romer-Friedman.

Brief of amici curiae filed on behalf of Students from the New York University School of Law Seminar on Critical Narratives in Civil Rights et al. by Peggy Cooper and Aderson B. Francois.

Brief of amici curiae filed on behalf of Howard University School of Law Fair Housing Clinic et al. by Aderson Bellegarde François and Valerie Schneider.

Brief of amici curiae filed on behalf of Sociologists, Social Psychologists, and Legal Scholars et al. by Eva Paterson, Allison Elgart, Mona Tawatao, Richard A. Rothschild, William C. Kennedy, Andrea Matsuoka, Rachel D. Godsil, David J. Berger, Megan E. Wall-Wolff, and Rebecca E. Wolitz.

Brief of amici curiae filed on behalf of National Association for the Advancement of Colored People et al. by Marshall Taylor, Khyla D. Craine, Stephen M. Dane, and Laura Arandes.

Brief of amici curiae filed on behalf of Henry G. Cisneros, Former Secretary of the United States Department of Housing and Urban Development et al. by Diane L. Houk and Alison Frick.

Brief of amici curiae filed on behalf of Constitutional Accountability Center by Douglas T. Kendall, Elizabeth B. Wydra, David H. Gans, and Brianne J. Gorod.

Brief of amici curiae filed on behalf of the National Black Law Students Association by Deborah N. Archer and Erika L. Wood.

Brief of amici curiae filed on behalf of the the Housing Equality Center of Pennsylvania by James Berry, Elizabeth Moreira, Mark A. Packman, Meredith R. Hiller, Jenna A. Hudson, and Daniel I. Wolf.

Brief of amici curiae filed on behalf of the United States by Solicitor General Verrilli, Acting Assistant Attorney General Gupta, Deputy Solicitor General Gershengorn, Assistant Solicitor General Harrington, Dennis J. Dimsey, April J. Anderson, Helen R. Kanovsky, Michelle Aronowitz, M. Casey Weissman-Vermeulen, and Ayelet R. Weiss.

Brief of amici curiae filed on behalf of Massachusetts et al. by Martha Coakley, Attorney General of Massachusetts, and Jonathan B. Miller and Genevieve C. Nadeau, Assistant Attorneys General, by Eric T. Schneiderman, Attorney General of New York, Barbara D. Underwood, Solicitor General, Cecelia C. Chang, Special Counsel to the Solicitor General, Kristen Clarke, Chief of the Civil Rights Bureau, Matthew W. Grieco, Assistant Solicitor General, and by the Attorneys General for their respective States as follows: Thomas C. Horne of Arizona, Kamala D. Harris of California, George Jepsen of Connecticut, Russell A. Suzuki of Hawaii, Lisa Madigan of Illinois, Lori Swanson of Minnesota, Chris Koster of Missouri, Joseph A. Foster of New Hampshire, Gary K. King of New Mexico, Roy Cooper of North Carolina, Ellen F. Rosenblum of Oregon, Sean D. Reyes of Utah, William H. Sorrell of Vermont, Mark R. Herring of Virginia, and Robert W. Ferguson of Washington.

Brief of amici curiae filed on behalf of AARP et al. by Susan Ann Silverstein.

Brief of amici curiae filed on behalf of National Fair Housing Alliance et al. by Morgan Williams, John P. Relman, and Sasha Samberg-Champion.

Brief of amici curiae filed on behalf of the Lawyers' Committee for Civil Rights Under Law Bill et al. by Lann Lee, Lindsay Nako, Julie Wilensky, Philip D. Tegeler, Megan Haberle, Joseph D. Rich, Thomas Silverstein, Alan Jenkins, Wade J. Henderson, and Lisa M. Bornstein.

Brief of amici curiae filed on behalf of Housing Scholars by Daniel R. Shulman, Stephen Menendian, and Daniel Costa.

Brief of amici curiae filed on behalf of Current and Former Members of Congress by Deepak Gupta and Jonathan E. Taylor, in support of affirmance.

Brief of amici curiae filed on behalf of Cities of San Francisco by Dennis J. Herrera, San Francisco City Attorney, Christine Van Aken, Chief of Appellate Litigation, and David T. Goldberg.

Brief of amici curiae filed on behalf of John R. Dunne et al. by Samuel R. Bagenstos.

Brief of amici curiae filed on behalf of Ian Ayres by Ian Ayres, Rachel J. Geman, and Jason L. Lichtman.

Brief of amici curiae filed on behalf the American Planning Association et al. by Edward Sullivan.

Brief of amici curiae filed on behalf NAACP Legal Defense & Educational Fund, Inc., by Sherrilyn Ifill, Leslie M. Proll, Janai Nelson, John Paul Schnapper-Casteras, Christina Swarns, Jin Hee Lee, and Rachel M. Kleinman.

Brief of amici curiae filed on behalf

Real Estate Professional Trade Organizations by Michael B. De Leeuw, Linda Riefberg, Rory Greebel, Michael J. Broadbent, and Cozen O'Connor.

Opposing Side (Petitioner / Appellant)

Brief of amici curiae filed on behalf of James P. Scanlan by Mr. Scanlan.

Brief of amici curiae filed on behalf of Gail Heriot et al. by Ms. Heriot and Anthony T. Caso.
Brief of amici curiae filed on behalf of
the Project on Fair Representation by William S. Consovoy, Thomas R. Mccarthy, and J. Michael Connolly.
Brief of amici curiae filed on behalf of the American Financial Services Association et al. By Andrew C. Glass and Paul F. Hancock.
Brief of amici curiae filed on behalf of American Civil Rights Union by Peter J. Ferrara.
Brief of amici curiae filed on behalf of National Association of Home Builders by Devala A. Janardan and Thomas J. Ward.
Brief of amici curiae filed on behalf of the American Insurance Association et al. by Kannon K. Shanmugam, Allison B. Jones, and A. Joshua Podoll.
Brief of amici curiae filed on behalf of the Consumer Data Industry Association et al. by Christopher A. Mohr.
Brief of amici curiae filed on behalf of Judicial Watch, Inc., et al. by Paul J. Orfanedes, Robert D. Popper, and Chris Fedeli.
Brief of amici curiae filed on behalf of Pacific Legal Foundation et al. by
Meriem L. Hubbard, Ralph W. Kasarda, Joshua P. Thompson, and Wencong Fa.
Brief of amici curiae filed on behalf of Texas Apartment Association by John Sepehri, Sean D. Jordan, Kent C. Sullivan, Peter C. Hanse, and Robert A. Lemus.
Brief of amici curiae filed on behalf of the Houston Housing Authority by Michael W. Skojec and Bryan J. Harrison.
Brief of amici curiae filed on behalf of National Leased Housing Association et al. by Harry J. Kelly, Brian J. Whittaker, and John C. Hayes, Jr.
Brief of amici curiae filed on behalf of Washington Legal Foundation by Cory L. Andrews and Richard A. Samp.
Brief of amici curiae filed on behalf of the American Bankers Association et al. by Lisa S. Blatt, Nancy L. Perkins, Anthony J. Franze, and Daniel Friedman.

IV. THE SUPREME COURT'S DECISION

"The issue here is whether, under a proper interpretation of the FHA, housing decisions with a disparate impact are prohibited. . . .

An important and appropriate means of ensuring that disparate-impact liability is properly limited is to give housing authorities and private developers leeway to state and explain the valid interest served by their policies. . . .

It would be paradoxical to construe the FHA to impose onerous costs on actors who encourage revitalizing dilapidated housing in our Nation's cities merely because some other priority might seem preferable. . . .

In a similar vein, a disparate-impact claim that relies on a statistical disparity must fail if the plaintiff cannot point to a defendant's policy or policies causing that disparity. . . .

The litigation at issue here provides an example. From the standpoint of determining advantage or disadvantage to racial minorities, it seems difficult to say as a general matter that a decision to build low-income housing in a blighted inner-city neighborhood instead of a suburb is discriminatory, or vice versa. If those sorts of judgments are subject to challenge without adequate safeguards, then there is a danger that potential defendants may adopt racial quotas—a circumstance that itself raises serious constitutional concerns. . . .

It must be noted further that, even when courts do find liability under a disparate-impact theory, their remedial orders must be consistent with the Constitution. . . .

The Court holds that disparate-impact claims are cognizable under the Fair Housing Act upon considering its results-oriented language, the Court's interpretation of similar language in Title VII and the ADEA, Congress' ratification of disparate-impact claims in 1988 against the backdrop of the unanimous view of nine Courts of Appeals, and the statutory purpose. . . .

In light of the longstanding judicial interpretation of the FHA to encompass disparate-impact claims and congressional reaffirmation of that result, residents and policymakers have come to rely on the availability of disparate-impact claims. . . .

The Court acknowledges the Fair Housing Act's continuing role in moving the Nation toward a more integrated society.

The judgment of the Court of Appeals . . . is affirmed, and the case is remanded . . . ."

V. JUSTICE VOTE

5 Pro ACLU Side vs. 4 Con Opposing Side

ACLU Side (Respondent / Appellee)

1. Kennedy, A. – Wrote majority opinion
2. Kagan, E. – Joined majority opinion
3. Breyer, S. – Joined majority opinion
4. Ginsburg, R. – Joined majority opinion
5. Sotomayor, S. – Joined majority opinion

Opposing Side (Petitioner / Appellant)

1. Alito, S. – Wrote dissenting opinion
2. Thomas, C. – Wrote dissenting opinion, joined Alito's dissent
3. Scalia, A. – Joined Alito's dissent
4. Roberts, J. – Joined Alito's dissent

VI. A WIN OR LOSS FOR THE ACLU?

The ACLU filed as amicus curiae urging affirmance; the Supreme Court affirmed the Court of Appeals' decision by a 5-4 vote, giving the ACLU an apparent win.

1141. Obergefell v. Hodges

(Decided June 26, 2015; 135 S.Ct. 2584; 576 U.S. _)

I. ISSUE

A. Issues Discussed

Federalism

B. Legal Question Presented

"The first [question], presented by the cases from Michigan and Kentucky, is whether the Fourteenth Amendment requires a State to license a marriage between two people of the same sex. The second [question], presented by the cases from Ohio, Tennessee, and, again, Kentucky, is whether the Fourteenth Amendment requires a State to recognize a same-sex marriage licensed and performed in a State which does grant that right."

C. Supreme Court's Answer

"The Court . . . holds same-sex couples may exercise the fundamental right to marry in all States. It follows that the Court also must hold—and it now does hold—that there is no lawful basis for a State to refuse to recognize a lawful same-sex marriage performed in another State on the ground of its same-sex character."

II. CASE SUMMARY

A. Background

"These cases come from Michigan, Kentucky, Ohio, and Tennessee, States that define marriage as a union between one man and one woman. The petitioners are 14 same-sex couples and two men whose same-sex partners are deceased. The respondents are state officials responsible for enforcing the laws in question. The petitioners claim the respondents violate the Fourteenth Amendment by denying them the right to marry or to have their marriages, lawfully performed in another State, given full recognition.

Petitioners filed these suits in United States District Courts in their home States. Each District Court ruled in their favor. . . . The respondents appealed the decisions against them to the United States Court of Appeals for the Sixth Circuit. It consolidated the cases and reversed the judgments of the District Courts. The Court of Appeals held that a State has no constitutional obligation to license same-sex marriages or to recognize same-sex marriages performed out of State."

The Supreme Court granted certiorari to review the case.

B. Counsel of Record / ACLU Attorney

ACLU Side (Petitioner / Appellant): Mary L. Bonauto argued the cause for appellants.

Douglas Hallward–Driemeier argued the cause for appellants.

Brief filed by Freda J. Levenson and Drew S. Dennis of the ACLU of Ohio, Inc., and James D. Esseks, Steven R. Shapiro, Joshua A. Block, Chase B. Strangio, Leslie Cooper, Ria Tabacco Mar, and Louise Melling of the American Civil Liberties Union Foundation, and William E. Sharp of the American Civil Liberties Union of Kentucky, and Jeffrey L. Fisher, Brian Wolfman, Daniel J. Canon, Laura E. Landenwich, L. Joe Dunman, Shannon Fauver, Dawn Elliott, Susan L. Sommer, M. Currey Cook, Omar Gonzalez–Pagan, Alphonse A. Gerhardstein, Jennifer L. Branch, Jacklyn Gonzales Martin, Adam Gingold Gerhardstein, Jon W. Davidson, Paul D. Castillo, Camilla B. Taylor, Ellen Essig Katz, Lisa T. Meeks, Kenneth M. Mogill, Dana M. Nessel, Mary L. Bonauto, Carole M. Stanyar, and Robert A. Sedler, Abby R. Rubenfeld, William L. Harbison, Phillip F. Cramer, J. Scott Hickman, John L. Farringer, Maureen T. Holland, Regina M. Lambert, Christopher Thomas Brown, Justin G. Florence, Shannon P. Minter, David C. Codell, Christopher F. Stoll, Amy Whelan, Asaf Orr, Paul S. Kellogg, Samira A. Omerovic, Emerson A. Siegle, John T. Dey, Joshua E. Goldstein.

Solicitor General Verrilli, Jr. argued the cause for the United States as amicus curiae.

Opposing Side (Respondent / Appellee): John J. Bursch argued the cause for appellees.

Solicitor General Joseph F. Whalen argued the cause for appellees.

Brief filed by Michael Dewine, Attorney General of Ohio, Eric E. Murphy, State Solicitor, Stephen P. Carney and Peter T. Reed, Deputy Solicitors, Herbert H. Slatery III, Attorney General, State of Tennessee, Martha A. Campbell and Kevin G. Steiling, Deputy Attorneys General, Alexander S. Rieger, Assistant Attorney General, Office of the Attorney General, Bill Schuette, Michigan Attorney General, Aaron D. Lindstrom, Solicitor General, B. Eric Restuccia, Deputy Solicitor General, Ann Sherman, Assistant Solicitor General, John J. Bursch, Special Assistant Attorney General, Leigh Gross Latherow, William H. Jones, Jr., and Gregory L. Monge.

III. AMICI CURIAE

ACLU Side (Petitioner / Appellant)

Brief of amici curiae filed on behalf of the County of Cuyahoga, Ohio by Majeed G. Makhlouf, Director of Law of Cuyahoga County, Awatef Assad and Ruchi V. Asher, Assistant Law Directors, and Doron M. Kalir.

Brief of amici curiae filed on behalf of Columbia Law School Sexuality and Gender Law Clinic by Henry P. Monaghan and Suzanne B. Goldberg.

Brief of amici curiae filed on behalf of OutServe-Servicemembers Legal Defense Network et al. by Abbe David Lowell and Christopher D. Man.

Brief of amici curiae filed on behalf of the State of Hawaii by Russell A. Suzuki, Attorney General of Hawaii, Girard D. Lau, Solicitor General, Kimberly T. Guidry, First Deputy Solicitor General, and Robert T. Nakatsuji, Deputy Solicitor General.

Brief of amici curiae filed on behalf of Indiana University by D. Lucetta Pope, Jane Dall Wilson, Daniel E. Pulliam, Jon Laramore, Jacqueline A. Simmons, and Kiply S. Drew.

Brief of amici curiae filed on behalf of BiLaw by Kyle C. Velte.

Brief of amici curiae filed on behalf of Services and Advocacy for Gay, Lesbian, Bisexual and Transgender Elders et al. by Jonathan Jacob Nadler, Rachael A. Harris, Lauren S. Kuley, and Brandon Román.

Brief of amici curiae filed on behalf of the Cleveland Choral Arts Association Inc., A/K/A the North Coast Men's Chorus by Harlan D. Karp and Tina R. Haddad.

Brief of amici curiae filed on behalf of Elected Officials and Former Officeholders of Michigan et al. byMark Totten, David Pepper, Gregory L. Diskant, Travis J. Tu, Jonah M. Knobler, Jenny Ma, and D. Brandon Trice.

Brief of amici curiae filed on behalf of Langley Hill Friends Meeting et al. by J.E. Mcneil and Daniel P. O' Connor.

Brief of amici curiae filed on behalf of Survivors of Sexual Orientation Change Therapies by Sanford Jay Rosen, Gay Crosthwait Grunfeld, and Benjamin Bien-Kahn.

Brief of amici curiae filed on behalf of California Council

of Churches et al. by Stacey Marie Kaplan and Eric Alan Isaacson.

Brief of amici curiae filed on behalf of President of the House of Deputies of the Episcopal Church et al. by Jeffrey S. Trachtman, Norman C. Simon, Jason M. Moff, and Kurt M. Denkl.

Brief of amici curiae filed on behalf of Conflict of Law Scholars by Tobias Barrington Wolff, Robert A. Long, and Daniel E. Matro.

Brief of amici curiae filed on behalf of Family Equality Council et al. by Katherine Keating, Tracy M. Talbot, Berrie Goldman, Robert J. Esposito, William J. Hibsher, and Emily Hecht-Mcgowan.

Brief of amici curiae filed on behalf of Equality Ohio et al. by Alana C. Jochum and Alan B. Morrison.

Brief of amici curiae filed on behalf of Bay Area Lawyers for Individual Freedom et al. by Jerome C. Roth and Amelia L.B. Sargent.

Brief of amici curiae filed on behalf of Kenneth B. Mehlman et al. by Sean R. Gallagher, Reginald J. Brown, Stacy A. Carpenter, Seth P. Waxman, Bennett L. Cohen, Paul R.Q. Wolfson, and Dina B. Mishra.

Brief of amici curiae filed on behalf of the American Humanist Association et al. by Monica L. Miller and Elizabeth L. Hileman.

Brief of amici curiae filed on behalf of National Women's Law Center et al. by Emily J. Martin, Nan D. Hunter, Marcia D. Greenberger, Elizabeth Johnston, Barbara B. Brown, Stephen B. Kinnaird, Jennifer S. Baldocchi, Jeffrey S. Haber, Betsey Boutelle, Peter T. Brejcha, Courtney T. Dethomas, Jenifer Q. Doan, Michaela Dudley, Rebecca D. Farber, Cameron W. Fox, Amanda L. Fretto, Bridget A. Gordon, Scott M. Klausner, Judith M. Kline, David B. Lyons, Ashley N. Mays, Eleanor K. Mercado, Brian P. Moran, Beth C. Mueller, Sean M. Smith, Mor Wetzler, and Misty Wright.

Brief of amici curiae filed on behalf of the Organization of American Historians by Catherine E. Stetson, Erica Knievel Songer, Mary Helen Wimberly, Madeline H. Gitomer, and Katherine J. Duncan.

Brief of amici curiae filed on behalf of 379 Employers and Organizations Representing Employers by Meghan Rhea, Susan Baker Manning, Michael L. Whitlock, Amanda D. Smith, John A. Polito, and Jawad Muaddi.

Brief of amici curiae filed on behalf of Institute for Justice by William H. Mellor,

Dana Berliner, Jeffrey T. Rowes, Robert J. Mcnamara, and Robert Everett Johnson.

Brief of amici curiae filed on behalf of the Alliance: State Advocates for Women's Rights and Gender Equality by Lisa M. Stone, Janet Chung, David Ward, Kathleen M. O'Sullivan, Abha Khanna, and David A. Perez.

Brief of amici curiae filed on behalf of GLMA et al. by Hector Vargas, Nicholas M. O'Donnell, and Caitlin C. Fahey.

Brief of amici curiae filed on behalf of American Sociological Association by Carmine D. Boccuzzi, Jr., Mark A. Lightner, Grant A. Bermann, and Alexandra Eber.

Brief of amici curiae filed on behalf of the Commonwealth of Virginia by

Mark R. Herring, Attorney General of Virginia, Cynthia E. Hudson, Chief Deputy Attorney General, Cynthia V. Bailey, Deputy Attorney General, Allyson K. Tysinger, Senior Assistant Attorney General, Carly L. Rush, Assistant Attorney General, Stuart A. Raphael, Solicitor General, and Trevor S. Cox, Deputy Solicitor General.

Brief of amici curiae filed on behalf of Scholars of the Constitutional Rights of Children by Catherine E. Smith, Lauren Fontana, Susannah W. Pollvogt, and Tanya Washington.

Brief of amici curiae filed on behalf of the National Family Civil Rights Center by Douglas J. Callahan.

Brief of amici curiae filed on behalf of the Human Rights Campaign et al. by Dale Carpenter, Steve Sanders, Roberta A. Kaplan, Andrew J. Ehrlich, and Jaren Janghorbani.

Brief of amici curiae filed on behalf of Constitutional Accountability Center by Douglas T. Kendall, Elizabeth B. Wydra, David H. Gans, and Judith E. Schaeffer.

Brief of amici curiae filed on behalf of Kristin M. Perry et al. by David Boies, Joshua I. Schiller, Theodore B. Olson, Matthew D. Mcgill, Amir C. Tayrani, Chantale Fiebig, Theodore J. Boutrous, Jr., Theane Evangelis, Enrique A. Monagas, Abbey Hudson, Thomas B. Shuttleworth, Robert E. Ruloff, Charles B. Lustig, Andrew M. Hendrick, and Erik C. Porcaro.

Brief of amici curiae filed on behalf of the United States by Solicitor General Verrilli, Acting Associate Attorney General Delery, Acting Assistant Attorneys General Gupta and Mizer, Deputy Solicitor General Gershengorn, Deputy Assistant Attorneys General Brinkmann, Friel, and Karlan, Assistant Solicitor General Feigin, Diana K. Flynn, Douglas N. Letter, Sharon M. Mcgowan, Michael Jay Singer, Robert A. Koch, Abby C. Wright, and Jeffrey E. Sandberg.

Brief of amici curiae filed on behalf of the American Psychological Association et al. by Nathalie F.P. Gilfoyle, Paul M. Smith, and Aaron M. Panner.

Brief of amici curiae filed on behalf of Anti-Defamation League et al. by Steven M. Freeman, Seth M. Marnin, Miriam L. Zeidman, David L. Barkey, Hilarie Bass, Elliot H. Scherker, Brigid F. Cech Samole, Gregory E. Ostfeld, and James P. Madigan.

Brief of amici curiae filed on behalf of PFLAG, Inc., by Andrew J. Davis and Jiyun Cameron Lee.

Brief of amici curiae filed on behalf of the Leadership Conference on Civil and Human Rights et al. by Wade J. Henderson, Lisa M. Bornstein, Matthew M. Hoffman, Abigail Hemani, Joshua M. Daniels, Kelly Phipps, Stephen M. Hoeplinger, Brian W. Cook, Ted Koehler, Beaudre D. Barnes, Matthew S. Williams, and Valerie A. Haggans.

Brief of amici curiae filed on behalf of Conflict of Laws and Family Law Professors by Joanna L. Grossman, Sean M. Selegue, Trenton H. Norris, Marjory A. Gentry, John S. Throckmorton, and Emily H. Wood.

Brief of amici curiae filed on behalf of the Donaldson Adoption Institute et al. by Aaron M. Tidman, A.W. Phinney III, Jonathan A. Shapiro, Kelly L. Frey, and Mina Nasseri.

Brief of amici curiae filed on behalf of the Liberty Education Forum by Craig Engle, Thorne Maginnis, Arent Fox, and Brett G. Kappel.

Brief of amici curiae filed on behalf of American Public Health Association et al. by Sheree R. Kanner, Kenneth Y. Choe, Margia K. Corner, Elizabeth C. Lockwood, Boris Bershteyn, David W. Skaar, Thomas Cummins, Daniel Bruner, Román J. Rodriguez, Michael Springer, Sam Auld, Audrey Feldman, Kevin C. Hu, and Stefanie E. Neale.

Brief of amici curiae filed on behalf of Hon. Lawrence J. Korb et al. By Eamon P. Joyce, Carter G. Phillips, Joseph R. Guerra, John T. Hebden, Julia G. Mirabella, and Christopher A. Eiswerth.

Brief of amici curiae filed on behalf of 167 Members of the U.S. House of Representatives et al. by Heather C. Sawyer, Joseph F. Tringali, Joshua C. Polster, Elisa Y. Lee, and Aidan T. Grano.

Brief of amici curiae filed on behalf of Howard University School of Law Civil Rights Clinic by Aderson B. François and Benjamin G. Shatz.

Brief of amici curiae filed on behalf of Law Enforcement Officers et al. by Hunter T. Carter and Matthew S. Trokenheim.

Brief of amici curiae filed on behalf of Legal Services NYC by Owen C. Pell, Kimberly A. Haviv, Harold W. Williford, and Alice Tsier.

Brief of amici curiae filed on behalf of Family Law Scholars by Joan Heifetz Hollinger, Courtney Joslin, E. Joshua Rosenkranz, Mark S. Davies, and Jeremy Peterman.

Brief of amici curiae filed on behalf of Freedom to Marry by Jonathan P. Schneller, Dimitri Portnoi, Anton Metlitsky, Walter Dellinger, and Jonathan D. Hacker.

Brief of amici curiae filed on behalf of the American Academy of Matrimonial Lawyers et al. by Diana Raimi and Brian C. Vertz.

Brief of amici curiae filed on behalf of Americans United for Separation of Church and State by Ayesha N. Khan, Alex J. Luchenitser, Charles A. Rothfeld, Miriam R. Nemetz, Richard B. Katskee, Hannah Y.S. Chanoine, Frank M. Dickerson, Emily C.R. Vermylen, Rebecca M. Klein, and Linda X. Shi.

Brief of amici curiae filed on behalf of the State of Massachusetts et al. by Maura Healey, Attorney General of Massachusetts, Jonathan B. Miller, Genevieve C. Nadeau, and Amanda R. Mangaser, Assistant Attorneys General, and by the Attorneys General for their respective jurisdictions as follows: Kamala D. Harris of California, George Jepsen of Connecticut, Matthew P. Denn of Delaware, Karl A. Racine of the District of Columbia, Lisa Madigan of Illinois, Tom Miller of Iowa, Janet T. Mills of Maine, Brian E. Frosh of Maryland, Joseph A. Foster of New Hampshire, Hector H. Balderas of New Mexico, Eric T. Schneiderman of New York, Ellen F. Rosenblum of Oregon, Kathleen G. Kane of Pennsylvania, Peter F. Kilmartin of Rhode Island, William H. Sorrell of Vermont, and Robert W. Ferguson of Washington.

Brief of amici curiae filed on behalf of the Honorable John K. Olson by G. Eric Brunstad, Jr., Dennis H. Hranitzky, Mark P. DiPerna, Kate M. O'Keeffe, Victoria Campbell Fitzpatrick, Mayer B. Grashin, Kevin P. Brost, Negin Hadaghian, and Rabia Muqaddam.

Brief of amici curiae filed on behalf of Marriage Equality USA by John A. Lewis and Martin N. Buchanan.

Brief of amici curiae filed on behalf of LGBT Student Organizations at Undergraduate, Graduate, and Professional Schools by Andrew Melzer, Deborah Marcuse, and David Tracey.

Brief of amici curiae filed on behalf of the State of Minnesota by Lori Swanson, Attorney General of Minnesota, Alan I. Gilbert, Solicitor General, and Jacob Campion, Assistant Attorney General.

Brief of amici curiae filed on behalf of Garden State Equality by Lawrence S. Lustberg and Joseph A. Pace.

Brief of amici curiae filed on behalf of 226 U.S. Mayors et al. by Michael N. Feuer, Los Angeles City Attorney, James P. Clark, Thomas H. Peters, Blithe Smith Bock, Lisa S. Berger, Juliann Anderson, Dennis Herrera, San Francisco City Attorney, Ronald P. Flynn, Christine Van Aken, Mollie M. Lee, Stephen R. Patton, Chicago City Corporation Counsel, and Zachary E. Carter, New York City Corporation Counsel.

Brief of amici curiae filed on behalf of NAACP Legal Defense & Educational Fund, Inc., et al. by Sherrilyn Ifill, John Paul Schnapper-Casteras, Janai Nelson, Christina Swarns, Jin Hee Lee, Rachel M. Kleinman, Marshall W. Taylor, and Khyla D. Craine.

Brief of amici curiae filed on behalf of the Mattachine Society of Washington, D.C., by Paul M. Thompson, Lisa A. Linsky, Melissa Nott Davis, Michael R. Huttenlocher, Mary D. Hallerman, Ryan O. Leske, and Krista Meany.

Brief of amici curiae filed on behalf of Professors Laurence H. Tribe et al. by Christopher J. Wright, Timothy J. Simeone, and Stephen W. Miller.

Brief of amici curiae filed on behalf of Campaign for Southern Equality et al. by Meghann K. Burke, W.O. Brazil III, S. Luke Largess, Jacob H. Sussman, John W. Gresham, Robert B. Mcduff, Cristina Alonso, Justin S. Wales, Namrata S. Joshi, Sylvia H. Walbolt, Joanna Garcia, and M. Derek Harris.

Brief of amici curiae filed on behalf of Cato Institute et al. by William N. Eskridge Jr., and Ilya Shapiro.

Brief of amici curiae filed on behalf of Douglas Laycock et al. by Mr. Laycock and Mr. Berg.

Brief of amici curiae filed on behalf of Human Rights Watch et al. by James D. Ross, Anna M. Pohl, Marie-Claude Jean-Baptiste, Richard L. Levine, Jay Minga, and Robert T. Vlasis III.

Brief of amici curiae filed on behalf of Historians of Marriage et al. by Jessica M. Weisel, Daniel McNeel Lane, Jr., Matthew E. Pepping, and Pratik A. Shah.

Brief of amici curiae filed on behalf of Ninety-two Plaintiffs in Marriage Cases in Alabama et al. by Wesley R. Powell, Mary J. Eaton, Sameer Advani, and Richard D. Bernstein.

Brief of amici curiae filed on behalf of Gary J. Gates by Adam P. Romero, Scott Ballenger, Melissa Arbus Sherry, and Angela Walker.

Brief of amici curiae filed on behalf of Foreign and Comparative Law Experts Harold Hongju Koh et al. by Noah B. Novogrodsky, Ruth N. Borenstein, and Marc A. Hearron.

Brief of amici curiae filed on behalf of Constitutional Law Scholars Ashutosh Bhagwat et al. by Geoffrey R. Stone, Lori Alvino Mcgill, and Diane M. Soubly.

Brief of amici curiae filed on behalf of Carlos A. Ball, Distinguished Professor of Law, Rutgers University by Mr. Ball, Paul J. Hall, Jeff Degroot, George Gigounas, and Jesse Medlong.

Brief of amici curiae filed on behalf of the American Federation of Labor and Congress of Industrial Organizations et al. by Lynn K. Rhinehart, H. Craig Becker, Alice O'Brien, Jason Walta, Kari Greenwood, Judith A. Scott, Nicole G. Berner, and Patrick J. Szymanski.

Brief of amici curiae filed on behalf of Experiential Learning Lab at New York University School of Law by Aderson Bellegarde François and Peggy Cooper Davis.

Brief of amici curiae filed on behalf of Chris Kluwe et al. by Timothy R. Holbrook and John A. Dragseth.

Brief of amici curiae filed on behalf of Legal Scholars Stephen Clark et al. by Andrew Koppelman, Ilya Somin, Joseph P. Lombardo, Eric S. Silvestri, Brittany L. Viola, and Sara T. Ghadir.

Opposing Side (Respondent / Appellee)

Brief of amici curiae filed on behalf of Robert J. Bentley, Governor of Alabama by David B. Byrne, Jr., Algert S. Agricola, Jr., and Adam J. MacLeod.

Brief of amici curiae filed on behalf of Dr. Paul Mchugh by Gerard V. Bradley.

Brief of amici curiae filed on behalf of Professor Daniel N. Robinson, Ph.D., by Kevin T. Snider.

Brief of amici curiae filed on behalf of Scholars of History and Related Disciplines by Charles J. Cooper, Howard C. Nielson, Jr., and Howard N. Slugh.

Brief of amici curiae filed on behalf of Ryan T. Anderson, Ph.D., by Michael F. Smith.

Brief of amici curiae filed on behalf of Dawn Stefanowicz et al. by David Boyle.

Brief of amici curiae filed on behalf of Heather Barwick et al. by David Boyle.

Brief of amici curiae filed on behalf of the State of South Carolina by Alan Wilson, Attorney General of South Carolina, Brendan Mcdonald and Ian Weschler, Assistant Attorneys General, Robert D. Cook, Solicitor General, and J. Emory Smith, Jr., Deputy Solicitor General.

Brief of amici curiae filed on behalf of Robert Oscar Lopez et al. by David Boyle.

Brief of amici curiae filed on behalf of 54 International and Comparative Law Experts from 27 Countries et al. by Lynn D. Wardle, Elizabeth A. Clark,

W. Cole Durham Jr., Robert T. Smith, and Donlu D. Thayer.

Brief of amici curiae filed on behalf of Family Trust Foundation of Kentucky, Inc., A/K/A The Family Foundation by Stanton L. Cave.

Brief of amici curiae filed on behalf of the Ruth Institute et al. by Sharee S. Langenstein.

Brief of amici curiae filed on behalf of North Carolina Values Coalition et al. by Deborah J. Dewart.

Brief of amici curiae filed on behalf of the Family Research by Council Paul Benjamin Linton and Christopher M. Gacek.

Brief of amici curiae filed on behalf of United States Conference of Catholic Bishops by Anthony R. Picarello, Jr., Jeffrey Hunter Moon, Michael F. Moses, and Hillary E. Byrnes.

Brief of amici curiae filed on behalf of Liberty Scholars et al. by David R. Upham.

Brief of amici curiae filed on behalf of Lary S. Larson by Sean J. Coletti.

Brief of amici curiae filed on behalf of CatholicVote.org Education Fund by Patrick T. Gillen.

Brief of amici curiae filed on behalf of Organizations that Promote Biological Parenting by Timothy Tardibono.

Brief of amici curiae filed on behalf of Scholars of Originalism by William C. Duncan.

Brief of amici curiae filed on behalf of Parents and Friends of Ex-Gays & Gays by Dean R. Broyles.

Brief of amici curiae filed on behalf of Wyoming Legislators et al. by Herbert K. Doby and Nathaniel S. Hibben.

Brief of amici curiae filed on behalf of David A. Robinson by Mr. Robinson.

Brief of amici curiae filed on behalf of Public Affairs Campaign et al. by John C. Eastman and Anthony T. Caso.

Brief of amici curiae filed on behalf of Algirdas M. Liepas by Mr. Liepas.

Brief of amici curiae filed on behalf of the National Coalition of Black Pastors and Christian Leaders by William R. Wagner, John S. Kane, Richard Thompson, and Erin Mersino.

Brief of amici curiae filed on behalf of American College of Pediatricians et al. by David C. Walker.

Brief of amici curiae filed on behalf of 100 Scholars of Marriage by Gene C. Schaerr.

Brief of amici curiae filed on behalf of Tri Valley Law, P.C., by Marc A. Greendorfer.

Brief of amici curiae filed on behalf of Organizations and Scholars of Gender-Diverse Parenting by Cecilia M. Wood and Edward H. Trent.

Brief of amici curiae filed on behalf of Catholic Answers by Charles S. Limandri, Paul M. Jonna, and Jeffrey M. Trissell.

Brief of amici curiae filed on behalf of 47 Scholars by Robert P. George.

Brief of amici curiae filed on behalf of Scholars of the Welfare of Women, Children, and Underprivileged Populations by Lynne Marie Kohm, John C. Eastman, and Anthony T. Caso.

Brief of amici curiae filed on behalf of Major Religious Organizations by Carl H. Esbeck, Alexander Dushku, R. Shawn Gunnarson, and Kirton McConkie.

Brief of amici curiae filed on behalf of Leaders of the 2012 Republican National Convention Committee on the Platform et al. by James Bopp, Jr. and Anita Y. Milanovich

Brief of amici curiae filed on behalf of Religious Organizations, Public Speakers, and Scholars Concerned About Free Speech by Jeffrey C. Mateer, Kelly J. Shackelford, Hiram S. Sasser III, Matthew J. Kacsmaryk, and Justin E. Butterfield.

Brief of amici curiae filed on behalf of the Committee for Justice by Curt Levey and Meir Katz.

Brief of amici curiae filed on behalf of the State of Louisiana et al. by James D. "Buddy" Caldwell, Attorney General of Louisiana, S. Kyle Duncan, Special Assistant Attorney General, Sean D. Reyes, Attorney General of Utah, Parker Douglas, Federal Solicitor, Ken Paxton, Attorney General of Texas, and by the Attorneys General for their respective States as follows: Craig W. Richards of Alaska, Mark Brnovich of Arizona, Leslie Rutledge of Arkansas, Samuel S. Olens of Georgia, Lawrence G. Wasden of Idaho, Derek Schmidt of Kansas, Timothy C. Fox of Montana, Dave Bydalek of Nebraska, Wayne Stenehjem of North Dakota, E. Scott Pruitt of Oklahoma, Marty J. Jackley of South Dakota, and Patrick Morissey of West Virginia.

Brief of amici curiae filed on behalf of Theodore Coates by Mr. Coates.

Brief of amici curiae filed on behalf of Texas Eagle Forum by Andrew L. Schlafly.

Brief of amici curiae filed on behalf of Scholars of Fertility and Marriage by James R. Tate in support of affirmance.

Brief of amici curiae filed on behalf of Richard A. Lawrence by Mr. Lawrence.

Brief of amici curiae filed on behalf of Mike Huckabee Policy Solutions by Jeffrey S. Wittenbrink.

Brief of amici curiae filed on behalf of Foundation for Moral Law by John A. Eidsmoe.

Brief of amici curiae filed on behalf of Public Advocate of the U.S. et al. by Michael Connelly, William J. Olson, Herbert W. Titus, Jeremiah L. Morgan, J. Mark Brewer, Kerry L. Morgan, Mark J. Fitzgibbons, and James N. Clymer.

Brief of amici curiae filed on behalf of the State of Alabama by Luther Strange, Attorney General of Alabama, Andrew L. Brasher, Solicitor General, Douglas G. Wardlow, David A. Cortman, James A. Campbell, and David Austin R. Nimocks.

Brief of amici curiae filed on behalf of Southeastern Legal Foundation by Shannon Lee Goessling and Kimberly Stewart Hermann.

Brief of amici curiae filed on behalf of Earl M. Maltz et al. by Herbert G. Grey.

Brief of amici curiae filed on behalf of Jason Feliciano et al. by Sandra F. Gilbert.

Brief of amici curiae filed on behalf of

Judicial Watch, Inc., by James F. Peterson and Meredith L. Di Liberto.

Brief of amici curiae filed on behalf of the International Conference of Evangelical Endorsers by Arthur A. Schulcz, Sr.

Brief of amici curiae filed on behalf of the Lighted Candle Society by John L. Harmer and George M. Weaver.

Brief of amici curiae filed on behalf of

Concerned Women for America by Steven W. Fitschen.

Brief of amici curiae filed on behalf of Institute for Marriage and Public Policy et al. by Teresa Stanton Collett.

Brief of amici curiae filed on behalf of Protectmarriage.Com – Yes On 8 et al. by Andrew P. P Ugno.

Brief of amici curiae filed on behalf of 57 Members of U.S. Congress by D. John Sauer.

Brief of amici curiae filed on behalf of Jon Simmons by Kevin E. Green.

Brief of amici curiae filed on behalf of Texas Values by Jonathan M. Saenz, David S. Lill, and Jared R. Woodfill.

Brief of amici curiae filed on behalf of Dr. Judith Reisman et al. by Mathew D. Staver and Mary E. McAlister.

Brief of amici curiae filed on behalf of Same-Sex Attracted Men and Their Wives by Darrin K. Johns.

Brief of amici curiae filed on behalf of David Boyle by Mr. Boyle.

Brief of amici curiae filed on behalf of Agudath Israel of America by Mordechai Biser and Larry Loigman.

Brief of amici curiae filed on behalf of Family Trust Foundation of Kentucky, Inc., A/K/A the Family Foundation by Stanton L. Cave.

Brief of amici curiae filed on behalf of Idaho Governor C.L. "Butch" Otter by Thomas C. Perry and Gene C. Schaerr.

Brief of amici curiae filed on behalf of Citizens United for the Individual Freedom to Define Marriage by D'Arcy Winston Straub in support of neither party and affirmance.

Brief of amici curiae filed on behalf of Eagle Forum Education & Legal Defense Fund Lawrence by J. Joseph in support of neither party suggesting the absence of jurisdiction.

Mae Kuykendall et al. by Ms. Kuykendall and Michael T. Worley in support of neither party and urging affirmance on question 1.

Brief of amici curiae filed on behalf of Professor W. Burlette Carter by Ms. Carter in support of neither party.

Brief of amici curiae filed on behalf of F the General Conference of Seventh-Day Adventists et al. by Todd Mcfarland, Eric C. Rassbach, Hannah C. Smith, Asma T. Uddin, and Andrew G. Schultz in support of neither party.

IV. THE SUPREME COURT'S DECISION

"The history of marriage is one of both continuity and change. . . .

Against this background, the legal question of same-sex marriage arose. . . .

After years of litigation, legislation, referenda, and the discussions that attended these public acts, the States are now divided on the issue of same-sex marriage. . . .

Under the Due Process Clause of the Fourteenth Amendment, no State shall 'deprive any person of life, liberty, or property, without due process of law.' . . .

[T]he Court has long held the right to marry is protected by the Constitution. . . .

This analysis compels the conclusion that same-sex couples may exercise the right to marry. The four principles and traditions to be discussed demonstrate that the reasons marriage is fundamental under the Constitution apply with equal force to same-sex couples.

A first premise of the Court's relevant precedents is that the right to personal choice regarding marriage is inherent in the concept of individual autonomy. . . .

A second principle in this Court's jurisprudence is that the right to marry is fundamental because it supports a two-person union unlike any other in its importance to the committed individuals. . . .

A third basis for protecting the right to marry is that it safeguards children and families . . . .

Fourth and finally, . . . traditions make clear that marriage is a keystone of our social order. . . .

These considerations lead to the conclusion that the right to marry is a fundamental right inherent in the liberty of the person, and under the Due Process and Equal Protection Clauses of the Fourteenth Amendment couples of the same-sex may not be deprived of that right and that liberty. The Court now holds that same-sex couples may exercise the fundamental right to marry. No longer may this liberty be denied to them. Baker v. Nelson must be and now is overruled, and the State laws challenged by Petitioners in these cases are now held invalid to the extent they exclude same-sex couples from civil marriage on the same terms and conditions as opposite-sex couples. . . .

These cases also present . . . whether the Constitution requires States to recognize same-sex marriages . . . performed out of State. As made clear by the case of Obergefell and Arthur, and by that of DeKoe and Kostura, the recognition bans inflict substantial and continuing harm on same-sex couples. . . .

The Court, in this decision, holds same-sex couples may exercise the fundamental right to marry in all States. It follows that the Court also must hold—and it now does hold—that there is no lawful basis for a State to refuse to recognize a lawful same-sex marriage performed in another State on the ground of its same-sex character. . . .

The judgment of the Court of Appeals for the Sixth Circuit is reversed."

V. JUSTICE VOTE

5 Pro ACLU Side vs. 4 Con Opposing Side

ACLU Side (Petitioner / Appellant)

1. Kennedy, A. – Wrote majority opinion
2. Kagan, E. – Joined majority opinion
3. Breyer, S. – Joined majority opinion
4. Ginsburg, R. – Joined majority opinion
5. Sotomayor, S. – Joined majority opinion

Opposing Side (Respondent / Appellee)

1. Alito, S. – Wrote dissenting opinion
2. Thomas, C. – Wrote dissenting opinion, joined Roberts' dissent, joined Scalia's dissent, joined Alito's dissent
3. Scalia, A. – Wrote dissenting opinion, joined Roberts' dissent, joined Thomas' dissent, joined Alito's dissent
4. Roberts, J. – Wrote dissenting opinion

VI. A WIN OR LOSS FOR THE ACLU?

The ACLU served as counsel for appellants urging reversal of the judgment of the Court of Appeals; the Supreme Court reversed in a 5-4 vote, giving the ACLU an apparent win.

1142. Arizona State Legislature v. Arizona Indep. Redistricting Comm'n

(Decided June 29, 2015; 135 S.Ct. 2652; 576 U.S. _)

I. ISSUE

A. Issues Discussed

Voting rights

B. Legal Question Presented

"(1) Does the Arizona Legislature have standing to bring this suit? (2) Do the Elections Clause of the United States Constitution and 2 U.S.C. § 2a(c) permit Arizona's use of a commission to adopt congressional districts?"

C. Supreme Court's Answer

"We hold, first, that the Arizona Legislature, having lost authority to draw congressional districts, has standing to contest the constitutionality of Proposition 106. Next, we hold that lawmaking power in Arizona includes the initiative process, and that both § 2a(c) and the Elections Clause permit use of the AIRC in congressional districting in the same way the Commission is used in districting for Arizona's own Legislature."

II. CASE SUMMARY

A. Background

"This case concerns an endeavor by Arizona voters to address the problem of partisan gerrymandering . . . .

In 2000, Arizona voters adopted an initiative, Proposition 106, aimed at 'ending the practice of gerrymandering and improving voter and candidate participation in elections.' . . .

The Arizona Legislature challenged the map the Commission adopted in January 2012 for congressional districts. Recognizing that the voters could control redistricting for state legislators, the Arizona Legislature sued the AIRC in federal court seeking a declaration that the Commission and its map for congressional districts violated the 'Elections Clause' of the U.S. Constitution. . . .

A three-judge District Court held, unanimously, that the Arizona Legislature had standing to sue; dividing two to one, the Court rejected the Legislature's complaint on the merits."

The Supreme Court postponed jurisdiction and reviewed the case.

B. Counsel of Record / ACLU Attorney

ACLU Side (Respondent / Appellee): Seth P. Waxman argued the cause for appellee. With him on the briefs were Mary O'Grady, Joseph N. Roth, Joseph A. Kanefield, Brunn W. Roysden III, Seth P. Waxman, Paul R.Q. Wolfson, Thomas G. Sprankling, Joshua M. Koppel, Jason D. Hirsch, and Ari J. Savitzky.

Assistant Solicitor General Feigin argued the cause for the United States as amicus curiae.

Opposing Side (Petitioner / Appellant): Paul D. Clement argued the cause for appellant. With him on the brief were Peter A. Gentala, Pele Peacock Fischer, Lesli M. H. Sorensen, Gregrey G. Jernigan, Paul D. Clement, George W. Hicks, Jr., Taylor

Meehan, Raymond P. Tolentino, Joshua W. Carden, and Marshall R. Hunt.

III. AMICI CURIAE

ACLU Side (Respondent / Appellee)

Brief of amici curiae filed on behalf of the Campaign Legal Center, the League of Women Voters of the United States, the American Civil Liberties Union, Common Cause, and Democracy 21 by J. Gerald Hebert, Paul M. Smith, Jessica Ring Amunson, Michelle R. Singer, Sean J. Young, Steven R. Shapiro, Matthew Coles, Dale E. Ho, Julie Ebenstein, Arthur N. Eisenberg, and Lloyd Leonard.

Brief of amici curiae filed on behalf of the United States by Solicitor General Verrilli, Acting Assistant Attorneys General Branda and Gupta, Deputy Solicitor General Gershengorn, Assistant Solicitor General Feigin, Assistant Solicitor General Feigin, Michael S. Raab, Tovah R. Calderon, Daniel Tenny, and Bonnie I. Robin-Vergeer.

Brief of amici curiae filed on behalf of Nathaniel Persily et al. by Mr Persily.

Brief of amici curiae filed on behalf of Thomas Mann et al. by Jaclyn L. Dilauro, Eugene A. Sokoloff, and Ira M. Feinberg.

Brief of amici curiae filed on behalf of State and Local Elected Officials by H. Rodgin Cohen, Richard C. Pepperman II, C. Megan Bradley, Jared P. Roscoe, Christopher J. Miller, and Charles E. Moulins.

Brief of amici curiae filed on behalf of Former Gov. Jim Edgar, et al. by Carter G. Phillips, Tacy F. Flint, Jeffrey T. Green, David H. Hoffman, Elizabeth L. Maxeiner, and Sarah O'Rourke Schrup.

Brief of amici curiae filed on behalf of Former California Governors George Deukmejian et al. by Steven A. Merksamer, Marguerite Mary Leoni, Christopher E. Skinnell, Nielsen Merksamer, Theodore B. Olson, Amir C. Tayrani, and Scott G. Stewart.

Brief of amici curiae filed on behalf of Historians of Congressional Redistricting by Robert A. Atkins, Andrew J. Ehrlich, Michael L. Nadler, and Justin Levitt.

Brief of amici curiae filed on behalf of Jack N. Rakove et al. by Charles A. Rothfeld and Joseph P. Minta.

Brief of amici curiae filed on behalf of the State of Washington et al. by Robert W. Ferguson, Attorney General of Washington, Noah G. Purcell, Solicitor General, Rebecca Ripoli Glasgow and Jay D. Geck, Deputy Solicitors General, and by the Attorneys General for their respective States as follows: Kamala D. Harris of California, Cynthia H. Coffman of Colorado, George Jepsen of Connecticut, Russell A. Suzuki of Hawaii, Lawrence G. Wasden of Idaho, Maura Healey of Massachusetts, Jim Hood of Mississippi, Hector H. Balderas of New Mexico, Eric T. Schneiderman of New York, Ellen F. Rosenblum of Oregon, Kathleen G. Kane of Pennsylvania, and Mark R. Herring of Virginia.

Brief of amici curiae filed on behalf of California Citizens Redistricting Commission by Marian M. Johnston.

Brief of amici curiae filed on behalf of Members of Congress by John P. Elwood, Jeremy C. Marwell, and Kathleen C. Neace.

Brief of amici curiae filed on behalf of League of Women Voters of Arizona et al. by Timothy M. Hogan, Andrew S. Gordon, Melissa A. Soliz, Shelley Tolman, Joseph R. Palmore, Deanne E. Maynard, and Joe P. Sparks.

Brief of amici curiae filed on behalf of the Brennan Center for Justice at N.Y.U. School of Law by Wendy Weiser, Michael Li, Tomas Lopez, Brent Ferguson, and Conor Colasurdo.

Opposing Side (Petitioner / Appellant)

Brief of amici curiae filed on behalf of National Conference of State Legislatures by Susan Parnas Frederick, Mark A. Packman, Jenna A. Hudson, and Kristiné M. Hansen.

Brief of amici curiae filed on behalf of Coolidge-Reagan Foundation by Michael T. Morleyk and Dan Backer.

IV. THE SUPREME COURT'S DECISION

"[T]he threshold question: Does the Arizona Legislature have standing to bring this suit? . . .

Our conclusion that the Arizona Legislature has standing fits . . . . Proposition 106, together with the Arizona Constitution's ban on efforts to undermine the purposes of an initiative, would 'completely nullif[y]' any vote by the Legislature, now or 'in the future,' purporting to adopt a redistricting plan.

This dispute, in short, 'will be resolved . . . in a concrete factual context conducive to a realistic appreciation of the consequences of judicial action.' Accordingly, we proceed to the merits. . . .

On the merits, we instructed the parties to address this question: Do the Elections Clause of the United States Constitution and 2 U.S.C. § 2a(c) permit Arizona's use of a commission to adopt congressional districts? . . .

Three decisions compose the relevant case law . . . .

In sum, our precedent teaches that redistricting is a legislative function, to be performed in accordance with the State's prescriptions for lawmaking, which may include the referendum and the Governor's veto. The exercise of the initiative, we acknowledge, was not at issue in our prior decisions. But as developed below, we see no constitutional barrier to a State's empowerment of its people by embracing that form of lawmaking. . . .

We take up next the statute the Court asked the parties to address, 2 U.S.C. § 2a(c), a measure modeled on the Reapportionment Act Congress passed in 1911. Section 2a(c), we hold, permits use of a commission to adopt Arizona's congressional districts. . . .

Invoking the Elections Clause, the Arizona Legislature instituted this lawsuit to disempower the State's voters from serving as the legislative power for redistricting purposes. But the Clause surely was not adopted to diminish a State's authority to determine its own lawmaking processes. . . .

The people of Arizona turned to the initiative to curb the practice of gerrymandering and, thereby, to ensure that Members of Congress would have 'an habitual recollection of their dependence on the people.' In so acting, Arizona voters sought to restore 'the core principle of republican government,' namely, 'that the voters should choose their representatives, not the other way around.' The Elections Clause does not hinder that endeavor.

For the reasons stated, the judgment of the United States District Court for the District of Arizona is affirmed."

V. JUSTICE VOTE

5 Pro ACLU Side vs. 4 Con Opposing Side

ACLU Side (Respondent / Appellee)

1. Ginsburg, R. – Wrote majority opinion
2. Kagan, E. – Joined majority opinion
3. Breyer, S. – Joined majority opinion
4. Kennedy, A. – Joined majority opinion
5. Sotomayor, S. – Joined majority opinion

Opposing Side (Petitioner / Appellant)

1. Alito, S. – Joined Roberts' dissent
2. Thomas, C. – Wrote dissenting opinion, joined Roberts' dissent and Scalia's dissent
3. Scalia, A. – Wrote dissenting opinion, joined Roberts' dissent and Thomas' dissent
4. Roberts, J. – Wrote dissenting opinion

VI. A WIN OR LOSS FOR THE ACLU?

The ACLU filed as amicus curiae urging affirmance; the Supreme Court affirmed the District Court's decision by a 5-4 vote, giving the ACLU an apparent win.

1143. Hurst v. Florida

(Decided January 12, 2016; 136 S.Ct. 616; 577 U.S. _)

I. ISSUE

A. Issues Discussed

Criminal procedure

B. Legal Question Presented

"[W]hether Florida's capital sentencing scheme violates the Sixth Amendment in light of Ring."

C. Supreme Court's Answer

"We hold this sentencing scheme unconstitutional. The Sixth Amendment requires a jury, not a judge, to find each fact necessary to impose a sentence of death. A jury's mere recommendation is not enough."

II. CASE SUMMARY

A. Background

"A Florida jury convicted Timothy Lee Hurst of murdering his co-worker, Cynthia Harrison. A penalty-phase jury recommended that Hurst's judge impose a death sentence. Notwithstanding this recommendation, Florida law required the judge to hold a separate hearing and determine whether sufficient aggravating circumstances existed to justify imposing the death penalty. The judge so found and sentenced Hurst to death. . . .

The Florida Supreme Court affirmed 4 to 3. As relevant here, the court rejected Hurst's argument that his sentence violated the Sixth Amendment in light of Ring, 536 U.S. 584. Ring, the court recognized, 'held that capital defendants are entitled to a jury determination of any fact on which the legislature conditions an increase in the maximum punishment.' But the court considered Ring inapplicable in light of this Court's repeated support of Florida's capital sentencing scheme in pre-Ring cases. Specifically, in Hildwin, this Court held that the Sixth Amendment 'does not require that the specific findings authorizing the imposition of the sentence of death be made by the jury.' The Florida court noted that we have 'never expressly overruled Hildwin, and did not do so in Ring.'"

The Supreme Court granted certiorari to review the case.

B. Counsel of Record / ACLU Attorney

ACLU Side (Petitioner / Appellant): Seth P. Waxman argued the cause for appellants. With him on the brief were Nancy A. Daniels, Public Defender of Leon County, David A. Davis Assistant Public Defender, Mark E. Olive, Catherine M.A. Carroll, David M. Lehn, Francesco Valentini, Eric F. Fletcher, and Allison Trzop.

Opposing Side (Respondent / Appellee): Allen Winsor, Solicitor General of Florida argued the cause for appellee. With him on the brief were Pamela Jo Bondi, Attorney General of Florida, Carolyn M. Snurkowski, Associate Deputy Attorney General, Allen Winsor, Solicitor General, and by Denise Harle, Rachel Nordby, and Osvaldo Vazquez, Deputy Solicitors General.

III. AMICI CURIAE

ACLU Side (Petitioner / Appellant)

Brief of amici curiae filed on behalf of the American Civil Liberties Union, the ACLU of Florida, and the Constitutional Accountability Center by Elizabeth B. Wydra, Brianne J. Gorod, Clifford M. Sloan, Paul M. Kerlin, Marisa B. Van Saanen, James C. Altman, Brian W. Stull, Cassandra Stubbs, Steven R. Shapiro, and Nancy G. Abudu.

Brief of amici curiae filed on behalf of the American Bar Association by Rory K. Little, Thomas J. Tynan, Saurish Bhattacharjee, and William C. Hubbard.

Brief of amici curiae filed on behalf of Former Justices of the Supreme Court of Florida by Karen M. Gottlieb and Stephen K. Harper.

Brief of amici curiae filed on behalf of Former Florida Circuit Court Judges by Stuart L. Hartstone and Sonya Rudenstine.

Opposing Side (Respondent / Appellee)

Brief of amici curiae filed on behalf of the State of Alabama et al. by Luther Strange, Attorney General of Alabama, Andrew L. Brasher, Solicitor General, Megan A. Kirkpatrick, Deputy Solicitor General, and Tim Fox, Attorney General of Montana.

IV. THE SUPREME COURT'S DECISION

"The Sixth Amendment provides: 'In all criminal prosecutions, the accused shall enjoy the right to a speedy and public trial, by an impartial jury . . . .' This right, in conjunction with the Due Process Clause, requires that each element of a crime be proved to a jury beyond a reasonable doubt. In Apprendi v. New Jersey, 530 U.S. 466 (2000), this Court held that any fact that 'expose[s] the defendant to a greater punishment than that authorized by the jury's guilty verdict' is an 'element' that must be submitted to a jury. . . .

In Ring, we concluded that Arizona's capital sentencing scheme violated Apprendi's rule because the State allowed a judge to find the facts necessary to sentence a defendant to death. . . .

The analysis the Ring Court applied to Arizona's sentencing scheme applies equally to Florida's. Like Arizona at the time of Ring, Florida does not require the jury to make the critical findings necessary to impose the death penalty. Rather, Florida requires a judge to find these facts. Although Florida incorporates an advisory jury verdict that Arizona lacked, we have previously made clear that this distinction is immaterial . . . .

As with Timothy Ring, the maximum punishment Timothy Hurst could have received without any judge-made findings was life in prison without parole. As with Ring, a judge increased Hurst's authorized punishment based on her own factfinding. In light of Ring, we hold that Hurst's sentence violates the Sixth Amendment. . .

Without contesting Ring's holding, Florida offers a bevy of arguments for why Hurst's sentence is constitutional. None holds water. . . .

The Sixth Amendment protects a defendant's right to an impartial jury. This right required Florida to base Timothy Hurst's death sentence on a jury's verdict, not a judge's factfinding. Florida's sentencing scheme, which required the judge alone to find the existence of an aggravating circumstance, is therefore unconstitutional.

The judgment of the Florida Supreme Court is reversed, and the case is remanded . . . ."

V. JUSTICE VOTE

8 Pro ACLU Side vs. 1 Con Opposing Side

ACLU Side (Petitioner / Appellant)

1. Sotomayor, S. – Wrote majority opinion
2. Kagan, E. – Joined majority opinion
3. Thomas, C. – Joined majority opinion
4. Breyer, S. – Wrote concurring opinion
5. Scalia, A. – Joined majority opinion
6. Kennedy, A. – Joined majority opinion
7. Ginsburg, R. – Joined majority opinion
8. Roberts, J. – Joined majority opinion

Opposing Side (Respondent / Appellee)

1. Alito, S. – Wrote dissenting opinion

VI. A WIN OR LOSS FOR THE ACLU?

The ACLU filed as amicus curiae urging reversal of the judgment of the Florida Supreme Court; the Supreme Court reversed in an 8-1 vote, giving the ACLU an apparent win.

1144. Montgomery v. Louisiana

(Decided January 25, 2016; 136 S.Ct. 718; 577 U.S. _)

I. ISSUE

A. Issues Discussed

Criminal procedure

B. Legal Question Presented

"In Miller v. Alabama, 567 U.S. –––– (2012), the Court held that a juvenile convicted of a homicide offense could not be sentenced to life in prison without parole absent consideration of the juvenile's special circumstances in light of the principles and purposes of juvenile sentencing. In the wake of Miller, the question has arisen whether its holding is retroactive to juvenile offenders whose convictions and sentences were final when Miller was decided."

C. Supreme Court's Answer

"The Court now holds that Miller announced a substantive rule of constitutional law. . . .

Giving Miller retroactive effect . . . does not require States to relitigate sentences . . . in every case where a juvenile offender received mandatory life without parole. A State may remedy a Miller violation by permitting juvenile homicide offenders to be considered for parole, rather than by resentencing them."

II. CASE SUMMARY

A. Background

"In 1963, Montgomery killed Charles Hurt, a deputy sheriff . . . . Montgomery was 17 years old . . . . He was . . . sentenced to death, but the Louisiana Supreme Court reversed . . . after finding that public prejudice had prevented a fair trial.

Montgomery was retried. The jury returned a verdict of 'guilty without capital punishment.' Under Louisiana law, this verdict required . . . a sentence of life without parole. The sentence was automatic upon the jury's verdict, so Montgomery had no opportunity to present mitigation evidence to justify a less severe sentence. . . .

Almost 50 years after Montgomery was first taken into custody, this Court decided Miller v. Alabama. Miller held that mandatory life without parole for juvenile homicide offenders violates the Eighth Amendment's prohibition on "cruel and unusual punishments." . . .

After this Court issued its decision in Miller, Montgomery sought collateral review of his mandatory life-without-parole sentence. . . .

The trial court denied Montgomery's motion on the ground that Miller is not retroactive on collateral review. Montgomery then filed an application for a supervisory writ. The Louisiana Supreme Court denied the application. The court relied on its earlier decision in State v. Tate, which held that Miller does not have retroactive effect in cases on state collateral review. . . .

This Court granted Montgomery's petition for certiorari."

B. Counsel of Record / ACLU Attorney

ACLU Side (Petitioner / Appellant): Opposing Side (Respondent / Appellee): Mark D. Plaisance argued the cause for appellants. With him on the brief were Lindsay Jarrell Blouin, Sean Collins, Marsha Levick, Emily C. Keller, Jean W. Strout, and Jeffrey J. Pokorak.

Deputy Solicitor General Dreeben argued the cause for the United States as amicus curiae. S. Kyle Duncan argued the cause for appellee. With him on the brief were James D. "Buddy" Caldwell, Attorney General of Louisiana, Trey Phillips, First Assistant Attorney General, Colin A. Clark, Assistant Attorney General, Hillar C. Moore III, East Baton Rouge District Attorney, Dylan C. Alge, Assistant District Attorney, and Kyle Duncan.

Richard D. Bernstein argued the cause for Court-appointed amicus curiae against jurisdiction.

III. AMICI CURIAE

ACLU Side (Petitioner / Appellant)

Brief of amici curiae filed on behalf of the American Civil Liberties Union and the ACLU of Louisiana by Steven R. Shapiro, Brandon J. Buskey, Ezekiel R. Edwards, and Candice C. Sirmon.

Brief of amici curiae filed on behalf of the United States by Solicitor General Verrilli, Assistant Attorney General Caldwell, Deputy Solicitor General Dreeben, Assistant Solicitor General Saharsky, and Robert A. Parker.

Brief of amici curiae filed on behalf of the Administration of Criminal Law by Deborah Gramiccioni, Robert L. Littlehale, and Damon C. Andrews in support of jurisdiction.

Brief of amici curiae filed on behalf of Certain Family Members of Victims Killed by Youths by Angela C. Vigil, Elizabeth L. Yingling and Carlos R. Perez-Toro.

Brief of amici curiae filed on behalf of Former Juvenile Court Judges by Douglas T. Kendall, Elizabeth B. Wydra, and Brianne J. Gorod.

Brief of amici curiae filed on behalf of the Equal Justice Initiative on behalf of Dozens Sentenced to Die in Prison When They Were Children by Bryan A. Stevenson, Alicia A. D'Addario, and John W. Dalton.

Brief of amici curiae filed on behalf of American Bar Association by Lawrence A. Wojcik, Kenneth L. Schmetterer, Katherine E. Chambers, Amanda E. Reagan, and William C. Hubbard.

Brief of amici curiae filed on behalf of Pascal F. Calogero, Jr., et al. by Keith Nordyke, Stephen M. Nickelsburg, Adam C. Goldstein, Alexander M. Feldman, Katie Barlow, Carlisle Overbey, and Amy Montour.

Brief of amici curiae filed on behalf of Northwestern University School of Law's Children and Family Justice Center et al. by Shobha L. Mahadev, Scott F. Main, Steven A. Drizin, Laura H. Nirider, and Megan G. Crane.

Brief of amici curiae filed on behalf of Professor Douglas A. Berman by Matthew C. Corcoran and Chad A. Readler.

Opposing Side (Respondent / Appellee)

Brief of amici curiae filed on behalf of Richard D. Bernstein argued the cause for Court-appointed amicus curiae against jurisdiction by Richard D. Bernstein, Stuart R. Lombardi, Jonathan D. Waisnor, Richard D. Bernstein, Frank Scaduto, Joanne T. Pedone, and Kyle A. Mathews.

Brief of amici curiae filed on behalf of the State of Michigan et al. by Bill Schuette, Attorney General of Michigan, Aaron D. Lindstrom, Solicitor General, B. Eric Restuccia, Deputy Solicitor General, and by the Attorneys General for their respective jurisdictions as follows: Luther Strange of Alabama, Leslie Rutledge of Arkansas, George Jepsen of Connecticut, Gregory F. Zoeller of Indiana, Derek Schmidt of Kansas, Douglas J. Peterson of Nebraska, Timothy C. Fox of Montana, Adam Paul Laxalt of Nevada, Joseph A. Foster of New Hampshire, Peter F. Kilmartin of Rhode Island, Alan Wilson of South Carolina, Marty J. Jackley of South Dakota, Ken Paxton of Texas, Sean D. Reyes of Utah, and Peter K. Michael of Wyoming.

Brief of amici curiae filed on behalf of Becky Wilson et al. by John J. Park, Jr.

Brief of amici curiae filed on behalf of the National District Attorneys Association et al. by John C. Neiman, Jr. and Kasdin Miller Mitchell.

Brief of amici curiae filed on behalf of the Criminal Justice Legal Foundation by Kent S. Scheidegger.

IV. THE SUPREME COURT'S DECISION

"Amicus argues that a State is under no obligation to give a new rule of constitutional law retroactive effect in its own collateral review proceedings. As those proceedings are created by state law . . . , it is for state courts to define applicable principles of retroactivity. . . .

If, however, the Constitution establishes a rule and requires . . . retroactive application, then a state court's refusal to give the rule retroactive effect is reviewable . . . . Amicus' argument therefore hinges on the premise that this Court's retroactivity precedents are not a constitutional mandate.

Justice O'Connor's plurality opinion in Teague v. Lane set forth a framework for retroactivity in cases on federal collateral review. Under Teague, a new constitutional rule of criminal procedure does not apply . . . to convictions that were final when the new rule was announced. Teague recognized, however, two categories of rules that are not subject to its general retroactivity bar. First, . . . new substantive rules of constitutional law. . . . Second, . . . new "'watershed rules of criminal procedure' implicating the fundamental fairness and accuracy of the criminal proceeding."

It is undisputed, then, that Teague requires the retroactive application of new substantive and watershed procedural rules in federal habeas proceedings. Amicus, however, contends that Teague was an interpretation of the federal habeas statute, not a constitutional command. . . .

This leads to the question whether Miller's prohibition on mandatory life without parole for juvenile offenders indeed did announce a new substantive rule that . . . must be retroactive. . . .

The Court now holds that Miller announced a substantive rule of constitutional law. . . .

Giving Miller retroactive effect . . . does not require States to relitigate sentences . . . in every case where a juvenile offender received mandatory life without parole. A State may remedy a Miller violation by permitting juvenile homicide offenders to be considered for parole, rather than by resentencing them. . . .

Extending parole eligibility to juvenile offenders does not impose an onerous burden on the States, nor does it disturb the finality of state convictions. . . .

Henry Montgomery has spent each day of the past 46 years knowing he was condemned to die in prison. Perhaps it can be established that . . . this fate was a just and proportionate punishment . . . . In light of what this Court has said in Roper, Graham, and Miller about how children are constitutionally different from adults in their level of culpability, however, prisoners like Montgomery must be given the opportunity to show their crime did not reflect irreparable corruption; and, if it did not, their hope for some years of life outside prison walls must be restored.

The judgment of the Supreme Court of Louisiana is reversed, and the case is remanded . . . ."

V. JUSTICE VOTE

6 Pro ACLU Side vs. 3 Con Opposing Side

ACLU Side (Petitioner / Appellant)

1. Kennedy, A. – Wrote majority opinion
2. Kagan, E. – Joined majority opinion
3. Breyer, S. – Joined majority opinion
4. Ginsburg, R. – Joined majority opinion
5. Sotomayor, S. – Joined majority opinion
6. Roberts, J. – Joined majority opinion

Opposing Side (Respondent / Appellee)

1. Alito, S. – Joined Scalia's dissent
2. Thomas, C. – Wrote dissenting opinion, joined Scalia's dissent
3. Scalia, A. – Wrote dissenting opinion

VI. A WIN OR LOSS FOR THE ACLU?

The ACLU filed as amicus curiae urging reversal of the judgment of the Supreme Court of Louisiana; the Supreme Court reversed in a 6-3 vote, giving the ACLU an apparent win.

1145. Evenwel v. Abbott

(Decided April 4, 2016; 136 S.Ct. 1120; 578 U.S. _)

I. ISSUE

A. Issues Discussed

Voting rights, census

B. Legal Question Presented

Whether "a State may draw its legislative districts based on total population."

C. Supreme Court's Answer

"We hold, based on constitutional history, this Court's decisions, and longstanding practice, that a State may draw its legislative districts based on total population."

II. CASE SUMMARY

A. Background

"After the 2010 census, Texas redrew its State Senate districts using a total-population baseline. . . . Once it became clear that the new Senate map, S148, would not receive preclearance in advance of the 2012 elections, the U.S. District Court for the Western District of Texas drew an interim Senate map, S164, which also equalized the total population of each district. On direct appeal, this Court observed that the District Court had failed to 'take guidance from the State's recently enacted plan in drafting an interim plan,' and therefore vacated the District Court's map.

The District Court, on remand, again used census data to draw districts so that each included roughly the same size total population. Texas used this new interim map, S172, in the 2012 elections, and, in 2013, the Texas Legislature adopted S172 as the permanent Senate map. . . .

Appellants Sue Evenwel and Edward Pfenninger live in Texas Senate districts . . . with particularly large eligible- and registered-voter populations. Contending that basing apportionment on total population dilutes their votes in relation to voters in other Senate districts, in violation of the one-person, one-vote principle of the Equal Protection Clause, appellants filed suit . . . . They . . . sought a permanent injunction barring use of the existing Senate map in favor of a map that would equalize the voter population in each district.

The case was referred to a three-judge District Court for hearing and decision. That court dismissed the complaint for failure to state a claim on which relief could be granted."

The Supreme Court noted probable jurisdiction.

B. Counsel of Record / ACLU Attorney

ACLU Side (Respondent / Appellee): Scott A. Keller, Solicitor General of Texas argued the cause for appellee. With him on the briefs were Ken Paxton, Attorney General, Charles E. Roy, First Assistant Attorney General, Matthew H. Frederick, Deputy Solicitor General, and Lisa Bennett, Assistant Solicitor General.

Deputy Solicitor General Gershengorn argued the cause for the United States as amicus curiae.

Opposing Side (Petitioner / Appellant): William S. Consovoy argued the cause for appellant. With him on the briefs were Meredith B. Parenti, Thomas R. McCarthy, and J. Michael Connolly.

III. AMICI CURIAE

ACLU Side (Respondent / Appellee)

Brief of amici curiae filed on behalf of the American Civil Liberties Union and the ACLU of Texas by Rebecca L. Robertson, Satinder Singh, Sean J. Young, Steven R. Shapiro, Matthew A. Coles, and Dale E. Ho.

Brief of amici curiae filed on behalf of the United States by Solicitor General Verrilli, Principal Deputy Assistant Attorney General Gupta, Deputy Solicitor General Gershengorn, Ann O'Connell, Assistant Solicitor General, Mark L. Gross, and Erin Aslan.

Brief of amici curiae filed on behalf of Common Cause by

Emmet J. Bondurant and Jeremy D. Farris.

Brief of amici curiae filed on behalf of the Texas Senate Hispanic Caucus et al. by Nina Perales, Thomas A. Saenz, and John Paul Salmon.

Brief of amici curiae filed on behalf of the Democratic National Committee by Robert F. Bauer, Marc Erik Elias, and William B. Stafford.

Brief of amici curiae filed on behalf of Former Directors of the U.S. Census Bureau by J. Gerald Hebert, Trevor Potter, Anita S. Earls, Paul M. Smith, Jessica Ring Amunson, and Mark P. Gaber.

Brief of amici curiae filed on behalf of the Brennan Center for Justice at N.Y.U. School of Law by Wendy R. Weiser, Sidney S. Rosdeitcher, Michael C. Li, Robert A. Atkins, Pietro Signoracci, and Elizabeth M. Gary.

Brief of amici curiae filed on behalf of NAACP Legal Defense & Educational Fund, Inc., by Sherrilyn Ifill, Janai Nelson, Christina Swarns, Leah C. Aden, Liliana Zaragoza, Coty Montag, John Paul Schnapper-Casteras, Walter Dellinger, Bradley N. Garcia, Jason Zarrow, and Danielle C. Gray.

Brief of amici curiae filed on behalf of Constitutional Accountability Center by Douglas T. Kendall, Elizabeth B. Wydra, David H. Gans, and Brianne J. Gorod.

Brief of amici curiae filed on behalf of Texas Senators by Chad Dunn, Scott Brazil, Abbie J. Kamin, and Martin J. Siegel.

Brief of amici curiae filed on behalf of Carl E. Heastie in his Official Capacity as Speaker of the New York State Assembly by C. Daniel Chill and Elaine M. Reich.

Brief of amici curiae filed on behalf of Direct Action for Rights and Equality (Dare) et al. by Peter Wagner, Aleks Kajstura, Brenda Wright, Adam Lioz, and Scott Novakowski.

Brief of amici curiae filed on behalf of the City of New York by Zachary W. Carter, New York City Corporation Cousel, Richard Dearin, Cecelia Chang, Kathy Park, and Celia Rhoads.

Brief of amici curiae filed on behalf of the Hispanic National Bar Association et al. by Robert T. Maldonado, Cynthia D. Mares, Peter Karanjia, and Alison Schary.

Brief of amici curiae filed on behalf of the Children's Defense Fund et al. by Robert Brandon, Jon Sherman, Architа Taylor, Cory D. Szczepanik, David R. Carpenter, Jose Sanchez, and Cameron F. Kerry.

Brief of amici curiae filed on behalf of Hawaii Reapportionment Case Plaintiffs (David P. Brostrom, Andrew Walden) by Robert H. Thomas, Anna H. Oshiro, and Mark M. Murakami.

Brief of amici curiae filed on behalf of the State of New York et al. by Eric T. Schneiderman, Attorney General of New York, Barbara D. Underwood, Solicitor General, Steven C. Wu, Deputy Solicitor General, Judith N. Vale Assistant Solicitor General, and by the Attorneys General for their respective States as follows: Craig W. Richards of Alaska, Kamala D. Harris of California, Matthew P. Denn of Delaware, Douglas S. Chin of Hawaii, Lisa Madigan of Illinois, Gregory F. Zoeller of Indiana, Tom Miller of Iowa, Janet T. Mills of Maine, Brian E. Frosh of Maryland, Maura Healey of Massachusetts, Bill Schuette of Michigan, Lori Swanson of Minnesota, Jim Hood of Mississippi, Joseph A. Foster of New Hampshire, Wayne Stenehjem of North Dakota, Ellen F. Rosenblum of Oregon, Peter F. Kilmartin of Rhode Island, William H. Sorrell of Vermont, Mark R. Herring of Virginia, and Robert W. Ferguson of Washington.

Brief of amici curiae filed on behalf of City of Los Angeles et al. by Michael N. Feuer, Los Angeles City Attorney, James P. Clark, Valerie L. Flores, Harit U. Trivedi, Strefan E. Fauble, Mary C. Wickham, Los Angeles Interim County Counsel, Lester J. Tolnai, Gregory L. Diskant, Jonah M. Knobler, Kathrina Szymborski, Thomas J. Faughnan, Judy W. Whitehurst, Vicki Kozikoujekian, Timothy T. Coates, Dennis J. Herrerra, San Francisco City Attorney, Christine Van Aken, Cathy Hampton, Atlanta City Attorney, Laura Burton, Christopher Walker, Adam Loukx, Toledo City Law Director, Cristal C. Brisco, South Bend City Corporation Counsel, David L. Minchello, Plainfield City Corporation Counsel, Anita Alvarez, Cook County State's Attorney, Daniel F. Gallagher, Paul A. Castiglione, Kent S. Ray, Stephen R. Patton, Chicago City Corporation Counsel, George A. Nilson, Baltimore City Solicitor, William R. Phelan, Jr., Barbara A. Langhenry, Cleveland City Director of Law, Margaret D. Plane, Salt Lake City Attorney, Marc A. Mckithen, Trenton Acting City Attorney, Alberto G. Santos, Kearney Town Mayor, and Rebecca J. Bertram, Bridgeton City Solicitor.

Brief of amici curiae filed on behalf of Harris County, Texas by Vince Ryan, Harris County Attorney, C. Robert Heath, and Gunnar P. Seaquist.

Brief of amici curiae filed on behalf of Nathaniel Persily et al. by Mr. Persily.

Brief of amici curiae filed on behalf of Lawyers' Committee for Civil Rights Under Law by Linda C. Goldstein, Neil A. Steiner, Rachel B. Swartz, Cara Schmidt, Mari C. Stonebraker, Diana C. Wang, and G. Eric Brunstad, Jr.

Brief of amici curiae filed on behalf of the Leadership Conference on Civil and Human Rights et al. by Wade J. Henderson, Lisa M. Bornstein, Matthew M. Hoffman, and Andrew Kim.

Opposing Side (Petitioner / Appellant)

Brief of amici curiae filed on behalf of the American Civil Rights Union by Kaylan L. Phillips.

Brief of amici curiae filed on behalf of Eagle Forum Education & Legal Defense Fund, Inc., by Lawrence J. Joseph.

Brief of amici curiae filed on behalf of Project 21 by David B. Rivkin, Jr., Andrew M. Grossman, and Richard B. Raile.

Brief of amici curiae filed on behalf of Tennessee State Legislators et al. by Linda Carver, Whitlow Knight, and John J. Park, Jr.

Brief of amici curiae filed on behalf of the Cato Institute by Manuel S. Klausner and Ilya Shapiro.

Brief of amici curiae filed on behalf of Mountain States Legal Foundation by Steven J. Lechner and Jeffrey W. McCoy.

Brief of amici curiae filed on behalf of Demographers Peter A. Morrison et al. by C. Dean Mcgrath, Jr., Bradley A. Benbrook, and Stephen M. Duvernay.

Brief of amici curiae filed on behalf of Center for Constitutional

Jurisprudence by John C. Eastman and Anthony T. Caso.
Brief of amici curiae filed on behalf of Immigration Reform Law Institute by Dale L. Wilcox.
Brief of amici curiae filed on behalf of Judicial Watch, Inc., et al. by Robert D. Popper, Chris Fedeli, and Lauren M. Burke.
Brief of amici curiae filed on behalf of the City of Yakima, Washington by Francis S. Floyd and John A. Safarli.

IV. THE SUPREME COURT'S DECISION

"The parties and the United States advance different positions in this case. As they did before the District Court, appellants insist that the Equal Protection Clause requires jurisdictions to draw state and local legislative districts with equal voter-eligible populations, thus protecting 'voter equality,' i.e., 'the right of eligible voters to an equal vote.' . . . Texas responds that jurisdictions may, consistent with the Equal Protection Clause, design districts using any population baseline—including total population and voter-eligible population—so long as the choice is rational and not invidiously discriminatory. . . . Sharing Texas' position . . . , the United States urges us not to address Texas' separate assertion that the Constitution allows States to use alternative population baselines, including voter-eligible population. . . .

In agreement with Texas and the United States, we reject appellants' attempt to locate a voter-equality mandate in the Equal Protection Clause. As history, precedent, and practice demonstrate, it is plainly permissible for jurisdictions to measure equalization by the total population of state and local legislative districts. . . .

Consistent with constitutional history, this Court's past decisions reinforce the conclusion that States and localities may comply with the one-person, one-vote principle by designing districts with equal total populations. . . .

What constitutional history and our prior decisions strongly suggest, settled practice confirms. Adopting voter-eligible apportionment as constitutional command would upset a well-functioning approach to districting that all 50 States and countless local jurisdictions have followed for decades, even centuries. Appellants have shown no reason for the Court to disturb this longstanding use of total population. . . .

In sum, the rule appellants urge has no mooring in the Equal Protection Clause. The Texas Senate map, we therefore conclude, complies with the requirements of the one-person, one-vote principle. Because history, precedent, and practice suffice to reveal the infirmity of appellants' claims, we need not and do not resolve whether, as Texas now argues, States may draw districts to equalize voter-eligible population rather than total population. . . .

[T]he judgment of the United States District Court for the Western District of Texas is affirmed."

V. JUSTICE VOTE

8 Pro ACLU Side vs. 0 Con Opposing Side

ACLU Side (Respondent / Appellee)

1. Ginsburg, R. – Wrote majority opinion
2. Alito, S. – Wrote concurring opinion
3. Kagan, E. – Joined majority opinion
4. Thomas, C. – Wrote concurring opinion, joined Alito's concurrence in part
5. Breyer, S. – Joined majority opinion
6. Kennedy, A. – Joined majority opinion
7. Sotomayor, S. – Joined majority opinion
8. Roberts, J. – Joined majority opinion

Vacant Seat

VI. A WIN OR LOSS FOR THE ACLU?

The ACLU filed as amicus curiae urging affirmance; the Supreme Court affirmed the United States District Court for the Western District of Texas' decision by an 8-0 vote, giving the ACLU an apparent win.

1146. Zubik v. Burwell

(Decided May 16, 2016; 136 S.Ct. 1557; 578 U.S. _)

I. ISSUE

A. Issues Discussed

1st Amendment, religion

B. Legal Question Presented

"Following oral argument, the Court requested supplemental briefing from the parties addressing 'whether contraceptive coverage could be provided to petitioners' employees, through petitioners' insurance companies, without any such notice from petitioners.'"

C. Supreme Court's Answer

"In light of the positions asserted by the parties in their supplemental briefs, the Court vacates the judgments below and remands to the respective United States Courts of Appeals for the Third, Fifth, Tenth, and D.C. Circuits. Given the gravity of the dispute and the substantial clarification and refinement in the positions of the parties, the parties on remand should be afforded an opportunity to arrive at an approach going forward that accommodates petitioners' religious exercise while at the same time ensuring that women covered by petitioners' health plans 'receive full and equal health coverage, including contraceptive coverage.'"

II. CASE SUMMARY

A. Background

"Petitioners are primarily nonprofit organizations that provide health insurance to their employees. Federal regulations require petitioners to cover certain contraceptives as part of their health plans, unless petitioners submit a form either to their insurer or to the Federal Government, stating that they object on religious grounds to providing contraceptive coverage. Petitioners allege that submitting this notice substantially burdens the exercise of their religion, in violation of the Religious Freedom Restoration Act of 1993."

The Supreme Court granted certiorari to review the case.

B. Counsel of Record / ACLU Attorney

ACLU Side (Respondent / Appellee): Solicitor General Verrilli argued the cause for appellee. With him on the brief were Principal Deputy Assistant Attorney General Mizer, Deputy Solicitors General Gershengorn and Kneedler, Assistant Solicitor General Fletcher, Mark B. Stern, Alisa B. Klein, Adam C. Jed, Patrick G. Nemeroff, Megan Barbero, and Joshua Salzman.

Opposing Side (Petitioner / Appellant): Paul D. Clement argued the cause for appellant in Nos. 15-35, 15-105, 15-119, 15-191. With him on the brief were David A. Cortman, Gregory S. Baylor, Jordan W. Lorence, Kevin H. Theriot, Matthew S. Bowman, Rory T. Gray, Bradley S. Tupi, Carl C. Scherz, Laurence A. Hansen, Kevin C. Walsh, Paul D. Clement, Erin E. Murphy, Robert M. Bernstein, Mark Rienzi, Eric C. Rassbach, Hannah C. Smith, Diana M. Verm, Adèle Auxier Keim, Daniel H. Blomberg, Kenneth R. Wynne.

Noel J. Francisco argued the cause for appellant in Nos. 14-1418, 14-1453, 14-1505. With him on the brief were Paul M. Pohl, John D. Goetz, Leon F. Dejulius, Jr., Ira M. Karoll, Robert J. Muise, David Yerushalmi, Noel J. Francisco, David T. Raimer, and Anthony J. Dick.

III. AMICI CURIAE

ACLU Side (Respondent / Appellee)

Brief of amici curiae filed on behalf of the American Civil Liberties Union, the Leadership Conference on Civil and Human Rights, the NAACP Legal Defense & Educational Fund, Inc., the National Coalition on Black Civic Participation, and the National Urban League by Daniel Mach, Heather L. Weaver, Brigitte Amiri, Louise Melling, Jennifer Lee, and Steven R. Shapiro.

Brief of amici curiae filed on behalf of the American Humanist Association by Gordon Gamm.

Brief of amici curiae filed on behalf of Harvard Law School Center for Health Law and Policy Innovation, et al. by Carmel Shachar and Robert Greenwald.

Brief of amici curiae filed on behalf of Church-State Scholars by Elizabeth Sepper, Catherine Weiss, Natalie J. Kraner, and Meg Slachetka.

Brief of amici curiae filed on behalf of the Ovarian Cancer Research Fund Alliance et al. by Jessica B. Livingston, Jessica L. Ellsworth, Michelle A. Kisloff,
Andrew S. Furlow, and Lowell M. Zeta.

Brief of amici curiae filed on behalf of Baptist Joint Committee for Religious Liberty by K. Hollyn Hollman, Douglas Laycock, and Jennifer Hawks.

Brief of amici curiae filed on behalf of Compassion & Choices by Jon B. Eisenberg, Lisa Perrochet, and Kevin Díaz.

Brief of amici curiae filed on behalf of National Women's Law Center et al. by Marcia D. Greenberger, Gretchen Borchelt, Leila Abolfazli, Charles E. Davidow, Priyanka K. Wityk, Abel Mcdonnell, and Luke J. O'Brien.

Brief of amici curiae filed on behalf of Norman Dorsen et al. by Burt Neuborne and Mr. Dorsen, both pro se.

Brief of amici curiae filed on behalf of American Jewish Committee Hanna et al. by Liebman Dershowitz and Marc D. Stern.

Brief of amici curiae filed on behalf of American College of Obstetricians and Gynecologists et al. by Sara Needleman Kline, Jennifer L.A. Blasdell, Bruce H. Schneider, and Michele L. Pahmer.

Brief of amici curiae filed on behalf of National Latina Institute for Reproductive Health et al. by Candace D. Gibson, Sarah E. Burns, and Sarah Samuels Wheeler.

Brief of amici curiae filed on behalf of Catholics for Choice et al. by Leslie C. Griffin.

Brief of amici curiae filed on behalf of Former State Attorneys General et al. by by Wesley R. Powell, Mary J. Eaton, Sarah M. Wastler, Derek Hammond, and Matthew J. Sorensen.

Brief of amici curiae filed on behalf of Foreign and International Law Experts Lawrence O. Gostin et al. by Aram A. Schvey, Marjorie E. Sheldon, and Boaz I. Cohen.

Brief of amici curiae filed on behalf of 240 Students, Faculty, and Staff at Religiously Affiliated Universities Richard B. Katskee,
Gregory M. Lipper, and Natacha Y. Lam.

Brief of amici curiae filed on behalf of American Academy of Pediatrics by Thomas E. Gorman, Asim M. Bhansali, Philip J. Tassin, and Julie Duncan Garcia.

Brief of amici curiae filed on behalf of Scholars of Religious Liberty Sarah Barringer et al. by Tejinder Singh and
Martin S. Lederman.

Brief of amici curiae filed on behalf of Health Policy Experts by Marcy Wilder, Sheree Kanner, Allison Holt, Madeline Gitomer, and Nathaniel G. Foell.

Brief of amici curiae filed on behalf of the Anti-Defamation League et al. by Steven M. Freeman, David L. Barkey, Michael Lieberman, Derek L. Shaffer, Victoria F. Maroulis, and Carolyn Homer Thomas.

Brief of amici curiae filed on behalf of Black Women's Health Imperative by Mark A. Packman, Kami E. Quinn, Jenna A. Hudson, Tamra B. Ferguson, Kristiné M. Hansen, and Marnie L. Glaeberman.

Brief of amici curiae filed on behalf of the Guttmacher Institute et al. by Walter Dellinger, Dawn Johnson, Anna-Rose Mathieson, and Ben Feuer.

Brief of amici curiae filed on behalf of Lambda Legal Defense and Education Fund, Inc., et al. Camilla B. Taylor, Kyle A. Palazzolo, Hayley Gorenberg, Omar Gonzalez-Pagan, Aisha N. Davis, Jennifer C. Pizer, and Jon W. Davidson.

Brief of amici curiae filed on behalf of 123 Members of the United States Congress by Gary W. Kubek, Harriet M. Antczak, David A. O'Neil, and Renee Cipro.

Brief of amici curiae filed on behalf of Military Historians by Elizabeth B. Wydra, Brianne J. Gorod, and David H. Gans.

Brief of amici curiae filed on behalf of the National Health Law Program et al. by Jane Perkins and Dipti Singh.

Brief of amici curiae filed on behalf of the State of California et al. by Kamala D. Harris, Attorney General of California, Edward C. Dumont, Solicitor General, Mark Breckler, Chief Assistant Attorney General, Angela Sierra, Senior Assistant Attorney General, Janill L. Richards, Principal Deputy Solicitor General, Nancy A. Beninati, Supervising Deputy Attorney General, Gregory D. Brown, Deputy Solicitor

General, Samuel P. Siegel, Associate Deputy Solicitor General, Lisa C. Ehrlich, Deputy Attorney General, and by the Attorneys General for their respective jurisdictions as follows: George Jepsen of Connecticut, Matthew P. Denn of Delaware, Karl A. Racine of the District of Columbia, Douglas S. Chin of Hawaii, Lisa Madigan of Illinois, Tom Miller of Iowa, Brian E. Frosh of Maryland, Maura Healey of Massachusetts, Lori Swanson of Minnesota, Joseph A. Foster of New Hampshire, Hector Balderas of New Mexico, Eric T. Schneiderman of New York, Ellen F. Rosenblum of Oregon, Peter F. Kilmartin of Rhode Island, William H. Sorrell of Vermont, Mark R. Herring of Virginia, and Robert W. Ferguson of Washington.

Brief of amici curiae filed on behalf of the Honorable Robert C. "Bobby" Scott by Marci A. Hamilton.

Brief of amici curiae filed on behalf of the Center for Inquiry et al. by Nicholas J. Little, Ronald A. Lindsay, Edward Tabash, and Amanda Knief.

Opposing Side (Petitioner / Appellant)

Brief of amici curiae filed on behalf of Orthodox Jewish Rabbis by Howard N. Slugh.

Brief of amici curiae filed on behalf of United States Conference of Catholic Bishops et al. by Anthony R. Picarello, Jr., Jeffrey Hunter Moon, Michael F. Moses, and Hillary E. Byrnes.

Brief of amici curiae filed on behalf of CNS International Ministries, Inc., et al. by Timothy Belz, J. Matthew Belz, and David R. Melton.

Brief of amici curiae filed on behalf of the Breast Cancer Prevention Institute by Catherine W. Short, Allison K. Aranda, Nikolas T. Nikas, and Dorinda C. Bordlee.

Brief of amici curiae filed on behalf of Residents and Families of Residents at Homes of the Little Sisters of the Poor by Dwight G. Duncan and Colbe Mazzarella.

Brief of amici curiae filed on behalf of the School of the Ozarks, Inc. D/B/A College of the Ozarks by Virginia L. Fry, Ginger K. Gooch, Mark G. Arnold, and Joann T. Sandifer.

Brief of amici curiae filed on behalf of Justice and Freedom Fund by James L. Hirsen and Deborah J. Dewart.

Brief of amici curiae filed on behalf of Ethics and Public Policy Center by Daniel P. Collins, Zachary Briers, and Ankur Mandhania.

Brief of amici curiae filed on behalf of the State of Texas et al. Ken Paxton, Attorney General of Texas, Charles E. Roy, First Assistant Attorney General, Scott A. Keller, Solicitor General, J. Campbell Barker, Deputy Solicitor General, Michael P. Murphy, Assistant Solicitor General, Michael Dewine, Attorney General of Ohio, and by the Attorneys General for their respective States as follows: Luther Strange of Alabama, Mark Brnovich of Arizona, Leslie Rutledge of Arkansas, Cynthia Coffman of Colorado, Pamela Jo Bondi of Florida, Samuel S. Olens of Georgia, Lawrence G. Wasden of Idaho, Derek Schmidt of Kansas, Bill Schuette of Michigan, Timothy C. Fox of Montana, Douglas J. Peterson of Nebraska, Adam Paul Laxalt of Neveda, E. Scott Pruitt of Oklahoma, Alan Wilson of South Carolina, Marty J. Jackley of South Dakota, Sean D. Reyes of Utah, Patrick Morrisey of West Virginia, and Brad D. Schimel of Wisconsin.

Brief of amici curiae filed on behalf of the Southern Baptist Theological Seminary et al. by Miles E. Coleman, Jay T. Thompson, and Derek Gaubatz.

Brief of amici curiae filed on behalf of Christian Legal Society et al. by Robert K. Smith, Michael A. Greene, Elliot Shackelford, Kimberlee Wood Colby, Matthew T. Martens, Reginald J. Brown, and Ashley E. Bashur.

Brief of amici curiae filed on behalf of the Lukumi Babalu Aye, Inc., et al. by Vincent M. Wagner, Aaron M. Streett, and J. Matthew Schmitten.

Brief of amici curiae filed on behalf of Christian and Missionary Alliance Foundation, Inc., et al. by Kelly J. Shackelford, Jeffrey C. Mateer, Hiram S. Sasser III, Matthew J. Kacsmaryk, Justin E. Butterfield, Jeremiah G. Dys, Stephanie N. Phillips, Brian D. Boyle, Gregory F. Jacob, Matthew J. Sheehan, and Brittney M. Lane.

Brief of amici curiae filed on behalf of 207 Members of Congress by Robert K. Kelner, Richard A. Hertling, Zachary G. Parks, Shruti C. Barker, and Carol A. Szurkowski.

Brief of amici curiae filed on behalf of the National Jewish Commission on Law and Public Affairs ("COLPA") by Dennis Rapps, Nathan Lewin, and Alyza D. Lewin.

Brief of amici curiae filed on behalf of Eagle Forum Education & Legal Defense Fund, Inc., by Lawrence J. Joseph.

Brief of amici curiae filed on behalf of Former Justice Department Officials by Michael W. Mcconnell, Mark E. Schneider, Jay P. Lefkowitz, and Steven J. Menash.

Brief of amici curiae filed on behalf of the Cato Institute et al. by Josh Blackman, Erin Morrow Hawley, Ilya Shapiro, Jayme Weber, and Joshua Hawley.

Brief of amici curiae filed on behalf of
National Association of Evangelicals et al. by Alexander Dushku, R. Shawn Gunnarson, Justin W Starr, and Kirton Mcconkie.

Brief of amici curiae filed on behalf of 50 Catholic Theologians and Ethicists by D. John Sauer, Mary Catherine Hodes, and Michael C. Martinich-Sauter.

Brief of amici curiae filed on behalf of Association of American Physicians & Surgeons et al. by Denise M. Burke, Mailee R. Smith, Anna R. Paprocki, and Mary E. Harned.

Brief of amici curiae filed on behalf of Constitutional Law Scholars by Ryan A. Shores and William J. Haun.

Brief of amici curiae filed on behalf of Women Speak for Themselves by Helen M. Alvaré.

Brief of amici curiae filed on behalf of Liberty Counsel by Mathew D. Staver, Anita L. Staver, Horatio G. Mihet, and Mary E. McAlister.

Brief of amici curiae filed on behalf of The Council For Christian Colleges and Universities and Matthew T. Nelson, John J. Bursch, and Conor B. Dugan.

Brief of amici curiae filed on behalf of The Knights of Columbus by L. Martin Nussbaum, Eric N. Kniffin, Ian S. Speir, John A. Marrella, and Beth M. Elfrey.

Brief of amici curiae filed on behalf of Bart Stupak et al. by John C. Eastman, Anthony T. Caso, and Cristen Wohlgemuth.

Brief of amici curiae filed on behalf of Dominican Sisters of Mary, Mother of the Eucharist et al. by Eileen J. O'Connor, Robert S. Logan, Carrie Severino, and Jonathan Keim.

Brief of amici curiae filed on behalf of the Thomas More Law

Center by Erin Elizabeth Mersino and Kate Oliveri.
Brief of amici curiae filed on behalf of ACNA Jurisdiction of the Armed Forces and Chaplaincy et al. by Scott W. Gaylord.
Brief of amici curiae filed on behalf of Eternal Word Television Network by S. Kyle Duncan.
Brief of amici curiae filed on behalf of David Boyle by Mr. Boyle.
Brief of amici curiae filed on behalf of Thirteen Law Professors by John D. Adams and Matthew A. Fitzgerald.
Brief of amici curiae filed on behalf of the International Conference of Evangelical Chaplain Endorsers by Arthur A. Schulcz, Sr.
Brief of amici curiae filed on behalf of Concerned Women for America by Steven W. Fitschen supporting reversal.
Brief of amici curiae filed on behalf of Michael J. New, Ph.D., Associate Scholar, Charlotte Lozier Institute by Thomas M. Messner and David R. Langdon.
Brief of amici curiae filed on behalf of American Center for Law and Justice by Mark Goldfeder, Jay Alan Sekulow, Stuart J. Roth, Walter M. Weber, Francis J. Manion, and Geoffrey R. Surtees.
Brief of amici curiae filed on behalf of U.S. Justice Foundation et al. by Michael Connelly, Herbert W. Titus, William J. Olson, Jeremiah L. Morgan, and John S. Miles.
Brief of amici curiae filed on behalf of Carmelite Sisters of the Most Sacred Heart of Los Angeles et al. by Robert E. Dunn, Autum L. Flores, Thomas G. Hungar, and Mary G. H. Lang.
Brief of amici curiae filed on behalf of the Catholic Benefits Association by L. Martin Nussbaum, Eric N. Kniffin, and Ian S. Speir.
Brief of amici curiae filed on behalf of Religious Institutions by Todd R. Mcfarland, Gene C. Schaerr, Dwayne Leslie, E.R. Lanier, and Uleses C. Henderson, Jr.

IV. THE SUPREME COURT'S DECISION

"[T]he Court requested supplemental briefing . . . addressing 'whether contraceptive coverage could be provided to petitioners' employees, through petitioners' insurance companies, without any such notice from petitioners.' Both petitioners and the Government now confirm that such an option is feasible. . . .

In light of the positions asserted by the parties in their supplemental briefs, the Court vacates the judgments below and remands to the respective United States Courts of Appeals for the Third, Fifth, Tenth, and D.C. Circuits. Given the gravity of the dispute and the substantial clarification and refinement in the positions of the parties, the parties on remand should be afforded an opportunity to arrive at an approach going forward that accommodates petitioners' religious exercise while at the same time ensuring that women covered by petitioners' health plans 'receive full and equal health coverage, including contraceptive coverage.' We anticipate that the Courts of Appeals will allow the parties sufficient time to resolve any outstanding issues between them.

The Court finds the foregoing approach more suitable than addressing the significantly clarified views of the parties in the first instance. Although there may still be areas of disagreement . . . on issues of implementation, the importance of those areas of potential concern is uncertain, as is the necessity of this Court's involvement . . . . This Court has taken similar action in other cases in the past. . . .

The Court expresses no view on the merits of the cases. In particular, the Court does not decide whether petitioners' religious exercise has been substantially burdened, whether the Government has a compelling interest, or whether the current regulations are the least restrictive means . . . .

Nothing . . . is to affect the ability of the Government to ensure that women covered by petitioners' health plans 'obtain, without cost, the full range of FDA approved contraceptives.' Through this litigation, petitioners have made the Government aware of their view that they meet 'the requirements for exemption from the contraceptive coverage requirement on religious grounds.' Nothing . . . 'precludes the Government from relying on this notice, to the extent it considers it necessary, to facilitate the provision of full contraceptive coverage' going forward. . . .

The judgments of the Courts of Appeals are vacated, and the cases are remanded . . . ."

V. JUSTICE VOTE

0 Pro ACLU Side vs. 8 Con Opposing Side

Opposing Side (Petitioner / Appellant)

1. Alito, S. – Per curiam opinion
2. Kagan, E. – Per curiam opinion
3. Thomas, C. – Per curiam opinion
4. Breyer, S. – Per curiam opinion
5. Kennedy, A. – Per curiam opinion
6. Ginsburg, R. – Joined Sotomayor's concurrence
7. Sotomayor, S. – Wrote concurring opinion
8. Roberts, J. – Per curiam opinion

Vacant Seat

VI. A WIN OR LOSS FOR THE ACLU?

The ACLU filed as amicus curiae urging affirmance; the Supreme Court vacated the Courts of Appeals' decisions by an 8-0 vote expressing no opinion on the merits, giving the ACLU an apparent loss.

1147. Simmons v. Himmelreich

(Decided June 6, 2016; 136 S.Ct. 1843; 578 U.S. _)

I. ISSUE

A. Issues Discussed

Civil procedure

B. Legal Question Presented

"The Federal Tort Claims Act (FTCA) . . . procedural provisions are contained in a single chapter of the United States Code, Chapter 171. But an 'Exceptions' section of the FTCA dictates that 'the provisions of [Chapter 171] . . . shall not apply' to certain categories of claims. At issue in this case is whether one of the 'provisions of [Chapter 171]'—the so-called judgment bar provision, § 2676—might nonetheless apply to one of the excepted claims."

C. Supreme Court's Answer

"We conclude it does not."

II. CASE SUMMARY

A. Background

"This case began with two suits filed by Walter Himmelreich. In each, Himmelreich alleged that he had been severely beaten by a fellow inmate in federal prison and that the beating was the result of prison officials' negligence. . . . Himmelreich was incarcerated for producing child pornography. His assailant had warned prison officials that he would "smash" a pedophile if given the opportunity but was nonetheless released into the general prison population, where he assaulted Himmelreich.

Himmelreich filed a first suit . . . . The District Court granted the Government's motion to dismiss. (Neither party here challenges the outcome of that first suit.) . . .

Himmelreich filed a second suit, this one a constitutional tort suit against individual Bureau of Prison employees rather than against the United States. Ordinarily, the FTCA would have nothing to say about such claims. But after the dismissal of Himmelreich's first suit, the individual employee defendants argued that Himmelreich's second suit was foreclosed by the FTCA's judgment bar provision, according to which a judgment in an FTCA suit forecloses any future suit against individual employees. [T]he District Court agreed and granted summary judgment in favor of the individual prison employees. . . .

The Sixth Circuit reversed, holding that the judgment bar provision did not apply to Himmelreich's suit."

The Supreme Court granted certiorari to review the case.

B. Counsel of Record / ACLU Attorney

ACLU Side (Respondent / Appellee): Christian Vergonis argued the cause for appellee. With him on the briefs were Yaakov M. Roth, David T. Raimer, and Jordan Von Bokern.

Opposing Side (Petitioner / Appellant): Assistant Solicitor General Martinez argued the cause for appellant. With him on the brief were Solicitor General Verrilli, Principal Deputy Assistant Attorney General Mizer, Deputy Solicitor General Gershengorn, Mark B. Stern, Edward Himmelfarb, and Imran R. Zaid.

III. AMICI CURIAE

ACLU Side (Respondent / Appellee)

Brief of amici curiae filed on behalf of Public Citizen, Inc., and the American Civil Liberties Union by Steven R. Shapiro, Allison M. Zieve, and Scott L. Nelson.

Brief of amici curiae filed on behalf of Professors Gregory Sisk et al. by Mr. Sisk.

Opposing Side (Petitioner / Appellant)

No briefs of amici curiae were filed in support of appellant.

IV. THE SUPREME COURT'S DECISION

"The FTCA's provisions are contained in two areas of the United States Code. One, 28 U.S.C. § 1346(b), gives federal district courts exclusive jurisdiction over tort claims against the United States for the acts of its employees '[s]ubject to the provisions of chapter 171' of Title 28. Chapter 171 . . . comprises the remaining provisions of the FTCA.

Chapter 171 contains an array of provisions. Some provisions govern how FTCA claims are to be adjudicated. . . . Other provisions limit plaintiffs' remedies outside the FTCA. . . .

The District Court in this case relied on one such remedies-limiting provision of Chapter 171, the judgment bar provision. Under the judgment bar provision, once a plaintiff receives a judgment . . . in an FTCA suit, he generally cannot proceed with a suit against an individual employee based on the same underlying facts. . . .

The parties disagree . . . about whether the judgment bar provision of Chapter 171 'shall not apply' to claims in one of the 'Exceptions' categories. The Government maintains that the judgment bar provision does apply to such claims. In that case, it applied to Himmelreich's first suit and would preclude any future actions, including his second suit. Himmelreich urges that it does not apply. On that reading, there is no reason he cannot proceed with his second suit. . . .

Himmelreich is correct. . . .

Nothing about the 'Exceptions' section or the judgment bar provision gives us any reason to doubt the plain-text result in this case. . . .

Given the clarity of the 'Exceptions' section's command, a reader might be forgiven for wondering how there could be any confusion about the statute's operation. The main source of uncertainty . . . is United States v. Smith, 499 U.S. 160 (1991). . . .

In light of the unique language of the Liability Reform Act, Smith is distinguishable from this case. Nothing in the text of the judgment bar provision compels the same result. . . .

The Government's remaining counterargument amounts to a parade of horribles that it believes will come to pass if every provision of Chapter 171 'shall not apply' to the 'Exceptions' categories . . . .

We decline to ignore the text of the statute to achieve . . . imprudently restrictive results. Accordingly, we read '[t]he provisions of this chapter . . . shall not apply' as it was written. The judgment bar provision . . . does not apply to the categories of claims in the 'Exceptions' sections of the FTCA. We therefore affirm the judgment of the Court of Appeals and remand . . . ."

V. JUSTICE VOTE

8 Pro ACLU Side vs. 0 Con Opposing Side

ACLU Side (Respondent / Appellee)

1. Sotomayor, S. – Wrote majority opinion
2. Alito, S. – Joined majority opinion
3. Kagan, E. – Joined majority opinion
4. Thomas, C. – Joined majority opinion
5. Breyer, S. – Joined majority opinion
6. Kennedy, A. – Joined majority opinion
7. Ginsburg, R. – Joined majority opinion
8. Roberts, J. – Joined majority opinion

Vacant Seat

VI. A WIN OR LOSS FOR THE ACLU?

The ACLU filed as amicus curiae urging affirmance; the Supreme Court affirmed the Court of Appeals' decision by an 8-0 vote, giving the ACLU an apparent win.

1148. Williams v. Pennsylvania

(Decided June 9, 2016; 136 S.Ct. 1899; 579 U.S. _)

I. ISSUE

A. Issues Discussed

Criminal procedure, death penalty

B. Legal Question Presented

"[W]hether the justice's denial of the recusal motion and his subsequent judicial participation violated the Due Process Clause of the Fourteenth Amendment."

C. Supreme Court's Answer

"This Court's precedents set forth an objective standard that requires recusal when the likelihood of bias on the part of the judge "is too high to be constitutionally tolerable." Applying this standard, the Court concludes that due process compelled the justice's recusal."

II. CASE SUMMARY

A. Background

"In this case, the Supreme Court of Pennsylvania vacated the decision of a postconviction court, which had granted relief to a prisoner convicted of first-degree murder and sentenced to death. One of the justices on the State Supreme Court had been the district attorney who gave his official approval to seek the death penalty in the prisoner's case. The justice in question denied the prisoner's motion for recusal and participated in the decision to deny relief."

The Supreme Court granted certiorari to review the case.

B. Counsel of Record / ACLU Attorney

ACLU Side (Petitioner / Appellant): Stuart B. Lev argued the cause for appellants. With him on the brief were Leigh M. Skipper, Chief Federal Defender for the Eastern District of Pennsylvania, Shawn Nolan, Matthew C. Lawry, Timothy P. Kane, and Katherine E. Ensler.

Opposing Side (Respondent / Appellee): Philadelphia City Deputy District Attorney Ronald Eisenberg, argued the cause for appellee. With him on the brief were Hugh J. Burns, Jr., Appeals Unit Chief, George D. Mosee, Jr., First Assistant District Attorney, and R. Seth Williams, District Attorney.

III. AMICI CURIAE

ACLU Side (Petitioner / Appellant)

Brief of amici curiae filed on behalf of the American Civil Liberties Union and the ACLU of Pennsylvania by Mary Catherine Roper, Witold J. Walczak, Anna Arceneaux, Cassandra Stubbs, and Steven R. Shapiro.

Brief of amici curiae filed on behalf of Constitutional Accountability Center by Elizabeth B. Wydra and Brianne J. Gorod.

Brief of amici curiae filed on behalf of Former Judges with Prosecutorial Experience by Gavin Reinke, Alan P. Solow, and David Winkler.

Brief of amici curiae filed on behalf of the Ethics Bureau at Yale et al. by Lawrence J. Fox.

Brief of amici curiae filed on behalf of the American Bar Association by Paulette Brown.

Brief of amici curiae filed on behalf of Former Appellate Court Jurists by Virginia E. Sloan, Jeffrey T. Green, Sarah Turberville, Kyle J. Fiet, and David E. Kronenberg.

Brief of amici curiae filed on behalf of Brennan Center for Justice at NYU School of Law et al. by Matthew Menendez, Daniel F. Kolb, David B. Toscano, Jeremy T. Adler, Brian Richichi, and Ronald J. Krock.

Brief of amici curiae filed on behalf of the American Academy of Appellate Lawyers by Wendy Cole Lascher and Charles A. Bird.

Opposing Side (Respondent / Appellee)

No briefs of amici curiae were filed in support of appellee.

IV. THE SUPREME COURT'S DECISION

"Williams contends that Chief Justice Castille's decision as district attorney to seek a death sentence against him barred the chief justice from later adjudicating Williams's petition . . . .

The Court's due process precedents do not set forth a specific test governing recusal when, as here, a judge had prior involvement in a case as a prosecutor. [H]owever, the principles on which these precedents rest dictate the rule that must control in the circumstances here. The Court now holds that under the Due Process Clause there is an impermissible risk of actual bias when a judge earlier had significant, personal involvement as a prosecutor in a critical decision regarding the defendant's case.

Due process guarantees 'an absence of actual bias' on the part of a judge. [A]n unconstitutional potential for bias exists when the same person serves as both accuser and adjudicator in a case. . . .

The due process guarantee that 'no man can be a judge in his own case' would have little substance if it did not disqualify a former prosecutor from sitting in judgment of a prosecution in which he or she had made a critical decision. . . .

The involvement of multiple actors and the passage of time do not relieve the former prosecutor of the duty to withdraw in order to ensure the neutrality of the judicial process . . . .

This leads to the question whether Chief Justice Castille's authorization to seek the death penalty against Williams amounts to significant, personal involvement in a critical trial decision. The Court now concludes that it was a significant, personal involvement; and, as a result, Chief Justice Castille's failure to recuse from Williams's case presented an unconstitutional risk of bias. . . .

Chief Justice Castille's significant, personal involvement in a critical decision in Williams's case gave rise to an unacceptable risk of actual bias. This risk so endangered the appearance of neutrality that his participation in the case 'must be forbidden if the guarantee of due process is to be adequately implemented.' . . .

Chief Justice Castille's participation in Williams's case was an error that affected the State Supreme Court's whole adjudicatory framework below. Williams must be granted an opportunity to present his claims to a court unburdened by any 'possible temptation . . . not to hold the balance . . . between the State and the accused.' . . .

Where a judge has had an earlier significant, personal involvement as a prosecutor in a critical decision in the defendant's case, the risk of actual bias in the judicial proceeding rises to an unconstitutional level. Due process entitles Terrance Williams to 'a proceeding in which he may present his case with assurance' that no member of the court is 'predisposed to find against him.'

The judgment of the Supreme Court of Pennsylvania is vacated, and the case is remanded . . . ."

V. JUSTICE VOTE

5 Pro ACLU Side vs. 3 Con Opposing Side

ACLU Side (Petitioner / Appellant)

1. Kennedy, A. – Wrote majority opinion
2. Kagan, E. – Joined majority opinion
3. Breyer, S. – Joined majority opinion
4. Ginsburg, R. – Joined majority opinion
5. Sotomayor, S. – Joined majority opinion

Opposing Side (Respondent / Appellee)

1. Alito, S. – Joined Roberts' dissent
2. Thomas, C. – Wrote dissenting opinion
3. Roberts, J. – Wrote dissenting opinion

Vacant Seat

VI. A WIN OR LOSS FOR THE ACLU?

The ACLU filed as amicus curiae urging reversal of the judgment of the Supreme Court of Pennsylvania; the Supreme Court vacated in a 5-3 vote, giving the ACLU an apparent win.

1149. Utah v. Strieff

(Decided June 20, 2016; 136 S.Ct. 2056; 579 U.S. _)

I. ISSUE

A. Issues Discussed

4th Amendment

B. Legal Question Presented

"To enforce the Fourth Amendment's prohibition against 'unreasonable searches and seizures,' this Court has at times required courts to exclude evidence obtained by unconstitutional police conduct. But the Court has also held that . . . the link between the unconstitutional conduct and the discovery of the evidence is too attenuated to justify suppression. The question in this case is whether this attenuation doctrine applies when an officer makes an unconstitutional investigatory stop; learns during that stop that the suspect is subject to a valid arrest warrant; and proceeds to arrest the suspect and seize incriminating evidence during a search incident to that arrest."

C. Supreme Court's Answer

"We hold that the evidence the officer seized as part of the search incident to arrest is admissible because the officer's discovery of the arrest warrant attenuated the connection between the unlawful stop and the evidence seized incident to arrest."

II. CASE SUMMARY

A. Background

"[S]omeone called the . . . police's drug-tip line to report 'narcotics activity' at a particular residence. Narcotics detective Douglas Fackrell investigated the tip. . . . He observed visitors who left a few minutes after arriving at the house. These visits were sufficiently frequent to raise his suspicion that the occupants were dealing drugs.

One of those visitors was respondent Edward Strieff. Officer Fackrell observed Strieff exit the house . . . . Officer Fackrell detained Strieff, identified himself, and asked Strieff what he was doing at the residence. . . .

Officer Fackrell requested Strieff's identification, and Strieff produced his Utah identification card. Officer Fackrell relayed Strieff's information to a police dispatcher, who reported that Strieff had an outstanding arrest warrant for a traffic violation. Officer Fackrell then arrested Strieff pursuant to that warrant. When Officer Fackrell searched Strieff incident to the arrest, he discovered a baggie of methamphetamine and drug paraphernalia.

The State charged Strieff with unlawful possession of methamphetamine and drug paraphernalia. Strieff moved to suppress the evidence, arguing that the evidence was inadmissible because it was derived from an unlawful investigatory stop. . . .

The trial court . . . admitted the evidence. . . .

Strieff conditionally pleaded guilty to reduced charges of attempted possession of a controlled substance and possession of drug paraphernalia, but reserved his right to appeal the trial court's denial of the suppression motion. The Utah Court of Appeals affirmed.

The Utah Supreme Court reversed."

The Supreme Court granted certiorari to review the case.

B. Counsel of Record / ACLU Attorney

ACLU Side (Respondent / Appellee): Joan C. Watt argued the cause for appellee. With her on the briefs were Stuart Banner and Patrick L. Anderson.

Opposing Side (Petitioner / Appellant): Utah Solicitor General Tyler R. Green argued the cause for appellant. With him on the briefs were Sean D. Reyes, Attorney General of Utah, Laura B. Dupaix, Deputy Solicitor General, Thomas B. Brunker, Criminal Appeals Director, and Jeffrey S. Gray, Search & Seizure Section Director.

Assistant Solicitor General Bash argued the cause for the United States as amicus curiae.

III. AMICI CURIAE

ACLU Side (Respondent / Appellee)

Brief of amici curiae filed on behalf of the American Civil Liberties Union and the National Association of Criminal Defense Lawyers by Steven R. Shapiro, Jeffrey L. Fisher, Michael B. Kimberly, and Matthew A. Warin.

Brief of amici curiae filed on behalf of the Electronic Privacy Information Center (EPIC) et al. by Marc Rotenberg, Alan Butler, Caitriona Fitzgerald, Claire Gartland, and Aimee Thomson.

Brief of amici curiae filed on behalf of the Southwestern Law Student Tracy E. Labrusciano et al. by Norman M. Garland and Michael M. Epstein.

Opposing Side (Petitioner / Appellant)

Brief of amici curiae filed on behalf of the United States by Solicitor General Verrilli, Assistant Attorney General Caldwell, Deputy Solicitor General Dreeben, Assistant Solicitor General Bash, and David M. Lieberman.

Brief of amici curiae filed on behalf of the Criminal Justice Legal Foundation by Kent S. Scheidegger.

Brief of amici curiae filed on behalf of the State of Michigan et al. by Bill Schuette, Attorney General of Michigan, Aaron D. Lindstrom,Solicitor General, Kathryn M. Dalzell, Assistant Solicitor General, and by the Attorneys General for their respective States as follows: Luther Strange of Alabama, Mark Brnovich of Arizona, Leslie Rutledge of Arkansas, Cynthia Coffman of Colorado, Pamela Jo Bondi of Florida, Douglas S. Chin of Hawaii, Lisa Madigan of Illinois, Gregory F. Zoeller of Indiana, Derek Schmidt of Kansas, Jack Conway of Kentucky, James D. "Buddy" Caldwell of Louisiana, Janet T. Mills of Maine, Douglas F. Gansler of Maryland, Timothy C. Fox of Montana, Douglas J. Peterson of Nebraska, John J. Hoffman of New Jersey, Adam Paul Laxalt of Nevada, Wayne Stenehjem of North Dakota, Michael DeWine of Ohio, Ellen F. Rosenblum of Oregon, E. Scott Pruitt of Oklahoma, Bruce R. Beemer of Pennsylvania, Peter F. Kilmartin of Rhode Island, Alan Wilson of South Carolina, Marty J. Jackley of South Dakota, Herbert Slatery III of Tennessee, Ken Paxton of Texas, Patrick Morrisey of West Virginia, and Peter K. Michael of Wyoming.

IV. THE SUPREME COURT'S DECISION

"The Fourth Amendment protects '[t]he right of the people to be secure in their persons, houses, papers, and effects, against unreasonable searches and seizures.' . . . In the 20th century, . . . the exclusionary rule . . . became the principal judicial remedy to deter Fourth Amendment violations. . . .

But the significant costs of this rule have led us to deem it 'applicable only . . . where its deterrence benefits outweigh its substantial social costs.' . . .

We have accordingly recognized several exceptions . . . . [A] t issue here, is the attenuation doctrine: Evidence is admissible when the connection between unconstitutional police conduct and the evidence is remote or has been interrupted by some intervening circumstance, so that 'the interest protected by the constitutional guarantee that has been violated would not be served by suppression of the evidence obtained.' . . .

It remains for us to address whether the discovery of a valid arrest warrant was a sufficient intervening event . . . . First, we look to the 'temporal proximity' . . . to determine how closely the discovery of evidence followed the unconstitutional search. Second, we consider 'the presence of intervening circumstances.' Third, and 'particularly' significant, we examine 'the purpose and flagrancy of the official misconduct.' In evaluating these factors, we assume without deciding (because the State conceded the point) that Officer Fackrell lacked reasonable suspicion to initially stop Strieff. And, because we ultimately conclude that the warrant breaks the causal chain, we also have no need to decide whether the warrant's existence alone would make the initial stop constitutional even if Officer Fackrell was unaware of its existence. . . .

Applying these factors, we hold that the evidence discovered on Strieff's person was admissible because the unlawful stop was sufficiently attenuated by the pre-existing arrest warrant. Although the illegal stop was close in time to Strieff's arrest, that consideration is outweighed by two factors supporting the State. The outstanding arrest warrant for Strieff's arrest is a critical intervening circumstance that is wholly independent of the illegal stop. The discovery of that warrant broke the causal chain between the unconstitutional stop and the discovery of evidence by compelling Officer Fackrell to arrest Strieff. And, it is especially significant that there is no evidence that Officer Fackrell's illegal stop reflected flagrantly unlawful police misconduct. . . .

We hold that the evidence Officer Fackrell seized as part of his search incident to arrest is admissible because his discovery of the arrest warrant attenuated the connection between the unlawful stop and the evidence seized from Strieff incident to arrest. The judgment of the Utah Supreme Court, accordingly, is reversed."

V. JUSTICE VOTE

3 Pro ACLU Side vs. 5 Con Opposing Side

ACLU Side (Respondent / Appellee)

1. Kagan, E. – Wrote dissenting opinion
2. Ginsburg, R. – Joined Kagan's dissent, joined Sotomayor's dissent in part
3. Sotomayor, S. – Wrote dissenting opinion

Opposing Side (Petitioner / Appellant)

1. Thomas, C. – Wrote majority opinion
2. Alito, S. – Joined majority opinion
3. Breyer, S. – Joined majority opinion
4. Kennedy, A. – Joined majority opinion
5. Roberts, J. – Joined majority opinion

Vacant Seat

VI. A WIN OR LOSS FOR THE ACLU?

The ACLU filed as amicus curiae urging affirmance; the Supreme Court reversed the Utah Supreme Court's decision by a 5-3 vote, giving the ACLU an apparent loss.

1150. Birchfield v. North Dakota

(Decided June 23, 2016; 136 S.Ct. 2160; 579 U.S. _)

I. ISSUE

A. Issues Discussed

4th Amendment

B. Legal Question Presented

"[W]hether motorists lawfully arrested for drunk driving may be convicted of a crime or otherwise penalized for refusing to take a warrantless test measuring the alcohol in their bloodstream."

C. Supreme Court's Answer

"Having assessed the effect of BAC tests on privacy interests and the need for such tests, we conclude that the Fourth Amendment permits warrantless breath tests incident to arrests for drunk driving. The impact of breath tests on privacy is slight, and the need for BAC testing is great.

We reach a different conclusion with respect to blood tests. Blood tests are significantly more intrusive, and their reasonableness must be judged in light of the availability of the less invasive alternative of a breath test. Respondents have offered no satisfactory justification for demanding the more intrusive alternative without a warrant."

II. CASE SUMMARY

A. Background

"[A] state trooper arrested Birchfield for driving while impaired, gave the usual Miranda warnings, . . . advised him of his obligation under North Dakota law to undergo BAC testing, and informed him . . . that refusing to take the test would expose him to criminal penalties. . . .

Birchfield refused to let his blood be drawn. . . . The [c]ourt . . . imposed a sentence . . . .

On appeal, the North Dakota Supreme Court affirmed. . . .

[O]fficers read Bernard Minnesota's implied consent advisory, which . . . informs motorists that it is a crime under state law to refuse to submit to a legally required BAC test. . . .

The officers asked Bernard to take a breath test. After he refused, prosecutors charged him with test refusal . . . .

The Minnesota District Court dismissed . . . on the ground that the warrantless breath test . . . was not permitted . . . . The Minnesota Court of Appeals reversed, and the State Supreme Court affirmed . . . .

[An] officer arrested Beylund for driving while impaired and took him to a nearby hospital. There he read Beylund North Dakota's implied consent advisory, informing him that test refusal in these circumstances is itself a crime. . . . Beylund agreed to have his blood drawn . . . which revealed a blood alcohol concentration of 0.250%, more than three times the legal limit.

Given the test results, Beylund's driver's license was suspended . . . . Beylund . . . to a North Dakota District Court, principally arguing that his consent to the blood test was coerced . . . . The District Court rejected this argument, and Beylund again appealed.

The North Dakota Supreme Court affirmed."

The Supreme Court granted certiorari to review the case.

B. Counsel of Record / ACLU Attorney

ACLU Side (Petitioner / Appellant): Charles A. Rothfeld argued the cause for appellants. With him on the brief was Dan Herbel, Eugene R. Fidell, Andrew J. Pincus, Michael B. Kimberly, and Paul W. Hughes.

Opposing Side (Respondent / Appellee): Thomas R. McCarthy argued the cause for appellee in Nos. 14-468 and 14-1507. Kathryn Keena, Assistant Dakota County Attorney, argued the cause for appellee in No. 14-1470. With them on the brief were William S. Consovoy, J. Michael Connolly, Bryan K. Weir, Patrick Strawbridge, Michael Park, and Brian David Grosinger, Assistant State's Attorney of North Dakota.

Deputy Solicitor General Gershengorn argued the cause for the United States as amicus curiae.

III. AMICI CURIAE

ACLU Side (Petitioner / Appellant)

Brief of amici curiae filed on behalf of the American Civil Liberties Union by Steven R. Shapiro, Catherine E. Stetson, Daniel J.T. Schuker, and Andrew D. Selbst.

Brief of amici curiae filed on behalf of the the DUI Defense Lawyers Association by Daniel J. Koewler, Ted Vosk, Evan Levow, Charles Ramsay, Mike Vang, and Linda Callahan.

Brief of amici curiae filed on behalf of the Downsize DC Foundation et al. by Michael Connelly, Robert J. Olson, Herbert W. Titus, John S. Miles, and Jeremiah L. Morgan.

Brief of amici curiae filed on behalf of the National College for DUI Defense et al. by Donald J. Ramsell, Leonard R. Stamm, and Jeffrey T. Green.

Opposing Side (Respondent / Appellee)

Brief of amici curiae filed on behalf of the California District Attorneys Association by Mark Zahner, Michael J. Yraceburn, and Stewart Hicks, Traffic Safety Resource Prosecutor.

Brief of amici curiae filed on behalf of the United States by Solicitor General Verrilli, Assistant Attorney General Caldwell, Deputy Solicitor General Dreeben, Assistant Solicitor General Kovner, and Thomas E. Booth.

Brief of amici curiae filed on behalf of the State of New Jersey et al. by Robert Lougy, Acting Attorney General of New Jersey, Jennifer E. Kmieciak, Deputy Attorney General, by Claudia Joy Demitro, Garima Joshi, and Ian C. Kennedy, Lila B. Leonard, Deputy Attorneys General, Bruce R. Beemer, First Deputy Attorney General of Pennsylvania, and by the Attorneys General for their respective States as follows: Luther Strange of Alabama, Craig W. Richards of Alaska, Leslie Rutledge of Arkansas, Cynthia H. Coffman of Colorado, Douglas S. Chin of Hawaii, Derek Schmidt of Kansas, Jeff Landry of Louisiana, Timothy C. Fox of Montana, Hector Baldares of New Mexico, Peter F. Kilmartin of Rhode Island, Alan Wilson of South Carolina, Marty J. Jackley of South Dakota, Ken Paxton of Texas, Sean D. Reyes of Utah, William H. Sorrell of Vermont, and Brad D. Schimel of Wisconsin.

Brief of amici curiae filed on behalf of the Council of State Government et al. by Lisa Soronen, Gregory G. Garre,

Jonathan Y. Ellis, and Benjamin W. Snyder.
Brief of amici curiae filed on behalf of Mothers Against Drunk Driving by Adam W. Vanek, David Venderbush, Kirk T. Bradley, and Brianna Kadjo.
Brief of amici curiae filed on behalf of the National District Attorneys Association et al. by Kay Chopard Cohen.

IV. THE SUPREME COURT'S DECISION

"The [Fourth] Amendment . . . prohibits 'unreasonable searches,' and . . . the taking of a blood sample or the administration of a breath test is a search. The question, then, is whether the warrantless searches at issue here were reasonable. . . .

We . . . consider how the search-incident-to-arrest doctrine applies . . . .

We begin by considering the impact of breath and blood tests on individual privacy interests . . . .

Years ago we said that breath tests do not 'implicat[e] significant privacy concerns.' . . .

Blood tests are a different matter. . . .

Having assessed the impact of breath and blood testing on privacy interests, we now look to the States' asserted need to obtain BAC readings for persons arrested for drunk driving. . . .

The [g]overnment ha[s] a 'paramount interest . . . in preserving the safety of . . . public highways.' . . .

Having assessed the effect of BAC tests on privacy interests and the need for such tests, we conclude that the Fourth Amendment permits warrantless breath tests incident to arrests for drunk driving. . . .

We reach a different conclusion with respect to blood tests. . . .

Because breath tests are significantly less intrusive than blood tests and in most cases amply serve law enforcement interests, we conclude that a breath test, but not a blood test, may be administered as a search incident to a lawful arrest for drunk driving. . . .

[W]e must address respondents' alternative argument that such tests are justified based on the driver's legally implied consent to submit to them. . . .

[W]e conclude that motorists cannot be deemed to have consented to submit to a blood test on pain of committing a criminal offense. . . .

Our remaining task is to apply our legal conclusions to the three cases before us. . . .

[W]e conclude that Birchfield was threatened with an unlawful search and that the judgment affirming his conviction must be reversed.

Bernard, on the other hand, was criminally prosecuted for refusing a warrantless breath test. That test was a permissible search incident to Bernard's arrest for drunk driving . . . .

Because voluntariness of consent to a search must be 'determined from the totality of all the circumstances,' we leave it to the state court on remand to reevaluate Beylund's consent . . . .

We accordingly reverse the judgment of the North Dakota Supreme Court in No. 14–1468 and remand . . . . We affirm the judgment of the Minnesota Supreme Court in No. 14–1470. And we vacate the judgment of the North Dakota Supreme Court in No. 14–1507 and remand . . . ."

V. JUSTICE VOTE

7 Pro ACLU Side vs. 1 Con Opposing Side

ACLU Side (Petitioner / Appellant)

1. Alito, S. – Wrote majority opinion
2. Kagan, E. – Joined majority opinion
3. Breyer, S. – Joined majority opinion
4. Kennedy, A. – Joined majority opinion
5. Ginsburg, R. – Joined Sotomayor's opinion
6. Sotomayor, S. – Wrote opinion concurring in part and dissenting in part
7. Roberts, J. – Joined majority opinion

Opposing Side (Respondent / Appellee)

1. Thomas, C. – Wrote concurring in part and dissenting in part

Vacant Seat

VI. A WIN OR LOSS FOR THE ACLU?

The ACLU filed as amicus curiae urging reversal of the judgment of the North Dakota Supreme Court; the Supreme Court reversed in a 7-1 vote, giving the ACLU an apparent win.

1151. Fisher v. Univ. of Texas at Austin

(Decided June 23, 2016; 136 S.Ct. 2198; 579 U.S. _)

I. ISSUE

A. Issues Discussed

Race

B. Legal Question Presented

"[W]hether the race-conscious admissions program at the University of Texas is lawful under the Equal Protection Clause."

C. Supreme Court's Answer

"The University has . . . met its burden of showing that the admissions policy it used at the time it rejected petitioner's application was narrowly tailored."

II. CASE SUMMARY

A. Background

"The University of Texas at Austin . . . relies upon a complex system of admissions . . . .

In 1996, the Court of Appeals . . . invalidated th[e] admissions system, holding that any consideration of race in college admissions violates the Equal Protection Clause.

One year later the University adopted a new admissions policy. . . .

The University used this admissions system until 2003, when this Court decided . . . companion cases . . . . In Gratz, this Court struck down the University of Michigan's undergraduate system of admissions, which at the time allocated predetermined points to racial minority candidates. In Grutter, however, the Court upheld the University of Michigan Law School's system of holistic review . . . .

[T]he University . . . requested permission to begin taking race into consideration . . . . The University has continued to use that admissions policy . . . .

Although the University's new admissions policy was a direct result of Grutter, it is not identical . . . .

Petitioner Abigail Fisher applied for admission . . . . Petitioner's application was rejected.

Petitioner then filed suit alleging that the . . . holistic-review process disadvantaged her and other Caucasian applicants . . . . The District Court entered summary judgment in the University's favor, and the Court of Appeals affirmed.

This Court granted certiorari and vacated the judgment of the Court of Appeals . . . . The Court remanded the case for the Court of Appeals to assess the parties' claims . . . .

Without further remanding to the District Court, the Court of Appeals again affirmed . . . summary judgment in the University's favor. This Court granted certiorari . . . ."

B. Counsel of Record / ACLU Attorney

ACLU Side (Respondent / Appellee): Gregory G. Garre argued the cause for appellee. With him on the briefs were Patricia C. Ohlendorf, Douglas Laycock, James C. Ho, Andrew P. Legrand, Maureen E. Mahoney, J. Scott Ballenger, Nicole Ries Fox, Lori Alvino Mcgill, and Katya S. Cronin.

Solicitor General Verrilli argued the cause for the United States as amicus curiae.

Opposing Side (Petitioner / Appellant): Bert W. Rein argued the cause for appellant. With him on the brief were William S. Consovoy, Thomas R. Mccarthy, J. Michael Connolly, Paul M. Terrill, and Claire J. Evans.

III. AMICI CURIAE

ACLU Side (Respondent / Appellee)

Brief of amici curiae filed on behalf of the American Civil Liberties Union and the ACLU of Texas by Rebecca L. Robertson, Dennis D. Parker, Sarah Hinger, Matthew A. Coles, and Steven R. Shapiro.

Brief of amici curiae filed on behalf of the Family of Heman Sweatt by Allan Van Fleet and Nicholas Grimmer.

Brief of amici curiae filed on behalf of the New York Law School Racial Justice Project by Deborah N. Archer, Stephen J. Ellmann, and Erika L. Wood.

Brief of amici curiae filed on behalf of Nationwide Coalition of Educators et al. by Larry H. James, Christina L. Corl, Sharon L. Davies, and Kwame Christian.

Brief of amici curiae filed on behalf of Richard Lempert by Sylvia Royce.

Brief of amici curiae filed on behalf of Professor W. Burlette Carter by Ms. Carter.

Brief of amici curiae filed on behalf of Human Rights Advocates et al. by Constance De La Vega and Neil A.F. Popović.

Brief of amici curiae filed on behalf of Coalition of Bar Associations of Color by Jonathan M. Cohen, Adrian C. Azer, Michelle A. Price, John J. Girgenti, and Marnie L. Glaeberman.

Brief of amici curiae filed on behalf of American Council on Education et al. by Peter G. Mcdonough, Martin Michaelson, Elizabeth B. Meers, and Joel D. Buckman.

Brief of amici curiae filed on behalf of the College Board et al. by Arthur L. Coleman, Teresa E. Taylor, Scott R. Palmer, Joan Van Tol, C. Mitchell Brown, and Richard W. Riley.

Brief of amici curiae filed on behalf of the American Educational Research Association et al. by Angelo N. Ancheta, Jonathan Weissglass, and Kristin M. Garcia.

Brief of amici curiae filed on behalf of the State of California by Kamala D. Harris, Attorney General of California, Edward C. Dumont, Solicitor General, Mark Breckler, Chief Assistant Attorney General, Angela Sierra, Senior Assistant Attorney General, Nancy A. Beninati, Supervising Deputy Attorney General, and Antonette Benita Cordero and Rebekah Fretz, Deputy Attorneys General.

Brief of amici curiae filed on behalf of 823 Social Scientists by Liliana M. Garces.

Brief of amici curiae filed on behalf of the University of North Carolina at Chapel Hill by David Mclean Parker, Stephen Keadey, Kara Ellice Simmons, Maura O'Keefe, Michael Y. Scudder, Jr., Patrick J. Fitzgerald, Lara A. Flath, Marianne H. Combs, and Lisa Gilford.

Brief of amici curiae filed on behalf of the New York State Bar Association by David P. Miranda, David H. Tennant, and Jena R. Rotheim.

Brief of amici curiae filed on behalf of Society of American Law Teachers by Marc A. Hearron, David D. Cross, and Bryan J. Leitch.

Brief of amici curiae filed on behalf of Intercultural Development Research Association (IDRA) by David G. Hinojosa.

Brief of amici curiae filed on behalf of Constitutional Law Scholars et al. by Elizabeth B. Wydra, David H. Gans, and Brianne J. Gorod.

Brief of amici curiae filed on behalf of Ruben Hinojosa, Member of Congress et al. by Steven D. Gordon.

Brief of amici curiae filed on behalf of the Black Student Alliance at the University of Texas at Austin et al. by Sherrilyn Ifill, John Paul Schnapper-Casteras, Janai Nelson, Christina Swarns, Jin Hee Lee, Rachel M. Kleinman, Monique Lin-Luse, Deuel Ross, and Liliana Zaragoza.

Brief of amici curiae filed on behalf of Association of American Law Schools by Pamelal S. Karlan, Jeffrey L. Fisher, and Brian Wolfman.

Brief of amici curiae filed on behalf of 53 Current Members of the Texas State Senate and House of Representatives by Robin A. Lenhardt, Michelle Adams, John Brittain, Eric L. Lewis, and Jeffrey D. Robinson.

Brief of amici curiae filed on behalf of Current and Former Student Body Presidents of University of Texas at Austin by Megan L. Anderson, Gray Plant Mooty, Felicia R. Reid, Natasha J. Baker, and Erin E. Dolly.

Brief of amici curiae filed on behalf of Kimberly West-Faulcon by Ms. West-Faulcon.

Brief of amici curiae filed on behalf of the American Jewish Committee et al. by Richard C. Godfrey, Martin L. Roth, and Russell King.

Brief of amici curiae filed on behalf of Association of American Medical Colleges et al. by Frank R. Trinity, Heather J. Alarcon, Jonathan S. Franklin, Robert Burgoyne, and John W. Akin.
Brief of amici curiae filed on behalf of the New York University School of Law Seminar on Critical Narratives in Civil Rights by Aderson Bellegarde François and Peggy Cooper Davis.
Brief of amici curiae filed on behalf of Leading Public Research Universities the University of Delaware et al. by Ryan Rutledge, Walter Dellinger, Danielle C. Gray, Raghav Ahuja.
Brief of amici curiae filed on behalf of Brown University et al. by Paul M. Smith and Elizabeth C. Bullock.
Brief of amici curiae filed on behalf of the United States by Solicitor General Verrilli, Principal Deputy Assistant Attorney General Gupta, Deputy Solicitor General Gershengorn, Assistant Solicitor General Anders, Diana K. Flynn, Tovah R. Calderon, Paul S. Koffsky, Acting Principal Deputy General Counsel for the Department of Defense, Stevan E. Bunnell, General Counsel for the Department of Homeland Security, James Cole, Jr., General Counsel for the Department of Education, William B. Schultz, General Counsel for the Department of Health and Human Services, Kelly R. Welsh, General Counsel for the Department of Commerce, and M. Patricia Smith, Solicitor for the Department of Labor.
Brief of amici curiae filed on behalf of the American Psychological Association by Nathalie F. P. Gilfoyle, Lisa S. Blatt, R. Reeves Anderson, and Jenna L. Goldstein.
Brief of amici curiae filed on behalf of the President and the Chancellors of the University of California by Charles F. Robinson, Karen J. Petrulakis, Margaret L. Wu, Elisabeth C. Yap, Bradley S. Phillips, John F. Muller, and Christopher M. Patti.
Brief of amici curiae filed on behalf of Fortune-100 et al. by Caroline M. Decell, Michael E. Stewart, David W. Debruin, Matthew S. Hellman, Ann Marie Hanrahan, Judith H. Jones, Laureen E. Seeger, Bruce Sewell, Paul M. Liebenson, Mareilé Cusack, James M. Rooney, Lawrence P. Tu, Neal A. Rubin, Sharon R. Barner, William F. Lloyd, Sharon E. Underberg, Marie Oh Huber, Marcus V. Brown, Darryl M. Bradford, Michelle Banks, Alex Dimitrief, Bradford A. Berenson, Jacqueline A. White, Michael Ullmann, Brian J. Cadwallader, Deborah H. Telman, Mark Zemelman, Edward A. Ryan, Michael Holston, Thomas W. Burt, Susan C. Levy, Sheila C. Cheston, Maureen F. Del Duca, Louise Pentland, Tony West, Markus Green, Timothy P. Harris, Teresa Burroff, Kimberly R. Phillips, Susan Z. Haller, Lucy Lee Helm, David C. Phelan, Lizbeth S. O'Shaughnessy, Kenneth D. Greisman, Deborah P. Majoras, Joseph D. Heyd, Gayla Thal,Thomas Newton Bolling, Charles D. Gill, Michael D. Fricklas, Daniel M. Mandil, Karen Roberts, John Howard, Bob Markowski, and Don H. Liu.
Brief of amici curiae filed on behalf of National Association of Basketball Coaches et al. by Richard D. Batchelder, Jr., Samira A. Omerovic, and Matthew T. Henshon.
Brief of amici curiae filed on behalf of Empirical Scholars by Iván Espinoza-Madrigal, Oren M. Sellstrom, Matthew Cregor, A.W. Phinney III, Yalonda T. Howze, Colin G. Van Dyke, and Mathilda S. Mcgee-Tubb.
Brief of amici curiae filed on behalf of Harvard University by Robert W. Iuliano, Ara B. Gershengorn, Matthew T. Fox, Felicia H. Ellsworth, Eric F. Fletcher,
Seth P. Waxman, Paul R.Q. Wolfson, Kelly P. Dunbar, Debo P. Adegbile, and Adriel I. Cepeda Derieux.
Brief of amici curiae filed on behalf of the Civil Rights Clinic and the Education Rights Center at Howard University School of Law by E. Christi Cunningham and Aderson Bellegarde François.
Brief of amici curiae filed on behalf of the National Education Association et al. by Judith A. Scott, David Strom, William Lurye, Alice O'Brien, Jason Walta, Lubna A. Alam, Harold Craig Becker, and Lynn Rhinehart.
Brief of amici curiae filed on behalf of United Negro College Fund et al. by Desireé C. Boykin, Nicole Lazarre, David E. Schwartz, Richard W. Kidd, Melinda M. Hightower, Ashly Nikkole Davis, Tatum Ji, and Christine A. Kuveke.
Brief of amici curiae filed on behalf of F California Institute of Technology et al. by Jeffrey A. Udell, Ellen V. Holloman, Jeremy M. King, and Kyle C. Bisceglie.
Brief of amici curiae filed on behalf of National Association for the Advancement of Colored People Texas State Conference of the NAACP by Anthony P. Ashton, Andrew L. Deutsch, Fredrick H.L. McClure, Bradford M. Berry, Khyla D. Craine, Victor Goode, and Gary L. Bledsoe.
Brief of amici curiae filed on behalf of Dupont et al. by Stacy L. Fox, Donald B. Ayer, Beth Heifetz, Meghan E. Greenfield, and Sarah A. Hunger.
Brief of amici curiae filed on behalf of Amherst College et al. by Susan Sturm, Haran Tae, Charles S. Sims, and John E. Roberts.
Brief of amici curiae filed on behalf of Professors Cedric Merlin Powell et al. by Junis L. Baldon and Miles R. Harrison.
Brief of amici curiae filed on behalf of U.S. Senators Harry Reid et al. by Mitchell Y. Mirviss and Maria E. Rodriguez.
Brief of amici curiae filed on behalf of F Teach for America et al. by Errol B. Taylor, Patricia Astorga, Christopher Delaubenfels, and Christopher Almon.
Brief of amici curiae filed on behalf of the American Association for Access, Equity and Diversity et al. by Dean Sparlin, Marilynn L. Schuyler, Joseph D. Weiner, Michael L. Childers, Emily A. Mcnee, and Matthew J. Camardella.
Brief of amici curiae filed on behalf of Anti-Defamation League by Steven M. Freeman, Seth M. Marnin, Cheryl R. Drazin, Mark S. Finkelstein, Lisa H. Bebchick, and Samuel P. Groner.
Brief of amici curiae filed on behalf of the American Bar Association by Theodore V. Wells, Jr., Sidney S. Rosdeitcher, Jaren Janghorbani, Jennifer H. Wu, Yahonnes Cleary, and Paulette Brown urging affirmance.
Brief of amici curiae filed on behalf of Religious Organizations and Campus Ministries et al. by Annan Finch and Melissa Hart.
Brief of amici curiae filed on behalf of the University of Michigan by Timothy G. Lynch, Maya R. Kobersy, John P. Elwood, and Gregory F. Miller.
Brief of amici curiae filed on behalf of 39 Undergraduate and Graduate Student Organizations Within the University of California by Kimberly Thomas Rapp, Keith Wurster, Travis

Silva, Monte Cooper, Robert A. Rosenfeld, Andrew Ardinger, Amisha R. Patel, and Naomi J. Mower.

Brief of amici curiae filed on behalf of Six Educational Nonprofit Organizations by Lawrence S. Lustberg and Avram D. Frey.

Brief of amici curiae filed on behalf of the Asian American Legal Defense and Education Fund et al. by Kenneth Kimerling, Margaret Fung, Dean Richlin, Hemmie Chang, Catherine Deneke, Sarah Burg, Alice Yu, and Amanda Hainsworth.

Brief of amici curiae filed on behalf of Dean Robert Post by Carter G. Phillips, Joseph R. Guerra, Joshua J. Fougere, and Nicholas J. Giles.

Brief of amici curiae filed on behalf of the National School Boards Association et al. by Francisco M. Negrón, Jr., Naomi Gittins, Pratik A. Shah, Hyland Hunt, and Adam N. Tabor.

Brief of amici curiae filed on behalf of the State of Massachusetts et al. by Maura Healey, Attorney General of Massachusetts, Elizabeth N. Dewar, Assistant State Solicitor, by Genevieve C. Nadeau, Jared Rinehimer, Kimberly Strovink, and Max Weinstein, Assistant Attorneys General, and by the Attorneys General for their respective jurisdictions as follows: George Jepsen of Connecticut, Matthew P. Denn of Delaware, Karl A. Racine of the District of Columbia, Douglas S. Chin of Hawaii, Lisa Madigan of Illinois, Tom Miller of Iowa, Janet T. Mills of Maine, Brian E. Frosh of Maryland, Jim Hood of Mississippi, Hector H. Balderas of New Mexico, Eric T. Schneiderman of New York, Roy Cooper of North Carolina, Ellen F. Rosenblum of Oregon, Peter F. Kilmartin of Rhode Island, William H. Sorrell of Vermont, Mark R. Herring of Virginia, and Robert W. Ferguson of Washington.

Brief of amici curiae filed on behalf of Experimental Psychologists by Jerry Kang, John V. Wintermute, and Rachel D. Godsil.

Brief of amici curiae filed on behalf of David Boyle by Mr. Boyle.

Brief of amici curiae filed on behalf of Boston Bar Association et al. by Jonathan M. Albano.

Brief of amici curiae filed on behalf of Cecilia Polanco et al. by Jon M. Greenbaum, Brenda Shum, Jack Holtzman, Christine Bischof, Reed N. Colfax, and Laura Arandes.

Brief of amici curiae filed on behalf of Social and Organizational Psychologists by Eva Paterson, Allison S. Elgart, David J. Berger, Lisa A. Davis, David A. Brown, and Stephen Menendian.

Brief of amici curiae filed on behalf of National Women's Law Center et al. by Marcia D. Greenberger, Emily J. Martin, Fatima Goss Graves, Mary L. Bonauto, Susan L. Sommer, Charles A. Rothfeld, Andrew J. Pincus, Paul W. Hughes, Michael B. Kimberly, and Eugene R. Fidell.

Brief of amici curiae filed on behalf of Lt. Gen. Julius W. Becton, Jr., et al. by Joe R. Reeder, Robert P. Charrow, Michael M. Purpura, and Kenji M. Price.

Brief of amici curiae filed on behalf of the Leadership Conference on Civil and Human Rights et al. by Wade Henderson, Lisa M. Bornstein, Richard Cohen, Rhonda Brownstein, Brigida Benitez, and Kathryn J. Gainey.

Brief of amici curiae filed on behalf of Members of Asian Americans Advancing Justice et al. by Albert Giang, Andrew Esbenshade, Laboni A. Hoq, and Nicole Gon Ochi.

Brief of amici curiae filed on behalf of National and Texas Latino Organizations by Marisa Bono, Celina Moreno, John Paul Salmon, Juan Cartagena, and Joanna Elise Cuevas Ingram.

Brief of amici curiae filed on behalf of Legal Scholars Defending Diversity in Higher Education by Shakira D. Pleasant and Vinay Harpalani.

Opposing Side (Petitioner / Appellant)

Brief of amici curiae filed on behalf of Jonathan Zell by Mr. Zell.

Brief of amici curiae filed on behalf of the Center for Individual Rights by Michael E. Rosman.

Brief of amici curiae filed on behalf of Gail Heriot et al. by Ms. Heriot and Peter N. Kirsanow.

Brief of amici curiae filed on behalf of the Cato Institute by Ilya Shapiro, David B. Rivkin, Jr., Andrew M. Grossman, and Mark W. Delaquil.

Brief of amici curiae filed on behalf of the American Center for Law and Justice by Jay Alan Sekulow, Stuart J. Roth, Colby M. May, and Walter M. Weber.

Brief of amici curiae filed on behalf of California Association of Scholars by John C. Eastman, Anthony T. Caso, and Cristen A. Wohlgemuth.

Brief of amici curiae filed on behalf of the Asian American Legal Foundation et al. by John C. Eastman, Lee C. Cheng, Alan Tse, Gordon M. Fauth, Jr., and Rosanne L. Mah.

Brief of amici curiae filed on behalf of the Judicial Education Project by Carrie Severino, Bradley A. Benbrook, and Stephen M. Duvernay.

Brief of amici curiae filed on behalf of Southeastern Legal Foundation by Kimberly Stewart Hermann and John J. Park, Jr.

Brief of amici curiae filed on behalf of Mountain States Legal Foundation by Steven J. Lechner and Jeffrey W. McCoy.

Brief of amici curiae filed on behalf of Indiana Tech Law School Amicus Project by Adam Lamparello.

Brief of amici curiae filed on behalf of Judicial Watch, Inc., by Paul J. Orfanedes and Chris Fedeli.

Brief of amici curiae filed on behalf of James F. Blumstein by Mr. Blumstein.

Brief of amici curiae filed on behalf of Pacific Legal Foundation by Meriem L. Hubbard, Joshua P. Thompson, and Wencong Fa.

Brief of amici curiae filed on behalf of David Orentlicher by Mr. Orentlicher in support of neither party.

Brief of amici curiae filed on behalf of Richard D. Kahlenberg by Meredith B. Parenti in support of neither party.

IV. THE SUPREME COURT'S DECISION

"[P]etitioner makes four arguments. First, she argues that the University has not articulated its compelling interest with sufficient clarity. . . .

Petitioner's contention that the University's goal was insufficiently concrete is rebutted by the record.

Second, petitioner argues that the University has no need to consider race because it had already 'achieved critical mass' by

2003 using the Top Ten Percent Plan and race-neutral holistic review. . . .

Though a college must continually reassess . . . , here that assessment appears to have been done with care, and a reasonable determination was made that the University had not yet attained its goals.

Third, petitioner argues that considering race was not necessary because such consideration has had only a "minimal impact' in advancing the [University's] compelling interest.' . . .

The fact that race consciousness played a role in only a small portion of admissions decisions should be a hallmark of narrow tailoring, not evidence of unconstitutionality.

Petitioner's final argument is that 'there are numerous other available race-neutral means of achieving' the University's compelling interest. [H]owever, . . . at the time of petitioner's application, none of her proposed alternatives was a workable means for the University to attain the benefits of diversity it sought. . . .

Petitioner's final suggestion is to uncap the Top Ten Percent Plan, and admit more—if not all—the University's students through a percentage plan. As an initial matter, petitioner overlooks the fact that the Top Ten Percent Plan, though facially neutral, cannot be understood apart from its basic purpose, which is to boost minority enrollment. . . .

[A]lthough it may be true that the Top Ten Percent Plan in some instances may provide a path out of poverty for those who excel at schools lacking in resources, the Plan cannot serve as the admissions solution that petitioner suggests. . . .

In short, none of petitioner's suggested alternatives—nor other proposals considered or discussed in the course of this litigation—have been shown to be 'available' and 'workable' means through which the University could have met its educational goals, as it understood and defined them in 2008. The University has thus met its burden of showing that the admissions policy it used at the time it rejected petitioner's application was narrowly tailored. . . .

The Court's affirmance of the University's admissions policy today does not necessarily mean the University may rely on that same policy without refinement. It is the University's ongoing obligation to engage in constant deliberation and continued reflection regarding its admissions policies.

The judgment of the Court of Appeals is affirmed."

V. JUSTICE VOTE

4 Pro ACLU Side vs. 3 Con Opposing Side

ACLU Side (Respondent / Appellee)

1. Kennedy, A. – Wrote majority opinion
2. Breyer, S. – Joined majority opinion
3. Ginsburg, R. – Joined majority opinion
4. Sotomayor, S. – Joined majority opinion

Opposing Side (Petitioner / Appellant)

1. Alito, S. – Wrote dissenting opinion
2. Thomas, C. – Wrote dissenting opinion, joined Alito's dissent
3. Roberts, J. – Joined Alito's dissent

Kagan, E. – Took no part in the decision.

Vacant Seat

VI. A WIN OR LOSS FOR THE ACLU?

The ACLU filed as amicus curiae urging affirmance; the Supreme Court affirmed the Court of Appeals' decision by a 4-3 vote, giving the ACLU an apparent win.

1152. Whole Woman's Health v. Hellerstedt

(Decided June 27, 2016; 136 S.Ct. 2292; 579 U.S. _)

I. ISSUE

A. Issues Discussed

Privacy

B. Legal Question Presented

"[W]hether two provisions of Texas' House Bill 2 violate the Federal Constitution as interpreted in Casey."

C. Supreme Court's Answer

"We conclude that neither of these provisions confers medical benefits sufficient to justify the burdens upon access that each imposes. Each places a substantial obstacle in the path of women seeking a previability abortion, each constitutes an undue burden on abortion access, and each violates the Federal Constitution."

II. CASE SUMMARY

A. Background

"In July 2013, the Texas Legislature enacted House Bill 2 . . . . In September (before the new law took effect), a group of Texas abortion providers filed an action . . . seeking facial invalidation of the law's admitting-privileges provision. In late October, the District Court granted the injunction. But three days later, the Fifth Circuit vacated the injunction . . . .

The Fifth Circuit subsequently upheld the provision . . . .

On April 6, one week after the Fifth Circuit's decision, petitioners, a group of abortion providers . . . filed the present lawsuit . . . . They sought an injunction preventing enforcement of the admitting-privileges provision as applied to physicians at two abortion facilities . . . . They also sought an injunction prohibiting enforcement of the surgical-center provision . . . . They claimed that the admitting-privileges provision and the surgical-center provision violated the Constitution's Fourteenth Amendment, as interpreted in Casey. . . .

[T]he District Court determined that the surgical-center requirement 'imposes an undue burden on the right of women . . . to seek a previability abortion,' and that the 'admitting-privileges requirement, . . . in conjunction with the ambulatory-surgical-center requirement, imposes an undue burden on the right of women . . . to seek a previability abortion.' . . . On August 29, 2014, the court enjoined the enforcement of the two provisions. . . .

On October 2, 2014, . . . the Court of Appeals stayed the District Court's injunction. Within the next two weeks, this Court vacated the Court of Appeals' stay . . . thereby leaving in effect the District Court's injunction . . . . The Court of Appeals then heard Texas' appeal.

On June 9, 2015, the Court of Appeals reversed the District Court on the merits."

The Supreme Court granted certiorari to review the case.

B. Counsel of Record / ACLU Attorney

ACLU Side (Petitioner / Appellant): Stephanie Toti argued the cause for appellants. With her on the brief were J. Alexander Lawrence, Marc A. Hearron, Jan Soifer, Patrick J. O'Connell, David Brown, Janet Crepps, Julie Rikelman, and Leah M. Litman.

Solicitor General Verrilli argued the cause for the United States as amicus curiae.

Opposing Side (Respondent / Appellee): Scott A. Keller argued the cause for appellee. With him on the brief were Ken Paxton, Attorney General of Texas, Charles E. Roy, First Assistant Attorney General, Scott A. Keller, Solicitor General, J. Campbell Barker, Deputy Solicitor General, and Beth Klusmann and Michael P. Murphy, Assistant Solicitors General.

III. AMICI CURIAE

ACLU Side (Petitioner / Appellant)

Brief of amici curiae filed on behalf of the American Civil Liberties Union, the ACLU of Alabama, and the ACLU of Wisconsin by Randall C. Marshall, Laurence J. Dupuis, Andrew D. Beck, Jennifer Dalven, and Steven R. Shapiro.

Brief of amici curiae filed on behalf of the United States by Solicitor General Verrilli, Principal Deputy Assistant Attorney General Mizer, Deputy Solicitor General Gershengorn, Assistant Solicitor General Goldenberg, Douglas N. Letter, Mark B. Stern, Alisa B. Klein, and William E. Havemann.

Brief of amici curiae filed on behalf of Theologians and Ethicists by Craig E. Countryman, Caroline K. Simons, James N. Sebel, and Holly K. Victorson.

Brief of amici curiae filed on behalf of Kate Banfield et al. by Michael J. Dell, Scott Ruskay-Kidd, and Sarah C. White.

Brief of amici curiae filed on behalf of Law Professors Melissa Murray et al. by Daralyn J. Durie and Alexandra H. Moss.

Brief of amici curiae filed on behalf of Republican Majority for Choice et al. by Catherine M. Foti, Robert M. Radick, and Ashley C. Burns.

Brief of amici curiae filed on behalf of Health Economists by Asim M. Bhansali and Paven Malhotra.

Brief of amici curiae filed on behalf of Advocates for Youth by Abbey J. Marr, Christopher J. Wright, Elizabeth Austin Bonner, and Elizabeth B. Uzelac.

Brief of amici curiae filed on behalf of Experts in Health Policy by Judith L. Lichtman, Sarah Lipton-Lubet, Deanne K. Cevasco, Michael Y. Jo, Justin Florence, Aaron M. Katz, and Carolyn L. Redding.

Brief of amici curiae filed on behalf of Institute for Women's Policy Research et al. by Susan J. Kohlmann, Katya Jestin, Alison I. Stein, and Matthew S. Hellman.

Brief of amici curiae filed on behalf of Constitutional Accountability Center by Elizabeth B. Wydra, David H. Gans, and Brianne J. Gorod.

Brief of amici curiae filed on behalf of Jane's Due Process, Inc., by Susan Hays.

Brief of amici curiae filed on behalf of Public Health Deans, Department Chairs, and Faculty et al. by Shannon Rose Selden, Kaitlin T. Farrell, and Holly S. Norgard.

Brief of amici curiae filed on behalf of National Physicians Alliance et al. by Boris Bershteyn, Michael K. Krouse, Daniel G. Dobies, Sara Haji, and Stefanie E. Neale.

Brief of amici curiae filed on behalf of Scientists et al. by Nicholas J. Little, Ronald A. Lindsay, and Edward Tabash.

Brief of amici curiae filed on behalf of Society of Hospital Medicine et al. by Clifton S. Elgarten, Keith J. Harrison, and A. Xavier Baker.

Brief of amici curiae filed on behalf of Social Science Researchers by Anton Metlitsky, Walter Dellinger, Darcy M. Meals, and Jeremy R. Girton.

Brief of amici curiae filed on behalf of American College of Obstetricians and Gynecologists et a. by Kimberly A. Parker, Sonya L. Lebsack, Skye L. Perryman, and Jessica E. Notebaert.

Brief of amici curiae filed on behalf of Constitutional Law Scholars Ashutosh Bhagwat et al. by Geoffrey R. Stone, Gillian E. Metzger, and Lori Alvino McGill.

Brief of amici curiae filed on behalf of the Texas Association Against Sexual Assault et al. by Christopher Kaiser, Lisa Hill Fenning, Paul Rodney, Hannah Sibiski, and Sarah Warlick.

Brief of amici curiae filed on behalf of National Network of Abortion Funds et al. by Matthew S. Trokenheim, Allen G. Reiter, and Meera Chandramouli.

Brief of amici curiae filed on behalf of Janice Macavoy et al. by Allan J. Arffa, Alexia D. Korberg, Brian K. Steinwascher, and Rebecca L. Orel.

Brief of amici curiae filed on behalf of the New York City Bar Association by Katharine ES Bodde.

Brief of amici curiae filed on behalf of Information Society Project at Yale Law School by Priscilla J. Smith.

Brief of amici curiae filed on behalf of National Abortion Federation by Lisa M. Brown, Heather D. Shumaker, Janice M. Mac Avoy, Stephen M. Juris, Jennifer L. Colyer, Jesse R. Loffler, and Andrew B. Cashmore.

Brief of amici curiae filed on behalf of Physicians for Reproductive Health by Thomas M. Bondy, Susannah Landes Weaver, E. Joshua Rosenkranz, and Sarah M. Sternlieb.

Brief of amici curiae filed on behalf of Lambda Legal Defense and Education Fund, Inc., et al. by Camilla B. Taylor, Kyle A. Palazzolo, Kara N. Ingelhart, Susan L. Sommer, Jennifer C. Pizer, and

Omar Gonzalez-Pagan.

Brief of amici curiae filed on behalf of 163 Members of Congress by Claude G. Szyfer, Robert Abrams, Joel T. Dodge, Julie L. Goldman, and Pamela S. Takefman.

Brief of amici curiae filed on behalf of the State of New York et al. by Eric T. Schneiderman, Attorney General of New York, Barbara D. Underwood, Solicitor General, Andrea Oser, Deputy Solicitor General, Claude S. Platton, Senior Assistant Solicitor General, and by the Attorneys General for their respective jurisdictions as follows: Kamala D. Harris of California, George Jepsen of Connecticut, Matthew P. Denn of

Delaware, Karl A. Racine of the District of Columbia, Douglas S. Chin of Hawaii, Lisa Madigan of Illinois, Tom Miller of Iowa, Janet T. Mills of Maine, Brian E. Frosh of Maryland, Maura Healey of Massachusetts, Ellen F. Rosenblum of Oregon, William H. Sorrell of Vermont, Mark R. Herring of Virginia, and Robert W. Ferguson of Washington.

Brief of amici curiae filed on behalf of Historians Eileen Boris, et al. by Kevin M. Fong and Christine A. Scheuneman.

Brief of amici curiae filed on behalf of Planned Parenthood Federation of America et al. by Carrie Y. Flaxman and Helene T. Krasnoff.

Brief of amici curiae filed on behalf of National Women's Law Center et al. by Mary Beth Forshaw, Jayma M. Meyer, Isaac M. Rethy, Michelle S. Kallen, Marcia D. Greenberger, Gretchen Borchelt, Emily J. Martin, and Rachel Easter.

Brief of amici curiae filed on behalf of National Center for Lesbian Rights et al. by Shannon Minter, Julianna S. Gonen, Amy Whelan, Christopher F. Stoll, Sanford Jay Rosen, and Margot Mendelson urging reversal.

Brief of amici curiae filed on behalf of Twelve Organizations Dedicated to the Fight for Reproductive Justice by Wesley R. Powell, Mary J. Eaton, Timothy J. Mcginn, Sarah M. Wastler, Lara S. Kasten, and Allison R. Klein.

Brief of amici curiae filed on behalf of National Latina Institute for Reproductive Health et al. By Ana Rodriguez Defrates, Madeline M. Gomez, Timothy P. Harkness, Freshfields Bruckhaus, and Cynthia Soohoo.

Brief of amici curiae filed on behalf of Experts and Organizations Supporting Survivors of Intimate Partner Violence by Jill D. Bowman, Sara L. Ainsworth, Lisa M. Stone, and David Ward.

Brief of amici curiae filed on behalf of Medical Staff Professionals by Philip H. Lebowitz, Erin M. Duffy, Katharyn I. Christian Mcgee, Alison Taylor Rosenblum, and Erica Fruiterman.

Brief of amici curiae filed on behalf of the Honorable Wendy Davis et al. by Rani Habash and Linda C. Goldstein.

Brief of amici curiae filed on behalf of Ten Pennsylvania Abortion Care Providers David S. Cohen, Thomas E. Zemaitis, Susan J. Frietsche, and Tara R. Pfeifer.

Brief of amici curiae filed on behalf of Judson Memorial Church et al. by Eugene M. Gelernter and Sheng T. Li.

Brief of amici curiae filed on behalf of Freedom and Individual Rights in Medicine (FIRM) et al. by Atara Miller and Erin Culbertson.

Brief of amici curiae filed on behalf of National Advocates for Pregnant Women et al. by Sarah E. Burns, Sarah Samuels Wheeler, Lynn M. Paltrow, and Laura A. Hecht-Felella.

Brief of amici curiae filed on behalf of the City of New York et al. by Zachary W. Carter, Corporation Counsel, Richard Dearing, Cecelia Chang, Jane L. Gordon, and Devin Slack.

Brief of amici curiae filed on behalf of Service Women's Action Network et al. by Agnès Dunogué, Laura Caldwell, and Jae Young Jeong.

Brief of amici curiae filed on behalf of Business Leaders by Alan S. Gilbert, Leah R. Bruno, Shannon Y. Shin, and Jacqueline A. Giannini.

Opposing Side (Respondent / Appellee)

Brief of amici curiae filed on behalf of National Right to Life Committee by James Bopp, Jr. and Richard E. Coleson.

Brief of amici curiae filed on behalf of University Faculty for Life et al. by Jonathan F. Mitchell.

Brief of amici curiae filed on behalf of Former Abortion Providers by Linda Boston Schlueter.

Brief of amici curiae filed on behalf of the State of Wisconsin by Brad D. Schimel, Attorney General of Wisconsin, Misha Tseytlin, Solicitor General, and Daniel P. Lennington and Luke N. Berg, Deputy Solicitors

General.

Brief of amici curiae filed on behalf of Right to Life Advocates, Inc., by Richard W. Schmude.

Brief of amici curiae filed on behalf of United States Conference of Catholic Bishops et al. by Anthony R. Picarello, Jr., Jeffrey Hunter Moon, and Michael F. Moses.

Brief of amici curiae filed on behalf of The American Center for Law and Justice et al. by Thomas P. Monaghan, Francis J. Manion, Cece Heil, Geoffrey R. Surtees, Jay Alan Sekulow, Stuart J. Roth, Colby M. May, and Walter M. Weber.

Brief of amici curiae filed on behalf of Legal Center for Defense of Life by Andrew L. Schlafly.

Brief of amici curiae filed on behalf of 3,348 Women Injured by Abortion et al. by Allan E. Parker, Jr., R. Clayton Trotter, and Kathleen Cassidy Goodman.

Brief of amici curiae filed on behalf of Democrats for Life et al. by Steven W. Fitschen.

Brief of amici curiae filed on behalf of Justice and Freedom Fund by James L. Hirsen and Deborah J. Dewart.

Brief of amici curiae filed on behalf of Priests for Life by Robert Joseph Muise and David Yerushalmi.

Brief of amici curiae filed on behalf of Live Action by Stephen L. Braga.

Brief of amici curiae filed on behalf of Texas Eagle Forum et al. by Lawrence J. Joseph.

Brief of amici curiae filed on behalf of American Association of Pro-Life Obstetricians and Gynecologists et al. by David A. Cortman, Kevin H. Theriot, and Steven H. Aden.

Brief of amici curiae filed on behalf of Illinois Right to Life by Thomas L. Brejcha and Jocelyn Floyd.

Brief of amici curiae filed on behalf of More Than 450 Bipartisan and Bicameral State Legislators and Lieutenant Governors by Denise M. Burke, Mailee R. Smith, Nikolas T. Nikas, and Dorinda C. Bordlee.

Brief of amici curiae filed on behalf of Physicians with Experience Treating Women in Rural or Emergency Settings by Teresa Stanton Collett.

Brief of amici curiae filed on behalf of 174 United States Senators and Members of the United States House of Representatives by Charles J. Cooper, Howard C. Nielson Jr., and Brian W. Barnes.

Brief of amici curiae filed on behalf of Center for Constitutional Jurisprudence et al. by Joshua Hawley, Erin Hawley, Kimberlee Colby, Michael K. Whitehead, Jonathan R. Whitehead, John C. Eastman, Anthony T. Caso, and Cristen Wohlgemuth.

Brief of amici curiae filed on behalf of

Bipartisan and Bicameral Coalition of 121 Texas Legislators by Erin Glenn Busby, Michelle S. Stratton, and Craig Enoch.

Brief of amici curiae filed on behalf of CatholicVote.org Legal Defense Fund et al. by Stephen G. Gilles.

Brief of amici curiae filed on behalf of 24 Scholars of Federalism by D. John Sauer, Mary Catherine Hodes, and Michael C. Martinich-Sauter.

Brief of amici curiae filed on behalf of Operation Rescue et al. by Mathew D. Staver, Anita L. Staver, Horatio G. Mihet, and Mary E. McAlister.

Brief of amici curiae filed on behalf of the State of Indiana et al. by Gregory F. Zoeller, Attorney General of Indiana, Thomas M. Fisher, Solicitor General, Jonathan Sichtermann, Deputy Attorney General, Mike Dewine, Attorney General Of Ohio, Eric E. Murphy, State Solicitor, Stephen P. Carney and Peter T. Reed, Deputy Solicitors, and by the Attorneys General for their respective States as follows: Luther Strange of Alabama, Mark Brnovich of Arizona, Leslie Rutledge of Arkansas, Pamela Jo Bondi of Florida, Sam Olens of Georgia, Lawrence G. Wasden of Idaho, Derek Schmidt of Kansas, Jeff Landry of Louisiana, Bill Schuette of Michigan, Jim Hood of Mississippi, Tim Fox of Montana, Douglas J. Peterson of Nebraska, Adam Paul Laxalt of Nevada, Wayne Stenehjem of North Dakota, E. Scott Pruitt of Oklahoma, Alan Wilson of South Carolina, Marty J. Jackley of South Dakota, Herbert H. Slatery III of Tennessee, Sean Reyes of Utah, Patrick Morrisey of West Virginia, and Peter K. Michael of Wyoming.

Brief of amici curiae filed on behalf of Texas Values et al. by Jonathan M. Saenz, David S. Lill, and Cleta Mitchell.

Brief of amici curiae filed on behalf of Association of American Physicians and Surgeons, Inc., by Gene C. Schaerr and S. Kyle Duncan.

Brief of amici curiae filed on behalf of CitizenLink et al. by Randall L. Wenger and Jeremy L. Samek.

Brief of amici curiae filed on behalf of And Then There Were None by Stephen Casey.

Brief of amici curiae filed on behalf of Conservative Legal Defense and Education Fund et al. by Michael Connelly, William J. Olson, Herbert W. Titus, Jeremiah L. Morgan, and J. Mark Brewer.

Brief of amici curiae filed on behalf of David Boyle by Mr. Boyle.

Brief of amici curiae filed on behalf of African-American and Hispanic-American Organizations by Morse Tan.

Brief of amici curiae filed on behalf of the Governors of Texas et al. by Greg Abbott, Governor of Texas, James D. Blacklock, Kim K. Reynolds, Lt. Governor of Iowa, and by the Governors of their respective States as follows: Robert Bentley of Alabama, Asa Hutchinson of Arkansas, Terry E. Branstad of Iowa, Matthew G. Bevin of Kentucky, John Bel Edwards of Louisiana, Paul R. LePage of Maine, Phil Bryant of Mississippi, Pete Ricketts of Nebraska, and Dennis M. Gaugaard of South Dakota.

Brief of amici curiae filed on behalf of Concerned Women for America by Kenneth A. Klukowski.

Brief of amici curiae filed on behalf of the Legal Defense for Unborn Children by Alan Ernest in support of neither party.

Brief of amici curiae filed on behalf of Facility Guidelines Institute by Charles A. Sims, Edward S. Kornreich, Andrew S. Wellin, Julia B. Bienstock, and Walter Vernon in support of neither party.

IV. THE SUPREME COURT'S DECISION

"Before turning to the constitutional question, we must consider the Court of Appeals' procedural grounds for holding that (but for the challenge to the provisions of H.B. 2 as applied to McAllen and El Paso) petitioners were barred from bringing their constitutional challenges. . . .

In sum, . . . none of petitioners' claims are barred by res judicata. [W]e conclude that the Court of Appeals' procedural ruling was incorrect. . . . We consequently proceed to consider the merits of petitioners' claims. . . .

Unlike in Gonzales, the relevant statute here does not set forth any legislative findings. Rather, one is left to infer that the legislature sought to further a constitutionally acceptable objective (namely, protecting women's health). For a district court to give significant weight to evidence in the judicial record in these circumstances is consistent with this Court's case law. [T]he District Court did so here. It did not simply substitute its own judgment for that of the legislature. It considered the evidence in the record . . . . It then weighed the asserted benefits against the burdens. We hold that, in so doing, the District Court applied the correct legal standard. . . .

Pre-existing Texas law already contained numerous detailed regulations covering abortion facilities, including a requirement that facilities be inspected at least annually. The record contains nothing to suggest that H.B. 2 would be more effective than pre-existing Texas law at deterring wrongdoers . . . from criminal behavior. . . .

We agree with the District Court that the surgical-center requirement, like the admitting-privileges requirement, provides few, if any, health benefits for women, poses a substantial obstacle to women seeking abortions, and constitutes an 'undue burden' on their constitutional right to do so. . . .

We consider three additional arguments that Texas makes and deem none persuasive. . . .

[T]he judgment of the Court of Appeals is reversed, and the case is remanded . . . ."

V. JUSTICE VOTE

5 Pro ACLU Side vs. 3 Con Opposing Side

ACLU Side (Petitioner / Appellant)

1. Breyer, S. – Wrote majority opinion
2. Kagan, E. – Joined majority opinion
3. Kennedy, A. – Joined majority opinion
4. Ginsburg, R. – Wrote concurring opinion
5. Sotomayor, S. – Joined majority opinion

Opposing Side (Respondent / Appellee)

1. Alito, S. – Wrote dissenting opinion
2. Thomas, C. – Wrote dissenting opinion, joined Alito's dissent
3. Roberts, J. – Joined Alito's dissent

Vacant Seat

VI. A WIN OR LOSS FOR THE ACLU?

The ACLU filed as amicus curiae urging reversal of the judgment of the Court of Appeals; the Supreme Court reversed in a 5-3 vote, giving the ACLU an apparent win.

1153. Fry v. Napoleon Community Schools

(Decided February 22, 2017; 137 S.Ct. 743; 580 U.S. _)

I. ISSUE

A. Issues Discussed

Civil rights, federal, regulation

B. Legal Question Presented

"The Individuals with Disabilities Education Act . . . ensures that children with disabilities receive needed special education services. One of its provisions, § 1415(l), addresses the Act's relationship with other laws protecting those children. Section 1415(l) makes clear that nothing in the IDEA 'restrict[s] or limit[s] the rights [or] remedies' that other federal laws . . . confer . . . . At the same time, the section states that if a suit brought under such a law 'seek[s] relief that is also available under' the IDEA, the plaintiff must first exhaust the IDEA's administrative procedures. In this case, we consider the scope of that exhaustion requirement."

C. Supreme Court's Answer

"We hold that exhaustion is not necessary when the gravamen of the plaintiff's suit is something other than the denial of the IDEA's core guarantee—what the Act calls a 'free appropriate public education.'"

II. CASE SUMMARY

A. Background

"E.F. is a child with a severe form of cerebral palsy . . . . When E.F. was five years old, her parents . . . obtained a trained service dog for her, as recommended by her pediatrician. The dog, a goldendoodle named Wonder, 'help[s E.F.] to live as independently as possible' . . . .

But when the Frys sought permission for Wonder to join E.F. in kindergarten, officials at Ezra Eby Elementary School refused the request. [T]he Frys . . . began homeschooling her.

[T]he Frys filed a complaint with the U.S. Department of Education's Office for Civil Rights . . . , charging . . . exclusion of E.F.'s service animal violated her rights . . . . OCR agreed. . . .

[S]chool officials at last agreed . . . . But . . . the Frys became concerned . . . . Accordingly, the Frys found a different public school . . . .

The Frys then filed this suit . . . .

The District Court granted the school districts' motion to dismiss the suit . . . . A divided panel of the Court of Appeals for the Sixth Circuit affirmed . . . ."

The Supreme Court granted certiorari to review the case.

B. Counsel of Record / ACLU Attorney

ACLU Side (Petitioner / Appellant): Samuel R. Bagenstos, Cooperating Attorney of the American Civil Liberties Union Fund of Michigan, argued the cause for appellant. With him on the brief were Jill M. Wheaton, James F. Hermon, Michael J. Steinberg of the American Civil Liberties Union, Fund of Michigan, and Steven R. Shapiro, Susan P. Mizner, and Claudia Center of the American Civil Liberties Union Foundation.

Assistant Solicitor General Martinez argued the cause for the United States as amicus curiae.

Opposing Side (Respondent / Appellee): Neal Kumar Katyal argued the cause for appellee. With him on the brief were Thomas P. Schmidt, Timothy J. Mullins, Kenneth B. Chapie, Eugene A. Sokoloff, and Mitchell P. Reich.

III. AMICI CURIAE

ACLU Side (Petitioner / Appellant)

Brief of amici curiae filed on behalf of Psychiatric Service Dog Partners, Inc., et al. by John J. Ensminger.

Brief of amici curiae filed on behalf of the United States by Acting Solicitor General Gershengorn, Principal Deputy Assistant Attorney General Gupta, Counselor to the Solicitor General Gornstein, Assistant Solicitor General Martinez, Sharon M. Mcgowan, Jennifer Levin Eichhorn, James Cole, Jr., General Counsel for the U.S. Department of Education, Francisco Lopez, Jessica Wolland, and Rhonda Weiss.

Brief of amici curiae filed on behalf of National Disability Rights Network et al. by Tauna M. Szymanski, Ronald M. Hager, Cliff Zucker, Laura J. Miller, and Samantha Crane.

Brief of amici curiae filed on behalf of Professor Thomas Hehir et al. by Ira A. Burnim, Lewis Bossing, Aaron M. Panner, Joshua Hafenbrack, and Frederick Gaston Hall.

Brief of amici curiae filed on behalf of the Council of Parent Attorneys and Advocates et al. by Alexis Casillas, Alice K. Nelson, Catherine Merino Reisman, Ellen Saideman, and Selene Almazan-Altobelli.

Brief of amici curiae filed on behalf of Hon. Lowell P. Weicker, Jr., by Arlene B. Mayerson, Sasha Samberg-Champion, and Michael G. Allen.

Brief of amici curiae filed on behalf of the States of Illinois of Minnesota by Lisa Madigan, Attorney General of Illinois, David Franklin, Solicitor General, Brett E. Legner, Deputy Solicitor General, Meghan P. Carter, Assistant Attorney General, and Lori Swanson, Attorney General of Minnesota.

Brief of amici curiae filed on behalf of Autism Speaks by Gary Mayerson, Jean Marie Brescia, Dan Unumb, and Caroline J. Heller.

Opposing Side (Respondent / Appellee)

Brief of amici curiae filed on behalf of National School Boards Association et al. by Francisco M. Negrón, Jr., Thomas B. Allen, W. Joseph Scholler, and Alexander L. Ewing.

IV. THE SUPREME COURT'S DECISION

"Section 1415(l) requires that a plaintiff exhaust the IDEA's procedures before filing an action under the ADA, the Rehabilitation Act, or similar laws when . . . her suit 'seek[s] relief that is also available' under the IDEA. We first hold that to meet that statutory standard, a suit must seek relief for the denial of a FAPE, because that is the only 'relief' the IDEA makes 'available.' We next conclude that in determining whether a suit indeed 'seeks' relief for such a denial, a court should look to the substance, or gravamen, of the plaintiff's complaint. . . .

In this Court, the parties have reached substantial agreement about what 'relief' the IDEA makes 'available' for children with disabilities—and about how the Sixth Circuit went wrong . . . .

[Section] 1415(l)'s exhaustion rule hinges on whether a lawsuit seeks relief for the denial of a free appropriate public education. If a lawsuit charges such a denial, the plaintiff cannot escape § 1415(l) merely by bringing her suit under a statute other than the IDEA . . . . Rather, that plaintiff must first submit her case to an IDEA hearing officer . . . . But if, in a suit brought under a different statute, . . . then exhaustion of the IDEA's procedures is not required. . . . A complaint seeking redress for . . . other harms, independent of any FAPE denial, is not subject to § 1415(l)'s exhaustion rule because, once again, the only 'relief' the IDEA makes 'available' is relief for the denial of a FAPE. . . .

Still, an important question remains: How is a court to tell when a plaintiff 'seeks' relief for the denial of a FAPE and when she does not? Here, too, the parties have found some common ground: By looking, they both say, to the 'substance' of, rather than the labels used in, the plaintiff's complaint. And here, too, we agree with that view: What matters is the crux—or, in legal-speak, the gravamen—of the plaintiff's complaint, setting aside any attempts at artful pleading. . . .

The Court of Appeals did not undertake the analysis we have just set forward. As noted above, it asked whether E.F.'s injuries were . . . 'educational' in nature. . . . That is not the same as asking whether the gravamen of E.F.'s complaint charges, and seeks relief for, the denial of a FAPE. . . . We lack some important information on that score, . . . so we remand the issue to the court below. . . .

[O]n remand, the court below should establish whether . . . the Frys invoked the IDEA's dispute resolution process before bringing . . . suit. [T]he court should decide whether their actions reveal that the gravamen of their complaint is . . . denial of a FAPE, thus necessitating further exhaustion.

With these instructions . . . , we vacate the judgment of the Court of Appeals and remand . . . ."

V. JUSTICE VOTE

8 Pro ACLU Side vs. 0 Con Opposing Side

ACLU Side (Petitioner / Appellant)

1. Kagan, E. – Wrote majority opinion
2. Alito, S. – Wrote concurring opinion
3. Thomas, C. – Joined Alito's concurrence
4. Breyer, S. – Joined majority opinion
5. Kennedy, A. – Joined majority opinion
6. Ginsburg, R. – Joined majority opinion
7. Sotomayor, S. – Joined majority opinion
8. Roberts, J. – Joined majority opinion

Vacant Seat

VI. A WIN OR LOSS FOR THE ACLU?

The ACLU argued the cause for appellant urging reversal of the judgment of the Court of Appeals; the Supreme Court vacated in an 8-0 vote, giving the ACLU an apparent win.

1154. Pena-Rodriguez v. Colorado

(Decided March 6, 2017; 137 S.Ct. 855; 580 U.S. _)

I. ISSUE

A. Issues Discussed

Race, criminal procedure

B. Legal Question Presented

"[W]hether there is an exception to the no-impeachment rule when, after the jury is discharged, a juror comes forward with compelling evidence that another juror made clear and explicit statements indicating that racial animus was a significant motivating factor in his or her vote to convict."

C. Supreme Court's Answer

"[T]he Court now holds that where a juror makes a clear statement that indicates he or she relied on racial stereotypes or animus to convict a criminal defendant, the Sixth Amendment requires that the no-impeachment rule give way in order to permit the trial court to consider the evidence of the juror's statement and any resulting denial of the jury trial guarantee."

II. CASE SUMMARY

A. Background

"The State charged petitioner with harassment, unlawful sexual contact, and attempted sexual assault on a child. Before the jury was empaneled, members of the venire were repeatedly asked whether they believed that they could be fair and impartial in the case. . . . None of the empaneled jurors expressed any reservations based on racial or any other bias. And none asked to speak with the trial judge.

After a 3-day trial, the jury found petitioner guilty of unlawful sexual contact and harassment, but it failed to reach a verdict on the attempted sexual assault charge. . . .

Following the discharge of the jury, petitioner's counsel entered the jury room to discuss the trial with the jurors. As the room was emptying, two jurors remained to speak with counsel in private. They stated that, during deliberations, another juror had expressed anti-Hispanic bias toward petitioner and petitioner's alibi witness. Petitioner's counsel reported this to the court and, with the court's supervision, obtained sworn affidavits from the two jurors. . . .

After reviewing the affidavits, the trial court acknowledged . . . apparent bias. But the court denied petitioner's motion for a new trial, noting that '[t]he actual deliberations that occur among the jurors are protected from inquiry under [Colorado Rule of Evidence] 606(b).' . . .

The verdict deemed final, petitioner was sentenced to two years' probation and was required to register as a sex offender. A divided panel of the Colorado Court of Appeals affirmed petitioner's conviction . . .

The Colorado Supreme Court affirmed by a vote of 4 to 3."

The Supreme Court granted certiorari to review the case.

B. Counsel of Record / ACLU Attorney

ACLU Side (Petitioner / Appellant): Jeffrey L. Fisher argued the cause for appellants. With him on the brief were Jonathan D. Rosen, Pamela S. Karlan, and Brian Wolfman.

Opposing Side (Respondent / Appellee): Frederick R. Yarger, Solicitor General of Colorado, argued the cause for appellee. With him on the brief were Cynthia H. Coffman, Attorney General of Colorado, L. Andrew Cooper, Deputy Attorney General, Glenn P. Roper, Deputy Solicitor General, Katharine J. Gillespie and Stephanie Lindquist Scoville, Senior Assistant Attorneys General, and Majid Yazdi and Molly E. McNab, Assistant Attorneys General.

Assistant to the Solicitor General Kovner argued the cause for the United States as amicus curiae.

III. AMICI CURIAE

ACLU Side (Petitioner / Appellant)

Brief of amici curiae filed on behalf of NAACP Legal Defense & Educational Fund, Inc., the National Association of Criminal Defense Lawyers, and the American Civil Liberties Union by Sherrilyn Ifill, John Paul Schnapper- Casteras, Janai Nelson, Christina Swarns, Jin Hee Lee, Liliana Zaragoza, R. Reeves Anderson, Holly E. Sterrett, Barbara Bergman, and Steven R. Shapiro.

Brief of amici curiae filed on behalf of the

United Mexican States by Gregory J. Kuykendall and Amy P. Knight.

Brief of amici curiae filed on behalf of Constitutional Accountability Center by Elizabeth B. Wydra, Brianne J. Gorod, and David H. Gans.

Brief of amici curiae filed on behalf of National Association of Federal Defenders by Donna F. Coltharp, Sarah S. Gannett, Daniel L. Kaplan, David A. Strauss, Sarah M. Konsky, Matthew S. Hellman, Josh M. Parker, and Michael A. Scodro.

Brief of amici curiae filed on behalf of Professors of Law by Lisa Kern Griffin and Marc A. Goldman.

Brief of amici curiae filed on behalf of Professor Cedric Merlin Powell of the Univesity of Louisville Brandeis School of Law by Junis L. Baldon, Mark A. Flores, and Miles R. Harrison.

Brief of amici curiae filed on behalf of the Hispanic National Bar Association by Robert T. Maldonado, Peter Karanjia, and Jason Harrow.

Brief of amici curiae filed on behalf of Center on the Administration of Criminal Law by Deborah L. Gramiccioni, David A. Barrett, Joshua J. Libling, and Yotam Barkai.

Opposing Side (Respondent / Appellee)

Brief of amici curiae filed on behalf of the United States by Acting Solicitor General Gershengorn, Assistant Attorney General Caldwell, Deputy Solicitor General Dreeben, Assistant to the Solicitor General Kovner, and William A. Glaser.

IV. THE SUPREME COURT'S DECISION

"Some version of the no-impeachment rule is followed in every State and the District of Columbia. . . .

This case lies at the intersection of the Court's decisions endorsing the no-impeachment rule and its decisions seeking to eliminate racial bias in the jury system. The two lines of precedent, however, need not conflict. . . .

[T]he Court now holds that where a juror makes a clear statement that indicates he or she relied on racial stereotypes or animus to convict a criminal defendant, the Sixth Amendment requires that the no-impeachment rule give way in order to permit the trial court to consider the evidence of the juror's statement and any resulting denial of the jury trial guarantee. . . .

To qualify, the statement must tend to show that racial animus was a significant motivating factor in the juror's vote to convict. Whether that threshold showing has been satisfied is a matter committed to the substantial discretion of the trial court in light of all the circumstances, including the content and timing of the alleged statements and the reliability of the proffered evidence.

The practical mechanics of acquiring and presenting such evidence will no doubt be shaped and guided by state rules of professional ethics and local court rules, both of which often limit counsel's post-trial contact with jurors. . . . These limits seek to provide jurors some protection when they return to their daily affairs after the verdict has been entered. But while a juror can always tell counsel they do not wish to discuss the case, jurors in some instances may come forward of their own accord.

That is what happened here. In this case the alleged statements by a juror were egregious and unmistakable in their reliance on racial bias. Not only did juror H.C. deploy a dangerous racial stereotype to conclude petitioner was guilty and his alibi witness should not be believed, but he also encouraged other jurors to join him in convicting on that basis. . . .

With the understanding that they were under no obligation to speak out, the jurors approached petitioner's counsel . . . to relay their concerns . . . . A similar pattern is common in cases involving juror allegations of racial bias. . . .

While the trial court concluded that Colorado's Rule 606(b) did not permit it even to consider the resulting affidavits, the Court's holding today removes that bar. When jurors disclose an instance of racial bias as serious as the one involved in this case, the law must not wholly disregard its occurrence. . . .

The judgment of the Supreme Court of Colorado is reversed, and the case is remanded . . . ."

V. JUSTICE VOTE

5 Pro ACLU Side vs. 3 Con Opposing Side

ACLU Side (Petitioner / Appellant)

1. Kennedy, A. – Wrote majority opinion

2. Kagan, E. – Joined majority opinion
3. Breyer, S. – Joined majority opinion
4. Ginsburg, R. – Joined majority opinion
5. Sotomayor, S. – Joined majority opinion

Opposing Side (Respondent / Appellee)

1. Alito, S. – Wrote dissenting opinion
2. Thomas, C. – Wrote dissenting opinion, joined Alito's dissent
3. Roberts, J. – Joined Alito's dissent

Vacant Seat

VI. A WIN OR LOSS FOR THE ACLU?

The ACLU filed as amicus curiae urging reversal of the judgment of the Supreme Court of Colorado; the U.S. Supreme Court reversed in a 5-3 vote, giving the ACLU an apparent win.

1155. Moore v. Texas

(Decided March 28, 2017; 137 S.Ct. 1039; 581 U.S. _)

I. ISSUE

A. Issues Discussed

8th Amendment, death penalty

B. Legal Question Presented

"[W]hether the CCA's adherence to superseded medical standards and its reliance on Briseno comply with the Eighth Amendment and this Court's precedents."

C. Supreme Court's Answer

"As we instructed in Hall, adjudications of intellectual disability should be 'informed by the views of medical experts.' That instruction cannot sensibly be read to give courts leave to diminish the force of the medical community's consensus. Moreover, the several factors Briseno set out as indicators of intellectual disability are an invention of the CCA untied to any acknowledged source. Not aligned with the medical community's information, and drawing no strength from our precedent, the Briseno factors 'creat[e] an unacceptable risk that persons with intellectual disability will be executed.' Accordingly, they may not be used, as the CCA used them, to restrict qualification of an individual as intellectually disabled."

II. CASE SUMMARY

A. Background

"Bobby James Moore fatally shot a store clerk during a botched robbery. He was convicted of capital murder and sentenced to death. Moore challenged his death sentence on the ground that he was intellectually disabled and therefore exempt from execution. A state habeas court made detailed factfindings and determined that, under this Court's decisions . . . Moore qualified as intellectually disabled. For that reason, the court concluded, Moore's death sentence violated the Eighth Amendment's proscription of 'cruel and unusual punishments.' The habeas court therefore recommended that Moore be granted relief.

The Texas Court of Criminal Appeals (CCA) declined to adopt the judgment recommended by the state habeas court."

The Supreme Court granted certiorari to review the case.

B. Counsel of Record / ACLU Attorney

ACLU Side (Petitioner / Appellant): Clifford M. Sloan argued the cause for appellants. With him on the brief were Alex Blaszczuk, Peter Horn, Luke Varley, Lauryn K. Fraas, Donald P. Salzman, Michael A. McIntosh, and Brendan B. Gants.

Opposing Side (Respondent / Appellee): Scott A. Keller, Solicitor General of Texas, argued the cause for appellee. With him on the brief were Ken Paxton, Attorney General of Texas, Jeffrey C. Mateer, First Assistant Attorney General, Matthew H. Frederick, Deputy Solicitor General, and Rance Craft and Michael P. Murphy, Assistant Solicitors General.

III. AMICI CURIAE

ACLU Side (Petitioner / Appellant)

Brief of amici curiae filed on behalf of the American Civil Liberties Union and the ACLU of Texas by Jeffery P. Robinson, Rebecca L. Robertson, Brian W. Stull, Cassandra Stubbs, Anna Arceneaux, and Steven R. Shapiro.

Brief of amici curiae filed on behalf of International Organizations Interested in Medical Expertise, Psychiatry and Criminal Justice by Paul Hessler.

Brief of amici curiae filed on behalf of American Psychological Association et al. by Nathalie F. P. Gilfoyle, Deanne Ottaviano, Paul M. Smith, J. Douglas Wilson, and Emily A. Bruemmer.

Brief of amici curiae filed on behalf of the American Bar Association by Danielle Spinelli, Catherine M. A. Carroll, Ari J. Savitzky, Robbie Manhas, Paulette Brown.

Brief of amici curiae filed on behalf of the American Association on Intellectual and Developmental Disabilities (AAIDD) et al. by James W. Ellis, Ann M. Delpha, Carol M. Suzuki, Steven K. Homer, David J. Stout, and April Land.

Brief of amici curiae filed on behalf of the Constitution Project by Virginia E. Sloan, Sarah Turberville, Meir Feder, and Ian Samuel.

Opposing Side (Respondent / Appellee)

Brief of amici curiae filed on behalf of the State of Arizona et al. by Mark Brnovich, Attorney General of Arizona, John R. Lopez IV, Solicitor General, Lacey Stover Gard, Chief Counsel for the Capital Litigation Section, Jeffrey L. Sparks, Assistant Attorney General, and by the Attorneys General for their respective States as follows: Luther Strange of Alabama, Leslie Rutledge of Arkansas, Cynthia H. Coffman of Colorado, Pamela Jo Bondi of Florida, Sam Olens of Georgia, Lawrence G. Wasden of Idaho, Derek Schmidt of Kansas, Jeff Landry of Louisiana, Chris Koster of Missouri, Adam Paul Laxalt of Nevada, E. Scott Pruitt of Oklahoma, Bruce R. Beemer of Pennsylvania, Alan Wilson of South Carolina, Herbert H. Slatery III of Tennessee, and Sean D. Reyes of Utah.

Brief of amici curiae filed on behalf of the Criminal Justice Legal Foundation by Kent S. Scheidegger and Kymberlee Stapleton.

IV. THE SUPREME COURT'S DECISION

"The Eighth Amendment prohibits 'cruel and unusual punishments,' and 'reaffirms the duty of the government to respect the dignity of all persons.' . . .

In Atkins v. Virginia, we held that the Constitution 'restrict[s] . . . the State's power to take the life of' any intellectually disabled individual. . . .

In Hall v. Florida, we held that a State cannot refuse to entertain other evidence of intellectual disability when a defendant has an IQ score above 70. . . .

The CCA's conclusion that Moore's IQ scores established that he is not intellectually disabled is irreconcilable with Hall. Hall instructs that, where an IQ score is close to, but above, 70, courts must account for the test's 'standard error of measurement.' . . .

Moore's score of 74, adjusted for the standard error of measurement, yields a range of 69 to 79 . . . . Because the lower end of Moore's score range falls at or below 70, the CCA had to move on to consider Moore's adaptive functioning. . . .

The CCA's consideration of Moore's adaptive functioning also deviated from prevailing clinical standards and from the older clinical standards the court claimed to apply.

In concluding that Moore did not suffer significant adaptive deficits, the CCA overemphasized Moore's perceived adaptive strengths. . . .

The CCA furthermore concluded that Moore's record of academic failure, along with the childhood abuse and suffering he endured, detracted from a determination that his intellectual and adaptive deficits were related. Those traumatic experiences, however, count in the medical community as 'risk factors' for intellectual disability. . . .

The CCA also departed from clinical practice by requiring Moore to show that his adaptive deficits were not related to 'a personality disorder.' . . .

The CCA's attachment to the seven Briseno evidentiary factors further impeded its assessment of Moore's adaptive functioning. . . .

By rejecting the habeas court's application of medical guidance and clinging to the standard it laid out in Briseno, including the wholly nonclinical Briseno factors, the CCA failed adequately to inform itself of the 'medical community's diagnostic framework,' Because Briseno pervasively infected the CCA's analysis, the decision of that court cannot stand. . . .

[T]he judgment of the Texas Court of Criminal Appeals is vacated, and the case is remanded . . . ."

V. JUSTICE VOTE

5 Pro ACLU Side vs. 3 Con Opposing Side

ACLU Side (Petitioner / Appellant)

1. Ginsburg, R. – Wrote majority opinion
2. Kagan, E. – Joined majority opinion
3. Breyer, S. – Joined majority opinion
4. Kennedy, A. – Joined majority opinion
5. Sotomayor, S. – Joined majority opinion

Opposing Side (Respondent / Appellee)

1. Alito, S. – Joined Roberts' dissent
2. Thomas, C. – Joined Roberts' dissent
3. Roberts, J. – Wrote dissenting opinion

Vacant Seat

VI. A WIN OR LOSS FOR THE ACLU?

The ACLU filed as amicus curiae urging reversal of the judgment of the Texas Court of Criminal Appeals; the Supreme Court vacated in a 5-3 vote, giving the ACLU an apparent win.

1156. Bank of America Corp. v. City of Miami

(Decided May 1, 2017; 137 S.Ct. 1296; 581 U.S. _)

I. ISSUE

A. Issues Discussed

Race, federal

B. Legal Question Presented

"[W]hether, as the Court of Appeals had in effect held, the amended complaints satisfied the FHA's zone-of-interests and proximate-cause requirements."

C. Supreme Court's Answer

"We hold that the City's claimed injuries fall within the zone of interests that the FHA arguably protects. Hence, the City is an 'aggrieved person' able to bring suit under the statute. We also hold that, to establish proximate cause under the FHA, a plaintiff must do more than show that its injuries foreseeably flowed from the alleged statutory violation. The lower court decided these cases on the theory that foreseeability is all that the statute requires, so we vacate and remand for further proceedings."

II. CASE SUMMARY

A. Background

"The Fair Housing Act (FHA or Act) forbids [racially discriminatory housing practices.]

The statute allows any 'aggrieved person' to file a civil action seeking damages for a violation of the statute. And it defines an 'aggrieved person' to include 'any person who . . . claims to have been injured by a discriminatory housing practice.'

The City of Miami claims that two banks, Bank of America and Wells Fargo, intentionally issued riskier mortgages on less favorable terms to African-American and Latino customers than they issued to similarly situated white, non-Latino customers, in violation of §§ 3604(b) and 3605(a). . . . The City claims that those practices violate the FHA and that it is entitled to damages . . . .

The District Court dismissed the complaints on the grounds that (1) the harms alleged, being economic and not discriminatory, fell outside the zone of interests the FHA protects; (2) the complaints fail to show a sufficient causal connection between the City's injuries and the Banks' discriminatory conduct; and (3) the complaints fail to allege unlawful activity occurring within the

Act's 2-year statute of limitations. The City then filed amended complaints (the complaints now before us) and sought reconsideration. The District Court held that the amended complaints could solve only the statute of limitations problem. It consequently declined to reconsider the dismissals.

The Court of Appeals reversed the District Court."

The Supreme Court granted certiorari to review the case.

B. Counsel of Record

ACLU Side (Respondent / Appellee): Robert S. Peck argued the cause for appellee. With him on the briefs were Victoria Méndez, Henry J. Hunnefeld, Erwin Chemerinsky, Rachel Geman, Daniel E. Seltz, Joel Liberson, Howard Liberson, Sherrie R. Savett, Sarah R. Schalman-Bergen, and Patrick F. Madden. Curtis E. Gannon argued the cause for the United States as amici curiae.

Opposing Side (Petitioner / Appellant): Neal Kumar Katyal argued the cause for appellant. With her on the briefs were David J. Zimmer, William M. Jay, Thomas M. Hefferon, Matthew S. Sheldon, Andrew Kim, David S. Norris, Paul F. Hancock, Olivia Kelman, Andrew C. Glass, Frederick Liu, Colleen E. Roh Sinzdak, Morgan L. Goodspeed, Daniel J.T. Schuker, Carol A. Licko, and John F. O'Sullivan.

III. AMICI CURIAE

ACLU Side (Respondent / Appellee)

Brief of amici curiae filed on behalf of the Lawyers' Committee for Civil Rights Under Law and the National Fair Housing Alliance, et al., including the American Civil Liberties Union, by Joseph D. Rich, Thomas Silverstein, Morgan Williams, Joseph M. Sellers, Brian Corman, Steven R. Shapiro, Sandra S. Park, Rachel E. Goodman, Stuart T. Rossman, Philip D. Tegeler, Megan Haberle, Wade J. Henderson, Lisa M. Bornstein, Jocelyn Larkin, and Lindsay Nako.

Brief of amici curiae filed on behalf of the United States by Tonya Robinson, Michelle Aronowitz, Jeanine Worden, Kathleen Pennington, M. Casey Weissman-Vermeulen, Ayelet Weiss, Acting Solicitor General Ian Heath Gershengorn, Principal Deputy Assistant Attorney General Vanita Gupta, Counselor to the Solicitor General Irving L. Gornstein, Assistant to the Solicitor General Curtis E. Gannon, Sharon M. McGowan, and April J. Anderson.

Brief of amici curiae filed on behalf of the NAACP Legal Defense & Educational Fund, Inc., by Sherrilyn Ifill, Ajmel Quereshi, John Paul Schnapper-Casteras, Janai Nelson, Christina Swarns, and Liliana Zaragoza.

Brief of amici curiae filed on behalf of the Constitutional Accountability Center by Elizabeth B. Wydra, Brianne J. Gorod, David H. Gans, and Brian R. Frazelle.

Brief of amici curiae filed on behalf of the National Association of Counties et al. by Lisa Soronen, Deepak Gupta, Rachel S. Bloomekatz, and Matthew Spurlock.

Brief of amici curiae filed on behalf of Anita Trafficante et al. by John P. Relman, Sasha Samberg-Champion, Michael G. Allen, and Stephen M. Dane.

Brief of amici curiae filed on behalf of AARP et al. by William Alvarado Rivera and Susan Ann Silverstein.

Brief of amici curiae filed on behalf of the Fraternal Order of Police, Miami Lodge 20 et al. by Debra L. Greenberger, Diane L. Houk, Robert D. Klausner, and Richard A. Sicking.

Brief of amici curiae filed on behalf of Asian Americans Advancing Justice | AAJC et al. by Cecelia Chang, Eugene Chay, Juan Cartagena, Martha Padro, Jose L. Perez, and Karla McKanders.

Brief of amici curiae filed on behalf of the City and County of Los Angeles et al. by Michael N. Feuer, James P. Clark, Dennis J. Herrera, Christine Van Aken, and Aileen N. McGrath.

Brief of amici curiae filed on behalf of Housing Scholars by Justin Steil, Alan M. White, and Franklin Siegel.

Brief of amici curiae filed on behalf of Current and Former Members of Congress by Thomas J. Henderson, Saba Bireda, Felicia Gilbert, and James E. Richardson.

Opposing Side (Petitioner / Appellant)

Brief of amici curiae filed on behalf of the Chamber of Commerce of the United States of America et al. by Kate Comerford Todd, Steven P. Lehotsky, Colleen Reppen Shiel, H. Rodgin Cohen, John J. Liolos, Brent J. McIntosh, and Jeffrey B. Wall.

Brief of amici curiae filed on behalf of the American Bankers Association et al. by Robert A. Long, Jr., Andrew M. Smith, and David M. Zionts.

Brief of amici curiae filed on behalf of the Cato Institute by Thaya Brook Knight, Ilya Shapiro, and Steven G. Bradbury.

Brief of amici curiae filed on behalf of DRI–The Voice of the Defense Bar by Laura E. Proctor, Matthew T. Nelson, Gaëtan Gerville-Réache, and Carly A. Zagaroli.

IV. THE SUPREME COURT'S DECISION

"To satisfy the Constitution's restriction of this Court's jurisdiction to 'Cases' and 'Controversies,' a plaintiff must demonstrate constitutional standing. To do so, the plaintiff must show an 'injury in fact' that is 'fairly traceable' to the defendant's conduct and 'that is likely to be redressed by a favorable judicial decision.' This Court has also referred to a plaintiff's need to satisfy 'prudential' or 'statutory' standing requirements. . . . In answering that question, we presume that a statute ordinarily provides a cause of action 'only to plaintiffs whose interests fall within the zone of interests protected by the law invoked.' We have added that '[w]hether a plaintiff comes within 'the zone of interests' is an issue that requires us to determine, using traditional tools of statutory interpretation, whether a legislatively conferred cause of action encompasses a particular plaintiff's claim.'

Here, we conclude that the City's claims of financial injury in their amended complaints . . . satisfy the 'cause-of-action' (or 'prudential standing') requirement. . . .

The upshot is that the City alleges economic injuries that arguably fall within the FHA's zone of interests, as we have previously interpreted that statute. Principles of stare decisis compel our adherence to those precedents in this context. And principles of statutory interpretation require us to respect Congress' decision to ratify those precedents when it reenacted the relevant statutory text. . . .

The remaining question is one of causation: Did the Banks'

allegedly discriminatory lending practices proximately cause the City to lose property-tax revenue and spend more on municipal services? The Eleventh Circuit concluded that the answer is 'yes' because the City plausibly alleged that its financial injuries were foreseeable results of the Banks' misconduct. We conclude that foreseeability alone is not sufficient to establish proximate cause under the FHA, and therefore vacate the judgment below. . . .

We conclude that the Eleventh Circuit erred in holding that foreseeability is sufficient to establish proximate cause under the FHA. . . .

The parties have asked us to draw the precise boundaries of proximate cause under the FHA and to determine on which side of the line the City's financial injuries fall. We decline to do so. . . . The lower courts should define, in the first instance, the contours of proximate cause under the FHA and decide how that standard applies to the City's claims for lost property-tax revenue and increased municipal expenses. . . .

The judgments of the Court of Appeals for the Eleventh Circuit are vacated, and the cases are remanded . . . ."

V. JUSTICE VOTE

5 Pro ACLU Side vs. 3 Con Opposing Side

ACLU Side (Respondent / Appellee)

1. Breyer, S. – Wrote majority opinion
2. Kagan, E. – Joined majority opinion
3. Ginsburg, R. – Joined majority opinion
4. Sotomayor, S. – Joined majority opinion
5. Roberts, J. – Joined majority opinion

Opposing Side (Petitioner / Appellant)

1. Alito, S. – Joined Thomas' opinion
2. Thomas, C. – Wrote opinion concurring in part and dissenting in part
3. Kennedy, A. – Joined Thomas' opinion

Gorsuch, N. – Took no part in the decision.

VI. A WIN OR LOSS FOR THE ACLU?

The ACLU filed as amicus curiae urging affirmance; the Supreme Court vacated the Court of Appeals' decision by a 5-3 vote, giving the ACLU an apparent win.

1157. County of Los Angeles v. Mendez

(Decided May 30, 2017; 137 S.Ct. 1539; 581 U.S. _)

I. ISSUE

A. Issues Discussed

4th Amendment

B. Legal Question Presented

"If law enforcement officers make a 'seizure' of a person using force that is judged to be reasonable based on a consideration of the circumstances relevant to that determination, may the officers nevertheless be held liable for injuries caused by the seizure on the ground that they committed a separate Fourth Amendment violation that contributed to their need to use force?"

C. Supreme Court's Answer

"We hold that the Fourth Amendment provides no basis for such a rule. A different Fourth Amendment violation cannot transform a later, reasonable use of force into an unreasonable seizure."

II. CASE SUMMARY

A. Background

"[D]eputies from the Los Angeles County Sheriff's Department were searching for a parolee-at-large named Ronnie O'Dell. A felony arrest warrant had been issued for O'Dell . . . . The task force received word . . . O'Dell had been seen on a bicycle at a home in Lancaster, California, owned by Paula Hughes, and the officers then mapped out a plan for apprehending O'Dell. . . . During this briefing, it was announced that a man named Angel Mendez lived in the backyard . . . with . . . Jennifer Garcia (now Mrs. Jennifer Mendez). Deputy Pederson heard this announcement, but at trial Deputy Conley testified that he did not remember it. . . .

Deputies Conley and Pederson, with guns drawn, searched the rear of the residence . . . .

Mendez and Garcia were in the shack . . . napping . . . . The deputies did not have a search warrant and did not knock and announce . . . . When Deputy Conley opened the wooden door . . . , Mendez thought it was Ms. Hughes and rose from the bed, picking up [a] BB gun so he could stand up and place it on the floor. [When the deputies entered, he was holding the BB gun, and it was 'point[ing] somewhat south towards Deputy Conley.' Deputy Conley yelled, 'Gun!' and the deputies immediately opened fire, discharging a total of 15 rounds. Mendez and Garcia 'were shot multiple times and suffered severe injuries,' and Mendez's right leg was later amputated below the knee. O'Dell was not . . . anywhere on the property. . . .

Mendez and his wife . . . filed suit . . . against . . . the County of Los Angeles and Deputies Conley and Pederson. As relevant here, they pressed three Fourth Amendment claims. . . .

After a bench trial, the District Court ruled largely in favor of respondents. . . .

The Court of Appeals affirmed in part and reversed in part."

The Supreme Court granted certiorari to review the case.

B. Counsel of Record / ACLU Attorney

ACLU Side (Respondent / Appellee): Leonard Feldman argued the cause for appellee. With him on the briefs were Eric Schnapper, Rachel Lee, and Sara Berry.

Opposing Side (Petitioner / Appellant): E. Joshua Rosenkranz argued the cause for appellant. With him on the briefs were Mary C. Wickham, Rodrigo A. Castro-Silva, Jennifer Lehman, Thomas C. Hurrell, Melinda Cantrall, Thomas M. Bondy, Andrew D. Silverman, Matthew L. Bush, Cynthia B. Stein, Benjamin F. Aiken, and Logan Dwyer.

Assistant Solicitor General Saharsky argued the cause for the United States as amicus curiae.

III. AMICI CURIAE

ACLU Side (Respondent / Appellee)

Brief of amici curiae filed on behalf of the American Civil Liberties Union and the ACLU of Southern California by Peter Bibring, Adrienna Wong, Melanie P. Ochoa, Catherine A. Wagner, David D. Cole, Ezekiel R. Edwards, and Jeffrey P. Robinson.

Brief of amici curiae filed on behalf of the Georgetown University Law Center Chapter of the Black Law Students Association by Aderson B. Francois.

Brief of amici curiae filed on behalf of the Rutherford Institute by John W. Whitehead, Douglas R. McKusick, and Anand Agneshwar.

Brief of amici curiae filed on behalf of National Association for the Advancement of Colored People et al. by William Harry Ehlies, Anita S. Earls, Ian A. Mance, Bradford M. Berry, and Khyla D. Craine.

Brief of amici curiae filed on behalf of National Police Accountability Project by Cynthia Heenan, Julia Yoo, Christopher Wimmer, Joshua Paulson, and Jeff Dominic Price.

Opposing Side (Petitioner / Appellant)

Brief of amici curiae filed on behalf of the United States by Acting Solicitor General Francisco, Acting Assistant Attorney General Branda, Deputy Solicitor General Dreeben, Assistant Solicitor General Saharsky, Douglas N. Letter, Barbara L. Herwig, and Edward Himmelfarb.

Brief of amici curiae filed on behalf of Los Angeles County Police Chiefs' Association by J. Scott Tiedemann and Leighton Davis Henderson.

Brief of amici curiae filed on behalf of National Association of Counties et al. by Lisa Sorenen, Daniel P. Collins, Mark R. Yohalem and Seth Fortin.

Brief of amici curiae filed on behalf of Major County Sheriffs' Association by Joseph John Summerill IV, Gaëtan Gerville-Réache, and Conor B. Dugan.

Brief of amici curiae filed on behalf of California State Sheriffs' Association et al. by Martin J. Mayer, James R. Touchstone, and Krista MacNevin Jee.

IV. THE SUPREME COURT'S DECISION

"The Ninth Circuit's provocation rule permits an excessive force claim under the Fourth Amendment 'where an officer intentionally or recklessly provokes a violent confrontation, if the provocation is an independent Fourth Amendment violation.' The rule comes into play after a forceful seizure has been judged to be reasonable under Graham. Once a court has made that determination, the rule instructs the court to ask whether the law enforcement officer violated the Fourth Amendment in some other way in the course of events leading up to the seizure. If so, that separate Fourth Amendment violation may 'render the officer's otherwise reasonable defensive use of force unreasonable as a matter of law.'

The provocation rule . . . is incompatible with our excessive force jurisprudence. The rule's fundamental flaw is that it uses another constitutional violation to manufacture an excessive force claim where one would not otherwise exist. . . .

'Excessive force claims . . . are evaluated for objective reasonableness based upon the information the officers had when the conduct occurred.' That inquiry is dispositive: When an officer carries out a seizure that is reasonable, taking into account all relevant circumstances, there is no valid excessive force claim.

The basic problem with the provocation rule is that it fails to stop there. Instead, the rule provides a novel and unsupported path to liability in cases in which the use of force was reasonable. Specifically, it instructs courts to look back in time to see if there was a different Fourth Amendment violation that is somehow tied to the eventual use of force. . . .

This approach mistakenly conflates distinct Fourth Amendment claims. Contrary to this approach, the objective reasonableness analysis must be conducted separately for each search or seizure that is alleged to be unconstitutional. An excessive force claim is a claim that a law enforcement officer carried out an unreasonable seizure through a use of force that was not justified under the relevant circumstances. It is not a claim that an officer used reasonable force after committing a distinct Fourth Amendment violation such as an unreasonable entry. . . .

The Court of Appeals also held that 'even without relying on [the] provocation theory, the deputies are liable for the shooting under basic notions of proximate cause.' . . .

Unfortunately, the Court of Appeals' proximate cause analysis appears to have been tainted by the same errors that cause us to reject the provocation rule. . . .

For these reasons, the judgment of the Court of Appeals is vacated, and the case is remanded . . . ."

V. JUSTICE VOTE

0 Pro ACLU Side vs. 8 Con Opposing Side

Opposing Side (Petitioner / Appellant)

1. Alito, S. – Wrote majority opinion
2. Kagan, E. – Joined majority opinion
3. Thomas, C. – Joined majority opinion
4. Breyer, S. – Joined majority opinion
5. Kennedy, A. – Joined majority opinion
6. Ginsburg, R. – Joined majority opinion
7. Sotomayor, S. – Joined majority opinion
8. Roberts, J. – Joined majority opinion

Gorsuch, N. – Took no part in the decision.

VI. A WIN OR LOSS FOR THE ACLU?

The ACLU filed as amicus curiae urging affirmance; the Supreme Court vacated the Court of Appeals' decision by an 8-0 vote, giving the ACLU an apparent loss.

1158. Advocate Health Care Network v. Stapleton

(Decided June 5, 2017; 137 S.Ct. 1652; 581 U.S. _)

I. ISSUE

A. Issues Discussed

Regulation

B. Legal Question Presented

"The Employee Retirement Income Security Act of 1974 (ERISA) exempts 'church plan[s]' from its otherwise-comprehensive regulation of employee benefit plans. Under the statute, certain plans for the employees of churches or church-affiliated nonprofits count as 'church plans' even though not actually administered by a church. The question presented here is whether a church must have originally established such a plan for it to so qualify."

C. Supreme Court's Answer

"ERISA, we hold, does not impose that requirement."

II. CASE SUMMARY

A. Background

"Petitioners identify themselves as three church-affiliated nonprofits that run hospitals . . . . They offer defined-benefit pension plans to their employees. Those plans were established by the hospitals themselves—not by a church—and are managed by internal employee-benefits committees.

ERISA generally obligates private employers offering pension plans to adhere to an array of rules . . . . But . . . , Congress made an important exception. '[C]hurch plan[s]' have never had to comply with ERISA's requirements. . . .

The three federal agencies responsible for administering ERISA have long read . . . provisions . . . to exempt plans like the hospitals' from the statute's mandates. . . .

The three cases before us are part of a recent wave of litigation challenging the agencies' view. Respondents, current and former employees of the hospitals, filed class actions alleging that their employers' pension plans do not fall within ERISA's church-plan exemption (and thus must satisfy the statute's requirements). . . . The District Courts handling the cases agreed with the employees' position, and therefore held that the hospitals' plans must comply with ERISA.

The Courts of Appeals for the Third, Seventh, and Ninth Circuits affirmed . . . ."

The Supreme Court granted certiorari to review the case.

B. Counsel of Record / ACLU Attorney

ACLU Side (Respondent / Appellee): James A. Feldman argued the cause for appellee. With him on the briefs were Lynn Lincoln Sarko, Matthew Gerend,

Laura R. Gerber, Ron Kilgard, Laurie Ashton, Karen L. Handorf, Michelle C. Yau, Julie G. Reiser, and Mary J. Bortscheller.

Opposing Side (Petitioner / Appellant): Lisa S. Blatt argued the cause for appellant. With her on the briefs were Elisabeth S. Theodore, Sally L. Pei, Amy L. Blaisdell, Daniel J. Schwartz, Heather M. Mehta, Jeffrey J. Greenbaum, James M. Hirschhorn, Katherine M. Lieb, Barry S. Landsberg, Harvey L. Rochman, Joanna S. Mccallum, and David L. Shapiro.

Deputy Solicitor General Stewart argued the cause for the United States as amicus curiae.

III. AMICI CURIAE

ACLU Side (Respondent / Appellee)

Opposing Side (Petitioner / Appellant)

Brief of amici curiae filed on behalf of Americans United for Separation of Church and State, American Civil Liberties Union, ACLU of Illinois, ACLU of Northern CalIfornia Foundation, Inc., ACLU of New Jersey, and People for the American Way Foundation by David Cole, Daniel Mach, Louise Melling, Brigitte Amiri, Richard B. Katskee, Bradley Girard, Elliot M. Mincberg, and Diane Laviolette.

Brief of amici curiae filed on behalf of National Employment Lawyers Association by Matthew C. Koski, Brian Wolfman, and Wyatt G. Sassman.

Brief of amici curiae filed on behalf of Pension Rights Center by Norman P. Stein and Karen W. Ferguson.

Brief of amici curiae filed on behalf of AARP et al. by William Alvarado Rivera and Mary Ellen Signorille.

Brief of amici curiae filed on behalf of Professor Daniel I. Halperin by Mr. Halperin and Marc I. Machiz.

Opposing Side (Petitioner / Appellant)

Brief of amici curiae filed on behalf of the United States by Deputy Solicitor General Kneedler, Acting Assistant Attorney General Branda, Assistant Solicitor General Fletcher, Mark B. Stern, Alisa B. Klein, and Nicolas Y. Riley.

Brief of amici curiae filed on behalf of Church Alliance by G. Daniel Miller, Laurence A. Hansen, and Hugh S. Balsam.

Brief of amici curiae filed on behalf of Council for Christian Colleges & Universities et al. by Robert E. Dunn, Daniel Nowicki, Helgi C. Walker, Rebekah Perry Ricketts, Hiram S. Sasser III, Matthew J. Kacsmaryk, and Katherine C. Yarger.

Brief of amici curiae filed on behalf of the American Center for Law and Justice by Jay Alan Sekulow, Stuart J. Roth, Colby M. May, and Walter M. Weber.

Brief of amici curiae filed on behalf of Alliance Defending Freedom et al. by Kristen Waggoner, David Cortman, Erik Stanley, Jordan Lorence, Shay Dvoretzky, Emily J. Kennedy, and Thomas Brejcha.

Brief of amici curiae filed on behalf of Saint Elizabeth Medical Center, Inc., by Richard G. Meyer, Mark D. Guilfoyle, and Mark R. Hervey.

Brief of amici curiae filed on behalf of Church Defendant by Robert W. Rachal, Howard Shapiro, Stacey C. S. Cerrone, and Madeline Chimento Rea.

Brief of amici curiae filed on behalf of Christian Legal Society et al. by Carl H. Esbeck, Steven W. Fitschen, Kimberlee Wood Colby, and Frederick Claybrook, Jr.

Brief of amici curiae filed on behalf of United States Conference of Catholic Bishops et al. by Anthony R. Picarello, Jr., Jeffrey

Hunter Moon, Michael F. Moses, Matthew L. Giuliano, Hillary E. Byrnes, Paul D. Clement, Erin E. Murphy, and Robert M. Bernstein.

Brief of amici curiae filed on behalf of the Catholic Health Association of the United States by Lisa J. Gilden, Mark E. Chopko, Marissa Parker, and Brandon Riley.

Brief of amici curiae filed on behalf of the Becket Fund for Religious Liberty by Eric Rassbach.

Brief of amici curiae filed on behalf of the General Conference of Seventh-Day Adventists by Todd R. Mcfarland, Gene C. Schaerr, S. Kyle Duncan, and Stephen S. Schwartz.

Brief of amici curiae filed on behalf of the Illinois Conference of the United Church of Christ et al. by Bradley J. Andreozzi, Emily T. Broach, and Matthew M. Morrissey.

IV. THE SUPREME COURT'S DECISION

"The dispute in these cases about what counts as a 'church plan' hinges on the combined meaning of paragraph (A) and subparagraph (C)(i). . . .

Under paragraph (A), a "church plan' means a plan established and maintained . . . by a church.'

Under subparagraph (C)(i), '[a] plan established and maintained . . . by a church . . . includes a plan maintained by [a principal-purpose] organization.'

The parties agree that under those provisions, a 'church plan' need not be maintained by a church; it may instead be maintained by a principal-purpose organization. But the parties differ as to whether a plan maintained by that kind of organization must still have been established by a church to qualify for the church-plan exemption. The hospitals say no: The effect of subparagraph (C)(i) was to bring within the church-plan definition all pension plans maintained by a principal-purpose organization, regardless of who first established them. The employees say yes: Subparagraph (C)(i) altered only the requirement that a pension plan be maintained by a church, while leaving intact the church-establishment condition. We conclude that the hospitals have the better of the argument. . . .

[K]eeping the church-establishment requirement would have prevented some plans run by pension boards—the very entities the employees say Congress most wanted to benefit—from qualifying as 'church plans' under ERISA. No argument the employees have offered here supports that goal-defying (much less that text-defying) statutory construction. . . .

ERISA provides (1) that a 'church plan' means a 'plan established and maintained . . . by a church' and (2) that a 'plan established and maintained . . . by a church' is to 'include[ ] a plan maintained by' a principal-purpose organization. Under the best reading of the statute, a plan maintained by a principal-purpose organization therefore qualifies as a 'church plan,' regardless of who established it. We accordingly reverse the judgments of the Courts of Appeals."

V. JUSTICE VOTE

0 Pro ACLU Side vs. 8 Con Opposing Side

Opposing Side (Petitioner / Appellant)

1. Kagan, E. – Wrote majority opinion
2. Alito, S. – Joined majority opinion
3. Thomas, C. – Joined majority opinion
4. Breyer, S. – Joined majority opinion
5. Kennedy, A. – Joined majority opinion
6. Ginsburg, R. – Joined majority opinion
7. Sotomayor, S. – Wrote concurring opinion
8. Roberts, J. – Joined majority opinion

Gorsuch, N. – Took no part in the decision.

VI. A WIN OR LOSS FOR THE ACLU?

The ACLU filed as amicus curiae urging affirmance; the Supreme Court reversed the Court of Appeals' decision by an 8-0 vote, giving the ACLU an apparent loss.

1159. Sessions v. Morales-Santana

(Decided June 12, 2017; 137 S.Ct. 1678; 582 U.S. _)

I. ISSUE

A. Issues Discussed

Immigration/citizenship, gender

B. Legal Question Presented

Whether a law with different requirements for unwed mothers and fathers to confer U.S.-citizenship on children is unconstitutional.

C. Supreme Court's Answer

"We hold that the gender line Congress drew is incompatible with the requirement that the Government accord to all persons 'the equal protection of the laws.' Nevertheless, we cannot convert § 1409(c)'s exception for unwed mothers into the main rule displacing § 1401(a)(7) (covering married couples) and § 1409(a) (covering unwed fathers). We must therefore leave it to Congress to select, going forward, a physical-presence requirement . . . uniformly applicable to all children born abroad with one U.S.-citizen and one alien parent, wed or unwed."

II. CASE SUMMARY

A. Background

"This case concerns a gender-based differential in the law governing acquisition of U.S. citizenship by a child born abroad, when one parent is a U.S. citizen, the other, a citizen of another nation. The main rule appears in 8 U.S.C. § 1401(a)(7) (1958 ed.), now § 1401(g) (2012 ed.). Applicable to married couples, § 1401(a)(7) requires a period of physical presence in the United States for the U.S.-citizen parent. The requirement, as initially prescribed, was ten years' physical presence prior to the child's birth; currently, the requirement is five years prebirth. That main rule is rendered applicable to unwed U.S.-citizen fathers by § 1409(a). Congress ordered an exception, however, for unwed U.S.-citizen mothers. Contained in § 1409(c), the exception allows an unwed mother to transmit her citizenship to a child born abroad if she has lived in the United States for just one year prior to the child's birth. . . .

Luis Ramón Morales-Santana, was born in the Dominican Republic when his father was just 20 days short of meeting § 1401(a)(7)'s physical-presence requirement. Opposing removal to the Dominican Republic, Morales-Santana asserts that the equal protection principle implicit in the Fifth Amendment entitles him to citizenship stature. . . .

An immigration judge rejected Morales-Santana's claim to citizenship derived from the U.S. citizenship of his father, and ordered Morales-Santana's removal to the Dominican Republic. In 2010, Morales-Santana moved to reopen the proceedings . . . . The Board of Immigration Appeals (BIA) denied the motion.

The United States Court of Appeals for the Second Circuit reversed the BIA's decision."

The Supreme Court granted certiorari to review the case.

B. Counsel of Record / ACLU Attorney

ACLU Side (Respondent / Appellee): Stephen A. Broome argued the cause for appellee. With him on the briefs were Kathleen M. Sullivan, Todd Anten, Justin T. Reinheimer, and Ellyde R. Thompson.

Opposing Side (Petitioner / Appellant): Deputy Solicitor General Kneedler argued the cause for appellant. With him on the briefs were Acting Solicitor General Gershengorn, Principal Deputy Assistant Attorney General Mizer, Assistant Solicitor General Harrington, Donald E. Keener, and Andrew C. MacLachlan.

III. AMICI CURIAE

ACLU Side (Respondent / Appellee)

Brief of amici curiae filed on behalf of the American Civil Liberties Union, the New York Civil Liberties Union, the National Immigration Law Center, and the National Women's Law Center by Jennifer Chang Newell, Cecillia D. Wang, Arthur N. Eisenberg, Sandra S. Park, Lee Gelernt, Lenora M. Lapidus, and Steven R. Shapiro.

Brief of amici curiae filed on behalf of Constitutional Law, Federal Courts, Citizenship, and Remedies Scholars by Judith Resnik, Stephen I. Vladeck, and Meir Feder.

Brief of amici curiae filed on behalf of Professors of History, Political Science, and Law by Kristin A. Collins, Catherine E. Stetson, Jessica K. Jacobs, and Jasmeet K. Ahuja.

Brief of amici curiae filed on behalf of Equality Now et al. by William R. Stein, Scott H. Christensen, Jason S. Cohen, Steven A. Hammond, Alyssa M. Johnson, Martha F. Davis, Shelby R. Quast, and Antonia Kirkland.

Brief of amici curiae filed on behalf of the National Immigrant Justice Center et al. by Charles Roth.

Brief of amici curiae filed on behalf of Population and Family Scholars Peter K. Stris, Elizabeth Rogers Brannen, and Suzanne B. Goldberg.

Brief of amici curiae filed on behalf of Scholars on Statelessness by Max Gitter, Rishi Zutshi, and Eric Jordan.

Opposing Side (Petitioner / Appellant)

No briefs of amici curiae were filed in support of appellant.

IV. THE SUPREME COURT'S DECISION

"Because § 1409 treats sons and daughters alike, Morales-Santana does not suffer discrimination on the basis of his gender. He complains, instead, of gender-based discrimination against his father, who was unwed at the time of Morales-Santana's birth and was not accorded the right an unwed U.S.-citizen mother would have to transmit citizenship to her child. . . .

Successful defense of legislation that differentiates on the basis of gender . . . requires an 'exceedingly persuasive justification.' . . .

In sum, the Government has advanced no 'exceedingly persuasive' justification for § 1409(a) and (c)'s gender-specific residency and age criteria. Those disparate criteria, we hold, cannot withstand inspection under a Constitution that requires the Government to respect the equal dignity and stature of its male and female citizens. . . .

While the equal protection infirmity in retaining a longer physical-presence requirement for unwed fathers than for unwed mothers is clear, this Court is not equipped to grant the relief . . . .

Although extension of benefits is customary in federal benefit cases, all indicators in this case point in the opposite direction. Put to the choice, Congress, we believe, would have abrogated § 1409(c)'s exception, preferring preservation of the general rule. . . .

The gender-based distinction infecting §§ 1401(a)(7) and 1409(a) and (c), we hold, violates the equal protection principle, as the Court of Appeals correctly ruled. For the reasons stated, however, we must adopt the remedial course Congress likely would have chosen 'had it been apprised of the constitutional infirmity.' Although the preferred rule in the typical case is to extend favorable treatment, this is hardly the typical case. Extension here would render the special treatment Congress prescribed in § 1409(c), the one-year physical-presence requirement for U.S.-citizen mothers, the general rule, no longer an exception. Section 1401(a)(7)'s longer physical-presence requirement, applicable to a substantial majority of children born abroad to one U.S.-citizen parent and one foreign-citizen parent, therefore, must hold sway. Going forward, Congress may address the issue and settle on a uniform prescription that neither favors nor disadvantages any person on the basis of gender. In the interim, as the Government suggests, § 1401(a)(7)'s now-five-year requirement should apply, prospectively, to children born to unwed U.S.-citizen mothers.

The judgment of the Court of Appeals for the Second Circuit is affirmed in part and reversed in part, and the case is remanded . . . ."

V. JUSTICE VOTE

8 Pro ACLU Side vs. 0 Con Opposing Side

ACLU Side (Respondent / Appellee)

1. Ginsburg, R. – Wrote majority opinion
2. Alito, S. – Joined Thomas' concurrence
3. Kagan, E. – Joined majority opinion
4. Thomas, C. – Wrote concurring opinion
5. Breyer, S. – Joined majority opinion
6. Kennedy, A. – Joined majority opinion
7. Sotomayor, S. – Joined majority opinion

8. Roberts, J. – Joined majority opinion

Gorsuch, N. – Took no part in the decision.

VI. A WIN OR LOSS FOR THE ACLU?

The ACLU filed as amicus curiae urging affirmance; the Supreme Court affirmed in part and reversed in part the Court of Appeals' decision by an 8-0 vote, giving the ACLU an apparent win.

1160. Packingham v. North Carolina

(Decided June 19, 2017; 137 S.Ct. 1730; 582 U.S. _)

I. ISSUE

A. Issues Discussed

1st Amendment, press, speech, association

B. Legal Question Presented

"In 2008, North Carolina enacted a statute making it a felony for a registered sex offender to gain access to a number of websites, including commonplace social media websites like Facebook and Twitter. The question presented is whether that law is permissible under the First Amendment's Free Speech Clause, applicable to the States under the Due Process Clause of the Fourteenth Amendment."

C. Supreme Court's Answer

"It is well established that, as a general rule, the Government 'may not suppress lawful speech as the means to suppress unlawful speech.' That is what North Carolina has done here. Its law must be held invalid."

II. CASE SUMMARY

A. Background

"North Carolina law makes it a felony for a registered sex offender 'to access a commercial social networking Web site where the sex offender knows that the site permits minor children to become members or to create or maintain personal Web pages.' . . .

[Section] 14–202.5 applies to about 20,000 people in North Carolina and the State has prosecuted over 1,000 people for violating it. . . .

In 2002, petitioner Lester Gerard Packingham . . . was required to register as a sex offender . . . . As a registered sex offender, petitioner was barred under § 14–202.5 from gaining access to commercial social networking sites.

In 2010, a state court dismissed a traffic ticket against petitioner. In response, he logged on to Facebook.com and posted [a] statement on his personal profile . . . .

At the time, a member of the Durham Police Department was investigating registered sex offenders who were thought to be violating § 14–202.5. . . .

Petitioner was indicted by a grand jury for violating § 14–202.5. The trial court denied his motion to dismiss the indictment on the grounds that the charge against him violated the First Amendment. Petitioner was ultimately convicted and given a suspended prison sentence. At no point during trial or sentencing did the State allege that petitioner contacted a minor—or committed any other illicit act—on the Internet.

Petitioner appealed to the Court of Appeals of North Carolina. That court struck down § 14–202.5 on First Amendment grounds . . . ."

The Supreme Court granted certiorari to review the case.

B. Counsel of Record / ACLU Attorney

ACLU Side (Petitioner / Appellant): David T. Goldberg argued the cause for appellants. With him on the brief were Glenn Gerding, Appellate Defender of North Carolina, David T. Goldberg, Jeffrey L. Fisher, and Pamela S. Karlan.

Opposing Side (Respondent / Appellee): Robert C. Montgomery, Senior Deputy Attorney General of North Carolina argued the cause for appellee. With him on the brief were Josh Stein, Attorney General, John F. Maddrey, Solicitor General, Robert C. Montgomery, Senior Deputy Attorney General, Daniel P. O'Brien, Special Deputy Attorney General, and Anne Murray Middleton, Special Deputy Attorney General.

III. AMICI CURIAE

ACLU Side (Petitioner / Appellant)

Brief of amici curiae filed on behalf of the Cato Institute, the American Civil Liberties Union, and the American Civil Liberties Union of North Carolina by Jason D. Hirsch, Ari J. Savitzky, Molly M. Jennings, Mark C. Fleming, Esha Bhandari, Lee Rowland, Christopher A. Brook, Ilya Shapiro, and Devin Watkins.

Brief of amici curiae filed on behalf of the Reporters Committee for Freedom of the Press et al. by J. Joshua Wheeler, Bruce D. Brown, Gregg P. Leslie, and Selina MacLaren.

Brief of amici curiae filed on behalf of the National Association of Criminal Defense Lawyers by Jeffrey T. Green, Jonathan D. Hacker, Deanna M. Rice, and Kimya Saied.

Brief of amici curiae filed on behalf of Association for the Treatment of Sexual Abusers et al. by John J. Korzen.

Brief of amici curiae filed on behalf of Electronic Frontier Foundation et al. by David G. Post, Emma Llansó, Adam Schwartz, Jonathan Sherman, Perry M. Grossman, and Charles Duan.

Brief of amici curiae filed on behalf of Electronic Privacy Information Center (EPIC) et al. by Marc Rotenberg and Alan Butler.

Opposing Side (Respondent / Appellee)

Brief of amici curiae filed on behalf of the State of Louisiana et al. by Jeff Landry, Attorney General of Louisiana, Elizabeth Murrill, Solicitor General, Colin Clark, Deputy Solicitor General, Andrea Barient, Assistant Attorney General, and by the Attorneys General for their respective States as follows: Mark Brnovich of Arizona, Cynthia H. Coffman of Colorado, Douglas S. Chin of Hawaii, Curtis T. Hill, Jr., of Indiana, Bill Schuette of Michigan, Lori Swanson of Minnesota, Adam Paul Laxalt of Nevada, Josh Shapiro of Pennsylvania, Ken Paxton of Texas, Peter F. Kilmartin of Rhode Island, Alan Wilson of South Carolina, and Brad D. Schimel of Wisconsin.

Brief of amici curiae filed on behalf of Stop Child Predators et al.

by Melissa Arbus Sherry and Charles Dameron.
Brief of amici curiae filed on behalf of Council of State Governments et al. by Lisa Soronen, John C. Neiman, Jr., and Braxton Thrash.

IV. THE SUPREME COURT'S DECISION

"A fundamental principle of the First Amendment is that all persons have access to places where they can speak and listen, and then, after reflection, speak and listen once more. The Court has sought to protect the right to speak in this spatial context. . . .

While in the past there may have been difficulty in identifying the most important places (in a spatial sense) for the exchange of views, today the answer is clear. It is cyberspace—the 'vast democratic forums of the Internet' in general, and social media in particular. . . .

This case is one of the first this Court has taken to address the relationship between the First Amendment and the modern Internet. As a result, the Court must exercise extreme caution before suggesting that the First Amendment provides scant protection for access to vast networks in that medium. . . .

This background informs the analysis of the North Carolina statute at issue. Even making the assumption that the statute is content neutral and thus subject to intermediate scrutiny, the provision cannot stand. . . .

In sum, to foreclose access to social media altogether is to prevent the user from engaging in the legitimate exercise of First Amendment rights. It is unsettling to suggest that only a limited set of websites can be used even by persons who have completed their sentences. Even convicted criminals—and in some instances especially convicted criminals—might receive legitimate benefits from these means for access to the world of ideas, in particular if they seek to reform and to pursue lawful and rewarding lives. . . .

It is well established that, as a general rule, the Government 'may not suppress lawful speech as the means to suppress unlawful speech.' That is what North Carolina has done here. Its law must be held invalid.

The judgment of the North Carolina Supreme Court is reversed, and the case is remanded . . . ."

V. JUSTICE VOTE

8 Pro ACLU Side vs. 0 Con Opposing Side

ACLU Side (Petitioner / Appellant)

1. Kennedy, A. – Wrote majority opinion
2. Alito, S. – Wrote concurring opinion
3. Kagan, E. – Joined majority opinion
4. Thomas, C. – Joined Alito's concurrence
5. Breyer, S. – Joined majority opinion
6. Ginsburg, R. – Joined majority opinion
7. Sotomayor, S. – Joined majority opinion
8. Roberts, J. – Joined Alito's concurrence

Gorsuch, N. – Took no part in the decision.

VI. A WIN OR LOSS FOR THE ACLU?

The ACLU filed as amicus curiae urging reversal of the judgment of the North Carolina Supreme Court; the Supreme Court reversed in an 8-0 vote, giving the ACLU an apparent win.

1161. Matal v. Tam

(Decided June 19, 2017; 137 S.Ct. 1744; 582 U.S. _)

I. ISSUE

A. Issues Discussed

1st Amendment, press, speech, association

B. Legal Question Presented

Whether "[t]he Patent and Trademark Office (PTO) [properly] denied [a trademark] application based on a provision of federal law prohibiting the registration of trademarks that may 'disparage . . . or bring . . . into contemp[t] or disrepute' any 'persons, living or dead.'"

C. Supreme Court's Answer

"We now hold that this provision violates the Free Speech Clause of the First Amendment. It offends a bedrock First Amendment principle: Speech may not be banned on the ground that it expresses ideas that offend."

II. CASE SUMMARY

A. Background

"Simon Tam is the lead singer of The Slants.' He chose this moniker in order to 'reclaim' and 'take ownership' of stereotypes about people of Asian ethnicity. The group 'draws inspiration for its lyrics from childhood slurs and mocking nursery rhymes' and has given its albums names such as 'The Yellow Album' and 'Slanted Eyes, Slanted Hearts.'

Tam sought federal registration of 'THE SLANTS,' on the principal register, but an examining attorney at the PTO rejected the request, applying the PTO's two-part framework and finding that 'there is . . . a substantial composite of persons who find the term in the applied-for mark offensive.' . . .

Tam contested the denial of registration before the examining attorney and before the PTO's Trademark Trial and Appeal Board (TTAB) but to no avail. Eventually, he took the case to federal court, where the en banc Federal Circuit ultimately found the disparagement clause facially unconstitutional under the First Amendment's Free Speech Clause."

The Supreme Court granted certiorari to review the case.

B. Counsel of Record / ACLU Attorney

ACLU Side (Respondent / Appellee): John C. Connell argued the cause for appellee. With him on the brief were Stuart Banner, Eugene Volokh, Ronald D. Coleman, and Joel G. MacMull.

Opposing Side (Petitioner / Appellant): Deputy Solicitor General Stewart argued the cause for appellant. With him on the brief were Acting Solicitor General Gershengorn, Principal Deputy Assistant Attorney General Mizer, Assistant Solicitor General Saharsky, Douglas N. Letter, Mark R. Freeman, Daniel Tenny, Joshua M. Salzman, General Counsel for the U.S. Patent and Trademark Office Sarah Harris, Solicitor Nathan K. Kelley, Deputy Solicitor Thomas W. Krause, and Christina J. Hieber,

Thomas L. Casagrande, Molly R. Silfen, and Mary Beth Walker, Associate Solicitors.

III. AMICI CURIAE

ACLU Side (Respondent / Appellee)

Brief of amici curiae filed on behalf of the American Civil Liberties Union, the ACLU of the Nation's Capital, the ACLU Foundation of Oregon, the Asian American Legal Defense and Education Fund, the Asian Pacific American Network of Oregon, The Chinese American Citizens Alliance, Portland Lodge, the Portland Japanese American Citizens League, and the Oregon Commission on Asian and Pacific Islander Affairs by Mathew W. dos Santos, Lee Rowland, Esha Bhandari, Vera Eidelman, Arthur B. Spitzer, Scott Michelman, and David Cole.

Brief of amici curiae filed on behalf of the American Center for Law and Justice by Jay Alan Sekulow, Stuart J. Roth, Colby M. May, and Walter M. Weber.

Brief of amici curiae filed on behalf of Pacific Legal Foundation by Joshua P. Thompson and Caleb R. Trotter.

Brief of amici curiae filed on behalf of Constitutional Law Professors by Rodney A. Smolla, Floyd Abrams, Fria Kermani, and Kathleen E. Farley.

Brief of amici curiae filed on behalf of Professors Edward Lee et al. by Mr. Lee.

Brief of amici curiae filed on behalf of Alliance Defending Freedom by David A. Cortman, Rory T. Gray, Kristen Wagonner, and Kevin H. Theriot.

Brief of amici curiae filed on behalf of the Chamber of Commerce of the United States of America by Lily Fu Claffee, Kate Comerford Todd, Warren Postman, Eugene Scalia, Amir C. Tayrani, and Michael R. Huston.

Brief of amici curiae filed on behalf of Pro-Football, Inc., by Robert L. Raskopf, Todd Anten, Jessica A. Rose, Lisa S. Blatt, Robert A. Garrett, and Stephen K. Wirth.

Brief of amici curiae filed on behalf of Justice and Freedom Fund by James L. Hirsen and Deborah J. Dewart.

Brief of amici curiae filed on behalf of San Francisco Dykes on Bikes Women's Motorcycle Contingent, Inc., by Brooke Oliver, Tobias Barrington Wolff, Mark A. Lemley, and Michael A. Feldman.

Brief of amici curiae filed on behalf of the Thomas Jefferson Center for the Protection of Free Expression et al. by David Greene, Daniel Nazer, J. Joshua Wheeler, and Clayton N. Hansen.

Brief of amici curiae filed on behalf of the American Jewish Committee by Kannon K. Shanmugam, Allison Jones Rushing, and William T. Marks.

Brief of amici curiae filed on behalf of the Rutherford Institute et al. by John W. Whitehead, Douglas R. McKusick, Joseph Colangelo, Megan L. Brown, Joshua S. Turner, Christopher J. Kelly, Dwayne D. Sam, and John T. Lin.

Brief of amici curiae filed on behalf of the International Trademark Association by Lawrence K. Nodine, Robert D. Carrol, Anthony J. Dreyer, Andrew L. Green, and John W. Crittenden.

Brief of amici curiae filed on behalf of the Cato Institute et al. by by Ilya Shapiro and Thomas A. Berry.

Brief of amici curiae filed on behalf of the Becket Fund for Religious Liberty by Mark L. Rienzi and Adèle Auxier Keim.

Brief of amici curiae filed on behalf of Professor Hugh C. Hansen by Mr. Hansen.

Brief of amici curiae filed on behalf of Law Professors Gregory Dolin et al. by Mr. Dolin and Matthew J. Dowd.

Brief of amici curiae filed on behalf of Erik Brunetti by John R. Sommer and Devon A. Beckwith.

Brief of amici curiae filed on behalf of First Amendment Lawyers Association by Marc J. Randazza.

Opposing Side (Petitioner / Appellant)

Brief of amici curiae filed on behalf of Amanda Blackhorse et al. by Adam G. Yoffie, Jesse A. Witten, Tore T. Debella, and Patrick H. Thompson.

Brief of amici curiae filed on behalf of Native American Organizations by Richard A. Guest, Larry S. Gondelman, Brandi A. Taylor, Charles A. Rothfeld, Andrew J. Pincus, Paul W. Hughes, and Michael B. Kimberly

Brief of amici curiae filed on behalf of Law Professors by Christine Haight Farley and Rebecca Tushnet.

Brief of amici curiae filed on behalf of the Fred T. Korematsu Center for Law and Equality et al. by Robert S. Chang, William C. Rava, Elvira Castillo, David A. Perez, Cara Wallace, and Dane Westermeyer.

Brief of amici curiae filed on behalf of the New York Intellectual Property Law Association by Walter E. Hanley, Jr., Charles R. Macedo, David P. Goldberg, Dyan Finguerra-DuCharme, Danielle E. Tepper, Pina M. Campagna, Kathleen E. McCarthy, Robert J. Rando, Michael C. Cannata, Stephen J. Smirti, Jr., Frank Misiti, William Thomashower, and Robert M. Isackson in support of neither party.

Brief of amici curiae filed on behalf of Public Knowledge by Charles Duan, Phillip R. Malone, and Jef Pearlman in support of neither party.

Brief of amici curiae filed on behalf of Certain Members of Congress by John T. Johnson and John Dragseth in support of neither party.

Brief of amici curiae filed on behalf of American Intellectual Property Law Association by Mark L. Whitaker and Paul M. Smith in support of neither party.

Brief of amici curiae filed on behalf of Public Citizen, Inc., by Scott L. Nelson, Allison M. Zieve, and Julie A. Murray in support of neither party.

Brief of amici curiae filed on behalf of the American Bar Association by Jonathan S. Jennings, Theodore H. Davis, Jr., Thomas L. Stoll, Jacquelyn R. McPeak, and Linda A. Klein in support of neither party.

Brief of amici curiae filed on behalf of Asian Americans Advancing Justice | AAJC et al. by Cecelia Chang, Daniel J. Kornstein, and Alanna Small in support of neither party.

IV. THE SUPREME COURT'S DECISION

"Because the disparagement clause applies to marks that disparage the members of a racial or ethnic group, we must decide whether the clause violates the Free Speech Clause of the First

Amendment. And at the outset, we must consider three arguments that would either eliminate any First Amendment protection or result in highly permissive rational-basis review. Specifically, the Government contends (1) that trademarks are government speech, not private speech, (2) that trademarks are a form of government subsidy, and (3) that the constitutionality of the disparagement clause should be tested under a new 'government-program' doctrine. . . .

Trademarks are private, not government, speech. . . .

We next address the Government's argument that this case is governed by cases in which this Court has upheld the constitutionality of government programs that subsidized speech expressing a particular viewpoint. . . .

Unlike the present case, the decisions on which the Government relies all involved cash subsidies . . . .

Cases like Rust and Finley are not instructive in analyzing the constitutionality of restrictions on speech imposed in connection with such services. . . .

Finally, the Government urges us to sustain the disparagement clause under a new doctrine that would apply to 'government-program' cases. . . .

[T]he disparagement clause cannot be saved by analyzing it as a type of government program in which some content- and speaker-based restrictions are permitted. . . .

Having concluded that the disparagement clause cannot be sustained under our government-speech or subsidy cases or under the Government's proposed 'government-program' doctrine, we must confront a dispute between the parties on the question whether trademarks are commercial speech and are thus subject to the relaxed scrutiny outlined in Central Hudson Gas & Elec. Corp. v. Public Serv. Comm'n of N. Y., 447 U.S. 557 (1980). . . .

We need not resolve . . . debate between the parties because the disparagement clause cannot withstand even Central Hudson review. . . .

[W]e hold that the disparagement clause violates the Free Speech Clause of the First Amendment. The judgment of the Federal Circuit is affirmed."

V. JUSTICE VOTE

8 Pro ACLU Side vs. 0 Con Opposing Side

ACLU Side (Respondent / Appellee)

1. Alito, S. – Wrote majority opinion
2. Kagan, E. – Joined Kennedy's concurrnce
3. Thomas, C. – Wrote concurring opinion
4. Breyer, S. – Joined majority opinion
5. Kennedy, A. – Wrote conurring opinion
6. Ginsburg, R. – Joined Kennedy's concurrence
7. Sotomayor, S. – Joined Kennedy's concurrence
8. Roberts, J. – Joined majority opinion

Gorsuch, N. – Took no part in the decision.

VI. A WIN OR LOSS FOR THE ACLU?

The ACLU filed as amicus curiae urging affirmance; the Supreme Court affirmed the Court of Appeals' decision by an 8-0 vote, giving the ACLU an apparent win.

1162. Ziglar v. Abbasi

(Decided June 19, 2017; 137 S.Ct. 1843; 582 U.S. _)

I. ISSUE

A. Issues Discussed

Immunity, prison

B. Legal Question Presented

"The first question to be discussed is whether petitioners can be sued for damages under Bivens and the ensuing cases in this Court defining the reach and the limits of that precedent. . . .

One [further question, whether] petitioners are subject to liability for civil conspiracy under 42 U.S.C. § 1985(3)."

C. Supreme Court's Answer

"[T]he question with respect to the Bivens claims is whether to allow an action for money damages in the absence of congressional authorization. [T]he Court answers that question in the negative as to the detention policy claims. As to the prisoner abuse claim, . . . the Court remands to allow the Court of Appeals to consider the claim in light of the Bivens analysis . . . .

The question with respect to the § 1985(3) claim is whether a reasonable officer in petitioners' position would have known the alleged conduct was an unlawful conspiracy. [T]he Court answers that question, too, in the negative."

II. CASE SUMMARY

A. Background

"Respondents are six men of Arab or South Asian descent. Five are Muslims. Each was illegally in this country, arrested during the course of the September 11 investigation, and detained [then] removed from the United States. . . .

Respondents . . . challenge is to the conditions of their confinement and the reasons or motives for imposing those conditions. The gravamen of their claims was that the Government had no reason to suspect them of any connection to terrorism, and thus had no legitimate reason to hold them for so long in . . . harsh conditions.

Seeking to invoke the Court's decision in Bivens, respondents brought four claims under the Constitution itself. . . .

Respondents also brought a claim under 42 U.S.C. § 1985(3), which . . . alleged that petitioners conspired . . . to hold respondents in harsh conditions because of their actual or apparent race, religion, or national origin. . . .

The District Court dismissed the claims against the Executive Officials but allowed the claims against the Wardens to go forward. The Court of Appeals affirmed in most respects as to the Wardens . . . . As to the Executive Officials, however, the Court of Appeals reversed, reinstating respondents' claims. . . . The Court of Appeals declined to rehear . . . en banc . . . ."

The Supreme Court granted certiorari to review the case.

B. Counsel of Record / ACLU Attorney

ACLU Side (Respondent / Appellee): Rachel Meeropol argued the cause for appellee. With her on the brief were Nancy L. Kestenbaum, Joanne Sum-Ping, Jennifer L. Robbins, Matthew Q. Verdin,

David M. Zionts, Michael Winger, Baher A. Azmy, Shayana Kadidal, and Alexander A. Reinert.

Opposing Side (Petitioner / Appellant): Jeffrey A. Lamken argued the cause for appellant in 15-1363. With him on the briefs was William Alden McDaniel, Jr.

Acting Solicitor General Gershengorn argued the cause for appellant in15-1358 and 15-1359.

III. AMICI CURIAE

ACLU Side (Respondent / Appellee)

Brief of amici curiae filed on behalf of the American Civil Liberties Union, American Immigration Council, National Immigration Project of the National Lawyers Guild, National Police Accountability Project, and Northwest Immigrant Rights Project by Trina Realmuto, Kristin Macleod-Ball, Matthew E. Price, Marina K. Jenkins, Tassity S. Johnson, Michael E. Stewart, Hina Shamsi, Lee Gelernt, Dror Ladin, David Cole, Jonathan Hafetz, Matt Adams, Mary A. Kenney, Julia Yoo, Eugene Iredale, and Johnathan H. Feinberg.

Brief of amici curiae filed on behalf of Professors of Civil Procedure by Allan Ides and Simona Gross.

Brief of amici curiae filed on behalf of Commonwealth Lawyers Association by Gary A. Isaac, Logan A. Steiner, and Jed W. Glickstein.

Brief of amici curiae filed on behalf of Medical and Other Scientific and Health-Related Professionals by Kami Lizarraga, Glenda Bleiberg, Elizabeth Velez, Jessica Djilani, Jay Minga, Alexandria Swette, Nigar Shaikh, and Eric Ordway.

Brief of amici curiae filed on behalf of Immigration Detention Advocacy Organizations by Ranjana Natarajan, Brian J. Murray, and William R. Weaver.

Brief of amici curiae filed on behalf of the American Association for Justice by Julie Braman Kane and Jeffrey R. White.

Brief of amici curiae filed on behalf of Former Correctional Officials by Joshua Colangelo-Bryan, Daniel Goldberger, Jeremy Schlosser, Andrew S. Pollis, and Avidan Y. Cover.

Brief of amici curiae filed on behalf of Americans United for Separation of Church and State et al. by Eliot Mincberg, Diane Laviolette, Richard B. Katskee, and Bradley Girard.

Brief of amici curiae filed on behalf of Asian Americans Advancing Justice et al. by Diala Shamas, Amna Akbar, Catherine E. Stetson, Yuri Fuchs, and Shirin Sinnar.

Brief of amici curiae filed on behalf of Karen Korematsu et al. by Robert L. Rusky, Eric K. Yamamoto, and Joseph Margulies.

Opposing Side (Petitioner / Appellant)

Brief of amici curiae filed on behalf of Former U.S. Attorneys General William P. Barr et al. by Richard A. Samp and Mark S. Chenoweth.

IV. THE SUPREME COURT'S DECISION

"The first question to be discussed is whether petitioners can be sued for damages under Bivens and the ensuing cases in this Court defining the reach and the limits of that precedent. . . .

[F]irst to the Bivens claims challenging the conditions of confinement . . . the 'detention policy claims.' [T]he question is whether, having considered the relevant special factors in the whole context of the detention policy claims, the Court should extend a Bivens-type remedy to those claims. . . .

The Court of Appeals . . . should have held that this was a new Bivens context. Had it done so, it would have recognized that a special factors analysis was required. . . .

[T]he Court now holds that those factors show that whether a damages action should be allowed is a decision for the Congress to make, not the courts. . . .

For all of these reasons, the Court of Appeals erred by allowing respondents' detention policy claims to proceed under Bivens. . . .

One of respondents' claims under Bivens requires a different analysis: the prisoner abuse claim against the MDC's warden, Dennis Hasty. . . .

Given the absence of a comprehensive presentation by the parties, and the fact that the Court of Appeals did not conduct the analysis, the Court declines to perform the special factors analysis itself. The better course is to vacate the judgment below, allowing . . . remand. . . .

One issue remains to be addressed: the claim that petitioners are subject to liability for civil conspiracy under 42 U.S.C. § 1985(3). Unlike the prisoner abuse claim just discussed, this claim implicates the activities of all the petitioners . . . .

Petitioners are entitled to qualified immunity with respect to . . . 42 U.S.C. § 1985(3). . . .

[T]he question with respect to the Bivens claims is whether to allow an action for money damages in the absence of congressional authorization. [T]he Court answers that question in the negative as to the detention policy claims. As to the prisoner abuse claim, . . . the Court remands to allow the Court of Appeals to consider the claim in light of the Bivens analysis . . . .

The question with respect to the § 1985(3) claim is whether a reasonable officer in petitioners' position would have known the alleged conduct was an unlawful conspiracy. [T]he Court answers that question, too, in the negative.

The judgment of the Court of Appeals is reversed as to all of the claims except the prisoner abuse claim against Warden Hasty. The judgment of the Court of Appeals with respect to that claim is vacated, and that case is remanded . . . ."

V. JUSTICE VOTE

2 Pro ACLU Side vs. 4 Con Opposing Side

ACLU Side (Respondent / Appellee)

1. Breyer, S. – Wrote dissenting opinion
2. Ginsburg, R. – Joined Breyer's dissent

Opposing Side (Petitioner / Appellant)

1. Kennedy, A. – Wrote majority opinion
2. Alito, S. – Joined majority opinion
3. Thomas, C. – Wrote concurring opinion
4. Roberts, J. – Joined majority opinion

Gorsuch, N. – Took no part in the decision.
Sotomayor, S – Took no part in the decision.
Kagan, E – Took no part in the decision.

VI. A WIN OR LOSS FOR THE ACLU?

The ACLU filed as amicus curiae urging affirmance; the Supreme Court reversed in part and vacated in part the Court of Appeals' decision by a 4-2 vote, giving the ACLU an apparent loss.

1163. Weaver v. Massachusetts

(Decided June 22, 2017; 137 S.Ct. 1899; 582 U.S. _)

I. ISSUE

A. Issues Discussed

Criminal procedure

B. Legal Question Presented

"In the direct review context, the underlying constitutional violation—the courtroom closure—has been treated by this Court as a structural error, i.e., an error entitling the defendant to automatic reversal without any inquiry into prejudice. The question is whether invalidation of the conviction is required here as well, or if the prejudice inquiry is altered when the structural error is raised in the context of an ineffective-assistance-of-counsel claim."

C. Supreme Court's Answer

"[P]etitioner must show prejudice in order to obtain a new trial. [H]e has not made the required showing."

II. CASE SUMMARY

A. Background

"During petitioner's trial on state criminal charges, the courtroom was occupied by potential jurors and closed to the public for two days of the jury selection process. Defense counsel neither objected to the closure at trial nor raised the issue on direct review. And the case comes to the Court on the assumption that, in failing to object, defense counsel provided ineffective assistance. . . .

Five years later, petitioner filed a motion for a new trial in Massachusetts state court. As relevant here, he argued that his attorney had provided ineffective assistance by failing to object to the courtroom closure. [T]he court held that petitioner was not entitled to relief.

Petitioner appealed the denial of the motion for a new trial to the Massachusetts Supreme Judicial Court. [T]he court rejected petitioner's claim of ineffective assistance of counsel."

The Supreme Court granted certiorari to review the case.

B. Counsel of Record / ACLU Attorney

ACLU Side (Petitioner / Appellant): Michael B. Kimberly argued the cause for appellants. With him on the brief were Ruth Greenberg, Eugene R. Fidell, Michael B. Kimberly, Charles A. Rothfeld, Andrew J. Pincus, and Paul W. Hughes.

Opposing Side (Respondent / Appellee): Randall E. Ravitz, Assistant Attorney General of Massuchusetts, argued the cause for appellee. With him on the brief were Maura Healey, Attorney General, Elizabeth N. Dewar, State Solicitor, Thomas E. Bocian, Assistant Attorney General, and John P. Zanini, Special Assistant Attorney General.

Assistant Solicitor General O'Connell argued the cause for the United States as amicus curiae.

III. AMICI CURIAE

ACLU Side (Petitioner / Appellant)

Brief of amici curiae filed on behalf of the American Civil Liberties Union and the ACLU of Massachusetts by Matthew R. Segal, Sarah R. Wunsch, Brian W. Stull, Cassandra Stubbs, Anna Arceneaux, and David D. Cole.

Brief of amici curiae filed on behalf of National Association of Criminal Defense Lawyers by David M. Porter and Stuart Banner.

Brief of amici curiae filed on behalf of the Reporters Committee for Freedom of the Press et al. by Bruce W. Sanford, Mark I. Bailen, Bruce D. Brown, Gregg P. Leslie, and Selina Maclaren.

Brief of amici curiae filed on behalf of Massachusetts Association of Criminal Defense Lawyers by Joshua Asher, Chauncey Wood, Kirsten Mayer, and Daniel E. Fine.

Brief of amici curiae filed on behalf of the Stein Center for Law and Ethics et al. by Lawrence J. Fox.

Opposing Side (Respondent / Appellee)

Brief of amici curiae filed on behalf of the United States by Acting Solicitor General Wall, Acting Assistant Attorney General Blanco, Deputy Solicitor General Dreeben, Assistant Solicitor General O'Connell, and David M. Lieberman.

Brief of amici curiae filed on behalf of the Criminal Justice Legal Foundation by Kent S. Scheidegger and Kymberlee C. Stapleton.

Brief of amici curiae filed on behalf of the State of Arkansas et al. by Leslie Rutledge, Attorney General of Arkansas, Lee Rudofsky, Solicitor General, Nicholas J. Bronini, Deputy Solicitor General, Kevin T. Kane, Chief State's Attorney of Connecticut, and by the Attorneys General for their respective States as follows: Steven T. Marshall of Alabama, Mark Brnovich of Arizona, Cynthia H. Coffman of Colorado, Matthew P. Denn of Delaware, Pamela Jo Bondi of Florida, Christopher M. Carr of Georgia, Douglas S. Chin of Hawaii, Lawrence G. Wasden of Idaho, Curtis T. Hill, Jr., of Indiana, Derek Schmidt of Kansas, Andy Beshear of Kentucky, Jeff Landry of Louisiana, Janet T. Mills of Maine, Brian E. Frosh of Maryland, Bill Schuette of Michigan, Jim Hood of Mississippi, Joshua D. Hawley of Missouri, Timothy C. Fox of Montana, Douglas J. Peterson of Nebraska, Adam Paul Laxalt of Nevada, Hector H. Balderas of New Mexico, Josh Stein of North Carolina, Wayne Stenehjem of North Dakota, Michael DeWine of Ohio, Mike Hunter of Oklahoma, Josh Shapiro of Pennsylvania, Peter F. Kilmartin of Rhode Island, Alan Wilson of South Carolina, Marty J. Jackley of South Dakota, Herbert H. Slatery III of Tennessee, Ken Paxton of Texas, Sean D. Reyes of Utah, Robert W. Ferguson of Washington, Patrick Morrisey of West Virginia, Brad D. Schimel of Wisconsin, and Peter K. Michael of Wyoming.

IV. THE SUPREME COURT'S DECISION

"This case requires a discussion, and the proper application, of two doctrines: structural error and ineffective assistance of counsel. The two doctrines are intertwined; for the reasons an error is deemed structural may influence the proper standard used to evaluate an ineffective-assistance claim premised on the failure to object to that error. . . .

For these purposes, . . . one point is critical: An error can count as structural even if the error does not lead to fundamental unfairness in every case. . . .

[A] violation of the right to a public trial is a structural error. . . .

The Court now turns to the proper remedy for addressing the violation of a structural right, and in particular the right to a public trial. . . .

To obtain relief on the basis of ineffective assistance of counsel, the defendant as a general rule bears the burden to meet two standards. First, the defendant must show deficient performance—that the attorney's error was 'so serious that counsel was not functioning as the 'counsel' guaranteed the defendant by the Sixth Amendment.' Second, the defendant must show that the attorney's error 'prejudiced the defense.' . . .

In sum, '[a]n ineffective-assistance claim can function as a way to escape rules of waiver and forfeiture . . . ,' thus undermining the finality of jury verdicts. For this reason, the rules governing ineffective-assistance claims 'must be applied with scrupulous care.' . . .

The final inquiry concerns the ineffective-assistance claim . . . . Although the case comes on the assumption that petitioner has shown deficient performance by counsel, he has not shown prejudice . . . .

In sum, petitioner has not shown a reasonable probability of a different outcome but for counsel's failure to object, and he has not shown that counsel's shortcomings led to a fundamentally unfair trial. He is not entitled to a new trial. . . .

In the criminal justice system, the constant, indeed unending, duty of the judiciary is to seek and to find the proper balance between the necessity for fair and just trials and the importance of finality of judgments. When a structural error is preserved and raised on direct review, the balance is in the defendant's favor . . . . When a structural error is raised in the context of an ineffective-assistance claim, however, finality concerns are far more pronounced. For this reason, and in light of the other circumstances . . . , petitioner must show prejudice in order to obtain a new trial. [H]e has not made the required showing. The judgment of the Massachusetts Supreme Judicial Court is affirmed."

V. JUSTICE VOTE

2 Pro ACLU Side vs. 7 Con Opposing Side

ACLU Side (Petitioner / Appellant)

1. Kagan, E. – Joined Breyer's dissent
2. Breyer, S. – Wrote dissenting opinion

Opposing Side (Respondent / Appellee)

1. Kennedy, A. – Wrote majority opinion
2. Alito, S. – Wrote concurring opinion
3. Thomas, C. – Wrote concurring opinion
4. Gorsuch, N. – Joined Thomas' concurrence, joined Alito's concurrence
5. Ginsburg, R. – Joined majority opinion
6. Sotomayor, S. – Joined majority opinion
7. Roberts, J. – Joined majority opinion

VI. A WIN OR LOSS FOR THE ACLU?

The ACLU filed as amicus curiae urging reversal of the judgment of the Massachusetts Supreme Judicial Court; the Supreme Court affirmed in a 7-2 vote, giving the ACLU an apparent loss.

1164. Hernandez v. Mesa

(Decided June 26, 2017; 137 S.Ct. 2003; 582 U.S. _)

I. ISSUE

A. Issues Discussed

4th Amendment, immunity

B. Legal Question Presented

"This case involves a tragic cross-border incident in which a United States Border Patrol agent standing on United States soil shot and killed a Mexican national standing on Mexican soil. The three questions presented concern whether the parents of the victim of that shooting may assert claims for damages against the agent under Bivens v. Six Unknown Fed. Narcotics Agents, 403 U.S. 388 (1971); whether the shooting violated the victim's Fourth Amendment rights; and whether the agent is entitled to qualified immunity on a claim that the shooting violated the victim's Fifth Amendment rights."

C. Supreme Court's Answer

"The facts alleged in the complaint depict a disturbing incident resulting in a heartbreaking loss of life. Whether petitioners may recover damages . . . depends on questions that are best answered by the Court of Appeals in the first instance."

II. CASE SUMMARY

A. Background

"Sergio Adrián Hernández Güereca, a 15-year-old Mexican national, was with a group of friends in the cement culvert that separates El Paso, Texas, from Ciudad Juarez, Mexico. . . . The international boundary runs down the middle of the culvert, and at the top of the embankment on the United States side is a fence. . . . Hernández and his friends were playing a game in which they ran up the embankment on the United States side, touched the fence, and then ran back down. At some point, Border Patrol Agent Jesus Mesa, Jr., arrived on the scene by bicycle and detained one of Hernández's friends in United States territory . . . . Hernández ran across the international boundary into Mexican territory . . . . While in United States territory, Mesa then fired at least two shots across the border at Hernández. One shot struck Hernández in the face and killed him. . . . Hernández was unarmed and unthreatening....

The Department of Justice investigated [and] concluded ... 'the agent did not act inconsistently with [Customs and Border Patrol] policy or training regarding use of force.' ...

Petitioners—Hernández's parents—brought suit. Among other claims, petitioners brought claims against Mesa for damages under Bivens, alleging that Mesa violated Hernández's rights under the Fourth and Fifth Amendments. The United States District Court for the Western District of Texas granted Mesa's motion to dismiss. A panel of the Court of Appeals for the Fifth Circuit affirmed in part and reversed in part....

On rehearing en banc, the Court of Appeals unanimously affirmed the District Court's dismissal of petitioners' claims against Mesa."

The Supreme Court granted certiorari to review the case.

B. Counsel of Record / ACLU Attorney

ACLU Side (Petitioner / Appellant): Robert C. Hilliard argued the cause for appellants. With him on the brief were Steve D. Shadowen, Cristobal M. Galindo, Stephen I. Vladeck, Deepak Gupta, Jonathan E. Taylor, Rachel Bloomekatz, Matthew W. H. Wessler, Matthew Spurlock, and Leah M. Litman.

Opposing Side (Respondent / Appellee): Randolph J. Ortega argued the cause for appellee. With him on the brief were Gabriel Perez, Felix Valenzuela, and Louis Elias Lopez, Jr.

Deputy Solicitor General Kneedler argued the cause for federal appellees. With him on the brief were Acting Solicitor General Gershengorn, Counselor to the Solicitor General Gornstein, Assistant Solicitor General Fletcher, Principal Deputy Assistant Attorney General Mizer, Mark B. Stern, Mary Hampton Mason, and Henry C. Whitaker.

III. AMICI CURIAE

ACLU Side (Petitioner / Appellant)

Brief of amici curiae filed on behalf of the American Civil Liberties Union, the ACLU Foundation of San Diego & Imperial Counties, the ACLU Foundation of Texas, the ACLU Foundation of Arizona, and the ACLU of New Mexico by Rebecca L. Robertson, Edgar Saldivar, Kathleen E. Brody, Daniel J. Pochoda, Brenda Munoz Furnish, Elisabeth V. Bechtold, Maria M. Sanchez, Andre I. Segura, Lee Gelernt, Cecillia D. Wang, Cody Wofsy, Mitra Ebadolahi, and David Loy.

Brief of amici curiae filed on behalf of Constitutional Law Scholars by Jeffrey L. Bleich, Kelly D. Fair, David R. Simonton, Joseph D. Lee, Andrew C. Rubenstein, and Nicholas D. Fram.

Brief of amici curiae filed on behalf of the Government of the United Mexican States by Donald Francis Donovan and Carl J. Micarelli.

Brief of amici curiae filed on behalf of Constitutional Accountability Center by Elizabeth B. Wydra, Brianne J. Gorod, and David H. Gans.

Brief of amici curiae filed on behalf of Professors James E. Pfander et al. by Mr. Pfander, Sarah O'Rourke Schrup, and Jeffrey T. Green.

Brief of amici curiae filed on behalf of the American Immigration Council et al. by Mary A. Kenney, Matthew E. Price, Marina K. Jenkins, Tassity S. Johnson, Michael E. Stewart, Trina Realmuto, Matt Adams, Julia Yoo, Eugene Iredale, and Johnathan H. Feinberg.

Brief of amici curiae filed on behalf of Ten Law Professors by James R. Saywell, Louis K. Fisher, and Julia Fong Sheketoff.

Brief of amici curiae filed on behalf of Former Officials of U.S. Customs and Border Protection Agency by Kelsi Brown Corkran, Thomas M. Bondy, Rachel Wainer Apter, and Elizabeth G. Bentley.

Brief of amici curiae filed on behalf of Border Scholars by Ethan D. Dettmer, Eli M. Lazarus, Shailey Jain, Courtney J. Chin, Priyah Kaul, and Joshua S. Lipshutz.

Brief of amici curiae filed on behalf of Restore the Fourth, Inc., by Mahesha P. Subbaraman.

Brief of amici curiae filed on behalf of Legal Historians by Richard L. Aynes.

Brief of amici curiae filed on behalf of Border Action Network et al. By Nancy Winkelman and Emily Daly.

Brief of amici curiae filed on behalf of Amnesty International USA et al. by Hope Metcalf, Diala Shamas, and Brent M. Rosenthal.

Brief of amici curiae filed on behalf of Former Police Chiefs by Peter Karanjia and Jason Harrow.

Brief of amici curiae filed on behalf of Mexican Jurists, Practitioners, and Scholars by Carmine D. Boccuzzi, Jr., Howard S. Zelbo, William R. Thomas, and David I. Feinstein.

Opposing Side (Respondent / Appellee)

Brief of amici curiae filed on behalf of APA Watch by Lawrence J. Joseph.

Brief of amici curiae filed on behalf of the Criminal Justice Legal Foundation by Kent S. Scheidegger and Kymberlee C. Stapleton.

Brief of amici curiae filed on behalf of Professor Gregory C. Sisk by Ari J. Savitzky, David Sapir Lesser, and Sarah Mortazavi in support of neither party.

IV. THE SUPREME COURT'S DECISION

"The Court turns first to the Bivens question, which is 'antecedent' to the other questions presented....

The Court of Appeals ... has not had the opportunity to consider how the reasoning and analysis in Abbasi may bear on this case. And the parties have not had the opportunity to brief and argue its significance. In these circumstances, it is appropriate for the Court of Appeals, rather than this Court, to address the Bivens question in the first instance....

The Fourth Amendment question in this case ... is sensitive and may have consequences that are far reaching. It would be imprudent for this Court to resolve that issue when, in light of the intervening guidance provided in Abbasi, doing so may be unnecessary to resolve this particular case.

With respect to petitioners' Fifth Amendment claim, the ... en banc Court of Appeals ... erred in granting qualified immunity based on those facts....

Mesa and the Government contend that Mesa is entitled to

qualified immunity even if Mesa was uncertain about Hernández's nationality and his ties to the United States at the time of the shooting. The Government also argues that, in any event, petitioners' claim is cognizable only under the Fourth Amendment, and not under the Fifth Amendment. This Court declines to address these arguments in the first instance. . . .

The facts alleged in the complaint depict a disturbing incident resulting in a heartbreaking loss of life. Whether petitioners may recover damages . . . depends on questions that are best answered by the Court of Appeals in the first instance.

The judgment of the Court of Appeals is vacated, and the case is remanded . . . ."

V. JUSTICE VOTE

3 Pro ACLU Side vs. 5 Con Opposing Side

ACLU Side (Petitioner / Appellant)

1. Thomas, C. – Wrote dissenting opinion
2. Breyer, S. – Wrote dissenting opinion
3. Ginsburg, R. – Joined Breyer's dissent

Opposing Side (Respondent / Appellee)

1. Alito, S. – Per curiam decision
2. Kagan, E. – Per curiam decision
3. Kennedy, A. – Per curiam decision
4. Sotomayor, S. – Per curiam decision
5. Roberts, J. – Per curiam decision

Gorsuch, N. – Took no part in the decision.

VI. A WIN OR LOSS FOR THE ACLU?

The ACLU filed as amicus curiae urging reversal of the judgment of the Court of Appeals; the Supreme Court vacated in a 5-3 per curiam decision, giving the ACLU an apparent loss.

1165. Trinity Lutheran Church of Columbia, Inc. v. Comer

(Decided June 26, 2017; 137 S.Ct. 2012; 582 U.S. _)

I. ISSUE

A. Issues Discussed

1st Amendment, religion

B. Legal Question Presented

"The [Missouri] Department [of Natural Resources] had a policy of categorically disqualifying churches and other religious organizations from receiving grants under its playground resurfacing program. The question presented is whether the Department's policy violated the rights of Trinity Lutheran [Church] under the Free Exercise Clause of the First Amendment."

C. Supreme Court's Answer

"The State has pursued its preferred policy to the point of expressly denying a qualified religious entity a public benefit solely because of its religious character. Under our precedents, that goes too far. The Department's policy violates the Free Exercise Clause."

II. CASE SUMMARY

A. Background

"The Missouri Department of Natural Resources offers state grants to help public and private schools, nonprofit daycare centers, and other nonprofit entities purchase rubber playground surfaces made from recycled tires. Trinity Lutheran Church applied for such a grant for its preschool and daycare center and would have received one, but for the fact that Trinity Lutheran is a church. The Department had a policy of categorically disqualifying churches and other religious organizations from receiving grants under its playground resurfacing program. . . .

Trinity Lutheran sued the Director of the Department in Federal District Court. The Church alleged that the Department's failure to approve the Center's application, pursuant to its policy of denying grants to religiously affiliated applicants, violates the Free Exercise Clause of the First Amendment. Trinity Lutheran sought declaratory and injunctive relief prohibiting the Department from discriminating against the Church on that basis in future grant applications.

The District Court granted the Department's motion to dismiss. . . .

The Court of Appeals for the Eighth Circuit affirmed. . . .
Rehearing en banc was denied by an equally divided court."
The Supreme Court granted certiorari to review the case.

B. Counsel of Record / ACLU Attorney

ACLU Side (Respondent / Appellee): James R. Layton, Solicitor General of Missouri, argued the cause for appellee. With him on the briefs were Chris Koster, Attorney General, and James B. Farnsworth, Assistant Attorney General.

Opposing Side (Petitioner / Appellant): David A Cortman argued the cause for appellant. With him on the briefs were Erik W. Stanley, Kevin H. Theriot, Michael K. Whitehead, Jonathan R. Whitehead, Rory T. Gray, and Jordan W. Lorence.

III. AMICI CURIAE

ACLU Side (Respondent / Appellee)

Brief of amici curiae filed on behalf of American Civil Liberties Union, ACLU of Missouri, American Humanist Association, Center for Inquiry, Freedom from Religion Foundation, and People for the American Way Foundation by Daniel Mach, Heather L. Weaver, Anthony E. Rothert, Jared O. Freedman, Samuel F. Jacobson, Steven R. Shapiro, and Louise Melling.

Brief of amici curiae filed on behalf of Religious and Civil Rights Organizations by Richard B. Katskee, Alex J. Luchenitser, Andrew J. Pincus, Seth M. Marnin, David L. Barkey, Jeffrey I. Pasek, and Eugene R. Fidell.

Brief of amici curiae filed on behalf of Legal and Religious Historians by Steven K. Green and Douglas B. Mishkin.

Brief of amici curiae filed on behalf of Baptist Joint Committee for Religious Liberty et al. by K. Hollyn Hollman and Jennifer L. Hawks.

Brief of amici curiae filed on behalf of Lambda Legal Defense and Education Fund, Inc., by Susan L. Sommer, Jennifer C.

Pizer, and Camilla B. Taylor.

Brief of amici curiae filed on behalf of the National Education Association by Alice O'Brien, Kristen L. Hollar, and John M. West. Brief of amici curiae filed on behalf of American Jewish Committee by Brian C. Walsh, Robert L. Newmark, D. Bruce La Pierre, and Marc D. Stern in support of neither party.

Opposing Side (Petitioner / Appellant)

Brief of amici curiae filed on behalf of World Vision, Inc., by Eugene Volokh.

Brief of amici curiae filed on behalf of the American Center for Law and Justice by Jay Alan Sekulow, Stuart J. Roth, Colby M. May, and Walter M. Weber.

Brief of amici curiae filed on behalf of the Union of Orthodox Jewish Congregations of America by Michael Helfand and Nathan J. Diament.

Brief of amici curiae filed on behalf of Justice and Freedom Fund by James L. Hirsen and Deborah J. Dewart.

Brief of amici curiae filed on behalf of the Becket Fund for Religious Liberty by Luke W. Goodrich, Hannah C. Smith, and Michael W. McConnell.

Brief of amici curiae filed on behalf of Ethics & Religious Liberty Commission by Michael Lee Francisco.

Brief of amici curiae filed on behalf of Association of Christian Schools International et al. by Thomas G. Hungar, Russell B. Balikian, Chad R. Mizelle, Benjamin J. Cassady, Kevin J. Barber, and Nathan H. Jack.

Brief of amici curiae filed on behalf of the Bronx Household of Faith by Allison B. Jones and William T. Marks.

Brief of amici curiae filed on behalf of Institutional Religious Freedom Alliance by C. Kevin Marshall, Ryan J. Watson, and Joshua I. Hammack.

Brief of amici curiae filed on behalf of American Association of Christian Schools by Matthew T. Martens, Ashley E. Bashur, William Osberghaus, Daniel Hartman, and Kevin Gallagher.

Brief of amici curiae filed on behalf of Members of Congress by Ryan L. Bangert, Helena H. Henry, Aaron M. Streett, Benjamin A. Geslison, and J. Mark Little.

Brief of amici curiae filed on behalf of Council for Christian Colleges and Universities et al. by Gene C. Schaerr and S. Kyle Duncan.

Brief of amici curiae filed on behalf of Institute for Justice by Richard D. Komer, Timothy D. Keller, and Michael E. Bindas.

Brief of amici curiae filed on behalf of Douglas County School District et al. by Douglas Laycock, James M. Lyons, L. Martin Nussbaum, Eric V. Hall, Paul D. Clement, George W. Hicks, and Andrew N. Ferguson.

Brief of amici curiae filed on behalf of the National Association of Evangelicals by Mark F. (Thor) Hearne II and Stephen S. Davis.

Brief of amici curiae filed on behalf of Pacific Legal Foundation by Meriem L. Hubbard, Wencong Fa, and Raymond J. Nhan.

Brief of amici curiae filed on behalf of the State of Nevada et al. by Adam Paul Laxalt, Attorney General of Nevada, Lawrence Vandyke, Solicitor General, Joseph Tartakovsky, Deputy Solicitor General, and by the Attorneys General for their respective States as follows: Luther Strange of Alabama, Mark Brnovich of Arizona, Leslie Rutledge of Arkansas, Pamela Jo Bondi of Florida, Sam Olens of Georgia, Jeff Landry of Louisiana, Bill Schuette of Michigan, Tim Fox of Montana, Douglas J. Peterson of Nebraska, Michael DeWine of Ohio, E. Scott Pruitt of Oklahoma, Alan Wilson of South Carolina, Marty J. Jackley of South Dakota, Ken Paxton of Texas, Sean Reyes of Utah, Patrick Morrisey of West Virginia, and Brad D. Schimel of Wisconsin.

Brief of amici curiae filed on behalf of the General Council of the Assemblies of God by Joshua D. Hawley, Erin Morrow Hawley, and Darryl P. Rains.

Brief of amici curiae filed on behalf of Belmont Abbey College by Joseph J. Lobue, Brendan C. McNamara, and Mark L. Rienzi.

Brief of amici curiae filed on behalf of Law and Religion Practitioners by Mark Goldfeder, Anton Sorkin, David I. Schoen, and Elliot Pasik.

Brief of amici curiae filed on behalf of the Cato Institute by Ilya Shapiro and Jayme Weber.

Brief of amici curiae filed on behalf of Christian Legal Society et al. by Thomas C. Berg, Travis Weber, and Kimberlee Wood Colby.

Brief of amici curiae filed on behalf of the State of Colorado by Cynthia H. Coffman, Attorney General of Colorado, Frederick R. Yarger, Solicitor General, David Blake, Chief Deputy Attorney General, and Glenn E. Roper, Deputy Solicitor General.

Brief of amici curiae filed on behalf of United States Conference of Catholic Bishops et al. by Anthony R. Picarello, Jr., Jeffrey Hunter Moon, Michael F. Moses, Hillary E. Byrnes, Paul J. Zidlicky, Edward McNicholas, HL Rogers, Eric D. McArthur, Benjamin Beaton, Alexander Dushku, Kevin P. Garvey, R. Shawn Gunnarson, Cormac A. Early, and Tyler McClay.

Brief of amici curiae filed on behalf of Liberty Counsel et al. by Mathew D. Staver, Anita L. Staver, Horatio G. Mihet, and Mary E. McAlister.

Brief of amici curiae filed on behalf of Wallbuilders, Inc., by Steven W. Fitschen.

IV. THE SUPREME COURT'S DECISION

"The First Amendment provides, in part, that 'Congress shall make no law respecting an establishment of religion, or prohibiting the free exercise thereof.' The parties agree that the Establishment Clause of that Amendment does not prevent Missouri from including Trinity Lutheran in the Scrap Tire Program. That does not, however, answer the question under the Free Exercise Clause, because we have recognized that there is 'play in the joints' between what the Establishment Clause permits and the Free Exercise Clause compels. . . .

In recent years, when this Court has rejected free exercise challenges, the laws in question have been neutral and generally applicable without regard to religion. We have been careful to distinguish such laws from those that single out the religious for disfavored treatment. . . .

The Department's policy expressly discriminates against otherwise eligible recipients by disqualifying them from a public benefit solely because of their religious character. [S]uch a policy imposes a penalty on the free exercise of religion that triggers the most exacting scrutiny. . . .

It is true the Department has not criminalized the way Trinity Lutheran worships or told the Church that it cannot subscribe to a certain view of the Gospel. But, as the Department itself acknowledges, the Free Exercise Clause protects against "indirect coercion or penalties on the free exercise of religion, not just outright prohibitions.' . . .

In this case, there is no dispute that Trinity Lutheran is put to the choice between being a church and receiving a government benefit. The rule is simple: No churches need apply. . . .

The State in this case expressly requires Trinity Lutheran to renounce its religious character in order to participate in an otherwise generally available public benefit program, for which it is fully qualified. Our cases make clear that such a condition imposes a penalty on the free exercise of religion that must be subjected to the 'most rigorous' scrutiny. . . .

The State has pursued its preferred policy to the point of expressly denying a qualified religious entity a public benefit solely because of its religious character. Under our precedents, that goes too far. The Department's policy violates the Free Exercise Clause. . . .

The judgment of the United States Court of Appeals for the Eighth Circuit is reversed, and the case is remanded . . . ."

V. JUSTICE VOTE

2 Pro ACLU Side vs. 7 Con Opposing Side

ACLU Side (Respondent / Appellee)

1. Ginsburg, R. – Joined Sotomayor's dissent
2. Sotomayor, S. – Wrote dissenting opinion

Opposing Side (Petitioner / Appellant)

1. Roberts, J. – Wrote majority opinion
2. Alito, S. – Joined majority opinion
3. Kagan, E. – Joined majority opinion
4. Thomas, C. – Wrote concurring opinion, joined Gorsuch's concurrence
5. Breyer, S. – Wrote concurring opinion
6. Gorsuch, N. – Wrote concurring opinion, joined Thomas' concurrence
7. Kennedy, A. – Joined majority opinion

VI. A WIN OR LOSS FOR THE ACLU?

The ACLU filed as amicus curiae urging affirmance; the Supreme Court reversed the Court of Appeals' decision by a 7-2 vote, giving the ACLU an apparent loss.

1166. Davila v. Davis

(Decided June 26, 2017; 137 S.Ct. 2058; 582 U.S. _)

I. ISSUE

A. Issues Discussed

Criminal procedure

B. Legal Question Presented

"In Martinez v. Ryan, 566 U.S. 1 (2012), and Trevino v. Thaler, 569 U.S. 413 (2013), this Court announced a narrow exception to Coleman's general rule. That exception treats ineffective assistance by a prisoner's state postconviction counsel as cause to overcome the default of a single claim—ineffective assistance of trial counsel—in a single context—where the State effectively requires a defendant to bring that claim in state postconviction proceedings rather than on direct appeal. The question in this case is whether we should extend that exception to allow federal courts to consider a different kind of defaulted claim—ineffective assistance of appellate counsel."

C. Supreme Court's Answer

"We decline to do so."

II. CASE SUMMARY

A. Background

"[A] group . . . gathered at Annette Stevenson's home to celebrate her granddaughter's birthday. Petitioner Erick Daniel Davila, believing he had seen a member of a rival street gang at the celebration, fired a rifle at the group . . . . He shot and killed Annette and her 5-year-old granddaughter Queshawn, and he wounded three other children and one woman.

After the police arrested petitioner, he confessed to the killings. He stated that he . . . was trying to kill Annette's son (and Queshawn's father) Jerry Stevenson and the other 'guys on the porch.' The other 'guys on the porch' were, apparently, women.

The State indicted petitioner for capital murder . . . . In response to the jury's request for clarification . . . , the trial court proposed instructing the jury on transferred intent. Under that doctrine, the jury could find petitioner guilty of murder if it determined that he intended to kill one person but instead killed a different person. Petitioner's counsel objected . . . . The trial court overruled the objection and submitted the instruction to the jury. The jury convicted petitioner of capital murder, and the trial court sentenced petitioner to death. . . .

Petitioner appealed . . . . The Texas Court of Criminal Appeals affirmed petitioner's conviction and sentence. . . .

Petitioner . . . sought habeas relief . . . . The Texas Court of Criminal Appeals denied relief. . . .

Petitioner then sought habeas relief in Federal District Court under 28 U.S.C. § 2254. . . .

The District Court denied petitioner's § 2254 petition. . . . The Court of Appeals for the Fifth Circuit denied a certificate of appealability . . . ."

The Supreme Court granted certiorari to review the case.

B. Counsel of Record / ACLU Attorney

ACLU Side (Petitioner / Appellant): Seth Kretzer argued the cause for appellants. With him on the brief were William R. Peterson and Jonathan Landers.

Opposing Side (Respondent / Appellee): Scott A. Keller, Solicitor General of Texas, argued the cause for appellee. With him on the brief were Ken Paxton, Attorney General, Jeffrey C. Mateer, First Assistant Attorney General, J. Campbell Barker, Deputy

Solicitor General, and Heather Gebelin Hacker and Jason R. LaFond, Assistant Solicitors General.

III. AMICI CURIAE

ACLU Side (Petitioner / Appellant)

Brief of amici curiae filed on behalf of the National Association of Criminal Defense Lawyers and the American Civil Liberties Union by Barbara E. Bergman, David D. Cole, Seth P. Waxman, Catherine M.A. Carroll, Robbie Manhas, Hyun Gyo Chung, Brian W. Stull, Cassandra Stubbs, and Rebecca L. Robertson.

Opposing Side (Respondent / Appellee)

Brief of amici curiae filed on behalf of the Criminal Justice Legal Foundation by Kent S. Scheidegger and Kymberlee C. Stapleton.

Brief of amici curiae filed on behalf of the State of Nevada et al. by Adam Paul Laxalt, Attorney General of Nevada, Joseph Tartakovsky, Deputy Solicitor General, Jeffrey M. Conner, Assistant Solicitor General, Jordan T. Smith, Assistant Solicitor General, and by the Attorneys General for their respective States as follows: Steven T. Marshall of Alabama, Mark Brnovich of Arizona, Leslie Rutledge of Arkansas, Cynthia Coffman of Colorado, Matthew P. Denn of Delaware, Pamela Jo Bondi of Florida, Christopher M. Carr of Georgia, Lawrence G. Wasden of Idaho, Curtis T. Hill, Jr., of Indiana, Derek Schmidt of Kansas, Andy Beshear of Kentucky, Jeff Landry of Louisiana, Bill Schuette of Michigan, Jim Hood of Mississippi, Joshua D. Hawley of Missouri, Timothy C. Fox of Montana, Doug Peterson of Nebraska, Wayne Stenehjem of North Dakota, Michael DeWine of Ohio, Mike Hunter of Oklahoma, Ellen F. Rosenblum of Oregon, Alan Wilson of South Carolina, Marty J. Jackley of South Dakota, Herbert H. Slatery III of Tennessee, Sean Reyes of Utah, Robert W. Ferguson of Washington, Patrick Morrisey of West Virginia, Brad D. Schimel of Wisconsin, and Peter K. Michael of Wyoming.

IV. THE SUPREME COURT'S DECISION

"Our decision in this case is guided by two fundamental tenets of federal review of state convictions. First, a state prisoner must exhaust available state remedies before presenting his claim to a federal habeas court. . . .

Second, a federal court may not review federal claims . . . procedurally defaulted in state court . . . .

A state prisoner may overcome the prohibition . . . if he can show 'cause' to excuse his failure to comply with the state procedural rule and 'actual prejudice . . . .' . . .

It has long been the rule that attorney error is an objective external factor providing cause for excusing a procedural default only if that error amounted to a deprivation of the constitutional right to counsel. [I]n Coleman, this Court held that attorney error committed in the course of state postconviction proceedings—for which the Constitution does not guarantee the right to counsel . . . —cannot supply cause to excuse a procedural default that occurs in those proceedings.

In Martinez, this Court announced a narrow, 'equitable . . . qualification' of the rule in Coleman that applies where state law requires prisoners to raise claims of ineffective assistance of trial counsel 'in an initial-review collateral proceeding,' rather than on direct appeal. . . .

Petitioner asks us to extend Martinez to allow a federal court to hear a substantial, but procedurally defaulted, claim of ineffective assistance of appellate counsel when a prisoner's state postconviction counsel provides ineffective assistance by failing to raise that claim. We decline to do so. . . .

Petitioner argues that allowing a claim of ineffective assistance of appellate counsel to evade review is just as concerning as allowing a claim of ineffective assistance of trial counsel to evade review. We do not agree. . . .

Finally, the Court in Martinez grounded its decision in part on the belief that its narrow exception was unlikely to impose significant systemic costs. The same cannot be said of petitioner's proposed extension. . . .

Adopting petitioner's argument could flood the federal courts with defaulted claims . . . .

Expanding Martinez would not only impose significant costs on the federal courts, but would also aggravate the harm to federalism that federal habeas review necessarily causes. . . .

Not only would these burdens on the federal courts and our federal system be severe, but the benefit would—as a systemic matter—be small. . . .Given that petitioner's proposed rule would likely generate high systemic costs and low systemic benefits, and that the unique concerns of Martinez are not implicated in cases like his, we do not think equity requires an expansion of Martinez. . . .

For the foregoing reasons, we affirm the judgment of the Court of Appeals."

V. JUSTICE VOTE

4 Pro ACLU Side vs. 5 Con Opposing Side

ACLU Side (Petitioner / Appellant)

1. Kagan, E. – Joined Breyer's dissent
2. Breyer, S. – Wrote dissenting opinion
3. Ginsburg, R. – Joined Breyer's dissent
4. Sotomayor, S. – Joined Breyer's dissent

Opposing Side (Respondent / Appellee)

1. Thomas, C. – Wrote majority opinion
2. Alito, S. – Joined majority opinion
3. Gorsuch, N. – Joined majority opinion
4. Kennedy, A. – Joined majority opinion
5. Roberts, J. – Joined majority opinion

VI. A WIN OR LOSS FOR THE ACLU?

The ACLU filed as amicus curiae urging reversal of the judgment of the Court of Appeals; the Supreme Court affirmed in a 5-4 vote, giving the ACLU an apparent loss.

1167. Trump v. Int'l Refugee Assistance Project

(Decided June 26, 2017; 137 S.Ct. 2080; 582 U.S. _)

I. ISSUE

A. Issues Discussed

Immigration/Citizenship

B. Legal Question Presented

Whether the Court should grant the stay applications pending review on the merits.

C. Supreme Court's Answer

"We accordingly grant the Government's stay applications in part and narrow the scope of the injunctions as to § 2(c). . . .

The Government's application to stay the injunction with respect to §§ 6(a) and (b) is accordingly granted in part."

II. CASE SUMMARY

A. Background

"These cases involve challenges to Executive Order No. 13780, Protecting the Nation From Foreign Terrorist Entry Into the United States. The order alters practices concerning the entry of foreign nationals into the United States by, among other things, suspending entry of nationals from six designated countries for 90 days. Respondents challenged the order in two separate lawsuits. They obtained preliminary injunctions barring enforcement of several of its provisions, including the 90-day suspension of entry. The injunctions were upheld in large measure by the Courts of Appeals.

The Government filed separate petitions for certiorari, as well as applications to stay the preliminary injunctions entered by the lower courts."

B. Counsel of Record / ACLU Attorney

ACLU Side (Respondent / Appellee): Omar C. Jadwat, Lee Gelernt, Hina Shamsi, Hugh Handeyside, Sarah L. Mehta, Spencer E. Amdur, David Cole, Daniel Mach, Heather L. Weaver, Cecillia D. Wang, and Cody H. Wofsy of the American Civil Liberties Union Foundation, and David Rocah, Deborah A. Jeon, Sonia Kumar, and Nicholas Taichi Steiner of the American Civil Liberties Union Foundation of Maryland, and Karen C. Tumlin, Nicholas Espíritu, Melissa S. Keaney, Esther Sung, Marielena Hincapié, and Justin B. Cox filed briefs for appellee.

Opposing Side (Petitioner / Appellant): Acting Solicitor General Wall, Acting Assistant Attorney General Readler, Deputy Solicitor General Kneedler, Deputy Assistant Attorney General Mooppan, Assistant Solicitor General Bond, Special Counsel Flentje, Douglas N. Letter, Sharon Swingle, H. Thomas Byron III, Lowell V. Sturgill, Jr., and Anne Murphy filed briefs for appellant.

III. AMICI CURIAE

ACLU Side (Respondent / Appellee)

Brief of amici curiae filed on behalf of the Roderick and Solange MacArthur Justice Center by Amir H. Ali.

Brief of amici curiae filed on behalf of Interfaith Coalition by Robert D. Fram, Robert Long, Ligia Markman, Karun Tilak, Michael Baker, and Andrew Guy.

Brief of amici curiae filed on behalf of T.A., a United States Citizen of Yemeni Descent, by Shaimaa M. Hussein, D. Nicole Guntner, Matthew R. Dollan, and Richard D. Bernstein.

Brief of amici curiae filed on behalf of National CIS Council 119 by Muhammad U. Faridi, Elizabeth Riordan Hurley, Michael N. Fresco, and James R. Parks.

Brief of amici curiae filed on behalf of Chicago et al. by Nick Kahlon, Edward N. Siskel, Chicago City Corporation Counsel, Benna Ruth Solomon, Deputy Corporation Counsel, Andrew W. Worseck, Chief Assistant Corporation Counsel, Jonathon D. Byrer, Assistant Corporation Counsel, Michael N. Feuer, City Attorney, Zachary W. Carter, New York City Corporation Counsel, Sozi Pedro Tulante, Philadelphia City Solicitor, Carl Newman, Sara K. Hornstra, Ryan P. Poscablo, Brian Neff, Eliberty Lopez, John Daniel Reaves, and Mark Muedeking.

Brief of amici curiae filed on behalf of the Cato Institute by Daniel Braun, Peter Jaffe, Brent Wible, David Y. Livshiz, and Karen Wiswall.

Brief of amici curiae filed on behalf of International Law Scholars et al. by Elisabeth C. Frost, Amanda R. Callais, and Aaron X. Fellmeth.

Brief of amici curiae filed on behalf of Freedom from Religion Foundation by Rebecca S. Markert.

Brief of amici curiae filed on behalf of Civil Rights Organizations by Lynne Bernabei and Alan R. Kabat.

Brief of amici curiae filed on behalf of David Boyle by Mr. Boyle.

Brief of amici curiae filed on behalf of the Decalogue Society of Lawyers by Jonathan Lubin.

Brief of amici curiae filed on behalf of Constitutional Law Scholars by Alexandra M. Walsh, Kieran Gostin, Roxana C. Guidero, Michael J. Zydney, and Ilya Somin.

Brief of amici curiae filed on behalf of International Lawyers for International Law by Curtis FJ Doebbler.

Brief of amici curiae filed on behalf of the Anti-Defamation League et al. by John B. Harris and Lily Landsman-Roos.

Brief of amici curiae filed on behalf of the Japanese American Citizens League by George T. Frampton, Jr., Thomas Frampton, Joseph N. Roth, and Walter Dellinger.

Brief of amici curiae filed on behalf of Khizr Khan by John W. Keker, Dan Jackson, and R. Adam Lauridsen.

Brief of amici curiae filed on behalf of 37 Appellate Lawyers by Charles A. Bird.

Brief of amici curiae filed on behalf of American Jewish Committee by Marc D. Stern, Adam S. Lurie, Vijaya R. Palaniswamy, Caitlin K. Potratz, John W. Akin, and Ishita Kala.

Brief of amici curiae filed on behalf of KARAMAH by Fatema Merchant, Sean M. Cuddihy, Imad S. Matini, Abraham

J. Shanedling, Amber Thomson, James McGinnis, David Douglass, Scott Maberry, Daniel L. Brown, Saleema Snow, and Aisha Rahman.

Brief of amici curiae filed on behalf of Episcopal Bishops by Michael R. Scott and Amit D. Ranade.

Brief of amici curiae filed on behalf of Constitutional Law Scholars by Roberta A. Kaplan and Joshua Matz.

Brief of amici curiae filed on behalf of International Labor Organizations by Lynn K. Rhinehart, Harold C. Becker, Matthew J. Ginsburg, Nicole G. Berner, Deborah L. Smith, Leo Gertner, Trisha Pande, Judith Rivlin, David J. Strom, Jody Calemine, Joseph E. Kolick, Jr., Niraj R. Ganatra, Ava Barbour, Mario Martínez, Nicholas Clark, and Richard J. Brean.

Brief of amici curiae filed on behalf of Scholars of Federal Jurisdiction by Stephen I. Vladeck, Omar A. Khan, Jamie Dycus, Adriel I. Cepeda Derieux, Ryan Chabot, Seth P. Waxman, and Mark C. Fleming.

Brief of amici curiae filed on behalf of the State of New York et al. by Eric T. Schneiderman, Attorney General of New York, Barbara D. Underwood, Solicitor General, Anisha S. Dasgupta, Deputy Solicitor General, Zainab A. Chaudhry, Assistant Attorney General, Lisa Madigan Attorney General of Illinois, David L. Franklin, Solicitor General, Brett E. Legner, Deputy Solicitor General, and by the Attorneys General for their respective jurisdictions as follows: Xavier Becerra of California, George Jepsen of Connecticut, Matthew P. Denn of Delaware, Karl A. Racine of the District of Columbia, Thomas J. Miller of Iowa, Janet T. Mills of Maine, Brian E. Frosh of Maryland, Maura Healey of Massachusetts, Hector Balderas of New Mexico, Josh Stein of North Carolina, Ellen F. Rosenblum of Oregon, Josh Shapiro of Pennsylvania, Peter F. Kilmartin of Rhode Island, Thomas J. Donovan, Jr., of Vermont, Mark R. Herring of Virginia, and Bob Ferguson of Washington.

Brief of amici curiae filed on behalf of Professors of Federal Courts Jurisprudence et al. by Catherine Y. Kim, Judith Resnik, Burt Neuborne, Lucas Guttentag, Fred A. Rowley, Jr., Mark R. Yohalem, John L. Schwab, and Susan S. Har.

Brief of amici curiae filed on behalf of the Foundation for the Children of Iran et al. by Brian T. Burgess, Kevin P. Martin, Nicholas K. Mitrokostas, William B. Brady, and Eileen L. Morrison.

Brief of amici curiae filed on behalf of Pars Equality Center et al. by Kristen Clarke, Jon Greenbaum, Mateya Kelley, Cyrus Mehri, Joanna K. Wasik, Lisa S. Blatt, John A. Freedman, R. Stanton Jones, Samuel M. Witten, Sally L. Pei, Sonia Tabriz, Stephen K. Wirth, Christopher M. Odell, Adrienne D. Boyd, David P. Gersch, Nancy L. Perkins, Allison B. Rumsey, Ronald A. Schechter, Robert N. Weiner, and Susan S. Hu.

Brief of amici curiae filed on behalf of Tahirih Justice Center et al. by Scott L. Winkelman, Luke Van Houwelingen, Dalal Hasan, Avi Rutschman, and Justin D. Kingsolver.

Brief of amici curiae filed on behalf of the United States Conference of Catholic Bishops et al. by Anthony R. Picarello, Jr., Jeffrey Hunter Moon, Carlos Ortiz Miranda, Theodore J. Boutrous Jr., Ethan D. Dettmer, and Joshua S. Lipshutz.

Brief of amici curiae filed on behalf of the Port of Seattle by William B. Adams, Ellyde R. Thompson, and Owen F. Roberts.

Brief of amici curiae filed on behalf of Members of Congress by Elizabeth B. Wydra, Brianne J. Gorod, David H. Gans, Peter Karanjia, Geoffrey Brounell, Victor A. Kovner, and Raymond H. Brescia.

Brief of amici curiae filed on behalf of Colleges and Universities by Thomas J. Perrelli, Lindsay C. Harrison, and Tassity S. Johnson.

Brief of amici curiae filed on behalf of Members of the Clergy et al. by Gillian B. Gillers, Kristi L. Graunke, Naomi R. Tsu, Richard B. Katskee, Eric Rothschild, and Andrew L. Nellis.

Brief of amici curiae filed on behalf of American-Arab Anti-Discrimination Committee by Abed A. Ayoub, Samer E. Khalaf, Yolanda C. Rondon, Anton G. Hajjar, Christopher J. Wright, Adrienne E. Fowler, and E. Austin Bonner.

Brief of amici curiae filed on behalf of Immigration Law Professors et al. by Mark A. Aronchick and Robert A. Wiygul.

Brief of amici curiae filed on behalf of American Professional Society on the Abuse of Children by Mary Kelly Persyn.

Brief of amici curiae filed on behalf of 161 Technology Companies by Andrew J. Pincus, Paul W. Hughes, and John T. Lewis.

Brief of amici curiae filed on behalf of Karen Korematsu et al. by Robert S. Chang, Lorraine K. Bannai, Pratik A. Shah, Eric K. Yamamoto, Fred T. Korematsu, Robert L. Rusky, Dale Minami, Donald K. Tamaki, Peter Irons, Leigh-Ann K. Miyasato, Martine E. Cicconi, Robert A. Johnson, Alice Hsu, Jessica M. Weisel, and Rodney L. Kawakami.

Brief of amici curiae filed on behalf of the Association of Art Museum Directors et al. by Antonio J. Perez-Marques, Avi Gesser, Kelsey Clark, Joseph Garmon, Jennifer Prevete, and Ilan Stein.

Brief of amici curiae filed on behalf of PEN American Center et al. by Robert D. Balin, Abigail B. Everdell, Jaya Kasibhatla, and Robert Corn-Revere.

Brief of amici curiae filed on behalf of Social Science Scholars by Robert Reeves Anderson, Anton A. Ware, George F. Langendorf, Aziz Huq, Farhana Khera, Johnathan Smith, and Sirine Shebaya.

Brief of amici curiae filed on behalf of American Council on Education et al. by Brad D. Brian, Michael R. Doyen, Chad Golder, and Adele M. El-Khouri.

Brief of amici curiae filed on behalf of Muslim Justice League et al. by Benjamin G. Shatz, Amy B. Briggs, John W. McGuinness, Sirena P. Castillo, Matthew D. Bottomly, Olufunmilayo Showole, and Ketakee R. Kane.

Brief of amici curiae filed on behalf of Human Rights First et al. by G. Eric Brunstad, Jr.

Brief of amici curiae filed on behalf of Immigration Equality et al. by Eric J. Gorman, Matthew E. Sloan, Noelle M. Reed, Allison B. Holcombe, Richard A. Schwartz, Alyssa J. Clover, Sarah Grossnickle, Jonathan Fombonne, Jennifer H. Berman, Joseph M. Sandman, Brittany Ellenberg, Aaron Morris, Virginia M. Goggin, and Glenn Magpantay.

Brief of amici curiae filed on behalf of Former National Security Officials by Phil Spector, Harold Hongju Koh, Hope Metcalf, Matthew S. Blumenthal, Jonathan Freiman, Tahlia Townsend,

William J. Murphy, and John J. Connolly.
Brief of amici curiae filed on behalf of NAACP Legal Defense & Educational Fund, Inc., by Sherrilyn A. Ifill, Ajmel Quereshi, Janai S. Nelson, Christopher Kemmitt, Samuel Spital, and Jin Hee Lee.
Brief of amici curiae filed on behalf of the American Bar Association by Sidney S. Rosdeitcher, Aidan Synnott, Arianna Markel, and Hilarie Bass.
Brief of amici curiae filed on behalf of Massachusetts Technology Leadership Council, Inc., by Christopher Hart, Michael B. Keating, Kristyn M. DeFilipp, and Daniel L. McFadden.
Brief of amici curiae filed on behalf of the Association of American Medical Colleges et al. by Frank R. Trinity, Amber R. Sterling, Joshua David Rogaczewski, Jennifer S. Geetter, and Matthew M. Girgenti.
Brief of amici curiae filed on behalf of Certain Immigrant Rights Organizations by Harrison (Buzz) Frahn, Reena T. Mittelman, Adrienne V. Baxley, Tomi Mendel, and Alan C. Turner.
Brief of amici curiae filed on behalf of Executive Branch Officials by Matthew L. Bush, Robert M. Loeb, Kelsi Brown Corkran, Thomas M. Bondy, Chris Richart, and Alec Schierenbeck.
Brief of amici curiae filed on behalf of Refugee Organizations by Christopher Mortweet, K. Ruby Bielik, Richard P. Bress, Alexandra Shechtel, Alan Billharz, Jayne Fleming, James C. Martin, Donna M. Doblick, and Devin M. Misour.
Brief of amici curiae filed on behalf of Interfaith Group of Religious and Interreligious Organizations by Purvi G. Patel, Jennifer K. Brown, Amanda Aikman, Joseph R. Palmore, Marc A. Hearron, Sophia M. Brill, and Sandeep N. Nandivada.
Brief of amici curiae filed on behalf of Syrian Asylee Ahmad M. by Vincent Levy, Gregory Dubinsky, Matthew V.H. Noller, and Kevin D. Benish.
Brief of amici curiae filed on behalf of the National Education Association by Alice O'Brien, Emma Leheny, Lubna A. Alam, and Sean Goldhammer.
Brief of amici curiae filed on behalf of Immigration Law Scholars by Deborah Anker, Sabrineh Ardalan, Philip L. Torrey, Fatma Marouf, Geoffrey Hoffman, Alan Hyde, and Karla McKander.
Brief of amici curiae filed on behalf of the National Asian Pacific American Bar Association et al. by Tina R. Matsuoka, Navdeep Singh, Meredith S.H. Higashi, Rachana Pathak, Albert Giang, James W. Kim, Andrew J. Genz, and Philip J. Levine.
Brief of amici curiae filed on behalf of New York University by Terrance J. Nolan, Steven E. Obus, Seth D. Fiur, Tiffany M. Woo, and Lary A. Rappaport.
Brief of amici curiae filed on behalf of Advocates for Human Rights et al. by Alina Das and Nancy Morawetz.
Brief of amici curiae filed on behalf of Hussam Ayloush et al. by Lena F. Masri, Gadeir I. Abbas, Jethro Eisenstein, Michael Price, and Faiza Patel.
Brief of amici curiae filed on behalf of Howard University School of Law Civil Rights Clinic et al. by Darin Johnson and Karla McKanders.
Brief of amici curiae filed on behalf of Janet A. Napolitano et al. by Michael J. Gottlieb, Joshua Riley, Isra J. Bhatty, and J. Wells Harrell.

Opposing Side (Petitioner / Appellant)

Brief of amici curiae filed on behalf of Professor Victor Williams by Mr. Williams.
Brief of amici curiae filed on behalf of American Center for Law and Justice by Edward L. White III, Erik M. Zimmerman, Francis J. Manion, Geoffrey R. Surtees, Jay Alan Sekulow, Stuart J. Roth, Colby M. May, Andrew J. Ekonomou, Jordan Sekulow, Craig L. Parshall, Matthew R. Clark, and Benjamin P. Sisney.
Brief of amici curiae filed on behalf of the State of Texas et al. by Ken Paxton, Attorney General of Texas, Jeffrey C. Mateer, First Assistant Attorney General, Scott A. Keller, Solicitor General, J. Campbell Barker, Deputy Solicitor General, Ari Cuenin, Assistant Solicitor General, and by the Attorneys General for their respective States as follows: Steve Marshall of Alabama, Mark Brnovich of Arizona, Leslie Rutledge of Arkansas, Pamela Jo Bondi of Florida, Derek Schmidt of Kansas, Jeff Landry of Louisiana, Phil Bryant of Mississippi, Joshua D. Hawley of Missouri, Wayne Stenehjem of North Dakota, Michael DeWine of Ohio, Mike Hunter of Oklahoma, Alan Wilson of South Carolina, Marty J. Jackley of South Dakota, Herbert H. Slatery III of Tennessee, and Patrick Morrisey of West Virginia .
Brief of amici curiae filed on behalf of Eagle Forum Education & Legal Defense Fund by Lawrence J. Joseph.
Brief of amici curiae filed on behalf of the American Civil Rights Union by Kenneth A. Klukowski.
Brief of amici curiae filed on behalf of the Zionist Organization of America (ZOA) by Elizabeth Berney.
Brief of amici curiae filed on behalf of National Security Experts Andrew C. McCarthy et al. by David Yerushalmi and Robert Joseph Muise.
Brief of amici curiae filed on behalf of Citizens United et al. by Michael Boos, William J. Olson, Herbert W. Titus, Jeremiah L. Morgan, Robert J. Olson, and Joseph W. Miller.
Brief of amici curiae filed on behalf of Immigration Reform Law Institute by Christopher J. Hajec, Michael M. Hethmon, Elizabeth A. Hohenstein, Mark S. Venezia, and Julie B. Axelrod.
Brief of amici curiae filed on behalf of Southeastern Legal Foundation by Kimberly S. Hermann, William S. Consovoy, and J. Michael Connolly.
Brief of amici curiae filed on behalf of American Legislators in Support of Judicial Restraint by Erin Elizabeth Mersino, William Wagner, and John Kane.
Brief of amici curiae filed on behalf of Scholars of Mormon History & Law by Anna-Rose Mathieson and Ben Feuer in support of neither party.
Brief of amici curiae filed on behalf of the Becket Fund for Religious Liberty by Mark L. Rienzi, Eric C. Rassbach, Hannah C. Smith, Diana M. Verm, Joseph C. Davis, and Rachel N. Busick in support of neither party.
Brief of amici curiae filed on behalf of Public Policy Legal Institute et al. by Barnaby W. Zall, Allen Dickerson, and Zac Morgan in support of neither party.

Brief of amici curiae filed on behalf of the Criminal Justice Legal Foundation by Kent S. Scheidegger and Kymberlee Stapleton in support of neither party.

Brief of amici curiae filed on behalf of Hardwired Global et al. by Bruce D. Abramson and Gregory Dolin in support of neither party.

IV. THE SUPREME COURT'S DECISION

"In IRAP, the Government argues that respondent Doe lacks standing to challenge § 2(c). The Government also contends that Doe's Establishment Clause claim fails on the merits. . . . At the very least, the Government argues, the injunction is too broad.

In Hawaii, the Government likewise argues that respondents Hawaii and Dr. Elshikh lack standing and that (at a minimum) the injunction should be narrowed. . . .

In addition to seeking certiorari, the Government asks the Court to stay the injunctions entered below . . . . According to the Government, it is likely to suffer irreparable harm unless a stay issues. . . .

To begin, we grant both of the Government's petitions for certiorari and consolidate the cases for argument. . . . In addition to the issues identified in the petitions, the parties are directed to address the following question: 'Whether the challenges to § 2(c) became moot on June 14, 2017.' . . .

We now turn to the preliminary injunctions barring enforcement of the § 2(c) entry suspension. We grant the Government's applications to stay the injunctions, to the extent the injunctions prevent enforcement of § 2(c) with respect to foreign nationals who lack any bona fide relationship with a person or entity in the United States. We leave the injunctions entered by the lower courts in place with respect to respondents and those similarly situated, as specified in this opinion. . . .

We accordingly grant the Government's stay applications in part and narrow the scope of the injunctions as to § 2(c). The injunctions remain in place only with respect to parties similarly situated to Doe, Dr. Elshikh, and Hawaii. . . .

The Hawaii injunction extends beyond § 2(c) to bar enforcement of the § 6(a) suspension of refugee admissions and the § 6(b) refugee cap. In our view, the equitable balance struck above applies in this context as well. An American individual or entity that has a bona fide relationship with a particular person seeking to enter the country as a refugee can legitimately claim concrete hardship if that person is excluded. . . .

The Government's application to stay the injunction with respect to §§ 6(a) and (b) is accordingly granted in part. Section 6(a) may not be enforced against an individual seeking admission as a refugee who can credibly claim a bona fide relationship with a person or entity in the United States. Nor may § 6(b); that is, such a person may not be excluded pursuant to § 6(b), even if the 50,000–person cap has been reached or exceeded. As applied to all other individuals, the provisions may take effect. . . .

Accordingly, the petitions for certiorari are granted, and the stay applications are granted in part."

V. JUSTICE VOTE

0 Pro ACLU Side vs. 9 Con Opposing Side

Opposing Side (Petitioner / Appellant)

1. Alito, S. – Joined Thomas' opinion
2. Kagan, E. – Per curiam decision
3. Thomas, C. – Wrote opinion concurring in part and dissenting in part
4. Breyer, S. – Per curiam decision
5. Gorsuch, N. – Joined Thomas' opinion
6. Kennedy, A. – Per curiam decision
7. Ginsburg, R. – Per curiam decision
8. Sotomayor, S. – Per curiam decision
9. Roberts, J. – Per curiam decision

VI. A WIN OR LOSS FOR THE ACLU?

The ACLU served as counsel for appellees urging the court to keep the injunctions in place; the Supreme Court partially granted the stay applications to narrow the injunctions by a 9-0 vote, giving the ACLU an apparent loss.

1168. District of Columbia v. Wesby

(Decided January 22, 2018; 138 S.Ct. 577; 583 U.S. _)

I. ISSUE

A. Issues Discussed

4th Amendment, immunity

B. Legal Question Presented

"[T]wo questions: whether the officers had probable cause to arrest the partygoers, and whether the officers were entitled to qualified immunity."

C. Supreme Court's Answer

"[W]e reverse the D.C. Circuit's holding that the officers lacked probable cause to arrest. Accordingly, the District and its officers are entitled to summary judgment on all of the partygoers' claims."

II. CASE SUMMARY

A. Background

"Around 1 a.m. . . . the District's Metropolitan Police Department received a complaint about loud music and illegal activities at a [vacant] house in Northeast D.C. . . .

[T]he officers knocked on the front door . . . . One of the partygoers opened the door . . . .

After interviewing all 21 [people in the house], the officers did not get a clear or consistent story. . . . Two of the women working the party said that a woman named 'Peaches' or 'Tasty' was renting the house and had given them permission to be there. . . .

An officer asked the woman to call Peaches . . . . Peaches answered . . . . At first, Peaches claimed to be renting . . . . When the sergeant again asked her who had given her permission to use the house, Peaches became evasive and hung up. . . . The officers eventually got Peaches on the phone again, and she admitted that she did not have permission . . . .

The officers then contacted the owner. He told them that he had been trying to negotiate a lease with Peaches, but they had not reached an agreement. . . . At that point, the officers arrested the 21 partygoers for unlawful entry [and] charge them with disorderly conduct. [T]he charges were eventually dropped. . . .

Respondents, 16 of the 21 partygoers, sued the District and five of the arresting officers. . . .

On cross-motions for summary judgment, the District Court awarded partial summary judgment to the partygoers. . . .

The jury awarded the partygoers a total of $680,000 in compensatory damages. . . .

On appeal, a divided panel of the D.C. Circuit affirmed. . . .

The D.C. Circuit denied rehearing en banc over the dissent of four judges. . . ."

The Supreme Court granted certiorari to review the case.

B. Counsel of Record / ACLU Attorney

ACLU Side (Respondent / Appellee): Nathaniel P. Garrett argued the cause for appellee. With him on the briefs were Gregory L. Lattimer, Charlotte H. Taylor, and Julia Fong Sheketof.

Opposing Side (Petitioner / Appellant): Todd S. Kim, Solicitor General of the District of Columbia argued the cause for appellant. With him on the briefs were Karl A. Racine, Attorney General, Loren L. Alikhan, Deputy Solicitor General, and Carl J. Schifferle, Assistant Attorney General.

Assistant Solicitor General Parker argued the cause for the United States as amicus curiae.

III. AMICI CURIAE

ACLU Side (Respondent / Appellee)

Brief of amici curiae filed on behalf of the American Civil Liberties Union and the American Civil Liberties Union of the District of Columbia by Cecillia D. Wang, Ezekiel R. Edwards, Arthur B. Spitzer, Scott Michelman, Andrew J. Pincus, and Eugene R. Fidell.

Opposing Side (Petitioner / Appellant)

Brief of amici curiae filed on behalf of the United States by Acting Solicitor General Wall, Acting Assistant Attorney General Readler, Deputy Solicitor General Dreeben, Assistant Solicitor General Kovner, Douglas N. Letter, Barbara L. Herwig, and H. Thomas Byron II.

Brief of amici curiae filed on behalf of the National Association of Counties et al. by Lisa Soronen and John J. Korzen.

Brief of amici curiae filed on behalf of the State of Utah et al. by Sean D. Reyes, Attorney General of Utah, Tyler R. Green, Solicitor General, Kyle J. Kaiser and Meb W. Anderson, Assistant Attorneys General, and by the Attorneys General for their respective States as follows: Steven T. Marshall of Alabama, Leslie Rutledge of Arkansas, Douglas S. Chin of Hawaii, Lisa Madigan of Illinois, Curtis T. Hill, Jr., of Indiana, Derek Schmidt of Kansas, Andy Beshear of Kentucky, Jeff Landry of Louisiana, Brian E. Frosh of Maryland, Bill Schuette of Michigan, Jim Hood of Mississippi, Doug Peterson of Nebraska, Adam Paul Laxalt of Nevada, Gordon J. MacDonald of New Hampshire, Christopher S. Porrino of New Jersey, Michael DeWine of Ohio, Mike Hunter of Oklahoma, Ellen F. Rosenblum of Oregon, Josh Shapiro of Pennsylvania, Peter F. Kilmartin of Rhode Island, Alan Wilson of South Carolina, Herbert H. Slatery III of Tennessee, Ken Paxton of Texas, Patrick Morrisey of West Virginia, and Brad D. Schimel of Wisconsin.

IV. THE SUPREME COURT'S DECISION

"The Fourth Amendment protects '[t]he right of the people to be secure in their persons, houses, papers, and effects, against unreasonable searches and seizures.' . . . A warrantless arrest is reasonable if the officer has probable cause to believe that the suspect committed a crime in the officer's presence. . . .

There is no dispute that the partygoers entered the house against the will of the owner. Nonetheless, the partygoers contend that the officers lacked probable cause to arrest them because the officers had no reason to believe that they 'knew or should have known' their 'entry was unwanted.' We disagree. Considering the totality of the circumstances, the officers made an 'entirely reasonable inference' that the partygoers were knowingly taking advantage of a vacant house as a venue for their late-night party. . . .

Taken together, the condition of the house and the conduct of the partygoers allowed the officers to make several "commonsense conclusions about human behavior." Most homeowners do not live in near-barren houses. And most homeowners do not invite people over to use their living room as a strip club, to have sex in their bedroom, to smoke marijuana inside, and to leave their floors filthy. The officers could thus infer that the partygoers knew their party was not authorized. . . .

The partygoers' answers to the officers' questions also suggested their guilty state of mind. When the officers asked who had given them permission to be there, the partygoers gave vague and implausible responses. . . .

Viewing these circumstances as a whole, a reasonable officer could conclude that there was probable cause to believe the partygoers knew they did not have permission to be in the house. . . .

[W]e reverse the D.C. Circuit's holding that the officers lacked probable cause to arrest. Accordingly, the District and its officers are entitled to summary judgment on all of the partygoers' claims. . . .

Our conclusion that the officers had probable cause to arrest the partygoers is sufficient to resolve this case. But where, as here, the Court of Appeals erred on both the merits of the constitutional claim and the question of qualified immunity, 'we have discretion to correct its errors at each step.' We exercise that discretion here because the D.C. Circuit's analysis, if followed elsewhere, would 'undermine the values qualified immunity seeks to promote.' . . .

The judgment of the D.C. Circuit is therefore reversed, and the case is remanded . . . ."

V. JUSTICE VOTE

0 Pro ACLU Side vs. 9 Con Opposing Side

Opposing Side (Petitioner / Appellant)

1. Thomas, C. – Wrote majority opinion
2. Alito, S. – Joined majority opinion
3. Kagan, E. – Joined majority opinion
4. Breyer, S. – Joined majority opinion
5. Gorsuch, N. – Joined majority opinion
6. Kennedy, A. – Joined majority opinion

7. Ginsburg, R. – Wrote concurring opinion
8. Sotomayor, S. – Wrote concurring opinion
9. Roberts, J. – Joined majority opinion

VI. A WIN OR LOSS FOR THE ACLU?

The ACLU filed as amicus curiae urging affirmance; the Supreme Court reversed the Court of Appeals' decision by a 9-0 vote, giving the ACLU an apparent loss.

1169. Class v. United States

(Decided February 21, 2018; 138 S.Ct. 798; 583 U.S. _)

I. ISSUE

A. Issues Discussed

Criminal procedure

B. Legal Question Presented

"Does a guilty plea bar a criminal defendant from later appealing his conviction on the ground that the statute of conviction violates the Constitution?"

C. Supreme Court's Answer

"In our view, a guilty plea by itself does not bar that appeal."

II. CASE SUMMARY

A. Background

"In September 2013, a federal grand jury indicted petitioner, Rodney Class, for possessing firearms in his locked jeep, which was parked in a lot on the grounds of the United States Capitol in Washington, D.C. . . . Soon thereafter, Class, appearing pro se, asked the Federal District Court for the District of Columbia to dismiss the indictment. . . . Class alleged that the statute, § 5104(e), violates the Second Amendment. He also raised a due process claim . . . . [T]he District Court denied both claims.

Several months later, Class pleaded guilty to 'Possession of a Firearm on U.S. Capitol Grounds, in violation of 40 U.S.C. § 5104(e).' The Government agreed to drop related charges.

A written plea agreement set forth the terms of Class' guilty plea, including several categories of rights that he expressly agreed to waive. . . . At the same time, the plea agreement expressly enumerated categories of claims that Class could raise on appeal . . . .

The agreement said nothing about the right to raise on direct appeal a claim that the statute of conviction was unconstitutional. . . .

Several days later, Class appealed his conviction to the Court of Appeals for the District of Columbia Circuit. Class was appointed an amicus to aid him in presenting his arguments. He repeated his constitutional claims . . . . The Court of Appeals held that Class could not raise his constitutional claims because, by pleading guilty, he had waived them"

The Supreme Court granted certiorari to review the case.

B. Counsel of Record / ACLU Attorney

ACLU Side (Petitioner / Appellant): Jessica R. Amunson argued the cause for appellants. With her on the brief were Erica L. Ross, Joshua M. Parker, Corinne M. Smith, and Leonard R. Powell.

Opposing Side (Respondent / Appellee): Assistant Solicitor General Feigin argued the cause for the United States. With him on the brief were Acting Solicitor General Wall, Acting Assistant Attorney General Blanco, Deputy Solicitor General Dreeben, and John-Alex Romano.

III. AMICI CURIAE

ACLU Side (Petitioner / Appellant)

Brief of amici curiae filed on behalf of the National Association of Criminal Defense Lawyers and the American Civil Liberties Union by Jonathan Hacker, David D. Cole, Daniel N. Lerman, Kathleen Shen, Ruthanne M. Deutsch, and Hyland Hunt.

Brief of amici curiae filed on behalf of Albert W. Alschuler by Matthew J. Silveira, Stephen J. Petrany, and Mr. Alschuler.

Brief of amici curiae filed on behalf of the Innocence Project by M. Chris Fabricant, Vanessa Potkin, James C. Dugan, Timothy J. McGinn, Steven J. Ballew, Patricia O. Haynes, and Elizabeth J. Jonas.

Opposing Side (Respondent / Appellee)

No briefs of amici curiae were filed in support of the United States.

IV. THE SUPREME COURT'S DECISION

"The question is whether a guilty plea by itself bars a federal criminal defendant from challenging the constitutionality of the statute of conviction on direct appeal. We hold that it does not. Class did not relinquish his right to appeal the District Court's constitutional determinations simply by pleading guilty. As we shall explain, this holding flows directly from this Court's prior decisions. . . .

In sum, the claims at issue here do not fall within any of the categories of claims that Class' plea agreement forbids him to raise on direct appeal. They challenge the Government's power to criminalize Class' (admitted) conduct. They thereby call into question the Government's power to "constitutionally prosecute" him. A guilty plea does not bar a direct appeal . . . .

We are not convinced by the three . . . arguments that the Government and the dissent make in reply.

First, the Government contends that by entering a guilty plea, Class inherently relinquished his constitutional claims. The Government is correct that a guilty plea does implicitly waive some claims, including some constitutional claims. However, . . . Class' valid guilty plea does not, by itself, bar direct appeal of his constitutional claims in these circumstances. . . .

Second, the Government and the dissent point to Rule 11(a)(2) of the Federal Rules of Criminal Procedure, which governs 'conditional' guilty pleas. . . .

We . . . hold that Rule 11(a)(2) cannot resolve this case.

Third, the Government argues that Class 'expressly waived' his right to appeal his constitutional claim. . . .

We do not see why the District Court Judge's statement should bar Class' constitutional claims. . . . Under these circumstances, Class' acquiescence neither expressly nor implicitly waived his right to appeal his constitutional claims. . . .

For these reasons, we hold that Rodney Class may pursue his constitutional claims on direct appeal. The contrary judgment of the Court of Appeals for the District of Columbia Circuit is reversed, and the case is remanded . . . ."

V. JUSTICE VOTE

6 Pro ACLU Side vs. 3 Con Opposing Side

ACLU Side (Petitioner / Appellant)

1. Breyer, S. – Wrote majority opinion
2. Kagan, E. – Joined majority opinion
3. Gorsuch, N. – Joined majority opinion
4. Ginsburg, R. – Joined majority opinion
5. Sotomayor, S. – Joined majority opinion
6. Roberts, J. – Joined majority opinion

Opposing Side (Respondent / Appellee)

1. Alito, S. – Wrote dissenting opinion
2. Thomas, C. – Joined Alito's dissent
3. Kennedy, A. – Joined Alito's dissent

VI. A WIN OR LOSS FOR THE ACLU?

The ACLU filed as amicus curiae urging reversal of the judgment of the Court of Appeals; the Supreme Court reversed in a 6-3 vote, giving the ACLU an apparent win.

1170. Jennings v. Rodriguez

(Decided February 27, 2018; 138 S.Ct. 830; 583 U.S. _)

I. ISSUE

A. Issues Discussed

Immigration/Citizenship

B. Legal Question Presented

"U.S. immigration law authorizes the Government to detain certain aliens seeking admission into the country under §§ 1225(b)(1) and (b)(2). It also authorizes the Government to detain certain aliens already in the country pending the outcome of removal proceedings under §§ 1226(a) and (c). The primary issue is the proper interpretation of §§ 1225(b), 1226(a), and 1226(c)."

C. Supreme Court's Answer

"[W]e hold that, subject only to express exceptions, §§ 1225(b) and 1226(c) authorize detention until the end of applicable proceedings. And . . . we hold that there is no justification for any of the procedural requirements that the Court of Appeals layered onto § 1226(a) without any arguable statutory foundation."

II. CASE SUMMARY

A. Background

"Respondent Alejandro Rodriguez is a Mexican citizen [and] lawful permanent resident of the United States. In April 2004, after Rodriguez was convicted of a drug offense and theft . . . , the Government detained . . . and sought to remove him . . . . In July 2004, an Immigration Judge ordered Rodriguez deported . . . . Rodriguez . . . appeal[ed] to the Board of Immigration Appeals, but five months later the Board agreed that Rodriguez was subject to mandatory removal. . . . Rodriguez [sought] review, [in] the Court of Appeals for the Ninth Circuit . . . .

In May 2007, . . . he filed a habeas petition . . . alleging that he was entitled to a bond hearing to determine whether his continued detention was justified. Rodriguez's case was consolidated with another, similar case . . . and together they moved for class certification. The District Court denied their motion, but the Court of Appeals for the Ninth Circuit reversed. It concluded that the proposed class met the certification requirements . . . and it remanded . . . .

The District Court . . . organized the class into four subclasses . . . . On appeal, the Court of Appeals held that the § 1231(a) subclass had been improperly certified, but it affirmed the certification of the other three subclasses. . . .

Rodriguez . . . argued that the relevant statutory provisions—§§ 1225(b), 1226(a), and 1226(c)—do not authorize 'prolonged' detention in the absence of an individualized bond hearing at which the Government proves by clear and convincing evidence that the class member's detention remains justified. . . .

[T]he District Court entered a permanent injunction in line with the relief sought by respondents, and the Court of Appeals affirmed."

The Supreme Court granted certiorari to review the case.

B. Counsel of Record / ACLU Attorney

ACLU Side (Respondent / Appellee): Ahilan T. Arulanantham of the ACLU Foundation of Southern California argued the cause for appellee. With him on the briefs were Mark H. Haddad, Sean A. Commons, Wen W. Shen, Jayashri Srikantiah, and Judy Rabinovitz, Michael K.T. Tan, Cecillia D. Wang, and Steven R. Shapiro of the ACLU Immigrants' Rights Project, and Michael Kaufman of the ACLU Foundation of Southern California.

Opposing Side (Petitioner / Appellant): Malcolm L. Stewart argued the cause for appellant. With him on the briefs were Acting Solicitor General Gershengorn, Principal Deputy Assistant Attorney General Mizer, Deputy Solicitor General Kneedler, Deputy Assistant Attorney General Fresco, Assistant Solicitor General Tripp, Sarah S. Wilson, and Erez R. Reuveni.

III. AMICI CURIAE

ACLU Side (Respondent / Appellee)

Brief of amici curiae filed on behalf of Asian Americans Advancing Justice by Laboni A. Hoq, Christopher M. Lapinig, Anjan Choudhury, John F. Muller, David J. Feder, Joon S. Hur, Anoop Prasad, Jenny Zhao, Kevin Lo, Cecelia Chang, Eugene F. Chay, Javeria Jamil, Andrew Kang, and Van Huynh.

Brief of amici curiae filed on behalf of National Immigration Project of the National Lawyers Guild et al. by Sejal Zota, David C. Frederick, and Joshua D. Branson.

Brief of amici curiae filed on behalf of National Immigration Project of the National Lawyers Guild et al. by Sejal Zota, Steven A. Hirsch, Daniel Purcell, Travis Silva, and Katherine Brady.

Brief of amici curiae filed on behalf of American Immigration Council et al. by Paul R.Q. Wolfson, Mark C. Fleming, and Sameer Ahmed.

Brief of amici curiae filed on behalf of National Association of Criminal Defense Lawyers et al. by James J. Farrell and James H. Moon.

Brief of amici curiae filed on behalf of Detained Legal Services Providers by Charles Roth, Karen Zwick, Brian J. Murray, and Joshua S. Stillman.

Brief of amici curiae filed on behalf of 43 Social Science Researchers and Professors by Nina Rabin, Kelsi Brown Corkran, Morton Dubin, and Kelly M. Daley.

Brief of amici curiae filed on behalf of Professors of Constitutional Law et al. by Dennis B. Auerbach, David M. Zionts, and Philip J. Levitz.

Brief of amici curiae filed on behalf of Human Rights First et al. by Eleanor Acer, Robyn Barnard, Eugene M. Gelernter, Jo Backer Laird, Jared S. Buszin, and Michael N. Fresco.

Brief of amici curiae filed on behalf of Americans for Immigrant Justice et al. by Anthony Enriquez and Alina Das.

Brief of amici curiae filed on behalf of Nine Retired Immigration Judges et al. by Brian R. Matsui, Seth W. Lloyd, and James J. Beha II.

Brief of amici curiae filed on behalf of the United Nations High Commissioner for Refugees by Alice Farmer, Amy Mason Saharia, and Ana C. Reyes.

Brief of amici curiae filed on behalf of American Bar Association by Jeffrey L. Bleich, Ian R. Barker, Peter Z. Stockburger, Benjamin P. Harbuck, Andrew M. Legolvan, and Linda A. Klein.

Brief of amici curiae filed on behalf of Americans for Immigrant Justice et al. by Anthony Enriquez and Alina Das.

Brief of amici curiae filed on behalf of Professors Stephen H. Legomsky et al. by Douglas Hallward-Driemeier, Jonathan Ference-Burke, David Rhinesmith, Lindsey Sullivan, Justin Florence, and Aaron Katz.

Brief of amici curiae filed on behalf of the State of California et al. by Xavier Becerra, Attorney General of California, Edward C. DuMont, Solicitor General, Michael J. Mongan, Deputy Solicitor General, Samuel P. Siegel and Max Carter-Oberstone, Associate Deputy Solicitors General, and by the Attorneys General for their respective States as follows: Maura Healey of Massachusetts, Eric T. Schneiderman of New York, Ellen F. Rosenblum of Oregon, Peter F. Kilmartin of Rhode Island, Thomas J. Donovan, Jr., of Vermont, and Robert W. Ferguson of Washington.

Brief of amici curiae filed on behalf of County of Santa Clara, California et al. by James R. Williams, Santa Clara County Counsel, Greta S. Hansen, Chief Assistant County Counsel, Kavita Narayan, Deputy County Counsel, Lorraine Van Kirk, Deputy County Counsel, Donna R. Ziegller, Alameda County Counsel, Anne L. Morgan, Austin City Attorney, David E. Ralph, Baltimore Acting City Solicitor, G. Nicholas (Nick) Herman, Carrboro Town General Counsel, Ralph D. Karpinos, Chapel Hill Town Attorney, Stephen R. Patton, Chicago City Corporation Counsel, Paula Boggs Muething, Cincinnati City Solicitor, Kristin M. Bronson, Denver City Attorney, Karl A. Racine, Attorney General of the District of Columbia, Dan Satterberg, King County Prosecuting Attorney, Susan L. Segal, Minneapolis City Attorney, Barbara J. Parker, Oakland City Attorney, Tracy Reeve, Portland City Attorney, Margaret D. Plane, Salt Lake City Attorney, Dennis J. Herrera, San Francisco City Attorney, Richard Doyle, San Jose City Attorney, John C. Beiers, San Mateo County Counsel, Peter S. Holmes, Seattle City Attorney, and Michael Rankin, Tucson City Attorney.

Brief of amici curiae filed on behalf of Eagle Forum Education & Defense Fund by Lawrence J. Joseph.

Opposing Side (Petitioner / Appellant)

Brief of amici curiae filed on behalf of 29 U.S. Representatives et al. by Richard A. Samp and Mark S. Chenoweth.

IV. THE SUPREME COURT'S DECISION

"When 'a serious doubt' is raised about the constitutionality of an act of Congress, 'it is a cardinal principle that this Court will first ascertain whether a construction of the statute is fairly possible by which the question may be avoided.' Relying on this canon of constitutional avoidance, the Court of Appeals construed §§ 1225(b), 1226(a), and 1226(c) to limit the permissible length of an alien's detention without a bond hearing....

The Court of Appeals misapplied the canon ... because its interpretations of the three provisions at issue here are implausible. [W]e hold that, subject only to express exceptions, §§ 1225(b) and 1226(c) authorize detention until the end of applicable proceedings. And ... we hold that there is no justification for any of the procedural requirements that the Court of Appeals layered onto § 1226(a) without any arguable statutory foundation....

In sum, §§ 1225(b)(1) and (b)(2) mandate detention ... throughout the completion of ... proceedings .... Of course, other provisions of the immigration statutes do authorize detention 'pending' other proceedings or 'until' a certain point. But there is no 'canon of interpretation that forbids interpreting different words used in different parts of the same statute to mean roughly the same thing.' ...

While the language of §§ 1225(b)(1) and (b)(2) is quite clear, § 1226(c) is even clearer....

We hold that § 1226(c) mandates detention ... and that detention may end prior to the conclusion of removal proceedings 'only if' the alien is released for witness-protection purposes....

Finally, ... § 1226(a) authorizes the Attorney General to arrest and detain an alien 'pending a decision on whether the alien is to be removed ....' As long as the detained alien is not covered by § 1226(c), the Attorney General 'may release' the alien on 'bond ... or conditional parole.' ...

The Court of Appeals ordered the Government to provide procedural protections that go well beyond the initial bond hearing.... Nothing in § 1226(a)'s text ... even remotely supports the imposition of either of those requirements. Nor does § 1226(a)'s text even hint that the length of detention prior to a bond hearing must specifically be considered in determining whether the alien should be released....

Because the Court of Appeals erroneously concluded that periodic bond hearings are required under the immigration provisions at issue here, it had no occasion to consider respondents' constitutional arguments on their merits. Consistent with our role as 'a court of review, not of first view,' we do not reach those arguments. Instead, we remand the case to the Court of Appeals to consider them . . . .

Before the Court of Appeals addresses those claims, however, it should reexamine whether respondents can continue litigating their claims as a class. . . .

We reverse the judgment of the . . . Court of Appeals for the Ninth Circuit and remand . . . ."

V. JUSTICE VOTE

3 Pro ACLU Side vs. 5 Con Opposing Side

ACLU Side (Respondent / Appellee)

1. Breyer, S. – Wrote dissenting opinion
2. Ginsburg, R. – Joined Breyer's dissent
3. Sotomayor, S. – Joined Breyer's dissent

Opposing Side (Petitioner / Appellant)

1. Alito, S. – Wrote majority opinion
2. Thomas, C. – Wrote concurring opinion
3. Gorsuch, N. – Joined Thomas' concurrence in part
4. Kennedy, A. – Joined majority opinion
5. Roberts, J. – Joined majority opinion

Kagan, E. – Took no part in the decision.

VI. A WIN OR LOSS FOR THE ACLU?

The ACLU argued the cause for appellee urging affirmance; the Supreme Court reversed the Court of Appeals' decision by a 5-3 vote, giving the ACLU an apparent loss.

1171. Ayestas v. Davis

(Decided March 21, 2018; 138 S.Ct. 1080; 584 U.S. _)

I. ISSUE

A. Issues Discussed

Criminal procedure, death penalty

B. Legal Question Presented

"Petitioner Carlos Ayestas, who was convicted of murder and sentenced to death in a Texas court, argues that he was wrongfully denied funding for investigative services needed to prove his entitlement to federal habeas relief. Petitioner moved for funding under 18 U.S.C. § 3599(f), which makes funds available if they are 'reasonably necessary,' but petitioner's motion was denied. . . .

[The question is] whether the lower courts applied the correct legal standard in denying the funding request."

C. Supreme Court's Answer

"We hold that the lower courts applied the wrong legal standard . . . ."

II. CASE SUMMARY

A. Background

"In 1997, petitioner was convicted of capital murder in a Texas court. . . .

The jury unanimously concluded that petitioner should be sentenced to death, and a capital sentence was imposed. Petitioner secured new counsel to handle his appeal, and his conviction and sentence were affirmed by the Texas Court of Criminal Appeals in 1998. . . .

While petitioner's direct appeal was still pending, a third legal team filed a habeas petition . . . in state court. . . . Petitioner's quest for state habeas relief ended unsuccessfully in 2008.

In 2009, represented by a fourth set of attorneys, petitioner filed a federal habeas petition under 28 U.S.C. § 2254, and . . . allege[d] that his right to the effective assistance of counsel at trial was violated because his attorneys failed to . . . search for mitigation evidence. . . .

Among the obstacles standing between petitioner and federal habeas relief, however, was the fact that he never raised this trial-level ineffective-assistance-of-counsel claim in state court. The District Court therefore held that the claim was barred by procedural default, and the Fifth Circuit affirmed.

Petitioner sought review in [the U.S. Supreme] Court, and we vacated the decision below and remanded for reconsideration in light of two of our subsequent decisions . . . .

The District Court refused the funding request and . . . denied petitioner's habeas petition. . . .

On appeal, the Fifth Circuit held that a COA was not needed for review of the funding issue, but it rejected that claim for essentially the same reasons as the District Court . . . . With respect to petitioner's other claims, including his claim of ineffective assistance of trial counsel, the Fifth Circuit refused to issue a COA."

The Supreme Court granted certiorari to review the case.

B. Counsel of Record / ACLU Attorney

ACLU Side (Petitioner / Appellant): Lee B. Kovarsky argued the cause for appellants. With him on the brief were Meaghan Vergow, Deanna M. Rice, Paul T. Stepnowsky, Jason Zarrow, Samantha Goldstein, Kimya Saied, Kathryn A. Clifford, Callie Heller, Jared Tyler, and Sheri Lynn Johnson.

Opposing Side (Respondent / Appellee): Scott A. Keller, Solicitor General of Texas, argued the cause for appellee. With him on the brief were Ken Paxton, Attorney General, Jeffrey C. Mateer, First Assistant Attorney General, J. Campbell Barker, Deputy Solicitor General, and Beth Klusmann and Jason R. LaFond, Assistant Solicitors General.

III. AMICI CURIAE

ACLU Side (Petitioner / Appellant)

Brief of amici curiae filed on behalf of the National Association of Criminal Defense Lawyers and the American Civil Liberties Union by David A. Strauss, Sarah M. Konsky, Barbara E. Bergman, Jessica Ring Amunson, Matthew S. Hellman, Andrew C. Noll, David D. Cole, and Brian W. Stull.

Brief of amici curiae filed on behalf of the Constitution Project by Eugene A. Sokoloff.

Brief of amici curiae filed on behalf of the American Bar Association by Clifford M. Sloan, Donald P. Salzman, Brendan B. Gants, and Linda A. Klein.

Brief of amici curiae filed on behalf of the Capital Punishment Center of the University of Texas at Austin School of Law by Jordan M. Steiker, Jim Marcus, Thea Posel, and Raoul D. Schonemann.

Opposing Side (Respondent / Appellee)

Brief of amici curiae filed on behalf of the State of Arizona et al. by Mark Brnovich, Attorney General of Arizona, Dominic E. Draye, Solicitor General, Lacey Stover Gard, Chief Counsel of the Capital Litigation Section, J.D. Nielsen, Assistant Attorney General, Kevin T. Kane, Chief State's Attorney of Connecticut, and by the Attorneys General for their respective States as follows: Leslie Rutledge of Arkansas, Christopher M. Carr of Georgia, Lawrence G. Wasden of Idaho, Curtis T. Hill, Jr., of Indiana, Derek Schmidt of Kansas, Jeff Landry of Louisiana, Joshua D. Hawley of Missouri, Timothy C. Fox of Montana, Douglas J. Peterson of Nebraska, Adam Paul Laxalt of Nevada, Alan Wilson of South Carolina, Patrick Morrisey of West Virginia, and Brad D. Schimel of Wisconsin.

IV. THE SUPREME COURT'S DECISION

"Satisfied that we have jurisdiction, we turn to the question whether the Court of Appeals applied the correct legal standard when it affirmed the denial of petitioner's funding request.

Section 3599(a) authorizes federal courts to provide funding to a party who is facing the prospect of a death sentence and is 'financially unable to obtain adequate representation or investigative, expert, or other reasonably necessary services.' . . .

Here we are concerned not with legal representation but with services provided by experts, investigators, and the like. Such services must be 'reasonably necessary for the representation of the [applicant]' in order to be eligible for funding. . . .

Section 3599 appears to use the term 'necessary' to mean something less than essential. . . . What the statutory phrase calls for, we conclude, is a determination by the district court, in the exercise of its discretion, as to whether a reasonable attorney would regard the services as sufficiently important, guided by the considerations we set out more fully below. . . .

A natural consideration informing the exercise of that discretion is the likelihood that the contemplated services will help the applicant win relief. . . .

To be clear, a funding applicant must not be expected to prove that he will be able to win relief if given the services he seeks. But the 'reasonably necessary' test requires an assessment of the likely utility of the services requested, and § 3599(f) cannot be read to guarantee that an applicant will have enough money to turn over every stone. . . .

We conclude that the Fifth Circuit's interpretation of § 3599(f) is not a permissible reading of the statute. We therefore vacate the judgment below and remand . . . ."

V. JUSTICE VOTE

9 Pro ACLU Side vs. 0 Con Opposing Side

ACLU Side (Petitioner / Appellant)

1. Alito, S. – Wrote majority opinion
2. Kagan, E. – Joined majority opinion
3. Thomas, C. – Joined majority opinion
4. Breyer, S. – Joined majority opinion
5. Gorsuch, N. – Joined majority opinion
6. Kennedy, A. – Joined majority opinion
7. Ginsburg, R. – Joined Sotomayor's concurrence
8. Sotomayor, S. – Wrote concurring opinion
9. Roberts, J. – Joined majority opinion

VI. A WIN OR LOSS FOR THE ACLU?

The ACLU filed as amicus curiae urging reversal of the judgment of the Court of Appeals; the Supreme Court vacated in a 9-0 vote, giving the ACLU an apparent win.

1172. Byrd v. United States

(Decided May 14, 2018; 138 S.Ct. 1518; 584 U.S. _)

I. ISSUE

A. Issues Discussed

4th Amendment

B. Legal Question Presented

"[W]hether a driver has a reasonable expectation of privacy in a rental car when he or she is not listed as an authorized driver on the rental agreement."

C. Supreme Court's Answer

"The Court now holds that, as a general rule, someone in otherwise lawful possession and control of a rental car has a reasonable expectation of privacy in it even if the rental agreement does not list him or her as an authorized driver."

II. CASE SUMMARY

A. Background

"In September 2014, Pennsylvania State Troopers pulled over a car driven by petitioner Terrence Byrd. Byrd was the only person in the car. In the course of the traffic stop the troopers learned that the car was rented and that Byrd was not listed on the rental agreement as an authorized driver. For this reason, the troopers told Byrd they did not need his consent to search the car, including its trunk where he had stored personal effects. A search of the trunk uncovered body armor and 49 bricks of heroin.

The evidence was turned over to federal authorities, who charged Byrd with distribution and possession of heroin with the intent to distribute in violation of 21 U.S.C. § 841(a)(1) and possession of body armor by a prohibited person in violation of 18 U.S.C. § 931(a)(1). Byrd moved to suppress the evidence as the fruit of an unlawful search. The United States District Court for the Middle District of Pennsylvania denied the motion, and the Court of Appeals for the Third Circuit affirmed. Both courts concluded that, because Byrd was not listed on the rental agreement, he lacked a reasonable expectation of privacy in the car.

Based on this conclusion, it appears that both the District Court and Court of Appeals deemed it unnecessary to consider whether the troopers had probable cause to search the car."

The Supreme Court granted certiorari to review the case.

B. Counsel of Record / ACLU Attorney

ACLU Side (Petitioner / Appellant): Robert M. Loeb argued the cause for appellants. With him on the brief were Heidi R. Freese, Frederick W. Ulrich, Joshua Rosenkranz, Robert M. Loeb, Thomas M. Bondy, Jeremy Peterman, Charles W. Tyler, and Logan Q. Dwyer.

Opposing Side (Respondent / Appellee): Assistant to the Solicitor General Feigin argued the cause for the United States. With him on the brief were Solicitor General Francisco, Acting Assistant Attorney General Cronan, Deputy Solicitor General Dreeben, Assistant Solicitor General Liu, and Thomas E. Booth.

III. AMICI CURIAE

ACLU Side (Petitioner / Appellant)

Brief of amici curiae filed on behalf of the American Civil Liberties Union and the National Association of Criminal Defense Lawyers by David D. Cole, Jeffrey T. Green, Rachel Wainer Apter, Michael B. Buschbacher, and Joshua L. Dratel.

Brief of amici curiae filed on behalf of Southwestern Law Student Lindsey N. Ursua et al. by Norman M. Garland and Michael M. Epstein.

Brief of amici curiae filed on behalf of Restore the Fourth, Inc., by Mahesha P. Subbaraman.

Brief of amici curiae filed on behalf of National Motorists Association by Aaron M. Panner and Thomas B. Bennett.

Brief of amici curiae filed on behalf of the National Association for Public Defense et al. by Janet Moore, Daniel L. Kaplan, Donna F. Coltharp, Sarah S. Gannett, David Debold, Lochlan F. Shelfer, Monica L. Haymond, Benjamin Hayes, and Andrew P. Legrand.

Brief of amici curiae filed on behalf of Electronic Privacy Information Center (EPIC) by Marc Rotenberg and Alan Butler.

Brief of amici curiae filed on behalf of Professor Morgan A. Cloud by Sarah M. Shalf.

Brief of amici curiae filed on behalf of Fourth Amendment Scholars by Matthew A. Abee and A. Mattison Bogan.

Opposing Side (Respondent / Appellee)

Brief of amici curiae filed on behalf of the State of Arizona et al. by Mark Brnovich, Attorney General of Arizona, Dominic Draye, Solicitor General, Andrew G. Pappas, and by the Attorneys General for their respective States as follows: Leslie Rutledge of Arkansas, Matt Denn of Delaware, Lawrence G. Wasden of Idaho, Curtis T. Hill, Jr., of Indiana, Andy Beshear of Kentucky, Doug Peterson of Nebraska, Adam Paul Laxalt of Nevada, Christopher S. Porrino of New Jersey, Michael DeWine of Ohio, Mike Hunter of Oklahoma, Josh Shapiro of Pennsylvania, Alan Wilson of South Carolina, Herbert H. Slattery III of Tennessee, and Sean D. Reyes of Utah.

IV. THE SUPREME COURT'S DECISION

"Few protections are as essential to individual liberty as the right to be free from unreasonable searches and seizures. . . .

This concern attends the search of an automobile. The Court has acknowledged, however, that there is a diminished expectation of privacy in automobiles . . . .

Whether a warrant is required is a separate question from the one the Court addresses here, which is whether the person claiming a constitutional violation 'has had his own Fourth Amendment rights infringed by the search and seizure which he seeks to challenge.' . . .

Reference to property concepts . . . aids the Court in assessing the precise question here: Does a driver of a rental car have a reasonable expectation of privacy in the car when he or she is not listed as an authorized driver on the rental agreement? . . .

On the one hand, . . . a person need not always have a recognized common-law property interest in the place searched to be able to claim a reasonable expectation of privacy in it. . . .

On the other hand, it is also clear that legitimate presence on the premises of the place searched, standing alone, is not enough to accord a reasonable expectation of privacy . . . .

This general property-based concept guides resolution of this case. . . .

Here, the Government contends that drivers who are not listed on rental agreements always lack an expectation of privacy in the automobile based on the rental company's lack of authorization alone. This per se rule rests on too restrictive a view of the Fourth Amendment's protections. Byrd, by contrast, contends that the sole occupant of a rental car always has an expectation of privacy in it based on mere possession and control. There is more to recommend Byrd's proposed rule than the Government's; but, without qualification, it would include within its ambit thieves and others who . . . would not have a reasonable expectation of privacy. . . .

The proper course is to remand for the argument and potentially further factual development to be considered in the first instance by the Court of Appeals or by the District Court. . . .

[T]he Court now holds, that the mere fact that a driver in lawful possession or control of a rental car is not listed on the rental agreement will not defeat his or her otherwise reasonable expectation of privacy. The Court leaves for remand two of the Government's arguments . . . .

The judgment of the Court of Appeals is vacated, and the case is remanded . . . ."

V. JUSTICE VOTE

9 Pro ACLU Side vs. 0 Con Opposing Side

ACLU Side (Petitioner / Appellant)

1. Kennedy, A. – Wrote majority opinion
2. Alito, S. – Wrote concurring opinion
3. Kagan, E. – Joined majority opinion
4. Thomas, C. – Wrote concurring opinion
5. Breyer, S. – Joined majority opinion
6. Gorsuch, N. – Joined Thomas' concurrence
7. Ginsburg, R. – Joined majority opinion

8. Sotomayor, S. – Joined majority opinion
9. Roberts, J. – Joined majority opinion

VI. A WIN OR LOSS FOR THE ACLU?

The ACLU filed as amicus curiae urging reversal of the judgment of the Court of Appeals; the Supreme Court vacated in a 9-0 vote, giving the ACLU an apparent win.

1173. Epic Systems Corp. v. Lewis

(Decided May 21, 2018; 138 S.Ct. 1612; 584 U.S. _)

I. ISSUE

A. Issues Discussed

Regulation

B. Legal Question Presented

"Should employees and employers be allowed to agree that any disputes between them will be resolved through one-on-one arbitration? Or should employees always be permitted to bring their claims in class or collective actions, no matter what they agreed with their employers?"

C. Supreme Court's Answer

"In the Federal Arbitration Act, Congress has instructed federal courts to enforce arbitration agreements according to their terms—including terms providing for individualized proceedings. Nor can we agree with the employees' suggestion that the National Labor Relations Act (NLRA) offers a conflicting command. . . . This Court has never read a right to class actions into the NLRA . . . . Far from conflicting, the Arbitration Act and the NLRA have long enjoyed separate spheres of influence and neither permits this Court to declare the parties' agreements unlawful."

II. CASE SUMMARY

A. Background

"The three cases before us differ in detail but not in substance. Take Ernst & Young LLP v. Morris. There Ernst & Young and one of its junior accountants, Stephen Morris, entered into an agreement providing that they would arbitrate any disputes that might arise between them. The agreement stated that the employee could choose the arbitration provider and that the arbitrator could 'grant any relief that could be granted by . . . a court' in the relevant jurisdiction. The agreement also specified individualized arbitration, with claims 'pertaining to different [e]mployees [to] be heard in separate proceedings.'

After his employment ended, and despite having agreed to arbitrate claims against the firm, Mr. Morris sued Ernst & Young in federal court. He alleged that the firm had misclassified its junior accountants as professional employees and violated the federal Fair Labor Standards Act (FLSA) and California law by paying them salaries without overtime pay. Although the arbitration agreement provided for individualized proceedings, Mr. Morris sought to litigate the federal claim on behalf of a nationwide class under the FLSA's collective action provision, 29 U.S.C. § 216(b). He sought to pursue the state law claim as a class action under Federal Rule of Civil Procedure 23.

Ernst & Young replied with a motion to compel arbitration. The district court granted the request, but the Ninth Circuit reversed this judgment"

The Supreme Court granted certiorari to review the cases.

B. Counsel of Record / ACLU Attorney

ACLU Side (Respondent / Appellee): Daniel R. Ortiz argued the cause for appellee in Nos. 16-285 and 16-300. With him on the briefs were David C. Zoeller, William E. Parsons, Caitlin M. Madden, Katelynn M. Williams, Toby J. Heytens, and Adam Hansen.

Richard F. Griffin, Jr., argued the cause for appellant in 16-307.

Opposing Side (Petitioner / Appellant): Paul D. Clement argued the cause for appellants in Nos. 16-285 and 16-300. With him on the briefs were Thomas P. Schmidt, Neal Kumar Katyal, Frederick Liu, Colleen E. Roh Sinzdak, and Daniel J.T. Schuker.

Acting Solicitor General Wall argued the cause for the United States as amicus curiae in support of appellants in 16-285 and 16-300, and appellees in 16-307.

III. AMICI CURIAE

ACLU Side (Respondent / Appellee)

Brief of amici curiae filed on behalf of NAACP Legal Defense & Educational Fund, Inc., Impact Fund, and 30 Civil Rights Organizations, including the American Civil Liberties Union, by Sherrilyn Ifill, Janai Nelson, Samuel Spital, Raymond Audain, Jocelyn D. Larkin, and Lindsay Nako.

Brief of amici curiae filed on behalf of National Academy of Arbitrators by Matthew W. Finkin.

Brief of amici curiae filed on behalf of Ten International Labor Unions et al. by Nicole G. Berner, Claire Prestel, Michael Rubin, Eric P. Brown, Judith Rivlin, David J. Strom, Jody Calemine, Mark Schneider, Bradley T. Raymond, Alice O'Brien, Matthew C. Koski, Catherine K. Ruckelshaus, Nicholas W. Clark, Richard J. Brean, Niraj R. Ganatra, and Cliff Palefsky.

Brief of amici curiae filed on behalf of Constitutional Accountability Center by Elizabeth B. Wydra, Brianne J. Gorod, and Brian R. Frazelle.

Brief of amici curiae filed on behalf of Labor Law Professors by Matthew W. Finkin, David C. Frederick, Jeremy S.B. Newman, and Benjamin D. Margo.

Brief of amici curiae filed on behalf of the State of Maryland et al. by Brian E. Frosh, Attorney General of Maryland, Steven M. Sullivan, Solicitor General, Patrick B. Hughes, Assistant Attorney General, and by the Attorneys General for their respective jurisdictions as follows: Xavier Becerra of California, George Jepsen of Connecticut, Matthew P. Denn of Delaware, Karl A. Racine of the District of Columbia, Lisa Madigan of Illinois, Thomas J. Miller of Iowa, Maura Healey of Massachusetts, Lori Swanson of Minnesota, Eric T. Schneiderman of New York, Josh Stein of North Carolina, Ellen F. Rosenblum of Oregon, Josh Shapiro of Pennsylvania, Peter F. Kilmartin of Rhode Island, Thomas J. Donovan, Jr., of Vermont, Mark R. Herring of Virginia, and Robert W.

Ferguson of Washington.
Brief of amici curiae filed on behalf of the Main Street Alliance et al. by Samuel R. Bagenstos and Kate Andrias.
Brief of amici curiae filed on behalf of American Association for Justice by Jeffrey R. White, Deepak Gupta, and Matthew Wessler.
Brief of amici curiae filed on behalf of Public Citizen, Inc., by Scott L. Nelson and Allison M. Zieve.
Brief of amici curiae filed on behalf of Susan Fowler by Chris Baker.
Brief of amici curiae filed on behalf of New York Taxi Workers Alliance by Jeanne Mirer.

Opposing Side (Petitioner / Appellant)

Brief of amici curiae filed on behalf of the United States by Acting Solicitor General Wall, Deputy Solicitor General Stewart, and Assistant Solicitor General Kedem.
Brief of amici curiae filed on behalf of the Equal Employment Advisory Council by Rae T. Vann.
Brief of amici curiae filed on behalf of the National Association of Manufacturers et al. by Henry D. Lederman, Michael J. Lotito, Linda E. Kelly, Patrick N. Forrest, Leland P Frost, Edward F. Berbarie, Robert F. Friedman, and Sean M. McCrory.
Brief of amici curiae filed on behalf of the Retail Litigation Center, Inc., by Deborah R. White and Adam G. Unikowsky.
Brief of amici curiae filed on behalf of the Chamber of Commerce of the United States of America by Kate Comerford Todd, Warren Postman, Andrew J. Pincus, Evan M. Tager, Archis A. Parasharami, and Matthew A. Waring.
Brief of amici curiae filed on behalf of the Business Roundtable by Maria Ghazal, William M. Jay, and Andrew Kim.
Brief of amici curiae filed on behalf of the Employers Group by George S. Howard, Jr., Steven Zadravecz, Beth Heifetz, and Anthony J. Dick.
Brief of amici curiae filed on behalf of Washington Legal Foundation by Richard A. Samp and Mark S. Chenoweth.
Brief of amici curiae filed on behalf of Pacific Legal Foundation by Deborah J. La Fetra.
Brief of amici curiae filed on behalf of HR Policy Association by Allyson N. Ho, John C. Sullivan, and Sam S. Shaulson.
Brief of amici curiae filed on behalf of Atlantic Legal Foundation by Martin S. Kaufman.
Brief of amici curiae filed on behalf of Law Professors by Thomas R. McCarthy and J. Michael Connolly.
Brief of amici curiae filed on behalf of Mortgage Bankers Association et al. by Germán A. Salazar, Stephen A. Fogdall, and Arleigh P. Helfer III.
Brief of amici curiae filed on behalf of International Association of Defense Counsel by Mary-Christine Sungaila and Alex R. Stevens.
Brief of amici curiae filed on behalf of the American Staffing Association et al. by Garrett R. Ferencz, Timothy O'Donnell, Melissa A. Siebert, Bonnie K. DelGobbo, John B. Lewis, Dustin M. Dow, Stephen C. Dwyer, Jason B. Klimpl, Kathryn S. Bernard, Craig S. Hopewell, Angelo I. Amador, Kevin W. Shaughnessy, Joyce Ackerbaum Cox, and Jennifer Hankes Painter.
Brief of amici curiae filed on behalf of Bristol Farms by Steven Katz.
Brief of amici curiae filed on behalf of New England Legal Foundation by Benjamin G. Robbins and Martin J. Newhouse.
Brief of amici curiae filed on behalf of DRI–The Voice of the Defense Bar by John E. Cuttino, David M. Axelrad, Felix Shafir, and John F. Querio in support of petitioners in Nos. 16-285 and 16-300 and respondent in No. 16-307.
Brief of amici curiae filed on behalf of Council on Labor Law Equality et al. by Ron Chapman, Jr., Brian E. Hayes, and Christopher C. Murray.

IV. THE SUPREME COURT'S DECISION

"We begin with the Arbitration Act and the question of its saving clause. . . .

The law of precedent teaches that like cases should generally be treated alike . . . . At the end of our encounter with the Arbitration Act, then, it appears just as it did at the beginning: a congressional command requiring us to enforce, not override, the terms of the arbitration agreements before us. . . .

But that's not the end of it. Even if the Arbitration Act normally requires us to enforce arbitration agreements like theirs, the employees reply that the NLRA overrides that guidance . . . .

This argument faces a stout uphill climb. When confronted with two Acts of Congress allegedly touching on the same topic, this Court is not at 'liberty to pick and choose among congressional enactments' and must instead strive "to give effect to both." . . .

A close look at the employees' best evidence of a potential conflict turns out to reveal no conflict . . . .

What all the[] textual and contextual clues indicate, our precedents confirm. In many cases over many years, this Court has heard and rejected efforts to conjure conflicts between the Arbitration Act and other federal statutes. . . .

The employees rejoin that our precedential story is complicated by some of this Court's cases interpreting Section 7 itself. But, as it turns out, this Court's Section 7 cases have usually involved just what you would expect from the statute's plain language: efforts by employees related to organizing and collective bargaining in the workplace, not the treatment of class or collective actions in court or arbitration proceedings. . . .

With so much against them . . . , the employees end by seeking shelter in Chevron. . . .

Where, as here, the canons supply an answer, 'Chevron leaves the stage.' . . .

The policy may be debatable but the law is clear: Congress has instructed that arbitration agreements like those before us must be enforced as written. While Congress is of course always free to amend this judgment, we see nothing suggesting it did so in the NLRA—much less that it manifested a clear intention to displace the Arbitration Act. Because we can easily read Congress's statutes to work in harmony, that is where our duty lies. The judgments in Epic, No. 16–285, and Ernst & Young, No. 16–300, are reversed, and the cases are remanded for further proceedings consistent with this opinion. The judgment in Murphy Oil, No. 16–307, is affirmed."

V. JUSTICE VOTE

4 Pro ACLU Side vs. 5 Con Opposing Side

ACLU Side (Respondent / Appellee)

1. Kagan, E. – Joined Ginsburg's dissent
2. Breyer, S. – Joined Ginsburg's dissent
3. Ginsburg, R. – Wrote dissenting opinion
4. Sotomayor, S. – Joined Ginsburg's dissent

Opposing Side (Petitioner / Appellant)

1. Gorsuch, N. – Wrote majority opinion
2. Alito, S. – Joined majority opinion
3. Thomas, C. – Wrote concurring opinion
4. Kennedy, A. – Joined majority opinion
5. Roberts, J. – Joined majority opinion

VI. A WIN OR LOSS FOR THE ACLU?

The ACLU filed as amicus curiae urging affirmance in Nos. 16-285 and 16-300 and reversal in No. 16-307; the Supreme Court reversed the Court of Appeals' decisions in Nos. 16-285 and 16-300 and affirmed in No. 16-307 by a 5-4 vote, giving the ACLU an apparent loss.

1174. Masterpiece Cakeshop, Ltd. v. Colorado Civil Rights Comm'n

(Decided June 4, 2018; 138 S.Ct. 1719; 584 U.S. _)

I. ISSUE

A. Issues Discussed

1st Amendment, religion

B. Legal Question Presented

Whether the Colorado Civil Rights Commission violated the U.S. Constitution through its order that a bakery's refusal to create a cake for a same-sex couple because of the shop owner's religion objection to same-sex marriage was unlawful.

C. Supreme Court's Answer

"[W]hatever the outcome of some future controversy involving facts similar to these, the Commission's actions here violated the Free Exercise Clause [of the First Amendment]; and its order must be set aside."

II. CASE SUMMARY

A. Background

"In 2012 a same-sex couple visited Masterpiece Cakeshop, a bakery in Colorado, to make inquiries about ordering a cake for their wedding reception. The shop's owner told the couple that he would not create a cake for their wedding because of his religious opposition to same-sex marriages—marriages the State of Colorado itself did not recognize at that time. The couple filed a charge with the Colorado Civil Rights Commission alleging discrimination on the basis of sexual orientation in violation of the Colorado Anti–Discrimination Act.

The Commission determined that the shop's actions violated the Act and ruled in the couple's favor. The Colorado state courts affirmed the ruling and its enforcement order . . . ."

The Supreme Court granted certiorari to review the case.

B. Counsel of Record / ACLU Attorney

ACLU Side (Respondent / Appellee): David D. Cole of the American Civil Liberties Union Foundation argued the cause for appellees Charlie Craig and David Mullins. With him on the briefs were Paula Greisen, and Mark Silverstein and Sara R. Neel of the American Civil Liberties Union Foundation of Colorado, and Ria Tabacco Mar, James D. Esseks, Leslie Cooper, Rachel Wainer Apter, Louise Melling, Rose A. Saxe, Lee Rowland, Amanda W. Shanor, and Daniel Mach of the American Civil Liberties Union Foundation.

Frederick R. Yarger, Solicitor General of Colorado, argued the cause for appellee Colorado Civil Rights Commission. With him on the briefs were Cynthia H. Coffman, Attorney General, Vincent E. Morscher, Deputy Attorney General, Glenn E. Roper, Deputy Solicitor General, Stacy L. Worthington, Senior Assistant Attorney General, and Grant T. Sullivan, Assistant Solicitor General.

Opposing Side (Petitioner / Appellant): Kristen Kellie Waggoner argued the cause for appellant. With her on the briefs were David A. Cortman, Rory T. Gray, Nicolle H. Martin, Jeremy D. Tedesco, James A. Campbell, and Jonathan A. Scruggs.

Solicitor General Francisco argued the cause for the United States as amicus curiae.

III. AMICI CURIAE

ACLU Side (Respondent / Appellee)

Brief of amici curiae filed on behalf of Legal Scholars in Support of Equality by Kyle C. Velte and Barbara J. Cox.

Brief of amici curiae filed on behalf of Freedom of Speech Scholars by Steven H. Shiffrin.

Brief of amici curiae filed on behalf of Services and Advocacy for Gay, Lesbian, Bisexual and Transgender Elders et al. by Jonathan Jacob Nadler, Marques P.D. Richeson, and Dylan J. Yépez.

Brief of amici curiae filed on behalf of American Unity Fund et al. by Dale Carpenter and Eugene Volokh.

Brief of amici curiae filed on behalf of Scholars of the Constitutional Rights and Interests of Children by Catherine E. Smith, Lauren Fontana, Angela Onwuachi-Willig, Tanya M. Washington, and Barbara Bennett Woodhouse.

Brief of amici curiae filed on behalf of Freedom from Religion Foundation by Rebecca S. Markert, Elizabeth Cavell, Andrew Seidel, Patrick Elliott, and Sam Grover.

Brief of amici curiae filed on behalf of the General Synod of the United Church of Christ et al. by Heather E. Kimmel, K. Hollyn Hollman, Jennifer L. Hawks, Douglas Hallward-Driemeier, Emerson Siegle, John McClain, Mary E. Kostel, Donald C. Clark, Jr., and Phillip H. Harris.

Brief of amici curiae filed on behalf of First Amendment Scholars by Elizabeth B. Wydra, Brianne J. Gorod, David H.

Gans, and Ashwin P. Phatak.

Brief of amici curiae filed on behalf of the Center for Inquiry et al. by Nicholas J. Little and Edward Tabash.

Brief of amici curiae filed on behalf of the National Women's Law Center et al. by Fatima Goss Graves, Emily J. Martin, Gretchen Borchelt, Sunu Chandy, Sarah David Heydemann, Anna P. Engh, Lauren K. Moxley, and Melissa Murray.

Brief of amici curiae filed on behalf of Chefs, Bakers, and Restaurateurs by Sarah Warbelow, Pratik A. Shah, and Martine E. Cicconi.

Brief of amici curiae filed on behalf of Washington Lawyers' Committee for Civil Rights and Urban Affairs et al. by Jonathan M. Smith, Matthew Handley, Matthew J. MacLean, Michael S. McNamara, and Jessica T. Nyman.

Brief of amici curiae filed on behalf of Church-State Scholars by Roberta A. Kaplan and Joshua Matz.

Brief of amici curiae filed on behalf of GLBTQ Legal Advocates & Defenders et al. by Shannon P. Minter, Christopher F. Stoll, Catherine R. Connors, Nolan L. Reichl, Mary L. Bonauto and Gary D. Buseck.

Brief of amici curiae filed on behalf of the Transgender Law Center et al. by Flor Bermudez, Lynly S. Egyes, Clifford M. Sloan, Caroline S. Van Zile, Brendan B. Gants, and Sydney P. Sgambato.

Brief of amici curiae filed on behalf of Colorado Organizations et al. by Evan Wolfson, Lino S. Lipinsky De Orlov, Peter Z. Stockburger, Eric Y. Wu, Melissa Hart, Craig J. Konnoth, and Scott Skinner-Thompson.

Brief of amici curiae filed on behalf of Americans United for Separation of Church and State et al. by Steven M. Freeman, David L. Barkey, Rachel G. Bresner, Miriam Zeidman, Elliot M. Mincberg, Diane LaViolette, Richard B. Katskee, Kelly M. Percival, and Claire L. Hillan.

Brief of amici curiae filed on behalf of OutServe-SLDN, Inc., et al. by Nima H. Mohebbi, Samuel Duimovich, Michael E. Bern, Matthew Peters, and Peter Perkowski.

Brief of amici curiae filed on behalf of the American Psychological Association et al. by Nathalie F.P. Gilfoyle, Deanne M. Ottaviano, Anne B. Camper, Jessica Ring Amunson, Emily L. Chapuis, and Tassity S. Johnson.

Brief of amici curiae filed on behalf of the American Bar Association by Donald B. Verrilli, Jr., Ginger D. Anders, Chad Golder, Jordan D. Segall, Allyson R. Bennett, and Hilarie Bass.

Brief of amici curiae filed on behalf of Floyd Abrams et al. by Dimitri D. Portnoi, Jamie Crooks, and Walter Dellinger.

Brief of amici curiae filed on behalf of the Main Street Alliance et al. by Charles C. Sipos, Nicola C. Menaldo, and Luke Rona.

Brief of amici curiae filed on behalf of Thirty-Seven Businesses and Organizations by Robert Cohen, Jonathan B. Sallet, Sarah D. Gordon, and Laura Lane-Steele.

Brief of amici curiae filed on behalf of Ilan H. Meyer, PhD., et al. by Adam P. Romero, Stephen B. Kinnaird, Randall V. Johnston, Peter S. Larson, Scott M. Klausner, Ji Hae Kim, Miri Song, and Serli Polatoglu.

Brief of amici curiae filed on behalf of the Central Conference of American Rabbis et al. by Jeffrey S. Trachtman, Norman C. Simon, Jason M. Moff, Kurt M. Denk, Evie Spanos, and Timur Tusiray.

Brief of amici curiae filed on behalf of Corporate Law Professors by Kent Greenfield, Andrew D. Silverman, and Daniel A. Rubens.

Brief of amici curiae filed on behalf of the Civil Rights Forum by Lawrence A. Organ, Navruz Avloni, Julianne K. Stanford, and Noah B. Baron.

Brief of amici curiae filed on behalf of Professor Tobias B. Wolff by Mr. Wolff.

Brief of amici curiae filed on behalf of 211 Members of Congress by Peter T. Barbur, Charles E. Loeser, and Nathalie J.K. Baker.

Brief of amici curiae filed on behalf of Former Representative Tony Coelho et al. by Sanford Jay Rosen.

Brief of amici curiae filed on behalf of 15 Faith and Civil Rights Organizations by Robin L. Muir, Johnathan J. Smith, Sirine Shebaya, Jessica L. Ellsworth, Kaitlin E. Welborn, David S. Victorson, Katherine Franke, and Elizabeth Reiner Platt.

Brief of amici curiae filed on behalf of National LGBTQ Task Force et al. by Candace Bond-Theriault, Marc A. Hearron, and Ruth N. Borenstein.

Brief of amici curiae filed on behalf of Canadian Civil Liberties Association et al. by Maureen P. Alger, Kyle Wong, and L. Alyssa Chen.

Brief of amici curiae filed on behalf of Public Accommodation Law Scholars by Elizabeth Sepper, Catherine Weiss, Natalie J. Kraner, Rey Lambert, and Meg Slachetka.

Brief of amici curiae filed on behalf of Denver Metro Chamber of Commerce et al. by Alan E. Schoenfeld, John F. Walsh, Reginald J. Brown, Paul R.Q. Wolfson, and Emily F. Gomez.

Brief of amici curiae filed on behalf of Service Employees International Union by Nicole G. Berner, Claire Prestel, Stacey Leyton, and Rebecca Lee.

Brief of amici curiae filed on behalf of Scholars of Behavioral Science and Economics by Adam W. Hofmann and Josephine K. Mason.

Brief of amici curiae filed on behalf of the State of Massachusetts et al. by

Brief of amici curiae filed on behalf of Maura Healey, Attorney General of Massachusetts, Elizabeth N. Dewar, State Solicitor, by David C. Kravitz, Genevieve C. Nadeau, and Jon Burke, Assistant Attorneys General, Douglas S. Chin, Attorney General of Hawaii, Clyde J. Wadsworth, Solicitor General, Kaliko'Onalani D. Fernandes, Deputy Solicitor General, and by the Attorneys General for their respective jurisdictions as follows: Xavier Becerra of California, George Jepsen of Connecticut, Matthew P. Denn of Delaware, Karl A. Racine of the District of Columbia, Lisa Madigan of Illinois, Thomas J. Miller of Iowa, Janet T. Mills of Maine, Brian E. Frosh of Maryland, Lori Swanson of Minnesota, Hector Balderas of New Mexico, Eric T. Schneiderman of New York, Josh Stein of North Carolina, Ellen F. Rosenblum of Oregon, Peter F. Kilmartin of Rhode Island, Thomas J. Donovan, Jr., of Vermont, Mark R. Herring of Virginia, and Robert W. Ferguson of Washington.

Brief of amici curiae filed on behalf of Tanenbaum Center for Interreligious Understanding by Daniel Lawrence Greenberg, Robert J. Ward, Holly H. Weiss, Jennifer M. Opheim, Randall

Adams, Mark Garibyan, and Brian Lanciault.

Brief of amici curiae filed on behalf of NAACP Legal Defense & Educational Fund, Inc., by Sherrilyn A. Ifill, Coty Montag, John Paul Schnapper-Casteras, Janai S. Nelson, and Samuel Spital.

Brief of amici curiae filed on behalf of Transgender Legal Defense and Education Fund by John D. Winter, Jeffrey S. Ginsberg, Lauren M. Capaccio, Peter Shakro, Jillian T. Weiss, Amy K.W. Helfant, Donna M. Levinsohn, and Sean P. Madden.

Brief of amici curiae filed on behalf of Lambda Legal Defense and Education Fund, Inc., et al. by Shelbi Day, Denise Brogan-Kator, Jennifer C. Pizer, and Nancy C. Marcus.

Brief of amici curiae filed on behalf of the County of Santa Clara et al. by James R. Williams, Santa Clara County Counsel, Greta S. Hansen, Laura S. Trice, Julie Wilensky, Julia B. Spiegel, Lynnette K. Miner, Zachary W. Carter, New York City Corporation Counsel, Richard Dearing, Claude S. Platton, Benjamin Welikson, Michael N. Feuer, Los Angeles City Attorney, James P. Clark, Thomas P. Peters, Blithe Smith Bock, and Shaun Dabby Jacobs.

Brief of amici curiae filed on behalf of Lawyers' Committee for Civil Rights Under Law et al. by Kristen Clarke, Jon Greenbaum, Dariely Rodriguez, Dorian Spence, Ilana H. Eisenstein, Courtney Gilligan Saleski, Ethan H. Townsend, Paul Schmitt, Adam Steene, and Jeffrey DeGroot.

Brief of amici curiae filed on behalf of the National League of Cities et al. by D. Bruce La Pierre, Brian C. Walsh, and Lisa E. Soronen.

Opposing Side (Petitioner / Appellant)

Brief of amici curiae filed on behalf of the United States by Acting Solicitor General Wall, Acting Assistant Attorney General Readler, Acting Assistant Attorney General Gore, Deputy Assistant Attorney General Mooppan, Assistant Solicitor General Goodspeed, Special Counsel Treene, Counsel to the Assistant Attorney General Lucas, and Lowell V. Sturgill Jr.

Brief of amici curiae filed on behalf of Billy Graham Evangelistic Association by Stuart J. Lark.

Brief of amici curiae filed on behalf of Indiana Family Institute, Inc., et al. by James Bopp, Jr., Richard E. Coleson and Corrine L. Youngs.

Brief of amici curiae filed on behalf of Southeastern Legal Foundation et al. by Kimberly S. Hermann and John J. Park, Jr.

Brief of amici curiae filed on behalf of Rev. Patrick Mahoney et al. by Thomas P. Monaghan and Walter M. Weber.

Brief of amici curiae filed on behalf of Ryan T. Anderson, Ph.D., et al. by Charles S. LiMandri, Paul M. Jonna, and Jeffrey M. Trissell.

Brief of amici curiae filed on behalf of the Cato Institute et al. by Manuel S. Klausner, Ilya Shapiro, and David McDonald.

Brief of amici curiae filed on behalf of the Thomas More Society by Thomas Brejcha, Jocelyn Floyd, and Joan M. Mannix.

Brief of amici curiae filed on behalf of Independence Law Center by Randall L. Wenger and Jeremy L. Samek.

Brief of amici curiae filed on behalf of North Carolina Values Coalition et al. by Tami Fitzgerald, Travis Weber, and Deborah J. Dewart.

Brief of amici curiae filed on behalf of the Foundation for Moral Law by John Eidsmoe.

Brief of amici curiae filed on behalf of Law and Economics Scholars by Sean P. Gates, Richard A. Epstein, and David A. Shaneyfelt.

Brief of amici curiae filed on behalf of United States Conference of Catholic Bishops et al. by Anthony R. Picarello, Jr., Jeffrey Hunter Moon, Michael F. Moses, Hillary E. Byrnes, and John J. Bursch.

Brief of amici curiae filed on behalf of the National Black Religious Broadcasters et al. by David H. Thompson.

Brief of amici curiae filed on behalf of William Jack et al. by Michael Lee Francisco.

Brief of amici curiae filed on behalf of Mark Regnerus et al. by Joseph E. Holland and Edward H. Trent.

Brief of amici curiae filed on behalf of the Becket Fund for Religious Liberty by Eric C. Rassbach, Mark L. Rienzi, Eric S. Baxter, Hannah C. Smith, Diana M. Verm, and Stephanie Hall Barclay.

Brief of amici curiae filed on behalf of Utah Republican State Senators by Michael K. Erickson and William C. Duncan.

Brief of amici curiae filed on behalf of Agudath Israel of America by Abba Cohen, Andrew Weinstock, Mordechai Biser, and Jeffrey I. Zuckerman.

Brief of amici curiae filed on behalf of International Christian Photographers et al. by Michael J. Norton, W. Michael Clark, and David M. Hyams.

Brief of amici curiae filed on behalf of 34 Legal Scholars by David R. Langdon.

Brief of amici curiae filed on behalf of Public Advocate of the United States et al. by Joseph W. Miller, William J. Olson, Herbert W. Titus, Jeremiah L. Morgan, Robert J. Olson, Michael Boos, and James N. Clymer.

Brief of amici curiae filed on behalf of 33 Family Policy Organizations by David French.

Brief of amici curiae filed on behalf of Christian Business Owners Supporting Religious Freedom by Erin Elizabeth Mersino, William Wagner, and John Kane.

Brief of amici curiae filed on behalf of Center for Constitutional Jurisprudence et al. by John C. Eastman and Anthony T. Caso.

Brief of amici curiae filed on behalf of Sherif Girgis by Robert P. George.

Brief of amici curiae filed on behalf of Richard Lawrence by Mr. Lawrence.

Brief of amici curiae filed on behalf of C12 Group et al. by Richard Baker.

Brief of amici curiae filed on behalf of American College of Pediatricians et al. by Nikolas T. Nikas, Dorinda C. Bordlee, Madeline Moreira, Catherine W. Short, and Roger G. Brooks.

Brief of amici curiae filed on behalf of Ethics & Religious Liberty Commission of the Southern Baptist Convention et al. by Michael K. Whitehead.

Brief of amici curiae filed on behalf of United States Senators and Representatives by Jonathan R. Whitehead.

Brief of amici curiae filed on behalf of Legal Scholar Adam J.

Macleod by Jennifer Bursch and Robert Tyler.
Brief of amici curiae filed on behalf of Liberty Counsel by Mathew D. Staver, Anita L. Staver, Horatio G. Mihet, and Mary E. McAlister.
Brief of amici curiae filed on behalf of Aaron and Melissa Klein by Tyler Smith, Herbert G. Grey, Kelly J. Shackelford, Hiram S. Sasser III, Kenneth A. Klukowski, and Stephanie N. Taub.
Brief of amici curiae filed on behalf of the National Jewish Commission on Law and Public Affairs ("COLPA") by Dennis Rapps, Nathan Lewin, and Alyza D. Lewin.
Brief of amici curiae filed on behalf of Christian Legal Society et al. by Thomas C. Berg and Douglas Laycock.
Brief of amici curiae filed on behalf of Professors Christopher R. Green et al. by Mr. Green and David R. Upham.
Brief of amici curiae filed on behalf of 479 Creative Professionals by Nathan W. Kellum.
Brief of amici curiae filed on behalf of Freedom X et al. by William J. Becker, Jr.
Brief of amici curiae filed on behalf of the Restoring Religious Freedom Project by Mark Goldfeder, Anton Sorkin, and David I. Schoen.
Brief of amici curiae filed on behalf of CatholicVote.org by Scott W. Gaylord.
Brief of amici curiae filed on behalf of Concerned Women for America by Steven W. Fitschen.
Brief of amici curiae filed on behalf of the National Legal Foundation et al. by Frederick W. Claybrook, Jr.
Brief of amici curiae filed on behalf of First Amendment Lawyers Association by D. Gill Sperlein, Robert Corn-Revere, and Ronald G. London.
Brief of amici curiae filed on behalf of the State of Texas et al. by Ken Paxton, Attorney General of Texas, Jeffrey C. Mateer, First Assistant Attorney General, Scott A. Keller, Solicitor General, J. Campbell Barker, Deputy Solicitor General, Michael P. Murphy and John C. Sullivan, Assistant Solicitors General, M. Stephen Pitt, General Counsel to the Governor of Kentucky, Brent A. Davis Chief Counsel to the Governor of Maine, and by the Attorneys General for their respective States as follows: Steve Marshall of Alabama, Mark Brnovich of Arizona, Leslie Rutledge of Arkansas, Lawrence G. Wasden of Idaho, Jeff Landry of Louisiana, Joshua D. Hawley of Missouri, Tim Fox of Montana, Doug Peterson of Nebraska, Adam Paul Laxalt of Nevada, Wayne Stenehjem of North Dakota, Mike Hunter of Oklahoma, Alan Wilson of South Carolina, Marty J. Jackley of South Dakota, Herbert H. Slatery III of Tennessee, Sean D. Reyes of Utah, Patrick Morrisey of West Virginia, and Brad Schimel of Wisconsin.
Brief of amici curiae filed on behalf of Christian Law Association by David C. Gibbs, Jr.
Brief of amici curiae filed on behalf of Cake Artists by Aaron M. Streett, Benjamin A. Geslison, J. Mark Little, Evan A. Young, and Samantha Kuhn in support of neither party.
Brief of amici curiae filed on behalf of Council for Christian Colleges and Universities (CCCU) et al. by Gene C. Schaerr and Michael T. Worley in support of neither party.
Brief of amici curiae filed on behalf of Institute for Justice by Robert J. McNamara and Paul M. Sherman in support of neither party.
Brief of amici curiae filed on behalf of David Boyle by Mr. Boyle in support of neither party.

IV. THE SUPREME COURT'S DECISION

"Our society has come to the recognition that gay persons and gay couples cannot be treated as social outcasts or as inferior in dignity and worth. For that reason the laws and the Constitution can, and in some instances must, protect them in the exercise of their civil rights. The exercise of their freedom on terms equal to others must be given great weight and respect by the courts. At the same time, the religious and philosophical objections to gay marriage are protected views and in some instances protected forms of expression. . . .

The neutral and respectful consideration to which Phillips was entitled was compromised here . . . . The Civil Rights Commission's treatment of his case has some elements of a clear and impermissible hostility toward the sincere religious beliefs that motivated his objection. . . .

For the reasons just described, the Commission's treatment of Phillips' case violated the State's duty under the First Amendment not to base laws or regulations on hostility to a religion or religious viewpoint. . . .

The Commission's hostility was inconsistent with the First Amendment's guarantee that our laws be applied in a manner that is neutral toward religion. Phillips was entitled to a neutral decisionmaker who would give full and fair consideration to his religious objection as he sought to assert it in all of the circumstances in which this case was presented, considered, and decided. In this case the adjudication concerned a context that may well be different going forward . . . . However later cases raising these or similar concerns are resolved in the future, for these reasons the rulings of the Commission and of the state court that enforced the Commission's order must be invalidated.

The outcome of cases like this in other circumstances must await further elaboration in the courts, all in the context of recognizing that these disputes must be resolved with tolerance, without undue disrespect to sincere religious beliefs, and without subjecting gay persons to indignities when they seek goods and services in an open market.

The judgment of the Colorado Court of Appeals is reversed."

V. JUSTICE VOTE

2 Pro ACLU Side vs. 7 Con Opposing Side

ACLU Side (Respondent / Appellee)

1. Ginsburg, R. – Wrote dissenting opinion
2. Sotomayor, S. – Joined Ginsburg's dissent

Opposing Side (Petitioner / Appellant)

1. Kennedy, A. – Wrote majority opinion
2. Alito, S. – Joined Gorsuch's concurrence
3. Kagan, E. – Wrote concurring opinion
4. Thomas, C. – Wrote concurring opinion
5. Breyer, S. – Joined Kagan's concurrence
6. Gorsuch, N. – Wrote concurring opinion, joined Thomas' concurrence

7. Roberts, J. – Joined majority opinion

VI. A WIN OR LOSS FOR THE ACLU?

The ACLU argued the cause for the private appellees urging affirmance; the Supreme Court reversed the Colorado Court of Appeals' decision by a 7-2 vote, giving the ACLU an apparent loss.

1175. Husted v. A. Philip Randolph Institute

(Decided June 11, 2018; 138 S.Ct. 1833; 584 U.S. _)

I. ISSUE

A. Issues Discussed

Voting rights

B. Legal Question Presented

Whether Ohio's law on removing voters from their voter registration list comports with the National Voter Registration Act of 1993 (NVRA) or the Help America Vote Act of 2002 (HAVA).

C. Supreme Court's Answer

"[W]e hold that Ohio law does not violate the Failure-to-Vote Clause. . . .

We similarly reject respondents' argument that Ohio violates other provisions of the NVRA and HAVA."

II. CASE SUMMARY

A. Background

"At issue in today's case is an Ohio law that aims to keep the State's voting lists up to date by removing the names of those who have moved out of the district where they are registered. Ohio uses the failure to vote for two years as a rough way of identifying voters who may have moved, and it then sends a preaddressed, postage prepaid card to these individuals asking them to verify that they still reside at the same address. Voters who do not return this card and fail to vote in any election for four more years are presumed to have moved and are removed from the rolls. . . .

A pair of advocacy groups and an Ohio resident (respondents here) think that Ohio's Supplemental Process violates the NVRA and HAVA. They sued petitioner, Ohio's Secretary of State, seeking to enjoin this process. Respondents alleged, first, that Ohio removes voters who have not actually moved, thus purging the rolls of eligible voters. They also contended that Ohio violates the NVRA's Failure-to-Vote Clause because the failure to vote plays a prominent part in the Ohio removal scheme: Failure to vote for two years triggers the sending of a return card, and if the card is not returned, failure to vote for four more years results in removal.

The District Court rejected both . . . arguments and entered judgment for the Secretary. . . .

A divided panel of the Court of Appeals for the Sixth Circuit reversed."

The Supreme Court granted certiorari to review the case.

B. Counsel of Record / ACLU Attorney

ACLU Side (Respondent / Appellee): Paul M. Smith argued the cause for appellee. With him on the briefs were Stuart C. Naifeh, Naila S. Awan, Cameron A. Bell, Brenda Wright, and Dale E. Ho, Sophia Lin Lakin, Theresa J. Lee, Cecillia D. Wang, Julie A. Ebenstein, T. Alora Thomas, Rachel Wainer Apter, and David D. Cole of the American Civil Liberties Union Foundation, and Freda Levenson, Daniel P. Tokaji, Paul Moke, and Richard Saphire of the ACLU of Ohio.

Opposing Side (Petitioner / Appellant): Eric E. Murphy, State Solicitor of Ohio, argued the cause for appellant. With him on the briefs were Michael DeWine, Attorney General, Michael J. Hendershot, Chief Deputy Solicitor, and Steven T. Voigt, Principal Assistant Attorney General.

Solicitor General Francisco argued the cause for the United States as amicus curiae.

III. AMICI CURIAE

ACLU Side (Respondent / Appellee)

Brief of amici curiae filed on behalf of the Libertarian Party of Ohio et al. by Mark R. Brown and Oliver Hall.

Brief of amici curiae filed on behalf of Constitutional Accountability Center by Elizabeth B. Wydra, Brianne J. Gorod, and David H. Gans.

Brief of amici curiae filed on behalf of American History Professors by Brittany N. Lovejoy, Patrick K. O'Brien, Richard P. Bress, Ryan C. Grover, and Savannah K. Burgoyne.

Brief of amici curiae filed on behalf of Libertarian National Committee by Thomas G. Saunders, Ari J. Savitzky, Janine M. Lopez, Katherine V. Mackey, and Jason D. Hirsch.

Brief of amici curiae filed on behalf of the League of Women Voters of the United States et al. by Wendy R. Weiser, Myrna Pérez, Jonathan Brater, John A. Freedman, Peter J. Schildkraut, Elisabeth S. Theodore, Jeremy Karpatkin, and Andrew W. Beyer.

Brief of amici curiae filed on behalf of National Association for the Advancement of Colored People et al. by Martin L. Saad, Kathleen K. Sheridan, John C. Vazquez, Christopher N. Moran, Gilda R. Daniels, Judith Browne Dianis, Donita Judge, Eileen Ma, Andrew Hairston, Bradford M. Berry, Janette M. Louard, Khyla D. Craine, James Workman, and H. Lee Thompson.

Brief of amici curiae filed on behalf of Senator Sherrod Brown by Steven A. Hirsch and David J. Silbert.

Brief of amici curiae filed on behalf of Certain Members of the Congressional Black Caucus by Linda C. Goldstein and Neil Steiner.

Brief of amici curiae filed on behalf of National Disability Rights Network et al. by Paul M. Smith, Danielle Lang, William Alvarado Rivera, Daniel B. Kohrman, Renata E. B. Strause, Ellis Jacobs, Nicole G. Berner, and Claire Prestel.

Brief of amici curiae filed on behalf of Common Cause by Emmet J. Bondurant, Jason J. Carter, Chad K. Lennon, and Allegra Chapman.

Brief of amici curiae filed on behalf of Eric H. Holder, Jr., et al. by Samuel R. Bagenstos.

Brief of amici curiae filed on behalf of the State of New York et al. by Eric T. Schneiderman, Attorney General of New York,

Barbara D. Underwood, Solicitor General, Steven C. Wu, Deputy Solicitor General, Seth M. Rokosky, Assistant Solicitor General, and by the Attorneys General for their respective jurisdictions as follows: Xavier Becerra of California, George Jepsen of Connecticut, Matthew P. Denn of Delaware, Karl A. Racine of the District of Columbia, Douglas S. Chin of Hawaii, Lisa Madigan of Illinois, Thomas J. Miller of Iowa, Andy Beshear of Kentucky, Brian E. Frosh of Maryland, Hector Balderas of New Mexico, Ellen F. Rosenblum of Oregon, and Bob Ferguson of Washington.

Brief of amici curiae filed on behalf of Asian Americans Advancing Justice | AAJC et al. by Brigida Benitez, Jessica I. Rothschild, Niyati Shah, Terry Ao Minnis, John Yang, Erin Hustings, Jose Perez, and Joanna E. Cuevas Ingram.

Brief of amici curiae filed on behalf of Public Citizen, Inc., by Scott L. Nelson and Allison M. Zieve.

Brief of amici curiae filed on behalf of Current and Former Ohio Elections Officials by Rachel Bloomekatz.

Brief of amici curiae filed on behalf of VoteVets Action Fund by Deborah N. Archer and Aderson B. Francois.

Brief of amici curiae filed on behalf of the Lawyers' Committee for Civil Rights Under Law et al. by Kristen Clarke, Jon M. Greenbaum, Ezra D. Rosenberg, Brendan Downes, Michael C. Keats, Michele L. Pahmer, and Daniel N. Bertaccini.

Brief of amici curiae filed on behalf of NAACP Legal Defense and Educational Fund, Inc., et al. by Sherrilyn A. Ifill, Janai S. Nelson, Samuel Spital, Leah C. Aden, Thomas M. Bondy, John Paul Schnapper-Casteras, Khai Lequang, Melanie D. Phillips, Emily K. Brown, Ethan M. Scapellati, Kristina Pieper Trautmann, and Daniel Robertson.

Opposing Side (Petitioner / Appellant)

Brief of amici curiae filed on behalf of the United States by Acting Solicitor General Wall, Acting Assistant Attorney General Gore, Deputy Solicitor General Stewart, and Assistant Solicitor General Fletcher.

Brief of amici curiae filed on behalf of the Buckeye Institute by Robert Alt, Michael A. Carvin, and Anthony J. Dick.

Brief of amici curiae filed on behalf of Eagle Forum Education & Legal Defense Fund by Lawrence J. Joseph.

Brief of amici curiae filed on behalf of the State of Georgia et al. by Christopher M. Carr, Attorney General of Georgia, Sarah Hawkins Warren, Solicitor General, Andrew A. Pinson, Deputy Solicitor General, and by the Attorneys General for their respective States as follows: Derek Schmidt of Kansas, Adam Paul Laxalt of Nevada, Sean Reyes of Utah, Ken Paxton of Texas, Joshua D. Hawley of Missouri, Herbert H. Slatery III of Tennessee, Patrick Morrisey of West Virginia, Steve Marshall of Alabama, Marty J. Jackley of South Dakota, Jeff Landry of Louisiana, Alan Wilson of South Carolina, Lawrence G. Wasden of Idaho, Curtis T. Hill, Jr., of Indiana, Tim Fox of Montana, Bill Schuette of Michigan, and Mike Hunter of Oklahoma.

Brief of amici curiae filed on behalf of Judicial Watch, Inc., by Robert D. Popper, Chris Fedeli, Lauren M. Burke, and Eric W. Lee.

Brief of amici curiae filed on behalf of American Civil Rights Union by J. Christian Adams, Kaylan L. Phillips, and Noel H. Johnson.

Brief of amici curiae filed on behalf of Former Attorneys of the Civil Rights Division of the United States Department of Justice by William S. Consovoy, J. Michael Connolly, and Cameron T. Norris.

Brief of amici curiae filed on behalf of Landmark Legal Foundation et al. by Michael J. O'Neill, Matthew C. Forys, Linda Carver Whitlow Knight, and Richard P. Hutchison.

Brief of amici curiae filed on behalf of National Conference of State Legislatures et al. by Lisa E. Soronen and Joshua P. Davis.

IV. THE SUPREME COURT'S DECISION

"[S]ubsection (d), the provision of the NVRA that directly addresses the procedures that a State must follow before removing a registrant from the rolls on change-of-residence grounds, provides that a State may remove a registrant who '(i) has failed to respond to a notice and "('ii) has not voted or appeared to vote . . . during the period beginning on the date of the notice and ending on the day after the date of the second general election for Federal office that occurs after the date of the notice' (about four years). Not only are States allowed to remove registrants who satisfy these requirements, but federal law makes this removal mandatory.

Ohio's Supplemental Process follows subsection (d) to the letter. . . .

Respondents argue . . . that, even if Ohio's process complies with subsection (d), it nevertheless violates the Failure-to-Vote Clause . . . . Respondents point out that Ohio's Supplemental Process uses a person's failure to vote twice: once as the trigger for sending return cards and again as one of the requirements for removal. . . .

We reject this argument because the Failure-to-Vote Clause . . . forbids the use of nonvoting as the sole criterion for removing a registrant, and Ohio does not use it that way. Instead, . . . Ohio removes registrants only if they have failed to vote and have failed to respond to a notice. . . .

Respondents and the dissent advance an alternative interpretation of the Failure-to-Vote Clause, but that reading is inconsistent with both the text of the clause and the clarification of its meaning in § 21083(a)(4)(A). . . .

Respondents put forth one additional argument regarding the Failure-to-Vote Clause. In essence, it boils down to this. So many properly registered voters simply discard return cards upon receipt that the failure to send them back is worthless as evidence that the addressee has moved. . . .

This argument is based on a dubious empirical conclusion that the NVRA and HAVA do not allow us to indulge. . . .

For all these reasons, we hold that Ohio law does not violate the Failure-to-Vote Clause. . . .

Nothing in the two dissents changes our analysis of the statutory language. . . .

The dissents have a policy disagreement, not just with Ohio, but with Congress. But this case presents a question of statutory interpretation, not a question of policy. We have no authority to second-guess Congress or to decide whether Ohio's Supplemental Process is the ideal method for keeping its voting rolls up to date.

The only question before us is whether it violates federal law. It does not.

The judgment of the Sixth Circuit is reversed."

V. JUSTICE VOTE

4 Pro ACLU Side vs. 5 Con Opposing Side

ACLU Side (Respondent / Appellee)

1. Kagan, E. – Joined Breyer's dissent
2. Breyer, S. – Wrote dissenting opinion
3. Ginsburg, R. – Joined Breyer's dissent
4. Sotomayor, S. – Wrote dissenting opinion, joined Breyer's dissent

Opposing Side (Petitioner / Appellant)

1. Alito, S. – Wrote majority opinion
2. Thomas, C. – Wrote concurring opinion
3. Gorsuch, N. – Joined majority opinion
4. Kennedy, A. – Joined majority opinion
5. Roberts, J. – Joined majority opinion

VI. A WIN OR LOSS FOR THE ACLU?

The ACLU served as counsel for appellee urging affirmance; the Supreme Court reversed the Court of Appeals' decision by a 5-4 vote, giving the ACLU an apparent loss.

1176. Gill v. Whitford

(Decided June 18, 2018; 138 S.Ct. 1916; 585 U.S. _)

I. ISSUE

A. Issues Discussed

Voting rights

B. Legal Question Presented

"[T]wo threshold questions . . . : what is necessary to show standing in a case of this sort, and whether those claims are justiciable."

C. Supreme Court's Answer

"Here we do not decide the latter question because the plaintiffs in this case have not shown standing under the theory upon which they based their claims for relief."

II. CASE SUMMARY

A. Background

"The State of Wisconsin, like most other States, entrusts to its legislature the periodic task of redrawing the boundaries of the State's legislative districts. A group of Wisconsin Democratic voters filed a complaint in the District Court, alleging that the legislature carried out this task with an eye to diminishing the ability of Wisconsin Democrats to convert Democratic votes into Democratic seats in the legislature. The plaintiffs asserted that, in so doing, the legislature had infringed their rights under the First and Fourteenth Amendments. . . .

The election officials moved to dismiss the complaint. They argued, among other things, that the plaintiffs lacked standing to challenge the constitutionality of Act 43 as a whole because, as individual voters, their legally protected interests extend only to the makeup of the legislative districts in which they vote. A three-judge panel of the District Court denied the defendants' motion. . . .

The case proceeded to trial . . . .

At the close of evidence, the District Court concluded—over the dissent of Judge Griesbach—that the plaintiffs had proved a violation of the First and Fourteenth Amendments. . . .

Regarding standing, the court held that the plaintiffs had a 'cognizable equal protection right against state-imposed barriers on [their] ability to vote . . . for the party of [their] choice.' . . .

The District Court enjoined the defendants from using the Act 43 map in future elections and ordered them to have a remedial districting plan . . . no later than November 1, 2017. The defendants appealed directly to this Court . . . . [The U.S. Supreme Court] stayed the District Court's judgment and postponed consideration of . . . jurisdiction."

B. Counsel of Record / ACLU Attorney

ACLU Side (Respondent / Appellee): Paul M. Smith argued the cause for appellee. With him on the briefs were Jessica Ring Amunson, Michele Odorizzi, Douglas M. Poland, Peter G. Earle, J. Gerald Hebert, Danielle M. Lang, Nicholas O. Stephanopoulos, Ruth M. Greenwood, and Annabelle E. Harless.

Opposing Side (Petitioner / Appellant): Misha Tseytlin, Solicitor General of Wisconsin, argued the cause for appellant. With him on the briefs were Brad D. Schimel, Attorney General, Kevin M. Leroy, Deputy Solicitor General, Ryan J. Walsh, Chief Deputy Solicitor General, Amy C. Miller, Assistant Solicitor General, and Brian P. Keenan, Assistant Attorney General.

Erin E. Murphy argued the cause for the Wisconsin State Senate et al. as amicus curiae.

III. AMICI CURIAE

ACLU Side (Respondent / Appellee)

Brief of amici curiae filed on behalf of the American Civil Liberties Union, the New York Civil Liberties Union, and the ACLU of Wisconsin Foundation by T. Alora Thomas, Theresa J. Lee, Dale E. Ho, Cecillia D. Wang, David D. Cole, Laurence J. Dupuis, Karyn L. Rotker, Perry M. Grossman, Arthur N. Eisenberg, and Samuel Issacharoff.

Brief of amici curiae filed on behalf of Heather K. Gerken et al. by Kevin K. Russell and Ms. Gerken.

Brief of amici curiae filed on behalf of Eric S. Lander by Reed Witherby.

Brief of amici curiae filed on behalf of American Jewish Committee et al. by David Leit, Natalie J. Kraner, Eric Weiner, and Brandon Fierro.

Brief of amici curiae filed on behalf of E NAACP Legal Defense & Educational Fund, Inc., et al. by Sherrilyn A. Ifill, Janai S. Nelson, Samuel Spital, Leah C. Aden, Justin Levitt, and Laura W. Brill.

Brief of amici curiae filed on behalf of 44 Election Law, Scientific Evidence, and Empirical Legal Scholars Andrew Chin.

Brief of amici curiae filed on behalf of Professor Norman Dorsen by Burt Neuborne and Mr. Dorsen (1930-2017).
Brief of amici curiae filed on behalf of Historians by Clifford M. Sloan and Brendan B. Gants.
Brief of amici curiae filed on behalf of Senators John McCain et al. by Kathryn Cahoy, KeAndra Barlow, Mark W. Mosier, Ryan Mowery, and Alec Webley.
Brief of amici curiae filed on behalf of Law Professors by Pamela S. Karlan, Jeffrey L. Fisher, and David T. Goldberg.
Brief of amici curiae filed on behalf of Political Geography Scholars by Richard H. Pildes, Tacy F. Flint, Jason G. Marsico, and Jeffrey T. Green.
Brief of amici curiae filed on behalf of Professor D. Theodore Rave by Mr. Rave.
Brief of amici curiae filed on behalf of Political Science Professors by Robert A. Atkins, Nicholas Groombridge, Andrew J. Ehrlich, Pietro Signoracci, and Michael Pernick.
Brief of amici curiae filed on behalf of the Brennan Center for Justice at N.Y.U. School of Law by Wendy R. Weiser, Michael C. Li, Daniel I. Weiner, Brent Ferguson, Thomas P. Wolf, Anton Metlitsky, Bradley N. Garcia, and Samantha M. Goldstein.
Brief of amici curiae filed on behalf of Republican Statewide Officials Sen. Bill Brock et al. by Charles Fried, David C. Frederick, Daniel V. Dorris, and Matthew R. Huppert.
Brief of amici curiae filed on behalf of the State of Oregon et al. by Ellen F. Rosenblum, Attorney General of Oregon, Benjamin Gutman, Solicitor General, by Erin K. Galli, Jona J. Maukonen, Cecil Reniche-Smith, and Jordan R. Silk, Assistant Attorneys General, and by the Attorneys General for their respective jurisdictions as follows: Jahna Lindemuth of Alaska, Xavier Becerra of California, George Jepsen of Connecticut, Matthew P. Denn of Delaware, Karl A. Racine of the District of Columbia, Douglas S. Chin of Hawaii, Lisa Madigan of Illinois, Thomas J. Miller of Iowa, Andy Beshear of Kentucky, Janet T. Mills of Maine, Maura Healey of Massachusetts, Lori Swanson of Minnesota, Hector Balderas of New Mexico, Eric T. Schneiderman of New York, Peter F. Kilmartin of Rhode Island, Thomas J. Donovan, Jr., of Vermont, and Robert W. Ferguson of Washington.
Brief of amici curiae filed on behalf of League of Conservation Voters et al. by Cary E. Adickman, Madeline H. Gitomer, Hunter J. Kendrick, Ira M. Feinberg, and Susan M. Crawford.
Brief of amici curiae filed on behalf of Center for Media and Democracy by Theodore R. Boehm, Joseph H. Yeager, Jr., Harmony A. Mappes, Dulany Lucetta Pope, Matthew B. Harris, Jeffrey P. Justman, and Juliana Yanez.
Brief of amici curiae filed on behalf of the Georgia State Conference of the NAACP et al. by Kristen Clarke, Jon Greenbaum, Ezra D. Rosenberg, Julie Houk, John Powers, William V. Custer, and Jennifer B. Dempsey.
Brief of amici curiae filed on behalf of California Citizens Redistricting Commission et al. by Benjamin R. Fliegel and Brian A. Sutherland.
Brief of amici curiae filed on behalf of Represent.Us et al. by Scott Greytak, Atara Miller, Daniel M. Perry, Alison Bonelli, Conor Colasurdo, Taryn Gallup, Alexandra Paslawsky, and Erik Wilson.
Brief of amici curiae filed on behalf of Current Members of Congress et al. by Elizabeth B. Wydra, Brianne J. Gorod, and David H. Gans.
Brief of amici curiae filed on behalf of Constitutional Law Professors by Daniel H. Bromberg and Kathleen M. Sullivan.
Brief of amici curiae filed on behalf of Bipartisan Group of 65 Current and Former State Legislators by Vincent Levy, Gregory Dubinsky, Matthew V.H. Noller, Kevin D. Benish, and Timothy W. Grinsell.
Brief of amici curiae filed on behalf of Common Cause by Emmet J. Bondurant, Edwin M. Speas, Jr., Gregory L. Diskant, Jonah M. Knobler, Peter A. Nelson, and Elena Steiger Reich.
Brief of amici curiae filed on behalf of the League of Women Voters by Lloyd Leonard, Kathleen R. Hartnett, and Brent K. Nakamura.
Brief of amici curiae filed on behalf of Fairvote by Andrew Spencer, David O'Brien, Justin A. Nelson, and Alejandra C. Salinas.
Brief of amici curiae filed on behalf of Election Law and Constitutional Law Scholars by Bradley S. Phillips.
Brief of amici curiae filed on behalf of International Municipal Lawyers Association et al. by Charles W. Thompson, Jr., Amanda Kellar Karras, Nestor M. Davidson, and Paul A. Diller.
Brief of amici curiae filed on behalf of Bipartisan Group of Current and Former Members of Congress by Jason D. Hirsch, Stephanie Simon, Christopher D. Dodge, Seth P. Waxman, Jonathan Cedarbaum, Ari J. Savitzky, and David Stoopler.
Brief of amici curiae filed on behalf of David Boyle by Mr. Boyle.
Brief of amici curiae filed on behalf of Robin Best et al. by Steven J. Hyman, Alan E. Sash, Jacqueline C. Gerrald, and Tracy A. Burnett.

Opposing Side (Petitioner / Appellant)

Brief of amici curiae filed on behalf of Wisconsin State Senate et al. by Kevin St. John, Paul D. Clement, Erin E. Murphy, and Michael D. Lieberman.
Brief of amici curiae filed on behalf of Republican National Committee by John R. Phillippe, Jr., Michael T. Morley, and Dalton L. Oldham.
Brief of amici curiae filed on behalf of Judicial Watch, Inc., et al. by Robert D. Popper, Chris Fedeli, Lauren M. Burke, and Eric W. Lee.
Brief of amici curiae filed on behalf of Tennessee State Senators by John L. Ryder, Pablo Adrian Varela, and Linda Carver Whitlow Knight.
Brief of amici curiae filed on behalf of the Wisconsin Institute for Law & Liberty by Richard M. Esenberg, Douglas R. Cox, Amir C. Tayrani, Brian M. Lipshutz, and David W. Casazza.
Brief of amici curiae filed on behalf of the Majority Leader and Temporary President of the New York State Senate by David L. Lewis.
Brief of amici curiae filed on behalf of the State of Texas et al. by Ken Paxton Attorney General of Texas, Jeffrey C. Mateer, First Assistant Attorney General, Scott A. Keller, Solicitor General, Matthew H. Frederick, Deputy Solicitor General, Kristofer S. Monson, Assistant Solicitor General, and by the Attorneys General for their respective States as follows: Steve Marshall of Alabama, Mark Brnovich of Arizona, Leslie Rutledge of Arkansas, Christopher M. Carr of Georgia, Curtis T. Hill, Jr.,

of Indiana, Derek Schmidt of Kansas, Jeff Landry of Louisiana, Bill Schuette of Michigan, Joshua D. Hawley of Missouri, Adam Paul Laxalt of Nevada, Michael DeWine of Ohio, Mike Hunter of Oklahoma, Alan Wilson of South Carolina, Sean D. Reyes of Utah, and Patrick Morrisey of West Virginia.

Brief of amici curiae filed on behalf of Southeastern Legal Foundation by Kimberly S. Hermann and John J. Park, Jr.

Brief of amici curiae filed on behalf of the Legacy Foundation by Thomas J. Josefiak, J. Michael Bayes, Shawn Toomey Sheehy, and Steven P. Saxe.

Brief of amici curiae filed on behalf of Republican State Leadership Committee by Matthew Raymer, Efrem M. Braden, Katherine L. McKnight, and Richard B. Raile.

Brief of amici curiae filed on behalf of Wisconsin Manufacturers & Commerce by Jordan C. Corning, Eric M. McLeod, and Joseph S. Diedrich.

Brief of amici curiae filed on behalf of the National Republican Congressional Committee by Jason Torchinsky, J. Michael Bayes, Shawn Toomey Sheehy, Phillip M. Gordon, and P. Christopher Winkelman.

Brief of amici curiae filed on behalf of the American Civil Rights Union et al. by J. Christian Adams and Kaylan L. Phillips.

Brief of amici curiae filed on behalf of Eric Mcghee by Christopher S. Elmendorf, Daniel F. Kolb, Lynn E. Busath, John Hammond Heath, and Elizabeth A. Tippett in support of neither party.

Brief of amici curiae filed on behalf of Bernard Grofman et al. by Thomas M. Bondy, Avi Daniel Rosenblit, E. Joshua Rosenkranz, Rachel Wainer Apter, and Hannah Garden-Monheit in support of neither party.

Brief of amici curiae filed on behalf of the Plaintiffs in the Maryland Redistricting Litigation, Benisek v. Lamone (formerly Shapiro v. Mcmanus) by Michael B. Kimberly and Paul W. Hughes in support of neither party.

IV. THE SUPREME COURT'S DECISION

"Over the past five decades this Court has been repeatedly asked to decide what judicially enforceable limits, if any, the Constitution sets on the gerrymandering of voters along partisan lines. Our previous attempts at an answer have left few clear landmarks for addressing the question. . . .

At argument . . . , counsel for the plaintiffs argued that this Court can address . . . partisan gerrymandering because it must: The Court should exercise its power here because it is the 'only institution . . .' capable of 'solv[ing] this problem.' Such invitations must be answered with care. . . .

Our considerable efforts in Gaffney, Bandemer, Vieth, and LULAC leave unresolved whether such claims may be brought in cases involving allegations of partisan gerrymandering. In particular, two threshold questions remain: what is necessary to show standing in a case of this sort, and whether those claims are justiciable. Here we do not decide the latter question because the plaintiffs in this case have not shown standing under the theory upon which they based their claims for relief.

To ensure that the Federal Judiciary respects 'the proper—and properly limited—role of the courts in a democratic society,' a plaintiff may not invoke federal-court jurisdiction unless he can show 'a personal stake in the outcome of the controversy.' . . . We enforce that requirement by insisting that a plaintiff satisfy the familiar three-part test for Article III standing: that he '(1) suffered an injury in fact, (2) that is fairly traceable to the challenged conduct of the defendant, and (3) that is likely to be redressed by a favorable judicial decision.' Foremost among these requirements is injury in fact . . . .

The plaintiffs argue that their legal injury is not limited to the injury that they have suffered as individual voters, but extends also to the statewide harm to their interest 'in their collective representation in the legislature' . . . . But our cases to date have not found that this presents an individual and personal injury of the kind required for Article III standing. . . .

In cases where a plaintiff fails to demonstrate Article III standing, we usually direct the dismissal of the plaintiff's claims. This is not the usual case. It concerns an unsettled kind of claim this Court has not agreed upon, the contours and justiciability of which are unresolved. Under the circumstances, and in light of the plaintiffs' allegations . . . , we decline to direct dismissal.

We therefore remand the case to the District Court so that the plaintiffs may have an opportunity to prove concrete and particularized injuries using evidence—unlike the bulk of the evidence presented thus far—that would tend to demonstrate a burden on their individual votes. . . . We express no view on the merits of the plaintiffs' case. We caution, however, that 'standing is not dispensed in gross': A plaintiff's remedy must be tailored to redress the plaintiff's particular injury.

The judgment of the District Court is vacated, and the case is remanded . . . ."

V. JUSTICE VOTE

0 Pro ACLU Side vs. 9 Con Opposing Side

Opposing Side (Petitioner / Appellant)

1. Roberts, J. – Wrote majority opinion
2. Alito, S. – Joined majority opinion
3. Kagan, E. – Wrote concurring opinion
4. Thomas, C. – Wrote concurring opinion
5. Breyer, S. – Joined Kagan's concurrence
6. Gorsuch, N. – Joined Thomas' concurrence
7. Kennedy, A. – Joined majority opinion
8. Ginsburg, R. – Joined Kagan's concurrence
9. Sotomayor, S. – Joined Kagan's concurrence

VI. A WIN OR LOSS FOR THE ACLU?

The ACLU filed as amicus curiae urging affirmance; the Supreme Court vacated the District Court's decision by a 9-0 vote, giving the ACLU an apparent loss.

1177. Benisek v. Lamone

(Decided June 18, 2018; 138 S.Ct. 1942; 585 U.S. _)

I. ISSUE

A. Issues Discussed

Voting rights

B. Legal Question Presented

Whether the District Court abused its discretion in denying a preliminary injunction regarding an electoral district map.

C. Supreme Court's Answer

"In these particular circumstances, we conclude that the District Court's decision denying a preliminary injunction cannot be regarded as an abuse of discretion."

II. CASE SUMMARY

A. Background

"This appeal arises from the denial of a motion for a preliminary injunction in the District Court. Appellants are several Republican voters, plaintiffs below, who allege that Maryland's Sixth Congressional District was gerrymandered in 2011 for the purpose of retaliating against them for their political views.

In May 2017, six years after the Maryland General Assembly redrew the Sixth District, plaintiffs moved the District Court to enjoin Maryland's election officials from holding congressional elections under the 2011 map. They asserted that 'extend[ing] this constitutional offense'—i.e., the alleged gerrymander—'into the 2018 election would be a manifest and irreparable injury.' In order to allow time for the creation of a new districting map, plaintiffs urged the District Court to enter a preliminary injunction by August 18, 2017.

On August 24, 2017, the District Court denied plaintiffs' motion and stayed further proceedings pending this Court's disposition of partisan gerrymandering claims in Gill v. Whitford, No. 16-1161. The District Court found that plaintiffs had failed to show a likelihood of success on the merits sufficient to warrant a preliminary injunction. . . ."

The Supreme Court granted certiorari to review the case.

B. Counsel of Record / ACLU Attorney

ACLU Side (Petitioner / Appellant): Michael B. Kimberly argued the cause for appellants. With him on the brief was Paul W. Hughes.

Opposing Side (Respondent / Appellee): Steven M. Sullivan, Solicitor General of Maryland, argued the cause for appellee. With him on the brief were Brian E. Frosh, Attorney General, Adam D. Snyder, Deputy Chief of Litigation, and Sarah W. Rice, Jennifer L. Katz, and Andrea W. Trento, Assistant Attorneys General.

III. AMICI CURIAE

ACLU Side (Petitioner / Appellant)

Brief of amici curiae filed on behalf of the American Civil Liberties Union, the ACLU of Maryland, and the New York Civil Liberties Union by David D. Cole, Arthur N. Eisenberg, Perry M. Grossman, Samuel Issacharof, Theresa J. Lee, T. Alora Thomas, Emily Rong Zhang, Dale E. Ho, Cecillia D. Wang, and Deborah A. Jeon.

Brief of amici curiae filed on behalf of Common Cause by Gregory L. Diskant, Jonah M. Knobler, Peter A. Nelson, Elena Steiger Reich, Emmet J. Bondurant, and Benjamin W. Thorpe.

Brief of amici curiae filed on behalf of Bipartisan Current and Former Members of Congress by Elizabeth B. Wydra, Brianne J. Gorod, and David H. Gans.

Brief of amici curiae filed on behalf of International Municipal Lawyers Association et al. by Charles W. Thompson, Jr., Amanda Kellar Karras, G. Michael Parsons, Jr., and Corey W. Roush.

Brief of amici curiae filed on behalf of Professor Michael Kang by Daniel F. Kolb, Russell M. Anello, Edith Beerdsen, Reagan T. Lynch, and Elizabeth A. Tippett.

Brief of amici curiae filed on behalf of the Campaign Legal Center et al. by Nicholas O. Stephanopoulos, Allison J. Riggs, Jaclyn Maffetore, Paul M. Smith, Ruth M. Greenwood, and Annabelle E. Harless.

Brief of amici curiae filed on behalf of Judicial Watch, Inc., et al. by T. Russell Nobile, Robert D. Popper, and Chris Fedel.

Brief of amici curiae filed on behalf of the Brennan Center for Justice at N.Y.U. School of Law by Wendy R. Weiser, Vincent Levy, Michael C. Li, Gregory Dubinsky, Thomas P. Wolf, and Matthew V.H. Noller.

Brief of amici curiae filed on behalf of the National Association for the Advancement of Colored People, Inc., et al. by Kristen Clarke, Jon Greenbaum, Ezra D. Rosenberg, Julie Houk, John Powers, William V. Custer, Jennifer B. Dempsey, Bradford M. Berry, Janette M. Louard, and Khyla D. Craine.

Brief of amici curiae filed on behalf of Governors Lawrence Joseph Hogan Jr., et al. by Brian A. Sutherland, Benjamin R. Fliegel, James C. Martin, Colin E. Wrabley, Devin M. Misour, and M. Patrick Yingling.

Brief of amici curiae filed on behalf of Stephen M. Shapiro by Alan B. Morrison.

Opposing Side (Respondent / Appellee)

Brief of amici curiae filed on behalf of Senator Joseph B. Scarnati, III by Jason Torchinsky, Phillip M. Gordon, Brian S. Paszamant, and John P. Wixted.

Brief of amici curiae filed on behalf of the State of Wisconsin by Brad D. Schimel, Attorney General of Wisconsin, Misha Tseytlin, Solicitor General, Kevin M. Leroy, Deputy Solicitor General, Amy C. Miller, Assistant Solicitor General, and Brian P. Keenan, Assistant Attorney General.

Brief of amici curiae filed on behalf of the Freedom Partners Chamber of Commerce by Douglas R. Cox, Amir C. Tayrani, David W. Casazza, and Brian M. Lipshutz.

Brief of amici curiae filed on behalf of the State of Michigan et al. by Bill Schuette, Attorney General of Michigan, Aaron D. Lindstrom, Solicitor General, and by the Attorneys General for their respective States as follows: Leslie Rutledge of Arkansas, Cynthia Coffman of Colorado, Christopher M. Carr of Georgia, Curtis T. Hill, Jr., of Indiana, Jeff Landry of Louisiana, Joshua D. Hawley of Missouri, Michael DeWine of Ohio, Mike Hunter of Oklahoma, Alan Wilson of South Carolina, Ken Paxton of Texas, and Sean D. Reyes of Utah.

IV. THE SUPREME COURT'S DECISION

"Plaintiffs ask this Court to vacate the District Court's order and remand for further consideration of whether a preliminary injunction is appropriate.

We now note our jurisdiction and review the District Court's decision for an abuse of discretion, keeping in mind that a preliminary injunction is 'an extraordinary remedy never awarded as of right.' As a matter of equitable discretion, a preliminary injunction does not follow as a matter of course from a plaintiff's showing of a likelihood of success on the merits. Rather, a court must also consider whether the movant has shown 'that he is likely to suffer irreparable harm in the absence of preliminary relief, that the balance of equities tips in his favor, and that an injunction is in the public interest.'

Plaintiffs made no such showing below. Even if we assume . . . that plaintiffs were likely to succeed on the merits of their claims, the balance of equities and the public interest tilted against their request for a preliminary injunction.

First, a party requesting a preliminary injunction must generally show reasonable diligence. . . . In this case, appellants did not move for a preliminary injunction in the District Court until six years, and three general elections, after the 2011 map was adopted . . . .

Second, a due regard for the public interest in orderly elections supported the District Court's discretionary decision to deny a preliminary injunction and to stay the proceedings. . . .

On top of this time constraint was the legal uncertainty surrounding any potential remedy for the plaintiffs' asserted injury. At the time the District Court made its decision, the appeal in Gill was pending before this Court. The District Court recognized that our decision in Gill had the potential to 'shed light on critical questions in this case' . . . . In the District Court's view, 'charging ahead' and adjudicating the plaintiffs' claims in that fluctuating legal environment, when firmer guidance from this Court might have been forthcoming, would have been a mistake. . . . In these particular circumstances, we conclude that the District Court's decision denying a preliminary injunction cannot be regarded as an abuse of discretion.

The order of the District Court is affirmed."

V. JUSTICE VOTE

0 Pro ACLU Side vs. 9 Con Opposing Side

Opposing Side (Respondent / Appellee)

1. Alito, S. – Per curiam decision
2. Kagan, E. – Per curiam decision
3. Thomas, C. – Per curiam decision
4. Breyer, S. – Per curiam decision
5. Gorsuch, N. – Per curiam decision
6. Kennedy, A. – Per curiam decision
7. Ginsburg, R. – Per curiam decision
8. Sotomayor, S. – Per curiam decision
9. Roberts, J. – Per curiam decision

VI. A WIN OR LOSS FOR THE ACLU?

The ACLU filed as amicus curiae urging reversal of the judgment of the District Court; the Supreme Court affirmed in a 9-0 per curiam decision, giving the ACLU an apparent loss.

1178. Carpenter v. United States

(Decided June 22, 2018; 138 S.Ct. 2206; 585 U.S. _)

I. ISSUE

A. Issues Discussed

4th Amendment

B. Legal Question Presented

"[W]hether the Government conducts a search under the Fourth Amendment when it accesses historical cell phone records that provide a comprehensive chronicle of the user's past movements."

C. Supreme Court's Answer

"[W]e hold that an individual maintains a legitimate expectation of privacy in the record of his physical movements as captured through CSLI. The location information obtained from Carpenter's wireless carriers was the product of a search."

II. CASE SUMMARY

A. Background

"[P]olice officers arrested four men suspected of robbing a series of . . . stores in Detroit. One of the men confessed that, over the previous four months, the group . . . had robbed nine different stores . . . . The suspect identified 15 accomplices . . . and gave the FBI some of their cell phone numbers; the FBI then reviewed his call records to identify additional numbers . . . .

Based on that information, the prosecutors applied for court orders under the Stored Communications Act to obtain cell phone records . . . . Federal Magistrate Judges issued two orders directing Carpenter's wireless carriers . . . to disclose 'cell/site sector [information] for [Carpenter's] telephone[ ] . . . during the four-month period when the string of robberies occurred. . . . Altogether the Government obtained 12,898 location points cataloging Carpenter's movements—an average of 101 data points per day. . . .

Prior to trial, Carpenter moved to suppress the cell-site data provided by the wireless carriers. He argued that the Government's seizure of the records violated the Fourth Amendment because they had been obtained without a warrant supported by probable cause. The District Court denied the motion.

At trial, seven of Carpenter's confederates pegged him as

the leader of the operation. In addition, FBI agent Christopher Hess offered expert testimony about the cell-site data. . . . In the Government's view, the location records clinched the case: They confirmed that Carpenter was 'right where the . . . robbery was at the exact time of the robbery.' . . . Carpenter was convicted on all but one of the firearm counts and sentenced to more than 100 years in prison.

The Court of Appeals for the Sixth Circuit affirmed."

The Supreme Court granted certiorari to review the case.

B. Counsel of Record / ACLU Attorney

ACLU Side (Petitioner / Appellant): Nathan Freed Wessler of the American Civil Liberties Union Foundation argued the cause for appellants. With him on the brief were Ben Wizner, Brett Max Kaufman, David D. Cole, and Cecillia D. Wang of the American Civil Liberties Union Foundation, Daniel S. Korobkin, Michael J. Steinberg, and Kary L. Moss of the American Civil Liberties Union Fund of Michigan, Jeffrey L. Fisher, and Harold Gurewitz.

Opposing Side (Respondent / Appellee): Deputy Solicitor General Dreeben argued the cause for the United States. With him on the brief were Solicitor General Francisco, Acting Assistant Attorney General Blanco, Assistant Solicitor General Prelogar, and Jenny C. Ellickson.

III. AMICI CURIAE

ACLU Side (Petitioner / Appellant)

Brief of amici curiae filed on behalf of Data & Society Research Institute et al. by Marcia Hofmann, Andrew D. Selbst, and Kendra Albert.

Brief of amici curiae filed on behalf of the Competitive Enterprise Institute et al. by Ilya Shapiro, Manuel S. Klausner, Jim Harper, Ryan C. Radia, and Curt Levey.

Brief of amici curiae filed on behalf of the Center for Democracy and Technology by Andrew J. Pincus.

Brief of amici curiae filed on behalf of Electronic Privacy Information Center (EPIC) et al. by Marc Rotenberg, Alan Butler, and John Davisso.

Brief of amici curiae filed on behalf of the Rutherford Institute by John W. Whitehead, Douglas R. McKusick, D. Alicia Hickok, and Mark D. Taticchi.

Brief of amici curiae filed on behalf of the Center for Competitive Politics et al. by Allen Dickerson and Zac Morgan.

Brief of amici curiae filed on behalf of Empirical Fourth Amendment Scholars by Sarah O'Rourke Schrup and Jeffrey T. Green.

Brief of amici curiae filed on behalf of Scholars of the History and Original Meaning of the Fourth Amendment by Elizabeth B. Wydra, Brianne J. Gorod, and Brian R. Frazelle.

Brief of amici curiae filed on behalf of the Reporters Committee for Freedom of the Press et al. by Bruce D. Brown, Caitlin Vogus, and Selina MacLaren.

Brief of amici curiae filed on behalf of Restore the Fourth, Inc., by Mahesha P. Subbaraman.

Brief of amici curiae filed on behalf of Institute for Justice et al. by Wesley Hottot and Robert P. Frommer.

Brief of amici curiae filed on behalf of Electronic Frontier Foundation et al. by Andrew Crocker, Jennifer Lynch, and Jamie Williams.

Brief of amici curiae filed on behalf of Scholars of Criminal Procedure and Privacy by Andrew G. Ferguson, Harry Sandick, Kathrina Szymborski, and Jared Buszin.

Brief of amici curiae filed on behalf of United States Justice Foundation et al. by Joseph W. Miller, Robert J. Olson, Herbert W. Titus, William J. Olson, Jeremiah L. Morgan, Michael Boos, and J. Mark Brewer.

Brief of amici curiae filed on behalf of Technology Experts by Brian Willen, Jack Mellyn, Samuel Dippo, Alex Abdo, and Jameel Jaffer.

Opposing Side (Respondent / Appellee)

Brief of amici curiae filed on behalf of Michael Varco by Mr. Varco.

Brief of amici curiae filed on behalf of the State of Alabama et al. by Pamela Jo Bondi, Attorney General of Florida, Amit Agarwal, Solicitor General, Denise M. Harle and Jordan E. Pratt, Deputy Solicitors General, and by the Attorneys General for their respective States as follows: Steve Marshall of Alabama, Mark Brnovich of Arizona, Cynthia H. Coffman of Colorado, Lawrence G. Wasden of Idaho, Curtis T. Hill, Jr., of Indiana, Derek Schmidt of Kansas, Andy Beshear of Kentucky, Brian E. Frosh of Maryland, Bill Schuette of Michigan, Timothy C. Fox of Montana, Doug Peterson of Nebraska, Gordon J. MacDonald of New Hampshire, Hector H. Balderas of New Mexico, Mike Hunter of Oklahoma, Josh Shapiro of Pennsylvania, Alan Wilson of South Carolina, Herbert H. Slatery III of Tennessee, and Peter K. Michael of Wyoming.

Brief of amici curiae filed on behalf of Professor Orin S. Kerr by Mr. Kerr.

Brief of amici curiae filed on behalf of National District Attorneys Association by Nelson O. Bunn, Jr., John M. Castellano, Linda Cantoni, and Karen J. Friedman.

Brief of amici curiae filed on behalf of Technology Companies by Seth P. Waxman, Jonathan G. Cedarbaum, Catherine M.A. Carroll, and Robbie Manhas in support of neither party.

IV. THE SUPREME COURT'S DECISION

"Although no single rubric definitively resolves which expectations of privacy are entitled to protection, the analysis is informed by historical understandings 'of what was deemed an unreasonable search and seizure when [the Fourth Amendment] was adopted.' . . .

The case before us involves the Government's acquisition of wireless carrier cell-site records revealing the location of Carpenter's cell phone whenever it made or received calls. This sort of digital data—personal location information maintained by a third party—does not fit neatly under existing precedents. Instead, requests for cell-site records lie at the intersection of two lines of cases, both of which inform our understanding of the privacy interests at stake.

The first set of cases addresses a person's expectation of privacy in his physical location and movements. . . .

In a second set of decisions, the Court has drawn a line between what a person keeps to himself and what he shares with others. . . .

We decline to extend Smith and Miller to cover these novel circumstances. Given the unique nature of cell phone location records, the fact that the information is held by a third party does not by itself overcome the user's claim to Fourth Amendment protection. Whether the Government employs its own surveillance technology as in Jones or leverages the technology of a wireless carrier, we hold that an individual maintains a legitimate expectation of privacy in the record of his physical movements as captured through CSLI. The location information obtained from Carpenter's wireless carriers was the product of a search. . . .

Having found that the acquisition of Carpenter's CSLI was a search, we also conclude that the Government must generally obtain a warrant supported by probable cause before acquiring such records. . . .

[However, w]hile police must get a warrant when collecting CSLI to assist in the mine-run criminal investigation, the rule we set forth does not limit their ability to respond to an ongoing emergency. . . .

We decline to grant the state unrestricted access to a wireless carrier's database of physical location information. . . . The Government's acquisition of the cell-site records here was a search under that Amendment.

The judgment of the Court of Appeals is reversed, and the case is remanded . . . ."

V. JUSTICE VOTE

5 Pro ACLU Side vs. 4 Con Opposing Side

ACLU Side (Petitioner / Appellant)

1. Roberts, J. – Wrote majority opinion
2. Kagan, E. – Joined majority opinion
3. Breyer, S. – Joined majority opinion
4. Ginsburg, R. – Joined majority opinion
5. Sotomayor, S. – Joined majority opinion

Opposing Side (Respondent / Appellee)

1. Alito, S. – Wrote dissenting opinion, joined Kennedy's dissent
2. Thomas, C. – Wrotre dissenting opinion, joined Kennedy's dissent, joined Alito's dissent
3. Gorsuch, N. – Wrote dissenting opinion
4. Kennedy, A. – Wrote dissenting opinion

VI. A WIN OR LOSS FOR THE ACLU?

The ACLU argued the cause for appellants urging reversal of the judgment of the Court of Appeals; the Supreme Court reversed in a 5-4 vote, giving the ACLU an apparent win.

1179. Trump v. Hawaii

(Decided June 26, 2018; 138 S.Ct. 2392; 585 U.S. _)

I. ISSUE

A. Issues Discussed

Immigration/Citizenship, 1st Amendment, religion

B. Legal Question Presented

"[W]hether the President had authority under the [Immigration and Nationality] Act to issue the Proclamation [restricting entry to the United States by nationals of select countries], and whether the entry policy violates the Establishment Clause of the First Amendment."

C. Supreme Court's Answer

"The Proclamation is squarely within the scope of Presidential authority under the INA. . . .

Under these circumstances, the Government has set forth a sufficient national security justification to survive rational basis review. We express no view on the soundness of the policy. We simply hold today that plaintiffs have not demonstrated a likelihood of success on the merits of their constitutional claim."

II. CASE SUMMARY

A. Background

"[T]he Immigration and Nationality Act . . .vests the President with authority to restrict the entry of aliens whenever he finds that their entry 'would be detrimental to the interests of the United States.' [T]he President concluded that it was necessary to impose entry restrictions on nationals of countries that do not share adequate information for an informed entry determination, or that otherwise present national security risks. The plaintiffs . . . , respondents here, challenged the application of those entry restrictions to certain aliens abroad. . . .

Plaintiffs in this case are the State of Hawaii, three individuals (Dr. Ismail Elshikh, John Doe # 1, and John Doe # 2), and the Muslim Association of Hawaii. The State operates the University of Hawaii system, which recruits students and faculty from the designated countries. The three individual plaintiffs are U.S. citizens or lawful permanent residents who have relatives from Iran, Syria, and Yemen applying for immigrant or nonimmigrant visas. The Association is a nonprofit organization that operates a mosque in Hawaii.

Plaintiffs challenged the Proclamation . . . on several grounds. [T]hey argued that the Proclamation contravenes provisions in the Immigration and Nationality Act (INA). Plaintiffs . . . claimed that the Proclamation violates the Establishment Clause of the First Amendment, because it was motivated not by . . . national security but by animus toward Islam.

The District Court granted a nationwide preliminary injunction barring enforcement of the entry restrictions. . . .

The Court of Appeals affirmed."

The Supreme Court granted certiorari to review the case.

B. Counsel of Record / ACLU Attorney

ACLU Side (Respondent / Appellee)

Neal Kumar Katyal argued the cause for appellee. With him on the briefs were Russell A. Suzuki, Acting Attorney General of Hawaii, Clyde J. Wadsworth, Solicitor General, Deirdre Marie-Iha, Donna H. Kalama, Kimberly T. Guidry, Robert T. Nakatsuji, Kaliko'onalani D. Fernandes, and Kevin M. Richardson, Deputy Attorneys General, Colleen E. Roh Sinzdak, Mitchell P. Reich, Elizabeth Hagerty, Sundeep Iyer, and Reedy C. Swanson.

Opposing Side (Petitioner / Appellant):

Solicitor General Francisco argued the cause for appellant. With him on the briefs were Acting Assistant Attorney General Readler, Deputy Solicitors General Wall and Kneedler, Deputy Assistant Attorney General Mooppan, Assistants to the Solicitor General Bond and Huston, Sharon Swingle, and H. Thomas Byron III.

III. AMICI CURIAE

ACLU Side (Respondent / Appellee)

Brief of amici curiae filed on behalf of Plaintiffs in International Refugee Assistance Project v. Trump by Karen C. Tumlin, Nicholas Espiritu, Melissa S. Keaney, Esther Sung, Marielena Hincapié, Justin B. Cox, Linda Evarts, Kathryn Claire Meyer, Deepa Alagesan, and Mariko Hirose, and Omar C. Jadwat, Lee Gelernt, Hina Shamsi, Hugh Handeyside, Sarah L. Mehta, David Hausman, Cecillia D. Wang, Cody H. Wofsy, Spencer E. Amdur, David Cole, Daniel Mach, and Heather L. Weaver of the American Civil Liberties Union Foundation, and David Rocah, Deborah A. Jeon, Sonia Kumar, and Nicholas Taichi Steiner of the American Civil Liberties Union Foundation of Maryland.

Brief of amici curiae filed on behalf of the Cato Institute by Daniel Braun, Peter Jaffe, Lauren Kaplin, Justin Simeone, David Y. Livshiz, Cameron C. Russell, and Karen Wiswall.

Brief of amici curiae filed on behalf of Khizr Khan by Dan Jackson.

Brief of amici curiae filed on behalf of Immigration Equality et al. by Eric J. Gorman, Matthew E. Sloan, Noelle M. Reed, Richard A. Schwartz, Allison B. Holcombe, Alyssa J. Clover, Sarah Grossnickle, Jennifer H. Berman, Joseph M. Sandman, Brittany Ellenberg, Aaron Morris, Nishan Bhaumik, Virginia M. Goggin, and Glenn D. Magpantay.

Brief of amici curiae filed on behalf of William Webster et al. by Shaimaa M. Hussein, Matthew R. Dollan, John L. Brennan, Ravi Chanderraj, and Richard D. Bernstein.

Brief of amici curiae filed on behalf of the Roderick & Solange MacArthur Justice Center by Amir H. Ali.

Brief of amici curiae filed on behalf of 36 Appellate Lawyers by Charles A. Bird, Richard A. Derevan, Jon B. Eisenberg, Kathryn E. Karcher, Wendy Cole Lascher, Robin Meadow, Susan Alexander, Robert Bacon, Charles Bonneau, Orly Degani, Jay-Allen Eisen, David Ettinger, Dennis Fischer, Paul Fogel, Cliff Gardner, Robert Gerstein, Howard Goodfriend, Joseph Grodin, Mark Harrison, Mark Alan Hart, Laurie Hepler, Steven Hirsch, Charity Kenyon, Todd Lundell, Eric Multhaup, Bradley Pauley, Barbara Ravitz, Kent Richland, Amitai Schwartz, Elisabeth Semel, Charles Sevilla, Catherine Smith, Cindy Tobisman, Michael Traynor, Kathryn Mickle Werdegar, Douglas Young.

Brief of amici curiae filed on behalf of the Association of American Medical Colleges et al. by Frank R. Trinity, Amber R. Sterling, Joshua David Rogaczewski, Jennifer S. Geetter, and Matthew M. Girgenti.

Brief of amici curiae filed on behalf of Former Executive Branch Officials by Matthew L. Bush, Robert M. Loeb, Kelsi Brown Corkran, Thomas M. Bondy, Chris Richart, and Alec Schierenbeck.

Brief of amici curiae filed on behalf of National League of Cities et al. by Lisa E. Soronen and Stuart Banner.

Brief of amici curiae filed on behalf of Civil Rights Organizations by Lynne Bernabei and Alan R. Kabat.

Brief of amici curiae filed on behalf of American Council on Education et al. by Brad D. Brian, Michael R. Doyen, Chad Golder, and Adele M. El-Khouri.

Brief of amici curiae filed on behalf of Labor Organizations by Nicole G. Berner, Deborah L. Smith, Leo Gertner, Barbara J. Chisholm, Kristin M. García, Judith Rivlin, Niraj R. Ganatra, Ava Barbour, Mario Martínez, Nicholas Clark, David J. Strom, Jody Calemine, Alice O'Brien, Emma Leheny, and Lubna A. Alam.

Brief of amici curiae filed on behalf of the National Immigrant Justice Center et al. by Charles Roth, Robert N. Hochman, and Nathaniel C. Love.

Brief of amici curiae filed on behalf of Muslim Justice League et al. by Benjamin G. Shatz, Amy B. Briggs, John W. McGuinness, Sirena P. Castillo, Olufunmilayo O. Showole, Ketakee R. Kane, Matthew D. Bottomly, and Eve L. Torres.

Brief of amici curiae filed on behalf of Mickey Edwards et al. by Tadhg Dooley, Benjamin M. Daniels, and Richard Luedeman.

Brief of amici curiae filed on behalf of Members of Congress by Peter Karanjia, Geoffrey Brounell, Elizabeth B. Wydra, Brianne J. Gorod, David H. Gans, Victor A. Kovner, and Raymond H. Brescia.

Brief of amici curiae filed on behalf of Karen Korematsu et al. by Robert S. Chang, Lorraine K. Bannai, Pratik A. Shah, Martine E. Ciccon, Eric K. Yamamoto, Fred T. Korematsu, Robert L. Rusky, Dale Minami, Donald K. Tamaki, Peter Irons, Leigh-Ann K. Miyasato, Robert A. Johnson, Alice Hsu, Jessica M. Weisel, and Rodney L. Kawakami.

Brief of amici curiae filed on behalf of Immigration, Family, and Constitutional Law Professors by Robert A. Wiygul and Mark A. Aronchick.

Brief of amici curiae filed on behalf of PEN America et al. by Robert D. Balin, Abigail B. Everdell, and Robert Corn-Revere.

Brief of amici curiae filed on behalf of NAACP Legal Defense & Educational Fund, Inc., by Sherrilyn A. Ifill, Ajmel Quereshi, Janai S. Nelson, Christopher Kemmitt, Samuel Spital, and Jin Hee Lee.

Brief of amici curiae filed on behalf of American Jewish Committee by Marc D. Stern, Adam S. Lurie, Vijaya R.

Palaniswamy, Caitlin K. Potratz, John W. Akin, and Stephen A. Cobb.

Brief of amici curiae filed on behalf of Retired Generals and Admirals of the U.S. Armed Forces by Hardy Vieux, Donald Francis Donovan, Carl J. Micarelli, Aasiya F.M. Glover, Alice N. Barrett, and Sarah Lee.

Brief of amici curiae filed on behalf of the Anti-Defamation League et al. by John B. Harris and Caren Decter.

Brief of amici curiae filed on behalf of Pars Equality Center et al. by Kristen Clarke, Jon Greenbaum, Mateya Kelley, Cyrus Mehri, U.W. Clemon, Joanna K. Wasik, Lisa S. Blatt, John A. Freedman, R. Stanton Jones, Samuel M. Witten, Sally L. Pei, Stephen K. Wirth, Lindsey D. Carson, Melissa Raggi, Katelyn A. Horne, and Amanda Claire Hoover.

Brief of amici curiae filed on behalf of Tahirih Justice Center et al. by Anne Elise Herold Li, Scott L. Winkelman, Luke Van Houwelingen, and Avi Rutschman.

Brief of amici curiae filed on behalf of the National Asian Pacific American Bar Association et al. by Tina R. Matsuoka, Navdeep Singh, Meredith S.H. Higashi, Rachana Pathak, Albert Giang, James W. Kim, Cathy Zeman Scheineson, and Llewelyn M. Engel.

Brief of amici curiae filed on behalf of Immigration Law Scholars on the Text and Structure of the Immigration and Nationality Act by Deborah Anker, Sabrineh Ardalan, Philip L. Torrey, and Fatma Marouf.

Brief of amici curiae filed on behalf of the State of New York et al. by Eric T. Schneiderman, Attorney General of New York, Barbara D. Underwood, Solicitor General, Anisha S. Dasgupta, Deputy Solicitor General, Zainab A. Chaudhry, Assistant Solicitor General, and by the Attorneys General for their respective jurisdictions as follows: Xavier Becerra of California, George Jepsen of Connecticut, Matthew P. Denn of Delaware, Karl A. Racine of the District of Columbia, Lisa Madigan of Illinois, Thomas J. Miller of Iowa, Janet T. Mills of Maine, Brian E. Frosh of Maryland, Maura Healey of Massachusetts, Gurbir S. Grewal of New Jersey, Hector Balderas of New Mexico, Ellen F. Rosenblum of Oregon, Patrick F. Kilmartin of Rhode Island, Thomas J. Donovan, Jr., of Vermont, Mark R. Herring of Virginia, and Robert Ferguson of Washington.

Brief of amici curiae filed on behalf of International Law Scholars et al. by Bruce V. Spiva, Elisabeth C. Frost, Amanda R. Callais, and Aaron X. Fellmeth.

Brief of amici curiae filed on behalf of Eblal Zakzok et al. by Robert A. Atkins, Liza Velazquez, Andrew J. Ehrlich, Steven C. Herzog, Meredith A. Arfa, Jeffrey J. Recher, Katherine K. Fell, Faiza Patel, Michael Price, Lena F. Masri, Gadeir Abbas, Carolyn Homer, and Ahmed Mohamed.

Brief of amici curiae filed on behalf of Professors of Federal Courts Jurisprudence et al. by Catherine Y. Kim, Judith Resnik, Burt Neuborne, Lucas Guttentag, Meir Feder, Rasha Gerges Shields, Rajeev Muttreja, and Amanda K. Rice.

Brief of amici curiae filed on behalf of Plaintiffs in International Refugee Assistance Project v. Trump by Karen C. Tumlin, Nicholas Espíritu, Melissa S. Keaney, Esther Sung, Marielena Hincapié, Omar C. Jadwat, Lee Gelernt, Hina Shamsi, Hugh Handeyside, Sarah L. Mehta, and David Hausman.

Brief of amici curiae filed on behalf of E the Japanese American Citizens League by George T. Frampton, Jr., Thomas Frampton, Joseph N. Roth, and Walter Dellinger.

Brief of amici curiae filed on behalf of the Association of Art Museum Directors et al. by Sharon Katz, Avi Gesser, Kelsey Clark, and Jennifer Prevete.

Brief of amici curiae filed on behalf of Plaintiffs in Iranian Alliances Across Borders v. Trump by Johnathan Smith, Sirine Shebaya, Mark H. Lynch, Mark W. Mosier, Karun Tilak, John W. Sorrenti, Jose E. Arvelo, Kathryn Cahoy, Rebecca G. Van Tassell, Richard B. Katskee, Eric Rothschild, Kelly M. Percival, and Andrew L. Nellis.

Brief of amici curiae filed on behalf of Massachusetts Technology Leadership Council, Inc., by Christopher Escobedo Hart, Michael B. Keating, Kristyn M. DeFilipp, and Daniel L. McFadden.

Brief of amici curiae filed on behalf of Evan McMullin et al. by R. Reeves Anderson, John B. Bellinger III, Elliott C. Mogul, and Kaitlin Konkel.

Brief of amici curiae filed on behalf of Colleges and Universities by Thomas J. Perrelli, Lindsay C. Harrison, and Tassity S. Johnson.

Brief of amici curiae filed on behalf of Federal Courts Scholars by Sarah M. Konsky, Matthew S. Hellman, Andrew C. Noll, and Kathryn L. Wynbrandt.

Brief of amici curiae filed on behalf of Janet A. Napolitano and Other Forner Federal Immigration Officials by Michael J. Gottlieb, Joshua Riley, and J. Wells Harrell.

Brief of amici curiae filed on behalf of Freedom from Religion Foundation by Rebecca S. Markert.

Brief of amici curiae filed on behalf of Scholars of Immigration Law by Peter Margulies, Shoba Sivaprasad Wadhia, Alan E. Schoenfeld, Ben Gifford, and Francisco Unger.

Brief of amici curiae filed on behalf of Interfaith Group of Religious and Interreligious Organizations by Purvi G. Patel, Jennifer K. Brown, Amanda Aikman, Joseph R. Palmore, Marc A. Hearron, Sophia M. Brill, and Sandeep N. Nandivada.

Brief of amici curiae filed on behalf of Immigrant Rights Organizations by Alan C. Turner, Harrison (Buzz) Frahn, Reena T. Mittelman, Adrienne V. Baxley, and Tomi Mendel.

Brief of amici curiae filed on behalf of American-Arab Anti-Discrimination Committee by Abed A. Ayoub, Samer E. Khalaf, Yolanda C. Rondon, Anton G. Hajjar, Christopher J. Wright, Adrienne E. Fowler, and E. Austin Bonner.

Brief of amici curiae filed on behalf of Constitutional Law Scholars by Ilya Somin, Michael J. Zydney Mannheimer, Barry R. Levy, H. Thomas Watson, and Kirk C. Jenkins.

Brief of amici curiae filed on behalf of the United States Conference of Catholic Bishops et al. by Anthony R. Picarello, Jr., Jeffrey Hunter Moon, Carlos Ortiz Miranda, Theodore J. Boutrous Jr, Ethan D. Dettmer, and Joshua S. Lipshutz.

Brief of amici curiae filed on behalf of New York University by Terrance J. Nolan, Steven E. Obus, Seth D. Fiur, Tiffany M. Woo, Om V. Alladi, and Lary A. Rappaport.

Brief of amici curiae filed on behalf of National Association of Muslim Lawyers et al. by Adeel A. Mangi, Michael F. Buchanan, Aron Fischer, Lachlan S. Campbell-Verduyn, Michael R. McDonald, A. Robert Quirk, and Jessica Rice.

Brief of amici curiae filed on behalf of City of Chicago et al. by Nick Kahlon, Edward N. Siskel, Chicago City Corporation Counsel, Benna Ruth Solomon, Deputy Corporation Counsel, Andrew W. Worseck, Chief Assistant Corporation Counsel, Sara K. Hornstra, Jonathon D. Byrer, Assistant Corporation Counsel, Ryan P. Poscablo, Brian Neff, Michael N. Feuer, Los Angeles City Attorney, Zachary W. Carter, New York City Corporation Counsel, Marcel S. Pratt, Philadelphia City Acting Solicitor, and John Daniel Reaves.

Brief of amici curiae filed on behalf of Episcopal Bishops by Jake Ewart and Michael R. Scott.

Brief of amici curiae filed on behalf of U.S. Companies by Andrew J. Pincus and Paul W. Hughes.

Brief of amici curiae filed on behalf of American Bar Association by Danielle Spinelli, Kevin M. Lamb, and Hilarie Bass.

Brief of amici curiae filed on behalf of Former National Security Officials by Phillip Spector, Jonathan Freiman, Tahlia Townsend, Harold Hongju Koh, Matthew S. Blumenthal, William J. Murphy, and John J. Connolly.

Brief of amici curiae filed on behalf of Constitutional Law Scholars by Roberta A. Kaplan and Joshua Matz.

Opposing Side (Petitioner / Appellant)

Brief of amici curiae filed on behalf of Great Lakes Justice Center by William Wagner, John S. Kane, and Erin Elizabeth Mersino.

Brief of amici curiae filed on behalf of the Foundation for Moral Law by John Eidsmoe and Matthew J. Clark.

Brief of amici curiae filed on behalf of Liberty, Life, and Law Foundation by Deborah J. Dewart.

Brief of amici curiae filed on behalf of National Security Experts Andrew C. McCarthy et al. by David Yerushalmi and Robert Joseph Muise.

Brief of amici curiae filed on behalf of the State of Texas et al. by Ken Paxton, Attorney General of Texas, Jeffrey C. Mateer, First Assistant Attorney General, Scott A. Keller, Solicitor General, Ari Cuenin, Assistant Solicitor General, Phil Bryant Governor of Mississippi, Brent Davis, Chief Counsel to the Governor of Maine, and by the Attorneys General for their respective States as follows: Steve Marshall of Alabama, Mark Brnovich of Arizona, Leslie Rutledge of Arkansas, Pamela Jo Bondi of Florida, Curtis T. Hill, Jr., of Indiana, Derek Schmidt of Kansas, Jeff Landry of Louisiana, Joshua D. Hawley of Missouri, Michael DeWine of Ohio, Mike Hunter of Oklahoma, Alan Wilson of South Carolina, Marty J. Jackley of South Dakota, and Patrick Morrisey of West Virginia.

Brief of amici curiae filed on behalf of Eagle Forum Education & Legal Defense Fund by Lawrence J. Joseph.

Brief of amici curiae filed on behalf of American Center for Law and Justice by Edward L. White III, Erik M. Zimmerman, Francis J. Manion, Geoffrey R. Surtees, Jay Alan Sekulow, Stuart J. Roth, Colby M. May, Andrew J. Ekonomou, Jordan Sekulow, Craig L. Parshall, Matthew R. Clark, and Benjamin P. Sisney.

Brief of amici curiae filed on behalf of Center for Constitutional Jurisprudence by John C. Eastman and Anthony T. Caso.

Brief of amici curiae filed on behalf of Immigration Reform Law Institute by Christopher J. Hajec, Julie B. Axelrod, Michael M. Hethmon, Elizabeth A. Hohenstein, and Mark S. Venezia.

Brief of amici curiae filed on behalf of Citizens United et al. by Joseph W. Miller, William J. Olson, Herbert W. Titus, Robert J. Olson, and Jeremiah L. Morgan.

Brief of amici curiae filed on behalf of the American Civil Rights Union by Kenneth A. Klukowski.

Brief of amici curiae filed on behalf of Southeastern Legal Foundation by Kimberly S. Hermann, William S. Consovoy, and J. Michael Connolly.

Brief of amici curiae filed on behalf of the Zionist Organization of America (ZOA) by Elizabeth Berney.

Brief of amici curiae filed on behalf of Scholars of Mormon History & Law by Anna-Rose Mathieson and Ben Feuer in support of neither party.

Brief of amici curiae filed on behalf of the Becket Fund for Religious Liberty by Eric C. Rassbach, Mark L. Rienzi, Diana M. Verm, and Joseph C. Davis in support of neither party.

Brief of amici curiae filed on behalf of Alliance Defending Freedom by Kristen K. Waggoner, Jonathan A. Scruggs, David A. Cortman, and Rory T. Gray in support of neither party.

Brief of amici curiae filed on behalf of Christian Legal Society et al. by Kimberlee Wood Colby in support of neither party.

IV. THE SUPREME COURT'S DECISION

"Before addressing the merits of plaintiffs' statutory claims, we consider whether we have authority to do so. . . .

[W]e may assume without deciding that plaintiffs' statutory claims are reviewable, notwithstanding consular nonreviewability or any other statutory nonreviewability issue . . . .

The INA establishes numerous grounds on which an alien abroad may be inadmissible . . . . Congress has also delegated to the President authority to suspend or restrict the entry of aliens in certain circumstances. The principal source of that authority, § 1182(f), enables the President to 'suspend the entry of all aliens or any class of aliens' whenever he 'finds' that their entry 'would be detrimental to the interests of the United States.' . . .

By its plain language, § 1182(f) grants the President broad discretion to suspend the entry of aliens into the United States. The President lawfully exercised that discretion based on his findings . . . that entry of the covered aliens would be detrimental to the national interest. And plaintiffs' attempts to identify a conflict with other provisions in the INA, and their appeal to the statute's purposes and legislative history, fail to overcome the clear statutory language. . . .

The Proclamation is squarely within the scope of Presidential authority under the INA. Indeed, neither dissent even attempts any serious argument to the contrary, despite the fact that plaintiffs' primary contention . . . was that the Proclamation violated the statute. . . .

We now turn to plaintiffs' claim that the Proclamation was issued for the unconstitutional purpose of excluding Muslims. . . .

Under these circumstances, the Government has set forth a sufficient national security justification to survive rational basis review. We express no view on the soundness of the policy. We simply hold today that plaintiffs have not demonstrated a likelihood of success on the merits of their constitutional claim. . . .

Because plaintiffs have not shown that they are likely to succeed on the merits of their claims, we reverse the grant of the preliminary injunction as an abuse of discretion. The case now returns to the lower courts for such further proceedings as may be appropriate. Our disposition of the case makes it unnecessary to consider the propriety of the nationwide scope of the injunction issued by the District Court.

The judgment of the Court of Appeals is reversed, and the case is remanded . . . ."

V. JUSTICE VOTE

4 Pro ACLU Side vs. 5 Con Opposing Side

ACLU Side (Respondent / Appellee)

1. Kagan, E. – Joined Breyer's dissent
2. Breyer, S. – Wrote dissenting opinion
3. Ginsburg, R. – Joined Sotomayor's dissent
4. Sotomayor, S. – Wrote dissenting opinion

Opposing Side (Petitioner / Appellant)

1. Roberts, J. – Wrote majority opinion
2. Alito, S. – Joined majority opinion
3. Thomas, C. – Wrote concurring opinion
4. Gorsuch, N. – Joined majority opinion
5. Kennedy, A. – Wrote concurring opinion

VI. A WIN OR LOSS FOR THE ACLU?

The ACLU filed as amicus curiae urging affirmance; the Supreme Court reversed the Court of Appeals' decision by a 5-4 vote, giving the ACLU an apparent loss.

1180. Janus v. American Federation of State, County, and Municipal Employees, Council 31

(Decided June 27, 2018; 138 S.Ct. 2448; 585 U.S. _)

I. ISSUE

A. Issues Discussed

1st Amendment, press, speech, association

B. Legal Question Presented

Whether the court should "overrule Abood and hold that public-sector agency-fee arrangements are unconstitutional."

C. Supreme Court's Answer

"We conclude that this arrangement violates the free speech rights of nonmembers by compelling them to subsidize private speech on matters of substantial public concern. . . .

Abood is therefore overruled."

II. CASE SUMMARY

A. Background

"Under the Illinois Public Labor Relations Act (IPLRA), employees of the State . . . are permitted to unionize. . . .

Employees who decline to join the union are not assessed full union dues but must instead pay what is generally called an 'agency fee,' which amounts to a percentage of the union dues. . . .

Petitioner Mark Janus is employed by the Illinois Department of Healthcare and Family Services . . . . The employees in his unit are among the 35,000 public employees in Illinois who are represented by respondent American Federation of State, County, and Municipal Employees, Council 31 (Union). Janus refused to join the Union . . . .

[I]t was the Governor who initially challenged the statute authorizing the imposition of agency fees. . . . Janus and two other state employees . . . moved to intervene . . . .

Respondents moved to dismiss the Governor's challenge for lack of standing, contending that the agency fees did not cause him any personal injury. The District Court agreed that the Governor could not maintain the lawsuit, but it held that petitioner and the other individuals who had moved to intervene had standing because the agency fees unquestionably injured them. Accordingly, . . . the court dismissed the Governor as a plaintiff, while simultaneously allowing petitioner and the other employees to file their own complaint. . . .

The amended complaint claims that all 'nonmember fee deductions are coerced political speech' and that 'the First Amendment forbids coercing any money from the nonmembers.' Respondents moved to dismiss the amended complaint . . . . The District Court granted the motion, and the Court of Appeals for the Seventh Circuit affirmed."

The Supreme Court granted certiorari to review the case.

B. Counsel of Record / ACLU Attorney

ACLU Side (Respondent / Appellee): David L. Franklin, Solicitor General of Illinois, argued the cause for appellee state respondents. With him on the briefs were Lisa Madigan, Attorney General, Brett E. Legner, Deputy Solicitor General, and Frank H. Bieszczat, Jane Flanagan, Sarah A. Hunger, Richard S. Huszagh, Lindsay Beyer Payne, and Andrew Tonelli, Assistant Attorneys General.

David C. Frederick argued the cause for appellee AFSCME Council 31. With him on the briefs were John M. West, Judith E. Rivlin, Teague P. Paterson, Derek T. Ho, and Benjamin S. Softness.

Opposing Side (Petitioner / Appellant): William L. Messenger argued the cause for appellant. With him on the briefs were Dan K. Webb, Joseph J. Torres, Lawrence R. Desideri, Jacob H. Huebert, Jeffrey M. Schwab, and Aaron B. Solem.

Solicitor General Francisco argued the cause for the United States as amicus curiae.

III. AMICI CURIAE

ACLU Side (Respondent / Appellee)

Brief of amici curiae filed on behalf of the American Civil Liberties Union by David D. Cole and Amanda W. Shanor.

Brief of amici curiae filed on behalf of the American Federation of Labor and Congress of Industrial Organizations by Lynn K. Rhinehart, Harold C. Becker, James B. Coppess, and Matthew J. Ginsburg.

Brief of amici curiae filed on behalf of Workers Rasheedah Gray et al. by Catherine K. Ruckelshaus and Ceilidh Gao.

Brief of amici curiae filed on behalf of Public Citizen, Inc., by Scott L. Nelson and Allison M. Zieve.

Brief of amici curiae filed on behalf of Governor Tom Wolf et al. by Samuel R. Bagenstos, Denise J. Smyler, General Counsel to the Governor of Pennsylvania, Joshua Civin, Montgomery County Public Schools General Counsel, Matthew Ruyak, Sacramento Interim City Attorney, James R. Williams, Santa Clara County Counsel, Andra M. Donovan, San Diego Unified School District General Counsel, Jeremy Farrell, Jersey City Corporation Counsel, and Zach Klein, Columbus City Attorney.

Brief of amici curiae filed on behalf of Steve Bullock, Governor of Montana by Raphael Graybill, Karl Englund, Deepak Gupta, Matthew W.H. Wessler, and Daniel Townsend.

Brief of amici curiae filed on behalf of Chabot Las-Positas Faculty Association et al. by Robert J. Bezemek.

Brief of amici curiae filed on behalf of Economists et al. by Dan Jackson.

Brief of amici curiae filed on behalf of Senators Sheldon Whitehouse et al. by Peter Karanjia and Eric Feder.

Brief of amici curiae filed on behalf of Republican Current and Former State and Local Officeholders by Elizabeth B. Wydra, Brianne J. Gorod, and David H. Gans.

Brief of amici curiae filed on behalf of the Laborers' International Union of North America by Laurence E. Gold, Theodore T. Green, and Lisa W. Pau.

Brief of amici curiae filed on behalf of Los Angeles County's Department of Health Services by Mary C. Wickham, Los Angeles County Counsel, Nicole G. Berner, Salvatore J. Russo, Daniel Rosenthal, and Walter Kamiat.

Brief of amici curiae filed on behalf of Professor Benjamin I. Sachs by Joseph M. Sellers and Miriam R. Nemeth.

Brief of amici curiae filed on behalf of the National Education Association et al. by Alice O'Brien, Jason Walta, Kristen L. Hollar, Risa L. Lieberwitz, Aaron Nisenson, and Nancy Long.

Brief of amici curiae filed on behalf of United States Conference of Catholic Bishops by Anthony R. Picarello, Jr.

Brief of amici curiae filed on behalf of the International Association of Fire Fighters by Thomas A. Woodley, Douglas L. Steele, Megan K. Mechak, and John W. Stewart.

Brief of amici curiae filed on behalf of American Federation of Teachers by Rhonda Weingarten, David J. Strom, Mark Richard, Kevin K. Russell, and Erica Oleszczuk Evans.

Brief of amici curiae filed on behalf of Fifteen Unions et al. by Pamela S. Karlan, Jeffrey L. Fisher, David T. Goldberg, Gregg Mclean Adam, and Gary M. Messing.

Brief of amici curiae filed on behalf of Crown Building Maintenance Co. & Crown Energy Services, Inc. d/b/a Able Services et al. by Michael P. Abate.

Brief of amici curiae filed on behalf of 24 Past Presidents of the D.C. Bar by John W. Nields, Jr., and Philip J. Levitz.

Brief of amici curiae filed on behalf of National Conference on Public Employee Retirement Systems by Arthur Liou, Mollie Simons, and Robert D. Klausner.

Brief of amici curiae filed on behalf of the National Fraternal Order of Police by Larry H. James and Joel A. D'Alba.

Brief of amici curiae filed on behalf of Mayor Eric Garcetti et al. by Donald B. Verrilli, Jr., and Dahlia Mignouna.

Brief of amici curiae filed on behalf of International Brotherhood of Teamsters by Bradley Raymond, Stephen P. Berzon, Scott A. Kronland, and Andrew Kushner.

Brief of amici curiae filed on behalf of the New York City Municipal Labor Committee by Harry Greenberg, Robin Roach, District Council 37 General Counsel, Alan M. Klinger, Dina Kolker, and David J. Kahne.

Brief of amici curiae filed on behalf of the State of California by Xavier Becerra, Attorney General of California, Edward C. Dumont, Solicitor General, Thomas S. Patterson, Senior Assistant Attorney General, Aimee Feinberg and Samuel P. Siegel, Deputy Solicitors General, and Alexandra Robert Gordon, Deputy Attorney General.

Brief of amici curiae filed on behalf of the American Federation of Government Employees by Justin B. Weiner, Jordan A. Rice, David A. Borer, Andres M. Grajales, Jeffrey A. Lamken, Michael G. Pattillo, Jr., and Eric R. Nitz.

Brief of amici curiae filed on behalf of New York City Sergeants Benevolent Association by Stephen P. Younger and Jonathan D. Schenker.

Brief of amici curiae filed on behalf of the Human Rights Campaign et al. by Laura B. Heiman, Steven E. Fineman, Jason L. Lichtman, Katherine I. McBride, Sharon McGowan, Natalie Nardecchia, Gregory R. Nevins, and Sarah Warbelow.

Brief of amici curiae filed on behalf of Professors Cynthia L. Estlund et al. by Richard J. Brean and Samuel Estreicher.

Brief of amici curiae filed on behalf of Professors Eugene Volokh et al. by Gregory Silbert, Adam B. Banks, and Samuel J. Zeitlin.

Brief of amici curiae filed on behalf of Labor Law & Labor Relations Professors by Matthew T. Bodie, Charlotte Garden, and Fred Korematsu.

Brief of amici curiae filed on behalf of Faith in Public Life et al. by Eric Alan Isaacson.

Brief of amici curiae filed on behalf of Constitutional Law Scholars by Andrew J. Pincus.

Brief of amici curiae filed on behalf of National Women's Law Center et al. by Fatima Goss Graves, Emily J. Martin, Sunu Chandy, Sarah David Heydemann, Vanita Gupta, Seema Nanda, Michael Zubrensky, Matthew S. Hellman, Emily A. Bruemmer, Jonathan A. Langlinais, David A. Strauss, and Sarah M. Konsky.

Brief of amici curiae filed on behalf of the State of New York et al. by Eric T. Schneiderman, Attorney General of New York, Barbara D. Underwood, Solicitor General, Anisha S. Dasgupta, Deputy Solicitor General, Philip V. Tisne, Assistant Solicitor General, and by the Attorneys General for their respective jurisdictions as follows: Jahna Lindemuth of Alaska, George Jepsen of Connecticut, Matthew P. Denn of Delaware,

Karl A. Racine of the District of Columbia, Douglas S. Chin of Hawaii, Thomas J. Miller of Iowa, Andy Beshear of Kentucky, Janet T. Mills of Maine, Brian E. Frosh of Maryland, Maura Healey of Massachusetts, Lori Swanson of Minnesota, Gurbir S. Grewal of New Jersey, Hector H. Balderas of New Mexico, Josh Stein of North Carolina, Ellen F. Rosenblum of Oregon, Josh Shapiro of Pennsylvania, Peter F. Kilmartin of Rhode Island, Thomas J. Donovan, Jr., of Vermont, Mark R. Herring of Virginia, and Robert W. Ferguson of Washington.

Brief of amici curiae filed on behalf of the City of New York by Zachary W. Carter, New York City Corporation Counsel, Richard Dearing, Jason Anton, and Noah Kazis.

Brief of amici curiae filed on behalf of the International Association of Machinists and Aerospace Workers, AFL-CIO by Mark Schneider.

Brief of amici curiae filed on behalf of Child Protective Service Workers and Their Representatives by J. Carl Cecere.

Opposing Side (Petitioner / Appellant)

Brief of amici curiae filed on behalf of the United States by Solicitor General Francisco, Deputy Solicitor General Wall, Assistant Solicitor General Michel, Nicholas C. Geale, Acting Solictor for the Department of Labor, Arthur F. Rosenfeld, Senior Counselor, and Jeffrey Lupardo.

Brief of amici curiae filed on behalf of James Madison Center for Free Speech, Inc., by James Bopp, Jr., and Richard E. Coleson.

Brief of amici curiae filed on behalf of the Cato Institute et al. by Karen R. Harned, Luke Wake, Ilya Shapiro, and Trevor Burrus.

Brief of amici curiae filed on behalf of Pacific Legal Foundation et al. by Deborah J. La Fetra.

Brief of amici curiae filed on behalf of the State of Michigan et al. by Bill Schuette, Attorney General of Michigan, Aaron D. Lindstrom, Solicitor General, Kathryn M. Dalzell, Assistant Solicitor General, and by the Attorneys General for their respective States as follows: Steve Marshall of Alabama, Mark Brnovich of Arizona, Leslie Rutledge of Arkansas, Pamela Jo Bondi of Florida, Christopher M. Carr of Georgia, Lawrence G. Wasden of Idaho, Curtis T. Hill, Jr., of Indiana, Derek Schmidt of Kansas, Jeff Landry of Louisiana, Joshua D. Hawley of Missouri, Douglas J. Peterson of Nebraska, Adam Paul Laxalt of Nevada, Mike Hunter of Oklahoma, Alan Wilson of South Carolina, Herbert H. Slatery III of Tennessee, Ken Paxton of Texas, Sean D. Reyes of Utah, Patrick Morrisey of West Virginia, and Brad Schimel of Wisconsin.

Brief of amici curiae filed on behalf of Center for Constitutional Jurisprudence by John C. Eastman and Anthony T. Caso.

Brief of amici curiae filed on behalf of the Rutherford Institute by John W. Whitehead, Douglas R. McKusick, D. Alicia Hickok, and Mark D. Taticch.

Brief of amici curiae filed on behalf of the Competitive Enterprise Institute by Sam Kazman, Andrew M. Grossman, Mark W. Delaquil, and Randal J. Meyer.

Brief of amici curiae filed on behalf of the American Center for Law and Justice by Jay Alan Sekulow, Stuart J. Roth, Colby M. May, and Walter M. Weber.

Brief of amici curiae filed on behalf of Gregory J. Hartnett et al. by Nathan J. McGrath.

Brief of amici curiae filed on behalf of the Buckeye Institute for Public Policy Solutions et al. by Robert Alt, Kimberly S. Hermann, and John J. Park, Jr.

Brief of amici curiae filed on behalf of Landmark Legal Foundation by Matthew C. Forys, Michael J. O'Neill, and Richard P. Hutchison.

Brief of amici curiae filed on behalf of the Center on National Labor Policy, Inc., et al. by Michael J. Lotito, Brendan J. Fitzgerald, and Michael E. Avakian.

Brief of amici curiae filed on behalf of Mackinac Center for Public Policy by Patrick J. Wright.

Brief of amici curiae filed on behalf of California Public-School Teachers by Terence J. Pell, Michael E. Rosman, Paul B. Green, Michael A. Carvin, Anthony J. Dick, William D. Coglianese, and Vivek Suri.

Brief of amici curiae filed on behalf of Jason R. Barclay et al. by David L. Applegate.

Brief of amici curiae filed on behalf of Rebecca Friedrichs et al. by James G. Abernathy, David M.S. Dewhirst, and Hannah S. Sells.

Brief of amici curiae filed on behalf of Atlantic Legal Foundation by Martin S. Kaufman.

Brief of amici curiae filed on behalf of 1851 Center for Constitutional Law by Maurice A. Thompson and Christopher P. Finney.

Brief of amici curiae filed on behalf of Employees of the State of Minnesota Court System by J. Michael Connolly, Thomas R. McCarthy, and Caroline A. Cook.

Brief of amici curiae filed on behalf of Jane Ladley et al. by Nathan J. McGrath.

Brief of amici curiae filed on behalf of the Becket Fund for Religious Liberty by Eric Baxter, Eric Rassbach, Adèle Auxier Keim, Joseph C. Davis, and Daniel Ortner.

Brief of amici curiae filed on behalf of the James Madison Institute by Joseph W. Jacquot, Andrew E. Underkofler, Joshua M. Hawkes, and Nicholas J. P. Meros.

Brief of amici curiae filed on behalf of the Freedom Foundation by James G. Abernathy.

Brief of amici curiae filed on behalf of Corporate Law Professors by Anna-Rose Mathieson and Ben Feuer in support of neither party.

Brief of amici curiae filed on behalf of Charles Fried et al. by Seth P. Waxman, Christopher E. Babbitt, Blake C. Roberts, Albinas J. Prizgintas, John Byrnes, Robbie Manhas, and Claire H. Chung in support of neither party.

Brief of amici curiae filed on behalf of Certified Public Accountants by Virginia A. Seitz in support of neither party.

IV. THE SUPREME COURT'S DECISION

"In Abood, the Court upheld the constitutionality of an agency-shop arrangement like the one now before us, but in more recent cases we have recognized that this holding is 'something of an anomaly' . . . . We have [previously left] for another day the question whether Abood should be overruled.

We now address that question. We first consider whether Abood's holding is consistent with standard First Amendment principles. . . .

Because the compelled subsidization of private speech seriously impinges on First Amendment rights, it cannot be casually allowed. . . .

Whatever may have been the case . . . when Abood was handed down, it is now undeniable that 'labor peace' can readily be achieved 'through means significantly less restrictive of associational freedoms' than the assessment of agency fees. . . .

In addition . . . , Abood cited 'the risk of 'free riders'' as justification for agency fees. . . .

We . . . hold that agency fees cannot be upheld on free-rider grounds. . . .

In short, the Union has offered no basis for concluding that Abood is supported by the original understanding of the First Amendment. . . .

The principal defense of Abood . . . is based on our decision in Pickering, 391 U.S. 563 . . . .

Pickering is a poor fit indeed. . . .

Even if we were to apply . . . Pickering, Illinois' agency-fee arrangement would not survive. . . .

[W]e conclude that public-sector agency-shop arrangements violate the First Amendment, and Abood erred in concluding otherwise. There remains the question whether stare decisis nonetheless counsels against overruling Abood. It does not. . . .

For these reasons, States and public-sector unions may no longer extract agency fees from nonconsenting employees. . . .

Neither an agency fee nor any other payment to the union may be deducted from a nonmember's wages, nor may any other attempt be made to collect such a payment, unless the employee affirmatively consents to pay. By agreeing to pay, nonmembers are waiving their First Amendment rights . . . .

Abood was wrongly decided and is now overruled. The judgment of the United States Court of Appeals for the Seventh Circuit is reversed, and the case is remanded . . . ."

V. JUSTICE VOTE

4 Pro ACLU Side vs. 5 Con Opposing Side

ACLU Side (Respondent / Appellee)

1. Kagan, E. – Wrote dissenting opinion
2. Breyer, S. – Joined Kagan's dissent
3. Ginsburg, R. – Joined Kagan's dissent
4. Sotomayor, S. – Wrote dissenting opinion, joined Kagan's dissent

Opposing Side (Petitioner / Appellant)

1. Alito, S. – Wrote majority opinion
2. Thomas, C. – Joined majority opinion
3. Gorsuch, N. – Joined majority opinion
4. Kennedy, A. – Joined majority opinion
5. Roberts, J. – Joined majority opinion

VI. A WIN OR LOSS FOR THE ACLU?

The ACLU filed as amicus curiae urging affirmance; the Supreme Court reversed the Court of Appeals' decision by a 5-4 vote, giving the ACLU an apparent loss.

1181. Timbs v. Indiana

(Decided February 20, 2019; 139 S.Ct. 682; 586 U.S. _)

I. ISSUE

A. Issues Discussed

Civil rights, state

B. Legal Question Presented

"Is the Eighth Amendment's Excessive Fines Clause an 'incorporated' protection applicable to the States under the Fourteenth Amendment's Due Process Clause?"

C. Supreme Court's Answer

"This safeguard, we hold, is 'fundamental to our scheme of ordered liberty,' with 'dee[p] root[s] in [our] history and tradition.' The Excessive Fines Clause is therefore incorporated by the Due Process Clause of the Fourteenth Amendment."

II. CASE SUMMARY

A. Background

"Tyson Timbs pleaded guilty in Indiana state court to dealing in a controlled substance and conspiracy to commit theft. The trial court sentenced him to one year of home detention and five years of probation, which included a court-supervised addiction-treatment program. The sentence also required Timbs to pay fees and costs totaling $ 1,203. At the time of Timbs's arrest, the police seized his vehicle, a Land Rover SUV Timbs had purchased for about $ 42,000. Timbs paid for the vehicle with money he received from an insurance policy when his father died.

The State engaged a private law firm to bring a civil suit for forfeiture of Timbs's Land Rover, charging that the vehicle had been used to transport heroin. After Timbs's guilty plea in the criminal case, the trial court held a hearing on the forfeiture demand. Although finding that Timbs's vehicle had been used to facilitate violation of a criminal statute, the court denied the requested forfeiture, observing that Timbs had recently purchased the vehicle for $ 42,000, more than four times the maximum $ 10,000 monetary fine assessable against him for his drug conviction. Forfeiture of the Land Rover, the court determined, would be grossly disproportionate to the gravity of Timbs's offense, hence unconstitutional under the Eighth Amendment's Excessive Fines Clause. The Court of Appeals of Indiana affirmed that determination, but the Indiana Supreme Court reversed. The Indiana Supreme Court did not decide whether the forfeiture would be excessive. Instead, it held that the Excessive Fines Clause constrains only federal action and is inapplicable to state impositions."

The Supreme Court granted certiorari to review the case.

B. Counsel of Record / ACLU Attorney

ACLU Side (Petitioner / Appellant): Wesley P. Hottot argued the cause for appellants. With him on the brief were Samuel B. Gedge, Scott G. Bullock, and Darpana M. Sheth.

Opposing Side (Respondent / Appellee): Thomas M. Fisher, Solicitor General of Indiana, argued the cause for appellee. With him on the brief were Curtis T. Hill, Jr., Attorney General, Kian J. Hudson, Deputy Solicitor General, and Aaron T. Craft and Julia C. Payne, Deputy Attorneys General.

III. AMICI CURIAE

ACLU Side (Petitioner / Appellant)

Brief of amici curiae filed on behalf of the American Civil Liberties Union, the R Street Institute, the Fines and Fees Justice Center, and the Southern Poverty Law Center by Charles Duan, Nila Bala, Lisa Foster, Joanna Weiss, Samuel Brooke, Danielle E. Davis, Nusrat J. Choudhury, Orion Danjuma, Amreeta Mathai, Dennis D. Parker, Mariana Kovel, Ezekiel Edwards, and David Cole.

Brief of amici curiae filed on behalf of the Constitutional Accountability Center by Elizabeth B. Wydra, Brianne J. Gorod, David H. Gans, and Brian R. Frazelle.

Brief of amici curiae filed on behalf of Judicial Watch, Inc., et al. by Chris Fedeli.

Brief of amici curiae filed on behalf of the Institute for Free Speech by Allen Dickerson, Zac Morgan, and Owen Yeates.

Brief of amici curiae filed on behalf of NAACP Legal Defense & Educational Fund, Inc., by Sherrilyn A. Ifill, Janai S. Nelson, Samuel Spital, and Daniel S. Harawa.

Brief of amici curiae filed on behalf of the Rutherford Institute by John W. Whitehead, Douglas R. McKusick, D. Alicia Hickok, Mark D. Taticchi, S. Vance Wittie, and Matthew C. Sapp.

Brief of amici curiae filed on behalf of the American Bar Association by Robert N. Weiner, Andrew T. Tutt, and Robert M. Carlson.

Brief of amici curiae filed on behalf of the DKT Liberty Project et al. by Jessica Ring Amunson, Jonathan A. Langlinais, Clark M. Neily III, Jay R. Schweikert, Shana-Tara O'Toole, Timothy Sandefur, Aditya Dynar, Wylie Stecklow, and Kevin Golembiewski.

Brief of amici curiae filed on behalf of the National Association of Criminal Defense Lawyers by Jeffrey T. Green, Michael B. Buschbacher, and Ray Mangum.

Brief of amici curiae filed on behalf of Pacific Legal Foundation by Lawrence G. Salzman, Anthony L. François, and Christina M. Martin.

Brief of amici curiae filed on behalf of Juvenile Law Center et al. by Marsha L. Levick, Jessica Feierman, Lisa Swaminathan, and Nadia Mozaffar.

Brief of amici curiae filed on behalf of Drug Policy Alliance et al. by Vincent Levy, Daniel M. Sullivan, Lauren Giudice, and Evan H. Stein.

Brief of amici curiae filed on behalf of Foundation for Moral Law by John A. Eidsmoe.

Brief of amici curiae filed on behalf of the American Civil Rights Union by Kenneth A. Klukowski.

Brief of amici curiae filed on behalf of the Chamber of Commerce of the United States of America by Daryl Joseffer, Michael B. Schon, Bert W. Rein, Carol A. Laham, and Andrew G. Woodson.

Brief of amici curiae filed on behalf of Scholars by Eugene Volokh.

Brief of amici curiae filed on behalf of Indiana Criminal Defense Lawyers by James T. Giles, Jed M. Silversmith, and William B. Shields.

Brief of amici curiae filed on behalf of Cause of Action Institute by John J. Vecchione, Julie A. Smith, and Cynthia F. Crawford.

Opposing Side (Respondent / Appellee)

Brief of amici curiae filed on behalf of the National Association of Counties et al. by Lisa Soronen and Lawrence Rosenthal.

Brief of amici curiae filed on behalf of Eighth Amendment Scholars by David Schulmeister and Nicholas M. McLean in support of neither party.

IV. THE SUPREME COURT'S DECISION

"The question presented: Is the Eighth Amendment's Excessive Fines Clause an 'incorporated' protection applicable to the States under the Fourteenth Amendment's Due Process Clause? Like the Eighth Amendment's proscriptions of 'cruel and unusual punishment' and '[e]xcessive bail,' the protection against excessive fines guards against abuses of government's punitive or criminal-law-enforcement authority. This safeguard, we hold, is 'fundamental to our scheme of ordered liberty,' with 'dee[p] root[s] in [our] history and tradition.' The Excessive Fines Clause is therefore incorporated by the Due Process Clause of the Fourteenth Amendment. . . .

In short, the historical and logical case for concluding that the Fourteenth Amendment incorporates the Excessive Fines Clause is overwhelming. Protection against excessive punitive economic sanctions secured by the Clause is, to repeat, both 'fundamental to our scheme of ordered liberty' and 'deeply rooted in this Nation's history and tradition.' . . .

The State of Indiana does not meaningfully challenge the case for incorporating the Excessive Fines Clause as a general matter. Instead, the State argues that the Clause does not apply to its use of civil in rem forfeitures because, the State says, the Clause's specific application to such forfeitures is neither fundamental nor deeply rooted.

In Austin v. United States, 509 U.S. 602 (1993), however, this Court held that civil in rem forfeitures fall within the Clause's protection when they are at least partially punitive. Austin arose in the federal context. But when a Bill of Rights protection is incorporated, the protection applies "identically to both the Federal Government and the States.' McDonald, 561 U.S., at 766. Accordingly, to prevail, Indiana must persuade us either to overrule our decision in Austin or to hold that, in light of Austin, the Excessive Fines Clause is not incorporated because the Clause's application to civil in rem forfeitures is neither fundamental nor deeply rooted. The first argument is not properly before us, and the second misapprehends the nature of our incorporation inquiry. . . .

For the reasons stated, the judgment of the Indiana Supreme Court is vacated, and the case is remanded . . . ."

V. JUSTICE VOTE

9 Pro ACLU Side vs. 0 Con Opposing Side

ACLU Side (Petitioner / Appellant)

1. Ginsburg, R. – Wrote majority opinion
2. Alito, S. – Joined majority opinion
3. Kagan, E. – Joined majority opinion
4. Thomas, C. – Wrote concurring opinion
5. Breyer, S. – Joined majority opinion
6. Gorsuch, N. – Wrote concurring opinion
7. Kavanaugh, B. – Joined majority opinion
8. Sotomayor, S. – Joined majority opinion
9. Roberts, J. – Joined majority opinion

VI. A WIN OR LOSS FOR THE ACLU?

The ACLU filed as amicus curiae urging reversal of the judgment of the Indiana Supreme Court; the U.S. Supreme Court vacated in a 9-0 vote, giving the ACLU an apparent win.

1182. Nielsen v. Preap

(Decided March 19, 2019; 139 S.Ct. 954; 586 U.S. _)

I. ISSUE

A. Issues Discussed

Immigration/Citizenship

B. Legal Question Presented

Whether "criminal aliens who are not arrested immediately upon release are thereby exempt from mandatory detention under § 1226(c)."

C. Supreme Court's Answer

"[N]either the statute's text nor its structure supports" the contention that "criminal aliens who are not arrested immediately upon release are thereby exempt from mandatory detention under § 1226(c)."

II. CASE SUMMARY

A. Background

"Respondents in the two cases before us are aliens who were detained under § 1226(c)(2)'s mandatory-detention requirement—and thus denied a bond hearing—pending a decision on their removal. Though all respondents had been convicted of criminal offenses covered in §§ 1226(c)(1)(A)–(D), none were arrested by immigration officials immediately after their release from criminal custody. Indeed, some were not arrested until several years later.

Respondent Mony Preap . . . is a lawful permanent resident with two drug convictions that qualify him for mandatory detention under § 1226(c). Though he was released from criminal custody in 2006, immigration officials did not detain him until 2013, when he was released from jail after an arrest for another offense. . . .

Although the named plaintiffs in Preap were not taken into custody on immigration grounds until years after their release from criminal custody, the District Court certified a broad class comprising all aliens in California "who . . . were not or will not have been taken into custody by the government immediately upon their release from criminal custody for a [s]ection 1226(c)(1) offense." The District Court granted a preliminary injunction . . . The Court of Appeals for the Ninth Circuit affirmed.

Khoury, the other case now before us, involves habeas petitions and a class-action complaint filed in the Western District of Washington. . . . The District Court granted summary judgment for respondents, and the Ninth Circuit again affirmed, citing its decision on the same day in Preap."

The Supreme Court granted certiorari to review the cases.

B. Counsel of Record / ACLU Attorney

ACLU Side (Respondent / Appellee): Cecillia Wang of the American Civil Liberties Union Foundation argued the cause for appellee. With her on the brief were Matt Adams, Robert Pauw, Devin T. Theriot-Orr, Lucas Guttentag, Anoop Prasad, Jingni (Jenny) Zhao, Daniel Purcell, and Grace Y. Yang, and Michael K.T. Tan, Judy Rabinovitz, Omar C. Jadwat, and David D. Cole of the American Civil Liberties Union Foundation, Emily Chiang of the American Civil Liberties Union Foundation of Washington, and Vasudha Talla of the American Civil Liberties Foundation of Northern California.

Opposing Side (Petitioner / Appellant): Assistant Solicitor General Tripp argued the cause for appellant. With him on the brief were Solicitor General Francisco, Acting Assistant Attorney General Readler, Deputy Solicitor General Kneedler, and Troy D. Liggett.

III. AMICI CURIAE

ACLU Side (Respondent / Appellee)

Brief of amici curiae filed on behalf of National Immigrant Justice Center by Charles G. Roth, Elaine J. Goldenberg, and Celia R. Choy.

Brief of amici curiae filed on behalf of Administrative and Immigration Law Professors by Deanna M. Rice and Anton Metlitsky.

Brief of amici curiae filed on behalf of Constitutional and Immigration Law Professors by Mark C. Fleming and Annaleigh E. Curtis.

Brief of amici curiae filed on behalf of Former INS and DHS General Counsels by Matthew E. Price.

Brief of amici curiae filed on behalf of Members of Congress by Geoffrey H. Yost, Ward A. Penfold, Diana Rogosa, Alexa Graumlich, Eric Ormsby, Marissa Rhoades, Jayashri Srikantiah, and Jennifer L. Stark.

Brief of amici curiae filed on behalf of Advancement Project et al. by Alina Das and Jessica Rofé.

Opposing Side (Petitioner / Appellant)

Brief of amici curiae filed on behalf of U.S. Reps. Andy Biggs et al. by Richard A. Samp and Marc B. Robertson.

Brief of amici curiae filed on behalf of Immigration Reform Law Institute by Christopher J. Hajec and Elizabeth A. Hohenstein.

Brief of amici curiae filed on behalf of the Criminal Justice Legal Foundation by Kent S. Scheidegger and Kymberlee C. Stapleton.

IV. THE SUPREME COURT'S DECISION

"Respondents contend that they are not properly subject to § 1226(c)'s mandatory-detention scheme, but instead are entitled to the bond hearings available to those held under the general arrest and release authority provided in § 1226(a). . . .

But neither the statute's text nor its structure supports this argument. In fact, both cut the other way. . . .

Respondents protest that reading § 1226(c) in the manner set forth here would render key language superfluous, lead to anomalies, and violate the canon of constitutional avoidance. We answer these objections in turn. . . .

According to respondents, the Government's reading of § 1226(c) flouts the interpretive canon against surplusage . . . .

In short, we read the 'when released' directive to apply when there is a release. In other situations, it is simply not relevant. . . .

Finally, respondents perch their reading of § 1226(c)—unsteadily, as it turns out—on the canon of constitutional avoidance. . . .

Here the text of § 1226 cuts clearly against respondents' position, . . . making constitutional avoidance irrelevant.

We emphasize that respondents' arguments here have all been statutory. Even their constitutional concerns are offered as just another pillar in an argument for their preferred reading of the language of § 1226(c)—an idle pillar here because the statute is clear. While respondents might have raised a head-on constitutional challenge to § 1226(c), they did not. Our decision today on the meaning of that statutory provision does not foreclose as-applied challenges—that is, constitutional challenges to applications of the statute as we have now read it. . . .

The judgments of the Court of Appeals for the Ninth Circuit are reversed, and the cases are remanded . . . ."

V. JUSTICE VOTE

5 Pro ACLU Side vs. 4 Con Opposing Side

ACLU Side (Respondent / Appellee)

1. Kagan, E. – Joined Breyer's dissent
2. Breyer, S. – Wrote dissenting opinion
3. Ginsburg, R. – Joined Breyer's dissent
4. Sotomayor, S. – Joined Breyer's dissent

Opposing Side (Petitioner / Appellant)

1. Alito, S. – Wrote majority opinion
2. Thomas, C. – Wrote concurring opinion
3. Gorsuch, N. – Joined Thomas' concurrence
4. Kavanaugh, B. – Wrote concurring opinion
5. Roberts, J. – Joined majority opinion

VI. A WIN OR LOSS FOR THE ACLU?

The ACLU served as counsel for appellees urging affirmance; the Supreme Court reversed the Court of Appeals' decisions by a 5-4 vote, giving the ACLU an apparent loss.

1183. Bucklew v. Precythe

(Decided April 1, 2019; 139 S.Ct. 1112; 587 U.S. _)

I. ISSUE

A. Issues Discussed

Death penalty, 8th Amendment

B. Legal Question Presented

Whether the State of Missouri was entitled to summary judgment on Bucklew's claim that Missouri's lethal injection method is unconstitutional as applied to him.

C. Supreme Court's Answer

"[T]he State was entitled to summary judgment on Mr. Bucklew's Eighth Amendment claim."

II. CASE SUMMARY

A. Background

"Russell Bucklew concedes that the State of Missouri lawfully convicted him of murder and a variety of other crimes. He acknowledges that the U.S. Constitution permits a sentence of execution for his crimes. He accepts, too, that the State's lethal injection protocol is constitutional in most applications. But because of his unusual medical condition, he contends the protocol is unconstitutional as applied to him. Mr. Bucklew raised this claim for the first time less than two weeks before his scheduled execution. He received a stay of execution and five years to pursue the argument, but in the end neither the district court nor the Eighth Circuit found it supported by the law or evidence. Now, Mr. Bucklew asks [the U.S. Supreme Court] to overturn those judgments."

The Supreme Court granted certiorari to review the case.

B. Counsel of Record / ACLU Attorney

ACLU Side (Petitioner / Appellant): Robert N. Hochman argued the cause for appellants. With him on the brief was Cheryl A. Pilate, Raechel J. Bimmerle, Lawrence P. Fogel, Steven J. Horowitz, Kelly J. Huggins, Suzanne B. Notton, Matthew J. Saldaña, and Heather B. Sultanian.

Opposing Side (Respondent / Appellee): D. John Sauer, State Solicitor of Maine, argued the cause for appellee. With him on the brief were Joshua D. Hawley, Attorney General, Joshua M. Divine, Julie Marie Blake, and Peter T. Reed, Deputy Solicitors, and Michael Joseph Spillane, Assistant Attorney General.

III. AMICI CURIAE

ACLU Side (Petitioner / Appellant)

Brief of amici curiae filed on behalf of the American Civil Liberties Union and the ACLU of Missouri by David D. Cole, Amanda W. Shanor, Anthony E. Rothert Gillian Wilcox, Jessie Steffan, Sandra L. Babcock, Cassandra Stubbs, Anna Arceneaux, Olivia Ensign, and Steven M. Watt.

Brief of amici curiae filed on behalf of Pharmacy, Medicine, and Health Policy Experts Jessica L. Ellsworth, Philip Katz, Lynn

W. Mehler, and Lowell M. Zeta.

Brief of amici curiae filed on behalf of Former Corrections Officials by Tejinder Singh and Erica Oleszczuk Evans.

Brief of amici curiae filed on behalf of Scholars and Academics of Constitutional Law by Bruce H. Schneider, David J. Kahne, and Emily L. Kuznick.

Brief of amici curiae filed on behalf of Megan McCracken et al. by Ginger D. Anders, Christopher M. Lynch, and Dahlia Mignouna.

Brief of amici curiae filed on behalf of Former Judges et al. by Jennifer Merrigan and John Mills.

Opposing Side (Respondent / Appellee)

Brief of amici curiae filed on behalf of the State of Texas et al. by Ken Paxton, Attorney General of Texas, Jeffrey C. Mateer, First Assistant Attorney General, Scott A. Keller, Solicitor General, Heather Gebelin Hacker, Assistant Solicitor General, and by the Attorneys General for their respective States as follows: Steve Marshall of Alabama, Mark Brnovich of Arizona, Leslie Rutledge of Arkansas Cynthia H. Coffman of Colorado, Pamela Jo Bondi of Florida, Christopher M. Carr of Georgia, Lawrence G. Wasden of Idaho, Curtis T. Hill, Jr., of Indiana, Derek Schmidt of Kansas, Jeff Landry of Louisiana, Jim Hood of Mississippi, Doug Peterson of Nebraska, Alan Wilson of South Carolina, Herbert H. Slatery III of Tennessee, Sean D. Reyes of Utah, and Peter K. Michael of Wyoming.

Brief of amici curiae filed on behalf of Arizona Voice for Crime Victims, Inc., by Paul G. Cassell, Daniel Nowicki, Allyson N. Ho, and Daniel Chen.

Brief of amici curiae filed on behalf of the Association for Accessible Medicines by Jeffrey K. Francer, Brian T. Burgess, Jaime A. Santos, and Andrew Kim in support of neither party.

Brief of amici curiae filed on behalf of American Medical Association by Leonard A. Nelson and Erin G. Sutton in support of neither party.

IV. THE SUPREME COURT'S DECISION

"We begin with Mr. Bucklew's suggestion that the test for lethal injection protocol challenges announced in Baze and Glossip should govern only facial challenges, not as-applied challenges like his. . . .

Having (re)confirmed that anyone bringing a method of execution claim alleging the infliction of unconstitutionally cruel pain must meet the Baze-Glossip test, we can now turn to the question whether Mr. Bucklew is able to satisfy that test. Has he identified a feasible and readily implemented alternative method of execution the State refused to adopt without a legitimate reason, even though it would significantly reduce a substantial risk of severe pain? Because the case comes to us after the entry of summary judgment, this appeal turns on whether Mr. Bucklew has shown a genuine issue of material fact warranting a trial. . . .

In sum, even if execution by nitrogen hypoxia were a feasible and readily implemented alternative to the State's chosen method, Mr. Bucklew has still failed to present any evidence suggesting that it would significantly reduce his risk of pain. For that reason as well, the State was entitled to summary judgment on Mr. Bucklew's Eighth Amendment claim. . . .

'Both the State and the victims of crime have an important interest in the timely enforcement of a sentence.' Those interests have been frustrated in this case. Mr. Bucklew committed his crimes more than two decades ago. He exhausted his appeal and separate state and federal habeas challenges more than a decade ago. Yet since then he has managed to secure delay through lawsuit after lawsuit. He filed his current challenge just days before his scheduled execution. That suit has now carried on for five years and yielded two appeals to the Eighth Circuit, two 11th-hour stays of execution, and plenary consideration in this Court. And despite all this, his suit in the end amounts to little more than an attack on settled precedent, lacking enough evidence even to survive summary judgment—and on not just one but many essential legal elements set forth in our case law and required by the Constitution's original meaning.

The people of Missouri, the surviving victims of Mr. Bucklew's crimes, and others like them deserve better. . . . If litigation is allowed to proceed, federal courts 'can and should' protect settled state judgments from 'undue interference' by invoking their 'equitable powers' to dismiss or curtail suits that are pursued in a 'dilatory' fashion or based on 'speculative' theories.

The judgment of the court of appeals is affirmed."

V. JUSTICE VOTE

4 Pro ACLU Side vs. 5 Con Opposing Side

ACLU Side (Petitioner / Appellant)

1. Kagan, E. – Joined Breyer's dissent in part
2. Breyer, S. – Wrote dissenting opinion
3. Ginsburg, R. – Joined Breyer's dissent in part
4. Sotomayor, S. – Wrote dissenting opinion, joined Breyer's dissent in part

Opposing Side (Respondent / Appellee)

1. Gorusch, N. – Wrote majority opinion
2. Alito, S. – Joined majority opinion
3. Thomas, C. – Wrote concurring opinion
4. Kavanaugh, B. – Wrote concurring opinion
5. Roberts, J. – Joined majority opinion

VI. A WIN OR LOSS FOR THE ACLU?

The ACLU filed as amicus curiae urging reversal of the judgment of the Court of Appeals; the Supreme Court affirmed in a 5-4 vote, giving the ACLU an apparent loss.

1184. Nieves v. Bartlett

(Decided May 28, 2019; 139 S.Ct. 1715; 587 U.S. _)

I. ISSUE

A. Issues Discussed

1st Amendment, press, speech, association

B. Legal Question Presented

"[W]hether probable cause to make an arrest defeats a claim that the arrest was in retaliation for speech protected by the First

Amendment."

C. Supreme Court's Answer

"[W]e conclude that the no-probable-cause requirement should not apply when a plaintiff presents objective evidence that he was arrested when otherwise similarly situated individuals not engaged in the same sort of protected speech had not been."

II. CASE SUMMARY

A. Background

"Bartlett was arrested during 'Arctic Man,' a weeklong winter sports festival held in the remote Hoodoo Mountains near Paxson, Alaska. . . .

The State ultimately dismissed the criminal charges against Bartlett, and Bartlett then sued the officers under 42 U.S.C. § 1983 . . . . As relevant here, he claimed that the officers violated his First Amendment rights by arresting him in retaliation for his speech. The protected speech, according to Bartlett, was his refusal to speak with [Sergeant] Nieves earlier in the evening and his intervention in [Trooper] Weight's discussion with the underage partygoer. The officers responded that they arrested Bartlett because he interfered with an investigation and initiated a physical confrontation with Weight. The District Court granted summary judgment for the officers. The court determined that the officers had probable cause to arrest Bartlett and held that the existence of probable cause precluded Bartlett's First Amendment retaliatory arrest claim.

The Ninth Circuit disagreed."

The Supreme Court granted certiorari to review the case.

B. Counsel of Record / ACLU Attorney

ACLU Side (Respondent / Appellee): Zane D. Wilson argued the cause for appellee. With him on the brief were Jeffrey L. Fisher, Pamela S. Karlan, Kerri L. Barsh, and Tyler P. Broker.

Opposing Side (Petitioner / Appellant): Dario Borghesan argued the cause for appellant. With him on the brief were Jahna Lindemuth, Attorney General of Alaska, Anna R. Jay, and Stephanie Galbraith Moore.

Principal Deputy Solicitor General Wall argued the cause for the United States as amicus curiae.

III. AMICI CURIAE

ACLU Side (Respondent / Appellee)

Brief of amici curiae filed on behalf of the National Police Accountability Project, Roderick & Solange MacArthur Justice Center, American Civil Liberties Union, and ACLU of Alaska by David D. Cole, Esha Bhandari, and David M. Shapiro.

Brief of amici curiae filed on behalf of Three Individual Activists by Michelle Otero Valdés and Megen Madison Gold.

Brief of amici curiae filed on behalf of the First Amendment Foundation et al. by Ginger D. Anders and Christopher M. Lynch.

Brief of amici curiae filed on behalf of Constitutional Accountability Center by Elizabeth B. Wydra, Brianne J. Gorod, and Brian R. Frazelle.

Brief of amici curiae filed on behalf of Institute for Justice by Paul M. Sherman, Michael B. Kimberly, and Matthew A. Waring.

Brief of amici curiae filed on behalf of Institute for Free Speech by Allen Dickerson, Floyd Abrams, Kathleen E. Farley, and Benjamin A. Taylor.

Brief of amici curiae filed on behalf of National Press Photographers Association by Robert D. Balin, Abigail B. Everdell, Charles S. Sims, and Mickey H. Osterreicher.

Brief of amici curiae filed on behalf of the Rutherford Institute by John W. Whitehead, Douglas R. McKusick, Erin Glenn Busby, and Lisa R. Eskow.

Opposing Side (Petitioner / Appellant)

Brief of amici curiae filed on behalf of the United States by Solicitor General Francisco, Acting Assistant Attorney General Readler, Principal Deputy Solicitor General Wall, Assistant Solicitor General Huston, Barbara L. Herwig, and Lowell V. Sturgill, Jr.

Brief of amici curiae filed on behalf of National Association of Counties et al. by Lisa E. Soronen, Sean R. Gallagher, Bennett L. Cohen, and Britton St. Onge.

Brief of amici curiae filed on behalf of the District of Columbia et. al. by Karl A. Racine, Attorney General for the District of Columbia, Loren L. Alikhan, Solicitor General, Caroline S. Van Zile, Deputy Solicitor General, Carl J. Schifferle, Senior Assistant Attorney General, and by the Attorneys General for their respective States as follows: Cynthia H. Coffman of Colorado, Curtis T. Hill, Jr., of Indiana, Janet T. Mills of Maine, Tim Fox of Montana, Mike Hunter of Oklahoma, Peter F. Kilmartin of Rhode Island, Lawrence G. Wasden of Idaho, Derek Schmidt of Kansas, Jeff Landry of Louisiana, Jim Hood of Mississippi, Hector Balderas of New Mexico, Josh Shapiro of Pennsylvania, Alan Wilson of South Carolina, Sean D. Reyes of Utah, and Peter K. Michael of Wyoming.

IV. THE SUPREME COURT'S DECISION

"We are asked to resolve whether probable cause to make an arrest defeats a claim that the arrest was in retaliation for speech protected by the First Amendment. . . .

'[A]s a general matter the First Amendment prohibits government officials from subjecting an individual to retaliatory actions' for engaging in protected speech. . . .

To prevail on such a claim, a plaintiff must establish a 'causal connection' between the government defendant's 'retaliatory animus' and the plaintiff's 'subsequent injury.' . . . Thus, Hartman requires plaintiffs in retaliatory prosecution cases to show more than the subjective animus of an officer and a subsequent injury; plaintiffs must also prove as a threshold matter that the decision to press charges was objectively unreasonable because it was not supported by probable cause. . . .

Adopting Hartman's no-probable-cause rule in this closely related context addresses . . . familiar concerns. Absent such a showing, a retaliatory arrest claim fails. But if the plaintiff establishes the absence of probable cause, 'then the Mt. Healthy test governs: The plaintiff must show that the retaliation was a substantial or motivating factor behind the [arrest], and, if that showing is made, the defendant can prevail only by showing that the [arrest] would have been initiated without respect to retaliation.' . . .

Although probable cause should generally defeat a retaliatory arrest claim, a narrow qualification is warranted for circumstances where officers have probable cause to make arrests, but typically exercise their discretion not to do so. . . .

For those reasons, we conclude that the no-probable-cause requirement should not apply when a plaintiff presents objective evidence that he was arrested when otherwise similarly situated individuals not engaged in the same sort of protected speech had not been. . . .

In light of the foregoing, Bartlett's retaliation claim cannot survive summary judgment. As an initial matter, the record contains insufficient evidence of retaliation on the part of Trooper Weight. . . .

In any event, Bartlett's claim against both officers cannot succeed because they had probable cause to arrest him. . . .

Because there was probable cause to arrest Bartlett, his retaliatory arrest claim fails as a matter of law. Accordingly, the judgment of the United States Court of Appeals for the Ninth Circuit is reversed, and the case is remanded . . . ."

V. JUSTICE VOTE

1 Pro ACLU Side vs. 8 Con Opposing Side

ACLU Side (Respondent / Appellee)

1. Sotomayor, S. – Wrote dissenting opinion

Opposing Side (Petitioner / Appellant)

1. Roberts, J. – Wrote majority opinion
2. Alito, S. – Joined majority opinion
3. Kagan, E. – Joined majority opinion
4. Thomas, C. – Wrote concurring opinion
5. Breyer, S. – Joined majority opinion
6. Gorsuch, N. – Wrote opinion concurring in part and dissenting in part
7. Kavanaugh, B. – Joined majority opinion
8. Ginsburg, R. – Wrote opinion concurring in part and dissenting in part

VI. A WIN OR LOSS FOR THE ACLU?

The ACLU filed as amicus curiae urging affirmance; the Supreme Court reversed the Court of Appeals' decision by an 8-1 vote, giving the ACLU an apparent loss.

1185. Manhattan Community Access Corp. v. Halleck

(Decided June 17, 2019; 139 S.Ct. 1921; 587 U.S. _)

I. ISSUE

A. Issues Discussed

1st Amendment, press, speech, association

B. Legal Question Presented

"[W]hether MNN—even though it is a private entity—nonetheless is a state actor when it operates [cable] public access channels. In other words, is operation of public access channels on a cable system a traditional, exclusive public function?"

C. Supreme Court's Answer

"Under the state-action doctrine as it has been articulated and applied by our precedents, we conclude that operation of public access channels on a cable system is not a traditional, exclusive public function. Moreover, a private entity such as MNN who opens its property for speech by others is not transformed by that fact alone into a state actor. In operating the public access channels, MNN is a private actor, not a state actor, and MNN therefore is not subject to First Amendment constraints on its editorial discretion."

II. CASE SUMMARY

A. Background

"Time Warner . . . operates a cable system in Manhattan. Under state law, Time Warner must set aside some channels on its cable system for public access. New York City (the City) has designated a private nonprofit corporation named Manhattan Neighborhood Network, commonly referred to as MNN, to operate Time Warner's public access channels in Manhattan. . . .

DeeDee Halleck and Jesus Papoleto Melendez produced public access programming in Manhattan. They made a film about MNN's alleged neglect of the East Harlem community. Halleck submitted the film to MNN for airing on MNN's public access channels, and MNN later televised the film. Afterwards, MNN fielded multiple complaints about the film's content. In response, MNN temporarily suspended Halleck from using the public access channels.

Halleck and Melendez soon became embroiled in another dispute with MNN staff. . . . MNN ultimately suspended Halleck and Melendez from all MNN services and facilities.

Halleck and Melendez then sued MNN . . . . The two producers claimed that MNN violated their First Amendment free-speech rights when MNN restricted their access to the public access channels because of the content of their film.

MNN moved to dismiss the producers' First Amendment claim . . . . The District Court . . . dismissed the producers' First Amendment claim.

The Second Circuit reversed in relevant part."

The Supreme Court granted certiorari to review the case.

B. Counsel of Record / ACLU Attorney

ACLU Side (Respondent / Appellee): Paul W. Hughes argued the cause for appellee. With him on the brief were Robert T. Perry, Eugene Volokh, Eugene R. Fidell, Michael B. Kimberly, Andrew J. Pincus, and Charles A. Rothfeld.

Opposing Side (Petitioner / Appellant): Michael B. de Leeuw argued the cause for appellant. With him on the brief were Tamar S. Wise, Stuart A. Shorenstein, Jesse R. Loffler, and Cozen O'Connor.

III. AMICI CURIAE

ACLU Side (Respondent / Appellee)

Brief of amici curiae filed on behalf of the American Civil Liberties Union, New York Civil Liberties Union, and National Coalition Against Censorship by Arthur N. Eisenberg, Amanda Shanor, David D. Cole, and Vera Eidelman.

Brief of amici curiae filed on behalf of the Alliance for Community Media et al. by Nancy L. Werner, James N. Horwood, Tillman L. Lay, Peter J. Hopkins, Jeffrey M. Bayne, and Amanda C. Drennen.

Brief of amici curiae filed on behalf of the National Police Accountability Project by David M. Shapiro and Daniel M. Greenfield.

Brief of amici curiae filed on behalf of the Knight First Amendment Institute at Columbia University by Katherine Fallow and Jameel Jaffer.

Brief of amici curiae filed on behalf of the New York County Lawyers Association by Elliot Dolby Shields, Ilyssa S. Fuchs, Robert Rickner, and Carolyn A. Kubitschek.

Opposing Side (Petitioner / Appellant)

Brief of amici curiae filed on behalf of the Cato Institute by Ilya Shapiro, David Debold, Trevor Burrus, Vince Eisinger, Grace Hart, and Clifford Hwang.

Brief of amici curiae filed on behalf of Chicago Access Corporation by Jim McVane, Erin E. Murphy, and Michael D. Lieberman.

Brief of amici curiae filed on behalf of Pacific Legal Foundation by Daniel M. Ortner, James M. Manley, Berin Szóka, and Thomas A. Berry.

Brief of amici curiae filed on behalf of Electronic Frontier Foundation by David Greene in support of neither party.

Brief of amici curiae filed on behalf of Internet Association by Chad Golder and Lauren E. Ross in support of neither party.

Brief of amici curiae filed on behalf of NCTA – the Internet & Television Association by Rick C. Chessen, Neal M. Goldberg, Michael S. Schooler, Diane B. Burstein, Howard J. Symons, and Jessica Ring Amunson in support of neither party.

Brief of amici curiae filed on behalf of the Chamber of Commerce of the United States of America by Daryl Joseffer, Jonathan D. Urick, Catherine E. Stetson, Colleen E. Roh Sinzdak, and Benjamin A. Field in support of neither party.

IV. THE SUPREME COURT'S DECISION

"[T]he Free Speech Clause prohibits only governmental abridgment of speech. The Free Speech Clause does not prohibit private abridgment of speech. . . .

Here, the producers claim that MNN, a private entity, restricted their access to MNN's public access channels because of the content of the producers' film. The producers have advanced a First Amendment claim against MNN. The threshold problem with that First Amendment claim is a fundamental one: MNN is a private entity. . . .

[T]he producers assert that MNN is nonetheless a state actor subject to First Amendment constraints on its editorial discretion. Under this Court's cases, a private entity can qualify as a state actor in a few limited circumstances . . . .

The producers' primary argument here falls into the first category: The producers contend that MNN exercises a traditional, exclusive public function when it operates the public access channels on Time Warner's cable system in Manhattan. We disagree. . . .

In short, operating public access channels on a cable system is not a traditional, exclusive public function within the meaning of this Court's cases. . . .

In sum, we conclude that MNN is not subject to First Amendment constraints on how it exercises its editorial discretion with respect to the public access channels. To be sure, MNN is subject to state-law constraints on its editorial discretion (assuming those state laws do not violate a federal statute or the Constitution). If MNN violates those state laws, or violates any applicable contracts, MNN could perhaps face state-law sanctions or liability of some kind. We of course take no position on any potential state-law questions. We simply conclude that MNN, as a private actor, is not subject to First Amendment constraints on how it exercises editorial discretion over the speech and speakers on its public access channels. . . .

MNN is a private entity that operates public access channels on a cable system. Operating public access channels on a cable system is not a traditional, exclusive public function. A private entity such as MNN who opens its property for speech by others is not transformed by that fact alone into a state actor. Under the text of the Constitution and our precedents, MNN is not a state actor subject to the First Amendment. We reverse in relevant part the judgment of the Second Circuit, and we remand . . . ."

V. JUSTICE VOTE

4 Pro ACLU Side vs. 5 Con Opposing Side

ACLU Side (Respondent / Appellee)

1. Kagan, E. – Joined Sotomayor's dissent
2. Breyer, S. – Joined Sotomayor's dissent
3. Ginsburg, R. – Joined Sotomayor's dissent
4. Sotomayor, S. – Wrote dissenting opinion

Opposing Side (Petitioner / Appellant)

1. Kavanaugh, B. – Wrote majority opinion
2. Alito, S. – Joined majority opinion
3. Thomas, C. – Joined majority opinion
4. Gorsuch, N. – Joined majority opinion
5. Roberts, J. – Joined majority opinion

VI. A WIN OR LOSS FOR THE ACLU?

The ACLU filed as amicus curiae urging affirmance; the Supreme Court reversed the Court of Appeals' decision by a 5-4 vote, giving the ACLU an apparent loss.

1186. Gamble v. United States

(Decided June 17, 2019; 139 S.Ct. 1960; 587 U.S. _)

I. ISSUE

A. Issues Discussed

Criminal procedure

B. Legal Question Presented

"[W]hether to overrule a longstanding interpretation of the Double Jeopardy Clause of the Fifth Amendment. That Clause provides that no person may be 'twice put in jeopardy' 'for the same offence.' . . .

We have long held that a crime under one sovereign's laws is not 'the same offence' as a crime under the laws of another sovereign. Under this 'dual-sovereignty' doctrine, a State may prosecute a defendant under state law even if the Federal Government has prosecuted him for the same conduct under a federal statute.

Or the reverse may happen, as it did here."

C. Supreme Court's Answer

"Today we affirm that precedent" in deciding to uphold the prior interpretation of the Double Jeopardy Clause.

II. CASE SUMMARY

A. Background

"In November 2015, a local police officer in Mobile, Alabama, pulled Gamble over for a damaged headlight. Smelling marijuana, the officer searched Gamble's car, where he found a loaded 9-mm handgun. Since Gamble had been convicted of second-degree robbery, his possession of the handgun violated an Alabama law providing that no one convicted of 'a crime of violence' 'shall own a firearm or have one in his or her possession.' . . . After Gamble pleaded guilty to this state offense, federal prosecutors indicted him for the same instance of possession under a federal law—one forbidding those convicted of 'a crime punishable by imprisonment for a term exceeding one year . . . to ship or transport in interstate or foreign commerce, or possess in or affecting commerce, any firearm or ammunition.'

Gamble moved to dismiss on one ground: The federal indictment was for 'the same offence' as the one at issue in his state conviction and thus exposed him to double jeopardy. But because th[e U.S. Supreme] Court has long held that two offenses 'are not the 'same offence'' for double jeopardy purposes if 'prosecuted by different sovereigns,' the District Court denied Gamble's motion to dismiss. Gamble then pleaded guilty to the federal offense while preserving his right to challenge the denial of his motion to dismiss on double jeopardy grounds. But on appeal the Eleventh Circuit affirmed, citing the dual-sovereignty doctrine. [The U.S. Supreme Court] granted certiorari to determine whether to overturn that doctrine."

B. Counsel of Record / ACLU Attorney

ACLU Side (Petitioner / Appellant): Louis A. Chaiten argued the cause for appellants. With him on the brief was Barre C. Dumas, Robert N. Stander, Emmett E. Robinson, and Amanda K. Rice.

Opposing Side (Respondent / Appellee): Assistant Solicitor General Feigin argued the cause for the United States. With him on the brief were Acting Solicitor General Wall, Assistant Attorney General Benczkowski, Assistant Solicitor General Ellickson, and Ross B. Goldman.

Kyle D. Hawkins, Solicitor General of Texas, argued the cause for Texas et al. as amicus curiae.

III. AMICI CURIAE

ACLU Side (Petitioner / Appellant)

Brief of amici curiae filed on behalf of the Constitutional Accountability Center, Cato Institute, American Civil Liberties Union, and American Civil Liberties Union of Alabama by Ilya Shapiro, Elizabeth B. Wydra, Jay R. Schweikert, Brianne J. Gorod, Ashwin P. Phatak, David Cole, Somil Trivedi, Ezekiel R. Edwards, and Randall Marshall.

Brief of amici curiae filed on behalf of Law Professors by Paul G. Cassell and Stuart Banner.

Brief of amici curiae filed on behalf of the U.S. Navy-Marine Corps Appellate Defense Division by Lt Daniel E. Rosinski, JAGC for the U.S. Navy-Marine Corps Appellate Defense, Rebecca S. Snyder, Deputy Director of the U.S. Navy-Marine Corps Appellate Defense Division, Lt Salomee G. Briggs of the U.S. Coast Guard Appellate Defense Division, CDR John C. Reardon, Chief Counsel for the U.S. Coast Guard Defense Services Division, Maj Shane A. McCammon, Deputy Chief of the U.S. Air Force Appellate Defense Division, Col Jane E. Boomer, Chief Counsel of the U.S. Air Force Appellate Defense Division, LTC Christopher D. Carrier, JA for the U.S. Army Defense Appellate Division, and COL Elizabeth G. Marotta, JA Chief Counsel for the U.S. Army Defense Appellate Division.

Brief of amici curiae filed on behalf of Senator Orrin Hatch by Adam G. Unikowsky and Michael E. Stewart.

Brief of amici curiae filed on behalf of the National Association of Criminal Defense Lawyers by David M. Porter, Jonathan L. Marcus, Paul M. Kerlin, Ryan J. Travers, and Sylvia Tsakos.

Brief of amici curiae filed on behalf of Curiae Criminal Procedure Professors et al. by Stephen E. Henderson, George C. Thomas III, Michael J. Z. Mannheimer, Kiel Brennan-Marquez, Barry R. Levy, and Peder K. Batalden.

Brief of amici curiae filed on behalf of Criminal Defense Experts by Paul D. Clement, George W. Hicks, Jr., and Lauren N. Beebe.

Brief of amici curiae filed on behalf of the Rutherford Institute by John W. Whitehead, Douglas R. McKusick, and Elliott Harding.

Opposing Side (Respondent / Appellee)

Brief of amici curiae filed on behalf of the State of Texas et al. by Ken Paxton, Attorney General of Texas, Jeffrey C. Mateer, First Assistant Attorney General, Kyle D. Hawkins, Solicitor General, J. Campbell Barker, Deputy Solicitor General, Eric A. White and Ari Cuenin, Assistant Solicitors General, Kevin T. Kane, Chief State's Attorney of Connecticut, and by the Attorneys General for their respective States as follows:

Steve Marshall of Alabama, Mark Brnovich of Arizona, Leslie Rutledge of Arkansas, Xavier Becerra of California, Cynthia H. Coffman of Colorado, Pamela Jo Bondi of Florida, Christopher M. Carr of Georgia, Lawrence G. Wasden of Idaho, Lisa Madigan of Illinois, Tom Miller of Iowa, Derek Schmidt of Kansas, Jeff Landry of Louisiana, Brian E. Frosh of Maryland, Maura Healey of Massachusetts, Bill Schuette of Michigan, Tim Fox of Montana, Doug Peterson of Nebraska, Gurbir S. Grewal of New Jersey, Hector H. Balderas of New Mexico, Barbara D. Underwood of New York, Joshua H. Stein of North Carolina, Michael DeWine of Ohio, Mike Hunter of Oklahoma, Ellen F. Rosenblum of Oregon, Josh Shapiro of Pennsylvania, Peter Kilmartin of Rhode Island, Alan Wilson of South Carolina, Marty J. Jackley of South Dakota, Sean Reyes of Utah, Thomas J. Donovan, Jr., of Vermont, Mark R. Herring of Virginia, Robert W. Ferguson of Washington, Patrick Morrisey of West Virginia, and Brad Schimel of Wisconsin.

Brief of amici curiae filed on behalf of National Indigenous Women's Resource Center by Sarah Deer, Mary Kathryn Nagle, Wilson K. Pipestem, Abi Fain, and Jordan Harmon.

Brief of amici curiae filed on behalf of National Association of Counties et al. by Lisa Soronen, Gordon D. Todd, Joshua J. Fougere, Spencer D. Driscoll, and Audry M. Klossner.

Brief of amici curiae filed on behalf of Howard University School of Law Thurgood Marshall Civil Rights Center by Justin Hansford and Adam Harris Kurland in support of neither party.

IV. THE SUPREME COURT'S DECISION

"Gamble contends that the Double Jeopardy Clause must forbid successive prosecutions by different sovereigns because that is what the founding-era common law did. But before turning to that historical claim, . . . we review the Clause's text and some of the cases Gamble asks us to overturn. . . .

We see no reason to abandon the sovereign-specific reading of the phrase 'same offence,' from which the dual-sovereignty rule immediately follows. . . .

Our cases reflect the same reading. A close look at them reveals how fidelity to the Double Jeopardy Clause's text does more than honor the formal difference between two distinct criminal codes. It honors the substantive differences between the interests that two sovereigns can have in punishing the same act. . . .

All told, this evidence does not establish that those who ratified the Fifth Amendment took it to bar successive prosecutions under different sovereigns' laws . . . .

Gamble's core claim is that early English cases reflect an established common-law rule barring domestic prosecution following a prosecution for the same act under a different sovereign's laws. But from the very dawn of the common law in medieval England until the adoption of the Fifth Amendment in 1791, there is not one reported decision barring a prosecution based on a prior trial under foreign law. We repeat: Gamble has not cited and we have not found a single pre-Fifth Amendment case in which a foreign acquittal or conviction barred a second trial in a British or American court. Given this void, Gamble faces a considerable challenge in convincing us that the Fifth Amendment was originally understood to establish such a bar. . . .

Surveying the pre-Fifth Amendment cases in 1959, we concluded that their probative value was 'dubious' due to 'confused and inadequate reporting.' Our assessment was accurate then, and the passing years have not made those early cases any clearer or more valuable. . . .

Not to worry, Gamble responds: Whatever the English courts actually did prior to adoption of the Fifth Amendment, by that time the early English cases were widely thought to support his view. This is a curious argument indeed. It would have us hold that the Fifth Amendment codified a common-law right that existed in legend, not case law. In any event, the evidence that this right was thought to be settled is very thin. . . .

Besides appealing to the remote past, Gamble contends that recent changes—one doctrinal, one practical—blunt the force of stare decisis here. They do not. . . .

The judgment of the Court of Appeals for the Eleventh Circuit is affirmed."

V. JUSTICE VOTE

2 Pro ACLU Side vs. 7 Con Opposing Side

ACLU Side (Petitioner / Appellant)

1. Gorsuch, N. – Wrote dissenting opinion
2. Ginsburg, R. – Wrote disenting opinion

Opposing Side (Respondent / Appellee)

1. Alito, S. – Wrote majority opinion
2. Kagan, E. – Joined majority opinion
3. Thomas, C. – Joined majority opinion
4. Breyer, S. – Joined majority opinion
5. Kavanaugh, B. – Joined majority opinion
6. Sotomayor, S. – Joined majority opinion
7. Roberts, J. – Joined majority opinion

VI. A WIN OR LOSS FOR THE ACLU?

The ACLU filed as amicus curiae urging reversal of the judgment of the Court of Appeals; the Supreme Court affirmed in a 7-2 vote, giving the ACLU an apparent loss.

1187. American Legion v. American Humanist Ass'n

(Decided June 20, 2019; 139 S.Ct. 2067; 588 U.S. _)

I. ISSUE

A. Issues Discussed

1st Amendment, religion

B. Legal Question Presented

Whether the Bladensburg Cross on public land violates the Establishment Clause of the First Amendment.

C. Supreme Court's Answer

"[W]e conclude that the Bladensburg Cross does not violate the Establishment Clause."

II. CASE SUMMARY

A. Background

"Since 1925, the Bladensburg Peace Cross (Cross) has stood as a tribute to 49 area soldiers who gave their lives in the First World War. Eighty-nine years after the dedication of the Cross, respondents filed this lawsuit, claiming that they are offended by the sight of the memorial on public land and that its presence there and the expenditure of public funds to maintain it violate the Establishment Clause of the First Amendment. To remedy this violation, they asked a federal court to order the relocation or demolition of the Cross or at least the removal of its arms. The Court of Appeals for the Fourth Circuit agreed that the memorial is unconstitutional and remanded for a determination of the proper remedy."

The Supreme Court granted certiorari to review the case.

B. Counsel of Record / ACLU Attorney

ACLU Side (Respondent / Appellee): Monica L. Miller argued the cause and filed the brief for appellee.

Opposing Side (Petitioner / Appellant): Michael A. Carvin argued the cause for appellant in No. 17-1717. With him on the brief were Kelly J. Shackelford, Hiram S. Sasser III, Kenneth A. Klukowski, Roger L. Byron, Christopher DiPompeo, Kaytlin L. Roholt, Daniel D. Benson, and Chris Pagliarella.

Neal Kumar Katyal argued the cause for appellant in No. 18-18. With him on the brief were Adrian R. Gardner, William C. Dickerson, Tracey A. Harvin, Mitchell P. Reich, and Benjamin A. Field.

Acting Solicitor General Wall argued the cause for the United States as amicus curiae.

III. AMICI CURIAE

ACLU Side (Respondent / Appellee)

Brief of amici curiae filed on behalf of Religious and Civil-Rights Organizations, including the American Civil Liberties Union and the American Civil Liberties Union of Maryland, by Steven M. Freeman, David L. Barkey, Amy Feinman, Samir Kalra, Suhag A. Shukla, Richard B. Katskee, Patrick Grubel, Daniel Mach, Heather L. Weaver, Elliot M. Mincberg, Diane Laviolette, Deborah A. Jeon, and Jeffrey I. Pasek.

Brief of amici curiae filed on behalf of Law Professors by Christopher C. Lund.

Brief of amici curiae filed on behalf of the Jewish War Veterans of the United States of America, Inc., by David A. Strauss, Sarah M. Konsky, Matthew S. Hellman, Caroline C. Cease, Zachary S. Blau, and Harvey Weiner.

Brief of amici curiae filed on behalf of Muslim Advocates by Johnathan J. Smith, Sirine Shebaya, Nimra H. Azmi, R. Stanton Jones, Stuart W. Turner, Matthew H. Horton, and Andrew T. Tutt.

Brief of amici curiae filed on behalf of Historians et al. by Steven K. Green, Charles A. Rothfeld, Andrew J. Pincus, Paul W. Hughes, and Michael B. Kimberly.

Brief of amici curiae filed on behalf of the Military Religious Freedom Foundation et al. by Sarah M. Shalf.

Brief of amici curiae filed on behalf of Freedom from Religion Foundation et al. by Gregory M. Lipper, Robert M. Loeb, Howard M. Ullman, Rochelle F. Swartz, Chad J. Smith, and Kristopher L. Peerali.

Brief of amici curiae filed on behalf of Baptist Joint Committee for Religious Liberty et al. by K. Hollyn Hollman, Douglas Laycock, and Jennifer L. Hawks.

Brief of amici curiae filed on behalf of Professors Walter Dellinger et al. by Martin S. Lederman in support of neither party.

Opposing Side (Petitioner / Appellant)

Brief of amici curiae filed on behalf of the United States by Acting Solicitor General Wall, Assistant Attorney General Clark, Deputy Solicitor General Kneedler, Assistant Solicitor General Liu, Andrew C. Mergen, Lowell V. Sturgill, Jr., and Joan M. Pepin.

Brief of amici curiae filed on behalf of American Association of Christian Schools et al. by William Wagner, Erin Elizabeth Mersino, Katherine L. Henry, and John S. Kane.

Brief of amici curiae filed on behalf of the Town of Taos, New Mexico by David C. McDonald, R. Timothy McCrum, and Elizabeth B. Dawson.

Brief of amici curiae filed on behalf of Thomas More Law Center by Erin J. Kuenzig and Richard Thompson.

Brief of amici curiae filed on behalf of Justice and Freedom Fund by James L. Hirsen and Deborah J. Dewart.

Brief of amici curiae filed on behalf of the Wisconsin Institute for Law & Liberty by Richard M. Esenberg and Anthony F. LoCoco.

Brief of amici curiae filed on behalf of the Foundation for Moral Law by John Eidsmoe.

Brief of amici curiae filed on behalf of the State of Maryland by Brian E. Frosh, Attorney General of Maryland and John R. Grimm, Assistant Attorney General.

Brief of amici curiae filed on behalf of Retired Generals et al. by Edwin Meese III, 75Th U.S. Attorney General, Aaron M. Streett, Jonathan P. Havens, and Cornelius M. Sweers.

Brief of amici curiae filed on behalf of the Utah Highway Patrol Association by Frank D. Mylar, Jessica L. Wagner, John S. Ehrett, Allyson N. Ho, Bradley G. Hubbard, Elizabeth A. Kiernan, and Katherine C. Yarger.

Brief of amici curiae filed on behalf of Citizens United et al. by Michael Boos, Matthew D. McGill, Andrew G. I. Kilberg, and Travis S. Andrews.

Brief of amici curiae filed on behalf of Medal of Honor Recipients by Brian H. Pandya, Megan L. Brown, A. Louisa Brooks, Wesley E. Weeks, Bethany A. Corbin, Krystal B. Swendsboe, Tatiana Sainati, and Jeremy J. Broggi.

Brief of amici curiae filed on behalf of Public Advocate of the United States et al. by Joseph W. Miller, Herbert W. Titus, William J. Olson, Jeremiah L. Morgan, James N. Clymer, and J. Mark Brewer.

Brief of amici curiae filed on behalf of National Association of Counties et al. by Lisa Soronen, Paul J. Zidlicky, Michael B. Buschbacher, Christopher S. Ross, Linda C. Emery, Mark Muedeking, Charles W. Thompson, Jr., and Mike Belarmino.

Brief of amici curiae filed on behalf of the Center for Constitutional Jurisprudence by John C. Eastman and Anthony T. Caso.

Brief of amici curiae filed on behalf of Family Research Council by Travis Weber, Alexandra McPhee, and Benjamin Eastburn.

Brief of amici curiae filed on behalf of the National Jewish Commission on Law and Public Affairs ("COLPA") et al. by Dennis Rapps, Nathan Lewin, and Alyza D. Lewin.

Brief of amici curiae filed on behalf of Family Members of Soldiers Named on the Peace Cross by Zachary G. Parks, Carol A. Szurkowski, Elizabeth N. Ertle, and Justin W. Burnam.

Brief of amici curiae filed on behalf of Judicial Watch, Inc., by James F. Peterson and Meredith L. Di Liberto

Brief of amici curiae filed on behalf of Major General Patrick Brady et al. by Kristen K. Waggoner, John J. Bursch, David A. Cortman, H. Woodruff Turner, Jenna M. Lorence, and Wesley A. Prichard.

Brief of amici curiae filed on behalf of Veterans of Foreign Wars of the United States et al. by Paul D. Clement and Erin E. Murphy. Brief of amici curiae filed on behalf of American Center for Law & Justice et al. by Francis J. Manion, Geoffrey R. Surtees, Edward L. White III, Erik M. Zimmerman, Jay Alan Sekulow, Stuart J. Roth, Walter M. Weber, and Jordan Sekulow.

Brief of amici curiae filed on behalf of Liberty Counsel by Mathew D. Staver, Anita L. Staver, Horatio G. Mihet, and Mary E. McAlister.

Brief of amici curiae filed on behalf of the Rutherford Institute by John W. Whitehead, Michael J. Lockerby, and Douglas R. McKusick.

Brief of amici curiae filed on behalf of the Cato Institute by Ilya Shapiro, Trevor Burrus, and Michael B. Finch.

Brief of amici curiae filed on behalf of West Virginia et al. by Patrick Morrisey, Attorney General of West Virginia, Lindsay S. See, Solicitor General, Zachary A. Viglianco, Assistant Attorney General, and by the Attorneys General for their respective States as follows: Steve Marshall of Alabama, Kevin G. Clarkson of Alaska, Mark Brnovich of Arizona, Leslie Rutledge of Arkansas, Cynthia H. Coffman of Colorado, Pamela J. Bondi of Florida, Christopher M. Carr of Georgia, Lawrence G. Wasden of Idaho, Curtis T. Hill, Jr., of Indiana, Derek Schmidt of Kansas, Andy Beshear of Kentucky, Jeff Martin Landry of Louisiana, Bill Schuette of Michigan, Jim Hood of Mississippi, Josh Hawley of Missouri, Tim Fox of Montana, Doug Peterson of Nebraska, Wayne Stenehjem of North Dakota, Michael DeWine of Ohio, Mike Hunter of Oklahoma, Peter F. Kilmartin of Rhode Island, Alan Wilson of South Carolina, Marty Jackley of South Dakota, Herbert H. Slatery III of Tennessee, Ken Paxton of Texas, Sean Reyes of Utah, Mark R. Herring of Virginia, Brad Schimel of Wisconsin, and Peter K. Michael of Wyoming.

Brief of amici curiae filed on behalf of the Becket Fund for Religious Liberty by Luke W. Goodrich, Eric C. Rassbach, Joseph C. Davis, Nicholas R. Reaves, and Michael W. Mcconnell.

Brief of amici curiae filed on behalf of Lieutenant Colonel Kamal S. Kalsi, D.O., by Tejinder Singh.

Brief of amici curiae filed on behalf of Jewish Coalition for Religious Liberty by Howard Slugh, Daniel P. Kearney, Jr., Kevin Gallagher, Christopher Danello, Andrew Miller, and Paul Vanderslice.

Brief of amici curiae filed on behalf of the American Civil Rights Union by John J. Park, Jr.

Brief of amici curiae filed on behalf of Various Professors by Stephen C. Piepgrass, James K. Trefil, Ryan J. Strasser, and Christopher W. Carlson.

Brief of amici curiae filed on behalf of 84 United States Senators and Members of the United States House of Representatives by Charles J. Cooper, David H. Thompson, and Haley N. Proctor.

Brief of amici curiae filed on behalf of Veterans in Defense of Liberty et al. by Steven W. Fitschen, Frederick W. Claybrook, Jr., James A. Davids, and David A. Bruce.

Brief of amici curiae filed on behalf of the Islam & Religious Freedom Action Team of the Religious Freedom Institute by Miles E. Coleman.

Brief of amici curiae filed on behalf of CatholicVote.org Education Fund by Scott W. Gaylord.

Brief of amici curiae filed on behalf of Maryland Elected Officials et al. by Thomas R. McCarthy and Jeffrey M. Harris.

Brief of amici curiae filed on behalf of the Military Order of the Purple Heart by William R. Suhre, Matthew J. Dowd, and Robert J. Scheffel.

Brief of amici curiae filed on behalf of Religious Denominations et al. by Alexander Dushku, Gene C. Schaerr, R. Shawn Gunnarson, Erik S. Jaffe, Michael T. Worley, and James A. Heilpern.

IV. THE SUPREME COURT'S DECISION

"The Establishment Clause of the First Amendment provides that 'Congress shall make no law respecting an establishment of religion.' While the concept of a formally established church is straightforward, pinning down the meaning of a 'law respecting an establishment of religion' has proved to be a vexing problem. . . . Lemon ambitiously attempted to distill from the Court's existing case law a test that would bring order and predictability to Establishment Clause decisionmaking. . . .

For at least four reasons, the Lemon test presents particularly daunting problems in cases, including the one now before us, that involve the use, for ceremonial, celebratory, or commemorative purposes, of words or symbols with religious associations. Together, these considerations counsel against efforts to evaluate such cases under Lemon and toward application of a presumption of constitutionality for longstanding monuments, symbols, and practices. . . .

While the Lemon Court ambitiously attempted to find a grand unified theory of the Establishment Clause, in later cases, we have taken a more modest approach that focuses on the particular issue at hand and looks to history for guidance. . . .

Applying these principles, we conclude that the Bladensburg

Cross does not violate the Establishment Clause. . . .

The cross is undoubtedly a Christian symbol, but that fact should not blind us to everything else that the Bladensburg Cross has come to represent. For some, that monument is a symbolic resting place for ancestors who never returned home. For others, it is a place for the community to gather and honor all veterans and their sacrifices for our Nation. For others still, it is a historical landmark. For many of these people, destroying or defacing the Cross that has stood undisturbed for nearly a century would not be neutral and would not further the ideals of respect and tolerance embodied in the First Amendment. For all these reasons, the Cross does not offend the Constitution. . . .

We reverse the judgment of the Court of Appeals for the Fourth Circuit and remand . . . ."

V. JUSTICE VOTE

2 Pro ACLU Side vs. 7 Con Opposing Side

ACLU Side (Respondent / Appellee)

1. Ginsburg, R. – Wrote dissenting opinion
2. Sotomayor, S. – Joined Ginsburg's dissent

Opposing Side (Petitioner / Appellant)

1. Alito, S. – Wrote majority opinion
2. Kagan, E. – Wrote concurring opinion, joined Breyer's concurrence
3. Thomas, C. – Wrote concurring opinion, joined Gorsuch's concurrence
4. Breyer, S. – Wrote concurring opinion
5. Gorsuch, N. – Wrote concurring opinion
6. Kavanaugh, B. – Wrote concurring opinion
7. Roberts, J. – Joined majority opinion

VI. A WIN OR LOSS FOR THE ACLU?

The ACLU filed as amicus curiae urging affirmance; the Supreme Court reversed the Court of Appeals' decision by a 7-2 vote, giving the ACLU an apparent loss.

1188. Gundy v. United States

(Decided June 20, 2019; 139 S.Ct. 2116; 588 U.S. _)

I. ISSUE

A. Issues Discussed

Governmental authority

B. Legal Question Presented

"The nondelegation doctrine bars Congress from transferring its legislative power to another branch of Government. This case requires us to decide whether 34 U.S.C. § 20913(d), enacted as part of the Sex Offender Registration and Notification Act (SORNA), violates that doctrine."

C. Supreme Court's Answer

"We hold it does not. Under § 20913(d), the Attorney General must apply SORNA's registration requirements as soon as feasible to offenders convicted before the statute's enactment. That delegation easily passes constitutional muster."

II. CASE SUMMARY

A. Background

"Congress has sought . . . to combat sex crimes and crimes against children through sex-offender registration schemes. In 1994, Congress first conditioned certain federal funds on States' adoption of registration laws . . . . Two years later, Congress strengthened those standards . . . . By that time, every State and the District of Columbia had enacted a sex-offender registration law. . . .

SORNA makes 'more uniform and effective' the prior 'patchwork' of sex-offender registration systems. . . . To that end, SORNA covers more sex offenders, and imposes more onerous registration requirements . . . . The Act also backs up those requirements with new criminal penalties. . . .

Section 20913 . . . elaborates the '[i]nitial registration' requirements for sex offenders. . . . .

Subsection (d) . . . focuses on . . . pre-Act offenders. Many of these individuals were unregistered at the time of SORNA's enactment, either because pre-existing law did not cover them or because they had successfully evaded that law . . . .

The final rule, . . . reiterated that SORNA applies to all pre-Act offenders. . . .

Petitioner Herman Gundy is a pre-Act offender. . . . After his release from prison in 2012, Gundy came to live in New York. But he never registered there as a sex offender. A few years later, he was convicted for failing to register . . . . He argued . . . that Congress unconstitutionally delegated legislative power when it authorized the Attorney General to 'specify the applicability' of SORNA's registration requirements to pre-Act offenders. The District Court and Court of Appeals for the Second Circuit rejected that claim . . . ."

The Supreme Court granted certiorari to review the case.

B. Counsel of Record / ACLU Attorney

ACLU Side (Petitioner / Appellant): Sarah Baumgartel argued the cause for appellants. With her on the brief were Jeffrey L. Fisher, David T. Goldberg, Pamela S. Karlan, Yuanchung Lee, Barry D. Leiwant, and Edward S. Zas.

Opposing Side (Respondent / Appellee): Principal Deputy Solicitor General Wall argued the cause for the United States. With him on the brief were Solicitor General Francisco, Assistant Attorney General Benczkowski, Assistant Solicitor General Bond, and Sonja M. Ralston.

III. AMICI CURIAE

ACLU Side (Petitioner / Appellant)

Brief of amici curiae filed on behalf of the American Civil Liberties Union by David D. Cole, Amanda W. Shanor, Jeffery P. Robinson, and Ezekiel R. Edwards.

Brief of amici curiae filed on behalf of the Cato Institute et al. by Ilya Shapiro, Trevor Burrus, and Reilly Stephens.

Brief of amici curiae filed on behalf of the National Association of Federal Defenders by Sarah S. Gannett, Daniel L. Kaplan,

Donna F. Coltharp, and John P. Rhodes.
Brief of amici curiae filed on behalf of the Competitive Enterprise Institute et al. by Sam Kazman and Devin Watkins.
Brief of amici curiae filed on behalf of Pacific Legal Foundation by Thomas A. Berry, Anthony L. François, Timothy R. Snowball, Todd Gaziano, and Mark Miller.
Brief of amici curiae filed on behalf of the National Association of Criminal Defense Lawyers by Donald M. Falk.
Brief of amici curiae filed on behalf of the New Civil Liberties Alliance by Philip Hamburger, Mark Chenoweth, Margaret A. Little, and Jonathan F. Mitchell.
Brief of amici curiae filed on behalf of Center for Constitutional Jurisprudence by John C. Eastman and Anthony T. Caso.
Brief of amici curiae filed on behalf of Downsize DC Foundation et al. by Joseph W. Miller, Herbert W. Titus, William J. Olson, Jeremiah L. Morgan, and Robert J. Olson.
Brief of amici curiae filed on behalf of Institute for Justice by Sheldon Gilbert and Dana Berliner.
Brief of amici curiae filed on behalf of Scholars Whose Work Includes Sex Offense Studies by Sean Hecker.
Brief of amici curiae filed on behalf of William D. Araiza et al. by Andrew D. Silverman, Benjamin Chagnon, and Alison M. Kilmartin.
Brief of amici curiae filed on behalf of the Becket Fund for Religious Liberty by Eric Rassbach and Diana M. Verm.

Opposing Side (Respondent / Appellee)

No briefs of amici curiae were filed in support of appellee.

IV. THE SUPREME COURT'S DECISION

"Article I of the Constitution provides that '[a]ll legislative Powers herein granted shall be vested in a Congress of the United States.' Accompanying that assignment of power to Congress is a bar on its further delegation. . . . So we have held, time and again, that a statutory delegation is constitutional as long as Congress 'lay[s] down by legislative act an intelligible principle to which the person or body authorized to [exercise the delegated authority] is directed to conform.'

Given that standard, a nondelegation inquiry always begins (and often almost ends) with statutory interpretation. The constitutional question is whether Congress has supplied an intelligible principle to guide the delegee's use of discretion. . . . Only after a court has determined a challenged statute's meaning can it decide whether the law sufficiently guides executive discretion to accord with Article I. And indeed, once a court interprets the statute, it may find that the constitutional question all but answers itself.

That is the case here, because § 20913(d) does not give the Attorney General anything like the 'unguided' and 'unchecked' authority that Gundy says. . . . This Court has already interpreted § 20913(d) . . . to require the Attorney General to apply SORNA to all pre-Act offenders as soon as feasible. And revisiting that issue yet more fully today, we reach the same conclusion. . . . Gundy's constitutional claim must fail. Section 20913(d)'s delegation falls well within permissible bounds. . . .

Now that we have determined what § 20913(d) means, we can consider whether it violates the Constitution. The question becomes: Did Congress make an impermissible delegation when it instructed the Attorney General to apply SORNA's registration requirements to pre-Act offenders as soon as feasible? Under this Court's long-established law, that question is easy. Its answer is no. . . .

It is wisdom and humility alike that this Court has always upheld such 'necessities of government.' . . . We therefore affirm the judgment of the Court of Appeals."

V. JUSTICE VOTE

3 Pro ACLU Side vs. 5 Con Opposing Side

ACLU Side (Petitioner / Appellant)

1. Thomas, C. – Joined Gorsuch's dissent
2. Gorsuch, N. – Wrote dissenting opinion
3. Roberts, J. – Joined Gorsuch's dissent

Opposing Side (Respondent / Appellee)

1. Kagan, E. – Wrote majority opinion
2. Alito, S. – Wrote concurring opinion
3. Breyer, S. – Joined majority opinion
4. Ginsburg, R. – Joined majority opinion
5. Sotomayor, S. – Joined majority opinion

Kavanaugh, B. – Took no part in the decision

VI. A WIN OR LOSS FOR THE ACLU?

The ACLU filed as amicus curiae urging reversal of the judgment of the Court of Appeals; the Supreme Court affirmed in a 5-3 vote, giving the ACLU an apparent loss.

1189. McDonough v. Smith

(Decided June 20, 2019; 139 S.Ct. 2149; 588 U.S. _)

I. ISSUE

A. Issues Discussed

Civil rights

B. Legal Question Presented

When did the statute of limitations begin to run on McDonough's § 1983 claim regarding fabricated evidence?

C. Supreme Court's Answer

"The statute of limitations for McDonough's § 1983 claim alleging that he was prosecuted using fabricated evidence began to run when the criminal proceedings against him terminated in his favor—that is, when he was acquitted at the end of his second trial."

II. CASE SUMMARY

A. Background

"Edward McDonough alleges that . . . Youel Smith fabricated evidence and used it to pursue criminal charges against him. McDonough was acquitted, then sued Smith under 42 U.S.C. § 1983. The courts below, concluding that the limitations period for McDonough's fabricated-evidence claim began to run when the evidence was used against him, determined that the claim was untimely. . . .

Against Smith, McDonough asserted two different constitutional claims: one for fabrication of evidence, and one for malicious prosecution without probable cause. The District Court dismissed the malicious prosecution claim as barred by prosecutorial immunity, though timely. It dismissed the fabricated-evidence claim, however, as untimely.

McDonough appealed to the U. S. Court of Appeals for the Second Circuit, which affirmed."

The Supreme Court granted certiorari to review the case.

B. Counsel of Record / ACLU Attorney

ACLU Side (Petitioner / Appellant): Neal Kumar Katyal argued the cause for appellants. With him on the brief were Thomas P. Schmidt, Brian D. Premo, Joel B. Rudin, Katherine B. Wellington, Matthew J. Higgins, and Erin R. Chapman.

Principal Deputy Solicitor General Wall argued the cause for the United States as amicus curiae.

Opposing Side (Respondent / Appellee): Thomas J. O'Connor argued the cause for appellee. With him on the brief were Matthew S. Hellman, Julian J. O. Ginos, David M. Manners-Weber, David A. Strauss, and Sarah M. Konsky.

III. AMICI CURIAE

ACLU Side (Petitioner / Appellant)

Brief of amici curiae filed on behalf of the Center on the Administration of Criminal Law at NYU School of Law, the American Civil Liberties Union, the New York Civil Liberties Union, and the Brennan Center for Justice at NYU School of Law by Courtney M. Oliva, Mark W. Mosier, Rafael Reyneri, James O. Strawbridge, Priya Raghavan, Philip Desgranges, Christopher Dunn, Mariana Kovel, Ezekiel Edwards, David Cole, and Somil Trivedi.

Brief of amici curiae filed on behalf of the United States by Solicitor General Francisco, Assistant Attorney General Hunt, Deputy Solicitor General Wall, Assistant Solicitor General Ellis, Barbara Herwig, Dana L. Kaersvang, and Richard Montague.

Brief of amici curiae filed on behalf of the Criminal Justice Institute of Harvard Law School by Ronald S. Sullivan Jr.

Brief of amici curiae filed on behalf of Cause of Action Institute by John J. Vecchione, John E. McGlothlin II, and Michael R. Geske.

Brief of amici curiae filed on behalf of Criminal Defense Organizations et al. by R. Stanton Jones, Andrew T. Tutt, Samuel F. Callahan, and Graham W. White.

Brief of amici curiae filed on behalf of Constitutional Accountability Center by Elizabeth B. Wydra, Brianne J. Gorod, and Brian R. Frazelle.

Brief of amici curiae filed on behalf of Federal Courts Scholars by Jon Loevy, Steven Art, David B. Owens, Tony Balkissoon, Julia Rickert, and Megan Pierce.

Brief of amici curiae filed on behalf of St. Thomas More Lawyers Guild of Rochester, New York by John M. Regan, Jr.

Brief of amici curiae filed on behalf of the Innocence Network by Benjamin Gruenstein, Yonatan Even, Jonathan L. Baker, and Michael W. Marvin.

Opposing Side (Respondent / Appellee)

Brief of amici curiae filed on behalf of the International Municipal Lawyers Association et al. by Lisa Soronen and Geoffrey P. Eaton.

Brief of amici curiae filed on behalf of the State of Indiana et al. by Curtis T. Hill, Jr., Attorney General of Indiana, Thomas M. Fisher, Solicitor General, Kian J. Hudson, Deputy Solicitor General, Aaron T. Craft and Julia C. Payne, Deputy Attorneys General, and by the Attorneys General for their respective States as follows: Leslie Rutledge of Arkansas, Jeff Landry of Louisiana, Doug Peterson of Nebraska, Dave Yost of Ohio, Alan Wilson of South Carolina, and Ken Paxton of Texas.

IV. THE SUPREME COURT'S DECISION

"The statute of limitations for a fabricated-evidence claim like McDonough's does not begin to run until the criminal proceedings against the defendant (i.e., the § 1983 plaintiff) have terminated in his favor. This conclusion follows both from the rule for the most natural common-law analogy (the tort of malicious prosecution) and from the practical considerations that have previously led this Court to defer accrual of claims that would otherwise constitute an untenable collateral attack on a criminal judgment. . . .

The question here is when the statute of limitations began to run. Although courts look to state law for the length of the limitations period, the time at which a § 1983 claim accrues 'is a question of federal law,' 'conforming in general to common-law tort principles.' . . .

Common-law malicious prosecution requires showing, in part, that a defendant instigated a criminal proceeding with improper purpose and without probable cause. The essentials of McDonough's claim are similar: His claim requires him to show that the criminal proceedings against him—and consequent deprivations of his liberty—were caused by Smith's malfeasance in fabricating evidence. At bottom, both claims challenge the integrity of criminal prosecutions undertaken 'pursuant to legal process.'

We follow the analogy where it leads: McDonough could not bring his fabricated-evidence claim under § 1983 prior to favorable termination of his prosecution. . . .

Only once the criminal proceeding has ended in the defendant's favor, or a resulting conviction has been invalidated within the meaning of Heck, will the statute of limitations begin to run. . . .

Smith's counterarguments do not sway the result. . . .

The statute of limitations for McDonough's § 1983 claim alleging that he was prosecuted using fabricated evidence began to run when the criminal proceedings against him terminated in his favor—that is, when he was acquitted at the end of his second trial. The judgment of the United States Court of Appeals for the Second Circuit is therefore reversed, and the case is remanded . . . ."

V. JUSTICE VOTE

6 Pro ACLU Side vs. 3 Con Opposing Side

ACLU Side (Petitioner / Appellant)

1. Sotomayor, S. – Wrote majority opinion
2. Alito, S. – Joined majority opinion
3. Breyer, S. – Joined majority opinion
4. Kavanaugh, B. – Joined majority opinion
5. Ginsburg, R. – Joined majority opinion
6. Roberts, J. – Joined majority opinion

Opposing Side (Respondent / Appellee)

1. Kagan, E. – Joined Thomas' dissent
2. Thomas, C. – Wrote dissenting opinion
3. Gorsuch, N. – Joined Thomas' dissent

VI. A WIN OR LOSS FOR THE ACLU?

The ACLU filed as amicus curiae urging reversal of the judgment of the Court of Appeals; the Supreme Court reversed in a 6-3 vote, giving the ACLU an apparent win.

1190. Iancu v. Brunetti

(Decided June 24, 2019; 139 S.Ct. 2294; 588 U.S. _)

I. ISSUE

A. Issues Discussed

1st Amendment, press, speech, association

B. Legal Question Presented

Whether "the Lanham Act's prohibition[] on [trademark] registration . . . applying to marks that '[c]onsist[ ] of or comprise[ ] immoral[ ] or scandalous matter,'" violates the First Amendment.

C. Supreme Court's Answer

"[O]nce the 'immoral or scandalous' bar is interpreted fairly, it must be invalidated. . . . It . . . violates the First Amendment."

II. CASE SUMMARY

A. Background

"Respondent Erik Brunetti is an artist and entrepreneur who founded a clothing line that uses the trademark FUCT. According to Brunetti, the mark . . . is pronounced as four letters, one after the other: F-U-C-T. But you might read it differently and, if so, you would hardly be alone. . . . That common perception caused difficulties for Brunetti when he tried to register his mark with the U. S. Patent and Trademark Office (PTO).

Generally, a trademark is eligible for registration, and receipt of . . . benefits, if it is 'used in commerce.' But the Act directs the PTO to 'refuse[ ] registration' of certain marks. . . .

This case involves [one] of the Lanham Act's prohibitions on registration—one applying to marks that '[c]onsist[ ] of or comprise[ ] immoral[ ] or scandalous matter.' . . . To determine whether a mark fits in the category, the PTO asks whether a 'substantial composite of the general public' would find the mark 'shocking to the sense of truth, decency, or propriety'; 'giving offense to the conscience or moral feelings'; 'calling out for condemnation'; 'disgraceful'; 'offensive'; 'disreputable'; or 'vulgar.'

. . .

Both a PTO examining attorney and the PTO's Trademark Trial and Appeal Board decided that Brunetti's mark flunked that test.

. . .

Brunetti then brought a facial challenge to the 'immoral or scandalous' bar in the Court of Appeals for the Federal Circuit. That court found the prohibition to violate the First Amendment."

The Supreme Court granted certiorari to review the case.

B. Counsel of Record / ACLU Attorney

ACLU Side (Respondent / Appellee): John R. Sommer argued the cause for appellee. With him on the brief were Megan E. Gray and Devon A. Beckwith.

Opposing Side (Petitioner / Appellant): Deputy Solicitor General Stewart argued the cause for appellant. With him on the brief were Solicitor General Francisco, Assistant Attorney General Hunt, Assistant Solicitor General Liu, Mark R. Freeman, Daniel Tenny, Joshua M. Salzman, Sarah Harris, General Counsel for the U.S. Patent and Trademark Office, Thomas W. Krause, Solicitor, and Christina J. Hieber, Thomas L. Casagrande, Mary Beth Walker, and Molly R. Silfen, Associate Solicitors.

III. AMICI CURIAE

ACLU Side (Respondent / Appellee)

Brief of amici curiae filed on behalf of the American Civil Liberties Union and the ACLU of the District of Columbia by Arthur B. Spitzer, David D. Cole, Emerson Sykes, Vera Eidelman, Esha Bhandari, and Jennesa Calvo-Friedman.

Brief of amici curiae filed on behalf of Pacific Legal Foundation by Caleb R. Trotter, Joshua P. Thompson, and Daniel M. Ortner.

Brief of amici curiae filed on behalf of Simon Tam by Stuart Banner.

Brief of amici curiae filed on behalf of Professors Barton Beebe et al. by Joshua J. Bone and William M. Jay.

Brief of amici curiae filed on behalf of the Rutherford Institute by John W. Whitehead, Douglas R. McKusick, Megan L. Brown, Scott B. Wilkens, Christopher J. Kelly, and Wesley E. Weeks.

Brief of amici curiae filed on behalf of the Cato Institute et al. by Thomas Berry, Ilya Shapiro, and Trevor Burrus.

Brief of amici curiae filed on behalf of the International Trademark Association by David Donahue, Claudia Ray, David H. Bernstein, Jeremy Feigelson, Pooja A. Boisture, Michael C. McGregor, and Jaime M. Freilich.

Opposing Side (Petitioner / Appellant)

Brief of amici curiae filed on behalf of Kurt M. Anderson by Mr. Anderson, pro se.

Brief of amici curiae filed on behalf of the American Intellectual Property Law Association by Sheldon H. Klein and Theodore H. Davis Jr., in support of neither party.

Brief of amici curiae filed on behalf of New York Intellectual

Property Law Association by Michael Carl Cannata, Frank Misiti, Stephen J. Smirti, Jr., Peter G. Thurlow, Dyan Finguerra-DuCharme, William Thomashower, Kamilah M. Holder, Robert J. Rando, Aron Fischer, Reece Brassler, and Kathleen E. McCarthy in support of neither party.

IV. THE SUPREME COURT'S DECISION

"This Court first considered a First Amendment challenge to a trademark registration restriction in Tam, just two Terms ago. There, the Court declared unconstitutional the Lanham Act's ban on registering marks that 'disparage' any 'person[ ], living or dead.' The eight-Justice Court divided evenly between two opinions and could not agree on the overall framework for deciding the case. . . . But all the Justices agreed on two propositions. First, if a trademark registration bar is viewpoint-based, it is unconstitutional. And second, the disparagement bar was viewpoint-based.

The Justices thus found common ground in a core postulate of free speech law: The government may not discriminate against speech based on the ideas or opinions it conveys. . . . Slightly different explanations, then, but a shared conclusion: Viewpoint discrimination doomed the disparagement bar.

If the 'immoral or scandalous' bar similarly discriminates on the basis of viewpoint, it must also collide with our First Amendment doctrine. . . .

It is viewpoint-based. . . .

The facial viewpoint bias in the law results in viewpoint-discriminatory application. . . .

How, then, can the Government claim that the 'immoral or scandalous' bar is viewpoint-neutral? . . .

[O]nce the 'immoral or scandalous' bar is interpreted fairly, it must be invalidated. The Government just barely argues otherwise. . . . But in any event, the 'immoral or scandalous' bar is substantially overbroad. There are a great many immoral and scandalous ideas in the world (even more than there are swearwords), and the Lanham Act covers them all. It therefore violates the First Amendment.

We accordingly affirm the judgment of the Court of Appeals."

V. JUSTICE VOTE

6 Pro ACLU Side vs. 3 Con Opposing Side

ACLU Side (Respondent / Appellee)

1. Kagan, E. – Wrote majority opinion
2. Alito, S. – Wrote concurring opinion
3. Thomas, C. – Joined majority opinion
4. Gorsuch, N. – Joined majority opinion
5. Kavanaugh, B. – Joined majority opinion
6. Ginsburg, R. – Joined majority opinion

Opposing Side (Petitioner / Appellant)

1. Breyer, S. – Wrote opinion concurring in part and dissenting in part, joined Sotomayor's opinion
2. Sotomayor, S. – Wrote opinion concurring in part and dissenting in part
3. Roberts, J. – Wrote opinion concurring in part and dissenting in part

VI. A WIN OR LOSS FOR THE ACLU?

The ACLU filed as amicus curiae urging affirmance; the Supreme Court affirmed the Court of Appeals' decision by a 6-3 vote, giving the ACLU an apparent win.

1191. Rucho v. Common Cause

(Decided June 27, 2019; 139 S.Ct. 2484; 588 U.S. _)

I. ISSUE

A. Issues Discussed

Voting rights

B. Legal Question Presented

"[W]hether claims of excessive partisanship in districting are 'justiciable'—that is, properly suited for resolution by the federal courts. . . . The districting plans at issue here are highly partisan, by any measure. The question is whether the courts below appropriately exercised judicial power when they found them unconstitutional as well."

C. Supreme Court's Answer

"We conclude that partisan gerrymandering claims present political questions beyond the reach of the federal courts. Federal judges have no license to reallocate political power between the two major political parties, with no plausible grant of authority in the Constitution, and no legal standards to limit and direct their decisions."

II. CASE SUMMARY

A. Background

"Voters and other plaintiffs in North Carolina and Maryland challenged their States' congressional districting maps as unconstitutional partisan gerrymanders. The North Carolina plaintiffs complained that the State's districting plan discriminated against Democrats; the Maryland plaintiffs complained that their State's plan discriminated against Republicans. The plaintiffs alleged that the gerrymandering violated the First Amendment, the Equal Protection Clause of the Fourteenth Amendment, the Elections Clause, and Article I, § 2, of the Constitution. The District Courts in both cases ruled in favor of the plaintiffs, and the defendants appealed directly to this Court."

The Supreme Court postponed jurisdiction to review the cases.

B. Counsel of Record / ACLU Attorney

ACLU Side (Respondent / Appellee): Emmet J. Bondurant II argued the cause for appellees Common Cause et al. With him on the brief were Gregory L. Diskant, Jonah M. Knobler, Peter A. Nelson, Elena Steiger Reich, Benjamin W. Thorpe, Edwin M. Speas, Jr., Steven B. Epstein, Caroline P. Mackie, and Richard H. Pildes.

Allison J. Riggs argued the cause for appellees League of Women Voters of North Carolina et al. With her on the brief were Nicholas Stephanopoulos, Jaclyn Maffetore, Paul M. Smith, Ruth M. Greenwood, Annabelle E. Harless, Jessica Ring

Amunson, and Sam Hirsch.

Opposing Side (Petitioner / Appellant): Paul D. Clement argued the cause for appellant. With him on the brief were Phillip J. Strach, Michael D. McKnight, Erin E. Murphy, and Andrew C. Lawrence.

III. AMICI CURIAE

ACLU Side (Respondent / Appellee)

Brief of amici curiae filed on behalf of the American Civil Liberties Union, New York Civil Liberties Union, ACLU of North Carolina, and ACLU of Maryland by David D. Cole, Perry M. Grossman, Arthur N. Eisenberg, Adriel I. Cepeda Derieux, Dale E. Ho, Jennesa Calvo-Friedman, Christopher Brook, Samuel Issacharoff, and Deborah A. Jeon.

Brief of amici curiae filed on behalf of Colleagues of Professor Norman Dorsen by Burt Neuborne.

Brief of amici curiae filed on behalf of First Amendment Clinic at Duke Law by H. Jefferson Powell and Nicole J. Ligon.

Brief of amici curiae filed on behalf of Eric S. Lander by H. Reed Witherby.

Brief of amici curiae filed on behalf of Stephen M. Shapiro by Mr. Shapiro and Michael R. Geroe.

Brief of amici curiae filed on behalf of Professor D. Theodore Rave by Mr. Rave.

Brief of amici curiae filed on behalf of First Amendment and Election Law Scholars by Bradley S. Phillips and Gregory D. Phillips.

Brief of amici curiae filed on behalf of Professors Wesley Pegden et al. by Tacy F. Flint, Jason G. Marsico, and Martha C. Clarke.

Brief of amici curiae filed on behalf of the Brennan Center for Justice at N.Y.U. School of Law by Wendy R. Weiser, Michael C. Li, Daniel I. Weiner, Thomas P. Wolf, Yurij Rudensky, Anton Metlitsky, Bradley N. Garcia, and Samantha M. Goldstein.

Brief of amici curiae filed on behalf of Bipartisan Group of Current and Former Members of the House of Representatives by Meghan Kaler, Seth P. Waxman, Jonathan G. Cedarbaum, Ari Savitzky, David Stoopler, Anuradha Sivaram, and Rebecca Cooper.

Brief of amici curiae filed on behalf of Professors Christopher Elmendorf et al. by Mr. Elmendorf, Mark A. Packman, Jenna A. Hudson, Samantha R. Miller, and Alison D. Gaske.

Brief of amici curiae filed on behalf of Constitutional Accountability Center by Elizabeth B. Wydra, Brianne J. Gorod, and David H. Gans.

Brief of amici curiae filed on behalf of Senator Sheldon Whitehouse by Kathryn Cahoy, Mark W. Mosier, Ryan Mowery, and Kathleen Choi.

Brief of amici curiae filed on behalf of the State of Oregon et al. by Ellen F. Rosenblum, Attorney General of Oregon, Benjamin Gutman, Solicitor General, Jordan R. Silk, Assistant Attorney General, and by the Attorneys General for their respective jurisdictions as follows: Xavier Becerra of California, Philip J. Weiser of Colorado, William Tong of Connecticut, Kathleen Jennings of Delaware, Clare E. Connors of Hawaii, Thomas J. Miller of Iowa, Andy Beshear of Kentucky, Aaron M. Frey of Maine, Maura Healey of Massachusetts, Dana Nessel of Michigan, Keith Ellison of Minnesota, Jim Hood of Mississippi, Gurbir S. Grewal of New Jersey, Letitia James of New York, Aaron D. Ford of Nevada, Hector Balderas of New Mexico.

Brief of amici curiae filed on behalf of 27 Election Law, Scientific Evidence, and Empirical Legal Scholars by Andrew Chin.

Brief of amici curiae filed on behalf of the American Jewish Committee by Marc D. Stern, Richard A. Rosen, Peter Sandel, Elizabeth J. Grossman, and Melina Meneguin Layerenza.

Brief of amici curiae filed on behalf of Political Science Professors by Brian A. Sutherland and Justin McGuirk.

Brief of amici curiae filed on behalf of Governors Arnold Schwarzenegger et al. by David A. Schwarz and Bruce A. Wessel.

Brief of amici curiae filed on behalf of Democracy North Carolina et al. by Jonathan K. Youngwood, Isaac Rethy, and Joshua C. Polster.

Brief of amici curiae filed on behalf of NAACP Legal Defense & Educational Fund, Inc., et al. by Sherrilyn A. Ifill, Janai S. Nelson, Samuel Spital, Leah C. Aden, Justin Levitt, Jennifer A. Holmes, Laura W. Brill, and Nicholas F. Daum.

Brief of amici curiae filed on behalf of Historians by Richard W. Clary, Amanda R. Bakowski, and Samantha Hall.

Brief of amici curiae filed on behalf of the Lawyers' Committee for Civil Rights Under Law by Robert E. Harrington, Erik R. Zimmerman, Travis S. Hinman, David Barkan, Kristen Clarke, Jon M. Greenbaum, Ezra D. Rosenberg, John Powers, Oliver J. Richards, Alex Pechette, Qiuyi Wu, and John Dragseth.

Brief of amici curiae filed on behalf of International Municipal Lawyers Association et al. by Charles W. Thompson, Jr., Amanda Kellar Karras, and G. Michael Parsons, Jr.

Brief of amici curiae filed on behalf of Anti-Defamation League et al. by David Leit and Natalie J. Kraner.

Brief of amici curiae filed on behalf of Professor Michael Kang by James P. Rouhandeh, David B. Toscano, Thomas Dec, and Amanda Rae Schwarzenbart.

Brief of amici curiae filed on behalf of Mathematicians et al. by Guy-Uriel E. Charles, Deepak Gupta, and Daniel Wilf-Townsend.

Brief of amici curiae filed on behalf of the Floyd Abrams Institute for Freedom of Expression by Mr. Abrams, Francesca L. Procaccini, David Schulz, and Charles Sims.

Opposing Side (Petitioner / Appellant)

Brief of amici curiae filed on behalf of the National Republican Redistricting Trust by Edward D. Greim and Lucinda H. Luetkemeyer.

Brief of amici curiae filed on behalf of the American Civil Rights Union et al. by Kimberly S. Hermann and John J. Park, Jr.

Brief of amici curiae filed on behalf of the Public Interest Legal Foundation by J. Christian Adams and Kaylan Phillips.

Brief of amici curiae filed on behalf of the Republican National Committee et al. by Jason Torchinsky, Dennis W. Polio, J. Justin Riemer, and P. Christopher Winkelman.

Brief of amici curiae filed on behalf of Members of Congress From the North Carolina Delegation by Misha Tseytlin and W.

Alex Smith.

Brief of amici curiae filed on behalf of Texas House Representative Carl Isett by James E. Trainor III and Joseph M. Nixon.

Brief of amici curiae filed on behalf of Speaker Michael C. Turzai, in his Official Capacity as Constitutional Officer of the Pennsylvania House of Representatives by Kathleen A. Gallagher, Russell D. Giancola, Carolyn Batz McGee, Robert J. Tucker, E. Mark Braden, Katherine L. McKnight, Richard B. Raile, and Patrick T. Lewis.

Brief of amici curiae filed on behalf of Wisconsin State Senate et al. by Kevin St. John, Adam K. Mortara, Joshua P. Ackerman, and Taylor A.R. Meehan.

Brief of amici curiae filed on behalf of the State of Texas et al. by Ken Paxton Attorney General of Texas, Jeffrey C. Mateer, First Assistant Attorney General, Kyle D. Hawkins, Solicitor General, Matthew H. Frederick, Deputy Solicitor General, Kristofer S. Monson, Assistant Solicitor General, and by the Attorneys General for their respective States as follows: Steve Marshall of Alabama, Leslie Rutledge of Arkansas, Christopher M. Carr of Georgia, Curtis T. Hill, Jr., of Indiana, Jeff Landry of Louisiana, Dave Yost of Ohio, Mike Hunter of Oklahoma, Alan Wilson of South Carolina, and Sean D. Reyes of Utah.

Brief of amici curiae filed on behalf of Judicial Watch, Inc., et al. by Robert D. Popper and Eric W. Lee in support of neither party.

Brief of amici curiae filed on behalf of David Orentlicher by Mr. Orentlicher in support of neither party.

Brief of amici curiae filed on behalf of Bernard Grofman et al. by Thomas M. Bondy, Hannah Garden-Monheit, Elizabeth R. Cruikshank, and E. Joshua Rosenkranz in support of neither party.

IV. THE SUPREME COURT'S DECISION

"In these cases we are asked to decide an important question of constitutional law. 'But before we do so, we must find that the question is presented in a 'case' or 'controversy' that is, in James Madison's words, 'of a Judiciary Nature.'' . . .

The question here is whether there is an 'appropriate role for the Federal Judiciary' in remedying the problem of partisan gerrymandering—whether such claims are claims of legal right, resolvable according to legal principles, or political questions that must find their resolution elsewhere. . . .

As we summed up last Term in Gill, our 'considerable efforts in Gaffney, Bandemer, Vieth, and LULAC leave unresolved whether . . . claims [of legal right] may be brought in cases involving allegations of partisan gerrymandering.' Two 'threshold questions' remained: standing, which we addressed in Gill, and 'whether [such] claims are justiciable.' . . .

In considering whether partisan gerrymandering claims are justiciable, we are mindful of Justice Kennedy's counsel in Vieth: Any standard for resolving such claims must be grounded in a 'limited and precise rationale' and be 'clear, manageable, and politically neutral.' . . .

As noted, the question is one of degree: How to 'provid[e] a standard for deciding how much partisan dominance is too much.' . . . If federal courts are to 'inject [themselves] into the most heated partisan issues' by adjudicating partisan gerrymandering claims, they must be armed with a standard that can reliably differentiate unconstitutional from 'constitutional political gerrymandering.' . . .

Appellees and the dissent propose a number of 'tests' for evaluating partisan gerrymandering claims, but none meets the need for a limited and precise standard that is judicially . . . manageable. . . .

We conclude that partisan gerrymandering claims present political questions beyond the reach of the federal courts. Federal judges have no license to reallocate political power between the two major political parties, with no plausible grant of authority in the Constitution, and no legal standards to limit and direct their decisions. . . .

No one can accuse this Court of having a crabbed view of the reach of its competence. But we have no commission to allocate political power and influence in the absence of a constitutional directive or legal standards to guide us in the exercise of such authority. 'It is emphatically the province and duty of the judicial department to say what the law is.' In this rare circumstance, that means our duty is to say 'this is not law.'

The judgments of the United States District Court for the Middle District of North Carolina and the United States District Court for the District of Maryland are vacated, and the cases are remanded with instructions to dismiss for lack of jurisdiction."

V. JUSTICE VOTE

4 Pro ACLU Side vs. 5 Con Opposing Side

ACLU Side (Respondent / Appellee)

1. Kagan, E. – Wrote dissenting opinion
2. Breyer, S. – Joined Kagan's dissent
3. Ginsburg, R. – Joined Kagan's dissent
4. Sotomayor, S. – Joined Kagan's dissent

Opposing Side (Petitioner / Appellant)

1. Roberts, J. – Wrote majority opinion
2. Alito, S. – Joined majority opinion
3. Thomas, C. – Joined majority opinion
4. Gorsuch, N. – Joined majority opinion
5. Kavanaugh, B. – Joined majority opinion

VI. A WIN OR LOSS FOR THE ACLU?

The ACLU filed as amicus curiae urging affirmance; the Supreme Court vacated the District Courts' decisions by a 5-4 vote, giving the ACLU an apparent loss.

1192. Mitchell v. Wisconsin

(Decided June 27, 2019; 139 S.Ct. 2525; 588 U.S. _)

I. ISSUE

A. Issues Discussed

4th Amendment

B. Legal Question Presented

"'[W]hether a statute authorizing a blood draw from an unconscious motorist provides an exception to the Fourth Amendment warrant requirement.'"

C. Supreme Court's Answer

"In such cases, we hold, the exigent-circumstances rule almost always permits a blood test without a warrant. [W]hen a driver is unconscious, the general rule is that a warrant is not needed."

II. CASE SUMMARY

A. Background

"Officer Alexander Jaeger . . . received a report that petitioner Gerald Mitchell, appearing ,. . . drunk, had climbed into a van and driven off. Jaeger soon found Mitchell wandering . . . . Mitchell could hardly stand . . . . Jaeger judged a field sobriety test hopeless, if not dangerous, and gave Mitchell a preliminary breath test. It registered a BAC level of 0.24%, triple the legal limit . . . . Jaeger arrested Mitchell for operating a vehicle while intoxicated and . . . drove him to a police station for a more reliable breath test using better equipment. . . .

Mitchell's condition continued to deteriorate—so much so that by the time the squad car had reached the station, he was too lethargic even for a breath test. Jaeger therefore drove Mitchell to a nearby hospital for a blood test; Mitchell lost consciousness on the ride over and had to be wheeled in. Even so, Jaeger read aloud to a slumped Mitchell the standard statement giving drivers a chance to refuse BAC testing. Hearing no response, Jaeger asked hospital staff to draw a blood sample. Mitchell remained unconscious while the sample was taken, and analysis of his blood showed that his BAC, about 90 minutes after his arrest, was 0.222%.

Mitchell was charged with violating two related drunk-driving provisions. He moved to suppress the results of the blood test on the ground that it violated his Fourth Amendment right against 'unreasonable searches' because it was conducted without a warrant. Wisconsin chose to rest its response on the notion that its implied-consent law . . . rendered the blood test a consensual one . . . . In the end, the trial court denied Mitchell's motion to suppress, and a jury found him guilty of the charged offenses. . . . The Wisconsin Supreme Court affirmed Mitchell's convictions . . . ."

The Supreme Court granted certiorari to review the case.

B. Counsel of Record / ACLU Attorney

ACLU Side (Petitioner / Appellant): Andrew R. Hinkel, Wisconsin Assistant State Public Defender, argued the cause for appellants. With him on the brief was Ginger D. Anders, Celia R. Choy, and Dane P. Shikman.

Opposing Side (Respondent / Appellee): Hannah S. Jurss, Assistant Attorney General of Wisconsin, argued the cause for appellee. With her on the brief were Joshua L. Kaul, Attorney General, Anthony D. Russomanno, and Michael C. Sanders, Assistant Attorney General.

III. AMICI CURIAE

ACLU Side (Petitioner / Appellant)

Brief of amici curiae filed on behalf of the American Civil Liberties Union and ACLU of Wisconsin by David D. Cole, Jennesa Calvo-Friedman, Ezekiel R. Edwards, Jason D. Williamson, Brandon J. Buskey, and Nathan Freed Wessler.

Brief of amici curiae filed on behalf of California DUI Lawyers Association by Donald J. Bartell and Lara J. Gressley.

Brief of amici curiae filed on behalf of the National College for DUI Defense by Donald J. Ramsell, Michelle Behan, Fleming Kanan Whited III, and Andrew Mishlove.

Brief of amici curiae filed on behalf of the Rutherford Institute et al. by John W. Whitehead, Douglas R. McKusick, Ilya Shapiro, Clark M. Neily III, Trevor Burrus, Jay R. Schweikert, D. Alicia Hickok, Mark D. Taticchi, D. Alexander Harrell, and Matthew C. Sapp.

Brief of amici curiae filed on behalf of Restore the Fourth, Inc., by Mahesha P. Subbaraman.

Brief of amici curiae filed on behalf of the DKT Liberty Project et al. by Jessica Ring Amunson and Andrew C. Noll.

Brief of amici curiae filed on behalf of DUI Defense Lawyers Association by D. Timothy Huey and Gregory A. Willis.

Opposing Side (Respondent / Appellee)

Brief of amici curiae filed on behalf of National Conference of State Legislatures et al. by Lisa Soronen, Lauren S. Kuley, Keith Bradley, and Brent Owen.

Brief of amici curiae filed on behalf of Mothers Against Drunk Driving by Dawn Diaz, Theane Evangelis, Lauren M. Blas, and Stephanie Balitzer.

Brief of amici curiae filed on behalf of League of Wisconsin Municipalities et al. by Douglas Hoffer, Eau Claire Deputy City Attorney, Carol Nawrocki, Legal Counsel for the Wisconsin Towns Association, and Claire Silverman, Legal Counsel for the League of Wisconsin Municipalities.

Brief of amici curiae filed on behalf of the State of Colorado et al. by Philip J. Weiser, Attorney General of Colorado, Eric R. Olson, Solicitor General, Daniel E. Rauch, Counsel to the Attorney General, L. Andrew Cooper, Deputy Attorney General, and by the Attorneys General for their respective States as follows: Ashley Moody of Florida, Christopher M. Carr of Georgia, Lawrence G. Wasden of Idaho, Kwame Raoul of Illinois, Curtis T. Hill, Jr., of Indiana, Thomas J. Miller of Iowa, Andy Beshear of Kentucky, Jeff Landry of Louisiana, Brian E. Frosh of Maryland, Keith Ellison of Minnesota, Timothy C. Fox of Montana, Joshua H. Stein of North Carolina, Dave Yost of Ohio, Mike Hunter of Oklahoma, Ellen F. Rosenblum of Oregon, Alan Wilson of South Carolina, and Jason R. Ravnsborg of South Dakota.

IV. THE SUPREME COURT'S DECISION

"In considering Wisconsin's implied-consent law, we do not write on a blank slate. 'Our prior opinions have referred approvingly to the general concept of implied-consent laws that impose civil penalties and evidentiary consequences on motorists who refuse to comply.' But our decisions have not rested on the idea that these laws do what their popular name might seem to suggest—that is, create actual consent to all the searches they authorize. Instead, we have based our decisions on the precedent regarding the specific constitutional claims in each case, while keeping in mind the wider regulatory scheme developed over the years to combat drunk driving. That scheme is centered on legally specified BAC limits for drivers—limits enforced by the BAC tests promoted by implied-consent laws. . . .

Because the 'standard evidentiary breath test is conducted after a motorist is arrested and transported to a police station or another appropriate facility, the important question here is what officers may do when a driver's unconsciousness (or stupor) eliminates any reasonable opportunity for that kind of breath test. . . .

The Fourth Amendment guards the 'right of the people to be secure in their persons . . . against unreasonable searches' and provides that 'no Warrants shall issue, but upon probable cause.' A blood draw is a search of the person, so we must determine if its administration here without a warrant was reasonable. . . . In McNeely, we considered how the exigent-circumstances exception applies to the broad category of cases in which a police officer has probable cause to believe that a motorist was driving under the influence of alcohol . . . . [W]e address how the exception bears on . . . unconscious drivers. In those cases, the need for a blood test is compelling, and an officer's duty to attend to more pressing needs may leave no time to seek a warrant. . . .

When police have probable cause to believe a person has committed a drunk-driving offense and the driver's unconsciousness or stupor requires him to be taken to the hospital or similar facility before police have a reasonable opportunity to administer a standard evidentiary breath test, they may almost always order a warrantless blood test to measure the driver's BAC without offending the Fourth Amendment. We do not rule out the possibility that in an unusual case a defendant would be able to show that his blood would not have been drawn if police had not been seeking BAC information, and that police could not have reasonably judged that a warrant application would interfere with other pressing needs or duties. Because Mitchell did not have a chance to attempt to make that showing, a remand for that purpose is necessary. . . .

The judgment of the Supreme Court of Wisconsin is vacated, and the case is remanded . . . ."

V. JUSTICE VOTE

4 Pro ACLU Side vs. 5 Con Opposing Side

ACLU Side (Petitioner / Appellant)

1. Kagan, E. – Joined Sotomayor's dissent
2. Gorsuch, N. – Wrote dissenting opinion
3. Ginsburg, R. – Joined Sotomayor's dissent
4. Sotomayor, S. – Wrote dissenting opinion

Opposing Side (Respondent / Appellee)

1. Alito, S. – Wrote plurality opinion
2. Thomas, C. – Wrote concurring opinion
3. Breyer, S. – Joined majority opinion
4. Kavanaugh, B. – Joined majority opinion
5. Roberts, J. – Joined majority opinion

VI. A WIN OR LOSS FOR THE ACLU?

The ACLU filed as amicus curiae urging reversal of the judgment of the Court of Appeals; the Supreme Court vacated in a 5-4 vote, giving the ACLU an apparent loss.

1193. Dep't of Commerce v. New York

(Decided June 27, 2019; 139 S.Ct. 2551; 588 U.S. _)

I. ISSUE

A. Issues Discussed

Census

B. Legal Question Presented

"[W]hether the Secretary [of Commerce] violated the Enumeration Clause of the Constitution, the Census Act, or otherwise abused his discretion" by reinstating the citizenship question on the 2020 census.

C. Supreme Court's Answer

"[T]he VRA enforcement rationale—the sole stated reason—seems to have been contrived.

We are presented, in other words, with an explanation for agency action that is incongruent with what the record reveals about the agency's priorities and decisionmaking process. . . .

In these unusual circumstances, the District Court was warranted in remanding to the agency, and we affirm that disposition."

II. CASE SUMMARY

A. Background

"[T]he Constitution requires an 'Enumeration' of the population every 10 years, to be made 'in such Manner' as Congress 'shall by Law direct.' In the Census Act, Congress delegated to the Secretary of Commerce the task of conducting the decennial census . . . .

There have been 23 decennial censuses from the first census in 1790 to the most recent in 2010. Every census between 1820 and 2000 (with the exception of 1840) asked at least some of the population about their citizenship or place of birth. . . .

In 2010, [a]ll households received the same questionnaire . . . . The more detailed demographic questions previously asked on the long-form questionnaire, including the question about citizenship, were instead asked in the American Community Survey (or ACS), which is sent each year to a rotating sample of about 2.6% of households.

In March 2018, Secretary of Commerce . . . Ross announced in a memo that he had decided to reinstate a question about citizenship on the 2020 decennial census questionnaire. . . .

Shortly after the Secretary announced his decision, two groups of plaintiffs filed suit in Federal District Court in New York, challenging the decision on several grounds. . . .

The Government moved to dismiss . . . . The District Court dismissed the Enumeration Clause claim but allowed the other claims to proceed. . . .

The District Court held a bench trial and issued findings of fact and conclusions of law on respondents' statutory and equal protection claims. . . . The court granted judgment to respondents on their statutory claims, vacated the Secretary's decision, and enjoined him from reinstating the citizenship question until he cured the legal errors the court had identified."

The Supreme Court granted certiorari to review the case.

B. Counsel of Record / ACLU Attorney

ACLU Side (Respondent / Appellee): Dale E. Ho of the American Civil Liberties Union Foundation argued the cause for appellee New York Immigration Coalition et al. With him on the brief were John A. Freedman, David P. Gersch, David J. Weiner, Elisabeth S. Theodore, and Samuel F. Callahan, and Christopher Dunn and Perry M. Grossman of the New York Civil Liberties Union Foundation, and Adriel I. Cepeda Derieux, Cecillia D. Wang, Jonathan Topaz, David D. Cole, Sarah Brannon, Davin M. Rosborough, and Ceridwen Cherry of the American Civil Liberties Union Foundation.

Barbara D. Underwood, Solicitor General of New York, argued the cause for appellee New York et al. With her on the brief were Letitia James, Attorney General, Steven C. Wu, Deputy Solicitor General, Judith N. Vale, Senior Assistant Solicitor General, Scott A. Eisman, Assistant Solicitor General, Matthew Colangelo, Chief Counsel for Federal Initiatives, Elena Goldstein, Acting Bureau Chief for the Civil Rights Bureau, Matthew Jerzyk, Central Falls City Solicitor, Edward N. Siskel, Chicago City Corporation Counsel, Zachary M. Klein, Columbus City Attorney, Dennis J. Herrera, San Francisco City and County Attorney, Rolando L. Rios, Cameron and Hidalgo Counties Special Counsel, Jo Anne Bernal, El Paso County Attorney, Charles J. McKee, Monterey County Counsel, John Daniel Reaves, General Counsel for the U.S. Conference of Mayors, Zachary W. Carter, New York City Corporation Counsel, Marcel S. Pratt, Philadelphia City Solicitor, Cris Meyer, Phoenix City Attorney, Yvonne S. Hilton, Pittsburgh City Solicitor, Jeffrey Dana, Providence City Solicitor, Peter S. Holmes, Seattle City Attorney, and the Attorneys General for their respective jurisdictions as follows: Phil Weiser of Colorado, William Tong of Connecticut, Kathleen Jennings of Delaware, Karl A. Racine of the District of Columbia, Kwame Raoul of Illinois, Thomas J. Miller of Iowa, Brian E. Frosh of Maryland, Maura Healey of Massachesetts, Keith Ellison of Minnesota, Gurbir S. Grewal of New Jersey, Hector H. Balderas of New Mexico, Joshua H. Stein of North Carolina, Ellen F. Rosenblum of Oregon, Josh Shapiro of Pennsylvania, Peter F. Neronha of Rhode Island, Thomas J. Donovan, Jr., of Vermont, and Robert W. Ferguson of Washington.

Douglas N. Letter argued the cause for the United States House of Representatives as amicus curiae.

Opposing Side (Petitioner / Appellant): Solicitor General Francisco argued the cause for appellant. With him on the brief were Assistant Attorney General Hunt, Deputy Solicitor General Wall, Deputy Assistant Attorney General Moopan, Assistant Solicitor General Joshi, Mark B. Stern, Gerard J. Sinzdak, Peter B. Davidson, General Counsel for the Department of Commerce, and David Dewhirst, Senior Counsel to the General Counsel.

III. AMICI CURIAE

ACLU Side (Respondent / Appellee)

Brief of amici curiae filed on behalf of the United States House of Representatives by Neal Kumar Katyal, Jonathan L. Backer, Joshua A. Geltzer, Amy L. Marshak, Mary B. McCord, Douglas N. Letter, General Counsel for the United States House of Representatives, Todd B. Tatleman, Deputy General Counsel, and Brooks M. Hanner, Assistant General Counsel.

Brief of amici curiae filed on behalf of the KIPP Foundation et al. by Anthony C. Thompson, Vincent M. Southerland, and Deborah N. Archer.

Brief of amici curiae filed on behalf of National School Boards Association et al. by Francisco M. Negrón, Jr., Richard P. Bress, Samir Deger-Sen, and Cherish A. Drain.

Brief of amici curiae filed on behalf of Businesses and Business Organizations by Alexander H. Southwell, Lee R. Crain, Stuart F. Delery, and Joshua M. Wesneski.

Brief of amici curiae filed on behalf of Natural Resources Defense Council by Ian Fein and Michael E. Wall.

Brief of amici curiae filed on behalf of Norman Y. Mineta et al. by Robert S. Chang, Lorraine K. Bannai, Pratik A. Shah, Z.W. Julius Chen, Geoffrey J. Derrick, Lena F. Masri, Gadeir Abbas, Ahmed M. Mohamed, Alice Hsu, and Robert H. Pees.

Brief of amici curiae filed on behalf of the State of California by Xavier Becerra, Attorney General of California, Edward C. Dumont, Solicitor General, Michael J. Mongan, Deputy Solicitor General, Anthony R. Hakl III, Supervising Deputy Attorney General, Gabrielle D. Boutin and R. Matthew Wise, Deputy Attorneys General, and Kristin A. Liska, Associate Deputy Solicitor General.

Brief of amici curiae filed on behalf of Current Members of Congress et al. by Elizabeth B. Wydra, Brianne J. Gorod, and David H. Gans.

Brief of amici curiae filed on behalf of Electronic Privacy Information Center (EPIC) et al. by Marc Rotenberg, Alan Butler, John Davisson, and Megan Iorio.

Brief of amici curiae filed on behalf of Amici Curiae Plaintiffs in Kravitz et al. v. United States Department of Commerce et al. No. 18- 1041 (D. Md.) by P. Benjamin Duke, Karun Tilak, Shankar Duraiswamy, and Daniel Grant.

Brief of amici curiae filed on behalf of the American Statistical Association et al. by Nicholas S. Brod, Kyle M. Druding, and Ira M. Feinberg.

Brief of amici curiae filed on behalf of the Nielsen Company (US), LLC by George D. Callard, Eric M. Rubenstein, Ishan K. Bhabha, James T. Dawson, Alison I. Stein, and Ali M. Arain.

Brief of amici curiae filed on behalf of the Catholic Charities of the Archdiocese of New York et al. by Eamon P. Joyce, Qais Ghafary, and David S. Kanter.

Brief of amici curiae filed on behalf of the Arab American Institute by Maya M. Berry, Ryan J. Suto, Jason C. Beekman, and Harsh K. Voruganti.

Brief of amici curiae filed on behalf of the Council of the Great

City Schools by Julie Wright Halbert, John W. Borkowski, and Aleksandra O. Rushing.

Brief of amici curiae filed on behalf of Harris County, Texas et al. by Terence O'Rourke, Scott Lemond, and Susan Hays.

Brief of amici curiae filed on behalf of the Leadership Conference on Civil and Human Rights et al. by Vanita Gupta, Corrine Yu, Michael Zubrensky, Wendy R. Weiser, Thomas P. Wolf, Kelly M. Percival, Alan E. Schoenfeld, Claire M. Guehenno, Tara E. Levens, and David E. Rudin.

Brief of amici curiae filed on behalf of NAACP Legal Defense & Educational Fund, Inc., by Sherrilyn A. Ifill, Janai S. Nelson, Samuel Spital, Leah C. Aden, Aaron Sussman, J. Zachery Morris, David J. Zimmer, Joshua J. Bone, Tiffany Mahmood, William Uhr, and Madeline DiLascia.

Brief of amici curiae filed on behalf of Lawyers for Civil Rights et al. by Iván Espinoza-Madrigal, Oren M. Sellstrom, Lauren Sampson, Yalonda T. Howze, Reena I. Thadhani, Mathilda S. McGee-Tubb, and Amanda L. Clairmont.

Brief of amici curiae filed on behalf of 190 Bipartisan Elected Officials et al. by Jeffrey M. Wice, Robert A. Atkins, Yahonnes Cleary, Johan E. Tatoy, David Giller, Michael Pernick, Robert H. Rankin, Melina Meneguin Layerenza, and Apeksha S. Vora.

Brief of amici curiae filed on behalf of Former Census Bureau Directors by Matthew D. Ingber, Andrew J. Pincus, Michael B. Kimberly, and Colleen M. Campbell.

Brief of amici curiae filed on behalf of Foundations and Philanthropy-Serving Organizations by Edward A. Friedman, Bruce S. Kaplan, Anne E. Beaumont, and John N. Orsini.

Brief of amici curiae filed on behalf of Former Federal District Judges by Derek T. Ho and T. Dietrich Hill.

Brief of amici curiae filed on behalf of National Asian Pacific American Bar Association et al. by Albert Giang, Ziwei Hu, Miguel A. Gradilla, Navdeep Singh, Meredith Higashi, Rachana Pathak, Jerry Vattamala, and Patricia Yan.

Brief of amici curiae filed on behalf of International Municipal Lawyers Association (IMLA) et al. by Amanda Kellar, Elizabeth Kellar, and John J. Korzen.

Brief of amici curiae filed on behalf of County of Santa Clara et al. by Michael N. Feuer, Los Angeles City Attorney, James P. Clark, Kathleen Kenealy, Valerie Flores, Michael Dundas, James R. Williams, Santa Clara County Counsel, Greta S. Hansen, Danielle L. Goldstein, Raphael N. Rajendra, Andre M. Davis, Baltimore City Solicitor, Charles Parkin, Long Beach City Attorney, Michael J. Mais, Barbara J. Parker, Oakland City Attorney, Maria Bee, Erin Bernstein, Malia McPherson, Susana Alcala Wood, Sacramento City Attorney, Dan Satterberg, King County Prosecuting Attorney, H. Kevin Wright, Laurie Webb Daniel, Charles L. Coleman III, David I. Holtzman, John C. Beiers, San Mateo County Counsel, John D. Nibbelin, Sue Ann Salmon Evans, Keith A. Yeomans, and Dannis Woliver Kelley.

Brief of amici curiae filed on behalf of Central Valley Immigrant Integration Collaborative et al. by Nicholas Espiritu and Joanna Elise Cuevas Ingram.

Brief of amici curiae filed on behalf of Legal Services NYC et al. by Gideon A. Schor, Chul Pak, Adam Burrowbridge, Paul Harper, and Tasha Thomas.

Brief of amici curiae filed on behalf of John R. Dunne et al. by Samuel R. Bagenstos and Justin Levitt.

Brief of amici curiae filed on behalf of Common Cause et al. by Suzanne Almeida, Gregory L. Diskant, Aron Fischer, Benjamin F. Jackson, and Jacob Newman.

Brief of amici curiae filed on behalf of Historians and Social Scientists Margo Anderson et al. by Daniel E. Alperstein, Brian A. Sutherland, Adam D. Brownrout, and Emily F. Lynch.

Brief of amici curiae filed on behalf of the City of San Jose et al. by John F. Libby, Barry S. Landsberg, Ronald B. Turovsky, Andrew C. Case, Ana G. Guardado, Kristen Clarke, Jon M. Greenbaum, Ezra D. Rosenberg, and Dorian L. Spence.

Brief of amici curiae filed on behalf of Nicholas Bagley et al. by Roberta A. Kaplan, Julie E. Fink, Joshua Matz, and Matthew J. Craig.

Brief of amici curiae filed on behalf of National Council of Nonprofits et al. by Tim Delaney and Tiffany Gourley Carter.

Brief of amici curiae filed on behalf of the California Legislature by Robin B. Johansen.

Brief of amici curiae filed on behalf of LatinoJustice PRLDEF et al. by Juan Cartagena, Jorge L. Vasquez, Esperanza Segarra, Donald E. Frechette, Alexandra J. Cavaliere, Ernesto R. Palomo, Hugh S. Balsam, Wasim K. Bleibel, and Gregory T. Noorigian.

Opposing Side (Petitioner / Appellant)

Brief of amici curiae filed on behalf of Ronald A. Cass et al. by Mr. Cass.

Brief of amici curiae filed on behalf of the State of Oklahoma et al. by Mike Hunter, Attorney General of Oklahoma, Mithun Mansinghani, Solicitor General, Matt Bevin, Governor of Kentucky, Phil Bryant, Governor of Mississippi, and by the Attorneys General for their respective States as follows: Steve Marshall of Alabama, Leslie Rutledge of Arkansas, Ashley Moody of Florida, Chris Carr of Georgia, Curtis T. Hill, Jr., of Indiana, Derek Schmidt of Kansas, Jeff Landry of Louisiana, Eric S. Schmitt of Missouri, Tim Fox of Montana, Doug Peterson of Nebraska, Alan Wilson of South Carolina, Jason R. Ravnsborg of South Dakota, Ken Paxton of Texas, and Patrick Morrisey of West Virginia.

Brief of amici curiae filed on behalf of Project on Fair Representation by William S. Consovoy and Bryan K. Weir.

Brief of amici curiae filed on behalf of Eagle Forum Education & Legal Defense Fund by Lawrence J. Joseph.

Brief of amici curiae filed on behalf of the Public Interest Legal Foundation by J. Christian Adams and Kaylan Phillips.

Brief of amici curiae filed on behalf of the Republican National Committee et al. by Jason Torchinsky, Dennis W. Polio, P. Christopher Winkelman, and J. Justin Riemer.

Brief of amici curiae filed on behalf of Citizens United et al. by Joseph W. Miller, William J. Olson, Herbert W. Titus, Jeremiah L. Morgan, and Robert J. Olson.

Brief of amici curiae filed on behalf of Judicial Watch, Inc., et al. by Robert D. Popper and Eric W. Lee.

Brief of amici curiae filed on behalf of Immigration Reform Law Institute by Christopher J. Hajec and Mark S. Venezia.

Brief of amici curiae filed on behalf of the Becket Fund for

Religious Liberty by Kayla A. Toney, Eric S. Baxter, and Joseph C. Davis in support of neither party.

IV. THE SUPREME COURT'S DECISION

"The Enumeration Clause of the Constitution does not provide a basis to set aside the Secretary's decision. . . .

In light of the early understanding of and long practice under the Enumeration Clause, we conclude that it permits Congress, and by extension the Secretary, to inquire about citizenship on the census questionnaire. . . .

We now consider the District Court's determination that the Secretary's decision must be set aside because it rested on a pretextual basis, which the Government conceded below would warrant a remand to the agency. . . .

Altogether, the evidence tells a story that does not match the explanation the Secretary gave for his decision. In the Secretary's telling, Commerce was simply acting on a routine data request from another agency. Yet the materials before us indicate that Commerce went to great lengths to elicit the request from DOJ (or any other willing agency). And unlike a typical case in which an agency may have both stated and unstated reasons for a decision, here the VRA enforcement rationale—the sole stated reason—seems to have been contrived.

We are presented, in other words, with an explanation for agency action that is incongruent with what the record reveals about the agency's priorities and decisionmaking process. It is rare to review a record as extensive as the one before us when evaluating informal agency action—and it should be. But having done so for the sufficient reasons we have explained, we cannot ignore the disconnect between the decision made and the explanation given. . . . If judicial review is to be more than an empty ritual, it must demand something better than the explanation offered for the action taken in this case.

In these unusual circumstances, the District Court was warranted in remanding to the agency, and we affirm that disposition. We do not hold that the agency decision here was substantively invalid. But agencies must pursue their goals reasonably. Reasoned decisionmaking under the Administrative Procedure Act calls for an explanation for agency action. What was provided here was more of a distraction. . . .

The judgment of the United States District Court for the Southern District of New York is affirmed in part and reversed in part, and the case is remanded . . . ."

V. JUSTICE VOTE

5 Pro ACLU Side vs. 4 Con Opposing Side

ACLU Side (Respondent / Appellee)

1. Roberts, J. – Wrote majority opinion
2. Kagan, E. – Joined Breyer's opinion
3. Breyer, S. – Wrote opinion concurring in part and dissenting in part
4. Ginsburg, R. – Joined Breyer's opinion
5. Sotomayor, S. – Joined Breyer's opinion

Opposing Side (Petitioner / Appellant)

1. Alito, S. – Wrote opinion concurring in part and dissenting in part
2. Thomas, C. – Wrote opinion concurring in part and dissenting in part
3. Gorsuch, N. – Joined Thomas' opinion
4. Kavanaugh, B. – Joined Thomas' opinion

VI. A WIN OR LOSS FOR THE ACLU?

The ACLU served as counsel for appellees urging affirmance; the Supreme Court affirmed in part and reversed in part the District Court's decision by a 5-4 vote, giving the ACLU an apparent win.[1]

1 The U.S. Suprme Court issued a fractured opinion on the various issues in the case, but the outcome was considered a victory for the ACLU side. The vote listed here represents the decision that the rationale for the census question appeared "contrived," Part V of the decision.

THE FIRST 100 YEARS OF THE

ACLU

A COMPENDIUM OF ADVOCACY BEFORE THE UNITED STATES SUPREME COURT

VOLUME 2 OF 3

1920—2020

CONCEIVED AND COMPILED BY
STEVEN C. MARKOFF

CASE SUMMARY EDITOR
JESSICA PIERUCCI

FOREWORD BY
ERWIN CHEMERINSKY

A GENUINE RARE BIRD BOOK

Rare Bird Books
6044 North Figueroa Street
Los Angeles, California 90042
rarebirdbooks.com

FIRST HARDCOVER EDITION

ISBN-13: 978-1-64428-510-7 [THREE-VOLUME SLIPCASE SET]
ISBN-13: 978-1-64428-511-4 [VOLUME ONE]
ISBN-13: 978-1-64428-512-1 [VOLUME TWO]
ISBN-13: 978-1-64428-513-8 [VOLUME THREE]

For more information, address:
Rare Bird Books Subsidiary Rights Department
6044 North Figueroa Street
Los Angeles, California 90042

Printed in China

10 9 8 7 6 5 4 3 2 1

Library of Congress Cataloging-in-Publication Data available upon request

Appendix C

ACLU/U.S. Supreme Court Case Summaries

continued from Volume I

423. County of Los Angeles v. Davis

(Decided March 27, 1979; 440 U.S. 625)

I. ISSUE

A. Issues Discussed

Civil rights, race, employment discrimination, Fourteenth Amendment

B. Legal Question Presented

"[W]hether the use of arbitrary employment criteria, racially exclusionary in operation, but not purposefully discriminatory, violates 42 U.S.C. § 1981 and, if so, whether the imposition of minimum hiring quotas for fully qualified minority applicants is an appropriate remedy in this employment discrimination case."

C. Supreme Court's Answer

This controversy has become moot and the judgment below must be vacated.

II. CASE SUMMARY

A. Background

"In 1969, persons seeking employment with the Los Angeles County Fire Department were required to take a written civil service examination and a physical-agility test. Applicants were ranked according to their performance on the two tests and selected for job interviews on the basis of their scores. Those who passed their oral interviews were then placed on a hiring-eligibility list. Because blacks and Hispanics did poorly on the written examination, this method of screening job applicants proved to have a disparate impact on minority hiring.

The County of Los Angeles has not used the written civil service examination as a ranking device since 1969. The county desisted, prior to the commencement of this litigation, because it felt that the test had a disparate adverse impact on minority hiring, because it feared that this impact might violate Title VII of the Civil Rights Act of 1964, . . . and because it wished, in any event, to increase minority representation in the Fire Department.

In 1971, the county replaced the 1969 procedure with a new method of screening job applicants. A new written test was designed expressly to eliminate cultural bias. The test was to be given and graded on a pass-fail basis for the sole purpose of screening out illiterates. Five hundred of the passing applicants were to be selected at random for oral interviews and physical-agility tests. Passing applicants were to be ranked solely on the basis of the results of the physical-agility test and the oral interview.

An examination was conducted, pursuant to this plan, in January 1972. Ninety-seven percent of the applicants passed the written test. There was no disparate adverse impact on minorities and this use of the written examination has not been challenged in this litigation.

After administration of the written test, but before the random selection could be made, an action was filed in state court against the county charging that the random-selection process violated provisions of the county charter and civil service regulations. The county was enjoined from using the random-selection method pending trial on the merits.

For a time the hiring process came to a halt. The eligibility list drawn from the 1969 examination had been exhausted. The county was unable to devise a nonrandom method of screening job applicants and the county lacked the resources to interview all of the applicants who had passed the 1972 examination.

As a consequence of this unintended hiring freeze, vacancies in the County Fire Department increased and the manpower needs of the Department became critical. Finally, to break the logjam, the County Department of Personnel proposed to interview those applicants who had received the top 544 scores on the 1972 written test. Of this number, 492 were white, 10 black, and 33 Mexican-American. The applicants were not to be ranked on the basis of the test results, however, and the interviews were not intended to eliminate the remaining applicants from consideration. The purpose was solely to expedite the hiring of sufficient firefighters to meet the immediate urgent requirements of the Fire Department. But when minority representatives objected to the plan, it was abandoned, uneffectuated, prior to the commencement of this litigation.

In January 1973, respondents, representing present and future black and Mexican-American applicants to the Fire Department, brought a class action against the County of Los Angeles, the Board of Supervisors of the County of Los Angeles, and the Civil Service Commission of the County of Los Angeles (petitioners). Respondents charged that petitioners' 1969 hiring procedures violated 42 U.S.C. § 1981. Respondents also charged that petitioners' plan to interview those applicants who had received the top 544 scores on the 1972 written test violated 42 U.S.C. § 1981.

The District Court found that petitioners had acted without discriminatory intent. Nonetheless, the District Court held that because the 1969 and 1972 written examinations had not been validated as predictive of job performance, petitioners' employment practices had violated 42 U.S.C. § 1981. The court permanently enjoined all future discrimination and mandated good-faith affirmative-action efforts. The court also entered a remedial hiring order whereby at least 20% of all new firefighter recruits were required to be black and another 20% were required to be Mexican-American until the percentage of blacks and Mexican-Americans in the Los Angeles County Fire Department was commensurate with their percentage in Los Angeles County.

The Court of Appeals reversed the District Court with respect to the 1969 examination: The Court of Appeals held that respondents did not have standing to seek relief on account of the 1969 civil service examination because the plaintiff class, as certified by the District Court, consisted only of present and future job applicants and did not include any persons who had in any way been affected by the 1969 test. The Court of Appeals affirmed, however, the District Court's holding with respect to the 1972 proposal to use an unvalidated civil service examination."

The Supreme Court granted certiorari to review the case, vacated, and remanded.

B. Counsel of Record / ACLU Attorney

ACLU Side (Respondent / Appellee): A. Thomas Hunt argued the cause for appellee.

Opposing Side (Petitioner / Appellant): William F. Stewart argued the cause for appellant.

III. AMICI CURIAE

ACLU Side (Respondent / Appellee)

Brief of amici curiae filed on behalf of the ACLU, et al., by Bruce J. Ennis, Burt Neuborne, E. Richard Larson, Fred Okrand, and Paul Hoffman.

Additional briefs of amicus curiae were filed on behalf of the Lawyers' Committee for Civil Rights Under Law, the NAACP Legal Defense and Educational Fund, Inc., and Incorporated Mexican American Government Employees, et al.

Opposing Side (Petitioner / Appellant)

Briefs of amici curiae were filed on behalf of the City and County of San Francisco, the California Organization of Police and Sheriffs, the Equal Employment Advisory Council, the Anti-Defamation League of B'nai B'rith, and the Pacific Legal Foundation.

IV. THE SUPREME COURT'S DECISION

"The only question remaining in this case, then, concerns petitioners' 1972 plan to interview the top 544 scorers on the 1972 written examination in order to fill temporary emergency manpower needs. We find that this controversy became moot during the pendency of this litigation.

'Simply stated, a case is moot when the issues presented are no longer 'live' or the parties lack a legally cognizable interest in the outcome.' [J]urisdiction, properly acquired, may abate if the case becomes moot because (1) it can be said with assurance that 'there is no reasonable expectation . . .' that the alleged violation will recur, and (2) interim relief or events have completely and irrevocably eradicated the effects of the alleged violation. When both conditions are satisfied it may be said that the case is moot because neither party has a legally cognizable interest in the final determination of the underlying questions of fact and law.

The burden of demonstrating mootness 'is a heavy one.' Nevertheless, that burden is fully met on this record.

The first condition is met because there can be no reasonable expectation that petitioners will use an unvalidated civil service examination for the purposes contemplated in 1972. . . . Petitioners considered employing such a procedure in 1972 only because of a temporary emergency shortage of firefighters and only because petitioners then had no alternative means of screening job applicants. Those conditions were unique, are no longer present, and are unlikely to recur because, since the commencement of this litigation, petitioners have succeeded in instituting an efficient and nonrandom method of screening job applicants and increasing minority representation in the Fire Department. . . .

There has been no suggestion by any of the parties, nor is there any reason to believe, that petitioners would significantly alter their present hiring practices if the injunction were dissolved. . . . Under these circumstances we believe that this aspect of the case has 'lost its character as a present, live controversy of the kind that must exist if [the Court is] to avoid advisory opinions on abstract propositions of law.'

The second condition of mootness is met because petitioners' compliance during the five years since 1973 with the District Court's decree and their hiring of over 50% of new recruits from minorities has completely cured any discriminatory effects of the 1972 proposal. Indeed, it is extremely doubtful, from this record, that the 1972 proposal had any discriminatory effects to redress. The plan . . . was never carried out. [T]here has been no finding that any minority job applicant was excluded from employment as a result of the proposal. . . .

All of these circumstances, taken together, persuade us that, whatever might have been the case at the time of trial, the controversy has become moot during the pendency of this litigation. Accordingly, we vacate the judgment of the Court of Appeals and remand to that court for entry of an appropriate order directing the District Court to dismiss the action as moot."

V. JUSTICE VOTE

4 Pro ACLU Side vs. 5 Con Opposing Side

ACLU Side (Respondent / Appellee)

1. Stewart, P. – Wrote dissenting opinion
2. Rehnquist, W. – Joined Stewart's dissent
3. Powell, L. – Wrote dissenting opinion
4. Burger, W. – Joined Powell's dissent

Opposing Side (Petitioner / Appellant)

1. Brennan, W. – Wrote majority opinion
2. White, B. – Joined majority opinion
3. Marshall, T. – Joined majority opinion
4. Blackmun, H. – Joined majority opinion
5. Stevens, J. – Joined majority opinion

VI. A WIN OR LOSS FOR THE ACLU?

The ACLU filed as amicus curiae urging affirmance; the Supreme Court vacated the judgment of the Court of Appeals for the Ninth Circuit in a 5-4 vote, giving the ACLU an apparent loss.

424. Delaware v. Prouse

(Decided March 27, 1979; 440 U.S. 648)

I. ISSUE

A. Issues Discussed

4th Amendment

B. Legal Question Presented

"[W]hether it is an unreasonable seizure under the Fourth and Fourteenth Amendments to stop an automobile, being driven on a public highway, for the purpose of checking the driving license of the operator and the registration of the car, where there is neither probable cause to believe nor reasonable suspicion that the car is being driven contrary to the laws governing the operation of motor vehicles or that either the car or any of its occupants is subject to seizure or detention in connection with the violation of any other applicable law."

C. Supreme Court's Answer

"[W]e hold that except in those situations in which there is at least articulable and reasonable suspicion that a motorist is unlicensed or that an automobile is not registered, or that either the vehicle or an occupant is otherwise subject to seizure for violation of law, stopping an automobile and detaining the driver in order to check his driver's license and the registration of the automobile are unreasonable under the Fourth Amendment."

II. CASE SUMMARY

A. Background

"At 7:20 p. m. on November 30, 1976, a New Castle County, Del., patrolman in a police cruiser stopped the automobile occupied by respondent. The patrolman smelled marihuana smoke as he was walking toward the stopped vehicle, and he seized marihuana in plain view on the car floor. Respondent was subsequently indicted for illegal possession of a controlled substance. At a hearing on respondent's motion to suppress the marihuana seized as a result of the stop, the patrolman testified that prior to stopping the vehicle he had observed neither traffic or equipment violations nor any suspicious activity, and that he made the stop only in order to check the driver's license and registration. The patrolman was not acting pursuant to any standards, guidelines, or procedures pertaining to document spot checks, promulgated by either his department or the State Attorney General. Characterizing the stop as 'routine,' the patrolman explained, 'I saw the car in the area and wasn't answering any complaints, so I decided to pull them off.' The trial court granted the motion to suppress, finding the stop and detention to have been wholly capricious and therefore violative of the Fourth Amendment.

The Delaware Supreme Court affirmed, noting first that '[t]he issue of the legal validity of systematic, roadblock-type stops of a number of vehicles for license and vehicle registration check is *not* now before the Court.' The court held that 'a random stop of a motorist in the absence of specific articulable facts which justify the stop by indicating a reasonable suspicion that a violation of the law has occurred is constitutionally impermissible and violative of the Fourth and Fourteenth Amendments to the United States Constitution.' [The U.S. Supreme Court] granted certiorari" to review the case.

B. Counsel of Record

ACLU Side (Respondent / Appellee): David M. Lukoff argued the cause for appellee. With him on the brief were Charles S. Sims of the American Civil Liberties Union Foundation, and Richard E. Fairbanks, Jr., Richard M. Baumeister, Lawrence M. Sullivan, Frank Askin, and Eric Neisser.

Opposing Side (Petitioner / Appellant): Charles M. Oberly III argued the cause for appellant. With him on the brief were Richard R. Wier, Jr., Attorney General of Delaware, and Carolyn Berger, Fred S. Silverman, and Kathleen Molyneux, Deputy Attorneys General.

III. AMICI CURIAE

ACLU Side (Respondent / Appellee)

No briefs of amici curiae were filed in support of appellee.

Opposing Side (Petitioner / Appellant)

Brief of amici curiae filed on behalf of Americans for Effective Law Enforcement, Inc., et al. by Frank Carrington, Wayne W. Schmidt, Glen R. Murphy, and James P. Costello.

IV. THE SUPREME COURT'S DECISION

"The Fourth and Fourteenth Amendments are implicated in this case because stopping an automobile and detaining its occupants constitute a 'seizure' within the meaning of those Amendments .... Thus, the permissibility of a particular law enforcement practice is judged by balancing its intrusion on the individual's Fourth Amendment interests against its promotion of legitimate governmental interests....

Given the alternative mechanisms available, both those in use and those that might be adopted, we are unconvinced that the incremental contribution to highway safety of the random spot check justifies the practice under the Fourth Amendment....

The marginal contribution to roadway safety possibly resulting from a system of spot checks cannot justify subjecting every occupant of every vehicle on the roads to a seizure—limited in magnitude compared to other intrusions but nonetheless constitutionally cognizable—at the unbridled discretion of law enforcement officials.... This kind of standardless and unconstrained discretion is the evil the Court has discerned when in previous cases it has insisted that the discretion of the official in the field be circumscribed, at least to some extent....

An individual operating or traveling in an automobile does not lose all reasonable expectation of privacy simply because the automobile and its use are subject to government regulation.... Were the individual subject to unfettered governmental intrusion every time he entered an automobile, the security guaranteed by the Fourth Amendment would be seriously circumscribed....

Accordingly, we hold that except in those situations in which there is at least articulable and reasonable suspicion that a motorist is unlicensed or that an automobile is not registered, or that either the vehicle or an occupant is otherwise subject to seizure for violation of law, stopping an automobile and detaining the driver in order to check his driver's license and the registration of the automobile are unreasonable under the Fourth Amendment. This holding does not preclude the State of Delaware or other States from developing methods for spot checks that involve less intrusion or that do not involve the unconstrained exercise of discretion. Questioning of all oncoming traffic at roadblock-type stops is one possible alternative. We hold only that persons in automobiles on public roadways may not for that reason alone have their travel and privacy interfered with at the unbridled discretion of police officers. The judgment below is affirmed."

V. JUSTICE VOTE

8 Pro ACLU Side vs. 1 Con Opposing Side

ACLU Side (Respondent / Appellee)

1. White, B. – Wrote majority opinion
2. Brennan, W. – Joined majority opinion
3. Marshall, T. – Joined majority opinion
4. Stewart, P. – Joined majority opinion
5. Powell, L. – Joined Blackmun's concurrence
6. Burger, W. – Joined majority opinion
7. Blackmun, H. – Wrote concurring opinion
8. Stevens, J. – Joined majority opinion

Opposing Side (Petitioner / Appellant)

1. Rehnquist, W. – Wrote dissenting opinion

VI. A WIN OR LOSS FOR THE ACLU?

The ACLU served as counsel for appellee urging affirmance of the judgment of the Supreme Court of Delaware; the U.S. Supreme Court affirmed, in an 8-1 vote, giving the ACLU an apparent win.

425. FCC v. Midwest Video Corp.

(Decided April 2, 1979; 440 U.S. 689)

I. ISSUE

A. Issues Discussed

Governmental authority, regulation, First Amendment

B. Legal Question Presented

"[W]hether [the challenged FCC] rules are 'reasonably ancillary to the effective performance of the Commission's various responsibilities for the regulation of television broadcasting,' and hence within the Commission's statutory authority."

C. Supreme Court's Answer

The challenged FCC rules are not within the FCC's statutory authority.

II. CASE SUMMARY

A. Background

"In May 1976, the Federal Communications Commission promulgated rules requiring cable television systems that have 3,500 or more subscribers and carry broadcast signals to develop, at a minimum, a 20-channel capacity by 1986, to make available certain channels for access by third parties, and to furnish equipment and facilities for access purposes. . . . Under the rules, cable operators are deprived of all discretion regarding who may exploit their access channels and what may be transmitted over such channels. System operators are specifically enjoined from exercising any control over the content of access programming except that they must adopt rules proscribing the transmission on most access channels of lottery information and commercial matter. . . . Finally, the rules circumscribe what operators may charge for privileges of access and use of facilities and equipment. . . .

The Commission's capacity and access rules were challenged on jurisdictional grounds in the course of the rulemaking proceedings. In its 1976 Order, the Commission rejected such comments on the ground that the regulations further objectives that it might properly pursue in its supervision over broadcasting. Specifically, the Commission maintained that its rules would promote 'the achievement of longstanding communications regulatory objectives by increasing outlets for local self-expression and augmenting the public's choice of programs.' . . .

On petition for review, the Eighth Circuit set aside the Commission's access, channel capacity, and facilities rules as beyond the agency's jurisdiction. The Court was of the view that the regulations were not reasonably ancillary to the Commission's jurisdiction over broadcasting, a jurisdictional condition established by past decisions of [the Supreme] Court. The rules amounted to an attempt to impose common-carrier obligations on cable operators, the Court said, and thus ran counter to the statutory command that broadcasters themselves may not be treated as common carriers. Furthermore, the Court made plain its belief that the regulations presented grave First Amendment problems."

The Supreme Court granted certiorari to review the case and affirmed.

B. Counsel of Record / ACLU Attorney

ACLU Side (Petitioner / Appellant): Deputy Solicitor General Lawrence C. Wallace argued the cause for appellant FCC in No. 77-1575 and in support of appellants in Nos. 77-1648 and 77-1662 under the Court's Rule 21(4). With him on the briefs were Solicitor General Wade H. McCree, Jr., Richard A. Allen, David J. Saylor, Daniel M. Armstrong, Keith H. Fagan, and Julian R. Rush, Jr.

Burt Neuborne, Bruce J. Ennis, Michael Botein, and David M. Rice filed a brief for appellant ACLU in No. 77-1648.

Edward J. Kuhlmann, Jeffrey H. Olson, and Charles M. Firestone filed a brief for appellants National Black Media Coalition, et al., in No. 77-1662.

Opposing Side (Respondent / Appellee): George H. Shapiro argued the cause for appellee Midwest Video Corp. in all cases. With him on the briefs were Harry M. Plotkin and Alan Auckenthaler.

III. AMICI CURIAE

ACLU Side (Petitioner / Appellant)

Brief of amici curiae filed on behalf of the Motion Picture Association of America by James Bouras, Fritz E. Attaway, Arthur Scheiner, and Stuart F. Feldstein.

Opposing Side (Respondent / Appellee)

Brief of amici curiae filed on behalf of the Teleprompter Corp., et al., by Lee Loevinger and Jay E. Ricks.

IV. THE SUPREME COURT'S DECISION

"The Commission derives its regulatory authority from the Communications Act of 1934 . . . . The Act preceded the advent of cable television and understandably does not expressly provide for the regulation of that medium. But it is clear that Congress meant to confer 'broad authority' on the Commission, so as 'to maintain, through appropriate administrative control, a grip on the dynamic aspects of radio transmission.' To that end, Congress subjected to regulation 'all interstate and foreign communication by wire or radio.' . . .

We agree with respondents that recognition of agency jurisdiction to promulgate the access rules would require an extension of this Court's prior decisions. Our holding in Midwest Video sustained the Commission's authority to regulate cable television with a purpose affirmatively to promote goals pursued in the regulation of television broadcasting; and the plurality's analysis of the origination requirement stressed the requirement's nexus to such goals. But the origination rule did not abrogate the cable operators' control over the composition of their programming, as do the access rules. It compelled operators only to assume a more positive role in that regard, one comparable to that fulfilled by television broadcasters. Cable operators had become enmeshed in the field of television broadcasting, and, by requiring them to engage in the functional equivalent of broadcasting, the Commission had sought 'only to ensure that they satisfactorily met community needs within the context of their undertaking.' . . .

The language of § 3(h) is unequivocal; it stipulates that broadcasters shall not be treated as common carriers. As we see it, § 3(h), consistently with the policy of the Act to preserve editorial control of programming in the licensee, forecloses any discretion in the Commission to impose access requirements amounting to common-carrier obligations on broadcast systems. The provision's background manifests a congressional belief that the intrusion worked by such regulation on the journalistic integrity of broadcasters would overshadow any benefits associated with the resulting public access. It is difficult to deny, then, that forcing broadcasters to develop a 'nondiscriminatory system for controlling access . . . is precisely what Congress intended to avoid through § 3(h) of the Act.' . . .

That limitation is not one having peculiar applicability to television broadcasting. Its force is not diminished by the variant technology involved in cable transmissions. Cable operators now share with broadcasters a significant amount of editorial discretion regarding what their programming will include. As the Commission, itself, has observed, 'both in their signal carriage decisions and in connection with their origination function, cable television systems are afforded considerable control over the content of the programming they provide.' . . .

The exercise of jurisdiction in Midwest Video, it has been said, 'strain[ed] the outer limits' of Commission authority. In light of the hesitancy with which Congress approached the access issue in the broadcast area, and in view of its outright rejection of a broad right of public access on a common-carrier basis, we are constrained to hold that the Commission exceeded those limits in promulgating its access rules. The Commission may not regulate cable systems as common carriers, just as it may not impose such obligations on television broadcasters. We think authority to compel cable operators to provide common carriage of public-originated transmissions must come specifically from Congress."

The Supreme Court affirmed the judgment of the Court of Appeals for the Eighth Circuit.

V. JUSTICE VOTE

3 Pro ACLU Side vs. 6 Con Opposing Side

ACLU Side (Petitioner / Appellant)

1. Stevens, J. – Wrote dissenting opinion
2. Brennan, W. – Joined dissenting opinion
3. Marshall, T. – Joined dissenting opinion

Opposing Side (Respondent / Appellee)

1. White, B. – Wrote majority opinion
2. Burger, W. – Joined majority opinion
3. Stewart, P. – Joined majority opinion
4. Blackmun, H. – Joined majority opinion
5. Powell, L. – Joined majority opinion
6. Rehnquist, W. – Joined majority opinion

VI. A WIN OR LOSS FOR THE ACLU?

The ACLU filed as petitioner, and the ACLU case was one of the cases combined in this decision, urging reversal; the Supreme Court affirmed the ruling of the Court of Appeals for the Eighth Circuit in a 6-3 vote, giving the ACLU an apparent loss.

426. Burch v. Louisiana

(Decided April 17, 1979; 441 U.S. 130)

I. ISSUE

A. Issues Discussed

Criminal procedure, Sixth Amendment, Fourteenth Amendment

B. Legal Question Presented

"[W]hether conviction by a nonunanimous six-person jury in a state criminal trial for a nonpetty offense as contemplated by . . . Louisiana law violates the rights of an accused to trial by jury guaranteed by the Sixth and Fourteenth Amendments."

C. Supreme Court's Answer

A nonunanimous criminal conviction by a six-person jury for a nonpetty offense violates the right to a trial by jury.

II. CASE SUMMARY

A. Background

"Petitioners, an individual and a Louisiana corporation, were jointly charged in two counts with the exhibition of two obscene motion pictures. Pursuant to Louisiana law, they were tried before a six-person jury, which found both petitioners guilty as charged. A poll of the jury after verdict indicated that the jury had voted unanimously to convict petitioner Wrestle, Inc., and had voted 5-1 to convict petitioner Burch. Burch was sentenced to two consecutive 7-month prison terms, which were suspended, and fined $1,000; Wrestle, Inc., was fined $600 on each count.

Petitioners appealed their convictions to the Supreme Court of Louisiana, where they argued that the provisions of Louisiana law permitting conviction by a nonunanimous six-member jury violated the rights of persons accused of nonpetty criminal offenses to trial by jury guaranteed by the Sixth and Fourteenth Amendments. Though acknowledging that the issue was 'close,' the court held that conviction by a nonunanimous six-person jury did not offend the Constitution. The court concluded that none of this Court's decisions precluded use of a nonunanimous six-person jury. . . .

Since the Louisiana Supreme Court believed that conviction by a nonunanimous six-person jury was not necessarily foreclosed by this Court's decisions, it stated that it preferred to 'indulg[e] in the presumption of federal constitutionality which must be afforded to provisions of our state constitution.'"

The Supreme Court granted certiorari to review the case, affirmed in part, and reversed in part.

B. Counsel of Record / ACLU Attorney

ACLU Side (Petitioner / Appellant): Jack Peebles argued the cause for appellant.

Opposing Side (Respondent / Appellee): Louise Korns argued the cause for appellee.

III. AMICI CURIAE

ACLU Side (Petitioner / Appellant)

Brief of amici curiae filed on behalf of the ACLU, et al., by Leon Friedman and Bruce J. Ennis.

Opposing Side (Respondent / Appellee)

No briefs of amici curiae were filed in support of appellee.

IV. THE SUPREME COURT'S DECISION

"We believe that conviction by a nonunanimous six-member jury in a state criminal trial for a nonpetty offense deprives an accused of his constitutional right to trial by jury. [B]ecause trial by jury in 'serious' criminal cases is 'fundamental to the American scheme of justice' and essential to due process of law, the Fourteenth Amendment guarantees a state criminal defendant the right to a jury trial in any case which, if tried in a federal court, would require a jury under the Sixth Amendment.

[T]he Williams Court observed that the jury's essential feature lies in the 'interposition between the accused and his accuser of the commonsense judgment of a group of laymen, and in the community participation and shared responsibility that results from that group's determination of guilt or innocence.' These purposes could be fulfilled, the Court believed, so long as the jury was of a sufficient size to promote group deliberation, free from outside intimidation, and to provide a fair possibility that a cross section of the community would be represented on it. [T]here is 'little reason to think that these goals are in any meaningful sense less likely to be achieved when the jury numbers six, than when it numbers 12—particularly if the requirement of unanimity is retained.' (emphasis added).

[I]n Ballew v. Georgia, we considered whether a jury of less than six members passes constitutional scrutiny . . . . The Court, in separate opinions, held that conviction by a unanimous five-person jury in a trial for a nonpetty offense deprives an accused of his right to trial by jury. While readily admitting that the line between six members and five was not altogether easy to justify, at least five Members of the Court believed that reducing a jury to five persons in nonpetty cases raised sufficiently substantial doubts as to the fairness of the proceeding and proper functioning of the jury to warrant drawing the line at six.

We thus have held that the Constitution permits juries of less than 12 members, but that it requires at least 6. And we have approved the use of certain nonunanimous verdicts in cases involving 12-person juries. [T]his case lies at the intersection of our decisions concerning jury size and unanimity. . . . But having already departed from the strictly historical requirements of jury trial, it is inevitable that lines must be drawn somewhere if the substance of the jury trial right is to be preserved. . . .

However, much the same reasons that led us in Ballew to decide that use of a five-member jury threatened the fairness of the proceeding and the proper role of the jury, lead us to conclude now that conviction for a nonpetty offense by only five members of a six-person jury presents a similar threat to preservation of the substance of the jury trial guarantee and justifies our requiring verdicts rendered by six-person juries to be unanimous.

[O]n this record, any benefits that might accrue by allowing five members of a six-person jury to render a verdict, as compared with requiring unanimity of a six-member jury, are speculative, at best. More importantly, we think that when a State has reduced the size of its juries to the minimum number of jurors permitted by the Constitution, the additional authorization of nonunanimous verdicts by such juries sufficiently threatens the constitutional principles that led to the establishment of the size threshold that any countervailing interest of the State should yield.

The judgment of the Louisiana Supreme Court affirming the conviction of petitioner Burch is, therefore, reversed, and its judgment affirming the conviction of petitioner Wrestle, Inc., is affirmed. The case is remanded to the Louisiana Supreme Court for proceedings not inconsistent with this opinion."

V. JUSTICE VOTE

9 Pro ACLU Side vs. 0 Con Opposing Side

ACLU Side (Petitioner / Appellant)

1. Rehnquist, W. – Wrote majority opinion
2. Burger, W. – Joined majority opinion
3. White, B. – Joined majority opinion
4. Blackmun, H. – Joined majority opinion
5. Powell, L. – Joined majority opinion
6. Stevens, J. – Wrote concurring opinion
7. Stewart, P. – Joined Brennan's opinion
8. Brennan, W. – Wrote opinion concurring in part and dissenting in part
9. Marshall, T. – Joined Brennan's opinion

VI. A WIN OR LOSS FOR THE ACLU?

The ACLU filed as amicus curiae urging reversal of petitioner Burch's conviction; the Supreme Court reversed Burch's conviction and affirmed Wrestle, Inc.'s in a 9-0 vote, giving the ACLU an apparent win.

427. Caban v. Mohammed

(Decided April 24, 1979; 441 U.S. 380)

I. ISSUE

A. Issues Discussed

Civil rights, gender, Fourteenth Amendment, equal protection

B. Legal Question Presented

Does §111 of the New York Domestic Relations Law unconstitutionally discriminate against unmarried fathers in violation of the Equal Protection Clause of the Fourteenth Amendment?

C. Supreme Court's Answer

The law unconstitutionally discriminates against unmarried fathers in violation of the Equal Protection Clause of the Fourteenth Amendment.

II. CASE SUMMARY

A. Background

Appellant Abdiel Caban, and Appellee Marie Mohammed were the parents of two children, David and Denise, born out of wedlock. Appellant, who was identified as the father on the birth certificates, contributed to the children's support.

"In December 1973, Mohammed took the two children and left the appellant to take up residence with appellee Kazim Mohammed, whom she married on January 30, 1974. For the next nine months, she took David and Denise each weekend to visit her mother, Delores Gonzales, who lived one floor above Caban. Because of his friendship with Gonzales, Caban was able to see the children each week when they came to visit their grandmother.

In September 1974, Gonzales left New York to take up residence in her native Pureto Rico. At the Mohammeds' request, the grandmother took David and Denise with her. According to appellees, they planned to join the children in Puerto Rico as soon as they had saved enough money to start a business there. During the children's stay with their grandmother, Mrs. Mohammed kept in touch with David and Denise by mail; Caban communicated with the children through his parents, who also resided in Puerto Rico. In November 1975, he went to Puerto Rico, where Gonzales willingly surrendered the children to Caban with the understanding that they would be returned after a few days. Caban, however, returned to New York with the children. When Mrs. Mohammed learned that the children were in Caban's custody, she attempted to retrieve them with the aid of a police officer. After this attempt failed, the appellees instituted custody proceedings in the New York Family Court, which placed the children in the temporary custody of the Mohammeds and gave Caban and his new wife, Nina, visiting rights.

In January 1976, appellees filed a petition under § 110 of the New York Domestic Relations Law to adopt David and Denise. In March, the Cabans cross-petitioned for adoption. After the Family Court stayed the custody suit pending the outcome of the adoption proceedings, a hearing was held on the petition and cross petition before a Law Assistant to a New York Surrogate in Kings County, N.Y. At this hearing, both the Mohammeds and the Cabans were represented by counsel and were permitted to present and cross-examine witnesses.

The Surrogate granted the Mohammeds' petition to adopt the children, thereby cutting off all of appellant's parental rights and obligations. In his opinion, the Surrogate noted the limited right under New York law of unwed fathers in adoption proceedings: 'Although a putative Father's consent to such an adoption is not a legal necessity, he is entitled to an opportunity to be heard in opposition to the proposed stepfather adoption.' Moreover, the court stated that the appellant was foreclosed from adopting David and Denise, as the natural mother had withheld her consent. Thus, the court considered the evidence presented by the Cabans only insofar as it reflected upon the Mohammeds' qualifications as prospective parents. The Surrogate found them well qualified and granted their adoption petition.

The New York Supreme Court, Appellate Division, affirmed.... The New York Court of Appeals dismissed the appeal ...."

The Supreme Court granted certiorari to review the case and reversed.

B. Counsel of Record / ACLU Attorney

ACLU Side (Petitioner / Appellant): Robert H. Silk argued the cause for appellant.

Opposing Side (Respondent / Appellee): Morris Schulslaper argued the cause for appellee.

Irwin M. Strum, Assistant Attorney General of New York, argued the cause for the Attorney General of New York as amicus curiae, by special leave of court.

III. AMICI CURIAE

ACLU Side (Petitioner / Appellant)

Brief of amici curiae filed on behalf of the ACLU by Martin Guggenheim, Rena K. Uviller, and Bruce J. Ennis.

Brief of amici curiae filed on behalf of Community Action for Legal Services, Inc., by Louise Gruner Gans.

Brief of amici curiae filed on behalf of the Legal Aid Society of New York City by John E. Kirklin and Kalman Finkel.

Opposing Side (Respondent / Appellee)

Brief of amici curiae filed on behalf of the Attorney General of New York by Irwin M. Strum, Assistant Attorney General, Louis J. Lefkowitz, Attorney General, pro se, Samuel A. Hirshowitz, First Assistant Attorney General, and Warren M. Goidel and Neil S. Solon, Assistant Attorneys General.

IV. THE SUPREME COURT'S DECISION

"[T]he New York Court of Appeals has stated unequivocally that the question whether consent is required is entirely separate from that of the best interests of the child. Indeed, the Surrogate's decision in the present case, affirmed by the New York Court of Appeals, was based upon the assumption that there was a distinctive difference between the rights of Abdiel Caban, as the unwed father of David and Denise, and Maria Mohammed, as the unwed mother of the children: Adoption by Abdiel was held to be impermissible in the absence of Maria's consent, whereas adoption by Maria could be prevented by Abdiel only if he could show that the Mohammeds' adoption of the children would not be in the children's best interests. Accordingly, it is clear that § 111 treats unmarried parents differently according to their sex. . . .

Gender-based distinctions 'must serve important governmental objectives and must be substantially related to achievement of those objectives' in order to withstand judicial scrutiny under the Equal Protection Clause. The question before us, therefore, is whether the distinction in § 111 between unmarried mothers and unmarried fathers bears a substantial relation to some important state interest. . . .

In sum, we believe that § 111 is another example of 'overbroad generalizations' in gender-based classifications. The effect of New York's classification is to discriminate against unwed fathers even when their identity is known and they have manifested a significant paternal interest in the child. The facts of this case illustrate the harshness of classifying unwed fathers as being invariably less qualified and entitled than mothers to exercise a concerned judgment as to the fate of their children. Section 111 both excludes some loving fathers from full participation in the decision whether their children will be adopted and, at the same time, enables some alienated mothers arbitrarily to cut off the paternal rights of fathers. We conclude that this undifferentiated distinction between unwed mothers and unwed fathers, applicable in all circumstances where adoption of a child of theirs is at issue, does not bear a substantial relationship to the State's asserted interests.

The judgment of the New York Court of Appeals is reversed."

V. JUSTICE VOTE

5 Pro ACLU Side vs. 4 Con Opposing Side

ACLU Side (Petitioner / Appellant)

1. Powell, L. – Wrote majority opinion
2. Brennan, W. – Joined majority opinion
3. White, B. – Joined majority opinion
4. Marshall, T. – Joined majority opinion
5. Blackmun, H. – Joined majority opinion

Opposing Side (Respondent / Appellee)

1. Stewart, P. – Wrote dissenting opinion
2. Stevens, J. – Wrote dissenting opinion
3. Burger, W. – Joined Stevens' dissent
4. Rehnquist, W. – Joined Stevens' dissent

VI. A WIN OR LOSS FOR THE ACLU?

The ACLU filed as amicus curiae urging reversal; the Supreme Court reversed the ruling of the Court of Appeals of New York in a 5-4 vote, giving the ACLU an apparent win.

428. Bell v. Wolfish

(Decided May 14, 1979; 441 U.S. 520)

I. ISSUE

A. Issues Discussed

Criminal justice, prisons, Fifth Amendment, Fourth Amendment, First Amendment

B. Legal Question Presented

Does subjecting pretrial detainees to the conditions and restrictions at the Metropolitan Correctional Center violate the liberty, due process, and privacy of detainees as protected by the First, Fourth, and Fifth Amendments?

C. Supreme Court's Answer

The conditions and restrictions at the correctional facility do not violate the constitutional rights of pretrial detainees.

II. CASE SUMMARY

A. Background

"When the [Metropolitan Correctional Center (MCC)] opened in August 1975, the planned capacity was 449 inmates, an increase of 50% over the former West Street facility. Despite some dormitory accommodations, the MCC was designed primarily to house these inmates in 389 rooms, which originally were intended for single occupancy. While the MCC was under construction, however, the number of persons committed to pretrial detention began to rise at an 'unprecedented' rate. The Bureau of Prisons took several steps to accommodate this unexpected flow of persons assigned to the facility, but despite these efforts, the inmate population at the MCC rose above its planned capacity within a short time after its opening. To provide sleeping space for this increased population, the MCC replaced the single bunks in many of the individual rooms and dormitories with double bunks. Also, each week some newly arrived inmates had to sleep on cots in the common areas until they could be transferred to residential rooms as space became available.

On November 28, 1975, less than four months after the MCC had opened, the named respondents initiated this action by filing in the District Court a petition for a writ of habeas corpus. . . . The petition served up a veritable potpourri of complaints that implicated virtually every facet of the institution's conditions and practices. Respondents charged, inter alia, that they had been deprived of their statutory and constitutional rights because of overcrowded conditions, undue length of confinement, improper searches, inadequate recreational, educational, and employment opportunities, insufficient staff, and objectionable restrictions on the purchase and receipt of personal items and books."

"This lawsuit was brought as a class action in the United States District Court for the Southern District of New York to challenge numerous conditions of confinement and practices at the Metropolitan Correctional Center (MCC), a federally operated short-term custodial facility in New York City designed primarily to house pretrial detainees. The District Court, in the words of the Court of Appeals for the Second Circuit, 'intervened broadly into almost every facet of the institution' and enjoined no fewer than

20 MCC practices on constitutional and statutory grounds. The Court of Appeals largely affirmed the District Court's constitutional rulings and in the process held that under the Due Process Clause of the Fifth Amendment, pretrial detainees may 'be subjected to only those 'restrictions and privations' which 'inhere in their confinement itself or which are justified by compelling necessities of jail administration.'"

The Supreme Court granted certiorari to review the case and reversed.

B. Counsel of Record / ACLU Attorney

ACLU Side (Respondent / Appellee): Phylis Skloot Bamberger argued the cause for appellee.

Opposing Side (Petitioner / Appellant): Deputy Solicitor General Andrew L. Fey argued the cause for appellant.

III. AMICI CURIAE

ACLU Side (Respondent / Appellee)

Brief of amici curiae filed on behalf of the National Prison Project of the ACLU Foundation by Ralph I. Knowles, Jr., and Alvin J. Bronstein.

Brief of amici curiae filed on behalf of the NAACP Legal Defense and Educational Fund, Inc , by Jack Greenberg, James M. Nabrit, III, and Joel Berger.

Opposing Side (Petitioner / Appellant)

No briefs of amici curiae were filed in support of appellant.

IV. THE SUPREME COURT'S DECISION

"Our fundamental disagreement with the Court of Appeals is that we fail to find a source in the Constitution for its compelling-necessity standard. Both the Court of Appeals and the District Court seem to have relied on the 'presumption of innocence' as the source of the detainee's substantive right to be free from conditions of confinement that are not justified by compelling necessity. But the presumption of innocence provides no support for such a rule.

[W]hat is at issue when an aspect of pretrial detention that is not alleged to violate any express guarantee of the Constitution is challenged, is the detainee's right to be free from punishment, and his understandable desire to be as comfortable as possible during his confinement, both of which may conceivably coalesce at some point. It seems clear that the Court of Appeals did not rely on the detainee's right to be free from punishment, but even if it had that right does not warrant adoption of that court's compelling-necessity test. . . .

The rooms provide more than adequate space for sleeping. During the remainder of the time, the detainees are free to move between their rooms and the common area. While 'double-bunking' may have taxed some of the equipment or particular facilities in certain of the common areas, this does not mean that the conditions at the MCC failed to meet the standards required by the Constitution. Our conclusion in this regard is further buttressed by the detainees' length of stay at the MCC. Nearly all of the detainees are released within 60 days. We simply do not believe that requiring a detainee to share toilet facilities and this admittedly rather small sleeping place with another person for generally a maximum period of 60 days violates the Constitution. . . .

We conclude that a prohibition against receipt of hardback books unless mailed directly from publishers, book clubs, or bookstores does not violate the First Amendment rights of MCC inmates. That limited restriction is a rational response by prison officials to an obvious security problem. It hardly needs to be emphasized that hardback books are especially serviceable for smuggling contraband into an institution; money, drugs, and weapons easily may be secreted in the binding. . . . Our conclusion that this limited restriction on receipt of hardback books does not infringe the First Amendment rights of MCC inmates is influenced by several other factors. The rule operates in a neutral fashion, without regard to the content of the expression. . . . The restriction, as it is now before us, allows soft-bound books and magazines to be received from any source and hardback books to be received from publishers, bookstores, and book clubs. In addition, the MCC has a 'relatively large' library for use by inmates. . . .

Inmates at the MCC were not permitted to receive packages from outside the facility containing items of food or personal property, except for one package of food at Christmas. This rule was justified by MCC officials on three grounds. First, officials testified to 'serious' security problems that arise from the introduction of such packages into the institution, the 'traditional file in the cake kind of situation' as well as the concealment of drugs 'in heels of shoes and seams of clothing.' As in the case of the 'publisher-only' rule, the warden testified that if such packages were allowed, the inspection process necessary to ensure the security of the institution would require a 'substantial and inordinate amount of available staff time.' Second, officials were concerned that the introduction of personal property into the facility would increase the risk of thefts, gambling, and inmate conflicts, the 'age-old problem of you have it and I don't.' Finally, they noted storage and sanitary problems that would result from inmates' receipt of food packages. . . .

Inmates at all Bureau of Prisons facilities, including the MCC, are required to expose their body cavities for visual inspection as a part of a strip search conducted after every contact visit with a person from outside the institution. . . . Admittedly, this practice instinctively gives us the most pause. However, assuming for present purposes that inmates, both convicted prisoners and pretrial detainees, retain some Fourth Amendment rights upon commitment to a corrections facility, we nonetheless conclude that these searches do not violate that Amendment. The Fourth Amendment prohibits only unreasonable searches, and under the circumstances, we do not believe that these searches are unreasonable.

[W]e think that these particular restrictions and practices were reasonable responses by MCC officials to legitimate security concerns. Respondents simply have not met their heavy burden of showing that these officials have exaggerated their response to the genuine security considerations that actuated these restrictions and practices. And as might be expected of restrictions applicable to pretrial detainees, these restrictions were of only limited duration so far as the MCC pretrial detainees were concerned. . . .

The judgment of the Court of Appeals is, accordingly, reversed, and the case is remanded for proceedings consistent with this opinion."

V. JUSTICE VOTE

3 Pro ACLU Side vs. 6 Con Opposing Side

ACLU Side (Respondent / Appellee)

1. Marshall, T. – Wrote dissenting opinion
2. Stevens, J. – Wrote dissenting opinion
3. Brennan, W. – Joined Stevens' dissent

Opposing Side (Petitioner / Appellant)

1. Rehnquist, W. – Wrote majority opinion
2. Burger, W. – Joined majority opinion
3. Stewart, P. – Joined majority opinion
4. White, B. – Joined majority opinion
5. Blackmun, H. – Joined majority opinion
6. Powell, L. – Wrote opinion concurring in part and dissenting in part

VI. A WIN OR LOSS FOR THE ACLU?

The ACLU filed as amicus curiae urging affirmance; the Supreme Court reversed the ruling of the Court of Appeals for the Second Circuit in a 6-3 vote, giving the ACLU an apparent loss.

429. Greenholtz v. Inmates of the Nebraska Penal and Correctional Complex

(Decided May 29, 1979; 442 U.S. 1)

I. ISSUE

A. Issues Discussed

Criminal, justice, prisons, Fourteenth Amendment, due process

B. Legal Question Presented

"[W]hether the Due Process Clause of the Fourteenth Amendment applies to discretionary parole-release determinations made by the Nebraska Board of Parole, and, if so, whether the procedures the Board currently provides meet constitutional requirements."

C. Supreme Court's Answer

The procedures for parole comply with due process given that parole is discretionary and inmates were provided due process when deprived of their liberty and incarcerated.

II. CASE SUMMARY

A. Background

"Inmates of the Nebraska Penal and Correctional Complex brought a class action under 42 U.S.C. § 1983 claiming that they had been unconstitutionally denied parole by the Board of Parole. The suit was filed against the individual members of the Board. One of the claims of the inmates was that the statutes and the Board's procedures denied them procedural due process. . . .

The procedures used by the Board to determine whether to grant or deny discretionary parole arise partly from statutory provisions and partly from the Board's practices. Two types of hearings are conducted: initial parole review hearings and final parole hearings. At least once each year initial review hearings must be held for every inmate, regardless of parole eligibility. At the initial review hearing, the Board examines the inmate's entire preconfinement and postconfinement record. Following that examination it provides an informal hearing; no evidence as such is introduced, but the Board interviews the inmate and considers any letters or statements that he wishes to present in support of a claim for release.

If the Board determines . . . that he is not yet a good risk for release, it denies parole, informs the inmate why release was deferred and makes recommendations designed to help correct any deficiencies observed. It also schedules another initial review hearing to take place within one year. If the Board determines from the file and the initial review hearing that the inmate is a likely candidate for release, a final hearing is scheduled. The Board then notifies the inmate of the month in which the final hearing will be held; the exact day and time is posted on a bulletin board that is accessible to all inmates on the day of the hearing. At the final parole hearing, the inmate may present evidence, call witnesses and be represented by private counsel of his choice. It is not a traditional adversary hearing since the inmate is not permitted to hear adverse testimony or to cross-examine witnesses who present such evidence. However, a complete tape recording of the hearing is preserved. If parole is denied, the Board furnishes a written statement of the reasons for the denial within 30 days. . . .

The District Court held that the procedures used by the Parole Board did not satisfy due process. . . .

On appeal, the Court of Appeals for the Eighth Circuit agreed with the District Court that the inmate had a Morrissey type, conditional liberty interest at stake and also found a statutorily defined, protectible interest in Neb.Rev.Stat. § 83-1,114 (1976). The Court of Appeals, however, modified the procedures required by the District Court . . . ."

The procedures defined by the Court of Appeals conflicted with the decisions of other Courts of Appeals. The Supreme Court granted certiorari to resolve the conflict and reversed.

B. Counsel of Record / ACLU Attorney

ACLU Side (Respondent / Appellee): Brian K. Ridenour argued the cause for appellee.

Opposing Side (Petitioner / Appellant): Ralph H. Gillan, Assistant Attorney General of Nebraska, argued the cause for appellant.

William Alsup argued the cause for the United States, as amicus curiae, by special leave of Court.

III. AMICI CURIAE

ACLU Side (Respondent / Appellee)

Brief of amici curiae filed on behalf of the National Prison Project of the ACLU Foundation by Alvin J. Bronstein and Dean Hill Rivkin.

Brief of amici curiae filed on behalf of the Jerome N. Frank Legal Services Organization, et al., by Robert L. Weinberg, Scott Blake Harris, Pierce O'Donnell, Laurie D. Zelon, Judith Resnik, Dennis E. Curtis, and Peter Goldberger.

Opposing Side (Petitioner / Appellant)

Brief of amici curiae filed on behalf of the United States by Wade H. McCree, Jr. Solicitor General, Philip B. Heymann, Assistant Attorney General, Frank H. Easterbrook, Deputy Solicitor General, William G. Otis, and Andrew S. Gordon.

Brief of amici curiae filed on behalf of the State of California by Evelle J. Younger, Attorney General, Jack R. Winkler, Chief Assistant Attorney General – Criminal Division, Edward P. O'Brien, Assistant Attorney General, and John T. Murphy and Karl S. Mayer, Deputy Attorneys General.

Brief of amici curiae filed on behalf of the State of Oklahoma by Larry Derryberry, Attorney General, and John F. Fischer, II, Assistant Attorney General.

IV. THE SUPREME COURT'S DECISION

"There is no constitutional or inherent right of a convicted person to be conditionally released before the expiration of a valid sentence. The natural desire of an individual to be released is indistinguishable from the initial resistance to being confined. But the conviction, with all its procedural safeguards, has extinguished that liberty right: 'given a valid conviction, the criminal defendant has been constitutionally deprived of his liberty.'

Decisions of the Executive Branch, however serious their impact, do not automatically invoke due process protection; there simply is no constitutional guarantee that all executive decision-making must comply with standards that assure error-free determinations. This is especially true with respect to the sensitive choices presented by the administrative decision to grant parole release.

A state may, as Nebraska has, establish a parole system, but it has no duty to do so. Moreover, to insure that the state-created parole system serves the public interest purposes of rehabilitation and deterrence, the state may be specific or general in defining the conditions for release and the factors that should be considered by the parole authority. . . .

The fallacy in respondents' position is that parole release and parole revocation are quite different. There is a crucial distinction between being deprived of a liberty one has, as in parole, and being denied a conditional liberty that one desires.

[W]e find nothing in the due process concepts as they have thus far evolved that requires the Parole Board to specify the particular 'evidence' in the inmate's file or at his interview on which it rests the discretionary determination that an inmate is not ready for conditional release. The Board communicates the reason for its denial as a guide to the inmate for his future behavior. To require the parole authority to provide a summary of the evidence would tend to convert the process into an adversary proceeding and to equate the Board's parole-release determination with a guilt determination. . . . The Nebraska procedure affords an opportunity to be heard, and when parole is denied it informs the inmate in what respects he falls short of qualifying for parole; this affords the process that is due under these circumstances. The Constitution does not require more.

Accordingly, the judgment of the Court of Appeals is reversed and the case is remanded for further proceedings consistent with this opinion."

V. JUSTICE VOTE

4 Pro ACLU Side vs. 5 Con Opposing Side

ACLU Side (Petitioner / Appellant)

1. Marshall, T. – Wrote opinion dissenting in part
2. Stevens, J. – Joined Marshall's opinion
3. Brennan, W. – Joined Marshall's opinion
4. Powell, L. – Wrote opinion concurring in part and dissenting in part

Opposing Side (Respondent / Appellee)

1. Burger, W. – Wrote majority opinion
2. White, B. – Joined majority opinion
3. Stewart, P. – Joined majority opinion
4. Blackmun, H. – Joined majority opinion
5. Rehnquist, W. – Joined majority opinion

VI. A WIN OR LOSS FOR THE ACLU?

The ACLU filed as amicus curiae urging affirmance; the Supreme Court reversed the ruling of the Court of Appeals for the Eight Circuit in a 5-4 vote, giving the ACLU an apparent loss.

430. Dunaway v. New York

(Decided June 5, 1979; 442 U.S. 200)

I. ISSUE

A. Issues Discussed

Criminal justice, Fourth Amendment, involuntary confessions

B. Legal Question Presented

Did police violate the Fourth Amendment when, without probable cause to arrest petitioner, they took him into custody, transported him to the police station, and detained him there for interrogation?

C. Supreme Court's Answer

The police violated petitioner's Fourth Amendment rights and his statements made during interrogation are, therefore, inadmissible.

II. CASE SUMMARY

A. Background

"On August 10, 1971, Detective Anthony Fantigrossi of the Rochester Police was told by another officer that an informant had supplied a possible lead implicating petitioner in [a] crime. Fantigrossi questioned the supposed source of the lead—a jail inmate awaiting trial for burglary—but learned nothing that supplied 'enough information to get a warrant' for petitioner's arrest. Nevertheless, Fantigrossi ordered other detectives to 'pick up' petitioner and 'bring him in.' Three detectives located petitioner at a neighbor's house on the morning of August 11. Petitioner was taken into custody; although he was not told he was under arrest, he would have been physically restrained if he had attempted to leave. He was driven to police headquarters in a police car and placed in an interrogation room, where he was questioned by officers after being given the warnings required by Miranda v. Arizona. Petitioner waived counsel and eventually made statements and drew sketches that incriminated him in the crime.

At petitioner's jury trial for attempted robbery and felony murder, his motions to suppress the statements and sketches were denied, and he was convicted. On appeal, both the Appellate Division of the Fourth Department and the New York Court of Appeals initially affirmed the conviction without opinion. However, [the Supreme] Court granted certiorari, vacated the judgment, and remanded the case for further consideration in light of the Court's supervening decision in Brown v. Illinois. . . .

The County Court determined after a supplementary suppression hearing that Dunaway's motion to suppress should have been granted. . . . A divided Appellate Division reversed. Although agreeing that the police lacked probable cause to arrest petitioner, the majority relied on the Court of Appeals' reaffirmation, subsequent to the County Court's decision, that '[l]aw enforcement officials may detain an individual upon reasonable suspicion for questioning for a reasonable and brief period of time under carefully controlled conditions which are ample to protect the individual's Fifth and Sixth Amendment rights.' . . . The Court of Appeals dismissed petitioner's application for leave to appeal."

The Supreme Court granted certiorari to review the case and reversed.

B. Counsel of Record / ACLU Attorney

ACLU Side (Petitioner / Appellant): Edward John Nowak argued the cause and for appellant.

Opposing Side (Respondent / Appellee): Melvin Bressler argued the cause for appellee.

III. AMICI CURIAE

ACLU Side (Petitioner / Appellant)

Brief of amici curiae filed on behalf of the ACLU, et al., by Richard Emery and Joel M. Gora.

Opposing Side (Respondent / Appellee)

No briefs of amici curiae were filed in support of appellee.

IV. THE SUPREME COURT'S DECISION

"There can be little doubt that petitioner was 'seized' in the Fourth Amendment sense when he was taken involuntarily to the police station. And respondent State concedes that the police lacked probable cause to arrest petitioner before his incriminating statement during interrogation. [T]he detention of petitioner was in important respects indistinguishable from a traditional arrest. Petitioner was not questioned briefly where he was found. Instead, he was taken from a neighbor's home to a police car, transported to a police station, and placed in an interrogation room. He was never informed that he was 'free to go'; indeed, he would have been physically restrained if he had refused to accompany the officers or had tried to escape their custody. The application of the Fourth Amendment's requirement of probable cause does not depend on whether an intrusion of this magnitude is termed an 'arrest' under state law. The mere facts that petitioner was not told he was under arrest, was not 'booked,' and would not have had an arrest record if the interrogation had proved fruitless, while not insignificant for all purposes, obviously do not make petitioner's seizure even roughly analogous to the narrowly defined intrusions involved in Terry and its progeny. Indeed, any 'exception' that could cover a seizure as intrusive as that in this case would threaten to swallow the general rule that Fourth Amendment seizures are 'reasonable' only if based on probable cause.

[T]he conclusion that detention for custodial interrogation—regardless of its label—intrudes so severely on interests protected by the Fourth Amendment as necessarily to trigger the traditional safeguards against illegal arrest. We accordingly hold that the Rochester police violated the Fourth and Fourteenth Amendments when, without probable cause, they seized petitioner and transported him to the police station for interrogation. . . .

Brown identified several factors to be considered 'in determining whether the confession is obtained by exploitation of an illegal arrest the temporal proximity of the arrest and the confession, the presence of intervening circumstances, . . . and, particularly, the purpose and flagrancy of the official misconduct . . . .' Examining the case before it, the Court readily concluded that the State had failed to sustain its burden of showing the confession was admissible. In the 'less than two hours' that elapsed between the arrest and the confession 'there was no intervening event of significance whatsoever.' Furthermore, the arrest without probable cause had a 'quality of purposefulness' in that it was an 'expedition for evidence' admittedly undertaken 'in the hope that something might turn up.' . . .

Satisfying the Fifth Amendment is only the 'threshold' condition of the Fourth Amendment analysis required by Brown. No intervening events broke the connection between petitioner's illegal detention and his confession. To admit petitioner's confession in such a case would allow 'law enforcement officers to violate the Fourth Amendment with impunity, safe in the knowledge that they could wash their hands in the 'procedural safeguards' of the Fifth.'

Reversed."

V. JUSTICE VOTE

6 Pro ACLU Side vs. 2 Con Opposing Side

ACLU Side (Petitioner / Appellant)

1. Brennan, W. – Wrote majority opinion
2. Stewart, P. – Joined majority opinion
3. White, B. – Wrote concurring opinion
4. Marshall, T. – Joined majority opinion
5. Blackmun, H. – Joined majority opinion
6. Stevens, J. – Wrote concurring opinion

Opposing Side (Respondent / Appellee)

1. Rehnquist, W. – Wrote dissenting opinion
2. Burger, W. – Joined Rehnquist's dissent

Powell, L – Took no part in the decision

VI. A WIN OR LOSS FOR THE ACLU?

The ACLU filed as amicus curiae urging reversal; the U.S. Supreme Court reversed the ruling of the Appellate Division of the Supreme Court of New York in a 6-2 vote, giving the ACLU an apparent win.

431. Davis v. Passman

(Decided June 5, 1979; 442 U.S. 228)

I. ISSUE

A. Issues Discussed

Civil rights, gender, Fifth Amendment, due process

B. Legal Question Presented

"[W]hether a cause of action and a damages remedy can . . . be implied directly under the Constitution when the Due Process Clause of the Fifth Amendment is violated."

C. Supreme Court's Answer

A cause of action and damages remedy can be implied under the Due Process Clause of the Fifth Amendment.

II. CASE SUMMARY

A. Background

"At the time this case commenced, respondent Otto E. Passman was a United States Congressman from the Fifth Congressional District of Louisiana. On February 1, 1974, Passman hired petitioner Shirley Davis as a deputy administrative assistant. Passman subsequently terminated her employment, effective July 31, 1974, writing Davis that, although she was 'able, energetic and a very hard worker,' he had concluded 'that it was essential that the understudy to my Administrative Assistant be a man.'

Davis brought suit in the United States District Court for the Western District of Louisiana, alleging that Passman's conduct discriminated against her 'on the basis of sex in violation of the United States Constitution and the Fifth Amendment thereto.' Davis sought damages in the form of backpay. Jurisdiction for her suit was founded on 28 U.S.C. § 1331(a), which provides in pertinent part that federal 'district courts shall have original jurisdiction of all civil actions wherein the matter in controversy exceeds the sum or value of $10,000 . . . and arises under the Constitution . . . of the United States . . . .'

The District Court [ruled] that Davis had 'no private right of action.' A panel of the Court of Appeals for the Fifth Circuit reversed. The panel concluded that a cause of action for damages arose directly under the Fifth Amendment; that, taking as true the allegations in Davis' complaint, Passman's conduct violated the Fifth Amendment; and that Passman's conduct was not shielded by the Speech or Debate Clause of the Constitution.

The Court of Appeals for the Fifth Circuit, sitting en banc, reversed the decision of the panel. The en banc court did not reach the merits, nor did it discuss the application of the Speech or Debate Clause. The court instead held that 'no right of action may be implied from the Due Process Clause of the fifth amendment.' . . . Noting that Congress had failed to create a damages remedy for those in Davis' position, the court also concluded that 'the proposed damage remedy is not constitutionally compelled' so that it was not necessary to 'countermand the clearly discernible will of Congress' and create such a remedy."

The Supreme Court granted certiorari to review the case and reversed.

B. Counsel of Record / ACLU Attorney

ACLU Side (Petitioner / Appellant): Sana F. Shtasel argued the cause for appellant, pro hac vice, by special leave of Court.

Opposing Side (Respondent / Appellee): A. Richard Gear argued the cause for appellee.

III. AMICI CURIAE

ACLU Side (Petitioner / Appellant)

Brief of amici curiae filed on behalf of the ACLU by Burt Neuborne, Bruce J. Ennis, Charles S. Sims, Michael P. Zweig, and Jerry Chasen.

Brief of amicus curiae filed on behalf of the Honorable Morris Udall, the Honorable Patricia Schroeder, the Honorable Charles Rose, Winnie Burrell, Carla Kish, Bruce Kriegman, the Honorable Les Aucoin, the Honorable Berkley Bedell, the Honorable David E. Bonior, the Honorable William M. Brodhead, the Honorable George E. Brown, Jr., the Honorable John H. Buchanan, Jr., the Honorable Yvonne Brathwaite Burke, the Honorable Robert Carr, the Honorable John Conyers, the Honorable Ronald V. Dellums, the Honorable Thomas Downey, the Honorable Robert F. Drinan, the Honorable Don Edwards, the Honorable Dante B. Fascell, the Honorable Dale E. Kildee, the Honorable William Lehman, the Honorable Edward J. Markey, the Honorable George Miller, the Honorable Anthony Moffett, the Honorable Richard Nolan, the Honorable Leon Panetta, the Honorable Don J. Pease, the Honorable Fred Richmond, the Honorable Bruce F. Vento, the Honorable Harold L. Volkmer, and the Honorable Ted Weiss, by Albert J. Beveridge, III, and Roderic V. O. Boggs.

Opposing Side (Respondent / Appellee)

No briefs of amici curiae were filed in support of appellee.

IV. THE SUPREME COURT'S DECISION

"We hold first that, pretermitting the question whether respondent's conduct is shielded by the Speech or Debate Clause, petitioner asserts a constitutionally protected right; second, that petitioner has stated a cause of action which asserts this right; and third, that relief in damages constitutes an appropriate form of remedy.

[A] damages remedy is surely appropriate in this case. . . . Relief in damages would be judicially manageable, for the case presents a focused remedial issue without difficult questions of valuation or causation. Litigation under Title VII of the Civil Rights Act of 1964 has given federal courts great experience evaluating claims for backpay due to illegal sex discrimination. Moreover since respondent is no longer a Congressman, equitable relief in the form of reinstatement would be unavailing. And there are available no other alternative forms of judicial relief. For Davis, as for Bivens [v. Six Unknown Named Agents], 'it is damages or nothing.' . . .

Finally, the Court of Appeals appeared concerned that, if a damages remedy were made available to petitioner, the danger existed 'of deluging federal courts with claims . . . .' We do not perceive the potential for such a deluge. [A] plaintiff seeking a damages remedy under the Constitution must first demonstrate that his constitutional rights have been violated. We do not hold that every tort by a federal official may be redressed in damages. And, of course, were Congress to create equally effective alternative remedies, the need for damages relief might be obviated. . . . We conclude, therefore, that in this case, as in Bivens, if petitioner is able to prevail on the merits, she should be able to redress her injury in damages, a 'remedial mechanism normally available in the federal courts.' . . .

We hold today that the Court of Appeals for the Fifth Circuit, en banc, must be reversed because petitioner has a cause of action under the Fifth Amendment, and because her injury may be redressed by a damages remedy. The Court of Appeals did not consider, however, whether respondent's conduct was shielded by the Speech or Debate Clause of the Constitution. Accordingly, we do not reach this question. And, of course, we express no opinion as to the merits of petitioner's complaint.

The judgment of the Court of Appeals is reversed and the case is remanded for further proceedings consistent with this opinion."

V. JUSTICE VOTE

5 Pro ACLU Side vs. 4 Con Opposing Side

ACLU Side (Petitioner / Appellant)

1. Brennan, W. – Wrote majority opinion
2. White, B. – Joined majority opinion
3. Marshall, T. – Joined majority opinion
4. Stevens, J. – Joined majority opinion
5. Blackmun, H. – Joined majority opinion

Opposing Side (Respondent / Appellee)

1. Stewart, P. – Wrote dissenting opinion
2. Powell, L. – Wrote dissenting opinion, joined Burger's dissent
3. Burger, W. – Wrote dissenting opinion, joined Powell's dissent
4. Rehnquist, W. – Joined Burger's dissent, joined Stewart's dissent, joined Powell's dissent

VI. A WIN OR LOSS FOR THE ACLU?

The ACLU filed as amicus curiae urging reversal; the Supreme Court reversed the ruling of the Court of Appeals for the Fifth Circuit in a 5-4 vote, giving the ACLU an apparent win.

432. Personnel Administrator of Massachusetts v. Feeney

(Decided June 5, 1979; 442 U.S. 256)

I. ISSUE

A. Issues Discussed

Gender, military

B. Legal Question Presented

"[W]hether Massachusetts, in granting an absolute lifetime preference to veterans, has discriminated against women in violation of the Equal Protection Clause of the Fourteenth Amendment."

C. Supreme Court's Answer

The veterans' preference statute does not violate the Equal Protection Clause of the Fourteenth Amendment.

II. CASE SUMMARY

A. Background

"This case presents a challenge to the constitutionality of the Massachusetts veterans' preference statute, Mass.Gen.Laws Ann., ch. 31, § 23, on the ground that it discriminates against women in violation of the Equal Protection Clause of the Fourteenth Amendment. Under ch. 31, § 23, all veterans who qualify for state civil service positions must be considered for appointment ahead of any qualifying nonveterans. The preference operates overwhelmingly to the advantage of males.

The appellee Helen B. Feeney is not a veteran. She brought this action pursuant to 42 U.S.C. § 1983, alleging that the absolute preference formula established in ch. 31, § 23, inevitably operates to exclude women from consideration for the best Massachusetts civil service jobs and thus unconstitutionally denies them the equal protection of the laws. The three-judge District Court agreed, one judge dissenting. . . .

Upon an appeal taken by the Attorney General of Massachusetts, this Court vacated the judgment and remanded the case for further consideration in light of our intervening decision in Washington v. Davis, 426 U.S. 229. . . .

Upon remand, the District Court, one judge concurring and one judge again dissenting, concluded that a veterans' hiring preference is inherently nonneutral because it favors a class from which women have traditionally been excluded, and that the consequences of the Massachusetts absolute-preference formula for the employment opportunities of women were too inevitable to have been 'unintended.' Accordingly, the court reaffirmed its original judgment. The Attorney General again appealed to this Court pursuant to 28 U.S.C. § 1253, and probable jurisdiction of the appeal was noted."

B. Counsel of Record

ACLU Side (Respondent / Appellee): Richard P. Ward argued the cause for appellee. With him on the brief were John Reinstein of the Massachusetts Civil Liberties Union Foundation, Stephen B. Perlman, Eleanor D. Acheson, and John H. Mason.

Opposing Side (Petitioner / Appellant): Thomas R. Kiley, Assistant Attorney General of Massachusetts, argued the cause for appellants. With him on the brief were Francis X. Bellotti, Attorney General, and Edward F. Vena, Assistant Attorney General.

III. AMICI CURIAE

ACLU Side (Respondent / Appellee)

Brief of amici curiae filed on behalf of the National Organization for Women et al. by Samuel J. Rabinove and Phyllis N. Segal.

Brief of amici curiae filed on behalf of the United States Office of Personnel Management et al., by Deanne Siemer, not taking a stance on the challenged statute's validity.

Opposing Side (Petitioner / Appellant)

Brief of amici curiae filed on behalf of the United States by Solicitor General McCree, Deputy Solicitor General Easterbrook, and William C. Bryson

Brief of amici curiae filed on behalf of the American Legion by John J. Curtin, Jr.

Brief of amici curiae filed on behalf of the Washington Legal Foundation by Paul D. Kamenar.

IV. THE SUPREME COURT'S DECISION

"The equal protection guarantee of the Fourteenth Amendment does not take from the States all power of classification. Most laws classify, and many affect certain groups unevenly, even though the law itself treats them no differently from all other members of the class described by the law. . . .

The cases of Washington v. Davis and Arlington Heights v. Metropolitan Housing Dev. Corp. recognize that when a neutral law has a disparate impact . . . , an unconstitutional purpose may still be at work. But those cases signaled no departure from the settled rule that the Fourteenth Amendment guarantees equal laws, not equal results. . . .

When a statute gender-neutral on its face is challenged on the ground that its effects upon women are disproportionably adverse, a twofold inquiry is thus appropriate. The first question is whether the statutory classification is indeed neutral in the sense that it is not gender-based. If the classification itself, covert of overt, is not based upon gender, the second question is whether the adverse effect reflects invidious gender-based discrimination. . . .

The distinction made by ch. 31, § 23, is, as it seems to be, quite simply between veterans and nonveterans, not between men and women. . . .

The dispositive question, then, is whether the appellee has shown that a gender-based discriminatory purpose has, at least in some measure, shaped the Massachusetts veterans' preference legislation. [S]he points to two basic factors which in her view distinguish ch. 31, § 23, from the neutral rules at issue in the Washington v. Davis and Arlington Heights cases. The first is the nature of the preference, which is said to be demonstrably gender-biased in the sense that it favors a status reserved . . . to men. The second concerns the impact of the absolute lifetime preference upon the employment opportunities of women, an impact claimed to be too inevitable to have been unintended. . . .

The appellee's ultimate argument rests upon the presumption, common to the criminal and civil law, that a person intends the natural and foreseeable consequences of his voluntary actions. . . .

This rhetorical question implies that a negative answer is obvious, but it is not. . . .

Veterans' hiring preferences represent an awkward—and, many argue, unfair—exception to the widely shared view that merit and merit alone should prevail in the employment policies of government. . . . But the Fourteenth Amendment 'cannot be made a refuge from ill-advised . . . laws.' The substantial edge granted to veterans by ch. 31, § 23, may reflect unwise policy. The appellee, however, has simply failed to demonstrate that the law in any way reflects a purpose to discriminate on the basis of sex.

The judgment is reversed, and the case is remanded . . . ."

V. JUSTICE VOTE

2 Pro ACLU Side vs. 7 Con Opposing Side

ACLU Side (Respondent / Appellee)

1. Marshall, T. – Wrote dissenting opinion
2. Brennan, W. – Joined Marshall's dissent

Opposing Side (Petitioner / Appellant)

1. Stewart, P. – Wrote majority opinion
2. Rehnquist, W. – Joined majority opinion
3. Burger, W. – Joined majority opinion
4. White, B. – Joined Stevens' concurrence
5. Blackmun, H. – Joined majority opinion
6. Powell, L. – Joined majority opinion
7. Stevens, J. – Wrote concurring opinion

VI. A WIN OR LOSS FOR THE ACLU?

The ACLU served as counsel for appellee urging affirmance; the Supreme Court reversed the District Court's decision by a 7-2 vote, giving the ACLU an apparent loss.

433. Babbitt v. United Farm Workers National Union

(Decided June 5, 1979; 442 U.S. 289)

I. ISSUE

A. Issues Discussed

Governmental authority, unions, First Amendment, Fourteenth Amendment

B. Legal Question Presented

Was it proper for the District Court to set aside Arizona's farm labor statute as unconstitutional?

C. Supreme Court's Answer

The District Court improperly set aside Arizona's farm labor statute as unconstitutional because only challenges to certain provisions of the statute presented justiciable controversies.

II. CASE SUMMARY

A. Background

In 1972, the Arizona Legislature enacted the Arizona Agricultural Employment Relations Act which creates "procedures governing the election of employee bargaining representatives, establishes various rights of agricultural employers and employees, proscribes a range of employer and union practices, and establishes a civil and criminal enforcement scheme to ensure compliance with the substantive provisions of the Act.

Appellees—the United Farm Workers National Union (UFW), an agent of the UFW, named farmworkers, and a supporter of the UFW—commenced suit in federal court to secure a declaration of the unconstitutionality of various sections of the Act, as well as of the entire Act, and an injunction against its enforcement. A three-judge District Court was convened to entertain the action. [T]he court determined that appellees' challenges were presently justiciable. Reaching the merits of some of the claims, the court ruled unconstitutional five distinct provisions of the Act. Specifically, the court disapproved the section specifying election procedures, § 23-1389, on the ground that, by failing to account for seasonal employment peaks, it precluded the consummation of elections before most workers dispersed and hence frustrated the associational rights of agricultural employees. The court was also of the view that the Act restricted unduly the class of employees technically eligible to vote for bargaining representatives and hence burdened the Workers' freedom of association in this second respect.

The court, moreover, ruled violative of the First and Fourteenth Amendments the provision limiting union publicity directed at consumers of agricultural products, § 23-1385(B)(8) . . . . The court also struck down the statute's criminal penalty provision, § 23-1392, on vagueness grounds, and held unconstitutional the provision excusing the employer from furnishing to a labor organization any materials, information, time, or facilities to enable the union to communicate with the employer's employees. § 23-1385(C). . . . Finally, the court disapproved a provision construed as mandating compulsory arbitration, § 23-1393 (B), on the ground that it denied employees due process and the right to a jury trial, which the District Court found guaranteed by the Seventh Amendment. The remainder of the Act fell 'by reason of its inseparability and inoperability apart from the provisions found to be invalid.'"

The Supreme Court granted certiorari to review the case and reversed.

B. Counsel of Record / ACLU Attorney

ACLU Side (Respondent / Appellee): Jerome Cohen argued the cause for appellee.

Opposing Side (Petitioner / Appellant): Rex E. Lee, Special Assistant Attorney General of Arizona, argued the cause for appellant.

III. AMICI CURIAE

ACLU Side (Respondent / Appellee)

Brief of amici curiae filed on behalf of the ACLU of Southern California, et al., by Mark D. Rosenbaum, Fred Okrand, and Dennis M. Perluss.

Brief of amici curiae filed on behalf of the American Federation of Labor and Congress of Industrial Organizations by J. Albert Woll and Laurence Gold.

Brief of amici curiae filed on behalf of the Agricultural Labor Relations Board by Marvin J. Brenner and Ellen Lake.

Opposing Side (Petitioner / Appellant)

Brief of amici curiae filed on behalf of the Agricultural Producers Labor Committee, et al., by Joseph Herman.

IV. THE SUPREME COURT'S DECISION

"We conclude that the challenges to two of the provisions specifically invalidated did not present a case or controversy within the jurisdiction of a federal court and hence should not have been adjudicated. Although the attacks on two other provisions were justiciable, we conclude that the District Court should have abstained from deciding the federal issues posed until material, unresolved questions of state law were determined by the Arizona courts. Finally, we believe that the District Court properly reached the merits of the fifth provision but erred in invalidating it. Accordingly, we reverse the judgment of the District Court. . . .

A plaintiff who challenges a statute must demonstrate a realistic danger of sustaining a direct injury as a result of the statute's operation or enforcement. . . . Examining the claims adjudicated by the three-judge court against the foregoing principles, it is our view that the challenges to the provisions regulating election procedures, consumer publicity, and criminal sanctions—but only those challenges—present a case or controversy.

[The Arizona Agricultural Employment Relations Act] authorizes imposition of criminal sanctions against '[a]ny person . . . who violates any provision' of the Act. [It] is clear that appellees desire to engage at least in consumer publicity campaigns prohibited by the Act; accordingly, we think their challenge to the precision of the criminal penalty provision, itself, was properly entertained by the District Court and may be raised here on appeal. If the provision were truly vague, appellees should not be expected to pursue their collective activities at their peril.

[T]he District Court should have postponed resolution of appellees' challenge to the criminal penalty provision. [W]e conclude that the District Court erred in entertaining all aspects of appellees' challenge to the consumer publicity section without the benefit of a construction thereof by the Arizona courts. We are sensitive to appellees' reluctance to repair to the Arizona courts after extensive litigation in the federal arena. We nevertheless hold that in this case the District Court should not have adjudicated substantial constitutional claims with respect to statutory provisions that are patently ambiguous on their face. . . .

The merits of appellees' challenge to the statutory election procedures remain to be considered. . . . As we see it, however, these general complaints that the statutory election procedures are ineffective are matters for the Arizona Legislature and not the federal courts. . . .

The statutory procedures need be pursued only if farmworkers desire to designate exclusive bargaining representatives and to compel their employer to bargain-rights that are conferred by statute rather than the Federal Constitution. Accordingly, at this time, we are unable to discern any First Amendment difficulty with the Arizona statutory election scheme, whether or not the procedures are as fair or efficacious as appellees would like.

Reversed and remanded."

V. JUSTICE VOTE

2 Pro ACLU Side vs. 7 Con Opposing Side

ACLU Side (Respondent / Appellee)

1. Brennan, W. – Wrote opinion concurring in part and dissenting in part
2. Marshall, T. – Joined Brennan's opinion

Opposing Side (Petitioner / Appellant)

1. White, B. – Wrote majority opinion
2. Burger, W. – Joined majority opinion
3. Stewart, P. – Joined majority opinion
4. Blackmun, H. – Joined majority opinion
5. Powell, L. – Joined majority opinion
6. Rehnquist, W. – Joined majority opinion
7. Stevens, J. – Joined majority opinion

VI. A WIN OR LOSS FOR THE ACLU?

The ACLU filed as amicus curiae urging affirmance; the Supreme Court reversed and remanded the ruling of the District Court of Arizona in a 7-2 vote, giving the ACLU an apparent loss.

434. Great American Federal Savings & Loan Association v. Novotny

(Decided June 11, 1979; 442 U.S. 366)

I. ISSUE

A. Issues Discussed

Civil rights, gender

B. Legal Question Presented

Does respondent, who was allegedly fired due to his support for female employees who he alleged were denied equal protection, have a cause of action against his employer under Title VII of the Civil Rights Act of 1964 through 42 U.S.C. § 1985(3)?

C. Supreme Court's Answer

Respondent does not have a cause of action through 42 U.S.C. § 1985(3).

II. CASE SUMMARY

A. Background

Respondent, John Novotny, worked for the Great American Federal Savings and Loan Association (Association). He was "secretary of the Association, a member of its board of directors, and a loan officer." He believed that the Association was denying equal opportunity to female employees, and he "expressed support for the female employees at a meeting of the board of directors." Shortly thereafter, "he was not re-elected as secretary, he was not re-elected to the board, and he was fired. . . .

Novotny filed a complaint with the Equal Employment Opportunity Commission under Title VII of the Civil Rights Act of 1964. After receiving a right-to-sue letter, he brought this lawsuit against the Association and its directors in the District Court for the Western District of Pennsylvania. He claimed damages under 42 U.S.C. § 1985(3), contending that he had been injured as the result of a conspiracy to deprive him of equal protection of and equal privileges and immunities under the laws. The District

Court granted the defendants' motion to dismiss. It held that § 1985(3) could not be invoked because the directors of a single corporation could not, as a matter of law and fact, engage in a conspiracy.

Novotny appealed. After oral argument before a three-judge panel, the case was reargued before the en banc Court of Appeals for the Third Circuit, which unanimously reversed the District Court's judgment. The Court of Appeals ruled that Novotny had stated a cause of action under § 1985(3). It held that conspiracies motivated by an invidious animus against women fall within § 1985(3), and that Novotny, a male allegedly injured as a result of such a conspiracy, had standing to bring suit under that statutory provision. It ruled that Title VII could be the source of a right asserted in an action under § 1985(3), and that intracorporate conspiracies come within the intendment of the section. Finally, the court concluded that its construction of §

1985(3) did not present any serious constitutional problem."

The Supreme Court granted certiorari to review the case, vacated, and remanded.

B. Counsel of Record / ACLU Attorney

ACLU Side (Respondent / Appellee): Stanley M. Stein argued the cause for appellee.

Deputy Solicitor General Lawrence G. Wallace argued the cause for the United States, as amicus curiae, by special leave of Court.

Opposing Side (Petitioner / Appellant): Eugene K. Connors argued the cause for appellant.

III. AMICI CURIAE

ACLU Side (Respondent / Appellee)

Brief of amici curiae filed on behalf of the ACLU, et al., by Judith Levin, Margaret L. Moses, Isabelle Katz Pinzler, and Thomas Harvey.

Brief of amici curiae filed on behalf of the United States, et al., by Solicitor General Wade H. McCree, Jr., Assistant Attorney General Drew S. Days, III, Assistant to the Solicitor General Louis F. Claiborne, Walter W. Barnett, Joan F. Hartman, Mildred M. Matesich, Issie L. Jenkins,

Opposing Side (Petitioner / Appellant)

Avrum M. Goldberg and William R. Weissman.

IV. THE SUPREME COURT'S DECISION

"[T]he Court found that § 1985(3) did provide a cause of action for damages caused by purely private conspiracies. . . . Under Title VII, cases of alleged employment discrimination are subject to a detailed administrative and judicial process designed to provide an opportunity for nonjudicial and nonadversary resolution of claims. . . .

If a violation of Title VII could be asserted through § 1985(3), a complainant could avoid most if not all of these detailed and specific provisions of the law. Section 1985(3) expressly authorizes compensatory damages; punitive damages might well follow. The plaintiff or defendant might demand a jury trial. The short and precise time limitations of Title VII would be grossly altered. Perhaps most importantly, the complaint could completely bypass the administrative process, which plays such a crucial role in the scheme established by Congress in Title VII. . . .

Section 1985(3), by contrast, creates no rights. It is a purely remedial statute, providing a civil cause of action when some otherwise defined federal right—to equal protection of the laws or equal privileges and immunities under the laws—is breached by a conspiracy in the manner defined by the section. Thus, we are not faced in this case with a question of implied repeal. The right Novotny claims under § 704(a) did not even arguably exist before the passage of Title VII. The only question here, therefore, is whether the rights created by Title VII may be asserted within the remedial framework of § 1985(3).

[W]e conclude that § 1985(3) may not be invoked to redress violations of Title VII. It is true that a § 1985(3) remedy would not be coextensive with Title VII, since a plaintiff in an action under § 1985(3) must prove both a conspiracy and a group animus that Title VII does not require. While this incomplete congruity would limit the damage that would be done to Title VII, it would not eliminate it. Unimpaired effectiveness can be given to the plan put together by Congress in Title VII only by holding that deprivation of a right created by Title VII cannot be the basis for a cause of action under § 1985(3).

Accordingly, the judgment of the Court of Appeals is vacated, and the case is remanded to that Court for further proceedings consistent with this opinion."

V. JUSTICE VOTE

3 Pro ACLU Side vs. 6 Con Opposing Side

ACLU Side (Respondent / Appellee)

1. White B. – Wrote dissenting opinion
2. Marshall, T. – Joined White's dissent
3. Brennan, W. – Joined White's dissent

Opposing Side (Petitioner / Appellant)

1. Stewart, P. – Wrote majority opinion
2. Burger, W. – Joined majority opinion
3. Blackmun, H. – Joined majority opinion
4. Powell, L. – Wrote concurring opinion
5. Rehnquist, W. – Joined majority opinion
6. Stevens, J. – Wrote concurring opinion

VI. A WIN OR LOSS FOR THE ACLU?

The ACLU filed as amicus curiae urging affirmance; the Supreme Court reversed the ruling of the Court of Appeals for the Third Circuit in a 6-3 vote, giving the ACLU an apparent loss.

435. Southeastern Community College v. Davis

(Decided June 11, 1979; 442 U.S. 397)

I. ISSUE

A. Issues Discussed

Civil rights, discrimination

B. Legal Question Presented

"Whether § 504 of the Rehabilitation Act of 1973, which prohibits discrimination against an 'otherwise qualified handicapped individual' in federally funded programs 'solely by reason of his handicap,' forbids professional schools from imposing physical qualifications for admission to their clinical training programs."

C. Supreme Court's Answer

The school's physical qualifications for admission to the nursing program do not violate § 504.

II. CASE SUMMARY

A. Background

Respondent Davis, who suffered from a serious hearing disability, sought admission to Southeastern Community College's nursing program. The school rejected respondent's application because the Executive Director of the North Carolina Board of Nursing believed "respondent's hearing disability made it unsafe for her to practice as a nurse. In addition, it would be impossible for respondent to participate safely in the normal clinical training program, and those modifications that would be necessary to enable safe participation would prevent her from realizing the benefits of the program." Respondent challenged the decision and, after additional consideration, the school again rejected respondent. "Respondent then filed suit in the United States District Court for the Eastern District of North Carolina, alleging both a violation of § 504 of the Rehabilitation Act of 1973 and a denial of equal protection and due process." Section 504 "prohibits discrimination against an 'otherwise qualified handicapped individual' in federally funded programs 'solely by reason of his handicap.'"

The District Court ruled in favor of petitioner. It concluded that respondent's "'handicap actually prevents her from safely performing in both her training program and her proposed profession.' . . . Based on these findings, the District Court concluded that respondent was not an 'otherwise qualified handicapped individual' protected against discrimination by § 504."

The Court of Appeals for the Fourth Circuit reversed, ruling that in light of intervening regulations, § 504 required petitioner "'to reconsider [respondent's] application for admission to the nursing program without regard to her hearing ability.' It concluded that the District Court had erred in taking respondent's handicap into account in determining whether she was 'otherwise qualified' for the program, rather than confining its inquiry to her 'academic and technical qualifications.' The Court of Appeals also suggested that § 504 required 'affirmative conduct' on the part of Southeastern to modify its program to accommodate the disabilities of applicants, 'even when such modifications become expensive.'"

The Supreme Court granted certiorari to review the case and reversed.

B. Counsel of Record / ACLU Attorney

ACLU Side (Respondent / Appellee): Marc P. Charmatz argued the cause for appellee.

Opposing Side (Petitioner / Appellant): Eugene Gressman argued the cause for appellant.

III. AMICI CURIAE

ACLU Side (Respondent / Appellee)

Brief of amici curiae filed on behalf of the ACLU, et al., by Bruce J. Ennis, George Kannar, Charles S. Sims, Robert M. Levy, Steven R. Shapiro, Fred Okrand, and Sam Rosenwein.

Additional briefs of amici curiae were filed on behalf of the United States, the State of California, the American Coalition of Citizens with Disabilities, et al., the California Association for the Physically Handicapped, et al., the Center for Independent Living, et al., the Institute for Public Representation, et al., the New York City Council of Organizations Serving the Deaf, et al., the American Association for the Advancement of Science, et al., and the Board of Governors of the University of North Carolina.

Opposing Side (Petitioner / Appellant)

A brief of amici curiae was filed by the Attorneys General for their respective States as follows: Francis X. Bellotti for Massachusetts, J. Marshall Coleman for Virginia, Robert K. Corbin for Arizona, Carl R. Ajello for Connecticut, Richard S. Gebelein for Delaware, Jim Smith for Florida, Arthur K. Bolton for Georgia, Wayne Minami for Hawaii, David H. Leroy for Idaho, Theodore L. Sendak for Indiana, Tom Miller for Iowa, Robert T. Stephan for Kansas, William J. Guste, Jr., for Louisiana, Stephen H. Sachs for Maryland, A. F. Summer for Mississippi, John D. Ashcroft for Missouri, Michael T. Greely for Montana, Paul L. Douglas for Nebraska, Thomas D. Rath for New Hampshire, John J. Degnan for New Jersey, Robert Abrams for New York, Rufus L. Edmisten for North Carolina, Allen I. Olson for North Dakota, William J. Brown for Ohio, Jan Eric Cartwright for Oklahoma, James A. Redden for Oregon, Daniel R. McLeod for South Carolina, William M. Leech, Jr. for Tennessee, Mark White for Texas, Slade Gorton for Washington, Chauncey H. Browning, Jr. for West Virginia, and Bronson C. LaFollette for Wisconsin.

Additional briefs of amici curiae were filed on behalf of the Association of American Medical Colleges, the Board of Trustees of Prince George's Community College, the Equal Employment Advisory Council, the National Institute for Independent Colleges and Universities, et al., the American Council on Education, the Commonwealth of Pennsylvania, and the American Council on Education.

IV. THE SUPREME COURT'S DECISION

"Section 504 by its terms does not compel educational institutions to disregard the disabilities of handicapped individuals or to make substantial modifications in their programs to allow disabled persons to participate. Instead, it requires only that an 'otherwise qualified handicapped individual' not be excluded from participation in a federally funded program 'solely by reason of his handicap,' indicating only that mere possession of a handicap is not a permissible ground for assuming an inability to function in a particular context. . . .

Although an agency's interpretation of the statute under which it operates is entitled to some deference, 'this deference is constrained by our obligation to honor the clear meaning of a statute, as revealed by its language, purpose, and history.' Here, neither the language, purpose, nor history of § 504 reveals an intent to impose an affirmative-action obligation on all recipients of federal funds. Accordingly, we hold that even if [the Department of Health, Education, and Welfare (HEW)] has attempted to create such an obligation itself, it lacks the authority to do so. . . .

In this case, however, it is clear that Southeastern's unwillingness to make major adjustments in its nursing program does not constitute such discrimination. [T]he purpose of its program was to train persons who could serve the nursing profession in all customary ways. This type of purpose, far from reflecting any animus against handicapped individuals is shared by many if not most of the institutions that train persons to render professional service. It is undisputed that respondent could not participate in Southeastern's nursing program unless the standards were substantially lowered. Section 504 imposes no requirement upon an educational institution to lower or to effect substantial modifications of standards to accommodate a handicapped person.

[W]e hold that there was no violation of § 504 when Southeastern concluded that respondent did not qualify for admission to its program. Nothing in the language or history of § 504 reflects an intention to limit the freedom of an educational institution to require reasonable physical qualifications for admission to a clinical training program. Nor has there been any showing in this case that any action short of a substantial change in Southeastern's program would render unreasonable the qualifications it imposed.

Accordingly, we reverse the judgment of the court below, and remand for proceedings consistent with this opinion."

V. JUSTICE VOTE

0 Pro ACLU Side vs. 9 Con Opposing Side

Opposing Side (Petitioner / Appellant)

1. Powell, L. – Wrote majority opinion
2. Stewart, P. – Joined majority opinion
3. White B. – Joined majority opinion
4. Burger, W. – Joined majority opinion
5. Blackmun, H. – Joined majority opinion
6. Stevens, J. – Joined majority opinion
7. Brennan, W. – Joined majority opinion

8. Marshall, T. – Joined majority opinion
9. Rehnquist, W. – Joined majority opinion

VI. A WIN OR LOSS FOR THE ACLU?

The ACLU filed as amicus curiae urging affirmance; the Supreme Court reversed the ruling of the Court of Appeals for the Fourth Circuit in a 9-0 vote, giving the ACLU an apparent loss.

436. Torres v. Puerto Rico

(Decided June 18, 1979; 442 U.S. 465)

I. ISSUE

A. Issues Discussed

Criminal justice, drugs, Fourth Amendment, search and seizure

B. Legal Question Presented

Was the search pursuant to Public Law 22 constitutional?

C. Supreme Court's Answer

The search was an unconstitutional violation of appellant's Fourth Amendment rights.

II. CASE SUMMARY

A. Background

In 1976, Appellant Terry Torres, a Florida resident, flew from Miami to San Juan, Puerto Rico. Upon his arrival, police officers searched his luggage at the airport without a warrant or probable cause to suspect that he was carrying anything illegal. This search was pursuant to a Puerto Rico statute, Public Law 22, authorizing "police to search the luggage of any person arriving in Puerto Rico from the United States. . . . The search revealed one ounce of marihuana, a wooden pipe bearing marijuana residue, and approximately $250,000 in cash. Torres was charged, tried, and convicted of violating § 404 of the Controlled Substances Act of Puerto Rico. . . .

On appeal to the Supreme Court of Puerto Rico, Torres contended that the search pursuant to Public Law 22 violated the federal constitutional prohibition against unreasonable searches. Only seven of the eight justices of the Puerto Rico Supreme Court participated in considering the appeal; four of the seven concluded that Public Law 22 violated the Fourth Amendment. Three justices held Public Law 22 constitutional. Article V, § 4, of the Puerto Rico Constitution provides that no law may be held unconstitutional except by a majority of all the members of the Supreme Court. Accordingly, there being only a minority of the justices so holding, the court entered a judgment stating: 'The search of appellant's belongings being based on the provisions of Act No. 22 of August 6, 1975, and considering the absence of the majority vote required by the Constitution to annul said Act, the judgment appealed is affirmed."

The Supreme Court granted certiorari and reversed.

B. Counsel of Record / ACLU Attorney

ACLU Side (Petitioner / Appellant): Joseph Remcho argued the cause for appellant.

Opposing Side (Respondent / Appellee): Roberto Armstrong, Jr. argued the cause for appellee.

III. AMICI CURIAE

ACLU Side (Petitioner / Appellant)

Brief of amici curiae filed on behalf of the ACLU by Bruce J. Ennis.

Opposing Side (Respondent / Appellee)

No briefs of amici curiae were filed in support of appellee.

IV. THE SUPREME COURT'S DECISION

"The search of appellant's baggage pursuant to Public Law 22 did not satisfy the requirements of the Fourth Amendment as we heretofore have construed it. First, the grounds for a search must satisfy objective standards which ensure that the invasion of personal privacy is justified by legitimate governmental interests. The governmental interests to be served in the detection or prevention of crime are subject to traditional standards of probable cause to believe that incriminating evidence will be found. Yet Public Law 22 does not require, and the officers who made the search challenged here did not have, probable cause for such belief.

Second, a warrant is normally a prerequisite to a search unless exigent circumstances make compliance with this requirement impossible. Yet, Public Law 22 requires no warrant, and none was obtained before appellant's bags were searched. . . .

The decisions on which Puerto Rico seeks to erect its theory of 'intermediate boundaries' do not reflect any geographical element of Fourth Amendment doctrine, however, but are based on a variety of considerations which have no bearing on this case. Public Law 22 cannot be justified by any analogy to customs searches at a functional equivalent of the international border of the United States. The authority of the United States to search the baggage of arriving international travelers is based on its inherent sovereign authority to protect its territorial integrity. By reason of that authority, it is entitled to require that whoever seeks entry must establish the right to enter and to bring into the country whatever he may carry. Puerto Rico has no sovereign authority to prohibit entry into its territory; as with all international ports of entry, border and customs control for Puerto Rico is conducted by federal officers. Congress has provided by statute that Puerto Rico must accord to all citizens of the United States the privileges and immunities of its own residents.

Public Law 22 also may not be sustained by analogy to state inspection provisions designed to implement health and safety legislation. By a vote of four to three the Puerto Rico Supreme Court rejected appellee's attempt to characterize Public Law 22 as a health and safety measure, finding instead that it was enacted for the purpose of enforcing criminal laws. In any event, health and safety inspections are subject to the Fourth Amendment warrant requirement unless they fall within one of its recognized exceptions, and must be based on a 'plan containing specific neutral criteria.' . . .

In any event, Puerto Rico's law enforcement needs are indistinguishable from those of many states. Puerto Rico is not unique because it is an island; like Puerto Rico, neither Alaska nor Hawaii are contiguous to the continental body of the United States. Moreover, the majority of all the states have borders which coincide in part with the international frontier of the United States; virtually all have international airport facilities subject to federal customs controls.

We therefore hold that the search pursuant to Public Law 22 violated constitutional guarantees; accordingly, evidence obtained in the search of appellant's luggage should have been suppressed. The judgment of the Supreme Court of Puerto Rico is therefore reversed, and the case is remanded to that court for further proceedings not inconsistent with this opinion."

V. JUSTICE VOTE

9 Pro ACLU Side vs. 0 Con Opposing Side

ACLU Side (Petitioner / Appellant)

1. Burger, W. – Wrote majority opinion
2. White B. – Joined majority opinion
3. Powell, L. – Joined majority opinion
4. Rehnquist, W. – Joined majority opinion
5. Stevens, J. – Joined majority opinion
6. Brennan, W. – Wrote concurring opinion
7. Marshall, T. – Joined Brennan's concurrence
8. Stewart, P. – Joined Brennan's concurrence
9. Blackmun, H. – Joined Brennan's concurrence

VI. A WIN OR LOSS FOR THE ACLU?

The ACLU filed as amicus curiae urging reversal; the U.S. Supreme Court reversed the ruling of the Supreme Court of Puerto Rico in a 9-0 vote, giving the ACLU an apparent win.

437. Michigan v. DeFillippo

(Decided June 25, 1979; 443 U.S. 31)

I. ISSUE

A. Issues Discussed

Criminal Justice, Fourth Amendment, Fourteenth Amendment

B. Legal Question Presented

"[W]hether an arrest made in good-faith reliance on an ordinance, which at the time had not been declared unconstitutional, is valid regardless of a subsequent judicial determination of its unconstitutionality."

C. Supreme Court's Answer

An arrest is valid when made in good-faith reliance on an ordinance that is subsequently declared unconstitutional.

II. CASE SUMMARY

A. Background

Respondent was found by Detroit police officers in an alley with a woman after officers were called over the radio "to investigate to persons reportedly appearing to be intoxicated in an alley." When asked for identification, respondent gave inconsistent and evasive responses. He was then arrested for violating a Detroit ordinance providing "that a police officer may stop and question an individual if he has reasonable cause to believe that the individual's behavior warrants further investigation for criminal activity," and making it "unlawful for any person stopped pursuant thereto to refuse to identify himself and produce evidence of his identity." During the search incident to the arrest, the officers discovered drugs on respondent's person. He was subsequently charged with a drug offense, but not with violating the city ordinance.

The trial court denied respondent's motion to suppress the evidence obtained in the search. The Michigan Court of Appeals reversed, holding that the ordinance "was unconstitutionally vague." Therefore, the court determined, both the search and arrest were invalid and the evidence obtained in the search should have been suppressed on federal constitutional grounds even though it was obtained as a result of an arrest pursuant to a "presumptively valid ordinance."

The Supreme Court granted certiorari to review the case and reversed.

B. Counsel of Record / ACLU Attorney

ACLU Side (Respondent / Appellee): James C. Howarth argued the cause for appellee.

Opposing Side (Petitioner / Appellant): Timothy A. Baughman argued the cause for appellant.

III. AMICI CURIAE

ACLU Side (Respondent / Appellee)

Brief of amici curiae filed on behalf of the ACLU Fund of Michigan by Edward M. Wise.

Brief of amici curiae filed on behalf of California Attorneys for Criminal Justice, et al., by John J. Cleary and Ephraim Margolin.

Brief of amici curiae filed on behalf of the National Legal Aid and Defender Association by Quin Denvir and Laurance S. Smith.

Opposing Side (Petitioner / Appellant)

Brief of amici curiae filed on behalf of the State of California by Evelle J. Younger, Attorney General, Jack R. Winkler, Chief Assistant Attorney General, Daniel J. Kremer, Assistant Attorney General, Harley D. Mayfield, Deputy Attorney General, and Karl Phaler, Deputy Attorney General.

Brief of amici curiae filed on behalf of Americans for Effective Law Enforcement, Inc., et al., by James P. Costello, John Fennig, Richard J. Vittenson, Richard F. Mayer, Frank Carrington, Wayne W. Schmidt, Glen R. Murphy, and Thomas Hendrickson.

IV. THE SUPREME COURT'S DECISION

"Under the Fourth and Fourteenth Amendments, an arresting officer may, without a warrant search a person validly arrested. The constitutionality of a search incident to an arrest does not depend on whether there is any indication that the person arrested possesses weapons or evidence. The fact of a lawful arrest, standing alone, authorizes a search. Here the officer effected the arrest of respondent for his refusal to identify himself; contraband drugs were found as a result of the search of respondent's person incidental to that arrest. If the arrest was valid when made, the search was valid and the illegal drugs are admissible in evidence.

Whether an officer is authorized to make an arrest ordinarily depends, in the first instance, on state law. Respondent does not contend, however, that the arrest was not authorized by Michigan law. His sole contention is that since the arrest was for allegedly violating a Detroit ordinance later held unconstitutional, the search was likewise invalid. . . .

The validity of the arrest does not depend on whether the suspect actually committed a crime; the mere fact that the suspect is later acquitted of the offense for which he is arrested is irrelevant to the validity of the arrest. We have made clear that the kinds and degree of proof and the procedural requirements necessary for a conviction are not prerequisites to a valid arrest. . . .

This Court repeatedly has explained that 'probable cause' to justify an arrest means facts and circumstances within the officer's knowledge that are sufficient to warrant a prudent person, or one of reasonable caution, in believing, in the circumstances shown, that the suspect has committed, is committing, or is about to commit an offense.

On this record there was abundant probable cause to satisfy the constitutional prerequisite for an arrest. At that time, of course, there was no controlling precedent that this ordinance was or was not constitutional, and hence the conduct observed violated a presumptively valid ordinance. A prudent officer, in the course of determining whether respondent had committed an offense under all the circumstances shown by this record, should not have been required to anticipate that a court would later hold the ordinance unconstitutional. . . .

The subsequently determined invalidity of the Detroit ordinance on vagueness grounds does not undermine the validity of the arrest made for violation of that ordinance, and the evidence discovered in the search of respondent should not have been suppressed. Accordingly, the case is remanded for further proceedings not inconsistent with this opinion."

V. JUSTICE VOTE

3 Pro ACLU Side vs. 6 Con Opposing Side

ACLU Side (Respondent / Appellee)

1. Brennan, W. – Wrote dissenting opinion
2. Marshall, T. – Joined Brennan's dissent
3. Stevens, J. – Joined Brennan's dissent

Opposing Side (Petitioner / Appellant)

1. Burger, W. – Wrote majority opinion
2. Stewart, P. – Joined majority opinion
3. White B. – Joined majority opinion
4. Powell, L. – Joined majority opinion
5. Rehnquist, W. – Joined majority opinion
6. Blackmun, H. – Wrote concurring opinion

VI. A WIN OR LOSS FOR THE ACLU?

The ACLU filed as amicus curiae urging affirmance; the Supreme Court reversed the ruling of the Michigan Court of Appeals in a 6-3 vote, giving the ACLU an apparent loss.

438. Califano v. Westcott

(Decided June 25, 1979; 443 U.S. 76)

I. ISSUE

A. Issues Discussed

Civil rights, gender, Fifth Amendment, Fourteenth Amendment, due process

B. Legal Question Presented

Does providing benefits to families where the father is unemployed, but not when the mother is unemployed, violate the Due Process Clause of the Fifth Amendment?

C. Supreme Court's Answer

This method of distributing benefits is unconstitutional and was appropriately remedied by extending the program to cover unemployment of parents of either gender.

II. CASE SUMMARY

A. Background

"Section 407 of the Social Security Act, part of the Aid to Families with Dependent Children program, provides benefits to families whose dependent children have been deprived of parental support because of the unemployment of the father, but does not provide such benefits when the mother becomes unemployed."

Appellees were two couples who each had an infant, and had satisfied all the requirements for the benefits except for the fact that the unemployed parent was the mother. Both couples had been denied benefits because the unemployed person was female. They instituted a class action suit in federal district court to challenge the gender qualification.

"The United States District Court for the District of Massachusetts held that this distinction violates the Due Process Clause of the Fifth Amendment, and ordered that benefits be paid to families deprived of support because of the unemployment of the mother to the same extent they are paid to families deprived of support because of the unemployment of the father. . . .

Although the Commissioner originally had agreed that this was the appropriate remedy, he later sought modification of the District Court's order, so as to effect a more limited extension of the AFDC–UF program. The Commissioner requested that he be permitted to pay benefits 'only to those families where needy children have been deprived of parental support or care by the unemployment of the family's principal wage-earner.' (emphasis added). This modification, he argued, would accomplish a gender-neutral extension of the program at a much lower cost. On August 9, 1978, the District Court denied the Commissioner's motion, believing that 'any reformulation of the statutory scheme

. . . which goes beyond the remedy already ordered in this case is properly left to Congressional action.'"

The Supreme Court granted certiorari to review the case and affirmed.

B. Counsel of Record / ACLU Attorney

ACLU Side (Respondent / Appellee): Henry A. Freedman argued the cause for appellee.

Opposing Side (Petitioner / Appellant): William H. Alsup argued the cause for appellant in No. 78-437. Paul W. Johnson argued the cause for appellant in No. 78-689.

III. AMICI CURIAE

ACLU Side (Respondent / Appellee)

Brief of amici curiae filed on behalf of the ACLU, et al., by Ruth Bader Ginsburg, Diana A. Steele, Phyllis N. Segal, Nancy Duff Campell, and Rosalind M. Gordon.

Brief of amici curiae filed on behalf of Cathy Stevens, Rosalie McRoberts, and Sonja Smith, by Stephan Landsman, Anthony Touschner, Charles E. Guerrier, and Barbara Kaye Besser.

Opposing Side (Petitioner / Appellant)

No briefs of amici curiae were filed in support of appellant.

IV. THE SUPREME COURT'S DECISION

"For mothers who are the primary providers for their families, and who are unemployed, § 407 is obviously gender biased, for it deprives them and their families of benefits solely on the basis of their sex . . . . AFDC-UF benefits are not 'fringe benefits,' nor are they a type of social assistance paid without regard to need. Rather, they are subsistence payments made available as a last resort to families that would otherwise lack basic necessities. The deprivation imposed by the Act, moreover, is not a mere procedural barrier, . . . but is an absolute bar to qualification for aid. We therefore reject the contention that the classification imposed by it does not discriminate on the basis of gender. . . .

Even if the actual purpose of the gender qualification was to deal with the problem of paternal desertion, it does not appear that the classification is substantially related to the achievement of that goal. . . . There is no evidence, in the legislative history or elsewhere, that a father has less incentive to desert in a family where the mother is the breadwinner and becomes unemployed, than in a family where the father is the breadwinner and becomes unemployed. In either case, the family's need will be equally great, and the father will be equally subject to pressure to leave the home to make the family eligible for benefits. . . .

We conclude that the gender classification of § 407 is not substantially related to the attainment of any important and valid statutory goals. It is, rather, part of the 'baggage of sexual stereotypes,' that presumes the father has the 'primary responsibility to provide a home and its essentials,' while the mother is the 'center of home and family life.' Legislation that rests on such presumptions, without more, cannot survive scrutiny under the Due Process Clause of the Fifth Amendment. . . .

The remedy the Commissioner proposes . . . undeniably would be cheaper than the remedy the District Court decreed, in part because it would terminate some current recipients' eligibility. Although cost may prove a dispositive factor in other contexts, we do not regard it as controlling here. . . . This Court, in any event, is ill-equipped both to estimate the relative costs of various types of coverage, and to gauge the effect that different levels of expenditures would have upon the alleviation of human suffering. Under these circumstances, any fine-tuning of AFDC coverage along 'principal wage-earner' lines is properly left to the democratic branches of the Government. In sum, we believe the District Court, in an effort to render the AFDC-UF program gender neutral, adopted the simplest and most equitable extension possible.

The judgment of the District Court accordingly is affirmed."

V. JUSTICE VOTE

5 Pro ACLU Side vs. 4 Con Opposing Side

ACLU Side (Respondent / Appellee)

1. Blackmun, H. – Wrote majority opinion
2. Brennan, W. – Joined majority opinion
3. White, B. – Joined majority opinion
4. Marshall, T. – Joined majority opinion
5. Stevens, J. – Joined majority opinion

Opposing Side (Petitioner / Appellant)

1. Powell, L. – Wrote opinion concurring in part and dissenting in part
2. Stewart, P. – Joined Powell's opinion
3. Burger, W. – Joined Powell's opinion
4. Rehnquist, W. – Joined Powell's opinion

VI. A WIN OR LOSS FOR THE ACLU?

The ACLU filed as amicus curiae urging affirmance; the Supreme Court affirmed the ruling of the District Court of Massachusetts in a 5-4 vote, giving the ACLU an apparent win.

439. Smith v. Daily Mail Publishing Co.

(Decided June 26, 1979; 443 U.S. 97)

I. ISSUE

A. Issues Discussed

First Amendment, freedoms of press, speech, and association, Fourteenth Amendment

B. Legal Question Presented

"[W]hether a West Virginia statute violates the First and Fourteenth Amendments of the United States Constitution by making it a crime for a newspaper to publish, without the written approval of the juvenile court, the name of any youth charged as a juvenile offender."

C. Supreme Court's Answer

The statute violates the First and Fourteenth Amendments.

II. CASE SUMMARY

A. Background

Respondent newspapers published articles which contained the name of a juvenile who had been arrested for allegedly killing another youth. Respondents "learned of the shooting by monitoring routinely the police band radio frequency." They obtained the name of the juvenile arrested "simply by asking various witnesses, the police, and as assistant prosecuting attorney who were at the school." Respondents were indicted for violating a West Virginia statute which made "it a crime for a newspaper to publish, without the written approval of the juvenile court, the name of any youth charged as a juvenile offender. . . .

Respondents then filed an original-jurisdiction petition with the West Virginia Supreme Court of Appeals, seeking a writ of prohibition against the prosecuting attorney and the Circuit Court Judges of Kanawha County, petitioners here. Respondents alleged that the indictment was based on a statute that violated the First and Fourteenth Amendments of the United States Constitution and several provisions of the State's Constitution and requested an order prohibiting the county officials from taking any action on the indictment.

The West Virginia Supreme Court of Appeals issued the writ of prohibition. Relying on holdings of [the Supreme] Court, it held that the statute abridged the freedom of the press. The court reasoned that the statute operated as a prior restraint on speech and that the State's interest in protecting the identity of the juvenile offender did not overcome the heavy presumption against the constitutionality of such prior restraints."

The Supreme Court granted certiorari to review the case and affirmed.

B. Counsel of Record / ACLU Attorney

ACLU Side (Respondent / Appellee): Floyd Abrams argued the cause for appellee.

Opposing Side (Petitioner / Appellant): Cletus B. Hanley, Special Assistant Attorney General of West Virginia, argued the cause for appellant.

III. AMICI CURIAE

ACLU Side (Respondent / Appellee)

Brief of amici curiae filed on behalf of the ACLU by Bruce J. Ennis, Charles S. Sims, and George Kannar.

Brief of amici curiae filed on behalf of the American Society of Newspaper Editors, et al., by Richard M. Schmidt, Jr., Ian D. Volner, and David M. Rickless.

Brief of amici curiae filed on behalf of the Chicago Tribune Company by Don H. Reuben, Lawrence Gunnels, and James A. Klenk.

Brief of amici curiae filed on behalf of the American Newspaper Publishers Association by Arthur B. Hanson, Frank M. Northam, Mitchell W. Dale, and Arthur D. McKey.

Opposing Side (Petitioner / Appellant)

Brief of amici curiae filed on behalf of the Juvenile Defender Attorney Program, et al., by Paul Raymond Stone and Charles R. Garten.

IV. THE SUPREME COURT'S DECISION

"[I]f a newspaper lawfully obtains truthful information about a matter of public significance then state officials may not constitutionally punish publication of the information, absent a need to further a state interest of the highest order. These cases involved situations where the government itself provided or made possible press access to the information. That factor is not controlling. Here respondents relied upon routine newspaper reporting techniques to ascertain the identity of the alleged assailant. A free press cannot be made to rely solely upon the sufferance of government to supply it with information. If the information is lawfully obtained, as it was here, the state may not punish its publication except when necessary to further an interest more substantial than is present here. . . .

The sole interest advanced by the State to justify its criminal statute is to protect the anonymity of the juvenile offender. It is asserted that confidentiality will further his rehabilitation because publication of the name may encourage further antisocial conduct and also may cause the juvenile to lose future employment or suffer other consequences for this single offense. In Davis v. Alaska, similar arguments were advanced by the State to justify not permitting a criminal defendant to impeach a prosecution witness on the basis of his juvenile record. We said there that 'we do not and need not challenge the State's interest as a matter of its own policy in the administration of criminal justice to seek to preserve the anonymity of a juvenile offender.' However, we concluded that the State's policy must be subordinated to the defendant's Sixth Amendment right of confrontation. The important rights created by the First Amendment must be considered along with the rights of defendants guaranteed by the Sixth Amendment. Therefore, the reasoning of Davis that the constitutional right must prevail over the state's interest in protecting juveniles applies with equal force here.

The magnitude of the State's interest in this statute is not sufficient to justify application of a criminal penalty to respondents. Moreover, the statute's approach does not satisfy constitutional requirements. The statute does not restrict the electronic media or any form of publication, except 'newspapers,' from printing the names of youths charged in a juvenile proceeding. In this very case, three radio stations announced the alleged assailant's name before the Daily Mail decided to publish it. Thus, even assuming the statute served a state interest of the highest order, it does not accomplish its stated purpose. [T]here is no evidence to demonstrate that the imposition of criminal penalties is necessary to protect the confidentiality of juvenile proceedings . . .

There is no issue before us of unlawful press access to confidential judicial proceedings, there is no issue here of privacy or prejudicial pretrial publicity. At issue is simply the power of a state to punish the truthful publication of an alleged juvenile delinquent's name lawfully obtained by a newspaper. The asserted state interest cannot justify the statute's imposition of criminal sanctions on this type of publication. Accordingly, the judgment of the West Virginia Supreme Court of Appeals is affirmed."

V. JUSTICE VOTE

8 Pro ACLU Side vs. 0 Con Opposing Side

ACLU Side (Respondent / Appellee)

1. Burger, W. – Wrote majority opinion
2. Marshall, T. – Joined majority opinion
3. Stevens, J. – Joined majority opinion
4. Brennan, W. – Joined majority opinion
5. Stewart, P. – Joined majority opinion
6. Blackmun, H. – Joined majority opinion
7. Rehnquist, W. – Wrote concurring opinion
8. White B. – Joined majority opinion

Powell, L – Took no part in the decision

VI. A WIN OR LOSS FOR THE ACLU?

The ACLU filed as amicus curiae urging affirmance; the U.S. Supreme Court affirmed the ruling of the Supreme Court of Appeals of West Virginia in an 8-0 vote, giving the ACLU an apparent win.

440. Baker v. McCollan

(Decided June 26, 1979; 443 U.S. 137)

I. ISSUE

A. Issues Discussed

Governmental authority, immunity, Fourteenth Amendment, warrants

B. Legal Question Presented

"[W]hether an allegation of simple negligence is sufficient to state a cause of action under § 1983," which imposes civil liability on a person who, under color of state law, subjects another to the deprivation "of a right 'secured by the Constitution and laws.'"

C. Supreme Court's Answer

This allegation is not sufficient to state a cause of action under § 1983.

II. CASE SUMMARY

A. Background

Respondent Linnie Carl McCollan's brother, Leonard McCollan, "procured a duplicate of Linnie's driver's license, identical to the original in every respect except that, . . . 'Leonard's picture graced it instead of Linnie's.'" Leonard was arrested on narcotics charges, booked in Linnie's name, and released on bond. An arrest warrant intended for the Leonard was subsequently issued in Linnie's name. Pursuant to that warrant, Linnie, over his protest, was taken into custody and detained in jail for several days before the error was discovered and he was released.

"Respondent brought this damages action 'pursuant to the Fourteenth Amendment to the United States Constitution and . . . [§] 1983.' After each party had rested his case, the United States District Court for the Northern District of Texas directed a verdict in favor of Sheriff Baker and his surety, Transamerica Insurance Co., without articulating its reasons. The Court of Appeals for the Fifth Circuit reversed." The Court of Appeals "determined that a jury could reasonably conclude that the sheriff had behaved unreasonably" in failing to immediately identify the error and release Linnie by not promptly comparing the photograph or fingerprints of Leonard with those of Linnie.

The Supreme Court granted certiorari to review the case and reversed.

B. Counsel of Record / ACLU Attorney

ACLU Side (Respondent / Appellee): Douglas R. Larson argued the cause for appellee.

Opposing Side (Petitioner / Appellant): A. W. Sorelle III argued the cause for appellant.

III. AMICI CURIAE

ACLU Side (Respondent / Appellee)

Brief of amici curiae filed on behalf of the ACLU by Leon Friedman, Bruce J. Ennis, Charles S. Sims, George Kannar, Alan H. Levine, Harold C. Hirschman, Gary S. Gilden, and Robert M. Mark.

Opposing Side (Petitioner / Appellant)

No briefs of amici curiae were filed in support of appellant.

IV. THE SUPREME COURT'S DECISION

"The first inquiry in any § 1983 suit . . . is whether the plaintiff has been deprived of a right 'secured by the Constitution and laws.' If there has been no such deprivation, the state of mind of the defendant is wholly immaterial. We think that respondent has failed to satisfy this threshold requirement of § 1983 and thus defer once again consideration of the question whether simple negligence can give rise to § 1983 liability.

[T]he Fourth Amendment requires the States to provide a fair and reliable determination of probable cause as a condition for any significant pretrial restraint of liberty. The probable-cause determination 'must be made by a judicial officer either before or promptly after arrest.' Since an adversary hearing is not required, and since the probable cause standard for pretrial detention is the same as that for arrest, a person arrested pursuant to a warrant issued by a magistrate on a showing of probable-cause is not constitutionally entitled to a separate judicial determination that there is probable cause to detain him pending trial. . . .

The Fourteenth Amendment does not protect against all deprivations of liberty. It protects only against deprivations of liberty accomplished 'without due process of law.' A reasonable division of functions between law enforcement officers, committing magistrates, and judicial officers—all of whom may be potential defendants in a § 1983 action—is entirely consistent with 'due process of law.' Given the requirements that arrest be made only on probable cause and that one detained be accorded a speedy trial, we do not think a sheriff executing an arrest warrant is required by the Constitution to investigate independently every claim of innocence, whether the claim is based on mistaken identity or a defense such as lack of requisite intent. Nor is the official charged with maintaining custody of the accused named in the warrant required by the Constitution to perform an error-free investigation of such a claim. The ultimate determination of such claims of innocence is placed in the hands of the judge and the jury. . . .

Section 1983 imposes liability for violations of rights protected by the Constitution, not for violations of duties of care arising out of tort law. Remedy for the latter type of injury must be sought in state court under traditional tort-law principles. Just as '[m]edical malpractice does not become a constitutional violation merely because the victim is a prisoner,' false imprisonment does not become a violation of the Fourteenth Amendment merely because the defendant is a state official.

Having been deprived of no rights secured under the United States Constitution, respondent had no claim cognizable under § 1983. The judgment of the Court of Appeals for the Fifth Circuit is therefore reversed."

V. JUSTICE VOTE

3 Pro ACLU Side vs. 6 Con Opposing Side

ACLU Side (Respondent / Appellee)

1. Marshall, T. – Wrote dissenting opinion, joined Stevens' dissent
2. Stevens, J. – Wrote dissenting opinion
3. Brennan, W. – Joined Stevens' dissent

Opposing Side (Petitioner / Appellant)

1. Rehnquist, W. – Wrote majority opinion
2. Burger, W. – Joined majority opinion
3. Stewart, P. – Joined majority opinion
4. White B. – Joined majority opinion
5. Blackmun, H. – Wrote concurring opinion
6. Powell, L. – Joined majority opinion

VI. A WIN OR LOSS FOR THE ACLU?

The ACLU filed as amicus curiae urging affirmance; the Supreme Court reversed the ruling of the Court of Appeals for the Fifth Circuit in a 6-3 vote, giving the ACLU an apparent loss.

441. United Steelworkers of America v. Weber

(Decided June 27, 1979; 443 U.S. 193)

I. ISSUE

A. Issues Discussed

Civil rights, race

B. Legal Question Presented

"[W]hether Congress, in Title VII of the Civil Rights Act of 1964, 78 Stat., 253, as amended, 42 U.S.C. § 2000e et seq., left employers and unions in the private sector free to take [certain] race-conscious steps to eliminate manifest racial imbalances in traditionally segregated job categories."

C. Supreme Court's Answer

Employers can create race-conscious affirmative action plans such as the plan implemented here.

II. CASE SUMMARY

A. Background

"In 1974, petitioner United Steelworkers of America (USWA) and petitioner Kaiser Aluminum & Chemical Corp. (Kaiser) entered into a master collective-bargaining agreement covering terms and conditions of employment at 15 Kaiser plants. The agreement contained, inter alia, an affirmative action plan designed to eliminate conspicuous racial imbalances in Kaiser's then almost exclusively white craft-work forces. Black craft-hiring goals were set for each Kaiser plant equal to the percentage of blacks in the respective local labor forces. To enable plants to meet these goals, on-the-job training programs were established to teach unskilled production workers—black and white—the skills necessary to become craftworkers. The plan reserved for black employees 50% of the openings in these newly created in-plant training programs.

This case arose from the operation of the plan at Kaiser's plant in Gramercy, La. Until 1974, Kaiser hired as craftworkers for that plant only persons who had had prior craft experience. Because blacks had long been excluded from craft unions, few were able to present such credentials. As a consequence, prior to 1974 only 1.83% (5 out of 273) of the skilled craftworkers at the Gramercy plant were black, even though the work force in the Gramercy area was approximately 39% black.

Pursuant to the national agreement Kaiser altered its craft-hiring practice in the Gramercy plant. Rather than hiring already trained outsiders, Kaiser established a training program to train its production workers to fill craft openings. Selection of craft trainees was made on the basis of seniority, with the proviso that at least 50% of the new trainees were to be black until the percentage of black skilled craftworkers in the Gramercy plant approximated the percentage of blacks in the local labor force.

During 1974, the first year of the operation of the Kaiser-USWA affirmative action plan, 13 craft trainees were selected from Gramercy's production work force. Of these, seven were black and six white. The most senior black selected into the program had less seniority than several white production workers whose bids for admission were rejected. Thereafter one of those white production workers, respondent Brian Weber (hereafter respondent), instituted this class action in the United States District Court for the Eastern District of Louisiana.

The complaint alleged that the filling of craft trainee positions at the Gramercy plant pursuant to the affirmative action program had resulted in junior black employees' receiving training in preference to senior white employees, thus discriminating against respondent and other similarly situated white employees in violation of §§ 703(a) and (d) of Title VII. The District Court held that the plan violated Title VII, entered a judgment in favor of the plaintiff class, and granted a permanent injunction prohibiting Kaiser and the USWA 'from denying plaintiffs, Brian F. Weber and all other members of the class, access to on-the-job training programs on the basis of race.' A divided panel of the Court of

Appeals for the Fifth Circuit affirmed, holding that all employment preferences based upon race, including those preferences incidental to bona fide affirmative action plans, violated Title VII's prohibition against racial discrimination in employment."

The Supreme Court granted certiorari to review the case and reversed.

B. Counsel of Record / ACLU Attorney

ACLU Side (Petitioner / Appellant): Michael H. Gottesman argued the cause for appellant in No. 78-432.

Noyes Thompson Powers argued the cause for appellant in No. 78-435.

Deputy Solicitor General Lawrence C. Wallace argued the cause for appellant in No. 78-436.

Opposing Side (Respondent / Appellee): Michael R. Fontham argued the cause for appellees in all cases.

III. AMICI CURIAE

ACLU Side (Petitioner / Appellant)

Brief of amici curiae filed on behalf of the ACLU, et al., by E. Richard Larson, Burt Neuborne, Bruce J. Ennis, and Frank Askin.

Brief of amici curiae filed on behalf of the Honorable Patricia Schroeder, Member of Congress, the ACLU Women's Rights Project, et al., by Eileen M. Stein, Donna R. Lenhoff, Pat Eames, and Susan Silber.

Additional briefs of amici curiae were filed on behalf of the Affirmative Action Coordinating Center, et al., the American Federation of State, County and Municipal Employees, AFL-CIO, et al., the Asian American Legal Defense and Education Fund, et al., the California Fair Employment Practice Commission, et al., the Lawyers' Committee for Civil Rights Under Law, the NAACP, the NAACP Legal Defense and Educational Fund, Inc., et al., the National Medical Association, Inc., et al., the National Puerto Rican Coalition, et al.,the National Union of Hospital and Health Care Employees, RWDSU, AFL-CIO, the Women's Caucus, District 31 of the United Steelworkers of America., the American G.I. Forum, et al., the United Electrical, Radio and Machine Workers of America, the National Coordinating Committee for Trade Union Action and Democracy, Women's Equal Rights Legal Defense and Educational Fund, the City of Los Angeles, the National Coordinating Committee for Trade Union Action and Democracy, and the Equal Employment Advisory Council.

Opposing Side (Respondent / Appellee)

Briefs of amici curiae were filed on behalf of the California Correctional Officers Association, the Government Contract Employers Association, the Pacific Legal Foundation, the Polish American Congress, et al., the Southeastern Legal Foundation, Inc., the United States Justice Foundation, the Anti-Defamation League of B'nai B'rith, et al., the Committee on Academic Nondiscrimination and Integrity, the Pacific Civil Liberties League, the Washington Legal Foundation, and the Great Plains Legal Foundation.

IV. THE SUPREME COURT'S DECISION

"We hold that Title VII does not prohibit such race-conscious affirmative action plans. . . . Respondent argues that Congress intended in Title VII to prohibit all race-conscious affirmative action plans. . . . Respondent's argument is not without force. But it overlooks the significance of the fact that the Kaiser-USWA plan is an affirmative action plan voluntarily adopted by private parties to eliminate traditional patterns of racial segregation. In this context respondent's reliance upon a literal construction of §§ 703(a) and (d) and upon McDonald is misplaced. . . . The prohibition against racial discrimination in §§ 703(a) and (d) of Title VII must therefore be read against the background of the legislative history of Title VII and the historical context from which the Act arose. Examination of those sources makes clear that an interpretation of the sections that forbade all race-conscious affirmative action would 'bring about an end completely at variance with the purpose of the statute' and must be rejected.

Congress' primary concern in enacting the prohibition against racial discrimination in Title VII of the Civil Rights Act of 1964 was with 'the plight of the Negro in our economy.' Before 1964, blacks were largely relegated to 'unskilled and semi-skilled jobs.' Because of automation the number of such jobs was rapidly decreasing. As a consequence, 'the relative position of the Negro worker [was] steadily worsening. In 1947 the nonwhite unemployment rate was only 64 percent higher than the white rate; in 1962 it was 124 percent higher.' Congress considered this a serious social problem. . . .

Given this legislative history, we cannot agree with respondent that Congress intended to prohibit the private sector from taking effective steps to accomplish the goal that Congress designed Title VII to achieve. The very statutory words intended as a spur or catalyst to cause 'employers and unions to self-examine and to self-evaluate their employment practices and to endeavor to eliminate, so far as possible, the last vestiges of an unfortunate and ignominious page in this country's history,' cannot be interpreted as an absolute prohibition against all private, voluntary, race-conscious affirmative action efforts to hasten the elimination of such vestiges. . . .

Title VII could not have been enacted into law without substantial support from legislators in both Houses who traditionally resisted federal regulation of private business. . . . Clearly, a prohibition against all voluntary, race-conscious, affirmative action efforts would disserve these ends. Such a prohibition would augment the powers of the Federal Government and diminish traditional management prerogatives while at the same time impeding attainment of the ultimate statutory goals. In view of this legislative history and in view of Congress' desire to avoid undue federal regulation of private businesses, use of the word 'require' rather than the phrase 'require or permit' in § 703(j) fortifies the conclusion that Congress did not intend to limit traditional business freedom to such a degree as to prohibit all voluntary, race-conscious affirmative action.

We therefore hold that Title VII's prohibition in §§ 703(a) and (d) against racial discrimination does not condemn all private, voluntary, race-conscious affirmative action plans. . . .

It suffices to hold that the challenged Kaiser-USWA affirmative action plan falls on the permissible side of the line. The purposes of the plan mirror those of the statute. [T]he plan does not unnecessarily trammel the interests of the white employees. The plan does not require the discharge of white workers and their replacement with new black hirees. Nor does the plan create an absolute bar to the advancement of white employees; half of those trained in the program will be white. Moreover, the plan is a temporary measure; it is not intended to maintain racial balance, but simply to eliminate a manifest racial imbalance. Preferential selection of craft trainees at the Gramercy plant will end as soon as the percentage of black skilled craftworkers in the Gramercy plant approximates the percentage of blacks in the local labor force.

We conclude, therefore, that the adoption of the Kaiser-USWA plan for the Gramercy plant falls within the area of discretion left by Title VII to the private sector voluntarily to adopt affirmative action plans designed to eliminate conspicuous racial imbalance in traditionally segregated job categories. Accordingly, the judgment of the Court of Appeals for the Fifth Circuit is reversed."

V. JUSTICE VOTE

5 Pro ACLU Side vs. 2 Con Opposing Side

ACLU Side (Petitioner / Appellant)

1. Brennan, W. – Wrote majority opinion
2. Stewart, P. – Joined majority opinion
3. White, B. – Joined majority opinion
4. Marshall, T. – Joined majority opinion
5. Blackmun, H. – Wrote concurring opinion

Opposing Side (Respondent / Appellee)

1. Rehnquist, W. – Wrote dissenting opinion
2. Burger, W. – Wrote dissenting opinion, joined Rehnquist's dissent

Powell, L. Took no part in the decision
Stevens, J – Took no part in the decision

VI. A WIN OR LOSS FOR THE ACLU?

The ACLU filed as amicus curiae urging reversal; the Supreme Court reversed the ruling of the Court of Appeals for the Fifth Circuit in a 5-2 vote, giving the ACLU an apparent win.

442. Gannett Co. v. DePasquale

(Decided July 2, 1979; 443 U.S. 368)

I. ISSUE

A. Issues Discussed

Criminal procedure, justiciability, right to a hearing, freedom of speech

B. Legal Question Presented

"[W]hether members of the public have an independent constitutional right to insist upon access to a pretrial judicial proceeding, even though the accused, the prosecutor, and the trial judge all have agreed to the closure of that proceeding in order to assure a fair trial."

C. Supreme Court's Answer

The public does not have an independent constitutional right to access to a pretrial proceeding where the judge, prosecutor, and accused agreed to close the proceeding to assure a fair trial.

II. CASE SUMMARY

A. Background

Defendants in a trial who had been charged with murder, robbery, and grand larceny "requested that the public and the press be excluded from the hearing" concerning the admissibility of certain evidence in their trial. Defendants argued that the "buildup of adverse publicity had jeopardized the ability of the defendants to receive a fair trial." The prosecutor did not oppose the motion. A reporter employed by petitioner newspaper, Gannet Co., whose newspapers had given extensive coverage of the crime and the pre-trial proceedings, made no objection even though she was in the courtroom "at the time of the closure motion." Respondent DePasquale, the trial judge, granted defendant's motion. The next day, the reporter "wrote a letter to the trial judge asserting a "right to cover this hearing" and requesting that "we . . . be given access to the transcript.' The judge responded later the same day. He stated that the suppression hearing had concluded and that any decision on immediate release of the transcript had been reserved. The petitioner then moved the court to set aside its exclusionary order."

The trial judge "refused to vacate his exclusion order or grant the petitioner immediate access to a transcript of the pretrial hearing. "[T]he judge ruled that the interest of the press and the public was outweighed in this case by the defendants' right to a fair trial." Petitioner immediately filed a lawsuit "challenging the closure orders on First, Sixth, and Fourteenth Amendment grounds." The New York Supreme Court, Appellate Division, Fourth Department vacated the orders and "held that the exclusionary orders transgressed the public's vital interest in open judicial proceedings and further constituted an unlawful prior restraint in violation of the First and Fourteenth Amendments." On appeal, the New York Court of Appeals "upheld the exclusion of the press and the public from the pretrial proceeding."

The Supreme Court granted certiorari to review the case and affirmed.

B. Counsel of Record / ACLU Attorney

ACLU Side (Petitioner / Appellant): Robert C. Bernius argued the cause for appellant.

Opposing Side (Respondent / Appellee): Bernard Kobroff argued the cause for appellee.

III. AMICI CURIAE

ACLU Side (Petitioner / Appellant)

Brief of amici curiae filed on behalf of the ACLU, et al., by David Rudenstine, Steven R. Shapiro, Bruce J. Ennis, and Joel M. Gora.

Additional briefs of amici curiae were filed on behalf of the American Newspaper Publishers Association, et al., the Deadline Club, the New York City Chapter of the Society of Professional Journalists, Sigma Delta Chi, et al., the Reporters Committee for Freedom of the Press, et al., and the New York Times Company.

Opposing Side (Respondent / Appellee)

No briefs of amici curiae were filed in support of appellee.

IV. THE SUPREME COURT'S DECISION

"This Court has long recognized that adverse publicity can endanger the ability of a defendant to receive a fair trial. To safeguard the due process rights of the accused, a trial judge has an affirmative constitutional duty to minimize the effects of prejudicial pretrial publicity. And because of the Constitution's pervasive concern for these due process rights, a trial judge may surely take protective measures even when they are not strictly and inescapably necessary.

Publicity concerning pretrial suppression hearings such as the one involved in the present case poses special risks of unfairness. The whole purpose of such hearings is to screen out unreliable or illegally obtained evidence and insure that this evidence does not become known to the jury. Publicity concerning the proceedings at a pretrial hearing, however, could influence public opinion against a defendant and inform potential jurors of inculpatory information wholly inadmissible at the actual trial. . . .

The Sixth Amendment, applicable to the States through the Fourteenth, surrounds a criminal trial with guarantees such as the rights to notice, confrontation, and compulsory process that have as their overriding purpose the protection of the accused from prosecutorial and judicial abuses. Among the guarantees that the Amendment provides to a person charged with the commission of a criminal offense, and to him alone, is the 'right to a speedy and public trial, by an impartial jury.' The Constitution nowhere mentions any right of access to a criminal trial on the part of the public; its guarantee, like the others enumerated, is personal to the accused. . . .

There is no question that the Sixth Amendment permits and even presumes open trials as a norm. But the issue here is whether the Constitution requires that a pretrial proceeding such as this one be opened to the public, even though the participants in the litigation agree that it should be closed to protect the defendants' right to a fair trial. . . . In conspicuous contrast with some of the early state constitutions that provided for a public right to open civil and criminal trials, the Sixth Amendment confers the right to a public trial only upon a defendant and only in a criminal case. . . .

Several factors lead to the conclusion that the actions of the trial judge here were consistent with any right of access the petitioner may have had under the First and Fourteenth Amendments. First, none of the spectators present in the courtroom, including the reporter employed by the petitioner, objected when the defendants made the closure motion. . . . Furthermore, any denial of access in this case was not absolute but only temporary. Once the danger of prejudice had dissipated, a transcript of the suppression hearing was made available. The press and the public then had a full opportunity to scrutinize the suppression hearing. [T]he press here had the opportunity to inform the public of the details of the pretrial hearing accurately and completely. Under these circumstances, any First and Fourteenth Amendment right of the petitioner to attend a criminal trial was not violated.

[W]e are asked to hold that the Constitution itself gave the petitioner an affirmative right of access to this pretrial proceeding, even though all the participants in the litigation agreed that it should be closed to protect the fair-trial rights of the defendants.

For all of the reasons discussed in this opinion, we hold that the Constitution provides no such right. Accordingly, the judgment of the New York Court of Appeals is affirmed."

V. JUSTICE VOTE

4 Pro ACLU Side vs. 5 Con Opposing Side

ACLU Side (Petitioner / Appellant)

1. Blackmun, H. – Wrote opinion concurring in part and dissenting in part
2. Brennan, W. – Joined Blackmun's opinion
3. White, B. – Joined Blackmun's opinion
4. Marshall, T. – Joined Blackmun's opinion

Opposing Side (Respondent / Appellee)

1. Stewart, P. – Wrote majority opinion
2. Rehnquist, W. – Wrote concurring opinion
3. Burger, W. – Wrote concurring opinion
4. Powell, L. – Wrote concurring opinion
5. Stevens, J. – Joined majority opinion

VI. A WIN OR LOSS FOR THE ACLU?

The ACLU filed as amicus curiae urging reversal; the Supreme Court affirmed the ruling of the New York Court of Appeals in a 5-4 vote, giving the ACLU an apparent loss.

443. Columbus Board of Education v. Penick

(Decided July 2, 1979; 443 U.S. 449)

I. ISSUE

A. Issues Discussed

Civil rights, racial discrimination

B. Legal Question Presented

Whether a systemwide remedy for racial discrimination in schools was appropriate in this circumstance where the lower courts concluded the facts supported a finding that segregation was maintained by a segregative and unconstitutional aim?

C. Supreme Court's Answer

Systemwide desegregation was appropriate here, where the facts supported a finding of persistent segregation.

II. CASE SUMMARY

A. Background

"The public schools of Columbus, Ohio, are highly segregated by race. . . . Fourteen named students in the Columbus school system brought this case on June 22, 1973, against the Columbus Board of Education, the State Board of Education, and the appropriate local and state officials. The second amended complaint, filed on October 22, 1974, charged that the Columbus defendants had pursued and were pursuing a course of conduct having the purpose and effect of causing and perpetuating segregation in the public schools, contrary to the Fourteenth Amendment. . . .

Trial of the case began more than a year later, consumed 36 trial days, produced a record containing over 600 exhibits and a transcript in excess of 6,600 pages, and was completed in June 1976. . . . The District Court's ultimate conclusion was that at the time of trial the racial segregation in the Columbus school system 'directly resulted from [the Board's] intentional segregative acts and omissions,' in violation of the Equal Protection Clause of the Fourteenth Amendment. Accordingly, judgment was entered against the local and state defendants enjoining them from continuing to discriminate on the basis of race in operating the Columbus public schools and ordering the submission of a systemwide desegregation plan. . . . The Board subsequently presented a plan that complied with the District Court's guidelines and that was embodied in a judgment entered on October 7. The plan was stayed pending appeal to the Court of Appeals.

Based on its own examination of the extensive record, the Court of Appeals affirmed the judgments entered against the local defendants."

The Supreme Court granted certiorari to review the case and affirmed.

B. Counsel of Record / ACLU Attorney

ACLU Side (Respondent / Appellee): Thomas I. Atkins argued the cause for appellee.

Assistant Attorney General Drew S. Days, III, argued the cause for the United States, as amicus curiae, by special leave of Court.

Opposing Side (Petitioner / Appellant): Samuel H. Porter argued the cause for appellant.

III. AMICI CURIAE

ACLU Side (Respondent / Appellee)

Brief of amici curiae filed on behalf of the ACLU, et al., by Burt Neuborne, E. Richard Larson, Robert Allen Sedler, Winn Newman, and Carole W. Wilson.

Brief of amici curiae filed on behalf of the United States by Assistant Attorney General Drew S. Days, III, Acting Solicitor General Lawrence G. Wallace, Assistant to the Solicitor General Sara Sun Beale, Brian K. Landsberg, and Robert J. Reinstein.

Additional briefs of amicus curiae were filed on behalf of the Fair Housing Council of Bergen County, New Jersey, the NAACP Legal Defense and Educational Fund, Inc., et al., the National Education Association, et al., and the American Jewish Congress.

Opposing Side (Petitioner / Appellant)

Brief of amici curiae filed on behalf of the Delaware State Board of Education, et al., by Richard S. Gebelein, Attorney General of Delaware, Regina M. Small, Deputy Attorney General, Mason E. Turner, Jr., James T. McKinstry, and Philip B. Kurland.

Brief of amici curiae filed on behalf of the Neighborhood School Coordinating Committee, et al., by Charles E. Brown and Ira Owen Kane.

Brief of amici curiae filed on behalf of the Cleveland, Ohio City School District by George I. Meisel, Charles F. Clarke, William C. Hartman, James P. Murphy, and John H. Bustamante.

IV. THE SUPREME COURT'S DECISION

"We have discovered no reason, however, to disturb the judgment of the Court of Appeals, based on the findings and conclusions of the District Court, that the Board's conduct at the time of trial and before not only was animated by an unconstitutional, segregative purpose, but also had current, segregative impact that was sufficiently systemwide to warrant the remedy ordered by the District Court. . . . Proof of purposeful and effective maintenance of a body of separate black schools in a substantial part of the system itself is prima facie proof of a dual school system and supports a finding to this effect absent sufficient contrary proof by the Board, which was not forthcoming in this case.

[T]he Columbus Board has been under a continuous constitutional obligation to disestablish its dual school system and that it has failed to discharge this duty. Under the Fourteenth Amendment and the cases that have construed it, the Board's duty to dismantle its dual system cannot be gainsaid. . . .The Board's continuing 'affirmative duty to disestablish the dual school system' is therefore beyond question, and it has pointed to nothing in the record persuading us that at the time of trial the dual school system and its effects had been disestablished. The Board does not appear to challenge the finding of the District Court that at the time of trial most blacks were still going to black schools and most whites to white schools. Whatever the Board's current purpose with respect to racially separate education might be, it knowingly continued its failure to eliminate the consequences of its past intentionally segregative policies. The Board 'never actively set out to dismantle this dual system.' . . .

These matters included the general practice of assigning black teachers only to those schools with substantial black student populations, a practice that was terminated only in 1974 as the result of a conciliation agreement with the Ohio Civil Rights Commission; the intentionally segregative use of optional attendance zones, discontiguous attendance areas, and boundary changes; and the selection of sites for new school construction that had the foreseeable and anticipated effect of maintaining the racial separation of the schools. The court generally noted that '[s]ince the 1954 Brown decision, the Columbus defendants or their predecessors were adequately put on notice of the fact that action was required to correct and to prevent the increase in' segregation, yet failed to heed their duty to alleviate racial separation in the schools.

[W]e cannot fault the conclusion of the District Court and the Court of Appeals that at the time of trial there was systemwide segregation in the Columbus schools that was the result of recent and remote intentionally segregative actions of the Columbus Board. . . . On this record, however, there is no apparent reason to disturb the factual findings and conclusions entered by the District Court and strongly affirmed by the Court of Appeals after its own examination of the record. . . .

Nor do we perceive any misuse of Keyes, where we held that purposeful discrimination in a substantial part of a school system furnishes a sufficient basis for an inferential finding of a system-wide discriminatory intent unless otherwise rebutted, and that given the purpose to operate a dual school system one could infer a connection between such a purpose and racial separation in other parts of the school system. There was no undue reliance here on the inferences permitted by Keyes, or upon those recognized by Swann. Furthermore, the Board was given ample opportunity to counter the evidence of segregative purpose and current, systemwide impact, and the findings of the courts below were against it in both respects.

Because the District Court and the Court of Appeals committed no prejudicial errors of fact or law, the judgment appealed from must be affirmed."

V. JUSTICE VOTE

7 Pro ACLU Side vs. 2 Con Opposing Side

ACLU Side (Respondent / Appellee)

1. White, B. – Wrote majority opinion
2. Brennan, W. – Joined majority opinion
3. Marshall, T. – Joined majority opinion
4. Blackmun, H. – Joined majority opinion
5. Stevens, J. – Joined majority opinion
6. Burger, W. – Wrote concurring opinion, joined Stewart's concurrence
7. Stewart, P. – Wrote concurring opinion

Opposing Side (Petitioner / Appellant)

1. Powell, L. – Wrote dissenting opinion, joined Rehnquist's dissent
2. Rehnquist, W. – Wrote dissenting opinion

VI. A WIN OR LOSS FOR THE ACLU?

The ACLU filed as amicus curiae urging affirmance; the Supreme Court affirmed the ruling of the Court of Appeals for the Sixth Circuit in a 7-2 vote, giving the ACLU an apparent win.

444. Bellotti v. Baird

(Decided July 2, 1979; 443 U.S. 622)

I. ISSUE

A. Issues Discussed

Privacy, civil rights, state

B. Legal Question Presented

Whether the Massachusetts statute limiting abortion access for minors, Mass.Gen.Laws Ann., ch. 112, § 12S, is constitutional.

C. Supreme Court's Answer

"Although it satisfies constitutional standards in large part, § 12S falls short of them in two respects: First, it permits judicial authorization for an abortion to be withheld from a minor who is found by the superior court to be mature and fully competent to make this decision independently. Second, it requires parental consultation or notification in every instance, without affording the pregnant minor an opportunity to receive an independent judicial determination that she is mature enough to consent or that an abortion would be in her best interests."

II. CASE SUMMARY

A. Background

"On August 2, 1974, the Legislature of the Commonwealth of Massachusetts passed, over the Governor's veto, an Act pertaining to abortions performed within the State. According to its title, the statute was intended to regulate abortions 'within present constitutional limits.' Shortly before the Act was to go into effect, the class action from which these appeals arise was commenced in the District Court to enjoin, as unconstitutional, the provision of the Act now codified as Mass.Gen.Laws Ann., ch. 112, § 12S. . . .

Physicians performing abortions in the absence of the consent required by § 12S are subject to injunctions and criminal penalties.

A three-judge District Court was convened . . . .

[T]he District Court issued an opinion invalidating § 12S. . . .

Appellants sought review in this Court, and [the Supreme Court] vacated the judgment of the District Court, concluding that it should have abstained and certified to the Supreme Judicial Court of Massachusetts appropriate questions concerning the meaning of § 12S, pursuant to existing procedure in that State.

On remand, the District Court certified nine questions to the Supreme Judicial Court. These were answered . . . .

Following the judgment of the Supreme Judicial Court, appellees returned to the District Court and obtained a stay of the enforcement of § 12S until its constitutionality could be determined. [T]he District Court again declared § 12S unconstitutional and enjoined its enforcement. . . .

Appellants sought review in this Court a second time, and [the U.S. Supreme Court] noted probable jurisdiction."

B. Counsel of Record

ACLU Side (Respondent / Appellee): Joseph J. Balliro argued the cause for appellees in both cases. With him on the brief was Joan C. Schmidt.

John H. Henn also argued the cause for appellees in both cases. With him on the brief were and John Reinstein of the Civil Liberties Union of Massachusetts, Scott C. Moriearty, Sandra L. Lynch, and Loyd M. Starrett

Opposing Side (Petitioner / Appellant): Garrick F. Cole, Assistant Attorney General of Massachusetts, argued the cause for appellants in No. 78-329. With him on the briefs were Francis X. Bellotti, Attorney General, pro se, and Michael B. Meyer and Thomas R. Kiley, Assistant Attorneys General. Brian A. Riley argued the cause for appellant in No. 78-330. With him on the brief was Thomas P. Russell.

III. AMICI CURIAE

ACLU Side (Respondent / Appellee)

Brief of amici curiae filed on behalf of the Planned Parenthood Federation of America, Inc., et al. by Eve W. Paul, Harriet F. Pilpel, and Sylvia A. Law.

Opposing Side (Petitioner / Appellant)

Brief of amici curiae filed on behalf of the Catholic League for Religious and Civil Rights et al. by Stuart D. Hubbell and Robert A. Destro.

Brief of amici curiae filed on behalf of Americans United for Life, Inc., et al., by Victor G. Rosenblum, Dennis J. Horan, and John D. Gorby.

Brief of amici curiae filed on behalf of the United States Catholic Conference by George E. Reed and Patrick F. Geary.

IV. THE SUPREME COURT'S DECISION

"We have recognized three reasons justifying the conclusion that the constitutional rights of children cannot be equated with those of adults: the peculiar vulnerability of children; their inability to make critical decisions in an informed, mature manner; and the importance of the parental role . . . .

With these principles in mind, we consider the specific constitutional questions presented by these appeals. In § 12S, Massachusetts has attempted to reconcile the constitutional right of a woman . . . to choose to terminate her pregnancy . . . with the special interest of the State in encouraging an unmarried pregnant minor to seek the advice of her parents in making the important decision . . . .

But we are concerned here with a constitutional right to seek an abortion. The abortion decision differs in important ways from other decisions that may be made during minority. The need to preserve the constitutional right and the unique nature of the abortion decision, especially when made by a minor, require a State to act with particular sensitivity when it legislates to foster parental involvement in this matter. . . .

For these reasons, as we held in Planned Parenthood of Central Missouri v. Danforth, 428 U.S., at 74, 'the State may not impose a blanket provision . . . requiring the consent of a parent or person in loco parentis as a condition for abortion of an unmarried minor during the first 12 weeks of her pregnancy.' . . . We therefore conclude that if the State decides to require a pregnant minor to obtain one or both parents' consent to an abortion, it also must provide an alternative procedure whereby authorization for the abortion can be obtained.

A pregnant minor is entitled in such a proceeding to show either: (1) that she is mature enough and well enough informed to make her abortion decision, in consultation with her physician, independently of her parents' wishes; or 2) that even if she is not able to make this decision independently, the desired abortion would be in her best interests. . . .

It is against these requirements that § 12S must be tested. . . .

Although it satisfies constitutional standards in large part, § 12S falls short of them in two respects: First, it permits judicial authorization for an abortion to be withheld from a minor who is found by the superior court to be mature and fully competent to make this decision independently. Second, it requires parental consultation or notification in every instance, without affording the pregnant minor an opportunity to receive an independent judicial determination that she is mature enough to consent or that an abortion would be in her best interests. Accordingly, we affirm the judgment of the District Court insofar as it invalidates this statute and enjoins its enforcement.

Affirmed."

V. JUSTICE VOTE

8 Pro ACLU Side vs. 1 Con Opposing Side

ACLU Side (Respondent / Appellee)

1. Powell, L. – Wrote majority opinion
2. Brennan, W. – Joined Stevens' concurrence
3. Marshall, T. – Joined Stevens' concurrence
4. Stewart, P. – Joined majority opinion
5. Rehnquist, W. – Wrote concurring opinion
6. Burger, W. – Joined majority opinion
7. Blackmun, H. – Joined Stevens' concurrence
8. Stevens, J. – Wrote concurring opinion

Opposing Side (Petitioner / Appellant)

1. White, B. – Wrote dissenting opinion

VI. A WIN OR LOSS FOR THE ACLU?

The ACLU served as counsel for appellees urging affirmance; the Supreme Court affirmed District Court's decision by an 8-1 vote, giving the ACLU an apparent win.

445. Washington v. Washington State Commercial Passenger Fishing Vessel Ass'n

(Decided July 2, 1979; 443 U.S. 658)

I. ISSUE

A. Issues Discussed

Governmental authority, regulation

B. Legal Question Presented

What is the nature of the right of Indians to fish in the State of Washington under treaties entered in 1854 and 1855?

C. Supreme Court's Answer

There is a present right to fish and any Washington state law commands to the contrary cannot override this right.

II. CASE SUMMARY

A. Background

"To extinguish the last group of conflicting claims to lands lying west of the Cascade Mountains and north of the Columbia River in what is now the State of Washington, the United States entered into a series of treaties with Indian tribes in 1854 and 1855. The Indians relinquished their interest in most of the Territory in exchange for monetary payments. In addition, certain relatively small parcels of land were reserved for their exclusive use, and they were afforded other guarantees, including protection of their 'right of taking fish, at all usual and accustomed grounds and stations . . . in common with all citizens of the Territory.' . . .

The Indians understood that non-Indians would also have the right to fish at their off-reservation fishing sites. But this was not understood as a significant limitation on their right to take fish. . . . The parties accordingly did not see the need and did not intend to regulate the taking of fish by either Indians or non-Indians, nor was future regulation foreseen.

Indeed, for several decades after the treaties were signed, Indians continued to harvest most of the fish taken from the waters of Washington, and they moved freely about the Territory and later the State in search of that resource. The size of the fishery resource continued to obviate the need during the period to regulate the taking of fish by either Indians or non-Indians. Not until major economic developments in canning and processing occurred in the last few years of the 19th century did a significant non-Indian fishery develop. It was as a consequence of these developments, rather than of the treaty, that non- Indians began to dominate the fisheries and eventually to exclude most Indians from participating in it—a trend that was encouraged by the onset of often discriminatory state regulation in the early decades of the 20th century. . . .

Unfortunately, that resource has now become scarce, and the meaning of the Indians' treaty right to take fish has accordingly become critical. The United States Court of Appeals for the Ninth Circuit and the Supreme Court of the State of Washington have issued conflicting decisions on its meaning.

[In the federal litigation, the District Court] held that the Indians were then entitled to a 45% to 50% share of the harvestable fish that will at some point pass through recognized tribal fishing grounds in the case area. The share was to be calculated on a river-by-river, run-by-run basis, subject to certain adjustments. Fish caught by Indians for ceremonial and subsistence purposes as well as fish caught within a reservation were excluded from the calculation of the tribes' share. In addition, in order to compensate for fish caught outside of the case area, i. e., beyond the State's jurisdiction, the court made an 'equitable adjustment' to increase the allocation to the Indians. The court left it to the individual tribes involved to agree among themselves on how best to divide the Indian share of runs that pass through the usual and accustomed grounds of more than one tribe, and it postponed until a later date the proper accounting for hatchery-bred fish. With a slight modification, the Court of Appeals for the Ninth Circuit affirmed, and [the Supreme Court] denied certiorari.

The injunction entered by the District Court required the Department of Fisheries (Fisheries) to adopt regulations protecting the Indians' treaty rights. After the new regulations were promulgated, however, they were immediately challenged by private citizens in suits commenced in the Washington state courts. The State Supreme Court, in two cases that are here in consolidated form in No. 77–983, ultimately held that Fisheries could not comply with the federal injunction. . . .

Because of the widespread defiance of the District Court's orders, this litigation has assumed unusual significance. [The Supreme Court] granted certiorari in the state and federal cases to interpret this important treaty provision and thereby to resolve the conflict between the state and federal courts regarding what, if any, right the Indians have to a share of the fish, to address the implications of international regulation of the fisheries in the area, and to remove any doubts about the federal court's power to enforce its orders."

B. Counsel of Record / ACLU Attorney

ACLU Side (Petitioner / Appellant in No. 77-983, Respondent / Appellee in Nos. 78-119 and 78-139):

Louis F. Claiborne argued the cause for the United States.
Mason D. Morisset argued the cause for the Indian Tribes.
Michael Taylor filed a brief for the Quinault Indian Nation.
James B. Hovis filed a brief for the Yakima Nation.

Opposing Side (Respondent / Appellee in No. 77-983, Petitioner / Appellant in Nos. 78-119 and 78-139):

Slade Gorton, Attorney General of Washington, argued the cause for the State of Washington.
Philip A. Lacovara argued the cause for the Associations of Non-Indian Fishermen.
Richard W. Pierson and Dale L. Kingman filed a brief for the Washington State Commercial Passenger Fishing Vessel Association.

III. AMICI CURIAE

ACLU Side (Petitioner / Appellant in No. 77-983, Respondent / Appellee in Nos. 78-119 and 78-139):

Brief of amici curiae filed on behalf of the ACLU, et al., by David H. Getches, Burt Neuborne, Stephen L. Pevar, George Kannar, Charles S. Sims, and Bruce J. Ennis.
Brief of amici curiae filed on behalf of the Nez Perce Tribe of Idaho by Arthur Lazarus, Jr., Robert E. Strom, W. Richard West, Jr., and LeRoy W. Wilder.
Brief of amici curiae filed on behalf of the American Friends Service Committee, et al., by Frederick L. Noland.
Brief of amici curiae, discussing the implications of diffuse control of fisheries and need for congressional intervention, filed on behalf of the American Institute of Fishery Research Biologists by J. Carl Mundt and Henry H. Happel, III.

Opposing Side (Respondent / Appellee in No. 77-983, Petitioner / Appellant in Nos. 78-119 and 78-139):

Brief of amici curiae filed on behalf of the Pacific Seafood Processors Association by Paul W. Steere and Ronald T. Schaps.
Brief of amici curiae filed on behalf of the Northwest Steelhead and Salmon Council of Trout Unlimited by Don S. Willner.
Brief of amici curiae filed on behalf of the Pacific Legal Foundation by Ronald A. Zumbrun and John H. Findley.

IV. THE SUPREME COURT'S DECISION

"In our view, the purpose and language of the treaties are unambiguous; they secure the Indians' right to take a share of each run of fish that passes through tribal fishing areas. But our prior decisions provide an even more persuasive reason why this interpretation is not open to question. For notwithstanding the bitterness that this litigation has engendered, the principal issue involved is virtually a 'matter decided' by our previous holdings.

The Court has interpreted the fishing clause in these treaties on six prior occasions. In all of these cases the Court placed a relatively broad gloss on the Indians' fishing rights and—more or less explicitly—rejected the State's 'equal opportunity' approach; in the earliest and the three most recent cases, moreover, we adopted essentially the interpretation that the United States is reiterating here. . . .

Whether Game and Fisheries may be ordered actually to promulgate regulations having effect as a matter of state law may well be doubtful. But the District Court may prescind that problem by assuming direct supervision of the fisheries if state recalcitrance or state-law barriers should be continued. It is therefore absurd to argue, as do the fishing associations, both that the state agencies may not be ordered to implement the decree and also that the District Court may not itself issue detailed remedial orders as a substitute for state supervision. The federal court unquestionably has the power to enter the various orders that state official and private parties have chosen to ignore, and even to displace local enforcement of those orders if necessary to remedy the violations of federal law found by the court. Even if those orders may have been erroneous in some respects, all parties have an unequivocal obligation to obey them while they remain in effect.

In short, we trust that the spirit of cooperation motivating the Attorney General's representation will be confirmed by the conduct of state officials. But if it is not, the District Court has the power to undertake the necessary remedial steps and to enlist the aid of the appropriate federal law enforcement agents in carrying out those steps. Moreover, the comments by the Court of Appeals strongly imply that it is prepared to uphold the use of stern measures to require respect for federal-court orders.

The judgments of the Court of Appeals for the Ninth Circuit and the Supreme Court of the State of Washington are vacated and the respective causes are remanded to those courts for further proceedings not inconsistent with this opinion, except that the judgment in United States v. Washington, 573 F.2d 1118 (the International Fisheries case) is affirmed."

V. JUSTICE VOTE

6 Pro ACLU Side vs. 3 Con Opposing Side

ACLU Side (Petitioner / Appellant in No. 77-983, Respondent / Appellee in Nos. 78-119 and 78-139):

1. Stevens, J. – Wrote majority opinion
2. Brennan, W. – Joined majority opinion
3. White, B. – Joined majority opinion
4. Blackmun, H. – Joined majority opinion
5. Marshall, T. – Joined majority opinion
6. Burger, W. – Joined majority opinion

Opposing Side(Respondent / Appellee in No. 77-983, Petitioner / Appellant in Nos. 78-119 and 78-139):

1. Powell, L. – Wrote dissenting opinion
2. Stewart, P. – Joined Powell's dissent
3. Rehnquist, W. – Joined Powell's dissent

VI. A WIN OR LOSS FOR THE ACLU?

The ACLU filed as amicus curiae urging reversal in No. 77-983 and affirmance in Nos. 78-119 and 78-139; the U.S. Supreme Court vacated the Supreme Court of State of Washington's judgment in No. 77-983, vacated the Court of Appeals for the Ninth Circuit's judgment in No. 78-139, and affirmed the Court of Appeals for the Ninth Circuit's judgment in No. 78-119 in a 6-3 vote, giving ACLU an apparent win.

446. Roberts v. United States

(Decided April 15, 1980; 445 U.S. 552)

I. ISSUE

A. Issues Discussed

Criminal procedure, drugs, self-incrimination, criminal conspiracy, First Amendment, Fourteenth Amendment

B. Legal Question Presented

"[W]hether the District Court properly considered, as one factor in imposing sentence, the petitioner's refusal to cooperate with officials investigating a criminal conspiracy in which he was a confessed participant."

C. Supreme Court's Answer

The District Court properly considered petitioner's refusal to cooperate with officials as one factor when imposing a sentence.

II. CASE SUMMARY

A. Background

Petitioner Winfield Roberts accompanied Cecilia Payne to the office of the United States Attorney for the District of Columbia one day in June 1975. Government surveillance previously had revealed that a green Jaguar owned by Payne was used to transport heroin within the District. Payne told investigators that she occasionally lent the Jaguar to petitioner, who was waiting outside in the hall. At Payne's suggestion, the investigators asked petitioner if he would answer some questions. Although petitioner was present voluntarily, the investigators gave him the warnings required by Miranda v. Arizona. They also told him that he was free to leave. When petitioner indicated that he would stay, the investigators asked whether he knew 'Boo' Thornton, then the principal target of the heroin investigation. Petitioner admitted that he had delivered heroin to Thornton on several occasions. Confessing also that he had discussed drug transactions with Thornton in certain intercepted telephone conversations, petitioner explained the meaning of code words used in the conversations. When asked to name suppliers, however, petitioner gave evasive answers. Although the investigators warned petitioner that the extent of his cooperation would bear on the charges brought against him, he provided no further information.

Petitioner was indicted on one count of conspiring to distribute heroin, 21 U.S.C. §§ 841, 846, and four counts of using a telephone to facilitate the distribution of heroin, 21 U.S.C. § 843(b). He retained a lawyer, who rejected the Government's continued efforts to enlist petitioner's assistance. In March 1976, petitioner entered a plea of guilty to the conspiracy count and received a sentence of 4 to 15 years' imprisonment, 3 years' special parole, and a $5,000 fine. The Court of Appeals vacated the conviction on the ground that the terms of the plea agreement were inadequately disclosed to the District Court.

On remand, petitioner pleaded guilty to two counts of telephone misuse under an agreement that permitted the Government to seek a substantial sentence. The Government filed a memorandum recommending two consecutive sentences of 16 to 48 months each and a $5,000 fine. . . .

At the sentencing hearing, defense counsel noted that petitioner had been incarcerated for two years pending appeal and that codefendant Thornton had been sentenced to probation. Counsel argued that petitioner should receive concurrent sentences that would result in his immediate release. He directed the court's attention to petitioner's voluntary confession, explaining that petitioner had refused to identify other members of the conspiracy because he 'wasn't that involved in it.' The prosecutor responded that the request for probation was 'ironic' in light of petitioner's refusal to cooperate in the investigation over the course of 'many, many years, knowing what he faces.' Thus, the Government could not ask the court 'to take into account some extenuating and mitigating circumstances, that the defendant has cooperated. . . .' Stressing the seriousness of the offense and the absence of excuse or mitigation, the Government recommended a substantial prison term.

The District Court imposed consecutive sentences of one to four years on each count and a special parole term of three years, but it declined to impose a fine. The court explained that these sentences were appropriate because petitioner was on parole from a bank robbery conviction at the time of the offenses, and because he was a dealer who had refused to cooperate with the Government. Petitioner again appealed, contending for the first time that the sentencing court should not have considered his failure to cooperate. The Court of Appeals for the District of Columbia Circuit vacated the special parole term but otherwise affirmed the judgment."

The Supreme Court granted certiorari to review the case and affirmed.

B. Counsel of Record / ACLU Attorney

ACLU Side (Petitioner / Appellant): Allan M. Palmer argued the cause for appellant.

Opposing Side (Respondent / Appellee): Stephen M. Shapiro argued the cause for the United States.

III. AMICI CURIAE

ACLU Side (Petitioner / Appellant): Brief of amici curiae filed on behalf of the ACLU by Bruce J. Ennis, Jr.

Opposing Side (Respondent / Appellee): No briefs of amici curiae were filed in support of appellee.

IV. THE SUPREME COURT'S DECISION

"Petitioner insists that he had a constitutional right to remain silent, and that no adverse inferences can be drawn from the exercise of that right. We find this argument singularly unpersuasive. The Fifth Amendment privilege against compelled self-incrimination is not self-executing. At least where the Government has no substantial reason to believe that the requested disclosures are likely to be incriminating, the privilege may not be relied upon unless it is invoked in a timely fashion.

[P]etitioner 'did not assert his privilege or in any manner suggest that he withheld his testimony because there was any ground for fear of self-incrimination. His assertion of it here is evidently an afterthought.' [T]he privilege 'must be deemed waived if not in some manner fairly brought to the attention of the tribunal which must pass upon it.' Thus, if petitioner believed that his failure to cooperate was privileged, he should have said so at a time when the sentencing court could have determined whether his claim was legitimate.

Petitioner would avoid the force of this elementary rule by arguing that Miranda warnings supplied additional protection for his right to remain silent. But the right to silence described in those warnings derives from the Fifth Amendment and adds nothing to it. Although Miranda's requirement of specific warnings creates a limited exception to the rule that the privilege must be claimed, the exception does not apply outside the context of the inherently coercive custodial interrogations for which it was designed. The warnings protect persons who, exposed to such interrogation without the assistance of counsel, otherwise might be unable to make a free and informed choice to remain silent. . . .

Petitioner has identified nothing that might have impaired his 'free choice to admit, to deny, or to refuse to answer.' . . . We conclude that the District Court committed no constitutional error. If we were to invalidate petitioner's sentence on the record before us, we would sanction an unwarranted interference with a function traditionally vested in the trial courts. Accordingly, the judgment of the Court of Appeals is affirmed."

V. JUSTICE VOTE

1 Pro ACLU Side vs. 8 Con Opposing Side

ACLU Side (Petitioner / Appellant)

1. Marshall, T. – Wrote dissenting opinion

Opposing Side (Respondent / Appellee)

1. Powell, L. – Wrote majority opinion
2. Brennan, W. – Wrote concurring opinion
3. White, B. – Joined majority opinion
4. Blackmun, H. – Joined majority opinion
5. Burger, W. – Joined majority opinion
6. Stewart, P. – Joined majority opinion
7. Rehnquist, W. – Joined majority opinion
8. Stevens, J. – Joined majority opinion

VI. A WIN OR LOSS FOR THE ACLU?

The ACLU filed as amicus curiae urging reversal; the Supreme Court affirmed the Court of Appeals' judgment in an 8-1 vote, giving the ACLU an apparent loss.

447. Owen v. City of Independence

(Decided April 16, 1980; 445 U.S. 622)

I. ISSUE

A. Issues Discussed

Governmental authority, immunity, civil rights, Fourteenth Amendment

B. Legal Question Presented

"[W]hether local governments, although not entitled to an absolute immunity, should be afforded some form of official immunity in § 1983 suits."

C. Supreme Court's Answer

Local governments are not immune from liability for suits under § 1983.

II. CASE SUMMARY

A. Background

In 1967, petitioner George Owen was appointed "to an indefinite term as Chief of Police. In 1972, Owen and a new City Manager, Lyle W. Alberg, engaged in a dispute over petitioner's administration of the Police Department's property room. In March of that year, a handgun, which the records of the Department's property room stated had been destroyed, turned up in Kansas City in possession of a felon. This discovery prompted Alberg to initiate an investigation of the management of the property room. . . .

On the evening of April 17, 1972, the City Council held its regularly scheduled meeting. After completion of the planned agenda, Councilman Roberts read a statement he had prepared on the investigation. Among other allegations, Roberts charged that petitioner had misappropriated Police Department property for his own use, that narcotics and money had 'mysteriously disappeared' from his office, that traffic tickets had been manipulated, that high ranking police officials had made 'inappropriate' requests affecting the police court, and that 'things have occurred causing the unusual release of felons.' At the close of his statement, Roberts moved that the investigative reports be released to the news media and turned over to the prosecutor for presentation to the grand jury, and that the City Manager 'take all direct and appropriate action' against those persons 'involved in illegal, wrongful, or gross inefficient activities brought out in the investigative reports.' After some discussion, the City Council passed Roberts' motion with no dissents and one abstention.

City Manager Alberg discharged petitioner the very next day. Petitioner was not given any reason for his dismissal . . . . The local press gave prominent coverage both to the City Council's action and petitioner's dismissal, linking the discharge to the investigation. As instructed by the City Council, Alberg referred the investigative reports and witness statements to the Prosecuting Attorney of Jackson County, Mo., for consideration by a grand jury. The results of the audit and investigation were never released to the public, however. The grand jury subsequently returned a 'no true bill,' and no further action was taken by either the City Council or City Manager Alberg. . . .

Petitioner named the city of Independence, City Manager Alberg, and the present members of the City Council in their official capacities as defendants in this suit. Alleging that he was discharged without notice of reasons and without a hearing in violation of his constitutional rights to procedural and substantive due process, petitioner sought declaratory and injunctive relief, including a hearing on his discharge, backpay from the date of discharge, and attorney's fees. The District Court, after a bench trial, entered judgment for respondents.

The Court of Appeals initially reversed the District Court. Although it agreed with the District Court that under Missouri law petitioner possessed no property interest in continued employment as Police Chief, the Court of Appeals concluded that the city's allegedly false public accusations had blackened petitioner's name and reputation, thus depriving him of liberty without due process of law. That the stigmatizing charges did not come from the City Manager and were not included in the official discharge notice was, in the court's view, immaterial. What was important, the court explained, was that 'the official actions of the city council released charges against [petitioner] contemporaneous and, in the eyes of the public, connected with that discharge.'"

After an initial review by the Supreme Court and remand to the Court of Appeals, the Court granted certiorari a second time in light of its decision in Monell v. New York City Dept. of Social Services, and reversed.

B. Counsel of Record / ACLU Attorney

ACLU Side (Petitioner / Appellant): Irving Achtenberg argued the cause for appellant.

Opposing Side (Respondent / Appellee): Richard G. Carlisle argued the cause for appellee.

III. AMICI CURIAE

ACLU Side (Petitioner / Appellant)

Brief of amici curiae filed on behalf of the ACLU, et al., by Bruce J. Ennis, Oscar G. Chase, and Nancy Stearns.

Brief of amici curiae filed on behalf of the National Education Association, et al., by Michael H. Gottesman, Robert M. Weinberg, David Rubin, William E. Caldwell, John B. Jones, Jr., Norman Redlich, William L. Robinson, and Norman Chachkin.

Opposing Side (Respondent / Appellee)

No briefs of amici curiae were filed in support of appellee.

IV. THE SUPREME COURT'S DECISION

"Our rejection of a construction of § 1983 that would accord municipalities a qualified immunity for their good faith constitutional violations is compelled both by the legislative purpose in enacting the statute and by considerations of public policy. The central aim of the Civil Rights Act was to provide protection to those persons wronged by the '[m]isuse of power, possessed by virtue of state law and made possible only because the wrongdoer is clothed with the authority of state law.' . . .

In sum, our decision holding that municipalities have no immunity from damages liability flowing from their constitutional violations harmonizes well with developments in the common law and our own pronouncements on official immunities under § 1983. Doctrines of tort law have changed significantly over the past century, and our notions of governmental responsibility should properly reflect that evolution. No longer is individual 'blameworthiness' the acid test of liability; the principle of equitable loss-spreading has joined fault as a factor in distributing the costs of official misconduct.

We believe that today's decision, together with prior precedents in this area, properly allocates these costs among the three principals in the scenario of the § 1983 cause of action: the victim of the constitutional deprivation; the officer whose conduct caused the injury; and the public, as represented by the municipal entity. The innocent individual who is harmed by an abuse of governmental authority is assured that he will be compensated for his injury. The offending official, so long as he conducts himself in good faith, may go about his business secure in the knowledge that a qualified immunity will protect him from personal liability for damages that are more appropriately chargeable to the populace as a whole. And the public will be forced to bear only the costs of injury inflicted by the 'execution of a government's policy or custom, whether made by its lawmakers or by those whose edicts or acts may fairly be said to represent official policy'

Reversed."

V. JUSTICE VOTE

5 Pro ACLU Side vs. 4 Con Opposing Side

ACLU Side (Petitioner / Appellant)

1. Brennan, W. – Wrote majority opinion
2. White, B. – Joined majority opinion
3. Blackmun, H. – Joined majority opinion
4. Marshall, T. – Joined majority opinion
5. Stevens, J. – Joined majority opinion

Opposing Side (Respondent / Appellee)

1. Powell, L. – Wrote dissenting opinion
2. Burger, W. – Joined Powell's dissent
3. Stewart, P. – Joined Powell's dissent
4. Rehnquist, W. – Joined Powell's dissent

VI. A WIN OR LOSS FOR THE ACLU?

The ACLU filed as amicus curiae urging reversal; the Supreme Court reversed the ruling of the Court of Appeals in a 5-4 vote, giving the ACLU an apparent win.

448. Carlson v. Green

(Decided April 22, 1980; 446 U.S. 14)

I. ISSUE

A. Issues Discussed

Governmental authority, due process, equal protection, Eighth Amendment

B. Legal Question Presented

"(1) Is a remedy available directly under the Constitution [for the death of respondent's son], given that respondent's allegations could also support a suit against the United States under the Federal Tort Claims Act? And (2) if so, is survival of the cause of action governed by federal common law or by state statutes?"

C. Supreme Court's Answer

A remedy is available under the Constitution even though one is available under the Federal Tort Claims Act and survival of the cause of action is governed by federal common law.

II. CASE SUMMARY

A. Background

"Respondent brought this suit in the District Court for the Southern District of Indiana on behalf of the estate of her deceased son, Joseph Jones, Jr., alleging that he suffered personal injuries from which he died because the petitioners, federal prison officials, violated his due process, equal protection, and Eighth Amendment rights. . . .

The District Court held that under Estelle v. Gamble, the allegations . . . pleaded a violation of the Eighth Amendment's proscription against infliction of cruel and unusual punishment, giving rise to a cause of action for damages under Bivens v. Six Unknown Fed. Narcotics Agents. The court recognized that the decedent could have maintained this action if he had survived, but dismissed the complaint because in its view the damages remedy as a matter of federal law was limited to that provided by Indiana's survivorship and wrongful-death laws and, as the court construed those laws, the damages available to Jones' estate failed to meet § 1331(a)'s $10,000 jurisdictional-amount requirement. The Court of Appeals for the Seventh Circuit agreed that an Eighth Amendment violation was pleaded under Estelle and that a cause of action was stated under Bivens, but reversed the holding that § 1331(a)'s jurisdictional-amount requirement was not met. Rather, the Court of Appeals held that § 1331(a) was satisfied because 'whenever the relevant state survival statute would abate a Bivens -type action brought against defendants whose conduct results in death, the federal common law allows survival of the action.' The court reasoned that the Indiana law, if applied, would 'subvert' 'the policy of allowing complete vindication of constitutional rights' by making it 'more advantageous for a tortfeasor to kill rather than to injure.'"

The Supreme Court granted certiorari to review the case and affirmed.

B. Counsel of Record / ACLU Attorney

ACLU Side (Respondent / Appellee): Michael E. Deutsch argued the cause for appellee.

Opposing Side (Petitioner / Appellant): Deputy Solicitor General Kenneth S. Geller argued the cause for appellant.

III. AMICI CURIAE

ACLU Side (Respondent / Appellee)

Brief of amici curiae filed on behalf of the ACLU Foundation, Inc., et al., by Alvin J. Bronstein, Bruce J. Ennis, and William E. Hellerstein.

Brief of amici curiae filed on behalf of the Lawyers' Committee for Civil Rights Under Law by John B. Jones, Jr., Norman Redlich, William L. Robinson, Norman J. Chachkin, and Richard S. Kohn.

Opposing Side (Petitioner / Appellant)

No briefs of amici curiae were field in support of appellee.

IV. THE SUPREME COURT'S DECISION

"[W]e have here no explicit congressional declaration that persons injured by federal officers' violations of the Eighth Amendment may not recover money damages from the agents but must be remitted to another remedy, equally effective in the view of Congress. Petitioners point to nothing in the Federal Tort Claims Act (FTCA) or its legislative history to show that Congress meant to pre-empt a Bivens remedy or to create an equally effective remedy for constitutional violations. . . . Plainly FTCA is not a sufficient protector of the citizens' constitutional rights, and without a clear congressional mandate we cannot hold that Congress relegated respondent exclusively to the FTCA remedy. . . .

Bivens actions are a creation of federal law and, therefore, the question whether respondent's action survived Jones' death is a question of federal law. Petitioners, however, would have us fashion a federal rule of survivorship that incorporates the survivorship laws of the forum State, at least where the state law is not inconsistent with federal law. Respondent argues, on the other hand, that only a uniform federal rule of survivorship is compatible with the goal of deterring federal officials from infringing federal constitutional rights in the manner alleged in respondent's complaint. We agree with respondent. Whatever difficulty we might have resolving the question were the federal involvement less clear, we hold that only a uniform federal rule of survivorship will suffice to redress the constitutional deprivation here alleged and to protect against repetition of such conduct.

In short, we agree with and adopt the reasoning of the Court of Appeals:

'The essentiality of the survival of civil rights claims for complete vindication of constitutional rights is buttressed by the need for uniform treatment of those claims, at least when they are against federal officials. As this very case illustrates, uniformity cannot be achieved if courts are limited to applicable state law. Here the relevant Indiana statute would not permit survival of the claim, while in Beard, the Illinois statute permitted survival of the Bivens action. The liability of federal agents for violation of constitutional rights should not depend upon where the violation occurred. . . . In sum, we hold that whenever the relevant state survival statute would abate a Bivens-type action brought against defendants whose conduct results in death, the federal common law allows survival of the action.'

Robertson v. Wegmann, holding that a § 1983 action would abate in accordance with Louisiana survivorship law is not to the contrary. There the plaintiff's death was not caused by the acts of the defendants upon which the suit was based. Moreover, Robertson expressly recognized that to prevent frustrations of the deterrence goals of § 1983 . . . ; '[a] state official contemplating illegal activity must always be prepared to face the prospect of a § 1983 action being filed against him.' A federal official contemplating unconstitutional conduct similarly must be prepared to face the prospect of a Bivens action. A uniform rule that claims such as respondent's survive the decedent's death is essential if we are not to 'frustrate in [an] important way the achievement' of the goals of Bivens actions.

Affirmed."

V. JUSTICE VOTE

7 Pro ACLU Side vs. 2 Con Opposing Side

ACLU Side (Respondent / Appellee)

1. Brennan, W. – Wrote majority opinion
2. White, B. – Joined majority opinion
3. Blackmun, H. – Joined majority opinion
4. Marshall, T. – Joined majority opinion
5. Powell, L. – Wrote concurring opinion
6. Stevens, J. – Joined majority opinion
7. Stewart, P. – Joined Powell's concurrence

Opposing Side (Petitioner / Appellant)

1. Rehnquist, W. – Wrote dissenting opinion
2. Burger, W. – Wrote dissenting opinion

VI. A WIN OR LOSS FOR THE ACLU?

The ACLU filed as amicus curiae urging affirmance; the Supreme Court affirmed the Court of Appeals' judgment in a 7-2 vote, giving the ACLU an apparent win.

449. Wengler v. Druggists Mutual Insurance Co.

(Decided April 22, 1980; 446 U.S. 142)

I. ISSUE

A. Issues Discussed

Civil rights, gender, Fourteenth Amendment, equal protection

B. Legal Question Presented

Does a Missouri statute which allows widows to automatically receive benefits from a husband's work-related death while widowers must prove incapacitation or dependence on a wife's wages to receive the same benefits, violate the Equal Protection Clause of the Fourteenth Amendment?

C. Supreme Court's Answer

The statute violates the Equal Protection Clause, but can be cured at the state Supreme Court level either by making the benefits automatic for both genders or requiring proof from both genders.

II. CASE SUMMARY

A. Background

"On February 11, 1977, Ruth Wengler, wife of appellant Paul J. Wengler, died in a work-related accident in the parking lot of her employer, appellee Dicus Prescription Drugs, Inc. Appellant filed a claim for death benefits under Mo.Rev.Stat. § 287.240 (Supp.1979), under which a widower is not entitled to death benefits unless he either is mentally or physically incapacitated from wage earning or proves actual dependence on his wife's earnings. In contrast, a widow qualifies for death benefits without having to prove actual dependence on her husband's earnings.

Appellant stipulated that he was neither incapacitated nor dependent on his wife's earnings, but argued that, owing to its disparate treatment of similarly situated widows and widowers, § 287.240 violated the Equal Protection Clause of the Fourteenth Amendment to the United States Constitution. The claim was administratively denied, but the Circuit Court of Madison County reversed, holding that § 287.240 violated the Equal Protection Clause because the statutory restriction on a widower's recovery of death benefits did not also apply to a surviving wife. Dicus and its insurer, appellee Druggists Mutual Insurance Co., were ordered to pay death benefits to appellant in the appropriate amount.

The Missouri Supreme Court, distinguishing certain cases in this Court, reversed the Circuit Court's decision. The equal protection challenge to § 287.240 failed because 'the substantive difference in the economic standing of working men and women justifies the advantage that [§ 287.240] administratively gives to a widow.'"

The Supreme Court granted certiorari to review the case and reversed.

B. Counsel of Record / ACLU Attorney

ACLU Side (Petitioner / Appellant): John W. Reid, II, argued the cause for appellant.

Opposing Side (Respondent / Appellee): Ralph C. Kleinschmidt argued the cause for appellee.

III. AMICI CURIAE

ACLU Side (Petitioner / Appellant)

Brief of amici curiae filed on behalf of the ACLU, et al., by Ruth Bader Ginsberg.

Brief of amici curiae filed on behalf of the United States by Solicitor General Wade H. McCree, Jr., Assistant Attorney General Drew S. Days, III, Assistant to the Solicitor General Stuart A. Smith, Brain K. Landsberg, and Mark L. Gross.

Opposing Side (Respondent / Appellee)

No briefs of amici curiae were filed in support of appellee.

IV. THE SUPREME COURT'S DECISION

"The Missouri law indisputably mandates gender-based discrimination. Although the Missouri Supreme Court was of the view that the law favored, rather than disfavored, women, it is apparent that the statute discriminates against both men and women. The provision discriminates against a woman covered by the Missouri workers' compensation system since, in the case of her death, benefits are payable to her spouse only if he is mentally or physically incapacitated or was to some extent dependent upon her. . . .

The Missouri law, as the Missouri courts recognized, also discriminates against men who survive their employed wives' dying in work-related accidents. To receive benefits, the surviving male spouse must prove his incapacity or dependency. The widow of a deceased wage earner, in contrast, is presumed dependent and is guaranteed a weekly benefit for life or until remarriage. . . .

However the discrimination is described in this case, our precedents require that gender-based discriminations must serve important governmental objectives and that the discriminatory means employed must be substantially related to the achievement of those objectives. . . .

Thus we conclude that the Supreme Court of Missouri erred in upholding the constitutional validity of § 287.240. We are left with the question whether the defect should be cured by extending the presumption of dependence to widowers or by eliminating it for widows. Because state legislation is at issue, and because a remedial outcome consonant with the state legislature's overall purpose is preferable, we believe that state judges are better positioned to choose an appropriate method of remedying the constitutional violation. Accordingly, we reverse the decision of the Supreme Court of Missouri and remand the case to that court for further proceedings not inconsistent with this opinion."

V. JUSTICE VOTE

8 Pro ACLU Side vs. 1 Con Opposing Side

ACLU Side (Petitioner / Appellant)

1. White, B. – Wrote majority opinion
2. Burger, W. – Joined majority opinion
3. Brennan, W. – Joined majority opinion
4. Stewart, P. – Joined majority opinion
5. Marshall, T. – Joined majority opinion
6. Blackmun, H. – Joined majority opinion
7. Powell, L. – Joined majority opinion
8. Stevens, J. – Wrote concurring opinion

Opposing Side (Respondent / Appellee)

1. Rehnquist, W. – Wrote dissenting opinion

VI. A WIN OR LOSS FOR THE ACLU?

The ACLU filed as amicus curiae urging reversal; The U.S. Supreme Court reversed the ruling of the Supreme Court of Missouri in an 8-1 vote, giving the ACLU an apparent win.

450. United States v. Mendenhall

(Decided May 27, 1980; 446 U.S. 544)

I. ISSUE

A. Issues Discussed

Fourth Amendment, search and seizure

B. Legal Question Presented

"[W]hether any right of the respondent guaranteed by the Fourth Amendment was violated in the circumstances presented by this case."

C. Supreme Court's Answer

The officers did not violate respondent's Fourth Amendment rights in this case.

II. CASE SUMMARY

A. Background

"The respondent arrived at the Detroit Metropolitan Airport on a commercial airline flight from Los Angeles early in the morning on February 10, 1976. As she disembarked from the airplane, she was observed by two agents of the DEA, who were present at the airport for the purpose of detecting unlawful traffic in narcotics. After observing the respondent's conduct, which appeared to the agents to be characteristic of persons unlawfully carrying narcotics, the agents approached her . . . , identified themselves as federal agents, and asked to see her identification and airline ticket. The respondent produced her driver's license, which was in the name of Sylvia Mendenhall, and, in answer to a question of one of the agents, stated that she resided at the address appearing on the license. The airline ticket was issued in the name of 'Annette Ford.' When asked why the ticket bore a name different from her own, the respondent stated that she 'just felt like using that name.' In response to a further question, the respondent indicated that she had been in California only two days. Agent Anderson then specifically identified himself as a federal narcotics agent and, according to his testimony, the respondent 'became quite shaken, extremely nervous. She had a hard time speaking.'

After returning the airline ticket and driver's license to her, Agent Anderson asked the respondent if she would accompany him to the airport DEA office for further questions. She did so . . . . At the office the agent asked the respondent if she would allow a search of her person and handbag and told her that she had the right to decline the search if she desired. She responded: 'Go ahead.' She then handed Agent Anderson her purse, which contained a receipt for an airline ticket that had been issued to 'F. Bush' three days earlier for a flight from Pittsburgh through Chicago to Los Angeles. The agent asked whether this was the ticket that she had used for her flight to California, and the respondent stated that is was.

A female police officer then arrived to conduct the search of the respondent's person. [T]he policewoman again asked the respondent if she consented to the search, and the respondent replied that she did. The policewoman explained that the search would require that the respondent remove her clothing. The respondent stated that she had a plane to catch and was assured by the policewoman that if she were carrying no narcotics, there would be no problem. The respondent then began to disrobe without further comment. As the respondent removed her clothing, she took from her undergarments two small packages, one of which appeared to contain heroin, and handed both to the policewoman. The agents then arrested the respondent for possessing heroin.

It was on the basis of this evidence that the District Court denied the respondent's motion to suppress. . . .

The Court of Appeals reversed the respondent's subsequent conviction . . . .

On rehearing en banc of the present case, the Court of Appeals reaffirmed its original decision, stating simply that the respondent had not validly consented to the search 'within the meaning of [McCaleb].'"

The Supreme Court granted certiorari to review the case, reversed, and remanded.

B. Counsel of Record / ACLU Attorney

ACLU Side (Respondent / Appellee): F. Randall Karfonta argued the cause for appellee.

Opposing Side (Petitioner / Appellant): Deputy Solicitor General Andrew L. Frey argued the cause for the United States.

III. AMICI CURIAE

ACLU Side (Respondent / Appellee)

Brief of amici curiae filed on behalf of the ACLU by Charles S. Sims, Bruce J. Ennis, Jr., Edna D. Wells, and Helene M. Freeman.

Brief of amici curiae filed on behalf of the National Legal Aid and Defender Association by Terence F. MacCarthy and Carol A. Brook.

Opposing Side (Petitioner / Appellant)

Brief of amici curiae filed on behalf of Americans for Effective Law Enforcement, Inc., by Fred E. Inbau, Wayne W. Schmidt, Frank G. Carrington, Jr., and James P. Manak.

IV. THE SUPREME COURT'S DECISION

"The Fourth Amendment's requirement that searches and seizures be founded upon an objective justification, governs all seizures of the person, 'including seizures that involve only a brief detention short of traditional arrest.' Accordingly, if the respondent was 'seized' when the DEA agents approached her on the concourse and asked questions of her, the agents' conduct in doing so was constitutional only if they reasonably suspected the respondent of wrongdoing. But '[o]bviously, not all personal intercourse between policemen and citizens involves 'seizures' of persons. Only when the officer, by means of physical force or show of authority, has in some way restrained the liberty of a citizen may we conclude that a 'seizure' has occurred.' . . .

On the facts of this case, no 'seizure' of the respondent occurred. The events took place in the public concourse. The agents wore no uniforms and displayed no weapons. They did not summon the respondent to their presence, but instead approached her and identified themselves as federal agents. They requested, but did not demand to see the respondent's identification and ticket. Such conduct, without more, did not amount to an intrusion upon any constitutionally protected interest. The respondent was not seized simply by reason of the fact that the agents approached her, asked her if she would show them her ticket and identification, and posed to her a few questions. Nor was it enough to establish a seizure that the person asking the questions was a law enforcement official. . . .

We also reject the argument that the only inference to be drawn from the fact that the respondent acted in a manner so contrary to her self-interest is that she was compelled to answer the agents' questions. It may happen that a person makes statements to law enforcement officials that he later regrets, but the issue in such cases is not whether the statement was self-protective, but rather whether it was made voluntarily. . . .

Although we have concluded that the initial encounter between the DEA agents and the respondent on the concourse at the Detroit Airport did not constitute an unlawful seizure, it is still arguable that the respondent's Fourth Amendment protections were violated when she went from the concourse to the DEA office. Such a violation might in turn infect the subsequent search of the respondent's person. . . .

On the other hand, it is argued that the incident would reasonably have appeared coercive to the respondent, who was 22 years old and had not been graduated from high school. It is additionally suggested that the respondent, a female and a Negro, may have felt unusually threatened by the officers, who were white males. While these factors were not irrelevant, neither were they decisive, and the totality of the evidence in this case was plainly adequate to support the District Court's finding that the respondent voluntarily consented to accompany the officers to the DEA office. . . .

We conclude that the District Court's determination that the respondent consented to the search of her person 'freely and voluntarily' was sustained by the evidence and that the Court of Appeals was, therefore, in error in setting it aside. Accordingly, the judgment of the Court of Appeals is reversed, and the case is remanded to that court for further proceedings."

V. JUSTICE VOTE

4 Pro ACLU Side vs. 5 Con Opposing Side

ACLU Side (Respondent / Appellee)

1. White, B. – Wrote dissenting opinion
2. Marshall, T. – Joined White's dissent
3. Brennan, W. – Joined White's dissent
4. Stevens, J. – Joined White's dissent

Opposing Side (Petitioner / Appellant)

1. Stewart, P. – Wrote majority opinion
2. Burger, W. – Joined Powell's concurrence
3. Blackmun, H. – Joined Powell's concurrence
4. Powell, L. – Wrote concurring opinion
5. Rehnquist, W. – Joined majority opinion

VI. A WIN OR LOSS FOR THE ACLU?

The ACLU, as amicus curiae, urged affirmance of the Sixth Circuit Court of Appeals' judgment; the Supreme Court reversed and remanded in a 5-4 vote, giving the ACLU an apparent loss.

451. Gomez v. Toledo

(Decided May 27, 1980; 446 U.S. 635)

I. ISSUE

A. Issues Discussed

Civil rights, qualified immunity

B. Legal Question Presented

"[W]hether, in an action brought under 42 U.S.C. § 1983 against a public official whose position might entitle him to qualified immunity, a plaintiff must allege that the official has acted in bad faith in order to state a claim for relief or, alternatively, whether the defendant must plead good faith as an affirmative defense."

C. Supreme Court's Answer

A plaintiff does not need to allege bad faith against a public official in a § 1983 action where the official may be entitled to qualified immunity. The defendant has the burden of pleading good faith as an affirmative defense.

II. CASE SUMMARY

A. Background

"Petitioner Carlos Rivera Gomez brought this action against respondent, the Superintendent of the Police of the Commonwealth of Puerto Rico, contending that respondent had violated his right to procedural due process by discharging him from employment with the Police Department's Bureau of Criminal Investigation. . . . Petitioner had been employed as an agent with the Puerto Rican police since 1968. In April 1975, he submitted a sworn statement to his supervisor in which he asserted that two other agents had offered false evidence for use in a criminal case under their investigation. As a result of this statement, petitioner was immediately transferred from the Criminal Investigation Corps for the Southern Area to Police Headquarters in San Juan, and a few weeks later to the Police Academy in Gurabo, where he was given no investigative authority. In the meantime respondent ordered an investigation of petitioner's claims, and the Legal Division of the Police Department concluded that all of petitioner's factual allegations were true.

In April 1976, while still stationed at the Police Academy, petitioner was subpoenaed to give testimony in a criminal case arising out of the evidence that petitioner had alleged to be false. At the trial petitioner, appearing as a defense witness, testified that the evidence was in fact false. As a result of this testimony, criminal charges, filed on the basis of information furnished by respondent, were brought against petitioner for the allegedly unlawful wiretapping of the agents' telephones. Respondent suspended petitioner in May 1976 and discharged him without a hearing in July. In October, the District Court of Puerto Rico found no probable cause to believe that petitioner was guilty of the allegedly unlawful wiretapping and, upon appeal by the prosecution, the Superior Court affirmed. Petitioner in turn sought review of his discharge before the Investigation, Prosecution, and Appeals Commission of Puerto Rico, which, after a hearing, revoked the discharge order rendered by respondent and ordered that petitioner be reinstated with back pay.

[P]etitioner brought this suit for damages, contending that his discharge violated his right to procedural due process, and that it had caused him anxiety, embarrassment, and injury to his reputation in the community. In his answer, respondent denied a number of petitioner's allegations of fact and asserted several affirmative defenses. Respondent then moved to dismiss the complaint for failure to state a cause of action, see Fed.Rule Civ.Proc. 12(b)(6), and the District Court granted the motion. Observing that respondent was entitled to qualified immunity for acts done in good faith within the scope of his official duties, it concluded that petitioner was required to plead as part of his claim for relief that, in committing the actions alleged, respondent was motivated by bad faith. The absence of any such allegation, it held, required dismissal of the complaint. The United States Court of Appeals for the First Circuit affirmed."

The Supreme Court granted certiorari to review the case and reversed.

B. Counsel of Record / ACLU Attorney

ACLU Side (Petitioner / Appellant): Michael Avery argued the cause for appellant.

Opposing Side (Respondent / Appellee): Federico Cedo Alzamora argued the cause for appellee.

III. AMICI CURIAE

ACLU Side (Petitioner / Appellant)

Brief of amici curiae filed on behalf of the ACLU by Leon Friedman, Charles S. Sims, and Bruce J. Ennis.

Opposing Side (Respondent / Appellee)

No briefs of amici curiae were filed in support of appellee.

IV. THE SUPREME COURT'S DECISION

"In certain limited circumstances, we have held that public officers are entitled to a qualified immunity from damages liability under [42 U.S.C.] § 1983. This conclusion has been based on an unwillingness to infer from legislative silence a congressional intention to abrogate immunities that were both 'well established at common law' and 'compatible with the purposes of the Civil Rights Act.' . . .

Nothing in the language or legislative history of § 1983, however, suggests that in an action brought against a public official whose position might entitle him to immunity if he acted in good faith, a plaintiff must allege bad faith in order to state a claim for relief. By the plain terms of § 1983, two—and only two—allegations are required in order to state a cause of action under that statute. First, the plaintiff must allege that some person has deprived him of a federal right. Second, he must allege that the person who has deprived him of that right acted under color of state or territorial law. . . .

Moreover, this Court has never indicated that qualified immunity is relevant to the existence of the plaintiff's cause of action; instead we have described it as a defense available to the official in question. . . .

Our conclusion as to the allocation of the burden of pleading is supported by the nature of the qualified immunity defense. As our decisions make clear, whether such immunity has been established depends on facts peculiarly within the knowledge and control of the defendant. . . . To impose the pleading burden on the plaintiff would ignore this elementary fact and be contrary to the established practice in analogous areas of the law.

The decision of the Court of Appeals is reversed, and the case is remanded to that court for further proceedings consistent with this opinion."

V. JUSTICE VOTE

9 Pro ACLU Side vs. 0 Con Opposing Side

ACLU Side (Petitioner / Appellant)

1. Marshall, T. – Wrote majority opinion
2. Burger, W. – Joined majority opinion
3. Brennan, W. – Joined majority opinion
4. Stewart, P. – Joined majority opinion
5. White, B. – Joined majority opinion
6. Blackmun, H. – Joined majority opinion
7. Powell, L – Joined majority opinion
8. Stevens, J. – Joined majority opinion
9. Rehnquist, W. – Wrote concurring opinion

VI. A WIN OR LOSS FOR THE ACLU?

The ACLU filed as amicus curiae urging reversal; the Supreme Court reversed the ruling of the Court of Appeals for the First Circuit in a 9-0 vote, giving the ACLU an apparent win.

452. Supreme Court of Virginia v. Consumers Union of the United States, Inc.

(Decided June 2, 1980; 446 U.S. 719)

I. ISSUE

A. Issues Discussed

Civil Rights, immunity, First Amendment, Fourteenth Amendment

B. Legal Question Presented

"[W]hether the Supreme Court of Virginia (Virginia Court) and its chief justice are officially immune from suit in an action brought under 42 U.S.C. § 1983 challenging the Virginia Court's disciplinary rules governing the conduct of attorneys and whether attorney's fees were properly awarded under the Civil Rights Attorney's Fees Awards Act of 1976, 42 U.S.C. § 1988, against the Virginia Court and its chief justice in his official capacity."

C. Supreme Court's Answer

The Supreme Court of Virginia and its chief justice are immune from suit here because the court was acting in its legislative capacity, and the award of attorney's fees was improper given the Court's immunity.

II. CASE SUMMARY

A. Background

The Supreme Court of Virginia, acting as a regulatory authority for Virginia licensed attorneys, published the Virginia Code of Professional Responsibility. When appellee the Consumers Union of the United States, Inc., attempted to compile a directory of legal services listing information about attorneys in the area, many attorneys "declined to supply the requested information for fear of violating the Bar Code's strict prohibition against attorney advertising." Appellees brought suit claiming, in part, that the Supreme Court of Virginia and its chief justice violated appellee's "First and Fourteenth Amendment rights to gather, publish, and receive factual information concerning attorneys" and requested "a permanent injunction against the enforcement and operation" of the offensive portion of the Code.

After the District Court declared the attorney advertising prohibition unconstitutional, in part, and an appeal was taken to the U.S. Supreme Court, the U.S. Supreme Court decided Bates v. State Bar of Arizona, holding "that enforcement of a ban on attorney advertising would violate the First and Fourteenth Amendment rights of attorneys seeking to advertise the fees they charged for certain routine legal services. In light of Bates, the judgment below was vacated and the case was remanded for further consideration."

On remand, the district court declared the ban on attorney advertising unconstitutional, and granted a permanent injunction against its enforcement. The district court also ordered that certain appellants, in their official capacity, pay attorney's fees for the appellees, pursuant to the Civil Rights Attorney's Fees Awards Act of 1976, citing the Virginia Supreme Court's denial of the State Bar's recommendation to amend the Code, and its failure to conform to the precedent set by Bates v. State Bar of Arizona.

The U.S. Supreme Court granted certiorari, vacated the decision, and remanded the case.

B. Counsel of Record / ACLU Attorney

ACLU Side (Respondent / Appellee): Ellen Broadman argued the cause for appellee.

Opposing Side (Petitioner / Appellant): J. Marshall Coleman, Attorney General of Virginia, argued the cause for appellant.

III. AMICI CURIAE

ACLU Side (Respondent / Appellee)

Brief of amici curiae filed on behalf of the ACLU, et al., by Burt Neuborne, Bruce J. Ennis, Jr., Manuel deQuintana, Edna D. Wells, and Stephen Bricker.

Opposing Side (Petitioner / Appellant)

Brief of amici curiae filed on behalf of the State of South Carolina by Daniel R. McLeod, Attorney General of South Carolina, joined by the Attorneys General of Arizona, Delaware, Florida, Illinois, Kansas, Louisiana, Maryland, Michigan, Missouri, Nebraska, Nevada, New Mexico, North Carolina, North Dakota, Rhode Island, Tennessee, Texas, Utah, West Virginia, Wisconsin, and Wyoming.

Brief of amici curiae filed on behalf of the Conference of Chief Justices in support of the jurisdictional statement by Philip B. Kurland.

IV. THE SUPREME COURT'S DECISION

"The District Court below referred to the issuance of the Code as a judicial function, but this is not conclusive upon us for the purpose of deciding whether issuance of the Code is a judicial act entitled to immunity under § 1983. [We] must inquire whether the Virginia Court and its chief justice are immune from suit for acts performed in their legislative capacity. . . .

In any event, in this case the Virginia Court claims inherent power to regulate the Bar, and as the dissenting judge below indicated, the Virginia Court is exercising the State's entire legislative power with respect to regulating the Bar, and its members are the State's legislators for the purpose of issuing the Bar Code. Thus the Virginia Court and its members are immune from suit when acting in their legislative capacity. . . .

If the sole basis for appellees' § 1983 action against the Virginia Court and its chief justice were the issuance of, or failure to amend, the challenged rules, legislative immunity would foreclose suit against appellants. As has been pointed out, however, the Virginia Court performs more than a legislative role with respect to the State Bar Code. It also hears appeals from lower court decisions in disciplinary cases, a traditional adjudicative task; and in addition, it has independent enforcement authority of its own. . . . If prosecutors and law enforcement personnel cannot be proceeded against for declaratory relief, putative plaintiffs would have to await the institution of state-court proceedings against them in order to assert their federal constitutional claims. This is not the way the law has developed, and, because of its own inherent and statutory enforcement powers, immunity does not shield the Virginia Court and its chief justice from suit in this case. . . .

Because appellees properly prevailed in their § 1983 action, the Civil Rights Attorney's Fees Awards Act, 42 U.S.C. § 1988, authorized the District Court, 'in its discretion,' to award them 'a reasonable attorney's fee,' which may be recovered from state officials sued in their official capacities. . . . We are unable to agree that attorney's fees should have been awarded for the reasons relied on by the District Court. Although the Virginia Court and its chief justice were subject to suit in their direct enforcement role, they were immune in their legislative roles. Yet the District Court's award of attorney's fees in this case was premised on acts or omissions for which appellants enjoyed absolute legislative immunity. This was error.

[W]e hold that it was an abuse of discretion to award fees because the Virginia Court failed to exercise its rulemaking authority in a manner that satisfied the District Court. We therefore vacate the award of attorney's fees and remand for further proceedings consistent with this opinion."

V. JUSTICE VOTE

0 Pro ACLU Side vs. 8 Con Opposing Side

Opposing Side (Petitioner / Appellant)

1. White, B. – Wrote majority opinion
2. Burger, W. – Joined majority opinion

3. Brennan, W. – Joined majority opinion
4. Stewart, P. – Joined majority opinion
5. Marshall, T. – Joined majority opinion
6. Blackmun, H. – Joined majority opinion
7. Stevens, J. – Joined majority opinion
8. Rehnquist, W. – Joined majority opinion

Powell, L – Took no part in the decision

VI. A WIN OR LOSS FOR THE ACLU?

The ACLU filed as amicus curiae urging affirmance; the Supreme Court vacated and remanded the ruling of the District Court for the Eastern District of Virginia in an 8-0 vote, giving the ACLU an apparent loss.

453. PruneYard Shopping Center v. Robins

(Decided June 9, 1980; 447 U.S. 74)

I. ISSUE

A. Issues Discussed

Free speech, Taking Clause, First Amendment, Fifth Amendment, Fourteenth Amendment

B. Legal Question Presented

"[W]hether state constitutional provisions, which permit individuals to exercise free speech and petition rights on the property of a privately owned shopping center to which the public is invited, violate the shopping center owner's property rights under the Fifth and Fourteenth Amendments or his free speech rights under the First and Fourteenth Amendments."

C. Supreme Court's Answer

The state constitutional provisions expanding free speech rights for individuals do not violate the shopping center owner's rights under the U.S. Constitution.

II. CASE SUMMARY

A. Background

"Appellant PruneYard is a privately owned shopping center in the city of Campbell, Cal. It covers approximately 21 acres . . . . The PruneYard is open to the public for the purpose of encouraging the patronizing of its commercial establishments. It has a policy not to permit any visitor or tenant to engage in any publicly expressive activity, including the circulation of petitions, that is not directly related to its commercial purposes. This policy has been strictly enforced in a nondiscriminatory fashion. . . .

Appellees are high school students who sought to solicit support for their opposition to a United Nations resolution against 'Zionism.' On a Saturday afternoon they set up a card table in a corner of PruneYard's central courtyard. They distributed pamphlets and asked passersby to sign petitions, which were to be sent to the President and Members of Congress. Their activity was peaceful and orderly and so far as the record indicates was not objected to by PruneYard's patrons.

Soon after appellees had begun soliciting signatures, a security guard informed them that they would have to leave because their activity violated PruneYard regulations. The guard suggested that they move to the public sidewalk at the PruneYard's perimeter. Appellees immediately left the premises and later filed this lawsuit in the California Superior Court of Santa Clara County. They sought to enjoin appellants from denying them access to the PruneYard for the purpose of circulating their petitions.

The Superior Court held that appellees were not entitled under either the Federal or California Constitution to exercise their asserted rights on the shopping center property. . . . The California Court of Appeal affirmed.

The California Supreme Court reversed, holding that the California Constitution protects 'speech and petitioning, reasonably exercised, in shopping centers even when the centers are privately owned'"

The U.S. Supreme Court granted certiorari to review the case and affirmed the judgment of the Supreme Court of California.

B. Counsel of Record / ACLU Attorney

ACLU Side (Respondent / Appellee): Philip L. Hammer argued the cause for appellee.

Assistant to the Solicitor General Elinor Hadley Stillman argued the cause for the United States, as amicus curiae, by special leave of court.

Opposing Side (Petitioner / Appellant): Max L. Gillam, Jr., argued the cause for appellant.

III. AMICI CURIAE

ACLU Side (Respondent / Appellee)

Brief of amici curiae filed on behalf of the ACLU of Northern California, et al., by Susan L. Paulus, Susan M. Popik, Margaret C. Grosby, Alan L. Schlosser, Amitai Schwartz, Charles S. Sims, Edna D. Wells, and Burt Neuborne.

Brief of amici curiae filed on behalf of the American Federation of Labor and Congress of Industrial Organizations by J. Albert Woll, Laurence Gold, and George Kaufmann.

Brief of amici curiae filed on behalf of the American Jewish Congress, et al., by Nathan Z. Dershowitz, Victoria B. Elger, and Marc D. Stern.

Brief of amici curiae filed on behalf of the People's Lobby, Inc., by Roger Jon Diamond.

Brief of amici curiae filed on behalf of the United States by Assistant to the Solicitor General Elinor Hadley Stillman, Solicitor General Wade H. McCree, Jr., and Deputy Solicitor General Lawrence G. Wallace.

Opposing Side (Petitioner / Appellant)

Brief of amici curiae filed on behalf of the Homart Development Company by Laurence M. Cohen, Martin K. Denis, and Charles H. May, II.

Brief of amici curiae filed on behalf of the International Council of Shopping Centers by John R. Reilly, Dean L. Overman, Edward C. Maeder, and Peter N. Kyros, Jr.

Brief of amici curiae filed on behalf of the Taubman Company, Inc., et al., by Joseph H. Moless, Jr., and Philip B. Kurland.

Brief of amici curiae filed on behalf of the Pacific Legal Foundation by Ronald A. Zumbrun, Thomas E. Hookano,

Elleene A. Kirkland, and Christopher H. Collins.

IV. THE SUPREME COURT'S DECISION

"Appellants first contend that Lloyd Corp. v. Tanner prevents the State from requiring a private shopping center owner to provide access to persons exercising their state constitutional rights of free speech and petition when adequate alternative avenues of communication are available. . ..

Our reasoning in Lloyd, however, does not ex proprio vigore [by its own force] limit the authority of the State to exercise its police power or its sovereign right to adopt in its own Constitution individual liberties more expansive than those conferred by the Federal Constitution. . . .

Appellants next contend that a right to exclude others underlies the Fifth Amendment guarantee against the taking of property without just compensation and the Fourteenth Amendment guarantee against the deprivation of property without due process of law. . . .

Here the requirement that appellants permit appellees to exercise state-protected rights of free expression and petition on shopping center property clearly does not amount to an unconstitutional infringement of appellants' property rights under the Taking Clause. There is nothing to suggest that preventing appellants from prohibiting this sort of activity will unreasonably impair the value or use of their property as a shopping center. The PruneYard is a large commercial complex that covers several city blocks, contains numerous separate business establishments, and is open to the public at large. The decision of the California Supreme Court makes it clear that the PruneYard may restrict expressive activity by adopting time, place, and manner regulations that will minimize any interference with its commercial functions. Appellees were orderly, and they limited their activity to the common areas of the shopping center. In these circumstances, the fact that they may have 'physically invaded' appellants' property cannot be viewed as determinative. . . .

Appellants finally contend that a private property owner has a First Amendment right not to be forced by the State to use his property as a forum for the speech of others. [T]he shopping center by choice of its owner is not limited to the personal use of appellants. It is instead a business establishment that is open to the public to come and go as they please. The views expressed by members of the public in passing out pamphlets or seeking signatures for a petition thus will not likely be identified with those of the owner. Second, no specific message is dictated by the State to be displayed on appellants' property. There consequently is no danger of governmental discrimination for or against a particular message. Finally, as far as appears here appellants can expressly disavow any connection with the message by simply posting signs in the area where the speakers or handbillers stand. Such signs, for example, could disclaim any sponsorship of the message and could explain that the persons are communicating their own messages by virtue of state law. . . .

We conclude that neither appellants' federally recognized property rights nor their First Amendment rights have been infringed by the California Supreme Court's decision recognizing a right of appellees to exercise state-protected rights of expression and petition on appellants' property. The judgment of the Supreme Court of California is therefore affirmed."

V. JUSTICE VOTE

9 Pro ACLU Side vs. 0 Con Opposing Side

ACLU Side (Respondent / Appellee)

1. Rehnquist, W. – Wrote majority opinion
2. Burger, W. – Joined majority opinion
3. Brennan, W. – Joined majority opinion
4. Stewart, P. – Joined majority opinion
5. Marshall, T. – Wrote concurring opinion
6. Stevens, J. – Joined majority opinion
7. White, B. – Wrote concurring opinion, joined Powell's concurrence
8. Powell, L. – Wrote concurring opinion
9. Blackmun, H. – Wrote concurring opinion

VI. A WIN OR LOSS FOR THE ACLU?

The ACLU, as amicus curiae, urged affirmance of the Supreme Court of California's judgment; the U.S. Supreme Court affirmed in a 9-0 vote, giving the ACLU an apparent win.

454. Maine v. Thiboutot

(Decided June 25, 1980; 448 U.S. 1)

I. ISSUE

A. Issues Discussed

Civil rights, attorney's fees

B. Legal Question Presented

"(1) [W]hether [42 U.S.C.] § 1983 encompasses claims based on purely statutory violations of federal law, and (2) if so, whether attorney's fees under [42 U.S.C.] § 1988 may be awarded to the prevailing party in such an action."

C. Supreme Court's Answer

Section 1983 encompasses claims based on purely statutory violations of federal law and attorney's fees may be awarded in such actions.

II. CASE SUMMARY

A. Background

"Respondents, Lionel and Joline Thiboutot, are married and have eight children, three of whom are Lionel's by a previous marriage. The Maine Department of Human Services notified Lionel that, in computing the Aid to Families with Dependent Children (AFDC) benefits to which he was entitled for the three children exclusively his, it would no longer make allowance for the money spent to support the other five children, even though Lionel is legally obligated to support them. Respondents, challenging the State's interpretation of 42 U.S.C. § 602(a)(7), exhausted their state administrative remedies and then sought judicial review of the administrative action in the State Superior Court. By amended complaint, respondents also claimed relief under § 1983 for themselves and others similarly situated. The Superior Court's judgment enjoined petitioners from enforcing the challenged rule and ordered them to adopt new regulations, to notify class members of the new regulations, and to pay the correct amounts retroactively to respondents and prospectively to eligible class members. The court, however, denied respondents' motion for attorney's fees. The Supreme Judicial Court of Maine concluded that respondents had no entitlement to attorney's fees under state law, but were eligible for attorney's fees pursuant to the Civil Rights Attorney's Fees Awards Act of 1976."

The U.S. Supreme Court granted certiorari to review the case and affirmed.

B. Counsel of Record / ACLU Attorney

ACLU Side (Respondent / Appellee): Robert Edmond Mittel argued the cause for appellee.

Opposing Side (Petitioner / Appellant): James Eastman Smith, Assistant Attorney General of Maine, argued the cause for appellant.

III. AMICI CURIAE

ACLU Side (Respondent / Appellee)

Brief of amici curiae filed on behalf of the ACLU, et al., by Charles S. Sims and Bruce J. Ennis.

Brief of amici curiae filed on behalf of the Volunteer Lawyers Project of the Boston Bar Association, et al., by Carol Goodman, Samuel Hoar, Kenneth W. Simons, and Leonard G. Learner.

Opposing Side (Petitioner / Appellant)

Edward G. Biester, Jr., Attorney General, and Robert E. Kelly and Allen C. Warshaw, Deputy Attorneys General, filed a brief of amici curiae on behalf of the Commonwealth of Pennsylvania, joined by officials for their respective States as follows: Francis X. Bellotti, Attorney General of Massachusetts, and Garrick F. Cole, Assistant Attorney General; John J. Degnan, Attorney General of New Jersey, and Andrea Silkowitz, Deputy Attorney General; Thomas D. Rath, Attorney General of New Hampshire; M. Jerome Diamond, Attorney General of Vermont, and Benson Scotch, Assistant Attorney General; Dennis J. Roberts, II, Attorney General of Rhode Island, Allen P. Rubine, Deputy Attorney General, and John S. Foley and Eileen G. Cooney, Special Assistant Attorneys General; and Richard S. Gebelein, Attorney General of Delaware, and Regina M. Small, State Solicitor.

IV. THE SUPREME COURT'S DECISION

"The question before us is whether the phrase 'and laws,' as used in § 1983, means what it says, or whether it should be limited to some subset of laws. Given that Congress attached no modifiers to the phrase, the plain language of the statute undoubtedly embraces respondents' claim that petitioners violated the Social Security Act.

Even were the language ambiguous, however, any doubt as to its meaning has been resolved by our several cases suggesting, explicitly or implicitly, that the § 1983 remedy broadly encompasses violations of federal statutory as well as constitutional law. . . .

Petitioners next argue that, even if this claim is within § 1983, Congress did not intend statutory claims to be covered by the Civil Rights Attorney's Fees Awards Act of 1976 . . . . Once again, . . . the plain language provides an answer. The statute states that fees are available in any § 1983 action. Since we hold that this statutory action is properly brought under § 1983, and since § 1988 makes no exception for statutory § 1983 actions, § 1988 plainly applies to this suit. . . . It follows . . . that the fee provision is part of the § 1983 remedy whether the action is brought in federal or state court.

Affirmed."

V. JUSTICE VOTE

6 Pro ACLU Side vs. 3 Con Opposing Side

ACLU Side (Respondent / Appellee)

1. Brennan, W. – Wrote majority opinion
2. Marshall, T. – Joined majority opinion
3. Stewart, P. – Joined majority opinion
4. White, B. – Joined majority opinion
5. Blackmun, H. – Joined majority opinion
6. Stevens, J. – Joined majority opinion

Opposing Side (Petitioner / Appellant)

1. Powell, L. – Wrote dissenting opinion
2. Burger, W. – Joined Powell's dissent
3. Rehnquist, W. – Joined Powell's dissent

VI. A WIN OR LOSS FOR THE ACLU?

The ACLU filed as amicus curiae urging affirmance; the U.S. Supreme Court affirmed the ruling of the Supreme Judicial Court of Maine in a 6-3 vote, giving the ACLU an apparent win.

455. Harris v. McRae

(Decided June 30, 1980; 448 U.S. 297)

I. ISSUE

A. Issues Discussed

Right to privacy, abortion, Due Process Clause, Free Exercise Clause, Establishment Clause, First Amendment, Fifth Amendment

B. Legal Question Presented

"The statutory question is whether Title XIX requires a State that participates in the Medicaid program to fund the cost of medically necessary abortions for which federal reimbursement is unavailable under the Hyde Amendment. The constitutional question, which arises only if Title XIX imposes no such requirement, is whether the Hyde Amendment, by denying public funding for certain medically necessary abortions, contravenes the liberty or equal protection guarantees of the Due Process Clause of the Fifth Amendment, or either of the Religion Clauses of the First Amendment."

C. Supreme Court's Answer

Title XIX does not require states participating in the Medicaid program to fund medically necessary abortions, and denying this funding does not contravene the Due Process Clause or Establishment Clause. The plaintiffs do not have standing to raise a challenge under the Free Exercise Clause.

II. CASE SUMMARY

A. Background

"The Medicaid program was created in 1965, when Congress added Title XIX to the Social Security Act for the purpose of providing federal financial assistance to States that choose to reimburse certain costs of medical treatment for needy persons. Although participation in the Medicaid program is entirely optional, once a State elects to participate, it must comply with the requirements of Title XIX. . . .

Since September 1976, Congress has prohibited—either by an amendment to the annual appropriations bill for the Department of Health, Education, and Welfare or by a joint resolution—the use of any federal funds to reimburse the cost of abortions under the Medicaid program except under certain specified circumstances. This funding restriction is commonly known as the 'Hyde Amendment,' after its original congressional sponsor, Representative Hyde. . . .

On September 30, 1976, the day on which Congress enacted the initial version of the Hyde Amendment, these consolidated cases were filed in the District Court for the Eastern District of New York. The plaintiffs—Cora McRae, a New York Medicaid recipient then in the first trimester of a pregnancy that she wished to terminate, the New York City Health and Hospitals Corp., a public benefit corporation that operates 16 hospitals, 12 of which provide abortion services, and others—sought to enjoin the enforcement of the funding restriction on abortions. They alleged that the Hyde Amendment violated the First, Fourth, Fifth, and Ninth Amendments of the Constitution insofar as it limited the funding of abortions to those necessary to save the life of the mother, while permitting the funding of costs associated with childbirth. Although the sole named defendant was the Secretary of Health, Education, and Welfare, the District Court permitted Senators James L. Buckley and Jesse A. Helms and Representative Henry J. Hyde to intervene as defendants.

After a hearing, the District Court entered a preliminary injunction prohibiting the Secretary from enforcing the Hyde Amendment and requiring him to continue to provide federal reimbursement for abortions under the standards applicable before the funding restriction had been enacted. Although stating that it had not expressly held that the funding restriction was unconstitutional, since the preliminary injunction was not its final judgment, the District Court noted that such a holding was 'implicit' in its decision granting the injunction. The District Court also certified the McRae case as a class action on behalf of all pregnant or potentially pregnant women in the State of New York eligible for Medicaid and who decide to have an abortion within the first 24 weeks of pregnancy, and of all authorized providers of abortion services to such women.

The Secretary then brought an appeal to [the Supreme] Court. After deciding Beal v. Doe, and Maher v. Roe, [the Supreme Court] vacated the injunction of the District Court and remanded the case for reconsideration in light of those decisions.

On remand, . . . the District Court concluded that the Hyde Amendment, though valid under the Establishment Clause, violates the equal protection component of the Fifth Amendment's Due Process Clause and the Free Exercise Clause of the First Amendment. With regard to the Fifth Amendment, the District Court noted that when an abortion is 'medically necessary to safeguard the pregnant woman's health, . . . the disentitlement to [M]edicaid assistance impinges directly on the woman's right to decide, in consultation with her physician and in reliance on his judgment, to terminate her pregnancy in order to preserve her health.' The court concluded that the Hyde Amendment violates the equal protection guarantee because, in its view, the decision of Congress to fund medically necessary services generally but only certain medically necessary abortions serves no legitimate governmental interest. As to the Free Exercise Clause of the First Amendment, the court held that insofar as a woman's decision to seek a medically necessary abortion may be a product of her religious beliefs under certain Protestant and Jewish tenets, the funding restrictions of the Hyde Amendment violate that constitutional guarantee as well.

Accordingly, the District Court ordered the Secretary to '[c]ease to give effect' to the various versions of the Hyde Amendment insofar as they forbid payments for medically necessary abortions. It further directed the Secretary to '[c]ontinue to authorize the expenditure of federal matching funds [for such abortions].' In addition, the court recertified the McRae case as a nationwide class action on behalf of all pregnant and potentially pregnant women eligible for Medicaid who wish to have medically necessary abortions, and of all authorized providers of abortions for such women."

The Supreme Court granted certiorari to review the case and reversed.

B. Counsel of Record / ACLU Attorney

ACLU Side (Respondent / Appellee): Rhonda Copelon argued the cause for appellee. With her on the briefs were Nancy Stearns, Sylvia Law, Ellen K. Sawyer, Janet Benshoof, Judith Levin, Harriet Pilpel, and Eve Paul.

Opposing Side (Petitioner / Appellant): Solicitor General Wade H. McCree, Jr., argued the cause for appellant. With him on the briefs were Alice Daniel, Peter Buscemi, and Eloise E. Davies.

III. AMICI CURIAE

ACLU Side (Respondent / Appellee)

Brief of amici curiae filed on behalf of the American Ethical Union, et al., by Leo Pfeffer.

Brief of amici curiae filed on behalf of for the Association of Legal Aid Attorneys of the City of New York - District 65 - U.A.W., et al., by Barbara Ellen Handschu, Jane Barrett, Marilyne Mason, and Deborah Weimer.

Brief of amici curiae filed on behalf of the National Organization for Women, et al., by Phyllis N. Segal, and Judith I. Avner.

Brief of amici curiae filed on behalf of the United Presbyterian

Church of the U.S.A. by Sanford Jay Rosen and Kathleen J. Purcell.

Brief of amici curiae filed on behalf of the National Council of Churches of Christ in the U.S.A. by Sanford Jay Rosen and Kathleen J. Purcell.

Brief of amici curiae filed on behalf of the Bergen-Passaic Health Systems Agency, et al., by Randall W. Westreich and David Ben Asher.

Opposing Side (Petitioner / Appellant)

Brief of amici curiae filed on behalf of Representative Jim Wright, et al., by John T. Noonan, Jr., and William B. Ball.

Brief of amici curiae filed on behalf of the United States Catholic Conference by Wilfred R. Caron, Patrick F. Geary, and George E. Reed.

Brief of amici curiae filed on behalf of the Coalition for Human Justice by James G. Kolb.

Brief of amici curiae filed on behalf of the Attorney General of the State of New York, et al., by Robert Abrams, Attorney General, Shirley Adelson Siegel, Solicitor General, Peter Bienstock, Bureau Chief, Civil Rights Bureau, Assistant Attorney General, and Arnold D Fleischer and Barbara E. Levy, Assistant Attorneys General.

Brief of amici curiae filed on behalf of the Legal Defense Fund for Unborn Children by Alan Ernest.

IV. THE SUPREME COURT'S DECISION

"The appellees assert that the funding restrictions of the Hyde Amendment violate several rights secured by the Constitution—(1) the right of a woman, implicit in the Due Process Clause of the Fifth Amendment, to decide whether to terminate a pregnancy, (2) the prohibition under the Establishment Clause of the First Amendment against any 'law respecting an establishment of religion,' and (3) the right to freedom of religion protected by the Free Exercise Clause of the First Amendment. The appellees also contend that, quite apart from substantive constitutional rights, the Hyde Amendment violates the equal protection component of the Fifth Amendment. . . .

The financial constraints that restrict an indigent woman's ability to enjoy the full range of constitutionally protected freedom of choice are the product not of governmental restrictions on access to abortions, but rather of her indigency. Although Congress has opted to subsidize medically necessary services generally, but not certain medically necessary abortions, the fact remains that the Hyde Amendment leaves an indigent woman with at least the same range of choice in deciding whether to obtain a medically necessary abortion as she would have had if Congress had chosen to subsidize no health care costs at all. We are thus not persuaded that the Hyde Amendment impinges on the constitutionally protected freedom of choice . . . .

Although the liberty protected by the Due Process Clause affords protection against unwarranted government interference with freedom of choice in the context of certain personal decisions, it does not confer an entitlement to such funds as may be necessary to realize all the advantages of that freedom. To hold otherwise would mark a drastic change in our understanding of the Constitution. . . . To translate the limitation on governmental power implicit in the Due Process Clause into an affirmative funding obligation would require Congress to subsidize the medically necessary abortion of an indigent woman even if Congress had not enacted a Medicaid program to subsidize other medically necessary services. Nothing in the Due Process Clause supports such an extraordinary result. Whether freedom of choice that is constitutionally protected warrants federal subsidization is a question for Congress to answer, not a matter of constitutional entitlement. Accordingly, we conclude that the Hyde Amendment does not impinge on the due process liberty . . . .

The appellees also argue that the Hyde Amendment contravenes rights secured by the Religion Clauses of the First Amendment. . . .

It is well settled that 'a legislative enactment does not contravene the Establishment Clause if it has a secular legislative purpose, if its principal or primary effect neither advances nor inhibits religion, and if it does not foster an excessive governmental entanglement with religion.' . . . That the Judaeo-Christian religions oppose stealing does not mean that a State or the Federal Government may not, consistent with the Establishment Clause, enact laws prohibiting larceny. . . . In sum, we are convinced that the fact that the funding restrictions in the Hyde Amendment may coincide with the religious tenets of the Roman Catholic Church does not, without more, contravene the Establishment Clause. . . .

We need not address the merits of the appellees' arguments concerning the Free Exercise Clause, because the appellees lack standing to raise a free exercise challenge to the Hyde Amendment. The named appellees fall into three categories: (1) the indigent pregnant women who sued on behalf of other women similarly situated, (2) the two officers of the Women's Division, and (3) the Women's Division itself. The named appellees in the first category lack standing to challenge the Hyde Amendment on free exercise grounds because none alleged, much less proved, that she sought an abortion under compulsion of religious belief. Although the named appellees in the second category did provide a detailed description of their religious beliefs, they failed to allege either that they are or expect to be pregnant or that they are eligible to receive Medicaid. These named appellees, therefore, lack the personal stake in the controversy needed to confer standing to raise such a challenge to the Hyde Amendment. . . .

The guarantee of equal protection under the Fifth Amendment is not a source of substantive rights or liberties, but rather a right to be free from invidious discrimination in statutory classifications and other governmental activity. It is well settled that where a statutory classification does not itself impinge on a right or liberty protected by the Constitution, the validity of classification must be sustained unless 'the classification rests on grounds wholly irrelevant to the achievement of [any legitimate governmental] objective.' . . .

For the reasons stated above, we have already concluded that the Hyde Amendment violates no constitutionally protected substantive rights. We now conclude as well that it is not predicated on a constitutionally suspect classification. . . .

The remaining question then is whether the Hyde Amendment is rationally related to a legitimate governmental objective. It is the Government's position that the Hyde Amendment bears a rational relationship to its legitimate interest in protecting the potential life of the fetus. We agree. . . .

For the reasons stated in this opinion, we hold that a State that participates in the Medicaid program is not obligated under Title XIX to continue to fund those medically necessary abortions for which federal reimbursement is unavailable under the Hyde Amendment. We further hold that the funding restrictions of the Hyde Amendment violate neither the Fifth Amendment nor the Establishment Clause of the First Amendment. It is also our view that the appellees lack standing to raise a challenge to the Hyde Amendment under the Free Exercise Clause of the First Amendment. Accordingly, the judgment of the District Court is reversed, and the case is remanded to that court for further proceedings consistent with this opinion."

V. JUSTICE VOTE

4 Pro ACLU Side vs. 5 Con Opposing Side

ACLU Side (Respondent / Appellee)

1. Brennan, W. – Wrote dissenting opinion
2. Marshall, T. – Wrote dissenting opinion, joined Brennan's dissent
3. Blackmun, H. – Wrote dissenting opinion, joined Brennan's dissent
4. Stevens, J. – Wrote dissenting opinion

Opposing Side (Petitioner / Appellant)

1. Stewart, P. – Wrote majority opinion
2. Buger, W. – Joined majority opinion
3. White, B. – Wrote concurring opinion
4. Powell, L. – Joined majority opinion
5. Rehnquist, W. – Joined majority opinion

VI. A WIN OR LOSS FOR THE ACLU?

The ACLU, as counsel, urged affirmance of the judgment of the District Court for the Eastern District of New York; the Supreme Court reversed and remanded in a 5-4 vote, giving the ACLU an apparent loss.

456. Fullilove v. Klutznick

(Decided July 2, 1980; 448 U.S. 448)

I. ISSUE

A. Issues Discussed

Civil rights, race, Fifth Amendment, Fourteenth Amendment

B. Legal Question Presented

Whether the Minority Business Enterprise (MBE) provision of the Public Works Employment Act of 1977 is constitutional.

C. Supreme Court's Answer

The MBE provision is constitutional.

II. CASE SUMMARY

A. Background

"In May 1977, Congress enacted the Public Works Employment Act of 1977, which . . . authorized an additional $4 billion appropriation for federal grants . . . to state and local government entities for use in local public works projects. Among the changes made was the addition of the provision that has become the focus of this litigation. Section 103(f)(2) of the 1977 Act, referred to as the 'minority business enterprise' or 'MBE' provision . . . ." This provision requires that at least ten percent of each grant be allocated for businesses owned by minority members, defined by the Act as "Negroes, Spanish-speaking, Orientals, Indians, Eskimos, and Aleuts."

"On November 30, 1977, petitioners filed a complaint in the United States District Court for the Southern District of New York seeking declaratory and injunctive relief to enjoin enforcement of the MBE provision. . . . Petitioners are several associations of construction contractors and subcontractors, and a firm engaged in heating, ventilation,

and air conditioning work. Their complaint alleged that they had sustained economic injury due to enforcement of the 10% MBE requirement and that the MBE provision on its face violated the Equal Protection Clause of the Fourteenth Amendment, the equal protection component of the Due Process Clause of the Fifth Amendment, and various statutory anti-discrimination provisions.

After a hearing held the day the complaint was filed, the District Court denied a requested temporary restraining order and scheduled the matter for an expedited hearing on the merits. On December 19, 1977, the District Court issued a memorandum opinion upholding the validity of the MBE program and denying the injunctive relief sought.

The United States Court of Appeals for the Second Circuit affirmed, holding that 'even under the most exacting standard of review the MBE provision passes constitutional muster.' Considered in the context of many years of governmental efforts to remedy past racial and ethnic discrimination, the court found it 'difficult to imagine' any purpose for the program other than to remedy such discrimination."

The Supreme Court granted certiorari to review the case and affirmed.

B. Counsel of Record / ACLU Attorney

ACLU Side (Respondent / Appellee): Assistant Attorney General Drew S. Days, III, argued the cause for appellee Secretary of Commerce.

Allen G. Schwartz argued the cause for appellee City of New York.

Opposing Side (Petitioner / Appellant): Robert G. Benisch argued the cause for appellants Fullilove, et al.

Robert J. Hickey argued the cause for appellant General Building Contractors of New York State, Inc.

III. AMICI CURIAE

ACLU Side (Respondent / Appellee)

Brief of amici curiae filed on behalf of the ACLU, et al., by E. Richard Larson, Edna D. Wells, Burt Neuborne, Bruce J. Ennis, Frank Askin, and Robert Sedler.

Additional briefs of amici curiae were filed on behalf of Alpha Kappa Alpha Sorority, Inc., the American Savings & Loan League, Inc., et al., the Asian American Legal Defense and Education Fund, Inc., the Lawyers' Committee for Civil Rights Under Law, the Mexican American/Hispanic Contractors and Truckers Association, Inc., et al., the Minority Contractors Assistance Project, Inc., the NAACP, et al., the NAACP Legal Defense and Educational Fund, Inc., et al., the National Bar Association, Inc., et al., the Affirmative Action Coordinating Center, et al., the Minority Contractors Association, Inc., and the National Conference of Black Mayors, Inc.

Opposing Side (Petitioner / Appellant)

Brief of amici curiae filed on behalf of the Equal Employment Advisory Council by Kenneth C. McGuiness, Douglas S. McDowell, and Daniel R. Levinson.

Brief of amici curiae filed on behalf of the Pacific Legal Foundation by Sandra M. Robertson, Ronald A. Zumbrun, and John H. Findley.

Brief of amici curiae filed on behalf of the Anti-Defamation League of B'nai B'rith by Robert A. Helman, Gary T. Johnson, Justin J. Finger, Jeffrey P. Sinensky, and Richard A Weisz.

IV. THE SUPREME COURT'S DECISION

"A program that employs racial or ethnic criteria, even in a remedial context, calls for close examination; yet we are bound to approach our task with appropriate deference to the Congress, a co-equal branch charged by the Constitution with the power to 'provide for the . . . general Welfare of the United States' and 'to enforce, by appropriate legislation,' the equal protection guarantees of the Fourteenth Amendment. . . .

The clear objective of the MBE provision is disclosed by our necessarily extended review of its legislative and administrative background. The program was designed to ensure that, to the extent federal funds were granted under the Public Works Employment Act of 1977, grantees who elect to participate would not employ procurement practices that Congress had decided might result in perpetuation of the effects of prior discrimination which had impaired or foreclosed access by minority businesses to public contracting opportunities. The MBE program does not mandate the allocation of federal funds according to inflexible percentages solely based on race or ethnicity. . . .

The legislative history of the MBE provision shows that there was a rational basis for Congress to conclude that the subcontracting practices of prime contractors could perpetuate the prevailing impaired access by minority businesses to public contracting opportunities, and that this inequity has an effect on interstate commerce. Thus Congress could take necessary and proper action to remedy the situation. . . . We conclude that in this respect the objectives of the MBE provision are within the scope of the Spending Power. . . .

A more specific challenge to the MBE program is the charge that it impermissibly deprives nonminority businesses of access to at least some portion of the government contracting opportunities generated by the Act. It must be conceded that by its objective of remedying the historical impairment of access, the MBE provision can have the effect of awarding some contracts to MBE's which otherwise might be awarded to other businesses, who may themselves be innocent of any prior discriminatory actions. Failure of nonminority firms to receive certain contracts is, of course, an incidental consequence of the program, not part of its objective; similarly, past impairment of minority-firm access to public contracting opportunities may have been an incidental consequence of 'business as usual' by public contracting agencies and among prime contractors. . . .

Another challenge to the validity of the MBE program is the assertion that it is underinclusive - that it limits its benefit to specified minority groups rather than extending its remedial objectives to all businesses whose access to government contracting is impaired by the effects of disadvantage or discrimination. Such an extension would, of course, be appropriate for Congress to provide; it is not a function for the courts. . . .

Congress, after due consideration, perceived a pressing need to move forward with new approaches in the continuing effort to achieve the goal of equality of economic opportunity. In this effort, Congress has necessary latitude to try new techniques such as the limited use of racial and ethnic criteria to accomplish remedial objectives; this is especially so in programs where voluntary cooperation with remedial measures is induced by placing conditions on federal expenditures. That the program may press the outer limits of congressional authority affords no basis for striking it down.

This opinion does not adopt, either expressly or implicitly, the formulas of analysis articulated in such cases as University of California Regents v. Bakke. However, our analysis demonstrates that the MBE provision would survive judicial review under either 'test' articulated in the several Bakke opinions. The MBE provision of the Public Works Employment Act of 1977 does not violate the Constitution.

Affirmed."

V. JUSTICE VOTE

6 Pro ACLU Side vs. 3 Con Opposing Side

ACLU Side (Respondent / Appellee)

1. Burger, W. – Wrote majority opinion
2. White, B. – Joined majority opinion
3. Powell, L. – Wrote concurring opinion
4. Marshall, T. – Wrote concurring opinion
5. Brennan, W. – Joined Marshall's concurrence
6. Blackmun, H. – Joined Marshall's concurrence

Opposing Side (Petitioner / Appellant)

1. Stewart, P. – Wrote dissenting opinion
2. Rehnquist, W. – Joined Stewart's dissent
3. Stevens, J. – Wrote dissenting opinion

VI. A WIN OR LOSS FOR THE ACLU?

The ACLU filed as amicus curiae urging affirmance; the Supreme Court affirmed the ruling of the Court of Appeals for the Second Circuit in a 6-3 vote, giving the ACLU an apparent win.

457. Richmond Newspapers, Inc. v. Virginia

(Decided July 2, 1980; 448 U.S. 555)

I. ISSUE

A. Issues Discussed

Criminal procedure, due process, freedom of speech and of the press, First Amendment

B. Legal Question Presented

"[W]hether the right of the public and press to attend criminal trials is guaranteed under the United States Constitution."

C. Supreme Court's Answer

Absent an overriding interest, criminal trials must be open to the public.

II. CASE SUMMARY

A. Background

"In March 1976, one Stevenson was indicted for the murder of a hotel manager who had been found stabbed to death on December 2, 1975. Tried promptly in July 1976, Stevenson was convicted of second-degree murder in the Circuit Court of Hanover County, Va. The Virginia Supreme Court reversed the conviction in October 1977, holding that a bloodstained shirt purportedly belonging to Stevenson had been improperly admitted into evidence.

[After two subsequent mistrials,] Stevenson was tried in the same court for a fourth time beginning on September 11, 1978. Present in the courtroom when the case was called were appellants Wheeler and McCarthy, reporters for appellant Richmond Newspapers, Inc. Before the trial began, counsel for the defendant moved that it be closed to the public. . . .

The trial judge, who had presided over two of the three previous trials, asked if the prosecution had any objection to clearing the courtroom. The prosecutor stated he had no objection and would leave it to the discretion of the court. [T]he trial judge then announced: '[T]he statute gives me that power specifically and the defendant has made the motion.' He then ordered 'that the Courtroom be kept clear of all parties except the witnesses when they testify.' The record does not show that any objections to the closure order were made by anyone present at the time, including appellants Wheeler and McCarthy.

Later that same day, however, appellants sought a hearing on a motion to vacate the closure order. . . . At the closed hearing, counsel for appellants observed that no evidentiary findings had been made by the court prior to the entry of its closure order and pointed out that the court had failed to consider any other, less drastic measures within its power to ensure a fair trial. . . . The court denied the motion to vacate and ordered the trial to continue the following morning 'with the press and public excluded.'

What transpired when the closed trial resumed the next day was disclosed . . . by an order of the court entered September 12, 1978:

'[I]n the absence of the jury, the defendant by counsel made a Motion that a mis-trial be declared, which motion was taken under advisement.

'At the conclusion of the Commonwealth's evidence, the attorney for the defendant moved the Court to strike the Commonwealth's evidence on grounds stated to the record, which Motion was sustained by the Court.

'And the jury having been excused, the Court doth find the accused NOT GUILTY of Murder, as charged in the Indictment, and he was allowed to depart.'

On September 27, 1978, the trial court granted appellants' motion to intervene nunc pro tunc in the Stevenson case. Appellants then petitioned the Virginia Supreme Court for writs of mandamus and prohibition and filed an appeal from the trial court's closure order. On July 9, 1979, the Virginia Supreme Court dismissed the mandamus and prohibition petitions and, finding no reversible error, denied the petition for appeal."

The U.S. Supreme Court granted certiorari to review the case and reversed the judgment of the Supreme Court of Virginia.

B. Counsel of Record / ACLU Attorney

ACLU Side (Petitioner / Appellant): Laurence H. Tribe argued the cause for appellant.

Opposing Side (Respondent / Appellee): J. Marshall Coleman, Attorney General of Virginia, argued the cause for appellee.

III. AMICI CURIAE

ACLU Side (Petitioner / Appellant)

Brief of amici curiae filed on behalf of the ACLU, et al., by Stephen Bricker, Edna D. Wells, and Bruce J. Ennis.

Additional briefs of amici curiae were filed on behalf of the State of New Jersey, the American Newspaper Publishers Association, et al., the Reporters Committee for Freedom of the Press, et al., and the Washington Post, et al.

Opposing Side (Respondent / Appellee)

No briefs of amici curiae were filed in support of appellee.

IV. THE SUPREME COURT'S DECISION

"[T]he historical evidence demonstrates conclusively that at the time when our organic laws were adopted, criminal trials both here and in England had long been presumptively open. This is no quirk of history; rather, it has long been recognized as an indispensable attribute of an Anglo-American trial. . . .

Despite the history of criminal trials being presumptively open since long before the Constitution, the State presses its contention that neither the Constitution nor the Bill of Rights contains any provision which by its terms guarantees to the public the right to attend criminal trials. Standing alone, this is correct, but there remains the question whether, absent an explicit provision, the Constitution affords protection against exclusion of the public from criminal trials. . . .

The First Amendment, in conjunction with the Fourteenth,

prohibits governments from 'abridging the freedom of speech, or of the press; or the right of the people peaceably to assemble, and to petition the Government for a redress of grievances.' These expressly guaranteed freedoms share a common core purpose of assuring freedom of communication on matters relating to the functioning of government. Plainly it would be difficult to single out any aspect of government of higher concern and importance to the people than the manner in which criminal trials are conducted . . . .

The right of access to places traditionally open to the public, as criminal trials have long been, may be seen as assured by the amalgam of the First Amendment guarantees of speech and press; and their affinity to the right of assembly is not without relevance. From the outset, the right of assembly was regarded not only as an independent right but also as a catalyst to augment the free exercise of the other First Amendment rights with which it was deliberately linked by the draftsmen. . . .

We hold that the right to attend criminal trials is implicit in the guarantees of the First Amendment; without the freedom to attend such trials, which people have exercised for centuries, important aspects of freedom of speech and 'of the press could be eviscerated.' . . .

Absent an overriding interest articulated in findings, the trial of a criminal case must be open to the public. Accordingly, the judgment under review is reversed"

V. JUSTICE VOTE

7 Pro ACLU Side vs. 1 Con Opposing Side

ACLU Side (Petitioner / Appellant)

1. Burger, W. – Wrote majority opinion
2. White, B. – Wrote concurring opinion
3. Stevens, J. – Wrote concurring opinion
4. Brennan, W. – Wrote concurring opinion
5. Marshall, T. – Joined Brennan's concurrence
6. Stewart, P. – Wrote concurring opinion
7. Blackmun, H. – Wrote concurring opinion

Opposing Side (Respondent / Appellee)

1. Rehnquist, W. – Wrote dissenting opinion

Powell, L – Took no part in the decision

VI. A WIN OR LOSS FOR THE ACLU?

The ACLU, as amicus curiae, urged reversal of the Supreme Court of Virginia's judgment; the U.S. Supreme Court reversed in a 7-1 vote, giving the ACLU an apparent win.

458. Dennis v. Sparks

(Decided November 17, 1980; 449 U.S. 24)

I. ISSUE

A. Issues Discussed

Civil rights, injunctions, judicial immunity

B. Legal Question Presented

Are individuals who allegedly bribed a judge to issue an injunction against respondent protected by judicial immunity, or can they be held liable for damages resulting from the injunction?

C. Supreme Court's Answer

The individuals can be held liable and are not protected by judicial immunity.

II. CASE SUMMARY

A. Background

"In January 1973, a judge of the 229th District Court of Duval County, Tex., enjoined the production of minerals from certain oil leases owned by respondents. In June 1975, the injunction was dissolved by an appellate court as having been illegally issued. Respondents then filed a complaint in the United States District Court purporting to state a cause of action for damages under 42 U.S.C. § 1983. Defendants were the Duval County Ranch Co., Inc., which had obtained the injunction, the sole owner of the corporation, the judge who entered the injunction, and the two individual sureties on the injunction bond, one of whom is now petitioner in this Court. Essentially, the claim was that the injunction had been corruptly issued as the result of a conspiracy between the judge and the other defendants, thus causing a deprivation of property, i. e., two years of oil production, without due process of law.

All defendants moved to dismiss, the judge asserting judicial immunity and the other defendants urging dismissal for failure to allege action 'under color' of state law, a necessary component of a § 1983 cause of action. The District Court concluded that because the injunction was a judicial act within the jurisdiction of the state court, the judge was immune from liability in a § 1983 suit, whether or not the injunction had issued as the result of a corrupt conspiracy. Relying on Haldane v. Chagnon, the District Court also ruled that with the dismissal of the judge the remaining defendants could not be said to have conspired under color of state law within the meaning of § 1983. The action against them was accordingly dismissed 'for failure to state a claim upon which relief can be granted.'

In a per curiam opinion, a panel of the Court of Appeals for the Fifth Circuit affirmed . . . . The case was reconsidered en banc, prior Circuit authority was overruled and the District Court judgment was reversed insofar as it had dismissed claims against the defendants other than the judge. The court ruled that there was no good reason in law, logic, or policy for conferring immunity on private persons who persuaded the immune judge to exercise his jurisdiction corruptly. Because the judgment below was inconsistent with the rulings of other Courts of Appeals and involves an important issue, [the Supreme Court] granted the petition for certiorari [and affirmed.]"

B. Counsel of Record / ACLU Attorney

ACLU Side (Respondent / Appellee): Garland F. Smith argued the cause for appellee.

Opposing Side (Petitioner / Appellant): Finley L. Edmonds argued the cause for appellant.

III. AMICI CURIAE

ACLU Side (Respondent / Appellee)

Brief of amici curiae filed on behalf of the ACLU by Suzanne M. Lynn.

Opposing Side (Petitioner / Appellant)

Brief of amici curiae filed on behalf of the State of Florida by Jim Smith, Attorney General, and Gerald B. Curington, Assistant Attorney General.

Brief of amici curiae filed on behalf of the State of Texas by Mark White, Attorney General, John W. Fainter, Jr., First Assistant Attorney General, and Laura S. Martin and Lonny F. Zwiener, Assistant Attorneys General.

IV. THE SUPREME COURT'S DECISION

"Based on the doctrine expressed in Bradley v. Fisher, this Court has consistently adhered to the rule that 'judges defending against § 1983 actions enjoy absolute immunity from damages liability for acts performed in their judicial capacities.' The courts below concluded that the judicial immunity doctrine required dismissal of the § 1983 action against the judge who issued the challenged injunction, and as the case comes to us, the judge has been properly dismissed from the suit on immunity grounds. It does not follow, however, that the action against the private parties accused of conspiring with the judge must also be dismissed. . . .

Private persons, jointly engaged with state official in the challenged action, are acting 'under color' of law for purposes of § 1983 actions. [H]ere the allegations were that an official act of the defendant judge was the product of a corrupt conspiracy involving bribery of the judge. Under these allegations, the private parties conspiring with the judge were acting under color of state law; and it is of no consequence in this respect that the judge himself is immune from damages liability. Immunity does not change the character of the judge's action or that of his co-conspirators. . . .

It is urged that if petitioner and other private co-conspirators of the judge are to be subject to § 1983 damages actions and if a case such as this is to go to trial, the charge of conspiracy and judicial corruption will necessarily be aired and decided, the consequence being that the judge, though not a party and immune from liability, will be heavily involved, very likely as a witness forced to testify about and defend his judicial conduct. [T]here is no . . . constitutionally based privilege immunizing judges from being required to testify about their judicial conduct in third-party litigation. Nor has any demonstration been made that, historically, the doctrine of judicial immunity not only protected the judge from liability but also excused him from responding as a witness when his co-conspirators are sued. . . .

Judicial immunity arose because it was in the public interest to have judges who were at liberty to exercise their independent judgment about the merits of a case without fear of being mulcted for damages should an unsatisfied litigant be able to convince another tribunal that the judge acted not only mistakenly but with malice and corruption. In terms of undermining a judge's independence and his judicial performance, the concern that his conduct will be examined in a collateral proceeding against those with whom he allegedly conspired, a proceeding in which he cannot be held liable for damages and which he need not defend, is not of the same order of magnitude as the prospects of being a defendant in a damages action from complaint to verdict with the attendant possibility of being held liable for damages if the factfinder mistakenly upholds the charge of malice or of a corrupt conspiracy with others. [W]e agree with the Court of Appeals that the potential harm to the public from denying immunity to private coconspirator is outweighed by the benefits of providing a remedy against those private persons who participate in subverting the judicial process, and in so doing, inflict injury on other persons.

The judgment of the Court of Appeals is affirmed."

V. JUSTICE VOTE

9 Pro ACLU Side vs. 0 Con Opposing Side

ACLU Side (Respondent / Appellee)

1. White, B. – Wrote majority opinion
2. Brennan, W. – Joined majority opinion
3. Blackmun, H. – Joined majority opinion
4. Marshall, T. – Joined majority opinion
5. Powell, L – Joined majority opinion
6. Stevens, J. – Joined majority opinion
7. Stewart, P. – Joined majority opinion
8. Rehnquist, W. – Joined majority opinion
9. Burger, W. – Joined majority opinion

VI. A WIN OR LOSS FOR THE ACLU?

The ACLU filed as amicus curiae urging affirmance; the Supreme Court affirmed the Court of Appeals' judgment in a 9-0 vote, giving the ACLU an apparent win.

459. Allen v. McCurry

(Decided December 9, 1980; 449 U.S. 90)

I. ISSUE

A. Issues Discussed

Criminal justice, Fourth Amendment, collateral estoppel

B. Legal Question Presented

"[W]hether the unavailability of federal habeas corpus prevented the police officers from raising the state courts' partial rejection of McCurry's constitutional claim as a collateral estoppel defense to the § 1983 suit against them for damages."

C. Supreme Court's Answer

Collateral estoppel can be a defense to suits under § 1983, including where the plaintiff is barred from federal habeas corpus relief.

II. CASE SUMMARY

A. Background

"McCurry was charged with possession of heroin and assault with intent to kill."

"At a hearing before his criminal trial in a Missouri court, the respondent, Willie McCurry, invoked the Fourth and Fourteenth Amendments to suppress evidence that had been seized by the police. The trial court denied the suppression motion in part, and McCurry was subsequently convicted after a jury trial. The conviction was later affirmed on appeal. Because he did not assert that the state courts had denied him a 'full and fair opportunity' to litigate his search and seizure claim, McCurry was barred by [the Supreme] Court's decision in Stone v. Powell from seeking a writ of habeas corpus in a federal district court. Nevertheless, he sought federal-court redress for the alleged constitutional violation by bringing a damages suit under 42 U.S.C. § 1983 against the officers who had entered his home and seized the evidence in question. . . .

The complaint alleged a conspiracy to violate McCurry's Fourth Amendment rights, an unconstitutional search and seizure of his house, and an assault on him by unknown police officers after he had been arrested and handcuffed. The petitioners moved for summary judgment. The District Court apparently understood the gist of the complaint to be the allegedly unconstitutional search and seizure and granted summary judgment, holding that collateral estoppel prevented McCurry from relitigating the search-and-seizure question already decided against him in the state courts.

The Court of Appeals reversed the judgment and remanded the case for trial. The appellate court said it was not holding that collateral estoppel was generally inapplicable in a § 1983 suit raising issues determined against the federal plaintiff in a state criminal trial. But noting that Stone v. Powell barred McCurry from federal habeas corpus relief, and invoking 'the special role of the federal courts in protecting civil rights,' the court concluded that the § 1983 suit was McCurry's only route to a federal forum for his constitutional claim and directed the trial court to allow him to proceed to trial unencumbered by collateral estoppel."

The Supreme Court granted certiorari to review the case and reversed.

B. Counsel of Record / ACLU Attorney

ACLU Side (Respondent / Appellee): Jeffrey J. Shank argued the cause for appellee.

Opposing Side (Petitioner / Appellant): John J. FitzGibbon argued the cause for appellant.

III. AMICI CURIAE

ACLU Side (Respondent / Appellee)

Brief of amici curiae filed on behalf of the ACLU of Eastern Missouri by Michael A. Wolff.

Opposing Side (Petitioner / Appellant)

Brief of amici curiae filed on behalf of Americans for Effective Law Enforcement, Inc., et al., by Stephen H. Sachs, Attorney General of Maryland, Emory A. Plitt, Jr., Assistant Attorney General, George P. Agnost, Fred E. Inbau, Wayne W. Schmidt, and James P. Manak.

IV. THE SUPREME COURT'S DECISION

"[T]he Court has eliminated the requirement of mutuality in applying collateral estoppel to bar relitigation of issues decided earlier in federal-court suits, and has allowed a litigant who was not a party to a federal case to use collateral estoppel 'offensively' in a new federal suit against the party who lost on the decided issue in the first case. But one general limitation the Court has repeatedly recognized is that the concept of collateral estoppel cannot apply when the party against whom the earlier decision is asserted did not have a 'full and fair opportunity' to litigate that issue in the earlier case.

[R]es judicata and collateral estoppel not only reduce unnecessary litigation and foster reliance on adjudication, but also promote the comity between state and federal courts that has been recognized as a bulwark of the federal system.

[N]othing in the language or legislative history of § 1983 proves any congressional intent to deny binding effect to a state-court judgment or decision when the state court, acting within its proper jurisdiction, has given the parties a full and fair opportunity to litigate federal claims, and thereby has shown itself willing and able to protect federal rights. And nothing in the legislative history of § 1983 reveals any purpose to afford less deference to judgments in state criminal proceedings than to those in state civil proceedings. There is, in short, no reason to believe that Congress intended to provide a person claiming a federal right an unrestricted opportunity to relitigate an issue already decided in state court simply because the issue arose in a state proceeding in which he would rather not have been engaged at all. . . .

The Court of Appeals erred in holding that McCurry's inability to obtain federal habeas corpus relief upon his Fourth Amendment claim renders the doctrine of collateral estoppel inapplicable to his § 1983 suit. Accordingly, the judgment is reversed, and the case is remanded to the Court of Appeals for proceedings consistent with this opinion."

V. JUSTICE VOTE

3 Pro ACLU Side vs. 6 Con Opposing Side

ACLU Side (Respondent / Appellee)

1. Blackmun, H. – Wrote dissenting opinion
2. Marshall, T. – Joined dissenting opinion
3. Brennan, W. – Joined dissenting opinion

Opposing Side (Petitioner / Appellant)

1. Stewart, P. – Wrote majority opinion
2. Burger, W. – Joined majority opinion
3. White, B. – Joined majority opinion
4. Powell, L. – Joined majority opinion
5. Rehnquist, W. – Joined majority opinion
6. Stevens, J. – Joined majority opinion

VI. A WIN OR LOSS FOR THE ACLU?

The ACLU filed as amicus curiae urging affirmance; the Supreme Court reversed the ruling of the Court of Appeals in a 6-3 vote, giving the ACLU an apparent loss.

460. United States v. DiFrancesco

(Decided December 9, 1980; 449 U.S. 117)

I. ISSUE

A. Issues Discussed

Criminal procedure, Fifth Amendment, Organized Crime Control Act of 1970

B. Legal Question Presented

Does the section of the Organized Crime Control Act of 1970 which authorizes the government to appeal the criminal sentence imposed upon a "dangerous special offender," violate the Double Jeopardy Clause of the Fifth Amendment?

C. Supreme Court's Answer

The section of the Organized Crime Control Act of 1970 does not violate the Double Jeopardy Clause.

II. CASE SUMMARY

A. Background

The Organized Crime Control Act of 1970, 18 U.S.C. § 3576, grants the United States the right, under certain circumstances, to appeal the sentence imposed on a "dangerous special offender." In 1977, at a trial in a federal district court, respondent Eugene DiFrancesco was convicted of federal racketeering offenses. "At another jury trial in 1978—before a different judge in the same District—based on an indictment returned prior to the racketeering indictment, respondent was convicted of damaging federal property, . . . of unlawfully storing explosive materials, . . . and of conspiring to commit those offenses . . . .

Respondent was first sentenced, in March 1978, on his convictions at the later trial. He received eight years on the charge for damaging federal property and five years on the conspiracy charge, these sentences to be served concurrently, and one year on the unlawful storage charge, to be served consecutively to the other sentences. This made a total of nine years' imprisonment. In April, respondent was sentenced as a dangerous special offender under § 3575 to two 10-year terms on the racketeering counts upon which he was convicted at the earlier trial; the court specified that these sentences were to be served concurrently with each other and with the sentences imposed in March. The dangerous special offender charge and sentences thus resulted in an additional punishment of only about one year.

Respondent appealed the judgments of conviction to the Court of Appeals for the Second Circuit, and the United States sought review, under § 3576, of the sentences imposed upon respondent as a dangerous special offender. The Court of Appeals unanimously affirmed the judgments of conviction. By a divided vote, however, the court dismissed the Government's appeal on double jeopardy grounds."

The Supreme Court granted certiorari to review the case and reversed.

B. Counsel of Record / ACLU Attorney

ACLU Side (Respondent / Appellee): Edgar C. DeMoyer argued the cause for appellee.

Opposing Side (Petitioner / Appellant): Deputy Solicitor General Andrew L. Frey argued the cause for the United States.

III. AMICI CURIAE

ACLU Side (Respondent / Appellee)

Brief of amici curiae filed on behalf of the ACLU by Martin Michaelson.

Brief of amici curiae filed on behalf of the State Public Defender of California by Quin Denvir and Laurance S. Smith.

Opposing Side (Petitioner / Appellant)

No briefs of amici curiae were filed in support of appellant.

IV. THE SUPREME COURT'S DECISION:

"The exaltation of form over substance is to be avoided. The Court has said that in the double jeopardy context it is the substance of the action that is controlling, and not the label given that action. Congress could have achieved the purpose of § 3576 by a slightly different statute whose constitutionality would be unquestionable. Congress might have provided that a defendant found to be a dangerous special offender was to receive a specified mandatory term, but that the trial court then could recommend a lesser sentence to the court of appeals, which would be free to accept the recommendation or to reject it. That scheme would offer no conceivable base for a double jeopardy objection. Yet the impact on the defendant would be exactly the same as, and possibly worse than, the impact under § 3576 as written. No double jeopardy policy is advanced by approving one of these procedures and declaring the other unconstitutional.

It is perhaps worth noting . . . that § 3576 represents a considered legislative attempt to attack a specific problem in our criminal justice system, that is, the tendency on the part of some trial judges 'to mete out light sentences in cases involving organized crime management personnel.' Section 3576 was Congress' response to that plea. The statute is limited in scope and is narrowly focused on the problem so identified. It is not an example of 'Government oppression' against which the Double Jeopardy Clause stands guard. . . .

We conclude that § 3576 withstands the constitutional challenge raised in the case before us. The judgment of the Court of Appeals is reversed, and the case is remanded for further proceedings consistent with this opinion."

V. JUSTICE VOTE

4 Pro ACLU Side vs. 5 Con Opposing Side

ACLU Side (Respondent / Appellee)

1. Brennan, W. – Wrote dissenting opinion
2. Stevens, J. – Wrote dissenting opinion, joined Brennan's dissent
3. Marshall, T. – Joined Brennan's dissent
4. White, B. – Joined Brennan's dissent

Opposing Side (Petitioner / Appellant)

1. Blackmun, H. – Wrote majority opinion
2. Powell, L. – Joined majority opinion
3. Stewart, P. – Joined majority opinion
4. Rehnquist, W. – Joined majority opinion
5. Burger, W. – Joined majority opinion

VI. A WIN OR LOSS FOR THE ACLU?

The ACLU filed as amicus curiae urging affirmance; the Supreme Court reversed the Court of Appeals in a 5-4 vote, giving the ACLU an apparent loss.

461. Delta Air Lines, Inc. v. August

(Decided March 9, 1981; 450 U.S. 346)

I. ISSUE

A. Issues Discussed

Civil rights, race, Federal Rules of Civil Procedure

B. Legal Question Presented

"[W]hether the words 'judgment finally obtained by the offeree' as used in [Rule 68 of the Federal Rules of Civil Procedure] should be construed to encompass a judgment against the offeree as well as a judgment in favor of the offeree."

C. Supreme Court's Answer

This rule does not apply when the judgment is against the offeree.

II. CASE SUMMARY

A. Background

"Respondent Rosemary August (plaintiff) filed a complaint against petitioner Delta Air Lines, Inc. (defendant), alleging that she had been discharged from her position as a flight attendant solely because of her race in violation of Title VII of the Civil Rights Act of 1964. She sought reinstatement, approximately $20,000 in backpay, attorney's fees, and costs. A few months after the complaint was filed, defendant made a formal offer of judgment to plaintiff in the amount of $450. The offer was refused, the case was tried, and plaintiff lost. The district court entered judgment in favor of defendant and directed that each party bear its own costs. Defendant then moved for modification of the judgment, contending that under Rule 68 [of the Federal Rules of Civil Procedure] the plaintiff should be required to pay the costs incurred by defendant after the offer of judgment had been refused. The district court denied the motion on the ground that the $450 offer had not been made in a good-faith attempt to settle the case and therefore did not trigger the cost-shifting provisions of Rule 68. The Court of Appeals affirmed on the same ground, holding that Rule 68 applied only if the defendant's settlement offer was sufficient 'to justify serious consideration by the plaintiff.'"

The Supreme Court granted certiorari to review the case and affirmed.

B. Counsel of Record / ACLU Attorney

ACLU Side (Respondent / Appellee): Susan Margaret Vance argued the cause for appellee.

Elinor Hadley Stillman argued the cause for the United States, as amicus curiae, by special leave of Court.

Opposing Side (Petitioner / Appellant): E. Allan Kovar argued the cause for appellant.

III. AMICI CURIAE

ACLU Side (Respondent / Appellee)

Brief of amici curiae filed on behalf of the ACLU by E. Richard Larson and Bruce J. Ennis.

Brief of amici curiae filed on behalf of the United States, et al., by Elinor Hadley Stillman, Solicitor General Wade H. McCree, Jr., Deputy Solicitor General Wallace, Leroy D. Clark, Joseph T. Eddins, Lutz Alexander Prager, and Warren Bo Duplinsky.

Brief of amici curiae filed on behalf of the Lawyers' Committee for Civil Rights Under Law by John B. Jones, Jr., Norman Redlich, William L. Robinson, Norman J. Chachkin, and Beatrice Rosenberg.

Brief of amici curiae filed on behalf of the Lawyers' Committee for Civil Rights Under Law, of Chicago, by Martha A. Mills and Sybille C. Fritzsche.

Brief of amici curiae filed on behalf of the NAACP by Aldus S. Mitchell and Sophia H. Hall.

Opposing Side (Petitioner / Appellant)

Brief of amici curiae filed on behalf of the Equal Employment Advisory Council by Robert E. Williams, Douglas S. McDowell, and Daniel R. Levinson.

IV. THE SUPREME COURT'S DECISION

"[I]f we limit our analysis to the text of the Rule itself, it is clear that it applies only to offers made by the defendant and only to judgments obtained by the plaintiff. It therefore is simply inapplicable to this case because it was the defendant that obtained the judgment. . . .

Our interpretation of the Rule is consistent with its purpose. The purpose of Rule 68 is to encourage the settlement of litigation. . . . We cannot reasonably conclude that the drafters of the Federal Rules intended on the one hand affirmatively to grant the district judge discretion to deny costs to the prevailing party under Rule 54(d) and then on the other hand to give defendants—and only defendants—the power to take away that discretion by performing a token act. . . . If a plaintiff chooses to reject a reasonable offer, then it is fair that he not be allowed to shift the cost of continuing the litigation to the defendant in the event that his gamble produces an award that is less than or equal to the amount offered. But it is hardly fair or evenhanded to make the plaintiff's rejection of an utterly frivolous settlement offer a watershed event that transforms a prevailing defendant's right to costs in the discretion of the trial judge into an absolute right to recover the costs incurred after the offer was made. [T]he only purpose served by these state offer-of-judgment rules was to penalize prevailing plaintiffs who had rejected reasonable settlement offers without good cause. . . .

Although defendant's petition for certiorari presented the question of the District Judge's abuse of discretion in denying defendants costs under Rule 54(d), that question was not raised in the Court of Appeals and is not properly before us. We therefore affirm the judgment of the Court of Appeals."

V. JUSTICE VOTE

6 Pro ACLU Side vs. 3 Con Opposing Side

ACLU Side (Respondent / Appellee)

1. Stevens, J. – Wrote majority opinion
2. Marshall, T. – Joined majority opinion
3. White, B. – Joined majority opinion
4. Brennan, W. – Joined majority opinion
5. Blackmun, H. – Joined majority opinion
6. Powell, L. – Wrote concurring opinion

Opposing Side (Petitioner / Appellant)

1. Rehnquist, W. – Wrote dissenting opinion
2. Stewart, P. – Joined Rehnquist's dissent
3. Burger, W. – Joined Rehnquist's dissent

VI. A WIN OR LOSS FOR THE ACLU?

The ACLU filed as amicus curiae urging affirmance; the Supreme Court affirmed the ruling of the Court of Appeals in a 6-3 vote, giving the ACLU an apparent win.

462. Kirchberg v. Feenstra

(Decided March 23, 1981; 450 U.S. 455)

I. ISSUE

A. Issues Discussed

Civil rights, gender

B. Legal Question Presented

"In this appeal we consider the constitutionality of a now superseded Louisiana statute that gave a husband, as 'head and master' of property jointly owned with his wife, the unilateral right to dispose of such property without his spouse's consent."

C. Supreme Court's Answer

"By granting the husband exclusive control over the disposition of community property, Art. 2404 clearly embodies the type of express gender-based discrimination that we have found unconstitutional absent a showing that the classification is tailored to further an important governmental interest. . . .

Because appellant has failed to offer such a justification, and because the State . . . has apparently abandoned any claim that an important government objective was served by the statute, we affirm the judgment of the Court of Appeals invalidating Art. 2404."

II. CASE SUMMARY

A. Background

"In 1974, . . . Mr. Feenstra retained appellant Karl Kirchberg, an attorney, to represent him. Mr. Feenstra signed a $3,000 promissory note in prepayment . . . . As security . . . , Mr. Feenstra executed a mortgage . . . on the home he jointly owned with his wife. Mrs. Feenstra was not informed of the mortgage . . . because . . . former Art. 2404 of the Louisiana Civil Code Ann., gave her husband exclusive control over . . . community property. . . .

Mrs. Feenstra first learned of the existence of the mortgage in 1976, when appellant Kirchberg threatened to foreclose on her home unless she paid him the amount outstanding . . . .

Kirchberg . . . filed this action . . . seeking a declaratory judgment against Mrs. Feenstra . . . . Mrs. Feenstra alleged . . . a second counterclaim challenging the constitutionality of the statutory scheme . . . .

While Mrs. Feenstra's appeal . . . was pending . . . , the Louisiana Legislature . . . abandoned the 'head and master' concept embodied in Art. 2404 . . . . These provisions, however, did not take effect until January 1, 1980, and the Court of Appeals was therefore required to consider whether Art. 2404 . . . violated the Equal Protection Clause of the Fourteenth Amendment. . . .

The court . . . concluded that Art. 2404 violated the Equal Protection Clause. However, because . . . retroactive application of its decision 'would create a substantial hardship with respect to property rights and obligations within the State of Louisiana,' the decision was limited to prospective application. Only Kirchberg appealed . . . ."

The Supreme Court granted certiorari to review the case.

B. Counsel of Record

ACLU Side (Respondent / Appellee): Barbara Hausman-Smith argued the cause and filed a brief for appellee.

Opposing Side (Petitioner / Appellant): Alan Ford Schoenberger argued the cause pro hac vice for appellant. With him on the brief was Karl J. Kirchberg, pro se.

III. AMICI CURIAE

ACLU Side (Respondent / Appellee)

Brief of amici curiae filed on behalf of NOW Legal Defense and Education Fund, American Civil Liberties Union Women's Rights Project, American Jewish Committee, American Jewish Congress, Institute for Women Today, National Center on Women and Family Law, National Coalition of American Nuns, Unitarian Universalist Women's Federation, Women's Equity Action League, Women's Legal Defense Fund by Sybil H. Pollet, Phyllis N. Segal, and Kim E. Greene.

Opposing Side (Petitioner / Appellant)

No briefs of amici curiae were filed in support of appellant.

IV. THE SUPREME COURT'S DECISION

"By granting the husband exclusive control over the disposition of community property, Art. 2404 clearly embodies the type of express gender-based discrimination that we have found unconstitutional absent a showing that the classification is tailored to further an important governmental interest. In defending the constitutionality of Art. 2404, appellant Kirchberg does not claim that the provision serves any such interest. Instead, appellant attempts to distinguish this Court's decisions . . . by arguing that appellee Feenstra, as opposed to the disadvantaged individuals in those cases, could have taken steps to avoid the discriminatory impact of Art. 2404. . . .

By focusing on steps that Mrs. Feenstra could have taken to preclude her husband from mortgaging their home without her consent, however, appellant overlooks the critical question: Whether Art. 2404 substantially furthers an important government interest. . . . Because appellant has failed to offer such a justification, and because the State, by declining to appeal from the decision below, has apparently abandoned any claim that an important government objective was served by the statute, we affirm the judgment of the Court of Appeals invalidating Art. 2404. . . .

Appellant's final contention is that even if Art. 2404 violates the Equal Protection Clause of the Fourteenth Amendment, the mortgage he holds on the Feenstra home is nonetheless valid because the Court of Appeals limited its ruling to prospective application. . . .

We decline to address appellant's concerns about the potential impact of the Court of Appeals' decision on other mortgages executed pursuant to Art. 2404. The only question properly before us is whether the decision of the Court of Appeals applies to the mortgage in this case, and on that issue we find no ambiguity. . . . Thus, the dispute between the parties at its core involves the validity of a single mortgage, and in passing on the constitutionality of Art. 2404, the Court of Appeals clearly intended to resolve that controversy adversely to appellant.

Accordingly, the judgment of the Court of Appeals is affirmed."

V. JUSTICE VOTE

9 Pro ACLU Side vs. 0 Con Opposing Side

ACLU Side (Respondent / Appellee)

1. Marshall, T. – Wrote majority opinion
2. Burger, W. – Joined majority opinion
3. Brennan, W. – Joined majority opinion
4. White, B. – Joined majority opinion
5. Blackmun, H. – Joined majority opinion
6. Powell, L. – Joined majority opinion
7. Stevens, J. – Joined majority opinion
8. Stewart, P. – Wrote concurring opinion
9. Rehnquist, W. – Joined Stewart's concurrence

VI. A WIN OR LOSS FOR THE ACLU?

The ACLU filed as amicus curiae urging affirmance; the Supreme Court affirmed the Court of Appeals' decision by a 9-0 vote, giving the ACLU an apparent win.

463. Michael M. v. Superior Court of Sonoma County

(Decided March 23, 1981; 450 U.S. 464)

I. ISSUE

A. Issues Discussed

Civil rights, gender, Fourteenth Amendment, equal protection

B. Legal Question Presented

"[W]hether California's 'statutory rape' law, § 261.5 of the California Penal Code, violates the Equal Protection Clause of the Fourteenth Amendment."

C. Supreme Court's Answer

California's statutory rape law does not violate the Equal Protection Clause of the Fourteenth Amendment.

II. CASE SUMMARY

A. Background

Petitioner, Michael M., a 17 1/2-year-old male, was charged with violating California's statutory rape law, California Penal Code § 261.5. The law defined "unlawful sexual intercourse as 'an act of sexual intercourse accomplished with a female no the wife of the perpetrator, where the female is under the age of 18 years.' . . . The evidence, adduced at a preliminary hearing showed that at approximately midnight on June 3, 1978, petitioner and two friends approached Sharon, a 16 1/2-year-old female, and her sister as they waited at a bus stop. Petitioner and Sharon, who had already been drinking, moved away from the others and began to kiss. After being struck in the face for rebuffing petitioner's initial advances, Sharon submitted to sexual intercourse with petitioner. Prior to trial, petitioner sought to set aside the information on both state and federal constitutional grounds, asserting that § 261.5 unlawfully discriminated on the basis of gender. The trial court and the California Court of Appeal denied petitioner's request for relief and petitioner sought review in the Supreme Court of California.

The Supreme Court held that 'section 261.5 discriminates on the basis of sex because only females may be victims, and only males may violate the section.' The court then subjected the classification to 'strict scrutiny,' stating that it must be justified by a compelling state interest. It found that the classification was 'supported not by mere social convention but by the immutable physiological fact that it is the female exclusively who can become pregnant.' Canvassing 'the tragic human costs of illegitimate teenage pregnancies,' including the large number of teenage abortions, the increased medical risk associated with teenage pregnancies, and the social consequences of teenage childbearing, the court concluded that the State has a compelling interest in preventing such pregnancies. Because males alone can 'physiologically cause the result which the law properly seeks to avoid,' the court further held that the gender classification was readily justified as a means of identifying offender and victim."

The Supreme Court granted certiorari to review the case and affirmed.

B. Counsel of Record / ACLU Attorney

ACLU Side (Petitioner / Appellant): Gregory F. Jilka argued the cause for appellant.

Opposing Side (Respondent / Appellee): Sandy R. Kriegler, Deputy Attorney General of California, argued the cause for appellee.

III. AMICI CURIAE

ACLU Side (Petitioner / Appellant)

Brief of amici curiae filed on behalf of the ACLU, et al., by Charles S. Sims and Bruce J. Ennis, Jr.

Brief of amici curiae filed on behalf of the Women's Legal Defense Fund by John W. Karr and Elkanah J. Burns.

Opposing Side (Respondent / Appellee)

Brief of amici curiae filed on behalf of the United States by Solicitor General Wade H. McCree, Jr., Assistant Attorney General Heymann, Assistant Solicitor General Levander, and Sara Criscitelli.

IV. THE SUPREME COURT'S DECISION

"We are satisfied not only that the prevention of illegitimate pregnancy is at least one of the 'purposes' of the statute, but also that the State has a strong interest in preventing such pregnancy. At the risk of stating the obvious, teenage pregnancies, which have increased dramatically over the last two decades, have significant social, medical, and economic consequences for both the mother and her child, and the State. . . .

We similarly reject petitioner's argument that § 261.5 is impermissibly overbroad because it makes unlawful sexual intercourse with prepubescent females, who are, by definition, incapable of becoming pregnant. Quite apart from the fact that the statute could well be justified on the grounds that very young females are particularly susceptible to physical injury from sexual intercourse, it is ludicrous to suggest that the Constitution requires the California Legislature to limit the scope of its rape statute to older teenagers and exclude young girls.

There remains only petitioner's contention that the statute is unconstitutional as it is applied to him because he, like Sharon, was under 18 at the time of sexual intercourse. Petitioner argues that the statute is flawed because it presumes that as between two persons under 18, the male is the culpable aggressor. We find petitioner's contentions unpersuasive. Contrary to his assertions, the statute does not rest on the assumption that males are generally the aggressors. It is instead an attempt by a legislature to prevent illegitimate teenage pregnancy by providing an additional deterrent for men. The age of the man is irrelevant since young men are as capable as older men of inflicting the harm sought to be prevented. [T]he statute instead reasonably reflects the fact that the consequences of sexual intercourse and pregnancy fall more heavily on the female than on the male.

Accordingly, the judgment of the California Supreme Court is affirmed."

V. JUSTICE VOTE

4 Pro ACLU Side vs. 5 Con Opposing Side

ACLU Side (Petitioner / Appellant)

1. Brennan, W. – Wrote dissenting opinion
2. White, B. – Joined Brennan's dissent
3. Marshall, T. – Joined Brennan's dissent
4. Stevens, J. – Wrote dissenting opinion

Opposing Side (Respondent / Appellee)

1. Rehnquist, W. – Wrote majority opinion
2. Burger, W. – Joined majority opinion
3. Powell, L. – Joined majority opinion
4. Stewart, P. – Wrote concurring opinion
5. Blackmun, H. – Wrote concurring opinion

VI. A WIN OR LOSS FOR THE ACLU?

The ACLU filed as amicus curiae urging reversal; the U.S. Supreme Court affirmed the ruling of the Supreme Court of California in a 5-4 vote, giving the ACLU an apparent loss.

464. Thomas v. Review Board of the Indiana Employment Security Division

(Decided April 6, 1981; 450 U.S. 707)

I. ISSUE

A. Issues Discussed

First Amendment, free exercise of religion

B. Legal Question Presented

"[W]hether the State's denial of unemployment compensation benefits to the petitioner, a Jehovah's Witness who terminated his job because his religious beliefs forbade participation in the production of armaments, constituted a violation of his First Amendment right to free exercise of religion."

C. Supreme Court's Answer

The State's denial of unemployment compensation benefits violated petitioner's First Amendment right to free exercise of religion.

II. CASE SUMMARY

A. Background

"Thomas, a Jehovah's Witness, was hired initially to work in the roll foundry at Blaw-Knox. The function of that department was to fabricate sheet steel for a variety of industrial uses. On his application form, he listed his membership in the Jehovah's Witnesses, and noted that his hobbies were Bible study and Bible reading. However, he placed no conditions on his employment; and he did not describe his religious tenets in any detail on the form.

Approximately a year later, the roll foundry closed, and Blaw-Knox transferred Thomas to a department that fabricated turrets for military tanks. On his first day at this new job, Thomas realized that the work he was doing was weapons related. He checked the bulletin board where in-plant openings were listed, and discovered that all of the remaining departments at Blaw-Knox were engaged directly in the production of weapons. Since no transfer to another department would resolve his problem, he asked for a layoff. When that request was denied, he quit, asserting that he could not work on weapons without violating the principles of his religion. The record does not show that he was offered any nonweapons work by his employer, or that any such work was available.

Upon leaving Blaw-Knox, Thomas applied for unemployment compensation benefits under the Indiana Employment Security Act. . . .

The referee concluded . . . that Thomas' termination was not based upon a 'good cause [arising] in connection with [his] work,' as required by the Indiana unemployment compensation statute. Accordingly, he was held not entitled to benefits. The Review Board adopted the referee's findings and conclusions, and affirmed the denial of benefits.

The Indiana Court of Appeals, accepting the finding that Thomas terminated his employment 'due to his religious convictions,' reversed the decision of the Review Board, and held that § 22-4-15-1, as applied, improperly burdened Thomas' right to the free exercise of his religion. Accordingly, it ordered the Board to extend benefits to Thomas.

The Supreme Court of Indiana, dividing 3-2, vacated the decision of the Court of Appeals, and denied Thomas benefits."

The U.S. Supreme Court granted certiorari and reversed the judgment of the Supreme Court of Indiana.

B. Counsel of Record / ACLU Attorney

ACLU Side (Petitioner / Appellant): Blanca Bianchi de la Torre argued the cause for appellant.

Opposing Side (Respondent / Appellee): William E. Daily argued the cause for appellee.

III. AMICI CURIAE

ACLU Side (Petitioner / Appellant)

Brief of amici curiae filed on behalf of the ACLU by Judith Levin, Tom Gerety, and Charles S. Sims.

Brief of amici curiae filed on behalf of the American Jewish Congress by Nathan Z. Dershowitz.

Brief of amici curiae filed on behalf of the Jewish Peace Fellowship, et al., by Leo Pfeffer.

Brief of amici curiae filed on behalf of Americans United for Separation of Church and State Fund, Inc., by Lee Boothby.

Opposing Side (Respondent / Appellee)

No briefs of amici curiae were filed in support of appellee.

IV. THE SUPREME COURT'S DECISION

"Only beliefs rooted in religion are protected by the Free Exercise Clause, which, by its terms, gives special protection to the exercise of religion. The determination of what is a 'religious' belief or practice is more often than not a difficult and delicate task, as the division in the Indiana Supreme Court attests. However, the resolution of that question is not to turn upon a judicial perception of the particular belief or practice in question; religious beliefs need not be acceptable, logical, consistent, or comprehensible to others in order to merit First Amendment protection. . . .

In reaching its conclusion, the Indiana court seems to have placed considerable reliance on the facts that Thomas was 'struggling' with his beliefs and that he was not able to 'articulate' his belief precisely. . . .

The narrow function of a reviewing court in this context is to determine whether there was an appropriate finding that petitioner terminated his work because of an honest conviction that such work was forbidden by his religion. Not surprisingly, the record before the referee and the Review Board was not made with an eye to the microscopic examination often exercised in appellate judicial review. However, judicial review is confined to the facts as found and conclusions drawn. On this record, it is clear that Thomas terminated his employment for religious reasons. . . .

There is no evidence in the record to indicate that the number of people who find themselves in the predicament of choosing between benefits and religious beliefs is large enough to create 'widespread unemployment,' or even to seriously affect unemployment—and no such claim was advanced by the Review Board. Similarly, although detailed inquiry by employers into applicants' religious beliefs is undesirable, there is no evidence in the record to indicate that such inquiries will occur in Indiana, or that they have occurred in any of the states that extend benefits to people in the petitioner's position. Nor is there any reason to believe that the number of people terminating employment for religious reasons will be so great as to motivate employers to make such inquiries.

Neither of the interests advanced is sufficiently compelling to justify the burden upon Thomas' religious liberty. Accordingly, Thomas is entitled to receive benefits . . . ."

The U.S. Supreme Court reversed the judgment of the Supreme Court of Indiana.

V. JUSTICE VOTE

8 Pro ACLU Side vs. 1 Con Opposing Side

ACLU Side (Petitioner / Appellant)

1. Burger, W. – Wrote majority opinion
2. Brennan, W. – Joined majority opinion
3. Stewart, P. – Joined majority opinion
4. White, B. – Joined majority opinion
5. Marshall, T. – Joined majority opinion
6. Powell, L. – Joined majority opinion
7. Stevens, J. – Joined majority opinion
8. Blackmun, H. – Wrote concurring opinion

Opposing Side (Respondent / Appellee)

1. Rehnquist, W. – Wrote dissenting opinion

VI. A WIN OR LOSS FOR THE ACLU?

The ACLU, as amicus curiae, urged reversal of the Supreme Court of Indiana's judgment; the U.S. Supreme Court reversed in an 8-1 vote, giving the ACLU an apparent win.

465. Steagald v. United States

(Decided April 21, 1981; 451 U.S. 204)

I. ISSUE

A. Issues Discussed

Civil rights, drugs, Fourth Amendment, search and seizure, warrants

B. Legal Question Presented

"[W]hether, under the Fourth Amendment, a law enforcement officer may legally search for the subject of an arrest warrant in the home of a third party without first obtaining a search warrant."

C. Supreme Court's Answer

A law enforcement officer may not legally search for the subject of an arrest warrant in a third party's home without a search warrant, absent exigent circumstances or consent.

II. CASE SUMMARY

A. Background

"In early January 1978, an agent of the Drug Enforcement Administration (DEA) was contacted in Detroit, Mich., by a confidential informant who suggested that he might be able to locate Ricky Lyons, a federal fugitive wanted on drug charges. . . . Lyons was the subject of a 6-month-old arrest warrant."

The informant supplied a telephone number and DEA agents, after contacting the telephone company to determine the corresponding address, "drove to the address supplied by the telephone company to search for Lyons. The officers observed two men standing outside the house to be searched. These men were Hoyt Gaultney and petitioner Gary Steagald. The officers approached with guns drawn, frisked both men, and, after demanding identification, determined that neither man was Lyons. Several agents proceeded to the house. Gaultney's wife answered the door, and informed the agents that she was alone in the house. She was told to place her hands against the wall and was guarded in that position while one agent searched the house. Ricky Lyons was not found, but during the search of the house the agent observed what he believed to be cocaine. Upon being informed of this discovery, Agent Goodowens sent an officer to obtain a search warrant and in the meantime conducted a second search of the house, which uncovered additional incriminating evidence. During a third search conducted pursuant to a search warrant, the agents uncovered 43 pounds of cocaine. Petitioner was arrested and indicted on federal drug charges.

Prior to trial, petitioner moved to suppress all evidence uncovered during the various searches on the ground that it was illegally obtained because the agents had failed to secure a search warrant before entering the house. Agent Goodowens testified at the suppression hearing that there had been no 'physical hinderance' preventing him from obtaining a search warrant and that he did not do so because he believed that the arrest warrant for Ricky Lyons was sufficient to justify the entry and search. The District Court agreed with this view, and denied the suppression motion. Petitioner was convicted, and renewed his challenge to the search in his appeal. A divided Court of Appeals for the Fifth Circuit affirmed the District Court's denial of petitioner's suppression motion."

The Supreme Court granted certiorari to review the case and reversed.

B. Counsel of Record / ACLU Attorney

ACLU Side (Petitioner / Appellant): John Richard Young, by appointment of the court, argued the cause for appellant.

Opposing Side (Respondent / Appellee): Deputy Solicitor General Andrew L. Frey argued the cause for the United States.

III. AMICI CURIAE

ACLU Side (Petitioner / Appellant)

Brief of amici curiae filed on behalf of the ACLU, et al., by John McNally and Charles S. Sims.

Opposing Side (Respondent / Appellee)

No briefs of amici curiae were filed in support of appellee.

IV. THE SUPREME COURT'S DECISION

"[W]hether the arrest warrant issued in this case adequately safeguarded the interests protected by the Fourth Amendment depends upon what the warrant authorized the agents to do. [T]he agents . . . relied on the warrant as legal authority to enter the home of a third person based on their belief that Ricky Lyons might be a guest there. . . . Thus, while the warrant in this case may have protected Lyons from an unreasonable seizure, it did absolutely nothing to protect petitioner's privacy interest in being free from an unreasonable invasion and search of his home. . . . In the absence of exigent circumstances, we have consistently held that such judicially untested determinations are not reliable enough to justify an entry into a person's home to arrest him without a warrant, or a search of a home for objects in the absence of a search warrant.

[T]wo distinct interests were implicated by the search at issue here—Ricky Lyons' interest in being free from an unreasonable seizure and petitioner's interest in being free from an unreasonable search of his home. Because the arrest warrant for Lyons addressed only the former interest, the search of petitioner's home was no more reasonable from petitioner's perspective than it would have been if conducted in the absence of any warrant. Since warrantless searches of a home are impermissible absent consent or exigent circumstances, we conclude that the instant search violated the Fourth Amendment. . . .

An arrest warrant, to the extent that it is invoked as authority to enter the homes of third parties, suffers from the same infirmity. Like a writ of assistance, it specifies only the object of a search—in this case, Ricky Lyons—and leaves to the unfettered discretion of the police the decision as to which particular homes should be searched. We do not believe that the Framers of the Fourth Amendment would have condoned such a result. . . . Any warrant requirement impedes to some extent the vigor with which the Government can seek to enforce its laws, yet the Fourth Amendment recognizes that this restraint is necessary in some cases to protect against unreasonable searches and seizures. We conclude that this is such a case. The additional burden imposed on the police by a warrant requirement is minimal. In contrast, the right protected—that of presumptively innocent people to be secure in their homes from unjustified, forcible intrusions by the Government—is weighty. Thus, in order to render the instant search reasonable under the Fourth Amendment, a search warrant was required.

Accordingly, the judgment of the Court of Appeals is reversed, and the case is remanded to that court for further proceedings consistent with this opinion."

V. JUSTICE VOTE

7 Pro ACLU Side vs. 2 Con Opposing Side

ACLU Side (Petitioner / Appellant)

1. Marshall, T. – Wrote majority opinion
2. Stevens, J. – Joined majority opinion
3. Brennan, W. – Joined majority opinion
4. Stewart, P. – Joined majority opinion
5. Blackmun, H. – Joined majority opinion
6. Powell, L. – Joined majority opinion
7. Burger, W. – Concurred in the judgment

Opposing Side (Respondent / Appellee)

1. Rehnquist, W. – Wrote dissenting opinion
2. White, B. – Joined Rehnquist's dissent

VI. A WIN OR LOSS FOR THE ACLU?

The ACLU filed as amicus curiae urging reversal; the Supreme Court reversed and remanded the ruling of the Court of Appeals for the Fifth Circuit in a 7-2 vote, giving the ACLU an apparent win.

466. Ball v. James

(Decided April 29, 1981; 451 U.S. 355)

I. ISSUE

A. Issues Discussed

Civil rights, voting, Fourteenth Amendment, equal protection

B. Legal Question Presented

"[W]hether the peculiarly narrow function of [the water reclamation district in Arizona, a] local governmental body and the special relationship of one class of citizens to that body releases it from the strict demands of the one-person, one-vote principle of the Equal Protection Clause of the Fourteenth Amendment."

C. Supreme Court's Answer

The district does not have to follow the one-person, one-vote principle.

II. CASE SUMMARY

A. Background

"The public entity at issue here is the Salt River Project Agricultural Improvement and Power District, which stores and delivers untreated water to the owners of land comprising 236,000 acres in central Arizona. The District, formed as a governmental entity in 1937, subsidizes its water operations by selling electricity, and has become the supplier of electric power for hundreds of thousands of people in an area including a large part of metropolitan Phoenix. . . . Under the new statutory scheme, which is essentially the one at issue in this case, the legislature allowed the district to limit voting for its directors to voters, otherwise regularly qualified under state law, who own land within the district, and to apportion voting power among those landowners according to the number of acres owned. . . .

This lawsuit was brought by a class of registered voters who live within the geographic boundaries of the District, and who own either no land or less than an acre of land within the District. The complaint alleged that the District enjoys such governmental powers as the power to condemn land, to sell tax-exempt bonds, and to levy taxes on real property. It also alleged that because the District sells electricity to virtually half the population of Arizona, and because, through its water operations, it can exercise significant influence on flood control and environmental management within its boundaries, the District's policies and actions have a substantial effect on all people who live within the District, regardless of property ownership. Seeking declaratory and injunctive relief, the appellees claimed that the acreage-based scheme for electing directors of the District violates the Equal Protection Clause of the Fourteenth Amendment. [T]he District Court for the District of Arizona held the District voting scheme constitutional and dismissed the complaint. A divided panel of the Court of Appeals for the Ninth Circuit reversed."

The Supreme Court granted certiorari to review the case and reversed.

B. Counsel of Record / ACLU Attorney

ACLU Side (Respondent / Appellee): Bruce E. Meyerson argued the cause for appellee.

Opposing Side (Petitioner / Appellant): Rex E. Lee argued the cause for appellant.

III. AMICI CURIAE

ACLU Side (Respondent / Appellee)

Brief of amici curiae filed on behalf of the Arizona Civil Liberties Union, et al., by Noel Fidel.

Opposing Side (Petitioner / Appellant)

No briefs of amici curiae were filed in support of appellant.

IV. THE SUPREME COURT'S DECISION

"[T]he District simply does not exercise the sort of governmental powers that invoke the strict demands of Reynolds. The District cannot impose ad valorem property taxes or sales taxes. It cannot enact any laws governing the conduct of citizens, nor does it administer such normal functions of government as the maintenance of streets, the operation of schools, or sanitation, health, or welfare services. [N]either the existence nor size of the District's power business affects the legality of its property-based voting scheme. [S]ince the electric power functions were stipulated to be incidental to the water functions which are the District's primary purpose, they cannot change the character of that enterprise. . . .

In this case, the parties have stipulated that the primary legislative purpose of the District is to store, conserve, and deliver water for use by District landowners, that the sole legislative reason for making water projects public entities was to enable them to raise revenue through interest-free bonds, and that the development and sale of electric power was undertaken not for the primary purpose of providing electricity to the public, but 'to support the primary irrigation functions by supplying power for reclamation uses and by providing revenues which could be applied to increase the amount and reduce the cost of water to Association subscribed lands.'

[A]ccording to the stipulation of the parties, the subscriptions of land which made the Association and then the District possible might well have never occurred had not the subscribing landowners been assured a special voice in the conduct of the District's business. Therefore, . . . the State could rationally limit the vote to landowners. Moreover, Arizona could rationally make the weight of their vote dependent upon the number of acres they own, since that number reasonably reflects the relative risks they incurred as landowners and the distribution of the benefits and the burdens of the District's water operations.

The judgment of the Court of Appeals is reversed, and the case is remanded for further proceedings consistent with this opinion."

V. JUSTICE VOTE

4 Pro ACLU Side vs. 5 Con Opposing Side

ACLU Side (Respondent / Appellee)

1. White, B. – Wrote dissenting opinion
2. Brennan, W. – Joined White's dissent
3. Marshall, T. – Joined White's dissent
4. Blackmun, H. – Joined White's dissent

Opposing Side (Petitioner / Appellant)

1. Stewart, P. – Wrote majority opinion
2. Burger, W. – Joined majority opinion
3. Powell, L. – Wrote concurring opinion
4. Rehnquist, W. – Joined majority opinion
5. Stevens, J. – Joined majority opinion

VI. A WIN OR LOSS FOR THE ACLU?

The ACLU filed as amicus curiae urging affirmance; the Supreme Court reversed the ruling of the Court of Appeals for the Ninth Circuit in a 5-4 vote, giving the ACLU an apparent loss.

467. University of Texas v. Camenisch

(Decided April 29, 1981; 451 U.S. 390)

I. ISSUE

A. Issues Discussed

Civil rights, injunctions, mootness, disabilities

B. Legal Question Presented

Should a preliminary injunction have issued in a suit by a deaf student alleging that a state university violated § 504 of the Rehabilitation Act of 1973 by refusing to pay for a sign-language interpreter?

C. Supreme Court's Answer

The question whether the preliminary injunction was proper is now moot, but the case must be remanded for a trial on the merits to determine who should pay for the interpreter.

II. CASE SUMMARY

A. Background

Respondent "Camenisch, a deaf graduate student at the University of Texas" alleged "that the University had violated § 504 of the Rehabilitation Act of 1973" by refusing to provide him with sign-language interpreter services. The University denied the respondent's request for such services on the grounds that he did not meet the university's established criteria for financial assistance to graduate students and therefore should pay for his own interpreter. The District Court for the Western District of Texas issued a preliminary injunction, ordering the university to provide the interpreter services, irrespective of the student's ability to pay for them. The Court of Appeals for the Fifth Circuit affirmed the District Court's preliminary injunction. "By the time the Court of Appeals had acted, the University had obeyed the injunction by paying for Camenisch's interpreter, and Camenisch had been graduated. The Court of Appeals, however, rejected a suggestion that the case was therefore moot. The court said: '[A] justiciable issue remains: whose responsibility is it to pay for this interpreter?'"

The Supreme Court granted certiorari, vacated the decision, and remanded the case.

B. Counsel of Record / ACLU Attorney

ACLU Side (Respondent / Appellee): Stephen J. Pollak argued the cause for appellee.

Peter Buscemi argued the cause for the United States, as amicus curiae, by special leave of Court.

Opposing Side (Petitioner / Appellant): Lonny F. Zwiener, Assistant Attorney General of Texas, argued the cause for appellant.

III. AMICI CURIAE

ACLU Side (Respondent / Appellee)

Brief of amici curiae filed on behalf of the ACLU, et al., by Marcia Robinson Lowry, George Kannar, and Robert Levy.

Brief of amici curiae filed on behalf of the United States by Peter Buscemi, Solicitor General Wade H. McCree, Jr., Acting Assistant Attorney General Furner, Jessica Dunsay Silver, and Irving L. Gornstein.

Additional briefs of amici curiae were filed on behalf of the Equal Employment Advisory Council, the American Coalition of Citizens with Disabilities, et al., the Deaf Counseling, Advocacy and Referral Agency, Inc., et al., the Legal Action Center of the City of New York, Inc., and the Michigan Rehabilitation Association, et al.

Opposing Side (Petitioner / Appellant)

Brief of amici curiae filed on behalf of the American Council on Education, et al., by Christien Topping Milliken, R. Claire Guthrie, and Sheldon Elliot Steinbach.

IV. THE SUPREME COURT'S DECISION

"The present case is replete with circumstances indicating the necessity for a full trial on the merits in the nisi prius court [court of original jurisdiction], where a preliminary injunction has become moot and an injunction bond has been issued. The proceedings here bear the marks of the haste characteristic of a request for a preliminary injunction: the parties have relied on a short stipulation of facts, and even the legal theories on which the University has relied have seemed to change from one level of the proceeding to another. [T]he question whether a preliminary injunction should have been issued here is moot, because the terms of the injunction, as modified by the Court of Appeals, have been fully and irrevocably carried out. The question whether the University must pay for the interpreter remains for trial on the merits. Until such a trial has taken place, it would be inappropriate for this Court to intimate any view on the merits of the lawsuit.

The judgment of the Court of Appeals is therefore vacated, and the case is remanded to the District Court for further proceedings consistent with this opinion."

V. JUSTICE VOTE

9 Pro ACLU Side vs. 0 Con Opposing Side

ACLU Side (Respondent / Appellee)

1. Stewart, P. – Wrote majority opinion
2. Burger, W. – Wrote concurring opinion
3. Rehnquist, W. – Joined majority opinion
4. Brennan, W. – Joined majority opinion
5. White, B. – Joined majority opinion
6. Blackmun, H. – Joined majority opinion
7. Powell, L. – Joined majority opinion
8. Marshall, T. – Joined majority opinion
9. Stevens, J. – Joined majority opinion

VI. A WIN OR LOSS FOR THE ACLU?

The ACLU filed as amicus curiae urging reversal; the Supreme Court vacated and remanded the ruling of the United States Court of Appeals for the Fifth Circuit in a unanimous vote, giving the ACLU an apparent win.

468. Parratt v. Taylor

(Decided May 18, 1981; 451 U.S. 527)

I. ISSUE

A. Issues Discussed

Criminal justice, prisons, Fourteenth Amendment, due process

B. Legal Question Presented

Was respondent deprived of any right, privilege, or immunity such that he could state a claim for relief under 42 U.S.C. § 1983?

C. Supreme Court's Answer

Although respondent was deprived of property, his particular deprivation is not sufficient to state a claim for relief under 42 U.S.C. § 1983.

II. CASE SUMMARY

A. Background

"The respondent is an inmate at the Nebraska Penal and Correctional Complex who ordered by mail certain hobby materials valued at $23.50. The hobby materials were lost and respondent brought suit under 42 U.S.C. § 1983 to recover their value. . . . Respondent claimed that his property was negligently lost by prison officials in violation of his rights under the Fourteenth Amendment to the United States Constitution. More specifically, he claimed that he had been deprived of property without due process of law.

The United States District Court for the District of Nebraska entered summary judgment for respondent, and the United States Court of Appeals for the Eighth Circuit affirmed in a per curiam order."

The Supreme Court granted certiorari to review the case and reversed.

B. Counsel of Record / ACLU Attorney

ACLU Side (Respondent / Appellee): Kevin Colleran, by appointment of the Court, argued the cause for appellee.

Opposing Side (Petitioner / Appellant): J. Kirk Brown, Assistant Attorney General of Nebraska, argued the cause for appellant.

III. AMICI CURIAE

ACLU Side (Respondent / Appellee)

Brief of amici curiae filed on behalf of the ACLU by Charles S. Sims, Bruce J. Ennis, Jr., and Gary Gilden.

Brief of amici curiae filed on behalf of the Edwin F. Mandel Legal Aid Clinic by Gary H. Palm.

Opposing Side (Petitioner / Appellant)

Briefs of amici curiae were filed on behalf of the State of Arizona, et al., the State of Hawaii, Americans for Effective Law Enforcement, Inc., et al., the Commonwealth of Massachusetts, the State of New Jersey, and the State of Texas.

IV. THE SUPREME COURT'S DECISION

"We have . . . recognized that postdeprivation remedies made available by the State can satisfy the Due Process Clause. In such cases, the normal predeprivation notice and opportunity to be heard is pretermitted if the State provides a postdeprivation remedy. . . .

Application of the principles recited above to this case leads us to conclude the respondent has not alleged a violation of the Due Process Clause of the Fourteenth Amendment. Although he has been deprived of property under color of state law, the deprivation did not occur as a result of some established state procedure. Indeed, the deprivation occurred as a result of the unauthorized failure of agents of the State to follow established state procedure. There is no contention that the procedures themselves are inadequate nor is there any contention that it was practicable for the State to provide a predeprivation hearing. Moreover, the State of Nebraska has provided respondent with the means by which he can receive redress for the deprivation. The State provides a remedy to persons who believe they have suffered a tortuous loss at the hands of the State. Through this tort claims procedure the State hears and pays claims of prisoners housed in its penal institutions. This procedure was in existence at the time of the loss here in question but respondent did not use it. It is argued that the State does not adequately protect the respondent's interests because it provides only for an action against the State as opposed to its individual employees, it contains no provisions for punitive damages, and there is no right to a trial by jury. Although the state remedies may not provide the respondent with all the relief which may have been available if he could have proceeded under §1983, that does not mean that the state remedies are not adequate to satisfy the requirements of due process. The remedies provided could have fully compensated the respondent for the property loss he suffered, and we hold that they are sufficient to satisfy the requirements of due process. . . .

Accordingly, the judgment of the Court of Appeals is reversed."

V. JUSTICE VOTE

1 Pro ACLU Side vs. 8 Con Opposing Side

ACLU Side (Respondent / Appellee)

1. Marshall, T. – Wrote opinion concurring in part and dissenting in part

Opposing Side (Petitioner / Appellant)

1. Rehnquist, W. – Wrote majority opinion
2. Burger, W. – Joined majority opinion
3. Brennan, W. – Joined majority opinion
4. Stevens, J. – Joined majority opinion
5. Stewart, P – Wrote concurring opinion
6. White, B. – Joined Blackmun's concurrence
7. Blackmun, H. – Wrote concurring opinion
8. Powell, L. – Wrote concurring opinion

VI. A WIN OR LOSS FOR THE ACLU?

The ACLU filed as amicus curiae urging affirmance; the Supreme Court reversed the ruling of the Court of Appeals for the Eighth Circuit in an 8-1 vote, giving the ACLU an apparent loss.

469. Little v. Streater

(Decided June 1, 1981; 452 U.S. 1)

I. ISSUE

A. Issues Discussed

Fourteenth Amendment, due process, equal protection, paternity

B. Legal Question Presented

"[W]hether a Connecticut statute which provides that in paternity actions the cost of blood grouping tests is to be borne by the party requesting them, violates the Due Process and Equal Protection Clauses of the Fourteenth Amendment when applied to deny such tests to indigent defendants."

C. Supreme Court's Answer

The statute denies due process in this circumstance, where it prevents an indigent defendant from using the blood grouping test in his paternity case.

II. CASE SUMMARY

A. Background

"On May 21, 1975, appellee Gloria Streater, while unmarried, gave birth to a female child, Kenyatta Chantel Streater. As a requirement stemming from her child's receipt of public assistance, appellee identified appellant Walter Little as the child's father to the Connecticut Department of Social Services. The Department then provided an attorney for appellee to bring a paternity suit against appellant in the Court of Common Pleas at New Haven to establish his liability for the child's support.

At the time the paternity action was commenced, appellant was incarcerated in the Connecticut Correctional Institution at Enfield. Through his counsel, who was provided by a legal aid organization, appellant moved the trial court to order blood grouping tests on appellee and her child pursuant to Conn.Gen. Stat. § 52-184 (1977), which . . . includes the provision that '[t]he costs of making such tests shall be chargeable against the party making the motion.' Appellant asserted that he was indigent and asked that the State be ordered to pay for the tests. The trial court granted the motion insofar as it sought blood grouping tests but denied the request that they be furnished at the State's expense.

For 'financial reasons,' no blood grouping tests were performed even though they had been authorized. The paternity action was tried to the court on September 28, 1978. Both appellee and appellant, who was still a state prisoner, testified at trial. After listening to the testimony, the court found that appellant was the child's father. Following a subsequent hearing on damages, the court entered judgment against appellant in the amount of $6,974.48, which included the 'lying-in' expenses of appellee and the child, 'accrued maintenance' through October 31, 1978, and the 'costs of suit plus reasonable attorney's fees.' In addition, appellant was ordered to pay child support at the rate of $2 per month—$1 toward the arrearage amount of $6,974.48 and $1 toward a current monthly award of $163.58—directly to Connecticut's Department of Finance and Control.

The Appellate Session of the Connecticut Superior Court affirmed the trial court's judgment . . . .

Thereafter, appellant's petition for certification was denied by the Connecticut Supreme Court."

The U.S. Supreme Court granted certiorari to review the case, reversed, and remanded.

B. Counsel of Record / ACLU Attorney

ACLU Side (Petitioner / Appellant): Jon C. Blue argued the cause for appellant.

Opposing Side (Respondent / Appellee): Stephen J. McGovern, Assistant Attorney General of Connecticut, argued the cause for appellee.

III. AMICI CURIAE

ACLU Side (Petitioner / Appellant)

Brief of amici curiae filed on behalf of the ACLU, et al., by Charles S. Sims and Bruce J. Ennis, Jr.

Opposing Side (Respondent / Appellee)

No briefs of amici curiae were filed in support of appellee.

IV. THE SUPREME COURT'S DECISION

"Due process, 'unlike some legal rules, is not a technical conception with a fixed content unrelated to time, place and circumstances.' Rather, it is 'flexible and calls for such procedural protections as the particular situation demands.' . . .

The ability of blood grouping tests to exonerate innocent putative fathers was confirmed by a 1976 report developed jointly by the American Bar Association and the American Medical Association. . . . These systems were found to be 'reasonable' in cost and to provide a 91% cumulative probability of negating paternity for erroneously accused Negro men and 93% for white men. . . .

Appellant emphasizes that, unlike a common dispute between private parties, the State's involvement in this paternity proceeding was considerable and manifest, giving rise to a constitutional duty. Because appellee's child was a recipient of public assistance, Connecticut law compelled her, upon penalty of fine and imprisonment for contempt, 'to disclose the name of the putative father under oath and to institute an action to establish the paternity of said child.' The State's Attorney General automatically became a party to the action, and any settlement agreement required his approval or that of the Commissioner of Human Resources or Commissioner of Income Maintenance. The State referred this mandatory paternity suit to appellee's lawyer 'for prosecution' and paid his fee as well as all costs of the litigation. In addition, the State will be the recipient of the monthly support payments to be made by appellant pursuant to the trial court's judgment. 'State action' has undeniably pervaded this case. Accordingly, appellant need not, and does not, contend that Connecticut has a constitutional obligation to fund blood tests for an indigent's defense in ordinary civil litigation between private parties. . . .

Under Connecticut law . . . the defendant in a paternity suit is placed at a distinct disadvantage in that his testimony alone is insufficient to overcome the plaintiff's prima facie case. Among the most probative additional evidence the defendant might offer are the results of blood grouping tests, but if he is indigent, the State essentially denies him that reliable scientific proof by requiring that he bear its cost. In substance, the State has created an adverse presumption regarding the defendant's testimony by elevating the weight to be accorded the mother's imputation of him. . . . Yet not only is the State inextricably involved in paternity litigation such as this and responsible for an imbalance between the parties, it in effect forecloses what is potentially a conclusive means for an indigent defendant to surmount that disparity and exonerate himself. Such a practice is irreconcilable with the command of the Due Process Clause. . . .

We hold that, in these specific circumstances, the application of Conn.Gen.Stat. § 46b-168 (1981) to deny appellant blood grouping tests because of his lack of financial resources violated the due process guarantee of the Fourteenth Amendment. Accordingly, the judgment of the Appellate Session of the Connecticut Superior Court is reversed, and the case is remanded for further proceedings not inconsistent with this opinion."

V. JUSTICE VOTE

9 Pro ACLU Side vs. 0 Con Opposing Side

ACLU Side (Petitioner / Appellant)

1. Burger, W. – Wrote majority opinion
2. Brennan, W. – Joined majority opinion
3. Stevens, J. – Joined majority opinion
4. White, B. – Joined majority opinion
5. Powell, L. – Joined majority opinion
6. Rehnquist, W. – Joined majority opinion
7. Marshall, T. – Joined majority opinion
8. Stewart, P. – Joined majority opinion
9. Blackmun, H. – Joined majority opinion

VI. A WIN OR LOSS FOR THE ACLU?

The ACLU, as amicus curiae, urged reversal of the Appellate Session of the Connecticut Superior Court's judgment; the Supreme Court reversed and remanded in a 9-0 vote, giving the ACLU an apparent win.

470. Lassiter v. Department of Social Services

(Decided June 1, 1981; 452 U.S. 18)

I. ISSUE

A. Issues Discussed

Civil rights, Fourteenth Amendment, due process, child custody

B. Legal Question Presented

Does the Due Process Clause of the Fourteenth Amendment requires a state to furnish an indigent parent court-appointed counsel in a proceeding to terminate the parent's parental rights?

C. Supreme Court's Answer

The Due Process Clause does not require court-appointed counsel for indigent parents in proceedings to terminate parental rights.

II. CASE SUMMARY

A. Background

As an infant, petitioner's son was deemed a neglected child and placed in the custody of the Durham County Department of Social Services. Petitioner Abby Gail Lassiter was later convicted of murder and sentenced to "25 to 40 years of imprisonment." The "Department petitioned the court to terminate Ms. Lassiter's parental rights." Although Ms. Lassiter attended her termination of parental rights hearing, she did not inform the lawyer her mother had retained for her murder case about the proceeding and attended the proceeding without a lawyer, "The hearing opened, apparently at the judge's instance, with a discussion of whether Ms. Lassiter should have more time in which to find legal assistance. Since the court concluded that she 'has had ample opportunity to seek and obtain counsel prior to the hearing of this matter, and [that] her failure to do so is without just cause,' the court did not postpone the proceedings. Ms. Lassiter did not aver that she was indigent, and the court did not appoint counsel for her." The court terminated Ms. Lassiter's parental rights at the hearing.

"On appeal, Ms. Lassiter argued only that, because she was indigent, the Due Process Clause of the Fourteenth Amendment entitled her to the assistance of counsel, and that the trial court had therefore erred in not requiring the State to provide counsel for her. The North Carolina Court of Appeals decided that '[w]hile this State action does invade a protected area of individual privacy, the invasion is not so serious or unreasonable as to compel us to hold that appointment of counsel for indigent parents is constitutionally mandated.' The Supreme Court of North Carolina summarily denied Ms. Lassiter's application for discretionary review,"

The Supreme Court granted certiorari to review the due process issue and affirmed.

B. Counsel of Record / ACLU Attorney

ACLU Side (Petitioner / Appellant): Leowen Evans argued the cause for appellant, pro hac vice, by special leave of Court.

Opposing Side (Respondent / Apellee):

Thomas Russell Odom argued the cause for appellee.

Steven Mansfield Shaber, Assistant Attorney General of North Carolina, argued the cause for the State of North Carolina, as amicus curiae, by special leave of Court.

III. AMICI CURIAE

ACLU Side (Petitioner / Appellant)

Brief of amici curiae filed on behalf of the North Carolina Civil Liberties Union by Douglas A. Scott and Robert S. Payne.

Brief of amici curiae filed on behalf of the National Center on Women and Family Law, Inc., et al., by Louise Gruner Gans, Catherine P. Mitchell, Jean Schneider, Edward N. Simon, Pamela Dru Sutton, Laurie Woods, and Phyllis Gelman.

Brief of amici curiae filed on behalf of the National Legal Aid and Defender Association by David R. Lundberg and Kenneth J. Falk.

Brief of amici curiae filed on behalf of the American Bar Association by Reece Smith, Jr., Robert M. Horowitz, Mark Hardin, and Howard Davidson.

Opposing Side (Respondent / Appellee)

Brief of amici curiae filed on behalf of the State of North Carolina, et al., by Rufus L. Edmisten, Attorney General of North Carolina, and Steven Mansfield Shaber, Assistant Attorney General; Richard S. Gebelein, Attorney General of Delaware, and Regina Mullen Small, State Solicitor; Bill Allain, Attorney General of Mississippi, and Jim R. Bruce, Special Assistant Attorney General; Jim Smith, Attorney General of Florida, and Sidney H. McKenzie, Assistant Attorney General; Richard R. Bryan, Attorney General of Nevada, and Claudia K. Cormier, Deputy Attorney General; and Steve Clark, Attorney General of Arkansas, and Robert R. Ross, Deputy Attorney General.

IV. THE SUPREME COURT'S DECISION

"For all its consequence, 'due process' has never been, and perhaps can never be, precisely defined. '[U]nlike some legal rules,' this Court has said, due process 'is not a technical conception with a fixed content unrelated to time, place and circumstances.' Rather, the phrase expresses the requirement of 'fundamental fairness,' a requirement whose meaning can be as opaque as its importance is lofty. Applying the Due Process Clause is therefore an uncertain enterprise which must discover what 'fundamental fairness' consists of in a particular situation by first considering any relevant precedents and then by assessing the several interests that are at stake. [T]he Court's precedents speak with one voice about what 'fundamental fairness' has meant when the Court has considered the right to appointed counsel, and we thus draw from them the presumption that an indigent litigant has a right to appointed counsel only when, if he loses, he may be deprived of his physical liberty. It is against this presumption that all the other elements in the due process decision must be measured.

[W]e hold that the trial court did not err in failing to appoint counsel for Ms. Lassiter. . . . In its Fourteenth Amendment, our Constitution imposes on the States the standards necessary to ensure that judicial proceedings are fundamentally fair. A wise public policy, however, may require that higher standards be adopted than those minimally tolerable under the Constitution. Informed opinion has clearly come to hold that an indigent parent is entitled to the assistance of appointed counsel not only in parental termination proceedings, but in dependency and neglect proceedings as well. Most significantly, 33 States and the District of Columbia provide statutorily for the appointment of counsel in termination cases. The Court's opinion today in no way implies that the standards increasingly urged by informed public opinion and now widely followed by the States are other than enlightened and wise.

For the reasons stated in this opinion, the judgment is affirmed."

V. JUSTICE VOTE

4 Pro ACLU Side vs. 5 Con Opposing Side

ACLU Side (Petitioner / Appellant)

1. Blackmun, H. – Wrote dissenting opinion
2. Brennan, W. – Joined Blackmun's dissent
3. Marshall, T. – Joined Blackmun's dissent
4. Stevens, J. – Wrote dissenting opinion

Opposing Side (Respondent / Appellee)

1. Stewart, P. – Wrote majority opinion
2. White, B. – Joined majority opinion
3. Powell, L. – Joined majority opinion
4. Rehnquist, W. – Joined majority opinion
5. Burger, W. – Wrote concurring opinion

VI. A WIN OR LOSS FOR THE ACLU?

The ACLU filed as amicus curiae urging reversal; the Supreme Court affirmed the ruling of the Court of Appeals of North Carolina in a 5-4 vote, giving the ACLU an apparent loss.

471. Schad v. Borough of Mount Ephraim

(Decided June 1, 1981; 452 U.S. 61)

I. ISSUE

A. Issues Discussed

First Amendment, Fourteenth Amendment, free speech

B. Legal Question Presented

Whether the "imposition of criminal penalties under an ordinance prohibiting all live entertainment, including nonobscene, nude dancing, violated [the appellants'] rights of free expression guaranteed by the First and Fourteenth Amendments of the United States Constitution."

C. Supreme Court's Answer

The ordinance prohibiting live entertainment violates First and Fourteenth Amendments.

II. CASE SUMMARY

A. Background

"In 1973, appellants began operating an adult bookstore in the commercial zone in the Borough of Mount Ephraim in Camden County, N.J. The store sold adult books, magazines, and films. Amusement licenses shortly issued permitting the store to install coin-operated devices by virtue of which a customer could sit in a booth, insert a coin, and watch an adult film. In 1976, the store introduced an additional coin-operated mechanism permitting the customer to watch a live dancer, usually nude, performing behind a glass panel. Complaints were soon filed against appellants charging that the bookstore's exhibition of live dancing violated § 99-15B of Mount Ephraim's zoning ordinance . . . .

Appellants were found guilty in the Municipal Court and fines were imposed. Appeal was taken to the Camden County Court, where a trial de novo was held on the record made in the Municipal Court and appellants were again found guilty. The County Court first rejected appellants' claim that the ordinance was being selectively and improperly enforced against them because other establishments offering live entertainment were permitted in the commercial zones. Those establishments, the court held, were permitted, nonconforming uses that had existed prior to the passage of the ordinance. In response to appellants' defense based on the First and Fourteenth Amendments, the court recognized that 'live nude dancing is protected by the First Amendment' but was of the view that 'First Amendment guarantees are not involved' since the case 'involves solely a zoning ordinance' under which '[l]ive entertainment is simply not a permitted use in any establishment' whether the entertainment is a nude dance or some other form of live presentation. . . . The Appellate Division of the Superior Court of New Jersey affirmed appellants' convictions in a per curiam opinion . . . . The Supreme Court of New Jersey denied further review."

The U.S. Supreme Court granted certiorari to review the case and reversed and remanded the judgment of the Supreme Court of New Jersey.

B. Counsel of Record / ACLU Attorney

ACLU Side (Petitioner / Appellant): Robert E. Levy argued the cause for appellant.

Opposing Side (Respondent / Appellee): Arnold N. Fishman argued the cause for appellee.

III. AMICI CURIAE

ACLU Side (Petitioner / Appellant)

Brief of amici curiae filed on behalf of the ACLU, et al., by Jerry Kay, Charles S. Sims, and Bruce J. Ennis.

Opposing Side (Respondent / Appellee)

Brief of amici curiae filed on behalf of Morality in Media, Inc., by Anthony H. Atlas, Paul J. McGeady, and Terence Carroll.

IV. THE SUPREME COURT'S DECISION

"The power of local governments to zone and control land use is undoubtedly broad and its proper exercise is an essential aspect of achieving a satisfactory quality of life in both urban and rural communities. But the zoning power is not infinite and unchallengeable; it 'must be exercised within constitutional limits.' . .

Mount Ephraim has not adequately justified its substantial restriction of protected activity. None of the justifications asserted in this Court was articulated by the state courts and none of them withstands scrutiny. First, the Borough contends that permitting live entertainment would conflict with its plan to create a commercial area that caters only to the 'immediate needs' of its residents and that would enable them to purchase at local stores the few items they occasionally forgot to buy outside the Borough. No evidence was introduced below to support this assertion, and it is difficult to reconcile this characterization of the Borough's commercial zones with the provisions of the ordinance. . . .

Mount Ephraim contends that it may selectively exclude commercial live entertainment from the broad range of commercial uses permitted in the Borough for reasons normally associated with zoning in commercial districts, that is, to avoid the problems that may be associated with live entertainment, such as parking, trash, police protection, and medical facilities. The Borough has presented no evidence, and it is not immediately apparent as a matter of experience, that live entertainment poses problems of this nature more significant than those associated with various permitted uses . . . .

The Borough also suggests that § 99-15B is a reasonable 'time, place, and manner' restriction; yet it does not identify the municipal interests making it reasonable to exclude all commercial live entertainment but to allow a variety of other commercial uses in the Borough. . . .

Accordingly, the convictions of these appellants are infirm, and the judgment of the Appellate Division of the Superior Court of New Jersey is reversed and the case is remanded for further proceedings not inconsistent with this opinion."

V. JUSTICE VOTE

7 Pro ACLU Side vs. 2 Con Opposing Side

ACLU Side (Petitioner / Appellant)

1. White, B. – Wrote majority opinion
2. Brennan, W. – Joined majority opinion
3. Stewart, P. – Joined Powell's concurrence
4. Marshall, T. – Joined majority opinion
5. Blackmun, H. – Wrote concurring opinion
6. Powell, L. – Wrote concurring opinion
7. Stevens, J. – Wrote concurring opinion

Opposing Side (Respondent / Appellee)

1. Burger, W. – Wrote dissenting opinion
2. Rehnquist, W. – Joined Burger's dissent

VI. A WIN OR LOSS FOR THE ACLU?

The ACLU, as amicus curiae, urged reversal of the Supreme Court of New Jersey's judgment; the Supreme Court reversed and remanded in a 7-2 vote, giving the ACLU an apparent win.

472. Gulf Oil Co. v. Bernard

(Decided June 1, 1981; 452 U.S. 89)

I. ISSUE

A. Issues Discussed

Class actions, First Amendment, freedom of speech, Federal Rules of Civil Procedure

B. Legal Question Presented

What is the "scope of a district court's authority to limit communications from named plaintiffs and their counsel to prospective class members, during the pendency of a class action"?

C. Supreme Court's Answer

The district court exceeded its authority to limit communications to prospective class members in this case.

II. CASE SUMMARY

A. Background

"In April 1976, Gulf and the Equal Employment Opportunity Commission (EEOC) entered into a conciliation agreement involving alleged discrimination against black and female employees at the Port Arthur refinery. Gulf agreed to cease various allegedly discriminatory practices, to undertake an affirmative-action program covering hiring and promotion, and to offer backpay to alleged victims of discrimination based on a set formula. Gulf began to send notices to the 643 employees eligible for backpay, stating the exact amount available to each person in return for execution within 30 days of a full release of all discrimination claims dating from the relevant time period.

Approximately one month after the signing of the conciliation agreement, on May 18, 1976, respondents filed this class action in the United States District Court for the Eastern District of Texas, on behalf of all black present and former employees, and rejected applicants for employment, at the refinery. They alleged racial discrimination in employment and sought injunctive, declaratory, and monetary relief, based on Title VII of the Civil Rights Act of 1964, and the Civil Rights Act of 1866. . . . Through this lawsuit, the named plaintiffs sought to vindicate the alleged rights of many of the employees who were receiving settlement offers from Gulf under the conciliation agreement.

On May 27, Gulf filed a motion in the District Court seeking an order limiting communications by parties and their counsel with class members. An accompanying brief described the EEOC conciliation agreement, asserting that 452 of the 643 employees entitled to backpay under that agreement had signed releases and been paid by the time the class action was filed. Gulf stated that after it was served in the case, it ceased sending backpay offers and release forms to class members. It then asserted that a lawyer for respondents Ulysses Gene Thibodeaux, had attended a meeting of 75 class members on May 22, where he had discussed the case and recommended that the employees not sign the releases sent under the conciliation agreement. Gulf added that Thibodeaux reportedly had advised employees to return checks they already had received, since they could receive at least double the amounts involved through the class action.

The court entered a temporary order prohibiting all communications concerning the case from parties or their counsel to potential or actual class members. The order listed several examples of communications that were covered, but stated that it was not limited to these examples. It was not based on any findings of fact.

[The court subsequently modified the order.] On appeal . . . respondents argued that the limitations on communications imposed by the District Court were beyond the power granted the court in Federal Rule of Civil Procedure 23(d) and were unconstitutional under the First Amendment. A divided panel of the United States Court of Appeals for the Fifth Circuit affirmed the District Court. . . .

The Fifth Circuit granted a rehearing en banc, and reversed the panel decision concerning the order limiting communications."

The Supreme Court granted certiorari to review the case and affirmed the judgment of the Fifth Circuit Court of Appeals.

B. Counsel of Record / ACLU Attorney

ACLU Side (Respondent / Appellee): Jack Greenberg argued the cause for appellee.

Opposing Side (Petitioner / Appellant): William G. Duck argued the cause for appellant.

III. AMICI CURIAE

ACLU Side (Respondent / Appellee)

Brief of amici curiae filed on behalf of the ACLU Fund of the National Capital Area, et al., by Arthur B. Spitzer and Kenneth J. Guido, Jr.

Brief of amici curiae filed on behalf of the United States, et al., by Wade H. McCree, Jr., Solicitor General, James P. Turner, Acting Assistant Attorney General, Lawrence G. Wallace, Deputy Solicitor General, Harlon L. Dalton, Assistant to the Solicitor General, Jessica Dunsay Silver, Carol E. Heckman, and Leroy D. Clark.

Brief of amici curiae filed on behalf of the Association of Trial Lawyers of America by Mayo L. Coiner and Harry M. Philo.

Brief of amici curiae filed on behalf of the Chicago Council of Lawyers by Richard F. Watt, Ellen J. Morgan, and Martha A. Mills.

Opposing Side (Petitioner / Appellant)

Brief of amici curiae filed on behalf of the Hudson Pulp and Paper Corporation by Stuart Rothman and George C. Smith.

Brief of amici curiae filed on behalf of the Tallahassee Memorial Hospital by William F. Kaspers and John D. Buchanan, Jr.

IV. THE SUPREME COURT'S DECISION

"In the present case, we are faced with the unquestionable assertion by respondents that the order created at least potential difficulties for them as they sought to vindicate the legal rights of a class of employees. The order interfered with their efforts to inform potential class members of the existence of this lawsuit, and may have been particularly injurious—not only to respondents but to the class as a whole—because the employees at that time were being pressed to decide whether to accept a backpay offer from Gulf that required them to sign a full release of all liability for discriminatory acts. In addition, the order made it more difficult for respondents, as the class representatives, to obtain information about the merits of the case from the persons they sought to represent.

Because of these potential problems, an order limiting communications between parties and potential class members should be based on a clear record and specific findings that reflect a weighing of the need for a limitation and the potential interference with the rights of the parties. Only such a determination can ensure that the court is furthering, rather than hindering, the policies embodied in the Federal Rules of Civil Procedure, especially Rule 23. In addition, such a weighing—identifying the potential abuses being addressed—should result in a carefully drawn order that limits speech as little as possible, consistent with the rights of the parties under the circumstances. . . .

In the present case, one looks in vain for any indication of a careful weighing of competing factors. Indeed, in this respect, the District Court failed to provide any record useful for appellate review. The court made neither factual findings nor legal arguments supporting the need for this sweeping restraint order. . . .

We conclude that the imposition of the order was an abuse of discretion. The record reveals no grounds on which the District Court could have determined that it was necessary or appropriate to impose this order. . . .

Accordingly, the judgment below is affirmed."

V. JUSTICE VOTE

9 Pro ACLU Side vs. 0 Con Opposing Side

ACLU Side (Respondent / Appellee)

1. Powell, L. – Wrote majority opinion
2. Brennan, W. – Joined majority opinion
3. Stevens, J. – Joined majority opinion
4. Blackmun, H. – Joined majority opinion
5. Marshall, T. – Joined majority opinion
6. Stewart, P. – Joined majority opinion
7. Rehnquist, W. – Joined majority opinion
8. Burger, W. – Joined majority opinion
9. White, B. – Joined majority opinion

VI. A WIN OR LOSS FOR THE ACLU?

The ACLU, as amicus curiae, urged affirmance of the Fifth Circuit Court of Appeals' judgment; the Supreme Court affirmed in a 9-0 vote, giving the ACLU an apparent win.

473. Minnick v. California Department of Corrections

(Decided June 1, 1981; 452 U.S. 105)

I. ISSUE

A. Issues Discussed

Civil rights, race, Fourteenth Amendment, equal protection

B. Legal Question Presented

"[W]hether the writ [of certiorari] should be dismissed because the judgment [below] did not finally determine the legal status of the challenged plan."

C. Supreme Court's Answer

The writ of certiorari should be dismissed because the constitutional issues should not be decided until the proceedings below are concluded.

II. CASE SUMMARY

A. Background

In 1975, petitioners, Minnick and Darden, two white male correctional officers employed by the California Department of Corrections (CDC), and the California Correction Officers Association, filed suit in California state court against respondents, CDC, alleging that the Department's "affirmative-action plan unlawfully discriminated against white males and that the individual petitioners had been denied promotions because they were white. . . . After a trial at which over 30 witnesses testified, the case was argued at length and submitted to the trial judge for decision on November 23, 1976. At that time the Supreme Court of California had only recently held in Bakke v. University of California Regents, 553 P.2d 1152 (1976), that the Equal Protection Clause of the Fourteenth Amendment to the United States Constitution prohibited a state university from giving any consideration to an applicant's race in making admissions decisions." On that basis, the trial court enjoined "respondents 'from considering as a factor for employment or for the promotion of a candidate his sex, race or national origin.' . . .

Respondents appealed to the California Court of Appeal. While their appeal was pending, [the U.S. Supreme] Court issued its decision in University of California Regents v. Bakke, 438 U.S. 265. . . . With the guidance of [the U.S. Supreme] Court's decision in Bakke, the California Court of Appeal reversed the judgment and the injunction entered by the trial court . . . ."

The U.S. Supreme Court granted certiorari to review the case, then decided upon further review to dismiss the writ of certiorari.

B. Counsel of Record / ACLU Attorney

ACLU Side (Respondent / Appellee): Stuart R. Pollak argued the cause for appellee.

Opposing Side (Petitioner / Appellant): Ronald Yank argued the cause for appellant.

III. AMICI CURIAE

ACLU Side (Respondent / Appellee)

Brief of amici curiae filed on behalf of the ACLU by E. Richard Larson, Isabelle Katz Pinzler, and Bruce J. Ennis.

Additional briefs of amici curiae were filed on behalf of the United States, et al., the New York State Department of Correctional Services, the City of Detroit, and the California Department of Fair Employment and Housing, et al.

Opposing Side (Petitioner / Appellant)

Briefs of amici curiae were filed on behalf of the Anti-Defamation League of B'nai B'rith, the Pacific Legal Foundation, and the Equal Employment Advisory Council.

IV. THE SUPREME COURT'S DECISION

"Accordingly, because of significant developments in the law—and perhaps in the facts as well—and because of significant ambiguities in the record concerning both the extent to which race or sex has been used as a factor in making promotions and the justification for such use, we conclude that we should not address the constitutional issues until the proceedings in the trial court are finally concluded and the state appellate courts have completed their review of the trial court record.

Accordingly, the writ of certiorari is dismissed."

V. JUSTICE VOTE

8 Pro ACLU Side vs. 1 Con Opposing Side

ACLU Side (Petitioner / Appellant)

1. Stevens, J. – Wrote majority opinion
2. Burger, W. – Joined majority opinion
3. White, B. – Joined majority opinion
4. Marshall, T. – Joined majority opinion
5. Blackmun, H. – Joined majority opinion
6. Powell, L. – Joined majority opinion
7. Rehnquist, W. – Wrote concurring opinion
8. Brennan, W. – Wrote concurring opinion

Opposing Side (Respondent / Appellee)

1. Stewart, P. – Wrote dissenting opinion

VI. A WIN OR LOSS FOR THE ACLU?

The ACLU filed as amicus curiae urging affirmance of the California Court of Appeal's decision; the Supreme Court refused to overturn the California Court of Appeal's decision by dismissing the writ of certiorari in an 8-1 vote, giving the ACLU an apparent win.

474. McDaniel v. Sanchez

(Decided June 1, 1981; 452 U.S. 130)

I. ISSUE

A. Issues Discussed

Civil rights, voting, Voting Rights Act

B. Legal Question Presented

"[W]hether the preclearance requirement of § 5 of the Voting Rights Act of 1965, as amended, applies to a reapportionment plan submitted to a Federal District Court by the legislative body of a covered jurisdiction in response to a judicial determination that the existing apportionment of its electoral districts is unconstitutional."

C. Supreme Court's Answer

The preclearance requirement applies to the reapportionment plan at issue in this case.

II. CASE SUMMARY

A. Background

"In January 1978, four Mexican-American residents of Kleberg County brought this class action against various county officials alleging that the apportionment of . . . four commissioners' precincts denied individual residents of the larger precincts a vote of equal weight, and unconstitutionally diluted the voting strength of the county's substantial Mexican-American population. After a trial, the District Court rejected the plaintiffs' claim that the county's apportionment plan unconstitutionally diluted the voting power of Mexican-Americans as a class, but held that individual voters were denied equal representation because of the substantial disparity in the number of residents in each commissioners' precinct. The District Court therefore directed the county officials to submit a proposed reapportionment plan to the court . . . .

Pursuant to the District Court's order, the Commissioners Court undertook the task of devising a new apportionment plan. . . . Respondents objected to the proposed plan. . . . After an evidentiary hearing, the District Court rejected both of respondents' factual contentions, and held as a matter of law that the Voting Rights Act did not require preclearance. The court entered an order approving the new plan and authorizing the Commissioners Court to conduct the 1980 primary and general elections under it.

Without expressing any opinion with respect to the constitutionality of the new plan, the Court of Appeals vacated the District Court's order in a per curiam opinion."

The Supreme Court granted certiorari to review the case and affirmed.

B. Counsel of Record / ACLU Attorney

ACLU Side (Respondent / Appellee): Robert J. Parmley argued the cause for appellee.

Deputy Solicitor General Lawrence G. Wallace argued the cause for the United States, as amicus curiae, by special leave of Court.

Opposing Side (Petitioner / Appellant): Richard A. Hall argued the cause for appellant.

III. AMICI CURIAE

ACLU Side (Respondent / Appellee)

Brief of amici curiae filed on behalf of the ACLU by Neil Bradley, Laughlin McDonald, Christopher Coates, Bruce J. Ennis, and E. Richard Larson.

Brief of amici curiae filed on behalf of the United States by Wade H. McCree, Jr., Solicitor General, James P. Turner, Acting Assistant Attorney General, Lawrence G. Wallace, Deputy Solicitor General, Harriet S. Shapiro, Assistant to the Solicitor General, Jessica Dunsay Silver, and Carol E. Heckman.

Brief of amici curiae filed on behalf of the Lawyers' Committee for Civil Rights Under Law by John B. Jones, Jr., Norman Redlich, William L. Robinson, Norman J. Chachkin, and Beatrice Rosenberg.

Opposing Side (Petitioner / Appellant)

No briefs of amici curiae were filed in support of appellant.

IV. THE SUPREME COURT'S DECISION

"In this case, we are concerned only with the question whether the reapportionment plan submitted to the District Court should be considered a legislative plan for purposes of preclearance under § 5. . . . The preclearance procedure is designed to forestall the danger that local decisions to modify voting practices will impair minority access to the electoral process. The federal interest in preventing local jurisdictions from making changes that adversely affect the rights of minority voters is the same whether a change is required to remedy a constitutional violation or is merely the product of a community's perception of the desirability of responding to new social patterns. . . .

As we construe the congressional mandate, it requires that whenever a covered jurisdiction submits a proposal reflecting the policy choices of the elected representatives of the people—no matter what constraints have limited the choices available to them—the preclearance requirement of the Voting Rights Act is applicable. It was, therefore, error for the District Court to act on the county's proposed plan before it had been submitted to the Attorney General or the United States District Court for the District of Columbia for preclearance.

The judgment of the Court of Appeals is therefore affirmed."

V. JUSTICE VOTE

7 Pro ACLU Side vs. 2 Con Opposing Side

ACLU Side (Petitioner / Appellant)

1. Stevens, J. – Wrote majority opinion
2. Burger, W. – Joined majority opinion
3. Brennan, W. – Joined majority opinion
4. White, B. – Joined majority opinion
5. Marshall, T. – Joined majority opinion
6. Blackmun, H. – Joined majority opinion
7. Powell, L. – Wrote concurring opinion

Opposing Side (Respondent / Appellee)

1. Stewart, P. – Wrote dissenting opinion
2. Rehnquist, W. – Joined Stewart's dissent

VI. A WIN OR LOSS FOR THE ACLU?

The ACLU filed as amicus curiae urging affirmance; the Supreme Court affirmed the ruling of the Court of Appeals for the Fifth Circuit in a 7-2 vote, giving the ACLU an apparent win.

475. County of Washington v. Gunther

(Decided June 8, 1981; 452 U.S. 161)

I. ISSUE

A. Issues Discussed

Civil rights, gender, Title VII of the Civil Rights Act of 1964, sex-based wage discrimination, equal pay.

B. Legal Question Presented

"[W]hether § 703(h) of Title VII of the Civil Rights Act of 1964, restricts Title VII's prohibition of sex-based wage discrimination to claims of equal pay for equal work."

C. Supreme Court's Answer

Sex-based wage discrimination claims under Title VII need not be restricted to claims of equal pay for equal work.

II. CASE SUMMARY

A. Background

"This case arises over the payment by petitioner, County of Washington, Or., of substantially lower wages to female guards in the female section of the county jail than it paid to male guards in the male section of the jail. . . .

Respondents filed suit against petitioners in Federal District Court under Title VII, 42 U.S.C. § 2000e et seq., seeking backpay and other relief. They alleged that they were paid unequal wages for work substantially equal to that performed by male guards, and in the alternative, that part of the pay differential was attributable to intentional sex discrimination. The latter allegation was based on a claim that, because of intentional discrimination, the county set the pay scale for female guards, but not for male guards, at a level lower than that warranted by its own survey of outside markets and the worth of the jobs.

After trial, the District Court found that the male guards supervised more than 10 times as many prisoners per guard as did the female guards, and that the females devoted much of their time to less valuable clerical duties. It therefore held that respondents' jobs were not substantially equal to those of the male guards, and that respondents were thus not entitled to equal pay. The Court of Appeals affirmed on that issue, and respondents do not seek review of the ruling.

The District Court also dismissed respondents claim that the discrepancy in pay between the male and female guards was attributable in part to intentional sex discrimination. It held as a matter of law that a sex-based wage discrimination claim cannot be brought under Title VII unless it would satisfy the equal work standard of the Equal Pay Act of 1963, 29 U.S.C. § 206(d). . . .

The Court of Appeals reversed, holding that persons alleging sex discrimination 'are not precluded from suing under Title VII to protect . . . discriminatory compensation practices' merely because their jobs were not equal to higher paying jobs held by members of the opposite sex. The court remanded to the District Court with instructions to take evidence on respondents' claim that part of the difference between their rate of pay and that of the male guards is attributable to sex discrimination."

The Supreme Court granted certiorari to review the intentional sex discrimination claim, and affirmed.

B. Counsel of Record / ACLU Attorney

ACLU Side (Respondent / Appellee): Carol A. Hewitt argued the cause for appellee.

Assistant to the Solicitor General Barry Sullivan argued the cause for the United States, et al., as amicus curiae, by special leave of Court.

Opposing Side (Petitioner / Appellant): Lawrence R. Derr argued the cause for appellant.

III. AMICI CURIAE

ACLU Side (Respondent / Appellee)

Brief of amici curiae filed on behalf of the ACLU, et al., by Mary L. Heen, Bruce J. Ennis, Jr., Isabelle Katz Pinzler, E. Richard Larson, and Joan E. Bertin.

Brief of amici curiae filed on behalf of the United States, et al., by Leroy D. Clark, Philip B. Sklover, Vincent J. Blackwood, Susan Buckingham Reilly, Wade H. McCree, Jr., Solicitor General, James P. Turner, Acting Assistant Attorney General, Lawrence G. Wallace, Deputy Solicitor General, Barry Sullivan, Assistant to the Solicitor General, Walter W. Barnett, and Neil H. Cogan.

Brief of amici curiae filed on behalf of the American Federation of Labor and Congress of Industrial Organizations, et al., by Richard B. Sobol, Michael B. Trister, Laurence Gold, J. Albert Woll, Winn Newman, Carole Wilson, John Fillion, Robert Tobias, John Bufe, Susan Silber, and Catherine Waelder.

Brief of amici curiae filed on behalf of the Lawyers' Committee for Civil Rights Under Law, et al., by John B. Jones, Jr., Norman Redlich, William L. Robinson, Norman J. Chachkin, Beatrice Rosenberg, and Richard T. Seymour.

Opposing Side (Petitioner / Appellant)

Brief of amici curiae filed on behalf of the Equal Employment Advisory Council, et al., by Kenneth C. McGuiness, Robert E. Williams, Douglas S. McDowell, and Edward E. Potter.

Brief of amici curiae filed on behalf of the American Society for Personnel Administration discussing the "comparable worth" concept, not taking a stance on the merits of the case, by Lawrence Z. Lorber. Thaddeus Holt, and Robin M. Schachter.

IV. THE SUPREME COURT'S DECISION

"We emphasize at the outset the narrowness of the question before us in this case. [R]espondents seek to prove, by direct evidence, that their wages were depressed because of intentional sex discrimination, consisting of setting the wage scale for female guards, but not for male guards, at a level lower than its own survey of outside markets and the worth of the jobs warranted. The narrow question in this case is whether such a claim is precluded by the last sentence of § 703(h) of Title VII, called the 'Bennett Amendment.' . . . The Bennet Amendment . . . provides:

'It shall not be an unlawful employment practice under this subchapter for any employer to differentiate upon the basis of sex in determining the amount of the wages or compensation paid or to be paid to employees of such employer if such differentiation is authorized by the provisions of section 206(d) of title 29.' . . .

Petitioners argue that the purpose of the Bennett Amendment was to restrict Title VII sex-based wage discrimination claims to those that could also be brought under the Equal Pay Act, and thus that claims not arising from 'equal work' are precluded. Respondents, in contrast, argue that the Bennett Amendment was designed merely to incorporate the four affirmative defenses of the Equal Pay Act into Title VII for sex-based wage discrimination claims. Respondents thus contend that claims for sex-based wage discrimination can be brought under Title VII even though no member of the opposite sex holds an equal but higher paying job, provided that the challenged wage rate is not based on seniority, merit, quantity or quality of production, or 'any other factor other than sex.' The Court of Appeals found respondents' interpretation the 'more persuasive.' While recognizing that the language and legislative history of the provision are not unambiguous, we conclude that the Court of Appeals was correct. . . .

Our interpretation of the Bennett Amendment draws additional support from the remedial purposes of Title VII and the Equal Pay Act. Section 703 (a) of Title VII makes it unlawful for an employer 'to fail or refuse to hire or to discharge any individual, or otherwise to discriminate against any individual with respect to his compensation, terms, conditions, or privileges of employment' because of such individual's sex. (emphasis added). As Congress itself has indicated, a 'broad approach' to the definition of equal employment opportunity is essential to overcoming and undoing the effect of discrimination. We must therefore avoid interpretations of Title VII that deprive victims of discrimination of a remedy, without clear congressional mandate. . . .

We do not decide in this case the precise contours of lawsuits challenging sex discrimination in compensation under Title VII. It is sufficient to note that respondents' claims of discriminatory undercompensation are not barred by § 703(h) of Title VII merely because respondents do not perform work equal to that of male jail guards. The judgment of the Court of Appeals is therefore affirmed."

V. JUSTICE VOTE

5 Pro ACLU Side vs. 4 Con Opposing Side

ACLU Side (Respondent / Appellee)

1. Brennan, W. – Wrote majority opinion
2. White, B. – Joined majority opinion
3. Marshall, T. – Joined majority opinion
4. Blackmun, H. – Joined majority opinion
5. Stevens, J. – Joined majority opinion

Opposing Side (Petitioner / Appellant)

1. Rehnquist, W. – Wrote dissenting opinion
2. Burger, W. – Joined Rehnquist's dissent
3. Stewart, P. – Joined Rehnquist's dissent
4. Powell, L. – Joined Rehnquist's dissent

VI. A WIN OR LOSS FOR THE ACLU?

The ACLU filed as amicus curiae urging affirmance; the Supreme Court affirmed the ruling of the Court of Appeals in a 5-4 vote, giving the ACLU an apparent win.

476. Heffron v. International Society for Krishna Consciousness, Inc.

(Decided June 22, 1981; 452 U.S. 640)

I. ISSUE

A. Issues Discussed

First Amendment, freedoms of press, speech, and association), Fourteenth Amendment

B. Legal Question Presented

"[W]hether a State, consistent with the First and Fourteenth Amendments, may require a religious organization desiring to distribute and sell religious literature and to solicit donations at a state fair to conduct those activities only at an assigned location within the fairgrounds even though application of the rule limits the religious practices of the organization."

C. Supreme Court's Answer

This requirement is constitutional as applied to religious organizations.

II. CASE SUMMARY

A. Background

A Minnesota law allowed the Minnesota Agricultural Society to create rules regulating the annual state fair. Rule 6.05 required organizations wishing to sell or distribute goods and written materials to confine themselves to an assigned location within the fairgrounds. "Although the Rule does not prevent organizational representatives from walking about the fairgrounds and communicating the organization's views with fair patrons in face-to-face discussions, it does require that any exhibitor conduct its sales, distribution, and fund solicitation operations from a booth rented from the Society. Space in the fairgrounds is rented to all comers in a nondiscriminatory fashion on a first-come, first-served basis with the rental charge based on the size and location of the booth. The Rule applies alike to nonprofit, charitable, and commercial enterprises.

[R]espondents International Society for Krishna Consciousness, Inc. (ISKCON), an international religious society espousing the views of the Krishna religion . . . filed suit against numerous state officials seeking a declaration that Rule 6.05, both on its face and as applied, violated respondents' rights under the First Amendment, and seeking injunctive relief prohibiting enforcement of the Rule against ISKCON and its members. Specifically, ISKCON asserted that the Rule would suppress the practice of Sankirtan, one of its religious rituals, which enjoins its members to go into public places to distribute or sell religious literature and to solicit donations for the support of the Krishna religion. The trial court . . . granted the state officials' motion for summary judgment, upholding the constitutionality of Rule 6.05. . . .

On appeal, the Minnesota Supreme Court reversed, holding that Rule 6.05, as applied to respondents, unconstitutionally restricted the Krishnas' religious practice of Sankirtan. The court rejected the Society's proffered justifications for the Rule as inadequate to warrant the restriction. Furthermore, the application of Rule 6.05 to ISKCON was not essential to the furtherance of the State's interests in that those interests could be served by means less restrictive of respondents' First Amendment rights."

The Supreme Court granted certiorari to review the case and reversed.

B. Counsel of Record / ACLU Attorney

ACLU Side (Respondent / Appellee): Laurence H. Tribe argued the cause for appellee.

Opposing Side (Petitioner / Appellant): Kent G. Harbison, Special Assistant Attorney General of Minnesota, argued the cause for appellant.

III. AMICI CURIAE

ACLU Side (Respondent / Appellee)

Brief of amici curiae filed on behalf of the ACLU, et al., by Albert N. Podell, Bruce J. Ennis, Jr., and Charles S. Sims.

Brief of amici curiae filed on behalf of the American Federation of Labor and Congress of Industrial Organizations by J. Albert Woll, Marsha Berzon, and Laurence Gold.

Brief of amici curiae filed on behalf of the Gujarat Cultural Association, Inc., et al., by John Jordan.

Brief of amici curiae filed on behalf of the India Cultural Society of New Jersey, et al., by Fletcher N. Baldwin, Jr.

Opposing Side (Petitioner / Appellant)

Brief of amici curiae filed on behalf of the State of New York by Robert Abrams, Attorney General, Shirley Adelson Siegel, Solicitor General, and Thomas J. Maroney and George M. Levy, Assistant Attorneys General.

Brief of amici curiae filed on behalf of the State of Ohio by William J. Brown, Attorney General, and Gary Elson Brown, Special Assistant Attorney General.

Brief of amici curiae filed on behalf of the County of Los Angeles by John H. Larson, DeWitt W. Clinton, and Mary F. Wawro.

IV. THE SUPREME COURT'S DECISION

"For Rule 6.05 to be valid as a place and manner restriction, it must also be sufficiently clear that alternative forums for the expression of respondents' protected speech exist despite the effects of the Rule. . . . First, the Rule does not prevent ISKCON from practicing Sankirtan anywhere outside the fairgrounds. More importantly, the Rule has not been shown to deny access within the forum in question. Here, the Rule does not exclude ISKCON from the fairgrounds, nor does it deny that organization the right to conduct any desired activity at some point within the forum. Its members may mingle with the crowd and orally propagate their views. The organization may also arrange for a booth and distribute and sell literature and solicit funds from that location on the fairgrounds itself. The Minnesota State Fair is a limited public forum in that it exists to provide a means for a great number of exhibitors temporarily to present their products or views, be they commercial, religious, or political, to a large number of people in an efficient fashion. Considering the limited functions of the Fair and the combined area within which it operates, we are unwilling to say that Rule 6.05 does not provide ISKCON and other organizations with an adequate means to sell and solicit on the fairgrounds. The First Amendment protects the right of every citizen to 'reach the minds of willing listeners and to do so there must be opportunity to win their attention.' Rule 6.05 does not unnecessarily limit that right within the fairgrounds.

The judgment of the Supreme Court of Minnesota is reversed, and the case is remanded for further proceedings not inconsistent with this opinion."

V. JUSTICE VOTE

4 Pro ACLU Side vs. 5 Con Opposing Side

ACLU Side (Petitioner / Appellant)

1. Blackmun, H. – Wrote opinion concurring in part and dissenting in part
2. Brennan, W. – Wrote opinion concurring in part and dissenting in part
3. Marshall, T. – Joined Brennan's opinion
4. Stevens, J. – Joined Brennan's opinion

Opposing Side (Respondent / Appellee)

1. White, B. – Wrote majority opinion
2. Burger, W. – Joined majority opinion
3. Stewart, P. – Joined majority opinion
4. Powell, L. – Joined majority opinion
5. Rehnquist, W. – Joined majority opinion

VI. A WIN OR LOSS FOR THE ACLU?

The ACLU filed as amicus curiae urging affirmance; the U.S. Supreme Court reversed the ruling of the Supreme Court of Minnesota in a 5-4 vote, giving the ACLU an apparent loss.

477. Michigan v. Summers

(Decided June 22, 1981; 452 U.S. 692)

I. ISSUE

A. Issues Discussed

Criminal procedure, Fourth Amendment, search and seizure, warrants

B. Legal Question Presented

"[W]hether the initial detention of respondent violated his constitutional right to be secure against an unreasonable seizure of his person."

C. Supreme Court's Answer

The initial detention of respondent did not violate his constitutional right to be secure against an unreasonable seizure of his person.

II. CASE SUMMARY

A. Background

"As Detroit police officers were about to execute a warrant to search a house for narcotics, they encountered respondent descending the front steps. They requested his assistance in gaining entry and detained him while they searched the premises. After finding narcotics in the basement and ascertaining that respondent owned the house, the police arrested him, searched his person, and found in his coat pocket an envelope containing 8.5 grams of heroin.

Respondent was charged with possession of the heroin found on his person. He moved to suppress the heroin as the product of an illegal search in violation of the Fourth Amendment, and the trial judge granted the motion and quashed the information. That order was affirmed by a divided panel of the Michigan Court of Appeals and by the Michigan Supreme Court over the dissent of three of its justices."

The U.S. Supreme Court granted certiorari to review the case and reversed.

B. Counsel of Record / ACLU Attorney

ACLU Side (Respondent / Appellee): Gerald M. Lorence argued the cause for appellee.

Bruce J. Ennis, Jr., argued the cause for the ACLU, as amicus curiae, by special leave of court.

Opposing Side (Petitioner / Appellant): Timothy A. Baughman argued the cause for appellant.

Elliott Schulder argued the cause for the United States, as amicus curiae, by special leave of Court.

III. AMICI CURIAE

ACLU Side (Respondent / Appellee)

Brief of amici curiae filed on behalf of the ACLU by Bruce J. Ennis, Jr., Mary L. Heen, Chares S. Sims, and Lawrence Herman.

Opposing Side (Petitioner / Appellant)

Brief of amici curiae filed on behalf of the United States by Elliott Schulder, Solicitor General Wade H. McCree, Jr., Assistant Attorney General Philip B. Heymann, and Deputy Solicitor General Andrew L. Frey.

IV. THE SUPREME COURT'S DECISION

"[S]ome seizures significantly less intrusive than an arrest have withstood scrutiny under the reasonableness standard embodied in the Fourth Amendment. In these cases the intrusion on the citizen's privacy 'was so much less severe' than that involved in a traditional arrest that 'the opposing interests in crime prevention and detection and in the police officer's safety' could support the seizure as reasonable. . . .

Of prime importance in assessing the intrusion is the fact that the police had obtained a warrant to search respondent's house for contraband. A neutral and detached magistrate had found probable cause to believe that the law was being violated in that house and had authorized a substantial invasion of the privacy of the persons who resided there. The detention of one of the residents while the premises were searched, although admittedly a significant restraint on his liberty, was surely less intrusive than the search itself. Indeed, we may safely assume that most citizens—unless they intend flight to avoid arrest—would elect to remain in order to observe the search of their possessions. Furthermore, the type of detention imposed here is not likely to be exploited by the officer or unduly prolonged in order to gain more information, because the information the officers seek normally will be obtained through the search and not through the detention. Moreover, because the detention in this case was in respondent's own residence, it could add only minimally to the public stigma associated with the search itself and would involve neither the inconvenience nor the indignity associated with a compelled visit to the police station. . . .

If the evidence that a citizen's residence is harboring contraband is sufficient to persuade a judicial officer that an invasion of the citizen's privacy is justified, it is constitutionally reasonable to require that citizen to remain while officers of the law execute a valid warrant to search his home. Thus, for Fourth Amendment purposes, we hold that a warrant to search for contraband founded on probable cause implicitly carries with it the limited authority to detain the occupants of the premises while a proper search is conducted.

Because it was lawful to require respondent to reenter and to remain in the house until evidence establishing probable cause to arrest him was found, his arrest and the search incident thereto were constitutionally permissible. The judgment of the Supreme Court of Michigan must therefore be reversed."

V. JUSTICE VOTE

3 Pro ACLU Side vs. 6 Con Opposing Side

ACLU Side (Respondent / Appellee)

1. Stewart, P. – Wrote dissenting opinion
2. Brennan, W. – Joined Stewart's dissent
3. Marshall, T. – Joined Stewart's dissent

Opposing Side (Petitioner / Appellant)

1. Stevens, J. – Wrote majority opinion
2. Burger, W. – Joined majority opinion
3. White, B. – Joined majority opinion
4. Blackmun, H. – Joined majority opinion
5. Powell, L. – Joined majority opinion
6. Rehnquist, W. – Joined majority opinion

VI. A WIN OR LOSS FOR THE ACLU?

The ACLU, as amicus curiae, urged affirmance of the Michigan Supreme Court's judgment; the Supreme Court reversed in a 6-3 vote, giving the ACLU an apparent loss.

478. Rostker v. Goldberg

(Decided June 25, 1981; 453 U.S. 57)

I. ISSUE

A. Issues Discussed

Civil rights, gender

B. Legal Question Presented

"The question presented is whether the Military Selective Service Act violates the Fifth Amendment to the United States Constitution in authorizing the President to require the registration of males and not females."

C. Supreme Court's Answer

"[W]e conclude that Congress acted well within its constitutional authority when it authorized the registration of men, and not women, under the Military Selective Service Act."

II. CASE SUMMARY

A. Background

"Congress is given the power under the Constitution 'To raise and support Armies,' 'To provide and maintain a Navy,' and 'To make Rules for the Government and Regulation of the land and naval Forces.' Pursuant to this grant of authority Congress has enacted the Military Selective Service Act. Section 3 . . . empowers the President, by proclamation, to require the registration of 'every male citizen' and male resident aliens between the ages of 18 and 26. . . .

Registration for the draft under § 3 was discontinued in 1975. In early 1980, President Carter determined that it was necessary to reactivate the draft registration process. . . .

Congress agreed that it was necessary to reactivate the registration process, and allocated funds for that purpose in a Joint Resolution . . . . The Resolution did not allocate all the funds originally requested by the President, but only those necessary to register males. . . . Congress . . . declined to amend the MSSA to permit the registration of women.

On July 2, 1980, the President, by Proclamation, ordered the registration of specified groups of young men pursuant to the authority conferred by § 3 of the Act. Registration was to commence on July 21, 1980. . . .

On Friday, July 18, 1980, three days before registration was to commence, the District Court issued an opinion finding that the Act violated the Due Process Clause of the Fifth Amendment and permanently enjoined the Government from requiring registration . . . .

Saturday, July 19, 1980, Justice BRENNAN, acting in his capacity as Circuit Justice for the Third Circuit, stayed the District Court's order enjoining commencement of registration. Registration began the next Monday. On December 1, 1980, [the Supreme Court] noted probable jurisdiction."

B. Counsel of Record

ACLU Side (Respondent / Appellee): Donald L. Weinberg argued the cause for appellee. With him on the brief were Laurence H. Tribe, Harold E. Kohn, Stuart H. Savett, Donald L. Weinberg, and Isabelle Katz Pinzler, Bruce J. Ennis, and Diana A. Steele of the American Civil Liberties Union Foundation.

Opposing Side (Petitioner / Appellant): Solicitor General McCree argued the cause for appellant. With him on the briefs were Assistant Attorney General Daniel, Acting Assistant Attorney General Martin, Deputy Solicitor General Claiborne, Barbara E. Etkind, William Kanter, and Mark H. Gallant.

III. AMICI CURIAE

ACLU Side (Respondent / Appellee)

Brief of amici curiae filed on behalf of Congressman Robert W. Kastenmeier et al. by Daniel Marcus.

Brief of amici curiae filed on behalf of Men's Rights, Inc., by Paul Kenney.

Brief of amici curiae filed on behalf of the National Organization for Women by Barbara A. Brown, Thomas J. Hart, Phyllis N. Segal, and Judith I. Avner.

Brief of amici curiae filed on behalf of the Women's Equity Action League Educational and Legal Defense Fund et al. by Judith L. Lichtman.

Opposing Side (Petitioner / Appellant)

Brief of amici curiae filed on behalf of the Orthodox Jewish Coalition on the Draft by Dennis Rapps and A. David Stern.

Brief of amici curiae filed on behalf of Stacy Acker et al. by Nathan Lewin.

Brief of amici curiae filed on behalf of Congressman Lawrence P. McDonald et al. by Daniel J. Popeo and Paul D. Kamenar.

IV. THE SUPREME COURT'S DECISION

"Whenever called upon to judge the constitutionality of an Act of Congress—'the gravest and most delicate duty that this Court is called upon to perform,'—the Court accords 'great weight to the decisions of Congress.' . . .

This is not, however, merely a case involving the customary deference accorded congressional decisions. The case arises in the context of Congress' authority over national defense and military affairs, and perhaps in no other area has the Court accorded Congress greater deference. . . .

In such a case, we cannot ignore Congress' broad authority conferred by the Constitution to raise and support armies when we are urged to declare unconstitutional its studied choice of one alternative in preference to another for furthering that goal. . . .

This case is quite different from several of the gender-based discrimination cases we have considered in that, despite appellees' assertions, Congress did not act 'unthinkingly' or 'reflexively and not for any considered reason.' The question of registering women for the draft not only received considerable national attention and was the subject of wide-ranging public debate, but also was extensively considered by Congress in hearings, floor debate, and in committee. . . .

The foregoing clearly establishes that the decision to exempt women from registration was not the "accidental by-product of a traditional way of thinking about females." . . .

In holding the MSSA constitutionally invalid the District Court relied heavily on the President's decision to seek authority to register women and the testimony of members of the Executive Branch and the military in support of that decision. . . .

In sum, Congress carefully evaluated the testimony that 80,000 women conscripts could be usefully employed in the event of a draft and rejected it in the permissible exercise of its constitutional responsibility. The District Court was quite wrong in undertaking an independent evaluation of this evidence, rather than adopting an appropriately deferential examination of Congress' evaluation of that evidence.

In light of the foregoing, we conclude that Congress acted well within its constitutional authority when it authorized the registration of men, and not women, under the Military Selective Service Act. The decision of the District Court holding otherwise is accordingly reversed."

V. JUSTICE VOTE

3 Pro ACLU Side vs. 6 Con Opposing Side

ACLU Side (Respondent / Appellee)

1. White, B. – Wrote dissenting opinion
2. Marshall, T. – Wrote dissenting opinion
3. Brennan, W. – Joined White's and Marshall's dissents

Opposing Side (Petitioner / Appellant)

1. Rehnquist, W. – Wrote majority opinion
2. Burger, W. – Joined majority opinion
3. Powell, L. – Joined majority opinion
4. Stewart, P. – Joined majority opinion
5. Blackmun, H. – Joined majority opinion
6. Stevens, J. – Joined majority opinion

VI. A WIN OR LOSS FOR THE ACLU?

The ACLU served as counsel for appellee urging affirmance; the Supreme Court reversed the District Court's decision by a 6-3 vote, giving the ACLU an apparent loss.

479. California Medical Ass'n v. Federal Election Commission

(Decided June 26, 1981; 453 U.S. 182)

I. ISSUE

A. Issues Discussed

First Amendment, Fifth Amendment, political speech, equal protection

B. Legal Question Presented

"[W]hether provisions of the Federal Election Campaign Act of 1971 . . . limiting the amount an unincorporated association may contribute to a multicandidate political committee violate the First Amendment or the equal protection component of the Fifth Amendment."

C. Supreme Court's Answer

The contribution limits do not violate the First Amendment or the Fifth Amendment.

II. CASE SUMMARY

A. Background

"The California Medical Association (CMA) is a not-for-profit unincorporated association of approximately 25,000 doctors residing in California. In 1976, CMA formed the California Medical Political Action Committee (CALPAC). CALPAC is registered as a political committee with the Federal Election Commission, and is subject to the provisions of the Federal Election Campaign Act relating to multicandidate political committees. One such provision, 2 U.S.C. § 441a(a)(1)(C), prohibits individuals and unincorporated associations such as CMA from contributing more than $5,000 per calendar year to any multicandidate political committee such as CALPAC. A related provision of the Act, 2 U.S.C. § 441a(f), makes it unlawful for political committees such as CALPAC knowingly to accept contributions exceeding this limit.

In October 1978, the Federal Election Commission found 'reason to believe' that CMA had violated the Act by making annual contributions to CALPAC in excess of $5,000, and that CALPAC had unlawfully accepted such contributions. When informal conciliation efforts failed, the Commission in April 1979 authorized its staff to institute a civil enforcement action against CMA and CALPAC to secure compliance with the contribution limitations of the Act. In early May 1979, after receiving formal notification of the Commission's impending enforcement action, CMA and CALPAC, together with two individual members of these organizations, filed this declaratory judgment action in the United States District Court for the Northern District of California challenging the constitutionality of the statutory contribution limitations upon which the Commission's enforcement action was to be based. Several weeks later, the Commission filed its enforcement action in the same District Court. In this second suit, CMA and CALPAC pleaded as affirmative defenses the same constitutional claims raised in their declaratory judgment action.

On May 17, 1979, pursuant to the special expedited review provisions of the Act . . . , the District Court certified the constitutional questions raised in appellants' declaratory judgment action to the Court of Appeals for the Ninth Circuit. In the meantime, pretrial discovery and preparation in the Commission's enforcement action continued in the District Court. In May 1980, a divided Court of Appeals, sitting en banc, rejected appellants' constitutional claims and upheld the $5,000 limit on annual contributions by unincorporated associations to multicandidate political committees."

The Supreme Court granted certiorari to review the case and affirmed.

B. Counsel of Record / ACLU Attorney

ACLU Side (Petitioner / Appellant): Frederick C. Zimmerman argued the cause for appellant.

Opposing Side (Respondent / Appellee): Charles N. Steele argued the cause for appellee.

III. AMICI CURIAE

ACLU Side (Petitioner / Appellant)

Brief of amici curiae filed on behalf of the ACLU by Bruce J. Ennis, Jr., Charles S. Sims, and Arthur Eisenberg.

Opposing Side (Respondent / Appellee)

Brief of amici curiae filed on behalf of Common Cause by Louis R. Cohen, A. Stephen Hut, Jr., Roger M. Witten, Bruce E. Coolidge, Andrew N. Vollmer, Kenneth J. Guido, Jr., Donald J. Simon, and Ellen G. Block.

IV. THE SUPREME COURT'S DECISION

"If the First Amendment rights of a contributor are not infringed by limitations on the amount he may contribute to a campaign organization which advocates the views and candidacy of a particular candidate, the rights of a contributor are similarly not impaired by limits on the amount he may give to a multicandidate political committee, such as CALPAC, which advocates the views and candidacies of a number of candidates. . . .

Appellants' claim of unfair treatment ignores the plain fact that the statute as a whole imposes far fewer restrictions on individuals and unincorporated associations than it does on corporations and unions. Persons subject to the restrictions of § 441a(a)(1)(C) may make unlimited expenditures on political speech; corporations and unions, however, may make only the limited contributions authorized by § 441b(b)(2). Furthermore, individuals and unincorporated associations may contribute to candidates, to candidates' committees, to national party committees, and to all other political committees while corporations and unions are absolutely barred from making any such contributions. In addition, multicandidate political committees are generally unrestricted in the manner and scope of their solicitations; the segregated funds that unions and corporations may establish pursuant to § 441b(b)(2)

(C) are carefully limited in this regard. The differing restrictions placed on individuals and unincorporated associations, on the one hand, and on unions and corporations, on the other, reflect a judgment by Congress that these entities have differing structures and purposes, and that they therefore may require different forms of regulation in order to protect the integrity of the electoral process. Appellants do not challenge any of the restrictions on the corporate and union political activity, yet these restrictions entirely undermine appellants' claim that because of § 441a(a)(1)(C), the Act discriminates against individuals and unincorporated associations in the exercise of their First Amendment rights.

Accordingly, we conclude that the $5,000 limitation on the amount that persons may contribute to multicandidate political committees violates neither the First nor the Fifth Amendment. The judgment of the Court of Appeals is therefore affirmed."

V. JUSTICE VOTE

4 Pro ACLU Side vs. 5 Con Opposing Side

ACLU Side (Petitioner / Appellant)

1. Stewart, P. – Wrote dissenting opinion
2. Burger, W. – Joined Stewart's dissent
3. Powell, L. – Joined Stewart's dissent
4. Rehnquist, W. – Joined Stewart's dissent

Opposing Side (Respondent / Appellee)

1. Marshall, T. – Wrote majority opinion
2. Brennan, W. – Joined majority opinion
3. White, B. – Joined majority opinion
4. Stevens, J. – Joined majority opinion
5. Blackmun, H. – Wrote concurring opinion

VI. A WIN OR LOSS FOR THE ACLU?

The ACLU filed as amicus curiae urging reversal of the judgment of the Court of Appeals for the Ninth Circuit; the Supreme Court affirmed in a 5-4 vote, giving the ACLU an apparent loss.

480. New York v. Belton

(Decided July 1, 1981; 453 U.S. 454)

I. ISSUE

A. Issues Discussed

Criminal procedure, Fourth Amendment, search and seizure, due process

B. Legal Question Presented

"When the occupant of an automobile is subjected to a lawful custodial arrest, does the constitutionally permissible scope of a search incident to his arrest include the passenger compartment of the automobile in which he was riding?"

C. Supreme Court's Answer

A search incident to the arrest of the occupant of an automobile can include a search of the passenger compartment of the automobile and containers within the passenger compartment.

II. CASE SUMMARY

A. Background

"On April 9, 1978, Trooper Douglas Nicot, a New York State policeman driving an unmarked car on the New York Thruway, was passed by another automobile traveling at an excessive rate of speed. Nicot gave chase, overtook the speeding vehicle, and ordered its driver to pull it over to the side of the road and stop. There were four men in the car, one of whom was Roger Belton, the respondent in this case. The policeman asked to see the driver's license and automobile registration, and discovered that none of the men owned the vehicle or was related to its owner. Meanwhile, the policeman had smelled burnt marihuana and had seen on the floor of the car an envelope marked 'Supergold' that he associated with marihuana. He therefore directed the men to get out of the car, and placed them under arrest for the unlawful possession of marihuana. He patted down each of the men and 'split them up into four separate areas of the Thruway at this time so they would not be in physical touching area of each other.' He then picked up the envelope marked 'Supergold' and found that it contained marihuana. After giving the arrestees the warnings required by Miranda v. Arizona the state policeman searched each one of them. He then searched the passenger compartment of the car. On the back seat he found a black leather jacket belonging to Belton. He unzipped one of the pockets of the jacket and discovered cocaine. Placing the jacket in his automobile, he drove the four arrestees to a nearby police station.

Belton was subsequently indicted for criminal possession of a controlled substance. In the trial court he moved that the cocaine the trooper had seized from the jacket pocket be suppressed. The court denied the motion. Belton then pleaded guilty to a lesser included offense, but preserved his claim that the cocaine had been seized in violation of the Fourth and Fourteenth Amendments. The Appellate Division of the New York Supreme Court upheld the constitutionality of the search and seizure . . . .

The New York Court of Appeals reversed, holding that '[a] warrantless search of the zippered pockets of an unaccessible jacket may not be upheld as a search incident to a lawful arrest where there is no longer any danger that the arrestee or a confederate might gain access to the article.'"

The Supreme Court granted certiorari to review the case and reversed the judgment of the New York Court of Appeals.

B. Counsel of Record / ACLU Attorney

ACLU Side (Respondent / Appellee): Paul J. Cambria, Jr., argued the cause for appellee.

Opposing Side (Petitioner / Appellant): James R. Harvey argued the cause for appellant.

Andrew L. Frey, Deputy Solicitor General, argued the cause for the United States, as amicus curiae, by special leave of Court.

III. AMICI CURIAE

ACLU Side (Respondent / Appellee)

Brief of amici curiae filed on behalf of the ACLU, et al., by Richard Emery, Charles S. Sims, and Bruce J. Ennis, Jr.

Opposing Side (Petitioner / Appellant)

Brief of amici curiae filed on behalf of the United States by Deputy Solicitor General Andrew L. Frey, Solicitor General Wade H. McCree, Jr., Acting Assistant Attorney General John C. Keeney, and Assistant to the Solicitor General Elliott Schulder.

IV. THE SUPREME COURT'S DECISION

"When a person cannot know how a court will apply a settled principle to a recurring factual situation, that person cannot know the scope of his constitutional protection, nor can a policeman know the scope of his authority. . . . Our reading of the cases suggests the generalization that articles inside the relatively narrow compass of the passenger compartment of an automobile are in fact generally, even if not inevitably, within 'the area into which an arrestee might reach in order to grab a weapon or evidentiary ite[m].' . . . Accordingly, we hold that when a policeman has made a lawful custodial arrest of the occupant of an automobile, he may, as a contemporaneous incident of that arrest, search the passenger compartment of that automobile.

It follows from this conclusion that the police may also examine the contents of any containers found within the passenger compartment, for if the passenger compartment is within reach of the arrestee, so also will containers in it be within his reach. Such a container may, of course, be searched whether it is open or closed, since the justification for the search is not that the arrestee has no privacy interest in the container, but that the lawful custodial arrest justifies the infringement of any privacy interest the arrestee may have. Thus, while the Court in Chimel held that the police could not search all the drawers in an arrestee's house simply because the police had arrested him at home, the Court noted that drawers within an arrestee's reach could be searched because of the danger their contents might pose to the police. . . .

It is not questioned that the respondent was the subject of a lawful custodial arrest on a charge of possessing marihuana. The search of the respondent's jacket followed immediately upon that arrest. The jacket was located inside the passenger compartment of the car in which the respondent had been a passenger just before he was arrested. The jacket was thus within the area which we have concluded was 'within the arrestee's immediate control' . . . . The search of the jacket, therefore, was a search incident to a lawful custodial arrest, and it did not violate the Fourth and Fourteenth Amendments. Accordingly, the judgment is reversed."

V. JUSTICE VOTE

3 Pro ACLU Side vs. 6 Con Opposing Side

ACLU Side (Respondent / Appellee)

1. Brennan, W. – Wrote dissenting opinion
2. White, B. – Wrote dissenting opinion
3. Marshall, T. – Joined Brennan's dissent, joined White's dissent

Opposing Side (Petitioner / Appellant)

1. Stevens, J. – Wrote majority opinion
2. Burger, W. – Joined majority opinion
3. Blackmun, H. – Joined majority opinion
4. Powell, L. – Joined majority opinion
5. Rehnquist, W. – Wrote concurring opinion
6. Stevens, J. – Wrote concurring opinion

VI. A WIN OR LOSS FOR THE ACLU?

The ACLU, as amicus curiae, urged affirmance of the New York Court of Appeals' judgment; the Supreme Court reversed in a 6-3 vote, giving the ACLU an apparent loss.

481. Metromedia, Inc. v. City of San Diego

(Decided July 2, 1981; 453 U.S. 490)

I. ISSUE

A. Issues Discussed

First Amendment, freedoms of press, speech, and association

B. Legal Question Presented

Whether "an ordinance of the city of San Diego, Cal., imposing substantial prohibitions on the erection of outdoor advertising displays within the city" is constitutional.

C. Supreme Court's Answer

The ordinance infringes on freedom of speech and is unconstitutional.

II. CASE SUMMARY

A. Background

"Stating that its purpose was 'to eliminate hazards to pedestrians and motorists brought about by distracting sign displays' and 'to preserve and improve the appearance of the City,' San Diego enacted an ordinance to prohibit 'outdoor advertising display signs.' . . . The ordinance provides two kinds of exceptions to the general prohibition: onsite signs and signs falling within 12 specified categories. . . .

Appellants are companies that were engaged in the outdoor advertising business in San Diego at the time the ordinance was passed. Each owns a substantial number of outdoor advertising displays (approximately 500 to 800) within the city. These signs are all located in areas zoned for commercial and industrial purposes, most of them on property leased by the owners to appellants for the purpose of maintaining billboards. Each sign has a remaining useful income-producing life of over 25 years, and each sign has a fair market value of between $2,500 and $25,000. Space on the signs was made available to 'all comers' and the copy on each sign changed regularly, usually monthly. . . .

Appellants brought suit in state court to enjoin enforcement of the ordinance. . . . On cross-motions for summary judgment, the trial court held that the ordinance was an unconstitutional exercise of the city's police power and an abridgment of appellants' First Amendment rights. The California Court of Appeal affirmed on the first ground alone and did not reach the First Amendment argument. [T]he California Supreme Court reversed."

The U.S. Supreme Court granted certiorari to review the case and reversed the decision of the California Supreme Court.

B. Counsel of Record / ACLU Attorney

ACLU Side (Petitioner / Appellant): Floyd Abrams argued the cause for appellant.

Opposing Side (Respondent / Appellee): C. Alan Sumption argued the cause for appellee.

III. AMICI CURIAE

ACLU Side (Petitioner / Appellant)

Brief of amici curiae filed on behalf of the ACLU by Nadine Strossen, Deborah J. Stavile, Charles S. Sims, and Bruce J. Ennis, Jr.

Additional briefs of amici curiae were filed on behalf of the American Newspaper Publishers Association, the Outdoor Advertising Association of America, and the Pacific Legal Foundation.

Opposing Side (Respondent / Appellee)

Brief of amici curiae filed on behalf of the United States by Solicitor General Wade H. McCree, Jr., Assistant Attorney General James W. Moorman, Deputy Solicitor General Louis F. Claiborne, Assistant to the Solicitor General Edwin S. Kneedler, F. Kaid Benfield, and Edward J. Shawaker.

Additional briefs of amici curiae were filed on behalf of the City and County of San Francisco, the State of Hawaii, et al., the City of Alameda, et al., and the National Institute of Municipal Law Officers.

IV. THE SUPREME COURT'S DECISION

"Billboards, . . . like other media of communication, combine communicative and noncommunicative aspects. As with other media, the government has legitimate interests in controlling the noncommunicative aspects of the medium, but the First and Fourteenth Amendments foreclose a similar interest in controlling the communicative aspects.

[W]e reject appellees' suggestion that the ordinance may be appropriately characterized as a reasonable 'time, place, and manner' restriction. The ordinance does not generally ban billboard advertising as an unacceptable 'manner' of communicating information or ideas; rather, it permits various kinds of signs. Signs that are banned are banned everywhere and at all times. We have observed that time, place, and manner restrictions are permissible if 'they are justified without reference to the content of the regulated speech, . . . serve a significant governmental interest, and . . . leave open ample alternative channels for communication of the information.' Here, it cannot be assumed that 'alternative channels' are available, for the parties stipulated to just the opposite: 'Many businesses and politicians and other persons rely upon outdoor advertising because other forms of advertising are insufficient, inappropriate and prohibitively expensive.' . . .

There can be no question that a prohibition on the erection of billboards infringes freedom of speech: The exceptions do not create the infringement, rather the general prohibition does. But the exceptions to the general prohibition are of great significance in assessing the strength of the city's interest in prohibiting billboards. We conclude that by allowing commercial establishments to use billboards to advertise the products and services they offer, the city necessarily has conceded that some communicative interests, e. g., onsite commercial advertising, are stronger than its competing interests in esthetics and traffic safety. It has nevertheless banned all noncommercial signs except those specifically excepted. . . .

Governmental interests are only revealed and given concrete force by the steps taken to meet those interests. If the city has concluded that its official interests are not as strong as private interests in commercial communications, may it nevertheless claim that those same official interests outweigh private interests in noncommercial communications? Our answer, which is consistent with our cases, is in the negative. . . .

Because the San Diego ordinance reaches too far into the realm of protected speech, we conclude that it is unconstitutional on its face. The judgment of the California Supreme Court is reversed, and the case is remanded to that court."

V. JUSTICE VOTE

6 Pro ACLU Side vs. 3 Con Opposing Side

ACLU Side (Petitioner / Appellant)

1. White, B. – Wrote majority opinion
2. Stewart, P. – Joined majority opinion
3. Marshall, T. – Joined majority opinion
4. Powell, L. – Joined majority opinion
5. Brennan, W. – Wrote concurring opinion
6. Blackmun, H. – Joined Brennan's concurrence

Opposing Side (Respondent / Appellee)

1. Stevens, J. – Wrote dissenting opinion
2. Burger, W. – Wrote dissenting opinion
3. Rehnquist, W. – Wrote dissenting opinion

VI. A WIN OR LOSS FOR THE ACLU?

The ACLU filed as amicus curiae urging reversal; the U.S. Supreme Court reversed the ruling of the California Supreme Court in a 6-3 vote, giving the ACLU an apparent win.

482. Washington v. Chrisman

(Decided January 13, 1982; 455 U.S. 1)

I. ISSUE

A. Issues Discussed

Criminal procedure, Fourth Amendment, search and seizure

B. Legal Question Presented

"[W]hether a police officer may, consistent with the Fourth Amendment, accompany an arrested person into his residence and seize contraband discovered there in plain view."

C. Supreme Court's Answer

A police officer may, consistent with the Fourth Amendment, accompany an arrested person into his residence and seize contraband discovered there in plain view.

II. CASE SUMMARY

A. Background

"On the evening of January 21, 1978, Officer Daugherty of the Washington State University police department observed Carl Overdahl, a student at the University, leave a student dormitory carrying a half-gallon bottle of gin. Because Washington law forbids possession of alcoholic beverages by persons under 21 and Overdahl appeared to be under age, the officer stopped him and asked for identification. Overdahl said that his identification was in his dormitory room and asked if the officer would wait while he went to retrieve it. The officer answered that under the circumstances he would have to accompany Overdahl, to which Overdahl replied 'O.K.'

Overdahl's room was approximately 11 by 17 feet and located on the 11th floor of the dormitory. Respondent Chrisman, Overdahl's roommate, was in the room when the officer and Overdahl entered. The officer remained in the open doorway, leaning against the doorjamb while watching Chrisman and Overdahl. He observed that Chrisman, who was in the process of placing a small box in the room's medicine cabinet, became nervous at the sight of an officer.

Within 30 to 45 seconds after Overdahl entered the room, the officer noticed seeds and a small pipe lying on a desk 8 to 10 feet from where he was standing. From his training and experience, the officer believed the seeds were marihuana and the pipe was of a type used to smoke marihuana. He entered the room and examined the pipe and seeds, confirming that the seeds were marihuana and observing that the pipe smelled of marihuana.

The officer informed Overdahl and Chrisman of their rights under Miranda v. Arizona; each acknowledged that he understood his rights and indicated that he was willing to waive them. Officer Daugherty then asked whether the students had any other drugs in the room. The respondent handed Daugherty the box he had been carrying earlier, which contained three small plastic bags filled with marihuana and $112 in cash. At that point, Officer Daugherty called by radio for a second officer; on his arrival, the two students were told that a search of the room would be necessary. The officers explained to Overdahl and Chrisman that they had an absolute right to insist that the officers first obtain a search warrant, but that they could voluntarily consent to the search. Following this explanation, which was given in considerable detail, the two students conferred in whispers for several minutes before announcing their consent; they also signed written forms consenting to the search of the room. The search yielded more marihuana and a quantity of lysergic acid diethylamide (LSD), both controlled substances.

Respondent was charged with one count of possessing more than 40 grams of marihuana and one count of possessing LSD, both felonies. A pretrial motion to suppress the evidence seized in the room was denied; respondent was convicted of both counts. On appeal, the Washington Court of Appeals affirmed the convictions, upholding the validity of the search.

The Supreme Court of Washington reversed."

The U.S. Supreme Court granted certiorari to review the case and reversed the judgment of the Supreme Court of Washington.

B. Counsel of Record / ACLU Attorney

ACLU Side (Respondent / Appellee): Robert F. Patrick argued the cause for appellee.

Opposing Side (Petitioner / Appellant): Ronald R. Carpenter argued the cause for appellant.

III. AMICI CURIAE

ACLU Side (Respondent / Appellee)

Briefs of amici curiae filed on behalf of the ACLU of Washington by Timothy K. Ford.

Opposing Side (Petitioner / Appellant)

Brief of amici curiae filed on behalf of Americans for Effective Law Enforcement, Inc., by Fred E. Inbau, Wayne W. Schmidt, and James P. Manak.

Brief of amici curiae filed on behalf of the Legal Foundation of America, et al., by David Crump, Susan E. Waite, Gray Miller, Richard F. Callaway, and Michael C. Kuhn.

IV. THE SUPREME COURT'S DECISION

"The 'plain view' exception to the Fourth Amendment warrant requirement permits a law enforcement officer to seize what clearly is incriminating evidence or contraband when it is discovered in a place where the officer has a right to be. Here, the officer had placed Overdahl under lawful arrest, and therefore was authorized to accompany him to his room for the purpose of obtaining identification. The officer had a right to remain literally at Overdahl's elbow at all times; nothing in the Fourth Amendment is to the contrary.

The central premise of the opinion of the Supreme Court of Washington is that Officer Daugherty was not entitled to accompany Overdahl from the public corridor of the dormitory into his room, absent a showing that such 'intervention' was required by 'exigent circumstances.' We disagree with this novel reading of the Fourth Amendment. The absence of an affirmative indication that an arrested person might have a weapon available or might attempt to escape does not diminish the arresting officer's authority to maintain custody over the arrested person. Nor is that authority altered by the nature of the offense for which the arrest was made.

Every arrest must be presumed to present a risk of danger to the arresting officer. There is no way for an officer to predict reliably how a particular subject will react to arrest or the degree of the potential danger. Moreover, the possibility that an arrested person will attempt to escape if not properly supervised is obvious. . . .

We hold, therefore, that it is not 'unreasonable' under the Fourth Amendment for a police officer, as a matter of routine, to monitor the movements of an arrested person, as his judgment dictates, following the arrest. The officer's need to ensure his own safety—as well as the integrity of the arrest—is compelling. Such surveillance is not an impermissible invasion of the privacy or personal liberty of an individual who has been arrested.

[R]egardless of where the officer was positioned with respect to the threshold, he did not abandon his right to be in the room whenever he considered it essential. Accordingly, he had the right to act as soon as he observed the seeds and pipe. This is a classic instance of incriminating evidence found in plain view when a police officer, for unrelated but entirely legitimate reasons, obtains lawful access to an individual's area of privacy. The Fourth Amendment does not prohibit seizure of evidence of criminal conduct found in these circumstances. . . .

Since the seizure of the marihuana and pipe was lawful, we have no difficulty concluding that this evidence and the contraband subsequently taken from respondent's room were properly admitted at his trial. Respondent voluntarily produced three bags of marihuana after being informed of his rights under Miranda v. Arizona. He then consented, in writing, to a search of the room, after being advised that his consent must be voluntary and that he had an absolute right to refuse consent and demand procurement of a search warrant. The seizure of the drugs pursuant to respondent's valid consent did not violate the Fourth Amendment.

The judgment of the Supreme Court of Washington is reversed, and the case is remanded for further proceedings not inconsistent with this opinion."

V. JUSTICE VOTE

3 Pro ACLU Side vs. 6 Con Opposing Side

ACLU Side (Petitioner / Appellant)

1. White, B. – Wrote dissenting opinion
2. Brennan, W. – Joined White's dissent
3. Marshall, T. – Joined White's dissent

Opposing Side (Respondent / Appellee)

1. Burger, W. – Wrote majority opinion
2. Blackmun, H. – Joined majority opinion
3. Powell, L. – Joined majority opinion
4. Rehnquist, W. – Joined majority opinion
5. Stevens, J. – Joined majority opinion
6. O'Connor, S. – Joined majority opinion

VI. A WIN OR LOSS FOR THE ACLU?

The ACLU, as amicus curiae, urged affirmance of the judgment of the Supreme Court of Washington; the U.S. Supreme Court reversed in a 6-3 vote, giving the ACLU an apparent loss.

483. Smith v. Phillips

(Decided January 25, 1982; 455 U.S. 209)

I. ISSUE

A. Issues Discussed

Fourteenth Amendment, due process

B. Legal Question Presented

Was due process of law denied to respondent either by the juror's act of applying for a job at the District Attorney's Office or by the prosecutors' failure to disclose the juror's job application?

C. Supreme Court's Answer

The respondent was not denied due process either by the juror's act or prosecutor's failure to disclose the application.

II. CASE SUMMARY

A. Background

"Respondent's original motion to vacate his conviction was based on the fact that a juror in respondent's case, one John Dana Smith, submitted during the trial an application for employment as a major felony investigator in the District Attorney's Office. Smith had learned of the position from a friend who had contacts within the office and who had inquired on Smith's behalf without mentioning Smith's name or the fact that he was a juror in respondent's trial. . . .

During later inquiry about the status of Smith's application, the friend mentioned that Smith was a juror in respondent's case. The attorney to whom the friend disclosed this fact promptly informed his superior, and his superior in turn informed the Assistant District Attorney in charge of hiring investigators. The following day, more than one week before the end of respondent's trial, the assistant informed the two attorneys actually prosecuting respondent that one of the jurors had applied to the office for employment as an investigator.

The two prosecuting attorneys conferred about the application but concluded that, in view of Smith's statements during voir dire, there was no need to inform the trial court or defense counsel of the application. They did instruct attorneys in the office not to contact Smith until after the trial had ended, and took steps to insure that they would learn no information about Smith that had not been revealed during voir dire. When the jury retired to deliberate on November 20th, three alternate jurors were available to substitute for Smith, and neither the trial court nor the defense counsel knew of his application. The jury returned its verdict on November 21st.

The District Attorney first learned of Smith's application on December 4th. Five days later, after an investigation to verify the information, he informed the trial court and defense counsel of the application and the fact that its existence was known to attorneys in his office at some time before the conclusion of the trial. Respondent's attorney then moved to set aside the verdict. . . .

In his application for federal habeas relief, respondent contended that he had been denied due process of law under the Fourteenth Amendment to the United States Constitution by Smith's conduct. The District Court found insufficient evidence to demonstrate that Smith was actually biased. Nonetheless, the court imputed bias to Smith because 'the average man in Smith's position would believe that the verdict of the jury would directly affect the evaluation of his job application.' Accordingly, the court ordered respondent released unless the State granted him a new trial within 90 days.

The United States Court of Appeals for the Second Circuit affirmed by a divided vote."

The Supreme Court granted certiorari to review the case and reversed the judgment of the Second Circuit Court of Appeals.

B. Counsel of Record / ACLU Attorney

ACLU Side (Respondent / Appellee): William M. Kunstler argued the cause for appellee.

Opposing Side (Petitioner / Appellant): Robert M. Pitler argued the cause for appellant.

III. AMICI CURIAE

ACLU Side (Respondent / Appellee)

Brief of amici curiae filed on behalf of the ACLU by Charles S. Sims, Bruce J. Ennis, Jr., and Richard M. Zuckerman.

Opposing Side (Petitioner / Appellant)

No briefs of amici curiae were filed in support of appellant.

IV. THE SUPREME COURT'S DECISION

"In argument before this Court, respondent has relied primarily on reasoning adopted by the District Court. He contends that a court cannot possibly ascertain the impartiality of a juror by relying solely upon the testimony of the juror in question. Given the human propensity for self-justification, respondent argues, the law must impute bias to jurors in Smith's position. We disagree. . . .

Due process means a jury capable and willing to decide the case solely on the evidence before it, and a trial judge ever watchful to prevent prejudicial occurrences and to determine the effect of such occurrences when they happen. Such determinations may properly be made at a hearing like that ordered in Remmer and held in this case.

The District Court and the Court of Appeals disregarded this doctrine.

[T]he Court of Appeals did not rely upon the District Court's imputation of bias. Indeed, it did not even reach the question of juror bias, holding instead that the prosecutors' failure to disclose Smith's application, without more, violated respondent's right to due process of law. . . .

The Court . . . recognize[s] that the aim of due process 'is not punishment of society for the misdeeds of the prosecutor but avoidance of an unfair trial to the accused.' . . .

In light of this principle, it is evident that the Court of Appeals erred when it concluded that prosecutorial misconduct alone requires a new trial. We do not condone the conduct of the prosecutors in this case. Nonetheless, . . . Smith's conduct did not impair his ability to render an impartial verdict. . . .

Accordingly, the judgment of the Court of Appeals is reversed."

V. JUSTICE VOTE

3 Pro ACLU Side vs. 6 Con Opposing Side

ACLU Side (Respondent / Appellee)

1. Marshall, T. – Wrote dissenting opinion
2. Brennan, W. – Joined dissenting opinion
3. Stevens, J. – Joined dissenting opinion

Opposing Side (Petitioner / Appellant)

1. Rehnquist, W. – Wrote majority opinion
2. Burger, W. – Joined majority opinion
3. White, B. – Joined majority opinion
4. Blackmun, H. – Joined majority opinion
5. Powell, L. – Joined majority opinion
6. O'Connor, S. – Wrote concurring opinion

VI. A WIN OR LOSS FOR THE ACLU?

The ACLU, as amicus curiae, urged affirmance of the Second Circuit Court of Appeals' judgment; the Supreme Court reversed in a 6-3 vote, giving the ACLU an apparent loss.

484. Murphy v. Hunt

(Decided March 2, 1982; 455 U.S. 478)

I. ISSUE

A. Issues Discussed

Criminal justice, Sixth Amendment, Eighth Amendment, Fourteenth Amendment, bail, mootness

B. Legal Question Presented

Does a provision of the Nebraska state constitution prohibiting pre-trial bail for certain sexual offense charges violate a defendant's federal constitutional rights under the Sixth, Eighth, and Fourteenth Amendments?

C. Supreme Court's Answer

The issue is moot because the defendant has already been tried and convicted and he only requested injunctive and declaratory relief; he did not bring a class action or seek damages for the pre-trial detention.

II. CASE SUMMARY

A. Background

"Appellee Hunt was charged with first-degree sexual assault on a child and three counts of first-degree forcible sexual assault. [H]is request for bail was denied. [T]he Nebraska

Constitution provides in relevant part: 'All persons shall be bailable . . . except for treason, sexual offenses involving penetration by force or against the will of the victim, and murder, where the proof is evident or the presumption great.' . . .

On June 9, 1980, pending trial on the charges against him, Hunt filed a complaint under 42 U.S.C. § 1983 in the United States District Court for the District of Nebraska. He claimed that Art. I, § 9, of the State Constitution, limiting bail in cases of first-degree sexual offenses, violated his federal constitutional rights to be free from excessive bail and cruel and unusual punishment, to due process and equal protection of the laws, and to the effective assistance of counsel under the Sixth, Eighth, and Fourteenth Amendments. He sought declaratory and injunctive relief only. On October 17, 1980, the District Court dismissed Hunt's civil rights complaint. Hunt appealed to the Court of Appeals for the Eighth Circuit.

Meanwhile, . . . he was found guilty of two of the three first-degree forcible sexual assault charges against him. [Then,] Hunt was convicted of first-degree sexual assault on a child. . . . Hunt appealed each of these convictions to the Nebraska Supreme Court and each of these appeals remains pending before that court.

On May 13, 1981, the Court of Appeals for the Eighth Circuit decided Hunt's appeal from the dismissal of his § 1983 claim. The court reversed the District Court and held that the exclusion of violent sexual offenses from bail before trial violates the Excessive Bail Clause of the Eighth Amendment of the United States Constitution."

The Supreme Court granted certiorari to review the case and vacated the Court of Appeals' judgment.

B. Counsel of Record / ACLU Attorney

ACLU Side (Respondent / Appellee): Bennett G. Hornstein argued the cause for appellee.

Opposing Side (Petitioner / Appellant): Terry R. Schaaf, Assistant Attorney General of Nebraska, argued the cause for appellant.

III. AMICI CURIAE

ACLU Side (Respondent / Appellee)

Brief of amici curiae filed on behalf of the ACLU by Irvin B. Nathan and David P. Towey.

Brief of amici curiae filed on behalf of the National Legal Aid and Defender Association, et al., by Sheldon Portman.

Brief of amici curiae filed on behalf of the State Public Defender of California by Quin Denvir and David R. Lipson.

Brief of amici curiae filed on behalf of the Legal Foundation of America by David Crump.

Opposing Side (Petitioner / Appellant)

Brief of amici curiae filed on behalf of Laws at Work, et al., by James P. Manak, G. Joseph Bertain, Jr., Lloyd F. Dunn, George Nicholson, Robert L. Toms, Donald E. Santarelli, William C. Summers, Jack Yelverton, George Deukmejian, Attorney General of California, and Richard S. Gebelein, Attorney General of Delaware.

Brief of amici curiae filed on behalf of the Washington Legal Foundation by Daniel J. Popeo, Paul D. Kamenar, and Nicholas E. Calio.

IV. THE SUPREME COURT'S DECISION

"In general a case becomes moot 'when the issues presented are no longer 'live' or the parties lack a legally cognizable interest in the outcome.' It would seem clear that under this general rule Hunt's claim to pretrial bail was moot once he was convicted. The question was no longer live because even a favorable decision on it would not have entitled Hunt to bail. For the same reason, Hunt no longer had a legally cognizable interest in the result in this case. He had not prayed for damages nor had he sought to represent a class of pretrial detainees. . . .

The Court has never held that a mere physical or theoretical possibility was sufficient . . . . If this were true, virtually any matter of short duration would be reviewable. Rather, we have said that there must be a 'reasonable expectation' or a 'demonstrated probability' that the same controversy will recur involving the same complaining party. We detect no such level of probability in this case. All we know from the record is that Hunt has been convicted on three separate offenses and that his counsel was willing to stipulate that, for the purposes of Hunt's eligibility for bail, the proof of guilt was evident and the presumption great. Based on these two facts, we cannot say that there exists a 'reasonable expectation' or 'demonstrated probability' that Hunt will ever again be in this position. There is no reason to expect that all three of Hunt's convictions will be overturned on appeal. Hunt's willingness to stipulate that the proof against him was 'evident' does not encourage us to believe otherwise. . . .

We have no reason to believe that Hunt will once again be in a position to demand bail before trial.

Accordingly, we find that the case presented is now moot. Indeed, it was moot at the time of the decisions of both the District Court and the Court of Appeals. The judgment of the Court of Appeals is vacated, and the case is remanded to the Court of Appeals with instructions that the complaint be dismissed."

V. JUSTICE VOTE

1 Pro ACLU Side vs. 8 Con Opposing Side

ACLU Side (Respondent / Appellee)

1. White, B. – Wrote dissenting opinion

Opposing Side (Petitioner / Appellant)

1. Burger, W. – Per curiam opinion
2. Brennan, W. – Per curiam opinion
3. Marshall, T. – Per curiam opinion
4. Blackmun, L. – Per curiam opinion
5. Powell, L. – Per curiam opinion
6. Rehnquist, W. – Per curiam opinion
7. Stevens, J. – Per curiam opinion
8. O'Connor, S. – Per curiam opinion

VI. A WIN OR LOSS FOR THE ACLU?

The ACLU filed a brief of amici curiae urging affirmance; the Supreme Court vacated and remanded the ruling of the Court of Appeals in an 8-1 vote, giving the ACLU an apparent loss.

485. Santosky v. Kramer

(Decided March 24, 1982; 455 U.S. 745)

I. ISSUE

A. Issues Discussed

Civil rights, state's rights, Fourteenth Amendment, due process, parental rights

B. Legal Question Presented

Does a state law requiring only "fair preponderance of evidence" to support the termination of parental rights violate the Due Process Clause of the Fourteenth Amendment?

C. Supreme Court's Answer

The fair preponderance standard violates the Due Process Clause; due process requires "at least clear and convincing evidence" to terminate parental rights.

II. CASE SUMMARY

A. Background

"Petitioners John Santosky II and Annie Santosky are the natural parents of Tina and John III. In November 1973, after incidents reflecting parental neglect, respondent Kramer, Commissioner of the Ulster County Department of Social Services, initiated a neglect proceeding under Fam.Ct.Act § 1022 and removed Tina from her natural home. About 10 months later, he removed John III and placed him with foster parents. On the day John was taken, Annie Santosky gave birth to a third child, Jed. When Jed was only three days old, respondent transferred him to a foster home on the ground that immediate removal was necessary to avoid imminent danger to his life or health.

In October 1978, respondent petitioned the Ulster County Family Court to terminate petitioners' parental rights in the three children. Petitioners challenged the constitutionality of the 'fair preponderance of the evidence' standard specified in Fam.Ct.Act § 622. The Family Court Judge rejected this constitutional challenge and weighed the evidence under the statutory standard. . . . The judge later held a dispositional hearing and ruled that the best interests of the three children required permanent termination of the Santoskys' custody.

Petitioners appealed, again contesting the constitutionality of § 622's standard of proof. The New York Supreme Court, Appellate Division, affirmed, holding application of the preponderance-of-the-evidence standard 'proper and constitutional.' That standard, the court reasoned, 'recognizes and seeks to balance rights possessed by the child . . . with those of the natural parents . . . .' The New York Court of Appeals then dismissed petitioners' appeal to that court 'upon the ground that no substantial constitutional question is directly involved.'"

The Supreme Court granted certiorari to review the case, vacated the decision, and remanded the case.

B. Counsel of Record / ACLU Attorney

ACLU Side (Petitioner / Appellant): Martin Guggenheim argued the cause for appellant.

Opposing Side (Respondent / Appellee): Steven Scavuzzo argued the cause for appellee, pro hac vice, by special leave of Court.

III. AMICI CURIAE

ACLU Side (Petitioner / Appellant)

Brief of amici curiae filed on behalf of the ACLU Children's Rights Project, et al., by Margaret Hayman, Abigail A. Jones, Marcia Robinson Lowry, George Kannar, and Steven R. Shapiro.

Brief of amici curiae filed on behalf of the Community Action for Legal Services, Inc., et al., by Louise Gruner Gans, Catherine P. Mitchell, Norman Siegel, Gary Connor, Louise Gruner Gans, Daniel Greenberg, Carolyn Kubitshek, Jean Schneider, Edward N. Simon, and Arnold Rothbaum.

Opposing Side (Respondent / Appellee)

Brief of amici curiae filed on behalf of the State of New York by Robert Abrams, Attorney General, Shirley Adelson Siegel, Solicitor General, and Lawrence J. Logan and Robert J. Schack, Assistant Attorneys General.

Brief of amici curiae filed on behalf of the State of Oregon by Dave Frohnmayer, Attorney General, William F. Gary, Solicitor General, and Jan Peter Londahl, Assistant Attorney General.

IV. THE SUPREME COURT'S DECISION

"Under New York law, the State may terminate, over parental objection, the rights of parents in their natural child upon a finding that the child is 'permanently neglected.' The New York Family Court Act § 622 requires that only a 'fair preponderance of the evidence' support that finding. Thus, in New York, the factual certainty required to extinguish the parent-child relationship is no greater than that necessary to award money damages in an ordinary civil action.

Today we hold that the Due Process Clause of the Fourteenth Amendment demands more than this. Before a State may sever completely and irrevocably the rights of parents in their natural child, due process requires that the State support its allegations by at least clear and convincing evidence. . . .

The fundamental liberty interest of natural parents in the care, custody, and management of their child does not evaporate simply because they have not been model parents or have lost temporary custody of their child to the State. Even when blood relationships are strained, parents retain a vital interest in preventing the irretrievable destruction of their family life. If anything, persons faced with forced dissolution of their parental rights have a more critical need for procedural protections than do those resisting state intervention into ongoing family affairs. When the State moves to destroy weakened familial bonds, it must provide the parents with fundamentally fair procedures. . . .

The logical conclusion of this balancing process is that the 'fair preponderance of the evidence' standard prescribed by Fam. Ct. Act § 622 violates the Due Process Clause of the Fourteenth Amendment. . . . The next question, then, is whether a 'beyond a reasonable doubt' or a 'clear and convincing' standard is constitutionally mandated. . . .

We, of course, express no view on the merits of petitioners' claims. At a hearing conducted under a constitutionally proper standard, they may or may not prevail. Without deciding the outcome under any of the standards we have approved, we vacate the judgment of the Appellate Division and remand the case for further proceedings not inconsistent with this opinion."

V. JUSTICE VOTE

5 Pro ACLU Side vs. 4 Con Opposing Side

ACLU Side (Petitioner / Appellant)

1. Blackmun, H. – Wrote majority opinion
2. Powell, L. – Joined majority opinion
3. Stevens, J. – Joined majority opinion
4. Brennan, W. – Joined majority opinion
5. Marshall, T. – Joined majority opinion

Opposing Side (Respondent / Appellee)

1. Rehnquist, W. – Wrote dissenting opinion

2. Burger, W. – Joined dissenting opinion
3. White, B. – Joined dissenting opinion
4. O'Connor, S. – Joined dissenting opinion

VI. A WIN OR LOSS FOR THE ACLU?

The ACLU filed a brief of amici curiae urging reversal; the Supreme Court reversed the lower court's ruling in a 5-4 vote, giving the ACLU an apparent win.

486. Larson v. Valente

(Decided April 21, 1982; 456 U.S. 228)

I. ISSUE

A. Issues Discussed

First Amendment, religion, Establishment Clause

B. Legal Question Presented

"[W]hether a Minnesota statute, imposing certain registration and reporting requirements upon only those religious organizations that solicit more than fifty per cent of their funds from nonmembers, discriminates against such organizations in violation of the Establishment Clause of the First Amendment."

C. Supreme Court's Answer

The fifty percent rule violates the Establishment Clause.

II. CASE SUMMARY

A. Background

Minnesota amended its charitable solicitation law in 1978 to exempt only religious organizations which solicited more than fifty percent of their contributions from members and affiliated organizations from filing "an extensive annual report" detailing the organization's finances. Prior to the amendment, all religious organizations were exempt from the reporting requirement. Religious organizations which received more than fifty percent of their revenue from nonmembers were required to register with the state, file financial disclosure forms, and be subjected to closer state scrutiny under the amended law.

Individual appellees, members of the Holy Spirit Association for the Unification of World Christianity ("Unification Church"), brought suit in the District Court for the District of Minnesota seeking "a declaration that the Act, on its face and as applied to them through [the] fifty per cent rule, constituted an abridgment of their First Amendment rights of expression and free exercise of religion, as well as a denial of their right to equal protection of the laws, guaranteed by the Fourteenth Amendment." After winning in trial court, the Court of Appeals for the Eighth Circuit vacated and remanded the lower court's favorable ruling. The Court of Appeals concluded that the "fifty per cent rule should be stricken," but organizations should not enjoy the religious organization exemption solely by claiming to be religious. Instead, the court determined that "proof of religious-organization status was required in order to gain the exemption."

The Supreme Court granted certiorari to review the case and affirmed.

B. Counsel of Record / ACLU Attorney

ACLU Side (Respondent / Appellee): Barry A. Fisher argued the cause for appellee.

Opposing Side (Petitioner / Appellant): Larry Salustro argued the cause for appellant.

III. AMICI CURIAE

ACLU Side (Respondent / Appellee)

Brief of amici curiae filed on behalf of the ACLU, et al., by Charles S. Sims and Bruce J. Ennis.

Brief of amici curiae filed on behalf of the American Jewish Congress by Nathan Z. Dershowitz.

Brief of amici curiae filed on behalf of the Americans United for Separation of Church and State Fund, Inc. by Lee Boothby.

Brief of amici curiae filed on behalf of the Center for Law and Religious Freedom of the Christian Legal Society by Robert L. Toms.

Brief of amici curiae filed on behalf of the General Conference of Seventh-Day Adventists, et al., by John W. Baker and Robert W. Nixon.

Brief of amici curiae filed on behalf of the Greater Minneapolis Association of Evangelicals by Thomas Stephen Neuberger and Thomas W. Strahan.

Opposing Side (Petitioner / Appellant)

No briefs of amici curiae were filed in support of appellant.

IV. THE SUPREME COURT'S DECISION

"The clearest command of the Establishment Clause is that one religious denomination cannot be officially preferred over another. . . .

Since Everson v. Board of Education, 330 U.S. 1 (1947), this Court has adhered to the principle, clearly manifested in the history and logic of the Establishment Clause, that no State can 'pass laws which aid one religion' or that 'prefer one religion over another.' . . .

The fifty per cent rule . . . clearly grants denominational preferences of the sort consistently and firmly deprecated in our precedents. Consequently, that rule must be invalidated unless it is justified by a compelling governmental interest, and unless it is closely fitted to further that interest. . . .

Appellants assert, and we acknowledge, that the State of Minnesota has a significant interest in protecting its citizens from abusive practices in the solicitation of funds for charity, and that this interest retains importance when the solicitation is conducted by a religious organization. We thus agree with the Court of Appeals that the Act, 'viewed as a whole, has a valid secular purpose,' and we will therefore assume, arguendo, that the Act generally is addressed to a sufficiently 'compelling' governmental interest. But our inquiry must focus more narrowly, upon the distinctions drawn by [the law], itself: Appellants must demonstrate that the challenged fifty per cent rule is closely fitted to further the interest that it assertedly serves.

Appellants argue that [the law's] distinction between contributions solicited from members and from nonmembers is eminently sensible. They urge that members are reasonably assumed to have significant control over the solicitation of contributions from themselves to their organization, and over the expenditure of the funds that they contribute, as well. . . .

We reject the argument, for it wholly fails to justify the only aspect of [the law], under attack—the selective fifty per cent rule. Appellants' argument is based on three distinct premises: that members of a religious organization can and will exercise supervision and control over the organization's solicitation activities when membership contributions exceed fifty per cent; that membership control, assuming its existence, is an adequate safeguard against abusive solicitations of the public by the organization; and that the need for public disclosure rises in proportion with the percentage of nonmember contributions. Acceptance of all three of these premises is necessary to appellants' conclusion, but we find no substantial support for any of them in the record. . . .

In sum, we conclude that the fifty per cent rule . . . is not closely fitted to the furtherance of any compelling governmental interest asserted by appellants, and that the provision therefore violates the Establishment Clause. Indeed, we think that [the] fifty per cent rule sets up precisely the sort of official denominational preference that the Framers of the First Amendment forbade. Accordingly, we hold that appellees cannot be compelled to register and report under the Act on the strength of that provision.

The judgment of the Court of Appeals is affirmed."

V. JUSTICE VOTE

5 Pro ACLU Side vs. 4 Con Opposing Side

ACLU Side (Respondent / Appellee)

1. Brennan, W. – Wrote majority opinion
2. Marshall, T. – Joined majority opinion
3. Blackmun, H. – Joined majority opinion
4. Powell, L. – Joined majority opinion
5. Stevens, J. – Wrote concurring opinion

Opposing Side (Petitioner / Appellant)

1. Rehnquist, W. – Wrote dissenting opinion, joined White's dissent
2. Burger, W. – Joined Rehnquist's dissent
3. O'Connor, S. – Joined Rehnquist's dissent
4. White, B. – Wrote dissenting opinion, joined Rehnquist's dissent

V. A WIN OR LOSS FOR THE ACLU?

The ACLU filed a brief of amicus curiae urging affirmance; the Supreme Court affirmed the ruling of the Eighth Circuit Court of Appeals in a 5-4 vote, giving the ACLU an apparent win.

487. Oregon v. Kennedy

(Decided May 24, 1982; 456 U.S. 667)

I. ISSUE

A. Issues Discussed

Criminal procedure, Fifth Amendment, double jeopardy

B. Legal Question Presented

Does prosecutorial misconduct that unintentionally leads to a mistrial bar a retrial under the Double Jeopardy Clause of the Fifth Amendment?

C. Supreme Court's Answer

A retrial is barred by double jeopardy only in circumstances where the misconduct was intended to provoke a mistrial.

II. CASE SUMMARY

A. Background

"Respondent was charged with the theft of an oriental rug. During his first trial, the State called an expert witness on the subject of Middle Eastern rugs to testify as to the value and the identity of the rug in question. On cross-examination, respondent's attorney apparently attempted to establish bias on the part of the expert witness by asking him whether he had filed a criminal complaint against respondent. The witness eventually acknowledged this fact, but explained that no action had been taken on his complaint. On redirect examination, the prosecutor sought to elicit the reasons why the witness had filed a complaint against respondent, but the trial court sustained a series of objections to this line of inquiry. [The prosecutor ultimately asked,] 'Is that because he is a crook?' The trial court then granted respondent's motion for a mistrial.

When the State later sought to retry respondent, he moved to dismiss the charges because of double jeopardy. After a hearing at which the prosecutor testified, the trial court found as a fact that 'it was not the intention of the prosecutor in this case to cause a mistrial.' On the basis of this finding, the trial court held that double jeopardy principles did not bar retrial, and respondent was then tried and convicted.

Respondent then successfully appealed to the Oregon Court of Appeals, which sustained his double jeopardy claim. . . .

The Court of Appeals accepted the trial court's finding that it was not the intent of the prosecutor to cause a mistrial. Nevertheless, the court held that retrial was barred because the prosecutor's conduct in this case constituted what it viewed as 'overreaching.' Although the prosecutor intended to rehabilitate the witness, the Court of Appeals expressed the view that the question was in fact 'a direct personal attack on the general character of the defendant.'"

The Supreme Court granted certiorari to review the case and reversed.

B. Counsel of Record / ACLU Attorney

ACLU Side (Respondent / Appellee): Donald C. Walker argued the cause for appellee.

Opposing Side (Petitioner / Appellant): Dave Frohnmayer, Attorney General of Oregon, argued the cause for appellant.

Samuel A. Alito, Jr., argued the cause for the United States, as amicus curiae, by special leave of Court.

III. AMICI CURIAE

ACLU Side (Respondent / Appellee)

Brief of amici curiae filed on behalf of the ACLU Foundation of Oregon, Inc., by Jennifer Friesen.

Opposing Side (Petitioner / Appellant)

Brief of amici curiae filed on behalf of the United States by Rex E. Lee, Solicitor General, D. Lowell Jensen, Assistant Attorney General Andrew L., Frey, Deputy Solicitor General, Samuel A. Alito, Jr., Assistant to the Solicitor General, and David B. Smith.

IV. THE SUPREME COURT'S DECISION

"Prosecutorial conduct that might be viewed as harassment or overreaching, even if sufficient to justify a mistrial on defendant's motion, . . . does not bar retrial absent intent on the part of the prosecutor to subvert the protections afforded by the Double Jeopardy Clause. A defendant's motion for a mistrial constitutes 'a deliberate election on his part to forgo his valued right to have his guilt or innocence determined before the first trier of fact.' . . . Only where the governmental conduct in question is intended to 'goad' the defendant into moving for a mistrial may a defendant raise the bar of double jeopardy to a second trial after having succeeded in aborting the first on his own motion.

Were we to embrace the broad and somewhat amorphous standard adopted by the Oregon Court of Appeals, we are not sure that criminal defendants as a class would be aided. . . .

Because of the confusion which these varying statements of the standard in question have occasioned in other courts, we deem it best to acknowledge the confusion and its justifiability in the light of these statements from previous decisions. We do not by this opinion lay down a flat rule that, where a defendant in a criminal trial successfully moves for a mistrial, he may not thereafter invoke the bar of double jeopardy against a second trial. But we do hold that the circumstances under which such a defendant may invoke the bar of double jeopardy in a second effort to try him are limited to those cases in which the conduct giving rise to the successful motion for a mistrial was intended to provoke the defendant into moving for a mistrial.

Since the Oregon trial court found, and the Oregon Court of Appeals accepted, that the prosecutorial conduct culminating in the termination of the first trial in this case was not so intended by the prosecutor, that is the end of the matter for purposes of the Double Jeopardy Clause of the Fifth Amendment to the United States Constitution. The judgment of the Oregon Court of Appeals is reversed, and the cause is remanded for further proceedings not inconsistent with this opinion."

V. JUSTICE VOTE

0 Pro ACLU Side vs. 9 Con Opposing Side

Opposing Side (Petitioner / Appellant)

1. Rehnquist, W. – Wrote majority opinion
2. Burger, W. – Joined majority opinion
3. White, B. – Joined majority opinion
4. O'Connor, S. – Joined majority opinion
5. Powell, L. – Wrote concurring opinion
6. Stevens, J. – Wrote concurring opinion
7. Brennan, W. – Wrote concurring opinion, joined Stevens' concurring opinion
8. Marshall, T. – Joined Brennan's concurrence, joined Stevens' concurrence
9. Blackmun, H. – Joined Stevens' concurrence

VI. A WIN OR LOSS FOR THE ACLU?

The ACLU filed as amicus curiae urging affirmance; the Supreme Court reversed the ruling of the Oregon Court of Appeals in a 9-0 vote, giving the ACLU an apparent loss.

488. United Steelworkers v. Sadlowski

(Decided June 14, 1982; 457 U.S. 102)

I. ISSUE

A. Issues Discussed

Governmental authority, unions, First Amendment, Labor-Management Reporting and Disclosure Act of 1959

B. Legal Question Presented

"[W]hether § 101(a)(2) of the Labor-Management Reporting and Disclosure Act of 1959 (LMRDA) . . . precludes the membership of a union from adopting a rule that prohibits candidates for union office from accepting campaign contributions from nonmembers."

C. Supreme Court's Answer

The LMRDA does not preclude a union from adopting a rule prohibiting candidates for union office from accepting campaign contributions from nonmembers.

II. CASE SUMMARY

A. Background

In 1978, petitioner, the United Steelworkers of America ("USWA"), adopted a rule prohibiting candidates running for union offices from accepting campaign contributions from people who are not members of the union. The union also created a committee with final decision-making power to enforce the "outsider rule."

Respondent Sadlowski was a member of the United Steelworkers of America. He lost a 1977 election for union office in which most of his financial support came from outside sources prior to the adoption of the "outsider rule." Sadlowski and other union members brought a suit against petitioner in the United States District Court for the District of Columbia claiming that the "outsider rule" violated the "right to sue" provision of the Labor-Management Reporting and Disclosure Act of 1959 (LMRDA), § 101(a)(4), which forbids unions from limiting the rights of its members to institute an action in any court or agency. The District Court ruled in favor of Sadlowski.

The Court of Appeals for the District of Columbia Circuit affirmed the lower court's finding that the "outsider rule" "violated the right-to-sue provision. However, it chose not to decide whether this violation alone justified an injunction restraining enforcement of the entire rule. It accepted respondents' argument, first raised on appeal, that the outsider rule also violated the § 101(a)(2) 'freedom of speech and assembly' provision, and that this violation justified the injunction."

The Supreme Court granted certiorari to review the case and reversed.

B. Counsel of Record / ACLU Attorney

ACLU Side (Respondent / Appellee): Joseph L. Rauh, Jr. argued the cause for appellee.

Opposing Side (Petitioner / Appellant): Michael H. Gottesman argued the cause for appellant.

III. AMICI CURIAE

ACLU Side (Respondent / Appellee)

Brief of amici curiae filed on behalf of the ACLU by Charles S. Sims.

Opposing Side (Petitioner / Appellant)

No briefs of amici curiae were filed in support of appellant.

IV. THE SUPREME COURT'S DECISION

"At the outset, we address respondents' contention that this case can be resolved simply by reference to First Amendment law. Respondents claim that § 101(a)(2) confers upon union members rights equivalent to the rights established by the First Amendment.

[H]istory reveals that Congress modeled Title I after the Bill of Rights, and that the legislators intended § 101(a)(2) to restate a principal First Amendment value—the right to speak one's mind without fear of reprisal. However, there is absolutely no indication that Congress intended the scope of § 101(a)(2) to be identical to the scope of the First Amendment. Rather, Congress' decision to include a proviso covering 'reasonable' rules refutes that proposition. . . .

To determine whether a union rule is valid under the statute, we first consider whether the rule interferes with an interest protected by the first part of § 101(a)(2). If it does, we then determine whether the rule is 'reasonable' and thus sheltered by the proviso to § 101(a)(2). . . .

Applying this form of analysis here, we conclude that the outsider rule is valid. Although it may limit somewhat the ability of insurgent union members to wage an effective campaign, an interest deserving some protection under the statute, it is rationally related to the union's legitimate interest in reducing outsider interference with union affairs. . . .

Although the outsider rule may implicate rights protected by §101(a)(2), it serves a legitimate purpose that is clearly protected under the statute. The union adopted the rule because it wanted to ensure that nonmembers do not unduly influence union affairs. . . .

The language of the rule contains no reference to litigation. In addition, the debates leading up to the passage of the rule do not contain any indication that the union intended the rule to apply in this context. But what is most persuasive, the Campaign Contribution Administrative Committee—which was given authority to make final and binding interpretations of the outsider rule—has issued an opinion concerning the impact of the outsider rule on the right to sue. In this opinion, it holds that 'the limitations imposed by Section 27 do not apply to the financing of lawsuits by non-members for the purpose of asserting the legal rights of candidates or other union members in connection with elections.' . . .

We hold that USWA's rule prohibiting candidates for union office from accepting campaign contributions from nonmembers does not violate §101(a)(2). Although it may interfere with rights Congress intended to protect, it is rationally related to a legitimate and protected purpose, and thus is sheltered by the proviso to §101(a)(2). We reverse the decision below and remand for further proceedings consistent with this opinion."

V. JUSTICE VOTE

4 Pro ACLU Side vs. 5 Con Opposing Side

ACLU Side (Respondent / Appellee)

1. White, B. – Wrote dissenting opinion
2. Burger, W. – Joined White's dissent
3. Brennan, W. – Joined White's dissent
4. Blackmun, H. – Joined White's dissent

Opposing Side (Petitioner / Appellant)

1. Marshall, T. – Wrote majority opinion
2. Powell, L. – Joined majority opinion
3. Rehnquist, W. – Joined majority opinion
4. Stevens, J. – Joined majority opinion
5. O'Connor, S. – Joined majority opinion

VI. A WIN OR LOSS FOR THE ACLU?

The ACLU filed a brief of amici curiae urging affirmance; the Supreme Court reversed the lower court's ruling in a 5-4 vote, giving the ACLU an apparent loss.

489. Middlesex County Ethics Committee v. Garden State Bar Association

(Decided June 21, 1982; 457 U.S. 423)

I. ISSUE

A. Issues Discussed

Civil rights, state's rights, abstention

B. Legal Question Presented

"[W]hether a federal court should abstain from considering a challenge to the constitutionality of disciplinary rules that are the subject of pending state disciplinary proceedings within the jurisdiction of the New Jersey Supreme Court."

C. Supreme Court's Answer

The federal court should abstain in this circumstance.

II. CASE SUMMARY

A. Background

The New Jersey Constitution grants "the State Supreme Court with the responsibility for licensing and disciplining attorneys admitted to practice law in the State." Complaints against attorneys move through a "three-tier procedure" in the court.

"Respondent Lennox Hinds, a member of the New Jersey Bar, served as executive director of the National Conference of Black Lawyers at the time of his challenged conduct. Hinds represented Joanne Chesimard in a civil proceeding challenging her conditions of confinement in jail. In 1977 Chesimard went to trial in state court for the murder of a policeman. Respondent Hinds was not a counsel of record for Chesimard in the murder case. However, at the outset of the criminal trial Hinds took part in a press conference, making statements critical of the trial and of the trial judge's judicial temperament and racial insensitivity."

The Middlesex County Ethics Committee concluded there was probable cause to believe that respondent had violated the Disciplinary Rules of the Code of Professional Responsibility by making statements "prejudicial to the administration of justice." Instead of answering these charges within ten days of this determination as required by the ethics rules, "Hinds and the three respondent organizations filed suit in the United States District Court for the District of New Jersey contending that the disciplinary rules violated respondents' First Amendment rights. . . .

The District Court granted petitioner's motion to dismiss based on Younger v. Harris, concluding that '[t]he principles of comity and federalism dictate that the federal court abstain so that the state is afforded the opportunity to interpret its rules in the face of a constitutional challenge.' At respondents' request the District Court reopened the case to allow respondents an opportunity to establish bad faith, harassment, or other extraordinary circumstance which would constitute an exception to Younger abstention. After two days of hearings the District Court found no evidence to justify an exception to the Younger abstention doctrine and dismissed the federal-court complaint.

A divided panel of the United States Court of Appeals for the Third Circuit reversed on the ground that the state bar disciplinary proceedings did not provide a meaningful opportunity to adjudicate constitutional claims."

The Supreme Court granted certiorari to review the case and reversed.

B. Counsel of Record / ACLU Attorney

ACLU Side (Respondent / Appellee): Morton Stavis argued the cause for appellee.

Opposing Side (Petitioner / Appellant): Mary Ann Burgess, Assistant Attorney General of New Jersey, argued the cause for appellant.

III. AMICI CURIAE

ACLU Side (Respondent / Appellee)

Brief of amici filed on behalf of the ACLU by Charles S. Sims and Arthur N. Eisenberg.

Brief of amici curiae filed on behalf of the National Alliance Against Racist and Political Repression by Max D. Stern and Roger Rice.

Brief of amici curiae filed on behalf of the NAACP Legal Defense and Educational Fund, Inc., et al., by Jack Greenberg, James M. Nabrit III, Charles Stephen Ralston, Gail J. Wright, and Bill Lann Lee.

Opposing Side (Petitioner / Appellant)

No briefs of amici curiae were filed in support of appellant.

IV. THE SUPREME COURT'S DECISION:

"Younger v. Harris, supra, and its progeny espouse a strong federal policy against federal-court interference with pending state judicial proceedings absent extraordinary circumstances. The policies underlying Younger abstention have been frequently reiterated by this Court. The notion of 'comity' includes 'a proper respect for state functions, a recognition of the fact that the entire country is made up of a Union of separate state governments, and a continuance of the belief that the National Government will fare best if the States and their institutions are left free to perform their separate functions in their separate ways.' Minimal respect for the state processes, of course, precludes any presumption that the state courts will not safeguard federal constitutional rights. . . .

The importance of the state interest in the pending state judicial proceedings and in the federal case calls Younger abstention into play. So long as the constitutional claims of respondents can be determined in the state proceedings and so long as there is no showing of bad faith, harassment, or some other extraordinary circumstance that would make abstention inappropriate, the federal courts should abstain. . . .

Respondents have not challenged the findings of the District Court that there was no bad faith or harassment on the part of petitioner and that the state rules were not 'flagrantly and patently' unconstitutional. We see no reason to disturb these findings, and no other extraordinary circumstances have been presented to indicate that abstention would not be appropriate. . . .

Because respondent Hinds had an 'opportunity to raise and have timely decided by a competent state tribunal the federal issues involved,' and because no bad faith, harassment, or other exceptional circumstances dictate to the contrary, federal courts should abstain from interfering with the ongoing proceedings. Accordingly, the judgment of the United States Court of Appeals for the Third Circuit is reversed, and the case is remanded for further proceedings consistent with this opinion."

V. JUSTICE VOTE

0 Pro ACLU Side vs. 9 Con Opposing Side

Opposing Side (Petitioner / Appellant)

1. Burger, W. – Wrote majority opinion
2. White, B. – Joined majority opinion

3. Powell, L. – Joined majority opinion
4. Rehnquist, W. – Joined majority opinion
5. O'Connor, S. – Joined majority opinion
6. Marshall, T. – Wrote concurring opinion
7. Blackmun, H. – Joined Marshall's concurrence
8. Stevens, J. – Joined Marshall's concurrence
9. Brennan, W. – Wrote concurring opinion, joined Marshall's concurrence

VI. A WIN OR LOSS FOR THE ACLU?

The ACLU filed as amicus curiae urging affirmance; the Supreme Court reversed and remanded the ruling of the Court of Appeals for the Third Circuit in a 9-0 vote, giving the ACLU an apparent loss.

490. Taylor v. Alabama

(Decided June 23, 1982; 457 U.S. 687)

I. ISSUE

A. Issues Discussed

Criminal justice, Fourth Amendment, Fifth Amendment

B. Legal Question Presented

"[W]hether petitioner's confession should have been suppressed as the fruit of an illegal arrest."

C. Supreme Court's Answer

Petitioner's confession should have been suppressed as the fruit of an illegal arrest.

II. CASE SUMMARY

A. Background

Petitioner Omar Taylor was arrested without a warrant in connection with a 1978 grocery store robbery in Montgomery, Alabama. "An individual who was at that time incarcerated on unrelated charges told a police officer that 'he had heard that [petitioner] Omar Taylor was involved in the robbery.' This individual had never before given similar information to this officer, did not tell the officer where he had heard this information, and did not provide any details of the crime. This tip was insufficient to give the police probable cause to obtain a warrant or to arrest petitioner."

The petitioner was given his Miranda warnings and taken to the station. "At the station, he was fingerprinted, readvised of his Miranda rights, questioned, and placed in a lineup. The victims of the robbery were unable to identify him in the lineup. The police told petitioner that his fingerprints matched those on some grocery items that had been handled by one of the participants in the robbery. After a short visit with his girlfriend and a male companion, petitioner signed a waiver-of- rights form and executed a written confession. The form and the signed confession were admitted into evidence.

Petitioner objected to the admission of this evidence at his trial. He argued that his warrantless arrest was not supported by probable cause, that he had been involuntarily transported to the police station, and that the confession must be suppressed as the fruit of this illegal arrest. The trial court overruled this objection, and petitioner was convicted. On appeal, the Alabama Court of Criminal Appeals reversed . . . . The Alabama Supreme Court reversed the Court of Criminal Appeals."

The Supreme Court granted certiorari to review the case and reversed.

B. Counsel of Record / ACLU Attorney

ACLU Side (Petitioner / Appellant): Robert M. Beno argued the cause for appellant.

Opposing Side (Respondent / Appellee): Thomas R. Allison argued the cause for appellee.

III. AMICI CURIAE

ACLU Side (Petitioner/Appellant):
Opposing Side (Respondent/Appellee):
Brief of amici curiae filed on behalf of the ACLU by Arthur F. Mathews, James E. Coleman, Jr., Fern B. Kaplan, and Nicholas S. Zeppos Brief of amici curiae filed on behalf of Americans for Effective Law Enforcement, Inc., et al., by Fred E. Inbau, Wayne W. Schmidt, James P. Manak, Patrick F. Healy, William K. Lambie, Richard J. Brzeczek, Frank G. Carrington, William C. Summers, Courtney A. Evans, Robert K. Corbin, Attorney General of Arizona, and Steven J. Twist, Chief Assistant Attorney General, Tyrone C. Fahner, Attorney General of Illinois, and Melbourne Noel, Chief Assistant Attorney General, and William L. Parker, Jr.

IV. THE SUPREME COURT'S DECISION

"In Brown v. Illinois, supra, and Dunaway v. New York, supra, the police arrested suspects without probable cause. The suspects were transported to police headquarters, advised of their Miranda rights, and interrogated. They confessed within two hours of their arrest. This court held that the confessions were not admissible at trial, reasoning that a confession obtained through custodial interrogation after an illegal arrest should be excluded unless intervening events break the causal connection between the illegal arrest and the confession so that the confession is 'sufficiently an act of free will to purge the primary taint.' This Court identified several factors that should be considered in determining whether a confession has been purged of the taint of the illegal arrest: '[the] temporal proximity of the arrest and the confession, the presence of intervening circumstances, . . . and, particularly, the purpose and flagrancy of the official misconduct.' . . .

In Brown and Dunaway, this Court firmly established that the fact that the confession may be 'voluntary' for purposes of the Fifth Amendment, in the sense that Miranda warnings were given and understood, is not by itself sufficient to purge the taint of the illegal arrest. In this situation, a finding of 'voluntariness' for purposes of the Fifth Amendment is merely a threshold requirement for Fourth Amendment analysis. . . .

This case is a virtual replica of both Brown and Dunaway. Petitioner was arrested without probable cause in the hope that something would turn up, and he confessed shortly thereafter without any meaningful intervening event. The State's arguments to the contrary are unpersuasive. . . .

In sum, petitioner's confession was the fruit of his illegal arrest. Under our decisions in Brown v. Illinois and Dunaway v. New York, the confession clearly should not have been admitted at his trial. Accordingly, we reverse the decision of the Alabama Supreme Court and remand this case for further proceedings not inconsistent with this opinion."

V. JUSTICE VOTE

5 Pro ACLU Side vs. 4 Con Opposing Side

ACLU Side (Petitioner / Appellant)

1. Marshall, T. – Wrote majority opinion
2. Brennan, W. – Joined majority opinion
3. White, B. – Joined majority opinion
4. Blackmun H. – Joined majority opinion
5. Stevens, J. – Joined majority opinion

Opposing Side (Respondent / Appellee)

1. O'Connor, S. – Wrote dissenting opinion
2. Burger, W. – Joined O'Connor's dissent
3. Powell, L. – Joined O'Connor's dissent
4. Rehnquist, W. – Joined O'Connoer's dissent

VI. A WIN OR LOSS FOR THE ACLU?

The ACLU filed as amicus curiae urging reversal; the Supreme Court reversed the ruling of the Alabama Supreme Court in a 5-4 vote, giving the ACLU an apparent win.

491. Board of Education v. Pico

(Decided June 25, 1982; 457 U.S. 853)

I. ISSUE

A. Issues Discussed

First Amendment, freedom of speech

B. Legal Question Presented

"[W]hether the First Amendment imposes limitations upon the exercise by a local school board of its discretion to remove library books from high school and junior high school libraries."

C. Supreme Court's Answer

The school board may not remove library books solely because the board disapproves of the books' content.

II. CASE SUMMARY

A. Background

"Petitioners are the Board of Education of the Island Trees Union Free School District No. 26, in New York, [and individual Board members Ahrens, Martis, Fasulo, Hughes, Melchers, Michaels, and Nessim.] The Board is a state agency charged with responsibility for the operation and administration of the public schools within the Island Trees School District, including the Island Trees High School and Island Trees Memorial Junior High School. . . .When this suit was brought, [respondents] Pico, Gold, Yarris, and Rieger were students at the High School, and [respondent] Sochinski was a student at the Junior High School.

In September 1975, petitioners Ahrens, Martin, and Hughes attended a conference sponsored by Parents of New York United (PONYU), a politically conservative organization of parents concerned about education legislation in the State of New York. At the conference these petitioners obtained lists of books described by Ahrens as 'objectionable,' and by Martin as 'improper fare for school students.' It was later determined that the High School library contained nine of the listed books, and that another listed book was in the Junior High School library. In February 1976, at a meeting with the Superintendent of Schools and the Principals of the High School and Junior High School, the Board gave an 'unofficial direction' that the listed books be removed from the library shelves and delivered to the Board's offices, so that Board members could read them. When this directive was carried out, it became publicized, and the Board issued a press release justifying its action. It characterized the removed books as 'anti-American, anti-Christian, anti-Sem[i]tic, and just plain filthy,' and concluded that '[i]t is our duty, our moral obligation, to protect the children in our schools from this moral danger as surely as from physical and medical dangers.'

A short time later, the Board appointed a 'Book Review Committee,' consisting of four Island Trees parents and four members of the Island Trees schools staff, to read the listed books and to recommend to the Board whether the books should be retained . . . . In July, the Committee made its final report to the Board, recommending that five of the listed books be retained . . . . The Board substantially rejected the Committee's report . . . , deciding that only one book should be returned to the High School library without restriction, that another should be made available subject to parental approval, but that the remaining nine books should 'be removed from elementary and secondary libraries and [from] use in the curriculum.' . . .

Respondents reacted to the Board's decision by bringing the present action under 42 U.S.C. § 1983 in the United States District Court for the Eastern District of New York. . . .

Respondents claimed that the Board's actions denied them their rights under the First Amendment. They asked the court for a declaration that the Board's actions were unconstitutional, and for preliminary and permanent injunctive relief ordering the Board to return the nine books to the school libraries and to refrain from interfering with the use of those books in the schools' curricula.

The District Court granted summary judgment in favor of petitioners. . . .

A three-judge panel of the United States Court of Appeals for the Second Circuit reversed the judgment of the District Court, and remanded the action for a trial on respondents' allegations."

The Supreme Court granted certiorari to review the case and affirmed the judgment of the Second Circuit Court of Appeals.

B. Counsel of Record / ACLU Attorney

ACLU Side (Respondent / Appellee): Alan H. Levine, New York Civil Liberties Union, argued the cause for appellee. With him on the brief were Steven R. Shapiro, Burt Neuborne, Alan Azzara, Bruce J. Ennis, Jr., and Charles S. Sims.

Opposing Side (Petitioner / Appellant): George W. Lipp, Jr., argued the cause for appellant. With him on the briefs was David S. J. Rubin.

III. AMICI CURIAE

ACLU Side (Respondent / Appellee)

Opposing Side (Petitioner / Appellant)

Briefs of amici curiae were on behalf of the American Federation of Labor and Congress of Industrial Organizations, et al., the American Library Association, et al., the Anti-Defamation League of B'nai B'rith, the Association of American Publishers, Inc., et al., the Authors League of America, Inc., the National Education Association, New York State United Teachers, the American Jewish Congress, et al., the Long Island Library Association Coalition and P. E. N. American Center. Brief of amici curiae filed on behalf of Charles H. Keating, Jr., et al., by Bruce A. Taylor and Fredrick D. Merrill.

Brief of amici curiae filed on behalf of the Legal Foundation of America by David Crump, Susan E. Waite, and Timothy T. Cooper.

IV. THE SUPREME COURT'S DECISION

"The Court has long recognized that local school boards have broad discretion in the management of school affairs. Epperson v. Arkansas reaffirmed that, by and large, 'public education in our Nation is committed to the control of state and local authorities,' and that federal courts should not ordinarily 'intervene in the resolution of conflicts which arise in the daily operation of school systems.' Tinker v. Des Moines School Dist. noted that we have 'repeatedly emphasized . . . the comprehensive authority of the States and of school officials . . . to prescribe and control conduct in the schools.' We have also acknowledged that public schools are vitally important 'in the preparation of individuals for participation as citizens,' and as vehicles for 'inculcating fundamental values necessary to the maintenance of a democratic political system.' We are therefore in full agreement with petitioners that local school boards must be permitted 'to establish and apply their curriculum in such a way as to transmit community values,' and that 'there is a legitimate and substantial community interest in promoting respect for authority and traditional values be they social, moral, or political.'

At the same time, however, we have necessarily recognized that the discretion of the States and local school boards in matters of education must be exercised in a manner that comports with the transcendent imperatives of the First Amendment. . . .

In sum, just as access to ideas makes it possible for citizens generally to exercise their rights of free speech and press in a meaningful manner, such access prepares students for active and effective participation in the pluralistic, often contentious society in which they will soon be adult members. Of course all First Amendment rights accorded to students must be construed 'in light of the special characteristics of the school environment.' But the special characteristics of the school library make that environment especially appropriate for the recognition of the First Amendment rights of students.

A school library, no less than any other public library, is 'a place dedicated to quiet, to knowledge, and to beauty.' . . . Petitioners emphasize the inculcative function of secondary education, and argue that they must be allowed unfettered discretion to 'transmit community values' through the Island Trees schools. But that sweeping claim overlooks the unique role of the school library. It appears from the record that use of the Island Trees school libraries is completely voluntary on the part of students. Their selection of books from these libraries is entirely a matter of free choice; the libraries afford them an opportunity at self-education and individual enrichment that is wholly optional. Petitioners might well defend their claim of absolute discretion in matters of curriculum by reliance upon their duty to inculcate community values. But we think that petitioners' reliance upon that duty is misplaced where, as here, they attempt to extend their claim of absolute discretion beyond the compulsory environment of the classroom, into the school library and the regime of voluntary inquiry that there holds sway.

[N]othing in our decision today affects in any way the discretion of a local school board to choose books to add to the libraries of their schools. Because we are concerned in this case with the suppression of ideas, our holding today affects only the discretion to remove books. In brief, we hold that local school boards may not remove books from school library shelves simply because they dislike the ideas contained in those books and seek by their removal to 'prescribe what shall be orthodox in politics, nationalism, religion, or other matters of opinion.' Such purposes stand inescapably condemned by our precedents."

The Supreme Court affirmed the judgment of the Second Circuit Court of Appeals.

V. JUSTICE VOTE

5 Pro ACLU Side vs. 4 Con Opposing Side

ACLU Side (Respondent / Appellee)

1. Brennan, W. – Wrote majority opinion
2. Marshall, T. – Joined majority opinion
3. Stevens, J. – Joined majority opinion
4. Blackmun H. – Wrote concurring opinion
5. White, B. – Wrote concurring opinion

Opposing Side (Petitioner / Appellant)

1. Burger, W. – Wrote dissenting opinion, joined Rehnquist's dissent
2. Powell, L. – Wrote dissenting opinion, joined Burger's dissent, joined Rehnquist's dissent
3. O'Connor, S. – Wrote dissenting opinion, joined Burger's dissent
4. Rehnquist, W. – Wrote dissenting opinion, joined Burger's dissent

V. A WIN OR LOSS FOR THE ACLU?

The ACLU, as counsel, urged affirmance of the judgment of the Second Circuit Court of Appeals; the Supreme Court affirmed in a 5-4 vote, giving the ACLU an apparent win.

492. Board Of Education v. Rowley

(Decided June 28, 1982; 458 U.S. 176)

I. ISSUE

A. Issues Discussed

Governmental authority, education

B. Legal Question Presented

Does the Education of the Handicapped Act require a State to "maximize the potential of handicapped children 'commensurate with the opportunity provided to other children'"?

C. Supreme Court's Answer

The Act requires "free appropriate public education" for handicapped children, but this does not require the State to maximize a handicapped child's potential commensurate with other children.

II. CASE SUMMARY

A. Background

Respondent Amy Rowley was a deaf student. Handicapped students, including deaf students, are able to obtain "a free appropriate public education" funded by federal money allocated to states through the Education of the Handicapped Act (Act) and governed by the strict rules and procedures of the Act. With the participation of the parents or guardian of affected children and school officials, States are required to submit an annual individualized educational program (IEP) for each child. Under the Act, respondent had been provided with a hearing aid and a tutor. When her parents' request for an interpreter was denied, respondent, through her parents, filed a case in the District Court for the Southern District of New York, requesting that the child be provided with a qualified sign-language interpreter in all of her academic classes because they alleged the lack of interpreter denied respondent of "free appropriate public education" required by the Act. The District Court found in favor of respondent, holding that a "free appropriate public education" meant that she was entitled to "'an opportunity to achieve [her] full potential commensurate with the opportunity provided to other children.'" The "Court of Appeals for the Second Circuit affirmed."

The Supreme Court granted certiorari to review the case and reversed.

B. Counsel of Record / ACLU Attorney

ACLU Side (Respondent / Appellee): Michael A. Chatoff argued the cause for appellee.

Elliott Schulder argued the cause for the United States, as amicus curiae, by special leave of Court.

Opposing Side (Petitioner / Appellant): Raymond G. Kuntz argued the cause for appellant.

III. AMICI CURIAE

ACLU Side (Respondent / Appellee)

Brief of amici curiae filed on behalf of the ACLU by Charles S. Sims.

Brief of amici curiae filed on behalf of the United States by Elliott Schulder, Solicitor General Lee, Assistant Attorney General Reynolds, Walter W. Barnett, and Louise A. Lerner.

Additional briefs of amici curiae were filed on behalf of the Association for Retarded Citizens of the United States, et al., the Maryland Advocacy Unit for the Developmentally Disabled, Inc., et al., the National Association of the Deaf, et al, the New York State Commission on the Quality of Care for the Mentally Disabled, Protection and Advocacy System, and the United Cerebral Palsy Associations, Inc., et al.

Opposing Side (Petitioner / Appellant)

Brief of amici curiae filed on behalf of the National School Boards Association, et al., by Norman H. Gross, Gwendolyn H. Gregory, Thomas A. Shannon, and August W. Steinhilber.

IV. THE SUPREME COURT'S DECISION

"We previously have cautioned that courts lack the 'specialized knowledge and experience' necessary to resolve 'persistent and difficult questions of educational policy.' We think that Congress shared that view when it passed the Act. As already demonstrated, Congress' intention was not that the Act displace the primacy of States in the field of education, but that States receive funds to assist them in extending their educational systems to the handicapped. Therefore, once a court determines that the requirements of the Act have been met, questions of methodology are for resolution by the States. . . .

Entrusting a child's education to state and local agencies does not leave the child without protection. Congress sought to protect individual children by providing for parental involvement in the development of state plans and policies, and in the formulation of the child's individual educational program. . . .

Applying these principles to the facts of this case, we conclude that the Court of Appeals erred in affirming the decision of the District Court. Neither the District Court nor the Court of Appeals found that petitioners had failed to comply with the procedures of the Act, and the findings of neither court would support a conclusion that Amy's educational program failed to comply with the substantive requirements of the Act. On the contrary, the District Court found that the 'evidence firmly establishes that Amy is receiving an 'adequate' education, since she performs better than the average child in her class and is advancing easily from grade to grade.' In light of this finding, and of the fact that Amy was receiving personalized instruction and related services calculated by the Furnace Woods school administrators to meet her educational needs, the lower courts should not have concluded that the Act requires the provision of a sign-language interpreter. Accordingly, the decision of the Court of Appeals is reversed, and the case is remanded for further proceedings consistent with this opinion."

V. JUSTICE VOTE

3 Pro ACLU Side vs. 6 Con Opposing Side

ACLU Side (Respondent / Appellee)

1. White, B. – Wrote dissenting opinion
2. Brennan, W. – Joined White's dissent
3. Marshall, T. – Joined White's dissent

Opposing Side (Petitioner / Appellant)

1. Rehnquist, W. – Wrote majority opinion
2. Burger, W. – Joined majority opinion
3. Blackmun, H. – Wrote concurring opinion
4. Powell, L. – Joined majority opinion
5. Stevens, J. – Joined majority opinion
5. O'Connor, S. – Joined majority opinion

VI. A WIN OR LOSS FOR THE ACLU?

The ACLU filed as amicus curiae urging affirmance; the Supreme Court reversed the Court of Appeals in a 6-3 vote, giving the ACLU an apparent loss.

493. Washington v. Seattle School District No. 1

(Decided June 30, 1982; 458 U.S. 457)

I. ISSUE

A. Issues Discussed

Civil rights, race, Fourteenth Amendment, equal protection

B. Legal Question Presented

"[W]hether an elected local school board may use the Fourteenth Amendment to defend its program of busing for integration from attack by the State."

C. Supreme Court's Answer

The school board may use the Fourteenth Amendment to defend its busing program, however, the initiative passed to prevent busing violates the Equal Protection Clause of the Fourteenth Amendment.

II. CASE SUMMARY

A. Background

In 1978, Appellee Seattle School District No. 1 enacted the "Seattle Plan" for desegregation of its schools. The plan made "extensive use of busing and mandatory reassignments." Subsequently, opponents of mandatory desegregation drafted statewide Initiative 350 to terminate the use of mandatory busing for purposes of racial integration in the public schools of the state of Washington. The initiative prohibited school boards from requiring "any student to attend a school other than the school which is geographically nearest or next nearest the student's place of residence." It "set out, however, a number of broad exceptions to this requirement," including assignment for special educational programs, or if the nearest school "is unfit or inadequate because of overcrowding, unsafe conditions or lack of physical facilities."

After the initiative passed, the Seattle School District No. 1 school officials, together with two other districts, brought suit against appellant, the State of Washington, in "District Court for the Western District of Washington, challenging the constitutionality of Initiative 350 under the Equal Protection Clause of the Fourteenth Amendment."

The District Court held the initiative unconstitutional on the ground that it established an "impermissible racial classification," among other concerns, and "permanently enjoined implementation of the initiative's restrictions." The Court of Appeals for the Ninth Circuit affirmed, entirely on the basis of the District Court's "impermissible racial classification" rationale.

The Supreme Court granted certiorari to review the case and affirmed.

B. Counsel of Record / ACLU Attorney

ACLU Side (Respondent / Appellee): Michael W. Hoge argued the cause for appellee. With him on the brief for appellee Seattle School District No. 1, et al., were Camden M. Hall and David J. Burman.

Phillip L. Burton, Frederick L. Noland, Thomas A. Lemly, and William H. Neukom filed a brief for appellee the American Civil Liberties Union, et al.

Ladd Leavens filed a brief for appellee East Pasco Neighborhood Council, et al.

Opposing Side (Petitioner / Appellant): Kenneth O. Eikenberry, Attorney General of Washington, argued the cause for appellant. With him on the briefs were Malachy R. Murphy, Deputy Attorney General, Thomas F. Carr, Senior Assistant Attorney General and Timothy R. Malone, Assistant Attorney General.

Solicitor General Lee, Assistant Attorney General Reynolds, Deputy Solicitor General Wallace, and Richard G. Wilkins filed a brief for the United States.

III. AMICI CURIAE

ACLU Side (Respondent / Appellee)

Briefs of amici curiae were filed on behalf of Grant L. Anderson, et al., the League of Women Voters of Seattle, et al., the NAACP Legal Defense and Educational Fund, the Washington Education Association, the National School Boards Association, and the Seattle Chapter Japanese American Citizens League.

Opposing Side (Petitioner / Appellant)

No briefs of amici curiae were filed in support of appellant.

IV. THE SUPREME COURT'S DECISION

"Initiative 350, however, works something more than the 'mere repeal' of a desegregation law by the political entity that created it. It burdens all future attempts to integrate Washington schools in districts throughout the State, by lodging decision making authority over the question at a new and remote level of government. . . .

It would be equally questionable for a community to require that laws or ordinances 'designed to ameliorate race relations or to protect racial minorities,' be confirmed by popular vote of the electorate as a whole, while comparable legislation is exempted from a similar procedure. The amendment addressed in Hunter [v. Erikson]—and, as we have explained, the legislation at issue here—was less obviously pernicious than are these examples, but was no different in principle. . . .

In reaching this conclusion, we do not undervalue the magnitude of the State's interest in its system of education. Washington could have reserved to state officials the right to make all decisions in the areas of education and student assignment. It has chosen, however, to use a more elaborate system; having done so, the State is obligated to operate that system within the confines of the Fourteenth Amendment. That, we believe, it has failed to do.

Accordingly, the judgment of the Court of Appeals is affirmed."

V. JUSTICE VOTE

5 Pro ACLU Side vs. 4 Con Opposing Side

ACLU Side (Respondent / Appellee)

1. Blackmun, H. – Wrote majority opinion
2. Brennan, W. – Joined majority opinion
3. Marshall, T. – Joined majority opinion
4. Stevens, J. – Joined majority opinion
5. White, B. – Joined majority opinion

Opposing Side (Petitioner / Appellant)

1. Powell, L. Wrote dissenting opinion
2. Burger, W. – Joined Powell's dissent
3. O'Connor, S. – Joined Powell's dissent
4. Rehnquist, W. – Joined Powell's dissent

VI. A WIN OR LOSS FOR THE ACLU?

The ACLU, as counsel, urged affirmance of the judgment of the Court of Appeals; the Supreme Court affirmed in a 5-4 vote, giving the ACLU an apparent win.

494. Mississippi Univ. for Women v. Hogan

(Decided July 1, 1982; 458 U.S. 718)

I. ISSUE

A. Issues Discussed

Civil rights, gender

B. Legal Question Presented

"[W]hether a state statute that excludes males from enrolling in a state-supported professional nursing school violates the Equal Protection Clause of the Fourteenth Amendment."

C. Supreme Court's Answer

"[W]e conclude that the State's policy of excluding males from MUW's School of Nursing violates the Equal Protection Clause of the Fourteenth Amendment . . . ."

II. CASE SUMMARY

A. Background

"In 1884, the Mississippi Legislature created the Mississippi Industrial Institute and College for the Education of White Girls of the State of Mississippi, now the oldest state-supported all-female college in the United States. The school, known today as Mississippi University for Women (MUW), has from its inception limited its enrollment to women.

In 1971, MUW established a School of Nursing . . . . The School of Nursing has its own faculty and administrative officers and establishes its own criteria for admission.

Respondent, Joe Hogan, is a registered nurse but does not hold a baccalaureate degree in nursing. . . . In 1979, Hogan applied for admission to the MUW School of Nursing's baccalaureate program. Although he was otherwise qualified, he was denied admission to the School of Nursing solely because of his sex. . . .

Hogan filed an action in the United States District Court for the Northern District of Mississippi, claiming the single-sex admissions policy of MUW's School of Nursing violated the Equal Protection Clause of the Fourteenth Amendment. Hogan sought injunctive and declaratory relief, as well as compensatory damages.

Following a hearing, the District Court denied preliminary injunctive relief. . . . When Hogan offered no further evidence, the District Court entered summary judgment in favor of the State.

The Court of Appeals for the Fifth Circuit reversed . . . ."

The Supreme Court granted certiorari to review the case.

B. Counsel of Record

ACLU Side (Respondent / Appellee): Wilbur O. Colom argued the cause for appellee. With him on the briefs were W. Wayne Drinkwater, Jr., and Shirley Payne of the American Civil Liberties Union of Mississippi.

Opposing Side (Petitioner / Appellant): Hunter M. Gholson argued the cause for appellants. With him on the briefs were Bill Attain, Attorney General of Mississippi, and Ed Davis Noble, Jr., Assistant Attorney General.

III. AMICI CURIAE

ACLU Side (Respondent / Appellee)

Brief of amici curiae filed on behalf of the National Women's Law Center et al. by Zona Fairbanks Hostetler, Suellen Terrill Keiner, Phyllis N. Segal, Marcia D. Greenberger, and Judith L. Lichtman.

Opposing Side (Petitioner / Appellant)

No briefs of amici curiae were filed on behalf of appellants.

IV. THE SUPREME COURT'S DECISION

"Because the challenged policy expressly discriminates among applicants on the basis of gender, it is subject to scrutiny under the Equal Protection Clause of the Fourteenth Amendment. . . . Our decisions also establish that the party seeking to uphold a statute that classifies individuals on the basis of their gender must carry the burden of showing an 'exceedingly persuasive justification' for the classification. The burden is met only by showing at least that the classification serves 'important governmental objectives and that the discriminatory means employed' are 'substantially related to the achievement of those objectives.' . . .

The State's primary justification for maintaining the single-sex admissions policy of MUW's School of Nursing is that it compensates for discrimination against women and, therefore, constitutes educational affirmative action. As applied to the School of Nursing, we find the State's argument unpersuasive. . . .

The policy is invalid also because it fails the second part of the equal protection test, for the State has made no showing that the gender-based classification is substantially and directly related to its proposed compensatory objective. To the contrary, MUW's policy of permitting men to attend classes as auditors fatally undermines its claim that women, at least those in the School of Nursing, are adversely affected by the presence of men. . . .

Thus, considering both the asserted interest and the relationship between the interest and the methods used by the State, we conclude that the State has fallen far short of establishing the 'exceedingly persuasive justification' needed to sustain the gender-based classification. Accordingly, we hold that MUW's policy of denying males the right to enroll for credit in its School of Nursing violates the Equal Protection Clause of the Fourteenth Amendment. . . .

In an additional attempt to justify its exclusion of men from MUW's School of Nursing, the State contends that MUW is the direct beneficiary 'of specific congressional legislation which, on its face, permits the institution to exist as it has in the past.' . . .

The fact that the language of § 901(a)(5) applies to MUW provides the State no solace: '[A] statute apparently governing a dispute cannot be applied by judges, consistently with their obligations under the Supremacy Clause, when such an application of the statute would conflict with the Constitution.' . . .

Because we conclude that the State's policy of excluding males from MUW's School of Nursing violates the Equal Protection Clause of the Fourteenth Amendment, we affirm the judgment of the Court of Appeals."

V. JUSTICE VOTE

5 Pro ACLU Side vs. 4 Con Opposing Side

ACLU Side (Respondent / Appellee)

1. O'Connor, S. – Wrote majority opinion
2. Brennan, W. – Joined majority opinion
3. White, B. – Joined majority opinion
4. Marshall, T. – Joined majority opinion
5. Stevens, J. – Joined majority opinion

Opposing Side (Petitioner / Appellant)

1. Rehnquist, W. – Joined Powell's dissent
2. Burger, W. – Wrote dissenting opinion
3. Powell, L. – Wrote dissenting opinion
4. Blackmun, H. – Wrote dissenting opinion

VI. A WIN OR LOSS FOR THE ACLU?

The ACLU served as counsel for appellee urging affirmance; the Supreme Court affirmed the Court of Appeals' decision by a 5-4 vote, giving the ACLU an apparent win.

495. New York v. Ferber

(Decided July 2, 1982; 458 U.S. 747)

I. ISSUE

A. Issues Discussed

1st Amendment, press, speech, association, obscenity

B. Legal Question Presented

"'To prevent the abuse of children who are made to engage in sexual conduct for commercial purposes, could the New York State Legislature, consistent with the First Amendment, prohibit the dissemination of material which shows children engaged in sexual conduct, regardless of whether such material is obscene?'"

C. Supreme Court's Answer

"We hold that [the New York child pornography law] § 263.15 sufficiently describes a category of material the production and distribution of which is not entitled to First Amendment protection. . . .

[W]e [further] hold that § 263.15 is not substantially overbroad. We consider this the paradigmatic case of a state statute whose legitimate reach dwarfs its arguably impermissible applications."

II. CASE SUMMARY

A. Background

"This case arose when Paul Ferber, the proprietor of a Manhattan bookstore specializing in sexually oriented products, sold two films to an undercover police officer. The films are devoted almost exclusively to depicting young boys masturbating. Ferber was indicted on two counts of violating § 263.10 and two counts of violating § 263.15, the two New York laws controlling dissemination of child pornography. After a jury trial, Ferber was acquitted of the two counts of promoting an obscene sexual performance, but found guilty of the two counts under § 263.15, which did not require proof that the films were obscene. Ferber's convictions were affirmed without opinion by the Appellate Division of the New York State Supreme Court.

The New York Court of Appeals reversed . . . ."

The Supreme Court granted certiorari to review the case.

B. Counsel of Record

ACLU Side (Respondent / Appellee): Herald Price Fahringer argued the cause for appellee. With him on the brief was Paul J. Cambria, Jr.

Opposing Side (Petitioner / Appellant): Robert M. Pitler argued the cause for appellant. With him on the briefs was Mark Dwyer.

III. AMICI CURIAE

ACLU Side (Respondent / Appellee)

Brief of amici curiae filed on behalf of the American Booksellers Association, Inc., Association of American Publishers, Inc., Council for Periodical Distributors Associations, Freedom to Read Foundation, International Periodical Distributors Association, Inc., National Association of College Stores, Inc.,

American Civil Liberties Union, the Association of American University Presses, Inc., New York Civil Liberties Union and St. Martin's Press, Incorporated by Michael A. Bamberger and Jeffrey A. Mitchell.

Opposing Side (Petitioner / Appellant)

Brief of amici curiae filed on behalf of Covenant House by Edmund J. Burns, Gregory A. Loken, and William A. Cahill, Jr.
Brief of amici curiae filed on behalf of Morality in Media, Inc., by John J. Walsh.
Brief of amici curiae filed on behalf of Charles H. Keating, Jr., et al. by Bruce A. Taylor.

IV. THE SUPREME COURT'S DECISION

"The Court of Appeals proceeded on the assumption that the standard of obscenity incorporated in § 263.10, which follows the guidelines enunciated in *Miller v. California*, 413 U.S. 15 (1973), constitutes the appropriate line dividing protected from unprotected expression by which to measure a regulation directed at child pornography. . . .

The Court of Appeals' assumption was not unreasonable . . . . This case, however, constitutes our first examination of a statute directed at and limited to depictions of sexual activity involving children. . . .

[W]e are persuaded that the States are entitled to greater leeway in the regulation of pornographic depictions of children. . . .

The test for child pornography is separate from the obscenity standard enunciated in Miller, but may be compared to it for the purpose of clarity. The Miller formulation is adjusted in the following respects: A trier of fact need not find that the material appeals to the prurient interest of the average person; it is not required that sexual conduct portrayed be done so in a patently offensive manner; and the material at issue need not be considered as a whole. . . .

We hold that § 263.15 sufficiently describes a category of material the production and distribution of which is not entitled to First Amendment protection. It is therefore clear that there is nothing unconstitutionally 'underinclusive' about a statute that singles out this category of material for proscription. It also follows that the State is not barred by the First Amendment from prohibiting the distribution of unprotected materials produced outside the State. . . .

It remains to address the claim that the New York statute is unconstitutionally overbroad . . . .

The scope of the First Amendment overbreadth doctrine, . . . must be carefully tied to the circumstances in which facial invalidation of a statute is truly warranted. . . .

Applying these principles, we hold that § 263.15 is not substantially overbroad. We consider this the paradigmatic case of a state statute whose legitimate reach dwarfs its arguably impermissible applications. . . .

Because § 263.15 is not substantially overbroad, it is unnecessary to consider its application to material that does not depict sexual conduct of a type that New York may restrict consistent with the First Amendment. As applied to Paul Ferber and to others who distribute similar material, the statute does not violate the First Amendment as applied to the States through the Fourteenth. The judgment of the New York Court of Appeals is reversed, and the case is remanded . . . ."

V. JUSTICE VOTE

0 Pro ACLU Side vs. 9 Con Opposing Side

Opposing Side (Petitioner / Appellant)

1. White, B. – Wrote majority opinion
2. Rehnquist, W. – Joined majority opinion
3. Burger, W. – Joined majority opinion
4. Powell, L. – Joined majority opinion
5. O'Connor, S. – Wrote concurring opinion
6. Blackmun, H. – Concurred in the result
7. Brennan, W. – Wrote concurring opinion
8. Marshall, T. – Joined Brennan's concurrence.
9. Stevens, J. – Wrote concurring opinion

VI. A WIN OR LOSS FOR THE ACLU?

The ACLU filed as amicus curiae urging affirmance; the Supreme Court reversed the New York Court of Appeals' decision by a 9-0 vote, giving the ACLU an apparent loss.

496. NAACP v. Claiborne Hardware Co.

(Decided July 2, 1982; 458 U.S. 886)

I. ISSUE

A. Issues Discussed

First Amendment, freedoms of press, speech, and association

B. Legal Question Presented

Can the NAACP, Mississippi Action for Progress, and others be held liable for damages resulting from a boycott of white merchants?

C. Supreme Court's Answer

They cannot be held liable for damages resulting from the boycott.

II. CASE SUMMARY

A. Background

In 1966, several hundred black citizens attended a meeting of a local branch of the National Association for the Advancement of Colored People (NAACP) and voted to launch a boycott against white merchants in Claiborne County, Mississippi. The purpose of the boycott was to secure compliance with a list of "demands for racial equality and integration," after their initial "complaints did not receive a satisfactory response."

In 1969, respondents, various white merchants, filed suit in Chancery Court of Hinds County for injunctive relief and damages against petitioners, NAACP, Mississippi Action for Progress, and a number of individuals who had participated in the boycott.

The Chancery Court "heard the testimony of 144 witnesses during an 8-month trial." In 1976, the court imposed damages liability and issued a permanent injunction, holding petitioners "jointly and severally liable" for respondents' lost earnings from 1966 to 1972, based on several theories of liability. Petitioners appealed to the Mississippi Supreme Court, which upheld the imposition of liability on the basis of "the tort of malicious interference" theory. The court held that the entire boycott was unlawful and affirmed petitioners' liability for damages "resulting from the boycott" on the ground that petitioners had agreed to "effectuate the boycott through force, violence, and threats."

The Supreme Court granted certiorari to review the case and reversed.

B. Counsel of Record / ACLU Attorney

ACLU Side (Petitioner / Appellant): Lloyd N. Cutler argued the cause for appellant.

Opposing Side (Respondent / Appellee): Grover Rees III argued the cause for appellee.

III. AMICI CURIAE

ACLU Side (Petitioner / Appellant)

Brief of amici curiae filed on behalf of the ACLU by John Vanderstar, Charles S. Sims, and Phyllis N. Segal.

Brief of amici curiae filed on behalf of the American Federation of Labor and Congress of Industrial Organizations by J. Albert Woll, Laurence Gold and George Kaufmann.

Brief of amici curiae filed on behalf of the American Jewish Congress by Paul S. Berger, David Bonderman, Leonard B. Simon, and Nathan Z. Dershowitz.

Opposing Side (Respondent / Appellee)

No briefs of amici curiae were filed in support of appellee.

IV. THE SUPREME COURT'S DECISION

"At times the difference between lawful and unlawful collective action may be identified easily by reference to its purpose. In this case, however, petitioners' ultimate objectives were unquestionably legitimate. The charge of illegality—like the claim of constitutional protection—derives from the means employed by the participants to achieve those goals. The use of speeches, marches, and threats of social ostracism cannot provide the basis for a damages award. But violent conduct is beyond the pale of constitutional protection.

The taint of violence colored the conduct of some of the petitioners. They, of course, may be held liable for the consequences of their violent deeds. The burden of demonstrating that it colored the entire collective effort, however, is not satisfied by evidence that violence occurred or even that violence contributed to the success of the boycott. A massive and prolonged effort to change the social, political, and economic structure of a local environment cannot be characterized as a violent conspiracy simply by reference to the ephemeral consequences of relatively few violent acts. Such a characterization must be supported by findings that adequately disclose the evidentiary basis for concluding that specific parties agreed to use unlawful means, that carefully identify the impact of such unlawful conduct, and that recognize the importance of avoiding the imposition of punishment for constitutionally protected activity. The burden of demonstrating that fear rather than protected conduct was the dominant force in the movement is heavy. . . . The findings of the chancellor, framed largely in the light of two legal theories rejected by the Mississippi Supreme Court, are constitutionally insufficient to support the judgment that all petitioners are liable for all losses resulting from the boycott.

The judgment is reversed. The case is remanded for further proceedings not inconsistent with this opinion."

V. JUSTICE VOTE

8 Pro ACLU Side vs. 0 Con Opposing Side

ACLU Side (Petitioner / Appellant)

1. Stevens, J. – Wrote majority opinion
2. Rehnquist, W. – Concurred in the result
3. White, B. – Joined majority opinion
4. Powell, L. – Joined majority opinion
5. Burger, W. – Wrote majority opinion
6. O'Connor, S. – Joined majority opinion
7. Blackmun, H. – Joined majority opinion
8. Brennan, W. – Joined majority opinion

Marshall, T. Took no part in the case.

VI. A WIN OR LOSS FOR THE ACLU?

The ACLU filed as amicus curiae urging reversal; the U.S. Supreme Court reversed the Mississippi Supreme Court's judgment in an 8-0 vote giving the ACLU an apparent win.

497. Larkin v. Grendel's Den, Inc.

(Decided December 13, 1982; 459 U.S. 116)

I. ISSUE

A. Issues Discussed

First Amendment, Establishment Clause, Fourteenth Amendment, due process

B. Legal Question Presented

"[W]hether a Massachusetts statute, which vests in the governing bodies of churches and schools the power effectively to veto applications for liquor licenses within a five hundred foot radius of the church or school, violates the Establishment Clause of the First Amendment or the Due Process Clause of the Fourteenth Amendment."

C. Supreme Court's Answer

The statute violates the Establishment Clause of the First Amendment.

II. CASE SUMMARY

A. Background

"Appellee operates a restaurant located in the Harvard Square area of Cambridge, Mass. The Holy Cross Armenian Catholic Parish is located adjacent to the restaurant; the back walls of the two buildings are ten feet apart. In 1977, appellee applied to the Cambridge License Commission for approval of an alcoholic beverages license for the restaurant.

Section 16C of Chapter 138 of the Massachusetts General Laws provides: 'Premises . . . located within a radius of five hundred feet of a church or school shall not be licensed for the sale of alcoholic beverages if the governing body of such church or school files written objection thereto.'

Holy Cross Church objected to appellee's application, expressing concern over 'having so many licenses so near' (emphasis in original). The License Commission voted to deny the application, citing only the objection of Holy Cross Church and noting that the church 'is within 10 feet of the proposed location.'

On appeal, the Massachusetts Alcoholic Beverages Control Commission upheld the License Commission's action. . . .

Appellee then sued the License Commission and the Beverages Control Commission in United States District Court. Relief was sought on the grounds that § 16C, on its face and as applied, violated the Equal Protection and Due Process Clauses of the Fourteenth Amendment, the Establishment Clause of the First Amendment, and the Sherman Act. . . .

The District Court held that § 16C violated the Due Process Clause and the Establishment Clause and held § 16C void on its face [but] rejected appellee's equal protection arguments . . . .

A panel of the First Circuit, in a divided opinion, reversed the District Court on the Due Process and Establishment Clause arguments . . . .

Appellee's motion for rehearing en banc was granted and the en banc court, in a divided opinion, affirmed the District Court's judgment on Establishment Clause grounds."

The Supreme Court granted certiorari to review the case and affirmed the judgment of the First Circuit Court of Appeals.

B. Counsel of Record / ACLU Attorney

ACLU Side (Respondent / Appellee): Laurence H. Tribe argued the cause for appellee.

Opposing Side (Petitioner / Appellant): Gerald J. Caruso, Assistant Attorney General of Massachusetts, argued the cause, pro hac vice, for appellant.

III. AMICI CURIAE

ACLU Side (Respondent / Appellee)

Brief of amici curiae filed on behalf of the ACLU, et al., by Charles S. Sims and John Reinstein.

Opposing Side (Petitioner / Appellant)

No briefs of amici curiae were filed in support of appellant.

IV. THE SUPREME COURT'S DECISION

"Appellants contend that the State may, without impinging on the Establishment Clause of the First Amendment, enforce what it describes as a 'zoning' law in order to shield schools and places of divine worship from the presence nearby of liquor dispensing establishments. It is also contended that a zone of protection around churches and schools is essential to protect diverse centers of spiritual, educational, and cultural enrichment. It is to that end that the State has vested in the governing bodies of all schools, public or private, and all churches, the power to prevent the issuance of liquor licenses for any premises within 500 feet of their institutions.

Plainly schools and churches have a valid interest in being insulated from certain kinds of commercial establishments, including those dispensing liquor. Zoning laws have long been employed to this end, and there can be little doubt about the power of a state to regulate the environment in the vicinity of schools, churches, hospitals, and the like by exercise of reasonable zoning laws. . . .

However, § 16C is not simply a legislative exercise of zoning power. As the Massachusetts Supreme Judicial Court concluded, § 16C delegates to private, nongovernmental entities power to veto certain liquor license applications. . . .

The purposes of the First Amendment guarantees relating to religion were twofold: to foreclose state interference with the practice of religious faiths, and to foreclose the establishment of a state religion familiar in other Eighteenth Century systems. Religion and government, each insulated from the other, could then coexist. . . .

The churches' power under the statute is standardless, calling for no reasons, findings, or reasoned conclusions. That power may therefore be used by churches to promote goals beyond insulating the church from undesirable neighbors; it could be employed for explicitly religious goals, for example, favoring liquor licenses for members of that congregation or adherents of that faith. . . .

Section 16C substitutes the unilateral and absolute power of a church for the reasoned decisionmaking of a public legislative body acting on evidence and guided by standards, on issues with significant economic and political implications. The challenged statute thus enmeshes churches in the processes of government and creates the danger of '[p]olitical fragmentation and divisiveness on religious lines.' Ordinary human experience and a long line of cases teach that few entanglements could be more offensive to the spirit of the Constitution.

The judgment of the Court of Appeals is affirmed."

V. JUSTICE VOTE

8 Pro ACLU Side vs. 1 Con Opposing Side

ACLU Side (Respondent / Appellee)

1. Burger, W. – Wrote majority opinion
2. Brennan, W. – Joined majority opinion
3. White, B. – Joined majority opinion
4. Marshall, T. – Joined majority opinion
5. Blackmun, H. – Joined majority opinion
6. Powell, L. – Joined majority opinion
7. Stevens, J. – Joined majority opinion
8. O'Connor, S. – Joined majority opinion

Opposing Side (Petitioner / Appellant)

1. Rehnquist, W. – Wrote dissenting opinion

VI. A WIN OR LOSS FOR THE ACLU?

The ACLU, as amicus curiae, urged affirmance of the First Circuit Court of Appeals' judgment; the Supreme Court affirmed in an 8-1 vote, giving the ACLU an apparent win.

498. Minneapolis Star & Tribune Co. v. Minnesota Commissioner of Revenue

(Decided March 29, 1983; 460 U.S. 575)

I. ISSUE

A. Issues Discussed

First Amendment, freedom of the press

B. Legal Question Presented

Does a State possess the "power to impose a special tax on the press and, by enacting exemptions, to limit its effect to only a few newspapers"?

C. Supreme Court's Answer

This tax violates the First Amendment by limiting the freedom of the press.

II. CASE SUMMARY

A. Background

"Since 1967, Minnesota has imposed a sales tax on most sales of goods for a price in excess of a nominal sum. In general, the tax applies only to retail sales. . . ,

The appellant, Minneapolis Star and Tribune Company 'Star Tribune,' is the publisher of a morning newspaper and an evening newspaper in Minneapolis. From 1967 until 1971, it enjoyed an exemption from the sales and use tax provided by Minnesota for periodic publications. In 1971, however, while leaving the exemption from the sales tax in place, the legislature amended the scheme to impose a 'use tax' on the cost of paper and ink products consumed in the production of a publication. Ink and paper used in publications became the only items subject to the use tax that were components of goods to be sold at retail. In 1974, the legislature again amended the statute, this time to exempt the first $100,000 worth of ink and paper consumed by a publication in any calendar year, in effect giving each publication an annual tax credit of $4,000. . . .

After the enactment of the $100,000 exemption, 11 publishers, producing 14 of the 388 paid circulation newspapers in the State, incurred a tax liability in 1974. Star Tribune was one of the 11, and, of the $893,355 collected, it paid $608,634, or roughly two-thirds of the total revenue raised by the tax. In 1975, 13 publishers, producing 16 out of 374 paid circulation papers, paid a tax. That year, Star Tribune again bore roughly two-thirds of the total receipts from the use tax on ink and paper.

Star Tribune instituted this action to seek a refund of the use taxes it paid from January 1, 1974, to May 31, 1975. It challenged the imposition of the use tax on ink and paper used in publications as a violation of the guarantees of freedom of the press and equal protection in the First and Fourteenth Amendments. The Minnesota Supreme Court upheld the tax against the federal constitutional challenge."

The Supreme Court granted certiorari to review the case and reversed.

B. Counsel of Record / ACLU Attorney

ACLU Side (Petitioner / Appellant): Lawrence C. Brown argued the cause for appellant.

Opposing Side (Respondent / Appellee): Paul R. Kempainen, Special Assistant Attorney General of Minnesota, argued the cause for appellee.

III. AMICI CURIAE

ACLU Side (Petitioner / Appellant)

Brief of amici curiae filed on behalf of the ACLU, et al., by Peter W. Schroth and Charles S. Sims.

Brief of amici curiae filed on behalf of Knight-Ridder Newspapers, Inc., et al., by Philip A. Lacovara, W. Terry Maguire, and Pamela J. Riley.

Opposing Side (Respondent / Appellee)

No briefs of amici curiae were filed in support of appellee.

IV. THE SUPREME COURT'S DECISION

"Clearly, the First Amendment does not prohibit all regulation of the press. It is beyond dispute that the States and the Federal Government can subject newspapers to generally applicable economic regulations without creating constitutional problems. Minnesota, however, has not chosen to apply its general sales and use tax to newspapers. Instead, it has created a special tax that applies only to certain publications protected by the First Amendment. Although the State argues now that the tax on paper and ink is part of the general scheme of taxation, the use tax provision . . . is facially discriminatory, singling out publications for treatment that is, to our knowledge, unique in Minnesota tax law.

Minnesota's treatment of publications differs from that of other enterprises in at least two important respects: it imposes a use tax that does not serve the function of protecting the sales tax, and it taxes an intermediate transaction rather than the ultimate retail sale. A use tax ordinarily serves to complement the sales tax by eliminating the incentive to make major purchases in States with lower sales taxes; it requires the resident who shops out-of-state to pay a use tax equal to the sales tax savings. Minnesota designed its overall use tax scheme to serve this function. . . . But the use tax on ink and paper serves no such complementary function; it applies to all uses, whether or not the taxpayer purchased the ink and paper instate, and it applies to items exempt from the sales tax. . . .

There is substantial evidence that differential taxation of the press would have troubled the Framers of the First Amendment. . . .

A power to tax differentially, as opposed to a power to tax generally, gives a government a powerful weapon against the taxpayer selected. When the State imposes a generally applicable tax, there is little cause for concern. We need not fear that a government will destroy a selected group of taxpayers by burdensome taxation if it must impose the same burden on the rest of its constituency. When the State singles out the press, though, the political constraints that prevent a legislature from passing crippling taxes of general applicability are weakened, and the threat of burdensome taxes becomes acute. That threat can operate as effectively as a censor to check critical comment by the press, undercutting the basic assumption of our political system that the press will often serve as an important restraint on government. . . .

Minnesota's ink and paper tax violates the First Amendment not only because it singles out the press, but also because it targets a small group of newspapers. The effect of the $100,000 exemption enacted in 1974 is that only a handful of publishers pay any tax at all, and even fewer pay any significant amount of tax. The State explains this exemption as part of a policy favoring an 'equitable' tax system, although there are no comparable exemptions for small enterprises outside the press. Again, there is no legislative history supporting the State's view of the purpose of the amendment. Whatever the motive of the legislature in this case, we think that recognizing a power in the State not only to single out the press but also to tailor the tax so that it singles out a few members of the press presents such a potential for abuse that no interest suggested by Minnesota can justify the scheme. . . .

Since Minnesota has offered no satisfactory justification for its tax on the use of ink and paper, the tax violates the First Amendment, and the judgment below is reversed."

V. JUSTICE VOTE

8 Pro ACLU Side vs. 1 Con Opposing Side

ACLU Side (Petitioner / Appellant)

1. O'Connor, S. – Wrote majority opinion
2. Burger, W. – Joined majority opinion
3. Brennan, W. – Joined majority opinion
4. Marshall, T. – Joined majority opinion
5. Powell, L. – Joined majority opinion
6. Stevens, J. – Joined majority opinion
7. Blackmun, H. – Joined majority opinion
8. White, B. – Wrote concurring in part and dissenting in part

Opposing Side (Respondent / Appellee)

1. Rehnquist, W. – Wrote dissenting opinion

VI. A WIN OR LOSS FOR THE ACLU?

The ACLU, as amicus curiae, urged reversal of the Supreme Court of Minnesota's judgment; the U.S. Supreme Court reversed in an 8-1 vote, giving the ACLU an apparent win.

499. United States Postal Service Board of Governors v. Aikens

(Decided April 4, 1983; 460 U.S. 711)

I. ISSUE

A. Issues Discussed

Civil rights, race, Fourteenth Amendment, employment discrimination

B. Legal Question Presented

Did the District Court err in ordering respondent to produce "proof of discriminatory intent" by his employer and to show, prima facie, that he was "as qualified or more qualified" than others promoted over him?

C. Supreme Court's Answer

The District Court erred in imposing these requirements and the judgment must therefore be vacated.

II. CASE SUMMARY

A. Background

"Respondent Louis Aikens filed suit under Title VII of the Civil Rights Act of 1964, . . . claiming that petitioner, the United States Postal Service, discriminated against him on account of his race. Aikens, who is black, claimed that the Postal Service had discriminatorily refused to promote him to higher positions in the Washington, D.C. Post Office where he had been employed since 1937. After a bench trial, the District Court entered judgment in favor of the Postal Service, but the Court of Appeals reversed. [The Supreme Court] vacated the Court of Appeals' judgment and remanded for reconsideration in light of Texas Department of Community Affairs v. Burdine.

On remand, the Court of Appeals reaffirmed its earlier holding that the District Court had erred in requiring Aikens to offer direct proof of discriminatory intent. It also held that the District Court erred in requiring Aikens to show, as part of his prima facie case, that he was 'as qualified or more qualified' than the people who were promoted."

The Supreme Court granted certiorari to review the case, vacated the judgment, and remanded the case.

B. Counsel of Record / ACLU Attorney

ACLU Side (Respondent / Appellee): Jack Greenberg argued the cause for appellee.

Opposing Side (Petitioner / Appellant): Deputy Solicitor General Wallace argued the cause for appellant.

III. AMICI CURIAE

ACLU Side (Respondent / Appellee)

Brief of amici curiae filed on behalf of the ACLU, et al., by Joan E. Bertin, Mary L. Heen, E. Richard Larson, and Isabelle Katz Pinzler.

Brief of amici curiae filed on behalf of the NOW Legal Defense and Education Fund, et al., by James E. Daniels, Paul A. Crotty, and Phyllis N. Segal.

Opposing Side (Petitioner / Appellant)

Brief of amici curiae filed on behalf of the Chamber of Commerce of the United States by Stephen A. Bokat.

Brief of amici curiae filed on behalf of the Equal Employment Advisory Council by Robert E. Williams, Douglas S. McDowell, and Edward E. Potter.

Brief of amici curiae filed on behalf of the American Federation of Labor and Congress of Industrial Organizations by J. Albert Woll, Robert M. Weinberg, Michael H. Gottesman, and Laurence Gold.

IV. THE SUPREME COURT'S DECISION

"On the state of the record at the close of the evidence, the District Court in this case should have proceeded to this specific question directly, just as district courts decide disputed questions of fact in other civil litigation. As we stated in [Texas Department of Community Affairs v.] Burdine:

'The plaintiff retains the burden of persuasion. [H]e may succeed in this either directly by persuading the court that a discriminatory reason more likely motivated the employer or indirectly by showing that the employer's proffered explanation is unworthy of credence.' . . .

The District Court erroneously thought that respondent was required to submit direct evidence of discriminatory intent and erroneously focused on the question of prima facie case rather than directly on the question of discrimination. Thus we cannot be certain that its findings of fact in favor of the Postal Service were not influenced by its mistaken view of the law. We accordingly vacate the judgment of the Court of Appeals, and remand the case to the District Court so that it may decide on the basis of the evidence before it whether the Postal Service discriminated against Aikens."

V. JUSTICE VOTE

0 Pro ACLU Side vs. 9 Con Opposing Side

Opposing Side (Petitioner / Appellant)

1. Rehnquist, W. – Wrote majority opinion
2. Stevens, J. – Joined majority opinion
3. White, B. – Joined majority opinion
4. Powell, L. – Joined majority opinion
5. Burger, W. – Joined majority opinion
6. O'Connor, S. – Joined majority opinion
7. Marshall, T. – Concurred in the judgment
8. Blackmun, H. – Wrote concurring opinion
9. Brennan, W. – Joined Blackmun's concurrence

VI. A WIN OR LOSS FOR THE ACLU?

The ACLU filed as amicus curiae urging affirmance; the Supreme Court vacated the Court of Appeals' judgment in a 9-0, vote giving the ACLU an apparent loss.

500. Kush v. Rutledge

(Decided April 4, 1983; 460 U.S. 719)

I. ISSUE

A. Issues Discussed

Civil rights, race, Eleventh Amendment

B. Legal Question Presented

Was Rutledge, a white football player, entitled to recover damages under 42 USC § 1985(2) against "the Arizona State University athletic director, head football coach, and assistant football coach" for engaging in "conspiracy to intimidate potential witness in a federal lawsuit"?

C. Supreme Court's Answer

Rutledge's ability to recover damages under § 1985(2) is not limited by his lack of allegations of invidious discrimination in alleging conspiracy to intimidate witnesses.

II. CASE SUMMARY

A. Background

"Respondent is a white football player of unknown political affiliation who seeks to recover damages under 42 U.S.C. § 1985(2) (1976) for an alleged conspiracy to intimidate potential witnesses in a federal lawsuit. . . . In both federal and state tribunals, respondent Rutledge has asserted a variety of common-law and statutory claims against Arizona State University and its officials arising out of incidents that occurred while he was a member of the college football squad. One of his claims is that three of the petitioners—the Arizona State University athletic director, head football coach, and assistant football coach—engaged in a conspiracy to intimidate and threaten various potential material witnesses in order to prevent them from testifying 'freely, fully and truthfully' in his lawsuit in federal court.

The District Court granted a motion to dismiss the entire complaint on the grounds that the action was barred by the Eleventh Amendment and that respondent had failed to allege a violation of his civil rights. . . . The Court of Appeals affirmed the dismissal of all claims against the university and its Board of Regents and of the vicarious liability claims against petitioner Miller, remanded for further proceedings on the other state-law tort claims against petitioners, and affirmed the dismissal of all federal civil rights claims against petitioners except the one at issue here.

The Court of Appeals construed respondent's allegations of witness intimidation, as containing two components—obstruction of justice at the state level, and interference with federal litigation. The former was not actionable under the second part of § 1985(2), the court held, because 'there exists no sufficient allegation of racial or class-based invidiously discriminatory animus.' The court acknowledged that this Court's decision in Griffin v. Breckenridge, supra, had interpreted a portion of § 1985(3) to include such a requirement in order to avoid the constitutional issues that would have attended enactment of a general federal tort law. It decided that the same principles applied to claims based on private conspiracies to obstruct justice in state court proceedings.

But the Court of Appeals concluded that no allegations of class-based animus were required under the first part of § 1985(2), which proscribes intimidation of witnesses in the federal courts. It relied on the plain language of the Civil Rights Act of 1871 and on the legislative history. Noting the federal government's unquestioned constitutional authority to protect the processes of its own courts, and the absence of any need to limit the first part of § 1985(2) to avoid creating a general federal tort law, the Court of Appeals declined to impose the limitation set forth in Griffin v. Breckenridge."

The Supreme Court granted certiorari to review the case and affirmed.

B. Counsel of Record / ACLU Attorney

ACLU Side (Respondent / Appellee): Robert Ong Hing argued the cause for appellee.

Opposing Side (Petitioner / Appellant): Michael L. Gallagher argued the cause for appellant.

III. AMICI CURIAE

ACLU Side (Respondent / Appellee)

Brief of amici curiae filed on behalf of the ACLU, et al., by Charles S. Sims.

Opposing Side (Petitioner / Appellant)

No briefs of amici curiae briefs were filed in support of appellant.

IV. THE SUPREME COURT'S DECISION

"The remaining two categories [of 42 U.S.C. § 1985] encompass underlying activity that is not institutionally linked to federal interests and that is usually of primary state concern. The second part of § 1985(2) applies to conspiracies to obstruct the course of justice in state courts, and the first part of § 1985(3) provides a cause of action against two or more persons who 'conspire or go in disguise on the highway or on the premises of another.' Each of these portions of the statute contains language requiring that the conspirators' actions be motivated by an intent to deprive their victims of the equal protection of the laws.

This limiting language was construed in Griffin v. Breckenridge, a case in which a unanimous Court held that § 1985(3) applies to purely private conspiracies. . . .

Although Griffin itself arose under the first clause of § 1985(3), petitioners argue that its reasoning should be applied to the remaining portions of § 1985 as well. We cannot accept that argument for three reasons. First, the scope of the Griffin opinion is carefully confined to the portion of § 1985(3) now before us. There is no suggestion in the opinion that its reasoning applies to any other portion of § 1985. Second, the analysis in the Griffin opinion relied heavily on the fact that the sponsors of the 1871 bill added the 'equal protection' language in response to objections that the 'enormous sweep of the original language' vastly extended federal authority and displaced state control over private conduct. That legislative background does not apply to the portions of the statute that prohibit interference with federal officers, federal courts, or federal elections. Third, and of greatest importance, the statutory language that provides the textual basis for the 'class-based, invidiously discriminatory animus' requirement simply does not appear in the portion of the statute that applies to this case.

Given the structure of § 2 of the 1871 Act, it is clear that Congress did not intend to impose a requirement of class-based animus on persons seeking to prove a violation of their rights under the first clause of §1985(2). The legislative history supports the conclusion we have drawn from the language of the statute. Protection of the processes of the federal courts was an essential component of Congress' solution to disorder and anarchy in the Southern States. Neither proponents nor opponents of the bill had any doubt that the Constitution gave Congress the power to prohibit intimidation of parties, witnesses, and jurors in federal courts.

The judgment of the Court of Appeals is affirmed."

V. JUSTICE VOTE

9 Pro ACLU Side vs. 0 Con Opposing Side

ACLU Side (Respondent / Appellee)

Opposing Side (Petitioner / Appellant)

1. Stevens, J. – Wrote majority opinion
2. White, B. – Joined majority opinion
3. Powell, L. – Joined majority opinion
4. Burger, W. – Joined majority opinion
5. O'Connor, S. – Joined majority opinion
6. Rehnquist, W. – Joined majority opinion
7. Blackmun, H. – Joined majority opinion
8. Marshall, T. – Joined majority opinion
9. Brennan, W. – Joined majority opinion

VI. A WIN OR LOSS FOR THE ACLU?

The ACLU filed as amicus curiae urging affirmance; the Supreme Court affirmed the Court of Appeals' judgment in a 9-0 vote giving the ACLU an apparent win.

501. Anderson v. Celebrezze

(Decided April 19, 1983; 460 U.S. 780)

I. ISSUE

A. Issues Discussed

Civil rights, voting rights, ballot access, First Amendment, Fourteenth Amendment.

B. Legal Question Presented

"[W]hether Ohio's early filing deadline place an unconstitutional burden on the voting and associational rights of Anderson's supporters."

C. Supreme Court's Answer

The early filing deadline places an unconstitutional burden on voting and associational rights of supporters of independent candidates, such as Anderson's supporters.

II. CASE SUMMARY

A. Background

"On April 24, 1980, petitioner John Anderson announced that he was an independent candidate for the office of President of the United States. . . . On April 24, however, it was already too late for Anderson to qualify for a position on the ballot in Ohio and certain other states because the statutory deadlines for filing a statement of candidacy had already passed. . . . On May 16, 1980, Anderson's supporters tendered a nominating petition containing approximately 14,500 signatures and a statement of candidacy to respondent Celebrezze, the Ohio Secretary of State. These documents would have entitled Anderson to a place on the ballot if they had been filed on or before March 20, 1980. Respondent refused to accept the petition solely because it had not been filed within the time required by § 3513.257 of the Ohio Revised Code. Three days later Anderson and three voters, two registered in Ohio and one in New Jersey, commenced this action in the United States District Court for the Southern District of Ohio, challenging the constitutionality of Ohio's early filing deadline for independent candidates. The District Court granted petitioners' motion for summary judgment and ordered respondent to place Anderson's name on the general election ballot.

The District Court held that the statutory deadline was unconstitutional on two grounds. It imposed an impermissible burden on the First Amendment rights of Anderson and his Ohio supporters and diluted the potential value of votes that might be cast for him in other States. Moreover, by requiring an independent to declare his candidacy in March without mandating comparable action by the nominee of a political party, the State violated the Equal Protection Clause of the Fourteenth Amendment. . . .

The Court of Appeals reversed. . . . It held that Ohio's early deadline 'ensures that voters making the important choice of their next president have the opportunity for a careful look at the candidates, a chance to see how they withstand the close scrutiny of a political campaign.'"

The Supreme Court granted certiorari to review the case and reversed.

B. Counsel of Record / ACLU Attorney

ACLU Side (Petitioner / Appellant): George T. Frampton, Jr. argued the cause for appellant.

Opposing Side (Respondent / Appellee): Joel S. Taylor argued the cause for appellee.

III. AMICI CURIAE

ACLU Side (Petitioner / Appellant)

Opposing Side (Respondent / Appellee)

Brief of amici curiae filed on behalf of the ACLU, et al., by Arthur N. Eisenberg, Charles S. Sims, Bruce Campbell, and John C. Armor.

Brief of amici curiae filed on behalf of the Libertarian National Committee by Paul S. Allen. No briefs of amici curiae were filed in support of appellee.

IV. THE SUPREME COURT'S DECISION

"Our primary concern is with the tendency of ballot access restrictions 'to limit the field of candidates from which voters might choose.' Therefore, '[i]n approaching candidate restrictions, it is essential to examine in a realistic light the extent and nature of their impact on voters.' . . .

The State identifies three separate interests that it seeks to further by its early filing deadline for independent Presidential candidates: voter education, equal treatment for partisan and independent candidates, and political stability. . . .

There can be no question about the legitimacy of the State's interest in fostering informed and educated expressions of the popular will in a general election. Moreover, the Court of Appeals correctly identified that interest as one of the concerns that motivated the Framers' decision not to provide for direct popular election of the President. We are persuaded, however, that the State's important and legitimate interest in voter education does not justify the specific restriction on participation in a Presidential election that is at issue in this case. . . .

We also find no merit in the State's claim that the early filing deadline serves the interest of treating all candidates alike. It is true that a candidate participating in a primary election must declare his candidacy on the same date as an independent. But both the burdens and the benefits of the respective requirements are materially different, and the reasons for requiring early filing for a primary candidate are inapplicable to independent candidates in the general election. . . .

Moreover, the early deadline for filing as an independent may actually impair the State's interest in preserving party harmony. . . .

We conclude that Ohio's March filing deadline for independent candidates for the office of President of the United States cannot be justified by the State's asserted interest in protecting political stability. . . .

We began our inquiry by noting that our primary concern is not the interest of candidate Anderson, but rather, the interests of the voters who chose to associate together to express their support for Anderson's candidacy and the views he espoused. Under any realistic appraisal, the 'extent and nature' of the burdens Ohio has placed on the voters' freedom of choice and freedom of association, in an election of nationwide importance, unquestionably outweigh the State's minimal interest in imposing a March deadline.

The judgment of the Court of Appeals is reversed."

V. JUSTICE VOTE

5 Pro ACLU Side vs. 4 Con Opposing Side

ACLU Side (Petitioner / Appellant)

1. Stevens, J. – Wrote majority opinion
2. Burger, W. – Joined majority opinion
3. Brennan, W. – Joined majority opinion
4. Marshall, T. – Joined majority opinion
5. Blackmun, H. – Joined majority opinion

Opposing Side (Respondent / Appellee)

1. Rehnquist, W. – Wrote dissenting opinion
2. White, B. – Joined Rehnquist's dissent
3. Powell, L. – Joined Rehnquist's dissent
4. O'Connor, S. – Joined Rehnquist's dissent

VI. A WIN OR LOSS FOR THE ACLU?

The ACLU filed as amicus curiae urging reversal; the Supreme Court reversed the judgment of the Court of Appeals for the Sixth Circuit in a 5-4 vote, giving the ACLU an apparent win.

502. Connick v. Myers

(Decided April 20, 1983; 461 U.S. 138)

I. ISSUE

A. Issues Discussed

First Amendment, freedoms of speech, press, and association, Fourteenth Amendment

B. Legal Question Presented

"[W]hether the First and Fourteenth Amendments prevent the discharge of a state employee for circulating a questionnaire concerning internal office affairs."

C. Supreme Court's Answer

The state employee's discharge for circulating a questionnaire concerning internal office affairs did not violate the First Amendment or Fourteenth Amendment.

II. CASE SUMMARY

A. Background

"The respondent, Sheila Myers, was employed as an Assistant District Attorney in New Orleans for five and a half years. She served at the pleasure of petitioner Harry Connick, the District Attorney for Orleans Parish. . . .

In the early part of October, 1980, Myers was informed that she would be transferred to prosecute cases in a different section of the criminal court. Myers was strongly opposed to the proposed transfer and expressed her view to several of her supervisors, including Connick. Despite her objections, on October 6 Myers was notified that she was being transferred. Myers again spoke with Dennis Waldron, one of the first assistant district attorneys, expressing her reluctance to accept the transfer. A number of other office matters were discussed and Myers later testified that, in response to Waldron's suggestion that her concerns were not shared by others in the office, she informed him that she would do some research on the matter.

That night Myers prepared a questionnaire soliciting the views of her fellow staff members concerning office transfer policy, office morale, the need for a grievance committee, the level of confidence in supervisors, and whether employees felt pressured to work in political campaigns. Early the following morning, Myers . . . met with Connick who urged her to accept the transfer. She said she would 'consider' it. Connick then left the office. Myers then distributed the questionnaire to 15 assistant district attorneys. Shortly after noon, Dennis Waldron learned that Myers was distributing the survey. He immediately phoned Connick and informed him that Myers was creating a "mini-insurrection" within the office. Connick returned to the office and told Myers that she was being terminated because of her refusal to accept the transfer. She was also told that her distribution of the questionnaire was considered an act of insubordination. . . .

Myers filed suit under 42 U.S.C. § 1983, contending that her employment was wrongfully terminated because she had exercised her constitutionally-protected right of free speech. The District Court agreed, ordered Myers reinstated, and awarded backpay, damages, and attorney's fees. The District Court found that although Connick informed Myers that she was being fired because of her refusal to accept a transfer, the facts showed that the questionnaire was the real reason for her termination. The court then proceeded to hold that Myers' questionnaire involved matters of public concern and that the state had not 'clearly demonstrated' that the survey 'substantially interfered' with the operations of the District Attorney's office.

Connick appealed to the United States Court of Appeals for the Fifth Circuit, which affirmed on the basis of the District Court's opinion."

The Supreme Court granted certiorari to review the case and reversed.

B. Counsel of Record / ACLU Attorney

ACLU Side (Respondent / Appellee): George M. Strickler, Jr., argued the cause for appellee.

Opposing Side (Petitioner / Appellant): William F. Wessel argued the cause for appellant.

III. AMICI CURIAE

ACLU Side (Respondent / Appellee)

Brief of amici curiae filed on behalf of the ACLU, et al., by Mark C. Rosenblum, Nadine Strossen, and Charles S. Sims.

Brief of amici curiae filed on behalf of the National Education Association, et al., by Robert H. Chanin, Laurence Gold, and Marsha S. Berzon.

Opposing Side (Petitioner / Appellant)

No briefs of amici curiae were filed in support of appellant.

IV. THE SUPREME COURT'S DECISION

"Myers' questionnaire touched upon matters of public concern in only a most limited sense; her survey, in our view, is most accurately characterized as an employee grievance concerning internal office policy. The limited First Amendment interest involved here does not require that Connick tolerate action which he reasonably believed would disrupt the office, undermine his authority, and destroy close working relationships. Myers' discharge therefore did not offend the First Amendment. We reiterate, however, the caveat we expressed in Pickering: 'Because of the enormous variety of fact situations in which critical statements by . . . public employees may be thought by their superiors . . . to furnish grounds for dismissal, we do not deem it either appropriate or feasible to attempt to lay down a general standard against which all such statements may be judged.'

Our holding today is grounded in our longstanding recognition that the First Amendment's primary aim is the full protection of speech upon issues of public concern, as well as the practical realities involved in the administration of a government office. Although today the balance is struck for the government, this is no defeat for the First Amendment. For it would indeed be a Pyrrhic victory for the great principles of free expression if the Amendment's safeguarding of a public employee's right, as a citizen, to participate in discussions concerning public affairs were confused with the attempt to constitutionalize the employee grievance that we see presented here. The judgment of the Court of Appeals is reversed."

V. JUSTICE VOTE

4 Pro ACLU Side vs. 5 Con Opposing Side

ACLU Side (Respondent / Appellee)

1. Brennan, W. – Wrote dissenting opinion
2. Marshall, T. – Joined Brennan's dissent
3. Blackmun, H. – Joined Brennan's dissent
4. Stevens, J. – Joined Brennan's dissent

Opposing Side (Petitioner / Appellant)

1. White, B. – Wrote majority opinion
2. Powell, L. – Joined majority opinion
3. Burger, W. – Joined majority opinion
4. O'Connor, S. – Joined majority opinion
5. Rehnquist, W. – Joined majority opinion

VI. A WIN OR LOSS FOR THE ACLU?

The ACLU filed as amicus curiae urging affirmance; the Supreme Court reversed the Court of Appeals' judgment in a 5-4 vote giving ACLU an apparent loss.

503. United States v. Grace

(Decided April 20, 1983; 461 U.S. 171)

I. ISSUE

A. Issues Discussed

First Amendment, freedom of speech

B. Legal Question Presented

"[W]hether 40 U.S.C. § 13k, which prohibits, among other things, the 'display [of] any flag, banner, or device designed or adapted to bring into public notice any party, organization, or movement' in the United States Supreme Court building and on its grounds, violates the First Amendment."

C. Supreme Court's Answer

40 U.S.C. § 13k violates the First Amendment as applied to sidewalks outside the Supreme Court building.

II. CASE SUMMARY

A. Background

"In May 1978 appellee Thaddeus Zywicki, standing on the sidewalk in front of the Supreme Court building, distributed leaflets to passerby. The leaflets were reprints of a letter to the editor of the Washington Post from a United States Senator concerning the removal of unfit judges from the bench. A Supreme Court police officer approached Zywicki and told him, accurately, that Title 40 of the United States Code prohibited the distribution of leaflets on the Supreme Court grounds, which includes the sidewalk. Zywicki left."

Zywicki returned a second and third time in 1980 to distribute leaflets for other causes, encountered police, and left after police indicated he would be arrested for violating Title 40. Before the third attempt, "Zywicki had consulted with an attorney concerning the legality of his activities and had been informed that the Superior Court for the District of Columbia had construed the statute that prohibited leafletting to prohibit only conduct done with the specific intent to influence, impede, or obstruct the administration of justice. . . .

Around noon on March 17, 1980, appellee Mary Grace entered upon the sidewalk in front of the Court and began to display a four foot by two and a half foot sign on which was inscribed the verbatim text of the First Amendment. A Court police officer approached Grace and informed her that she would have to go across the street if she wished to display the sign. Grace was informed that Title 40 of the United States Code prohibited her conduct and that if she did not cease she would be arrested. Grace left the grounds.

On May 13, 1980, Zywicki and Grace filed the present suit in the United States District Court for the District of Columbia. They sought an injunction against continued enforcement of 40 U.S.C. § 13k and a declaratory judgment that the statute was unconstitutional on its face. On August 7, 1980, the District Court dismissed the complaint for failure to exhaust administrative remedies. Appellees took an appeal, arguing that the District Court's action was improper and that the Court of Appeals should grant the relief requested in the complaint.

The Court of Appeals determined that the District Court's dismissal for failure to exhaust administrative remedies was erroneous and went on to strike down § 13k on its face as an unconstitutional restriction on First Amendment rights in a public place."

The Supreme Court granted certiorari to review the case and affirmed.

B. Counsel of Record / ACLU Attorney

ACLU Side (Respondent / Appellee): Sebastian K. D. Graber argued the cause for appellee.

Opposing Side (Petitioner / Appellant): Solicitor General Lee argued the cause for appellant.

III. AMICI CURIAE

ACLU Side (Respondent / Appellee)

Brief of amici curiae filed on behalf of the ACLU, et al., by A. Stephen Hut, Jr., Arthur B. Spitzer, and Charles S. Sims.

Brief of amici curiae filed on behalf of the League of United Latin American Citizens by Robert L. Gnaizda, Sidney M. Wolinsky, and Anita P. Arriola.

Opposing Side (Petitioner / Appellant)

No briefs of amici curiae filed in support of appellant.

IV. THE SUPREME COURT'S DECISION

"There is no doubt that as a general matter peaceful picketing and leafletting are expressive activities involving 'speech' protected by the First Amendment.

It is also true that 'public places' historically associated with the free exercise of expressive activities, such as streets, sidewalks, and parks, are considered, without more, to be 'public forums.' . . .

Publicly owned or operated property does not become a 'public forum' simply because members of the public are permitted to come and go at will. . . . There is little doubt that in some circumstances the Government may ban the entry on to public property that is not a 'public forum' of all persons except those who have legitimate business on the premises. . . .

The prohibitions imposed by § 13k technically cover the entire grounds of the Supreme Court as defined in § 13p. That section describes the Court grounds as extending to the curb of each of the four streets enclosing the block on which the building is located. Included within this small geographical area, therefore, are not only the building, the plaza and surrounding promenade, lawn area, and steps, but also the sidewalks. The sidewalks comprising the outer boundaries of the Court grounds are indistinguishable from any other sidewalks in Washington, D.C., and we can discern no reason why they should be treated any differently. Sidewalks, of course, are among those areas of public property that traditionally have been held open to the public for expressive activities and are clearly within those areas of public property that may be considered, generally without further inquiry, to be public forum property. . . . The public sidewalks forming the perimeter of the Supreme Court grounds, in our view, are public forums and should be treated as such for First Amendment purposes. . . .

We thus perceive insufficient justification for § 13k's prohibition of carrying signs, banners, or devices on the public sidewalks surrounding the building. We hold that under the First Amendment the section is unconstitutional as applied to those sidewalks. Of course, this is not to say that those sidewalks, like other sidewalks, are not subject to reasonable time, place, and manner restrictions, either by statute or by regulations issued pursuant to 40 U.S.C. § 13l.

The judgment below is accordingly affirmed to the extent indicated by this opinion and is otherwise vacated."

V. JUSTICE VOTE

7 Pro ACLU Side vs. 2 Con Opposing Side

ACLU Side (Respondent / Appellee)

1. White, B. – Wrote majority opinion
2. Burger, W. – Joined majority opinion
3. Brennan, W. – Joined majority opinion
4. Blackmun, H. – Joined majority opinion
5. Powell, L. – Joined majority opinion
6. Rehnquist, W. – Joined majority opinion
7. O'Connor, S. – Joined majority opinion

Opposing Side (Petitioner / Appellant)

1. Marshall, T. – Wrote opinion concurring in part and dissenting in part
2. Stevens, J. – Wrote opinion concurring in part and dissenting in part

VI. A WIN OR LOSS FOR THE ACLU?

The ACLU, as amicus curiae, urged affirmance of the Court of Appeals' judgment; the Supreme Court affirmed in part and vacated in part in a 7-2 vote, giving the ACLU an apparent win.

504. Martinez v. Bynum

(Decided May 2, 1983; 461 U.S. 321)

I. ISSUE

A. Issues Discussed

Civil rights, state's rights, Fourteenth Amendment, residence requirements

B. Legal Question Presented

Is Texas Education Code § 21.031(d) a bona fide residence requirement or did it violate the Equal Protection Clause of the Fourteenth Amendment?

C. Supreme Court's Answer

The statute is a bona fide residence requirement and does not violate the Equal Protection Clause.

II. CASE SUMMARY

A. Background

"Roberto Morales was born in 1969 in McAllen, Texas, and is thus a United States citizen by birth. His parents are Mexican citizens who reside in Reynosa, Mexico. He left Reynosa in 1977 and returned to McAllen to live with his sister, petitioner Oralia Martinez, for the primary purpose of attending school in the McAllen Independent School District. Although Martinez is now Morales's custodian, she is not—and does not desire to become—his guardian. As a result, Morales is not entitled to tuition-free admission to the McAllen schools. Section 21.031(b) and (c) of the Texas Education Code would require the local school authorities to admit him if he or 'his parent, guardian, or the person having lawful control of him' resided in the school district, Tex. Educ.Code Ann. § 21.031(b) and (c), but § 21.031(d) denies tuition-free admission for a minor who lives apart from a 'parent, guardian, or other person having lawful control of him under an order of a court' if his presence in the school district is 'for the primary purpose of attending the public free schools.' Respondent McAllen Independent School District therefore denied Morales's application for admission in the fall of 1977.

In December 1977 Martinez, as next friend of Morales, and four other adult custodians of school-age children instituted the present action in the United States District Court for the Southern District of Texas . . . . Plaintiffs initially alleged that § 21.031(d), both on its face and as applied by defendants, violated certain provisions of the Constitution, including the Equal Protection Clause, the Due Process Clause, and the Privileges and Immunities Clause. Plaintiffs also sought preliminary and permanent injunctive relief.

The District Court denied a preliminary injunction in August 1978. It found 'that the school boards . . . have been more than liberal in finding that certain children are not living away from parents and residing in the school district for the sole purpose of attending school.' The evidence 'conclusively' showed 'that children living within the school districts with someone other than their parents or legal guardians will be admitted to school if any reason exists for such situation other than that of attending school only.'

Plaintiffs subsequently amended the complaint to narrow their claims. They now seek only 'a declaration that . . . § 21.031(d) is unconstitutional on its face,' an injunction prohibiting defendants from denying the children admission to school pursuant to § 21.031(d), restitution of certain tuition payments, costs, and attorney's fees. After a hearing on the merits, the District Court granted judgment for the defendants. The court concluded that § 21.031(d) was justified by the State's 'legitimate interest in protecting and preserving the quality of its educational system and the right of its own bona fide residents to attend state schools on a preferred tuition basis.' In an appeal by two plaintiffs, the United States Court of Appeals for the Fifth Circuit affirmed."

The Supreme Court granted certiorari to review the case and affirmed.

B. Counsel of Record / ACLU Attorney

ACLU Side (Petitioner / Appellant): Edward J. Tuddenham argued the cause for appellant.

Opposing Side (Respondent / Appellee): Richard L. Arnett, Special Assistant Attorney General of Texas, argued the cause for appellee.

III. AMICI CURIAE

ACLU Side (Petitioner / Appellant)

Brief of amici curiae filed on behalf of the ACLU, et al., by Robert S. Ogden, Jr., and Charles S. Sims.

Opposing Side (Respondent / Appellee)

Brief of amici curiae filed on behalf of the Texas Association of School Boards, et al., by David Crump.

IV. THE SUPREME COURT'S DECISION

"The central question we must decide here is whether § 21.031(d) is a bona fide residence requirement. Although the meaning may vary according to context, 'residence' generally requires both physical presence and an intention to remain. As the Supreme Court of Maine explained over a century ago:

'When . . . a person voluntarily takes up his abode in a given place, with intention to remain permanently, or for an indefinite period of time; or, to speak more accurately, when a person takes up his abode in a given place, without any present intention to remove therefrom, such place of abode becomes his residence . . . .'

Section 21.031 is far more generous than this traditional standard. It compels a school district to permit a child such as Morales to attend school without paying tuition if he has a bona fide intention to remain in the school district indefinitely, for he then would have a reason for being there other than his desire to attend school: his intention to make his home in the district. Thus § 21.031 grants the benefits of residency to all who satisfy the traditional requirements. The statute goes further and extends these benefits to many children even if they (or their families) do not intend to remain in the district indefinitely. As long as the child is not living in the district for the sole purpose of attending school, he satisfies the statutory test. For example, if a person comes to Texas to work for a year, his children will be eligible for tuition-free admission to the public schools. Or if a child comes to Texas for six months for health reasons, he would qualify for tuition-free education. In short, § 21.031 grants the benefits of residency to everyone who satisfies the traditional residence definition and to some who legitimately could be classified as nonresidents. Since there is no indication that this extension of the traditional definition has any impermissible basis, we certainly cannot say that § 21.031(d) violates the Constitution. . . .

The Constitution permits a State to restrict eligibility for tuition-free education to its bona fide residents. We hold that § 21.031 is a bona fide residence requirement that satisfies constitutional standards. The judgment of the Court of Appeals accordingly is affirmed."

V. JUSTICE VOTE

1 Pro ACLU Side vs. 8 Con Opposing Side

ACLU Side (Petitioner / Appellant)

1. Marshall, T. – Wrote dissenting opinion

Opposing Side (Respondent / Appellee)

1. Powell, L. – Wrote majority opinion
2. Blackmun, H. – Joined majority opinion
3. Burger, W. – Joined majority opinion
4. O'Connor, S. – Joined majority opinion
5. Stevens, J. – Joined majority opinion
6. White, B. – Joined majority opinion
7. Rehnquist, W. – Joined majority opinion
8. Brennan, W. – Wrote concurring opinion

VI. A WIN OR LOSS FOR THE ACLU?

The ACLU filed as amicus curiae urging reversal; the Supreme Court affirmed the Court of Appeals' judgment in an 8-1 vote giving the ACLU an apparent loss.

505. Kolender v. Lawson

(Decided May 2, 1983; 461 U.S. 352)

I. ISSUE

A. Issues Discussed

Criminal Justice, Fourth Amendment, vagueness

B. Legal Question Presented

Is the California Penal Code § 647(e), which "requires persons who loiter or wander on the streets to provide a 'credible and reliable' identification and to account for their presence when requested by a peace officer" during a Terry stop, unconstitutionally vague?

C. Supreme Court's Answer

The statute is unconstitutionally vague.

II. CASE SUMMARY

A. Background

California Penal Code § 647(e) "requires persons who loiter or wander on the streets to provide a 'credible and reliable' identification and to account for their presence when requested by a peace officer" during a Terry stop.

"Appellee Edward Lawson was detained or arrested on approximately 15 occasions between March 1975 and January 1977 pursuant to Cal.Penal Code § 647(e). Lawson was prosecuted only twice, and was convicted once. The second charge was dismissed.

Lawson then brought a civil action in the District Court for the Southern District of California seeking a declaratory judgment that § 647(e) is unconstitutional, a mandatory injunction seeking to restrain enforcement of the statute, and compensatory and punitive damages against the various officers who detained him. The District Court found that § 647(e) was overbroad because 'a person who is stopped on less than probable cause cannot be punished for failing to identify himself.' The District Court enjoined enforcement of the statute, but held that Lawson could not recover damages because the officers involved acted in the good faith belief that each detention or arrest was lawful.

Appellant H.A. Porazzo, Deputy Chief Commander of the California Highway Patrol, appealed the District Court decision to the Court of Appeals for the Ninth Circuit. Lawson cross-appealed, arguing that he was entitled to a jury trial on the issue of damages against the officers. The Court of Appeals affirmed the District Court determination as to the unconstitutionality of § 647(e). The appellate court determined that the statute was unconstitutional in that it violates the Fourth Amendment's proscription against unreasonable searches and seizures, it contains a vague enforcement standard that is susceptible to arbitrary enforcement, and it fails to give fair and adequate notice of the type of conduct prohibited. Finally, the Court of Appeals reversed the District Court as to its holding that Lawson was not entitled to a jury trial to determine the good faith of the officers in his damages action against them, and remanded the case to the District Court for trial."

The Supreme Court granted certiorari to review the case and affirmed.

B. Counsel of Record / ACLU Attorney

ACLU Side (Respondent / Appellee): ACLU attorney Mark D. Rosenbaum, by invitation of the Court, argued the cause as amicus curiae in support of the judgment below. With him on the brief were Dennis M. Perluss, Fred Okrand, Mary Ellen Gale, Robert H. Lynn, and Charles S. Sims.

Opposing Side (Petitioner / Appellant): A. Wells Petersen, Deputy Attorney General of California, argued the cause for appellants. With him on the briefs were George Deukmejian, Attorney General, Robert H. Philibosian, Chief Assistant Attorney General, Daniel J. Kremer, Assistant Attorney General, and Jay M. Bloom, Deputy Attorney General.

III. AMICI CURIAE

ACLU Side (Respondent / Appellee)

Briefs of amici curiae were filed on behalf of the California Attorneys for Criminal Justice, the Center for Constitutional Rights, the National Lawyers Guild, et al., and the State Public Defender of California.

Opposing Side (Petitioner / Appellant)

Briefs of amici curiae were filed on behalf of the Wayne County Prosecutor's Office, the Appellate Committee of the California District Attorneys Association, and Americans for Effective Law Enforcement Inc., et al.

IV. THE SUPREME COURT'S DECISION

"Our Constitution is designed to maximize individual freedoms within a framework of ordered liberty. Statutory limitations on those freedoms are examined for substantive authority and content as well as for definiteness or certainty of expression. . . .

Appellants stress the need for strengthened law enforcement tools to combat the epidemic of crime that plagues our Nation. The concern of our citizens with curbing criminal activity is certainly a matter requiring the attention of all branches of government. As weighty as this concern is, however, it cannot justify legislation that would otherwise fail to meet constitutional standards for definiteness and clarity. Section 647(e), as presently construed, requires that 'suspicious' persons satisfy some undefined identification requirement, or face criminal punishment. Although due process does not require 'impossible standards' of clarity, this is not a case where further precision in the statutory language is either impossible or impractical. . . .

We conclude § 647(e) is unconstitutionally vague on its face because it encourages arbitrary enforcement by failing to describe with sufficient particularity what a suspect must do in order to satisfy the statute. Accordingly, the judgment of the Court of Appeals is affirmed, and the case is remanded for further proceedings consistent with this opinion."

V. JUSTICE VOTE

7 Pro ACLU Side vs. 2 Con Opposing Side

ACLU Side (Respondent / Appellee)

1. O'Connor, S. – Wrote majority opinion
2. Blackmun, H. – Joined majority opinion
3. Burger, W. – Joined majority opinion
4. Powell, L. – Joined majority opinion
5. Stevens, J. – Joined majority opinion
6. Marshall, T. – Joined majority opinion
7. Brennan, W. – Wrote concurring opinion

Opposing Side (Petitioner / Appellant)

1. White, B. – Wrote dissenting opinion
2. Rehnquist, W. – Joined White's dissent

VI. A WIN OR LOSS FOR THE ACLU?

The ACLU filed and argued as amicus curiae urging affirmance; the Supreme Court affirmed the Court of Appeals' judgment in a 7-2 vote giving the ACLU an apparent win.

506. Boston Firefighters Union, Local 718 v. Boston Chapter, NAACP

(Decided May 16, 1983; 461 U.S. 477)

I. ISSUE

A. Issues Discussed

Civil rights, race

B. Legal Question Presented

"Having previously found discriminatory exclusion of racial minorities from a city's police and fire departments, and having previously established a program of relief designed to remedy the effects of that discrimination, did the district court properly exercise its discretion when, in order to prevent the substantial eradication of the court's remedial efforts, it prohibited the reduction of current proportionate representation of minority officers when the city undertook a massive and unforeseen program of seniority-based layoffs?"[1]

C. Supreme Court's Answer

"In light of these changed circumstances, we vacate the judgment of the Court of Appeals and remand for consideration of mootness in light of 1982 Mass. Acts, ch. 190, § 25."

II. CASE SUMMARY

A. Background

"In these cases, the United States Court of Appeals for the First Circuit upheld the District Court's August 7, 1981 orders enjoining the Boston Police and Fire Departments from laying off policemen and firefighters in a manner that would reduce the percentage of minority officers below the level obtaining at the commencement of layoffs in July, 1981. These orders had the effect of partially superseding the operation of the state's statutory last-hired, first-fired scheme for civil service layoffs, Mass.Gen. Laws Ann. ch. 31, § 39."

B. Counsel of Record

ACLU Side (Respondent / Appellee): James S. Dittmar argued the cause for appellees in all cases. With him on the brief were Judith Bernstein Tracy, Peggy A. Wiesenberg, and Gerald Gillerman.

Opposing Side (Petitioner / Appellant): John F. McMahon argued the cause for appellants in Nos. 82-185 and 82-246 and filed briefs for appellant in No. 82-185. Thomas A. Barnico, Assistant Attorney General of Massachusetts, argued the cause pro hac vice for appellants in No. 82-259. With him on the briefs were Francis X. Bellotti, Attorney General, Thomas R. Kiley, First Assistant Attorney General, E. Michael Sloman, Assistant Attorney General, and Marc S. Seigle, Special Assistant Attorney General. Kevin P. Phillips fied a brief for appellant in No. 82-246.

1 Brief for Respondents at i, Boston Firefighters Union, Local 718 v. Boston Chapter, NAACP, 461 U.S. 477 (1983) (Nos. 82-185, 82-246, 82-259).

III. AMICI CURIAE

ACLU Side (Respondent / Appellee)

Brief of amici curiae filed on behalf of the National Black Police Association, American Civil Liberties Union, and ACLU of Massachusetts by Jon C. Dubin, E. Richard Larson, Burt Neuborne, and Paulette M. Caldwell.

Brief of amici curiae filed on behalf of the National Bar Association, Inc., et al. by J. Clay Smith, Jr., and Herbert O. Reid, Sr.

Brief of amici curiae filed on behalf of the City of Detroit by O. Peter Sherwood, Clyde E. Murphy, and Barry L. Goldstein.

Brief of amici curiae filed on behalf of the League of United Latin American Citizens et al. by Joaquin G. Avila, Morris J. Baller, and Carmen A. Estrada.

Brief of amici curiae filed on behalf of the Officers For Justice et al. by Robert L. Harris and Eva Jefferson Paterson.

Brief of amici curiae filed on behalf of the National Organization for Women et al. by Judith I. Avner and Anne E. Simon.

Brief of amici curiae filed on behalf of the National Education Association by Robert H. Chanin, Richard B. Sobol, and Michael B. Trister.

Brief of amici curiae filed on behalf of Robert Lipshutz et al. by Mr. Lipshutz, pro se.

Brief of amici curiae filed on behalf of the NAACP Legal Defense and Educational Fund, Inc., by Jack Greenberg and Eric Schnapper.

Brief of amici curiae filed on behalf of the Affirmative Action Coordinating Center et al. by Arthur Kinoy and Michael Ratner.

Opposing Side (Petitioner / Appellant)

Brief of amici curiae filed on behalf of the United States by Solicitor General Lee, Assistant Attorney General Reynolds, Deputy Solicitor General Wallace, Deputy Assistant Attorney General Cooper, Carter G. Phillips, Brian K. Landsberg, Walter W. Barnett, and Dennis J. Dimsey.

Brief of amici curiae filed on behalf of the Equal Employment Advisory Council by Robert E. Williams, Douglas S. McDowell, and Daniel R. Levinson.

Brief of amici curiae filed on behalf of the American Federation of Labor and Congress of Industrial Organizations et al. by J. Albert Woll, Michael H. Gottesman, Robert M. Weinberg, George H. Cohen, and Laurence Gold.

Brief of amici curiae filed on behalf of the International Association of Firefighters, AFL-CIO by Edward J. Hickey, Jr., Michael S. Wolly, and Erick J. Genser.

Brief of amici curiae filed on behalf of the AntiDefamation League of B'nai B'rith by Robert A. Helman, Michele Odorizzi, Daniel M. Harris, Justin J. Finger, Jeffrey P. Sinensky, and Meyer Eisenberg.

Brief of amici curiae filed on behalf of the Washington Legal Foundation by Daniel J. Popeo, Paul D. Kamenar, and Nicholas E. Calio.

Brief of amici curiae filed on behalf of the Detroit Police Officers Association by Walter S. Nussbaum and Donald J. Mooney, Jr.

Brief of amici curiae filed on behalf of the Pacific Legal Foundation by Ronald A. Zumbrun and John H. Findley.

IV. THE SUPREME COURT'S DECISION

"Following the Court of Appeals' decision, Massachusetts enacted legislation providing the City of Boston with new revenues, requiring reinstatement of all police and firefighters laid off during the reductions in force, securing these personnel against future layoffs for fiscal reasons, and requiring the maintenance of minimum staffing levels in the police and fire departments through June 30, 1983. In light of these changed circumstances, we vacate the judgment of the Court of Appeals and remand for consideration of mootness in light of 1982 Mass. Acts, c. 190, § 25."

V. JUSTICE VOTE

0 Pro ACLU Side vs. 8 Con Opposing Side

Opposing Side (Petitioner / Appellant)

1. Rehnquist, W. – Per curiam decision
2. Burger, W. – Per curiam decision
3. Powell, L. – Per curiam decision
4. O'Connor, S. – Per curiam decision
5. Blackmun, H. – Per curiam decision
6. Brennan, W. – Per curiam decision
7. White, B. – Per curiam decision
8. Stevens, J. – Per curiam decision

Marshall, T – Took no part in the decision

VI. A WIN OR LOSS FOR THE ACLU?

The ACLU filed as amicus curiae urging affirmance; the Supreme Court vacated the Court of Appeals' decision by a per curiam 8-0 decision, giving the ACLU an apparent loss.

507. Bob Jones University v. United States

(Decided May 24, 1983; 461 U.S. 574)

I. ISSUE

A. Issues Discussed

First Amendment, Free Exercise Clause, Establishment Clause, civil rights, race

B. Legal Question Presented

"[W]hether petitioners, nonprofit private schools that prescribe and enforce racially discriminatory admissions standards on the basis of religious doctrine, qualify as tax-exempt organizations under § 501(c)(3) of the Internal Revenue Code of 1954."

C. Supreme Court's Answer

Petitioners cannot qualify as tax-exempt organizations while enforcing racially discriminatory admissions standards on the basis of religious doctrine.

II. CASE SUMMARY

A. Background

"Until 1970, the Internal Revenue Service granted tax-exempt status to private schools, without regard to their racial admissions policies, under § 501(c)(3) of the Internal Revenue Code, and granted charitable deductions for contributions to such schools....

On January 12, 1970, a three-judge District Court for the District of Columbia issued a preliminary injunction prohibiting the IRS from according tax-exempt status to private schools in Mississippi that discriminated as to admissions on the basis of race. Thereafter, in July 1970, the IRS concluded that it could 'no longer legally justify allowing tax-exempt status [under § 501(c)(3)] to private schools which practice racial discrimination.' At the same time, the IRS announced that it could not 'treat gifts to such schools as charitable deductions for income tax purposes.' By letter dated November 30, 1970, the IRS formally notified private schools, including those involved in this litigation, of this change in policy, 'applicable to all private schools in the United States at all levels of education.'

On June 30, 1971, the three-judge District Court issued its opinion on the merits of the Mississippi challenge. That court approved the IRS' amended construction of the Tax Code....

Bob Jones University is a nonprofit corporation.... Its purpose is 'to conduct an institution of learning..., giving special emphasis to the Christian religion and the ethics revealed in the Holy Scriptures.' The corporation operates a school with an enrollment of approximately 5,000 students, from kindergarten through college and graduate school. Bob Jones University is not affiliated with any religious denomination, but is dedicated to the teaching and propagation of its fundamentalist Christian religious beliefs. It is both a religious and educational institution. Its teachers are required to be devout Christians, and all courses at the University are taught according to the Bible. Entering students are screened as to their religious beliefs, and their public and private conduct is strictly regulated by standards promulgated by University authorities.

The sponsors of the University genuinely believe that the Bible forbids interracial dating and marriage. To effectuate these views, Negroes were completely excluded until 1971. From 1971 to May 1975, the University accepted no applications from unmarried Negroes, but did accept applications from Negroes married within their race.

Following the decision of the United States Court of Appeals for the Fourth Circuit in McCrary v. Runyon, prohibiting racial exclusion from private schools, the University revised its policy. Since May 29, 1975, the University has permitted unmarried Negroes to enroll; but a disciplinary rule prohibits interracial dating and marriage.

[O]n April 16, 1975, the IRS notified the University of the proposed revocation of its tax-exempt status. On January 19, 1976, the IRS officially revoked the University's tax-exempt status, effective as of December 1, 1970, the day after the University was formally notified of the change in IRS policy. The University subsequently filed returns under the Federal Unemployment Tax Act for the period from December 1, 1970, to December 31, 1975, and paid a tax totalling $21.00 on one employee for the calendar year of 1975. After its request for a refund was denied, the University instituted the present action, seeking to recover the $21.00 it had paid to the IRS. The Government counterclaimed for unpaid federal unemployment taxes for the taxable years 1971 through 1975, in the amount of $489,675.59, plus interest.

The United States District Court for the District of South Carolina held that revocation of the University's tax-exempt status exceeded the delegated powers of the IRS, was improper under the IRS rulings and procedures, and violated the University's rights under the Religion Clauses of the First Amendment. . . .

The Court of Appeals for the Fourth Circuit, in a divided opinion, reversed. . . . In the court's view, Bob Jones University did not meet this requirement, since its 'racial policies violated the clearly defined public policy, rooted in our Constitution, condemning racial discrimination and, more specifically, the government policy against subsidizing racial discrimination in education, public or private.' . . . Finally, the Court of Appeals rejected petitioner's arguments that the revocation of the tax exemption violated the Free Exercise and Establishment Clauses of the First Amendment."

The Supreme Court granted certiorari to review the case and affirmed the judgment of the Fourth Circuit Court of Appeals.

B. Counsel of Record / ACLU Attorney

ACLU Side (Respondent / Appellee): Assistant Attorney General Reynolds argued the cause for the United States.

William T. Coleman, Jr., pro se, by invitation of the Court, argued the cause as amicus curiae.

Opposing Side (Petitioner / Appellant): William Bentley Ball argued the cause for appellant.

III. AMICI CURIAE

ACLU Side (Respondent / Appellee)

Brief of amici curiae filed on behalf of the ACLU, et al., by Nadine Strossen, E. Richard Larson, and Samuel Rabinove.

Brief of amici curiae filed on behalf of William T. Coleman, Jr., by William T. Coleman, Jr., pro se, Richard C. Warmer, Donald T. Bliss, John W. Stamper, Ira M. Feinberg, and Eric Schnapper.

Additional briefs of amici curiae were filed on behalf of the Anti-Defamation League of B'nai B'rith, Independent Sector, the International Human Rights Law Group, the Lawyers' Committee for Civil Rights Under Law, the National Association for the Advancement of Colored People, et al., the NAACP Legal Defense and Educational Fund, Inc., the National Association of Independent Schools, the North Carolina Association of Black Lawyers, the United Church of Christ, Lawrence E. Lewy, Laurence H. Tribe, and Bernard Wolfman.

Opposing Side (Petitioner / Appellant)

Briefs of amici curiae were filed on behalf of the American Baptist Churches in the U.S.A., et al., the Center for Law and Religious Freedom of the Christian Legal Society, the National Association of Evangelicals, National Jewish Commission on Law and Public Affairs, and Congressman Trent Lott.

IV. THE SUPREME COURT'S DECISION

"In Revenue Ruling 71-447, the IRS formalized the policy, first announced in 1970, that § 170 and § 501(c)(3) embrace the common-law 'charity' concept. Under that view, to qualify for a tax exemption pursuant to § 501(c)(3), an institution must show, first, that it falls within one of the eight categories expressly set forth in that section, and second, that its activity is not contrary to settled public policy. . . .

When the Government grants exemptions or allows deductions all taxpayers are affected; the very fact of the exemption or deduction for the donor means that other taxpayers can be said to be indirect and vicarious 'donors.' Charitable exemptions are justified on the basis that the exempt entity confers a public benefit—a benefit which the society or the community may not itself choose or be able to provide, or which supplements and advances the work of public institutions already supported by tax revenues. . . . The institution's purpose must not be so at odds with the common community conscience as to undermine any public benefit that might otherwise be conferred. . . .

We are bound to approach these questions with full awareness that determinations of public benefit and public policy are sensitive matters with serious implications for the institutions affected; a declaration that a given institution is not 'charitable' should be made only where there can be no doubt that the activity involved is contrary to a fundamental public policy. But there can no longer be any doubt that racial discrimination in education violates deeply and widely accepted views of elementary justice. . . .

Petitioners contend that, regardless of whether the IRS properly concluded that racially discriminatory private schools violate public policy, only Congress can alter the scope of § 170 and § 501(c)(3). Petitioners accordingly argue that the IRS overstepped its lawful bounds in issuing its 1970 and 1971 rulings. . . .

On the record before us, there can be no doubt as to the national policy. In 1970, when the IRS first issued the ruling challenged here, the position of all three branches of the Federal Government was unmistakably clear. . . . We therefore hold that the IRS did not exceed its authority when it announced its interpretation of § 170 and § 501(c)(3) in 1970 and 1971. . . .

Petitioners contend that, even if the Commissioner's policy is valid as to nonreligious private schools, that policy cannot constitutionally be applied to schools that engage in racial discrimination on the basis of sincerely held religious beliefs. As to such schools, it is argued that the IRS construction of § 170 and § 501(c)(3) violates their free exercise rights under the Religion Clauses of the First Amendment. . . .

The governmental interest at stake here is compelling. [T] he Government has a fundamental, overriding interest in eradicating racial discrimination in education—discrimination that prevailed, with official approval, for the first 165 years of this Nation's history. That governmental interest substantially outweighs whatever burden denial of tax benefits places on petitioners' exercise of their religious beliefs. . . .

The remaining issue is whether the IRS properly applied its policy to these petitioners. . . . Petitioner Bob Jones University . . . contends that it is not racially discriminatory. It emphasizes that it now allows all races to enroll, subject only to its restrictions on the conduct of all students, including its prohibitions of association between men and women of different races, and of interracial marriage. Although a ban on intermarriage or interracial dating applies to all races, decisions of this Court firmly establish that discrimination on the basis of racial affiliation and association is a form of racial discrimination. We therefore find that the IRS properly applied Revenue Ruling 71-447 to Bob Jones University.

The judgments of the Court of Appeals are, accordingly, affirmed."

V. JUSTICE VOTE

8 Pro ACLU Side vs. 1 Con Opposing Side

ACLU Side (Respondent / Appellee)

1. Burger, W. – Wrote majority opinion
2. Brennan, W. – Joined majority opinion
3. White, B. – Joined majority opinion
4. Marshall, T. – Joined majority opinion
5. Stevens, J. – Joined majority opinion
6. O'Connor, S. – Joined majority opinion
7. Powell, L. – Wrote concurring opinion
8. Blackmun, H. – Joined majority opinion

Opposing Side (Petitioner / Appellant)

1. Rehnquist, W. – Wrote dissenting opinion

VI. A WIN OR LOSS FOR THE ACLU?

The ACLU, as amicus curiae, urged affirmance of the judgment of the Fourth Circuit Court of Appeals; the Supreme Court affirmed in an 8-1 vote, giving the ACLU an apparent win.

508. Illinois v. Gates

(Decided June 8, 1983; 462 U.S. 213)

I. ISSUE

A. Issues Discussed

Criminal justice, Fourth Amendment, Fourteenth Amendement, warrants

B. Legal Question Presented

"[W]hether respondents' rights under the Fourth and Fourteenth Amendments were violated by the search of their car and house."

C. Supreme Court's Answer

Respondents' Fourth and Fourteenth Amendment rights were not violated because the search warrant was supported by probable cause.

II. CASE SUMMARY

A. Background

"On May 3, 1978, the Bloomingdale Police Department received by mail an anonymous handwritten letter [alledging that Lance and Susan Gates, respondents, were drug dealers with] over $100,000 worth of drugs in their basement [and detailing predicted future activites]. . . . Chief of Police . . . Mader [investigated the couple and] learned from a police officer assigned to O'Hare Airport that 'L. Gates' had made a reservation on Eastern Airlines flight 245 to West Palm Beach, Fla., scheduled to depart from Chicago on May 5 at 4:15 p.m.

Mader then made arrangements with an agent of the Drug Enforcement Administration for surveillance of the May 5 Eastern Airlines flight. [The surveillance revealed activities in line with those discussed in the anonymous letter.]

Mader signed an affidavit . . . and submitted it to a judge of the Circuit Court of DuPage County, together with a copy of the anonymous letter. The judge of that court thereupon issued a search warrant for the Gates' residence and for their automobile. The judge, in deciding to issue the warrant, could have determined that the modus operandi of the Gates had been substantially corroborated. As the anonymous letter predicted, Lance Gates had flown from Chicago to West Palm Beach late in the afternoon of May 5th, had checked into a hotel room registered in the name of his wife, and, at 7:00 a.m. the following morning, had headed north, accompanied by an unidentified woman, out of West Palm Beach on an interstate highway used by travelers from South Florida to Chicago in an automobile bearing a license plate issued to him.

At 5:15 a.m. on March 7th, only 36 hours after he had flown out of Chicago, Lance Gates, and his wife, returned to their home in Bloomingdale, driving the car in which they had left West Palm Beach some 22 hours earlier. The Bloomingdale police were awaiting them, searched the trunk of the Mercury, and uncovered approximately 350 pounds of marijuana. A search of the Gates' home revealed marijuana, weapons, and other contraband. The Illinois Circuit Court ordered suppression of all these items, on the ground that the affidavit submitted to the Circuit Judge failed to support the necessary determination of probable cause to believe that the Gates' automobile and home contained the contraband in question. This decision was affirmed in turn by the Illinois Appellate Court and by a divided vote of the Supreme Court of Illinois."

The Supreme Court granted certiorari to review the case and reversed.

B. Counsel of Record / ACLU Attorney

ACLU Side (Respondent / Appellee): James W. Reilley reargued the cause for appellee.

Opposing Side (Petitioner / Appellant): Paul P. Biebel, Jr., First Assistant Attorney General of Illinois, reargued the cause for appellant.

Solicitor General Lee argued the cause on reargument for the United States, as amicus curiae, by special leave of Court.

III. AMICI CURIAE

ACLU Side (Respondent / Appellee)

Brief of amici curiae filed on behalf of the ACLU, et al., by Charles S. Sims and Burt Neuborne.

Additional briefs of amici curiae were filed on behalf of the Association of Trial Lawyers of America, the Illinois State Bar Association, the New York Criminal Bar Association, the Legal Internship Program, Georgetown University Law Center, the American Bar Association, the Committee on Criminal Law of the Association of the Bar of the City of New York, the National Association of Criminal Defense Lawyers, et al., and the National Legal Aid and Defender Association.

Opposing Side (Petitioner / Appellant)

Brief of amici curiae filed on behalf of the United States by Solicitor General Lee, Assistant Attorney General Jensen, Deputy Solicitor General Frey, Kathryn A. Oberly, Geoffrey S. Stewart, and Robert J. Erickson, Mr. Jensen, Alan I. Horowitz, and David B. Smith.

Additional briefs of amici curiae were filed on behalf of the State of California, Americans for Effective Law Enforcement, Inc., et al., Laws at Work, et al., the Commonwealth of Virginia, the State of Florida, et al., and the National District Attorneys Association, Inc.

IV. THE SUPREME COURT'S DECISION

"[T]he anonymous letter contained a range of details relating not just to easily obtained facts and conditions existing at the time of the tip, but to future actions of third parties ordinarily not easily predicted. The letter writer's accurate information as to the travel plans of each of the Gates was of a character likely obtained only from the Gateses themselves, or from someone familiar with their not entirely ordinary travel plans. If the informant had access to accurate information of this type a magistrate could properly conclude that it was not unlikely that he also had access to reliable information of the Gates' alleged illegal activities. Of course, the Gates' travel plans might have been learned from a talkative neighbor or travel agent; under the 'two-pronged test' developed from Spinelli, the character of the details in the anonymous letter might well not permit a sufficiently clear inference regarding the letterwriter's 'basis of knowledge.' But, as discussed previously, probable cause does not demand the certainty we associate with formal trials. It is enough that there was a fair probability that the writer of the anonymous letter had obtained his entire story either from the Gates or someone they trusted. And corroboration of major portions of the letter's predictions provides just this probability. It is apparent, therefore, that the judge issuing the warrant had a 'substantial basis for . . . conclud[ing]' that probable cause to search the Gates' home and car existed. The judgment of the Supreme Court of Illinois therefore must be reversed."

V. JUSTICE VOTE

3 Pro ACLU Side vs. 6 Con Opposing Side

ACLU Side (Respondent / Appellee)

1. Stevens, J. – Wrote dissenting opinion
2. Brennan, W. – Wrote dissenting opinion, joined Stevens' dissent
3. Marshall, T. – Joined Brennan's dissent

Opposing Side (Petitioner / Appellant)

1. Rehnquist, W. – Wrote majority opinion
2. Blackmun, H. – Joined majority opinion
3. Burger, W. – Joined majority opinion
4. Powell, L. – Joined majority opinion
5. O'Connor, S. – Joined majority opinion
6. White, B. – Wrote concurring opinion

VI. A WIN OR LOSS FOR THE ACLU?

The ACLU filed as amicus curiae urging affirmance; the U.S. Supreme Court reversed the Illinois Supreme Court's judgment in a 6-3 vote, giving the ACLU an apparent loss.

509. Chappell v. Wallace

(Decided June 13, 1983; 462 U.S. 296)

I. ISSUE

A. Issues Discussed

Governmental authority, military

B. Legal Question Presented

"[W]hether enlisted military personnel may maintain suits to recover damages from superior officers for injuries sustained as a result of violations of constitutional rights in the course of military service."

C. Supreme Court's Answer

Enlisted military personnel may not maintain a suit to recover damages from superior officers for alleged violations of constitutional rights because of the unique military structure.

II. CASE SUMMARY

A. Background

"Respondents are five enlisted men who serve in the United States Navy on board a combat naval vessel. Petitioners are the Commanding Officer of the vessel, four lieutenants and three noncommissioned officers.

Respondents brought action against these officers seeking damages, declaratory judgment, and injunctive relief. Respondents alleged that because of their minority race petitioners failed to assign them desirable duties, threatened them, gave them low performance evaluations, and imposed penalties of unusual severity. Respondents claimed, inter alia, that the actions complained of 'deprived [them] of [their] rights under the Constitution and laws of the United States, including the right not to be discriminated against because of [their] race, color or previous condition of servitude . . . .' Respondents also alleged a conspiracy among petitioners to deprive them of rights in violation of 42 U.S.C. § 1985.

The United States District Court for the Southern District of California dismissed the complaint on the grounds that the actions respondents complained of were nonreviewable military decisions, that petitioners were entitled to immunity and that respondents had failed to exhaust their administrative remedies.

The United States Court of Appeals for the Ninth Circuit reversed. The Court of Appeals assumed that Bivens v. Six Unknown Named Agents of Federal Bureau of Narcotics, authorized the award of damages for the constitutional violations alleged in their complaint, unless the actions complained of were either not reviewable or petitioners were immune from suit. The Court of Appeals set out certain tests for determining whether the actions at issue are reviewable by a civilian court and, if so, whether petitioners are nonetheless immune from suit. The case was remanded to the District Court for application of these tests."

The Supreme Court granted certiorari to review the case and reversed.

B. Counsel of Record / ACLU Attorney

ACLU Side (Respondent / Appellee): John Murcko, by appointment of the Court, argued the cause for appellee.

Opposing Side (Petitioner / Appellant): Assistant Attorney General McGrath argued the cause for appellant.

III. AMICI CURIAE

ACLU Side (Respondent / Appellee)

Brief of amici curiae filed on behalf of the ACLU by Nanette Dembitz and Burt Neuborne.

Brief of amici curiae filed on behalf of the Bill of Rights Foundation, Inc., by Leonard B. Boudin.

Brief of amici curiae filed on behalf of the Lawyers' Committee for Civil Rights Under Law by Barry Sullivan.

Brief of amici curiae filed on behalf of the NAACP Legal Defense and Educational Fund, Inc., by Jack Greenberg, James M. Nabritt, III, Steven L. Winter, and Steven J. Phillips.

Opposing Side (Petitioner / Appellant)

Brief of amici curiae filed on behalf of the Naval Reserve Association by Mitchell L. Lathrop and Terrence L. Bingman.

Brief of amici curiae filed on behalf of the Washington Legal Foundation by Daniel J. Popeo, Paul D. Kamenar, and Nicholas E. Calio.

IV. THE SUPREME COURT'S DECISION

"Congress' authority in this area, and the distance between military and civilian life, was summed up by the Court in Orloff v. Willoughby . . . '[J]udges are not given the task of running the Army. The responsibility for setting up channels through which . . . grievances can be considered and fairly settled rests upon the Congress and upon the President of the United States and his subordinates. The military constitutes a specialized community governed by a separate discipline from that of the civilian. Orderly government requires that the judiciary be as scrupulous not to interfere with legitimate Army matters as the Army must be scrupulous not to intervene in judicial matters.' . . .

The special status of the military has required, the Constitution has contemplated, Congress has created, and this Court has long recognized two systems of justice, to some extent parallel: one for civilians and one for military personnel. The special nature of military life—the need for unhesitating and decisive action by military officers and equally disciplined responses by enlisted personnel—would be undermined by a judicially created remedy exposing officers to personal liability at the hands of those they are charged to command. . . .

Also, Congress, the constitutionally authorized source of authority over the military system of justice, has not provided a damages remedy for claims by military personnel that constitutional rights have been violated by superior officers. Any action to provide a judicial response by way of such a remedy would be plainly inconsistent with Congress' authority in this field.

Taken together, the unique disciplinary structure of the Military Establishment and Congress' activity in the field constitute 'special factors' which dictate that it would be inappropriate to provide enlisted military personnel a Bivens-type remedy against their superior officers. . . .

We hold that enlisted military personnel may not maintain a suit to recover damages from a superior officer for alleged constitutional violations. The judgment of the Court of Appeals is reversed, and the case is remanded for further proceedings consistent with this opinion."

V. JUSTICE VOTE

0 Pro ACLU Side vs. 9 Con Opposing Side

Opposing Side (Petitioner / Appellant)

1. Burger, W. – Wrote majority opinion
2. Marshall, T. – Joined majority opinion
3. Brennan, W. – Joined majority opinion
4. White, B. – Joined majority opinion
5. Powell, L. – Joined majority opinion
6. Rehnquist, W. – Joined majority opinion
7. O'Connor, S. – Joined majority opinion
8. Stevens, J. – Joined majority opinion
9. Blackmun, H. – Joined majority opinion

VI. A WIN OR LOSS FOR THE ACLU?

The ACLU filed as amicus curiae urging affirmance; the Supreme Court reversed the Court of Appeals' judgment in a 9-0 vote giving the ACLU an apparent loss.

510. Haring v. Prosise

(Decided June 13, 1983; 462 U.S. 306)

I. ISSUE

A. Issues Discussed

Criminal justice, drugs, Fourth Amendment

B. Legal Question Presented

"[W]hether Prosise's § 1983 action to redress an alleged Fourth Amendment violation is barred by the judgment of conviction entered in state court following his guilty plea."

C. Supreme Court's Answer

The § 1983 action is not barred by Prosise's guilty plea.

II. CASE SUMMARY

A. Background

"On April 27, 1978, pursuant to a plea agreement, Prosise pleaded guilty in the Circuit Court for Arlington County, Va., to one count of manufacturing phencyclidine. The Commonwealth then called one witness, Detective Henry Allen of the Arlington County Police Department. Allen testified that on September 7, 1977, he responded to a radio call directing him to an Arlington apartment which turned out to be leased to Prosise. By the time he arrived, two uniformed officers had placed Prosise under arrest for the possession of a controlled substance. After entering the apartment, Allen noticed various chemicals in the apartment as well as a quantity of what he believed to be phencyclidine. A warrant was later obtained for a search of the apartment. Allen and Detective Petti then conducted a search which led to the seizure of devices and chemicals used to manufacture phencyclidine, receipts for such chemicals, a paper containing a formula for making phencyclidine, and two buckets containing traces of the substance.

At the conclusion of Allen's testimony, the judge accepted Prosise's guilty plea, finding that it had been entered voluntarily and intelligently and that it had a sufficient basis in fact. On June 23, 1978, the court denied Prosise's motion to withdraw his plea and sentenced him to 25 years' imprisonment.

On January 23, 1979, while under confinement in the Arlington Detention Center, Prosise filed a pro se action under 42 U.S.C. § 1983 against Lt. Gilbert A. Haring and various other members of the Arlington County Police Department who had participated in the search of his apartment. His complaint alleged that the officers had unlawfully searched his apartment prior to obtaining a search warrant, and that after obtaining the warrant the officers conducted a search that exceeded the scope of the warrant.

The District Court granted summary judgment for defendants on the ground that Prosise's guilty plea to the charge of manufacturing phencyclidine barred his § 1983 claim. . . . The Court of Appeals reversed and remanded for further proceedings."

The Supreme Court granted certiorari to review the case and affirmed.

B. Counsel of Record / ACLU Attorney

ACLU Side (Respondent / Appellee): Norman A. Townsend argued the cause for appellee.

Opposing Side (Petitioner / Appellant): David R. Lasso argued the cause for appellant.

III. AMICI CURIAE

ACLU Side (Respondent / Appellee)

Brief of amici curiae filed on behalf of the ACLU by Charles S. Sims and Burt Neuborne.

Brief of amici curiae filed on behalf of the University of Virginia School of Law Post-Conviction Assistance Project by Stephen A. Saltzburg.

Opposing Side (Petitioner / Appellant)

Brief of amici curiae filed on behalf of Americans for Effective Law Enforcement, Inc., et al., by Fred E. Inbau, Wayne W. Schmidt, James P. Manak, Evelle J. Younger, Daniel B. Hales, and David Crump.

IV. THE SUPREME COURT'S DECISION

"Under our past decisions, as the District Court correctly recognized, a guilty plea results in the defendant's loss of any meaningful opportunity he might otherwise have had to challenge the admissibility of evidence obtained in violation of the Fourth Amendment. It does not follow, however, that a guilty plea is a 'waiver' of antecedent Fourth Amendment claims that may be given effect outside the confines of the criminal proceeding. The defendant's rights under the Fourth Amendment are not among the trial rights that he necessarily waives when he knowingly and voluntarily pleads guilty. . . .

Defendants who have pleaded guilty and who wish to bring a § 1983 claim would be forced to bring that claim in state court, if at all. Not only have petitioners failed to advance any compelling justification for a rule confining the litigation of constitutional claims to a state forum, but such a rule would be wholly contrary to one of the central concerns which motivated the enactment of § 1983, namely, the 'grave congressional concern that the state courts had been deficient in protecting federal rights.'

We conclude that respondent's conviction in state court does not preclude him from now seeking to recover damages under 42 U.S.C. § 1983 for an alleged Fourth Amendment violation that was never considered in the state proceedings. Accordingly, the judgment of the Court of Appeals is affirmed."

V. JUSTICE VOTE

9 Pro ACLU Side vs. 0 Con Opposing Side

ACLU Side (Respondent / Appellee)

1. Marshall, T. – Wrote majority opinion
2. Burger, W. – Joined majority opinion
3. Brennan, W. – Joined majority opinion
4. White, B. – Joined majority opinion
5. Powell, L. – Joined majority opinion
6. Rehnquist, W. – Joined majority opinion
7. O'Connor, S. – Joined majority opinion
8. Stevens, J. – Joined majority opinion
9. Blackmun, H. – Joined majority opinion

VI. A WIN OR LOSS FOR THE ACLU?

The ACLU filed as amicus curiae urging affirmance; the Supreme Court affirmed the Court of Appeals' judgment in a 9-0 vote giving the ACLU an apparent win.

511. Bush v. Lucas

(Decided June 13, 1983; 462 U.S. 367)

I. ISSUE

A. Issues Discussed

First amendment, freedoms of press, speech, and association, employment

B. Legal Question Presented

Whether a federal employee can receive nonstatutory damages for the violation of his First Amendment rights by his superior where Congress has provided a comprehensive remedial scheme for claims arising within the employment relationship.

C. Supreme Court's Answer

The federal employee cannot receive nonstatutory damages because Congress has provided a comprehensive remedial scheme for grievances arising from this type of employment relationship.

II. CASE SUMMARY

A. Background

"Petitioner Bush is an aerospace engineer employed at the George C. Marshall Space Flight Center, a major facility operated by the National Aeronautics and Space Administration in Alabama. Respondent Lucas is the Director of the Center. In 1974 the facility was reorganized and petitioner was twice reassigned to new positions. He objected to both reassignments and sought formal review by the Civil Service Commission. In May and June 1975, while some of his administrative appeals were pending, he made a number of public statements, including two televised interviews, that were highly critical of the agency. . . .

In August 1975 an adverse personnel action was initiated to remove petitioner from his position. Petitioner was charged with 'publicly mak[ing] intemperate remarks which were misleading and often false, evidencing a malicious attitude towards Management and generating an environment of sensationalism demeaning to the Government, the National Aeronautics and Space Administration and the personnel of the George C. Marshall Space Flight Center, thereby impeding Government efficiency and economy and adversely affecting public confidence in the Government service.' He was also informed that his conduct had undermined morale at the Center and caused disharmony and disaffection among his fellow employees. Petitioner had the opportunity to file a written response and to make an oral presentation to agency officials. Respondent then determined that petitioner's statements were false and misleading and that his conduct would justify removal, but that the lesser penalty of demotion was appropriate for a 'first offense.' He approved a reduction in grade from GS-14 to GS-12, which decreased petitioner's annual salary by approximately $9,716.

Petitioner exercised his right to appeal to the Federal Employee Appeals Authority. After a three-day public hearing, the Authority upheld some of the charges and concluded that the demotion was justified. It specifically determined that a number of petitioner's public statements were misleading and that, for three reasons, they 'exceeded the bounds of expression protected by the First Amendment.' . . .

Two years after the Appeals Authority's decision, petitioner requested the Civil Service Commission's Appeals Review Board to reopen the proceeding. The Board reexamined petitioner's First Amendment claim and [determined that] the nature and extent of proven disruption to the agency's operations did not 'justify abrogation of the exercise of free speech.' The Board recommended that petitioner be restored to his former position, retroactively to November 30, 1975, and that he receive back pay. . . .

While his administrative appeal was pending, petitioner filed an action against respondent in state court in Alabama seeking to recover damages for defamation and violation of his constitutional rights. Respondent removed the lawsuit to the United States District Court for the Northern District of Alabama, which granted respondent's motion for summary judgment. . . . The United States Court of Appeals for the Fifth Circuit affirmed. [The Supreme Court] vacated that court's judgment, and directed that it reconsider the case in the light of [the] intervening decision in Carlson v. Green, 446 U.S. 14 (1980). The Court of Appeals again affirmed the judgment against petitioner. It adhered to its previous conclusion 'that plaintiff had no cause of action for damages under the First Amendment for retaliatory demotion in view of the available remedies under the Civil Service Commission regulations.'"

The Supreme Court granted certiorari to review the case and affirmed.

B. Counsel of Record / ACLU Attorney

ACLU Side (Petitioner / Appellant): William Harvey Elrod, Jr., argued the cause for appellant

Opposing Side (Respondent / Appellee): Deputy Solicitor General Geller argued the cause for appellee.

III. AMICI CURIAE

ACLU Side (Petitioner / Appellant)

Brief of amici curiae filed on behalf of the ACLU by Charles B. Wayne and Mark H. Lynch.

Brief of amici curiae filed on behalf of the American Federation of Labor and Congress of Industrial Organizations, et al., by J. Albert Woll, Marsha Berzon, Laurence Gold, Edward J. Hickey, Erick Genser, James Rosa, and David Barr.

Brief of amici curiae filed on behalf of the National Treasury Employees Union by John F. Bufe, Lois G. Williams, and Michael David Fox.

Brief of amici curiae filed on behalf of Representative Schroeder, et al., by John C. Keeney, Jr., Joseph M. Hassett, and Peter Raven-Hansen.

Opposing Side (Respondent / Appellee)

No briefs of amici curiae were filed in support of appellee.

IV. THE SUPREME COURT'S DECISION

"[W]e assume, a federal right has been violated and Congress has provided a less than complete remedy for the wrong. If we were writing on a clean slate, we might answer the question whether to supplement the statutory scheme in either of two quite simple ways. We might adopt the common-law approach to the judicial recognition of new causes of action and hold that it is the province of the judiciary to fashion an adequate remedy for every wrong that can be proved in a case over which a court has jurisdiction. Or we might start from the premise that federal courts are courts of limited jurisdiction whose remedial powers do not extend beyond the granting of relief expressly authorized by Congress. Under the former approach, petitioner would obviously prevail; under the latter, it would be equally clear that he would lose. . . .

In the Standard Oil case, [t]he Court refused to create a damages remedy, which would be 'the instrument for determining and establishing the federal fiscal and regulatory policies which the Government's executive arm thinks should prevail in a situation not covered by traditionally established liabilities.' . . .

Given the history of the development of civil service remedies and the comprehensive nature of the remedies currently available, it is clear that the question we confront today is quite different from the typical remedial issue confronted by a common-law court. The question is not what remedy the court should provide for a wrong that would otherwise go unredressed. It is whether an elaborate remedial system that has been constructed step by step, with careful attention to conflicting policy considerations, should be augmented by the creation of a new judicial remedy for the constitutional violation at issue. That question obviously cannot be answered simply by noting that existing remedies do not provide complete relief for the plaintiff. The policy judgment should be informed by a thorough understanding of the existing regulatory structure and the respective costs and benefits that would result from the addition of another remedy for violations of employees' First Amendment rights. . . .

Thus, we do not decide whether or not it would be good policy to permit a federal employee to recover damages from a supervisor who has improperly disciplined him for exercising his First Amendment rights. As we did in Standard Oil, we decline 'to create a new substantive legal liability without legislative aid and as at the common law,' because we are convinced that Congress is in a better position to decide whether or not the public interest would be served by creating it. The judgment of the Court of Appeals is affirmed."

V. JUSTICE VOTE

0 Pro ACLU Side vs. 9 Con Opposing Side

Opposing Side (Respondent / Appellee)

1. Stevens, J. – Wrote majority opinion
2. Burger, W. – Joined majority opinion
3. Brennan, W. – Joined majority opinion
4. White, B. – Joined majority opinion
5. Powell, L. – Joined majority opinion
6. Rehnquist, W. – Joined majority opinion
7. O'Connor, S. – Joined majority opinion
8. Marshall, T. – Wrote concurring opinion
9. Blackmun, H. – Joined Marshall's concurrence

VI. A WIN OR LOSS FOR THE ACLU?

The ACLU filed as amicus curiae urging reversal; the Supreme Court affirmed the Court of Appeals' judgment in a 9-0 vote giving ACLU an apparent loss.

512. City of Akron v. Akron Center for Reproductive Health, Inc.

(Decided June 15, 1983; 462 U.S. 416)

I. ISSUE

A. Issues Discussed

Fourteenth Amendment, right to privacy, abortion rights

B. Legal Question Presented

Is an Ohio ordinance, which regulates the performance of abortions, constitutional?

C. Supreme Court's Answer

The portions of the ordinance challenged before the Supreme Court are all unconstitutional.

II. CASE SUMMARY

A. Background

"In February 1978 the city council of Akron enacted Ordinance No. 160–1978, entitled 'Regulation of Abortions.' The ordinance sets forth 17 provisions that regulate the performance of abortions, five of which are at issue in this case:

(i) Section 1870.03 requires that all abortions performed after the first trimester of pregnancy be performed in a hospital.

(ii) Section 1870.05 sets forth requirements for notification of and consent by parents before abortions may be performed on unmarried minors.

(iii) Section 1870.06 requires that the attending physician make certain specified statements to the patient 'to insure that the consent for an abortion is truly informed consent.'

(iv) Section 1870.07 requires a 24-hour waiting period between the time the woman signs a consent form and the time the abortion is performed.

(v) Section 1870.16 requires that fetal remains be 'disposed of in a humane and sanitary manner.'

A violation of any section of the ordinance is punishable as a criminal misdemeanor. If any provision is invalidated, it is to be severed from the remainder of the ordinance. The ordinance became effective on May 1, 1978.

On April 19, 1978, a lawsuit challenging virtually all of the ordinance's provisions was filed in the District Court for the Northern District of Ohio. The plaintiffs, respondents and cross-petitioners in this Court, were three corporations that operate abortion clinics in Akron and a physician who has performed abortions at one of the clinics. The defendants, petitioners and cross-respondents here, were the city of Akron and three city officials ('Akron'). . . . On April 27, 1978, the District Court preliminarily enjoined enforcement of the ordinance.

In August 1979, after hearing evidence, the District Court ruled on the merits. It found that plaintiffs lacked standing to challenge seven provisions of the ordinance, none of which is before this Court. The District Court invalidated four provisions, including § 1870.05 (parental notice and consent), § 1870.06(B) (requiring disclosure of facts concerning the woman's pregnancy, fetal development, the complications of abortion, and agencies available to assist the woman), and § 1870.16 (disposal of fetal remains). The court upheld the constitutionality of the remainder of the ordinance, including § 1870.03 (hospitalization for abortions after the first trimester), § 1870.06(C) (requiring disclosure of the particular risks of the woman's pregnancy and the abortion technique to be employed), and § 1870.07 (24-hour waiting period).

All parties appealed some portion of the District Court's judgment. The Court of Appeals for the Sixth Circuit affirmed in part and reversed in part. It affirmed the District Court's decision that § 1870.03's hospitalization requirement is constitutional. It also affirmed the ruling that §§ 1870.05, 1870.06(B), and 1870.16

are unconstitutional. The Court of Appeals reversed the District Court's decision on §§ 1870.06(C) and 1870.07, finding these provisions to be unconstitutional."

The Supreme Court granted certiorari to review the case, reversed the Court of Appeals decision upholding the hospitalization requirement, but affirmed the remainder the decision holding other aspects of the ordinance unconstitutional.

B. Counsel of Record / ACLU Attorney

ACLU Side (Respondent / Appellee in No. 81-746, Petitioner / Appellant in No. 81-1172): Stephan Landsman argued the cause for appellee in No. 81-746 and appellant in No. 81-1172. With him on the briefs were Janet Benshoof, Suzanne M. Lynn, Nan D. Hunter, Lois J. Lipton, and Gordon Beggs.

Opposing Side (Petitioner / Appellant in No. 81-746, Respondent / Appellee in No. 81-1172): Alan G. Segedy argued the cause for appellant in No. 81-746 and appellee in No. 81-1172.

Solicitor General Rex E. Lee argued the cause for the United States, as amicus curiae, by special leave of Court.

III. AMICI CURIAE

ACLU Side (Respondent / Appellee in No. 81-746, Petitioner / Appellant in No. 81-1172):

Briefs of amici curiae were filed on behalf of the American Psychological Association, and the Committee for Abortion Rights and Against Sterilization Abuse, et al., California Women Lawyers, et al., Certain Religious Organizations, the College of American Pathologists, the American College of Obstetricians and Gynecologists, et al., the American Public Health Association, the National Abortion Federation, the NAACP Legal Defense and Educational Fund, Inc., the National Organization for Women, et al., the Planned Parenthood Federation of America, Inc., et al., Women Lawyers of Sacramento, et al., and Certain Law Professors

Opposing Side (Petitioner / Appellant in No. 81-746, Respondent / Appellee in No. 81-1172):

Brief of amici curiae filed on behalf of the United States by Solicitor General Rex E. Lee, Assistant Attorney General McGrath, and Deputy Solicitor General Geller.

Briefs of amici curiae urging reversal were filed on behalf of Feminists for Life, and the United Families Foundation, et al., Womankind, Inc., Americans United for Life, the Catholic League for Religious and Civil Rights, Lawyers for Life, and the Legal Defense Fund for Unborn Children.

IV. THE SUPREME COURT'S DECISION

"We believe that the courts below misinterpreted this Court's prior decisions, and we now hold that § 1870.03 is unconstitutional. . . .

We reaffirm today, that a State's interest in health regulation becomes compelling at approximately the end of the first trimester. The existence of a compelling state interest in health, however, is only the beginning of the inquiry. The State's regulation may be upheld only if it is reasonably designed to further that state interest. . . . By preventing the performance of D & E abortions in an appropriate nonhospital setting, Akron has imposed a heavy, and unnecessary, burden on women's access to a relatively inexpensive, otherwise accessible, and safe abortion procedure. Section 1870.03 has 'the effect of inhibiting . . . the vast majority of abortions after the first 12 weeks,' and therefore unreasonably infringes upon a woman's constitutional right to obtain an abortion. . . .

We turn next to § 1870.05(B), the provision prohibiting a physician from performing an abortion on a minor pregnant woman under the age of 15 unless she obtains 'the informed written consent of one of her parents or her legal guardian' or unless the minor obtains 'an order from a court having jurisdiction over her that the abortion be performed or induced.' . . . We . . . affirm the Court of Appeals' judgment that § 1870.05(B) is unconstitutional. . . .

'[I]n order to insure that the consent for an abortion is truly informed consent,' the woman must be 'orally informed by her attending physician' of the status of her pregnancy, the development of her fetus, the date of possible viability, the physical and emotional complications that may result from an abortion, and the availability of agencies to provide her with assistance and information with respect to birth control, adoption, and childbirth. § 1870.06(B). In addition, the attending physician must inform her 'of the particular risks associated with her own pregnancy and the abortion technique to be employed [and] other information which in his own medical judgment is relevant to her decision as to whether to have an abortion or carry her pregnancy to term.' § 1870.06(C). . . . The Court of Appeals concluded that both provisions were unconstitutional. We affirm. . . .

The Akron ordinance prohibits a physician from performing an abortion until 24 hours after the pregnant woman signs a consent form. § 1870.07. . . . We find that Akron has failed to demonstrate that any legitimate state interest is furthered by an arbitrary and inflexible waiting period. There is no evidence suggesting that the abortion procedure will be performed more safely. Nor are we convinced that the State's legitimate concern that the woman's decision be informed is reasonably served by requiring a 24-hour delay as a matter of course. . . .

Section 1870.16 of the Akron ordinance requires physicians performing abortions to 'insure that the remains of the unborn child are disposed of in a humane and sanitary manner.' The Court of Appeals found that the word 'humane' was impermissibly vague as a definition of conduct subject to criminal prosecution. . . . Because § 1870.16 fails to give a physician 'fair notice that his contemplated conduct is forbidden,' we agree that it violates the Due Process Clause. . . .

We affirm the judgment of the Court of Appeals invalidating those sections of Akron's 'Regulations of Abortions' ordinance that deal with parental consent, informed consent, a 24-hour waiting period, and the disposal of fetal remains. The remaining portion of the judgment, sustaining Akron's requirement that all second-trimester abortions be performed in a hospital, is reversed."

V. JUSTICE VOTE

6 Pro ACLU Side vs. 3 Con Opposing Side

ACLU Side (Respondent / Appellee in No. 81-746, Petitioner / Appellant in No. 81-1172):

1. Powell, L. – Wrote majority opinion
2. Burger, W. – Joined majority opinion
3. Brennan, W. – Joined majority opinion
4. Marshall, T. – Joined majority opinion
5. Blackmun, H. – Joined majority opinion
6. Stevens, J. – Joined majority opinion

Opposing Side (Petitioner / Appellant in No. 81-746, Respondent / Appellee in No. 81-1172):

1. O'Connor, S. – Wrote dissenting opinion
2. White, B. – Joined O'Connor's dissent
3. Rehnquist, W. – Joined O'Connor's dissent

VI. A WIN OR LOSS FOR THE ACLU?

The ACLU, as counsel of record, urged affirmance of the judgment of the Court of Appeals for the Sixth Circuit with reversal as to the hospitalization requirement; the Supreme Court affirmed in part and reversed in part in accordance with the ACLU's arguments in a 6-3 vote, giving the ACLU an apparent win.

513. United States v. Place

(Decided June 20, 1983; 462 U.S. 696)

I. ISSUE

A. Issues Discussed

Criminal procedure, Fourth Amendment, search and seizure

B. Legal Question Presented

"[W]hether the Fourth Amendment prohibits law enforcement authorities from temporarily detaining personal luggage for exposure to a trained narcotics detection dog on the basis of reasonable suspicion that the luggage contains narcotics."

C. Supreme Court's Answer

"[U]nder all of the circumstances of this case, the seizure, of respondent's luggage was unreasonable under the Fourth Amendment."

II. CASE SUMMARY

A. Background

"Respondent Raymond J. Place's behavior aroused the suspicions of law enforcement officers as he waited in line at the Miami International Airport to purchase a ticket to New York's La Guardia Airport. As Place proceeded to the gate for his flight, the agents approached him and requested his airline ticket and some identification. Place complied with the request and consented to a search of the two suitcases he had checked. Because his flight was about to depart, however, the agents decided not to search the luggage.

Prompted by Place's parting remark that he had recognized that they were police, the agents inspected the address tags on the checked luggage and noted discrepancies in the two street addresses. Further investigation revealed that neither address existed and that the telephone number Place had given the airline belonged to a third address on the same street. On the basis of their encounter with Place and this information, the Miami agents called Drug Enforcement Administration (DEA) authorities in New York to relay their information about Place.

Two DEA agents waited for Place at the arrival gate at La Guardia Airport in New York. There again, his behavior aroused the suspicion of the agents. . . . They identified themselves as federal narcotics agents, to which Place responded that he knew they were 'cops' and had spotted them as soon as he had deplaned. One of the agents informed Place that, based on their own observations and information obtained from the Miami authorities, they believed that he might be carrying narcotics. After identifying the bags as belonging to him, Place stated that a number of police at the Miami Airport had surrounded him and searched his baggage. The agents responded that their information was to the contrary. The agents requested and received identification from Place—a New Jersey driver's license, on which the agents later ran a computer check that disclosed no offenses, and his airline ticket receipt. When Place refused to consent to a search of his luggage, one of the agents told him that they were going to take the luggage to a federal judge to try to obtain a search warrant and that Place was free to accompany them. Place declined, but obtained from one of the agents telephone numbers at which the agents could be reached.

The agents then took the bags to Kennedy Airport, where they subjected the bags to a 'sniff test' by a trained narcotics detection dog. The dog reacted positively to the smaller of the two bags but ambiguously to the larger bag. Approximately 90 minutes had elapsed since the seizure of respondent's luggage. Because it was late on a Friday afternoon, the agents retained the luggage until Monday morning, when they secured a search warrant from a Magistrate for the smaller bag. Upon opening that bag, the agents discovered 1,125 grams of cocaine.

Place was indicted for possession of cocaine with intent to distribute... In the District Court, Place moved to suppress the contents of the luggage . . . , claiming that the warrantless seizure of the luggage violated his Fourth Amendment rights. The District Court denied the motion. . . . Place pleaded guilty to the possession charge, reserving the right to appeal the denial of his motion to suppress.

On appeal of the conviction, the United States Court of Appeals for the Second Circuit reversed."

The Supreme Court granted certiorari to review the case and affirmed the judgment of the Second Circuit Court of Appeals.

B. Counsel of Record / ACLU Attorney

ACLU Side (Respondent / Appellee): James D. Clark argued the cause for appellee.

Opposing Side (Petitioner / Appellant): Alan I. Horowitz argued the cause for the United States.

III. AMICI CURIAE

ACLU Side (Respondent / Appellee)

Opposing Side (Petitioner / Appellant)

Brief of amici curiae filed on behalf of the ACLU, et al., by Richard Emery and Charles S. Sims. Brief of amici curiae filed on behalf of Americans for Effective Law Enforcement, Inc., et al., by Fred E. Inbau, Wayne W. Schmidt, James P. Manak, Evelle J. Younger, and Howard G. Berringer.

IV. THE SUPREME COURT'S DECISION

"In this case, the Government asks us to recognize the reasonableness under the Fourth Amendment of warrantless seizures of personal luggage from the custody of the owner on the basis of less than probable cause, for the purpose of pursuing a limited course of investigation, short of opening the luggage, that would quickly confirm or dispel the authorities' suspicion. Specifically, we are asked to apply the principles of Terry v. Ohio, supra, to permit such seizures on the basis of reasonable, articulable suspicion, premised on objective facts, that the luggage contains contraband or evidence of a crime. In our view, such application is appropriate. . . .

We must balance the nature and quality of the intrusion on the individual's Fourth Amendment interests against the importance of the governmental interests alleged to justify the intrusion. When the nature and extent of the detention are minimally intrusive of the individual's Fourth Amendment interests, the opposing law enforcement interests can support a seizure based on less than probable cause.

We examine first the governmental interest offered as a justification for a brief seizure of luggage from the suspect's custody for the purpose of pursuing a limited course of investigation. The Government contends that, where the authorities possess specific and articulable facts warranting a reasonable belief that a traveler's luggage contains narcotics, the governmental interest in seizing the luggage briefly to pursue further investigation is substantial. We agree.

[W]e conclude that when an officer's observations lead him reasonably to believe that a traveler is carrying luggage that contains narcotics, the principles of Terry and its progeny would permit the officer to detain the luggage briefly to investigate the circumstances that aroused his suspicion, provided that the investigative detention is properly limited in scope.

[W]e must reject the Government's suggestion that the point at which probable cause for seizure of luggage from the person's presence becomes necessary is more distant than in the case of a Terry stop of the person himself. The premise of the Government's argument is that seizures of property are generally less intrusive than seizures of the person. While true in some circumstances, that premise is faulty on the facts we address in this case. . . .

The length of the detention of respondent's luggage alone precludes the conclusion that the seizure was reasonable in the absence of probable cause. Although we have recognized the reasonableness of seizures longer than the momentary ones . . . , the brevity of the invasion of the individual's Fourth Amendment interests is an important factor in determining whether the seizure is so minimally intrusive as to be justifiable on reasonable suspicion. Moreover, in assessing the effect of the length of the detention, we take into account whether the police diligently pursue their investigation. We note that here the New York agents knew the time of Place's scheduled arrival at La Guardia, had ample time to arrange for their additional investigation at that location, and thereby could have minimized the intrusion on respondent's Fourth Amendment interests. Thus, although we decline to adopt any outside time limitation for a permissible Terry stop, we have never approved a seizure of the person for the prolonged 90-minute period involved here and cannot do so on the facts presented by this case. . . .

We conclude that, under all of the circumstances of this case, the seizure of respondent's luggage was unreasonable under the Fourth Amendment. Consequently, the evidence obtained from the subsequent search of his luggage was inadmissible, and Place's conviction must be reversed. The judgment of the Court of Appeals, accordingly, is affirmed."

V. JUSTICE VOTE

9 Pro ACLU Side vs. 0 Con Opposing Side

ACLU Side (Respondent / Appellee)

Opposing Side (Petitioner / Appellant)

1. O'Connor, S. – Wrote majority opinion
2. Burger, W. – Joined majority opinion
3. White, B. – Joined majority opinion
4. Powell, L. – Joined majority opinion
5. Rehnquist, W. – Joined majority opinion
6. Stevens, J. – Joined majority opinion
7. Brennan, W. – Wrote concurring opinion
8. Marshall, T. – Joined Blackmun's concurrence, joined Brennan's concurrence
9. Blackmun, H. – Wrote concurring opinion

VI. A WIN OR LOSS FOR THE ACLU?

The ACLU, as amicus curiae, urged affirmance of the Second Circuit Court of Appeals' judgment; the Supreme Court affirmed in a 9-0 vote, giving the ACLU an apparent win.

514. Bolger v. Youngs Drug Products Corp.

(Decided June 24, 1983; 463 U.S. 60)

I. ISSUE

A. Issues Discussed

Civil rights, privacy, First Amendment, commercial speech

B. Legal Question Presented

Whether "Title 39 U.S.C. § 3001(e)(2) [which] prohibits the mailing of unsolicited advertisements for contraceptives" violates the First Amendment "as applied to appellee's mailings."

C. Supreme Court's Answer

Section § 3001(e)(2) violates the First Amendment as applied to appellee's mailings.

II. CASE SUMMARY

A. Background

"Section 3001(e)(2) states that "[a]ny unsolicited advertisement of matter which is designed, adapted, or intended for preventing conception is nonmailable matter, shall not be carried or delivered by mail, and shall be disposed of as the Postal Service directs . . . ." As interpreted by Postal Service regulations, the statutory provision does not apply to unsolicited advertisements in which the mailer has no commercial interest. In addition to the civil consequences of a violation of § 3001(e)(2), 18 U.S.C. § 1461 makes it a crime knowingly to use the mails for anything declared by § 3001(e) to be nonmailable.

Appellee Youngs Drug Products Corporation (Youngs) is engaged in the manufacture, sale and distribution of contraceptives. Youngs markets its products primarily through sales to chain warehouses and wholesale distributors, who in turn sell contraceptives to retail pharmacists, who then sell those products to individual customers. . . . This litigation resulted from Youngs' decision to undertake a campaign of unsolicited mass mailings to members of the public. . . .

In 1979 the Postal Service traced to a wholesaler of Youngs' products an allegation of an unsolicited mailing of contraceptive advertisements. The Service warned the wholesaler that the mailing violated 39 U.S.C. § 3001(e)(2). Subsequently, Youngs contacted the Service and furnished it with copies of Youngs' three types of proposed mailings, stating its view that the statute could not constitutionally restrict the mailings. The Service rejected Youngs' legal argument and notified the company that the proposed mailings would violate § 3001(e). Youngs then brought this action for declaratory and injunctive relief in the United States District Court for the District of Columbia. It claimed that the statute, as applied to its proposed mailings, violated the First Amendment and that Youngs and its wholesaler were refraining from distributing the advertisements because of the Service's warning.

The District Court determined that § 3001(e)(2), by its plain language, prohibited all three types of proposed mailings. The Court then addressed the constitutionality of the statute as applied to these mailings. Finding all three types of materials to be commercial solicitations, the Court considered the constitutionality of the statute within the framework established by [the Supreme] Court for analyzing restrictions imposed on commercial speech. The Court concluded that the statutory prohibition was more extensive than necessary to the interests asserted by the government, and it therefore held that the Statute's absolute ban on the three type of mailings violated the First Amendment."

The Supreme Court granted certiorari to review the case and affirmed.

B. Counsel of Record / ACLU Attorney

ACLU Side (Respondent / Appellee): Jerold S. Solovy argued the cause for appellee.

Opposing Side (Petitioner / Appellant): David A. Strauss argued the cause for appellant.

III. AMICI CURIAE

ACLU Side (Respondent / Appellee): Brief of amici curiae filed on behalf of the ACLU by Michael L. Burack, Charles S. Sims, and Janet Benshoof.

Brief of amici curiae filed on behalf of the Planned Parenthood Federation of America, Inc., et al., by Robert D. Joffe, Eve W. Paul, and Dara Klassel.

Opposing Side (Petitioner / Appellant): No briefs of amici curiae were filed in support of appellant.

IV. THE SUPREME COURT'S DECISION

"Title 39 U.S.C. § 3001(e)(2) prohibits the mailing of unsolicited advertisements for contraceptives. The District Court held that, as applied to appellee's mailings, the statute violates the First Amendment. We affirm.

[T]he Government asserts that the statute (1) shields recipients of mail from materials that they are likely to find offensive and (2) aids parents' efforts to control the manner in which their children become informed about sensitive and important subjects such as birth control. The first of these interests carries little weight. In striking down a state prohibition of contraceptive advertisements in Carey v. Population Services International, supra, we stated that offensiveness was 'classically not [a] justificatio[n] validating the suppression of expression protected by the First Amendment. At least where obscenity is not involved, we have consistently held that the fact that protected speech may be offensive to some does not justify its suppression.' We specifically declined to recognize a distinction between commercial and noncommercial speech that would render this interest a sufficient justification for a prohibition of commercial speech. . . .

The second interest asserted by the Government—aiding parents' efforts to discuss birth control with their children—is undoubtedly substantial. '[P]arents have an important 'guiding role' to play in the upbringing of their children . . . which presumptively includes counseling them on important decisions.' As a means of effectuating this interest, however, § 3001(e)(2) fails to withstand scrutiny. . . .

We thus conclude that the justifications offered by appellants are insufficient to warrant the sweeping prohibition on the mailing of unsolicited contraceptive advertisements. As applied to appellee's mailings, § 3001(e)(2) is unconstitutional. The judgment of the District Court is therefore affirmed."

V. JUSTICE VOTE

8 Pro ACLU Side vs. 0 Con Opposing Side

ACLU Side (Respondent / Appellee)

1. Marshall, T. – Wrote majority opinion
2. Burger, W. – Joined majority opinion
3. White, B. – Joined majority opinion
4. Blackmun, H. – Joined majority opinion
5. Powell, L. – Joined majority opinion
6. Rehnquist, W. – Wrote concurring opinion

7. Stevens, J. – Wrote concurring opinion
8. O'Connor, S. – Joined Rehnquist's concurrence

Brennan, W – Took no part in the decision

VI. A WIN OR LOSS FOR THE ACLU?

The ACLU filed as amicus curiae urging affirmance; the Supreme Court affirmed the ruling of the District Court for the District of Columbia in an 8-0 vote, giving the ACLU an apparent win.

515. Shaw v. Delta Air Lines, Inc.

(Decided June 24, 1983; 463 U.S. 85)

I. ISSUE

A. Issues Discussed

Governmental authority, regulation, preemption

B. Legal Question Presented

Whether "New York's Human Rights Law [that] forbids discrimination in employment, including discrimination in employee benefit plans on the basis of pregnancy," and New York's "Disability Benefits Law [that] requires employers to pay sick-leave benefits to employees unable to work because of pregnancy or other nonoccupational disabilities," are "pre-empted by the federal Employee Retirement Income Security Act of 1974 (ERISA) ."

C. Supreme Court's Answer

"New York's Human Rights Law is preempted with respect to ERISA benefit plans only insofar as it prohibits practices that are lawful under federal law. [T]he Disability Benefits Law is not pre-empted by ERISA, although New York may not enforce its provisions through regulation of ERISA covered benefit plans."

II. CASE SUMMARY

A. Background

"The federal Employee Retirement Income Security Act of 1974 subjects to federal regulation plans providing employees with fringe benefits. ERISA is a comprehensive statute designed to promote the interests of employees and their beneficiaries in employee benefit plans. . . . ERISA does not mandate that employers provide any particular benefits, and does not itself proscribe discrimination in the provision of employee benefits.

Section 514(a) of ERISA, pre-empts 'any and all State laws insofar as they may now or hereafter relate to any employee benefit plan' covered by ERISA. . . .

Appellees in this litigation, Delta Air Lines, Inc., and other airlines (Airlines), . . . provided their employees with various medical and disability benefits through welfare plans subject to ERISA. These plans, prior to the effective date of the Pregnancy Discrimination Act, did not provide benefits to employees disabled by pregnancy as required by the New York Human Rights Law and the State's Disability Benefits Law. Appellees brought three separate federal declaratory judgment actions against appellant state agencies and officials, alleging that the Human Rights Law was pre-empted by ERISA. The Airlines in their action alleged that the Disability Benefits Law was similarly pre-empted.

The United States District Court in each case held that the Human Rights Law was pre-empted, at least insofar as it required the provision of pregnancy benefits prior to the effective date of the Pregnancy Discrimination Act. With respect to the Airlines' challenge to the Disability Benefits Law, the District Court construed § 4(b)(3) of ERISA as exempting from the federal statute 'those provisions of an employee plan which are maintained to comply with' state disability insurance laws. Because it concluded that the Airlines would have provided pregnancy benefits solely to comply with the Disability Benefits Law, the court dismissed the portion of their complaint seeking relief from that law.

The United States Court of Appeals for the Second Circuit affirmed as to the Human Rights Law. . . . With respect to the Disability Benefits Law, the Court of Appeals had concluded earlier that § 4(b)(3)'s exemption from pre-emption applied only when a benefit plan, 'as an integral unit,' is maintained solely to comply with a disability law. The court remanded for inquiries into whether the Airlines provided disability benefits through plans constituting separate administrative units, in which event the Disability Benefits Law would be enforceable, or through portions of comprehensive benefit plans, in which case ERISA regulation would be exclusive."

The Supreme Court granted certiorari to review the cases, affirmed in part, and vacated and remanded in part.

B. Counsel of Record / ACLU Attorney

ACLU Side (Petitioner / Appellant): Deborah Bachrach, Assistant Attorney General of New York, argued the cause for appellant.

Opposing Side (Respondent / Appellee): Gordon Dean Booth, Jr., argued the cause for appellee.

III. AMICI CURIAE

ACLU Side (Petitioner / Appellant)

Brief of amici curiae filed on behalf of the ACLU, et al., by Mary L. Heen, Joan E. Bertin, and Isabelle Katz Pinzler.

Brief of amici curiae filed on behalf of the Commonwealth of Pennsylvania, et al., by LeRoy S. Zimmerman, Attorney General and Ellen M. Doyle.

Brief of amici curiae filed on behalf of the American Federation of Labor and Congress of Industrial Organizations, et al., by J. Albert Woll, Marsha Berzon, Laurence Gold, and John Fillion.

Opposing Side (Respondent / Appellee)

Brief of amici curiae filed on behalf of the United States by Solicitor General Lee, Stuart A. Smith, T. Timothy Ryan, Jr., Kerry L. Adams, and John A. Bryson.

Brief of amici curiae filed on behalf of the ERISA Industry Committee, et al., by Eugene B. Granof and George J. Pantos.

Brief of amici curiae filed on behalf of Westinghouse Electric Corporation by Walter P. DeForest and Stuart I. Saltman.

IV. THE SUPREME COURT'S DECISION

"[W]hile the State may not require an employer to alter its ERISA plan, it may force the employer to choose between providing disability benefits in a separately administered plan and including the state-mandated benefits in its ERISA plan. If the State is not satisfied that the ERISA plan comports with the requirements of its disability insurance law, it may compel the employer to maintain a separate plan that does comply. The Court of Appeals erred, therefore, in holding that appellants are not at all free to enforce the Disability Benefits Law against those appellees that provide disability benefits as part of multibenefit plans. . . .

We hold that New York's Human Rights Law is preempted with respect to ERISA benefit plans only insofar as it prohibits practices that are lawful under federal law. To this extent, the judgments of the Court of Appeals are affirmed. To the extent the Court of Appeals held any more of the Human Rights Law pre-empted, we vacate its judgments and remand the cases.

We further hold that the Disability Benefits Law is not pre-empted by ERISA, although New York may not enforce its provisions through regulation of ERISA covered benefit plans. We therefore vacate the Court of Appeals' judgment in the Airlines' case on this ground and remand that case for further proceedings consistent with this opinion."

V. JUSTICE VOTE

9 Pro ACLU Side vs. 0 Con Opposing Side

ACLU Side (Petitioner / Appellant)

1. Blackmun, H. – Wrote majority opinion
2. Burger, W. – Joined majority opinion
3. Brennan, W. – Joined majority opinion
4. White, B. – Joined majority opinion
5. Marshall, T. – Joined majority opinion
6. Powell, L. – Joined majority opinion
7. Rehnquist, W. – Joined majority opinion
8. Stevens, J. – Joined majority opinion
9. O'Connor, S. – Joined majority opinion

VI. A WIN OR LOSS FOR THE ACLU?

The ACLU filed as amicus curiae urging reversal; the Supreme Court affirmed in part, but also vacated and remanded in part the lower court's ruling in a 9-0 vote; giving the ACLU an apparent win.

516. City of Revere v. Massachusetts General Hospital

(Decided June 27, 1983; 463 U.S. 239)

I. ISSUE

A. Issues Discussed

Governmental authority, regulation

B. Legal Question Presented

"[W]hether a municipality's constitutional duty to obtain necessary medical care for a person injured by the municipality's police in the performance of their duties includes a corresponding duty to compensate the provider of that medical care."

C. Supreme Court's Answer

The constitutional duty to ensure persons injured by police in the performance of police duties receive prompt medical care does not include a constitutional duty to compensate the medical care provider.

II. CASE SUMMARY

A. Background

"On September 20, 1978, members of the police force of petitioner city of Revere, Mass., responded to a report of a breaking and entering in progress. At the scene they sought to detain a man named Patrick M. Kivlin, who attempted to flee. When repeated commands to stop and a warning shot failed to halt Kivlin's flight, an officer fired at Kivlin and wounded him. The officers summoned a private ambulance. It took Kivlin, accompanied by one officer, to the emergency room of respondent Massachusetts General Hospital (MGH) in Boston. Kivlin was hospitalized at MGH from September 20 until September 29. Upon his release, Revere police served him with an arrest warrant that had been issued on September 26. Kivlin was arraigned and released on his own recognizance.

On October 18, MGH sent the Chief of Police of Revere a bill for $7,948.50 for its services to Kivlin. The Chief responded immediately by a letter denying responsibility for the bill. On October 27, Kivlin returned to MGH for further treatment. He was released on November 10; the bill for services rendered during this second stay was $5,360.41.

In January 1979, MGH sued Revere in state court to recover the full cost of its hospital services rendered to Kivlin. The Superior Court for the County of Suffolk dismissed the complaint. MGH appealed, and the Supreme Judicial Court of Massachusetts transferred the case to its own docket.

The Supreme Judicial Court reversed in part, holding 'that the constitutional prohibition against cruel and unusual punishment, embodied in the Eighth Amendment to the United States Constitution [as applied to the States through the Fourteenth Amendment], requires that Revere be liable to the hospital for the medical services rendered to Kivlin during his first stay at the hospital.' The court apparently believed that such a rule was needed to ensure that persons in police custody receive necessary medical attention."

The Supreme Court granted certiorari to review the case and reversed.

B. Counsel of Record / ACLU Attorney

ACLU Side (Petitioner / Appellant): Ira H. Zaleznik argued the cause for appellant.

Opposing Side (Respondent / Appellee): Michael Broad argued the cause for appellee.

III. AMICI CURIAE

ACLU Side (Petitioner / Appellant)

Brief of amici curiae filed on behalf of the ACLU, et al., by Charles S. Sims, Burt Neuborne, and John Reinstein.

Brief of amici curiae filed on behalf of the City of Fitchburg, et al., by Paul R. Devin.

Brief of amici curiae filed on behalf of the Washington Legal Foundation by Daniel J. Popeo, Paul D. Kamenar, and Nicholas E. Calio.

Opposing Side (Respondent / Appellee)

Brief of amici curiae filed on behalf of the Massachusetts Hospital Association, Inc., by William T. McGrail.

IV. THE SUPREME COURT'S DECISION

"The Eighth Amendment's proscription of cruel and unusual punishments is violated by 'deliberate indifference to serious medical needs of prisoners.' As MGH acknowledges, on the facts of this case the relevant constitutional provision is not the Eighth Amendment but is, instead, the Due Process Clause of the Fourteenth Amendment. . . . Because there had been no formal adjudication of guilt against Kivlin at the time he required medical care, the Eighth Amendment has no application. . . .

The Due Process Clause, however, does require the responsible government or governmental agency to provide medical care to persons, such as Kivlin, who have been injured while being apprehended by the police. In fact, the due process rights of a person in Kivlin's situation are at least as great as the Eighth Amendment protections available to a convicted prisoner. . . . And as long as the governmental entity ensures that the medical care needed is in fact provided, the Constitution does not dictate how the cost of that care should be allocated as between the entity and the provider of the care. That is a matter of state law.

If, of course, the governmental entity can obtain the medical care needed for a detainee only by paying for it, then it must pay. There are, however, other means by which the entity could meet its obligation. Many hospitals are subject to federal or state laws that require them to provide care to indigents. . . .

In short, the injured detainee's constitutional right is to receive the needed medical treatment; how the city of Revere obtains such treatment is not a federal constitutional question. . . . For these reasons, the judgment of the Supreme Judicial Court is reversed."

V. JUSTICE VOTE

9 Pro ACLU Side vs. 0 Con Opposing Side

ACLU Side (Petitioner / Appellant)

1. Blackmun, H. – Wrote majority opinion
2. Brennan, W. – Joined majority opinion
3. Powell, L. – Joined majority opinion
4. Burger, W. – Joined majority opinion
5. Marshall, T. – Joined majority opinion
6. O'Connor, S. – Joined majority opinion
7. Rehnquist, W. – Wrote concurring opinion
8. White, B. – Joined Rehnquist's concurrence
9. Stevens, J. – Wrote concurring opinion

VI. A WIN OR LOSS FOR THE ACLU?

The ACLU filed as amicus curiae urging reversal; the U.S. Supreme Court reversed the ruling of the Supreme Judicial Court of Massachusetts in a 9-0 vote, giving the ACLU an apparent win.

517. Jones v. United States

(Decided June 29, 1983; 463 U.S. 354)

I. ISSUE

A. Issues Discussed

Criminal procedure, insanity defense, Fourth Amendment, due process

B. Legal Question Presented

"[W]hether petitioner, who was committed to a mental hospital upon being acquitted of a criminal offense by reason of insanity, must be released because he has been hospitalized for a period longer than he might have served in prison had he been convicted."

C. Supreme Court's Answer

After acquittal for a crime by reason of insanity, petitioner can be confined in a mental hospital for a period longer than the time he would have served in prison for the crime.

II. CASE SUMMARY

A. Background

"In the District of Columbia a criminal defendant may be acquitted by reason of insanity if his insanity . . . . If he successfully invokes the insanity defense, he is committed to a mental hospital. The statute provides several ways of obtaining release. Within 50 days of commitment the acquittee is entitled to a judicial hearing to determine his eligibility for release . . . . Alternatively, the acquittee is entitled to a judicial hearing every six months at which he may establish by a preponderance of the evidence that he is entitled to release.

Independent of its provision for the commitment of insanity acquittees, the District of Columbia also has adopted a civil-commitment procedure, under which an individual may be committed upon clear and convincing proof by the Government that he is mentally ill and likely to injure himself or others. The individual may demand a jury in the civil-commitment proceeding. Once committed, a patient may be released at any time upon certification of recovery by the hospital chief of service. Alternatively, the patient is entitled after the first 90 days, and subsequently at 6-month intervals, to request a judicial hearing at which he may gain his release by proving by a preponderance of the evidence that he is no longer mentally ill or dangerous. . . .

On September 19, 1975, petitioner was arrested for attempting to steal a jacket from a department store. . . . The court ordered petitioner committed to St. Elizabeths, a public hospital for the mentally ill, for a determination of his competency to stand trial. On March 2, 1976, a hospital psychologist submitted a report to the court stating that petitioner was competent to stand trial, that petitioner suffered from 'Schizophrenia, paranoid type,' and that petitioner's alleged offense was 'the product of his mental disease.' The court ruled that petitioner was competent to stand trial. Petitioner subsequently decided to plead not guilty by reason of insanity. The Government did not contest the plea, and it entered into a stipulation of facts with petitioner. On March 12, 1976, the Superior Court found petitioner not guilty by reason of insanity and committed him to St. Elizabeths . . . .

On May 25, 1976, the court held the 50-day hearing . . . . The court . . . found that 'the defendant-patient is mentally ill and as a result of his mental illness, at this time, he constitutes a danger to himself or others.' Petitioner was returned to St. Elizabeths. Petitioner obtained new counsel and, following some procedural confusion, a second release hearing was held on February 22, 1977. By that date petitioner had been hospitalized for more than one year, the maximum period he could have spent in prison if he had been convicted. On the basis he demanded that he be released unconditionally or recommitted pursuant to the civil-commitment standards in § 21-545 (b), including a jury trial and proof by clear and convincing evidence of his mental illness and dangerousness. The Superior Court denied petitioner's request for a civil-commitment hearing, reaffirmed the findings made at the May 25, 1976, hearing, and continued petitioner's commitment to St. Elizabeths.

Petitioner appealed to the District of Columbia Court of Appeals. A panel of the court affirmed the Superior Court, but then granted rehearing and reversed. Finally, the court heard the case en banc and affirmed the judgment of the Superior Court."

The Supreme Court granted certiorari to review the case and affirmed.

B. Counsel of Record / ACLU Attorney

ACLU Side (Petitioner / Appellant): Silas J. Wasserstrom argued the cause for appellant.

Opposing Side (Respondent / Appellee): Joshua I. Schwartz argued the cause for the United States.

III. AMICI CURIAE

ACLU Side (Petitioner / Appellant)

Brief of amici curiae filed on behalf of the ACLU, et al., by Michael L. Burack, M. Carolyn Cox, Arthur B. Spitzer, and Charles S. Sims.

Brief of amici curiae filed on behalf of the Department of the Public Advocate, Division of Mental Health Advocacy, State of New Jersey, by Joseph H. Rodriquez, Michael L. Perlin, Stanley C. Van Ness, and John J. Ensminger.

Brief of amici curiae filed on behalf of the Georgia Legal Services Program, Inc., by Robert B. Remar.

Opposing Side (Respondent / Appellee)

No briefs of amici curiae were filed in support of appellee.

IV. THE SUPREME COURT'S DECISION

"We turn first to the question whether the finding of insanity at the criminal trial is sufficiently probative of mental illness and dangerousness to justify commitment. A verdict of not guilty by reason of insanity establishes two facts: (i) the defendant committed an act that constitutes a criminal offense, and (ii) he committed the act because of mental illness. Congress has determined that these findings constitute an adequate basis for hospitalizing the acquittee as a dangerous and mentally ill person. . . . The fact that a person has been found, beyond a reasonable doubt, to have committed a criminal act certainly indicates dangerousness. . . . We therefore conclude that a finding of not guilty by reason of insanity is a sufficient foundation for commitment of an insanity acquittee for the purposes of treatment and the protection of society. . . .

The remaining question is whether petitioner nonetheless is entitled to his release because he has been hospitalized for a period longer than he could have been incarcerated if convicted. . . . The purpose of commitment following an insanity acquittal, like that of civil commitment, is to treat the individual's mental illness and protect him and society from his potential dangerousness. The committed acquittee is entitled to release when he has recovered his sanity or is no longer dangerous. . . .

As he was not convicted, he may not be punished. His confinement rests on his continuing illness and dangerousness. Thus, under the District of Columbia statute, no matter how serious the act committed by the acquittee, he may be released within 50 days of his acquittal if he has recovered. In contrast, one who committed a less serious act may be confined for a longer period if he remains ill and dangerous. There simply is no necessary correlation between severity of the offense and length of time necessary for recovery. The length of the acquittee's hypothetical criminal sentence therefore is irrelevant to the purposes of his commitment. . . .

We hold that when a criminal defendant establishes by a preponderance of the evidence that he is not guilty of a crime by reason of insanity, the Constitution permits the Government, on the basis of the insanity judgment, to confine him to a mental institution until such time as he has regained his sanity or is no longer a danger to himself or society. This holding accords with the widely and reasonably held view that insanity acquittees constitute a special class that should be treated differently from other candidates for commitment. . . .

The judgment of the District of Columbia Court of Appeals is affirmed."

V. JUSTICE VOTE

4 Pro ACLU Side vs. 5 Con Opposing Side

ACLU Side (Petitioner / Appellant)

1. Brennan, W. – Wrote dissenting opinion
2. Marshall, T. – Joined Brennan's dissent
3. Blackmun, H. – Joined Brennan's dissent
4. Stevens, J. – Wrote dissenting opinion

Opposing Side (Respondent / Appellee)

1. Powell, L. – Wrote majority opinion
2. Burger, W. – Joined majority opinion
3. White, B. – Joined majority opinion
4. O'Connor, S. – Joined majority opinion
5. Rehnquist, W. – Joined majority opinion

VI. A WIN OR LOSS FOR THE ACLU?

The ACLU filed as amicus curiae urging reversal; the Supreme Court affirmed the ruling of the District of Columbia Court of Appeals in a 5-4 vote, giving the ACLU an apparent loss.

518. United States v. Sells Engineering, Inc.

(Decided June 30, 1983; 463 U.S. 418)

I. ISSUE

A. Issues Discussed

Criminal procedure, court documents

B. Legal Question Presented

"[U]nder what conditions attorneys for the Civil Division of the Justice Department, their paralegal and secretarial staff, and all other necessary assistants, may obtain access to grand jury materials, compiled with the assistance and knowledge of other Justice Department attorneys, for the purpose of preparing and pursuing a civil suit."

C. Supreme Court's Answer

"[S]uch access is permissible only when the Government moves for court-ordered disclosure under Federal Rule of Criminal Procedure 6(e)(3)(C)(i) and makes the showing of particularized need required by that Rule."

II. CASE SUMMARY

A. Background

"Respondents Peter A. Sells and Fred R. Witte were officers of respondent Sells Engineering, Inc. That company had contracts with the United States Navy to produce airborne electronic devices designed to interfere with enemy radar systems. In 1974, a Special Agent of the Internal Revenue Service began a combined criminal and civil administrative investigation of respondents. The Agent issued administrative summonses for certain corporate records of Sells Engineering. When the corporation refused to comply, the Agent obtained a district court order enforcing the summonses. Enforcement was stayed, however, pending appeal.

While the enforcement case was pending in the Court of Appeals, a federal grand jury was convened to investigate charges of criminal fraud on the Navy and of evasion of federal income taxes. The grand jury subpoenaed, and respondents produced, many of the same materials that were the subject of the IRS administrative summonses. The grand jury indicted all three respondents on two counts of conspiracy to defraud the United States and nine counts of tax fraud. Respondents moved to dismiss the indictment, alleging grand jury misuse for civil purposes. Before the motion was decided, however, the parties reached a plea bargain. The individual respondents each pleaded guilty to one count of conspiracy to defraud the Government by obstructing an IRS investigation. All other counts were dismissed, and respondents withdrew their charges of grand jury misuse.

Thereafter, the Government moved for disclosure of all grand jury materials to attorneys in the Justice Department's Civil Division, their paralegal and secretarial assistants, and certain Defense Department experts, for use in preparing and conducting a possible civil suit against respondents under the False Claims Act. Respondents opposed the disclosure, renewing their allegations of grand jury misuse. The District Court granted the requested disclosure, concluding that attorneys in the Civil Division are entitled to disclosure as a matter of right under Rule 6(e)(3)(A)(i). The Court also stated that disclosure to Civil Division attorneys and their non-attorney assistants was warranted because the Government had shown particularized need for disclosure. The Court of Appeals vacated and remanded, holding that Civil Division attorneys could obtain disclosure only by showing particularized need under Rule 6(e)(3)(C)(i), and that the District Court had not applied a correct standard of particularized need."

The Supreme Court granted certiorari to review the case and affirmed.

B. Counsel of Record / ACLU Attorney

ACLU Side (Respondent / Appellee): Arlington Ray Robbins argued the cause for appellee.

Opposing Side (Petitioner / Appellant): Douglas Letter argued the cause for the United States.

III. AMICI CURIAE

ACLU Side (Respondent / Appellee)

Brief of amici curiae filed on behalf of the ACLU, et al., by Thomas E. Holliday, Fred Okrand, Charles S. Sims, and Burt Neuborne.

Brief of amici curiae filed on behalf of the American Bar Association by Morris Harrell and Richard L. Aynes.

Brief of amici curiae filed on behalf of General Motors Corporation by Erwin N. Griswold and Otis M. Smith.

Brief of amici curiae filed on behalf of Miller Brewing Company by Thomas J. Donnelly.

Opposing Side (Petitioner / Appellant)

Brief of amici curiae filed on behalf of the District Attorney of Suffolk County, New York, by Patrick Henry, pro se, Mark D. Cohen, and James J. O'Rourke.

IV. THE SUPREME COURT'S DECISION

"The question in this case is under what conditions attorneys for the Civil Division of the Justice Department, their paralegal and secretarial staff, and all other necessary assistants, may obtain access to grand jury materials, compiled with the assistance and knowledge of other Justice Department attorneys, for the purpose of preparing and pursuing a civil suit. We hold that such access is permissible only when the Government moves for court-ordered disclosure under Federal Rule of Criminal Procedure 6(e)(3)(C)(i) and makes the showing of particularized need required by that Rule. . . .

Rule 6(e) of the Federal Rules of Criminal Procedure codifies the traditional rule of grand jury secrecy. Paragraph 6(e)(2) provides that grand jurors, Government attorneys and their assistants, and other personnel attached to the grand jury are forbidden to disclose matters occurring before the grand jury. Witnesses are not under the prohibition unless they also happen to fit into one of the enumerated classes. Paragraph 6(e)(3) sets forth four exceptions to this nondisclosure rule.

Subparagraph 6(e)(3)(A) contains two authorizations for disclosure as a matter of course, without any court order. First, under subparagraph 6(e)(3)(A)(i), disclosure may be made without a court order to 'an attorney for the government for use in the performance of such attorney's duty' (referred to hereinafter as '(A)(i) disclosure'). . . .

The Government contends that all attorneys in the Justice Department qualify for automatic disclosure of grand jury materials under (A)(i), regardless of the nature of the litigation in which they intend to use the materials. We hold that (A)(i) disclosure is limited to use by those attorneys who conduct the criminal matters to which the materials pertain. This conclusion is mandated by the general purposes and policies of grand jury secrecy, by the limited policy reasons why Government attorneys are granted access to grand jury materials for criminal use, and by the legislative history of Rule 6(e). . . .

Rule 6(e) was never intended to grant free access to grand jury materials to attorneys not working on the criminal matters to which the materials pertain. The Advisory Committee's explanation strongly suggests that automatic access to grand jury materials is available only to those attorneys for the Government who would be entitled to appear before the grand jury. . . .

The Court of Appeals correctly held that disclosure to government attorneys and their assistants for use in a civil suit is permissible only with a court order under Rule 6(e)(3)(C)(i), and that the District Court did not apply correctly the particularized need standard for issuance of such an order. Accordingly, the judgment of the Court of Appeals is affirmed."

V. JUSTICE VOTE

5 Pro ACLU Side vs. 4 Con Opposing Side

ACLU Side (Respondent / Appellee)

1. Brennan, W. – Wrote majority opinion
2. Blackmun, H. – Joined majority opinion
3. Marshall, T. – Joined majority opinion
4. White, B. – Joined majority opinion
5. Stevens, J. – Joined majority opinion

Opposing Side (Petitioner / Appellant)

1. Burger, W. – Wrote dissenting opinion
2. O'Connor, S. – Joined Burger's dissent
3. Rehnquist, W. – Joined Burger's dissent
4. Powell, L. – Joined Burger's dissent

VI. A WIN OR LOSS FOR THE ACLU?

The ACLU filed as amicus curiae urging affirmance; The Supreme Court affirmed the ruling of the Court of Appeals for the Ninth Circuit in a 5-4 vote, giving the ACLU an apparent win.

519. Guardians Ass'n v. Civil Service Commission

(Decided July 1, 1983; 463 U.S. 582)

I. ISSUE

A. Issues Discussed

Civil rights, race, Title VI of the Civil Rights Act of 1964, damages

B. Legal Question Presented

"[W]hether the private plaintiffs in this case need to prove discriminatory intent to establish a violation of Title VI of the Civil Rights Act of 1964, . . . and administrative implementing regulations promulgated thereunder."

C. Supreme Court's Answer

The private plaintiffs need not prove discriminatory intent to establish a violation of Title VI, but the plaintiffs can only receive declaratory and injunctive relief for the violation, no compensatory relief is available to them.

II. CASE SUMMARY

A. Background

"This class action involves a challenge by black and Hispanic police officers, petitioners here, to several written examinations administered by New York City between 1968 and 1970 that were used to make entry-level appointments to the city's police department (the 'Department') through October 1974. The District Court found that the challenged examinations had a discriminatory impact on the scores and pass-rates of blacks and Hispanics and were not job-related. These findings were not disturbed in the Court of Appeals.

[T]he District Court held that, although petitioners had failed to prove that the respondents had acted with discriminatory intent, the use of the exams violated Title VII, because the tests had a disparate impact upon minorities and were not proven by respondents to be job-related.

[After various appeals, the Second Circuit Court of Appeals] affirmed the relief under Title VII but reversed as to Title VI. All three members of the panel agreed that the award of Title VI relief could not be sustained, but the panel divided on the rationale for this conclusion"

The Supreme Court granted certiorari to review the case and affirmed.

B. Counsel of Record / ACLU Attorney

ACLU Side (Petitioner / Appellant): Christopher Crowley argued the cause for appellant.

Opposing Side (Respondent / Appellee): Leonard Koerner argued the cause for appellee.

III. AMICI CURIAE

ACLU Side (Petitioner / Appellant)

Brief of amici curiae filed on behalf of the ACLU, et al., by Arthur N. Eisenberg and E. Richard Larson.

Brief of amicus curiae filed on behalf of the Asian American Legal Defense and Education Fund, et al., by Vilma S. Martinez, Morris J. Baller, and Roger L. Waldman.

Brief of amici curiae filed on behalf of the NAACP by Thomas I. Atkins and Michael H. Sussman.

Opposing Side (Respondent / Appellee)

Brief of amici curiae filed on behalf of the Equal Employment Advisory Council by Robert E. Williams, Douglas S. McDowell, and Thomas R. Bagby.

IV. THE SUPREME COURT'S DECISION

"The threshold issue before the Court is whether the private plaintiffs in this case need to prove discriminatory intent to establish a violation of Title VI of the Civil Rights Act of 1964 . . . . I conclude, as do four other Justices, in separate opinions, that the Court of Appeals erred in requiring proof of discriminatory intent. However, I conclude that the judgment below should be affirmed on other grounds, because, in the absence of proof of discriminatory animus, compensatory relief should not be awarded to private Title VI plaintiffs; unless discriminatory intent is shown, declaratory and limited injunctive relief should be the only available private remedies for Title VI violations. There being four other Justices who would affirm the judgment of the Court of Appeals, that judgment is accordingly affirmed. . . .

Although the Court of Appeals erred in construing Title VI, it does not necessarily follow that its judgment should be reversed. As an alternative ground for affirmance, respondents defend the judgment on the basis that there is no private right of action available under Title VI that will afford petitioners the relief that they seek. I agree that the relief denied petitioners under Title VII is unavailable to them under Title VI, at least where no intentional discrimination has been proved, as is the case here.

[I]t is apparent to me that the only proper Title VI relief granted by the District Court is the order directing the respondents to take actions and make disclosures intended to insure that future hiring practices will be nondiscriminatory and valid. However, this relief is wholly sustainable under the District Court's findings and conclusions with respect to petitioners' Title VII claim, and all members of the class will fully benefit from it. There is thus no need to disturb the judgment of the Court of Appeals. . . .

In conclusion, for the reasons expressed above, I am convinced that discriminatory intent is not an essential element of a Title VI violation, but that a private plaintiff should recover only injunctive, noncompensatory relief for a defendant's unintentional violations of Title VI. Such relief should not include an award of constructive seniority. Albeit on different grounds, the judgment below is affirmed."

V. JUSTICE VOTE

4 Pro ACLU Side vs. 5 Con Opposing Side

ACLU Side (Petitioner / Appellant)

1. Stevens, J. – Wrote dissenting opinion
2. Blackmun, H. – Joined Stevens' dissent
3. Brennan, W. – Joined Stevens' dissent
4. Marshall, T. – Wrote dissenting opinion

Opposing Side (Respondent / Appellee)

1. White, B. – Wrote majority opinion
2. Rehnquist, W. – Joined Powell's concurrence in part, wrote opinion concurring in judgment
3. Powell, L. – Wrote concurring opinion
4. Burger, W. – Joined Powell's concurrence
5. O'Connor, S. – Wrote concurring opinion

VI. A WIN OR LOSS FOR THE ACLU?

The ACLU filed as amicus curiae urging reversal; the Supreme Court affirmed the ruling of the Court of Appeals for the Second Circuit in a 5-4 vote, giving the ACLU an apparent loss.

520. United Brotherhood of Carpenters v. Scott

(Decided July 5, 1983; 463 U.S. 825)

I. ISSUE

A. Issues Discussed

Civil rights, federal rights, First Amendment, freedom of association, conspiracy

B. Legal Question Presented

What is "the scope of the cause of action made available by 42 U.S.C. § 1985(3) to those injured by conspiracies formed 'for the purpose of depriving, either directly or indirectly, any person or class of persons of the equal protection of the laws, or of equal privileges and immunities under the laws.'"

C. Supreme Court's Answer

The cause of action does not extend to this circumstance where the conspiracy alleged relates to the First Amendment but lacks state action and is based on economic views.

II. CASE SUMMARY

A. Background

"A.A. Cross Construction Co., Inc. (Cross), contracted with the Department of the Army to construct the Alligator Bayou Pumping Station and Gravity Drainage Structure on the Taylor Bayou Hurricane Levee near Port Arthur, Texas. In accordance with its usual practice, Cross hired workers for the project without regard to union membership. Some of them were from outside the Port Arthur area. Employees of Cross were several times warned by local residents that Cross's practice of hiring non-union workers was a matter of serious concern to many in the area and that it could lead to trouble. According to the District Court, the evidence showed that at a January 15, 1975, meeting of the Executive Committee of the Sabine Area Building and Construction Trades Council a citizen protest against Cross's hiring practices was discussed and a time and place for the protest were chosen. On the morning of January 17, a large group assembled at the entrance to the Alligator Bayou construction site. . . . From this gathering several truckloads of men emerged, drove on to the construction site, assaulted and beat Cross employees, and burned and destroyed construction equipment. The District Court found that continued violence was threatened 'if the nonunion workers did not leave the area or concede to union policies and principles.' The violence and vandalism delayed construction and led Cross to default on its contract with the Army.

The plaintiffs in this case, after amendment of the complaint, were respondents Scott and Matthews—two Cross employees who had been beaten, and the company itself. The Sabine Area

Building and Trades Council, 25 local unions, and various individuals were named as defendants. Plaintiffs asserted that defendants had conspired to deprive plaintiffs of their legally protected rights, contrary to 42 U.S.C. § 1985(3). The case was tried to the court. A permanent injunction was entered, and damages were awarded against 11 of the local unions, $5000 each to the individual plaintiffs and $112,385.14 to Cross, plus attorney's fees in the amount of $25,000. . . .

The Court of Appeals, sitting en banc, except for setting aside for failure of proof the judgment against eight of the eleven local unions, affirmed the judgment of the District Court[,] holding that the purpose of the conspiracy was to deprive plaintiffs of their First Amendment right not to associate with a union. The Court of Appeals went on to hold that § 1985(3) reached conspiracies motivated either by political or economic bias. Thus petitioners' conspiracy to harm the nonunion employees of a non-unionized contractor embodied the kind of class-based animus contemplated by § 1985(3) as construed in Griffin."

The Supreme Court granted certiorari to review the case and reversed.

B. Counsel of Record / ACLU Attorney

ACLU Side (Respondent / Appellee): Robert Q. Keith argued the cause for appellee.

Opposing Side (Petitioner / Appellant): Laurence Gold argued the cause for appellant.

III. AMICI CURIAE

ACLU Side (Respondent / Appellee)

Brief of amici curiae filed on behalf of the ACLU by Burt Neuborne.

Additional briefs of amici curiae were filed on behalf of Associated Builders & Contractors, Inc., the Chamber of Commerce of the United States, the Legal Foundation of America, and the National Right to Work Legal Defense Foundation.

Opposing Side (Petitioner / Appellant)

No briefs of amici curiae were filed in support of appellant.

IV. THE SUPREME COURT'S DECISION

"We do not disagree with the District Court and the Court of Appeals that there was a conspiracy, an act done in furtherance thereof, and a resultant injury to persons and property. Contrary to the Court of Appeals, however, we conclude that an alleged conspiracy to infringe First Amendment rights is not a violation of § 1985(3) unless it is proved that the State is involved in the conspiracy or that the aim of the conspiracy is to influence the activity of the State. We also disagree with the Court of Appeals' view that there was present here the kind of animus that § 1985(3) requires. . . .

The Court of Appeals accordingly erred in holding that § 1985(3) prohibits wholly private conspiracies to abridge the right of association guaranteed by the First Amendment. Because of that holding the Court of Appeals found it unnecessary to determine whether respondents' action could be sustained under § 1985(3) as involving a conspiracy to deprive respondents of rights, privileges, or immunities under state law or those protected against private action by the Federal Constitution or federal statutory law. Conceivably, we could remand for consideration of these possibilities, or we ourselves could consider them. We take neither course, for in our view the Court of Appeals should also be reversed on the dispositive ground that § 1985(3)'s requirement that there must be 'some racial, or perhaps otherwise class-based, invidiously discriminatory animus behind the conspirators' action,' was not satisfied in this case. . . .

Because the facts in Griffin revealed an animus against Negroes and those who supported them, a class-based, invidious discrimination which was the central concern of Congress in enacting § 1985(3), the Court expressly declined to decide 'whether a conspiracy motivated by invidiously discriminatory intent other than racial bias would be actionable under the portion of § 1985(3) before us.' Both courts below answered that question; both held that the section not only reaches conspiracies other than those motivated by racial bias but also forbids conspiracies against workers who refuse to join a union. We disagree with the latter conclusion and do not affirm the former.

[W]e find no convincing support in the legislative history for the proposition that the provision was intended to reach conspiracies motivated by bias towards others on account of their economic views, status, or activities. Such a construction would extend § 1985(3) into the economic life of the country in a way that we doubt that the 1871 Congress would have intended when it passed the provision in 1871. . . .

Economic and commercial conflicts, we think, are best dealt with by statutes, federal or state, specifically addressed to such problems, as well as by the general law proscribing injuries to persons and property. If we have misconstrued the intent of the 1871 Congress, or, in any event, if Congress now prefers to take a different tack, the Court will, of course, enforce any statute within the power of Congress to enact.

Accordingly, the judgment of the Court of Appeals is reversed."

V. JUSTICE VOTE

4 Pro ACLU Side vs. 5 Con Opposing Side

ACLU Side (Respondent / Appellee)

1. Blackmun, H. – Wrote dissenting opinion
2. Brennan, W. – Joined Blackmun's dissent
3. Marshall, T. – Joined Blackmun's dissent
4. O'Connor, S. – Joined Blackmun's dissent

Opposing Side (Petitioner / Appellant)

1. White, B. – Wrote majority opinion
2. Rehnquist, W. – Joined majority opinion
3. Powell, L. – Joined majority opinion
4. Burger, W. – Joined majority opinion
5. Stevens, J. – Joined majority opinion

VI. A WIN OR LOSS FOR THE ACLU?

The ACLU filed as amicus curiae urging affirmance; the Supreme Court reversed the ruling of the Court of Appeals in a 5-4 vote, giving the ACLU an apparent loss.

521. Barefoot v. Estelle

(Decided July 6, 1983; 463 U.S. 880)

I. ISSUE

A. Issues Discussed

Criminal justice, death penalty, criminal procedure, stay of execution, cruel and unusual punishment

B. Legal Question Presented

"[W]hether the District Court erred on the merits in rejecting the petition for habeas corpus filed by petitioner, and whether the Court of Appeals for the Fifth Circuit correctly denied a stay of execution of the death penalty pending appeal of the District Court's judgment."

C. Supreme Court's Answer

Neither the District Court nor the Court of Appeals erred in this circumstance.

II. CASE SUMMARY

A. Background

"On November 14, 1978, petitioner was convicted of the capital murder of a police officer in Bell County, Texas. A separate sentencing hearing before the same jury was then held to determine whether the death penalty should be imposed. [The jury decided to impose] the death penalty.

On appeal to the Texas Court of Criminal Appeals, petitioner urged, among other submissions, that the use of psychiatrists at the punishment hearing to make predictions about petitioner's future conduct was unconstitutional because psychiatrists, individually and as a class, are not competent to predict future dangerousness.... The court rejected all of these contentions and affirmed the conviction and sentence....

Petitioner's execution was scheduled for September 17, 1980. On July 29, [the Supreme] Court granted a stay of execution pending the filing and disposition of a petition for certiorari, which was filed and then denied on June 29, 1981. Petitioner's execution was again scheduled by the state courts.... An application for habeas corpus to the Texas Court of Criminal Appeals was denied..., whereafter a petition for habeas corpus was filed in the United States District Court for the Western District of Texas.... The District Court stayed petitioner's execution pending action on the petition.... On November 9, 1982, the District Court filed its findings and conclusions, rejecting each of the several grounds asserted by petitioner. The writ was accordingly denied; also, the stay of petitioner's death sentence was vacated. The District Court, however, granted petitioner's motion to proceed in forma pauperis and issued a certificate of probable cause pursuant to 28 U.S.C. § 2253, which provides that an appeal may not be taken to the Court of Appeals from the final order in a habeas corpus proceeding where the detention complained of arises out of process issued by a state court 'unless the Justice or Judge who rendered the order or a Circuit Justice or Judge issues a certificate of probable cause.' Notice of appeal was filed on November 24, 1982.

At this point, the Texas courts set January 25, 1983, as the new execution date. A petition for habeas corpus and motion for stay of execution were then denied by the Texas Court of Criminal Appeals on December 21, 1982, and another motion for stay of execution was denied by the same court on January 11, 1983.

On January 14, petitioner moved the Court of Appeals for the Fifth Circuit to stay his execution pending consideration of his appeal from the denial of his petition for habeas corpus. On ... January 20, the Court of Appeals issued an opinion and judgment denying the stay.... The court concluded that since the petition had no substantial merit, a stay should be denied.

Petitioner then filed an application for stay of execution with the Circuit Justice for the Fifth Circuit, who referred the matter to the [Supreme] Court."

The Supreme Court granted certiorari to review the case and affirmed.

B. Counsel of Record / ACLU Attorney

ACLU Side (Petitioner / Appellant): Will Gray argued the cause for appellant.

Jack Greenberg argued the cause for the NAACP Legal Defense and Educational Fund, Inc., as amicus curiae, by special leave of Court.

Opposing Side (Respondent / Appellee): Douglas M. Becker, Assistant Attorney General of Texas argued the cause for appellee.

III. AMICI CURIAE

ACLU Side (Petitioner / Appellant)

Brief of amici curiae filed on behalf of the Texas Civil Liberties Union, et al., by Gerald H. Goldstein, Maury Maverick, and Burt Neuborne.

Brief of amici curiae filed on behalf of the NAACP Legal Defense and Educational Fund, Inc., by Jack Greenberg, James M. Nabrit III, Joel Berger, John Charles Boger, Deborah Fins, James S. Liebman, and Anthony G. Amsterdam.

Brief of amici curiae filed on behalf of the American Psychiatric Association by Joel I. Klein.

Brief of amici curiae filed on behalf of the American Bar Association by Morris Harrell, Marna S. Tucker, E. Barrett Prettyman, Jr., and Paul J. Larkin, Jr.

Opposing Side (Respondent / Appellee)

Brief of amici curiae filed on behalf of the Washington Legal Foundation by Daniel J. Popeo, Paul D. Kamenar, and Nicholas E. Calio.

IV. THE SUPREME COURT'S DECISION

"Although the Court of Appeals did not formally affirm the judgment of the District Court, there is no question that the Court of Appeals ruled on the merits of the appeal.... It would have been advisable, once the court had addressed the merits and arrived at these conclusions, to verify the obvious by expressly affirming the judgment of the District Court, as well as to deny the stay. The court's failure to do so, however, does not conflict with Garrison and related cases....

Furthermore, the Texas Court of Criminal Appeals could find

no fault with the mode of examining the two psychiatrists under Texas law: 'The trial court did not err by permitting the doctors to testify on the basis of the hypothetical question. The use of hypothetical questions in the examination of expert witnesses is a well-established practice. That the experts had not examined appellant went to the weight of their testimony, not to its admissibility.'

Like the Court of Criminal Appeals, the District Court, and the Court of Appeals, we reject petitioner's constitutional arguments against the use of hypothetical questions. Although cases such as this involve the death penalty, we perceive no constitutional barrier to applying the ordinary rules of evidence governing the use of expert testimony. . . .

In sum, we affirm the judgment of the District Court. There is no doubt that the psychiatric testimony increased the likelihood that petitioner would be sentenced to death, but this fact does not make that evidence inadmissible, any more than it would with respect to other relevant evidence against any defendant in a criminal case. At bottom, to agree with petitioner's basic position would seriously undermine and in effect overrule Jurek v. Texas. Petitioner conceded as much at oral argument. We are not inclined, however, to overturn the decision in that case.

The judgment of the District Court is affirmed."

V. JUSTICE VOTE

3 Pro ACLU Side vs. 6 Con Opposing Side

ACLU Side (Petitioner / Appellant)

1. Blackmun, H. – Wrote dissenting opinion
2. Marshall, T. – Wrote dissenting opinion, joined Blackmun's dissent
3. Brennan, W. – Joined Marshall's dissent, joined Blackmun's dissent

Opposing Side (Respondent / Appellee)

1. White, B. – Wrote majority opinion
2. Powell, L. – Joined majority opinion
3. Burger, W. – Joined majority opinion
4. O'Connor, S. – Joined majority opinion
5. Rehnquist, W. – Joined majority opinion
6. Stevens, J. – Wrote concurring opinion

VI. A WIN OR LOSS FOR THE ACLU?

The ACLU filed as amicus curiae, urging reversal; the Supreme Court affirmed the District Court's judgment in a 6-3 vote giving the ACLU an apparent loss.

522. Arizona Governing Committee for Tax Deferred Annuity & Deferred Compensation Plans v. Norris

(Decided July 16, 1983; 463 U.S. 1073)

I. ISSUE

A. Issues Discussed

Civil rights, gender, Civil Rights Act of 1964, Fourteenth Amendment

B. Legal Question Presented

"[W]hether Title VII of the Civil Rights Act of 1964 . . . prohibits an employer from offering its employees the option of receiving retirement benefits from one of several companies selected by the employer, all of which pay a woman lower monthly retirement benefits than a man who has made the same contributions; and whether, if so, the relief awarded by the District Court was proper."

C. Supreme Court's Answer

Title VII prohibits an employer from only offering retirement benefit options which pay a lower monthly benefit to a women than a man, however, the damages in this case should only be prospective, not retroactive.

II. CASE SUMMARY

A. Background

"Arizona is authorized by Ariz.Rev.Stat.Ann. § 38-871 to investigate, approve and contract for tax deferred compensation and annuity programs for its employees. Norris' class, which was certified, consists of all female employees of Arizona who have enrolled in, or will enroll in, the plan.

The plan is offered to all employees on a voluntary basis. It is funded entirely by employee contributions. The employees are offered one of three options. First, an employee may elect the lump sum option. This option allows one to withdraw at once all of the accumulated annuity. Second, the employee may elect to receive a fixed sum for a fixed period of time. The third option—the life annuity contract—is the one in question here. The employee may elect to receive a certain amount of money each month for life. Arizona selects the companies with which the employee must contract. All the companies selected by Arizona use sex-segregated mortality tables in computing the monthly amounts due under the life annuity contract.

Norris challenged the plan as violative of Title VII and the Fourteenth Amendment. The district court agreed that the plan violates Title VII. The court held that the plan does not violate the Fourteenth Amendment because the discrimination was not intentional. The court enjoined Arizona from using sex-segregated actuarial tables and ordered that future annuity payments to women equal the payments to similarly situated men."[1] The Court of Appeals for the Ninth Circuit affirmed.

---

1 Norris v. Arizona Governing Committee for Tax Deferred Annuity & Deferred Compenation Plans, 671 F.2d 330 (9th Cir. 1982).

The Supreme Court granted certiorari to review the case, affirmed in part, and reversed in part.

B. Counsel of Record / ACLU Attorney

ACLU Side (Respondent / Appellee): Amy Jo Gittler argued the cause for appellee.

Opposing Side (Petitioner / Appellant): John L. Endicott, Special Assistant Attorney General of Arizona, argued the cause for appellant.

III. AMICI CURIAE

ACLU Side (Respondent / Appellee)

Brief of amici curiae filed on behalf of the ACLU, et al., by Mary L. Heen, Burt Neuborne, Isabelle Katz Pinzler, Joan E. Bertin, and Charles S. Sims.

Additional briefs of amici curiae were filed on behalf of the American Association of University Professors, et al., the American Federation of Labor and Congress of Industrial Organizations, et al., the American Nurses' Association, the Lawyers' Committee for Civil Rights Under Law, et al., Eight Individual Actuaries, and the National Insurance Consumer Organization.

Opposing Side (Petitioner / Appellant)

Briefs of amici curiae were filed on behalf of the State of Florida, the New York State Teachers' Retirement System, the American Council of Life Insurance, the Equal Employment Advisory Council, the Teachers Insurance and Annuity Association, et al., and the National Association of Insurance Commissioners.

Brief of amici curiae filed on behalf of the American Academy of Actuaries by Lawrence J. Latto, Stephen J. Hadley, and William D. Hager urging the Supreme Court to grant the writ of certiorari in the case.

IV. THE SUPREME COURT'S DECISION

"Petitioners in this case administer a deferred compensation plan for employees of the State of Arizona. The respondent class consists of all female employees who are enrolled in the plan or will enroll in the plan in the future. Certiorari was granted to decide whether Title VII of the Civil Rights Act of 1964 . . . prohibits an employer from offering its employees the option of receiving retirement benefits from one of several companies selected by the employer, all of which pay a woman lower monthly retirement benefits than a man who has made the same contributions; and whether, if so, the relief awarded by the District Court was proper. The Court holds that this practice does constitute discrimination on the basis of sex in violation of Title VII, and that all retirement benefits derived from contributions made after the decision today must be calculated without regard to the sex of the beneficiary. This position is expressed in Parts I, II, and III of the opinion of Justice MARSHALL, which are joined by Justice BRENNAN, Justice WHITE, Justice STEVENS, and Justice O'CONNOR. The Court further holds that benefits derived from contributions made prior to this decision may be calculated as provided by the existing terms of the Arizona plan. This position is expressed in Part III of the opinion of Justice POWELL, which is joined by THE CHIEF JUSTICE, Justice BLACKMUN, Justice REHNQUIST, and Justice O'CONNOR. Accordingly, the judgment of the Court of Appeals is affirmed in part, reversed in part, and the case is remanded for further proceedings consistent with this opinion. The Clerk is directed to issue the judgment August 1, 1983."

V. JUSTICE VOTE

5 Pro ACLU Side vs. 4 Con Opposing Side

ACLU Side (Respondent / Appellee)

1. Marshall, T. – Wrote concurring opinion
2. Brennan, W. – Joined Marshall's concurrence
3. White, B. – Joined Marshall's concurrence
4. Stevens, J. – Joined Marshall's concurrence
5. O'Connor, S. – Wrote concurring opinion, joined Marshall's concurrence in part, joined Powell's opinion in part

Opposing Side (Petitioner / Appellant)

1. Powell, L. – Wrote opinion dissenting in part and concurring in part
2. Burger, W. – Joined Powell's opinion
3. Rehnquist, W. – Joined Powell's opinion
4. Blackmun, H. – Joined Powell's opinion

VI. A WIN OR LOSS FOR THE ACLU?

The ACLU filed as amicus curiae urging affirmance; the Supreme Court affirmed in part, reversed in part, and remanded the ruling of the Court of Appeals for the Federal District Court in a 5-4 vote, giving the ACLU an apparent win.

523. Migra v. Warren City School District Board of Education

(Decided January 23, 1984; 465 U.S. 75)

I. ISSUE

A. Issues Discussed

Governmental authority, civil procedure, claim preclusion, First Amendment, Fifth Amendment, Fourteenth Amendment

B. Legal Question Presented

Does a state court judgment have a claim preclusive effect over a subsequent suit in federal court?

C. Supreme Court's Answer

The application of claim preclusion here must be determined by state law. The case is remanded to apply Ohio claim preclusion law to this case.

II. CASE SUMMARY

A. Background

"Petitioner, Dr. Ethel D. Migra, was employed by the Warren [Ohio] City School District Board of Education . . . . Her employment was on an annual basis under written contracts for successive school years.

On April 17, 1979, at a regularly scheduled meeting, the Board, with all five of its members present, unanimously adopted a resolution renewing Dr. Migra's employment as supervisor for the 1979-1980 school year. Being advised of this, she accepted the renewed appointment by letter dated April 18 delivered to a member of the Board on April 23. . . .

The Board, however, held a special meeting, called by its President, on the morning of April 24. [F]our of the five members of the Board were present. The President first read Dr. Migra's acceptance letter. Then . . . a motion was made and adopted, by a vote of three to one, not to renew Petitioner's employment for the 1979-1980 school year. Dr. Migra was given written notice of this nonrenewal and never received a written contract of employment for that year. . . .

Petitioner brought suit in the Court of Common Pleas of Trumbull County, Ohio, against the Board and its three members who had voted not to renew her employment. The complaint . . . presented . . . essentially two causes of action, namely, breach of contract by the Board, and wrongful interference by the individual members with petitioner's contract of employment. The state court . . . awarded Dr. Migra reinstatement to her position and compensatory damages. . . . The Ohio Court of Appeals, Eleventh District, in an unreported opinion, affirmed the judgment of the Court of Common Pleas. Review was denied by the Supreme Court of Ohio.

In July 1980, Dr. Migra filed the present action in the United States District Court for the Northern District of Ohio against the Board, its then individual members, and the Superintendent of Schools. Her complaint alleged that Dr. Migra had become the director of a commission appointed by the Board to fashion a voluntary plan for the desegregation of the District's elementary schools; that she had prepared a social studies curriculum; that the individual defendants objected to and opposed the curriculum and resisted the desegregation plan; that hostility and ill will toward petitioner developed; and that, as a consequence, the individual defendants determined not to renew petitioner's contract of employment. . . . Dr. Migra claimed that the Board's actions were intended to punish her for the exercise of her First Amendment rights. She also claimed that the actions deprived her of property without due process and denied her equal protection. Her federal claim thus arose under the First, Fifth and Fourteenth Amendments and 42 U.S.C. §§ 1983 and 1985. She requested injunctive relief and compensatory and punitive damages. [D]efendants moved for summary judgment on the basis of res judicata and the bar of the statute of limitations.

The District Court granted summary judgment for the defendants and dismissed the complaint. The United States Court of Appeals for the Sixth Circuit, by a short unreported order, affirmed."

The Supreme Court granted certiorari to review the case, vacated, and remanded.

B. Counsel of Record / ACLU Attorney

ACLU Side (Petitioner / Appellant): John R. Vintilla argued the cause for appellant.

Opposing Side (Respondent / Appellee): James L. Messenger argued the cause for appellee.

III. AMICI CURIAE

ACLU Side (Petitioner / Appellant)

Brief of amici curiae filed on behalf of the ACLU, et al., by Charles S. Sims, Burt Neuborne, Gordon Beggs, and Barbara Besser.

Brief of amici curiae filed on behalf of the Edwin F. Mandel Legal Aid Clinic by Gary H. Palm.

Brief of amici curiae filed on behalf of the National Education Association by Joy L. Koletsky and Robert H. Chanin.

Opposing Side (Respondent / Appellee)

Brief of amici curiae filed on behalf of the State of Maryland, et al., by Stephen H. Sachs, Attorney General of Maryland, Diana G. Motz and Frederick G. Savage, Assistant Attorneys General, and Sheldon Elliot Steinbach.

IV. THE SUPREME COURT'S DECISION

"In the present litigation, petitioner does not claim that the state court would not have adjudicated her federal claims had she presented them in her original suit in state court. Alternatively, petitioner could have obtained a federal forum for her federal claim by litigating it first in a federal court. Section 1983, however, does not override state preclusion law and guarantee petitioner a right to proceed to judgment in state court on her state claims and then turn to federal court for adjudication of her federal claims. We hold, therefore, that petitioner's state-court judgment in this litigation has the same claim preclusive effect in federal court that the judgment would have in the Ohio state courts. . . .

In 1968, the Supreme Court of Ohio twice dealt with the question of what constitutes a cause of action for preclusion purposes. In each of these cases, although a second action against the defendant was permitted, the court clearly was developing a broader and more expansive attitude toward claim preclusion. In addition, the Ohio Supreme Court in 1970 adopted Rule 13 of the Ohio Rules of Civil Procedure establishing compulsory counterclaim provision like its federal counterpart in Rule 13 of the Federal Rules of Civil Procedure.

Then, in 1982, the Supreme Court of Ohio, adopted what appears to be a broad doctrine of preclusion indeed, although in a defensive, not offensive, context. . . . In reading the opinion of the District Court in the present litigation, we are unable to determine whether that court was applying what it thought was the Ohio law of preclusion. The opinion cites a Sixth Circuit opinion that purported to enunciate Ohio law, and also relied on precedents from other federal Courts of Appeals applying both federal and state law. Our holding today makes clear that Ohio state preclusion law is to be applied to this case. Prudence also dictates that it is the District Court, in the first instance, not this Court, that should interpret Ohio preclusion law and apply it.

The judgment of the Court of Appeals, accordingly, is vacated and the case is remanded to that court so that it may instruct the District Court to conduct such further proceedings as are required by, and are consistent with, this opinion."

V. JUSTICE VOTE

9 Pro ACLU Side vs. 0 Con Opposing Side

ACLU Side (Petitioner / Appellant)

1. Blackmun, H. – Wrote majority opinion
2. Brennan, W. – Joined majority opinion
3. Marshall, T. – Joined majority opinion
4. Rehnquist, W. – Joined majority opinion
5. Stevens, J. – Joined majority opinion
6. O'Connor, S. – Joined majority opinion
7. White, B. – Wrote concurring opinion
8. Burger, W. – Joined White's concurrence
9. Powell, L. – Joined White's concurrence

VI. A WIN OR LOSS FOR THE ACLU?

The ACLU filed as amicus curiae urging reversal; the Supreme Court vacated the ruling of the Court of Appeals for the Sixth Circuit in a 9-0 vote; giving the ACLU an apparent win.

524. Flanagan v. United States

(Decided February 21, 1984; 465 U.S. 259)

I. ISSUE

A. Issues Discussed

Criminal procedure, Fifth Amendment, Sixth Amendment

B. Legal Question Presented

Whether "a District Court's pretrial disqualification of defense counsel in a criminal prosecution is . . . immediately appealable under 28 U.S.C. § 1291."

C. Supreme Court's Answer

The pretrial disqualification of defense counsel is not immediately appealable.

II. CASE SUMMARY

A. Background

"Petitioners are four police officers . . . . A federal grand jury in the Eastern District of Pennsylvania indicted petitioners in September 1981. The indictment alleged that petitioners had conspired to make arrests without probable cause and had unlawfully arrested and abused eight people. . . .

Prior to the return of the indictment, petitioners had retained the law firm of Sprague and Rubenstone to act as joint counsel. Petitioners decided to continue the joint representation after the indictment was handed down, even though the indictment did not make the same allegations against all petitioners. Petitioners Keweshan, Landis, and McNamee, however, moved to sever their case from petitioner Flanagan's, arguing that the government's evidence against Flanagan alone was so much greater than the evidence against them that severance was necessary to avoid prejudicial spillover. . . . The Government responded by moving to disqualify Sprague and Rubenstone from its multiple representation of petitioners . . . . In early December 1981, following a hearing and briefing on the Government's motion, the District Court disqualified the law firm from participation in the case. . . .

Petitioners appealed to the United States Court of Appeals for the Third Circuit, which affirmed the decision of the District Court in June 1982. Although jurisdiction was not challenged, the Court of Appeals noted that it had jurisdiction under 28 U.S.C. § 1291 because the disqualification order was appealable prior to trial as a collateral order . . . . The court went on to hold that the disqualification order was proper because an actual conflict of interest was very likely to arise. In July 1982 the court denied rehearing but stayed issuance of the mandate to permit filing of a petition for a writ of certiorari in [the Supreme] Court."

The Supreme Court granted certiorari to review the case and reversed.

B. Counsel of Record / ACLU Attorney

ACLU Side (Petitioner / Appellant): Edward H. Rubenstone argued the cause for appellant.

Opposing Side (Respondent / Appellee): Deputy Solicitor General Frey argued the cause for the United States.

III. AMICI CURIAE

ACLU Side (Petitioner / Appellant)

Brief of amici curiae filed on behalf of the ACLU by James D. Crawford, Burt Neuborne, and Charles S. Sims.

Brief of amici curiae filed on behalf of the National Association of Criminal Defense Lawyers, et al., by Eugene G. Iredale and James M. Shellow.

Opposing Side (Respondent / Appellee)

No briefs of amici curiae were filed in support of appellee.

IV. THE SUPREME COURT'S DECISION

"'Finality as a condition of review is an historic characteristic of federal appellate procedure.' Thus, the jurisdictional statute applicable to this case limits the jurisdiction of the courts of appeals to appeals from 'final decisions of the district courts.' This final judgment rule requires that 'a party must ordinarily raise all claims of error in a single appeal following final judgment on the merits.' In a criminal case the rule prohibits appellate review until conviction and imposition of sentence. . . .

An order disqualifying counsel lacks the critical characteristics that make orders denying bail reduction or refusing to dismiss on double jeopardy or Speech or Debate grounds immediately appealable. Unlike a request for bail reduction, a constitutional objection to counsel's disqualification is in no danger of becoming moot upon conviction and sentence. Moreover, it cannot be said that the right petitioners assert, whether based on the Due Process Clause of the Fifth Amendment or on the Assistance of Counsel Clause of the Sixth Amendment, is a right not to be tried. . . .

Nothing about a disqualification order distinguishes it from the run of pretrial judicial decisions that affect the rights of criminal defendants yet must await completion of trial court proceedings for review. Such an order fails to satisfy the stringent conditions for qualification as an immediately appealable collateral order, and the overriding policies against interlocutory review in criminal cases apply in full. The exceptions to the final judgment rule in criminal cases are rare. An order disqualifying counsel is not one.

The judgment of the Court of Appeals is accordingly reversed. On remand the appeal should be dismissed."

V. JUSTICE VOTE

9 Pro ACLU Side vs. 0 Con Opposing Side

ACLU Side (Petitioner / Appellant)

1. O'Connor, S. – Wrote majority opinion
2. Rehnquist, W. – Joined majority opinion
3. Powell, L. – Joined majority opinion
4. Blackmun, H. – Joined majority opinion
5. Burger, W. – Joined majority opinion
6. Marshall, T. – Joined majority opinion
7. White, B. – Joined majority opinion
8. Brennan, W. – Joined majority opinion
9. Stevens, J. – Joined majority opinion

VI. A WIN OR LOSS FOR THE ACLU?

The ACLU filed as amicus curiae urging reversal; the Supreme Court reversed the ruling of the Court of Appeals for the Third Circuit in a 9-0 vote, giving the ACLU an apparent win.

525. Lynch v. Donnelly

(Decided March 5, 1984; 465 U.S. 668)

I. ISSUE

A. Issues Discussed

First Amendment, religious displays, Establishment Clause

B. Legal Question Presented

"[W]hether the Establishment Clause of the First Amendment prohibits a municipality from including a crèche, or Nativity scene, in its annual Christmas display."

C. Supreme Court's Answer

The Establishment Clause does not prohibit the crèche.

II. CASE SUMMARY

A. Background

"Each year, in cooperation with the downtown retail merchants' association, the City of Pawtucket, Rhode Island, erects a Christmas display as part of its observance of the Christmas holiday season. The display is situated in a park owned by a nonprofit organization and located in the heart of the shopping district.... The Pawtucket display comprises many of the figures and decorations traditionally associated with Christmas, including ... the crèche at issue here. All components of this display are owned by the City.

The crèche, which has been included in the display for 40 or more years, consists of the traditional figures, including the Infant Jesus, Mary and Joseph, angels, shepherds, kings, and animals....

Respondents, Pawtucket residents and individual members of the Rhode Island affiliate of the American Civil Liberties Union, and the affiliate itself, brought this action in the United States District Court for Rhode Island, challenging the City's inclusion of the crèche in the annual display. The District Court held that the City's inclusion of the crèche in the display violates the Establishment Clause, which is binding on the states through the Fourteenth Amendment.... The City was permanently enjoined from including the crèche in the display.

A divided panel of the Court of Appeals for the First Circuit affirmed."

The Supreme Court granted certiorari to review the case and reversed.

B. Counsel of Record / ACLU Attorney

ACLU Side (Respondent / Appellee): Amato A. DeLuca argued the cause for appellee. With him on the briefs were Sandra A. Blanding, Burt Neuborne, E. Richard Larson, and Norman Dorsen.

Opposing Side (Petitioner / Appellant): William F. McMahon argued the cause for appellant. With him on the briefs were Richard P. McMahon and Spencer W. Viner.

Solicitor General Lee argued the cause for the United States, as amicus curiae, by special leave of Court.

III. AMICI CURIAE

ACLU Side (Respondent / Appellee)

Brief of amici curiae filed on behalf of the American Jewish Committee, et al., by Samuel Rabinove.

Brief of amici curiae filed on behalf of the Anti-Defamation League of B'nai B'rith, et al., by Justin J. Finger, Alan Dershowitz, Meyer Eisenberg, Jeffrey P. Sinensky, Nathan Z. Dershowitz, and Marc Stern.

Opposing Side (Petitioner / Appellant)

Brief of amici curiae filed on behalf of the Coalition for Religious Liberty, et al., by James J. Knicely and John W. Whitehead.

Brief of amici curiae filed on behalf of the Legal Foundation of America by David Crump.

Brief of amici curiae filed on behalf of the Washington Legal Foundation by Daniel J. Popeo, Paul D. Kamenar, and Nicholas E. Calio.

Brief of amici curiae filed on behalf of the United States by Solicitor General Lee, Assistant Attorney General McGrath, Deputy Solicitor General Bator, Deputy Assistant Attorney General Kuhl, and Kathryn A. Oberly.

IV. THE SUPREME COURT'S DECISION

"In our modern, complex society, whose traditions and constitutional underpinnings rest on and encourage diversity and pluralism in all areas, an absolutist approach in applying the Establishment Clause is simplistic and has been uniformly rejected by the Court.

Rather than mechanically invalidating all governmental conduct or statutes that confer benefits or give special recognition to religion in general or to one faith—as an absolutist approach would dictate—the Court has scrutinized challenged legislation or official conduct to determine whether, in reality, it establishes a religion or religious faith, or tends to do so. . . .

In the line-drawing process we have often found it useful to inquire whether the challenged law or conduct has a secular purpose, whether its principal or primary effect is to advance or inhibit religion, and whether it creates an excessive entanglement of government with religion. . . .

The narrow question is whether there is a secular purpose for Pawtucket's display of the crèche. The display is sponsored by the City to celebrate the Holiday and to depict the origins of that Holiday. These are legitimate secular purposes. . . .

We are satisfied that the City has a secular purpose for including the crèche, that the City has not impermissibly advanced religion, and that including the crèche does not create excessive entanglement between religion and government. . . .

Of course the crèche is identified with one religious faith but no more so than the examples we have set out from prior cases in which we found no conflict with the Establishment Clause. It would be ironic, however, if the inclusion of a single symbol of a particular historic religious event, as part of a celebration acknowledged in the Western World for 20 centuries, and in this country by the people, by the Executive Branch, by the Congress, and the courts for two centuries, would so 'taint' the City's exhibit as to render it violative of the Establishment Clause. To forbid the use of this one passive symbol—the crèche—at the very time people are taking note of the season with Christmas hymns and carols in public schools and other public places, and while the Congress and Legislatures open sessions with prayers by paid chaplains would be a stilted over-reaction contrary to our history and to our holdings. If the presence of the crèche in this display violates the Establishment Clause, a host of other forms of taking official note of Christmas, and of our religious heritage, are equally offensive to the Constitution. . . .

We hold that, notwithstanding the religious significance of the crèche, the City of Pawtucket has not violated the Establishment Clause of the First Amendment. Accordingly, the judgment of the Court of Appeals is reversed."

V. JUSTICE VOTE

4 Pro ACLU Side vs. 5 Con Opposing Side

ACLU Side (Respondent / Appellee)

1. Brennan, W. – Wrote dissenting opinion
2. Marshall, T. – Joined Brennan's dissent
3. Stevens, J. – Joined Brennan's dissent, joined Blackmun's dissent
4. Blackmun, H. – Wrote dissenting opinion, joined Brennan's dissent

Opposing Side (Petitioner / Appellant)

1. Burger, W. – Wrote majority opinion
2. White, B. – Joined majority opinion
3. Powell, L. – Joined majority opinion
4. Rehnquist, W. – Joined majority opinion
5. O'Connor, S. – Wrote concurring opinion

VI. A WIN OR LOSS FOR THE ACLU?

The ACLU, as counsel of record, urged affirmance of the judgment of the Court of Appeals for the First Circuit; the Supreme Court reversed in a 5-4 vote, giving the ACLU an apparent loss.

526. Heckler v. Mathews

(Decided March 5, 1984; 465 U.S. 728)

I. ISSUE

A. Issues Discussed

Civil rights, gender, Fifth Amendment, equal protection, due process

B. Legal Question Presented

Did the extension of the gender-based classification of Congress' pension-offset violate the Fifth Amendment?

C. Supreme Court's Answer

The extension does not violate the Fifth Amendment.

II. CASE SUMMARY

A. Background

"Califano v. Goldfarb, 430 U.S. 199 (1977), held that a gender-based classification in the spousal-benefit provisions of the Social Security Act violated the right to the equal protection of the laws guaranteed by the Due Process Clause of the Fifth Amendment. In this case, the United States District Court for the Northern District of Alabama held that amendments to the Act, adopted in 1977 partly in response to [the Supreme Court] decision, unjustifiably revive the gender-based classification that was invalidated in Goldfarb and therefore also violate the Fifth Amendment. . . .

Appellee Mathews retired from his job with the United States Postal Service on October 18, 1977. His wife, who had retired from her job a few months earlier, was fully insured under the Social Security Act. In December 1977, Mathews applied for husband's benefits on his wife's account. On review of the application, the Social Security Administration (SSA) informed Mathews that he was entitled to spousal benefits of $153.30 per month but that, because, as appellee acknowledged, he was not dependent upon his wife for one-half of his support, this amount would be entirely offset by his $573 per month Postal Service pension in accordance with § 334(b)(2) of the 1977 Amendments, 42 U.S.C. § 402(c)(2). After a hearing, an administrative law judge (ALJ) affirmed the SSA's initial decision. The ALJ's decision was in turn affirmed by the Appeals Council of the Department of Health and Human Services and thereby became the final decision of the Secretary.

Mathews then brought this class action against the Secretary in the United States District Court for the Northern District of Alabama under § 205(g) of the Act, 42 U.S.C. 405(g). The complaint alleged that application of the pension offset provision of the 1977 Amendments to Mathews and other nondependent men but not to similarly situated nondependent women violated the Due Process Clause of the Fifth Amendment and sought a declaratory judgment to that effect. Appellee also contended that the severability clause of the 1977 Amendments was unconstitutional. The District Court certified a nationwide class . . . .

Shortly thereafter, the District Court filed an opinion holding both the pension offset exception of § 334(g)(1)(B) and the severability clause of § 334(g)(3) unconstitutional. . . . Accordingly, the court . . . ordered the Secretary to pay Mathews and the rest of the plaintiff class full spousal benefits without regard to dependency and without offsetting the amount of their government pensions."

The Supreme Court granted certiorari to review the case and reversed.

B. Counsel of Record / ACLU Attorney

ACLU Side (Respondent / Appellee): John R. Benn argued the cause for appellee.

Opposing Side (Petitioner / Appellant): Mark I. Levy argued the cause for appellant.

III. AMICI CURIAE

ACLU Side (Respondent / Appellee)

Opposing Side (Petitioner / Appellant)

Brief of amici curiae filed on behalf of the ACLU, et al., by Isabelle Katz Pinzler, Burt Neuborne, and Nancy Duff Campbell.

Additional briefs of amici curiae were filed on behalf of the Louisiana Public Service Commission, Southeastern Legal Foundation, Inc., Utilities: Houston Lighting and Power Company, et al., the American Public Power Association, the Mountain States Legal Foundation, Central Hudson Gas & Electric Corporation, Arkansas Power & Light Company, et al., Mississippi Power & Light Company, the State of Texas, the Potomac Electric Power Company, the Duke Power Company, et al., Southern Company Services, Inc., et al., and Florida Power & Light Company.

Brief of amici curiae filed on behalf of the Legal Foundation of America by David Crump and Susan E. Waite urging reversal in part and affirmance in part of the judgment of the District Court. Briefs of amici curiae were filed on behalf of Windfarms, Ltd., Hawaii Sugar Planters' Association, Hoffman-La Roche, Inc., et al, the Energy Law Institute and the State of Maine, the State of Maryland, et al., the National Alliance for Hydroelectric Energy, et al., the American Paper Institute, Inc., Windfarms, Ltd., et al., the California Public Utilities Commission, California Energy Resources Conservation and Development Commission, the County of Onondaga, New York, the Department of Energy of the State of Oregon, and the American Federation of Government Employees, AFL-CIO, et al.

IV. THE SUPREME COURT'S DECISION

"Congress adopted the pension offset requirement to prevent the serious fiscal drain that it concluded would result from payment of unreduced benefits to the new class of recipients made eligible by the decision in Goldfarb. Nevertheless, in an effort to protect the reliance interests of individuals who had planned their retirement before the March 1977 Goldfarb decision and the resulting amendments to the Act, Congress exempted from the offset requirement those individuals eligible for spousal benefits under the Act 'as it was in effect and being administered in January 1977.' There can be no dispute that in January 1977 men were eligible for benefits only upon a showing of dependency whereas women were subject to no such requirement. . . .

Consistent with the plain import of these provisions, Senator Long, then Chairman of the Senate Finance Committee and principal manager of the bill in the Senate, explained that the exception clause was meant 'to afford . . . protection to those who anticipated receiving their spouses benefits prior to March 1977 without providing it also to those [who] would qualify only as a result of [the Goldfarb] decision.' Appellee's proposed interpretation of the exception provision would defeat this clearly expressed intention and, by rendering the offset requirement applicable to very few applicants, frustrate the congressional aim of preventing a major fiscal drain on the Social Security trust fund. Accordingly, we reject appellee's construction of the Act and conclude that the exception to the offset provision applies to otherwise eligible men only when they can show dependency on their wives for one-half of their support. . . .

By reviving for a five-year period the eligibility criteria in effect in January 1977, the exception is narrowly tailored to protect only those individuals who made retirement plans prior to the changes in the law that occurred after that date. Individuals who were eligible for spousal benefits before the law changed and who retire within five years of the statute's enactment may reasonably be assumed to have begun planning for their retirement prior to the adoption of the offset provision. . . .

The exception to the pension offset requirement set out in § 334(g)(1) of the 1977 Amendments to the Social Security Act, while temporarily reviving the gender-based classification invalidated in Califano v. Goldfarb, is directly and substantially related to the important governmental interest of protecting individuals who planned their retirements in reasonable reliance on the law in effect prior to that decision. Accordingly, the judgment of the District Court is reversed."

V. JUSTICE VOTE

0 Pro ACLU Side vs. 9 Con Opposing Side

Opposing Side (Petitioner / Appellant)

1. Brennan, W. – Wrote majority opinion
2. Rehnquist, W. – Joined majority opinion
3. Powell, L. – Joined majority opinion
4. Blackmun, H. – Joined majority opinion
5. Burger, W. – Joined majority opinion
6. Marshall, T. – Joined majority opinion
7. White, B. – Joined majority opinion
8. O'Connor, S. – Joined majority opinion
9. Stevens, J. – Joined majority opinion

VI. A WIN OR LOSS FOR THE ACLU?

The ACLU filed as amicus curiae urging affirmance; the Supreme Court reversed the ruling of the District Court for the Northern District of Alabama in a 9-0 vote, giving the ACLU an apparent loss.

527. Blum v. Stenson

(Decided March 21, 1984; 465 U.S. 886)

I. ISSUE

A. Issues Discussed

Civil procedure, civil rights

B. Legal Question Presented

"The two issues in this case are whether Congress intended fee awards to nonprofit legal service organizations to be calculated according to cost or to prevailing market rates, and whether, and under what circumstances, an upward adjustment of an award based on prevailing market rates is appropriate under § 1988."

C. Supreme Court's Answer

"The Civil Rights Attorney's Fees Awards Act of 1976, 42 U.S.C. § 1988, authorizes district courts to award a reasonable attorney's fee to prevailing civil rights litigants. In enacting the statute, Congress directed that attorney's fees be calculated according to standards currently in use under other fee-shifting statutes . . . .

Respondents . . . have failed to carry their burden of justifying entitlement to an upward adjustment."

II. CASE SUMMARY

A. Background

"Throughout this litigation, respondents were represented by attorneys from The Legal Aid Society of New York, a private nonprofit law office. In November 1980, respondents filed a request for attorney's fees for the period December 1978 through the end of the litigation. Their three attorneys sought payment for some 809 hours of work at rates varying from $95 to $105 per hour. This amounted to approximately $79,312. Respondents' total fee request, however, reflected a 50% increase in that fee. In their brief to the District Court, respondents explained that such an increase was necessary to compensate for the complexity of the case, the novelty of the issues, and the 'great benefit' achieved. The total requested fee amounted to approximately $118,968. Petitioner opposed the fee award on the grounds that the rates were exorbitant, the number of hours charged were unreasonable and duplicative, and the 50% 'bonus' was improper.

Petitioner submitted no evidence to support its claim that the hours and rates charged by respondents were unreasonable. . . .

The District Court held that both the hours expended and the rates charged were reasonable. It also held that the fee calculated by multiplying the number of hours times the hourly rates should be increased by the requested 50% because of the quality of representation, the complexity of the issues, the riskiness of success, and the 'great benefit to the large class' that was achieved. The District Court awarded respondents the requested fee of $118,968.

The Court of Appeals affirmed in an unpublished opinion."

The Supreme Court granted certiorari to review the case.

B. Counsel of Record

ACLU Side (Respondent / Appellee): Leon Silverman argued the cause for appellee. With him on the brief were Kalman Finkel, Arthur J. Fried, John E. Kirklin, and Linda R. Blumkin.

Opposing Side (Petitioner / Appellant): Melvyn R. Leventhal, Deputy First Assistant Attorney General of New York, argued the cause for appellant. With him on the briefs were Robert Abrams, Attorney General, Dennis H. Allee, First Assistant Attorney General, Peter H. Schiff, George D. Zuckerman, Deputy Solicitor General, and Marion R. Buchbinder and Frederick K. Mehlman, Assistant Attorneys General.

III. AMICI CURIAE

ACLU Side (Respondent / Appellee)

Brief of amici curiae filed on behalf of the NAACP Legal Defense and Educational Fund, Inc., Lawyers' Committee for Civil Rights Under Law, Puerto Rican Legal Defense and Education Fund, Inc., Mexican American Legal Defense and Educational Fund, and American Civil Liberties Union by Jack Greenberg, James M. Nabrit III, Charles Stephen Ralston, Steven L. Winter, Fred N. Fishman, Robert H. Kapp, Norman Redlich, William L. Robinson, Norman J. Chachkin, E. Richard Larson, Burt Neuborne, Kenneth Kimerling, Joaquin G. Avila, and Morris J. Baller.

Brief of amici curiae filed on behalf of the Alliance for Justice by Laura Macklin.

Brief of amici curiae filed on behalf of the California Coalition of Welfare Rights Organizations by Mary S. Burdick and Richard A. Rothschild.

Brief of amici curiae filed on behalf of the National Education Association et al. by Michael H. Gottesman, Robert M. Weinberg, Julia Penny Clark, Robert H. Chanin, and Lawrence A. Poltrock.

Brief of amici curiae filed on behalf of the New York State Bar Association et al. by Haliburton Fales II; and for Oliver Hill et al. by Armand Derfner and Stephen P. Berzon.

Opposing Side (Petitioner / Appellant)

Brief of amici curiae filed on behalf of the United States by Solicitor General Lee, Assistant Attorney General McGrath, Deputy Solicitor General Geller, Deputy Assistant Attorney General Kuhl, Joshua I. Schwartz, William Kanter, and Mark W. Pennak.

Brief of amici curiae filed on behalf of the State of Alabama et al. by Kenneth O. Eikenberry, Attorney General of Washington, and Thomas F. Carr, Senior Assistant Attorney General, and by the Attorneys General for their respective States as follows: Charles A. Graddick of Alabama, Norman C. Gorsuch of Alaska, Robert K. Corbin of Arizona, Duane Woodard of Colorado, Joseph Lieberman of Connecticut, Jim Smith of Florida, Michael J. Bowers of Georgia, Tany S. Hong of Hawaii, Jim Jones of Idaho, Neil Hartigan of Illinois, Linley E. Pearson of Indiana, Thomas J. Miller of Iowa, Robert T. Stephan of Kansas, William J. Guste, Jr., of Louisiana, Stephen H. Sachs of Maryland, Frank J. Kelley of Michigan, Hubert H. Humphrey III of Minnesota, John D. Ashcroft of Missouri, Michael T. Greely of Montana, Paul L. Douglas of Nebraska, Brian McKay of Nevada, Gregory H. Smith of New Hampshire, Irwin I. Kimmelman of New Jersey, Rufus L. Edmisten of North Carolina, Robert O. Wefald of North Dakota, Anthony J. Celebrezze, Jr., of Ohio, Michael Turpen of Oklahoma, David B. Frohnmayer of Oregon, LeRoy S. Zimmerman of Pennsylvania, Dennis J. Roberts I of Rhode Island, Mark V. Meierhenry of South Dakota, William M. Leech, Jr., of Tennessee, David L. Wilkinson of Utah, John J. Easton of Vermont, Gerald L. Baliles of Virginia, Chauncey H. Browning of West Virginia, Bronson C. La Follette of Wisconsin, and Archie G. McClintock of Wyoming.

Brief of amici curiae filed on behalf of r the Commonwealth of Massachusetts by Francis X. Bellotti, Attorney General, Thomas R. Kiley, First Assistant Attorney General, and Judith S. Yogman and Carl Valvo, Assistant Attorneys General.

IV. THE SUPREME COURT'S DECISION

"Petitioner argues that the use of prevailing market rates to calculate attorneys fees under § 1988 leads to exorbitant fee awards and provides windfalls to civil rights counsel contrary to the express intent of Congress. To avoid this result, petitioner urges this Court to require that all fee awards under § 1988 be calculated according to the cost of providing legal services rather than according to the prevailing market rate. . . .

Resolution . . . begins and ends with an interpretation of the attorney's fee statute. The Civil Rights Attorney's Fees Awards Act of 1976, 42 U.S.C. § 1988, authorizes district courts to award a reasonable attorney's fee to prevailing civil rights litigants. . . . Congress directed that attorney's fees be calculated according to standards currently in use under other fee-shifting statutes . . . .

We address now the second question presented: whether a 50% upward adjustment in the fee was—as petitioner argues—an abuse of discretion by the District Court. Petitioner makes two separate but related arguments. First, she asserts that a reasonable attorney's fee is calculated by multiplying the reasonable number of hours expended times a reasonable hourly rate and that any upward adjustment of that fee is improper. In the alternative, she argues that the 50% upward adjustment in this case constitutes a clear abuse of discretion. . . .

On this record, . . . any upward adjustment for the contingent nature of the litigation was unjustified.

In sum, we reiterate what was said in Hensley: 'where a plaintiff has obtained excellent results, his attorney should recover a fully compensatory fee. Normally this will encompass all hours reasonably expended on the litigation, and indeed in some cases of exceptional success an enhancement award may be justified.' We therefore reject petitioner's argument that an upward adjustment to an attorney's fee is never appropriate under § 1988. On the record before us, however, respondent established only that hourly rates ranging from $95 per hour to $105 per hour for the full 809.75 hours billed were reasonable. This resulted in a charge of $79,312. Respondents introduced no evidence that enhancement was necessary to provide fair and reasonable compensation. They therefore have failed to carry their burden of justifying entitlement to an upward adjustment. On this record, we conclude that the fee of $79,312 was 'fully compensatory.' Accordingly, the judgment below is reversed only insofar as the fee award was increased by the sum of $39,656."

V. JUSTICE VOTE

9 Pro ACLU Side vs. 0 Con Opposing Side

ACLU Side (Respondent / Appellee)

1. Powell, L. – Wrote majority opinion
2. Rehnquist, W. – Joined majority opinion
3. Burger, W. – Joined majority opinion
4. O'Connor, S. – Joined majority opinion
5. Blackmun, H. – Joined majority opinion
6. Brennan, W. – Wrote concurring opinion
7. White, B. – Joined majority opinion
8. Marshall, T. – Joined Brennan's concurrence
9. Stevens, J. – Joined majority opinion

VI. A WIN OR LOSS FOR THE ACLU?

The ACLU filed as amicus curiae urging affirmance; the Supreme Court affirmed in part and reversed in part the Court of Appeals' decision by a 9-0 vote, giving the ACLU an apparent win.

528. Escambia County v. McMillan

(Decided March 27, 1984; 466 U.S. 48)

I. ISSUE

A. Issues Discussed

Civil rights, race, voting rights, First, Thirteenth, Fourteenth, and Fifteenth Amendments

B. Legal Question Presented

"[W]hether the evidence of discriminatory intent in the record before the District Court was adequate to support the finding that the at-large [voting] system violated the Fourteenth Amendment."

C. Supreme Court's Answer

Declining to decide the issue, the Court vacated the judgment below and remanded the case.

II. CASE SUMMARY

A. Background

"Appellees, black voters of Escambia County, Florida, filed suit in the District Court, alleging that the at-large system for electing the five members of the Board of County Commissioners violated appellees' rights under the First, Thirteenth, Fourteenth and Fifteenth Amendments, the Civil Rights Act of 1957, and the Voting Rights Act. Appellees contended that the at-large system operated to 'dilute' their voting strength.

The District Court entered judgment for appellees. That court found that the at-large system used by the County discriminated against black voters and had been retained at least in part for discriminatory purposes. The court concluded that the system violated appellees' rights under the Fourteenth and Fifteenth Amendments and the Voting Rights Act. The District Court ordered that the five commissioners be elected from single-member districts.

The Court of Appeals affirmed the District Court's judgment, concluding that the at-large election system violated the Fourteenth Amendment and that the District Court's remedy was appropriate. As the finding of a Fourteenth Amendment violation was adequate to support the District Court's judgment, the Court of Appeals did not review the District Court's conclusion that the at-large system also violated the Fifteenth Amendment and the Voting Rights Act."

The Supreme Court granted certiorari to review the case, vacated the judgment, and remanded the case.

B. Counsel of Record / ACLU Attorney

ACLU Side (Respondent / Appellee): Larry T. Menefee argued the cause for appellee.

Opposing Side (Petitioner / Appellant): Charles S. Rhyne argued the cause for appellant.

III. AMICI CURIAE

ACLU Side (Respondent / Appellee)

Brief of amici curiae filed on behalf of the ACLU by Laughlin McDonald, Neil Bradley, Christopher Coates, Burt Neuborne, and E. Richard Larson.

Brief of amici curiae filed on behalf of the Lawyers' Committee for Civil Rights Under Law by Fred N. Fishman, Robert H. Kapp, Norman Redlich, William L. Robinson, and Frank R. Parker.

Opposing Side (Petitioner / Appellant)

No briefs of amici curiae were filed in support of appellant.

IV. THE SUPREME COURT'S DECISION

"This appeal presents the question whether the evidence of discriminatory intent in the record before the District Court was adequate to support the finding that the at-large system violated the Fourteenth Amendment. We decline to decide this question. As the Court of Appeals noted, the District Court's judgment rested alternatively upon the Voting Rights Act. Moreover, the 1982 amendments to that Act were not before the Court of Appeals. Affirmance on the statutory ground would moot the constitutional issues presented by the case. It is a well-established principle governing the prudent exercise of this Court's jurisdiction that normally the Court will not decide a constitutional question if there is some other ground upon which to dispose of the case.

The parties have not briefed the statutory question, and, in any event, that question should be decided in the first instance by the Court of Appeals. We conclude, therefore, that the proper course is to vacate the judgment of the Court of Appeals, and remand the case to that court for consideration of the question whether the Voting Rights Act provides grounds for affirmance of the District Court's judgment."

V. JUSTICE VOTE

1 Pro ACLU Side vs. 8 Con Opposing Side

ACLU Side (Respondent / Appellee)

1. Marshall, T. – Wrote dissenting opinion

Opposing Side (Petitioner / Appellant)

1. Brennan, W. – Per curiam opinion
2. Rehnquist, W. – Per curiam opinion
3. Powell, L. – Per curiam opinion
4. Burger, W. – Per curiam opinion
5. White, B. – Per curiam opinion
6. O'Connor, S. – Per curiam opinion
7. Stevens, J. – Per curiam opinion
8. Blackmun, H. – Per curiam opinion, but would disallow costs

VI. A WIN OR LOSS FOR THE ACLU?

The ACLU filed as amicus curiae urging affirmance; the Supreme Court vacated the ruling of the Court of Appeals in an 8-1 vote, giving the ACLU an apparent loss.

529. Oliver v. United States

(Decided April 17, 1984; 466 U.S. 170)

I. ISSUE

A. Issues Discussed

Fourth Amendment, search and seizure

B. Legal Question Presented

Whether the "open fields" doctrine is consistent with the Fourth Amendment and applicable to these two cases.

C. Supreme Court's Answer

The "open fields" doctrine is valid and applicable in these cases.

II. CASE SUMMARY

A. Background

"No. 82-15. Acting on reports that marihuana was being raised on the farm of petitioner Oliver, two narcotics agents of the Kentucky State Police went to the farm to investigate. Arriving at the farm, they drove past petitioner's house to a locked gate with a 'No Trespassing' sign. A footpath led around one side of the gate. The agents walked around the gate and along the road for several hundred yards, passing a barn and a parked camper. At that point, someone standing in front of the camper shouted: 'No hunting is allowed, come back up here.' The officers shouted back that they were Kentucky State Police officers, but found no one when they returned to the camper. The officers resumed their investigation of the farm and found a field of marihuana over a mile from petitioner's home.

Petitioner was arrested and indicted for 'manufactur[ing]' a 'controlled substance.' After a pretrial hearing, the District Court suppressed evidence of the discovery of the marihuana field. [T]he court found that petitioner had a reasonable expectation that the field would remain private because petitioner 'had done all that could be expected of him to assert his privacy in the area of farm that was searched.' . . . The Court of Appeals for the Sixth Circuit, sitting en banc, reversed the District Court. . . .

No. 82-1273. After receiving an anonymous tip that marihuana was being grown in the woods behind respondent Thornton's residence, two police officers entered the woods by a path between this residence and a neighboring house. They followed a footpath through the woods until they reached two marihuana patches fenced with chicken wire. Later, the officers determined that the patches were on the property of respondent, obtained a warrant to search the property, and seized the marihuana. On the basis of this evidence, respondent was arrested and indicted.

The trial court granted respondent's motion to suppress the fruits of the second search. The warrant for this search was premised on information that the police had obtained during their previous warrantless search, that the court found to be unreasonable. 'No Trespassing' signs and the secluded location of the marihuana patches evinced a reasonable expectation of privacy. Therefore, the court held, the open fields doctrine did not apply.

The Maine Supreme Judicial Court affirmed."

The Supreme Court granted certiorari to review both cases, affirmed the judgment of the Sixth Circuit Court of Appeals, and reversed the Maine Supreme Judicial Court.

B. Counsel of Record / ACLU Attorney

ACLU Side (Petitioner / Appellant in No. 82-15, Respondent / Appellee in No. 82-1273):

Frank E. Haddad, Jr., argued the cause for appellant in No. 82-15.

Donna L. Zeegers, by appointment of the Court, argued the cause and filed a brief for appellee in No. 82-1273.

Opposing Side (Respondent / Appellee in No. 82-15, Petitioner / Appellant in No. 82-1273):

Alan I. Horowitz argued the cause for the United States in No. 82-15.

Wayne S. Moss, Assistant Attorney General of Maine, argued the cause for appellant in No. 82-1273.

III. AMICI CURIAE

ACLU Side (Petitioner / Appellant in No. 82-15, Respondent / Appellee in No. 82-1273):

Brief of amici curiae filed in No. 82-15 on behalf of the ACLU of Northern California, et al., by Eric Neisser, Alan Schlosser, Amitai Schwartz, Joaquin G. Avila, Morris J. Baller, and John E. Huerta.

Brief of amici curiae filed in No. 82-15 on behalf of the California Farm Bureau Federation, et al., by Thomas F. Olson.

Opposing Side (Respondent / Appellee in No. 82-15, Petitioner / Appellant in No. 82-1273):

Brief of amici curiae filed in No. 82-15 on behalf of Americans for Effective Law Enforcement, Inc., et al., by Fred E. Inbau, Wayne W. Schmidt, and James P. Manak.

Brief of amici curiae filed in No. 82-15 on behalf of the State of California by John K. Van De Kamp, Attorney General, Harley D. Mayfield, Assistant Attorney General, and Jay M. Bloom, Deputy Attorney General.

Brief of amici curiae filed in No. 82-1273 on behalf of the State of Alabama, et al., by Charles A. Graddick, Attorney General of Alabama, and Joseph G.L. Marston III, Assistant Attorney General, and by the Attorneys General for Alaska, American Samoa, Arizona, Colorado, Delaware, Kansas, Kentucky, Nebraska, Utah, Vermont, West Virginia, Wisconsin, and Wyoming.

IV. THE SUPREME COURT'S DECISION

"As Justice Holmes explained for the Court in his characteristically laconic style: '[T]he special protection accorded by the Fourth Amendment to the people in their 'persons, houses, papers, and effects,' is not extended to the open fields. The distinction between the latter and the house is as old as the common law.' . . .

This interpretation of the Fourth Amendment's language is consistent with the understanding of the right to privacy expressed in our Fourth Amendment jurisprudence. Since Katz v. United States, the touchstone of Amendment analysis has been the question whether a person has a 'constitutionally protected reasonable expectation of privacy.' . . .

No single factor determines whether an individual legitimately may claim under the Fourth Amendment that a place should be free of government intrusion not authorized by warrant. In assessing the degree to which a search infringes upon individual privacy, the Court has given weight to such factors as the intention of the Framers of the Fourth Amendment, the uses to which the individual has put a location, and our societal understanding that certain areas deserve the most scrupulous protection from government invasion. These factors are equally relevant to determining whether the government's intrusion upon open fields without a warrant or probable cause violates reasonable expectations of privacy and is therefore a search proscribed by the Amendment.

In this light, the rule of Hester v. United States, supra, that we reaffirm today, may be understood as providing that an individual may not legitimately demand privacy for activities conducted out of doors in fields, except in the area immediately surrounding the home. . . .

In contrast, open fields do not provide the setting for those intimate activities that the Amendment is intended to shelter from government interference or surveillance. There is no societal interest in protecting the privacy of those activities, such as the cultivation of crops, that occur in open fields. Moreover, as a practical matter these lands usually are accessible to the public and the police in ways that a home, an office, or commercial structure would not be. . . .

Nor is the government's intrusion upon an open field a 'search' in the constitutional sense because that intrusion is a trespass at common law. The existence of a property right is but one element in determining whether expectations of privacy are legitimate. . . .

The common law may guide consideration of what areas are protected by the Fourth Amendment by defining areas whose invasion by others is wrongful. The law of trespass, however, forbids intrusions upon land that the Fourth Amendment would not proscribe. For trespass law extends to instances where the exercise of the right to exclude vindicates no legitimate privacy interest. Thus, in the case of open fields, the general rights of property protected by the common law of trespass have little or no relevance to the applicability of the Fourth Amendment. . . .

We therefore affirm Oliver v. United States; Maine v. Thornton is reversed and remanded for further proceedings not inconsistent with this opinion."

V. JUSTICE VOTE

3 Pro ACLU Side vs. 6 Con Opposing Side

ACLU Side (Petitioner / Appellant in No. 82-15, Respondent / Appellee in No. 82-1273):

1. Marshall, T. – Wrote dissenting opinion
2. Brennan, W. – Joined Marshall's dissent
3. Stevens, J. – Joined Marshall's dissent

Opposing Side (Respondent / Appellee in No. 82-15, Petitioner / Appellant in No. 82-1273):

1. Powell, L. – Wrote majority opinion
2. Burger, W. – Joined majority opinion
3. Blackmun, H. – Joined majority opinion
4. Rehnquist, W. – Joined majority opinion
5. O'Connor, S. – Joined majority opinion
6. White, B. – Wrote concurring opinion

VI. A WIN OR LOSS FOR THE ACLU?

The ACLU, as amicus curiae, urged reversal of the Sixth Circuit Court of Appeals' judgment; the Supreme Court affirmed in a 6-3 vote, giving the ACLU an apparent loss.

530. Immigration & Naturalization Service v. Delgado

(Decided April 17, 1984; 466 U.S. 210)

I. ISSUE

A. Issues Discussed

Fourth Amendment, search and seizure, immigration

B. Legal Question Presented

Whether INS factory surveys constitute the seizure of a work force, and of the individuals questioned under the Fourth Amendment.

C. Supreme Court's Answer

The factory surveys are not seizures under the Fourth Amendment.

II. CASE SUMMARY

A. Background

"Acting pursuant to two warrants, in January and September 1977, the [Immigration and Naturalization Service (INS)] conducted a survey of the work force at Southern California Davis Pleating Co. (Davis Pleating) in search of illegal aliens. The warrants were issued on a showing of probable cause by the INS that numerous illegal aliens were employed at Davis Pleating, although neither of the search warrants identified any particular illegal aliens by name. A third factory survey was conducted with the employer's consent in October 1977, at Mr. Pleat, another garment factory.

At the beginning of the surveys several agents positioned themselves near the buildings' exits, while other agents dispersed throughout the factory to question most, but not all, employees at their work stations. . . . Moving systematically through the factory, the agents approached employees and, after identifying themselves, asked them from one to three questions relating to their citizenship. If the employee gave a credible reply that he was a United States citizen, the questioning ended, and the agent moved on to another employee. If the employee gave an unsatisfactory response or admitted that he was an alien, the employee was asked to produce his immigration papers. During the survey, employees continued with their work and were free to walk around within the factory.

Respondents are four employees questioned in one of the three surveys. In 1978 respondents and their union representative, the International Ladies Garment Workers' Union, filed two actions, later consolidated, in the United States District Court for the Central District of California challenging the constitutionality of INS factory surveys and seeking declaratory and injunctive relief. Respondents argued that the factory surveys violated their Fourth Amendment right to be free from unreasonable searches or seizures and the equal protection component of the Due Process Clause of the Fifth Amendment.

[T]he District Court ruled that none of the respondents had been detained under the Fourth Amendment during the factory surveys, either when they were questioned or otherwise. Accordingly, it granted summary judgment in favor of the INS.

The [Ninth Circuit] Court of Appeals reversed."

The Supreme Court granted certiorari to review the case and reversed.

B. Counsel of Record / ACLU Attorney

ACLU Side (Respondent / Appellee): Henry R. Fenton argued the cause for appellee.

Opposing Side (Petitioner / Appellant): Deputy Solicitor General Frey argued the cause for appellant.

III. AMICI CURIAE

ACLU Side (Respondent / Appellee)

Brief of amici curiae filed on behalf of the ACLU by David M. Brodsky, Burt Neuborne, and Charles S. Sims.

Brief of amici curiae filed on behalf of the Mexican American Legal Defense and Education Fund, Inc., et al., by Michael Kantor and Alan Diamond.

Opposing Side (Petitioner / Appellant)

No briefs of amici curiae were filed in support of appellant.

IV. THE SUPREME COURT'S DECISION

"The Fourth Amendment does not proscribe all contact between the police and citizens, but is designed 'to prevent arbitrary and oppressive interference by enforcement officials with the privacy and personal security of individuals.' Given the diversity of encounters between police officers and citizens, however, the Court has been cautious in defining the limits imposed by the Fourth Amendment on encounters between the police and citizens. As we have noted elsewhere: 'Obviously, not all personal intercourse between policemen and citizens involves 'seizures' of persons. Only when the officer, by means of physical force or show of authority, has restrained the liberty of a citizen may we conclude that a 'seizure' has occurred.' . . .

Unless the circumstances of the encounter are so intimidating as to demonstrate that a reasonable person would have believed he was not free to leave if he had not responded, one cannot say that the questioning resulted in a detention under the Fourth Amendment. But if the person refuses to answer and the police take additional steps . . . to obtain an answer, then the Fourth Amendment imposes some minimal level of objective justification to validate the detention or seizure. . . .

We reject the claim that the entire work forces of the two factories were seized for the duration of the surveys when the INS placed agents near the exits of the factory sites. Ordinarily, when people are at work their freedom to move about has been meaningfully restricted, not by the actions of law enforcement officials, but by the workers' voluntary obligations to their employers. The record indicates that when these surveys were initiated, the employees were about their ordinary business, operating machinery and performing other job assignments. While the surveys did cause some disruption, including the efforts of some workers to hide, the record also indicates that workers were not prevented by the agents from moving about the factories.

Respondents argue, however, that the stationing of agents near the factory doors showed the INS's intent to prevent people from leaving. But there is nothing in the record indicating that this is what the agents at the doors actually did. The obvious purpose of the agents' presence at the factory doors was to insure that all persons in the factories were questioned. . . . Likewise, the mere possibility that they would be questioned if they sought to leave the buildings should not have resulted in any reasonable apprehension by any of them that they would be seized or detained in any meaningful way. Since most workers could have had no reasonable fear that they would be detained upon leaving, we conclude that the work forces as a whole were not seized. . . .

Accordingly, the judgment of the Court of Appeals is reversed."

V. JUSTICE VOTE

2 Pro ACLU Side vs. 7 Con Opposing Side

ACLU Side (Respondent / Appellee)

1. Brennan, W. – Wrote opinion concurring in part and dissenting in part
2. Marshall, T. – Joined Brennan's opinion

Opposing Side (Petitioner / Appellant)

1. Rehnquist, W. – Wrote majority opinion
2. Burger, W. – Joined majority opinion
3. White, B. – Joined majority opinion
4. Blackmun, H. – Joined majority opinion
5. Stevens, J. – Wrote concurring opinion
6. O'Connor, S. – Joined majority opinion
7. Powell, L. – Wrote concurring opinion

VI. A WIN OR LOSS FOR THE ACLU?

The ACLU, as amicus curiae, urged affirmance of the Ninth Circuit Court of Appeals' judgment; the Supreme Court reversed in a 7-2 vote, giving the ACLU an apparent loss.

531. Justices of Boston Municipal Court v. Lydon

(Decided April 18, 1984; 466 U.S. 294)

I. ISSUE

A. Issues Discussed

Criminal procedure, Fifth Amendment, double jeopardy

B. Legal Question Presented

Whether "the trial de novo of respondent Lydon, pursuant to Massachusetts' 'two- tier' system for trying minor crimes, would violate his right not to be placed twice in jeopardy for the same crime."

C. Supreme Court's Answer

The trial de novo under the two-tier system does not violate the Double Jeopardy Clause.

II. CASE SUMMARY

A. Background

"Under Massachusetts law, a defendant charged with certain crimes in Boston Municipal Court may elect either a bench trial or a jury trial. If a defendant chooses a jury and is convicted, he has the normal appellate process open to him, while a defendant dissatisfied with the results of a bench trial, if he elects that course, has an absolute right to a trial de novo before a jury. A convicted defendant who has chosen a bench trial need not allege error at that trial to obtain de novo review. On the other hand, he may not rely upon error at the bench trial to obtain reversal of his conviction; his only recourse is a trial de novo.

Respondent Michael Lydon was arrested after breaking into an automobile in Boston. . . . Lydon elected to undergo a first-tier bench trial and was convicted. The trial judge rejected Lydon's claim that the prosecution had introduced no evidence that Lydon intended to steal from the car and that his actions were as consistent with activities not covered by the complaint. Lydon was sentenced to two years in jail.

Lydon requested a trial de novo in the jury session of the Boston Municipal Court. . . . Before the jury trial commenced, Lydon moved to dismiss the charge against him on the ground that no evidence of the element of intent had been presented at the bench trial. He contended that retrial was therefore barred under the principles of Burks v. United States, which held that the Double Jeopardy Clause bars a second trial when a reviewing court reverses a conviction on the ground that the evidence presented at the first trial was legally insufficient.

After the motion to dismiss was denied, Lydon sought relief in the single justice session of the Supreme Judicial Court of Massachusetts. The single justice issued a stay of the de novo trial and reported two questions to the full bench . . . .

On review by the Supreme Judicial Court, the court initially noted that the single justice did not sit as a reviewing court in determining the sufficiency of the evidence and that any conclusion reached by him on that issue 'was made for the purpose of reporting clearly framed questions to the full bench and is not an adjudication of the rights of the parties in this case.' The Massachusetts court then found Lydon's double jeopardy argument to be without merit. . . . The court concluded that '[a] defendant is not placed in double jeopardy merely because his only avenue of relief from a conviction based on insufficient evidence at a voluntarily sought bench trial is a trial de novo.' . . .

Lydon then filed a petition for a writ of habeas corpus in the United States District Court for the District of Massachusetts. First addressing the question of its jurisdiction, the District Court held that Lydon was 'in custody' for purposes of 28 U.S.C. § 2254(b) and that he had exhausted his state remedies because there was no state remedy available to him short of submitting to a second trial. On the merits, the District Court viewed Burks v. United States, supra, as 'bestow[ing] a constitutional right upon defendants not to be retried when the initial conviction rests on insufficient evidence,' and thought that this holding foreclosed a second trial if the evidence against Lydon at the bench trial was insufficient. After reviewing the transcript of the bench trial, the District Court concluded that there was insufficient evidence of intent to support a conviction and ordered the writ to issue. On appeal, a divided Court of Appeals for the First Circuit affirmed in all respects."

The Supreme Court granted certiorari to review the case and reversed.

B. Counsel of Record / ACLU Attorney

ACLU Side (Respondent / Appellee): David B. Rossman argued the cause for appellee.

Opposing Side (Petitinoer / Appellant):
Barbara A. H. Smith, Assistant Attorney General of Massachusetts, argued the cause for appellant.

III. AMICI CURIAE

ACLU Side (Respondent / Appellee)

Brief of amici curiae filed on behalf of the ACLU, et al., by Eric D. Blumenson, Burt Neuborne, Charles S. Sims, John Reinstein, and Marjorie Heins.

Opposing Side (Petitioner / Appellant)

No briefs of amici curiae were filed in support of appellant.

IV. THE SUPREME COURT'S DECISION

"Our cases have recognized three separate guarantees embodied in the Double Jeopardy Clause: It protects against a second prosecution for the same offense after acquittal, against a second prosecution for the same offense after conviction, and against multiple punishments for the same offense. The primary goal of barring reprosecution after acquittal is to prevent the State from mounting successive prosecutions and thereby wearing down the defendant. . . . The primary purpose of foreclosing a second prosecution after conviction, on the other hand, is to prevent a defendant from being subjected to multiple punishments for the same offense. . . .

The Double Jeopardy Clause is not an absolute bar to successive trials. The general rule is that the Clause does not bar reprosecution of a defendant whose conviction is overturned on appeal. . . .

A number of features of the Massachusetts system persuade us that it does not constitute 'governmental oppression of the sort against which the Double Jeopardy Clause was intended to protect,' even when a defendant convicted at the first tier claims insufficiency of the evidence. . . . The defendant's right to obtain de novo review without alleging error is significant in that it ameliorates one of the concerns underlying our opinion in Burks. . . .

As the dissent in the Court of Appeals recognized, the two-tier system affords benefits to defendants that are unavailable in a more conventional system. In traditional systems, a convicted defendant may seek reversal only on matters of law; in the Massachusetts system a defendant is given two opportunities to be acquitted on the facts. If he is acquitted at the first trial, he cannot be retried. . . .

Accordingly, we reverse the judgment of the Court of Appeals."

V. JUSTICE VOTE

0 Pro ACLU Side vs. 9 Con Opposing Side

Opposing Side (Petitioner / Appellant)

1. White, B. – Wrote majority opinion
2. Rehnquist, W. – Joined majority opinion
3. Blackmun, H. – Joined majority opinion
4. O'Connor, S. – Wrote concurring opinion
5. Brennan, W. – Wrote concurring opinion
6. Marshall, T. – Joined Brennan's concurrence
7. Stevens, J. – Wrote concurring opinion
8. Powell, L. – Wrote concurring opinion
9. Burger, W. – Joined Powell's concurrence

VI. A WIN OR LOSS FOR THE ACLU?

The ACLU filed as amicus curiae urging affirmance; the Supreme Court reversed the ruling of the Court of Appeals for the First Circuit in a 9-0 vote, giving the ACLU an apparent loss.

532. Palmore v. Sidoti

(Decided April 25, 1984; 466 U.S. 429)

I. ISSUE

A. Issues Discussed

Civil rights, race, child custody

B. Legal Question Presented

Do the effects of racial prejudice justify removing a child from the custody of her natural mother?

C. Supreme Court's Answer

"The effects of racial prejudice, however real, cannot justify a racial classification removing an infant child from the custody of its natural mother found to be an appropriate person to have such custody."

II. CASE SUMMARY

A. Background

"When petitioner Linda Sidoti Palmore and respondent Anthony J. Sidoti, both Caucasians, were divorced in May 1980 in Florida, the mother was awarded custody of their 3-year-old daughter.

In September 1981 the father sought custody of the child by filing a petition to modify the prior judgment because of changed conditions. The change was that the child's mother was then cohabiting with a Negro, Clarence Palmore, Jr., whom she married two months later.

[T]he court made a finding that 'there is no issue as to either party's devotion to the child, adequacy of housing facilities, or respectability of the new spouse of either parent.'

The court then addressed the recommendations of the court counselor, who had made an earlier report 'in [another] case coming out of this circuit also involving the social consequences of an interracial marriage.' From this vague reference to that earlier case, the court turned to the present case and noted the counselor's recommendation for a change in custody because '[t]he wife [petitioner] has chosen for herself and for her child, a life-style unacceptable to the father and to society.... The child... is, or at school age will be, subject to environmental pressures not of choice.'

The court then concluded that the best interests of the child would be served by awarding custody to the father. The court's rationale is contained in the following: 'The father's evident resentment of the mother's choice of a black partner is not sufficient to wrest custody from the mother. It is of some significance, however, that the mother did see fit to bring a man into her home and carry on a sexual relationship with him without being married to him. Such action tended to place gratification of her own desires ahead of her concern for the child's future welfare. This Court feels that despite the strides that have been made in bettering relations between the races in this country, it is inevitable that Melanie will, if allowed to remain in her present situation and attains school age and thus more vulnerable to peer pressures, suffer from the social stigmatization that is sure to come.'

The Second District Court of Appeal affirmed without opinion, thus denying the Florida Supreme Court jurisdiction to review the case."

The Supreme Court granted certiorari to review the case and reversed the judgment of the Second District Court of Appeal.

B. Counsel of Record / ACLU Attorney

ACLU Side (Petitioner / Appellant): Robert J. Shapiro argued the cause for appellant.

Opposing Side (Respondent / Appellee): John E. Hawtrey argued the cause for appellee.

III. AMICI CURIAE

ACLU Side (Petitioner / Appellant)

Brief of amici curiae filed on behalf of the ACLU, et al., by Burt Neuborne, William D. Zabel, Marcia Robinson Lowry, Thomas I. Atkins, Ira G. Greenberg, and Samuel Rabinove.

Brief of amici curiae filed on behalf of the United States by Solicitor General Lee, Assistant Attorney General Reynolds, Deputy Solicitor General Wallace, Deputy Assistant Attorney General Cooper, Kathryn A. Oberly, and Brian K. Landsberg.

Brief of amici curiae filed on behalf of Leigh Earls, et al., by Jay L. Carlson, James P. Tuite, Roderic V. O. Boggs, James D. Weill, Justin J. Finger, Jeffrey P. Sinensky, Leslie K. Shedlin, and Marc D. Stern.

Brief of amici curiae filed on behalf of the Women's Legal Defense Fund, et al., by Sally Katzen, Lynn Bregman, and Nancy Polikoff.

Opposing Side (Respondent / Appellee)

No briefs of amici curiae were filed in support of appellee.

IV. THE SUPREME COURT'S DECISION

"The judgment of a state court determining or reviewing a child custody decision is not ordinarily a likely candidate for review by this Court. However, the court's opinion, after stating that the 'father's evident resentment of the mother's choice of a black partner is not sufficient' to deprive her of custody, then turns to what it regarded as the damaging impact on the child from remaining in a racially mixed household. This raises important federal concerns arising from the Constitution's commitment to eradicating discrimination based on race....

The court correctly stated that the child's welfare was the controlling factor. But that court was entirely candid and made no effort to place its holding on any ground other than race. Taking the court's findings and rationale at face value, it is clear that the outcome would have been different had petitioner married a Caucasian male of similar respectability.

A core purpose of the Fourteenth Amendment was to do away with all governmentally imposed discrimination based on race. Classifying persons according to their race is more likely to reflect racial prejudice than legitimate public concerns; the race, not the person, dictates the category. Such classifications are subject to the most exacting scrutiny; to pass constitutional muster, they must be justified by a compelling governmental interest and must be 'necessary... to the accomplishment' of their legitimate purpose....

It would ignore reality to suggest that racial and ethnic prejudices do not exist or that all manifestations of those prejudices have been eliminated. There is a risk that a child living with a stepparent of a different race may be subject to a variety of pressures and stresses not present if the child were living with parents of the same racial or ethnic origin.

The question, however, is whether the reality of private biases and the possible injury they might inflict are permissible considerations for removal of an infant child from the custody of its natural mother. We have little difficulty concluding that they are not. The Constitution cannot control such prejudices but neither can it tolerate them. Private biases may be outside the reach of the law, but the law cannot, directly or indirectly, give them effect....

Whatever problems racially mixed households may pose for children in 1984 can no more support a denial of constitutional rights than could the stresses that residential integration was thought to entail in 1917. The effects of racial prejudice, however real, cannot justify a racial classification removing an infant child from the custody of its natural mother found to be an appropriate person to have such custody.

The judgment of the District Court of Appeal is reversed."

V. JUSTICE VOTE

9 Pro ACLU Side vs. 0 Con Opposing Side

ACLU Side (Petitioner / Appellant)

1. Burger, W. – Wrote majority opinion
2. White, B. – Joined majority opinion
3. Rehnquist, W. – Joined majority opinion
4. O'Connor, S. – Joined majority opinion
5. Stevens, J. – Joined majority opinion
6. Brennan, W. – Joined majority opinion
7. Marshall, T. – Joined majority opinion
8. Blackmun, H. – Joined majority opinion
9. Powell, L. – Joined majority opinion

VI. A WIN OR LOSS FOR THE ACLU?

The ACLU, as amicus curiae, urged reversal of the District Court of Appeal's judgment; the Supreme Court reversed in a 9-0 vote, giving the ACLU an apparent win.

533. Bose Corp. v. Consumers Union, Inc.

(Decided April 30, 1984; 466 U.S. 485)

I. ISSUE

A. Issues Discussed

First Amendment, defamation, judicial power, civil procedure

B. Legal Question Presented

"[W]hether the Court of Appeals erred when it refused to apply the clearly-erroneous standard of Rule 52(a) to the District Court's 'finding' of actual malice."

C. Supreme Court's Answer

The Court of Appeals did not err in refusing to apply the clearly-erroneous standard of Rule 52(a).

II. CASE SUMMARY

A. Background

"In the May 1970 issue of its magazine, Consumer Reports, respondent published a seven-page article evaluating the quality of numerous brands of medium-priced loudspeakers. In a boxed-off section occupying most of two pages, respondent commented on 'some loudspeakers of special interest,' one of which was the Bose 901—an admittedly 'unique and unconventional' system that had recently been placed on the market by petitioner. After describing the system and some of its virtues, and after noting that a listener 'could pinpoint the location of various instruments much more easily with a standard speaker than with the Bose system,' respondent's article made the following statements:

'Worse, individual instruments heard through the Bose system seemed to grow to gigantic proportions and tended to wander about the room. For instance, a violin appeared to be 10 feet wide and a piano stretched from wall to wall. With orchestral music, such effects seemed inconsequential. But we think they might become annoying when listening to soloists.'

After stating opinions concerning the overall sound quality, the article concluded: 'We think the Bose system is so unusual that a prospective buyer must listen to it and judge it for himself. We would suggest delaying so big an investment until you were sure the system would please you after the novelty value had worn off.'

Petitioner took exception to numerous statements made in the article, and when respondent refused to publish a retraction, petitioner commenced this product disparagement action in the United States District Court for the District of Massachusetts. . . . In its lengthy, detailed opinion on the merits of the case, the District Court ruled in respondent's favor on most issues. Most significantly, the District Court ruled that the petitioner is a 'public figure' . . . and therefore the First Amendment, as interpreted in New York Times Co. v. Sullivan, precludes recovery in this product disparagement action unless the petitioner proved by clear and convincing evidence that respondent made a false disparaging statement with 'actual malice.' . . . Judgment was entered for petitioner on the product disparagement claim.

The United States Court of Appeals for the First Circuit reversed."

The Supreme Court granted certiorari to review the case and affirmed.

B. Counsel of Record / ACLU Attorney

ACLU Side (Respondent / Appellee): Michael N. Pollet argued the cause for appellee.

Opposing Side (Petitioner / Appellant): Charles Hieken argued the cause for appellant.

III. AMICI CURIAE

ACLU Side (Respondent / Appellee)

Brief of amici curiae filed on behalf of the ACLU, et al., by James F. McHugh, Charles S. Sims, and John Reinstein.

Brief of amici curiae filed on behalf of the New York Times Company, et al., by Floyd Abrams, Dean Ringel, Devereux Chatillon, Robert Sack, Alice Neff Lucan, Corydon B. Dunham, David Otis Fuller, Jr., W. Terry Maguire, Richard M. Schmidt, Jr., R. Bruce Rich, and Peter C. Gould.

Opposing Side (Petitioner / Appellant)

No briefs of amici curiae were filed in support of appellant.

IV. THE SUPREME COURT'S DECISION

"The statement in this case represents the sort of inaccuracy that is commonplace in the forum of robust debate to which the New York Times rule applies. 'Realistically, . . . some error is inevitable; and the difficulties of separating fact from fiction convinced the Court in New York Times, Butts, Gertz, and similar cases to limit liability to instances where some degree of culpability is present in order to eliminate the risk of undue self-censorship and the suppression of truthful material.' '[E]rroneous statement is inevitable in free debate, and . . . must be protected if the freedoms of expression are to have the 'breathing space' that they 'need . . . to survive.'"

The Court of Appeals entertained some doubt concerning the ruling that the New York Times rule should be applied to a claim of product disparagement based on a critical review of a loud-speaker system. We express no view on that ruling, but having accepted it for purposes of deciding this case, we agree with the Court of Appeals that the difference between hearing violin sounds move around the room and hearing them wander back and forth fits easily within the breathing space that gives life to the First Amendment. We may accept all of the purely factual findings of the District Court and nevertheless hold as a matter of law that the record does not contain clear and convincing evidence that Seligson or his employer prepared the loud-speaker article with knowledge that it contained a false statement, or with reckless disregard of the truth.

It may well be that in this case, the 'finding' of the District Court on the actual-malice question could have been set aside under the clearly-erroneous standard of review, and we share the concern of the Court of Appeals that the statements at issue tread the line between fact and opinion. Moreover, the analysis of the central legal question before us may seem out of place in a case involving a dispute about the sound quality of a loudspeaker. But though the question presented reaches us on a somewhat peculiar wavelength, we reaffirm the principle of independent appellate review that we have applied uncounted times before. We hold that the clearly-erroneous standard of Rule 52(a) of the Federal Rules of Civil Procedure does not prescribe the standard of review to be applied in reviewing a determination of actual malice in a case governed by New York Times Co. v. Sullivan. Appellate judges in such a case must exercise independent judgment and determine whether the record establishes actual malice with convincing clarity.

The judgment of the Court of Appeals is affirmed."

V. JUSTICE VOTE

6 Pro ACLU Side vs. 3 Con Opposing Side

ACLU Side (Respondent / Appellee)

1. Stevens, J. – Wrote majority opinion
2. Brennan, W. – Joined majority opinion
3. Marshall, T. – Joined majority opinion
4. Blackmun, H. – Joined majority opinion
5. Powell, L. – Joined majority opinion
6. Burger, W. – Concurred in the judgment without an opinion

Opposing Side (Petitioner / Appellant)

1. White, B. – Wrote dissenting opinion
2. Rehnquist, W. – Wrote dissenting opinion
3. O'Connor, S. – Joined Rehnquist's dissent

VI. A WIN OR LOSS FOR THE ACLU?

The ACLU filed as amicus curiae urging affirmance, the Supreme Court affirmed the Court of Appeals for the First Circuit's decision in a 6-3 vote, giving the ACLU an apparent win.

534. Pulliam v. Allen

(Decided May 14, 1984; 466 U.S. 522)

I. ISSUE

A. Issues Discussed

Governmental authority, judicial immunity, Fourteenth Amendment

B. Legal Question Presented

"[W]hether Judicial Immunity Bars the Award of Attorney's Fees Pursuant to 42 U.S.C. § 1988 Against a Member of the Judiciary Acting in his Judicial Capacity."

C. Supreme Court's Answer

"Judicial immunity is no bar to the award of attorney's fees under 42 U.S.C. § 1988."

II. CASE SUMMARY

A. Background

Respondents were arrested for the nonincarcerable misdemeanors of "using abusive and insulting language" and "being drunk in public." Petitioner, a Magistrate in Virginia, imposed bail, and when respondents were unable to pay bail petitioner committed them to jail. "The District Court found it to be petitioner's practice to require bond for nonincarcerable offenses. The court declared the practice to be a violation of due process and equal protection and enjoined it. The court also found that respondents, having substantially prevailed on their claims, were entitled to costs, including reasonable attorney's fees, in accordance with § 1988. It directed respondents to submit a request for costs to petitioner within 10 days. Petitioner did not appeal this order.

Respondents submitted a request for fees and costs totaling \$7,691.09. The fee component of this figure was \$7,038. Petitioner filed objections and prayed 'that the Court reduce the request of Plaintiffs for attorney's fees.' The court found the fees figure reasonable and granted fees and costs in the requested amount.

Petitioner took an appeal from the order awarding attorney's fees against her. She argued that, as a judicial officer, she was absolutely immune from an award of attorney's fees. The Court of Appeals reviewed the language and legislative history of § 1988. It concluded that a judicial officer is not immune from an award of attorney's fees in an action in which prospective relief properly is awarded against her. Since the court already had determined that judicial immunity did not extend to injunctive and declaratory relief under § 1983, the court concluded that prospective relief properly had been awarded against petitioner. It therefore affirmed the award of attorney's fees."

The Supreme Court granted certiorari to review the case and affirmed.

B. Counsel of Record / ACLU Attorney

ACLU Side (Respondent / Appellee): Deborah Chasen Wyatt argued the cause for appellee.

Opposing Side (Petitioner / Appellant): Gerald L. Baliles, Attorney General of Virginia, argued the cause for appellant.

III. AMICI CURIAE

ACLU Side (Respondent / Appellee)

Brief of amici curiae filed on behalf of the ACLU, et al., by Burt Neuborne and E. Richard Larson.

Brief of amici curiae filed on behalf of the National Association of Criminal Defense Lawyers by J. Lloyd Snook III.

Opposing Side (Petitioner / Appellant)

Brief of amici curiae filed on behalf of the State of Minnesota, et al., by Hubert H. Humphrey III, Attorney General of Minnesota, Kent G. Harbison, Chief Deputy Attorney General, Douglas C. Blomgren and D. Douglas Blanke, Special Assistant Attorneys General, and the Attorneys General for Alabama, Alaska, Arizona, Arkansas, California, Colorado, Connecticut, Delaware, Florida, Georgia, Hawaii, Idaho, Illinois, Indiana, Iowa, Kansas, Kentucky, Louisiana, Maine, Maryland, Massachusetts, Michigan, Mississippi, Missouri, Montana, Nebraska, Nevada, New Hampshire, New Jersey, New York, North Carolina, North Dakota, Ohio, Oklahoma, Oregon, Pennsylvania, Rhode Island, South Carolina, South Dakota, Tennessee, Texas, Utah, Vermont, Washington, West Virginia, Wisconsin, and Wyoming.

Brief of amici curiae filed on behalf of the American Bar Association by Morris Harrell, W. Ervin James, and Phillip J. Roth.

Brief of amici curiae filed on behalf of the Conference of Chief Justices by Paul L. Friedman and Michael D. Sullivan.

Brief of amici curiae filed on behalf of the Honorable Lawrence H. Cooke, Chief Judge of the State of New York, by Paul A. Feigenbaum, Michael Colodner, and Kenneth Falk.

Brief of amici curiae filed on behalf of the Honorable Abraham J. Gafni, Court Administrator of Pennsylvania, by Howland W. Abramson and Charles W. Johns.

IV. THE SUPREME COURT'S DECISION

"Our own experience is fully consistent with the common law's rejection of a rule of judicial immunity from prospective relief. We never have had a rule of absolute judicial immunity from prospective relief, and there is no evidence that the absence of that immunity has had a chilling effect on judicial independence. None of the seminal opinions on judicial immunity, either in England or in this country, has involved immunity from injunctive relief. No Court of Appeals ever has concluded that immunity bars injunctive relief against a judge. At least seven Circuits have indicated affirmatively that there is no immunity bar to such relief, and in situations where in their judgment an injunction against a judicial officer was necessary to prevent irreparable injury to a petitioner's constitutional rights, courts have granted that relief. . . .

We conclude that judicial immunity is not a bar to prospective injunctive relief against a judicial officer acting in her judicial capacity. In so concluding, we express no opinion as to the propriety of the injunctive relief awarded in this case. Petitioner did not appeal the award of injunctive relief against her. The Court of Appeals therefore had no opportunity to consider whether respondents had an adequate remedy at law, rendering equitable relief inappropriate, or whether the order itself should have been more narrowly tailored. On the record before us and without the benefit of the Court of Appeals' assessment, we are unwilling to speculate about these possibilities. We proceed, therefore, to the question whether judicial immunity bars an award of attorney's fees, under § 1988, to one who succeeds in obtaining injunctive relief against a judicial officer. . . .

Congress has made clear in § 1988 its intent that attorney's fees be available in any action to enforce a provision of § 1983. The legislative history of the statute confirms Congress' intent that an attorney's fee award be available even when damages would be barred or limited by 'immunity doctrines and special defenses, available only to public officials.' . . .

Congress' intent could hardly be more plain. Judicial immunity is no bar to the award of attorney's fees under 42 U.S.C. § 1988.

The judgment of the Court of Appeals, allowing the award of attorney's fees against petitioner, is therefore affirmed."

V. JUSTICE VOTE

5 Pro ACLU Side vs. 4 Con Opposing Side

ACLU Side (Respondent / Appellee)

1. Blackmun, H. – Wrote majority opinion
2. Brennan, W. – Joined majority opinion
3. White, B. – Joined majority opinion
4. Marshall, T. – Joined majority opinion
5. Stevens, J. – Joined majority opinion

Opposing Side (Petitioner / Appellant)

1. Powell, L. – Wrote dissenting opinion
2. Burger, W. – Joined Powell's dissent
3. Rehnquist, W. – Joined Powell's dissent
4. O'Connor, S. – Joined Powell's dissent

VI. A WIN OR LOSS FOR THE ACLU?

The ACLU filed as amicus curiae urging affirmance; the Supreme Court affirmed the Court of Appeals for the Fourth Circuit's decision in a 5-4 vote, giving the ACLU an apparent win.

535. United States v. Cronic

(Decided May 14, 1984; 466 U.S. 648)

I. ISSUE

A. Issues Discussed

Criminal procedure

B. Legal Question Presented

"The Court of Appeals reversed the conviction because it concluded that respondent did not 'have the Assistance of Counsel for his defence' that is guaranteed by the Sixth Amendment to the Constitution. . . . The question presented . . . is whether the Court of Appeals has correctly interpreted the Sixth Amendment."

C. Supreme Court's Answer

"This case is not one in which the surrounding circumstances make it unlikely that the defendant could have received the effective assistance of counsel. The criteria used by the Court of Appeals do not demonstrate that counsel failed to function in any meaningful sense as the Government's adversary. Respondent can therefore make out a claim of ineffective assistance only by pointing to specific errors made by trial counsel."

II. CASE SUMMARY

A. Background

"Respondent and two associates were indicted on mail fraud charges involving the transfer of over $9,400,000 in checks between banks in Tampa, Fla., and Norman, Okla., during a 4-month period in 1975. Shortly before the scheduled trial date, respondent's retained counsel withdrew. The court appointed a young lawyer with a real estate practice to represent respondent, but allowed him only 25 days for pretrial preparation, even though it had taken the Government over four and one-half years to investigate the case and it had reviewed thousands of documents during that investigation. The two codefendants agreed to testify for the Government; respondent was convicted on 11 of the 13 counts in the indictment and received a 25-year sentence.

The Court of Appeals reversed the conviction because it concluded that respondent did not 'have the Assistance of Counsel for his defence' that is guaranteed by the Sixth Amendment to the Constitution."

The Supreme Court granted certiorari to review the case.

B. Counsel of Record

ACLU Side (Respondent / Appellee): Steven Duke, by appointment of the Court, argued the cause and filed a brief for appellee.

Opposing Side (Petitioner / Appellant): Edwin S. Kneedler argued the cause for the United States. With him on the briefs were Solicitor General Lee, Assistant Attorney General Trott, Deputy Solicitor General Frey, and John Fichter De Pue.

III. AMICI CURIAE

ACLU Side (Respondent / Appellee)

Brief of amici curiae filed on behalf of the National Legal Aid and Defender Association, the Association of Trial Lawyers of America, and the American Civil Liberties Union by Richard J. Wilson, David S. Shrager, Charles S. Sims, and Burt Neuborne.

Brief of amici curiae filed on behalf of the National Association of Criminal Defense Lawyers et al. by John J. Cleary.

Opposing Side (Petitioner / Appellant)

No briefs of amici curiae were filed in support of appellant.

IV. THE SUPREME COURT'S DECISION

"An accused's right to be represented by counsel is a fundamental component of our criminal justice system. . . . 'Of all the rights that an accused person has, the right to be represented by counsel is by far the most pervasive for it affects his ability to assert any other rights he may have.'

The special value of the right to the assistance of counsel explains why '[i]t has long been recognized that the right to counsel is the right to the effective assistance of counsel.' . . .

The Court of Appeals did not find that respondent was denied the presence of counsel at a critical stage of the prosecution. Nor did it find, based on the actual conduct of the trial, that there was a breakdown in the adversarial process that would justify a presumption that respondent's conviction was insufficiently reliable to satisfy the Constitution. The dispositive question in this case therefore is whether the circumstances surrounding respondent's representation—and in particular the five criteria identified by the Court of Appeals—justified such a presumption. . . .

The five factors listed in the Court of Appeals' opinion are relevant to an evaluation of a lawyer's effectiveness in a particular case, but neither separately nor in combination do they provide a basis for concluding that competent counsel was not able to provide this respondent with the guiding hand that the Constitution guarantees. . . .

Neither the period of time that the Government spent investigating the case, nor the number of documents that its agents reviewed during that investigation, is necessarily relevant to the question whether a competent lawyer could prepare to defend the case in 25 days. . . .

That conclusion is not undermined by the fact that respondent's lawyer was young, that his principal practice was in real estate, or that this was his first jury trial. . . .

The three other criteria—the gravity of the charge, the complexity of the case, and the accessibility of witnesses—are all matters that may affect what a reasonably competent attorney could be expected to have done under the circumstances, but none identifies circumstances that in themselves make it unlikely that respondent received the effective assistance of counsel. . . .

The criteria used by the Court of Appeals do not demonstrate that counsel failed to function in any meaningful sense as the Government's adversary. Respondent can therefore make out a claim of ineffective assistance only by pointing to specific errors made by trial counsel. In this Court, respondent's present counsel argues that the record would support such an attack, but we leave that claim—as well as the other alleged trial errors raised by respondent which were not passed upon by the Court of Appeals—for the consideration of the Court of Appeals on remand.

The judgment is reversed, and the case is remanded . . . ."

V. JUSTICE VOTE

0 Pro ACLU Side vs. 9 Con Opposing Side

Opposing Side (Petitioner / Appellant)

1. Stevens, J. – Wrote majority opinion
2. Rehnquist, W. – Joined majority opinion
3. Burger, W. – Joined majority opinion
4. Powell, L. – Joined majority opinion
5. O'Connor, S. – Joined majority opinion
6. Blackmun, H. – Joined majority opinion
7. Brennan, W. – Joined majority opinion
8. White, B. – Joined majority opinion
9. Marshall, T. – Concurred in the judgment

VI. A WIN OR LOSS FOR THE ACLU?

The ACLU filed as amicus curiae urging affirmance; the Supreme Court reversed the Court of Appeals' decision by a 9-0 vote, giving the ACLU an apparent loss.

536. Welsh v. Wisconsin

(Decided May 15, 1984; 466 U.S. 740)

I. ISSUE

A. Issues Discussed

Criminal justice, Fourth Amendment, search and seizure, warrants

B. Legal Question Presented

"[W]hether, and if so under what circumstances, the Fourth Amendment prohibits the police from making a warrantless night entry of a person's home in order to arrest him for a nonjailable traffic offense."

C. Supreme Court's Answer

A warrantless night entry of a person's home to arrest him for driving while intoxicated is prohibited by the Fourth Amendment.

II. CASE SUMMARY

A. Background

"Shortly before 9 o'clock on the rainy night of April 24, 1978, a lone witness, Randy Jablonic, observed a car being driven erratically. After changing speeds and veering from side to side, the car eventually swerved off the road and came to a stop in an open field. No damage to any person or property occurred. Concerned about the driver and fearing that the car would get back on the highway, Jablonic drove his truck up behind the car so as to block it from returning to the road. Another passerby also stopped at the scene, and Jablonic asked her to call the police. Before the police arrived, however, the driver of the car emerged from his vehicle, approached Jablonic's truck, and asked Jablonic for a ride home. Jablonic instead suggested that they wait for assistance in removing or repairing the car. Ignoring Jablonic's suggestion, the driver walked away from the scene.

A few minutes later, the police arrived and questioned Jablonic. He told one officer what he had seen, specifically noting that the driver was either very inebriated or very sick. The officer checked the motor vehicle registration of the abandoned car and learned that it was registered to the petitioner, Edward G. Welsh. In addition, the officer noted that the petitioner's residence was a short distance from the scene, and therefore easily within walking distance.

Without securing any type of warrant, the police proceeded to the petitioner's home, arriving about 9 p.m. When the petitioner's stepdaughter answered the door, the police gained entry into the house. Proceeding upstairs to the petitioner's bedroom, they found him lying naked in bed. At this point, the petitioner was placed under arrest for driving or operating a motor vehicle while under the influence of an intoxicant, in violation of Wis. Stat. § 346.63(1) (1977). The petitioner was taken to the police station, where he refused to submit to a breath-analysis test. . . .

As a result of these events, the petitioner was subjected to two separate but related proceedings: one concerning his refusal to submit to a breath test and the other involving the alleged code violation for driving while intoxicated. . . .

As noted, in this case the petitioner refused to submit to a breath test; he subsequently filed a timely request for a refusal hearing. Before that hearing was held, however, the State filed a criminal complaint against the petitioner for driving while intoxicated. The petitioner responded by filing a motion to dismiss the complaint, relying on his contention that the underlying arrest was invalid. [T]he trial court concluded that the criminal complaint would not be dismissed because the existence of both probable cause and exigent circumstances justified the warrantless arrest. . . .

As expected, after the refusal hearing, the trial court concluded that the arrest of the petitioner was lawful and that the petitioner's refusal to take the breath test was therefore unreasonable. Accordingly, the court issued an order suspending the petitioner's operating license for 60 days. On appeal, the suspension order was vacated by the Wisconsin Court of Appeals. Contrary to the trial court, the appellate court concluded that the warrantless arrest of the petitioner in his home violated the Fourth Amendment because the State, although demonstrating probable cause to arrest, had not established the existence of exigent circumstances. The petitioner's refusal to submit to a breath test was therefore reasonable. The Supreme Court of Wisconsin in turn reversed the Court of Appeals, relying on the existence of three factors that it believed constituted exigent circumstances: the need for 'hot pursuit' of a suspect, the need to prevent physical harm to the offender and the public, and the need to prevent destruction of evidence."

The Supreme Court granted certiorari to review the case, vacated, and remanded.

B. Counsel of Record / ACLU Attorney

ACLU Side (Petitioner / Appellant): Gordon Brewster Baldwin argued the cause for appellant.

Opposing Side (Respondent / Appellee): Stephen W. Kleinmaier, Assistant Attorney General of Wisconsin, argued the cause for appellee.

III. AMICI CURIAE

ACLU Side (Petitioner / Appellant)

Brief of amici curiae filed on behalf of the Wisconsin Civil Liberties Union Foundation by Charles F. Kahn, Jr.

Opposing Side (Respondent / Appellee)

No briefs of amici curiae were filed in support of appellee.

IV. THE SUPREME COURT'S DECISION

"It is axiomatic that the 'physical entry of the home is the chief evil against which the wording of the Fourth Amendment is directed.' . . . It is not surprising, therefore, that the Court has recognized, as 'a 'basic principle of Fourth Amendment law[,]' that searches and seizures inside a home without a warrant are presumptively unreasonable.' . . .

Before agents of the government may invade the sanctity

of the home, the burden is on the government to demonstrate exigent circumstances that overcome the presumption of unreasonableness that attaches to all warrantless home entries. When the government's interest is only to arrest for a minor offense, that presumption of unreasonableness is difficult to rebut, and the government usually should be allowed to make such arrests only with a warrant issued upon probable cause by a neutral and detached magistrate. . . .

We . . . hold that an important factor to be considered when determining whether any exigency exists is the gravity of the underlying offense for which the arrest is being made. Moreover, although no exigency is created simply because there is probable cause to believe that a serious crime has been committed, application of the exigent-circumstances exception in the context of a home entry should rarely be sanctioned when there is probable cause to believe that only a minor offense, such as the kind at issue in this case, has been committed.

Application of this principle to the facts of the present case is relatively straightforward. The petitioner was arrested in the privacy of his own bedroom for a noncriminal, traffic offense. The State attempts to justify the arrest by relying on the hot-pursuit doctrine, on the threat to public safety, and on the need to preserve evidence of the petitioner's blood-alcohol level. On the facts of this case, however, the claim of hot pursuit is unconvincing because there was no immediate or continuous pursuit of the petitioner from the scene of a crime. Moreover, because the petitioner had already arrived home, and had abandoned his car at the scene of the accident, there was little remaining threat to the public safety. Hence, the only potential emergency claimed by the State was the need to ascertain the petitioner's blood-alcohol level. [A] warrantless home arrest cannot be upheld simply because evidence of the petitioner's blood-alcohol level might have dissipated while the police obtained a warrant. To allow a warrantless home entry on these facts would be to approve unreasonable police behavior that the principles of the Fourth Amendment will not sanction. . . .

The Supreme Court of Wisconsin let stand a warrantless, nighttime entry into the petitioner's home to arrest him for a civil traffic offense. Such an arrest, however, is clearly prohibited by the special protection afforded the individual in his home by the Fourth Amendment. The petitioner's arrest was therefore invalid, the judgment of the Supreme Court of Wisconsin is vacated, and the case is remanded for further proceedings not inconsistent with this opinion."

V. JUSTICE VOTE

6 Pro ACLU Side vs. 3 Con Opposing Side

ACLU Side (Petitioner / Appellant)

1. Brennan, W. – Wrote majority opinion
2. Marshall, T. – Joined majority opinion
3. Stevens, J. – Joined majority opinion
4. O'Connor, S. – Joined majority opinion
5. Powell, L. – Joined majority opinion
6. Blackmun, H. – Wrote concurring opinion

Opposing Side (Respondent / Appellee)

1. Burger, W. – Wrote separate statement urging dismissal of the writ of certiorari
2. White, B. – Wrote dissenting opinion
3. Rehnquist, W. – Joined White's dissent

VI. A WIN OR LOSS FOR THE ACLU?

The ACLU filed as amicus curiae urging reversal; the Supreme Court vacated and remanded the Wisconsin Supreme Court's decision in a 6-3 vote, giving the ACLU an apparent win.

537. Members of the City Council of Los Angeles v. Taxpayers for Vincent

(Decided May 15, 1984; 466 U.S. 789)

I. ISSUE

A. Issues Discussed

First Amendment, freedoms of press, speech, and association

B. Legal Question Presented

Whether § 28.04 of the Los Angeles Municipal Code, which "prohibits the posting of signs on public property, . . . abridges appellees' freedom of speech within the meaning of the First Amendment."

C. Supreme Court's Answer

Section 28.04 is not unconstitutional as applied to appellees.

II. CASE SUMMARY

A. Background

"Section 28.04 of the Los Angeles Municipal Code prohibits the posting of signs on public property. . . . In March 1979, Roland Vincent was a candidate for election to the Los Angeles City Council. A group of his supporters, known as Taxpayers for Vincent (Taxpayers) entered into a contract with a political sign service company known as Candidates' Outdoor Graphics Service (COGS) to fabricate and post signs with Vincent's name on them. COGS produced 15 44-inch cardboard signs and attached them to utility poles . . . . The signs' message was: 'Roland Vincent—City Council.'

Acting under the authority of § 28.04 of the Municipal Code, employees of the city's Bureau of Street Maintenance routinely removed all posters attached to utility poles and similar objects covered by the ordinance, including the COGS signs.

On March 12, 1979, Taxpayers and COGS filed this action in the United States District Court for the Central District of California . . . . They sought an injunction against enforcement of the ordinance as well as compensatory and punitive damages. After engaging in discovery, the parties filed cross-motions for summary judgment on the issue of liability. The District Court entered findings of fact, concluded that the ordinance was constitutional, and granted the City's motion. . . .

The Court of Appeals did not question any of the District Court's findings of fact, but it rejected some of its conclusions of law. . . . In its appeal to [the Supreme] Court the City challenges the Court of Appeals' holding that § 28.04 is unconstitutional on its face. Taxpayers and COGS defend that holding and also contend that the ordinance is unconstitutional as applied to their posting of political campaign signs on the crossarms of utility poles."

The Supreme Court granted certiorari to review the case, reversed, and remanded.

B. Counsel of Record / ACLU Attorney

ACLU Side (Respondent / Appellee): Wayne S. Canterbury argued the cause for appellee.

Opposing Side (Petitioner / Appellant): Anthony Saul Alperin argued the cause for appellant.

III. AMICI CURIAE

ACLU Side (Respondent / Appellee)

Brief of amici curiae filed on behalf of the ACLU, et al., by Alan L. Schlosser, Amitai Schwartz, Fred Okrand, and Neil H. O'Donnell.

Opposing Side (Petitioner / Appellant)

Brief of amici curiae filed on behalf of the City of Antioch by William R. Galstan.

Brief of amici curiae filed on behalf of the National Institute of Municipal Law Officers by J. Lamar Shelley, John W. Witt, Henry W. Underhill, Jr., Benjamin L. Brown, Roy D. Bates, James B. Brennan, Roger F. Cutler, Clifford D. Pierce, Jr., Walter M. Powell, Frederick A.O. Schwarz, Jr., William H. Taube, William I. Thornton, Jr., Max P. Zall, and Charles S. Rhyne.

IV. THE SUPREME COURT'S DECISION

"Appellees have simply failed to demonstrate a realistic danger that the ordinance will significantly compromise recognized First Amendment protections of individuals not before the Court. It would therefore be inappropriate in this case to entertain an overbreadth challenge to the ordinance.

[A]ppellees' attack on the ordinance is basically a challenge to the ordinance as applied to their activities. We therefore limit our analysis of the constitutionality of the ordinance to the concrete case before us, and now turn to the arguments that it is invalid as applied to the expressive activity of Taxpayers and COGS. . . .

The application of the ordinance to appellees' expressive activities surely raises the question whether the ordinance abridges their 'freedom of speech' within the meaning of the First Amendment . . . . In this case, taxpayers and COGS do not dispute that it is within the constitutional power of the City to attempt to improve its appearance, or that this interest is basically unrelated to the suppression of ideas. Therefore the critical inquiries are whether that interest is sufficiently substantial to justify the effect of the ordinance on appellees' expression, and whether that effect is no greater than necessary to accomplish the City's purpose. . . .

The problem addressed by this ordinance—the visual assault on the citizens of Los Angeles presented by an accumulation of signs posted on public property—constitutes a significant substantive evil within the City's power to prohibit. . . . With respect to signs posted by appellees . . . it is the tangible medium of expressing the message that has the adverse impact on the appearance of the landscape. [T]he application of the ordinance in this case responds precisely to the substantive problem which legitimately concerns the City. The ordinance curtails no more speech than is necessary to accomplish its purpose. . . .

Any constitutionally mandated exception to the City's total prohibition against temporary signs on public property would necessarily rest on a judicial determination that the City's traffic control and safety interests had little or no applicability within the excepted category, and that the City's interests in esthetics are not sufficiently important to justify the prohibition in that category. But the findings of the District Court provide no basis for questioning the substantiality of the esthetic interest at stake, or for believing that a uniquely important form of communication has been abridged for the categories of expression engaged in by Taxpayers and COGS.

Therefore, we accept the City's position that it may decide that the esthetic interest in avoiding 'visual clutter' justifies a removal of signs creating or increasing that clutter. The findings of the District Court that COGS signs add to the problems addressed by the ordinance and, if permitted to remain, would encourage others to post additional signs, are sufficient to justify application of the ordinance to these appellees. . . .

We hold that on this record these interests are sufficiently substantial to justify this content-neutral, impartially administered prohibition against the posting of appellees' temporary signs on public property and that such an application of the ordinance does not create an unacceptable threat to the 'profound national commitment to the principle that debate on public issues should be uninhibited, robust, and wide-open.'

The judgment of the Court of Appeals is reversed, and the case is remanded to that Court."

V. JUSTICE VOTE

3 Pro ACLU Side vs. 6 Con Opposing Side

ACLU Side (Respondent / Appellee)

1. Brennan, W. – Wrote dissenting opinion
2. Marshall, T. – Joined Brennan's dissent
3. Blackmun, H. – Joined Brennan's dissent

Opposing Side (Petitioner / Appellant)

1. Stevens, J. – Joined majority opinion
2. Burger, W. – Joined majority opinion
3. White, B. – Joined majority opinion
4. Rehnquist, W. – Joined majority opinion
5. O'Connor, S. – Joined majority opinion
6. Powell, L. – Joined majority opinion

VI. A WIN OR LOSS FOR THE ACLU?

The ACLU filed as amicus curiae urging affirmance; the Supreme Court reversed the Court of Appeals for the Ninth Circuit in a 6-3 vote, giving the ACLU an apparent loss.

538. Seattle Times Co. v. Rhinehart

(Decided May 21, 1984; 467 U.S. 20)

I. ISSUE

A. Issues Discussed

First Amendment, freedoms of press, speech, and association

B. Legal Question Presented

"[W]hether parties to a civil litigation have a First Amendment right to disseminate, in advance of trial, information gained through the pretrial discovery process."

C. Supreme Court's Answer

Parties to a civil litigation do not have a First Amendment right to disseminate, in advance of trial, information gained exclusively through pretrial discovery, where that information is protected by an order issued on a showing of good cause.

II. CASE SUMMARY

A. Background

"Respondent Rhinehart is the spiritual leader of a religious group, the Aquarian Foundation. . . . Aquarian beliefs include life after death and the ability to communicate with the dead through mediums. Rhinehart is the primary Aquarian medium.

In recent years, the Seattle Times and the Walla Walla Union-Bulletin have published stories about Rhinehart and the Foundation. . . . The five articles that appeared in 1973 focused on Rhinehart and the manner in which he operated the foundation. They described seances conducted by Rhinehart in which people paid him to put them in touch with deceased relatives and friends. The articles also stated that Rhinehart had sold magical 'stones' that had been 'expelled' from his body. One article referred to Rhinehart's conviction, which was later vacated, for sodomy. The four articles that appeared in 1978 concentrated on an 'extravaganza' sponsored by Rhinehart at the Walla Walla State Penitentiary. The articles stated that he had treated 1,100 inmates to a 6-hour-long show, during which he gave away between $35,000 and $50,000 in cash and prizes. One article described a 'chorus line of girls [who] shed their gowns and bikinis and sang . . .' The two articles that appeared in 1979 referred to a purported connection between Rhinehart and Lou Ferrigno, star of the popular television program, The Incredible Hulk.

Rhinehart brought this action in the Washington Superior Court [alleging] that the articles contained statements that were 'fictional and untrue,' and that the defendants—petitioners here—knew, or should have known, they were false. [During discovery, respondents] opposed the motion [to compel], arguing in particular that compelled production of the identities of the Foundation's donors and members would violate the First Amendment rights of members and donors to privacy, freedom of religion, and freedom of association. Respondents also moved for a protective order preventing petitioners from disseminating any information gained through discovery.

[T]he trial court initially granted the motion to compel and ordered respondents to identify all donors who made contributions during the five years preceding the date of the complaint, along with the amounts donated. [After respondents] renewed their motion for a protective order . . . , the trial court issued a protective order covering all information obtained through the discovery process that pertained to 'the financial affairs of the various plaintiffs, the names and addresses of Aquarian Foundation members, contributors, or clients, and the names and addresses of those who have been contributors, clients, or donors to any of the various plaintiffs.' . . . Respondents appealed from the trial court's production order, and petitioners appealed from the protective order. The Supreme Court of Washington affirmed both."

The U.S. Supreme Court granted certiorari to review the case and affirmed.

B. Counsel of Record / ACLU Attorney

ACLU Side (Petitioner / Appellant): Evan L. Schwab argued the cause for appellant.

Opposing Side (Respondent / Appellee): Malcolm L. Edwards argued the cause for appellee.

III. AMICI CURIAE

ACLU Side (Petitioner / Appellant)

Brief of amici curiae filed on behalf of the ACLU, et al., by James C. Goodale, John G. Koeltl, Burt Neuborne, Charles S. Sims, W. Terry Maguire, Anthony Epstein, Erwin G. Krasnow, Bruce W. Sanford, J. Laurent Scharff, Richard M. Schmidt, Jr., and Donald F. Luke.

Opposing Side (Respondent / Appellee)

No briefs of amici curiae were filed in support of appellee.

IV. THE SUPREME COURT'S DECISION

"The critical question that this case presents is whether a litigant's freedom comprehends the right to disseminate information that he has obtained pursuant to a court order that both granted him access to that information and placed restraints on the way in which the information might be used. In addressing that question it is necessary to consider whether the 'practice in question [furthers] an important or substantial governmental interest unrelated to the suppression of expression' and whether 'the limitation of First Amendment freedoms [is] no greater than is necessary or essential to the protection of the particular governmental interest involved.' . . .

As in all civil litigation, petitioners gained the information they wish to disseminate only by virtue of the trial court's discovery processes. . . . A litigant has no First Amendment right of access to information made available only for purposes of trying his suit. Thus, continued court control over the discovered information does not raise the same specter of government censorship that such control might suggest in other situations.

[T]he provision for protective orders in the Washington Rules requires, in itself, no heightened First Amendment scrutiny. . . . Rule 26(c) confers broad discretion on the trial court to decide when a protective order is appropriate and what degree of protection is required. The Legislature of the State of Washington, following the example of the Congress in its approval of the Federal

Rules of Civil Procedure, has determined that such discretion is necessary, and we find no reason to disagree. The trial court is in the best position to weigh fairly the competing needs and interests of parties affected by discovery. The unique character of the discovery process requires that the trial court have substantial latitude to fashion protective orders. . . .

The facts in this case illustrate the concerns that justifiably may prompt a court to issue a protective order. As we have noted, the trial court's order allowing discovery was extremely broad. It compelled respondents—among other things—to identify all persons who had made donations over a 5-year period to Rhinehart and the Aquarian Foundation, together with the amounts donated. In effect the order would compel disclosure of membership as well as sources of financial support. The Supreme Court of Washington found that dissemination of this information would 'result in annoyance, embarrassment and even oppression.' It is sufficient for purposes of our decision that the highest court in the State found no abuse of discretion in the trial court's decision to issue a protective order pursuant to a constitutional state law. We therefore hold that where, as in this case, a protective order is entered on a showing of good cause as required by Rule 26(c), is limited to the context of pretrial civil discovery, and does not restrict the dissemination of the information if gained from other sources, it does not offend the First Amendment.

The judgment accordingly is affirmed."

V. JUSTICE VOTE

0 Pro ACLU Side vs. 9 Con Opposing Side

Opposing Side (Respondent / Appellee)

1. Powell, L. – Wrote majority opinion
2. Burger, W. – Joined majority opinion
3. White, B. – Joined majority opinion
4. Blackmun, H. – Joined majority opinion
5. Rehnquist, W. – Joined majority opinion
6. Stevens, J. – Joined majority opinion
7. O'Connor, S. – Joined majority opinion
8. Brennan, W. – Wrote concurring opinion
9. Marshall, T. – Joined Brennan's concurrence

VI. A WIN OR LOSS FOR THE ACLU?

The ACLU filed as amicus curiae urging reversal; the Supreme Court affirmed the Washington Supreme Court decision in a 9-0 vote, giving the ACLU an apparent loss.

539. Hishon v. King & Spalding

(Decided May 22, 1984; 467 U.S. 69)

I. ISSUE

A. Issues Discussed

Civil rights, gender, First Amendment, Fourteenth Amendment

B. Legal Question Presented

"[W]hether the District Court properly dismissed a Title VII complaint alleging that a law partnership discriminated against petitioner, a woman lawyer employed as an associate, when it failed to invite her to become a partner."

C. Supreme Court's Answer

The District Court erred in dismissing the Title VII complaint.

II. CASE SUMMARY

A. Background

"In 1972 petitioner Elizabeth Anderson Hishon accepted a position as an associate with respondent, a large Atlanta law firm established as a general partnership. When this suit was filed in 1980, the firm had more than 50 partners and employed approximately 50 attorneys as associates. Up to that time, no woman had ever served as a partner at the firm.

Petitioner alleges that the prospect of partnership was an important factor in her initial decision to accept employment with respondent. She alleges that respondent used the possibility of ultimate partnership as a recruiting device to induce petitioner and other young lawyers to become associates at the firm. According to the complaint, respondent represented that advancement to partnership after five or six years was 'a matter of course' for associates 'who receive[d] satisfactory evaluations' and that associates were promoted to partnership 'on a fair and equal basis.' Petitioner alleges that she relied on these representations when she accepted employment with respondent. The complaint further alleges that respondent's promise to consider her on a 'fair and equal basis' created a binding employment contract.

In May 1978 the partnership considered and rejected Hishon for admission to the partnership; one year later, the partners again declined to invite her to become a partner. Once an associate is passed over for partnership at respondent's firm, the associate is notified to begin seeking employment elsewhere. Petitioner's employment as an associate terminated on December 31, 1979. . . .

Hishon filed a charge with the Equal Employment Opportunity Commission on November 19, 1979, claiming that respondent had discriminated against her on the basis of her sex in violation of Title VII of the Civil Rights Act of 1964. Ten days later the Commission issued a notice of right to sue, and on February 27, 1980, Hishon brought this action in the United States District Court for the Northern District of Georgia. She sought declaratory and injunctive relief, backpay, and compensatory damages 'in lieu of reinstatement and promotion to partnership.' This, of course, negates any claim for specific performance of the contract alleged.

The District Court dismissed the complaint on the ground that Title VII was inapplicable to the selection of partners by a partnership. A divided panel of the United States Court of Appeals for the Eleventh Circuit affirmed."

The Supreme Court granted certiorari to review the case and reversed.

B. Counsel of Record / ACLU Attorney

ACLU Side (Petitioner / Appellant): Emmet J. Bondurant argued the cause for appellant.

Deputy Solicitor General Bator argued the cause for the United States, as amicus curiae, by special leave of Court.

Opposing Side (Respondent / Appellee): Charles Morgan, Jr., argued the cause for appellee.

III. AMICI CURIAE

ACLU Side (Petitioner / Appellant)

Brief of amici curiae filed on behalf of the ACLU by Samuel Estreicher, Burt Neuborne, Isabelle Katz Pinzler, E. Richard Larson, Charles S. Sims, and Mary L. Heen.

Brief of amici curiae filed on behalf of the United States, et al., by Deputy Solicitor General Bator, Solicitor General Lee, Assistant Attorney General Reynolds, David A. Strauss, Brian K. Landsberg, James W. Clute, and Philip B. Sklover.

Additional briefs of amici curiae were filed on behalf of the American Association of University Women, et al., the Anti-Defamation League of B'nai B'rith, et al., California Women Lawyers, the Dallas Association of Black Women Attorneys, et al., the NAACP Legal Defense and Education Fund, Inc., the Women's Bar Association of Illinois, et al., the Women's Bar Association of Massachusetts, and Robert Abrams, et al.

Opposing Side (Respondent / Appellee)

Brief of amici curiae filed on behalf of the New England Legal Foundation by Joseph D. Alviani.

IV. THE SUPREME COURT'S DECISION

"The contractual relationship of employment triggers the provision of Title VII governing 'terms, conditions, or privileges of employment.' Title VII in turn forbids discrimination on the basis of 'race, color, religion, sex, or national origin.'

Because the underlying employment relationship is contractual, it follows that the 'terms, conditions, or privileges of employment' clearly include benefits that are part of an employment contract. Here, petitioner in essence alleges that respondent made a contract to consider her for partnership. Indeed, this promise was allegedly a key contractual provision which induced her to accept employment. If the evidence at trial establishes that the parties contracted to have petitioner considered for partnership, that promise clearly was a term, condition, or privilege of her employment. Title VII would then bind respondent to consider petitioner for partnership as the statute provides, i.e., without regard to petitioner's sex. . . .

Petitioner's claim that a contract was made, however, is not the only allegation that would qualify respondent's consideration of petitioner for partnership as a term, condition, or privilege of employment. An employer may provide its employees with many benefits that it is under no obligation to furnish by any express or implied contract. . . . A benefit that is part and parcel of the employment relationship may not be doled out in a discriminatory fashion, even if the employer would be free under the employment contract simply not to provide the benefit at all. Those benefits that comprise the 'incidents of employment,' may not be afforded in a manner contrary to Title VII. [T]he opportunity to become a partner was part and parcel of an associate's status as an employee at respondent's firm . . . .

A benefit need not accrue before a person's employment is completed to be a term, condition, or privilege of that employment relationship. [R]espondent argues that Title VII categorically exempts partnership decisions from scrutiny. However, respondent points to nothing in the statute or the legislative history that would support such a per se exemption. When Congress wanted to grant an employer complete immunity, it expressly did so. Although . . . the activities of lawyers may make a 'distinctive contribution . . . to the ideas and beliefs of our society,' respondent has not shown how its ability to fulfill such a function would be inhibited by a requirement that it consider petitioner for partnership on her merits. . . .

We conclude that petitioner's complaint states a claim cognizable under Title VII. Petitioner therefore is entitled to her day in court to prove her allegations. The judgment of the Court of Appeals is reversed, and the case is remanded for further proceedings consistent with this opinion."

V. JUSTICE VOTE

9 Pro ACLU Side vs. 0 Con Opposing Side

ACLU Side (Petitioner / Appellant)

1. Burger, W. – Wrote majority opinion
2. Brennan, W. – Joined majority opinion
3. White, B. – Joined majority opinion
4. Marshall, T. – Joined majority opinion
5. Blackmun, H. – Joined majority opinion
6. Rehnquist, W. – Joined majority opinion
7. Stevens, J. – Joined majority opinion
8. O'Connor, S. – Joined majority opinion
9. Powell, L. – Wrote concurring opinion

VI. A WIN OR LOSS FOR THE ACLU?

The ACLU filed as amicus curiae urging reversal; the Supreme Court reversed the Court of Appeals for the Eleventh Circuit's decision in a 9-0 vote, giving the ACLU an apparent win.

540. United States v. Gouveia

(Decided May 29, 1984; 467 U.S. 180)

I. ISSUE

A. Issues Discussed

Sixth Amendment, right to counsel, prisons

B. Legal Question Presented

Whether prisoners were "constitutionally entitled to the appointment of counsel while they were in administrative segregation and before any adversary judicial proceedings had been initiated against them."

C. Supreme Court's Answer

The right to appointment of counsel attaches only after adversary judicial proceedings are initiated against the accused, including when the accused is a prisoner in administrative segregation.

II. CASE SUMMARY

A. Background

"Respondents William Gouveia, Robert Ramirez, Adolpho Reynoso, and Philip Segura were convicted of murdering a fellow inmate at a federal prison in Lompoc, Cal. Respondents Robert Mills and Richard Pierce were convicted of a later murder of another inmate at the same institution. Prison officials placed each respondent in administrative detention shortly after the murders, and they remained there for an extended period of time before they were eventually indicted on criminal charges. On appeal of respondents' convictions, the en banc Court of Appeals for the Ninth Circuit held by divided vote that they had a Sixth Amendment right to an attorney during the period in which they were held in administrative detention before the return of indictments against them, and that because they had been denied that right, their convictions had to be overturned and their indictments dismissed."

The Supreme Court granted certiorari to review the case and reversed.

B. Counsel of Record / ACLU Attorney

ACLU Side (Respondent / Appellee): Charles P. Diamond, by appointment of the Court, argued the cause for appellees, Mills et al. Joel Levine, by appointment of the Court, argued the cause for appellees Gouveia et al.

Opposing Side (Petitioner / Appellant): Deputy Solicitor General Frey argued the cause for the United States.

III. AMICI CURIAE

ACLU Side (Respondent / Appellee)

Brief of amici curiae filed on behalf of the ACLU Foundation by Richard F. Ziegler and Charles S. Sims.

Brief of amici curiae filed on behalf of the National Legal Aid and Defender Association by Richard J. Wilson.

Opposing Side (Petitioner / Appellant)

No briefs of amici curiae filed on behalf of appellant.

IV. THE SUPREME COURT'S DECISION

"The Sixth Amendment guarantees that '[i]n all criminal prosecutions, the accused shall enjoy the right . . . to have the Assistance of Counsel for his defence.' [O]ur cases have long recognized that the right to counsel attaches only at or after the initiation of adversary judicial proceedings against the defendant. . . .

That interpretation of the Sixth Amendment right to counsel is consistent not only with the literal language of the Amendment, which requires the existence of both a 'criminal prosecutio[n]' and an 'accused,' but also with the purposes which we have recognized that the right to counsel serves. We have recognized that the 'core purpose' of the counsel guarantee is to assure aid at trial, 'when the accused [is] confronted with both the intricacies of the law and the advocacy of the public prosecutor.' . . .

Although we have extended an accused's right to counsel to certain 'critical' pretrial proceedings, we have done so recognizing that at those proceedings, 'the accused [is] confronted, just as at trial, by the procedural system, or by his expert adversary, or by both,' in a situation where the results of the confrontation 'might well settle the accused's fate and reduce the trial itself to a mere formality.'

Thus, given the plain language of the Amendment and its purpose of protecting the unaided layman at critical confrontations with his adversary, our conclusion that the right to counsel attaches at the initiation of adversary judicial criminal proceedings 'is far from a mere formalism.' It is only at that time 'that the government has committed itself to prosecute, and only then that the adverse positions of government and defendant have solidified. It is then that a defendant finds himself faced with the prosecutorial forces of organized society, and immersed in the intricacies of substantive and procedural criminal law.' . . .

Thus, at bottom, the [Court of Appeals] majority's concern is that because an inmate suspected of a crime is already in prison, the prosecution may have little incentive promptly to bring formal charges against him, and that the resulting preindictment delay may be particularly prejudicial to the inmate, given the problems inherent in investigating prison crimes, such as the transient nature of the prison population and the general reluctance of inmates to cooperate. But applicable statutes of limitations protect against the prosecution's bringing stale criminal charges against any defendant and, beyond that protection, the Fifth Amendment requires the dismissal of an indictment, even if it is brought within the statute of limitations, if the defendant can prove that the Government's delay in bringing the indictment was a deliberate device to gain an advantage over him and that it caused him actual prejudice in presenting his defense. Those protections apply to criminal defendants within and without the prison walls, and we decline to depart from our traditional interpretation of the Sixth Amendment right to counsel in order to provide additional protections for respondents here.

We conclude that the Court of Appeals was wrong in holding that respondents were constitutionally entitled to the appointment of counsel while they were in administrative segregation and before any adversary judicial proceedings had been initiated against them. Accordingly, we reverse the judgment of the Court of Appeals and remand for further proceedings consistent with this opinion."

V. JUSTICE VOTE

1 Pro ACLU Side vs. 8 Con Opposing Side

ACLU Side (Respondent / Appellee)

1. Marshall, T. – Wrote dissenting opinion

Opposing Side (Petitioner / Appellant)

1. Rehnquist, W. – Wrote majority opinion
2. Burger, W. – Joined majority opinion
3. White, B. – Joined majority opinion
4. Blackmun, H. – Joined majority opinion
5. Powell, L. – Joined majority opinion
6. O'Connor, S. – Joined majority opinion
7. Stevens, J. – Wrote concurring opinion
8. Brennan, W. – Joined Stevens' concurrence

VI. A WIN OR LOSS FOR THE ACLU?

The ACLU, as amicus curiae, urged affirmance of the Ninth Circuit Court of Appeals' judgment; the Supreme Court reversed and remanded in an 8-1 vote, giving the ACLU an apparent loss.

541. New York v. Uplinger

(Decided May 30, 1984; 467 U.S. 246)

I. ISSUE

A. Issues Discussed

Civil rights, privacy, First Amendment, equal protection, due process

B. Legal Question Presented

Is a New York statute "which prohibits loitering 'in a public place for the purpose of engaging, or soliciting another person to engage, in deviate sexual intercourse or other sexual behavior of a deviate nature" unconstitutional?

C. Supreme Court's Answer

Declining to decide the question, the Court dismissed the writ of certiorari as improvidently granted.

II. CASE SUMMARY

A. Background

The Supreme Court "granted certiorari to review a decision of the New York Court of Appeals concerning N.Y. Penal Law § 240.35 (3), which prohibits loitering 'in a public place for the purpose of engaging, or soliciting another person to engage, in deviate sexual intercourse or other sexual behavior of a deviate nature.' Respondents, charged with violating the statute, challenged its constitutionality and the Court of Appeals sustained their claim. The court concluded that § 240.35 (3) is 'a companion statute to the consensual sodomy statute . . . which criminalized acts of deviate sexual intercourse between consenting adults' and noted that it had previously held the latter statute unconstitutional in People v. Onofre, 415 N.E.2d 936 (1980), which [the Supreme Court] declined to review. Construing the loitering statute as intended 'to punish conduct anticipatory to the act of consensual sodomy,' the Court of Appeals reasoned that '[i]nasmuch as the conduct ultimately contemplated by the loitering statute may not be deemed criminal, we perceive no basis upon which the State may continue to punish loitering for that purpose.'"

The Supreme Court granted certiorari to review, then dismissed the writ of certiorari as improvidently granted.

B. Counsel of Record / ACLU Attorney

ACLU Side (Respondent / Appellee): William H. Gardner argued the cause for appellee.

Opposing Side (Petitioner / Appellant): Richard J. Arcara argued the cause for appellant.

III. AMICI CURIAE

ACLU Side (Respondent / Appellee)

Brief of amici curiae filed on behalf of the ACLU, et al., by Steven R. Shapiro, Burt Neuborne, and Charles S. Sims.

Additional briefs of amici curiae were filed on behalf of the American Association for Personal Privacy, et al., the American Psychological Association, et al., the Committee on Sex and Law of the Association of the Bar of the City of New York, et al., the Attorney General of the State of New York, the Center for Constitutional Rights, et al., National Association of Business Councils, et al., and the Lambda Legal Defense and Education Fund, Inc.

Opposing Side (Petitioner / Appellant)

No briefs of amici curiae were filed in support of appellant.

IV. THE SUPREME COURT'S DECISION

"Petitioner challenges the decision of the Court of Appeals on the ground that the loitering statute is a valid exercise of the State's power to control public order. Respondents, on the other hand, defend the decision by arguing that the statute is unconstitutionally vague and overboard on its face and that, as applied, it violates their First Amendment, equal protection, and due process rights. We decline to address these arguments, however, because examination of the case, after full briefing and oral argument, has convinced us that the writ of certiorari was improvidently granted.

As the diverse arguments presented in the briefs have demonstrated, the opinion of the Court of Appeals is fairly subject to varying interpretations, leaving us uncertain as to the precise federal constitutional issue the court decided. Moreover, whatever the constitutional basis of the Court of Appeals' decision, it was clearly premised on the court's earlier decision in People v. Onofre, and for that reason a meaningful evaluation of the decision below would entail consideration of the questions decided in that case. Petitioner does not, however, challenge the decision of the New York Court of Appeals in that case.

Under these circumstances, we are persuaded that this case provides an inappropriate vehicle for resolving the important constitutional issues raised by the parties. We therefore dismiss the writ of certiorari as improvidently granted."

V. JUSTICE VOTE

5 Pro ACLU Side vs. 4 Con Opposing Side

ACLU Side (Respondent / Appellee)

1. Brennan, W. – Per curiam decision
2. Powell, L. – Per curiam decision
3. Marshall, T. – Per curiam decision
4. Blackmun, H. – Per curiam decision
5. Stevens, J. – Wrote concurring opinion

Opposing Side (Petitioner / Appellant)

1. White, B. – Wrote dissenting opinion
2. Burger, W. – Joined dissenting opinion
3. O'Connor, S. – Joined dissenting opinion
4. Rehnquist, W. – Joined dissenting opinion

VI. A WIN OR LOSS FOR THE ACLU?

The ACLU filed as amicus curiae urging affirmance; the Supreme Court dismissed the writ of certiorari as improvidently granted in a 5-4 vote, giving the ACLU an apparent win.

542. Immigration & Naturalization Service v. Stevic

(Decided June 5, 1984; 467 U.S. 407)

I. ISSUE

A. Issues Discussed

Immigration

B. Legal Question Presented

"[W]hether a deportable alien must demonstrate a clear probability of persecution in order to obtain . . . relief under § 243(h) of the Immigration and Nationality Act of 1952, as amended by § 203(e) of the Refugee Act of 1980," which gives "the Attorney General . . . statutory authority to withhold the deportation of an alien upon a finding that the alien would be subject to persecution in the country to which he would be deported."

C. Supreme Court's Answer

The alien must demonstrate "a clear probability of persecution" to obtain relief under § 243(h).

II. CASE SUMMARY

A. Background

"Respondent, a Yugoslavian citizen, entered the United States in 1976 to visit his sister, then a permanent resident alien residing in Chicago. Petitioner, the Immigration and Naturalization Service (INS), instituted deportation proceedings against respondent when he overstayed his 6-week period of admission. Respondent admitted that he was deportable and agreed to depart voluntarily by February 1977. In January 1977, however, respondent married a United States citizen who obtained approval of a visa petition on his behalf. Shortly thereafter, respondent's wife died in an automobile accident. The approval of respondent's visa petition was automatically revoked, and petitioner ordered respondent to surrender for deportation to Yugoslavia.

Respondent moved to reopen the deportation proceedings in August 1977, seeking relief under § 243(h) of the Immigration and Naturalization Act, which then provided: 'The Attorney General is authorized to withhold deportation of any alien within the United States to any country in which in his opinion the alien would be subject to persecution on account of race, religion, or political opinion and for such period of time as he deems to be necessary for such reason.'

Respondent's supporting affidavit stated that he had become active in an anti-Communist organization after his marriage in early 1977, that his father-in-law had been imprisoned in Yugoslavia because of membership in that organization, and that he feared imprisonment upon his return to Yugoslavia.

In October 1979, the Immigration Judge denied respondent's motion to reopen without conducting an evidentiary hearing. The Board of Immigration Appeals (BIA) upheld that action . . . . After receiving notice to surrender for deportation in February 1981, respondent filed his second motion to reopen. . . . Although additional written material was submitted in support of the second motion, like the first, it was denied without a hearing. . . .

The United States Court of Appeals for the Second Circuit reversed and remanded for a plenary hearing under a different standard of proof. Specifically, it held that respondent no longer had the burden of showing 'a clear probability of persecution,' but instead could avoid deportation by demonstrating a 'well-founded fear of persecution.' The latter language is contained in a definition of the term 'refugee' adopted by a United Nations Protocol to which the United States has adhered since 1968. The Court of Appeals held that the Refugee Act of 1980 changed the standard of proof that an alien must satisfy to obtain relief under § 243(h), concluding that Congress intended to abandon the 'clear probability of persecution' standard and substitute the 'well-founded fear of persecution' language of the Protocol as the standard."

The Supreme Court granted certiorari to review the case and reversed the judgment of the Second Circuit Court of Appeals.

B. Counsel of Record / ACLU Attorney

ACLU Side (Respondent / Appellee): Ann L. Ritter argued the cause for appellee.

Opposing Side (Petitioner / Appellant): Deputy Solicitor General Geller argued the cause for appellant.

III. AMICI CURIAE

ACLU Side (Respondent / Appellee)

Brief of amici curiae filed on behalf of the ACLU, et al., by Burt Neuborne, E. Richard Larson, and David Carliner.

Additional briefs of amici curiae were filed on behalf of the American Immigration Lawyers Association, the American Jewish Committee, et al., Amnesty International USA, the Committee on Migration and Refugee Affairs of the American Council of Voluntary Agencies for Foreign Service, et al., the Lawyers Committee for International Human Rights, the National Immigration Project of the National Lawyers Guild, Inc., and the United Nations High Commissioner for Refugees.

Opposing Side (Petitioner / Appellant)

No briefs of amici curiae were filed in support of appellant.

IV. THE SUPREME COURT'S DECISION

"Legislation enacted by the Congress in 1950, 1952, and 1965 authorized the Attorney General to withhold deportation of an otherwise deportable alien if the alien would be subject to persecution upon deportation. At least before 1968, it was clear that an alien was required to demonstrate a 'clear probability of persecution' or a 'likelihood of persecution' in order to be eligible for withholding of deportation under § 243(h) of the Immigration and Nationality Act of 1952. . . .

In 1968 the United States acceded to the United Nations Protocol Relating to the Status of Refugees. The Protocol bound parties to comply with the substantive provisions of Articles 2 through 34 of the United Nations Convention Relating to the Status of Refugees with respect to 'refugees' as defined in Article 1.2 of the Protocol.

Article 1.2 of the Protocol defines a 'refugee' as an individual who 'owing to a well-founded fear of being persecuted for reasons of race, religion, nationality, membership of a particular social group or political opinion, is outside the country of his nationality and is unable or, owing to such fear, is unwilling to avail himself of the protection of that country; or who, not having a nationality and being outside the country of his former habitual residence, is unable or, owing to such fear, is unwilling to return to it.' . . .

Petitioner argues that persecution must be more likely than not for a fear of persecution to be considered 'well founded.' The positions of respondent and several amici curiae are somewhat amorphous. Respondent seems to maintain that a fear of persecution is 'well founded' if the evidence establishes some objective basis in reality for the fear. This would appear to mean that so long as the fear is not imaginary—i. e., if it is founded in reality at all—it is 'well founded.' A more moderate position is that so long as an objective situation is established by the evidence, it need not be shown that the situation will probably result in persecution, but it is enough that persecution is a reasonable possibility. . . .

The Court of Appeals' decision rests on the mistaken premise that every alien who qualifies as a 'refugee' under the statutory definition is also entitled to a withholding of deportation under § 243(h). We find no support for this conclusion in either the language of § 243(h), the structure of the amended Act, or the legislative history.

The judgment of the Court of Appeals is reversed, and the cause is remanded for further proceedings consistent with this opinion"

V. JUSTICE VOTE

0 Pro ACLU Side vs. 9 Con Opposing Side

Opposing Side (Petitioner / Appellant)

1. Stevens, J. – Wrote majority opinion
2. Brennan, W. – Joined majority opinion
3. Rehnquist, W. – Joined majority opinion
4. Burger, W. – Joined majority opinion
5. Powell, L. – Joined majority opinion
6. O'Connor, S. – Joined majority opinion
7. Blackmun, H. – Joined majority opinion
8. White, B. – Joined majority opinion
9. Marshall, T. – Joined majority opinion

VI. A WIN OR LOSS FOR THE ACLU?

The ACLU, as amicus curiae, urged affirmance of the judgment of the Second Circuit Court of Appeals; the Supreme Court reversed in a 9-0 vote, giving the ACLU an apparent loss.

543. Capital Cities Cable, Inc. v. Crisp

(Decided June 18, 1984; 467 U.S. 691)

I. ISSUE

A. Issues Discussed

First Amendment, freedoms of speech, association, and press, preemption

B. Legal Question Presented

"[W]hether Oklahoma may require cable television operators in that State to delete all advertisements for alcoholic beverages contained in the out-of-state signals that they retransmit by cable to their subscribers."

C. Supreme Court's Answer

Oklahoma may not require cable television operators in the State to delete all alcohol advertisements from out-of-state signals.

II. CASE SUMMARY

A. Background

"Since 1959, it has been lawful to sell and consume alcoholic beverages in Oklahoma. The State Constitution, however, . . . prohibits the advertising of such beverages, except by means of strictly regulated on-premises signs. For several years, pursuant to this authority, Oklahoma has prohibited television broadcasting stations in the State from broadcasting alcoholic beverage commercials as part of their locally produced programming and has required these stations to block out all such advertising carried on national network programming. At the same time, the Oklahoma Attorney General has ruled—principally because of the practical difficulties of enforcement—that the ban does not apply to alcoholic beverage advertisements appearing in newspapers, magazines, and other publications printed outside Oklahoma but sold and distributed in the State. Consequently, out-of-state publications may be delivered to Oklahoma subscribers and sold at retail outlets within the State, even though they contain advertisements for alcoholic beverages. Until 1980, Oklahoma applied a similar policy to cable television operators who were permitted to retransmit out-of-state signals containing alcoholic beverage commercials to their subscribers. In March of that year, however, the Oklahoma Attorney General issued an opinion in which he concluded that the retransmission of out-of-state alcoholic beverage commercials by cable television systems operating in the State would be considered a violation of the advertising ban. Respondent Crisp, Director of the Oklahoma Alcoholic Beverage Control Board, thereafter warned Oklahoma cable operators, including petitioners, that they would be criminally prosecuted if they continued to carry such out-of-state advertisements over their systems.

Petitioners, operators of several cable television systems in Oklahoma, filed this suit in March 1981 in the United States District Court for the Western District of Oklahoma, seeking declaratory and injunctive relief. They alleged that the Oklahoma policy violated the Commerce and Supremacy Clauses, the First and Fourteenth Amendments, and the Equal Protection Clause of the Fourteenth Amendment. Following an evidentiary hearing, the District Court granted petitioners a preliminary injunction and subsequently entered summary judgment and a permanent injunction in December 1981. . . . On appeal, the Court of Appeals for the Tenth Circuit reversed, holding that, while the wine commercials at issue were protected by the First Amendment, the state ban was a valid restriction on commercial speech."

The Supreme Court granted certiorari to review the case and reversed.

B. Counsel of Record / ACLU Attorney

ACLU Side (Petitioner / Appellant): Brent N. Rushforth argued the cause for appellant.

Michael W. McConnell argued the cause, pro hac vice, for the Federal Communications Commission, as amicus curiae, by special leave of Court.

Opposing Side (Respondent / Appellee): Robert L. McDonald, First Assistant Attorney General of Oklahoma, argued the cause for appellee.

III. AMICI CURIAE

ACLU Side (Petitioner / Appellant)

Brief of amici curiae filed on behalf of the ACLU, et al., by John G. Koeltl, James C. Goodale, Burt Neuborne, and Charles S. Sims.

Brief of amici curiae filed on behalf of the Federal Communications Commission by Michael W. McConnell, Solicitor General Lee, Deputy Solicitor General Bator, Richard G. Wilkins, Bruce E. Fein, and C. Grey Pash, Jr.

Additional briefs of amici curiae were filed on behalf of the National Association of Broadcasters, et al., the National Cable Television Association, Inc., et al., the American Newspaper Publishers Association, et al., the American Advertising Federation, et al., and the Turner Broadcasting System, Inc., et al.

Opposing Side (Respondent / Appellee)

Briefs of amici curiae filed on behalf of S.A.N.E., Inc. and the State of Mississippi.

IV. THE SUPREME COURT'S DECISION

"[A]pplication of Oklahoma's advertising ban to out-of-state signals carried by cable operators in that State is designed principally to further the State's interest in discouraging consumption of intoxicating liquor. . . . When this limited interest is measured against the significant interference with the federal objective of ensuring widespread availability of diverse cable services throughout the United States—an objective that will unquestionably be frustrated by strict enforcement of the Oklahoma statute—it is clear that the State's interest is not of the same stature as the goals identified in the FCC's rulings and regulations. As in Midcal Aluminum, therefore, we hold that when, as here, a state regulation squarely conflicts with the accomplishment and execution of the full purposes of federal law, and the State's central power under the Twenty-first Amendment of regulating the times, places, and manner under which liquor may be imported and sold is not directly implicated, the balance between state and federal power tips decisively in favor of the federal law, and enforcement of the state statute is barred by the Supremacy Clause. . . .

We conclude that the application of Oklahoma's alcoholic beverage advertising ban to out-of-state signals carried by cable operators in that State is pre-empted by federal law and that the Twenty-first Amendment does not save the regulation from pre-emption. The judgment of the Court of Appeals is reversed."

V. JUSTICE VOTE

9 Pro ACLU Side vs. 0 Con Opposing Side

ACLU Side (Petitioner / Appellant)

1. Brennan, W. – Wrote majority opinion
2. Marshall T. – Joined majority opinion
3. Burger, W. – Joined majority opinion
4. White, B. – Joined majority opinion
5. Powell, L. – Joined majority opinion
6. Rehnquist, W. – Joined majority opinion
7. O'Connor, S. – Joined majority opinion
8. Stevens, J. – Joined majority opinion
9. Blackmun, H. – Joined majority opinion

VI. A WIN OR LOSS FOR THE ACLU?

The ACLU filed as amicus curiae urging reversal; the Supreme Court reversed the judgment of the Court of Appeals in a 9-0 vote, giving the ACLU an apparent win.

544. Secretary of State of Maryland. v. Joseph H. Munson Co.

(Decided June 26, 1984; 467 U.S. 947)

I. ISSUE

A. Issues Discussed

First Amendment, freedom of speech, overbreadth

B. Legal Question Presented

"[W]hether a Maryland statute with a . . . percentage limitation [on charitable fundraising], but with provisions that render it more 'flexible' than the Schaumburg ordinance [previously held unconstitutional by the Supreme Court], can withstand constitutional attack."

C. Supreme Court's Answer

The statute is unconstitutionally overbroad.

II. CASE SUMMARY

A. Background

"Joseph H. Munson Co., Inc. (Munson), an Indiana corporation, instituted this action in the Circuit Court for Anne Arundel County, Md., seeking declaratory and injunctive relief against the Secretary of State of Maryland (Secretary). Munson is a professional for-profit fundraiser in the business of promoting fundraising events and giving advice to customers on how those events should be conducted. Its Maryland customers include various chapters of the Fraternal Order of Police (FOP).

Section 103A et seq. . . . concern[s] charitable organizations. Section 103D prohibits such an organization, in connection with any fundraising activity, from paying or agreeing to pay as expenses more than 25% of the amount raised. Munson in its complaint alleged that it regularly charges an FOP chapter an amount in excess of 25% of the gross raised for the event it promotes. Munson also alleged that the Secretary had informed it that it was subject to § 103D and would be prosecuted if it failed to comply with the provisions of that statute.

In its initial complaint, filed March 7, 1978, Munson took the position that its contracts with the FOP should not be subject to § 103A et seq. The Circuit Court dismissed that challenge for failure to exhaust administrative remedies. The court concluded, however, that Munson could attack the statutes as an improper delegation of legislative authority, in violation of the Maryland Constitution. Munson then amended its complaint to allege that the statutes effected an unconstitutional infringement on its right to free speech and assembly under the First and Fourteenth Amendments of the United States Constitution.

The Secretary questioned Munson's standing to assert its claims. He urged that § 103D is directed to acts of charitable organizations and, therefore, that only an organization of that kind can challenge the statute's constitutionality. . . .

The Circuit Court did not address the standing argument, but upheld the statute on the merits. . . .

Munson appealed to the Court of Special Appeals of Maryland. The Secretary did not take a cross-appeal. The Court of Special Appeals affirmed the judgment of the Circuit Court.

Both Munson and the Secretary then petitioned the Court of Appeals of Maryland for writs of certiorari. Munson challenged the validity of the statute and the Secretary challenged Munson's standing. The court granted both petitions and, by a unanimous vote, reversed the judgment of the Court of Special Appeals. . . .

On the merits, the court concluded that Schaumburg required that the Maryland statute be ruled unconstitutional."

The Supreme Court granted certiorari to review the case and affirmed.

B. Counsel of Record / ACLU Attorney

ACLU Side (Respondent / Appellee): Yale L. Goldberg argued the cause for appellee.

Opposing Side (Petitioner / Appellant): Diana G. Motz, Assistant Attorney General of Maryland, argued the cause for appellant.

III. AMICI CURIAE

ACLU Side (Respondent / Appellee)

Brief of amici curiae filed on behalf of the ACLU, et al., by Robert B. Hummel, Thomas J. McGrew, Charles S. Sims, and Arthur B. Spitzer.

Brief of amici curiae filed on behalf of Independent Sector, et al., by Adam Yarmolinsky, Stephen T. Owen, and Michael B. Jennison.

Brief of amici curiae filed on behalf of Box Office, Inc., by Barry A. Fisher, Robert C. Moest, and David Grosz.

Opposing Side (Petitioner / Appellant)

Brief of amici curiae filed on behalf of the State of Connecticut, et al., by Francis X. Bellotti, Attorney General of Massachusetts, and Catharine W. Hantzis, Leslie G. Espinoza, and Dana L. Mason, Assistant Attorneys General, Joseph I. Lieberman, Attorney General of Connecticut, Neil F. Hartigan, Attorney General of Illinois, Robert T. Stephan, Attorney General of Kansas, Irwin I. Kimmelman, Attorney General of New Jersey, Robert Abrams, Attorney General of New York, LeRoy S. Zimmerman, Attorney General of Pennsylvania, Mark Meierhenry, Attorney General of South Dakota, and William M. Leech, Jr., Attorney General of Tennessee.

IV. THE SUPREME COURT'S DECISION

"The Court in Schaumburg determined first that charitable solicitations are so intertwined with speech that they are entitled to the protections of the First Amendment . . . .

Because the percentage limitation restricted the ways in which charities might engage in solicitation activity, the Court concluded that it was a 'direct and substantial limitation on protected activity that cannot be sustained unless it serves a sufficiently strong, subordinating interest that the Village is entitled to protect.' In addition, in order to be valid, the limitation would have to be a 'narrowly drawn regulatio[n] designed to serve [the] interes[t] without unnecessarily interfering with First Amendment freedoms.'

Although the Court in Schaumburg recognized that the Village had legitimate interests in protecting the public from fraud, crime, and undue annoyance, it rejected the limitation because it was not a precisely tailored means of accommodating those interests. . . .

Schaumburg left open the primary question now before this Court—whether the constitutional deficiencies in a percentage limitation on funds expended in solicitation are remedied by the possibility of an administrative waiver of the limitation for a charity that can demonstrate financial necessity. . . .

The Secretary urges that even though there may remain charities whose First Amendment activity is limited by the statute, we should not strike down the statute on its face because, with the waiver provision, it no longer is 'substantially overbroad.' We are not persuaded. . . . While there no doubt are organizations that have high fundraising costs not due to protected First Amendment activity and that, therefore, should not be heard to complain that their activities are prohibited, this statute cannot distinguish those organizations from charities that have high costs due to protected First Amendment activities. The flaw in the statute is not simply that it includes within its sweep some impermissible applications, but that in all its applications it operates on a fundamentally mistaken premise that high solicitation costs are an accurate measure of fraud. That the statute in some of its applications actually prevents the misdirection of funds from the organization's purported charitable goal is little more than fortuitous. It is equally likely that the statute will restrict First Amendment activity that results in high costs but is itself a part of the charity's goal or that is simply attributable to the fact that the charity's cause proves to be unpopular. On the other hand, if an organization indulges in fraud, there is nothing in the percentage limitation that prevents it from misdirecting funds. In either event, the percentage limitation, though restricting solicitation costs, will have done nothing to prevent fraud. . . .

The possibility of a waiver may decrease the number of impermissible applications of the statute, but it does nothing to remedy the statute's fundamental defect. We conclude that, regardless of the waiver provision, Schaumburg requires that the percentage limitation in the Maryland statute be rejected. . . .

We agree with the Court of Appeals of Maryland that § 103D is unconstitutionally overbroad. The judgment of that court therefore is affirmed."

V. JUSTICE VOTE

5 Pro ACLU Side vs. 4 Con Opposing Side

ACLU Side (Respondent / Appellee)

1. Blackmun, H. – Wrote majority opinion
2. Brennan, W. – Joined majority opinion
3. White, B. – Joined majority opinion
4. Marshall T. – Joined majority opinion
5. Stevens, J. – Wrote concurring opinion

Opposing Side (Petitioner / Appellant)

1. Rehnquist, W. – Wrote dissenting opinion
2. Burger, W. – Joined Rehnquist's dissent
3. Powell, L. – Joined Rehnquist's dissent
4. O'Connor, S. – Joined Rehnquist's dissent

VI. A WIN OR LOSS FOR THE ACLU?

The ACLU, as amicus curiae, urged affirmance of the judgment of the Maryland Court of Appeals; the Supreme Court affirmed in a 5-4 vote, giving the ACLU an apparent win.

545. Burnett v. Grattan

(Decided June 27, 1984; 468 U.S. 42)

I. ISSUE

A. Issues Discussed

Civil rights, race, liability, Civil Rights Act

B. Legal Question Presented

"[W]hether a state law, establishing a procedure for administrative resolution of employment discrimination complaints, provides an appropriate statute of limitations for actions brought under the Reconstruction–Era Civil Rights Acts."

C. Supreme Court's Answer

The state law statute of limitations for administrative actions is inappropriate for actions brought under the Civil Rights Act.

II. CASE SUMMARY

A. Background

"Respondents James Grattan and Adrienne Hedman were employees of Coppin State College, a predominantly [black] college in Maryland. Their primary responsibility was to recruit students of diverse ethnic backgrounds to attend the school. Respondents received notice in June 1976 that their contracts would not be renewed because the college 'was not satisfied with the recruitment efforts of the Minority Affairs office.' In response, respondents, who are white, filed complaints of racial discrimination with the federal Equal Employment Opportunity Commission. While those claims were pending, they filed suit in state court in February 1977 . . . . In October 1981, on leave of the court, respondents filed an amended complaint, specifically alleging that they were victims of racial discrimination, and, in Hedman's case, gender discrimination, in violation of 42 U.S.C. §§ 1981, 1983, 1985, 1986, and the Equal Protection Clause of the Fourteenth Amendment, and that their discharge also violated the First Amendment and various provisions of the Maryland Constitution. Petitioners removed the action from state to federal court. Thereafter, they filed a motion to dismiss on the ground that respondents' claims were barred by the applicable statute of limitations.

Because the federal statutes under which respondents sued do not themselves contain a statute of limitations, the District Court borrowed a limitations period from a state statute prohibiting discriminatory practices in employment. . . . Because Respondents' complaint had been filed more than six months after their cause of action accrued, the District Court dismissed the suit as time-barred.

The Court of Appeals for the Fourth Circuit . . . found the 6–month period selected by the District Court inappropriate for suits brought under the Civil Rights Acts because the state law 'governed the limitation of administrative proceedings which were informal, investigatory and conciliatory in nature.' The Court of Appeals applied Maryland's 3–year statute of limitations for all civil actions for which the Code does not otherwise provide a limitations period. [T]he Court of Appeals held that the action was not time-barred, and remanded to the District Court."

The Supreme Court granted certiorari to review the case and affirmed.

B. Counsel of Record / ACLU Attorney

ACLU Side (Respondent / Appellee): Sheldon H. Laskin argued the cause for appellee.

Opposing Side (Petitioner / Appellant): Paul F. Strain, Deputy Attorney General of Maryland, argued the cause for appellant.

III. AMICI CURIAE

ACLU Side (Respondent / Appellee)

Brief of amici curiae filed on behalf of the ACLU by Leon Friedman, Charles S. Sims, and Burt Neuborne.

Opposing Side (Petitioner / Appellant)

Brief of amici curiae filed on behalf of the League of Kansas Municipalities by Neil R. Shortlidge.

IV. THE SUPREME COURT'S DECISION

"In the Civil Rights Acts, Congress established causes of action arising out of rights and duties under the Constitution and federal statutes. These causes of action exist independent of any other legal or administrative relief that may be available as a matter of federal or state law. . . . An appropriate limitations period must be responsive to these characteristics of litigation under the federal statutes. A state law is not 'appropriate' if it fails to take into account practicalities that are involved in litigating federal civil rights claims and policies that are analogous to the goals of the Civil Rights Acts.

Applying these criteria for disqualifying a particular state law, we begin with the observation that borrowing an administrative statute of limitations ignores the dominant characteristic of civil rights actions: they belong in court. Assuring the full availability of a judicial forum necessitates attention to the practicalities of litigation. . . . The practical difficulties facing an aggrieved person who invokes administrative remedies are strikingly different. . . .

The divergence between the goals of the federal civil rights statutes and of the state employment discrimination administrative statute is clear in the present case. The goals of the federal statutes are compensation of persons whose civil rights have been violated, and prevention of the abuse of state power. That these are not the goals of the statute empowering Maryland's administrative agency to resolve employment discrimination complaints is apparent both because the remedial authority of the agency is limited, and because the state scheme does not create a private right of action. The stated goal of the state administrative procedure is the prompt identification and resolution of employment disputes. The administrative scheme, including a short statute of limitations, encourages conciliation and private settlement through the agency's intervention in live disputes. . . .

In sum, the Court of Appeals properly applied the tests established by our prior cases for determining whether a particular state statute of limitations should control a suit brought under the Civil Rights Acts. Both the practical differences between the administrative proceeding contemplated by the Maryland statute and a civil action in a federal court, and the divergence in the objectives of the state administrative procedure to resolve employment discrimination suits and a federal cause of action to vindicate constitutional rights, lead us to conclude that borrowing the limitations period from Maryland's Article 49B was inappropriate. The judgment of the Court of Appeals is therefore affirmed."

V. JUSTICE VOTE

9 Pro ACLU Side vs. 0 Con Opposing Side

ACLU Side (Respondent / Appellee)

1. Marshall, T. – Wrote majority opinion
2. Brennan, W. – Joined majority opinion
3. White, B. – Joined majority opinion
4. Stevens, J. – Joined majority opinion
5. Blackmun, H. – Joined majority opinion
6. Powell, L. – Wrote concurring opinion
7. Rehnquist, W. – Wrote concurring opinion
8. Burger, W. – Joined Rehnquist's concurrence
9. O'Connor, S. – Joined Rehnquist's concurrence

VI. A WIN OR LOSS FOR THE ACLU?

The ACLU filed as amicus curiae urging affirmance; the Supreme Court affirmed the judgment of the Court of Appeals in a 9-0 vote, giving the ACLU an apparent win.

546. Davis v. Scherer

(Decided June 28, 1984; 468 U.S. 183)

I. ISSUE

A. Issues Discussed

Civil rights, qualified immunity, employment

B. Legal Question Presented

Whether "a state official loses his qualified immunity from suit for deprivation of federal constitutional rights if he is found to have violated the clear command of a state administrative regulation."

C. Supreme Court's Answer

The state officials did not lose qualified immunity here where rights were not clearly established at the time of the alleged violation.

II. CASE SUMMARY

A. Background

"The present controversy arose when appellee Gregory Scherer, who was employed by the Florida Highway Patrol as a radio-teletype operator, applied for permission from the Patrol to work as well for the Escambia County Sheriff's Office as a reserve deputy. To avoid conflicts of interest, an order of the Florida Department of Highway Safety and Motor Vehicles required that proposed outside employment of Patrol members be approved by the Department. A letter from appellee's troop commander, Capt. K.S. Sconiers, dated September 1, 1977, granted appellee permission to accept the part-time work. The letter noted that permission would be rescinded 'should [the] employment interfere . . . with your duties with [the] department.' Later that month, Capt. Sconiers informed appellee by memorandum that permission to accept the employment was revoked. As Capt. Sconiers explained at trial, his superiors in the Highway Patrol had determined that appellee's reserve deputy duties could conflict with his duties at the Highway Patrol.

Appellee continued to work at the second job, despite the revocation of permission." Various discussions and letters back and forth led to appellee's dismissal because of his refusal to quit the second job. Subsequently, "appellee filed an appeal with the Florida Career Service Commission. Before the Commission had heard appellee's administrative appeal from his dismissal, appellee and the Department settled the dispute. The settlement reinstated appellee with backpay. But friction between appellee and his superiors continued, and in January 1979, after appellee was suspended from the Patrol, he resigned 'to avoid further harassment and to remove a cloud over his employability.'

Appellee then filed the present suit against appellants in the United States District Court for the Northern District of Florida, seeking relief under 42 U.S.C. § 1983. Appellee's complaint alleged that appellants in 1977 had violated the Due Process Clause of the Fourteenth Amendment by discharging appellee from his job without a formal pretermination or a prompt post-termination hearing. Appellee requested a declaration that his rights had been violated and an award of money damages.

The District Court granted the requested relief for violation of appellee's Fourteenth Amendment rights. . . .

Five days after entry of the District Court's order, the Court of Appeals for the Fifth Circuit decided Weisbrod v. Donigan, 651 F.2d 334 (1981). The Court of Appeals there held that Florida officials in 1978 had violated no well-established due process rights in discharging a permanent state employee without a pretermination or a prompt post-termination hearing. On motion for reconsideration, the District Court found that Weisbrod required it to vacate its prior holding that appellants had forfeited their immunity by violating appellee's clearly established constitutional rights. The court nevertheless reaffirmed its award of monetary damages. . . .

The Court of Appeals affirmed on the basis of the District Court's opinion. [The Supreme Court] noted probable jurisdiction to consider whether the Court of Appeals properly had declared the Florida statute unconstitutional and denied appellants' claim of qualified immunity."

The Supreme Court granted certiorari to review the case and reversed.

B. Counsel of Record / ACLU Attorney

ACLU Side (Respondent / Appellee): Bruce S. Rogow argued the cause for appellee.

Opposing Side (Petitioner / Appellant): Mitchell D. Franks argued the cause for appellant.

Richard G. Wilkins argued the cause for the United States, as amicus curiae, by special leave of Court.

III. AMICI CURIAE

ACLU Side (Respondent / Appellee)

Brief of amici curiae filed on behalf of the ACLU by Michael S. Helfer, Burt Neuborne, and Charles S. Sims.

Opposing Side (Petitioner / Appellant)

Brief of amici curiae filed on behalf of the United States by Richard G. Wilkins, Solicitor General Lee, Acting Assistant Attorney General Willard, Deputy Solicitor General Geller, Barbara L. Herwig, and John F. Cordes.

IV. THE SUPREME COURT'S DECISION

A. "We acknowledge of course that officials should conform their conduct to applicable statutes and regulations. For that reason, it is an appealing proposition that the violation of such provisions is a circumstance relevant to the official's claim of qualified immunity. But in determining what circumstances a court may consider in deciding claims of qualified immunity, we choose 'between the evils inevitable in any available alternative.' Appellee's submission, if adopted, would disrupt the balance that our cases strike between the interests in vindication of citizens' constitutional rights and in public officials' effective performance of their duties. The qualified immunity doctrine recognizes that officials can act without fear of harassing litigation only if they reasonably can anticipate when their conduct may give rise to liability for damages and only if unjustified lawsuits are quickly terminated.

[It is not] always fair, or sound policy, to demand official compliance with statute and regulation on pain of money damages. Such officials as police officers or prison wardens, to say nothing of higher level executives who enjoy only qualified immunity, routinely make close decisions in the exercise of the broad authority that necessarily is delegated to them. These officials are subject to a plethora of rules, 'often so voluminous, ambiguous, and contradictory, and in such flux that officials can only comply with or enforce them selectively.' In these circumstances, officials should not err always on the side of caution. '[O]fficials with a broad range of duties and authority must often act swiftly and firmly at the risk that action deferred will be futile or constitute virtual abdication of office.' . . .

A plaintiff who seeks damages for violation of constitutional or statutory rights may overcome the defendant official's qualified immunity only by showing that those rights were clearly established at the time of the conduct at issue. As appellee has made no such showing, the judgment of the Court of Appeals is reversed, and the case is remanded for proceedings consistent with this opinion."

V. JUSTICE VOTE

4 Pro ACLU Side vs. 5 Con Opposing Side

ACLU Side (Respondent / Appellee)

1. Brennan, W. – Wrote opinion concurring in part and dissenting in part
2. Marshall T. – Joined Brennan's opinion
3. Blackmun, H. – Joined Brennan's opinion
4. Stevens, J. – Joined Brennan's opinion

Opposing Side (Petitioner / Appellant)

1. Powell, L. – Wrote majority opinion
2. Burger, W. – Joined majority opinion
3. White, B. – Joined majority opinion
4. Rehnquist, W. – Joined majority opinion
5. O'Connor, S. – Joined majority opinion

VI. A WIN OR LOSS FOR THE ACLU?

The ACLU filed as amicus curiae urging affirmance; the Supreme Court reversed the ruling of the Court of Appeals in a 5-4 vote giving the ACLU an apparent loss.

547. Clark v. Community for Creative Non-Violence

(Decided June 29, 1984; 468 U.S. 288)

I. ISSUE

A. Issues Discussed

First Amendment, freedom of speech

B. Legal Question Presented

"[W]hether a National Park Service regulation prohibiting camping in certain parks violates the First Amendment when applied to prohibit demonstrators from sleeping in Lafayette Park and the Mall in connection with a demonstration intended to call attention to the plight of the homeless."

C. Supreme Court's Answer

The regulation does not violate the First Amendment when applied to prohibit the demonstrators from sleeping in Lafayette Park and the Mall.

II. CASE SUMMARY

A. Background

"The Interior Department, through the National Park Service, is charged with responsibility for the management and maintenance of the National Parks and is authorized to promulgate rules and regulations for the use of the parks in accordance with the purposes for which they were established. The network of National Parks includes the National Memorial-core parks, Lafayette Park and the Mall, which are set in the heart of Washington, D.C., and which are unique resources that the Federal Government holds in trust for the American people. . . .

Under the regulations involved in this case, camping in National Parks is permitted only in campgrounds designated for that purpose. No such campgrounds have ever been designated in Lafayette Park or the Mall. . . .

Demonstrations for the airing of views or grievances are permitted in the Memorial-core parks, but for the most part only by Park Service permits. Temporary structures may be erected for demonstration purposes but may not be used for camping.

In 1982, the Park Service issued a renewable permit to respondent Community for Creative Non-Violence (CCNV) to conduct a wintertime demonstration in Lafayette Park and the Mall for the purpose of demonstrating the plight of the homeless. The permit authorized the erection of two symbolic tent cities: 20 tents in Lafayette Park that would accommodate 50 people and 40 tents in the Mall with a capacity of up to 100. The Park Service, however, relying on the above regulations, specifically denied CCNV's request that demonstrators be permitted to sleep in the symbolic tents.

CCNV and several individuals then filed an action to prevent the application of the no-camping regulations to the proposed demonstration, which, it was claimed, was not covered by the regulation. It was also submitted that the regulations were unconstitutionally vague, had been discriminatorily applied, and could not be applied to prevent sleeping in the tents without violating the First Amendment. The District Court granted summary judgment in favor of the Park Service. The Court of Appeals, sitting en banc, reversed. The 11 judges produced 6 opinions. Six of the judges believed that application of the regulations so as to prevent sleeping in the tents would infringe the demonstrators' First Amendment right of free expression. The other five judges disagreed and would have sustained the regulations as applied to CCNV's proposed demonstration."

The Supreme Court granted certiorari to review the case and reversed.

B. Counsel of Record / ACLU Attorney

ACLU Side (Respondent / Appellee): Burt Neuborne argued the cause for appellee. With him on the brief were Charles S. Sims, Laura Macklin, Arthur B. Spitzer, and Elizabeth Symonds.

Opposing Side (Petitioner / Appellant): Deputy Solicitor General Bator argued the cause for appellant. With him on the briefs were Solicitor General Lee, Assistant Attorney General McGrath, Alan I. Horowitz, Leonard Schaitman, and Katherine S. Gruenheck.

III. AMICI CURIAE

ACLU Side (Respondent / Appellee)

Brief of amici curiae filed on behalf of the National Coalition for the Homeless by Ogden Northrop Lewis.

Opposing Side (Petitioner / Appellant)

No briefs of amici curiae were filed in support of appellant.

IV. THE SUPREME COURT'S DECISION

"We need not differ with the view of the Court of Appeals that overnight sleeping in connection with the demonstration is expressive conduct protected to some extent by the First Amendment. . . . Expression, whether oral or written or symbolized by conduct, is subject to reasonable time, place, or manner restrictions. We have often noted that restrictions of this kind are valid provided that they are justified without reference to the content of the regulated speech, that they are narrowly tailored to serve a significant governmental interest, and that they leave open ample alternative channels for communication of the information.

It is also true that a message may be delivered by conduct that is intended to be communicative and that, in context, would reasonably be understood by the viewer to be communicative. Symbolic expression of this kind may be forbidden or regulated if the conduct itself may constitutionally be regulated, if the regulation is narrowly drawn to further a substantial governmental interest, and if the interest is unrelated to the suppression of free speech.

Petitioners submit, as they did in the Court of Appeals, that the regulation forbidding sleeping is defensible either as a time, place, or manner restriction or as a regulation of symbolic conduct. We agree with that assessment. . . . That sleeping, like the symbolic tents themselves, may be expressive and part of the message delivered by the demonstration does not make the ban any less a limitation on the manner of demonstrating, for reasonable time, place, or manner regulations normally have the purpose and direct effect of limiting expression but are nevertheless valid. Neither does the fact that sleeping, arguendo, may be expressive conduct, rather than oral or written expression, render the sleeping prohibition any less a time, place, or manner regulation. To the contrary, the Park Service neither attempts to ban sleeping generally nor to ban it everywhere in the parks. It has established areas for camping and forbids it elsewhere, including Lafayette Park and the Mall. Considered as such, we have very little trouble concluding that the Park Service may prohibit overnight sleeping in the parks involved here.

The requirement that the regulation be content-neutral is clearly satisfied. The courts below accepted that view, and it is not disputed here that the prohibition on camping, and on sleeping specifically, is content-neutral and is not being applied because of disagreement with the message presented. Neither was the regulation faulted, nor could it be, on the ground that without overnight sleeping the plight of the homeless could not be communicated in other ways. The regulation otherwise left the demonstration intact, with its symbolic city, signs, and the presence of those who were willing to take their turns in a day-and-night vigil.

Respondents do not suggest that there was, or is, any barrier to delivering to the media, or to the public by other means, the intended message concerning the plight of the homeless.

It is also apparent to us that the regulation narrowly focuses on the Government's substantial interest in maintaining the parks in the heart of our Capital in an attractive and intact condition, readily available to the millions of people who wish to see and enjoy them by their presence. . . .

We are unmoved by the Court of Appeals' view that the challenged regulation is unnecessary, and hence invalid, because there are less speech-restrictive alternatives that could have satisfied the Government interest in preserving park lands. . . . We do not believe . . . that either United States v. O'Brien or the time, place, or manner decisions assign to the judiciary the authority to replace the Park Service as the manager of the Nation's parks or endow the judiciary with the competence to judge how much protection of park lands is wise and how that level of conservation is to be attained.

Accordingly, the judgment of the Court of Appeals is reversed."

V. JUSTICE VOTE

2 Pro ACLU Side vs. 7 Con Opposing Side

ACLU Side (Respondent / Appellee)

1. Marshall T. – Wrote dissenting opinion
2. Brennan, W. – Joined Marshall's dissent

Opposing Side (Petitioner / Appellant)

1. White, B. – Wrote majority opinion
2. Burger, W. – Wrote concurring opinion
3. Blackmun, H. – Joined majority opinion
4. Powell, L. – Joined majority opinion
5. Rehnquist, W. – Joined majority opinion
6. Stevens, J. – Joined majority opinion
7. O'Connor, S. – Joined majority opinion

VI. A WIN OR LOSS FOR THE ACLU?

The ACLU, as counsel, urged affirmance of the judgment of the Court of Appeals; the Supreme Court reversed in a 7-2 vote, giving the ACLU an apparent loss.

548. Hobby v. United States

(Decided July 2, 1984; 468 U.S. 339)

I. ISSUE

A. Issues Discussed

Fifth Amendment, due process, jury selection

B. Legal Question Presented

"[W]hether discrimination in the selection of federal grand jury foremen, resulting in the underrepresentation of Negroes and women in that position, requires reversal of the conviction of a white male defendant and dismissal of the indictment against him."

C. Supreme Court's Answer

The alleged discrimination does not require reversal of the conviction or dismissal of the indictment.

II. CASE SUMMARY

A. Background

"Petitioner, a white male, was indicted on one count of conspiring to defraud the United States of funds appropriated under the Comprehensive Employment and Training Act of 1973 . . . . Prior to trial in the United States District Court for the Eastern District of North Carolina, petitioner moved for dismissal of the indictment against him 'due to improper selection of grand jurors.' In particular, he alleged that the grand jury selection plan 'exclude[d] citizens from service . . . on account of race, color, economic status and occupation, in violation of . . . the Fifth and Sixth Amendments of the United States Constitution.'

At an evidentiary hearing on the motion to dismiss, petitioner introduced the testimony of a statistical social science consultant regarding the characteristics of the persons selected as grand jury foremen or deputy foremen in the Eastern District of North Carolina between 1974 and 1981. The expert witness reported that none of the 15 grand juries empaneled during this 7-year period had had a Negro or female foreman. Of the 15 deputies appointed during this interval, so this expert testified, had been Negroes and had been women. From these data the expert witness concluded that Negroes and women were underrepresented among grand jury foremen and deputy foremen serving in the Eastern District of North Carolina. Rejecting petitioner's claim of discrimination in the selection process, the District Court denied petitioner's motion to dismiss the indictment, and petitioner was convicted after a jury trial.

The United States Court of Appeals for the Fourth Circuit affirmed."

The Supreme Court granted certiorari to review the case and affirmed the judgment of the Fourth Circuit Court of Appeals.

B. Counsel of Record / ACLU Attorney

ACLU Side (Petitioner / Appellant): Daniel H. Pollitt argued the cause for appellant.

Opposing Side (Respondent / Appellee): Joshua I. Schwartz argued the cause for the United States.

III. AMICI CURIAE

ACLU Side (Petitioner / Appellant)

Brief of amici curiae filed on behalf of the ACLU, et al., by William Van Alstyne, Sara Sun Beale, Burt Neuborne, and Charles S. Sims.

Brief of amici curiae filed on behalf of the NAACP Legal Defense and Educational Fund, Inc., by Jack Greenberg, James M. Nabrit III, and Charles Stephen Ralston.

Opposing Side (Respondent / Appellee)

No briefs of amici curiae were filed in support of appellee.

IV. THE SUPREME COURT'S DECISION

"Discrimination in the selection of grand jury foremen—as distinguished from discrimination in the selection of the grand jury itself—does not in any sense threaten the interests of the defendant protected by the Due Process Clause. Unlike the grand jury itself, the office of grand jury foreman is not a creature of the Constitution; instead, the post of foreman was originally instituted by statute for the convenience of the court. . . .

Only by setting aside his conviction and dismissing the indictment against him, petitioner urges, will this Court deter future purposeful exclusion of minorities and women from the post of federal grand jury foreman. . . . However, we decline petitioner's invitation to embark upon the course of vacating criminal convictions because of discrimination in the selection of foremen. Less Draconian measures will suffice to rectify the problem.

In no sense do we countenance a purposeful exclusion of minorities or women from appointment as foremen of federal grand juries. We are fully satisfied that the district judges charged with the appointment of grand jury foremen will see to it that no citizen is excluded from consideration for service in that position on account of race, color, religion, sex, national origin, or economic status. . . .

We hold that, assuming discrimination entered into the selection of federal grand jury foremen, such discrimination does not warrant the reversal of the conviction of, and dismissal of the indictment against, a white male bringing a claim under the Due Process Clause. Accordingly, the judgment of the United States Court of Appeals for the Fourth Circuit is affirmed."

V. JUSTICE VOTE

3 Pro ACLU Side vs. 6 Con Opposing Side

ACLU Side (Petitioner / Appellant)

1. Marshall, T. – Wrote dissenting opinion
2. Brennan, W. – Joined Marshall's dissent
3. Stevens, J. – Wrote dissenting opinion, joined Marshall's dissent

Opposing Side (Respondent / Appellee)

1. Burger, W. – Wrote majority opinion
2. White, B. – Joined majority opinion
3. Blackmun, H. – Joined majority opinion
4. Powell, L. – Joined majority opinion
5. Rehnquist, W. – Joined majority opinion
6. O'Connor, S. – Joined majority opinion

VI. A WIN OR LOSS FOR THE ACLU?

The ACLU, as amicus curiae, urged reversal of the judgment of the Fourth Circuit Court of Appeals; the Supreme Court affirmed in a 6-3 vote, giving the ACLU an apparent loss.

549. FCC v. League of Women Voters

(Decided July 2, 1984; 468 U.S. 364)

I. ISSUE

A. Issues Discussed

First Amendment, freedoms of press, speech, and association

B. Legal Question Presented

"[W]hether Congress, by imposing [a] restriction [which prohibits editorializing in 'noncommercial educational broadcasting'], has passed a "law ... abridging the freedom of speech, or of the press" in violation of the First Amendment of the Constitution."

C. Supreme Court's Answer

The restriction violates the First Amendment.

II. CASE SUMMARY

A. Background

"Congress set out in 1967 to support and promote the development of noncommercial, educational broadcasting stations. A keystone of Congress' program was the Public Broadcasting Act of 1967, . . . which established the Corporation for Public Broadcasting, a nonprofit corporation authorized to disburse federal funds to noncommercial television and radio stations in support of station operations and educational programming. Section 399 of that Act, as amended by the Public Broadcasting Amendments Act of 1981, . . . forbids any 'noncommercial educational broadcasting station which receives a grant from the Corporation' to 'engage in editorializing.'

Appellee Pacifica Foundation is a nonprofit corporation that owns and operates several noncommercial educational broadcasting stations in five major metropolitan areas. Its licensees have received and are presently receiving grants from the Corporation and are therefore prohibited from editorializing by the terms of § 399, as originally enacted and as recently amended. In April 1979, appellees brought this suit in the United States District Court for the Central District of California challenging the constitutionality of former § 399.

[After an initial decision in the case that was subsequently vacated, the] District Court granted summary judgment in favor of appellees, holding that § 399's ban on editorializing violated the First Amendment."

The Supreme Court granted certiorari to review the case and affirmed.

B. Counsel of Record / ACLU Attorney

ACLU Side (Respondent / Appellee): Frederic D. Woocher argued the cause for appellee.

Opposing Side (Petitioner / Appellant): Samuel A. Alito, Jr., argued the cause for appellant.

III. AMICI CURIAE

ACLU Side (Respondent / Appellee)

Brief of amici curiae filed on behalf of the ACLU by Burt Neuborne and Charles S. Sims.

Brief of amici curiae filed on behalf of CBS, Inc., et al., by J. Roger Wollenberg, Timothy B. Dyk, Erwin G. Krasnow, and J. Laurent Scharff.

Brief of amici curiae filed on behalf of the National Black Media Coalition by Charles M. Firestone.

Brief of amici curiae filed on behalf of the Public Broadcasting Service, et al., by Lawrence A. Horn, Nancy H. Hendry, and Theodore D. Frank.

Opposing Side (Petitioner / Appellant)

Brief of amici curiae filed on behalf of Mobil Corporation by Larry S. Solomon.

IV. THE SUPREME COURT'S DECISION

"[A]lthough the Government's interest in ensuring balanced coverage of public issues is plainly both important and substantial, we have, at the same time, made clear that broadcasters are engaged in a vital and independent form of communicative activity. As a result, the First Amendment must inform and give shape to the manner in which Congress exercises its regulatory power in this area.

[T]he restriction imposed by § 399 is specifically directed at a form of speech—namely, the expression of editorial opinion—that lies at the heart of First Amendment protection. . . . Section 399 . . . singles out noncommercial broadcasters and denies them the right to address their chosen audience on matters of public importance. . . . The regulation impermissibly sweeps within its prohibition a wide range of speech by wholly private stations on topics that do not take a directly partisan stand or that have nothing whatever to do with federal, state, or local government. . . .

The patent overinclusiveness and underinclusiveness of § 399's ban 'undermines the likelihood of a genuine [governmental] interest' in preventing private groups from propagating their own views via public broadcasting. . . .

In conclusion, we emphasize that our disposition of this case rests upon a narrow proposition. We do not hold that the Congress or the FCC is without power to regulate the content, timing, or character of speech by noncommercial educational broadcasting stations. Rather, we hold only that the specific interests sought to be advanced by § 399's ban on editorializing are either not sufficiently substantial or are not served in a sufficiently limited manner to justify the substantial abridgment of important journalistic freedoms which the First Amendment jealously protects.

Accordingly, the judgment of the District Court is affirmed."

V. JUSTICE VOTE

5 Pro ACLU Side vs. 4 Con Opposing Side

ACLU Side (Respondent / Appellee)

1. Brennan, W. – Wrote majority opinion
2. Blackmun, H. – Joined majority opinion
3. O'Connor, S. – Joined majority opinion
4. Powell, L. – Joined majority opinion
5. Marshall T. – Joined majority opinion

Opposing Side (Petitioner / Appellant)

1. Rehnquist, W. – Wrote dissenting opinion
2. Burger, W. – Joined Rehnquist's dissent
3. White, B. – Wrote dissenting opinion, joined Rehnquist's dissent
4. Stevens, J. – Wrote dissenting opinion

VI. A WIN OR LOSS FOR THE ACLU?

The ACLU filed as amicus curiae urging affirmance; the Supreme Court affirmed the judgment of the District Court in a 5-4 vote, giving the ACLU an apparent win.

550. Berkemer v. McCarty

(Decided July 2, 1984; 468 U.S. 420)

I. ISSUE

A. Issues Discussed

Criminal procedure, right to remain silent, right to counsel, custodial interrogation

B. Legal Question Presented

"First, does our decision in Miranda v. Arizona, 384 U.S. 436 (1966), govern the admissibility of statements made during custodial interrogation by a suspect accused of a misdemeanor traffic offense? Second, does the roadside questioning of a motorist detained pursuant to a traffic stop constitute custodial interrogation for the purposes of the doctrine enunciated in Miranda?"

C. Supreme Court's Answer

Miranda governs the admissibility of statements made during custodial interrogation by a suspect accused of a misdemeanor traffic offense. Roadside questioning of a motorist detained pursuant to a traffic stop is not custodial interrogation for the purposes of Miranda.

II. CASE SUMMARY

A. Background

"On the evening of March 31, 1980, Trooper Williams of the Ohio State Highway Patrol observed respondent's car weaving in and out of a lane on Interstate Highway 270. After following the car for two miles, Williams forced respondent to stop and asked him to get out of the vehicle. When respondent complied, Williams noticed that he was having difficulty standing. At that point, 'Williams concluded that [respondent] would be charged with a traffic offense and, therefore, his freedom to leave the scene was terminated.' However, respondent was not told that he would be taken into custody. Williams then asked respondent to perform a field sobriety test, commonly known as a 'balancing test.' Respondent could not do so without falling.

While still at the scene of the traffic stop, Williams asked respondent whether he had been using intoxicants. Respondent replied that 'he had consumed two beers and had smoked several joints of marijuana a short time before.' Respondent's speech was slurred, and Williams had difficulty understanding him. Williams thereupon formally placed respondent under arrest and transported him in the patrol car to the Franklin County Jail.

At the jail, respondent was given an intoxilyzer test to determine the concentration of alcohol in his blood. The test did not detect any alcohol whatsoever in respondent's system. Williams then resumed questioning respondent in order to obtain information for inclusion in the State Highway Patrol Alcohol Influence Report. Respondent answered affirmatively a question whether he had been drinking. When then asked if he was under the influence of alcohol, he said, 'I guess, barely.' Williams next asked respondent to indicate on the form whether the marihuana he had smoked had been treated with any chemicals. In the section of the report headed 'Remarks,' respondent wrote, 'No ang[el] dust or PCP in the pot. Rick McCarty.'

At no point in this sequence of events did Williams or anyone else tell respondent that he had a right to remain silent, to consult with an attorney, and to have an attorney appointed for him if he could not afford one. . . .

Respondent was charged with operating a motor vehicle while under the influence of alcohol and/or drugs . . . . Respondent moved to exclude the various incriminating statements he had made to Trooper Williams on the ground that introduction into evidence of those statements would violate the Fifth Amendment insofar as he had not been informed of his constitutional rights prior to his interrogation. When the trial court denied the motion, respondent pleaded 'no contest' and was found guilty. . . .

On appeal to the Franklin County Court of Appeals, respondent renewed his constitutional claim. [T]he Court of Appeals rejected respondent's argument and affirmed his conviction. The Ohio Supreme Court dismissed respondent's appeal on the ground that it failed to present a 'substantial constitutional question.'

Respondent then filed an action for a writ of habeas corpus in the District Court for the Southern District of Ohio. The District Court dismissed the petition . . . .

A divided panel of the Court of Appeals for the Sixth Circuit reversed, holding that 'Miranda warnings must be given to all individuals prior to custodial interrogation, whether the offense investigated be a felony or a misdemeanor traffic offense.' (emphasis in original)."

The Supreme Court granted certiorari to review the case and affirmed.

B. Counsel of Record / ACLU Attorney

ACLU Side (Respondent / Appellee): R. William Meeks argued the cause for appellee.

Opposing Side (Petitioner / Appellant): Alan C. Travis argued the cause for appellant.

III. AMICI CURIAE

ACLU Side (Respondent / Appellee)

Brief of amici curiae filed on behalf of the ACLU, et al., by Jacob D. Fuchsberg and Charles S. Sims.

Opposing Side (Petitioner / Appellant)

Brief of amici curiae filed on behalf of the State of Ohio by Anthony J. Celebrezze, Jr., Attorney General, and Richard David Drake, Assistant Attorney General.

IV. THE SUPREME COURT'S DECISION

"We hold . . . that a person subjected to custodial interrogation is entitled to the benefit of the procedural safeguards enunciated in Miranda regardless of the nature or severity of the offense of which he is suspected or for which he was arrested.

The implication of this holding is that the Court of Appeals was correct in ruling that the statements made by respondent at the County Jail were inadmissible. There can be no question that respondent was 'in custody' at least as of the moment he was formally placed under arrest and instructed to get into the police car. Because he was not informed of his constitutional rights at that juncture, respondent's subsequent admissions should not have been used against him. . . .

To assess the admissibility of the self-incriminating statements made by respondent prior to his formal arrest, we are obliged to address a second issue concerning the scope of our decision in Miranda: whether the roadside questioning of a motorist detained pursuant to a routine traffic stop should be considered 'custodial interrogation.' . . . Turning to the case before us, we find nothing in the record that indicates that respondent should have been given Miranda warnings at any point prior to the time Trooper Williams placed him under arrest. . . . We conclude, in short, that respondent was not taken into custody for the purposes of Miranda until Williams arrested him. Consequently, the statements respondent made prior to that point were admissible against him. . . .

We are left with the question of the appropriate remedy. In his brief, petitioner contends that, if we agree with the Court of Appeals that respondent's post-arrest statements should have been suppressed, but conclude that respondent's pre-arrest statements were admissible, we should reverse the Court of Appeals' judgment on the ground that the state trial court's erroneous refusal to exclude the postarrest admissions constituted 'harmless error.' [P]etitioner argues that the statements made by respondent at the police station 'were merely recitations of what respondent had already admitted at the scene of the traffic arrest,' and therefore were unnecessary to his conviction. We reject this proposed disposition of the case . . . .

Accordingly, the judgment of the Court of Appeals is affirmed."

V. JUSTICE VOTE

9 Pro ACLU Side vs. 0 Con Opposing Side

ACLU Side (Respondent / Appellee)

1. Marshall, T. – Wrote majority opinion
2. Brennan, W. – Joined majority opinion
3. Burger, W. – Joined majority opinion
4. White, B. – Joined majority opinion
5. Powell, L. – Joined majority opinion
6. Rehnquist, W. – Joined majority opinion
7. O'Connor, S. – Joined majority opinion

8. Blackmun, H. – Joined majority opinion
9. Stevens, J. – Wrote concurring opinion

VI. A WIN OR LOSS FOR THE ACLU?

The ACLU filed as amicus curiae urging affirmance; the Supreme Court affirmed the judgment of the Court of Appeals in a 9-0 vote, giving the ACLU an apparent win.

551. Roberts v. United States Jaycees

(Decided July 3, 1984; 468 U.S. 609)

I. ISSUE

A. Issues Discussed

Civil rights, gender, First Amendment, freedom of association

B. Legal Question Presented

Whether "by requiring the United States Jaycees to admit women as full voting members, the Minnesota Human Rights Act violates the First and Fourteenth Amendment rights of the organization's members."

C. Supreme Court's Answer

The Minnesota Human Rights Act does not violate the First or Fourteenth Amendment rights of the United States Jaycees by requiring the organization to admit women as full voting members.

II. CASE SUMMARY

A. Background

"The United States Jaycees (Jaycees) . . . is a nonprofit membership corporation, incorporated in Missouri with national headquarters in Tulsa, Okla. The objective of the Jaycees, as set out in its bylaws, is to pursue 'such educational and charitable purposes as will promote and foster the growth and development of young men's civic organizations in the United States . . . .'

The organization's bylaws establish seven classes of membership, including individual or regular members, associate individual members, and local chapters. Regular membership is limited to young men between the ages of 18 and 35, while associate membership is available to individuals or groups ineligible for regular membership, principally women and older men. An associate member, whose dues are somewhat lower than those charged regular members, may not vote, hold local or national office, or participate in certain leadership training and awards programs. . . .

In 1974 and 1975, respectively, the Minneapolis and St. Paul chapters of the Jaycees began admitting women as regular members. Currently, the memberships and boards of directors of both chapters include a substantial proportion of women. As a result, the two chapters have been in violation of the national organization's bylaws for about 10 years. The national organization has imposed a number of sanctions on the Minneapolis and St. Paul chapters for violating the bylaws, including denying their members eligibility for state or national office or awards programs, and refusing to count their membership in computing votes at national conventions.

In December 1978, the president of the national organization advised both chapters that a motion to revoke their charters would be considered at a forthcoming meeting of the national board of directors in Tulsa. Shortly after receiving this notification, members of both chapters filed charges of discrimination with the Minnesota Department of Human Rights. The complaints alleged that the exclusion of women from full membership required by the national organization's bylaws violated the Minnesota Human Rights Act (Act) . . . .

The . . . Minnesota Human Rights Department hearing examiner . . . ordered the national organization to cease and desist from discriminating against any member or applicant for membership on the basis of sex and from imposing sanctions on any Minnesota affiliate for admitting women. The Jaycees then filed a renewed complaint in the District Court, which in turn certified to the Minnesota Supreme Court the question whether the Jaycees organization is a 'place of public accommodation' within the meaning of the State's Human Rights Act.

With the record of the administrative hearing before it, the Minnesota Supreme Court answered that question in the affirmative. . . . Subsequently, the Jaycees amended its complaint in the District Court to add a claim that the Minnesota Supreme Court's interpretation of the Act rendered it unconstitutionally vague and overbroad. The federal suit then proceeded to trial, after which the District Court entered judgment in favor of the state officials. On appeal, a divided Court of Appeals for the Eighth Circuit reversed."

The Supreme Court granted certiorari to review the case and reversed.

B. Counsel of Record / ACLU Attorney

ACLU Side (Petitioner / Appellant): Richard L. Varco, Jr., Special Assistant Attorney General of Minnesota, argued the cause for the appellant.

Opposing Side (Respondent / Appellee): Carl D. Hall, Jr. argued the cause for the appellee.

III. AMICI CURIAE

ACLU Side (Petitioner / Appellant)

Brief of amici curiae filed on behalf of the ACLU, et al., by Laurence H. Tribe, Burt Neuborne, Isabelle Katz, Pinzler, E. Richard Larson, and Charles S. Sims.

Additional briefs of amici curiae were filed on behalf of the State of New York, et al., the Alliance for Women Membership, Community Business Leaders, NAACP Legal Defense and Educational Fund, Inc., National League of Cities, et al., National Organization for Women, et al., and the Women's Issues Network, Inc.

Opposing Side (Respondent / Appellee)

Briefs of amici curiae filed on behalf of the Boy Scouts of America, the Conference of Private Organizations, and Rotary International.

IV. THE SUPREME COURT'S DECISION

"Our decisions have referred to constitutionally protected 'freedom of association' in two distinct senses. In one line of decisions, the Court has concluded that choices to enter into and maintain certain intimate human relationships must be secured against undue intrusion by the State because of the role of such relationships in safeguarding the individual freedom that is central to our constitutional scheme. In this respect, freedom of association receives protection as a fundamental element of personal liberty. In another set of decisions, the Court has recognized a right to associate for the purpose of engaging in those activities protected by the First Amendment—speech, assembly, petition for the redress of grievances, and the exercise of religion. The Constitution guarantees freedom of association of this kind as an indispensable means of preserving other individual liberties.

[T]he local chapters of the Jaycees are neither small nor selective. Moreover, much of the activity central to the formation and maintenance of the association involves the participation of strangers to that relationship. Accordingly, we conclude that the Jaycees chapters lack the distinctive characteristics that might afford constitutional protection to the decision of its members to exclude women. We turn therefore to consider the extent to which application of the Minnesota statute to compel the Jaycees to accept women infringes the group's freedom of expressive association.

An individual's freedom to speak, to worship, and to petition the government for the redress of grievances could not be vigorously protected from interference by the State unless a correlative freedom to engage in group effort toward those ends were not also guaranteed. . . . Consequently, we have long understood as implicit in the right to engage in activities protected by the First Amendment a corresponding right to associate with others in pursuit of a wide variety of political, social, economic, educational, religious, and cultural ends. . . .

The right to associate for expressive purposes is not, however, absolute. Infringements on that right may be justified by regulations adopted to serve compelling state interests, unrelated to the suppression of ideas, that cannot be achieved through means significantly less restrictive of associational freedoms. We are persuaded that Minnesota's compelling interest in eradicating discrimination against its female citizens justifies the impact that application of the statute to the Jaycees may have on the male members' associational freedoms.

[E]ven if enforcement of the Act causes some incidental abridgment of the Jaycees' protected speech, that effect is no greater than is necessary to accomplish the State's legitimate purposes. As we have explained, acts of invidious discrimination in the distribution of publicly available goods, services, and other advantages cause unique evils that government has a compelling interest to prevent—wholly apart from the point of view such conduct may transmit. Accordingly, like violence or other types of potentially expressive activities that produce special harms distinct from their communicative impact, such practices are entitled to no constitutional protection. In prohibiting such practices, the Minnesota Act therefore 'responds precisely to the substantive problem which legitimately concerns' the State and abridges no more speech or associational freedom than is necessary to accomplish that purpose. . . .

The judgment of the Court of Appeals is reversed."

V. JUSTICE VOTE

7 Pro ACLU Side vs. 0 Con Opposing Side

ACLU Side (Petitioner / Appellant)

1. Brennan, W. – Wrote majority opinion
2. Stevens, J. – Joined majority opinion
3. Marshall, T. – Joined majority opinion
4. Powell, L. – Joined majority opinion
5. Rehnquist, W. – Concurred in the judgment
6. White, B. – Joined majority opinion
7. O'Connor, S. – Wrote concurring opinion

Burger, W. – Took no part in the decision
Blackmun, H. – Took no part in the decision

VI. A WIN OR LOSS FOR THE ACLU?

The ACLU filed as amicus curiae urging reversal; the Supreme Court reversed the Court of Appeals' ruling in a 7-0 vote, giving the ACLU an apparent win.

552. New Jersey v. T.L.O.

(Decided January 15, 1985; 469 U.S. 325)

I. ISSUE

A. Issues Discussed

Fourth Amendment, search and seizure, privacy, schools

B. Legal Question Presented

Did the warrantless search of a fourteen-year-old high school student's purse by the Assistant Vice Principal violate the Fourth Amendment?

C. Supreme Court's Answer

The search did not violate the Fourth Amendment.

II. CASE SUMMARY

A. Background

"On March 7, 1980, a teacher at Piscataway High School in Middlesex County, N.J., discovered two girls smoking in a lavatory. One of the two girls was the respondent T.L.O., who at that time was a 14-year-old high school freshman. Because smoking in the lavatory was a violation of a school rule, the teacher took the two girls to the Principal's office, where they met with Assistant Vice Principal Theodore Choplick. In response to questioning by Mr. Choplick, T.L.O.'s companion admitted that she had violated the rule. T.L.O., however, denied that she had been smoking in the lavatory and claimed that she did not smoke at all.

Mr. Choplick asked T.L.O. to come into his private office and demanded to see her purse. Opening the purse, he found a pack of cigarettes, which he removed from the purse and held before

T.L.O. as he accused her of having lied to him. As he reached into the purse for the cigarettes, Mr. Choplick also noticed a package of cigarette rolling papers. In his experience, possession of rolling papers by high school students was closely associated with the use of marihuana. Suspecting that a closer examination of the purse might yield further evidence of drug use, Mr. Choplick proceeded to search the purse thoroughly. The search revealed a small amount of marihuana, a pipe, a number of empty plastic bags, a substantial quantity of money in one-dollar bills, an index card that appeared to be a list of students who owed T.L.O. money, and two letters that implicated T.L.O. in marihuana dealing.

Mr. Choplick notified T.L.O.'s mother and the police, and turned the evidence of drug dealing over to the police. At the request of the police, T.L.O.'s mother took her daughter to police headquarters, where T.L.O. confessed that she had been selling marihuana at the high school. On the basis of the confession and the evidence seized by Mr. Choplick, the State brought delinquency charges against T.L.O. in the Juvenile and Domestic Relations Court of Middlesex County. Contending that Mr. Choplick's search of her purse violated the Fourth Amendment, T.L.O. moved to suppress the evidence found in her purse as well as her confession, which, she argued, was tainted by the allegedly unlawful search. The Juvenile Court denied the motion to suppress. . . . Having denied the motion to suppress, the court on March 23, 1981, found T.L.O. to be a delinquent . . . .

On appeal from the final judgment of the Juvenile Court, a divided Appellate Division affirmed the trial court's finding that there had been no Fourth Amendment violation, but vacated the adjudication of delinquency and remanded for a determination whether T.L.O. had knowingly and voluntarily waived her Fifth Amendment rights before confessing. T.L.O. appealed the Fourth Amendment ruling, and the Supreme Court of New Jersey reversed the judgment of the Appellate Division and ordered the suppression of the evidence found in T.L.O.'s purse."

The Supreme Court granted certiorari to review the case and reversed

B. Counsel of Record / ACLU Attorney

ACLU Side (Respondent / Appellee): Lois De Julio reargued the cause for appellee.

Opposing Side (Petitioner / Appellant): Allan J. Nodes, Deputy Attorney General of New Jersey, reargued the cause for appellant.

III. AMICI CURIAE

ACLU Side (Respondent / Appellee)

Brief of amici curiae filed on behalf of the ACLU, et al., by Mary L. Heen, Burt Neuborne, E. Richard Larson, Barry S. Goodman, and Charles S. Sims.

Brief of amici curiae filed on behalf of the Legal Aid Society of the City of New York, et al., by Janet Fink and Henry Weintraub.

Opposing Side (Petitioner / Appellant)

Brief of amici curiae filed on behalf of the United States by Solicitor General Lee, Deputy Solicitor General Frey, and Kathryn A. Oberly.

Brief of amici curiae filed on behalf of the National Association of Secondary School Principals, et al., by Ivan B. Gluckman.

Brief of amici curiae filed on behalf of the National School Boards Association by Gwendolyn H. Gregory, August W. Steinhilber, and Thomas A. Shannon.

Brief of amici curiae filed on behalf of the Washington Legal Foundation by Daniel J. Popeo and Paul D. Kamenar.

Brief of amici curiae filed on behalf of the New Jersey School Boards Association by Paula A. Mullaly and Thomas F. Scully.

IV. THE SUPREME COURT'S DECISION

"In determining whether the search at issue in this case violated the Fourth Amendment, we are faced initially with the question whether that Amendment's prohibition on unreasonable searches and seizures applies to searches conducted by public school officials. We hold that it does. . . .

To hold that the Fourth Amendment applies to searches conducted by school authorities is only to begin the inquiry into the standards governing such searches. Although the underlying command of the Fourth Amendment is always that searches and seizures be reasonable, what is reasonable depends on the context within which a search takes place. The determination of the standard of reasonableness governing any specific class of searches requires 'balancing the need to search against the invasion which the search entails.' . . .

It is evident that the school setting requires some easing of the restrictions to which searches by public authorities are ordinarily subject. The warrant requirement, in particular, is unsuited to the school environment: requiring a teacher to obtain a warrant before searching a child suspected of an infraction of school rules (or of the criminal law) would unduly interfere with the maintenance of the swift and informal disciplinary procedures needed in the schools. [W]e hold today that school officials need not obtain a warrant before searching a student who is under their authority.

The school setting also requires some modification of the level of suspicion of illicit activity needed to justify a search. Ordinarily, a search—even one that may permissibly be carried out without a warrant—must be based upon 'probable cause' to believe that a violation of the law has occurred. However, 'probable cause' is not an irreducible requirement of a valid search. The fundamental command of the Fourth Amendment is that searches and seizures be reasonable, and although 'both the concept of probable cause and the requirement of a warrant bear on the reasonableness of a search, . . . in certain limited circumstances neither is required.'

[T]he legality of a search of a student should depend simply on the reasonableness, under all the circumstances, of the search. Determining the reasonableness of any search involves a twofold inquiry: first, one must consider 'whether the . . . action was justified at its inception,' second, one must determine whether the search as actually conducted 'was reasonably related in scope to the circumstances which justified the interference in the first place,' Under ordinary circumstances, a search of a student by a teacher or other school official will be 'justified at its inception' when there are reasonable grounds for suspecting that the search will turn up evidence that the student has violated or is violating either the law or the rules of the school. Such a search will be permissible in its scope when the measures adopted are reasonably related to the objectives of the search and not excessively intrusive in light of the age and sex of the student and the nature of the infraction.

[I]t cannot be said that Mr. Choplick acted unreasonably when he examined T.L.O.'s purse to see if it contained cigarettes. [W]e cannot conclude that the search for marihuana was unreasonable in any respect.

Because the search resulting in the discovery of the evidence of marihuana dealing by T.L.O. was reasonable, the New Jersey Supreme Court's decision to exclude that evidence from T.L.O.'s juvenile delinquency proceedings on Fourth Amendment grounds was erroneous. Accordingly, the judgment of the Supreme Court of New Jersey is reversed."

V. JUSTICE VOTE

3 Pro ACLU Side vs. 6 Con Opposing Side

ACLU Side (Respondent / Appellee)

1. Stevens, J. – Wrote opinion concurring in part and dissenting in part
2. Brennan, W. – Wrote opinion concurring in part and dissenting in part, joined Stevens' opinion, in part
3. Marshall, T. – Joined Brennan's opinion, joined Stevens' opinion

Opposing Side (Petitioner / Appellant)

1. White, B. – Wrote majority opinion
2. Powell, L. – Wrote concurring opinion
3. Blackmun, H. – Wrote concurring opinion
4. Burger, W. – Joined majority opinion
5. Rehnquist, W. – Joined majority opinion
6. O'Connor, S. – Joined Powell's concurrence

VI. A WIN OR LOSS FOR THE ACLU?

The ACLU, as amicus curiae, urged affirmance of the judgment of the Supreme Court of New Jersey; the U.S. Supreme Court reversed in a 6-3 vote, giving the ACLU an apparent loss.

553. Federal Election Commission v. National Conservative Political Action Committee

(Decided March 18, 1985; 470 U.S. 480)

I. ISSUE

A. Issues Discussed

First Amendment, freedoms of press, speech, and association, elections

B. Legal Question Presented

Whether § 9012(f) of the Federal Election Campaign Act violates the First Amendment.

C. Supreme Court's Answer

Section 9012(f) violates the First Amendment.

II. CASE SUMMARY

A. Background

"The Presidential Election Campaign Fund Act (Fund Act), 26 U.S.C. § 9001 et seq., offers the Presidential candidates of major political parties the option of receiving public financing for their general election campaigns. If a Presidential candidate elects public financing, § 9012(f) makes it a criminal offense for independent 'political committees,' such as appellees National Conservative Political Action Committee (NCPAC) and Fund For A Conservative Majority (FCM), to expend more than $1,000 to further that candidate's election. A three-judge District Court for the Eastern District of Pennsylvania, in companion lawsuits brought respectively by the Federal Election Commission (FEC) and by the Democratic Party of the United States and the Democratic National Committee (DNC), held § 9012(f) unconstitutional on its face because it violated the First Amendment to the United States Constitution. These plaintiffs challenge that determination on this appeal, and the FEC also appeals from that part of the judgment holding that the Democratic Party and the DNC have standing under 26 U.S.C. § 9011(b)(1) to seek a declaratory judgment against appellees upholding the constitutionality of § 9012(f). [The Supreme Court] noted probable jurisdiction pursuant to the statutory appeal provision of § 9011(b)(2), which provides for a direct appeal to [the Supreme] Court from three-judge district courts convened in proceedings under § 9011(b)(1). [The Supreme Court] reverse[d] the judgment of the District Court on the issue of the standing of the Democratic Party and the DNC, but affirm its judgment as to the constitutional validity of § 9012(f)."

B. Counsel of Record / ACLU Attorney

ACLU Side (Respondent / Appellee): Robert R. Sparks, Jr., argued the cause for appellee in both cases.

Opposing Side (Petitioner / Appellant): Charles N. Steele argued the cause for appellant in No. 88-1032. Steven B. Fierson argued the cause for appellant in No. 83-1122.

III. AMICI CURIAE

ACLU Side (Respondent / Appellee)

Brief of amici curiae filed on behalf of the ACLU by Philip A. Lacovara, Ronald A. Stern, Charles S. Sims, and Arthur B. Spitzer.

Brief of amici curiae filed on behalf of the Gulf & Great Plains Legal Foundation, et al., by Wilkes C. Robinson.

Brief of amici curiae filed on behalf of the National Congressional Club by Brice M. Clagett and John R. Bolton.

Opposing Side (Petitioner / Appellant)

Brief of amici curiae filed on behalf of Common Cause by Roger M. Witten, William T. Lake, and Jana B. Singer.

IV. THE SUPREME COURT'S DECISION

"In view of our conclusion that the Democrats lack standing under the statute, there is no need to reach the Art. III issue decided by the District Court. Therefore, we turn to the merits of the FEC's appeal of its unsuccessful declaratory judgment action against the PACs. . . .

There can be no doubt that the expenditures at issue in this case produce speech at the core of the First Amendment. . . . Having concluded that the PAC's expenditures are entitled to full First Amendment protection, we now look to see if there is a sufficiently strong governmental interest served by § 9012(f)'s restriction on them and whether the section is narrowly tailored to the evil that may legitimately be regulated. The restriction involved here is not merely an effort by the Government to regulate the use of its own property, . . . or the dismissal of a speaker from Government employment . . . . It is a flat, across-the-board criminal sanction applicable to any 'committee, association, or organization' which spends more than $1,000 on this particular type of political speech. . . .

While in NRWC we held that the compelling governmental interest in preventing corruption supported the restriction of the influence of political war chests funneled through the corporate form, in the present cases we do not believe that a similar finding is supportable: when the First Amendment is involved, our standard of review is 'rigorous,' and the effort to link either corruption or the appearance of corruption to independent expenditures by PACs, whether large or small, simply does not pass this standard of review. Even assuming that Congress could fairly conclude that large-scale PACs have a sufficient tendency to corrupt, the overbreadth of § 9012(f) in these cases is so great that the section may not be upheld. We are not quibbling over fine-tuning of prophylactic limitations, but are concerned about wholesale restriction of clearly protected conduct.

The judgment of the District Court is affirmed as to the constitutionality of § 9012(f), but is reversed on the issue of the Democrats' standing, with instructions to dismiss their complaint for lack of standing."

V. JUSTICE VOTE

6 Pro ACLU Side vs. 3 Con Opposing Side

ACLU Side (Respondent / Appellee)

1. Rehnquist, W. – Wrote majority opinion
2. Burger, W. – Joined majority opinion
3. Blackmun, H. – Joined majority opinion
4. O'Connor, S. – Joined majority opinion
6. Powell, L. – Joined majority opinion
6. Stevens, J. – Wrote opinion concurring in part and dissenting in part

Opposing Side (Petitioner / Appellant)

1. White, B. – Wrote dissenting opinion
2. Marshall, T. – Wrote dissenting opinion, joined White's dissent, in part
3. Brennan, W. – Joined White's dissent, in part

VI. A WIN OR LOSS FOR THE ACLU?

The ACLU filed as amicus curiae urging affirmance of the District Court for the Eastern District of Pennsylvania ruling that § 9012(f) of the Federal Election Campaign Act is unconstitutional; the Supreme Court affirmed the ruling as to the constitutionality of the statute, but reversed as to the standing of the Democrats, by a 6-3 vote, giving the ACLU an apparent win.

554. Cleveland Board of Education v. Loudermill

(Decided March 19, 1985; 470 U.S. 532)

I. ISSUE

A. Issues Discussed

Fourteenth Amendment, due process, employment

B. Legal Question Presented

"[W]hat pretermination process must be accorded a public employee who can be discharged only for cause."

C. Supreme Court's Answer

A pretermination opportunity to respond is required by due process for a public employee who can be discharged only for cause.

II. CASE SUMMARY

A. Background

"In 1979 the Cleveland Board of Education, petitioner in No. 83-1362, hired respondent James Loudermill as a security guard. On his job application, Loudermill stated that he had never been convicted of a felony. Eleven months later, as part of a routine examination of his employment records, the Board discovered that in fact Loudermill had been convicted of grand larceny in 1968. By letter dated November 3, 1980, the Board's Business Manager informed Loudermill that he had been dismissed because of his dishonesty in filling out the employment application. Loudermill was not afforded an opportunity to respond to the charge of dishonesty or to challenge his dismissal. On November 13, the Board adopted a resolution officially approving the discharge.

Under Ohio law, Loudermill was a 'classified civil servant.' Such employees can be terminated only for cause, and may obtain administrative review if discharged. Pursuant to this provision, Loudermill filed an appeal with the Cleveland Civil Service Commission on November 12. The Commission appointed a referee, who held a hearing on January 29, 1981. Loudermill argued that he had thought that his 1968 larceny conviction was for a misdemeanor rather than a felony. The referee recommended reinstatement. On July 20, 1981, the full Commission heard argument and orally announced that it would uphold the dismissal. Proposed findings of fact and conclusions of law followed on August 10, and Loudermill's attorneys were advised of the result by mail on August 21.

Although the Commission's decision was subject to judicial review in the state courts, Loudermill instead brought the present suit in the Federal District Court for the Northern District of Ohio. The complaint alleged that § 124.34 was unconstitutional on its face because it did not provide the employee an opportunity to respond to the charges against him prior to removal. As a result, discharged employees were deprived of liberty and property without due process. The complaint also alleged that the provision was unconstitutional as applied because discharged employees were not given sufficiently prompt postremoval hearings.

Before a responsive pleading was filed, the District Court dismissed for failure to state a claim on which relief could be granted. . . .

The other case before us arises on similar facts and followed a similar course. . . .

Both employers petitioned for certiorari. Nos. 83–1362 and 83–1363. In a cross-petition, Loudermill sought review of the rulings adverse to him. No. 83–6392."

The Supreme Court granted certiorari to review the cases and affirmed.

B. Counsel of Record / ACLU Attorney

ACLU Side (Respondent / Appellee in Nos. 83-1362 and 83-1363, Petitioner / Appellant in No. 83-6392):

Robert M. Fertel, by appointment of the Court, argued the cause for appellee in Nos. 83-1362 and 83-1363 and appellant in No. 83-6392.

Opposing Side (Petitioner / Appellant in Nos. 83-1362 and 83-1363, Respondent / Appellee in No. 83-1362):

James G. Wyman argued the cause for appellant in Nos. 83-1362 and 83-1363 and appellee in No. 83-1362.

III. AMICI CURIAE

ACLU Side (Respondent / Appellee in Nos. 83-1362 and 83-1363, Petitioner / Appellant in No. 83-6392):

Brief of amici curiae filed on behalf of the ACLU of Cleveland Foundation by Gordon J. Beggs, Edward R. Stege, Jr., and Charles S. Sims.

Brief of amici curiae filed on behalf of the American Federation of State, County, and Municipal Employees, AFL-CIO, by Richard Kirschner.

Brief of amici curiae filed on behalf of the National Educational Association by Robert H. Chanin and Michael H. Gottesman.

Opposing Side (Petitioner / Appellant in Nos. 83-1362 and 83-1363, Respondent / Appellee in No. 83-1362):

Brief of amici curiae filed on behalf of the State of Ohio, et al., by Anthony J. Celebrezze, Jr., Attorney General of Ohio, and Gene W. Holliker and Christine Manuelian, Assistant Attorneys General; Charles A. Graddick, Attorney General of Alabama; Robert K. Corbin, Attorney General of Arizona; Tany S. Hong, Attorney General of Hawaii; Lindley E. Pearson, Attorney General of Indiana; Robert T. Stephen, Attorney General of Kansas; Frank J. Kelley, Attorney General of Michigan; Hubert H. Humphrey III, Attorney General of Minnesota; William A. Allain, Attorney General of Mississippi; Michael T. Greely, Attorney General of Montana; Brian McKay, Attorney General of Nevada; Gregory H. Smith, Attorney General of New Hampshire; Irwin I. Kimmelman, Attorney General of New Jersey; Robert WeFald, Attorney General of North Dakota; Michael Turpen, Attorney General of Oklahoma; David Frohnmayer, Attorney General of Oregon; LeRoy S. Zimmerman, Attorney General of Pennsylvania; Mark V. Meierhenry, Attorney General of South Dakota; Bronson C. La Follette, Attorney General of Wisconsin; and Archie G. McClintock, Attorney General of Wyoming.

Brief of amici curiae filed on behalf of the National School Boards Association by Gwendolyn H. Gregory and August W. Steinhilber.

IV. THE SUPREME COURT'S DECISION

"Respondents' federal constitutional claim depends on their having had a property right in continued employment. If they did, the State could not deprive them of this property without due process. . . . The Ohio statute plainly creates such an interest. . . . The statute plainly supports the conclusion, reached by both lower courts, that respondents possessed property rights in continued employment.

[T]he Due Process Clause provides that certain substantive rights—life, liberty, and property—cannot be deprived except pursuant to constitutionally adequate procedures. . . . The right to due process 'is conferred, not by legislative grace, but by constitutional guarantee. While the legislature may elect not to confer a property interest in [public] employment, it may not constitutionally authorize the deprivation of such an interest, once conferred, without appropriate procedural safeguards.' . . .

An essential principle of due process is that a deprivation of life, liberty, or property 'be preceded by notice and opportunity for hearing appropriate to the nature of the case.' . . . The need for some form of pretermination hearing, recognized in these cases, is evident from a balancing of the competing interests at stake. These are the private interests in retaining employment, the governmental interest in the expeditious removal of unsatisfactory employees and the avoidance of administrative burdens, and the risk of an erroneous termination. . . . The governmental interest in immediate termination does not outweigh [the competing] interests. [A]ffording the employee an opportunity to respond prior to termination would impose neither a significant administrative burden nor intolerable delays. Furthermore, the employer shares the employee's interest in avoiding disruption and erroneous decisions; and until the matter is settled, the employer would continue to receive the benefit of the employee's labors. It is preferable to keep a qualified employee on than to train a new one. A governmental employer also has an interest in keeping citizens usefully employed rather than taking the possibly erroneous and counterproductive step of forcing its employees onto the welfare rolls. Finally, in those situations where the employer perceives a significant hazard in keeping the employee on the job, it can avoid the problem by suspending with pay. . . .

The foregoing considerations indicate that the pretermination 'hearing,' though necessary, need not be elaborate. . . . The essential requirements of due process, and all that respondents seek or the Court of Appeals required, are notice and an opportunity to respond. The opportunity to present reasons, either in person or in writing, why proposed action should not be taken is a fundamental due process requirement. . . .

In his cross-petition Loudermill asserts, as a separate constitutional violation, that his administrative proceedings took too long. The Court of Appeals held otherwise, and we agree. The Due Process Clause requires provision of a hearing at a meaningful time.' At some point, a delay in the post-termination hearing would become a constitutional violation. In the present case, however, the complaint merely recites the course of proceedings and concludes that the denial of a 'speedy resolution' violated due process. This reveals nothing about the delay except that it stemmed in part from the thoroughness of the procedures. A 9-month adjudication is not, of course, unconstitutionally lengthy per se. Yet Loudermill offers no indication that his wait was unreasonably prolonged other than the fact that it took nine months. The chronology of the proceedings set out in the complaint, coupled with the assertion that nine months is too long to wait, does not state a claim of a constitutional deprivation. . . .

We conclude that all the process that is due is provided by a pretermination opportunity to respond, coupled with post-termination administrative procedures as provided by the Ohio statute. Because respondents allege in their complaints that they had no chance to respond, the District Court erred in dismissing for failure to state a claim. The judgment of the Court of Appeals is affirmed, and the case is remanded for further proceedings consistent with this opinion."

V. JUSTICE VOTE

8 Pro ACLU Side vs. 1 Con Opposing Side

ACLU Side (Respondent / Appellee in Nos. 83-1362 and 83-1363, Petitioner / Appellant in No. 83-6392):

1. White, B. – Wrote majority opinion
2. Burger, W. – Joined majority opinion
3. Blackmun, H. – Joined majority opinion
4. Powell, L. – Joined majority opinion
5. O'Connor, S. – Joined majority opinion
6. Stevens, J. – Joined majority opinion
7. Marshall, T. – Wrote concurring opinion
8. Brennan, W. – Wrote opinion concurring in part and dissenting in part

Opposing Side (Petitioner / Appellant in Nos. 83-1362 and 83-1363, Respondent / Appellee in No. 83-1362):

1. Rehnquist, W. – Wrote dissenting opinion

VI. A WIN OR LOSS FOR THE ACLU?

The ACLU filed as amicus curiae urging affirmance; the Supreme Court affirmed the Court of Appeals for the Sixth Circuit's decision by an 8-1 vote, giving the ACLU an apparent win.

555. Anderson v. City of Bessemer

(Decided March 19, 1985; 470 U.S. 564)

I. ISSUE

A. Issues Discussed

Civil rights, gender, employment discrimination

B. Legal Question Presented

"[W]hether the Court of Appeals erred in holding the District Court's finding of discrimination to be clearly erroneous."

C. Supreme Court's Answer

The Court of Appeals erred by misapplying the clearly erroneous standard to overturn the District Court's finding of discrimination.

II. CASE SUMMARY

A. Background

"Early in 1975, officials of respondent Bessemer City, North Carolina, set about to hire a new Recreation Director for the city. . . . A five-member committee selected by the Mayor was responsible for choosing the Recreation Director. Of the five members, four were men; the one woman on the committee, Mrs. Auddie Boone, served as the chairperson.

Eight persons applied for the position of Recreation Director. Petitioner, at the time a 39-year-old schoolteacher with college degrees in social studies and education, was the only woman among the eight. The selection committee reviewed the resumés submitted by the applicants and briefly interviewed each of the jobseekers. Following the interviews, the committee offered the position to Mr. Donald Kincaid, a 24-year-old who had recently graduated from college with a degree in physical education. All four men on the committee voted to offer the job to Mr. Kincaid; Mrs. Boone voted for petitioner.

Believing that the committee had passed over her in favor of a less qualified candidate solely because she was a woman, petitioner filed discrimination charges with the Charlotte District Office of the Equal Employment Opportunity

Commission. In July 1980 (five years after petitioner filed the charges), the EEOC's District Director found that there was reasonable cause to believe that petitioner's charges were true and invited the parties to attempt a resolution of petitioner's grievance through conciliation proceedings. The EEOC's efforts proved unsuccessful, and in due course, petitioner received a right-to-sue letter.

Petitioner then filed this Title VII action in the United States District Court for the Western District of North Carolina. After a 2-day trial . . . , the court [found] that petitioner was entitled to judgment because she had been denied the position of Recreation Director on account of her sex. . . . On the basis of its findings that petitioner was the most qualified candidate, that the committee had been biased against hiring a woman, and that the committee's explanations for its choice of Mr. Kincaid were pretextual, the court concluded that petitioner had met her burden of establishing that she had been denied the position of Recreation Director because of her sex. . . .

The Fourth Circuit reversed the District Court's finding of discrimination. In the view of the Court of Appeals, three of the District Court's crucial findings were clearly erroneous: the finding that petitioner was the most qualified candidate, the finding that petitioner had been asked questions that other applicants were spared, and the finding that the male committee members were biased against hiring a woman."

The Supreme Court granted certiorari to review the case and reversed.

B. Counsel of Record / ACLU Attorney

ACLU Side (Petitioner / Appellant): Jonathan Wallas argued the cause for appellant.

Carolyn S. Corwin argued the cause for the United States, et al., as amicus curiae, by special leave of Court.

Opposing Side (Respondent / Appellee): Philip M. Van Hoy argued the cause for appellee.

III. AMICI CURIAE

ACLU Side (Petitioner / Appellant)

Brief of amici curiae filed on behalf of the ACLU, et al., by Joan E. Bertin, E. Richard Larson, Burt Neuborne, and Isabelle Katz Pinzler.

Brief of amici curiae filed on behalf of the United States, et al., by Carolyn S. Corwin, Solicitor General Lee, Deputy Solicitor General Wallace, Johnny J. Butler, and Philip B. Sklover.

Opposing Side (Respondent / Appellee)

No briefs of amici curiae were filed in support of appellee.

IV. THE SUPREME COURT'S DECISION

"Because a finding of intentional discrimination is a finding of fact, the standard governing appellate review of a district court's finding of discrimination is that set forth in Federal Rule of Civil Procedure 52(a): 'Findings of fact shall not be set aside unless clearly erroneous, and due regard shall be given to the opportunity of the trial court to judge of the credibility of the witnesses.' The question before us, then, is whether the Court of Appeals erred in holding the District Court's finding of discrimination to be clearly erroneous. . . .

Our determination that the findings of the District Court regarding petitioner's qualifications, the conduct of her interview, and the bias of the male committee members were not clearly erroneous leads us to conclude that the court's finding that petitioner was discriminated against on account of her sex was also not clearly erroneous. The District Court's findings regarding petitioner's superior qualifications and the bias of the selection committee are sufficient to support the inference that petitioner was denied the position of Recreation Director on account of her sex. Accordingly, we hold that the Fourth Circuit erred in denying petitioner relief under Title VII.

In so holding, we do not assert that our knowledge of what happened 10 years ago in Bessemer City is superior to that of the Court of Appeals; nor do we claim to have greater insight than the Court of Appeals into the state of mind of the men on the selection committee who rejected petitioner for the position of Recreation Director. Even the trial judge, who has heard the witnesses directly and who is more closely in touch than the appeals court with the milieu out of which the controversy before him arises, cannot always be confident that he 'knows' what happened. Often, he can only determine whether the plaintiff has succeeded in presenting an account of the facts that is more likely to be true than not. Our task—and the task of appellate tribunals generally—is more limited still: we must determine whether the trial judge's conclusions are clearly erroneous. On the record before us, we cannot say that they are. Accordingly, the judgment of the Court of Appeals is reversed."

V. JUSTICE VOTE

9 Pro ACLU Side vs. 0 Con Opposing Side

ACLU Side (Petitioner / Appellant)

1. White, B. – Wrote majority opinion
2. Burger, W. – Joined majority opinion
3. Brennan, W. – Joined majority opinion
4. Marshall, T. – Joined majority opinion
5. Rehnquist, W. – Joined majority opinion
6. Stevens, J. – Joined majority opinion
7. O'Connor, S. – Joined majority opinion
8. Powell, L. – Wrote concurring opinion
9. Blackmun, H. – Wrote concurring opinion

VI. A WIN OR LOSS FOR THE ACLU?

The ACLU filed as amicus curiae urging reversal; the Supreme Court reversed the ruling of the Court of Appeals for the Fourth Circuit in a 9-0 vote, giving the ACLU an apparent win.

556. Lindahl v. Office of Personnel Management

(Decided March 20, 1985; 470 U.S. 768)

I. ISSUE

A. Issues Discussed

Governmental authority, regulation, judicial review, disabilities

B. Legal Question Presented

"The first [question] is whether § 8347(c) bars judicial review altogether of an MSPB judgment affirming the denial by OPM of a disability retirement claim, or bars review only of factual determinations while permitting review for alleged errors of law and procedure. If judicial review is available to the latter, limited extent, a second question arises: whether the United States Court of Appeals for the Federal Circuit has jurisdiction directly to review MSPB decisions in such cases, or whether an applicant whose appeal is rejected by the MSPB must instead file a Tucker Act claim in the United States Claims Court or a United States district court, from which an appeal could then be taken to the Federal Circuit."

C. Supreme Court's Answer

Section 8347(c) does not entirely bar judicial review of the judgment, but does bar review of the factual determinations in the judgment. The Court of Appeals for the Federal Circuit had jurisdiction to review the decision.

II. CASE SUMMARY

A. Background

"Until his retirement, the petitioner Wayne Lindahl served as a civilian security guard at the Mare Island Naval Shipyard in Vallejo, Cal. Lindahl suffers from acute and chronic bronchitis, allegedly aggravated in part by his exposure over the years to chemical irritants at Mare Island. In September 1979, the Department of the Navy informed Lindahl that he would be retired 'because your physical condition has disabled you to such an extent that you are unable to perform the full range of duties required of your position as a Police Officer.' Lindahl agreed with the Navy's assessment and chose not to contest his separation.

Both before and after his retirement, Lindahl took steps to apply for a disability retirement annuity. [The Office of Personnel Management (OPM)] denied Lindahl's claim several months after he had been retired on the ground that the evidence 'fails to establish that you have a disability severe enough to prevent useful, efficient, and safe performance of the essential duties of the position from which you are seeking retirement.' Pursuant to 5 U.S.C. § 8347(d), Lindahl appealed this decision to the [Merit Systems Protection Board (MSPB)]. The Board sustained OPM's denial, finding that Lindahl had not demonstrated by a preponderance of the evidence that he was disabled within the meaning of the [Civil Service] Retirement Act.

Lindahl then filed a complaint in the Court of Claims . . . . After Congress enacted the [Federal Courts Improvement Act (FCIA)] in 1982, Lindahl's case was transferred to the Federal Circuit. The OPM moved to dismiss, arguing in the alternative (1) that judicial review of legal and procedural questions, as well as of factual determinations, is altogether barred in Retirement Act cases by 5 U.S.C. § 8347(c); and (2) that the jurisdictional provisions of § 7703 are limited to 'employees,' that retired employees are no longer 'employees,' and that the Federal Circuit therefore lacks direct jurisdiction of appeals from MSPB decisions in Retirement Act cases. The MSPB intervened as an amicus curiae in support of Lindahl's reviewability and jurisdictional contentions.

The Federal Circuit sitting en banc dismissed Lindahl's appeal as barred by § 8347(c). The court concluded that the plain words of the subsection, along with the structure of the civil service laws and the import of the 1980 amendment, overcome the usual presumption favoring judicial review of administrative action."

The Supreme Court granted certiorari to review the case and reversed.

B. Counsel of Record / ACLU Attorney

ACLU Side (Petitioner / Appellant): John Murcko, by appointment of the Court, argued the cause for appellant.

Opposing Side (Respondent / Appellee): Edwin S. Kneedler argued the cause for appellee.

III. AMICI CURIAE

ACLU Side (Petitioner / Appellant)

Brief of amici curiae filed on behalf of the ACLU by Burt Neuborne.

Brief of amici curiae filed on behalf of the American Federation of Government Employees, AFL-CIO, by Stuart A. Kirsch and Mark D. Roth.

Brief of amici curiae filed on behalf of the National Association of Retired Federal Employees by Irving Kator, Joseph B. Scott, James H. Heller, and Michael J. Kator.

Opposing Side (Respondent / Appellee)

No briefs of amici curiae were filed in support of appellee.

IV. THE SUPREME COURT'S DECISION

"[Section] 8347(c) imposes a 'special and unusual restriction on judicial examination, and under it courts are not as free to review Commission retirement decisions as they would be if the 'finality' clause were not there.' . . .

The Federal Circuit . . . erred in concluding that § 8347(c), as amended, altogether bars judicial review of MSPB decisions in retirement disability cases. Accordingly, while the factual underpinnings of § 8347 disability determinations may not be judicially reviewed, such review is available to determine whether 'there has been a substantial departure from important procedural rights, a misconstruction of the governing legislation, or some like error 'going to the heart of the administrative determination.'' . . .

The respondent has skillfully parsed the legislative history and culled every possible nuance and ambiguity, but it has failed to advance a single argument why Congress would have intended to depart from the plain jurisdictional language in cases of disability retirement appeals and to require, instead, that such appeals be reviewed for legal and procedural error first by the Claims Court or a district court, and then all over again by the Federal Circuit. That Congress could not have intended such a wasteful exercise is reinforced by § 8347(d)(2), which explicitly provides that one subclass of disability retirement cases—those involving involuntary dismissals based on an individual's alleged mental disability—are appealable directly from the MSPB to the Federal Circuit. We can discern no reason why Congress would have intended that mental disability cases, which permit for evidentiary review, be channeled to an appellate forum, while intending that other retirement cases, which permit only for Scroggins review, be channeled to a trial forum for nonevidentiary review and then to the Federal Circuit for performance of the identical review. Moreover . . . , there frequently will be disputes—as in this case—as to whether an employee's retirement was involuntary or voluntary, and accordingly as to whether the appeal might properly be characterized as an adverse action, rather than as a simple disability retirement matter. In the absence of any indication in the legislative history or persuasive functional argument to the contrary, we cannot assume that Congress intended to create such a bizarre jurisdictional patchwork. Accordingly, we conclude that MSPB decisions concerning retirement disability claims are reviewable in the first instance by the Federal Circuit pursuant to the jurisdictional grants in 5 U.S.C. § 7703(b)(1) and 28 U.S.C. § 1295(a)(9).

The judgment of the Court of Appeals is reversed, and the case is remanded for further proceedings consistent with this opinion."

V. JUSTICE VOTE

5 Pro ACLU Side vs. 4 Con Opposing Side

ACLU Side (Petitioner / Appellant)

1. Brennan, W. – Wrote majority opinion
2. Marshall, T. – Joined majority opinion
3. Blackmun, H. – Joined majority opinion

4. Powell, L. – Joined majority opinion
5. Stevens, J. – Joined majority opinion

Opposing Side (Respondent / Appellee)

1. White, B. – Wrote dissenting opinion
2. Burger, W. – Joined White's dissent
3. Rehnquist, W. – Joined White's dissent
4. O'Connor, S. – Joined White's dissent

VI. A WIN OR LOSS FOR THE ACLU?

The ACLU filed as amicus curiae urging reversal; the Supreme Court reversed the ruling of the Court of Appeals for the Federal Circuit in a 5-4 vote, giving the ACLU an apparent win.

557. Tony and Susan Alamo Foundation v. Secretary of Labor

(Decided April 23, 1985; 471 U.S. 290)

I. ISSUE

A. Issues Discussed

Employment, First Amendment, Establishment Clause, Free Exercise Clause

B. Legal Question Presented

"[W]hether the minimum wage, overtime, and recordkeeping requirements of the Fair Labor Standards Act . . . apply to workers engaged in the commercial activities of a religious foundation, regardless of whether those workers consider themselves 'employees,' [and] whether application of the Act in this context violates the Religion Clauses of the First Amendment."

C. Supreme Court's Answer

The FLSA applies to the workers as they are "employees" for purposes of the Act and application of the FLSA in this context does not violate the establishment clause or free exercise clause.

II. CASE SUMMARY

A. Background

"The Tony and Susan Alamo Foundation is a nonprofit religious organization incorporated under the laws of California. Among its primary purposes, as stated in its Articles of Incorporation, are to 'establish, conduct and maintain an Evangelistic Church; to conduct religious services, to minister to the sick and needy, to care for the fatherless and to rescue the fallen, and generally to do those things needful for the promotion of Christian faith, virtue, and charity.' The Foundation does not solicit contributions from the public. It derives its income largely from the operation of a number of commercial businesses, which include service stations, retail clothing and grocery outlets, hog farms, roofing and electrical construction companies, a recordkeeping company, a motel, and companies engaged in the production and distribution of candy. These activities have been supervised by petitioners Tony and Susan Alamo, president and secretary-treasurer of the Foundation, respectively. The businesses are staffed largely by the Foundation's 'associates,' most of whom were drug addicts, derelicts, or criminals before their conversion and rehabilitation by the Foundation. These workers receive no cash salaries, but the Foundation provides them with food, clothing, shelter, and other benefits.

In 1977, the Secretary of Labor filed an action against the Foundation, the Alamos, and Larry La Roche, who was then the Foundation's vice president, alleging violations of the minimum wage, overtime, and recordkeeping provisions of the Fair Labor Standards Act with respect to approximately 300 associates. The United States District Court for the Western District of Arkansas held that the Foundation was an 'enterprise' within the meaning of 29 U.S.C. § 203(r), which defines that term as 'the related activities performed . . . by any person or persons for a common business purpose.' The District Court found that despite the Foundation's incorporation as a nonprofit religious organization, its businesses were 'engaged in ordinary commercial activities in competition with other commercial businesses.'

The District Court further ruled that the associates who worked in these businesses were 'employees' of the Alamos and of the Foundation within the meaning of the Act. The associates who had testified at trial had vigorously protested the payment of wages, asserting that they considered themselves volunteers who were working only for religious and evangelical reasons. Nevertheless, the District Court found that the associates were 'entirely dependent upon the Foundation for long periods.' Although they did not expect compensation in the form of ordinary wages, the District Court found, they did expect the Foundation to provide them 'food, shelter, clothing, transportation and medical benefits.' These benefits were simply wages in another form, and under the 'economic reality' test of employment the associates were employees. The District Court also rejected petitioners' arguments that application of the Act to the Foundation violated the Free Exercise and Establishment Clauses of the First Amendment, and the court found no evidence that the Secretary had engaged in unconstitutional discrimination against petitioners in bringing this suit.

The Court of Appeals for the Eighth Circuit affirmed the District Court's holding as to liability, but vacated and remanded as to the appropriate remedy. . . Like the District Court, the Court of Appeals also rejected petitioners' constitutional claims."

The Supreme Court granted certiorari to review the case and affirmed the judgment.

B. Counsel of Record / ACLU Attorney

ACLU Side (Respondent / Appellee): Charles Fried argued the cause for appellee.

Opposing Side (Petitioner / Appellant): Roy Gean, Jr., argued the cause for appellant.

III. AMICI CURIAE

ACLU Side (Respondent / Appellee)

Brief of amici curiae filed on behalf of the ACLU by Burt Neuborne and Charles S. Sims.

Opposing Side (Petitioner / Appellant)

No briefs of amici curiae were filed in support of appellant.

IV. THE SUPREME COURT'S DECISION

"In order for the Foundation's commercial activities to be subject to the Fair Labor Standards Act, two conditions must be satisfied. First, the Foundation's businesses must constitute an '[e]nterprise engaged in commerce or in the production of goods for commerce.' Second, the associates must be 'employees' within the meaning of the Act. While the statutory definition is exceedingly broad it does have its limits. An individual who, 'without promise or expectation of compensation, but solely for his personal purpose or pleasure, worked in activities carried on by other persons either for their pleasure or profit,' is outside the sweep of the Act. . . .

Petitioners contend that the Foundation is not an 'enterprise' within the meaning of the Act because its activities are not performed for 'a common business purpose.' In support of this assertion, petitioners point to the fact that the Internal Revenue Service has certified the Foundation as tax-exempt under 26 U.S.C. § 501(c)(3) . . . .

The Court has consistently construed the Act 'liberally to apply to the furthest reaches consistent with congressional direction' recognizing that broad coverage is essential to accomplish the goal of outlawing from interstate commerce goods produced under conditions that fall below minimum standards of decency. The statute contains no express or implied exception for commercial activities conducted by religious or other nonprofit organizations, and the agency charged with its enforcement has consistently interpreted the statute to reach such businesses. . . .

That the Foundation's commercial activities are within the Act's definition of 'enterprise' does not, as we have noted, end the inquiry. An individual may work for a covered enterprise and nevertheless not be an 'employee.' . . .

Relying on the affidavits and testimony of numerous associates, petitioners contend that the individuals who worked in the Foundation's businesses . . . expected no compensation for their labors. . . .

Nevertheless, these protestations, however sincere, cannot be dispositive. The test of employment under the Act is one of 'economic reality.' [I]n this case the associates were 'entirely dependent upon the Foundation for long periods, in some cases several years.' . . .

Petitioners further contend that application of the Act infringes on rights protected by the Religion Clauses of the First Amendment. Specifically, they argue that imposition of the minimum wage and recordkeeping requirements will violate the rights of the associates to freely exercise their religion and the right of the Foundation to be free of excessive government entanglement in its affairs. Neither of these contentions has merit. . . .

The Foundation's commercial activities, undertaken with a 'common business purpose,' are not beyond the reach of the Fair Labor Standards Act because of the Foundation's religious character, and its associates are 'employees' within the meaning of the Act because they work in contemplation of compensation. Like other employees covered by the Act, the associates are entitled to its full protection. Furthermore, application of the Act to the Foundation's commercial activities is fully consistent with the requirements of the First Amendment. The judgment below is accordingly affirmed."

V. JUSTICE VOTE

9 Pro ACLU Side vs. 0 Con Opposing Side

ACLU Side (Respondent / Appellee)

1. White, B. – Wrote majority opinion
2. Rehnquist, W. – Joined majority opinion
3. Burger, W. – Joined majority opinion
4. Brennan, W. – Joined majority opinion
5. Marshall, T. – Joined majority opinion
6. Blackmun, H. – Joined majority opinion
7. O'Connor, S. – Joined majority opinion
8. Stevens, J. – Joined majority opinion
9. Powell, L. – Joined majority opinion

VI. A WIN OR LOSS FOR THE ACLU?

The ACLU, as amicus curiae, urged affirmance of the Eighth Circuit Court of Appeals' judgment; the Supreme Court affirmed in a 9-0 vote, giving the ACLU an apparent win.

558. Zauderer v. Office of Disciplinary Counsel

(Decided May 28, 1985; 471 U.S. 626)

I. ISSUE

A. Issues Discussed

First Amendment, freedoms of press, speech, and association, attorney advertising

B. Legal Question Presented

"[W]hether a State may discipline an attorney for soliciting business by running newspaper advertisements containing nondeceptive illustrations and legal advice, and whether a State may seek to prevent potential deception of the public by requiring attorneys to disclose in their advertising certain information regarding fee arrangements."

C. Supreme Court's Answer

Attorney advertisements containing nondeceptive illustrations and legal advice are protected, however, the State may seek to prevent potential deception by requiring accurate disclosure of fee arrangements.

II. CASE SUMMARY

A. Background

"Appellant is an attorney practicing in Columbus, Ohio. Late in 1981, he sought to augment his practice by advertising in local newspapers. His first effort was a modest one: he ran a small advertisement in the Columbus Citizen Journal advising its readers that his law firm would represent defendants in drunken driving cases and that his clients' '[f]ull legal fee [would be] refunded if [they were] convicted of DRUNK DRIVING.' The advertisement appeared in the Journal for two days; on the second day, Charles Kettlewell, an attorney employed by the Office of Disciplinary Counsel of the Supreme Court of Ohio (appellee) telephoned appellant and informed him that the advertisement appeared to be an offer to represent criminal defendants on a contingent-fee basis, a practice prohibited by Disciplinary Rule 2-106(C) of the Ohio Code of Professional Responsibility. Appellant immediately withdrew the advertisement and in a letter to Kettlewell apologized for running it, also stating in the letter that he would decline to accept employment by persons responding to the ad.

Appellant's second effort was more ambitious. In the spring of 1982, appellant placed an advertisement in 36 Ohio newspapers publicizing his willingness to represent women who had suffered injuries resulting from their use of a contraceptive device known as the Dalkon Shield Intrauterine Device. The advertisement featured a line drawing of the Dalkon Shield accompanied by the question, "DID YOU USE THIS IUD?" The advertisement then related . . . information [about appellant's willingness to represent women who used the device.]

The advertisement was successful in attracting clients: appellant received well over 200 inquiries regarding the advertisement, and he initiated lawsuits on behalf of 106 of the women who contacted him as a result of the advertisement. The ad, however, also aroused the interest of the Office of Disciplinary Counsel. On July 29, 1982, the Office filed a complaint against appellant charging him with a number of disciplinary violations arising out of both the drunken driving and Dalkon Shield advertisements. . . .

The charges against appellant were heard by a panel of the Board of Commissioners on Grievances and Discipline of the Supreme Court of Ohio. . . . The panel found that appellant's use of advertising had violated a number of Disciplinary Rules. . . . The panel rejected appellant's arguments that Ohio's regulations regarding the content of attorney advertising were unconstitutional as applied to him. . . . The Supreme Court of Ohio, in turn, adopted the Board's findings that appellant's advertisements had violated the Disciplinary Rules specified by the hearing panel. The court also agreed with the Board that the application of Ohio's rules to appellant's advertisements did not offend the First Amendment. . . .

Contending that Ohio's Disciplinary Rules violate the First Amendment insofar as they authorize the State to discipline him for the content of his Dalkon Shield advertisement, appellant filed this appeal. Appellant also claims that the manner in which he was disciplined for running his drunken driving advertisement violated his right to due process."

The Supreme Court granted certiorari to review the case, affirmed in part, and reversed in part.

B. Counsel of Record / ACLU Attorney

ACLU Side (Petitioner / Appellant): Alan B. Morrison argued the cause for appellant.

Opposing Side (Respondent / Appellee): H. Bartow Farr III argued the cause for appellee.

III. AMICI CURIAE

ACLU Side (Petitioner / Appellant)

Brief of amici curiae filed onbehalf of the ACLU, et al., by Bruce Campbell and Charles S. Sims.

Opposing Side (Respondent / Appellee)

Brief of amici curiae filed on behalf of A.H. Robins Co., by E. Barrett Prettyman, Jr.

IV. THE SUPREME COURT'S DECISION

"Our recent decisions involving commercial speech have been grounded in the faith that the free flow of commercial information is valuable enough to justify imposing on would-be regulators the costs of distinguishing the truthful from the false, the helpful from the misleading, and the harmless from the harmful. The value of the information presented in appellant's advertising is no less than that contained in other forms of advertising—indeed, insofar as appellant's advertising tended to acquaint persons with their legal rights who might otherwise be shut off from effective access to the legal system, it was undoubtedly more valuable than many other forms of advertising. . . . An attorney may not be disciplined for soliciting legal business through printed advertising containing truthful and nondeceptive information and advice regarding the legal rights of potential clients. . . .

The application of DR 2-101(B)'s restriction on illustrations in advertising by lawyers to appellant's advertisement fails for much the same reasons as does the application of the self-recommendation and solicitation rules. The use of illustrations or pictures in advertisements serves important communicative functions: it attracts the attention of the audience to the advertiser's message, and it may also serve to impart information directly. Accordingly, commercial illustrations are entitled to the First Amendment protections afforded verbal commercial speech: restrictions on the use of visual media of expression in advertising must survive scrutiny under the Central Hudson test. . . .

The Supreme Court of Ohio issued a public reprimand incorporating by reference its opinion finding that appellant had violated Disciplinary Rules 2-101(A), 2-101(B), 2-101 (B)(15), 2-103(A), and 2-104(A). That judgment is affirmed to the extent that it is based on appellant's advertisement involving his terms of representation in drunken driving cases and on the omission of information regarding his contingent-fee arrangements in his Dalkon Shield advertisement. But insofar as the reprimand was based on appellant's use of an illustration in his advertisement in violation of DR 2-101(B) and his offer of legal advice in his advertisement in violation of DR 2-103(A) and 2-104(A), the judgment is reversed."

V. JUSTICE VOTE

8 Pro ACLU Side vs. 0 Con Opposing Side

ACLU Side (Petitioner / Appellant)

1. White, B. – Wrote majority opinion
2. Stevens, J. – Joined majority opinion
3. Blackmun, H. – Joined majority opinion
4. Brennan, W. – Wrote opinion concurring in part, concurring in the judgment in part, and dissenting in part
5. Marshall, T. – Joined Brennan's opinion
6. O'Connor, S. – Wrote opinion concurring in part, concurring in the judgment in part, and dissenting in part

7. Burger, W. – Joined O'Connor's opinion
8. Rehnquist, W. – Joined O'Connor's opinion

Powell, L. – Took no part in the decision

VI. A WIN OR LOSS FOR THE ACLU?

The ACLU filed as amicus curiae urging reversal; the U.S. Supreme Court affirmed in part and reversed in part the judgment of the Supreme Court of Ohio in an 8-0 vote giving ACLU an apparent win.

559. Oklahoma City v. Tuttle

(Decided June 3, 1985; 471 U.S. 808)

I. ISSUE

A. Issues Discussed

Civil rights, federal rights, municipal liability

B. Legal Question Presented

Whether "proof of a single incident of unconstitutional activity by a police officer could suffice to establish municipal liability."

C. Supreme Court's Answer

"Under the charge upheld by the Court of Appeals the jury could properly have imposed liability on the city based solely upon proof that it employed a non-policymaking officer who violated the Constitution."

II. CASE SUMMARY

A. Background

"On October 4, 1980, Officer Julian Rotramel, a member of the Oklahoma City police force, shot and killed Albert Tuttle outside the We'll Do Club, a bar in Oklahoma City. . . .

Respondent Rose Marie Tuttle is Albert Tuttle's widow, and the administratrix of his estate. She brought suit under § 1983 in the United States District Court, Western District of Oklahoma, against Rotramel and the city, alleging that their actions had deprived Tuttle of certain of his constitutional rights. . . .

The jury returned a verdict in favor of Rotramel but against the city, and awarded respondent $1,500,000 in damages. The city appealed to the Court of Appeals for the Tenth Circuit, arguing, inter alia, that the trial court had improperly instructed the jury on the standard for municipal liability. In particular, petitioner claimed it was error to instruct the jury that a municipality could be held liable for a 'policy' of 'inadequate training' based merely upon evidence of a single incident of unconstitutional activity. The Court of Appeals rejected petitioner's claims. [The Supreme Court] granted certiorari because the Court of Appeals' holding that proof of a single incident of unconstitutional activity by a police officer could suffice to establish municipal liability seemed to conflict with the decisions of other Courts of Appeals."

The Supreme Court reversed the Court of Appeals' decision.

B. Counsel of Record / ACLU Attorney

ACLU Side (Respondent / Appellee): Carl Hughes argued the cause for appellee.

Opposing Side (Petitioner / Appellant): Burck Bailey argued the cause for appellant.

III. AMICI CURIAE

ACLU Side (Respondent / Appellee)

Brief of amici curiae filed on behalf of the ACLU, et al., by Burt Neuborne and Charles S. Sims.

Opposing Side (Petitioner / Appellant)

Brief of amici curiae filed on behalf of the State of Oklahoma by Michael C. Turpen, Attorney General, and David W. Lee, Assistant Attorney General.

IV. THE SUPREME COURT'S DECISION

"[O]nly deprivations visited pursuant to municipal 'custom' or 'policy' could lead to municipal liability. . . . Respondent did not claim in the District Court that Oklahoma City had a 'custom' or 'policy' of authorizing its police force to use excessive force in the apprehension of suspected criminals, and the jury was not instructed on that theory of municipal liability. Rather, respondent's theory of liability was that the 'policy' in question was the city's policy of training and supervising police officers, and that this 'policy' resulted in inadequate training, and the constitutional violations alleged. . . .

Here the [jury] instructions allowed the jury to infer a thoroughly nebulous 'policy' of 'inadequate training' on the part of the municipal corporation from the single incident . . . . and at the same time sanctioned the inference that the 'policy' was the cause of the incident. . . . Proof of a single incident of unconstitutional activity is not sufficient to impose liability under Monell, unless proof of the incident includes proof that it was caused by an existing, unconstitutional municipal policy, which policy can be attributed to a municipal policymaker. . . . Under the charge upheld by the Court of Appeals the jury could properly have imposed liability on the city based solely upon proof that it employed a non-policymaking officer who violated the Constitution. The decision of the Court of Appeals is accordingly reversed."

V. JUSTICE VOTE

1 Pro ACLU Side vs. 7 Con Opposing Side

ACLU Side (Respondent / Appellee)

1. Stevens, J. – Wrote dissenting opinion

Opposing Side (Petitioner / Appellant)

1. Rehnquist, W. – Wrote majority opinion
2. Burger, W. – Joined majority opinion
3. White, B. – Joined majority opinion
4. O'Connor, S. – Joined majority opinion
5. Brennan, W. – Wrote concurring opinion
6. Marshall, T. – Joined Brennan's concurrence
7. Blackmun, H. – Joined Brennan's concurrence

Powell, L. – Took no part in the decision

VI. A WIN OR LOSS FOR THE ACLU?

The ACLU filed as amicus curiae urging affirmance; the Supreme Court reversed the judgment of the Court of Appeals in a 7-1 vote, giving the ACLU an apparent loss.

560. Wallace v. Jaffree

(Decided June 4, 1985; 472 U.S. 38)

I. ISSUE

A. Issues Discussed

First Amendment, Establishment Clause, prayer in schools

B. Legal Question Presented

"[W]hether § 16–1–20.1, [an Alabama statute] which authorizes a period of silence for 'meditation or voluntary prayer,' is a law respecting the establishment of religion within the meaning of the First Amendment."

C. Supreme Court's Answer

Alabama's statute allowing time for "voluntary prayer" is a law respecting the establishment of religion by the state and is therefore unconstitutional.

II. CASE SUMMARY

A. Background

"Appellee Ishmael Jaffree . . . filed a complaint on behalf of three of his minor children . . . 'seeking principally a declaratory judgment and an injunction restraining the Defendants . . . from maintaining or allowing the maintenance of regular religious prayer services or other forms of religious observances in the Mobile County Public Schools in violation of the First Amendment as made applicable to states by the Fourteenth Amendment to the United States Constitution.' The complaint further alleged . . . that the defendant teachers had 'on a daily basis' led their classes in saying certain prayers in unison . . . the appellees challenged the constitutionality of three Alabama statutes: §§ 16-1-20, 16-1-20.1, and 16-1-20.2.

[At] an evidentiary hearing on appellees' motion for a preliminary injunction, . . . State Senator Donald G. Holmes testified that he was the 'prime sponsor' of the bill that was enacted in 1981 as §16–1–20.1. He explained that the bill was an 'effort to return voluntary prayer to our public schools . . . .' Apart from [that] purpose . . . , Senator Holmes unequivocally testified that he had 'no other purpose in mind.' A week after the hearing, the District Court entered a preliminary injunction. The court held that appellees were likely to prevail on the merits because the enactment of §§ 16–1–20.1 and 16–1–20.2 did not reflect a clearly secular purpose."

Following a trial on the merits, the District Court reviewed "what it perceived to be newly discovered historical evidence, [and] concluded that 'the establishment clause of the first amendment to the United States Constitution does not prohibit the state from establishing a religion.' In a separate opinion, the District Court dismissed appellees' challenge to the three Alabama statutes because of a failure to state any claim for which relief could be granted. The court's dismissal of this challenge was also based on its conclusion that the Establishment Clause did not bar the States from establishing a religion.

The Court of Appeals consolidated the two cases; not surprisingly, it reversed. The Court of Appeals noted that this Court had considered and had rejected the historical arguments that the District Court found persuasive, and that the District Court had misapplied the doctrine of stare decisis. The Court of Appeals then held that the teachers' religious activities violated the Establishment Clause of the First Amendment."

The Supreme Court granted certiorari to review the case and affirmed.

B. Counsel of Record / ACLU Attorney

ACLU Side (Respondent / Appellee): Ronnie L. Williams argued the cause for appellee.

Opposing Side (Petitioner / Appellant): John S. Baker, Jr., argued the cause for appellant.

Deputy Solicitor General Bator argued the cause for the United States, as amicus curiae, by special leave of Court.

III. AMICI CURIAE

ACLU Side (Respondent / Appellee)

Brief of amici curiae filed on behalf of the ACLU, et al., by Jack D. Novik, Burt Neuborne, John Sexton, and Nathan Z. Dershowitz.

Briefs of amici curiae filed on behalf of the American Jewish Congress, et al., by Lowell P. Weicker, Jr.

Opposing Side (Petitioner / Appellant)

Brief of amici curiae filed on behalf of the United States by Deputy Solicitor General Bator, Solicitor General Lee, Assistant Attorney General Reynolds, Michael W. McConnell, and Brian K. Landsburg.

Additional briefs of amici curiae were filed on behalf of the State of Delaware, et al., the State of Connecticut, the Center for Judicial Studies, the Christian Legal Society, et al., the Freedom Council, the Legal Foundation of America, the Moral Majority, Inc., and Winston C. Anderson, et al.

IV. THE SUPREME COURT'S DECISION

"When the Court has been called upon to construe the breadth of the Establishment Clause, . . . '[e]very analysis in this area must begin with consideration of the cumulative criteria developed by the Court over many years. Three such tests may be gleaned from our cases. First, the statute must have a secular legislative purpose; second, its principal or primary effect must be one that neither advances nor inhibits religion; finally, the statute must not foster 'an excessive government entanglement with religion.'"

It is the first of these three criteria that is most plainly implicated by this case. . . . The sponsor of the bill that became § 16–1–20.1, Senator Donald Holmes, inserted into the legislative record—apparently without dissent—a statement indicating that the legislation was an 'effort to return voluntary prayer' to the public schools. Later Senator Holmes confirmed this purpose before the District Court. In response to the question whether he had any purpose for the legislation other than returning voluntary prayer to public schools, he stated: 'No, I did not have no other purpose in mind.' The State did not present evidence of any secular purpose. . . .

The legislative intent to return prayer to the public schools is, of course, quite different from merely protecting every student's right to engage in voluntary prayer during an appropriate moment of silence during the schoolday. The 1978 statute already protected that right, containing nothing that prevented any student from engaging in voluntary prayer during a silent minute of meditation. Appellants have not identified any secular purpose that was not fully served by § 16–1–20 before the enactment of § 16–1–20.1. Thus, only two conclusions are consistent with the text of § 16–1–20.1: (1) the statute was enacted to convey a message of state endorsement and promotion of prayer; or (2) the statute was enacted for no purpose. No one suggests that the statute was nothing but a meaningless or irrational act.

We must, therefore, conclude that the Alabama Legislature intended to change existing law and that it was motivated by the same purpose that the Governor's answer to the second amended complaint expressly admitted; that the statement inserted in the legislative history revealed; and that Senator Holmes' testimony frankly described. . . . The addition of 'or voluntary prayer' indicates that the State intended to characterize prayer as a favored practice. Such an endorsement is not consistent with the established principle that the government must pursue a course of complete neutrality toward religion. . . .

The well-supported concurrent findings of the District Court and the Court of Appeals—that § 16–1–20.1 was intended to convey a message of state approval of prayer activities in the public schools—make it unnecessary, and indeed inappropriate, to evaluate the practical significance of the addition of the words 'or voluntary prayer' to the statute. Keeping in mind, as we must, 'both the fundamental place held by the Establishment Clause in our constitutional scheme and the myriad, subtle ways in which Establishment Clause values can be eroded,' we conclude that § 16–1–20.1 violates the First Amendment.

The judgment of the Court of Appeals is affirmed."

V. JUSTICE VOTE

6 Pro ACLU Side vs. 3 Con Opposing Side

ACLU Side (Respondent / Appellee)

1. Stevens, J. – Wrote majority opinion
2. Powell, L. – Wrote concurring opinion
3. O'Connor, S. – Wrote concurring opinion
4. Brennan, W. – Joined majority opinion
5. Marshall, T. – Joined majority opinion
6. Blackmun, H. – Joined majority opinion

Opposing Side (Petitioner / Appellant)

1. Burger, W. – Wrote dissenting opinion
2. White, B. – Wrote dissenting opinion
3. Rehnquist, W. – Wrote dissenting opinion

VI. A WIN OR LOSS FOR THE ACLU?

The ACLU, as amicus curiae, urged affirmance of the judgment of the Court of Appeals; the Supreme Court affirmed in a 6-3 vote, giving the ACLU an apparent win.

561. Lowe v. Securities & Exchange Commission

(Decided June 10, 1985; 472 U.S. 181)

I. ISSUE

A. Issues Discussed

First Amendment, freedoms of press, speech, and association

B. Legal Question Presented:

"[W]hether petitioners may be permanently enjoined from publishing nonpersonalized investment advice and commentary in securities newsletters because they are not registered as investment advisers under § 203(c) of the Investment Advisers Act of 1940."

C. Supreme Court's Answer

The publications fall within the Act's exception for bona fide publications so petitioners need not be registered investment advisors under the Act to pubish their publications.

II. CASE SUMMARY

A. Background

"Christopher Lowe is the president and principal shareholder of Lowe Management Corporation. From 1974 until 1981, the corporation was registered as an investment adviser under the Act. During that period Lowe was convicted of misappropriating funds of an investment client, of engaging in business as an investment adviser without filing a registration application with New York's Department of Law, of tampering with evidence to cover up fraud of an investment client, and of stealing from a bank. Consequently, on May 11, 1981, the Securities and Exchange Commission (Commission), after a full hearing before an Administrative Law Judge, entered an order revoking the registration of the Lowe Management Corporation, and ordering Lowe not to associate thereafter with any investment adviser. . . .

A little over a year later, the Commission commenced this action by filing a complaint in the United States District Court for the Eastern District of New York, alleging that Lowe, the Lowe Management Corporation, and two other corporations, were violating the [Investment Advisors Act of 1940 (Act)], and that Lowe was violating the Commission's order. The principal charge in the complaint was that Lowe and the three corporations (petitioners) were publishing two investment newsletters and soliciting subscriptions for a stock-chart service. . . .

After determining that petitioners' publications were protected by the First Amendment, the District Court held that the Act must be construed to allow a publisher who is willing to comply with the existing reporting and disclosure requirements to register for the limited purpose of publishing such material and to engage in such publishing. A splintered panel of the Court of Appeals for the Second Circuit reversed."

The Supreme Court granted certiorari to review the case and reversed.

B. Counsel of Record / ACLU Attorney

ACLU Side (Petitioner / Appellant): Michael E. Schoeman argued the cause for appellant.

Opposing Side (Respondent / Appellee): Solicitor General Lee argued the cause for appellee.

III. AMICI CURIAE

ACLU Side (Petitioner / Appellant)

Brief of amici curiae filed on behalf of the American Federation of Labor and Congress of Industrial Organizations by Robert M. Weinberg and Laurence Gold.

Brief of amici curiae filed on behalf of the Association of American Publishers, Inc., by R. Bruce Rich and Lauren W. Field.

Brief of amici curiae filed on behalf of the Reporters Committee for Freedom of the Press, et al., by Benjamin W. Boley, Jack C. Landau, Robert S. Becker, Nancy J. Bregstein, Richard M. Wyner, Richard M. Schmidt, Richard N. Winfield, Robert J. Brinkmann, David Barr, and Bruce W. Sanford.

Opposing Side (Respondent / Appellee)

Brief of amici curiae filed on behalf of the ACLU by Michael R. Klein.

Brief of amici curiae filed on behalf of the North American Securities Administrators Association, Inc., by Harry F. Tepker, Jr., Joseph C. Long, H. Wayne Howell, and F. Daniel Bell III.

IV. THE SUPREME COURT'S DECISION

"The Act excludes several categories of persons from its definition of an investment adviser, lists certain investment advisers who need not be registered, and also authorizes the Commission to exclude 'such other person' as it may designate by rule or order.

One of the statutory exclusions is for 'the publisher of any bona fide newspaper, news magazine or business or financial publication of general and regular circulation.' . . . The language of the exclusion, read literally, seems to describe petitioners' newsletters. Petitioners are 'publishers of any bona fide newspaper, news magazine or business or financial publication.' [The publications] are published by those engaged solely in the publishing business and are not personal communications masquerading in the clothing of newspapers, news magazines, or financial publications. Moreover, there is no suggestion that they contained any false or misleading information, or that they were designed to tout any security in which petitioners had an interest. Further, petitioners' publications are 'of general and regular circulation.' Although the publications have not been "regular" in the sense of consistent circulation, the publications have been 'regular' in the sense important to the securities market: there is no indication that they have been timed to specific market activity, or to events affecting or having the ability to affect the securities industry.

The dangers of fraud, deception, or overreaching that motivated the enactment of the statute are present in personalized communications but are not replicated in publications that are advertised and sold in an open market. . . . As long as the communications between petitioners and their subscribers remain entirely impersonal and do not develop into the kind of fiduciary, person-to-person relationships that were discussed at length in the legislative history of the Act and that are characteristic of investment adviser-client relationships, we believe the publications are, at least presumptively, within the exclusion and thus not subject to registration under the Act.

We therefore conclude that petitioners' publications fall within the statutory exclusion for bona fide publications and that none of the petitioners is an 'investment adviser' as defined in the Act. It follows that neither their unregistered status, nor the Commission order barring Lowe from associating with an investment adviser, provides a justification for restraining the future publication of their newsletters. It also follows that we need not specifically address the constitutional question we granted certiorari to decide.

The judgment of the Court of Appeals is reversed."

V. JUSTICE VOTE

8 Pro ACLU Side vs. 0 Con Opposing Side

ACLU Side (Petitioner / Appellant)

1. Stevens, J. – Wrote majority opinion
2. Brennan, W. – Joined majority opinion
3. Marshall, T. – Joined majority opinion
4. Blackmun, H. – Joined majority opinion
5. O'Connor, S. – Joined majority opinion
6. White, B. – Wrote concurring opinion
7. Burger, W. – Joined White's concurrence
8. Rehnquist, W. – Joined White's concurrence

Powell, L – Took no part in the decision

VI. A WIN OR LOSS FOR THE ACLU?

The ACLU filed as amicus curiae urging reversal; the Supreme Court reversed the Court of Appeals for the Second Circuit's decision in an 8-0 vote, giving the ACLU an apparent win.

562. Western Air Lines, Inc. v. Criswell

(Decided June 17, 1985; 472 U.S. 400)

I. ISSUE

A. Issues Discussed

Civil rights, federal rights, employment discrimination

B. Legal Question Presented

"[W]hether the jury was properly instructed on the elements of the BFOQ [(bona fide occupational qualification)] defense."

C. Supreme Court's Answer

The jury was properly instructed on the BFOQ defense.

II. CASE SUMMARY

A. Background

"The petitioner, Western Air Lines, Inc., requires that its flight engineers retire at age 60. Although the Age Discrimination in Employment Act of 1967 (ADEA), 29 U.S.C. §§ 621-634, generally prohibits mandatory retirement before age 70, the Act provides an exception 'where age is a bona fide occupational qualification [BFOQ] reasonably necessary to the normal operation of the particular business.' . . .

In its commercial airline operations, Western operates a variety of aircraft [that] require three crew members in the cockpit: a captain, a first officer, and a flight engineer. 'The 'captain' is the pilot and controls the aircraft. . . . The 'first officer' is the copilot and assists the captain. The 'flight engineer' usually monitors a side-facing instrument panel. He does not operate the flight controls unless the captain and the first officer become incapacitated.'

A regulation of the Federal Aviation Administration (FAA) prohibits any person from serving as a pilot or first officer on a commercial flight 'if that person has reached his 60th birthday.' . . . At the same time, the FAA has refused to establish a mandatory retirement age for flight engineers. . . .

In 1978, respondents Criswell and Starley were captains operating DC-10s for Western. Both men celebrated their 60th birthdays in July 1978. Under the collective-bargaining agreement in effect between Western and the union, cockpit crew members could obtain open positions by bidding in order of seniority. In order to avoid mandatory retirement under the FAA's under-age-60 rule for pilots, Criswell and Starley applied for reassignment as flight engineers. Western denied both requests, ostensibly on the ground that both employees were members of the company's retirement plan which required all crew members to retire at age 60. For the same reason, respondent Ron, a career flight engineer, was also retired in 1978 after his 60th birthday. . . .

Criswell, Starley, and Ron brought this action against Western contending that the under-age-60 qualification for the position of flight engineer violated the ADEA. . . . The jury was instructed that the 'BFOQ defense is available only if it is reasonably necessary to the normal operation or essence of defendant's business.' The jury was informed that 'the essence of Western's business is the safe transportation of their passengers.' [The jury received additional instructions on ways to prove BFOQ.]

The jury rendered a verdict for the plaintiffs, and awarded damages. After trial, the District Court granted equitable relief, explaining in a written opinion why it found no merit in Western's BFOQ defense to the mandatory retirement rule.

On appeal, Western made various arguments attacking the verdict and judgment below, but the Court of Appeals affirmed in all respects. In particular, the Court of Appeals rejected Western's contention that the instruction on the BFOQ defense was insufficiently deferential to the airline's legitimate concern for the safety of its passengers."

The Supreme Court granted certiorari to review the case and affirmed.

B. Counsel of Record / ACLU Attorney

ACLU Side (Respondent / Appellee): Raymond C. Fay argued the cause for appellee.

Deputy Solicitor General Wallace argued the cause for the United States, et al., as amici curiae, by special leave of Court.

Opposing Side (Petitioner / Appellant): Gordon Dean Booth, Jr., argued the cause for appellant.

III. AMICI CURIAE

ACLU Side (Respondent / Appellee)

Opposing Side (Petitioner / Appellant)

Brief of amici curiae filed on behalf of the ACLU, et al., by Susan Deller Ross.

Brief of amici curiae filed on behalf of the American Association of Retired Persons by Alfred Miller and Harry P. Cohen.

Brief of amici curiae filed on behalf of the Flight Engineers International Association, American Airlines Chapter, AFL-CIO, by Asher Schwartz and David Rosen.

Brief of amici curiae filed on behalf of the United States, et al., by Deputy Solicitor General Wallace, Solicitor General Lee, Harriet S. Shapiro, Johnny J. Butler, and Philip B. Sklover.

Brief of amici curiae filed on behalf of the National Council on the Aging, Inc., et al., by Howard C. Eglit. Brief of amici curiae filed on behalf of the Air Line Pilots Association International, by Michael E. Abram and Jay P. Levy-Warren.

Brief of amici curiae filed on behalf of American Airlines, Inc., by Richard A. Malahowski.

Brief of amici curiae filed on behalf of Delta Air Lines, Inc., by James W. Callison, Robert S. Harkey, and Thomas J. Kassin.

Brief of amici curiae filed on behalf of the Equal Employment Advisory Council by Robert E. Williams, Douglas S. McDowell, and Thomas R. Bagby.

Brief of amici curiae filed on behalf of Pan American World Airways, Inc., by Robert S. Venning.

Brief of amici curiae filed on behalf of Trans World Airlines, Inc., by Henry J. Oechler, Jr., Donald I. Strauber, and Peter N. Hillman.

IV. THE SUPREME COURT'S DECISION

"Shortly after the passage of the [Age Discrimination in Employment] Act, the Secretary of Labor, who was at that time charged with its enforcement, adopted regulations declaring that the BFOQ exception to the ADEA has only 'limited scope and application' and 'must be construed narrowly.' . . . The restrictive language of the statute and the consistent interpretation of the administrative agencies charged with enforcing the statute convince us that, like its Title VII counterpart, the BFOQ exception 'was in fact meant to be an extremely narrow exception to the general prohibition' of age discrimination contained in the ADEA. . . .

In Usery v. Tamiami Trail Tours, Inc., 531 F.2d 224 (1976) . . . the Court of Appeals drew on its Title VII precedents, and concluded that two inquiries were relevant [in evaluating the BFOQ defense].

First, the court recognized that some job qualifications may be so peripheral to the central mission of the employer's business that no age discrimination can be 'reasonably necessary to the normal operation of the particular business.' . . . Second, the court recognized that the ADEA requires that age qualifications be something more than 'convenient' or 'reasonable'; they must be 'reasonably necessary . . . to the particular business,' and this is only so when the employer is compelled to rely on age as a proxy for the safety-related job qualifications validated in the first inquiry. . . .

However, Western claims that in several respects the instructions given below were insufficiently protective of public safety. Western urges that we interpret or modify the Tamiami standard to weigh these concerns in the balance.

[W]e are satisfied that the verdict is a consequence of a defect in Western's proof rather than a defect in the trial court's instructions. . . .

The judgment of the Court of Appeals is affirmed."

V. JUSTICE VOTE

8 Pro ACLU Side vs. 0 Con Opposing Side

ACLU Side (Respondent / Appellee)

1. Stevens, J. – Wrote majority opinion
2. Brennan, W. – Joined majority opinion
3. Marshall, T. – Joined majority opinion
4. Blackmun, H. – Joined majority opinion
5. O'Connor, S. – Joined majority opinion
6. White, B. – Joined majority opinion
7. Burger, W. – Joined majority opinion
8. Rehnquist, W. – Joined majority opinion

Powell, L – Took no part in the decision

VI. A WIN OR LOSS FOR THE ACLU?

The ACLU filed as amicus curiae urging affirmance; the Supreme Court affirmed the Court of Appeals for the Ninth Circuit's decision by an 8-0 vote, giving the ACLU an apparent win.

563. Maryland v. Macon

(Decided June 17, 1985; 472 U.S. 463)

I. ISSUE

A. Issues Discussed

Fourth Amendment, search and seizure, obscenity, exclusion of evidence

B. Legal Question Presented

"[W]hether allegedly obscene magazines purchased by undercover officers shortly before the warrantless arrest of a salesclerk must be excluded from evidence at the clerk's subsequent trial for distribution of obscene materials."

C. Supreme Court's Answer

The magazines should not be excluded from evidence.

II. CASE SUMMARY

A. Background

"On May 6, 1981, three Prince George's County police detectives went to the Silver News, Inc., an adult bookstore in Hyattsville, Maryland, as part of a police investigation of adult bookstores in the area. One of the detectives, who was not in uniform, entered the store, browsed for several minutes, and purchased two magazines from a clerk, Baxter Macon, with a marked $50 bill. The detective left the store and showed the two magazines to his fellow officers who were waiting nearby. Together they concluded that the magazines were obscene under the criteria previously used by them in warrant applications. The detectives returned to the store, arrested respondent Macon, who was the only attendant in the store, and retrieved from the cash register the $50 bill that had been used to make the purchase. The officers neglected to return the change received at the time of the purchase. Respondent escorted the remaining customers out and closed the bookstore before leaving with the detectives.

Prior to trial, Macon moved to suppress the magazines purchased by the officers and the $50 bill used to make the purchase. The trial judge denied the motion on the grounds that the purchase was not a seizure within the meaning of the Fourth Amendment and that the warrantless arrest was lawful. The magazines, but not the $50 bill, were subsequently introduced in evidence at trial. The jury found respondent guilty of distributing obscene materials. Respondent appealed, contending that a prior judicial determination of probable cause to believe the matter distributed was obscene was required to sustain a seizure and an arrest on charges related to obscenity. . . .

The Maryland Court of Special Appeals agreed that a warrant is required both to seize allegedly obscene materials and to arrest the distributor in order to provide a procedural safeguard for the First Amendment freedom of expression. . . . The court determined that the purchase of the magazines was a 'constructive' seizure and that the proper remedy was to exclude the magazines from evidence at the subsequent trial. Alternatively, the court held that the warrantless arrest of respondent on obscenity charges required the exclusion of the publications from evidence. The court accordingly reversed the conviction and ordered that the charges be dismissed because without the magazines the evidence was insufficient to sustain a conviction."

The Supreme Court granted certiorari to review the case and reversed the judgment of the Maryland Court of Appeals.

B. Counsel of Record / ACLU Attorney

ACLU Side (Respondent / Appellee): Burton W. Sandler argued the cause for appellee.

Opposing Side (Petitioner / Appellant): Deborah K. Chasanow argued the cause for appellant.

III. AMICI CURIAE

ACLU Side (Respondent / Appellee)

Brief of amici curiae filed on behalf of the ACLU by Burt Neuborne.

Brief of amici curiae filed on behalf of the American Booksellers Association, Inc., et al., by Michael A. Bamberger and Shirley Adelson Siegel.

Opposing Side (Petitioner / Appellant)

Brief of amici curiae filed on behalf of the United States by Solicitor General Lee, Assistant Attorney General Trott, and Deputy Solicitor General Frey.

IV. THE SUPREME COURT'S DECISION

"The First Amendment imposes special constraints on searches for and seizures of presumptively protected material, and requires that the Fourth Amendment be applied with 'scrupulous exactitude' in such circumstances. . . . A search occurs when 'an expectation of privacy that society is prepared to consider reasonable is infringed.' Here, respondent did not have any reasonable expectation of privacy in areas of the store where the public was invited to enter and to transact business. The mere expectation that the possibly illegal nature of a product will not come to the attention of the authorities, whether because a customer will not complain or because undercover officers will not transact business with the store, is not one that society is prepared to recognize as reasonable. The officer's action in entering the bookstore and examining the wares that were intentionally exposed to all who frequent the place of business did not infringe a legitimate expectation of privacy and hence did not constitute a search within the meaning of the Fourth Amendment.

Nor was the subsequent purchase a seizure within the meaning of the Fourth Amendment. A seizure occurs when 'there is some meaningful interference with an individual's possessory interests' in the property seized. Here, respondent voluntarily transferred any possessory interest he may have had in the magazines to the purchaser upon the receipt of the funds. . . .

The use of undercover officers is essential to the enforcement of vice laws. An undercover officer does not violate the Fourth Amendment merely by accepting an offer to do business that is freely made to the public. 'A government agent, in the same manner as a private person, may accept an invitation to do business and may enter upon the premises for the very purposes contemplated by the occupant.' . . .

The question remains whether respondent's warrantless arrest after the purchase of the magazines requires their exclusion at trial. Again, assuming, arguendo, that the warrantless arrest was an unreasonable seizure in violation of the Fourth Amendment—a question we do not decide—it yielded nothing of evidentiary value that was not already in the lawful possession of the police. 'The exclusionary rule enjoins the Government from benefiting from evidence it has unlawfully obtained; it does not reach backward to taint information that was in official hands prior to any illegality.' Here, the magazines were in police possession before the arrest, and the $50 bill, the only fruit of the arrest, was not introduced in evidence. . . .

Because the undercover agents did not obtain possession of the allegedly obscene magazines by means of an unreasonable search or seizure and the magazines were not the fruit of an arrest, lawful or otherwise, the magazines were properly admitted in evidence at respondent's trial for distribution of obscene materials. The judgment of the Maryland Court of Special Appeals is reversed."

V. JUSTICE VOTE

2 Pro ACLU Side vs. 7 Con Opposing Side

ACLU Side (Respondent / Appellee)

1. Brennan, W. – Wrote dissenting opinion
2. Marshall, T. – Joined Brennan's dissent

Opposing Side (Petitioner / Appellant)

1. O'Connor, S. – Wrote majority opinion
2. Burger, W. – Joined majority opinion
3. White, B. – Joined majority opinion
4. Blackmun, H. – Joined majority opinion
5. Powell, L. – Joined majority opinion
6. Rehnquist, W. – Joined majority opinion
7. Stevens, J. – Joined majority opinion

VI. A WIN OR LOSS FOR THE ACLU?

The ACLU, as amicus curiae, urged affirmance of the judgment of the Maryland Court of Appeals; the Supreme Court reversed in a 7-2 vote, giving the ACLU an apparent loss.

564. McDonald v. Smith

(Decided June 19, 1985; 472 U.S. 479)

I. ISSUE

A. Issues Discussed

First Amendment, Petition Clause

B. Legal Question Presented

"[W]hether the Petition Clause of the First Amendment provides absolute immunity to a defendant charged with expressing libelous and damaging falsehoods in letters to the President of the United States."

C. Supreme Court's Answer

The Petition Clause does not provide absolute immunity to the defendant.

II. CASE SUMMARY

A. Background

"In July 1981, respondent commenced a libel action against petitioner in state court under the common law of North Carolina. Respondent alleged that while he was being considered for the position of United States Attorney, petitioner wrote two letters to President Reagan. The complaint alleges that these letters 'contained false, slanderous, libelous, inflammatory and derogatory statements' concerning respondent. . . . Respondent alleged that petitioner knew that these accusations were false, and that petitioner maliciously intended to injure respondent by undermining his prospect of being appointed United States Attorney.

The complaint alleges that petitioner mailed copies of the letters to Presidential Adviser Edwin Meese, Senator Jesse Helms, Representative W. E. Johnston, and three other officials in the Executive and Legislative Branches. It further alleges that petitioner's letters had their intended effect: respondent was not appointed United States Attorney, his reputation and career as an attorney were injured, and he 'suffered humiliation, embarrassment, anxiety and mental anguish.' Respondent sought compensatory and punitive damages of $1 million.

Petitioner removed the case to the United States District Court on the basis of diversity of citizenship. He then moved for judgment on the pleadings on the ground that the Petition Clause of the First Amendment provides absolute immunity. The District Court agreed with petitioner that his communications fell 'within the general protection afforded by the petition clause,' but held that the Clause does not grant absolute immunity from liability for libel. The Fourth Circuit . . . affirmed."

The Supreme Court granted certiorari to review the case and affirmed the judgment of the Fourth Circuit Court of Appeals.

B. Counsel of Record / ACLU Attorney

ACLU Side (Petitioner / Appellant): Bruce J. Ennis, Jr., argued the cause for appellant.

Opposing Side (Respondent / Appellee): William A. Eagles argued the cause for appellee.

III. AMICI CURIAE

ACLU Side (Petitioner / Appellant)

Brief of amici curiae filed on behalf of the ACLU by Charles S. Sims.

Opposing Side (Respondent / Appellee)

No briefs of amici curiae were filed in support of appellee.

IV. THE SUPREME COURT'S DECISION

"The First Amendment guarantees 'the right of the people . . . to petition the Government for a redress of grievances.' The right to petition is cut from the same cloth as the other guarantees of that Amendment, and is an assurance of a particular freedom of expression. . . .

Although the values in the right of petition as an important aspect of self-government are beyond question, it does not follow that the Framers of the First Amendment believed that the Petition Clause provided absolute immunity from damages for libel. Early libel cases in state courts provide no clear evidence of the nature of the right to petition as it existed at the time the First Amendment was adopted; these cases reveal conflicting views of the privilege afforded expressions in petitions to government officials. . . .

Nothing presented to us suggests that the Court's decision not to recognize an absolute privilege in 1845 should be altered; we are not prepared to conclude, 140 years later, that the Framers of the First Amendment understood the right to petition to include an unqualified right to express damaging falsehoods in exercise of that right. . . .

To accept petitioner's claim of absolute immunity would elevate the Petition Clause to special First Amendment status. The Petition Clause, however, was inspired by the same ideals of liberty and democracy that gave us the freedoms to speak, publish, and assemble. These First Amendment rights are inseparable and there is no sound basis for granting greater constitutional protection to statements made in a petition to the President than other First Amendment expressions. . . .

We hold that the Petition Clause does not require the State to expand this privilege into an absolute one. The right to petition is guaranteed; the right to commit libel with impunity is not. The judgment of the Court of Appeals is therefore affirmed."

V. JUSTICE VOTE

0 Pro ACLU Side vs. 8 Con Opposing Side

Opposing Side (Respondent / Appellee)

1. Burger, W. – Wrote majority opinion
2. White, B. – Joined majority opinion
3. Rehnquist, W. – Joined majority opinion
4. Stevens, J. – Joined majority opinion
5. O'Connor, S. – Joined majority opinion
6. Brennan, W. – Wrote concurring opinion
7. Marshall, T. – Joined Brennan's concurrence
8. Blackmun, H. – Joined Brennan's concurrence

Powell, L. Took no part in decision

VI. A WIN OR LOSS FOR THE ACLU?

The ACLU, as amicus curiae, urged reversal of the judgment of the Court of Appeals for the Fourth Circuit; the Supreme Court affirmed in an 8-0 vote, giving the ACLU an apparent loss.

565. In re Snyder

(Decided June 24, 1985; 472 U.S. 634)

I. ISSUE

A. Issues Discussed

First Amendment, freedoms of press, speech, and association, bar admission, disbarment, attorney discipline

B. Legal Question Presented

Does a letter wherein an attorney criticizes the administration of justice in a "harsh" tone, constitute grounds upon which the attorney can be suspended from practice?

C. Supreme Court's Answer

The letter does not warrant suspension from the practice of law.

II. CASE SUMMARY

A. Background

"In March 1983, petitioner Robert Snyder was appointed by the Federal District Court for the District of North Dakota to represent a defendant under the Criminal Justice Act. After petitioner completed the assignment, he submitted a claim for $1,898.55 for services and expenses. The claim was reduced by the District Court to $1,796.05. . . .

Chief Judge Lay found the claim insufficiently documented, and he returned it with a request for additional information. Because of technical problems with his computer software, petitioner could not readily provide the information in the form requested by the Chief Judge. He did, however, file a supplemental application.

The secretary of the Chief Judge of the Circuit again returned the application, stating that the proffered documentation was unacceptable. Petitioner then discussed the matter with Helen Monteith, the District Court Judge's secretary, who suggested he write a letter expressing his view. Petitioner then wrote the letter that led to this case."

In a letter the Chief Judge described as "'totally disrespectful to the federal courts and to the judicial system,'" petitioner complained about the low pay for the representation and stated that he would not represent indigent criminal defendants under the Criminal Justice Act in the future. Although the Chief Judge would have dropped the issue if petitioner apologized, petitioner refused to do so. After a hearing, petitioner again refused to apologize for the letter and "was suspended from the practice of law in the federal courts in the Eighth Circuit for six months." Petitioner's "petition for rehearing en banc was denied."

The Supreme Court granted certiorari to review the case and reversed.

B. Counsel of Record / ACLU Attorney

ACLU Side (Petitioner / Appellant): David L. Peterson argued the cause for appellant.

Opposing Side (Respondent / Appellee): John J. Greer argued the cause for appellee.

III. AMICI CURIAE

ACLU Side (Petitioner / Appellant)

Brief of amici curiae filed on behalf of the ACLU by Erwin Chemerinsky and Charles S. Sims.

Brief of amici curiae filed on behalf of the Ohio State Bar Association by Frank E. Bazler and Albert L. Bell.

Brief of amici curiae filed on behalf of the National Association of Criminal Defense Lawyers, Inc., by Michael Pancer.

Opposing Side (Respondent / Appellee)

IV. THE SUPREME COURT'S DECISION

A. "Courts have long recognized an inherent authority to suspend or disbar lawyers. This inherent power derives from the lawyer's role as an officer of the court which granted admission. The standard for disciplining attorneys practicing before the courts of appeals is set forth in Federal Rule of Appellate Procedure 46: '(b) Suspension or Disbarment. When it is shown to the court that any member of its bar has been suspended or disbarred from practice in any other court of record, or has been guilty of conduct unbecoming a member of the bar of the court, he will be subject to suspension or disbarment by the court. The member shall be afforded an opportunity to show good cause, within such time as the court shall prescribe, why he should not be suspended or disbarred. Upon his response to the rule to show cause, and after hearing, if requested, or upon expiration of the time prescribed for a response if no response is made, the court shall enter an appropriate order' (Emphasis added.) . . .

We must examine the record in light of Rule 46 to determine whether the Court of Appeals' action is supported by the evidence. In the letter, petitioner declined to submit further documentation in support of his fee request, refused to accept further assignments under the Criminal Justice Act, and criticized the administration of the Act. Petitioner's refusal to submit further documentation in support of his fee request could afford a basis for declining to award a fee; however, the submission of adequate documentation was only a prerequisite to the collection of his fee, not an affirmative obligation required by his duties to a client or the court. Nor, as the Court of Appeals ultimately concluded, was petitioner legally obligated under the terms of the local plan to accept Criminal Justice Act cases. . . .

All persons involved in the judicial process—judges, litigants, witnesses, and court officers—owe a duty of courtesy to all other participants. The necessity for civility in the inherently contentious setting of the adversary process suggests that members of the bar cast criticisms of the system in a professional and civil tone. However, even assuming that the letter exhibited an unlawyerlike rudeness, a single incident of rudeness or lack of professional courtesy—in this context—does not support a finding of contemptuous or contumacious conduct, or a finding that a lawyer is 'not presently fit to practice law in the federal courts.' Nor does it rise to the level of 'conduct unbecoming a member of the bar' warranting suspension from practice.

Accordingly, the judgment of the Court of Appeals is reversed."

V. JUSTICE VOTE

8 Pro ACLU Side vs. 0 Con Opposing Side

ACLU Side (Petitioner / Appellant)

1. Burger, W. – Wrote majority opinion
2. Brennan, W. – Joined majority opinion
3. White, B. – Joined majority opinion
4. Marshall, T. – Joined majority opinion
5. Powell, L. – Joined majority opinion
6. Rehnquist, W. – Joined majority opinion
7. Stevens, J. – Joined majority opinion
8. O'Connor, S. – Joined majority opinion

Blackmun, H – Took no part in the decision

VI. A WIN OR LOSS FOR THE ACLU?

The ACLU filed as amicus curiae urging reversal; the Supreme Court reversed the decision of the Court of Appeals in an 8-0 vote, giving the ACLU an apparent win.

566. United States v. Albertini

(Decided June 24, 1985; 472 U.S. 675)

I. ISSUE

A. Issues Discussed

Military, 1st Amendment, press, speech, association

B. Legal Question Presented

"[W]hether respondent may be convicted for violating 18 U.S.C. § 1382, which makes it unlawful to reenter a military base after having been barred by the commanding officer."

C. Supreme Court's Answer

"Unless the statutory language is to be emptied of its ordinary meaning, respondent violated the terms of § 1382 when he reentered Hickam in 1981 contrary to the bar letter."

II. CASE SUMMARY

A. Background

"The events underlying this case date from 1972, when respondent and a companion entered Hickam Air Force Base (Hickam) in Hawaii ostensibly to present a letter to the commanding officer. Instead, they obtained access to secret Air Force documents and destroyed the documents by pouring animal blood on them. For these acts, respondent was convicted of conspiracy to injure Government property in violation of 18 U.S.C. §§ 371, 1361. Respondent also received a 'bar letter' from the Commander of Hickam informing him that he was forbidden to 'reenter the confines of this installation without the written permission of the Commander or an officer designated by him to issue a permit of reentry.' . . .

Respondent entered Hickam again on May 16, 1981, during the base's annual open house for Armed Forces Day. . . .

With four friends, respondent attended the open house in order to engage in a peaceful demonstration criticizing the nuclear arms race. . . .

An information filed on July 1, 1981, charged respondent with violating § 1382 . . . . Respondent was convicted after a bench trial and sentenced to three months' imprisonment. . . . The conviction must be reversed, the Court of Appeals held, because Hickam had been transformed into a temporary public forum during the open house, and the military could not exclude respondent from such a forum."

The Supreme Court granted certiorari to review the case.

B. Counsel of Record

ACLU Side (Respondent / Appellee): Charles S. Sims argued the cause for appellee. With him on the briefs were Gerard E. Lynch, Burt Neuborne (ACLU National Legal Director 1981-86), William A. Harrison, and Yvonne Chotzen.

Opposing Side (Petitioner / Appellant): David A. Strauss argued the cause for the United States. With him on the briefs were Solicitor General Lee, Assistant Attorney General Trott, Deputy Solicitor General Wallace, John F. De Pue, and Major Robert T. Lee.

III. AMICI CURIAE

ACLU Side (Respondent / Appellee)

No briefs of amici curiae were filed on behalf of appellee.

Opposing Side (Petitioner / Appellant)

No briefs of amici curiae were filed on behalf of the United States.

IV. THE SUPREME COURT'S DECISION

"Courts in applying criminal laws generally must follow the plain and unambiguous meaning of the statutory language. . . .

Turning to the statute involved here, we conclude that § 1382 applies to respondent's conduct. The relevant portion of the statute makes it unlawful for a person to reenter a military base after having been ordered not to do so by the commanding officer. Unless the statutory language is to be emptied of its ordinary meaning, respondent violated the terms of § 1382 when he reentered Hickam in 1981 contrary to the bar letter. Respondent, however, argues that § 1382 does not apply to his attendance at the open house for three reasons. First, he contends that § 1382 does not allow indefinite exclusion from a military base, but instead applies only when a person has reentered 'within a reasonable period of time after being ejected.' Second, respondent maintains that Congress did not intend § 1382 to apply when a military base is opened to the general public for purposes of attending an open house. Respondent finally argues that reentry is unlawful under § 1382 only if a person knows that his conduct violates an extant order not to return. None of these arguments is persuasive.

The legislative history of § 1382, although sparse, fully supports application of the statute to respondent. . . .

We find no merit to the reasons respondent offers for concluding he did not violate § 1382. . . .

Section 1382, we further conclude, applies during an open house. . . .

The final statutory argument advanced by respondent is that he did not violate § 1382 because he did not subjectively believe that his attendance at the open house was contrary to a valid order barring reentry. This argument misperceives the knowledge required for a violation of the statute. . . .

In holding that § 1382 cannot be applied during an open house, the Court of Appeals misapprehended the significance of Flower. . . .

Whether or not Hickam constituted a public forum on the day of the open house, the exclusion of respondent did not violate the First Amendment. . . .

Section 1382 is content-neutral and serves a significant Government interest by barring entry to a military base by persons whose previous conduct demonstrates that they are a threat to security. Application of a facially neutral regulation that incidentally burdens speech satisfies the First Amendment if it 'furthers an important or substantial governmental interest; if the governmental interest is unrelated to the suppression of free expression; and if the incidental restriction on alleged First Amendment freedoms is no greater than is essential to the furtherance of that interest.' . . .

[T]he judgment of the Court of Appeals is reversed, and the case is remanded . . . ."

V. JUSTICE VOTE

3 Pro ACLU Side vs. 6 Con Opposing Side

ACLU Side (Respondent / Appellee)

1. Stevens, J. – Wrote dissenting opinion
2. Brennan, W. – Joined Stevens' dissent
3. Marshall, T. – Joined Stevens' dissent

Opposing Side (Petitioner / Appellant)

1. O'Connor, S. – Wrote majority opinion
2. Rehnquist, W. – Joined majority opinion
3. Burger, W. – Joined majority opinion
4. Powell, L. – Joined majority opinion
5. Blackmun, H. – Joined majority opinion
6. White, B. – Joined majority opinion

VI. A WIN OR LOSS FOR THE ACLU?

The ACLU served as counsel for appellee urging affirmance; the Supreme Court reversed the Court of Appeals' decision by a 6-3 vote, giving the ACLU an apparent loss.

567. Jean v. Nelson

(Decided June 26, 1985; 472 U.S. 846)

I. ISSUE

A. Issues Discussed

Governmental authority, immigration, Fifth Amendment

B. Legal Question Presented

Can detained unadmitted immigrants invoke the Fifth Amendment to challenge the Government's failure to release them temporarily on parole?

C. Supreme Court's Answer

"[T]he Court of Appeals should not have reached and decided the parole question on constitutional grounds, but we affirm its judgment remanding the case to the District Court."

II. CASE SUMMARY

A. Background

"Petitioners, the named representatives of a class of undocumented and unadmitted aliens from Haiti, sued respondent Commissioner of the Immigration and Naturalization Service (INS). They alleged, inter alia, that they had been denied parole by INS officials on the basis of race and national origin. The en banc Eleventh Circuit concluded that any such discrimination concerning parole would not violate the Fifth Amendment to the United States Constitution because of the Government's plenary authority to control the Nation's borders. That court remanded the case to the District Court for consideration of petitioners' claim that their treatment violated INS regulations, which did not authorize consideration of race or national origin in determining whether or not an excludable alien should be paroled."

The Supreme Court granted certiorari to review the case.

B. Counsel of Record / ACLU Attorney

ACLU Side (Petitioner / Appellant): Ira J. Kurzban argued the cause for appellant.

Opposing Side (Respondent / Appellee): Solicitor General Lee argued the cause for appellee.

III. AMICI CURIAE

ACLU Side (Petitioner / Appellant)

Brief of amici curiae filed on behalf of the ACLU by Burt Neuborne and Charles S. Sims.

Additional briefs of amici curiae were filed on behalf of the American Immigration Lawyers Association, Amnesty International U.S.A., the Asian American Legal Defense and Education Fund, et al., Metropolitan Dade County, et al., the NAACP Legal Defense and Educational Fund, Inc., the National Association for the Advancement of Colored People, et al., the National Coalition for Haitian Refugees, et al., the Procedural Aspects of International Law Institute, et al., and the Lawyers Committee for International Human Rights, et al.

Opposing Side (Respondent / Appellee)

Brief of amici curiae filed on behalf of the Federation for American Immigration Reform by Robert E. Jensen.

Brief of amici curiae filed on behalf of the Washington Legal Foundation by Daniel J. Popeo and George C. Smith;

IV. THE SUPREME COURT'S DECISION

"Petitioners contend that the only adequate remedy is 'declaratory and injunctive relief' ordered by this Court, based upon the Fifth Amendment. The limited statutory remedy ordered by the court . . . petitioners contend, is insufficient. For their part respondents are also eager to have us reach the Fifth Amendment issue. Respondents wish us to hold that the equal protection component of the Fifth Amendment has no bearing on an unadmitted alien's request for parole.

'Prior to reaching any constitutional questions, federal courts must consider nonconstitutional grounds for decision.' This is a 'fundamental rule of judicial restraint.' Of course, the fact that courts should not decide constitutional issues unnecessarily does not permit a court to press statutory construction 'to the point of disingenuous evasion' to avoid a constitutional question. '[I]f there is one doctrine more deeply rooted than any other in the process of constitutional adjudication, it is that we ought not to pass on questions of constitutionality . . . unless such adjudication is unavoidable.'

[W]e affirm the en banc court's judgment insofar as it remanded to the District Court for a determination whether the INS officials are observing this limit upon their broad statutory discretion to deny parole to class members in detention. On remand the District Court must consider: (1) whether INS officials exercised their discretion under § 1182(d)(5)(A) to make individualized determinations of parole, and (2) whether INS officials exercised this broad discretion under the statutes and regulations without regard to race or national origin.

Petitioners protest, however, that such a nonconstitutional remedy will permit lower-level INS officials to commence parole revocation and discriminatory parole denial against class members who are currently released on parole. But these officials, while like all others bound by the provisions of the Constitution, are just as surely bound by the provisions of the statute and of the regulations. Respondents concede that the latter do not authorize discrimination on the basis of race and national origin. These class members are therefore protected by the terms of the Court of Appeals' remand from the very conduct which they fear. The fact that the protection results from the terms of a regulation or statute, rather than from a constitutional holding, is a necessary consequence of the obligation of all federal courts to avoid constitutional adjudication except where necessary.

The judgment of the Court of Appeals remanding the case to the District Court for consideration of petitioner's claims based on the statute and regulations is affirmed."

V. JUSTICE VOTE

2 Pro ACLU Side vs. 6 Con Opposing Side

ACLU Side (Petitioner / Appellant)

1. Marshall, T. – Wrote dissenting opinion
2. Brennan, W. – Joined Marshall's dissent

Opposing Side (Respondent / Appellee)

1. Rehnquist, W. – Wrote majority opinion
2. Burger, W. – Joined majority opinion
3. White, B. – Joined majority opinion
4. Blackmun, H. – Joined majority opinion
5. Stevens, J. – Joined majority opinion
6. O'Connor, S. – Joined majority opinion

Powell, L – Took no part in the decision

VI. A WIN OR LOSS FOR THE ACLU?

The ACLU filed as amicus curiae urging reversal; the Supreme Court affirmed the ruling of the Court of Appeals for the Eleventh Circuit in a 6-2 vote, giving the ACLU an apparent loss.

568. Atascadero State Hospital v. Scanlon

(Decided June 28, 1985; 473 U.S. 234)

I. ISSUE

A. Issues Discussed

Governmental authority, regulation, civil rights, Eleventh Amendment

B. Legal Question Presented

"[W]hether States and state agencies are subject to suit in federal court by litigants seeking retroactive monetary relief under § 504 of the Rehabilitation Act of 1973, 29 U.S.C. § 794, or whether such suits are proscribed by the Eleventh Amendment."

C. Supreme Court's Answer

States in this circumstance are immune from suit.

II. CASE SUMMARY

A. Background

"Respondent, Douglas James Scanlon, suffers from diabetes mellitus and has no sight in one eye. In November 1979 he filed suit against petitioners, Atascadero State Hospital and the California Department of Mental Health, in the United States District Court for the Central District of California, alleging that in 1978 the hospital denied him employment as a graduate student assistant recreational therapist solely because of his physical handicaps. Respondent charged that the hospital's discriminatory refusal to hire him violated § 504 of the Rehabilitation Act of 1973, as amended, 29 U.S.C. § 794, and certain state fair employment laws. Respondent sought compensatory, injunctive, and declaratory relief.

Petitioners moved for dismissal of the complaint. [T]he District Court granted petitioners' motion to dismiss the complaint on the ground that respondent's claims were barred by the Eleventh Amendment. On appeal, the United States Court of Appeals for the Ninth Circuit affirmed. It did not reach the question whether the Eleventh Amendment proscribed respondent's suit. Rather it affirmed the District Court on the ground that respondent failed to allege an essential element of a claim under § 504, namely, that a primary objective of the federal funds received by the defendants was to provide employment.

Respondent then sought review by [the Supreme] Court [which] granted certiorari, vacated the judgment of the Court of Appeals, and remanded the case for further consideration . . . . On remand, the Court of Appeals reversed the judgment of the District Court. It held that 'the Eleventh Amendment does not bar [respondent's] action because the State, if it has participated in and received funds from programs under the Rehabilitation Act, has implicitly consented to be sued as a recipient under 29 U.S.C. § 794.'"

The Supreme Court granted certiorari to review the case and reversed.

B. Counsel of Record / ACLU Attorney

ACLU Side (Respondent / Appellee): Marilyn Holle argued the cause for appellee.

Opposing Side (Petitioner / Appellant): James E. Ryan, Deputy Attorney General of California, argued the cause for appellant.

III. AMICI CURIAE

ACLU Side (Respondent / Appellee)

Brief of amici curiae filed on behalf of the ACLU Foundation, et al., by David L. Shapiro, Burt Neuborne, Charles S. Sims, Paul L. Hoffman, and Mark D. Rosenbaum.

Brief of amici curiae filed on behalf of Senator Cranston, et al., by Bonnie Milstein.

Brief of amici curiae filed on behalf of the Disability and Employment Advocacy Project of the Employment Law Center by Joan M. Graff and Robert Barnes.

Opposing Side (Petitioner / Appellant)

Brief of amici curiae filed on behalf of the United States by Solicitor General Lee, Assistant Attorney General Reynolds, Deputy Assistant Attorney General Cooper, Charles Fried, Christopher J. Wright, and Walter W. Barnett.

IV. THE SUPREME COURT'S DECISION

"The court properly recognized that the mere receipt of federal funds cannot establish that a State has consented to suit in federal court. The court erred, however, in concluding that because various provisions of the Rehabilitation Act are addressed to the States, a State necessarily consents to suit in federal court by participating in programs funded under the statute. We have decided today that the Rehabilitation Act does not evince an unmistakable congressional purpose, pursuant to § 5 of the Fourteenth Amendment, to subject unconsenting States to the jurisdiction of the federal courts. The Act likewise falls far short of manifesting a clear intent to condition participation in the programs funded under the Act on a State's consent to waive its constitutional immunity. Thus, where we view this statute as an enactment pursuant to the Spending Clause, Art. I, 8, we would hold that there was no indication that the State of California consented to federal jurisdiction. . . .

The provisions of the Rehabilitation Act fall far short of expressing an unequivocal congressional intent to abrogate the States' Eleventh Amendment immunity. Nor has the State of California specifically waived its immunity to suit in federal court. In view of these determinations, the judgment of the Court of Appeals must be reversed."

V. JUSTICE VOTE

4 Pro ACLU Side vs. 5 Con Opposing Side

ACLU Side (Respondent / Appellee)

1. Brennan, W. – Wrote dissenting opinion, joined Blackmun's dissent
2. Blackmun, H. – Wrote dissenting opinion, joined Brennan's dissent
3. Stevens, J. – Wrote dissenting opinion, joined Brennan's dissent and Blackmun's dissent
4. Marshall, T. – Joined Brennan's dissent and Blackmun's dissent

Opposing Side (Petitioner / Appellant)

1. Powell, L. – Wrote majority opinion
2. Burger, W. – Joined majority opinion
3. White, B. – Joined majority opinion
4. Rehnquist, W. – Joined majority opinion
5. O'Connor, S. – Joined majority opinion

VI. A WIN OR LOSS FOR THE ACLU?

The ACLU filed as amicus curiae urging affirmance; the Supreme Court reversed the ruling of the Court of Appeals for the Ninth Circuit in a 5-4 vote, giving the ACLU an apparent loss.

569. Walters v. National Ass'n of Radiation Survivors

(Decided June 28, 1985; 473 U.S. 305)

I. ISSUE

A. Issues Discussed

Governmental authority, regulation, Fifth Amendment, due process, First Amendment

B. Legal Question Presented

Does Title 38 U.S.C. § 3404(c) violate the First and Fifth Amendments by limiting "the fee that may be paid an attorney or agent who represents a veteran seeking benefits for service-connected death or disability"?

C. Supreme Court's Answer

Title 38 U.S.C. § 3404(c) does not violate the Fifth Amendment or First Amendment.

II. CASE SUMMARY

A. Background

"Title 38 U.S.C. § 3404(c) limits to $10 the fee that may be paid an attorney or agent who represents a veteran seeking benefits for service-connected death or disability. . . . Appellees contended in the District Court that the fee limitation provision of § 3404 denied them any realistic opportunity to obtain legal representation in presenting their claims to the VA and hence violated their rights under the Due Process Clause of the Fifth Amendment and under the First Amendment. The District Court agreed with the appellees on both of these grounds, and entered a nationwide 'preliminary injunction' barring appellants from enforcing the fee limitation."

The Supreme Court granted certiorari to review the case and reversed.

B. Counsel of Record / ACLU Attorney

ACLU Side (Respondent / Appellee): Gordon P. Erspamer and Robert L. Gnaizda argued the cause for appellee.

Opposing Side (Petitioner / Appellant): Mark I. Levy argued the cause for appellant.

III. AMICI CURIAE

ACLU Side (Respondent / Appellee)

Brief of amici curiae filed on behalf of the ACLU Foundation, et al., by Burt Neuborne, Charles S. Sims, Alan L. Schlosser, and Amitai Schwartz.

Additional briefs of amici curiae were filed on behalf of the American Veterans Committee, Inc., the Federal Bar Association, the Lawyers' Club of San Francisco, the National Association of Atomic Veterans, Vietnam Veterans of America, and Andrew Groza.

Opposing Side (Petitioner / Appellant)

Brief of amici curiae filed on behalf of Disabled American Veterans by Joseph C. Zengerle.

IV. THE SUPREME COURT'S DECISION

"[A]ppellees' First Amendment arguments, at base, are really inseparable from their due process claims. The thrust is that they have been denied 'meaningful access to the courts' to present their claims. This must be based in some notion that VA claimants, who presently are allowed to speak in court, and to have someone speak for them, also have a First Amendment right to pay their surrogate speaker; beyond that questionable proposition, however, even as framed appellees' argument recognizes that such a First Amendment interest would attach only in the absence of a 'meaningful' alternative. [Our] analysis of appellees' due process claim focused on substantially the same question—whether the process allows a claimant to make a meaningful presentation—and we concluded that appellees had such an opportunity under the present claims process, and that significant Government interests favored the limitation on 'speech' that appellees attack. Under those circumstances appellees' First Amendment claim has no independent significance. The decision of the District Court is accordingly reversed."

V. JUSTICE VOTE

3 Pro ACLU Side vs. 6 Con Opposing Side

ACLU Side (Respondent / Appellee)

1. Stevens, J. – Wrote dissenting opinion
2. Brennan, W. – Wrote dissenting opinion, joined Stevens' dissent
3. Marshall, T. – Joined Brennan's dissent, joined Stevens' dissent

Opposing Side (Petitioner / Appellant)

1. Rehnquist, W. – Wrote majority opinion
2. Burger, W. – Joined majority opinion
3. White, B. – Joined majority opinion
4. Blackmun, H. – Joined O'Connor's concurrence
5. Powell, L. – Joined majority opinion
6. O'Connor, S. – Wrote concurring opinion

VI. A WIN OR LOSS FOR THE ACLU?

The ACLU filed as amicus curiae urging affirmance; the Supreme Court reversed the ruling of the District Court for the Northern District of California in a 6-3 vote, giving the ACLU an apparent loss.

570. Aguilar v. Felton

(Decided July 1, 1985; 473 U.S. 402)

I. ISSUE

A. Issues Discussed

First Amendment, Establishment Clause, schools

B. Legal Question Presented

Whether the City of New York's use of "federal funds to pay the salaries of public employees who teach in parochial schools . . . violates the Establishment Clause of the First Amendment."

C. Supreme Court's Answer

The program violates the Establishment Clause.

II. CASE SUMMARY

A. Background

"The program at issue in this case, originally enacted as Title I of the Elementary and Secondary Education Act of 1965, authorizes the Secretary of Education to distribute financial assistance to local educational institutions to meet the needs of educationally deprived children from low-income families. The funds are to be appropriated in accordance with programs proposed by local educational agencies and approved by state educational agencies. . . .

Since 1966, the City of New York has provided instructional services funded by Title I to parochial school students on the premises of parochial schools. . . . The programs conducted at these schools include remedial reading, reading skills, remedial mathematics, English as a second language, and guidance services. These programs are carried out by regular employees of the public schools . . . who have volunteered to teach in the parochial schools. . . .

The City's Bureau of Nonpublic School Reimbursement makes teacher assignments, and the instructors are supervised by field personnel, who attempt to pay at least one unannounced visit per month. The field supervisors, in turn, report to program coordinators, who also pay occasional unannounced supervisory visits to monitor Title I classes in the parochial schools. The professionals involved in the program are directed to avoid involvement with religious activities that are conducted within the private schools and to bar religious materials in their classrooms. All material and equipment used in the programs funded under Title I are supplied by the Government and are used only in those programs. The professional personnel are solely responsible for the selection of the students. Additionally, the professionals are informed that contact with private school personnel should be kept to a minimum. Finally, the administrators of the parochial schools are required to clear the classrooms used by the public school personnel of all religious symbols. . . .

In 1978, six taxpayers commenced this action in the District Court for the Eastern District of New York, alleging that the Title I program administered by the City of New York violates the Establishment Clause. . . . The District Court granted appellants' motion for summary judgment . . . . A unanimous panel of the Court of Appeals for the Second Circuit reversed."

The Supreme Court granted certiorari to review the case and affirmed the judgment of the Court of Appeals.

B. Counsel of Record / ACLU Attorney

ACLU Side (Respondent / Appellee): Stanley Geller argued the cause for appellee.

Opposing Side (Petitioner / Appellant): Solicitor General Lee argued the cause for appellant.

III. AMICI CURIAE

ACLU Side (Respondent / Appellee)

Brief of amici curiae filed on behalf of the ACLU, et al., by Burt Neuborne, Charles Sims, and Marc D. Stern.

Brief of amici curiae filed on behalf of Americans United for Separation of Church and State, et al., by Lee Boothby.

Brief of amici curiae filed on behalf of the Anti-Defamation Leaque of B'nai B'rith by Justin J. Finger, Meyer Eisenberg, and Jeffrey P. Sinensky.

Opposing Side (Petitioner / Appellant)

Brief of amici curiae filed on behalf of the Council for American Private Education, et al., by Edward McGlynn Gaffney, Jr.

Brief of amici curiae filed on behalf of the Catholic League for Religious and Civil Rights by Steven Frederick McDowell.

Brief of amici curiae filed on behalf of Citizens for Educational Freedom by Charles E. Rice.

Brief of amici curiae filed on behalf of the National Jewish Commission on Law and Public Affairs by Nathan Lewin, Dennis Rapps, and Daniel D. Chazin.

Brief of amici curiae filed on behalf of Parents Rights, Inc., by John J. Donnelly.

Brief of amici curiae filed on behalf of the United States Catholic Conference by Wilfred R. Caron and Mark E. Chopko.

IV. THE SUPREME COURT'S DECISION

"The New York City programs challenged in this case are very similar to the programs we examined in Ball. In both cases, publicly funded instructors teach classes composed exclusively of private school students in private school buildings. In both cases, an overwhelming number of the participating private schools are religiously affiliated. In both cases, the publicly funded programs provide not only professional personnel, but also all materials and supplies necessary for the operation of the programs. Finally, the instructors in both cases are told that they are public school employees under the sole control of the public school system.

Appellants attempt to distinguish this case on the ground that the City of New York . . . has adopted a system for monitoring the religious content of publicly funded Title I classes in the religious schools. At best, the supervision in this case would assist in preventing the Title I program from being used, intentionally or unwittingly, to inculcate the religious beliefs of the surrounding parochial school. But appellants' argument fails in any event, because the supervisory system established by the City of New York inevitably results in the excessive entanglement of church and state, an Establishment Clause concern distinct from that addressed by the effects doctrine. Even where state aid to parochial institutions does not have the primary effect of advancing religion, the provision of such aid may nonetheless violate the Establishment Clause owing to the nature of the interaction of church and state in the administration of that aid. . . .

First, as noted above, the aid is provided in a pervasively sectarian environment. Second, because assistance is provided in the form of teachers, ongoing inspection is required to ensure the absence of a religious message. In short, the scope and duration of New York City's Title I program would require a permanent and pervasive state presence in the sectarian schools receiving aid.

This pervasive monitoring by public authorities in the sectarian schools infringes precisely those Establishment Clause values at the root of the prohibition of excessive entanglement. [T]he religious school, which has as a primary purpose the advancement and preservation of a particular religion must endure the ongoing presence of state personnel whose primary purpose is to monitor teachers and students in an attempt to guard against the infiltration of religious thought. . . .

Despite the well-intentioned efforts taken by the City of New York, the program remains constitutionally flawed owing to the nature of the aid, to the institution receiving the aid, and to the constitutional principles that they implicate—that neither the State nor Federal Government shall promote or hinder a particular faith or faith generally through the advancement of benefits or through the excessive entanglement of church and state in the administration of those benefits.

Affirmed."

V. JUSTICE VOTE

5 Pro ACLU Side vs. 4 Con Opposing Side

ACLU Side (Respondent / Appellee)

1. Brennan, W. – Wrote majority opinion
2. Marshall, T. – Joined majority opinion
3. Blackmun, H. – Joined majority opinion
4. Powell, L. – Wrote concurring opinion
5. Stevens, J. – Joined majority opinion

Opposing Side (Petitioner / Appellant)

1. Burger, W. – Wrote dissenting opinion
2. White, B. – Wrote dissenting opinion
3. O'Connor, S. – Wrote dissenting opinion
4. Rehnquist, W. – Wrote dissenting opinion, joined O'Connor's dissent, in part

VI. A WIN OR LOSS FOR THE ACLU?

The ACLU, as amicus curiae, urged affirmance of the Second Circuit Court of Appeals' judgment; the Supreme Court affirmed in a 5-4 vote, giving the ACLU an apparent win.

571. City of Cleburne v. Cleburne Living Center

(Decided July 1, 1985; 473 U.S. 432)

I. ISSUE

A. Issues Discussed

Civil rights, state's rights, zoning, Fourteenth Amendment, equal protection

B. Legal Question Presented

Did requiring "a special use permit for the operation of a group home for the mentally" disabled deprive respondents of equal protection of the law?

C. Supreme Court's Answer

Requiring the special use permit deprived respondents of equal protection.

II. CASE SUMMARY

A. Background

"In July 1980, respondent Jan Hannah purchased a building . . . with the intention of leasing it to Cleburne Living Center, Inc. (CLC), for the operation of a group home for the mentally retarded. . . . The city informed CLC that a special use permit would be required for the operation of a group home at the site, and CLC accordingly submitted a permit application. . . . After holding a public hearing on CLC's application, the City Council voted 3 to 1 to deny a special use permit.

CLC then filed suit in Federal District Court against the city and a number of its officials, alleging, inter alia, that the zoning ordinance was invalid on its face and as applied because it discriminated against the mentally retarded in violation of the equal protection rights of CLC and its potential residents. [T]he District Court held the ordinance and its application constitutional. . . .

The Court of Appeals for the Fifth Circuit reversed, determining that mental retardation was a quasi-suspect classification and that it should assess the validity of the ordinance under intermediate-level scrutiny. . . . Applying the test that it considered appropriate, the court held that the ordinance was invalid on its face because it did not substantially further any important governmental interests. The Court of Appeals went on to hold that the ordinance was also invalid as applied. Rehearing en banc was denied with six judges dissenting in an opinion urging en banc consideration of the panel's adoption of a heightened standard of review."

The Supreme Court granted certiorari to review the case, affirmed in part, and vacated in part.

B. Counsel of Record / ACLU Attorney

ACLU Side (Respondent / Appellee): Renea Hicks reargued the cause for appellee.

Opposing Side (Petitioner / Appellant): Earl Luna reargued the cause for appellant.

III. AMICI CURIAE

ACLU Side (Respondent / Appellee)

Brief of amici curiae filed on behalf of the ACLU, et al., by Burt Neuborne, Charles S. Sims, Robert M. Levy, Paul Hoffman, Stanley Fleishman, Joseph Lawrence, James Preis, and James C. Harrington.

Additional briefs of amici curiae were filed on behalf of the State of Connecticut, et al., the State of Pennsylvania, et al., the American Association on Mental Deficiency, et al., the Association for Retarded Citizens/USA, et al., the Disability Rights Education and Defense Fund, Disabled Peoples' International and Human Rights Advocates, Inc., and the National Conference of Catholic Charities, et al.

Opposing Side (Petitioner / Appellant)

Brief of amici curiae filed on behalf of the United States by Solicitor General Lee, Assistant Attorney General Reynolds, Deputy Solicitor General Fried, Deputy Assistant Attorney General Cooper, and Walter W. Barnett.

Brief of amici curiae filed on behalf of the Federation of Greater Baton Rouge Civic Associations, Inc., by Elliott W. Atkinson, Jr.

IV. THE SUPREME COURT'S DECISION

"[W]e conclude for several reasons that the Court of Appeals erred in holding mental retardation a quasi-suspect classification calling for a more exacting standard of judicial review than is normally accorded economic and social legislation. First, it is undeniable, and it is not argued otherwise here, that those who are mentally retarded have a reduced ability to cope with and function in the everyday world. . . . Second, the distinctive legislative response, both national and state, to the plight of those who are mentally retarded demonstrates not only that they have unique problems, but also that the lawmakers have been addressing their difficulties in a manner that belies a continuing antipathy or prejudice and a corresponding need for more intrusive oversight by the judiciary. . . . Third, the legislative response, which could hardly have occurred and survived without public support, negates any claim that the mentally retarded are politically powerless in the sense that they have no ability to attract the attention of the lawmakers. . . . Fourth, if the large and amorphous class of the mentally retarded were deemed quasi-suspect for the reasons given by the Court of Appeals, it would be difficult to find a principled way to distinguish a variety of other groups who have perhaps immutable disabilities setting them off from others, who cannot themselves mandate the desired legislative responses, and who can claim some degree of prejudice from at least part of the public at large. . . .

We turn to the issue of the validity of the zoning ordinance insofar as it requires a special use permit for homes for the mentally retarded. We inquire first whether requiring a special use permit for the Featherston home in the circumstances here deprives respondents of the equal protection of the laws. . . . Because in our view the record does not reveal any rational basis for believing that the Featherston home would pose any special threat to the city's legitimate interests, we affirm the judgment below insofar as it holds the ordinance invalid as applied in this case. . . .

The short of it is that requiring the permit in this case appears to us to rest on an irrational prejudice against the mentally retarded, including those who would occupy the Featherston facility and who would live under the closely supervised and highly regulated conditions expressly provided for by state and federal law.

The judgment of the Court of Appeals is affirmed insofar as it invalidates the zoning ordinance as applied to the Featherston home. The judgment is otherwise vacated, and the case is remanded."

V. JUSTICE VOTE

9 Pro ACLU Side vs. 0 Con Opposing Side

ACLU Side (Respondent / Appellee)

1. White, B. – Wrote majority opinion
2. Powell, L. – Joined majority opinion
3. Rehnquist, W. – Joined majority opinion
4. Stevens, J. – Wrote concurring opinion

5. O'Connor, S. – Joined majority opinion
6. Burger, W. – Joined Stevens' concurrence
7. Marshall, T. – Wrote opinion concurring in the judgment in part and dissenting in part
8. Brennan, W. – Joined Marshall's opinion
9. Blackmun, H. – Joined Marshall's opinion

VI. A WIN OR LOSS FOR THE ACLU?

The ACLU filed as amicus curiae urging affirmance; the Supreme Court affirmed in part the ruling of the Court of Appeals in a 9-3 vote, giving the ACLU an apparent win.

572. Cornelius v. NAACP Legal Defense and Educational Fund, Inc.

(Decided July 2, 1985; 473 U.S. 788)

I. ISSUE

A. Issues Discussed

First Amendment, freedoms of press, speech, and procedure

B. Legal Question Presented

"[W]hether the Federal Government violates the First Amendment when it excludes legal defense and political advocacy organizations from participation in the Combined Federal Campaign (CFC or Campaign), a charity drive aimed at federal employees."

C. Supreme Court's Answer

The government does not violate the First Amendment by excluding legal defense and political advocacy organizations from the CFC, so long as the exclusion remains viewpoint neutral.

II. CASE SUMMARY

A. Background

"The [Combined Federal Campaign (CFC)] is an annual charitable fund-raising drive conducted in the federal workplace during working hours largely through the voluntary efforts of federal employees. . . . From 1963 until 1982, [o]nly tax-exempt, nonprofit charitable organizations that were supported by contributions from the public and that provided direct health and welfare services to individuals were eligible to participate in the CFC. . . .

Each of the respondents attempts to influence public policy through one or more of the following means: political activity, advocacy, lobbying, or litigation on behalf of others. In 1980, two of the respondents—the NAACP Legal Defense and Educational Fund, Inc., and the Puerto Rican Legal Defense and Education Fund (the Legal Defense Funds)—joined by the NAACP Special Contribution Fund, for the first time sought to participate in the CFC. The Office of Personnel Management (OPM) . . . refused admission to the Legal Defense Funds. This action led to a series of three lawsuits, the third of which is before [the Supreme Court]. . . .

In response to the District Court's decision in NAACP I, President Reagan . . . issued Executive Order No. 12353, 3 CFR 139 (1983), to replace the 1961 Executive Order which had established the CFC. . . . Shortly thereafter, the President amended Executive Order No. 12353 to specify the purposes of the CFC and to identify groups whose participation would be consistent with those purposes. . . . The Order limited participation to 'voluntary, charitable, health and welfare agencies that provide or support direct health and welfare services to individuals or their families," and specifically excluded those '[a]gencies that seek to influence the outcomes of elections or the determination of public policy through political activity or advocacy, lobbying, or litigation on behalf of parties other than themselves.'

Respondents brought this action challenging their threatened exclusion under the new Executive Order. . . . The District Court dismissed the vagueness challenge and the Equal Protection claim on ripeness grounds. Those rulings were not appealed . . . . The District Court also held that respondents' exclusion from the designated contribution portion of the CFC was unconstitutional. The court reasoned that the CFC was a 'limited public forum' and that respondents' exclusion was content-based. Finding that the regulation was not narrowly drawn to support a compelling governmental interest, the District Court granted summary judgment to respondents and enjoined the denial of respondents' pending or future applications to participate in the solicitation of designated contributions.

The judgment was affirmed by a divided panel of the United States Court of Appeals for the District of Columbia Circuit. . . . An equally divided court denied the Government's request for rehearing en banc."

The Supreme Court granted certiorari to review the case and reversed.

B. Counsel of Record / ACLU Attorney

ACLU Side (Respondent / Appellee): Charles Stephen Ralston argued the cause for appellee.

Opposing Side (Petitioner / Appellant): Solicitor General Lee argued the cause for appellant.

III. AMICI CURIAE

ACLU Side (Respondent / Appellee)

Brief of amici curiae filed on behalf of the ACLU Foundation by E. Richard Larson, Burt Neuborne, Joseph M. Hassett, and Patricia A. Brannan.

Additional briefs of amici curiae were filed on behalf of the State of New York, the American Jewish Committee, et al., the Planned Parenthood Federation of America, Inc., and the National Committee for Responsive Philanthropy, Independent Sector, et al.

Opposing Side (Petitioner / Appellant)

Brief of amici curiae filed on behalf of the United Black Fund of America, et al., by Joseph B. Scott and Michael J. Kator.

IV. THE SUPREME COURT'S DECISION

"The conclusion that the solicitation which occurs in the CFC is protected speech merely begins our inquiry. Even protected speech is not equally permissible in all places and at all times. Nothing in the Constitution requires the Government freely to grant access to all who wish to exercise their right to free speech on every type of Government property without regard to the nature of the property or to the disruption that might be caused by the speaker's activities. [T]he Court has adopted a forum analysis as a means of determining when the Government's interest in limiting the use of its property to its intended purpose outweighs the interest of those wishing to use the property for other purposes. Accordingly, the extent to which the Government can control access depends on the nature of the relevant forum. . . .

An examination of the nature of the Government property involved strengthens the conclusion that the CFC is a nonpublic forum. The federal workplace, like any place of employment, exists to accomplish the business of the employer. . . . It follows that the Government has the right to exercise control over access to the federal workplace in order to avoid interruptions to the performance of the duties of its employees. In light of the Government policy in creating the CFC and its practice in limiting access, we conclude that the CFC is a nonpublic forum. . . .

Control over access to a nonpublic forum can be based on subject matter and speaker identity so long as the distinctions drawn are reasonable in light of the purpose served by the forum and are viewpoint-neutral. [T]he government violates the First Amendment when it denies access to a speaker solely to suppress the point of view he espouses on an otherwise includible subject.

[W]e . . . conclude that respondents may be excluded from the CFC. . . . The Government's decision to restrict access to a nonpublic forum need only be reasonable; it need not be the most reasonable or the only reasonable limitation. In contrast to a public forum, a finding of strict incompatibility between the nature of the speech or the identity of the speaker and the functioning of the nonpublic forum is not mandated. . . . Here, . . . the speakers have access to alternative channels, including direct mail and in-person solicitation outside the workplace, to solicit contributions from federal employees. . . .

We conclude that the Government does not violate the First Amendment when it limits participation in the CFC in order to minimize disruption to the federal workplace, to ensure the success of the fundraising effort, or to avoid the appearance of political favoritism without regard to the viewpoint of the excluded groups. Accordingly, we reverse the judgment of the Court of Appeals that the exclusion of respondents was unreasonable, and we remand this case for further proceedings consistent with this opinion."

V. JUSTICE VOTE

3 Pro ACLU Side vs. 4 Con Opposing Side

ACLU Side (Respondent / Appellee)

1. Blackmun, H. – Wrote dissenting opinion
2. Brennan, W. – Joined Blackmun's dissent
3. Stevens, J. – Wrote dissenting opinion

Opposing Side (Petitioner / Appellant)

1. O'Connor, S. – Wrote majority opinion
2. Burger, W. – Joined majority opinion
3. White, B. – Joined majority opinion
4. Rehnquist, W. – Joined majority opinion

Marshall, T – Took no part in the decision
Powell, L – Took no part in the decision

VI. A WIN OR LOSS FOR THE ACLU?

The ACLU filed as amicus curiae urging affirmance; the Supreme Court reversed the judgment of the Court of Appeals in a 4-3 vote, giving the ACLU an apparent loss.

573. Marek v. Chesny

(Decided July 27, 1985; 473 U.S. 1)

I. ISSUE

A. Issues Discussed

Civil rights, federal rights, attorney's fees

B. Legal Question Presented

"[W]hether attorney's fees incurred by a plaintiff, subsequent to an offer of settlement under Federal Rule of Civil Procedure 68 must be paid by the defendant under 42 U.S.C. § 1988 when the plaintiff recovers a judgment less than the offer."

C. Supreme Court's Answer

A defendant is not liable for attorney's fees incurred by a plaintiff under § 1988 subsequent to an offer of settlement where the plaintiff recovers a judgment less than the offer.

II. CASE SUMMARY

A. Background

"Petitioners, three police officers, in answering a call on a domestic disturbance, shot and killed respondent's adult son. Respondent, on his own behalf and as administrator of his son's estate, filed suit against the officers in the United States District Court under 42 U.S.C. § 1983 and state tort law.

Prior to trial, petitioners made a timely offer of settlement 'for a sum, including costs now accrued and attorney's fees, of ONE HUNDRED THOUSAND ($100,000) DOLLARS.' Respondent did not accept the offer. The case went to trial and respondent was awarded $5,000 on the state-law 'wrongful death' claim, $52,000 for the §1983 violation, and $3,000 in punitive damages.

Respondent filed a request for $171,692.47 in costs, including attorney's fees. This amount included costs incurred after the settlement offer. Petitioners opposed the claim for postoffer costs, relying on Federal Rule of Civil Procedure 68, which shifts to the plaintiff all 'costs' incurred subsequent to an offer of judgment not exceeded by the ultimate recovery at trial. Petitioners argued that attorney's fees are part of the 'costs' covered by Rule 68. The District Court agreed with petitioners and declined to award respondent 'costs, including attorney's fees, incurred after the offer of judgment.' The parties subsequently agreed that $32,000 fairly represented the allowable costs, including attorney's fees, accrued prior to petitioners' offer of settlement. Respondent appealed the denial of postoffer costs.

The Court of Appeals reversed. The court rejected what it termed the "rather mechanical linking up of Rule 68 and section 1988.' It stated that the District Court's reading of Rule 68 and § 1988, while 'in a sense logical,' would put civil rights plaintiffs and counsel in a 'predicament' that 'cuts against the grain of section 1988.' Plaintiffs' attorneys, the court reasoned, would be forced to "think very hard" before rejecting even an inadequate offer, and would be deterred from bringing good-faith actions because of the prospect of losing the right to attorney's fees if a settlement offer more favorable than the ultimate recovery were rejected."

The Supreme Court granted certiorari to review the case and reversed.

B. Counsel of Record / ACLU Attorney

ACLU Side (Respondent / Appellee): Victor J. Stone argued the cause for appellee.

Opposing Side (Petitioner / Appellant): Donald G. Peterson argued the cause for appellant.

Jerrold J. Ganzfried argued the cause for the United States, as amicus curiae, by special leave of Court.

III. AMICI CURIAE

ACLU Side (Respondent / Appellee)

Brief of amici curiae filed on behalf of the ACLU, et al., by Roger Pascal, Burt Neuborne, E. Richard Larson, and Harvey Grossman.

Additional briefs of amici curiae were filed on behalf of the Alliance for Justice, the Lawyers' Committee for Civil Rights Under Law, the Committee on the Federal Courts of the Association of the Bar of the City of New York, and the NAACP Legal Defense and Educational Fund, Inc.

Opposing Side (Petitioner / Appellant)

Brief of amici curiae filed on behalf of the United States by Jerrold J. Ganzfried, Solicitor General Lee, Acting Assistant Attorney General Willard, Deputy Solicitor General Geller, Deputy Assistant Attorney General Kuhl, Katheryn A. Oberly, Robert S. Greenspan, and Barbara S. Woodall.

Additional briefs of amici curiae were filed on behalf of the State of Florida, the City of New York, and the Equal Employment Advisory Council.

IV. THE SUPREME COURT'S DECISION

"At the time an offer is made, the plaintiff knows the amount in damages caused by the challenged conduct. The plaintiff also knows, or can ascertain, the costs then accrued. A reasonable determination whether to accept the offer can be made by simply adding these two figures and comparing the sum to the amount offered. Respondent is troubled that a plaintiff will not know whether the offer on the substantive claim would be exceeded at trial, but this is so whenever an offer of settlement is made. In any event, requiring itemization of damages separate from costs would not in any way help plaintiffs know in advance whether the judgment at trial will exceed a defendant's offer. . . .

Congress, of course, was well aware of Rule 68 when it enacted § 1988, and included attorney's fees as part of recoverable costs. The plain language of Rule 68 and § 1988 subjects such fees to the cost-shifting provision of Rule 68. Nothing revealed in our review of the policies underlying § 1988 constitutes 'the necessary clear expression of congressional intent' required 'to exempt [the] statute from the operation of' Rule 68. We hold that petitioners are not liable for costs of $139,692 incurred by respondent after petitioners' offer of settlement.

The judgment of the Court of Appeals is reversed."

V. JUSTICE VOTE

3 Pro ACLU Side vs. 6 Con Opposing Side

ACLU Side (Respondent / Appellee)

1. Brennan, W. – Wrote dissenting opinion
2. Blackmun, H. – Joined Brennan's dissent
3. Marshall, T. – Joined Brennan's dissent

Opposing Side (Petitioner / Appellant)

1. Burger, W. – Wrote majority opinion
2. White, B. – Joined majority opinion
3. Powell, L. – Wrote concurring opinion
4. Rehnquist, W. – Wrote concurring opinion
5. Stevens, J. – Joined majority opinion
6. O'Connor, S. – Joined majority opinion

VI. A WIN OR LOSS FOR THE ACLU?

The ACLU filed as amicus curiae urging affirmance; the Supreme Court reversed the judgment of the Court of Appeals for the Seventh Circuit in a 6-3 vote, giving the ACLU an apparent loss.

574. Miller v. Fenton

(Decided December 3, 1985; 474 U.S. 104)

I. ISSUE

A. Issues Discussed

Criminal procedure, Fourteenth Amendment, confessions, evidence

B. Legal Question Presented:

"[W]hether the voluntariness of a confession is an issue of fact entitled to the § 2254(d) presumption" that "state-court findings of fact 'shall be presumed to be correct' in a federal habeas corpus proceeding unless one of eight enumerated exceptions applies."

C. Supreme Court's Answer

This issue, "whether, under the totality of the circumstances, the challenged confession was obtained in a manner compatible with the requirements of the Constitution is a matter for independent federal determination.

II. CASE SUMMARY

A. Background

Police officers brought petitioner to the police station as a suspect in the murder of a 17-year-old girl. During a 58-minute long interrogation police officers made false statements about the victim to petitioner and one officer "stated that he did not consider petitioner to be a criminal because the perpetrator of the deed had a 'mental problem' and needed medical help rather than punishment. Eventually, petitioner fully confessed to the crime. After doing so, he lapsed into what Detective Boyce described as a 'state of shock.' . . .

The trial court rejected petitioner's motion to suppress the confession, and the jury found petitioner guilty of murder in the first degree. The Superior Court Appellate Division reversed, finding as a matter of law that the confession was the result of 'intense and mind bending psychological Compulsion' and therefore was impermissible under the Fourteenth Amendment's guarantee of due process. Over three dissents, the Supreme Court of New Jersey reversed again. After examining the 'totality of all the surrounding circumstances,' including petitioner's educational level, age, and awareness of his Miranda rights, the court found that the interrogation 'did not exceed proper bounds,' and that the resulting confession, being voluntary, had been properly admitted into evidence.

Petitioner then sought a writ of habeas corpus in the United States District Court for the District of New Jersey. That court dismissed the application without an evidentiary hearing. A divided panel of the Court of Appeals for the Third Circuit affirmed."

The Supreme Court granted certiorari to review the case and reversed.

B. Counsel of Record / ACLU Attorney

ACLU Side (Petitioner / Appellant): Paul Martin Klein argued the cause for appellant.

Opposing Side (Respondent / Appellee): Anne C. Paskow, Deputy Attorney General of New Jersey, argued the cause for appellee.

III. AMICI CURIAE

ACLU Side (Petitioner / Appellant)

Brief of amici curiae filed on behalf of the ACLU, et al., by Charles S. Sims.

Opposing Side (Respondent / Appellee)

No briefs of amici curiae were filed in support of appellee.

IV. THE SUPREME COURT'S DECISION

"Faced with statements extracted by beatings and other forms of physical and psychological torture, the Court held that confessions procured by means 'revolting to the sense of justice' could not be used to secure a conviction. On numerous subsequent occasions the Court has set aside convictions secured through the admission of an improperly obtained confession. [T]he Court's analysis has consistently been animated by the view that 'ours is an accusatorial and not an inquisitorial system,' and that, accordingly, tactics for eliciting inculpatory statements must fall within the broad constitutional boundaries imposed by the Fourteenth Amendment's guarantee of fundamental fairness. . . .

Without exception, the Court's confession cases hold that the ultimate issue of 'voluntariness' is a legal question requiring independent federal determination. . . .

In short, an unbroken line of cases, coming to the Supreme Court both on direct appeal and on review of applications to lower federal courts for a writ of habeas corpus, forecloses the Court of Appeals' conclusion that the 'voluntariness' of a confession merits something less than independent federal consideration. [T]he ultimate question whether, under the totality of the circumstances, the challenged confession was obtained in a manner compatible with the requirements of the Constitution is a matter for independent federal determination. . . .

After defending at length its conclusion that the voluntariness of a confession was entitled to the § 2254(d) presumption, and after carefully analyzing the petitioner's confession under that standard, the Court of Appeals suggested in a brief footnote that it [would reach the same result' even were it to give the issue plenary consideration. Inasmuch as it is not clear from this language that the court did in fact independently evaluate the admissibility of the confession, and because, in any event, we think that the case warrants fuller analysis under the appropriate standard, we reverse the decision below and remand for further proceedings consistent with this opinion."

V. JUSTICE VOTE

8 Pro ACLU Side vs. 1 Con Opposing Side

ACLU Side (Petitioner / Appellant)

1. O'Connor, S. – Wrote majority opinion
2. Brennan, W. – Joined majority opinion
3. Marshall, T. – Joined majority opinion
4. Stevens, J. – Joined majority opinion
5. Burger, W. – Joined majority opinion
6. Blackmun, H. – Joined majority opinion
7. Powell, L. – Joined majority opinion
8. White, B. – Joined majority opinion

Opposing Side (Respondent / Appellee)

1. Rehnquist, W. – Wrote dissenting opinion

VI. A WIN OR LOSS FOR THE ACLU?

The ACLU filed as amicus urging reversal; the Supreme Court reversed and remanded the ruling the Court of Appeals for the Third Circuit in an 8-1 vote, giving the ACLU an apparent win.

575. Wainwright v. Greenfield

(Decided January 14, 1986; 474 U.S. 284)

I. ISSUE

A. Issues Discussed

Criminal procedure, Fourteenth Amendment, due process, evidence

B. Legal Question Presented

"[W]hether . . . use of a defendant's silence [against him to show his sanity] violates the Due Process Clause of the Fourteenth Amendment as construed in Doyle v. Ohio."

C. Supreme Court's Answer

Use of defendant's silence against him to show his sanity violates due process.

II. CASE SUMMARY

A. Background

Respondent David Greenfield was arrested for sexual battery and given three separate Miranda warnings prior to interrogation. Throughout the interrogation, he exercised his right to remain silent and requested to speak with an attorney before answering questions. At trial, respondent "entered a plea of not guilty by reason of insanity."

"In his closing argument, over defense counsel's objection, the prosecutor reviewed the testimony of Officer Pilifant and Detective Jolley [describing respondent's interrogation] and suggested that respondent's repeated refusals to answer questions without first consulting an attorney demonstrated a degree of comprehension that was inconsistent with his claim of insanity. The jury found respondent guilty and the judge sentenced him to life imprisonment.

By a 2-to-1 vote, the Florida Court of Appeal for the Second District affirmed the conviction. . . . The Florida Supreme Court granted respondent's petition for certiorari and summarily remanded the case to the Court of Appeal for reconsideration in light of Clark v. State . . . . On reconsideration, the Court of Appeal adhered to its earlier decision.

Having exhausted his state remedies, respondent filed a petition for a writ of habeas corpus in the Federal District Court. The petition was referred to a Magistrate. . . . The Magistrate concluded that federal review of the claim was not foreclosed because counsel had objected to the prosecutor's closing argument and because the Florida Court of Appeal had rejected the claim on its merits. The Magistrate, however, agreed with the Florida courts' disposition of the merits and recommended that the habeas corpus petition be denied. The District Court accepted that recommendation.

The United States Court of Appeals for the Eleventh Circuit reversed. Disagreeing with two other Federal Courts of Appeals—but not with the position taken by the Florida Supreme Court in a case decided after this respondent had exhausted his state remedies—the Court of Appeals held that . . . respondent was entitled to a new trial."

The Supreme Court granted certiorari to review the case and affirmed.

B. Counsel of Record / ACLU Attorney

ACLU Side (Respondent / Appellee): James D. Whittemore, by appointment of the Court, argued the cause for appellee.

Opposing Side (Petitioner / Appellant): Ann Garrison Paschall, Assistant Attorney General of Florida, argued the cause for appellant.

III. AMICI CURIAE

ACLU Side (Respondent / Appellee)

Brief of amici curiae filed on behalf of the ACLU by Charles S. Sims and Jack D. Novik.

Brief of amici curiae filed on behalf of the Illinois Psychological Association by Donald Paull and Marilyn Martin.

Opposing Side (Petitioner / Appellant)

No briefs of amici curiae were filed in support of appellant.

IV. THE SUPREME COURT'S DECISION

"'[W]e have consistently explained Doyle as a case where the government had induced silence by implicitly assuring the defendant that his silence would not be used against him. [W]e explained that use of silence for impeachment was fundamentally unfair in Doyle because 'Miranda warnings inform a person of his right to remain silent and assure him, at least implicitly, that his silence will not be used against him. . . . Doyle bars the use against a criminal defendant of silence maintained after receipt of governmental assurances" . . .

We find no warrant for the claimed distinction in the reasoning of Doyle and of subsequent cases. The point of the Doyle holding is that it is fundamentally unfair to promise an arrested person that his silence will not be used against him and thereafter to breach that promise by using the silence to impeach his trial testimony. It is equally unfair to breach that promise by using silence to overcome a defendant's plea of insanity. In both situations, the State gives warnings to protect constitutional rights and implicitly promises that any exercise of those rights will not be penalized. In both situations, the State then seeks to make use of the defendant's exercise of those rights in obtaining his conviction. The implicit promise, the breach, and the consequent penalty are identical in both situations. . . .

The Attorney General's argument about the probative value of silence therefore fails entirely to meet the problem of fundamental unfairness that flows from the State's breach of its implied assurances. . . .

In Doyle, we held that Miranda warnings contain an implied promise, rooted in the Constitution, that 'silence will carry no penalty.' Our conclusion that it was fundamentally unfair for the Ohio prosecutor to breach that promise by using the defendants' postarrest, post-Miranda warnings silence to impeach their trial testimony requires us also to conclude that it was fundamentally unfair for the Florida prosecutor to breach the officers' promise to respondent by using his postarrest, post-Miranda warnings silence as evidence of his sanity.

The judgment of the Court of Appeals is affirmed."

V. JUSTICE VOTE

9 Pro ACLU Side vs. 0 Con Opposing Side

ACLU Side (Respondent / Appellee)

1. Stevens J. – Wrote majority opinion
2. Brennan, W. – Joined majority opinion
3. White, B. – Joined majority opinion
4. Marshall, T. – Joined majority opinion
5. Blackmun, H. – Joined majority opinion
6. Powell, L. – Joined majority opinion
7. O'Connor, S. – Joined majority opinion
8. Rehnquist, W. – Wrote concurring opinion
9. Burger, W. – Joined Rehnquist's concurrence

VI. A WIN OR LOSS FOR THE ACLU?

The ACLU filed as amicus curiae urging affirmance; the Supreme Court affirmed the judgment of the Court of Appeals for the Eleventh Circuit in a 9-0 vote, giving the ACLU an apparent win.

576. Witters v. Washington Department of Services for the Blind

(Decided January 27, 1986; 474 U.S. 481)

I. ISSUE

A. Issues Discussed

First Amendment, Establishment Clause

B. Legal Question Presented

Whether "the First Amendment precludes the State of Washington from extending assistance under a state vocational rehabilitation assistance program to a blind person studying at a Christian college and seeking to become a pastor, missionary, or youth director."

C. Supreme Court's Answer

The First Amendment does not preclude the State of Washington from providing assistance to a blind person pursuing religious education.

II. CASE SUMMARY

A. Background

"Petitioner Larry Witters applied in 1979 to the Washington Commission for the Blind for vocational rehabilitation services pursuant to Wash. Rev. Code § 74.16.181 (1981). That statute authorized the Commission, inter alia, to '[p]rovide for special education and/or training in the professions, business or trades' so as to 'assist visually handicapped persons to overcome vocational handicaps and to obtain the maximum degree of self-support and self-care.' Petitioner, suffering from a progressive eye condition, was eligible for vocational rehabilitation assistance under the terms of the statute. He was at the time attending Inland Empire School of the Bible, a private Christian college in Spokane, Washington, and studying the Bible, ethics, speech, and church administration in order to equip himself for a career as a pastor, missionary, or youth director.

The Commission denied petitioner aid. It relied on an earlier determination embodied in a Commission policy statement that '[t]he Washington State constitution forbids the use of public funds to assist an individual in the pursuit of a career or degree in theology or related areas' . . . . That ruling was affirmed by a state hearings examiner . . . . That ruling, in turn, was upheld on internal administrative appeal.

Petitioner then instituted an action in State Superior Court for review of the administrative decision; the court affirmed on the same state-law grounds cited by the agency. The State Supreme Court affirmed as well. The Supreme Court, however, declined to ground its ruling on the Washington Constitution. Instead, it explicitly reserved judgment on the state constitutional issue and chose to base its ruling on the Establishment Clause of the Federal Constitution."

The U.S. Supreme Court granted certiorari to review the case and reversed.

B. Counsel of Record / ACLU Attorney

ACLU Side (Respondent / Appellee): Timothy R. Malone, Assistant Attorney General for Washington, argued the cause for appellee.

Opposing Side (Petitioner / Appellant): Michael P. Farris argued the cause for appellant.

III. AMICI CURIAE

ACLU Side (Respondent / Appellee)

Brief of amici curiae filed on behalf of the ACLU, et al., by Charles B. Wiggins, Jack D. Novik, Charles S. Sims, and Burt Neuborne.

Brief of amici curiae filed on behalf of Americans United for Separation of Church and State by Lee Boothby and Walter E. Carson.

Brief of amici curiae filed on behalf of the Anti-Defamation League of B'nai B'rith, et al., by Ruti G. Teitel, Justin J. Finger, Jeffrey P. Sinensky, and Steven M. Freeman.

Opposing Side (Petitioner / Appellant)

Brief of amici curiae filed on behalf of the United States by Acting Solicitor General Fried, Acting Assistant Attorney General Willard, Michael C. McConnell, Anthony J. Steinmeyer, and Michael Jay Singer.

Brief of amici curiae filed on behalf of the American Jewish Committee by Samuel Rabinove and Richard T. Foltin.

Brief of amici curiae filed on behalf of the American Jewish Congress by Marc D. Stern and Ronald A. Krauss.

Brief of amici curiae filed on behalf of the Christian Legal Society, et al., by Samual Eric Hans Ericsson, Kimberly Wood Colby, and Forest D. Montgomery.

Brief of amici curiae filed on behalf of the Rutherford Institute, et al., by Larry L. Crain, Guy O. Farley, Jr., John W. Whitehead, James J. Knicely, Thomas O. Kotouc, Wendell R. Bird, and William B. Hollberg.

Brief of amici curiae filed on behalf of the National Legal Christian Foundation.

IV. THE SUPREME COURT'S DECISION

"We are guided, as was the court below, by the three-part test set out by this Court in Lemon . . . . Our analysis relating to the first prong of that test is simple: all parties concede the unmistakably secular purpose of the Washington program. That program was designed to promote the well-being of the visually handicapped through the provision of vocational rehabilitation services, and no more than a minuscule amount of the aid awarded under the program is likely to flow to religious education. No party suggests that the State's 'actual purpose' in creating the program was to endorse religion or that the secular purpose articulated by the legislature is merely 'sham.'

The answer to the question posed by the second prong of the

Lemon test is more difficult.... The question presented is whether, on the facts as they appear in the record before us, extension of aid to petitioner and the use of that aid by petitioner to support his religious education is a permissible transfer ... or is an impermissible 'direct subsidy.'

Certain aspects of Washington's program are central to our inquiry. As far as the record shows, vocational assistance provided under the Washington program is paid directly to the student, who transmits it to the educational institution of his or her choice. Any aid provided under Washington's program that ultimately flows to religious institutions does so only as a result of the genuinely independent and private choices of aid recipients. Washington's program is 'made available generally without regard to the sectarian-nonsectarian, or public-nonpublic nature of the institution benefited,' and is in no way skewed towards religion. ... In this case, the fact that aid goes to individuals means that the decision to support religious education is made by the individual, not by the State....

On the facts we have set out, it does not seem appropriate to view any aid ultimately flowing to the Inland Empire School of the Bible as resulting from a state action sponsoring or subsidizing religion. Nor does the mere circumstance that petitioner has chosen to use neutrally available state aid to help pay for his religious education confer any message of state endorsement of religion.... On the facts present here, we think the Washington program works no state support of religion prohibited by the Establishment Clause....

The judgment of the Washington Supreme Court is reversed, and the case is remanded for further proceedings not inconsistent with this opinion."

V. JUSTICE VOTE

0 Pro ACLU Side vs. 9 Con Opposing Side

Opposing Side (Petitioner / Appellant)

1. Marshall, T. – Wrote majority opinion
2. Burger, W. – Joined Powell's concurrence
3. Brennan, W. – Joined majority opinion
4. White, B. – Wrote concurring opinion
5. Blackmun, H. – Joined majority opinion
6. Powell, L. – Wrote concurring opinion
7. Rehnquist, W. – Joined Powell's concurrence
8. Stevens, J. – Joined majority opinion
9. O'Connor, S. – Wrote concurring opinion

VI. A WIN OR LOSS FOR THE ACLU?

The ACLU, as amicus curiae, urged affirmance of the judgment of the Supreme Court of Washington; the U.S. Supreme Court reversed and remanded in a 9-0 vote, giving the ACLU an apparent loss.

577. City of Renton v. Playtime Theatres, Inc.

(Decided February 25, 1986; 475 U.S. 41)

I. ISSUE

A. Issues Discussed

First Amendment, Fourteenth Amendment, freedoms of press, speech, and association, zoning ordinances

B. Legal Question Presented

Whether "a zoning ordinance . . . that prohibits adult motion picture theaters from locating within 1,000 feet of any residential zone, single- or multiple-family dwelling, church, park, or school" violates the First and Fourteenth Amendments.

C. Supreme Court's Answer

The zoning ordinance complies with the First and Fourteenth Amendments.

II. CASE SUMMARY

A. Background

"In May 1980, the Mayor of Renton, a city of approximately 32,000 people located just south of Seattle, suggested to the Renton City Council that it consider the advisability of enacting zoning legislation dealing with adult entertainment uses....

In April 1981, acting on the basis of the Planning and Development Committee's recommendation, the City Council enacted Ordinance No. 3526. The ordinance prohibited any 'adult motion picture theater' from locating within 1,000 feet of any residential zone, single- or multiple-family dwelling, church, or park, and within one mile of any school....

In early 1982, respondents acquired two existing theaters in downtown Renton, with the intention of using them to exhibit feature-length adult films. The theaters were located within the area proscribed by Ordinance No. 3526. At about the same time, respondents filed [a] lawsuit challenging the ordinance on First and Fourteenth Amendment grounds, and seeking declaratory and injunctive relief. While the federal action was pending, the City Council amended the ordinance in several respects, adding a statement of reasons for its enactment and reducing the minimum distance from any school to 1,000 feet.

In November 1982, the Federal Magistrate to whom respondents' action had been referred recommended the entry of a preliminary injunction against enforcement of the Renton ordinance and the denial of Renton's motions to dismiss and for summary judgment. The District Court adopted the Magistrate's recommendations and entered the preliminary injunction, and respondents began showing adult films at their two theaters in Renton. Shortly thereafter, the parties agreed to submit the case for a final decision on whether a permanent injunction should issue on the basis of the record as already developed.

The District Court then vacated the preliminary injunction, denied respondents' requested permanent injunction, and entered summary judgment in favor of Renton.... The Court of Appeals for the Ninth Circuit reversed."

The Supreme Court granted certiorari to review the case and reversed the judgment of the Ninth Circuit Court of Appeals.

B. Counsel of Record / ACLU Attorney

ACLU Side (Respondent / Appellee): Jack R. Burns argued the cause for appellee.

Opposing Side (Petitioner / Appellant): E. Barrett Prettyman, Jr., argued the cause for appellant.

III. AMICI CURIAE

ACLU Side (Respondent / Appellee)

Brief of amici curiae filed on behalf of the ACLU, et al., by David Utevsky, Jack D. Novik, and Burt Neuborne.

Brief of amici curiae filed on behalf of the American Booksellers Association, Inc., et al., by Michael A. Bamberger.

Brief of amici curiae filed on behalf of the Outdoor Advertising Association of America, Inc., et al., by Eric M. Rubin and Walter E. Diercks.

Opposing Side (Petitioner / Appellant)

Brief of amici curiae filed on behalf of Jackson County, Missouri, by Russell D. Jacobson.

Brief of amici curiae filed on behalf of the Freedom Council Foundation by Wendell R. Bird and Robert K. Skolrood.

Brief of amici curiae filed on behalf of the National Institute of Municipal Law Officers by George Agnost, Roy D. Bates, Benjamin L. Brown, J. Lamar Shelley, John W. Witt, Roger F. Cutler, Robert J. Alfton, James K. Baker, Barbara Mather, James D. Montgomery, Clifford D. Pierce, Jr., William H. Taube, William I. Thornton, Jr., and Charles S. Rhyne.

Brief of amici curiae filed on behalf of the National League of Cities, et al., by Benna Ruth Solomon, Joyce Holmes Benjamin, Beate Bloch, and Lawrence R. Velvel.

IV. THE SUPREME COURT'S DECISION

"In our view, the resolution of this case is largely dictated by our decision in Young v. American Mini Theatres, Inc., supra. There, although five Members of the Court did not agree on a single rationale for the decision, we held that the city of Detroit's zoning ordinance, which prohibited locating an adult theater within 1,000 feet of any two other 'regulated uses' or within 500 feet of any residential zone, did not violate the First and Fourteenth Amendments. The Renton ordinance, like the one in American Mini Theatres, does not ban adult theaters altogether, but merely provides that such theaters may not be located within 1,000 feet of any residential zone, single- or multiple-family dwelling, church, park, or school. The ordinance is therefore properly analyzed as a form of time, place, and manner regulation. . . .

The District Court's finding as to 'predominate' intent, left undisturbed by the Court of Appeals, is more than adequate to establish that the city's pursuit of its zoning interests here was unrelated to the suppression of free expression. The ordinance by its terms is designed to prevent crime, protect the city's retail trade, maintain property values, and generally 'protec[t] and preserv[e] the quality of [the city's] neighborhoods, commercial districts, and the quality of urban life,' not to suppress the expression of unpopular views. . . .

Finally, turning to the question whether the Renton ordinance allows for reasonable alternative avenues of communication, we note that the ordinance leaves some 520 acres, or more than five percent of the entire land area of Renton, open to use as adult theater sites. . . .

Respondents argue, however, that some of the land in question is already occupied by existing businesses, that 'practically none' of the undeveloped land is currently for sale or lease, and that in general there are no 'commercially viable' adult theater sites within the 520 acres left open by the Renton ordinance. . . .

We disagree with both the reasoning and the conclusion of the Court of Appeals. That respondents must fend for themselves in the real estate market, on an equal footing with other prospective purchasers and lessees, does not give rise to a First Amendment violation. . . .

In sum, we find that the Renton ordinance represents a valid governmental response to the 'admittedly serious problems' created by adult theaters. Renton has not used 'the power to zone as a pretext for suppressing expression,' but rather has sought to make some areas available for adult theaters and their patrons, while at the same time preserving the quality of life in the community at large by preventing those theaters from locating in other areas. This, after all, is the essence of zoning. . . . The judgment of the Court of Appeals is therefore reversed."

V. JUSTICE VOTE

2 Pro ACLU Side vs. 7 Con Opposing Side

ACLU Side (Respondent / Appellee)

1. Brennan, W. – Wrote dissenting opinion
2. Marshall, T. – Joined Brennan's dissent

Opposing Side (Petitioner / Appellant)

1. Rehnquist, W. – Wrote majority opinion
2. Burger, W. – Joined majority opinion
3. White, B. – Joined majority opinion
4. Powell, L. – Joined majority opinion
5. Stevens, J. – Joined majority opinion
6. O'Connor, S. – Joined majority opinion
7. Blackmun, H. – Concurred in the result

VI. A WIN OR LOSS FOR THE ACLU?

The ACLU, as amicus curiae, urged affirmance of the judgment of the Ninth Circuit Court of Appeals; the Supreme Court reversed in a 7-2 vote, giving the ACLU an apparent loss.

578. Malley v. Briggs

(Decided March 5, 1986; 475 U.S. 335)

I. ISSUE

A. Issues Discussed

Criminal justice, drugs, Fourth Amendment, Fourteenth Amendment, qualified immunity, absolute immunity

B. Legal Question Presented

What is "the degree of immunity accorded a defendant police officer in a damages action under 42 U.S.C. § 1983 when it is alleged that the officer caused the plaintiffs to be unconstitutionally arrested by presenting a judge with a complaint and a supporting affidavit which failed to establish probable cause."

C. Supreme Court's Answer

A police officer in this circumstance is entitled only to qualified immunity and this immunity does not shield the officer from damages liability here.

II. CASE SUMMARY

A. Background

"In December 1980, the Rhode Island State Police were conducting a court-authorized wiretap on the telephone of one Paul Driscoll, an acquaintance of respondents' daughter. [The police intercepted two calls they thought relevant to a charge of drug use.] On the basis of these two calls, petitioner drew up felony complaints charging that respondents and Paul Driscoll 'did unlawfully conspire to violate the uniform controlled substance act of the State of Rhode Island by having [marihuana] in their possession . . . .' These complaints were presented to a State District Court Judge in February 1981, after the wiretap of Driscoll's phone had been terminated. Accompanying the complaints were unsigned warrants for each respondent's arrest, and supporting affidavits describing the two intercepted calls and petitioner's interpretation of them. The judge signed warrants for the arrest of respondents and 20 other individuals charged by petitioner as a result of information gathered through the wiretap.

Respondents were arrested at their home shortly before six o'clock on the morning of March 19, 1981. They were taken to a police station, booked, held for several hours, arraigned, and released. Local and statewide newspapers published the fact that respondents, who are prominent members of their community, had been arrested and charged with drug possession. The charges against respondents were subsequently dropped when the grand jury to which the case was presented did not return an indictment.

Respondents brought an action under 42 U.S.C. § 1983 in the United States District Court for the District of Rhode Island charging, inter alia, that petitioner, in applying for warrants for their arrest, violated their rights under the Fourth and Fourteenth Amendments. The case was tried to a jury, and at the close of respondents' evidence, petitioner moved for and was granted a directed verdict. . . . The United States Court of Appeals for the First Circuit reversed, holding that an officer who seeks an arrest warrant by submitting a complaint and supporting affidavit to a judge is not entitled to immunity unless the officer has an objectively reasonable basis for believing that the facts alleged in his affidavit are sufficient to establish probable cause."

The Supreme Court granted certiorari to review the case and affirmed.

B. Counsel of Record / ACLU Attorney

ACLU Side (Respondent / Appellee): Leonard Decof argued the cause for appellee.

Opposing Side (Petitioner / Appellant): Ann M. Sheadel, Assistant Attorney General of Rhode Island, argued the cause for appellant.

III. AMICI CURIAE

ACLU Side (Respondent / Appellee)

Opposing Side (Petitioner / Appellant)

Brief of amici curiae filed on behalf of the ACLU, et al., by Steven P. Lockman, Jack D. Novik, Burt Neuborne, and Lynette Labinger.

Brief of amici curiae filed on behalf of the State of Minnesota, et al., by Hubert H. Humphrey III, Attorney General of Minnesota; Catharine F. Haukedahl, Special Assistant Attorney General; Charles A. Graddick, Attorney General of Alabama; Robert K. Corbin, Attorney General of Arizona; John K. Van de Kamp, Attorney General of California; Jim Smith, Attorney General of Florida; Michael J. Bowers, Attorney General of Georgia; Corinne Watanabe, Acting Attorney General of Hawaii; Jim Jones, Attorney General of Idaho; Linley E. Pearson, Attorney General of Indiana; Robert T. Stephan, Attorney General of Kansas; William J. Guste, Jr., Attorney General of Louisiana; Frank J. Kelley, Attorney General of Michigan; Edwin Lloyd Pittman, Attorney General of Mississippi; William L. Webster, Attorney General of Missouri; Mike Greely, Attorney General of Montana; Robert M. Spire, Attorney General of Nebraska; Brian McKay, Attorney General of Nevada; Stephen E. Merrill, Attorney General of New Hampshire; Irwin I. Kimmelman, Attorney General of New Jersey; Lacy H. Thornburg, Attorney General of North Carolina; Anthony J. Celebrezze, Jr., Attorney General of Ohio; David Frohnmayer, Attorney General of Oregon; LeRoy S. Zimmerman, Attorney General of Pennsylvania; T. Travis Medlock, Attorney General of South Carolina; W. J. Michael Cody, Attorney General of Tennessee; David L. Wilkinson, Attorney General of Utah; William G. Broaddus, Attorney General of Virginia; Bronson C. La Follette, Attorney General of Wisconsin; and A. G. McClintock, Attorney General of Wyoming.

Brief of amici curiae filed on behalf of Americans for Effective Law Enforcement, Inc., et al. by David Crump, Daniel B. Hales, Fred E. Inbau, Wayne W. Schmidt, and James P. Manak.

IV. THE SUPREME COURT'S DECISION

"Petitioner urges reversal on two grounds: first, that in this context, he is absolutely immune from liability for damages; second, that he is at least entitled to qualified immunity in this case. We reject both propositions and address first the absolute immunity issue. . . .

Defendants will not be immune if, on an objective basis, it is obvious that no reasonably competent officer would have concluded that a warrant should issue; but if officers of reasonable competence could disagree on this issue, immunity should be recognized. . . .

[W]e hold that the same standard of objective reasonableness that we applied in the context of a suppression hearing in Leon, supra, defines the qualified immunity accorded an officer whose request for a warrant allegedly caused an unconstitutional arrest. Only where the warrant application is so lacking in indicia of probable cause as to render official belief in its existence unreasonable will the shield of immunity be lost. . . .

We also reject petitioner's argument that if an officer is entitled to only qualified immunity in cases like this, he is nevertheless shielded from damages liability because the act of applying for a warrant is per se objectively reasonable, provided that the officer believes that the facts alleged in his affidavit are true. Petitioner insists that he is entitled to rely on the judgment of a judicial officer in finding that probable cause exists and hence issuing the warrant. This view of objective reasonableness is at odds with our development of that concept . . . . It is true that in an ideal system an unreasonable request for a warrant would be harmless, because no judge would approve it. But ours is not an ideal system, and it is possible that a magistrate, working under docket pressures, will fail to perform as a magistrate should. We find it reasonable to require the officer applying for the warrant to minimize this danger by exercising reasonable professional judgment.

The judgment of the Court of Appeals is affirmed, and the case is remanded for further proceedings consistent with this opinion."

V. JUSTICE VOTE

7 Pro ACLU Side vs. 2 Con Opposing Side

ACLU Side (Respondent / Appellee)

1. White, B. – Wrote majority opinion
2. Burger, W. – Joined majority opinion
3. Brennan, W. – Joined majority opinion
4. Marshall, T. – Joined majority opinion
5. Blackmun, H. – Joined majority opinion
6. Stevens, J. – Joined majority opinion
7. O'Connor, S. – Joined majority opinion

Opposing Side (Petitioner / Appellant)

1. Powell, L. – Wrote opinion concurring in part and dissenting in part
2. Rehnquist, W. – Joined Powell's opinion

VI. A WIN OR LOSS FOR THE ACLU?

The ACLU filed as amicus curiae urging affirmance of the judgment of the Court of Appeals; the Supreme Court affirmed in a 7-2 vote, giving the ACLU an apparent win.

579. Pembaur v. City of Cincinnati

(Decided March 25, 1986; 475 U.S. 469)

I. ISSUE

A. Issues Discussed

Civil rights, federal rights, Fourth Amendment, Fourteenth Amendment, municipal liability

B. Legal Question Presented

"[W]hether, and in what circumstances, a decision by municipal policymakers on a single occasion may satisfy" the Monell requirement that "municipal liability under 42 U.S.C. § 1983 is limited to deprivations of federally protected rights caused by action taken 'pursuant to official municipal policy of some nature . . . .'"

C. Supreme Court's Answer

The county can be held liable under § 1983 in this case.

II. CASE SUMMARY

A. Background

"Bertold Pembaur is a licensed Ohio physician and the sole proprietor of the Rockdale Medical Center . . . . During the spring of 1977, Simon Leis, the Hamilton County Prosecutor, began investigating charges that Pembaur fraudulently had accepted payments from state welfare agencies for services not actually provided to patients. A grand jury was convened . . . . In April, the grand jury charged Pembaur in a six-count indictment.

During the investigation, the grand jury issued subpoenas for the appearance of two of Pembaur's employees. When these employees failed to appear as directed, the Prosecutor obtained capiases for their arrest and detention from the Court of Common Pleas of Hamilton County.

On May 19, 1977, two Hamilton County Deputy Sheriffs attempted to serve the capiases at Pembaur's clinic. [Pembaur blocked them from entering beyond the reception area and additional police officers arrived at the scene.] After a final attempt to persuade Pembaur voluntarily to allow them to enter, the Deputy Sheriffs tried unsuccessfully to force the door. City police officers, who had been advised of the County Prosecutor's instructions to 'go in and get' the witnesses, obtained an axe and chopped down the door. The Deputy Sheriffs then entered and searched the clinic. Two individuals who fit descriptions of the witnesses sought were detained, but turned out not to be the right persons.

After this incident, the Prosecutor obtained an additional indictment against Pembaur for obstructing police in the performance of an authorized act. Although acquitted of all other charges, Pembaur was convicted for this offense. The Ohio Court of Appeals reversed . . . . The Ohio Supreme Court reversed and reinstated the conviction. . . .

On April 20, 1981, Pembaur filed the present action in the United States District Court for the Southern District of Ohio . . . . Pembaur sought damages under 42 U.S.C. § 1983, alleging that the county and city police had violated his rights under the Fourth and Fourteenth Amendments. . . . The District Court awarded judgment to the defendants and dismissed the complaint in its entirety. . . .

The Court of Appeals for the Sixth Circuit upheld the dismissal of Pembaur's claims against Whalen and Hamilton County, but reversed the dismissal of his claim against the city of Cincinnati on the ground that the District Court's findings concerning the policies followed by the Cincinnati police were clearly erroneous.

The Court of Appeals affirmed the District Court's dismissal of Pembaur's claim against Hamilton County, but on different grounds. . . . Pembaur petitioned for certiorari to review only the dismissal of his claim against Hamilton County."

The Supreme Court granted certiorari to review the case and reversed.

B. Counsel of Record / ACLU Attorney

ACLU Side (Petitioner / Appellant): Robert E. Manley argued the cause for appellant.

Opposing Side (Respondent / Appellee): Roger E. Friedmann argued the cause for appellee.

III. AMICI CURIAE

ACLU Side (Petitioner / Appellant)

Brief of amici curiae filed on behalf of the ACLU, et al., by Jack D. Novik, Burt Neuborne, and Bruce Campbell.

Opposing Side (Respondent / Appellee)

No briefs of amici curiae were filed in support of appellee.

IV. THE SUPREME COURT'S DECISION

"[T]ortious conduct, to be the basis for municipal liability under § 1983, must be pursuant to a municipality's 'official policy' . . . . The 'official policy' requirement was intended to distinguish acts of the municipality from acts of employees of the municipality, and thereby make clear that municipal liability is limited to action for which the municipality is actually responsible.

[W]e hasten to emphasize that not every decision by municipal officers automatically subjects the municipality to § 1983 liability. Municipal liability attaches only where the decision maker possesses final authority to establish municipal policy with respect to the action ordered. . . .

We hold that municipal liability under § 1983 attaches where—and only where—a deliberate choice to follow a course of action is made from among various alternatives by the official or officials responsible for establishing final policy with respect to the subject matter in question. . . .

Applying this standard to the case before us, we have little difficulty concluding that the Court of Appeals erred in dismissing petitioner's claim against the county. The Deputy Sheriffs who attempted to serve the capiases at petitioner's clinic found themselves in a difficult situation. Unsure of the proper course of action to follow, they sought instructions from their supervisors. The instructions they received were to follow the orders of the County Prosecutor. The Prosecutor made a considered decision based on his understanding of the law and commanded the officers forcibly to enter petitioner's clinic. That decision directly caused the violation of petitioner's Fourth Amendment rights. . . .

In ordering the Deputy Sheriffs to enter petitioner's clinic the County Prosecutor was acting as the final decision maker for the County, and the county may therefore be held liable under § 1983.

The decision of the Court of Appeals is reversed, and the case is remanded for further proceedings consistent with this opinion."

V. JUSTICE VOTE

6 Pro ACLU Side vs. 3 Con Opposing Side

ACLU Side (Petitioner / Appellant)

1. Brennan, W. – Wrote majority opinion
2. Marshall, T. – Joined majority opinion
3. Blackmun, H. – Joined majority opinion
4. White, B. – Wrote concurring opinion
5. Stevens, J. – Wrote concurring opinion
6. O'Connor, S. – Wrote concurring opinion

Opposing Side (Respondent / Appellee)

1. Powell, L. – Wrote dissenting opinion
2. Rehnquist, W. – Joined Powell's dissent
3. Burger, W. – Joined Powell's dissent

VI. A WIN OR LOSS FOR THE ACLU?

The ACLU filed a brief as amicus curiae urging reversal; the Supreme Court reversed the judgment of the Court of Appeals for the Sixth Circuit in a 6-3 vote, giving the ACLU an apparent win.

580. Goldman v. Weinberger

(Decided March 25, 1986; 475 U.S. 503)

I. ISSUE

A. Issues Discussed

First Amendment, Free Exercise Clause, military

B. Legal Question Presented

Whether "the Free Exercise Clause of the First Amendment to the United States Constitution permits [petitioner] to wear a yarmulke while in uniform, notwithstanding an Air Force regulation mandating uniform dress for Air Force personnel."

C. Supreme Court's Answer

The First Amendment does not prohibit the Air Force regulation that prevents petitioner from wearing a yarmulke while in uniform.

II. CASE SUMMARY

A. Background

"Petitioner S. Simcha Goldman contends that the Free Exercise Clause of the First Amendment to the United States Constitution permits him to wear a yarmulke while in uniform, notwithstanding an Air Force regulation mandating uniform dress for Air Force personnel. The District Court for the District of Columbia permanently enjoined the Air Force from enforcing its regulation against petitioner and from penalizing him for wearing his yarmulke. The Court of Appeals for the District of Columbia Circuit reversed on the ground that the Air Force's strong interest in discipline justified the strict enforcement of its uniform dress requirements. . . .

Petitioner Goldman is an Orthodox Jew and ordained rabbi. In 1973, he was accepted into the Armed Forces Health Professions Scholarship Program and placed on inactive reserve status in the Air Force while he studied clinical psychology . . . . After completing his Ph.D. in psychology, petitioner entered active service in the United States Air Force as a commissioned officer, in accordance with a requirement that participants in the scholarship program serve one year of active duty for each year of subsidized education. Petitioner was stationed at March Air Force Base in Riverside, California, and served as a clinical psychologist at the mental health clinic on the base."

The Supreme Court granted certiorari to review the case and affirmed the judgment of the Court of Appeals.

B. Counsel of Record / ACLU Attorney

ACLU Side (Petitioner / Appellant): Nathan Lewin argued the cause for appellant. With him on the briefs were David J. Butler and Dennis Rapps.

Opposing Side (Respondent / Appellee): Kathryn A. Oberly argued the cause for appellee. With her on the brief were Solicitor General Fried, Assistant Attorney General Willard, Deputy Solicitor General Geller, and Anthony J. Steinmeyer.

III. AMICI CURIAE

ACLU Side (Petitioner / Appellant)

Brief of amici curiae filed by the American Jewish Congress on behalf of itself, the Synagogue Council of America, and the ACLU, by Ronald A. Krauss and Marc D. Stern.

Brief of amici curiae filed on behalf of the American Jewish Committee, et al., by Samuel Eric Hans Ericsson, Kimberlee Wood Colby, Samuel Rabinove, and Richard T. Foltin.

Brief of amici curiae filed on behalf of the Anti-Defamation League of B'nai B'rith by Daniel P. Levitt, Justin J. Finger, and Jeffrey P. Sinensky.

Brief of amici curiae filed on behalf of the Catholic League for Religious and Civil Rights by Steven Frederick McDowell.

Brief of amici curiae filed on behalf of the Rutherford Institute, et al., by W. Charles Bundren, Guy O. Farley, Jr., John W. Whitehead, Thomas O. Kotouc, Wendell R. Bird, and William B. Hollberg.

Opposing Side (Respondent / Appellee)

No briefs of amici curiae were filed in support of appellee.

IV. THE SUPREME COURT'S DECISION

"Our review of military regulations challenged on First Amendment grounds is far more deferential than constitutional review of similar laws or regulations designed for civilian society. The military need not encourage debate or tolerate protest to the extent that such tolerance is required of the civilian state by the First Amendment; to accomplish its mission the military must foster instinctive obedience, unity commitment, and esprit de corps. . . .

The considered professional judgment of the Air Force is that the traditional outfitting of personnel in standardized uniforms encourages the subordination of personal preferences and identities in favor of the overall group mission. Uniforms encourage a sense of hierarchical unity by tending to eliminate outward individual distinctions except for those of rank. . . .

Petitioner Goldman contends that the Free Exercise Clause of the First Amendment requires the Air Force to make an exception to its uniform dress requirements for religious apparel unless the accouterments create a 'clear danger' of undermining discipline and esprit de corps. He asserts that in general, visible but 'unobtrusive' apparel will not create such a danger and must therefore be accommodated. . . .

The Air Force has drawn the line essentially between religious apparel that is visible and that which is not, and we hold that those portions of the regulations challenged here reasonably and evenhandedly regulate dress in the interest of the military's perceived need for uniformity. The First Amendment therefore does not prohibit them from being applied to petitioner even though their effect is to restrict the wearing of the headgear required by his religious beliefs.

The judgment of the Court of Appeals is affirmed."

V. JUSTICE VOTE

4 Pro ACLU Side vs. 5 Con Opposing Side

ACLU Side (Petitioner / Appellant)

1. Brennan, W. – Wrote dissenting opinion
2. Marshall, T. – Joined Brennan's dissent and O'Connor's dissent
3. Blackmun, H. – Wrote dissenting opinion
4. O'Connor, S. – Wrote dissenting opinion

Opposing Side (Respondent / Appellee)

1. Rehnquist, W. – Wrote majority opinion
2. Burger, W. – Joined majority opinion
3. White, B. – Joined Stevens' concurrence
4. Powell, L. – Joined Stevens' concurrence
5. Stevens, J. – Wrote concurring opinion

VI. A WIN OR LOSS FOR THE ACLU?

The ACLU, as amicus curiae, urged reversal of the judgment of the Court of Appeals for the District of Columbia Circuit; the Supreme Court affirmed in a 5-4 vote, giving the ACLU an apparent loss.

581. Bender v. Williamsport Area School District

(Decided March 25, 1986; 475 U.S. 534)

I. ISSUE

A. Issues Discussed

First Amendment, religion, standing, jurisdiction

B. Legal Question Presented

"Whether one member of a School Board has standing to appeal from a declaratory judgment against the Board."

C. Supreme Court's Answer

The member of the School Board does not have standing to appeal the judgment against the Board.

II. CASE SUMMARY

A. Background

"In September 1981 a group of high school students in Williamsport, Pennsylvania, formed a club called 'Petros' for the purpose of promoting 'spiritual growth and positive attitudes in the lives of its members.' The group asked the Principal of the high school for permission to meet on school premises during student activity periods . . . . On November 16, 1981, the Principal and the Superintendent met with representatives of Petros and advised them that 'based on the Solicitor's legal opinion, their request must be denied.' . . . The students thereafter wrote a letter to the Chairman of the Williamsport Area School Board appealing the Superintendent's decision. At a meeting held January 19, 1982, the Board upheld the Superintendent's decision and 'denied the appeal on the basis of the Solicitor's opinion.' . . .

On June 2, 1982, 10 of the students filed suit in the United States District Court . . . . The complaint alleged that the defendants' refusal to recognize Petros and to allow it to meet on the same basis as other student groups because of its religious activities violated the First Amendment. The complaint prayed for declaratory and injunctive relief. . . . The final order entered by the District Court was a ruling 'in favor of the plaintiffs and against the defendants on plaintiffs' freedom of speech claim' No injunction was entered, and no relief was granted against any defendant in his individual capacity. The District Court, in effect, merely held that the Board's attorney was incorrect in his legal advice.

The School District did not challenge the judgment of the District Court in any way. It made no motion for a stay and took no appeal. Instead, it decided to comply with the judgment and to allow Petros to conduct the meetings it had requested.

However, John C. Youngman, Jr., who was then still a member of the Board, did file a timely notice of appeal. [T]he majority of the Court of Appeals held 'that the particular circumstances disclosed by this record and present at the Williamsport Area High School lead to the inexorable conclusion that the constitutional balance of interests tilts against permitting the Petros activity to be conducted within the school as a general activity program.'"

The Supreme Court granted certiorari to review the case, vacated, and remanded.

B. Counsel of Record / ACLU Attorney

ACLU Side (Respondent / Appellee): John C. Youngman, Jr., pro se, argued the cause for appellee.

Opposing Side (Petitioner / Appellant): James M. Smart, Jr., argued the cause for appellant.

Deputy Solicitor General Fried argued the cause for the United States, as amicu curiae, urging reversal.

III. AMICI CURIAE

ACLU Side (Respondent / Appellee)

Brief of amici curiae filed on behalf of the ACLU, et al., by Jack D. Novik, Charles S. Sims, Burt Neuborne, Stefan Presser, and Joy L. Koletsky.

Additional briefs of amici curiae were filed on behalf of the American Association of School Administrators, the American Jewish Committee, et al., the American Jewish Congress, et al., Kiwanis International, et al., and the Anti-Defamation League of B'nai B'rith, et al.

Opposing Side (Petitioner / Appellant)

Brief of amici curiae filed on behalf of the United States by Deputy Solicitor General Fried, Solicitor General Lee, Acting Assistant Attorney General Willard, Michael W. McConnell, Anthony J. Steinmeyer, and Robert V. Zener.

Additional briefs of amici curiae were filed on behalf of the Ad Hoc Group of State Education Officials, School Administrators, and School Board Members, the Catholic League for Religious and Civil Rights, the Concerned Women for American Education and Legal Defense Foundation, Inter-Varsity Christian Fellowship of the U.S.A., the Rutherford Institute, et al., the Baptist Joint Committee on Public Affairs, et al., and the United States Catholic Conference.

IV. THE SUPREME COURT'S DECISION:

"Federal courts are not courts of general jurisdiction; they have only the power that is authorized by Article III of the Constitution and the statutes enacted by Congress pursuant thereto. . . . '[A]t an irreducible minimum, Art. III requires the party who invokes the court's authority to 'show that he personally has suffered some actual or threatened injury as a result of the putatively illegal conduct of the defendant,' and that the injury 'fairly can be traced to the challenged action' and 'is likely to be redressed by a favorable decision." . . .

Since the judgment against Mr. Youngman was not in his individual capacity, he had no standing to appeal in that capacity. . . . As a member of the School Board sued in his official capacity Mr. Youngman has no personal stake in the outcome of the litigation and therefore did not have standing to file the notice of appeal. . . . The reasons why Mr. Youngman may not take an appeal in his individual capacity also foreclose an appeal in his capacity as a parent. . . . Having failed to assert his parental interest in the District Court—or to adduce any factual support for that interest in this Court—Mr. Youngman has no right to prosecute an appeal in his capacity as a parent.

We therefore hold that because the Court of Appeals was without jurisdiction to hear the appeal, it was without authority to decide the merits. Accordingly, the judgment of the Court of Appeals is vacated, and the case is remanded with instructions to dismiss the appeal for want of jurisdiction."

V. JUSTICE VOTE

4 Pro ACLU Side vs. 5 Con Opposing Side

ACLU Side (Respondent / Appellee)

1. Powell, L. – Wrote dissenting opinion
2. Burger, W. – Wrote dissenting opinion
3. Rehnquist, W. – Joined Burger's dissent
4. White, B. – Joined Burger's dissent

Opposing Side (Petitioner / Appellant)

1. Stevens, J. – Wrote majority opinion
2. Blackmun, H. – Joined majority opinion

3. O'Connor, S. – Joined majority opinion
4. Brennan, W. – Joined majority opinion
5. Marshall, T. – Wrote concurring opinion

VI. A WIN OR LOSS FOR THE ACLU?

The ACLU filed as amicus curiae urging affirmance of the judgment of the Court of Appeals; the Supreme Court reversed in a 5-4 vote, giving the ACLU an apparent loss.

582. Holbrook v. Flynn

(Decided March 26, 1986; 475 U.S. 560)

I. ISSUE

A. Issues Discussed

Criminal procedure

B. Legal Question Presented

"[W]hether a criminal defendant was denied his constitutional right to a fair trial when, at his trial with five codefendants, the customary courtroom security force was supplemented by four uniformed state troopers sitting in the first row of the spectators' section."

C. Supreme Court's Answer

"All a federal court may do in such a situation is look at the scene presented to jurors and determine whether what they saw was so inherently prejudicial as to pose an unacceptable threat to defendant's right to a fair trial; if the challenged practice is not found inherently prejudicial and if the defendant fails to show actual prejudice, the inquiry is over. Respondent has failed to carry his burden here."

II. CASE SUMMARY

A. Background

"On August 14, 1975, nine masked men [committed an armed robbery]. . . .

In April 1976, respondent and his five codefendants were brought to trial . . . . [R]espondent's counsel noted the presence of four uniformed state troopers, sitting in the first row of the spectators' section . . . . Counsel immediately complained to the judge . . . . Justice Giannini replied that the troopers were present because the Committing Squad . . . was overextended at that time. [T]he judge agreed to see whether they might be made to wear civilian clothes . . . .

Justice Giannini announced that he had 'received a report that it is not practical . . .' for the four troopers to dress in civilian clothes. . . . He noted that . . . defendants would in no way be prejudiced. . . . Jury selection began. . . .

[R]espondent sought interlocutory review in the Rhode Island Supreme Court of Justice Giannini's ruling. [T]he Supreme Court . . . granted respondent's petition. . . .

After completing jury selection, . . . the justice concluded that the presence of the troopers would not affect defendants' ability to receive a fair trial.

The trial . . . ended with verdicts acquitting three defendants and convicting respondent and two others. On appeal, the Rhode Island Supreme Court affirmed the convictions. . . .

Respondent then brought this habeas proceeding in Federal District Court. [T]he District Court for the District of Rhode Island entertained the petition and rejected all the claims therein. . . .

The Court of Appeals, however, reversed this dismissal. . . . The court ordered that the writ of habeas corpus be granted."

The Supreme Court granted certiorari to review the case.

B. Counsel of Record

ACLU Side (Respondent / Appellee): George Kannar of the American Civil Liberties Union argued the cause for appellee. With him on the briefs were Charles S. Sims and Burt Neuborne of American Civil Liberties Union.

Opposing Side (Petitioner / Appellant): Thomas More Dickinson, Special Assistant Attorney General of Rhode Island, argued the cause for appellants. With him on the brief were Arlene Violet, Attorney General, and John Austin Murphy.

III. AMICI CURIAE

ACLU Side (Respondent / Appellee)

No briefs of amici curiae were filed in support of appellee.

Opposing Side (Petitioner / Appellant)

Brief of amici curiae filed on behalf of the State of California by John K. Van de Kamp, Attorney General, Karl S. Mayer, Assistant Attorney General, and Robert E. Niver, Deputy Attorney General.

IV. THE SUPREME COURT'S DECISION

"Central to the right to a fair trial, guaranteed by the Sixth and Fourteenth Amendments, is the principle that 'one accused of a crime is entitled to have his guilt or innocence determined solely on the basis of the evidence introduced at trial, and not on grounds of official suspicion, indictment, continued custody, or other circumstances not adduced as proof at trial.' This does not mean, however, that every practice tending to single out the accused from everyone else in the courtroom must be struck down. . . .

The first issue to be considered here is thus whether the conspicuous, or at least noticeable, deployment of security personnel in a courtroom during trial is the sort of inherently prejudicial practice that, like shackling, should be permitted only where justified by an essential state interest specific to each trial. We do not believe that it is. . . .

The courtroom security force in this case consisted of four uniformed state troopers, two Deputy Sheriffs, and six Committing Squad officers. Though respondent does not concede that the deployment of the uniformed Committing Squad officers was proper, his focus at every stage of his habeas proceedings has been exclusively on the prejudice he attributes to the four state troopers. The only question we need answer is thus whether the presence of these four uniformed and armed officers was so inherently prejudicial that respondent was thereby denied his constitutional right to a fair trial. . . .

While, in our supervisory capacity, we might express a preference that officers providing courtroom security in federal courts not be easily identifiable by jurors as guards, we are much more constrained when reviewing a constitutional challenge to a state-court proceeding. All a federal court may do in such a situation is look at the scene presented to jurors and determine whether what they saw was so inherently prejudicial as to pose an unacceptable threat to defendant's right to a fair trial; if the challenged practice is not found inherently prejudicial and if the defendant fails to show actual prejudice, the inquiry is over. Respondent has failed to carry his burden here.

The judgment of the Court of Appeals is reversed."

V. JUSTICE VOTE

0 Pro ACLU Side vs. 9 Con Opposing Side

Opposing Side (Petitioner / Appellant)

1. Marshall, T. – Wrote majority opinion
2. Rehnquist, W. – Joined majority opinion
3. Burger, W. – Wrote concurring opinion
4. Powell, L. – Joined majority opinion
5. O'Connor, S. – Joined majority opinion
6. Blackmun, H. – Joined majority opinion
7. Brennan, W. – Joined majority opinion
8. White, B. – Joined majority opinion
9. Stevens, J. – Joined majority opinion

VI. A WIN OR LOSS FOR THE ACLU?

The ACLU served as counsel for appellee urging affirmance; the Supreme Court reversed the Court of Appeals' decision by a 9-0 vote, giving the ACLU an apparent loss.

583. Evans v. Jeff D.

(Decided April 21, 1986; 475 U.S. 717)

I. ISSUE

A. Issues Discussed

Civil procedure

B. Legal Question Presented

"[W]hether attorney's fees must be assessed when the case has been settled by a consent decree granting prospective relief to the plaintiff class but providing that the defendants shall not pay any part of the prevailing party's fees or costs."

C. Supreme Court's Answer

"We hold that the District Court has the power, in its sound discretion, to refuse to award fees."

II. CASE SUMMARY

A. Background

"The petitioners are the Governor and other public officials of the State of Idaho responsible for the education and treatment of children who suffer from emotional and mental handicaps. Respondents are a class of such children ....

The factual allegations ... described deficiencies in both the educational programs and the health care services provided respondents....

[T]he District Court ... appoint[ed] Charles Johnson ... for the sole purpose of instituting and prosecuting the action. ... Johnson was employed by the Idaho Legal Aid Society, Inc., a private, nonprofit corporation that provides free legal services ....

[P]etitioners presented respondents with a ... settlement proposal. [T]he proposal 'offered virtually all of the injunctive relief [they] had sought in their complaint.' ... [H]owever, petitioners' offer included ... a waiver by respondents of any claim to fees or costs.... Johnson ... determined that his ethical obligation to his clients mandated acceptance ....

Johnson filed a written motion requesting the District Court to approve the settlement 'except for the provision on costs and attorney's fees' .... [T]he District Court approved the settlement and denied the motion to submit a costs bill.

When respondents appealed from the order denying attorney's fees and costs, petitioners filed a motion requesting the District Court to suspend or stay their obligation to comply with the substantive terms of the settlement. [T]he District Court ... granted the motion. The Court of Appeals, however, ... invalidated the fee waiver and left standing the remainder of the settlement ...."

The Supreme Court granted certiorari to review the case.

B. Counsel of Record

ACLU Side (Respondent / Appellee): William T. Coleman, Jr., argued the cause for appellees. With him on the brief were Aaron S. Bayer, Howard A. Belodoff, and Charles Johnson III.

Opposing Side (Petitioner / Appellant): James Thomas Jones, Attorney General of Idaho, argued the cause for appellants. With him on the briefs were John J. McMahon, Chief Deputy Attorney General, and Michael De Angelo and James Wickham, Deputy Attorneys General. Deputy Solicitor General Wallace argued the cause for the United States as amicus curiae.

III. AMICI CURIAE

ACLU Side (Respondent / Appellee)

Brief of amici curiae filed on behalf of the NAACP Legal Defense and Educational Fund, Inc., Lawyers' Committee for Civil Rights Under Law, American Civil Liberties Union, and Legal Aid Society of New York by James Robertson, Harold R. Tyler, Jr., Norman Redlich, William L. Robinson, Norman J. Chachkin, Kalman Finkel, Helaine M. Barnett, John E. Kirklin, Julius LeVonne Chambers, Charles Stephen Ralston, Steven L. Winter, E. Richard Larson, amd Burt Neuborne.

Brief of amici curiae filed on behalf of the Committee on Legal Assistance of the Association of the Bar of the City of New York by Allan L. Gropper.

Opposing Side (Petitioner / Appellant)

Brief of amici curiae filed on behalf of the United States by Deputy Solicitor General Wallace, Acting Solicitor General Fried, Acting Assistant Attorney General Willard, Deputy Solicitor General Geller, Kathryn A. Oberly, John F. Cordes, and Douglas Letter.

Brief of amici curiae filed on behalf of the State of Alabama et al. by Francis X. Bellotti, Attorney General of Massachusetts, and Ellen Janos and Carl Valvo, Assistant Attorneys General, Charles A. Graddick, Attorney General of Alabama, Harold Brown, Attorney General of Alaska, Robert K. Corbin, Attorney General of Arizona, and Anthony Ching, Solicitor General, John Steven Clark, Attorney General of Arkansas, John Van de Kamp, Attorney General of California, Duane Woodard, Attorney General of Colorado, Charles M. Oberly, Attorney General of Delaware, Jim Smith, Attorney General of Florida, Michael J. Bowers, Attorney General of Georgia, Richard G. Opper, Attorney General of Guam, Corinne Watanabe, Acting Attorney General of Hawaii, Linley E. Pearson, Attorney General of Indiana, Thomas J. Miller, Attorney General of Iowa, Robert T. Stephan, Attorney General of Kansas, David L. Armstrong, Attorney General of Kentucky, William J. Guste, Jr., Attorney General of Louisiana, James E. Tierney, Attorney General of Maine, Stephen H. Sachs, Attorney General of Maryland, Frank J. Kelley, Attorney General of Michigan, Hubert H. Humphrey III, Attorney General of Minnesota, Edwin Lloyd Pittman, Attorney General of Mississippi, William L. Webster, Attorney General of Missouri, Mike Greely, Attorney General of Montana, Brian McKay, Attorney General of Nevada, Stephen E. Merrill, Attorney General of New Hampshire, Irwin I. Kimmelman, Attorney General of New Jersey, Lacy H. Thornburg, Attorney General of North Carolina, Nicholas Spaeth, Attorney General of North Dakota, Anthony J. Celebrezze, Jr., Attorney General of Ohio, Michael Turpen, Attorney General of Oklahoma, David Frohnmayer, Attorney General of Oregon, Leroy S. Zimmerman, Attorney General of Pennsylvania, Hector Rivera-Cruz, Attorney General of Puerto Rico, Arlene Violet, Attorney General of Rhode Island, Travis Medlock, Attorney General of South Carolina, Mark V. Meierhenry, Attorney General of South Dakota, W. J. Michael Cody, Attorney General of Tennessee, Jim Mattox, Attorney General of Texas, David L. Wilkinson, Attorney General of Utah, Jeffrey Amestoy, Attorney General of Vermont, William J. Broaddus, Attorney General of Virginia, Victor G. Schneider, Acting Attorney General of the Virgin Islands, Kenneth O. Eikenberry, Attorney General of Washington, Charlie Brown, Attorney General of West Virginia, Bronson C. La Follette, Attorney General of Wisconsin, and A. G. McClintock, Attorney General of Wyoming.

Brief of amici curiae filed on behalf of the City of New York by Frederick A. O. Schwarz, Jr., Leonard Koerner, and Paul T. Rephen.

Brief of amici curiae filed on behalf of the Council of State Governments et al. by Benna Ruth Solomon and J. Phillip Jordan.

Brief of amici curiae filed on behalf of the Equal Employment Advisory Council by Robert E. Williams, Douglas S. McDowell, and Thomas R. Bagby.

IV. THE SUPREME COURT'S DECISION

"To begin with, the Court of Appeals' decision rested on an erroneous view of the District Court's power to approve settlements in class actions. . . . Rule 23(e) does not give the court the power, in advance of trial, to modify a proposed consent decree and order its acceptance over either party's objection. . . . The question we must decide, therefore, is whether the District Court had a duty to reject the proposed settlement because it included a waiver of statutorily authorized attorney's fees.

That duty . . . derives ultimately from the Fees Act rather than from the strictures of professional ethics. . . . Plainly, Johnson had no ethical obligation to seek a statutory fee award. His ethical duty was to serve his clients loyally and competently. Since the proposal to settle the merits was more favorable than the probable outcome of the trial, Johnson's decision to recommend acceptance was consistent with the highest standards of our profession. The District Court, therefore, correctly concluded that approval of the settlement involved no breach of ethics in this case.

The defect, if any, in the negotiated fee waiver must be traced not to the rules of ethics but to the Fees Act. . . .

The question this case presents, then, is whether the Fees Act requires a district court to disapprove a stipulation seeking to settle a civil rights class action under Rule 23 when the offered relief equals or exceeds the probable outcome at trial but is expressly conditioned on waiver of statutory eligibility for attorney's fees. [W]e are not persuaded that Congress has commanded that all such settlements must be rejected by the District Court. Moreover, on the facts of record in this case, we are satisfied that the District Court did not abuse its discretion by approving the fee waiver. . . .

The text of the Fees Act provides no support for the proposition that Congress intended to ban all fee waivers offered in connection with substantial relief on the merits. . . .

We conclude, therefore, that it is not necessary to construe the Fees Act as embodying a general rule prohibiting settlements conditioned on the waiver of fees . . . .

The question remains whether the District Court abused its discretion in this case by approving a settlement which included a complete fee waiver. . . .

In this case, the District Court did not abuse its discretion in upholding a fee waiver which secured broad injunctive relief, relief greater than that which plaintiffs could reasonably have expected to achieve at trial.

The judgment of the Court of Appeals is reversed."

V. JUSTICE VOTE

3 Pro ACLU Side vs. 6 Con Opposing Side

ACLU Side (Respondent / Appellee)

1. Brennan, W. – Wrote dissenting opinion
2. Marshall, T. – Joined Brennan's dissent
3. Blackmun, H. – Joined Brennan's dissent

Opposing Side (Petitioner / Appellant)

1. Stevens, J. – Wrote majority opinion
2. Rehnquist, W. – Joined majority opinion
3. Burger, W. – Joined majority opinion
4. Powell, L. – Joined majority opinion
5. O'Connor, S. – Joined majority opinion
6. White, B. – Joined majority opinion

VI. A WIN OR LOSS FOR THE ACLU?

The ACLU filed as amicus curiae urging affirmance; the Supreme Court reversed the Court of Appeals' decision by a 6-3 vote, giving the ACLU an apparent loss.

584. Philadelphia Newspapers, Inc. v. Hepps

(Decided April 21, 1986; 475 U.S. 767)

I. ISSUE

A. Issues Discussed

First Amendment, freedom of speech, defamation

B. Legal Question Presented

"[W]here a newspaper publishes speech of public concern, [whether] a private-figure plaintiff [can] recover damages without also showing that the statements at issue are false."

C. Supreme Court's Answer

"[A]t least where a newspaper publishes speech of public concern, a private- figure plaintiff cannot recover damages without also showing that that statements at issue are false."

II. CASE SUMMARY

A. Background

"Maurice S. Hepps is the principal stockholder of General Programming, Inc. (GPI), a corporation that franchises a chain of stores—known at the relevant time as 'Thrifty' stores—selling beer, soft drinks, and snacks. Mr. Hepps, GPI, and a number of its franchisees are the appellees here. Appellant Philadelphia Newspapers, Inc., owns the Philadelphia Inquirer (Inquirer). The Inquirer published a series of articles, authored by appellants William Ecenbarger and William Lambert, containing the statements at issue here. The general theme of the five articles, which appeared in the Inquirer between May 1975 and May 1976, was that appellees had links to organized crime and used some of those links to influence the State's governmental processes, both legislative and administrative. . . .

Appellees brought suit for defamation against appellants in a Pennsylvania state court. Consistent with Gertz, Pennsylvania requires a private figure who brings a suit for defamation to bear the burden of proving negligence or malice by the defendant in publishing the statements at issue. As to falsity, Pennsylvania follows the common law's presumption that an individual's reputation is a good one. Statements defaming that person are therefore presumptively false, although a publisher who bears the burden of proving the truth of the statements has an absolute defense.

The parties first raised the issue of burden of proof as to falsity before trial, but the trial court reserved its ruling on the matter. Appellee Hepps testified at length that the statements at issue were false and he extensively cross-examined the author of the stories as to the veracity of the statements at issue. After all the evidence had been presented by both sides, the trial court concluded that Pennsylvania's statute giving the defendant the burden of proving the truth of the statements violated the Federal Constitution. The trial court therefore instructed the jury that the plaintiffs bore the burden of proving falsity. . . . The jury ruled for appellants and therefore awarded no damages to appellees.

Pursuant to Pennsylvania statute the appellees here brought an appeal directly to the Pennsylvania Supreme Court. That court viewed Gertz as simply requiring the plaintiff to show fault in actions for defamation. It concluded that a showing of fault did not require a showing of falsity, held that to place the burden of showing truth on the defendant did not unconstitutionally inhibit free debate, and remanded the case for a new trial."

The Supreme Court granted certiorari to review the case and reversed.

B. Counsel of Record / ACLU Attorney

ACLU Side (Petitioner / Appellant): David H. Marion argued the cause for appellant.

Opposing Side (Respondent / Appellee): Ronald H. Surkin argued the cause for appellee.

III. AMICI CURIAE

ACLU Side (Petitioner / Appellant)

Brief of amici curiae filed on behalf of the ACLU, et al., by John G. Koeltl, James C. Goodale, Burt Neuborne, Jack D. Novick, Stefan Presser, Bruce W. Sanford, W. Terry Maguire, R. Bruce Rich, Robert D. Sack, and Alice Neff Lucan.

Additional briefs of amici curiae were filed on behalf of the American Federation of Labor and Congress of Industrial Organizations, Capital Cities Communications, Inc., et al., and Print and Broadcast Media, et al.

Opposing Side (Respondent / Appellee)

Brief of amici curiae filed on behalf of the American Legal Foundation by Daniel J. Popeo.

IV. THE SUPREME COURT'S DECISION

"Our opinions to date have chiefly treated the necessary showings of fault rather than of falsity. Nonetheless, as one might expect given the language of the Court in New York Times, a public-figure plaintiff must show the falsity of the statements at issue in order to prevail in a suit for defamation.

Here, as in Gertz, the plaintiff is a private figure and the newspaper articles are of public concern. In Gertz, as in New York Times, the common-law rule was superseded by a constitutional rule. We believe that the common law's rule on falsity—that the defendant must bear the burden of proving truth—must similarly fall here to a constitutional requirement that the plaintiff bear the burden of showing falsity, as well as fault, before recovering damages.

There will always be instances when the factfinding process will be unable to resolve conclusively whether the speech is true or false; it is in those cases that the burden of proof is dispositive. Under a rule forcing the plaintiff to bear the burden of showing falsity, there will be some cases in which plaintiffs cannot meet their burden despite the fact that the speech is in fact false. The plaintiff's suit will fail despite the fact that, in some abstract sense, the suit is meritorious. Similarly, under an alternative rule placing the burden of showing truth on defendants, there would be some cases in which defendants could not bear their burden despite the fact that the speech is in fact true. Those suits would succeed despite the fact that, in some abstract sense, those suits are unmeritorious. Under either rule, then, the outcome of the suit will sometimes be at variance with the outcome that we would desire if all speech were either demonstrably true or demonstrably false.

This dilemma stems from the fact that the allocation of the burden of proof will determine liability for some speech that is true and some that is false, but all of such speech is unknowably true or false. Because the burden of proof is the deciding factor only when the evidence is ambiguous, we cannot know how much of the speech affected by the allocation of the burden of proof is true and how much is false. In a case presenting a configuration of speech and plaintiff like the one we face here, and where the scales are in such an uncertain balance, we believe that the Constitution requires us to tip them in favor of protecting true speech. To ensure that true speech on matters of public concern is not deterred we hold that the common-law presumption that defamatory speech is false cannot stand when a plaintiff seeks damages against a media defendant for speech of public concern. . . .

For the reasons stated above, the judgment of the Pennsylvania Supreme Court is reversed, and the case is remanded for further proceedings not inconsistent with this opinion."

V. JUSTICE VOTE

5 Pro ACLU Side vs. 4 Con Opposing Side

ACLU Side (Petitioner / Appellant)

1. O'Connor, S. – Wrote majority opinion
2. Brennan, W. – Wrote concurring opinion
3. Marshall, T. – Joined majority opinion
4. Blackmun, H. – Joined Brennan's concurrence
5. Powell, L. – Joined majority opinion

Opposing Side (Respondent / Appellee)

1. Stevens, J. – Wrote dissenting opinion
2. Burger, W. – Joined Stevens' dissent
3. White, B. – Joined Stevens' dissent
4. Rehnquist, W. – Joined Stevens' dissent

VI. A WIN OR LOSS FOR THE ACLU?

The ACLU, as amicus curiae, urged reversal of the Supreme Court of Pennsylvania's judgment; the U.S. Supreme Court reversed and remanded in a 5-4 vote, giving the ACLU an apparent win.

585. Smalis v. Pennsylvania

(Decided May 5, 1986; 476 U.S. 140)

I. ISSUE

A. Issues Discussed

Criminal procedure, Fifth Amendment, double jeopardy

B. Legal Question Presented

"[W]hether the Double Jeopardy Clause bars the prosecution from appealing this ruling" which "dismissed certain charges against petitioners on the ground that the evidence presented was legally insufficient to support a conviction."

C. Supreme Court's Answer

The Double Jeopardy Clause bars the prosecution from appealing the ruling.

II. CASE SUMMARY

A. Background

"Petitioners, husband and wife, owned a building housing a restaurant and some apartments that burned under suspicious circumstances, killing two of the tenants. Petitioners were charged with various crimes in connection with this fire, including criminal homicide, reckless endangerment, and causing a catastrophe. They opted for a bench trial, and at the close of the prosecution's case in chief challenged the sufficiency of the evidence by filing a demurrer pursuant to Pennsylvania Rule of Criminal Procedure 1124(a)(1). The trial court sustained petitioners' demurrer to charges of murder, voluntary manslaughter, and causing a catastrophe . . . .

The Commonwealth sought review of this ruling in the Superior Court of Pennsylvania, but a panel of that court quashed the appeal, holding it barred by the Double Jeopardy Clause. The Superior Court granted review en banc and affirmed. . . . The Commonwealth appealed to the Supreme Court of Pennsylvania, which reversed."

The U.S. Supreme Court granted certiorari to review the case and reversed.

B. Counsel of Record / ACLU Attorney

ACLU Side (Petitioner / Appellant): Norma Chase argued the cause for appellant.

Opposing Side (Respondent / Appellee): Robert L. Eberhardt argued the cause for appellee.

Deputy Solicitor General Frey argued the cause for the United States, as amicus curiae, by special leave of Court.

III. AMICI CURIAE

ACLU Side (Petitioner / Appellant)

Opposing Side (Respondent / Appellee)

Brief of amici curiae filed on behalf of the ACLU, et al., by Charles S. Sims. Brief of amici curiae filed on behalf of the United States by Deputy Solicitor General Frey, Solicitor General Fried, Assistant Attorney General Trott, and Alan I. Horowitz.

IV. THE SUPREME COURT'S DECISION:

"The Pennsylvania Supreme Court erred in holding that, for purposes of considering a plea of double jeopardy, a defendant who demurs at the close of the prosecution's case in chief 'elects to seek dismissal on grounds unrelated to his factual guilt or innocence.' What the demurring defendant seeks is a ruling that, as a matter of law, the State's evidence is insufficient to establish his factual guilt. Our past decisions, which we are not inclined to reconsider at this time, hold that such a ruling is an acquittal under the Double Jeopardy Clause. United States v. Scott does not overturn these precedents; indeed, it plainly indicates that the category of acquittals includes 'judgment[s] . . . by the court that the evidence is insufficient to convict.'

The Commonwealth argues that its appeal is nonetheless permissible under Justices of Boston Municipal Court v. Lydon because resumption of petitioners' bench trial following a reversal on appeal would simply constitute 'continuing jeopardy.' But Lyndon teaches that '[a]cquittals, unlike convictions, terminate the initial jeopardy.' Thus, whether the trial is to a jury or to the bench, subjecting the defendant to postacquittal factfinding proceedings going to guilt or innocence violates the Double Jeopardy Clause.

When a successful postacquittal appeal by the prosecution would lead to proceedings that violate the Double Jeopardy Clause, the appeal itself has no proper purpose. Allowing such an appeal would frustrate the interest of the accused in having an end to the proceedings against him. The Superior Court was correct, therefore, in holding that the Double Jeopardy Clause bars a postacquittal appeal by the prosecution not only when it might result in a second trial, but also if reversal would translate into 'further proceedings of some sort, devoted to the resolution of factual issues going to the elements of the offense charged.'

We hold, therefore, that the trial judge's granting of petitioners' demurrer was an acquittal under the Double Jeopardy Clause, and that the Commonwealth's appeal was barred because reversal would have led to further trial proceedings.

The judgment of the Pennsylvania Supreme Court is reversed."

V. JUSTICE VOTE

9 Pro ACLU Side vs. 0 Con Opposing Side

ACLU Side (Petitioner / Appellant)

1. White, B. – Wrote the majority opinion
2. Rehnquist, W. – Joined majority opinion
3. Powell, L. – Joined majority opinion
4. Brennan, W. – Joined majority opinion
5. Stevens, J. – Joined majority opinion
6. Blackmun, H. – Joined majority opinion
7. Burger, W. – Joined majority opinion
8. Marshall, T. – Joined majority opinion
9. Brennan, W. – Joined majority opinion

VI. A WIN OR LOSS FOR THE ACLU?

The ACLU filed as amicus curiae urging reversal of the judgment of the Pennsylvania Supreme Court; the U.S. Supreme Court reversed in a 9-0 vote, giving the ACLU an apparent win.

586. California v. Ciraolo

(Decided May 19, 1986; 476 U.S. 207)

I. ISSUE

A. Issues Discussed

Fourth Amendment, search and seizure

B. Legal Question Presented

"[W]hether the Fourth Amendment is violated by aerial observation without a warrant from an altitude of 1,000 feet of a fenced-in backyard within the curtilage of a home."

C. Supreme Court's Answer

The Fourth Amendment is not violated by aerial observation of a fenced-in backyard without a warrant at an altitude of 1,000 feet.

II. CASE SUMMARY

A. Background

"On September 2, 1982, Santa Clara Police received an anonymous telephone tip that marijuana was growing in respondent's backyard. Police were unable to observe the contents of respondent's yard from ground level because of a 6-foot outer fence and a 10-foot inner fence completely enclosing the yard. Later that day, Officer Shutz, who was assigned to investigate, secured a private plane and flew over respondent's house at an altitude of 1,000 feet, within navigable airspace; he was accompanied by Officer Rodriguez. Both officers were trained in marijuana identification. From the overflight, the officers readily identified marijuana plants 8 feet to 10 feet in height growing in a 15- by 25-foot plot in respondent's yard; they photographed the area with a standard 35mm camera.

On September 8, 1982, Officer Shutz obtained a search warrant on the basis of an affidavit describing the anonymous tip and their observations; a photograph depicting respondent's house, the backyard, and neighboring homes was attached to the affidavit as an exhibit. The warrant was executed the next day and 73 plants were seized; it is not disputed that these were marijuana.

After the trial court denied respondent's motion to suppress the evidence of the search, respondent pleaded guilty to a charge of cultivation of marijuana. The California Court of Appeal reversed, however, on the ground that the warrantless aerial observation of respondent's yard which led to the issuance of the warrant violated the Fourth Amendment. . . . The California Supreme Court denied the State's petition for review."

The Supreme Court granted certiorari to review the case and reversed.

B. Counsel of Record / ACLU Attorney

ACLU Side (Respondent / Appellee): Marshall Warren Krause, by appointment of the Court, argued the cause for appellee.

Opposing Side (Petitioner / Appellant): Laurence K. Sullivan, Deputy Attorney General of California, argued the cause for appellant.

III. AMICI CURIAE

ACLU Side (Respondent / Appellee)

Brief of amici curiae filed on behalf of the ACLU, et al., by C. Douglas Floyd, Alan L. Schlosser, and Charles S. Sims.
Brief of amici curiae filed on behalf of the Civil Liberties Monitoring Project by Amitai Schwartz.
Brief of amici curaie filed on behalf of the National Association of Criminal Defense Lawyers by John Kenneth Zwerling.

Opposing Side (Petitioner / Appellant)

Brief of amici curiae filed on behalf of the State of Indiana, et al., by Linley E. Pearson, Attorney General of Indiana, William E. Daily and Lisa M. Paunicka, Deputy Attorneys General, Charles A. Graddick, Attorney General of Alabama, Charles M. Oberly, Attorney General of Delaware, Michael J. Bowers, Attorney General of Georgia, Neil F. Hartigan, Attorney General of Illinois, Robert T. Stephan, Attorney General of Kansas, David L. Armstrong, Attorney General of Kentucky, William J. Guste, Jr., Attorney General of Louisiana, James E. Tierney, Attorney General of Maine, Francis X. Bellotti, Attorney General of Massachusetts, William L. Webster, Attorney General of Missouri, Robert M. Spire, Attorney General-Designate of Nebraska, Brian McKay, Attorney General of Nevada, Stephen E. Merrill, Attorney General of New Hampshire, Paul Bardacke, Attorney General of New Mexico, Anthony Celebrezze, Attorney General of Ohio, LeRoy S. Zimmerman, Attorney General of Pennsylvania, Travis Medlock, Attorney General of South Carolina, Jeffrey Amestoy, Attorney General of Vermont, Gerald L. Baliles, Attorney General of Virginia, Kenneth O. Eikenberry, Attorney General of Washington, and Archie G. McClintock, Attorney General of Wyoming.
Brief of amici curiae filed on behalf of Americans for Effective Law Enforcement Inc., et al., by Fred E. Inbau, Wayne W. Schmidt, James P. Manak, David Crump, and Daniel B. Hales.
Brief of amici curiae filed on behalf of the Criminal Justice Legal Foundation by Christopher N. Heard.
Brief of amici curiae filed on behalf of the Washington Legal Foundation by Daniel J. Popeo and George C. Smith.

IV. THE SUPREME COURT'S DECISION

"The touchstone of Fourth Amendment analysis is whether a person has a 'constitutionally protected reasonable expectation of privacy.' [F]irst, has the individual manifested a subjective expectation of privacy in the object of the challenged search? Second, is society willing to recognize that expectation as reasonable?

Clearly—and understandably—respondent has met the test of manifesting his own subjective intent and desire to maintain privacy as to his unlawful agricultural pursuits. However, we need not address that issue, for the State has not challenged the finding of the California Court of Appeal that respondent had such an expectation. It can reasonably be assumed that the 10-foot fence was placed to conceal the marijuana crop from at least street-level views. So far as the normal sidewalk traffic was concerned, this fence served that purpose, because respondent 'took normal precautions to maintain his privacy.'

Yet a 10-foot fence might not shield these plants from the eyes of a citizen or a policeman perched on the top of a truck or a two-level bus. Whether respondent therefore manifested a subjective expectation of privacy from all observations of his backyard, or whether instead he manifested merely a hope that no one would observe his unlawful gardening pursuits, is not entirely clear in these circumstances. Respondent appears to challenge the authority of government to observe his activity from any vantage point or place if the viewing is motivated by a law enforcement purpose, and not the result of a casual, accidental observation.

We turn, therefore, to the second inquiry . . . , whether that expectation is reasonable. In pursuing this inquiry, we must keep in mind that '[t]he test of legitimacy is not whether the individual chooses to conceal assertedly 'private' activity,' but instead 'whether the government's intrusion infringes upon the personal and societal values protected by the Fourth Amendment.' . . .

The Fourth Amendment protection of the home has never been extended to require law enforcement officers to shield their eyes when passing by a home on public thoroughfares. Nor does the mere fact that an individual has taken measures to restrict some views of his activities preclude an officer's observations from a public vantage point where he has a right to be and which renders the activities clearly visible. . . .

In an age where private and commercial flight in the public airways is routine, it is unreasonable for respondent to expect that his marijuana plants were constitutionally protected from being observed with the naked eye from an altitude of 1,000 feet. The Fourth Amendment simply does not require the police traveling in the public airways at this altitude to obtain a warrant in order to observe what is visible to the naked eye.

Reversed."

V. JUSTICE VOTE

4 Pro ACLU Side vs. 4 Con Opposing Side

ACLU Side (Respondent / Appellee)

1. Powell, L. – Wrote dissenting opinion
2. Brennan, W. – Joined Powell's dissent
3. Marshall, T. – Joined Powell's dissent
4. Blackmun, H. – Joined Powell's dissent

Opposing Side (Petitioner / Appellant)

1. Burger, W. – Wrote majority opinion
2. White, B. – Joined majority opinion
3. Rehnquist, W. – Joined majority opinion
4. Stevens, J. – Joined majority opinion
5. O'Connor, S. – Joined majority opinion

VI. A WIN OR LOSS FOR THE ACLU?

The ACLU, as amicus curiae, urged affirmance of the judgment of the California Court of Appeal; the Supreme Court reversed in a 5-4 vote, giving the ACLU an apparent loss.

587. Bowen v. City of New York

(Decided June 2, 1986; 476 U.S. 467)

I. ISSUE

A. Issues Discussed

Governmental authority, regulation, class actions

B. Legal Question Presented

"[W]hether the District Court correctly included within the class (i) claimants who had received a final decision on their individual claims for benefits more than 60 days prior to the filing of this action, and (ii) other claimants who had not exhausted their administrative remedies."

C. Supreme Court's Answer

The District Court correctly included both classes of claimants in the class action.

II. CASE SUMMARY

A. Background

"The Federal Government provides benefits to disabled persons under two distinct programs administered by the Social Security Administration (SSA). The Social Security Disability Insurance Program (SSD) . . . pays benefits to disabled persons who have contributed to the program and who suffer from a mental or physical disability. The Supplemental Security Income Program (SSI) . . . provides benefits to indigent disabled persons. . . .

On February 8, 1983, respondents . . . brought this class action against the Secretary and the Commissioner of SSA. They sought relief on behalf of all individuals residing in the State who had applied for or received SSD or SSI benefits on or after April 1, 1980, who had been found by petitioners to have a severe mental impairment, and whose applications for benefits either had been or were to be denied, or whose benefits had been or were to be terminated, based on petitioners' determination that the claimants were capable of substantial gainful employment.

The gravamen of respondents' complaint was that petitioners had adopted an unlawful, unpublished policy under which countless deserving claimants were denied benefits. . . . Respondents contended that failure to make the policy known to claimants denied the individual plaintiffs and class members due process of law.

[T]he District Court held that from 1978 until at least the early months of 1983, SSA followed the covert policy alleged by respondents and that the policy was illegal. . . . The District Court certified a class, and decided that the class properly included claimants who had not exhausted administrative remedies. . . . Similarly, the District Court decided that the class properly included those who had not complied with the requirement that a claimant seek judicial review within 60 days of the Secretary's final decision or 'within such further time as the Secretary may allow.' . . . The Court of Appeals for the Second Circuit affirmed. . . . On petition for rehearing, the same panel of the Court of Appeals, per Judge Newman, denied rehearing."

The Supreme Court granted certiorari to review the case and affirmed.

B. Counsel of Record / ACLU Attorney

ACLU Side (Respondent / Appellee): Frederick A.O. Schwarz, Jr., argued the cause for appellee.

Opposing Side (Petitioner / Appellant): Edwin S. Kneedler argued the cause for appellant.

III. AMICI CURIAE

ACLU Side (Respondent / Appellee)

Brief of amici curiae filed on behalf of the ACLU, et al., by Burt Neuborne and Charles S. Sims.

Additional briefs of amici curiae were filed on behalf of the State of Alabama, et al., the City of Chicago, the American Bar Association, the American Psychiatric Association, the Association of the Bar of the City of New York, and the National Institute of Municipal Law Officers.

Opposing Side (Petitioner / Appellant)

No briefs of amici curiae were filed in support of appellant.

IV. THE SUPREME COURT'S DECISION:

"In addition to serving its customary purpose, the statute of limitations embodied in § 405(g) is a mechanism by which Congress was able to move cases to speedy resolution in a bureaucracy that processes millions of claims annually. Thus, the limitation serves both the interest of the claimant and the interest of the Government. Tolling, in the rare case such as this, does not undermine the purpose of the 60-day limitations period when viewed in connection with the underlying statute. Rather, it serves the purpose of the Act where, as the Court of Appeals stated, 'the Government's secretive conduct prevents plaintiffs from knowing of a violation of rights . . . .' Tolling of the 60-day limitations period was appropriate in this case, and the District Court properly included in the class claimants who had received a final decision from the Secretary, but who did not seek judicial review within the statutory 60-day time period. . . .

Petitioners correctly assert that, had class members exhausted administrative remedies, some might have received benefits despite the illegal policy. It also is likely that many may have been disqualified for reasons having nothing to do with the illegal policy. Such observations, however, merely serve to remind us why exhaustion is the rule in the vast majority of cases; they do not aid the Court in deciding when exhaustion should be excused. We hold that the District Court did not err in waiving exhaustion in this case either with respect to those claimants whose time to pursue further administrative appeals had lapsed, or with respect to those claimants who still had time to pursue administrative remedies. . . .

Government agencies administering complex programs that bridge both state and federal bureaucracies necessarily will take certain actions pursuant to policies unknown to the public. We do not suggest that every internal policy that is found to be inconsistent with legal requirements, and arguably touches upon the outcome of a class of cases, will justify tolling the statute of limitations or excusing exhaustion. But, whatever the outer bounds of our holding today, this case falls well within them. While 'hard' cases may arise, this is not one of them.

Moreover, we are aware that administrative inconvenience may result from our decision today. But the Secretary had the capability and the duty to prevent the illegal policy found to exist by the District Court. The claimants here were denied the fair and neutral procedure required by the statute and regulations, and they are now entitled to pursue that procedure. The judgment of the Court of Appeals is affirmed."

V. JUSTICE VOTE

9 Pro ACLU Side vs. 0 Con Opposing Side

ACLU Side (Respondent / Appellee)

1. Powell, L. – Wrote majority opinion
2. Rehnquist, W. – Joined majority opinion
3. Brennan, W. – Joined majority opinion
4. Stevens, J. – Joined majority opinion
5. Blackmun, H. – Joined majority opinion
6. Burger, W. – Joined majority opinion
7. Marshall, T. – Joined majority opinion
8. Brennan, W. – Joined majority opinion
9. White, B. – Joined majority opinion

VI. A WIN OR LOSS FOR THE ACLU?

The ACLU filed as amicus curiae urging affirmance of the judgment of the Court of Appeals; the Supreme Court affirmed in a 9-0 vote, giving the ACLU an apparent win.

588. City of Los Angeles v. Preferred Communications, Inc.

(Decided June 2, 1986; 476 U.S. 488)

I. ISSUE

A. Issues Discussed

First Amendment, freedoms of press, speech, and association

B. Legal Question Presented

Did the City of Los Angeles violate the First Amendment by refusing to grant respondent a cable television franchise?

C. Supreme Court's Answer

The case implicates the First Amendment, but must be remanded to determine whether there was a violation of the First Amendment.

II. CASE SUMMARY

A. Background

"Respondent Preferred Communications, Inc., sued petitioners City of Los Angeles (City) and the Department of Water and Power (DWP) in the United States District Court for the Central District of California. The complaint alleged a violation of respondent's rights under the First and Fourteenth Amendments, and under §§ 1 and 2 of the Sherman Act, by reason of the City's refusal to grant respondent a cable television franchise and of DWP's refusal to grant access to DWP's poles or underground conduits used for power lines. The District Court dismissed the complaint for failure to state a claim upon which relief could be granted. See Fed.Rule Civ.Proc. 12(b)(6). The Court of Appeals for the Ninth Circuit affirmed with respect to the Sherman Act, but reversed as to the First Amendment claim. . . .

Respondent's complaint against the City and DWP alleged . . . the following facts: Respondent asked Pacific Telephone and Telegraph (PT & T) and DWP for permission to lease space on their utility poles in order to provide cable television service in the south central area of Los Angeles. These utilities responded that they would not lease the space unless respondent first obtained a cable television franchise from the City. Respondent asked the City for a franchise, but the City refused to grant it one, stating that respondent had failed to participate in an auction that was to award a single franchise in the area.

The complaint further alleged that cable operators are First Amendment speakers, that there is sufficient excess physical capacity and economic demand in the south central area of Los Angeles to accommodate more than one cable company, and that the City's auction process allowed it to discriminate among franchise applicants based on which one it deemed to be the 'best.' Based on these and other factual allegations, the complaint alleged that the City and DWP had violated the Free Speech Clause of the First Amendment, as made applicable to the State by the Fourteenth Amendment, §§ 1 and 2 of the Sherman Act, the California Constitution, and certain provisions of state law."

The Supreme Court granted certiorari on the First Amendment issue and affirmed.

B. Counsel of Record / ACLU Attorney

ACLU Side (Respondent / Appellee): Harold R. Farrow argued the cause for appellee.

Opposing Side (Petitioner / Appellant): Edward J. Perez argued the cause for appellant.

III. AMICI CURIAE

ACLU Side (Respondent / Appellee)

Brief of amici curiae filed on behalf of the ACLU, et al., by Charles S. Sims, Burt Neuborne, Antonia Cordero, and Paul Hoffman.

Additional briefs of amici curiae were filed on behalf of Best View Cablevision, Inc., the United States, et al., the American Cable Publishers Institute, Inc., the Guam Cable TV, the Mid-America Legal Foundation, the Motion Picture Association of America, Inc., the National Cable Television Association, Inc., the National Satellite Cable Association, the Nor-West Cable Communications Partnership, et al., Space, the Satellite Television Industry Association, Inc., and Tele-Communications, Inc., et al.

Brief of amici curiae filed by Nicholas W. Carlin, without permission of either party, discussing trespass and easements in cable operations.

Opposing Side (Petitioner / Appellant)

Briefs of amici curiae were filed on behalf of the State of Connecticut, the city of Brookfield, Wisconsin, the city of

New York, the city of Palo Alto, California, et al., Mountain States Telephone and Telegraph Co., et al., the National Association of Broadcasters, the National Federation of Local Cable Programmers, et al., the National Institute of Municipal Law Officers, the National League of Cities, et al., the Office of Communication of United Church of Christ, et al., and Wisconsin Bell, Inc.

IV. THE SUPREME COURT'S DECISION

"We agree with the Court of Appeals that respondent's complaint should not have been dismissed, and we therefore affirm the judgment of that court; but we do so on a narrower ground than the one taken by it. The well-pleaded facts in the complaint include allegations of sufficient excess physical capacity and economic demand for cable television operators in the area which respondent sought to serve. The City, while admitting the existence of excess physical capacity on the utility poles, the rights-of-way, and the like, justifies the limit on franchises in terms of minimizing the demand that cable systems make for the use of public property. . . .

We do think that the activities in which respondent allegedly seeks to engage plainly implicate First Amendment interests. . . . Thus, through original programming or by exercising editorial discretion over which stations or programs to include in its repertoire, respondent seeks to communicate messages on a wide variety of topics and in a wide variety of formats. . . . Cable television partakes of some of the aspects of speech and the communication of ideas as do the traditional enterprises of newspaper and book publishers, public speakers, and pamphleteers. . . .

Of course, the conclusion that respondent's factual allegations implicate protected speech does not end the inquiry. 'Even protected speech is not equally permissible in all places and at all times.' Moreover, where speech and conduct are joined in a single course of action, the First Amendment values must be balanced against competing societal interests. We do not think, however, that it is desirable to express any more detailed views on the proper resolution of the First Amendment question raised by respondent's complaint and the City's responses to it without a fuller development of the disputed issues in the case. We think that we may know more than we know now about how the constitutional issues should be resolved when we know more about the present uses of the public utility poles and rights-of-way and how respondent proposes to install and maintain its facilities on them. . . .

We affirm the judgment of the Court of Appeals reversing the dismissal of respondent's complaint by the District Court, and remand the case to the District Court so that petitioners may file an answer and the material factual disputes between the parties may be resolved."

V. JUSTICE VOTE

9 Pro ACLU Side vs. 0 Con Opposing Side

ACLU Side (Respondent / Appellee)

1. Rehnquist, W. – Wrote majority opinion
2. Burger, W. – Joined majority opinion
3. White, B. – Joined majority opinion
4. Powell, L. – Joined majority opinion
5. Brennan, W. – Joined majority opinion
6. Stevens, J. – Joined majority opinion
7. Blackmun, H. – Wrote concurring opinion
8. O'Connor, S. – Joined Blackmun's concurrence
9. Marshall, T. – Joined Blackmun's concurrence

VI. A WIN OR LOSS FOR THE ACLU?

The ACLU filed as amicus curiae urging affirmance; the Supreme Court affirmed the judgment of the Court of Appeals in a 9-0 vote, giving the ACLU an apparent win.

589. Thornburgh v. American College of Obstetricians and Gynecologists

(Decided June 11, 1986; 476 U.S. 747)

I. ISSUE

A. Issues Discussed

Privacy, abortion, injunctions

B. Legal Question Presented

Do the challenged provisions of the Pennsylvania Abortion Control Act of 1982 violate the Constitution?

C. Supreme Court's Answer

The Court of Appeals correctly held the challenged provisions unconstitutional.

II. CASE SUMMARY

A. Background

"In 1981, abortion legislation was proposed in the Pennsylvania House as an amendment to a pending Senate bill to outlaw 'tough-guy competitions.' The suggested amendment, aimed at limiting abortions, was patterned after a model statute developed by a Chicago-based, nonprofit anti-abortion organization. The bill underwent further change in the legislative process but, when passed, was vetoed by the Governor. Finally, the 1982 Act was formulated, enacted, and approved.

After the passage of the Act, but before its effective date, the present litigation was instituted in the United States District Court for the Eastern District of Pennsylvania. . . . Alleging that the Act violated the United States Constitution, the plaintiffs, pursuant to 42 U.S.C. § 1983, sought declaratory and injunctive relief. The defendants named in the complaint were the Governor of the Commonwealth, other Commonwealth officials, and the District Attorney for Montgomery County, Pa. . . .

Relying substantially on the opinions of the respective Courts of Appeals in Akron Center for Reproductive Health, Inc. v. City of Akron . . . and in Planned Parenthood Assn. of Kansas City v. Ashcroft . . . the District Court concluded that, with one exception, the plaintiffs had failed to establish a likelihood of success on the merits and thus were not entitled to preliminary injunctive relief [to prevent enforcement of the Act].

Appellees appealed from the denial of the preliminary injunction, and appellants cross-appealed with respect to the single statutory provision as to which the District Court had allowed relief. The Third Circuit then granted appellees' motion to enjoin enforcement of the entire Act pending appeal. [T]he court withheld judgment pending the anticipated decisions by [the Supreme] Court in Akron, supra, Ashcroft, supra, and Simopoulos v. Commonwealth .... After reargument in light of those decisions, the Court of Appeals ... ruled that various provisions of the Act were unconstitutional. Appellants' petition for rehearing en banc was denied, with four judges voting to grant the petition."

The Supreme Court granted certiorari to review the case and affirmed.

B. Counsel of Record / ACLU Attorney

ACLU Side (Respondent / Appellee): Kathryn Kolbert argued the cause for appellee.

Opposing Side (Petitioner / Appellant): Andrew S. Gordon, Senior Deputy Attorney General of Pennsylvania, argued the cause for appellant.

III. AMICI CURIAE

ACLU Side (Respondent / Appellee)

Brief of amici curiae filed on behalf of the ACLU, et al., by Nan D. Hunter, Janet Benshoof, and Suzanne M. Lynn.

Additional briefs of amici curiae were filed on behalf of the Attorney General of New York, the American Medical Association, et al., the Center for Constitutional Rights, et al., the National Abortion Federation, the National Abortion Rights Action League, et al., the National Family Planning and Reproductive Health Association, Inc., the National Organization for Women, et al., the Planned Parenthood Federation of America, Inc., et al., the American Psychological Association, the Women's Lawyers' Association of Los Angeles, California, et al., ,the Unitarian Universalist Association, et al., and Senator Bob Packwood, et al.,

Opposing Side (Petitioner / Appellant)

Briefs of amici curiae were filed on behalf of the United States, the National Right to Life Committee, Inc., the United States Catholic Conference, Senator Gordon J. Humphrey, et al., Watson D. Bowes, Jr., et al., Olivia Gans, et al., and John D. Lane, et al.

IV. THE SUPREME COURT'S DECISION

"In the years since this Court's decision in Roe, States and municipalities have adopted a number of measures seemingly designed to prevent a woman, with the advice of her physician, from exercising her freedom of choice. . . . But the constitutional principles that led this Court to its decisions in 1973 still provide the compelling reason for recognizing the constitutional dimensions of a woman's right to decide whether to end her pregnancy. '[I]t should go without saying that the vitality of these constitutional principles cannot be allowed to yield simply because of disagreement with them.' The States are not free, under the guise of protecting maternal health or potential life, to intimidate women into continuing pregnancies. Appellants claim that the statutory provisions before us today further legitimate compelling interests of the Commonwealth. Close analysis of those provisions, however, shows that they wholly subordinate constitutional privacy interests and concerns with maternal health in an effort to deter a woman from making a decision that, with her physician, is hers to make. . . .

Constitutional rights do not always have easily ascertainable boundaries, and controversy over the meaning of our Nation's most majestic guarantees frequently has been turbulent. As judges, however, we are sworn to uphold the law even when its content gives rise to bitter dispute. We recognized at the very beginning of our opinion in Roe that abortion raises moral and spiritual questions over which honorable persons can disagree sincerely and profoundly. But those disagreements did not then and do not now relieve us of our duty to apply the Constitution faithfully.

Our cases long have recognized that the Constitution embodies a promise that a certain private sphere of individual liberty will be kept largely beyond the reach of government. That promise extends to women as well as to men. Few decisions are more personal and intimate, more properly private, or more basic to individual dignity and autonomy, than a woman's decision—with the guidance of her physician and within the limits specified in Roe—whether to end her pregnancy. A woman's right to make that choice freely is fundamental. Any other result, in our view, would protect inadequately a central part of the sphere of liberty that our law guarantees equally to all.

The Court of Appeals correctly invalidated the specified provisions of Pennsylvania's 1982 Abortion Control Act. Its judgment is affirmed."

V. JUSTICE VOTE

5 Pro ACLU Side vs. 4 Con Opposing Side

ACLU Side (Respondent / Appellee)

1. Blackmun, H. – Wrote majority opinion
2. Marshall, T. – Joined majority opinion
3. Brennan, W. – Joined majority opinion
4. Powell, L. – Joined majority opinion
5. Stevens, J. – Wrote concurring opinion

Opposing Side (Petitioner / Appellant)

1. Burger, W. – Wrote dissenting opinion
2. White, B. – Wrote dissenting opinion
3. O'Connor, S. – Wrote dissenting opinion
4. Rehnquist, W. – Joined White's dissent and O'Connor's dissent

VI. A WIN OR LOSS FOR THE ACLU?

The ACLU, as amicus curiae, urged affirmance of the judgment of the Third Circuit Court of Appeals; the Supreme Court affirmed in a 5-4 vote, giving the ACLU an apparent win.

590. Memphis Community School District v. Stachura

(Decided June 25, 1986; 477 U.S. 299)

I. ISSUE

A. Issues Discussed

Civil rights, damages

B. Legal Question Presented

"[W]hether 42 U.S.C. § 1983 authorizes an award of compensatory damages based on the factfinder's assessment of the value or importance of a substantive constitutional right."

C. Supreme Court's Answer

Compensatory damages under § 1983 cannot be based on the factfinder's assessment of the value or importance of a substantive constitutional right.

II. CASE SUMMARY

A. Background

"Respondent Edward Stachura is a tenured teacher in the Memphis, Michigan, public schools. When the events that led to this case occurred, respondent taught seventh-grade life science, using a textbook that had been approved by the School Board. The textbook included a chapter on human reproduction. During the 1978-1979 school year, respondent spent six weeks on this chapter. As part of their instruction, students were shown pictures of respondent's wife during her pregnancy. Respondent also showed the students two films concerning human growth and sexuality. These films were provided by the County Health Department, and the Principal of respondent's school had approved their use. Both films had been shown in past school years without incident.

After the showing of the pictures and the films, a number of parents complained to school officials about respondent's teaching methods. These complaints, which appear to have been based largely on inaccurate rumors about the allegedly sexually explicit nature of the pictures and films, were discussed at an open School Board meeting held on April 23, 1979. Following the advice of the School Superintendent, respondent did not attend the meeting, during which a number of parents expressed the view that respondent should not be allowed to teach in the Memphis school system. The day after the meeting, respondent was suspended with pay. The School Board later confirmed the suspension, and notified respondent that an 'administration evaluation' of his teaching methods was underway. No such evaluation was ever made. Respondent was reinstated the next fall, after filing this lawsuit.

Respondent sued the School District, the Board of Education, various Board members and school administrators, and two parents who had participated in the April 23 School Board meeting. The complaint alleged that respondent's suspension deprived him of both liberty and property without due process of law and violated his First Amendment right to academic freedom. Respondent sought compensatory and punitive damages under 42 U.S.C. § 1983 for these constitutional violations. . . .

In addition to this instruction on the standard elements of compensatory damages, the court explained that punitive damages could be awarded, and described the standards governing punitive awards. [A]t respondent's request and over petitioners' objection, the court charged that damages also could be awarded based on the value or importance of the constitutional rights that were violated . . . .

The jury found petitioners liable, and awarded a total of $275,000 in compensatory damages and $46,000 in punitive damages. The District Court entered judgment notwithstanding the verdict as to one of the defendants, reducing the total award to $266,750 in compensatory damages and $36,000 in punitive damages. [T[he Court of Appeals for the Sixth Circuit affirmed."

The Supreme Court granted certiorari on the issue of damages, reversed, and remanded.

B. Counsel of Record / ACLU Attorney

ACLU Side (Respondent / Appellee): Jeffrey A. Heldt argued the cause for appellee.

Opposing Side (Petitioner / Appellant): Patrick J. Berardo argued the cause for appellant.

III. AMICI CURIAE

ACLU Side (Respondent / Appellee)

Brief of amici curiae filed on behalf of the ACLU by Charles S. Sims and Stuart H. Singer.

Opposing Side (Petitioner / Appellant)

Brief of amici curiae filed on behalf of the United States by Solicitor General Fried, Assistant Attorney General Willard, Deputy Solicitor General Geller, Bruce N. Kuhlik, and Barbara L. Herwig.

Brief of amici curiae filed on behalf of the National Schools Boards Association by Gwendolyn H. Gregory, August W. Steinhilber, and Thomas A. Shannon.

IV. THE SUPREME COURT'S DECISION

"We have repeatedly noted that 42 U.S.C. § 1983 creates "a species of tort liability' in favor of persons who are deprived of 'rights, privileges, or immunities secured' to them by the Constitution.' Accordingly, when § 1983 plaintiffs seek damages for violations of constitutional rights, the level of damages is ordinarily determined according to principles derived from the common law of torts. . . . Consequently, 'the basic purpose' of § 1983 damages is 'to compensate persons for injuries that are caused by the deprivation of constitutional rights.' . . .

The jurors in this case were told that, in determining how much was necessary to 'compensate [respondent] for the deprivation' of his constitutional rights, they should place a money value on the 'rights' themselves by considering such factors as the particular right's 'importance . . . in our system of government,' its role in American history, and its 'significance . . . in the context of the activities' in which respondent was engaged. These factors focus, not on compensation for provable injury, but on the jury's subjective perception of the importance of constitutional rights as an abstract matter. Carey establishes that such an approach is impermissible. The constitutional right transgressed in Carey—the right to due process of law—is central to our system of ordered liberty. . . .

Respondent further argues that the challenged instructions authorized a form of 'presumed' damages—a remedy that is both compensatory in nature and traditionally part of the range of tort law remedies. Alternatively, respondent argues that the erroneous instructions were at worst harmless error.

Neither argument has merit. Presumed damages are a substitute for ordinary compensatory damages, not a supplement for an award that fully compensates the alleged injury. . . . Nor can we find that the erroneous instructions were harmless. When damages instructions are faulty and the verdict does not reveal the means by which the jury calculated damages, '[the] error in the charge is difficult, if not impossible, to correct without retrial, in light of the jury's general verdict.' . . . For these reasons, the case must be remanded for a new trial on compensatory damages. . . .

The judgment of the Court of Appeals is reversed, and the case is remanded for further proceedings consistent with this opinion."

V. JUSTICE VOTE

0 Pro ACLU Side vs. 9 Con Opposing Side

Opposing Side (Petitioner / Appellant)

1. Powell, L. – Wrote majority opinion
2. Burger, W. – Joined majority opinion
3. Brennan, W. – Joined Marshall's concurrence
4. White, B. – Joined majority opinion
5. Rehnquist, W. – Joined majority opinion
6. Stevens, J. – Joined Marshall's concurrence
7. O'Connor, S. – Joined majority opinion
8. Marshall, T. – Wrote concurring opinion
9. Blackmun, H. – Joined Marshall's concurrence

VI. A WIN OR LOSS FOR THE ACLU?

The ACLU filed as amicus curiae urging affirmance of the judgment of the Sixth Circuit Court of Appeals; the Supreme Court reversed and remanded in a 9-0 vote, giving the ACLU an apparent loss.

591. Kimmelman v. Morrison

(Decided June 26, 1986; 477 U.S. 365)

I. ISSUE

A. Issues Discussed

Criminal procedure, Fourth Amendment, Sixth Amendment, Fourteenth Amendment, ineffective assistance of counsel

B. Legal Question Presented

"[W]hether the restrictions on federal habeas review of Fourth Amendment claims announced in Stone v. Powell should be extended to Sixth Amendment claims of ineffective assistance of counsel where the principal allegation and manifestation of inadequate representation is counsel's failure to file a timely motion to suppress evidence allegedly obtained in violation of the Fourth Amendment."

C. Supreme Court's Answer

The restrictions on Fourth Amendment claims in Stone v. Powell do not extend to Sixth Amendment claims of ineffective assistance of counsel.

II. CASE SUMMARY

A. Background

"Respondent, Neil Morrison, was convicted by the State of New Jersey of raping a 15-year-old girl. . . . The State . . . called as a witness Detective Dolores Most, one of the officers who investigated the rape complaint. Most testified that she accompanied the victim to Morrison's apartment building a few hours after the rape. Morrison was not at home, but another tenant in the building let them into respondent's one-room apartment. While there, Most stated, she seized a sheet from respondent's bed.

At this point in the testimony respondent's counsel objected to the introduction of the sheet and to any testimony concerning it on the ground that Most had seized it without a search warrant. New Jersey Court Rules, however, require that suppression motions be made within 30 days of indictment unless the time is enlarged by the trial court for good cause. Because the 30-day deadline had long since expired, the trial judge ruled that counsel's motion was late. Defense counsel explained to the court that he had not heard of the seizure until the day before, when trial began, and that his client could not have known of it because the police had not left a receipt for the sheet. The prosecutor responded that defense counsel, who had been on the case from the beginning, had never asked for any discovery. Had trial counsel done so, the prosecutor observed, police reports would have revealed the search and seizure. The prosecutor stated further that one month before trial he had sent defense counsel a copy of the laboratory report concerning the tests conducted on stains and hairs found on the sheets.

Asked repeatedly by the trial court why he had not conducted any discovery, respondent's attorney asserted that it was the State's obligation to inform him of its case against his client, even though he made no request for discovery. The judge rejected this assertion and stated: 'I hate to say it, but I have to say it, that you were remiss. I think this evidence was there and available to you for examination and inquiry.' . . . The trial judge, in rendering his verdict, . . . declared his conclusion that the State had proved its case beyond a reasonable doubt.

After trial, respondent dismissed his attorney and retained new counsel for his appeal. On appeal, respondent alleged ineffective assistance of counsel and error in the trial court's refusal to entertain the suppression motion during trial.

[After numerous appeals,] [r]espondent then sought a writ of habeas corpus in Federal District Court, again raising claims of ineffective assistance of counsel and erroneous admission of illegally seized evidence. The District Court ruled that because respondent did not allege that the State had denied him an opportunity to litigate his Fourth Amendment claim fully and fairly, direct consideration of this claim on federal habeas review was barred by Stone v. Powell. The District Court did find respondent's ineffective-assistance claim meritorious. . . . The District Court then determined that . . . respondent had been prejudiced by counsel's ineffectiveness and issued a conditional writ of habeas corpus ordering Morrison's release unless New Jersey should retry him. . . .

Relying on both the language of Stone and the different natures of Fourth and Sixth Amendment claims, the Court of Appeals concluded that Stone should not be extended to bar federal habeas consideration of Sixth Amendment claims based on counsel's alleged failure competently to litigate Fourth Amendment claims.

Because Strickland had recently been decided by [the Supreme] Court, the Court of Appeals reviewed the District Court's determination of ineffective assistance under Strickland's test. The Court of Appeals determined that respondent's trial counsel had been 'grossly ineffective,' but vacated and remanded for the District Court to consider whether, under the standards set forth in Strickland, supra, respondent had been prejudiced by his attorney's incompetence."

The Supreme Court granted certiorari to review the case and affirmed.

B. Counsel of Record / ACLU Attorney

ACLU Side (Respondent / Appellee): William E. Staehle, by appointment of the Court, argued the cause for appellee.

Opposing Side (Petitioner / Appellant): Allan J. Nodes argued the cause for appellant.

III. AMICI CURIAE

ACLU Side (Respondent / Appellee)

Brief of amici curiae filed on behalf of the ACLU, et al., by Leon Friedman, Charles S. Sims, and Burt Neuborne.

Opposing Side (Petitioner / Appellant)

No briefs of amici curiae were filed in support of appellant.

IV. THE SUPREME COURT'S DECISION

"[W]e reject petitioners' argument that Stone's restriction on federal habeas review of Fourth Amendment claims should be extended to Sixth Amendment ineffective-assistance-of-counsel claims which are founded primarily on incompetent representation with respect to a Fourth Amendment issue. Where a State obtains a criminal conviction in a trial in which the accused is deprived of the effective assistance of counsel, the 'State . . . unconstitutionally deprives the defendant of his liberty.' The defendant is thus 'in custody in violation of the Constitution,' and federal courts have habeas jurisdiction over his claim. We hold that federal courts may grant habeas relief in appropriate cases, regardless of the nature of the underlying attorney error. . . .

At the time Morrison's lawyer decided not to request any discovery, he did not—and, because he did not ask, could not—know what the State's case would be. While the relative importance of witness credibility vis-à-vis the bedsheet and related expert testimony is pertinent to the determination whether respondent was prejudiced by his attorney's incompetence, it sheds no light on the reasonableness of counsel's decision not to request any discovery. We therefore agree with the District Court and the Court of Appeals that the assistance rendered respondent by his trial counsel was constitutionally deficient. . . .

While the existing record proved adequate for our application of Strickland's competency standard, it is incomplete with respect to prejudice. No evidentiary hearing has ever been held on the merits of respondent's Fourth Amendment claim. Because the State has not conceded the illegality of the search and seizure, it is entitled to an opportunity to establish that Officer Most's search came within one of the exceptions we have recognized to the Fourth Amendment's prohibition against warrantless searches. Even if not, respondent may be unable to show that absent the evidence concerning the bedsheet there is a reasonable probability that the trial judge would have had a reasonable doubt as to his guilt. If respondent could not make this showing, a matter on which we express no view, there would of course be no need to hold an evidentiary hearing on his Fourth Amendment claim.

The judgment of the Court of Appeals is affirmed."

V. JUSTICE VOTE

9 Pro ACLU Side vs. 0 Con Opposing Side

ACLU Side (Respondent / Appellee)

1. Brennan, W. – Wrote majority opinion
2. White, B. – Joined majority opinion
3. Marshall, T. – Joined majority opinion
4. Blackmun, H. – Joined majority opinion
5. Stevens, J. – Joined majority opinion
6. O'Connor, S. – Joined majority opinion
7. Powell, L. – Wrote concurring opinion
8. Burger, W. – Joined Powell's concurrence
9. Rehnquist, W. – Joined Powell's concurrence

VI. A WIN OR LOSS FOR THE ACLU?

The ACLU filed as amicus curiae urging affirmance of the judgment of the Court of Appeals; the Supreme Court affirmed in a 9-0 vote, giving the ACLU an apparent win.

592. Murray v. Carrier

(Decided June 26, 1986; 477 U.S. 478)

I. ISSUE

A. Issues Discussed

Criminal procedure, Sixth Amendment, Fourteenth Amendment, ineffective assistance of counsel

B. Legal Question Presented

"[W]hether a federal habeas petitioner can show cause for a procedural default by establishing that competent defense counsel inadvertently failed to raise the substantive claim of error rather than deliberately withholding it for tactical reasons."

C. Supreme Court's Answer

The petitioner cannot show cause for procedural default in this circumstance and the claim must be dismissed for failure to show cause for the default.

II. CASE SUMMARY

A. Background

"Respondent Clifford Carrier was convicted of rape and abduction by a Virginia jury in 1977. Before trial, respondent's court-appointed counsel moved for discovery of the victim's statements to police describing 'her assailants, the vehicle the assailants were driving, and the location of where the alleged rape took place.' The presiding judge denied the motion by letter to counsel after examining the statements in camera and determining that they contained no exculpatory evidence. Respondent's counsel made a second motion to discover the victim's statements immediately prior to trial, which the trial judge denied for the same reason after conducting his own in camera examination.

After respondent was convicted, his counsel filed a notice of appeal to the Virginia Supreme Court assigning seven errors, of which the fifth was:

'Did the trial judge err by not permitting defendant's counsel to examine the written statements of the victim prior to trial, and during the course of the trial?'

Without consulting respondent, counsel subsequently submitted the required petition for appeal but failed to include this claim, notwithstanding that Virginia Supreme Court Rule 5:21 provides that '[o]nly errors assigned in the petition for appeal will be noticed by this Court and no error not so assigned will be admitted as a ground for reversal of a decision below.' The Virginia Supreme Court refused the appeal and [the Supreme] Court denied certiorari.

A year later respondent, by this time proceeding pro se, filed a state habeas corpus petition claiming that he had been denied due process of law by the prosecution's withholding of the victim's statements. . . . The state habeas court dismissed the petition . . . and the Virginia Supreme Court denied certiorari.

Respondent next filed a pro se habeas petition in the District Court for the Eastern District of Virginia, renewing his due process discovery claim as grounds for relief. . . . The District Court [held] the discovery claim barred by the procedural default and indicat[ed] that respondent should establish cause for that default in the state courts. . . . A divided panel of the Court of Appeals reversed and remanded. . . . The State sought rehearing, and the en banc Court of Appeals adopted the panel majority's decision, with four judges dissenting."

The Supreme Court granted certiorari to review the case and reversed.

B. Counsel of Record / ACLU Attorney

ACLU Side (Respondent / Appellee): Sherman L. Cohn, by appointment of the Court, argued the cause for appellee.

Opposing Side (Petitioner / Appellant): Jerry P. Slonaker argued the cause for appellant.

Deputy Solicitor General Frey argued the cause for the United States, as amicus curiae, by special leave of Court.

III. AMICI CURIAE

ACLU Side (Respondent / Appellee)

Brief of amici curiae filed on behalf of the ACLU, et al., by Larry W. Yackle, Charles S. Sims, and Burt Neuborne.

Opposing Side (Petitioner / Appellant)

Brief of amici curiae filed on behalf of the United States by Deputy Solicitor General Frey, Acting Solicitor General Fried, Assistant Attorney General Trott, Edwin S. Kneedler, and Kathleen A. Felton.

Additional briefs of amici curiae were filed on behalf of the State of Idaho, et al., the State of Florida, and the Legal Foundation of America, et al.

IV. THE SUPREME COURT'S DECISION:

"[T]he question of cause for a procedural default does not turn on whether counsel erred or on the kind of error counsel may have made. So long as a defendant is represented by counsel whose performance is not constitutionally ineffective under the standard established in Strickland v. Washington, supra, we discern no inequity in requiring him to bear the risk of attorney error that results in a procedural default. Instead, we think that the existence of cause for a procedural default must ordinarily turn on whether the prisoner can show that some objective factor external to the defense impeded counsel's efforts to comply with the State's procedural rule. Without attempting an exhaustive catalog of such objective impediments to compliance with a procedural rule, we note that a showing that the factual or legal basis for a claim was not reasonably available to counsel, or that 'some interference by officials' made compliance impracticable, would constitute cause under this standard.

Similarly, if the procedural default is the result of ineffective assistance of counsel, the Sixth Amendment itself requires that responsibility for the default be imputed to the State, which may not 'conduc[t] trials at which persons who face incarceration must defend themselves without adequate legal assistance.' Ineffective assistance of counsel, then, is cause for a procedural default. However, we think that the exhaustion doctrine, which is 'principally designed to protect the state courts' role in the enforcement of federal law and prevent disruption of state judicial proceedings,' generally requires that a claim of ineffective assistance be presented to the state courts as an independent claim before it may be used to establish cause for a procedural default. The question whether there is cause for a procedural default does not pose any occasion for applying the exhaustion doctrine when the federal habeas court can adjudicate the question of cause—a question of federal law—without deciding an independent and unexhausted constitutional claim on the merits. But if a petitioner could raise his ineffective assistance claim for the first time on federal habeas in order to show cause for a procedural default, the federal habeas court would find itself in the anomalous position of adjudicating an unexhausted constitutional claim for which state court review might still be available. The principle of comity that underlies the exhaustion doctrine would be ill served by a rule that allowed a federal district court 'to upset a state court conviction without an opportunity to the state courts to correct a constitutional violation.'

[W]e hold that counsel's failure to raise a particular claim on appeal is to be scrutinized under the cause and prejudice standard when that failure is treated as a procedural default by the state courts. Attorney error short of ineffective assistance of counsel does not constitute cause for a procedural default even when that default occurs on appeal rather than at trial. To the contrary, cause for a procedural default on appeal ordinarily requires a showing of some external impediment preventing counsel from constructing or raising the claim. . . .

Respondent has never alleged any external impediment that might have prevented counsel from raising his discovery claim in his petition for review, and has disavowed any claim that counsel's performance on appeal was so deficient as to make out an ineffective assistance claim. Respondent's petition for federal habeas review of his procedurally defaulted discovery claim must therefore be dismissed for failure to establish cause for the default, unless it is determined on remand that the victim's statements contain material that would establish respondent's actual innocence.

The judgment of the Court of Appeals is reversed, and the case is remanded for further proceedings consistent with this opinion."

V. JUSTICE VOTE

2 Pro ACLU Side vs. 7 Con Opposing Side

ACLU Side (Respondent / Appellee)

1. Brennan, W. – Wrote dissenting opinion
2. Marshall, T. – Joined Brennan's dissent

Opposing Side (Petitioner / Appellant)

1. O'Connor, S. – Wrote majority opinion
2. Burger, W. – Joined majority opinion
3. Rehnquist, W. – Joined majority opinion
4. White, B. – Joined majority opinion
5. Powell, L. – Joined majority opinion
6. Stevens, J. – Wrote concurring opinion
7. Blackmun, H. – Joined Stevens' concurrence

VI. A WIN OR LOSS FOR THE ACLU?

The ACLU filed as amicus curiae urging affirmance of the judgment of the Court of Appeals; the Supreme Court reversed in a 7-2 vote, giving the ACLU and apparent loss.

593. Ohio Civil Rights Commission v. Dayton Christian Schools, Inc.

(Decided June 27, 1986; 477 U.S. 619)

I. ISSUE

A. Issues Discussed

First Amendment, freedom of religion, discrimination, abstention

B. Legal Question Presented

Whether the district court should have abstained under Younger v. Harris.

C. Supreme Court's Answer

The district court should have abstained under Younger v. Harris.

II. CASE SUMMARY

A. Background

"Appellee Dayton Christian Schools, Inc. (Dayton), and various individuals brought an action in the United States District Court for the Southern District of Ohio under 42 U.S.C. § 1983, seeking to enjoin a pending state administrative proceeding brought against Dayton by appellant Ohio Civil Rights Commission (Commission). Dayton asserted that the Free Exercise and Establishment Clauses of the First Amendment prohibited the Commission from exercising jurisdiction over it or from punishing it for engaging in employment discrimination. The District Court refused to issue the injunction on grounds that any conflict between the First Amendment and the administrative proceedings was not yet ripe, and that in any case the proposed action of the Commission violated neither the Free Exercise Clause nor the Establishment Clause of the First Amendment, as made applicable to the States by the Fourteenth Amendment. The Court of Appeals for the Sixth Circuit reversed, holding that the exercise of jurisdiction and the enforcement of the statute would impermissibly burden appellees' rights under the Free Exercise Clause and would result in excessive entanglement under the Establishment Clause. . . .

Dayton is a private nonprofit corporation that provides education at both the elementary and secondary school levels. . . . The charter . . . includes a section entitled 'Statement of Faith,' which serves to restrict membership on the board and the educational staff to persons who subscribe to a particular set of religious beliefs. The Statement of Faith requires each board or staff member to be a born-again Christian and to reaffirm his or her belief annually . . . .

The board has elaborated these requirements to include a belief in the internal resolution of disputes through the 'Biblical chain of command.' The core of this doctrine, rooted in passages from the New Testament, is that one Christian should not take another Christian into courts of the State. Teachers are expected to present any grievance they may have to their immediate supervisor, and to acquiesce in the final authority of the board, rather than to pursue a remedy in civil court. The board has sought to ensure compliance with this internal dispute resolution doctrine by making it a contractual condition of employment.

Linda Hoskinson was employed as a teacher at Dayton during the 1978-1979 school year. She subscribed to the Statement of Faith and expressly agreed to resolve disputes internally through the Biblical chain of command. In January 1979, she informed her principal, James Rakestraw, that she was pregnant. After consulting with his superiors, Rakestraw informed Hoskinson that her employment contract would not be renewed at the end of the school year because of Dayton's religious doctrine that mothers should stay home with their preschool age children. Instead of appealing this decision internally, Hoskinson contacted an attorney who sent a letter to Dayton's superintendent, Claude Schindler, threatening litigation based on state and federal sex discrimination laws if Dayton did not agree to rehire Hoskinson for the coming school year."

The Supreme Court granted certiorari to review the case and reversed.

B. Counsel of Record / ACLU Attorney

ACLU Side (Petitioner / Appellant): Kathleen McManus argued the cause for appellant.

Opposing Side (Respondent / Appellee): William Bentley Ball argued the cause for appellee.

III. AMICI CURIAE

ACLU Side (Petitioner / Appellant)

Brief of amici curiae filed on behalf of the ACLU, et al., by Joan E. Bertin, George Kannar, Charles S. Sims, Isabelle Katz Pinzler, and Burt Neuborne.

Opposing Side (Respondent / Appellee)

Briefs of amici curiae were filed on behalf of the American Jewish Committee, et al., Americans United for Separation of Church and State, the Associated Christian Conciliation Services, the Catholic Conference of Ohio, Concerned Women of America, the Council on Religious Freedom by Lee Boothby and Rolland Truman; for the General Conference of Seventh-day Adventists, the Gulf & Great Plains Legal Foundation, the National Jewish Commission on Law and Public Affairs ("COLPA"), the Rutherford Institute et al., the United States Catholic Conference, the American Jewish Congress, and the Catholic League for Religious and Civil Rights, et al.

IV. THE SUPREME COURT'S DECISION

"We hold that we have appellate jurisdiction under 28 U.S.C. § 1254(2) to review the decision of the Court of Appeals. That statute authorizes an appeal to this Court 'by a party relying on a State statute held by a court of appeals to be invalid as repugnant to the Constitution.' This authority embraces cases holding a state statute unconstitutional as applied to the facts of the case. Here there is no doubt that the decision by the Court of Appeals satisfies this test. The court expressly held that Ohio Rev. Code Ann. § 4112.02 et seq. is repugnant to the Free Exercise and Establishment Clauses as applied to authorize the administrative body to investigate the charges against Dayton and to decide whether to impose sanctions.

Having taken jurisdiction over the decision below, we now turn to whether the District Court should have exercised jurisdiction over the case itself. We conclude that the District Court should have abstained from adjudicating this case under Younger v. Harris. . . .

We have no doubt that the elimination of prohibited sex discrimination is a sufficiently important state interest to bring the present case within the ambit of the cited authorities. We also have no reason to doubt that Dayton will receive an adequate opportunity to raise its constitutional claims. Dayton contends that the mere exercise of jurisdiction over it by the state administrative body violates its First Amendment rights. But we have repeatedly rejected the argument that a constitutional attack on state procedures themselves 'automatically vitiates the adequacy of those procedures for purposes of the Younger-Huffman line of cases.' Even religious schools cannot claim to be wholly free from some state regulation. We therefore think that however Dayton's constitutional claim should be decided on the merits, the Commission violates no constitutional rights by merely investigating the circumstances of Hoskinson's discharge in this case, if only to ascertain whether the ascribed religious-based reason was in fact the reason for the discharge. . . .

Section 4112.06 of Ohio Rev. Code Ann. provides that any 'respondent claiming to be aggrieved by a final order of the commission . . . may obtain judicial review thereof.' Dayton cites us to no Ohio authority indicating that this provision does not authorize judicial review of claims that agency action violates the United States Constitution.

The judgment of the Court of Appeals is therefore reversed, and the case remanded for further proceedings consistent with this opinion."

V. JUSTICE VOTE

9 Pro ACLU Side vs. 0 Con Opposing Side

ACLU Side (Petitioner / Appellant)

1. Rehnquist W. – Wrote majority opinion
2. Burger, W. – Joined majority opinion
3. White, B. – Joined majority opinion
4. Powell, L. – Joined majority opinion
5. O'Connor, S. – Joined majority opinion
6. Stevens, J. – Wrote concurring opinion
7. Brennan, W. – Joined Stevens' concurrence
8. Marshall, T. – Joined Stevens' concurrence
9. Blackmun, H. – Joined Stevens' concurrence

VI. A WIN OR LOSS FOR THE ACLU?

The ACLU, as amicus curiae, urged reversal of the judgment of the Court of Appeals; the Supreme Court reversed in a 9-0 vote, giving the ACLU an apparent win.

594. New Mexico v. Earnest

(Decided June 27, 1986; 477 U.S. 648)

I. ISSUE

A. Issues Discussed

Criminal procedure, Sixth Amendment, mistrial, evidence

B. Legal Question Presented

Whether the retrial after a mistrial was appropriate is defendant's case and whether any procedures in the retrial are grounds for a new trial.

C. Supreme Court's Answer

The Court vacated the judgment below and remanded the case for further proceedings, in a per curiam decision.

II. CASE SUMMARY

A. Background

"Ralph Rodney Earnest (defendant), Phillip Boeglin (Boeglin), and Perry Connor (Connor) were charged with murder, conspiracy to commit murder, kidnapping, conspiracy to distribute a controlled substance (methamphetamines), and possession of a controlled substance (methamphetamines). Defendant, Boeglin, and Connor were each tried separately. During the course of defendant's trial before a jury, a mistrial was declared. Defendant was subsequently retried, convicted on all counts and sentenced to life imprisonment for the murder, eighteen years for conspiracy to commit murder (with nine years suspended), nine years for kidnapping, eighteen months for conspiracy to distribute a controlled substance and three years for possession of a controlled substance. All of these sentences were to run consecutively to each other and consecutively to the life sentence. From this judgment and sentence, defendant appeal[ed]."[1] The Supreme Court of New Mexico reversed and remanded.

The Supreme Court granted certiorari to review the case and vacated the judgment below.

B. Counsel of Record / ACLU Attorney

ACLU Side (Respondent / Appellee): J. Thomas Sullivan argued the cause for appellee.

Opposing Side (Petitioner / Appellant): Paul Bardacke, Attorney General of New Mexico, argued the cause for appellant.

III. AMICI CURIAE

ACLU Side (Respondent / Appellee)

Brief of amici curiae filed on behalf of the ACLU, et al., by Burt Neuborne and Charles S. Sims.

Brief of amici curiae filed on behalf of the New Mexico Public Defender Department by David Stafford and Susan Gibbs.

Opposing Side (Petitioner / Appellant)

Brief of amici curiae filed on behalf of the State of Indiana, et al., by Linley E. Pearson, Attorney General of Indiana, and William E. Daily and Lisa M. Paunicka, Deputy Attorneys General; Robert K. Corbin, Attorney General of Arizona; John J. Kelly, Chief State's Attorney of Connecticut; Charles M. Oberly, Attorney General of Delaware; Richard Opper, Attorney General of Guam; Corinne K. A. Watanabe, Attorney General of Hawaii; Jim Jones, Attorney General of Idaho; Neil F. Hartigan, Attorney General of Illinois; William J. Guste, Jr., Attorney General of Louisiana; Mike Greeley, Attorney General of Montana; Irwin I. Kimmelman, Attorney General of New Jersey; Anthony Celebrezze, Attorney General of Ohio; Michael Turpen, Attorney General of Oklahoma; Travis Medlock, Attorney General of South Carolina; W.J. Michael Cody, Attorney General of Tennessee; Jim Mattox, Attorney General of Texas; David L. Wilkinson, Attorney General of Utah; Jeffrey Amestoy, Attorney General of Vermont; William G. Broaddus, Attorney General of Virginia; Bronson C. La Follette, Attorney General of Wisconsin; and Archie G. McClintock, Attorney General of Wyoming.

IV. THE SUPREME COURT'S DECISION

"We vacate the judgment of the Supreme Court of New Mexico and remand for further proceedings not inconsistent with the opinion in Lee v. Illinois."

V. JUSTICE VOTE

0 Pro ACLU Side vs. 9 Con Opposing Side

Opposing Side (Petitioner / Appellant)

1. Burger, W. – Per curiam decision
2. White, B. – Per curiam decision
3. Stevens, J. – Per curiam decision
4. Blackmun, H. – Per curiam decision
5. Brennan, W. – Per curiam decision
6. Marshall, T. – Per curiam decision
7. Rehnquist, W. – Wrote concurring opinion
8. O'Connor, S. – Joined Rehnquist's concurrence
9. Powell, L. – Joined Rehnquist's concurrence

VI. A WIN OR LOSS FOR THE ACLU?

The ACLU filed as amicus curiae urging affirmance; the Supreme Court vacated and remanded the ruling of the New Mexico Supreme Court in a 9-0 vote, giving the ACLU an apparent loss.

595. Press-Enterprise Co. v. Superior Court

(Decided June 30, 1986; 478 U.S. 1)

I. ISSUE

A. Issues Discussed

First Amendment, right to a fair trial, closed court proceedings

B. Legal Question Presented

"[W]hether petitioner has a First Amendment right of access to the transcript of a preliminary hearing growing out of a criminal prosecution."

C. Supreme Court's Answer

Petitioner's First Amendment right to access the transcript of a preliminary hearing is governed by the "substantial probability" test.

II. CASE SUMMARY

A. Background

"On December 23, 1981, the State of California filed a complaint in the Riverside County Municipal Court, charging Robert Diaz with 12 counts of murder and seeking the death penalty. The complaint alleged that Diaz, a nurse, murdered 12 patients by

1 State v. Earnest, 703 P.2d 872 (N.M. 1985).

administering massive doses of the heart drug lidocaine. The preliminary hearing on the complaint commenced on July 6, 1982. Diaz moved to exclude the public from the proceedings under Cal. Penal Code Ann. § 868, which requires such proceedings to be open unless 'exclusion of the public is necessary in order to protect the defendant's right to a fair and impartial trial.' The Magistrate granted the unopposed motion, finding that closure was necessary because the case had attracted national publicity and 'only one side may get reported in the media.'

The preliminary hearing continued for 41 days. . . . At the conclusion of the hearing, petitioner Press-Enterprise Company asked that the transcript of the proceedings be released. The Magistrate refused and sealed the record.

On January 21, 1983, the State moved in Superior Court to have the transcript of the preliminary hearing released to the public; petitioner later joined in support of the motion. Diaz opposed the motion, contending that release of the transcript would result in prejudicial pretrial publicity. The Superior Court found that the information in the transcript was 'as factual as it could be,' and that the facts were neither 'inflammatory' nor 'exciting,' but that there was, nonetheless, 'a reasonable likelihood that release of all or any part of the transcripts might prejudice defendant's right to a fair and impartial trial.'

Petitioner then filed a peremptory writ of mandate with the Court of Appeal. That court originally denied the writ but, after being so ordered by the California Supreme Court, set the matter for a hearing. Meanwhile, Diaz waived his right to a jury trial and the Superior Court released the transcript. After holding that the controversy was not moot, the Court of Appeal denied the writ of mandate.

The California Supreme Court thereafter denied petitioner's peremptory writ of mandate, holding that there is no general First Amendment right of access to preliminary hearings."

The Supreme Court granted certiorari to review the case and reversed.

B. Counsel of Record / ACLU Attorney

ACLU Side (Petitioner / Appellant): James D. Ward argued the cause for appellant.

Opposing Side (Respondent / Appellee): Joyce Ellen Manulis Reikes argued the cause for appellee.

III. AMICI CURIAE

ACLU Side (Petitioner / Appellant)

Brief of amici curiae filed on behalf of the ACLU, et al., by Robert S. Warren, Rex S. Heinke, and Charles S. Sims.

Brief of amici curiae filed on behalf of the District Attorney, County of Riverside, by Grover C. Trask II, pro se.

Brief of amici curiae filed on behalf of the State of California by John K. Van de Kamp, Attorney General, Andrea Sheridan Ordin and Steve White, Chief Assistant Attorneys General, and Marian M. Johnston, Deputy Attorney General.

Brief of amici curiae filed on behalf of the American Newspaper Publishers Association, et al., by Bruce W. Sanford, Lee Levine, W. Terry Maguire, Richard M. Schmidt, Jr., George A. Vradenburg III, Lawrence Gunnels, Mark L. Tuft, Robert D. Sack, Alice Neff Lucan, E. Susan Garsh, Harvey L. Lipton, Norton L. Armour, Robert J. Brinkmann, Lois J. Schiffer, Samuel E. Klein, Nancy H. Hendry, Jane E. Kirtley, Alexander Wellford, P. Cameron De Vore, and Carol D. Melamed.

Brief of amici curiae filed on behalf of Copley Press, Inc., et al., by Harold W. Fuson, Jr., Judith R. Epstein, Edward J. McIntyre, William A. Niese, Donald L. Zachary, Mark L. Tuft, Lawrence Gunnels, Robert N. Landes, Kenneth M. Vittor, and Jonathan Kotler.

Opposing Side (Respondent / Appellee)

No briefs of amici curiae were filed in support of appellee.

IV. THE SUPREME COURT'S DECISION

"Plainly the defendant has a right to a fair trial but, as we have repeatedly recognized, one of the important means of assuring a fair trial is that the process be open to neutral observers.

The right to an open public trial is a shared right of the accused and the public, the common concern being the assurance of fairness. . . . If the interest asserted is the right of the accused to a fair trial, the preliminary hearing shall be closed only if specific findings are made demonstrating that, first, there is a substantial probability that the defendant's right to a fair trial will be prejudiced by publicity that closure would prevent and, second, reasonable alternatives to closure cannot adequately protect the defendant's fair trial rights.

The California Supreme Court, interpreting its access statute, concluded that 'the magistrate shall close the preliminary hearing upon finding a reasonable likelihood of substantial prejudice.' As the court itself acknowledged, the 'reasonable likelihood' test places a lesser burden on the defendant than the 'substantial probability' test which we hold is called for by the First Amendment. Moreover, the court failed to consider whether alternatives short of complete closure would have protected the interests of the accused. . . .

The standard applied by the California Supreme Court failed to consider the First Amendment right of access to criminal proceedings. Accordingly, the judgment of the California Supreme Court is reversed."

V. JUSTICE VOTE

7 Pro ACLU Side vs. 2 Con Opposing Side

ACLU Side (Petitioner / Appellant)

1. Burger, W. – Wrote majority opinion
2. Brennan, W. – Joined majority opinion
3. White, B. – Joined majority opinion
4. Marshall, T. – Joined majority opinion
5. Blackmun, H. – Joined majority opinion
6. Powell, L. – Joined majority opinion
7. O'Connor, S. – Joined majority opinion

Opposing Side (Respondent / Appellee)

1. Stevens, J. – Wrote dissenting opinion
2. Rehnquist, W. – Joined Stevens' dissent, in part

VI. A WIN OR LOSS FOR THE ACLU?

The ACLU, as amicus curiae, urged reversal of the judgment of the California Supreme Court; the U.S. Supreme Court reversed in a 7-2 vote, giving the ACLU an apparent win.

596. Davis v. Bandemer

(Decided June 30, 1986; 478 U.S. 109)

I. ISSUE

A. Issues Discussed

Justiciable controversy, vote dilution, equal protection

B. Legal Question Presented

Whether the case was justiciable and whether there was an equal protection violation in the reapportionment.

C. Supreme Court's Answer

The case was justiciable but the evidence did not show an equal protection violation.

II. CASE SUMMARY

A. Background

"The Indiana Legislature, also known as the 'General Assembly,' consists of a House of Representatives and a Senate. . . . Reapportionment is required every 10 years and is based on the federal decennial census. There is no prohibition against more frequent reapportionments.

In early 1981, the General Assembly initiated the process of reapportioning the State's legislative districts pursuant to the 1980 census. At this time, there were Republican majorities in both the House and the Senate, and the Governor was Republican. Bills were introduced in both Houses, and a reapportionment plan was duly passed and approved by the Governor. . . .

In early 1982, this suit was filed by several Indiana Democrats (here the appellees) against various state officials (here the appellants), alleging that the 1981 reapportionment plans constituted a political gerrymander intended to disadvantage Democrats. Specifically, they contended that the particular district lines that were drawn and the mix of single-member and multimember districts were intended to and did violate their right, as Democrats, to equal protection under the Fourteenth Amendment. . . .

On December 13, 1984, a divided District Court issued a decision declaring the reapportionment to be unconstitutional, enjoining the appellants from holding elections pursuant to the 1981 redistricting, ordering the General Assembly to prepare a new plan, and retaining jurisdiction over the case. . . .

The defendants appealed, seeking review of the District Court's rulings that the case was justiciable and that, if justiciable, an equal protection violation had occurred."

The Supreme Court granted certiorari to review the case and reversed.

B. Counsel of Record / ACLU Attorney

ACLU Side (Respondent / Appellee): Theodore R. Boehm argued the cause for appellee.

Opposing Side (Petitioner / Appellant): William M. Evans argued the cause for appellant.

III. AMICI CURIAE

ACLU Side (Respondent / Appellee)

Brief of amici curiae filed on behalf of the ACLU, et al., by Arthur N. Eisenberg, Burt Neuborne, Charles S. Sims, and Lawrence M. Reuben.

Brief of amici curiae filed on behalf of Common Cause by Philip Heymann.

Brief of amici curiae filed on behalf of the Republican National Committee by Roger Allan Moore, E. Mark Braden, Michael A. Hess, James R. Parrinello, and Marguerite Mary Leoni.

Opposing Side (Petitioner / Appellant)

Brief of amici curiae filed on behalf of the Assembly of the State of California by Joseph Remcho and Charles C. Marson.

Brief of amici curiae filed on behalf of the Mexican American Legal Defense and Educational Fund by Jose Garza, Antonia Hernandez, and John E. Huerta.

Brief of amici curiae filed on behalf of the Senate of the State of California by Allan Browne.

Brief of amici curiae filed on behalf of the California Democratic Congressional Delegation Richard C. Borow, Jonathan H. Steinberg, and Daniel Hays Lowenstein.

IV. THE SUPREME COURT'S DECISION

"We decline to overturn the District Court's finding of discriminatory intent as clearly erroneous. . . . As long as redistricting is done by a legislature, it should not be very difficult to prove that the likely political consequences of the reapportionment were intended. . . .

We do not accept, however, the District Court's legal and factual basis for concluding that the 1981 Act visited a sufficiently adverse effect on the appellees' constitutionally protected rights to make out a violation of the Equal Protection Clause. [U]nconstitutional discrimination occurs only when the electoral system is arranged in a manner that will consistently degrade a voter's or a group of voters' influence on the political process as a whole. . . . Relying on a single election to prove unconstitutional discrimination is unsatisfactory. [T]he District Court erred in concluding that the 1981 Act violated the Equal Protection Clause. . . .

In sum, we hold that political gerrymandering cases are properly justiciable under the Equal Protection Clause. We also conclude, however, that a threshold showing of discriminatory vote dilution is required for a prima facie case of an equal protection violation. In this case, the findings made by the District Court of an adverse effect on the appellees do not surmount the threshold requirement. Consequently, the judgment of the District Court is reversed."

V. JUSTICE VOTE

2 Pro ACLU Side vs. 7 Con Opposing Side

ACLU Side (Respondent / Appellee)

1. Powell, L. – Wrote opinion concurring in part and dissenting in part
2. Stevens, J. – Joined Powell's opinion

Opposing Side (Petitioner / Appellant)

1. White, B. – Wrote majority opinion
2. Brennan, W. – Joined majority opinion
3. Marshall, T. – Joined majority opinion
4. Blackmun, H. – Joined majority opinion
5. Burger, W. – Wrote concurring opinion, joined O'Connor's concurrence
6. O'Connor, S. – Wrote concurring opinion
7. Rehnquist, W. – Wrote concurring opinion

VI. A WIN OR LOSS FOR THE ACLU?

The ACLU, as amicus curiae, urged affirmance of the judgment of the District Court; the Supreme Court reversed in a 7-2 vote, giving the ACLU an apparent loss.

597. Posadas de Puerto Rico Associates v. Tourism Company of Puerto Rico

(Decided July 1, 1986; 478 U.S. 328)

I. ISSUE

A. Issues Discussed

First Amendment, freedom of speech, commercial speech

B. Legal Question Presented

Whether "a Puerto Rico statute and regulations restricting advertising of casino gambling aimed at the residents of Puerto Rico" is constitutional.

C. Supreme Court's Answer

The statute and regulations are not unconstitutional.

II. CASE SUMMARY

A. Background

"Appellant sought a declaratory judgment that the statute and regulations, both facially and as applied by the Tourism Company, impermissibly suppressed commercial speech in violation of the First Amendment and the equal protection and due process guarantees of the United States Constitution. The Superior Court held that the advertising restrictions had been unconstitutionally applied to appellant's past conduct. But the court adopted a narrowing construction of the statute and regulations and held that, based on such a construction, both were facially constitutional. The Supreme Court of Puerto Rico dismissed an appeal on the ground that it 'd[id] not present a substantial constitutional question.' . . .

In 1948, the Puerto Rico Legislature legalized certain forms of casino gambling. . . . The Act also provided that '[n]o gambling room shall be permitted to advertise or otherwise offer their facilities to the public of Puerto Rico.' . . . In 1975, appellant Posadas de Puerto Rico Associates, a partnership organized under the laws of Texas, obtained a franchise to operate a gambling casino and began doing business under the name Condado Holiday Inn Hotel and Sands Casino. In 1978, appellant was twice fined by the Tourism Company for violating the advertising restrictions in the Act and implementing regulations. Appellant protested the fines in a series of letters to the Tourism Company. . . . Appellant then filed a declaratory judgment action against the Tourism Company in the Superior Court of Puerto Rico, San Juan Section, seeking a declaration that the Act and implementing regulations, both facially and as applied by the Tourism Company, violated appellant's commercial speech rights under the United States Constitution."

The Supreme Court granted certiorari to review the case and affirmed.

B. Counsel of Record / ACLU Attorney

ACLU Side (Petitioner / Appellant): Maria Milagros Soto argued the cause for appellant.

Opposing Side (Respondent / Appellee): Lino J. Saldana argued the cause for appellee.

III. AMICI CURIAE

ACLU Side (Petitioner / Appellant)

Brief of amici curiae filed on behalf of the ACLU by M. Margaret McKeown, Burt Neuborne, and Charles S. Sims.

Brief of amici curiae filed on behalf of the American Association of Advertising Agencies, Inc., by David S. Versfelt and C. Evan Stewart.

Brief of amici curiae filed on behalf of the American Broadcasting Companies, Inc., et al., by Carl R. Ramey, Timothy B. Dyk, Sally Katzen, Valerie G. Schulte, and L. Stanley Paige.

Brief of amici curiae filed on behalf of the American Federation of Labor and Congress of Industrial Organizations by Robert M. Weinberg, Peter O. Shinevar, and Laurence Gold.

Brief of amici curiae filed on behalf of the American Newspaper Publishers Association by P. Cameron DeVore, Marshall J. Nelson, and W. Terry Maguire.

Brief of amici curiae filed on behalf of the National Broadcasting Co., Inc., by Floyd Abrams, Dean Ringel, Corydon B. Dunham, and Howard Monderer.

Brief of amici curiae filed on behalf of the Atlantic City Casino Association by Herbert J. Miller, Jr., and David O. Stewart.

Brief of amici curiae filed on behalf of the Association of National Advertisers. Inc., by Gilbert H. Weil.

Opposing Side (Respondent / Appellee)

No briefs of amici curiae were filed in support of appellee.

IV. THE SUPREME COURT'S DECISION

"We hold that we have jurisdiction to review the decision of the Supreme Court of Puerto Rico. . . .

Because this case involves the restriction of pure commercial speech which does 'no more than propose a commercial transaction,' our First Amendment analysis is guided by the general principles identified in Central Hudson Gas & Electric Corp. v. Public Service Comm'n of New York. Under Central Hudson, commercial speech receives a limited form of First Amendment protection so long as it concerns a lawful activity and is not misleading or fraudulent. Once it is determined that the First Amendment applies to the particular kind of commercial speech at issue, then the speech may be restricted only if the government's interest in doing so is substantial, the restrictions directly advance the government's asserted interest, and the restrictions are no more extensive than necessary to serve that interest.

[W]e conclude that the statute and regulations at issue in this case, as construed by the Superior Court, pass muster under each prong of the Central Hudson test. We therefore hold that the Supreme Court of Puerto Rico properly rejected appellant's First Amendment claim. . . .

Appellant also makes the related argument that, having chosen to legalize casino gambling for residents of Puerto Rico, the legislature is prohibited by the First Amendment from using restrictions on advertising to accomplish its goal of reducing demand for such gambling. We disagree. In our view, appellant has the argument backwards. [I]t is precisely because the government could have enacted a wholesale prohibition of the underlying conduct that it is permissible for the government to take the less intrusive step of allowing the conduct, but reducing the demand through restrictions on advertising. . . .

For the foregoing reasons, the decision of the Supreme Court of Puerto Rico that, as construed by the Superior Court, § 8 of the Games of Chance Act of 1948 and the implementing regulations do not facially violate the First Amendment or the due process or equal protection guarantees of the Constitution, is affirmed."

V. JUSTICE VOTE

4 Pro ACLU Side vs. 5 Con Opposing Side

ACLU Side (Petitioner / Appellant)

1. Brennan, W. – Wrote dissenting opinion
2. Stevens, J. – Wrote dissenting opinion
3. Marshall, T. – Joined Brennan's dissent and Stevens' dissent
4. Blackmun, H. – Joined Brennan's dissent and Stevens' dissent

Opposing Side (Respondent / Appellee)

1. Rehnquist, W. – Wrote majority opinion
2. Burger, W. – Joined majority opinion
3. Powell, L. – Joined majority opinion
4. O'Connor, S. – Joined majority opinion
5. White, B. – Joined majority opinion

VI. A WIN OR LOSS FOR THE ACLU?

The ACLU, as amicus curiae, urged reversal of the judgment of Supreme Court of Puerto Rico; the U.S. Supreme Court affirmed in a 5-4 vote, giving the ACLU an apparent loss.

598. Rose v. Clark

(Decided July 2, 1986; 478 U.S. 570)

I. ISSUE

A. Issues Discussed

Criminal procedure, jury instructions

B. Legal Question Presented

"[W]hether the harmless-error standard of Chapman v. California applies to jury instructions that violate the principles of Sandstrom v. Montana and Francis v. Franklin."

C. Supreme Court's Answer

The harmless-error standard of Chapman applies to the jury instructions in this case and case must be remanded to review the error under this standard.

II. CASE SUMMARY

A. Background

Respondent was charged with two murders and, at his trial, "argued that he was either insane or incapable of forming the requisite criminal intent. To support this argument, respondent introduced evidence that he was suffering from amnesia and could not remember the events of the night of the murders. In addition, some testimony suggested that respondent had been drinking heavily the entire day before the murders. Finally, two defense psychiatrists testified that respondent was legally insane at the time the murders were committed because his depression concerning his recent breakup with Joy Faulk [one of the deceased] made it impossible for him to conform his conduct to the law.

At the close of trial, the court instructed the jury on the elements of both first- and second-degree murder. [The court included an instruction that] 'All homicides are presumed to be malicious in the absence of evidence which would rebut the implied presumption.' . . . The jury found respondent guilty of first-degree murder for killing Faulk and of second-degree murder for killing Browning.

The Tennessee Court of Criminal Appeals affirmed the convictions, rejecting respondent's argument that the jury instructions had impermissibly shifted the burden of proof as to malice. Respondent then sought habeas corpus relief in the Middle District of Tennessee. The District Court held that the malice instruction had violated respondent's right to have his guilt proved beyond a reasonable doubt, as that right was defined in Sandstrom v. Montana. The court went on to find that the error could not be deemed harmless because respondent had 'relied upon a mens rea defense' in contesting his guilt.

The Court of Appeals for the Sixth Circuit affirmed. The court agreed that the malice instruction was unconstitutional under Sandstrom. Turning to the question whether the error was harmless, the court reasoned that because respondent contested malice at his trial, an erroneous burden-shifting instruction could not be harmless under governing precedent."

The Supreme Court granted certiorari to review the case, vacated, and remanded.

B. Counsel of Record / ACLU Attorney

ACLU Side (Respondent / Appellee): Scott Daniel argued the cause for appellee.

Opposing Side (Petitioner / Appellant): W. J. Michael Cody, Attorney General of Tennessee, argued the cause for appellant.

Paul J. Larkin, Jr., argued the cause for the United States, as amicus curiae, by special leave of Court.

III. AMICI CURIAE

ACLU Side (Respondent / Appellee)

Brief of amici curiae filed on behalf of the ACLU, et al., by Burt Neuborne and Charles S. Sims.

Brief of amici curiae filed on behalf of the National Association of Criminal Defense Lawyers, et al., by Kim Robert Fawcett and Stephen A. Saltzburg.

Opposing Side (Petitioner / Appellant)

Brief of amici curiae filed on behalf of the United States by Paul J. Larkin, Jr., Solicitor General Fried, Assistant Attorney General Trott, and Deputy Solicitor General Frey.

Brief of amici curiae filed on behalf of the State of California by John K. Van de Kamp, Attorney General of California, Steve White, Chief Assistant Attorney General, and Ronald E. Niver and David D. Salmon, Deputy Attorneys General.

IV. THE SUPREME COURT'S DECISION

"'[W]e have repeatedly reaffirmed the principle that an otherwise valid conviction should not be set aside if the reviewing court may confidently say, on the whole record, that the constitutional error was harmless beyond a reasonable doubt.' . . . Apart from the challenged malice instruction, the jury in this case was clearly instructed that it had to find respondent guilty beyond a reasonable doubt as to every element of both first- and second-degree murder. . . .

We therefore find that the error at issue here—an instruction that impermissibly shifted the burden of proof on malice—is not 'so basic to a fair trial' that it can never be harmless. . . . For purposes of deciding this case, it is enough to recognize that in some cases that inference is overpowering. It would further neither justice nor the purposes of the Sandstrom rule to reverse a conviction in such a case. We accordingly hold that Chapman's harmless-error standard applies in cases such as this one. . . . The Court of Appeals has not yet applied Chapman to the facts of this case. We therefore remand to that court for determination of whether the error committed in this case was harmless beyond a reasonable doubt.

The judgment of the Court of Appeals is vacated, and the case is remanded for further proceedings consistent with this opinion."

V. JUSTICE VOTE

3 Pro ACLU Side vs. 6 Con Opposing Side

ACLU Side (Respondent / Appellee)

1. Blackmun, H. – Wrote dissenting opinion
2. Marshall, T. – Joined Blackmun's dissent
3. Brennan, W. – Joined Blackmun's dissent

Opposing Side (Petitioner / Appellant)

1. Powell, L. – Wrote majority opinion
2. Burger, W. – Wrote concurring opinion
3. White, B. – Joined majority opinion
4. Rehnquist, W. – Joined majority opinion
5. O'Connor, S. – Joined majority opinion
6. Stevens, J. – Wrote concurring opinion

VI. A WIN OR LOSS FOR THE ACLU?

The ACLU, as amicus curiae, urged affirmance of the judgment of the Court of Appeals; the Supreme Court vacated and remanded in a 6-3 vote, giving the ACLU an apparent loss.

599. Arcara v. Cloud Books Inc.

(Decided July 7, 1986; 478 U.S. 697)

I. ISSUE

A. Issues Discussed

First Amendment

B. Legal Question Presented

"[W]hether the First Amendment bars enforcement of a statute authorizing closure of premises found to be used as a place for prostitution and lewdness because the premises are also used as an adult bookstore."

C. Supreme Court's Answer

The First Amendment does not bar closure of the premises.

II. CASE SUMMARY

A. Background

"Respondents own and operate the 'Village Books and News Store' in Kenmore, New York. The establishment characterizes itself as an "adult" bookstore and sells sexually explicit books and magazines with booths available for the viewing of sexually explicit movies. . . . During September and October 1982, the Erie County Sheriff's Department conducted an undercover investigation into reported illicit sexual activities occurring on respondents' premises. A Deputy Sheriff personally observed instances of masturbation, fondling, and fellatio by patrons on the premises of the store, all within the observation of the proprietor. He also observed instances of solicitation of prostitution, and was himself solicited on at least four occasions by men who offered to perform sexual acts in exchange for money. The Deputy Sheriff reported that the management of the 'Village Books and News Store' was fully aware of the sexual activity on the premises. . . . The results of the undercover investigation formed the basis of a civil complaint against respondents seeking closure of the premises under § 2321 of the New York Public Health Law. . . .

Respondents answered the complaint by denying the allegations of the Deputy Sheriff that sexual activities occurred on the premises with respondents' knowledge, and also by asserting that a closure of the premises would impermissibly interfere with their First Amendment right to sell books on the premises.

Respondents moved for partial summary judgment on these First Amendment grounds, and also advanced an argument that the statute was not intended to reach establishments other than houses of prostitution in the traditional sense. The Trial Division of the New York Supreme Court, Special Term, denied the motion for summary judgment, holding that the statute was applicable to respondents; it rejected respondents' First Amendment claims as well, reasoning that the closure order sought did not involve a prior restraint of materials presumptively protected by the First Amendment. It also held that respondents' bookselling activities could not be employed as 'a curtain behind which illegal activity can be freely encouraged and conducted.'

The Appellate Division, Fourth Department, affirmed. . . . The New York Court of Appeals reversed. That court agreed that the Public Health Law applied to establishments other than houses of prostitution, but reversed on First Amendment grounds."

The Suprme Court granted certiorari to review the case and reversed.

B. Counsel of Record / ACLU Attorney

ACLU Side (Respondent / Appellee): Paul John Cambria, Jr., argued the cause for appellee.

Opposing Side (Petitioner / Appellant): John J. DeFranks argued the cause for appellant.

III. AMICI CURIAE

ACLU Side (Respondent / Appellee)

Brief of amici curiae filed on behalf of the ACLU, et al., by Steven R. Shapiro, Burt Neuborne, and Charles S. Sims.

Opposing Side (Petitioner / Appellant)

Brief of amici curiae filed on behalf of the city of Santa Ana, California, by Edward Cooper and James J. Clancy.

Brief of amici curiae filed on behalf of the city of New York by Frederick A. O. Schwarz, Jr., and Leonard Koerner.

IV. THE SUPREME COURT'S DECISION

"First Amendment values may not be invoked by merely linking the words 'sex' and 'books.' [R]espondents argue that the statutory closure remedy impermissibly burdens its First Amendment protected bookselling activities. The severity of this burden is dubious at best, and is mitigated by the fact that respondents remain free to sell the same materials at another location. In any event, this argument proves too much, since every civil and criminal remedy imposes some conceivable burden on First Amendment protected activities. . . .

It is true that the closure order in this case would require respondents to move their bookselling business to another location. Yet we have not traditionally subjected every criminal and civil sanction imposed through legal process to 'least restrictive means' scrutiny simply because each particular remedy will have some effect on the First Amendment activities of those subject to sanction. Rather, we have subjected such restrictions to scrutiny only where it was conduct with a significant expressive element that drew the legal remedy in the first place, as in O'Brien, or where a statute based on a nonexpressive activity has the inevitable effect of singling out those engaged in expressive activity, as in Minneapolis Star. This case involves neither situation, and we conclude the First Amendment is not implicated by the enforcement of a public health regulation of general application against the physical premises in which respondents happen to sell books.

The New York Court of Appeals thus misread O'Brien, which has no relevance to a statute directed at imposing sanctions on nonexpressive activity. The legislation providing the closure sanction was directed at unlawful conduct having nothing to do with books or other expressive activity. Bookselling in an establishment used for prostitution does not confer First Amendment coverage to defeat a valid statute aimed at penalizing and terminating illegal uses of premises. The legislature properly sought to protect the environment of the community by directing the sanction at premises knowingly used for lawless activities.

The judgment of the New York Court of Appeals is reversed."

V. JUSTICE VOTE

3 Pro ACLU Side vs. 6 Con Opposing Side

ACLU Side (Respondent / Appellee)

1. Blackmun, H. – Wrote dissenting opinion
2. Brennan, W. – Joined Blackmun's dissent
3. Marshall, T. – Joined Blackmun's dissent

Opposing Side (Petitioner / Appellant)

1. Burger, W. – Wrote majority opinion
2. White, B. – Joined majority opinion
3. Powell, L. – Joined majority opinion
4. Rehnquist, W. – Joined majority opinion
5. Stevens, J. – Joined O'Connor's concurrence
6. O'Connor, S. – Wrote concurring opinion

VI. A WIN OR LOSS FOR THE ACLU?

The ACLU, as amicus curiae, urged affirmance of the judgment of the Court of Appeals; the Supreme Court reversed in a 6-3 vote, giving the ACLU an apparent loss.

600. Munro v. Socialist Workers Party

(Decided December 10, 1986; 479 U.S. 189)

I. ISSUE

A. Issues Discussed

First Amendment, Fourteenth Amendment, elections, voting rights, freedom of association

B. Legal Question Presented

Whether the requirement "that a minor-party candidate for partisan office receive at least 1% of all votes cast for that office in the State's primary election before the candidate's name will be placed on the general election ballot . . . violates the First and Fourteenth Amendments to the United States Constitution."

C. Supreme Court's Answer

The requirement does not violate the First Amendment or Fourteenth Amendment.

II. CASE SUMMARY

A. Background

"The State of Washington requires that a minor-party candidate for partisan office receive at least 1% of all votes cast for that office in the State's primary election before the candidate's name will be placed on the general election ballot. . . .

The events giving rise to this action occurred in 1983, after the state legislature authorized a special primary election to be held on October 11, 1983, to fill a vacancy in the office of United States Senator. Appellee Dean Peoples qualified to be placed on the primary election ballot as the nominee of appellee Socialist Workers Party (Party). Also appearing on that ballot were 32 other candidates. At the primary, Mr. Peoples received approximately nine one-hundredths of one percent of the total votes cast for the office, and, accordingly, the State did not place his name on the general election ballot.

Appellees (Peoples, the Party, and two registered voters) commenced this action in United States District Court, alleging that § 29.18.110 abridged their rights secured by the First and Fourteenth Amendments. The District Court entered judgment denying appellees relief, but the Court of Appeals for the Ninth Circuit reversed, holding that § 29.18.110, as applied to candidates for statewide offices, was unconstitutional."

The Supreme Court granted certiorari to review the case and reversed.

B. Counsel of Record / ACLU Attorney

ACLU Side (Respondent / Appellee): Daniel Hoyt Smith argued the cause for appellee.

Opposing Side (Petitioner / Appellant): James M. Johnson, Senior Assistant Attorney General of Washington, argued the cause for appellant.

III. AMICI CURIAE

ACLU Side (Respondent / Appellee)

Brief of amici curiae filed on behalf of the ACLU Foundation, et al., by Jack D. Novik, Burt Neuborne and David J. Burman.

Brief of amici curiae filed on behalf of the Libertarian Party of Washington by James J. Featherstone and Richard E. Gardiner.

Opposing Side (Petitioner / Appellant)

No briefs of amici curiae were filed in support of appellant.

IV. THE SUPREME COURT'S DECISION

"Restrictions upon the access of political parties to the ballot impinge upon the rights of individuals to associate for political purposes, as well as the rights of qualified voters to cast their votes effectively . . . . These associational rights, however, are not absolute and are necessarily subject to qualification if elections are to be run fairly and effectively. . . .

We have never required a State to make a particularized showing of the existence of voter confusion, ballot overcrowding, or the presence of frivolous candidacies prior to the imposition of reasonable restrictions on ballot access. . . . Such a requirement would necessitate that a State's political system sustain some level of damage before the legislature could take corrective action. Legislatures, we think, should be permitted to respond reasonably to potential deficiencies in the electoral process with foresight rather than reactively . . . .

The State of Washington was clearly entitled to raise the ante for ballot access, to simplify the general election ballot, and to avoid the possibility of unrestrained factionalism at the general election. . . . Washington has chosen a vehicle by which minor-party candidates must demonstrate voter support that serves to promote the very First Amendment values that are threatened by overly burdensome ballot access restrictions. It can hardly be said that Washington's voters are denied freedom of association because they must channel their expressive activity into a campaign at the primary as opposed to the general election. It is true that voters must make choices as they vote at the primary, but there are no state-imposed obstacles impairing voters in the exercise of their choices. Washington simply has not substantially burdened the 'availability of political opportunity.' . . .

Here, because Washington affords a minor-party candidate easy access to the primary election ballot and the opportunity for the candidate to wage a ballot-connected campaign, we conclude that the magnitude of § 29.18.110's effect on constitutional rights is slight when compared to the restrictions we upheld in Jenness and American Party. Accordingly, Washington did not violate the Constitution by denying appellee Peoples a position on the general election ballot on November 8, 1983.

The judgment of the Court of Appeals for the Ninth Circuit is therefore reversed."

V. JUSTICE VOTE

2 Pro ACLU Side vs. 7 Con Opposing Side

ACLU Side (Respondent / Appellee)

1. Marshall, T. – Wrote dissenting opinion
2. Brennan, W. – Joined Marshall's dissent

Opposing Side (Petitioner / Appellant)

1. White, B. – Wrote majority opinion
2. Rehnquist, W. – Joined majority opinion
3. Blackmun, H. – Joined majority opinion
4. Powell, L. – Joined majority opinion
5. Stevens, J. – Joined majority opinion
6. O'Connor, S. – Joined majority opinion
7. Scalia, A. – Joined majority opinion

VI. A WIN OR LOSS FOR THE ACLU?

The ACLU, as amicus curiae, urged affirmance of the judgment of the Court of Appeals; the Supreme Court reversed in a 2-7 vote, giving the ACLU an apparent loss.

601. Federal Election Commission v. Massachusetts Citizens For Life, Inc.

(Decided December 15, 1986; 479 U.S. 238)

I. ISSUE

A. Issues Discussed

First Amendment, political speech

B. Legal Question Presented

"[W]hether appellee Massachusetts Citizens for Life, Inc. (MCFL), a nonprofit, nonstock corporation, by financing certain activity with its treasury funds, has violated the restriction on independent spending contained in § 441b [and] whether application of that section to MCFL's conduct is constitutional."

C. Supreme Court's Answer

MCFL violated § 441b, but the section is unconstitutional as applied to MCFL.

II. CASE SUMMARY

A. Background

2 U.S.C. § 441b "prohibits corporations from using treasury funds to make an expenditure 'in connection with' any federal election, and requires that any expenditure for such purpose be financed by voluntary contributions to a separate segregated fund."

Massachusetts Citizens for Life, Inc. "was incorporated in January 1973 as a nonprofit, nonstock corporation under Massachusetts law. . . . In September 1978, MCFL prepared and distributed a 'Special Edition' prior to the September 1978 primary elections. . . . The front page of the publication was headlined 'EVERYTHING YOU NEED TO KNOW TO VOTE PRO–LIFE,' and readers were admonished that '[n]o pro-life candidate can win in November without your vote in September.' 'VOTE PRO–LIFE' was printed in large boldfaced letters on the back page, and a coupon was provided to be clipped and taken to the polls to remind voters of the name of the 'pro-life' candidates. Next to the exhortation to vote 'pro-life' was a disclaimer: 'This special election edition does not represent an endorsement of any particular candidate.' . . .

A complaint was filed with the Commission alleging that the 'Special Edition' was a violation of § 441b. The complaint maintained that the Edition represented an expenditure of funds from a corporate treasury to distribute to the general public a campaign flyer on behalf of certain political candidates. The FEC found reason to believe that such a violation had occurred, initiated an investigation, and determined that probable cause existed to believe that MCFL had violated the Act. After conciliation efforts failed, the Commission filed a complaint in the District Court under § 437g(a)(6)(A), seeking a civil penalty and other appropriate relief.

Both parties moved for summary judgment. The District Court granted MCFL's motion, holding that: (1) the election publications could not be regarded as 'expenditures' under § 441b(b)(2); (2) the 'Special Edition' was exempt from the statutory prohibition by virtue of § 431(9)(B)(i), which in general exempts news commentary distributed by a periodical publication unaffiliated with any candidate or political party; and (3) if the statute applied to MCFL, it was unconstitutional as a violation of the First Amendment.

On appeal, the Court of Appeals for the First Circuit held that the statute was applicable to MCFL, but affirmed the District Court's holding that the statute as so applied was unconstitutional."

The Supreme Court granted certiorari to review the case and affirmed.

B. Counsel of Record / ACLU Attorney

ACLU Side (Respondent / Appellee): Francis H. Fox argued the cause for appellee.

Opposing Side (Petitioner / Appellant): Charles N. Steele argued the cause for appellant.

III. AMICI CURIAE

ACLU Side (Respondent / Appellee)

Brief of amici curiae filed on behalf of the ACLU, et al., by Marjorie Heins, Burt Neuborne, and Jack Novik.

Brief of amici curiae filed on behalf of the Catholic League for Religious and Civil Rights by Steven Frederick McDowell.

Brief of amici curiae filed on behalf of the Chamber of Commerce of the United States by Judith K. Richmond, Stephen A. Bokat, Robin S. Conrad, and Jan W. Baran.

Brief of amici curiae filed on behalf of the Home Builders Association of Massachusetts by Wayne S. Henderson.

Brief of amici curiae filed on behalf of the National Rifle Association of America by James J. Featherstone and Richard E. Gardiner.

Brief of amici curiae filed on behalf of Joseph M. Scheidler, et al., by Edward R. Grant and Maura K. Quinlan.

Brief of amici curiae filed on behalf of the Reporters Committee for Freedom of the Press, et al., by Jane E. Kirtley, David Barr, Nancy H. Hendry, J. Laurent Scharff, and Bruce W. Sanford.

Opposing Side (Petitioner / Appellant)

Brief of amici curiae filed on behalf of Common Cause by Roger M. Witten, William T. Lake, Carol F. Lee, and Archibald Cox.

IV. THE SUPREME COURT'S DECISION

"The 'Special Edition' . . . falls squarely within §441(b), for it represents express advocacy of the election of particular candidates distributed to members of the general public. . . . We must therefore determine whether the prohibition of §441(b) burdens political speech, and if so, whether such a burden is justified by a compelling state interest. . . .

Our conclusion is that § 441b's restriction of independent spending is unconstitutional as applied to MCFL, for it infringes protected speech without a compelling justification for such infringement. We acknowledge the legitimacy of Congress' concern that organizations that amass great wealth in the economic marketplace not gain unfair advantage in the political marketplace.

Regardless of whether that concern is adequate to support application of § 441b to commercial enterprises, a question not before us, that justification does not extend uniformly to all corporations. Some corporations have features more akin to voluntary political associations than business firms, and therefore should not have to bear burdens on independent spending solely because of their incorporated status.

In particular, MCFL has three features essential to our holding that it may not constitutionally be bound by § 441b's restriction on independent spending. First, it was formed for the express purpose of promoting political ideas, and cannot engage in business activities. . . . Second, it has no shareholders or other persons affiliated so as to have a claim on its assets or earnings. . . . Third, MCFL was not established by a business corporation or a labor union, and it is its policy not to accept contributions from such entities. . . .

It may be that the class of organizations affected by our holding today will be small. That prospect, however, does not diminish the significance of the rights at stake. Freedom of speech plays a fundamental role in a democracy; as this Court has said, freedom of thought and speech 'is the matrix, the indispensable condition, of nearly every other form of freedom.' Our pursuit of other governmental ends, however, may tempt us to accept in small increments a loss that would be unthinkable if inflicted all at once. For this reason, we must be as vigilant against the modest diminution of speech as we are against its sweeping restriction. Where at all possible, government must curtail speech only to the degree necessary to meet the particular problem at hand, and must avoid infringing on speech that does not pose the danger that has prompted regulation. In enacting the provision at issue in this case, Congress has chosen too blunt an instrument for such a delicate task.

The judgment of the Court of Appeals is affirmed."

V. JUSTICE VOTE

9 Pro ACLU Side vs. 0 Con Opposing Side

ACLU Side (Respondent / Appellee)

1. Brennan, W. – Wrote majority opinion
2. O'Connor, S. – Wrote concurring opinion
3. Powell, L. – Joined majority opinion
4. Scalia, A. – Joined majority opinion
5. Marshall, T. – Joined majority opinion

Opposing Side (Petitioner / Appellant)

1. Rehnquist, W. – Wrote opinion concurring in part and dissenting in part
2. White, B. –Wrote dissenting opinion, Joined Rehnquist's opinion
3. Blackmun, H. – Joined Rehnquist's opinion
4. Stevens, J. – Joined Rehnquist's opinion

VI. A WIN OR LOSS FOR THE ACLU?

The ACLU, as amicus curiae, urged affirmance of the judgment of the Court of Appeals; the Supreme Court affirmed in a 5-4 vote, giving the ACLU an apparent win.

602. California Federal Savings & Loan Association v. Guerra

(Decided January 13, 1987; 479 U.S. 272)

I. ISSUE

A. Issues Discussed

Civil Right Act, gender discrimination, employment discrimination

B. Legal Question Presented

"[W]hether Title VII of the Civil Rights Act of 1964, as amended by the Pregnancy Discrimination Act of 1978, pre-empts a state statute that requires employers to provide leave and reinstatement to employees disabled by pregnancy."

C. Supreme Court's Answer

Title VII does not preempt the California statute.

II. CASE SUMMARY

A. Background

"Petitioner California Federal Savings & Loan Association (Cal Fed) is a federally chartered savings and loan association based in Los Angeles; it is an employer covered by both Title VII and § 12945(b)(2). Cal Fed has a facially neutral leave policy that permits employees who have completed three months of service to take unpaid leaves of absence for a variety of reasons, including disability and pregnancy. Although it is Cal Fed's policy to try to provide an employee taking unpaid leave with a similar position upon returning, Cal Fed expressly reserves the right to terminate an employee who has taken a leave of absence if a similar position is not available.

Lillian Garland was employed by Cal Fed as a receptionist for several years. In January 1982, she took a pregnancy disability leave. When she was able to return to work in April of that year, Garland notified Cal Fed, but was informed that her job had been filled and that there were no receptionist or similar positions available. Garland filed a complaint with respondent Department of Fair Employment and Housing, which issued an administrative accusation against Cal Fed on her behalf. Respondent charged Cal Fed with violating § 12945(b)(2) of the FEHA. Prior to the scheduled hearing before respondent Fair Employment and Housing Commission, Cal Fed, joined by petitioners Merchants and Manufacturers Association and the California Chamber of Commerce, brought this action in the United States District Court for the Central District of California.

They sought a declaration that § 12945(b)(2) is inconsistent with and pre-empted by Title VII and an injunction against enforcement of the section. The District Court granted petitioners' motion for summary judgment. . . .

The United States Court of Appeals for the Ninth Circuit reversed. It held that 'the district court's conclusion that section 12945(b)(2) discriminates against men on the basis of pregnancy defies common sense, misinterprets case law, and flouts Title VII and the PDA.' Based on its own reading of Newport News, the Court of Appeals found that the PDA does not 'demand that state law be blind to pregnancy's existence.' The court held that in enacting the PDA Congress intended 'to construct a floor beneath which pregnancy disability benefits may not drop-not a ceiling above which they may not rise.' Because it found that the California statute furthers the goal of equal employment opportunity for women, the Court of Appeals concluded: 'Title VII does not preempt a state law that guarantees pregnant women a certain number of pregnancy disability leave days, because this is neither inconsistent with, nor unlawful under, Title VII.'"

The Supreme Court granted certiorari to review the case and affirmed.

B. Counsel of Record / ACLU Attorney

ACLU Side (Respondent / Appellee): Marian M. Johnston, Deputy Attorney General of California, argued the cause for appellee.

Opposing Side (Petitioner / Appellant): Theodore B. Olson argued the cause for appellant.

III. AMICI CURIAE

ACLU Side (Respondent / Appellee)

Brief of amici curiae filed on behalf of the ACLU, et al., by Joan E. Bertin, Isabelle Katz Pinzler, George Kannar, and Charles S. Sims, in support of neither party, urging the court to determine that the state statute is not preempted by Title VII and that both pregnant women and others experiencing an inability to work should be treated the same to comply with Title VII.

Additional briefs of amici curiae were filed on behalf of the State of Connecticut, et al., the American Federation of Labor and Congress of Industrial Organizations, California Women Lawyers, et al., Equal Rights Advocates, et al., Human Rights Advocates, et al., the National Conference of State Legislatures, et al., the Coalition for Reproductive Equality in the Workplace, et al., and Lillian Garland.

The National Organization for Women, et al., filed a brief of amici curiae in support of neither party, urging that the Court should find employers must comply with both the state and federal law.

Opposing Side (Petitioner / Appellant)

Brief of amici curiae filed on behalf of the United States by Solicitor General Fried, Assistant Attorney General Reynolds, Deputy Solicitor General Geller, Deputy Assistant Attorney General Carvin, Richard J. Lazarus, Brian K. Landsberg, David K. Flynn, and Mary E. Mann.

Brief of amici curiae filed on behalf of the Equal Employment Advisory Council by Robert E. Williams, Douglas S. McDowell, and Lorence L. Kessler.

Brief of amici curiae filed on behalf of the Chamber of Commerce of the United States by Robin S. Conrad and Paula J. Connelly.

IV. THE SUPREME COURT'S DECISION:

"In determining whether a state statute is preempted by federal law and therefore invalid under the Supremacy Clause of the Constitution, our sole task is to ascertain the intent of Congress. . . . In two sections of the 1964 Civil Rights Act, §§ 708 and 1104, Congress has indicated that state laws will be pre-empted only if they actually conflict with federal law. . . . Accordingly, there is no need to infer congressional intent to pre-empt state laws from the substantive provisions of Title VII; these two sections provide a 'reliable indicium of congressional intent with respect to state authority' to regulate employment practice.

[S]ubject to certain limitations, we agree with the Court of Appeals' conclusion that Congress intended the PDA to be 'a floor beneath which pregnancy disability benefits may not drop-not a ceiling above which they may not rise.' . . .

Thus, petitioners' facial challenge to § 12945(b)(2) fails. The statute is not pre-empted by Title VII, as amended by the PDA, because it is not inconsistent with the purposes of the federal statute, nor does it require the doing of an act which is unlawful under Title VII.

The judgment of the Court of Appeals is affirmed."

V. JUSTICE VOTE

6 Pro ACLU Side vs. 3 Con Opposing Side

ACLU Side (Respondent / Appellee)

1. Marshall T. – Wrote majority opinion
2. Stevens J. – Wrote concurring opinion
3. Scalia, A. – Wrote concurring opinion
4. Brennan, W. – Joined majority opinion
5. Blackmun, H. – Joined majority opinion
6. O'Connor, S. – Joined majority opinion

Opposing Side (Petitioner / Appellant)

1. White, B. – Wrote dissenting opinion
2. Rehnquist W. – Joined White's dissent
3. Powell, L. – Joined White's dissent

VI. A WIN OR LOSS FOR THE ACLU?

The ACLU, as amicus curiae, urged the Supreme Court to vacate the judgment of the Court of Appeals; the Supreme Court affirmed in a 6-3 vote, but determined that the state statute was not preempted by Title VII, giving the ACLU an apparent win.

603. Colorado v. Bertine

(Decided January 14, 1987; 479 U.S. 367)

I. ISSUE

A. Issues Discussed

Criminal procedure, Fourth Amendment, search and seizure, inventory searches

B. Legal Question Presented

"[W]hether the Fourth Amendment prohibits the State from proving . . . charges [of drug possession with intent to distribute] with the evidence discovered during the inventory of Bertine's van."

C. Supreme Court's Answer

The Fourth Amendment does not prohibit admission of the evidence to prove drug possession.

II. CASE SUMMARY

A. Background

"On February 10, 1984, a police officer in Boulder, Colorado, arrested respondent Steven Lee Bertine for driving while under the influence of alcohol. After Bertine was taken into custody and before the arrival of a tow truck to take Bertine's van to an impoundment lot, a backup officer inventoried the contents of the van. The officer opened a closed backpack in which he found controlled substances, cocaine paraphernalia, and a large amount of cash. Bertine was subsequently charged with driving while under the influence of alcohol, unlawful possession of cocaine with intent to dispense, sell, and distribute, and unlawful possession of methaqualone. . . . The backup officer inventoried the van in accordance with local police procedures . . . .

After Bertine was charged with the offenses described above, he moved to suppress the evidence found during the inventory search on the ground, inter alia, that the search of the closed backpack and containers exceeded the permissible scope of such a search under the Fourth Amendment. The Colorado trial court ruled that probable cause supported Bertine's arrest and that the police officers had made the decisions to impound the vehicle and to conduct a thorough inventory search in good faith. . . . On the State's interlocutory appeal, the Supreme Court of Colorado affirmed."

The U.S. Supreme Court granted certiorari to review the case and reversed.

B. Counsel of Record / ACLU Attorney

ACLU Side (Respondent / Appellee): Cary C. Lacklen argued the cause for appellee.

Opposing Side (Petitioner / Appellant): John M. Haried argued the cause for appellant.

Richard J. Lazarus argued the cause for the United States as amicus curiae urging reversal.

III. AMICI CURIAE

ACLU Side (Respondent / Appellee)

Brief of amici curiae filed on behalf of the ACLU, et al., by Larry W. Yackle and George Kannar.

Brief of amici curiae filed on behalf of the Colorado Criminal Defense Bar, Inc., et al., by John M. Richilano and Mary G. Allen.

Opposing Side (Petitioner / Appellant)

Brief of amici curiae filed on behalf of the United States by Richard J. Lazarus, Solicitor General Fried, Assistant Attorney General Trott, and Deputy Solicitor General Bryson.

IV. THE SUPREME COURT'S DECISION

"[I]nventory searches are now a well-defined exception to the warrant requirement of the Fourth Amendment. The policies behind the warrant requirement are not implicated in an inventory search, nor is the related concept of probable cause . . . .

In Opperman, this Court assessed the reasonableness of an inventory search of the glove compartment in an abandoned automobile impounded by the police. We found that inventory procedures serve to protect an owner's property while it is in the custody of the police, to insure against claims of lost, stolen, or vandalized property, and to guard the police from danger. In light of these strong governmental interests and the diminished expectation of privacy in an automobile, we upheld the search. . . .

In . . . Lafayette, a police officer conducted an inventory search of the contents of a shoulder bag in the possession of an individual being taken into custody. In deciding whether this search was reasonable, we recognized that the search served legitimate governmental interests similar to those identified in Opperman. We determined that those interests outweighed the individual's Fourth Amendment interests and upheld the search.

In the present case, as in Opperman and Lafayette, there was no showing that the police, who were following standardized procedures, acted in bad faith or for the sole purpose of investigation. In addition, the governmental interests justifying the inventory searches in Opperman and Lafayette are nearly the same as those which obtain here. . . .

While both Opperman and Lafayette are distinguishable from the present case on their facts, we think that the principles enunciated in those cases govern the present one.

The judgment of the Supreme Court of Colorado is therefore reversed."

V. JUSTICE VOTE

2 Pro ACLU Side vs. 7 Con Opposing Side

ACLU Side (Respondent / Appellee)

1. Marshall, T. – Wrote dissenting opinion
2. Brennan, W. – Joined Marshall's dissent

Opposing Side (Petitioner / Appellant)

1. Rehnquist, W. – Wrote majority opinion
2. White B. – Joined majority opinion
3. Blackmun, H. – Wrote concurring opinion
4. Powell, L. – Joined Blackmun's concurrence
5. Stevens, J. – Joined majority opinion
6. O'Connor, S. – Joined Blackmun's concurrence
7. Scalia, A. – Joined majority opinion

VI. A WIN OR LOSS FOR THE ACLU?

The ACLU, as amicus curiae, urged affirmance of the judgment of the Supreme Court of Colorado; the U.S. Supreme Court reversed in a 7-2 vote, giving the ACLU an apparent loss.

604. Wimberly v. Labor and Industrial Relations Commission of Missouri

(Decided January 21, 1987; 479 U.S. 511)

I. ISSUE

A. Issues Discussed

Disability, employment discrimination, pregnancy

B. Legal Question Presented

Whether the "Federal Unemployment Tax Act, 26 U.S.C. § 3304(a)(12), . . . prohibit[s] a State from disqualifying unemployment compensation claimants who leave their jobs because of pregnancy, when the State imposes the same disqualification on all claimants who leave their jobs for a reason not causally connected to their work or their employer."

C. Supreme Court's Answer

The Act does not prohibit a State from disqualifying unemployment compensation claimants in this circumstance.

II. CASE SUMMARY

A. Background

"In August 1980, after having been employed by the J.C. Penney Company for approximately three years, petitioner requested a leave of absence on account of her pregnancy. Pursuant to its established policy, the J.C. Penney Company granted petitioner a 'leave without guarantee of reinstatement,' meaning that petitioner would be rehired only if a position was available when petitioner was ready to return to work. Petitioner's child was born on November 5, 1980. On December 1, 1980, when petitioner notified J.C. Penney that she wished to return to work, she was told that there were no positions open.

Petitioner then filed a claim for unemployment benefits. The claim was denied by the Division of Employment Security (Division) pursuant to Mo.Rev.Stat. § 288.050.1(1) (Supp.1984), which disqualifies a claimant who 'has left his work voluntarily without good cause attributable to his work or to his employer.' . . . Petitioner appealed the decision to the Division's appeals tribunal, which, after a full evidentiary hearing, entered findings of fact and conclusions of law affirming the deputy's decision. The Labor and Industrial Relations Commission denied petitioner's petition for review.

Petitioner then sought review in the Circuit Court of Jackson County, Missouri. The court concluded that § 288.050.1(1) was inconsistent with 26 U.S.C. § 3304(a)(12) . . . and therefore could not be enforced. [The court] reversed the Commission's decision and remanded for entry of an award. The Missouri Court of Appeals affirmed. . . .

The Missouri Supreme Court reversed, with three judges dissenting. The court held that previous state appellate decisions had correctly interpreted Mo.Rev.Stat. § 288.050.1(1) (Supp.1984) as disqualifying all claimants who, like petitioner, leave work 'for reasons that, while perhaps legitimate and necessary from a personal standpoint, were not causally connected to the claimant's work or employer.'"

The U.S. Supreme Court granted certiorari to review the case and affirmed.

B. Counsel of Record / ACLU Attorney

ACLU Side (Petitioner / Appellant): Julie S. Levin argued the cause for appellant.

Opposing Side (Respondent / Appellee): Michael L. Boicourt, Assistant Attorney General of Missouri, argued the cause for appellee.

Christopher J. Wright argued the cause for the United States, as amicus curiae, by special leave of Court.

III. AMICI CURIAE

ACLU Side (Petitioner / Appellant)

Brief of amici curiae filed on behalf of the ACLU, et al., by Joan E. Bertin and Isabelle Katz Pinzler, in support of neither party and urging the Court to remand the case for a determination of whether the actions at issued denied appellant unemployment insurance in violation of 26 U.S.C. § 3304(a)(12).

Brief of amici curiae filed on behalf of Equal Rights Advocates, et al., by Judith E. Kurtz and Lorraine L. Loder.

Opposing Side (Respondent / Appellee)

Brief of amici curiae filed on behalf of the United States by Christopher J. Wright, Solicitor General Fried, Assistant Attorney General Willard, Deputy Solicitor General Ayer, John F. Cordes, Marleigh D. Dover, George R. Salem, Allen H. Feldman, Carol A. De Deo, Barbara J. Johnson, and Jeffrey A. Hennemuth.

IV. THE SUPREME COURT'S DECISION

"According to petitioner, § 3304(a)(12) affirmatively requires States to provide unemployment benefits to women who leave work because of pregnancy when they are next [sic] available and able to work, regardless of the State's treatment of other similarly situated claimants.

Contrary to petitioner's assertions, the plain import of the language of § 3304(a)(12) is that Congress intended only to prohibit States from singling out pregnancy for unfavorable treatment. [I]f a State adopts a neutral rule that incidentally disqualifies pregnant or formerly pregnant claimants as part of a larger group, the neutral application of that rule cannot readily be characterized as a decision made 'solely on the basis of pregnancy.' [P] etitioner can point to nothing in the Committee Reports, or elsewhere in the statute's legislative history, that evidences congressional intent to mandate preferential treatment for women on account of pregnancy. . . .

Thus, the agency's interpretation of the statute, like its legislative history, confirms what is clear from the statute's plain language: that § 3304(a)(12) prohibits discrimination but does not mandate preferential treatment.

Because § 3304(a)(12) does not require States to afford preferential treatment to women on account of pregnancy, the judgment of the Missouri Supreme Court is affirmed."

V. JUSTICE VOTE

0 Pro ACLU Side vs. 8 Con Opposing Side

Opposing Side (Respondent / Appellee)

1. O'Connor, S. – Wrote majority opinion
2. Rehnquist, W. – Joined majority opinion
3. White, B. – Joined majority opinion
4. Powell, L. – Joined majority opinion
5. Scalia, A. – Joined majority opinion
6. Brennan, W. – Joined majority opinion
7. Marshall, T. – Joined majority opinion
8. Stevens, J. – Joined majority opinion

Blackmun, H – Took no part in the decision

VI. A WIN OR LOSS FOR THE ACLU?

The ACLU, as amicus curiae, urged remand of the judgment of the Missouri Supreme Court for additional determinations; the U.S. Supreme Court affirmed in an 8-0 vote, giving the ACLU an apparent loss.

605. California v. Brown

(Decided January 27, 1987; 479 U.S. 538)

I. ISSUE

A. Issues Discussed

Due process, death penalty, Eighth Amendment, Fourteenth Amendment, jury instructions

B. Legal Question Presented

"[W]hether an instruction informing jurors that they 'must not be swayed by mere sentiment, conjecture, sympathy, passion, prejudice, public opinion or public feeling' during the penalty phase of a capital murder trial violates the Eighth and Fourteenth Amendments to the United States Constitution."

C. Supreme Court's Answer

The instruction does not violate the Eighth Amendment or Fourteenth Amendment.

II. CASE SUMMARY

A. Background

"Respondent Albert Brown was found guilty by a jury of forcible rape and first-degree murder in the death of 15-year-old Susan J. At the penalty phase, the State presented evidence that respondent had raped another young girl some years prior to his attack on Susan J. Respondent presented the testimony of several family members, who recounted respondent's peaceful nature and expressed disbelief that respondent was capable of such a brutal crime. Respondent also presented the testimony of a psychiatrist, who stated that Brown killed his victim because of his shame and fear over sexual dysfunction. Brown himself testified, stating that he was ashamed of his prior criminal conduct and asking for mercy from the jury.

California Penal Code Ann. § 190.3 (West Supp.1987) provides that capital defendants may introduce at the penalty phase any evidence 'as to any matter relevant to . . . mitigation . . . including, but not limited to, the nature and circumstances of the present offense, . . . and the defendant's character, background, history, mental condition and physical condition.' The trial court instructed the jury to consider the aggravating and mitigating circumstances and to weigh them in determining the appropriate penalty. But the court cautioned the jury that it 'must not be swayed by mere sentiment, conjecture, sympathy, passion, prejudice, public opinion or public feeling.' Respondent was sentenced to death.

On automatic appeal, the Supreme Court of California reversed the sentence of death. Over two dissents on this point, the majority opinion found that the instruction at issue here violates the Federal Constitution: "federal constitutional law forbids an instruction which denies a capital defendant the right to have the jury consider any

'sympathy factor' raised by the evidence when determining the appropriate penalty . . . ." the court ruled that the instruction 'is calculated to divert the jury from its constitutional duty to consider 'any [sympathetic] aspect of the defendant's character or record,' whether or not related to the offense for which he is on trial, in deciding the appropriate penalty.'"

The U.S. Supreme Court granted certiorari to review the jury instruction and reversed.

B. Counsel of Record / ACLU Attorney

ACLU Side (Respondent / Appellee): Monica Knox argued the cause for appellee.

Opposing Side (Petitioner / Appellant): Jay M. Bloom, Supervising Deputy Attorney General of California, argued the cause for appellant.

III. AMICI CURIAE

ACLU Side (Respondent / Appellee)

Brief of amici curiae filed on behalf of the ACLU, et al., by Paul W. Cane, Jr., and Paul Hoffman.

Opposing Side (Petitioner / Appellant)

Brief of amici curiae filed on behalf of the Criminal Justice Legal Foundation by Christopher N. Heard.

IV. THE SUPREME COURT'S DECISION

"We think that the California Supreme Court improperly focused solely on the word 'sympathy' to determine that the instruction interferes with the jury's consideration of mitigating evidence. 'The question, however, is not what the State Supreme Court declares the meaning of the charge to be, but rather what a reasonable juror could have understood the charge as meaning.' To determine how a reasonable juror could interpret an instruction, we 'must focus initially on the specific language challenged.' If the specific instruction fails constitutional muster, we then review the instructions as a whole to see if the entire charge delivered a correct interpretation of the law. In this case, we need not reach the second step of analysis because we hold that a reasonable juror would not interpret the challenged instruction in a manner that would render it unconstitutional. . . .

An instruction prohibiting juries from basing their sentencing decisions on factors not presented at the trial, and irrelevant to the issues at the trial, does not violate the United States Constitution.

It serves the useful purpose of confining the jury's imposition of the death sentence by cautioning it against reliance on extraneous emotional factors, which, we think, would be far more likely to turn the jury against a capital defendant than for him. And to the extent that the instruction helps to limit the jury's consideration to matters introduced in evidence before it, it fosters the Eighth Amendment's 'need for reliability in the determination that death is the appropriate punishment in a specific case.' Indeed, by limiting the jury's sentencing considerations to record evidence, the State also ensures the availability of meaningful judicial review, another safeguard that improves the reliability of the sentencing process.

We hold that the instruction challenged in this case does not violate the provisions of the Eighth and Fourteenth Amendments to the United States Constitution. The judgment of the Supreme Court of California is therefore reversed, and the cause is remanded for further proceedings not inconsistent with this opinion."

V. JUSTICE VOTE

4 Pro ACLU Side vs. 5 Con Opposing Side

ACLU Side (Respondent / Appellee)

1. Brennan, W. – Wrote dissenting opinion
2. Marshall, T. – Joined Brennan's dissent, in part, joined Blackmun's dissent
3. Stevens, J. – Joined Brennan's dissent, in part
5. Blackmun, H. – Wrote dissenting opinion

Opposing Side (Petitioner / Appellant)

1. Rehnquist, W. – Wrote majority opinion
2. White, B. – Joined majority opinion
3. Powell, L. – Joined majority opinion
4. Scalia, A. – Joined majority opinion
5. O'Connor, S. – Wrote concurring opinion

VI. A WIN OR LOSS FOR THE ACLU?

The ACLU, as amicus curiae, urged affirmance of the judgment of the Supreme Court of California; the U.S. Supreme Court reversed and remanded in a 5-4 vote, giving the ACLU an apparent loss.

606. City of Springfield v. Kibbe

(Decided February 25, 1987; 480 U.S. 257)

I. ISSUE

A. Issues Discussed

Civil rights, federal rights, municipal liability

B. Legal Question Presented

"[W]hether consistently with our decision in Monell v. New York City Dept. of Social Services, a municipality can be held liable under 42 U.S.C. § 1983 for inadequate training of its employees."

C. Supreme Court's Answer

The Supreme Court declined to decide the question, dismissing the writ of certiorari as improvidently granted.

II. CASE SUMMARY

A. Background

"Appellee Lois Thurston Kibbe, administratrix of the estate of Clinton Thurston, filed this suit under 42 U.S.C. § 1983 alleging that appellant City of Springfield and a number of its police officers deprived Thurston of his civil rights in a motor vehicle pursuit that ended with a police officer shooting Thurston in the head, causing his death. The jury returned verdicts against the police officer who fired the fatal shot and against the City, but found for three other officers. It awarded one dollar in compensatory damages and five hundred dollars in punitive damages against the officer and compensatory damages in the amount of fifty thousand dollars against the City. Appellant challenges the district court's refusal to grant either a directed verdict or judgment notwithstanding the verdict, and also claims error in the jury charge."[1] The Court of Appeals for the First Circuit affirmed.

The Supreme Court granted certiorari to review the case, then dismissed the writ of certiorari as improvidently granted.

B. Counsel of Record / ACLU Attorney

ACLU Side (Respondent / Appellee): Terry Scott Nagel argued the cause for appellee.

Opposing Side (Petitioner / Appellant): Edward M. Pikula argued the cause for appellant.

III. AMICI CURIAE

ACLU Side (Respondent / Appellee)

Brief of amici curiae filed on behalf of the ACLU, et al., by Marjorie Heins, Jack D. Novik, Howard Friedman, Michael Avery, and Donald Rudovsky.

Brief of amici curiae filed on behalf of the National Association for the Advancement of Colored People by Grover G. Hankins.

Opposing Side (Petitioner / Appellant)

Brief of amici curiae filed on behalf of the U.S. Conference of Mayors by Benna Ruth Solomon and David O. Stewart.

IV. THE SUPREME COURT'S DECISION

"The case having now been fully briefed and orally argued, we conclude that we cannot reach the negligence question. Although petitioner city of Springfield argues here that a heightened negligence standard does not suffice under Monell's requirement of a municipal policy, it appears that in the District Court petitioner did not object to the jury instruction stating that gross negligence would suffice, and indeed proposed its own instruction to the same effect. Nor did it argue for a higher standard than gross negligence in the Court of Appeals. It has informed us of no special circumstances explaining its failure to preserve this

1 Kibbe v. City of Springfield, 777 F.2d 801 (1st Cir. 1985).

question.

We ordinarily will not decide questions not raised or litigated in the lower courts. That rule has special force where the party seeking to argue the issue has failed to object to a jury instruction, since Rule 51 of the Federal Rules of Civil Procedure provides that '[n]o party may assign as error the giving . . . [of] an instruction unless he objects thereto before the jury retires to consider its verdict.' Here, our inability to reach the negligence issue makes this case an inappropriate vehicle for resolving the inadequate training question, because of the close interrelationship between the two matters, and the other questions presented are not of sufficient importance to warrant our review independently. . . .

For these reasons, we have concluded that the writ should be dismissed as improvidently granted."

V. JUSTICE VOTE

5 Pro ACLU Side vs. 4 Con Opposing Side

ACLU Side (Respondent / Appellee)

1. Brennan, W. – Per curiam decision
2. Marshall, T. – Per curiam decision
3. Stevens, J. – Per curiam decision
4. Scalia, A. – Per curiam decision
5. Blackmun, H. – Per curiam decision

Opposing Side (Petitioner / Appellant)

1. O'Connor, S. – Wrote dissenting opinion
2. Rehnquist, W. – Joined O'Connor's dissent
3. Powell, L. – Joined O'Connor's dissent
4. White, B. – Joined O'Connor's dissent

VI. A WIN OR LOSS FOR THE ACLU?

The ACLU filed as amicus curiae urging affirmance; the Supreme Court determined that the writ of certiorari should be dismissed, in a 5-4 vote, thus allowing the lower court's opinion to stand and giving the ACLU an apparent win.

607. Arizona v. Hicks

(Decided March 3, 1987; 480 U.S. 321)

I. ISSUE

A. Issues Discussed

Fourth Amendment, search and seizure, plain view doctrine

B. Legal Question Presented

"[W]hether th[e] 'plain view' doctrine may be invoked when the police have less than probable cause to believe that the item in question is evidence of a crime or is contraband."

C. Supreme Court's Answer

The plain view doctrine may not be applied when an item in plain view is moved absent probable cause.

II. CASE SUMMARY

A. Background

"On April 18, 1984, a bullet was fired through the floor of respondent's apartment, striking and injuring a man in the apartment below. Police officers arrived and entered respondent's apartment to search for the shooter, for other victims, and for weapons. They found and seized three weapons, including a sawed-off rifle, and in the course of their search also discovered a stocking-cap mask.

One of the policemen, Officer Nelson, noticed two sets of expensive stereo components, which seemed out of place in the squalid and otherwise ill-appointed four-room apartment. Suspecting that they were stolen, he read and recorded their serial numbers—moving some of the components, including a Bang and Olufsen turntable, in order to do so—which he then reported by phone to his headquarters. On being advised that the turntable had been taken in an armed robbery, he seized it immediately. It was later determined that some of the other serial numbers matched those on other stereo equipment taken in the same armed robbery, and a warrant was obtained and executed to seize that equipment as well. Respondent was subsequently indicted for the robbery.

The state trial court granted respondent's motion to suppress the evidence that had been seized. The Court of Appeals of Arizona affirmed. It was conceded that the initial entry and search, although warrantless, were justified by the exigent circumstance of the shooting. The Court of Appeals viewed the obtaining of the serial numbers, however, as an additional search, unrelated to that exigency. Relying upon a statement in Mincey v. Arizona, that a 'warrantless search must be 'strictly circumscribed by the exigencies which justify its initiation,'' the Court of Appeals held that the police conduct violated the Fourth Amendment, requiring the evidence derived from that conduct to be excluded. Both courts—the trial court explicitly and the Court of Appeals by necessary implication—rejected the State's contention that Officer Nelson's actions were justified under the 'plain view' doctrine of Coolidge v. New Hampshire, supra. The Arizona Supreme Court denied review, and the State filed this petition."

The Supreme Court granted certiorari to review the case and affirmed.

B. Counsel of Record / ACLU Attorney

ACLU Side (Respondent / Appellee): John W. Rood III, by appointment of the Court, argued the cause for appellee.

Opposing Side (Petitioner / Appellant): Linda A. Akers, Assistant Attorney General of Arizona, argued the cause for appellant.

III. AMICI CURIAE

ACLU Side (Respondent / Appellee)

Brief of amici curiae filed on behalf of the ACLU Foundation by William J. Taylor, G. Scott Emblidge, George Kannar, and Burt Neuborne.

Opposing Side (Petitioner / Appellant)

Brief of amici curiae filed on behalf of Americans for Effective Law Enforcement, Inc., et al., by David Crump, Daniel B. Hales, William C. Summers, Jack E. Yelverton, Fred E. Inbau,

Wayne W. Schmidt, and James P. Manak.

IV. THE SUPREME COURT'S DECISION

"Officer Nelson's moving of the equipment . . .did constitute a 'search' separate and apart from the search for the shooter, victims, and weapons that was the lawful objective of his entry into the apartment. Merely inspecting those parts of the turntable that came into view during the latter search would not have constituted an independent search, because it would have produced no additional invasion of respondent's privacy interest. But taking action, unrelated to the objectives of the authorized intrusion, which exposed to view concealed portions of the apartment or its contents, did produce a new invasion of respondent's privacy unjustified by the exigent circumstance that validated the entry. . . . It matters not that the search uncovered nothing of any great personal value to respondent—serial numbers rather than (what might conceivably have been hidden behind or under the equipment) letters or photographs. A search is a search, even if it happens to disclose nothing but the bottom of a turntable. . . .

The remaining question is whether the search was 'reasonable' under the Fourth Amendment. . . . We now hold that probable cause is required. To say otherwise would be to cut the 'plain view' doctrine loose from its theoretical and practical moorings. . . . We do not say, of course, that a seizure can never be justified on less than probable cause. We have held that it can—where, for example, the seizure is minimally intrusive and operational necessities render it the only practicable means of detecting certain types of crime. No special operational necessities are relied on here, however—but rather the mere fact that the items in question came lawfully within the officer's plain view. That alone cannot supplant the requirement of probable cause. . . .

For the reasons stated, the judgment of the Court of Appeals of Arizona is affirmed."

V. JUSTICE VOTE

6 Pro ACLU Side vs. 3 Con Opposing Side

ACLU Side (Respondent / Appellee)

1. Scalia, A. – Wrote majority opinion
2. Brennan, W. – Joined majority opinion
3. White, B. – Wrote concurring opinion
4. Marshall, T. – Joined majority opinion
5. Blackmun, H. – Joined majority opinion
6. Stevens, J. – Joined majority opinion

Opposing Side (Petitioner / Appellant)

1. Powell, L. – Wrote dissenting opinion, joined O'Connor's dissent
2. O'Connor, S. – Wrote dissenting opinion, joined Powell's dissent
3. Rehnquist, W. – Joined Powell's dissent, joined O'Connor's dissent

VI. A WIN OR LOSS FOR THE ACLU?

The ACLU, as amicus curiae, urged affirmance of the judgment of the Court of Appeals of Arizona; the Supreme Court affirmed in a 6-3 vote, giving the ACLU an apparent win.

608. Town of Newton v. Rumery

(Decided March 9, 1987; 480 U.S. 386)

I. ISSUE

A. Issues Discussed

Civil rights, waiver of constitutional rights, criminal procedure

B. Legal Question Presented

"[W]hether a court properly may enforce an agreement in which a criminal defendant releases his right to file an action under 42 U.S.C. § 1983 in return for a prosecutor's dismissal of pending criminal charges."

C. Supreme Court's Answer

A court may properly enforce this agreement.

II. CASE SUMMARY

A. Background

"Barrett arrested Rumery and accused him of tampering with a witness in violation of N.H.Rev.Stat.Ann. § 641:5(I)(b) (1986), a Class B felony.

Rumery promptly retained Stephen Woods, an experienced criminal defense attorney. Woods contacted Brian Graf, the Deputy County Attorney for Rockingham County. He warned Graf that he 'had better [dismiss] these charges, because we're going to win them and after that we're going to sue.' After further discussions, Graf and Woods reached an agreement, under which Graf would dismiss the charges against Rumery if Rumery would agree not to sue the town, its officials, or Deary for any harm caused by the arrest. . . .

Woods drafted an agreement in which Rumery agreed to release any claims he might have against the town, its officials, or Deary if Graf agreed to dismiss the criminal charges (the release-dismissal agreement). After Graf approved the form of the agreement, Woods presented it to Rumery. Although Rumery's recollection of the events was quite different, the District Court found that Woods discussed the agreement with Rumery in his office for about an hour and explained to Rumery that he would forgo all civil actions if he signed the agreement. Three days later, on June 6, 1983, Rumery returned to Woods' office and signed the agreement. The criminal charges were dropped.

Ten months later, on April 13, 1984, Rumery filed an action under § 1983 in the Federal District Court for the District of New Hampshire. He alleged that the town and its officers had violated his constitutional rights by arresting him, defaming him, and imprisoning him falsely. The defendants filed a motion to dismiss, relying on the release-dismissal agreement as an affirmative defense. Rumery argued that the agreement was unenforceable because it violated public policy. The court rejected Rumery's argument and concluded that a 'release of claims under section 1983 is valid . . . if it results from a decision that is voluntary, deliberate and informed.' . . . The court then dismissed Rumery's suit.

On appeal, the Court of Appeals for the First Circuit reversed. It adopted a per se rule invalidating release-dismissal agreements."

The Supreme Court granted certiorari to review the case and reversed.

B. Counsel of Record / ACLU Attorney

ACLU Side (Respondent / Appellee): Charles P. Bauer argued the cause for appellee.

Opposing Side (Petitioner / Appellant): Donald E. Gardner argued the cause for appellant.

III. AMICI CURIAE

ACLU Side (Respondent / Appellee)

Brief of amici curiae filed on behalf of the ACLU, et al., by John H. Henn, John Reinstein, and Jack D. Novik.

Opposing Side (Petitioner / Appellant)

Brief of amici curiae filed on behalf of Americans for Effective Law Enforcement, Inc., et al., by Daniel B. Hales, William C. Summers, Jack E. Yelverton, Fred E. Inbau, Wayne W. Schmidt, and James P. Manak.

Brief of amici curiae filed on behalf of the town of Milton, Massachusetts, by Philip M. Cronin.

IV. THE SUPREME COURT'S DECISION

"We agree that some release-dismissal agreements may not be the product of an informed and voluntary decision. The risk, publicity, and expense of a criminal trial may intimidate a defendant, even if he believes his defense is meritorious. But this possibility does not justify invalidating all such agreements. . . . For example, it is well settled that plea bargaining does not violate the Constitution even though a guilty plea waives important constitutional rights. We see no reason to believe that release-dismissal agreements pose a more coercive choice than other situations we have accepted. . . .

Turning to the agreement presented by this case, we conclude that the District Court's decision to enforce the agreement was correct. [I]t is clear that Rumery voluntarily entered the agreement. Moreover, in this case the prosecutor had an independent, legitimate reason to make this agreement directly related to his prosecutorial responsibilities. The agreement foreclosed both the civil and criminal trials concerning Rumery, in which Deary would have been a key witness. She therefore was spared the public scrutiny and embarrassment she would have endured if she had had to testify in either of those cases. Both the prosecutor and the defense attorney testified in the District Court that this was a significant consideration in the prosecutor's decision.

In sum, we conclude that this agreement was voluntary, that there is no evidence of prosecutorial misconduct, and that enforcement of this agreement would not adversely affect the relevant public interests. . . .

We reverse the judgment of the Court of Appeals and remand the case to the District Court for dismissal of the complaint."

V. JUSTICE VOTE

4 Pro ACLU Side vs. 5 Con Opposing Side

ACLU Side (Respondent / Appellee)

1. Stevens, J. – Wrote dissenting opinion
2. Brennan, W. – Joined Stevens' dissent
3. Marshall, T. – Joined Stevens' dissent
4. Blackmun, H. – Joined Stevens' dissent

Opposing Side (Petitioner / Appellant)

1. Powell, L. – Wrote majority opinion
2. Rehnquist, W. – Joined majority opinion
3. White, B. – Joined majority opinion
4. Scalia, A. – Joined majority opinion
5. O'Connor, S. – Wrote concurring opinion

VI. A WIN OR LOSS FOR THE ACLU?

The ACLU, as amicus curiae, urged affirmance of the judgment of the Court of Appeals; the Supreme Court reversed and remanded in a 5-4 vote, giving the ACLU an apparent loss.

609. Immigration & Naturalization Service v. Cardoza-Fonseca

(Decided March 9, 1987; 480 U.S. 421)

I. ISSUE

A. Issues Discussed

Immigration, asylum, statutory construction

B. Legal Question Presented

Whether a refugee seeking asylum is required to show it is "more likely than not" the refugee would be persecuted if returned to his country of origin.

C. Supreme Court's Answer

The refugee does not need to meet this standard to show a "well-founded fear of persecution."

II. CASE SUMMARY

A. Background

"Respondent is a 38–year–old Nicaraguan citizen who entered the United States in 1979 as a visitor. After she remained in the United States longer than permitted, and failed to take advantage of the Immigration and Naturalization Service's (INS) offer of voluntary departure, the INS commenced deportation proceedings against her. Respondent conceded that she was in the country illegally, but requested withholding of deportation pursuant to § 243(h) and asylum as a refugee pursuant to § 208(a). . . .

The Immigration Judge applied the same standard in evaluating respondent's claim for withholding of deportation under § 243(h) as he did in evaluating her application for asylum under § 208(a). He found that she had not established 'a clear probability of persecution' and therefore was not entitled to either form of relief. On appeal, the Board of Immigration Appeals (BIA) agreed that respondent had 'failed to establish that she would suffer persecution within the meaning of section 208(a) or 243(h) of the Immigration and Nationality Act.'

In the Court of Appeals for the Ninth Circuit, respondent did not challenge the BIA's decision that she was not entitled to withholding of deportation under § 243(h), but argued that she was eligible for consideration for asylum under § 208(a), and contended that the Immigration Judge and BIA erred in applying the 'more likely than not' standard of proof from § 243(h) to her § 208(a) asylum claim. Instead, she asserted, they should have applied the 'well-founded fear' standard, which she considered to be more generous. The court agreed. Relying on both the text and the structure of the Act, the court held that the 'well-founded fear' standard which governs asylum proceedings is different, and in fact more generous, than the 'clear probability' standard which governs withholding of deportation proceedings. Agreeing with the Court of Appeals for the Seventh Circuit, the court interpreted the standard to require asylum applicants to present "specific facts' through objective evidence to prove either past persecution or 'good reason' to fear future persecution.' The court remanded respondent's asylum claim to the BIA to evaluate under the proper legal standard."

The Supreme Court granted certiorari to review the case and affirmed.

B. Counsel of Record / ACLU Attorney

ACLU Side (Respondent / Appellee): Dana Marks Keener argued the cause for appellee.

Opposing Side (Petitioner / Appellant): Deputy Solicitor General Wallace argued the cause for appellant.

III. AMICI CURIAE

ACLU Side (Respondent / Appellee)

Brief of amici curiae filed on behalf of the ACLU, et al., by Carol Leslie Wolchok, Burt Neuborne, Lucas Guttentag, Jack Novik, and Robert N. Weiner.

Brief of amici curiae filed on behalf of the United Nations High Commissioner for Refugees by Ralph G. Steinhardt

Brief of amici curiae filed on behalf of the American Immigration

Lawyers Association by Ira J. Kurzban.

Brief of amici curiae filed on behalf of the International Human Rights Law Group, et al., by E. Edward Bruce.

Brief of amici curiae filed on behalf of the Lawyers Committee for Human Rights, et al., by Richard F. Ziegler, Arthur C. Helton, Samuel Rabinove, Richard T. Foltin, Ruti G. Teitel, Steven M. Freeman, and Richard J. Rubin.

Opposing Side (Petitioner / Appellant)

No briefs of amici curiae were filed in support of appellant.

IV. THE SUPREME COURT'S DECISION

"The different emphasis of the two standards which is so clear on the face of the statute is significantly highlighted by the fact that the same Congress simultaneously drafted § 208(a) and amended § 243(h). In doing so, Congress chose to maintain the old standard in § 243(h), but to incorporate a different standard in § 208(a). . . . The question whether Congress intended the two standards to be identical is a pure question of statutory construction for the courts to decide. Employing traditional tools of statutory construction, we have concluded that Congress did not intend the two standards to be identical. . . .

Our analysis of the plain language of the Act, its symmetry with the United Nations Protocol, and its legislative history, lead inexorably to the conclusion that to show a 'well-founded fear of persecution,' an alien need not prove that it is more likely than not that he or she will be persecuted in his or her home country. We find these ordinary canons of statutory construction compelling, even without regard to the longstanding principle of construing any lingering ambiguities in deportation statutes in favor of the alien.

Deportation is always a harsh measure; it is all the more replete with danger when the alien makes a claim that he or she will be subject to death or persecution if forced to return to his or her home country. In enacting the Refugee Act of 1980 Congress sought to 'give the United States sufficient flexibility to respond to situations involving political or religious dissidents and detainees throughout the world.' Our holding today increases that flexibility by rejecting the Government's contention that the Attorney General may not even consider granting asylum to one who fails to satisfy the strict § 243(h) standard. Whether or not a 'refugee' is eventually granted asylum is a matter which Congress has left for the Attorney General to decide. But it is clear that Congress did not intend to restrict eligibility for that relief to those who could prove that it is more likely than not that they will be persecuted if deported.

The judgment of the Court of Appeals is affirmed."

V. JUSTICE VOTE

6 Pro ACLU Side vs. 3 Con Opposing Side

ACLU Side (Respondent / Appellee)

1. Stevens, J. – Wrote majority opinion
2. Brennan, W. – Joined majority opinion
3. O'Connor, S. – Joined majority opinion
4. Marshall, T. – Joined majority opinion
5. Blackmun, H. – Wrote concurring opinion
6. Scalia, A. – Wrote concurring opinion

Opposing Side (Petitioner / Appellant)

1. Powell, L. – Wrote dissenting opinion
2. White, B. – Joined Powell's dissent
3. Rehnquist, W. – Joined Powell's dissent

VI. A WIN OR LOSS FOR THE ACLU?

The ACLU, as amicus curiae, urged affirmance of the judgment of the Ninth Circuit Court of Appeals; the Supreme Court affirmed in a 6-3 vote, giving the ACLU an apparent win.

610. Johnson v. Transportation Agency

(Decided March 25, 1987; 480 U.S. 616)

I. ISSUE

A. Issues Discussed

Gender, civil rights

B. Legal Question Presented

"[W]hether in making [a] promotion the [Transportation Agency of Santa Clara County, California] impermissibly took into account the sex of the applicants in violation of Title VII of the Civil Rights Act of 1964."

C. Supreme Court's Answer

"We . . . hold that the Agency appropriately took into account as one factor the sex of Diane Joyce in determining that she should be promoted . . . . The decision to do so was made pursuant to an affirmative action plan that represents a moderate, flexible, case-by-case approach to effecting a gradual improvement in the representation of minorities and women in the Agency's work force. Such a plan is fully consistent with Title VII . . . ."

II. CASE SUMMARY

A. Background

"Respondent, Transportation Agency of Santa Clara County, California, unilaterally promulgated an Affirmative Action Plan applicable to promotions of employees. In selecting applicants for the promotional position of road dispatcher, the Agency, pursuant to the Plan, passed over petitioner Paul Johnson, a male employee, and promoted a female employee applicant, Diane Joyce. The question for decision is whether in making the promotion the Agency impermissibly took into account the sex of the applicants in violation of Title VII of the Civil Rights Act of 1964. The District Court for the Northern District of California, in an action filed by petitioner following receipt of a right-to-sue letter from the Equal Employment Opportunity Commission (EEOC), held that respondent had violated Title VII. The Court of Appeals for the Ninth Circuit reversed."

The Supreme Court granted certiorari to review the case.

B. Counsel of Record

ACLU Side (Respondent / Appellee): Steven Woodside argued the cause for appellees. With him on the brief for respondent Transportation Agency, Santa Clara County, California, were Ann Miller Ravel, James Rumble, and Morris J. Bailer. David A. Rosenfeld filed a brief for respondent Service Employees International Union Local 715.

Opposing Side (Petitioner / Appellant): Constance E. Brooks argued the cause for appellant. With her on the briefs was James L. Dawson.

III. AMICI CURIAE

ACLU Side (Respondent / Appellee)

Brief of amici curiae filed on behalf of the NOW Legal Defense and Education Fund, National Organization for Women, American Civil Liberties Union, California Women Lawyers, Employment Law Center, Equal Rights Advocates, Federally Employed Women Legal and Education Fund, League of Women Voters of the United States, NAACP Legal Defense and Educational Fund, National Women's Law Center; Northwest Women's Law Center, Women Employed, Women's Equity Action League, Women's Law Project, Women's Legal Defense Fund by Marsha Levick, Claudia Withers, Emily J. Spitzer, and Judith L. Lichtman.

Brief of amici curiae filed on behalf of the State of California et al. by John K. Van de Kamp, Attorney General, Andrea Sheridan Ordin, Chief Assistant Attorney General, Marian M. Johnston, Supervising Deputy Attorney General, Beverly Tucker, Deputy Attorney General, Jim Jones, Attorney General of Idaho, William J. Guste, Jr., Attorney General of Louisiana, Stephen H. Sachs, Attorney General of Maryland, Frank J. Kelley, Attorney General of Michigan, Hubert H. Humphrey III, Attorney General of Minnesota, Robert M. Spire, Attorney General of Nebraska, Robert Abrams, Attorney General of New York, David Frohnmayer, Attorney General of Oregon, Bronson C. La Follette, Attorney General of Wisconsin, and Elisabeth S. Shuster.

Brief of amici curiae filed on behalf of the American Federation of Labor and Congress of Industrial Organizations by David Silberman and Laurence Gold.

Brief of amici curiae filed on behalf of the American Society for Personnel Administration by Lawrence Z. Lorber and J. Robert Kirk.

Brief of amici curiae filed on behalf of the National League of Cities et al. by Cynthia M. Pols, John J. Gunther, Carolyn F. Corwin, Bruce N. Kuhlik, and Frederic Lee Ruck.

Brief of amici curiae filed on behalf of the Equal Employment Advisory Council by Robert E. Williams, Douglas S. McDowell, and Thomas R. Bagby.

Brief of amici curiae filed on behalf of the city of Detroit et al. by Daniel B. Edelman, James R. Murphy, Charles L. Reischel, Frederick N. Merkin, and Robert Cramer.

Brief of amici curiae filed on behalf of the Lawyers' Committee for Civil Rights Under Law et al. by Harold R. Tyler, Jr., James Robertson, Norman Redlich, William L. Robinson, Richard T. Seymour, James D. Crawford, Antonia Hernandez, Grover G. Hankins, and Kenneth Kimerling.

Opposing Side (Petitioner / Appellant)

Brief of amici curiae filed on behalf of the United States by Solicitor General Fried, Assistant Attorney General Reynolds, Deputy Solicitor General Ayer, Deputy Assistant Attorney General Carvin, Roger Clegg, and David K. Flynn.

Brief of amici curiae filed on behalf of the Mid-Atlantic Legal Foundation by Richard B. McGlynn and Douglas Foster.

Brief of amici curiae filed on behalf of the Pacific Legal Foundation et al. by Ronald A. Zumbrun, John H. Findley, and Anthony T. Caso.

IV. THE SUPREME COURT'S DECISION

"As a preliminary matter, we note that petitioner bears the burden of establishing the invalidity of the Agency's Plan. . . .

In reviewing the employment decision at issue in this case, we must first examine whether that decision was made pursuant to a plan prompted by concerns similar to those of the employer in Weber. Next, we must determine whether the effect of the Plan on males and nonminorities is comparable to the effect of the Plan in that case. . . .

Given the obvious imbalance in the Skilled Craft category, and given the Agency's commitment to eliminating such imbalances, it was plainly not unreasonable for the Agency to determine that it was appropriate to consider as one factor the sex of Ms. Joyce in making its decision. The promotion of Joyce thus satisfies the first requirement enunciated in Weber, since it was undertaken to further an affirmative action plan designed to eliminate Agency work force imbalances in traditionally segregated job categories.

We next consider whether the Agency Plan unnecessarily trammeled the rights of male employees or created an absolute bar to their advancement. [T]he Plan sets aside no positions for women. . . .

In evaluating the compliance of an affirmative action plan with Title VII's prohibition on discrimination, we must be mindful of 'this Court's and Congress' consistent emphasis on 'the value of voluntary efforts to further the objectives of the law." The Agency in the case before us has undertaken such a voluntary effort, and has done so in full recognition of both the difficulties and the potential for intrusion on males and nonminorities. . . .

We therefore hold that the Agency appropriately took into account as one factor the sex of Diane Joyce in determining that she should be promoted to the road dispatcher position. The decision to do so was made pursuant to an affirmative action plan that represents a moderate, flexible, case-by-case approach to effecting a gradual improvement in the representation of minorities and women in the Agency's work force. Such a plan is fully consistent with Title VII, for it embodies the contribution that voluntary employer action can make in eliminating the vestiges of discrimination in the workplace. Accordingly, the judgment of the Court of Appeals is affirmed."

V. JUSTICE VOTE

6 Pro ACLU Side vs. 3 Con Opposing Side

ACLU Side (Respondent / Appellee)

1. Brennan, W. – Wrote majority opinion
2. Powell, L. – Joined majority opinion
3. Blackmun, H. – Joined majority opinion
4. Marshall, T. – Joined majority opinion
5. O'Connor, S. – Wrote concurring opinion
6. Stevens, J. – Wrote concurring opinion

Opposing Side (Petitioner / Appellant)

1. Rehnquist, W. – Joined Scalia's dissent
2. White, B. – Wrote dissenting opinion, joined Scalia's dissent in part
3. Scalia, A. – Wrote dissenting opinion

VI. A WIN OR LOSS FOR THE ACLU?

The ACLU filed as amicus curiae urging affirmance; the Supreme Court affirmed the Court of Appeals' decision by a 6-3 vote, giving the ACLU an apparent win.

611. O'Connor v. Ortega

(Decided March 31, 1987; 480 U.S. 709)

I. ISSUE

A. Issues Discussed

Fourth Amendment, search and seizure, right to privacy

B. Legal Question Presented

"First, we must determine whether the respondent, a public employee, had a reasonable expectation of privacy in his office, desk, and file cabinets at his place of work. Second, we must address the appropriate Fourth Amendment standard for a search conducted by a public employer in areas in which a public employee is found to have a reasonable expectation of privacy."

C. Supreme Court's Answer

A public employee has a reasonable expectation of privacy in his desk and file cabinets. The appropriate Fourth Amendment standard in this circumstance is an inquiry to determine reasonableness.

II. CASE SUMMARY

A. Background

"Dr. Magno Ortega, a physician and psychiatrist, held the position of Chief of Professional Education at Napa State Hospital (Hospital) for 17 years, until his dismissal from that position in 1981. . . . In July 1981, Hospital officials . . . became concerned about possible improprieties in Dr. Ortega's management of the residency program. In particular, the Hospital officials were concerned with Dr. Ortega's acquisition of an Apple II computer for use in the residency program. The officials thought that Dr. Ortega may have misled Dr. O'Connor into believing that the computer had been donated, when in fact the computer had been financed by the possibly coerced contributions of residents. Additionally, the Hospital officials were concerned with charges that Dr. Ortega had sexually harassed two female Hospital employees, and had taken inappropriate disciplinary action against a resident. . . .

At some point during the investigation, Mr. Friday made the decision to enter Dr. Ortega's office. The specific reason for the entry into Dr. Ortega's office is unclear from the record. The petitioners claim that the search was conducted to secure state property. Initially, petitioners contended that such a search was pursuant to a Hospital policy of conducting a routine inventory of state property in the office of a terminated employee. At the time of the search, however, the Hospital had not yet terminated Dr. Ortega's employment; Dr. Ortega was still on administrative leave. Apparently, there was no policy of inventorying the offices of those on administrative leave. Before the search had been initiated, however, petitioners had become aware that Dr. Ortega had taken the computer to his home. Dr. Ortega contends that the purpose of the search was to secure evidence for use against him in administrative disciplinary proceedings.

The resulting search of Dr. Ortega's office was quite thorough. The investigators entered the office a number of times and seized several items from Dr. Ortega's desk and file cabinets, including a Valentine's Day card, a photograph, and a book of poetry all sent to Dr. Ortega by a former resident physician. These items were later used in a proceeding before a hearing officer of the California State Personnel Board to impeach the credibility of the former resident, who testified on Dr. Ortega's behalf. The investigators also seized billing documentation of one of Dr. Ortega's private patients under the California Medicaid program. The investigators did not otherwise separate Dr. Ortega's property from state property because, as one investigator testified, '[t]rying to sort State from non-State, it was too much to do, so I gave it up and boxed it up.' Thus, no formal inventory of the property in the office was ever made. Instead, all the papers in Dr. Ortega's office were merely placed in boxes, and put in storage for Dr. Ortega to retrieve.

Dr. Ortega commenced this action against petitioners in Federal District Court under 42 U.S.C. § 1983, alleging that the search of his office violated the Fourth Amendment. On cross-motions for summary judgment, the District Court granted petitioners' motion for summary judgment. The District Court . . . concluded that the search was proper because there was a need to secure state property in the office. The Court of Appeals for the Ninth Circuit affirmed in part and reversed in part, concluding that Dr. Ortega had a reasonable expectation of privacy in his office. While the Hospital had a procedure for office inventories, these inventories were reserved for employees who were departing or were terminated. The Court of Appeals also concluded—albeit without explanation—that the search violated the Fourth Amendment. The Court of Appeals held that the record justified a grant of partial summary judgment for Dr. Ortega on the issue of liability for an unlawful search, and it remanded the case to the District Court for a determination of damages."

The Supreme Court granted certiorari to review the case and reversed.

B. Counsel of Record / ACLU Attorney

ACLU Side (Respondent / Appellee): Joel I. Klein, by invitation of the Court, argued the cause and filed a brief as amicus curiae in support of the judgment below. Magno J. Ortega, pro se, filed a brief as appellee.

Opposing Side (Petitioner / Appellant): Jeffrey T. Miller argued the cause for appellant.

III. AMICI CURIAE

ACLU Side (Respondent / Appellee)

Brief of amici curiae filed on behalf of the ACLU, et al., by Peter W. Morgan, Jack Novik, Burt Neuborne, and Michael Simpson.

Brief of amici curiae filed on behalf of the American Federation of State, County, and Municipal Employees, AFL-CIO, by Richard Kirschner.

Opposing Side (Petitioner / Appellant)

Brief of amici curiae filed on behalf of the United States by Solicitor General Fried, Assistant Attorney General Willard, Deputy Solicitor General Geller, Alan I. Horowitz, Barbara L. Herwig, and John P. Schnitker.

IV. THE SUPREME COURT'S DECISION

"The Fourth Amendment protects the 'right of the people to be secure in their persons, houses, papers, and effects, against unreasonable searches and seizures . . . .' Our cases establish that Dr. Ortega's Fourth Amendment rights are implicated only if the conduct of the Hospital officials at issue in this case infringed 'an expectation of privacy that society is prepared to consider reasonable.' . . .

Within the workplace context, this Court has recognized that employees may have a reasonable expectation of privacy against intrusions by police. As with the expectation of privacy in one's home, such an expectation in one's place of work is 'based upon societal expectations that have deep roots in the history of the Amendment.'

[W]e recognize that the undisputed evidence suggests that Dr. Ortega had a reasonable expectation of privacy in his desk and file cabinets. . . .

In the case of searches conducted by a public employer, we must balance the invasion of the employees' legitimate expectations of privacy against the government's need for supervision, control, and the efficient operation of the workplace.

[W]e conclude that the 'special needs, beyond the normal need for law enforcement make the . . . probable cause requirement impracticable,' for legitimate work-related, noninvestigatory intrusions as well as investigations of work-related misconduct. . . . We hold, therefore, that public employer intrusions on the constitutionally protected privacy interests of government employees for noninvestigatory, work-related purposes, as well as for investigations of work-related misconduct, should be judged by the standard of reasonableness under all the circumstances. Under this reasonableness standard, both the inception and the scope of the intrusion must be reasonable: 'Determining the reasonableness of any search involves a twofold inquiry: first, one must consider 'whether the . . . action was justified at its inception,' second, one must determine whether the search as actually conducted 'was reasonably related in scope to the circumstances which justified the interference in the first place." . . .

On remand, . . . the District Court must determine the justification for the search and seizure, and evaluate the reasonableness of both the inception of the search and its scope.

Accordingly, the judgment of the Court of Appeals is reversed, and the case is remanded to that court for further proceedings consistent with this opinion."

V. JUSTICE VOTE

4 Pro ACLU Side vs. 5 Con Opposing Side

ACLU Side (Respondent / Appellee)

1. Blackmun, H. – Wrote dissenting opinion
2. Brennan, W. – Joined Blackmun's dissent
3. Marshall, T. – Joined Blackmun's dissent
4. Stevens, J. – Joined Blackmun's dissent

Opposing Side (Petitioner / Appellant)

1. O'Connor, S. – Wrote majority opinion
2. Rehnquist, W. – Joined majority opinion

3. White, B. – Joined majority opinion
4. Powell, L. – Joined majority opinion
5. Scalia, A. – Wrote concurring opinion

VI. A WIN OR LOSS FOR THE ACLU?

The ACLU, as amicus curiae, urged affirmance of the judgment of the Court of Appeals; the Supreme Court reversed and remanded in a 5-4 vote, giving the ACLU an apparent loss.

612. Corp. for the Presiding Bishop of the Church of Jesus Christ of Latter-Day Saints v. Amos

(Decided March 31, 1987; 483 U.S. 327)

I. ISSUE

A. Issues Discussed

Civil rights, federal, 1st Amendment, religion

B. Legal Question Presented

"Section 702 of the Civil Rights Act of 1964 exempts religious organizations from Title VII's prohibition against discrimination in employment on the basis of religion. The question presented is whether applying the § 702 exemption to the secular nonprofit activities of religious organizations violates the Establishment Clause of the First Amendment."

C. Supreme Court's Answer

Applying the § 702 exemption does not violate the Establishment Clause.

II. CASE SUMMARY

A. Background

"The Deseret Gymnasium (Gymnasium) in Salt Lake City, Utah, is a nonprofit facility, open to the public, run by the Corporation of the Presiding Bishop of The Church of Jesus Christ of Latter-day Saints (CPB), and the Corporation of the President of The Church of Jesus Christ of Latter-day Saints (COP). The CPB and the COP are religious entities associated with The Church of Jesus Christ of Latter-day Saints (Church), an unincorporated religious association sometimes called the Mormon or LDS Church.

Appellee Mayson worked at the Gymnasium for some 16 years as an assistant building engineer and then as building engineer. He was discharged in 1981 because he failed to qualify for a temple recommend, that is, a certificate that he is a member of the Church and eligible to attend its temples.

Mayson and others purporting to represent a class of plaintiffs brought an action against the CPB and the COP alleging, among other things, discrimination on the basis of religion in violation of § 703 of the Civil Rights Act of 1964. . . .

The court concluded that Mayson's case involves nonreligious activity. . . .

Finding that § 702 impermissibly sponsors religious organizations by granting them 'an exclusive authorization to engage in conduct which can directly and immediately advance religious tenets and practices,' the court declared the statute unconstitutional as applied to secular activity. The court entered summary judgment in favor of Mayson . . . . After further briefing and argument the court affirmed its prior determination . . . ."

The Supreme Court granted certiorari to review the case.

B. Counsel of Record

ACLU Side (Respondent / Appellee): David B. Watkiss of the American Civil Liberties Union, Utah Chapter, argued the cause for appellees in both cases. With him on the brief were John E. Harvey, Elizabeth T. Dunning of the ACLU, Utah Chapter, and John A. Powell and Joan E. Bertin of the ACLU Foundation.

Opposing Side (Petitioner / Appellant): Rex E. Lee argued the cause for appellants in No. 86-179. With him on the briefs were Wilford W. Kirton, Jr., Dan S. Bushnell, M. Karlynn Hinman, Benjamin W. Heineman, Jr., Carter G. Phillips, and Ronald S. Flagg. Assistant Attorney General Reynolds argued the cause for the United States in No. 86-401. With him on the briefs were Solicitor General Fried, Deputy Solicitor General Ayer, Deputy Assistant Attorney General Carvin, and Andrew J. Pincus.

III. AMICI CURIAE

ACLU Side (Respondent / Appellee)

Brief of amici curiae filed on behalf of the American Federation of Labor and Congress of Industrial Organizations et al. by Michael H. Gottesman, Robert M. Weinberg, David M. Silberman, and Laurence Gold.

Brief of amici curiae filed on behalf of the Anti-Defamation League of B'nai B'rith by Harold P. Weinberger, Justin J. Finger, Jeffrey P. Sinensky, Jill L. Kahn, Ruti G. Tietel, and Meyer Eisenberg.

Brief of amici curiae filed on behalf of the Employment Law Center of the Legal Aid Society of San Francisco by Joan M. Graff, Robert Barnes, and Robert E. Borton.

Brief of amici curiae filed on behalf of the Women's Legal Defense Fund et al. by Donna Lenhof.

Opposing Side (Petitioner / Appellant)

Brief of amici curiae filed on behalf of the American Association of Presidents of Independent Colleges and Universities et al. by Edward McGlynn Gaffney, Jr.

Brief of amici curiae filed on behalf of the American Jewish Congress by Marc D. Stern and Amy Adelson.

Brief of amici curiae filed on behalf of the Baptist Joint Committee on Public Affairs by Donald R. Brewer and Oliver S. Thomas.

Brief of amici curiae filed on behalf of the Catholic League for Religious and Civil Rights by Steven Frederick McDowell.

Brief of amici curiae filed on behalf of the Christian Legal Society et al. by Michael W. McConnell, Michael J. Woodruff, Samuel E. Ericsson, Kimberlee W. Colby, Philip E. Draheim, and Forest D. Montgomery

Brief of amici curiae filed on behalf of the General Conference of Seventh-day Adventists by Warren L. Johns, Walter E. Carson, and Melvin B. Sabey.

Brief of amici curiae filed on behalf of the National Jewish

Commission on Law and Public Affairs by Nathan Lewin and Dennis Rapps.

Brief of amici curiae filed on behalf of the United States Catholic Conference by John A. Liekweg and Mark E. Chopko.

Brief of amici curiae filed on behalf of the Council on Religious Freedom by Lee Boothby, James M. Parker, Robert W. Nixon, and Rolland Truman.

Brief of amici curiae filed on behalf of Concerned Women of America by Jordan W. Lorence.

IV. THE SUPREME COURT'S DECISION

"'This Court has long recognized that the government may (and sometimes must) accommodate religious practices and that it may do so without violating the Establishment Clause.' . . . At some point, accommodation may devolve into 'an unlawful fostering of religion,' but these are not such cases, in our view.

The private appellants contend that we should not apply the three-part Lemon approach, which is assertedly unsuited to judging the constitutionality of exemption statutes such as § 702. [W]e need not reexamine Lemon as applied in this context, for the exemption involved here is in no way questionable under the Lemon analysis.

Lemon requires first that the law at issue serve a 'secular legislative purpose.' . . .

We agree with the District Court that this purpose does not violate the Establishment Clause.

The second requirement under Lemon is that the law in question have 'a principal or primary effect . . . that neither advances nor inhibits religion.' . . .

[I]t suffices to hold—as we now do—that as applied to the nonprofit activities of religious employers, § 702 is rationally related to the legitimate purpose of alleviating significant governmental interference with the ability of religious organizations to define and carry out their religious missions.

It cannot be seriously contended that § 702 impermissibly entangles church and state; the statute effectuates a more complete separation of the two and avoids the kind of intrusive inquiry into religious belief that the District Court engaged in in this case. The statute easily passes muster under the third part of the Lemon test.

The judgment of the District Court is reversed, and the cases are remanded . . . ."

V. JUSTICE VOTE

0 Pro ACLU Side vs. 9 Con Opposing Side

Opposing Side (Petitioner / Appellant)

1. White, B. – Wrote majority opinion
2. Rehnquist, W. – Joined majority opinion
3. Powell, L. – Joined majority opinion
4. Stevens, J. – Joined majority opinion
5. Scalia, A. – Joined majority opinion
6. Brennan, W. – Wrote concurring opinion
7. Marshall, T. – Joined Brennan's concurrence
8. Blackmun, H. – Wrote concurring opinion
9. O'Connor, S. – Wrote concurring opinion

VI. A WIN OR LOSS FOR THE ACLU?

The ACLU served as counsel for appellee urging affirmance; the Supreme Court reversed the Court of Appeals' decision by a 9-0 vote, giving the ACLU an apparent loss.

613. Arkansas Writers' Project, Inc. v. Ragland

(Decided April 22, 1987; 481 U.S. 221)

I. ISSUE

A. Issues Discussed

First Amendment, freedoms of speech and of the press

B. Legal Question Presented

"[W]hether a state sales tax scheme that taxes general interest magazines, but exempts newspapers and religious, professional, trade, and sports journals, violates the First Amendment's guarantee of freedom of the press."

C. Supreme Court's Answer

The sales tax scheme violates the First Amendment.

II. CASE SUMMARY

A. Background

"Since 1935, Arkansas has imposed a tax on receipts from sales of tangible personal property. . . . Numerous items are exempt from the state sales tax, however. These include '[g]ross receipts or gross proceeds derived from the sale of newspapers,' and 'religious, professional, trade and sports journals and/or publications printed and published within this State . . . when sold through regular subscriptions.

Appellant Arkansas Writers' Project, Inc. publishes Arkansas Times, a general interest monthly magazine with a circulation of approximately 28,000. The magazine includes articles on a variety of subjects, including religion and sports. It is printed and published in Arkansas, and is sold through mail subscriptions, coin-operated stands, and over-the-counter sales. In 1980, following an audit, appellee Commissioner of Revenue assessed tax on sales of Arkansas Times. Appellant initially contested the assessment, but eventually reached a settlement with the State and agreed to pay the tax beginning in October 1982. However, appellant reserved the right to renew its challenge if there were a change in the tax law or a court ruling drawing into question the validity of Arkansas' exemption structure.

Subsequently, in Minneapolis Star & Tribune Co. v. Minnesota Comm'r of Revenue, 460 U.S. 575 (1983), this Court held unconstitutional a Minnesota tax on paper and ink used in the production of newspapers. In January 1984, relying on this authority, appellant sought a refund of sales tax paid since October 1982, asserting that the magazine exemption must be construed to include Arkansas Times. It maintained that subjecting Arkansas Times to the sales tax, while sales of newspapers and other magazines were exempt, violated the First and Fourteenth Amendments. The Commissioner denied appellant's claim for refund.

Having exhausted available administrative remedies, appellant filed a complaint in the Chancery Court for Pulaski County, Arkansas, seeking review of the Commissioner's decision. The complaint also stated a claim under 42 U.S.C. §§ 1983 and 1988 for injunctive relief and attorney's fees. The parties stipulated that Arkansas Times is not a 'newspaper' or a 'religious, professional, trade or sports Journal' and that, during the relevant time period, appellant had paid $15,838.22 in sales tax. The Chancery Court granted appellant summary judgment, construing § 84-1904(j) to create two categories of tax-exempt magazines sold through subscriptions, one for religious, professional, trade, and sports journals, and one for publications published and printed within the State of Arkansas. Because Arkansas Times came within the second category, the court held that the magazine was exempt from sales tax and appellant was entitled to a refund. The court determined that resolution of the dispute on statutory grounds made it unnecessary to address the constitutional issues raised in appellant's § 1983 claim.

The Arkansas Supreme Court reversed the decision of the Chancery Court. It construed § 84-1904(j) as creating a single exemption and held that, in order to qualify for this exemption, a magazine had to be a 'religious, professional, trade, or sports periodical.' Concluding that 'neither party has questioned the constitutionality of the exemption,' the State Supreme Court failed to address appellant's First and Fourteenth Amendment claims.

On petition for rehearing, the court issued a supplementary opinion in which it acknowledged that appellant had pursued its constitutional claims and that they 'should have been discussed' in the court's original opinion. It rejected appellant's claims of discriminatory treatment, reasoning that exemptions granted to other publications need not be considered, because: '[I]t would avail [appellant] nothing if it wins its argument . . . . It is immaterial that an exemption in favor of some other taxpayer may be invalid, as discriminatory. If so, it is the exemption that would fall, not the tax against the [Arkansas] Times.'

As to appellant's First Amendment objections, the court noted that this Court has held that 'the owners of newspapers are not immune from any of the 'ordinary forms of taxation' for support of the government.' In contrast to Minneapolis Star, supra, and Grosjean, supra, the Arkansas Supreme Court concluded that the Arkansas sales tax was a permissible 'ordinary form of taxation.'"

The Supreme Court granted certiorari to review the case and reversed.

B. Counsel of Record / ACLU Attorney

ACLU Side (Petitioner / Appellant): Anne Owings Wilson argued the cause for appellant.

Opposing Side (Respondent / Appellee): John Steven Clark argued the cause for appellee.

III. AMICI CURIAE

ACLU Side (Petitioner / Appellant)

Brief of amici curiae filed on behalf of the ACLU Foundation, et al., by Jack

Novik and Philip E. Kaplan.

Brief of amici curiae filed on behalf of the City & Regional Magazine Association by Donald M. Middlebrooks.

Brief of amici curiae filed on behalf of the Magazine Publishers Co., et al., by Edward Soto, Gerald B. Cope, Jr., W. Terry Maguire, and Parker Thomson.

Brief of amici curiae filed on behalf of Time Inc., by E. Barrett Prettyman, Jr., David J. Saylor, and John

G. Roberts, Jr.

Brief of amici curiae filed on behalf of the Times Mirror Co. et al. by Rex S.

Heinke, William A. Niese, and Jeffrey S. Klein.

Opposing Side (Respondent / Appellee)

Brief of amici curiae filed on behalf of the Territory of American Samoa, et al., by the Attorneys General for their respective jurisdictions as follows: Thomas J. Miller of Iowa, Leulumoega S. Lutu of American Samoa, Joseph Liberman of Connecticut, Jim Smith of Florida, Corinne K. A. Watanabe of Hawaii, Jim Jones of Idaho, William J. Guste, Jr., of Louisiana, Hubert H. Humphrey III of Minnesota, Michael Turpen of Oklahoma, LeRoy S. Zimmerman of Pennsylvania, T. Travis Medlock of South Carolina, Mark V. Meierhenry of South Dakota, Jim Mattox of Texas, David L. Wilkinson of Utah, and Jeffrey L. Amestoy of Vermont.

Brief of amici curiae filed on behalf of the State of Maryland by Stephen H. Sachs, Attorney General, Ralph S. Tyler III, Assistant Attorney General, and Carmen M. Shepard, Special Assistant Attorney General.

IV. THE SUPREME COURT'S DECISION

"Our cases clearly establish that a discriminatory tax on the press burdens rights protected by the First Amendment. . . . Arkansas faces a heavy burden in attempting to defend its content-based approach to taxation of magazines. In order to justify such differential taxation, the State must show that is regulation is necessary to serve a compelling state interest and is narrowly drawn to achieve that end. . . .

Because we hold today that the State's selective application of its sales tax to magazines is unconstitutional and therefore invalid, our ruling eliminates the differential treatment of newspapers and magazines. Accordingly, we need not decide whether a distinction between different types of periodicals presents an additional basis for invalidating the sales tax, as applied to the press. . . .

In the Chancery Court, appellant asserted its First and Fourteenth Amendment claims under 42 U.S.C. § 1983, as well as a corresponding entitlement to attorney's fees under § 1988. Because this Court has found a constitutional violation, appellant urges us to consider its cause of action under § 1983 and order an award of attorney's fees. However, the state courts have not yet indicated whether they will exercise jurisdiction over this claim and we therefore remand to give them an opportunity to do so. . . .

We stated in Minneapolis Star that '[a] tax that singles out the press, or that targets individual publications within the press, places a heavy burden on the State to justify its action.' In this case, Arkansas has failed to meet this heavy burden. It has advanced no compelling justification for selective, content-based taxation of certain magazines, and the tax is therefore invalid under the First Amendment. Accordingly, we reverse the judgment of the Arkansas Supreme Court and remand for proceedings not inconsistent with this opinion."

V. JUSTICE VOTE

7 Pro ACLU Side vs. 2 Con Opposing Side

ACLU Side (Petitioner / Appellant)

1. Marshall, T. – Wrote majority opinion
2. Brennan, W. – Joined majority opinion
3. White, B. – Joined majority opinion
4. Blackmun, H. – Joined majority opinion
5. Powell, L. – Joined majority opinion
6. O'Connor, S. – Joined majority opinion
7. Stevens, J. – Wrote concurring opinion

Opposing Side (Respondent / Appellee)

1. Scalia, A. – Wrote dissenting opinion
2. Rehnquist, W. – Joined Scalia's dissent

VI. A WIN OR LOSS FOR THE ACLU?

The ACLU, as amicus curiae, urged reversal of the judgment of the Arkansas Supreme Court; the U.S. Supreme Court reversed and remanded in a 7-2 vote, giving the ACLU an apparent win.

614. Meese v. Keene

(Decided April 28, 1987; 481 U.S. 465)

I. ISSUE

A. Issues Discussed

First Amendment, freedom of speech

B. Legal Question Presented

Whether "Congress violated the First Amendment by using the term 'political propaganda' as the statutory name for [a] regulated category of expression."

C. Supreme Court's Answer

Congress did not violate the First Amendment by labeling a regulated category of expression "political propaganda."

II. CASE SUMMARY

A. Background

"The Foreign Agents Registration Act . . . uses the term 'political propaganda,' as defined in the Act, to identify those expressive materials that must comply with the Act's registration, filing, and disclosure requirements. . . .

Appellee, an attorney and a member of the California State Senate, does not want the Department of Justice and the public to regard him as the disseminator of foreign political propaganda, but wishes to exhibit three Canadian motion picture films that have been so identified. The films, distributed by the NFBC, deal with the subjects of nuclear war and acid rain. Appellee brought suit in the Federal District Court for the Eastern District of California on March 24, 1983, to enjoin the application of the Act to these three films. On May 23, 1983, the District Court denied appellants' motion to dismiss and granted appellee's motion for a preliminary injunction. The injunction prohibited appellants from designating the films as 'political propaganda' and from subjecting them to the labeling and reporting requirements of the Act. . . .

On September 12, 1985, the District Court granted summary judgment for appellee and a permanent injunction against enforcement of any portion of the Act which incorporates the term 'political propaganda.' The District Court opined that the term 'propaganda' is a semantically slanted word of reprobation; that the use of such a denigrating term renders the regulated materials unavailable to American citizens who wish to use them as a means of personal expression; and that since there was no compelling state interest to justify the use of such a pejorative label, it was an unnecessary, and therefore invalid, abridgment of speech. The court amended its judgment on October 29, 1985, limiting the permanent injunction against enforcement of the Act to the three films at issue in this case."

The Supreme Court granted certiorari to review the case and reversed.

B. Counsel of Record / ACLU Attorney

ACLU Side (Respondent / Appellee): John G. Donhoff, Jr., argued the cause for appellee.

Opposing Side (Petitioner / Appellant): Deputy Solicitor General Ayer argued the cause for the United States.

III. AMICI CURIAE

ACLU Side (Respondent / Appellee)

Brief of amici curiae filed on behalf of the ACLU, et al., by Daniel Marcus, Susan W. Shaffer, Charles S. Sims, Robert Abrams, Attorney General of New York, O. Peter Sherwood, Solicitor General, Lawrence S. Kahn, Deputy Solicitor General, and Sanford M. Cohen, Assistant Attorney General.

Brief of amici curiae filed on behalf of the Freedom to Read Foundation by Robert Steven Chapman.

Brief of amici curiae filed on behalf of Playboy Enterprises, Inc., et al., by Bruce J. Ennis, Jr., Burton Joseph, and Maxwell J. Lillienstein.

Opposing Side (Petitioner / Appellant)

Brief of amici curiae filed on behalf of the Washington Legal Foundation, et al., by Daniel J. Popeo and George C. Smith.

IV. THE SUPREME COURT'S DECISION

"According to the District Court, the denigration of speech to which the label 'political propaganda' has been attached constitutes 'a conscious attempt to place a whole category of materials beyond the pale of legitimate discourse,' and is therefore an unconstitutional abridgment of that speech. We find this argument unpersuasive, indeed, untenable, for three reasons.

First, the term 'political propaganda' does nothing to place regulated expressive materials 'beyond the pale of legitimate discourse.' . . .

Second, the reasoning of the District Court is contradicted by history. The statutory definition of 'political propaganda' has been on the books for over four decades. We should presume that the people who have a sufficient understanding of the law to know that the term 'political propaganda' is used to describe the regulated category also know that the definition is a broad, neutral one rather than a pejorative one. Given this long history, it seems obvious that if the fear of misunderstanding had actually interfered with the exhibition of a significant number of foreign-made films, that effect would be disclosed in the record. . . .

Third, Congress' use of the term 'political propaganda' does not lead us to suspend the respect we normally owe to the Legislature's power to define the terms that it uses in legislation. We have no occasion here to decide the permissible scope of Congress' 'right to speak'; we simply view this particular choice of language, statutorily defined in a neutral and evenhanded manner, as one that no constitutional provision prohibits the Congress from making. . . .

The judgment of the District Court is reversed, and the case is remanded for further proceedings consistent with this opinion."

V. JUSTICE VOTE

3 Pro ACLU Side vs. 5 Con Opposing Side

ACLU Side (Respondent / Appellee)

1. Blackmun, H. – Wrote dissenting opinion
2. Brennan, W. – Joined dissenting opinion
3. Marshall, T. – Joined dissenting opinion

Opposing Side (Petitioner / Appellant)

1. Stevens, J. – Wrote majority opinion
2. Rehnquist, W. – Joined majority opinion
3. White, B. – Joined majority opinion
4. Powell, L. – Joined majority opinion
5. O'Connor, S. – Joined majority opinion

Scalia, A – Took no part in the decision

VI. A WIN OR LOSS FOR THE ACLU?

The ACLU, as amicus curiae, urged affirmance of the judgment of the District Court; the Supreme Court reversed in a 5-3 vote, giving the ACLU an apparent loss.

615. Pope v. Illinois

(Decided May 4, 1987; 481 U.S. 497)

I. ISSUE

A. Issues Discussed

First Amendment, obscenity, Fourteenth Amendment

B. Legal Question Presented

"[W]hether, in a prosecution for the sale of allegedly obscene materials, the jury may be instructed to apply community standards in deciding the value question" of "whether the work, taken as a whole, lacks serious literary, artistic, political, or scientific value" when applying the Miller test for obscenity.

C. Supreme Court's Answer

The jury should apply a reasonable person standard, not a community standard.

II. CASE SUMMARY

A. Background

"On July 21, 1983, Rockford, Illinois, police detectives purchased certain magazines from the two petitioners, each of whom was an attendant at an adult bookstore. Petitioners were subsequently charged separately with the offense of 'obscenity' for the sale of these magazines. Each petitioner moved to dismiss the charges against him on the ground that the then-current version of the Illinois obscenity statute, Ill.Rev.Stat., ch. 38, ¶ 11–20 (1983), violated the First and Fourteenth Amendments to the United States Constitution. Both petitioners argued, among other things, that the statute was unconstitutional in failing to require that the value question be judged 'solely on an objective basis as opposed to reference [sic] to contemporary community standards.' Both trial courts rejected this contention and instructed the respective juries to judge whether the material was obscene by determining how it would be viewed by ordinary adults in the whole State of Illinois. Both petitioners were found guilty, and both appealed to the Illinois Appellate Court, Second District. That court also rejected petitioners' contention that the issue of value must be determined on an objective basis and not by reference to contemporary community standards. The Illinois Supreme Court denied review . . . ."

The Supreme Court granted certiorari to review the case, vacated, and remanded.

B. Counsel of Record / ACLU Attorney

ACLU Side (Petitioner / Appellant): Glenn A. Stanko argued the cause for appellant.

Opposing Side (Respondent / Appellee): Sally Louise Dilgart, Assistant Attorney General of Illinois, argued the cause for appellee.

III. AMICI CURIAE

ACLU Side (Petitioner / Appellant)

Brief of amici curiae filed on behalf of the ACLU, et al., by Bruce J. Ennis, Jr., David W. Ogden, Harvey Grossman, Jane M. Whicher, Jack Novik, and David Goldstein.

Briefs of amici curiae filed on behalf of the American Booksellers Association, Inc., et al., by Michael A. Bamberger, R. Bruce Rich, Roger L. Funk, and Maxwell J. Lillienstein.

Brief of amici curiae filed on behalf of Volunteer Lawyers for the Arts, Inc. by Irwin Karp and I. Fred Koenigsberg.

Opposing Side (Respondent / Appellee)

Brief of amici curiae filed on behalf of the city of Santa Ana, California by Edward Cooper and James J. Clancy.

IV. THE SUPREME COURT'S DECISION

"In Miller itself, the Court was careful to point out that '[t]he First Amendment protects works which, taken as a whole, have serious literary, artistic, political, or scientific value, regardless of whether the government or a majority of the people approve of the ideas these works represent.' Just as the ideas a work represents need not obtain majority approval to merit protection, neither, insofar as the First Amendment is concerned, does the value of the work vary from community to community based on the degree of local acceptance it has won. The proper inquiry is not whether an ordinary member of any given community would find serious literary, artistic, political, or scientific value in allegedly obscene material, but whether a reasonable person would find such value in the material, taken as a whole. The instruction at issue in this case was therefore unconstitutional. [I]n the present cases the jurors were not precluded from considering the question of value: they were informed that, to convict, they must find, among other things, that the magazines petitioners sold were utterly without redeeming social value. While it was error to instruct the juries to use a state community standard in considering the value question, if a reviewing court concludes that no rational juror, if properly instructed, could find value in the magazines, the convictions should stand.

Although we plainly have the authority to decide whether, on the facts of a given case, a constitutional error was harmless under the standard of Chapman v. California, we do so sparingly. In this case, the Illinois Appellate Court has not considered the harmless error issue. We therefore vacate its judgment and remand so that it may do so."

V. JUSTICE VOTE

5 Pro ACLU Side vs. 4 Con Opposing Side

ACLU Side (Petitioner / Appellant)

1. White, B. – Wrote majority opinion
2. Rehnquist, W. – Joined majority opinion
3. Powell, L. – Joined majority opinion
4. O'Connor, S. – Joined majority opinion
5. Scalia, A. – Wrote concurring opinion

Opposing Side (Respondent / Appellee)

1. Brennan, W. – Wrote dissenting opinion, joined Stevens' dissent, in part
2. Stevens, J. – Wrote dissenting opinion
3. Marshall, T. – Joined Stevens' dissent
4. Blackmun, H. – Wrote opinion concurring in part and dissenting in part, joined Stevens' dissent, in part

VI. A WIN OR LOSS FOR THE ACLU?

The ACLU filed as amicus curiae urging reversal of the judgment of the Illinois Appellate Court; the Supreme Court vacated in a 5-4 vote, giving the ACLU an apparent win.

616. Board of Directors of Rotary Int'l v. Rotary Club of Duarte

(Decided May 4, 1987; 481 U.S. 537)

I. ISSUE

A. Issues Discussed

Gender, First Amendment, press, speech, association

B. Legal Question Presented

"[W]hether a California statute that requires California Rotary Clubs to admit women members violates the First Amendment."

C. Supreme Court's Answer

"We . . . hold that application of the Unruh Act to California Rotary Clubs does not violate the right of expressive association afforded by the First Amendment."

II. CASE SUMMARY

A. Background

"Rotary International (International) is a nonprofit corporation . . . . Individual members belong to a local Rotary Club rather than to International. . . .

Individuals are admitted to membership in a Rotary Club according to a 'classification system.' The purpose of this system is to ensure 'that each Rotary Club includes a representative of every worthy and recognized business, professional, or institutional activity in the community.' . . . There is no limit to the number of clergymen, journalists, or diplomats who may be admitted to membership.

Subject to these requirements, each local Rotary Club is free to adopt its own rules and procedures for admitting new members. . . .

Membership in Rotary Clubs is open only to men. . . . Although women are not admitted to membership, they are permitted to attend meetings, give speeches, and receive awards. . . .

In 1977 the Rotary Club of Duarte, California, admitted Donna Bogart, Mary Lou Elliott, and Rosemary Freitag to active membership. International notified the Duarte Club that admitting women members is contrary to the Rotary constitution. After an internal hearing, International's board of directors revoked the charter of the Duarte Club and terminated its membership in Rotary International. The Duarte Club's appeal to the International Convention was unsuccessful.

The Duarte Club and two of its women members filed a complaint in the California Superior Court for the County of Los Angeles. [T]he court entered judgment for International.

The California Court of Appeal reversed."

The Supreme Court granted certiorari to review the case.

B. Counsel of Record

ACLU Side (Respondent / Appellee): Judith Resnik argued the cause for appellees. With her on the brief were Carol Agate, Sanford K. Smith, Blanche C. Bersch, Paul Hoffman, and Fred Okrand.

Marian M. Johnston argued the cause for intervenor State of California. With her on the brief were John K. Van de Kamp, Attorney General, Andrea Sheridan Ordin, Chief Assistant Attorney General, and Beverly Tucker, Deputy Attorney General.

Opposing Side (Petitioner / Appellant): William P. Sutter argued the cause for appellants. With him on the briefs were Peter F. Lovato III and Wm. John Kennedy.

III. AMICI CURIAE

ACLU Side (Respondent / Appellee)

Brief of amici curiae filed on behalf of the Kiwanis Club of Ridgewood, Inc. and Julie Fletcher by Marcia K. Baer and Julie Fletcher on behalf of American Civil Liberties Union of New Jersey.

Brief of amici curiae filed on behalf of the State of Minnesota et al. by Hubert H. Humphrey III, Attorney General of Minnesota, Richard S. Slowes, Assistant Solicitor General, and Peter M. Ackerberg, Special Assistant Attorney General, and for the Attorneys General for their respective States as follows: Joseph I. Lieberman of Connecticut, Neil F. Hartigan of Illinois, William J. Guste of Louisiana, W. Cary Edwards of New Jersey, Anthony J. Celebrezze, Jr., of Ohio, Dave Frohnmayer of Oregon, Jim Mattox of Texas, David L. Wilkinson of Utah, and Donald S. Hanaway of Wisconsin.

Brief of amici curiae filed on behalf of the city of New York et al. by Doron Gopstein and Leonard Koerner.

Brief of amici curiae filed on behalf of the American Jewish Congress et al. by Marc D. Stern.

Brief of amici curiae filed on behalf of the Anti-defamation League of B'nai B'rith by Abigail T. Kelman, Justin J. Finger, Jeffrey P. Sinensky, Steven M. Freeman, and Meyer Eisenberg.

Brief of amici curiae filed on behalf of California Women Lawyers et al. by Lorraine L. Loder and Fredric D. Woocher.

Brief of amici curiae filed on behalf of the Lloyd Lyons Club by Maria J. McGeorge and Allen T. Murphy, Jr.

Brief of amici curiae filed on behalf of the Rotary Club of Seattle et al. by M. Margaret McKeown and Eugene C. Chellis.

Brief of amici curiae filed on behalf of the Employment Law Center of the Legal Aid Society of San Francisco by Joan M. Graff and Douglas R. Young.

Opposing Side (Petitioner / Appellant)

Brief of amici curiae filed on behalf of the Boy Scouts of America by Ronald C. Redcay, George A. Davidson, and David K. Park.

Brief of amici curiae filed on behalf of the Conference of Private Organizations by Thomas P. Ondeck.

Brief of amici curiae filed on behalf of the Legal Foundation of America by Jean F. Powers and David Crump.

Brief of amici curiae filed on behalf of Pilot Club International et al. by Stephen G. Seliger.

IV. THE SUPREME COURT'S DECISION

"In *Roberts v. United States Jaycees,* we upheld against First Amendment challenge a Minnesota statute that required the Jaycees to admit women as full voting members. *Roberts* provides the framework for analyzing appellants' constitutional claims. As we observed in *Roberts,* our cases have afforded constitutional protection to freedom of association in two distinct senses. First, the Court has held that the Constitution protects against unjustified government interference with an individual's choice to enter into and maintain certain intimate or private relationships. Second, the Court has upheld the freedom of individuals to associate for the purpose of engaging in protected speech or religious activities. In many cases, government interference with one form of protected association will also burden the other form of association. In *Roberts* we determined the nature and degree of constitutional protection by considering separately the effect of the challenged state action on individuals' freedom of private association and their freedom of expressive association. We follow the same course in this case. . . .

The evidence in this case indicates that the relationship among Rotary Club members is not the kind of intimate or private relation that warrants constitutional protection. . . .

We therefore conclude that application of the Unruh Act to local Rotary Clubs does not interfere unduly with the members' freedom of private association. . . .

The Court also has recognized that the right to engage in activities protected by the First Amendment implies 'a corresponding right to associate with others in pursuit of a wide variety of political, social, economic, educational, religious, and cultural ends.' . . .

Even if the Unruh Act does work some slight infringement on Rotary members' right of expressive association, that infringement is justified because it serves the State's compelling interest in eliminating discrimination against women. . . . We therefore hold that application of the Unruh Act to California Rotary Clubs does not violate the right of expressive association afforded by the First Amendment. . . .

Finally, appellants contend that the Unruh Act is unconstitutionally vague and overbroad. We conclude that these contentions were not properly presented to the state courts. . . .

The judgment of the Court of Appeal of California is affirmed."

V. JUSTICE VOTE

7 Pro ACLU Side vs. 0 Con Opposing Side

Opposing Side (Petitioner / Appellant)

1. Powell, L. – Wrote majority opinion
2. Brennan, W. – Joined majority opinion
3. Marshall, T. – Joined majority opinion
4. White, B. – Joined majority opinion
5. Stevens, J. – Joined majority opinion
6. Rehnquist, W. – Joined majority opinion
7. Scalia, A. – Concurred in the judgment

Blackmun, H. – Took no part in the decision.
O'Connor, S. – Took no part in the decision.

VI. A WIN OR LOSS FOR THE ACLU?

The ACLU filed as amicus curiae urging affirmance; the Supreme Court affirmed the California Court of Appeal's decision by a 7-0 vote, giving the ACLU an apparent win.

617. Pennsylvania v. Finley

(Decided May 18, 1987; 481 U.S. 551)

I. ISSUE

A. Issues Discussed

Right to counsel, due process, equal protection

B. Legal Question Presented

Whether the constitutional right to counsel in criminal proceedings extends beyond the first appeal of right.

C. Supreme Court's Answer

The constitutional right to counsel does not extend beyond the first appeal of right.

II. CASE SUMMARY

A. Background

"In 1975 respondent was convicted of second-degree murder by the Court of Common Pleas of Philadelphia County. She was sentenced to life imprisonment. Her appointed trial attorney appealed the conviction to the Supreme Court of Pennsylvania. That court unanimously affirmed the conviction. Having failed on direct appeal, respondent, proceeding pro se, sought relief from the trial court under the Pennsylvania Post Conviction Hearing Act. She raised the same issues that the Supreme Court of Pennsylvania had rejected on the merits. The trial court denied relief, but the State Supreme Court reversed, holding that respondent was entitled, under state law, to appointed counsel in her postconviction proceedings. On remand, the trial court appointed counsel. Counsel reviewed the trial record and consulted with respondent. He concluded that there were no arguable bases for collateral relief. Accordingly, he advised the trial court in writing of his conclusion and requested permission to withdraw. The trial court conducted an independent review of the record and agreed that there were no issues even arguably meritorious. The court thus dismissed the petition for postconviction relief.

Respondent acquired new appointed counsel and pursued an appeal to the Superior Court. Over a dissent, that court concluded that the conduct of the counsel in the trial court's postconviction proceedings violated respondent's constitutional rights. The court held that 'Pennsylvania law concerning procedures to be followed when a court-appointed attorney sees no basis for an appeal is derived from the seminal case of' Anders v. California, 386 U.S. 738 (1967). In Anders, this Court held that when an attorney appointed to represent an indigent defendant on direct appeal finds a case wholly frivolous:

'[H]e should so advise the court and request permission to withdraw. That request must, however, be accompanied by a brief referring to anything in the record that might arguably support the appeal. A copy of counsel's brief should be furnished the indigent and time allowed him to raise any points that he chooses; the court—not counsel—then proceeds, after a full examination of all the proceedings, to decide whether the case is wholly frivolous.'

The Superior Court held that respondent's postconviction counsel had failed to follow these procedures, and it therefore remanded the case to the Court of Common Pleas for further proceedings."

The Supreme Court granted certiorari to review the case and reversed.

B. Counsel of Record / ACLU Attorney

ACLU Side (Respondent / Appellee): Catherine M. Harper, by appointment of the Court, argued the cause for appellee.

Opposing Side (Petitioner / Appellant): Gaele McLaughlin Barthold argued the cause for appellant.

III. AMICI CURIAE

ACLU Side (Respondent / Appellee)

Brief of amici curiae filed on behalf of the ACLU, et al., by Larry W. Yackle, Alvin J. Bronstein, Vivian O. Berger, David Goldstein, and Stefan Presser.

Brief of amici curiae filed on behalf of the National Legal Aid and Defender Association by David P. Bergschneider.

Opposing Side (Petitioner / Appellant)

Linley E. Pearson, Attorney General of Indiana, and William E. Daily and Lisa M. Paunicka, Deputy Attorneys General, filed a brief for the State of Indiana, et al., as amici curiae, joined by officials for their respective States as follows: John Van de Kamp, Attorney General of California, John J. Kelly, Chief State's Attorney for Connecticut, Charles M. Oberly, Attorney General of Delaware, Jim Smith, Attorney General of Florida, Corinne K. A. Watanabe, Attorney General of Hawaii, Jim Jones, Attorney General of Idaho, Robert T. Stephan, Attorney General of Kansas, David L. Armstrong, Attorney General of Kentucky, William J. Guste, Jr., Attorney General of Louisiana, William L. Webster, Attorney General of Missouri, Travis Medlock, Attorney General of South Carolina, Mary Sue Terry, Attorney General of Virginia, Bronson C. LaFollette, Attorney General of Wisconsin, and Archie G. McClintock, Attorney General of Wyoming.

IV. THE SUPREME COURT'S DECISION

"We think that the court below improperly relied on the United States Constitution to extend the Anders procedures to postconviction proceedings. The holding in Anders was based on the underlying constitutional right to appointed counsel established in Douglas v. California, 372 U.S. 353 (1963). Relying on 'that equality demanded by the Fourteenth Amendment,' the Douglas Court held that denial of counsel to indigents on first appeal as of right amounted to unconstitutional discrimination against the poor. In Anders, the Court held that in order to protect the 'constitutional requirement of substantial equality and fair process' set out in Douglas, appointed appellate counsel must follow the procedures described above when a case appears to be frivolous. . . .

We have never held that prisoners have a constitutional right to counsel when mounting collateral attacks upon their convictions, and we decline to so hold today. Our cases establish that the right to appointed counsel extends to the first appeal of right, and no further. Thus, we have rejected suggestions that we establish a right to counsel on discretionary appeals. We think that since a defendant has no federal constitutional right to counsel when pursuing a discretionary appeal on direct review of his conviction, a fortiori, he has no such right when attacking a conviction that has long since become final upon exhaustion of the appellate process. . . .

At bottom, the decision below rests on a premise that we are unwilling to accept—that when a State chooses to offer help to those seeking relief from convictions, the Federal Constitution dictates the exact form such assistance must assume. On the contrary, in this area States have substantial discretion to develop and implement programs to aid prisoners seeking to secure postconviction review. In Pennsylvania, the State has made a valid choice to give prisoners the assistance of counsel without requiring the full panoply of procedural protections that the Constitution requires be given to defendants who are in a fundamentally different position—at trial and on first appeal as of right. In this context, the Constitution does not put the State to the difficult choice between affording no counsel whatsoever or following the strict procedural guidelines ennunciated in Anders. The judgment of the Superior Court is reversed, and the cause is remanded for further proceedings not inconsistent with this opinion."

V. JUSTICE VOTE

3 Pro ACLU Side vs. 6 Con Opposing Side

ACLU Side (Respondent / Appellee)

1. Brennan, W. – Wrote dissenting opinion
2. Marshall, T. – Joined Brennan's dissent
3. Stevens, J. – Wrote dissenting opinion

Opposing Side (Petitioner / Appellant)

1. Rehnquist, W. – Wrote majority opinion
2. White, B. – Joined majority opinion
3. Powell, L. – Joined majority opinion
4. O'Connor, S. – Joined majority opinion
5. Scalia, A. – Joined majority opinion
6. Blackmun, H. – Wrote concurring opinion

VI. A WIN OR LOSS FOR THE ACLU?

The ACLU, as amicus curiae, urged affirmance of the judgment of the Pennsylvania Superior Court; the Supreme Court reversed in a 6-3 vote, giving the ACLU an apparent loss.

618. United States v. Salerno

(Decided May 26, 1987; 481 U.S. 739)

I. ISSUE

A. Issues Discussed

Criminal justice, Eighth Amendment, Fifth Amendment, detention, due process, bail

B. Legal Question Presented

Whether the "Bail Reform Act of 1984 [which] allows a federal court to detain an arrestee pending trial if the Government demonstrates by clear and convincing evidence after an adversary hearing that no release conditions 'will reasonably assure . . . the safety of any other person and the community'" is unconstitutional.

C. Supreme Court's Answer

The Bail Reform Act of 1984 is constitutional.

II. CASE SUMMARY

A. Background

"The Bail Reform Act of 1984 (Act) allows a federal court to detain an arrestee pending trial if the Government demonstrates by clear and convincing evidence after an adversary hearing that no release conditions 'will reasonably assure . . . the safety of any other person and the community.' . . .

Respondents Anthony Salerno and Vincent Cafaro were arrested on March 21, 1986, after being charged in a 29-count indictment alleging various Racketeer Influenced and Corrupt Organizations Act (RICO) violations, mail and wire fraud offenses, extortion, and various criminal gambling violations. The RICO counts alleged 35 acts of racketeering activity, including fraud, extortion, gambling, and conspiracy to commit murder. At respondents' arraignment, the Government moved to have Salerno and Cafaro detained pursuant to § 3142(e), on the ground that no condition of release would assure the safety of the community or any person. . . . The District Court granted the Government's detention motion, concluding that the Government had established by clear and convincing evidence that no condition or combination of conditions of release would ensure the safety of the community or any person . . . . Respondents appealed, contending that to the extent that the Bail Reform Act permits pretrial detention on the ground that the arrestee is likely to commit future crimes, it is unconstitutional on its face. Over a dissent, the United States Court of Appeals for the Second Circuit agreed."

The Supreme Court granted certiorari to review the case and reversed.

B. Counsel of Record / ACLU Attorney

ACLU Side (Respondent / Appellee): Anthony M. Cardinale argued the cause for appellee.

Opposing Side (Petitioner / Appellant): Solicitor General Fried argued the cause for the United States.

III. AMICI CURIAE

ACLU Side (Respondent / Appellee)

Brief of amici curiae filed on behalf of the ACLU, et al., by William J. Genego, Dennis E. Curtis, Mark Rosenbaum, Paul Hoffman, Richard Emery, Martin Guggenheim, Alvin Bronstein, and David Goldstein.

Brief of amici curiae filed on behalf of the National Association of Criminal Defense Lawyers by Jon May and Mark King Leban.

Brief of amici curiae filed on behalf of the Public Defender Service by Cheryl M. Long, James Klein, and David A. Reiser.

Opposing Side (Petitioner / Appellant)

Brief of amici curiae filed on behalf of the American Bar Association by Eugene C. Thomas, Charles G. Cole, and David A. Schlueter.

IV. THE SUPREME COURT'S DECISION:

"In our society liberty is the norm, and detention prior to trial or without trial is the carefully limited exception. We hold that the provisions for pretrial detention in the Bail Reform Act of 1984 fall within that carefully limited exception. The Act authorizes the detention prior to trial of arrestees charged with serious felonies who are found after an adversary hearing to pose a threat to the safety of individuals or to the community which no condition of release can dispel. The numerous procedural safeguards . . . must attend this adversary hearing. We are unwilling to say that this congressional determination, based as it is upon that primary concern of every government—a concern for the safety and indeed the lives of its citizens—on its face violates either the Due Process Clause of the Fifth Amendment or the Excessive Bail Clause of the Eighth Amendment.

The judgment of the Court of Appeals is therefore reversed."

V. JUSTICE VOTE

3 Pro ACLU Side vs. 6 Con Opposing Side

ACLU Side (Respondent / Appellee)

1. Marshall, T. – Wrote dissenting opinion
2. Brennan, W. – Joined Marshall's dissent
3. Stevens, J. – Wrote dissenting opinion

Opposing Side (Petitioner / Appellant)

1. Rehnquist, W. – Wrote majority opinion
2. Powell, L. – Joined majority opinion
3. White, B. – Joined majority opinion
4. O'Connor, S. – Joined majority opinion
5. Blackmun, H. – Joined majority opinion
6. Scalia, A. – Joined majority opinion

VI. A WIN OR LOSS FOR THE ACLU?

The ACLU filed as amicus curiae urging affirmance of the judgment of the Court of Appeals; the Supreme Court reversed in a 6-3 vote, giving the ACLU an apparent loss.

619. Hilton v. Braunskill

(Decided May, 26, 1987; 481 U.S. 770)

I. ISSUE

A. Issues Discussed

Habeas corpus, prisoner release

B. Legal Question Presented

Under Federal Rules of Appellate Procedure 23(c) and 23(d), "what factors these provisions allow a court to consider in determining whether to release a state prisoner pending appeal of a district court order granting habeas relief."

C. Supreme Court's Answer

The court is not restricted to only considering risk of flight, and instead can consider the various factors usually considered in determining whether to stay a judgment, when determining whether to release a prisoner pending appeal of a decision to grant habeas relief.

II. CASE SUMMARY

A. Background

"Federal Rule of Appellate Procedure 23(c) provides that, when the Government appeals a decision granting a writ of habeas corpus, the habeas petitioner shall be released from custody 'unless the court or justice or judge rendering the decision, or the court of appeals or the Supreme Court, or a judge or justice of either court shall otherwise order.' Federal Rule of Appellate Procedure 23(d) states that initial orders issued pursuant to Rule 23(c) shall 'govern review in the court of appeals and in the Supreme Court unless for special reasons shown . . . the order shall be modified, or an independent order respecting custody, enlargement or surety shall be made.' In this case, we are asked to decide what factors these provisions allow a court to consider in determining whether to release a state prisoner pending appeal of a district court order granting habeas relief.

In January 1981, respondent Dana Braunskill was convicted in the Superior Court of New Jersey, Law Division, of sexual assault and unlawful possession of a weapon, . . . and was sentenced to eight years' imprisonment. The Appellate Division of the Superior Court affirmed the convictions, and the New Jersey Supreme Court denied review.

Respondent then, in 1985, filed a petition for a writ of habeas corpus in the United States District Court for the District of New Jersey. Finding that respondent's Sixth Amendment rights had been violated at his trial, the District Court granted respondent's petition and ordered that 'a writ of habeas corpus shall issue unless within 30 days the State of New Jersey shall afford [respondent] a new trial.' Petitioners subsequently moved the District Court to stay its order pending appeal. Relying on Carter v. Rafferty, 781 F.2d 993, 997 (CA3 1986), the District Court determined that it could grant petitioners' request only if they demonstrated that there was risk that respondent would not appear for subsequent proceedings. The court found that petitioners had failed to make such a showing and denied the motion.

Petitioners then filed a motion in the United States Court of Appeals for the Third Circuit, seeking a stay of the District Court's order releasing respondent. The Court of Appeals denied the motion by order dated May 27, 1986."

The Supreme Court granted certiorari to review the case, vacated, and remanded.

B. Counsel of Record / ACLU Attorney

ACLU Side (Respondent / Appellee): Mark H. Friedman argued the cause for appellee.

Opposing Side (Petitioner / Appellant): John G. Holl argued the cause for appellant.

III. AMICI CURIAE

ACLU Side (Respondent / Appellee)

Brief of amici curiae filed on behalf of the ACLU, et al., by Leon Friedman, Brian Neary, Alvin Bronstein, and Eric Neisser.

Brief of amici curiae filed on behalf of the Coastal States Organization, et al., by David C. Slade.

Opposing Side (Petitioner / Appellant)

Brief of amici curiae filed on behalf of the United States by Solicitor General Fried, Assistant Attorney General Weld, Deputy Solicitor General Bryson, and Paul J. Larkin, Jr.

IV. THE SUPREME COURT'S DECISION

"In deciding under Rules 23(c) and (d) whether to stay pending appeal a district court order granting relief to a habeas petitioner, federal courts are not restricted to considering only the petitioner's risk of flight.

"In Carter v. Rafferty, supra, the authority governing the Court of Appeals decision in this case, the court held that federal courts deciding whether to release a successful habeas petitioner pending appeal may consider the petitioner's risk of flight, but not his danger to the community. . . .

We do not believe that federal courts, in deciding whether to stay pending appeal a district court order granting relief to a habeas petitioner, are as restricted as the Carter court thought. Rule 23(c) undoubtedly creates a presumption of release from custody in such cases, but that presumption may be overcome if the judge rendering the decision, or an appellate court or judge, 'otherwise orders.'

[W]e think that a court making an initial custody determination under Rule 23(c) should be guided not only by the language of the Rule itself but also by the factors traditionally considered in deciding whether to stay a judgment in a civil case. There is presumption in favor of enlargement of the petitioner with or without surety, but it may be overcome if the traditional stay factors tip the balance against it. A court reviewing an initial custody determination pursuant to Rule 23(d) must accord a presumption of correctness to the initial custody determination made pursuant to Rule 23(c), whether that order directs release or continues custody, but that presumption, too, may be overcome if the traditional stay factors so indicate. The construction of Rule 23 we here adopt accords both the court making the initial custody determination and the court reviewing that determination considerably more latitude than that apparently thought appropriate by the Court of Appeals for the Third Circuit in this case. . . .

We think that the District Court and the Court of Appeals, in relying on the latter's decision in Carter v. Rafferty, supra, took too limited a view of the discretion allowed to federal courts under Rules 23(c) and (d) in staying pending appeal an order directing the release of a habeas petitioner. We therefore vacate the judgment of the Court of Appeals denying petitioner's application for a stay in this case, and remand the case to that court for further proceedings consistent with this opinion."

V. JUSTICE VOTE

3 Pro ACLU Side vs. 6 Con Opposing Side

ACLU Side (Respondent / Appellee)

1. Marshall, T. – Wrote dissenting opinion
2. Brennan, W. – Joined Marshall's dissent
3. Blackmun, H. – Joined Marshall's dissent

Opposing Side (Petitioner / Appellant)

1. Rehnquist, W. – Wrote majority opinion
2. White, B. – Joined majority opinion
3. Powell, L. – Joined majority opinion
4. Stevens, J. – Joined majority opinion
5. O'Connor, S. – Joined majority opinion
6. Scalia, A. – Joined majority opinion

VI. A WIN OR LOSS FOR THE ACLU?

The ACLU, as amicus curiae, urged affirmance of the judgment of the Court of Appeals; the Supreme Court vacated in a 6-3 vote, giving the ACLU an apparent loss.

620. United States v. Mendoza-Lopez

(Decided May 26, 1987; 481 U.S. 828)

I. ISSUE

A. Issues Discussed

Due process, immigration, deportation

B. Legal Question Presented

"[W]hether an alien who is prosecuted under 8 U.S.C. § 1326 for illegal entry following deportation may assert in that criminal proceeding the invalidity of the underlying deportation order."

C. Supreme Court's Answer

The alien may assert the invalidity of the underlying deportation order.

II. CASE SUMMARY

A. Background

"Respondents, Jose Mendoza-Lopez and Angel Landeros-Quinones, were arrested at separate locations in Lincoln, Nebraska, on October 23, 1984, by agents of the Immigration and Naturalization Service. On October 30, 1984, they were transported to Denver, Colorado, where a group deportation hearing was held for respondents along with 11 other persons, all of whom were, like respondents, Mexican nationals.

After the hearing, respondents were ordered deported and were bused to El Paso, Texas. They were deported from El Paso on November 1, 1984. Each received, at the time of his deportation, a copy of Form I–294, which advised, in both Spanish and English, that a return to the United States without permission following deportation would constitute a felony.

On December 12, 1984, both respondents were once again separately arrested in Lincoln, Nebraska. They were subsequently indicted by a grand jury in the District of Nebraska . . . . Respondents moved in the District Court to dismiss their indictments, on the ground that they were denied fundamentally fair deportation hearings. They contended that the Immigration Law Judge inadequately informed them of their right to counsel at the hearing, and accepted their unknowing waivers of the right to apply for suspension of deportation.

The District Court ruled that respondents could collaterally attack their previous deportation orders. It rejected their claims that they were not adequately informed of their right to counsel. It found, however, that respondents had apparently failed to understand the Immigration Judge's explanation of suspension of deportation. The District Court concluded that respondents had not made knowing and intelligent waivers of their rights to apply for suspension of deportation or their rights to appeal, finding it 'inconceivable that they would so lightly waive their rights to appeal, and thus to the relief they now claim entitlement, [sic] if they had been fully apprised of the ramifications of such a choice.' Holding that the 'failure to overcome these defendants' lack of understanding about the proceedings, which is apparent from listening to the tape recording, totally undermined the reliability of the proceedings' and that 'substantial justice was not done,' the District Court dismissed the indictments in both cases.

The Court of Appeals for the Eighth Circuit affirmed."

The Supreme Court granted certiorari to review the case and affirmed.

B. Counsel of Record / ACLU Attorney

ACLU Side (Respondent / Appellee): Kathy Goudy, by appointment of the Court, argued the cause for appellee.

Opposing Side (Petitioner / Appellant): Christopher J. Wright argued the cause for the United States.

III. AMICI CURIAE

ACLU Side (Respondent / Appellee)

Brief of amici curiae filed on behalf of the ACLU, et al., by Richard F. Ziegler, Lucas Guttentag, Alvin J. Bronstein, and Kip Steinberg.

Brief of amici curiae filed on behalf of the American Immigration Lawyers Association by Susan M. Lydon and Bill Ong Hing.

Opposing Side (Petitioner / Appellant)

No briefs of amici curiae were filed in support of appellant.

IV. THE SUPREME COURT'S DECISION

"The text and background of § 1326 . . . indicate no congressional intent to sanction challenges to deportation orders in proceedings under § 1326. . . . That Congress did not intend the validity of the deportation order to be contestable in a §1326 prosecution does not end our inquiry. If the statute envisions that a court may impose a criminal penalty for reentry after any deportation, regardless of how violative of the rights the alien the deportation proceeding may have been, the statute does not comport with the constitutional requirement of due process. . . .

The fundamental procedural defects of the deportation hearing in this case rendered direct review of the Immigration Judge's determination unavailable to respondents. . . . Persons charged with crime are entitled to have the factual and legal determinations upon which convictions are based subjected to the scrutiny of an impartial judicial officer. . . .

Because respondents were deprived of their rights to appeal, and of any basis to appeal since the only relief for which they would have been eligible was not adequately explained to them, the deportation proceeding in which these events occurred may not be used to support a criminal conviction, and the dismissal of the indictments against them was therefore proper. The judgment of the Court of Appeals is affirmed."

V. JUSTICE VOTE

5 Pro ACLU Side vs. 4 Con Opposing Side

ACLU Side (Respondent / Appellee)

1. Marshall, T. – Wrote majority opinion
2. Brennan, W. – Joined majority opinion
3. Blackmun, H. – Joined majority opinion
4. Powell, L. – Joined majority opinion
5. Stevens, J. – Joined majority opinion

Opposing Side (Petitioner / Appellant)

1. Rehnquist, W. – Wrote dissenting opinion
2. White, B. – Joined Rehnquist's dissent
3. O'Connor, S. – Joined Rehnquist's dissent
4. Scalia, A. – Wrote dissenting opinion

VI. A WIN OR LOSS FOR THE ACLU?

The ACLU, as amicus curiae, urged affirmance of the judgment of the Court of Appeals; the Supreme Court affirmed in a 5-4 vote, giving the ACLU an apparent win.

621. United States v. Hohri

(Decided June 1, 1987; 482 U.S. 64)

I. ISSUE

A. Issues Discussed

Civil rights, jurisdiction, Fourteenth Amendment

B. Legal Question Presented

"[W]hich court—the Court of Appeals for the Federal Circuit or the appropriate regional Court of Appeals—has jurisdiction over an appeal from a Federal District Court's decision of a case raising both a nontax claim under the Little Tucker Act and a claim under the Federal Tort Claims Act (FTCA)."

C. Supreme Court's Answer

A case raising both a nontax claim under the Little Tucker Act and an FTCA claim must be appealed to the Federal Circuit.

II. CASE SUMMARY

A. Background

"During World War II, the Government of the United States removed approximately 120,000 Japanese-Americans from their homes and placed them in internment camps. Respondents are an organization of Japanese-Americans and 19 individuals-former internees and their representatives. They filed this action in the United States District Court for the District of Columbia, seeking damages and declaratory relief for the tangible and intangible injuries suffered because of this incident. Jurisdiction was based on, inter alia, the Little Tucker Act, 28 U.S.C. § 1346(a)(2), and the FTCA, 28 U.S.C. § 1346(b). The District Court concluded that all claims were barred either by sovereign immunity or the applicable statute of limitations.

Respondents appealed to the Court of Appeals for the District of Columbia Circuit. That court reversed the District Court's dismissal of certain claims under the Little Tucker Act. First, the court concluded that it, rather than the Court of Appeals for the Federal Circuit, had jurisdiction over the appeal. It noted that 28 U.S.C. § 1295(a)(2) generally grants the Federal Circuit exclusive jurisdiction of appeals in cases involving nontax claims under the Little Tucker Act. But it concluded that Congress did not intend the Federal Circuit to hear appeals of such cases when they also included FTCA claims. On the merits, the court concluded that the statute of limitations did not begin to run on certain of respondents' Little Tucker Act claims until 1980, when Congress created the Commission on Wartime Relocation and Internment of Civilians. Chief Judge Markey, sitting by designation pursuant to 28 U.S.C. § 291(b), filed a dissent, disagreeing with the court's jurisdictional analysis as well as its decision as to the statute of limitations. A petition for rehearing en banc was denied by a 6-to-5 vote. Judge Bork, joined by four other judges, filed a dissent from denial of the petition, in which he disagreed with both of the court's conclusions."

The Supreme Court granted certiorari to review the case, vacated, and remanded.

B. Counsel of Record / ACLU Attorney

ACLU Side (Respondent / Appellee): Benjamin L. Zelenko argued the cause for appellee.

Opposing Side (Petitioner / Appellant): Solicitor General Fried argued the cause for the United States.

III. AMICI CURIAE

ACLU Side (Respondent / Appellee)

Brief of amici curiae filed on behalf of the ACLU, et al., by Fred Okrand, Paul L. Hoffman, and Dougas E. Mirell.

Brief of amici curiae filed on behalf of the State of California, et al., by John K. Van de Kamp, Attorney General of California, Warren Price III, Attorney General of Hawaii, Corinne K. A. Watanabe, First Deputy Attorney General, and Steven S. Michaels, Deputy Attorney General.

Brief of amici curiae filed on behalf of the American Friends Service Committee, et al., by David Kairys.

Brief of amici curiae filed on behalf of Fred Korematsu, et al., by Dale Minami, Peggy Nagae, and Ruti G. Teitel.

Opposing Side (Petitioner / Appellant)

No briefs of amici curiae were filed in support of appellant.

IV. THE SUPREME COURT'S DECISION:

"[T]he Federal Circuit has exclusive appellate jurisdiction of a case raising only a nontax claim under the Little Tucker Act . . . the appropriate regional Court of Appeals . . . has exclusive appellate jurisdiction . . . of a case raising only a claim under the FTCA.

This case presents claims under both the Little Tucker Act and the FTCA, a situation not specifically addressed by § 1295(a)(2). Resolution of this problem turns on interpretation of the second clause of this subsection, the so-called 'except clause.' [T]he except clause was directed at cases raising only one claim; it strains the language to apply the except clause to cases raising multiple claims, some within and some not within the except clause. . . .

We conclude that Congress intended for centralized determination of nontax Little Tucker Act claims to predominate over regional adjudication of FTCA claims. We hold that a mixed case, presenting both a nontax Little Tucker Act claim and an FTCA claim, may be appealed only to the Federal Circuit. . . .

We vacate the judgment of the Court of Appeals, and remand the case to that court, with instructions to transfer the case to the Federal Circuit."

V. JUSTICE VOTE

0 Pro ACLU Side vs. 8 Con Opposing Side

Opposing Side (Petitioner / Appellant)

1. Powell, L. – Wrote majority opinion
2. White, B. – Joined majority opinion
3. O'Connor, S. – Joined majority opinion
4. Rehnquist, W. – Joined majority opinion
5. Brennan, W. – Joined majority opinion
6. Stevens, J. – Joined majority opinion
7. Marshall, T. – Joined majority opinion
8. Blackmun, H. – Wrote concurring opinion

Scalia, A – Took no part in the decision

VI. A WIN OR LOSS FOR THE ACLU?

The ACLU filed as amicus curiae urging affirmance of the judgment of the Court of Appeals for the District of Columbia Circuit; the Supreme Court vacated and remanded in an 8-0 vote, giving the ACLU an apparent loss.

622. O'Lone v. Estate of Shabazz

(Decided June 9, 1987; 482 U.S. 342)

I. ISSUE

A. Issues Discussed

Criminal justice, prisons, First Amendment, religion

B. Legal Question Presented

What is the appropriate "standard of review for prison regulations claimed to inhibit the exercise of constitutional rights"?

C. Supreme Court's Answer

Where prison officials acted reasonably, the Court should not substitute its judgment for that of prison officials, even in matters of alleged violations of constitutional rights.

II. CASE SUMMARY

A. Background

"Respondents, members of the Islamic faith, were prisoners in New Jersey's Leesburg State Prison. They challenged policies adopted by prison officials which resulted in their inability to attend Jumu'ah, a weekly Muslim congregational service regularly held in the main prison building and in a separate facility known as 'the Farm.' Jumu'ah is commanded by the Koran and must be held every Friday after the sun reaches its zenith and before the Asr, or afternoon prayer. . . .

Respondents filed suit under 42 U.S.C. § 1983, alleging that the prison policies unconstitutionally denied them their Free Exercise rights under the First Amendment, as applied to the States through the Fourteenth Amendment. The District Court . . . concluded that no constitutional violation had occurred. . . . The Court of Appeals, sua sponte hearing the case en banc, decided that its earlier decision relied upon by the District Court was not sufficiently protective of prisoners' free exercise rights . . . . The case was remanded to the District Court for reconsideration under the standards enumerated in the opinion."

The Supreme Court granted certiorari to review the case and reversed.

B. Counsel of Record / ACLU Attorney

ACLU Side (Respondent / Appellee): James Katz argued the cause for appellee.

Opposing Side (Petitioner / Appellant): Laurie M. Hodian, Deputy Attorney General of New Jersey, argued the cause for appellant.

Roger Clegg argued the cause for the United States, as amicus curiae, by special leave of Court.

III. AMICI CURIAE

ACLU Side (Respondent / Appellee)

Brief of amici curiae filed on behalf of the ACLU, et al., by Eric Neisser, Alvin J. Bronstein, David B. Goldstein, Edward I. Koren, and Elizabeth Alexander.

Brief of amici curiae filed on behalf of the American Jewish Congress, et al., by Marc D. Stern and Amy Adelson.

Brief of amici curiae filed on behalf of the Catholic League for Religious and Civil Rights, et al., by Steven Frederick McDowell.

Brief of amici curiae filed on behalf of the Christian Legal Society, et al., by Michael J. Woodruff and Samuel E. Ericsson.

Brief of amici curiae filed on behalf of the Prisoners' Rights Project of the Legal Aid Society of the city of New York, et al., by Philip L. Weinstein, David A. Lewis, and Stephen M. Latimer.

Brief of amici curiae filed on behalf of Imam Jamil Abdullah Al-Amin, et al., by Ellen J. Winner, James G. Abourezk, and Albert P. Mokhiber.

Brief of amici curiae filed on behalf of Len Marek, et al., by Steven C. Moore and Walter R. Echo-Hawk.

Opposing Side (Petitioner / Appellant)

Brief of amici curiae filed on behalf of the United States by Roger Clegg, Solicitor General Fried, Assistant Attorney General Weld, and Deputy Solicitor General Bryson.

Brief of amici curiae filed on behalf of the Commonwealth of Pennsylvania, et al., by LeRoy S. Zimmerman, Attorney General of Pennsylvania; Amy Zapp, Deputy Attorney General of Pennsylvania; John G. Knorr III, Senior Deputy Attorney General of Pennsylvania; Andrew S. Gordon, Chief Deputy Attorney General of Pennsylvania; Charles A. Graddick, Attorney General of Alabama; Ronald W. Lorensen, Acting Attorney General of Alaska; Robert K. Corbin, Attorney General of Arizona; Steven Clark, Attorney General of Arkansas; John K. Van de Kamp, Attorney General of California; Duane Woodard, Attorney General of Colorado; Charles M. Oberly III, Attorney General of Delaware; Jim Smith, Attorney General of Florida; Corinne K. A. Watanabe, Attorney General of Hawaii; James T. Jones, Attorney General of Idaho; Linley E. Pearson, Attorney General of Indiana; Robert P. Stephan, Attorney General of Kansas; William J. Guste, Jr., Attorney General of Louisiana; Stephen H. Sachs, Attorney General of Maryland; Francis X. Bellotti, Attorney General of Massachusetts; Frank J. Kelley, Attorney General of Michigan; Hubert H. Humphrey III, Attorney General of Minnesota; Lloyd Pittman, Attorney General of Mississippi; William L. Webster, Attorney General of Missouri; Robert M. Spire, Attorney General of Nebraska; Brian McKay, Attorney General of Nevada; Lacy H. Thornburg, Attorney General of North Carolina; Nicholas J. Spaeth, Attorney General of North Dakota; Anthony J. Celebrezze Jr., Attorney General of Ohio; Dave Frohnmayer, Attorney General of Oregon; T. Travis Medlock, Attorney General of South Carolina; Mark V. Meierhenryl, Attorney General of South Dakota; W.J. Michael Cody, Attorney General of Tennessee; Mary Sue Terry, Attorney General of Virginia; Kenneth O. Eikenberry, Attorney General of Washington; A.G. McClintock, Attorney General of Wyoming; and James R. Murphy, Acting Corporate Counsel of the District of Columbia.

IV. THE SUPREME COURT'S DECISION

"Inmates clearly retain protections afforded by the First Amendment, including its directive that no law shall prohibit the free exercise of religion. Second, '[l]awful incarceration brings about the necessary withdrawal or limitation of many privileges and rights, a retraction justified by the considerations underlying our penal system.' . . . '[W]hen a prison regulation impinges on inmates' constitutional rights, the regulation is valid if it is reasonably related to legitimate penological interests.' . . .

We think the Court of Appeals decision in this case was wrong when it established a separate burden on prison officials to prove 'that no reasonable method exists by which [prisoners'] religious rights can be accommodated without creating bona fide security problems.' Though the availability of accommodations is relevant to the reasonableness inquiry, we have rejected the notion that 'prison officials . . . have to set up and then shoot down every conceivable alternative method of accommodating the claimant's constitutional complaint.' By placing the burden on prison officials to disprove the availability of alternatives, the approach articulated by the Court of Appeals fails to reflect the respect and deference that the United States Constitution allows for the judgment of prison administrators.

Turning to consideration of the policies challenged in this case, we think the findings of the District Court establish clearly that prison officials have acted in a reasonable manner. . . .

We take this opportunity to reaffirm our refusal, even where claims are made under the First Amendment, to 'substitute our judgment on . . . difficult and sensitive matters of institutional administration,' for the determinations of those charged with the formidable task of running a prison. Here the District Court decided that the regulations alleged to infringe constitutional rights were reasonably related to legitimate penological objectives. We agree with the District Court, and it necessarily follows that the regulations in question do not offend the Free Exercise Clause of the First Amendment to the United States Constitution. The judgment of the Court of Appeals is therefore reversed."

V. JUSTICE VOTE

4 Pro ACLU Side vs. 5 Con Opposing Side

ACLU Side (Respondent / Appellee)

1. Brennan, W. – Wrote dissenting opinion
2. Marshall, T. – Joined Brennan's dissent
3. Blackmun, H. – Joined Brennan's dissent
4. Stevens, J. – Joined Brennan's dissent

Opposing Side (Petitioner / Appellant)

1. Rehnquist, W. – Wrote majority opinion
2. White, B. – Joined majority opinion
3. Powell, L. – Joined majority opinion
4. O'Connor, S. – Joined majority opinion
5. Scalia, A. – Joined majority opinion

VI. A WIN OR LOSS FOR THE ACLU?

The ACLU filed as amicus curiae urging affirmance of the judgment of the Court of Appeals; the Supreme Court reversed in a 5-4 vote, giving the ACLU an apparent loss.

623. Miller v. Florida

(Decided June 9, 1987; 482 U.S. 423)

I. ISSUE

A. Issues Discussed

Criminal procedure, Ex Post Facto Clause

B. Legal Question Presented

"[W]hether application of . . . amended guidelines in petitioner's case [to sentence petitioner to a longer prison term than would have been imposed at the time the crime was committed,] is unconstitutional by virtue of the Ex Post Facto Clause."

C. Supreme Court's Answer

The application of amended sentencing guidelines violated the Ex Post Facto Clause.

II. CASE SUMMARY

A. Background

"At the time petitioner committed the crime for which he was convicted, Florida's sentencing guidelines would have resulted in a presumptive sentence of 3½ to 4½ years' imprisonment. At the time petitioner was sentenced, the revised guidelines called for a presumptive sentence of 5½ to 7 years in prison. The trial court applied the guidelines in effect at the time of sentencing and imposed a 7-year sentence. . . .

Petitioner was convicted in August 1984 on counts of sexual battery with slight force, a second-degree felony, . . . burglary with an assault, a felony of the 'first degree punishable by . . . life,' . . . and petit theft, a misdemeanor . . . . On April 25, 1984, when these offenses were committed, the sentencing guidelines adopted October 1, 1983, were still in effect. On May 8, 1984, however, the Supreme Court of Florida proposed several revisions to the sentencing guidelines. In June 1984 the Florida Legislature adopted the recommended changes, and the legislation implementing the revised guidelines became effective July 1, 1984. When petitioner was sentenced on October 2, 1984, therefore, these revised sentencing guidelines were the guidelines then in effect. . . .

At petitioner's sentencing hearing on October 2, 1984, the State contended that the revised guidelines should apply in determining petitioner's sentence. Alternatively, the State argued that if the sentencing judge applied the earlier guidelines, he should depart from the guidelines' range and impose a 7-year sentence. The sentencing judge, rejecting petitioner's ex post facto argument, ruled that the revised guidelines should apply. Concluding that he would 'stay within the new guidelines,' the judge imposed a 7-year term of imprisonment for the sexual assault count. Petitioner received a concurrent 7-year sentence on the burglary count, and time served on the misdemeanor charge.

On appeal, the Florida District Court of Appeal . . . vacated petitioner's sentence and remanded for resentencing in accordance with the sentencing guidelines in effect at the time the offense was committed. . . . The Supreme Court of Florida reversed."

The U.S. Supreme Court granted certiorari to review the case and reversed.

B. Counsel of Record / ACLU Attorney

ACLU Side (Petitioner / Appellant): Anthony Calvello argued the cause for appellant.

Opposing Side (Respondent / Appellee): Joy B. Shearer, Assistant Attorney General of Florida, argued the cause for appellee.

III. AMICI CURIAE

ACLU Side (Petitioner / Appellant)

Brief of amici curiae filed on behalf of the ACLU, et al., by Gerald D. Stern and Alvin Bronstein.

Opposing Side (Respondent / Appellee)

No briefs of amici curiae were filed in support of appellee.

IV. THE SUPREME COURT'S DECISION

"Article I of the United States Constitution provides that neither Congress nor any State shall pass any 'ex post facto Law.' [T]o fall within the ex post facto prohibition, two critical elements must be present: first, the law 'must be retrospective . . .'; and second, 'it must disadvantage the offender affected by it.' [N]o ex post facto violation occurs if a change does not alter 'substantial personal rights,' but merely changes 'modes of procedure which do not affect matters of substance.' . . .

A law is retrospective if it 'changes the legal consequences of acts completed before its effective date.' Application of the revised guidelines law in petitioner's case clearly satisfies this standard. . . .

Petitioner plainly has been 'substantially disadvantaged' by the change in sentencing laws. To impose a 7-year sentence under the old guidelines, the sentencing judge would have to depart from the presumptive sentence range of 3 1/2-4 1/2 years. As a result, the sentencing judge would have to provide clear and convincing reasons in writing for the departure, on facts proved beyond a reasonable doubt, and his determination would be reviewable on appeal. By contrast, because a 7-year sentence is within the presumptive range under the revised law, the trial judge did not have to provide any reasons, convincing or otherwise, for imposing the sentence, and his decision was unreviewable. Thus, even if the revised guidelines law did not 'technically . . . increase . . . the punishment annexed to [petitioner's] crime,'' it foreclosed his ability to challenge the imposition of a sentence longer than his presumptive sentence under the old law. Petitioner therefore was 'substantially disadvantaged' by the retrospective application of the revised guidelines to his crime. . . .

Although the distinction between substance and procedure might sometimes prove elusive, here the change at issue appears to have little about it that could be deemed procedural. The 20% increase in points for sexual offenses in no wise [sic] alters the method to be followed in determining the appropriate sentence; it simply inserts a larger number into the same equation. The comments of the Florida Supreme Court acknowledge that the sole reason for the increase was to punish sex offenders more heavily: the amendment was intended to, and did, increase the 'quantum of punishment' for category 2 crimes. . . .

The law at issue in this case, like the law in Weaver, 'makes more onerous the punishment for crimes committed before its enactment.' Accordingly, we find that Florida's revised guidelines law, 1984 Fla. Laws, ch. 84-328, is void as applied to petitioner, whose crime occurred before the law's effective date. We reverse the judgment of the Supreme Court of Florida, and remand the case for further proceedings not inconsistent with this opinion."

V. JUSTICE VOTE

9 Pro ACLU Side vs. 0 Con Opposing Side

ACLU Side (Petitioner / Appellant)

1. O'Connor, S. – Wrote majority opinion
2. Rehnquist, W. – Joined majority opinion
3. Brennan, W. – Joined majority opinion
4. White, B. – Joined majority opinion
5. Marshall, T. – Joined majority opinion
6. Blackmun, H. – Joined majority opinion
7. Powell, L. – Joined majority opinion
8. Stevens, J. – Joined majority opinion
9. Scalia, A. – Joined majority opinion

VI. A WIN OR LOSS FOR THE ACLU?

The ACLU filed as amicus curiae urging reversal of the judgment of the Florida Supreme Court; the U.S. Supreme Court reversed in a unanimous 9-0 vote, giving the ACLU an apparent win.

624. City of Houston v. Hill

(Decided June 15, 1987; 482 U.S. 451)

I. ISSUE

A. Issues Discussed

First Amendment, freedom of speech

B. Legal Question Presented

"[W]hether a municipal ordinance that makes it unlawful to interrupt a police officer in the performance of his or her duties is unconstitutionally overbroad under the First Amendment."

C. Supreme Court's Answer

The ordinance is unconstitutionally overbroad.

II. CASE SUMMARY

A. Background

"Appellee Raymond Wayne Hill is a lifelong resident of Houston, Texas. At the time this lawsuit began, he worked as a paralegal and as executive director of the Houston Human Rights League. A member of the board of the Gay Political Caucus, which he helped found in 1975, Hill was also affiliated with a Houston radio station, and had carried city and county press passes since 1975. He lived in Montrose, a 'diverse and eclectic neighborhood' that is the center of gay political and social life in Houston.

The incident that sparked this lawsuit occurred in the Montrose area on February 14, 1982. Hill observed a friend, Charles Hill, intentionally stopping traffic on a busy street, evidently to enable a vehicle to enter traffic. Two Houston police officers, one of whom was named Kelley, approached Charles and began speaking with him. According to the District Court, 'shortly thereafter' Hill began shouting at the officers 'in an admitted attempt to divert Kelley's attention from Charles Hill.' Hill first shouted: 'Why don't you pick on somebody your own size?' After Officer Kelley responded: '[A]re you interrupting me in my official capacity as a Houston police officer?' Hill then shouted: 'Yes, why don't you pick on somebody my size?' Hill was arrested under Houston Code of Ordinances § 34-11(a), for 'wilfully or intentionally interrupt[ing] a city policeman . . . by verbal challenge during an investigation.' Charles Hill was not arrested. Hill was then acquitted after a nonjury trial in Municipal Court. . . .

Following his acquittal in the Charles Hill incident, Hill brought the suit in the Federal District Court for the Southern District of Texas, seeking (1) a declaratory judgment that § 34-11(a) was unconstitutional both on its face and as it had been applied to him, (2) a permanent injunction against any attempt to enforce the ordinance, (3) an order expunging the records of his arrests under the ordinance, and (4) damages and attorney's fees under 42 U.S.C. §§ 1983 and 1988.

At trial, Hill introduced records provided by the city regarding both the frequency with which arrests had been made for violation of the ordinance and the type of conduct with which those arrested had been charged. He also introduced evidence and testimony concerning the arrests of several reporters under the ordinance. Finally, Hill introduced evidence regarding his own experience with the ordinance, under which he has been arrested four times since 1975, but never convicted.

The District Court held that Hill's evidence did not demonstrate that the ordinance had been unconstitutionally applied. The court also rejected Hill's contention that the ordinance was unconstitutionally vague or overbroad on its face. . . .

A panel of the Court of Appeals reversed. The city's suggestion for rehearing en banc was granted, and the Court of Appeals, by a vote of 8-7, upheld the judgment of the panel."

The Supreme Court granted certiorari to review the case and affirmed.

B. Counsel of Record / ACLU Attorney

ACLU Side (Respondent / Appellee): Charles Alan Wright argued the cause for appellee.

Opposing Side (Petitioner / Appellant): Robert J. Collins argued the cause for appellant.

III. AMICI CURIAE

ACLU Side (Respondent / Appellee)

Brief of amici curiae filed on behalf of the ACLU, et al., by Alvin Bronstein, David Goldstein, Burt Neuborne, James Harrington, and Bruce Griffiths.

Opposing Side (Petitioner / Appellant)

No briefs of amici curiae were filed in support of appellant.

IV. THE SUPREME COURT'S DECISION

"The elements of First Amendment overbreadth analysis are familiar. Only a statute that is substantially overbroad may be invalidated on its face. . . .

The city's principal argument is that the ordinance does not inhibit the exposition of ideas, and that it bans 'core criminal conduct' not protected by the First Amendment. In its view, the application of the ordinance to Hill illustrates that the police employ it only to prohibit such conduct, and not 'as a subterfuge to control or dissuade free expression.' Since the ordinance is 'content-neutral,' and since there is no evidence that the city has applied the ordinance to chill particular speakers or ideas, the city concludes that the ordinance is not substantially overbroad.

We disagree with the city's characterization for several reasons. First, the enforceable portion of the ordinance deals not with core criminal conduct, but with speech. . . . Second, contrary to the city's contention, the First Amendment protects a significant amount of verbal criticism and challenge directed at police officers. 'Speech is often provocative and challenging . . . . [But it] is nevertheless protected against censorship or punishment, unless shown likely to produce a clear and present danger of a serious substantive evil that rises far above public inconvenience, annoyance, or unrest.' . . .

Houston's ordinance criminalizes a substantial amount of constitutionally protected speech, and accords the police unconstitutional discretion in enforcement. The ordinance's plain language is admittedly violated scores of times daily yet only some individuals—those chosen by the police in their unguided discretion—are arrested. Far from providing the 'breathing space' that 'First Amendment freedoms need . . . to survive,' the ordinance is susceptible of regular application to protected expression. We conclude that the ordinance is substantially overbroad, and that the Court of Appeals did not err in holding it facially invalid. . . .

Today's decision reflects the constitutional requirement that, in the face of verbal challenges to police action, officers and municipalities must respond with restraint. We are mindful that the preservation of liberty depends in part upon the maintenance of social order. But the First Amendment recognizes, wisely we think, that a certain amount of expressive disorder not only is inevitable in a society committed to individual freedom, but must itself be protected if that freedom would survive. We therefore affirm the judgment of the Court of Appeals."

V. JUSTICE VOTE

8 Pro ACLU Side vs. 1 Con Opposing Side

ACLU Side (Respondent / Appellee)

1. Brennan, W. – Wrote majority opinion
2. White, B. – Joined majority opinion
3. Marshall, T. – Joined majority opinion
4. Blackmun, H. – Wrote concurring opinion
5. Stevens, J. – Joined majority opinion
6. Scalia, A. – Wrote concurring opinion, joined Powell's opinion, in part
7. Powell, L. – Wrote opinion concurring in part and dissenting in part
8. O'Connor, S. – Joined Powell's opinion

Opposing Side (Petitioner / Appellant)

1. Rehnquist, W. – Wrote dissenting opinion, joined Powell's opinion, in part

VI. A WIN OR LOSS FOR THE ACLU?

The ACLU, as amicus curiae, urged affirmance of the judgment of the Fifth Circuit Court of Appeals; the Supreme Court affirmed in an 8-1 vote, giving the ACLU an apparent win.

625. Edwards v. Aguillard

(Decided June 19, 1987; 482 U.S. 578)

I. ISSUE

A. Issues Discussed

First Amendment, creation science, religion in schools, Establishment Clause

B. Legal Question Presented

"[W]hether Louisiana's 'Balanced Treatment for Creation-Science and Evolution-Science in Public School Instruction' Act (Creationism Act), is facially invalid as violative of the Establishment Clause of the First Amendment."

C. Supreme Court's Answer

The Creationism Act is unconstitutional.

II. CASE SUMMARY

A. Background

"The Creationism Act forbids the teaching of the theory of evolution in public schools unless accompanied by instruction in 'creation science.' No school is required to teach evolution or creation science. If either is taught, however, the other must also be taught. . . .

Appellees, who include parents of children attending Louisiana public schools, Louisiana teachers, and religious leaders, challenged the constitutionality of the Act in District Court, seeking an injunction and declaratory relief. Appellants, Louisiana officials charged with implementing the Act, defended on the ground that the purpose of the Act is to protect a legitimate secular interest, namely, academic freedom. Appellees attacked the Act as facially invalid because it violated the Establishment Clause and made a motion for summary judgment. The District Court granted the motion. The court held that there can be no valid secular reason for prohibiting the teaching of evolution, a theory historically opposed by some religious denominations. The court further concluded that 'the teaching of 'creation science' and 'creationism,' as contemplated by the statute, involves teaching 'tailored to the principles' of a particular religious sect or group of sects.' The District Court therefore held that the Creationism Act violated the Establishment Clause either because it prohibited the teaching of evolution or because it required the teaching of creation science with the purpose of advancing a particular religious doctrine.

The Court of Appeals affirmed. . . . A suggestion for rehearing en banc was denied over a dissent."

The Supreme Court granted certiorari to review the case and affirmed.

B. Counsel of Record / ACLU Attorney

ACLU Side (Respondent / Appellee): Jay Topkis argued the cause for appellee. With him on the briefs were John DiGiulio, Samuel I, Rosenberg, Allen Blumstein, Gerald E. Harper, Jack D. Novik, Burt Neuborne, Norman Dorsen, John Sexton, and Ron Wilson.

Opposing Side (Petitioner / Appellant): Wendell R. Bird, Special Assistant Attorney General of Georgia, argued the cause for appellant. With him on the briefs were A. Morgan Brian, Jr., and Thomas T. Anderson, Special Assistant Attorneys General, Kendall L. Vick, and Patricia Nalley Bowers, Assistant Attorney General of Louisiana.

III. AMICI CURIAE

ACLU Side (Respondent / Appellee)

Brief of amici curiae filed on behalf of the Rabbinical Alliance of America, et al., by F. Tayton Dencer, John W. Whitehead, Larry L. Crain, the Honorable William E. Dannemeyer, and the Honorable Robert K. Dornan.

Brief of amici curiae filed on behalf of Reverand Bill McLean, et al., by Philip E. Kaplan and Karen L. Ardnt.

Brief of amici curiae filed on behalf of the State of New York, et al., by Robert Abrams, Attorney General of New York, O. Peter Sherwood, Solicitor General, Paul M. Glickman, Jane Levine, Suzanne Lynn, and Marla Tepper, Assistant Attorneys General, and Neil F. Hartigan, Attorney General of Illinois.

Brief of amici curiae filed on behalf of the American Association of University Professors, et al., by Ann H. Franke, Jacqueline W. Mintz, and Sheldon E. Steinbach.

Brief of amici curiae filed on behalf of the American Federation of Teachers, AFL-CIO, by Bruce A. Miller and Stuart M. Israel.

Brief of amici curiae filed on behalf of the American Jewish Congress et al. by Marvin E. Frankel, Marc D. Stern, and Ronald A. Krauss.

Brief of amici curiae filed on behalf of Americans United for Separation of Church and State, et al., by Lee Boothby, Samuel Rabinove, Richard T. Foltin, and James M. Parker.

Brief of amici curiae filed on behalf of the Anti-Defamation League of B'nai B'rith, et al., by Ruti G. Teitel, Justin J. Finger, Jeffrey P. Sinensky, and Steven M. Freeman.

Brief of amici curiae filed on behalf of the National Academy of Sciences by Barry H. Garfinkel and Mark Herlihy

Brief of amici curiae filed on behalf of the New York Committee for Public Education and Religious Liberty by Leo Pfeffer.

Brief of amici curiae filed on behalf of People for the American Way, et al., by Timothy B. Dyk, A. Douglas Melamed, and Kerry W. Kircher.

Brief of amici curiae filed on behalf of the Spartacist League, et al., by Rachel H. Wolkenstein.

Brief of amici curiae filed on behalf of 72 Nobel Laureates, et al., by Walter B. Slocombe.

Opposing Side (Petitioner / Appellant)

Brief of amici curiae filed on behalf of the Catholic League for Religious and Civil Rights by Steven Frederick McDowell.

Brief of amici curiae filed on behalf of the Christian Legal Society, et al., by Michael J. Woodruff, Kimberlee W. Colby, Samuel E. Ericsson, and Forest D. Montgomery.

Brief of amici curiae filed on behalf of Concerned Women for America by Michael P. Farris and Jordan W. Lorence.

IV. THE SUPREME COURT'S DECISION

"While the Court is normally deferential to a State's articulation of a secular purpose, it is required that the statement of such purpose be sincere and not a sham. . . . It is clear from the legislative history that the purpose of the legislative sponsor, Senator Bill Keith, was to narrow the science curriculum. . . . It is equally clear that requiring schools to teach creation science with evolution does not advance academic freedom. . . .

Furthermore, the goal of basic 'fairness' is hardly furthered by the Act's discriminatory preference for the teaching of creation science and against the teaching of evolution. . . . The Act forbids school boards to discriminate against anyone who 'chooses to be a creation-scientist' or to teach 'creationism,' but fails to protect those who choose to teach evolution or any other non-creation science theory, or who refuse to teach creation science.

If the Louisiana Legislature's purpose was solely to maximize th comprehensiveness and effectiveness of science instruction, it would have encouraged the teaching of all scientific theories about the origins of humankind. But under the Act's requirements, teachers who were once free to teach any and all facets of this subject are now unable to do so. Moreover, the Act fails even to ensure that creation science will be taught, but instead requires the teaching of this theory only when the theory of evolution is taught. Thus we agree with the Court of Appeals' conclusion that the Act does not serve to protect academic freedom, but has the distinctly different purpose of discrediting 'evolution by counter-balancing its teaching at every turn with the teaching of creationism . . . .'

We do not imply that a legislature could never require that scientific critiques of prevailing scientific theories be taught. [T]eaching a variety of scientific theories about the origins of humankind to schoolchildren might be validly done with the clear secular intent of enhancing the effectiveness of science instruction. But because the primary purpose of the Creationism Act is to endorse a particular religious doctrine, the Act furthers religion in violation of the Establishment Clause. . . .

The Louisiana Creationism Act advances a religious doctrine by requiring either the banishment of the theory of evolution from public school classrooms or the presentation of a religious viewpoint that rejects evolution in its entirety. The Act violates the Establishment Clause of the First Amendment because it seeks to employ the symbolic and financial support of government to achieve a religious purpose. The judgment of the Court of Appeals therefore is affirmed."

V. JUSTICE VOTE

7 Pro ACLU Side vs. 2 Con Opposing Side

ACLU Side (Respondent / Appellee)

1. Brennan, W. – Wrote majority opinion
2. White, B. – Wrote concurring opinion
3. Marshall, T. – Joined majority opinion
4. Blackmun, H. – Joined majority opinion
5. Stevens, J. – Joined majority opinion
6. O'Connor, S. – Joined Powell's concurrence
7. Powell, L. – Wrote concurring opinion

Opposing Side (Petitioner / Appellant)

1. Scalia, A. – Wrote dissenting opinion
2. Rehnquist, W. – Joined Scalia's dissent

VI. A WIN OR LOSS FOR THE ACLU?

The ACLU, as counsel of record, urged affirmance of the judgment of the Court of Appeals; the Supreme Court affirmed in a 7-2 vote, giving the ACLU an apparent win.

626. New York v. Burger

(Decided June 19, 1987; 482 U.S. 691)

I. ISSUE

A. Issues Discussed

Criminal justice, Fourth Amendment, search and seizure

B. Legal Question Presented

"[W]hether the warrantless search of an automobile junkyard, conducted pursuant to a statute authorizing such a search, falls within the exception to the warrant requirement for administrative inspections of pervasively regulated industries."

C. Supreme Court's Answer

The warrantless search falls within the exception for administrative inspections of pervasively regulated industries.

II. CASE SUMMARY

A. Background

"Respondent Joseph Burger is the owner of a junkyard in Brooklyn, N.Y. . . . At approximately noon on November 17, 1982, Officer Joseph Vega and four other plainclothes officers, all members of the Auto Crimes Division of the New York City Police Department, entered respondent's junkyard to conduct an inspection pursuant to N.Y.Veh. & Traf.Law § 415-a5. On any given day, the Division conducts from 5 to 10 inspections of vehicle dismantlers, automobile junkyards, and related businesses.

Upon entering the junkyard, the officers asked to see Burger's license and his 'police book'—the record of the automobiles and vehicle parts in his possession. Burger replied that he had neither a license nor a police book. The officers then announced their intention to conduct a § 415-a5 inspection. Burger did not object. In accordance with their practice, the officers copied down the Vehicle Identification Numbers (VINs) of several vehicles and parts of vehicles that were in the junkyard. After checking these numbers against a police computer, the officers determined that respondent was in possession of stolen vehicles and parts. Accordingly, Burger was arrested and charged with five counts of possession of stolen property and one count of unregistered operation as a vehicle dismantler, in violation of § 415-a1.

In the Kings County Supreme Court, Burger moved to suppress the evidence obtained as a result of the inspection, primarily on the ground that § 415-a5 was unconstitutional. After a hearing, the court denied the motion. . . . When respondent moved for reconsideration in light of a recent decision of the Appellate

Division, People v. Pace, the court granted reargument. Upon reconsideration, the court distinguished the situation in Pace from that in the instant case. . . . The court therefore reaffirmed its earlier determination in the instant case that § 415-a5 was constitutional. For the same reasons, the Appellate Division affirmed.

The New York Court of Appeals, however, reversed."

The Supreme Court granted certiorari to review the case and reversed.

B. Counsel of Record / ACLU Attorney

ACLU Side (Respondent / Appellee): Stephen R. Mahler argued the cause for appellee.

Opposing Side (Petitioner / Appellant): Elizabeth Holtzman argued the cause for appellant.

III. AMICI CURIAE

ACLU Side (Respondent / Appellee)

Brief of amici curiae filed on behalf of the ACLU, et al., Richard Emery, Gerard E. Lynch, and Alvin J. Bronstein.

Opposing Side (Petitioner / Appellant)

No briefs of amici curiae were filed in support of appellant.

IV. THE SUPREME COURT'S DECISION

"The Court long has recognized that the Fourth Amendment's prohibition on unreasonable searches and seizures is applicable to commercial premises, as well as to private homes. An owner or operator of a business thus has an expectation of privacy in commercial property, which society is prepared to consider to be reasonable. . . . An expectation of privacy in commercial premises, however, is different from, and indeed less than, a similar expectation in an individual's home. This expectation is particularly attenuated in commercial property employed in 'closely regulated' industries. The Court observed in Marshall v. Barlow's, Inc.: 'Certain industries have such a history of government oversight that no reasonable expectation of privacy, could exist for a proprietor over the stock of such an enterprise.' . . .

Because the owner or operator of commercial premises in a 'closely regulated' industry has a reduced expectation of privacy, the warrant and probable-cause requirements, which fulfill the traditional Fourth Amendment standard of reasonableness for a government search, have lessened application in this context. Rather, we conclude that, as in other situations of 'special need,' where the privacy interests of the owner are weakened and the government interests in regulating particular businesses are concomitantly heightened, a warrantless inspection of commercial premises may well be reasonable within the meaning of the Fourth Amendment. . . .

Searches made pursuant to § 415-a5, in our view, clearly fall within this established exception to the warrant requirement for administrative inspections in 'closely regulated' businesses. . . . The New York regulatory scheme satisfies the three criteria necessary to make reasonable warrantless inspections pursuant to § 415-a5. First, the State has a substantial interest in regulating the vehicle-dismantling and automobile-junkyard industry because motor vehicle theft has increased in the State and because the problem of theft is associated with this industry. . . . Second, regulation of the vehicle-dismantling industry reasonably serves the State's substantial interest in eradicating automobile theft. . . . Third, § 415-a5 provides a 'constitutionally adequate substitute for a warrant.' Finally, the 'time, place, and scope' of the inspection is limited, to place appropriate restraints upon the discretion of the inspecting officers. . . . A search conducted pursuant to § 415-a5, therefore, clearly falls within the well-established exception to the warrant requirement for administrative inspections of 'closely regulated' businesses. . . .

Accordingly, the judgment of the New York Court of Appeals is reversed, and the case is remanded to that court for further proceedings not inconsistent with this opinion."

V. JUSTICE VOTE

3 Pro ACLU Side vs. 6 Con Opposing Side

ACLU Side (Respondent / Appellee)

1. Brennan, W. – Wrote dissenting opinion
2. Marshall, T. – Joined Brennan's dissent
3. O'Connor, S. – Joined all but Part III of Brennan's dissent

Opposing Side (Petitioner / Appellant)

1. Blackmun, H. – Wrote majority opinion
2. Rehnquist, W. – Joined majority opinion
3. White, B. – Joined majority opinion
4. Powell, L. – Joined majority opinion
5. Stevens, J. – Joined majority opinion
6. Scalia, A. – Joined majority opinion

VI. A WIN OR LOSS FOR THE ACLU?

The ACLU filed a brief, as amicus curiae, urging affirmance of the judgment of the New York Court of Appeals; the Supreme Court reversed in a 6-3 vote, giving the ACLU an apparent loss.

627. Kentucky v. Stincer

(Decided June 19, 1987; 482 U.S. 730)

I. ISSUE

A. Issues Discussed

Fourteenth Amendment, due process, Sixth Amendment, Confrontation Clause

B. Legal Question Presented

"[W]hether the exclusion of a defendant from a hearing held to determine the competency of two child witnesses to testify violates the defendant's rights under the Confrontation Clause of the Sixth Amendment or the Due Process Clause of the Fourteenth Amendment."

C. Supreme Court's Answer

Defendant's exclusion from the competency hearing did not violate defendant's right under either the Confrontation Clause or the Due Process Clause.

II. CASE SUMMARY

A. Background

"Respondent Sergio Stincer was indicted in the Circuit Court of Christian County, Ky., and charged with committing first-degree sodomy with T. G., an 8-year-old girl, N. G., a 7-year-old girl, and B. H., a 5-year-old boy . . . . After a jury was sworn, but before the presentation of evidence, the court conducted an in-chambers hearing to determine if the two young girls were competent to testify. Over his objection, respondent, but not his counsel (a public defender), was excluded from this hearing.

The two children were examined separately and the judge, the prosecutor, and respondent's counsel asked questions of each girl to determine if she were capable of remembering basic facts and of distinguishing between telling the truth and telling a lie. . . . The two children were not asked about the substance of the testimony they were to give at trial. The court ruled that the girls were competent to testify. Respondent's counsel did not object to these rulings.

Before each of the girls began her substantive testimony in open court, the prosecutor repeated some of the basic questions regarding the girl's background that had been asked at the competency hearing. . . .

On cross-examination, respondent's counsel asked each girl questions designed to determine if she could remember past events and if she knew the difference between the truth and a lie. Some of these questions were similar to those that had been asked at the competency hearing. After the testimony of the girls was concluded, counsel did not request that the trial court reconsider its ruling that the girls were competent to testify. The jury convicted respondent of first-degree sodomy for engaging in deviate sexual intercourse and fixed his sentence at 20 years' imprisonment.

On appeal to the Supreme Court of Kentucky, respondent argued, among other things, that his exclusion from the competency hearing of the two girls denied him due process and violated his Sixth Amendment right to confront the witnesses against him. The Kentucky Supreme Court, by a divided vote, agreed that, under the Sixth Amendment of the Federal Constitution and under § 11 of the Bill of Rights of the Kentucky Constitution (the right 'to meet the witnesses face to face'), respondent had an absolute right to be present at the competency hearing because the hearing' was a crucial phase of the trial.'"

The U.S. Supreme Court granted certiorari to review the case and reversed.

B. Counsel of Record / ACLU Attorney

ACLU Side (Respondent / Appellee): Mark A. Posnansky, by appointment of the Court, argued the cause for appellee.

Opposing Side (Petitioner / Appellant): Penny R. Warren, Assistant Attorney General of Kentucky, argued the cause for appellant.

III. AMICI CURIAE

ACLU Side (Respondent / Appellee)

Brief of amici curiae filed on behalf of the ACLU by George Kannar.

Brief of amici curiae filed on behalf of the National Association of Criminal Defense Lawyers by Nancy Hollander.

Opposing Side (Petitioner / Appellant)

Brief of amici curiae filed on behalf of the State of Arkansas, et al., by Steve Clark, Attorney General of Arkansas, and Rodney A. Smolla, joined by the Attorneys General for their respective jurisdictions as follows: Don Siegelman of Alabama, Charles M. Oberly III of Delaware, Robert A. Butterworth of Florida, Charles Troutman of Guam, Jim Jones of Idaho, Linley E. Pearson of Indiana, Neil F. Hartigan of Illinois, Robert T. Stephan of Kansas, William J. Guste, Jr., of Louisiana, Frank J. Kelley of Michigan, Hubert H. Humphrey III of Minnesota, Edwin L. Pittman of Mississippi, William L. Webster of Missouri, Mike Greely of Montana, Brian McKay of Nevada, Stephen E. Merrill of New Hampshire, W. Cary Edwards of New Jersey, Hal Stratton of New Mexico, Lacy H. Thornburg of North Carolina, Nicholas Spaeth of North Dakota, Dave Frohnmayer of Oregon, LeRoy S. Zimmerman of Pennsylvania, James E. O'Neil of Rhode Island, T. Travis Medlock of South Carolina, Roger A. Tellinghuisen of South Dakota, W. J. Michael Cody of Tennessee, Jeffrey Amestoy of Vermont, J'Ada Finch-Sheen of the Virgin Islands, Charles G. Brown of West Virginia, and Donald J. Hanaway of Wisconsin.

Brief of amici curiae filed on behalf of the Appellate Committee of the California District Attorneys Association by Ira Reiner and Harry B. Sondheim.

Brief of amici curiae filed on behalf of the American Psychological Association by Donald N. Bersoff.

IV. THE SUPREME COURT'S DECISION

"The Commonwealth argues that respondent's exclusion from the competency hearing of the two children did not violate the Confrontation Clause because a competency hearing is not 'a stage of trial where evidence or witnesses are being presented to the trier of fact.' . . .

Instead of attempting to characterize a competency hearing as a trial or pretrial proceeding, it is more useful to consider whether excluding the defendant from the hearing interferes with his opportunity for effective cross-examination. No such interference occurred when respondent was excluded from the competency hearing of the two young girls in this case. After the trial court determined that the two children were competent to testify, they appeared and testified in open court. At that point, the two witnesses were subject to full and complete cross-examination, and were so examined. Respondent was present throughout this cross-examination and was available to assist his counsel as necessary. There was no Kentucky rule of law, nor any ruling by the trial court, that restricted respondent's ability to cross-examine the witnesses at trial. Any questions asked during the competency hearing, which respondent's counsel attended and in which he participated, could have been repeated during direct examination and cross-examination of the witnesses in respondent's presence. . . .

Because respondent had the opportunity for full and effective cross-examination of the two witnesses during trial, and because of the nature of the competency hearing at issue in this case, we conclude that respondent's rights under the Confrontation Clause were not violated by his exclusion from the competency hearing of the two girls. . . .

Respondent argues that his rights under the Due Process Clause of the Fourteenth Amendment were violated by his exclusion from the competency hearing. The Court has assumed that, even in situations where the defendant is not actually confronting witnesses or evidence against him, he has a due process right 'to be present in his own person whenever his presence has a relation, reasonably substantial, to the fulness of his opportunity to defend against the charge.' Although the Court has emphasized that this privilege of presence is not guaranteed 'when presence would be useless, or the benefit but a shadow,' due process clearly requires that a defendant be allowed to be present 'to the extent that a fair and just hearing would be thwarted by his absence.' Thus, a defendant is guaranteed the right to be present at any stage of the criminal proceeding that is critical to its outcome if his presence would contribute to the fairness of the procedure.

We conclude that respondent's due process rights were not violated by his exclusion from the competency hearing in this case. We emphasize, again, the particular nature of the competency hearing. No question regarding the substantive testimony that the two girls would have given during trial was asked at that hearing. All the questions, instead, were directed solely to each child's ability to recollect and narrate facts, to her ability to distinguish between truth and falsehood, and to her sense of moral obligation to tell the truth. Thus, although a competency hearing in which a witness is asked to discuss upcoming substantive testimony might bear a substantial relationship to a defendant's opportunity better to defend himself at trial, that kind of inquiry is not before us in this case.

Respondent has given no indication that his presence at the competency hearing in this case would have been useful in ensuring a more reliable determination as to whether the witnesses were competent to testify. He has presented no evidence that his relationship with the children, or his knowledge of facts regarding their background, could have assisted either his counsel or the judge in asking questions that would have resulted in a more assured determination of competency. On the record of this case, therefore, we cannot say that respondent's rights under the Due Process Clause of the Fourteenth Amendment were violated by his exclusion from the competency hearing. . . .

The judgment of the Supreme Court of Kentucky is reversed."

V. JUSTICE VOTE

3 Pro ACLU Side vs. 6 Con Opposing Side

ACLU Side (Respondent / Appellee)

1. Marshall, T. – Wrote dissenting opinion
2. Brennan, W. – Joined Marshall's dissent
3. Stevens, J. – Joined Marshall's dissent

Opposing Side (Petitioner / Appellant)

1. Blackmun, H. – Wrote majority opinion
2. Rehnquist, W. – Joined majority opinion
3. White, B. – Joined majority opinion
4. Powell, L. – Joined majority opinion
5. O'Connor, S. – Joined majority opinion
6. Scalia, A. – Joined majority opinion

VI. A WIN OR LOSS FOR THE ACLU?

The ACLU, as amicus curiae, urged affirmance of the judgment of the Kentucky Supreme Court; the U.S. Supreme Court reversed in a 6-3 vote, giving the ACLU an apparent loss.

628. Bowen v. Gilliard

(Decided June 25, 1987; 483 U.S. 587)

I. ISSUE

A. Issues Discussed

Civil rights, federal

B. Legal Question Presented

"Congress amended the statute authorizing Federal Aid to Families with Dependent Children (AFDC) to require that a family's eligibility for benefits must take into account . . . the income of all parents, brothers, and sisters living in the same home. The principal question presented . . . is whether that requirement violates the Fifth Amendment to the United States Constitution when it is applied to . . . a child for whom child support payments are being made by a noncustodial parent."

C. Supreme Court's Answer

"The provisions at issue do not violate the Due Process Clause" of the Fifth Amendment.

II. CASE SUMMARY

A. Background

"This litigation began in 1970. . . . The District Court . . . granted classwide relief. We affirmed that judgment. No constitutional question was decided at that time.

Congress amended the AFDC program in 1975 to require . . . that applicants for assistance must assign to the State any right to receive child support payments . . . . In response, North Carolina amended its laws . . . .

In 1983, the Secretary of Health and Human Services proposed certain amendments . . . .

The Secretary's proposal was not enacted in 1983, but one of the provisions in the Deficit Reduction Act of 1984 (DEFRA) established a standard filing unit for the AFDC program. . . .

Because the 1984 amendment forced families to include in the filing unit children for whom support payments were being received, the practical effect was that many families' total income was reduced. . . . In sum, if the assigned support exceeded $50 plus the difference in the benefit level caused by adding the child or children receiving support, the family would suffer; if less than $50 and the difference in the benefit level was collected as support, it would not. . . .

After North Carolina adopted regulations to comply with the 1984 amendments, some members of the class that had earlier obtained relief filed a motion to reopen the 1971 decree and obtain further relief on behalf of the class. . . . The District Court found that North Carolina's and the Department of Health and Human Services' regulations were in conformance with the statute, but concluded that the statutory scheme violated both the Due Process Clause and the Takings Clause of the Fifth Amendment."

The Supreme Court granted certiorari to review the case.

B. Counsel of Record

ACLU Side (Respondent / Appellee): Jane R. Wettach argued the cause for appellees in both cases. With her on the brief were Lucie E. White, Julius LeVonne Chambers, Eric Schnapper, and Jean M. Cary.

Opposing Side (Petitioner / Appellant): Deputy Solicitor General Lauber argued the cause for appellant in No. 86-509. With him on the briefs were Solicitor General Fried, Assistant Attorney General Willard, Jerrold J. Ganzfried, and William Kanter.

Catherine C. McLamb, Assistant Attorney General of North Carolina, argued the cause for appellants in No. 86-564. With her on the briefs were Lacy H. Thornburg, Attorney General, and Lemuel W. Hinton, Assistant Attorney General.

III. AMICI CURIAE

ACLU Side (Respondent / Appellee)

Brief of amici curiae filed on behalf of the American Civil Liberties Union, the Food Research Action Center, and the National Legal Aid and Defender Association by

Joan E. Bertin, John A. Powell, and Lucy Billings.

Brief of amici curiae filed on behalf of Juvenile and Family Court Judges by Thomas J. Madden.

Brief of amici curiae filed on behalf of the NOW Legal Defense and Education Fund et al. by Sally F. Goldfarb, Sarah E. Burns, and Marsha Levick.

Opposing Side (Petitioner / Appellant)

No briefs of amici curiae were filed in support of appellant.

IV. THE SUPREME COURT'S DECISION

"The precepts that govern our review of appellees' due process and equal protection challenges to this program are similar to those we have applied . . . to other parts of the Social Security Act:

'[O]ur review is deferential. 'Governmental decisions to spend money to improve the general public welfare in one way and not another are 'not confided to the courts. The discretion belongs to Congress unless the choice is clearly wrong, a display of arbitrary power, not an exercise of judgment." . . .

It was . . . rational for Congress to adjust the AFDC program to reflect the fact that support money generally provides significant benefits for entire family units. . . .

We conclude that the District Court erred in subjecting the DEFRA amendment to any form of heightened scrutiny. . . .

Last Term we rejected a constitutional challenge to a provision in the Federal Food Stamp Program . . . . We held that the guarantee of equal treatment in the Due Process Clause of the Fifth Amendment was not violated by the statutory requirement that generally treated parents, children, and siblings who lived together as a single household . . . .

In light of this, we concluded in Lyng that the 'District Court erred in judging the constitutionality of the statutory distinction under 'heightened scrutiny." In this case the District Court committed the same error. . . . The provisions at issue do not violate the Due Process Clause. . . .

Aside from holding that the amendment violated the Due Process Clause of the Fifth Amendment and its equal protection component, the District Court invalidated the DEFRA amendments as a taking of private property without just compensation. . . .

In evaluating whether governmental regulation of property constitutes a 'taking' we have 'eschewed the development of any set formula . . . and have relied instead on ad hoc, factual inquiries into the circumstances of each particular case.' . . .

Here, each of these three factors refutes the conclusion that there has been a taking. . . .

The law does not require any custodial parent to apply for AFDC benefits. Surely it is reasonable to presume that a parent who does make such an application does so because she or he is convinced that the family as a whole—as well as each child committed to her or his custody—will be better off with the benefits than without. In making such a decision, the parent is not taking a child's property without just compensation; nor is the State doing so when it responds to that decision by supplementing the collections of support money with additional AFDC benefits. . . .

The judgment of the District Court is reversed."

V. JUSTICE VOTE

3 Pro ACLU Side vs. 6 Con Opposing Side

ACLU Side (Respondent / Appellee)

1. Brennan, W. – Wrote dissenting opinion
2. Marshall, T. – Joined Brennan's dissent
3. Blackmun, H. – Wrote dissenting opinion

Opposing Side (Petitioner / Appellant)

1. Stevens, J. – Wrote majority opinion
2. Powell, L. – Joined majority opinion
3. Rehnquist, W. – Joined majority opinion
4. White, B. – Joined majority opinion
5. Scalia, A. – Joined majority opinion
6. O'Connor, S. – Joined majority opinion

VI. A WIN OR LOSS FOR THE ACLU?

The ACLU filed as amicus curiae urging affirmance; the Supreme Court reversed the District Court's decision by a 6-3 vote, giving the ACLU an apparent loss.

629. Anderson v. Creighton

(Decided June 25, 1987; 483 U.S. 635)

I. ISSUE

A. Issues Discussed

Criminal justice, Fourth Amendment, governmental liability, qualified immunity

B. Legal Question Presented

"[W]hether a federal law enforcement officer who participates in a search that violates the Fourth Amendment may be held personally liable for money damages if a reasonable officer could have believed that the search comported with the Fourth Amendment."

C. Supreme Court's Answer

The officer may not be held personally liable if a reasonable officer could have believed the search comported with the Fourth Amendment.

II. CASE SUMMARY

A. Background

"Petitioner Russell Anderson is an agent of the Federal Bureau of Investigation. On November 11, 1983, Anderson and other state and federal law enforcement officers conducted a warrantless search of the home of respondents, the Creighton family. The search was conducted because Anderson believed that Vadaain Dixon, a man suspected of a bank robbery committed earlier that day, might be found there. He was not.

The Creightons later filed suit against Anderson in a Minnesota state court, asserting among other things a claim for money damages under the Fourth Amendment. After removing the suit to Federal District Court, Anderson filed a motion to dismiss or for summary judgment, arguing that the Bivens claim was barred by Anderson's qualified immunity from civil damages liability. Before any discovery took place, the District Court granted summary judgment on the ground that the search was lawful, holding that the undisputed facts revealed that Anderson had had probable cause to search the Creighton's home and that his failure to obtain a warrant was justified by the presence of exigent circumstances.

The Creightons appealed to the Court of Appeals for the Eighth Circuit, which reversed."

The Supreme Court granted certiorari to review the case, vacated, and remanded.

B. Counsel of Record / ACLU Attorney

ACLU Side (Respondent / Appellee): John P. Sheehy argued the cause pro hac vice for appellee.

Opposing Side (Petitioner / Appellant): Andrew J. Pincus argued the cause for appellant.

III. AMICI CURIAE

ACLU Side (Respondent / Appellee)

Brief of amici curiae filed on behalf of the ACLU by David Rudovsky, Jack D. Novik, and Michael Avery.

Opposing Side (Petitioner / Appellant)

No briefs of amici curiae were filed in support of appellant.

IV. THE SUPREME COURT'S DECISION

"[G]overnment officials performing discretionary functions with a qualified immunity, [are shielded] from civil damages liability as long as their actions could reasonably have been thought consistent with the rights they are alleged to have violated. [W]hether an official protected by qualified immunity may be held personally liable for an allegedly unlawful official action generally turns on the 'objective legal reasonableness' of the action, assessed in light of the legal rules that were 'clearly established' at the time it was taken. . . .

The relevant question . . . is . . . whether a reasonable officer could have believed Anderson's warrantless search to be lawful, in light of clearly established law and the information the searching officers possessed. Anderson's subjective beliefs about the search are irrelevant.

The principles of qualified immunity that we reaffirm today require that Anderson be permitted to argue that he is entitled to summary judgment on the ground that, in light of the clearly established principles governing warrantless searches, he could, as a matter of law, reasonably have believed that the search of the Creightons' home was lawful. . . .

The general rule of qualified immunity is intended to provide government officials with the ability 'reasonably [to] anticipate when their conduct may give rise to liability for damages.' Where that rule is applicable, officials can know that they will not be held personally liable as long as their actions are reasonable in light of current American law. That security would be utterly defeated if officials were unable to determine whether they were protected by the rule without entangling themselves in the vagaries of the English and American common law. . . . We therefore decline to make an exception to the general rule of qualified immunity for cases involving allegedly unlawful warrantless searches of innocent third parties' homes in search of fugitives.

For the reasons stated, we vacate the judgment of the Court of Appeals and remand the case for further proceedings consistent with this opinion."

V. JUSTICE VOTE

3 PRO ACLU SIDE VS. 6 CON OPPOSING SIDE

ACLU Side (Respondent / Appellee)

1. Stevens, J. – Wrote dissenting opinion
2. Brennan, W. – Joined Steven's dissent
3. Marshall, T. – Joined Steven's dissent

Opposing Side (Petitioner / Appellant)

1. Scalia, A. – Wrote majority opinion
2. Rehnquist, W. – Joined majority opinion
3. White, B. – Joined majority opinion
4. Blackmun, H. – Joined majority opinion
5. Powell, L. – Joined majority opinion
6. O'Connor, S. – Joined majority opinion

VI. A WIN OR LOSS FOR THE ACLU?

The ACLU filed as amicus curiae urging affirmance of the judgment of the Court of Appeals; the Supreme Court reversed in a 6-3 vote, giving the ACLU an apparent loss.

630. Greer v. Miller

(Decided June 26, 1987; 483 U.S. 756)

I. ISSUE

A. Issues Discussed

Fourteenth Amendment, Due Process Clause, Miranda

B. Legal Question Presented

"[W]hether a prosecutor's question at trial concerning a criminal defendant's postarrest silence require reversal of the defendant's conviction."

C. Supreme Court's Answer

The improper question was cured at trial such that it does not require reversal of the conviction.

II. CASE SUMMARY

A. Background

"In 1980, Neil Gorsuch was kidnaped, robbed, and murdered after leaving a bar in Jacksonville, Illinois. Three men were charged with the crimes: Randy Williams, Clarence Armstrong, and the respondent, Charles Miller. Williams confessed, and later entered into a plea agreement under which most of the charges against him were dropped in return for his testimony at the separate trials of Armstrong and Miller.

At Miller's trial, Williams testified that he, his brother, and Armstrong had met Gorsuch in a tavern on the evening of February 8. Armstrong offered the victim a ride back to his hotel, and the four men left together at about 1:30 a.m. After Williams' brother was dropped off, Armstrong began beating Gorsuch in the back seat of the car. According to Williams' testimony, the group stopped briefly at Williams' parents' home to pick up a shotgun, and the men then drove to the trailer home where Miller was staying. Williams testified that Miller joined the group, and that they then traveled to a bridge on an isolated road. Williams stated that once there each of the three men shot Gorsuch in the head with the shotgun.

Respondent Miller took the stand on his own behalf and told a different story. On direct examination he testified that he had taken no part in the crime, but that Armstrong and Williams had come to the trailer home after the murder was committed seeking Miller's advice. Miller testified that Armstrong confessed that he and Williams had beaten and robbed Gorsuch, and that they had killed him to avoid being identified as the perpetrators.

The prosecutor began his cross-examination of Miller as follows:

'Q: Mr. Miller, how old are you?

'A: 23.

'Q: Why didn't you tell this story to anybody when you got arrested?'

Defense counsel immediately objected. Out of the hearing of the jury, Miller's lawyer requested a mistrial on the ground that the prosecutor's question violated Miller's right to remain silent after arrest. The trial judge denied the motion, but immediately sustained the objection and instructed the jury to 'ignore [the] question, for the time being.' The prosecutor did not pursue the issue further, nor did he mention it during his closing argument. At the conclusion of the presentation of evidence, defense counsel did not renew his objection or request an instruction concerning the prosecutor's question. Moreover, the judge specifically instructed the jury to 'disregard questions . . . to which objections were sustained.' Miller was convicted of murder, aggravated kidnaping, and robbery, and sentenced to 80 years in prison. . . .

The Illinois Appellate Court . . . reversed the conviction, concluding that the evidence against Miller 'was not so overwhelming as to preclude all reasonable doubts about the effect of the prosecutor's comment.' The Supreme Court of Illinois disagreed and reinstated the trial court's decision. . . .

Miller then filed a petition for a writ of habeas corpus in the Federal District Court for the Central District of Illinois. The District Court denied the petition, finding 'no possibility that the prosecutor's questioning on post-arrest silence could have contributed to the conviction.' A divided panel of the Court of Appeals for the Seventh Circuit reversed the District Court's decision as did the full court on reargument en banc."

The Supreme Court granted certiorari to review the case and reversed the judgment of the Seventh Circuit Court of Appeals.

B. Counsel of Record / ACLU Attorney

ACLU Side (Respondent / Appellee): Gary R. Peterson argued the cause for appellee.

Opposing Side (Petitioner / Appellant): Mark L. Rotert, Assistant Attorney General of Illinois, argued the cause for appellant.

III. AMICI CURIAE

ACLU Side (Respondent / Appellee)

Brief of amici curiae filed on behalf of the ACLU, et al., by Leon Friedman, Vivian O. Berger, and Harvey Grossman.

Opposing Side (Petitioner / Appellant)

No briefs of amici curiae were filed in support of appellant.

IV. THE SUPREME COURT'S DECISION

"The starting point of our analysis is Doyle v. Ohio. . . . The Court noted that postarrest silence may not be particularly probative of guilt. We also found that because Miranda warnings contain an implicit assurance 'that silence will carry no penalty,' "it does not comport with due process to permit the prosecution during the trial to call attention to [the defendant's] silence at the time of arrest and to insist that because he did not speak about the facts of the case at that time, as he was told he need not do, an unfavorable inference might be drawn as to the truth of his trial testimony." Accordingly, the Court in Doyle held that 'the use for impeachment purposes of petitioners' silence, at the time of arrest and after receiving Miranda warnings, violated the Due Process Clause of the Fourteenth Amendment.' . . .

There is no question that Miller received the 'implicit assurance' of Miranda warnings in this case. Thus, this prerequisite of a Doyle violation was met. But the holding of Doyle is that the Due Process Clause bars 'the use for impeachment purposes' of a defendant's postarrest silence.

[T]he trial court in this case did not permit the inquiry that Doyle forbids. Instead, the court explicitly sustained an objection to the only question that touched upon Miller's postarrest silence. No further questioning or argument with respect to Miller's silence occurred, and the court specifically advised the jury that it should disregard any questions to which an objection was sustained. . . . The fact of Miller's postarrest silence was not submitted to the jury as evidence from which it was allowed to draw any permissible inference, and thus no Doyle violation occurred in this case.

The sequence of events in this case—a single question, an immediate objection, and two curative instructions—clearly indicates that the prosecutor's improper question did not violate Miller's due process rights. The Illinois Supreme Court's determination that the properly admitted evidence at trial 'was sufficient to prove defendant's guilt beyond a reasonable doubt,' further supports this result. . . .

We reverse the judgment of the Court of Appeals for the Seventh Circuit and remand for proceedings consistent with this opinion."

V. JUSTICE VOTE

3 Pro ACLU Side vs. 6 Con Opposing Side

ACLU Side (Respondent / Appellee)

1. Brennan, W. – Wrote dissenting opinion
2. Marshall, T. – Joined Brennan's dissent
3. Blackmun, H. – Joined Brennan's dissent

Opposing Side (Petitioner / Appellant)

1. Powell, L. – Wrote majority opinion
2. Rehnquist, W. – Joined majority opinion
3. White, B. – Joined majority opinion
4. O'Connor, S. – Joined majority opinion
5. Scalia, A. – Joined majority opinion
6. Stevens, J. – Wrote concurring opinion

VI. A WIN OR LOSS FOR THE ACLU?

The ACLU, as amicus curiae, urged affirmance of the judgment of the Seventh Circuit Court of Appeals; the Supreme Court reversed in a 6-3 vote, giving the ACLU an apparent loss.

631. Griffin v. Wisconsin

(Decided June 26, 1987; 483 U.S. 868)

I. ISSUE

A. Issues Discussed

Fourth Amendment, search and seizure

B. Legal Question Presented

Whether a search without a warrant or probable cause of the home of petitioner, a probationer, violated the Fourth Amendment.

C. Supreme Court's Answer

The search of petitioner's home did not violate the Fourth Amendment.

II. CASE SUMMARY

A. Background

"On September 4, 1980, Griffin, who had previously been convicted of a felony, was convicted in Wisconsin state court of resisting arrest, disorderly conduct, and obstructing an officer. He was placed on probation.

Wisconsin law puts probationers in the legal custody of the State Department of Health and Social Services and renders them 'subject . . . to . . . conditions set by the court and rules and regulations established by the department.' One of the Department's regulations permits any probation officer to search a probationer's home without a warrant as long as his supervisor approves and as long as there are 'reasonable grounds' to believe the presence of contraband—including any item that the probationer cannot possess under the probation conditions. . . .

On April 5, 1983, while Griffin was still on probation, Michael Lew, the supervisor of Griffin's probation officer, received information from a detective on the Beloit Police Department that there were or might be guns in Griffin's apartment. Unable to secure the assistance of Griffin's own probation officer, Lew, accompanied by another probation officer and three plainclothes policemen, went to the apartment. When Griffin answered the door, Lew told him who they were and informed him that they were going to search his home. During the subsequent search—carried out entirely by the probation officers under the authority of Wisconsin's probation regulation—they found a handgun.

Griffin was charged with possession of a firearm by a convicted felon, which is itself a felony. He moved to suppress the evidence seized during the search. The trial court denied the motion, concluding that no warrant was necessary and that the search was reasonable. A jury convicted Griffin of the firearms violation, and he was sentenced to two years' imprisonment. The conviction was affirmed by the Wisconsin Court of Appeals.

On further appeal, the Wisconsin Supreme Court also affirmed."

The U.S. Supreme Court granted certiorari to review the case and affirmed the judgment of the Supreme Court of Wisconsin.

B. Counsel of Record / ACLU Attorney

ACLU Side (Petitioner / Appellant): Alan G. Habermehl, by appointment of the Court argued the cause for appellant.

Opposing Side (Respondent / Appellee): Barry M. Levenson, Assistant Attorney General of Wisconsin, argued the cause for appellee.

III. AMICI CURIAE

ACLU Side (Petitioner / Appellant)

Brief of amici curiae filed on behalf of the ACLU, et al., by Arthur Eisenberg.

Opposing Side (Respondent / Appellee)

Brief of amici curiae filed on behalf of the United States by Solicitor General Fried, Assistant Attorney General Weld,

Deputy Solicitor General Bryson, Richard G. Taranto, and Kathleen A. Felton.

Brief of amici curiae filed on behalf of the People of the State of California by John K. Van de Kamp, Attorney General, Steve White, Chief Assistant Attorney General, and Ronald E. Niver and Stan M. Helfman, Deputy Attorneys General.

Brief of amici curiae filed on behalf of the State of New York, et al., by Robert Abrams, Attorney General of New York, O. Peter Sherwood, Solicitor General, Lawrence S. Kahn, Deputy Solicitor General, Judith T. Kramer, Assistant Attorney General, Robert K. Corbin, Attorney General of Arizona, John J. Kelly, Chief State's Attorney of Connecticut, Charles M. Oberly III, Attorney General of Delaware, Robert A. Butterworth, Attorney General of Florida, James T. Jones, Attorney General of Idaho, Neil F. Hartigan, Attorney General of Illinois, Linley E. Pearson, Attorney General of Indiana, Frank J. Kelley, Attorney General of Michigan, Hubert H. Humphrey III, Attorney General of Minnesota, Stephen E. Merrill, Attorney General of New Hampshire, E. Cary Edwards, Attorney General of New Jersey, Lacy H. Thornburg, Attorney General of North Carolina, and T. Travis Medlock, Attorney General of South Carolina.

IV. THE SUPREME COURT'S DECISION

"We think the Wisconsin Supreme Court correctly concluded that this warrantless search did not violate the Fourth Amendment. . . . As his sentence for the commission of a crime, Griffin was committed to the legal custody of the Wisconsin State Department of Health and Social Services, and thereby made subject to that Department's rules and regulations. The search of Griffin's home satisfied the demands of the Fourth Amendment because it was carried out pursuant to a regulation that itself satisfies the Fourth Amendment's reasonableness requirement under well-established principles. . . .

A State's operation of a probation system, like its operation of a school, government office or prison, or its supervision of a regulated industry, likewise presents 'special needs' beyond normal law enforcement that may justify departures from the usual warrant and probable-cause requirements. Probation, like incarceration, is 'a form of criminal sanction imposed by a court upon an offender after verdict, finding, or plea of guilty.' . . .

These restrictions are meant to assure that the probation serves as a period of genuine rehabilitation and that the community is not harmed by the probationer's being at large. . . .

A warrant requirement would interfere to an appreciable degree with the probation system, setting up a magistrate rather than the probation officer as the judge of how close a supervision the probationer requires. Moreover, the delay inherent in obtaining a warrant would make it more difficult for probation officials to respond quickly to evidence of misconduct and would reduce the deterrent effect that the possibility of expeditious searches would otherwise create. By way of analogy, one might contemplate how parental custodial authority would be impaired by requiring judicial approval for search of a minor child's room. . . .

We think that the probation regime would also be unduly disrupted by a requirement of probable cause. . . . First, even more than the requirement of a warrant, a probable-cause requirement would reduce the deterrent effect of the supervisory arrangement. The probationer would be assured that so long as his illegal (and perhaps socially dangerous) activities were sufficiently concealed as to give rise to no more than reasonable suspicion, they would go undetected and uncorrected. . . .

The search of Griffin's residence was 'reasonable' within the meaning of the Fourth Amendment because it was conducted pursuant to a valid regulation governing probationers. This conclusion makes it unnecessary to consider whether, as the court below held and the State urges, any search of a probationer's home by a probation officer is lawful when there are 'reasonable grounds' to believe contraband is present. For the foregoing reasons, the judgment of the Wisconsin Supreme Court is affirmed."

V. JUSTICE VOTE

4 Pro ACLU Side vs. 5 Con Opposing Side

ACLU Side (Petitioner / Appellant)

1. Blackmun, H. – Wrote dissenting opinion
2. Marshall, T. – Joined Blackmun's dissent, joined Stevens' dissent
3. Brennan, W. – Joined Blackmun's dissent, in part
4. Stevens, J. – Wrote dissenting opinion, joined Blackmun's dissent, in part

Opposing Side (Respondent / Appellee)

1. Scalia, A. – Wrote majority opinion
2. Rehnquist, W. – Joined majority opinion
3. White, B. – Joined majority opinion
4. Powell, L. – Joined majority opinion
5. O'Connor, S. – Joined majority opinion

VI. A WIN OR LOSS FOR THE ACLU?

The ACLU, as amicus curiae, urged reversal of the judgment of the Supreme Court of Wisconsin; the U.S. Supreme Court affirmed in a 5-4 vote, giving the ACLU an apparent loss.

632. Church of Scientology of California v. Internal Revenue Service

(Decided November 10, 1987; 484 U.S. 9)

I. ISSUE

A. Issues Discussed

Governmental authority, tax information

B. Legal Question Presented

Whether "the Haskell Amendment removes from the classification of 'return information' all data which do not identify a particular taxpayer, and, [whether] 5 U.S.C. § 552(b)—requiring that '[a]ny reasonably segregable portion' of a record be provided to a requester after deletion of the portions which are exempt—compels respondent to redact 'return information' in its files where possible so as to bring that material within the terms of the

Haskell Amendment."

C. Supreme Court's Answer

Removal of identifying information from confidential documents does not remove the documents from protection simply because information identifying individual taxpayers is removed.

II. CASE SUMMARY

A. Background

"Section 6103 of the Internal Revenue Code 26 U.S.C. § 6103, lays down a general rule that 'returns' and 'return information' as defined therein shall be confidential. 'Return information' is elaborately defined in § 6103(b) (2); immediately after that definition appears the following proviso, known as the Haskell Amendment:

'[B]ut such term does not include data in a form which cannot be associated with, or otherwise identify, directly or indirectly, a particular taxpayer.'

Petitioner Church of Scientology of California, seeking disclosure under the Freedom of Information Act, contends that the Haskell Amendment excepts from the definition of 'return information' all material in the files of the Internal Revenue Service (IRS) which can be redacted to delete those parts which would identify a particular taxpayer. Respondent IRS in opposition argues that the mere redaction of identifying data will not, by virtue of the Haskell Amendment, take the material out of the definition of 'return information.' . . .

Petitioner filed a request with respondent under the Freedom of Information Act (FOIA), 5 U.S.C. § 552, for the production of numerous documents. . . . Dissatisfied by the slow response to its request, petitioner filed suit in the United States District Court for the District of Columbia to compel release of the materials. . . .

The District Court, after an in camera review of representative documents, held that respondent had correctly limited its search for and disclosure of materials requested by petitioner. Petitioner appealed that decision to the United States Court of Appeals for the District of Columbia Circuit. [T]he Court of Appeals sua sponte undertook en banc review of the meaning of the Haskell Amendment and the modification it works upon § 6103(b)(2). The Court of Appeals concluded that, by using the words 'in a form,' Congress contemplated 'not merely the deletion of an identifying name or symbol on a document that contains return information, but agency reformulation of the return information into a statistical study or some other composite product . . . .' Thus, the court held, before respondent may produce documents otherwise protected, the Haskell Amendment requires that some modification have occurred in the form of the data contained in the documents. '[M]ere deletion of the taxpayer's name or other identifying data is not enough, since that would render the reformulation requirement entirely duplicative of the nonidentification requirement.'"

The Supreme Court granted certiorari to review the case and affirmed.

B. Counsel of Record / ACLU Attorney

ACLU Side (Petitioner / Appellant): Michael Lee Hertzberg argued the cause for appellant.

Opposing Side (Respondent / Appellee): Deputy Solicitor General Lauber argued the cause for appellee.

III. AMICI CURIAE

ACLU Side (Petitioner / Appellant)

Brief of amici curiae filed on behalf of the ACLU, et al., by John A. Powell, Stephen K. Strong, and David F. Stobaugh.

Brief of amici curiae filed on behalf of Professor John L. Neufeld, et al., by David C. Vladeck and Alan B. Morrison.

Opposing Side (Respondent / Appellee)

No briefs of amici curiae were filed in support of appellee.

IV. THE SUPREME COURT'S DECISION

"Petitioner asserts that the segregation requirement of the FOIA, § 552(b), directs respondent to remove the identifiers from such documents as these and that, once the materials are purged of such identifiers, they must be disclosed because they no longer constitute return information described in § 6103(b)(2).

We find no support for petitioner's arguments in either the language of § 6103 or in its legislative history. In addition to the returns themselves, which are protected from disclosure by § 6103(b)(1), § 6103(b)(2) contains an elaborate description of the sorts of information related to returns that respondent is compelled to keep confidential. If the mere removal of identifying details from return information sufficed to put the information 'in a form' envisioned by the Haskell Amendment, the remainder of the categories included in § 6103(b)(2) would often be irrelevant. The entire section could have been prefaced by the simple instruction to respondent that the elimination of identifiers would shift related tax data outside the realm of protected return information. . . .

The legislative history of the Tax Reform Act of 1976, Pub. L. 94-455, 90 Stat. 1520, of which the amendments to § 6103 are a part, also indicates that Congress did not intend the statute to allow the disclosure of otherwise confidential return information merely by the redaction of identifying details. . . . Petitioner's suggestion that the Haskell Amendment was intended to modify the restrictions of § 6103 by making all nonidentifying return information eligible for disclosure would mean that the Amendment was designed to undercut the legislation' s primary purpose of limiting access to tax filings. . . .

We thus hold that, as with a return itself, removal of identification from return information would not deprive it of protection under § 6103(b). Since such deletion would not make otherwise protected return information discloseable, respondent has no duty under the FOIA to undertake such redaction. The judgment of the Court of Appeals is accordingly affirmed."

V. JUSTICE VOTE

0 Pro ACLU Side vs. 6 Con Opposing Side

Opposing Side (Respondent / Appellee)

1. Rehnquist, W. – Wrote majority opinion
2. White, B. – Joined majority opinion
3. O'Connor, S. – Joined majority opinion
4. Marshall, T. – Joined majority opinion

5. Stevens, J. – Joined majority opinion
6. Blackmun, H. – Joined majority opinion

Brennan, W. Took no part in the decision
Scalia, A. Took no part in the decision
Vacant Seat

VI. A WIN OR LOSS FOR THE ACLU?

The ACLU filed as amicus curiae urging reversal of the judgment of the Court of Appeals; the Supreme Court affirmed in a 6-0 vote, giving the ACLU an apparent loss.

633. Karcher v. May

(Decided December 1, 1987; 484 U.S. 72)

I. ISSUE

A. Issues Discussed

First Amendment, Establishment Clause, standing, jurisdiction

B. Legal Question Presented

"[W]hether public officials who have participated in a lawsuit solely in their official capacities may appeal an adverse judgment after they have left office."

C. Supreme Court's Answer

The former public officials may not appeal an adverse judgment after they have left office when they intervened in the case in their official capacities.

II. CASE SUMMARY

A. Background

"In December 1982 the New Jersey Legislature enacted, over the Governor's veto, a statute requiring the State's primary and secondary public school educators to permit their students to observe a minute of silence before the start of each schoolday. . . .

The New Jersey Attorney General immediately announced that he would not defend the statute if it were challenged. The statute became effective December 17, 1982, and within a month appellees—a New Jersey public school teacher, several public school students, and parents of public school students—challenged its constitutionality in federal court. Appellees sued under 42 U.S.C. § 1983, alleging that the statute violated the Establishment Clause of the First Amendment and seeking both declaratory and injunctive relief. They named as defendants the New Jersey Department of Education, its Commissioner, and two township boards of education.

When it became apparent that neither the Attorney General nor the named defendants would defend the statute, Karcher and Orechio, as Speaker of the New Jersey General Assembly and President of the New Jersey Senate, respectively, sought and obtained permission to intervene as defendants on behalf of the legislature. Appellees entered into a stipulation dismissing the suit against the named defendants, but the District Court refused to accept the stipulation out of concern for the effect it might have on the jurisdictional posture of the case. The legislature, through its presiding officers, carried the entire burden of defending the statute.

After a 5-day trial, the District Court declared the New Jersey statute unconstitutional. . . .

Karcher and Orechio appealed from the District Court's judgment in their official capacities as Speaker of the New Jersey General Assembly and President of the New Jersey Senate. The named defendants filed letters with the Court of Appeals stating that they would not participate in the appeal, except to the extent necessary to protect themselves from having to pay attorney's fees.

The Court of Appeals affirmed the District Court's declaratory judgment by a divided vote. . . .

On January 14, 1986, Karcher and Orechio lost their posts as presiding legislative officers. Charles Hardwick replaced Karcher as Speaker of the New Jersey General Assembly. John Russo succeeded Orechio as President of the New Jersey Senate.

A March 19, 1986, notice appealing the judgment of the Court of Appeals to [the Supreme] Court was filed on behalf of 'Alan J. Karcher, as Speaker of the New Jersey General Assembly; the New Jersey General Assembly; Carmen A. Orechio, as President of the New Jersey Senate and the New Jersey Senate.' By letter dated May 6, 1986, appellants' counsel informed [the Supreme Court] that Senate President Russo and General Assembly Speaker Hardwick were withdrawing the legislature's appeal, but that Karcher desired to continue the appeal. Appellees moved to dismiss the appeal on the ground that the legislature's withdrawal left the Court without a case or controversy. [The Supreme Court] postponed consideration of the jurisdictional question to the hearing of the case on the merits."

The Supreme Court reviewed the case and ultimately dismissed the appeal for lack of jurisdiction.

B. Counsel of Record / ACLU Attorney

ACLU Side (Respondent / Appellee): Norman L. Cantor argued the cause for appellee. With him on the briefs were Richard M. Altman, John A. Powell, and Eric Neisser.

Opposing Side (Petitioner / Appellant): Rex E. Lee argued the cause for appellant. With him on the briefs were William W. Robertson, Dean A. Gaver, Robert P. Zoller, and Carter G. Phillips.

III. AMICI CURIAE

ACLU Side (Respondent / Appellee)

Brief of amici curiae filed on behalf of the American Association of School Administrators by David S. Tatel, Walter A. Smith, Jr., and Elizabeth B. Heffernan.

Brief of amici curiae filed on behalf of the American Jewish Congress, et al., by Sheldon H. Elsen and Clement J. Colucci.

Brief of amici curiae filed on behalf of Americans United for Separation of Church and State, et al., by Lee Boothby and James M. Parker.

Brief of amici curiae filed on behalf of the Anti-Defamation League of B'nai B'rith, et al., by Ruti G. Teitel, Justin J. Finger, Meyer Eisenberg, Jeffrey P. Sinensky, and Steven M. Freeman.

Brief of amici curiae filed on behalf of the New Jersey Council of Churches, et al., by Donald L. Drakeman.

Brief of amici curiae filed on behalf of the New Jersey Education Association by James R. Zazzali and Kenneth I. Nowak.

Opposing Side (Petitioner / Appellant)

Brief of amici curiae filed on behalf of the United States by Solicitor General Fried, Assistant Attorney General Reynolds, Deputy Solicitor General Ayer, Deputy Assistant Attorney General Carvin, Andrew J. Pincus, David K. Flynn, and Dennis J. Dimsey.

Brief of amici curiae filed on behalf of the State of Connecticut, et al., by Joseph I. Lieberman, Attorney General of Connecticut, Barney Lapp, Henry S. Cohn, and Carl J. Schuman, Assistant Attorneys General, and by the Attorneys General for their respective States as follows: Robert K. Corbin of Arizona, Charles M. Oberly III of Delaware, Linley E. Pearson of Indiana, William J. Guste, Jr., of Louisiana, Frank J. Kelley of Michigan, Brian McKay of Nevada, and Hal Stratton of New Mexico.

Brief of amici curiae filed on behalf of the Catholic League for Religious and Civil Rights by Steven Frederick McDowell.

Brief of amici curiae filed on behalf of the Rutherford Institute, et al., by John W. Whitehead, David E. Morris, Alfred J. Lindh, Ira W. Still III, William B. Hollberg, Randall A. Pentiuk, Thomas W. Strahan, John F. Southworth, Jr., and W. Charles Bundren.

Brief of amici curiae filed on behalf of Ronald Sokalski, et al., by Rex E. Lee, Carter G. Phillips, Richard G. Wilkins, Michael J. Woodruff, and Samuel E. Ericsson.

IV. THE SUPREME COURT'S DECISION

"[W]e have consistently applied the general rule that one who is not a party or has not been treated as a party to a judgment has no right to appeal therefrom.

Karcher and Orechio intervened in this lawsuit in their official capacities as presiding officers on behalf of the New Jersey Legislature. They do not appeal the judgment in those capacities. Indeed, they could not, for they no longer hold those offices. The authority to pursue the lawsuit on behalf of the legislature belongs to those who succeeded Karcher and Orechio in office. . . . The current presiding officers have informed us that the New Jersey Legislature is not an appellant in this case. . . .

The course of proceedings in this case from the District Court to this Court make it clear that the only party-intervenor in this case was the incumbent New Jersey Legislature. At the District Court hearing on their oral motion to intervene, Karcher and Orechio represented to both the court and their opponents that they were intervening on behalf of the legislature and not as individual legislators. . . .

In sum, Karcher and Orechio participated in this lawsuit in their official capacities as presiding officers of the New Jersey Legislature, but since they no longer hold those offices, they lack authority to pursue this appeal on behalf of the legislature. Karcher and Orechio as individual legislators and as representatives of the 200th New Jersey Legislature are not 'parties' entitled to appeal the Court of Appeals' judgment under 28 U.S.C. § 1254(2). Accordingly, we must dismiss their appeal for want of jurisdiction."

V. JUSTICE VOTE

8 Pro ACLU Side vs. 0 Con Opposing Side

ACLU Side (Respondent / Appellee)

1. O'Connor, S. – Wrote majority opinion
2. Rehnquist, W. – Joined majority opinion
3. Brennan, W. – Joined majority opinion
4. Marshall, T. – Joined majority opinion
5. Blackmun, H. – Joined majority opinion
6. Stevens, J. – Joined majority opinion
7. Scalia, A. – Joined majority opinion
8. White, B. – Wrote concurring opinion

Vacant Seat

VI. A WIN OR LOSS FOR THE ACLU?

The ACLU, as counsel for appellee, urged dismissal; the Supreme Court dismissed the appeal from the circuit court by an 8-0 vote, giving the ACLU an apparent win.

634. Deakins v. Monaghan

(Decided January 12, 1988; 484 U.S. 193)

I. ISSUE

A. Issues Discussed

Civil rights, federal rights, Fourth Amendment, Fifth Amendment, Sixth Amendment, Fourteenth Amendment, abstention

B. Legal Question Presented

"[W]hether the District Court, under Younger v. Harris, was required to abstain from adjudicating respondents' claims for injunctive relief, and, if so, whether the court had the discretion to dismiss, rather than to stay, respondents' additional claims for damages and attorney's fees."

C. Supreme Court's Answer

The injunctive relief claim is moot and the District Court should have stayed the additional claims.

II. CASE SUMMARY

A. Background

"Respondents William Monaghan, Theodore DeSantis, and John James are in the construction business together. They jointly own respondents Foundations & Structures, Inc. (F & S), and MJD Construction Company, Inc., New Jersey corporations, and William E. Monaghan Associates, a New Jersey general partnership. On October 4, 1984, petitioner Albert G. Palentchar, a criminal investigator for the State of New Jersey, applied to the Honorable Samuel T. Lenox, Jr., . . . for a warrant to search the Tuckahoe, N.J., premises of F & S . . . . Judge Lenox found probable cause and issued a warrant authorizing the seizure of documents . . . .

The following morning, Palentchar and eight other New Jersey law enforcement officers, all petitioners here, executed the warrant. The search lasted approximately eight hours. In their federal complaint, respondents allege that, in addition to seizing hundreds of documents, petitioners barricaded the sole exit from the premises, searched all departing vehicles, recorded the serial numbers on F & S machinery, detained in one room all persons on the premises at the time of the search until they produced identification, threatened to tear apart respondents' homes if the documents were not discovered, and engaged in a number of other unlawful activities. . . .

Respondents' attorneys arrived while the search was in progress and challenged the adequacy under New Jersey law of the inventory procedure. To resolve the dispute, respondents' counsel and petitioner Deakins telephoned Judge Lenox, who ordered all seized materials sealed pending his assessment of the procedure. . . . In the course of this examination, counsel identified numerous documents that they contended were either outside the scope of the warrant or protected by the attorney-client or attorney-work-product privilege. The State disagreed, and the disputed documents were resealed under the authority of Judge Lenox's original sealing order.

On December 27, while the documents were still under seal, respondents instituted this civil rights action under 42 U.S.C. § 1983 in the United States District Court for the District of New Jersey. [P]etitioners moved to dismiss the complaint, arguing that the existence of an ongoing state grand jury investigation required the federal court to abstain from adjudicating disputes arising out of that investigation. Respondents countered with a motion for a preliminary injunction directing the return of the documents.

While all this was taking place in federal court, Judge Lenox, at the State's behest, entered an ex parte order directing respondents to show cause why he should not lift the seal and make the documents available to the state officials conducting the grand jury investigation. Three days before the scheduled hearing on that order to show cause, the District Court issued a temporary restraining order staying discovery in the federal action and directing the State not to lift the seal before the District Court disposed of the motions pending before it. Several months later, on August 6, 1985, the District Court granted petitioners' motion to dismiss on abstention grounds and denied respondents' motion for a preliminary injunction.

On appeal, the Court of Appeals for the Third Circuit affirmed the District Court's denial of the preliminary injunction but reversed the judgment dismissing the complaint. . . .

After the Court of Appeals rendered its judgment, the state grand jury returned an indictment against three of the respondents . . . . The Superior Court has since held that certain documents were seized in violation of the attorney-client privilege and has ordered their return. Still pending before that court are motions seeking the return of other documents seized. In light of these developments, all six respondents represent, through common counsel, that they do not wish to pursue their claims for equitable relief in federal court. They wish to withdraw these claims from their federal complaint and seek injunctive relief exclusively in the state proceedings initiated by the indictment. Respondents also represent that, if the complaint were remanded to the District Court, they would seek a stay of all federal proceedings on the damages claims pending resolution of the state proceedings."

The Supreme Court granted certiorari to review the case, affirmed in part, vacated in part, and remanded.

B. Counsel of Record / ACLU Attorney

ACLU Side (Respondent / Appellee): Edward N. Fitzpatrick argued the cause for appellee.

Opposing Side (Petitioner / Appellant): Larry R. Etzweiler, Deputy Attorney General of New Jersey, argued the cause for appellant.

III. AMICI CURIAE

ACLU Side (Respondent / Appellee)

Brief of amici curiae filed on behalf of the ACLU, et al., by Frank Askin, Eric Neisser, and John A. Powell.

Opposing Side (Petitioner / Appellant)

No briefs of amici curiae were filed in support of appellant.

IV. THE SUPREME COURT'S DECISION

"Because this case was rendered moot in part by respondents' willingness permanently to withdraw their equitable claims from their federal action, a dismissal with prejudice is indicated. . . .

Our conclusion that the issue concerning respondents' equitable claims is now moot does not prevent our consideration of the propriety of the District Court's dismissal of respondents' claims for monetary relief. . . .

In reversing the District Court's dismissal of the claims for damages and attorney's fees, the Court of Appeals applied the Third Circuit rule that requires a District Court to stay rather than dismiss claims that are not cognizable in the parallel state proceeding. The Third Circuit rule is sound. It allows a parallel state proceeding to go forward without interference from its federal sibling, while enforcing the duty of federal courts 'to assume jurisdiction where jurisdiction properly exists.' . . .

Because respondents' claims for equitable relief are moot, we vacate the portion of the Court of Appeals' judgment addressing those claims and remand with instructions to dismiss the claims for equitable relief with prejudice. We affirm the portion of the Court of Appeals' judgment reversing the District Court's dismissal of respondents' claims for monetary relief and attorney's fees."

V. JUSTICE VOTE

8 Pro ACLU Side vs. 0 Con Opposing Side

ACLU Side (Respondent / Appellee)

1. Blackmun, H. – Wrote majority opinion
2. Rehnquist, W. – Joined majority opinion
3. Brennan, W. – Joined majority opinion
4. Marshall, T. – Joined majority opinion
5. Stevens, J. – Joined majority opinion
6. Scalia, A. – Joined majority opinion
7. White, B. – Wrote concurring opinion
8. O'Connor, S. – Joined White's concurrence

Vacant Seat

VI. A WIN OR LOSS FOR THE ACLU?

The ACLU filed as amicus curiae urging affirmance of the judgment of the Court of Appeals for the Third Circuit; the Supreme Court affirmed in part, vacated in part, and remanded, giving the ACLU an apparent win.

635. Hazelwood School District v. Kuhlmeier

(Decided January 13, 1988; 484 U.S. 260)

I. ISSUE

A. Issues Discussed

First Amendment, freedom of speech

B. Legal Question Presented

To what extent may educators "exercise editorial control over the contents of a high school newspaper produced as part of the school's journalism curriculum"?

C. Supreme Court's Answer

The principal's decision to not allow two pages of the student newspaper to go to print was an exercise of proper editorial control and did not infringe students' First Amendment rights.

II. CASE SUMMARY

A. Background

"Petitioners are the Hazelwood School District in St. Louis County, Missouri; various school officials; Robert Eugene Reynolds, the principal of Hazelwood East High School; and Howard Emerson, a teacher in the school district. Respondents are three former Hazelwood East students who were staff members of Spectrum, the school newspaper. They contend that school officials violated their First Amendment rights by deleting two pages of articles from the May 13, 1983, issue of Spectrum.

Spectrum was written and edited by the Journalism II class at Hazelwood East. . . . The practice at Hazelwood East during the spring 1983 semester was for the journalism teacher to submit page proofs of each Spectrum issue to Principal Reynolds for his review prior to publication. On May 10, Emerson delivered the proofs of the May 13 edition to Reynolds, who objected to two of the articles scheduled to appear in that edition. One of the stories described three Hazelwood East students' experiences with pregnancy; the other discussed the impact of divorce on students at the school. . . . Accordingly, he directed Emerson to withhold from publication the two pages containing the stories on pregnancy and divorce. He informed his superiors of the decision, and they concurred. Respondents subsequently commenced this action in the United States District Court for the Eastern District of Missouri seeking a declaration that their First Amendment rights had been violated, injunctive relief, and monetary damages. After a bench trial, the District Court denied an injunction, holding that no First Amendment violation had

occurred. . . . The Court of Appeals for the Eighth Circuit reversed."

The Supreme Court granted certiorari to review the case and reversed.

B. Counsel of Record / ACLU Attorney

ACLU Side (Respondent / Appellee): Leslie D. Edwards argued the cause and filed a brief for appellee.

Opposing Side (Petitioner / Appellant): Robert P. Baine, Jr., argued the cause for appellant.

III. AMICI CURIAE

ACLU Side (Respondent / Appellee)

Briefs of amici curiae filed on behalf of the ACLU, et al., by Janet L. Benshoof, John A. Powell, Steven R. Shapiro, and Frank Susman.

Brief of amici curiae filed on behalf of the American Society of Newspaper Editors, et al., by Richard M. Schmidt, Jr.

Brief of amici curiae filed on behalf of People for the American Way by Marvin E. Frankel.

Brief of amici curiae filed on behalf of the NOW Legal Defense and Education Fund, et al., by Martha L. Minow, Sarah E. Burns, and Marsha Levick.

Brief of amici curiae filed on behalf of the Planned Parenthood Federation of America, Inc., et al., by Eve W. Paul.

Brief of amici curiae filed on behalf of the Student Press Law Center, et al., by J. Marc Abrams.

Opposing Side (Petitioner / Appellant)

Brief of amici curiae filed on behalf of the Pacific Legal Foundation by Ronald A. Zumbrun and Anthony T. Caso.

Brief of amici curiae filed on behalf of the National School Boards Association, et al., by Gwendolyn H. Gregory, August W. Steinhilber, Thomas A. Shannon, and Ivan B. Gluckman.

Brief of amici curiae filed on behalf of the School Board of Dade County, Florida, by Frank A. Howard, Jr., and Johnny Brown.

IV. THE SUPREME COURT'S DECISION

"[T]he First Amendment rights of students in the public schools 'are not automatically coextensive with the rights of adults in other settings,' and must be 'applied in light of the special characteristics of the school environment.' . . .

We deal first with the question whether Spectrum may appropriately be characterized as a forum for public expression. [S]chool facilities may be deemed to be public forums only if school authorities have 'by policy or by practice' opened those facilities 'for indiscriminate use by the general public,' or by some segment of the public, such as student organizations. . . .

School officials did not evince either 'by policy or by practice,' any intent to open the pages of Spectrum to 'indiscriminate use,' by its student reporters and editors, or by the student body generally. Instead, they 'reserve[d] the forum for its intended purpos[e],' as a supervised learning experience for journalism students. Accordingly, school officials were entitled to regulate the contents of Spectrum in any reasonable manner. . . .

The question whether the First Amendment requires a school to tolerate particular student speech—the question that we addressed in Tinker —is different from the question whether the First Amendment requires a school affirmatively to promote particular student speech. [W]e conclude that the standard articulated in Tinker for determining when a school may punish student expression need not also be the standard for determining when a school may refuse to lend its name and resources to the dissemination of student expression. Instead, we hold that educators do not offend the First Amendment by exercising editorial control over the style and content of student speech in school-sponsored expressive activities so long as their actions are reasonably related to legitimate pedagogical concerns. . . . It is only when the decision to censor a school-sponsored publication, theatrical production, or other vehicle of student expression has no valid educational purpose that the First Amendment is so 'directly and sharply implicate[d],' as to require judicial intervention to protect students' constitutional rights. . . .

We also conclude that Principal Reynolds acted reasonably in requiring the deletion from the May 13 issue of Spectrum of the pregnancy article, the divorce article, and the remaining articles that were to appear on the same pages of the newspaper.

[W]e cannot reject as unreasonable Principal Reynolds' conclusion that neither the pregnancy article nor the divorce article was suitable for publication in Spectrum. Reynolds could reasonably have concluded that the students who had written and edited these articles had not sufficiently mastered those portions of the Journalism II curriculum that pertained to the treatment of controversial issues and personal attacks, the need to protect the privacy of individuals whose most intimate concerns are to be revealed in the newspaper, and 'the legal, moral, and ethical restrictions imposed upon journalists within [a] school community' that includes adolescent subjects and readers. Finally, we conclude that the principal's decision to delete two pages of Spectrum, rather than to delete only the offending articles or to require that they be modified, was reasonable under the circumstances as he understood them. Accordingly, no violation of First Amendment rights occurred. The judgment of the Court of Appeals for the Eighth Circuit is therefore reversed."

V. JUSTICE VOTE

3 Pro ACLU Side vs. 5 Con Opposing Side

ACLU Side (Respondent / Appellee)

1. Brennan, W. – Wrote dissenting opinion
2. Marshall, T. – Joined Brennan's dissent
3. Blackmun, H. – Joined Brennan's dissent

Opposing Side (Petitioner / Appellant)

1. White, B. – Wrote majority opinion
2. Rehnquist, W. – Joined majority opinion
3. Stevens, J. – Joined majority opinion
4. O'Connor, S. – Joined majority opinion
5. Scalia, A. – Joined majority opinion

   Vacant Seat

VI. A WIN OR LOSS FOR THE ACLU?

The ACLU, as amicus curiae, urged affirmance of the judgment of the Court of Appeals; the Supreme Court reversed in a 5-3 vote, giving the ACLU an apparent loss.

636. Virginia v. American Booksellers Ass'n, Inc.

(Decided January 25, 1988; 484 U.S. 383)

I. ISSUE

A. Issues Discussed

First Amendment, freedom of speech, obscenity

B. Legal Question Presented

Whether "the following Virginia statute: 'It shall be unlawful for any person . . . to knowingly display for commercial purpose in a manner whereby juveniles may examine and peruse' visual or written material that 'depicts sexually explicit nudity, sexual conduct or sadomasochistic abuse and which is harmful to juveniles,'" is unconstitutional.

C. Supreme Court's Answer

The Court certified two questions to the Virginia Supreme Court to aid in determining the constitutionality of the statute.

II. CASE SUMMARY

A. Background

"The Virginia Code's current definition of 'harmful to juveniles' is a modification of the Miller definition of obscenity, adapted for juveniles. The statute reads in relevant part:

"Harmful to Juveniles' means that quality of any description or presentation, in whatever form, of nudity, sexual conduct, sexual excitement, or sadomasochistic abuse, when it (a) predominately appeals to the prurient, shameful or morbid interest of juveniles, (b) is patently offensive to prevailing standards in the adult community as a whole with respect to what is suitable material for juveniles, and (c) is, when taken as a whole, lacking in serious literary, artistic, political or scientific value for juveniles.'

In 1985, Virginia amended its law to make it also a crime 'to knowingly display for commercial purpose in a manner whereby juveniles may examine and peruse' the aforementioned materials, even if these materials are not actually sold to any juvenile.

Plaintiffs made a facial challenge to the 1985 amendment in the United States District Court for the Eastern District of Virginia. They asserted that the 1985 amendment was fundamentally different from the prior statute in that it burdens the First Amendment rights of adults, as to whom at least some of the covered works are not obscene. . . . Plaintiffs brought suit under 42 U.S.C. § 1983 against the Arlington County Chief of Police. Pursuant to 28 U.S.C. § 2403(b), the Virginia Attorney General intervened. . . .

Plaintiffs moved for a preliminary injunction, and defendants moved to dismiss or abstain. . . . The trial court denied defendant's motion to dismiss the case and declined to abstain. On the merits, it held as a factual matter that the statute would cover between 5 and 25 percent of a typical bookseller's inventory. Further, the court agreed with plaintiffs as to the alternatives available to comply with the law, rejecting defendants' suggestion that a bookseller could avoid criminal prosecution by merely tagging the materials or placing them behind 'blinder' racks. The court reasoned from this that the 1985 amendment placed significant burdens on adult First Amendment rights by restricting adult access to nonobscene works. It concluded that the 1985 amendment was overbroad, and permanently enjoined its enforcement.

The Court of Appeals for the Fourth Circuit affirmed."

The Supreme Court granted certiorari to review the case and certified questions to the Virginia Supreme Court.

B. Counsel of Record / ACLU Attorney

ACLU Side (Respondent / Appellee): Paul M. Bator argued the cause for appellee.

Opposing Side (Petitioner / Appellant): Richard B. Smith, Assistant Attorney General of Virginia, argued the cause for appellant.

III. AMICI CURIAE

ACLU Side (Respondent / Appellee)

Brief of amici curiae filed on behalf of the ACLU, et al., by Charles S. Sims, John A. Powell, and Steven R. Shapiro.

Brief of amici curiae filed on behalf of the Freedom to Read Foundation by Bruce J. Ennis and David W. Ogden.

Brief of amici curiae filed on behalf of Jean M. Auel, et al., by R. Bruce Rich.

Opposing Side (Petitioner / Appellant)

Brief of amici curiae filed on behalf of the city of Minneapolis by Robert J. Alfton and David M. Gross.

Brief of amici curiae filed on behalf of the Institute for Youth Advocacy by Gregory A. Loken.

Brief of amici curiae filed on behalf of the National Legal Foundation by Paul S. McConnell and Robert K. Skolrood.

IV. THE SUPREME COURT'S DECISION

"We first address plaintiffs' standing to bring suit. The State argued before the District Court that plaintiffs lacked standing to bring a pre-enforcement facial challenge, alleging that plaintiffs did not suffer sufficient harm, and what harm they did suffer was economic, not speech related. Further, the State argued that plaintiffs' challenge was premature, having been made before the statute became effective. . . .

We are not troubled by the pre-enforcement nature of this suit. The State has not suggested that the newly enacted law will not be enforced, and we see no reason to assume otherwise. We conclude that plaintiffs have alleged an actual and well-founded fear that the law will be enforced against them. Further, the alleged danger of this statute is, in large measure, one of self-censorship; a harm that can be realized even without an actual prosecution. . . .

We have concluded that we should not attempt to decide the constitutional issues presented without first having the Virginia Supreme Court's interpretation of key provisions of the statute. Several factors combine in a unique way to counsel that course.

At oral argument the State's attorney conceded that if the statute is read as plaintiffs contend, not only is it unconstitutional but its enforcement should, as a normative matter, be enjoined. Indeed, he seemingly conceded that if any of the books introduced as plaintiffs' exhibits below is covered by the statute, plaintiffs should prevail. However, the State argues that the statute's coverage is much narrower than plaintiffs allege or the courts below found. It contends that the statute covers only a very few 'borderline' obscene works, and none of the exhibits introduced by plaintiffs. . . .

Under these unusual circumstances, where it appears the State will decline to defend a statute if it is read one way and where the nature and substance of plaintiffs' constitutional challenge is drastically altered if the statute is read another way, it is essential that we have the benefit of the law's authoritative construction from the Virginia Supreme Court. . . .

Pursuant to Rule 5:42 of the Virginia Supreme Court, we respectfully certify to that court the following questions:

1. Does the phrase 'harmful to juveniles' as used in Virginia Code 18.2-390 and 18.2-391 (1982 and Supp. 1987), properly construed, encompass any of the books introduced as plaintiffs' exhibits below, and what general standard should be used to determine the statute's reach in light of juveniles' differing ages and levels of maturity?

2. What meaning is to be given to the provision of Virginia Code 18.2-391(a) (Supp. 1987) making it unlawful 'to knowingly display for commercial purpose in a manner whereby juveniles may examine or peruse' certain materials? Specifically, is the provision complied with by a plaintiff bookseller who has a policy of not permitting juveniles to examine and peruse materials covered by the statute and who prohibits such conduct when observed, but otherwise takes no action regarding the display of restricted materials? If not, would the statute be complied with if the store's policy were announced or otherwise manifested to the public?"

V. JUSTICE VOTE

0 Pro ACLU Side vs. 8 Con Opposing Side

Opposing Side (Petitioner / Appellant)

1. Brennan, W. – Wrote majority opinion
2. Rehnquist, W. – Joined majority opinion
3. White, B. – Joined majority opinion
4. Marshall, T. – Joined majority opinion
5. Blackmun, H. – Joined majority opinion
6. O'Connor, S. – Joined majority opinion
7. Scalia, A. – Joined majority opinion
8. Stevens, J. – Wrote opinion concurring in part and dissenting in part

Vacant Seat

VI. A WIN OR LOSS FOR THE ACLU?

The ACLU filed as amicus curiae urging affirmance; the U.S. Supreme Court certified two questions and remanded the matter to the Virginia Supreme Court in an 8-0 vote, giving the ACLU an apparent loss.

637. Department of the Navy v. Egan

(Decided February 23, 1988; 484 U.S. 518)

I. ISSUE

A. Issues Discussed

National security, security clearance

B. Legal Question Presented

"[W]hether the Merit Systems Protection Board (Board) has authority by statute to review the substance of an underlying decision to deny or revoke a security clearance in the course of reviewing an adverse action."

C. Supreme Court's Answer

The Board does not have the authority to review the substance of an underlying decision to deny or revoke a security clearance.

II. CASE SUMMARY

A. Background

"Respondent Thomas M. Egan lost his laborer's job at the Trident Naval Refit Facility in Bremerton, Wash., when he was denied a required security clearance. . . . On February 16, 1983, the Director of the Naval Civilian Personnel Command issued a letter of intent to deny respondent a security clearance. . . . Respondent was informed that he had a right to respond to the proposed security-clearance denial. On May 6, he answered the Navy's letter of intent . . . . The Director, after reviewing this response, concluded that the information provided did not sufficiently explain, mitigate, or refute the reasons on which the proposed denial was based. Accordingly, respondent's security clearance was denied.

Respondent took an appeal to the Personnel Security Appeals Board, but his removal was effected before that Board acted (which it eventually did by affirming the denial of clearance).

Without a security clearance, respondent was not eligible for the job for which he had been hired. Reassignment to a nonsensitive position at the facility was not possible because there was no nonsensitive position there. Accordingly, the Navy issued a notice of proposed removal, and respondent was placed on administrative leave pending final decision. Respondent did not reply to the notice. On July 15, 1983, he was informed that his removal was effective July 22.

Respondent, pursuant to 5 U.S.C. § 7513(d), sought review by the Merit Systems Protection Board. Under § 7513(a), an agency may remove an employee 'only for such cause as will promote the efficiency of the service.' The statute, together with § 7701 to which § 7513(d) specifically refers, provides the employee with a number of procedural protections, including notice, an opportunity to respond and be represented by counsel, and a decision in writing. The employee, unless he is a nonveteran in the excepted service, may appeal the agency's decision to the Board, as respondent did, which is to sustain the action if it is 'supported by a preponderance of the evidence.' The stated 'cause' for respondent's removal was his failure to meet the requirements for his position due to the denial of security clearance. Before the Board, the Government argued that the Board's review power was limited to determining whether the required removal procedures had been followed and whether a security clearance was a condition for respondent's position. It contended that the Board did not have the authority to judge the merits of the underlying security-clearance determination.

The Board's presiding official reversed the agency's decision, ruling that the Board did have authority to review the merits. . . .

The Navy petitioned for full Board review of the presiding official's ruling. In a unanimous decision, the Board reversed the presiding official's ruling and sustained the agency's removal action. . . . Respondent, pursuant to § 7703, appealed to the Court of Appeals for the Federal Circuit. By a divided vote, that court reversed the Board's decision that it had no authority to review the merits of a security-clearance determination underlying a removal. . . . The court then remanded the case to the Board for such review, stating that the question of an appropriate remedy, should the Board now rule that a security clearance was improperly denied, was not yet ripe."

The Supreme Court granted certiorari to review the case and reversed.

B. Counsel of Record / ACLU Attorney

ACLU Side (Respondent / Appellee): William J. Nold argued the cause for appellee.

Opposing Side (Petitioner / Appellant): Deputy Solicitor General Cohen argued the cause for appellant.

III. AMICI CURIAE

ACLU Side (Respondent / Appellee)

Brief of amici curiae filed on behalf of the ACLU Foundation, et al., by John A. Powell, Helen Hershkoff, and Steven R. Shapiro.

Brief of amici curiae filed on behalf of the American Federation of Labor and Congress of Industrial Organizations by George Kaufmann and Laurence Gold.

Brief of amici curiae filed on behalf of the National Federation of Federal Employees by Patrick J. Riley.

Brief of amici curiae filed on behalf of Ralph B. Bogdanowicz by Stuart A. Kirsch and Mark D. Roth

Opposing Side (Petitioner / Appellant)

Brief of amici curiae filed on behalf of the Washington Legal Foundation by Daniel J. Popeo, Paul D. Kamenar, and Todd Natkin.

IV. THE SUPREME COURT'S DECISION

"It should be obvious that no one has a 'right' to a security clearance. The grant of a clearance requires an affirmative act of discretion on the part of the granting official. The general standard is that a clearance may be granted only when 'clearly consistent with the interests of the national security.' A clearance does not equate with passing judgment upon an individual's character. Instead, it is only an attempt to predict his possible future behavior and to assess whether, under compulsion of circumstances or for other reasons, he might compromise sensitive information. . . .

As noted above, this must be a judgment call. The Court also has recognized 'the generally accepted view that foreign policy was the province and responsibility of the Executive.' 'As to these areas of Art. II duties the courts have traditionally shown the utmost deference to Presidential responsibilities.' Thus, unless Congress specifically has provided otherwise, courts traditionally have been reluctant to intrude upon the authority of the Executive in military and national security affairs. . . .

The Act by its terms does not confer broad authority on the Board to review a security-clearance determination. . . . We do not agree that respondent would have received greater procedural protections under § 7532 than he received in the present case. Respondent received notice of the reasons for the proposed denial, an opportunity to inspect all relevant evidence, a right to respond, a written decision, and an opportunity to appeal to the Personnel Security Appeals Board. Until the time of his removal, he remained on full-pay status. His removal was subject to Board review that provided important protections outlined above. In contrast, had he been removed under § 7532, he would have received notice to 'the extent that the head of the agency determines that the interests of national security permit,' a hearing before an agency board, and a decision by the head of the agency. He could have been suspended without pay pending the outcome. He would not have been entitled to any review outside the agency, and, once removed, he would have been barred from employment with the agency. In short, § 7532, instead, provides a procedure that is harsh and drastic both for the employee and for the agency head, who must act personally in suspending and removing the employee.

Respondent's argument that the Board's decision in this case creates an anomaly seems to come down to his contention that, had he been removed under § 7532 , he would have been entitled to a trial-type hearing prior to his removal. Even assuming he would be entitled to such a hearing under § 7532, however, we would still consider the two procedures not anomalous, but merely different. As explained above, we doubt whether removal under § 7532, even as envisioned by respondent, would have amounted to 'more' procedural protection.

The judgment of the Court of Appeals is reversed."

V. JUSTICE VOTE

3 Pro ACLU Side vs. 5 Con Opposing Side

ACLU Side (Respondent / Appellee)

1. White, J. – Wrote dissenting opinion
2. Brennan, W. – Joined White's dissent
3. Marshall, T. – Joined White's dissent

Opposing Side (Petitioner / Appellant)

1. Blackmun, H. – Wrote majority opinion
2. Rehnquist, W. – Joined majority opinion
3. Stevens, J. – Joined majority opinion
4. O'Connor, S. – Joined majority opinion
5. Scalia, A. – Joined majority opinion

Kennedy, A – Took no part in the decision

VI. A WIN OR LOSS FOR THE ACLU?

The ACLU, as amicus curiae, urged affirmance of the judgment of the Court of Appeals; the Supreme Court reversed in a 5-3 vote, giving the ACLU an apparent loss.

638. Pennell v. City of San Jose

(Decided February 24, 1988; 485 U.S. 1)

I. ISSUE

A. Issues Discussed

Fifth Amendment, Takings Clause, Fourteenth Amendment, due process, equal protection

B. Legal Question Presented

Whether "a rent control ordinance enacted by the city of San Jose, California, that allows a hearing officer to consider, among other factors, the 'hardship to a tenant' when determining whether to approve a rent increase proposed by a landlord" violates the takings clause, due process, clause, or equal protection clause.

C. Supreme Court's Answer

The ordinance does not facially violate the due process clause or equal protection clause, and the takings clause challenge is premature.

II. CASE SUMMARY

A. Background

"This case involves a challenge to a rent control ordinance enacted by the city of San Jose, California, that allows a hearing officer to consider, among other factors, the 'hardship to a tenant' when determining whether to approve a rent increase proposed by a landlord. Appellants Richard Pennell and the Tri-County Apartment House Owners Association sued in the Superior Court of Santa Clara County seeking a declaration that the ordinance, in particular the 'tenant hardship' provisions, are 'facially unconstitutional and therefore . . . illegal and void.' The Superior Court entered judgment on the pleadings in favor of appellants, sustaining their claim that the tenant hardship provisions violated the Takings Clause of the Fifth Amendment, as made applicable to the States by the Fourteenth Amendment. The California Court of Appeal affirmed this judgment but the Supreme Court of California reversed, each by a divided vote."

The U.S. Supreme Court granted certiorari to review the case and affirmed the judgment of the Supreme Court of California.

B. Counsel of Record / ACLU Attorney

ACLU Side (Respondent / Appellee): Joan R. Gallo argued the cause for appellee.

Opposing Side (Petitioner / Appellant): Harry D. Miller argued the cause for appellant.

III. AMICI CURIAE

ACLU Side (Respondent / Appellee)

Briefs of amici curiae filed on behalf of the ACLU, et al., by John A. Powell, Steven R. Shapiro, Helen Hershkoff, Paul L. Hoffman, and Mark Rosenbaum.

Brief of amici curiae filed on behalf of the American Federation of Labor and Congress of Industrial Organizations by Robert M. Weinberg and Laurence Gold.

Brief of amici curiae filed on behalf of the Asian Law Alliance, et al., by Brenton Rogozen.

Brief of amici curiae filed on behalf of the Center for Constitutional Rights by Frank E. Deale.

Brief of amici curiae filed on behalf of the National Housing Law Project by David B. Bryson.

Brief of amici curiae filed on behalf of the National Institute of Municipal Law Officers by William I. Thornton, Jr., Roger F. Cutler, Roy D. Bates, and William H. Taube.

Brief of amici curiae filed on behalf of the U.S. Conference of Mayors, et al., by Benna Ruth Solomon and H. Bartow Farr III.

Brief of amici curiae filed on behalf of the city of Santa Monica, et al., by Joseph Lawrence, Karl M. Manheim, Joel M. Levy, Hadassa K. Gilbert, Manuela Albuquerque, Raymond E. Ott, Mary Jo Levinger, Marc G. Hynes, Jayne W. Williams, K. Duane Lyders, Louise H. Renne, Roger T. Picquet, Steven A. Amerikaner, Mark G. Sellers, and John M. Powers.

Opposing Side (Petitioner / Appellant)

Brief of amici curiae filed on behalf of the California Association of Realtors by William M. Pfeiffer.

Brief of amici curiae filed on behalf of the National Apartment Association, et al., by Jon D. Smock, Wilbur H. Haines III, and Jeffrey J. Gale.

Brief of amici curiae filed on behalf of the National Association of Realtors by William D. North.

Brief of amici curiae filed on behalf of the National Multi Housing Council by Lawrence B. Simons and Michael E. Fine.

Brief of amici curiae filed on behalf of the Rent Stabilization Association of New York City, Inc., et al., by Erwin N. Griswold.

Brief of amici curiae filed on behalf of the Washington Legal Foundation by Daniel J. Popeo, Paul D. Kamenar, and Todd Natkin.

Brief of amici curiae filed on behalf of the Competitive Enterprise Institute by Sam Kazman.

Brief of amici curiae filed on behalf of the National Association of Home Builders, et al., by Gus Bauman.

IV. THE SUPREME COURT'S DECISION

"[A]ppellants contend, the additional reduction of rent on grounds of hardship accomplishes a transfer of the landlord's property to individual hardship tenants; the Ordinance forces private individuals to shoulder the 'public' burden of subsidizing their poor tenants' housing. As appellants point out, '[i]t is axiomatic that the Fifth Amendment's just compensation provision is 'designed to bar Government from forcing some people alone to bear public burdens which, in all fairness and justice, should be borne by the public as a whole."

We think it would be premature to consider this contention on the present record. As things stand, there simply is no evidence that the 'tenant hardship clause' has in fact ever been relied upon by a hearing officer to reduce a rent below the figure it would have been set at on the basis of the other factors set forth in the Ordinance. In addition, there is nothing in the Ordinance requiring that a hearing officer in fact reduce a proposed rent increase on grounds of tenant hardship. . . .

Appellants also urge that the mere provision in the Ordinance that a hearing officer may consider the hardship of the tenant in finally fixing a reasonable rent renders the Ordinance 'facially invalid' under the Due Process and Equal Protection Clauses, even though no landlord ever has its rent diminished by as much as one dollar because of the application of this provision. The standard for determining whether a state price-control regulation is constitutional under the Due Process Clause is well established: 'Price control is 'unconstitutional . . . if arbitrary, discriminatory, or demonstrably irrelevant to the policy the legislature is free to adopt . . . .' In other contexts we have recognized that the government may intervene in the marketplace to regulate rates or prices that are artificially inflated as a result of the existence of a monopoly or near monopoly or a discrepancy between supply and demand in the market for a certain product. Accordingly, appellants do not dispute that the Ordinance's asserted purpose of 'prevent[ing] excessive and unreasonable rent increases' caused by the 'growing shortage of and increasing demand for housing in the City of San Jose,' is a legitimate exercise of appellees' police powers. They do argue, however, that it is 'arbitrary, discriminatory, or demonstrably irrelevant,' for appellees to attempt to accomplish the additional goal of reducing the burden of housing costs on low-income tenants by requiring that 'hardship to a tenant' be considered in determining the amount of excess rent increase that is 'reasonable under the circumstances' pursuan to § 5703.28. As appellants put it, '[t]he objective of alleviating individual tenant hardship is . . . not a 'policy the legislature is free to adopt' in a rent control ordinance.'

We reject this contention, however, because we have long recognized that a legitimate and rational goal of price or rate regulation is the protection of consumer welfare. Indeed, a primary purpose of rent control is the protection of tenants. Here, the Ordinance establishes a scheme in which a hearing officer considers a number of factors in determining the reasonableness of a proposed rent increase which exceeds eight percent and which exceeds the amount deemed reasonable . . . . We accordingly find that the Ordinance, which so carefully considers both the individual circumstances of the landlord and the tenant before determining whether to allow an additional increase in rent over and above certain amounts that are deemed reasonable, does not on its face violate the Fourteenth Amendment's Due Process Clause.

We also find that the Ordinance does not violate the Amendment's Equal Protection Clause. Here again, the standard is deferential; appellees need only show that the classification scheme embodied in the Ordinance is 'rationally related to a legitimate state interest.' As we stated in Vance v. Bradley, 'we will not overturn [a statute that does not burden a suspect class or a fundamental interest] unless the varying treatment of different groups or persons is so unrelated to the achievement of any combination of legitimate purposes that we can only conclude that the legislature's actions were irrational.' In light of our conclusion above that the Ordinance's tenant hardship provisions are designed to serve the legitimate purpose of protecting tenants, we can hardly conclude that it is irrational for the Ordinance to treat certain landlords differently on the basis of whether or not they have hardship tenants. . . .

For the foregoing reasons, we hold that it is premature to consider appellants' claim under the Takings Clause and we reject their facial challenge to the Ordinance under the Due Process and Equal Protection Clauses of the Fourteenth Amendment. The judgment of the Supreme Court of California is accordingly affirmed."

V. JUSTICE VOTE

6 Pro ACLU Side vs. 2 Con Opposing Side

ACLU Side (Respondent / Appellee)

1. Rehnquist, W. – Wrote majority opinion
2. Brennan, W. – Joined majority opinion
3. White, B. – Joined majority opinion
4. Marshall, T. – Joined majority opinion
5. Blackmun, H. – Joined majority opinion
6. Stevens, J. – Joined majority opinion

Opposing Side (Petitioner / Appellant)

1. Scalia, A. – Wrote opinion concurring in part and dissenting in part
2. O'Connor, S. – Joined Scalia's opinion

Kennedy, A – Took no part in the decision

VI. A WIN OR LOSS FOR THE ACLU?

The ACLU, as amicus curiae, urged affirmance of the judgment of the Supreme Court of California; the U.S. Supreme Court affirmed in a 6-2 vote, giving the ACLU an apparent win.

639. Hustler Magazine, Inc. v. Falwell

(Decided February 24, 1988; 485 U.S. 46)

I. ISSUE

A. Issues Discussed

First Amendment, freedom of speech, intentional infliction of emotional distress

B. Legal Question Presented

Whether an award for damages for intentional infliction of emotional distress in this case "is consistent with the First and Fourteenth Amendments of the United States Constitution."

C. Supreme Court's Answer

Respondent cannot recover damages for intentional infliction of emotional distress in this case.

II. CASE SUMMARY

A. Background

"Petitioner Hustler Magazine, Inc., is a magazine of nationwide circulation. Respondent Jerry Falwell, a nationally known minister who has been active as a commentator on politics and public affairs, sued petitioner and its publisher, petitioner Larry Flynt, to recover damages for invasion of privacy, libel, and intentional infliction of emotional distress. The District Court directed a verdict against respondent on the privacy claim, and submitted the other two claims to a jury. The jury found for petitioners on the defamation claim, but found for respondent on the claim for intentional infliction of emotional distress and awarded damages. . . .

The inside front cover of the November 1983 issue of Hustler Magazine featured a 'parody' of an advertisement for Campari Liqueur that contained the name and picture of respondent and was entitled 'Jerry Falwell talks about his first time.' This parody was modeled after actual Campari ads that included interviews with various celebrities about their 'first times.' Although it was apparent by the end of each interview that this meant the first time they sampled Campari, the ads clearly played on the sexual double entendre of the general subject of 'first times.' Copying the form and layout of these Campari ads, Hustler's editors chose respondent as the featured celebrity and drafted an alleged 'interview' with him in which he states that his 'first time' was during a drunken incestuous rendezvous with his mother in an outhouse. The Hustler parody portrays respondent and his mother as drunk and immoral, and suggests that respondent is a hypocrite who preaches only when he is drunk. In small print at the bottom of the page, the ad contains the disclaimer, 'ad parody—not to be taken seriously.' The magazine's table of contents also lists the ad as 'Fiction; Ad and Personality Parody.' . . .

On appeal, the United States Court of Appeals for the Fourth Circuit affirmed the judgment against petitioners. . . . Petitioners then filed a petition for rehearing en banc, but this was denied by a divided court."

The Supreme Court granted certiorari to review the case and reversed.

B. Counsel of Record / ACLU Attorney

ACLU Side (Petitioner / Appellant): Alan L. Isaacman argued the cause for appellant.

Opposing Side (Respondent / Appellee): Norman Roy Grutman argued the cause for appellee.

III. AMICI CURIAE

ACLU Side (Petitioner / Appellant)

Brief of amici curiae filed on behalf of the ACLU Foundation, et al., by Harriette K. Dorsen, John A. Powell, and Steven R. Shapiro.

Additional briefs of amici curiae were filed on behalf of the Association of American Editorial Cartoonists, et al., the Association of American Publishers, Inc., Home Box Office, Inc., the Law & Humanities Institute, the Reporters Committee for Freedom of the Press, et al., Richmond

Newspapers, Inc., et al., and Volunteer Lawyers for the Arts, Inc.

Opposing Side (Respondent / Appellee)

No briefs of amici curiae were filed in support of appellee.

IV. THE SUPREME COURT'S DECISION

"Since New York Times Co. v. Sullivan, we have consistently ruled that a public figure may hold a speaker liable for the damage to reputation caused by publication of a defamatory falsehood, but only if the statement was made 'with knowledge that it was false or with reckless disregard of whether it was false or not.' . . .

We conclude that public figures and public officials may not recover for the tort of intentional infliction of emotional distress by reason of publications such as the one here at issue without showing in addition that the publication contains a false statement of fact which was made with 'actual malice,' i.e., with knowledge that the statement was false or with reckless disregard as to whether or not it was true. This is not merely a 'blind application' of the New York Times standard, it reflects our considered judgment that such a standard is necessary to give adequate 'breathing space' to the freedoms protected by the First Amendment.

Here it is clear that respondent Falwell is a 'public figure' for purposes of First Amendment law. The jury found against respondent on his libel claim when it decided that the Hustler ad parody could not 'reasonably be understood as describing actual facts about [respondent] or actual events in which [he] participated.' The Court of Appeals interpreted the jury's finding to be that the ad parody 'was not reasonably believable,' and in accordance with our custom we accept this finding. Respondent is thus relegated to his claim for damages awarded by the jury for the intentional infliction of emotional distress by 'outrageous' conduct. But for reasons heretofore stated this claim cannot, consistently with the First Amendment, form a basis for the award of damages when the conduct in question is the publication of a caricature such as the ad parody involved here. The judgment of the Court of Appeals is accordingly reversed."

V. JUSTICE VOTE

8 Pro ACLU Side vs. 0 Con Opposing Side

ACLU Side (Petitioner / Appellant)

1. Rehnquist, W. – Wrote majority opinion
2. Brennan, W. – Joined majority opinion
3. Marshall, T. – Joined majority opinion
4. Blackmun, H. – Joined majority opinion
5. Stevens, J. – Joined majority opinion
6. O'Connor, S. – Joined majority opinion
7. Scalia, A. – Joined majority opinion
8. White, B. – Wrote concurring opinion

Kennedy, A – Took no part in the decision

VI. A WIN OR LOSS FOR THE ACLU?

The ACLU, as amicus curiae, urged reversal of the judgment of the Court of Appeals; the Supreme Court reversed in an 8-0 vote, giving the ACLU an apparent win.

640. Boos v. Barry

Decided March 22, 1988; 485 U.S. 312)

I. ISSUE

A. Issues Discussed

First Amendment, political speech, freedoms of speech and association

B. Legal Question Presented

[W]hether a provision of the District of Columbia Code, § 22-1115, violates the First Amendment."

C. Supreme Court's Answer

The display clause violates the First Amendment and is therefore unconstitutional, while the congregation clause does not violate the First Amendment.

II. CASE SUMMARY

A. Background

"District of Columbia Code, § 22-1115 . . . prohibits the display of any sign within 500 feet of a foreign embassy if that sign tends to bring that foreign government into 'public odium' or 'public disrepute.' It also prohibits any congregation of three or more persons within 500 feet of a foreign embassy. . . .

Petitioners are three individuals who wish to carry signs critical of the Governments of the Soviet Union and Nicaragua on the public sidewalks within 500 feet of the embassies of those Governments in Washington, D.C. . . . All of the petitioners also wish to congregate with two or more other persons within 500 feet of official foreign buildings.

Asserting that D.C.Code § 22-1115 (1981) prohibited them from engaging in these expressive activities, petitioners, together with respondent Father R. David Finzer, brought a facial First Amendment challenge to that provision in the District Court for the District of Columbia. . . . The District Court granted respondents' motion for summary judgment . . . . A divided panel of the Court of Appeals for the District of Columbia affirmed."

The Supreme Court granted certiorari to review the case and reversed as to the display clause, but affirmed as to the congregation clause.

B. Counsel of Record / ACLU Attorney

ACLU Side (Petitioner / Appellant): Raymond D. Battocchi argued the cause for appellant.

Opposing Side (Respondent / Appellee): Edward E. Schwab argued the cause for appellee.

Edwin S. Kneedler argued the cause for the United States, as amicus curiae, by special leave of Court.

III. AMICI CURIAE

ACLU Side (Petitioner / Appellant)

Brief of amici curiae filed on behalf of the ACLU, et al., by Arthur B. Spitzer, John A. Powell, and Elizabeth Symonds.

Brief of amici curiae filed on behalf of the American Jewish Congress by Joel H. Levy, Marc D. Stern, Lois C. Waldman, and Amy Adelson.
Brief of amici curiae filed on behalf of the Legal Affairs Council, et al., by Wyatt B. Durrette, Jr.
Brief of amici curiae filed on behalf of the Washington Legal Foundation, et al., by Daniel J. Popeo and Paul D. Kamenar.

Opposing Side (Respondent / Appellee)

Brief of amici curiae filed on behalf of the United States by Edwin S. Kneedler, Solicitor General Fried, Assistant Attorney General Willard, Deputy Solicitor General Wallace, Anthony J. Steinmeyer, and Barbara Biddle.
Brief of amici curiae filed on behalf of Geraldine M. Lipkin, et al., by Seth P. Waxman.

IV. THE SUPREME COURT'S DECISION

"[T]he display clause is content-based. The clause is justified only by reference to the content of speech. Respondents and the United States do not point to the 'secondary effects' of picket signs in front of embassies. They do not point to congestion, to interference with ingress or egress, to visual clutter, or to the need to protect the security of embassies. Rather, they rely on the need to protect the dignity of foreign diplomatic personnel by shielding them from speech that is critical of their governments. This justification focuses only on the content of the speech and the direct impact that speech has on its listeners. The emotive impact of speech on its audience is not a 'secondary effect.' Because the display clause regulates speech due to its potential primary impact, we conclude it must be considered content-based. . . .

Our cases indicate that as a content-based restriction on political speech in a public forum, § 22-1115 must be subjected to the most exacting scrutiny. Thus, we have required the State to show that the 'regulation is necessary to serve a compelling state interest and that it is narrowly drawn to achieve that end.' . . . Relying on congressional judgment in this delicate area, we conclude that the availability of alternatives such as § 112 amply demonstrates that the display clause is not crafted with sufficient precision to withstand First Amendment scrutiny. It may serve an interest in protecting the dignity of foreign missions, but it is not narrowly tailored; a less restrictive alternative is readily available. Thus, even assuming for present purposes that the dignity interest is 'compelling,' we hold that the display clause of § 22-1115 is inconsistent with the First Amendment. . . .

The Court of Appeals, we must first observe, read the congregation clause as distinct from the display clause, so the constitutional infirmity of the latter need not affect the former. Second, the Court of Appeals followed the lead of several earlier decisions, and concluded that the statute permits the dispersal only of congregations that are directed at an embassy; it does not grant 'police the power to disperse for reasons having nothing to do with the nearby embassy.' Finally, the Court of Appeals further circumscribed police discretion by holding that the statute permits dispersal 'only when the police reasonably believe that a threat to the security or peace of the embassy is present.' . . .

So narrowed, the congregation clause withstands First Amendment overbreadth scrutiny. It does not reach a substantial amount of constitutionally protected conduct; it merely regulates the place and manner of certain demonstrations. Unlike a general breach of the peace statute, the congregation clause is site specific; it applies only within 500 feet of foreign embassies. Moreover, the congregation clause does not prohibit peaceful congregations; its reach is limited to groups posing a security threat. As we have noted, 'where demonstrations turn violent, they lose their protected quality as expression under the First Amendment.' These two limitations prevent the congregation clause from reaching a substantial amount of constitutionally protected conduct and make the clause consistent with the First Amendment. . . .

The intended function of § 22-1116 is largely pre-empted by our conclusion that the display clause is invalid. Viewing the section in this way eliminates any potential unequal treatment of nonlabor and labor congregations. Accordingly, in our view, § 22-1116 does not violate the Equal Protection Clause. . . .

We conclude that the display clause of § 22-1115 is unconstitutional on its face. It is a content-based restriction on political speech in a public forum, and it is not narrowly tailored to serve a compelling state interest. We also conclude that the congregation clause, as narrowed by the Court of Appeals, is not facially unconstitutional. Accordingly, the judgment of the Court of Appeals is reversed in part and affirmed in part."

V. JUSTICE VOTE

5 Pro ACLU Side vs. 3 Con Opposing Side

ACLU Side (Petitioner / Appellant)

1. O'Connor, S. – Wrote majority opinion
2. Brennan, W. – Wrote concurring opinion
3. Marshall, T. – Joined Brennan's concurrence
4. Stevens, J. – Joined majority opinion
5. Scalia, A. – Joined majority opinion

Opposing Side (Respondent / Appellee)

1. Rehnquist, W. – Wrote opinion concurring in part and dissenting in part
2. White, B. – Joined Rehnquist's opinion
3. Blackmun, H. – Joined Rehnquist's opinion

Kennedy, A – Took no part in the decision

VI. A WIN OR LOSS FOR THE ACLU?

The ACLU, as amicus curiae, urged reversal of the judgment of the Court of Appeals; the Supreme Court reversed in part and affirmed in part in a 5-3 vote, giving the ACLU an apparent win.

641. Lyng v. Northwest Indian Cemetery Protective Ass'n

(Decided April 19, 1988; 485 U.S. 439)

I. ISSUE

A. Issues Discussed

First Amendment, Free Exercise Clause

B. Legal Question Presented

"[W]hether the First Amendment's Free Exercise Clause prohibits the Government from permitting timber harvesting in, or constructing a road through, a portion of a National Forest that has traditionally been used for religious purposes by members of three American Indian tribes in northwestern California."

C. Supreme Court's Answer

The First Amendment does not prohibit the Government from permitting timber harvesting or road construction in the area.

II. CASE SUMMARY

A. Background

"As part of a project to create a paved 75-mile road linking two California towns, Gasquet and Orleans, the United States Forest Service has upgraded 49 miles of previously unpaved roads on federal land. . . .

In 1977, the Forest Service issued a draft environmental impact statement that discussed proposals for upgrading an existing unpaved road that runs through the Chimney Rock area. . . . The study concluded that constructing a road along any of the available routes 'would cause serious and irreparable damage to the sacred areas which are an integral and necessary part of the belief systems and lifeway of Northwest California Indian peoples.' Accordingly, the report recommended that the G–O road not be completed.

In 1982, the Forest Service decided not to adopt this recommendation . . . . At about the same time, the Forest Service adopted a management plan allowing for the harvesting of significant amounts of timber in this area of the forest. . . .

After exhausting their administrative remedies, respondents . . . challenged both the roadbuilding and timber-harvesting decisions in the United States District Court for the Northern District of California. . . .

After a trial, the District Court issued a permanent injunction prohibiting the Government from constructing the Chimney Rock section of the G–O road or putting the timber-harvesting management plan into effect. . . .

While an appeal was pending before the United States Court of Appeals for the Ninth Circuit, Congress enacted the California Wilderness Act of 1984. Under that statute, much of the property covered by the Forest Service's management plan is now designated a wilderness area, which means that commercial activities such as timber harvesting are forbidden. The statute exempts a narrow strip of land, coinciding with the Forest Service's proposed route for the remaining segment of the G–O road, from the wilderness designation. . . .

A panel of the Ninth Circuit affirmed in part. . . . By a divided decision, the District Court's constitutional ruling was also affirmed. [T]he majority found that construction of the Chimney Rock section of the G–O road would have significant, though largely indirect, adverse effects on Indian religious practices. The majority concluded that the Government had failed to demonstrate a compelling interest in the completion of the road, and that it could have abandoned the road without thereby creating 'a religious preserve for a single group in violation of the establishment clause.' The majority apparently applied the same analysis to logging operations that might be carried out in portions of the Chimney Rock area not covered by the California Wilderness Act."

The Supreme Court granted certiorari to review the case, reversed, and remanded.

B. Counsel of Record / ACLU Attorney

ACLU Side (Respondent / Appellee): Marilyn B. Miles argued the cause for appellee.

Opposing Side (Petitioner / Appellant): Andrew J. Pincus argued the cause for appellant.

III. AMICI CURIAE

ACLU Side (Respondent / Appellee)

Brief of amici curiae filed on behalf of the ACLU Foundation, et al., by John A. Powell, Steven R. Shapiro, Paul L. Hoffman, Mark D. Rosenbaum, Alan L. Schlosser, Edward M. Chen, Matthew A. Coles, and Stephen L. Pevar.

Brief of amici curiae filed on behalf of the American Jewish Congress, et al., by Marc D. Stern, Lois C. Waldman, and Amy Adelson.

Brief of amici curiae filed on behalf of the Christian Legal Society, et al., by Michael J. Woodruff, Samuel Rabinove, Richard T. Foltin, and Jordan Lorence.

Brief of amici curiae filed on behalf of the National Congress of American Indians, et al., by Steven C. Moore.

Opposing Side (Petitioner / Appellant)

Brief of amici curiae filed on behalf of the State of Hawaii, et al., by Kenneth O. Eikenberry, Attorney General of Washington, Timothy R. Malone, Nixon Handy, and Mark S. Green, Assistant Attorneys General, Warren Price III, Attorney General of Hawaii, Roger A. Tellinghuisen, Attorney General of South Dakota, and David Wilkinson, Attorney General of Utah.

Brief of amici curiae filed on behalf of the Colorado Mining Association, et al., by Lawrence E. Stevens and Patrick J. Garver.

Brief of amici curiae filed on behalf of the Howonquet Community Association, et al., by Ronald A. Zumbrun and Robin L. Rivett.

Brief of amici curiae filed on behalf of the city of Williams, Arizona, by Gary Verburg.

IV. THE SUPREME COURT'S DECISION

"[R]espondents contend that the burden on their religious practices is heavy enough to violate the Free Exercise Clause unless the Government can demonstrate a compelling need to complete the G–O road or to engage in timber harvesting in the Chimney Rock area. We disagree. . . .

Whatever may be the exact line between unconstitutional prohibitions on the free exercise of religion and the legitimate conduct by government of its own affairs, the location of the line cannot depend on measuring the effects of a governmental action on a religious objector's spiritual development. The Government does not dispute, and we have no reason to doubt, that the logging and road-building projects at issue in this case could have devastating effects on traditional Indian religious practices. Those practices are intimately and inextricably bound up with the unique features of the Chimney Rock area, which is known to the Indians as the 'high country.' Individual practitioners use this area for personal spiritual development; some of their activities are believed to be critically important in advancing the welfare of the Tribe, and indeed, of mankind itself. The Indians use this area, as they have used it for a very long time, to conduct a wide variety of specific rituals that aim to accomplish their religious goals. According to their beliefs, the rituals would not be efficacious if conducted at other sites than the ones traditionally used, and too much disturbance of the area's natural state would clearly render any meaningful continuation of traditional practices impossible. To be sure, the Indians themselves were far from unanimous in opposing the G–O road, and it seems less than certain that construction of the road will be so disruptive that it will doom their religion. Nevertheless, we can assume that the threat to the efficacy of at least some religious practices is extremely grave. . . .

Except for abandoning its project entirely, and thereby leaving the two existing segments of road to dead-end in the middle of a National Forest, it is difficult to see how the Government could have been more solicitous. Such solicitude accords with 'the policy of the United States to protect and preserve for American Indians their inherent right of freedom to believe, express, and exercise the traditional religions of the American Indian . . . including but not limited to access to sites, use and possession of sacred objects, and the freedom to worship through ceremonials and traditional rites.' . . .

The decision of the court below, according to which the First Amendment precludes the Government from completing the G–O road or from permitting timber harvesting in the Chimney Rock area, is reversed. In order that the District Court's injunction may be reconsidered in light of this holding, and in the light of any other relevant events that may have intervened since the injunction issued, the case is remanded for further proceedings consistent with this opinion."

V. JUSTICE VOTE

3 Pro ACLU Side vs. 5 Con Opposing Side

ACLU Side (Respondent / Appellee)

1. Brennan, W. – Wrote dissenting opinion
2. Marshall, T. – Joined Brennan's dissent
3. Blackmun, H. – Joined Brennan's dissent

Opposing Side (Petitioner / Appellant)

1. O'Connor, S. – Wrote majoity opinion
2. Rehnquist, W. – Joined majority opinion
3. White, B. – Joined majority opinion
4. Stevens, J. – Joined majority opinion
5. Scalia, A. – Joined majority opinion

Kennedy, A – Took no part in the decision

VI. A WIN OR LOSS FOR THE ACLU?

The ACLU, as amicus curiae, urged affirmance of the judgment of the Court of Appeals; the Supreme Court reversed in a 5-3 vote, giving the ACLU an apparent loss.

642. Traynor v. Turnage

(Decided April 20, 1988; 485 U.S. 535)

I. ISSUE

A. Issues Discussed

Governmental regulation, civil rights, veterans' benefits, discrimination

B. Legal Question Presented

"[W]hether the Veterans' Administration's decision [to not extend the time for recovered alcoholics to use their educational benefits as veterans] is subject to judicial review and, if so, whether that decision violates § 504 of the Rehabilitation Act of 1973, which requires that federal programs not discriminate against handicapped individuals solely because of their handicap."

C. Supreme Court's Answer

The decision is subject to judicial review and does not violate § 504 of the Rehabilitation Act.

II. CASE SUMMARY

A. Background

"Veterans who have been honorably discharged from the United States Armed Forces are entitled to receive educational assistance benefits under the Veterans' Readjustment Benefit Act of 1966 ('GI Bill') to facilitate their readjustment to civilian life. These benefits generally must be used within 10 years following discharge or release from active duty. Veterans may obtain an extension of the 10–year delimiting period, however, if they were prevented from using their benefits earlier by 'a physical or mental disability which was not the result of [their] own willful misconduct.'

Petitioners are honorably discharged veterans who did not exhaust their educational benefits during the decade following their military service. They sought to continue to receive benefits after the expiration of the 10–year delimiting period on the ground that they had been disabled by alcoholism during much of that period. The Veterans' Administration determined that petitioners' alcoholism constituted 'willful misconduct' under 38 CFR § 3.301(c)(2) (1987), and accordingly denied the requested extensions.

Petitioner Traynor sought review of the Veterans' Administration's decision in the United States District Court for the Southern District of New York. The District Court held that it was not foreclosed from exercising jurisdiction over the case . . . . The court rejected Traynor's claim that the Veterans' Administration's refusal to extend his delimiting period violated the Due Process Clause and the equal protection component of the Fifth Amendment. However, the court concluded that alcoholism is a handicap within the meaning of the Rehabilitation

Act, and that the Veterans' Administration therefore had engaged in the sort of discrimination on the basis of handicap that is forbidden by that Act.

A divided panel of the Court of Appeals for the Second Circuit reversed on the ground that § 211(a) barred judicial review of the Rehabilitation Act claim. . . .

Meanwhile, petitioner McKelvey sought review of the Veterans' Administration's decision in the District Court for the District of Columbia. The District Court exercised jurisdiction over McKelvey's claims . . . . The court then invalidated 38 CFR § 3.301(c)(2) (1987) as contrary to the Rehabilitation Act. . . .

On appeal, the Court of Appeals for the District of Columbia Circuit agreed that judicial review was not foreclosed by § 211(a) . . . . On the merits, however, the Court of Appeals reversed, holding that the Veterans' Administration could consistently with the Rehabilitation Act distinguish between veterans who are at least to some extent responsible for their disabilities and veterans who are not."

The Supreme Court granted certiorari to review the case and reversed.

B. Counsel of Record / ACLU Attorney

ACLU Side (Petitioner / Appellant): Keith A. Teel argued the cause for appellant. With him on the briefs were Margaret K. Brooks, Catherine H. O'Neill, John A. Powell, Arthur B. Spitzer, Elizabeth Symonds, and Steven R. Shapiro.

Opposing Side (Respondent / Appellee): Jerrold J. Ganzfried argued the cause for appellee. With him on the brief were Solicitor General Fried, Assistant Attorney General Willard, Deputy Solicitor General Wallace, Anthony J. Steinmeyer, and Robert V. Zener.

III. AMICI CURIAE

ACLU Side (Petitioner / Appellant)

Brief of amici curiae filed on behalf of the National Council on Alcoholism, Inc., by Elizabeth Bartholet.

Brief of amici curiae filed on behalf of the American Medical Association, et al., by Benjamin W. Heineman, Jr., Carter G. Phillips, and Joel I. Klein.

Brief of amici curiae filed on behalf of Vietnam Veterans of America by Samuel M. Sipe, Jr., and Barton F. Stichman.

Opposing Side (Respondent / Appellee)

No briefs of amici curiae were filed in support of appellee.

IV. THE SUPREME COURT'S DECISION

"The text and legislative history of § 211(a) . . . provide no clear and convincing evidence of any congressional intent to preclude a suit claiming that § 504 of the Rehabilitation Act, a statute applicable to all federal agencies, has invalidated an otherwise valid regulation issued by the Veterans' Administration and purporting to have the force of law. . . . Permitting these cases to go forward will not undermine the purposes of § 211(a) . . . . Of course, if experience proves otherwise, the Veterans' Administration is fully capable of seeking appropriate relief from Congress.

Accordingly, we conclude that the question whether a Veterans' Administration regulation violates the Rehabilitation Act is not foreclosed from judicial review by § 211(a). We therefore turn to the merits of petitioners' Rehabilitation Act claim.

[W]e hold that a construction of § 1662(a)(1) that reflects the original congressional intent that primary alcoholics not be excused from the 10-year delimiting period for utilizing 'GI Bill' benefits is not inconsistent with the prohibition on discrimination against the handicapped contained in § 504 of the Rehabilitation Act. Accordingly, since we 'are not at liberty to pick and choose among congressional enactments . . . when two statutes are capable of co-existence,' we must conclude that the earlier, more specific provisions of § 1662(a)(1) were neither expressly nor implicitly repealed by the later, more general provisions of § 504. . . .

This litigation does not require the Court to decide whether alcoholism is a disease whose course its victims cannot control. It is not our role to resolve this medical issue, on which the authorities remain sharply divided. Our task is to decide whether Congress intended, in enacting § 504 of the Rehabilitation Act, to reject the position taken on the issue by the Veterans' Administration and by Congress itself only one year earlier. In our view, it is by no means clear that § 504 and the characterization of primary alcoholism as a willfully incurred disability are in irreconcilable conflict. If petitioners and their proponents continue to believe that this position is erroneous, their arguments are better presented to Congress than to the courts.

The judgment of the Court of Appeals for the District of Columbia Circuit in No. 86-737 is affirmed. The judgment of the Court of Appeals for the Second Circuit in No. 86-622 is reversed, and the case is remanded for further proceedings consistent with this opinion."

V. JUSTICE VOTE

3 Pro ACLU Side vs. 4 Con Opposing Side

ACLU Side (Petitioner / Appellant)

1. Blackmun, H. – Wrote opinion concurring in part and dissenting in part
2. Brennan, W. – Joined Blackmun's opinion
3. Marshall, T. – Joined Blackmun's opinion

Opposing Side (Respondent / Appellee)

1. White, B. – Wrote majority opinion
2. Rehnquist, W. – Joined majority opinion
3. Stevens, J. – Joined majority opinion
4. O'Connor, S. – Joined majority opinion

Scalia, A – Took no part in the decision
Kennedy, A – Took no part in the decision

VI. A WIN OR LOSS FOR THE ACLU?

The ACLU filed as counsel, representing petitioner and urging reversal of the Court of Appeals for the District of Columbia Circuit; the Supreme Court affirmed in a 4-3 vote, giving the ACLU an apparent loss.

643. Edward J. DeBartolo Corp. v. Florida Gulf Coast Building & Construction Trades Council

(Decided April 20, 1988; 485 U.S. 568)

I. ISSUE

A. Issues Discussed

Statutory construction, First Amendment, freedom of speech, National Labor Relations Act

B. Legal Question Presented

Did Congress intend, when it drafted § 8(b)(4) of the National Labor Relations Act, to proscribe a union's distribution of handbills urging customers not to patronize stores in a mall until the construction workers performing construction work at the mall were paid fair wages?

C. Supreme Court's Answer

Section 8(b)(4) was not intended to prevent the distribution of handbills in this circumstance.

II. CASE SUMMARY

A. Background

"This case centers around the respondent union's peaceful handbilling of the businesses operating in a shopping mall in Tampa, Florida, owned by petitioner, the Edward J. DeBartolo Corporation (DeBartolo). The union's primary labor dispute was with H.J. High Construction Company (High) over alleged substandard wages and fringe benefits. High was retained by the H.J. Wilson Company (Wilson) to construct a department store in the mall, and neither DeBartolo nor any of the other 85 or so mall tenants had any contractual right to influence the selection of contractors.

The union, however, sought to obtain their influence upon Wilson and High by distributing handbills asking mall customers not to shop at any of the stores in the mall 'until the Mall's owner publicly promises that all construction at the Mall will be done using contractors who pay their employees fair wages and fringe benefits.' . . .

After DeBartolo failed to convince the union to alter the language of the handbills to state that its dispute did not involve DeBartolo or the mall lessees other than Wilson and to limit its distribution to the immediate vicinity of Wilson's construction site, it filed a complaint with the National Labor Relations Board (Board), charging the union with engaging in unfair labor practices under § 8(b)(4) of the National Labor Relations Act (NLRA) . . . . The Board's General Counsel issued a complaint, but the Board eventually dismissed it, concluding that the handbilling was protected by the publicity proviso of § 8(b)(4). The Court of Appeals for the Fourth Circuit affirmed the Board, but [the Supreme] Court reversed in Edward J. DeBartolo Corp. v. NLRB, 463 U.S. 147 (1983). There, we concluded that the handbilling did not fall within the proviso's limited scope of exempting 'publicity intended to inform the public that the primary employer's product is 'distributed by' the secondary employer' because DeBartolo and the other tenants, as opposed to Wilson, did not distribute products of High. Since there had not been a determination below whether the union's handbilling fell within the prohibition of § 8(b)(4), and, if so, whether it was protected by the First Amendment, we remanded the case.

On remand, the Board held that the union's handbilling was proscribed by § 8(b)(4)(ii)(B). . . . The Board observed that it need not inquire whether the prohibition of this handbilling raised serious questions under the First Amendment, for 'the statute's literal language and the applicable case law require[d]' a finding of a violation. Finally, it reiterated its longstanding position that 'as a congressionally created administrative agency, we will presume the constitutionality of the Act we administer.'

The Court of Appeals for the Eleventh Circuit denied enforcement of the Board's order."

The Supreme Court granted certiorari to review the case and affirmed.

B. Counsel of Record / ACLU Attorney

ACLU Side (Respondent / Appellee): Laurence Gold argued the cause for appellee.

Opposing Side (Petitioner / Appellant): Lawrence M. Cohen argued the cause for appellant.

Deputy Solicitor General Cohen argued the cause for the United States, as amicus curiae, by special leave of the Court.

III. AMICI CURIAE

ACLU Side (Respondent / Appellee)

Brief of amici curiae filed on behalf of the ACLU Foundation by John A. Powell, Helen Hershkoff, Steven R. Shapiro, C. Edwin Baker, Robert A. Bush, and Ira L. Gottlieb.

Opposing Side (Petitioner / Appellant)

Brief of amici curiae field on behalf of the United States by Deputy Solicitor General Cohen, Solicitor General Fried, Rosemary M. Collyer, Norton J. Come, Linda Sher, and Carmel P. Ebb.

Brief of amici curiae filed on behalf of the American Retail Federation by Jack L. Whitacre.

Brief of amici curiae filed on behalf of the Chamber of Commerce of the United States by Edward B. Miller and Stephen A. Bokat.

Brief of amici curiae filed on behalf of the International Council of Shopping Centers, Inc., by Edward J. Sack and Stephanie McEvily.

IV. THE SUPREME COURT'S DECISION

"We agree with the Court of Appeals and respondents that this case calls for the invocation of the Catholic Bishop rule, for the Board's construction of the statute, as applied in this case, poses serious questions of the validity of § 8(b)(4) under the First Amendment. The handbills involved here truthfully revealed the existence of a labor dispute and urged potential customers of the mall to follow a wholly legal course of action, namely, not to patronize the retailers doing business in the mall. The handbilling was peaceful. No picketing or patrolling was involved. On its face, this was expressive activity arguing that substandard wages should be opposed by abstaining from shopping in a mall where such wages were paid. Had the union simply been leafletting the public generally, including those entering every shopping mall in town, pursuant to an annual educational effort against substandard pay, there is little doubt that legislative proscription of such leaflets would pose a substantial issue of validity under the First Amendment. The same may well be true in this case, although here the handbills called attention to a specific situation in the mall allegedly involving the payment of unacceptably low wages by a construction contractor. . . .

Because there was not the required 'clearest indication in the legislative history,' we rejected the Board's interpretation that limited expressive activities. Again, in Catholic Bishop, we independently determined whether the Board's jurisdiction extended to parochial schools in the face of a substantial First Amendment challenge, although the Board itself had previously considered the First Amendment challenge and presumably interpreted the statute cognizable of those limits.

We follow this course here and conclude, as did the Court of Appeals, that the section is open to a construction that obviates deciding whether a congressional prohibition of handbilling on the facts of this case would violate the First Amendment.

The case turns on whether handbilling such as involved here must be held to 'threaten, coerce, or restrain any person' to cease doing business with another, within the meaning of § 8(b)(4)(ii)(B). . . . Our decision in Tree Fruits, however, makes untenable the notion that any kind of handbilling, picketing, or other appeals to a secondary employer to cease doing business with the employer involved in the labor dispute is 'coercion' within the meaning of § 8(b)(4)(ii)(B) if it has some economic impact on the neutral. . . .

In our view, interpreting § 8(b)(4) as not reaching the handbilling involved in this case is not foreclosed either by the language of the section or its legislative history. That construction makes unnecessary passing on the serious constitutional questions that would be raised by the Board's understanding of the statute. Accordingly, the judgment of the Court of Appeals is affirmed."

V. JUSTICE VOTE

8 Pro ACLU Side vs. 0 Con Opposing Side

ACLU Side (Respondent / Appellee)

1. White, B. – Wrote majority opinion
2. Rehnquist, C. – Joined majority opinion
3. Blackmun, H. – Joined majority opinion
4. O'Connor, S. – Concurred in the judgment without an opinion
5. Scalia, A. – Concurred in the judgment without an opinion
6. Stevens, J. – Joined majority opinion
7. Brennan, W. – Joined majority opinion
8. Marshall, T. – Joined majority opinion

Kennedy, A – Took no part in the decision

VI. A WIN OR LOSS FOR THE ACLU?

The ACLU, as amicus curiae, urged affirmance of the judgment of the Court of Appeals; the Supreme Court affirmed in an 8-0 vote, giving the ACLU an apparent win.

644. United States v. Providence Journal Co.

(Decided May 2, 1988; 485 U.S. 693)

I. ISSUE

A. Issues Discussed

Criminal contempt, prosecution

B. Legal Question Presented

Did the special prosecutor possess the authority to represent the United States before the Supreme Court?

C. Supreme Court's Answer

The writ of certiorari is dismissed because the special prosecutor did not have the authority to represent the United States before the Supreme Court.

II. CASE SUMMARY

A. Background

"On November 8, 1985, Raymond J. Patriarca, son of Raymond L.S. Patriarca, by then deceased, filed suit against the Federal Bureau of Investigation (FBI), its Director, the Department of Justice, the Attorney General of the United States, the Providence Journal Company (Journal), and WJAR Television Ten (WJAR), seeking to enjoin further dissemination of logs and memoranda compiled from 1962 to 1965 during the course of illegal electronic surveillance of the plaintiff's father. [T]he Chief Judge entered a temporary restraining order barring publication of the logs and memoranda and set a hearing for Friday, November 15. . . .

During the evening of November 13, respondent Charles M. Hauser, executive editor of the Journal, was first advised of the restraining order. After discussing with other Journal executives the perils of noncompliance, Hauser decided to publish a story based on the logs and memoranda. . . . Patriarca forthwith filed a motion to have the Journal and Hauser adjudged in criminal contempt.

Patriarca, however, declined to prosecute the contempt motion, and the District Court decided not to ask the United States Attorney to pursue the matter because of his representation of the federal defendants in the underlying civil action. Invoking Federal Rule of Criminal Procedure 42(b), the District Court appointed William A. Curran of the Rhode Island Bar as 'prosecuting attorney with full authority to prosecute' the pending contempt motion. On Curran's application, the District Court then ordered respondents to show cause why they should not be adjudged in criminal contempt.

Following a hearing on February 10, 1986, the District Court found respondents in criminal contempt of the order entered on November 13. . . . Respondents appealed, and the United

States Court of Appeals for the First Circuit reversed the judgment of contempt. . . . The Court of Appeals, then sitting en banc, summarily modified the panel's opinion, holding that even those subject to a transparently invalid order must make a good-faith effort to seek emergency appellate relief. It ruled, however, that the publisher may proceed to publish and challenge the constitutionality of the order in the contempt proceeding if timely access to the appellate court is not available or if a timely decision is not forthcoming. The court was not convinced that respondents could have obtained emergency relief before the publisher had to make a final decision whether to run the story the following day, and found it unfair to subject respondents to substantial sanctions for failing to follow the newly announced procedures."

The Supreme Court granted certiorari to review the case, determined the special prosecutor could not represent the case before the Supreme Court, and dismissed the writ of certiorari.

B. Counsel of Record / ACLU Attorney

ACLU Side (Respondent / Appellee): Floyd Abrams argued the cause for appellee.

Opposing Side (Petitioner / Appellant): Robert D. Parrillo argued the cause for the appellant.

III. AMICI CURIAE

ACLU Side (Respondent / Appellee)

Brief of amici curiae filed on behalf of the ACLU, et al., by John A. Powell, Steven R. Shapiro, Lynette Labinger, Martha Minow, Kathleen M. Sullivan, and Marjorie Heins.

Brief of amici curiae filed on behalf of the American Newspaper Publishers Association, et al., by James C. Goodale and John G. Koeltl.

Opposing Side (Petitioner / Appellant)

Brief of amici curiae filed on behalf of the United States by Solicitor General Fried, Assistant Attorney General Willard, Deputy Solicitor General Bryson, Edwin S. Kneedler, and Douglas N. Letter.

Brief of amici curiae filed on behalf of the Washington Legal Foundation, et al., by Daniel J. Popeo and Michael P. McDonald.

IV. THE SUPREME COURT'S DECISION

"If the plain statutory language of § 518(a) were not reason enough to persuade us to accept respondents' objections and dismiss the writ of certiorari, we observe that the salutary policies that support § 518(a) could be undermined by, and anomalous consequences could result from, the approach urged upon the Court by the special prosecutor and the Solicitor General. Among the reasons for reserving litigation in this Court to the Attorney General and the Solicitor General, is the concern that the United States usually should speak with one voice before this Court, and with a voice that reflects not the parochial interests of a particular agency, but the common interests of the Government and therefore of all the people. Without the centralization of the decision whether to seek certiorari, this Court might well be deluged with petitions from every federal prosecutor, agency, or instrumentality, urging as the position of the United States, a variety of inconsistent positions shaped by the immediate demands of the case sub judice, rather than by longer term interests in the development of the law. . . .

We conclude that a criminal contempt prosecution brought to vindicate the authority of the Judiciary and to punish disobedience of a court order is a suit 'in which the United States is interested,' within the meaning of § 518(a), regardless of who is appointed by the district court to prosecute the action. In this case, the special prosecutor filed a petition for a writ of certiorari without the authorization of the Solicitor General, and thus without authorization to appear on behalf of the United States. Absent a proper representative of the Government, as a petitioner in this criminal prosecution, jurisdiction is lacking and the writ of certiorari, heretofore granted, is now dismissed."

V. JUSTICE VOTE

6 Pro ACLU Side vs. 2 Con Opposing Side

ACLU Side (Respondent / Appellee)

1. Blackmun, H. – Wrote majority opinion
2. Brennan, W. – Joined majority opinion
3. White, B. – Joined majority opinion
4. Marshall, T. – Joined majority opinion
5. O'Connor, S. – Joined majority opinion
6. Scalia, A. – Wrote concurring opinion

Opposing Side (Petitioner / Appellant)

1. Stevens, J. – Wrote dissenting opinion
2. Rehnquist, W. – Joined Stevens' dissent

Kennedy, A – Took no part in the decision

VI. A WIN OR LOSS FOR THE ACLU?

The ACLU filed as amicus curiae urging affirmance; the Supreme Court dismissed the writ of certiorari by a 6-2 vote, thus allowing the judgment of the Court of Appeals to stand, giving the ACLU an apparent win.

645. Meyer v. Grant

(Decided June 6, 1988; 486 U.S. 414)

I. ISSUE

A. Issues Discussed

First Amendment, political speech, voting, initiatives

B. Legal Question Presented

Whether "[o]ne section of the state law regulating the initiative process [that] makes it a felony to pay petition circulators" is unconstitutional.

C. Supreme Court's Answer

The section making it a felony to pay petitioner circulators is unconstitutional.

II. CASE SUMMARY

A. Background

"Under Colorado law, proponents of an initiative measure must submit the measure to the State Legislative Council and the Legislative Drafting Office for review and comment. . . . After approval . . . , the proponents of the measure then have six months to obtain the necessary signatures . . . . If the signature requirements are met, the petitions may be filed with the Secretary of State, and the measure will appear on the ballot at the next general election.

State law requires that the persons who circulate the approved drafts of the petitions for signature be registered voters. . . . The payment of petition circulators is punished as a felony.

Appellees are proponents of an amendment to the Colorado Constitution . . . . Based on their own experience as petition circulators, as well as that of other unpaid circulators, appellees concluded that they would need the assistance of paid personnel to obtain the required number of signatures within the allotted time. They then brought this action under 42 U.S.C. § 1983 against the Secretary of State and the Attorney General of Colorado seeking a declaration that the statutory prohibition against the use of paid circulators violates their rights under the First Amendment.

After a brief trial, the District Judge entered judgment upholding the statute on alternative grounds. . . . A divided panel of the Court of Appeals affirmed for the reasons stated by the District Court. After granting rehearing en banc, however, the court reversed. The en banc majority concluded that the record demonstrated that petition circulators engage in the communication of ideas while they are obtaining signatures and that the available pool of circulators is necessarily smaller if only volunteers can be used. . . . The Court of Appeals then rejected the State's asserted justifications for the ban. . . . Having decided to confer the right, the State was obligated to do so in a manner consistent with the Constitution because . . . this case involves 'core political speech.'"

The Supreme Court granted certiorari to review the case and affirmed.

B. Counsel of Record / ACLU Attorney

ACLU Side (Respondent / Appellee): William C. Danks argued the cause for appellee.

Opposing Side (Petitioner / Appellant): Maurice G. Knaizer, First Assistant Attorney General of Colorado, argued the cause for appellant.

III. AMICI CURIAE

ACLU Side (Respondent / Appellee)

Brief of amici curiae filed on behalf of the ACLU, et al., by James J. Sandman, Steven R. Shapiro, and John A. Powell.

Brief of amici curiae filed on behalf of the Washington Legal Foundation, et al., by Daniel J. Popeo and Paul D. Kamenar.

Opposing Side (Petitioner / Appellant)

No briefs of amici curiae were filed in support of appellant.

IV. THE SUPREME COURT'S DECISION

"We fully agree with the Court of Appeals' conclusion that this case involves a limitation on political expression subject to exacting scrutiny. . . . We agree with the Court of Appeals' conclusion that the statute trenches upon an area in which the importance of First Amendment protections is 'at its zenith.' For that reason the burden that Colorado must overcome to justify this criminal law is well-nigh insurmountable. . . .

We are not persuaded by the State's arguments that the prohibition is justified by its interest in making sure that an initiative has sufficient grass roots support to be placed on the ballot, or by its interest in protecting the integrity of the initiative process. As the Court of Appeals correctly held, the former interest is adequately protected by the requirement that no initiative proposal may be placed on the ballot unless the required number of signatures has been obtained. . . . Other provisions of the Colorado statute deal expressly with the potential danger that circulators might be tempted to pad their petitions with false signatures. It is a crime to forge a signature on a petition, to make false or misleading statements relating to a petition, or to pay someone to sign a petition. Further, the top of each page of the petition must bear a statement printed in red ink warning potential signatories that it is a felony to forge a signature on a petition or to sign the petition when not qualified to vote and admonishing signatories not to sign the petition unless they have read and understand the proposed initiative. These provisions seem adequate to the task of minimizing the risk of improper conduct in the circulation of a petition, especially since the risk of fraud or corruption, or the appearance thereof, is more remote at the petition stage of an initiative than at the time of balloting.

'[L]egislative restrictions on advocacy of the election or defeat of political candidates are wholly at odds with the guarantees of the First Amendment.' That principle applies equally to 'the discussion of political policy generally or advocacy of the passage or defeat of legislation.' The Colorado statute prohibiting the payment of petition circulators imposes a burden on political expression that the State has failed to justify. The Court of Appeals correctly held that the statute violates the First and Fourteenth Amendments. Its judgment is therefore affirmed."

V. JUSTICE VOTE

9 Pro ACLU Side vs. 0 Con Opposing Side

ACLU Side (Respondent / Appellee)

1. Stevens, J. – Wrote majority opinion
2. Brennan, W. – Joined majority opinion
3. Kennedy, A. – Joined majority opinion
4. Rehnquist, W. – Joined majority opinion
5. White, B. – Joined majority opinion
6. O'Connor, S. – Joined majority opinion
7. Scalia, A. – Joined majority opinion
8. Marshall, T. – Joined majority opinion
9. Blackmun, H. – Joined majority opinion

VI. A WIN OR LOSS FOR THE ACLU?

The ACLU, as amicus curiae, urged affirmance of the judgment of the Court of Appeals; the Supreme Court affirmed in a 9-0 vote, giving the ACLU an apparent win.

646. Clark v. Jeter

(Decided June 6, 1988; 486 U.S. 456)

I. ISSUE

A. Issues Discussed

Equal protection, due process, child support

B. Legal Question Presented

Whether a Pennsylvania law that "an illegitimate child must prove paternity before seeking support from his or her father, and a suit to establish paternity ordinarily must be brought within six years of an illegitimate child's birth [whereas by] contrast, a legitimate child may seek support from his or her parents at any time" is constitutional.

C. Supreme Court's Answer

The law is unconstitutional under the Equal Protection Clause.

II. CASE SUMMARY

A. Background

"On September 22, 1983, petitioner Cherlyn Clark filed a support complaint in the Allegheny County Court of Common Pleas on behalf of her minor daughter, Tiffany, who was born out of wedlock on June 11, 1973. Clark named respondent Gene Jeter as Tiffany's father. The court ordered blood tests, which showed a 99.3% probability that Jeter is Tiffany's father.

Jeter moved to dismiss the complaint on the ground that it was barred by the 6–year statute of limitations for paternity actions. In her response, Clark contended that this statute is unconstitutional under the Equal Protection and Due Process Clauses of the Fourteenth Amendment. In the alternative, she argued that the statute was tolled by fraudulent and misleading actions of the welfare department, or by threats and assaults by Jeter.

The trial court upheld the statute of limitations . . . . The trial court also rejected Clark's argument that the statute should be tolled, specifically finding that any fear that Clark may have had of Jeter had subsided more than six years before she filed her support complaint. Therefore, the trial court entered judgment for Jeter.

Clark appealed to the Superior Court of Pennsylvania, again raising her constitutional challenges to the 6–year statute of limitations. Before the court decided her case, the Pennsylvania Legislature enacted an 18–year statute of limitations for actions to establish paternity. Pennsylvania thereby brought its law into compliance with a provision of the federal Child Support Enforcement Amendments of 1984 that requires all States participating in the federal child support program to have procedures to establish the paternity of any child who is less than 18 years old. The Superior Court concluded, however, that Pennsylvania's new 18–year statute of limitations did not apply retroactively, and that it would not revive Clark's cause of action in any event. It affirmed the trial court's conclusions that the 6–year statute of limitations was constitutional, and that Clark's tolling argument was without merit. Thereafter, the Superior Court denied Clark's motion for reargument. The Pennsylvania Supreme Court denied her petition for allowance of appeal."

The Supreme Court granted certiorari to review the case and reversed.

B. Counsel of Record / ACLU Attorney

ACLU Side (Petitioner / Appellant): Evalynn B. Welling argued the cause for appellant.

Opposing Side (Respondent / Appellee): Craig McClean argued the cause for appellee.

III. AMICI CURIAE

ACLU Side (Petitioner / Appellant)

Briefs of amici curiae filed on behalf of the ACLU Foundation, et al., by John A. Powell, Helen Hershkoff, Steven P. Shapiro, and Stefan Presser.

Brief of amici curiae filed on behalf of the Women's Legal Defense Fund, et al., by Erwin N. Griswold, Judith L. Lichtman, Donna R. Lenhoff, and James D. Weill.

Opposing Side (Respondent / Appellee)

No briefs of amici curiae were filed in support of appellee.

IV. THE SUPREME COURT'S DECISION

"This Court has developed a particular framework for evaluating equal protection challenges to statutes of limitations that apply to suits to establish paternity, and thereby limit the ability of illegitimate children to obtain support.

'First, the period for obtaining support . . . must be sufficiently long in duration to present a reasonable opportunity for those with an interest in such children to assert claims on their behalf. Second, any time limitation placed on that opportunity must be substantially related to the State's interest in avoiding the litigation of stale or fraudulent claims.'

[W]e conclude that Pennsylvania's 6-year statute of limitations violates the Equal Protection Clause. Even six years does not necessarily provide a reasonable opportunity to assert a claim on behalf of an illegitimate child. 'The unwillingness of the mother to file a paternity action on behalf of her child, which could stem from her relationship with the natural father or . . . from the emotional strain of having an illegitimate child, or even from the desire to avoid community and family disapproval, may continue years after the child is born. The problem may ben exacerbated if, as often happens, the mother herself is a minor.' Not all of these difficulties are likely to abate in six years. . . .

We do not rest our decision on this ground, however, for it is not entirely evident that six years would necessarily be an unreasonable limitations period for child support actions involving illegitimate children. We are, however, confident that the 6-year statute of limitations is not substantially related to Pennsylvania's interest in avoiding the litigation of stale or fraudulent claims. . . .

We conclude that the Pennsylvania statute does not withstand heightened scrutiny under the Equal Protection Clause. We therefore find it unnecessary to reach Clark's due process claim. The judgment of the Superior Court is reversed, and the case is remanded for further proceedings not inconsistent with this opinion."

V. JUSTICE VOTE

9 Pro ACLU Side vs. 0 Con Opposing Side

ACLU Side (Petitioner / Appellant)

1. O' Connor, S. – Wrote majority opinion
2. White, B. – Joined majority opinion
3. Brennan, W. – Joined majority opinion
4. Rehnquist, W. – Joined majority opinion
5. Stevens, J. – Joined majority opinion
6. Marshall, T. – Joined majority opinion
7. Blackmun, H. – Joined majority opinion
8. Scalia, A. – Joined majority opinion
9. Kennedy, A. – Joined majority opinion

VI. A WIN OR LOSS FOR THE ACLU?

The ACLU, as amicus curiae, urged reversal of the judgment of the Superior Court; the Supreme Court reversed in a 9-0 vote, giving the ACLU an apparent win.

647. City of Lakewood v. Plain Dealer Publishing Co.

(Decided June 17, 1988; 486 U.S. 750)

I. ISSUE

A. Issues Discussed

First Amendment, freedom of speech and of the press

B. Legal Question Presented

First, "whether the Newspaper may bring a facial challenge to the city's ordinance" which gives the mayor discretion to grant or deny permits for newsracks. Second, "whether the First Amendment is abridged" by the ordinance.

C. Supreme Court's Answer

The Newspaper may bring a facial challenge to the ordinance and the ordinance, by "giving the mayor unfettered discretion to deny a permit application and unbounded authority to condition the permit," is unconstitutional.

II. CASE SUMMARY

A. Background

"Prior to 1983, the city of Lakewood absolutely prohibited the private placement of any structure on public property. On the strength of that law, the city denied the Plain Dealer Publishing Company (Newspaper) permission to place its coin-operated newspaper dispensing devices on city sidewalks. In response, the Newspaper brought suit in the District Court for the Northern District of Ohio challenging the ordinance. The District Court adjudged the absolute prohibition unconstitutional, but delayed entering a permanent injunction to give the city time to amend its law.

Although the city could have appealed the District Court's judgment, it decided instead to adopt two ordinances permitting the placement of structures on city property under certain conditions. One of those ordinances specifically concerns newsracks. That ordinance gives the mayor the authority to grant or deny applications for annual newsrack permits. If the mayor denies an application, he is required to 'stat[e] the reasons for such denial.' In the event the mayor grants an application, the city issues an annual permit subject to several terms and conditions. Among them are: (1) approval of the newsrack design by the city's Architectural Board of Review; (2) an agreement by the newsrack owner to indemnify the city against any liability arising from the newsrack, guaranteed by a $100,000 insurance policy to that effect; and (3) any 'other terms and conditions deemed necessary and reasonable by the Mayor.'

Dissatisfied with the new ordinance, the Newspaper elected not to seek a permit, and instead amended its complaint in the District Court to challenge facially the law as amended. The District Court found the ordinance constitutional in its entirety, and entered judgment in the city's favor. The Court of Appeals for the Sixth Circuit reversed, finding the ordinance unconstitutional in three respects. First, it held that the ordinance gives the mayor unbounded discretion to grant or deny a permit application and to place unlimited additional terms and conditions on any permit that issues. Second, it concluded that in the absence of any express standards governing newsrack design, the design approval requirement effectively gives the Board unbridled discretion to deny applications. Finally, a majority of the panel decided that the indemnity and insurance requirements for newsrack owners violate the First Amendment because no similar burdens are placed on owners of other structures on public property. The court found that the foregoing provisions of the law were not severable, and therefore held the entire ordinance unconstitutional insofar as it regulates newsracks in commercial districts."

The Supreme Court granted certiorari to review the case and affirmed.

B. Counsel of Record / ACLU Attorney

ACLU Side (Respondent / Appellee): James P. Garner argued the cause for appellee.

Opposing Side (Petitioner / Appellant): Henry B. Fischer argued the cause for appellant.

III. AMICI CURIAE

ACLU Side (Respondent / Appellee)

Brief of amici curiae filed on behalf of the ACLU Foundation by Gordon J. Beggs, John A. Powell, Steven R. Shapiro, Bruce A. Campbell, and Paul L. Hoffman.

Brief of amici curiae filed on behalf of the American Newspaper Publishers Association, et al., by Robb M. Jones, Robert C. Bernius, Peter G. Stone, Lawrence W. Boes, William Niese, Boisfeuillet Jones, Jr., W. Terry Maguire, Tonda F. Rush, Harold W. Fuson, Jr., Alice Neff Lucan, and Norton L. Armour.

Opposing Side (Petitioner / Appellant)

Briefs of amici curiae filed on behalf of the National Institute of Municipal Law Officers by William I. Thornton, Jr., Roger F. Cutler, Roy D. Bates, William H. Taube, John W. Witt, Robert J. Alfton, James K. Baker, Joseph N. deRaismes, Frank B. Gummy III, Robert J. Mangler, Neal E. McNeill, Analeslie Muncy, Dante R. Pellegrini, Clifford D. Pierce, Jr., and Charles S. Rhyne.

Brief of amici curiae filed on behalf of the National League of Cities, et al., by Benna Ruth Solomon, Joyce Holmes Benjamin, Beate Bloch, and Peter Buscemi.

IV. THE SUPREME COURT'S DECISION

"At the outset, we confront the issue whether the Newspaper may bring a facial challenge to the city's ordinance. We conclude that it may.

[T]he First Amendment is certainly implicated by the city's circulation restriction; the question we must resolve is whether the First Amendment is abridged. . . .

It is apparent that the face of the ordinance itself contains no explicit limits on the mayor's discretion. Indeed, nothing in the law as written requires the mayor to do more than make the statement 'it is not in the public interest' when denying a permit application. Similarly, the mayor could grant the application, but require the newsrack to be placed in an inaccessible location without providing any explanation whatever. To allow these illusory 'constraints' to constitute the standards necessary to bound a licensor's discretion renders the guarantee against censorship little more than a high-sounding ideal. . . .

We hold those portions of the Lakewood ordinance giving the mayor unfettered discretion to deny a permit application and unbounded authority to condition the permit on any additional terms he deems 'necessary and reasonable,' to be unconstitutional. We need not resolve the remaining questions presented for review, as our conclusion regarding mayoral discretion will alone sustain the Court of Appeals' judgment if these portions of the ordinance are not severable from the remainder. Severability of a local ordinance is a question of state law, and is therefore best resolved below. Accordingly, we remand this cause to the Court of Appeals to decide whether the provisions of the ordinance we have declared unconstitutional are severable, and to take further action consistent with this opinion."

V. JUSTICE VOTE

4 Pro ACLU Side vs. 3 Con Opposing Side

ACLU Side (Respondent / Appellee)

1. Brennan, W. – Wrote majority opinion
2. Marshall, T. – Joined majority opinion
3. Blackmun, H. – Joined majority opinion
4. Scalia, A. – Joined majority opinion

Opposing Side (Petitioner / Appellant)

1. White, B. – Wrote dissenting opinion
2. Stevens, J. – Joined White's dissent
3. O'Connor, S. – Joined White's dissent

Rehnquist, W – Took no part in the decision
Kennedy, A – Took no part in the decision

VI. A WIN OR LOSS FOR THE ACLU?

The ACLU, as amicus curiae, urged affirmance of the judgment of the Court of Appeals; the Supreme Court affirmed in a 4-3 vote, giving the ACLU an apparent win.

648. New York State Club Ass'n v. City of New York

(Decided June 20, 1988; 487 U.S. 1)

I. ISSUE

A. Issues Discussed

First Amendment, freedom of association, equal protection

B. Legal Question Presented

Whether appellant has standing to challenge a New York antidiscrimination law and, if so, whether the law is unconstitutional on its face.

C. Supreme Court's Answer

Appellant has standing to challenge the law, but the law is not unconstitutional on its face.

II. CASE SUMMARY

A. Background

"In 1965, New York City adopted a Human Rights Law that prohibits discrimination by any 'place of public accommodation, resort or amusement.' . . . Yet the Law . . . exempted from its coverage various public educational facilities and 'any institution, club or place of accommodation which proves that it is in its nature distinctly private.' . . .

In 1984, New York City amended its Human Rights Law. The basic purpose of the amendment is to prohibit discrimination in certain private clubs that are determined to be sufficiently 'public' in nature that they do not fit properly within the exemption . . . . The specific change wrought by the amendment is to extend the antidiscrimination provisions of the Human Rights Law to any 'institution, club or place of accommodation [that] has more than four hundred members, provides regular meal service and regularly receives payment for dues, fees, use of space, facilities, services, meals or beverages directly or indirectly from or on behalf of nonmembers for the furtherance of trade or business.' Any such club 'shall not be considered in its nature distinctly private.' Nonetheless, the city also stated that any such club 'shall be deemed to be in its nature distinctly private' if it is 'a corporation incorporated under the benevolent orders law or described in the benevolent orders law but formed under any other law of this state, or a religious corporation incorporated under the education law or the religious corporations law.' . . .

Immediately after the 1984 Law became effective, the New York State Club Association filed suit against the city and some of its officers in state court, seeking a declaration that the Law is invalid on various state grounds and is unconstitutional on its face under the First and Fourteenth Amendments and requesting that defendants be enjoined from enforcing it. On cross-motions for summary judgment, the trial court upheld the Law against all challenges, including the federal constitutional challenges. The intermediate state appellate court affirmed this judgment on appeal . . . .

The State Club Association appealed this decision to the New York Court of Appeals, which affirmed in a unanimous opinion. The court rejected the First Amendment challenge to Local Law 63 . . . . It ruled that any infringement on associational rights is amply justified by the city's compelling interest in eliminating discrimination against women and minorities. In addition, the Law employs the least restrictive means to achieve its ends because it interferes with the policies and activities of private clubs only 'to the extent necessary to ensure that they do not automatically exclude persons from membership or use of the facilities on account of invidious discrimination.' The court denied relief on the equal protection claim without discussing it."

The Supreme Court granted certiorari to review the case and affirmed.

B. Counsel of Record / ACLU Attorney

ACLU Side (Respondent / Appellee): Peter L. Zimroth argued the cause for appellee.

Opposing Side (Petitioner / Appellant): Alan Mansfield argued the cause for appellant.

III. AMICI CURIAE

ACLU Side (Respondent / Appellee)

Briefs of amici curiae filed on behalf of the ACLU Foundation, et al., by Burt Neuborne, John A. Powell, Steven R. Shapiro, Isabelle Katz Pinzler, Arthur N. Eisenberg, Paul L. Hoffman, and Judith Resnik.

Additional briefs of amici curiae were filed on behalf of the Lawyer's Committee for Civil Rights Under Law, the State of New York, et al., the city of Chicago, the city of Los Angeles, et al., the city and county of San Francisco, the Licensing Board of the city of Boston, the American Bar Association, the Anti-Defamation League of B'nai B'rith, et al., the Committees on Civil Rights and Sex and Law of the Association of the Bar of the city of New York, the NOW Legal Defense and Education Fund, et al., and the U.S. Conference of Mayors, et al.

Opposing Side (Petitioner / Appellant)

Brief of amici curiae filed on behalf of the Conference of Private Organizations by Thomas P. Ondeck.

Brief of amici curiae filed on behalf of the Club Managers Association of America by John M. Wood and David Ferber.

Brief of amici curiae filed on behalf of the Francisca Club, et al., by Michael H. Salinsky and Kevin M. Fong.

IV. THE SUPREME COURT'S DECISION

"The initial question in this case is whether appellant has standing to challenge the constitutionality of Local Law 63 in this Court. We hold that it does. [T]he appellant consortium has standing to sue on behalf of its member associations as long as those associations would have standing to bring the same challenge to Local Law 63. In this regard, it is sufficient to note that appellant's member associations would have standing to bring this same suit on behalf of their own individual members, since those individuals 'are suffering immediate or threatened injury' to their associational rights as a result of the Law's enactment.

[A]ppellant brought this suit challenging the constitutionality of the 1984 Law on its face before any enforcement proceedings were initiated against any of its member associations. Although such facial challenges are sometimes permissible and often have been entertained, especially when speech protected by the First Amendment is at stake, to prevail on a facial attack the plaintiff must demonstrate that the challenged law either 'could never be applied in a valid manner' or that even though it may be validly applied to the plaintiff and others, it nevertheless is so broad that it 'may inhibit the constitutionally protected speech of third parties.' . . . We are unpersuaded that appellant is entitled to make either one of these two distinct facial challenges. . . .

On its face, Local Law 63 does not affect 'in any significant way' the ability of individuals to form associations that will advocate public or private viewpoints. It does not require the clubs 'to abandon or alter' any activities that are protected by the First Amendment. If a club seeks to exclude individuals who do not share the views that the club's members wish to promote, the Law erects no obstacle to this end. Instead, the Law merely prevents an association from using race, sex, and the other specified characteristics as shorthand measures in place of what the city considers to be more legitimate criteria for determining membership. . . . The facial attack based on the claim that Local Law 63 is invalid in all of its applications must therefore fail. . . .

A law is constitutional unless it is substantially overbroad.' To succeed in its challenge, appellant must demonstrate from the text of Local Law 63 and from actual fact that a substantial number of instances exist in which the Law cannot be applied constitutionally. Yet appellant has not identified those clubs for whom the antidiscrimination provisions will impair their ability to associate together or to advocate public or private viewpoints. . . . We therefore cannot conclude that the Law is substantially overbroad and must assume that 'whatever overbreadth may exist should be cured through case-by-case analysis of the fact situations to which its sanctions, assertedly, may not be applied.' . . .

The City Council's explanation for exempting benevolent orders and religious corporations from the Local Law 63's coverage reflects a view that these associations are different in kind, at least in the crucial respect of whether business activity is prevalent among them, from the associations on whose behalf appellant has brought suit. Appellant has the burden of showing that this view is erroneous and that the issue is not truly debatable, a burden that appellant has failed to carry. There is no evidence in the record to indicate that a detailed examination of the practices, purposes, and structures of benevolent orders and religious corporations would show them to be identical in this and other critical respects to the private clubs that are covered under the city's antidiscrimination provisions. Without any such showing, appellant's facial attack on the Law under the Equal Protection Clause must founder.

We therefore affirm the judgment below."

V. JUSTICE VOTE

9 Pro ACLU Side vs. 0 Con Opposing Side

ACLU Side (Respondent / Appellee)

1. White, B. – Wrote majority opinion
2. Rehnquist, W. – Joined majority opinion
3. Brennan, W. – Joined majority opinion
4. Marshall, T. – Joined majority opinion
5. Blackmun, H. – Joined majority opinion
6. Stevens, J. – Joined majority opinion
7. O'Connor, S. – Wrote concurring opinion
8. Kennedy, A. – Joined O'Connor's concurrence
9. Scalia, A. – Wrote concurring opinion

VI. A WIN OR LOSS FOR THE ACLU?

The ACLU, as amicus curiae, urged affirmance of the judgment of the Court of Appeals; the Supreme Court affirmed in a 9-0 vote, giving the ACLU an apparent win.

649. West v. Atkins

(Decided June 20, 1988; 487 U.S. 42)

I. ISSUE

A. Issues Discussed

Civil rights, state action, prisons

B. Legal Question Presented

"[W]hether a physician who is under contract with the State to provide medical services to inmates at a state-prison hospital on a part-time basis acts 'under color of state law,' within the meaning of 42 U.S.C. § 1983, when he treats an inmate."

C. Supreme Court's Answer

A physician under contract with the State to provide medical services to inmates acts "under color of state law" within the meaning of 42 U.S.C. § 1983 when treating an inmate.

II. CASE SUMMARY

A. Background

"Petitioner, Quincy West, tore his left Achilles tendon in 1983 while playing volleyball at Odom Correctional Center, the Jackson, N.C., state prison in which he was incarcerated. A physician under contract to provide medical care to Odom inmates examined petitioner and directed that he be transferred to Raleigh for orthopedic consultation at Central Prison Hospital, the acute-care medical facility operated by the State for its more than 17,500 inmates. Central Prison Hospital has one full-time staff physician, and obtains additional medical assistance under 'Contracts for Professional Services' between the State and area physicians.

Respondent, Samuel Atkins, M.D., a private physician, provided orthopedic services to inmates pursuant to one such contract. Under it, Doctor Atkins was paid approximately $52,000 annually to operate two 'clinics' each week at Central Prison Hospital, with additional amounts for surgery. Over a period of several months, he treated West's injury by placing his leg in a series of casts. West alleges that although the doctor acknowledged that surgery would be necessary, he refused to schedule it, and that he eventually discharged West while his ankle was still swollen and painful, and his movement still impeded. Because West was a prisoner in 'close custody,' he was not free to employ or elect to see a different physician of his own choosing.

Pursuant to 42 U.S.C. § 1983, West, proceeding pro se, commenced this action against Doctor Atkins in the United States District Court for the Eastern District of North Carolina for violation of his Eighth Amendment right to be free from cruel and unusual punishment. West alleged that Atkins was deliberately indifferent to his serious medical needs, by failing to provide adequate treatment.

[T]he District Court granted Doctor Atkins' motion for summary judgment. . . . A panel of the United States Court of Appeals for the Fourth Circuit vacated the District Court's judgment. . . . On en banc rehearing, however, a divided Court of Appeals affirmed the District Court's dismissal of West's complaint."

The Supreme Court granted certiorari to review the case and reversed.

B. Counsel of Record / ACLU Attorney

ACLU Side (Petitioner / Appellant): Adam Stein argued the cause for appellant.

Opposing Side (Respondent / Appellee): Jacob L. Safron, Special Deputy Attorney General of North Carolina, argued the cause for appellee.

III. AMICI CURIAE

ACLU Side (Petitioner / Appellant)

Brief of amici curiae filed on behalf of the ACLU Foundation, et al., by John Powell, Norman Smith, Elizabeth Alexander, Edward I. Koren, and Alvin J. Bronstein.

Brief of amici curiae filed on behalf of the American Public Health Association by William J. Rold.

Opposing Side (Respondent / Appellee)

No briefs of amici curiae were filed in support of appellee.

IV. THE SUPREME COURT'S DECISION

"To state a claim under § 1983, a plaintiff must allege the violation of a right secured by the Constitution and laws of the United States, and must show that the alleged deprivation was committed by a person acting under color of state law. . . . The only issue before us is whether petitioner has established the second essential element—that respondent acted under color of state law in treating West's injury. . . .

Doctor Atkins is authorized and obliged to treat prison inmates, such as West. He does so 'clothed with the authority of state law.' He is 'a person who may fairly be said to be a state actor.' It is only those physicians authorized by the State to whom the inmate may turn. Under state law, the only medical care West could receive for his injury was that provided by the State. If Doctor Atkins misused his power by demonstrating deliberate indifference to West's serious medical needs, the resultant deprivation was caused, in the sense relevant for state-action inquiry, by the State's exercise of its right to punish West by incarceration and to deny him a venue independent of the State to obtain needed medical care.

The fact that the State employed respondent pursuant to a contractual arrangement that did not generate the same benefits or obligations applicable to other 'state employees' does not alter the analysis. . . .

For the reasons stated above, we conclude that respondent's delivery of medical treatment to West was state action fairly attributable to the State, and that respondent therefore acted under color of state law for purposes of § 1983. Accordingly, we reverse the judgment of the Court of Appeals and remand the case for further proceedings consistent with this opinion."

V. JUSTICE VOTE

9 Pro ACLU Side vs. 0 Con Opposing Side

ACLU Side (Petitioner / Appellant)

1. Blackmun, H. – Wrote majority opinion
2. White, B. – Joined majority opinion
3. Rehnquist, W. – Joined majority opinion
4. Brennan, W. – Joined majority opinion
5. Marshall, T. – Joined majority opinion
6. Stevens, J. – Joined majority opinion
7. O'Connor, S. – Joined majority opinion
8. Kennedy, A. – Joined majority opinion
9. Scalia, A. – Wrote concurring opinion

VI. A WIN OR LOSS FOR THE ACLU?

The ACLU, as amicus curiae, urged reversal of the judgment of the Court of Appeals; the Supreme Court reversed in a 9-0 vote, giving the ACLU an apparent win.

650. United States Catholic Conference v. Abortion Rights Mobilization, Inc.

(Decided June 20, 1988; 487 U.S. 72)

I. ISSUE

A. Issues Discussed

Governmental authority, civil procedure, judicial power, jurisdiction

B. Legal Question Presented

"[W]hether a nonparty witness may defend against a civil contempt adjudication by challenging the subject-matter jurisdiction of the district court."

C. Supreme Court's Answer

A nonparty witness may defend against a civil contempt adjudication by challenging the court's subject-matter jurisdiction.

II. CASE SUMMARY

A. Background

"In the underlying action, Abortion Rights Mobilization, Inc., and others (ARM) sued to revoke the tax-exempt status of the Roman Catholic Church in the United States. ARM alleged that the Conferences had violated the rules governing their tax-exempt status by participating in political activities. . . . The Conferences were originally named as parties to this suit, but were later dismissed, leaving the Secretary of the Treasury and the Commissioner of Internal Revenue as the sole defendants.

ARM served subpoenas on the Conferences in 1983, seeking extensive documentary evidence to support its claims. A series of court orders to produce, intertwined with other procedural motions, were followed by objections and refusals. . . . After the Conferences informed the court that they could not 'in conscience, comply with the subpoenas in question,' the court, which had made detailed orders including orders limiting discovery at the behest of the Conferences, found the Conferences in civil contempt. The court assessed fines of $50,000 against each Conference for each day of further noncompliance. The Court of Appeals affirmed, stating that 'the witnesses have standing to question only whether the District Court has a colorable basis for exercising subject matter jurisdiction . . . .' The order was stayed pending appeal, and the stay remains in effect."

The Supreme Court granted certiorari to review the case and reversed.

B. Counsel of Record / ACLU Attorney

ACLU Side (Respondent / Appellee): Marshall Beil argued the cause for appellee.

Opposing Side (Petitioner / Appellant): Kevin T. Baine argued the cause for appellant.

Alan I. Horowitz argued the cause for the federal respondents in support of appellant pursuant to Court Rule 19.6.

III. AMICI CURIAE

ACLU Side (Respondent / Appellee)

Brief of amici curiae filed on behalf of the ACLU Foundation, et al., by Steven R. Shapiro, John A. Powell, Helen Hershkoff, C. Edwin Baker, and Arthur N. Eisenberg.

Brief of amici curiae filed on behalf of the National Abortion Rights Action League, et al., by Ellyn R. Weiss.

Brief of amici curiae filed on behalf of the National Association of Laity by Cletus P. Lyman.

Opposing Side (Petitioner / Appellant)

Brief of amici curiae filed on behalf of the Christian Legal Society by Michael J. Woodruff and Samuel E. Ericsson.

Brief of amici curiae filed on behalf of the National Council of Churches of Christ in the U.S.A., et al., by Edward McGlynn Gaffney, Jr., and Douglas Laycock.

Brief of amici curiae filed on behalf of the Rutherford Institute by William Bonner, John F. Southworth, Jr., Alfred J. Lindh, Ira W. Still III, William B. Hollberg, Randall A. Pentiuk, Thomas W. Strahan, James J. Knicely, John W. Whitehead, and David E. Morris.

IV. THE SUPREME COURT'S DECISION

"We hold that a nonparty witness can challenge the court's lack of subject-matter jurisdiction in defense of a civil contempt citation, notwithstanding the absence of a final judgment in the underlying action. Federal Rule of Civil Procedure 45 grants a district court the power to issue subpoenas as to witnesses and documents, but the subpoena power of a court cannot be more extensive than its jurisdiction. It follows that if a district court does not have subject-matter jurisdiction over the underlying action, and the process was not issued in aid of determining that jurisdiction, then the process is void and an order of civil contempt based on refusal to honor it must be reversed. . . .

The challenge in this case goes to the subject-matter jurisdiction of the court and hence its power to issue the order. . . .

Nothing we have said puts in question the inherent and legitimate authority of the court to issue process and other binding orders, including orders of discovery directed to nonparty witnesses, as necessary for the court to determine and rule upon its own jurisdiction, including jurisdiction over the subject matter.

Though the concurring opinion in the Court of Appeals indicated that the order of the District Court in the case before us might be sustained as an inquiry in aid of the court's jurisdiction over the subject matter, the record shows that the process was issued to obtain discovery on the merits of the litigation. It is a recognized and appropriate procedure for a court to limit discovery proceedings at the outset to a determination of jurisdictional matters, but that was not the objective of this discovery order, even by implication. Before the contempt order, the District Court twice ruled that it had subject-matter jurisdiction of the case.

Accordingly, on remand, the Court of Appeals must determine whether the District Court had subject-matter jurisdiction in the underlying action. If not, then the subpoenas duces tecum are void, and the civil contempt citation must be reversed 'in its entirety.' . . .

We hold that the Court of Appeals for the Second Circuit erred in limiting the Conferences' jurisdictional challenge to the argument that the District Court lacked even colorable jurisdiction to hear the suit. The judgment of the Court of Appeals is therefore reversed, and the case is remanded for further proceedings consistent with this opinion."

V. JUSTICE VOTE

1 Pro ACLU Side vs. 8 Con Opposing Side

ACLU Side (Respondent / Appellee)

1. Marshall, T. – Wrote dissenting opinion

Opposing Side (Petitioner / Appellant)

1. Kennedy, A. – Wrote majority opinion
2. Rehnquist, W. – Joined majority opinion
3. Brennan, W. – Joined majority opinion
4. White, B. – Joined majority opinion
5. Blackmun, H. – Joined majority opinion
6. Stevens, J. – Joined majority opinion
7. O'Connor, S. – Joined majority opinion
8. Scalia, A. – Joined majority opinion

VI. A WIN OR LOSS FOR THE ACLU?

The ACLU filed as amicus curiae urging affirmance of the judgment of the Court of Appeals; the Supreme Court reversed and remanded in an 8-1 vote, giving the ACLU an apparent loss.

651. Ross v. Oklahoma

(Decided June 22, 1988; 487 U.S. 81)

I. ISSUE

A. Issues Discussed

Sixth Amendment, Fourteenth Amendment, due process, jury selection, right to an impartial jury

B. Legal Question Presented

What are "the Sixth and Fourteenth Amendment implications of the trial court's failure to remove Huling for cause and petitioner's subsequent use of a peremptory challenge to strike Huling."

C. Supreme Court's Answer

The trial court erred in failing to remove Huling for cause, however, the error did not violate the Sixth Amendment or Fourteenth Amendment.

II. CASE SUMMARY

A. Background

"In the course of robbing a motel in Elk City, Oklahoma, petitioner killed a police officer. Petitioner was charged with first-degree murder, a capital offense. By statute, Oklahoma provides nine peremptory challenges to both parties in capital trials.

The jury selection began with the drawing of 12 names from the 150-person venire. Each of the 12 was examined individually by the court and counsel. Prospective jurors not excused for cause after the voir dire were provisionally seated. If a prospective juror was excused for cause, a replacement juror was called and examined. After 12 jurors had been provisionally seated, the parties exercised their peremptory challenges alternately beginning with the prosecution. When a juror was struck, a replacement juror was immediately selected and examined in the manner described above. Once a replacement was provisionally seated, the trial court called for the exercise of a challenge by the party whose turn it was. This procedure was repeated until each side had exercised or waived its nine peremptory challenges.

Darrell Huling's name was drawn to replace the juror excused by the defense with its fifth peremptory challenge. During voir dire, Huling initially indicated that he could vote to recommend a life sentence if the circumstances were appropriate. On further examination by defense counsel, Huling declared that if the jury found petitioner guilty, he would vote to impose death automatically. Defense counsel moved to have Huling removed for cause, arguing that Huling would not be able to follow the law at the penalty phase. The trial court denied the motion and Huling was provisionally seated. The defense then exercised its sixth peremptory challenge to remove Huling. The defense ultimately used all nine of its challenges. The prosecution used only five, waiving the remaining four.

None of the 12 jurors who actually sat and decided petitioner's fate was challenged for cause by defense counsel. Petitioner is black; the victim was white. At the close of jury selection, the defense objected 'to the composition of the twelve people, in that there were no black people called as jurymen in this case and the defendant feels he's denied a fair and impartial trial by his peers.' The trial court overruled the objection, and the trial commenced.

After two days of evidence, the parties gave closing arguments, the trial court instructed the jury, and deliberations began. The jury found petitioner guilty of first-degree murder. Following the presentation of evidence and arguments at a separate sentencing proceeding, the same jury found five aggravating circumstances and sentenced petitioner to death.

On appeal, the Oklahoma Court of Criminal Appeals rejected petitioner's argument that the trial court had committed reversible error in failing to excuse Huling for cause . . . ."

The Supreme Court granted certiorari to review the case and affirmed.

B. Counsel of Record / ACLU Attorney

ACLU Side (Petitioner / Appellant): Gary Peterson argued the cause for appellant.

Opposing Side (Respondent / Appellee): Robert A. Nance, Assistant Attorney General of Oklahoma, argued the cause for appellee.

III. AMICI CURIAE

ACLU Side (Petitioner / Appellant)

Brief of amici curiae filed on behalf of the ACLU by Moses Silverman, John A. Powell, Steven R. Shapiro, and Mandy Welch.

Opposing Side (Respondent / Appellee)

No briefs of amici curiae were filed in support of appellee.

IV. THE SUPREME COURT'S DECISION

"It is well settled that the Sixth and Fourteenth Amendments guarantee a defendant on trial for his life the right to an impartial jury. Had Huling sat on the jury that ultimately sentenced petitioner to death, and had petitioner properly preserved his right to challenge the trial court's failure to remove Huling for cause, the sentence would have to be overturned. But Huling did not sit. Petitioner exercised a peremptory challenge to remove him, and Huling was thereby removed from the jury as effectively as if the trial court had excused him for cause.

Any claim that the jury was not impartial, therefore, must focus not on Huling, but on the jurors who ultimately sat. None of those 12 jurors, however, was challenged for cause by petitioner, and he has never suggested that any of the 12 was not impartial. '[T]he Constitution presupposes that a jury selected from a fair cross section of the community is impartial, regardless of the mix of individual viewpoints actually represented on the jury, so long as the jurors can conscientiously and properly carry out their sworn duty to apply the law to the facts of the particular case.' Although at the close of jury selection petitioner did assert that the jury was not fair and impartial, this claim was based on the absence of blacks from the jury panel. Petitioner neither presses that claim before this Court nor suggests that the absence of blacks was in any way related to the failure to remove Huling for cause. We conclude that petitioner has failed to establish that the jury was not impartial. . . .

Petitioner relies heavily upon the Gray Court's statement that 'the relevant inquiry is 'whether the composition of the jury panel as a whole could possibly have been affected by the trial court's error.'' Petitioner points out that had he not used his sixth peremptory challenge to remove Huling, he could have removed another juror, including one who ultimately sat on the jury. Petitioner asserts, moreover, that had he used his sixth peremptory challenge differently, the prosecution may have exercised its remaining peremptory challenges differently in response, and consequently, the composition of the jury panel might have changed significantly.

Although we agree that the failure to remove Huling may have resulted in a jury panel different from that which would otherwise have decided the case, we do not accept the argument that this possibility mandates reversal. We decline to extend the rule of Gray beyond its context: the erroneous 'Witherspoon exclusion' of a qualified juror in a capital case. We think the broad language used by the Gray Court is too sweeping to be applied literally, and is best understood in the context of the facts there involved. One of the principal concerns animating the decision in Gray was the inability to know to a certainty whether the prosecution could and would have used a peremptory challenge to remove the erroneously excused juror. In the instant case, there is no need to speculate whether Huling would have been removed absent the erroneous ruling by the trial court; Huling was in fact removed and did not sit.

Petitioner was undoubtedly required to exercise a peremptory challenge to cure the trial court's error. But we reject the notion that the loss of a peremptory challenge constitutes a violation of the constitutional right to an impartial jury. We have long recognized that peremptory challenges are not of constitutional dimension. They are a means to achieve the end of an impartial jury. So long as the jury that sits is impartial, the fact that the defendant had to use a peremptory challenge to achieve that result does not mean the Sixth Amendment was violated. We conclude that no violation of petitioner's right to an impartial jury occurred. . . .

Petitioner relies on Logan and Hicks to support his claim of a denial of due process. The Logan Court held that because of the arbitrary application of a limitations period, Logan had been deprived of a state-provided cause of action in violation of due process. In Hicks, the Court overturned on due process grounds the sentence imposed on Hicks because the sentence had not been determined by the jury as required by Oklahoma law. Here, however, the requirement that the defendant use peremptory challenges to cure trial court errors is established by Oklahoma law, and petitioner received all that was due under Oklahoma law.

Although the trial court erred in failing to dismiss prospective juror Huling for cause, the error did not deprive petitioner of an impartial jury or of any interest provided by the State. '[T]he Constitution entitles a criminal defendant to a fair trial, not a perfect one.'

Affirmed."

V. JUSTICE VOTE

4 Pro ACLU Side vs. 5 Con Opposing Side

ACLU Side (Petitioner / Appellant)

1. Marshall, T. – Wrote dissenting opinion
2. Brennan, W. – Joined Marshall's dissent
3. Blackmun, H. – Joined Marshall's dissent
4. Stevens, J. – Joined Marshall's dissent

Opposing Side (Respondent / Appellee)

1. Rehnquist, W. – Wrote majority opinion
2. White, B. – Joined majority opinion
3. O'Connor, S. – Joined majority opinion
4. Scalia, A. – Joined majority opinion
5. Kennedy, A. – Joined majority opinion

VI. A WIN OR LOSS FOR THE ACLU?

The ACLU, as amicus curiae, urged reversal of the judgment of the Oklahoma Court of Criminal Appeals; the Supreme Court affirmed in a 5-4 vote, giving the ACLU an apparent loss.

652. Bank of Nova Scotia v. United States

(Decided June 22, 1988; 487 U.S. 250)

I. ISSUE

A. Issues Discussed

Criminal procedure, Fifth Amendment, Sixth Amendment, prosecutorial misconduct

B. Legal Question Presented

"[W]hether a district court may invoke its supervisory power to dismiss an indictment for prosecutorial misconduct in a grand jury investigation, where the misconduct does not prejudice the defendants."

C. Supreme Court's Answer

The district court may not dismiss an indictment for prosecutorial misconduct where the misconduct did not prejudice the defendants.

II. CASE SUMMARY

A. Background

"In 1982, after a 20-month investigation conducted before two successive grand juries, eight defendants, including petitioners William A. Kilpatrick, Declan J. O'Donnell, Sheila C. Lerner, and The Bank of Nova Scotia, were indicted on 27 counts. The first 26 counts charged all defendants with conspiracy and some of them with mail and tax fraud. Count 27 charged Kilpatrick with obstruction of justice. The United States District Court for the District of Colorado initially dismissed the first 26 counts for failure to charge a crime, improper pleading, and, as to charges against the bank, for failure to allege that the bank or its agents had the requisite knowledge and criminal intent. Kilpatrick was tried and convicted on the obstruction of justice count.

The Government appealed the dismissal of the first 26 counts. Before oral argument, however, the Court of Appeals granted a defense motion to remand the case to the District Court for a hearing on whether prosecutorial misconduct and irregularities in the grand jury proceedings were additional grounds for dismissal. United States District Judge Fred M. Winner first presided over the post-trial motions and granted a new trial to Kilpatrick on the obstruction of justice count. The cases were later reassigned to United States District Judge John L. Kane, Jr., to complete the posttrial proceedings. After 10 days of hearings, Judge Kane dismissed all 27 counts of the indictment. . . .

The Government appealed once again, and a divided panel of the Court of Appeals reversed the order of dismissal."

The Supreme Court granted certiorari to review the case and affirmed.

B. Counsel of Record / ACLU Attorney

ACLU Side (Petitioner / Appellant): James E. Nesland argued the cause for appellant.

Opposing Side (Respondent / Appellee): Deputy Solicitor General Bryson argued the cause for the United States.

III. AMICI CURIAE

ACLU Side (Petitioner / Appellant)

Brief of amici curiae filed on behalf of the ACLU, Foundation, et al., by John A. Powell, Helen Hershkoff, Steven R. Shapiro, Richard F. Ziegler, and Martha F. Davis.

Brief of amici curiae filed on behalf of the National Association of Criminal Defense Lawyers by Shelley I. Gilman and Larry S. Pozner.

Opposing Side (Respondent / Appellee)

No briefs of amici curiae were filed in support of appellee.

IV. THE SUPREME COURT'S DECISION

"We hold that, as a general matter, a district court may not dismiss an indictment for errors in grand jury proceedings unless such errors prejudiced the defendants. . . . We now hold that a federal court may not invoke supervisory power to circumvent the harmless-error inquiry prescribed by Federal Rule of Criminal Procedure 52(a). . . .

Having concluded that our customary harmless-error inquiry is applicable where, as in the cases before us, a court is asked to dismiss an indictment prior to the conclusion of the trial, we turn to the standard of prejudice that courts should apply in assessing such claims. We adopt for this purpose, at least where dismissal is sought for nonconstitutional error, the standard articulated by Justice O'Connor in her concurring opinion in United States v. Mechanik, supra. Under this standard, dismissal of the indictment is appropriate only 'if it is established that the violation substantially influenced the grand jury's decision to indict,' or if there is 'grave doubt' that the decision to indict was free from the substantial influence of such violations. . . .

We must address, however, whether, despite the grand jury's independence, there was any misconduct by the prosecution that otherwise may have influenced substantially the grand jury's decision to indict, or whether there is grave doubt as to whether the decision to indict was so influenced. Several instances of misconduct found by the District Court—that the prosecutors manipulated the grand jury investigation to gather evidence for use in civil audits; violated the secrecy provisions of Rule 6(e) by publicly identifying the targets and the subject matter of the grand jury investigation; and imposed secrecy obligations in violation of Rule 6(e) uponbgrand jury witnesses—might be relevant to an allegation of a purpose or intent to abuse the grand jury process. Here, however, it is plain that these alleged breaches could not have affected the charging decision. We have no occasion to consider them further. . . .

In considering the prejudicial effect of the foregoing instances of alleged misconduct, we note that these incidents occurred as isolated episodes in the course of a 20-month investigation, an investigation involving dozens of witnesses and thousands of documents. In view of this context, those violations that did occur do not, even when considered cumulatively, raise a substantial question, much less a grave doubt, as to whether they had a substantial effect on the grand jury's decision to charge.

Errors of the kind alleged in these cases can be remedied adequately by means other than dismissal. For example, a knowing violation of Rule 6 may be punished as a contempt of court. In addition, the court may direct a prosecutor to show cause why he should not be disciplined and request the bar or the Department of Justice to initiate disciplinary proceedings against him. The court may also chastise the prosecutor in a published opinion. Such remedies allow the court to focus on the culpable individual rather than granting a windfall to the unprejudiced defendant. . . .

We conclude that the District Court had no authority to dismiss the indictment on the basis of prosecutorial misconduct absent a finding that petitioners were prejudiced by such misconduct. The prejudicial inquiry must focus on whether any violations had an effect on the grand jury's decision to indict. If violations did substantially influence this decision, or if there is grave doubt that the decision to indict was free from such substantial influence, the violations cannot be deemed harmless. The record will not support the conclusion that petitioners can meet this standard. The judgment of the Court of Appeals is affirmed."

V. JUSTICE VOTE

1 Pro ACLU Side vs. 8 Con Opposing Side

ACLU Side (Petitioner / Appellant)

1. Marshall, T. – Wrote dissenting opinion

Opposing Side (Respondent / Appellee)

1. Kennedy, A. – Wrote majority opinion
2. Rehnquist, W. – Joined majority opinion
3. Brennan, W. – Joined majority opinion
4. White, B. – Joined majority opinion
5. Blackmun, H. – Joined majority opinion
6. Stevens, J. – Joined majority opinion
7. O'Connor, S. – Joined majority opinion
8. Scalia, A. – Wrote concurring opinion

VI. A WIN OR LOSS FOR THE ACLU?

The ACLU filed a brief as amicus curiae urging reversal of the judgment of the Court of Appeals; the Supreme Court affirmed in an 8-1 vote, giving the ACLU an apparent loss.

653. Schweiker v. Chilicky

(Decided June 24, 1988; 487 U.S. 412)

I. ISSUE

A. Issues Discussed

Governmental regulation, Social Security disability benefits

B. Legal Question Presented

"[W]hether the improper denial of Social Security disability benefis, allegedly resulting from violations of due process by government officials who administered the federal Social Security program, give rise to a cause of action for money damages against those officials."

C. Supreme Court's Answer

The improper denial of benefits here does not give rise to a cause of action for money damages against government officials administering the benefits system.

II. CASE SUMMARY

A. Background

"Under Title II of the Social Security Act (Act), the Federal Government provides disability benefits to individuals who have contributed to the Social Security program and who, because of a medically determinable physical or mental impairment, are unable to engage in substantial gainful work. . . .

Respondents are three individuals whose disability benefits under Title II were terminated pursuant to the CDR [continuing disability review] program in 1981 and 1982. Respondents Spencer Harris and Dora Adelerte appealed these determinations through the administrative process, were restored to disabled status, and were awarded full retroactive benefits. Respondent James Chilicky did not pursue these administrative remedies. Instead, he filed a new application for benefits about a year and a half after his benefits were stopped. His application was granted, and he was awarded one year's retroactive benefits; his application for the restoration of the other six months' benefits is apparently still pending. Because the terminations in these three cases occurred before the 1983 emergency legislation was enacted, respondents experienced delays of many months in receiving disability benefits to which they were entitled. All the respondents had been wholly dependent on their disability benefits, and all allege that they were unable to maintain themselves or their families in even a minimally adequate fashion after they were declared ineligible. Respondent James Chilicky was in the hospital recovering from open-heart surgery when he was informed that his heart condition was no longer disabling.

In addition to pursuing administrative remedies, respondents (along with several other individuals who have since withdrawn from the case) filed this lawsuit in the United States District Court for the District of Arizona. They alleged that petitioners—one Arizona and two federal officials who had policymaking roles in the administration of the CDR program—had violated respondents' due process rights. . . .

The District Court dismissed the case on the ground that petitioners were protected by a qualified immunity. Their alleged conduct, the court concluded, did not violate "clearly established statutory or constitutional rights of which a reasonable person would have known." . . .

Respondents appealed, pressing only their claims for money damages against petitioners in their individual capacities. These claims, noted the Court of Appeals, are 'predicated on the constitutional tort theory of Bivens v. Six Unknown Named Agents.' Petitioners argued that the District Court lacked subject matter jurisdiction because the procedures set forth in 42 U.S.C. § 405(g), which do not authorize judicial review in a case like this one, provide the exclusive means of judicial redress for actions 'arising under' the relevant provisions of the Act. The Court of Appeals rejected this argument, holding that subject matter jurisdiction existed because respondents' claims for emotional distress 'arose under' the Due Process Clause of the Fifth Amendment rather than under the statute. The Court of Appeals went on to affirm the District Court to the extent that it dismissed the claims involving acceleration of the CDR program and nonacquiescence in Ninth Circuit decisions. As to respondents' other claims, however, the Court of Appeals concluded that '[i]t cannot be determined as a matter of law that [respondents] could prove no state of facts . . . that resulted in violations of their due process rights and consequent damages.' The case was accordingly remanded for further proceedings, including a trial if necessary.

The petition for certiorari presented one question: 'Whether a Bivens remedy should be implied for alleged due process violations in the denial of social security disability benefits.'"

The Supreme Court granted certiorari to review the case and reversed.

B. Counsel of Record / ACLU Attorney

ACLU Side (Respondent / Appellee): Laurence H. Tribe argued the cause for appellee.

Opposing Side (Petitioner / Appellant): Solicitor General Fried argued the cause for appellant.

III. AMICI CURIAE

ACLU Side (Respondent / Appellee)

Brief of amici curiae filed on behalf of the ACLU Foundation, et al., by Steven R. Shapiro, John A. Powell, and Helen Hershkoff.

Brief of amici curiae filed on behalf of the National Mental Health Association, et al., by Daniel M. Taubman and Peter Komlos-Hrobsky.

Opposing Side (Petitioner / Appellant)

No briefs of amici curiae were filed in support of appellant.

IV. THE SUPREME COURT'S DECISION

"In 1971, this Court held that the victim of a Fourth Amendment violation by federal officers acting under color of their authority may bring suit for money damages against the officers in federal court. . . . So-called 'Bivens actions' for money damages against federal officers have subsequently been permitted under § 1331 for violations of the Due Process Clause of the Fifth Amendment, and the Cruel and Unusual Punishments Clause of the Eighth Amendment.

[T]he concept of 'special factors counselling hesitation in the absence of affirmative action by Congress' has proved to include an appropriate judicial deference to indications that congressional inaction has not been inadvertent. When the design of a Government program suggests that Congress has provided what it considers adequate remedial mechanisms for constitutional violations that may occur in the course of its administration, we have not created additional Bivens remedies. . . .

Congressional attention to problems that have arisen in the administration of CDR (including the very problems that gave rise to this case) has . . . been frequent and intense. Congress itself required that the CDR program be instituted. Within two years after the program began, Congress enacted emergency legislation providing for the continuation of benefits even after a finding of ineligibility by a state agency. Less than two years after passing that law, and fully aware of the results of extensive investigations of the practices that led to respondents' injuries, Congress again enacted legislation aimed at reforming the administration of CDR; that legislation again specifically addressed the problem that had provoked the earlier emergency legislation. At each step, Congress chose specific forms and levels of protection for the rights of persons affected by incorrect eligibility determinations under CDR. At no point did Congress choose to extend to any person the kind of remedies that respondents seek in this lawsuit. Thus, congressional unwillingness to provide consequential damages for unconstitutional deprivations of a statutory right is at least as clear in the context of this case as it was in Bush. . . .

We agree that suffering months of delay in receiving the income on which one has depended for the very necessities of life cannot be fully remedied by the 'belated restoration of back benefits.' The trauma to respondents, and thousands of others like them, must surely have gone beyond what anyone of normal sensibilities would wish to see imposed on innocent disabled citizens. Nor would we care to 'trivialize' the nature of the wrongs alleged in this case. Congress, however, has addressed the problems created by state agencies' wrongful termination of disability benefits. Whether or not we believe that its response was the best response, Congress is the body charged with making the inevitable compromises required in the design of a massive and complex welfare benefits program. Congress has discharged that responsibility to the extent that it affects the case before us, and we see no legal basis that would allow us to revise its decision.

Because the relief sought by respondents is unavailable as a matter of law, the case must be dismissed. The judgment of the Court of Appeals to the contrary is therefore reversed."

V. JUSTICE VOTE

3 Pro ACLU Side vs. 6 Con Opposing Side

ACLU Side (Respondent / Appellee)

1. Brennan, W. – Wrote dissenting opinion
2. Marshall, T. – Joined Brennan's dissent
3. Blackmun, H. – Joined Brennan's dissent

Opposing Side (Petitioner / Appellant)

1. O'Connor, S. – Wrote majority opinion
2. Rehnquist, W. – Joined majority opinion
3. White, B. – Joined majority opinion
4. Scalia, A. – Joined majority opinion
5. Kennedy, A. – Joined majority opinion
6. Stevens, J. – Wrote concurring opinion

VI. A WIN OR LOSS FOR THE ACLU?

The ACLU, as amicus curiae, urged affirmance of the judgment of the Court of Appeals; the Supreme Court reversed in a 6-3 vote, giving the ACLU an apparent loss.

654. Kadrmas v. Dickinson Public Schools

(Decided June 24, 1988; 487 U.S. 450)

I. ISSUE

A. Issues Discussed

Fourteenth Amendment, equal protection

B. Legal Question Presented

Whether "the Equal Protection Clause forbids a State to allow some local school boards, but not others, to assess a fee for transporting pupils between their homes and the public schools."

C. Supreme Court's Answer

This policy does not violate the Equal Protection Clause.

II. CASE SUMMARY

A. Background

"North Dakota is a sparsely populated State, with many people living on isolated farms and ranches. One result has been that some children, as late as the mid–20th century, were educated in 'the one-room school where, in many cases, there [we]re twenty or more pupils with one teacher attempting in crowded conditions and under other disadvantages to give instructions in all primary grades.' . . .

Since 1947, the legislature has authorized and encouraged thinly populated school districts to consolidate or 'reorganize' themselves into larger districts so that education can be provided more efficiently. . . . Appellee Dickinson Public Schools, which serves a relatively populous area, has chosen not to participate in such a reorganization. . . . Dickinson's School Board instituted door-to-door bus service and began charging a fee. During the period relevant to this case, about 13% of the students rode the bus; their parents were charged $97 per year for one child or $150 per year for two children. Such fees covered approximately 11% of the cost of providing the bus service, and the remainder was provided from state and local tax revenues.

In 1979, the State enacted the legislation at issue in this case. This statute expressly indicates that nonreorganized school districts, like Dickinson, may charge a fee for transporting students to school; such fees, however, may not exceed the estimated cost to the school district of providing the service. . . .

Appellants are a Dickinson schoolchild, Sarita Kadrmas, and her mother, Paula. The Kadrmas family, which also includes Mrs. Kadrmas' husband and two preschool children, lives about 16 miles from Sarita's school. Mr. Kadrmas works sporadically in the North Dakota oil fields, and the family's annual income at the time of trial was at or near the officially defined poverty level. Until 1985, the Kadrmas family had agreed each year to pay the fee for busing Sarita to school. Having fallen behind on these and other bills, however, the family refused to sign a contract obligating them to pay $97 for the 1985 school year. Accordingly, the school bus no longer stopped for Sarita, and the family arranged to transport her to school privately. The costs they incurred that year for Sarita's transportation exceeded $1,000, or about 10 times the fee charged by the school district for bus service. This arrangement continued until the spring of 1987, when Paula Kadrmas signed a bus service contract for the remainder of the 1986 school year and paid part of the fee. Mrs. Kadrmas later signed another contract for the 1987 school year, and paid about half of the fee for that period.

In September 1985, appellants, along with others who have since withdrawn from the case, filed an action in state court seeking to enjoin appellees—the Dickinson Public Schools and various school district officials—from collecting any fee for the bus service. The action was dismissed on the merits, and an appeal was taken to the Supreme Court of North Dakota. After rejecting a state-law challenge, which is not at issue here, the court considered appellants' claim that the busing fee violates the Equal Protection Clause of the Fourteenth Amendment. The court characterized the 1979 statute as 'purely economic legislation,' which 'must be upheld unless it is patently arbitrary and fails to bear a rational relationship to any legitimate government purpose.' The court then concluded 'that the charges authorized [by the statute] are rationally related to the legitimate governmental objective of allocating limited resources and that the statute does not discriminate on the basis of wealth so as to violate federal or state equal protection rights.' The court also rejected the contention that the distinction drawn by the statute between reorganized and nonreorganized school districts violates the Equal Protection Clause. The distinction, the court found, serves the legitimate objective of promoting reorganization 'by alleviating parental concerns regarding the cost of student transportation in the reorganized district.' Three justices dissented on state-law grounds."

The Supreme Court granted certiorari to review the case and affirmed.

B. Counsel of Record / ACLU Attorney

ACLU Side (Petitioner / Appellant): Duane Houdek argued the cause for appellant.

Opposing Side (Respondent / Appellee): George T. Dynes argued the cause and filed a brief for appellee.

III. AMICI CURIAE

ACLU Side (Petitioner / Appellant)

Brief of amici curiae filed on behalf of the ACLU Foundation, et al., by C. Edwin Baker, John A. Powell, Helen Hershkoff, Steven R. Shapiro, and Robert Vogel.

Brief of amici curiae filed on behalf of the Children's Defense Fund, et al., by Julius L. Chambers and John Charles Boger.

Opposing Side (Respondent / Appellee)

Brief of amici curiae filed on behalf of the United States by Solicitor General Fried, Assistant Attorney General Reynolds, Deputy Solicitor General Ayer, Deputy Assistant Attorney General Clegg, Paul J. Larkin, Jr., and David K. Flynn.

IV. THE SUPREME COURT'S DECISION

"Unless a statute provokes 'strict judicial scrutiny' because it interferes with a 'fundamental right' or discriminates against a 'suspect class,' it will ordinarily survive an equal protection attack so long as the challenged classification is rationally related to a legitimate governmental purpose. . . .

Applying the appropriate test—under which a statute is upheld if it bears a rational relation to a legitimate government objective—we think it is quite clear that a State's decision to allow local school boards the option of charging patrons a user fee for bus service is constitutionally permissible. The Constitution does not require that such service be provided at all, and it is difficult to imagine why choosing to offer the service should entail a constitutional obligation to offer it for free. No one denies that encouraging local school districts to provide school bus service is a legitimate state purpose or that such encouragement would be undermined by a rule requiring that general revenues be used to subsidize an optional service that will benefit a minority of the district's families. It is manifestly rational for the State to refrain from undermining its legitimate objective with such a rule. . . .

Appellants contend that, even without the application of strict or heightened scrutiny, the 1979 statute violates equal protection because it permits user fees for bus service only in nonreorganized school districts. This distinction, they say, can be given no rational justification whatsoever. [W]e conclude that appellants have failed to carry the 'heavy burden' of demonstrating that the challenged statute is both arbitrary and irrational. . . . Even if we assume, as appellants apparently do, that the State has forbidden reorganized school districts to charge user fees for bus service under any circumstances, it is evident that the legislature could conceivably have believed that such a policy would serve the legitimate purpose of fulfilling the reasonable expectations of those residing in districts with free busing arrangements imposed by reorganization plans. Because this purpose could have no application to nonreorganized districts, the legislature could just as rationally conclude that those districts should have the option of imposing user fees on those who take advantage of the service they are offered.

In sum, the statute challenged in this case discriminates against no suspect class and interferes with no fundamental right. Appellants have failed to carry the heavy burden of demonstrating that the statute is arbitrary and irrational. The Supreme Court of North Dakota correctly concluded that the statute does not violate the Equal Protection Clause of the Fourteenth Amendment, and its judgment is affirmed."

V. JUSTICE VOTE

4 Pro ACLU Side vs. 5 Con Opposing Side

ACLU Side (Petitioner / Appellant)

1. Marshall, T. – Wrote dissenting opinion
2. Brennan, W. – Joined Marshall's dissent
3. Stevens, J. – Wrote dissenting opinion
4. Blackmun, H. – Joined Stevens' dissent

Opposing Side (Respondent / Appellee)

1. O'Connor, S. – Wrote majority opinion
2. Rehnquist, W. – Joined majority opinion
3. White, B. – Joined majority opinion
4. Scalia, A. – Joined majority opinion
5. Kennedy, A. – Joined majority opinion

VI. A WIN OR LOSS FOR THE ACLU?

The ACLU, as amicus curiae, urged reversal of the judgment of the North Dakota Supreme Court; the U.S. Supreme Court affirmed in a 5-4 vote, giving the ACLU an apparent loss.

655. Frisby v. Schultz

(Decided June 27, 1988; 487 U.S. 474)

I. ISSUE

A. Issues Discussed

First Amendment, freedom of speech

B. Legal Question Presented

Does "an ordinance that completely bans picketing 'before or about' any residence" violate the First Amendment?

C. Supreme Court's Answer

The ordinance does not violate the First Amendment.

II. CASE SUMMARY

A. Background

"Brookfield, Wisconsin, is a residential suburb of Milwaukee with a population of approximately 4,300. The appellees, Sandra C. Schultz and Robert C. Braun, are individuals strongly opposed to abortion and wish to express their views on the subject by picketing on a public street outside the Brookfield residence of a doctor who apparently performs abortions at two clinics in neighboring towns. Appellees and others engaged in precisely that activity . . . .

The Town Board therefore resolved to enact an ordinance to restrict the picketing. On May 7, 1985, the town passed an ordinance that prohibited all picketing in residential neighborhoods except for labor picketing. But after reviewing this Court's decision in Carey v. Brown which invalidated a similar ordinance as a violation of the Equal Protection Clause, the town attorney instructed the police not to enforce the new ordinance and advised the Town Board that the ordinance's labor picketing exception likely rendered it unconstitutional. This ordinance was repealed on May 15, 1985, and replaced with the following flat ban on all residential picketing:

'It is unlawful for any person to engage in picketing before or about the residence or dwelling of any individual in the Town of Brookfield.' . . .

On May 18, 1985, appellees were informed by the town attorney that enforcement of the new, revised ordinance would begin on May 21, 1985. Faced with this threat of arrest and prosecution, appellees ceased picketing in Brookfield and filed this lawsuit in the United States District Court for the Eastern District of Wisconsin. . . .

The District Court granted appellees' motion for a preliminary injunction. The court concluded that the ordinance was not narrowly tailored enough to restrict protected speech in a public forum. The District Court's order specified that unless the appellants requested a trial on the merits within 60 days or appealed, the preliminary injunction would become permanent. Appellants requested a trial and also appealed the District Court's entry of a preliminary injunction.

A divided panel of the United States Court of Appeals for the Seventh Circuit affirmed. The Court of Appeals subsequently vacated this decision, however, and ordered a rehearing en banc. After rehearing, the Court of Appeals affirmed the judgment of the District Court by an equally divided vote."

The Supreme Court granted certiorari to review the case and reversed the judgment of the Seventh Circuit Court of Appeals.

B. Counsel of Record / ACLU Attorney

ACLU Side (Respondent / Appellee): Steven Frederick McDowell argued the cause for appellee.

Opposing Side (Petitioner / Appellant): Harold H. Fuhrman argued the cause for appellant.

III. AMICI CURIAE

ACLU Side (Respondent / Appellee)

Brief of amici curiae filed on behalf of the ACLU, et al., by Harrey Grossman, Jane M. Whicher, Jonathan K. Baum, John A. Powell, Steven R. Shapiro, and William Lynch.

Brief of amici curiae filed on behalf of the American Federation of Labor and Congress of Industrial Organizations by Marsha S. Berzon and Laurence Gold.

Brief of amici curiae filed on behalf of the Rutherford Institute, et al., by Robert R. Melnick, William Bonner, John F. Southworth, Jr., W. Charles Bundren, Alfred J. Lindh, Ira W. Still III, William B. Hollberg, Randall A. Pentiuk, Thomas W. Strahan, John W. Whitehead, A. Eric Johnston, and David E. Morris.

Brief of amici curiae filed on behalf of the American Life League, Inc., et al., by Charles E. Rice, Thomas Patrick Monaghan, and James M. Henderson, Sr.

Opposing Side (Petitioner / Appellant)

Brief of amici curiae filed on behalf of the National Institute of Municipal Law Officers by William I. Thornton, Jr., Roy D. Bates, William H. Taube, Roger F. Cutler, Robert J. Alfton, James K. Baker, Joseph N. deRaismes, Frank B. Gummey III, Robert J. Mangler, Neal E. McNeill, Analeslie Muncy, Dante R. Pellegrini, Clifford D. Pierce, Jr., Charles S. Rhyne, and Benjamin L. Brown.

Brief of amici curiae filed on behalf of the National League of Cities, et al., by Benna Ruth Solomon and Mark B. Rotenberg.

Brief of amici curiae filed on behalf of the Pacific Legal Foundation by Ronald A. Zumbrun and Robin L. Rivett.

IV. THE SUPREME COURT'S DECISION

"To ascertain what limits, if any, may be placed on protected speech, we have often focused on the 'place' of that speech, considering the nature of the forum the speaker seeks to employ. Our cases have recognized that the standards by which limitations on speech must be evaluated 'differ depending on the character of the property at issue.' Specifically, we have identified three types of fora: 'the traditional public forum, the public forum created by government designation, and the nonpublic forum.'

[T]he antipicketing ordinance must be judged against the stringent standards we have established for restrictions on speech in traditional public fora:

'In these quintessential public for[a], the government may not prohibit all communicative activity. For the State to enforce a content-based exclusion it must show that its regulation is necessary to serve a compelling state interest and that it is narrowly drawn to achieve that end. . . . The State may also enforce regulations of the time, place, and manner of expression which are content-neutral, are narrowly tailored to serve a significant government interest, and leave open ample alternative channels of communication.' . . .

The precise scope of the ban is not further described within the text of the ordinance, but in our view the ordinance is readily subject to a narrowing construction that avoids constitutional difficulties. Specifically, the use of the singular form of the words 'residence' and 'dwelling' suggests that the ordinance is intended to prohibit only picketing focused on, and taking place in front of, a particular residence. . . . Accordingly, we construe the ban to be a limited one; only focused picketing taking place solely in front of a particular residence is prohibited.

So narrowed, the ordinance permits the more general dissemination of a message. As appellants explain, the limited nature of the prohibition makes it virtually self-evident that ample alternatives remain:

'Protestors have not been barred from the residential neighborhoods. They may enter such neighborhoods, alone or in groups, even marching. . . . They may go door-to-door to proselytize their views. They may distribute literature in this manner . . . or through the mails. They may contact residents by telephone, short of harassment.'

We readily agree that the ordinance preserves ample alternative channels of communication and thus move on to inquire whether the ordinance serves a significant government interest. We find that such an interest is identified within the text of the ordinance itself: the protection of residential privacy. . . .

One important aspect of residential privacy is protection of the unwilling listener. Although in many locations, we expect individuals simply to avoid speech they do not want to hear, the home is different. . . . Thus, we have repeatedly held that individuals are not required to welcome unwanted speech into their own homes and that the government may protect this freedom. . . .

Because the picketing prohibited by the Brookfield ordinance is speech directed primarily at those who are presumptively unwilling to receive it, the State has a substantial and justifiable interest in banning it. The nature and scope of this interest make the ban narrowly tailored. The ordinance also leaves open ample alternative channels of communication and is content neutral. Thus, largely because of its narrow scope, the facial challenge to the ordinance must fail. The contrary judgment of the Court of Appeals is reversed."

V. JUSTICE VOTE

3 Pro ACLU Side vs. 6 Con Opposing Side

ACLU Side (Respondent / Appellee)

1. Brennan, W. – Wrote dissenting opinion
2. Marshall, T. – Joined Brennan's dissent
3. Stevens, J. – Wrote dissenting opinion

Opposing Side (Petitioner / Appellant)

1. O'Connor, S. – Wrote majority opinion
2. Rehnquist, W. – Joined majority opinion
3. Blackmun, H. – Joined majority opinion
4. Scalia, A. – Joined majority opinion
5. Kennedy, A. – Joined majority opinion
6. White, B. – Wrote concurring opinion

VI. A WIN OR LOSS FOR THE ACLU?

The ACLU, as amicus curiae, urged affirmance of the judgment of the Seventh Circuit Court of Appeals; the Supreme Court reversed in a 6-3 vote, giving the ACLU an apparent loss.

656. Murray v. United States

(Decided June 27, 1988; 487 U.S. 533)

I. ISSUE

A. Issues Discussed

Criminal justice, drugs, Fourth Amendment, Sixth Amendment, search and seizure, warrants

B. Legal Question Presented

"[W]hether, . . . assuming evidence obtained pursuant to an independently obtained search warrant, the portion of such evidence that had been observed in plain view at the time of a prior illegal entry must be suppressed."

C. Supreme Court's Answer

The case must be vacated and remanded to determine "whether the warrant-authorized search of the warehouse was an independent source of the challenged evidence."

II. CASE SUMMARY

A. Background

"Both cases arise out of the conviction of petitioner Michael F. Murray, petitioner James D. Carter, and others for conspiracy to possess and distribute illegal drugs. . . . Based on information received from informants, federal law enforcement agents had been surveilling petitioner Murray and several of his co-conspirators. At about 1:45 p.m. on April 6, 1983, they observed Murray drive a truck and Carter drive a green camper, into a warehouse in South Boston. When the petitioners drove the vehicles out about 20 minutes later, the surveilling agents saw within the warehouse two individuals and a tractor-trailer rig bearing a long, dark container. Murray and Carter later turned over the truck and camper to other drivers, who were in turn followed and ultimately arrested, and the vehicles lawfully seized. Both vehicles were found to contain marijuana.

After receiving this information, several of the agents converged on the South Boston warehouse and forced entry. They found the warehouse unoccupied, but observed in plain view numerous burlap-wrapped bales that were later found to contain marijuana. They left without disturbing the bales, kept the warehouse under surveillance, and did not reenter it until they had a search warrant. In applying for the warrant, the agents did not mention the prior entry, and did not rely on any observations made during that entry. When the warrant was issued—at 10:40 p.m., approximately eight hours after the initial entry—the agents immediately reentered the warehouse and seized 270 bales of marijuana and notebooks listing customers for whom the bales were destined.

Before trial, petitioners moved to suppress the evidence found in the warehouse. The District Court denied the motion, rejecting petitioners' arguments that the warrant was invalid because the agents did not inform the Magistrate about their prior warrantless entry, and that the warrant was tainted by that entry. The First Circuit affirmed, assuming for purposes of its decision that the first entry into the warehouse was unlawful."

The Supreme Court granted certiorari to review the case, vacated, and remanded.

B. Counsel of Record / ACLU Attorney

ACLU Side (Petitioner / Appellant): A. Raymond Randolph argued the cause for appellant.

Opposing Side (Respondent / Appellee): Roy T. Englert, Jr. argued the cause for the United States.

III. AMICI CURIAE

ACLU Side (Petitioner / Appellant)

Brief of amici curiae filed on behalf of the ACLU, et al., by Larry W. Yackle, John A. Powell, David B. Goldstein, and John Reinstein.

Opposing Side (Respondent / Appellee)

No briefs of amici curiae were filed in support of appellee.

IV. THE SUPREME COURT'S DECISION

"Knowledge that the marijuana was in the warehouse was assuredly acquired at the time of the unlawful entry. But it was also acquired at the time of entry pursuant to the warrant, and if that later acquisition was not the result of the earlier entry there is no reason why the independent source doctrine should not apply. Invoking the exclusionary rule would put the police (and society) not in the same position they would have occupied if no violation occurred, but in a worse one. . . .

The ultimate question, therefore, is whether the search pursuant to warrant was in fact a genuinely independent source of the information and tangible evidence at issue here. This would not have been the case if the agents' decision to seek the warrant was prompted by what they had seen during the initial entry, or if information obtained during that entry was presented to the Magistrate and affected his decision to issue the warrant. . . .

The District Court found that the agents did not reveal their warrantless entry to the Magistrate, and that they did not include in their application for a warrant any recitation of their observations in the warehouse. It did not, however, explicitly find that the agents would have sought a warrant if they had not earlier entered the warehouse. The Government concedes this in its brief. To be sure, the District Court did determine that the purpose of the warrantless entry was in part 'to guard against the destruction of possibly critical evidence,' and one could perhaps infer from this that the agents who made the entry already planned to obtain that 'critical evidence' through a warrant-authorized search. That inference is not, however, clear enough to justify the conclusion that the District Court's findings amounted to a determination of independent source.

Accordingly, we vacate the judgment and remand these cases to the Court of Appeals with instructions that it remand to the District Court for determination whether the warrant-authorized search of the warehouse was an independent source of the challenged evidence in the sense we have described."

V. JUSTICE VOTE

4 Pro ACLU Side vs. 3 Con Opposing Side

ACLU Side (Petitioner / Appellant)

1. Scalia, A. – Wrote majority opinion
2. Rehnquist, W. – Joined majority opinion
3. White, B. – Joined majority opinion
4. Blackmun, H. – Joined majority opinion

Opposing Side (Respondent / Appellee)

1. Marshall, T. – Wrote dissenting opinion
2. O'Connor, S. – Joined Marshall's dissent
3. Stevens, J. – Wrote dissenting opinion, joined Marshall's dissent

Brennan, W – Took no part in the decision
Kennedy, A – Took no part in the decision

VI. A WIN OR LOSS FOR THE ACLU?

The ACLU filed a brief as amicus curiae urging reversal of the judgment of the Court of Appeals; the Supreme Court vacated and remanded in a 4-3 vote, giving the ACLU an apparent win.

657. Bowen v. Kendrick

(Decided June 29, 1988; 487 U.S. 589)

I. ISSUE

A. Issues Discussed

First Amendment, religion, Establishment Clause

B. Legal Question Presented

Whether "a federal grant program that provides funding for services relating to adolescent sexuality and pregnancy . . . violated the Establishment Clause of the First Amendment insofar as it provided for the involvement of religious organizations in the federally funded programs."

C. Supreme Court's Answer

The case must be remanded to determine whether the program violates the Establishment Clause "as applied."

II. CASE SUMMARY

A. Background

"The Adolescent Family Life Act (AFLA or Act) . . . is essentially a scheme for providing grants to public or nonprofit private organizations or agencies 'for services and research in the area of premarital adolescent sexual relations and pregnancy.' . . .

In 1983, this lawsuit against the Secretary was filed in the United States District Court for the District of Columbia by appellees, a group of federal taxpayers, clergymen, and the American Jewish Congress. Seeking both declaratory and injunctive relief, appellees challenged the constitutionality of the AFLA on the grounds that on its face and as applied the statute violates the Religion Clauses of the

First Amendment. Following cross-motions for summary judgment, the District Court held for appellees and declared that the AFLA was invalid both on its face and as applied 'insofar as religious organizations are involved in carrying out the programs and purposes of the Act.'"

The Supreme Court granted certiorari to review the case and reversed.

B. Counsel of Record / ACLU Attorney

ACLU Side (Respondent / Appellee): Janet Benshoof argued the cause for appellees in Nos. 87-253, 87-431, and 87-775 and appellants in No. 87-462. With her on the briefs were Lynn M. Paltrow, Nan D. Hunter, Rachael N. Pine, and Bruce J. Ennis, Jr.

Opposing Side (Petitioner / Appellant): Solicitor General Fried argued the cause for appellant in Nos. 87-253 and 87-431, and for the federal appellee in No. 87-462. With him on the briefs were Assistant Attorney General Willard, Acting Assistant Attorney General Spears, Deputy Solicitor General Ayer, Deputy Assistant Attorney General Cynkar, Lawrence S. Robbins, Michael Jay Singer, Jay S. Bybee, and Theodore C. Hirt.

Michael W. McConnell argued the cause for appellant in No. 87-775. With him on the briefs were Edward R. Grant, Clarke D. Forsythe, Paul Arneson, and Michael J. Woodruff.

III. AMICI CURIAE

ACLU Side (Respondent / Appellee)

Brief of amici curiae filed on behalf of the American Public Health Association, et al., by John H. Hall, Nadine Taub, and Judith Levin.

Brief of amici curiae filed on behalf of the Baptist Joint Committee on Public Affairs, et al. by Oliver S. Thomas.

Brief of amici curiae filed on behalf of the Committee for Public Education and Religious Liberty by Leo Pfeffer.

Brief of amici curiae filed on behalf of the Council on Religious Freedom by Lee Boothby, Robert W. Nixon, and Rolland Truman.

Brief of amici curiae filed on behalf of the National Coalition for Public Education and Religious Liberty, et al., by David B. Isbell, David H. Remes, and Herman Schwartz.

Brief of amici curiae filed on behalf of the NOW Legal Defense and Education Fund, et al., by Sarah E. Burns and Marsha Levick.

Brief of amici curiae filed on behalf of the Anti-Defamation League of B'nai B'rith, et al., by Ruti G. Teitel, Justin J. Finger, Jeffrey P. Sinensky, Meyer Eisenberg, and Steven M. Freeman.

Brief of amici curiae filed on behalf of the Unitarian Universalist Association, et al., by Patricia Hennessey.

Opposing Side (Petitioner / Appellant)

Brief of amici curiae filed on behalf of the Attorney General of Arizona, et al., by Gary B. Born and James S. Campbell.

Brief of amici curiae filed on behalf of the Catholic League for Religious and Civil Rights, et al., by Steven Frederick McDowell.

Brief of amici curiae filed on behalf of the Institute for Youth Advocacy by Gregory A. Loken.

Brief of amici curiae filed on behalf of the National Jewish Commission on Law and Public Affairs by Nathan Lewin and Dennis Rapps

Brief of amici curiae filed on behalf of the National Right to Life Committee, Inc., by James Bopp, Jr.

Brief of amici curiae filed on behalf of the Rutherford Institute, et al., by John W. Whitehead, David E. Morris, Alfred J. Lindh, Ira W. Still III, William B. Hollberg, Randall A. Pentiuk, Thomas W. Strahan, William Bonner, John F. Southworth, Jr., and W. Charles Bundren.

Brief of amici curiae filed on behalf of the United States Catholic Conference by Mark E. Chopko and Philip H. Harris.

Brief of amici curiae filed on behalf of Catholic Charities, U.S.A., et al., by Patrick Francis Geary.

IV. THE SUPREME COURT'S DECISION

"The District Court in this lawsuit held the AFLA unconstitutional both on its face and as applied. Few of our cases in the Establishment Clause area have explicitly distinguished between facial challenges to a statute and attacks on the statute as applied. . . .

This said, we turn to consider whether the District Court was correct in concluding that the AFLA was unconstitutional on its face. As in previous cases involving facial challenges on Establishment Clause grounds, we assess the constitutionality of an enactment by reference to the three factors first articulated in Lemon v. Kurtzman. Under the Lemon standard, which guides '[t]he general nature of our inquiry in this area,' a court may invalidate a statute only if it is motivated wholly by an impermissible purpose, if its primary effect is the advancement of religion, or if it requires excessive entanglement between church and state. We consider each of these factors in turn.

As we see it, it is clear from the face of the statute that the AFLA was motivated primarily, if not entirely, by a legitimate secular purpose—the elimination or reduction of social and economic problems caused by teenage sexuality, pregnancy, and parenthood. . . .

As usual in Establishment Clause cases, the more difficult question is whether the primary effect of the challenged statute is impermissible. [W]e do not think that the absence of an express limitation on the use of federal funds for religious purposes means that the statute, on its face, has the primary effect of advancing religion.

This, of course, brings us to the third prong of the Lemon Establishment Clause 'test'—the question whether the AFLA leads to 'an excessive government entanglement with religion.' [G]rant monitoring does not amount to 'excessive entanglement,' at least in the context of a statute authorizing grants to religiously affiliated organizations that are not necessarily 'pervasively sectarian.'

In sum, in this somewhat lengthy discussion of the validity of the AFLA on its face, we have concluded that the statute has a valid secular purpose, does not have the primary effect of advancing religion, and does not create an excessive entanglement of church and state. We note, as is proper given the traditional presumption in favor of the constitutionality of statutes enacted by Congress, that our conclusion that the statute does not violate the Establishment Clause is consistent with the conclusion Congress reached in the course of its deliberations on the AFLA. . . . For the foregoing reasons we conclude that the AFLA does not violate the Establishment Clause 'on its face.' . . .

We turn now to consider whether the District Court correctly ruled that the AFLA was unconstitutional as applied. . . . On the merits of the 'as applied' challenge, it seems to us that the District Court did not follow the proper approach in assessing appellees' claim that the Secretary is making grants under the Act that violate the Establishment Clause of the First Amendment. . . .

We conclude, first, that the District Court erred in holding that the AFLA is invalid on its face, and second, that the court should consider on remand whether particular AFLA grants have had the primary effect of advancing religion. Should the court conclude that the Secretary's current practice does allow such grants, it should devise a remedy to insure that grants awarded by the Secretary comply with the Constitution and the statute. The judgment of the District Court is accordingly reversed."

V. JUSTICE VOTE

4 Pro ACLU Side vs. 5 Con Opposing Side

ACLU Side (Respondent / Appellee)

1. Blackmun, H. – Wrote dissenting opinion
2. Brennan, W. – Joined Blackmun's dissent
3. Marshall, T. – Joined Blackmun's dissent
4. Stevens, J. – Joined Blackmun's dissent

Opposing Side (Petitioner / Appellant)

1. Rehnquist, W. – Wrote majority opinion
2. O'Connor, S. – Wrote concurring opinion
3. Kennedy, A. – Wrote concurring opinion
4. Scalia, A. – Joined Kennedy's concurrence
5. White, B. – Joined majority opinion

VI. A WIN OR LOSS FOR THE ACLU?

The ACLU, as counsel of record, urged affirmance of the judgment of the District Court for the District of Columbia; the Supreme Court reversed in a 5-4 vote, giving the ACLU an apparent loss.

658. Watson v. Fort Worth Bank & Trust

(Decided June 29, 1988; 487 U.S. 977)

I. ISSUE

A. Issues Discussed

Employment discrimination, evidentiary standards

B. Legal Question Presented

"[W]hat evidentiary standards should be applied under Title VII of the Civil Rights Act of 1964 in determining whether an employer's practice of committing promotion decisions to the subjective discretion of supervisory employees has led to illegal discrimination."

C. Supreme Court's Answer

The employment practice may properly be analyzed using disparate impact analysis.

II. CASE SUMMARY

A. Background

"Petitioner Clara Watson, who is black, was hired by respondent Fort Worth Bank and Trust (the Bank) as a proof operator in August 1973. In January 1976, Watson was promoted to a position as teller in the Bank's drive-in facility. In February 1980, she sought to become supervisor of the tellers in the main lobby; a white male, however, was selected for this job. Watson then sought a position as supervisor of the drive-in bank, but this position was given to a white female. In February 1981, after Watson had served for about a year as a commercial teller in the Bank's main lobby, and informally as assistant to the supervisor of tellers, the man holding that position was promoted. Watson applied for the vacancy, but the white female who was the supervisor of the drive-in bank was selected instead. Watson then applied for the vacancy created at the drive-in; a white male was selected for that job. The Bank, which has about 80 employees, had not developed precise and formal criteria for evaluating candidates for the positions for which Watson unsuccessfully applied. It relied instead on the subjective judgment of supervisors who were acquainted with the candidates and with the nature of the jobs to be filled. All the supervisors involved in denying Watson the four promotions at issue were white.

Watson filed a discrimination charge with the Equal Employment Opportunity Commission (EEOC). After exhausting her administrative remedies, she filed this lawsuit in the United States District Court for the Northern District of Texas. She alleged that the Bank had unlawfully discriminated against blacks in hiring, compensation, initial placement, promotions, terminations, and other terms and conditions of employment. On Watson's motion under Federal Rule of Civil Procedure 23, the District Court certified a class consisting of 'blacks who applied to or were employed by [respondent] on or after October 21, 1979 or who may submit employment applications to [respondent] in the future.' The District Court later decertified this broad class . . . .

The District Court addressed Watson's individual claims under the evidentiary standards that apply in a discriminatory treatment case. It concluded, on the evidence presented at trial, that Watson had established a prima facie case of employment discrimination, but that the Bank had met its rebuttal burden by presenting legitimate and nondiscriminatory reasons for each of the challenged promotion decisions. The court also concluded that Watson had failed to show that these reasons were pretexts for racial discrimination. Accordingly, the action was dismissed.

A divided panel of the United States Court of Appeals for the Fifth Circuit affirmed in part."

The Supreme Court granted certiorari to review the case, vacated the judgment of the Court of Appeals, and remanded the case.

B. Counsel of Record / ACLU Attorney

ACLU Side (Petitioner / Appellant): Art Brender argued the cause for appellant.

Opposing Side (Respondent / Appellee): Bruce W. McGee argued the cause for appellee.

III. AMICI CURIAE

ACLU Side (Petitioner / Appellant)

Brief of amici curiae filed on behalf of the ACLU, et al., by Deborah A. Ellis, Isabelle Katz Pinzler, and Joan E. Bertin.

Brief of amici curiae filed on behalf of the State of Texas, et al., by Jim Mattox, Attorney General, Mary F. Keller, Executive Assistant Attorney General, and James C. Todd.

Brief of amici curiae filed on behalf of the American Psychological Association by Donald N. Bersoff.

Brief of amici curiae filed on behalf of the Lawyers' Committee for Civil Rights Under Law by John Townsend Rich, Conrad K. Harper, Stuart J. Land, Norman Redlich, William L. Robinson, Judith A. Winston, and Richard T. Seymour.

Brief of amici curiae filed on behalf of the NAACP Legal Defense and Educational Fund, Inc., et al., by Bill Lann Lee, Stephen M. Cutler, Joan M. Graff, Patricia A. Shiu, Julius LeVonne Chambers, Ronald L. Ellis, Charles Stephen Ralston, Antonia Hernandez, and E. Richard Larson.

Opposing Side (Respondent / Appellee)

Brief of amici curiae filed on behalf of the United States by Solicitor General Fried, Assistant Attorney General Reynolds, Deputy Solicitor General Ayer, Deputy Assistant Attorney General Clegg, David K. Flynn, and Charles A. Shanor.
Brief of amici curiae filed on behalf of the Equal Employment Advisory Council by Robert E. Williams, Douglas S. McDowell, Edward E. Potter, and Garen E. Dodge.
Brief of amici curiae filed on behalf of the American Society for Personnel Administration, et al., by Lawrence Z. Lorber and J. Robert Kirk.
Brief of amici curiae filed on behalf of the Landmark Legal Foundation by Jerald L. Hill and Mark J. Bredemeier.
Brief of amici curiae filed on behalf of the Merchants and Manufacturers Association by Paul Grossman.

IV. THE SUPREME COURT'S DECISION

"We conclude . . . that subjective or discretionary employment practices may be analyzed under the disparate impact approach in appropriate cases. . . .

We granted certiorari to determine whether the court below properly held disparate impact analysis inapplicable to a subjective or discretionary promotion system, and we now hold that such analysis may be applied. We express no opinion as to the other rulings of the Court of Appeals.

Neither the District Court nor the Court of Appeals has evaluated the statistical evidence to determine whether petitioner made out a prima facie case of discriminatory promotion practices under disparate impact theory. It may be that the relevant data base is too small to permit any meaningful statistical analysis, but we leave the Court of Appeals to decide in the first instance, on the basis of the record and the principles announced today, whether this case can be resolved without further proceedings in the District Court. The judgment of the Court of Appeals is vacated, and the case is remanded for further proceedings consistent with this opinion."

V. JUSTICE VOTE

8 Pro ACLU Side vs. 0 Con Opposing Side

ACLU Side (Petitioner / Appellant)

1. O'Connor, S. – Wrote majority opinion
2. Rehnquist, W. – Joined majority opinion
3. Brennan, W. – Joined Blackmun's concurrence
4. White, B. – Joined majority opinion
5. Marshall, T. – Joined Blackmun's concurrence
6. Blackmun, H. – Wrote concurring opinion
7. Scalia, A. – Joined majority opinion
8. Stevens, J. – Wrote concurring opinion

Kennedy, A – Took no part in the decision

VI. A WIN OR LOSS FOR THE ACLU?

The ACLU, as amicus curiae, urged reversal of the judgment of the Court of Appeals; the Supreme Court vacated the judgment in an 8-0 vote, giving the ACLU an apparent win.

659. Penson v. Ohio

(Decided November 29, 1988; 488 U.S. 75)

I. ISSUE

A. Issues Discussed

Criminal procedure, due process, right to an attorney

B. Legal Question Presented

"'May a State appellate court refuse to provide counsel to brief and argue an indigent criminal defendant's first appeal as of right on the basis of a conclusory statement by the appointed attorney on appeal that the case has no merit and that he will file no brief?'"

C. Supreme Court's Answer

The State appellate court erred in allowing counsel to withdraw based on a conclusory statement that the case had no merit and not appointing new counsel after finding arguable claims.

II. CASE SUMMARY

A. Background

"Petitioner is indigent. After a trial in the Montgomery County, Ohio, Court of Common Pleas, he and two codefendants were found guilty of several serious crimes. Petitioner was sentenced to a term of imprisonment of 18 to 28 years. On January 8, 1985, new counsel was appointed to represent him on appeal. Counsel filed a timely notice of appeal.

On June 2, 1986, petitioner's appellate counsel filed with the Montgomery County, Ohio, Court of Appeals a document captioned 'Certification of Meritless Appeal and Motion.' . . .

A week later, the Court of Appeals entered an order allowing appellate counsel to withdraw and granting petitioner 30 days in which to file an appellate brief pro se. The order further specified that the court would thereafter 'independently review the record thoroughly to determine whether any error exists requiring reversal or modification of the sentence . . . .' . . .

In due course, and without the assistance of any advocacy for petitioner, the Court of Appeals made its own examination of the record to determine whether petitioner received 'a fair trial and whether any grave or prejudicial errors occurred therein.' . . . In reviewing the record and the briefs filed by counsel on behalf of petitioner's codefendants, the court found 'several arguable claims.' Indeed, the court concluded that plain error had been committed in the jury instructions concerning one count. The court therefore reversed petitioner's conviction and sentence on that count but affirmed the convictions and sentences on the remaining counts. It concluded that petitioner 'suffered no prejudice' as a result of 'counsel's failure to give a more conscientious examination of the record' because the court had thoroughly examined the record and had received the benefit of arguments advanced by counsel for petitioner's two codefendants. Petitioner appealed the judgment of the Court of Appeals to the Ohio Supreme Court, which dismissed the appeal."

The Supreme Court granted certiorari to review the case and reversed.

B. Counsel of Record / ACLU Attorney

ACLU Side (Petitioner / Appellant): Gregory L. Ayers, by appointment of the Court, argued the cause for appellant.

Opposing Side (Respondent / Appellee): Mark B. Robinette argued the cause for appellee.

III. AMICI CURIAE

ACLU Side (Petitioner / Appellant)

Brief of amici curiae filed on behalf of the ACLU, et al., by Larry W. Yackle, John A. Powell, Steven R. Shapiro, and Kim Robert Fawcett.

Brief of amici curiae filed on behalf of the National Association of Criminal Defense Lawyers by Bruce S. Rogow.

Brief of amici curiae filed on behalf of the Ohio Association of Criminal Defense Lawyers by Gloria A. Eyerly and Harry R. Reinhart.

Opposing Side (Respondent / Appellee)

No briefs of amici curiae were filed in support of appellee.

IV. THE SUPREME COURT'S DECISION

"Approximately a quarter of a century ago, in Douglas v. California, this Court recognized that the Fourteenth Amendment guarantees a criminal appellant the right to counsel on a first appeal as of right. We held that a procedure in which appellate courts review the record and 'appoint counsel if in their opinion' the assistance of counsel 'would be helpful to the defendant or the court,' is an inadequate substitute for guaranteed representation. Four years later, in Anders v. California, we held that a criminal appellant may not be denied representation on appeal based on appointed counsel's bare assertion that he or she is of the opinion that there is no merit to the appeal.

The Anders opinion did, however, recognize that in some circumstances counsel may withdraw without denying the indigent appellant fair representation provided that certain safeguards are observed: Appointed counsel is first required to conduct 'a conscientious examination' of the case. If he or she is then of the opinion that the case is wholly frivolous, counsel may request leave to withdraw. The request 'must, however, be accompanied by a brief referring to anything in the record that might arguably support the appeal.' Once the appellate court receives this brief, it must then itself conduct 'a full examination of all the proceeding[s] to decide whether the case is wholly frivolous.' Only after this separate inquiry, and only after the appellate court finds no nonfrivolous issue for appeal, may the court proceed to consider the appeal on the merits without the assistance of counsel. On the other hand, if the court disagrees with counsel—as the Ohio Court of Appeals did in this case—and concludes that there are nonfrivolous issues for appeal, 'it must, prior to decision, afford the indigent the assistance of counsel to argue the appeal.'

It is apparent that the Ohio Court of Appeals did not follow the Anders procedures when it granted appellate counsel's motion to withdraw, and that it committed an even more serious error when it failed to appoint new counsel after finding that the record supported several arguably meritorious grounds for reversal of petitioner's conviction and modification of his sentence. As a result, petitioner was left without constitutionally adequate representation on appeal. . . .

By proceeding to decide the merits of petitioner's appeal without appointing new counsel to represent him, the Ohio Court of Appeals deprived both petitioner and itself of the benefit of an adversary examination and presentation of the issues. . . .

The State nonetheless maintains that even if the Court of Appeals erred in granting the motion to withdraw and in failing to appoint new counsel, the court's conclusion that petitioner suffered 'no prejudice' indicates both that petitioner has failed to show prejudice . . . and also that any error was harmless . . . . In either event, in the State's view, the Court of Appeals' affirmance of petitioner's conviction should stand. We disagree.

The primary difficulty with the State's argument is that it proves too much. . . . Under the State's theory, if on reviewing the bare appellate record a court would ultimately conclude that the conviction should not be reversed, then the indigent criminal appellant suffers no prejudice by being denied his right to counsel. Similarly, however, if on reviewing the record the court would find a basis for reversal, then the criminal defendant also suffers no prejudice. In either event, the criminal appellant is not harmed and thus has no basis for complaint. Thus, adopting the State's view would render meaningless the protections afforded by Douglas and Anders. . . .

Finally, it is important to emphasize that the denial of counsel in this case left petitioner completely without representation during the appellate court's actual decisional process. . . .

The judgment of the Court of Appeals is accordingly reversed, and the case is remanded to that court for further proceedings not inconsistent with this opinion."

V. JUSTICE VOTE

8 Pro ACLU Side vs. 1 Con Opposing Side

ACLU Side (Petitioner / Appellant)

1. Stevens, J. – Wrote majority opinion
2. Brennan, W. – Joined majority opinion
3. White, B. – Joined majority opinion
4. Marshall, T. – Joined majority opinion
5. Blackmun, H. – Joined majority opinion
6. O'Connor, S. – Wrote concurring opinion
7. Scalia, A. – Joined majority opinion
8. Kennedy, A. – Joined majority opinion

Opposing Side (Respondent / Appellee)

1. Rehnquist, W. – Wrote dissenting opinion

VI. A WIN OR LOSS FOR THE ACLU?

The ACLU, as amicus curiae, urged reversal of the judgment of the Court of Appeals; the Supreme Court reversed in an 8-1 vote, giving the ACLU an apparent win.

660. Carlucci v. Doe

(Decided December 6, 1988; 488 U.S. 93)

I. ISSUE

A. Issues Discussed

Federal regulation, employment termination

B. Legal Question Presented

"[W]hether the National Security Agency (NSA) invoked the proper statutory authority when it terminated respondent John Doe, an NSA employee."

C. Supreme Court's Answer

The NSA invoked proper statutory authority to terminate respondent.

II. CASE SUMMARY

A. Background

"This case began in 1982 when John Doe, a cryptographic material control technician at NSA for 16 years, disclosed to NSA officials that he had engaged in homosexual relationships with foreign nationals. Doe was notified of his proposed removal pursuant to Chapter 370 of the PMM, which governs NSA's procedures for removal for cause. The notification letter of Virginia C. Jenkins, Director of Civilian Personnel, was dated November 23, 1982, and explained that Doe's 'indiscriminate personal conduct with unidentified foreign nationals' makes impossible his continued—and essential to NSA employment—access to classified information. The notice also advised Doe of his adjudicatory rights to contest the decision, which rights he exercised through counsel, including in his answer the results of a psychiatric evaluation as to his security threat. Pursuant to 50 U.S.C. § 832(b), the NSA Director convened a board of appraisal, which ultimately concluded that Doe's access to classified material was 'clearly inconsistent with the national security.' After a hearing before the Director, Doe was notified that his security clearance was being revoked. Because this clearance is a condition of NSA employment, the Director, pursuant to the authority delegated to him under the 1959 NSA Act, removed Doe. Relying on 5 U.S.C. § 7532, Doe then requested a hearing before the Secretary of Defense, claiming that the 1959 NSA Act does not authorize removals and that he could only be discharged by the Secretary after a hearing before that official or his designee. Both the Secretary and the Director replied that Doe's removal was 'for cause' under Chapter 370 of the PMM and was not pursuant to the Secretary's § 7532 summary authority.

Doe brought suit in the District Court challenging his removal on constitutional and statutory grounds. He charged, inter alia, that the 1959 NSA Act's appointment authority delegated by the Secretary of Defense to the NSA Director does not include the authority to remove employees; hence NSA is required to apply 5 U.S.C. § 7532's termination procedures that guarantee NSA employees a preremoval hearing before the Secretary or his designee, the NSA Director. The District Court denied this argument and granted summary judgment for petitioners. . . . The Court of Appeals reversed as to the optional applicability of § 7532 and vacated the remainder of the District Court's decision."

The Supreme Court granted certiorari to review the case and reversed.

B. Counsel of Record / ACLU Attorney

ACLU Side (Respondent / Appellee): John G. Gill, Jr., argued the cause for appellee.

Opposing Side (Petitioner / Appellant): Michael K. Kellogg argued the cause for appellant.

III. AMICI CURIAE

ACLU Side (Respondent / Appellee)

Brief of amici curiae filed on behalf of the ACLU Foundation by David I. Shapiro, George Kaufmann, Peter W. Morgan, John A. Powell, and Steven R. Shapiro.

Opposing Side (Petitioner / Appellant)

No briefs of amici curiae were filed in support of appellant.

IV. THE SUPREME COURT'S DECISION

"The 1959 NSA Act authorizes the Secretary of Defense, or his designee, 'to establish such positions, and to appoint thereto, without regard to the civil service laws, such officers and employees, in the National Security Agency, as may be necessary to carry out the functions of such agency.' . . . Although the 1959 NSA Act does not refer to termination, the Court has held, as a matter of statutory interpretation, that, absent a 'specific provision to the contrary, the power of removal from office is incident to the power of appointment.' Neither the Court of Appeals nor respondent questions this general proposition, nor have they shown that Congress expressly or impliedly indicated a contrary purpose in the 1959 NSA Act or its subsequent amendments.

The Court of Appeals, however, held that removals for national security reasons must occur under either 5 U.S.C. § 7532 or 50 U.S.C. § 833 and that because NSA disclaimed reliance on § 833, resort to § 7532 rather than NSA's for-cause removal regulations was mandatory. In our view, however, § 833 and § 7532 are not the exclusive means to remove NSA employees for national security reasons, but instead contemplate alternative recourse to NSA's ordinary removal mechanisms pursuant to the 1959 NSA Act. . . .

We thus agree with the conclusion of the Merit Systems Protection Board in a similar case that 'section 7532 is not the exclusive basis for removals based upon security clearance revocations,' and with the Court of Appeals for the Federal Circuit that '[t]here is nothing in the text of section 7532 or in its legislative history to suggest that its procedures were intended to preempt section 7513 procedures whenever the removal could be taken under section 7532. The language of section 7532 is permissive.'

Accordingly, the judgment of the Court of Appeals is reversed, and the case is remanded for further proceedings consistent with this opinion."

V. JUSTICE VOTE

0 Pro ACLU Side vs. 9 Con Opposing Side

Opposing Side (Petitioner / Appellant)

1. White, B. – Wrote majority opinion
2. Kennedy, A. – Joined majority opinion
3. Marshall, T. – Joined majority opinion
4. Rehnquist, W. – Joined majority opinion
5. Blackmun, H. – Joined majority opinion
6. O'Connor, S. – Joined majority opinion
7. Brennan, W. – Joined majority opinion
8. Scalia, A. – Joined majority opinion
9. Stevens, J. – Joined majority opinion

VI. A WIN OR LOSS FOR THE ACLU?

The ACLU, as amicus curiae, urged affirmance of the judgment of the Court of Appeals; the Supreme Court reversed in a 9-0 vote, giving the ACLU an apparent loss.

661. Owens v. Okure

(Decided January 10, 1989; 488 U.S. 235)

I. ISSUE

A. Issues Discussed

Civil rights, statute of limitations

B. Legal Question Presented

"[W]hat limitations period should apply to a § 1983 action where a State has one or more statutes of limitations for certain enumerated intentional torts, and a residual statute for all other personal injury actions."

C. Supreme Court's Answer

"We hold that the residual or general personal injury statute of limitations applies."

II. CASE SUMMARY

A. Background

"On November 13, 1985, respondent Tom U.U. Okure brought suit in the District Court for the Northern District of New York, seeking damages under § 1983 from petitioners Javan Owens and Daniel G. Lessard, two State University of New York (SUNY) police officers. Okure alleged that, on January 27, 1984, the officers unlawfully arrested him on the SUNY campus in Albany and charged him with disorderly conduct. The complaint stated that Okure was 'forcibly transported' to a police detention center, 'battered and beaten by [the police officers] and forced to endure great emotional distress, physical harm, and embarrassment.' As a result of the arrest and beating, Okure claimed, he 'sustained personal injuries, including broken teeth and a sprained finger, mental anguish, shame, humiliation, legal expenses and the deprivation of his constitutional rights.'

The officers moved to dismiss the complaint, which had been filed 22 months after the alleged incident, as time barred. They contended that § 1983 actions were governed by New York's 1-year statute of limitations covering eight intentional torts: 'assault, battery, false imprisonment, malicious prosecution, libel, slander, false words causing special damages, [and] a violation of the right of privacy.'

The District Court denied the motion to dismiss. Borrowing 'a narrowly drawn statute which is applicable only to certain intentional torts,' the court stated, was inconsistent with this Court's endorsement of 'a simple, broad characterization of all § 1983 claims.' Moreover, a 1-year statute of limitations on § 1983 claims 'would improperly restrict the scope of § 1983 and controvert federal policy.' The court concluded that New York's 3-year residual statute of limitations for claims of personal injury not embraced by specific statutes of limitations was applicable to § 1983 actions, and that Okure's complaint was therefore timely. The court then certified an interlocutory appeal on this question pursuant to 28 U.S.C. § 1292(b) (1982 ed., Supp. IV) and Rule 5(a) of the Federal Rules of Appellate Procedure.

The Court of Appeals for the Second Circuit granted permission for the appeal and affirmed. It stated that Wilson's description of § 1983 claims as general personal injury actions required a statute of limitations 'expansive enough to accommodate the diverse personal injury torts that section 1983 has come to embrace.' As between the two New York statutes of limitations, the court observed: 'By nature, section 214(5) is general; section 215(3) is more specific and exceptional. This dichotomy survives no matter how many similar intentional torts are judicially added to those enumerated in section 215(3).' The Court of Appeals favored § 214(5) for another reason: its 3-year period of limitations 'more faithfully represents the federal interest in providing an effective remedy for violations of civil rights than does the restrictive one year limit.' Injuries to personal rights are not 'necessarily apparent to the victim at the time they are inflicted,' the court explained, and '[e]ven where the injury itself is obvious, the constitutional dimensions of the tort may not be.'"

The Supreme Court granted certiorari to review the case and affirmed.

B. Counsel of Record / ACLU Attorney

ACLU Side (Respondent / Appellee): Kenneth Kimerling argued the cause for appellees. With him on the brief were Arthur N. Eisenberg, John A. Powell, Steven Shapiro, Helen Hershkoff, and Joseph M. Brennan.

Opposing Side (Petitioner / Appellant): Peter H. Schiff, Deputy Solicitor General of New York, argued the cause for appellants. With him on the briefs were Robert Abrams, Attorney General, O. Peter Sherwood, Solicitor General, and Charles R. Fraser, Assistant Attorney General.

III. AMICI CURIAE

ACLU Side (Respondent / Appellee)

No briefs of amici curiae were filed in support of appellee.

Opposing Side (Petitioner / Appellant)

Brief of amici curiae filed on behalf of the State of Nebraska, et al., by Robert M. Spire, Attorney General of Nebraska, and Mark D. Starr, Assistant Attorney General; Joseph B. Meyer, Attorney General of Wyoming; John Steven Clark, Attorney General of Arkansas; Robert H. Henry, Attorney General of Oklahoma and David Lee, Assistant Attorney General; Roger

A. Tellinghuisen, Attorney General of South Dakota; Donald J. Hanaway, Attorney General of Wisconsin; T. Travis Medlock, Attorney General of South Carolina; Robert T. Stephan, Attorney General of Kansas; and William L. Webster, Attorney General of Missouri.

Brief of amici curiae filed on behalf of the city of New York by Peter L. Zimroth, Leonard J. Koerner, Edward F. X. Hart, and John P. Woods.

IV. THE SUPREME COURT'S DECISION

"In choosing between the two alternatives endorsed by the Courts of Appeals—the intentional torts approach and the general or residual personal injury approach—we are mindful that ours is essentially a practical inquiry. Our decision in Wilson that one 'simple broad characterization' of all § 1983 actions was appropriate under § 1988 was, after all, grounded in the realization that the potential applicability of different state statutes of limitations had bred chaos and uncertainty. Thus, our task today is to provide courts with a rule for determining the appropriate personal injury limitations statute that can be applied with ease and predictability in all 50 States.

A rule endorsing the choice of the state statute of limitations for intentional torts would be manifestly inappropriate. . . . Were we to call upon courts to apply the state statute of limitations governing intentional torts, we would succeed only in transferring the present confusion over the choice among multiple personal injury provisions to a choice among multiple intentional tort provisions.

In marked contrast to the multiplicity of state intentional tort statutes of limitations, every State has one general or residual statute of limitations governing personal injury actions. Some States have a general provision which applies to all personal injury actions with certain specific exceptions. Others have a residual provision which applies to all actions not specifically provided for, including personal injury actions. Whichever form they take, these provisions are easily identifiable by language or application. . . . Potential § 1983 plaintiffs and defendants therefore can readily ascertain, with little risk of confusion or unpredictability, the applicable limitations period in advance of filing a § 1983 action. . .

The Court of Appeals therefore correctly applied New York's 3-year statute of limitations governing general personal injury actions to respondent Okure's claim. Our decision in Wilson promised an end to the confusion over what statute of limitations to apply to § 1983 actions; with today's decision, we hope to fulfill Wilson's promise. Accordingly, the judgment of the Court of Appeals is affirmed."

V. JUSTICE VOTE

9 Pro ACLU Side vs. 0 Con Opposing Side

ACLU Side (Respondent / Appellee)

1. Marshall, T. – Wrote majority opinion
2. Rehnquist, W. – Joined majority opinion
3. Brennan, W. – Joined majority opinion
4. White, B. – Joined majority opinion
5. Blackmun, H. – Joined majority opinion
6. Stevens, J. – Joined majority opinion
7. O'Connor, S. – Joined majority opinion
8. Scalia, A. – Joined majority opinion
9. Kennedy, A. – Joined majority opinion

VI. A WIN OR LOSS FOR THE ACLU?

The ACLU, as counsel for appellee, urged affirmance of the judgment of the Court of Appeals for the Second Circuit; the Supreme Court affirmed in a 9-0 vote, giving the ACLU an apparent win.

662. Florida v. Riley

(Decided January 23, 1989; 488 U.S. 445)

I. ISSUE

A. Issues Discussed

Fourth Amendment, search and seizure, warrants

B. Legal Question Presented

"'[W]hether surveillance of the interior of a partially covered greenhouse in a residential backyard from the vantage point of a helicopter located 400 feet above the greenhouse constitutes a 'search' for which a warrant is required under the Fourth Amendment and Article I, § 12 of the Florida Constitution.'"

C. Supreme Court's Answer

This method of surveillance is not a "search" for which a warrant is required under the Fourth Amendment.

II. CASE SUMMARY

A. Background

"Respondent Riley lived in a mobile home located on five acres of rural property. A greenhouse was located 10 to 20 feet behind the mobile home. Two sides of the greenhouse were enclosed. The other two sides were not enclosed but the contents of the greenhouse were obscured from view from surrounding property by trees, shrubs, and the mobile home. The greenhouse was covered by corrugated roofing panels, some translucent and some opaque. At the time relevant to this case, two of the panels, amounting to approximately 10% of the roof area, were missing. A wire fence surrounded the mobile home and the greenhouse, and the property was posted with a 'DO NOT ENTER' sign.

This case originated with an anonymous tip to the Pasco County Sheriff's office that marijuana was being grown on respondent's property. When an investigating officer discovered that he could not see the contents of the greenhouse from the road, he circled twice over respondent's property in a helicopter at the height of 400 feet. With his naked eye, he was able to see through the openings in the roof and one or more of the open sides of the greenhouse and to identify what he thought was marijuana growing in the structure. A warrant was obtained based on these observations, and the ensuing search revealed marijuana growing in the greenhouse. Respondent was charged with possession of marijuana under Florida law. The trial court granted his motion to suppress; the Florida Court of Appeals reversed but certified the case to the Florida Supreme Court, which quashed the decision of the Court of Appeals and reinstated the trial court's suppression order."

The U.S. Supreme Court granted certiorari to review the case and reversed.

B. Counsel of Record / ACLU Attorney

ACLU Side (Respondent / Appellee): Marc H. Salton argued the cause for appellee.

Opposing Side (Petitioner / Appellant): Parker D. Thomson, Special Assistant Attorney General of Florida, argued the cause for appellant.

III. AMICI CURIAE

ACLU Side (Respondent / Appellee)

Brief of amici curiae filed on behalf of the ACLU, et al., by Kent L. Richland, Pamela Victorine, John A. Powell, Steve R. Shapiro, Paul Hoffman, Joan W. Howarth, and James K. Green.

Brief of amici curiae filed on behalf of Community Outreach to Vietnam Era Returnees, Inc., by Deborah C. Wyatt.

Brief of amici curiae filed on behalf of the National Association of Criminal Defense Lawyers by Milton Hirsch.

Brief of amici curiae filed on behalf of the California Attorneys for Criminal Justice, et al., by Ronald M. Sinoway.

Opposing Side (Petitioner / Appellant)

Brief of amici curiae filed on behalf of the State of Indiana, et al., by Linley E. Pearson, Attorney General of Indiana, and Lisa M. Paunicka, Deputy Attorney General, Don Siegelman, Attorney General of Alabama, Robert K. Corbin, Attorney General of Arizona, John Steven Clark, Attorney General of Arkansas, John J. Kelly, Chief State's Attorney of Connecticut, Charles M. Oberly, Attorney General of Delaware, Warren Price III, Attorney General of Hawaii, Jim Jones, Attorney General of Idaho, Neil F. Hartigan, Attorney General of Illinois, Robert T. Stephan, Attorney General of Kansas, Frederic J. Cowan, Attorney General of Kentucky, Frank J. Kelley, Attorney General of Michigan, Hubert H. Humphrey III, Attorney General of Minnesota, William L. Webster, Attorney General of Missouri, Robert M. Spire, Attorney General of Nebraska, Lacy H. Thornburg, Attorney General of North Carolina, Anthony J. Celebrezze, Jr., Attorney General of Ohio, Dave Frohnmayer, Attorney General of Oregon, Travis Medlock, Attorney General of South Carolina, Roger A. Tellinghuisen, Attorney General of South Dakota, David L. Wilkinson, Attorney General of Utah, Jeffrey Amestoy, Attorney General of Vermont, Don Hanaway, Attorney General of Wisconsin, and Joseph B. Meyer, Attorney General of Wyoming.

Brief of amici curiae filed on behalf of the Airborne Law Enforcement Association, Inc., by Ellen M. Condon and Paul J. Marino.

IV. THE SUPREME COURT'S DECISION

"As a general proposition, the police may see what may be seen 'from a public vantage point where [they have] a right to be.' Thus the police, like the public, would have been free to inspect the backyard garden from the street if their view had been unobstructed. They were likewise free to inspect the yard from the vantage point of an aircraft flying in the navigable airspace as this plane was. 'In an age where private and commercial flight in the public airways is routine, it is unreasonable for respondent to expect that his marijuana plants were constitutionally protected from being observed with the naked eye from an altitude of 1,000 feet. The Fourth Amendment simply does not require the police traveling in the public airways at this altitude to obtain a warrant in order to observe what is visible to the naked eye.'

We arrive at the same conclusion in the present case. [O] n the facts before us, [it does not] make a difference for Fourth Amendment purposes that the helicopter was flying at 400 feet when the officer saw what was growing in the greenhouse through the partially open roof and sides of the structure. We would have a different case if flying at that altitude had been contrary to law or regulation. But helicopters are not bound by the lower limits of the navigable airspace allowed to other aircraft. Any member of the public could legally have been flying over Riley's property in a helicopter at the altitude of 400 feet and could have observed Riley's greenhouse. The police officer did no more. . . .

Neither is there any intimation here that the helicopter interfered with respondent's normal use of the greenhouse or of other parts of the curtilage. As far as this record reveals, no intimate details connected with the use of the home or curtilage were observed, and there was no undue noise, and no wind, dust, or threat of injury. In these circumstances, there was no violation of the Fourth Amendment.

The judgment of the Florida Supreme Court is accordingly reversed."

V. JUSTICE VOTE

4 Pro ACLU Side vs. 5 Con Opposing Side

ACLU Side (Respondent / Appellee)

1. Brennan, W. – Wrote dissenting opinion
2. Marshall, T. – Joined Brennan's dissent
3. Stevens, J. – Joined Brennan's dissent
4. Blackmun, H. – Wrote dissenting opinion

Opposing Side (Petitioner / Appellant)

1. White, B. – Wrote majority opinion
2. Rehnquist, W. – Joined majority opinion
3. Scalia, A. – Joined majority opinion
4. Kennedy, A. – Joined majority opinion
5. O'Connor, S. – Wrote concurring opinion

VI. A WIN OR LOSS FOR THE ACLU?

The ACLU, as amicus curiae, urged affirmance of the judgment of the Florida Supreme Court; the U.S. Supreme Court reversed in a 5-4 vote, giving the ACLU an apparent loss.

663. City of Richmond v. J.A. Croson Co.

(Decided January 23, 1989; 488 U.S. 469)

I. ISSUE

A. Issues Discussed

Racial quotas, discrimination

B. Legal Question Presented

Did the city of Richmond have a compelling governmental interest that justified the adoption of a Minority Business Utilization Plan?

C. Supreme Court's Answer

The city did not have a compelling state interest to justify adopting a Minority Business Utilization Plan.

II. CASE SUMMARY

A. Background

"On April 11, 1983, the Richmond City Council adopted the Minority Business Utilization Plan (the Plan). The Plan required prime contractors to whom the city awarded construction contracts to subcontract at least 30% of the dollar amount of the contract to one or more Minority Business Enterprises (MBE's). The 30% set-aside did not apply to city contracts awarded to minority-owned prime contractors. . . . The Director also promulgated 'purchasing procedures' to be followed in the letting of city contracts in accordance with the Plan. . . .

There was no direct evidence of race discrimination on the part of the city in letting contracts or any evidence that the city's prime contractors had discriminated against minority-owned subcontractors. Opponents of the ordinance questioned both its wisdom and its legality. They argued that a disparity between minorities in the population of Richmond and the number of prime contracts awarded to MBE's had little probative value in establishing discrimination in the construction industry. . . .

[Croson placed the only bid for a project in 1983. The company did not comply with the Plan and the city refused to grant a waiver of the Plan. As a result, the city rejected the bid and opened the project for rebidding.] Croson [then] brought this action under 42 U.S.C. § 1983 in the Federal District Court for the Eastern District of Virginia, arguing that the Richmond ordinance was unconstitutional on its face and as applied in this case.

The District Court upheld the Plan in all respects. In its original opinion, a divided panel of the Fourth Circuit Court of Appeals affirmed. . . .

Croson sought certiorari from [the Supreme] Court. We granted the writ, vacated the opinion of the Court of Appeals, and remanded the case for further consideration in light of our intervening decision in Wygant v. Jackson Board of Education.

On remand, a divided panel of the Court of Appeals struck down the Richmond set-aside program as violating both prongs of strict scrutiny under the Equal Protection Clause of the Fourteenth Amendment."

The Supreme Court granted certiorari to review the case and affirmed.

B. Counsel of Record / ACLU Attorney

ACLU Side (Petitioner / Appellant): John Payton argued the cause for appellant.

Opposing Side (Respondent / Appellee): Walter H. Ryland argued the cause for appellee.

III. AMICI CURIAE

ACLU Side (Petitioner / Appellant)

Brief of amici curiae filed on behalf of the ACLU, et al., by Edward M. Chen, Steven R. Shapiro, John A. Powell, and John Hart Ely.

Additional briefs of amici curiae were filed on behalf of the State of Maryland, the State of Michigan, the State of New York, et al., the Alpha Kappa Alpha Sorority, et al., the city of San Francisco, California, et al., the Lawyer's Committee for Civil Rights under Law, et al., the Maryland Legislative Black Caucus, the Minority Business Enterprise Legal Defense and Education Fund, Inc., et al., the NAACP Legal Defense and Educational Fund, Inc., and the National League of Cities et al.

Opposing Side (Respondent / Appellee)

Briefs of amici curiae were filed on behalf of the United States, the Anti-Defamation League of B'nai B'rith, Associated Specialty Contractors, Inc., the Equal Employment Advisory Council, the Mountain States Legal Foundation, the Pacific Legal Foundation, the Southeastern Legal Foundation, Inc., and the Washington Legal Foundation, et al.

IV. THE SUPREME COURT'S DECISION

"The parties and their supporting amici fight an initial battle over the scope of the city's power to adopt legislation designed to address the effects of past discrimination. Relying on our decision in Wygant, appellee argues that the city must limit any race-based remedial efforts to eradicating the effects of its own prior discrimination. This is essentially the position taken by the Court of Appeals below. Appellant argues that our decision in Fullilove is controlling, and that as a result the city of Richmond enjoys sweeping legislative power to define and attack the effects of prior discrimination in its local construction industry. We find that neither of these two rather stark alternatives can withstand analysis. . . .

The Equal Protection Clause of the Fourteenth Amendment provides that '[n]o State shall . . . deny to any person within its jurisdiction the equal protection of the laws.' (Emphasis added.) As this Court has noted in the past, the 'rights created by the first section of the Fourteenth Amendment are, by its terms, guaranteed to the individual. The rights established are personal rights.' The Richmond Plan denies certain citizens the opportunity to compete for a fixed percentage of public contracts based solely upon their race. To whatever racial group these citizens belong, their 'personal rights' to be treated with equal dignity and respect are implicated by a rigid rule erecting race as the sole criterion in an aspect of public decisionmaking.

Absent searching judicial inquiry into the justification for such race-based measures, there is simply no way of determining what classifications are 'benign' or 'remedial' and what classifications are in fact motivated by illegitimate notions of racial inferiority or simple racial politics. . . .

We think it clear that the factual predicate offered in support of the Richmond Plan suffers from the same two defects identified as fatal in Wygant. The District Court found the city council's 'findings sufficient to ensure that, in adopting the Plan, it was remedying the present effects of past discrimination in the construction industry.' Like the 'role model' theory employed in Wygant, a generalized assertion that there has been past discrimination in an entire industry provides no guidance for a legislative body to determine the precise scope of the injury it seeks to remedy. It 'has no logical stopping point.' 'Relief" for such an ill-defined wrong could extend until the percentage of public contracts awarded to MBE's in Richmond mirrored the percentage of minorities in the population as a whole. . . .

In sum, none of the evidence presented by the city points to any identified discrimination in the Richmond construction industry. We, therefore, hold that the city has failed to demonstrate a compelling interest in apportioning public contracting opportunities on the basis of race. . . .

As noted by the court below, it is almost impossible to assess whether the Richmond Plan is narrowly tailored to remedy prior discrimination since it is not linked to identified discrimination in any way. . . .

Nothing we say today precludes a state or local entity from taking action to rectify the effects of identified discrimination within its jurisdiction. If the city of Richmond had evidence before it that nonminority contractors were systematically excluding minority businesses from subcontracting opportunities it could take action to end the discriminatory exclusion. Where there is a significant statistical disparity between the number of qualified minority contractors willing and able to perform a particular service and the number of such contractors actually engaged by the locality or the locality's prime contractors, an inference of discriminatory exclusion could arise. Under such circumstances, the city could act to dismantle the closed business system by taking appropriate measures against those who discriminate on the basis of race or other illegitimate criteria. . . .

Nor is local government powerless to deal with individual instances of racially motivated refusals to employ minority contractors. Where such discrimination occurs, a city would be justified in penalizing the discriminator and providing appropriate relief to the victim of such discrimination. . . .

Because the city of Richmond has failed to identify the need for remedial action in the awarding of its public construction contracts, its treatment of its citizens on a racial basis violates the dictates of the Equal Protection Clause. Accordingly, the judgment of the Court of Appeals for the Fourth Circuit is affirmed."

V. JUSTICE VOTE

3 Pro ACLU Side vs. 6 Con Opposing Side

ACLU Side (Petitioner / Appellant)

1. Marshall, T. – Wrote dissenting opinion
2. Brennan, W. – Joined Marshall's dissent, joined Blackmun's dissent
3. Blackmun, H. – Wrote a dissenting opinion, joined Marshall's dissent

Opposing Side (Respondent / Appellee)

1. O'Connor, S. – Wrote majority opinion
2. Rehnquist, W. – Joined majority opinion
3. White, B. – Joined majority opinion
4. Stevens, J. – Wrote concurring opinion
5. Kennedy, A. – Wrote concurring opinion
6. Scalia, A. – Wrote concurring opinion

VI. A WIN OR LOSS FOR THE ACLU?

The ACLU, as amicus curiae, urged reversal of the judgment of the Court of Appeals; the Supreme Court affirmed in a 6-3 vote, giving the ACLU an apparent loss.

664. Texas Monthly, Inc. v. Bullock

(Decided February 21, 1989; 489 U.S. 1)

I. ISSUE

A. Issues Discussed

First Amendment, religion, Establishment Clause, Free Exercise Clause

B. Legal Question Presented

"[W]hether [a religious periodical] exemption [from Texas sales tax] violates the Establishment Clause or the Free Press Clause of the First Amendment when the State denies a like exemption for other publications."

C. Supreme Court's Answer

The exemption violates the First Amendment.

II. CASE SUMMARY

A. Background

"Prior to October 2, 1984, Texas exempted from its sales and use tax magazine subscriptions running half a year or longer and entered as second class mail. This exemption was repealed as of October 2, 1984, before being reinstated effective October 1, 1987. Throughout this 3-year period, Texas continued to exempt from its sales and use tax periodicals published or distributed by a religious faith consisting entirely of writings promulgating the teaching of the faith, along with books consisting solely of writings sacred to a religious faith.

Appellant Texas Monthly, Inc., publishes a general interest magazine of the same name. Appellant is not a religious faith, and its magazine does not contain only articles promulgating the teaching of a religious faith. Thus, it was required during this 3-year period to collect and remit to the State the applicable sales tax on the price of qualifying subscription sales. In 1985, appellant paid sales taxes of $149,107.74 under protest and sued to recover those payments in state court.

The District Court of Travis County, Texas, ruled that an exclusive exemption for religious periodicals had 'no basis . . . other than the promotion of religion itself, a prohibited reason' under the Establishment Clause. The court also found the exemption unconstitutional because it discriminated on the basis of the content of publications, presumably in violation of the Free Press Clause. . . .

The Court of Appeals, Third Supreme Judicial District of Texas, reversed by a 2-to-1 vote."

The Supreme Court granted certiorari to review the case and reversed.

B. Counsel of Record / ACLU Attorney

ACLU Side (Petitioner / Appellant): Roger James George, Jr., argued the cause for appellant.

Opposing Side (Respondent / Appellee): Harriet D. Burke, Assistant Attorney General of Texas, argued the cause for appellee.

III. AMICI CURIAE

ACLU Side (Petitioner / Appellant)

Brief of amici curiae filed on behalf of the ACLU, et al., by James C. Harrington, Steven R. Shapiro, and John A. Powell.

Brief of amici curiae filed on behalf of the American Booksellers Association, Inc., by Maxwell J. Lillienstein.

Brief of amici curiae filed on behalf of the Magazine Publishers of America, Inc., by Eli D. Minton and James R. Cregan.

Opposing Side (Respondent / Appellee)

No briefs of amici curiae were filed in support of appellee.

IV. THE SUPREME COURT'S DECISION

"Texas' sales tax exemption for periodicals published or distributed by a religious faith and consisting wholly of writings promulgating the teaching of the faith lacks sufficient breadth to pass scrutiny under the Establishment Clause. Every tax exemption constitutes a subsidy that affects nonqualifying taxpayers, forcing them to become 'indirect and vicarious 'donors." Insofar as that subsidy is conferred upon a wide array of nonsectarian groups as well as religious organizations in pursuit of some legitimate secular end, the fact that religious groups benefit incidentally does not deprive the subsidy of the secular purpose and primary effect mandated by the Establishment Clause. However, when government directs a subsidy exclusively to religious organizations that is not required by the Free Exercise Clause and that either burdens nonbeneficiaries markedly or cannot reasonably be seen as removing a significant state-imposed deterrent to the free exercise of religion, as Texas has done, it 'provide[s] unjustifiable awards of assistance to religious organizations' and cannot but 'conve[y] a message of endorsement' to slighted members of the community. This is particularly true where, as here, the subsidy is targeted at writings that promulgate the teachings of religious faiths. It is difficult to view Texas' narrow exemption as anything but state sponsorship of religious belief, regardless of whether one adopts the perspective of beneficiaries or of uncompensated contributors. . . . Because Texas' sales tax exemption for periodicals promulgating the teaching of any religious sect lacks a secular objective that would justify this preference along with similar benefits for nonreligious publications or groups, and because it effectively endorses religious belief, the exemption manifestly fails this test. . . .

In this case, the State has adduced no evidence that the payment of a sales tax by subscribers to religious periodicals or purchasers of religious books would offend their religious beliefs or inhibit religious activity. The State therefore cannot claim persuasively that its tax exemption is compelled by the Free Exercise Clause in even a single case, let alone in every case. . . .

On the record before us, neither the Free Exercise Clause nor the Establishment Clause prevents Texas from withdrawing its current exemption for religious publications if it chooses not to expand it to promote some legitimate secular aim. . . .

We conclude that Texas' sales tax exemption for religious publications violates the First Amendment, as made applicable to the States by the Fourteenth Amendment. Accordingly, the judgment of the Texas Court of Appeals is reversed, and the case is remanded for further proceedings."

V. JUSTICE VOTE

6 Pro ACLU Side vs. 3 Con Opposing Side

ACLU Side (Petitioner / Appellant)

1. Brennan, W. – Wrote majority opinion
2. Stevens, J. – Joined majority opinion
3. Marshall, T. – Joined majority opinion
4. O'Connor, S. – Joined Blackmun's concurrence
5. White, B. – Wrote concurring opinion
6. Blackmun, H. – Wrote concurring opinion

Opposing Side (Respondent / Appellee)

1. Scalia, A. – Wrote dissenting opinion
2. Rehnquist, W. – Joined dissenting opinion
3. Kennedy, A. – Joined dissenting opinion

VI. A WIN OR LOSS FOR THE ACLU?

The ACLU filed as amicus curiae urging reversal of the judgment of the Texas Court of Appeals; the Supreme Court reversed in a 6-3 vote, giving the ACLU an apparent win.

665. Fort Wayne Books, Inc. v. Indiana

(Decided February 21, 1989; 489 U.S. 46)

I. ISSUE

A. Issues Discussed

First Amendment, obscenity, Fourteenth Amendment, RICO

B. Legal Question Presented

Whether Indiana's RICO statute is unconstitutional and whether the pretrial seizure of books violated the First Amendment.

C. Supreme Court's Answer

Indiana's RICO statute is not unconstitutionally vague as applied, but the pretrial seizure of books violated the First Amendment.

II. CASE SUMMARY

A. Background

"We have before us two decisions of the Indiana courts, involving the application of that State's Racketeer Influenced and Corrupt Organizations (RICO) and Civil Remedies for Racketeering Activity (CRRA) Acts to cases involving bookstores containing allegedly obscene materials. . . .

Petitioner in No. 87–470, Fort Wayne Books, Inc., and two other corporations each operated an 'adult bookstore' in Fort Wayne, Indiana. On March 19, 1984, the State of Indiana and a local prosecutor, respondents here, filed a civil action against the three corporations and certain of their employees alleging that defendants had engaged in a pattern of racketeering activity by repeatedly violating the state laws barring the distribution of obscene books and films, thereby violating the State's RICO law.

[R]espondents asked the Allen County Circuit Court 'to immediately seize . . . all property 'subject to forfeiture' as set forth in [the CRRA] complaint.' . . . The trial court, ex parte, heard testimony in support of the petition and had supporting exhibits before it. On the same day, the court entered an order finding that probable cause existed to conclude that Fort Wayne Books was violating the State RICO law, and directing the immediate seizure of the real estate, publications, and other personal property comprising each of the three bookstores operated by the corporate defendants. The court's order authorized the county sheriff to padlock the stores. This was done, and a few days later, the contents of the stores were hauled away by law enforcement officials. No trial date on the CRRA complaint was ever set.

Following the March 1984 seizure of the bookstores, Fort Wayne Books sought to vacate the ex parte seizure order. An adversarial hearing on a motion to vacate the order based on federal constitutional grounds failed to yield relief. Other efforts to obtain some measure of relief also failed. The trial court did, however, certify the constitutional issues to the Indiana Court of Appeals. In June 1985, that court held that the relevant RICO/CRRA provisions were violative of the United States Constitution. The Indiana Supreme Court reversed, upholding the constitutionality of the CRRA statute as a general proposition and the pretrial seizure of Fort Wayne Books' store as a specific matter.

[The U.S. Supreme Court] granted Fort Wayne's petition for certiorari, for the purpose of considering the substantial constitutional issues raised by the pretrial seizure. . . .

In No. 87–614, an investigation of adult bookstores in Howard County, Indiana, led prosecutors there, in April 1985, to charge petitioner Sappenfield with six counts of distribution of obscene matter, in violation of Ind.Code § 35- 49–3–1 (1988). In addition employing the 1984 amendments to the Indiana RICO statute discussed above, prosecutors used these alleged predicate acts of obscenity as a basis for filing two charges of RICO violations against petitioner. The obscenity charges were Class A misdemeanors under Indiana law, the racketeering offenses Class C felonies.

The trial court dismissed the two RICO counts on the ground that the RICO statute was unconstitutionally vague as applied to obscenity predicate offenses. The Indiana Court of Appeals reversed and reinstated the charges against petitioner. Relying on the Indiana Supreme Court's opinion under review here in No. 87–470, 4447 Corp. v. Goldsmith, supra, the Court of Appeals held that 'Indiana's RICO statute is not unconstitutional as applied to the State's obscenity statute.' The Indiana Supreme

Court declined to review this holding of the Indiana Court of Appeals.

[The U.S. Supreme Court] granted certiorari, and consolidated this case with No. 87–470, to consider the common and separate issues presented by both cases."

B. Counsel of Record / ACLU Attorney

ACLU Side (Petitioner / Appellant): John H. Weston argued the cause for appellant.

Opposing Side (Respondent / Appellee): Stephen Goldsmith, pro se, argued the cause for appellee.

III. AMICI CURIAE

ACLU Side (Petitioner / Appellant)

Brief of amici curiae filed on behalf of the ACLU, et al., by Marvin E. Frankel, Jeffrey S. Trachtman, John A. Powell, Steven R. Shapiro, and Richard A. Waples.

Brief of amici curiae filed on behalf of the American Booksellers Association, Inc., et al. by Michael A. Bamberger and Jonathan B. Piper.

Brief of amici curiae filed on behalf of PHE, Inc., by Bruce J. Ennis, Jr., and David W. Ogden.

Brief of amici curiae filed on behalf of the Video Software Dealers Association by Charles B. Ruttenberg and Theodore D. Frank.

Brief of amici curiae filed on behalf of the Spartacist League, et al., by Rachel H. Wolkenstein.

Opposing Side (Respondent / Appellee)

Brief of amici curiae filed on behalf of the United States by Solicitor General Fried, Acting Assistant Attorney General Dennis, Deputy Solicitor General Bryson, and Michael K. Kellogg.

Brief of amici curiae filed on behalf of Robert K. Corbin, Attorney General of Arizona, by Mr. Corbin, pro se, and Bruce A. Taylor.

Brief of amici curiae filed on behalf of Tom Collins, County Attorney of the County of Maricopa, Arizona, by Benjamin W. Bull.

Brief of amici curiae filed on behalf of Morality in Media, Inc., by John J. Walsh and Paul J. McGeady.

Brief of amici curiae filed on behalf of James J. Clancy, et al., by Mr. Clancy, pro se.

Brief of amici curiae filed on behalf of the National District Attorneys' Association by G. Robert Blakey.

IV. THE SUPREME COURT'S DECISION

"[W]e deal first with No. 87–614. [P]etitioners claim is that certain particulars of the Indiana RICO law render the prosecution of petitioner under that statute unconstitutional. . . . It is true, as petitioner argues, that the punishments available in a RICO prosecution are different from those for obscenity violations. But we fail to see how this difference renders the RICO statute void for vagueness. . . . It may be true that the stiffer RICO penalties will provide an additional deterrent to those who might otherwise sell obscene materials . . . . The mere assertion of some possible self-censorship resulting from a statute is not enough to render an antiobscenity law unconstitutional under our precedents. . . . Consequently, we find no constitutional bar to the State's inclusion of substantive obscenity violations among the predicate offenses under its RICO statute. . . . We consequently affirm the judgment in No. 87–614. . . .

We reverse, however, the judgment in No. 87–470 sustaining the pretrial seizure order.

[T]his Court has repeatedly held that rigorous procedural safeguards must be employed before expressive materials can be seized as 'obscene.' [T]he Court established that pretrial seizures of expressive materials could only be undertaken pursuant to a 'procedure 'designed to focus searchingly on the question of obscenity.'' . . .

While a single copy of a book or film may be seized and retained for evidentiary purposes based on a finding of probable cause, the publication may not be taken out of circulation completely until there has been a determination of obscenity after an adversary hearing.

Thus, while the general rule under the Fourth Amendment is that any and all contraband, instrumentalities, and evidence of crimes may be seized on probable cause (and even without a warrant in various circumstances), it is otherwise when materials presumptively protected by the First Amendment are involved. . . .

We do not question the holding of the court below that adding obscenity-law violations to the list of RICO predicate crimes was not a mere ruse to sidestep the First Amendment. And for the purpose of disposing of this case, we assume without deciding that bookstores and their contents are forfeitable . . . when it is proved that these items are property actually used in, or derived from, a pattern of violations of the State's obscenity laws. Even with these assumptions, though, we find the seizure at issue here unconstitutional. It is incontestable that these proceedings were begun to put an end to the sale of obscenity at the three bookstores named in the complaint, and hence we are quite sure that the special rules applicable to removing First Amendment materials from circulation are relevant here. . . . As noted above, our cases firmly hold that mere probable cause to believe a legal violation has transpired is not adequate to remove books or films from circulation. The elements of a RICO violation other than the predicate crimes remain to be established in this case. . . . Therefore, the pretrial seizure at issue here was improper. . . .

While we accept the Indiana Supreme Court's finding that Indiana's RICO law is not 'pretextual' as applied to obscenity offenses, it is true that the State cannot escape the constitutional safeguards of our prior cases by merely recategorizing a pattern of obscenity violations as 'racketeering.' . . .

Here, literally thousands of books and films were carried away and taken out of circulation by the pretrial order. Yet it remained to be proved whether the seizure was actually warranted under the Indiana CRRA and RICO statutes. If we are to maintain the regard for First Amendment values expressed in our prior decisions dealing with interrupting the flow of expressive materials, the judgment of the Indiana Court must be reversed. . . .

For the reasons given above, the judgment in No. 87–470 is reversed, and the case is remanded for further proceedings. The judgment in No. 87–614 is affirmed, and it too is remanded for further proceedings."

V. JUSTICE VOTE

9 Pro ACLU Side vs. 0 Con Opposing Side

ACLU Side (Petitioner / Appellant)

1. White, B. – Wrote majority opinion
2. Rehnquist, W. – Joined majority opinion
3. Scalia, A. – Joined majority opinion
4. Kennedy, A. – Joined majority opinion
5. Blackmun, H. – Wrote concurring opinion
6. O'Connor, S. – Wrote opinion concurring in part and dissenting in part
7. Stevens, J. – Wrote opinion concurring in part and dissenting in part
8. Marshall, T. - Joined Stevens' opinion
9. Brennan, W. – Joined Stevens' opinion

VI. A WIN OR LOSS FOR THE ACLU?

The ACLU filed as amicus curiae urging reversal of the judgment of the Supreme Court of Indiana; the U.S. Supreme Court reversed in part and affirmed in part in a 9-0 vote, giving the ACLU an apparent win.

666. DeShaney v. Winnebago County Department of Social Services

(Decided February 22, 1989; 489 U.S. 189)

I. ISSUE

A. Issues Discussed

Fourteenth Amendment, due process

B. Legal Question Presented

Whether petitioner's social workers' "failure to act deprived [petitioner] of his liberty in violation of the Due Process Clause of the Fourteenth Amendment to the United States Constitution."

C. Supreme Court's Answer

The State had no duty to act under the Due Process Clause.

II. CASE SUMMARY

A. Background

"The facts of this case are undeniably tragic. Petitioner Joshua DeShaney was born in 1979. In 1980, a Wyoming court granted his parents a divorce and awarded custody of Joshua to his father, Randy DeShaney. The father shortly thereafter moved to Neenah, a city located in Winnebago County, Wisconsin, taking the infant Joshua with him. There he entered into a second marriage, which also ended in divorce.

The Winnebago County authorities first learned that Joshua DeShaney might be a victim of child abuse in January 1982, when his father's second wife complained to the police, at the time of their divorce, that he had previously 'hit the boy causing marks and [was] a prime case for child abuse.' The Winnebago County Department of Social Services (DSS) interviewed the father, but he denied the accusations, and DSS did not pursue them further. In January 1983, Joshua was admitted to a local hospital with multiple bruises and abrasions. The examining physician suspected child abuse and notified DSS, which immediately obtained an order from a Wisconsin juvenile court placing Joshua in the temporary custody of the hospital. Three days later, the county convened an ad hoc 'Child Protection Team'—consisting of a pediatrician, a psychologist, a police detective, the county's lawyer, several DSS case-workers, and various hospital personnel—to consider Joshua's situation. At this meeting, the Team decided that there was insufficient evidence of child abuse to retain Joshua in the custody of the court. The Team did, however, decide to recommend several measures to protect Joshua, including enrolling him in a preschool program, providing his father with certain counselling services, and encouraging his father's girlfriend to move out of the home. Randy DeShaney entered into a voluntary agreement with DSS in which he promised to cooperate with them in accomplishing these goals.

Based on the recommendation of the Child Protection Team, the juvenile court dismissed the child protection case and returned Joshua to the custody of his father. A month later, emergency room personnel called the DSS caseworker handling Joshua's case to report that he had once again been treated for suspicious injuries. The caseworker concluded that there was no basis for action. For the next six months, the caseworker made monthly visits to the DeShaney home, during which she observed a number of suspicious injuries on Joshua's head; she also noticed that he had not been enrolled in school, and that the girlfriend had not moved out. The caseworker dutifully recorded these incidents in her files, along with her continuing suspicions that someone in the DeShaney household was physically abusing Joshua, but she did nothing more. In November 1983, the emergency room notified DSS that Joshua had been treated once again for injuries that they believed to be caused by child abuse. On the caseworker's next two visits to the DeShaney home, she was told that Joshua was too ill to see her. Still DSS took no action.

In March 1984, Randy DeShaney beat 4-year-old Joshua so severely that he fell into a life-threatening coma. Emergency brain surgery revealed a series of hemorrhages caused by traumatic injuries to the head inflicted over a long period of time. Joshua did not die, but he suffered brain damage so severe that he is expected to spend the rest of his life confined to an institution for the profoundly retarded. Randy DeShaney was subsequently tried and convicted of child abuse.

Joshua and his mother brought this action under 42 U.S.C. § 1983 in the United States District Court for the Eastern District of Wisconsin against respondents Winnebago County, DSS, and various individual employees of DSS. The complaint alleged that respondents had deprived Joshua of his liberty without due process of law, in violation of his rights under the Fourteenth Amendment, by failing to intervene to protect him against a risk of violence at his father's hands of which they knew or should have known. The District Court granted summary judgment for respondents.

The Court of Appeals for the Seventh Circuit affirmed . . . ,"

The Supreme Court granted certiorari to review the case and affirmed.

B. Counsel of Record / ACLU Attorney

ACLU Side (Petitioner / Appellant): Donald J. Sullivan argued the cause for appellant.

Opposing Side (Respondent / Appellee): Mark J. Mingo argued the cause for appellee.

Deputy Solicitor General Ayer argued the cause for the United States, as amicus curiae, by special leave of Court.

III. AMICI CURIAE

ACLU Side (Petitioner / Appellant)

Brief of amici curiae filed on behalf of the ACLU Children's Rights Project, et al., by Christopher A. Hansen, Marcia Robinson Lowry, John A. Powell, Steven R. Shapiro, and Helen Hershkoff.

Brief of amici curiae filed on behalf of the Massachusetts Committee for Children and Youth by Laura L. Carroll.

Opposing Side (Respondent / Appellee)

Brief of amici curiae filed on behalf of Deputy Solicitor General Ayer, Solicitor General Fried, Assistant Attorney General Bolton, Roy T. Englert, Jr., Barbara L. Herwig, and John S. Koppel.

Brief of amici curiae filed on behalf of the State of New York, et al., by Robert Abrams, Attorney General of New York, O. Peter Sherwood, Solicitor General, Peter H. Schiff, Deputy Solicitor General, and Michael S. Buskus, Assistant Attorney General, Joseph I. Lieberman, Attorney General of Connecticut, J. Joseph Curran, Jr., Attorney General of Maryland, Dave Frohnmayer, Attorney General of Oregon, LeRoy S. Zimmerman, Attorney General of Pennsylvania, Donald J. Hanaway, Attorney General of Wisconsin, and Charles Hoornstra, Assistant Attorney General.

Brief of amici curiae filed on behalf of the National Association of Counties, et al., by Benna Ruth Solomon and Douglas A. Poe.

Brief of amici curiae filed on behalf of the National School Boards Association by Gwendolyn H. Gregory, August W. Steinhilber, and Thomas A. Shannon.

IV. THE SUPREME COURT'S DECISION

"The Due Process Clause of the Fourteenth Amendment provides that '[n]o State shall . . . deprive any person of life, liberty, or property, without due process of law.' Petitioners contend that the State deprived Joshua of his liberty interest in 'free[dom] from . . . unjustified intrusions on personal security,' by failing to provide him with adequate protection against his father's violence. The claim is one invoking the substantive rather than the procedural component of the Due Process Clause; petitioners do not claim that the State denied Joshua protection without according him appropriate procedural safeguards, but that it was categorically obligated to protect him in these circumstances.

But nothing in the language of the Due Process Clause itself requires the State to protect the life, liberty, and property of its citizens against invasion by private actors. . . . Its purpose was to protect the people from the State, not to ensure that the State protected them from each other. . . .

Consistent with these principles, our cases have recognized that the Due Process Clauses generally confer no affirmative right to governmental aid, even where such aid may be necessary to secure life, liberty, or property interests of which the government itself may not deprive the individual. . . . If the Due Process Clause does not require the State to provide its citizens with particular protective services, it follows that the State cannot be held liable under the Clause for injuries that could have been averted had it chosen to provide them. As a general matter, then, we conclude that a State's failure to protect an individual against private violence simply does not constitute a violation of the Due Process Clause.

Petitioners contend, however, that even if the Due Process Clause imposes no affirmative obligation on the State to provide the general public with adequate protective services, such a duty may arise out of certain 'special relationships' created or assumed by the State with respect to particular individuals. Petitioners argue that such a 'special relationship' existed here because the State knew that Joshua faced a special danger of abuse at his father's hands, and specifically proclaimed, by word and by deed, its intention to protect him against that danger. . . .

We reject this argument. . . . It may well be that, by voluntarily undertaking to protect Joshua against a danger it concededly played no part in creating, the State acquired a duty under state tort law to provide him with adequate protection against that danger. But the claim here is based on the Due Process Clause of the Fourteenth Amendment, which, as we have said many times, does not transform every tort committed by a state actor into a constitutional violation. . . .

Judges and lawyers, like other humans, are moved by natural sympathy in a case like this to find a way for Joshua and his mother to receive adequate compensation for the grievous harm inflicted upon them. But before yielding to that impulse, it is well to remember once again that the harm was inflicted not by the State of Wisconsin, but by Joshua's father. . . .

Affirmed."

V. JUSTICE VOTE

3 Pro ACLU Side vs. 6 Con Opposing Side

ACLU Side (Petitioner / Appellant)

1. Brennan, W. – Wrote dissenting opinion
2. Marshall, T. – Joined Brennan's dissent
3. Blackmun, H. – Wrote dissenting opinion, joined Brennan's dissent

Opposing Side (Respondent / Appellee)

1. Rehnquist, W. – Wrote majority opinion
2. White, B. – Joined majority opinion
3. Stevens, J. – Joined majority opinion
4. O'Connor, S. – Joined majority opinion
5. Scalia, A. – Joined majority opinion
6. Kennedy, A. – Joined majority opinion

VI. A WIN OR LOSS FOR THE ACLU?

The ACLU, as amicus curiae, urged reversal of the judgment of the Seventh Circuit Court of Appeals; the Supreme Court affirmed in a 6-3 vote, giving the ACLU an apparent loss.

667. City of Canton, Ohio v. Harris

(Decided February 28, 1989; 489 U.S. 378)

I. ISSUE

A. Issues Discussed

Civil rights, due process, police misconduct

B. Legal Question Presented

"[I]f a municipality can ever be liable under 42 U.S.C. § 1983 for constitutional violations resulting from its failure to train municipal employees."

C. Supreme Court's Answer

"We hold today that the inadequacy of police training may serve as the basis for § 1983 liability only where the failure to train amounts to deliberate indifference to the rights of persons with whom the police come into contact."

II. CASE SUMMARY

A. Background

"In April 1978, respondent Geraldine Harris was arrested by officers of the Canton Police Department. Mrs. Harris was brought to the police station in a patrol wagon.

When she arrived at the station, Mrs. Harris was found sitting on the floor of the wagon. She was asked if she needed medical attention, and responded with an incoherent remark. After she was brought inside the station for processing, Mrs. Harris slumped to the floor on two occasions. Eventually, the police officers left Mrs. Harris lying on the floor to prevent her from falling again. No medical attention was ever summoned for Mrs. Harris. After about an hour, Mrs. Harris was released from custody, and taken by an ambulance (provided by her family) to a nearby hospital. There, Mrs. Harris was diagnosed as suffering from several emotional ailments; she was hospitalized for one week and received subsequent outpatient treatment for an additional year.

Some time later, Mrs. Harris commenced this action alleging many state-law and constitutional claims against the city of Canton and its officials. Among these claims was one seeking to hold the city liable under 42 U.S.C. § 1983 for its violation of Mrs. Harris' right, under the Due Process Clause of the Fourteenth Amendment, to receive necessary medical attention while in police custody.

A jury trial was held on Mrs. Harris' claims. . . . At the close of the evidence, the District Court submitted the case to the jury, which rejected all of Mrs. Harris' claims except one: her § 1983 claim against the city resulting from its failure to provide her with medical treatment while in custody. . . .

On appeal, the Sixth Circuit [held] that 'a municipality is liable for failure to train its police force, [where] the plaintiff . . . prove[s] that the municipality acted recklessly, intentionally, or with gross negligence.' . . . However, the Court of Appeals reversed the judgment for respondent, and remanded this case for a new trial, because it found that certain aspects of the District Court's jury instructions might have led the jury to believe that it could find against the city on a mere respondeat superior theory. Because the jury's verdict did not state the basis on which it had ruled for Mrs. Harris on her § 1983 claim, a new trial was ordered."

The Supreme Court granted certiorari to review the case and vacated the judgment of the Court of Appeals.

B. Counsel of Record / ACLU Attorney

ACLU Side (Respondent / Appellee): David Rudovsky argued the cause for appellee.

Opposing Side (Petitioner / Appellant): Carter G. Phillips argued the cause for appellant.

III. AMICI CURIAE

ACLU Side (Respondent / Appellee)

Brief of amici curiae filed on behalf of the ACLU, et al., by John A. Powell, Steven R. Shapiro, Howard A. Friedman, and Michael Aaron Avery.

Opposing Side (Petitioner / Appellant)

Brief of amici curiae filed on behalf of the International City Management Association, et al., by Benna Ruth Solomon, Beate Bloch, and Richard K. Willard.

IV. THE SUPREME COURT'S DECISION

"We hold today that the inadequacy of police training may serve as the basis for § 1983 liability only where the failure to train in a relevant respect amounts to deliberate indifference to the constitutional rights of persons with whom the police come into contact. . . . Only where a municipality's failure to train its employees in a relevant respect evidences a 'deliberate indifference' to the rights of its inhabitants can such a shortcoming be properly thought of as a city 'policy or custom' that is actionable under § 1983. . . .

Moreover, for liability to attach in this circumstance the identified deficiency in a city's training program must be closely related to the ultimate injury. Thus in the case at hand, respondent must still prove that the deficiency in training actually caused the police officers' indifference to her medical needs. . . . To adopt lesser standards of fault and causation would open municipalities to unprecedented liability under § 1983. In virtually every instance where a person has had his or her constitutional rights violated by a city employee, a § 1983 plaintiff will be able to point to something the city 'could have done' to prevent the unfortunate incident. . . . Consequently, while claims such as respondent's—alleging that the city's failure to provide training to municipal employees resulted in the constitutional deprivation she suffered—are cognizable under § 1983, they can only yield liability against a municipality where that city's failure to train reflects deliberate indifference to the constitutional rights of its inhabitants. . . .

The final question here is whether this case should be remanded for a new trial, or whether, as petitioner suggests, we should conclude that there are no possible grounds on which respondent can prevail. It is true that the evidence in the record now does not meet the standard of § 1983 liability we have set forth above. But, the standard of proof the District Court ultimately imposed on respondent (which was consistent with Sixth Circuit precedent) was a lesser one than the one we adopt today. Whether respondent should have an opportunity to prove her case under the 'deliberate indifference' rule we have adopted is a matter for the Court of Appeals to deal with on remand. . . .

Consequently, for the reasons given above, we vacate the judgment of the Court of Appeals and remand this case for further proceedings consistent with this opinion."

V. JUSTICE VOTE

3 Pro ACLU Side vs. 6 Con Opposing Side

ACLU Side (Respondent / Appellee)

1. O'Connor, S. – Wrote opinion concurring in part and dissenting in part
2. Scalia, A. – Joined O'Connor's opinion
3. Kennedy, A. – Joined O'Connor's opinion

Opposing Side (Petitioner / Appellant)

1. White, B. – Wrote majority opinion
2. Rehnquist, W. – Joined majority opinion
3. Brennan, W. – Wrote concurring opinion
4. Marshall, T. – Joined majority opinion
5. Balckmun, H. – Joined majority opinion
6. Stevens, J. – Joined majority opinion

VI. A WIN OR LOSS FOR THE ACLU?

The ACLU, as amicus curiae, urged affirmance of the judgment of the Court of Appeals; the Supreme Court vacated in a 6-3 vote, giving the ACLU an apparent loss.

668. Blanton v. City of North Las Vegas, Nevada

(Decided March 6, 1989; 489 U.S. 538)

I. ISSUE

A. Issues Discussed

Sixth Amendment, right to a jury trial

B. Legal Question Presented

"[W]hether there is a constitutional right to a trial by jury for persons charged under Nevada law with driving under the influence of alcohol (DUI)."

C. Supreme Court's Answer

There is no constitutional right to a jury trial for a person charged under the Nevada DUI law.

II. CASE SUMMARY

A. Background

"DUI is punishable [in Nevada] by a minimum term of two days' imprisonment and a maximum term of six months' imprisonment. Alternatively, a trial court may order the defendant 'to perform 48 hours of work for the community while dressed in distinctive garb which identifies him as [a DUI offender].' The defendant also must pay a fine ranging from $200 to $1,000. In addition, the defendant automatically loses his driver's license for 90 days, and he must attend, at his own expense, an alcohol abuse education course. Repeat DUI offenders are subject to increased penalties.

Petitioners Melvin R. Blanton and Mark D. Fraley were charged with DUI in separate incidents. Neither petitioner had a prior DUI conviction. The North Las Vegas, Nevada, Municipal Court denied their respective pretrial demands for a jury trial. On appeal, the Eighth Judicial District Court denied Blanton's request for a jury trial but, a month later, granted Fraley's. Blanton then appealed to the Supreme Court of Nevada, as did respondent city of North Las Vegas with respect to Fraley. After consolidating the two cases along with several others raising the same issue, the Supreme Court concluded, inter alia, that the Federal Constitution does not guarantee a right to a jury trial for a DUI offense because the maximum term of incarceration is only six months and the maximum possible fine is $1,000."

The U.S. Supreme Court granted certiorari to review the case and affirmed.

B. Counsel of Record / ACLU Attorney

ACLU Side (Petitioner / Appellant): John J. Graves, Jr., argued the cause for appellant.

Opposing Side (Respondent / Appellee): Mark L. Zalaoras argued the cause for appellee.

III. AMICI CURIAE

ACLU Side (Petitioner / Appellant)

Brief of amici curiae filed on behalf of the ACLU, et al., by Dan C. Bowen and John A. Powell.

Opposing Side (Respondent / Appellee)

Brief of amici curiae filed on behalf of the United States by Solicitor General Fried, Acting Assistant Attorney General Dennis, Deputy Solicitor General Bryson, Michael R. Lazerwitz, and Louis M. Fischer.

Brief of amici curiae filed on behalf of the State of Nevada by Brian McKay, Attorney General, and Brian Randall Hutchins, Chief Deputy Attorney General.

Brief of amici curiae filed on behalf of the State of New Jersey by W. Cary Edwards, Attorney General, and Boris Moczula, Larry R. Etzweiler, and Cherrie Madden Black, Deputy Attorneys General.

Brief of amici curiae filed on behalf of the city of Las Vegas, Nevada, by George F. Ogilvie.

Brief of amici curiae filed on behalf of the Louisiana District Attorneys Association by Dorothy A. Pendergast.

IV. THE SUPREME COURT'S DECISION

"It has long been settled that 'there is a category of petty crimes or offenses which is not subject to the Sixth Amendment jury trial provision.' In determining whether a particular offense should be categorized as 'petty,' our early decisions focused on the nature of the offense and on whether it was triable by a jury at common law. In recent years, however, we have sought more 'objective indications of the seriousness with which society regards the offense.' '[W]e have found the most relevant such criteria in the severity of the maximum authorized penalty.'

[O]ur decision in Baldwin established that a defendant is entitled to a jury trial whenever the offense for which he is charged carries a maximum authorized prison term of greater than six months. The possibility of a sentence exceeding six months, we determined, is 'sufficiently severe by itself' to require the opportunity for a jury trial. As for a prison term of six months or less, we recognized that it will seldom be viewed by the defendant as 'trivial or 'petty.'' But we found that the disadvantages of such a sentence, 'onerous though they may be, may be outweighed by the benefits that result from speedy and inexpensive nonjury adjudications.' . . .

A defendant is entitled to a jury trial in such circumstances only if he can demonstrate that any additional statutory penalties, viewed in conjunction with the maximum authorized period of incarceration, are so severe that they clearly reflect a legislative determination that the offense in question is a 'serious' one. . . .

Applying these principles here, it is apparent that petitioners are not entitled to a jury trial. The maximum authorized prison sentence for first-time DUI offenders does not exceed six months. A presumption therefore exists that the Nevada Legislature views DUI as a 'petty' offense for purposes of the Sixth Amendment. Considering the additional statutory penalties as well, we do not believe that the Nevada Legislature has clearly indicated that DUI is a 'serious' offense. . . .

It was not error, therefore, to deny petitioners jury trials. Accordingly, the judgment of the Supreme Court of Nevada is affirmed."

V. JUSTICE VOTE

0 Pro ACLU Side vs. 9 Con Opposing Side

Opposing Side (Respondent / Appellee)

1. Marshall, T. – Wrote majority opinion
2. Kennedy, A. – Joined majority opinion
3. Rehnquist, W. – Joined majority opinion
4. White, B. – Joined majority opinion
5. Blackmun, H. – Joined majority opinion
6. O'Connor, S. – Joined majority opinion
7. Scalia, A. – Joined majority opinion
8. Stevens, J. – Joined majority opinion
9. Brennan, W. – Joined majority opinion

VI. A WIN OR LOSS FOR THE ACLU?

The ACLU, as amicus curiae, urged reversal of the judgment of the Nevada Supreme Court; the U.S. Supreme Court affirmed in a 9-0 vote, giving the ACLU an apparent loss.

669. Graham v. Connor

(Decided March 15, 1989; 490 U.S. 386)

I. ISSUE

A. Issues Discussed

Fourth Amendment, excessive force

B. Legal Question Presented

"[W]hat constitutional standard governs a free citizen's claim that law enforcement officials used excessive force in the course of making an arrest, investigatory stop, or other 'seizure' of his person."

C. Supreme Court's Answer

"We hold that such claims are properly analyzed under the Fourth Amendment's 'objective reasonableness' standard."

II. CASE SUMMARY

A. Background

"In this action under 42 U.S.C. § 1983, petitioner Dethorne Graham seeks to recover damages for injuries allegedly sustained when law enforcement officers used physical force against him during the course of an investigatory stop. . . . On November 12, 1984, Graham, a diabetic, felt the onset of an insulin reaction. He asked a friend, William Berry, to drive him to a nearby convenience store so he could purchase some orange juice to counteract the reaction. Berry agreed, but when Graham entered the store, he saw a number of people ahead of him in the checkout line. Concerned about the delay, he hurried out of the store and asked Berry to drive him to a friend's house instead.

Respondent Connor, an officer of the Charlotte, North Carolina, Police Department, saw Graham hastily enter and leave the store. The officer became suspicious that something was amiss and followed Berry's car. About one-half mile from the store, he made an investigative stop. Although Berry told Connor that Graham was simply suffering from a 'sugar reaction,' the officer ordered Berry and Graham to wait while he found out what, if anything, had happened at the convenience store. When Officer Connor returned to his patrol car to call for backup assistance, Graham got out of the car, ran around it twice, and finally sat down on the curb, where he passed out briefly.

In the ensuing confusion, a number of other Charlotte police officers arrived on the scene in response to Officer Connor's request for backup. One of the officers rolled Graham over on the sidewalk and cuffed his hands tightly behind his back, ignoring Berry's pleas to get him some sugar. Another officer said: 'I've seen a lot of people with sugar diabetes that never acted like this. Ain't nothing wrong with the M.F. but drunk. Lock the S.B. up.' Several officers then lifted Graham up from behind, carried him over to Berry's car, and placed him face down on its hood. Regaining consciousness, Graham asked the officers to check in his wallet for a diabetic decal that he carried. In response, one of the officers told him to 'shut up' and shoved his face down against the hood of the car. Four officers grabbed Graham and threw him headfirst into the police car. A friend of Graham's brought some orange juice to the car, but the officers refused to let him have it. Finally, Officer Connor received a report that Graham had done nothing wrong at the convenience store, and the officers drove him home and released him.

At some point during his encounter with the police, Graham sustained a broken foot, cuts on his wrists, a bruised forehead, and an injured shoulder; he also claims to have developed a loud ringing in his right ear that continues to this day. He commenced this action under 42 U.S.C. § 1983 against the individual officers involved in the incident, all of whom are respondents here, alleging that they had used excessive force in making the investigatory stop, in violation of 'rights secured to him under the Fourteenth Amendment to the United States Constitution and 42 U.S.C. § 1983.'

The case was tried before a jury. At the close of petitioner's evidence, respondents moved for a directed verdict. [T]he District Court granted respondents' motion for a directed verdict.

A divided panel of the Court of Appeals for the Fourth Circuit affirmed."

The Supreme Court granted certiorari to review the case and reversed.

B. Counsel of Record / ACLU Attorney

ACLU Side (Petitioner / Appellant): H. Gerald Beaver argued the cause for appellant.

Opposing Side (Respondent / Appellee): Mark I. Levy argued the cause for appellee.

III. AMICI CURIAE

ACLU Side (Petitioner / Appellant)

Brief of amici curiae filed on behalf of the ACLU, et al., by Steven R. Shapiro.

Briefs of amici curiae filed on behalf of the United States by Solicitor General Fried, Assistant Attorney General Reynolds, Deputy Assistant Attorney General Clegg, David L. Shapiro, Brian J. Martin, and David K. Flynn.

Opposing Side (Respondent / Appellee)

Brief of amici curiae filed on behalf of the State of North Carolina by Lacy H. Thornburg, Attorney General of North Carolina, Isaac T. Avery III, Special Deputy Attorney General, and Linda Anne Morris, Assistant Attorney General.

IV. THE SUPREME COURT'S DECISION

"Where, as here, the excessive force claim arises in the context of an arrest or investigatory stop of a free citizen, it is most properly characterized as one invoking the protections of the Fourth Amendment, which guarantees citizens the right 'to be secure in their persons . . . against unreasonable . . . seizures' of the person. . . .

Determining whether the force used to effect a particular seizure is 'reasonable' under the Fourth Amendment requires a careful balancing of "the nature and quality of the intrusion on the individual's Fourth Amendment interests" against the countervailing governmental interests at stake. . . . The 'reasonableness' of a particular use of force must be judged from the perspective of a reasonable officer on the scene, rather than with the 20/20 vision of hindsight. . . . As in other Fourth Amendment contexts, . . . the 'reasonableness' inquiry in an excessive force case is an objective one: the question is whether the officers' actions are 'objectively reasonable' in light of the facts and circumstances confronting them, without regard to their underlying intent or motivation. . . .

Because petitioner's excessive force claim is one arising under the Fourth Amendment, the Court of Appeals erred in analyzing it under the four-part Johnson v. Glick test. . . . Because the Court of Appeals reviewed the District Court's ruling on the motion for directed verdict under an erroneous view of the governing substantive law, its judgment must be vacated and the case remanded to that court for reconsideration of that issue under the proper Fourth Amendment standard."

V. JUSTICE VOTE

9 Pro ACLU Side vs. 0 Con Opposing Side

ACLU Side (Petitioner / Appellant)

1. Rehnquist, W. – Wrote majority opinion
2. White, B. – Joined majority opinion
3. Stevens, J. – Joined majority opinion
4. O'Connor, S. – Joined majority opinion
5. Scalia, A. – Joined majority opinion
6. Kennedy, A. – Joined majority opinion
7. Blackmun, H. – Wrote concurring opinion
8. Brennan, W. – Joined Blackmun's concurrence
9. Marshall, T. – Joined Blackmun's concurrence

VI. A WIN OR LOSS FOR THE ACLU?

The ACLU, as amicus curiae, urged reversal of the judgment of the Court of Appeals; the Supreme Court vacated in a 9-0 vote, giving the ACLU an apparent win.

670. Skinner v. Railway Labor Executives' Ass'n

(Decided March 21, 1989; 489 U.S. 602)

I. ISSUE

A. Issues Discussed

Fourth Amendment, drug testing, expectation of privacy, search and seizure, warrant requirement

B. Legal Question Presented

Whether "Federal Railroad Administration (FRA) . . . regulations that mandate blood and urine tests of employees who are involved in certain train accidents [and] regulations that do not require, but do authorize, railroads to administer breath and urine tests to employees who violate certain safety rules . . . violate the Fourth Amendment."

C. Supreme Court's Answer

The regulations do not violate the Fourth Amendment.

II. CASE SUMMARY

A. Background

"In July 1983, the FRA expressed concern that these industry efforts were not adequate to curb alcohol and drug abuse by railroad employees. . . . In view of the obvious safety hazards of drug and alcohol use by railroad employees, the FRA announced in June 1984 its intention to promulgate federal regulations on the subject. . . . To the extent pertinent here, two subparts of the regulations relate to testing. Subpart C, which is entitled 'Post-Accident Toxicological Testing,' is mandatory. It provides that railroads 'shall take all practicable steps to assure that all covered employees of the railroad directly involved . . . provide blood and urine samples for toxicological testing by FRA,' upon the occurrence of certain specified events. . . .

Subpart D of the regulations, which is entitled 'Authorization to Test for Cause,' is permissive. It authorizes railroads to require covered employees to submit to breath or urine tests in certain circumstances not addressed by Subpart C. . . .

Respondents, the Railway Labor Executives' Association and various of its member labor organizations, brought the instant suit in the United States District Court for the Northern District of California, seeking to enjoin the FRA's regulations on various statutory and constitutional grounds. In a ruling from the bench, the District Court granted summary judgment in petitioners' favor. . . . A divided panel of the Court of Appeals for the Ninth Circuit reversed."

The Supreme Court granted certiorari to review the case and reversed.

B. Counsel of Record / ACLU Attorney

ACLU Side (Respondent / Appellee): Lawrence M. Mann argued the cause for appellee.

Opposing Side (Petitioner / Appellant): Attorney General Thornburgh argued the cause for appellant.

III. AMICI CURIAE

ACLU Side (Respondent / Appellee)

Brief of amici curiae filed on behalf of the ACLU, et al., by James D. Holzhauer, John A. Powell, Stephen R. Shapiro, Harvey Grossman, and Edward M. Chen.

Brief of amici curiae filed on behalf of the American Federation of Labor and Congress of Industrial Organizations by David Silberman and Laurence Gold.

Brief of amici curiae filed on behalf of the Aircraft Owners & Pilots Association by Scott D. Raphael.

Opposing Side (Petitioner / Appellant)

Brief of amici curiae filed on behalf of the American Public Transit Association by Donald T. Bliss.

Brief of amici curiae filed on behalf of the Bendiner-Schlesinger Laboratory, et al., by David G. Evans and William J. Judge.

Brief of amici curiae filed on behalf of the California Employment Law Council by Victor Schachter.

Brief of amici curiae filed on behalf of the Equal Employment Advisory Council by Robert E. Williams, Douglas S. McDowell, Stephen C. Yohay, and Garen E. Dodge.

Brief of amici curiae filed on behalf of the National Railroad Passenger Corporation, et al., by Erwin N. Griswold.
Brief of amici curiae filed on behalf of the Pacific Legal Foundation by Ronald A. Zumbrun and Anthony T. Caso.
Brief of amici curiae filed on behalf of the Private Truck Council of America, Inc., et al., by Peter A. Susser, William H. Borghesani, Jr., G. William Frick, and Alan B. Friedlander.
Brief of amici curiae filed on behalf of Thomas Colley, et al., by John G. Kester, John J. Buckley, Jr., Stephen L. Urbanczyk, William C. Sammons, Stanley J. Glod, Charles I. Appler, Thomas L. Bright, Robert W. Katz, William L. Pope, and Bertram D. Fisher.

IV. THE SUPREME COURT'S DECISION

"Before we consider whether the tests in question are reasonable under the Fourth Amendment, we must inquire whether the tests are attributable to the Government or its agents, and whether they amount to searches or seizures.... The Government has removed all legal barriers to the testing authorized by Subpart D and indeed has made plain not only its strong preference for testing, but also its desire to share the fruits of such intrusions. In addition, it has mandated that the railroads not bargain away the authority to perform tests granted by Subpart D. These are clear indices of the Government's encouragement, endorsement, and participation, and suffice to implicate the Fourth Amendment.... Because it is clear that the collection and testing of urine intrudes upon expectations of privacy that society has long recognized as reasonable, the Federal Courts of Appeals have concluded unanimously, and we agree, that these intrusions must be deemed searches under the Fourth Amendment....

The FRA has prescribed toxicological tests, not to assist in the prosecution of employees, but rather 'to prevent accident and casualties in railroad operations that result from impairment of employees by alcohol or drugs.' This governmental interest in ensuring the safety of the traveling public and of the employees themselves plainly justifies prohibiting covered employees from using alcohol or drugs on duty, or while subject to being called for duty. This interest also 'require[s] and justif[ies] the exercise of supervision to assure that the restrictions are in fact observed.' The question that remains, then, is whether the Government's need to monitor compliance with these restrictions justifies the privacy intrusions at issue absent a warrant or individualized suspicion....

We conclude that the compelling Government interests served by the FRA's regulations would be significantly hindered if railroads were required to point to specific facts giving rise to a reasonable suspicion of impairment before testing a given employee. In view of our conclusion that, on the present record, the toxicological testing contemplated by the regulations is not an undue infringement on the justifiable expectations of privacy of covered employees, the Government's compelling interests outweigh privacy concerns....

Alcohol and drug tests conducted in reliance on the authority of Subpart D cannot be viewed as private action outside the reach of the Fourth Amendment. Because the testing procedures mandated or authorized by Subparts C and D effect searches of the person, they must meet the Fourth Amendment's reasonableness requirement. In light of the limited discretion exercised by the railroad employers under the regulations, the surpassing safety interests served by toxicological tests in this context, and the diminished expectation of privacy that attaches to information pertaining to the fitness of covered employees, we believe that it is reasonable to conduct such tests in the absence of a warrant or reasonable suspicion that any particular employee may be impaired. We hold that the alcohol and drug tests contemplated by Subparts C and D of the FRA's regulations are reasonable within the meaning of the Fourth Amendment. The judgment of the Court of Appeals is accordingly reversed."

V. JUSTICE VOTE

2 Pro ACLU Side vs. 7 Con Opposing Side

ACLU Side (Respondent / Appellee)

1. Marshall, T. – Wrote dissenting opinion
2. Brennan, W. – Joined Marshall's dissent

Opposing Side (Petitioner / Appellant)

1. Kennedy, A. – Wrote majority opinion
2. Rehnquist, W. – Joined majority opinion
3. White, B. – Joined majority opinion
4. Blackmun, H. – Joined majority opinion
5. O'Connor, S. – Joined majority opinion
6. Scalia, A. – Joined majority opinion
7. Stevens, J. – Wrote concurring opinion

VI. A WIN OR LOSS FOR THE ACLU?

The ACLU, as amicus curiae, urged affirmance of the judgment of the Court of Appeals; the Supreme Court reversed in a 7-2 vote, giving the ACLU an apparent loss.

671. National Treasury Employees Union v. Von Raab

(Decided March 21, 1989; 489 U.S. 656)

I. ISSUE

A. Issues Discussed

Fourth Amendment, search and seizure, government employment

B. Legal Question Presented

"[W]hether it violates the Fourth Amendment for the United States Customs Service to require a urinalysis test from employees who seek transfer or promotion to certain positions."

C. Supreme Court's Answer

Drug testing does not violate the Fourth Amendment as to employees engaged in interdiction of illegal drugs or carrying firearms.

II. CASE SUMMARY

A. Background

"In December 1985, respondent, the Commissioner of Customs, established a Drug Screening Task Force to explore the possibility of implementing a drug-screening program within the [United States Customs] Service. After extensive research and consultation with experts in the field, the task force concluded that 'drug screening through urinalysis is technologically reliable, valid and accurate.' Citing this conclusion, the Commissioner announced his intention to require drug tests of employees who applied for, or occupied, certain positions within the Service. . . .

In May 1986, the Commissioner announced implementation of the drug-testing program. Drug tests were made a condition of placement or employment for positions that meet one or more of three criteria. The first is direct involvement in drug interdiction or enforcement of related laws . . . . The second criterion is a requirement that the incumbent carry firearms . . . . The third criterion is a requirement for the incumbent to handle 'classified' material . . . .

The laboratory tests the sample for the presence of marijuana, cocaine, opiates, amphetamines, and phencyclidine. . . . Customs employees who test positive for drugs and who can offer no satisfactory explanation are subject to dismissal from the Service. Test results may not, however, be turned over to any other agency, including criminal prosecutors, without the employee's written consent. . . .

Petitioners, a union of federal employees and a union official, commenced this suit in the United States District Court for the Eastern District of Louisiana on behalf of current Customs Service employees who seek covered positions. Petitioners alleged that the Custom Service drug-testing program violated, inter alia, the Fourth Amendment. The District Court agreed. . . . The court enjoined the drug-testing program, and ordered the Customs Service not to require drug tests of any applicants for covered positions.

A divided panel of the United States Court of Appeals for the Fifth Circuit vacated the injunction."

The Supreme Court granted certiorari to review the case, affirmed the judgment in part, and vacated the judgment in part.

B. Counsel of Record / ACLU Attorney

ACLU Side (Petitioner / Appellant): Lois G. Williams argued the cause for appellant.

Opposing Side (Respondent / Appellee): Solicitor General Fried argued the cause for appellee.

III. AMICI CURIAE

ACLU Side (Petitioner / Appellant)

Brief of amici curiae filed on behalf of the ACLU, et al., by Stephen H. Sachs, Carl Willner, John A. Powell, Steven R. Shapiro, Arthur B. Spitzer, and Elizabeth Symonds.

Brief of amici curiae filed on behalf of the American Federation of Labor and Congress of Industrial Organizations, et al., by Joe Goldberg, David Silberman, Laurence Gold, Edward J. Hickey, Jr., Thomas A. Woodley, and Richard Kirschner.

Brief of amici curiae filed on behalf of the Coalition of California Utility Workers by Glenn Rothner.

Brief of amici curiae filed on behalf of the Fraternal Order of Police, Grand Lodge, by James E. Phillips and John R. Fisher.

Brief of amici curiae filed on behalf of the New Jersey State Lodge, Fraternal Order of Police, by Jay Rubenstein, Janemary S. Belsole, and Stuart Reiser.

Opposing Side (Respondent / Appellee)

Brief of amici curiae filed on behalf of the California Employment Law Council by Paul Grossman.

Brief of amici curiae filed on behalf of the College of American Pathologists by Jack R. Bierig.

Brief of amici curiae filed on behalf of the Equal Employment Advisory Council by Robert E. Williams, Douglas S. McDowell, Stephen C. Yohay, and Garen E. Dodge.

Brief of amici curiae filed on behalf of Pharmchem Laboratories, Inc., et al., by Nelson G. Dong.

Brief of amici curiae filed on behalf of the Washington Legal Foundation, et al., by Daniel J. Popeo, Paul D. Kamenar, and Vicki S. Marani.

Brief of amici curiae filed on behalf of the Chamber of Commerce of the United States of America by Paul R. Friedman and Stephen A. Bokat.

Brief of amici curiae filed on behalf of the Pacific Legal Foundation by Ronald A. Zumbrun and Anthony T. Caso.

IV. THE SUPREME COURT'S DECISION

"In Skinner v. Railway Labor Executives' Ass'n . . . we held that federal regulations requiring employees of private railroads to produce urine samples for chemical testing implicate the Fourth Amendment, as those tests invade reasonable expectations of privacy. Our earlier cases have settled that the Fourth Amendment protects individuals from unreasonable searches conducted by the Government, even when the Government acts as an employer, and, in view of our holding in Railway Labor Executives that urine tests are searches, it follows that the Customs Service's drug-testing program must meet the reasonableness requirement of the Fourth Amendment.

[O]ur cases establish that where a Fourth Amendment intrusion serves special governmental needs, beyond the normal need for law enforcement, it is necessary to balance the individual's privacy expectations against the Government's interests to determine whether it is impractical to require a warrant or some level of individualized suspicion in the particular context.

It is clear that the Customs Service's drug-testing program is not designed to serve the ordinary needs of law enforcement. Test results may not be used in a criminal prosecution of the employee without the employee's consent. The purposes of the program are to deter drug use among those eligible for promotion to sensitive positions within the Service and to prevent the promotion of drug users to those positions. These substantial interests, no less than the Government's concern for safe rail transportation at issue in Railway Labor Executives, present a special need that may justify departure from the ordinary warrant and probable-cause requirements. . . .

We hold that the suspicionless testing of employees who apply for promotion to positions directly involving the interdiction of illegal drugs, or to positions that require the incumbent to carry a firearm, is reasonable. The Government's compelling interests in preventing the promotion of drug users to positions where they might endanger the integrity of our Nation's borders or the life of the citizenry outweigh the privacy interests of those who seek promotion to these positions, who enjoy a diminished expectation of privacy by virtue of the special, and obvious, physical and ethical demands of those positions. We do not decide whether testing those who apply for promotion to positions where they would handle 'classified' information is reasonable because we find the record inadequate for this purpose.

The judgment of the Court of Appeals for the Fifth Circuit is affirmed in part and vacated in part, and the case is remanded for further proceedings consistent with this opinion."

V. JUSTICE VOTE

4 Pro ACLU Side vs. 5 Con Opposing Side

ACLU Side (Petitioner / Appellant)

1. Marshall, T. – Wrote dissenting opinion
2. Brennan, W. – Joined Marshall's dissent
3. Scalia, A. – Wrote dissenting opinion
4. Stevens, J. – Joined Scalia's dissent

Opposing Side (Respondent / Appellee)

1. Kennedy, A. – Wrote majority opinion
2. Rehnquist, W. – Joined majority opinion
3. White, B. – Joined majority opinion
4. Blackmun, H. – Joined majority opinion
5. O'Connor, S. – Joined majority opinion

VI. A WIN OR LOSS FOR THE ACLU?

The ACLU, as amicus curiae, urged reversal of the judgment of the Fifth Circuit Court of Appeals; the Supreme Court affirmed in part and vacated in part in a 5-4 vote, giving the ACLU an apparent loss.

672. Board of Estimate of New York v. Morris

(Decided March 22, 1989; 489 U.S. 688)

I. ISSUE

A. Issues Discussed

Fourteenth Amendment, Equal Protection Clause

B. Legal Question Presented

Whether "[b]ecause the [New York City] boroughs have widely disparate populations[,] yet each has equal representation on the [Board of Estimate,] this structure is inconsistent with the Equal Protection Clause of the Fourteenth Amendment."

C. Supreme Court's Answer

This voting structure is inconsistent with the Equal Protection Clause of the Fourteenth Amendment.

II. CASE SUMMARY

A. Background

"The Board of Estimate of the City of New York consists of three members elected citywide, plus the elected presidents of each of the city's five boroughs. Because the boroughs have widely disparate populations—yet each has equal representation on the board—the Court of Appeals for the Second Circuit held that this structure is inconsistent with the Equal Protection Clause of the Fourteenth Amendment. . . .

Appellees, residents and voters of Brooklyn, New York City's most populous borough, commenced this action against the city in December 1981. They charged that the city's charter sections that govern the composition of the Board of Estimate are inconsistent with the Equal Protection Clause of the Fourteenth Amendment as construed and applied in various decisions of this Court dealing with districting and apportionment for the purpose of electing legislative bodies. The District Court dismissed the complaint . . . because in its view the board is a nonelective, nonlegislative body. The Court of Appeals reversed. Because all eight officials on the board ultimately are selected by popular vote, the court concluded that the board's selection process must comply with the so-called 'one-person, one-vote' requirement of the reapportionment cases. The court remanded to the District Court to ascertain whether this compliance exists. [T]he District Court determined first, that applying [the Supreme] Court's methodology in Abate v. Mundt to the disparate borough populations produced a total deviation of 132.9% from voter equality among these electorates; and second, that the city's several explanations for this range neither require nor justify the electoral scheme's gross deviation from equal representation. The court thus found it unnecessary to hold that the deviation it identified was per se unconstitutional.

The Court of Appeals affirmed."

The Supreme Court granted certiorari to review the case and affirmed the judgment.

B. Counsel of Record / ACLU Attorney

ACLU Side (Respondent / Appellee): Richard D. Emery argued the cause for appellee. With him on the briefs were Paul W. Kahn, Arthur N. Eisenberg, John A. Powell, and Steven R. Shapiro.

Opposing Side (Petitioner / Appellant): Peter L. Zimroth argued the cause for appellants. With him on the briefs for appellants in No. 87-1022 were Leonard J. Koerner, Jeffrey D. Friedlander, Stephen J. McGrath, and Fay Leoussis. Philip G. Minardo filed briefs for appellant in No. 87-1112.

III. AMICI CURIAE

ACLU Side (Respondent / Appellee)

Brief of amici curiae filed on behalf of the Citizens Union of the city of New York by John V. Lindsay, Donald J. Cohn, and Alan Rothstein.

Brief of amici curiae filed on behalf of Peter F. Vallone, et al., by Peter F. Vallone, pro se, and Susan Belgard.

Opposing Side (Petitioner / Appellant)

Brief of amici curiae filed on behalf of the Staten Island League for Better Government by Michael Weinberger.
Brief of amici curiae filed on behalf of Abraham D. Beame, et al., by Edward N. Costikyan, Simon H. Rifkind, and Gerard E. Harper.
Brief of amici curiae filed on behalf of John J. Marchi by John J. Marchi, pro se, and David Jaffe.

BRIEF OF AMICI CURIAE FILED BY JOHN F. BANZHAF III, PRO SE. IV. THE SUPREME COURT'S DECISION

"As an initial matter, we reject the city's suggestion that because the Board of Estimate is a unique body wielding nonlegislative powers, board membership elections are not subject to review under the prevailing reapportionment doctrine. The equal protection guarantee of 'one-person, one-vote' extends not only to congressional districting plans, not only to state legislative districting, but also to local government apportionment. Both state and local elections are subject to the general rule of population equality between electoral districts. No distinction between authority exercised by state assemblies, and the general governmental powers delegated by these assemblies to local, elected officials, suffices to insulate the latter from the standard of substantial voter equality. . . .

These cases are based on the propositions that in this country the people govern themselves through their elected representatives and that 'each and every citizen has an inalienable right to full and effective participation in the political processes' of the legislative bodies of the Nation, State, or locality as the case may be. Since '[m]ost citizens can achieve this participation only as qualified voters through the election of legislators to represent them,' full and effective participation requires 'that each citizen have an equally effective voice in the election of members of his . . . legislature.' . . .

That the members of New York City's Board of Estimate trigger this constitutional safeguard is certain. All eight officials become members as a matter of law upon their various elections. The mayor, the comptroller, and the president of the city council, who constitute the board's citywide number, are elected by votes of the entire city electorate. Each of these three cast two votes . . . . Similarly, when residents of the city's five boroughs . . . elect their respective borough presidents, the elections decide each borough's representative on the board. These five members each have single votes on all board matters. . . .

The city presents in this Court nothing that was not considered below, arguing chiefly that the board, as presently structured, is essential to the successful government of a regional entity, the City of New York. The board, it is said, accommodates natural and political boundaries as well as local interests. Furthermore, because the board has been effective it should not be disturbed. All of this, the city urges, is supported by the city's history. The courts below, of course, are in a much better position than we to assess the weight of these arguments, and they concluded that the proffered governmental interests were either invalid or were not sufficient to justify a deviation of 132%, in part because the valid interests of the city could be served by alternative ways of constituting the board that would minimize the discrimination in voting power among the five boroughs. Their analysis is equally applicable to a 78% deviation, and we conclude that the city's proffered governmental interests do not suffice to justify such a substantial departure from the one-person, one-vote ideal.

Accordingly the judgment of the Court of Appeals is affirmed."

V. JUSTICE VOTE

9 Pro ACLU Side vs. 0 Con Opposing Side

ACLU Side (Respondent / Appellee)

1. White, B. – Wrote majority opinion
2. Brennan, W. – Wrote concurring opinion
3. Kennedy, A. – Joined majority opinion
4. Marshall, T. – Joined majority opinion
5. Blackmun, H. – Wrote concurring opinion
6. Stevens, J. – Joined Brennan's concurrence
7. O'Connor, S. – Joined majority opinion
8. Rehnquist, W. – Joined majority opinion
9. Scalia, A. – Joined majority opinion

VI. A WIN OR LOSS FOR THE ACLU?

The ACLU, as counsel, urged affirmance of the judgment of the Second Circuit Court of Appeals; the Supreme Court affirmed in a 9-0 vote, giving the ACLU an apparent win.

673. United States Department of Justice v. Reporters Committee for Freedom of the Press

(Decided March 22, 1989; 489 U.S. 749)

I. ISSUE

A. Issues Discussed

Right to privacy, Freedom of Information Act

B. Legal Question Presented

"[W]hether the disclosure of the content of [criminal identification records] to a third party 'could reasonably be expected to constitute an unwarranted invasion of personal privacy' within the meaning of the Freedom of Information Act (FOIA)."

C. Supreme Court's Answer

Disclosure of criminal identification records is an unwarranted invasion of personal privacy.

II. CASE SUMMARY

A. Background

"This case arises out of requests made by a CBS news correspondent and the Reporters Committee for Freedom of the Press (respondents) for information concerning the criminal records of four members of the Medico family. . . .

In their complaint in the District Court, respondents sought the rap sheet for the fourth, Charles Medico (Medico), insofar as it contained 'matters of public record.' The parties filed cross-motions for summary judgment. . . . The District Court granted the Department's motion for summary judgment . . . . The Court of Appeals reversed. . . . In response to rehearing petitions advising the court that, contrary to its original understanding, most States had adopted policies of refusing to provide members of the public with criminal-history summaries, the Court of Appeals modified its holding. . . .

In accordance with its initial opinion, it remanded the case to the District Court to determine whether the withheld information is publicly available at its source, and if so, whether the Department might satisfy its statutory obligation by referring respondents to the enforcement agency or agencies that had provided the original information. . . . The Court of Appeals denied rehearing en banc, with four judges dissenting."

The Supreme Court granted certiorari to review the case and reversed.

B. Counsel of Record / ACLU Attorney

ACLU Side (Petitioner / Appellant): Roy T. Englert, Jr., argued the cause for appellant.

Opposing Side (Respondent / Appellee): Kevin T. Baine argued the cause for appellee.

III. AMICI CURIAE

ACLU Side (Petitioner / Appellant)

Brief of amici curiae filed on behalf of the ACLU by John A. Powell, Kate Martin, Janlori Goldman, and Hope Nakamura.

Brief of amici curiae filed on behalf of the State of California by John K. Van de Kamp, Attorney General, N. Eugene Hill, Assistant Attorney General, Paul H. Dobson, Supervising Deputy Attorney General, and Ramon M. de la Guardia, Deputy Attorney General.

Brief of amici curiae filed on behalf of the Search Group, Inc., et al., by Robert R. Belair and Cathy Cravens Snell.

Opposing Side (Respondent / Appellee)

Brief of amici curiae filed on behalf of the American Newspaper Publishers Association, et al., by Richard J. Ovelmen and Laura Besvinick.

Brief of amici curiae filed on behalf of the National Association of Retired Federal Employees by Joseph B. Scott and Michael J. Kator.

Brief of amici curiae filed on behalf of Public Citizen, et al., by Patti A. Goldman, Alan B. Morrison, and Eric R. Glitzenstein.

IV. THE SUPREME COURT'S DECISION

"The privacy interest in a rap sheet is substantial. The substantial character of that interest is affected by the fact that in today's society the computer can accumulate and store information that would otherwise have surely been forgotten long before a person attains age 80, when the FBI's rap sheets are discarded. . . .

Both the general requirement that a court 'shall determine the matter de novo' and the specific reference to an 'unwarranted' invasion of privacy in Exemption 7(C) indicate that a court must balance the public interest in disclosure against the interest Congress intended the Exemption to protect. . . .

The privacy interest in maintaining the practical obscurity of rap-sheet information will always be high. When the subject of such a rap sheet is a private citizen and when the information is in the Government's control as a compilation, rather than as a record of 'what the Government is up to,' the privacy interest protected by Exemption 7(C) is in fact at its apex while the FOIA-based public interest in disclosure is at its nadir. Such a disparity on the scales of justice holds for a class of cases without regard to individual circumstances; the standard virtues of bright-line rules are thus present, and the difficulties attendant to ad hoc adjudication may be avoided. Accordingly, we hold as a categorical matter that a third party's request for law enforcement records or information about a private citizen can reasonably be expected to invade that citizen's privacy, and that when the request seeks no 'official information' about a Government agency, but merely records that the Government happens to be storing, the invasion of privacy is 'unwarranted.' The judgment of the Court of Appeals is reversed."

V. JUSTICE VOTE

9 Pro ACLU Side vs. 0 Con Opposing Side

ACLU Side (Petitioner / Appellant)

1. Stevens, J. – Wrote majority opinion
2. Rehnquist, W. – Joined majority opinion
3. White, B. – Joined majority opinion
4. Marshall, T. – Joined majority opinion
5. O'Connor, S. – Joined majority opinion
6. Scalia, A. – Joined majority opinion
7. Kennedy, A. – Joined majority opinion
8. Blackmun, H. – Wrote concurring opinion
9. Brennan, W. – Joined Blackmun's concurrence

VI. A WIN OR LOSS FOR THE ACLU?

The ACLU, as amicus curiae, urged reversal of the judgment of the Court of Appeals; the Supreme Court reversed in a 9-0 vote, giving the ACLU an apparent win.

674. Frazee v. Illinois Dep't of Employment Security

(Decided March 29, 1989; 489 U.S. 829)

I. ISSUE

A. Issues Discussed

1st Amendment, religion

B. Legal Question Presented

Whether "the denial of unemployment compensation benefits [for refusal to take a job requiring work on Sundays due to religious beliefs] violated the Free Exercise Clause of the First Amendment of the Constitution, as applied to the States through the Fourteenth Amendment."

C. Supreme Court's Answer

"The denial of unemployment compensation benefits violated the Free Exercise Clause of the First Amendment as applied to the States through the Fourteenth Amendment."

II. CASE SUMMARY

A. Background

"The Illinois Unemployment Insurance Act provides that '[a]n individual shall be ineligible for benefits if he has failed, without good cause, either to apply for available, suitable work when so directed . . . or to accept suitable work when offered him . . . .' In April 1984, William Frazee refused a temporary retail position offered him by Kelly Services because the job would have required him to work on Sunday. Frazee told Kelly that, as a Christian, he could not work on 'the Lord's day.' Frazee then applied to the Illinois Department of Employment Security for unemployment benefits claiming that there was good cause for his refusal to work on Sunday. His application was denied. Frazee appealed the denial of benefits to the Department of Employment Security's Board of Review, which also denied his claim. . . . The Circuit Court of the Tenth Judicial Circuit of Illinois, Peoria County, affirmed . . . .

Frazee's free exercise claim was again rejected by the Appellate Court of Illinois, Third District. . . . The Illinois Supreme Court denied Frazee leave to appeal.

The mandatory appellate jurisdiction of this Court was invoked under 28 U.S.C. § 1257(2), since the state court rejected a challenge to the constitutionality of Illinois' statutory 'good cause' requirement as applied in this case."

B. Counsel of Record

ACLU Side (Petitioner / Appellant): David A. French argued the cause for appellant. With him on the briefs was John W. Whitehead.

Opposing Side (Respondent / Appellee): Robert J. Ruiz, Solicitor General of Illinois, argued the cause for appellees. With him on the brief were Neil F. Hartigan, Attorney General, and Diane Curry Grapsas and Marcy I. Singer, Assistant Attorneys General.

III. AMICI CURIAE

ACLU Side (Petitioner / Appellant)

Brief of amici curiae filed on behalf of the American Jewish Congress on behalf of Itself and the Synagogue Council of America, the American Civil Liberties Union, the Christian Legal Society, the National Association of Evangelicals, the Lord's Day Alliance of the United States, and the Baptist Joint Committee on Public Affairs by Amy Adelson, Lois C. Waldman, Marc D. Stern, Jeremy S. Garber, and Sarah Barringer Gordon.

Brief of amici curiae filed on behalf of the Anti-Defamation League of B'nai B'rith by Steven M. Freeman, Meyer Eisenberg, Jeffrey P. Sinensky, Jill L. Kahn, and Richard E. Shevitz.

Brief of amici curiae filed on behalf of the the Council on Religious Freedom et al. by Lee Boothby, Samuel Rabinove, Richard T. Foltin, Robert W. Nixon, and Rolland Truman.

Brief of amici curiae filed on behalf of Robert Roesser et al. by Bruce N. Cameron.

Opposing Side (Respondent / Appellee)

No briefs of amici curiae were filed in support of appellee.

IV. THE SUPREME COURT'S DECISION

"We have had more than one occasion before today to consider denials of unemployment compensation benefits to those who have refused work on the basis of their religious beliefs. . . . In each of these cases, we concluded that the denial of unemployment compensation benefits violated the Free Exercise Clause of the First Amendment of the Constitution, as applied to the States through the Fourteenth Amendment.

It is true, as the Illinois court noted, that each of the claimants in those cases was a member of a particular religious sect, but none of those decisions turned on that consideration or on any tenet of the sect involved that forbade the work the claimant refused to perform. Our judgments in those cases rested on the fact that each of the claimants had a sincere belief that religion required him or her to refrain from the work in question. . . .

There is no doubt that '[o]nly beliefs rooted in religion are protected by the Free Exercise Clause.' Purely secular views do not suffice. Nor do we underestimate the difficulty of distinguishing between religious and secular convictions and in determining whether a professed belief is sincerely held. States are clearly entitled to assure themselves that there is an ample predicate for invoking the Free Exercise Clause. We do not face problems about sincerity or about the religious nature of Frazee's convictions, however. The courts below did not question his sincerity, and the State concedes it. . . .

The State offers no justification for the burden that the denial of benefits places on Frazee's right to exercise his religion. . . .

As was the case in Thomas where there was 'no evidence in the record to indicate that the number of people who find themselves in the predicament of choosing between benefits and religious beliefs is large enough to create 'widespread unemployment,' or even to seriously affect unemployment,' there is nothing before us in this case to suggest that Sunday shopping, or Sunday sporting, for that matter, will grind to a halt as a result of our decision today. And, as we have said in the past, there may exist state interests sufficiently compelling to override a legitimate claim to the free exercise of religion. No such interest has been presented here.

The judgment of the Appellate Court of Illinois for the Third District is therefore reversed, and the case is remanded . . . ."

V. JUSTICE VOTE

9 Pro ACLU Side vs. 0 Con Opposing Side

ACLU Side (Petitioner / Appellant)

1. White, B. – Wrote majority opinion
2. Kennedy, A. – Joined majority opinion
3. Rehnquist, W. – Joined majority opinion
4. Brennan, W. – Joined majority opinion
5. Scalia, A. – Joined majority opinion
6. Blackmun, H. – Joined majority opinion

7. Marshall, T. – Joined majority opinion
8. O'Connor, S. – Joined majority opinion
9. Stevens, J. – Joined majority opinion

VI. A WIN OR LOSS FOR THE ACLU?

The ACLU filed as amicus curiae urging reversal of the judgment of the Appellate Court of Illinois for the Third District; the Supreme Court reversed in a 9-0 vote, giving the ACLU an apparent win.

675. American Foreign Service Ass'n v. Garfinkel

(Decided April 18, 1989; 490 U.S. 153)

I. ISSUE

A. Issues Discussed

Nondisclosure agreements, judicial power

B. Legal Question Presented

"[W]hether § 630 impermissibly intrudes upon the Executive's authority to regulate the disclosure of national security information."

C. Supreme Court's Answer

The decision must be vacated and the case remanded for the District Court to decide the issues presented in this case in the first instance.

II. CASE SUMMARY

A. Background

"As a condition of obtaining access to classified information, employees in the Executive Branch are required to sign 'nondisclosure agreements' that detail the employees' obligation of confidentiality and provide for penalties in the event of unauthorized disclosure. Two such nondisclosure forms are at issue in this case. One, Standard Form 189, was devised by the Director of the Information Security Oversight Office (DISOO) (now appellee Garfinkel); the other, Form 4193, was created by the Director of Central Intelligence (DCI) (now appellee Webster). Both of these forms forbade employees to reveal classified or 'classifiable' information to persons not authorized to receive such information, and made clear that employees who disclosed information in violation of these agreements could lose their security clearances, their jobs, or both. . . .

Section 630 of the Continuing Resolution for Fiscal Year 1988, enacted by Congress in 1987, prohibited the expenditure of funds in fiscal year 1988 for the implementation or enforcement of Form 189, Form 4193, or any other form that violated one of its five subsections. In response to this statute, appellee Garfinkel ordered agencies to cease using Form 189, but several agencies nevertheless required approximately 43,000 employees to sign the form after § 630 was enacted. The DCI, in contrast, continued to require employees to sign Form 4193, but attached a paragraph to the form stating that the nondisclosure agreement would 'be implemented and enforced in a manner consistent with' the statute of which § 630 was a part. Three months after § 630 became law, the DCI replaced Form 4193 with Form 4355, which eliminated the term 'classifiable.'

Appellant American Foreign Service Association (AFSA) and several Members of Congress brought the present lawsuit challenging appellees' use of Forms 189 and 4193 on the ground that they violated § 630. They sought declaratory and injunctive relief that would (1) bar appellees from requiring employees to execute or sign Form 4193 during fiscal year 1988; (2) compel appellees to treat any Form 4193 agreement signed after December 22, 1987 (the effective date of § 630), as void; and (3) direct appellees to notify all employees who signed Form 189 or 4193 after December 22, 1987, that these agreements were void and that the terms of such forms signed before that date could not be enforced in fiscal year 1988. This lawsuit was consolidated with two other cases, brought by the National Federation of Federal Employees and the American Federation of Government Employees, which sought to enjoin the use of Forms 189 and 4193 because, among other things, they violated § 630 and because the term 'classifiable' was so vague and overbroad that it inhibited employees' speech in violation of the First Amendment.

The District Court for the District of Columbia concluded that appellant AFSA had standing to challenge the nondisclosure forms on behalf of its members, but that the Members of Congress lacked standing to challenge the use of the forms. The court then assumed that 'the Executive's actions since enactment of section 630 do not comply with the requirements of that legislation,' because the DCI had continued to require employees to sign Form 4193 for three months after enactment of § 630 despite § 630's specific prohibition on the use of that form. Acknowledging that, during that time, the DCI had added a paragraph to Form 4193 stating that the agreement would be enforced in a manner consistent with § 630, the District Court nevertheless concluded that this action was not "true to the congressional mandate from which it derives authority," and that review of the Executive's action under the Administrative Procedure Act, 5 U.S.C. § 706, 'likely' would show that the Executive's action was contrary to law. Having thus skirted the statutory question whether the Executive Branch's implementation of Forms 189 and 4193 violated § 630, the court proceeded to address appellees' argument that the lawsuit should be dismissed because § 630 was an unconstitutional interference with the President's authority to protect the national security. Concluding that § 630 'impermissibly restricts the President's power to fulfill obligations imposed upon him by his express constitutional powers and the role of the Executive in foreign relations,' the court entered summary judgment in favor of appellees."

The Supreme Court granted certiorari to review the case, vacated, and remanded.

B. Counsel of Record / ACLU Attorney

ACLU Side (Petitioner / Appellant): Patti A. Goldman argued the cause for appellants.

Opposing Side (Respondent / Appellee): Edwin S. Kneedler argued the cause for appellees.

III. AMICI CURIAE

ACLU Side (Petitioner / Appellant)

Brief of amici curiae filed on behalf of the ACLU by Kate Martin, Gary M. Stern, Steven R. Shapiro, and John A. Powell.

Brief of amici curiae filed on behalf of the American Federation of Labor and Congress of Industrial Organizations, et al., by Robert M. Weinberg, Walter Kamiat, Laurence Gold, George Kaufmann, Mark Roth, and Charles A. Hobbie.

Brief of amici curiae filed on behalf of the Government Accountability Project, et al., by Joseph B. Kennedy.

Brief of amici curiae filed on behalf of the Speaker and Leadership Group of the United States House of Representatives by Steven R. Ross and Charles Tiefer, urging the court to vacate the judgment below.

Brief of amici curiae filed on behalf of the United States Senate by Michael Davidson, Ken U. Benjamin, Jr., and Morgan J. Frankel, urging the court to vacate the judgment below as moot and unripe.

Opposing Side (Respondent / Appellee)

No briefs of amici curiae were filed in support of appellee.

IV. THE SUPREME COURT'S DECISION

"We decline to decide the merits of appellants' request for individualized notice to [former] employees . . . because the questions whether individual notice is required by § 630 and whether appellants' complaint can be read to request such notice for former employees are questions best addressed in the first instance by the District Court.

A second reason why we remand this case for further proceedings rather than ordering it dismissed is that appellants argue that the definition of 'classified information' now supplied by the DISOO does not comply with § 630. . . . It appears that, in order to press this issue, appellants would be forced to amend their complaint in order to take into account the new definition of the term 'classified.' Because the decision whether to allow this amendment is one for the District Court, and because appellants' argument raises a question of statutory interpretation not touched upon by the District Court, we leave these matters for that court to decide in the first instance. . . .

[S]ubsections (3), (4), and (5) of § 630, dealing with disclosure of classified information to Congress. Both appellants and appellees apparently agree that these subsections simply preserve pre-existing rights, rights guaranteed by other statutes and constitutional provisions. The only relief appellants request with respect to this portion of the case is notice to employees informing them that Forms 189 and 4193 did not alter those pre-existing rights. No actual instance in which an employee sought to disclose information to Congress, and was prohibited from doing so, has been brought to our attention. There thus exists a substantial possibility that this last portion of the case is not ripe . . . . We are not, however, disposed to decide for ourselves whether this is so. Since the District Court analyzed the interaction between § 630 and the Executive Branch's nondisclosure policy only in abbreviated fashion, we do not have the benefit of a lower court's interpretation of the statute and of Executive policy to help us decide whether the case is ready for decision or, if it is, to guide our own resolution of the merits. Again, therefore, we return these questions to the District Court to allow it to sort them out in the first instance.

Because part of the controversy has become moot but other parts of it may retain vitality, we vacate the judgment below and remand for further proceedings consistent with this opinion. [T]he District Court should not pronounce upon the relative constitutional authority of Congress and the Executive Branch unless it finds it imperative to do so. Particularly where, as here, a case implicates the fundamental relationship between the Branches, courts should be extremely careful not to issue unnecessary constitutional rulings. On remand, the District Court should decide first whether the controversy is sufficiently live and concrete to be adjudicated and whether it is an appropriate case for equitable relief, and then decide whether the statute and forms are susceptible of a reconciling interpretation; if they are not, the court may turn to the constitutional question whether § 630 impermissibly intrudes upon the Executive Branch's authority over national security information.

The judgment of the District Court for the District of Columbia is vacated, and the case is remanded for further proceedings consistent with this opinion."

V. JUSTICE VOTE

9 Pro ACLU Side vs. 0 Con Opposing Side

ACLU Side (Petitioner / Appellant)

Opposing Side (Respondent / Appellee)

1. Marshall, T. – Per curiam decision
2. Rehnquist, W. – Per curiam decision
3. Blackmun, H. – Per curiam decision
4. Scalia, A. – Per curiam decision
5. Stevens, J. – Per curiam decision
6. Brennan, W. – Per curiam decision
7. Kennedy, A. – Per curiam decision
8. White, B. – Per curiam decision
9. O'Connor, S. – Per curiam decision

VI. A WIN OR LOSS FOR THE ACLU?

The ACLU filed as amicus curiae urging reversal of the judgment of the District Court for the District of Columbia; the Supreme Court vacated and remanded in a 9-0 vote, giving the ACLU an apparent win.

676. Frank v. Minnesota Newspaper Ass'n, Inc.

(Decided April 25, 1989; 490 U.S. 225)

I. ISSUE

A. Issues Discussed

First Amendment, freedoms of press, speech, and association, due process

B. Legal Question Presented

Are the advertisement and prize list clauses in § 1302 valid under the First Amendment and Due Process Clause of the Fifth Amendment?

C. Supreme Court's Answer

"[T]here is no longer any live controversy on the issue whether the statute is constitutional as it applies to prize lists" and the judgment below is vacated.

II. CASE SUMMARY

A. Background

"Appellee filed suit in District Court to bar enforcement of 18 U.S.C. § 1302, based on the First Amendment and the Due Process Clause of the Fifth Amendment. The suit sought declaratory and injunctive relief against the Postmaster General, among others. Section 1302 prohibits the mailing of any 'publication of any kind containing any advertisement of any lottery, gift enterprise, or scheme of any kind offering prizes dependent in whole or in part upon lot or chance, or containing any list of the prizes drawn or awarded by means of any such lottery, gift enterprise, or scheme.' The District Court found § 1302 valid as applied to advertisements, but unconstitutional as applied to prize lists, because the statute could prevent the publication of prize lists in news reports. The District Court granted an injunction limited to the latter issue. Appellants sought review of the ruling on prize lists, and appellee cross-appealed from the ruling on advertisements."

The Supreme Court noted probable jurisdiction, then vacated the judgment below.

B. Counsel of Record / ACLU Attorney

ACLU Side (Respondent / Appellee): P. Cameron DeVore argued the cause for appellee.

Opposing Side (Petitioner / Appellant): Paul J. Larkin, Jr., argued the cause for appellant.

III. AMICI CURIAE

ACLU Side (Respondent / Appellee)

Brief of amici curiae filed on behalf of the ACLU, et al., by John P. Borger, Robert Hicks, and Steven R. Shapiro.

Brief of amici curiae filed on behalf of the Association of National Advertisers by Burt Neuborne and Gilbert H. Weil.

Brief of amici curiae filed on behalf of the American Newspaper Publishers Association, et al., by P. Cameron DeVore, Marshall J. Nelson, W. Terry Maguire, Rene P. Milam, Charles V. Hamm, and Jeanne S. Whiteing.

Opposing Side (Petitioner / Appellant)

No briefs of amici curiae were filed in support of appellant.

IV. THE SUPREME COURT'S DECISION

"After the Court had noted probable jurisdiction of both appeals, Congress passed two laws affecting the coverage of § 1302. Charity Games Advertising Clarification Act of 1988, § 2(a), Pub.L. 100-625, 102 Stat. 3205 (Nov. 7, 1988); Indian Gaming Regulatory Act, § 21, Pub.L. 100-497, 102 Stat. 2486 (Oct. 17, 1988). Although the first statute does not take effect until May 7, 1990, the parties agreed to dismiss the cross-appeal under this Court's Rule 53.

In this Court, appellants now take the position that the statute does not apply to the noncommercial publishing of prize lists. In light of this concession, appellee, the original plaintiff in the case, states its willingness to forgo any further claim to the declaratory and equitable relief sought in its complaint. In these circumstances, we conclude that there is no longer any live controversy on the issue whether the statute is constitutional as it applies to prize lists, and that this appeal is moot. There is no justification for our retaining jurisdiction of a civil case where no real controversy is before us. We therefore vacate the judgment below and remand for the District Court to dismiss the portions of the complaint remaining at issue on this appeal."

V. JUSTICE VOTE

3 Pro ACLU Side vs. 6 Con Opposing Side

ACLU Side (Respondent / Appellee)

1. Stevens, J. – Wrote dissenting opinion
2. White, B. – Dissented without an opinion
3. Marshall, T. – Dissented without an opinion

Opposing Side (Petitioner / Appellant)

1. Rehnquist, W. – Per curiam decision
2. Blackmun, H. – Per curiam decision
3. Scalia, A. – Per curiam decision
4. Brennan, W. – Per curiam decision
5. Kennedy, A. – Per curiam decision
6. O'Connor, S. – Per curiam decision

VI. A WIN OR LOSS FOR THE ACLU?

The ACLU filed as amicus curiae urging affirmance of the judgment of the District Court for the District of Minnesota; the Supreme Court vacated the judgment in a 6-3 vote, giving the ACLU an apparent loss.

677. Price-Waterhouse v. Hopkins

(Decided May 1, 1989; 490 U.S. 228)

I. ISSUE

A. Issues Discussed

Gender

B. Legal Question Presented

Whether "an employer who has allowed a discriminatory motive to play a part in an employment decision must prove by clear and convincing evidence that it would have made the same decision in the absence of discrimination."

C. Supreme Court's Answer

"We hold that when a plaintiff in a Title VII case proves that her gender played a motivating part in an employment decision, the defendant may avoid a finding of liability only by proving by a preponderance of the evidence that it would have made the same decision even if it had not taken the plaintiff's gender into account."

II. CASE SUMMARY

A. Background

"Ann Hopkins was a senior manager in an office of Price Waterhouse when she was proposed for partnership in 1982. She was neither offered nor denied admission to the partnership; instead, her candidacy was held for reconsideration the following year. When the partners in her office later refused to repropose her for partnership, she sued Price Waterhouse under Title VII of the Civil Rights Act of 1964, charging that the firm had discriminated against her on the basis of sex in its decisions regarding partnership. Judge Gesell in the Federal District Court for the District of Columbia ruled in her favor on the question of liability, and the Court of Appeals for the District of Columbia Circuit affirmed. [The Supreme Court] granted certiorari to resolve a conflict among the Courts of Appeals concerning the respective burdens of proof of a defendant and plaintiff in a suit under Title VII when it has been shown that an employment decision resulted from a mixture of legitimate and illegitimate motives."

B. Counsel of Record

ACLU Side (Respondent / Appellee): James H. Heller argued the cause for appellee. With him on the brief was Douglas B. Huron.

Opposing Side (Petitioner / Appellant): Kathryn A. Oberly argued the cause for appellant. With her on the briefs were Paul M. Bator, Douglas A. Poe, Eldon Olson, and Ulric R. Sullivan.

III. AMICI CURIAE

ACLU Side (Respondent / Appellee)

Brief of amici curiae filed on behalf of the NOW Legal Defense and Education Fund, American Civil Liberties Union, Women's Legal Defense Fund, American Association of University Women, Employment Law Center, Equal Rights Advocates, Inc., Greater Washington Area Chapter, Women Lawyers Division, National Bar Association, Institute for Research on Women's Health, Nadine Taub, National Coalition for Women's Mental Health, National Conference of Women's Bar Associations, National Organization for Women, National Women's Law Center, Northwest Women's Law Center, Organization of Pan Asian-American Women, San Francisco Women Lawyers Alliance, Women Employed, Women's Bar Association of Massachusetts, Women's Bar Association of the District of Columbia, and Women's Equity Action League by Donna R. Lenhoff, Claudia A. Withers, Sarah E. Burns, Lynn Hecht Schafran, Joan E. Bertin, and John A. Powell.

Brief of amici curiae filed on behalf of the American Federation of Labor and Congress of Industrial Organizations by Marsha S. Berzon and Laurence Gold.

Brief of amici curiae filed on behalf of the American Psychological Association by Donald N. Bersof.

Brief of amici curiae filed on behalf of the Committees on Civil Rights, Labor and Employment Law, and Sex and Law of the Association of the Bar of the City of New York by Jonathan Lang, Eugene S. Friedman, Arthur Leonard, and Colleen McMahon.

Opposing Side (Petitioner / Appellant)

Brief of amici curiae filed on behalf of the Equal Employment Advisory Council by Robert E. Williams and Douglas S. McDowell.

Brief of amici curiae filed on behalf of the United States by Solicitor General Fried, Assistant Attorney General Reynolds, Deputy Solicitor General Merrill, Deputy Assistant Attorney General Clegg, Brian J. Martin, and David K. Flynn urging the Supreme Court to vacate the lower court's judgment.

IV. THE SUPREME COURT'S DECISION

"The specification of the standard of causation under Title VII is a decision about the kind of conduct that violates that statute. According to Price Waterhouse, an employer violates Title VII only if it gives decisive consideration to an employee's gender, race, national origin, or religion in making a decision that affects that employee. . . . In Hopkins' view, on the other hand, an employer violates the statute whenever it allows one of these attributes to play any part in an employment decision. . . . We conclude that, as often happens, the truth lies somewhere in between. . . .

In passing Title VII, Congress made the simple but momentous announcement that sex, race, religion, and national origin are not relevant to the selection, evaluation, or compensation of employees. Yet, the statute does not purport to limit the other qualities and characteristics that employers may take into account in making employment decisions. . . .

The central point is this: while an employer may not take gender into account in making an employment decision (except in those very narrow circumstances in which gender is a BFOQ), it is free to decide against a woman for other reasons. We think these principles require that, once a plaintiff in a Title VII case shows that gender played a motivating part in an employment decision, the defendant may avoid a finding of liability only by proving that it would have made the same decision even if it had not allowed gender to play such a role. . . .

In saying that gender played a motivating part in an employment decision, we mean that, if we asked the employer at the moment of the decision what its reasons were and if we received a truthful response, one of those reasons would be that the applicant or employee was a woman. In the specific context of sex stereotyping, an employer who acts on the basis of a belief that a woman cannot be aggressive, or that she must not be, has acted on the basis of gender. . . .

The courts below held that an employer who has allowed a discriminatory impulse to play a motivating part in an employment decision must prove by clear and convincing evidence that it would have made the same decision in the absence of discrimination. We are persuaded that the better rule is that the employer must make this showing by a preponderance of the evidence. . . .

We hold that when a plaintiff in a Title VII case proves that her gender played a motivating part in an employment decision, the defendant may avoid a finding of liability only by proving by a preponderance of the evidence that it would have made the same decision even if it had not taken the plaintiff's gender into account. Because the courts below erred by deciding that the defendant must make this proof by clear and convincing evidence, we reverse the Court of Appeals' judgment against Price Waterhouse on liability and remand the case to that court for further proceedings."

V. JUSTICE VOTE

3 Pro ACLU Side vs. 6 Con Opposing Side

ACLU Side (Respondent / Appellee)

1. Kennedy, A. – Wrote dissenting opinion
2. Rehnquist, W. – Joined Kennedy's dissent
3. Scalia, A. – Joined Kennedy's dissent

Opposing Side (Petitioner / Appellant)

1. Brennan, W. – Wrote majority opinion
2. Blackmun, H. – Joined majority opinion
3. Marshall, T. – Joined majority opinion
4. Stevens, J. – Joined majority opinion
5. White, B. – Wrote concurring opinion
6. O'Connor, S. – Wrote concurring opinion

VI. A WIN OR LOSS FOR THE ACLU?

The ACLU filed as amicus curiae urging affirmance; the Supreme Court reversed the Court of Appeals' decision by a 6-3 vote, giving the ACLU an apparent loss.

678. Maleng v. Cook

(Decided May 15, 1989; 490 U.S. 488)

I. ISSUE

A. Issues Discussed

Criminal justice, prisons, habeas corpus

B. Legal Question Presented

"[W]hether a habeas petitioner remains 'in custody' under a conviction after the sentence imposed for it has fully expired, merely because of the possibility that the prior conviction will be used to enhance the sentences imposed for any subsequent crimes of which he is convicted."

C. Supreme Court's Answer

A habeas petitioner is not "in custody" after a sentence has fully expired, however, petitioner can still bring a habeas challenge here because he is in prison under different charges.

II. CASE SUMMARY

A. Background

"In 1958, respondent was convicted of robbery in Washington state court and sentenced to 20 years of imprisonment; this sentence expired by its terms in 1978. In 1976, while on parole from that sentence, he was convicted of two counts of assault and one count of aiding a prisoner to escape; in 1978, the State sentenced him to two life terms and one 10-year term on those convictions. These sentences were maximum terms under Washington's then-indeterminate sentencing scheme, with the minimum term to be set by the Board of Prison Terms and Paroles. Under Washington law, the 1958 conviction will increase by several years the mandatory minimum term which respondent will have to serve on his 1978 sentences.

In 1976 respondent was also convicted of bank robbery and conspiracy in federal court and sentenced to 30 years of imprisonment. He is currently serving his federal sentence in a federal penitentiary in California, but the State of Washington has lodged a detainer against him with federal prison authorities. Respondent is scheduled to begin serving the sentences imposed upon him by the Washington courts in 1978 at the expiration of his federal term.

In 1985, while in federal prison, respondent filed a pro se petition for habeas corpus relief in the United States District Court for the Western District of Washington. Respondent's petition listed the 1958 Washington conviction as the 'conviction under attack,' alleging that it was invalid because respondent had not been given a competency hearing, even though there was reasonable doubt as to his competency to stand trial. Respondent also alleged that the 1958 conviction had been used illegally to enhance his 1978 state sentences, which he had not yet begun to serve. The District Court dismissed the petition for lack of subject-matter jurisdiction, holding that respondent was not 'in custody' for the purposes of a habeas attack on the 1958 conviction because the sentence imposed for that conviction had already expired. The Court of Appeals for the Ninth Circuit reversed. The Court of Appeals held that respondent was still 'in custody' under the 1958 conviction, even though the sentence imposed for that conviction had expired, because it had been used to enhance the sentences imposed in 1978 for his 1976 state convictions, which he had yet to serve."

The Supreme Court granted certiorari to review the case and affirmed.

B. Counsel of Record / ACLU Attorney

ACLU Side (Respondent / Appellee): John B. Midgley argued the cause for appellee.

Opposing Side (Petitioner / Appellant): Kenneth O. Eikenberry, Attorney General of Washington, argued the cause for appellant.

III. AMICI CURIAE

ACLU Side (Respondent / Appellee)

Brief of amici curiae filed on behalf of the ACLU by Sheryl Gordon McCloud and John A. Powell.

Brief of amici curiae filed on behalf of the National Legal Aid and Defender Association by Alan Raphael.

Opposing Side (Petitioner / Appellant)

No briefs of amici curiae were filed in support of appellant.

IV. THE SUPREME COURT'S DECISION

"The federal habeas statute gives the United States district courts jurisdiction to entertain petitions for habeas relief only from persons who are 'in custody in violation of the Constitution or laws or treaties of the United States.' (emphasis added.) We have interpreted the statutory language as requiring that the habeas petitioner be 'in custody' under the conviction or sentence under attack at the time his petition is filed. . . . Our interpretation of the "in custody" language has not required that a prisoner be physically confined in order to challenge his sentence on habeas corpus. . . . We have never held, however, that a habeas petitioner may be 'in custody' under a conviction when the sentence imposed for that conviction has fully expired at the time his petition is filed. . . . While we have very liberally construed the 'in custody' requirement for purposes of federal habeas, we have never extended it to the situation where a habeas petitioner suffers no present restraint from a conviction. . . .

In this case, of course, the possibility of a sentence upon a subsequent conviction being enhanced because of the prior conviction actually materialized, but we do not think that requires any different conclusion. When the second sentence is imposed, it is pursuant to the second conviction that the petitioner is incarcerated and is therefore 'in custody.'

We do think, however, that respondent may challenge the sentences imposed upon him by the State of Washington in 1978, even though he is not presently serving them. . . .

We think that Braden and Peyton together require the conclusion that respondent in this case was 'in custody' under his 1978 state sentences at the time he filed. Since we think respondent's habeas petition, construed with the deference to which pro se litigants are entitled, can be read as asserting a challenge to the 1978 sentences, as enhanced by the allegedly invalid prior conviction, we affirm the Court of Appeals' finding that respondent has satisfied the 'in custody' requirement for federal habeas jurisdiction.

Our holding is limited to the narrow issue of 'custody' for subject-matter jurisdiction of the habeas court. We express no view on the extent to which the 1958 conviction itself may be subject to challenge in the attack upon the 1978 sentences which it was used to enhance.

The judgment of the Court of Appeals is affirmed."

V. JUSTICE VOTE

9 Pro ACLU Side vs. 0 Con Opposing Side

ACLU Side (Respondent / Appellee)

1. Rehnquist, W. – Per curiam decision
2. White, B. – Per curiam decision
3. O'Connor, S. – Per curiam decision
4. Scalia, A. – Per curiam decision
5. Kennedy, A. – Per curiam decision
6. Stevens, J. – Per curiam decision
7. Brennan, W. – Per curiam decision
8. Marshall, T. – Per curiam decision
9. Blackmun, H. – Per curiam decision

VI. A WIN OR LOSS FOR THE ACLU?

The ACLU filed as amicus curiae urging affirmance of the judgment of the Court of Appeals; the Supreme Court affirmed in a 9-0 vote, giving the ACLU an apparent win.

679. Wards Cove Packing Co. v. Atonio

(Decided June 5, 1989; 490 U.S. 642)

I. ISSUE

A. Issues Discussed

Employment discrimination, civil rights

B. Legal Question Presented

Whether plaintiffs successfully demonstrated a "disparate-impact" to show employment discrimination under Title VII of the Civil Rights Act of 1964.

C. Supreme Court's Answer

The statistical evidence did not establish a prima facie case of "disparate-impact," however, the case is remanded to determine whether the employer violated Title VII under the proper method of analysis.

II. CASE SUMMARY

A. Background

"Jobs at the canneries are of two general types: 'cannery jobs' on the cannery line, which are unskilled positions; and 'noncannery jobs,' which fall into a variety of classifications. Most noncannery jobs are classified as skilled positions. Cannery jobs are filled predominantly by nonwhites: Filipinos and Alaska Natives. . . . Noncannery jobs are filled with predominantly white workers, who are hired during the winter months from the companies' offices in Washington and Oregon. Virtually all of the noncannery jobs pay more than cannery positions. The predominantly white noncannery workers and the predominantly nonwhite cannery employees live in separate dormitories and eat in separate mess halls.

In 1974, respondents, a class of nonwhite cannery workers who were (or had been) employed at the canneries, brought this Title VII action against petitioners. Respondents alleged that a variety of petitioners' hiring/promotion practices—e.g., nepotism, a rehire preference, a lack of objective hiring criteria, separate hiring channels, a practice of not promoting from within—were responsible for the racial stratification of the work force and had denied them and other nonwhites employment as noncannery workers on the basis of race. Respondents also complained of petitioners' racially segregated housing and dining facilities. All of respondents' claims were advanced under both the disparate-treatment and disparate-impact theories of Title VII liability.

The District Court held a bench trial, after which it entered 172 findings of fact. . . . Judgment was entered for petitioners.

On appeal, a panel of the Ninth Circuit affirmed, but that decision was vacated when the Court of Appeals agreed to hear the case en banc. . . .

On remand, the panel applied the en banc ruling to the facts of this case. It held that respondents had made out a prima facie case of disparate impact in hiring for both skilled and unskilled noncannery positions. The panel remanded the case for further proceedings, instructing the District Court that it was the employer's burden to prove that any disparate impact caused by its hiring and employment practices was justified by business necessity. Neither the en banc court nor the panel disturbed the District Court's rejection of the disparate-treatment claims."

The Supreme Court granted certiorari to review the case and reversed.

B. Counsel of Record / ACLU Attorney

ACLU Side (Respondent / Appellee): Abraham A. Arditi argued the cause for appellee.

Opposing Side (Petitioner / Appellant): Douglas M. Fryer argued the cause for appellant.

III. AMICI CURIAE

ACLU Side (Respondent / Appellee)

Brief of amici curiae filed on behalf of the ACLU, et al., by Joan E. Bertin, Isabelle Katz Pinzler, and John A. Powell.

Brief of amici curiae filed on behalf of the Lawyers' Committee for Civil Rights Under Law by Nicholas DeB. Katzenbach, Alan E. Kraus, Conrad Harper, Stuart J. Land, Norman Redlich, Richard T. Seymour, and James C. Gray, Jr.

Brief of amici curiae filed on behalf of the National Association for the Advancement of Colored People by Grover G. Hankins and Alfred W. Blumrosen.

Brief of amici curiae filed on behalf of the NAACP Legal Defense and Educational Fund, Inc., et al., by Julius LeVonne Chambers, Charles Stephen Ralston, Ronald L. Ellis, Bill Lann Lee, Patrick O. Patterson, Jr., Theodore M. Shaw, Antonia Hernandez, and E. Richard Larson.

Opposing Side (Petitioner / Appellant)

Brief of amici curiae filed on behalf of the United States by Solicitor General Fried, Assistant Attorney General Reynolds, Deputy Assistant Attorney General Clegg, Richard G. Taranto, David K. Flynn, and Lisa J. Stark.

Brief of amici curiae filed on behalf of the American Society for Personnel Administration by Lawrence Z. Lorber and J. Robert Kirk.

Brief of amici curiae filed on behalf of the Chamber of Commerce of the United States by Glen D. Nager, Andrew M. Kramer, David A. Copus, Patricia A. Dunn, and Stephen A. Bokat.

Brief of amici curiae filed on behalf of the Equal Employment Advisory Council by Robert E. Williams, Douglas S. McDowell, and Edward E. Potter.

Brief of amici curiae filed on behalf of the Center for Civil Rights by Clint Bolick, Jerald L. Hill, and Mark J. Bredemeier.

IV. THE SUPREME COURT'S DECISION

"[W]e reverse the Court of Appeals' ruling that a comparison between the percentage of cannery workers who are nonwhite and the percentage of noncannery workers who are nonwhite makes out a prima facie case of disparate impact. Of course, this leaves unresolved whether the record made in the District Court will support a conclusion that a prima facie case of disparate impact has been established on some basis other than the racial disparity between cannery and noncannery workers. This is an issue that the Court of Appeals or the District Court should address in the first instance.

[O]n remand, the courts below are instructed to require, as part of respondents' prima facie case, a demonstration that specific elements of the petitioners' hiring process have a significantly disparate impact on nonwhites. . . .

If, on remand, respondents meet the proof burdens outlined above, and establish a prima facie case of disparate impact with respect to any of petitioners' employment practices, the case will shift to any business justification petitioners offer for their use of these practices. This phase of the disparate-impact case contains two components: first, a consideration of the justifications an employer offers for his use of these practices; and second, the availability of alternative practices to achieve the same business ends, with less racial impact. . . .

For the reasons given above, the judgment of the Court of Appeals is reversed, and the case is remanded for further proceedings consistent with this opinion."

V. JUSTICE VOTE

4 Pro ACLU Side vs. 5 Con Opposing Side

ACLU Side (Respondent / Appellee)

1. Blackmun, H. – Wrote dissenting opinion, joined Stevens' dissent
2. Stevens, J. – Wrote dissenting opinion
3. Brennan, W. – Joined Blackmun's dissent, joined Stevens' dissent
4. Marshall, T. – Joined Blackmun's dissent, joined Stevens' dissent

Opposing Side (Petitioner / Appellant)

1. White, B. – Wrote majority opinion
2. Rehnquist, W. – Joined majority opinion
3. O'Connor, S. – Joined majority opinion
4. Scalia, A. – Joined majority opinion
5. Kennedy, A. – Joined majority opinion

VI. A WIN OR LOSS FOR THE ACLU?

The ACLU, as amicus curiae, urged affirmance of the judgment of the Court of Appeals; the Supreme Court reversed in a 5-4 vote, giving the ACLU an apparent loss.

680. Martin v. Wilks

(Decided June 12, 1989; 490 U.S. 755)

I. ISSUE

A. Issues Discussed

Due process, employment discrimination

B. Legal Question Presented

Whether "white firefighters were precluded from challenging employment decisions taken pursuant to [consent] decrees, even though these firefighters had not been parties to the proceedings in which the decrees were entered."

C. Supreme Court's Answer

The firefighters can challenge employment decisions made pursuant to the decrees.

II. CASE SUMMARY

A. Background

"A group of white firefighters sued the city of Birmingham, Alabama (City), and the Jefferson County Personnel Board (Board) alleging that they were being denied promotions in favor of less qualified black firefighters. They claimed that the City and the Board were making promotion decisions on the basis of race in reliance on certain consent decrees, and that these decisions constituted impermissible racial discrimination in violation of the Constitution and federal statutes. The District Court held that the white firefighters were precluded from challenging employment decisions taken pursuant to the decrees, even though these firefighters had not been parties to the proceedings in which the decrees were entered. . . .

On appeal, the Eleventh Circuit reversed."

The Supreme Court granted certiorari to review the case and affirmed.

B. Counsel of Record / ACLU Attorney

ACLU Side (Petitioner / Appellant): James P. Alexander argued the cause for appellants in Nos. 87-1639 and 87-1668. Frank M. Young III and James C. Huckaby, Jr., filed a brief for appellants in No. 87-1639. Robert D. Joffe argued the cause for appellants in No. 87-1614.

Opposing Side (Respondent / Appellee): Raymond P. Fitzpatrick, Jr., argued the cause for appellees Wilks, et al. Deputy Solicitor General Merrill argued the cause for the United States.

III. AMICI CURIAE

ACLU Side (Petitioner / Appellant)

Brief of amici curiae filed on behalf of the ACLU, et al., by Steven R. Shapiro, John A. Powell, Michael J. Wahoske, Mark B. Rotenberg, and Leslie J. Anderson.

Brief of amici curiae filed on behalf of the State of Alabama, et al., by James M. Shannon, Attorney General of Massachusetts, Alice Daniel, Deputy Attorney General, and Jane S. Schacter and Peter Sacks, Assistant Attorneys General, Don Siegelman, Attorney General of Alabama, John Steven Clark, Attorney General of Arkansas, John Van de Kamp, Attorney General of California, Joseph I. Lieberman, Attorney General of Connecticut, Frederick D. Cooke, Corporation Counsel of the District of Columbia, Robert A. Butterworth, Attorney General of Florida, Michael J. Bowers, Attorney General of Georgia, Jim Jones, Attorney General of Idaho, Linley E. Pearson, Attorney General of Indiana, Thomas J. Miller, Attorney General of Iowa, Robert T. Stephan, Attorney General of Kansas, Frederic J. Cowan, Attorney General of Kentucky, William J. Guste, Jr., Attorney General of Louisiana, J. Joseph Curran, Jr., Attorney General of Maryland, Hubert H. Humphrey III, Attorney General of Minnesota, William L. Webster, Attorney General of Missouri, Mike Greely, Attorney General of Montana, Robert M. Spire, Attorney General of Nebraska, Brian McKay, Attorney General of Nevada, Stephen E. Merrill, Attorney General of New Hampshire, Cary Edwards, Attorney General of New Jersey, Robert Abrams, Attorney General of New York, Anthony J. Celebrezze, Jr., Attorney General of Ohio, Robert H. Henry, Attorney General of Oklahoma, James E. O'Neil, Attorney General of Rhode Island, T. Travis Medlock, Attorney General of South Carolina, Jim Mattox, Attorney General of Texas, Jeffrey Amestoy, Attorney General of Vermont, Mary Sue Terry, Attorney General of Virginia, Godfrey R. de Castro, Attorney General of the Virgin Islands, Charlie Brown, Attorney General of West Virginia, Donald J. Hanaway, Attorney General of Wisconsin, and Joseph B. Meyer, Attorney General of Wyoming.

Brief of amici curiae filed on behalf of the Equal Employment Advisory Council by Robert E. Williams and Douglas S. McDowell.

Brief of amici curiae filed on behalf of the National League of Cities, et al., by Benna Ruth Solomon, Beate Bloch, and Zachary D. Fasman.

Brief of amici curiae filed on behalf of the NAACP Legal Defense and Educational Fund, Inc., et al., by N. Thompson Powers, Ronald S. Cooper, Barry L. Goldstein, Julius LeVonne Chambers, and Ronald L. Ellis.

Opposing Side (Respondent / Appellee)

Briefs of amici curiae filed on behalf of the International Association of Fire Fighters, AFL-CIO, by Thomas A. Woodley and Michael S. Wolly.

Brief of amici curiae filed on behalf of the Pacific Legal Foundation by Ronald A. Zumbrun and Anthony T. Caso.

IV. THE SUPREME COURT'S DECISION

"A judgment or decree among parties to a lawsuit resolves issues as among them, but it does not conclude the rights of strangers to those proceedings. . . .

Joinder as a party, rather than knowledge of a lawsuit and an opportunity to intervene, is the method by which potential parties are subjected to the jurisdiction of the court and bound by a judgment or decree. The parties to a lawsuit presumably know better than anyone else the nature and scope of relief sought in the action, and at whose expense such relief might be granted. It makes sense, therefore, to place on them a burden of bringing in additional parties where such a step is indicated, rather than placing on potential additional parties a duty to intervene when they acquire knowledge of the lawsuit. . . .

No one can seriously contend that an employer might successfully defend against a Title VII claim by one group of employees on the ground that its actions were required by an earlier decree entered in a suit brought against it by another group, if the later group did not have adequate notice or knowledge of the earlier suit. . . .

For the foregoing reasons we affirm the decision of the Court of Appeals for the Eleventh Circuit. That court remanded the case for trial of the reverse discrimination claims. Petitioners point to language in the District Court's findings of fact and conclusions of law which suggests that respondents will not prevail on the merits. We agree with the view of the Court of Appeals, however, that the proceedings in the District Court may have been affected by the mistaken view that respondents' claims on the merits were barred to the extent they were inconsistent with the consent decree."

V. JUSTICE VOTE

4 Pro ACLU Side vs. 5 Con Opposing Side

ACLU Side (Petitioner / Appellant)

1. Stevens, J. – Wrote dissenting opinion
2. Brennan, W. – Joined Stevens' dissent
3. Marshall, T. – Joined Stevens' dissent
4. Blackmun, H. – Joined Stevens' dissent

Opposing Side (Respondent / Appellee)

1. Rehnquist, W. – Wrote majority opinion
2. White, B. – Joined majority opinion
3. O'Connor, S. – Joined majority opinion
4. Scalia, A. – Joined majority opinion
5. Kennedy, A. – Joined majority opinion

VI. A WIN OR LOSS FOR THE ACLU?

The ACLU, as amicus curiae, urging reversal of the judgment of the Court of Appeals; the Supreme Court affirmed in a 5-4 vote, giving the ACLU an apparent loss.

681. Will v. Michigan Department of State Police

(Decided June 15, 1989; 491 U.S. 58)

I. ISSUE

A. Issues Discussed

Civil rights, personhood of states and state actors

B. Legal Question Presented

"[W]hether a State, or an official of the State while acting in his or her official capacity, is a 'person' within the meaning of Rev.Stat. § 1979, 42 U.S.C. §1983."

C. Supreme Court's Answer

Neither a State nor an official of the State is a "person" within the meaning of § 1983.

II. CASE SUMMARY

A. Background

"Petitioner Ray Will filed suit in Michigan Circuit Court alleging various violations of the United States and Michigan Constitutions as grounds for a claim under § 1983. He alleged that he had been denied a promotion to a data systems analyst position with the Department of State Police for an improper reason, that is, because his brother had been a student activist and the subject of a 'red squad' file maintained by respondent. Named as defendants were the Department of State Police and the Director of State Police in his official capacity, also a respondent here.

The Circuit Court remanded the case to the Michigan Civil Service Commission for a grievance hearing. While the grievance was pending, petitioner filed suit in the Michigan Court of Claims raising an essentially identical § 1983 claim. The Civil Service Commission ultimately found in petitioner's favor, ruling that respondents had refused to promote petitioner because of 'partisan considerations.' On the basis of that finding, the state-court judge, acting in both the Circuit Court and the Court of Claims cases, concluded that petitioner had established a violation of the United States Constitution. The judge held that the Circuit Court action was barred under state law but that the Claims Court action could go forward. The judge also ruled that respondents were persons for purposes of § 1983.

The Michigan Court of Appeals vacated the judgment against the Department of State Police, holding that a State is not a person under § 1983, but remanded the case for determination of the possible immunity of the Director of State Police from liability for damages. The Michigan Supreme Court granted discretionary review and affirmed the Court of Appeals in part and reversed in part. The Supreme Court agreed that the State itself is not a person under § 1983, but held that a state official acting in his or her official capacity also is not such a person."

The U.S. Supreme Court granted certiorari to review the case and affirmed.

B. Counsel of Record / ACLU Attorney

ACLU Side (Petitioner / Appellant): William Burnham argued the cause for appellant. With him on the briefs were Clark Cunningham, Paul D. Reingold, John A. Powell, Helen Hershkoff, and Steven R. Shapiro.

Opposing Side (Respondent / Appellee): George H. Weller, Assistant Attorney General of Michigan, argued the cause for appellee. With him on the briefs were Frank J. Kelley, Attorney General, Louis J. Caruso, Solicitor General, and Thomas L. Casey, Assistant Solicitor General.

III. AMICI CURIAE

ACLU Side (Petitioner / Appellant)

Brief of amici curiae filed on behalf of the Lawyers' Committee for Civil Rights Under Law, et al., William A. Bradford, Jr.,

Conrad K. Harper, Stuart J. Land, Norman Redlich, William L. Robinson, and Antonia Hernandez.

Opposing Side (Respondent / Appellee)

Brief of amici curiae filed on behalf of the State of Tennessee, et al., by W. J. Michael Cody, Attorney General of Tennessee, and Michael W. Catalano, Deputy Attorney General, and by the Attorneys General for their respective jurisdictions as follows: Don Siegelman of Alabama, Robert K. Corbin of Arizona, John Steven Clark of Arkansas, John Van de Kamp of California, Duane Woodard of Colorado, Joseph Lieberman of Connecticut, Charles M. Oberly of Delaware, Robert Butterworth of Florida, Warren Pries III of Hawaii, Neil F. Hartigan of Illinois, Linley E. Pearson of Indiana, Thomas J. Miller of Iowa, Robert T. Stephan of Kansas, Frederic J. Cowan of Kentucky, William J. Guste, Jr., of Louisiana, J. Joseph Curran, Jr., of Maryland, Hubert H. Humphrey III of Minnesota, Michael C. Moore of Mississippi, William L. Webster of Missouri, Mike Greely of Montana, Robert M. Spire of Nebraska, Stephen E. Merrill of New Hampshire, Hal Stratton of New Mexico, Lacy H. Thornburg of North Carolina, Nicholas Spaeth of North Dakota, Anthony J. Celebrezze, Jr., of Ohio, Robert Henry of Oklahoma, LeRoy S. Zimmerman of Pennsylvania, Hector Rivera-Cruz of Puerto Rico, Travis Medlock of South Carolina, Roger A. Tellinghuisen of South Dakota, David L. Wilkinson of Utah, Jeffrey Amestoy of Vermont, Mary Sue Terry of Virginia, Kenneth O. Eikenberry of Washington, Charlie Brown of West Virginia, Don J. Hanaway of Wisconsin, and Joseph B. Meyer of Wyoming.

Brief of amici curiae filed on behalf of the National Governors' Association, et al., by Benna Ruth Solomon, Kenneth S. Geller, and Andrew J. Pincus.

IV. THE SUPREME COURT'S DECISION

"Petitioner filed the present § 1983 actions in Michigan state court, which places the question whether a State is a person under § 1983 squarely before us since the Eleventh Amendment does not apply in state courts. For the reasons that follow, we reaffirm today what we had concluded prior to Monell and what some have considered implicit in Quern: that a State is not a person within the meaning of § 1983. . . .

Section 1983 provides a federal forum to remedy many deprivations of civil liberties, but it does not provide a federal forum for litigants who seek a remedy against a State for alleged deprivations of civil liberties. The Eleventh Amendment bars such suits unless the State has waived its immunity, or unless Congress has exercised its undoubted power under § 5 of the Fourteenth Amendment to override that immunity. That Congress, in passing § 1983, had no intention to disturb the States' Eleventh Amendment immunity and so to alter the federal–state balance in that respect was made clear in our decision in Quern. Given that a principal purpose behind the enactment of § 1983 was to provide a federal forum for civil rights claims, and that Congress did not provide such a federal forum for civil rights claims against States, we cannot accept petitioner's argument that Congress intended nevertheless to create a cause of action against States to be brought in state courts, which are precisely the courts Congress sought to allow civil rights claimants to avoid through § 1983. . . .

Petitioner asserts, alternatively, that state officials should be considered 'persons' under § 1983 even though acting in their official capacities. In this case, petitioner named as defendant not only the Michigan Department of State Police but also the Director of State Police in his official capacity.

Obviously, state officials literally are persons. But a suit against a state official in his or her official capacity is not a suit against the official but rather is a suit against the official's office. As such, it is no different from a suit against the State itself. We see no reason to adopt a different rule in the present context, particularly when such a rule would allow petitioner to circumvent congressional intent by a mere pleading device.

We hold that neither a State nor its officials acting in their official capacities are 'persons' under § 1983. The judgment of the Michigan Supreme Court is affirmed."

V. JUSTICE VOTE

4 Pro ACLU Side vs. 5 Con Opposing Side

ACLU Side (Petitioner / Appellant)

1. Brennan, W. – Wrote dissenting opinion
2. Marshall, T. – Joined Brennan's dissent
3. Blackmun, H. – Joined Brennan's dissent
4. Stevens, J. – Wrote dissenting opinion, joined Brennan's dissent

Opposing Side (Respondent / Appellee)

1. White, B. – Wrote majority opinion
2. Rehnquist, W. – Joined majority opinion
3. O'Connor, S. – Joined majority opinion
4. Scalia, A. – Joined majority opinion
5. Kennedy, A. – Joined majority opinion

VI. A WIN OR LOSS FOR THE ACLU?

The ACLU, as counsel, urged reversal of the judgment of the Michigan Supreme Court; the U.S. Supreme Court affirmed in a 5-4 vote, giving the ACLU an apparent loss.

682. Quinn v. Millsap

(Decided June 15, 1989; 491 U.S. 95)

I. ISSUE

A. Issues Discussed

Fourteenth Amendment, equal protection

B. Legal Question Presented

Whether a law that the "governments of the city of St. Louis and St. Louis County may be reorganized by a vote of the electorate of the city and county upon a plan of reorganization drafted by a 'board of freeholders' . . . violates the Equal Protection Clause of the Fourteenth Amendment to the United States Constitution because it requires that every member of this official board own real property."

C. Supreme Court's Answer

The law violates the Equal Protection Clause.

II. CASE SUMMARY

A. Background

"The Constitution of the State of Missouri provides that the governments of the city of St. Louis and St. Louis County may be reorganized by a vote of the electorate of the city and county upon a plan of reorganization drafted by a 'board of freeholders.' Appellants contend that this provision violates the Equal Protection Clause of the Fourteenth Amendment to the United States Constitution because it requires that every member of this official board own real property. The Supreme Court of Missouri, without disputing appellants' premise that ownership of real property is a prerequisite for appointment to the board of freeholders, ruled that 'the Equal Protection Clause has no relevancy here' because the board 'exercises no general governmental powers.' . . .

In November 1987, appellants Robert J. Quinn, Jr., and Patricia J. Kampsen filed in the United States District Court for the Western District of Missouri a class-action complaint on behalf of all Missouri voters who did not own real property. Appellants claimed that § 30 violated the Equal Protection Clause of the Fourteenth Amendment on its face, insofar as it required ownership of real property in order to serve on the board that was to consider proposals for reorganizing the St. Louis city and county governments.

[I]n an order accompanying its memorandum, the state court entered a declaratory judgment that § 30 is valid both on its face and as applied to the present board.

The Missouri Supreme Court affirmed this judgment, but relied exclusively on its interpretation of the Equal Protection Clause."

The U.S. Supreme Court granted certiorari to review the case and reversed.

B. Counsel of Record / ACLU Attorney

ACLU Side (Petitioner / Appellant): Kevin M. O'Keefe argued the cause for appellant.

Opposing Side (Respondent / Appellee): Simon B. Buckner, Assistant Attorney General of Missouri, argued the cause for appellee.

III. AMICI CURIAE

ACLU Side (Petitioner / Appellant)

Brief of amici curiae filed on behalf of the ACLU of Eastern Missouri, et al., by Stanley E. Goldstein, Kathleen L. Wilde, Laughlin McDonald, and Neil Bradley.

Opposing Side (Respondent / Appellee)

No briefs of amici curiae were filed in support of appellee.

IV. THE SUPREME COURT'S DECISION:

"In their brief, appellees offer two justifications for a real-property requirement in this case. First, they contend that owners of real estate have a 'first-hand knowledge of the value of good schools, sewer systems and the other problems and amenities of urban life.' Second, they assert that a real-property owner 'has a tangible stake in the long term future of his area.' These two arguments, however, were precisely the ones that this Court rejected in Turner itself.

As to the first, the Court explained that an ability to understand the issues concerning one's community does not depend on ownership of real property. 'It cannot be seriously urged that a citizen in all other respects qualified to sit on a school board must also own real property if he is to participate responsibly in educational decisions.' Similarly indefensible is the proposition that someone otherwise qualified to sit on the board that proposes a reorganization of St. Louis government must be removed from consideration just because he does not own real property. . . .

Missouri cannot entirely exclude from eligibility for appointment to this board all persons who do not own real property, regardless of their other qualifications and their demonstrated commitment to their community.

In sum, we cannot agree with appellees that under the Equal Protection Clause, as previously construed by this Court, land-owners alone may be eligible for appointment to a body empowered to propose a wholesale revision of local government. 'Whatever objectives' Missouri may wish 'to obtain by [a] 'freeholder' requirement must be secured, in this instance at least, by means more finely tailored to achieve the desired goal.' Accordingly, a land-ownership requirement is unconstitutional here, just as it was in Turner and in Chappelle.

The judgment of the Missouri Supreme Court is reversed."

V. JUSTICE VOTE

9 Pro ACLU Side vs. 0 Con Opposing Side

ACLU Side (Petitioner / Appellant)

1. Blackmun, H. – Wrote majority opinion
2. Scalia, A. – Joined majority opinion
3. Brennan, W. – Joined majority opinion
4. Rehnquist, W. – Joined majority opinion
5. O'Connor, S. – Joined majority opinion
6. Kennedy, A. – Joined majority opinion
7. Stevens, J. – Joined majority opinion
8. Marshall, T. – Joined majority opinion
9. White, B. – Joined majority opinion

VI. A WIN OR LOSS FOR THE ACLU?

The ACLU, as amicus curiae, urged reversal of the judgment of the Missouri Supreme Court; the U.S. Supreme Court reversed in a 9-0 vote, giving the ACLU an apparent win.

683. Michael H. v. Gerald D.

(Decided June 15, 1989; 491 U.S. 110)

I. ISSUE

A. Issues Discussed

Fourteenth Amendment, due process, parental rights, equal protection

B. Legal Question Presented

Whether a state law that "a child born to a married woman living with her husband is presumed to be a child of the marriage . . . infringes upon the due process rights of a man who wishes to establish his paternity of a child born to the wife of another man [or] infringes upon the constitutional right of the child to maintain a relationship with her natural father."

C. Supreme Court's Answer

The state law does not violate the constitutional rights of the natural father or the child.

II. CASE SUMMARY

A. Background

"The facts of this case are, we must hope, extraordinary. On May 9, 1976, in Las Vegas, Nevada, Carole D., an international model, and Gerald D., a top executive in a French oil company, were married. The couple established a home in Playa del Rey, California, in which they resided as husband and wife when one or the other was not out of the country on business. In the summer of 1978, Carole became involved in an adulterous affair with a neighbor, Michael H. In September 1980, she conceived a child, Victoria D., who was born on May 11, 1981. Gerald was listed as father on the birth certificate and has always held Victoria out to the world as his daughter. Soon after delivery of the child, however, Carole informed Michael that she believed he might be the father.

In the first three years of her life, Victoria remained always with Carole, but found herself within a variety of quasi-family units. In October 1981, Gerald moved to New York City to pursue his business interests, but Carole chose to remain in California. At the end of that month, Carole and Michael had blood tests of themselves and Victoria, which showed a 98.07% probability that Michael was Victoria's father. [Carole then proceeded to take Victoria with her to spend varying amounts of time with Michael, Gerald, and another man, Scott.]

In November 1982, rebuffed in his attempts to visit Victoria, Michael filed a filiation action in California Superior Court to establish his paternity and right to visitation. In March 1983, the court appointed an attorney and guardian ad litem to represent Victoria's interests. Victoria then filed a cross-complaint asserting that if she had more than one psychological or de facto father, she was entitled to maintain her filial relationship, with all of the attendant rights, duties, and obligations, with both. In May 1983, Carole filed a motion for summary judgment. During this period, from March through July 1983, Carole was again living with Gerald in New York. In August, however, she returned to California, became involved once again with Michael, and instructed her attorneys to remove the summary judgment motion from the calendar.

For the ensuing eight months, when Michael was not in St. Thomas he lived with Carole and Victoria in Carole's apartment in Los Angeles and held Victoria out as his daughter. In April 1984, Carole and Michael signed a stipulation that Michael was Victoria's natural father. Carole left Michael the next month, however, and instructed her attorneys not to file the stipulation. In June 1984, Carole reconciled with Gerald and joined him in New York, where they now live with Victoria and two other children since born into the marriage.

In May 1984, Michael and Victoria, through her guardian ad litem, sought visitation rights for Michael pendente lite. . . .

On October 19, 1984, Gerald, who had intervened in the action, moved for summary judgment on the ground that under Cal. Evid.Code § 621 there were no triable issues of fact as to Victoria's paternity. This law provides that 'the issue of a wife cohabiting with her husband, who is not impotent or sterile, is conclusively presumed to be a child of the marriage.' The presumption may be rebutted by blood tests, but only if a motion for such tests is made, within two years from the date of the child's birth, either by the husband or, if the natural father has filed an affidavit acknowledging paternity, by the wife.

On January 28, 1985, . . . the Superior Court granted Gerald's motion for summary judgment, rejecting Michael's and Victoria's challenges to the constitutionality of § 621. . . .

After submission of briefs and a hearing, the California Court of Appeal affirmed the judgment of the Superior Court and upheld the constitutionality of the statute. It interpreted that judgment, moreover, as having denied permanent visitation rights under § 4601, regarding that as the implication of the Superior Court's reliance upon § 621 and upon an earlier California case which had held that once an assertion of biological paternity is 'determined to be legally impossible' under § 621, visitation against the wishes of the mother should be denied under § 4601.

The Court of Appeal denied Michael's and Victoria's petitions for rehearing, and, on July 30, 1987, the California Supreme Court denied discretionary review."

The Supreme Court granted certiorari to revew the case and affirmed.

B. Counsel of Record / ACLU Attorney

ACLU Side (Petitioner / Appellant): Robert A. W. Boraks argued the cause for appellant.

Opposing Side (Respondent / Appellee): Larry M. Hoffman argued the cause for appellee.

III. AMICI CURIAE

ACLU Side (Petitioner / Appellant)

Brief of amici curiae filed on behalf of the ACLU Foundation, et al., by Paul Hoffman, Joan Howarth, John A. Powell, Helen Hershkoff, Steven R. Shapiro, and Isabelle Katz Pinzler.

Brief of amici curiae filed on behalf of the National Council for Children's Rights by Michael L. Oddenino.

Opposing Side (Respondent / Appellee)

No briefs of amici curiae were filed in support of appellee.

IV. THE SUPREME COURT'S DECISION

"California law, like nature itself, makes no provision for dual fatherhood. Michael was seeking to be declared the father of Victoria. [T]he legal issue in the present case reduces to whether the relationship between persons in the situation of Michael and Victoria has been treated as a protected family unit under the historic practices of our society, or whether on any other basis it has been accorded special protection. We think it impossible to find that it has. In fact, quite to the contrary, our traditions have protected the marital family (Gerald, Carole, and the child they acknowledge to be theirs) against the sort of claim Michael asserts. . . .

We have found nothing in the older sources, nor in the older cases, addressing specifically the power of the natural father to assert parental rights over a child born into a woman's existing marriage with another man. Since it is Michael's burden to establish that such a power (at least where the natural father has established a relationship with the child) is so deeply embedded within our traditions as to be a fundamental right, the lack of evidence alone might defeat his case. But the evidence shows that even in modern times—when, as we have noted, the rigid protection of the marital family has in other respects been relaxed—the ability of a person in Michael's position to claim paternity has not been generally acknowledged. . . .

We have never had occasion to decide whether a child has a liberty interest, symmetrical with that of her parent, in maintaining her filial relationship. We need not do so here because, even assuming that such a right exists, Victoria's claim must fail. Victoria's due process challenge is, if anything, weaker than Michael's. Her basic claim is not that California has erred in preventing her from establishing that Michael, not Gerald, should stand as her legal father. Rather, she claims a due process right to maintain filial relationships with both Michael and Gerald. This assertion merits little discussion, for, whatever the merits of the guardian ad litem's belief that such an arrangement can be of great psychological benefit to a child, the claim that a State must recognize multiple fatherhood has no support in the history or traditions of this country. . . .

We apply . . . the ordinary 'rational relationship' test to Victoria's equal protection challenge. The primary rationale underlying § 621's limitation on those who may rebut the presumption of legitimacy is a concern that allowing persons other than the husband or wife to do so may undermine the integrity of the marital union. When the husband or wife contests the legitimacy of their child, the stability of the marriage has already been shaken. In contrast, allowing a claim of illegitimacy to be pressed by the child—or, more accurately, by a court-appointed guardian ad litem—may well disrupt an otherwise peaceful union. Since it pursues a legitimate end by rational means, California's decision to treat Victoria differently from her parents is not a denial of equal protection.

The judgment of the California Court of Appeal is affirmed."

V. JUSTICE VOTE

4 Pro ACLU Side vs. 5 Con Opposing Side

ACLU Side (Petitioner / Appellant)

1. Brennan, W. – Wrote dissenting opinion, joined White's dissent
2. Marshall, T. – Joined Brennan's dissent
3. Blackmun, H. – Joined Brennan's dissent
4. White, B. – Wrote dissenting opinion

Opposing Side (Respondent / Appellee)

1. Scalia, A. – Wrote majority opinion
2. Rehnquist, W. – Joined majority opinion
3. O'Connor, S. – Wrote concuring opinion
4. Kennedy, A. – Joined O'Connor's concurrence
5. Stevens, J. – Wrote concurring opinion

VI. A WIN OR LOSS FOR THE ACLU?

The ACLU, as amicus curiae, urged reversal of the judgment of the Court of Appeals; the Supreme Court affirmed in a 5-4 vote, giving the ACLU an apparent loss.

684. Patterson v. McLean Credit Union

(Decided June 15, 1989; 491 U.S. 164)

I. ISSUE

A. Issues Discussed

Civil rights, employment discrimination, racial discrimination

B. Legal Question Presented

"[W]hether petitioner's claim of racial harassment in her employment is actionable under § 1981, and whether the jury instruction given by the District Court on petitioner's § 1981 promotion claim was error."

C. Supreme Court's Answer

Petitioner's racial harassment claim is not actionable under § 1981. The jury instruction for the promotion claim was erroneous.

II. CASE SUMMARY

A. Background

"Petitioner Brenda Patterson, a black woman, was employed by respondent McLean Credit Union as a teller and a file coordinator, commencing in May 1972. In July 1982, she was laid off. After the termination, petitioner commenced this action in the United States District Court for the Middle District of North Carolina. She alleged that respondent, in violation of 14 Stat. 27, 42 U.S.C. § 1981, had harassed her, failed to promote her to an intermediate accounting clerk position, and then discharged her, all because of her race. Petitioner also claimed this conduct amounted to an intentional infliction of emotional distress, actionable under North Carolina tort law.

The District Court determined that a claim for racial harassment is not actionable under § 1981 and declined to submit that part of the case to the jury. The jury did receive and deliberate upon petitioner's § 1981 claims based on alleged discrimination in her discharge and the failure to promote her, and it found for respondent on both claims. As for petitioner's state law claim, the District Court directed a verdict for respondent on the ground that the employer's conduct did not rise to the level of outrageousness required to state a claim for intentional infliction of emotional distress under applicable standards of North Carolina law.

In the Court of Appeals, petitioner raised two matters which are relevant here. First, she challenged the District Court's refusal to submit to the jury her § 1981 claim based on racial harassment. Second, she argued that the District Court erred in instructing the jury that in order to prevail on her § 1981 claim of discriminatory failure to promote, she must show that she was better qualified than the white employee who she alleges was promoted in her stead. The Court of Appeals affirmed. On the racial harassment issue, the court held that, while instances of racial harassment 'may implicate the terms and conditions of employment under Title VII [of the Civil Rights Act of 1964] and of course may be probative of the discriminatory intent required to be shown in a § 1981 action,' racial harassment itself is not cognizable under § 1981 because 'racial harassment does not abridge the right to 'make' and 'enforce' contracts.' On the jury instruction issue, the court held that once respondent had advanced superior qualification as a legitimate nondiscriminatory reason for its promotion decision, petitioner had the burden of persuasion to show that respondent's justification was a pretext and that she was better qualified than the employee who was chosen for the job."

The Supreme Court granted certiorari to review the case, affirmed in part, vacated in part, and remanded.

B. Counsel of Record / ACLU Attorney

ACLU Side (Petitioner / Appellant): Julius LeVonne Chambers reargued the cause for appellant. Penda D. Hair argued the cause for appellant on the original argument.

Opposing Side (Respondent / Appellee): Roger S. Kaplan reargued the cause for appellee. H. Lee Davis, Jr., argued the cause for appellee on the original argument.

III. AMICI CURIAE

ACLU Side (Petitioner / Appellant)

Brief of amici curiae filed on behalf of the ACLU Foundation, et al., by Steven R. Shapiro, John A. Powell, Helen Hershoff, and Adam Stein.

Brief of amici curiae filed on behalf of the United States by Solicitor General Fried, Assistant Attorney General Reynolds, Deputy Solicitor General Ayer, Deputy Assistant Attorney General Clegg, Glen D. Nager, and Jessica Dunsay Silver.

Additional briefs of amici curiae were filed on behalf of 66 Members of the United States Senate, et al., the State of New York, et al., the American Bar Association, the American Jewish Congress, et al., the Association of the Bar of the City of New York, et al., the Center for Constitutional Rights, et al., the Lawyers' Committee for Civil Rights Under Law, Carol L. Bisharat, et al., Curtis and Sandy McCrary, and Eric Foner, et al.

Opposing Side (Respondent / Appellee)

Briefs of amici curiae were filed on behalf of the Equal Employment Advisory Council, J. Philip Anderegg, pro se, the Center for Civil Rights, and the Washington Legal Foundation, et al.

IV. THE SUPREME COURT'S DECISION

"[W]e agree with the Court of Appeals that petitioner's racial harassment claim is not actionable under § 1981. . . . With the exception perhaps of her claim that respondent refused to promote her to a position as an accountant, none of the conduct which petitioner alleges as part of the racial harassment against her involves either a refusal to make a contract with her or the impairment of her ability to enforce her established contract rights. Rather, the conduct which petitioner labels as actionable racial harassment is postformation conduct by the employer relating to the terms and conditions of continuing employment. . . .

Interpreting § 1981 to cover postformation conduct unrelated to an employee's right to enforce his or her contract, such as incidents relating to the conditions of employment, is not only inconsistent with that statute's limitation to the making and enforcement of contracts, but would also undermine the detailed and well-crafted procedures for conciliation and resolution of Title VII claims. . . .

Petitioner's claim that respondent violated § 1981 by failing to promote her, because of race, to a position as an intermediate accounting clerk is a different matter. . . . This brings us to the question of the District Court's jury instructions on petitioner's promotion claim. We think the District Court erred when it instructed the jury that petitioner had to prove that she was better qualified than the white employee who allegedly received the promotion. In order to prevail under § 1981, a plaintiff must prove purposeful discrimination. . . . Although petitioner retains the ultimate burden of persuasion, our cases make clear that she must also have the opportunity to demonstrate that respondent's proffered reasons for its decision were not its true reasons. In doing so, petitioner is not limited to presenting evidence of a certain type. This is where the District Court erred. The evidence which petitioner can present in an attempt to establish that respondent's stated reasons are pretextual may take a variety of forms. . . . It was, therefore, error for the District Court to instruct the jury that petitioner could carry her burden of persuasion only by showing that she was in fact better qualified than the white applicant who got the job. . . .

The law now reflects society's consensus that discrimination based on the color of one's skin is a profound wrong of tragic dimension. Neither our words nor our decisions should be interpreted as signaling one inch of retreat from Congress' policy to forbid discrimination in the private, as well as the public, sphere. Nevertheless, in the area of private discrimination, to which the ordinance of the Constitution does not directly extend, our role is limited to interpreting what Congress may do and has done. The statute before us, which is only one part of Congress' extensive civil rights legislation, does not cover the acts of harassment alleged here.

In sum, we affirm the Court of Appeals' dismissal of petitioner's racial harassment claim as not actionable under § 1981. The Court of Appeals erred, however, in holding that petitioner could succeed in her discriminatory promotion claim under § 1981 only by proving that she was better qualified for the position of intermediate accounting clerk than the white employee who in fact was promoted. The judgment of the Court of Appeals is therefore vacated insofar as it relates to petitioner's discriminatory promotion claim, and the case is remanded for further proceedings consistent with this opinion."

V. JUSTICE VOTE

4 Pro ACLU Side vs. 5 Con Opposing Side

ACLU Side (Petitioner / Appellant)

1. Brennan, W. – Wrote opinion concurring in part and dissenting in part
2. Marshall, T. – Joined Brennan's opinion
3. Blackmun, H. – Joined Brennan's opinion
4. Stevens, J. – Joined Brennan's opinion

Opposing Side (Respondent / Appellee)

1. Kennedy, A. – Wrote majority opinion
2. Rehnquist, W. – Joined majority opinion
3. White, B. – Joined majority opinion
4. O'Connor, S. – Joined majority opinion
5. Scalia, A. – Joined majority opinion

VI. A WIN OR LOSS FOR THE ACLU?

The ACLU, as amicus curiae, urged reversal of the judgment of the Court of Appeals; the Supreme Court affirmed in part, vacated in part, and remanded in a 5-4 vote, giving the ACLU an apparent loss.

685. Dellmuth v. Muth

(Decided June 15, 1989; 491 U.S. 223)

I. ISSUE

A. Issues Discussed

Federalism, immunity, Eleventh Amendment

B. Legal Question Presented

"[W]hether the Education of the Handicapped Act abrogates the States' Eleventh Amendment immunity from suit in the federal courts."

C. Supreme Court's Answer

The Act does not abrogate the States' Eleventh Amendment immunity from suit in federal court.

II. CASE SUMMARY

A. Background

"The Education of the Handicapped Act (EHA), enacts a comprehensive scheme to assure that handicapped children may receive a free public education appropriate to their needs. To achieve these ends, the Act mandates certain procedural requirements for participating state and local educational agencies. In particular, the Act guarantees to parents the right to participate in the development of an 'individualized education program' (IEP) for their handicapped child, and to challenge the appropriateness of their child's IEP in an administrative hearing with subsequent judicial review.

Alex Muth, the son of respondent Russell Muth (hereinafter respondent), is a bright child, but one handicapped within the meaning of the EHA by a language learning disability and associated emotional problems. Alex was enrolled in public school in the Central Bucks School District of Pennsylvania from 1980 to 1983. In the summer of 1983, respondent requested a statutory administrative hearing to challenge the district's IEP for Alex. In September, shortly before the hearing convened, respondent enrolled Alex in a private school for learning disabled children for the coming school year.

The hearing examiner found that Alex's original IEP was inappropriate and made a number of recommendations. Both respondent and the school district then appealed the decision to the secretary of education, as provided under Pennsylvania law. The secretary remanded the case to the hearing examiner with instructions to the school district to revise Alex's IEP. After the district did so, the hearing examiner issued a decision declaring the revised IEP appropriate, and the secretary affirmed that decision on October 24, 1984, more than a year after the original due process hearing.

While the administrative proceedings were underway, respondent brought this suit in the Eastern District of Pennsylvania. [R]espondent's complaint alleged that the district's IEP for Alex was inappropriate and that the Commonwealth's administrative proceedings had violated the procedural requirements of the EHA in two respects: the assignment of review to the secretary, an allegedly partial officer; and the delays occasioned by the secretary's remand to the hearing examiner. Respondent requested declaratory and injunctive relief, reimbursement for Alex's private-school tuition in 1983–1984, and attorney's fees.

The District Court found various procedural infirmities in Pennsylvania's administrative scheme and entered summary judgment on respondent's procedural claims. The court held a hearing to resolve the remaining issues in the case and to determine the proper remedy for the procedural violations. The court concluded that, while the district's proposed IEP for 1983–1984 had been appropriate within the meaning of the EHA, respondent was entitled to reimbursement for Alex's tuition that year because the procedural flaws had delayed the administrative process. The District Court further determined that the school district and the Commonwealth of Pennsylvania were jointly and severally liable, agreeing with respondent that the EHA abrogated Pennsylvania's Eleventh Amendment immunity from suit. The court also awarded attorney's fees, assessed jointly and severally against the school district and the Commonwealth.

The United States Court of Appeals for the Third Circuit affirmed."

The Supreme Court granted certiorari to review the case and reversed.

B. Counsel of Record / ACLU Attorney

ACLU Side (Respondent / Appellee): Martha A. Field argued the cause for appellee.

Opposing Side (Petitioner / Appellant): Maria Parisi Vickers, Chief Deputy Attorney General of Pennsylvania, argued the cause for appellant.

III. AMICI CURIAE

ACLU Side (Respondent / Appellee)

Brief of amici curiae filed on behalf of the ACLU, et al., by Minna J. Kotkin, Kathleen A. Sullivan, Herbert Semmel, and Elizabeth Lottman Schneider.

Opposing Side (Petitioner / Appellant)

Brief of amici curiae filed on behalf of the State of North Carolina by Lacy H. Thornburg, Attorney General, and Edwin M. Speas, Jr., Special Deputy Attorney General.

IV. THE SUPREME COURT'S DECISION

"To temper Congress' acknowledged powers of abrogation with due concern for the Eleventh Amendment's role as an essential component of our constitutional structure, we have applied a simple but stringent test: 'Congress may abrogate the States' constitutionally secured immunity from suit in federal court only by making its intention unmistakably clear in the language of the statute.' . . .

We cannot agree that the textual provisions on which the Court of Appeals relied, or any other provisions of the EHA, demonstrate with unmistakable clarity that Congress intended to abrogate the States' immunity from suit. The EHA makes no reference whatsoever to either the Eleventh Amendment or the States' sovereign immunity. Nor does any provision cited by the Court of Appeals address abrogation in even oblique terms, much less with the clarity Atascadero requires. The general statement of legislative purpose in the Act's preamble simply has nothing to do with the States' sovereign immunity. The 1986 amendment to the EHA deals only with attorney's fees, and does not alter or speak to what parties are subject to suit. Respondent conceded as much at oral argument, acknowledging that 'the 1986 EHA Amendments . . . are not directly relevant [here] because they concerned only attorney's fees.' Finally, 20 U.S.C. § 1415(e)(2), the centerpiece of the Court of Appeals' textual analysis, provides judicial review for aggrieved parties, but in no way intimates that the States' sovereign immunity is abrogated. As we made plain in Atascadero: 'A general authorization for suit in federal court is not the kind of unequivocal statutory language sufficient to abrogate the Eleventh Amendment.' . . .

This statutory structure lends force to the inference that the States were intended to be subject to damages actions for violations of the EHA. But such a permissible inference, whatever its logical force, would remain just that: a permissible inference. It would not be the unequivocal declaration which, we reaffirm today, is necessary before we will determine that Congress intended to exercise its powers of abrogation. . . .

We hold that the statutory language of the EHA does not evince an unmistakably clear intention to abrogate the States' constitutionally secured immunity from suit. The Eleventh Amendment bars respondent's attempt to collect tuition reimbursement from the Commonwealth of Pennsylvania. The judgment of the Court of Appeals is reversed, and the case is remanded for proceedings consistent with this opinion."

V. JUSTICE VOTE

4 Pro ACLU Side vs. 5 Con Opposing Side

ACLU Side (Respondent / Appellee)

1. Brennan, W. – Wrote dissenting opinion
2. Marshall, T. – Joined Brennan's dissent
3. Blackmun, H. – Wrote dissenting opinion, joined Brennan's dissent
4. Stevens, J. – Wrote dissenting opinion, joined Brennan's dissent

Opposing Side (Petitioner / Appellant)

1. Kennedy, A. – Wrote majority opinion
2. Rehnquist, W. – Joined majority opinion
3. White, B. – Joined majority opinion
4. O'Connor, S. – Joined majority opinion
5. Scalia, A. – Wrote concurring opinion

VI. A WIN OR LOSS FOR THE ACLU?

The ACLU, as amicus curiae, urged affirmance of the judgment of the Court of Appeals; the Supreme Court reversed in a 5-4 vote, giving the ACLU an apparent loss.

686. Texas v. Johnson

(Decided June 21, 1989; 491 U.S. 397)

I. ISSUE

A. Issues Discussed

First Amendment, freedom of speech, flag burning

B. Legal Question Presented

Whether respondent's conviction for "desecrating a flag . . . is consistent with the First Amendment."

C. Supreme Court's Answer

The conviction is not consistent with the First Amendment.

II. CASE SUMMARY

A. Background

"While the Republican National Convention was taking place in Dallas in 1984, respondent Johnson participated in a political demonstration dubbed the 'Republican War Chest Tour.' . . . The demonstration ended in front of Dallas City Hall, where Johnson unfurled the American flag, doused it with kerosene, and set it on fire. While the flag burned, the protestors chanted: 'America, the red, white, and blue, we spit on you.' . . . No one was physically injured or threatened with injury, though several witnesses testified that they had been seriously offended by the flag burning.

Of the approximately 100 demonstrators, Johnson alone was charged with a crime. The only criminal offense with which he was charged was the desecration of a venerated object in violation of Tex.Penal Code Ann. § 42.09 (a)(3) (1989). After a trial, he was convicted, sentenced to one year in prison, and fined $2,000. The Court of Appeals for the Fifth District of Texas at Dallas affirmed

Johnson's conviction, but the Texas Court of Criminal Appeals reversed, holding that the State could not, consistent with the First Amendment, punish Johnson for burning the flag in these circumstances. "

The Supreme Court granted certiorari to review the case and affirmed.

B. Counsel of Record / ACLU Attorney

ACLU Side (Respondent / Appellee): William M. Kunstler argued the cause for appellee.

Opposing Side (Petitioner / Appellant): Kathi Alyce Drew argued the cause for appellant.

III. AMICI CURIAE

ACLU Side (Respondent / Appellee)

Brief of amici curiae filed on behalf of the ACLU, et al., by Peter Linzer, James C. Harrington, and Steven R. Shapiro.

Brief of amici curiae filed on behalf of the Christic Institute, et al., by James C. Goodale.

Brief of amici curiae filed on behalf of Jasper Johns, et al., by Robert G. Sugarman and Gloria C. Phares.

Opposing Side (Petitioner / Appellant)

Brief of amici curiae filed on behalf of the Legal Affairs Council by Wyatt B. Durrette, Jr., and Bradley B. Cavedo.

Brief of amici curiae filed on behalf of the Washington Legal Foundation by Daniel J. Popeo and Paul D. Kamenar.

IV. THE SUPREME COURT'S DECISION

"The First Amendment literally forbids the abridgement only of 'speech,' but we have long recognized that its protection does not end at the written or spoken words. . . . In these circumstances, Johnson's burning of the flag was conduct 'sufficiently imbued with elements of communication,' to implicate the First Amendment. . . .

Texas claims that its interest in preventing breaches of the peace justifies Johnson's conviction for flag desecration. However, no disturbance of the peace actually occurred or threatened to occur because of Johnson's burning of the flag. . . . We thus conclude that the State's interest in maintaining order is not implicated on these facts. The State need not worry that our holding will disable it from preserving the peace. We do not suggest that the First Amendment forbids a State to prevent 'imminent lawless action.' And, in fact, Texas already has a statute specifically prohibiting breaches of the peace, which tends to confirm that Texas need not punish this flag desecration in order to keep the peace. . . .

It remains to consider whether the State's interest in preserving the flag as a symbol of nationhood and national unity justifies Johnson's conviction. . . . If there is a bedrock principle underlying the First Amendment, it is that the government may not prohibit the expression of an idea simply because society finds the idea itself offensive or disagreeable. . . . To conclude that the government may permit designated symbols to be used to communicate only a limited set of messages would be to enter territory having no discernible or defensible boundaries. Could the government, on this theory, prohibit the burning of state flags? Of copies of the Presidential seal? Of the Constitution? In evaluating these choices under the First Amendment, how would we decide which symbols were sufficiently special to warrant this unique status? To do so, we would be forced to consult our own political preferences, and impose them on the citizenry, in the very way that the First Amendment forbids us to do. . . . We do not consecrate the flag by punishing its desecration, for in doing so we dilute the freedom that this cherished emblem represents. . . .

Johnson was convicted for engaging in expressive conduct. The State's interest in preventing breaches of the peace does not support his conviction because Johnson's conduct did not threaten to disturb the peace. Nor does the State's interest in preserving the flag as a symbol of nationhood and national unity justify his criminal conviction for engaging in political expression. The judgment of the Texas Court of Criminal Appeals is therefore affirmed."

V. JUSTICE VOTE

5 Pro ACLU Side vs. 4 Con Opposing Side

ACLU Side (Respondent / Appellee)

1. Brennan, W. – Wrote majority opinion
2. Marshall, T. – Joined majority opinion
3. Blackmun, H. – Joined majority opinion
4. Scalia, A. – Joined majority opinion
5. Kennedy, A. – Wrote concurring opinion

Opposing Side (Petitioner / Appellant)

1. Rehnquist, W. – Wrote dissenting opinion
2. White, B. – Joined Rehnquist's dissent
3. O'Connor, S. – Joined Rehnquist's dissent
4. Stevens, J. – Wrote dissenting opinion

VI. A WIN OR LOSS FOR THE ACLU?

The ACLU, as amicus curiae, urged affirmance of the judgment of the Texas Court of Criminal Appeals; the Supreme Court affirmed in a 5-4 vote, giving the ACLU an apparent win.

687. Independent Federation of Flight Attendants v. Zipes

(Decided June 22, 1989; 491 U.S. 754)

I. ISSUE

A. Issues Discussed

Attorney's fees, civil rights

B. Legal Question Presented

"[U]nder what circumstances § 706(k) permits a court to award attorney's fees against intervenors who have not been found to have violated the Civil Rights Act or any other federal law."

C. Supreme Court's Answer

The court may award attorney's fees against intervenors in this circumstance only where their action "was frivolous, unreasonable, or without foundation."

II. CASE SUMMARY

A. Background

"Section 706(k) of the Civil Rights Act of 1964 provides in relevant part that a 'court, in its discretion, may allow the prevailing party, other than the [Equal Employment Opportunity] Commission or the United States, a reasonable attorney's fee as part of the costs.' . . .

This controversy began in 1970 when respondents, female flight attendants of Trans World Airlines, brought this class action against TWA claiming that its policy of terminating flight attendants who became mothers constituted sex discrimination that violated Title VII of the Civil Rights Act of 1964.

[After extended litigation, to] come, finally, to the aspect of this lengthy litigation giving rise to the issues now before us: Respondents' attorneys petitioned the District Court for an award of attorney's fees against petitioner under § 706(k) of the Civil Rights Act of 1964. The District Court held that '[u]nsuccessful Title VII union intervenors are, like unsuccessful Title VII defendants, consistently held responsible for attorneys' fees,' and thus awarded respondents a total of $180,915.84 in fees against petitioner—in addition to approximately $1.25 million it had earlier awarded against TWA from the settlement fund. A divided panel of the Court of Appeals affirmed."

The Supreme Court granted certiorari to review the case and reversed.

B. Counsel of Record / ACLU Attorney

ACLU Side (Respondent / Appellee): Aram A. Hartunian argued the cause for appellee.

Opposing Side (Petitioner / Appellant): Steven A. Fehr argued the cause for appellant.

III. AMICI CURIAE

ACLU Side (Respondent / Appellee)

Brief of amici curiae filed on behalf of the ACLU, et al., by Colleen K. Connell, Harvey Grossman, John A. Powell, and Steven R. Shapiro.

Opposing Side (Petitioner / Appellant)

Brief of amici curiae filed on behalf of the United States, et al., by Acting Solicitor General Bryson, Acting Assistant Attorney General Turner, Deputy Solicitor General Merrill, Deputy Assistant Attorney General Clegg, Dennis J. Dimsey, and Charles A. Shanor.

Brief of amici curiae filed on behalf of the Americans United for Life Legal Defense Fund by Edward R. Grant and Clarke D. Forsythe.

Brief of amici curiae filed on behalf of the International Association of Fire Fighters, AFL-CIO, by Thomas A. Woodley and Michael S. Wolly.

IV. THE SUPREME COURT'S DECISION

"Of course, an intervenor may sometimes raise an argument that brings into question not merely the appropriateness of the remedy but the plaintiff's very entitlement to relief. Here, for example, petitioner advanced one argument that would have prevented the District Court's approval of any relief for Subclass B respondents. But that an intervenor can advance the same argument as a defendant does not mean that the two must be treated alike for purposes of fee assessments. The central fact remains that petitioner litigated (and lost) not to avoid liability for violation of the law but to prevent TWA's bargaining away of its members' seniority rights in order to settle with respondents. It was entitled, like any litigant, to pursue that legitimate end through arguments that go to the merits no less than through arguments that go only to the scope of the relief. It would hardly serve the congressional policy in favor of 'vigorous' adversary proceedings to require intervenors to disguise or avoid their strongest arguments in order to escape liability for attorney's fees. Moreover, it is often quite difficult to separate arguments directed to the appropriate remedy from arguments directed to the existence or extent of past violations, so that making fees turn upon that distinction would violate our admonition that 'a request for attorney's fees should not result in a second major litigation.' . . .

Because the courts below incorrectly presumed that petitioner was liable for attorney's fees to respondents, and accordingly made no inquiry as to whether petitioner's intervention was frivolous, unreasonable, or without foundation, the judgment of the Court of Appeals is reversed, and the case is remanded for further proceedings consistent with this opinion."

V. JUSTICE VOTE

2 Pro ACLU Side vs. 6 Con Opposing Side

ACLU Side (Respondent / Appellee)

1. Marshall, T. – Wrote dissenting opinion
2. Brennan, W. – Joined Marshall's dissent

Opposing Side (Petitioner / Appellant)

1. Scalia, A. – Wrote majority opinion
2. Rehnquist, W. – Joined majority opinion
3. White, B. – Joined majority opinion
4. O'Connor, S. – Joined majority opinion
5. Kennedy, A. – Joined majority opinion
6. Blackmun, H. – Wrote concurring opinion

Stevens, J – Took no part in the decision

VI. A WIN OR LOSS FOR THE ACLU?

The ACLU, as amicus curiae, urged affirmance of the judgment of the Court of Appeals; the Supreme Court reversed in a 6-2 vote, giving the ACLU an apparent loss.

688. Murray v. Giarratano

(Decided June 23, 1989; 492 U.S. 1)

I. ISSUE

A. Issues Discussed

Criminal justice, death penalty, Eighth Amendment, right to counsel, Fourteenth Amendment, due process

B. Legal Question Presented

Whether "appointment of counsel upon request was necessary for [indigent death row] prisoners to enjoy their constitutional right to access to the courts in pursuit of state habeas corpus relief."

C. Supreme Court's Answer

The state is not required to appoint counsel upon request for indigent death row inmates in pursuit of state habeas corpus relief.

II. CASE SUMMARY

A. Background

"Joseph M. Giarratano is a Virginia prisoner under a sentence of death. He initiated this action under 42 U.S.C. § 1983, by pro se complaint in Federal District Court, against various state officials including Edward W. Murray who is the Director of the Virginia Department of Corrections. Some months later, the District Court certified a class comprising all current and future Virginia inmates awaiting execution who do not have and cannot afford counsel to pursue postconviction proceedings. The inmates asserted a number of constitutional theories for an entitlement to appointed counsel and the case was tried to the court.

[The District Court] ordered Virginia to develop a program for the appointment of counsel, upon request, to indigent death row inmates wishing to pursue habeas corpus in state court. . . .

On appeal to the United States Court of Appeals for the Fourth Circuit, a divided panel reversed the District Court's judgment that the Commonwealth was constitutionally required to provide personal attorneys to represent death row inmates in state collateral proceedings. But that court, en banc, subsequently reheard the case and affirmed the District Court."

The Supreme Court granted certiorari to review the case and reversed.

B. Counsel of Record / ACLU Attorney

ACLU Side (Respondent / Appellee): Gerald T. Zerkin argued the cause for appellee.

Opposing Side (Petitioner / Appellant): Robert Q. Harris, Assistant Attorney General of Virginia, argued the cause for appellant.

III. AMICI CURIAE

ACLU Side (Respondent / Appellee)

Brief of amici curiae filed on behalf of the ACLU, et al., by Elizabeth Alexander, Alvin J. Bronstein, Steven R. Shapiro, and John A. Powell.

Brief of amici curiae filed on behalf of the American Bar Association by Robert D. Raven, Ronald J. Tabak, George H. Kendall, and Clifford D. Stromberg.

Brief of amici curiae filed on behalf of the Maryland State Bar Association, et al., by John H. Blume.

Brief of amici curiae filed on behalf of the National Legal Aid & Defender Association, et al., by Ephraim Margolin and Steven M. Pesner.

Opposing Side (Petitioner / Appellant)

No briefs of amici curiae were filed in support of appellant.

IV. THE SUPREME COURT'S DECISION

"In Finley we ruled that neither the Due Process Clause of the Fourteenth Amendment nor the equal protection guarantee of 'meaningful access' required the State to appoint counsel for indigent prisoners seeking state postconviction relief. The Sixth and Fourteenth Amendments to the Constitution assure the right of an indigent defendant to counsel at the trial stage of a criminal proceeding, and an indigent defendant is similarly entitled as a matter of right to counsel for an initial appeal from the judgment and sentence of the trial court. But we held in Ross v. Moffitt that the right to counsel at these earlier stages of a criminal procedure did not carry over to a discretionary appeal provided by North Carolina law from the intermediate appellate court to the Supreme Court of North Carolina. We contrasted the trial stage of a criminal proceeding, where the State by presenting witnesses and arguing to a jury attempts to strip from the defendant the presumption of innocence and convict him of a crime, with the appellate stage of such a proceeding, where the defendant needs an attorney 'not as a shield to protect him against being 'haled into court' by the State and stripped of his presumption of innocence, but rather as a sword to upset the prior determination of guilt.' . . .

There is no inconsistency whatever between the holding of Bounds and the holding in Finley; the holding of neither case squarely decides the question presented in this case. For the reasons previously stated in this opinion, we now hold that Finley applies to those inmates under sentence of death as well as to other inmates, and that holding necessarily imposes limits on Bounds.

Petitioners and respondents disagree as to the practices currently in effect in Virginia state prisons with respect to death row prisoners. Respondents contend that these prisoners are denied adequate and timely access to a law library during the final weeks before the date set for their execution. If respondents are correct, the District Court on remand may remedy this situation without any need to enlarge the holding of Bounds.

The judgment of the Court of Appeals is reversed."

V. JUSTICE VOTE

4 Pro ACLU Side vs. 5 Con Opposing Side

ACLU Side (Respondent / Appellee)

1. Stevens, J. – Wrote dissenting opinion
2. Brennan, W. – Joined Stevens' dissent
3. Marshall, T. – Joined Stevens' dissent
4. Blackmun, H. – Joined Stevens' dissent

Opposing Side (Petitioner / Appellant)

1. Rehnquist, W. – Wrote majority opinion
2. White, B. – Joined majority opinion
3. O'Connor, S. – Wrote concurring opinion, joined Kennedy's concurrence
4. Scalia, A. – Joined majority opinion
5. Kennedy, A. – Wrote concurring opinion

VI. A WIN OR LOSS FOR THE ACLU?

The ACLU filed as amicus curiae urging affirmance of the judgment of the Court of Appeals; the Supreme Court reversed in a 5-4 vote, giving the ACLU an apparent loss.

689. Webster v. Reproductive Health Services

(Decided July 3, 1989; 492 U.S. 490)

I. ISSUE

A. Issues Discussed

First Amendment, Fourth Amendment, Ninth Amendment, Fourteenth Amendment, right to privacy, abortion rights

B. Legal Question Presented

Whether "a Missouri statute regulating the performance of abortions" is unconstitutional.

C. Supreme Court's Answer

The challenged provisions of the Missouri statute are either constitutional or not subject to review at this time.

II. CASE SUMMARY

A. Background

"In June 1986, the Governor of Missouri signed into law Missouri Senate Committee Substitute for House Bill No. 1596 (hereinafter Act or statute), which amended existing state law concerning unborn children and abortions. The Act consisted of 20 provisions, 5 of which are now before the Court. The first provision, or preamble, contains 'findings' by the state legislature that '[t]he life of each human being begins at conception,' and that 'unborn children have protectable interests in life, health, and well-being.' The Act further requires that all Missouri laws be interpreted to provide unborn children with the same rights enjoyed by other persons, subject to the Federal Constitution and this Court's precedents. Among its other provisions, the Act requires that, prior to performing an abortion on any woman whom a physician has reason to believe is 20 or more weeks pregnant, the physician ascertain whether the fetus is viable by performing 'such medical examinations and tests as are necessary to make a finding of the gestational age, weight, and lung maturity of the unborn child.' The Act also prohibits the use of public employees and facilities to perform or assist abortions not necessary to save the mother's life, and it prohibits the use of public funds, employees, or facilities for the purpose of 'encouraging or counseling' a woman to have an abortion not necessary to save her life.

In July 1986, five health professionals employed by the State and two nonprofit corporations brought this class action in the United States District Court for the Western District of Missouri to challenge the constitutionality of the Missouri statute. Plaintiffs, appellees in this Court, sought declaratory and injunctive relief on the ground that certain statutory provisions violated the First, Fourth, Ninth, and Fourteenth Amendments to the Federal Constitution. . . .

Plaintiffs filed this suit 'on their own behalf and on behalf of the entire class consisting of facilities and Missouri licensed physicians or other health care professionals offering abortion services or pregnancy counseling and on behalf of the entire class of pregnant females seeking abortion services or pregnancy counseling within the State of Missouri.' . . .

Several weeks after the complaint was filed, the District Court temporarily restrained enforcement of several provisions of the Act. Following a 3-day trial in December 1986, the District Court declared seven provisions of the Act unconstitutional and enjoined their enforcement. These provisions included the preamble; the 'informed consent' provision, which required physicians to inform the pregnant woman of certain facts before performing an abortion; the requirement that post-16-week abortions be performed only in hospitals; the mandated tests to determine viability; and the prohibition on the use of public funds, employees, and facilities to perform or assist nontherapeutic abortions, and the restrictions on the use of public funds, employees, and facilities to encourage or counsel women to have such abortions.

The Court of Appeals for the Eighth Circuit affirmed, with one exception not relevant to this appeal."

The Supreme Court granted certiorari to review the case and reversed.

B. Counsel of Record / ACLU Attorney

ACLU Side (Respondent / Appellee): Frank Susman argued the cause for appellee.

Opposing Side (Petitioner / Appellant): William L. Webster, Attorney General of Missouri, pro se, argued the cause for appellant.

Charles Fried argued the cause for the United States, as amicus curiae, urging reversal.

III. AMICI CURIAE

ACLU Side (Respondent / Appellee)

Brief of amici curiae filed on behalf of the ACLU, et al., by Burt Neuborne, Janet Benshoof, Rachael N. Pine, and Lynn M. Paltrow.

Additional briefs of amici curiae were filed on behalf of the American Jewish Congress, et al., the American Library Association, et al., the American Medical Association, et al., the American Psychological Association, the American Public Health Association, et al., Americans for Democratic Action, et al., Americans United for Separation of Church and State, the Association of Reproductive Health Professionals, et al., Bioethicists for Privacy, Catholics for a Free Choice, et al., the Center for Population Options, et al., the Committee on Civil Rights of the Bar of the City of New York, et al., 22 International Women's Health Organizations, the American Nurses' Association, et al., the National Coalition Against Domestic Violence, the National Family Planning and Reproductive Health Association, the National Association of Public Hospitals, Population-Environment Balance, et al., 281 American Historians, 2,887 Women Who Have Had Abortions, et al., the Attorney General of the State of California, et al., the California National Organization for Women, et al., the Canadian Abortion Rights Action League, et al., a Group of American Law Professors, the National Association of Women Lawyers, et al., the National Council of Negro Women, Inc., et al., the National Organization for Women, 77 Organizations Committed to Women's Equality, Certain Members of the Congress of the United States, 608 State Legislators from 32 States, and 167 Distinguished Scientists and Physicians.

Opposing Side (Petitioner / Appellant)

Brief of amici curiae filed on behalf of the United States by Charles Fried, Acting Solicitor General Bryson, Assistant Attorney General Bolton, Deputy Solictor General Merrill, Roger Clegg, Steven R. Valentine, and Michael K. Kellogg.

Additioanl briefs of amici curiae were filed on behalf of Alabama Lawyers for Unborn Children, Inc., the American Association of Prolife Obstetricians and Gynecologists, et al., the American Family Association, Inc., the American Life League, Inc., the Catholic Health Association of the United States, the Catholic Lawyers Guild of the Archdiocese of Boston, Inc., the Center for Judicial Studies, et al., Covenant House, et al., Focus On The Family, et al., the Holy Orthodox Church, the Knights of Columbus, the Lutheran Church-Missouri Synod, et al., the Missouri Catholic Conference, the National Legal Foundation, Right to Life Advocates, Inc., the Rutherford Institute, et al., the Southern Center for Law and Ethics, the Southwest Life and Law Center, Inc., the United States Catholic Conference, 127 Members of the Missouri General Assembly, James Joseph Lynch, Jr., Agudath Israel of America, the State of Louisiana, et al., Birthright, Inc., Congressman Christopher H. Smith, et al., American Collegians for Life, Inc., et al., Larry Joyce, Certain American State Legislators, Certain Members of the General Assembly of the Commonwealth of Pennsylvania, Catholics United for Life, et al., the American Academy of Medical Ethics, the National Right to Life Committee, Inc., the New England Christian Action Council, Inc., Edward Allen, Austin Vaughn, et al., Paul Marx, Bernard N. Nathanson, M.D., the Right to Life League of Southern California, Inc., the International Right to Life Federation, Feminists For Life of America, et al., the Association for Public Justice, et al., Christian Advocates Serving Evangelism, Free Speech Advocates, Human Life International, and Doctors for Life, et al.

IV. THE SUPREME COURT'S DECISION

"Decision of this case requires us to address four sections of the Missouri Act: (a) the preamble; (b) the prohibition on the use of public facilities or employees to perform abortions; (c) the prohibition on public funding of abortion counseling; and (d) the requirement that physicians conduct viability tests prior to performing abortions. We address these seriatim. . . .

It will be time enough for federal courts to address the meaning of the preamble should it be applied to restrict the activities of appellees in some concrete way. Until then, this Court 'is not empowered to decide . . . abstract propositions, or to declare, for the government of future cases, principles or rules of law which cannot affect the result as to the thing in issue in the case before it.' We therefore need not pass on the constitutionality of the Act's preamble. . . .

Nothing in the Constitution requires States to enter or remain in the business of performing abortions. Nor, as appellees suggest, do private physicians and their patients have some kind of constitutional right of access to public facilities for the performance of abortions. Indeed, if the State does recoup all of its costs in performing abortions, and no state subsidy, direct or indirect, is available, it is difficult to see how any procreational choice is burdened by the State's ban on the use of its facilities or employees for performing abortions. . . . Thus we uphold the Act's restrictions on the use of public employees and facilities for the performance or assistance of nontherapeutic abortions. . . .

A majority of the Court agrees with appellees that the controversy over § 188.205 [prohibiting public funding for abortion counseling] is now moot, because appellees' argument amounts to a decision to no longer seek a declaratory judgment that § 188.205 is unconstitutional and accompanying declarative relief. We accordingly direct the Court of Appeals to vacate the judgment of the District Court with instructions to dismiss the relevant part of the complaint. . . .

The tests that § 188.029 requires the physician to perform are designed to determine viability. The State here has chosen viability as the point at which its interest in potential human life must be safeguarded. It is true that the tests in question increase the expense of abortion, and regulate the discretion of the physician in determining the viability of the fetus. Since the tests will undoubtedly show in many cases that the fetus is not viable, the tests will have been performed for what were in fact second-trimester abortions. But we are satisfied that the requirement of these tests permissibly furthers the State's interest in protecting potential human life, and we therefore believe § 188.029 to be constitutional. . . .

Both appellants and the United States as amicus curiae have urged that we overrule our decision in Roe v. Wade. The facts of the present case, however, differ from those at issue in Roe. Here, Missouri has determined that viability is the point at which its interest in potential human life must be safeguarded. In Roe, on the other hand, the Texas statute criminalized the performance of all abortions, except when the mother's life was at stake. This case therefore affords us no occasion to revisit the holding of Roe, which was that the Texas statute unconstitutionally infringed the right to an abortion derived from the Due Process Clause, and we leave it undisturbed. To the extent indicated in our opinion, we would modify and narrow Roe and succeeding cases.

Because none of the challenged provisions of the Missouri Act properly before us conflict with the Constitution, the judgment of the Court of Appeals is reversed."

V. JUSTICE VOTE

4 Pro ACLU Side vs. 5 Con Opposing Side

ACLU Side (Respondent / Appellee)

1. Blackmun, H. – Wrote opinion concurring in part and dissenting in part
2. Brennan, W. – Joined Blackmun's opinion
3. Marshall, T. – Joined Blackmun's opinion
4. Stevens, J. – Wrote opinion concurring in part and dissenting in part

Opposing Side (Petitioner / Appellant)

1. Rehnquist, W. – Wrote majority opinion
2. White, B. – Joined majority opinion
3. O'Connor, S. – Wrote concurring opinion
4. Scalia, A. – Wrote concurring opinion
5. Kennedy, A. – Joined majority opinion

VI. A WIN OR LOSS FOR THE ACLU?

The ACLU, as amicus curiae, urged affirmance of the judgment of the Court of Appeals; the Supreme Court reversed in a 5-4 vote, giving the ACLU an apparent loss.

690. County of Allegheny v. American Civil Liberties Union Greater Pittsburgh Chapter

(Decided July 3, 1989; 492 U.S. 573)

I. ISSUE

A. Issues Discussed

First Amendment, Establishment Clause

B. Legal Question Presented

Whether "a crèche placed on the Grand Staircase of the Allegheny County Courthouse [and] a Chanukah menorah placed just outside the City-County Building, next to a Christmas tree and a sign saluting liberty [violate] the Establishment Clause of the First Amendment."

C. Supreme Court's Answer

The crèche violates the Establishment Clause, but the menorah does not violate the Establishment Clause.

II. CASE SUMMARY

A. Background

"This litigation concerns the constitutionality of two recurring holiday displays located on public property in downtown Pittsburgh. The first is a crèche placed on the Grand Staircase of the Allegheny County Courthouse. The second is a Chanukah menorah placed just outside the City–County Building, next to a Christmas tree and a sign saluting liberty. . . .

This litigation began on December 10, 1986, when respondents, the Greater Pittsburgh Chapter of the American Civil Liberties Union and seven local residents, filed suit against the county and the city, seeking permanently to enjoin the county from displaying the crèche in the county courthouse and the city from displaying the menorah in front of the City-County Building. Respondents claim that the displays of the crèche and the menorah each violate the Establishment Clause of the First Amendment, made applicable to state governments by the Fourteenth Amendment. . . .

On May 8, 1987, the District Court denied respondents' request for a permanent injunction. . . . Respondents appealed, and a divided panel of the Court of Appeals reversed. . . . Rehearing en banc was denied by a 6-to-5 vote."

The Supreme Court granted certiorari to review the case, affirmed in part, and reversed in part.

B. Counsel of Record / ACLU Attorney

ACLU Side (Respondent / Appellee): Roslyn M. Litman argued the cause for appellees. With her on the brief for appellees American Civil Liberties Union, et al., were Jon Pushinsky, James B. Lieber, John A. Powell, and Steven R. Shapiro. Ruti Teitel, Jeffrey P. Sinensky, Steven M. Freeman, Richard E. Shevitz, and Jill L. Kahn filed a brief for appellee Tunador.

Opposing Side (Petitioner / Appellant): Peter Buscemi argued the cause for appellants in Nos. 87-2050 and 88-96. With him on the briefs were George M. Janocsko, Robert L. McTiernan, D.R. Pellegrini, and George R. Specter. Nathan Lewin argued the cause for appellant in No. 88-90. With him on the briefs was Charles H. Saul.

III. AMICI CURIAE

ACLU Side (Respondent / Appellee)

Brief of amici curiae filed on behalf of the American Jewish Committee, et al., by Samuel Rabinove, Richard T. Foltin, James G. Greilsheimer, Alan M. Klinger, David A. Stein, Lauren G. Klein, and Lee Boothby.

Brief of amici curiae filed on behalf of the American Jewish Congress, et al., by Arlene Fickler, Marc D. Stern, Lois C. Waldman, and Amy Adelson.

Opposing Side (Petitioner / Appellant)

Brief of amici curiae filed on behalf of the United States by Solicitor General Fried, Deputy Solicitor General Ayer, and Michael K. Kellogg.

Brief of amici curiae filed on behalf of the city of Warren, Michigan, by Robert E. Williams.

Brief of amici curiae filed on behalf of Concerned Women for America by Jordan W. Lorence, Cimron Campbell, and Wendell R. Bird.

Brief of amici curiae filed on behalf of the National Jewish Commission on Law and Public Affairs by Dennis Rapps and A. David Stern

Brief of amici curiae filed on behalf of the National Legal Foundation by Douglas W. Davis, Robert K. Skolrood, and William C. Wood, Jr.

IV. THE SUPREME COURT'S DECISION

"The Establishment Clause [of the First Amendment], at the very least, prohibits government from appearing to take a position on questions of religious belief or from 'making adherence to a religion relevant in any way to a person's standing in the political community.' . . .

We turn first to the county's crèche display. There is no doubt, of course, that the crèche itself is capable of communicating a religious message. . . . Lynch teaches that government may celebrate Christmas in some manner and form, but not in a way that endorses Christian doctrine. Here, Allegheny County has transgressed this line. It has chosen to celebrate Christmas in a way that has the effect of endorsing a patently Christian message: Glory to God for the birth of Jesus Christ. Under Lynch, and the rest of our cases, nothing more is required to demonstrate a violation of the Establishment Clause. The display of the crèche in this context, therefore, must be permanently enjoined. . . . It is . . . incontrovertible that the Court's decision today, premised on the determination that the crèche display on the Grand Staircase demonstrates the county's endorsement of Christianity, does not represent a hostility or indifference to religion but, instead, the respect for religious diversity that the Constitution requires. . . .

The display of the Chanukah menorah in front of the City-County Building may well present a closer constitutional question. [T]he menorah here stands next to a Christmas tree and a sign saluting liberty. While no challenge has been made here to the display of the tree and the sign, their presence is obviously relevant in determining the effect of the menorah's display. . . . The Christmas tree, unlike the menorah, is not itself a religious symbol. Although Christmas trees once carried religious connotations, today they typify the secular celebration of Christmas. . . . Although the city has used a symbol with religious meaning as its representation of Chanukah, this is not a case in which the city has reasonable alternatives that are less religious in nature. It is difficult to imagine a predominantly secular symbol of Chanukah that the city could place next to its Christmas tree. . . .

Given all these considerations, it is not 'sufficiently likely that residents of Pittsburgh will perceive the combined display of the tree, the sign, and the menorah as an 'endorsement' or 'disapproval . . . of their individual religious choices.' . . . On the contrary, for purposes of the Establishment Clause, the city's overall display must be understood as conveying the city's secular recognition of different traditions for celebrating the winter-holiday season.

The conclusion here that, in this particular context, the menorah's display does not have an effect of endorsing religious faith does not foreclose the possibility that the display of the menorah might violate either the 'purpose' or 'entanglement' prong of the Lemon analysis. These issues were not addressed by the Court of Appeals and may be considered by that court on remand. . . .

Lynch v. Donnelly confirms, and in no way repudiates, the longstanding constitutional principle that government may not engage in a practice that has the effect of promoting or endorsing religious beliefs. The display of the crèche in the county courthouse has this unconstitutional effect. The display of the menorah in front of the City-County Building, however, does not have this effect, given its 'particular physical setting.' The judgment of the Court of Appeals is affirmed in part and reversed in part, and the cases are remanded for further proceedings."

V. JUSTICE VOTE

5 Pro ACLU Side vs. 4 Con Opposing Side

ACLU Side (Respondent / Appellee)

1. Blackmun, H. – Wrote majority opinion
2. Stevens, J. – Wrote opinion concurring in part and dissenting in part, joined O'Connor's opinion in part, joined Brennan's opinion
3. O'Connor, S. – Wrote concurring opinion
4. Brennan, W. – Wrote opinion concurring in part and dissenting in part, joined O'Connor's opinion in part, joined Stevens' opinion
5. Marshall, T. – Joined Brennan's opinion, joined Stevens' opinion

Opposing Side (Petitioner / Appellant)

1. Kennedy, A. – Wrote opinion concurring in part and dissenting in part
2. Rehnquist, W. – Joined Kennedy's opinion
3. White, B. – Joined Kennedy's opinion
4. Scalia, A. – Joined Kennedy's opinion

VI. A WIN OR LOSS FOR THE ACLU?

The ACLU, as a party of record and counsel of record, urged affirmance of the judgment of the Court of Appeals for the Third Circuit; the Supreme Court affirmed in part and reversed in part in a 5-4 vote, giving the ACLU an apparent win.

691. Spallone v. United States

(Decided January 10, 1990; 493 U.S. 265)

I. ISSUE

A. Issues Discussed

Civil rights, race, Fourteenth Amendment, judicial power, contempt of court

B. Legal Question Presented

"[W]hether it was a proper exercise of judicial power for the District Court to hold petitioners, four Yonkers city councilmembers, in contempt for refusing to vote in favor of legislation implementing a consent decree earlier approved by the city."

C. Supreme Court's Answer

It was improper for the District Court to hold the individual petitioners in contempt of court.

II. CASE SUMMARY

A. Background

"In 1980, the United States filed a complaint alleging, inter alia, that the two named defendants—the city of Yonkers and the Yonkers Community Development Agency—had intentionally engaged in a pattern and practice of housing discrimination, in violation of Title VIII of the Civil Rights Act of 1968, and the Equal Protection Clause of the Fourteenth Amendment. The Government and plaintiff-intervenor National Association for the Advancement of Colored People (NAACP) asserted that the city had, over a period of three decades, selected sites for subsidized housing in order to perpetuate residential racial segregation. The plaintiffs' theory was that the city had equated subsidized housing for families with minority housing, and thus disproportionately restricted new family housing projects to areas of the city—particularly southwest Yonkers—already predominately populated by minorities."

Litigation ensued and the District Court entered a decree ordering the city to take affirmative steps to remedy the discrimination. While litigation continued, the city delayed implementing provisions of the decree without "obtain[ing] any stay of the District Court's order."

"[P]rovisions of the order specified escalating daily amounts of fines in the event of contempt, and provided that if the legislation were not enacted before August 10, 1988, any councilmember who remained in contempt should be committed to the custody of the United States Marshal for imprisonment. The specified daily fines for the city were $100 for the first day, to be doubled for each consecutive day of noncompliance; the specified daily fine for members of the city council was $500 per day.

Notwithstanding the threat of substantial sanctions, on August 1 the city council defeated a resolution of intent to adopt the legislative package, known as the Affordable Housing Ordinance, by a vote of 4 to 3 (petitioners constituting the majority). On August 2, the District Court held a hearing to afford the city and the councilmembers an opportunity to show cause why they should not be adjudicated in contempt. It rejected the city's arguments, held the city in contempt, and imposed the coercive sanctions set forth in the July 26 order. After questioning the individual councilmembers as to the reasons for their negative votes, the court also held each of the petitioners in contempt and imposed sanctions. . . .

On August 9, the Court of Appeals stayed the contempt sanctions pending appeal. Shortly thereafter, the court affirmed the adjudications of contempt against both the city and the councilmembers, but limited the fines against the city so that they would not exceed $1 million per day. . . .

Both the city and the councilmembers requested [the Supreme] Court to stay imposition of sanctions pending filing and disposition of petitions for certiorari. We granted a stay as to petitioners, but denied the city's request. With the city's contempt sanction approaching $1 million per day, the city council finally enacted the Affordable Housing Ordinance on September 9, 1988, by a vote of 5 to 2, petitioners Spallone and Fagan voting no."

The Supreme Court granted certiorari to review the case and reversed.

B. Counsel of Record / ACLU Attorney

ACLU Side (Respondent / Appellee): Solicitor General Starr argued the cause for appellees in all cases.

Opposing Side (Petitioner / Appellant): James D. Harmon, Jr., argued the cause for appellants in all cases.

III. AMICI CURIAE

ACLU Side (Respondent / Appellee)

Brief of amici curiae filed on behalf of the ACLU, et al., by Steven R. Shapiro, Christopher A. Hansen, John A. Powell, Helen Hershkoff, and Arthur N. Eisenberg.

Opposing Side (Petitioner / Appellant)

Brief of amici curiae filed on behalf of the Save Yonkers Federation, Inc., by Henry Mark Holzer, Daniel J. Popeo, and Paul D. Kamenar.

IV. THE SUPREME COURT'S DECISION

"Petitioners contend that the District Court's order violates their rights to freedom of speech under the First Amendment, and they also contend that they are entitled as legislators to absolute immunity for actions taken in discharge of their legislative responsibilities. We find it unnecessary to reach either of these questions, because we conclude that the portion of the District Court's order of July 26 imposing contempt sanctions against petitioners if they failed to vote in favor of the court-proposed ordinance was an abuse of discretion under traditional equitable principles. . . .

Given that the city had entered a consent judgment committing itself to enact legislation implementing the longterm plan, we certainly cannot say it was an abuse of discretion for the District Court to have chosen contempt sanctions against the city, as opposed to petitioners, as a means of ensuring compliance. The city, as we have noted, was a party to the action from the beginning, had been found liable for numerous statutory and constitutional violations, and had been subjected to various elaborate remedial decrees which had been upheld on appeal. Petitioners, the individual city councilmembers, on the other hand, were not parties to the action, and they had not been found individually liable for any of the violations upon which the remedial decree was based. Although the injunctive portion of that decree was directed not only to the city but to 'its officers, agents, employees, successors and all persons in active concert or participation with any of them,' the remaining parts of the decree ordering affirmative steps were directed only to the city. . . .

We hold that the District Court, in view of the 'extraordinary' nature of the imposition of sanctions against the individual councilmembers, should have proceeded with such contempt sanctions first against the city alone in order to secure compliance with the remedial order. Only if that approach failed to produce compliance within a reasonable time should the question of imposing contempt sanctions against petitioners even have been considered. This limitation accords with the doctrine that a court must exercise '[t]he least possible power adequate to the end proposed.'

The judgment of the Court of Appeals is reversed."

V. JUSTICE VOTE

4 Pro ACLU Side vs. 5 Con Opposing Side

ACLU Side (Respondent / Appellee)

1. Brennan, W. – Wrote dissenting opinion
2. Marshall, T. – Joined Brennan's dissent
3. Blackmun, H. – Joined Brennan's dissent
4. Stevens, J. – Joined Brennan's dissent

Opposing Side (Petitioner / Appellant)

1. Rehnquist, W. – Wrote majority opinion
2. White, B. – Joined majority opinion
3. O'Connor, S. – Joined majority opinion
4. Scalia, A. – Joined majority opinion
5. Kennedy, A. – Joined majority opinion

VI. A WIN OR LOSS FOR THE ACLU?

The ACLU filed as amicus urging affirmance of the judgment of the Court of Appeals; the Supreme Court reversed in a 5-4 vote, giving the ACLU an apparent loss.

692. Jimmy Swaggart Ministries v. Board of Equalization of California

(Decided January 17, 1990; 493 U.S. 378)

I. ISSUE

A. Issues Discussed

First Amendment, Free Exercise Clause, Establishment Clause

B. Legal Question Presented

"[W]hether the Religion Clauses of the First Amendment prohibit a State from imposing a generally applicable sales and use tax on the distribution of religious materials by a religious organization."

C. Supreme Court's Answer

The First Amendment does not prohibit the State from imposing a generally applicable sales and use tax on religious materials distributed by a religious organization.

II. CASE SUMMARY

A. Background

"California's Sales and Use Tax Law requires retailers to pay a sales tax '[f]or the privilege of selling tangible personal property at retail.' . . .

The use tax, as a complement to the sales tax, reaches out-of-state purchases by residents of the State. It is 'imposed on the storage, use, or other consumption in this state of tangible personal property purchased from any retailer,' at the same rate as the sales tax (6 percent). . . . Neither the State Constitution nor the State Sales and Use Tax Law exempts religious organizations from the sales and use tax, apart from a limited exemption for the serving of meals by religious organizations.

During the tax period in question (1974 to 1981), appellant Jimmy Swaggart Ministries was a religious organization . . . . From 1974 to 1981, appellant conducted numerous 'evangelistic crusades' in auditoriums and arenas across the country in cooperation with local churches. During this period, appellant held 23 crusades in California . . . . Some of these services were recorded for later sale or broadcast. Appellant also sold religious books, tapes, records, and other religious and nonreligious merchandise at the crusades.

Appellant also published a monthly magazine, 'The Evangelist,' which was sold nationwide by subscription. . . .

In 1980, appellee Board of Equalization of the State of California (Board) informed appellant that religious materials were not exempt from the sales tax and requested appellant to register as a seller to facilitate reporting and payment of the tax. Appellant responded that it was exempt from such taxes under the First Amendment. . . .

Based on the Board's review of appellant's records, the parties stipulated 'that [appellant] sold for use in California tangible personal property for the period April 1, 1974, through December 31, 1981, measured by payment to [appellant] of $1,702,942.00 for mail order sales from Baton Rouge, Louisiana and $240,560.00 for crusade merchandise sales in California.' These figures represented the sales and use in California of merchandise with specific religious content . . . . Based on the sales figures for appellant's religious materials, the Board notified appellant that it owed sales and use taxes of $118,294.54, plus interest of $36,021.11, and a penalty of $11,829.45, for a total amount due of $166,145.10. Appellant did not contest the Board's assessment of tax liability for the sale and use of certain nonreligious merchandise . . . .

Appellant filed a petition for redetermination with the Board, reiterating its view that the tax on religious materials violated the First Amendment. Following a hearing and an appeal to the Board, the Board deleted the penalty but otherwise redetermined the matter without adjustment in the amount of $118,294.54 in taxes owing, plus $65,043.55 in interest. Pursuant to state procedural law, appellant paid the amount and filed a petition for redetermination and refund with the Board. The Board denied appellant's petition, and appellant brought suit in state court, seeking a refund of the tax paid.

The trial court entered judgment for the Board, ruling that appellant was not entitled to a refund of any tax. The California Court of Appeal affirmed, and the California Supreme Court denied discretionary review."

The Supreme Court granted certiorari to review the case and affirmed.

B. Counsel of Record / ACLU Attorney

ACLU Side (Respondent / Appellee): Richard E. Nielsen, Deputy Attorney General of California, argued the cause for appellee.

Opposing Side (Petitioner / Appellant): Michael W. McConnell argued the cause for appellant.

III. AMICI CURIAE

ACLU Side (Respondent / Appellee)

Brief of amici curiae filed on behalf of the ACLU by Steven R. Shapiro.

Brief of amici curiae filed on behalf of the National Conference of State Legislatures, et al., by Benna Ruth Solomon and Charles Rothfeld.

Opposing Side (Petitioner / Appellant)

Brief of amici curiae filed on behalf of the Association for Public Justice by Bradley P. Jacob.

Brief of amici curiae filed on behalf of the Evangelical Council for Financial Accountability, et al., by Samuel E. Ericsson, Michael J. Woodruff, and Forest D. Montgomery.

Brief of amici curiae filed on behalf of the International Society for Krishna Consciousness of California, Inc., by David M. Liberman, Robert C. Moest, and Barry A. Fisher.

Brief of amici curiae filed on behalf of the National Council of Churches of Christ in the U.S.A. by Douglas Laycock.

Brief of amici curiae filed on behalf of the National Taxpayers Union by Gale A. Norton.

Brief of amici curiae filed on behalf of the Watchtower Bible and Tract Society of New York, Inc., by James M. McCabe and Donald T. Ridley.

IV. THE SUPREME COURT'S DECISION

"There is no evidence in this case that collection and payment of the tax violates appellant's sincere religious beliefs. California's nondiscriminatory Sales and Use Tax Law requires only that appellant collect the tax from its California purchasers and remit the tax money to the State. The only burden on appellant is the claimed reduction in income resulting from the presumably lower demand for appellant's wares (caused by the marginally higher price) and from the costs associated with administering the tax. As the Court made clear in Hernandez, however, to the extent that imposition of a generally applicable tax merely decreases the amount of money appellant has to spend on its religious activities, any such burden is not constitutionally significant. . . .

We therefore conclude that the collection and payment of the generally applicable tax in this case imposes no constitutionally significant burden on appellant's religious practices or beliefs. The Free Exercise Clause accordingly does not require the State to grant appellant an exemption from its generally applicable sales and use tax. Although it is of course possible to imagine that a more onerous tax rate, even if generally applicable, might effectively choke off an adherent's religious practices, we face no such situation in this case. Accordingly, we intimate no views as to whether such a generally applicable tax might violate the Free Exercise Clause.

[B]ecause we find no excessive entanglement between government and religion in this case, we hold that the imposition of sales and use tax liability on appellant does not violate the Establishment Clause.

[W]e conclude that appellant's Commerce Clause and Due Process Clause argument is not properly before us. We thus express no opinion on the merits of the claim.

The judgment of the California Court of Appeal is affirmed."

V. JUSTICE VOTE

9 Pro ACLU Side vs. 0 Con Opposing Side

ACLU Side (Respondent / Appellee)

1. O'Connor, S. – Wrote majority opinion
2. Rehnquist, W. – Joined majority opinion
3. White, B. – Joined majority opinion
4. Scalia, A. – Joined majority opinion
5. Kennedy, A. – Joined majority opinion
6. Brennan, W. – Joined majority opinion
7. Marshall, T. – Joined majority opinion
8. Blackmun, H. – Joined majority opinion
9. Stevens, J. – Joined majority opinion

VI. A WIN OR LOSS FOR THE ACLU?

The ACLU, as amicus curiae, urged affirmance of the judgment of the California Court of Appeal; the Supreme Court affirmed in a 9-0 vote, giving the ACLU an apparent win.

693. Federal Trade Commission v. Superior Court Trial Lawyers Ass'n

(Decided January 22, 1990; 493 U.S. 411)

I. ISSUE

A. Issues Discussed

Antitrust, First Amendment, freedoms of press, speech, and association

B. Legal Question Presented

"Pursuant to a well-publicized plan, a group of lawyers agreed not to represent indigent criminal defendants in the District of Columbia Superior Court until the District of Columbia government increased the lawyers' compensation. The questions presented are whether the lawyers' concerted conduct violated § 5 of the Federal Trade Commission Act and, if so, whether it was nevertheless protected by the First Amendment to the Constitution."

C. Supreme Court's Answer

The conduct violated the Federal Trade Commission Act and was not protected by the First Amendment.

II. CASE SUMMARY

A. Background

"The burden of providing competent counsel to indigent defendants in the District of Columbia is substantial. During 1982, court-appointed counsel represented the defendant in approximately 25,000 cases. In the most serious felony cases, representation was generally provided by full-time employees of the District's Public Defender System (PDS). Less serious felony and misdemeanor cases constituted about 85 percent of the total caseload. In these cases, lawyers in private practice were appointed and compensated pursuant to the District of Columbia Criminal Justice Act (CJA). . . .

Bar organizations began as early as 1975 to express concern about the low fees paid to CJA lawyers. . . . On September 6, 1983, about 90 percent of the CJA regulars refused to accept any new assignments. . . . Within 10 days, the key figures in the District's criminal justice system 'became convinced that the system was on the brink of collapse because of the refusal of CJA lawyers to take on new cases.' On September 15, they hand-delivered a letter to the Mayor describing why the situation was expected to 'reach a crisis point' by early the next week and urging the immediate enactment of a bill increasing all CJA rates to $35 per hour. The Mayor promptly met with members of the strike committee and offered to support an immediate temporary increase to the $35 level as well as a subsequent permanent increase to $45 an hour for out-of-court time and $55 for in-court time.

At noon on September 19, 1983, over 100 CJA lawyers attended an SCTLA meeting and voted to accept the $35 offer and end the boycott. The city council's Judiciary Committee convened at 2 o'clock that afternoon. The committee recommended legislation increasing CJA fees to $35, and the council unanimously passed the bill on September 20. On September 21, the CJA regulars began to accept new assignments and the crisis subsided. . . .

The Federal Trade Commission (FTC) filed a complaint against SCTLA and four of its officers (respondents) alleging that they had 'entered into an agreement among themselves and with other lawyers to restrain trade by refusing to compete for or accept new appointments under the CJA program beginning on September 6, 1983, unless and until the District of Columbia increased the fees offered under the CJA program.' The complaint alleged that virtually all of the attorneys who regularly compete for or accept new appointments under the CJA program had joined the agreement. The FTC characterized respondents' conduct as 'a conspiracy to fix prices and to conduct a boycott' and concluded that they were engaged in 'unfair methods of competition in violation of Section 5 of the Federal Trade Commission Act.'

After a 3-week hearing, the ALJ found that the facts alleged in the complaint had been proved, and rejected each of the respondents' three legal defenses . . . . The ALJ's pragmatic moderation found no favor with the FTC. Like the ALJ, the FTC rejected each of respondents' defenses. . . . The Court of Appeals vacated the FTC order and remanded for a determination whether respondents possessed 'significant market power.'"

The Supreme Court granted certiorari to review the case, reversed in part, and remanded.

B. Counsel of Record / ACLU Attorney

ACLU Side (Petitioner / Appellant): Ernest J. Isenstadt argued the cause for appellant.

Opposing Side (Respondent / Appellee): Willard K. Tom argued the cause for appellee.

III. AMICI CURIAE

ACLU Side (Petitioner / Appellant)

Brief of amici curiae filed on behalf of the ACLU, et al., by William Warfield Ross, Gerald P. Norton, John A. Powell, Arthur B. Spitzer, and Elizabeth Symonds.

Brief of amici curiae filed on behalf of the State of South Dakota, et al., by Roger A. Tellinghuisen, Attorney General of South Dakota, and Jeffrey P. Hallem, Assistant Attorney General; Robert K. Corbin, Attorney General of Arizona; Douglas B. Baily, Attorney General of Alaska; Richard D. Monkman, Assistant Attorney General; Duane Woodard, Attorney General of Colorado; Thomas P. McMahon, First Assistant Attorney General of Delaware; Charles M. Oberly III, Attorney General of Delaware; David G. Culley, Deputy Attorney General of Delaware; Warren Price III, Attorney General of Hawaii; Thomas J. Miller, Attorney General of Iowa; John R. Perkins, Deputy Attorney General Iowa; Robert T. Stephan, Attorney General of Kansas; John W. Campbell, Deputy Attorney General of Kansas; Mark S. Braun, Assistant Attorney General of Kansas; Frederic J. Cowan, Attorney General of Kentucky; James M. Ringo, Assistant Attorney General of Kentucky; William J. Guste, Jr., Attorney General of Louisiana; Anne F. Benoit, Assistant Attorney General of Louisiana; J. Joseph Curran, Jr., Attorney General of Maryland; Michael F. Brockmeyer and Ellen S. Cooper, Assistant Attorneys General of Maryland; Robert M. Spire, Attorney General of Nebraska; Dale A. Comer, Assistant Attorney General of Nebraska; Jim Mattox, Attorney General of Texas; Mary F. Keller, First Assistant Attorney General of Texas; Lou McCreary, Executive Assistant Attorney General of Texas; Allene D. Evans, Assistant Attorney General of Texas; Donald J. Hanaway, Attorney General of Wisconsin; Mark E. Musolf, Deputy Attorney General of Wisconsin; Kevin J. O'Connor and Matthew J. Frank, Assistant Attorneys General of Wisconsin.

Brief of amici curiae filed on behalf of the National Association of Criminal Defense Lawyers by Rick Harris.

Opposing Side (Respondent / Appellee)

Brief of amici curiae filed on behalf of the American Medical Association by Jack R. Bierig and Carter G. Phillips.

Brief of amici curiae filed on behalf of the Washington Council of Lawyers, et al., by Andrew J. Pincus.

IV. THE SUPREME COURT'S DECISION

"As the ALJ, the FTC, and the Court of Appeals all agreed, respondents' boycott 'constituted a classic restraint of trade within the meaning of Section 1 of the Sherman Act.' As such, it also violated the prohibition against unfair methods of competition in § 5 of the FTC Act. Prior to the boycott CJA lawyers were in competition with one another, each deciding independently whether and how often to offer to provide services to the District at CJA rates. The agreement among the CJA lawyers was designed to obtain higher prices for their services and was implemented by a concerted refusal to serve an important customer in the market for legal services and, indeed, the only customer in the market for the particular services that CJA regulars offered. . . .

It is, of course, true that the city purchases respondents' services because it has a constitutional duty to provide representation to indigent defendants. It is likewise true that the quality of representation may improve when rates are increased. Yet neither of these facts is an acceptable justification for an otherwise unlawful restraint of trade. . . .

Respondents' concerted action in refusing to accept further CJA assignments until their fees were increased was thus a plain violation of the antitrust laws. The exceptions derived from Noerr and Claiborne Hardware have no application to respondents' boycott. For these reasons we reject the arguments made by respondents in the cross-petition. . . .

In sum, there is thus nothing unique about the 'expressive component' of respondents' boycott. A rule that requires courts to apply the antitrust laws 'prudently and with sensitivity' whenever an economic boycott has an 'expressive component' would create a gaping hole in the fabric of those laws. Respondents' boycott thus has no special characteristics meriting an exemption from the per se rules of antitrust law. . . .

Of course, some boycotts and some price-fixing agreements are more pernicious than others; some are only partly successful, and some may only succeed when they are buttressed by other causative factors, such as political influence. But an assumption that, absent proof of market power, the boycott disclosed by this record was totally harmless—when overwhelming testimony demonstrated that it almost produced a crisis in the administration of criminal justice in the District and when it achieved its economic goal—is flatly inconsistent with the clear course of our antitrust jurisprudence. Conspirators need not achieve the dimensions of a monopoly, or even a degree of market power any greater than that already disclosed by this record, to warrant condemnation under the antitrust laws. . . .

The judgment of the Court of Appeals is accordingly reversed insofar as that court held the per se rules inapplicable to the lawyers' boycott. The case is remanded for further proceedings consistent with this opinion."

V. JUSTICE VOTE

6 Pro ACLU Side vs. 3 Con Opposing Side

ACLU Side (Petitioner / Appellant)

1. Stevens, J. – Wrote majority opinion
2. Rehnquist, W. – Joined majority opinion
3. White, B. – Joined majority opinion
4. O'Connor, S. – Joined majority opinion
5. Scalia, A. – Joined majority opinion
6. Kennedy, A. – Joined majority opinion

Opposing Side (Respondent / Appellee)

1. Brennan, W. – Wrote opinion concurring in part and dissenting in part
2. Marshall, T. – Joined Brennan's opinion
3. Blackmun, H. – Wrote opinion concurring in part and dissenting in part

VI. A WIN OR LOSS FOR THE ACLU?

The ACLU filed as amicus curiae urging reversal of the judgment of the Court of Appeals; the Supreme Court reversed in part in a 6-3 vote, giving the ACLU an apparent win.

694. Holland v. Illinois

(Decided January 22, 1990; 493 U.S. 474)

I. ISSUE

A. Issues Discussed

Civil rights, race, Sixth Amendment, criminal justice, jury selection

B. Legal Question Presented

"(1) [W]hether a white defendant has standing to raise a Sixth Amendment challenge to the prosecutor's exercise of peremptory challenges to exclude all black potential jurors from his petit jury, and (2) whether such exclusion violates his Sixth Amendment right to trial by an impartial jury."

C. Supreme Court's Answer

The white defendant has standing in this case, however, the exclusion of black jurors through peremptory strikes does not violate his Sixth Amendment rights.

II. CASE SUMMARY

A. Background

"Petitioner Daniel Holland was charged in the Circuit Court of Cook County, Illinois, with aggravated kidnaping, rape, deviate sexual assault, armed robbery, and aggravated battery. According to his allegations, a venire of 30 potential jurors was assembled, 2 of whom were black. Petitioner's counsel objected to those of the State's peremptory challenges that struck the two black venire members from the petit jury, on the ground that petitioner had a Sixth Amendment right to 'be tried by a representative cross section of the community.' The trial judge overruled the objection, and petitioner was subsequently convicted of all except the aggravated battery charge. The convictions were reversed by the Illinois Appellate Court, First District, on grounds that are irrelevant here, but on further appeal by the State were reinstated by the Illinois Supreme Court, which rejected petitioner's Equal Protection Clause and Sixth Amendment challenges to the exclusion of the black jurors."

The Supreme Court granted certiorari to review the case and affirmed.

B. Counsel of Record / ACLU Attorney

ACLU Side (Petitioner / Appellant): Donald S. Honchell argued the cause for appellant.

Opposing Side (Respondent / Appellee): Inge Fryklund argued the cause for appellee.

III. AMICI CURIAE

ACLU Side (Petitioner / Appellant)

Brief of amici curiae filed on behalf of the ACLU, et al., by Steven R. Shapiro, Julius LeVonne Chambers, and Charles Stephen Ralston.

Opposing Side (Respondent / Appellee)

No briefs of amici curiae were filed in support of appellee.

IV. THE SUPREME COURT'S DECISION

"The threshold question is whether petitioner, who is white, has standing to raise a Sixth Amendment challenge to the exclusion of blacks from his jury. We hold that he does. . . .

The rule we announce today is not only the only plausible reading of the text of the Sixth Amendment, but we think it best furthers the Amendment's central purpose as well. Although the constitutional guarantee runs only to the individual and not to the State, the goal it expresses is jury impartiality with respect to both contestants: neither the defendant nor the State should be favored. This goal, it seems to us, would positively be obstructed by a petit jury cross-section requirement which, as we have described, would cripple the device of peremptory challenge. We have acknowledged that that device occupies 'an important position in our trial procedures,' and has indeed been considered 'a necessary part of trial by jury.' Peremptory challenges, by enabling each side to exclude those jurors it believes will be most partial toward the other side, are a means of 'eliminat[ing] extremes of partiality on both sides,' thereby 'assuring the selection of a qualified and unbiased jury.' . . .

Since only the Sixth Amendment claim, and not the equal protection claim, is at issue, the question before us is not whether the defendant has been unlawfully discriminated against because he was white, or whether the excluded jurors have been unlawfully discriminated against because they were black, but whether the defendant has been denied the right to 'trial . . . by an impartial jury.' The earnestness of this Court's commitment to racial justice is not to be measured by its willingness to expand constitutional provisions designed for other purposes beyond their proper bounds.

The judgment of the Illinois Supreme Court is affirmed."

V. JUSTICE VOTE

4 Pro ACLU Side vs. 5 Con Opposing Side

ACLU Side (Petitioner / Appellant)

1. Marshall, T. – Wrote dissenting opinion
2. Brennan, W. – Joined Marshall's dissent
3. Blackmun, H. – Joined Marshall's dissent
4. Stevens, J. – Wrote dissenting opinion

Opposing Side (Respondent / Appellee)

1. Scalia, A. – Wrote majority opinion
2. Rehnquist, W. – Joined majority opinion
3. White, B. – Joined majority opinion
4. O'Connor, S. – Joined majority opinion
5. Kennedy, A. – Wrote concurring opinion

VI. A WIN OR LOSS FOR THE ACLU?

The ACLU filed as amicus curiae urging reversal of the judgment of the Supreme Court of Illinois, the U.S. Supreme Court affirmed in a 5-4 vote, giving the ACLU an apparent loss.

695. Zinermon v. Burch

(Decided February 27, 1990; 494 U.S. 113)

I. ISSUE

A. Issues Discussed

Civil rights, Fourteenth Amendment, remedies

B. Legal Question Presented

Are the allegations in Burch's compliant sufficient to state a claim under 42 U.S.C. § 1983 despite the availability of alternative remedies?

C. Supreme Court's Answer

The allegations are sufficient to state a claim under 42 U.S.C. § 1983.

II. CASE SUMMARY

A. Background

"Respondent Darrell Burch brought this suit under 42 U.S.C. § 1983 against the 11 petitioners, who are physicians, administrators, and staff members at Florida State Hospital (FSH) in Chattahoochee, and others. Respondent alleges that petitioners deprived him of his liberty, without due process of law, by admitting him to FSH as a 'voluntary' mental patient when he was incompetent to give informed consent to his admission. Burch contends that in his case petitioners should have afforded him procedural safeguards required by the Constitution before involuntary commitment of a mentally ill person, and that petitioners' failure to do so violated his due process rights.

Petitioners argue that Burch's complaint failed to state a claim under § 1983 because, in their view, it alleged only a random, unauthorized violation of the Florida statutes governing admission of mental patients. Their argument rests on Parratt v. Taylor, 451 U.S. 527 (1981), where this Court held that a deprivation of a constitutionally protected property interest caused by a state employee's random, unauthorized conduct does not give rise to a § 1983 procedural due process claim, unless the State fails to provide an adequate postdeprivation remedy. The Court in those two cases reasoned that in a situation where the State cannot predict and guard in advance against a deprivation, a postdeprivation tort remedy is all the process the State can be expected to provide, and is constitutionally sufficient.

In the District Court, petitioners did not file an answer to Burch's complaint. They moved, instead, for dismissal under Rule 12(b)(6) of the Federal Rules of Civil Procedure. The court granted that motion, pointing out that Burch did not contend that Florida's statutory procedure for mental health placement was inadequate to ensure due process, but only that petitioners failed to follow the state procedure. Since the State could not have anticipated or prevented this unauthorized deprivation of Burch's liberty, the District Court reasoned, there was no feasible predeprivation remedy, and, under Parratt and Hudson, the State's postdeprivation tort remedies provided Burch with all the process that was due him.

On appeal, an Eleventh Circuit panel affirmed the dismissal . . . . The Court of Appeals, however, upon its own motion, ordered rehearing en banc. On that rehearing, the Eleventh Circuit reversed the District Court and remanded the case."

The Supreme Court granted certiorari to review the case and affirmed.

B. Counsel of Record / ACLU Attorney

ACLU Side (Respondent / Appellee): Richard M. Powers argued the cause for appellee.

Opposing Side (Petitioner / Appellant): Louis F. Hubener, Assistant Attorney General of Florida, argued the cause for appellee.

III. AMICI CURIAE

ACLU Side (Respondent / Appellee)

Brief of amici curiae filed on behalf of the ACLU, et al., by Leon Friedman and Steven R. Shapiro.

Brief of amici curiae filed on behalf of the American Orthopsychiatric Association, et al., by John Townsend Rich, James E. Kaplan, Ruth L. Henning, and Leonard S. Rubenstein.

Opposing Side (Petitioner / Appellant)

No briefs of amici curiae were filed in support of appellant.

IV. THE SUPREME COURT'S DECISION

"We conclude that petitioners cannot escape § 1983 liability by characterizing their conduct as a 'random, unauthorized' violation of Florida law which the State was not in a position to predict or avert, so that all the process Burch could possibly be due is a postdeprivation damages remedy. Burch, according to the allegations of his complaint, was deprived of a substantial liberty interest without either valid consent or an involuntary placement hearing, by the very state officials charged with the power to deprive mental patients of their liberty and the duty to implement procedural safeguards. Such a deprivation is foreseeable, due to the nature of mental illness, and will occur, if at all, at a predictable point in the admission process. Unlike Parratt and Hudson, this case does not represent the special instance of the Mathews due process analysis where postdeprivation process is all that is due because no predeprivation safeguards would be of use in preventing the kind of deprivation alleged.

We express no view on the ultimate merits of Burch's claim; we hold only that his complaint was sufficient to state a claim under § 1983 for violation of his procedural due process rights.

The judgment of the Court of Appeals is affirmed."

V. JUSTICE VOTE

5 Pro ACLU Side vs. 4 Con Opposing Side

ACLU Side (Respondent / Appellee)

1. Blackmun, H. – Wrote majority opinion
2. Brennan, W. – Joined majority opinion
3. White, B. – Joined majority opinion
4. Marshall, T. – Joined majority opinion
5. Stevens, J. – Joined majority opinion

Opposing Side (Petitioner / Appellant)

1. O'Connor, S. – Wrote dissenting opinion
2. Rehnquist, W. – Joined O'Connor's dissent
3. Scalia, A. – Joined O'Connor's dissent
4. Kennedy, A. – Joined O'Connor's dissent

VI. A WIN OR LOSS FOR THE ACLU?

The ACLU filed as amicus curiae urging affirmance of the judgment of the Court of Appeals; the Supreme Court affirmed in a 5-4 vote, giving the ACLU an apparent win.

696. United States v. Verdugo-Urquidez

(Decided February 28, 1990; 494 U.S. 259)

I. ISSUE

A. Issues Discussed

Fourth Amendment, search and seizure

B. Legal Question Presented

"[W]hether the Fourth Amendment applies to the search and seizure by United States agents of property that is owned by a nonresident alien and located in a foreign country."

C. Supreme Court's Answer

The Fourth Amendment does not apply to this search and seizure outside the United States.

II. CASE SUMMARY

A. Background

"Respondent Rene Martin Verdugo–Urquidez is a citizen and resident of Mexico. He is believed by the United States Drug Enforcement Agency (DEA) to be one of the leaders of a large and violent organization in Mexico that smuggles narcotics into the United States. Based on a complaint charging respondent with various narcotics-related offenses, the Government obtained a warrant for his arrest on August 3, 1985. In January 1986, Mexican police officers, after discussions with United States marshals, apprehended Verdugo–Urquidez in Mexico and transported him to the United States Border Patrol station in Calexico, California. There, United States marshals arrested respondent and eventually moved him to a correctional center in San Diego, California, where he remains incarcerated pending trial.

Following respondent's arrest, Terry Bowen, a DEA agent assigned to the Calexico DEA office, decided to arrange for searches of Verdugo–Urquidez's Mexican residences located in Mexicali and San Felipe. Bowen believed that the searches would reveal evidence related to respondent's alleged narcotics trafficking activities and his involvement in the kidnaping and torture-murder of DEA Special Agent Enrique Camarena Salazar (for which respondent subsequently has been convicted in a separate prosecution.). Bowen telephoned Walter White, the Assistant Special Agent in charge of the DEA office in Mexico City, and asked him to seek authorization for the search from the Director General of the Mexican Federal Judicial Police (MFJP). After several attempts to reach high ranking Mexican officials, White eventually contacted the Director General, who authorized the searches and promised the cooperation of Mexican authorities. Thereafter, DEA agents working in concert with officers of the MFJP searched respondent's properties in Mexicali and San Felipe and seized certain documents. In particular, the search of the Mexicali residence uncovered a tally sheet, which the Government believes reflects the quantities of marijuana smuggled by Verdugo–Urquidez into the United States.

The District Court granted respondent's motion to suppress evidence seized during the searches, concluding that the Fourth Amendment applied to the searches and that the DEA agents had failed to justify searching respondent's premises without a warrant. A divided panel of the Court of Appeals for the Ninth Circuit affirmed."

The Supreme Court granted certiorari to review the case and reversed.

B. Counsel of Record / ACLU Attorney

Opposing Side (Petitioner / Appellant): Michael Pancer argued the cause for appellee.

ACLU Side (Respondent / Appellee): Lawrence S. Robbins argued the cause for the United States.

III. AMICI CURIAE

ACLU Side (Respondent / Appellee)

Opposing Side (Petitioner / Appellant)

Brief of amici curiae filed on behalf of the ACLU, et al., by John A. Powell, Paul L. Hoffman, and David D. Cole. Brief of amici curiae filed on behalf of the Criminal Justice Legal Foundation by Kent S. Scheidegger.

IV. THE SUPREME COURT'S DECISION

"The Fourth Amendment . . . prohibits 'unreasonable searches and seizures' whether or not the evidence is sought to be used in a criminal trial, and a violation of the Amendment is 'fully accomplished' at the time of an unreasonable governmental intrusion. For purposes of this case, therefore, if there were a constitutional violation, it occurred solely in Mexico. . . .

What we know of the history of the drafting of the Fourth Amendment . . . suggests that its purpose was to restrict searches and seizures which might be conducted by the United States in domestic matters. . . . There is likewise no indication that the Fourth Amendment was understood by contemporaries of the Framers to apply to activities of the United States directed against aliens in foreign territory or in international waters. . . .

We think that the text of the Fourth Amendment, its history, and our cases discussing the application of the Constitution to aliens and extraterritorially require rejection of respondent's claim. At the time of the search, he was a citizen and resident of Mexico with no voluntary attachment to the United States, and the place searched was located in Mexico. Under these circumstances, the Fourth Amendment has no application.

For better or for worse, we live in a world of nation-states in which our Government must be able to 'functio[n] effectively in the company of sovereign nations.' Some who violate our laws may live outside our borders under a regime quite different from that which obtains in this country. Situations threatening to important American interests may arise half-way around the globe, situations which in the view of the political branches of our Government require an American response with armed force. If there are to be restrictions on searches and seizures which occur incident to such American action, they must be imposed by the political branches through diplomatic understanding, treaty, or legislation.

The judgment of the Court of Appeals is accordingly reversed."

V. JUSTICE VOTE

3 Pro ACLU Side vs. 6 Con Opposing Side

ACLU Side (Respondent / Appellee)

1. Brennan, W. – Wrote dissenting opinion
2. Blackmun, H. – Wrote dissenting opinion
3. Marshall, T. – Joined Brennan's dissent

Opposing Side (Petitioner / Appellant)

1. Rehnquist, W. – Wrote majority opinion
2. Kennedy, A. – Wrote concurring opinion
3. Stevens, J. – Wrote concurring opinion
4. White, B. – Joined majority opinion
5. O'Connor, S. – Joined majority opinion
6. Scalia, A. – Joined majority opinion

VI. A WIN OR LOSS FOR THE ACLU?

The ACLU, as amicus curiae, urged affirmance of the judgment of the Court of Appeals; the Supreme Court reversed in a 6-3 vote, giving the ACLU an apparent loss.

697. Michigan v. Harvey

(Decided March 5, 1990; 494 U.S. 344)

I. ISSUE

A. Issues Discussed

Criminal procedure, right to counsel, Fifth Amendment, Sixth Amendment, impeachment

B. Legal Question Presented

"[W]hether the prosecution may use a statement at trial, taken in violation of the Jackson prophylactic rule to impeach a defendant's false or inconsistent testimony."

C. Supreme Court's Answer

The prosecution may use a statement taken in violation of the Jackson prophylactic rule to impeach a defendant's false or inconsistent testimony.

II. CASE SUMMARY

A. Background

"Respondent Tyris Lemont Harvey was convicted of two counts of first-degree criminal sexual conduct in connection with the rape of Audrey Sharp on June 11, 1986. Harvey was taken into custody on July 2, 1986, and on that date, he made a statement to an investigating officer. He was arraigned later on July 2, and counsel was appointed for him. More than two months later, Harvey told another police officer that he wanted to make a second statement, but did not know whether he should talk to his lawyer. Although the entire context of the discussion is not clear from the record, the officer told respondent that he did not need to speak with his attorney, because 'his lawyer was going to get a copy of the statement anyway.' Respondent then signed a constitutional rights waiver form, on which he initialed the portions advising him of his right to remain silent, his right to have a lawyer present before and during questioning, and his right to have a lawyer appointed for him prior to any questioning. Asked whether he understood his constitutional rights, respondent answered affirmatively. He then gave a statement detailing his version of the events of June 11. . . .

On cross-examination, the prosecutor used Harvey's second statement to the police to impeach his testimony. Before doing so, the prosecutor stipulated that the statement 'was not subject to proper Miranda,' and therefore could not have been used in the case in chief. But because the statement was voluntary, the prosecutor argued that it could be used for impeachment under our decision in Harris v. New York, 401 U.S. 222 (1971). Defense counsel did not object, and the trial court permitted the questioning. The prosecutor then impeached certain of Harvey's statements . . . . The trial judge believed the victim's testimony and found respondent guilty as charged.

The Michigan Court of Appeals reversed the conviction. The court noted that if the second statement had been taken only in violation of the rules announced in Miranda v. Arizona, 384 U.S. 436, (1966), it could have been used to impeach Harvey's testimony. It held, however, that the statement was inadmissible even for impeachment purposes, because it was taken 'in violation of defendant's Sixth Amendment right to counsel.' Because the trial 'involved a credibility contest between defendant and the victim,' the court concluded that the impeachment was not harmless beyond a reasonable doubt. The Michigan Supreme Court denied leave to appeal, three justices dissenting . . . ."

The Supreme Court granted certiorari to review the case and reversed.

B. Counsel of Record / ACLU Attorney

ACLU Side (Respondent / Appellee): Robert M. Morgan argued the cause for appellee.

Opposing Side (Petitioner / Appellant): Timothy A. Baughman argued the cause for appellant.

III. AMICI CURIAE

ACLU Side (Respondent / Appellee)

Brief of amici curiae filed on behalf of the ACLU, et al., by Steven R. Shapiro.

Opposing Side (Petitioner / Appellant)

Brief of amici curiae filed on behalf of the United States by Acting Solicitor General Bryson and Assistant Attorney General Dennis.

IV. THE SUPREME COURT'S DECISION

"There is no reason for a different result in a Jackson case, where the prophylactic rule is designed to ensure voluntary, knowing, and intelligent waivers of the Sixth Amendment right to counsel rather than the Fifth Amendment privilege against self-incrimination or 'right to counsel.' We have mandated the exclusion of reliable and probative evidence for all purposes only when it is derived from involuntary statements. We have never prevented use by the prosecution of relevant voluntary statements by a defendant, particularly when the violations alleged by a defendant relate only to procedural safeguards that are 'not themselves rights protected by the Constitution,' but are instead measures designed to ensure that constitutional rights are protected. In such cases, we have decided that the 'search for truth in a criminal case' outweighs the 'speculative possibility' that exclusion of evidence might deter future violations of rules not compelled directly by the Constitution in the first place. . . .

Respondent and amici assert, alternatively, that the conduct of the police officer who took Harvey's second statement violated the 'core value' of the Sixth Amendment's constitutional guarantee, and under those circumstances, the second statement may not be used even for impeachment purposes. They contend that respondent was affirmatively misled as to his need for counsel, and his purported waiver is therefore invalid. But on the record before us, it is not possible to determine whether Harvey's waiver was knowing and voluntary. The state courts developed no record on that issue, and the Michigan Court of Appeals did not rest its holding on any such determination. . . . The Michigan court made no independent inquiry into whether there had been an otherwise valid waiver of the right to counsel, and respondent's counsel himself conceded that, putting aside the prosecutor's concession, the record is insufficient to determine whether there was a voluntary waiver of Sixth Amendment rights. In short, the issue was never litigated in this case.

Because respondent's counsel did not object at trial to the use of his second statement for impeachment purposes, the State had no occasion to offer evidence to establish that Harvey gave a knowing and voluntary waiver of his right to counsel under traditional standards. On remand, the Michigan courts are free to conduct a hearing on that question. It is the State's burden to show that a waiver is knowing and voluntary, and if all the circumstances in a particular case show that the police have engaged in a course of conduct which would render the waiver involuntary, the burden will not be satisfied. Those facts are not before us, however, and we need not consider the admissibility for impeachment purposes of a voluntary statement obtained in the absence of a knowing and voluntary waiver of the right to counsel.

The judgment of the Michigan Court of Appeals is reversed, and the case is remanded for further proceedings not inconsistent with this opinion."

V. JUSTICE VOTE

4 Pro ACLU Side vs. 5 Con Opposing Side

ACLU Side (Respondent / Appellee)

1. Stevens, J. – Wrote dissenting opinion
2. Brennan, W. – Joined Stevens' dissent
3. Marshall, T. – Joined Stevens' dissent
4. Blackmun, H. – Joined Stevens' dissent

Opposing Side (Petitioner / Appellant)

1. Rehnquist, W. – Wrote majority opinion
2. White, B. – Joined majority opinion
3. O'Connor, S. – Joined majority opinion
4. Scalia, A. – Joined majority opinion
5. Kennedy, A. – Joined majority opinion

VI. A WIN OR LOSS FOR THE ACLU?

The ACLU filed as amicus curiae urging affirmance of the judgment of the Court of Appeals; the Supreme Court reversed in a 5-4 vote, giving the ACLU an apparent loss.

698. Butterworth v. Smith

(Decided March 21, 1990; 494 U.S. 624)

I. ISSUE

A. Issues Discussed

First Amendment, freedom of speech

B. Legal Question Presented

Whether a statute which "prohibits a grand jury witness from ever disclosing testimony which he gave before that body" violates the First Amendment.

C. Supreme Court's Answer

The statute violates the First Amendment.

II. CASE SUMMARY

A. Background

"Respondent was a reporter for the Charlotte Herald-News in Charlotte County, Florida. While writing a series of newspaper articles, he obtained information relevant to alleged improprieties committed by the Charlotte County State Attorney's Office and Sheriff's Department. A special prosecutor appointed to investigate the allegations called respondent to testify before a special grand jury which had been convened as part of the investigation. At the time he testified, respondent was warned by the special prosecutor's staff not to reveal his testimony in any manner, and that such revelation could result in a criminal prosecution . . . .

After the grand jury terminated its investigation, respondent set out to publish a news story—and perhaps a book—about the subject matter of the investigation, a publication which would include respondent's testimony and experiences in dealing with the grand jury. He sued in the United States District Court for the Middle District of Florida, seeking a declaration that [Florida Statute] § 905.27 was an unconstitutional abridgment of speech, and an injunction preventing the State from prosecuting him. The District Court granted summary judgment to the State, holding that Florida was entitled to make the judgment that a permanent and total ban on the disclosure of witness testimony was necessary to the proper functioning of the grand jury, and that 'this is the exceptional case where a severe infringement on rights under the First Amendment is permissible.'

The United States Court of Appeals for the Eleventh Circuit reversed."

The Supreme Court granted certiorari to review the case and affirmed."

B. Counsel of Record / ACLU Attorney

ACLU Side (Respondent / Appellee): Gregg D. Thomas argued the cause for appellee.

Opposing Side (Petitioner / Appellant): George L. Waas, Assistant Attorney General of Florida, argued the cause for appellant.

III. AMICI CURIAE

ACLU Side (Respondent / Appellee)

Brief of amici curiae filed on behalf of the ACLU, et al., by M. David Gelfand, Terry E. Allbritton, James K. Green, and Steven R. Shapiro.

Brief of amici curiae filed on behalf of the Florida Press Association, et al., by Richard J. Ovelmen, Gregg D. Thomas, and Gary B. Pruitt.

Brief of amici curiae filed on behalf of the Reporters Committee for Freedom of the Press, et al., by Jane E. Kirtley, W. Terry Maguire, Richard M. Schmidt, Jr., Robert J. Brinkmann, Robert Litt, James Grossberg, J. Laurent Scharff, and Bruce Sanford.

Opposing Side (Petitioner / Appellant)

Brief of amici curiae filed on behalf of the Florida Prosecuting Attorneys Association by Arthur I. Jacobs.

Brief of amici curiae filed on behalf of the State of Arizona by Robert K. Corbin, Attorney General, Jessica Gifford Funkhouser, and Georgia B. Ellexson.

IV. THE SUPREME COURT'S DECISION

"Historically, the grand jury has served an important role in the administration of criminal justice. . . . At the same time, we have recognized that the invocation of grand jury interests is not 'some talisman that dissolves all constitutional protections.' . . .

When an investigation ends, there is no longer a need to keep information from the targeted individual in order to prevent his escape—that individual presumably will have been exonerated, on the one hand, or arrested or otherwise informed of the charges against him, on the other. There is also no longer a need to prevent the importuning of grand jurors since their deliberations will be over. Similarly, the concern that some witnesses will be deterred from presenting testimony due to fears of retribution is, we think, not advanced by this prohibition; any witness is free not to divulge his own testimony, and that part of the Florida statute which prohibits the witness from disclosing the testimony of another witness remains enforceable under the ruling of the Court of Appeals. . . .

Against the state interests which we have just evaluated must be placed the impact of Florida's prohibition on respondent's ability to make a truthful public statement. The effect is dramatic: before he is called to testify in front of the grand jury, respondent is possessed of information on matters of admitted public concern about which he was free to speak at will. After giving his testimony, respondent believes he is no longer free to communicate this information since it relates to the 'content, gist, or import' of his testimony. The ban extends not merely to the life of the grand jury but into the indefinite future. The potential for abuse of the Florida prohibition, through its employment as a device to silence those who know of unlawful conduct or irregularities on the part of public officials, is apparent.

We agree with the Court of Appeals that the interests advanced by the portion of the Florida statute struck down are not sufficient to overcome respondent's First Amendment right to make a truthful statement of information he acquired on his own. Its judgment is therefore affirmed."

V. JUSTICE VOTE

9 Pro ACLU Side vs. 0 Con Opposing Side

ACLU Side (Respondent / Appellee)

1. Rehnquist, W. – Wrote majority opinion
2. Scalia, A. – Wrote concurring opinion
3. O'Connor, S. – Joined majority opinion
4. Kennedy, A. – Joined majority opinion
5. Brennan, W. – Joined majority opinion
6. Marshall, T. – Joined majority opinion
7. Blackmun, H. – Joined majority opinion
8. Stevens, J. – Joined majority opinion
9. White, B. – Joined majority opinion

VI. A WIN OR LOSS FOR THE ACLU?

The ACLU, as amicus curiae, urged affirmance of the judgment of the Court of Appeals; the Supreme Court affirmed in a 9-0 vote, giving the ACLU an apparent win.

699. Austin v. Michigan Chamber of Commerce

(Decided March 27, 1990; 494 U.S. 652)

I. ISSUE

A. Issues Discussed

First Amendment, freedoms of speech, press, and association, Fourteenth Amendment, equal protection

B. Legal Question Presented

"[W]hether § 54(1) of the Michigan Campaign Finance Act, 1976 Mich.Pub. Acts 388, violates either the First or the Fourteenth Amendment to the Constitution."

C. Supreme Court's Answer

Section 541(1) of the Michigan Campaign Finance Act does not violate the First Amendment or the Fourteenth Amendment.

II. CASE SUMMARY

A. Background

"Section 54(1) of the Michigan Campaign Finance Act prohibits corporations from making contributions and independent expenditures in connection with state candidate elections. The issue before us is only the constitutionality of the State's ban on independent expenditures. The Act defines 'expenditure' as 'a payment, donation, loan, pledge, or promise of payment of money or anything of ascertainable monetary value for goods, materials, services, or facilities in assistance of, or in opposition to, the nomination or election of a candidate.' An expenditure is considered independent if it is 'not made at the direction of, or under the control of, another person and if the expenditure is not a contribution to a committee.' The Act exempts from this general prohibition against corporate political spending any expenditure made from a segregated fund. A corporation may solicit contributions to its political fund only from an enumerated list of persons associated with the corporation.

The Chamber, a nonprofit Michigan corporation, challenges the constitutionality of this statutory scheme. . . . In June 1985 Michigan scheduled a special election to fill a vacancy in the Michigan House of Representatives. Although the Chamber had established and funded a separate political fund, it sought to use its general treasury funds to place in a local newspaper an advertisement supporting a specific candidate. As the Act made such an expenditure punishable as a felony, the Chamber brought suit in District Court for injunctive relief against enforcement of the Act, arguing that the restriction on expenditures is unconstitutional under both the First and the Fourteenth Amendments.

The District Court upheld the statute. The Sixth Circuit reversed, reasoning that the expenditure restrictions as applied to the Chamber, violated the First Amendment."

The Supreme Court granted certiorari to review the case and reversed.

B. Counsel of Record / ACLU Attorney

ACLU Side (Respondent / Appellee): Richard D. McLellan argued the cause for appellee.

Opposing Side (Petitioner / Appellant): Louis J. Caruso, Solicitor General of Michigan, argued the cause for appellant.

III. AMICI CURIAE

ACLU Side (Respondent / Appellee)

Brief of amici curiae filed on behalf of the ACLU by Arthur B. Spitzer, John A. Powell, and Joel M. Gora.

Brief of amici curiae filed on behalf of the American Medical Association, et al., by Michael A. Nemeroff, Carter G. Phillips and Mark D. Hopson.

Brief of amici curiae filed on behalf of the Center for Public Interest Law by Robert C. Fellmeth

Brief of amici curiae filed on behalf of the Washington Legal Foundation, et al., by Daniel J. Popeo and Paul D. Kamenar.

Brief of amici curiae filed on behalf of the National Organization for Women, et al., by Thomas J. Hart and Lena S. Zezulin.

Opposing Side (Petitioner / Appellant)

Brief of amici curiae filed on behalf of the Federal Election Commission by Lawrence M. Noble and Richard B. Bader.

Brief of amici curiae filed on behalf of Common Cause by Roger M. Witten, Carol F. Lee, and Archibald Cox.

IV. THE SUPREME COURT'S DECISION

"To determine whether Michigan's restriction on corporate political expenditures may constitutionally be applied to the Chamber, we must ascertain whether it burdens the exercise of political speech and, if it does, whether it is narrowly tailored to serve a compelling state interest. . . .

Corporate wealth can unfairly influence elections when it is deployed in the form of independent expenditures, just as it can when it assumes the guise of political contributions. We therefore hold that the State has articulated a sufficiently compelling rationale to support its restriction on independent expenditures by corporations. . . .

We next turn to the question whether the Act is sufficiently narrowly tailored to achieve its goal. We find that the Act is precisely targeted to eliminate the distortion caused by corporate spending while also allowing corporations to express their political views. . . .

A valid distinction . . . exists between corporations that are part of the media industry and other corporations that are not involved in the regular business of imparting news to the public. Although the press' unique societal role may not entitle the press to greater protection under the Constitution, it does provide a compelling reason for the State to exempt media corporations from the scope of political expenditure limitations. We therefore hold that the Act does not violate the Equal Protection Clause. . . .

Michigan identified as a serious danger the significant possibility that corporate political expenditures will undermine the integrity of the political process, and it has implemented a narrowly tailored solution to that problem. By requiring corporations to make all independent political expenditures through a separate fund made up of money solicited expressly for political purposes, the Michigan Campaign Finance Act reduces the threat that huge corporate treasuries amassed with the aid of favorable state laws will be used to influence unfairly the outcome of elections. The Michigan Chamber of Commerce does not exhibit the characteristics identified in MCFL that would require the State to exempt it from a generally applicable restriction on independent corporate expenditures. We therefore reverse the decision of the Court of Appeals."

V. JUSTICE VOTE

3 Pro ACLU Side vs. 6 Con Opposing Side

ACLU Side (Respondent / Appellee)

1. Kennedy, A. – Wrote dissenting opinion
2. Scalia, A. – Wrote dissenting opinion, joined Kennedy's dissent
3. O'Connor, S. – Joined Kennedy's dissent

Opposing Side (Petitioner / Appellant)

1. Marshall T. – Wrote majority opinions
2. White, B. – Joined majority opinion
3. Blackmun, H. – Joined majority opinion
4. Rehnquist, W. – Joined majority opinion
5. Stevens, J. – Wrote concurring opinion
6. Brennan, W. – Wrote concurring opinion

VI. A WIN OR LOSS FOR THE ACLU?

The ACLU filed as amicus curiae urging affirmance of the judgment of the Court of Appeals; the Supreme Court reversed in a 6-3 vote, giving the ACLU an apparent loss.

700. Employment Division v. Smith

(Decided April 17, 1990; 494 U.S. 872)

I. ISSUE

A. Issues Discussed

First Amendment, free exercise of religion, drugs

B. Legal Question Presented

"[W]hether the Free Exercise Clause of the First Amendment permits the State of Oregon to include religiously inspired peyote use within the reach of its general criminal prohibition on the use of that drug, and thus permits the State to deny unemployment benefits to persons dismissed from their jobs because of such religiously inspired use."

C. Supreme Court's Answer

The Free Exercise Clause permits the State of Oregon to include religiously inspired peyote use within the reach of its general criminal prohibition on the use of that drug.

II. CASE SUMMARY

A. Background

"Oregon law prohibits the knowing or intentional possession of a 'controlled substance' unless the substance has been prescribed by a medical practitioner. . . . Persons who violate this provision by possessing a controlled substance listed on Schedule I are 'guilty of a Class B felony.' . . . Schedule I contains the drug peyote, a hallucinogen derived from the plant Lophophora williamsii Lemaire.

Respondents Alfred Smith and Galen Black (hereinafter respondents) were fired from their jobs with a private drug rehabilitation organization because they ingested peyote for sacramental purposes at a ceremony of the Native American Church, of which both are members. When respondents applied to petitioner Employment Division (hereinafter petitioner) for unemployment compensation, they were determined to be ineligible for benefits because they had been discharged for work-related 'misconduct.'

The Oregon Court of Appeals reversed that determination, holding that the denial of benefits violated respondents' free exercise rights under the First Amendment.

On appeal to the Oregon Supreme Court, . . . the court concluded that respondents were entitled to payment of unemployment benefits. [The U.S. Supreme Court] granted certiorari.

Before this Court in 1987, petitioner continued to maintain that the illegality of respondents' peyote consumption was relevant to their constitutional claim. We agreed, concluding that 'if a State has prohibited through its criminal laws certain kinds of religiously motivated conduct without violating the First Amendment, it certainly follows that it may impose the lesser burden of denying unemployment compensation benefits to persons who engage in that conduct.' We noted, however, that the Oregon Supreme Court had not decided whether respondents' sacramental use of peyote was in fact proscribed by Oregon's controlled substance law, and that this issue was a matter of dispute between the parties. Being 'uncertain about the legality of the religious use of peyote in Oregon,' we determined that it would not be 'appropriate for us to decide whether the practice is protected by the Federal Constitution.' Accordingly, we vacated the judgment of the Oregon Supreme Court and remanded for further proceedings.

On remand, the Oregon Supreme Court held that respondents' religiously inspired use of peyote fell within the prohibition of the Oregon statute, which 'makes no exception for the sacramental use' of the drug. It then considered whether that prohibition was valid under the Free Exercise Clause, and concluded that it was not. The court therefore reaffirmed its previous ruling that the State could not deny unemployment benefits to respondents for having engaged in that practice."

The U.S. Supreme Court again granted certiorari to review the case and reversed.

B. Counsel of Record / ACLU Attorney

ACLU Side (Respondent / Appellee): Craig J. Dorsay argued the cause for appellee.

Opposing Side (Petitioner / Appellant): Dave Frohnmayer, Attorney General of Oregon, argued the cause for appellant.

III. AMICI CURIAE

ACLU Side (Respondent / Appellee)

Brief of amici curiae filed on behalf of the ACLU, et al., by Steven R. Shapiro and John A. Powell.

Brief of amici curiae filed on behalf of the American Jewish Congress by Amy Adelson, Lois C. Waldman, and Marc D. Stern.

Brief of amici curiae filed on behalf of the Association on American Indian Affairs, et al., by Steven C. Moore and Jack Trope.

Brief of amici curiae filed on behalf of the Council on Religious Freedom by Lee Boothby and Robert W. Nixon.

Opposing Side (Petitioner / Appellant)

No briefs of amici curiae were filed in support of appellant.

IV. THE SUPREME COURT'S DECISION

"Now that the Oregon Supreme Court has confirmed that Oregon does prohibit the religious use of peyote, we proceed to consider whether that prohibition is permissible under the Free Exercise Clause. . . .

We have never held that an individual's religious beliefs excuse him from compliance with an otherwise valid law prohibiting conduct that the State is free to regulate. On the contrary, the record of more than a century of our free exercise jurisprudence contradicts that proposition. . . .

There being no contention that Oregon's drug law represents an attempt to regulate religious beliefs, the communication of religious beliefs, or the raising of one's children in those beliefs, the rule to which we have adhered ever since Reynolds plainly controls. 'Our cases do not at their farthest reach support the proposition that a stance of conscientious opposition relieves an objector from any colliding duty fixed by a democratic government.' . . .

Values that are protected against government interference through enshrinement in the Bill of Rights are not thereby banished from the political process. Just as a society that believes in the negative protection accorded to the press by the First Amendment is likely to enact laws that affirmatively foster the dissemination of the printed word, so also a society that believes in the negative protection accorded to religious belief can be expected to be solicitous of that value in its legislation as well. It is therefore not surprising that a number of States have made an exception to their drug laws for sacramental peyote use. But to say that a nondiscriminatory religious-practice exemption is permitted, or even that it is desirable, is not to say that it is constitutionally required, and that the appropriate occasions for its creation can be discerned by the courts. It may fairly be said that leaving accommodation to the political process will place at a relative disadvantage those religious practices that are not widely engaged in; but that unavoidable consequence of democratic government must be preferred to a system in which each conscience is a law unto itself or in which judges weigh the social importance of all laws against the centrality of all religious beliefs. . . .

Because respondents' ingestion of peyote was prohibited under Oregon law, and because that prohibition is constitutional, Oregon may, consistent with the Free Exercise Clause, deny respondents unemployment compensation when their dismissal results from use of the drug. The decision of the Oregon Supreme Court is accordingly reversed."

V. JUSTICE VOTE

3 Pro ACLU Side vs. 6 Con Opposing Side

ACLU Side (Respondent / Appellee)

1. Blackmun, H. – Wrote dissenting opinion, joined O'Connor's opinion in part
2. Brennan, W. – Joined Blackmun's dissent, joined O'Connor's opinion in part
3. Marshall, T. – Joined Blackmun's dissent, joined O'Connor's opinion in part

Opposing Side (Petitioner / Appellant)

1. Scalia, A. – Wrote majority opinion
2. O'Connor, S. – Wrote concurring opinion
3. Rehnquist, W. – Joined majority opinion
4. Stevens, J. – Joined majority opinion
5. Kennedy, A. – Joined majority opinion
6. White, B. – Joined majority opinion

VI. A WIN OR LOSS FOR THE ACLU?

The ACLU, as amicus curiae, urged affirmance of the judgment of the Supreme Court of Oregon; the U.S. Supreme Court reversed in a 6-3 vote, giving the ACLU an apparent loss.

701. Keller v. State Bar of California

(Decided June 4, 1990; 496 U.S. 1)

I. ISSUE

A. Issues Discussed

First Amendment, freedoms of speech and association

B. Legal Question Presented

Whether the use of State Bar of California "membership dues to finance certain ideological or political activities to which [members] were opposed violated [the members'] rights under the First Amendment of the United States Constitution."

C. Supreme Court's Answer

The use of bar membership dues for certain ideological or political activities violates the First Amendment rights of members.

II. CASE SUMMARY

A. Background

"The State Bar is an organization created under California law to regulate the State's legal profession. [M]embership and dues are required as a condition of practicing law in [the] State. . . . The association performs a variety of functions such as 'examining applicants for admission, formulating rules of professional conduct, disciplining members for misconduct, preventing unlawful practice of the law, and engaging in study and recommendation of changes in procedural law and improvement of the administration of justice.' Respondent also engages in a number of other activities which are the subject of the dispute in this case. '[T]he State Bar for many years has lobbied the Legislature and other governmental agencies, filed amicus curiae briefs in pending cases, held an annual conference of delegates at which issues of current interest are debated and resolutions approved, and engaged in a variety of education programs.' These activities are financed principally through the use of membership dues.

Petitioners, 21 members of the State Bar, sued in state court claiming that through these activities respondent expends mandatory dues payments to advance political and ideological causes to which they do not subscribe. Asserting that their compelled financial support of such activities violates their First and Fourteenth Amendment rights to freedom of speech and association, petitioners requested, inter alia, an injunction restraining respondent from using mandatory bar dues or the name of the State Bar to advance political and ideological causes or beliefs. The trial court granted summary judgment to respondent on the grounds that it is a governmental agency and therefore permitted under the First Amendment to engage in the challenged activities. The California Court of Appeal reversed . . . .

The Supreme Court of California reversed the Court of Appeal by a divided vote. The court reasoned that respondent's status as a public corporation, as well as certain of its other characteristics, made it a 'government agency.' It also expressed its belief that subjecting respondent's activities to First Amendment scrutiny would place an 'extraordinary burden' on its mission to promote the administration of justice. . . . The court concluded that 'the State Bar, considered as a government agency, may use dues for any purpose within the scope of its statutory authority.' With the exception of certain election campaigning conducted by respondent and its president, the court found that all of respondent's challenged activities fell within its statutory authority."

The U.S. Supreme Court granted certiorari to review the case and reversed.

B. Counsel of Record / ACLU Attorney

ACLU Side (Petitioner / Appellant): Anthony T. Caso argued the cause for appellant.

Opposing Side (Respondent / Appellee): Seth M. Hufstedler argued the cause for appellee.

III. AMICI CURIAE

ACLU Side (Petitioner / Appellant)

Brief of amici curiae filed on behalf of the ACLU by Steven R. Shapiro and John A. Powell.

Brief of amici curiae filed on behalf of the Ad Hoc Committee Opposing Lobbying and Certain Other Activities of a Mandatory Bar by James J. Bierbower.

Brief of amici curiae filed on behalf of the National Right to Work Legal Defense Foundation by Edwin Vieira.

Brief of amici curiae filed on behalf of the Washington Legal Foundation, et al., by Daniel J. Popeo, Paul D. Kamenar, and John C. Scully.

Brief of amici curiae filed on behalf of Robert E. Gibson by Herbert R. Kraft.

Brief of amici curiae filed by Trayton L. Lathrop, pro se.

Brief of amici curiae filed by Joseph W. Little, pro se.

Brief of amici curiae filed by Steven Levine, pro se.

Opposing Side (Respondent / Appellee)

Briefs of amici curiae urging affirmance were filed for the American Bar Association by L. Stanley Chauvin, Jr., Carter G. Phillips, and Mark D. Hopson;

Brief of amici curiae filed on behalf of the American Federation of Labor and Congress of Industrial Organizations by Marsha S. Berzon and Laurence Gold.

Brief of amici curiae filed on behalf of the Beverly Hills Bar Association, et al., by Ellis J. Horvitz and Peter Abrahams.

Brief of amici curiae filed on behalf of the California Legislature by Bion M. Gregory.

Brief of amici curiae filed on behalf of the Lawyers' Committee for the Administration of Justice by James J. Brosnahan.

Brief of amici curiae filed on behalf of the State Bar of Michigan, et al., by Michael Franck and Michael J. Karwoski.

Brief of amici curiae filed on behalf of the State Bar of Wisconsin, et al., by John S. Skilton, Barry S. Richard, and Stephen L. Tober.

IV. THE SUPREME COURT'S DECISION

A. "The State Bar of California was created, not to participate in the general government of the State, but to provide specialized professional advice to those with the ultimate responsibility of governing the legal profession. Its members and officers are such not because they are citizens or voters, but because they are lawyers. We think that these differences between the State Bar, on the one hand, and traditional government agencies and officials, on the other hand, render unavailing respondent's argument that it is not subject to the same constitutional rule with respect to the use of compulsory dues as are labor unions representing public and private employees.

[T]he guiding standard must be whether the challenged expenditures are necessarily or reasonably incurred for the purpose of regulating the legal profession or 'improving the quality of the legal service available to the people of the State.'

The Supreme Court of California decided that most of the activities complained of by petitioners were within the scope of the State Bar's statutory authority and were therefore not only permissible but could be supported by the compulsory dues of objecting members. The Supreme Court of California quoted the language of the relevant statute to the effect that the State Bar was authorized to 'aid in all matters pertaining to the advancement of the science of jurisprudence or to the improvement of the administration of justice.' Simply putting this language alongside our previous discussion of the extent to which the activities of the State Bar may be financed from compulsory dues might suggest that there is little difference between the two. But there is a difference, and that difference is illustrated by the allegations in petitioners' complaint as to the kinds of State Bar activities which the Supreme Court of California has now decided may be funded with compulsory dues.

Petitioners assert that the State Bar has engaged in, inter alia, lobbying for or against state legislation (1) prohibiting state and local agency employers from requiring employees to take polygraph tests; (2) prohibiting possession of armor-piercing handgun ammunition; (3) creating an unlimited right of action to sue anybody causing air pollution; and (4) requesting Congress to refrain from enacting a guest-worker program or from permitting the importation of workers from other countries. Petitioners' complaint also alleges that the conference of delegates funded and sponsored by the State Bar endorsed a gun control initiative, disapproved statements of a United States senatorial candidate regarding court review of a victim's bill of rights, endorsed a nuclear weapons freeze initiative, and opposed federal legislation limiting federal-court jurisdiction over abortions, public school prayer, and busing.

Precisely where the line falls between those State Bar activities in which the officials and members of the Bar are acting essentially as professional advisers to those ultimately charged with the regulation of the legal profession, on the one hand, and those activities having political or ideological coloration which are not reasonably related to the advancement of such goals, on the other, will not always be easy to discern. But the extreme ends of the spectrum are clear: Compulsory dues may not be expended to endorse or advance a gun control or nuclear weapons freeze initiative; at the other end of the spectrum petitioners have no valid constitutional objection to their compulsory dues being spent for activities connected with disciplining members of the Bar or proposing ethical codes for the profession. . . .

The judgment of the Supreme Court of California is reversed, and the case is remanded for further proceedings not inconsistent with this opinion."

V. JUSTICE VOTE

9 Pro ACLU Side vs. 0 Con Opposing Side

ACLU Side (Petitioner / Appellant)

1. Rehnquist, W. – Wrote majority opinion
2. White, B. – Joined majority opinion
3. Blackmun, H. – Joined majority opinion
4. Stevens, J. – Joined majority opinion
5. O'Connor, S. – Joined majority opinion
6. Scalia, A. – Joined majority opinion
7. Kennedy, A. – Joined majority opinion
8. Marshall, T. – Joined majority opinion
9. Brennan, W. – Joined majority opinion

VI. A WIN OR LOSS FOR THE ACLU?

The ACLU, as amicus curiae, urged reversal of the judgment of the Supreme Court of California; the U.S. Supreme Court reversed and remanded in a 9-0 vote, giving the ACLU an apparent win.

702. Illinois v. Perkins

(Decided June 4, 1990; 496 U.S. 292)

I. ISSUE

A. Issues Discussed

Miranda warnings, self-incrimination

B. Legal Question Presented

"[W]hether an undercover law enforcement officer must give Miranda warnings to an incarcerated suspect before asking him questions that may elicit an incriminating response."

C. Supreme Court's Answer

An undercover law enforcement officer is not required to give Miranda warnings before asking questions that may elicit an incriminating response.

II. CASE SUMMARY

A. Background

"On November 1984, Richard Stephenson was murdered in a suburb of East St. Louis, Illinois. The murder remained unsolved until March 1986, when one Donald Charlton told police that he had learned about a homicide from a fellow inmate at the Graham Correctional Facility, where Charlton had been serving a sentence for burglary. The fellow inmate was Lloyd Perkins, who is the respondent here. Charlton told police that, while at Graham, he had befriended respondent, who told him in detail about a murder that respondent had committed in East St. Louis. On hearing Charlton's account, the police recognized details of the Stephenson murder that were not well known, and so they treated Charlton's story as a credible one.

By the time the police heard Charlton's account, respondent had been released from Graham, but police traced him to a jail in Montgomery County, Illinois, where he was being held pending trial on a charge of aggravated battery, unrelated to the

Stephenson murder. The police wanted to investigate further respondent's connection to the Stephenson murder, but feared that the use of an eavesdropping device would prove impracticable and unsafe. They decided instead to place an undercover agent in the cellblock with respondent and Charlton. The plan was for Charlton and undercover agent John Parisi to pose as escapees from a work release program who had been arrested in the course of a burglary. Parisi and Charlton were instructed to engage respondent in casual conversation and report anything he said about the Stephenson murder.

Parisi, using the alias 'Vito Bianco,' and Charlton, both clothed in jail garb, were placed in the cellblock with respondent at the Montgomery County jail. The cellblock consisted of 12 separate cells that opened onto a common room. Respondent greeted Charlton who, after a brief conversation with respondent, introduced Parisi by his alias. Parisi told respondent that he 'wasn't going to do any more time' and suggested that the three of them escape. Respondent replied that the Montgomery County jail was 'rinky-dink' and that they could 'break out.' The trio met in respondent's cell later that evening, after the other inmates were asleep, to refine their plan. Respondent said that his girlfriend could smuggle in a pistol. Charlton said: 'Hey, I'm not a murderer, I'm a burglar. That's your guys' profession.' After telling Charlton that he would be responsible for any murder that occurred, Parisi asked respondent if he had ever 'done' anybody. Respondent said that he had and proceeded to describe at length the events of the Stephenson murder. Parisi and respondent then engaged in some casual conversation before respondent went to sleep. Parisi did not give respondent Miranda warnings before the conversations.

Respondent was charged with the Stephenson murder. Before trial, he moved to suppress the statements made to Parisi in the jail. The trial court granted the motion to suppress, and the State appealed. The Appellate Court of Illinois affirmed, holding that Miranda v. Arizona prohibits all undercover contacts with incarcerated suspects that are reasonably likely to elicit an incriminating response."

The Supreme Court granted certiorari to review the case and reversed.

B. Counsel of Record / ACLU Attorney

ACLU Side (Respondent / Appellee): Dan W. Evers, by appointment of the Court, argued the cause for appellee.

Opposing Side (Petitioner / Appellant): Marcia L. Friedl, Assistant Attorney General of Illinois, argued the cause for appellant.

Paul J. Larkin, Jr., argued the cause for the United State, as amicus curiae, by special leave of Court.

III. AMICI CURIAE

ACLU Side (Respondent / Appellee)

Brief of amici curiae filed on behalf of the ACLU, et al., by John A. Powell, William B. Rubenstein, and Harvey Grossman.

Opposing Side (Petitioner / Appellant)

Brief of amici curiae filed on behalf of the United States by Paul J. Larkin, Jr., Solicitor General Starr, Assistant Attorney General Dennis, and Deputy Solicitor General Bryson.

Brief of amici curiae filed on behalf of Americans for Effective Law Enforcement, Inc., et al., by Gregory U. Evans, Daniel B. Hales, George D. Webster, Jack E. Yelverton, Fred E. Inbau, Wayne W. Schmidt, Bernard J. Farber, and James P. Manak.

Brief of amici curiae filed on behalf of the Lincoln Legal Foundation, et al., by Joseph A. Morris, Donald D. Bernardi, Fred L. Foreman, Daniel M. Harrod, and Jack E. Yelverton.

IV. THE SUPREME COURT'S DECISION

"Conversations between suspects and undercover agents do not implicate the concerns underlying Miranda. The essential ingredients of a 'police-dominated atmosphere' and compulsion are not present when an incarcerated person speaks freely to someone whom he believes to be a fellow inmate. Coercion is determined from the perspective of the suspect. When a suspect considers himself in the company of cellmates and not officers, the coercive atmosphere is lacking. There is no empirical basis for the assumption that a suspect speaking to those whom he assumes are not officers will feel compelled to speak by the fear of reprisal for remaining silent or in the hope of more lenient treatment should he confess. . . .

Miranda forbids coercion, not mere strategic deception by taking advantage of a suspect's misplaced trust in one he supposes to be a fellow prisoner. As we recognized in Miranda: '[C]onfessions remain a proper element in law enforcement. Any statement given freely and voluntarily without any compelling influences is, of course, admissible in evidence.' Ploys to mislead a suspect or lull him into a false sense of security that do not rise to the level of compulsion or coercion to speak are not within Miranda's concerns. . . .

Respondent can seek no help from his argument that a bright-line rule for the application of Miranda is desirable. Law enforcement officers will have little difficulty putting into practice our holding that undercover agents need not give Miranda warnings to incarcerated suspects. The use of undercover agents is a recognized law enforcement technique, often employed in the prison context to detect violence against correctional officials or inmates, as well as for the purposes served here. The interests protected by Miranda are not implicated in these cases, and the warnings are not required to safeguard the constitutional rights of inmates who make voluntary statements to undercover agents.

We hold that an undercover law enforcement officer posing as a fellow inmate need not give Miranda warnings to an incarcerated suspect before asking questions that may elicit an incriminating response. The statements at issue in this case were voluntary, and there is no federal obstacle to their admissibility at trial. We now reverse and remand for proceedings not inconsistent with our opinion."

V. JUSTICE VOTE

1 Pro ACLU Side vs. 8 Con Opposing Side

ACLU Side (Respondent / Appellee)

1. Marshall, T. – Wrote dissenting opinion

Opposing Side (Petitioner / Appellant)

1. Kennedy, A. – Wrote majority opinion
2. Rehnquist, W. – Joined majority opinion
3. White, B. – Joined majority opinion
4. Blackmun, H. – Joined majority opinion
5. Stevens, J. – Joined majority opinion
6. O'Connor, S. – Joined majority opinion
7. Scalia, A. – Joined majority opinion
8. Brennan, W. – Wrote concurring opinion

VI. A WIN OR LOSS FOR THE ACLU?

The ACLU, as amicus curiae, urged affirmance of the judgment of the Appellate Court of Illinois; the Supreme Court reversed in an 8-1 vote, giving the ACLU an apparent loss.

703. United States v. Eichman

(Decided June 11, 1990; 496 U.S. 310)

I. ISSUE

A. Issues Discussed

First Amendment, flag burning

B. Legal Question Presented

"[W]hether appellees' prosecution for burning a United States flag in violation of the Flag Protection Act of 1989 is consistent with the First Amendment."

C. Supreme Court's Answer

The Flag Protection Act of 1989 is not consistent with the First Amendment.

II. CASE SUMMARY

A. Background

"In No. 89-1433, the United States prosecuted certain appellees for violating the Flag Protection Act of 1989, 103 Stat. 777, 18 U.S.C. § 700 (1988 ed. and Supp. I), by knowingly setting fire to several United States flags on the steps of the United States Capitol while protesting various aspects of the Government's domestic and foreign policy. In No. 89-1434, the United States prosecuted other appellees for violating the Act by knowingly setting fire to a United States flag in Seattle while protesting the Act's passage. In each case, the respective appellees moved to dismiss the flag-burning charge on the ground that the Act, both on its face and as applied, violates the First Amendment. Both the United States District Court for the Western District of Washington, and the United States District Court for the District of Columbia, following Johnson, supra, held the Act unconstitutional as applied to appellees and dismissed the charges."

The Supreme Court granted certiorari in both cases, consolidated the cases for review, and affirmed.

B. Counsel of Record / ACLU Attorney

ACLU Side (Respondent / Appellee): William M. Kunstler argued the cause for appellee.

Opposing Side (Petitioner / Appellant): Solicitor General Starr argued the cause for the United States.

III. AMICI CURIAE

ACLU Side (Respondent / Appellee)

Brief of amici curiae filed on behalf of the ACLU, et al., by Charles Fried, Kathleen M. Sullivan. Norman Dorsen, and Steven R. Shapiro.

Brief of amici curiae filed on behalf of the Association of Art Museum Directors, et al., by James C. Goodale.

Brief of amici curiae filed on behalf of the National Association for the Advancement of Colored People by Charles E. Carter.

Brief of amici curiae filed on behalf of People for the American Way, et al., by Timothy B. Dyk, Glen D. Nager, and Elliot M. Mincberg.

Brief of amici curiae filed on behalf of Jasper Johns, et al., by Robert G. Sugarman and Gloria C. Phares.

Opposing Side (Petitioner / Appellant)

Brief of amici curiae filed on behalf of the United States Senate by Michael Davidson, Ken U. Benjamin, Jr., and Morgan J. Frankel.

Brief of amici curiae filed on behalf of Senator Joseph R. Biden, Jr., by Kenneth S. Geller, Andrew J. Pincus, and Roy T. Englert, Jr.

Brief of amici curiae filed on behalf of Governor Mario M. Cuomo by Evan A. Davis.

Brief of amici curiae filed on behalf of the Southeastern Legal Foundation, Inc., by Robert L. Barr, Jr., and G. Stephen Parker.

Brief of amici curiae filed on behalf of the Speaker and Leadership Group of the United States House of Representatives by Steven R. Ross, Charles Tiefer, Michael L. Murray, Janina Jaruzelski, and Robert Michael Long.

IV. THE SUPREME COURT'S DECISION

"Last Term in Johnson, we held that a Texas statute criminalizing the desecration of venerated objects, including the United States flag, was unconstitutional as applied to an individual who had set such a flag on fire during a political demonstration. . . . After our decision in Johnson, Congress passed the Flag Protection Act of 1989. . . .

Although the Flag Protection Act contains no explicit content-based limitation on the scope of prohibited conduct, it is nevertheless clear that the Government's asserted interest is 'related 'to the suppression of free expression," and concerned with the content of such expression. The Government's interest in protecting the 'physical integrity' of a privately owned flag rests upon a perceived need to preserve the flag's status as a symbol of our Nation and certain national ideals. But the mere destruction or disfigurement of a particular physical manifestation of the symbol, without more, does not diminish or otherwise affect the symbol itself in any way. . . .

Government may create national symbols, promote them, and encourage their respectful treatment. But the Flag Protection Act of 1989 goes well beyond this by criminally proscribing expressive conduct because of its likely communicative impact.

We are aware that desecration of the flag is deeply offensive to many. But the same might be said, for example, of virulent ethnic and religious epithets, vulgar repudiations of the draft, and scurrilous caricatures. 'If there is a bedrock principle underlying the First Amendment, it is that the Government may not prohibit the expression of an idea simply because society finds the idea itself offensive or disagreeable.' Punishing desecration of the flag dilutes the very freedom that makes this emblem so revered, and worth revering. The judgments of the District Courts are affirmed."

V. JUSTICE VOTE

5 Pro ACLU Side vs. 4 Con Opposing Side

ACLU Side (Respondent / Appellee)

1. Brennan, W. – Wrote majority opinion
2. Marshall, T. – Joined majority opinion
3. Blackmun, H. – Joined majority opinion
4. Scalia, A. – Joined majority opinion
5. Kennedy, A. – Joined majority opinion

Opposing Side (Petitioner / Appellant)

1. Stevens, J. – Wrote dissenting opinion
2. White, B. – Joined Stevens' dissent
3. Rehnquist, W. – Joined Stevens' dissent
4. O'Connor, S. – Joined Stevens' dissent

VI. A WIN OR LOSS FOR THE ACLU?

The ACLU, as amicus curiae, urged affirmance of the judgments below; the Supreme Court affirmed in a 5-4 vote, giving the ACLU an apparent win.

704. Alabama v. White

(Decided June 11, 1990; 496 U.S. 325)

I. ISSUE

A. Issues Discussed

Criminal justice, drugs, Fourth Amendment, search and seizure

B. Legal Question Presented

"[W]hether [an anonymous] tip, as corroborated by independent police work, exhibited sufficient indicia of reliability to provide reasonable suspicion to make the investigatory stop."

C. Supreme Court's Answer

The tip, as corroborated, established reasonable suspicion for the investigatory stop of respondent's vehicle.

II. CASE SUMMARY

A. Background

"On April 22, 1987, at approximately 3 p.m., Corporal B.H. Davis of the Montgomery Police Department received a telephone call from an anonymous person, stating that Vanessa White would be leaving 235–C Lynwood Terrace Apartments at a particular time in a brown Plymouth station wagon with the right taillight lens broken, that she would be going to Dobey's Motel, and that she would be in possession of about an ounce of cocaine inside a brown attaché case. Corporal Davis and his partner, Corporal P. A. Reynolds, proceeded to the Lynwood Terrace Apartments. The officers saw a brown Plymouth station wagon with a broken right taillight in the parking lot in front of the 235 building. The officers observed respondent leave the 235 building, carrying nothing in her hands, and enter the station wagon. They followed the vehicle as it drove the most direct route to Dobey's Motel. When the vehicle reached the Mobile Highway, on which Dobey's Motel is located, Corporal Reynolds requested a patrol unit to stop the vehicle. The vehicle was stopped at approximately 4:18 p.m., just short of Dobey's Motel. Corporal Davis asked respondent to step to the rear of her car, where he informed her that she had been stopped because she was suspected of carrying cocaine in the vehicle. He asked if they could look for cocaine, and respondent said they could look. The officers found a locked brown attaché case in the car, and, upon request, respondent provided the combination to the lock. The officers found marijuana in the attaché case and placed respondent under arrest. During processing at the station, the officers found three milligrams of cocaine in respondent's purse.

Respondent was charged in Montgomery County Court with possession of marijuana and possession of cocaine. The trial court denied respondent's motion to suppress, and she pleaded guilty to the charges, reserving the right to appeal the denial of her suppression motion. The Court of Criminal Appeals of Alabama held that the officers did not have the reasonable suspicion necessary under Terry v. Ohio, 392 U.S. 1 (1968), to justify the investigatory stop of respondent's car, and that the marijuana and cocaine were fruits of respondent's unconstitutional detention. The court concluded that respondent's motion to dismiss should have been granted and reversed her conviction. The Supreme Court of Alabama denied the State's petition for writ of certiorari, two justices dissenting."

The U.S. Supreme Court granted certiorari to review the case and reversed.

B. Counsel of Record / ACLU Attorney

ACLU Side (Respondent / Appellee): David B. Byrne, Jr., by appointment of the Court, argued the cause for appellee.

Opposing Side (Petitioner / Appellant): Joseph G. L. Marston III, Assistant Attorney General of Alabama, argued the cause for appellant.

III. AMICI CURIAE

ACLU Side (Respondent / Appellee)

Brief of amici curiae filed on behalf of the ACLU, et al., by Steven R. Shapiro and David I. Schoen.

Opposing Side (Petitioner / Appellant)

Brief of amici curiae filed on behalf of Americans for Effective Law Enforcement, Inc., et al., by Gregory U. Evans, Daniel B. Hales, Joseph A. Morris, George D. Webster, Fred E. Inbau, Wayne W. Schmidt, Bernard J. Farber, William K. Lambie, and James P. Manak.

IV. THE SUPREME COURT'S DECISION

"Illinois v. Gates dealt with an anonymous tip in the probable-cause context. The Court there abandoned the "two-pronged test" of Aguilar v. Texas and Spinelli v. United States in favor of a "totality of the circumstances" approach to determining whether an informant's tip establishes probable cause. Gates made clear, however, that those factors that had been considered critical under Aguilar and Spinelli—an informant's 'veracity,' 'reliability,' and 'basis of knowledge'—remain 'highly relevant in determining the value of his report.' These factors are also relevant in the reasonable-suspicion context, although allowance must be made in applying them for the lesser showing required to meet that standard. . . .

As there was in Gates, however, in this case there is more than the tip itself. The tip was not as detailed, and the corroboration was not as complete, as in Gates, but the required degree of suspicion was likewise not as high. . . . Reasonable suspicion is a less demanding standard than probable cause not only in the sense that reasonable suspicion can be established with information that is different in quantity or content than that required to establish probable cause, but also in the sense that reasonable suspicion can arise from information that is less reliable than that required to show probable cause. . . . We there assumed that the unverified tip from the known informant might not have been reliable enough to establish probable cause, but nevertheless found it sufficiently reliable to justify a Terry stop. . . .

It is true that not every detail mentioned by the tipster was verified, such as the name of the woman leaving the building or the precise apartment from which she left; but the officers did corroborate that a woman left the 235 building and got into the particular vehicle that was described by the caller. With respect to the time of departure predicted by the informant, Corporal Davis testified that the caller gave a particular time when the woman would be leaving, but he did not state what that time was. He did testify that, after the call, he and his partner proceeded to the Lynwood Terrace Apartments to put the 235 building under surveillance. Given the fact that the officers proceeded to the indicated address immediately after the call and that respondent emerged not too long thereafter, it appears from the record before us that respondent's departure from the building was within the time frame predicted by the caller. As for the caller's prediction of respondent's destination, it is true that the officers stopped her just short of Dobey's Motel and did not know whether she would have pulled in or continued past it. But given that the 4-mile route driven by respondent was the most direct route possible to Dobey's Motel . . . we think respondent's destination was significantly corroborated. . . .

When significant aspects of the caller's predictions were verified, there was reason to believe not only that the caller was honest but also that he was well informed, at least well enough to justify the stop.

Although it is a close case, we conclude that under the totality of the circumstances the anonymous tip, as corroborated, exhibited sufficient indicia of reliability to justify the investigatory stop of respondent's car. We therefore reverse the judgment of the Court of Criminal Appeals of Alabama and remand the case for further proceedings not inconsistent with this opinion."

V. JUSTICE VOTE

3 Pro ACLU Side vs. 6 Con Opposing Side

ACLU Side (Respondent / Appellee)

1. Stevens, J. – Wrote dissenting opinion
2. Brennan, W. – Joined Stevens' dissent
3. Marshall, T. – Joined Stevens' dissent

Opposing Side (Petitioner / Appellant)

1. White, B. – Wrote majority opinion
2. Rehnquist, W. – Joined majority opinion
3. Blackmun, H. – Joined majority opinion
4. O'Connor, S. – Joined majority opinion
5. Scalia, A. – Joined majority opinion
6. Kennedy, A. – Joined majority opinion

VI. A WIN OR LOSS FOR THE ACLU?

The ACLU filed as amicus curiae urging affirmance of the judgment of the Court of Criminal Appeals of Alabama; the Supreme Court reversed in a 6-3 vote, giving the ACLU an apparent loss.

705. Milkovich v. Lorain Journal Co.

(Decided June 21, 1990; 497 U.S. 1)

I. ISSUE

A. Issues Discussed

First Amendment, defamation, freedom of speech

B. Legal Question Presented

Whether "the First Amendment . . . prohibit[s] the application of Ohio's libel laws to the alleged defamations contained in the article" at issue in this case.

C. Supreme Court's Answer

"[T]he First Amendment does not prohibit the application of Ohio's libel laws to the alleged defamations contained in the article."

II. CASE SUMMARY

A. Background

"Respondent J. Theodore Diadiun authored an article in an Ohio newspaper implying that petitioner Michael Milkovich, a local high school wrestling coach, lied under oath in a judicial proceeding about an incident involving petitioner and his team which occurred at a wrestling match. Petitioner sued Diadiun and the newspaper for libel, and the Ohio Court of Appeals affirmed a lower court entry of summary judgment against petitioner. This judgment was based in part on the grounds that the article constituted an 'opinion' protected from the reach of state defamation law by the First Amendment to the United States Constitution. . . .

This lawsuit is before us for the third time in an odyssey of litigation spanning nearly 15 years."

The Supreme Court granted certiorari to review the case and reversed.

B. Counsel of Record / ACLU Attorney

ACLU Side (Respondent / Appellee): Richard D. Panza argued the cause for appellee.

Opposing Side (Petitioner / Appellant): Brent L. English argued the cause for appellant.

III. AMICI CURIAE

ACLU Side (Respondent / Appellee)

Brief of amici curiae filed on behalf of the ACLU, et al., by Henry R. Kaufman.

Brief of amici curiae filed on behalf of Dow Jones & Co., et al., by Robert D. Sack, Richard J. Tofel, Richard M. Schmidt, Jr., Devereux Chatillon, Douglas P. Jacobs, Barbara L. Wartelle, Harvey L. Lipton, Laura R. Handman, Slade R. Metcalf, Richard J. Ovelmen, Deborah R. Linfield, Jane E. Kirtley, and Bruce W. Sanford.

Brief of amici curiae filed on behalf of the Ohio Newspaper Association, et al., by Louis A. Colombo, David L. Marburger, and Michael K. Farrell.

Opposing Side (Petitioner / Appellant)

No briefs of amici curiae were filed in support of appellant.

IV. THE SUPREME COURT'S DECISION

"We . . . think the connotation that petitioner committed perjury is sufficiently factual to be susceptible of being proved true or false. A determination of whether petitioner lied in this instance can be made on a core of objective evidence by comparing, inter alia, petitioner's testimony before the OHSAA board with his subsequent testimony before the trial court. As the Scott court noted regarding the plaintiff in that case: '[W]hether or not H. Don Scott did indeed perjure himself is certainly verifiable by a perjury action with evidence adduced from the transcripts and witnesses present at the hearing. Unlike a subjective assertion, the averred defamatory language is an articulation of an objectively verifiable event.' So too with petitioner Milkovich.

The numerous decisions . . . establishing First Amendment protection for defendants in defamation actions surely demonstrate the Court's recognition of the Amendment's vital guarantee of free and uninhibited discussion of public issues. But there is also another side to the equation; we have regularly acknowledged the 'important social values which underlie the law of defamation,' and recognize that '[s]ociety has a pervasive and strong interest in preventing and redressing attacks upon reputation.' . . .

We believe our decision in the present case holds the balance true. The judgment of the Ohio Court of Appeals is reversed, and the case remanded for further proceedings not inconsistent with this opinion. Reversed."

V. JUSTICE VOTE

2 Pro ACLU Side vs. 7 Con Opposing Side

ACLU Side (Respondent / Appellee)

1. Brennan, W. – Wrote dissenting opinion
2. Marshall, T. – Joined Brennan's dissent

Opposing Side (Petitioner / Appellant)

1. Rehnquist, W. – Wrote majority opinion
2. White, B. – Joined majority opinion
3. Blackmun, H. – Joined majority opinion
4. Stevens, J. – Joined majority opinion
5. O'Connor, S. – Joined majority opinion
6. Scalia, A. – Joined majority opinion
7. Kennedy, A. – Joined majority opinion

VI. A WIN OR LOSS FOR THE ACLU?

The ACLU filed as amicus curiae urging affirmance of the judgment of the Ohio Court of Appeals, the Supreme Court reversed in a 7-2 vote, giving the ACLU an apparent loss.

706. Cruzan v. Director, Missouri Department of Health

(Decided June 25, 1990; 497 U.S. 261)

I. ISSUE

A. Issues Discussed

Due process, right to die

B. Legal Question Presented

"[W]hether Cruzan has a right under the United States Constitution which would require the hospital to withdraw life-sustaining treatment from her under these circumstances."

C. Supreme Court's Answer

The state can require clear and convincing evidence of Cruzan's desire to withdraw life-sustaining treatment in order to withdraw the treatment because she is incompetent. The evidence provided here does not meet the clear and convincing evidence standard.

II. CASE SUMMARY

A. Background

"Petitioner Nancy Beth Cruzan was rendered incompetent as a result of severe injuries sustained during an automobile accident. Copetitioners Lester and Joyce Cruzan, Nancy's parents and coguardians, sought a court order directing the withdrawal of their daughter's artificial feeding and hydration equipment after it became apparent that she had virtually no chance of recovering her cognitive faculties. . . .

The [state] court found that a person in Nancy's condition had a fundamental right under the State and Federal Constitutions to refuse or direct the withdrawal of 'death prolonging procedures.' The court also found that Nancy's 'expressed thoughts at age twenty-five in somewhat serious conversation with a housemate friend that if sick or injured she would not wish to continue her life unless she could live at least halfway normally suggests that given her present condition she would not wish to continue on with her nutrition and hydration.'

The Supreme Court of Missouri reversed by a divided vote."

The U.S. Supreme Court granted certiorari to review the case and affirmed.

B. Counsel of Record / ACLU Attorney

ACLU Side (Petitioner / Appellant): William H. Colby argued the cause for appellants. With him on the briefs were David J. Waxse, Walter E. Williams, Edward J. Kelly III, John A. Powell, and Steven R. Shapiro.

Opposing Side (Respondent / Appellee): Robert L. Presson, Assistant Attorney General of Missouri, argued the cause for appellee Director, Missouri Department of Health, et al. With him on the brief were William L. Webster, Attorney General, and Robert Northcutt.

Thad C. McCanse, pro se, and David B. Mouton filed a brief for respondent guardian ad litem.

Solicitor General Starr argued the cause for the United States, as amicus curiae, by special leave of Court.

III. AMICI CURIAE

ACLU Side (Petitioner / Appellant)

Briefs of amici curiae were filed on behalf of the AIDS Civil Rights Project, the American Academy of Neurology, the American College of Physicians, the American Geriatrics Society, the American Hospital Association, the American Medical Association, et al., the Colorado Medical Society, et al., Concern for Dying, the Evangelical Lutheran Church in America, the General Board of Church and Society of the United Methodist Church, Missouri Hospitals, et al., the National Hospice Organization, the National Academy of Elder Law Attorneys, the Society of Critical Care Medicine, et al., the Society for the Right to Die, Inc., Wisconsin Bioethicists, et al., Barbara Burgoon, et al., John E. McConnell, et al, and the American Nurses Association, et al.

The SSM Health Care System, et al., filed a brief of amici curiae in support of neither appellant nor appellee.

Opposing Side (Respondent / Appellee)

Brief of amici curiae filed on behalf of the United States by Solicitor General Starr, Acting Assistant Attorney General Schiffer, Deputy Solicitor General Merrill, and Brian J. Martin.

Additional briefs of amici curiae were filed on behalf of Agudath Israel of America, the American Academy of Medical Ethics, the Association of American Physicians and Surgeons, et al., the Association for Retarded Citizens of the United States, et al., the Catholic Lawyers Guild of the Archdiocese of Boston, Inc., the District Attorney of Milwaukee County, Wisconsin, Doctors for Life, et al., Families for Life, et al., Focus on the Family, et al., Free Speech Advocates, et al., the International Anti-Euthanasia Task Force, et al., the Knights of Columbus, the National Right to Life Committee, Inc., the New Jersey Right to Life Committee, Inc., et al., the Rutherford Institute, et al., the United States Catholic Conference, the Value of Life Committee, Inc., and Elizabeth Sadowski, et al.

IV. THE SUPREME COURT'S DECISION

"This is the first case in which we have been squarely presented with the issue whether the United States Constitution grants what is in common parlance referred to as a 'right to die.' . . .

The Fourteenth Amendment provides that no State shall 'deprive any person of life, liberty, or property, without due process of law.' The principle that a competent person has a constitutionally protected liberty interest in refusing unwanted medical treatment may be inferred from our prior decisions. . . .

Petitioners go on to assert that an incompetent person should possess the same right in this respect as is possessed by a competent person. . . . The difficulty with petitioners' claim is that in a sense it begs the question: An incompetent person is not able to make an informed and voluntary choice to exercise a hypothetical right to refuse treatment or any other right. Such a 'right' must be exercised for her, if at all, by some sort of surrogate. Here, Missouri has in effect recognized that under certain circumstances a surrogate may act for the patient in electing to have hydration and nutrition withdrawn in such a way as to cause death, but it has established a procedural safeguard to assure that the action of the surrogate conforms as best it may to the wishes expressed by the patient while competent. Missouri requires that evidence of the incompetent's wishes as to the withdrawal of treatment be proved by clear and convincing evidence. The question, then, is whether the United States Constitution forbids the establishment of this procedural requirement by the State. We hold that it does not. . . .

The choice between life and death is a deeply personal decision of obvious and overwhelming finality. We believe Missouri may legitimately seek to safeguard the personal element of this choice through the imposition of heightened evidentiary requirements. It cannot be disputed that the Due Process Clause protects an interest in life as well as an interest in refusing life-sustaining medical treatment. . . .

In our view, Missouri has permissibly sought to advance these interests through the adoption of a 'clear and convincing' standard of proof to govern such proceedings. . . .

In sum, we conclude that a State may apply a clear and convincing evidence standard in proceedings where a guardian seeks to discontinue nutrition and hydration of a person diagnosed to be in a persistent vegetative state. . . .

No doubt is engendered by anything in this record but that Nancy Cruzan's mother and father are loving and caring parents. If the State were required by the United States Constitution to repose a right of 'substituted judgment' with anyone, the Cruzans would surely qualify. But we do not think the Due Process Clause requires the State to repose judgment on these matters with anyone but the patient herself. Close family members may have a strong feeling—a feeling not at all ignoble or unworthy, but not entirely disinterested, either—that they do not wish to witness the continuation of the life of a loved one which they regard as hopeless, meaningless, and even degrading. But there is no automatic assurance that the view of close family members will necessarily be the same as the patient's would have been had she been confronted with the prospect of her situation while competent. All of the reasons previously discussed for allowing Missouri to require clear and convincing evidence of the patient's wishes lead us to conclude that the State may choose to defer only to those wishes, rather than confide the decision to close family members.

The judgment of the Supreme Court of Missouri is affirmed."

V. JUSTICE VOTE

4 Pro ACLU Side vs. 5 Con Opposing Side

ACLU Side (Petitioner / Appellant)

1. Brennan, W. – Wrote dissenting opinion
2. Stevens, J. – Wrote dissenting opinion
3. Marshall, T. – Joined Brennan's dissent
4. Blackmun, H. – Joined Brennan's dissent

Opposing Side (Respondent / Appellee)

1. Rehnquist, W – Wrote majority opinion
2. O'Connor, S. – Wrote concurring opinion
3. Scalia, A. – Wrote concurring opinion
4. Kennedy, A. – Joined majority opinion
5. White, B. – Joined majority opinion

VI. A WIN OR LOSS FOR THE ACLU?

The ACLU, as counsel for petitioners, urged reversal of the judgment of the Supreme Court of Missouri; the U.S. Supreme Court affirmed in a 5-4 vote, giving the ACLU an apparent loss.

707. Hodgson v. Minnesota

(Decided June 25, 1990; 497 U.S. 417)

I. ISSUE

A. Issues Discussed

Civil rights, state, privacy

B. Legal Question Presented

Whether a Minnesota statute providing "that no abortion shall be performed on a woman under 18 years of age until at least 48 hours after both of her parents have been notified" is constitutional.

C. Supreme Court's Answer

"[W]e now conclude that the requirement of notice to both of the pregnant minor's parents is not reasonably related to legitimate state interests and that subdivision 2 is unconstitutional. A different majority of the Court, for reasons stated in separate opinions, concludes that subdivision 6 is constitutional."

II. CASE SUMMARY

A. Background

"A Minnesota statute provides, with certain exceptions, that no abortion shall be performed on a woman under 18 years of age until at least 48 hours after both of her parents have been notified. In subdivisions 2–4 of the statute the notice is mandatory unless (1) the attending physician certifies that an immediate abortion is necessary to prevent the woman's death and there is insufficient time to provide the required notice; (2) both of her parents have consented in writing; or (3) the woman declares that she is a victim of parental abuse or neglect, in which event notice of her declaration must be given to the proper authorities. The United States Court of Appeals for the Eighth Circuit, sitting en banc, unanimously held these provisions unconstitutional. In No. 88–1309, [the Supreme Court] granted the State's petition to review that holding. Subdivision 6 of the same statute provides that if a court enjoins the enforcement of subdivision 2, the same notice requirement shall be effective unless the pregnant woman obtains a court order permitting the abortion to proceed. By a vote of 7 to 3, the Court of Appeals upheld the constitutionality of subdivision 6. In No. 88–1125, [the Supreme Court] granted the plaintiffs' petition to review that holding."

B. Counsel of Record

ACLU Side (Petitioner / Appellant): Janet Benshoof of the American Civil Liberties Union Foundation argued the cause for appellants in No. 88-1125 and appellees in No. 88-1309. With her on the briefs were Rachel N. Pine, Lynn M. Paltrow, and John A. Powell of the ACLU Foundation, Kathryn Kolbert, Linda Ojala William Z. Pentelovitch, and Rebecca A. Palmer, and Simon Heller and Robert S. Hicks of the Minnesota Civil Liberties Union.

Opposing Side (Respondent / Appellee): John R. Tunheim, Chief Deputy Attorney General of Minnesota, argued the cause for appellees in No. 88-1125 and appellants in No. 88-1309. With him on the briefs were Hubert H. Humphrey III, Attorney General, Catharine F. Haukedahl, Solicitor General, Kenneth E. Raschke, Jr., Assistant Attorney General, and John B. Galus, Special Assistant Attorney General.

III. AMICI CURIAE

ACLU Side (Petitioner / Appellant)

Brief of amici curiae filed on behalf of the American Psychological Association et al. by Donald N. Bersoff and Mark D. Schneider.

Brief of amici curiae filed on behalf of the Anti-Defamation League of B'Nai B'rith et al. by Kenneth J. Bialkin, Peggy L. Kerr, Meyer Eisenberg, Justin. J. Finger, Jeffrey P. Sinensky, Steven M. Freeman, Jill L. Kahn, and Livia D. Thompson.

Brief of amici curiae filed on behalf of 274 Organizations in Support of Roe v. Wade by Kathleen M. Sullivan, Susan R. Estrich, Barbara Jordan, and Estelle H. Rogers.

Brief of amici curiae filed on behalf of the American College of Obstetricians and Gynecologists et al. by Cater G. Phillips, Elizabeth H. Esty, Ann E. Allen, Stephani E. Lawton, Laurie R. Rockett, and Joel I. Klein.

Brief of amici curiae filed on behalf of the Center for Population Options et al. by John H. Henn.

Brief of amici curiae filed on behalf of James Joseph Lynch, Jr., pro se.

Brief of amici curiae filed on behalf of 13 Individual Members of the Panel on Adolescent Pregnancy and Childbearing or the Committee on Child Development Research and Public Policy by Hannah E. M. Lieberman and Pamela H. Anderson.

Opposing Side (Respondent / Appellee)

Brief of amici curiae filed on behalf of the Association of American Physicians and Surgeons by Clarke D. Forsythe and Kent Masterson Brown.

Brief of amici curiae filed on behalf of the American Academy of Medical Ethics by Joseph W. Dellapenna.

Brief of amici curiae filed on behalf of the United States by Solicitor General Starr, Acting Assistant Attorney General Schiffer, Deputy Solicitor General Merrill, Paid J. Larkin, Jr., Stephen J. Marzen, and Steven R. Valentine.

Brief of amici curiae filed on behalf of the American Family Association, Inc., by Peggy M. Coleman.

Brief of amici curiae filed on behalf of the Catholic League for Religious and Civil Rights et al. by Nancy J. Gannon and Thomas W. Strahan.

Brief of amici curiae filed on behalf of the Elliot Institute for Social Sciences Research et al. by Stephen R. Kaufmann.

Brief of amici curiae filed on behalf of Focus on the Family et al. by H. Robert Showers.

Brief of amici curiae filed on behalf of the Knights of Columbus by Brendan V. Sullivan, Jr., Kevin J. Hasson, and Carl A. Anderson.

Brief of amici curiae filed on behalf of the Luthern Church-Missouri Synod by Philip E. Draheim.

Brief of amici curiae filed on behalf of the National Right to Life Committee, Inc., by James Bopp, Jr.

Brief of amici curiae filed on behalf of the United States Catholic Conference by Mark E. Chopko.

Brief of amici curiae filed on behalf of Members of the General Assembly of the Commonwealth of Pennsylvania by Maura K. Quinlin and Philip J. Murren.

Brief of amici curiae filed on behalf of the State of Louisiana et al. by William J. Guste, Jr., Attorney General of Louisiana, Jenifer Schaye and Meredith H. Lieux, Assistant Attorneys General, Jo Ann P. Levert, Thomas A. Rayner, Robert K. Corbin, Attorney General of Arizona, William L. Webster, Attorney General of Missouri, and Ernest D. Preate, Jr., Attorney General of Pennsylvania.

Brief of amici curiae filed on behalf of Representative Christopher H. Smith et al. by Mr. Bopp.

IV. THE SUPREME COURT'S DECISION

"There is a natural difference between men and women: Only women have the capacity to bear children. A woman's decision to conceive or to bear a child is a component of her liberty that is protected by the Due Process Clause of the Fourteenth Amendment to the Constitution. . . .

As we stated in Planned Parenthood of Central Mo. v. Danforth, 428 U.S. 52 (1976), the right to make this decision 'do[es] not mature and come into being magically only when one attains the state-defined age of majority.' Thus, the constitutional protection against unjustified state intrusion into the process of deciding whether or not to bear a child extends to pregnant minors as well as adult women. . . .

The Court has considered the constitutionality of statutes providing for parental consent or parental notification in six abortion cases decided during the last 14 years. . . .

Three separate but related interests—the interest in the welfare of the pregnant minor, the interest of the parents, and the interest of the family unit—are relevant to our consideration of the constitutionality of the 48-hour waiting period and the two-parent notification requirement. . . .

We think it is clear that a requirement that a minor wait 48 hours after notifying a single parent of her intention to get an abortion would reasonably further the legitimate state interest in ensuring that the minor's decision is knowing and intelligent. . . .

The 48-hour delay imposes only a minimal burden on the right of the minor to decide whether or not to terminate her pregnancy. . . .

It is equally clear that the requirement that both parents be notified, whether or not both wish to be notified or have assumed responsibility for the upbringing of the child, does not reasonably further any legitimate state interest. . . .

The judgment of the Court of Appeals in its entirety is affirmed."

V. JUSTICE VOTE

5 Pro ACLU Side vs. 4 Con Opposing Side

ACLU Side (Petitioner / Appellant)

1. Stevens, J. – Wrote majority opinion
2. Brennan, W. – Joined Marshall's opinion
3. Marshall, T. – Wrote opinion concurring in part and dissenting in part
4. Blackmun, H. – Joined Marshall's opinion
5. O'Connor, S. – Wrote concurring opinion

Opposing Side (Respondent / Appellee)

1. Kennedy, A. – Wrote opinion concurring in part and dissenting in part
2. Rehnquist, W. – Joined Kennedy's opinion
3. White, B. – Joined Kennedy's opinion
4. Scalia, A. – Wrote opinion concurring in part and dissenting in part

VI. A WIN OR LOSS FOR THE ACLU?

The ACLU served as counsel for appellant urging the court to declare sections 2-6 of the Minnesota statute unconstitutional; the Supreme Court found section 2 unconstitutional in a 5-4 vote, giving the ACLU an apparent win.[1]

708. Metro Broadcasting, Inc. v. FCC

(Decided June 27, 1990; 497 U.S. 547)

I. ISSUE

A. Issues Discussed

Civil rights, affirmative action, equal protection, racial discrimination, Fifth Amendment

1 *Timeline of Important Reproductive Freedom Cases Decided by the Supreme Court, ACLU*, https://www.aclu.org/other/timeline-important-reproductive-freedom-cases-decided-supreme-court (last visited Feb. 11, 2020) ("In *Hodgson v. Minnesota, the ACLU secured for teenagers the option of going to court to obtain authorization for an abortion, when they could not or would not comply with a parental notification law.*").

B. Legal Question Presented

"[W]hether certain minority preference policies of the Federal Communications Commission violate the equal protection component of the Fifth Amendment. The policies in question are (1) a program awarding an enhancement for minority ownership in comparative proceedings for new licenses, and (2) the minority 'distress sale' program, which permits a limited category of existing radio and television broadcast stations to be transferred only to minority-controlled firms."

C. Supreme Court's Answer

The minority preference policies comply with the Equal Protection Clause of the Fifth Amendment.

II. CASE SUMMARY

A. Background

"[T]he FCC adopted in May 1978 its Statement of Policy on Minority Ownership of Broadcasting Facilities . . . . First, the Commission pledged to consider minority ownership as one factor in comparative proceedings for new licenses. . . . Second, the FCC outlined a plan to increase minority opportunities to receive reassigned and transferred licenses through the so-called 'distress sale' policy. As a general rule, a licensee whose qualifications to hold a broadcast license come into question may not assign or transfer that license until the FCC has resolved its doubts in a noncomparative hearing. The distress sale policy is an exception to that practice, allowing a broadcaster whose license has been designated for a revocation hearing, or whose renewal application has been designated for hearing, to assign the license to an FCC-approved minority enterprise. The assignee must meet the FCC's basic qualifications, and the minority ownership must exceed 50 percent or be controlling. The buyer must purchase the license before the start of the revocation or renewal hearing, and the price must not exceed 75 percent of fair market value. These two Commission minority ownership policies are at issue today. . . .

In No. 89-453, petitioner Metro Broadcasting, Inc. (Metro), challenges the Commission's policy awarding preferences to minority owners in comparative licensing proceedings. . . . Prior to the Commission's completion of its Docket 86-484 inquiry, however, Congress enacted and the President signed into law the FCC appropriations legislation for fiscal year 1988. The measure prohibited the Commission from spending any appropriated funds to examine or change its minority ownership policies. Complying with this directive, the Commission closed its Docket 86-484 inquiry. The FCC also reaffirmed its grant of the license in this case to Rainbow Broadcasting. The case returned to the Court of Appeals, and a divided panel affirmed the Commission's order awarding the license to Rainbow. . . .

The dispute in No. 89-700 emerged from a series of attempts by Faith Center, Inc., the licensee of a Hartford, Connecticut, television station, to execute a minority distress sale. . . . A divided Court of Appeals invalidated the Commission's minority distress sale policy."

The Supreme Court granted certiorari to review the case and reversed.

B. Counsel of Record / ACLU Attorney

ACLU Side (Respondent / Appellee in No. 89-453, Petitioner / Appellant in No. 89-700): Daniel M. Armstrong argued the cause for the federal appellee in No. 89-453. Margot Polivy argued the cause for appellee Rainbow Broadcasting Co. J.Roger Wollengerg argued the cause for appellant in No. 89-700.

Opposing Side (Petitioner / Appellant in No. 89-453, Respondent / Appellee in No. 89-700): Gregory H. Guillot argued the cause for appellant in No. 89-453. Harry F. Cole argued the cause for appellees in No. 89-700.

III. AMICI CURIAE

ACLU Side (Respondent / Appellee in No. 89-453, Petitioner / Appellant in No. 89-700):

Brief of amici curiae filed in No. 89-453 and No. 89-700 on behalf of the ACLU by Burt Neuborne, Steven R. Shapiro, John A. Powell and Sarah E. Burns.

Briefs of amici curiae in No. 89-453 and No. 89-700 were filed on behalf of the Congressional Black Caucus, the National Association of Black Owned Broadcasters, Inc., and the National Bar Association.

Brief of amici curiae filed in No. 89-700 on behalf of the Committee to Promote Diversity.

Briefs of amici curiae in No. 89-453 were filed on behalf of the United States Senate, the American Jewish Committee, et al., Capital Cities/ABC, Inc., Cook Inlet Region, Inc., et al., Giles Television, Inc., the Lawyers' Committee for Civil Rights Under Law, the NAACP Legal Defense & Educational Fund, Inc., American Women in Radio and Television, Inc., and the National League of Cities, et al.

Opposing Side (Petitioner / Appellant in No. 89-453, Respondent / Appellee in No. 89-700):

Briefs of amici curiae in No. 89-453 were filed on behalf of the United States, Associated General Contractors of America, Inc., Galaxy Communications, Inc., the Mountain States Legal Foundation, et al., the Pacific Legal Foundation, and the Washington Legal Foundation.

Briefs of amici curiae in No. 89-700 were filed on behalf of the United States, the Pacific Legal Foundation, Southeastern Legal Foundation, Inc.

IV. THE SUPREME COURT'S DECISION

"We hold that the FCC minority ownership policies pass muster under the test we announce today. First, we find that they serve the important governmental objective of broadcast diversity. Second, we conclude that they are substantially related to the achievement of that objective. . . .

Congress found that 'the effects of past inequities stemming from racial and ethnic discrimination have resulted in a severe underrepresentation of minorities in the media of mass communications.' Congress and the Commission do not justify the minority ownership policies strictly as remedies for victims of this discrimination, however. Rather, Congress and the FCC have selected the minority ownership policies primarily to promote programming diversity, and they urge that such diversity is an important governmental objective that can serve as a constitutional basis for the preference policies. We agree. . . . We have long recognized that '[b]ecause of the scarcity of [electromagnetic] frequencies, the Government is permitted to put restraints on licensees in favor of others whose views should be expressed on this unique medium.' . . .

Against this background, we conclude that the interest in enhancing broadcast diversity is, at the very least, an important governmental objective and is therefore a sufficient basis for the Commission's minority ownership policies. Just as a 'diverse student body' contributing to a 'robust exchange of ideas' is a 'constitutionally permissible goal' on which a race-conscious university admissions program may be predicated, the diversity of views and information on the airwaves serves important First Amendment values. The benefits of such diversity are not limited to the members of minority groups who gain access to the broadcasting industry by virtue of the ownership policies; rather, the benefits redound to all members of the viewing and listening audience. . . .

We also find that the minority ownership policies are substantially related to the achievement of the Government's interest. One component of this inquiry concerns the relationship between expanded minority ownership and greater broadcast diversity; both the FCC and Congress have determined that such a relationship exists. . . . In short, the Commission established minority ownership preferences only after long experience demonstrated that race-neutral means could not produce adequate broadcasting diversity. . . .

The Commission's minority ownership policies bear the imprimatur of longstanding congressional support and direction and are substantially related to the achievement of the important governmental objective of broadcast diversity. The judgment in No. 89-453 is affirmed, the judgment in No. 89-700 is reversed, and the cases are remanded for proceedings consistent with this opinion."

V. JUSTICE VOTE

5 Pro ACLU Side vs. 4 Con Opposing Side

ACLU Side (Respondent / Appellee in No. 89-453, Petitioner / Appellant in No. 89-700):

1. Brennan, W. – Wrote majority opinion
2. White, B. – Joined majority opinion
3. Marshall, T. – Joined majority opinion
4. Blackmun, H. – Joined majority opinion
5. Stevens, J. – Wrote concurring opinion

Opposing Side (Petitioner / Appellant in No. 89-453, Respondent / Appellee in No. 89-700):

1. O'Connor, S. – Wrote dissenting opinion
2. Rehnquist, W. – Joined O'Connor's dissent
3. Scalia, A. – Joined O'Connor's dissent, joined Kennedy's dissent
4. Kennedy, A. – Wrote dissenting opinion, joined O'Connor's dissent

VI. A WIN OR LOSS FOR THE ACLU?

The ACLU filed as amicus curiae urging affirmance in No. 89-453 and reversal in No. 89-700; the Supreme Court affirmed the ruling of the Court of Appeals in No. 89-453 and reversed in No. 89-700 in a 5-4 vote, giving the ACLU an apparent win.

709. Walton v. Arizona

(Decided June 27, 1990; 497 U.S. 639)

I. ISSUE

A. Issues Discussed

Criminal justice, death penalty, Sixth Amendment, Eighth Amendment, Fourteenth Amendment

B. Legal Question Presented

Whether "the death sentence imposed by an Arizona trial court after a jury found petitioner Jeffrey Walton guilty of committing first-degree murder" is a valid sentence.

C. Supreme Court's Answer

The death sentence is a valid sentence.

II. CASE SUMMARY

A. Background

"Petitioner Walton and his two codefendants, Robert Hoover and Sharold Ramsey, went to a bar in Tucson, Arizona, on the night of March 2, 1986, intending to find and rob someone at random, steal his car, tie him up, and leave him in the desert while they fled the State in the car. In the bar's parking lot, the trio encountered Thomas Powell, a young, off-duty Marine. The three robbed Powell at gunpoint and forced him into his car which they then drove out into the desert. While driving out of Tucson, the three asked Powell questions about where he lived and whether he had any more money. When the car stopped, Ramsey told a frightened Powell that he would not be hurt. Walton and Hoover then forced Powell out of the car and had him lie face down on the ground near the car while they debated what to do with him. Eventually, Walton instructed Hoover and Ramsey to sit in the car and turn the radio up loud. Walton then took a .22 caliber derringer and marched Powell off into the desert. After walking a short distance, Walton forced Powell to lie down on the ground, placed his foot on Powell's neck, and shot Powell once in the head. Walton later told Hoover and Ramsey that he had shot Powell and that he had 'never seen a man pee in his pants before.' Powell's body was found approximately a week later, after Walton was arrested and led police to the murder site. A medical examiner determined that Powell had been blinded and rendered unconscious by the shot but was not immediately killed. Instead, Powell regained consciousness, apparently floundered about in the desert, and ultimately died from dehydration, starvation, and pneumonia approximately a day before his body was found.

A jury convicted Walton of first-degree murder after being given instructions on both premeditated and felony murder. . . . The court then concluded that there were 'no mitigating circumstances sufficiently substantial to call for leniency.' The court sentenced Walton to death.

The Arizona Supreme Court affirmed Walton's conviction and sentence."

The U.S. Supreme Court granted certiorari to review the case and affirmed.

B. Counsel of Record / ACLU Attorney

ACLU Side (Petitioner / Appellant): Timothy K. Ford argued the cause for appellant.

Opposing Side (Respondent / Appellee): Paul J. McMurdie, Assistant Attorney General of Arizona, argued the cause for appellee.

III. AMICI CURIAE

ACLU Side (Petitioner / Appellant)

Brief of amici curiae filed on behalf of the ACLU, et al., by John A. Powell, Michael Laurence, Welsh S. White, and Randy Hertz.

Opposing Side (Respondent / Appellee)

Brief of amici curiae filed on behalf of the Commonwealth of Pennsylvania, et al., by Ernest D. Preate, Jr., Attorney General of Pennsylvania; Robert A. Graci, Chief Deputy Attorney General; Mary Benefield Seiverling, Deputy Attorney General; John J. Kelly, Chief State's Attorney of Connecticut; Robert Butterworth, Attorney General of Florida; James T. Jones, Attorney General of Idaho; Neil F. Hartigan, Attorney General of Illinois; Robert T. Stephan, Attorney General of Kansas; Frederic J. Cowan, Attorney General of Kentucky; Michael C. Moore, Attorney General of Mississippi; William L. Webster, Attorney General of Missouri; Marc Racicot, Attorney General of Montana; Brian McKay, Attorney General of Nevada; John P. Arnold, Attorney General of New Hampshire; Hal Stratton, Attorney General of New Mexico; Lacy H. Thornburg, Attorney General of North Carolina; Anthony J. Celebrezze, Jr., Attorney General of Ohio; Robert H. Henry, Attorney General of Oklahoma; Roger A. Tellinghuisen, Attorney General of South Dakota; Kenneth O. Eikenberry, Attorney General of Washington; and Joseph B. Meyer, Attorney General of Wyoming.

IV. THE SUPREME COURT'S DECISION

"Walton's first argument is that every finding of fact underlying the sentencing decision must be made by a jury, not by a judge, and that the Arizona scheme would be constitutional only if a jury decides what aggravating and mitigating circumstances are present in a given case and the trial judge then imposes sentence based on those findings. . . . We repeatedly have rejected constitutional challenges to Florida's death sentencing scheme, which provides for sentencing by the judge, not the jury. . . . We thus conclude that the Arizona capital sentencing scheme does not violate the Sixth Amendment. . . .

Also unpersuasive is Walton's contention that the Arizona statute violates the Eighth and Fourteenth Amendments because it imposes on defendants the burden of establishing, by a preponderance of the evidence, the existence of mitigating circumstances sufficiently substantial to call for leniency. . . . So long as a State's method of allocating the burdens of proof does not lessen the State's burden to prove every element of the offense charged, or in this case to prove the existence of aggravating circumstances, a defendant's constitutional rights are not violated by placing on him the burden of proving mitigating circumstances sufficiently substantial to call for leniency. . . . We therefore reject Walton's argument that Arizona's allocation of the burdens of proof in a capital sentencing proceeding violates the Constitution. . . .

Walton's final contention is that the especially heinous, cruel, or depraved aggravating circumstance as interpreted by the Arizona courts fails to channel the sentencer's discretion as required by the Eighth and Fourteenth Amendments. . . .

In effect Walton challenges the proportionality review of the Arizona Supreme Court as erroneous and asks us to overturn it. This we decline to do, for we have just concluded that the challenged factor has been construed by the Arizona courts in a manner that furnishes sufficient guidance to the sentencer. This being so proportionality review is not constitutionally required, and we 'lawfully may presume that [Walton's] death sentence was not 'wantonly and freakishly' imposed—and thus that the sentence is not disproportionate within any recognized meaning of the Eighth Amendment.' Furthermore, the Arizona Supreme Court plainly undertook its proportionality review in good faith and found that Walton's sentence was proportional to the sentences imposed in cases similar to his. The Constitution does not require us to look behind that conclusion.

The judgment of the Arizona Supreme Court is affirmed."

V. JUSTICE VOTE

4 Pro ACLU Side vs. 5 Con Opposing Side

ACLU Side (Petitioner / Appellant)

1. Brennan, W. – Wrote dissenting opinion, joined Blackmun's dissent
2. Blackmun, H. – Wrote dissenting opinion
3. Stevens, J. – Wrote dissenting opinion, joined Blackmun's dissent
4. Marshall, T. – Joined Brennan's dissent, joined Blackmun's dissent

Opposing Side (Respondent / Appellee)

1. White, B. – Wrote majority opinion
2. O'Connor, S. – Joined majority opinion
3. Rehnquist, W. – Joined majority opinion
4. Scalia, A. – Wrote concurring opinion
5. Kennedy, A. – Joined majority opinion

VI. A WIN OR LOSS FOR THE ACLU?

The ACLU filed as amicus curiae urging reversal; the Supreme Court affirmed in a 5-4 vote, giving the ACLU an apparent loss.

710. United States v. Kokinda

(Decided June 27, 1990; 497 U.S. 720)

I. ISSUE

A. Issues Discussed

First Amendment, freedoms of press, speech, and association

B. Legal Question Presented

"[W]hether a United States Postal Service regulation that prohibits '[s]oliciting alms and contributions' on postal premises violates the First Amendment."

C. Supreme Court's Answer

The postal regulation, as applied in this case, does not violate the First Amendment.

II. CASE SUMMARY

A. Background

"The respondents in this case, Marsha B. Kokinda and Kevin E. Pearl, were volunteers for the National Democratic Policy Committee, who set up a table on the sidewalk near the entrance of the Bowie, Maryland, Post Office to solicit contributions, sell books and subscriptions to the organization's newspaper, and distribute literature addressing a variety of political issues. The postal sidewalk provides the sole means by which customers of the post office may travel from the parking lot to the post office building and lies entirely on Postal Service property. . . .

During the several hours that respondents were at the post office, postal employees received between 40 and 50 complaints regarding their presence. The record does not indicate the substance of the complaints with one exception. One individual complained 'because she knew the Girl Scouts were not allowed to sell cookies on federal property.' The Bowie postmaster asked respondents to leave, which they refused to do. Postal inspectors arrested respondents, seizing their table as well as their literature and other belongings.

Respondents were tried before a United States Magistrate in the District of Maryland and convicted of violating 39 CFR § 232.1(h)(1) (1989), which provides in relevant part:

'Soliciting alms and contributions, campaigning for election to any public office, collecting private debts, commercial soliciting and vending, and displaying or distributing commercial advertising on postal premises are prohibited.'

Respondent Kokinda was fined $50 and sentenced to 10 days' imprisonment; respondent Pearl was fined $100 and received a 30–day suspended sentence under that provision.

Respondents appealed their convictions to the District Court, asserting that application of § 232.1(h)(1) violated the First Amendment. The District Court affirmed their convictions, holding that the postal sidewalk was not a public forum and that the Postal Service's ban on solicitation is reasonable.

A divided panel of the United States Court of Appeals for the Fourth Circuit reversed. . . . The United States' petition for rehearing and a suggestion for rehearing en banc were denied."

The Supreme Court granted certiorari to review the case and reversed.

B. Counsel of Record / ACLU Attorney

ACLU Side (Respondent / Appellee): Jay Alan Sekulow argued the cause for appellee.

Opposing Side (Petitioner / Appellant): Deputy Solicitor General Roberts argued the cause for the United States.

III. AMICI CURIAE

ACLU Side (Respondent / Appellee)

Brief of amici curiae filed on behalf of the ACLU, et al., by Steven R. Shapiro.

Brief of amici curiae filed on behalf of the American Federation of Labor and Congress of Industrial Organizations by Marsha S. Berzon and Laurence Gold.

Brief of amici curiae filed on behalf of Free Speech Advocates by Thomas Patrick Monaghan.

Brief of amici curiae filed on behalf of the National Committee of the Libertarian Party, et al., by Frank M. Dunbaugh.

Brief of amici curiae filed on behalf of the International Society for Krishna Consciousness of California, Inc., by David M. Liberman.

Brief of amici curiae filed on behalf of Newport News Daily Press, et al., by Alice Neff Luca, Richard P. Holme, Lawrence J. Aldrich, Boisfeuillet Jones, Jr., Alexander Wellford, and David C. Kohler.

Brief of amici curiae filed on behalf of the Project for Public Spaces, Inc., by Andrew J. Ekonomou.

Opposing Side (Petitioner / Appellant)

No briefs of amici curiae were filed in support of appellant.

IV. THE SUPREME COURT'S DECISION

"Solicitation is a recognized form of speech protected by the First Amendment. . . . Respondents contend that although the sidewalk is on Postal Service property, because it is not distinguishable from the municipal sidewalk across the parking lot from the post office's entrance, it must be a traditional public forum and therefore subject to strict scrutiny. This argument is unpersuasive. The mere physical characteristics of the property cannot dictate forum analysis. . . . The postal sidewalk at issue does not have the characteristics of public sidewalks traditionally open to expressive activity. The municipal sidewalk that runs parallel to the road in this case is a public passageway. The Postal Service's sidewalk is not such a thoroughfare. Rather, it leads only from the parking area to the front door of the post office. . . .

The Postal Service has not expressly dedicated its sidewalks to any expressive activity. Indeed, postal property is expressly dedicated to only one means of communication: the posting of public notices on designated bulletin boards. No Postal Service regulation opens postal sidewalks to any First Amendment activity. . . .

Thus, the regulation at issue must be analyzed under the standards set forth for nonpublic fora: It must be reasonable and 'not an effort to suppress expression merely because public officials oppose the speaker's view.' Indeed, '[c]ontrol over access to a nonpublic forum can be based on subject matter and speaker identity so long as the distinctions drawn are reasonable in light of the purpose served by the forum and are viewpoint neutral.' 'The Government's decision to restrict access to a nonpublic forum need only be reasonable; it need not be the most reasonable or the only reasonable limitation.' . . .

Whether or not the Service permits other forms of speech, which may or may not be disruptive, it is not unreasonable to prohibit solicitation on the ground that it is unquestionably a particular form of speech that is disruptive of business. [T]he disruption and delay caused by solicitation rings of 'commonsense,' which is sufficient in this Court to uphold a regulation under reasonableness review. . . .

Clearly, the regulation does not discriminate on the basis of content or viewpoint. Indeed, '[n]othing suggests the Postal Service intended to discourage one viewpoint and advance another . . . . By excluding all . . . groups from engaging in [solicitation] the Postal Service is not granting to 'one side of a debatable public question . . . a monopoly in expressing its views." The Service's concern about losing customers because of the potentially unpleasant situation created by solicitation per se does not reveal 'an effort to suppress expression merely because public officials oppose the speaker's view.'

It is clear that this regulation passes constitutional muster under the Court's usual test for reasonableness. Accordingly, we conclude, as have the Courts of Appeals for the Third and Eleventh Circuits, that the Postal Service's regulation of solicitation is reasonable as applied.

The judgment of the Court of Appeals is reversed."

V. JUSTICE VOTE

4 Pro ACLU Side vs. 5 Con Opposing Side

ACLU Side (Respondent / Appellee)

1. Brennan, W. – Wrote dissenting opinion
2. Stevens, J. – Joined Brennan's dissent
3. Marshall, T. – Joined Brennan's dissent
4. Blackmun, H. – Joined Brennan's dissent in part

Opposing Side (Petitioner / Appellant)

1. O'Connor, S. – Wrote majority opinion
2. Rehnquist, W. – Joined majority opinion
3. White, B. – Joined majority opinion
4. Scalia, A. – Joined majority opinion
5. Kennedy, A. – Wrote concurring opinion

VI. A WIN OR LOSS FOR THE ACLU?

The ACLU filed as amicus curiae urging affirmance of the judgment of the Court of Appeals; the Supreme Court reversed in a 5-4 vote, giving the ACLU an apparent loss.

711. Idaho v. Wright

(Decided June 27, 1990; 497 U.S. 805)

I. ISSUE

A. Issues Discussed

Criminal procedure, Sixth Amendment, Confrontation Clause, juvenile witnesses, hearsay exceptions

B. Legal Question Presented

"[W]hether the admission at trial of certain hearsay statements made by a child declarant to an examining pediatrician violates a defendant's rights under the Confrontation Clause of the Sixth Amendment."

C. Supreme Court's Answer

The admission of the hearsay statements violated the Confrontation Clause.

II. CASE SUMMARY

A. Background

"Respondent Laura Lee Wright was jointly charged with Robert L. Giles of two counts of lewd conduct with a minor under 16, in violation of Idaho Code § 18-1508 (1987). The alleged victims were respondent's two daughters, one of whom was 5 1/2 and the other 2 ½ years old at the time the crimes were charged. . . .

At issue in this case is the admission at trial of certain statements made by the younger daughter to Dr. Jambura in response to questions he asked regarding the alleged abuse. . . .

Respondent and Giles were each convicted of two counts of lewd conduct with a minor under 16 and sentenced to 20 years' imprisonment. Each appealed only from the conviction involving the younger daughter. Giles contended that the trial court erred in admitting Dr. Jambura's testimony under Idaho's residual hearsay exception. The Idaho Supreme Court disagreed and affirmed his conviction. Respondent asserted that the admission of Dr. Jambura's testimony under the residual hearsay exception nevertheless violated her rights under the Confrontation Clause. The Idaho Supreme Court agreed and reversed respondent's conviction."

The U.S. Supreme Court granted certiorari to review the case and affirmed.

B. Counsel of Record / ACLU Attorney

ACLU Side (Respondent / Appellee): Rolf Michael Kehne argued the cause for appellee.

Opposing Side (Petitioner / Appellant): James T. Jones, Attorney General of Idaho, argued the cause for appellant.

Deputy Solicitor General Bryson argued the cause for the United States, as amicus curiae, by special leave of Court.

III. AMICI CURIAE

ACLU Side (Respondent / Appellee)

Brief of amici curiae filed on behalf of the ACLU by Margaret A. Berger and Steven R. Sharpiro.

Brief of amici curiae filed on behalf of the National Association of Criminal Defense Lawyers by Natman Schaye.

Brief of amici curiae filed on behalf of the American Professional Society on the Abuse of Children, et al., by Stephan E. Lawton, John E.B. Myers, Kirk B. Johnson, and Thomas R. Finn, in support of neither appellant nor appellee.

Opposing Side (Petitioner / Appellant)

Brief of amici curiae filed on behalf of the United States by Deputy Solicitor General Bryson, Solicitor General Starr, Assistant Attorney General Dennis, and Michael R. Dreeben.

Brief of amici curiae filed on behalf of the Commonwealth of Pennsylvania, et al., by Ernest D. Preate, Jr., Attorney General of Pennsylvania, and Marylou Barton, Chief Deputy Attorney General; Douglas B. Baily, Attorney General of Alaska; Robert K. Corbin, Attorney General of Arizona; Steve Clark, Attorney General of Arkansas; Duane Woodard, Attorney General of Colorado; Charles M. Oberly III, Attorney General of Delaware; Robert A. Butterworth, Attorney General of Florida; Neil F. Hartigan, Attorney General of Illinois; Linley E. Pearson, Attorney General of Indiana; Tom Miller, Attorney General of Iowa; Robert T. Stephan, Attorney General of Kansas; Frederic J. Cowan, Attorney General of Kentuck; William J. Guste, Jr., Attorney General of Louisiana; Joseph Curran, Jr., Attorney General of Maryland; James M. Shannon, Attorney General of Massachusetts; Frank J. Kelly, Attorney General of Michigan; Mike Moore, Attorney General of Mississippi; William L. Webster, Attorney General of Missouri; Marc Racicot, Attorney General of Montana; Robert M. Spire, Attorney General of Nebraska; Brian McKay, Attorney General of Nevada; John P. Arnold, Attorney General of New Hampshire; Robert Del Tufo, Attorney General Designate of New Jersey; Hal Stratton, Attorney General of New Mexico; Lacy H. Thornburg, Attorney General of North Carolina; Nicholas Spaeth, Attorney General of North Dakota; Robert H. Henry, Attorney General of Oklahoma; T. Travis Medlock, Attorney General of South Carolina; Roger A. Tellinghuisen, Attorney General of South Dakota; Paul Van Dam, Attorney General of Utah; Jeffrey L. Amestoy, Attorney General of Vermont; Godfrey R. de Castro, Attorney General of the Virgin Islands; Mary Sue Terry, Attorney General of Virginia; and Joseph B. Meyer, Attorney General of Wyoming.

IV. THE SUPREME COURT'S DECISION

"The Confrontation Clause of the Sixth Amendment, made applicable to the States through the Fourteenth Amendment, provides: 'In all criminal prosecutions, the accused shall enjoy the right . . . to be confronted with the witnesses against him.' . . .

Of the factors the trial court found relevant, only two relate to circumstances surrounding the making of the statements: whether the child had a motive to 'make up a story of this nature' and whether, given the child's age, the statements are of the type 'that one would expect a child to fabricate.' The other factors on which the trial court relied, however, such as the presence of physical evidence of abuse, the opportunity of respondent to commit the offense, and the older daughter's corroborating identification, relate instead to whether other evidence existed to corroborate the truth of the statement. These factors, as we have discussed, are irrelevant to a showing of the 'particularized guarantees of trustworthiness necessary for admission of hearsay statements under the Confrontation Clause.'

We think the Supreme Court of Idaho properly focused on the presumptive unreliability of the out-of-court statements and on the suggestive manner in which Dr. Jambura conducted the interview. Viewing the totality of the circumstances surrounding the younger daughter's responses to Dr. Jambura's questions, we find no special reason for supposing that the incriminating statements were particularly trustworthy. The younger daughter's last statement regarding the abuse of the older daughter, however, presents a closer question. According to Dr. Jambura, the younger daughter 'volunteered' that statement 'after she sort of clammed-up.' Although the spontaneity of the statement and the change in demeanor suggest that the younger daughter was telling the truth when she made the statement, we note that it is possible that '[i] f there is evidence of prior interrogation, prompting, or manipulation by adults, spontaneity may be an inaccurate indicator of trustworthiness.' Moreover, the statement was not made under circumstances of reliability comparable to those required, for example, for the admission of excited utterances or statements made for purposes of medical diagnosis or treatment. Given the presumption of inadmissibility accorded accusatory hearsay statements not admitted pursuant to a firmly rooted hearsay exception, we agree with the court below that the State has failed to show that the younger daughter's incriminating statements to the pediatrician possessed sufficient 'particularized guarantees of trustworthiness' under the Confrontation Clause to overcome that presumption.

The State does not challenge the Idaho Supreme Court's conclusion that the Confrontation Clause error in this case was not harmless beyond a reasonable doubt, and we see no reason to revisit the issue. We therefore agree with that court that respondent's conviction involving the younger daughter must be reversed and the case remanded for further proceedings. Accordingly, the judgment of the Supreme Court of Idaho is affirmed."

V. JUSTICE VOTE

5 Pro ACLU Side vs. 4 Con Opposing Side

ACLU Side (Respondent / Appellee)

1. O'Connor, S. – Wrote majority opinion
2. Brennan, W. – Joined majority opinion
3. Marshall, T. – Joined majority opinion
4. Stevens, J. – Joined majority opinion
5. Scalia, A. – Joined majority opinion

Opposing Side (Petitioner / Appellant)

1. Kennedy, A. – Wrote dissenting opinion
2. Rehnquist, W. – Joined Kennedy's dissent
3. White, B. – Joined Kennedy's dissent
4. Blackmun, H. – Joined Kennedy's dissent

VI. A WIN OR LOSS FOR THE ACLU?

The ACLU filed as amicus curiae urging affirmance of the judgment of the Idaho Supreme Court; the U.S. Supreme Court affirmed in a 5-4 vote, giving the ACLU an apparent win.

712. Board of Education of Oklahoma City v. Dowell

(Decided January 15, 1991; 498 U.S. 237)

I. ISSUE

A. Issues Discussed

Civil rights, race

B. Legal Question Presented

Whether "a desegregation decree remains in effect until a school district can show 'grievous wrong evoked by new and unforeseen conditions,' and 'dramatic changes in conditions unforseen at the time of the decree that . . . impose extreme and unexpectedly oppressive hardships on the obligor.'"

C. Supreme Court's Answer

"We hold that the Court of Appeals' test is more stringent than is required either by our cases dealing with injunctions or by the Equal Protection Clause of the Fourteenth Amendment."

II. CASE SUMMARY

A. Background

"Petitioner Board of Education of Oklahoma City sought dissolution of a decree entered by the District Court imposing a school desegregation plan. The District Court granted relief over the objection of respondents Robert L. Dowell et al., black students and their parents. The Court of Appeals for the Tenth Circuit reversed, holding that the Board would be entitled to such relief only upon "[n]othing less than a clear showing of grievous wrong evoked by new and unforeseen conditions . . . .""

The Supreme Court granted certiorari to review the case.

B. Counsel of Record

ACLU Side (Respondent / Appellee): Julius LeVonne Chambers argued the cause for appellees. With him on the brief were Charles Stephen Ralston, Norman J. Chachkin, Lewis Barber, Jr., Janell M. Byrd, and Anthony G. Amsterdam.

Opposing Side (Petitioner / Appellant): Ronald L. Day argued the cause for appellant. With him on the briefs were Laurie W. Jones and Charles J. Cooper.

Solicitor General Starr argued the cause for the United States as amicus curiae.

III. AMICI CURIAE

ACLU Side (Respondent / Appellee)

Brief of amici curiae filed on behalf of the Lawyers' Committee for Civil Rights Under Law, American Civil Liberties Union, and American Jewish Congress by Paul Vizcarrondo, Jr., Norman Redlich, Robert F. Mullen, John A. Powell, Steven R. Shapiro, and Marc D. Stern.

Brief of amici curiae filed on behalf of the American Jewish Committee et al. by Samuel Rabinove, Richard T. Foltin, and William B. Duffy, Jr.

Brief of amici curiae filed on behalf of the National Association for the Advancement of Colored People et al. by David J. Burman, William L. Taylor, and Susan M. Liss.

Brief of amici curiae filed on behalf of the National Education Association by Robert H. Chanin and Jeremiah A. Collins.

Opposing Side (Petitioner / Appellant)

Brief of amici curiae filed on behalf of the United States by Solicitor General Starr, Assistant Attorney General Dunne, Deputy Solicitor General Roberts, Deputy Assistant Attorney General Clegg, Lawrence S. Robbins, David K. Flynn, and Mark L. Gross.

Brief of amici curiae filed on behalf of the DeKalb County Board of Education by Rex E. Lee, Carter G. Phillips, Mark D. Hopson, Gary M. Sams, Charles L. Weatherly, and J. Stanley Hawkins.

Brief of amici curiae filed on behalf of the Intervenors in Carlin v. Board of Education of San Diego Unified School District by Elmer Enstrom, Jr.

Brief of amici curiae filed on behalf of the Landmark Legal Foundation Center for Civil Rights by Clint Bolick, Jerald L. Hill, Gary Lawson, Daniel Polsby, Charles E. Rice, Robert A. Anthony, Thomas C. Arthur, Peter J. Ferrara, Lino A. Graglia, and Henry Mark Holzer.

Brief of amici curiae filed on behalf of the Council of the Great City Schools et al. by David S. Tatel, Walter A. Smith, Jr., and Patricia A. Brannan.

Brief of amici curiae filed on behalf of the Mountain States Legal Foundation by William Perry Pendley.

IV. THE SUPREME COURT'S DECISION

"We must first consider whether respondents may contest the District Court's 1987 order dissolving the injunction which had imposed the desegregation decree. Respondents did not appeal from the District Court's 1977 order finding that the school system had achieved unitary status, and petitioner contends that the 1977 order bars respondents from contesting the 1987 order. We disagree, for the 1977 order did not dissolve the desegregation decree, and the District Court's unitariness finding was too ambiguous to bar respondents from challenging later action by the Board. . . .

The Court of Appeals relied upon language from this Court's decision in United States v. Swift and Co., for the proposition that a desegregation decree could not be lifted or modified absent a showing of 'grievous wrong evoked by new and unforeseen conditions.' It also held that 'compliance alone cannot become the basis for modifying or dissolving an injunction,' relying on United States v. W.T. Grant Co., 345 U.S. 629 (1953). We hold that its reliance was mistaken. . . .

A district court need not accept at face value the profession of a school board which has intentionally discriminated that it will cease to do so in the future. But in deciding whether to modify or dissolve a desegregation decree, a school board's compliance with previous court orders is obviously relevant. . . .

Petitioner urges that we reinstate the decision of the District Court terminating the injunction, but we think that the preferable course is to remand the case to that court so that it may decide, in accordance with this opinion, whether the Board made a sufficient showing of constitutional compliance as of 1985, when the SRP was adopted, to allow the injunction to be dissolved. The District Court should address itself to whether the Board had complied in good faith with the desegregation decree since it was entered, and whether the vestiges of past discrimination had been eliminated to the extent practicable. . . .

After the District Court decides whether the Board was entitled to have the decree terminated, it should proceed to decide respondent's challenge to the SRP. A school district which has been released from an injunction imposing a desegregation plan no longer requires court authorization for the promulgation of policies and rules regulating matters such as assignment of students and the like, but it of course remains subject to the mandate of the Equal Protection Clause of the Fourteenth Amendment. If the Board was entitled to have the decree terminated as of 1985, the District Court should then evaluate the Board's decision to implement the SRP under appropriate equal protection principles.

The judgment of the Court of Appeals is reversed, and the case is remanded . . . ."

V. JUSTICE VOTE

3 Pro ACLU Side vs. 5 Con Opposing Side

ACLU Side (Respondent / Appellee)

1. Marshall, T. – Wrote dissenting opinion
2. Blackmun, H. – Joined Marshall's dissent
3. Stevens, J. – Joined Marshall's dissent

Opposing Side (Petitioner / Appellant)

1. Rehnquist, W. – Wrote majority opinion
2. Kennedy, A. – Joined majority opinion
3. White, B. – Joined majority opinion
4. Scalia, A. – Joined majority opinion
5. O'Connor, S. – Joined majority opinion

Souter, D – Took no part in the decision.

VI. A WIN OR LOSS FOR THE ACLU?

The ACLU filed as amicus curiae urging affirmance; the Supreme Court reversed the Court of Appeals' decision by a 5-3 vote, giving the ACLU an apparent loss.

713. UAW v. Johnson Controls, Inc.

(Decided March 20, 1991; 499 U.S. 187)

I. ISSUE

A. Issues Discussed

Civil rights, gender, employment discrimination

B. Legal Question Presented

"May an employer exclude a fertile female employee from certain jobs because of its concern for the health of the fetus the woman might conceive?"

C. Supreme Court's Answer

An employer may not exclude fertile female employees in this way because this method of exclusion is discriminatory.

II. CASE SUMMARY

A. Background

"Respondent Johnson Controls, Inc., manufactures batteries. In the manufacturing process, the element lead is a primary ingredient. Occupational exposure to lead entails health risks, including the risk of harm to any fetus carried by a female employee.

Before the Civil Rights Act of 1964 became law, Johnson Controls did not employ any woman in a battery-manufacturing job. In June 1977, however, it announced its first official policy concerning its employment of women in lead-exposure work . . . . Johnson Controls 'stopped short of excluding women capable of bearing children from lead exposure,' but emphasized that a woman who expected to have a child should not choose a job in which she would have such exposure. The company also required a woman who wished to be considered for employment to sign a statement that she had been advised of the risk of having a child while she was exposed to lead. . . .

Five years later, in 1982, Johnson Controls shifted from a policy of warning to a policy of exclusion. . . . The policy defined 'women . . . capable of bearing children' as '[a]ll women except those whose inability to bear children is medically documented.' It further stated that an unacceptable work station was one where, 'over the past year,' an employee had recorded a blood lead level of more than 30 micrograms per deciliter or the work site had yielded an air sample containing a lead level in excess of 30 micrograms per cubic meter. . . .

In April 1984, petitioners filed in the United States District Court for the Eastern District of Wisconsin a class action challenging Johnson Controls' fetal-protection policy as sex discrimination that violated Title VII of the Civil Rights Act of 1964 . . . . Among the individual plaintiffs were petitioners Mary Craig, who had chosen to be sterilized in order to avoid losing her job, Elsie Nason, a 50-year-old divorcee, who had suffered a loss in compensation when she was transferred out of a job where she was exposed to lead, and Donald Penney, who had been denied a request for a leave of absence for the purpose of lowering his lead level because he intended to become a father. Upon stipulation of the parties, the District Court certified a class consisting of 'all past, present and future production and maintenance employees' in United Auto Workers bargaining units at nine of Johnson Controls' plants 'who have been and continue to be affected by [the employer's] Fetal Protection Policy implemented in 1982.'

The District Court granted summary judgment for defendant-respondent Johnson Controls. . . . The Court of Appeals for the Seventh Circuit, sitting en banc, affirmed the summary judgment by a 7-to-4 vote."

The Supreme Court granted certiorari to review the case and reversed.

B. Counsel of Record / ACLU Attorney

ACLU Side (Petitioner / Appellant): Marsha S. Berzon argued the cause for appellant.

Opposing Side (Respondent / Appellee): Stanley S. Jaspan argued the cause for appellee.

III. AMICI CURIAE

ACLU Side (Petitioner / Appellant)

Brief of amici curiae filed on behalf of the ACLU by Joan E. Bertin, Elisabeth A. Werby, and Isabelle Katz Pinzler.

Additional briefs of amici curiae were filed on behalf of the United States, et al., the State of California, et al., the Commonwealth of Massachusetts, et al., the American Public Health Association, et al., Equal Rights Advocates, et al., the NAACP Legal Defense and Educational Fund, Inc., et al., Trial Lawyers for Public Justice, the Association of the Bar of the City of New York, et al., and the National Resources Defense Council, Inc.

Opposing Side (Respondent / Appellee)

Briefs of amici curiae were filed on behalf of the Chamber of Commerce of the United States of America, Concerned Women for America, the Equal Employment Advisory Council, et al., the Industrial Hygiene Law Project, the National Safe Workplace Institute, the United States Catholic Conference, the Washington Legal Foundation, and the Pacific Legal Foundation, et al.

IV. THE SUPREME COURT'S DECISION

"The bias in Johnson Controls' policy is obvious. . . . Respondent's fetal-protection policy explicitly discriminates against women on the basis of their sex. The policy excludes women with childbearing capacity from lead-exposed jobs, and so creates a facial classification based on gender. . . .

Our conclusion is bolstered by the Pregnancy Discrimination Act (PDA), in which Congress explicitly provided that, for purposes of Title VII, discrimination "on the basis of sex" includes discrimination 'because of or on the basis of pregnancy, childbirth, or related medical conditions.' 'The Pregnancy Discrimination Act has now made clear that, for all Title VII purposes, discrimination based on a woman's pregnancy is, on its face, discrimination because of her sex.' In its use of the words 'capable of bearing children' in the 1982 policy statement as the criterion for exclusion, Johnson Controls explicitly classifies on the basis of potential for pregnancy. Under the PDA, such a classification must be regarded, for Title VII purposes, in the same light as explicit sex discrimination. Respondent has chosen to treat all its female employees as potentially pregnant; that choice evinces discrimination on the basis of sex. . . .

Our holding today that Title VII, as so amended, forbids sex-specific fetal-protection policies is neither remarkable nor unprecedented. Concern for a woman's existing or potential offspring historically has been the excuse for denying women equal employment opportunities. Congress in the PDA prohibited discrimination on the basis of a woman's ability to become pregnant. We do no more than hold that the PDA means what it says.

It is no more appropriate for the courts than it is for individual employers to decide whether a woman's reproductive role is more important to herself and her family than her economic role. Congress has left this choice to the woman as hers to make.

The judgment of the Court of Appeals is reversed, and the case is remanded for further proceedings consistent with this opinion."

V. JUSTICE VOTE

9 Pro ACLU Side vs. 0 Con Opposing Side

ACLU Side (Petitioner / Appellant)

1. Blackmun, H. – Wrote majority opinion
2. Marshall, T. – Joined majority opinion
3. Stevens, J. – Joined majority opinion
4. O'Connor, S. – Joined majority opinion
5. Souter, D. – Joined majority opinion
6. White, B. – Wrote concurring opinion
7. Rehnquist, W. – Joined White's concurrence
8. Kennedy, A. – Joined White's concurrence
9. Scalia, A. – Wrote concurring opinion

VI. A WIN OR LOSS FOR THE ACLU?

The ACLU filed as amicus curiae, urging reversal of the judgment of the Court of Appeals; the Supreme Court reversed in a 9-0 vote, giving the ACLU an apparent win.

714. Equal Employment Opportunity Commission v. Arabian American Oil Co.

(Decided March 26, 1991; 499 U.S. 244)

I. ISSUE

A. Issues Discussed

Civil rights, federal rights, employment discrimination, extraterritoriality

B. Legal Question Presented

"[W]hether Title VII applies extraterritorially to regulate the employment practices of United States employers who employ United States citizens abroad."

C. Supreme Court's Answer

Title VII does not apply extraterritorially to regulate employment practices of United States employers who employ United States citizens abroad.

II. CASE SUMMARY

A. Background

"Petitioner Boureslan is a naturalized United States citizen who was born in Lebanon. The respondents are two Delaware corporations, Arabian American Oil Company (Aramco), and its subsidiary, Aramco Service Company (ASC). Aramco's principal place of business is Dhahran, Saudi Arabia, and it is licensed to do business in Texas. ASC's principal place of business is Houston, Texas.

In 1979, Boureslan was hired by ASC as a cost engineer in Houston. A year later he was transferred, at his request, to work for Aramco in Saudi Arabia. Boureslan remained with Aramco in

Saudi Arabia until he was discharged in 1984. After filing a charge of discrimination with the Equal Employment Opportunity Commission (EEOC or Commission), he instituted this suit in the United States District Court for the Southern District of Texas against Aramco and ASC. He sought relief under both state law and Title VII of the Civil Rights Act of 1964, on the ground that he was harassed and ultimately discharged by respondents on account of his race, religion, and national origin.

Respondents filed a motion for summary judgment on the ground that the District Court lacked subject-matter jurisdiction over Boureslan's claim because the protections of Title VII do not extend to United States citizens employed abroad by American employers. The District Court agreed and dismissed Boureslan's Title VII claim; it also dismissed his state-law claims for lack of pendent jurisdiction and entered final judgment in favor of respondents. A panel for the Fifth Circuit affirmed. After vacating the panel's decision and rehearing the case en banc, the court affirmed the District Court's dismissal of Boureslan's complaint."

The Supreme Court granted certiorari to review the case and reversed.

B. Counsel of Record / ACLU Attorney

ACLU Side (Petitioner / Appellant): Solicitor General Starr argued the cause for appellant.

Opposing Side (Respondent / Appellee): Paul L. Friedman argued the case for appellee.

III. AMICI CURIAE

ACLU Side (Petitioner / Appellant)

Brief of amici curiae filed on behalf of the ACLU, et al., by Jane M. Picker, Sidney Picker, Jr., Isabelle Katz Pinzler, and John A. Powell.

Brief of amici curiae filed on behalf of the International Human Rights Law Group by Robert Plotkin and Steven M. Schneebaum.

Brief of amici curiae filed on behalf of the Lawyers' Committee for Civil Rights Under Law by Gary B. Born, Robert F. Mullen, David S. Tatel, Norman Redlich, Thomas J. Henderson, and Richard T. Seymour.

Brief of amici curiae filed on behalf of the NAACP Legal Defense and Educational Fund, Inc., et al., by Julius LeVonne Chambers and Charles Stephen Ralston.

Opposing Side (Respondent / Appellee)

Brief of amici curiae filed on behalf of the Equal Employment Advisory Council by Robert E. Williams, Douglas S. McDowell, and Edward E. Potter.

Brief of amici curiae filed on behalf of the Rule of Law Committee, et al., by Cecil J. Olmstead.

Brief of amici curiae filed on behalf of the Society for Human Resources Management by Kenneth Kirschner, John E. Parauda, and Lawrence Z. Lorber.

Brief of amici curiae filed on behalf of the Washington Legal Foundation by Jeffrey I. Zuckerman, Daniel J. Popeo, and Paul D. Kamenar.

IV. THE SUPREME COURT'S DECISION

"It is a longstanding principle of American law 'that legislation of Congress, unless a contrary intent appears, is meant to apply only within the territorial jurisdiction of the United States.' This 'canon of construction . . . is a valid approach whereby unexpressed congressional intent may be ascertained.' It serves to protect against unintended clashes between our laws and those of other nations which could result in international discord. . . . We assume that Congress legislates against the backdrop of the presumption against extraterritoriality. Therefore, unless there is 'the affirmative intention of the Congress clearly expressed, we must presume it 'is primarily concerned with domestic conditions.' . . .

The intent of Congress as to the extraterritorial application of this statute must be deduced by inference from boilerplate language which can be found in any number of congressional acts, none of which have ever been held to apply overseas. [W]e have repeatedly held that even statutes that contain broad language in their definitions of 'commerce' that expressly refer to 'foreign commerce' do not apply abroad. . . .

We are of the view that, even when considered in combination with petitioners' other arguments, the EEOC's interpretation is insufficiently weighty to overcome the presumption against extraterritorial application.

Our conclusion today is buttressed by the fact that '[w]hen it desires to do so, Congress knows how to place the high seas within the jurisdictional reach of a statute.' Congress' awareness of the need to make a clear statement that a statute applies overseas is amply demonstrated by the numerous occasions on which it has expressly legislated the extraterritorial application of a statute. . . .

Petitioners have failed to present sufficient affirmative evidence that Congress intended Title VII to apply abroad. Accordingly, the judgment of the Court of Appeals is affirmed."

V. JUSTICE VOTE

3 Pro ACLU Side vs. 6 Con Opposing Side

ACLU Side (Petitioner / Appellant)

1. Marshall, T. – Wrote dissenting opinion
2. Blackmun, H. – Joined Marshall's dissent
3. Stevens, J. – Joined Marshall's dissent

Opposing Side (Respondent / Appellee)

1. Rehnquist, W. – Wrote majority opinion
2. White, B. – Joined majority opinion
3. Souter, D. – Joined majority opinion
4. Kennedy, A. – Joined majority opinion
5. O'Connor, S. – Joined majority opinion
6. Scalia, A. – Wrote concurring opinion

VI. A WIN OR LOSS FOR THE ACLU?

The ACLU filed as amicus curiae urging reversal of the judgment of the Court of Appeals; the Supreme Court affirmed in a 6-3 vote; giving the ACLU an apparent loss.

715. Powers v. Ohio

(Decided April 1, 1991; 499 U.S. 400)

I. ISSUE

A. Issues Discussed

Equal protection, discrimination, jury selection

B. Legal Question Presented

"[W]hether, based on the Equal Protection Clause, a white defendant may object to the prosecution's peremptory challenges of black venirepersons."

C. Supreme Court's Answer

A white defendant may object to the prosecution's peremptory challenges of black venirepersons.

II. CASE SUMMARY

A. Background

"Petitioner Larry Joe Powers, a white man, was indicted in Franklin County, Ohio, on two counts of aggravated murder and one count of attempted aggravated murder. . . .

In the jury selection process, Powers objected when the prosecutor exercised his first peremptory challenge to remove a black venireperson. Powers requested the trial court to compel the prosecutor to explain, on the record, his reasons for excluding a black person. The trial court denied the request and excused the juror. The State proceeded to use nine more peremptory challenges, six of which removed black venirepersons from the jury. Each time the prosecution challenged a black prospective juror, Powers renewed his objections . . . . His objections were overruled. The record does not indicate that race was somehow implicated in the crime or the trial; nor does it reveal whether any black persons sat on petitioner's petit jury or if any of the nine jurors petitioner excused by peremptory challenges were black persons.

The empaneled jury convicted Powers on counts of murder, aggravated murder, and attempted aggravated murder, each with the firearm specifications, and the trial court sentenced him to a term of imprisonment of 53 years to life. Powers appealed his conviction to the Ohio Court of Appeals, contending that the prosecutor's discriminatory use of peremptories violated the Sixth Amendment's guarantee of a fair cross section in his petit jury, the Fourteenth Amendment's Equal Protection Clause, and Article I, §§ 10 and 16, of the Ohio Constitution. Powers contended that his own race was irrelevant to the right to object to the prosecution's peremptory challenges. The Court of Appeals affirmed the conviction, and the Supreme Court of Ohio dismissed Powers' appeal on the ground that it presented no substantial constitutional question."

The Supreme Court granted certiorari to review the case and reversed.

B. Counsel of Record / ACLU Attorney

ACLU Side (Petitioner / Appellant): Robert L. Lane, by appointment of the Court, argued the cause for appellant.

Opposing Side (Respondent / Appellee): Alan Craig Travis argued the cause for appellee.

III. AMICI CURIAE

ACLU Side (Petitioner / Appellant)

Brief of amici curiae filed on behalf of the ACLU, et al., by Barbara D. Underwood, Steven R. Shapiro, Julius LeVonne Chambers, and Charles Stephen Ralston.

Brief of amici curiae filed on behalf of the Criminal Justice Legal Foundation by Kent S. Scheidegger.

Brief of amici curiae filed on behalf of the Ohio Association of Criminal Defense Lawyers by Harry R. Reinhart and Kathleen S. Aynes.

Opposing Side (Respondent / Appellee)

No briefs of amici curiae were filed in support of appellee.

IV. THE SUPREME COURT'S DECISION

"For over a century, this Court has been unyielding in its position that a defendant is denied equal protection of the laws when tried before a jury from which members of his or her race have been excluded by the State's purposeful conduct. . . .

Because Powers is white, the State argues, he cannot object to the exclusion of black prospective jurors. This limitation on a defendant's right to object conforms neither with our accepted rules of standing to raise a constitutional claim nor with the substantive guarantees of the Equal Protection Clause and the policies underlying federal statutory law. . . .

We hold that the Equal Protection Clause prohibits a prosecutor from using the State's peremptory challenges to exclude otherwise qualified and unbiased persons from the petit jury solely by reason of their race, a practice that forecloses a significant opportunity to participate in civic life. An individual juror does not have a right to sit on any particular petit jury, but he or she does possess the right not to be excluded from one on account of race. . . .

The discriminatory use of peremptory challenges by the prosecution causes a criminal defendant cognizable injury, and the defendant has a concrete interest in challenging the practice. This is not because the individual jurors dismissed by the prosecution may have been predisposed to favor the defendant; if that were true, the jurors might have been excused for cause. Rather, it is because racial discrimination in the selection of jurors 'casts doubt on the integrity of the judicial process,' and places the fairness of a criminal proceeding in doubt. . . .

Both the excluded juror and the criminal defendant have a common interest in eliminating racial discrimination from the courtroom. A venireperson excluded from jury service because of race suffers a profound personal humiliation heightened by its public character. The rejected juror may lose confidence in the court and its verdicts, as may the defendant if his or her objections cannot be heard. This congruence of interests makes it necessary and appropriate for the defendant to raise the rights of the juror. And, there can be no doubt that petitioner will be a motivated, effective advocate for the excluded venirepersons' rights. Petitioner has much at stake in proving that his jury was improperly constituted due to an equal protection violation, for we have recognized that discrimination in the jury selection process may lead to the reversal of a conviction. . . .

We conclude that a defendant in a criminal case can raise the third-party equal protection claims of jurors excluded by the prosecution because of their race. . . .

It remains for the trial courts to develop rules, without unnecessary disruption of the jury selection process, to permit legitimate and well-founded objections to the use of peremptory challenges as a mask for race prejudice. In this case, the State concedes that, if we find the petitioner has standing to object to the prosecution's use of the peremptory challenges, the case should be remanded. We find that petitioner does have standing. The judgment is reversed, and the case is remanded for further proceedings not inconsistent with our opinion."

V. JUSTICE VOTE

7 Pro ACLU Side vs. 2 Con Opposing Side

ACLU Side (Petitioner / Appellant)

1. Kennedy, A. – Wrote majority opinion
2. White, B. – Joined majority opinion
3. Marshall, T. – Joined majority opinion
4. Blackmun, H. – Joined majority opinion
5. Stevens, J. – Joined majority opinion
6. O'Connor, S. – Joined majority opinion
7. Souter, D. – Joined majority opinion

Opposing Side (Respondent / Appellee)

1. Scalia, A. – Wrote dissenting opinion
2. Rehnquist, W. – Joined Scalia's dissent

VI. A WIN OR LOSS FOR THE ACLU?

The ACLU, as amicus curiae, urged reversal of the judgment of the Ohio Court of Appeals; the Supreme Court reversed in a 7-2 vote, giving the ACLU an apparent win.

716. County of Riverside v. McLaughlin

(Decided May 13, 1991; 500 U.S. 44)

I. ISSUE

A. Issues Discussed

Criminal justice, Fourth Amendment, probable cause

B. Legal Question Presented

"[W]hat constitutes a 'prompt' probable cause determination under Gerstein."

C. Supreme Court's Answer

A probable cause determination procedure is not presumptively "prompt" and is therefore subject to challenge when the regular practice allows determinations to extend beyond 48 hours after arrest.

II. CASE SUMMARY

A. Background

"This is a class action brought under 42 U.S.C. § 1983 challenging the manner in which the County of Riverside, California (County), provides probable cause determinations to persons arrested without a warrant. At issue is the County's policy of combining probable cause determinations with its arraignment procedures. Under County policy, which tracks closely the provisions of Cal.Penal Code Ann. § 825 (West 1985), arraignments must be conducted without unnecessary delay and, in any event, within two days of arrest. This 2–day requirement excludes from computation weekends and holidays. Thus, an individual arrested without a warrant late in the week may in some cases be held for as long as five days before receiving a probable cause determination. Over the Thanksgiving holiday, a 7–day delay is possible. . . .

In August 1987, Donald Lee McLaughlin filed a complaint in the United States District Court for the Central District of California, seeking injunctive and declaratory relief on behalf of himself and "all others similarly situated." The complaint alleged that McLaughlin was then currently incarcerated in the Riverside County Jail and had not received a probable cause determination. He requested "an order and judgment requiring that the defendants and the County of Riverside provide in-custody arrestees, arrested without warrants, prompt probable cause, bail and arraignment hearings." Shortly thereafter, McLaughlin moved for class certification.

[After resolving issues of plaintiff's standing, in] November 1988, the District Court certified a class comprising 'all present and future prisoners in the Riverside County Jail including those pretrial detainees arrested without warrants and held in the Riverside County Jail from August 1, 1987 to the present, and all such future detainees who have been or may be denied prompt probable cause, bail or arraignment hearings.'

In March 1989, plaintiffs asked the District Court to issue a preliminary injunction requiring the County to provide all persons arrested without a warrant a judicial determination of probable cause within 36 hours of arrest. The District Court issued the injunction, holding that the County's existing practice violated this Court's decision in Gerstein. . . .

On November 8, 1989, the Court of Appeals affirmed the order granting the preliminary injunction against Riverside County."

The Supreme Court granted certiorari to review the case, vacated, and remanded.

B. Counsel of Record / ACLU Attorney

ACLU Side (Respondent / Appellee): Dan Stormer argued the cause for appellee.

Opposing Side (Petitioner / Appellant): Timothy T. Coates argued the cause for appellant.

III. AMICI CURIAE

ACLU Side (Respondent / Appellee)

Brief of amici curiae filed on behalf of the ACLU by Robert M. Rotstein, John A. Powell, Paul L. Hoffman, and Judith Resnik.

Brief of amici curiae filed on behalf of the Youth Law Center by Mark I. Soler and Loran M. Warboys.

Opposing Side (Petitioner / Appellant)

Brief of amici curiae filed on behalf of the State of California by John K. Van de Kamp, Attorney General, Richard B. Iglehart, Chief Assistant Attorney General, Harley D. Mayfield, Senior Assistant Attorney General, and Robert M. Foster and Frederick R. Millar, Jr., Supervising Deputy Attorneys General.
Brief of amici curiae filed on behalf of the District Attorney, County of Riverside, California, by Grover C. Trask, II, pro se.
Brief of amici curiae filed on behalf of the State of Hawaii, et al., by Warren Price III, Attorney General of Hawaii, and Steven S. Michaels, Deputy Attorney General, Don Siegelman, Attorney General of Alabama, Ron Fields, Attorney General of Arkansas, John J. Kelly, Chief State's Attorney of Connecticut, Charles J. Oberly III, Attorney General of Delaware, James T. Jones, Attorney General of Idaho, Neil F. Hartigan, Attorney General of Illinois, Linley E. Pearson, Attorney General of Indiana, James E. Tierney, Attorney General of Maine, Frank J. Kelley, Attorney General of Michigan, Mike Moore, Attorney General of Mississippi, Marc Racicot, Attorney General of Montana, Robert M. Spire, Attorney General of Nebraska, Robert J. Del Tufo, Attorney General of New Jersey, John P. Arnold, Attorney General of New Hampshire, Hal Stratton, Attorney General of New Mexico, Brian McKay, Attorney General of Nevada, Lacy H. Thornburg, Attorney General of North Carolina, Robert H. Henry, Attorney General of Oklahoma, T. Travis Medlock, Attorney General of South Carolina, Roger A. Tellinghuisen, Attorney General of South Dakota, Jeffrey L. Amestoy, Attorney General of Vermont, and Joseph P. Meyer, Attorney General of Wyoming.
Brief of amici curiae filed on behalf of the County of Los Angeles, et al., by De Witt W. Clinton and Dixon M. Holston.
Brief of amici curiae filed on behalf of the California District Attorneys Association by Michael R. Capizzi.

IV. THE SUPREME COURT'S DECISION

"[S]tates have a strong interest in protecting public safety by taking into custody those persons who are reasonably suspected of having engaged in criminal activity, even where there has been no opportunity for a prior judicial determination of probable cause. On the other hand, prolonged detention based on incorrect or unfounded suspicion may unjustly 'imperil [a] suspect's job, interrupt his source of income, and impair his family relationships.'

[S]ome delays are inevitable. For example, where, as in Riverside County, the probable cause determination is combined with arraignment, there will be delays caused by paperwork and logistical problems. . . . In our view, the Fourth Amendment permits a reasonable postponement of a probable cause determination while the police cope with the everyday problems of processing suspects through an overly burdened criminal justice system.

But flexibility has its limits . . . . A state has no legitimate interest in detaining for extended periods individuals who have been arrested without probable cause. . . .

Unfortunately, as lower court decisions applying Gerstein have demonstrated, it is not enough to say that probable cause determinations must be 'prompt.' This vague standard simply has not provided sufficient guidance. Instead, it has led to a flurry of systemic challenges to city and county practices, putting federal judges in the role of making legislative judgments and overseeing local jailhouse operations.

Our task in this case is to articulate more clearly the boundaries of what is permissible under the Fourth Amendment. Although we hesitate to announce that the Constitution compels a specific time limit, it is important to provide some degree of certainty so that States and counties may establish procedures with confidence that they fall within constitutional bounds. [W]e believe that a jurisdiction that provides judicial determinations of probable cause within 48 hours of arrest will, as a general matter, comply with the promptness requirement of Gerstein. For this reason, such jurisdictions will be immune from systemic challenges. . . .

Where an arrested individual does not receive a probable cause determination within 48 hours, the calculus changes. In such a case, the arrested individual does not bear the burden of proving an unreasonable delay. Rather, the burden shifts to the government to demonstrate the existence of a bona fide emergency or other extraordinary circumstance. The fact that, in a particular case, it may take longer than 48 hours to consolidate pretrial proceedings does not qualify as an extraordinary circumstance. Nor, for that matter, do intervening weekends. A jurisdiction that chooses to offer combined proceedings must do so as soon as is reasonably feasible, but in no event later than 48 hours after arrest. . . .

Everyone agrees that the police should make every attempt to minimize the time a presumptively innocent individual spends in jail. One way to do so is to provide a judicial determination of probable cause immediately upon completing the administrative steps incident to arrest—i.e., as soon as the suspect has been booked, photographed, and fingerprinted. . . . For the reasons we have articulated, we conclude that Riverside County is entitled to combine probable cause determinations with arraignments. The record indicates, however, that the County's current policy and practice do not comport fully with the principles we have outlined. The County's current policy is to offer combined proceedings within two days, exclusive of Saturdays, Sundays, or holidays. As a result, persons arrested on Thursdays may have to wait until the following Monday before they receive a probable cause determination. The delay is even longer if there is an intervening holiday. Thus, the County's regular practice exceeds the 48-hour period we deem constitutionally permissible, meaning that the County is not immune from systemic challenges, such as this class action. . . .

The judgment of the Court of Appeals is vacated, and the case is remanded for further proceedings consistent with this opinion."

V. JUSTICE VOTE

4 Pro ACLU SIde vs. 5 Con Opposing Side

ACLU Side (Respondent / Appellee)

1. Scalia, A. – Wrote dissenting opinion
2. Marshall, T. – Wrote dissenting opinion

3. Blackmun, H. – Joined Marshall's dissent
4. Stevens, J. – Joined Marshall's dissent

Opposing Side (Petitioner / Appellant)

1. O'Connor, S. – Wrote majority opinion
2. White, B. – Joined majority opinion
3. Souter, D. – Joined majority opinion
4. Kennedy, A. – Joined majority opinion
5. Rehnquist, W. – Joined majority opinion

VI. A WIN OR LOSS FOR THE ACLU?

The ACLU filed as amicus curiae urging affirmance of the judgment of the Ninth Circuit Court of Appeals; the Supreme Court vacated and remanded in a 5-4 vote; giving the ACLU an apparent loss.

717. Rust v. Sullivan

(Decided May 23, 1991; 500 U.S. 173)

I. ISSUE

A. Issues Discussed

First Amendment, freedom of speech, Fifth Amendment, abortion rights

B. Legal Question Presented

Whether "Department of Health and Human Services (HHS) regulations which limit the ability of Title X fund recipients to engage in abortion-related activities" are constitutional.

C. Supreme Court's Answer

The regulations limiting abortion-related activities are constitutional.

II. CASE SUMMARY

A. Background

"In 1970, Congress enacted Title X of the Public Health Service Act (Act), . . . which provides federal funding for family-planning services. . . . Section 1008 of the Act, however, provides that '[n]one of the funds appropriated under this subchapter shall be used in programs where abortion is a method of family planning.' That restriction was intended to ensure that Title X funds would 'be used only to support preventive family planning services, population research, infertility services, and other related medical, informational, and educational activities.' . . .

In 1988, the Secretary promulgated new regulations designed to provide "clear and operational guidance' to grantees about how to preserve the distinction between Title X programs and abortion as a method of family planning.' . . . The regulations attach three principal conditions on the grant of federal funds for Title X projects. First, the regulations specify that a 'Title X project may not provide counseling concerning the use of abortion as a method of family planning or provide referral for abortion as a method of family planning.' . . . Second, the regulations broadly prohibit a Title X project from engaging in activities that 'encourage, promote or advocate abortion as a method of family planning.' . . . Third, the regulations require that Title X projects be organized so that they are 'physically and financially separate' from prohibited abortion activities. . . .

Petitioners are Title X grantees and doctors who supervise Title X funds suing on behalf of themselves and their patients. Respondent is the Secretary of HHS. After the regulations had been promulgated, but before they had been applied, petitioners filed two separate actions, later consolidated, challenging the facial validity of the regulations and seeking declaratory and injunctive relief to prevent implementation of the regulations. Petitioners challenged the regulations on the grounds that they were not authorized by Title X and that they violate the First and Fifth Amendment rights of Title X clients and the First Amendment rights of Title X health providers. After initially granting petitioners a preliminary injunction, the District Court rejected petitioners' statutory and constitutional challenges to the regulations and granted summary judgment in favor of the Secretary.

A panel of the Court of Appeals for the Second Circuit affirmed."

The Supreme Court granted certiorari to review the case and affirmed.

B. Counsel of Record / ACLU Attorney

ACLU Side (Petitioner / Appellant): Laurence H. Tribe argued the cause for appellants in both cases. With him on the briefs for appellants in No. 89-1391 were Kathleen M. Sullivan, Rachael N. Pine, Janet Benshoof, Lynn Paltrow, Kathryn Kolbert, Steven R. Shapiro, Norman Siegel, Arthur Eisenberg, Roger K. Evans, Laurie R. Rockett, and Peter J. Rubin. Robert Abrams, Attorney General of New York, O. Peter Sherwood, Solicitor General, Suzanne M. Lynn and Sanford M. Cohen, Assistant Attorneys General, Victor A. Kovner, Leonard J. Koerner, Lorna Bade Goodman, Gail Rubin, and Hillary Weisman filed briefs for appellants in No. 89-1392.

Opposing Side (Respondent / Appellee): Solicitor General Starr argued the cause and filed a brief for appellee in both cases. With him on the brief were Assistant Attorney General Gerson, Deputy Solicitor General Roberts, Jeffrey P. Minear, Anthony J. Steinmeyer, Lowell V. Sturgill, Jr., and Joel Mangel.

III. AMICI CURIAE

ACLU Side (Petitioner / Appellant)

Brief of amici curiae filed on behalf of the Commonwealth of Massachusetts, et al., by David D. Cole, James M. Shannon, Attorney General of Massachusetts, and Ruth A. Bourquin, Assistant Attorney General.

Brief of amici curiae filed on behalf of Anthony J. Celebrezze, Jr., Attorney General of Ohio, et al., by Anthony J. Celebrezze, pro se, Suzanne E. Mohr and Jack W. Decker, Assistant Attorneys General, and Rita S. Eppler, Douglas B. Baily, Attorney General of Alaska, John K. Van de Kamp, Attorney General of California, Clarine Nardi Riddle, Attorney General of Connecticut, Charles M. Oberly III, Attorney General of Delaware, Herbert O. Reid, Sr., Corporation Counsel for the District of Columbia, James E. Tierney, Attorney General of Maine, Hubert H. Humphrey III, Attorney General of Minnesota, Robert M. Spire, Attorney General of Nebraska,

Robert J. Del Tufo, Attorney General of New Jersey, Dave Frohnmayer, Attorney General of Oregon, Jim Mattox, Attorney General of Texas, Jeffrey L. Amestoy, Attorney General of Vermont, and Mary Sue Terry, Attorney General of Virginia.

Brief of amici curiae filed on behalf of the American College of Obstetricians and Gynecologists, et al., by Carter G. Phillips, Ann E. Allen, Kirk B. Johnson, Laurie R. Rockett, Joel I. Klein, and Jack R. Bierig.

Brief of amici curiae filed on behalf of the American Library Association, et al., by Bruce J. Ennis, Jr., and David W. Ogden.

Brief of amici curiae filed on behalf of the American Public Health Association, et al., by Larry M. Lavinsky, Charles S. Sims, Michele M. Ovesey, and Nadine Taub.

Brief of amici curiae filed on behalf of the Association of the Bar of the City of New York by Conrad K. Harper, Janice Goodman, and Diane S. Wilner.

Brief of amici curiae filed on behalf of the NAACP Legal Defense and Educational Fund, Inc., et al., by Julius LeVonne Chambers and Charles Stephen Ralston.

Brief of amici curiae filed on behalf of the National Association of Women Lawyers, et al., by James F. Fitzpatrick, L. Hope O'Keeffe, and Walter Dellinger.

Brief of amici curiae filed on behalf of the Planned Parenthood Federation of America, et al., by Dara Klassel, Eve W. Paul, and Barbara E. Otten.

Brief of Twenty-Two Biomedical Ethicists by Michael E. Fine and Douglas W. Smith.

Brief of amici curiae filed on behalf of Representative Patricia Schroeder, et al., by David M. Becker.

Brief of amici curiae filed on behalf of the NOW Legal Defense and Education Fund, et al., by John H. Hall, Sarah E. Burns, and Alison Wetherfield.

Opposing Side (Respondent / Appellee)

Brief of amici curiae filed on behalf of the American Academy of Medical Ethics by Carolyn B. Kuhl.

Brief of amici curiae filed on behalf of the Association of American Physicians and Surgeons by Clarke D. Forsythe and Kent Masterson Brown.

Brief of amici curiae filed on behalf of Feminists for Life of America, et al., by Edward R. Grant.

Brief of amici curiae filed on behalf of the Knights of Columbus by Carl A. Anderson.

Brief of amici curiae filed on behalf of the Rutherford Institute, et al., by Wm. Charles Bundren, John W. Whitehead, A. Eric Johnston, David E. Morris, Stephen E. Hurst, Joseph P. Secola, Thomas S. Neuberger, J. Brian Heller, Thomas W. Strahan, William Bonner, Larry Crain, and James Knicely.

Brief of amici curiae filed on behalf of the United States Catholic Conference by Mark E. Chopko and Phillip H. Harris.

Brief of amici curiae filed on behalf of Senator Gordon J. Humphrey, et al., by James Bopp, Jr., and Richard E. Coleson.

Brief of amici curiae filed on behalf of the American Life League, Inc., et al., by Robert L. Sassone.

Brief of amici curiae filed on behalf of Catholics United for Life, et al., by Thomas Patrick Monaghan, Jay Alan Sekulow, Walter M. Weber, Thomas A. Glessner, Charles E. Rice, and Michael J. Laird.

Brief of amici curiae filed on behalf of the National Right to Life Committee, Inc., et al., by James Bopp, Jr., and Richard E. Coleson.

IV. THE SUPREME COURT'S DECISION

"We need not dwell on the plain language of the statute because we agree with every court to have addressed the issue that the language is ambiguous. . . . The Secretary's construction of Title X may not be disturbed as an abuse of discretion if it reflects a plausible construction of the plain language of the statute and does not otherwise conflict with Congress' expressed intent. . . . We find that the Secretary amply justified his change of interpretation with a 'reasoned analysis.' . . . Having concluded that the plain language and legislative history are ambiguous as to Congress' intent in enacting Title X, we must defer to the Secretary's permissible construction of the statute.

[T]he 'program integrity' requirements embodied at § 59.9 of the regulations, mandating separate facilities, personnel, and records . . . are not inconsistent with the plain language of Title X. . . . While we do not think that the constitutional arguments made by petitioners in these cases are without some force, . . . we hold that they do not carry the day. Applying the canon of construction under discussion as best we can, we hold that the regulations promulgated by the Secretary do not raise the sort of 'grave and doubtful constitutional questions,' that would lead us to assume Congress did not intend to authorize their issuance. Therefore, we need not invalidate the regulations in order to save the statute from unconstitutionality. . . .

Petitioners contend that the regulations violate the First Amendment by impermissibly discriminating based on viewpoint because they prohibit 'all discussion about abortion as a lawful option—including counseling, referral, and the provision of neutral and accurate information about ending a pregnancy—while compelling the clinic or counselor to provide information that promotes continuing a pregnancy to term.' . . . The Government can, without violating the Constitution, selectively fund a program to encourage certain activities it believes to be in the public interest, without at the same time funding an alternative program which seeks to deal with the problem in another way. In so doing, the Government has not discriminated on the basis of viewpoint; it has merely chosen to fund one activity to the exclusion of the other. . . .

Individuals who are voluntarily employed for a Title X project must perform their duties in accordance with the regulation's restrictions on abortion counseling and referral. The employees remain free, however, to pursue abortion-related activities when they are not acting under the auspices of the Title X project. The regulations, which govern solely the scope of the Title X project's activities, do not in any way restrict the activities of those persons acting as private individuals. The employees' freedom of expression is limited during the time that they actually work for the project; but this limitation is a consequence of their decision to accept employment in a project, the scope of which is permissibly restricted by the funding authority. . . .

We turn now to petitioners' argument that the regulations violate a woman's Fifth Amendment right to choose whether to terminate her pregnancy. . . . The Government has no constitutional duty to subsidize an activity merely because the activity is constitutionally protected and may validly choose to fund childbirth over abortion and "implement that judgment by the allocation of public funds" for medical services relating to childbirth but not to those relating to abortion. . . .

Petitioners contend . . . that most Title X clients are effectively precluded by indigency and poverty from seeing a health-care provider who will provide abortion-related services. But once again, even these Title X clients are in no worse position than if Congress had never enacted Title X. 'The financial constraints that restrict an indigent woman's ability to enjoy the full range of constitutionally protected freedom of choice are the product not of governmental restrictions on access to abortion, but rather of her indigency.'

The Secretary's regulations are a permissible construction of Title X and do not violate either the First or Fifth Amendments to the Constitution. Accordingly, the judgment of the Court of Appeals is affirmed."

V. JUSTICE VOTE

4 Pro ACLU Side vs. 5 Con Opposing Side

ACLU Side (Petitioner / Appellant)

1. Blackmun, H. – Wrote dissenting opinion
2. Marshall, T. – Joined Blackmun's dissent
3. O'Connor, S. – Wrote dissenting opinion, joined Blackmun's dissent in part
4. Stevens, J. – Wrote dissenting opinion, joined Blackmun's dissent in part

Opposing Side (Respondent / Appellee)

1. Rehnquist, W. – Wrote majority opinion
2. White, B. – Joined majority opinion
3. Kennedy, A. – Joined majority opinion
4. Scalia, A. – Joined majority opinion
5. Souter, D. – Joined majority opinion

VI. A WIN OR LOSS FOR THE ACLU?

The ACLU, as counsel of record, urged reversal of the judgment of the Court of Appeals; the Supreme Court affirmed in a 5-4 vote, giving the ACLU an apparent loss.

718. Siegert v. Gilley

(Decided May 23, 1991; 500 U.S. 226)

I. ISSUE

A. Issues Discussed

Governmental authority, civil procedure, Fifth Amendment, due process

B. Legal Question Presented

"[W]hether the United States Court of Appeals for the District of Columbia Circuit properly directed dismissal of petitioner's Bivens claim on the grounds that he had not overcome respondent's claim of qualified immunity."

C. Supreme Court's Answer

The Court of Appeals properly directed dismissal of petitioner's Bivens claim.

II. CASE SUMMARY

A. Background

"Petitioner Frederick A. Siegert, a clinical psychologist, was employed at St. Elizabeths Hospital, a Federal Government facility in Washington, D.C., from November 1979 to October 1985. . . . In January 1985, respondent H. Melvyn Gilley became head of the division for which Siegert worked.

In August 1985, St. Elizabeths notified Siegert that it was preparing to terminate his employment. Siegert was informed that his 'proposed removal was based upon his inability to report for duty in a dependable and reliable manner, his failure to comply with supervisory directives, and cumulative charges of absence without approved leave.' After meeting with hospital officials, Siegert agreed to resign from the hospital and thereby avoid a termination that might damage his reputation.

Following his resignation from St. Elizabeths, Siegert began working as a clinical psychologist at a United States Army Hospital in Bremerhaven, West Germany. Because of the requirement that he be 'credentialed' to work in hospitals operated by the Army, Siegert signed a 'Credential Information Request Form' asking that St. Elizabeths Hospital provide to his prospective supervisor, Colonel William Smith, 'all information on job performance and the privileges' he had enjoyed while a member of its staff. . . .

In response to Siegert's request, Gilley notified the Army by letter that 'he could not recommend [Siegert] for privileges as a psychologist.' In that letter, Gilley wrote that he 'consider[ed] Dr. Siegert to be both inept and unethical, perhaps the least trustworthy individual I have supervised in my thirteen years at [St. Elizabeths].' After receiving this letter, the Army Credentials Committee told Siegert that since 'reports about him were 'extremely unfavorable' . . . the committee was . . . recommending that [Siegert] not be credentialed.'

After being denied credentials by the committee, Siegert was turned down for a position he sought with an Army hospital in Stuttgart. Siegert then returned to Bremerhaven where he was given provisional credentials, limited to his work with adults. Siegert filed administrative appeals with the Office of the Surgeon General to obtain full credentials. In December 1987, the Surgeon General denied Siegert's claims. Soon thereafter, his 'federal service employment [was] terminated.'

Upon learning of Gilley's letter in November 1986, Siegert filed suit in the United States District Court for the District of Columbia, alleging that Gilley's letter had caused him to lose his post as a psychologist at the Bremerhaven Army Hospital, and had rendered him unable to obtain other appropriate employment in the field. . . .

In December 1987, the District Court issued an order '[declining] to decide this matter on a Summary Judgment motion at this time.' Instead, the court determined that '[it] would like to see a more developed record,' and therefore ordered 'a limited amount of discovery.' In particular, the court directed the taking of the depositions of the parties and Colonel Smith.

Gilley filed a motion for reconsideration, asking the court to stay further discovery pending disposition of his qualified immunity claim. In June 1988, the District Court denied the motion, and in a written opinion found that Siegert's factual allegations were sufficient to state violations of a clearly established constitutional right. . . . Gilley appealed the denial of his qualified immunity defense to the Court of Appeals . . . .

A divided panel of the United States Court of Appeals for the District of Columbia Circuit reversed and remanded with instructions that the case be dismissed."

The Supreme Court granted certiorari to review the case and affirmed.

B. Counsel of Record / ACLU Attorney

ACLU Side (Petitioner / Appellant): Nina Kraut argued the cause for appellant.

Opposing Side (Respondent / Appellee): Michael R. Laserwitz argued the cause for appellee.

III. AMICI CURIAE

ACLU Side (Petitioner / Appellant)

Brief of amici curiae filed on behalf of the ACLU, et al., by David H. Remes, David Rudovsky, Steven R. Shapiro, and Arthur B. Spitzer.

Opposing Side (Respondent / Appellee)

No briefs of amici curiae were filed is support of appellee.

IV. THE SUPREME COURT'S DECISION

1"We granted certiorari in order to clarify the analytical structure under which a claim of qualified immunity should be addressed. We hold that the petitioner in this case failed to satisfy the first inquiry in the examination of such a claim; he failed to allege the violation of a clearly established constitutional right. . . . In this case, Siegert based his constitutional claim on the theory that Gilley's actions, undertaken with malice, deprived him of a 'liberty interest' secured by the Fifth Amendment . . . . A necessary concomitant to the determination of whether the constitutional right asserted by a plaintiff is 'clearly established' at the time the defendant acted is the determination of whether the plaintiff has asserted a violation of a constitutional right at all. Decision of this purely legal question permits courts expeditiously to weed out suits which fail the test without requiring a defendant who rightly claims qualified immunity to engage in expensive and time consuming preparation to defend the suit on its merits. . . .

Siegert failed not only to allege the violation of a constitutional right that was clearly established at the time of Gilley's actions, but also to establish the violation of any constitutional right at all. [We have held] that injury to reputation by itself was not a 'liberty' interest protected under the Fourteenth Amendment. . . . Defamation, by itself, is a tort actionable under the laws of most States, but not a constitutional deprivation. . . .

The Court of Appeals' majority concluded that the District Court should have dismissed petitioner's suit because he had not overcome the defense of qualified immunity asserted by respondent. By a different line of reasoning, we reach the same conclusion, and the judgment of the Court of Appeals is therefore affirmed."

V. JUSTICE VOTE

3 Pro ACLU Side vs. 6 Con Opposing Side

ACLU Side (Petitioner / Appellant)

1. Marshall, T. – Wrote dissenting opinion
2. Blackmun, H. – Joined Marshall's dissent
3. Stevens, J. – Joined parts II and III of Marshall's dissent

Opposing Side (Respondent / Appellee)

1. Rehnquist, W. – Wrote majority opinion
2. White, B. – Joined majority opinion
3. O'Connor, S. – Joined majority opinion
4. Scalia, A. – Joined majority opinion
5. Souter, D. – Joined majority opinion
6. Kennedy, A. – Wrote concurring opinion

VI. A WIN OR LOSS FOR THE ACLU?

The ACLU filed as amicus curiae urging reversal of the judgment of the Court of Appeals; the Supreme Court affirmed in a 6-3 vote, giving the ACLU an apparent loss.

719. Burns v. Reed

(Decided May 30, 1991; 500 U.S. 478)

I. ISSUE

A. Issues Discussed

Civil rights, prosecutorial immunity, Fourth Amendment, Fifth Amendment, Fourteenth Amendment

B. Legal Question Presented

"[W]hether a state prosecuting attorney is absolutely immune from liability for damages under 42 U.S.C. § 1983 for giving legal advice to the police and for participating in a probable-cause hearing."

C. Supreme Court's Answer

The attorney is absolutely immune from § 1983 liability for participating in the probable cause hearing, but not absolutely immune for giving legal advice to the police.

II. CASE SUMMARY

A. Background

"The relevant facts are not in dispute. On the evening of September 2, 1982, petitioner Cathy Burns called the Muncie, Indiana, police and reported that an unknown assailant had entered her house, knocked her unconscious, and shot and wounded her two sons while they slept. Two police officers, Paul Cox and Donald

Scroggins, were assigned to investigate the incident. The officers came to view petitioner as their primary suspect, even though she passed a polygraph examination and a voice stress test, submitted exculpatory handwriting samples, and repeatedly denied shooting her sons.

Speculating that petitioner had multiple personalities, one of which was responsible for the shootings, the officers decided to interview petitioner under hypnosis. . . . While under hypnosis, petitioner referred to the assailant as 'Katie' and also referred to herself by that name. The officers interpreted that reference as supporting their multiple-personality theory. As a result, they detained petitioner at the police station and sought respondent's advice about whether there was probable cause to arrest petitioner. After hearing about the statements that petitioner had made while under hypnosis, respondent told the officers that they 'probably had probable cause' to arrest petitioner. Based on that assurance, the officers placed petitioner under arrest.

The next day, respondent and Officer Scroggins appeared before a county court judge in a probable-cause hearing, seeking to obtain a warrant to search petitioner's house and car. During that hearing, Scroggins testified, in response to respondent's questioning, that petitioner had confessed to shooting her children. Neither the officer nor respondent informed the judge that the 'confession' was obtained under hypnosis or that petitioner had otherwise consistently denied shooting her sons. On the basis of the misleading presentation, the judge issued a search warrant.

Petitioner was charged under Indiana law with attempted murder of her sons. Before trial, however, the trial judge granted petitioner's motion to suppress the statements given under hypnosis. As a result, the prosecutor's office dropped all charges against petitioner.

On January 31, 1985, petitioner filed an action in the United States District Court for the Southern District of Indiana against respondent, Officers Cox and Scroggins, and others. She alleged that the defendants were liable under 42 U.S.C. § 1983 for violating her rights under the Fourth, Fifth, and Fourteenth Amendments to the United States Constitution, and she sought compensatory and punitive damages. Petitioner reached a settlement with several of the defendants, and the case proceeded to trial against respondent. After petitioner presented her case, the District Court granted respondent a directed verdict, finding that respondent was absolutely immune from liability for his conduct.

Petitioner appealed to the United States Court of Appeals for the Seventh Circuit. That court affirmed. It held that 'a prosecutor should be afforded absolute immunity for giving legal advice to police officers about the legality of their prospective investigative conduct. In a brief footnote, the court also held that respondent was absolutely immune from liability for his role in the probable-cause hearing."

The Supreme Court granted certiorari to review the case, affirmed in part, and reversed in part.

B. Counsel of Record / ACLU Attorney

ACLU Side (Petitioner / Appellant): Michael K. Sutherlin argued the cause for appellant.

Opposing Side (Respondent / Appellee): Robert S. Spear argued the cause for appellee.

Michael R. Lazerwitz argued the cause for the United States, as amicus curiae, by special leave of Court.

III. AMICI CURIAE

ACLU Side (Petitioner / Appellant)

Brief of amici curiae filed on behalf of the ACLU, et al., by Louis M. Bograd, Steven R. Shapiro, and Richard A. Waples.

Opposing Side (Respondent / Appellee)

Brief of amici curiae filed on behalf of the United States by Michael R. Lazerwitz, Solicitor General Starr, Assistant Attorney General Gerson, Deputy Solicitor General Shapiro, and Barbara L. Herwig.

Brief of amici curiae filed on behalf of the State of Wyoming, et al., by Joseph B. Meyer, Attorney General of Wyoming; Sylvia Lee Hackl, Senior Assistant Attorney General; Don Siegelman, Attorney General of Alabama; Douglas B. Baily, Attorney General of Alaska; Steve Clark, Attorney General of Arkansas; John K. Van de Kamp, Attorney General of California; Duane Woodard, Attorney General of Colorado; John J. Kelly, Chief State's Attorney of Connecticut; Herbert O. Reid, Sr., Corporation Counsel of the District of Columbia; Robert A. Butterworth, Attorney General of Florida; Warren Price III, Attorney General of Hawaii; Jim Jones, Attorney General of Idaho; Neil F. Hartigan, Attorney General of Illinois; Thomas J. Miller, Attorney General of Iowa; Frederic J. Cowan, Attorney General of Kentucky; James E. Tierney, Attorney General of Maine; Joseph Curran, Jr., Attorney General of Maryland; Frank J. Kelley, Attorney General of Michigan; Hubert H. Humphrey III, Attorney General of Minnesota; Mike Moore, Attorney General of Mississippi; William L. Webster, Attorney General of Missouri; Marc Racicot, Attorney General of Montana; Brian McKay, Attorney General of Nevada; John P. Arnold, Attorney General of New Hampshire; Robert J. Del Tufo, Attorney General of New Jersey; Lacy H. Thornburg, Attorney General of North Carolina; Robert H. Henry, Attorney General of Oklahoma; Ernest D. Preate, Jr., Attorney General of Pennsylvania; James E. O'Neil, Attorney General of Rhode Island; T. Travis Medlock, Attorney General of South Carolina; Roger A. Tellinghuisen, Attorney General of South Dakota; Charles W. Burson, Attorney General of Tennessee; Jim Mattox, Attorney General of Texas, and Paul Van Dam, Attorney General of Utah.

Brief of amici curiae filed on behalf of the California District Attorney Association by Edwin L. Miller, Jr. and Thomas F. McArdle.

IV. THE SUPREME COURT'S DECISION

"[P]rosecutors are absolutely immune from liability under § 1983 for their conduct in 'initiating a prosecution and in presenting the State's case,' insofar as that conduct is 'intimately associated with the judicial phase of the criminal process.' . . .

We now consider whether the absolute prosecutorial immunity recognized in Imbler is applicable to (a) respondent's participation in a probable cause hearing, which led to the issuance of a search warrant, and (b) respondent's legal advice to the police regarding the use of hypnosis and the existence of probable cause to arrest petitioner. . . .

We address first respondent's appearance as a lawyer for the State in the probable-cause hearing, where he examined a witness and successfully supported the application for a search warrant. The decision in Imbler leads to the conclusion that respondent is absolutely immune from liability in a § 1983 suit for that conduct. . . .

Turning to respondent's acts of providing legal advice to the police, we note first that neither respondent nor the court below has identified any historical or common-law support for extending absolute immunity to such actions by prosecutors. . . .

The next factor to be considered—risk of vexatious litigation—also does not support absolute immunity for giving legal advice. The Court of Appeals asserted that absolute immunity was justified because 'a prosecutor's risk of becoming entangled in litigation based on his or her role as a legal advisor to police officer is as likely as the risks associated with initiating and prosecuting a case.' We disagree. In the first place, a suspect or defendant is not likely to be as aware of a prosecutor's role in giving advice as a prosecutor's role in initiating and conducting a prosecution. But even if a prosecutor's role in giving advice to the police does carry with it some risk of burdensome litigation, the concern with litigation in our immunity cases is not merely a generalized concern with interference with an official's duties, but rather is a concern with interference with the conduct closely related to the judicial process. Absolute immunity is designed to free the judicial process from the harassment and intimidation associated with litigation. That concern therefore justifies absolute prosecutorial immunity only for actions that are connected with the prosecutor's role in judicial proceedings, not for every litigation-inducing conduct.

[W]e conclude that respondent has not met his burden of showing that the relevant factors justify an extension of absolute immunity to the prosecutorial function of giving legal advice to the police. . . .

For the foregoing reasons, we affirm in part and reverse in part the judgment of the Court of Appeals."

V. JUSTICE VOTE

9 Pro ACLU Side vs. 0 Con Opposing Side

ACLU Side (Petitioner / Appellant)

1. White, B. – Wrote the majority opinion
2. Rehnquist, W. – Joined majority opinion
3. Stevens, J. – Joined majority opinion
4. O'Connor, S. – Joined majority opinion
5. Kennedy, A. – Joined majority opinion
6. Souter, D. – Joined majority opinion
7. Scalia, A. – Wrote opinion concurring in part and dissenting in part
8. Blackmun, H. – Joined Scalia's opinion
9. Marshall, T. – Joined part III of Scalia's opinion

VI. A WIN OR LOSS FOR THE ACLU?

The ACLU filed as amicus curiae, urging reversal of the judgment of the Court of Appeals for the Seventh Circuit; the Supreme Court affirmed in part and reversed in part in a 9-0 vote, giving the ACLU an apparent win.

720. Edmonson v. Leesville Concrete Co.

(Decided June 3, 1991; 500 U.S. 614)

I. ISSUE

A. Issues Discussed

Governmental authority, civil procedure, Fifth Amendment, jury selection

B. Legal Question Presented

"[W]hether a private litigant in a civil case may use peremptory challenges to exclude jurors on account of their race."

C. Supreme Court's Answer

A private litigant in a civil case may not use peremptory challenges to exclude jurors on account of their race. The case must be remanded to determine whether the plaintiff established a prima facie case of racial discrimination.

II. CASE SUMMARY

A. Background

"Thaddeus Donald Edmonson, a construction worker, was injured in a jobsite accident at Fort Polk, Louisiana, a federal enclave. Edmonson sued Leesville Concrete Company for negligence in the United States District Court for the Western District of Louisiana, claiming that a Leesville employee permitted one of the company's trucks to roll backward and pin him against some construction equipment. Edmonson invoked his Seventh Amendment right to a trial by jury.

During voir dire, Leesville used two of its three peremptory challenges authorized by statute to remove black persons from the prospective jury. Citing [the Supreme Court] decision in Batson v. Kentucky, 476 U.S. 79 (1986), Edmonson, who is himself black, requested that the District Court require Leesville to articulate a race-neutral explanation for striking the two jurors. The District Court denied the request on the ground that Batson does not apply in civil proceedings. As empaneled, the jury included 11 white persons and 1 black person. The jury rendered a verdict for Edmonson, assessing his total damages at $90,000. It also attributed 80% of the fault to Edmonson's contributory negligence, however, and awarded him the sum of $18,000.

Edmonson appealed, and a divided panel of the Court of Appeals for the Fifth Circuit reversed, holding that our opinion in Batson applies to a private attorney representing a private litigant and that peremptory challenges may not be used in a civil trial for the purpose of excluding jurors on the basis of race. The Court of Appeals panel held that private parties become state actors when they exercise peremptory challenges and that to limit Batson to criminal cases 'would betray Batson's fundamental principle [that] the state's use, toleration, and approval of peremptory challenges based on race violates the equal protection clause.' The panel remanded to the trial court to consider whether Edmonson had established a prima facie case of racial discrimination under Batson.

The full court then ordered rehearing en banc. A divided en banc panel affirmed the judgment of the District Court, holding that a private litigant in a civil case can exercise peremptory challenges without accountability for alleged racial classifications. The court concluded that the use of peremptories by private litigants does not constitute state action and, as a result, does not implicate constitutional guarantees."

The Supreme Court granted certiorari to review the case and reversed.

B. Counsel of Record / ACLU Attorney

ACLU Side (Petitioner / Appellant): James B. Doyle argued the cause for appellant.

Opposing Side (Respondent / Appellee): John S. Baker, Jr., argued the cause for appellee.

III. AMICI CURIAE

ACLU Side (Petitioner / Appellant)

Brief of amici curiae filed on behalf of the ACLU by Steven R. Shapiro and John A. Powell.

Brief of amici curiae filed on behalf of the NAACP Legal Defense and Education Fund, Inc., et al., by Julius LeVonne Chambers, Eric Schnapper, Samuel Rabinove, Deval L. Patrick, Marc Goodheart, Robert F. Mullen, David S. Tatel, Norman Redlich, Thomas J. Henderson, and Richard J. Seymour.

Opposing Side (Respondent / Appellee)

Brief of amici curiae filed on behalf of the Defense Research Institute by Jeanmarie LoCoco and John J. Weigel.

Brief of amici curiae filed on behalf of Dixis Insurance Company by Suzanne N. Saunders.

Brief of amici curiae filed on behalf of the Louisiana Association of Defense Counsel by Joseph R. Ward, Jr. and Wood Brown III.

IV. THE SUPREME COURT'S DECISION

"The Constitution's protections of individual liberty and equal protection apply in general only to action by the government. Racial discrimination, though invidious in all contexts, violates the Constitution only when it may be attributed to state action. . . .

Peremptory challenges are permitted only when the government, by statute or decisional law, deems it appropriate to allow parties to exclude a given number of persons who otherwise would satisfy the requirements for service on the petit jury. . . . Without this authorization, granted by an Act of Congress itself, Leesville would not have been able to engage in the alleged discriminatory acts. . . . It cannot be disputed that, without the overt, significant participation of the government, the peremptory challenge system, as well as the jury trial system of which it is a part, simply could not exist. . . . The peremptory challenge is used in selecting an entity that is a quintessential governmental body, having no attributes of a private actor. . . . The selection of jurors represents a unique governmental function delegated to private litigants by the government and attributable to the government for purposes of invoking constitutional protections against discrimination by reason of race. . . .

Race discrimination within the courtroom raises serious questions as to the fairness of the proceedings conducted there. Racial bias mars the integrity of the judicial system, and prevents the idea of democratic government from becoming a reality. . . . To permit racial exclusion in this official forum compounds the racial insult inherent in judging a citizen by the color of his or her skin.

[A] litigant may raise a claim on behalf of a third party if the litigant can demonstrate that he or she has suffered a concrete, redressable injury, that he or she has a close relation with the third party, and that there exists some hindrance to the third party's ability to protect his or her own interests. All three of these requirements for third-party standing were held satisfied in the criminal context, and they are satisfied in the civil context as well. . . . Racial discrimination has no place in the courtroom, whether the proceeding is civil or criminal. . . . We conclude that courts must entertain a challenge to a private litigant's racially discriminatory use of peremptory challenges in a civil trial. . . .

The judgment is reversed, and the case is remanded for further proceedings consistent with our opinion."

V. JUSTICE VOTE

6 Pro ACLU Side vs. 3 Con Opposing Side

ACLU Side (Petitioner / Appellant)

1. Kennedy, A. – Wrote majority opinion
2. White, B. – Joined majority opinion
3. Marshall, T. – Joined majority opinion
4. Blackmun, H. – Joined majority opinion
5. Stevens, J. – Joined majority opinion
6. Souter, D. – Joined majority opinion

Opposing Side (Respondent / Appellee)

1. O'Connor, S. – Wrote dissenting opinion
2. Rehnquist, W. – Joined O'Connor's dissent
3. Scalia, A. – Wrote dissenting opinion, joined O'Connor's dissent

VI. A WIN OR LOSS FOR THE ACLU?

The ACLU filed as amicus curiae urging reversal of the judgment of the Court of Appeals; the Supreme Court reversed in a 6-3 vote, giving the ACLU an apparent win.

721. Clark v. *Roemer*

(Decided June 3, 1991; 500 U.S. 646)

I. ISSUE

A. Issues Discussed

Civil rights, voting rights, Section 5 of the Voting Rights Act of 1965, election discrimination

B. Legal Question Presented

"The case presents two discrete issues under § 5 of the Voting Rights Act. First, we must decide whether the District Court erred by not enjoining elections held for judgeships to which the Attorney General interposed valid § 5 objections. Second, we must determine whether the State's failure to preclear certain earlier voting changes under § 5 was cured by the Attorney General's preclearance of later, or related, voting changes."

C. Supreme Court's Answer

The District Court should have enjoined elections for judgeships with pending § 5 objections. The failure to preclear was not cured by the Attorney General's preclearance of later or related changes after the fact.

II. CASE SUMMARY

A. Background

"The Voting Rights Act of 1965, 42 U.S.C. § 1973 et seq., contains two major provisions governing discrimination in election practices. Section 2 addresses existing election procedures. It prohibits procedures that 'resul[t] in a denial or abridgement of the right of any citizen of the United States to vote on account of race or color . . . . Section 5 governs changes in voting procedures. In order to prevent changes that have a discriminatory purpose or effect, § 5 requires covered jurisdictions, such as Louisiana, to obtain preclearance by one of two methods before implementing new voting practices. Through judicial preclearance, a covered jurisdiction may obtain from the United States District Court for the District of Columbia a declaratory judgment that the voting change 'does not have the purpose and will not have the effect of denying or abridging the right to vote on account of race or color.' Through administrative preclearance, the jurisdiction may submit the change to the Attorney General of the United States. If the Attorney General 'has not interposed an objection within sixty days after such submission,' the State may enforce the change.

Appellants are black registered voters and a voting rights organization in Louisiana. They filed this suit in 1986 under §§ 2 and 5 of the Voting Rights Act of 1965, challenging the validity of Louisiana's multimember, at-large electoral scheme for certain appellate, district, and family court judges. Under § 2, appellants alleged that Louisiana's electoral scheme diluted minority voting strength. In an amended complaint filed in July 1987, appellants also alleged that Louisiana violated § 5 by failing to submit for preclearance a number of statutory and constitutional voting changes, many of them adopted in the late 1960's and 1970's. The § 2 portion of the case was assigned to a single District Court Judge; the § 5 allegations were heard by a three-judge District Court.

In response to the appellants' § 5 allegations, Louisiana submitted all of the unprecleared voting changes for administrative preclearance. In September 1988 and May 1989, the Attorney General granted preclearance for some of the changes, but objected to others. On June 18 and 20, 1990, Louisiana asked the Attorney General to reconsider his denial of preclearance for these seats, and proceeded with plans to hold elections for them in the fall of 1990. On July 23, 1990, appellants filed a motion asking the three-judge District Court to enjoin the elections for the unprecleared seats.

[After extensive litigation,] the three-judge District Court made its final pronouncement on the status of the unprecleared judgeships. The court divided the unprecleared electoral changes into two categories. Category one involved at-large judgeships in districts where, for the most part, the State had obtained administrative preclearance for later created judgeships. The three-judge District Court held that, despite his current objections, the Attorney General had precleared the earlier judgeships when he precleared the later, or related, voting changes. . . .

Category two under the court's ruling involved judgeships subject to valid objections by the Attorney General. Yet despite its holding that these unprecleared judgeships violated § 5, the court refused to enjoin the elections. It found 'the potential harm to all of the citizens of Louisiana [from such an injunction] outweigh[ed] the potential harm, if any, of allowing the elections to continue.' . . .

On October 29, 1990, appellants filed an emergency application in [the Supreme] Court to enjoin the November 6 and December 8 elections pending appeal. On November 2, we granted the application in part and enjoined the elections for the judgeships that the District Court conceded were uncleared. We did not overturn the District Court's refusal to enjoin elections for the judgeships that it considered precleared by implication.

On January 18, 1991, we noted probable jurisdiction. The next day, the State sought judicial preclearance for the electoral changes that the three-judge District Court found to be uncleared. That action is still pending in the United States District Court for the District of Columbia."

The Supreme Court granted certiorari to review the case and reversed.

B. Counsel of Record / ACLU Attorney

ACLU Side (Petitioner / Appellant): Robert B. McDuff argued the cause for appellant.

James A. Feldman argued the cause for the United States, as amicus curiae, by special leave of Court.

Opposing Side (Respondent / Appellee): Robert G. Pugh, Jr., argued the cause for appellee.

III. AMICI CURIAE

ACLU Side (Petitioner / Appellant)

Brief of amici curiae filed on behalf of the ACLU, et al., by Kathleen L. Wilde, Laughlin McDonald, and Neil Bradley.

Brief of amici curiae filed on behalf of the United States by James A. Feldman, Solicitor General Starr, Assistant Attorney General Dunne, Deputy Solicitor General Roberts, Deputy Assistant Attorney General Clegg, and Jessica Dunsay Silver.

Opposing Side (Respondent / Appellee)

No briefs of amici curiae were filed in support of appellee.

IV. THE SUPREME COURT'S DECISION

"Section 5 requires States to obtain either judicial or administrative preclearance before implementing a voting change. . . . Failure to obtain either judicial or administrative preclearance 'renders the change unenforceable.' . . .

The District Court ignored these principles altogether. It presented a number of reasons for not enjoining the elections, none of which we find persuasive. . . . Appellants displayed no lack of diligence in challenging elections for the unprecleared seats, and every participant in the process knew for over three years that the challenged seats were unprecleared, in violation of

§ 5. . . . Nor did the District Court's vague concerns about voter confusion and low voter turnout in a special election . . . justify its refusal to enjoin the illegal elections. Voters may be more confused and inclined to avoid the polls when an election is held in conceded violation of federal law. . . . Louisiana had with consistency ignored the mandate of § 5. The District Court should have enjoined the elections.

[T]he submission of legislation for administrative preclearance under § 5 defines the scope of the preclearance request. '[S]ubmission of a particular change does not encompass all prior changes—precleared or not—that have been made since the Act's effective date . . . .' 'A request for preclearance of certain identified changes in election practices which fails to identify other practices as new ones thus cannot be considered an adequate submission of the latter practices.' . . . In light of its legal errors, the District Court's finding that the Attorney General 'expressly approved' the prior uncleared changes cannot stand. . . .

The judgment is reversed, and the case is remanded for further proceedings consistent with this opinion."

V. JUSTICE VOTE

9 Pro ACLU Side vs. 0 Con Opposing Side

ACLU Side (Petitioner / Appellant)

1. Kennedy, A. – Wrote majority opinion
2. O'Connor, S. – Joined majority opinion
3. Scalia, A. – Joined majority opinion
4. Souter, D. – Joined majority opinion
5. Stevens, J. – Joined majority opinion
6. Blackmun, H. – Joined majority opinion
7. Marshall, T. – Joined majority opinion
8. Rehnquist, W. – Joined majority opinion
9. White, B. – Joined majority opinion

VI. A WIN OR LOSS FOR THE ACLU?

The ACLU filed as amicus curiae urging reversal of the judgment of the District Court for the Middle District of Louisiana; the Supreme Court reversed and remanded in a 9-0 vote, giving the ACLU an apparent win.

722. Renne v. Geary

(Decided June 17, 1991; 501 U.S. 312)

I. ISSUE

A. Issues Discussed

First Amendment, freedoms of press, speech, and association, Fourteenth Amendment, political party endorsements, justiciability

B. Legal Question Presented

"[W]hether § 6(b) [of the California Constitution] violates the First Amendment."

C. Supreme Court's Answer

The case is nonjusticable and must be dismissed.

II. CASE SUMMARY

A. Background

"Petitioners are the City and County of San Francisco, its board of supervisors, and certain local officials. The individual respondents are 10 registered voters residing in the City and County of San Francisco. They include the chairman and three members of the San Francisco Republican County Central Committee and one member of the San Francisco Democratic County Central Committee. Election Action, an association of voters, is also a respondent, but it asserts no interest in relation to the issues before us different from that of the individual voters. Hence, we need not consider it further.

Respondents filed this suit in the United States District Court for the Northern District of California. Their third cause of action challenged [Article II,] § 6(b) [of the California Constitution] and petitioners' acknowledged policy, based on that provision, of deleting any references to a party endorsement from the candidate statements included in voter pamphlets. As we understand it, petitioners print the pamphlets and pay the postage required to mail them to voters. The voter pamphlets contain statements prepared by candidates for office and arguments submitted by interested persons concerning other measures on the ballot. The complaint sought a declaration that Article II, § 6, is unconstitutional and an injunction preventing petitioners from editing candidate statements to delete references to party endorsements.

The District Court granted summary judgment for respondents on their third cause of action, declaring § 6(b) unconstitutional and enjoining petitioners from enforcing it. The court entered judgment on this claim pursuant to Federal Rule of Civil Procedure 54(b), and petitioners appealed. A Ninth Circuit panel reversed, but the en banc Court of Appeals affirmed the District Court's decision."

The Supreme Court granted certiorari to review the case and determined the case was not justiciable.

B. Counsel of Record / ACLU Attorney

ACLU Side (Respondent / Appellee): Arlo Hale Smith argued the cause for appellee.

Opposing Side (Petitioner / Appellant): Dennis Aftergut argued the cause for appellant.

III. AMICI CURIAE

ACLU Side (Respondent / Appellee)

Brief of amici curiae filed on behalf of the ACLU, et al., by Karl Olson, Steven R. Shapiro and Alan L. Schlosser.

Brief of amici curiae filed on behalf of the California Democratic Party, et al., by Cedric C. Chao.

Opposing Side (Petitioner / Appellant)

Brief of amici curiae filed on behalf of the California Judges Association by Jerome B. Falk, Jr., and Steven L. Mayer.

IV. THE SUPREME COURT'S DECISION

"Respondents have failed to demonstrate a live dispute involving the actual or threatened application of § 6(b) to bar particular speech. Respondents' generalized claim that petitioners have deleted party endorsements from candidate statements in past elections does not demonstrate a live controversy. . . . The allegation that the Democratic Committee has not endorsed candidates '[i]n elections since 1986' for fear of the consequences of violating § 6 provides insufficient indication of a controversy continuing at the time this litigation began or arising thereafter. . . . Nor can a ripe controversy be found in the fact that the Republican Committee endorsed candidates for nonpartisan elections in 1987, the year this suit was filed. . . . We also discern no ripe controversy in the allegations that respondents desire to endorse candidates in future elections, either as individual committee members or through their committees. . . . The record also contains no evidence of a credible threat that § 6(b) will be enforced, other than against candidates in the context of voter pamphlets. . . .

Postponing consideration of the questions presented until more concrete controversy arises also has the advantage of permitting the state courts further opportunity to construe § 6(b), and perhaps, in the process, to 'materially alter the question to be decided.' . . .

The free speech issues argued in the briefs filed here have fundamental and far-reaching import. For that very reason, we cannot decide the case based upon the amorphous and ill-defined factual record presented to us. . . .

The judgment is vacated and the case remanded with instructions to dismiss respondents' third cause of action without prejudice."

V. JUSTICE VOTE

3 Pro ACLU Side vs. 6 Con Opposing Side

ACLU Side (Respondent / Appellee)

1. White, B. – Wrote dissenting opinion
2. Marshall, T. – Wrote dissenting opinion
3. Blackmun, H. – Joined Marshall's dissent

Opposing Side (Petitioner / Appellant)

1. Kennedy, A. – Wrote majority opinion
2. Rehnquist, W. – Joined majority opinion
3. Stevens, J. – Wrote concurring opinion
4. O'Connor, S. – Joined majority opinion
5. Souter, D. – Joined majority opinion
6. Scalia, A. – Joined in all but Part II-B of the majority opinion

VI. A WIN OR LOSS FOR THE ACLU?

The ACLU filed as amicus curiae urging affirmance of the judgment of the Court of Appeals; the Supreme Court vacated and remanded in a 6-3 vote, giving the ACLU an apparent loss.

723. Florida v. Bostick

(Decided June 20, 1991; 501 U.S. 429)

I. ISSUE

A. Issues Discussed

Criminal justice, drugs, Fourth Amendment, search and seizure

B. Legal Question Presented

Whether the rule that "the Fourth Amendment permits police officers to approach individuals at random in airport lobbies and other public places to ask them questions and to request consent to search their luggage, so long as a reasonable person would understand that he or she could refuse to cooperate" applies on buses.

C. Supreme Court's Answer

The rule applies to buses.

II. CASE SUMMARY

A. Background

"In this case, two officers discovered cocaine when they searched a suitcase belonging to Terrance Bostick. . . .

'Two officers, complete with badges, insignia and one of them holding a recognizable zipper pouch, containing a pistol, boarded a bus bound from Miami to Atlanta during a stopover in Fort Lauderdale. Eyeing the passengers, the officers, admittedly without articulable suspicion, picked out the defendant passenger and asked to inspect his ticket and identification. The ticket, from Miami to Atlanta, matched the defendant's identification and both were immediately returned to him as unremarkable. However, the two police officers persisted and explained their presence as narcotics agents on the lookout for illegal drugs. In pursuit of that aim, they then requested the defendant's consent to search his luggage. Needless to say, there is a conflict in the evidence about whether the defendant consented to the search of the second bag in which the contraband was found and as to whether he was informed of his right to refuse consent. However, any conflict must be resolved in favor of the state, it being a question of fact decided by the trial judge.' . . .

Bostick was arrested and charged with trafficking in cocaine. He moved to suppress the cocaine on the grounds that it had been seized in violation of his Fourth Amendment rights. The trial court denied the motion but made no factual findings. Bostick subsequently entered a plea of guilty, but reserved the right to appeal the denial of the motion to suppress.

The Florida District Court of Appeal affirmed, but considered the issue sufficiently important that it certified a question to the Florida Supreme Court. . . . It ruled categorically that "an impermissible seizure result[s] when police mount a drug search on buses during scheduled stops and question boarded passengers without articulable reasons for doing so, thereby obtaining consent to search the passengers' luggage." The Florida Supreme Court thus adopted a per se rule that the Broward County Sheriff's practice of 'working the buses' is unconstitutional."

The U.S. Supreme Court granted certiorari to review the case and reversed.

B. Counsel of Record / ACLU Attorney

ACLU Side (Respondent / Appellee): Donald B. Ayer argued the cause for appellee.

Opposing Side (Petitioner / Appellant): Joan Fowler, Assistant Attorney General of Florida, argued the cause for appellant.

Solicitor General Starr argued the cause for the United States, as amici curiae, by special leave of Court.

III. AMICI CURIAE

ACLU Side (Respondent / Appellee)

Brief of amici curiae filed on behalf of the ACLU, et al., by Mary Irene Coombs, Steven R. Sharpiro, John A. Powell, James K. Green, Jefferey S. Weiner, and Robert G. Amsel.

Brief of amici curiae filed on behalf of Americans for Effective Law Enforcement by Fred E. Inbau, Wayne W. Schmidt, Bernard J. Farber, and James P. Manak.

Opposing Side (Petitioner / Appellant)

Brief of amici curiae filed on behalf of the United States by Solicitor General Starr, Assistant Attorney General Mueller, Deputy Solicitor General Bryson, Christopher J. Wright, and Kathleen A. Felton.

IV. THE SUPREME COURT'S DECISION

"Our cases make it clear that a seizure does not occur simply because a police officer approaches an individual and asks a few questions. So long as a reasonable person would feel free 'to disregard the police and go about his business,' the encounter is consensual and no reasonable suspicion is required. The encounter will not trigger Fourth Amendment scrutiny unless it loses its consensual nature. . . . There is no doubt that if this same encounter had taken place before Bostick boarded the bus or in the lobby of the bus terminal, it would not rise to the level of a seizure. . . .

Bostick's freedom of movement was restricted by a factor independent of police conduct—i.e., by his being a passenger on a bus. . . . In such a situation, the appropriate inquiry is whether a reasonable person would feel free to decline the officers' requests or otherwise terminate the encounter. This formulation follows logically from prior cases and breaks no new ground. We have said before that the crucial test is whether, taking into account all of the circumstances surrounding the encounter, the police conduct would 'have communicated to a reasonable person that he was not at liberty to ignore the police presence and go about his business.'

[W]e refrain from deciding whether or not a seizure occurred in this case. The trial court made no express findings of fact, and the Florida Supreme Court rested its decision on a single fact—that the encounter took place on a bus—rather than on the totality of the circumstances. We remand so that the Florida courts may evaluate the seizure question under the correct legal standard. We do reject, however, Bostick's argument that he must have been seized because no reasonable person would freely consent to a search of luggage that he or she knows contains drugs. This argument cannot prevail because the 'reasonable person' test presupposes an innocent person. . . .

We adhere to the rule that, in order to determine whether a particular encounter constitutes a seizure, a court must consider all the circumstances surrounding the encounter to determine whether the police conduct would have communicated to a reasonable person that the person was not free to decline the officers' requests or otherwise terminate the encounter. That rule applies to encounters that take place on a city street or in an airport lobby, and it applies equally to encounters on a bus. The Florida Supreme Court erred in adopting a per se rule.

The judgment of the Florida Supreme Court is reversed, and the case is remanded for further proceedings not inconsistent with this opinion."

V. JUSTICE VOTE

3 Pro ACLU Side vs. 6 Con Opposing Side

ACLU Side (Respondent / Appellee)

1. Marshall, T. – Wrote dissenting opinion
2. Stevens, J. – Joined Marshall's dissent
3. Blackmun, H. – Joined Marshall's dissent

Opposing Side (Petitioner / Appellant)

1. O'Connor, S. – Wrote majority opinion
2. Rehnquist, W. – Joined majority opinion
3. Scalia, A. – Joined majority opinion
4. Kennedy, A. – Joined majority opinion
5. White, B. – Joined majority opinion
6. Souter, D. – Joined majority opinion

VI. A WIN OR LOSS FOR THE ACLU?

The ACLU filed as amicus curiae urging affirmance of the judgment of the Florida Supreme Court; the U.S. Supreme Court reversed in a 6-3 vote, giving the ACLU an apparent loss.

724. Barnes v. Glen Theatre, Inc.

(Decided June 21, 1991; 501 U.S. 560)

I. ISSUE

A. Issues Discussed

First Amendment, obscenity, freedom of expression

B. Legal Question Presented

Whether "the First Amendment's guarantee of freedom of expression prevents the State of Indiana from enforcing its public indecency law to prevent [totally nude] dancing."

C. Supreme Court's Answer

Enforcement of the public indecency statute to prevent totally nude dancing does not violate the First Amendment.

II. CASE SUMMARY

A. Background

"Respondents are two establishments in South Bend, Indiana, that wish to provide totally nude dancing as entertainment, and individual dancers who are employed at these establishments. . . .

Respondents sued in the United States District Court for the Northern District of Indiana to enjoin the enforcement of the Indiana public indecency statute, asserting that its prohibition against complete nudity in public places violated the First Amendment. The District Court originally granted respondents' prayer for an injunction, finding that the statute was facially overbroad. The Court of Appeals for the Seventh Circuit reversed, deciding that previous litigation with respect to the statute in the Supreme Court of Indiana and this Court precluded the possibility of such a challenge, and remanded to the District Court in order for the plaintiffs to pursue their claim that the statute violated the First Amendment as applied to their dancing. On remand, the District Court concluded that 'the type of dancing these plaintiffs wish to perform is not expressive activity protected by the Constitution of the United States,' and rendered judgment in favor of the defendants. The case was again appealed to the Seventh Circuit, and a panel of that court reversed the District Court, holding that the nude dancing involved here was expressive conduct protected by the First Amendment. The Court of Appeals then heard the case en banc, and the court rendered a series of comprehensive and thoughtful opinions. The majority concluded that nonobscene nude dancing performed for entertainment is expression protected by the First Amendment, and that the public indecency statute was an improper infringement of that expressive activity because its purpose was to prevent the message of eroticism and sexuality conveyed by the dancers."

The Supreme Court granted certiorari to review the case and reversed.

B. Counsel of Record / ACLU Attorney

ACLU Side (Respondent / Appellee): Bruce J. Ennis, Jr., argued the cause for appellees. Lee J. Klein and Bradley J. Shafer filed a brief for appellees Glen Theatre, Inc., et al. Patrick Louis Baude and Charles A. Asher filed a brief for appellees Darlene Miller, et al.

Opposing Side (Petitioner / Appellant): Wayne E. Uhl, Deputy Attorney General of Indiana, argued the cause for appellants. With him on the briefs was Linley E. Pearson, Attorney General.

III. AMICI CURIAE

ACLU Side (Respondent / Appellee)

Brief of amici curiae filed on behalf of the ACLU, et al., by Spencer Neth, Thomas D. Buckley, Jr., Steven R. Sharpiro, and John A. Powell.

Brief of amici curiae filed on behalf of the Georgia on Premise & Lounage Association, Inc., by James A. Walrath.

Brief of amici curiae filed on behalf of People for the American Way, et al., by Timothy B. Dyk, Robert H. Klonoff, Patricia A. Dunn, Elliot M. Mincberg, Stephen F. Rohde, and Mary D. Dorman.

Brief of amici curiae filed by James J. Clancy, pro se, in support of neither appellants nor appellees.

Opposing Side (Petitioner / Appellant)

Brief of amici curiae filed on behalf of the State of Arizona, et al., by Robert K. Corbin, Attorney General of Arizona, and Steven J. Twist, Chief Assistant Attorney General, Clarine Nardi Riddle, Attorney General of Connecticut, and John J. Kelly, Chief State's Attorney, William L. Webster, Attorney General of Missouri, Lacy H. Thornburg, Attorney General of North Carolina, and Rosalie Simmonds Ballentine, Acting Attorney General of the Virgin Islands.

Brief of amici curiae filed on behalf of the American Family Association, Inc., et al., by Alan E. Sears, James Mueller, and Peggy M. Coleman.

Brief of amici curiae filed on behalf of the National Governors' Association, et al., by Benna Ruth Solomon and Peter Buscemi.

IV. THE SUPREME COURT'S DECISION

"We . . . hold that the Indiana statutory requirement that the dancers in the establishments involved in this case must wear pasties and G-strings does not violate the First Amendment. . . .

Several of our cases contain language suggesting that nude dancing of the kind involved here is expressive conduct protected by the First Amendment. . . .

Applying the four-part O'Brien test . . . , we find that Indiana's public indecency statute is justified despite its incidental limitations on some expressive activity. The public indecency statute is clearly within the constitutional power of the State and furthers substantial governmental interests. . . .

This and other public indecency statutes were designed to protect morals and public order. The traditional police power of the States is defined as the authority to provide for the public health, safety, and morals, and we have upheld such a basis for legislation. . . .

This interest is unrelated to the suppression of free expression. Some may view restricting nudity on moral grounds as necessarily related to expression. We disagree.

[W]e do not think that when Indiana applies its statute to the nude dancing in these nightclubs it is proscribing nudity because of the erotic message conveyed by the dancers. Presumably numerous other erotic performances are presented at these establishments and similar clubs without any interference from the State, so long as the performers wear a scant amount of clothing. Likewise, the requirement that the dancers don pasties and G-strings does not deprive the dance of whatever erotic message it conveys; it simply makes the message slightly less graphic. The perceived evil that Indiana seeks to address is not erotic dancing, but public nudity. The appearance of people of all shapes, sizes and ages in the nude at a beach, for example, would convey little if any erotic message, yet the State still seeks to prevent it. Public nudity is the evil the State seeks to prevent, whether or not it is combined with expressive activity. . . .

It is without cavil that the public indecency statute is 'narrowly tailored'; Indiana's requirement that the dancers wear at least pasties and G-strings is modest, and the bare minimum necessary to achieve the State's purpose.

The judgment of the Court of Appeals accordingly is reversed."

V. JUSTICE VOTE

4 Pro ACLU Side vs. 5 Con Opposing Side

ACLU Side (Respondent / Appellee)

1. White, B. – Wrote dissenting opinion
2. Marshall, T. – Joined White's dissent
3. Blackmun, H. – Joined White's dissent
4. Stevens, J. – Joined White's dissent

Opposing Side (Petitioner / Appellant)

1. Rehnquist, W. – Wrote majority opinion
2. Scalia, A. – Wrote concurring opinion
3. Souter, D. – Wrote concurring opinion
4. O'Connor, S. – Joined majority opinion
5. Kennedy, A. – Joined majority opinion

VI. A WIN OR LOSS FOR THE ACLU?

The ACLU, as amicus curiae, urged affirmance of the judgment of the Court of Appeals for the Seventh Circuit; the Supreme Court reversed in a 5-4 vote, giving the ACLU an apparent loss.

725. Harmelin v. Michigan

(Decided June 27, 1991; 501 U.S. 957)

I. ISSUE

A. Issues Discussed

Criminal justice, drugs, Eighth Amendment, cruel and unusual punishment

B. Legal Question Presented

Does a mandatory term of life in prison without the possibility of parole violate the Eighth Amendment's prohibition against cruel and unusual punishment if it does not allow for consideration of mitigating factors?

C. Supreme Court's Answer

A mandatory term of life in prison without the possibility of parole that does not allow for consideration of mitigating factors does not violate the Eighth Amendment.

II. CASE SUMMARY

A. Background

"Petitioner was convicted of possessing 672 grams of cocaine and sentenced to a mandatory term of life in prison without possibility of parole. The Michigan Court of Appeals initially reversed his conviction because evidence supporting it had been obtained in violation of the Michigan Constitution. On petition for rehearing, the Court of Appeals vacated its prior decision and affirmed petitioner's sentence, rejecting his argument that the sentence was 'cruel and unusual' within the meaning of the Eighth Amendment. The Michigan Supreme Court denied leave to appeal . . . ."

The U.S. Supreme Court granted certiorari to review the case and affirmed.

B. Counsel of Record / ACLU Attorney

ACLU Side (Petitioner / Appellant): Carla J. Johnson, by appointment of the Court, argued the cause for appellant.

Opposing Side (Respondent / Appellee): Richard Thompson argued the cause for appellee.

III. AMICI CURIAE

ACLU Side (Petitioner / Appellant)

Brief of amici curiae filed on behalf of the ACLU, et al., by Steven R. Shapiro.

Brief of amici curiae filed on behalf of the Criminal Defense Attorneys of Michigan, et al., by Neil N. Fink, Elizabeth L. Jacobs, and William Swor.

Opposing Side (Respondent / Appellee)

Brief of amici curiae filed on behalf of the United States by Solicitor General Starr, Acting Assistant Attorney General Mueller, Deputy Solicitor General Bryson, and James A. Feldman.

Brief of amici curiae filed on behalf of the State of Arizona by Robert K. Corbin, Attorney General, Jessica Gifford Funkhouser, and Vicki Gotkin Adler, Assistant Attorney General.

Brief of amici curiae filed on behalf of the State of Michigan by Frank J. Kelley, Attorney General, Gay Secor Hardy, Solicitor General, and K. Davison Hunter and Thomas C. Nelson, Assistant Attorneys General.

Brief of amici curiae filed on behalf of the National District Attorneys Association by Richard P. Ieyoub, Jack E. Yelverton, and James P. Manak.

Brief of amici curiae filed on behalf of the Prosecuting Attorneys Association of Michigan by Robert Weiss, John D. O'Hair, and Timothy A. Baughman.

Brief of amici curiae filed on behalf of the Washington Legal Foundation, et al., by Daniel J. Popeo and Paul D. Kamenar.

IV. THE SUPREME COURT'S DECISION

"We think it enough that those who framed and approved the Federal Constitution chose, for whatever reason, not to include within it the guarantee against disproportionate sentences that some State Constitutions contained. It is worth noting, however, that there was good reason for that choice . . . . While there are relatively clear historical guidelines and accepted practices that enable judges to determine which modes of punishment are 'cruel and unusual,' proportionality does not lend itself to such analysis. Neither Congress nor any state legislature has ever set out with the objective of crafting a penalty that is 'disproportionate'; yet . . . many enacted dispositions seem to be so—because they were made for other times or other places, with different social attitudes, different criminal epidemics, different public fears, and different prevailing theories of penology. . . .

Though the different needs and concerns of other States may

induce them to treat simple possession of 672 grams of cocaine as a relatively minor offense, nothing in the Constitution requires Michigan to follow suit. The Eighth Amendment is not a ratchet, whereby a temporary consensus on leniency for a particular crime fixes a permanent constitutional maximum, disabling the States from giving effect to altered beliefs and responding to changed social conditions. . . .

Petitioner claims that his sentence violates the Eighth Amendment for a reason in addition to its alleged disproportionality. He argues that it is 'cruel and unusual' to impose a mandatory sentence of such severity, without any consideration of so-called mitigating factors such as, in his case, the fact that he had no prior felony convictions. He apparently contends that the Eighth Amendment requires Michigan to create a sentencing scheme whereby life in prison without possibility of parole is simply the most severe of a range of available penalties that the sentencer may impose after hearing evidence in mitigation and aggravation.

[T]his claim has no support in the text and history of the Eighth Amendment. Severe, mandatory penalties may be cruel, but they are not unusual in the constitutional sense, having been employed in various forms throughout our Nation's history. . . .

It is true that petitioner's sentence is unique in that it is the second most severe known to the law; but life imprisonment with possibility of parole is also unique in that it is the third most severe. And if petitioner's sentence forecloses some 'flexible techniques' for later reducing his sentence, it does not foreclose all of them, since there remain the possibilities of retroactive legislative reduction and executive clemency. . . . But even where the difference is the greatest, it cannot be compared with death. We have drawn the line of required individualized sentencing at capital cases, and see no basis for extending it further.

The judgment of the Michigan Court of Appeals is affirmed."

V. JUSTICE VOTE

4 Pro ACLU Side vs. 5 Con Opposing Side

ACLU Side (Petitioner / Appellant)

1. White, B. – Wrote dissenting opinion
2. Blackmun, H. – Joined White's dissent, joined Stevens' dissent
3. Stevens, J. – Wrote dissenting opinion, joined White's dissent
4. Marshall T. – Wrote dissenting opinion

Opposing Side (Respondent / Appellee)

1. Scalia, A. – Wrote majority opinion
2. Rehnquist, W. – Joined majority opinion
3. Kennedy, A. – Wrote concurring opinion
4. O'Connor, S. – Joined Kennedy's concurrence
5. Souter, D. – Joined Kennedy's concurrence

VI. A WIN OR LOSS FOR THE ACLU?

The ACLU filed as amicus curiae urging reversal of the judgment of the Court of Appeals of Michigan; the Supreme Court affirmed in a 5-4 vote, giving the ACLU an apparent loss.

726. Gentile v. State Bar of Nevada

(Decided June 27, 1991; 501 U.S. 1030)

I. ISSUE

A. Issues Discussed

First Amendment, freedoms of press, speech, and association

B. Legal Question Presented

Whether application of Nevada Supreme Court Rule 177 in this case violates the First Amendment.

C. Supreme Court's Answer

"Nevada's application of Rule 177 in this case violates the First Amendment. . . . Furthermore, the Rule's safe harbor provision, Rule 177(3), appears to permit the speech in question, and Nevada's decision to discipline petitioner in spite of that provision raises concerns of vagueness and selective enforcement."

II. CASE SUMMARY

A. Background

"Hours after his client was indicted on criminal charges, petitioner Gentile, who is a member of the Bar of the State of Nevada, held a press conference. He made a prepared statement . . . and then he responded to questions. . . .

Some six months later, the criminal case was tried to a jury and the client was acquitted on all counts. The State Bar of Nevada then filed a complaint against petitioner, alleging a violation of Nevada Supreme Court Rule 177, a rule governing pretrial publicity almost identical to ABA Model Rule of Professional Conduct 3.6. . . . Rule 177(1) prohibits an attorney from making 'an extrajudicial statement that a reasonable person would expect to be disseminated by means of public communication if the lawyer knows or reasonably should know that it will have a substantial likelihood of materially prejudicing an adjudicative proceeding.' Rule 177(2) lists a number of statements that are 'ordinarily . . . likely' to result in material prejudice. Rule 177(3) provides a safe harbor for the attorney, listing a number of statements that can be made without fear of discipline notwithstanding the other parts of the Rule.

Following a hearing, the Southern Nevada Disciplinary Board of the State Bar found that Gentile had made the statements in question and concluded that he violated Rule 177. The board recommended a private reprimand. Petitioner appealed to the Nevada Supreme Court, waiving the confidentiality of the disciplinary proceeding, and the Nevada court affirmed the decision of the board."

The U.S. Supreme Court granted certiorari to review the case and reversed.

B. Counsel of Record / ACLU Attorney

ACLU Side (Petitioner / Appellant): Michael E. Tigar argued the cause for appellant.

Opposing Side (Respondent / Appellee): Robert H. Klonoff argued the cause for appellee.

III. AMICI CURIAE

ACLU Side (Petitioner / Appellant)

Brief of amici curiae filed on behalf of the ACLU, et al., by Leon Friedman, Steven R. Shapiro, John A. Powell, and Elliot Mincberg.

Brief of amici curiae filed on behalf of the American Newspaper Publishers Association, et al., by Alice Neff Lucan, Harold W. Fuson, Jr., Jane E. Kirtley, David M. Olive, Deborah R. Linfield, W. Terry Maguire, Rene P. Milam, Bruce W. Sanford, J. Laurent Scharff, Richard M. Schmidt, Jr., and Barbara Wartelle Wall.

Brief of amici curiae filed on behalf of Nevada Attorneys for Criminal Justice by Kevin M. Kelly.

Brief of amici curiae filed on behalf of the National Association of Criminal Defense Lawyers by William J. Genego.

Opposing Side (Respondent / Appellee)

Brief of amici curiae filed on behalf of the United States by Solicitor General Starr, Assistant Attorney General Mueller, Deputy Solicitor General Bryson, and Stephen J. Marzen.

Brief of amici curiae filed on behalf of the American Bar Association by John J. Curtin, Jr., and George A. Kuhlman.

IV. THE SUPREME COURT'S DECISION

"Nevada's application of Rule 177 in this case violates the First Amendment. Petitioner spoke at a time and in a manner that neither in law nor in fact created any threat of real prejudice to his client's right to a fair trial or to the State's interest in the enforcement of its criminal laws. Furthermore, the Rule's safe harbor provision, Rule 177(3), appears to permit the speech in question, and Nevada's decision to discipline petitioner in spite of that provision raises concerns of vagueness and selective enforcement. . . .

There is no question that speech critical of the exercise of the State's power lies at the very center of the First Amendment. Nevada seeks to punish the dissemination of information relating to alleged governmental misconduct, which only last Term we described as 'speech

which has traditionally been recognized as lying at the core of the First Amendment.'

The judicial system, and in particular our criminal justice courts, play a vital part in a democratic state, and the public has a legitimate interest in their operations. . . . Public awareness and criticism have even greater importance where, as here, they concern allegations of police corruption. . . .

Even if one were to accept respondent's argument that lawyers participating in judicial proceedings may be subjected, consistent with the First Amendment, to speech restrictions that could not be imposed on the press or general public, the judgment should not be upheld. The record does not support the conclusion that petitioner knew or reasonably should have known his remarks created a substantial likelihood of material prejudice . . . .

As interpreted by the Nevada Supreme Court, the Rule is void for vagueness . . . . Rule 177(3)(a) provides that a lawyer 'may state without elaboration . . . the general nature of the . . . defense.' Statements under this provision are protected '[n]otwithstanding subsection 1 and 2(a-f).' By necessary operation of the word 'notwithstanding,' the Rule contemplates that a lawyer describing the 'general nature of the . . . defense' 'without elaboration' need fear no discipline, even if he comments on '[t]he character, credibility, reputation or criminal record of a . . . witness,' and even if he 'knows or reasonably should know that [the statement] will have a substantial likelihood of materially prejudicing an adjudicative proceeding.' . . .

A lawyer seeking to avail himself of Rule 177(3)'s protection must guess at its contours. The right to explain the 'general' nature of the defense without 'elaboration' provides insufficient guidance because 'general' and 'elaboration' are both classic terms of degree. In the context before us, these terms have no settled usage or tradition of interpretation in law. The lawyer has no principle for determining when his remarks pass from the safe harbor of the general to the forbidden sea of the elaborated. . . .

The judgment of the Supreme Court of Nevada is reversed."

V. JUSTICE VOTE

5 Pro ACLU Side vs. 4 Con Opposing Side

ACLU Side (Petitioner / Appellant)

1. Kennedy, A. – Wrote majority opinion as to Parts III & VI, and concurring opinion as to Parts I, II, IV and V
2. Marshall, T. – Joined majority opinion as to Parts III & VI, joined Kennedy's concurring opinion
3. Blackmun, H. – Joined majority opinion as to Parts III & VI, joined Kennedy's concurring opinion
4. Stevens, J. – Joined majority opinion as to Parts III & VI, joined Kennedy's concurring opinion
5. O'Connor, S. – Wrote concurring opinion

Opposing Side (Respondent / Appellee)

1. Rehnquist, W. – Delivered majority opinion as to Parts I & II and dissenting opinion as to Part III
2. Scalia, A. – Joined Rehnquist's opinion
3. Souter, D. – Joined Rehnquist's opinion
4. White, B. – Joined Rehnquist's opinion

VI. A WIN OR LOSS FOR THE ACLU?

The ACLU filed as amicus curiae urging reversal of the judgment of the Nevada Supreme Court; the Supreme Court reversed in a 5-4 vote, giving the ACLU an apparent win.

727. Hafer v. Melo

(Decided November 5, 1991; 502 U.S. 21)

I. ISSUE

A. Issues Discussed

Civil rights, Eleventh Amendment, Fourteenth Amendment, § 1983

B. Legal Question Presented

"[W]hether state officers may be held personally liable for damages under § 1983 based upon actions taken in their official capacities."

C. Supreme Court's Answer

State officers may be held personally liable for damages udner § 1983 based upon actions taken in their official capacities.

II. CASE SUMMARY

A. Background

"In 1988, petitioner Barbara Hafer sought election to the post of auditor general of Pennsylvania. Respondents allege that during the campaign United States Attorney James West gave Hafer a list of 21 employees in the auditor general's office who secured their jobs through payments to a former employee of the office. They further allege that Hafer publicly promised to fire all employees on the list if elected.

Hafer won the election. Shortly after becoming auditor general, she dismissed 18 employees, including named respondent James Melo, Jr., on the basis that they 'bought' their jobs. Melo and seven other terminated employees sued Hafer and West in Federal District Court. They asserted state and federal claims, including a claim under § 1983, and sought monetary damages. Carl Gurley and the remaining respondents in this case also lost their jobs with the auditor general soon after Hafer took office. These respondents allege that Hafer discharged them because of their Democratic political affiliation and support for her opponent in the 1988 election. They too filed suit against Hafer, seeking monetary damages and reinstatement under § 1983.

After consolidating the Melo and Gurley actions, the District Court dismissed all claims. In relevant part, the court held that the § 1983 claims against Hafer were barred because, under Will, she could not be held liable for employment decisions made in her official capacity as auditor general.

The Court of Appeals for the Third Circuit reversed this portion of the District Court's decision. As to claims for reinstatement brought against Hafer in her official capacity, the court rested on [the Supreme Court's] statement in Will that state officials sued for injunctive relief in their official capacities are 'persons' subject to liability under § 1983. Turning to respondents' monetary claims, the court found that six members of the Gurley group had expressly sought damages from Hafer in her personal capacity. The remaining plaintiffs 'although not as explicit, signified a similar intent.' The court found this critical. While Hafer's power to hire and fire derived from her position as auditor general, it said, a suit for damages based on the exercise of this authority could be brought against Hafer in her personal capacity. Because Hafer acted under color of state law, respondents could maintain a § 1983 individual-capacity suit against her."

The Sarape Court granted certiorari to review the case and affirmed.

B. Counsel of Record / ACLU Attorney

ACLU Side (Respondent / Appellee): William Goldstein argued the cause for appellee.

Opposing Side (Petitioner / Appellant): Jerome R. Richter argued the cause for appellant.

III. AMICI CURIAE

ACLU Side (Respondent / Appellee)

Brief of amici curiae filed on behalf of the ACLU, et al., by Andrew J. Pincus, John A. Powell, and Steven R. Shapiro.

Brief of amici curiae filed on behalf of the American Federation of Labor and Congress of Industrial Organizations by Robert M. Weinberg, Andrew D. Roth, Walter Kamiat, and Laurence Gold.

Brief of amici curiae filed on behalf of Kenneth W. Fultz by Cletus P. Lyman.

Brief of amici curie filed on behalf of Nancy Haberstroh by Stephen R. Kaplan.

Opposing Side (Petitioner / Appellant)

Brief of amici curiae filed on behalf of the National Association of Counties, et al., by Richard Ruda.

IV. THE SUPREME COURT'S DECISION

"Will itself makes clear that the distinction between official-capacity suits and personal-capacity suits is more than 'a mere pleading device.' State officers sued for damages in their official capacity are not 'persons' for purposes of the suit because they assume the identity of the government that employs them. By contrast, officers sued in their personal capacity come to court as individuals. A government official in the role of personal-capacity defendant thus fits comfortably within the statutory term 'person.' . . .

Hafer seeks to overcome the distinction between official- and personal-capacity suits by arguing that § 1983 liability turns not on the capacity in which state officials are sued, but on the capacity in which they acted when injuring the plaintiff. Under Will, she asserts, state officials may not be held liable in their personal capacity for actions they take in their official capacity. Although one Court of Appeals has endorsed this view, we find it both unpersuasive as an interpretation of § 1983 and foreclosed by our prior decisions. . . .

To be sure, imposing personal liability on state officers may hamper their performance of public duties. But such concerns are properly addressed within the framework of our personal immunity jurisprudence. Insofar as respondents seek damages against Hafer personally, the Eleventh Amendment does not restrict their ability to sue in federal court.

We hold that state officials, sued in their individual capacities, are 'persons' within the meaning of § 1983. The Eleventh Amendment does not bar such suits, nor are state officers absolutely immune from personal liability under § 1983 solely by virtue of the 'official' nature of their acts.

The judgment of the Court of Appeals is affirmed."

V. JUSTICE VOTE

8 Pro ACLU Side vs. 0 Con Opposing Side

ACLU Side (Respondent / Appellee)

1. O'Connor, S. – Wrote majority opinion
2. Rehnquist, W. – Joined majority opinion
3. Stevens, J. – Joined majority opinion

4. Scalia, A. – Joined majority opinion
5. Kennedy, A. – Joined majority opinion
6. White, B. – Joined majority opinion
7. Blackmun, H. – Joined majority opinion
8. Souter, D. – Joined majority opinion

Thomas, C – Took no part in the decision

VI. A WIN OR LOSS FOR THE ACLU?

The ACLU filed as amicus curiae urging affirmance of the judgment of the Court of Appeals; the Supreme Court affirmed in an 8-0 vote, giving the ACLU an apparent win.

728. Simon & Schuster, Inc. v. Members of the New York State Crime Victims Board

(Decided December 10, 1991; 502 U.S. 105)

I. ISSUE

A. Issues Discussed

First Amendment, freedoms of press, speech, and association

B. Legal Question Presented

Whether "New York's 'Son of Sam' law [which] requires that an accused or convicted criminal's income from works describing his crime be deposited in an escrow account" violates the First Amendment.

C. Supreme Court's Answer

The Son of Sam law violates the First Amendment as not narrowly tailored to achieve its objective.

II. CASE SUMMARY

A. Background

"New York's 'Son of Sam' law requires that an accused or convicted criminal's income from works describing his crime be deposited in an escrow account. These funds are then made available to the victims of the crime and the criminal's other creditors. . . .

This case began in 1986, when the [New York State Crime Victims] Board first became aware of the contract between petitioner Simon & Schuster and admitted organized crime figure Henry Hill. . . .

On January 31, the Board notified Simon & Schuster: 'It has come to our attention that you may have contracted with a person accused or convicted of a crime for the payment of monies to such person.' The Board ordered Simon & Schuster to furnish copies of any contracts it had entered into with Hill, to provide the dollar amounts and dates of all payments it had made to Hill, and to suspend all payments to Hill in the future. Simon & Schuster complied with this order. By that time, Simon & Schuster had paid Hill's literary agent $96,250 in advances and royalties on Hill's behalf, and was holding $27,958 for eventual payment to Hill.

The Board reviewed the book and the contract, and on May 21, 1987, issued a proposed determination and order. The Board determined that [the book] Wiseguy was covered by § 632–a of the Executive Law, that Simon & Schuster had violated the law by failing to turn over its contract with Hill to the Board and by making payments to Hill, and that all money owed to Hill under the contract had to be turned over to the Board to be held in escrow for the victims of Hill's crimes. The Board ordered Hill to turn over the payments he had already received, and ordered Simon & Schuster to turn over all money payable to Hill at the time or in the future.

Simon & Schuster brought suit in August 1987, under 42 U.S.C. § 1983, seeking a declaration that the Son of Sam law violates the First Amendment and an injunction barring the statute's enforcement. After the parties filed cross-motions for summary judgment, the District Court found the statute to be consistent with the First Amendment. A divided Court of Appeals affirmed."

The Supreme Court granted certiorari to review the case and reversed.

B. Counsel of Record / ACLU Attorney

ACLU Side (Petitioner / Appellant): Ronald S. Rauchberg argued the cause for appellant.

Opposing Side (Respondent / Appellee): Howard L. Zwickel, Assistant Attorney General of New York, argued the cause for appellee..

III. AMICI CURIAE

ACLU Side (Petitioner / Appellant)

Brief of amici curiae filed on behalf of the ACLU, et al., by Leon Friedman, Steven R. Shapiro, John A. Powell, and Arthur N. Eisenberg.

Brief of amici curiae filed on behalf of the Association of American Publishers, Inc. by R. Bruce Rich and Robin E. Silverman.

Brief of amici curiae filed on behalf of the Motion Picture Association of America, Inc. by Richard M. Cooper, David E. Kendall, Laurence Shore, Simon Barsky, Gail Markels, and Walter J. Josiah, Jr.

Opposing Side (Respondent / Appellee)

Brief of amici curiae filed on behalf of the State of Florida, et al., by Robert A. Butterworth, Attorney General of Florida, and Louis F. Hubener and Charles A. Finkel, Assistant Attorneys General, and by the Attorneys General for their respective States as follows: Jimmy Evans of Alabama, Charles E. Cole of Alaska, Daniel E. Lungren of California, Gale E. Norton of Colorado, Richard Blumenthal of Connecticut, Charles M. Oberly III of Delaware, Michael J. Bowers of Georgia, Larry Echo-Hawk of Idaho, Roland W. Burris of Illinois, Linley E. Pearson of Indiana, Robert T. Stephan of Kansas, J. Joseph Curran, Jr. of Maryland, Scott Harshbarger of Massachusetts, Frank J. Kelley of Michigan, Hubert H. Humphrey III of Minnesota, Mike Moore of Mississippi, William L. Webster of Missouri, Marc Racicot of Montana, Don Stenberg of Nebraska, Frankie Sue Del Papa of Nevada, John P. Arnold of New Hampshire, Robert J. Del Tufo of New Jersey, Lacy H. Thornburg of North Carolina, Lee Fisher of Ohio, Robert H. Henry of Oklahoma, Ernest D. Preate, Jr. of Pennsylvania, T. Travis Medlock of South Carolina, Mark Barnett of South Dakota, Charles W. Burson of Tennessee, Paul Van Dam of Utah, Jeffrey L. Amestoy of Vermont, Mary Sue Terry of Virginia, and Joseph B. Meyer of Wyoming.

Brief of amici curiae filed on behalf of the Council of State Governments, et al., by Richard Ruda, Michael G. Dzialo, Steven K. Hoffman, Tanya S. Chutkan, and Randal S. Milch.

Brief of amici curiae filed on behalf of the United States by Solicitor General Starr, Assistant Attorneys General Gerson and Mueller, Deputy Solicitor General Shapiro, and Ronald J. Mann, uring a narrow decision.

Brief of amici curiae filed on behalf of the Crime Victims Legal Clinic by Judith Rowland.

Brief of amici curiae filed on behalf of the National Organization for Victim Assistance, et al., by Charles G. Brown III.

Brief of amici curiae filed on behalf of the Washington Legal Foundation, et al., by Daniel J. Popeo, Richard A. Samp, and Jonathan K. Van Patten.

IV. THE SUPREME COURT'S DECISION

"[T]he State has a compelling interest in ensuring that victims of crime are compensated by those who harm them. . . . The State's interest in preventing wrongdoers from dissipating their assets before victims can recover explains the existence of the State's statutory provisions for prejudgment remedies and orders of restitution. . . . The State likewise has an undisputed compelling interest in ensuring that criminals do not profit from their crimes. . . .

In short, the State has a compelling interest in compensating victims from the fruits of the crime, but little if any interest in limiting such compensation to the proceeds of the wrongdoer's speech about the crime. . . .

As a means of ensuring that victims are compensated from the proceeds of crime, the Son of Sam law is significantly over-inclusive. [T]he statute applies to works on any subject, provided that they express the author's thoughts or recollections about his crime, however tangentially or incidentally. In addition, the statute's broad definition of 'person convicted of a crime' enables the Board to escrow the income of any author who admits in his work to having committed a crime, whether or not the author was ever actually accused or convicted. . . .

We conclude simply that in the Son of Sam law, New York has singled out speech on a particular subject for a financial burden that it places on no other speech and no other income. The State's interest in compensating victims from the fruits of crime is a compelling one, but the Son of Sam law is not narrowly tailored to advance that objective. As a result, the statute is inconsistent with the First Amendment.

The judgment of the Court of Appeals is accordingly reversed."

V. JUSTICE VOTE

8 Pro ACLU Side vs. 0 Con Opposing Side

ACLU Side (Petitioner / Appellant)

1. O'Connor, S. – Wrote majority opinion
2. Rehnquist, W. – Joined majority opinion
3. Stevens, J. – Joined majority opinion
4. Scalia, A. – Joined majority opinion
5. White, B. – Joined majority opinion
6. Souter, D. – Joined majority opinion
7. Blackmun, H. – Wrote concurring opinion
8. Kennedy, A. – Wrote concurring opinion

Thomas, C – Took no part in the decision

VI. A WIN OR LOSS FOR THE ACLU?

The ACLU filed a brief as amicus curiae urging reversal of the judgment of the Court of Appeals; the Supreme Court reversed in an 8-0 vote, giving the ACLU an apparent win.

729. United States Department of State v. Ray

(Decided December 16, 1991; 502 U.S. 164)

I. ISSUE

A. Issues Discussed

Governmental authority, immigration, Fifth Amendment, Sixth Amendment

B. Legal Question Presented

"[W]hether . . . deletions [of names of Haitians who illegally attempted to emigrate to the United States] were authorized by FOIA Exemption 6, which provides that FOIA disclosure requirements do not apply to 'personnel and medical files and similar files the disclosure of which would constitute a clearly unwarranted invasion of personal privacy.'"

C. Supreme Court's Answer

The deletions were authorized because disclosure of the names was clearly unwarranted.

II. CASE SUMMARY

A. Background

"In response to this burgeoning 'illegal migration by sea of large numbers of undocumented aliens' from Haiti and other countries, President Reagan ordered the Coast Guard and the Secretary of State to intercept vessels carrying undocumented aliens and, except for passengers who qualified for refugee status, to return them to their point of origin. [T]he Secretary of State obtained an assurance from the Haitian Government that interdicted Haitians would 'not be subject to prosecution for illegal departure.' In order to monitor compliance with that assurance, State Department personnel conducted confidential interviews with a 'representative sample' of unsuccessful emigrants about six months after their involuntary return. All but one or two of the emigrants reported that they had not been harassed or prosecuted since their return to Haiti.

Respondents in this case are a Florida lawyer who represents undocumented Haitian nationals seeking political asylum in the United States and three of his clients. In immigration proceedings, respondents are attempting to prove that Haitians who immigrated illegally will face a well-founded fear of persecution if they return to their homeland and therefore are refugees entitled to asylum in this country. Relying in part on the evidence in the reports of the interviews with former passengers on vessels interdicted by the Coast Guard, the Government has taken the position in those proceedings that respondents' fear of persecution is not well founded.

In order to test the accuracy of the Government's assertion that undocumented Haitian nationals have not been persecuted upon their return to Haiti, respondents made a series of FOIA requests to three Government agencies for copies of reports of the interviews. [T]he net result of these requests was the production by the State Department of 25 documents . . . which describe a number of interviews with specific returnees and summarize the information that had been obtained during successive periods. . . . In 17 of the documents, the information related to individual interviews, but the names and other identifying information had been redacted before the documents were delivered to respondents. The only issue for [the Supreme Court] to decide is whether that redaction was lawful.

The District Court found that any invasion of privacy from the 'mere act of disclosure of names and addresses would be de minimis and little more than speculation' and was clearly outweighed by the public interest in the 'safe relocation of returned Haitians.' It therefore ordered the Department to produce the redacted information.

The Court of Appeals affirmed. For two reasons, however, it disagreed with the District Court's 'de minimis' characterization of the privacy interest at stake."

The Supreme Court granted certiorari to review the case and reversed.

B. Counsel of Record / ACLU Attorney

ACLU Side (Respondent / Appellee): Michael Dean Ray argued the cause, pro se.

Opposing Side (Petitioner / Appellant): Kent L. Jones argued the cause for appellant.

III. AMICI CURIAE

ACLU Side (Respondent / Appellee)

Brief of amici curiae filed on behalf of the ACLU, et al., by Debra A. Valentine, John A. Rogovin, Stephanie J. Parr, Marc Rotenberg, David L. Sobel, John A. Powell, Lucas Guttentag, Janlori Goldman, and Gary M. Stern.

Brief of amici curiae filed on behalf of the American Newspaper Publishers Association, et al., by Robb M. Jones, Lisa B. Singer, Robert C. Bernius, René P. Milam, Barbara Wartelle Wall, Jane E. Kirtley, Richard M. Schmidt, Bruce W. Sanford, Henry L. Baumann, Steve A. Bookshester, James E. Grossberg, and George Freeman.

Brief of amici curiae filed on behalf of the Lawyers Committee for Human Rights, et al., by Theresa A. Amato, David C. Vladeck, and Alan B. Morrison.

Opposing Side (Petitioner / Appellant)

No briefs of amici curiae were filed in support of appellant.

IV. THE SUPREME COURT'S DECISION

"The District Court and the Court of Appeals properly began their analysis by considering the significance of the privacy interest at stake. We are persuaded, however, that several factors, when considered together, make the privacy interest more substantial than the Court of Appeals recognized.

[T]he Court of Appeals appeared to assume that respondents sought only the names and addresses of the interviewees. But respondents sought—and the District Court ordered that the Government disclose—the unredacted interview summaries. As the Government points out, many of these summaries contain personal details about particular interviewees. . . .

We are also persuaded that the Court of Appeals gave insufficient weight to the fact that the interviews had been conducted pursuant to an assurance of confidentiality. We agree that such a promise does not necessarily prohibit disclosure, but it has a special significance in this case. Not only is it apparent that an interviewee who had been given such an assurance might have been willing to discuss private matters that he or she would not otherwise expose to the public—and therefore would regard a subsequent interview by a third party armed with that information as a special affront to his or her privacy—but, as discussed above, it is also true that the risk of mistreatment gives this group of interviewees an additional interest in assuring that their anonymity is maintained.

[W]e cannot overlook the fact that respondents plan to make direct contact with the individual Haitian returnees identified in the reports. As the Court of Appeals properly recognized, the intent to interview the returnees magnifies the importance of maintaining the confidentiality of their identities.

Although the interest in protecting the privacy of the redacted information is substantial, we must still consider the importance of the public interest in its disclosure. For unless the invasion of privacy is 'clearly unwarranted,' the public interest in disclosure must prevail.

[T]he Court of Appeals properly recognized that the public interest in knowing whether the State Department has adequately monitored Haiti's compliance with its promise not to prosecute returnees is cognizable under FOIA. We are persuaded, however, that this public interest has been adequately served by disclosure of the redacted interview summaries and that disclosure of the unredacted documents would therefore constitute a clearly unwarranted invasion of the interviewees' privacy. . . .

We are also unmoved by respondents' asserted interest in ascertaining the veracity of the interview reports. There is not a scintilla of evidence, either in the documents themselves or elsewhere in the record, that tends to impugn the integrity of the reports. We generally accord Government records and official conduct a presumption of legitimacy. . . .

On the record before us, we are satisfied that the proposed invasion of the serious privacy interest of the Haitian returnees is 'clearly unwarranted.'

The judgment of the Court of Appeals is reversed."

V. JUSTICE VOTE

0 Pro ACLU Side vs. 8 Con Opposing Side

Opposing Side (Petitioner / Appellant)

1. Stevens, J. – Wrote majority opinion
2. O'Connor, S. – Joined majority opinion
3. Rehnquist, W. – Joined majority opinion
4. Blackmun, H. – Joined majority opinion
5. White, B. – Joined majority opinion
6. Souter, D. – Joined majority opinion
7. Scalia, A. – Wrote concurring opinion
8. Kennedy, A. – Joined Scalia's concurrence

Thomas, C – Took no part in the decision

VI. A WIN OR LOSS FOR THE ACLU?

The ACLU filed a brief as amicus curiae urging affirmance of the judgment of the Court of Appeals; the Supreme Court reversed in an 8-0 vote, giving the ACLU an apparent loss.

730. Norman v. Reed

(Decided January 14, 1992; 502 U.S. 279)

I. ISSUE

A. Issues Discussed

First Amendment, freedoms of press, speech, and association, Fourteenth Amendment, elections

B. Legal Question Presented

"[W]hether §§ 10–2 and 10–5, as construed by the Supreme Court of Illinois, violate petitioners' right of access to the Cook County ballot."

C. Supreme Court's Answer

The statutes, as construed, violate petitioners' right of access to the Cook County ballot.

II. CASE SUMMARY

A. Background

"The Harold Washington Party (HWP or Party), named after the late mayor of Chicago, has been established in the city of Chicago since 1989. Petitioners were the principal organizers of an effort to expand the Party by establishing it in Cook County, and, as candidates for county office, they sought to run under the Party name in the November 1990 elections. . . .

Because the Party had previously engaged solely in Chicago municipal elections, petitioners were obliged to qualify as a 'new party' in Cook County in order to run under the Party name. Accordingly, § 10–2 required them to obtain 25,000 nominating signatures in order to designate candidates for the at-large offices. And since petitioners wished to field candidates for the county board seats allocated to the separate districts, they also had to collect 25,000 signatures from each district. Petitioners gathered 44,000 signatures on the city-district component of their petition, but only 7,800 on the suburban component.

After petitioners filed the petition with the county authorities and presented their slate of candidates for both at-large and district-specific seats, respondent Dorothy Reed and several other interested voters (collectively, Reed) filed objections to the slate with the Cook County Officers Electoral Board (Board or Electoral Board). The Board rejected most of Reed's claims. . . .

On appeal, the Circuit Court of Cook County affirmed the Board's ruling on the use of the HWP name, but on grounds different from the Board's. It ruled that while Evans had no statutory power to authorize the use of the Party name, § 10–2 implicitly confined the scope of § 10–5 to cases where two parties seeking to use the same name coexist in the same political subdivision. Since Cook County and the city of Chicago are separate subdivisions, the Circuit Court found no violation of the Election Code.

The Circuit Court nonetheless held that under the plain language of § 10–2, petitioners' failure to obtain 25,000 signatures for the suburban-district candidates doomed the entire slate, and it alternatively held that petitioners' failure to list Party candidates for judicial office compelled the same result. For these two independent reasons, the Circuit Court reversed the Board.

On review, the Supreme Court of Illinois held in a brief written order that § 10–5 prohibited petitioners from using the HWP name, and that their failure to gather enough signatures for the candidates in the suburban-district races disqualified the entire slate. . . .

Petitioners then applied for a stay from Justice Stevens, who, in his capacity as Circuit Justice, ordered the mandate of the Illinois Supreme Court to be 'stayed or, if necessary, recalled' pending further review by [the U.S. Supreme] Court."

The U.S. Supreme Court granted certiorari to review the case, affirmed in part, reversed in part, and remanded.

B. Counsel of Record / ACLU Attorney

ACLU Side (Petitioner / Appellant): R. Eugene Pincham and Kenneth L. Gillis argued the cause for appellants.

Opposing Side (Respondent / Appellee): Gregory A. Adamski argued the cause for appellees.

III. AMICI CURIAE

ACLU Side (Petitioner / Appellant)

Brief of amici curiae filed on behalf of the ACLU of Illinois by William T. Barker, Gerald E. Fradin, Harvey M. Grossman, John A. Powell, Steven R. Shapiro, and Arthur N. Eisenberg.

Brief of amici curiae filed on behalf of the Committee for Party Renewal by Robert E. Tait and Bradley A. Smith.

Opposing Side (Respondent / Appellee)

No briefs of amici curiae were in support of appellees.

IV. THE SUPREME COURT'S DECISION

"We start with Reed's contention that we should treat the controversy as moot because the election is over. We should not. Even if the issue before us were limited to petitioners' eligibility to use the Party name on the 1990 ballot, that issue would be worthy of resolution as 'capable of repetition, yet evading review.' . . .

Since petitioners chose to field candidates for the county board seats allocated to the separate districts and, as required by state law, used the 'component' (i. e., district specific) form of nominating petition, the State Supreme Court's construction of § 10–2 required petitioners to accumulate 50,000 signatures (25,000 from the city district and another 25,000 from the suburbs) to run any candidates in Cook County elections. The State may not do this in the face of Socialist Workers Party, which forbids it to require petitioners to gather twice as many signatures to field candidates in Cook County as they would need statewide. . . .

Illinois does not require a new party fielding candidates solely for statewide office to apportion its nominating signatures among the various counties or other political subdivisions of the State. Organizers of a new party could therefore win access to the statewide ballot, but not the Cook County ballot, by collecting all 25,000 signatures from the county's city district. But if the State deems it unimportant to ensure that new statewide parties enjoy any distribution of support, it requires elusive logic to demonstrate a serious state interest in demanding such a distribution for new local parties. Thus, as in Socialist Workers Party, the State's requirements for access to the statewide ballot become criteria in the first instance for judging whether rules of access to local ballots are narrow enough to pass constitutional muster. Reed has adduced no justification for the disparity here. . . .

In responding to Reed's objection that the HWP had not fielded candidates for any elected judicial offices in Cook County, the Circuit Court held that, under § 10–2, 'the exclusion of judicial candidates on the slate was a failure to fulfill the 'complete slate requirement' of the Election Code.' The court then overruled the Electoral Board and treated this failure as an alternative ground for invalidating the Party's entire slate.

We decline to consider whether that ruling was constitutional. The Supreme Court of Illinois itself did not address it and therefore did not decide whether, under Illinois law, the Party's omission of judicial candidates doomed the entire slate. We therefore remand these cases to that court for its prompt resolution of this issue.

The judgment of the State Supreme Court is affirmed in part and reversed in part, and the cases are remanded for further proceedings not inconsistent with this opinion."

V. JUSTICE VOTE

7 Pro ACLU Side vs. 1 Con Opposing Side

ACLU Side (Petitioner / Appellant)

1. Souter, D. – Wrote majority opinion
2. Rehnquist, W. – Joined majority opinion
3. Blackmun, H. – Joined majority opinion
4. White, B. – Joined majority opinion
5. O'Connor, S. – Joined majority opinion
6. Stevens, J. – Joined majority opinion
7. Kennedy, A. – Joined majority opinion

Opposing Side (Respondent / Appellee)

1. Scalia, A. – Wrote dissenting opinion

Thomas, C – Took no part in the decision

VI. A WIN OR LOSS FOR THE ACLU?

The ACLU filed a brief as amicus curiae urging reversal of the judgment of the Illinois Supreme Court; the U.S. Supreme Court affirmed in part, reversed in part, and remanded in a 7-1 vote, giving the ACLU an apparent win.

731. Immigration & Naturalization Service v. Doherty

(Decided January 15, 1992; 502 U.S. 314)

I. ISSUE

A. Issues Discussed

Governmental authority, immigration, criminal procedure

B. Legal Question Presented

"[W]hether the Attorney General abused his discretion in refusing to reopen the deportation proceedings against respondent to allow consideration of respondent's claims for asylum and withholding of deportation which he had earlier withdrawn."

C. Supreme Court's Answer

The Attorney General did not abuse his discretion by refusing to reopen the deportation proceedings.

II. CASE SUMMARY

A. Background

"Respondent is a native of Northern Ireland and a citizen of both Ireland and the United Kingdom. In May 1980, he and fellow members of the Provisional Irish Republican Army ambushed a car containing members of the British Army and killed British Army Captain Herbert Richard Westmacott. He was tried for the murder of Westmacott in Northern Ireland. Before the court returned a verdict, he escaped from the maximum security prison where he was held; the court found him guilty in absentia of murder and related charges and sentenced him to life imprisonment.

In 1982, respondent surreptitiously entered the United States under an alias. In June 1983, he was located by the Immigration and Naturalization Service (INS), which thereupon began deportation proceedings against him. Respondent applied for asylum under § 208 of the Immigration and Nationality Act . . . . The immigration proceedings were suspended to allow completion of extradition proceedings, which were initiated by the United States at the request of the United Kingdom.

In December 1984, United States District Judge Sprizzo, acting as an Extradition Magistrate under 18 U.S.C. § 3184, held that respondent was not extraditable because his crimes fell into the political offenses exception to the extradition treaty between the United States and the United Kingdom. . . .

When the extradition proceedings concluded, the deportation proceeding against respondent resumed. On September 12, 1986, at a hearing before the Immigration Judge, respondent conceded deportability and designated Ireland as the country to which he be deported pursuant to 8 U.S.C. § 1253(a). In conjunction with this designation, respondent withdrew his application for asylum and withholding of deportation. . . . On March 11, 1987, the Board of Immigration Appeals (BIA) affirmed the deportation order . . . .

The INS appealed the BIA's determination to the Attorney General pursuant to 8 CFR § 3.1(h)(iii) (1987). While the order to deport respondent to Ireland was being reviewed by the Attorney General, respondent filed a motion to reopen his deportation proceedings on the basis that the Irish Extradition Act, implemented by Ireland in December 1987, constituted new evidence requiring that his claims for withholding of deportation and asylum now be reopened. In June 1988, Attorney General Meese reversed the BIA and ordered respondent deported to the United Kingdom. . . .

The BIA granted respondent's motion to reopen, concluding that the 1987 Irish Extradition Act was a circumstance that respondent could not have been expected to anticipate, and that the result of his designation would now leave him to be extradited from Ireland to the United Kingdom, where he feared persecution. The BIA's decision to reopen was appealed by the INS and was reversed by Attorney General Thornburgh who found three independent grounds for denying Doherty's motion to reopen. The Court of Appeals for the Second Circuit . . . affirmed the Meese order, but by a divided vote reversed the Thornburgh order. . . . The Court of Appeals also held that Attorney General Thornburgh had erred in determining, on a motion for reopening, that respondent was not entitled to the ultimate relief requested."

The Supreme Court granted certiorari to review the case and reversed.

B. Counsel of Record / ACLU Attorney

ACLU Side (Respondent / Appellee): Mary Boresz Pike argued the cause for appellee.

Opposing Side (Petitioner / Appellant): Deputy Solicitor General Maureen E. Mahoney argued the cause for appellant.

III. AMICI CURIAE

ACLU Side (Respondent / Appellee)

Brief of amici curiae filed on behalf of the ACLU, et al., by David W. Rivkin, Michael W. Galligan, Geoffrey H. Coll, Philip L. Harvey, Mallika Dutt, Christine M. Bell, Lucas Guttentag, Steven R. Shapiro, Deborah Anker, and Carolyn Patty Blum.

Brief of amici curiae filed on behalf of Amnesty International, et al., by Jessica Eve Goldfarb, Joan Fitzpatrick, Laini Millar-Melnick, and Paul L. Hoffman.

Brief of amici curiae filed on behalf of the International Human Rights Law Group by Franklin G. Snyder and Philip L. Gordon.

Brief of amici curiae filed on behalf of Members of the United States Senate, et al., by Carolyn Patty Blum, Kevin R. Johnson, Joseph K. Brenner, and Kenneth P. Stern.

Brief of amici curiae filed on behalf of the United Nations High Commissioner for Refugees by O. Thomas Johnson, Jr., Andrew I. Schoenholtz, Julian Fleet, Fernando Chang-Muy, Guy S. Goodwin-Gill, and Ralph G. Steinhardt.

Opposing Side (Petitioner / Appellant)

No briefs of amici curiae were filed in support of appellant.

IV. THE SUPREME COURT'S DECISION

"There is no statutory provision for reopening of a deportation proceeding, and the authority for such motions derives solely from regulations promulgated by the Attorney General. The regulation with which we deal here, 8 CFR § 3.2 (1987), is couched solely in negative terms; it requires that under certain circumstances a motion to reopen be denied, but does not specify the conditions under which it shall be granted . . . . The granting of a motion to reopen is thus discretionary, and the Attorney General has 'broad discretion' to grant or deny such motions. . . .

The Attorney General determined that neither the denial of respondent's designation of Ireland as the country of deportation, nor the change in Irish extradition law, qualified as new material evidence to support reopening of respondent's deportation proceedings. . . . The Attorney General also decided that Ireland's implementation of its 1987 Extradition Act was neither relevant nor new. . . .

We hold . . . that it was well within [the Attorney General's] broad discretion in considering motions to reopen to decide that the material adduced by respondent could have been foreseen or anticipated at the time of the earlier proceeding. . . .

The Court of Appeals also took the view that since the BIA had granted the motion to reopen, the Attorney General was in some way limited in his authority to overturn that decision. But the BIA is simply a regulatory creature of the Attorney General, to which he has delegated much of his authority under the applicable statutes. He is the final administrative authority in construing the regulations, and in deciding questions under them. The mere fact that he disagrees with a conclusion of the BIA in construing or applying a regulation cannot support a conclusion that he abused his discretion. . . .

The Attorney General found, as an independent basis for denying reopening, that respondent had waived his claims for relief by withdrawing them at the first hearing to obtain a tactical advantage. We disagree with the Court of Appeals' rejection of this reason to deny reopening. [T]he Attorney General found that withdrawing a claim for a tactical advantage is not a reasonable explanation for failing to pursue the claim at an earlier hearing.

Precisely because an alien may qualify for one form of relief from deportation, but not another, the INS allows aliens to plead in the alternative in immigration proceedings. There was nothing which prevented respondent from bringing evidence in support of his asylum and withholding of deportation claims at his first deportation proceeding, in case the Attorney General did contest his designation of Ireland as the country to which he be deported. Respondent chose, however, to withdraw those claims, even when expressly questioned by the Immigration Judge.

The Court of Appeals rejected this ground for the Attorney General's denial of reopening on the ground that his reasoning was 'incompatible with any motion to reopen . . . .' It may be that the Attorney General has adopted a narrow, rather than a broad, construction of the regulations governing reopening, but nothing in the regulations forbids such a course. The Attorney General here held that respondent's decision to withdraw certain claims in the initial proceedings was a 'deliberate tactical decision,' and that under applicable regulations those claims could have been submitted at that time even though inconsistent with other claims made by respondent. We hold that this basis for the Attorney General's decision was not an abuse of discretion.

The judgment of the Court of Appeals is reversed."

V. JUSTICE VOTE

3 Pro ACLU Side vs. 5 Con Opposing Side

ACLU Side (Respondent / Appellee)

1. Scalia, A. – Wrote opinion concurring in part and dissenting in part
2. Souter, D. – Joined Scalia's opinion
3. Stevens, J. – Joined Scalia's opinion

Opposing Side (Petitioner / Appellant)

1. Rehnquist, W. – Wrote majority opinion
2. Kennedy, A. – Joined majority opinion
3. O'Connor, S. – Joined majority opinion
4. White, B. – Joined majority opinion
5. Blackmun, H. – Joined majority opinion

Thomas, C – Took no part in the decision

VI. A WIN OR LOSS FOR THE ACLU?

The ACLU filed a brief as amicus curiae urging affirmance of the judgment of the Court of Appeals for the Second Circuit; the Supreme Court reversed in an 8-0 vote, giving the ACLU an apparent loss.

732. Rufo v. Inmates of the Suffolk County Jail

(Decided January 15, 1992; 502 U.S. 367)

I. ISSUE

A. Issues Discussed

Criminal justice, prisons, consent decrees

B. Legal Question Presented

"[W]hether the courts below applied the correct standard in denying" the "motion of the sheriff of Suffolk County, Massachusetts, to modify a consent decree entered to correct unconstitutional conditions at the Suffolk County Jail."

C. Supreme Court's Answer

The courts below did not apply the correct standard and the cases must be remanded to correct these errors.

II. CASE SUMMARY

A. Background

"This litigation began in 1971 when inmates sued . . . claiming that inmates not yet convicted of the crimes charged against them were being held under unconstitutional conditions at what was then the Suffolk County Jail. . . .

The court permanently enjoined the government defendants: '(a) from housing at the Charles Street Jail after November 30, 1973 in a cell with another inmate, any inmate who is awaiting trial and (b) from housing at the Charles Street Jail after June 30, 1976 any inmate who is awaiting trial.' The defendants did not appeal.

In 1977, with the problems of the Charles Street Jail still unresolved, the District Court ordered defendants, including the Boston City Council, to take such steps and expend the funds reasonably necessary to renovate another existing facility as a substitute detention center. . . . The Court of Appeals ordered that the Charles Street Jail be closed on October 2, 1978, unless a plan was presented to create a constitutionally adequate facility for pretrial detainees in Suffolk County.

Four days before the deadline, the plan that formed the basis for the consent decree now before this Court was submitted to the District Court. . . . The court therefore allowed Suffolk County to continue housing its pretrial detainees at the Charles Street Jail.

Seven months later, the court entered a formal consent decree . . . . The decree specifically incorporated the provisions of the Suffolk County Detention Center, Charles Street Facility, Architectural Program, which—in the words of the consent decree—'sets forth a program which is both constitutionally adequate and constitutionally required.' . . .

Although the architectural program projected that construction of the new jail would be completed by 1983, work on the new facility had not been started by 1984. During the intervening years, the inmate population outpaced population projections. Litigation in the state courts ensued, and defendants were ordered to build a larger jail. . . . Construction started in 1987.

In July 1989, while the new jail was still under construction, the sheriff moved to modify the consent decree to allow the double bunking of male detainees in 197 cells, thereby raising the capacity of the new jail to 610 male detainees. . . .

The District Court refused to grant the requested modification . . . .

The District Court briefly stated that, even under the flexible modification standard adopted by other Courts of Appeals, the sheriff would not be entitled to relief because '[a] separate cell for each detainee has always been an important element of the relief sought in this litigation—perhaps even the most important element.' Finally, the court rejected the argument that the decree should be modified because the proposal complied with constitutional standards, reasoning that such a rule 'would undermine and discourage settlement efforts in institutional cases.' The District Court never decided whether the sheriff's proposal for double celling at the new jail would be constitutionally permissible.

The new Suffolk County Jail opened shortly thereafter.

The Court of Appeals affirmed, stating: '[W]e are in agreement with the well-reasoned opinion of the district court and see no reason to elaborate further.'"

The Supreme Court granted certiorari to review the case, vacated, and remanded.

B. Counsel of Record / ACLU Attorney

ACLU Side (Respondent / Appellee): Max D. Stern argued the cause for appellees in both cases.

Opposing Side (Petitioner / Appellant): Chester A. Janiak argued the cause for petitioners in No. 90-954. John T. Montgomery, First Assistant Attorney General of Massachusetts, argued the cause for petitioners in No. 90-1004.

III. AMICI CURIAE

ACLU Side (Respondent / Appellee)

Briefs of amici curiae filed on behalf of the ACLU, et al., by John A. Powell, Steven R. Shapiro, John Reinstein, Elizabeth Alexander, David C. Fathi, Alexa P. Freeman, and Alvin J. Bronstein.

Brief of amici curiae filed on behalf of Allen F. Breed, et al., by Sheldon Krantz.

Brief of amici curiae filed on behalf of the Center for Dispute Settlement by Susan P. Strum and C. Lani Guinier.

Brief of amici curiae filed on behalf of the Inmates of the Lorton Central Facility by Peter J. Nickles, Bruce N. Kuhlik, Alan A. Pemberton, and Michele J. Woods.

Brief of amici curiae filed on behalf of the Lawyers' Committee for Civil Rights Under Law of the Boston Bar Association by John C. Englander, Loretta M. Smith, Peter F. Young, and Ozell Hudson, Jr.

Opposing Side (Petitioner / Appellant)

Briefs of amici curiae filed on behalf of the State of New York by Attorney General Robert Abrams, Solicitor General O. Peter Sherwood, Deputy Solicitor General Lawrence S. Kahn, and Assistant Attorney General Barbara B. Butler.

Brief of amici curiae filed on behalf of the State of Tennessee, et al., by Charles W. Burson, Attorney General of Tennessee; Michael W. Catalano, Deputy Attorney General; Charles Cole, Attorney General of Alaska; Grant Woods, Attorney General of Arizona; Winston Bryant, Attorney General of Arkansas; Dan Lungren, Attorney General of California; Gale Norton, Attorney General of Colorado; Charles M. Oberly III, Attorney General of Delaware; Robert A. Butterworth, Attorney General of Florida; Michael J. Bowers, Attorney General of Georgia; Elizabeth Barrett-Anderson, Attorney General of Guam; Warren Price III, Attorney General of Hawaii; Larry EchoHawk, Attorney General of Idaho; Roland W. Burris, Attorney General of Illinois; Linley E. Pearson, Attorney General of Indiana; Bonnie Campbell, Attorney General of Iowa; Robert T. Stephan, Attorney General of Kansas; Fred Cowan, Attorney General of Kentucky; William J. Guste, Jr., Attorney General of Louisiana; Michael E. Carpenter, Attorney General of Maine; J. Joseph Curran, Jr., Attorney General of Maryland; Frank J. Kelley, Attorney General of Michigan; Hubert H. Humphrey III, Attorney General of Minnesota; Mike Moore, Attorney General of Mississippi; William L. Webster, Attorney General of Missouri; Frankie Sue Del Papa, Attorney General of Nevada; John P. Arnold, Attorney General of New Hampshire; Robert J. Del Tufo, Attorney General of New Jersey; Tom Udall, Attorney General of New Mexico; Lacy H. Thornburg, Attorney General of North Carolina; Nicholas Spaeth, Attorney General of North Dakota; Lee Fisher, Attorney General of Ohio; Robert H. Henry, Attorney General of Oklahoma; Dave Frohnmayer, Attorney General of Oregon; Ernest D. Preate, Jr., Attorney General of Pennsylvania; Hector Rivera-Cruz, Attorney General of Puerto Rico; James E. O'Neil, Attorney General of Rhode Island; T. Travis Medlock, Attorney General of South Carolina; Mark "Barney" Barnett, Attorney General of South Dakota; Paul Van Dam, Attorney General of Utah; Jeffrey L. Amestoy, Attorney General of Vermont; Rosalie Ballentine, Acting Attorney General of the Virgin Islands; Mary Sue Terry, Attorney General of Virginia; Ken Eikenberry, Attorney General of Washington; Mario Palumbo, Attorney General of West Virginia; and Joseph B. Meyer, Attorney General of Wyoming.

Brief of amici curiae filed on behalf of the City of New York by Victor A. Kovner, Leonard J. Koerner, Fay Leoussis, and Timothy J. O'Shaughnessy.

for the International City Management Association, et al., by Richard Ruda, Zachary D. Fasman, and Mark L. Gerchick.

Brief of amici curiae filed on behalf of Michael J. Ashe, Jr., Sheriff of Hampden County, et al., by Edward J. McDonough, Jr.

Brief of amici curiae filed on behalf of the United States by Solicitor General Starr, Assistant Attorney General Gerson, Deputy Solicitor General Shapiro, Harriet S. Shapiro, Robert E. Kopp, and Thomas M. Bondy.

IV. THE SUPREME COURT'S DECISION

"[T]he 'grievous wrong' language of Swift was not intended to take on a talismanic quality, warding off virtually all efforts to modify consent decrees. . . . There is thus little basis for concluding that Rule 60(b) misread the Swift opinion and intended that modifications of consent decrees in all cases were to be governed by the standard actually applied in Swift. That Rule, in providing that, on such terms as are just, a party may be relieved from a final judgment or decree where it is no longer equitable that the judgment have prospective application, permits a less stringent, more flexible standard. . . .

Although we hold that a district court should exercise flexibility in considering requests for modification of an institutional reform consent decree, it does not follow that a modification will be warranted in all circumstances. [A] party seeking modification of a consent decree bears the burden of establishing that a significant change in circumstances warrants revision of the decree. . . .

A party seeking modification of a consent decree may meet its initial burden by showing a significant change either in factual conditions or in law. . . .

Modification of a consent decree may be warranted when changed factual conditions make compliance with the decree substantially more onerous. . . .

The District Court was . . . in error in holding that even under a more flexible standard than its version of Swift required, modification of the single cell requirement was necessarily forbidden. . . . A consent decree must of course be modified if, as it later turns out, one or more of the obligations placed upon the parties has become impermissible under federal law.

[A] court should surely keep the public interest in mind in ruling on a request to modify based on a change in conditions making it substantially more onerous to abide by the decree. To refuse modification of a decree is to bind all future officers of the State, regardless of their view of the necessity of relief from one or more provisions of a decree that might not have been entered had the matter been litigated to its conclusion. The District Court seemed to be of the view that the problems of the fiscal officers of the State were only marginally relevant to the request for modification in this case. Financial constraints may not be used to justify the creation or perpetuation of constitutional violations, but they are a legitimate concern of government defendants in institutional reform litigation and therefore are appropriately considered in tailoring a consent decree modification.

To conclude, we hold that the Swift 'grievous wrong' standard does not apply to requests to modify consent decrees stemming from institutional reform litigation. Under the flexible standard we adopt today, a party seeking modification of a consent decree must establish that a significant change in facts or law warrants revision of the decree and that the proposed modification is suitably tailored to the changed circumstance. We vacate the decision below and remand the cases for further proceedings consistent with this opinion."

V. JUSTICE VOTE

2 Pro ACLU Side vs. 6 Con Opposing Side

ACLU Side (Petitioner / Appellant)

1. Stevens, J. – Wrote dissenting opinion
2. Blackmun, H. – Joined Stevens' dissent

Opposing Side (Respondent / Appellee)

1. White, B. – Wrote majority opinion
2. Rehnquist, W. – Joined majority opinion
3. Scalia, A. – Joined majority opinion
4. Kennedy, A. – Joined majority opinion
5. Souter, D. – Joined majority opinion
6. O'Connor, S. – Wrote concurring opinion

Thomas, C – Took no part in the decision

VI. A WIN OR LOSS FOR THE ACLU?

The ACLU filed a brief as amicus curiae urging affirmance of the judgment of the Court of Appeals for the First Circuit; the Supreme Court vacated and remanded in a 6-2 vote, giving the ACLU an apparent loss.

733. Hudson v. McMillian

(Decided February 25, 1992; 503 U.S. 1)

I. ISSUE

A. Issues Discussed

Criminal justice, Eighth Amendment, cruel and unusual punishment

B. Legal Question Presented

"[W]hether the use of excessive physical force against a prisoner may constitute cruel and unusual punishment when the inmate does not suffer serious injury."

C. Supreme Court's Answer

The use of excessive physical force against a prisoner may constitute cruel and unusual punishment even when the inmate does not suffer serious injury.

II. CASE SUMMARY

A. Background

"At the time of the incident that is the subject of this suit, petitioner Keith Hudson was an inmate at the state penitentiary in Angola, Louisiana. Respondents Jack McMillian, Marvin Woods, and Arthur Mezo served as corrections security officers at the Angola facility. During the early morning hours of October 30, 1983, Hudson and McMillian argued. Assisted by Woods, McMillian then placed Hudson in handcuffs and shackles, took the prisoner out of his cell, and walked him toward the penitentiary's 'administrative lockdown' area. Hudson testified that, on the way there, McMillian punched Hudson in the mouth, eyes, chest, and stomach while Woods held the inmate in place and kicked and punched him from behind. He further testified that Mezo, the supervisor on duty, watched the beating but merely told the officers 'not to have too much fun.' As a result of this episode, Hudson suffered minor bruises and swelling of his face, mouth, and lip. The blows also loosened Hudson's teeth and cracked his partial dental plate, rendering it unusable for several months.

Hudson sued the three corrections officers in Federal District Court under Rev.Stat. § 1979, 42 U.S.C. § 1983, alleging a violation of the Eighth Amendment's prohibition on cruel and unusual punishments and seeking compensatory damages. The parties consented to disposition of the case before a Magistrate, who found that McMillian and Woods used force when there was no need to do so and that Mezo expressly condoned their actions. The Magistrate awarded Hudson damages of $800.

The Court of Appeals for the Fifth Circuit reversed. It held that inmates alleging use of excessive force in violation of the Eighth Amendment must prove: (1) significant injury; (2) resulting 'directly and only from the use of force that was clearly excessive to the need'; (3) the excessiveness of which was objectively unreasonable; and (4) that the action constituted an unnecessary and wanton infliction of pain. The court determined that respondents' use of force was objectively unreasonable because no force was required. Furthermore, '[t]he conduct of McMillian and Woods qualified as clearly excessive and occasioned unnecessary and wanton infliction of pain.' However, Hudson could not prevail on his Eighth Amendment claim because his injuries were 'minor' and required no medical attention."

The Supreme Court granted certiorari to review the case and reversed.

B. Counsel of Record / ACLU Attorney

ACLU Side (Petitioner / Appellant): Alvin J. Bronstein argued the cause for appellant. With him on the briefs were John A. Powell, Steven R. Shapiro, Mark J. Lopez, and Elizabeth Alexander.

Deputy Solicitor General Roberts argued the cause for the United States, as amicus curiae, by special leave of Court.

Opposing Side (Respondent / Appellee): Harry McCall, Jr., Special Assistant Attorney General of Louisiana, argued the case for appellee. With him on the briefs were William J. Guste, Jr., Attorney General, Jonathan C. McCall, Special Assistant Attorney General, and Jenifer Schaye, Clifton O. Bingham, Jr., Houston C. Gascon III, and Joseph Erwin Kopsa, Assistant Attorneys General.

III. AMICI CURIAE

ACLU Side (Petitioner / Appellant)

Brief of amici curiae filed on behalf of the United States by Deputy Solicitor General Roberts, Solicitor General Starr, Assistant Attorneys General Dunne and Mueller, Acting Deputy Solicitor General Wright, and Ronald J. Mann.

Brief of amici curiae filed on behalf of Americans for Effective Law Enforcement, Inc., by Daniel B. Hales, Emory A. Plitt, Jr., Wayne W Schmidt, and James P. Manak.

Brief of amici curiae filed on behalf of the D. C. Prisoners' Legal Services Project, Inc., by Theodore A. Howard and Richard J. Arsenault.

Brief of amici curiae filed on behalf of Human Rights Watch by Cameron Clark.

Brief of amici curiae filed on behalf of the Prisoners' Legal Service of New York by John A. Gresham and Stephen M. Latimer.

Opposing Side (Respondent / Appellee)

Brief of amici curiae filed on behalf of the State of Texas, et al., by Dan Morales, Attorney General of Texas, Will Pryor, First Assistant Attorney General, Mary F. Keller, Deputy Attorney General, and Michael P. Hodge, Charles A. Palmer, Sharon Felfe, and Adrian L. Young, Assistant Attorneys General, joined by the Attorneys General for their respective States as follows: Warren Price III of Hawaii, Joseph B. Meyer of Wyoming, Frankie Sue Del Papa of Nevada, and Robert A. Butterworth of Florida.

IV. THE SUPREME COURT'S DECISION

"In Whitley v. Albers, 312 U.S. 312 (1986), the principal question before us was what legal standard should govern the Eighth Amendment claim of an inmate shot by a guard during a prison riot. We based our answer on the settled rule that 'the unnecessary and wanton infliction of pain . . . constitutes cruel and unusual punishment forbidden by the Eighth Amendment.'

[O]fficials confronted with a prison disturbance must balance the threat unrest poses to inmates, prison workers, administrators, and visitors against the harm inmates may suffer if guards use force. '[T]he question whether the measure taken inflicted unnecessary and wanton pain and suffering ultimately turns on 'whether force was applied in a good faith effort to maintain or restore discipline or maliciously and sadistically for the very purpose of causing harm.' [W]e hold that whenever prison officials stand accused of using excessive physical force in violation of the Cruel and Unusual Punishments Clause, the core judicial inquiry . . . whether force was applied in a good-faith effort to maintain or restore discipline, or maliciously and sadistically to cause harm. . . .

When prison officials maliciously and sadistically use force to cause harm, contemporary standards of decency always are violated. This is true whether or not significant injury is evident. Otherwise, the Eighth Amendment would permit any physical punishment, no matter how diabolic or inhuman, inflicting less than some arbitrary quantity of injury. . . . The extent of Hudson's injuries thus provides no basis for dismissal of his § 1983 claim. . . .

The judgment of the Court of Appeals is reversed."

V. JUSTICE VOTE

7 Pro ACLU Side vs. 2 Con Opposing Side

ACLU Side (Petitioner / Appellant)

1. O'Connor, S. – Wrote majority opinion
2. Rehnquist, W. – Joined majority opinion
3. White, B. – Joined majority opinion
4. Kennedy, A. – Joined majority opinion
5. Souter, D. – Joined majority opinion
6. Stevens, J. – Wrote concurring opinion
7. Blackmun, H. – Wrote concurring opinion

Opposing Side (Respondent / Appellee)

1. Thomas, C. – Wrote dissenting opinion
2. Scalia, A. – Joined Thomas' dissent

VI. A WIN OR LOSS FOR THE ACLU?

The ACLU, as counsel, urging reversal of the judgment of the Court of Appeals; the Supreme Court reversed in a 7-2 vote, giving the ACLU an apparent win.

734. Collins v. City of Harker Heights, Texas

(Decided February 26, 1992; 503 U.S. 115)

I. ISSUE

A. Issues Discussed

Civil rights, federal rights, Fourteenth Amendment

B. Legal Question Presented

"[W]hether § 1 of the Civil Rights Act of 1871, Rev.Stat. § 1979, 42 U.S.C. § 1983, provides a remedy for a municipal employee who is fatally injured in the course of his employment because the city customarily failed to train or warn its employees about known hazards in the workplace."

C. Supreme Court's Answer

"Even though the city's conduct may be actionable under state law, we hold that § 1983 does not apply because such conduct does not violate the Due Process Clause."

II. CASE SUMMARY

A. Background

"On October 21, 1988, Larry Michael Collins, an employee in the sanitation department of the City of Harker Heights, Texas, died of asphyxia after entering a manhole to unstop a sewer line. Petitioner, his widow, brought this action alleging that Collins 'had a constitutional right to be free from unreasonable risks of harm to his body, mind and emotions and a constitutional right to be protected from the city of Harker Heights' custom and policy of deliberate indifference toward the safety of its employees.' Her complaint alleged that the city violated that right by following a custom and policy of not training its employees about the dangers of working in sewer lines and manholes, not providing safety equipment at jobsites, and not providing safety warnings. The complaint also alleged that a prior incident had given the city notice of the risks of entering the sewer lines and that the city had systematically and intentionally failed to provide the equipment and training required by a Texas statute. The District Court dismissed the complaint on the ground that a constitutional violation had not been alleged. The Court of Appeals for the Fifth Circuit affirmed on a different theory. It did not reach the question whether the city had violated Collins' constitutional rights because it denied recovery on the ground that there had been no 'abuse of governmental power,' which the Fifth Circuit had found to be a necessary element of a § 1983 action."

The Supreme Court granted certiorari to review the case and affirmed.

B. Counsel of Record / ACLU Attorney

ACLU Side (Petitioner / Appellant): Sanford J. Rosen argued the cause for appellant.

Opposing Side (Respondent / Appellee): Lucas A. Powe, Jr. argued the case for appellee.

III. AMICI CURIAE

ACLU Side (Petitioner / Appellant)

Brief of amici curiae filed on behalf of the ACLU, et al., by Edward Tuddenham, J. Patrick Wiseman, Steven R. Shapiro, John A. Powell, and Helen Hershkoff.

Brief of amici curiae filed on behalf of the Association of Trial Lawyers of America by Jeffrey L. Needle and Michael C. Maher.

Brief of amici curiae filed on behalf of the National Education Association by Robert H. Chanin, Jeremiah A. Collins, and Andrew D. Roth.

Opposing Side (Respondent / Appellee)

Brief of amici curiae filed on behalf of the National League of Cities, et al., by Richard Ruda, Carter G. Phillips, Mark D. Hopson, and Jeffrey S. Steinberg.

IV. THE SUPREME COURT'S DECISION

"[P]roper analysis requires us to separate two different issues when a § 1983 claim is asserted against a municipality: (1) whether plaintiff's harm was caused by a constitutional violation, and (2) if so, whether the city is responsible for that violation. . . .

Petitioner's constitutional claim rests entirely on the Due Process Clause of the Fourteenth Amendment. [S]he relies on the substantive component of the Clause that protects individual liberty against 'certain government actions regardless of the fairness of the procedures used to implement them.'

As a general matter, the Court has always been reluctant to expand the concept of substantive due process because guideposts for responsible decision making in this uncharted area are scarce and open-ended. The doctrine of judicial self-restraint requires us to exercise the utmost care whenever we are asked to break new ground in this field. It is important, therefore, to focus on the allegations in the complaint to determine how petitioner describes the constitutional right at stake and what the city allegedly did to deprive her husband of that right.

A fair reading of petitioner's complaint does not charge the city with a willful violation of Collins' rights. . . . Instead, she makes the more general allegation that the city deprived him of life and liberty by failing to provide a reasonably safe work environment. . . . Neither the text nor the history of the Due Process Clause supports petitioner's claim that the governmental employer's duty to provide its employees with a safe working environment is a substantive component of the Due Process Clause. . . . Petitioner cannot maintain . . . that the city deprived Collins of his liberty when it made, and he voluntarily accepted, an offer of employment.

We also are not persuaded that the city's alleged failure to train its employees, or to warn them about known risks of harm, was an omission that can properly be characterized as arbitrary, or conscience shocking, in a constitutional sense. . . . The Due Process Clause 'is not a guarantee against incorrect or ill-advised personnel decisions.' Nor does it guarantee municipal employees a workplace that is free of unreasonable risks of harm.

Finally, we reject petitioner's suggestion that the Texas Hazard Communication Act supports her substantive due process claim. We assume that the Act imposed a duty on the city to warn its sanitation employees about the dangers of noxious gases in the sewers and to provide safety training and protective equipment to minimize those dangers. We also assume, as petitioner argues, that the Act created an entitlement that qualifies as a 'liberty interest' protected by the Due Process Clause. But even with these assumptions, petitioner's claim must fail for she has not alleged that the deprivation of this liberty interest was arbitrary in the constitutional sense. The reasons why the city's alleged failure to train and warn did not constitute a constitutionally arbitrary deprivation of Collins' life apply a fortiori to the less significant liberty interest created by the Texas statute.

In sum, we conclude that the Due Process Clause does not impose an independent federal obligation upon municipalities to provide certain minimal levels of safety and security in the workplace and the city's alleged failure to train or to warn its sanitation department employees was not arbitrary in a constitutional sense. The judgment of the Court of Appeals is therefore affirmed."

V. JUSTICE VOTE

0 Pro ACLU Side vs. 9 Con Opposing Side

Opposing Side (Respondent / Appellee)

1. Stevens, J. – Wrote majority opinion
2. Blackmun, H. – Joined majority opinion
3. White, B. – Joined majority opinion
4. Souter, D. – Joined majority opinion
5. Kennedy, A. – Joined majority opinion
6. O'Connor, S. – Joined majority opinion
7. Scalia, A. – Joined majority opinion
8. Rehnquist, W. – Joined majority opinion
9. Thomas, C. – Joined majority opinion

VI. A WIN OR LOSS FOR THE ACLU?

The ACLU filed as amicus curiae urging reversal of the judgment of the Court of Appeals; the Supreme Court affirmed in a 9-0 vote, giving the ACLU an apparent loss.

735. Dawson v. Delaware

(Decided March 9, 1992; 503 U.S. 159)

I. ISSUE

A. Issues Discussed

Criminal justice, death penalty, First Amendment, Fourteenth Amendment, Eighth Amendment, evidence

B. Legal Question Presented

"[W]hether the First and Fourteenth Amendments prohibit the introduction in a capital sentencing proceeding of the fact that the defendant was a member of an organization called the Aryan Brotherhood, where the evidence has no relevance to the issues being decided in the proceeding."

C. Supreme Court's Answer

The First and Fourteenth Amendments prohibit introduction of Aryan Brotherhood evidence here where it has no relevance to the issues being decided in the proceeding.

II. CASE SUMMARY

A. Background

After escaping from prison, David Dawson committed a string of crimes which led to his conviction for "first-degree murder, possession of a deadly weapon during the commission of a felony, and various other crimes. The trial court then conducted a penalty hearing before the jury to determine whether Dawson should be sentenced to death for the first-degree murder conviction. The prosecution gave notice that it intended to introduce (1) expert testimony regarding the origin and nature of the Aryan Brotherhood, as well as the fact that Dawson had the words 'Aryan Brotherhood' tattooed on the back of his right hand, (2) testimony that Dawson referred to himself as 'Abaddon' and had the name 'Abaddon' tattooed in red letters across his stomach, and (3) photographs of multiple swastika tattoos on Dawson's back and a picture of a swastika he had painted on the wall of his prison cell. Dawson argued that this evidence was inflammatory and irrelevant, and that its admission would violate his rights under the First and Fourteenth Amendments.

Before the penalty phase began, the parties agreed to a stipulation regarding the Aryan Brotherhood evidence. The stipulation provided that:

The Aryan Brotherhood refers to a white racist prison gang that began in the 1960's in California in response to other gangs of racial minorities. Separate gangs calling themselves the Aryan Brotherhood now exist in many state prisons including Delaware.'

In return for Dawson's agreement to the stipulation, the prosecution agreed not to call any expert witnesses to testify about the Aryan Brotherhood. Although Dawson agreed to the stipulation in order to avoid presentation of this expert testimony, it is apparent from the record and from the opinion of the Supreme Court of Delaware that he continued to assert that the admission of the stipulated facts into evidence violated the Constitution. At the penalty hearing, the prosecution read the stipulation to the jury and introduced evidence that Dawson had tattooed the words 'Aryan Brotherhood' on his hand. The trial judge permitted the prosecution to present the evidence related to the name "Abaddon" as well, but excluded all of the swastika evidence. In addition, the prosecution submitted proof of Dawson's lengthy criminal record. Dawson, in turn, presented mitigating evidence based on the testimony of two family members and on the fact that he had earned good time credits in prison for enrolling in various drug and alcohol programs. The jury found three statutory aggravating circumstances, each making Dawson eligible for the death penalty under Delaware law; it determined (1) that the murder was committed by an escaped prisoner, (2) that the murder was committed during the commission of a burglary, and (3) that the murder was committed for pecuniary gain. The jury further concluded that the aggravating evidence outweighed the mitigating evidence, and recommended that Dawson be sentenced to death. The trial court, bound by that recommendation, imposed the death penalty.

The Supreme Court of Delaware affirmed the convictions and the death sentence."

The U.S. Supreme Court granted certiorari to review the case, vacated, and remanded.

B. Counsel of Record / ACLU Attorney

ACLU Side (Petitioner / Appellant): Bernard J. O'Donnell argued the cause for appellant.

Opposing Side (Respondent / Appellee): Richard E. Fairbanks, Jr., argued the cause for appellee.

III. AMICI CURIAE

ACLU Side (Petitioner / Appellant)

Brief of amici curiae filed on behalf of the ACLU, et al., by Michael A. Bamberger, Stuart Altschuler, John A. Powell, Steven R. Shapiro, and Jonathan Lang.

Opposing Side (Respondent / Appellee)

Brief of amici curiae filed on behalf of the United States by Solicitor General Starr, Assistant Attorney General Mueller, Deputy Solicitor General Bryson, and Robert A. Long, Jr.

IV. THE SUPREME COURT'S DECISION

"[T]he First Amendment protects an individual's right to join groups and associate with others holding similar beliefs. [However,] in United States v. Abel, 469 U.S. 45 (1984), we held that the Government could impeach a defense witness by showing that both the defendant and the witness were members of the Aryan Brotherhood, and that members were sworn to lie on behalf of each other. We held the evidence admissible to show bias, even assuming that membership in the organization was among the associational freedoms protected by the First Amendment. . . . We therefore conclude that the Constitution does not erect a per se barrier to the admission of evidence concerning one's beliefs and associations at sentencing simply because those beliefs and associations are protected by the First Amendment.

[I]n this case, the receipt into evidence of the stipulation regarding his membership in the Aryan Brotherhood was constitutional error. Before the penalty hearing, the prosecution claimed that its expert witness would show that the Aryan Brotherhood is a white racist prison gang that is associated with drugs and violent escape attempts at prisons, and that advocates the murder of fellow inmates. If credible and otherwise admissible evidence to that effect had been presented, we would have a much different case. But, after reaching an agreement with Dawson, the prosecution limited its proof regarding the Aryan Brotherhood to the stipulation. The brief stipulation proved only that an Aryan Brotherhood prison gang originated in California in the 1960's, that it entertains white racist beliefs, and that a separate gang in the Delaware prison system calls itself the Aryan Brotherhood. We conclude that the narrowness of the stipulation left the Aryan Brotherhood evidence totally without relevance to Dawson's sentencing proceeding. . . .

Dawson's First Amendment rights were violated by the admission of the Aryan Brotherhood evidence in this case, because the evidence proved nothing more than Dawson's abstract beliefs. Delaware might have avoided this problem if it had presented evidence showing more than mere abstract beliefs on Dawson's part, but on the present record one is left with the feeling that the Aryan Brotherhood evidence was employed simply because the jury would find these beliefs morally reprehensible. Because Delaware failed to do more, we cannot find the evidence was properly admitted as relevant character evidence. . . .

The question whether the wrongful admission of the Aryan Brotherhood evidence at sentencing was harmless error is not before us at this time, and we therefore leave it open for consideration by the Supreme Court of Delaware on remand.

For the foregoing reasons, we vacate the judgment of the Supreme Court of Delaware and remand the case for further proceedings not inconsistent with this opinion."

V. JUSTICE VOTE

8 Pro ACLU Side vs. 1 Con Opposing Side

ACLU Side (Petitioner / Appellant)

1. Rehnquist, W. – Wrote majority opinion
2. White, B. – Joined majority opinion
3. Blackmun, H. – Wrote concurring opinion
4. Stevens, J. – Joined majority opinion
5. Souter, D. – Joined majority opinion
6. Kennedy, A. – Joined majority opinion
7. O'Connor, S. – Joined majority opinion
8. Scalia, A. – Joined majority opinion

Opposing Side (Respondent / Appellee)

1. Thomas, C. – Wrote dissenting opinion

VI. A WIN OR LOSS FOR THE ACLU?

The ACLU filed as amicus curiae urging reversal of the judgment of the Supreme Court of Delaware; the U.S. Supreme Court vacated and remanded in an 8-1 vote, giving the ACLU an apparent win.

736. Freeman v. Pitts

(Decided March 31, 1992; 503 U.S. 467)

I. ISSUE

A. Issues Discussed

Civil rights, race

B. Legal Question Presented

"Two principal questions are presented. The first is whether a district court may relinquish its supervision and control over those aspects of a school system in which there has been compliance with a desegregation decree if other aspects of the system remain in noncompliance. [T]he second question is whether the Court of Appeals erred in reversing the District Court's order providing for incremental withdrawal of supervision in all the circumstances of this case."

C. Supreme Court's Answer

"We hold that, in the course of supervising desegregation plans, federal courts have the authority to relinquish supervision and control of school districts in incremental stages, before full compliance has been achieved in every area of school operations. While retaining jurisdiction over the case, the court may determine that it will not order further remedies in areas where the school district is in compliance with the decree."

II. CASE SUMMARY

A. Background

"DeKalb County, Georgia, is a major suburban area of Atlanta. This case involves a court-ordered desegregation decree for the DeKalb County School System (DCSS). DCSS now serves some 73,000 students in kindergarten through high school and is the 32d largest elementary and secondary school system in the Nation.

DCSS has been subject to the supervision and jurisdiction of the United States District Court for the Northern District of Georgia since 1969, when it was ordered to dismantle its dual school system. In 1986, petitioners filed a motion for final dismissal. The District Court ruled that DCSS had not achieved unitary status in all respects but had done so in student attendance and three other categories. In its order the District Court relinquished remedial control as to those aspects of the system in which unitary status had been achieved, and retained supervisory authority only for those aspects of the school system in which the district was not in full compliance. The Court of Appeals for the Eleventh Circuit reversed, holding that a district court should retain full remedial authority over a school system until it achieves unitary status in six categories at the same time for several years."

The Supreme Court granted certiorari to review the case.

B. Counsel of Record

ACLU Side (Respondent / Appellee): Christopher A. Hansen of the American Civil Liberties Union Foundation argued the cause for appellee. With him on the briefs were Steven R.

Shapiro, Helen Hershkoff, and John A. Powell of the ACLU Foundation, Marcia Borowski, and Willie Abrams.

Opposing Side (Petitioner / Appellant): Rex E. Lee argued the cause for appellants. With her on the briefs were Carter G. Phillips, Mark D. Hopson, Gary M. Sams, Charles L. Weatherly, and J Stanley Hawkins.

Solicitor General Starr argued the cause for the United States as amicus curiae.

III. AMICI CURIAE

ACLU Side (Respondent / Appellee)

Brief of amici curiae filed on behalf of the American Civil Liberties Union of Georgia by Thomas A. Eaton and Gerald Weber.

Brief of amici curiae filed on behalf of the Lawyers' Committee for Civil Rights Under Law by Norman Redlich and Burke Marshal.

Brief of amici curiae filed on behalf of the NAACP, DeKalb County, Georgia, Branch et al. by William H. Allen and Elliott Schulder.

Opposing Side (Petitioner / Appellant)

Brief of amici curiae filed on behalf of the United States by Solicitor General Starr, Assistant Attorney General Dunne, Deputy Solicitor General Roberts, Deputy Assistant Attorney General Clegg, Ronald J Mann, David K. Flynn, and Lisa J Stark.

Brief of amici curiae filed on behalf of the Intervenors in Carlin v. Board of Education San Diego Unified School District by Elmer Enstrom, Jr.

Brief of amici curiae filed on behalf of the Southeastern Legal Foundation, Inc., by G. Stephen Parker.

Brief of amici curiae filed on behalf of plaintiff-intervenors by Charles S. Johnson III.

IV. THE SUPREME COURT'S DECISION

"Two principal questions are presented. The first is whether a district court may relinquish its supervision and control over those aspects of a school system in which there has been compliance with a desegregation decree if other aspects of the system remain in noncompliance. As we answer this question in the affirmative, the second question is whether the Court of Appeals erred in reversing the District Court's order providing for incremental withdrawal of supervision in all the circumstances of this case. . . .

The duty and responsibility of a school district once segregated by law is to take all steps necessary to eliminate the vestiges of the unconstitutional de jure system. . . .

We hold that, . . . federal courts have the authority to relinquish supervision and control of school districts in incremental stages, before full compliance has been achieved in every area of school operations. While retaining jurisdiction over the case, the court may determine that it will not order further remedies in areas where the school district is in compliance with the decree. . . .

We reach now the question whether the Court of Appeals erred in prohibiting the District Court from returning to DCSS partial control over some of its affairs. We decide that the Court of Appeals did err in holding that, as a matter of law, the District Court had no discretion to permit DCSS to regain control over student assignment, transportation, physical facilities, and extracurricular activities, while retaining court supervision over the areas of faculty and administrative assignments and the quality of education, where full compliance had not been demonstrated. . . .

We next consider whether retention of judicial control over student attendance is necessary or practicable to achieve compliance in other facets of the school system. . . .

[T]he District Court in this case stated that throughout the period of judicial supervision it has been impressed by the successes DCSS has achieved and its dedication to providing a quality education for all students . . . . With respect to those areas where compliance had not been achieved, the District Court did not find that DCSS had acted in bad faith or engaged in further acts of discrimination since the desegregation plan went into effect. This, though, may not be the equivalent of a finding that the school district has an affirmative commitment to comply in good faith with the entirety of a desegregation plan, and further proceedings are appropriate for this purpose as well.

The judgment is reversed, and the case is remanded to the Court of Appeals. It should determine what issues are open for its further consideration in light of the previous briefs and arguments of the parties and in light of the principles set forth in this opinion. Thereupon it should order further proceedings as necessary or order an appropriate remand to the District Court."

V. JUSTICE VOTE

0 Pro ACLU Side vs. 8 Con Opposing Side

Opposing Side (Petitioner / Appellant)

1. Kennedy, A. – Wrote majority opinion
2. Souter, D. – Wrote concurring opinion
3. Rehnquist, W. – Joined majority opinion
4. White, B. – Joined majority opinion
5. Scalia, A. – Wrote concurring opinion
6. Blackmun, H. – Wrote concurring opinion
7. O'Connor, S. – Joined Blackmun's concurrence
8. Stevens, J. – Joined Blackmun's concurrence

Thomas, C. – Took no part in the decision.

VI. A WIN OR LOSS FOR THE ACLU?

The ACLU served as counsel for appellee and filed as amicus curiae urging affirmance; the Supreme Court reversed the Court of Appeals' decision by an 8-0 vote, giving the ACLU an apparent loss.

737. Jacobson v. United States

(Decided April 6, 1992; 503 U.S. 540)

I. ISSUE

A. Issues Discussed

Criminal procedure, entrapment

B. Legal Question Presented

Whether "the Government . . . carried its burden of proving beyond reasonable doubt that petitioner was predisposed to break the law and hence was not entrapped."

C. Supreme Court's Answer

The Government did not prove that petitioner was predisposed to break the law and thus not entrapped.

II. CASE SUMMARY

A. Background

"On September 24, 1987, petitioner Keith Jacobson was indicted for violating a provision of the Child Protection Act of 1984 (Act), which criminalizes the knowing receipt through the mails of a 'visual depiction [that] involves the use of a minor engaging in sexually explicit conduct . . . .' Petitioner defended on the ground that the Government entrapped him into committing the crime through a series of communications from undercover agents that spanned the 26 months preceding his arrest. Petitioner was found guilty after a jury trial. The Court of Appeals affirmed his conviction, holding that the Government had carried its burden of proving beyond reasonable doubt that petitioner was predisposed to break the law and hence was not entrapped."

The Supreme Court granted certiorari to review the case and reversed.

B. Counsel of Record / ACLU Attorney

ACLU Side (Petitioner / Appellant): George H. Moyer, Jr., argued the cause for appellant.

Opposing Side (Respondent / Appellee): Paul J. Larkin, Jr., argued the cause for the United States.

III. AMICI CURIAE

ACLU Side (Petitioner / Appellant)

Brief of amici curiae filed on behalf of the ACLU, et al., by Bennett L. Gershman, Steven R. Shapiro, John A. Powell, and William B. Rubenstein.

Opposing Side (Respondent / Appellee)

Brief of amici curiae filed on behalf of Americans for Effective Law Enforcement, Inc., et al., by Gregory U. Evans, Daniel B. Hales, George D. Webster, Jack E. Yelverton, Fred E. Inbau, Wayne W. Schmidt, Bernard J. Farber, and James P. Manak.

Brief of amici curiae filed on behalf of the National Center for Missing and Exploited Children, et al., by H. Robert Showers and Judith Drazen Schretter.

Brief of amici curiae filed on behalf of Honorable Thomas J. Bliley, Jr., et al., by James P. Mueller, Michael J. Lockerby, and David E. Anderson.

IV. THE SUPREME COURT'S DECISION

"There can be no dispute about the evils of child pornography or the difficulties that laws and law enforcement have encountered in eliminating it. Likewise, there can be no dispute that the Government may use undercover agents to enforce the law. 'It is well settled that the fact that officers or employees of the Government merely afford opportunities or facilities for the commission of the offense does not defeat the prosecution.' . . . In their zeal to enforce the law, however, Government agents may not originate a criminal design, implant in an innocent person's mind the disposition to commit a criminal act, and then induce commission of the crime so that the Government may prosecute. . . .

Had the agents in this case simply offered petitioner the opportunity to order child pornography through the mails, and petitioner—who must be presumed to know the law—had promptly availed himself of this criminal opportunity, it is unlikely that his entrapment defense would have warranted a jury instruction.

But that is not what happened here. By the time petitioner finally placed his order, he had already been the target of 26 months of repeated mailings and communications from Government agents and fictitious organizations.

[T]he strong arguable inference is that, by waving the banner of individual rights and disparaging the legitimacy and constitutionality of efforts to restrict the availability of sexually explicit materials, the Government . . . exerted substantial pressure on petitioner to obtain and read such material as part of a fight against censorship and the infringement of individual rights. . . .

When the Government's quest for convictions leads to the apprehension of an otherwise law-abiding citizen who, if left to his own devices, likely would have never run afoul of the law, the courts should intervene.

Because we conclude that this is such a case, and that the prosecution failed, as a matter of law, to adduce evidence to support the jury verdict that petitioner was predisposed, independent of the Government's acts and beyond a reasonable doubt, to violate the law by receiving child pornography through the mails, we reverse the Court of Appeals' judgment affirming the conviction of Keith Jacobson."

V. JUSTICE VOTE

5 Pro ACLU Side vs. 4 Con Opposing Side

ACLU Side (Petitioner / Appellant)

1. White, B. – Wrote majority opinion
2. Blackmun, H. – Joined majority opinion
3. Stevens, J. – Joined majority opinion
4. Souter, D. – Joined majority opinion
5. Thomas, C. – Joined majority opinion

Opposing Side (Respondent / Appellee)

1. O'Connor, S. – Wrote dissenting opinion
2. Rehnquist, W. – Joined O'Connor's dissent
3. Kennedy, A. – Joined O'Connor's dissent
4. Scalia, A. – Joined O'Connor's dissent

VI. A WIN OR LOSS FOR THE ACLU?

The ACLU filed as amicus curiae urging reversal of the judgment of the Court of Appeals; the Supreme Court reversed in a 5-4 vote, giving the ACLU an apparent win.

738. Denton v. Hernandez

(Decided May 4, 1992; 504 U.S. 25)

I. ISSUE

A. Issues Discussed

Criminal justice, prisons, Fourteenth Amendment, judicial review

B. Legal Question Presented

"[W]hen an in forma pauperis claim may be dismissed as factually frivolous under § 1915(d)."

C. Supreme Court's Answer

"Because the frivolousness determination is a discretionary one, we . . . hold that a § 1915(d) dismissal is properly reviewed for an abuse of that discretion, and that it was error for the Court of Appeals to review the dismissal of Hernandez's claims de novo."

II. CASE SUMMARY

A. Background

"The federal in forma pauperis statute, codified at 28 U.S.C. § 1915, allows an indigent litigant to commence a civil or criminal action in federal court without paying the administrative costs of proceeding with the lawsuit. The statute protects against abuses of this privilege by allowing a district court to dismiss the case 'if the allegation of poverty is untrue, or if satisfied that the action is frivolous or malicious.' . . .

Petitioners are 15 officials at various institutions in the California penal system. Between 1983 and 1985, respondent Mike Hernandez, a state prisoner proceeding pro se, named petitioners as defendants in five civil rights suits filed in forma pauperis. . . .

The District Court determined that the five cases were related and referred them to a Magistrate, who recommended that the complaints be dismissed as frivolous. . . .

Hernandez appealed the dismissal of three of the five cases. Reviewing the dismissal de novo, the Court of Appeals for the Ninth Circuit reversed and remanded.

[The Supreme Court] granted petitioners' first petition for a writ of certiorari, vacated the judgment, and remanded the case to the Court of Appeals for consideration of our intervening decision in Neitzke v. Williams, 490 U.S. 319 (1989). On remand, the Court of Appeals reaffirmed its earlier decision. Judge Schroeder modified her original opinion to state that judicial notice was just 'one useful standard' for determining factual frivolousness under § 1915(d), but adhered to her position that the case could not be dismissed because no judicially noticeable fact could contradict Hernandez's claims of rape."

The Supreme Court granted a second writ of certiorari to review the case, vacated, and remanded.

B. Counsel of Record / ACLU Attorney

ACLU Side (Respondent / Appellee): Richard W. Nichols, by appointment of the Court, argued the cause for appellee.

Opposing Side (Petitioner / Appellant): James Ching, Supervising Deputy Attorney General of California, argued the cause for appellant.

III. AMICI CURIAE

ACLU Side (Respondent / Appellee)

Brief of amici curiae filed on behalf of the ACLU, et al., by Elizabeth Alexander, David C. Fathi, John A. Powell, Steven R. Shapiro, and Matthew Coles.

Opposing Side (Petitioner / Appellant)

Brief of amici curiae filed on behalf of the United States by Solicitor General Starr, Assistant Attorney General Mueller, and Deputy Solicitor General Roberts.

IV. THE SUPREME COURT'S DECISION

"In enacting the federal in forma pauperis statute, Congress 'intended to guarantee that no citizen shall be denied an opportunity to commence, prosecute, or defend an action, civil or criminal, in any court of the United States, solely because . . . poverty makes it impossible . . . to pay or secure the costs' of litigation. At the same time that it sought to lower judicial access barriers to the indigent, however, Congress recognized that 'a litigant whose filing fees and court costs are assumed by the public, unlike a paying litigant, lacks an economic incentive to refrain from filing frivolous, malicious, or repetitive lawsuits.' In response to this concern, Congress included subsection (d) as part of the statute, which allows the courts to dismiss an in forma pauperis complaint 'if satisfied that the action is frivolous or malicious.'

'[A] complaint, containing . . . both factual allegations and legal conclusions, is frivolous where it lacks an arguable basis either in law or in fact.' [T]he in forma pauperis statute . . . 'accords judges not only the authority to dismiss a claim based on an indisputably meritless legal theory, but also the unusual power to pierce the veil of the complaint's factual allegations and dismiss those claims whose factual contentions are clearly baseless.' . . .

We . . . reject the notion that a court must accept as 'having an arguable basis in fact' all allegations that cannot be rebutted by judicially noticeable facts. [A] court may dismiss a claim as factually frivolous only if the facts alleged are 'clearly baseless,' a category encompassing allegations that are 'fanciful,' 'fantastic,' and 'delusional.' As those words suggest, a finding of factual frivolousness is appropriate when the facts alleged rise to the level of the irrational or the wholly incredible, whether or not there are judicially noticeable facts available to contradict them. An in forma pauperis complaint may not be dismissed, however, simply because the court finds the plaintiff's allegations unlikely.

[W]e are confident that the district courts, who are 'all too familiar' with factually frivolous claims are in the best position to determine which cases fall into this category. . . . Because the frivolousness determination is a discretionary one, we . . . hold that a § 1915(d) dismissal is properly reviewed for an abuse of that discretion, and that it was error for the Court of Appeals to review the dismissal of Hernandez's claims de novo. . . .

Accordingly, we vacate the judgment below and remand the case for proceedings consistent with this opinion,"

V. JUSTICE VOTE

2 Pro ACLU Side vs. 7 Con Opposing Side

ACLU Side (Respondent / Appellee)

1. Stevens, J. – Wrote dissenting opinion
2. Blackmun, J. – Joined Stevens' dissent

Opposing Side (Petitioner / Appellant)

1. O'Connor, S. – Wrote majority opinion
2. Rehnquist, W. – Joined majority opinion
3. White, B. – Joined majority opinion
4. Scalia, A. – Joined majority opinion
5. Kennedy, A. – Joined majority opinion
6. Souter, D. – Joined majority opinion
7. Thomas, C. – Joined majority opinion

VI. A WIN OR LOSS FOR THE ACLU?

The ACLU filed as amicus curiae urging affirmance of the judgment of the Court of Appeals; the Supreme Court vacated and remanded in a 7-2 vote, giving the ACLU an apparent loss.

739. United States v. Burke

(Decided May 26, 1992; 504 U.S. 229)

I. ISSUE

A. Issues Discussed

Civil rights, gender, Title VII of the Civil Rights Act of 1964, federal taxation

B. Legal Question Presented

"[W]hether a payment received in settlement of a backpay claim under Title VII of the Civil Rights Act of 1964 . . . is excludable from the recipient's gross income under § 104(a)(2) of the federal Internal Revenue Code as 'damages received . . . on account of personal injuries.'"

C. Supreme Court's Answer

The payment is not excludable from gross income under the Internal Revenue Code.

II. CASE SUMMARY

A. Background

"In 1984, Judy A. Hutcheson, an employee of the Tennessee Valley Authority (TVA), filed a Title VII action in the United States District Court for the Eastern District of Tennessee alleging that TVA had discriminated unlawfully in the payment of salaries on the basis of sex. . . .

After the District Court denied cross-motions for summary judgment, the parties reached a settlement. TVA agreed to pay $4,200 to Hutcheson and a total of $5 million for the other affected employees, to be distributed under a formula based on length of service and rates of pay. Although TVA did not withhold taxes on the $4,200 for Hutcheson, it did withhold, pursuant to the agreement, federal income taxes on the amounts allocated to the other affected employees, including the three respondents here.

Respondents filed claims for refund of the taxes withheld from the settlement payments. The Internal Revenue Service (IRS) disallowed those claims. Respondents then brought a refund action in the United States District Court for the Eastern District of Tennessee, claiming that the settlement payments should be excluded from their respective gross incomes under § 104(a)(2) of the Internal Revenue Code as 'damages received (whether by suit or agreement and whether as lump sums or as periodic payments) on account of personal injuries or sickness.' The District Court ruled that, because respondents sought and obtained only back wages due them as a result of TVA's discriminatory underpayments rather than compensatory or other damages, the settlement proceeds could not be excluded from gross income as 'damages received . . . on account of personal injuries.'

The United States Court of Appeals for the Sixth Circuit, by a divided vote, reversed. The Court of Appeals concluded that exclusion under § 104(a)(2) turns on whether the injury and the claim are 'personal and tort-like in nature.' 'If the answer is in the affirmative,' the court held, 'then that is the beginning and end of the inquiry.' The court concluded that TVA's unlawful sex discrimination constituted a personal, tort-like injury to respondents, and rejected the Government's attempt to distinguish Title VII, which authorizes no compensatory or punitive damages, from other statutes thought to redress personal injuries. Thus, the court held, the award of backpay pursuant to Title VII was excludable from gross income under § 104(a)(2)."

The Supreme Court granted certiorari to review the case and reversed.

B. Counsel of Record / ACLU Attorney

ACLU Side (Respondent / Appellee): Joseph E. Finley argued the cause for appellee.

Opposing Side (Petitioner / Appellant): Jeffrey P. Minear argued the cause for the United States.

III. AMICI CURIAE

ACLU Side (Respondent / Appellee)

Brief of amici curiae filed on behalf of the ACLU, et al., by C. Cabell Chinnis, Jr., Alison C. Wetherfield, Martha F. Davis, Steven R. Shapiro, Isabelle Katz Pinzler, Julius L. Chambers, and Charles Stephen Ralston.

Brief of amici curiae filed on behalf of the American Association of Retired Persons by Steven S. Zaleznick, Cathy Ventrell-Monsees, Raymond C. Fay, and Thomas F. Joyce.

Brief of amici curiae filed on behalf of the Equal Employment Advisory Council by Robert E. Williams and Douglas S. McDowell.

Brief of amici curiae filed on behalf of Equal Rights Advocates, Inc., by Stephen V. Bomse, Nancy L. Davis, and Maria Blanco.

Brief of amici curiae filed on behalf of Women Employed, et al., by Michael B. Erp, Mary K. O'Melveny, and Stephen G. Seliger.

Brief of amici curiae filed on behalf of the National Employment Lawyers Association by Robert B. Fitzpatrick.

Brief of amici curiae filed on behalf of the National Women's Law Center by Walter J. Rockler.

Opposing Side (Petitioner / Appellant)

No briefs of amici curiae were filed in support of appellant.

IV. THE SUPREME COURT'S DECISION

"In order to come within the § 104(a)(2) income exclusion, respondents . . . must show that Title VII, the legal basis for their recovery of backpay, redresses a tort-like personal injury . . . .

It is beyond question that discrimination in employment on the basis of sex, race, or any of the other classifications protected by Title VII is, as respondents argue and this Court consistently has held, an invidious practice that causes grave harm to its victims. The fact that employment discrimination causes harm to individuals does not automatically imply, however, that there exists a tort-like 'personal injury' for purposes of federal income tax law.

Indeed, in contrast to the tort remedies for physical and nonphysical injuries discussed above, Title VII does not allow awards for compensatory or punitive damages; instead, it limits available remedies to backpay, injunctions, and other equitable relief. . . .

Notwithstanding a common-law tradition of broad tort damages and the existence of other federal antidiscrimination statutes offering similarly broad remedies, Congress declined to recompense Title VII plaintiffs for anything beyond the wages properly due them—wages that, if paid in the ordinary course, would have been fully taxable. Thus, we cannot say that a statute such as Title VII, whose sole remedial focus is the award of back wages, redresses a tort-like personal injury within the meaning of § 104(a)(2) and the applicable regulations.

Accordingly, we hold that the backpay awards received by respondents in settlement of their Title VII claims are not excludable from gross income as 'damages received . . . on account of personal injuries' under § 104(a)(2). The judgment of the Court of Appeals is reversed."

V. JUSTICE VOTE

2 Pro ACLU Side vs. 7 Con Opposing Side

ACLU Side (Respondent / Appellee)

1. O'Connor, S. – Wrote dissenting opinion
2. Thomas, C. – Joined O'Connor's dissent

Opposing Side (Petitioner / Appellant)

1. Blackmun, H. – Wrote majority opinion
2. Rehnquist, W. – Joined majority opinion
3. White, B. – Joined majority opinion
4. Stevens, J. – Joined majority opinion
5. Kennedy, A. – Joined majority opinion
6. Souter, D. – Wrote concurring opinion
7. Scalia, A. – Wrote concurring opinion

VI. A WIN OR LOSS FOR THE ACLU?

The ACLU filed as amicus curiae urging affirmance of the judgment of the Court of Appeals; the Supreme Court reversed in a 7-2 vote, giving the ACLU an apparent loss.

740. Burdick v. Takushi

(Decided June 8, 1992; 504 U.S. 428)

I. ISSUE

A. Issues Discussed

Voting rights, 1st Amendment, press, speech, association

B. Legal Question Presented

"[W]hether Hawaii's prohibition on write-in voting unreasonably infringes upon its citizens' rights under the First and Fourteenth Amendments."

C. Supreme Court's Answer

"We think that Hawaii's prohibition on write-in voting, considered as part of an electoral scheme that provides constitutionally sufficient ballot access, does not impose an unconstitutional burden upon the First and Fourteenth Amendment rights of the State's voters."

II. CASE SUMMARY

A. Background

"Petitioner is a registered voter in the city and county of Honolulu. In 1986, only one candidate filed nominating papers to run for the seat representing petitioner's district in the Hawaii House of Representatives. Petitioner wrote to state officials inquiring about Hawaii's write-in voting policy and received a copy of an opinion letter issued by the Hawaii Attorney General's Office stating that the State's election law made no provision for write-in voting.

Petitioner then filed this lawsuit, claiming that he wished to vote in the primary and general elections for a person who had not filed nominating papers and that he wished to vote in future elections for other persons whose names might not appear on the ballot. The United States District Court for the District of Hawaii concluded that the ban on write-in voting violated petitioner's First Amendment right of expression and association and entered a preliminary injunction ordering respondents to provide for the casting and tallying of write-in votes in the November 1986 general election. The District Court denied a stay pending appeal.

The Court of Appeals entered the stay, and vacated the judgment of the District Court . . . .

The United States District Court then granted petitioner's renewed motion for summary judgment and injunctive relief, but entered a stay pending appeal.

The Court of Appeals again reversed . . . ."

The Supreme Court granted certiorari to review the case.

B. Counsel of Record

ACLU Side (Petitioner / Appellant): Arthur N. Eisenberg of the New York Civil Liberties Union Foundation argued the cause for appellant. With him on the briefs were Steven R. Shapiro and John A. Powell of the American Civil Liberties Union Foundation, Carl Varady of the ACLU of Hawaii Foundation, Mary Blaine Johnston, Paul W. Kahn, Lawrence G. Sager, Burt Neuborne, and Alan B. Burdick.

Opposing Side (Respondent / Appellee): Steven S. Michaels, Deputy Attorney General of Hawaii, argued the cause for appellees. With him on the brief were Warren Price III, Attorney General and Girard D. Lau, Deputy Attorney General.

III. AMICI CURIAE

ACLU Side (Petitioner / Appellant)

Brief of amici curiae filed on behalf of Common Cause/ Hawaii by Stanley E. Levin.

Brief of amici curiae filed on behalf of the Hawaii Libertarian Party by Arlo Hale Smith.

Brief of amici curiae filed on behalf of the Socialist Workers Party by Edward Copeland and Eric M. Lieberman.

Brief of amici curiae filed on behalf of Andre Marrou et al. by James C. Linger.

Opposing Side (Respondent / Appellee)

Brief of amici curiae filed on behalf of the State of Arizona et al. by Frankie Sue Del Papa, Attorney General of Nevada, and Kateri Cavin, Deputy Attorney General, and by the Attorneys General for their respective jurisdictions as follows: Grant Woods of Arizona, Robert A Butterworth of Florida, Richard P. Ieyoub of Louisiana, Lacy H. Thornburg of North Carolina, Susan Brimer Loving of Oklahoma, Mark Barnett of South Dakota, Paul Van Dam of Utah, Joseph B. Meyer of Wyoming, and Robert Naraja of the Commonwealth of the Northern Mariana Islands.

IV. THE SUPREME COURT'S DECISION

"Petitioner proceeds from the erroneous assumption that a law that imposes any burden upon the right to vote must be subject to strict scrutiny. Our cases do not so hold. . . .

There is no doubt that the Hawaii election laws, like all election regulations, have an impact on the right to vote, but it can hardly be said that the laws at issue here unconstitutionally limit access to the ballot by party or independent candidates or unreasonably interfere with the right of voters to associate and have candidates of their choice placed on the ballot. . . .

Because he has characterized this as a voting rights rather than ballot access case, petitioner submits that the write-in prohibition deprives him of the opportunity to cast a meaningful ballot, conditions his electoral participation upon the waiver of his First Amendment right to remain free from espousing positions that he does not support, and discriminates against him based on the content of the message he seeks to convey through his vote. . . .

Petitioner's argument is based on two flawed premises. . . .

The appropriate standard for evaluating a claim that a state law burdens the right to vote is set forth in Anderson. Applying that standard, we conclude that, in light of the adequate ballot access afforded under Hawaii's election code, the State's ban on write-in voting imposes only a limited burden on voters' rights to make free choices and to associate politically through the vote. . . .

We turn next to the interests asserted by Hawaii to justify the burden imposed by its prohibition of write-in voting. Because we have already concluded that the burden is slight, the State need not establish a compelling interest to tip the constitutional scales in its direction. Here, the State's interests outweigh petitioner's limited interest in waiting until the eleventh hour to choose his preferred candidate. . . .

Indeed, the foregoing leads us to conclude that when a State's ballot access laws pass constitutional muster as imposing only reasonable burdens on First and Fourteenth Amendment rights—as do Hawaii's election laws—a prohibition on write-in voting will be presumptively valid, since any burden on the right to vote for the candidate of one's choice will be light and normally will be counterbalanced by the very state interests supporting the ballot access scheme. . . .

We think that Hawaii's prohibition on write-in voting, considered as part of an electoral scheme that provides constitutionally sufficient ballot access, does not impose an unconstitutional burden upon the First and Fourteenth Amendment rights of the State's voters. Accordingly, the judgment of the Court of Appeals is affirmed."

V. JUSTICE VOTE

3 Pro ACLU Side vs. 6 Con Opposing Side

ACLU Side (Petitioner / Appellant)

1. Kennedy, A. – Wrote dissenting opinion
2. Blackmun, H. – Joined Kennedy's dissent
3. Stevens, J. – Joined Kennedy's dissent

Opposing Side (Respondent / Appellee)

1. White, B. – Wrote majority opinion
2. Rehnquist, W. – Joined majority opinion
3. O'Connor, S. – Joined majority opinion
4. Scalia, A. – Joined majority opinion
5. Souter, D. – Joined majority opinion
6. Thomas, C. – Joined majority opinion

VI. A WIN OR LOSS FOR THE ACLU?

The ACLU served a counsel for appellant urging reversal of the judgment of the Court of Appeals; the Supreme Court affirmed in a 6-3 vote, giving the ACLU an apparent loss.

741. Ankenbrandt v. Richards

(Decided June 15, 1992; 504 U.S. 689)

I. ISSUE

A. Issues Discussed

Civil rights, scope of judicial power, juvenile rights, jurisdiction

B. Legal Question Presented

"[W]hether the federal courts have jurisdiction or should abstain in a case involving alleged torts committed by the former husband of petitioner and his female companion against petitioner's children, when the sole basis for federal jurisdiction is the diversity-of-citizenship provision of 28 U.S.C. § 1332."

C. Supreme Court's Answer

The federal courts have jurisdiction in this case.

II. CASE SUMMARY

A. Background

"Petitioner Carol Ankenbrandt, a citizen of Missouri, brought this lawsuit on September 26, 1989, on behalf of her daughters L.R. and S.R. against respondents Jon A. Richards and Debra Kesler, citizens of Louisiana, in the United States District Court for the Eastern District of Louisiana. Alleging federal jurisdiction based on the diversity-of-citizenship provision of § 1332, Ankenbrandt's complaint sought monetary damages for alleged sexual and physical abuse of the children committed by Richards and Kesler. Richards is the divorced father of the children and Kesler his female companion. On December 10, 1990, the District Court granted respondents' motion to dismiss this lawsuit. Citing In re Burrus, 136 U.S. 586 (1890), for the proposition that '[t]he whole subject of the domestic relations of husband and wife, parent and child, belongs to the laws of the States and not to the laws of the United States,' the court concluded that this case fell within what has become known as the 'domestic relations' exception to diversity jurisdiction, and that it lacked jurisdiction over the case. The court also invoked the abstention principles announced in Younger v. Harris, 401 U.S. 37 (1971), to justify its decision to dismiss the complaint without prejudice. The Court of Appeals affirmed in an unpublished opinion."

The Supreme Court granted certiorari to review the case and reversed.

B. Counsel of Record / ACLU Attorney

ACLU Side (Petitioner / Appellant): Richard Lynn Ducote argued the cause for appellant.

Opposing Side (Respondent / Appellee): Paul S. Weidenfeld argued the cause for appellee.

III. AMICI CURIAE

ACLU Side (Petitioner / Appellant)

Brief of amici curiae filed on behalf of the ACLU by Marcia Robinson Lowry, Steven R. Shapiro, and John A. Powell.

Opposing Side (Respondent / Appellee)

No briefs of amici curiae were filed in support of appellee.

IV. THE SUPREME COURT'S DECISION

"The domestic relations exception upon which the courts below relied to decline jurisdiction has been invoked often by the lower federal courts. The seeming authority for doing so originally stemmed from the announcement [in a prior case] that the federal courts have no jurisdiction over suits for divorce or the allowance of alimony. . . . The statements disclaiming jurisdiction over divorce and alimony decree suits, though technically dicta, formed the basis for excluding 'domestic relations' cases from the jurisdiction of the lower federal courts, a jurisdictional limitation those courts have recognized ever since. . . .

An examination of Article III . . . and our cases . . . makes clear that the Constitution does not exclude domestic relations cases from the jurisdiction otherwise granted by statute to the federal courts. . . .

We thus are content to rest our conclusion that a domestic relations exception exists as a matter of statutory construction not on the accuracy of the historical justifications on which it was seemingly based, but rather on Congress' apparent acceptance of this construction of the diversity jurisdiction provisions in the years prior to 1948, when the statute limited jurisdiction to 'suits of a civil nature at common law or in equity.' . . .

When Congress amended the diversity statute in 1948 to replace the law/equity distinction with the phrase 'all civil actions,' we presume Congress did so with full cognizance of the Court's nearly century-long interpretation of the prior statutes, which had construed the statutory diversity jurisdiction to contain an exception for certain domestic relations matters. With respect to the 1948 amendment, the Court has previously stated that 'no changes of law or policy are to be presumed from changes of language in the revision unless an intent to make such changes is clearly expressed.' . . .

Subsequently, this Court expanded the domestic relations exception to include decrees in child custody cases. [The] statement that '[t]he whole subject of the domestic relations of husband and wife, parent and child, belongs to the laws of the States and not to the laws of the United States,' has been interpreted by the federal courts to apply with equal vigor in suits brought pursuant to diversity jurisdiction. . . . We conclude, therefore, that the domestic relations exception, as articulated by this Court . . . divests the federal courts of power to issue divorce, alimony, and child custody decrees. Given the long passage of time without any expression of congressional dissatisfaction, we have no trouble today reaffirming the validity of the exception as it pertains to divorce and alimony decrees and child custody orders. . . .

We thus conclude that the Court of Appeals erred by affirming the District Court's rulings to decline jurisdiction based on the domestic relations exception to diversity jurisdiction . . . . The exception has no place in a suit such as this one, in which a former spouse sues another on behalf of children alleged to have been abused. Because the allegations in this complaint do not request the District Court to issue a divorce, alimony, or child custody decree, we hold that the suit is appropriate for the exercise of § 1332 jurisdiction given the existence of diverse citizenship between petitioner and respondents and the pleading of the relevant amount in controversy. Accordingly, we reverse the decision of the Court of Appeals and remand the case for further proceedings consistent with this opinion."

V. JUSTICE VOTE

9 Pro ACLU Side vs. 0 Con Opposing Side

ACLU Side (Petitioner / Appellant)

1. White, B. – Wrote majority opinion
2. Blackmun, H. – Wrote concurring opinion
3. Stevens, J. – Wrote concurring opinion
4. Souter, D. – Joined majority opinion
5. Kennedy, A. – Joined majority opinion
6. O'Connor, S. – Joined majority opinion
7. Scalia, A. – Joined majority opinion
8. Rehnquist, W. – Joined majority opinion
9. Thomas, C. – Joined Stevens' concurrence

VI. A WIN OR LOSS FOR THE ACLU?

The ACLU filed as amicus curiae urging reversal of the judgment of the Court of Appeals; the Supreme Court reversed in a 9-0 vote, giving the ACLU an apparent win.

742. Morgan v. Illinois

(Decided June 15, 1992; 504 U.S. 719)

I. ISSUE

A. Issues Discussed

Criminal justice, death penalty, jury selection, Fourteenth Amendment, Sixth Amendment

B. Legal Question Presented

"[W]hether, during voir dire for a capital offense, a state trial court may, consistent with the Due Process Clause of the Fourteenth Amendment, refuse inquiry into whether a potential juror would automatically impose the death penalty upon conviction of the defendant."

C. Supreme Court's Answer

The state trial court may not refuse inquiry into whether a potential juror would automatically impose the death penalty upon conviction of defendant.

II. CASE SUMMARY

A. Background

"Petitioner Derrick Morgan was convicted in Cook County, Illinois, of first-degree murder and sentenced to death. . . .

Three separate venires were required to be called before the jury was finally chosen. In accordance with Illinois law, the trial court, rather than the attorneys, conducted voir dire. The State, having elected to pursue capital punishment, requested inquiry permitted by Witherspoon v. Illinois, 391 U.S. 510 (1968), to determine whether any potential juror would in all instances refuse to impose the death penalty upon conviction of the offense. Accordingly, the trial court, over opposition from the defense, questioned each venire whether any member had moral or religious principles so strong that he or she could not impose the death penalty 'regardless of the facts.' Seventeen potential jurors were excused when they expressed substantial doubts about their ability to follow Illinois law in deciding whether to impose a sentence of death. All of the jurors eventually empaneled were also questioned individually under Witherspoon, each receiving and responding in the negative to this question or a slight variation: 'Would you automatically vote against the death penalty no matter what the facts of the case were?'

After seven members of the first venire had been questioned, including three who eventually became jurors, petitioner's counsel requested the trial court to ask all prospective jurors the following question: 'If you found Derrick Morgan guilty, would you automatically vote to impose the death penalty no matter what the facts are?' The trial court refused this request, stating that it had 'asked the question in a different vein substantially in that nature.' . . .

On appeal, the Illinois Supreme Court affirmed petitioner's conviction and death sentence, rejecting petitioner's claim that, pursuant to Ross v. Oklahoma, 487 U.S. 81 (1988), voir dire must include the 'life qualifying' or 'reverse-Witherspoon' question upon request."

The U.S. Supreme Court granted certiorari to review the case and reversed.

B. Counsel of Record / ACLU Attorney

ACLU Side (Petitioner / Appellant): Allen H. Andrews III argued the cause for appellant.

Opposing Side (Respondent / Appellee): Kenneth L. Gillis argued the cause for appellee.

III. AMICI CURIAE

ACLU Side (Petitioner / Appellant)

Brief of amici curiae filed on behalf of the ACLU, et al., by Robert L. Graham, Laura A. Kaster, Harvey Grossman, John A. Powell, Steven Shapiro, and Diann Rust-Tierney.

Brief of amici curiae filed on behalf of the National Association of Criminal Defense Lawyers by Andrea D. Lyon.

Opposing Side (Respondent / Appellee)

No briefs of amici curiae were filed in support of appellee.

IV. THE SUPREME COURT'S DECISION

"[D]ue process alone has long demanded that, if a jury is to be provided the defendant, regardless of whether the Sixth Amendment requires it, the jury must stand impartial and indifferent to the extent commanded by the Sixth Amendment. . . .

A juror who will automatically vote for the death penalty in every case will fail in good faith to consider the evidence of aggravating and mitigating circumstances as the instructions require him to do. . . . Therefore, based on the requirement of impartiality embodied in the Due Process Clause of the Fourteenth Amendment, a capital defendant may challenge for cause any prospective juror who maintains such views. If even one such juror is empanelled and the death sentence is imposed, the State is disentitled to execute the sentence. . . .

We deal here with petitioner's ability to exercise intelligently his complementary challenge for cause against those biased persons on the venire who as jurors would unwaveringly impose death after a finding of guilt. Were voir dire not available to lay bare the foundation of petitioner's challenge for cause against those prospective jurors who would always impose death following conviction, his right not to be tried by such jurors would be rendered as nugatory and meaningless as the State's right, in the absence of questioning, to strike those who would never do so. . . .

Petitioner was entitled, upon his request, to inquiry discerning those jurors who, even prior to the State's case in chief, had predetermined the terminating issue of his trial, that being whether to impose the death penalty. . . .

Because the 'inadequacy of voir dire' leads us to doubt that petitioner was sentenced to death by a jury empanelled in compliance with the Fourteenth Amendment, his sentence cannot stand. Accordingly, the judgment of the Illinois Supreme Court affirming petitioner's death sentence is reversed, and the case is remanded for further proceedings not inconsistent with this opinion."

V. JUSTICE VOTE

6 Pro ACLU Side vs. 3 Con Opposing Side

ACLU Side (Petitioner / Appellant)

1. White, B. – Wrote majority opinion
2. Blackmun, H. – Joined majority opinion
3. Stevens, J. – Joined majority opinion
4. O'Connor, S. – Joined majority opinion
5. Kennedy, A. – Joined majority opinion
6. Souter, D. – Joined majority opinion

Opposing Side (Respondent / Appellee)

1. Scalia, A. – Wrote dissenting opinion
2. Rehnquist, W. – Joined Scalia's dissent
3. Thomas, C. – Joined Scalia's dissent

VI. A WIN OR LOSS FOR THE ACLU?

The ACLU filed a brief as amicus curiae urging reversal of the judgment of the Illinois Supreme Court; the U.S. Supreme Court reversed in a 6-3 vote, giving the ACLU an apparent win.

743. Forsyth County v. Nationalist Movement

(Decided June 19, 1992; 505 U.S. 123)

I. ISSUE

A. Issues Discussed

First Amendment, freedoms of press, speech, and association, Fourteenth Amendment

B. Legal Question Presented

"[W]hether the free speech guarantees of the First and Fourteenth Amendments are violated by an assembly and parade ordinance that permits a government administrator to vary the fee for assembling or parading to reflect the estimated cost of maintaining public order."

C. Supreme Court's Answer

The ordinance violates the First and Fourteenth Amendments.

II. CASE SUMMARY

A. Background

"'As a direct result' of [two race relations demonstrations], the Forsyth County Board of Commissioners enacted Ordinance 34 on January 27, 1987. The ordinance recites that it is 'to provide for the issuance of permits for parades, assemblies, demonstrations, road closings, and other uses of public property and roads by private organizations and groups of private persons for private purposes.' The board of commissioners justified the ordinance by explaining that 'the cost of necessary and reasonable protection of persons participating in or observing said parades, assemblies, demonstrations, road closings and other related activities exceeds the usual and normal cost of law enforcement for which those participating should be held accountable and responsible.' The ordinance required the permit applicant to defray these costs by paying a fee, the amount of which was to be fixed 'from time to time' by the Board.

Ordinance 34 was amended on June 8, 1987, to provide that every permit applicant "shall pay in advance for such permit, for the use of the County, a sum not more than $1,000.00 for each day such parade, procession, or open air public meeting shall take place." In addition, the county administrator was empowered to "adjust the amount to be paid in order to meet the expense incident to the administration of the Ordinance and to the maintenance of public order in the matter licensed."

In January 1989, respondent The Nationalist Movement proposed to demonstrate in opposition to the federal holiday commemorating the birthday of Martin Luther King, Jr. In Forsyth County, the Movement sought to 'conduct a rally and speeches for one and a half to two hours' on the courthouse steps on a Saturday afternoon. The county imposed a $100 fee. The fee did not include any calculation for expenses incurred by law enforcement authorities, but was based on 10 hours of the county administrator's time in issuing the permit. The county administrator testified that the cost of his time was deliberately undervalued and that he did not charge for the clerical support involved in processing the application.

The Movement did not pay the fee and did not hold the rally. Instead, it instituted this action on January 19, 1989, in the United States District Court for the Northern District of Georgia, requesting a temporary restraining order and permanent injunction prohibiting Forsyth County from interfering with the Movement's plans. The District Court denied the temporary restraining order and injunction. . . .

The United States Court of Appeals for the Eleventh Circuit reversed [and] held: 'An ordinance which charges more than a nominal fee for using public forums for public issue speech, violates the First Amendment.' The court determined that a permit fee of up to $1,000 a day exceeded this constitutional threshold. . . .

The Court of Appeals then voted to vacate the panel's opinion and to rehear the case en banc. After further briefing, the court issued a per curiam opinion reinstating the panel opinion in its entirety."

The Supreme Court granted certiorari to review the case and affirmed.

B. Counsel of Record / ACLU Attorney

ACLU Side (Respondent / Appellee): Richard Barrett argued the cause for appellee.

Opposing Side (Petitioner / Appellant): Robert S. Stubbs III argued the cause for appellant.

III. AMICI CURIAE

ACLU Side (Respondent / Appellee)

Brief of amici curiae filed on behalf of the ACLU, et al., by Eric Neisser, Steven R. Shapiro, John A. Powell, and Elliot M. Mincberg.

Brief of amici curiae filed on behalf of the American Federation of Labor and Congress of Industrial Organizations by Marsha S. Berzon and Laurence Gold.

Brief of amici curiae filed on behalf of Public Citizen by David C. Vladeck and Alan B. Morrison.

Opposing Side (Petitioner / Appellant)

Brief of amici curiae filed on behalf of the City of Orlando, et al., by Jody M. Litchford.

IV. THE SUPREME COURT'S DECISION

"The Forsyth County ordinance requiring a permit and a fee before authorizing public speaking, parades, or assemblies in 'the archetype of a traditional public forum,' is a prior restraint on speech. Although there is a 'heavy presumption' against the validity of a prior restraint, the Court has recognized that government, in order to regulate competing uses of public forums, may impose a permit requirement on those wishing to hold a march, parade, or rally. Such a scheme, however, must meet certain constitutional requirements. It may not delegate overly broad licensing discretion to a government official. Further, any permit scheme controlling the time, place, and manner of speech must not be based on the content of the message, must be narrowly tailored to serve a significant governmental interest, and must leave open ample alternatives for communication. . . .

Respondent contends that the county ordinance is facially invalid because it does not prescribe adequate standards for the administrator to apply when he sets a permit fee. A government regulation that allows arbitrary application is 'inherently inconsistent with a valid time, place, and manner regulation because such discretion has the potential for becoming a means of suppressing a particular point of view.'

[T]he county has made clear how it interprets and implements the ordinance. The ordinance can apply to any activity on public property—from parades, to street corner speeches, to bike races—and the fee assessed may reflect the county's police and administrative costs. Whether or not, in any given instance, the fee would include any or all of the county's administrative and security expenses is decided by the county administrator. . . .

Based on the county's implementation and construction of the ordinance, it simply cannot be said that there are any 'narrowly drawn, reasonable and definite standards,' guiding the hand of the Forsyth County administrator. The decision how much to charge for police protection or administrative time—or even whether to charge at all—is left to the whim of the administrator. There are no articulated standards either in the ordinance or in the county's established practice. The administrator is not required to rely on any objective factors. He need not provide any explanation for his decision, and that decision is unreviewable. Nothing in the law or its application prevents the official from encouraging some views and discouraging others through the arbitrary application of fees. The First Amendment prohibits the vesting of such unbridled discretion in a government official. . . .

The Forsyth County ordinance contains more than the possibility of censorship through uncontrolled discretion. As construed by the county, the ordinance often requires that the fee be based on the content of the speech.

[T]he provision of the Forsyth County ordinance relating to fees is invalid because it unconstitutionally ties the amount of the fee to the content of the speech and lacks adequate procedural safeguards; no limit on such a fee can remedy these constitutional violations.

The judgment of the Court of Appeals is affirmed."

V. JUSTICE VOTE

5 Pro ACLU Side vs. 4 Con Opposing Side

ACLU Side (Respondent / Appellee)

1. Blackmun, H. – Wrote majority opinion
2. Stevens, J. – Joined majority opinion
3. O'Connor, S. – Joined majority opinion
4. Kennedy, A. – Joined majority opinion
5. Souter, D. – Joined majority opinion

Opposing Side (Petitioner / Appellant)

1. Rehnquist, W. – Wrote dissenting opinion
2. White, B. – Joined Rehnquist's dissent
3. Scalia, A. – Joined Rehnquist's dissent
4. Thomas, C. – Joined Rehnquist's dissent

VI. A WIN OR LOSS FOR THE ACLU?

The ACLU filed as amicus curiae urging affirmance of the judgment of the Court of Appeals; the Supreme Court affirmed in a 5-4 vote, giving the ACLU an apparent win.

744. Wright v. West

(Decided June 19, 1992; 505 U.S. 277)

I. ISSUE

A. Issues Discussed

Criminal procedure, habeas corpus, due process

B. Legal Question Presented

"[W]hether the Court of Appeals for the Fourth Circuit correctly applied our decision in Jackson v. Virginia, 443 U.S. 307 (1979), in concluding that the evidence against respondent Frank West was insufficient, as a matter of due process, to support his state-court conviction for grand larceny."

C. Supreme Court's Answer

The evidence was sufficient to support respondent's grand larceny conviction.

II. CASE SUMMARY

A. Background

"Between December 13 and December 26, 1978, someone broke into the Westmoreland County, Virginia, home of Angelo Cardova and stole items valued at approximately $3,500. On January 10, 1979, police conducted a lawful search of the Gloucester County, Virginia, home of West and his wife. They discovered several of the items stolen from the Cardova home . . . .

West was charged with grand larceny. Testifying at trial on his own behalf, he admitted to a prior felony conviction, but denied having taken anything from Cardova's house. [He gave confusing testimony describing how he acquired some of the items.]

The jury returned a guilty verdict, and West received a 10-year prison sentence. West petitioned for an appeal, contending (among other things) that the evidence was insufficient to support a finding of guilt beyond a reasonable doubt. In May 1980, the Supreme Court of Virginia refused the petition—a disposition indicating that the court found the petition without merit. Seven years later, West filed a petition for a writ of habeas corpus in the same court . . . The Supreme Court of Virginia again denied relief. West then filed a petition for a writ of habeas corpus in the District Court for the Eastern District of Virginia, which rejected both claims and denied relief.

The Court of Appeals for the Fourth Circuit reversed. . . . After the Fourth Circuit denied rehearing en banc by an equally divided court, the warden and the State Attorney General sought review in this Court on, among other questions, whether the Court of Appeals had applied Jackson correctly in this case."

The Supreme Court granted certiorari to review the case and reversed.

B. Counsel of Record / ACLU Attorney

ACLU Side (Respondent / Appellee): Steven H. Goldblatt argued the cause for appellee.

Opposing Side (Petitioner / Appellant): Donald R. Curry, Senior Assistant Attorney General of Virginia, argued the cause for appellant.

Maureen E. Mahoney, Deputy Solicitor General, argued the cause for the United States, as amicus curiae, by special leave of Court.

III. AMICI CURIAE

ACLU Side (Respondent / Appellee)

Brief of amici curiae filed on behalf of the ACLU, et al., by Leslie A. Harris, Steven R. Shapiro, and John A. Powell.

Brief of amici curiae filed on behalf of the State of New York, et al., by Robert Abrams, Attorney General of New York; Lee Fisher, Attorney General of Ohio; Jerry Boone, Solicitor General of New York; Peter H. Schiff, Deputy Solicitor General; and Martin A. Hotvet, Assistant Attorney General.

Brief of amici curiae filed on behalf of Senator Biden, et al., by William F. Sheehan and Christopher E. Palmer.

Brief of amici curiae filed on behalf of the American Bar Association by Talbot D'Alemberte and Seth P. Waxman.

Brief of amici curiae filed on behalf of Benjamin R. Civiletti, et al., by Douglas G. Robinson and James S. Liebman.

Brief of amici curiae filed on behalf of Gerald Gunther, et al., by Larry W. Yackle.

Opposing Side (Petitioner / Appellant)

Brief of amici curiae filed on behalf of the United States by Maureen E. Mahoney, Deputy Solicitor General, Solicitor General Starr, Assistant Attorney General Mueller, and Deputy Solicitor General Roberts.

Brief of amici curiae filed on behalf of the State of Florida, et al., by Robert A. Butterworth, Attorney General, and Richard B. Martell, Assistant Attorney General; Charles E. Cole, Attorney General of Alaska; Grant Woods, Attorney General of Arizona; Winston Bryant, Attorney General of Arkansas; Daniel E. Lungren, Attorney General of California; Gale A. Norton, Attorney General of Colorado; Richard N. Palmer, Chief State's Attorney of Connecticut; Charles M. Oberly III, Attorney General of Delaware; Michael J. Bowers, Attorney General of Georgia; Warren Price III, Attorney General of Hawaii; Larry EchoHawk, Attorney General of Idaho; Linley E. Pearson, Attorney General of Indiana; Bonnie J. Campbell, Attorney General of Iowa; Robert T. Stephen, Attorney General of Kansas; Chris Gorman, Attorney General of Kentucky; Joseph Curran, Jr., Attorney General of Maryland; Hubert H. Humphrey III, Attorney General of Minnesota; Michael C. Moore, Attorney General of Mississippi; William L. Webster, Attorney General of Missouri; Marc Racicot, Attorney General of Montana; Don Stenberg, Attorney General of Nebraska; Frankie Sue Del Papa, Attorney General of Nevada; John P. Arnold, Attorney General of New Hampshire; Robert J. Del Tufo, Attorney General of New Jersey; Tom Udall, Attorney General of New Mexico; Lacy H. Thornburg, Attorney General of North Carolina; Nicholas J. Spaeth, Attorney General of North Dakota; Susan B. Loving, Attorney General of Oklahoma; Charles S. Crookham, Attorney General of Oregon; Ernest D. Preate, Jr., Attorney General of Pennsylvania; Travis Medlock, Attorney General of South Carolina; Mark Barnett, Attorney General of South Dakota; Dan Morales, Attorney General of Texas; Paul Van Dam, Attorney General of Utah; Jeffrey L. Amestoy, Attorney General of Vermont; Kenneth O. Eikenberry, Attorney General of Washington; Mario J. Palumbo, Attorney General of West Virginia; and Joseph B. Meyer, Attorney General of Wyoming.

Brief of amici curiae filed on behalf of the Criminal Justice Legal Foundation by Kent S. Scheidegger.

IV. THE SUPREME COURT'S DECISION

"The case against West was strong. [O]ver 15 of the items stolen were recovered from West's home. On direct examination at trial, West said nothing more than that he frequently bought and sold items at different flea markets. He failed to offer specific information about how he had come to acquire any of the stolen items. . . .

As the trier of fact, the jury was entitled to disbelieve West's uncorroborated and confused testimony. In evaluating that testimony, moreover, the jury was entitled to discount West's credibility on account of his prior felony conviction and to take into account West's demeanor when testifying, which neither the Court of Appeals nor we may review. And if the jury did disbelieve West, it was further entitled to consider whatever it concluded to be perjured testimony as affirmative evidence of guilt. . . .

[W]e think it clear that the trial record contained sufficient evidence to support West's conviction. . . .

The judgment of the Court of Appeals is reversed, and the case is remanded for further proceedings consistent with this opinion."

V. JUSTICE VOTE

0 Pro ACLU Side vs. 9 Con Opposing Side

Opposing Side (Petitioner / Appellant)

1. Thomas, C. – Wrote majority opinion
2. Souter, D. – Wrote concurring opinion
3. Kennedy, A. – Wrote concurring opinion
4. Scalia, A. – Joined majority opinion
5. Rehnquist, W. – Joined majority opinion
6. White, B. – Wrote concurring opinion
7. O'Connor, S. – Wrote concurring opinion
8. Blackmun, H. – Joined O'Connor's concurrence
9. Stevens, J. – Joined O'Connor's concurrence

VI. A WIN OR LOSS FOR THE ACLU?

The ACLU filed a brief as amicus curiae urging affirmance of the judgment of the Court of Appeals; the Supreme Court reversed in a 9-0 vote, giving the ACLU an apparent loss.

745. R.A.V. v. City of St. Paul

(Decided June 22, 1992; 505 U.S. 377)

I. ISSUE

A. Issues Discussed

First Amendment, freedom of speech

B. Legal Question Presented

Whether the St. Paul Bias-Motivated Crime Ordinance violates the First Amendment.

C. Supreme Court's Answer

The ordinance violates the First Amendment.

II. CASE SUMMARY

A. Background

"In the predawn hours of June 21, 1990, petitioner and several other teenagers allegedly assembled a crudely made cross by taping together broken chair legs. They then allegedly burned the cross inside the fenced yard of a black family that lived across the street from the house where petitioner was staying. Although this conduct could have been punished under any of a number of laws, one of the two provisions under which respondent city of St. Paul chose to charge petitioner (then a juvenile) was the St. Paul Bias–Motivated Crime Ordinance, St. Paul, Minn., Legis.Code § 292.02 (1990), which provides:

'Whoever places on public or private property a symbol, object, appellation, characterization or graffiti, including, but not limited to, a burning cross or Nazi swastika, which one knows or has reasonable grounds to know arouses anger, alarm or resentment in others on the basis of race, color, creed, religion or gender commits disorderly conduct and shall be guilty of a misdemeanor.'

Petitioner moved to dismiss this count on the ground that the St. Paul ordinance was substantially overbroad and impermissibly content based and therefore facially invalid under the First Amendment. The trial court granted this motion, but the Minnesota Supreme Court reversed. That court rejected petitioner's overbreadth claim because, as construed in prior Minnesota cases, the modifying phrase 'arouses anger, alarm or resentment in others' limited the reach of the ordinance to conduct that amounts to 'fighting words,' i.e., 'conduct that itself inflicts injury or tends to incite immediate violence . . . ,' and therefore the ordinance reached only expression 'that the first amendment does not protect.' The court also concluded that the ordinance was not impermissibly content based because, in its view, 'the ordinance is a narrowly tailored means toward accomplishing the compelling governmental interest in protecting the community against bias-motivated threats to public safety and order.'"

The Supreme Court granted certiorari to review the case and reversed.

B. Counsel of Record / ACLU Attorney

ACLU Side (Petitioner / Appellant): Edward J. Cleary argued the cause for appellant.

Opposing Side (Respondent / Appellee): Tom Foley argued the cause for appellee.

III. AMICI CURIAE

ACLU Side (Petitioner / Appellant)

Brief of amici curiae filed on behalf of the ACLU, et al., by Steven R. Shapiro, John A. Powell, and Mark R. Anfinson.

Brief of amici curiae filed on behalf of the Association of American Publishers, et al., by Bruce J. Ennis.

Brief of amici curiae filed on behalf of the Center for Individual Rights by Gary B. Born and Michael P. McDonald.

Brief of amici curiae filed on behalf of the Patriot's Defense Foundation, Inc., by Charles R. Sheppard.

Opposing Side (Respondent / Appellee)

Briefs of amici curiae filed on behalf of the State of Minnesota, et al., by Hubert H. Humphrey III, Attorney General of Minnesota, and Richard S. Slowes, Assistant Attorney General, Jimmy Evans, Attorney General of Alabama, Grant Woods, Attorney General of Arizona, Richard Blumenthal, Attorney General of Connecticut, and John J. Kelly, Chief State's Attorney of Connecticut, Larry EchoHawk, Attorney General of Idaho, Roland W. Burris, Attorney General of Illinois, Robert T. Stephan, Attorney General of Kansas, J. Joseph Curran, Jr., Attorney General of Maryland, Scott Harshbarger, Attorney General of Massachusetts, Frank J. Kelley, Attorney General of Michigan, Robert J. Del Tufo, Attorney General of New Jersey, Lee I. Fisher, Attorney General of Ohio, Susan B. Loving, Attorney General of Oklahoma, T. Travis Medlock, Attorney General of South Carolina, Charles W. Burson, Attorney General of Tennessee, Mary Sue Terry, Attorney General of Virginia, and Paul Van Dam, Attorney General of Utah.

Brief of amici curiae filed on behalf of the Anti-Defamation League of B'nai B'rith by Allen I. Saeks, Jeffrey P. Sinensky, Steven M. Freeman, and Michael Lieberman.

Brief of amici curiae filed on behalf of the Asian American Legal Defense and Education Fund, et al., by Angelo N. Ancheta.

Brief of amici curiae filed on behalf of the Center for Democratic Renewal, et al., by Frank E. Deale.
Brief of amici curiae filed on behalf of the Criminal Justice Legal Foundation by Kent S. Scheidegger and Charles L. Hobson.
Brief of amici curiae filed on behalf of the League of Minnesota Cities, et al., by Carla J. Heyl, Robert J. Alfton, and Jerome J. Segal.
Brief of amici curiae filed on behalf of the National Association for the Advancement of Colored People, et al., by Ronald D. Maines, Dennis C. Hayes, Willie Abrams, and Kemp R. Harshman.
Brief of amici curiae filed on behalf of the National Black Women's Health Project by Catharine A. MacKinnon and Burke Marshall.
Brief of amici curiae filed on behalf of the National Institute of Municipal Law Officers, et al., by Richard Ruda, Michael J. Wahoske, and Mark B. Rotenberg.
Brief of amici curiae filed on behalf of People for the American Way by Richard S. Hoffman, Kevin J. Hasson, and Elliot M. Mincberg.

IV. THE SUPREME COURT'S DECISION

"In construing the St. Paul ordinance, we are bound by the construction given to it by the Minnesota court. Accordingly, we accept the Minnesota Supreme Court's authoritative statement that the ordinance reaches only those expressions that constitute 'fighting words' within the meaning of Chaplinsky. . . . Assuming, arguendo, that all of the expression reached by the ordinance is proscribable under the 'fighting words' doctrine, we nonetheless conclude that the ordinance is facially unconstitutional in that it prohibits otherwise permitted speech solely on the basis of the subjects the speech addresses.

[W]e conclude that, even as narrowly construed by the Minnesota Supreme Court, the ordinance is facially unconstitutional. Although the phrase in the ordinance, 'arouses anger, alarm or resentment in others,' has been limited by the Minnesota Supreme Court's construction to reach only those symbols or displays that amount to 'fighting words,' the remaining, unmodified terms make clear that the ordinance applies only to 'fighting words' that insult, or provoke violence, 'on the basis of race, color, creed, religion or gender.' Displays containing abusive invective, no matter how vicious or severe, are permissible unless they are addressed to one of the specified disfavored topics. Those who wish to use 'fighting words' in connection with other ideas—to express hostility, for example, on the basis of political affiliation, union membership, or homosexuality— are not covered. The First Amendment does not permit St. Paul to impose special prohibitions on those speakers who express views on disfavored subjects. . . .

The dispositive question in this case . . . is whether content discrimination is reasonably necessary to achieve St. Paul's compelling interests; it plainly is not. An ordinance not limited to the favored topics, for example, would have precisely the same beneficial effect. In fact the only interest distinctively served by the content limitation is that of displaying the city council's special hostility towards the particular biases thus singled out. That is precisely what the First Amendment forbids. The politicians of St. Paul are entitled to express that hostility—but not through the means of imposing unique limitations upon speakers who (however benightedly) disagree.

Let there be no mistake about our belief that burning a cross in someone's front yard is reprehensible. But St. Paul has sufficient means at its disposal to prevent such behavior without adding the First Amendment to the fire.

The judgment of the Minnesota Supreme Court is reversed, and the case is remanded for proceedings not inconsistent with this opinion."

V. JUSTICE VOTE

9 Pro ACLU Side vs. 0 Con Opposing Side

ACLU Side (Petitioner / Appellant)

1. Scalia, A. – Wrote majority opinion
2. Rehnquist, W. – Joined majority opinion
3. Kennedy, A. – Joined majority opinion
4. Souter, D. – Joined majority opinion
5. Thomas, C. – Joined majority opinion
6. White, B. – Wrote concurring opinion , joined Stevens' concurrence, in part
7. Blackmun, H. – Wrote concurring opinion, joined White's concurrence, joined Stevens' concurrence, in part
8. O'Connor, S. – Joined White's concurrence
9. Stevens, J. – Wrote concurring opinion, joined White's concurrence, in part

VI. A WIN OR LOSS FOR THE ACLU?

The ACLU, as amicus curiae, urged reversal of the judgment the Supreme Court of Minnesota; the U.S. Supreme Court reversed in a 9-0 vote, giving the ACLU an apparent win.

746. Lee v. Weisman

(Decided June 24, 1992; 505 U.S. 577)

I. ISSUE

A. Issues Discussed

First Amendment, Establishment Clause, Free Exercise Clause, prayer in schools

B. Legal Question Presented

"[W]hether including clerical members who offer prayers as part of the official school graduation ceremony is consistent with the Religion Clauses of the First Amendment, provisions the Fourteenth Amendment makes applicable with full force to the States and their school districts."

C. Supreme Court's Answer

This practice violates the Establishment Clause of the First Amendment.

II. CASE SUMMARY

A. Background

"Deborah Weisman graduated from Nathan Bishop Middle School, a public school in Providence, at a formal ceremony in June 1989. . . . Deborah's graduation was held on the premises of Nathan Bishop Middle School on June 29, 1989. Four days before the ceremony, Daniel Weisman, in his individual capacity as a Providence taxpayer and as next friend of Deborah, sought a temporary restraining order in the United States District Court for the District of Rhode Island to prohibit school officials from including an invocation or benediction in the graduation ceremony. The court denied the motion for lack of adequate time to consider it. Deborah and her family attended the graduation, where the prayers were recited. In July 1989, Daniel Weisman filed an amended complaint seeking a permanent injunction barring petitioners, various officials of the Providence public schools, from inviting the clergy to deliver invocations and benedictions at future graduations. We find it unnecessary to address Daniel Weisman's taxpayer standing, for a live and justiciable controversy is before us. Deborah Weisman is enrolled as a student at Classical High School in Providence and from the record it appears likely, if not certain, that an invocation and benediction will be conducted at her high school graduation.

The case was submitted on stipulated facts. The District Court held that petitioners' practice of including invocations and benedictions in public school graduations violated the Establishment Clause of the First Amendment, and it enjoined petitioners from continuing the practice. . . . On appeal, the United States Court of Appeals for the First Circuit affirmed."

The Supreme Court granted certiorari to review the case and affirmed.

B. Counsel of Record / ACLU Attorney

ACLU Side (Respondent / Appellee): Sandra A. Blanding argued the cause for appellee. With her on the brief were Steven R. Shapiro and John A. Powell.

Opposing Side (Petitioner / Appellant): Charles J. Cooper argued the cause for appellant. With him on the brief were Michael A. Carvin, Peter J. Ferrara, Robert J. Cynkar, Joseph A. Rotella, and Jay Alan Sekulow.

Solicitor General Starr argued the cause for the United States, as amicus curiae, by special leave of Court.

III. AMICI CURIAE

ACLU Side (Respondent / Appellee)

Brief of amici curiae filed on behalf of Americans for Religious Liberty by Ronald A. Lindsay.

Brief of amici curiae filed on behalf of the American Jewish Congress, et al., by Douglas Laycock.

Brief of amici curiae filed on behalf of the Council on Religious Freedom, et al., by Lee Boothby, Robert W. Nixon, Walter E. Carson, and Rolland Truman.

Brief of amici curiae filed on behalf of the National Coalition for Public Education and Religious Liberty, et al., by David B. Isbell and T. Jeremy Gunn.

Opposing Side (Petitioner / Appellant)

Brief of amici curiae filed on behalf of the United States by Solicitor General Starr, Assistant Attorney General Gerson, Deputy Solicitor General Roberts, Deputy Assistant Attorney General McGinnis, and Richard H. Seamon.

Brief of amici curiae filed on behalf of the State of Delaware by Charles M. Oberly III, Attorney General of Delaware, Michael F. Foster, Solicitor General, David S. Swayze, and David B. Ripsom.

Brief of amici curiae filed on behalf of the National School Boards Association by Gwendolyn H. Gregory, August W. Steinhilber, and Thomas A. Shannon.

Brief of amici curiae filed on behalf of the Institute in Basic Life Principles by Joe Reynolds.

Brief of amici curiae filed on behalf of the Board of Education of Alpine School District by Brinton R. Burbidge and Merrill F. Nelson.

Brief of amici curiae filed on behalf of the Christian Legal Society, et al., by Edward McGlynn Gaffney, Michael J. Woodruff, Samuel E. Ericsson, and Forest D. Montgomery.

Brief of amici curiae filed on behalf of the Clarendon Foundation by Kemp R. Harshman and Ronald D. Maines.

Brief of amici curiae filed on behalf of Concerned Women for America, et al., by James Matthew Henderson, Sr., Jordan Lorence, Mark N. Troobnick, and Thomas Patrick Monaghan.

Brief of amici curiae filed on behalf of Focus on the Family, et al., by Stephen H. Galebach and Laura D. Millman.

Brief of amici curiae filed on behalf of the Liberty Counsel by Mathew D. Staver.

Brief of amici curiae filed on behalf of the National Jewish Commission on Law and Public Affairs by Nathan Lewin and Dennis Rapps.

Brief of amici curiae filed on behalf of the National Legal Foundation by Robert K. Skolrood and Brian M. McCormick.

Brief of amici curiae filed on behalf of the Rutherford Institute, et al., by John W. Whitehead, Alexis I. Crow, A. Eric Johnston, Stephen E. Hurst, Joseph Secola, Thomas S. Neuberger, J. Brian Heller, Amy Dougherty, David Melton, Thomas W. Strahan, Robert R. Melnick, William Bonner, Larry Crain, W. Charles Bundren, and James Knicely.

Brief of amici curiae filed on behalf of Specialty Research Associates, Inc., et al., by Jordan Lorence.

Brief of amici curiae filed on behalf of the Southern Baptist Convention Christian Life Commission by Michael K. Whitehead and James M. Smart, Jr.

Brief of amici curiae filed on behalf of the United States Catholic Conference by Mark E. Chopko and Phillip H. Harris.

IV. THE SUPREME COURT'S DECISION

"The principle that government may accommodate the free exercise of religion does not supersede the fundamental limitations imposed by the Establishment Clause. It is beyond dispute that, at a minimum, the Constitution guarantees that government may not coerce anyone to support or participate in religion or its exercise, or otherwise act in a way which 'establishes a [state] religion or religious faith, or tends to do so.' The State's involvement in the school prayers challenged today violates these central principles. . . .

Finding no violation under these circumstances would place objectors in the dilemma of participating, with all that implies, or protesting. We do not address whether that choice is acceptable if the affected citizens are mature adults, but we think the State may not, consistent with the Establishment Clause, place primary and secondary school children in this position. . . .

The injury caused by the government's action, and the reason why Daniel and Deborah Weisman object to it, is that the State, in a school setting, in effect required participation in a religious exercise. It is, we concede, a brief exercise during which the individual can concentrate on joining its message, meditate on her own religion, or let her mind wander. But the embarrassment and the intrusion of the religious exercise cannot be refuted by arguing that these prayers, and similar ones to be said in the future, are of a de minimis character. To do so would be an affront to the rabbi who offered them and to all those for whom the prayers were an essential and profound recognition of divine authority. And for the same reason, we think that the intrusion is greater than the two minutes or so of time consumed for prayers like these. Assuming, as we must, that the prayers were offensive to the student and the parent who now object, the intrusion was both real and, in the context of a secondary school, a violation of the objectors' rights. That the intrusion was in the course of promulgating religion that sought to be civic or nonsectarian rather than pertaining to one sect does not lessen the offense or isolation to the objectors. At best it narrows their number, at worst increases their sense of isolation and affront. . . .

We recognize that, at graduation time and throughout the course of the educational process, there will be instances when religious values, religious practices, and religious persons will have some interaction with the public schools and their students. But these matters, often questions of accommodation of religion, are not before us. The sole question presented is whether a religious exercise may be conducted at a graduation ceremony in circumstances where, as we have found, young graduates who object are induced to conform. No holding by this Court suggests that a school can persuade or compel a student to participate in a religious exercise. That is being done here, and it is forbidden by the Establishment Clause of the First Amendment.

For the reasons we have stated, the judgment of the Court of Appeals is affirmed."

V. JUSTICE VOTE

5 Pro ACLU Side vs. 4 Con Opposing Side

ACLU Side (Respondent / Appellee)

1. Kennedy, A. – Wrote majority opinion
2. Blackmun, H. – Wrote concurring opinion
3. Souter, D. – Wrote concurring opinion
4. Stevens, J. – Joined Blackmun's concurrence, joined Souter's concurrence
5. O'Connor, S. – Joined Blackmun's concurrence, joined Souter's concurrence

Opposing Side (Petitioner / Appellant)

1. Scalia, A. – Wrote dissenting opinion
2. Rehnquist, W. – Joined Scalia's dissent
3. White, B. – Joined Scalia's dissent
4. Thomas, C. – Joined Scalia's dissent

VI. A WIN OR LOSS FOR THE ACLU?

The ACLU, as counsel of record, urged affirmance of the judgment of the Court of Appeals for the First Circuit; the Supreme Court affirmed in a 5-4 vote, giving the ACLU an apparent win.

747. International Society for Krishna Consciousness, Inc. v. Lee

(Decided June 26, 1992; 505 U.S. 672)

I. ISSUE

A. Issues Discussed

First Amendment, freedoms of press, speech, and association

B. Legal Question Presented

"[W]hether an airport terminal operated by a public authority is a public forum and whether a regulation prohibiting solicitation in the interior of an airport terminal violates the First Amendment."

C. Supreme Court's Answer

The airport terminal is a nonpublic forum and the prohibiton does not violate the First Amendment.

II. CASE SUMMARY

A. Background

"Petitioner International Society for Krishna Consciousness, Inc. (ISKCON), is a not-for-profit religious corporation whose members perform a ritual known as sankirtan. The ritual consists of "going into public places, disseminating religious literature and soliciting funds to support the religion." . . .

The Port Authority owns and operates three major airports in the greater New York City area . . . . Most space at the three airports is leased to commercial airlines, which bear primary responsibility for the leasehold. The Port Authority retains control over unleased portions, including La Guardia's Central Terminal Building, portions of Kennedy's International Arrivals Building, and Newark's North Terminal Building (we refer to these areas collectively as the 'terminals'). The terminals are generally accessible to the general public and contain various commercial establishments such as restaurants, snack stands, bars, newsstands, and stores of various types. Virtually all who visit the terminals do so for purposes related to air travel. These visitors principally include passengers, those meeting or seeing off passengers, flight crews, and terminal employees.

The Port Authority has adopted a regulation forbidding within the terminals the repetitive solicitation of money or distribution of literature. . . . The regulation governs only the terminals; the Port Authority permits solicitation and distribution on the sidewalks outside the terminal buildings. The regulation effectively prohibits ISKCON from performing sankirtan in the terminals. As a result, ISKCON brought suit seeking declaratory and injunctive relief under 42 U.S.C. § 1983, alleging that the regulation worked to deprive its members of rights guaranteed under the First Amendment. The District Court . . . granted ISKCON summary judgment.

The Court of Appeals affirmed in part and reversed in part."

The Supreme Court granted certiorari to review the case and affirmed.

B. Counsel of Record / ACLU Attorney

ACLU Side (Petitioner / Appellant): Barry A. Fisher argued the cause for appellant.

Opposing Side (Respondent / Appellee): Arthur P. Berg argued the cause for appellee.

III. AMICI CURIAE

ACLU Side (Petitioner / Appellant)

Brief of amici curiae filed on behalf of the ACLU, et al., by Steven R. Shapiro, John A. Powell, and Arthur N. Eisenberg.

Brief of amici curiae filed on behalf of the American Federation of Labor and Congress of Industrial Organizations by Marsha S. Berzon, Walter Kamiat, and Laurence Gold.

Brief of amici curiae filed on behalf of the American Jewish Congress, et al., by Bradley P. Jacob, Edward McGlynn Gaffney, Jr., Steven T. McFarland, and Thomas C. Berg.

Brief of amici curiae filed on behalf of the American Newspaper Publishers Association, et al., by Robert C. Bernius, Alice Neff Lucan, Rene P. Milam, Richard A. Bernstein, Barbara Wartelle Wall, John C. Fontaine, Cristina L. Mendoza, George Freeman, and Carol D. Malamed.

Brief of amici curiae filed on behalf of the American Tract Society, et al., by James Matthew Henderson, Sr., Mark N. Troobnick, Thomas Patrick Monaghan, and Charles E. Rice.

Brief of amici curiae filed on behalf of the Free Congress Foundation by Wendell R. Bird and David J. Myers.

Brief of amici curiae filed on behalf of Project Vote, et al., by Elliot M. Mincberg, Sonia A. Bacchus, Robert Plotkin, Elinor L. Colbourn, and Andrew J. Steinberg.

Opposing Side (Respondent / Appellee)

Brief of amici curiae filed on behalf of the Airports Association Council International-North America by Michael M. Conway.

Brief of amici curiae filed on behalf of the National Institute of Municipal Law Officers by Benjamin L. Brown, Analeslie Muncy, Robert J. Alfton, Frank B. Gummey III, Frederick S. Dean, Neal M. Janey, Victor J. Kaleta, Robert J. Mangler, Neal E. McNeill, Robert J. Watson, and Iris J. Jones.

Brief of amici curiae filed on behalf of Multimedia Newspaper Co., et al., by Carl F. Muller and Wallace K. Lightsey.

Brief of amici curiae filed on behalf of the Criminal Justice Legal Foundation by Kent S. Scheidegger and Charles L. Hobson.

IV. THE SUPREME COURT'S DECISION

"It is uncontested that the solicitation at issue in this case is a form of speech protected under the First Amendment. But it is also well settled that the government need not permit all forms of speech on property that it owns and controls. Where the government is acting as a proprietor, managing its internal operations, rather than acting as lawmaker with the power to regulate or license, its action will not be subjected to the heightened review to which its actions as a lawmaker may be subject.

[R]egulation of speech on government property that has traditionally been available for public expression is subject to the highest scrutiny. Such regulations survive only if they are narrowly drawn to achieve a compelling state interest. The second category of public property is the designated public forum, whether of a limited or unlimited character—property that the State has opened for expressive activity by part or all of the public. Regulation of such property is subject to the same limitations as that governing a traditional public forum. Finally, there is all remaining public property. Limitations on expressive activity conducted on this last category of property must survive only a much more limited review. . . .

The decision to create a public forum must instead be made 'by intentionally opening a nontraditional forum for public discourse.' [The] precedents foreclose the conclusion that airport terminals are public fora. [T]he tradition of airport activity does not demonstrate that airports have historically been made available for speech activity. [W]e think that neither by tradition nor purpose can the terminals be described as satisfying the standards we have previously set out for identifying a public forum.

The restrictions here challenged, therefore, need only satisfy a requirement of reasonableness. [W]e conclude that the solicitation ban is reasonable.

For the foregoing reasons, the judgment of the Court of Appeals sustaining the ban on solicitation in Port Authority terminals is affirmed."

V. JUSTICE VOTE

3 Pro ACLU Side vs. 6 Con Opposing Side

ACLU Side (Petitioner / Appellant)

1. Souter, D. – Wrote dissenting opinion, joined Kennedy's concurrence in part
2. Stevens, J. – Joined Souter's dissent, joined Kennedy's concurrence in part
3. Blackmun, H. – Joined Souter's dissent, joined Kennedy's concurrence in part

Opposing Side (Respondent / Appellee)

1. Rehnquist, W. – Wrote majority opinion
2. White, B. – Joined majority opinion
3. O'Connor, S. – Wrote concurring opinion
4. Scalia, A. – Joined majority opinion
5. Thomas, C. – Joined majority opinion
6. Kennedy, A. – Wrote concurring opinion

VI. A WIN OR LOSS FOR THE ACLU?

The ACLU filed as amicus curiae urging reversal of the judgment of the Court of Appeals; the Supreme Court affirmed in a 6-3 vote, giving the ACLU an apparent loss.

748. Planned Parenthood of Southeastern Pennsylvania v. Casey

(Decided June 29, 1992; 505 U.S. 833)

I. ISSUE

A. Issues Discussed

Fourteenth Amendment, First Amendment, abortion

B. Legal Question Presented

Whether "five provisions of the Pennsylvania Abortion Control Act of 1982" are constitutional, and whether Roe v. Wade should be overturned.

C. Supreme Court's Answer

All the provisions except the spousal notification provision are valid and the decision in Roe v. Wade is reaffirmed.

II. CASE SUMMARY

A. Background

"At issue in these cases are five provisions of the Pennsylvania Abortion Control Act of 1982, as amended in 1988 and 1989. . . . The Act requires that a woman seeking an abortion give her informed consent prior to the abortion procedure, and specifies that she be provided with certain information at least 24 hours before the abortion is performed. For a minor to obtain an abortion, the Act requires the informed consent of one of her parents, but provides for a judicial bypass option if the minor does not wish to or cannot obtain a parent's consent. Another provision of the Act requires that, unless certain exceptions apply, a married woman seeking an abortion must sign a statement indicating that she has notified her husband of her intended abortion. The Act exempts compliance with these three requirements in the event of a 'medical emergency,' which is defined in § 3203 of the Act. In addition to the above provisions regulating the performance of abortions, the Act imposes certain reporting requirements on facilities that provide abortion services.

Before any of these provisions took effect, the petitioners, who are five abortion clinics and one physician representing himself as well as a class of physicians who provide abortion services, brought this suit seeking declaratory and injunctive relief. Each provision was challenged as unconstitutional on its face. The District Court entered a preliminary injunction against the enforcement of the regulations, and, after a 3-day bench trial, held all the provisions at issue here unconstitutional, entering a permanent injunction against Pennsylvania's enforcement of them. The Court of Appeals for the Third Circuit affirmed in part and reversed in part, upholding all of the regulations except for the husband notification requirement."

The Supreme Court granted certiorari to review the case, affirmed in part, reversed in part, and remanded.

B. Counsel of Record / ACLU Attorney

ACLU Side (Petitioner/Appellant in No. 91-744, Respondent/Appellee in No. 91-902): Kathryn Kolbert argued the cause for appellants in No. 91-744 and appellees in No. 91-902. With her on the briefs were Janet Benshoof, Lynn M. Paltrow, Rachael N. Pine, Steven R. Shapiro, John A. Powell, Linda J. Wharton, and Carol E. Tracy. Ernest D. Preate, Jr., Attorney General of Pennsylvania, argued the cause for appellees in No. 91-744 and appellants in No. 91-902. With him on the brief were John G. Knorr III, Chief Deputy Attorney General, and Kate L. Mershimer, Senior Deputy Attorney General.

Opposing Side (Respondent/Appellee in No. 91-744, Petitioner/Appellant in No. 91-902): Solicitor General Starr argued the cause for the United States as amicus curiae in support of appellees in No. 91-744 and appellants in No. 91-902.

III. AMICI CURIAE

ACLU Side (Petitioner / Appellant in No. 91-744, Respondent / Appellee in No. 91-902):

Brief of amici curiae filed on behalf of the State of New York, et al., by Robert Abrams, Attorney General of New York, Jerry Boone, Solicitor General, Mary Ellen Burns, Chief Assistant Attorney General, and Sanford M. Cohen, Donna I. Dennis, Marjorie Fujiki, and Shelley B. Mayer, Assistant Attorneys General, and John McKernan, Governor of Maine, and Michael E. Carpenter, Attorney General, Richard Blumenthal, Attorney General of Connecticut, Charles M. Oberly III, Attorney General of Delaware, Warren Price III, Attorney General of Hawaii, Roland W. Burris, Attorney General of Illinois, Bonnie J. Campbell, Attorney General of Iowa, J. Joseph Curran, Jr., Attorney General of Maryland, Scott Harshbarger, Attorney General of Massachusetts, Frankie Sue Del Papa, Attorney General of Nevada, Robert J. Del Tufo, Attorney General of New Jersey, Tom Udall, Attorney General of New Mexico, Lacy H. Thornburg, Attorney General of North Carolina, James E. O'Neil, Attorney General of Rhode Island, Dan Morales, Attorney General of Texas, Jeffrey L. Amestoy, Attorney General of Vermont, and John Payton, Corporation Counsel of District of Columbia.

Brief of amici curiae filed on behalf of the City of New York, et al., by O. Peter Sherwood, Conrad Harper, Janice Goodman, Leonard J. Koerner, Lorna Bade Goodman, Gail Rubin, and Julie Mertus.

Brief of amici curiae filed on behalf of 178 Organizations by Pamela S. Karlan and Sarah Weddington.

Brief of amici curiae filed on behalf of the Alan Guttmacher Institute, et al., by Colleen K. Connell and Dorothy B. Zimbrakos.

Brief of amici curiae filed on behalf of the American College of Obstetricians and Gynecologists, et al., by Carter G. Phillips, Ann E. Allen, Laurie R. Rockett, Joel I. Klein, Nadine Taub, and Sarah C. Carey.

Brief of amici curiae filed on behalf of the American Psychological Association by David W. Ogden.

Brief of amici curiae filed on behalf of the NAACP Legal Defense and Educational Fund, Inc., et al., by Julius L. Chambers, Ronald L. Ellis, and Alice L. Brown.

Brief of amici curiae filed on behalf of the Pennsylvania Coalition Against Domestic Violence, et al., by Phyllis Gelman.

Brief of amici curiae filed on behalf of Representative Don Edwards, et al., by Walter Dellinger and Lloyd N. Cutler.

Brief of amici curiae filed on behalf of 250 American Historians by Sylvia A. Law.

Opposing Side (Respondent / Appellee in No. 91-744, Petitioner / Appellant in No. 91-902):

Brief of amici curiae filed on behalf of the United States by Solicitor General Starr, Assistant Attorney General Gerson, Paul J. Larkin, Jr., Thomas G. Hungar, and Alfred R. Mollin.

Brief of amici curiae filed on behalf of Certain American State Legislators by Pual Benjamin Linton.

Brief of amici curiae filed on behalf of Catholics United for Life, et al., by Thomas A. Glessner, Charles E. Rice, and Michael J. Laird.

Brief of amici curiae filed on behalf of Focus on the Family, et al., by Stephen H. Galebach, Gregory J. Granitto, Stephen W. Reed, David L. Llewellyn, Jr., Benjamin W. Bull, and Leonard J. Pranschke.

Brief of amici curiae filed on behalf of the State of Utah by R. Paul Van Dam, Attorney General, and Mary Anne Q. Wood, Special Assistant Attorney General.

Brief of amici curiae filed on behalf of the United States Catholic Conference, et al., by Mark E. Chopko, Phillip H. Harris, Michael K. Whitehead, and Forest D. Montgomery.

Brief of amici curiae filed on behalf of Representative Henry J. Hyde, et al., by Albert P. Blaustein and Kevin J. Todd.

Brief of amici curiae filed on behalf of the National Legal Foundation by Robert K. Skolrood.

Brief of amici curiae filed on behalf of the Knights of Columbia by Carl A. Anderson.

Brief of amici curiae filed on behalf of 19 Arizona Legislators by Ronald D. Maines.

Brief of amici curiae filed on behalf of the American Academy of Medical Ethics by Joseph W. Dellapenna.

Brief of amici curiae filed on behalf of the Rutherford Institute, et al., by Thomas W. Strahan, John W. Whitehead, Mr. Johnston, Stephen E. Hurst, Joseph Secola, Thomas S. Neuberger, J. Brian Heller, Amy Dougherty, Stanley R. Jones, David Melton, Robert R. Melnick, William Bonner, W. Charles Bundren, and James Knicely.

Brief of amici curiae filed on behalf of the American Association of Pro-Life Obstetricians and Gynecologists, et al., by William Bentley Ball, Philip J. Murren, and Maura K. Quinlan.

Brief of amici curaie filed on behalf of Texas Black Americans for Life by Lawrence J. Joyce and Craig H.Greenwood.

Brief of amici curiae filed on behalf of Feminists for Life of America, et al., by Keith A. Fournier, John G. Stepanovich, Christine Smith Torre, Theodore H. Amshoff, Jr., and Mary Dice Grenen.

Brief of amici curiae filed on behalf of the Southern Center for Law & Ethics by Tony G. Miller.

Brief of amici curiae filed on behalf of National Right to Life, Inc., by James Bopp, Jr., Richard E. Coleson, Robert A. Destro, and A. Eric Johnston.

Brief of amici curiae filed on behalf of the Life Issues Institute by James Bopp, Jr., and Richard E. Coleson.

Brief of amici curiae filed on behalf of Agudath Israel of America by David Zwiebel.

Brief of amici curiae filed on behalf of University Faculty for Life by Clarke D. Forsythe and Victor G. Rosenblum.

IV. THE SUPREME COURT'S DECISION

"After considering the fundamental constitutional questions resolved by Roe, principles of institutional integrity, and the rule of stare decisis, we are led to conclude this: the essential holding of Roe v. Wade should be retained and once again reaffirmed.

It must be stated at the outset and with clarity that Roe's essential holding, the holding we reaffirm, has three parts. First is a recognition of the right of the woman to choose to have an abortion before viability and to obtain it without undue interference from the State. Before viability, the State's interests are not strong enough to support a prohibition of abortion or the imposition of a substantial obstacle to the woman's effective right to elect the procedure. Second is a confirmation of the State's power to restrict abortions after fetal viability, if the law contains exceptions for pregnancies which endanger the woman's life or health. And third is the principle that the State has legitimate interests from the outset of the pregnancy in protecting the health of the woman and the life of the fetus that may become a child. These principles do not contradict one another; and we adhere to each. . . .

We give this summary:

(a) To protect the central right recognized by Roe v. Wade while at the same time accommodating the State's profound interest in potential life, we will employ the undue burden analysis . . . . An undue burden exists, and therefore a provision of law is invalid, if its purpose or effect is to place a substantial obstacle in the path of a woman seeking an abortion before the fetus attains viability.

(b) We reject the rigid trimester framework of Roe v. Wade. To promote the State's profound interest in potential life, throughout pregnancy the State may take measures to ensure that the woman's choice is informed, and measures designed to advance this interest will not be invalidated as long as their purpose is to persuade the woman to choose childbirth over abortion. These measures must not be an undue burden on the right.

(c) As with any medical procedure, the State may enact regulations to further the health or safety of a woman seeking an abortion. Unnecessary health regulations that have the purpose or effect of presenting a substantial obstacle to a woman seeking an abortion impose an undue burden on the right.

(d) Our adoption of the undue burden analysis does not disturb the central holding of Roe v. Wade, and we reaffirm that holding. Regardless of whether exceptions are made for particular circumstances, a State may not prohibit any woman from making the ultimate decision to terminate her pregnancy before viability.

(e) We also reaffirm Roe's holding that 'subsequent to viability, the State in promoting its interest in the potentiality of human life may, if it chooses, regulate, and even proscribe, abortion except where it is necessary, in appropriate medical judgment, for the preservation of the life or health of the mother.'

These principles control our assessment of the Pennsylvania statute, and we now turn to the issue of the validity of its challenged provisions. . . .

The Court of Appeals applied what it believed to be the undue burden standard and upheld each of the provisions except for the husband notification requirement. We agree generally with this conclusion, but refine the undue burden analysis in accordance with the principles articulated above.

[We] conclude that, as construed by the Court of Appeals, the medical emergency definition imposes no undue burden on a woman's abortion right.

[T]he right protected by Roe is a right to decide to terminate a pregnancy free of undue interference by the State. Because the informed consent requirement facilitates the wise exercise of that right, it cannot be classified as an interference with the right Roe protects. The informed consent requirement is not an undue burden on that right. . . .

Section 3209 of Pennsylvania's abortion law provides, except in cases of medical emergency, that no physician shall perform an abortion on a married woman without receiving a signed statement from the woman that she has notified her spouse that she is about to undergo an abortion. . . . Section 3209 embodies a view of marriage consonant with the common-law status of married women but repugnant to our present understanding of marriage and of the nature of the rights secured by the Constitution. Women do not lose their constitutionally protected liberty when they marry. The Constitution protects all individuals, male or female, married or unmarried, from the abuse of governmental power, even where that power is employed for the supposed benefit of a member of the individual's family. These considerations confirm our conclusion that § 3209 is invalid. . . .

Our cases establish, and we reaffirm today, that a State may require a minor seeking an abortion to obtain the consent of a parent or guardian, provided that there is an adequate judicial bypass procedure. . . .

Subsection (12) of the reporting provision requires the reporting of, among other things, a married woman's 'reason for failure to provide notice' to her husband. This provision in effect requires women, as a condition of obtaining an abortion, to provide the Commonwealth with the precise information we have already recognized that many women have pressing reasons not to reveal. Like the spousal notice requirement itself, this provision places an undue burden on a woman's choice, and must be invalidated for that reason. . . .

The judgment in No. 91–902 is affirmed. The judgment in No. 91–744 is affirmed in part and reversed in part, and the case is remanded for proceedings consistent with this opinion, including consideration of the question of severability."

V. JUSTICE VOTE

5 Pro ACLU Side vs. 4 Con Opposing Side

ACLU Side (Petitioner / Appellant in No. 91-744, Respondent / Appellee in No. 91-902):

1. O'Connor, S. – Co-wrote majority opinion
2. Kennedy, A. – Co-wrote majority opinion
3. Souter, D. – Co-wrote majority opinion
4. Stevens, J. – Wrote opinion concurring in part and dissenting in part
5. Blackmun, H. – Wrote opinion concurring in part and dissenting in part

Opposing Side (Respondent / Appellee in No. 91-744, Petitioner / Appellant in No. 91-902):

1. Rehnquist, W. – Wrote opinion concurring in part and dissenting in part, joined Scalia's opinion
2. Thomas, C. – Wrote opinion concurring in part and dissenting in part, joined Rehnquist's opinion
3. White, B. – Joined Rehnquist's opinion, joined Thomas' opinion
4. Scalia, A. – Joined Rehnquist's opinion, joined Thomas' opinion

VI. A WIN OR LOSS FOR THE ACLU?

The ACLU, as counsel for petitioners in No. 91-744 and respondents in No. 91-902, urged reversal in No. 91-744 and affirmance in No. 91-902, of the judgment of the Court of Appeals for the Third Circuit; the Supreme Court affirmed in part and reversed in part in No. 91-744 in a 5-4 vote and affirmed in No. 91-902, giving the ACLU an apparent win.

749. Soldal v. Cook County, Illinois

(Decided December 8, 1992; 506 U.S. 56)

I. ISSUE

A. Issues Discussed

Criminal justice, Fourth Amendment, search and seizure

B. Legal Question Presented

"[W]hether the seizure and removal of the Soldals' trailer home implicated their Fourth Amendment rights . . . ."

C. Supreme Court's Answer

The removal of the Soldals' trailer home was a "seizure" within the meaning of the Fourth Amendment and implicated their Fourth Amendment rights.

II. CASE SUMMARY

A. Background

"Edward Soldal and his family resided in their trailer home, which was located on a rented lot in the Willoway Terrace mobile home park in Elk Grove, Illinois. In May, 1987, Terrace Properties, the owner of the park, and Margaret Hale, its manager, filed an eviction proceeding against the Soldals in an Illinois state court. Under the Illinois Forcible Entry and Detainer Act, Ill.Rev.Stat., ch. 110, ¶ 9-101 et seq. (1991), a tenant cannot be dispossessed absent a judgment of eviction. The suit was dismissed on June 2, 1987. A few months later, in August 1987, the owner brought a second proceeding of eviction, claiming nonpayment of rent. The case was set for trial on September 22, 1987.

Rather than await judgment in their favor, Terrace Properties and Hale, contrary to Illinois law, chose to evict the Soldals forcibly two weeks prior to the scheduled hearing. On September 4, Hale notified the Cook County's Sheriff's Department that she was going to remove the trailer home from the park, and requested the presence of sheriff deputies to forestall any possible resistance. Later that day, two Terrace Properties employees arrived at the Soldals' home accompanied by Cook County Deputy Sheriff O'Neil. The employees proceeded to wrench the sewer and water connections off the side of the trailer home, disconnect the phone, tear off the trailer's canopy and skirting, and hook the home to a tractor. Meanwhile, O'Neil explained to Edward Soldal that "he was there to see that [Soldal] didn't interfere with [Willoway's] work."

By this time, two more deputy sheriffs had arrived at the scene and Soldal told them that he wished to file a complaint for criminal trespass. They referred him to Deputy Lieutenant Jones, who was in Hale's office. Jones asked Soldal to wait outside while he remained closeted with Hale and other Terrace Properties employees for over 20 minutes. After talking to a district attorney and making Soldal wait another half hour, Jones told Soldal that he would not accept a complaint because "it was between the landlord and the tenant . . . [and] they were going to go ahead and continue to move out the trailer." Throughout this period, the deputy sheriffs knew that Terrace Properties did not have an eviction order and that its actions were unlawful. Eventually, and in the presence of an additional two deputy sheriffs, the Willoway workers pulled the trailer free of its moorings and towed it onto the street. Later, it was hauled to a neighboring property.

On September 9, the state judge assigned to the pending eviction proceedings ruled that the eviction had been unauthorized and ordered Terrace Properties to return the Soldals' home to the lot. The home, however, was badly damaged. The Soldals brought this action under 42 U.S.C. § 1983, alleging a violation of their rights under the Fourth and Fourteenth Amendments. They claimed that Terrace Properties and Hale had conspired with Cook County deputy sheriffs to unreasonably seize and remove the Soldals' trailer home. The District Judge granted defendants' motion for summary judgment on the grounds that the Soldals had failed to adduce any evidence to support their conspiracy theory and, therefore, the existence of state action necessary under § 1983.

The Court of Appeals for the Seventh Circuit, construing the facts in petitioners' favor, accepted their contention that there was state action. However, it went on to hold that the

removal of the Soldals' trailer did not constitute a seizure for purposes of the Fourth Amendment or a deprivation of due process for purposes of the Fourteenth.

On rehearing, a majority of the Seventh Circuit, sitting en banc, reaffirmed the panel decision."

B. Counsel of Record / ACLU Attorney

ACLU Side (Petitioner / Appellant): John L. Stainthorp argued the cause for appellant.

Opposing Side (Respondent / Appellee): Kenneth L. Gillis argued the cause for appellee.

III. AMICI CURIAE

ACLU Side (Petitioner / Appellant)

Brief of amici curiae filed on behalf of the ACLU, et al., by James D. Holzhauer, Timothy S. Bishop, John A. Powell, Steven R. Shapiro, Harvey M. Grossman, and Alan K. Chen.

Opposing Side (Respondent / Appellee)

Brief of amici curiae filed on behalf of the National League of Cities, et al., by Richard Ruda, Carter G. Phillips, Mark D. Hopson, and Mark E. Haddad.

IV. THE SUPREME COURT'S DECISION

"The Fourth Amendment, made applicable to the States by the Fourteenth [Amendment], provides in pertinent part that the 'right of the people to be secure in their persons, houses, papers, and effects, against unreasonable searches and seizures, shall not be violated . . . .'

A 'seizure' of property. . . occurs when 'there is some meaningful interference with an individual's possessory interests in that property.' . . . As a result of the state action in this case, the Soldals' domicile was not only seized, it literally was carried away, giving new meaning to the term 'mobile home.' We fail to see how being unceremoniously dispossessed of one's home in the manner alleged to have occurred here can be viewed as anything but a seizure invoking the protection of the Fourth Amendment. Whether the Amendment was in fact violated is, of course, a different question that requires determining if the seizure was reasonable. That inquiry entails the weighing of various factors and is not before us. . . .

We do not agree with [the Court of Appeals for the Seventh Circuit's] interpretation of the Fourth Amendment. The Amendment protects the people from unreasonable searches and seizures of 'their persons, houses, papers, and effects.' This language surely cuts against the novel holding below, and our cases unmistakably hold that the Amendment protects property as well as privacy. . . .

We . . . see no justification for departing from our prior cases. In our view, the reason why an officer might enter a house or effectuate a seizure is wholly irrelevant to the threshold question whether the Amendment applies. What matters is the intrusion on the people's security from governmental interference. Therefore, the right against unreasonable seizures would be no less transgressed if the seizure of the house was undertaken to collect evidence, verify compliance with a housing regulation, effect an eviction by the police, or on a whim, for no reason at all. . . .

The complaint here alleges that respondents, acting under color of state law, dispossessed the Soldals of their trailer home by physically tearing it from its foundation and towing it to another lot. Taking these allegations as true, this was no 'garden-variety' landlord-tenant or commercial dispute. The facts alleged suffice to constitute a 'seizure' within the meaning of the Fourth Amendment, for they plainly implicate the interests protected by that provision. The judgment of the Court of Appeals is, accordingly, reversed, and the case is remanded for further proceedings consistent with this opinion."

V. JUSTICE VOTE

9 Pro ACLU Side vs. 0 Con Opposing Side

ACLU Side (Petitioner / Appellant)

1. White, B. – Wrote majority opinion
2. Blackmun, H. – Joined majority opinion

3. Stevens, J. – Joined majority opinion
4. Souter, D. – Joined majority opinion
5. Kennedy, A. – Joined majority opinion
6. O'Connor, S. – Joined majority opinion
7. Scalia, A. – Joined majority opinion
8. Rehnquist, W. – Joined majority opinion
9. Thomas, C. – Joined majority opinion

VI. A WIN OR LOSS FOR THE ACLU?

The ACLU filed as amicus curiae urging reversal of the judgment of the Court of Appeals; the Supreme Court reversed and remanded in a 9-0 vote, giving the ACLU an apparent win.

750. Crosby v. United States

(Decided January 13, 1993; 506 U.S. 255)

I. ISSUE

A. Issues Discussed

Criminal procedure, Fifth Amendment, Sixth Amendment

B. Legal Question Presented

"[W]hether Federal Rule of Criminal Procedure 43 permits the trial in absentia of a defendant who absconds prior to trial and is absent at its beginning."

C. Supreme Court's Answer

The rule does not permit a trial in absentia when the defendant is absent at the beginning of trial.

II. CASE SUMMARY

A. Background

"In April 1988, a federal grand jury in the District of Minnesota indicted petitioner Michael Crosby and others on a number of counts of mail fraud. . . . Crosby appeared before a federal magistrate on June 15, 1988, and, upon his plea of not guilty, was conditionally released from detention after agreeing to post a $100,000 bond and remain in the State. Subsequently, he attended pretrial conferences and hearings with his attorney and was advised that the trial was scheduled to begin on October 12.

Crosby did not appear on October 12, however, nor could he be found. . . . When the District Court raised the subject of conducting the trial in Crosby's absence, Crosby's attorney objected. Nevertheless, after several days of delay and a fruitless search for Crosby, the court, upon a formal request from the Government, decided that trial would commence on October 17. The court ordered Crosby's $100,000 bond forfeited and stated for the record its findings that Crosby had been given adequate notice of the trial date, that his absence was knowing and deliberate, and that requiring the Government to try Crosby separately from his codefendants would present extreme difficulty for the Government, witnesses, counsel, and the court. It further concluded that Crosby voluntarily had waived his constitutional right to be present during the trial, and that the public interest in proceeding with the trial in his absence outweighed his interest in being present during the proceedings. Trial began on October 17, with petitioner's counsel actively participating, and continued in Crosby's absence until November 18, when the jury returned verdicts of guilty on charges against Crosby and two of his codefendants. One codefendant was acquitted.

Approximately six months later, Crosby was arrested in Florida and brought back to Minnesota, where he was sentenced to 20 years in prison followed by 5 years on probation with specified conditions. Crosby's convictions were upheld by the Court of Appeals, which rejected his argument that Federal Rule of Criminal Procedure 43 forbids the trial in absentia of a defendant who is not present at the beginning of trial."

The Supreme Court granted certiorari to review the case and reversed.

B. Counsel of Record / ACLU Attorney

ACLU Side (Petitioner / Appellant): Mark D. Nyvold, by appointment of the court, argued the cause for appellant.

Opposing Side (Respondent / Appellee): Richard H. Seamon argued the cause for the United States.

III. AMICI CURIAE

ACLU Side (Petitioner / Appellant)

Brief of amici curiae filed on behalf of the ACLU by Steven R. Shapiro and John A. Powell.

Opposing Side (Respondent / Appellee)

No briefs of amici curiae were filed in support of appellee.

IV. THE SUPREME COURT'S DECISION

"Rule 43 provides in relevant part:

(a) PRESENCE REQUIRED. The defendant shall be present at the arraignment, at the time of the plea, at every stage of the trial including the impaneling of the jury and the return of the verdict, and at the imposition of sentence, except as otherwise provided by this rule.

(b) CONTINUED PRESENCE NOT REQUIRED. The further progress of the trial to and including the return of the verdict shall not be prevented and the defendant shall be considered to have waived the right to be present whenever a defendant, initially present,

'(1) is voluntarily absent after the trial has commenced . . . .'

The Government concedes that the Rule does not specifically authorize the trial in absentia of a defendant who was not present at the beginning of his trial. The Government argues, nonetheless, that 'Rule 43 does not purport to contain a comprehensive listing of the circumstances under which the right to be present may be waived.' . . .

The language, history, and logic of Rule 43 support a straightforward interpretation that prohibits the trial in absentia of a defendant who is not present at the beginning of trial. Because we find Rule 43 dispositive, we do not reach Crosby's claim that his trial in abstentia was also prohibited by the Constitution.

The judgment of the Court of Appeals is reversed, and the case is remanded for further proceedings consistent with this opinion."

V. JUSTICE VOTE

9 Pro ACLU Side vs. 0 Con Opposing Side

ACLU Side (Petitioner / Appellant)

1. Blackmun, H. – Wrote majority opinion
2. Rehnquist, W. – Joined majority opinion
3. Stevens, J. – Joined majority opinion
4. O'Connor, S. – Joined majority opinion
5. Scalia, A. – Joined majority opinion
6. Kennedy, A. – Joined majority opinion
7. Souter, D. – Joined majority opinion
8. Thomas, C. – Joined majority opinion
9. White, B. – Joined majority opinion

VI. A WIN OR LOSS FOR THE ACLU?

The ACLU filed a brief as amicus curiae urging reversal of the judgment of the Court of Appeals; the Supreme Court reversed in a 9-0 vote, giving the ACLU an apparent win.

751. Bray v. Alexandria Women's Health Clinic

(Decided January 13, 1993; 506 U.S. 263)

I. ISSUE

A. Issues Discussed

Civil rights, privacy, abortion

B. Legal Question Presented

"[W]hether the first clause of Rev.Stat. § 1980, 42 U.S.C. § 1985(3)—the surviving version of § 2 of the Civil Rights Act of 1871—provides a federal cause of action against persons obstructing access to abortion clinics."

C. Supreme Court's Answer

The clause does not provide a federal cause of action against persons obstruction access to abortion clinics.

II. CASE SUMMARY

A. Background

"Respondents are clinics that perform abortions and organizations that support legalized abortion and that have members who may wish to use abortion clinics. Petitioners are Operation Rescue, an unincorporated association whose members oppose abortion, and six individuals. Among its activities, Operation Rescue organizes antiabortion demonstrations in which participants trespass on, and obstruct general access to, the premises of abortion clinics. The individual petitioners organize and coordinate these demonstrations.

Respondents sued to enjoin petitioners from conducting demonstrations at abortion clinics in the Washington, D.C., metropolitan area. Following an expedited trial, the District Court ruled that petitioners had violated § 1985(3) by conspiring to deprive women seeking abortions of their right to interstate travel. The court also ruled for respondents on their pendent state-law claims of trespass and public nuisance. As relief on these three claims, the court enjoined petitioners from trespassing on, or obstructing access to, abortion clinics in specified Virginia counties and cities in the Washington, D.C., metropolitan area. Based on its § 1985(3) ruling and pursuant to 42 U.S.C. § 1988 , the court also ordered petitioners to pay respondents $27,687.55 in attorney's fees and costs.

The Court of Appeals for the Fourth Circuit affirmed . . . ."

The Supreme Court granted certiorari to review the case, reversed in part, vacated in part, and remanded.

B. Counsel of Record / ACLU Attorney

ACLU Side (Respondent / Appellee): Deborah A. Ellis reargued the cause for appellee. John H. Schafer originally argued the cause for appellee.

Opposing Side (Petitioner / Appellant): Jay Alan Sekulow reargued the cause for appellant.

Deputy Solicitor General Roberts reargued the cause for the United States, as amicus curiae, by special leave of Court.

III. AMICI CURIAE

ACLU Side (Respondent / Appellee)

Brief of amici curiae filed on behalf of the ACLU, et al., by Judith Levin, Steven R. Shapiro, John A. Powell, Burt Neuborne, and Elliot M. Mincberg.

Brief of amici curiae filed on behalf of the Attorney General of New York, et al., by Robert Abrams, Attorney General of New York, pro se; O. Peter Sherwood, Solicitor General; Sanford M. Cohen and Shelley B. Mayer, Assistant Attorneys General; and Mary Sue Terry, Attorney General of Virginia, pro se.

Brief of amici curiae filed on behalf of Falls Church, Virginia, by David R. Lasso.

Brief of amici curiae filed on behalf of the NAACP Legal Defense and Educational Fund, Inc., et al., by Julius L. Chambers, Charles Stephen Ralston, and Eric Schnapper.

Brief of amici curiae filed on behalf of the National Abortion Federation, et al., by Elaine Metlin, Roger K. Evans, and Eve W Paul.

Brief of amici curiae filed on behalf of 29 Organizations Committed to Women's Health and Women's Equality by Dawn Johnsen, Lois Eisner Murphy, and Marcy J. Wilder.

Opposing Side (Petitioner / Appellant)

Brief of amici curiae filed on behalf of the United States by Deputy Solicitor General Roberts, Solicitor General Starr, Assistant Attorney General Gerson, Paul J. Larkin, Jr., Barbara L. Herwig, and Lowell V. Sturgill, Jr.

Brief of amici curiae filed on behalf of American Victims of Abortion by James Bopp, Jr., and Richard E. Coleson.

Brief of amici curiae filed on behalf of Concerned Women for America by Andrew J. Ekonomou and Mark N. Troobnick.

Brief of amici curiae filed on behalf of Feminists for Life of America, et al., by Christine Smith Torre and Edward R. Grant.

Brief of amici curiae filed on behalf of the Free Congress Foundation by Eric A. Daly and Jordan Lorence.

Brief of amici curiae filed on behalf of the Rutherford Institute, et al., by John W Whitehead, Joseph P. Secola, and George J. Mercer.
Brief of amici curiae filed on behalf of the Southern Center for Law & Ethics by Albert L. Jordan.
Brief of amici curiae filed on behalf of Woman Exploited by Abortion, et al., by Samuel Brown Casey, Victor L. Smith, and David L. Llewellyn.
Brief of amici curiae filed on behalf of Daniel Berrigan, et al., by Wendall R. Bird and David J. Meyers.
Brief of amici curiae filed by James Joseph Lynch, Jr., pro se.
Brief of amici curiae filed on behalf of the National Right to Life Committee, Inc., et al., by James Bopp, Jr., and Barry A. Bostrom.
Brief of amici curiae filed on behalf of George Lucas, et al., by Lawrence J. Joyce and Craig H. Greenwood.

IV. THE SUPREME COURT'S DECISION

"To begin with, we reject the apparent conclusion of the District Court (which respondents make no effort to defend) that opposition to abortion constitutes discrimination against the 'class' of 'women seeking abortion.' Whatever may be the precise meaning of a 'class' for purposes of Griffin's speculative extension of § 1985(3) beyond race, the term unquestionably connotes something more than a group of individuals who share a desire to engage in conduct that the § 1985(3) defendant disfavors. Otherwise, innumerable tort plaintiffs would be able to assert causes of action under § 1985(3) by simply defining the aggrieved class as those seeking to engage in the activity the defendant has interfered with. This definitional ploy would convert the statute into the 'general federal tort law' it was the very purpose of the animus requirement to avoid. . . .

Some activities may be such an irrational object of disfavor that, if they are targeted, and if they also happen to be engaged in exclusively or predominantly by a particular class of people, an intent to disfavor that class can readily be presumed. A tax on wearing yarmulkes is a tax on Jews. But opposition to voluntary abortion cannot possibly be considered such an irrational surrogate for opposition to (or paternalism towards) women. Whatever one thinks of abortion, it cannot be denied that there are common and respectable reasons for opposing it, other than hatred of, or condescension toward (or indeed any view at all concerning), women as a class—as is evident from the fact that men and women are on both sides of the issue, just as men and women are on both sides of petitioners' unlawful demonstrations. . . .

Respondents have failed to show a conspiracy to violate the right of interstate travel for yet another reason: Petitioners' proposed demonstrations would not implicate that right. The federal guarantee of interstate travel does not transform state-law torts into federal offenses when they are intentionally committed against interstate travelers. Rather, it protects interstate travelers against two sets of burdens: 'the erection of actual barriers to interstate movement' and 'being treated differently' from intrastate travelers. . . . The other right alleged by respondents to have been intentionally infringed is the right to abortion. The District Court declined to rule on this contention, relying exclusively upon the right-of-interstate-travel theory; in our view it also is an inadequate basis for respondents' § 1985(3) claim. Whereas, unlike the right of interstate travel, the asserted right to abortion was assuredly 'aimed at' by the petitioners, deprivation of that federal right (whatever its contours) cannot be the object of a purely private conspiracy. . . .

Without a race- or class-based animus requirement, the 'hindrance' clause of this post-Civil War statute would have been an available weapon against the mass 'sit-ins' that were conducted for purposes of promoting desegregation in the 1960's—a wildly improbable result.

Even, moreover, if the 'hindrance'-clause claim did not fail for lack of class-based animus, it would still fail unless the 'hindrance' clause applies to a private conspiracy aimed at rights that are constitutionally protected only against official (as opposed to private) encroachment. . . .

Trespassing upon private property is unlawful in all States, as is, in many States and localities, intentionally obstructing the entrance to private premises. These offenses may be prosecuted criminally under state law, and may also be the basis for state civil damages. They do not, however, give rise to a federal cause of action simply because their objective is to prevent the performance of abortions, any more than they do so (as we have held) when their objective is to stifle free speech.

The judgment of the Court of Appeals is reversed in part and vacated in part, and the case is remanded for further proceedings consistent with this opinion."

V. JUSTICE VOTE

3 Pro ACLU Side vs. 6 Con Opposing Side

ACLU Side (Respondent / Appellee)

1. Stevens, J. – Wrote dissenting opinion
2. O'Connor, S. – Wrote dissenting opinion
3. Blackmun, H. – Joined Stevens' dissent, joined O'Connor's dissent

Opposing Side (Petitioner / Appellant)

1. Scalia, A. – Wrote majority opinion
2. Rehnquist, W. – Joined majority opinion
3. White, B. – Joined majority opinion
4. Kennedy, A. – Wrote concurring opinion
5. Thomas, C. – Joined majority opinion
6. Souter, D. – Wrote opinion concurring in part and dissenting in part

VI. A WIN OR LOSS FOR THE ACLU?

The ACLU filed as amicus curiae urging affirmance of the judgment of the Court of Appeals; the Supreme Court reversed in part and vacated in part in a 6-3 vote, giving the ACLU an apparent loss.

752. Brecht v. Abrahamson

(Decided April 21, 1993; 507 U.S. 619)

I. ISSUE

A. Issues Discussed

Criminal procedure, habeas corpus, Fourth Amendment, Fifth Amendment, Fourteenth Amendment

B. Legal Question Presented

'[W]hether the Chapman harmless-error standard applies in determining whether the prosecution's use for impeachment purposes of petitioner's post-Miranda silence, in violation of due process under Doyle v. Ohio, 426 U.S. 610 (1976), entitles petitioner to habeas corpus relief."

C. Supreme Court's Answer

The Chapman harmless-error standard does not apply. The Kotteakos standard applies and dictates the conclusion that petitioner is not entitled to habeas corpus relief.

II. CASE SUMMARY

A. Background

In a Wisconsin state court, Todd Brecht admitted shooting his brother-in-law, claiming it was accidental. Attempting to discredit Brecht's testimony, the State referenced that Brecht failed to tell anyone that the shooting was accidental before he was given his Miranda warnings. The State also referenced to his post-Miranda warning silence.

"The jury returned a guilty verdict, and petitioner was sentenced to life imprisonment. The Wisconsin Court of Appeals set the conviction aside on the ground that the State's references to petitioner's post-Miranda silence violated due process under Doyle v. Ohio, 426 U.S. 610 (1976), and that this error was sufficiently 'prejudicial' to require reversal. The Wisconsin Supreme Court reinstated the conviction. Although it agreed that the State's use of petitioner's post-Miranda silence was impermissible, the court determined that this error "was harmless beyond a reasonable doubt." . . .

Petitioner then sought a writ of habeas corpus under 28 U.S.C. § 2254, reasserting his Doyle claim. The District Court agreed that the State's use of petitioner's post-Miranda silence violated Doyle, but disagreed with the Wisconsin Supreme Court that this error was harmless beyond a reasonable doubt, and set aside the conviction. . . . The Court of Appeals for the Seventh Circuit reversed."

The Supreme Court granted certiorari to review the case and affirmed.

B. Counsel of Record / ACLU Attorney

ACLU Side (Petitioner / Appellant): Allen E. Shoenberger, by appointment of the Court, argued the cause for appellant.

Opposing Side (Respondent / Appellee): Sally L. Wellman, Assistant Attorney General of Wisconsin, argued the cause for appellee.

Attorney General Barr argued the cause for the United States, as amicus curiae, by special leave of Court.

III. AMICI CURIAE

ACLU Side (Petitioner / Appellant)

Brief of amici curiae filed on behalf of the ACLU, et al., by Steven R. Shapiro, John A. Powell, Leon Friedman, and Larry W Yackle.

Opposing Side (Respondent / Appellee)

Brief of amici curiae filed on behalf of the United States by Attorney General Barr, Solicitor General Starr, Assistant Attorney General Mueller, Deputy Solicitor General Roberts, Ronald J. Mann, and Vicki S. Marani.

Brief of amici curiae filed on behalf of the State of California, et al., by Daniel E. Lungren, Attorney General of California, George Williamson, Chief Assistant Attorney General, Dane R. Gillette, Deputy Attorney General, and Mark L. Krotoski, Special Assistant Attorney General; and James H. Evans, Attorney General of Alabama; Charles E. Cole, Attorney General of Alaska; Winston Bryant, Attorney General of Arkansas; Gale A. Norton, Attorney General of Colorado; Richard N. Palmer, Chief State's Attorney of Connecticut; Larry EchoHawk, Attorney General of Idaho; Linley E. Pearson, Attorney General of Indiana; Robert T. Stephan, Attorney General of Kansas; Chris Gorman, Attorney General of Kentucky; Richard P. Ieyoub, Attorney General of Louisiana; Frank J. Kelley, Attorney General of Michigan; Michael C. Moore, Attorney General of Mississippi; William L. Webster, Attorney General of Missouri; Marc Racicot, Attorney General of Montana; Don Stenberg, Attorney General of Nebraska; Frankie Sue Del Papa, Attorney General of Nevada; Robert J. Del Tufo, Attorney General of New Jersey; Lee Fisher, Attorney General of Ohio; Ernest D. Preate, Jr., Attorney General of Pennsylvania; Travis Medlock, Attorney General of South Carolina; Mark Barnett, Attorney General of South Dakota; Dan Morales, Attorney General of Texas; Paul Van Dam, Attorney General of Utah; Jeffrey L. Amestoy, Attorney General of Vermont; Kenneth O. Eikenberry, Attorney General of Washington; Mario J. Palumbo, Attorney General of West Virginia; and Joseph B. Meyer, Attorney General of Wyoming.

Brief of amici curiae filed on behalf of the County of Wayne, Michigan by John D. O'Hair, Timothy A. Baughman.

Brief of amici curiae filed on behalf of the Criminal Justice Legal Foundation by Kent S. Scheidegger and Charles L. Hobson.

IV. THE SUPREME COURT'S DECISION

"In Chapman v. California, 386 U.S. 18 (1967), we held that the standard for determining whether a conviction must be set aside because of federal constitutional error is whether the error 'was harmless beyond a reasonable doubt.' In this case we must decide whether the Chapman harmless-error standard applies in determining whether the prosecution's use for impeachment purposes of petitioner's post-Miranda silence, in violation of due process under Doyle v. Ohio, 426 U.S. 610 (1976), entitles petitioner to habeas corpus relief. We hold that it does not. Instead, the standard for determining whether habeas relief must be granted is whether the Doyle error 'had substantial and injurious effect or influence in determining the jury's verdict.' The Kotteakos harmless-error standard is better tailored to the nature and purpose of collateral review than the Chapman standard, and application of a less onerous harmless-error standard on habeas promotes the considerations underlying our habeas jurisprudence. Applying this standard, we conclude that petitioner is not entitled to habeas relief....

The first time petitioner claimed that the shooting was an accident was when he took the stand at trial. It was entirely proper—and probative—for the State to impeach his testimony by pointing out that petitioner had failed to tell anyone before the time he received his Miranda warnings at his arraignment about the shooting being an accident. Indeed, if the shooting was an accident, petitioner had every reason—including to clear his name and preserve evidence supporting his version of the events—to offer his account immediately following the shooting. On the other hand, the State's references to petitioner's silence after that point in time, or more generally to petitioner's failure to come forward with his version of events at any time before trial crossed the Doyle line. For it is conceivable that, once petitioner had been given his Miranda warnings, he decided to stand on his right to remain silent because he believed his silence would not be used against him at trial....

The State's references to petitioner's post-Miranda silence were infrequent, comprising less than two pages of the 900–page trial transcript in this case. And in view of the State's extensive and permissible references to petitioner's pre-Miranda silence—i.e., his failure to mention anything about the shooting being an accident to the officer who found him in the ditch, the man who gave him a ride to Winona, or the officers who eventually arrested him— its references to petitioner's post-Miranda silence were, in effect, cumulative. Moreover, the State's evidence of guilt was, if not overwhelming, certainly weighty. The path of the bullet through Mr. Hartman's body was inconsistent with petitioner's testimony that the rifle had discharged as he was falling. The police officers who searched the Hartmans' home found nothing in the downstairs hallway that could have caused petitioner to trip. The rifle was found outside the house (where Hartman was shot), not inside where petitioner claimed it had accidently fired, and there was a live round rammed in the gun's chamber, suggesting that petitioner had tried to fire a second shot. Finally, other circumstantial evidence, including the motive proffered by the State, also pointed to petitioner's guilt.

In light of the foregoing, we conclude that the Doyle error that occurred at petitioner's trial did not 'substantial[ly] . . . influence' the jury's verdict. Petitioner is therefore not entitled to habeas relief, and the judgment of the Court of Appeals is affirmed."

V. JUSTICE VOTE

4 Pro ACLU Side vs. 5 Con Opposing Side

ACLU Side (Petitioner / Appellant)

1. White, B. – Wrote dissenting opinion
2. Blackmun, H. – Wrote dissenting opinion, joined White's dissent
3. Souter, D. – Wrote dissenting opinion, joined White's dissent in part
4. O'Connor, S. – Wrote dissenting opinion

Opposing Side (Respondent / Appellee)

1. Rehnquist, W. – Wrote majority opinion
2. Stevens, J. – Wrote concurring opinion
3. Scalia, A. – Joined majority opinion
4. Kennedy, A. – Joined majority opinion
5. Thomas, C. – Joined majority opinion

VI. A WIN OR LOSS FOR THE ACLU?

The ACLU filed as amicus curiae urging reversal of the judgment of the Court of Appeals for the Seventh Circuit; the Supreme Court affirmed in a 5-4 vote, giving the ACLU an apparent loss.

753. Withrow v. Williams

(Decided April 21, 1993; 507 U.S. 680)

I. ISSUE

A. Issues Discussed

Criminal procedure, habeas corpus, Fourteenth Amendment, Fifth Amendment, self-incrimination, Fourth Amendment, search and seizure

B. Legal Question Presented

Whether "Stone's restriction on the exercise of federal habeas jurisdiction . . . extend[s] to a state prisoner's claim that his conviction rests on statements obtained in violation of the safeguards mandated by Miranda v. Arizona, 384 U.S. 436 (1966)."

C. Supreme Court's Answer

Stone's restriction does not extend to a state prisoner's claim that his conviction rests on statements obtained in violation of Miranda safeguards.

II. CASE SUMMARY

A. Background

Respondent, Robert Williams, was questioned by police regarding a murder. He was not read his Miranda rights and made several self-incriminating statements. Eventually, about 40 minutes into the questioning, the police gave Williams his Miranda warning. Williams waived his rights and made further self-incriminating statements.

"Before trial, Williams moved to suppress his responses to the interrogations . . . The court declined to suppress the statements . . . ruling that the police had given Williams a timely warning of his Miranda rights. A bench trial led to Williams's conviction on two counts each of first-degree murder and possession of a firearm during the commission of a felony and resulted in two concurrent life sentences. The Court of Appeals of Michigan affirmed . . . and the Supreme Court of Michigan denied leave to appeal. [The U.S. Supreme Court] denied the ensuing petition for writ of certiorari.

Williams then began this action pro se by petitioning for a writ of habeas corpus in the District Court, alleging a violation of his Miranda rights as the principal ground for relief. The District Court granted relief.... The Court of Appeals affirmed ...."

The Supreme Court granted certiorari to review the case, affirmed in part, reversed in part, and remanded.

B. Counsel of Record / ACLU Attorney

ACLU Side (Respondent / Appellee): Seth P. Waxman, by appointment of the Court, argued the cause for appellee.

Opposing Side (Petitioner / Appellant): Jeffrey Caminsky argued the cause for appellant.

Deputy Solicitor General Roberts argued the cause for the United States, as amicus curiae, by special leave of Court.

III. AMICI CURIAE

ACLU Side (Respondent / Appellee)

Brief of amici curiae filed on behalf of the ACLU, et al., by Larry W. Yackle, Steven R. Shapiro, Leslie A. Harris, and John A. Powell.

Brief of amici curiae filed on behalf of the American Bar Association by Talbot D'Alemberte and William J. Mertens.

Brief of amici curiae filed on behalf of the Police Foundation, et al., by Joseph D. Tydings and Michael Millemann.

Opposing Side (Petitioner / Appellant)

Brief of amici curiae filed on behalf of the United States by Deputy Solicitor General Roberts, Solicitor General Starr, Assistant Attorney General Mueller, and Ronald J. Mann.

Brief of amici curiae filed on behalf of the State of California, et al., by Daniel E. Lungren, Attorney General of California; George Williamson, Chief Assistant Attorney General; Donald E. De Nicola, Deputy Attorney General; Mark L. Krotoski, Special Assistant Attorney General; James H. Evans, Attorney General of Alabama; Charles E. Cole, Attorney General of Alaska; Grant Woods, Attorney General of Arizona; Winston Bryant, Attorney General of Arkansas; Gale A. Norton, Attorney General of Colorado; Richard N. Palmer, Chief State's Attorney of Connecticut; Charles M. Oberly III, Attorney General of Delaware; Robert A. Butterworth, Attorney General of Florida; Michael J. Bowers, Attorney General of Georgia; Warren Price III, Attorney General of Hawaii; Larry EchoHawk, Attorney General of Idaho; Linley E. Pearson, Attorney General of Indiana; Robert T. Stephan, Attorney General of Kansas; Chris Gorman, Attorney General of Kentucky; Richard P. Ieyoub, Attorney General of Louisiana; Scott Harshbarger, Attorney General of Massachusetts; Michael C. Moore, Attorney General of Mississippi; William L. Webster, Attorney General of Missouri; Marc Racicot, Attorney General of Montana; Don Stenberg, Attorney General of Nebraska; Frankie Sue Del Papa, Attorney General of Nevada; John P. Arnold, Attorney General of New Hampshire; Robert J. Del Tufo, Attorney General of New Jersey; Tom Udall, Attorney General of New Mexico; Lacy H. Thornburg, Attorney General of North Carolina; Lee Fisher, Attorney General of Ohio; T. Travis Medlock, Attorney General of South Carolina; Mark W. Barnett, Attorney General of South Dakota; Charles W. Burson, Attorney General of Tennessee; R. Paul Van Dam, Attorney General of Utah; Jeffrey L. Amestoy, Attorney General of Vermont; Mary Sue Terry, Attorney General of Virginia; Kenneth O. Eikenberry, Attorney General of Washington; Mario J. Palumbo, Attorney General of West Virginia; and Joseph B. Meyer, Attorney General of Wyoming.

Brief of amici curiae filed on behalf of Americans for Effective Law Enforcement, Inc., et al., by Thomas J. Charron, Bernard J. Farber, Fred E. Inbau, Wayne W. Schmidt, and James P. Manak.

Brief of amici curiae filed on behalf of the Criminal Justice Legal Foundation by Kent S. Scheidegger.

IV. THE SUPREME COURT'S DECISION

"We have made it clear that Stone's limitation on federal habeas relief was not jurisdictional in nature, but rested on prudential concerns counseling against the application of the Fourth Amendment exclusionary rule on collateral review. [T]he costs of applying the exclusionary rule on habeas were comparatively great. We reasoned that doing so would not only exclude reliable evidence and divert attention from the central question of guilt, but would also intrude upon the public interest ....

As we explained in Stone, the Mapp rule 'is not a personal constitutional right,' but serves to deter future constitutional violations; although it mitigates the juridical consequences of invading the defendant's privacy, the exclusion of evidence at trial can do nothing to remedy the completed and wholly extrajudicial Fourth Amendment violation. . . .

Miranda differs from Mapp in both respects. 'Prophylactic' though it may be, in protecting a defendant's Fifth Amendment privilege against self-incrimination, Miranda safeguards 'a fundamental trial right.' . . .

Finally, and most importantly, eliminating review of Miranda claims would not significantly benefit the federal courts in their exercise of habeas jurisdiction, or advance the cause of federalism in any substantial way. . . .

We thus fail to see how abdicating Miranda's bright-line (or, at least, brighter-line) rules in favor of an exhaustive totality-of-circumstances approach on habeas would do much of anything to lighten the burdens placed on busy federal courts. We likewise fail to see how purporting to eliminate Miranda issues from federal habeas would go very far to relieve such tensions as Miranda may now raise between the two judicial systems. Relegation of habeas petitioners to straight involuntariness claims would not likely reduce the amount of litigation, and each such claim would in any event present a legal question requiring an 'independent federal determination' on habeas. . . .

The judgment of the Court of Appeals is affirmed in part and reversed in part, and the case is remanded for further proceedings consistent with this opinion."

V. JUSTICE VOTE

5 Pro ACLU Side vs. 4 Con Opposing Side

ACLU Side (Respondent / Appellee)

1. Souter, D. – Wrote majority opinion
2. White, B. – Joined majority opinion
3. Blackmun, H. – Joined majority opinion
4. Stevens, J. – Joined majority opinion
5. Kennedy, A. – Joined majority opinion

Opposing Side (Petitioner / Appellant)

1. O'Connor, S. – Wrote opinion concurring in part and dissenting in part
2. Rehnquist, W. – Joined O'Connor's opinion
3. Scalia, A. – Wrote opinion concurring in part and dissenting in part
4. Thomas, C. – Joined Scalia's opinion

VI. A WIN OR LOSS FOR THE ACLU?

The ACLU filed a brief as amicus curiae urging affirmance of the judgment of the Court of Appeals; the Supreme Court reversed in part and affirmed in part in a 5-4 vote, giving the ACLU an apparent win.

754. Gilmore v. Taylor

(Decided June 7, 1993; 508 U.S. 333)

I. ISSUE

A. Issues Discussed

Criminal procedure, habeas corpus, Fourteenth Amendment

B. Legal Question Presented

Whether "the rule announced in Falconer was . . . dictated by prior precedent and is therefore [not] 'new' within the meaning of Teague v. Lane."

C. Supreme Court's Answer

The rule in Falconer was not dictated by prior precedent. The rule is new and cannot provide a basis for habeas in this case.

II. CASE SUMMARY

A. Background

"Respondent Kevin Taylor was convicted of murder by an Illinois jury and sentenced to 35 years' imprisonment. After his conviction and sentence became final, he sought federal habeas relief on the ground that the jury instructions given at his trial violated the Fourteenth Amendment's Due Process Clause. The Court of Appeals for the Seventh Circuit granted relief on the basis of its recent decision in Falconer v. Lane, 905 F.2d 1129 (1990), which held that the Illinois pattern jury instructions on murder and voluntary manslaughter [used in Taylor's case] were unconstitutional because they allowed a jury to return a murder verdict without considering whether the defendant possessed a mental state that would support a voluntary-manslaughter verdict instead."

The Supreme Court granted certiorari to review the case and reversed.

B. Counsel of Record / ACLU Attorney

ACLU Side (Respondent / Appellee): Lawrence C. Marshall, by appointment of the Court, argued the cause for appellee.

Opposing Side (Petitioner / Appellant): Mark E. Wilson, Assistant Attorney General of Illinois, argued the cause for appellant.

III. AMICI CURIAE

ACLU Side (Respondent / Appellee)

Brief of amici curiae filed on behalf of the ACLU, et al., by Larry W. Yackle, Steven R. Shapiro, Leslie A. Harris, John A. Powell, and Harvey Grossman.

Brief of amici curiae filed on behalf of Nicholas deB. Katzenbach, et al., by George N. Leighton and George H. Kendall.

Opposing Side (Petitioner / Appellant)

Brief of amici curiae filed on behalf of the Criminal Justice Legal Foundation Kent S. Scheidegger and Charles L. Hobson.

IV. THE SUPREME COURT'S DECISION

"Subject to two narrow exceptions, a case that is decided after a defendant's conviction and sentence become final may not provide the basis for federal habeas relief if it announces a 'new rule.' [A] decision announces a new rule 'if the result was not dictated by precedent existing at the time the defendant's conviction became final.' . . .

We begin our analysis with the actual flaw found by the Falconer court in the challenged jury instructions. It was not that they somehow lessened the State's burden of proof below that constitutionally required by cases such as In re Winship, 397 U. S. 358 (1970); nor was it that the instructions affirmatively misstated applicable state law. Rather, the flaw identified by the Falconer court was that when the jury instructions were read consecutively, with the elements of murder set forth before the elements of voluntary manslaughter, a juror could conclude that the defendant was guilty of murder after applying the elements of that offense without continuing on to decide whether the elements of voluntary manslaughter were also made out, so as to justify returning a verdict on that lesser offense instead.

In concluding that this defect violated due process, the Falconer court relied on Cupp v. Naughten . . . . We think Cupp is an unlikely progenitor of the rule announced in Falconer, a view now shared by the Seventh Circuit.

[R]espondent argues that the right to present a defense includes the right to have the jury consider it, and that confusing instructions on state law which prevent a jury from considering an affirmative defense therefore violate due process. But such an expansive reading of our cases would make a nullity of the rule reaffirmed in Estelle v. McGuire, supra, that instructional errors of state law generally may not form the basis for federal habeas relief. And the level of generality at which respondent invokes this line of cases is far too great to provide any meaningful guidance for purposes of our Teague inquiry.

For the foregoing reasons, we disagree with the Seventh Circuit and respondent that our precedent foreordained the result in Falconer, and therefore hold that the rule announced in Falconer is 'new' within the meaning of Teague. . . .

Because the rule announced in Falconer is 'new' within the meaning of Teague and does not fall into one of Teague's exceptions, it cannot provide the basis for federal habeas relief in respondent's case. The judgment of the Court of Appeals is therefore reversed."

V. JUSTICE VOTE

2 Pro ACLU Side vs. 7 Con Opposing Side

ACLU Side (Respondent / Appellee)

1. Blackmun, H. – Wrote dissenting opinion
2. Stevens, J. – Joined Blackmun's dissent

Opposing Side (Petitioner / Appellant)

1. Rehnquist, W. – Wrote majority opinion
2. Scalia, A. – Joined majority opinion
3. Kennedy, A. – Joined majority opinion
4. Thomas, C. – Joined majority opinion
5. Souter, D. – Joined majority opinion
6. O'Connor, S. – Wrote concurring opinion
7. White, B. – Joined O'Connor's concurrence

VI. A WIN OR LOSS FOR THE ACLU?

The ACLU filed a brief as amicus curiae urging affirmance of the judgment of the Court of Appeals; the Supreme Court reversed in a 7-2 vote, giving the ACLU an apparent loss.

755. Minnesota v. Dickerson

(Decided June 7, 1993; 508 U.S. 366)

I. ISSUE

A. Issues Discussed

Criminal justice, drugs, Fourth Amendment, search and seizure

B. Legal Question Presented

"[W]hether the Fourth Amendment permits the seizure of contraband detected through a police officer's sense of touch during a protective patdown search."

C. Supreme Court's Answer

The Fourth Amendment does not permit seizure of contraband in this circumstance.

II. CASE SUMMARY

A. Background

"On the evening of November 9, 1989, two Minneapolis police officers were patrolling an area on the city's north side in a marked squad car. At about 8:15 p.m., one of the officers observed respondent leaving a 12–unit apartment building on Morgan Avenue North. The officer, having previously responded to complaints of drug sales in the building's hallways and having executed several search warrants on the premises, considered the building to be a notorious 'crack house.' [R]espondent began walking toward the police but, upon spotting the squad car and making eye contact with one of the officers, abruptly halted and began walking in the opposite direction. His suspicion aroused, this officer watched as respondent turned and entered an alley on the other side of the apartment building. Based upon respondent's seemingly evasive actions and the fact that he had just left a building known for cocaine traffic, the officers decided to stop respondent and investigate further.

The officers pulled their squad car into the alley and ordered respondent to stop and submit to a patdown search. The search revealed no weapons, but the officer conducting the search did take an interest in a small lump in respondent's nylon jacket. The officer later testified:

'[A]s I pat-searched the front of his body, I felt a lump, a small lump, in the front pocket. I examined it with my fingers and it slid and it felt to be a lump of crack cocaine in cellophane.'

The officer then reached into respondent's pocket and retrieved a small plastic bag containing one fifth of one gram of crack cocaine. Respondent was arrested and charged in Hennepin County District Court with possession of a controlled substance.

Before trial, respondent moved to suppress the cocaine. The trial court . . . ruled that the officers' seizure of the cocaine did not violate the Fourth Amendment . . . . His suppression motion having failed, respondent proceeded to trial and was found guilty.

On appeal, the Minnesota Court of Appeals reversed. . . . The Minnesota Supreme Court affirmed. Like the Court of Appeals, the State Supreme Court held that both the stop and the frisk of respondent were valid under Terry, but found the seizure of the cocaine to be unconstitutional. The court expressly refused 'to extend the plain view doctrine to the sense of touch' on the grounds that 'the sense of touch is inherently less immediate and less reliable than the sense of sight' and that 'the sense of touch is far more intrusive into the personal privacy that is at the core of the [F]ourth [A]mendment.'"

The U.S. Supreme Court granted certiorari to review the case and affirmed.

B. Counsel of Record / ACLU Attorney

ACLU Side (Respondent / Appellee): Peter W. Gorman argued the cause for appellee

Opposing Side (Petitioner / Appellant): Michael O. Freeman argued the cause for appellant.

Richard H. Seamon argued the cause for the United States, as amicus curiae, by special leave of Court.

III. AMICI CURIAE

ACLU Side (Respondent / Appellee)

Brief of amici curiae filed on behalf of the ACLU, et al., by John F. Savarese, Stuart C. Berman, Steven R. Shapiro, and Deborah Gilman.

Brief of amici curiae filed on behalf of the National Association of Criminal Defense Lawyers by David M. Eldridge.

Opposing Side (Petitioner / Appellant)

Brief of amici curiae filed on behalf of the United States by Richard H. Seamon, Solicitor General Starr, Assistant Attorney General Mueller, Deputy Solicitor General Bryson, and Kathleen A. Felton.

Brief of amici curiae filed on behalf of Americans for Effective Law Enforcement, Inc., et al., by Fred Inbau, Wayne W. Schmidt, James P. Manak, Roy C. Kime, Richard M. Weintraub, and Robert H. Macy.

IV. THE SUPREME COURT'S DECISION

"Where, as here, 'an officer who is executing a valid search for one item seizes a different item,' this Court rightly 'has been sensitive to the danger . . . that officers will enlarge a specific authorization, furnished by a warrant or an exigency, into the equivalent of a general warrant to rummage and seize at will.'

[T]he officer's continued exploration of respondent's pocket after having concluded that it contained no weapon was unrelated to '[t]he sole justification of the search [under Terry:] . . . the protection of the police officer and others nearby.'' . . .

Although the officer was lawfully in a position to feel the lump in respondent's pocket, because Terry entitled him to place his hands upon respondent's jacket, the court below determined that the incriminating character of the object was not immediately apparent to him. Rather, the officer determined that the item was contraband only after conducting a further search, one not authorized by Terry or by any other exception to the warrant requirement. Because this further search of respondent's pocket was constitutionally invalid, the seizure of the cocaine that followed is likewise unconstitutional. . . .

For these reasons, the judgment of the Minnesota Supreme Court is affirmed."

V. JUSTICE VOTE

9 Pro ACLU Side vs. 0 Con Opposing Side

ACLU Side (Respondent / Appellee)

1. White, B. – Wrote majority opinion
2. Stevens, J. – Joined majority opinion
3. O'Connor, S. – Joined majority opinion
4. Scalia, A. – Wrote concurring opinion
5. Kennedy, A. – Joined majority opinion
6. Souter, D. – Joined majority opinion
7. Rehnquist, W. – Wrote opinion concurring in part and dissenting in part
8. Blackmun, H. – Joined Rehnquist's opinion
9. Thomas, C. – Joined Rehnquist's opinion

VI. A WIN OR LOSS FOR THE ACLU?

The ACLU filed as amicus curiae urging affirmance of the judgment of the Minnesota Supreme Court; the U.S. Supreme Court affirmed in a 9-0 vote, giving the ACLU an apparent win.

756. Lamb's Chapel v. Center Moriches Union Free School District

(Decided June 7, 1993; 508 U.S. 384)

I. ISSUE

A. Issues Discussed

First Amendment, freedoms of speech, press and association, Establishment Clause, Free Exercise Clause

B. Legal Question Presented

"[W]hether . . . it violates the Free Speech Clause of the First Amendment, made applicable to the States by the Fourteenth Amendment, to deny a church access to school premises to exhibit for public viewing and for assertedly religious purposes, a film series dealing with family and child-rearing issues faced by parents today."

C. Supreme Court's Answer

It violates the Free Speech Clause of the First Amendment for a school district to deny a church access to school premises for a film viewing where a school allows similar access for non-religious groups.

II. CASE SUMMARY

A. Background

"[T]he Board of Center Moriches Union Free School District (District) has issued rules and regulations with respect to the use of school property when not in use for school purposes. . . . Rule 7 . . . , consistent with the judicial interpretation of state law, provides that '[t]he school premises shall not be used by any group for religious purposes.' . . .

Petitioners (Church) are Lamb's Chapel, an evangelical church in the community of Center Moriches, and its pastor John Steigerwald. Twice the Church applied to the District for permission to use school facilities to show a six-part film series containing lectures by Doctor James Dobson. . . . The District denied the first application, saying that '[t]his film does appear to be church related and therefore your request must be refused.' The second application for permission to use school premises for showing the film series, which described it as a 'Family oriented movie—from a Christian perspective,' was denied using identical language.

The Church brought suit in the District Court, challenging the denial as a violation of the Freedom of Speech and Assembly Clauses, the Free Exercise Clause, and the Establishment Clause of the First Amendment, as well as the Equal Protection Clause of the Fourteenth Amendment. As to each cause of action, the Church alleged that the actions were undertaken under color of state law, in violation of 42 U.S.C. § 1983. The District Court granted summary judgment for respondents, rejecting all the Church's claims. . . . The Court of Appeals affirmed the judgment of the District Court 'in all respects.'"

The Supreme Court granted certiorari to review the case and reversed.

B. Counsel of Record / ACLU Attorney

ACLU Side (Petitioner / Appellant): Jay Alan Sekulow argued the cause for appellant.

Opposing Side (Respondent / Appellee): John W. Hoefling argued the cause for appellee.

Robert Abrams, Attorney General of New York, filed a brief, pro se.

III. AMICI CURIAE

ACLU Side (Petitioner / Appellant)

Brief of amici curiae filed on behalf of the ACLU, et al., by David H. Remes, T. Jeremy Gunn, Kif Augustine Adams, Steven R. Shapiro, John A. Powell, and Elliot M. Mincberg.

Brief of amici curiae filed on behalf of the United States by Solicitor General Starr, Assistant Attorney General Gerson, Deputy Solicitor General Roberts, Edward C. DuMont, Anthony J. Steinmeyer, and Lowell V. Sturgill, Jr.

Brief of amici curiae filed on behalf of the American Federation of Labor and Congress of Industrial Organizations by Robert M. Weinberg, Virginia A. Seitz, Laurence Gold, and Walter A. Kamiat.

Brief of amici curiae filed on behalf of the Christian Legal Society, et al., by Kimberlee Wood Colby, Steven T. McFarland, Bradley P. Jacob, Thomas C. Berg, Michael S. Paulsen, and Karon Owen Bowdre.

Brief of amici curiae filed on behalf of Concerned Women for America, et al., by Wendell R. Bird and David J. Myers.

Brief of amici curiae filed on behalf of the National Jewish Commission on Law and Public Affairs by Nathan Lewin and Dennis Rapps.

Brief of amici curiae filed on behalf of the Rutherford Institute by James J. Knicely and John W. Whitehead.

Opposing Side (Respondent / Appellee)

Brief of amici curiae filed on behalf of the New York State School Boards Association, et al., by Jay Worona, Pilar Sokol, and Louis Grument.

IV. THE SUPREME COURT'S DECISION

"There is no question that the District, like the private owner of property, may legally preserve the property under its control for the use to which it is dedicated. It is also common ground that the District need not have permitted after-hours use of its property for any of the uses permitted by N.Y. Educ. Law § 414. The District, however, did open its property for 2 of the 10 uses permitted by § 414. . . .

With respect to public property that is not a designated public forum open for indiscriminate public use for communicative purposes, we have said that '[c]ontrol over access to a nonpublic forum can be based on subject matter and speaker identity so long as the distinctions drawn are reasonable in light of the purpose served by the forum and are viewpoint neutral.' The Court of Appeals appeared to recognize that the total ban on using District property for religious purposes could survive First Amendment challenge only if excluding this category of speech was reasonable and viewpoint neutral. The court's conclusion in this case was that Rule 7 met this test. We cannot agree with this holding, for Rule 7 was unconstitutionally applied in this case. . . .

The film series involved here no doubt dealt with a subject otherwise permissible under Rule 10, and its exhibition was denied solely because the series dealt with the subject from a religious standpoint. The principle that has emerged from our cases 'is that the First Amendment forbids the government to regulate speech in ways that favor some viewpoints or ideas at the expense of others.' . . .

The showing of this film series would not have been during school hours, would not have been sponsored by the school, and would have been open to the public, not just to church members. The District property had repeatedly been used by a wide variety of private organizations. Under these circumstances . . . , there would have been no realistic danger that the community would think that the District was endorsing religion or any particular creed, and any benefit to religion or to the Church would have been no more than incidental. [P]ermitting District property to be used to exhibit the film series involved in this case would not have been an establishment of religion under the three-part test articulated in Lemon v. Kurtzman, 403 U.S. 602 (1971): The challenged governmental action has a secular purpose, does not have the principal or primary effect of advancing or inhibiting religion, and does not foster an excessive entanglement with religion. . . .

For the reasons stated in this opinion, the judgment of the Court of Appeals is reversed."

V. JUSTICE VOTE

9 Pro ACLU Side vs. 0 Con Opposing Side

ACLU Side (Petitioner / Appellant)

1. White, B. – Wrote majority opinion
2. Rehnquist, W. – Joined majority opinion
3. Blackmun, H. – Joined majority opinion
4. Stevens, J. – Joined majority opinion
5. O'Connor, S. – Joined majority opinion
6. Souter, D. – Joined in majority opinion
7. Kennedy, A. – Wrote concurring opinion
8. Scalia, A. – Wrote concurring opinion
9. Thomas, C. – Joined Scalia's concurrence

VI. A WIN OR LOSS FOR THE ACLU?

The ACLU filed as amicus curiae urging reversal of the judgment of the Court of Appeals; the Supreme Court reversed in a 9-0 vote, giving the ACLU an apparent win.

757. Wisconsin v. Mitchell

(Decided June 11, 1993; 508 U.S. 476)

I. ISSUE

A. Issues Discussed

Criminal procedure, hate crimes, penalty enhancements

B. Legal Question Presented

"[W]hether [a] penalty enhancement [for a race-based crime] is prohibited by the First and Fourteenth Amendments."

C. Supreme Court's Answer

A penalty enhancement for race-based crimes does not violate the First Amendment or Fourteenth Amendment.

II. CASE SUMMARY

A. Background

"On the evening of October 7, 1989, a group of young black men and boys, including Mitchell, gathered at an apartment complex in Kenosha, Wisconsin. Several members of the group discussed a scene from the motion picture 'Mississippi Burning,' in which a white man beat a young black boy who was praying. The group moved outside and Mitchell asked them: "Do you all feel hyped up to move on some white people?" Shortly thereafter, a young white boy approached the group on the opposite side of the street where they were standing. As the boy walked by, Mitchell said: "You all want to fuck somebody up? There goes a white boy; go get him." Mitchell counted to three and pointed in the boy's direction. The group ran toward the boy, beat him severely, and stole his tennis shoes. The boy was rendered unconscious and remained in a coma for four days.

After a jury trial in the Circuit Court for Kenosha County, Mitchell was convicted of aggravated battery. That offense ordinarily carries a maximum sentence of two years' imprisonment. But because the jury found that Mitchell had intentionally selected his victim because of the boy's race, the maximum sentence for Mitchell's offense was increased to seven years under § 939.645. That provision enhances the maximum penalty for an offense whenever the defendant '[i]ntentionally selects the person against whom the crime . . . is committed . . . because of the race, religion, color, disability, sexual orientation, national origin or ancestry of that person . . . .' The Circuit Court sentenced Mitchell to four years' imprisonment for the aggravated battery.

Mitchell unsuccessfully sought postconviction relief in the Circuit Court. Then he appealed his conviction and sentence, challenging the constitutionality of Wisconsin's penalty-enhancement provision on First Amendment grounds. The Wisconsin Court of Appeals rejected Mitchell's challenge, but the Wisconsin Supreme Court reversed."

The U.S. Supreme Court granted certiorari to review the case and reversed.

B. Counsel of Record / ACLU Attorney

ACLU Side (Petitioner / Appellant): James E. Doyle, Attorney General of Wisconsin, argued the cause for appellant.

Michael R. Dreeben argued the cause for the United States, as amicus curiae, by special leave of Court.

Opposing Side (Respondent / Appellee): Lynn S. Adelman argued the cause for appellee.

III. AMICI CURIAE

ACLU Side (Petitioner / Appellant)

Brief of amici curiae filed on behalf of the ACLU, et al., by Steven R. Shapiro and John A. Powell.

Brief of amici curiae filed on behalf of the United States by Michael R. Dreeben, Acting Solicitor General Bryson, Acting Assistant Attorneys General Keeney and Turner, Kathleen A. Felton, and Thomas E. Chandler.

Additional briefs of amici curiae were filed on behalf of the State of Ohio, et al., the City of Atlanta, et al., the Anti-Defamation League, et al., the Appellate Committee of the California District Attorneys Association, the California Association of Human Rights Organizations, et al., the Chicago Lawyers' Committee for Civil Rights Under Law, Inc., the Criminal Justice Legal Foundation, the Crown Heights Coalition, et al., the Jewish Advocacy Center, the Lawyers' Committee for Civil Rights of the San Francisco Bay Area, the National Asian Pacific American Legal Consortium, et al., the National Conference of State Legislatures, et al., the Lawyers' Committee for Civil Rights Under Law, and Congressman Charles E. Schumer, et al.

Opposing Side (Respondent / Appellee)

Brief of amici curiae filed on behalf of the ACLU of Ohio by Daniel T. Kobil, Sarah J. DeBruin, Benson A. Wolman, Kevin Francis O'Neil, and David Goldberger.

Additional briefs of amici curiae were filed on behalf of California Attorneys for Criminal Justice, the Center for Individual Rights, the National Association of Criminal Defense Lawyers, et al., the Ohio Public Defender, the Wisconsin Freedom of Information Council, the Reason Foundation, the Wisconsin Association of Criminal Defense Lawyers, Larry Alexander, et al., and the Wisconsin Inter-Racial and Inter-Faith Coalition for Freedom of Thought.

IV. THE SUPREME COURT'S DECISION

"Traditionally, sentencing judges have considered a wide variety of factors in addition to evidence bearing on guilt in determining what sentence to impose on a convicted defendant. The defendant's motive for committing the offense is one important factor. . . . But it is equally true that a defendant's abstract beliefs, however obnoxious to most people, may not be taken into consideration by a sentencing judge. . . .

Mitchell argues that the Wisconsin penalty-enhancement statute is invalid because it punishes the defendant's discriminatory motive, or reason, for acting. But motive plays the same role under the Wisconsin statute as it does under federal and state antidiscrimination laws, which we have previously upheld against constitutional challenge.

[T]he Wisconsin statute singles out for enhancement bias-inspired conduct because this conduct is thought to inflict greater individual and societal harm. . . . The State's desire to redress these perceived harms provides an adequate explanation for its penalty-enhancement provision over and above mere disagreement with offenders' beliefs or biases. . . .

Finally, there remains to be considered Mitchell's argument that the Wisconsin statute is unconstitutionally overbroad because of its 'chilling effect' on free speech. . . . We find no merit in this contention. . . .

For the foregoing reasons, we hold that Mitchell's First Amendment rights were not violated by the application of the Wisconsin penalty-enhancement provision in sentencing him. The judgment of the Supreme Court of Wisconsin is therefore reversed, and the case is remanded for further proceedings not inconsistent with this opinion."

V. JUSTICE VOTE

9 Pro ACLU Side vs. 0 Con Opposing Side

ACLU Side (Petitioner / Appellant)

1. Rehnquist, W. – Wrote majority opinion
2. Scalia, A. – Joined majority opinion
3. O'Connor, S. – Joined majority opinion
4. Thomas, C. – Joined majority opinion
5. White, B. – Joined majority opinion
6. Souter, D. – Joined majority opinion
7. Stevens, J. – Joined majority opinion
8. Kennedy, A. – Joined majority opinion
9. Blackmun, H. – Joined majority opinion

VI. A WIN OR LOSS FOR THE ACLU?

The ACLU, as amicus curiae, urged reversal of the judgment of the Supreme Court of Wisconsin; the U.S. Supreme Court reversed in a 9-0 vote, giving the ACLU an apparent win.

758. Church of Lukumi Babalu Aye, Inc. v. City of Hialeah

(Decided June 11, 1993; 508 U.S. 520)

I. ISSUE

A. Issues Discussed

First Amendment, Free Exercise Clause

B. Legal Question Presented

Whether city ordinances in Haileah, Florida, prohibiting the religious sacrifice of animals violate the Free Exercise Clause of the First Amendment.

C. Supreme Court's Answer

The city ordinances violate the Free Exercise Clause.

II. CASE SUMMARY

A. Background

"This case involves practices of the Santeria religion .... Sacrifices are performed at birth, marriage, and death rites, for the cure of the sick, for the initiation of new members and priests, and during an annual celebration. Animals sacrificed in Santeria rituals include chickens, pigeons, doves, ducks, guinea pigs, goats, sheep, and turtles. The animals are killed by the cutting of the carotid arteries in the neck. The sacrificed animal is cooked and eaten, except after healing and death rituals....

Petitioner Church of the Lukumi Babalu Aye, Inc. (Church), is a not-for-profit corporation organized under Florida law in 1973. The Church and its congregants practice the Santeria religion. . . . In April 1987, the Church leased land in the City of Hialeah, Florida. [T]he Church's goal was to bring the practice of the Santeria faith, including its ritual of animal sacrifice, into the open. The Church began the process of obtaining utility service and receiving the necessary licensing, inspection, and zoning approvals. Although the Church's efforts at obtaining the necessary licenses and permits were far from smooth, it appears that it received all needed approvals by early August 1987.

The prospect of a Santeria church in their midst was distressing to many members of the Hialeah community, and the announcement of the plans to open a Santeria church in Hialeah prompted the city council to hold an emergency public session on June 9, 1987. [The city proceeded to adopt numerous ordinances prohibiting animal sacrifice.]

Following enactment of these ordinances, the Church . . . filed this action pursuant to 42 U.S.C. § 1983 in the United States District Court for the Southern District of Florida. . . . Alleging violations of petitioners' rights under, inter alia, the Free Exercise Clause, the complaint sought a declaratory judgment and injunctive and monetary relief. The District Court granted summary judgment to the individual defendants, finding that they had absolute immunity for their legislative acts and that the ordinances and resolutions adopted by the council did not constitute an official policy of harassment, as alleged by petitioners.

After a 9–day bench trial on the remaining claims, the District Court ruled for the city, finding no violation of petitioners' rights under the Free Exercise Clause. . . . The Court of Appeals for the Eleventh Circuit affirmed in a one-paragraph per curiam opinion."

The Supreme Court granted certiorari to review the case and reversed.

B. Counsel of Record / ACLU Attorney

ACLU Side (Petitioner / Appellant): Douglas Laycock argued the cause for appellant. With him on the briefs were Jeanne Baker, Nina E. Vinik, Mitchell Horwich, Steven R. Shapiro, and Jorge A. Duarte.

Opposing Side (Respondent / Appellee): Richard G. Garrett argued the cause for appellee. With him on the brief were Stuart H. Singer and Steven M. Goldsmith.

III. AMICI CURIAE

ACLU Side (Petitioner / Appellant)

Brief of amici curiae filed on behalf of Americans United for Separation of Church and State, et al., by Edward McGlynn Gaffney, Jr., Steven T. McFarland, Bradley P. Jacob, and Michael W. McConnell.

Brief of amici curiae filed on behalf of the Council on Religious Freedom by Lee Boothby, Robert W. Nixon, Walter E. Carson, Harold Lance, and Rolland Truman.

Brief of amici curiae filed on behalf of the Rutherford Institute by Carl Howard Esbeck and John W. Whitehead.

Brief of amici curiae filed on behalf of the National Jewish Commission on Law and Public Affairs by Nathan Lewin, J. Jay Lobell, and Dennis Rapps.

Brief of amici curiae filed on behalf of the United States Catholic Conference by Mark E. Chopko, John A. Liekweg, and Michael F. Moses, in support of neither party.

Opposing Side (Respondent / Appellee)

Brief of amici curiae filed on behalf of the International Society for Animal Rights, et al., by Henry Mark Holzer and Lance J. Gotko.

Brief of amici curiae filed on behalf of People for the Ethical Treatment of Animals, et al., by Gary L. Francione.
Brief of amici curiae filed on behalf of the Washington Humane Society by E. Edward Bruce and Lars Noah.
Brief of amici curiae filed on behalf of the Humane Society of the United States, et al., by Peter Buscemi, Anita W. Coupe, Maureen Beyers, Michael T. Murray, Melissa Seide Rubin, Karen B. Forney, Roger A. Kindler, Eugene Underwood, Jr., and Joyce Tischler.
Brief of amici curiae filed on behalf of the Institute for Animal Rights Law, et al., by Henry Mark Holzer and Lance J. Gotko.

IV. THE SUPREME COURT'S DECISION

"In addressing the constitutional protection for free exercise of religion, our cases establish the general proposition that a law that is neutral and of general applicability need not be justified by a compelling governmental interest even if the law has the incidental effect of burdening a particular religious practice. Neutrality and general applicability are interrelated, and, as becomes apparent in this case, failure to satisfy one requirement is a likely indication that the other has not been satisfied. A law failing to satisfy these requirements must be justified by a compelling governmental interest and must be narrowly tailored to advance that interest. These ordinances fail to satisfy the Smith requirements. . . .

A law lacks facial neutrality if it refers to a religious practice without a secular meaning discernable from the language or context. Petitioners contend that three of the ordinances fail this test of facial neutrality because they use the words 'sacrifice' and 'ritual,' words with strong religious connotations. We agree that these words are consistent with the claim of facial discrimination, but the argument is not conclusive. . . .

In sum, the neutrality inquiry leads to one conclusion: The ordinances had as their object the suppression of religion. The pattern we have recited discloses animosity to Santeria adherents and their religious practices; the ordinances by their own terms target this religious exercise; the texts of the ordinances were gerrymandered with care to proscribe religious killings of animals but to exclude almost all secular killings; and the ordinances suppress much more religious conduct than is necessary in order to achieve the legitimate ends asserted in their defense. These ordinances are not neutral, and the court below committed clear error in failing to reach this conclusion. . . .

We conclude, in sum, that each of Hialeah's ordinances pursues the city's governmental interests only against conduct motivated by religious belief. The ordinances 'ha[ve] every appearance of a prohibition that society is prepared to impose upon [Santeria worshippers] but not upon itself.' This precise evil is what the requirement of general applicability is designed to prevent. . . .

A law burdening religious practice that is not neutral or not of general application must undergo the most rigorous of scrutiny. . . . A law that targets religious conduct for distinctive treatment or advances legitimate governmental interests only against conduct with a religious motivation will survive strict scrutiny only in rare cases. It follows from what we have already said that these ordinances cannot withstand this scrutiny. . . .

The Free Exercise Clause commits government itself to religious tolerance, and upon even slight suspicion that proposals for state intervention stem from animosity to religion or distrust of its practices, all officials must pause to remember their own high duty to the Constitution and to the rights it secures. Those in office must be resolute in resisting importunate demands and must ensure that the sole reasons for imposing the burdens of law and regulation are secular. Legislators may not devise mechanisms, overt or disguised, designed to persecute or oppress a religion or its practices. The laws here in question were enacted contrary to these constitutional principles, and they are void.

Reversed."

V. JUSTICE VOTE

9 Pro ACLU Side vs. 0 Con Opposing Side

ACLU Side (Petitioner / Appellant)

1. Kennedy, A. – Wrote majority opinion
2. Scalia, A. – Wrote concurring opinion
3. Souter, D. – Wrote concurring opinion
4. Blackmun, H. – Wrote concurring opinion
5. Rehnquist, W. – Joined Scalia's concurrence
6. Stevens, J. – Joined majority opinion
7. Thomas, C. – Joined majority opinion
8. O'Connor, S. – Joined Blackmun's concurrence
9. White, B. – Joined majority opinion

VI. A WIN OR LOSS FOR THE ACLU?

The ACLU, as counsel for petitioners, urged reversal of the judgment of the Court of Appeals for the Eleventh Circuit; the Supreme Court reversed in a 9-0 vote, giving the ACLU an apparent win.

759. Godinez v. Moran

(Decided June 24, 1993; 509 U.S. 389)

I. ISSUE

A. Issues Discussed

Criminal procedure, Fourteenth Amendment, competency to stand trial

B. Legal Question Presented

"[W]hether the competency standard for pleading guilty or waiving the right to counsel is higher than the competency standard for standing trial."

C. Supreme Court's Answer

The competency standard for pleading guilty or waiving the right to counsel is the same as the competency standard for standing trial.

II. CASE SUMMARY

A. Background

"On August 2, 1984, in the early hours of the morning, respondent entered the Red Pearl Saloon in Las Vegas, Nevada, and shot the bartender and a patron four times each with an automatic pistol. He then walked behind the bar and removed the cash register. Nine days later, respondent arrived at the apartment of his former wife and opened fire on her; five of his seven shots hit their target. Respondent then shot himself in the abdomen and attempted, without success, to slit his wrists. Of the four victims of respondent's gunshots, only respondent himself survived. On August 13, respondent summoned police to his hospital bed and confessed to the killings.

After respondent pleaded not guilty to three counts of first-degree murder, the trial court ordered that he be examined by a pair of psychiatrists, both of whom concluded that he was competent to stand trial. The State thereafter announced its intention to seek the death penalty. On November 28, 1984, 2 1/2 months after the psychiatric evaluations, respondent again appeared before the trial court. At this time respondent informed the court that he wished to discharge his attorneys and change his pleas to guilty. The reason for the request, according to respondent, was to prevent the presentation of mitigating evidence at his sentencing. . . .

The court advised respondent that he had a right both to the assistance of counsel and to self-representation, warned him of the 'dangers and disadvantages' of self-representation, inquired into his understanding of the proceedings and his awareness of his rights, and asked why he had chosen to represent himself. It then accepted respondent's waiver of counsel. The court also accepted respondent's guilty pleas, but not before it had determined that respondent was not pleading guilty in response to threats or promises, that he understood the nature of the charges against him and the consequences of pleading guilty, that he was aware of the rights he was giving up, and that there was a factual basis for the pleas. The trial court explicitly found that respondent was 'knowingly and intelligently' waiving his right to the assistance of counsel, and that his guilty pleas were 'freely and voluntarily' given.

On January 21, 1985, a three-judge court sentenced respondent to death for each of the murders. The Supreme Court of Nevada affirmed respondent's sentences for the Red Pearl Saloon murders, but reversed his sentence for the murder of his ex-wife and remanded for imposition of a life sentence without the possibility of parole.

On July 30, 1987, respondent filed a petition for postconviction relief in state court. Following an evidentiary hearing, the trial court rejected respondent's claim that he was 'mentally incompetent to represent himself,' concluding that 'the record clearly shows that he was examined by two psychiatrists both of whom declared [him] competent.' The Supreme Court of Nevada dismissed respondent's appeal, and [the U.S. Supreme Court] denied certiorari.

Respondent then filed a habeas petition in the United States District Court for the District of Nevada. The District Court denied the petition, but the Ninth Circuit reversed."

The Supreme Court granted certiorari to review the case and reversed.

B. Counsel of Record / ACLU Attorney

ACLU Side (Respondent / Appellee): Cal J. Potter III, by appointment of the Court, argued the cause for appellee.

Opposing Side (Petitioner / Appellant): David F. Sarnowski, Chief Deputy Attorney General of Nevada, argued the cause for appellant.

Amy L. Wax argued the cause for the United States, as amicus curiae, by special leave of Court.

III. AMICI CURIAE

ACLU Side (Respondent / Appellee)

Brief of amici curiae filed on behalf of the ACLU, et al., by Steven R. Shapiro, Diann Y. Rust-Tierney, John A. Powell, Susan N. Herman, and Bruce J. Winick.

Brief of amici curiae filed on behalf of the American Psychiatric Association, et al., by James W. Ellis, Barbara E. Bergman, and Christian G. Fritz.

Brief of amici curiae filed on behalf of the National Association of Criminal Defense Lawyers by Jon May.

Opposing Side (Petitioner / Appellant)

Brief of amici curiae filed on behalf of the United States by Amy L. Wax, Acting Solicitor General Bryson, Acting Assistant Attorney General Keeney, and Joel M. Gershowitz.

Brief of amici curiae filed on behalf of the Criminal Justice Legal Foundation by Kent S. Scheidegger and Charles L. Hobson.

IV. THE SUPREME COURT'S DECISION

"A criminal defendant may not be tried unless he is competent, and he may not waive his right to counsel or plead guilty unless he does so 'competently and intelligently.' . . . While we have described the standard for competence to stand trial, however, we have never expressly articulated a standard for competence to plead guilty or to waive the right to the assistance of counsel. . . .

In sum, all criminal defendants—not merely those who plead guilty—may be required to make important decisions once criminal proceedings have been initiated. And while the decision to plead guilty is undeniably a profound one, it is no more complicated than the sum total of decisions that a defendant may be called upon to make during the course of a trial. (The decision to plead guilty is also made over a shorter period of time, without the distraction and burden of a trial.) This being so, we can conceive of no basis for demanding a higher level of competence for those defendants who choose to plead guilty. If the Dusky standard is adequate for defendants who plead not guilty, it is necessarily adequate for those who plead guilty.

Nor do we think that a defendant who waives his right to the assistance of counsel must be more competent than a defendant who does not, since there is no reason to believe that the decision to waive counsel requires an appreciably higher level of mental functioning than the decision to waive other constitutional rights. . . .

A finding that a defendant is competent to stand trial . . . is not all that is necessary before he may be permitted to plead guilty or waive his right to counsel. In addition to determining that a defendant who seeks to plead guilty or waive counsel is competent, a trial court must satisfy itself that the waiver of his constitutional rights is knowing and voluntary. In this sense there is a 'heightened' standard for pleading guilty and for waiving the right to counsel, but it is not a heightened standard of competence. . . .

Requiring that a criminal defendant be competent has a modest aim: It seeks to ensure that he has the capacity to understand the proceedings and to assist counsel. While psychiatrists and scholars may find it useful to classify the various kinds and degrees of competence, and while States are free to adopt competency standards that are more elaborate than the Dusky formulation, the Due Process Clause does not impose these additional requirements. The judgment of the Court of Appeals is reversed, and the case is remanded for further proceedings consistent with this opinion."

V. JUSTICE VOTE

2 Pro ACLU Side vs. 7 Con Opposing Side

ACLU Side (Respondent / Appellee)

1. Blackmun, H. – Wrote dissenting opinion
2. Stevens, J. – Joined Blackmun's dissent

Opposing Side (Petitioner / Appellant)

1. Thomas, C. – Wrote majority opinion
2. Rehnquist, W. – Joined majority opinion
3. White, B. – Joined majority opinion
4. O'Connor, S. – Joined majority opinion
5. Souter, D. – Joined majority opinion
6. Kennedy, A. – Wrote concurring opinion
7. Scalia, A. – Joined Kennedy's concurrence

VI. A WIN OR LOSS FOR THE ACLU?

The ACLU filed as amicus curiae urging affirmance of the judgment of the Court of Appeals; the Supreme Court reversed in a 7-2 vote, giving the ACLU an apparent loss.

760. United States v. Edge Broadcasting Co.

(Decided June 25, 1993; 509 U.S. 418)

I. ISSUE

A. Issues Discussed

1st Amendment, press, speech, association

B. Legal Question Presented

"[W]hether federal statutes that prohibit the broadcast of lottery advertising by a broadcaster licensed to a State that does not allow lotteries, while allowing such broadcasting by a broadcaster licensed to a State that sponsors a lottery, are, as applied to respondent, consistent with the First Amendment."

C. Supreme Court's Answer

"[T]he statutes challenged here regulate commercial speech in a manner that does not violate the First Amendment . . . ."

II. CASE SUMMARY

A. Background

"States have long viewed [lotteries] as a hazard . . . . Congress has, since the early 19th century, sought to assist the States in controlling lotteries. . . . When the Louisiana Lottery moved its operations to Honduras, Congress passed the Act of Mar. 2, 1895, which outlawed the transportation of lottery tickets in interstate or foreign commerce. . . .

In 1975, Congress amended the statutory scheme to allow newspapers and broadcasters to advertise state-run lotteries if the newspaper is published in or the broadcast station is licensed to a State which conducts a state-run lottery. . . .

North Carolina does not sponsor a lottery . . . . Virginia, on the other hand, has chosen to legalize lotteries under a state monopoly and has entered the marketplace vigorously.

Respondent, Edge Broadcasting Company (Edge), owns and operates a radio station licensed by the Federal Communications Commission (FCC) to Elizabeth City, North Carolina. . . . Because Edge is licensed to serve a North Carolina community, the federal statute prohibits it from broadcasting advertisements for the Virginia lottery. . . .

Edge entered federal court in the Eastern District of Virginia, seeking a declaratory judgment that, as applied to it, §§ 1304 and 1307, together with corresponding FCC regulations, violated the First Amendment to the Constitution and the Equal Protection Clause of the Fourteenth, as well as injunctive protection against the enforcement of those statutes and regulations.

The District Court . . . held . . . that the statutes . . . did not directly advance the asserted governmental interest, failed the Central Hudson test in this respect, and hence could not be constitutionally applied to Edge. A divided Court of Appeals . . . affirmed in all respects . . . ."

The Supreme Court granted certiorari to review the case.

B. Counsel of Record

ACLU Side (Respondent / Appellee): Conrad M. Shumadine argued the cause for appellee. With him on the brief was Walter D. Kelley, Jr.

Opposing Side (Petitioner / Appellant): Paul J. Larkin, Jr., argued the cause for appellant. With him on the briefs were Solicitor General Starr, Acting Solicitor General Bryson, Assistant Attorney General Gerson, and Deputy Solicitor General Roberts.

III. AMICI CURIAE

ACLU Side (Respondent / Appellee)

Brief of amici curiae filed on behalf of the National Association of Broadcasters; American Association of Advertising Agencies, Inc.; American Civil Liberties Union; Dow Jones & Company; Gannett Co., Inc.; The Hearst Corporation; Magazine Publishers of America, Inc.; The Media Institute; Multimedia Broadcasting Company, Inc.; Newspaper Association of America; North Carolina Association of Broadcasters, Inc.; Post-Newsweek Stations, Inc.; Providence Journal Company; Society of Professional Journalists; Time Inc.; Tribune Company; and Westinghouse Broadcasting

Company, Inc., by P. Cameron Devore, Marshall J. Nelson, Sima F. Sarrafan, John Kamp, Steven R. Shapiro, John A. Powell, Stuart D. Karle, Barbara W. Wall, Victor F. Ganzi, Robert J. Hawley, Kenneth M. Vittor, Slade R. Metcalf, Richard E. Wiley, Daniel E. Troy, David P. Fleming, Roberta R. Brackman, John F. Sturm, Rene P. Milam, Wade H. Hargrove, Mark J. Prak, L. Stanley Paige, Michael B. Isaacs, Bruce W. Sanford, Henry S. Hoberman, Robert D. Lystad, Harry M. Johnston III, David D. Hiller And Charles J. Sennet, Martin P. Messinger, Bryan T. Mcginnis, Henry L. Baumann, and Steven A. Bookshester.

Brief of amici curiae filed on behalf of the the Association of National Advertisers, Inc., et al. by Burt Neuborne and Gilbert H. Weil.

Opposing Side (Petitioner / Appellant)

No briefs of amici curiae were filed in support of appellant.

IV. THE SUPREME COURT'S DECISION

"The Government argues first that gambling implicates no constitutionally protected right . . . ; it argues that we therefore need not proceed with a *Central Hudson* analysis. The Court of Appeals did not address this issue and neither do we, for the statutes are not unconstitutional under the standards of *Central Hudson* applied by the courts below. . . .

In Central Hudson, we set out the general scheme for assessing government restrictions on commercial speech. [W]e assume that Edge . . . would air nonmisleading advertisements about the Virginia lottery . . . . As to the second Central Hudson factor, . . . the Government has a substantial interest in supporting the policy of nonlottery States, as well as not interfering with the policy of States that permit lotteries. [W]e also agree that the statutes are no broader than necessary to advance the Government's interest and hence the fourth part of the Central Hudson test is satisfied.

The Court of Appeals, however, affirmed the District Court's holding that the statutes were invalid because, as applied to Edge, they failed to advance directly the governmental interest supporting them. . . . In our judgment, the courts below erred in that respect. . . .

The third Central Hudson factor asks whether the 'regulation directly advances the governmental interest asserted.' . . . The courts below . . . asked the wrong question . . . .

We have no doubt that the statutes directly advanced the governmental interest at stake . . . .

Left unresolved, of course, is the validity of applying the statutory restriction to Edge, an issue that we now address under the fourth Central Hudson factor, i.e., whether the regulation is more extensive than is necessary to serve the governmental interest. . . .

We have no doubt that the fit in this case was a reasonable one. . . .

Thus, even if it were proper to conduct a Central Hudson analysis of the statutes only as applied to Edge, we would not agree with the courts below that the restriction at issue here, which prevents Edge from broadcasting lottery advertising to its sizable radio audience in North Carolina, is rendered ineffective by the fact that Virginia radio and television programs can be heard in North Carolina. In our view, the restriction, even as applied only to Edge, directly advances the governmental interest within the meaning of Central Hudson. . . .

Because the statutes challenged here regulate commercial speech in a manner that does not violate the First Amendment, the judgment of the Court of Appeals is reversed."

V. JUSTICE VOTE

2 Pro ACLU Side vs. 7 Con Opposing Side

ACLU Side (Respondent / Appellee)

1. Stevens, J. – Wrote dissenting opinion
2. Blackmun, H. – Joined Stevens' dissent

Opposing Side (Petitioner / Appellant)

1. White, B. – Wrote majority opinion
2. Souter, D. – Wrote concurring opinion
3. Kennedy, A. – Joined Souter's concurrence
4. Rehnquist, W. – Joined majority opinion
5. Scalia, A. – Joined majority opinion in part
6. Thomas, C. – Joined majority opinion
7. O'Connor, S. – Joined majority opinion in part

VI. A WIN OR LOSS FOR THE ACLU?

The ACLU filed as amicus curiae urging affirmance; the Supreme Court reversed the Court of Appeals' decision by a 7-2 vote, giving the ACLU an apparent loss.

761. Alexander v. United States

(Decided June 28, 1993; 509 U.S. 544)

I. ISSUE

A. Issues Discussed

First Amendment, obscenity, Eighth Amendment, excessive fines

B. Legal Question Presented

Whether forfeiture of defendant's assets after his RICO conviction was consistent with both the First Amendment and the excessive fines clause of the Eighth Amendment

C. Supreme Court's Answer

The forfeiture was consistent with the First Amendment, but the case must be remanded to decide whether the forfeiture was an excessive fine under the Eighth Amendment.

II. CASE SUMMARY

A. Background

"After a full criminal trial, petitioner Ferris J. Alexander, owner of more than a dozen stores and theaters dealing in sexually explicit materials, was convicted on, inter alia, 17 obscenity counts and 3 counts of violating the Racketeer Influenced and Corrupt Organizations Act (RICO). . . .

Petitioner was sentenced to a total of six years in prison, fined $100,000, and ordered to pay the cost of prosecution, incarceration, and supervised release. In addition to these punishments, the District Court reconvened the same jury and conducted a forfeiture proceeding pursuant to § 1963(a)(2). At this proceeding, the Government sought forfeiture of the businesses and real estate that represented petitioner's interest in the racketeering enterprise, § 1963(a)(2)(A), the property that afforded petitioner influence over that enterprise, § 1963(a)(2)(D), and the assets and proceeds petitioner had obtained from his racketeering offenses, §§ 1963(a)(1), (3). The jury found that petitioner had an interest in 10 pieces of commercial real estate and 31 current or former businesses, all of which had been used to conduct his racketeering enterprise. Sitting without the jury, the District Court then found that petitioner had acquired a variety of assets as a result of his racketeering activities. The court ultimately ordered petitioner to forfeit his wholesale and retail businesses (including all the assets of those businesses) and almost $9 million in moneys acquired through racketeering activity.

The Court of Appeals affirmed the District Court's forfeiture order."

The Supreme Court granted certiorari to review the case, vacated, and remanded.

B. Counsel of Record / ACLU Attorney

ACLU Side (Petitioner / Appellant): John H. Weston argued the cause for appellant.

Opposing Side (Respondent / Appellee): Solicitor General Kenneth W. Starr argued the cause for appellee.

III. AMICI CURIAE

ACLU Side (Petitioner / Appellant)

Brief of amici curiae filed on behalf of the ACLU, et al., by Marvin E. Frankel, Jeffrey S. Trachman, Gregory A. Horowitz, Robert A. Culp, Steven R. Shapiro, Marjorie Heins, and Deborah Gilman.

Brief of amici curiae filed on behalf of the American Booksellers Foundation for Free Expression, et al., by Michael A. Bamberger and Margaret S. Determan.

Brief of amici curiae filed on behalf of the American Library Association, et al., by Bruce Rich, Linda Steinman, Bruce J. Ennis, Jr., David W. Ogden, and Ann M. Kappler.

Brief of amici curiae filed on behalf of Feminists for Free Expression by Helen M. Mickiewicz and Catherine Siemann.

Brief of amici curiae filed on behalf of the Video Software Dealers Association by Charles B. Ruttenberg, James P. Mercurio, and Theodore D. Frank.

Opposing Side (Respondent / Appellee)

Brief of amici curiae filed on behalf of Christian Legal Defense by Wendell R. Bird, David J. Myers, and Timothy W. Townsend.

Brief of amici curiae filed on behalf of the National Family Legal Foundation, et al., by Jams P. Mueller and Len L. Munsil.

Brief of amici curiae filed on behalf of Morality in Media, Inc., by Paul J. McGeady and Robert W. Peters.

Brief of amici curiae filed on behalf of the Religious Alliance Against Pornography, et al., by H. Robert Showers and Gene L. Malpas.

IV. THE SUPREME COURT'S DECISION

"Petitioner first contends that the forfeiture in this case, which effectively shut down his adult entertainment business, constituted an unconstitutional prior restraint on speech, rather than a permissible criminal punishment.

[T]he RICO forfeiture order in this case does not forbid petitioner from engaging in any expressive activities in the future, nor does it require him to obtain prior approval for any expressive activities. It only deprives him of specific assets that were found to be related to his previous racketeering violations. . . . He is perfectly free to open an adult bookstore or otherwise engage in the production and distribution of erotic materials; he just cannot finance these enterprises with assets derived from his prior racketeering offenses. . . .

In sum, we think that fidelity to our cases requires us to analyze the forfeiture here not as a prior restraint, but under normal First Amendment standards. So analyzing it, we find that petitioner's claim falls well short of the mark. He does not challenge either his 6–year jail sentence or his $100,000 fine as violative of the First Amendment. The first inquiry that comes to mind, then, is why, if incarceration for six years and a fine of $100,000 are permissible forms of punishment under the RICO statute, the challenged forfeiture of certain assets directly related to petitioner's racketeering activity is not. Our cases support the instinct from which this question arises; they establish quite clearly that the First Amendment does not prohibit either stringent criminal sanctions for obscenity offenses or forfeiture of expressive materials as punishment for criminal conduct. . . .

Petitioner also argues that the forfeiture order in this case—considered atop his 6-year prison term and $100,000 fine—is disproportionate to the gravity of his offenses and therefore violates the Eighth Amendment, either as a 'cruel and unusual punishment' or as an 'excessive fine.' . . . The in personam criminal forfeiture at issue here is clearly a form of monetary punishment no different, for Eighth Amendment purposes, from a traditional 'fine.' Accordingly, the forfeiture in this case should be analyzed under the Excessive Fines Clause. . . . It is in the light of the extensive criminal activities which petitioner apparently conducted through this racketeering enterprise over a substantial period of time that the question whether the forfeiture was 'excessive' must be considered. We think it preferable that this question be addressed by the Court of Appeals in the first instance.

For these reasons, we hold that RICO's forfeiture provisions, as applied in this case, did not violate the First Amendment, but that the Court of Appeals should have considered whether they resulted in an 'excessive' penalty within the meaning of the Eighth Amendment's Excessive Fines Clause. Accordingly, we vacate the judgment of the Court of Appeals and remand the case for further proceedings consistent with this opinion."

V. JUSTICE VOTE

4 Pro ACLU Side vs. 5 Con Opposing Side

ACLU Side (Petitioner / Appellant)

1. Kennedy, A. – Wrote dissenting opinion
2. Blackmun, H. – Joined Kennedy's dissent

3. Stevens, J. – Joined Kennedy's dissent
4. Souter, D. – Wrote opinion concurring in part and dissenting in part, joined Kennedy's dissent, in part

Opposing Side (Respondent / Appellee)

1. Rehnquist, W. – Wrote majority opinion
2. White, B. – Joined majority opinion
3. O'Connor, S. – Joined majority opinion
4. Scalia, A. – Joined majority opinion
5. Thomas, C. – Joined majority opinion

VI. A WIN OR LOSS FOR THE ACLU?

The ACLU filed as amicus curiae urging reversal of the judgment of the Court of Appeals; the Supreme Court affirmed in part and vacated in part in a 5-4 vote, giving the ACLU an apparent loss.

762. Austin v. United States

(Decided June 28, 1993; 509 U.S. 602)

I. ISSUE

A. Issues Discussed

Criminal justice, drugs, Eighth Amendment, Excessive Fines Clause

B. Legal Question Presented

"[W]hether the Excessive Fines Clause of the Eighth Amendment applies to forfeitures of property under 21 U.S.C. §§ 881(a)(4) and (a)(7)."

C. Supreme Court's Answer

The Excessive Fines Clause applies to property forfeitures under the statutes.

II. CASE SUMMARY

A. Background

"On August 2, 1990, petitioner Richard Lyle Austin was indicted on four counts of violating South Dakota's drug laws. Austin ultimately pleaded guilty to one count of possessing cocaine with intent to distribute and was sentenced by the state court to seven years' imprisonment. On September 7, the United States filed an in rem action in the United States District Court for the District of South Dakota seeking forfeiture of Austin's mobile home and auto body shop under 21 U.S.C. §§ 881(a)(4) and (a)(7). Austin filed a claim and an answer to the complaint.

On February 4, 1991, the United States made a motion, supported by an affidavit from Sioux Falls Police Officer Donald Satterlee, for summary judgment. According to Satterlee's affidavit, Austin met Keith Engebretson at Austin's body shop on June 13, 1990, and agreed to sell cocaine to Engebretson. Austin left the shop, went to his mobile home, and returned to the shop with two grams of cocaine which he sold to Engebretson. State authorities executed a search warrant on the body shop and mobile home the following day. They discovered small amounts of marijuana and cocaine, a .22 caliber revolver, drug paraphernalia, and approximately $4,700 in cash. In opposing summary judgment, Austin argued that forfeiture of the properties would violate the Eighth Amendment. The District Court rejected this argument and entered summary judgment for the United States.

The United States Court of Appeals for the Eighth Circuit 'reluctantly agree[d] with the government' and affirmed. Although it thought that 'the principle of proportionality should be applied in civil actions that result in harsh penalties,' and that the Government was 'exacting too high a penalty in relation to the offense committed,' the court felt constrained from holding the forfeiture unconstitutional. It cited [the Supreme] Court's decision in Calero–Toledo v. Pearson Yacht Leasing Co., 416 U.S. 663 (1974), for the proposition that, when the Government is proceeding against property in rem, the guilt or innocence of the property's owner 'is constitutionally irrelevant.' It then reasoned: 'We are constrained to agree with the Ninth Circuit that '[i]f the constitution allows in rem forfeiture to be visited upon innocent owners . . . the constitution hardly requires proportionality review of forfeitures.''"

The Supreme Court granted certiorari to review the case and reversed.

B. Counsel of Record / ACLU Attorney

ACLU Side (Petitioner / Appellant): Richard L. Johnson argued the cause for appellant.

Opposing Side (Respondent / Appellee): Miguel A. Estrada argued the cause for the United States.

III. AMICI CURIAE

ACLU Side (Petitioner / Appellant)

Brief of amici curiae filed on behalf of the ACLU by Gerard E. Lynch, Steven R. Shapiro, and John A. Powell.

Brief of amici curiae filed on behalf of the National Association of Criminal Defense Layers by David B. Smith and Justin M. Miller.

Opposing Side (Respondent / Appellee)

Brief of amici curiea filed on behalf of the American Alliance for Rights and Responsibilities by Roger L. Conner, Robert Teir, Edward S. G. Dennis, Jr., and Peter Buscemi.

Brief of amici curiae filed on behalf of the State of Arizona, et al., by Grant Woods, Attorney General of Arizona, Cameron H. Holmes, Assistant Attorney General, Sandra L. Janzen, Assistant Attorney General, Daniel E. Lungren, Attorney General of California, George Williamson, Chief Assistant Attorney, and Gary W. Schons, Senior, Assistant Attorney General, and the following Attorneys General for their respective states: Winston Bryant of Arkansas, Domenick Galluzzo of Connecticut, Robert A. Butterworth of Florida, Michael J. Bowers of Georgia, Robert A. Marks of Hawaii, Larry EechoHawk of Idaho, Robert T. Stephan of Kansas, Chris Gorman of Kentucky, Richard P. Ieyoub of Louisiana, Michael Carpenter of Maine, J. Joseph Curran, Jr., of Marlyand, Scott Harshbarger of Massachusetts, Frank J. Kelley of Michigan, Hubert H. Humphrey, III, of Minnesota, Michaelo Moore of Mississippi, Joseph P. Mazurek of Montana, Don Stenberg of

Nebraska, Frankie Sue Del Papa of Nevada, Jeffrey R. Howard of New Hampshire, Tom Udall of New Mexico, Michael F. Easley of North Carolina, Susan B. Loving of Oklahoma, Ernest D. Preate, Jr., of Pennsylvania, Jeffrey B. Pine of Rhode Island, T. Travis Medlock of South Carolina, Dan Morales of Texas, Jan Graham of Utah, Stephen D. Rosenthal of Virginia, Christine O. Gregoire of Washington, Joseph B. Meyer of Wyoming, and Rosalie Simmonds Ballentine of the Virgin Islands.

IV. THE SUPREME COURT'S DECISION

"The Court concluded that both the Eighth Amendment and §10 of the English Bill of Rights of 1689, from which it derives, were intended to prevent the government from abusing its power to punish, and therefore that 'the Excessive Fines Clause was intended to limit only those fines directly imposed by, and payable to, the government.' . . . The purpose of the Eighth Amendment, putting the Bail Clause to one side, was to limit the government's power to punish. The Cruel and Unusual Punishments Clause is self-evidently concerned with punishment. The Excessive Fines Clause limits the government's power to extract payments, whether in cash or in kind, 'as punishment for some offense.' 'The notion of punishment, as we commonly understand it, cuts across the division between the civil and the criminal law.' 'It is commonly understood that civil proceedings may advance punitive as well as remedial goals, and, conversely, that both punitive and remedial goals may be served by criminal penalties.' Thus, the question is not, as the United States would have it, whether forfeiture under §§ 881(a)(4) and (a)(7) is civil or criminal, but rather whether it is punishment. . . .

We need not exclude the possibility that a forfeiture serves remedial purposes to conclude that it is subject to the limitations of the Excessive Fines Clause. We, however, must determine that it can only be explained as serving in part to punish. . . . We turn, then, to consider whether, at the time the Eighth Amendment was ratified, forfeiture was understood at least in part as punishment and whether forfeiture under §§ 881(a)(4) and (a)(7) should be so understood today.

[C]onsider whether forfeitures under 21 U.S.C. §§ 881(a)(4) and (a)(7) are properly considered punishment today. We find nothing in these provisions or their legislative history to contradict the historical understanding of forfeiture as punishment. Unlike traditional forfeiture statutes, §§ 881(a)(4) and (a)(7) expressly provide an 'innocent owner' defense. These exemptions serve to focus the provisions on the culpability of the owner in a way that makes them look more like punishment, not less. In United States v. United States Coin & Currency, we reasoned that 19 U.S.C. § 1618, which provides that the Secretary of the Treasury is to return the property of those who do not intend to violate the law, demonstrated Congress' intent 'to impose a penalty only upon those who are significantly involved in a criminal enterprise.' The inclusion of innocent-owner defenses in §§ 881(a)(4) and (a)(7) reveals a similar congressional intent to punish only those involved in drug trafficking.

Furthermore, Congress has chosen to tie forfeiture directly to the commission of drug offenses. Thus, under § 881(a)(4), a conveyance is forfeitable if it is used or intended for use to facilitate the transportation of controlled substances, their raw materials, or the equipment used to manufacture or distribute them. . . .

In our view, neither argument withstands scrutiny. Concededly, we have recognized that the forfeiture of contraband itself may be characterized as remedial because it removes dangerous or illegal items from society. The Court, however, previously has rejected government's attempt to extend that reasoning to conveyances used to transport illegal liquor. . . . We previously have upheld the forfeiture of goods involved in customs violations as 'a reasonable form of liquidated damages.' But the dramatic variations in the value of conveyances and real property forfeitable under §§ 881(a)(4) and (a)(7) undercut any similar argument with respect to those provisions. . . .

Fundamentally, even assuming that §§ 881(a)(4) and (a)(7) serve some remedial purpose, the Government's argument must fail. '[A] civil sanction that cannot fairly be said solely to serve a remedial purpose, but rather can only be explained as also serving either retributive or deterrent purposes, is punishment, as we have come to understand the term.' In light of the historical understanding of forfeiture as punishment, the clear focus of §§ 881(a)(4) and (a)(7) on the culpability of the owner, and the evidence that Congress understood those provisions as serving to deter and to punish, we cannot conclude that forfeiture under §§ 881(a)(4) and (a)(7) serves solely a remedial purpose. We therefore conclude that forfeiture under these provisions constitutes 'payment to a sovereign as punishment for some offense,' and, as such, is subject to the limitations of the Eighth Amendment's Excessive Fines Clause. . . .

The judgment of the Court of Appeals is reversed, and the case is remanded to that court for further proceedings consistent with this opinion."

V. JUSTICE VOTE

9 Pro ACLU Side vs. 0 Con Opposing Side

ACLU Side (Petitioner / Appellant)

1. Blackmun, H. – Wrote majority opinion
2. Stevens, J. – Joined majority opinion
3. O'Connor, S. – Joined majority opinion
4. Souter, D. – Joined majority opinion
5. White, B. – Joined majority opinion
6. Kennedy, A. – Wrote concurring opinion
7. Rehnquist, W. – Joined Kennedy's concurrence
8. Thomas, C. – Joined Kennedy's concurrence
9. Scalia, A. – Wrote concurring opinion

VI. A WIN OR LOSS FOR THE ACLU?

The ACLU filed as amicus curiae urging reversal of the judgment of the Court of Appeals; the Supreme Court reversed in a 9-0 vote, giving the ACLU an apparent win.

763. Harris v. Forklift Systems, Inc.

(Decided November 9, 1993; 510 U.S. 17)

I. ISSUE

A. Issues Discussed

Title VII of the Civil Rights Act of 1965, sexual harassment

B. Legal Question Presented

"[W]hether conduct, to be actionable as 'abusive work environment' harassment . . . , must 'seriously affect [an employee's] psychological well-being' or lead the plaintiff to 'suffe[r] injury.'"

C. Supreme Court's Answer

The conduct does not have to seriously affect the employee's psychological well-being or lead the employee to suffer injury to be actionable as abusive work environment harassment.

II. CASE SUMMARY

A. Background

"Teresa Harris worked as a manager at Forklift Systems, Inc., an equipment rental company, from April 1985 until October 1987. Charles Hardy was Forklift's president.

The Magistrate found that, throughout Harris' time at Forklift, Hardy often insulted her because of her gender and often made her the target of unwanted sexual innuendos. Hardy told Harris on several occasions, in the presence of other employees, 'You're a woman, what do you know' and 'We need a man as the rental manager'; at least once, he told her she was 'a dumb ass woman.' Again in front of others, he suggested that the two of them 'go to the Holiday Inn to negotiate [Harris'] raise.' Hardy occasionally asked Harris and other female employees to get coins from his front pants pocket. He threw objects on the ground in front of Harris and other women, and asked them to pick the objects up. He made sexual innuendos about Harris' and other women's clothing.

In mid-August 1987, Harris complained to Hardy about his conduct. Hardy said he was surprised that Harris was offended, claimed he was only joking, and apologized. He also promised he would stop, and based on this assurance Harris stayed on the job. But in early September, Hardy began anew: While Harris was arranging a deal with one of Forklift's customers, he asked her, again in front of other employees, 'What did you do, promise the guy... some [sex] Saturday night?' On October 1, Harris collected her paycheck and quit.

Harris then sued Forklift, claiming that Hardy's conduct had created an abusive work environment for her because of her gender. The United States District Court for the Middle District of Tennessee, adopting the report and recommendation of the Magistrate, found this to be 'a close case,' but held that Hardy's conduct did not create an abusive environment....

The United States Court of Appeals for the Sixth Circuit affirmed in a brief unpublished decision."

The Supreme Court granted certiorari to review the case and reversed.

B. Counsel of Record / ACLU Attorney

ACLU Side (Petitioner / Appellant): Irwin Venick argued the cause for appellant.

Jeffrey P. Minear argued the cause for the United States, et al., as amicus curiae, by special leave of Court.

Opposing Side (Respondent / Appellee): Stanley M. Chernau argued the cause for appellee.

III. AMICI CURIAE

ACLU Side (Petitioner / Appellant)

Brief of amici curiae filed on behalf of the ACLU, et al., by Steven R. Shapiro, John A. Powell, and Lois C. Waldman.

Brief of amici curiae filed on behalf of the United States, et al., by Jeffrey P. Minear, Acting Solicitor General Bryson, Acting Assistant Attorney General Turner, Denis J. Dimsey, Thomas E. Chandler, Donald R. Livingston, Gwendolyn Young Reams, Carolyn L. Wheeler, and Dori K. Bernstein.

Additional briefs of amici curiae were filed on behalf of Femenists for Free Expression, the NAACP Legal Defense and Educational Fund, Inc., et al., the National Conference of Women's Bar Associations, et al., the National Employment Lawyers Association, the NOW Legal Defense and Education Fund, et al., the Southern States Police Benevolent Association, et al., the Women's Legal Defense Fund, et al., and the Employment Law Center, et al.

Opposing Side (Respondent / Appellee)

Brief of amici curiae filed on behalf of the Equal Employment Advisory Council by Robert E. Williams, Douglas S. McDowell, and Ann Elizabeth Reesman.

Brief of amici curiae filed on behalf of the American Psychological Association by Dort S. Bigg, in support of neither party.

IV. THE SUPREME COURT'S DECISION

"Title VII of the Civil Rights Act of 1964 makes it 'an unlawful employment practice for an employer . . . to discriminate against any individual with respect to his compensation, terms, conditions, or privileges of employment, because of such individual's race, color, religion, sex, or national origin.' . . . When the workplace is permeated with 'discriminatory intimidation, ridicule, and insult,' that is 'sufficiently severe or pervasive to alter the conditions of the victim's employment and create an abusive working environment,' Title VII is violated....

Certainly Title VII bars conduct that would seriously affect a reasonable person's psychological well being, but the statute is not limited to such conduct. So long as the environment would reasonably be perceived, and is perceived, as hostile or abusive there is no need for it also to be psychologically injurious.

This is not, and by its nature cannot be, a mathematically precise test. We need not answer today all the potential questions it raises, nor specifically address the EEOC's new regulations on this subject. But we can say that whether an environment is 'hostile' or 'abusive' can be determined only by looking at all the circumstances. These may include the frequency of the discriminatory conduct; its severity; whether it is physically threatening or humiliating, or a mere offensive utterance; and whether it unreasonably interferes with an employee's work performance. The effect on the employee's psychological well being is, of course, relevant to determining whether the plaintiff actually found the environment abusive. But while psychological harm, like any other relevant factor, may be taken into account, no single factor is required. . . .

We therefore reverse the judgment of the Court of Appeals, and remand the case for further proceedings consistent with this opinion."

V. JUSTICE VOTE

9 Pro ACLU Side vs. 0 Con Opposing Side

ACLU Side (Petitioner / Appellant)

1. O'Connor, S. – Wrote majority opinion
2. Scalia, A. – Wrote concurring opinion
3. Ginsburg, R. – Wrote concurring opinion
4. Kennedy, A. – Joined majority opinion
5. Souter, D. – Joined majority opinion
6. Thomas, C. – Joined majority opinion
7. Blackmun, H. – Joined majority opinion
8. Rehnquist, W. – Joined majority opinion
9. Stevens, J. – Joined majority opinion

VI. A WIN OR LOSS FOR THE ACLU?

The ACLU, as amicus curiae, urged reversal of the judgment of the Court of Appeals; the Supreme Court reversed and remanded in a 9-0 vote, giving the ACLU an apparent win .

764. United States v. James Daniel Good Real Property

(Decided December 13, 1993; 510 U.S. 43)

I. ISSUE

A. Issues Discussed

Criminal justice, drugs, Fifth Amendment, due process, notice and hearing, Fourth Amendment, search and seizure, property forfeiture

B. Legal Question Presented

"[W]hether, in the absence of exigent circumstances, the Due Process Clause of the Fifth Amendment prohibits the Government in a civil forfeiture case from seizing real property without first affording the owner notice and an opportunity to be heard."

C. Supreme Court's Answer

In the absence of exigent circumstances, due process prohibits the Government from seizing real property in civil forfeiture without first affording the owner notice and the opportunity to be heard.

II. CASE SUMMARY

A. Background

"On January 31, 1985, Hawaii police officers executed a search warrant at the home of claimant James Daniel Good. The search uncovered about 89 pounds of marijuana, marijuana seeds, vials containing hashish oil, and drug paraphernalia. About six months later, Good pleaded guilty to promoting a harmful drug in the second degree, in violation of Hawaii law. He was sentenced to one year in jail and five years' probation, and fined $1,000. Good was also required to forfeit to the State $3,187 in cash found on the premises.

On August 8, 1989, 4 1/2 years after the drugs were found, the United States filed an in rem action in the United States District Court for the District of Hawaii, seeking to forfeit Good's house and the 4-acre parcel on which it was situated. The United States sought forfeiture under 21 U.S.C. § 881(a)(7), on the ground that the property had been used to commit or facilitate the commission of a federal drug offense.

On August 18, 1989, in an ex parte proceeding, a United States Magistrate Judge found that the Government had established probable cause to believe Good's property was subject to forfeiture under § 881(a)(7). A warrant of arrest in rem was issued, authorizing seizure of the property. The warrant was based on an affidavit recounting the fact of Good's conviction and the evidence discovered during the January 1985 search of his home by Hawaii police.

The Government seized the property on August 21, 1989, without prior notice to Good or an adversary hearing. At the time of the seizure, Good was renting his home to tenants for $900 per month. The Government permitted the tenants to remain on the premises subject to an occupancy agreement, but directed the payment of future rents to the United States Marshal.

Good filed a claim for the property and an answer to the Government's complaint. He asserted that the seizure deprived him of his property without due process of law and that the forfeiture action was invalid because it had not been timely commenced under the statute. The District Court granted the Government's motion for summary judgment and entered an order forfeiting the property.

The Court of Appeals for the Ninth Circuit affirmed in part, reversed in part, and remanded for further proceedings. The court was unanimous in holding that the seizure of Good's property, without prior notice and a hearing, violated the Due Process Clause. In a divided decision, the Court of Appeals further held that the District Court erred in finding the action timely. The Court of Appeals ruled that the 5-year statute of limitations in 19 U.S.C. § 1621 is only an 'outer limit' for filing a forfeiture action, and that further limits are imposed by 19 U.S.C. §§ 1602 -1604. Those provisions, the court reasoned, impose a 'series of internal notification and reporting requirements,' under which 'customs agents must report to customs officers, customs officers must report to the United States attorney, and the Attorney General must 'immediately' and 'forthwith' bring a forfeiture action if he believes that one is warranted.' The Court of Appeals ruled that failure to comply with these internal reporting rules could require dismissal of the forfeiture action as untimely. The court remanded the case for a determination whether the Government had satisfied its obligation to make prompt reports."

The Supreme Court granted certiorari to review the case, affirmed in part, reversed in part, and remanded.

B. Counsel of Record / ACLU Attorney

ACLU Side (Respondent / Appellee): Christopher J. Yuen argued the cause for appellee.

Opposing Side (Petitioner / Appellant): Edwin S. Kneedler argued the cause for appellant.

III. AMICI CURIAE

ACLU Side (Respondent / Appellee)

Brief of amici curiae filed on behalf of the ACLU, et al., by Steven Alan Reiss, Richard A. Rothman, Katherine Oberlies, Lee P. Dranikoff, Steven R. Shapiro, and John A. Powell.

Brief of amici curiae filed on behalf of the Institute for Justice by William H. Mellor III, Clint Bolick, Dirk G. Roggeveen, and Scott G. Bullock.

Brief of amici curiae filed on behalf of the National Association of Criminal Defense Lawyers by Richard J. Troberman and E. E. Edwards III.

Opposing Side (Petitioner / Appellant)

Brief of amici curiae filed on behalf of the State of Kentucky, et al., by Chris Gorman, Attorney General of Kentucky, David A. Sexton, Assistant Attorney General, and the following Attorneys General for their respective states: Malaetasi Togafau of American Samoa, Grant Woods of Arizona, Daniel E. Lungren of California, Domenick J. Galluzzo of Connecticut, Pamela Carter of Indiana, Robert T. Stephan of Kansas, Richard P. Ieyoub of Louisiana, J. Joseph Curran, Jr., of Maryland, Scott Harshbarger of Massachusetts, Frank J. Kelley of Michigan, Mike Moore of Mississippi, Joseph P. Mazurek of Montana, Don Stenberg of Nebraska, Jeffrey R. Howard of New Hampshire, Tom Udall of New Mexico, Heidi Heitkamp of North Dakota, Ernest D. Preate, Jr., of Pennsylvania, Joseph B. Myer of Wyoming.

IV. THE SUPREME COURT'S DECISION

"Though the Fourth Amendment places limits on the Government's power to seize property for purposes of forfeiture, it does not provide the sole measure of constitutional protection that must be afforded property owners in forfeiture proceedings. So even assuming that the Fourth Amendment were satisfied in this case, it remains for us to determine whether the seizure complied with our well settled jurisprudence under the Due Process Clause. . . .

The right to prior notice and a hearing is central to the Constitution's command of due process. . . . We tolerate some exceptions to the general rule requiring predeprivation notice and hearing, but only in "extraordinary situations where some valid governmental interest is at stake that justifies postponing the hearing until after the event." . . .

In sum, based upon the importance of the private interest at risk and the absence of countervailing Government needs, we hold that the seizure of real property under § 881(a)(7) is not one of those extraordinary instances that justify the postponement of notice and hearing. Unless exigent circumstances are present, the Due Process Clause requires the Government to afford notice and a meaningful opportunity to be heard before seizing real property subject to civil forfeiture. . . . We agree with the Court of Appeals that no showing of exigent circumstances has been made in this case, and we affirm its ruling that the ex parte seizure of Good's real property violated due process. . . .

We hold that courts may not dismiss a forfeiture action filed within the 5-year statute of limitations for noncompliance with the internal timing requirements of §§ 1602-1604. The Government filed the action in this case within the five-year statute of limitations, and that sufficed to make it timely. We reverse the contrary holding of the Court of Appeals."

V. JUSTICE VOTE

5 Pro ACLU Side vs. 4 Con Opposing Side

ACLU Side (Respondent / Appellee)

1. Kennedy, A. – Wrote majority opinion
2. Blackmun, H. – Joined majority opinion
3. Stevens, J. – Joined majority opinion
4. Souter, D. – Joined majority opinion
5. Ginsburg, R. – Joined majority opinion

Opposing Side (Petitioner / Appellant)

1. Rehnquist, W. – Wrote opinion concurring in part and dissenting in part
2. Scalia, A. – Joined Rehnquist's opinion
3. O'Connor, S. – Wrote opinion concurring in part and dissenting in part, joined Rehnquist's opinion in part
4. Thomas, C. – Wrote opinion concurring in part and dissenting in part

VI. A WIN OR LOSS FOR THE ACLU?

The ACLU filed as amicus curiae urging affirmance of the judgment of the Court of Appeals; the Supreme Court affirmed in part in a 5-4 vote, giving the ACLU an apparent win.

765. Weiss v. United States

(Decided January 19, 1994; 510 U.S. 163)

I. ISSUE

A. Issues Discussed

Governmental authority, military, Fifth Amendment, due process, Appointments Clause

B. Legal Question Presented

"[W]hether the current method of appointing military judges violates the Appointments Clause of the Constitution, and whether the lack of a fixed term of office for military judges violates the Fifth Amendment's Due Process Clause."

C. Supreme Court's Answer

The current method of appointing military judges does not violate the Appointments Clause and the lack of fixed terms does not violate the Due Process Clause.

II. CASE SUMMARY

A. Background

"Petitioner Weiss, a United States Marine, pleaded guilty at a special court-martial to one count of larceny, in violation of Article 121 of the Uniform Code of Military Justice (UCMJ or Code), 10 U.S.C. § 921. He was sentenced to three months of confinement, partial forfeiture of pay, and a bad-conduct discharge. Petitioner Hernandez, also a Marine, pleaded guilty to the possession, importation, and distribution of cocaine, in violation of Article 112a, UCMJ, 10 U.S.C. § 912a, and conspiracy, in violation of Article 81, UCMJ, 10 U.S.C. § 881. He was sentenced to 25 years of confinement, forfeiture of all pay, a reduction in rank, and a dishonorable discharge. The convening authority reduced Hernandez' sentence to 20 years of confinement.

The Navy–Marine Corps Court of Military Review, in separate appeals, affirmed petitioners' convictions. The Court of Military Appeals granted plenary review in petitioner Weiss' case to address his contention that the judges in his case had no authority to convict him because their appointments violated the Appointments Clause, and their lack of a fixed term of office violated the Due Process Clause. Relying on its recent decision in United States v. Graf, 35 M.J. 450 (1992), cert. pending, No. 92–1102, in which the court unanimously held that due process does not require military judges to have a fixed term of office, the court rejected Weiss' due process argument. In a splintered decision, the court also rejected petitioner's Appointments Clause challenge.

Two of the five judges concluded that the initial appointment of military trial and appellate judges as commissioned officers is sufficient to satisfy the Appointments Clause. A separate appointment before taking on the duties of a military judge is unnecessary, according to the plurality, in part because the duties of a judge in the military justice system are germane to the duties that military officers already discharge. One judge concurred in the result only, concluding that the Appointments Clause does not apply to the military. The other two judges dissented separately. Both stressed the significant changes brought about by the Military Justice Act of 1968, particularly the duties added to the newly created office of military judge, and both concluded that the duties of a military judge are sufficiently distinct from the other duties performed by military officers to require a second appointment.

The Court of Military Appeals accordingly affirmed petitioner Weiss' conviction. Based on its decision in Weiss, the court, in an unpublished opinion, also affirmed petitioner Hernandez' conviction."

The Supreme Court granted certiorari to review both cases and affirmed.

B. Counsel of Record / ACLU Attorney

ACLU Side (Petitioner / Appellant): Alan B. Morrison argued the cause for appellant.

Opposing Side (Respondent / Appellee): Solicitor General Drew S. Days, III, argued the case for appellee.

III. AMICI CURIAE

ACLU Side (Petitioner / Appellant)

Brief of amici curiae filed on behalf of the ACLU, et al., by David B. Isabell, John Vanderstar, David H. Resnicoff, Steven R. Shapiro, and Arthur B. Spitzer.

Brief of amici curiae filed on behalf of the United States Air Force Appellate Defense Division by Robert I. Smith, Jay L. Cohen, and Frank J. Spinner.

Opposing Side (Respondent / Appellee)

No briefs of amici curiae were filed in support of appellee.

IV. THE SUPREME COURT'S DECISION

"Congress' treatment of military judges is . . . quite different from its treatment of those offices, such as Chairman of the Joint Chiefs of Staff, for which it wished to require a second appointment before already-commissioned officers could occupy them. This difference negates any permissible inference that Congress intended that military judges should receive a second appointment, but in a fit of absentmindedness forgot to say so.

[M]ilitary judges do not have any 'inherent judicial authority separate from a court-martial to which they have been detailed. When they act, they do so as a court-martial, not as a military judge. Until detailed to a specific court-martial, they have no more authority than any other military officer of the same grade and rank.' Military appellate judges similarly exercise judicial functions only when they are 'assigned' to a Court of Military Review. Neither military trial nor appellate judges, moreover, have a fixed term of office. Commissioned officers are assigned or detailed to the position of military judge by a Judge Advocate General for a period of time he deems necessary or appropriate, and then they may be reassigned to perform other duties. Even while serving as military trial judges, officers may perform, with the permission of the Judge Advocate General, duties unrelated to their judicial responsibilities. Whatever might be the case in civilian society, we think that the role of military judge is 'germane' to that of military officer.

In sum, we believe that the current scheme satisfies the Appointments Clause. It is quite clear that Congress has not required a separate appointment to the position of military judge, and we believe it equally clear that the Appointments Clause by its own force does not require a second appointment before military officers may discharge the duties of such a judge. . . .

Although a fixed term of office is a traditional component of the Anglo–American civilian judicial system, it has never been a part of the military justice tradition. . . . The entire system . . . is overseen by the Court of Military Appeals, which is composed entirely of civilian judges who serve for fixed terms of 15 years. That court has demonstrated its vigilance in checking any attempts to exert improper influence over military judges. . . . The absence of tenure as a historical matter in the system of military justice, and the number of safeguards in place to ensure impartiality, lead us to reject petitioners' due process challenge. Petitioners have fallen far short of demonstrating that the factors favoring fixed terms of office are so extraordinarily weighty as to overcome the balance achieved by Congress.

For the reasons stated, we reject the petitioners' Appointments Clause and Due Process Clause attacks on the judges who convicted them and those who heard their appeals. The judgments of the Court of Military Appeals are accordingly affirmed."

V. JUSTICE VOTE

0 Pro ACLU Side vs. 9 Con Opposing Side

Opposing Side (Respondent / Appellee)

1. Rehnquist, W. – Wrote majority opinion
2. Blackmun, H. – Joined majority opinion
3. Stevens, J. – Joined majority opinion
4. O'Connor, S. – Joined majority opinion
5. Kennedy, A. – Joined majority opinion
6. Scalia, A. – Wrote concurring opinion
7. Thomas, C. – Joined Scalia's concurrence
8. Souter, D. – Wrote concurring opinion
9. Ginsburg, R. – Wrote concurring opinion

VI. A WIN OR LOSS FOR THE ACLU?

The ACLU filed as amicus curiae urging reversal of the judgment of the United States Court of Military Appeals; the Supreme Court affirmed in a 9-0 vote, giving the ACLU an apparent loss.

766. National Organization for Women, Inc. v. Scheidler

(Decided January 24, 1994; 510 U.S. 249)

I. ISSUE

A. Issues Discussed

Government authority, civil procedure, First Amendment, RICO

B. Legal Question Presented

"[W]hether RICO requires proof that either the racketeering enterprise or the predicate acts of racketeering were motivated by an economic purpose."

C. Supreme Court's Answer

RICO does not require proof that racketeering activities were motivated by an economic purpose.

II. CASE SUMMARY

A. Background

"Petitioner National Organization for Women, Inc. (NOW), is a national nonprofit organization that supports the legal availability of abortion; petitioners Delaware Women's Health Organization, Inc. (DWHO), and Summit Women's Health Organization, Inc. (SWHO), are health care centers that perform abortions and other medical procedures. Respondents are a coalition of antiabortion groups called the Pro–Life Action Network (PLAN), Joseph Scheidler and other individuals and organizations that oppose legal abortion, and a medical laboratory that formerly provided services to the two petitioner health care centers.

Petitioners sued respondents in the United States District Court for the Northern District of Illinois, alleging violations of the Sherman Act, 26 Stat. 209, as amended, 15 U.S.C. § 1 et seq., and RICO's §§ 1962(a), (c), and (d), as well as several pendent state-law claims stemming from the activities of antiabortion protesters at the clinics. According to respondent Scheidler's congressional testimony, these protesters aim to shut down the clinics and persuade women not to have abortions. Petitioners sought injunctive relief, along with treble damages, costs, and attorney's fees. They later amended their complaint, and pursuant to local rules, filed a 'RICO Case Statement' that further detailed the enterprise, the pattern of racketeering, the victims of the racketeering activity, and the participants involved.

The amended complaint alleged that respondents were members of a nationwide conspiracy to shut down abortion clinics through a pattern of racketeering activity including extortion in violation of the Hobbs Act, 18 U.S.C. § 1951. Section 1951(b)(2) defines extortion as 'the obtaining of property from another, with his consent, induced by wrongful use of actual or threatened force, violence, or fear, or under color of official right.' Petitioners alleged that respondents conspired to use threatened or actual force, violence, or fear to induce clinic employees, doctors, and patients to give up their jobs, give up their economic right to practice medicine, and give up their right to obtain medical services at the clinics. Petitioners claimed that this conspiracy 'has injured the business and/or property interests of the [petitioners].' According to the amended complaint, PLAN constitutes the alleged racketeering 'enterprise' for purposes of § 1962(c).

The District Court dismissed the case pursuant to Federal Rule of Civil Procedure 12(b)(6). . . . The Court of Appeals affirmed."

The Supreme Court granted certiorari to review the case and reversed.

B. Counsel of Record / ACLU Attorney

ACLU Side (Petitioner / Appellant): Fay Clayton argued the cause for the appellant.

Miguel A. Estrada argued the cause for the United States, as amicus curiae, by special leave of Court.

Opposing Side (Respondent / Appellee): G. Robert Blakey argued the cause for appellee.

III. AMICI CURIAE

ACLU Side (Petitioner / Appellant)

Brief of amici curiae filed on behalf of the ACLU by Louis M. Bograd and Steven R. Shapiro. The ACLU filed an amicus brief in support of neither party, urging remand with enhanced clarity on RICO guidelines.

Brief of amici curiae filed on behalf of the United States by Miguel A. Estrada, Solicitor General Days, Acting Assistant Attorney General Keeney, Deputy Solicitor General Bryson, and Cynthia A. Young.

Brief of amici curiae filed on behalf of the State of New York, et al., by Robert Abrams, Attorney General of New York, Jerry Boone, Solicitor General, Sanford M. Cohen, Assistant Attorney General, and the following Attorneys General for their respective states: Richard Blumental of Connecticut, Roland W. Burris of Illinois, Michael F. Easley of North Carolina, Stephen D. Rosenthal of Virginia, Hubert H. Humphrey II of Minnesota, and Lee Fisher of Ohio.

Brief of amici curiae filed on behalf of the American Medical Association, et al., by Jack R. Bierig, Carter G. Phillips, Kirk B. Johnson, Edward B. Hirshfeld, Michael L. Ile, David F. Graham, Richard D. Raskin, and Ann E. Allen.

Brief of amici curiae filed on behalf of the National Abortion Federation, et al., by Elaine Metlin, Nancie A. Thomas, Celeste Lacy Davis, Eve W. Paul, and Roger K. Evans.

Brief of amici curiae filed on behalf of the Nation Network of Abortion Funds by Kathryn Kolbert and Eve C. Gartner.

Brief of amici curiae filed on behalf of the NOW Legal Defense and Education Fund, et al., by David I. Goldblatt, Charles S. Sims, Deborah A. Ellis, Harry W. Lipman, and Burt Neuborne.

Opposing Side (Respondent / Appellee)

Brief of amici curiae filed on behalf of People for the Ethical Treatment of Animals, Inc., et al., by Edward McGlynn Gaffney, Jr., Victor G. Rosenblum, and David Goldberger.

Brief of amici curiae filed on behalf of the Ohio Right to Life Society, Inc., et al., by David F. Forte.

Brief of amici curiae filed on behalf of the Southern Center for Law & Ethics, et al., by Steven T. McFarland, Bradley P. Jacob, Albert L. Jordan, and David Smolin.

Brief of amici curiae filed on behalf of Focus on the Family by Stephen W. Reed, Carmen K. Bullard, Theresa Schrempp, and Ronald E. McKinstry.

IV. THE SUPREME COURT'S DECISION

"Section 1962(c) makes it unlawful 'for any person employed by or associated with any enterprise engaged in, or the activities of which affect, interstate or foreign commerce, to conduct or participate, directly or indirectly, in the conduct of such enterprise's affairs through a pattern of racketeering activity or collection of unlawful debt.' Section 1961(1) defines 'pattern of racketeering activity' to include conduct that is 'chargeable' or 'indictable' under a host of state and federal laws. RICO broadly defines 'enterprise' in § 1961(4) to 'includ[e] any individual, partnership, corporation, association, or other legal entity, and any union or group of individuals associated in fact although not a legal entity.' Nowhere in either § 1962(c) or in the RICO definitions in § 1961 is there any indication that an economic motive is required.

[T]he 'enterprise' in subsection (c) connotes generally the vehicle through which the unlawful pattern of racketeering activity is committed, rather than the victim of that activity. [I]t need not have a property interest that can be acquired nor an economic motive for engaging in illegal activity; it need only be an association in fact that engages in a pattern of racketeering activity. . . .

We therefore hold that petitioners may maintain this action if respondents conducted the enterprise through a pattern of racketeering activity. The questions of whether the respondents committed the requisite predicate acts, and whether the commission of these acts fell into a pattern, are not before us. We hold only that RICO contains no economic motive requirement.

The judgment of the Court of Appeals is accordingly reversed."

V. JUSTICE VOTE

9 Pro ACLU Side vs. 0 Con Opposing Side

ACLU Side (Petitioner / Appellant)

1. Rehnquist, W. – Wrote majority opinion
2. Blackmun, H. – Joined majority opinion
3. Stevens, J. – Joined majority opinion
4. O'Connor, S. – Joined majority opinion
5. Scalia, A. – Joined majority opinion
6. Thomas, C. – Joined majority opinion
7. Ginsberg, R. – Joined majority opinion
8. Souter, D. – Wrote concurring opinion
9. Kennedy, A. – Joined concurring opinion

VI. A WIN OR LOSS FOR THE ACLU?

The ACLU filed as amicus curiae urging remand of the judgment of the Court of Appeals; the Supreme Court reversed in a 9-0 vote, giving the ACLU an apparent win.

767. Albright v. Oliver

(Decided January 24, 1994; 510 U.S. 266)

I. ISSUE

A. Issues Discussed

Criminal justice, drugs, Fourth Amendment, due process, Fourteenth Amendment

B. Legal Question Presented

Whether there is "a substantive right under the Due Process Clause of the Fourteenth Amendment to be free from criminal prosecution except upon probable cause."

C. Supreme Court's Answer

There is no substantive due process right implicated here, however, the decision is upheld under the Fourth Amendment

II. CASE SUMMARY

A. Background

"Illinois authorities issued an arrest warrant for petitioner Kevin Albright, charging him on the basis of a previously filed criminal information with the sale of a substance which looked like an illegal drug. When he learned of the outstanding warrant, petitioner surrendered to respondent, Roger Oliver, a police detective employed by the city of Macomb, but denied his guilt of such an offense. He was released after posting bond, one of the conditions of which was that he not leave the State without permission of the court.

At a preliminary hearing, respondent Oliver testified that petitioner sold the look-alike substance to Moore, and the court found probable cause to bind petitioner over for trial. At a later pretrial hearing, the court dismissed the criminal action against petitioner on the ground that the charge did not state an offense under Illinois law.

Albright then instituted this action under Rev.Stat. § 1979,

42 U.S.C. § 1983, against Detective Oliver in his individual and official capacities, alleging that Oliver deprived him of substantive due process under the Fourteenth Amendment—his 'liberty interest'—to be free from criminal prosecution except upon probable cause. The District Court granted respondent's motion to dismiss under Rule 12(b)(6) on the ground that the complaint did not state a claim under § 1983. The Court of Appeals for the Seventh Circuit affirmed . . . ."

The Supreme Court granted certiorari to review the case and affirmed, but on different grounds.

B. Counsel of Record / ACLU Attorney

ACLU Side (Petitioner / Appellant): John H. Bisbee argued the cause for appellant.

Opposing Side (Respondent / Appellee): James G. Sotos argued the cause for appellee.

III. AMICI CURIAE

ACLU Side (Petitioner / Appellant)

Brief of amici curiae filed on behalf of the ACLU, et al., by Leon Friedman, Steven R. Shapiro, John A. Powell, and Harvey Grossman.

Opposing Side (Respondent / Appellee)

Brief of amici curiae filed on behalf of the National League of Cities, et al., by Richard Ruda.

IV. THE SUPREME COURT'S DECISION

"We hold that it is the Fourth Amendment, and not substantive due process, under which petitioner Albright's claim must be judged.

Section 1983 'is not itself a source of substantive rights,' but merely provides a 'method for vindicating federal rights elsewhere conferred.' . . .

The protections of substantive due process have for the most part been accorded to matters relating to marriage, family, procreation, and the right to bodily integrity. Petitioner's claim to be free from prosecution except on the basis of probable cause is markedly different from those recognized in this group of cases. . . .

The Framers considered the matter of pretrial deprivations of liberty and drafted the Fourth Amendment to address it. The Fourth Amendment provides:

'The right of the people to be secure in their persons, houses, papers, and effects, against unreasonable searches and seizures, shall not be violated, and no Warrants shall issue, but upon probable cause, supported by Oath or affirmation, and particularly describing the place to be searched, and the persons or things to be seized.'

We have in the past noted the Fourth Amendment's relevance to the deprivations of liberty that go hand in hand with criminal prosecutions. We have said that the accused is not 'entitled to judicial oversight or review of the decision to prosecute.' But here petitioner was not merely charged; he submitted himself to arrest.

We express no view as to whether petitioner's claim would succeed under the Fourth Amendment, since he has not presented that question in his petition for certiorari. We do hold that substantive due process, with its 'scarce and open-ended' 'guideposts' can afford him no relief.

The judgment of the Court of Appeals is therefore affirmed."

V. JUSTICE VOTE

2 Pro ACLU Side vs. 7 Con Opposing Side

ACLU Side (Petitioner / Appellant)

1. Stevens, J. – Wrote dissenting opinion
2. Blackmun, H. – Joined Stevens' dissent

Opposing Side (Respondent / Appellee)

1. Rehnquist, W. – Wrote majority opinion
2. O'Connor, S. – Joined majority opinion
3. Scalia, A. – Wrote concurring opinion
4. Ginsburg, R. – Wrote concurring opinion
5. Kennedy, A. – Wrote concurring opinion
6. Thomas, C. – Joined Kennedy's concurrence
7. Souter, D. – Wrote concurring opinion

VI. A WIN OR LOSS FOR THE ACLU?

The ACLU filed as amicus curiae urging reversal of the judgment of the Court of Appeals; the Supreme Court affirmed in a 7-2 vote giving the ACLU an apparent loss.

768. Elder v. Holloway

(Decided February 23, 1994; 510 U.S. 510)

I. ISSUE

A. Issues Discussed

Criminal justice, Fourth Amendment, precedent

B. Legal Question Presented

"[W]hether an appellate court, reviewing a judgment according public officials qualified immunity from a damages suit charging violation of a federal right, must disregard relevant legal authority not presented to, or considered by, the court of first instance."

C. Supreme Court's Answer

"We hold that appellate review of qualified immunity dispositions is to be conducted in light of all relevant precedents, not simply those cited to, or discovered by, the district court."

II. CASE SUMMARY

A. Background

"In April 1987, police officers in Idaho learned that Charles Elder was wanted by Florida authorities. They set out to arrest Elder, but did not obtain an Idaho arrest warrant. The officers planned to apprehend Elder at his workplace, in a public area where a warrant is not required. Finding that Elder had already left his jobsite, the officers surrounded the house in which he resided and ordered him to come out. Elder suffered epileptic seizures during the episode, and an officer instructed him to crawl out of the house to avoid injury from falling. Elder, instead, walked through the doorway, immediately suffered another seizure, and fell on the concrete walk in front of the house. He sustained serious brain trauma and remains partially paralyzed. . . .

Alleging that the warrantless arrest violated his Fourth Amendment right to be secure against unreasonable seizure, Elder sued the arresting officers for damages under 42 U.S.C. § 1983. [As to one aspect of the decision,] the District Court 'found no controlling Idaho or Ninth Circuit case law.' The District Court accordingly granted summary judgment for the officers on qualified immunity grounds.

On appeal, the Ninth Circuit noticed precedent in point missed in the District Court: United States v. Al–Azzawy, 784 F.2d 890 (CA9 1985), cert. denied, 476 U.S. 1144 (1986). . . . Elder could not benefit from the rule reaffirmed in Al– Azzawy, the Court of Appeals believed, because that precedent had been unearthed too late. For the conclusion that cases unmentioned in the District Court could not control on appeal, the Court of Appeals relied on Davis v. Scherer, 468 U.S. 183 (1984) . . . . Just as appellants forfeit facts not presented to the court of first instance, the Ninth Circuit reasoned, so, in the peculiar context of civil rights qualified immunity litigation, a plaintiff may not benefit on appeal from precedent neither he nor the district court itself mentioned in the first instance . . . ."

The Supreme Court granted certiorari to review the case and reversed.

B. Counsel of Record / ACLU Attorney

ACLU Side (Petitioner / Appellant): Michael E. Tankersley argued the cause for appellant.

Opposing Side (Respondent / Appellee): James J. Davis argued the cause for appellee.

III. AMICI CURIAE

ACLU Side (Petitioner / Appellant)

Brief of amici curiae filed on behalf of the ACLU by Andrew J. Pincus and Steven R. Shapiro.

Opposing Side (Respondent / Appellee)

Brief of amici curiae filed on behalf of the State of Hawaii, et al., by Robert A. Marks, Attorney General of Hawaii, and Steven S. Michaels, Deputy Attorney General, and by the Attorneys General for their respective jurisdictions as follows: Charles M. Oberly III of Delaware, Larry EchoHawk of Idaho, Roland W Burris of Illinois, Robert T. Stephan of Kansas, Scott Harshbarger of Massachusetts, Joseph P. Mazurek of Montana, Ernest D. Preate, Jr., of Pennsylvania, Jefferey B. Pine of Rhode Island, Jeffrey L. Amestoy of Vermont, Joseph B. Meyer of Wyoming, and Malaetasi Togafau of American Samoa.

IV. THE SUPREME COURT'S DECISION

"We hold that appellate review of qualified immunity dispositions is to be conducted in light of all relevant precedents, not simply those cited to, or discovered by, the district court. . . .

The central purpose of affording public officials qualified immunity from suit is to protect them 'from undue interference with their duties and from potentially disabling threats of liability.' The rule announced by the Ninth Circuit does not aid this objective because its operation is unpredictable in advance of the district court's adjudication. Nor does the rule further the interests on the other side of the balance: deterring public officials' unlawful actions and compensating victims of such conduct. Instead, it simply releases defendants because of shortages in counsel's or the court's legal research or briefing.

In thinking its rule compelled by this Court's instruction, the Ninth Circuit misconstrued Davis v. Scherer. The Court held in Davis that an official's clear violation of a state administrative regulation does not allow a § 1983 plaintiff to overcome the official's qualified immunity. Only in this context is the Court's statement comprehensible: 'A plaintiff who seeks damages for violation of constitutional or statutory rights may overcome the defendant official's qualified immunity only by showing that those rights were clearly established . . . .' Davis, in short, concerned not the authorities a court may consider in determining qualified immunity, but this entirely discrete question: Is qualified immunity defeated where a defendant violates any clearly established duty, including one under state law, or must the clearly established right be the federal right on which the claim for relief is based? The Court held the latter.

Whether an asserted federal right was clearly established at a particular time, so that a public official who allegedly violated the right has no qualified immunity from suit, presents a question of law, not one of 'legal facts.' That question of law, like the generality of such questions, must be resolved de novo on appeal. A court engaging in review of a qualified immunity judgment should therefore use its 'full knowledge of its own [and other relevant] precedents.'

We leave it to the Court of Appeals to consider, in light of all relevant authority . . . , whether the respondent officers are entitled to prevail on their qualified immunity defense. We express no opinion on that ultimate issue, nor do we consider whether the officers' alternate plea of exigent circumstances is tenable.

For the reasons stated, the judgment of the Court of Appeals is reversed, and the case is remanded for further proceedings consistent with this opinion."

V. JUSTICE VOTE

9 Pro ACLU Side vs. 0 Con Opposing Side

ACLU Side (Petitioner / Appellant)

1. Ginsburg, R. – Wrote majority opinion
2. Rehnquist, W. – Joined majority opinion
3. O'Connor, S. – Joined majority opinion
4. Scalia, A. – Joined majority opinion
5. Kennedy, A. – Joined majority opinion
6. Thomas, C. – Joined majority opinion
7. Souter, D. – Joined majority opinion
8. Stevens, J. – Joined majority opinion
9. Blackmun, H. – Joined majority opinion

VI. A WIN OR LOSS FOR THE ACLU?

The ACLU filed as amicus curiae urging reversal of the judgment of the Court of Appeals; the Supreme Court reversed in a 9-0 vote, giving the ACLU an apparent win.

769. Campbell v. Acuff-Rose Music, Inc.

(Decided March 7, 1994; 510 U.S. 569)

I. ISSUE

A. Issues Discussed

Governmental regulation, copyright, First Amendment

B. Legal Question Presented

"[W]hether 2 Live Crew's commercial parody of Roy Orbison's song, 'Oh, Pretty Woman,' may be a fair use within the meaning of the Copyright Act of 1976, 17 U.S.C. § 107."

C. Supreme Court's Answer

"Because we hold that a parody's commercial character is only one element to be weighed in a fair use enquiry, and that insufficient consideration was given to the nature of parody in weighing the degree of copying, we reverse and remand."

II. CASE SUMMARY

A. Background

"In 1964, Roy Orbison and William Dees wrote a rock ballad called 'Oh, Pretty Woman' and assigned their rights in it to respondent Acuff–Rose Music, Inc. Acuff–Rose registered the song for copyright protection.

Petitioners Luther R. Campbell, Christopher Wongwon, Mark Ross, and David Hobbs are collectively known as 2 Live Crew, a popular rap music group. In 1989, Campbell wrote a song entitled 'Pretty Woman,' which he later described in an affidavit as intended, 'through comical lyrics, to satirize the original work . . . .' On July 5, 1989, 2 Live Crew's manager informed Acuff–Rose that 2 Live Crew had written a parody of 'Oh, Pretty Woman,' that they would afford all credit for ownership and authorship of the original song to Acuff–Rose, Dees, and Orbison, and that they were willing to pay a fee for the use they wished to make of it. Enclosed with the letter were a copy of the lyrics and a recording of 2 Live Crew's song. Acuff–Rose's agent refused permission, stating that 'I am aware of the success enjoyed by 'The 2 Live Crews,' but I must inform you that we cannot permit the use of a parody of 'Oh, Pretty Woman." Nonetheless, in June or July 1989, 2 Live Crew released records, cassette tapes, and compact discs of 'Pretty Woman' in a collection of songs entitled 'As Clean As They Wanna Be.' The albums and compact discs identify the authors of 'Pretty Woman' as Orbison and Dees and its publisher as Acuff–Rose.

Almost a year later, after nearly a quarter of a million copies of the recording had been sold, Acuff–Rose sued 2 Live Crew and its record company, Luke Skyywalker Records, for copyright infringement. The District Court granted summary judgment for 2 Live Crew . . . . The Court of Appeals for the Sixth Circuit reversed and remanded."

The Supreme Court granted certiorari to review the case and reversed.

B. Counsel of Record / ACLU Attorney

ACLU Side (Petitioner / Appellant): Bruce S. Rogow argued the cause for appellant.

Opposing Side (Respondent / Appellee): Sidney S. Rosdeitcher argued the cause for appellee.

III. AMICI CURIAE

ACLU Side (Petitioner / Appellant)

Brief of amici curiae filed on behalf of the ACLU by Steven F. Reich, Thomas A. Robertson, Leecia R. Eve, Steven R. Shapiro, Marjorie Heins, and John A. Powell.

Brief of amici curiae filed on behalf of Capitol Steps Production, Inc., et al., by William C. Lane, David Charles Masselli, and Tracy Ann Roman.

Brief of amici curiae filed on behalf of the Harvard Lampoon, Inc., by Robert H. Loeffler and Jonathan Band.

Brief of amici curiae filed on behalf of the PEN American Center by Leon Friedman.

Brief of amici curiae filed on behalf of Robert C. Berry, et al., by Alfred C. Yen.

Brief of amici curiae filed on behalf of Home Box Office, et al., by Daniel M. Waggoner, P. Cameron DeVore, Gregory J. Kopta, David Wright Tremaine, John S. Redpath, Sr., Stephen Sapienza, Steven Paul Mark, George Vradenburg, Bonnie Bogin, Lillian Laserson, Anne H. Egerton, Richard Cotton, and Michell Salem.

Opposing Side (Respondent / Appellee)

Brief of amici curiae filed on behalf of the National Music Publishers' Association, Inc., et al., by Marvin E. Frankel and Michael S. Oberman.

Brief of amici curiae filed on behalf of Fred Ebb, et al., by Stephen Rackow Kaye, Charles S. Sims, Jon A. Baumgarten, Paul H. Epstein, Christopher T. Meyer, and Susan L. Hochman.

Brief of amici curiae filed on behalf of Warner Bros. by Cary H. Sherman, Robert Alan Garrett, Preeta D. Bansal, Bernard R. Sorkin, and John A. Schulman, in support of neither party.

IV. THE SUPREME COURT'S DECISION

"It is uncontested here that 2 Live Crew's song would be an infringement of Acuff Rose's rights in 'Oh, Pretty Woman,' under the Copyright Act of 1976, but for a finding of fair use through parody. From the infancy of copyright protection, some opportunity for fair use of copyrighted materials has been thought necessary to fulfill copyright's very purpose, 'to promote the Progress of Science and useful Arts . . . .'

This Court has only once before even considered whether parody may be fair use, and that time issued no opinion because of the Court's equal division. Suffice it to say now that parody has an obvious claim to transformative value, as Acuff-Rose itself does not deny. Like less ostensibly humorous forms of criticism, it can provide social benefit, by shedding light on an earlier work, and, in the process, creating a new one. We thus line up with the courts that have held that parody, like other comment or criticism, may claim fair use under § 107. . . .

Here, the District Court held, and the Court of Appeals assumed, that 2 Live Crew's 'Pretty Woman' contains parody, commenting on and criticizing the original work, whatever it may have to say about society at large. As the District Court remarked, the words of 2 Live Crew's song copy the original's first line, but then 'quickly degenerat[e] into a play on words, substituting predictable lyrics with shocking ones . . . [that] derisively demonstrat[e] how bland and banal the Orbison song seems to them.' . . .

The threshold question when fair use is raised in defense of parody is whether a parodic character may reasonably be perceived. Whether, going beyond that, parody is in good taste or bad does not and should not matter to fair use. . . .

We think the Court of Appeals was insufficiently appreciative of parody's need for the recognizable sight or sound when it ruled 2 Live Crew's use unreasonable as a matter of law. It is true, of course, that 2 Live Crew copied the characteristic opening bass riff (or musical phrase) of the original, and true that the words of the first line copy the Orbison lyrics. But if quotation of the opening riff and the first line may be said to go to the 'heart' of the original, the heart is also what most readily conjures up the song for parody, and it is the heart at which parody takes aim. Copying does not become excessive in relation to parodic purpose merely because the portion taken was the original's heart. If 2 Live Crew had copied a significantly less memorable part of the original, it is difficult to see how its parodic character would have come through. . . .

It was error for the Court of Appeals to conclude that the commercial nature of 2 Live Crew's parody of 'Oh, Pretty Woman' rendered it presumptively unfair. No such evidentiary presumption is available to address either the first factor, the character and purpose of the use, or the fourth, market harm, in determining whether a transformative use, such as parody, is a fair one. The court also erred in holding that 2 Live Crew had necessarily copied excessively from the Orbison original, considering the parodic purpose of the use. We therefore reverse the judgment of the Court of Appeals and remand the case for further proceedings consistent with this opinion."

V. JUSTICE VOTE

9 Pro ACLU Side vs. 0 Con Opposing Side

ACLU Side (Petitioner / Appellant)

1. Souter, D. – Wrote majority opinion
2. Rehnquist, W. – Joined majority opinion
3. Blackmun, H. – Joined majority opinion
4. Stevens, J. – Joined majority opinion
5. O'Connor, S. – Joined majority opinion
6. Scalia, A. – Joined majority opinion
7. Thomas, C. – Joined majority opinion
8. Ginsburg, R. – Joined majority opinion
9. Kennedy, A. – Wrote concurring opinion

VI. A WIN OR LOSS FOR THE ACLU?

The ACLU filed a brief of amicus curiae urging reversal of the judgment of the Court of Appeals; the Supreme Court reversed in a 9-0 vote, giving ACLU an apparent win.

770. J.E.B. v. Alabama ex rel. T.B.

(Decided April 19, 1994; 511 U.S. 127)

I. ISSUE

A. Issues Discussed

Equal protection, gender discrimination, jury selection

B. Legal Question Presented

"[W]hether the Equal Protection Clause forbids intentional discrimination on the basis of gender, just as it prohibits discrimination on the basis of race."

C. Supreme Court's Answer

"Intentional discrimination on the basis of gender by state actors violates the Equal Protection Clause, particularly where, as here, the discrimination serves to ratify and perpetuate invidious, archaic, and overbroad stereotypes about the relative abilities of men and women."

II. CASE SUMMARY

A. Background

"On behalf of relator T. B., the mother of a minor child, respondent State of Alabama filed a complaint for paternity and child support against petitioner J.E.B. in the District Court of Jackson County, Alabama. On October 21, 1991, the matter was called for trial and jury selection began. The trial court assembled a panel of 36 potential jurors, 12 males and 24 females. After the court excused three jurors for cause, only 10 of the remaining 33 jurors were male. The State then used 9 of its 10 peremptory strikes to remove male jurors; petitioner used all but one of his strikes to remove female jurors. As a result, all the selected jurors were female.

Before the jury was empaneled, petitioner objected to the State's peremptory challenges on the ground that they were exercised against male jurors solely on the basis of gender, in violation of the Equal Protection Clause of the Fourteenth Amendment. Petitioner argued that the logic and reasoning of Batson v. Kentucky, which prohibits peremptory strikes solely on the basis of race, similarly forbids intentional discrimination on the basis of gender. The court rejected petitioner's claim and empaneled the all-female jury. The jury found petitioner to be the father of the child and the court entered an order directing him to pay child support. On post-judgment motion, the court reaffirmed its ruling that Batson does not extend to gender based peremptory challenges. The Alabama Court of Civil Appeals affirmed, relying on Alabama precedent. The Supreme Court of Alabama denied certiorari."

The Supreme Court granted certiorari to review the case and reversed.

B. Counsel of Record / ACLU Attorney

ACLU Side (Petitioner / Appellant): John F. Porter, III, argued the cause for appellant.

Michael R. Dreeben argued the cause for the United States, as amicus curiae, by special leave of Court.

Opposing Side (Respondent / Appellee): Lois B. Brasfield, Assistant Attorney General of Alabama, argued the cause for appellee.

III. AMICI CURIAE

ACLU Side (Petitioner / Appellant)

Brief of amici curiae filed on behalf of the National Women's Law Center, American Association of Univerity Women, ACLU, et al., by Marcia Greenberger, Myung J. Lee, Deborah L. Brake, David H. Coburn, Roderick L. Thomas, and Stephanie A. Philips.

Brief of amici curiae filed on behalf of the United States by Michael R. Dreeben, Solicitor General Days, Acting Assistant Attorneys General Keeney and Turner, and Deputy Solicitor General Bryson.

Opposing Side (Respondent / Appellee)

No briefs of amici curiae were filed in support of appellee.

IV. THE SUPREME COURT'S DECISION

"Equal opportunity to participate in the fair administration of justice is fundamental to our democratic system. It not only furthers the goals of the jury system. It reaffirms the promise of equality under the law—that all citizens, regardless of race, ethnicity, or gender, have the chance to take part directly in our democracy. When persons are excluded from participation in our democratic processes solely because of race or gender, this promise of equality dims, and the integrity of our judicial system is jeopardized.

In view of these concerns, the Equal Protection Clause prohibits discrimination in jury selection on the basis of gender, or on the assumption that an individual will be biased in a particular case for no reason other than the fact that the person happens to be a woman or happens to be a man. . . .

The judgment of the Court of Civil Appeals of Alabama is reversed, and the case is remanded to that court for further proceedings not inconsistent with this opinion."

V. JUSTICE VOTE

6 Pro ACLU Side vs. 3 Con Opposing Side

ACLU Side (Petitioner / Appellant)

1. Blackmun, H. – Wrote majority opinion
2. Stevens, J. – Joined majority opinion
3. O'Connor, S. – Wrote concurring opinion
4. Souter, D. – Joined majority opinion
5. Ginsburg, R. – Joined majority opinion
6. Kennedy, A. – Wrote concurring opinion

Opposing Side (Respondent / Appellee)

1. Rehnquist, W. – Wrote dissenting opinion, joined Scalia's dissent
2. Scalia, A. – Wrote dissenting opinion
3. Thomas, C. – Joined Scalia's dissent

VI. A WIN OR LOSS FOR THE ACLU?

The ACLU, as amicus curiae, urged reversal of the judgment of the Court of Civil Appeals of Alabama; the Supreme Court reversed in a 6-3 vote, giving the ACLU an apparent win.

771. Nichols v. United States

(Decided June 6, 1994; 511 U.S. 738)

I. ISSUE

A. Issues Discussed

Criminal justice, drugs, Sixth Amendment, Fourteenth Amendment

B. Legal Question Presented

"Whether the Constitution prohibits a sentencing court from considering a defendant's previous uncounseled misdemeanor conviction in sentencing him for a subsequent offense."

C. Supreme Court's Answer

The Constitution allows a sentencing court to consider a previous uncounseled misdemeanor conviction in sentencing for a subsequent offense.

II. CASE SUMMARY

A. Background

"In 1990, petitioner Nichols pleaded guilty to conspiracy to possess cocaine with intent to distribute, in violation of 21 U.S.C. § 846. Pursuant to the United States Sentencing Commission's Guidelines (Sentencing Guidelines), petitioner was assessed three criminal history points for a 1983 federal felony drug conviction. An additional criminal history point was assessed for petitioner's 1983 state misdemeanor conviction for driving under the influence (DUI), for which petitioner was fined $250 but was not incarcerated. This additional criminal history point increased petitioner's Criminal History Category from Category II to Category III. As a result, petitioner's sentencing range under the Sentencing Guidelines increased from 168-210 months (under Criminal History Category II) to 188-235 months (under Category III).

Petitioner objected to the inclusion of his DUI misdemeanor conviction in his criminal history score because he was not represented by counsel at that proceeding. He maintained that consideration of that uncounseled misdemeanor conviction in establishing his sentence would violate the Sixth Amendment as construed in Baldasar, supra. The United States District Court for the Eastern District of Tennessee found that petitioner's misdemeanor conviction was uncounseled and that, based on the record before it, petitioner had not waived his right to counsel. But the District Court rejected petitioner's Baldasar argument, explaining that in the absence of a majority opinion, Baldasar 'stands only for the proposition that a prior uncounseled misdemeanor conviction may not be used to create a felony with a prison term.' Because petitioner's offense was already defined as a felony, the District Court ruled that Baldasar was inapplicable to the facts of this case; thus, petitioner's constitutional rights were not violated by using his 1983 DUI conviction to enhance his sentence. It sentenced petitioner to the maximum term allowed by the Sentencing Guidelines under its interpretation of Baldasar, a term 25 months longer than if the misdemeanor conviction had not been considered in calculating petitioner's criminal history score.

A divided panel of the Court of Appeals for the Sixth Circuit affirmed. After reviewing the fractured decision in Baldasar and the opinions from other Courts of Appeals that had considered the issue, the court held that Baldasar limits the collateral use at sentencing of a prior uncounseled misdemeanor conviction only when the effect of such consideration is to convert a misdemeanor into a felony. The dissent, while recognizing that 'numerous courts have questioned whether [Baldasar] expresses any single holding, and, accordingly, have largely limited Baldasar to its facts,' nevertheless concluded that Baldasar proscribed the use of petitioner's prior uncounseled DUI conviction to enhance his sentence under the Sentencing Guidelines."

The Supreme Court granted certiorari to review the case and affirmed.

B. Counsel of Record / ACLU Attorney

ACLU Side (Petitioner / Appellant): William B. Mitchell Carter, by appointment of the Court, argued the cause for appellant.

Opposing Side (Respondent / Appellee): Deputy Solicitor General William C. Bryson argued the cause for appellee.

III. AMICI CURIAE

ACLU Side (Petitioner / Appellant)

Brief of amici curiae filed on behalf of the ACLU by Susan N. Herman and Steven R. Shapiro.

Opposing Side (Respondent / Appellee)

Brief of amici curiae filed on behalf of the Criminal Justice Legal Foundation by Kent S. Scheidegger and Charles L. Hobson.

IV. THE SUPREME COURT'S DECISION

"Five Members of the Court in Baldasar—the four dissenters and Justice Stewart— expressed continued adherence to Scott v. Illinois. There the defendant was convicted of shoplifting under a criminal statute which provided that the penalty for the offense should be a fine of not more than $500, a term of not more than one year in jail, or both. The defendant was in fact fined $50, but he contended that since imprisonment for the offense was authorized by statute, the Sixth and Fourteenth Amendments to the United States Constitution required Illinois to provide trial counsel. We rejected that contention, holding that so long as no imprisonment was actually imposed, the Sixth Amendment right to counsel did not obtain. We reasoned that the Court, in a number of decisions, had already expanded the language of the Sixth Amendment well beyond its obvious meaning, and that the line should be drawn between criminal proceedings which resulted in imprisonment, and those that did not.

We adhere to that holding today, but agree with the dissent in Baldasar that a logical consequence of the holding is that an uncounseled conviction valid under Scott may be relied upon to enhance the sentence for a subsequent offense, even though that sentence entails imprisonment. Enhancement statutes, whether in the nature of criminal history provisions such as those contained in the Sentencing Guidelines, or recidivist statutes which are common place in state criminal laws, do not change the penalty imposed for the earlier conviction. As pointed out in the dissenting opinion in Baldasar, '[t]his Court consistently has sustained repeat-offender laws as penalizing only the last offense committed by the defendant.' . . .

Sentencing courts have not only taken into consideration a defendant's prior convictions, but have also considered a defendant's past criminal behavior, even if no conviction resulted from that behavior. . . .

Thus, consistently with due process, petitioner in the present case could have been sentenced more severely based simply on evidence of the underlying conduct which gave rise to the previous DUI offense. And the state need prove such conduct only by a preponderance of the evidence. Surely, then, it must be constitutionally permissible to consider a prior uncounseled misdemeanor conviction based on the same conduct where that conduct must be proven beyond a reasonable doubt. . . .

Today we adhere to Scott v. Illinois, supra, and overrule Baldasar. Accordingly we hold, consistent with the Sixth and Fourteenth Amendments of the Constitution, that an uncounseled misdemeanor conviction, valid under Scott because no prison term was imposed, is also valid when used to enhance punishment at a subsequent conviction.

The judgment of the Court of Appeals is therefore affirmed."

V. JUSTICE VOTE

3 Pro ACLU Side vs. 6 Con Opposing Side

ACLU Side (Petitioner / Appellant)

1. Blackmun, H. – Wrote dissenting opinion
2. Ginsburg, R. – Wrote dissenting opinion, joined Blackmun's dissent
3. Stevens, J. – Joined Blackmun's dissent

Opposing Side (Respondent / Appellee)

1. Rehnquist, W. – Wrote majority opinion
2. O'Connor, S. – Joined majority opinion
3. Scalia, A. – Joined majority opinion
4. Kennedy, A. – Jointed majority opinion
5. Thomas, C. – Joined majority opinion
6. Souter, D. – Wrote concurring opinion

VI. A WIN OR LOSS FOR THE ACLU?

The ACLU filed as amicus curiae urging reversal of the judgment of the Court of Appeals; the Supreme Court affirmed in a 6-3 vote, giving the ACLU an apparent loss.

772. Farmer v. Brennan

(Decided June 6, 1994; 511 U.S. 825)

I. ISSUE

A. Issues Discussed

8th amendment, prison

B. Legal Question Presented

"A prison official's 'deliberate indifference' to a substantial risk of serious harm to an inmate violates the Eighth Amendment. This case requires us to define the term 'deliberate indifference' . . . ."

C. Supreme Court's Answer

"[S]ubjective recklessness as used in the criminal law is a familiar and workable standard that is consistent with the Cruel and Unusual Punishments Clause as interpreted in our cases, and we adopt it as the test for 'deliberate indifference' under the Eighth Amendment."

II. CASE SUMMARY

A. Background

"The dispute . . . stems from a civil suit brought by petitioner, Dee Farmer, alleging that respondents, federal prison officials, violated the Eighth Amendment by their deliberate indifference to petitioner's safety. Petitioner . . . has been diagnosed . . . as a transsexual . . . .

On March 9, 1989, petitioner was transferred for disciplinary reasons from the Federal Correctional Institute in Oxford, Wisconsin (FCI–Oxford), to the United States Penitentiary in Terre Haute, Indiana (USP–Terre Haute). . . . Within two weeks, . . . petitioner was beaten and raped by another inmate in petitioner's cell. Several days later, after petitioner claims to have reported the incident, officials returned petitioner to segregation to await . . . a hearing about petitioner's HIV-positive status.

Acting without counsel, petitioner then filed a Bivens complaint, alleging a violation of the Eighth Amendment. . . . [T]he complaint alleged that respondents either transferred petitioner to USP–Terre Haute or placed petitioner in its general population despite knowledge that the penitentiary had a violent environment and a history of inmate assaults, and despite knowledge that petitioner, as a transsexual who 'projects feminine characteristics,' would be particularly vulnerable . . . . This allegedly amounted to a deliberately indifferent failure to protect petitioner's safety, and thus to a violation of petitioner's Eighth Amendment rights. . . .

[T]he District Court denied petitioner's Rule 56(f) motion and granted summary judgment to respondents, concluding that there had been no deliberate indifference . . . .

The United States Court of Appeals for the Seventh Circuit summarily affirmed . . . ."

The Supreme Court granted certiorari to review the case.

B. Counsel of Record

ACLU Side (Petitioner / Appellant): Elizabeth Alexander of the National Prison Project of the American Civil Liberties Union Foundation argued the cause for appellants. With her on the brief were Alvin J. Bronstein, Ayesha N. Khan, and Marjorie Rifkin of the National Prison Project of the American Civil Liberties Union Foundation, and Steven R. Shapiro of the American Civil Liberties Union Foundation.

Opposing Side (Respondent / Appellee): Deputy Solicitor General Bender argued the cause for appellees. With him on the brief were Solicitor General Days, Assistant Attorney General Hunger, Amy L. Wax, Barbara L. Herwig, and Robert M. Loeb.

III. AMICI CURIAE

ACLU Side (Petitioner / Appellant)

Brief of amici curiae filed on behalf of the Montana Defender Project by Jeffrey T. Renz.

Brief of amici curiae filed on behalf of the D. C. Prisoners' Legal Services Project, Inc., by Alan A. Pemberton and Jonathan M. Smith.

Brief of amici curiae filed on behalf of Stop Prisoner Rape by Frank M. Dunbaugh.

Opposing Side (Respondent / Appellee)

Brief of amici curiae filed on behalf of the State of Maryland et al. by J. Joseph Curran, Jr., Attorney General of Maryland, and Andrew H. Baida, Assistant Attorney General, and by the Attorneys General and other officials for their respective States as follows: Jimmy Evans, Attorney General of Alabama, Charles E. Cole, Attorney General of Alaska, Grant Woods, Attorney General of Arizona, Winston Bryant, Attorney General of Arkansas, Daniel E. Lungren, Attorney General of California, Charles M. Oberly III, Attorney General of Delaware, Michael J. Bowers, Attorney General of Georgia, Robert A. Marks, Attorney General of Hawaii, Pamela Carter, Attorney General of Indiana, Robert T. Stephan, Attorney General of Kansas, Chris Gorman, Attorney General of Kentucky, Scott Harshbarger, Attorney General of Massachusetts, Frank J. Kelley, Attorney General of Michigan, Hubert H. Humphrey III, Attorney General of Minnesota, Mike Moore, Attorney General of Mississippi, Jay Nixon, Attorney General of Missouri, Don Stenberg, Attorney General of Nebraska, Frankie Sue Del Papa, Attorney General of Nevada, Jeffrey R. Howard, Attorney General of New Hampshire, Fred DeVesa, Acting Attorney General of New Jersey, Michael F. Easley, Attorney General of North Carolina, Heidi Heitkamp, Attorney General of North Dakota, Lee Fisher, Attorney General of Ohio, Susan B. Loving, Attorney General of Oklahoma, Theodore R. Kulongoski, Attorney General of Oregon, Ernest D. Preate, Jr., Attorney General of Pennsylvania, T. Travis Medlock, Attorney General of South Carolina, Mark Barnett, Attorney General of South Dakota, Charles W. Burson, Attorney General of Tennessee, Jan Graham, Attorney General of Utah, Jeffrey L. Amestoy, Attorney General of Vermont, Stephen D. Rosenthal, Attorney General of Virginia, James E. Doyle, Attorney General of Wisconsin, and Joseph B. Meyer, Attorney General of Wyoming.

IV. THE SUPREME COURT'S DECISION

"The Constitution 'does not mandate comfortable prisons,' but neither does it permit inhumane ones, and it is now settled that 'the treatment a prisoner receives in prison and the conditions under which he is confined are subject to scrutiny under the Eighth Amendment.' . . .

In particular, . . . 'prison officials have a duty . . . to protect prisoners from violence at the hands of other prisoners.' . . .

It is not, however, every injury suffered by one prisoner at the hands of another that translates into constitutional liability for prison officials responsible for the victim's safety. Our cases have held that a prison official violates the Eighth Amendment only when two requirements are met. First, the deprivation alleged must be, objectively, 'sufficiently serious' . . . .

The second requirement follows from the principle that 'only the unnecessary and wanton infliction of pain implicates the Eighth Amendment.' . . . The parties disagree, however, on the proper test for deliberate indifference, which we must therefore undertake to define. . . .

We reject petitioner's invitation to adopt an objective test for deliberate indifference. We hold instead that a prison official cannot be found liable under the Eighth Amendment for denying an inmate humane conditions of confinement unless the official knows of and disregards an excessive risk to inmate health or safety; the official must both be aware of facts from which the inference could be drawn that a substantial risk of serious harm exists, and he must also draw the inference. . . .

That said, subjective recklessness as used in the criminal law is a familiar and workable standard that is consistent with the Cruel and Unusual Punishments Clause as interpreted in our cases, and we adopt it as the test for 'deliberate indifference' under the Eighth Amendment. . . .

Under the test we adopt today, an Eighth Amendment claimant need not show that a prison official acted or failed to act believing that harm actually would befall an inmate; it is enough that the official acted or failed to act despite his knowledge of a substantial risk of serious harm. . . .

Accordingly, we . . . hold that a prison official may be held liable under the Eighth Amendment for denying humane conditions of confinement only if he knows that inmates face a substantial risk of serious harm and disregards that risk by failing to take reasonable measures to abate it. . . .

Against this backdrop, we consider whether the District Court's disposition of petitioner's complaint, summarily affirmed without briefing by the Court of Appeals for the Seventh Circuit, comports with Eighth Amendment principles. We conclude that the appropriate course is to remand. . . .

The judgment of the Court of Appeals is vacated, and the case is remanded . . . ."

V. JUSTICE VOTE

9 Pro ACLU Side vs. 0 Con Opposing Side

ACLU Side (Petitioner / Appellant)

1. Souter, D. – Wrote majority opinion
2. Kennedy, A. – Joined majority opinion
3. Rehnquist, W. – Joined majority opinion
4. Ginsburg, R. – Joined majority opinion
5. Scalia, A. – Joined majority opinion
6. Blackmun, H. – Wrote concurring opinion
7. Thomas, C. – Wrote concurring opinion
8. O'Connor, S. – Joined majority opinion
9. Stevens, J. – Wrote concurring opinion

VI. A WIN OR LOSS FOR THE ACLU?

The ACLU served as counsel for appellant urging reversal of the judgment of the Court of Appeals; the Supreme Court vacated in a 9-0 vote, giving the ACLU an apparent win.

773. City of Ladue v. Gilleo

(Decided June 13, 1994; 512 U.S. 43)

I. ISSUE

A. Issues Discussed

First Amendment, freedom of speech

B. Legal Question Presented

Whether an "ordinance of the City of Ladue [that] prohibits homeowners from displaying any signs on their property except 'residence identification' signs, 'for sale' signs, and signs warning of safety hazards . . . violates a Ladue resident's right to free speech."

C. Supreme Court's Answer

The ordinance violates a Ladue resident's right to free speech.

II. CASE SUMMARY

A. Background

"Respondent Margaret P. Gilleo owns one of the 57 single-family homes in the Willow Hill subdivision of Ladue. On December 8, 1990, she placed on her front lawn a 24- by 36-inch sign printed with the words 'Say No to War in the Persian Gulf, Call Congress Now.' After that sign disappeared, Gilleo put up another but it was knocked to the ground. When Gilleo reported these incidents to the police, they advised her that such signs were prohibited in Ladue. The city council denied her petitioner for a variance. Gilleo then filed this action under 42 U.S.C. § 1983 against the City, the Mayor, and members of the City Council, alleging that Ladue's sign ordinance violated her First Amendment right of free speech.

The District Court issued a preliminary injunction against enforcement of the ordinance. Gilleo then placed an 8.5- by 11-inch sign in the second story window of her home stating, 'For Peace in the Gulf.' The Ladue City Council responded to the injunction by repealing its ordinance and enacting a replacement. Like its predecessor, the new ordinance contains a general prohibition of 'signs' and defines that term broadly. The ordinance prohibits all signs except those that fall within 1 of 10 exemptions. Thus, 'residential identification signs' no larger than one square foot are allowed, as are signs advertising 'that the property is for sale, lease or exchange' and identifying the owner or agent. Also exempted are signs 'for churches, religious institutions, and schools,' '[c]ommercial signs in commercially or industrial zoned districts,' and on site signs advertising 'gasoline filling stations.' Unlike its predecessor, the new ordinance contains a lengthy 'Declaration of Findings, Policies, Interests, and Purposes,' part of which recites that the

'proliferation of an unlimited number of signs in private, residential, commercial, industrial, and public areas of the City of Ladue would create ugliness, visual blight and clutter, tarnish the natural beauty of the landscape as well as the residential and commercial architecture, impair property values, substantially impinge upon the privacy and special ambience of the community, and may cause safety and traffic hazards to motorists, pedestrians, and children.'

Gilleo amended her complaint to challenge the new ordinance, which explicitly prohibits window signs like hers. The District Court held the ordinance unconstitutional, and the Court of Appeals affirmed."

The Supreme Court granted certiorari to review the case and affirmed.

B. Counsel of Record / ACLU Attorney

ACLU Side (Respondent / Appellee): Gerald P. Greiman argued the cause for appellee. With him on the brief were Martin M. Green, Mitchell A. Margo, and Steven R. Shapiro.

Deputy Solicitor General Bender argued the cause for the United States, by special leave of Court.

Opposing Side (Petitioner / Appellant): Jordan B. Cherrick argued the cause for appellant. With him on the brief were Robert F. Schlafly and Jay A. Summerville.

III. AMICI CURIAE

ACLU Side (Respondent / Appellee)

Brief of amici curiae filed on behalf of the United States by Deputy Solicitor General Bender, Solicitor General Days, Assistant Attorney General Hunger, and Amy L. Wax.

Brief of amici curiae filed on behalf of the American Advertising Federation, et al., by Wallace S. Synder, Jeffrey L. Perlman, Richard E. Wiley, Lawrence W. Secrest, III, Howard H. Bell, Daniel E. Troy, John F. Kamp, David S. Versfelt, Kenneth M. Vittor, and Slade Metcalf.

Brief of amici curiae filed on behalf of the Association of National Advertisers, Inc., by Burn Neuborne and Gilbert H. Weil.

Brief of amici curiae filed on behalf of People for the American Way, et al., by Elliot M. Mincberg, Marc D. Stern, Timothy B. Dyk, Barbara McDowell, and David J. Schenck.

Brief of amici curiae filed on behalf of the Washington Legal Foundation, et al., by Daniel J. Popeo and Richard A. Samp.

Opposing Side (Petitioner / Appellant)

Brief of amici curiae filed on behalf of the State of Hawaii, et al., by J. Joseph Curran, Jr., Attorney General of Maryland, Jack Schwartz and Diane Krejsa, Assistant Attorneys General, and the following Attorneys General for their respective jurisdictions: Robert A. Marks of Hawaii, Pamela Carter of Indiana, Jeffrey R. Howard of New Hampshire, Fred DeVesa of New Jersey, Ernest D. Preate, Jr., of Pennsylvania, and Jeffrey L. Amestoy of Vermont.

Brief of amici curiae filed on behalf of the National Institute of Municipal Law officers, et al., by Richard Ruda, James I. Crowley, and Lee Fennell.

IV. THE SUPREME COURT'S DECISION

"While signs are a form of expression protected by the Free Speech Clause, they pose distinctive problems that are subject to municipalities' police powers. Unlike oral speech, signs take up space and may obstruct views, distract motorists, displace alternative uses for land, and pose other problems that legitimately call for regulation. It is common ground that governments may regulate the physical characteristics of signs—just as they can, within reasonable bounds and absent censorial purpose, regulate audible expression in its capacity as noise. However, because regulation of a medium inevitably affects communication itself, it is not surprising that we have had occasion to review the constitutionality of municipal ordinances prohibiting the display of certain outdoor signs. . . .

A special respect for individual liberty in the home has long been part of our culture and our law; that principle has special resonance when the government seeks to constrain a person's ability to speak there. Most Americans would be understandably dismayed, given that tradition, to learn that it was illegal to display from their window an 8- by 11-inch sign expressing their political views. Whereas the government's need to mediate among various competing uses, including expressive ones, for public streets and facilities is constant and unavoidable, its need to regulate temperate speech from the home is surely much less pressing.

Our decision that Ladue's ban on almost all residential signs violates the First Amendment by no means leaves the City powerless to address the ills that may be associated with residential signs. It bears mentioning that individual residents themselves have strong incentives to keep their own property values up and to prevent 'visual clutter' in their own yards and neighborhoods—incentives markedly different from those of persons who erect signs on others' land, in others' neighborhoods, or on public property. Residents' self-interest diminishes the danger of the 'unlimited' proliferation of residential signs that concerns the City of Ladue. We are confident that more temperate measures could in large part satisfy Ladue's stated regulatory needs without harm to the First Amendment rights of its citizens. As currently framed, however, the ordinance abridges those rights.

Accordingly, the judgment of the Court of Appeals is affirmed."

V. JUSTICE VOTE

9 Pro ACLU Side vs. 0 Con Opposing Side

ACLU Side (Respondent / Appellee)

1. Stevens, J. – Wrote majority opinion
2. O'Connor, S. – Wrote concurring opinion
3. Scalia, A. – Joined majority opinion
4. Kennedy, A. – Joined majority opinion
5. Thomas, C. – Joined majority opinion

6. Souter, D. – Joined majority opinion
7. Ginsburg, R. – Joined majority opinion
8. Blackmun, H. – Joined majority opinion
9. Rehnquist, W. – Joined majority opinion

VI. A WIN OR LOSS FOR THE ACLU?

The ACLU, as counsel for respondent, urged affirmance of the judgment of the Court of Appeals for the Eighth Circuit; the Supreme Court affirmed in a 9-0 vote, giving the ACLU an apparent win.

774. McFarland v. Scott

(Decided June 30, 1994; 512 U.S. 849)

I. ISSUE

A. Issues Discussed

Criminal justice, death penalty, Eighth Amendment, habeas corpus

B. Legal Question Presented

"[W]hether a capital defendant must file a formal habeas corpus petition in order to invoke this statutory right and to establish a federal court's jurisdiction to enter a stay of execution."

C. Supreme Court's Answer

A capital defendant is not required to file a formal habeas corpus petition to allow a federal court to enter a stay of execution.

II. CASE SUMMARY

A. Background

"Petitioner Frank Basil McFarland was convicted of capital murder on November 13, 1989, in the State of Texas and sentenced to death. The Texas Court of Criminal Appeals affirmed the conviction and sentence, and on June 7, 1993, [the Supreme] Court denied certiorari. Two months later, on August 16, 1993, the Texas trial court scheduled McFarland's execution for September 23, 1993. On September 19, McFarland filed a pro se motion requesting that the trial court stay or withdraw his execution date to allow the Texas Resource Center an opportunity to recruit volunteer counsel for his state habeas corpus proceeding. Texas opposed a stay of execution, arguing that McFarland had not filed an application for writ of habeas corpus and that the court thus lacked jurisdiction to enter a stay. The trial court declined to appoint counsel, but modified McFarland's execution date to October 27, 1993.

On October 16, 1993, the Resource Center informed the trial court that it had been unable to recruit volunteer counsel and asked the court to appoint counsel for McFarland. Concluding that Texas law did not authorize the appointment of counsel for state habeas corpus proceedings, the trial court refused either to appoint counsel or to modify petitioner's execution date. McFarland then filed a pro se motion in the Texas Court of Criminal Appeals requesting a stay and a remand for appointment of counsel. The court denied the motion without comment.

Having failed to obtain either the appointment of counsel or a modification of his execution date in state court, McFarland, on October 22, 1993, commenced the present action in the United States District Court for the Northern District of Texas by filing a pro se motion stating that he 'wish[ed] to challenge [his] conviction and sentence under [the federal habeas corpus statute.]" McFarland requested the appointment of counsel under 21 U.S.C. § 848(q)(4)(B) and a stay of execution to give that counsel time to prepare and file a habeas corpus petition.

The District Court denied McFarland's motion on October 25, 1993, concluding that because no 'post conviction proceeding' had been initiated pursuant to 28 U.S.C. § 2254 or § 2255, petitioner was not entitled to appointment of counsel and the court lacked jurisdiction to enter a stay of execution. The court later denied a certificate of probable cause to appeal.

On October 26, the eve of McFarland's scheduled execution, the Court of Appeals for the Fifth Circuit denied his application for stay. The court noted that federal law expressly authorizes federal courts to stay state proceedings while a federal habeas corpus proceeding is pending, but held that no such proceeding was pending, because a 'motion for stay and for appointment of counsel [is not] the equivalent of an application for habeas relief.' The court concluded that any other federal judicial interference in state-court proceedings was barred by the Anti-Injunction Act.

Shortly before the Court of Appeals ruled, a Federal Magistrate Judge located an attorney willing to accept appointment in McFarland's case and suggested that if the attorney would file a skeletal document entitled 'petition for writ of habeas corpus,' the District Court might be willing to appoint him and grant McFarland a stay of execution. The attorney accordingly drafted and filed a pro forma habeas petition, together with a motion for stay of execution and appointment of counsel. As in the Gosch case, despite the fact that Texas did not oppose a stay, the District Court found the petition to be insufficient and denied the motion for stay on the merits.

On October 27, 1993, [the Supreme] Court granted a stay of execution in McFarland's original suit pending consideration of his petition for certiorari."

The Supreme Court granted certiorari to review the case and reversed.

B. Counsel of Record / ACLU Attorney

ACLU Side (Petitioner / Appellant): Mandy Welch argued the cause for appelant.

Opposing Side (Respondent / Appellee): Margaret Portman Griffey, Assistant Attorney General of Texas, argued the cause for appellee.

III. AMICI CURIAE

ACLU Side (Petitioner / Appellant)

Brief of amici curiae filed on behalf of the ACLU, et al., by Larry W. Yackle, Steven R. Shapiro, and Diann Y. Rust-Tierney.

Brief of amici curiae filed on behalf of the American Bar Association by R. William Ide, III, Stephen H. Sachs, Michael A. Millemann, Michael A. Mello, John E. Smith, and David M. Shub.

Brief of amici curiae filed on behalf of the Texas Criminal Defense Lawyers Association, by Jim E. Lavine.

Opposing Side (Respondent / Appellee)

Brief of amici curiae filed on behalf of the Criminal Justice Legal Foundation by Kent S. Scheidegger and Charles L. Hobson.

Brief of amici curiae filed on behalf of the Tarrant, Bexar, Dallas, and Harris County District Attorneys by John B. Holmes, Jr., Steven C. Hilbig, Ed F. Shaughnessy, Tim Curry, Betty Marshall, Charles M. Mallin, Edward L. Wilkinson, and John Vance.

IV. THE SUPREME COURT'S DECISION

"Section 848(q)(4)(B) of Title 21 provides:

'In any post conviction proceeding under section 2254 or 2255 of title 28 seeking to vacate or set aside a death sentence, any defendant who is or becomes financially unable to obtain adequate representation or investigative, expert, or other reasonably necessary services shall be entitled to the appointment of one or more attorneys and the furnishing of such other services in accordance with paragraphs (5), (6), (7), (8), and (9).' (emphasis added).

On its face, this statute grants indigent capital defendants a mandatory right to qualified legal counsel and related services '[i]n any [federal] post conviction proceeding.' The express language does not specify, however, how a capital defendant's right to counsel in such a proceeding shall be invoked. . . .

Construing § 848(q)(4)(B) in light of its related provisions . . . indicates that the right to appointed counsel adheres prior to the filing of a formal, legally sufficient habeas corpus petition. . . .

This interpretation is the only one that gives meaning to the statute as a practical matter. Congress' provision of a right to counsel under § 848(q)(4)(B) reflects a determination that quality legal representation is necessary in capital habeas corpus proceedings in light of 'the seriousness of the possible penalty and . . . the unique and complex nature of the litigation.' An attorney's assistance prior to the filing of a capital defendant's habeas corpus petition is crucial, because '[t]he complexity of our jurisprudence in this area . . . makes it unlikely that capital defendants will be able to file successful petitions for collateral relief without the assistance of persons learned in the law.' . . .

Requiring an indigent capital petitioner to proceed without counsel in order to obtain counsel thus would expose him to the substantial risk that his habeas claims never would be heard on the merits. . . .

The language and purposes of § 848(q)(4)(B) and its related provisions establish that the right to appointed counsel includes a right to legal assistance in the preparation of a habeas corpus application. We therefore conclude that a 'post-conviction proceeding' within the meaning of § 848(q)(4)(B) is commenced by the filing of a death row defendant's motion requesting the appointment of counsel for his federal habeas corpus proceeding. McFarland filed such a motion and was entitled to the appointment of a lawyer. . . .

Federal courts cannot enjoin a state-court proceedings unless the intervention is authorized expressly by federal statute or falls under one of two other exceptions to the Anti-Injunction Act. . . . McFarland argues that his request for counsel in a 'post conviction proceeding' under § 848(q)(4)(B) initiated a 'habeas corpus proceeding' within the meaning of § 2251, and that the District Court thus had jurisdiction to enter a stay. Texas contends, in turn, that even if a 'post conviction proceeding' under § 848(q)(4)(B) can be triggered by a death row defendant's request for appointment of counsel, no 'habeas corpus proceeding' is 'pending' under § 2251, and thus no stay can be entered, until a legally sufficient habeas petition is filed.

The language of these two statutes indicates that the sections refer to the same proceeding. . . . We thus conclude that the two statutes must be read in pari materia to provide that once a capital defendant invokes his right to appointed counsel, a federal court also has jurisdiction under § 2251 to enter a stay of execution. Because § 2251 expressly authorizes federal courts to stay state-court proceedings 'for any matter involved in the habeas corpus proceeding,' the exercise of this authority is not barred by the Anti-Injunction Act. . . .

We conclude that a capital defendant may invoke this right to a counseled federal habeas corpus proceeding by filing a motion requesting the appointment of habeas counsel, and that a district court has jurisdiction to enter a stay of execution where necessary to give effect to that statutory right. McFarland filed a motion for appointment of counsel and for stay of execution in this case, and the District Court had authority to grant the relief he sought.

The judgment of the Court of Appeals is reversed."

V. JUSTICE VOTE

5 Pro ACLU Side vs. 4 Con Opposing Side

ACLU Side (Petitioner / Appellant)

1. Blackmun, H. – Wrote majority opinion
2. Stevens, J. – Joined majority opinion
3. Kennedy, A. – Joined majority opinion
4. Souter, D. – Joined majority opinion
5. Ginsburg, R. – Joined majority opinion

Opposing Side (Respondent / Appellee)

1. O'Connor, S. – Wrote opinion concurring in part and dissenting in part
2. Thomas, C. – Wrote dissenting opinion
3. Rehnquist, W. – Joined Thomas' dissent
4. Scalia, A. – Joined Thomas' dissent

VI. A WIN OR LOSS FOR THE ACLU?

The ACLU filed as amicus curiae urging reversal of the judgment of the Court of Appeals; the Supreme Court reversed in a 5-4 vote, giving the ACLU an apparent win.

775. Tuilaepa v. California

(Decided June 30, 1994; 512 U.S. 967)

I. ISSUE

A. Issues Discussed

Criminal procedure, death penalty, Eighth Amendment, cruel and unusual punishment

B. Legal Question Presented

"[W]hether three of the § 190.3 penalty-phase factors are unconstitutionally vague under decisions of this Court construing the Cruel and Unusual Punishments Clause of the Eighth Amendment, made applicable to the States by the Fourteenth Amendment."

C. Supreme Court's Answer

The three factors are not unconstitutionally vague.

II. CASE SUMMARY

A. Background

"In California, to sentence a defendant to death for first-degree murder the trier of fact must find the defendant guilty and also find one or more of 19 special circumstances listed in Cal. Penal Code Ann. § 190.2 (West 1988 and Supp.1994). The case then proceeds to the penalty phase, where the trier of fact must consider a number of specified factors in deciding whether to sentence the defendant to death. . . .

Petitioner Tuilaepa's case arises out of a murder he committed in Long Beach, California, in October 1986. Tuilaepa and an accomplice walked into the Wander Inn Bar in Long Beach, where a small crowd had gathered to watch Monday Night Football. Tuilaepa, who was carrying a .22-caliber rifle, approached the bartender, pointed the rifle at him, and demanded money from the cash register. After the bartender turned over the money, Tuilaepa and his accomplice began robbing the bar's patrons. When the accomplice demanded money from a man named Melvin Whiddon, Whiddon refused and knocked the accomplice to the floor. Tuilaepa shot Whiddon in the neck and next shot Whiddon's brother, Kelvin, who was standing nearby. Tuilaepa turned to another man, Bruce Monroe, and shot him in the stomach. As Tuilaepa and his accomplice ran toward the back door, they confronted Kenneth Boone. Tuilaepa shot Boone in the neck. Melvin Whiddon died at the scene from the gunshot wounds; the others suffered serious and in some cases permanent injuries.

The State sought the death penalty against Tuilaepa, charging him with the murder of Melvin Whiddon and one special circumstance under § 190.2: murder during the commission of a robbery. The jury found Tuilaepa guilty of first-degree murder and also found the special circumstance true. At the penalty phase, the trial judge instructed the jury to consider the relevant sentencing factors specified in § 190.3. The jury was unanimous in sentencing Tuilaepa to death.

Petitioner Proctor murdered Bonnie Stendal, a 55-year-old schoolteacher who lived in Burney, a small community in Shasta County, California. On a night in April 1982, Proctor entered Mrs. Stendal's home and beat her, causing numerous cuts and bruises on her face. Proctor stabbed Mrs. Stendal in the neck several times and inflicted seven stab wounds in the area of the right breast. Proctor raped Mrs. Stendal and committed further sexual assaults with a foreign object. After beating, torturing, and raping Mrs. Stendal, Proctor strangled her to death and dumped her body on the side of the road near Lake Britton, 12 miles from Burney. The body was found late the next afternoon, clad in a nightgown with hands tied behind the back.

The State sought the death penalty against Proctor, charging him with murder and a number of special circumstances under § 190.2 including murder during the commission of a rape, murder during the commission of a burglary, and infliction of torture during a murder. The jury found Proctor guilty of murder and found the three special circumstances true. After a mistrial at the penalty phase, Proctor's motion for change of venue was granted, and a new sentencing jury was empaneled in Sacramento County. The trial judge instructed the jury to consider the sentencing factors specified in § 190.3. The jury was unanimous in sentencing Proctor to death.

Petitioners appealed to the Supreme Court of California, which affirmed their convictions and death sentences."

The U.S. Supreme Court granted certiorari to review the cases and affirmed.

B. Counsel of Record / ACLU Attorney

ACLU Side (Petitioner / Appellant): Howard W. Gillingham argued the cause for appellant Tuilaepa.

Wendy C. Lascher, by appointment of the Court, argued the cause for appellant Proctor.

Opposing Side (Respondent / Appellee): Deputy Attorney General Prahl argued the cause for appellee.

III. AMICI CURIAE

ACLU Side (Petitioner / Appellant)

Brief of amici curiae filed on behalf of the ACLU by Michael Laurence, Paul L. Hoffman, and Mark Silverstein.

Brief of amici curiae filed on behalf of the California Appellate Project by Clifford Gardner, Melissa W. Johnson, Gail R. Weinheimer, Daniel N. Abrahamson, and Steven W. Parnes.

Opposing Side (Respondent / Appellee)

Brief of amici curiae filed on behalf of the Criminal Justice Legal Foundation by Kent S. Scheidegger.

IV. THE SUPREME COURT'S DECISION

"Petitioners contend that three of those Section 190.3 sentencing factors are unconstitutional and that, as a consequence, it was error to instruct their juries to consider them. Both Proctor and Tuilaepa challenge factor (a), which requires the sentencer to consider the 'circumstances of the crime of which the defendant was convicted in the present proceeding and the existence of any special circumstances found to be true.' Tuilaepa challenges two other factors as well: factor (b), which requires the sentencer to consider '[t]he presence or absence of criminal activity by the defendant which involved the use or attempted use of force or violence or the express or implied threat to use force or violence'; and factor (i),which requires the sentencer to consider '[t]he age of the defendant at the time of the crime.' We conclude that none of the three factors is defined in terms that violate the Constitution.

Petitioners' challenge to factor (a) is at some odds with settled principles, for our capital jurisprudence has established that the sentencer should consider the circumstances of the crime in deciding whether to impose the death penalty. We would be hard pressed to invalidate a jury instruction that implements what we have said the law requires. In any event, this California factor instructs the jury to consider a relevant subject matter and does so in understandable terms. The circumstances of the crime are a traditional subject for consideration by the sentencer, and an instruction to consider the circumstances is neither vague nor otherwise improper under our Eighth Amendment jurisprudence.

Tuilaepa also challenges factor (b), which requires the sentencer to consider the defendant's prior criminal activity. The objection fails for many of the same reasons. Factor (b) is phrased in conventional and understandable terms and rests in large part on a determination whether certain events occurred, thus asking the jury to consider matters of historical fact. . . . Both a backward looking and a forward looking inquiry are a permissible part of the sentencing process, however, and the States have considerable latitude in determining how to guide the sentencer's decision in this respect. Here, factor (b) is not vague.

Tuilaepa's third challenge is to factor (i), which requires the sentencer to consider '[t]he age of the defendant at the time of the crime.' This again is an unusual challenge in light of our precedents. The factual inquiry is of the most rudimentary sort, and there is no suggestion that the term 'age' is vague. . . . It is neither surprising nor remarkable that the relevance of the defendant's age can pose a dilemma for the sentencer. But difficulty in application is not equivalent to vagueness. Both the prosecution and the defense may present valid arguments as to the significance of the defendant's age in a particular case. . . . We find no constitutional deficiency in factor (i). . . .

Petitioners also suggest that the §190.3 sentencing factors are flawed because they do not instruct the sentencer how to weigh any of the facts it finds in deciding upon the ultimate sentence. . . . This argument, too, is foreclosed by our cases. A capital sentencer need not be instructed how to weigh any particular fact in the capital sentencing decision. . . .

The instructions to the juries in petitioners' cases directing consideration of factor (a), factor (b), and factor (i) did not violate the Constitution. The judgments of the Supreme Court of California are affirmed."

V. JUSTICE VOTE

1 Pro ACLU Side vs. 8 Con Opposing Side

ACLU Side (Petitioner / Appellant)

1. Blackmun, H. – Wrote dissenting opinion

Opposing Side (Respondent / Appellee)

1. Kennedy, A. – Wrote majority opinion
2. Rehnquist, W. – Joined majority opinion
3. O'Connor, S. – Joined majority opinion
4. Thomas, C. – Joined majority opinion
5. Stevens, J. – Wrote concurring opinion
6. Scalia, A. – Wrote concurring opinion
7. Souter, D. – Wrote concurring opinion
8. Ginsburg, R. – Joined Stevens' concurrence

VI. A WIN OR LOSS FOR THE ACLU?

The ACLU filed as amicus curiae urging reversal of the judgment of the Supreme Court of California; the U.S. Supreme Court affirmed in an 8-1 vote, giving the ACLU an apparent loss.

776. Lebron v. National Railroad Passenger Corp.

(Decided February 21, 1995; 513 U.S. 374)

I. ISSUE

A. Issues Discussed

First Amendment, freedoms of press, speech, and association

B. Legal Question Presented

"[W]hether actions of the National Railroad Passenger Corporation, commonly known as Amtrak, are subject to the constraints of the Constitution."

C. Supreme Court's Answer

Amtrak is part of the government for First Amendment purposes.

II. CASE SUMMARY

A. Background

"Petitioner, Michael A. Lebron, creates billboard displays that involve commentary on public issues, and that seemingly propel him into litigation. In August 1991, he contacted Transportation Displays, Incorporated (TDI), which manages the leasing of the billboards in Amtrak's Pennsylvania Station in New York City, seeking to display an advertisement on a billboard of colossal proportions, known to New Yorkers (or at least to the more Damon Runyonesque among them) as 'the Spectacular.' . . .

On November 30, 1992, Lebron signed a contract with TDI to display an advertisement on the Spectacular for two months beginning in January 1993. . . . Lebron declined to disclose the specific content of his advertisement throughout his negotiations with TDI, although he did explain to TDI that it was generally political. . . . Amtrak's vice president disapproved the advertisement, invoking Amtrak's policy, inherited from its predecessor as landlord of Penn Station, the Pennsylvania Railroad Company, 'that it will not allow political advertising on the [S]pectacular advertising sign.'

Lebron then filed suit against Amtrak and TDI, claiming, inter alia, that the refusal to place his advertisement on the Spectacular had violated his First and Fifth Amendment rights. After expedited discovery, the District Court ruled that Amtrak, because of its close ties to the Federal Government, was a Government actor, at least for First Amendment purposes, and that its rejection of Lebron's proposed advertisement as unsuitable for display in Penn Station had violated the First Amendment. The court granted Lebron an injunction and ordered Amtrak and TDI to display Lebron's advertisement on the Spectacular.

The United States Court of Appeals for the Second Circuit reversed."

The Supreme Court granted certiorari to review the case and reversed.

B. Counsel of Record / ACLU Attorney

ACLU Side (Petitioner / Appellant): David D. Cole argued the cause for appellant.

Opposing Side (Respondent / Appellee): Kevin T. Baine argued the cause for appellee.

III. AMICI CURIAE

ACLU Side (Petitioner / Appellant)

Brief of amici curiae filed on behalf of the ACLU by Stephen R. Shapiro, Adam S. Cohen, Marjorie Heins, and Arthur N. Eisenberg.

Brief of amici curiae filed on behalf of the NAACP Legal Defense and Educational Fund, Inc., et al., by James F. Fitzpatrick, Michael E. Korens, Elliot M. Mincberg, Lawrence S. Ottinger, Elaine R. Jones, Theodore M. Shaw, Bill Tamayo, Philip Thiatsu Nash, Marcia Greenberger, Deborah L. Brake, Kenneth Kimerling, Judith L. Lichtman, and Donna R. Lenhoff.

Opposing Side (Respondent / Appellee)

No briefs of amici curiae were filed in support of appellee.

IV. THE SUPREME COURT'S DECISION

"[I]t is not for Congress to make the final determination of Amtrak's status as a Government entity for purposes of determining the constitutional rights of citizens affected by its actions. . . .

Facing the question of Amtrak's status for the first time, we conclude that it is an agency or instrumentality of the United States for the purpose of individual rights guaranteed against the Government by the Constitution.

This conclusion seems to us in accord with public and judicial understanding of the nature of Government-created and -controlled corporations over the years. . . . That Government-created and -controlled corporations are for many purposes at least part of the Government itself has a strong basis, not merely in past practice and understanding, but in reason itself. It surely cannot be that government, state or federal, is able to evade the most solemn obligations imposed in the Constitution by simply resorting to the corporate form. . . .

Amtrak was created by a special statute, explicitly for the furtherance of federal governmental goals. [S]ix of the corporation's eight externally named directors . . . are appointed directly by the President of the United States—four of them . . . with the advice and consent of the Senate. . . .

We hold that where, as here, the Government creates a corporation by special law, for the furtherance of governmental objectives, and retains for itself permanent authority to appoint a majority of the directors of that corporation, the corporation is part of the Government for purposes of the First Amendment. We express no opinion as to whether Amtrak's refusal to display Lebron's advertisement violated that Amendment, but leave it to the Court of Appeals to decide that. The judgment of the Court of Appeals is reversed, and the case is remanded for further proceedings consistent with this opinion."

V. JUSTICE VOTE

8 Pro ACLU Side vs. 1 Con Opposing Side

ACLU Side (Petitioner / Appellant)

1. Scalia, A. – Wrote majority opinion
2. Rehnquist, W. – Joined majority opinion
3. Kennedy, A. – Joined majority opinion
4. Souter, D. – Joined majority opinion
5. Thomas, C. – Joined majority opinion
6. Stevens, J. – Joined majority opinion
7. Breyer, S. – Joined majority opinion
8. Ginsburg, R. – Joined majority opinion

Opposing Side (Respondent / Appellee)

1. O'Connor, S. – Wrote dissenting opinion

VI. A WIN OR LOSS FOR THE ACLU?

The ACLU filed a brief as amicus curiae urging reversal of the judgment of the Court of Appeals; the Supreme Court reversed in an 8-1 vote, giving the ACLU an apparent win.

777. O'Neal v. McAninch

(Decided February 21, 1995; 513 U.S. 432)

I. ISSUE

A. Issues Discussed

Criminal procedure, habeas corpus, trial error

B. Legal Question Presented

"[W]hether a federal habeas court should consider a trial error harmless when the court (1) reviews a state-court judgment from a criminal trial, (2) finds a constitutional error, and (3) is in grave doubt about whether or not that error is harmless."

C. Supreme Court's Answer

"We conclude that the uncertain judge should treat the error, not as if it were harmless, but as if it affected the verdict (i.e., as if it had a 'substantial and injurious effect or influence in determining the jury's verdict)."

II. CASE SUMMARY

A. Background

"Robert O'Neal filed a federal habeas corpus petition challenging his state-court convictions for murder and other crimes. The Federal District Court agreed with several of his claims of constitutional trial error. On appeal the Sixth Circuit disagreed with the District Court, with one important exception. That exception focused on possible jury 'confusion' arising out of a trial court instruction about the state of mind necessary for conviction combined with a related statement by a prosecutor. The Sixth Circuit assumed, for argument's sake, that the instruction (taken together with the prosecutor's statement) had indeed violated the Federal Constitution by misleading the jury. Nonetheless, the court disregarded the error on the ground that it was 'harmless.'

The court's opinion sets forth the standard normally applied by a federal habeas court in deciding whether or not this kind of constitutional 'trial' error is harmless, namely, whether the error 'had substantial and injurious effect or influence in determining the jury's verdict.' But, rather than ask directly whether the record's facts satisfied this standard, the court seemed to refer to a burden of proof. Its opinion says that the habeas petitioner must bear the 'burden of establishing' whether the error was prejudicial. As a practical matter, this statement apparently means that, if a judge is in grave doubt about the effect on the jury of this kind of error, the petitioner must lose. Thus, O'Neal might have lost in the Court of Appeals, not because the judges concluded that the error was harmless, but because the record of the trial left them in grave doubt about the effect of the error."

The Supreme Court granted certiorari to review the case, vacated, and remanded.

B. Counsel of Record / ACLU Attorney

ACLU Side (Petitioner / Appellant): Thomas R. Wetterer, Jr., argued the cause for appellant.

Opposing Side (Respondent / Appellee): Richard A. Cordray, State Solicitor of Ohio, argued the cause for appellee.

James A. Feldman argued the cause for the United States, as amicus curiae, by special leave of Court.

III. AMICI CURIAE

ACLU Side (Petitioner / Appellant)

Brief of amici curiae filed on behalf of the ACLU, et al., by Larry W. Yackle, Steven R. Shapiro, and James S. Liebman.

Brief of amici curiae filed on behalf of Timothy Scott Sherman by Andrew L. Frey, Roy T. Englert, Jr., James G. Duncan, Thomas Dilenge, and Stuart J. Robinson.

Brief of amici curiae filed on behalf of the National and Ohio Associations of Criminal Defense Lawyers by Harry R. Reinhart and Lawrence J. Fleming.

Opposing Side (Respondent / Appellee)

Brief of amici curiae filed on behalf of the United States by James A. Feldman, Solicitor General Days, Assistant Attorney General Harris, and Deputy Solicitor General Wallace.

Brief of amici curiae filed on behalf of the State of Maryland, et al., by J. Joseph Curran, Jr., Attorney General of Maryland, and Tarra DeShields-Minnis, Assistant Attorney General; and by the Attorneys General for their respective jurisdictions as follows: James H. Evans of Alabama, Bruce M. Botelho of Alaska, Grant Woods of Arizona, Winston Bryant of Arkansas, Daniel E. Lungren of California, Gale H. Norton of Colorado, John M. Bailey of Connecticut, Charles Oberly of Delaware, Robert A. Butterworth of Florida, Michael J. Bowers of Georgia, Robert A. Marks of Hawaii, Larry EchoHawk of Idaho, Roland W. Burris of Illinois, Pamela Carter of Indiana, Bonnie J. Campbell of Iowa, Robert T. Stephan of Kansas, Chris Gorman of Kentucky, Richard P. Ieyoub of Louisiana, Michael E. Carpenter of Maine, Scott Harshbarger of Massachusetts, Frank J. Kelley of Michigan, Hubert H. Humphrey III of Minnesota, Mike Moore of Mississippi, Jeremiah (Jay) Nixon of Missouri, Joseph P. Mazurek of Montana, Don Stenberg of Nebraska, Frankie Sue Del Papa of Nevada, Jeffrey R. Howard of New Hampshire, Deborah T. Poritz of New Jersey, Tom Udall of New Mexico, G. Oliver Koppel of New York, Michael F. Easley of North Carolina, Susan B. Loving of Oklahoma, Theodore R. Kulongoski of Oregon, Ernest D. Preate, Jr., of Pennsylvania, Pedro R. Pierluisi of Puerto Rico, Jeffrey B. Pine of Rhode Island, T. Travis Medlock of South Carolina, Mark Barnett of South Dakota, Charles Burson of Tennessee, Dan Morales of Texas, Jan Graham of Utah, Jeffrey L. Amestoy of Vermont, Rosalie Simmonds Ballentine of the Virgin Islands, James S. Gilmore III of Virginia, Christine O. Gregoire of Washington, Darrell V. McGraw, Jr. of West Virginia, James E. Doyle of Wisconsin, and Joseph B. Meyer of Wyoming.

IV. THE SUPREME COURT'S DECISION

"Our legal conclusion—that in cases of grave doubt as to harmlessness the petitioner must win—rests upon three considerations. First, precedent supports our conclusion. As this Court has stated, 'the original common-law harmless-error rule put the burden on the beneficiary of the error [here, the State] . . . to prove that there was no injury . . . .' . . .

Second, our conclusion is consistent with the basic purposes underlying the writ of habeas corpus. . . . Such a rule . . . both protects individuals from unconstitutional convictions and helps to guarantee the integrity of the criminal process by assuring that trials are fundamentally fair. [D]enying the writ in cases of grave uncertainty, would virtually guarantee that many, in fact, will be held in unlawful custody—contrary to the writ's most basic traditions and purposes. . . .

Third, our rule has certain administrative virtues. It is consistent with the way that courts have long treated important trial errors. . . .

The State makes one additional argument. It points to language in the habeas corpus statute . . . . We do not see what in the language of the statute tells a court that it should treat a violation as harmless when it is in grave doubt about its harmlessness.

[W]e conclude that, when a habeas court is in grave doubt as to the harmlessness of an error that affects substantial rights, it should grant relief. . . .

For these reasons, the judgment of the Court of Appeals is vacated, and the case is remanded for further proceedings consistent with this opinion."

V. JUSTICE VOTE

6 Pro ACLU Side vs. 3 Con Opposing Side

ACLU Side (Petitioner / Appellant)

1. Breyer, S. – Wrote majority opinion
2. Stevens, J. – Joined majority opinion
3. O'Connor, S. – Joined majority opinion
4. Kennedy, A. – Joined majority opinion
5. Souter, D. – Joined majority opinion
6. Ginsburg, R. – Joined majority opinion

Opposing Side (Respondent / Appellee)

1. Thomas, C. – Wrote dissenting opinion
2. Rehnquist, W. – Joined Thomas' dissent
3. Scalia, A. – Joined Thomas' dissent

VI. A WIN OR LOSS FOR THE ACLU?

The ACLU filed as amicus curiae urging reversal of the judgment of the Court of Appeals; the Supreme Court vacated in a 6-3 vote, giving the ACLU an apparent win.

778. United States v. National Treasury Employees Union

(Decided February 22, 1995; 513 U.S. 454)

I. ISSUE

A. Issues Discussed

First Amendment, freedoms of press, speech, and association

B. Legal Question Presented

Whether "a law that broadly prohibits federal employees from accepting any compensation for making speeches or writing articles . . . comports with the Constitution's command that 'Congress shall make no law . . . abridging the freedom of speech.'"

C. Supreme Court's Answer

The law violates the First Amendment as applied to respondents.

II. CASE SUMMARY

A. Background

"In 1989 Congress enacted a law that broadly prohibits federal employees from accepting any compensation for making speeches or writing articles. The prohibition applies even when neither the subject of the speech or article nor the person or group paying for it has any connection with the employee's official duties. . . .

Two unions and several career civil servants employed full-time by various Executive departments and agencies filed suit in the United States District Court for the District of Columbia to challenge the constitutionality of the honoraria ban. . . . Each of the individual respondents alleges that he or she has in the past received compensation for writing or speaking on various topics in full compliance with earlier ethics regulations. . . .

The District Court granted respondents' motion for summary judgment, held the statute 'unconstitutional insofar as it applies to Executive Branch employees of the United States government,' and enjoined the Government from enforcing the statute against any Executive Branch employee. . . .

The Court of Appeals affirmed. . . . Over two dissents, the Court of Appeals denied a petition for rehearing en banc."

The Supreme Court granted certiorari to review the case, affirmed in part, reversed in part, and remanded.

B. Counsel of Record / ACLU Attorney

ACLU Side (Respondent / Appellee): Gregory O'Duden argued the cause for appellee. With him on the briefs were Elaine Kaplan, Barbara A. Atkin, Mark D. Roth, Anne Wagner, John Vanderstar, Arthur Spitzer, and Steven R. Shapiro.

Opposing Side (Petitioner / Appellant): Deputy Solicitor General Paul Bender argued the cause for appellant. With him on the briefs were Solicitor General Days, Assistant Attorney General Hunger, Michael R. Dreeben, John C. Hoyle, and Alfred Mollin.

III. AMICI CURIAE

ACLU Side (Respondent / Appellee)

Brief of amici curiae filed on behalf of the Freedom to Read Foundation, et al., by R. Bruce Rich, Linda Steinman, Maria Pallante, Paul M. Smith, Bruce J. Ennis, Jr., Julie M. Carpenter, Elliot M. Mincberg, and Lawrence S. Ottinger.

Brief of amici curiae filed on behalf of Public Citizen, Inc., by Alan B. Morrison.

Brief of amici curiae filed on behalf of the Senior Executives Association by George J. Shaw, Jr., William L. Bransford, and Christopher M. Okay.

Brief of amici curiae filed on behalf of Peter Bollen by Stephen S. Ostrach and Todd S. Brilliant.

Opposing Side (Petitioner / Appellant)

Brief of amici curiae filed on behalf of Common Cause by Stephen F. Black, Hardy Callcott, Kenneth P. Stern, and Rebecca Arbogast.

IV. THE SUPREME COURT'S DECISION

"For three reasons, we agree with the Government's first suggestion—that the relief should be limited to the parties before the Court. First, although the occasional case requires us to entertain a facial challenge in order to vindicate a party's right not to be bound by an unconstitutional statute, we neither want nor need to provide relief to nonparties when a narrower remedy will fully protect the litigants. In this case, granting full relief to respondents—who include all Executive Branch employees below Grade GS-16—does not require passing on the applicability of § 501(b) to the senior executives who received a 25 percent salary increase that offsets the honoraria ban's disincentive to speak and write. Second, the Government conceivably might advance a different justification for an honoraria ban limited to more senior officials, thus presenting a different constitutional question than the one we decide today. Our policy of avoiding unnecessary adjudication of constitutional issues, therefore counsels against determining senior officials' rights in this case. Third, as the Court of Appeals recognized, its remedy required it to tamper with the text of the statute, a practice we strive to avoid.

Our obligation to avoid judicial legislation also persuades us to reject the Government's second suggestion—that we modify the remedy by crafting a nexus requirement for the honoraria ban. We cannot be sure that our attempt to redraft the statute to limit its coverage to cases involving an undesirable nexus between the speaker's official duties and either the subject matter of the speaker's expression or the identity of the payor would correctly identify the nexus Congress would have adopted in a more limited honoraria ban. We cannot know whether Congress accurately reflected its sense of an appropriate nexus in the terse, 33-word parenthetical statement with which it exempted series of speeches and articles from the definition of honoraria in the 1992 amendment, in an elaborate, nearly 600-word provision with which it later exempted Department of Defense military school faculty and students from the ban; or in neither. The process of drawing a proper nexus, even more than the defense of the statute's application to senior employees, would likely raise independent constitutional concerns whose adjudication is unnecessary to decide this case. We believe the Court of Appeals properly left to Congress the task of drafting a narrower statute.

Insofar as the judgment of the Court of Appeals affirms the injunction against enforcement of 501(b) against respondents, it is affirmed; insofar as it grants relief to parties not before the Court, it is reversed. The case is remanded for further proceedings consistent with this opinion."

V. JUSTICE VOTE

6 Pro ACLU Side vs. 3 Con Opposing SIde

ACLU Side (Respondent / Appellee)

1. Stevens, J. – Wrote majority opinion
2. Breyer, S. – Joined majority opinion
3. Ginsburg, R. – Joined majority opinion
4. Souter, D. – Joined majority opinion
5. O'Connor, S. – Wrote opinion concurring in part and dissenting in part
6. Kennedy, A. – Joined majority opinion

Opposing Side (Petitioner / Appellant)

1. Rehnquist, W. – Wrote dissenting opinion
2. Scalia, A. – Joined Rehnquist's dissent
3. Thomas, C. – Joined Rehnquist's dissent

VI. A WIN OR LOSS FOR THE ACLU?

The ACLU, as respondent's counsel, urged affirmance of the judgment of the Court of Appeals; the Supreme Court affirmed in part, reversed in part, and remanded the case in a 5-4 vote, giving the ACLU an apparent win.

779. Arizona v. Evans

(Decided March 1, 1995; 514 U.S. 1)

I. ISSUE

A. Issues Discussed

Fourth Amendment, search and seizure, exclusion of evidence

B. Legal Question Presented

"[W]hether evidence seized in violation of the Fourth Amendment by an officer who acted in reliance on a police record indicating the existence of an outstanding arrest warrant—a record that is later determined to be erroneous—must be suppressed by virtue of the exclusionary rule regardless of the source of the error."

C. Supreme Court's Answer

The evidence falls within the good faith exception to the exclusionary rule and therefore does not need to be suppressed at trial.

II. CASE SUMMARY

A. Background

"In January 1991, Phoenix police officer Bryan Sargent observed respondent Isaac Evans driving the wrong way on a one-way street in front of the police station. The officer stopped respondent and asked to see his driver's license. After respondent told him that his license had been suspended, the officer entered respondent's name into a computer data terminal located in his patrol car. The computer inquiry confirmed that respondent's license had been suspended and also indicated that there was an outstanding misdemeanor warrant for his arrest. Based upon the outstanding warrant, Officer Sargent placed respondent under arrest. While being handcuffed, respondent dropped a hand-rolled cigarette that the officers determined smelled of marijuana. Officers proceeded to search his car and discovered a bag of marijuana under the passenger's seat.

The State charged respondent with possession of marijuana. When the police notified the Justice Court that they had arrested him, the Justice Court discovered that the arrest warrant previously had been quashed and so advised the police. Respondent argued that because his arrest was based on a warrant that had been quashed 17 days prior to his arrest, the marijuana seized incident to the arrest should be suppressed as the fruit of an unlawful arrest. Respondent also argued that '[t]he 'good faith' exception to the exclusionary rule [was] inapplicable . . . because it was police error, not judicial error, which caused the invalid arrest.' . . .

The trial court granted the motion to suppress because it concluded that the State had been at fault for failing to quash the warrant. Presumably because it could find no 'distinction between State action, whether it happens to be the police department or not,' the trial court made no factual finding as to whether the Justice Court or Sheriff's Office was responsible for the continued presence of the quashed warrant in the police records.

A divided panel of the Arizona Court of Appeals reversed because it 'believe[d] that the exclusionary rule [was] not intended to deter justice court employees or Sheriff's Office employees who are not directly associated with the arresting officers or the arresting officers' police department.' Therefore, it concluded, 'the purpose of the exclusionary rule would not be served by excluding the evidence obtained in this case.'

The Arizona Supreme Court reversed."

The U.S. Supreme Court granted certiorari to review the case and reversed the judgment of the Arizona Supreme Court.

B. Counsel of Record / ACLU Attorney

ACLU Side (Respondent / Appellee): Carol A. Carrigan argued the cause for appellee.

Opposing Side (Petitioner / Appellant): Gerald Grant argued the cause for appellant.

III. AMICI CURIAE

ACLU Side (Respondent / Appellee)

Brief of amici curiae filed on behalf of the ACLU, et al., by Steven R. Shapiro, Alice L. Bendheim, and Tracey Maclin.

Brief of amici curiae filed on behalf of the National Association of Criminal Defense Lawyers by Ephraim Margolin and Barry P. Helft.

Opposing Side (Petitioner / Appellant)

Brief of amici curiae filed on behalf of the United States by Solicitor General Days, Assistant Attorney General Harris, Deputy Solicitor General Bryson, and Jeffrey P. Minear.

Brief of amici curiae filed on behalf of the State of Florida, et al., by Robert A. Butterworth, Attorney General for the State of

Florida, and Michael J. Neimand, Assistant Attorney General, and the following Attorneys General for their respective states: James H. Evans of Alabama, Bruce M. Botelho of Alaska, Larry EchoHawk of Idaho, Pamela Carter of Indiana, Robert T. Stephan of Kansas, Chris Gorman of Kentucky, Scott Harshbarger of Massachusetts, Joseph P. Mazurek of Montana, Lee Fisher of Ohio, T. Travis Medlock of South Carolina, Jeffrey L. Amestoy of Vermont, and James S. Gilmore, III, of Virginia.

Brief of amici curiae filed on behalf of Americans for Effective Law Enforcement, Inc., by Fred E. Inbau, Wayne W. Schmidt, James P. Manak, Roy C. Kime, Richard M. Weintraub, William C. O'Malley, and Bernard J. Farber.

Brief of amici curiae filed on behalf of the Washington Legal Foundation, et al., by Daniel J. Popeo, Paul D. Kamenar, and Paul J. Larkin, Jr.

IV. THE SUPREME COURT'S DECISION

"The Fourth Amendment states that '[t]he right of the people to be secure in their persons, houses, papers, and effects, against unreasonable searches and seizures, shall not be violated, and no Warrants shall issue, but upon probable cause, supported by Oath or affirmation, and particularly describing the place to be searched, and the persons or things to be seized.' We have recognized, however, that the Fourth Amendment contains no provision expressly precluding the use of evidence obtained in violation of its commands. . . .

'The question whether the exclusionary rule's remedy is appropriate in a particular context has long been regarded as an issue separate from the question whether the Fourth Amendment rights of the party seeking to invoke the rule were violated by police conduct.' The exclusionary rule operates as a judicially created remedy designed to safeguard against future violations of Fourth Amendment rights through the rule's general deterrent effect. As with any remedial device, the rule's application has been restricted to those instances where its remedial objectives are thought most efficaciously served. Where 'the exclusionary rule does not result in appreciable deterrence, then, clearly, its use . . . is unwarranted.'

In Leon, we applied these principles to the context of a police search in which the officers had acted in objectively reasonable reliance on a search warrant, issued by a neutral and detached Magistrate, that later was determined to be invalid. On the basis of three factors, we determined that there was no sound reason to apply the exclusionary rule as a means of deterring misconduct on the part of judicial officers who are responsible for issuing warrants. First, we noted that the exclusionary rule was historically designed 'to deter police misconduct rather than to punish the errors of judges and magistrates.' Second, there was 'no evidence suggesting that judges and magistrates are inclined to ignore or subvert the Fourth Amendment or that lawlessness among these actors requires the application of the extreme sanction of exclusion.' Third, and of greatest importance, there was no basis for believing that exclusion of evidence seized pursuant to a warrant would have a significant deterrent effect on the issuing judge or magistrate. . . .

If court employees were responsible for the erroneous computer record, the exclusion of evidence at trial would not sufficiently deter future errors so as to warrant such a severe sanction. First, as we noted in Leon, the exclusionary rule was historically designed as a means of deterring police misconduct, not mistakes by court employees. Second, respondent offers no evidence that court employees are inclined to ignore or subvert the Fourth Amendment or that lawlessness among these actors requires application of the extreme sanction of exclusion. To the contrary, the Chief Clerk of the Justice Court testified at the suppression hearing that this type of error occurred once every three or four years.

Finally, and most important, there is no basis for believing that application of the exclusionary rule in these circumstances will have a significant effect on court employees responsible for informing the police that a warrant has been quashed. Because court clerks are not adjuncts to the law enforcement team engaged in the often competitive enterprise of ferreting out crime they have no stake in the outcome of particular criminal prosecutions. The threat of exclusion of evidence could not be expected to deter such individuals from failing to inform police officials that a warrant had been quashed.

If it were indeed a court clerk who was responsible for the erroneous entry on the police computer, application of the exclusionary rule also could not be expected to alter the behavior of the arresting officer. As the trial court in this case stated: 'I think the police officer [was] bound to arrest. I think he would [have been] derelict in his duty if he failed to arrest.' The Chief Clerk of the Justice Court testified that this type of error occurred 'on[c] e every three or four years.' In fact, once the court clerks discovered the error, they immediately corrected it and then proceeded to search their files to make sure that no similar mistakes had occurred. There is no indication that the arresting officer was not acting objectively reasonably when he relied upon the police computer record. Application of the Leon framework supports a categorical exception to the exclusionary rule for clerical errors of court employees.

The judgment of the Supreme Court of Arizona is therefore reversed, and the case is remanded to that court for proceedings not inconsistent with this opinion."

V. JUSTICE VOTE

2 Pro ACLU Side vs. 7 Con Opposing Side

ACLU Side (Respondent / Appellee)

1. Stevens, J. – Wrote dissenting opinion, joined Ginsburg's dissent
2. Ginsburg, R. – Wrote dissenting opinion

Opposing Side (Petitioner / Appellant)

1. Rehnquist, W. – Wrote majority opinion
2. O'Connor, S. – Wrote concurring opinion
3. Scalia, A. – Joined majority opinion
4. Kennedy, A. – Joined majority opinion
5. Souter, D. – Wrote concurring opinion, joined O'Connor's concurrence

6. Thomas, C. – Joined majority opinion
7. Breyer, S. – Joined O'Connor's concurrence, joined Souter's concurrence

VI. A WIN OR LOSS FOR THE ACLU?

The ACLU, as amicus curiae, urged affirmance of the judgment of the Supreme Court of Arizona; the Supreme Court reversed in a 7-2 vote, giving the ACLU an apparent loss.

780. Swint v. Chambers County Commission

(Decided March 1, 1995; 514 U.S. 35)

I. ISSUE

A. Issues Discussed

Civil rights, drugs, jurisdiction

B. Legal Question Presented

Whether "the Eleventh Circuit lacked jurisdiction to rule on the county commission's liability at this interlocutory stage of the litigation."

C. Supreme Court's Answer

"[W]e conclude that the Eleventh Circuit lacked jurisdiction to rule on the county commission's liability at this interlocutory stage of the litigation."

II. CASE SUMMARY

A. Background

"On December 14, 1990, and again on March 29, 1991, law enforcement officers from Chambers County and the City of Wadley, Alabama, raided the Capri Club in Chambers County as part of a narcotics operation. The raids were conducted without a search warrant or an arrest warrant. Petitioners filed suit, alleging, among other claims for relief, violations of their federal civil rights. Petitioners named as defendants the county commission; the city of Wadley; and three individual defendants, Chambers County Sheriff James C. Morgan, Wadley Police Chief Freddie Morgan, and Wadley Police Officer Gregory Dendinger.

The five defendants moved for summary judgment on varying grounds. . . . The United States District Court for the Middle District of Alabama denied the motions for summary judgment. . . . Invoking the rule that an order denying qualified immunity is appealable before trial, the individual defendants immediately appealed. The city of Wadley and the Chambers County Commission also appealed, arguing, first, that the denial of their summary judgment motions—like the denial of the individual defendants' summary judgment motions—was immediately appealable as a collateral order . . . . Alternatively, the city and county commission urged the Eleventh Circuit Court of Appeals to exercise 'pendent appellate jurisdiction,' a power that court had asserted in earlier cases. Stressing the Eleventh Circuit's undisputed jurisdiction over the individual defendants' qualified immunity pleas, the city and county commission maintained that, in the interest of judicial economy, the court should resolve, simultaneously, the city's and commission's appeals.

The Eleventh Circuit affirmed in part and reversed in part the District Court's order denying summary judgment for the individual defendants."

The Supreme Court granted certiorari to review the case, vacated in part, and remanded.

B. Counsel of Record / ACLU Attorney

ACLU Side (Respondent / Appellee): Paul M. Smith argued the cause for appellees. With him on the briefs were Bruce J. Ennis, Donald B. Verrilli, Jr., James W Webb, Kendrick E. Webb, and Bart Harmon.

Opposing Side (Petitioner / Appellant): Robert B. McDuff argued the cause for appellant. With him on the briefs were Carlos A. Williams, Bryan Stevenson, and Bernard Harcourt.

Paul R. Q. Wolfson argued the cause for the United States, as amicus curiae, by special leave of Court.

III. AMICI CURIAE

ACLU Side (Respondent / Appellee)

Brief of amici curiae filed on behalf of the ACLU by Mitchell F. Dolin, Robert A. Long, Jr., T. Jeremy Gunn, Steven R. Shapiro, Michael A. Cooper, Herbert J. Hansell, Norman Redlich, Barbara R. Arwine, Thomas J. Henderson, and Sharon R. Vinick.

Brief of amici curiae filed on behalf of Jefferson County, Alabama, by Charles S. Wagner.

Brief of amici curiae filed on behalf of the National Association of Counties, et al., by Richard Ruda and James L. Crowley.

Opposing Side (Petitioner / Appellant)

Brief of amici curiae filed on behalf of the Southern States Police Benevolent Association by J. Michael McGuinness.

Brief of amici curiae filed on behalf of the United States by Paul R. Q. Wolfson, Solicitor General Days, Assistant Attorney General Patrick, Deputy Solicitor General Bender, Beth S. Brinkmann, Jessica Dunsay Silver, and Linda F. Thome.

IV. THE SUPREME COURT'S DECISION

"[There are] statutory instructions Congress has given to control the timing of appellate proceedings. The main rule on review of 'final decisions,' is followed by prescriptions for appeals from 'interlocutory decisions.' . . .

Congress' designation of the rule-making process as the way to define or refine when a district court ruling is 'final' and when an interlocutory order is appealable warrants the Judiciary's full respect.

Two decisions of this Court securely support the conclusion that the Eleventh Circuit lacked jurisdiction instantly to review the denial of the county commission's summary judgment motion: Abney v. United States, 431 U.S. 651 (1977), and United States v. Stanley, 483 U.S. 669 (1987). In Abney, we permitted appeal before trial of an order denying a motion to dismiss an indictment on double jeopardy grounds. Immediate appeal of that ruling, we held, fit within the Cohen collateral order doctrine.

But we further held that the Court of Appeals lacked authority to review simultaneously the trial court's rejection of the defendant's challenge to the sufficiency of the indictment. . . . The Eleventh Circuit's authority immediately to review the District Court's denial of the individual police officer defendants' summary judgment motions did not include authority to review at once the unrelated question of the county commission's liability. The District Court's preliminary ruling regarding the county did not qualify as a 'collateral order,' and there is no 'pendent party' appellate jurisdiction of the kind the Eleventh Circuit purported to exercise. We therefore vacate the relevant portion of the Eleventh Circuit's judgment and remand the case for proceedings consistent with this opinion."

V. JUSTICE VOTE

0 Pro ACLU Side vs. 9 Con Opposing Side

Opposing Side (Petitioner / Appellant)

1. Ginsburg, R. – Wrote majority opinion
2. Breyer, S. – Joined majority opinion
3. Thomas, C. – Joined majority opinion
4. Souter, D. – Joined majority opinion
5. O'Connor, S. – Joined majority opinion
6. Kennedy, A. – Joined majority opinion
7. Scalia, A. – Joined majority opinion
8. Rehnquist, W. – Joined majority opinion
9. Stevens, J. – Joined majority opinion

VI. A WIN OR LOSS FOR THE ACLU?

The ACLU filed as amicus curiae urging affirmance of the judgment of the Court of Appeals; the Supreme Court vacated and remanded in a 9-0 vote, giving the ACLU an apparent loss.

781. McIntyre v. Ohio Elections Commission

(Decided April 19, 1995; 514 U.S. 334)

I. ISSUE

A. Issues Discussed

First Amendment, freedoms of press, speech, and association

B. Legal Question Presented

"[W]hether an Ohio statute that prohibits the distribution of anonymous campaign literature is a 'law . . . abridging the freedom of speech' within the meaning of the First Amendment.'"

C. Supreme Court's Answer

The Ohio statute violates the First Amendment.

II. CASE SUMMARY

A. Background

"On April 27, 1988, Margaret McIntyre distributed leaflets to persons attending a public meeting at the Blendon Middle School in Westerville, Ohio. At this meeting, the superintendent of schools planned to discuss an imminent referendum on a proposed school tax levy. The leaflets expressed Mrs. McIntyre's opposition to the levy. There is no suggestion that the text of her message was false, misleading, or libelous. She had composed and printed it on her home computer and had paid a professional printer to make additional copies. Some of the handbills identified her as the author; others merely purported to express the views of 'CONCERNED PARENTS AND TAX PAYERS.' Except for the help provided by her son and a friend, who placed some of the leaflets on car windshields in the school parking lot, Mrs. McIntyre acted independently.

While Mrs. McIntyre distributed her handbills, an official of the school district, who supported the tax proposal, advised her that the unsigned leaflets did not conform to the Ohio election laws. Undeterred, Mrs. McIntyre appeared at another meeting on the next evening and handed out more of the handbills.

The proposed school levy was defeated at the next two elections, but it finally passed on its third try in November 1988. Five months later, the same school official filed a complaint with the Ohio Elections Commission charging that Mrs. McIntyre's distribution of unsigned leaflets violated § 3599.09(A) of the Ohio Code. The commission agreed and imposed a fine of $100.

The Franklin County Court of Common Pleas reversed. Finding that Mrs. McIntyre did not 'mislead the public nor act in a surreptitious manner,' the court concluded that the statute was unconstitutional as applied to her conduct. The Ohio Court of Appeals, by a divided vote, reinstated the fine. . . . The Ohio Supreme Court affirmed by a divided vote."

The Supreme Court granted certiorari to review the case and reversed.

B. Counsel of Record / ACLU Attorney

ACLU Side (Petitioner / Appellant): David Goldberger argued the cause for appellant. With him on the briefs were Steven R. Shapiro, Joel M. Gora, Barbara P. O'Toole, Roger Baldwin, Louis A. Jacobs, Kevin E. O'Neil, and George Q. Vaile.

Opposing Side (Respondent / Appellee): Assistant Attorney General of Ohio Andrew I. Sutter argued the cause for appellee. With him on the briefs were Attorney General Lee Fisher, Assistant Attorneys General Andrew S. Bergman, Robert A. Zimmerman, and James M. Harrison, State Solicitor Richard A. Cordray, and Simon B. Karas.

III. AMICI CURIAE

ACLU Side (Petitioner / Appellant)

Brief of amici curiae filed on behalf of the California Political Attorneys Association by Lowell Finley, Robert E. Leidigh, Charles H. Bell, Jr., and Darryl R. Wold.

Opposing Side (Respondent / Appellee)

Brief of amici curiae filed on behalf of the State of Tennessee, et al., by Charles W Burson, Attorney General of Tennessee, Michael E. Moore, Solicitor General, and Michael W Catalano, Associate Solicitor General, and by the Attorneys General for their respective States as follows: Jimmy Evans of Alabama, Bruce M. Botelho of Alaska, Winston Bryant of Arkansas,

Gale A. Norton of Colorado, Charles M. Oberly III of Delaware, Robert A. Butterworth of Florida, Larry EchoHawk of Idaho, Roland W. Burris of Illinois, Pamela Fanning Carter of Indiana, Chris Gorman of Kentucky, Richard P. Ieyoub of Louisiana, Frank J. Kelley of Michigan, Hubert H. Humphrey III of Minnesota, Mike Moore of Mississippi, Joseph P. Mazurek of Montana, Frankie Sue Del Papa of Nevada, Jeffrey R. Howard of New Hampshire, Deborah T. Poritz of New Jersey, Michael F. Easley of North Carolina, Heidi Heitkamp of North Dakota, Susan B. Loving of Oklahoma, T. Travis Medlock of South Carolina, Mark Barnett of South Dakota, Jeffrey L. Amestoy of Vermont, James S. Gilmore, III, of Virginia, Darrell V. McGraw, Jr., of West Virginia, James E. Doyle of Wisconsin, and Joseph B. Meyer or Wyoming.

Brief of amici curiae filed on behalf of the Council of State Governments, et al., by Richard Ruda and Lee Fennell.

IV. THE SUPREME COURT'S DECISION

"[A]n author's decision to remain anonymous, like other decisions concerning omissions or additions to the content of a publication, is an aspect of the freedom of speech protected by the First Amendment.

The freedom to publish anonymously extends beyond the literary realm. In Talley, the Court held that the First Amendment protects the distribution of unsigned handbills urging readers to boycott certain Los Angeles merchants who were allegedly engaging in discriminatory employment practices. . . . Writing for the Court, Justice Black noted that '[p]ersecuted groups and sects from time to time throughout history have been able to criticize oppressive practices and laws either anonymously or not at all.' Justice Black recalled England's abusive press licensing laws and seditious libel prosecutions, and he reminded us that even the arguments favoring the ratification of the Constitution advanced in the Federalist Papers were published under fictitious names. . . .

Under our Constitution, anonymous pamphleteering is not a pernicious, fraudulent practice, but an honorable tradition of advocacy and of dissent. Anonymity is a shield from the tyranny of the majority. It thus exemplifies the purpose behind the Bill of Rights, and of the First Amendment in particular: to protect unpopular individuals from retaliation—and their ideas from suppression—at the hand of an intolerant society. The right to remain anonymous may be abused when it shields fraudulent conduct. But political speech by its nature will sometimes have unpalatable consequences, and, in general, our society accords greater weight to the value of free speech than to the dangers of its misuse. Ohio has not shown that its interest in preventing the misuse of anonymous election-related speech justifies a prohibition of all uses of that speech. The State may, and does, punish fraud directly. But it cannot seek to punish fraud indirectly by indiscriminately outlawing a category of speech, based on its content, with no necessary relationship to the danger sought to be prevented. One would be hard pressed to think of a better example of the pitfalls of Ohio's blunderbuss approach than the facts of the case before us.

The judgment of the Ohio Supreme Court is reversed."

V. JUSTICE VOTE

7 Pro ACLU Side vs. 2 Con Opposing Side

ACLU Side (Petitioner / Appellant)

1. Stevens, J. – Wrote majority opinion
2. O'Connor, S. – Joined majority opinion
3. Kennedy, A. – Joined majority opinion
4. Souter, D. – Joined majority opinion
5. Breyer, S. – Joined majority opinion
6. Thomas, C. – Wrote concurring opinion
7. Ginsburg, R. – Wrote concurring opinion

Opposing Side (Respondent / Appellee)

1. Scalia, A. – Wrote dissenting opinion
2. Rehnquist, W. – Joined Scalia's dissent

VI. A WIN OR LOSS FOR THE ACLU?

The ACLU, as counsel to the petitioner, sought reversal of the judgment of the Ohio Supreme Court; the U.S. Supreme Court reversed in a 7-2 vote, giving the ACLU an apparent win.

782. City of Edmonds v. Oxford House, Inc.

(Decided May 15, 1995; 514 U.S. 725)

I. ISSUE

A. Issues Discussed

Regulation, civil rights, federal

B. Legal Question Presented

"[W]hether Edmonds' family composition rule qualifies as a 'restrictio[n] regarding the maximum number of occupants permitted to occupy a dwelling' within the meaning of the FHA's absolute exemption. 42 U.S.C. § 3607(b)(1)."

C. Supreme Court's Answer

"We hold that §3607(b)(1) does not exempt prescriptions of the family-defining kind, i. e., provisions designed to foster the family character of a neighborhood. Instead, § 3607(b)(1)'s absolute exemption removes from the FHA's scope only total occupancy limits, i. e., numerical ceilings that serve to prevent overcrowding in living quarters. . . .

Edmonds' zoning code provision describing who may compose a 'family' is not a maximum occupancy restriction exempt from the FHA under §3607(b)(1)."

II. CASE SUMMARY

A. Background

"In the summer of 1990, respondent Oxford House opened a group home in the City of Edmonds, Washington (City), for 10 to 12 adults recovering from alcoholism and drug addiction. The group home, called Oxford House–Edmonds, is located in a neighborhood zoned for single-family residences. Upon learning that Oxford House had leased and was operating a home in Edmonds, the City issued criminal citations to the owner and a resident of the house. The citations charged violation of the zoning code rule that defines who may live in single-family dwelling units. The occupants of such units must compose a 'family,' and family, under the City's defining rule, 'means an individual or two or more persons related by genetics, adoption, or marriage, or a group of five or fewer persons who are not related by genetics, adoption, or marriage.' Oxford House–Edmonds houses more than five unrelated persons, and therefore does not conform to the code.

Oxford House asserted reliance on the Fair Housing Act, which declares it unlawful '[t]o discriminate in the sale or rental, or to otherwise make unavailable or deny, a dwelling to any buyer or renter because of a handicap of . . . that buyer or renter.' . . .

Oxford House asked Edmonds to make a 'reasonable accommodation' by allowing it to remain in the single-family dwelling it had leased. . . .

Edmonds sued Oxford House in the United States District Court for the Western District of Washington . . . .

[T]he District Court held that ECDC § 21.30.010, defining 'family,' is exempt from the FHA . . . . The United States Court of Appeals for the Ninth Circuit reversed . . . ."

The Supreme Court granted certiorari to review the case.

B. Counsel of Record

ACLU Side (Respondent / Appellee): William F. Sheehan argued the cause for private appellees. With him on the briefs were Steven R. Shapiro of the American Civil Liberties Union Foundation, Robert I. Heller, Elizabeth M. Brown, David E. Jones, and John P. Relman. Deputy Solicitor General Bender argued the cause for appellee United States. With him on the brief were Solicitor General Days, Assistant Attorney General Patrick, Cornelia T. L. Pillard, Jessica Dunsay Silver, and Gregory B. Friel.

Opposing Side (Petitioner / Appellant): W. Scott Snyder argued the cause and filed briefs for appellant.

III. AMICI CURIAE

ACLU Side (Respondent / Appellee)

Brief of amici curiae filed on behalf of the Commonwealth of Massachusetts et al. by Scott Harshbarger, Attorney General of Massachusetts, and Stanley J. Eichner, Donna L. Palermino, and Leo T. Sorokin, Assistant Attorneys General, and by the Attorneys General for their respective jurisdictions as follows: Grant Woods of Arizona, Winston Bryant of Arkansas, Alan G. Lance of Idaho, Thomas J. Miller of Iowa, Richard P. Ieyoub of Louisiana, Frankie Sue Del Papa of Nevada, Tom Udall of New Mexico, Charles W. Burson of Tennessee, Dan Morales of Texas, Jan Graham of Utah, Rosalie Simmonds Ballantine of the Virgin Islands, and Darrell V. McGraw, Jr., of West Virginia.

Brief of amici curiae filed on behalf of the American Association on Mental Retardation et al. by Lois G. Williams, Jerrold J. Ganzfried, Gregg A. Hand, Leonard S. Rubenstein, and Ira A. Burnim.

Brief of amici curiae filed on behalf of the American Association of Retired Persons by Steven S. Zaleznick, Michael Schuster, Bruce B. Vignery, and Deborah M. Zuckerman.

Brief of amici curiae filed on behalf of the American Planning Association by Brian W. Blaesser and Daniel M. Lauber.

Brief of amici curiae filed on behalf of the American Society of Addiction Medicine et al. by Paul M. Smith, Seth P. Stein, Robert L. Schonfeld, Richard Taranto, and Carolyn I. Polowy.

Brief of amici curiae filed on behalf of the American Train Dispatchers Division of Brotherhood of Locomotive Engineers et al. by Lawrence M. Mann.

Brief of amici curiae filed on behalf of the National Fair Housing Alliance by Timothy C. Hester, Robert A. Long, Jr., and Christina T. Uhlrich.

Opposing Side (Petitioner / Appellant)

Brief of amici curiae filed on behalf of the City of Lubbock by Jean E. Shotts, Jr.

Brief of amici curiae filed on behalf of the City of Mountlake Terrace by Gregory G. Schrag.

Brief of amici curiae filed on behalf of the Township of Upper St. Clair by Robert N. Hackett.

Brief of amici curiae filed on behalf of the International City/County Management Association et al. by Richard Ruda, Lee Fennell, and Michael J. Wahoske.

Brief of amici curiae filed on behalf of the City of Fultondale by Palmer W. Norris and Fred Blanton, Jr.

Brief of amici curiae filed on behalf of the Pacific Legal Foundation by Ronald A. Zumbrun and Anthony T. Caso.

IV. THE SUPREME COURT'S DECISION

"Congress enacted § 3607(b)(1) against the backdrop of an evident distinction between municipal land-use restrictions and maximum occupancy restrictions. . . .

To limit land use to single-family residences, a municipality must define the term "family"; thus family composition rules are an essential component of single-family residential use restrictions.

Maximum occupancy restrictions, in contradistinction, cap the number of occupants per dwelling, typically in relation to available floor space or the number and type of rooms. . . .

We recognized this distinction between maximum occupancy restrictions and land-use restrictions in Moore v. East Cleveland, 431 U.S. 494 (1977). . . .

Section 3607(b)(1)'s language—'restrictions regarding the maximum number of occupants permitted to occupy a dwelling'—surely encompasses maximum occupancy restrictions. But the formulation does not fit family composition rules typically tied to land-use restrictions. In sum, rules that cap the total number of occupants in order to prevent overcrowding of a dwelling 'plainly and unmistakably' fall within § 3607(b)(1)'s absolute exemption from the FHA's governance; rules designed to preserve the family character of a neighborhood, fastening on the composition of households rather than on the total number of occupants living quarters can contain, do not. . . .

Turning specifically to the City's Community Development Code, we note that the provisions Edmonds invoked against Oxford House, ECDC §§ 16.20.010 and 21.30.010, are classic examples of a use restriction and complementing family composition rule. . . .

This space and occupancy standard is a prototypical maximum occupancy restriction. . . .

The parties have presented, and we have decided, only a threshold question: Edmonds' zoning code provision describing who may compose a 'family' is not a maximum occupancy restriction exempt from the FHA under § 3607(b)(1). It remains for the lower courts to decide whether Edmonds' actions against Oxford House violate the FHA's prohibitions against discrimination set out in §§ 3604(f)(1)(A) and (f)(3)(B). For the reasons stated, the judgment of the United States Court of Appeals for the Ninth Circuit is affirmed."

V. JUSTICE VOTE

6 Pro ACLU Side vs. 3 Con Opposing Side

ACLU Side (Respondent / Appellee)

1. Ginsburg, R. – Wrote majority opinion
2. Rehnquist, W. – Joined majority opinion
3. Stevens, J. – Joined majority opinion
4. O'Connor, S. – Joined majority opinion
5. Souter, D. – Joined majority opinion
6. Breyer, S. – Joined majority opinion

Opposing Side (Petitioner / Appellant)

1. Thomas, C. – Wrote dissenting opinion
2. Kennedy, A. – Joined Thomas' dissent
3. Scalia, A. – Joined Thomas' dissent

VI. A WIN OR LOSS FOR THE ACLU?

The ACLU served as counsel for appellees urging affirmance; the Supreme Court affirmed the Court of Appeals' decision by a 6-3 vote, giving the ACLU an apparent win.

783. U.S. Term Limits, Inc. v. Thornton

(Decided May 22, 1995; 514 U.S. 779)

I. ISSUE

A. Issues Discussed

Federalism, elections

B. Legal Question Presented

Whether § 3 of Amendment 73 of the Arkansas Constitution violates the Federal Constitution by creating qualifications for service in the United States Congress.

C. Supreme Court's Answer

Section 3 of Amendment 73 of the Arkansas Constitution violates the Federal Constitution.

II. CASE SUMMARY

A. Background

"Today's cases present a challenge to [Amendment 73] to the Arkansas State Constitution that prohibits the name of an otherwise-eligible candidate for Congress from appearing on the general election ballot if that candidate has already served three terms in the House of Representatives or two terms in the Senate. . . .

On November 13, 1992, respondent Bobbie Hill, on behalf of herself, similarly situated Arkansas 'citizens, residents, taxpayers and registered voters,' and the League of Women Voters of Arkansas, filed a complaint in the Circuit Court for Pulaski County, Arkansas, seeking a declaratory judgment that § 3 of Amendment 73 is 'unconstitutional and void.' . . . On cross-motions for summary judgment, the Circuit Court held that § 3 of Amendment 73 violated Article I of the Federal Constitution.

With respect to that holding, in a 5-to-2 decision, the Arkansas Supreme Court affirmed."

The Supreme Court granted certiorari to review the case and affirmed.

B. Counsel of Record / ACLU Attorney

ACLU Side (Respondent / Appellee): Louis R. Cohen argued the cause for appellees in both cases.

Solicitor General Drew S. Days, III, argued the cause for the United States, as amicus curiae, by special leave of Court.

Opposing Side (Petitioner / Appellant): J. Winston Bryant, Attorney General of Arkansas, argued the cause for appellants in No. 93-1828.

John G. Kester argued the cause for appellants in No. 93-1456.

III. AMICI CURIAE

ACLU Side (Respondent / Appellee)

Brief of amici curiae filed on behalf of the ACLU, et al., by Kevin J. Hamilton, Perkins Coie, and Steven R. Shapiro.

Brief of amici curiae filed on behalf of the United States by Solicitor General Days, Assistant Attorneys General Dellinger and Hunger, Deputy Solicitor General Bender, Paul R. Q. Wolfson, Douglas N. Letter, and Michael S. Raab.

Brief of amici curiae filed on behalf of the California Democratic Party by Daniel H. Lowenstein, Jonathan H. Steinberg, Elliot Brown, and George Waters.

Brief of amici curiae filed on behalf of the League of Women Voters of the United States, et al., by Fredric C. Tausend and Herbert E. Wilgis, III.

Brief of amici curiae filed on behalf of Henry J. Hyde by Charles A. Rothfield, David C. Crane, and Myles R. Hansen.

Opposing Side (Petitioner / Appellant)

Briefs of amici curiae were filed on behalf of the Alaska Committee for a Citizen Congress, et al., the Allied Educational Foundation, Governor John Engler, the State of Nebraska, et al., the State of Washington, Citizens for Term Limits, et al., the Citizens United Foundation, Congressional Term Limits Coalition, Inc., the Mountain States Legal Foundation, et al., People's Advocate, Inc., et al., the United States Justice Foundation, Virginians for Term Limits, et al., and the Washington Legal Foundation, et al.

IV. THE SUPREME COURT'S DECISION

"As the opinions of the Arkansas Supreme Court suggest, the constitutionality of Amendment 73 depends critically on the resolution of two distinct issues. The first is whether the Constitution forbids States to add to or alter the qualifications specifically enumerated in the Constitution. The second is, if the Constitution does so forbid, whether the fact that Amendment 73 is formulated as a ballot access restriction rather than as an outright disqualification is of constitutional significance.

[W]e reaffirm that the qualifications for service in Congress set forth in the text of the Constitution are 'fixed,' at least in the sense that they may not be supplemented by Congress. [T]he available historical and textual evidence, read in light of the basic principles of democracy underlying the Constitution and recognized by this Court in Powell, reveal the Framers' intent that neither Congress nor the States should possess the power to supplement the exclusive qualifications set forth in the text of the Constitution. . . .

The merits of term limits, or 'rotation,' have been the subject of debate since the formation of our Constitution, when the Framers unanimously rejected a proposal to add such limits to the Constitution. The cogent arguments on both sides of the question that were articulated during the process of ratification largely retain their force today. Over half the States have adopted measures that impose such limits on some offices either directly or indirectly, and the Nation as a whole, notably by constitutional amendment, has imposed a limit on the number of terms that the President may serve. Term limits, like any other qualification for office, unquestionably restrict the ability of voters to vote for whom they wish. On the other hand, such limits may provide for the infusion of fresh ideas and new perspectives, and may decrease the likelihood that representatives will lose touch with their constituents. It is not our province to resolve this longstanding debate.

We are, however, firmly convinced that allowing the several States to adopt term limits for congressional service would effect a fundamental change in the constitutional framework. Any such change must come not by legislation adopted either by Congress or by an individual State, but rather-as have other important changes in the electoral process 50—through the amendment procedures set forth in Article V. The Framers decided that the qualifications for service in the Congress of the United States be fixed in the Constitution and be uniform throughout the Nation. That decision reflects the Framers' understanding that Members of Congress are chosen by separate constituencies, but that they become, when elected, servants of the people of the United States. They are not merely delegates appointed by separate, sovereign States; they occupy offices that are integral and essential components of a single National Government. In the absence of a properly passed constitutional amendment, allowing individual States to craft their own qualifications for Congress would thus erode the structure envisioned by the Framers, a structure that was designed, in the words of the Preamble to our Constitution, to form a 'more perfect Union.'

The judgment is affirmed."

V. JUSTICE VOTE

5 Pro ACLU Side vs. 4 Con Opposing Side

ACLU Side (Respondent / Appellee)

1. Stevens, J. – Wrote majority opinion
2. Kennedy, A. – Wrote concurring opinion
3. Souter, D. – Joined majority opinion
4. Ginsburg, R. – Joined majority opinion
5. Breyer, S. – Joined majority opinion

Opposing Side (Petitioner / Appellant)

1. Thomas, C. – Wrote dissenting opinion
2. Rehnquist, W. – Joined Thomas' dissent
3. O'Connor, S. – Joined Thomas' dissent
4. Scalia, A. – Joined Thomas' dissent

VI. A WIN OR LOSS FOR THE ACLU?

The ACLU, as amicus curiae, urged affirmance of the judgment of the Supreme Court of Arkansas; the U.S. Supreme Court affirmed in a 5-4 vote, giving the ACLU an apparent win.

784. Wilson v. Arkansas

(Decided May 22, 1995; 514 U.S. 927)

I. ISSUE

A. Issues Discussed

Criminal justice, drugs, Fourth Amendment, search and seizure

B. Legal Question Presented

"[W]hether the common-law knock and announce principle forms a part of the Fourth Amendment reasonableness inquiry."

C. Supreme Court's Answer

The knock and announce principle is a factor in the reasonableness inquiry under the Fourth Amendment.

II. CASE SUMMARY

A. Background

"During November and December 1992, petitioner Sharlene Wilson made a series of narcotics sales to an informant acting at the direction of the Arkansas State Police. In late November, the informant purchased marijuana and methamphetamine at the home that petitioner shared with Bryson Jacobs. On December 30, the informant telephoned petitioner at her home and arranged to meet her at a local store to buy some marijuana. [P]etitioner produced a semiautomatic pistol at this meeting and waved it in the informant's face, threatening to kill her if she turned out to be working for the police. Petitioner then sold the informant a bag of marijuana.

The next day, police officers applied for and obtained warrants to search petitioner's home and to arrest both petitioner and Jacobs. Affidavits filed in support of the warrants set forth the details of the narcotics transactions and stated that Jacobs had previously been convicted of arson and firebombing. The search was conducted later that afternoon. Police officers found the main door to petitioner's home open. While opening an unlocked screen door and entering the residence, they identified themselves as police officers and stated that they had a warrant. Once inside the home, the officers seized marijuana, methamphetamine, valium, narcotics paraphernalia, a gun, and ammunition. They also found petitioner in the bathroom, flushing marijuana down the toilet. Petitioner and Jacobs were arrested and charged with delivery of marijuana, delivery of methamphetamine, possession of drug paraphernalia, and possession of marijuana.

Before trial, petitioner filed a motion to suppress the evidence seized during the search. Petitioner asserted that the search was invalid on various grounds, including that the officers had failed to 'knock and announce' before entering her home. The trial court summarily denied the suppression motion. After a jury trial, petitioner was convicted of all charges and sentenced to 32 years in prison.

The Arkansas Supreme Court affirmed petitioner's conviction on appeal."

The U.S. Supreme Court granted certiorari to review the case and reversed.

B. Counsel of Record / ACLU Attorney

ACLU Side (Petitioner / Appellant): John Wesley Hall, Jr., argued the cause for appellant.

Opposing Side (Respondent / Appellee): Winston Bryant, Attorney General of Arkansas, argued the cause for appellee.

Deputy Solicitor General Dreeben argued the cause for the United States, as amicus curiae, by special leave of Court.

III. AMICI CURIAE

ACLU Side (Petitioner / Appellant)

Brief of amici curiae filed on behalf of the ACLU, et al., by Tracey Maclin, Steven R. Shapiro, and Ephraim Margolin.

Opposing Side (Respondent / Appellee)

Brief of amici curiae filed on behalf of the United States by Deputy Solicitor General Dreeben, Solicitor General Days, Assistant Attorney General Harris, Paul A. Engelmayer, and Deborah Watson.

Brief of amici curiae filed on behalf of the State of California, et al., by Daniel E. Lungren, Attorney General of California, Richard Rochman, Assistant Attorney General, and Eleni M. Constantine, and by the Attorneys General for their respective jurisdictions as follows: Jeff Sessions of Alabama, Grant Woods of Arizona, Gale A. Norton of Colorado, M. Jane Brady of Delaware, Robert A. Butterworth of Florida, Margery S. Bronster of Hawaii, Alan G. Lance of Idaho, Jim Ryan of Illinois, Tom Miller of Iowa, Carla J. Stovall of Kansas, Chris Gorman of Kentucky, Andrew Ketterer of Maine, J. Joseph Curran, Jr., of Maryland, Frank J. Kelley of Michigan, Mike Moore of Mississippi, Jeremiah W. "Jay" Nixon of Missouri, Joseph P. Mazurek of Montana, Don Stenberg of Nebraska, Frankie Sue Del Papa of Nevada, Deborah T. Poritz of New Jersey, Dennis C. Vacco of New York, Michael F. Easley of North Carolina, Betty Montgomery of Ohio, Theodore R. Kulongoski of Oregon, Jeffrey B. Pine of Rhode Island, Charlie Condon of South Carolina, Mark Bennett of South Dakota, Dan Morales of Texas, Jan Graham of Utah, Jeffrey L. Amestoy of Vermont, and James S. Gilmore III of Virginia.

Brief of amici curiae filed on behalf of Wayne County, Michigan, by John D. O'Hair and Timothy A. Baughman.

Brief of amici curiae filed on behalf of Americans for Effective Law Enforcement, Inc., et al., by Fred E. Inbau, Wayne W. Schmidt, James P. Manak, Richard M. Weintraub, Robert L. Deschamps, and Bernard J. Farber.

IV. THE SUPREME COURT'S DECISION

"The common-law knock and announce principle was woven quickly into the fabric of early American law. . . . Our own cases have acknowledged that the common-law principle of announcement is 'embedded in Anglo-American law,' but we have never squarely held that this principle is an element of the reasonableness inquiry under the Fourth Amendment. We now so hold. [W] e hold that in some circumstances an officer's unannounced entry into a home might be unreasonable under the Fourth Amendment.

This is not to say, of course, that every entry must be preceded by an announcement. The Fourth Amendment's flexible requirement of reasonableness should not be read to mandate a rigid rule of announcement that ignores countervailing law enforcement interests. . . . We need not attempt a comprehensive catalog of the relevant countervailing factors here. For now, we leave to the lower courts the task of determining the circumstances under which an unannounced entry is reasonable under the Fourth Amendment. We simply hold that although a search or seizure of a dwelling might be constitutionally defective if police officers enter without prior announcement, law enforcement interests may also establish the reasonableness of an unannounced entry. . . .

Respondent contends that the judgment below should be affirmed because the unannounced entry in this case was justified for two reasons. First, respondent argues that police officers reasonably believed that a prior announcement would have placed them in peril, given their knowledge that petitioner had threatened a government informant with a semiautomatic weapon and that Mr. Jacobs had previously been convicted of arson and firebombing. Second, respondent suggests that prior announcement would have produced an unreasonable risk that petitioner would destroy easily disposable narcotics evidence.

These considerations may well provide the necessary justification for the unannounced entry in this case. Because the Arkansas Supreme Court did not address their sufficiency, however, we remand to allow the state courts to make any necessary findings of fact and to make the determination of reasonableness in the first instance. The judgment of the Arkansas Supreme Court is reversed, and the case is remanded for further proceedings not inconsistent with this opinion."

V. JUSTICE VOTE

9 Pro ACLU Side vs. 0 Con Opposing Side

ACLU Side (Petitioner / Appellant)

1. Thomas, C. – Wrote majority opinion
2. Souter, D. – Joined majority opinion

3. Ginsburg, R. – Joined majority opinion
4. Breyer, S. – Joined majority opinion
5. O'Connor, S. – Joined majority opinion
6. Scalia, A. – Joined majority opinion
7. Kennedy, A. – Joined majority opinion
8. Stevens, J. – Joined majority opinion
9. Rehnquist, W. – Joined majority opinion

VI. A WIN OR LOSS FOR THE ACLU?

The ACLU filed as amicus curiae urging reversal of the judgment of the Arkansas Supreme Court; the U.S. Supreme Court reversed in a 9-0 vote, giving the ACLU an apparent win.

785. Missouri v. Jenkins

(Decided June 12, 1995; 515 U.S. 70)

I. ISSUE

A. Issues Discussed

Civil rights, race, Fourteenth Amendment, school desegregation

B. Legal Question Presented

"(1) [W]hether the District Court exceeded its constitutional authority when it granted salary increases to virtually all instructional and noninstructional employees of the KCMSD, and (2) whether the District Court properly relied upon the fact that student achievement test scores had failed to rise to some unspecified level when it declined to find that the State had achieved partial unitary status as to the quality education programs."

C. Supreme Court's Answer

The salary increases were beyond the scope of the District Court's authority. The reliance upon student achievement test scores to determine whether the State has achieved partial unitary status was not appropriate.

II. CASE SUMMARY

A. Background

"As this school desegregation litigation enters its 18th year, we are called upon again to review the decisions of the lower courts. In this case, the State of Missouri has challenged the District Court's order of salary increases for virtually all instructional and noninstructional staff within the Kansas City, Missouri, School District (KCMSD) and the District Court's order requiring the State to continue to fund remedial 'quality education' programs because student achievement levels were still 'at or below national norms at many grade levels.' . . .

This case has been before the same United States District Judge since 1977. In that year, the KCMSD, the school board, and the children of two school board members brought suit against the State and other defendants. Plaintiffs alleged that the State, the surrounding suburban school districts (SSD's), and various federal agencies had caused and perpetuated a system of racial segregation in the schools of the Kansas City metropolitan area. . . .

The District Court's desegregation plan has been described as the most ambitious and expensive remedial program in the history of school desegregation. The annual cost per pupil at the KCMSD far exceeds that of the neighboring SSD's or of any school district in Missouri. Nevertheless, the KCMSD, which has pursued a 'friendly adversary' relationship with the plaintiffs, has continued to propose ever more expensive programs. As a result, the desegregation costs have escalated and now are approaching an annual cost of $200 million. . . .

With this background, we turn to the present controversy. First, the State has challenged the District Court's requirement that it fund salary increases for KCMSD instructional and noninstructional staff. The State claimed that funding for salaries was beyond the scope of the District Court's remedial authority. Second, the State has challenged the District Court's order requiring it to continue to fund the remedial quality education programs for the 1992–1993 school year.

The District Court rejected the State's arguments. . . . The Court of Appeals for the Eighth Circuit affirmed."

The Supreme Court granted certiorari to review the case and reversed.

B. Counsel of Record / ACLU Attorney

ACLU Side (Respondent / Appellee): Theodore M. Shaw argued the cause for appellees.

Deputy Solicitor General Paul Bender argued the cause for the United States, as amicus curiae, by special leave of Court.

Opposing Side (Petitioner / Appellant): John R. Munich argued the cause for appellant.

III. AMICI CURIAE

ACLU Side (Respondent / Appellee)

Brief of amici curiae filed on behalf of the ACLU, et al., by Christopher A. Hansen, Steven R. Shapiro, and Helen Hershkoff.

Brief of amici curiae filed on behalf of the United States by Deputy Solicitor General Bender, Solicitor General Days, Assistant Attorney General Patrick, Irving L. Gornstein, Dennis J. Dimsey and Mark L. Gross.

Brief of amici curiae filed on behalf of the Civic Council of Greater Kansas City by David F. Oliver.

Brief of amici curiae filed on behalf of the Lawyers' Committee for Civil Rights Under Law by Herbert J. Hansell, Barbara R. Arnwine, Carolyn A. Johnston, Michael S. Dicke, Matthew I. Kreeger, Jack W. Londen, Michael Cooper, and Thomas J. Henderson.

Brief of amici curiae filed on behalf of James D. Anderson, et al., by Kevin J. Hamilton, Julia L. Parsons, Stephen C. Willey, and Elizabeth K. Peck.

Brief of amici curiae filed on behalf of the National Urban League, et al., by William L. Taylor and Dianne M. Piche.

Opposing Side (Petitioner / Appellant)

Brief of amici curiae filed on behalf of Icelean Clark, et al., by Mark J. Bredemeier, Jerald L. Hill, Mark R. Levin, and Richard P. Hutchison.

IV. THE SUPREME COURT'S DECISION

"Proper analysis of the District Court's orders challenged here . . . must rest upon their serving as proper means to the end of restoring the victims of discriminatory conduct to the position they would have occupied in the absence of that conduct and their eventual restoration of 'state and local authorities to the control of a school system that is operating in compliance with the Constitution.' . . .

The District Court's remedial plan in this case . . . is not designed solely to redistribute the students within the KCMSD [Kansas City, Missouri School District] in order to eliminate racially identifiable schools within the KCMSD. Instead, its purpose is to attract nonminority students from outside the KCMSD schools. But this interdistrict goal is beyond the scope of the intradistrict violation identified by the District Court. In effect, the District Court has devised a remedy to accomplish indirectly what it admittedly lacks the remedial authority to mandate directly: the interdistrict transfer of students. . . .

Here, the District Court has done just that: created a magnet district of the KCMSD in order to serve the interdistrict goal of attracting nonminority students from the surrounding SSD's [suburban school districts] and redistributing them within the KCMSD. The District Court's pursuit of 'desegregative attractiveness' is beyond the scope of its broad remedial authority. . . .

Similar considerations lead us to conclude that the District Court's order requiring the State to continue to fund the quality education programs because student achievement levels were still 'at or below national norms at many grade levels' cannot be sustained. . . .

Although the District Court has determined that '[s]egregation has caused a system wide reduction in achievement in the schools of the KCMSD,' it never has identified the incremental effect that segregation has had on minority student achievement or the specific goals of the quality education programs. . . .

On remand, the District Court must bear in mind that its end purpose is not only 'to remedy the violation' to the extent practicable, but also 'to restore state and local authorities to the control of a school system that is operating in compliance with the Constitution.

The judgment of the Court of Appeals is reversed."

V. JUSTICE VOTE

4 Pro ACLU Side vs. 5 Con Opposing Side

ACLU Side (Respondent / Appellee)

1. Souter, D. – Wrote dissenting opinion
2. Stevens, J. – Joined Souter's dissent
3. Breyer, S. – Joined Souter's dissent
4. Ginsburg, R. – Wrote dissenting opinion, joined Souter's dissent

Opposing Side (Petitioner / Appellant)

1. Rehnquist, W. – Wrote majority opinion
2. O'Connor, S. – Wrote concurring opinion
3. Scalia, A. – Joined majority opinion
4. Kennedy, A. – Joined majority opinion
5. Thomas, C. – Wrote concurring opinion

VI. A WIN OR LOSS FOR THE ACLU?

The ACLU filed as amicus curiae urging affirmance of the judgment of the Court of Appeals; the Supreme Court reversed in a 5-4 vote, giving the ACLU an apparent loss.

786. Kimberlin v. Quinlan

(Decided June 12, 1995; 515 U.S. 321)

I. ISSUE

A. Issues Discussed

Criminal Justice, prisons, First Amendment, qualified immunity, interlocutory appeals

B. Legal Question Presented

"1. Whether plaintiffs in Bivens cases in which unlawful motive is an element of the alleged offense must satisfy a 'heightened pleading standard' to survive a motion to dismiss or for summary judgment based on an assertion of qualified immunity.

2. Whether plaintiffs in *Bivens* cases must produce, prior to discovery, 'direct,' as opposed to persuasive circumstantial, evidence of unlawful motive?"[1]

C. Supreme Court's Answer

The Supreme Court vacated the judgment for reconsideration below in light of a recent decision by the Supreme Court.

II. CASE SUMMARY

A. Background

"Kimberlin was interviewed by NBC News on the afternoon of Friday, November 4, 1988, four days before the presidential election, and he was scheduled to have another interview, this time with a group of reporters, at 7:00 p.m. that same day. However, before the second interview could take place, defendant J. Michael Quinlan, the Director of the Bureau of Prisons, cancelled the meeting and ordered Kimberlin to be placed in administrative detention where he remained until the next day. Two days after that, on Monday, November 7, the day before the presidential election, Kimberlin planned to address a conference of reporters in Washington, D.C. via telephone, but in the morning of that day he was again placed in detention, this time to be kept for seven days, until November 14. Kimberlin was placed in detention a third time, from December 22 until December 23, 1988.

Based on these events, Kimberlin has filed Bivens actions against two government officials, Bureau of Prisons Director Quinlan, and Loye W. Miller, Jr., at the time Director of Public Affairs of the Department of Justice, in their individual capacities, for violating his rights under the First and Fifth Amendments. It is plaintiff's claim that it was the defendants' purpose, when issuing or participating in the issuance of the first two detention orders, to prevent him from informing the press prior to the election about his transactions with Dan Quayle, and that the third

1 Brief of Petitioner at i, Kimberlin v. Quinlan, 515 U.S. 321 (1995) (No. 93-2068).

detention was ordered in retaliation for his previous contacts with the press. In their motion papers, the defendants contest plaintiff's claims. Specifically, they assert that Kimberlin's first detention was effected for his own safety, and that the second and third detentions were ordered because the correctional authorities were investigating whether he had violated prison rules against making third-party telephone calls.

In addition to the Bivens suit, Kimberlin has filed an action under the Federal Tort Claims Act (FTCA) against the United States and against Mr. Quinlan in his official capacity. It is charged in that action that the three detentions amounted to false imprisonment, and that Kimberlin's treatment by prison guards while he was in detention constituted assault and battery. Kimberlin also claims that prison officials monitored his telephone calls in violation of Title III of the Omnibus Crime Control and Safe Streets Act of 1968."[1]

The United States District Court for the District of Columbia dismissed the Fifth Amendment claims, denied the motion to dismiss as to the FTCA false imprisonment claim, granted the motion to dismiss as the the FTCA assault and battery claim, and denied the motion to dismiss as to the Title III claim.

The Supreme Court granted certiorari to review the case, vacated, and remanded.

B. Counsel of Record / ACLU Attorney

ACLU Side (Petitioner / Appellant): Howard T. Rosenblatt argued the cause for appellant.

Paul Bender, Deputy Solicitor General, argued the cause for the United States, as amicus curiae, by special leave of Court.

Opposing Side (Respondent / Appellee): Michael L. Martinez argued the cause for appellee.

III. AMICI CURIAE

ACLU Side (Petitioner / Appellant)

Brief of amici curiae filed on behalf of the ACLU, et al., by Anthony C. Epstein, Steven R. Shapiro, Mark D. Harris, Jodie L. Kelley, Arthur B. Spitzer, Leslie A. Brueckner, and Marc D. Stern.

Brief of amici curiae filed on behalf of the United States by Deputy Solicitor General Bender, Solicitor General Days, Assistant Attorney General Hunger, and Cornelia T. L. Pillard.

Opposing Side (Respondent / Appellee)

Brief of amici curiae filed on behalf of the State of Hawaii, et al., by Margery S. Bronster, Attorney General of Hawaii, and Girard D. Lau, Deputy Attorney General; Winston Bryant, Attorney General of Arkansas; Daniel E. Lungren, Attorney General of California; M. Jane Brady, Attorney General of Delaware; Alan G. Lance, Attorney General of Idaho; Pamela Carter, Attorney General of Indiana; Carla J. Stovall, Attorney General of Kansas; Chris Gorman, Attorney General of Kentucky; Hubert H. Humphrey III, Attorney General of Minnesota; Mike Moore, Attorney General of Mississippi; Jeremiah W Nixon, Attorney General of Missouri; Joseph P. Mazurek, Attorney General of Montana; Jeffrey R. Howard, Attorney General of New Hampshire; Victoria A. Graffeo, Attorney General of New York; Betty D. Montgomery, Attorney General of Ohio; Drew Edmondson, Attorney General of Oklahoma; Jeffrey B. Pine, Attorney General of Rhode Island; Mark Barnett, Attorney General of South Dakota; Jan Graham, Attorney General of Utah; Jeffrey L. Amestoy, Attorney General of Vermont; James S. Gilmore III, Attorney General of Virginia; James E. Doyle, Attorney General of Wisconsin; Richard Weil, Attorney General of the Commonwealth of the Northern Mariana Islands; and Alva A. Swan, Acting Attorney General of the Virgin Islands.

IV. THE SUPREME COURT'S DECISION

"PER CURIAM. The judgment is vacated, and the case is remanded to the United States Court of Appeals for the District of Columbia Circuit for further consideration in light of Johnson v. Jones, 515 U.S. 304."

V. JUSTICE VOTE

9 Pro ACLU Side vs. 0 Con Opposing Side

ACLU Side (Petitioner / Appellant)

1. Souter, D. – Per curiam decision
2. Thomas, C. – Per curiam decision
3. Ginsberg, R. – Per curiam decision
4. Breyer, S. – Per curiam decision
5. O'Connor, S. – Per curiam decision
6. Scalia, A. – Per curiam decision
7. Kennedy, A. – Per curiam decision
8. Stevens, J. – Per curiam decision
9. Rehnquist, W. – Per curiam decision

VI. A WIN OR LOSS FOR THE ACLU?

The ACLU filed as amicus curiae urging reversal of the judgment of the Court of Appeals; the Supreme Court vacated and remanded in a per curiam 9-0 vote, giving the ACLU an apparent win.

787. Sandin v. Conner

(Decided June 19, 1995; 515 U.S. 472)

I. ISSUE

A. Issues Discussed

Criminal justice, prisons, Fourteenth Amendment, due process

B. Legal Question Presented

Whether appellee held a liberty interest protected by the due process clause when he was disciplined while in prison serving his sentence.

C. Supreme Court's Answer

The state's action in disciplining appellee did not implicate a liberty interest protected by the due process clause.

1 Kimberlin v. Quinlan, 774 F. Supp. 1 (D. D.C. 1991).

II. CASE SUMMARY

A. Background

"DeMont Conner was convicted of numerous state crimes, including murder, kidnaping, robbery, and burglary, for which he is currently serving an indeterminate sentence of 30 years to life in a Hawaii prison. He was confined in the Halawa Correctional Facility, a maximum security prison in central Oahu. In August 1987, a prison officer escorted him from his cell to the module program area. The officer subjected Conner to a strip search, complete with an inspection of the rectal area. Conner retorted with angry and foul language directed at the officer. Eleven days later he received notice that he had been charged with disciplinary infractions. The notice charged Conner with 'high misconduct' for using physical interference to impair a correctional function, and 'low moderate misconduct' for using abusive or obscene language and for harassing employees.

Conner appeared before an adjustment committee on August 28, 1987. The committee refused Conner's request to present witnesses at the hearing, stating that '[w]itnesses were unavailable due to move [sic] to the medium facility and being short staffed on the modules.' At the conclusion of proceedings, the committee determined that Conner was guilty of the alleged misconduct. It sentenced him to 30 days' disciplinary segregation in the Special Holding Unit for the physical obstruction charge, and four hours segregation for each of the other two charges to be served concurrent with the 30 days. Conner's segregation began August 31, 1987, and ended September 29, 1987.

Conner sought administrative review within 14 days of receiving the committee's decision. Nine months later, the deputy administrator found the high misconduct charge unsupported and expunged Conner's disciplinary record with respect to that charge. But before the deputy administrator decided the appeal, Conner had brought this suit against the adjustment committee chair and other prison officials in the United States District Court for the District of Hawaii based on Rev.Stat. § 1979, 42 U.S.C. § 1983. His amended complaint prayed for injunctive relief, declaratory relief, and damages for, among other things, a deprivation of procedural due process in connection with the disciplinary hearing. The District Court granted summary judgment in favor of the prison officials.

The Court of Appeals for the Ninth Circuit reversed the judgment."

The Supreme Court granted certiorari to review the case and reversed.

B. Counsel of Record / ACLU Attorney

ACLU Side (Respondent / Appellee): Paul L. Hoffman argued the cause for appellee. With him on the brief were Gary L. Bostwick, Erwin Chemerinsky, and Peter Labrador.

Opposing Side (Petitioner / Appellant): Steven S. Michaels, First Deputy Attorney General of Hawaii, argued the cause for appellant. With him on the briefs were Margery S. Bronster, Attorney General of Hawaii, Robert A. Marks, former Attorney General, and Kathleen M. Sato, Deputy Attorney General.

III. AMICI CURIAE

ACLU Side (Respondent / Appellee)

Brief of amici curiae filed on behalf of the ACLU, et al., by Steven R. Shapiro, Carl Varady, Margaret Winter, Elizabeth Alexander, Ayesha Kahn, and Alvin J. Bronstein.

Brief of amici curiae filed on behalf of the Edwin F. Mandel Legal Aid Clinic by Gary H. Palm and Mark J. Heyrman.

Opposing Side (Petitioner / Appellant)

Brief of amici curiae filed on behalf of the State of New Hampshire, et al., by Jeffrey R. Howard, Attorney General of New Hampshire, Douglas N. Jones, Assistant Attorney General, and Eleni M. Constantine, and by the Attorneys General for their respective jurisdictions as follows: Grant Woods of Arizona, Winston Bryant of Arkansas, Donald E. Lungren of California, Gale A. Norton of Colorado, Robert A. Butterworth of Florida, Larry EchoHawk of Idaho, Roland W. Burris of Illinois, Bonnie J. Campbell of Iowa, Robert T. Stephan of Kansas, Richard P. Ieyoub of Louisiana, J. Joseph Curran, Jr., of Maryland, Scott Harshbarger of Massachusetts, Hubert H. Humphrey III of Minnesota, Mike Moore of Mississippi, Jeremiah W. Nixon of Missouri, Joseph P. Mazurek of Montana, Deborah T. Poritz of New Jersey, Frankie Sue Del Papa of Nevada, Tom Udall of New Mexico, G. Oliver Koppell of New York, Michael F. Easley of North Carolina, Heidi Heitkamp of North Dakota, Lee Fisher of Ohio, Susan B. Loving of Oklahoma, Theodore R. Kulongoski of Oregon, Ernest D. Preate, Jr., of Pennsylvania, T. Travis Medlock of South Carolina, Mark Barnett of South Dakota, Charles W. Burson of Tennessee, Jan Graham of Utah, Jeffrey L. Amestoy of Vermont, Rosalie S. Ballentine of the Virgin Islands, James S. Gilmore III of Virginia, Christine O. Gregoire of Washington, James E. Doyle of Wisconsin, and Joseph B. Meyer of Wyoming.

Brief of amici curiae filed on behalf of the Criminal Justice Legal Foundation by Kent S. Scheidegger and Charles L. Hobson.

IV. THE SUPREME COURT'S DECISION

"[W]e believe that the search for a negative implication from mandatory language in prisoner regulations has strayed from the real concerns undergirding the liberty protected by the Due Process Clause. The time has come to return to the due process principles we believe were correctly established and applied in Wolff and Meachum. Following Wolff, we recognize that States may under certain circumstances create liberty interests which are protected by the Due Process Clause. But these interests will be generally limited to freedom from restraint which, while not exceeding the sentence in such an unexpected manner as to give rise to protection by the Due Process Clause of its own force, nonetheless imposes atypical and significant hardship on the inmate in relation to the ordinary incidents of prison life. . . .

This case, though concededly punitive, does not present a dramatic departure from the basic conditions of Conner's indeterminate sentence. Although Conner points to dicta in cases implying that solitary confinement automatically triggers due process protection, this Court has not had the opportunity to address in an argued case the question whether disciplinary confinement of inmates itself implicates constitutional liberty interests. We hold that Conner's discipline in segregated confinement did not present the type of atypical, significant deprivation in which a State might conceivably create a liberty interest. . . .

Nor does Conner's situation present a case where the State's action will inevitably affect the duration of his sentence. Nothing in Hawaii's code requires the parole board to deny parole in the face of a misconduct record or to grant parole in its absence, even though misconduct is by regulation a relevant consideration. . . .

We hold, therefore, that neither the Hawaii prison regulation in question, nor the Due Process Clause itself, afforded Conner a protected liberty interest that would entitle him to the procedural protections set forth in Wolff. The regime to which he was subjected as a result of the misconduct hearing was within the range of confinement to be normally expected for one serving an indeterminate term of 30 years to life.

The judgment of the Court of Appeals is accordingly reversed."

V. JUSTICE VOTE

4 Pro ACLU Side vs. 5 Con Opposing Side

ACLU Side (Respondent / Appellee)

1. Ginsburg, R. – Wrote dissenting opinion
2. Breyer, S. – Wrote dissenting opinion
3. Stevens, J. – Joined Ginsburg's dissent
4. Souter, D. – Joined Breyer's dissent

Opposing Side (Petitioner / Appellant)

1. Rehnquist, W. – Wrote majority opinion
2. O'Connor, S. – Joined majority opinion
3. Scalia, A. – Joined majority opinion
4. Kennedy, A. – Joined majority opinion
5. Thomas, C. – Joined majority opinion

VI. A WIN OR LOSS FOR THE ACLU?

The ACLU filed as amicus curiae urging affirmance of the judgment of the Court of Appeals; the Supreme Court reversed in a 5-4 vote, giving the ACLU an apparent loss.

788. Hurley v. Irish-American Gay, Lesbian & Bisexual Group of Boston

(Decided June 19, 1995; 515 U.S. 557)

I. ISSUE

A. Issues Discussed

First Amendment, freedoms of speech, press, and association

B. Legal Question Presented

"[W]hether Massachusetts may require private citizens who organize a parade to include among the marchers a group imparting a message the organizers do not wish to convey."

C. Supreme Court's Answer

Requiring parade organizers to include a message they do not wish to convey in their parade violates the First Amendment.

II. CASE SUMMARY

A. Background

"[I]n 1947, [Boston] Mayor James Michael Curley himself granted authority to organize and conduct the St. Patrick's Day-Evacuation Day Parade to the petitioner South Boston Allied War Veterans Council, an unincorporated association of individuals elected from various South Boston veterans groups. Every year since that time, the Council has applied for and received a permit for the parade, which at times has included as many as 20,000 marchers and drawn up to 1 million watchers. No other applicant has ever applied for that permit. Through 1992, the city allowed the Council to use the city's official seal, and provided printing services as well as direct funding.

In 1992, a number of gay, lesbian, and bisexual descendants of the Irish immigrants joined together with other supporters to form the respondent organization, GLIB, to march in the parade as a way to express pride in their Irish heritage as openly gay, lesbian, and bisexual individuals, to demonstrate that there are such men and women among those so descended, and to express their solidarity with like individuals who sought to march in New York's St. Patrick's Day Parade. Although the Council denied GLIB's application to take part in the 1992 parade, GLIB obtained a state-court order to include its contingent, which marched 'uneventfully' among that year's 10,000 participants and 750,000 spectators.

In 1993, after the Council had again refused to admit GLIB to the upcoming parade, the organization and some of its members filed this suit . . . alleging violations of the State and Federal Constitutions and of the state public accommodations law . . . .

The court held that because the statute did not mandate inclusion of GLIB but only prohibited discrimination based on sexual orientation, any infringement on the Council's right to expressive association was only 'incidental' and 'no greater than necessary to accomplish the statute's legitimate purpose' of eradicating discrimination. Accordingly,

it ruled that 'GLIB is entitled to participate in the Parade on the same terms and conditions as other participants.'

The Supreme Judicial Court of Massachusetts affirmed . . . ."

The U.S. Supreme Court granted certiorari to review the case and reversed.

B. Counsel of Record / ACLU Attorney

ACLU Side (Petitioner / Appellant): Chester Darling argued the cause for appellant.

Opposing Side (Respondent / Appellee): John Ward argued the cause for appellee.

III. AMICI CURIAE

ACLU Side (Petitioner / Appellant)

Brief of amici curiae filed on behalf of the ACLU by Burt Neuborne, Steven R. Shapiro, and Marjorie Heins, in support of neither party, urging the court to vacate the judgment and remand the case.

Brief of amici curiae filed on behalf of the Boy Scouts of America by George A. Davidson, Carla A. Kerr, and David K. Park.

Brief of amici curiae filed on behalf of the Catholic War Veterans of the United States of America by Thomas Bolan.

Brief of amici curiae filed on behalf of the Center for Individual Rights, et al., by Michael P. McDonald, Gary B. Born, Thomas M. Clark, Bernard Roberts, Ernest L. Mathews, Jr., and Maura R. Cahill.

Brief of amici curiae filed on behalf of the Christian Legal Society, et al., by Steven T. McFarland, Samuel B. Casey, and Gregory S. Baylor.

Opposing Side (Respondent / Appellee)

Brief of amici curiae filed on behalf of the Anti-Defamation League, et al., by Walter A. Smith, Jr., Thomas N. Bulleit, Jr., William P. Flanagan, Thomas E. Joaquin, Ruth L. Lansner, Steven M. Freeman, Sally J. Greenberg, Arlene B. Mayerson, Beatrice Dohrn, Patricia Logue, Nancy A. Russell, Antonia Hernandez, Nancy Ramirez, Elizabeth Hendrickson, Kathryn Kendell, Juan A. Figueroa, Nina Perales, Alice, E. Zaft, Judist L. Lichtman, and Donna R. Lenhoff.

Brief of amici curiae filed on behalf of the Irish Lesbian and Gay Organization, et al., by Michael E. Deutsch, Paul O'Dwyer, R. Paul Wickes, Clare O'Brien, Mark A. Siemens, and Susan R. Schwaiger.

IV. THE SUPREME COURT'S DECISION

"The protected expression that inheres in a parade is not limited to its banners and songs . . . for the Constitution looks beyond written or spoken words as mediums of expression. Noting that '[s]ymbolism is a primitive but effective way of communicating ideas,' our cases have recognized that the First Amendment shields such acts as saluting a flag (and refusing to do so), wearing an armband to protest a war, displaying a red flag, and even '[m]arching, walking or parading' in uniforms displaying the swastika.

[A] private speaker does not forfeit constitutional protection simply by combining multifarious voices, or by failing to edit their themes to isolate an exact message as the exclusive subject matter of the speech. Nor, under our precedent, does First Amendment protection require a speaker to generate, as an original matter, each item featured in the communication. . . .

In the case before us, . . . the Massachusetts law has been applied in a peculiar way. Its enforcement does not address any dispute about the participation of openly gay, lesbian, or bisexual individuals in various units admitted to the parade. Petitioners disclaim any intent to exclude homosexuals as such, and no individual member of GLIB claims to have been excluded from parading as a member of any group that the Council has approved to march. Instead, the disagreement goes to the admission of GLIB as its own parade unit carrying its own banner. Since every participating unit affects the message conveyed by the private organizers, the state courts' application of the statute produced an order essentially requiring petitioners to alter the expressive content of their parade. Although the state courts spoke of the parade as a place of public accommodation, once the expressive character of both the parade and the marching GLIB contingent is understood, it becomes apparent that the state courts' application of the statute had the effect of declaring the sponsors' speech itself to be the public accommodation. Under this approach any contingent of protected individuals with a message would have the right to participate in petitioners' speech, so that the communication produced by the private organizers would be shaped by all those protected by the law who wished to join in with some expressive demonstration of their own. But this use of the State's power violates the fundamental rule of protection under the First Amendment, that a speaker has the autonomy to choose the content of his own message. . . .

True, the size and success of petitioners' parade makes it an enviable vehicle for the dissemination of GLIB's views, but that fact, without more, would fall far short of supporting a claim that petitioners enjoy an abiding monopoly of access to spectators. Considering that GLIB presumably would have had a fair shot (under neutral criteria developed by the city) at obtaining a parade permit of its own, respondents have not shown that petitioners enjoy the capacity to 'silence the voice of competing speakers,' as cable operators do with respect to program providers who wish to reach subscribers. Nor has any other legitimate interest been identified in support of applying the Massachusetts statute in this way to expressive activity like the parade. . . .

Our holding today rests not on any particular view about the Council's message but on the Nation's commitment to protect freedom of speech. Disapproval of a private speaker's statement does not legitimize use of the Commonwealth's power to compel the speaker to alter the message by including one more acceptable to others. Accordingly, the judgment of the Supreme Judicial Court is reversed, and the case is remanded for proceedings not inconsistent with this opinion."

V. JUSTICE VOTE

9 Pro ACLU Side vs. 0 Con Opposing Side

ACLU Side (Petitioner / Appellant)

1. Souter, D. – Wrote majority opinion
2. Thomas, C. – Joined majority opinion
3. Ginsburg, R. – Joined majority opinion
4. Breyer, S. – Joined majority opinion
5. O'Connor, S. – Joined majority opinion
6. Scalia, A. – Joined majority opinion
7. Kennedy, A. – Joined majority opinion
8. Stevens, J. – Joined majority opinion
9. Rehnquist, W. – Joined majority opinion

VI. A WIN OR LOSS FOR THE ACLU?

The ACLU, as amicus curiae, urged the Supreme Court to vacate and remand the judgment of the Supreme Judicial Court of Massachusetts; the Supreme Court reversed and remanded in a 9-0 vote, giving the ACLU an apparent win.

789. Capitol Square Review & Advisory Board v. Pinette

(Decided June 29, 1995; 515 U.S. 753)

I. ISSUE

A. Issues Discussed

First Amendment, freedom of speech, Establishment Clause

B. Legal Question Presented

"[W]hether a State violates the Establishment Clause when, pursuant to a religiously neutral state policy, it permits a private party to display an unattended religious symbol in a traditional public forum located next to its seat of government.

C. Supreme Court's Answer

A State does not violate the Establishment Clause by permitting a private party to display an unattended religious symbol in a traditional public forum located next to its seat of government.

II. CASE SUMMARY

A. Background

"Capitol Square is a 10-acre, state-owned plaza surrounding the statehouse in Columbus, Ohio. For over a century the square has been used for public speeches, gatherings, and festivals advocating and celebrating a variety of causes, both secular and religious. . . .

In November 1993, after reversing an initial decision to ban unattended holiday displays from the square during December 1993, the Board authorized the State to put up its annual Christmas tree. On November 29, 1993, the Board granted a rabbi's application to erect a menorah. That same day, the Board received an application from respondent Donnie Carr, an officer of the Ohio Ku Klux Klan, to place a cross on the square from December 8, 1993, to December 24, 1993. The Board denied that application on December 3, informing the Klan by letter that the decision to deny 'was made upon the advice of counsel, in a good faith attempt to comply with the Ohio and United States Constitutions, as they have been interpreted in relevant decisions by the Federal and State Courts.'

Two weeks later, having been unsuccessful in its effort to obtain administrative relief from the Board's decision, the Ohio Klan, through its leader Vincent Pinette, filed the present suit in the United States District Court for the Southern District of Ohio, seeking an injunction requiring the Board to issue the requested permit. The Board defended on the ground that the permit would violate the Establishment Clause. The District Court determined that Capitol Square was a traditional public forum open to all without any policy against freestanding displays; that the Klan's cross was entirely private expression entitled to full First Amendment protection; and that the Board had failed to show that the display of the cross could reasonably be construed as endorsement of Christianity by the State. The District Court issued the injunction and, after the Board's application for an emergency stay was denied, the Board permitted the Klan to erect its cross. The Board then received, and granted, several additional applications to erect crosses on Capitol Square during December 1993 and January 1994.

On appeal by the Board, the United States Court of Appeals for the Sixth Circuit affirmed the District Court's judgment."

The Supreme Court granted certiorari to review the case and affirmed.

B. Counsel of Record / ACLU Attorney

ACLU Side (Respondent / Appellee): Benson A. Wolman argued the cause for appellee. With him on the brief were David Goldberger, Barbara P. O'Toole, Steven R. Shapiro, Kevin Francis O'Neill, and Peter Joy.

Opposing Side (Petitioner / Appellant): Michael J. Renner argued the cause for appellant. With him on the briefs were Betty D. Montgomery, Attorney General of Ohio, and Christopher S. Cook, Andrew S. Bergman, Simon B. Karas, and Andrew I. Sutter, Assistant Attorneys General.

III. AMICI CURIAE

ACLU Side (Respondent / Appellee)

Brief of amici curiae filed on behalf of the American Center for Law & Justice by Jay Alan Sekulow, James M. Henderson, Sr., John P. Tuskey, and Keith A. Fournier.

Brief of amici curiae filed on behalf of the Chabad House of Western Michigan, Inc., et al., by Nathan Lewin.

Brief of amici curiae filed on behalf of the Christian Legal Society by Thomas C. Berg, Steven T. McFarland, Samuel B. Casey, Gregory S. Baylor, Douglas Laycock, and Kimberlee Wood Colby.

Brief of amici curiae filed on behalf of the Knights of Columbus Council 2961, et al., by Kevin J. Hasson and Pat A. Cipollone.

Brief of amici curiae filed on behalf of Liberty Counsel by Mathew D. Staver, Frederick H. Nelson, Nicole Arfaras Kerr, and Gina R. Perez Toro.

Opposing Side (Petitioner / Appellant)

Brief of amici curiae filed on behalf of the Town of Trumbell, Connecticut, et al., by Arthur A. Hiller, Martin B. Margulies, and Emanuel Margolis.

Brief of amici curiae filed on behalf of Americans United for Separation of Church and State, et al., by Steven K. Green, Julie A. Segal, Norman Dorsen, Samuel Rabinove, Elliot M. Mincberg, David Saperstein, John D. Shullenberger, and Richard T. Cassidy.

Brief of amici curiae filed on behalf of the Council on Religious Freedom, et al., by Lee Boothby, Walter E. Carson, Robert W. Nixon, and Rolland Truman.

Brief of amici curiae filed on behalf of the Freedom From Religion Foundation, Inc., by Robert R. Tiernan.

Brief of amici curiae filed on behalf of the American Jewish Congress, et al., by Marvin E. Frankel, Alan R. Friedman, Richard K. Milin, Marc D. Stern, Lois C. Waldman, Ruth Lansner, and Steve Freeman.

IV. THE SUPREME COURT'S DECISION

"Respondents' religious display in Capitol Square was private expression. Our precedent establishes that private religious speech, far from being a First Amendment orphan, is as fully protected under the Free Speech Clause as secular private expression. . . .

It is undeniable, of course, that speech which is constitutionally protected against state suppression is not thereby accorded a guaranteed forum on all property owned by the State. The right to use government property for one's private expression depends upon whether the property has by law or tradition been given the status of a public forum, or rather has been reserved for specific official uses. . . .

Petitioners do not claim that their denial of respondents' application was based upon a content-neutral time, place, or manner restriction. To the contrary, they concede—indeed it is the essence of their case—that the Board rejected the display precisely because its content was religious. Petitioners advance a single justification for closing Capitol Square to respondents' cross: the State's interest in avoiding official endorsement of Christianity, as required by the Establishment Clause. . . .

If Ohio is concerned about misperceptions, nothing prevents it from requiring all private displays in the Square to be identified as such. That would be a content-neutral 'manner' restriction that is assuredly constitutional. But the State may not, on the claim of misperception of official endorsement, ban all private religious speech from the public square, or discriminate against it by requiring religious speech alone to disclaim public sponsorship.

Religious expression cannot violate the Establishment Clause where it (1) is purely private and (2) occurs in a traditional or designated public forum, publicly announced and open to all on equal terms. Those conditions are satisfied here, and therefore the State may not bar respondents' cross from Capitol Square.

The judgment of the Court of Appeals is affirmed."

V. JUSTICE VOTE

7 Pro ACLU Side vs. 2 Con Opposing Side

ACLU Side (Respondent / Appellee)

1. Scalia, A. – Wrote majority opinion
2. O'Connor, S. – Wrote concurring opinion, joined O'Connor's concurrence
3. Souter, D. – Wrote concurring opinion, joined O'Connor's concurrence
4. Thomas, C. – Wrote concurring opinion
5. Rehnquist, W. – Joined majority opinion
6. Kennedy, A. – Joined majority opinion
7. Breyer, S. – Joined O'Connor's concurrence, joined Souter's concurrence

Opposing Side (Petitioner / Appellant)

1. Stevens, J. – Wrote dissenting opinion
2. Ginsburg, R. – Wrote dissenting opinion

VI. A WIN OR LOSS FOR THE ACLU?

The ACLU, as counsel for appellee, urged affirmance of the judgment of the Court of Appeals for the Sixth Circuit; the Supreme Court affirmed in a 7-2 vote, giving the ACLU an apparent win.

790. Rosenberger v. Rector & Visitors of the University of Virginia

(Decided June 29, 1995; 515 U.S. 819)

I. ISSUE

A. Issues Discussed

First Amendment, freedom of speech, Establishment Clause, separation of church and state

B. Legal Question Presented

Did the University of Virginia violate the First Amendment rights of its Christian magazine staff by denying them the same funding resources that it made available to secular student-run organization?

C. Supreme Court's Answer

The University violated the First Amendment by denying funding to the Christian magazine that is granted to secular student organizations.

II. CASE SUMMARY

A. Background

"The University of Virginia, an instrumentality of the Commonwealth for which it is named and thus bound by the First and Fourteenth Amendments, authorizes the payment of outside contractors for the printing costs of a variety of student publications. It withheld any authorization for payments on behalf of petitioners for the sole reason that their student paper 'primarily promotes or manifests a particular belie[f] in or about a deity or an ultimate reality.' That the paper did promote or manifest views within the defined exclusion seems plain enough. The challenge is to the University's regulation and its denial of authorization,

the case raising issues under the Speech and Establishment Clauses of the First Amendment. . . . The suit sought damages for the costs of printing the paper, injunctive and declaratory relief, and attorney's fees.

On cross-motions for summary judgment, the District Court ruled for the University, holding that denial of [Student Activities Fund] support was not an impermissible content or viewpoint discrimination against petitioners' speech, and that the University's Establishment Clause concern over its 'religious activities' was a sufficient justification for denying payment to third-party contractors. The court did not issue a definitive ruling on whether reimbursement, had it been made here, would or would not have violated the Establishment Clause.

The United States Court of Appeals for the Fourth Circuit, in disagreement with the District Court, held that the Guidelines did discriminate on the basis of content. It ruled that, while the State need not underwrite speech, there was a presumptive violation of the Speech Clause when viewpoint discrimination was invoked to deny third-party payment otherwise available to [Contracted Independent Organizations]. The Court of Appeals affirmed the judgment of the District Court nonetheless, concluding that the discrimination by the University was justified by the 'compelling interest in maintaining strict separation of church and state.'"

The Supreme Court granted certiorari to review the case and reversed.

B. Counsel of Record / ACLU Attorney

ACLU Side (Respondent / Appellee): John C. Jeffries, Jr., argued the cause for appellee.

Opposing Side (Petitioner / Appellant): Michael W. McConnell argued the cause for appellant.

III. AMICI CURIAE

ACLU Side (Respondent / Appellee)

Brief of amici curiae filed on behalf of the ACLU, et al., by Marjorie Heins, Steven R. Shapiro, and Stephen B. Pershing.

Additional briefs of amici curiae were filed on behalf of Americans United for Separation of Church and State, et al., the Baptist Joint Committee on Public Affairs, et al., the Council on Religious Freedom, the National School Boards Association, the Pacific Legal Foundation, and the Student Press Law Center.

Opposing Side (Petitioner / Appellant)

Brief of amici curiae filed on behalf of the Commonwealth of Virginia, the American Center for Law and Justice, the Catholic League for Religious and Civil Rights, the Christian Legal Society, et al., and Intercollegiate Studies Institute.

IV. THE SUPREME COURT'S DECISION

"It is axiomatic that the government may not regulate speech based on its substantive content or the message it conveys. Other principles follow from this precept. In the realm of private speech or expression, government regulation may not favor one speaker over another. Discrimination against speech because of its message is presumed to be unconstitutional. . . . When the government targets not subject matter, but particular views taken by speakers on a subject, the violation of the First Amendment is all the more blatant. Viewpoint discrimination is thus an egregious form of content discrimination. The government must abstain from regulating speech when the specific motivating ideology or the opinion or perspective of the speaker is the rationale for the restriction. . . .

The University's denial of [Wide Awake Productions'] request for third-party payments in the present case is based upon viewpoint discrimination . . . . The distinction between the University's own favored message and the private speech of students is evident in the case before us. The University itself has taken steps to ensure the distinction in the agreement each CIO must sign. The University declares that the student groups eligible for SAF support are not the University's agents, are not subject to its control, and are not its responsibility. Having offered to pay the third-party contractors on behalf of private speakers who convey their own messages, the University may not silence the expression of selected viewpoints.

[W]e hold that the regulation invoked to deny SAF support, both in its terms and in its application to these petitioners, is a denial of their right of free speech guaranteed by the First Amendment. It remains to be considered whether the violation following from the University's action is excused by the necessity of complying with the Constitution's prohibition against state establishment of religion. . . .

To obey the Establishment Clause, it was not necessary for the University to deny eligibility to student publications because of their viewpoint. The neutrality commanded of the State by the separate Clauses of the First Amendment was compromised by the University's course of action. The viewpoint discrimination inherent in the University's regulation required public officials to scan and interpret student publications to discern their underlying philosophic assumptions respecting religious theory and belief. That course of action was a denial of the right of free speech and would risk fostering a pervasive bias or hostility to religion, which could undermine the very neutrality the Establishment Clause requires. There is no Establishment Clause violation in the University's honoring its duties under the Free Speech Clause.

The judgment of the Court of Appeals must be, and is, reversed."

V. JUSTICE VOTE

4 Pro ACLU Side vs. 5 Con Opposing Side

ACLU Side (Respondent / Appellee)

1. Souter, D. – Wrote dissenting opinion
2. Stevens, J. – Joined Souter's dissent
3. Ginsburg, R. – Joined Souter's dissent
4. Breyer, S. – Joined Souter's dissent

Opposing Side (Petitioner / Appellant)

1. Kennedy, A. – Wrote majority opinion
2. O'Connor, S. – Wrote concurring opinion
3. Thomas, C. – Wrote concurring opinion
4. Rehnquist, W. – Joined majority opinion
5. Scalia, A. – Joined majority opinion

VI. A WIN OR LOSS FOR THE ACLU?

The ACLU, as amicus curiae, urged affirmance of the judgment of the Court of Appeals for the Fourth Circuit; the Supreme Court reversed in a 5-4 vote, giving the ACLU an apparent loss.

791. Miller v. Johnson

(Decided June 29, 1995; 515 U.S. 900)

I. ISSUE

A. Issues Discussed

Voting rights, race

B. Legal Question Presented

"[W]hether Georgia's new Eleventh District gives rise to a valid equal protection claim under the principles announced in Shaw, and, if so, whether it can be sustained nonetheless as narrowly tailored to serve a compelling governmental interest."

C. Supreme Court's Answer

"In our view, the District Court applied the correct analysis, and its finding that race was the predominant factor motivating the drawing of the Eleventh District was not clearly erroneous. . . .

Whether or not in some cases compliance with the [Voting Rights] Act, standing alone, can provide a compelling interest independent of any interest in remedying past discrimination, it cannot do so here."

II. CASE SUMMARY

A. Background

"In 1965, the Attorney General designated Georgia a covered jurisdiction under § 4(b) of the Voting Rights Act. In consequence, § 5 of the Act requires Georgia to obtain either administrative preclearance by the Attorney General or approval by the United States District Court for the District of Columbia of any change in a 'standard, practice, or procedure with respect to voting' made after November 1, 1964. . . .

Between 1980 and 1990, one of Georgia's 10 congressional districts was a majority-black district, that is, a majority of the district's voters were black. The 1990 Decennial Census indicated that Georgia's population of 6,478,216 persons, 27% of whom are black, entitled it to an additional eleventh congressional seat, prompting Georgia's General Assembly to redraw the State's congressional districts. . . .

Elections were held under the new congressional redistricting plan on November 4, 1992, and black candidates were elected to Congress from all three majority-black districts. On January 13, 1994, appellees, five white voters from the Eleventh District, filed this action against various state officials (Miller Appellants) in the United States District Court for the Southern District of Georgia. . . .

A majority of the District Court panel agreed that the Eleventh District was invalid under Shaw, with one judge dissenting. . . .

Appellants filed notices of appeal and requested a stay of the District Court's judgment, which [the U.S. Supreme Court] granted pending the filing and disposition of the appeals in this litigation, [and] later noted probable jurisdiction."

B. Counsel of Record

ACLU Side (Petitioner / Appellant): Elaine R. Jones, Norman J. Chachkin, Jacqueline Berrien, and Gerald R. Weber of the American Civil Liberties Union of Georgia, and Lauglin McDonald, Neil Bradley, Maha Zaki, and Mary Wyckoff of the American Civil Liberties Union Foundation, Inc. filed briefs for appellants Abrams et al. David F. Walbert, Special Assistant Attorney General of Georgia, argued the cause for the state and private appellants. With him on the briefs for appellants Miller et al. were Michael J. Bowers, Attorney General, and Dennis R. Dunn, Senior Assistant Attorney General. Solicitor General Days argued the cause for the United States. With him on the briefs were Assistant Attorney General Patrick, Deputy Solicitor General Bender, James A. Feldman, Steven H. Rosenbaum, and Miriam R. Eisenstein.

Opposing Side (Respondent / Appellee): A. Lee Parks argued the cause for appellees. With him on the brief was Larry H. Chesin.

III. AMICI CURIAE

ACLU Side (Petitioner / Appellant)

Brief of amici curiae filed on behalf of the State of Texas et al. by Dan Morales, Attorney General of Texas, Jorge Vega, First Assistant Attorney General, and Renea Hicks, State Solicitor, and Michael F. Easley, Attorney General of North Carolina.

Brief of amici curiae filed on behalf of the Congressional Black Caucus by A. Leon Higginbotham, Jr.

Brief of amici curiae filed on behalf of the Democratic National Committee et al. by Wayne Arden and Donald J. Simon.

Brief of amici curiae filed on behalf of the Georgia Association of Black Elected Officials by Eben Moglen and Pamela S. Karlan.

Brief of amici curiae filed on behalf of the Lawyers' Committee for Civil Rights Under Law by Michael A. Cooper, Herbert J. Hansell, Thomas J. Henderson, Brenda Wright, J. Gerald Hebert, Nicholas deB. Katzenbach, and Alan E. Kraus.

Brief of amici curiae filed on behalf of the Mexican American Legal Defense and Educational Fund et al. by Charisse R. Lillie, Karen Narasaki, Wade Henderson, Dennis Courtland Hayes, Kim Gandy, Deborah Ellis, Rodney G. Gregory, Elliot Mincberg, and Donna R. Lenhoff.

Brief of amici curiae filed on behalf of the National Voting Rights Institute by Jamin Raskin.

Opposing Side (Respondent / Appellee)

Brief of amici curiae filed on behalf of the Anti-Defamation League by F. Peter Phillips, Jeffrey P. Sinensky, Steven M. Freeman, Debbie N. Kaminer, and Martin E. Karlinsky.

Brief of amici curiae filed on behalf of the Washington Legal Foundation et al. by Daniel J. Popeo and Richard A. Samp.

Brief of amici curiae filed on behalf of Ruth O. Shaw et al. by Robinson O. Everett and Clifford Dougherty.

Brief of amici curiae filed on behalf of A. J. Pate by William C. Owens, Jr.

IV. THE SUPREME COURT'S DECISION

"Finding that the 'evidence of the General Assembly's intent to racially gerrymander the Eleventh District is overwhelming, and practically stipulated by the parties involved,' the District Court held that race was the predominant, overriding factor in drawing the Eleventh District. . . . Appellants' conception of the constitutional violation misapprehends our holding in *Shaw* and the equal protection precedent upon which *Shaw* relied.

Shaw recognized a claim 'analytically distinct' from a vote dilution claim. . . .

The logical implication, as courts applying Shaw have recognized, is that parties may rely on evidence other than bizarreness to establish race-based districting.

Our reasoning in Shaw compels this conclusion. We recognized in Shaw that, outside the districting context, statutes are subject to strict scrutiny under the Equal Protection Clause not just when they contain express racial classifications, but also when, though race neutral on their face, they are motivated by a racial purpose or object. . . .

Shaw applied these same principles to redistricting. . . .

In sum, we make clear that parties alleging that a State has assigned voters on the basis of race are neither confined in their proof to evidence regarding the district's geometry and makeup nor required to make a threshold showing of bizarreness. Today's litigation requires us further to consider the requirements of the proof necessary to sustain this equal protection challenge. . . .

Federal-court review of districting legislation represents a serious intrusion on the most vital of local functions. It is well settled that 'reapportionment is primarily the duty and responsibility of the State.' . . .

In our view, the District Court applied the correct analysis, and its finding that race was the predominant factor motivating the drawing of the Eleventh District was not clearly erroneous. . . .

Race was, as the District Court found, the predominant, overriding factor explaining the General Assembly's decision to attach to the Eleventh District various appendages containing dense majority-black populations. As a result, Georgia's congressional redistricting plan cannot be upheld unless it satisfies strict scrutiny, our most rigorous and exacting standard of constitutional review. . . .

To satisfy strict scrutiny, the State must demonstrate that its districting legislation is narrowly tailored to achieve a compelling interest. . . . Whether or not in some cases compliance with the Act, standing alone, can provide a compelling interest independent of any interest in remedying past discrimination, it cannot do so here. . . .

The judgment of the District Court is affirmed, and the cases are remanded . . . ."

V. JUSTICE VOTE

4 Pro ACLU Side vs. 5 Con Opposing Side

ACLU Side (Petitioner / Appellant)

1. Ginsburg, R. – Wrote dissenting opinion
2. Souter, D. – Joined Ginsburg's dissent in part
3. Breyer, S. – Joined Ginsburg's dissent
4. Stevens, J. – Wrote dissenting opinion, joined Ginsburg's dissent

Opposing Side (Respondent / Appellee)

1. Kennedy, A. – Wrote majority opinion
2. Rehnquist, W. – Joined majority opinion
3. O'Connor, S. – Wrote concurring opinion
4. Scalia, A. – Joined majority opinion
5. Thomas, C. – Joined majority opinion

VI. A WIN OR LOSS FOR THE ACLU?

The ACLU served as counsel for appellants urging reversal of the judgment of the Court of Appeals; the Supreme Court affirmed in a 5-4 vote, giving the ACLU an apparent loss.

792. National Labor Relations Board v. Town & Country Electric, Inc.

(Decided November 28, 1995; 516 U.S. 85)

I. ISSUE

A. Issues Discussed

Unions, discrimination

B. Legal Question Presented

"Can a worker be a company's 'employee,' within the terms of the National Labor Relations Act, if at the same time, a union pays that worker to help the union organize the company?"

C. Supreme Court's Answer

Yes, the worker can be a company's employee at the same time as the union pays the worker to organize the company.

II. CASE SUMMARY

A. Background

"The relevant background is the following: Town & Country Electric, Inc., a nonunion electrical contractor, wanted to hire several licensed Minnesota electricians for construction work in Minnesota. Town & Country (through an employment agency) advertised for job applicants, but it refused to interview 10 of 11 union applicants (including two professional union staff) who responded to the advertisement. Its employment agency hired the one union applicant whom Town & Country interviewed, but he was dismissed after only a few days on the job.

The members of the International Brotherhood of Electrical Workers, Locals 292 and 343) (Union), filed a complaint with the National Labor Relations Board claiming that Town & Country and the employment agency had refused to interview (or retain) them because of their union membership. An Administrative Law Judge ruled in favor of the Union members, and the Board affirmed that ruling.

In the course of its decision, the Board determined that all 11 job applicants (including the two Union officials and the one member briefly hired) were 'employees' as the Act defines that word. The Board recognized that under well-established law, it made no difference that the 10 members who were simply applicants were never hired. Neither, in the Board's view, did it matter (with respect to the meaning of the word 'employee') that the Union members intended to try to organize the company if they secured the advertised jobs, nor that the Union would pay them while they set about their organizing. The Board then rejected the company's fact-based explanations for its refusals to interview or to retain these 11 'employees' and held that the company had committed 'unfair labor practices' by discriminating on the basis of union membership.

The United States Court of Appeals for the Eighth Circuit reversed the Board. It held that the Board had incorrectly interpreted the statutory word 'employee.' In the court's view, that key word does not cover (and therefore the Act does not protect from antiunion discrimination) those who work for a company while a union simultaneously pays them to organize that company. For this threshold reason the court refused to enforce the Board's order."

The Supreme Court granted certiorari to review the case, vacated, and remanded.

B. Counsel of Record / ACLU Attorney

ACLU Side (Petitioner / Appellant): Deputy Solicitor General Lawrence G. Wallace argued the cause for appellant.

Opposing Side (Respondent / Appellee): James K. Pease, Jr., argued the cause for appellee.

III. AMICI CURIAE

ACLU Side (Petitioner / Appellant)

Brief of amici curiae filed on behalf of the ACLU by Steven R. Shapiro, Helen Hershkoff, Lewis Maltby, and Alan Hyde.

Brief of amici curiae filed on behalf of the International Brotherhood of Boilermakers, Iron Ship Builders, Blacksmiths, Forgers & Helpers, AFL-CIO, CFL, by Michael T. Manley, G. Gordon Atcheson, John J. Blake, Michael J. Stapp, and Charles R. Schwartz.

Opposing Side (Respondent / Appellee)

Brief of amici curiae filed on behalf of Associated Builders and Contractors, Inc., et al., by Maurice Baskin, Jan S. Amundson, and Quentin Riegel.

Brief of amici curiae filed on behalf of the Associated General Contractors of America by Joe F. Canterbury, Jr., Frederic Gover, Michael E. Kennedy, and William A. Isokait.

Brief of amici curiae filed on behalf of the Chamber of Commerce of the United States by Marshall B. Babson, Stanley R. Strauss, Stephen A. Bokat, Robin S. Conrad, and Mona C. Zeiberg.

Brief of amici curiae filed on behalf of the Labor Policy Association by Robert E. Williams and Daniel V. Yager.

IV. THE SUPREME COURT'S DECISION

"The Act seeks to improve labor relations ('eliminate the causes of certain substantial obstructions to the free flow of commerce,') in large part by granting specific sets of rights to employers and to employees. This case grows out of a controversy about rights that the Act grants to 'employees,' namely, rights 'to self-organization, to form, join, or assist labor organizations, to bargain collectively . . . and to engage in other concerted activities for the purpose of collective bargaining or other mutual aid or protection.' We granted certiorari to decide only that part of the controversy that focuses upon the meaning of the word 'employee,' a key term in the statute, since these rights belong only to those workers who qualify as 'employees' as that term is defined in the Act.

[S]ervice to the union for pay does not 'involve abandonment of . . . service' to the company. . . . Common sense suggests that as a worker goes about his or her ordinary tasks during a working day, say, wiring sockets or laying cable, he or she is subject to the control of the company employer, whether or not the union also pays the worker. The company, the worker, the union, all would expect that to be so. And, that being so, that union and company interests or control might sometimes differ should make no difference. . . .

This is not to say that the law treats paid union organizers like other company employees in every labor law context. For instance, the Board states that, at least sometimes, a paid organizer may not share a sufficient 'community of interest' with other employees (as to wages, hours, and working conditions) to warrant inclusion in the same bargaining unit. We need not decide this matter. Nor do we express any view about any of the other matters Town & Country raised before the Court of Appeals, such as whether or not Town & Country's conduct (in refusing to interview, or to retain, 'employees' who were on the union's payroll) amounted to an unfair labor practice. We hold only that the Board's construction of the word 'employee' is lawful; that term does not exclude paid union organizers. . . .

For these reasons the judgment of the Court of Appeals is vacated, and the case is remanded for further proceedings consistent with this opinion."

V. JUSTICE VOTE

9 Pro ACLU Side vs. 0 Con Opposing Side

ACLU Side (Petitioner / Appellant)

1. Breyer, S. – Wrote majority opinion
2. Ginsburg, R. – Joined majority opinion
3. Thomas, C. – Joined majority opinion
4. Souter, D. – Joined majority opinion
5. O'Connor, S. – Joined majority opinion
6. Kennedy, A. – Joined majority opinion
7. Stevens, J. – Joined majority opinion
8. Rehnquist, W. – Joined majority opinion
9. Scalia, A. – Joined majority opinion

VI. A WIN OR LOSS FOR THE ACLU?

The ACLU, as amicus curiae, urged reversal of the judgment of the Court of Appeals; the Supreme Court vacated and remanded in a 9-0 vote, giving the ACLU an apparent win.

793. United States v. Chesapeake & Potomac Telephone Co. of Virginia

(Decided February 27, 1996; 516 U.S. 415)

I. ISSUE

A. Issues Discussed

First Amendment, freedoms of press, speech, and association

B. Legal Question Presented

Does 47 U.S.C. § 533(b) of the Cable Communications Policy Act of 1984, which makes it "unlawful for any common carrier . . . to provide video programming directly to subscribers in its telephone service area," violate the First Amendment's protection of free speech?

C. Supreme Court's Answer

"The judgment is vacated and the cases are remanded to the United States Court of Appeals for the Fourth Circuit for consideration of the question whether they are moot."

II. CASE SUMMARY

A. Background

"At issue in this case is the constitutionality of 47 U.S.C. § 533(b), which provides, in pertinent part:

(1) It shall be unlawful for any common carrier, subject in whole or in part to subchapter II of this chapter, to provide video programming directly to subscribers in its telephone service area, either directly or indirectly through an affiliate owned by, operated by, controlled by, or under common control with the common carrier.

(2) It shall be unlawful for any common carrier, subject in whole or in part to subchapter II of this chapter, to provide channels of communication or pole line conduit space, or other rental arrangements, to any entity which is directly or indirectly owned by, operated by, controlled by, or under common control with such common carrier, if such facilities or arrangements are to be used for, or in connection with, the provision of video programming directly to subscribers in the telephone service area of the common carrier.

47 U.S.C. § 533(b)(1), (2). This provision, enacted as part of the Cable Communications Policy Act of 1984 (the '1984 Cable Act'), Pub.L. No. 98–549, 98 Stat. 2779 (codified at 47 U.S.C. § 521 et seq.), essentially prohibits local telephone companies from offering, with editorial control, cable television services to their common carrier subscribers. In a thorough opinion, the district court found the statute to violate the First Amendment. . . .

Chesapeake and Potomac Telephone Company of Virginia ('C & P') applied for a cable franchise from the City of Alexandria ('City'). It is undisputed that the City denied this application solely upon its belief that any grant of such a franchise would violate 47 U.S.C. § 533(b). Thereafter, C & P and Bell Atlantic Video Systems, both wholly-owned subsidiaries of Bell Atlantic Corporation, brought suit in federal district court in Virginia against the United States, the Federal Communications Commission ('FCC') and the Attorney General (collectively the 'Government defendants') seeking to invalidate Section 533(b) as itself violative of the First Amendment and seeking to enjoin its enforcement. Subsequently, the National Cable Television Association ('NCTA') sought, and was granted, permission to intervene as a defendant. Cross-motions for summary judgment were filed. Ultimately, the district court granted plaintiffs' motion for summary judgment. It declared 47 U.S.C. § 533(b) unconstitutional both facially and as applied to plaintiffs and enjoined the Government defendants from enforcing the provision."[1]

The Court of Appeals for the Fourth Circuit affirmed the district court.

The Supreme Court granted certiorari to review the case and vacated the decision of the Court of Appeals.

B. Counsel of Record / ACLU Attorney

ACLU Side (Respondent / Appellee): Laurence H. Tribe argued the cause for appellees in both cases.

Opposing Side (Petitioner / Appellant): Deputy Solicitor General Lawrence G. Wallace argued the cause for appellants in both cases.

III. AMICI CURIAE

ACLU Side (Respondent / Appellee)

Brief of amici curiae filed on behalf of the ACLU, et al., by Burt Neuborne and Steven R. Shapiro.

Brief of amici curiae filed on behalf of Bellsouth Corporation by Walter H. Alford, John F. Beasley, William Barfield, and Roger M. Flynt, Jr.

Brief of amici curiae filed on behalf of East Ascension Telephone Co. by Richard A. Epstein.

Brief of amici curiae filed on behalf of GTE Corp. by M. Edward Whelan III, John F. Raposa, and Richard A. Cordray.

Brief of amici curiae filed on behalf of Mets Fans United/Virginia Consumers for Cable Choice, et al., by Samuel A. Simon. Brief of amici curiae filed on behalf of the United States Telephone Association, et al., by Mary McDermott, Linda Kent, Charles D. Cosson, Michael W. McConnell, Kenneth S. Geller, H. Thomas Byron, III, David Cosson, L. Marie Guillory, Thomas P. Hester, Kelly R. Welsh, Thomas E. Taylor, Christopher J. Wilson, Michael J. Shortley, III, Ellyn Elise Crutcher, Owen E. MacBride, Lisa M. Zaina, Morrison Des. Webb, John M. Clarke, John P. Walsh, Richard W. Odgers, Lucille, M. Mates, Alan F. Ciamporcero, James D. Ellis, Liam S. Coonan, Kelly M. Murray, Mary W. Marks, Martin E. Grambow, Madelyn M. Dematteo, and Alfred J. Brunetti.

Brief of amici curiae filed on behalf of U.S. West, Inc. by Loyd N. Cutler, Louis R. Cohen, William T. Lake, Steven M. Dunne, Lynn Charytan, Charles P. Russ, III, Stuart S. Cunckel, David S. Sather, and Norton Cutler.

Opposing Side (Petitioner / Appellant)

Brief of amici curiae filed on behalf of the California Cable Television Association by Bruce D. Sokler, Frank W. Lloyd, III, James J. Valentino, Spencer R. Kaitz, and Jeffrey Sinsheimer.

Brief of amici curiae filed on behalf of the Consumer Federation of America, et al., by Gigi B. Sohn, Andrew Jay Schwartzman, and Bradley Stillman.

IV. THE SUPREME COURT'S DECISION

"The judgment is vacated and the cases are remanded to the United States Court of Appeals for the Fourth Circuit for consideration of the question whether they are moot."

V. JUSTICE VOTE

0 Pro ACLU Side vs. 9 Con Opposing Side

Opposing Side (Petitioner / Appellant)

1. Rehnquist, W. – Per curiam decision
2. Stevens, J. – Per curiam decision
3. O'Connor, S. – Per curiam decision
4. Scalia, A. – Per curiam decision
5. Kennedy, A. – Per curiam decision
6. Souter, D. – Per curiam decision
7. Thomas, C. – Per curiam decision

1 Chesapeake & Potomac Telephone Co. of Virginia v. United States, 42 F.3d 181 (4th Cir. 1994).

8. Ginsburg, R. – Per curiam decision
9. Breyer, S. – Per curiam decision

VI. A WIN OR LOSS FOR THE ACLU?

The ACLU filed as amicus curiae urging affirmance of the judgment of the Court of Appeals; the Supreme Court vacated and remanded in a 9-0 vote, giving the ACLU an apparent loss.

794. Wisconsin v. City of New York

(Decided March 20, 1996; 517 U.S. 1)

I. ISSUE

A. Issues Discussed

Census, reapportionment

B. Legal Question Presented

Whether the decision of "the Secretary of Commerce . . . to use a particular statistical adjustment that had been designed to correct an undercount in the initial enumeration" of the census violated the Constitution and related statutory provisions.

C. Supreme Court's Answer

The decision of the Secretary of Commerce was constitutional.

II. CASE SUMMARY

A. Background

"The Constitution requires an 'actual Enumeration' of the population every 10 years and vests Congress with the authority to conduct that census 'in such Manner as they shall by Law direct.' . . . The Constitution provides that the results of the census shall be used to apportion the Members of the House of Representatives among the States. . . .

There have been 20 decennial censuses in the history of the United States. Although each was designed with the goal of accomplishing an 'actual Enumeration' of the population, no census is recognized as having been wholly successful in achieving that goal. . . . It is thought that these errors have resulted in a net 'undercount' of the actual American population in every decennial census. . . . Since at least 1940, the Census Bureau has thought that the undercount affects some racial and ethnic minority groups to a greater extent than it does whites. . . .

In preparing for the 1990 census, the Bureau and the task forces also looked into the possibility of using large-scale statistical adjustment to compensate for the undercount and differential undercount. Although the Bureau had previously considered that possibility (most recently in 1980), it always had decided instead to rely upon more traditional methodology and the results of the enumeration. . . .

In the context of the census, the initial enumeration of the entire population (the 'capture') would be followed by the post-enumeration survey (PES) (the 'recapture') of certain representative geographical areas. The Bureau would then compare the results of the PES to the results of the initial enumeration for those areas targeted by the PES, in order to determine a rate of error . . . . That rate of error would be extrapolated to the entire population, and thus would be used to statistically adjust the results of the initial enumeration.

[I]n October 1987, the Department of Commerce announced that the 1990 census would not be statistically adjusted.

In November 1988, several plaintiffs (including a number of the respondents in this action) brought suit in the United States District Court for the Eastern District of New York, arguing that the Secretary's decision against statistical adjustment of the 1990 census was unconstitutional and contrary to federal law. The parties entered into an interim stipulation providing, inter alia, that the Secretary would reconsider the possibility of a statistical adjustment.

In July 1991, the Secretary issued his decision not to use the PES to adjust the 1990 census. . . . The plaintiffs returned to court. The District Court concluded that the Secretary's decision violated neither the Constitution nor federal law.

Respondents appealed, arguing that the District Court had adopted the wrong standard of review for their constitutional claim, and the Court of Appeals for the Second Circuit reversed by a divided vote."

The Supreme Court granted certiorari to review the consolidated cases and reversed.

B. Counsel of Record / ACLU Attorney

ACLU Side (Respondent / Appellee): Robert S. Rifkind argued the cause for the appellee.

Opposing Side (Petitioner / Appellant): Drew S. Days, III, Solicitor General, argued the cause for the federal appellants.

James E. Doyle, Attorney General of Wisconsin, argued the cause for the state appellants.

III. AMICI CURIAE

ACLU Side (Respondent / Appellee)

Brief of amici curiae filed on behalf of the Lawyers Committee for Civil Rights Under Law, the ACLU, et al., by Jonathan L. Greenblatt, Margaret Hahn-Dupont, Paul C. Saunders, Herbert J. Hansell, Norman Redlich, Barbara R. Arnwine, Thomas J. Henderson, Christopher A. Hansen, Stevn R. Shapiro, Samuel Rabinove, Elaine R. Jones, Theodore M. Shaw, Charles Stephen Ralston, and Arthur N. Eisenberg.

Brief of amici curiae filed on behalf of the city of Detroit by Linda D. Fegins and Phyliss A. James.

Opposing Side (Petitioner / Appellant)

Brief of amici curiae filed on behalf of the Commonwealth of Pennsylvania by Thomas W. Corbett, Jr., Attorney General, and John G. Knorr, III, Chief Deputy Attorney General.

Brief of amici curiae filed on behalf of United States Senator Herb Kohl, et al., by Brady C. Williamson and Debbie K. Lerner.

IV. THE SUPREME COURT'S DECISION

"We think that the Court of Appeals erred in holding the 'one person-one vote' standard of Wesberry and its progeny applicable to the action at hand. For several reasons, the 'good-faith effort to achieve population equality' required of a State conducting intrastate redistricting does not translate into a requirement that the Federal Government conduct a census that is as accurate as possible. First, we think that the Court of Appeals understated the significance of the two differences that it recognized between state redistricting cases and the instant action. The court failed to recognize that the Secretary's decision was made pursuant to Congress' direct delegation of its broad authority over the census. The court also undervalued the significance of the fact that the Constitution makes it impossible to achieve population equality among interstate districts. . . .

Rather than the standard adopted by the Court of Appeals, we think that it is the standard established by this Court in Montana and Franklin that applies to the Secretary's decision not to adjust. The text of the Constitution vests Congress with virtually unlimited discretion in conducting the decennial 'actual Enumeration,' and notwithstanding the plethora of lawsuits that inevitably accompany each decennial census, there is no basis for thinking that Congress' discretion is more limited than the text of the Constitution provides. Through the Census Act, Congress has delegated its broad authority over the census to the Secretary. Hence, so long as the Secretary's conduct of the census is 'consistent with the constitutional language and the constitutional goal of equal representation,' it is within the limits of the Constitution. In light of the Constitution's broad grant of authority to Congress, the Secretary's decision not to adjust need bear only a reasonable relationship to the accomplishment of an actual enumeration of the population, keeping in mind the constitutional purpose of the census. . . .

Turning finally to review the Secretary's conclusion that the PES-based adjustment would not improve distributive accuracy, we need note only that the Secretary's conclusion is supported by the reasoning of some of his advisers, and was therefore a reasonable choice in an area where technical experts disagree. . . .

The Constitution confers upon Congress the responsibility to conduct an 'actual Enumeration' of the American public every 10 years, with the primary purpose of providing a basis for apportioning political representation among the States. Here, the Secretary of Commerce, to whom Congress has delegated its constitutional authority over the census, determined that in light of the constitutional purpose of the census, an 'actual Enumeration' would best be achieved without the PES-based statistical adjustment of the results of the initial enumeration. We find that conclusion entirely reasonable. Therefore we hold that the Secretary's decision was well within the constitutional bounds of discretion over the conduct of the census provided to the Federal Government. The judgment of the Court of Appeals is reversed."

V. JUSTICE VOTE

0 Pro ACLU Side vs. 9 Con Opposing Side

Opposing Side (Petitioner / Appellant)

1. Rehnquist, W. – Wrote majority opinion
2. Breyer, S. – Joined majority opinion
3. Ginsburg, R. – Joined majority opinion
4. Thomas, C. – Joined majority opinion
5. Souter, D. – Joined majority opinion
6. O'Connor, S. – Joined majority opinion
7. Kennedy, A. – Joined majority opinion
8. Stevens, J. – Joined majority opinion
9. Scalia, A. – Joined majority opinion

VI. A WIN OR LOSS FOR THE ACLU?

The ACLU, as amicus curiae, urged affirmance of the judgment of the Court of Appeals; the Supreme Court reversed in a 9-0 vote, giving the ACLU an apparent loss.

795. Morse v. Republican Party of Virginia

(Decided March 27, 1996; 517 U.S. 186)

I. ISSUE

A. Issues Discussed

Voting rights, poll tax

B. Legal Question Presented

"[W]hether § 5 of the Act required preclearance of the Party's decision to exact [a party nomination] fee and whether appellants were permitted to challenge it as a poll tax prohibited by § 10."

C. Supreme Court's Answer

Section 5 required preclearance of the party nomination fee and appellants were permitted to challenge the fee as a poll tax under § 10.

II. CASE SUMMARY

A. Background

"On December 16, 1993, the Republican Party of Virginia (Party) issued a call for a state convention to be held on June 3, 1994, to nominate the Republican candidate for United States Senator. The call invited all registered voters in Virginia to participate in local mass meetings, canvasses, or conventions to be conducted by officials of the Party. Any voter could be certified as a delegate to the state convention by a local political committee upon payment of a registration fee of $35 or $45 depending on the date of certification. Over 14,000 voters paid the fee and took part in the convention.

In response to the call, appellants Bartholomew, Enderson, and Morse sought to become delegates to the convention. As a registered voter in Virginia willing to declare his or her intent to support the Party's nominee, each was eligible to participate upon payment of the registration fee. Bartholomew and Enderson refused to pay the fee and did not become delegates; Morse paid the fee with funds advanced by supporters of the eventual nominee.

On May 2, 1994, appellants filed a complaint in the United States District Court for the Western District of Virginia alleging that the imposition of the registration fee violated §§ 5 and 10 of the Voting Rights Act, 79 Stat. 439, 442, as amended, 42 U.S.C. §§ 1973c and 1973h, as well as the Equal Protection Clause of the Fourteenth Amendment and the Twenty-fourth Amendment to the Constitution. They sought an injunction preventing the Party from imposing the fee and ordering it to return the fee paid by Morse. As §§ 5 and 10 require, a three-judge District Court was convened to consider the statutory claims. That court remanded the two constitutional claims to a single-judge District Court, and, after expedited briefing and argument, granted the Party's motion to dismiss the § 5 and § 10 claims."

The Supreme Court granted certiorari to review the case and reversed.

B. Counsel of Record / ACLU Attorney

ACLU Side (Petitioner / Appellant): Pamela S. Karlan argued the cause for the appellants.

Paul Bender, Deputy Solicitor General, argued the cause for the United States, as amicus curiae, by special leave of Court.

Opposing Side (Respondent / Appellee): E. Duncan Getchell, Jr., argued the cause for the appellees.

III. AMICI CURIAE

ACLU Side (Petitioner / Appellant)

Brief of amici curiae filed on behalf of the Lawyers' Committee for Civil Rights Under Law and the ACLU by Donald B. Verrilli, Jr., Stuart M. Rennert, Michael A. Cooper, Herbert J. Hansell, Norman Redlich, Barbara R. Arnwine, Thomas J. Henderson, Brenda Wright, Todd A. Cox, and Laughlin McDonald.

Brief of amici curiae filed on behalf of the United States by Deputy Solicitor General Paul Bender, Solicitor General Drew S. Days, III, Assistant Attorney General Deval L. Patrick, Richard H. Seamon, Steven H. Rosenbaum, and Samuel R. Bagenstos.

Brief of amici curiae filed on behalf of the National Association for the Advancement of Colored People by Dennis Courtland Hayes, Willie Abrams, and Ronald D. Maines.

Opposing Side (Respondent / Appellee)

Brief of amici curiae filed on behalf of the Commonwealth of Virginia by James S. Gilmore, III, Attorney General of Virginia, David E. Anderson, Chief Deputy Attorney General, John Paul Woodley, Jr., and William H. Hurd, Deputy Attorneys General, and Maureen Riley Matsen, Assistant Attorney General.

IV. THE SUPREME COURT'S DECISION

"The Party does not question the validity of the Attorney General's regulation. That regulation unambiguously provides that when a political party makes a change affecting voting, § 5 requires preclearance if two conditions are satisfied: The change must relate to 'a public electoral function of the party' and the party must be 'acting under authority explicitly or implicitly granted by a covered jurisdiction.' The Party does not deny that the delegate fee is a change that relates to a public electoral function of the Party. It argues, instead, that the regulation did not apply when it selected its nominee for United States Senator at a convention because it was not 'acting under authority' granted by Virginia. We disagree. The District Court erred in its application of the regulation, because the Party exercised delegated state power when it certified its nominee for automatic placement on Virginia's general election ballot. . . .

The Party's activities fall directly within the scope of the regulation. We next conclude, based on the language and structure of the Act, and the historical background which informed the Congress that enacted it, that § 5 of its own force covers changes in electoral practices such as the Party's imposition of a filing fee for delegates to its convention. . . .

A fair reading of the text of § 5 unquestionably supports the conclusion that by imposing its filing fee the Party sought to administer a 'voting qualification or prerequisite to voting, or standard, practice, or procedure with respect to voting different from that in force or effect on November 1, 1968.' . . .

The imposition by an established political party—that is to say, a party authorized by state law to determine the method of selecting its candidates for elective office and also authorized to have those candidates' names automatically appear atop the general election ballot—of a new prerequisite to voting for the party's nominees is subject to § 5's preclearance requirement. . . .

The District Court dismissed appellants' claim under § 10 of the Act because that section only authorizes enforcement proceedings brought by the Attorney General and does not expressly mention private actions. . . . Since § 10 is, by its terms, a statute designed for enforcement of the guarantees of the Fourteenth and Fifteenth Amendments, Congress must have intended it to provide private remedies. . . . Without reaching the merits, the District Court dismissed appellants' claim because it held there was no private cause of action under § 10. Since we hold that this conclusion is incorrect, we postpone any consideration of the merits until after they have been addressed by the District Court.

The judgment of the District Court is reversed, and the case is remanded for further proceedings consistent with this opinion."

V. JUSTICE VOTE

5 Pro ACLU Side vs. 4 Con Opposing Side

ACLU Side (Petitioner / Appellant)

1. Stevens, J. – Wrote majority opinion
2. Ginsburg, R. – Joined majority opinion
3. Breyer, S. – Wrote concurring opinion
4. Souter, D. – Joined Breyer's concurrence
5. O'Connor, S. – Joined Breyer's concurrence

Opposing Side (Respondent / Appellee)

1. Scalia, A. – Wrote dissenting opinion, joined Thomas' dissent
2. Thomas, C. – Wrote dissenting opinion, joined Scalia's dissent
3. Kennedy, A. – Wrote dissenting opinion, joined Thomas' dissent
4. Rehnquist, W. – Joined Kennedy's dissent, joined Thomas' dissent

VI. A WIN OR LOSS FOR THE ACLU?

The ACLU, as amicus curiae, urged reversal of the judgment of the District Court; the Supreme Court reversed and remanded in a 5-4 vote, giving the ACLU an apparent win.

796. United States v. Armstrong

(Decided May 13, 1996; 517 U.S. 456)

I. ISSUE

A. Issues Discussed

Racial discrimination, selective prosecution

B. Legal Question Presented

Whether respondents made "the showing necessary for a defendant to be entitled to discovery on a claim that the prosecuting attorney singled him out for prosecution on the basis of his race."

C. Supreme Court's Answer

"[R]espondents failed to satisfy the threshold showing: They failed to show that the Government declined to prosecute similarly situated suspects of other races."

II. CASE SUMMARY

A. Background

"In April 1992, respondents were indicted in the United States District Court for the Central District of California on charges of conspiring to possess with intent to distribute more than 50 grams of cocaine base (crack) and conspiring to distribute the same, . . . and federal firearms offenses. For three months prior to the indictment, agents of the Federal Bureau of Alcohol, Tobacco, and Firearms and the Narcotics Division of the Inglewood, California, Police Department had infiltrated a suspected crack distribution ring by using three confidential informants. . . .

In response to the indictment, respondents filed a motion for discovery or for dismissal of the indictment, alleging that they were selected for federal prosecution because they are black. In support of their motion, they offered only an affidavit by a 'Paralegal Specialist,' employed by the Office of the Federal Public Defender representing one of the respondents. The only allegation in the affidavit was that, in every one of the 24 § 841 or § 846 cases closed by the office during 1991, the defendant was black. Accompanying the affidavit was a 'study' listing the 24 defendants, their race, whether they were prosecuted for dealing cocaine as well as crack, and the status of each case. . . .

The District Court granted the motion. It ordered the Government (1) to provide a list of all cases from the last three years in which the Government charged both cocaine and firearms offenses, (2) to identify the race of the defendants in those cases, (3) to identify what levels of law enforcement were involved in the investigations of those cases, and (4) to explain its criteria for deciding to prosecute those defendants for federal cocaine offenses.

The Government moved for reconsideration of the District Court's discovery order. . . .

The District Court denied the motion for reconsideration. When the Government indicated it would not comply with the court's discovery order, the court dismissed the case.

A divided three-judge panel of the Court of Appeals for the Ninth Circuit reversed, holding that, because of the proof requirements for a selective-prosecution claim, defendants must 'provide a colorable basis for believing that 'others similarly situated have not been prosecuted'' to obtain discovery. The Court of Appeals voted to rehear the case en banc, and the en banc panel affirmed the District Court's order of dismissal, holding that 'a defendant is not required to demonstrate that the government has failed to prosecute others who are similarly situated.'"

The Supreme Court granted certiorari to review the case and reversed.

B. Counsel of Record / ACLU Attorney

ACLU Side (Respondent / Appellee): Barbara E. O'Connor argued the cause for appellee.

Opposing Side (Petitioner / Appellant): Drew S. Days, III, Solicitor General, argued the cause for appellant.

III. AMICI CURIAE

ACLU Side (Respondent / Appellee)

Brief of amici curiae filed on behalf of the NAACP Legal Defense & Educational Fund, Inc., and the ACLU by Steven R. Shapiro, Elaine R. Jones, Theodore M. Shaw, George H. Kendall, and L. Song Richardson.

Brief of amici curiae filed on behalf of former law enforcement officials and police organizations, et al., by David Cole and Julius Lobel.

Brief of amici curiae filed on behalf of the National Association of Criminal Defense Lawyers by Gerald R. Smith, Judy Clarke, Nancy Hollander, and Barbara Bergman.

Opposing Side (Petitioner / Appellant)

Brief of amici curiae filed on behalf of the Criminal Justice Legal Foundation by Kent F. Scheidegger.

Brief of amici curiae filed on behalf of the Washington Legal Foundation, et al., by Daniel J. Popeo and Richard A. Samp.

IV. THE SUPREME COURT'S DECISION

"A selective-prosecution claim is not a defense on the merits to the criminal charge itself, but an independent assertion that the prosecutor has brought the charge for reasons forbidden by the Constitution. . . .

The requirements for a selective-prosecution claim draw on 'ordinary equal protection standards.' The claimant must demonstrate that the federal prosecutorial policy 'had a discriminatory effect and that it was motivated by a discriminatory purpose.' To establish a discriminatory effect in a race case, the claimant must show that similarly situated individuals of a different race were not prosecuted. . . .

Having reviewed the requirements to prove a selective-prosecution claim, we turn to the showing necessary to obtain discovery in support of such a claim. If discovery is ordered, the Government must assemble from its own files documents which might corroborate or refute the defendant's claim. Discovery thus imposes many of the costs present when the Government must respond to a prima facie case of selective prosecution. It will divert prosecutors' resources and may disclose the Government's prosecutorial strategy. The justifications for a rigorous standard for the elements of a selective-prosecution claim thus require a correspondingly rigorous standard for discovery in aid of such a claim. . . . In this case we consider what evidence constitutes 'some evidence tending to show the existence' of the discriminatory effect element. . . .

In the case before us, respondents' 'study' did not constitute 'some evidence tending to show the existence of the essential elements of' a selective-prosecution claim. The study failed to identify individuals who were not black and could have been prosecuted for the offenses for which respondents were charged, but were not so prosecuted. This omission was not remedied by respondents' evidence in opposition to the Government's motion for reconsideration. The newspaper article, which discussed the discriminatory effect of federal drug sentencing laws, was not relevant to an allegation of discrimination in decisions to prosecute. Respondents' affidavits, which recounted one attorney's conversation with a drug treatment center employee and the experience of another attorney defending drug prosecutions in state court, recounted hearsay and reported personal conclusions based on anecdotal evidence. The judgment of the Court of Appeals is therefore reversed, and the case is remanded for proceedings consistent with this opinion."

V. JUSTICE VOTE

1 Pro ACLU Side vs. 8 Con Opposing Side

ACLU Side (Respondent / Appellee)

1. Stevens, J. – Wrote dissenting opinion

Opposing Side (Petitioner / Appellant)

1. Rehnquist, W. – Wrote majority opinion
2. Scalia, A. – Joined majority opinion
3. O'Connor, S. – Joined majority opinion
4. Thomas, C. – Joined majority opinion
5. Kennedy, A. – Joined majority opinion
6. Ginsburg, R. – Wrote concurring opinion
7. Souter, D. – Wrote concurring opinion
8. Breyer, S. – Wrote concurring opinion

VI. A WIN OR LOSS FOR THE ACLU?

The ACLU, as amicus curiae, urged affirmance of the judgment of the Court of Appeals; the Supreme Court reversed and remanded in an 8-1 vote, giving the ACLU an apparent loss.

797. 44 Liquormart, Inc. v. Rhode Island

(Decided May 13, 1996; 517 U.S. 484)

I. ISSUE

A. Issues Discussed

First Amendment, freedom of speech, commercial speech, Twenty-first Amendment

B. Legal Question Presented

Whether "Rhode Island's statutory prohibition against advertisements that provide the public with accurate information about retail prices of alcoholic beverages is . . . invalid."

C. Supreme Court's Answer

"Rhode Island's statutory prohibition against advertisements that provide the public with accurate information about retail prices of alcoholic beverages is . . . invalid [because] such an advertising ban is an abridgment of speech protected by the First Amendment and that it is not shielded from constitutional scrutiny by the Twenty-first Amendment."

II. CASE SUMMARY

A. Background

"In 1956, the Rhode Island Legislature enacted two separate prohibitions against advertising the retail price of alcoholic beverages. The first applies to vendors licensed in Rhode Island as well as to out-of-state manufacturers, wholesalers, and shippers. It prohibits them from 'advertising in any manner whatsoever' the price of any alcoholic beverage offered for sale in the State; the only exception is for price tags or signs displayed with the merchandise within licensed premises and not visible from the street. The second statute applies to the Rhode Island news media. It contains a categorical prohibition against the publication or broadcast of any advertisements—even those referring to sales in other States—that 'make reference to the price of any alcoholic beverages.' . . .

Petitioners 44 Liquormart, Inc. (44 Liquormart), and Peoples Super Liquor Stores, Inc. (Peoples), are licensed retailers of alcoholic beverages. Petitioner 44 Liquormart operates a store in Rhode Island and petitioner Peoples operates several stores in Massachusetts that are patronized by Rhode Island residents. Peoples uses alcohol price advertising extensively in Massachusetts, where such advertising is permitted, but Rhode Island newspapers and other media outlets have refused to accept such ads.

Complaints from competitors about an advertisement placed by 44 Liquormart in a Rhode Island newspaper in 1991 generated enforcement proceedings that in turn led to the initiation of this litigation. The advertisement did not state the price of any alcoholic beverages. Indeed, it noted that 'State law prohibits advertising liquor prices.' The ad did, however, state the low prices at which peanuts, potato chips, and Schweppes mixers were being offered, identify various brands of packaged liquor, and include the word 'WOW' in large letters next to pictures of vodka and rum bottles. Based on the conclusion that the implied reference to bargain prices for liquor violated the statutory ban on price advertising, the Rhode Island Liquor Control Administrator assessed a $400 fine.

After paying the fine, 44 Liquormart, joined by Peoples, filed this action against the administrator in the Federal District Court seeking a declaratory judgment that the two statutes and the administrator's implementing regulations violate the First Amendment and other provisions of federal law. . . .

In his findings of fact, the District Judge first noted that there was a pronounced lack of unanimity among researchers who have studied the impact of advertising on the level of consumption of alcoholic beverages. . . . After summarizing the testimony of the expert witnesses for both parties, he found 'as a fact that Rhode Island's off-premises liquor price advertising ban has no significant impact on levels of alcohol consumption in Rhode Island.'

As a matter of law, he concluded that the price advertising ban was unconstitutional because it did not 'directly advance' the State's interest in reducing alcohol consumption and was 'more extensive than necessary to serve that interest.' . . .

The Court of Appeals reversed."

The Supreme Court granted certiorari to review the case and reversed.

B. Counsel of Record / ACLU Attorney

ACLU Side (Petitioner / Appellant): Evan T. Lawson argued the cause for the appellant.

Opposing Side (Respondent / Appellee): Rebecca Tedford Partington, Special Assistant Attorney General, argued the cause for appellee.

III. AMICI CURIAE

ACLU Side (Petitioner / Appellant)

Brief of amici curiae filed on behalf of the ACLU, et al., by Steven R. Shapiro and Marjorie Heins.

Additional briefs of amici curiae were filed on behalf of the American Advertising Federation, et al., the Association of National Advertisers, Inc., et al., the Beer Institute, et al., the Institute for Justice, the Newspaper Association of America, and the Washington Legal Foundation, et al.

Opposing Side (Respondent / Appellee)

Brief of amici curiae filed on behalf of the Council of State Governments, et al., by Richard Ruda and Lee Fennell.

Brief of amici curiae filed on behalf of the Malt Beverage Distributors Association of Pennsylvania by Mary Lou Hogan.

IV. THE SUPREME COURT'S DECISION

"As our review of the case law reveals, Rhode Island errs in concluding that all commercial speech regulations are subject to a similar form of constitutional review simply because they target a similar category of expression. The mere fact that messages propose commercial transactions does not in and of itself dictate the constitutional analysis that should apply to decisions to suppress them.

When a State regulates commercial messages to protect consumers from misleading, deceptive, or aggressive sales practices, or requires the disclosure of beneficial consumer information, the purpose of its regulation is consistent with the reasons for according constitutional protection to commercial speech and therefore justifies less than strict review. However, when a State entirely prohibits the dissemination of truthful, nonmisleading commercial messages for reasons unrelated to the preservation of a fair bargaining process, there is far less reason to depart from the rigorous review that the First Amendment generally demands. . . .

Precisely because bans against truthful, nonmisleading commercial speech rarely seek to protect consumers from either deception or overreaching, they usually rest solely on the offensive assumption that the public will respond 'irrationally' to the truth. The First Amendment directs us to be especially skeptical of regulations that seek to keep people in the dark for what the government perceives to be their own good. That teaching applies equally to state attempts to deprive consumers of accurate information about their chosen products . . . .

In this case, there is no question that Rhode Island's price advertising ban constitutes a blanket prohibition against truthful, nonmisleading speech about a lawful product. There is also no question that the ban serves an end unrelated to consumer protection. Accordingly, we must review the price advertising ban with 'special care,' mindful that speech prohibitions of this type rarely survive constitutional review.

[E]ven under the less than strict standard that generally applies in commercial speech cases, the State has failed to establish a 'reasonable fit' between its abridgment of speech and its temperance goal. It necessarily follows that the price advertising ban cannot survive the more stringent constitutional review that Central Hudson itself concluded was appropriate for the complete suppression of truthful, nonmisleading commercial speech. . . .

As is clear, the text of the Twenty-first Amendment supports the view that, while it grants the States authority over commerce that might otherwise be reserved to the Federal Government, it places no limit whatsoever on other constitutional provisions. . . Accordingly, we now hold that the Twenty-first Amendment does not qualify the constitutional prohibition against laws abridging the freedom of speech embodied in the First Amendment. The Twenty-first Amendment, therefore, cannot save Rhode Island's ban on liquor price advertising. . . .

Because Rhode Island has failed to carry its heavy burden of justifying its complete ban on price advertising, we conclude that R.I. Gen. Laws §§ 3–8–7 and 3–8–8.1 (1989), as well as Regulation 32 of the Rhode Island Liquor Control Administration, abridge speech in violation of the First Amendment as made applicable to the States by the Due Process Clause of the Fourteenth Amendment. The judgment of the Court of Appeals is therefore reversed."

V. JUSTICE VOTE

9 Pro ACLU Side vs. 0 Con Opposing Side

ACLU Side (Petitioner / Appellant)

1. Stevens, J. – Wrote majority opinion
2. Breyer, S. – Joined O'Connor's concurrence
3. Ginsburg, R. – Joined majority opinion
4. Thomas, C. – Wrote concurring opinion
5. Souter, D. – Joined O'Connor's concurrence
6. O'Connor, S. – Wrote concurring opinion
7. Kennedy, A. – Joined majority opinion
8. Rehnquist, W. – Joined O'Connor's concurrence
9. Scalia, A. – Wrote concurring opinion

VI. A WIN OR LOSS FOR THE ACLU?

The ACLU, as amicus curiae, urged reversal of the judgment of the Court of Appeals; the Supreme Court reversed in a 9-0 vote, giving the ACLU an apparent win.

798. Romer v. Evans

(Decided May 20, 1996; 517 U.S. 620)

I. ISSUE

A. Issues Discussed

Fourteenth Amendment, equal protection, sexual orientation discrimination

B. Legal Question Presented

Whether Amendment 2 to the Colorado Constitution, which "prohibits all legislative, executive or judicial action at any level of state or local government designed to protect" homosexual persons violates the Equal Protection Clause of the Fourteenth Amendment.

C. Supreme Court's Answer

Amendment 2 violates the Equal Protection Clause.

II. CASE SUMMARY

A. Background

"The enactment challenged in this case is an amendment to the Constitution of the State of Colorado, adopted in a 1992 statewide referendum. The parties and the state courts refer to it as 'Amendment 2,' its designation when submitted to the voters. The impetus for the amendment and the contentious campaign that preceded its adoption came in large part from [anti-discrimination] ordinances that had been passed in various Colorado municipalities. . . . Amendment 2 repeals these ordinances to the extent they prohibit discrimination on the basis of 'homosexual, lesbian or bisexual orientation, conduct, practices or relationships.'

Yet Amendment 2, in explicit terms, does more than repeal or rescind these provisions. It prohibits all legislative, executive or judicial action at any level of state or local government designed to protect the named class, a class we shall refer to as homosexual persons or gays and lesbians. . . .

Soon after Amendment 2 was adopted, this litigation to declare its invalidity and enjoin its enforcement was commenced in the District Court for the City and County of Denver. Among the plaintiffs (respondents here) were homosexual persons, some of them government employees. They alleged that enforcement of Amendment 2 would subject them to immediate and substantial risk of discrimination on the basis of their sexual orientation. Other plaintiffs (also respondents here) included the three municipalities whose ordinances we have cited and certain other governmental entities which had acted earlier to protect homosexuals from discrimination but would be prevented by Amendment 2 from continuing to do so. Although Governor Romer had been on record opposing the adoption of Amendment 2, he was named in his official capacity as a defendant, together with the Colorado Attorney General and the State of Colorado.

The trial court granted a preliminary injunction to stay enforcement of Amendment 2, and an appeal was taken to the Supreme Court of Colorado. Sustaining the interim injunction and remanding the case for further proceedings, the State Supreme Court held that Amendment 2 was subject to strict scrutiny under the Fourteenth Amendment because it infringed the fundamental right of gays and lesbians to participate in the political process. . . . On remand, the . . . trial court . . . enjoined enforcement of Amendment 2, and the Supreme Court of Colorado, in a second opinion, affirmed the ruling."

The U.S. Supreme Court granted certiorari to review the case and affirmed.

B. Counsel of Record / ACLU Attorney

ACLU Side (Respondent / Appellee): Jean E. Dubofsky argued the cause for appellees. With her on the brief for appellees Evans, et al., were Roderick M. Hills, Jr., Matthew Coles, Steven R. Shapiro, Clyde J. Wadsworth, Suzanne B. Goldberg, Jeanne Winer, Gregory A. Eurich, David H. Miller, Darlene M. Ebert, Joseph N. de Raismes III, and Walter A. Smith, Jr.

Edward M. Caswall and John P. Worcester filed a brief for appellees City of Aspen, et al.

Opposing Side (Petitioner / Appellant): Timothy M. Tymkovich, Solicitor General of Colorado, argued the cause for appellants. With him on the briefs were Gale A. Norton, Attorney General, Stephen K. ErkenBrack, Chief Deputy Attorney General, John Daniel Dailey and Paul Farley, Deputy Attorneys General, and Rex E. Lee and Carter G. Phillips, Special Assistant Attorneys General.

III. AMICI CURIAE

ACLU Side (Respondent / Appellee)

Brief of amici curiae filed on behalf of the State of Oregon, et al., by Theodore R. Kulongoski, Attorney General of Oregon, Thomas A. Balmer, Deputy Attorney General, Virginia L. Linder, Solicitor General, Michael D. Reynolds, Assistant Solicitor General, and Rives Kistler, Assistant Attorney General, Thomas J. Miller, Attorney General of Iowa, J. Joseph Curran, Jr., Attorney General of Maryland, Scott Harshbarger, Attorney General of Massachusetts, Hubert H. Humphrey III, Attorney General of Minnesota, Frankie Sue Del Papa, Attorney General of Nevada, Christine O. Gregoire, Attorney General of Washington, and Garland Pinkston, Jr., Acting Corporation Counsel of the District of Columbia.

Brief of amici curiae filed on behalf of the City of Atlanta, et al., by Louise H. Renne, Dennis Aftergut, Burk E. Delventhal, Julia M. C. Friedlander, Mary Carole Cooney, Robin Joy Shahar, Neal M. Janey, Stephen H. Clark, James K. Hahn, David I. Schulman, Eunice Gibson, Paul A. Crotty, Leonard A. Kerner, Jeffrey L. Rogers, Linda Meng, Janet E. Halley, Mark H. Sidran, Henry W Underhill, Jr., Benna Ruth Solomon, and Susan S. Sher.

Brief of amici curiae filed on behalf of Affirmation: United Methodists for Gay, Lesbian and Bisexual Concerns, et al., by Celeste McCollough and Matthew L. Hess.

Brief of amici curiae filed on behalf of the American Bar Association by George E. Bushnell, Jr.

Brief of amici curiae filed on behalf of the American Association on Mental Retardation, et al., by James W Ellis and Maureen A. Sanders.

Brief of amici curiae filed on behalf of the American Federation of State, County and Municipal Employees, AFL-CIO, by John C. Dempsey, Robert D. Lenhard, and Larry P. Weinberg.
Brief of amici curiae filed on behalf of the American Friends Service Committee, et al., by Stark Ritchie.
Brief of amici curiae filed on behalf of the American Psychological Association, et al., by Paul M. Smith, James L. McHugh, Jr., and Richard G. Taranto.
Brief of amici curiae filed on behalf of the Asian American Legal Defense and Education Fund, et al., by Eben Moglen and Pamela S. Karlan.
Brief of amici curiae filed on behalf of the Colorado Bar Association, et al., by Frank I. Michelman, Teri Al Little, Tracey K. Merwise, Roger W. Doughty, Stephen V. Bomse, Martha Minow, and Frances A. Koncilja.
Brief of amici curiae filed on behalf of the Gay and Lesbian Lawyers of Philadelphia by Cletus P. Lyman.
Brief of amici curiae filed on behalf of the NAACP Legal Defense and Educational Fund, Inc., et al., by Eric Schnapper, Elaine R. Jones, Theodore M. Shaw, Victor A. Bolde, Antonia Hernandez, Catherine Powell, Judith L. Lichtman, and Donna R. Lenhoff.
Brief of amici curiae filed on behalf of the National Bar Association by J. Clay Smith, Jr.
Brief of amici curiae filed on behalf of the National Education Association, et al., by Robert H. Chanin and John M. West.
Brief of amici curiae filed on behalf of James E. Andrews by Eric J. Graninger.
Brief of amici curiae filed on behalf of Laurence H. Tribe, et al., by Laurence H. Tribe, pro se, John Hart Ely, pro se, Philip B. Kurland, pro se, Kathleen M. Sullivan, pro se, and Gerald Gunther, pro se.
Brief of amici curiae filed on behalf of the Human Rights Campaign Fund, et al., by Philip Chai R. Feldblum.

Opposing Side (Petitioner / Appellant)

Brief of amici curiae filed on behalf of the State of Alabama, et al., by Charles J. Cooper, Richard F. Duncan, and the Attorneys General for their respective States as follows: Jeff Sessions of Alabama, Daniel E. Lungren of California, Alan G. Lance of Idaho, Don Stenberg of Nebraska, Charles Molony Condon of South Carolina, Mark Barnett of South Dakota, and James S. Gilmore, III, of Virginia.
Brief of amici curiae filed on behalf of the American Center for Law and Justice Family Life Project by Jay Alan Sekulow, John P. Tuskey, James M. Henderson, Sr., and Keith A. Fournier.
Brief of amici curiae filed on behalf of the Christian Legal Society, et al., by Steven T. McFarland, Samuel B. Casey, Gregory S. Baylor, Carl Howard Esbeck, and John K. Hulston Hall.
Brief of amici curiae filed on behalf of Colorado for Family Values by Robert K. Skolrood, Herbert W. Titus, and Barry C. Hodge.
Brief of amici curiae filed on behalf of Concerned Women for America, Inc., by David J. Myers and Wendell R. Bird.
Brief of amici curiae filed on behalf of Equal Rights, Not Special Rights, Inc., by Michael A. Carvin, William L. McGrath, and Robert H. Bork.
Brief of amici curiae filed on behalf of the Family Research Council by Melissa Wells-Petry.
Brief of amici curiae filed on behalf of the Pacific Legal Foundation by Anthony T. Caso and Deborah J. La Fetra.
Brief of amici curiae filed on behalf of the Oregon Citizens Alliance, et al., by Lawrence J. Hall, Melanie E. Mansell, and Gordon L. Cummings.

IV. THE SUPREME COURT'S DECISION

"The Fourteenth Amendment's promise that no person shall be denied the equal protection of the laws must coexist with the practical necessity that most legislation classifies for one purpose or another, with resulting disadvantage to various groups or persons. We have attempted to reconcile the principle with the reality by stating that, if a law neither burdens a fundamental right nor targets a suspect class, we will uphold the legislative classification so long as it bears a rational relation to some legitimate end.

Amendment 2 fails, indeed defies, even this conventional inquiry. First, the amendment has the peculiar property of imposing a broad and undifferentiated disability on a single named group, an exceptional and, as we shall explain, invalid form of legislation. Second, its sheer breadth is so discontinuous with the reasons offered for it that the amendment seems inexplicable by anything but animus toward the class it affects; it lacks a rational relationship to legitimate state interests. . . .

The primary rationale the State offers for Amendment 2 is respect for other citizens' freedom of association, and in particular the liberties of landlords or employers who have personal or religious objections to homosexuality. Colorado also cites its interest in conserving resources to fight discrimination against other groups. The breadth of the amendment is so far removed from these particular justifications that we find it impossible to credit them. We cannot say that Amendment 2 is directed to any identifiable legitimate purpose or discrete objective. It is a status-based enactment divorced from any factual context from which we could discern a relationship to legitimate state interests; it is a classification of persons undertaken for its own sake, something the Equal Protection Clause does not permit. '[C]lass legislation . . . [is] obnoxious to the prohibitions of the Fourteenth Amendment . . . .'

We must conclude that Amendment 2 classifies homosexuals not to further a proper legislative end but to make them unequal to everyone else. This Colorado cannot do. A State cannot so deem a class of persons a stranger to its laws. Amendment 2 violates the Equal Protection Clause, and the judgment of the Supreme Court of Colorado is affirmed."

V. JUSTICE VOTE

6 Pro ACLU Side vs. 3 Con Opposing Side

ACLU Side (Respondent / Appellee)

1. Kennedy, A. – Wrote majority opinion
2. Stevens, J. – Joined majority opinion
3. O'Connor, S. – Joined majority opinion
4. Souter, D. – Joined majority opinion
5. Ginsburg, R. – Joined majority opinion
6. Breyer, S. – Joined majority opinion

Opposing Side (Petitioner / Appellant)

1. Scalia, A. – Wrote dissenting opinion
2. Rehnquist, W. – Joined Scalia's dissent
3. Thomas, C. – Joined Scalia's dissent

VI. A WIN OR LOSS FOR THE ACLU?

The ACLU, as co-counsel for respondents, urged affirmance of the judgment of the Supreme Court of Colorado; the U.S. Supreme Court affirmed in a 6-3 vote, giving the ACLU an apparent win.

799. Ornelas v. United States

(Decided May 28, 1996; 517 U.S. 690)

I. ISSUE

A. Issues Discussed

Fourth Amendment, search and seizure

B. Legal Question Presented

Whether the Court of Appeals should have used a de novo standard of review for reasonable suspicion and probable cause determinations below.

C. Supreme Court's Answer

"We . . . hold that as a general matter determinations of reasonable suspicion and probable cause should be reviewed de novo on appeal."

II. CASE SUMMARY

A. Background

"Petitioners each pleaded guilty to possession of cocaine with intent to distribute. They reserved their right to appeal the District Court's denial of their motion to suppress the cocaine found in their car. The District Court had found reasonable suspicion to stop and question petitioners as they entered their car, and probable cause to remove one of the interior panels where a package containing two kilograms of cocaine was found. . . .

The Court of Appeals reviewed deferentially the District Court's determinations of reasonable suspicion and probable cause; it would reverse only upon a finding of 'clear error.' The court found no clear error in the reasonable-suspicion analysis and affirmed that determination. With respect to the probable-cause finding, however, the court remanded the case for a determination on whether Luedke was credible when testifying about the loose panel.

On remand, the Magistrate Judge expressly found the testimony credible. The District Court accepted the finding, and once again ruled that probable cause supported the search. The Seventh Circuit held that determination not clearly erroneous."

The Supreme Court granted certiorari to review the case, vacated, and remanded.

B. Counsel of Record / ACLU Attorney

ACLU Side (Petitioner / Appellant): Robert G. LeBell argued the cause for appellants.

Opposing Side (Respondent / Appellee): Cornelia T. L. Pillard argued the cause for appellee.

Peter D. Isakoff argued the cause as amicus curiae, by special leave of Court.

III. AMICI CURIAE

ACLU Side (Petitioner / Appellant)

Brief of amici curiae filed on behalf of the ACLU, et al., by Tracey Maclin, Steven R. Shapiro, and Barbara E. Bergman.

Opposing Side (Respondent / Appellee)

Brief of amici curiae filed by Peter D. Isakoff and David A. Hickerson.

Brief of amici curiae filed on behalf of Fred E. Inbau, Wayne W. Schmidt, James P. Manak, and Bernard J. Farber.

IV. THE SUPREME COURT'S DECISION

"The Court of Appeals, in adopting its deferential standard of review here, reasoned that de novo review for warrantless searches would be inconsistent with the "great deference" paid when reviewing a decision to issue a warrant. We cannot agree. The Fourth Amendment demonstrates a 'strong preference for searches conducted pursuant to a warrant,' and the police are more likely to use the warrant process if the scrutiny applied to a magistrate's probable-cause determination to issue a warrant is less than that for warrantless searches. Were we to eliminate this distinction, we would eliminate the incentive.

We therefore hold that as a general matter determinations of reasonable suspicion and probable cause should be reviewed de novo on appeal. Having said this, we hasten to point out that a reviewing court should take care both to review findings of historical fact only for clear error and to give due weight to inferences drawn from those facts by resident judges and local law enforcement officers.

A trial judge views the facts of a particular case in light of the distinctive features and events of the community; likewise, a police officer views the facts through the lens of his police experience and expertise. The background facts provide a context for the historical facts, and when seen together yield inferences that deserve deference. For example, what may not amount to reasonable suspicion at a motel located alongside a transcontinental highway at the height of the summer tourist season may rise to that level in December in Milwaukee. That city is unlikely to have been an overnight stop selected at the last minute by a traveler coming from California to points east. The 85-mile width of Lake Michigan blocks any further eastward progress. And while the city's salubrious summer climate and seasonal attractions bring many tourists at that time of year, the same is not true in December. Milwaukee's average daily high temperature in that month is 31 degrees and its average daily low is 17 degrees; the percentage of possible sunshine is only 38 percent. It is a reasonable inference that a Californian stopping in Milwaukee in December is either there to transact business or to visit family or friends. The background facts, though rarely the subject of explicit findings, inform the judge's assessment of the historical facts.

In a similar vein, our cases have recognized that a police officer may draw inferences based on his own experience in deciding whether probable cause exists. To a layman the sort of loose panel below the back seat armrest in the automobile involved in this case may suggest only wear and tear, but to Officer Luedke, who had searched roughly 2,000 cars for narcotics, it suggested that drugs may be secreted inside the panel. An appeals court should give due weight to a trial court's finding that the officer was credible and the inference was reasonable.

We vacate the judgments and remand the case to the Court of Appeals to review de novo the District Court's determinations that the officer had reasonable suspicion and probable cause in this case."

V. JUSTICE VOTE

8 Pro ACLU Side vs. 1 Con Opposing Side

ACLU Side (Petitioner / Appellant)

1. Rehnquist, W. – Wrote majority opinion
2. Breyer, S. – Joined majority opinion
3. Ginsburg, R. – Joined majority opinion
4. Thomas, C. – Joined majority opinion
5. Souter, D. – Joined majority opinion
6. O'Connor, S. – Joined majority opinion
7. Kennedy, A. – Joined majority opinion
8. Stevens, J. – Joined majority opinion

Opposing Side (Respondent / Appellee)

1. Scalia, A. – Wrote dissenting opinion

VI. A WIN OR LOSS FOR THE ACLU?

The ACLU, as amicus curiae, urged reversal of the judgment of the Court of Appeals; the Supreme Court vacated and remanded in an 8-1 vote, giving the ACLU an apparent win.

800. Loving v. United States

(Decided June 3, 1996; 517 U.S. 748)

I. ISSUE

A. Issues Discussed

Separation of powers, death penalty

B. Legal Question Presented

What is "the authority of the President, in [the United States'] system of separated powers, to prescribe aggravating factors that permit a court-martial to impose the death penalty upon a member of the Armed Forces convicted of murder."

C. Supreme Court's Answer

The President has the power to prescribe aggravating factors that permit a court-martial to impose the death penalty.

II. CASE SUMMARY

A. Background

"On December 12, 1988, petitioner Dwight Loving, an Army private stationed at Fort Hood, Texas, murdered two taxicab drivers from the nearby town of Killeen. He attempted to murder a third, but the driver disarmed him and escaped. Civilian and Army authorities arrested Loving the next afternoon. He confessed.

After a trial, an eight-member general court-martial found Loving guilty of, among other offenses, premeditated murder and felony murder under Article 118 of the Uniform Code of Military Justice (UCMJ). In the sentencing phase of the trial, the court-martial found three aggravating factors: (1) that the premeditated murder of the second driver was committed during the course of a robbery; (2) that Loving acted as the triggerman in the felony murder of the first driver; and (3) that Loving, having been found guilty of the premeditated murder, had committed a second murder, also proved at the single trial. The court-martial sentenced Loving to death. The commander who convened the court-martial approved the findings and sentence. The United States Army Court of Military Review and the United States Court of Appeals for the Armed Forces (formerly the United States Court of Military Appeals (CMA)) affirmed, relying on United States v. Curtis, 32 M.J. 252(CMA), cert. denied, 502 U.S. 952 (1991), to reject Loving's claims that the President lacked authority to promulgate the aggravating factors that enabled the court-martial to sentence him to death."

The Supreme Court granted certiorari to review the case and affirmed.

B. Counsel of Record / ACLU Attorney

ACLU Side (Petitioner / Appellant): John H. Blume argued the cause for appellant.

Opposing Side (Respondent / Appellee): Deputy Solicitor General Edwin S. Kneedler argued the cause for the United States.

III. AMICI CURIAE

ACLU Side (Petitioner / Appellant)

Brief of amici curiae filed on behalf of the ACLU by Ronald W. Meister, Steven R. Shapiro, and Diann Y. Rust-Tierney.

Brief of amici curiae filed on behalf of Public Citizen, Inc., by Alan B. Morrison, Eugene R. Fidell, and David C. Vladeck.

Brief of amici curiae filed on behalf of Marci A. Hamilton, et al., by Marci A. Hamilton, pro se, and David Schoenbrod, pro se.

Brief of amici curiae filed on behalf of the United States Navy-Marine Corps Appellate Defense Division by Phillip Del Grissom, John Francis Havranek, and Howard Barry Goodman.

Opposing Side (Respondent / Appellee)

Brief of amici curiae filed on behalf of the Criminal Legal Foundation by Kent S. Scheidegger and Charles L. Hobson.

IV. THE SUPREME COURT'S DECISION

"In 1950, Congress confronted the problem of what criminal jurisdiction would be appropriate for Armed Forces of colossal size, stationed on bases that in many instances were small societies unto themselves. Congress, confident in the procedural protections of the UCMJ, gave to courts-martial jurisdiction of the crime of murder. It further declared the law that service members who commit premeditated and felony murder may be sentenced to death by a court-martial. There is nothing in the constitutional scheme or our traditions to prohibit Congress from delegating the prudent and proper implementation of the capital murder statute to the President acting as Commander in Chief. . . .

It is hard to deem lawless a delegation giving the President broad discretion to prescribe rules on this subject. From the early days of the Republic, the President has had congressional authorization to intervene in cases where courts-martial decreed death. It would be contradictory to say that Congress cannot further empower him to limit by prospective regulation the circumstances in which courtsmartial can impose a death sentence. Specific authority to make rules for the limitation of capital punishment contributes more toward principled and uniform military sentencing regimes than does case-by-case intervention, and it provides greater opportunity for congressional oversight and revision.

Separation-of-powers principles are vindicated, not disserved, by measured cooperation between the two political branches of the Government, each contributing to a lawful objective through its own processes. The delegation to the President as Commander in Chief of the authority to prescribe aggravating factors was in all respects consistent with these precepts, and the promulgation of RCM 1004 was well within the delegated authority. Loving's sentence was lawful, and the judgment of the Court of Appeals of the Armed Forces is affirmed."

V. JUSTICE VOTE

0 Pro ACLU Side vs. 9 Con Opposing Side

Opposing Side (Respondent / Appellee)

1. Kennedy, A. – Wrote majority opinion
2. Rehnquist, W. – Joined majority opinion
3. Breyer, S. – Joined Stevens' concurrence
4. Ginsburg, R. – Joined Stevens' concurrence
5. Souter, D. – Joined Stevens' concurrence
6. Thomas, C. – Wrote concurring opinion
7. O'Connor, S. – Joined Scalia's concurrence
8. Stevens, J. – Wrote concurring opinion
9. Scalia, A. – Wrote concurring opinion

VI. A WIN OR LOSS FOR THE ACLU?

The ACLU, as amicus curiae, urged reversal of the judgment of the Court of Appeals; the Supreme Court affirmed in a 9-0 vote, giving the ACLU an apparent loss.

801. Whren v. United States

(Decided June 10, 1996; 517 U.S. 806)

I. ISSUE

A. Issues Discussed

Fourth Amendment, search and seizure

B. Legal Question Presented

"[W]hether the temporary detention of a motorist who the police have probable cause to believe has committed a civil traffic violation is inconsistent with the Fourth Amendment's prohibition against unreasonable seizures, unless a reasonable officer would have been motivated to stop the car by a desire to enforce the traffic laws."

C. Supreme Court's Answer

The stop here is consistent with the Fourth Amendment.

II. CASE SUMMARY

A. Background

"On the evening of June 10, 1993, plainclothes vice-squad officers of the District of Columbia Metropolitan Police Department were patrolling a 'high drug area' of the city in an unmarked car. Their suspicions were aroused when they passed a dark Pathfinder truck with temporary license plates and youthful occupants waiting at a stop sign, the driver looking down into the lap of the passenger at his right. The truck remained stopped at the intersection for what seemed an unusually long time—more than 20 seconds. When the police car executed a U-turn in order to head back toward the truck, the Pathfinder turned suddenly to its right, without signaling, and sped off at an 'unreasonable' speed. The policemen followed, and in a short while overtook the Pathfinder when it stopped behind other traffic at a red light. They pulled up alongside, and Officer Ephraim Soto stepped out and approached the driver's door, identifying himself as a police officer and directing the driver, petitioner Brown, to put the vehicle in park. When Soto drew up to the driver's window, he immediately observed two large plastic bags of what appeared to be crack cocaine in petitioner Whren's hands. Petitioners were arrested, and quantities of several types of illegal drugs were retrieved from the vehicle.

Petitioners were charged in a four-count indictment with violating various federal drug laws, including 21 U.S.C. §§ 844(a) and 860(a). At a pretrial suppression hearing, they challenged the legality of the stop and the resulting seizure of the drugs. They argued that the stop had not been justified by probable cause to believe, or even reasonable suspicion, that petitioners were engaged in illegal drug-dealing activity; and that Officer Soto's asserted ground for approaching the vehicle—to give the driver a warning concerning traffic violations—was pretextual. The District Court denied the suppression motion, concluding that 'the facts of the stop were not controverted,' and '[t]here was nothing to really demonstrate that the actions of the officers were contrary to a normal traffic stop.'

Petitioners were convicted of the counts at issue here. The Court of Appeals affirmed the convictions, holding with respect to the suppression issue that, 'regardless of whether a police officer subjectively believes that the occupants of an automobile may be engaging in some other illegal behavior, a traffic stop is permissible as long as a reasonable officer in the same circumstances could have stopped the car for the suspected traffic violation.'"

The Supreme Court granted certiorari to review the case and affirmed.

B. Counsel of Record / ACLU Attorney

ACLU Side (Petitioner / Appellant): Lisa Burget Wright argued the cause for appellants.

Opposing Side (Respondent / Appellee): James A. Feldman argued the cause for the United States.

III. AMICI CURIAE

ACLU Side (Petitioner / Appellant)

Brief of amici curiae filed on behalf of the ACLU by Steven R. Shapiro and Susan N. Herman.

Brief of amici curiae filed on behalf of the National Association of Criminal Defense Lawyers by Walter B. Nash, III, and Gregory J. Kuykendall.

Opposing Side (Respondent / Appellee)

Brief of amici curiae filed on behalf of the Criminal Justice Legal Foundation by Kent S. Scheidegger and Charles L. Hobson.

Brief of amici curiae filed on behalf of the California District Attorney's Association by Jeff Rubin, Thomas J. Orloff, Richard S. Michaels, and William M. Baldwin.

Brief of amici curiae filed on behalf of the State of California, et al., by Daniel E. Lungren, Attorney General of California, George Williamson, Chief Assistant Attorney General, Ronald A. Bass, Senior Assistant Attorney General, Joan Killeen, Supervising Deputy Attorney General, Catherine A. Rivlin, Supervising Deputy Attorney General, and Christina V. Kuo, Deputy Attorney General, and the following Attorneys General for their respective states: M. Jane Brady of Delaware, Thomas J. Miller of Iowa, Carla J. Stovall of Kansas, J. Joseph Curran, Jr., of Maryland, Mike Moore of Mississippi, Frankie Sue Del Papa of Nevada, Deborah T. Poritz of New Jersey, Dennis C. Vacco of New York, Michael F. Easley of North Carolina, Betty D. Montgomery of Ohio, W. A. Drew Edmondson of Oklahoma, Charles W. Burson of Tennessee, and Jan Graham of Utah.

IV. THE SUPREME COURT'S DECISION

"The Fourth Amendment guarantees '[t]he right of the people to be secure in their persons, houses, papers, and effects, against unreasonable searches and seizures.' Temporary detention of individuals during the stop of an automobile by the police, even if only for a brief period and for a limited purpose, constitutes a 'seizure' of 'persons' within the meaning of this provision. . . .

We think [the precedent] cases foreclose any argument that the constitutional reasonableness of traffic stops depends on the actual motivations of the individual officers involved. We of course agree with petitioners that the Constitution prohibits selective enforcement of the law based on considerations such as race. But the constitutional basis for objecting to intentionally discriminatory application of laws is the Equal Protection Clause, not the Fourth Amendment. Subjective intentions play no role in ordinary, probable-cause Fourth Amendment analysis. . . .

It is of course true that in principle every Fourth Amendment case, since it turns upon a 'reasonableness' determination, involves a balancing of all relevant factors. With rare exceptions not applicable here, however, the result of that balancing is not in doubt where the search or seizure is based upon probable cause. . . .

Where probable cause has existed, the only cases in which we have found it necessary actually to perform the 'balancing' analysis involved searches or seizures conducted in an extraordinary manner, unusually harmful to an individual's privacy or even physical interests . . . . The making of a traffic stop out of uniform does not remotely qualify as such an extreme practice, and so is governed by the usual rule that probable cause to believe the law has been broken 'outbalances' private interest in avoiding police contact. . . .

For the run-of-the-mine case, which this surely is, we think there is no realistic alternative to the traditional common-law rule that probable cause justifies a search and seizure. . . .

Here the District Court found that the officers had probable cause to believe that petitioners had violated the traffic code. That rendered the stop reasonable under the Fourth Amendment, the evidence thereby discovered admissible, and the upholding of the convictions by the Court of Appeals for the District of Columbia Circuit correct. The judgment is affirmed."

V. JUSTICE VOTE

0 Pro ACLU Side vs. 9 Con Opposing Side

Opposing Side (Respondent / Appellee)

1. Scalia, A. – Wrote majority opinion
2. Kennedy, A. – Joined majority opinion
3. Rehnquist, W. – Joined majority opinion
4. Breyer, S. – Joined majority opinion
5. Ginsburg, R. – Joined majority opinion
6. Thomas, C. – Joined majority opinion
7. Souter, D. – Joined majority opinion
8. O'Connor, S. – Joined majority opinion
9. Stevens, J. – Joined majority opinion

VI. A WIN OR LOSS FOR THE ACLU?

The ACLU, as amicus curiae, urged reversal of the judgment of the Court of Appeals; the Supreme Court affirmed in a 9-0 vote, giving the ACLU an apparent loss.

802. Shaw v. Hunt

(Decided June 13, 1996; 517 U.S. 899)

I. ISSUE

A. Issues Discussed

Fourteenth Amendment, racial gerrymandering, redistricting

B. Legal Question Presented

Whether North Carolina's redistricting plan violates the Equal Protection Clause of the Fourteenth Amendment.

C. Supreme Court's Answer

The redistricting plan violates the Equal Protection Clause.

II. CASE SUMMARY

A. Background

"This suit is here for a second time. In Shaw v. Reno, 509 U.S. 630 (1993) (Shaw I), [the Supreme Court] held that plaintiffs whose complaint alleged that the deliberate segregation of voters into separate and bizarre-looking districts on the basis of race stated a claim for relief under the Equal Protection Clause of the Fourteenth Amendment. We remanded the case for further consideration by the District Court. That court held that the North Carolina redistricting plan did classify voters by race, but that the classification survived strict scrutiny and therefore did not offend the Constitution. . . .

After the 1990 census, North Carolina's congressional delegation increased from 11 to 12 members. The State General Assembly adopted a reapportionment plan, Chapter 601, that included one majority-black district, District 1, located in the northeastern region of the State. The legislature then submitted the plan to the Attorney General of the United States for preclearance under § 5 of the Voting Rights Act of 1965. The Assistant Attorney General for Civil Rights, acting on the Attorney General's behalf, objected to the proposed plan because it failed 'to give effect to black and Native American voting strength' in 'the south-central to southeastern part of the state' and opined that the State's reasons for not creating a second majority-minority district appeared 'to be pretextual.' Duly chastened, the legislature revised its districting scheme to include a second majority-black district. The new plan, Chapter 7, located the minority district, District 12, in the north-central or Piedmont region, not in the south-central or southeastern region identified in the Justice Department's objection letter. The Attorney General nonetheless precleared the revised plan.

By anyone's measure, the boundary lines of Districts 1 and 12 are unconventional. A map portrays the districts' deviance far better than words . . . .

Five North Carolinians commenced the present action in the United States District Court for the Eastern District of North Carolina against various state officials. Following [the Supreme Court's] reversal of the District Court's dismissal of their complaint in Shaw I, the District Court allowed a number of individuals to intervene, 11 on behalf of the plaintiffs and 22 for the defendants. After a 6–day trial, the District Court unanimously found 'that the Plan's lines were deliberately drawn to produce one or more districts of a certain racial composition.' A majority of the court held that the plan was constitutional, nonetheless, because it was narrowly tailored to further the State's compelling interests in complying with §§ 2 and 5 of the Voting Rights Act, 42 U.S.C. §§ 1973, 1973c."

The Supreme Court granted certiorari to review the case and reversed.

B. Counsel of Record / ACLU Attorney

ACLU Side (Respondent / Appellee): Edwin M. Speas, Jr., Senior Deputy Attorney General of North Carolina, argued the cause for appellees Hunt, et al., in both cases.

Julius L. Chambers argued the cause for appellees Gingles, et al., in both cases.

Deputy Solicitor General Paul Bender argued the cause for the United States, as amicus curiae, by special leave of Court.

Opposing Side (Petitioner / Appellant): Robinson O. Everett and Thomas A. Farr argued the cause for appellants.

III. AMICI CURIAE

ACLU Side (Respondent / Appellee)

Brief of amici curiae filed on behalf of the ACLU, et al., by Laughlin McDonald, Neil Bradley, Maha S. Zaki, Steven R. Shapiro, Paul C. Saunders, Herbert J. Hansell, Barbara R. Arnwine, Thomas J. Henderson, Todd Cox, and Brenda Wright.

Brief of amici curiae filed on behalf of the United States by Deputy Solicitor General Bender, Solicitor General Days, Assistant Attorney General Deval L. Patrick, Beth S. Brinkmann, Steven H Rosenbaum, and Miriam R. Eisenstein.

Brief of amici curiae filed on behalf of the North Carolina Legislative Black Caucus, et al., by Pamela S. Karlan and Eben Moglen.

Brief of amici curiae filed on behalf of the Congressional Black Caucus, et al., by Marcella David, A. Leon Higginbotham, Jr., Gregory A. Clarick, Terri James, and Debo P. Adegbile.

Opposing Side (Petitioner / Appellant)

Brief of amici curiae filed on behalf of the Pacific Legal Foundation by Anthony T. Caso and Deborah J. La Fetra.

IV. THE SUPREME COURT'S DECISION

"Racial classifications are antithetical to the Fourteenth Amendment, whose 'central purpose' was 'to eliminate racial discrimination emanating from official sources in the States.' While appreciating that a racial classification causes 'fundamental injury' to the 'individual rights of a person,' we have recognized that, under certain circumstances, drawing racial distinctions is permissible where a governmental body is pursuing a 'compelling state interest.' A State, however, is constrained in how it may pursue that end: '[T]he means chosen to accomplish the State's asserted purpose must be specifically and narrowly framed to accomplish that purpose.' North Carolina, therefore, must show not only that its redistricting plan was in pursuit of a compelling state interest, but also that 'its districting legislation is narrowly tailored to achieve [that] compelling interest.'

Appellees point to three separate compelling interests to sustain District 12: to eradicate the effects of past and present discrimination; to comply with § 5 of the Voting Rights Act; and to comply with § 2 of that Act. . . .

In this suit, the District Court found that an interest in ameliorating past discrimination did not actually precipitate the use of race in the redistricting plan. . . . Appellees, to support their claim that the plan was drawn to remedy past discrimination, rely on passages from two reports prepared for this litigation by a historian and a social scientist. Obviously these reports, both dated March 1994, were not before the General Assembly when it enacted Chapter 7. And there is little to suggest that the legislature considered the historical events and social-science data that the reports recount, beyond what individual members may have recalled from personal experience. We certainly cannot say on the basis of these reports that the District Court's findings on this point were clearly erroneous.

Appellees devote most of their efforts to arguing that the race-based redistricting was constitutionally justified by the State's duty to comply with the Voting Rights Act. The District Court agreed and held that compliance with §§ 2 and 5 of the Act could be, and in this suit was, a compelling state interest. In Miller, we expressly left open the question whether under the proper circumstances compliance with the Voting Rights Act, on its own, could be a compelling interest. Here once again we do not reach that question because we find that creating an additional majority-black district was not required under a correct reading of § 5 and that District 12, as drawn, is not a remedy narrowly tailored to the State's professed interest in avoiding § 2 liability.

With respect to § 5 of the Voting Rights Act, we believe our decision in Miller forecloses the argument, adopted by the District Court, that failure to engage in the race-based districting would have violated that section. In Miller, we considered an equal protection challenge to Georgia's Eleventh Congressional District. As appellees do here, Georgia contended that its redistricting plan was necessary to meet the Justice Department's preclearance demands. The Justice Department had interposed an objection to a prior plan that created only two majority-minority districts. We held that the challenged congressional plan was not required by a correct reading of § 5 and therefore compliance with that law could not justify race-based districting.

We believe the same conclusion must be drawn here. . . .

We assume, arguendo, for the purpose of resolving this suit, that compliance with § 2 could be a compelling interest, and we likewise assume, arguendo, that the General Assembly believed a second majority-minority district was needed in order not to violate § 2, and that the legislature at the time it acted had a strong basis in evidence to support that conclusion. We hold that even with the benefit of these assumptions, the North Carolina plan does not survive strict scrutiny because the remedy—the creation of District 12—is not narrowly tailored to the asserted end. . . .

For the foregoing reasons, the judgment of the District Court is reversed."

V. JUSTICE VOTE

4 Pro ACLU Side vs. 5 Con Opposing Side

ACLU Side (Respondent / Appellee)

1. Stevens, J. – Wrote dissenting opinion
2. Souter, D. – Wrote dissenting opinion
3. Ginsburg, R. – Joined Stevens' dissent in part, joined Souter's dissent
4. Breyer, S. – Joined Stevens' dissent in part, joined Souter's dissent

Opposing Side (Petitioner / Appellant)

1. Rehnquist, W. – Wrote majority opinion
2. Scalia, A. – Joined majority opinion
3. O'Connor, S. – Joined majority opinion
4. Thomas, C. – Joined majority opinion
5. Kennedy, A. – Joined majority opinion

VI. A WIN OR LOSS FOR THE ACLU?

The ACLU, as amicus curiae, urged affirmance of the judgment of the Court of Appeals; the Supreme Court reversed in a 5-4 vote, giving the ACLU an apparent loss.

803. Lane v. Pena

(Decided June 20, 1996; 518 U.S. 187)

I. ISSUE

A. Issues Discussed

Discrimination, government immunity

B. Legal Question Presented

"[W]hether Congress has waived the Federal Government's sovereign immunity against awards of monetary damages for violations of" § 504(a) of the Rehabilitation Act of 1973.

C. Supreme Court's Answer

Congress has not waived the Federal Government's sovereign immunity against awards of monetary damages for violations of § 504(a) of Rehabilitation Act of 1973.

II. CASE SUMMARY

A. Background

"Petitioner James Griffin Lane entered the [United States Merchant Marine] Academy as a first-year student in July 1991 after meeting the Academy's requirements for appointment, including passing a physical examination conducted by the Department of Defense. During his first year at the Academy, however, Lane was diagnosed by a private physician as having diabetes mellitus. Lane reported the diagnosis to the Academy's Chief Medical Officer. The Academy's Physical Examination Review Board conducted a hearing in September 1992 to determine Lane's 'medical suitability' to continue at the Academy, following which the Board reported to the Superintendent of the Academy that Lane suffered from insulin-dependent diabetes.

In December 1992, Lane was separated from the Academy on the ground that his diabetes was a 'disqualifying condition,' rendering him ineligible to be commissioned for service in the Navy/Merchant Marine Reserve Program or as a Naval Reserve Officer. After unsuccessfully challenging his separation before the Maritime Administrator, Lane brought suit in Federal District Court against the Secretary of the Department of Transportation and other defendants, alleging that his separation from the Academy violated § 504(a) of the Rehabilitation Act, 29 U.S.C. § 794(a). He sought reinstatement to the Academy, compensatory damages, attorney's fees, and costs.

The District Court granted summary judgment in favor of Lane, concluding that his separation from the Academy solely on the basis of his diabetes violated the Act. The court ordered Lane reinstated to the Academy, and the Government did not dispute the propriety of this injunctive relief. The Government did, however, dispute the propriety of a compensatory damages award, claiming that the United States was protected against a damages suit by the doctrine of sovereign immunity. The District Court disagreed; it ruled that Lane was entitled to a compensatory damages award against the Government for its violation of § 504(a), but deferred resolution of the specific amount of damages due.

Shortly thereafter, however, the Court of Appeals for the District of Columbia Circuit ruled in Dorsey v. United States Dept. of

Labor, 41 F.3d 1551 (1994), that the Act did not waive the Federal Government's sovereign immunity against monetary damages for violations of § 504(a). The court denied compensatory damages based on the absence, in any statutory text, of an 'unequivocal expression' of congressional intent to waive the Government's immunity as to monetary damages, and this Court's instruction that waivers of sovereign immunity may not be implied.

In light of Dorsey, the District Court vacated its prior order to the extent that it awarded damages to Lane and held that Lane was not entitled to a compensatory damages award against the Federal Government. Lane appealed. The Court of Appeals for the District of Columbia Circuit first rejected Lane's request for initial en banc review to reconsider Dorsey, then granted the Government's motion for summary affirmance."

The Supreme Court granted certiorari to review the case and affirmed.

B. Counsel of Record / ACLU Attorney

ACLU Side (Petitioner / Appellant): Walter A. Smith, Jr., argued the cause for appellant. With him on the briefs were Daniel B. Kohrman, Audrey J. Anderson, Arthur B. Spitzer, and Steven R. Shapiro.

Opposing Side (Respondent / Appellee): Beth S. Brinkmann argued the cause for appellees. With her on the brief were Solicitor General Days, Assistant Attorney General Hunger, Deputy Solicitor General Bender, Barbara C. Biddle, Deborah Ruth Kant, and Christine N. Kohl.

III. AMICI CURIAE

ACLU Side (Petitioner / Appellant)

Brief of amici curiae filed on behalf of the American Association of Retired Persons, et al., by Linda D. Kilb, Arlene B. Mayerson, Vicki Laden, Jennifer Middleton, and Patricia Shiu.

Brief of amici curiae filed on behalf of the American Diabetes Association by Michael A. Greene and Jerry W. Lee.

Opposing Side (Respondent / Appellee)

No briefs of amici curiae were filed in support of appellee.

IV. THE SUPREME COURT'S DECISION

"The clarity of expression necessary to establish a waiver of the Government's sovereign immunity against monetary damages for violations of § 504 is lacking in the text of the relevant provisions. . . .

Given the existence of a statutory provision that is directed precisely to the remedies available for violations of § 504, it would be a curious application of our sovereign immunity jurisprudence to conclude, as the dissent appears to do, that the lack of clear reference to Executive agencies in any express remedies provision indicates congressional intent to subject the Federal Government to monetary damages. . . .

Section 1003(a) is not so free from ambiguity that we can comfortably conclude, based thereon, that Congress intended to subject the Federal Government to awards of monetary damages for violations of § 504(a) of the Act. Given the care with which Congress responded to our decision in Atascadero by crafting an unambiguous waiver of the States' Eleventh Amendment immunity in § 1003, it would be ironic indeed to conclude that that same provision 'unequivocally' establishes a waiver of the Federal Government's sovereign immunity against monetary damages awards by means of an admittedly ambiguous reference to 'public . . . entit[ies]' in the remedies provision attached to the unambiguous waiver of the States' sovereign immunity.

For the reasons stated, the judgment of the Court of Appeals for the District of Columbia Circuit is affirmed."

V. JUSTICE VOTE

2 Pro ACLU Side vs. 7 Con Opposing Side

ACLU Side (Petitioner / Appellant)

1. Stevens, J. – Wrote dissenting opinion
2. Breyer, S. – Joined Stevens' dissent

Opposing Side (Respondent / Appellee)

1. O'Connor, S. – Wrote majority opinion
2. Ginsburg, R. – Joined majority opinion
3. Thomas, C. – Joined majority opinion
4. Souter, D. – Joined majority opinion
5. Rehnquist, W. – Joined majority opinion
6. Scalia, A. – Joined majority opinion
7. Kennedy, A. – Joined majority opinion

VI. A WIN OR LOSS FOR THE ACLU?

The ACLU, as counsel of record, urged reversal of the judgment of the Court of Appeals for the District of Columbia Circuit; the Supreme Court affirmed in a 7-2 vote, giving the ACLU an apparent loss.

804. United States v. Ursery

(Decided June 24, 1996; 518 U.S. 267)

I. ISSUE

A. Issues Discussed

Fifth Amendment, double jeopardy

B. Legal Question Presented

Whether civil property forfeitures constitute "punishment" for purposes of the Double Jeopardy Clause.

C. Supreme Court's Answer

Civil property forfeitures do not constitute "punishment" for purposes of the Double Jeopardy Clause and are therefore permitted.

II. CASE SUMMARY

A. Background

"No. 95-345: Michigan Police found marijuana growing adjacent to respondent Guy Ursery's house, and discovered marijuana seeds, stems, stalks, and a grow light within the house. The United States instituted civil forfeiture proceedings against the house, alleging that the property was subject to forfeiture under 84 Stat.

1276, as amended, 21 U.S.C. § 881(a)(7), because it had been used for several years to facilitate the unlawful processing and distribution of a controlled substance. Ursery ultimately paid the United States $13,250 to settle the forfeiture claim in full. Shortly before the settlement was consummated, Ursery was indicted for manufacturing marijuana, in violation of § 841(a)(1). A jury found him guilty, and he was sentenced to 63 months in prison.

The Court of Appeals for the Sixth Circuit by a divided vote reversed Ursery's criminal conviction, holding that the conviction violated the Double Jeopardy Clause of the Fifth Amendment of the United States Constitution. . . .

No. 95-346: Following a jury trial, Charles Wesley Arlt and James Wren were convicted of: conspiracy to aid and abet the manufacture of methamphetamine, in violation of 21 U.S.C. § 846; conspiracy to launder monetary instruments, in violation of 18 U.S.C. § 371; and numerous counts of money laundering, in violation of § 1956. The District Court sentenced Arlt to life in prison and a 10-year term of supervised release, and imposed a fine of $250,000. Wren was sentenced to life imprisonment and a 5-year term of supervised release.

Before the criminal trial had started, the United States had filed a civil in rem complaint against various property seized from, or titled to, Arlt and Wren, or Payback Mines, a corporation controlled by Arlt. . . . The parties agreed to defer litigation of the forfeiture action during the criminal prosecution. More than a year after the conclusion of the criminal trial, the District Court granted the Government's motion for summary judgment in the civil forfeiture proceeding.

Arlt and Wren appealed the decision in the forfeiture action, and the Court of Appeals for the Ninth Circuit reversed, holding that the forfeiture violated the Double Jeopardy Clause."

The Supreme Court granted certiorari to review both cases and reversed.

B. Counsel of Record / ACLU Attorney

ACLU Side (Respondent / Appellee): Jeffry K. Finer and Lawrence S. Robbins argued the cause for appellees.

Opposing Side (Petitioner / Appellant): Deputy Solicitor General Michael R. Dreeben argued the cause for the United States in both cases.

III. AMICI CURIAE

ACLU Side (Respondent / Appellee)

Brief of amici curiae filed on behalf of the ACLU by Susan N. Herman, Gerard E. Lynch, Stacy Caplow, and Steven R. Shapiro.

Brief of amici curiae filed on behalf of Americans for Effective Law Enforcement, Inc., et al., by Fred E. Inbau, Wayne W. Schmidt, James P. Manak, Richard M. Weintraub, Roy C. Kime, and Bernard J. Farber.

Brief of amici curiae filed on behalf of the National Association of Criminal Defense Lawyers by Richard J. Troberman, Brooks R. Fudenberg, Tamara R. Piety, and David B. Smith.

Brief of amici curiae filed on behalf of Advocates for Highway and Auto Safety, et al., by Henry M. Jasny.

Opposing Side (Petitioner / Appellant)

Brief of amici curiae filed on behalf of the State of Connecticut, et al., by John M. Bailey, Chief State's Attorney of Connecticut, and Mary H. Lesser, Assistant State's Attorney, and by the Attorneys General for their respective jurisdictions as follows: Jeff Sessions of Alabama, Bruce M. Botelho of Alaska, Grant Woods of Arizona, Winston Bryant of Arkansas, Daniel E. Lungren of California, Gale A. Norton of Colorado, M. Jane Brady of Delaware, Robert A. Butterworth of Florida, Michael J. Bowers of Georgia, Margery S. Bronster of Hawaii, Alan G. Lance of Idaho, Jim Ryan of Illinois, Pamela Carter of Indiana, Tom Miller of Iowa, Carla J. Stovall of Kansas, A. B. Chandler III of Kentucky,Richard P. Ieyoub of Louisiana, Andrew Ketterer of Maine, J. Joseph Curran, Jr., of Maryland, Scott Harshbarger of Massachusetts, Frank J. Kelley of Michigan, Hubert H. Humphrey III of Minnesota, Mike Moore of Mississippi, Joseph P. Mazurek of Montana, Don Stenberg of Nebraska, Frankie Sue Del Papa of Nevada, Jeffrey R. Howard of New Hampshire, Deborah T. Poritz of New Jersey, Tom Udall of New Mexico, Dennis C. Vacco of New York, Michael F. Easley of North Carolina, Heidi Heitkamp of North Dakota, Betty D. Montgomery of Ohio, Drew Edmondson of Oklahoma, Theodore R. Kulongoski of Oregon, Thomas W. Corbett, Jr., of Pennsylvania, Pedro R. Pierluisi of Puerto Rico, Jeffrey B. Pine of Rhode Island, Charles Molony Condon of South Carolina, Mark W. Barnett of South Dakota, Charles W. Burson of Tennessee, Dan Morales of Texas, Jan Graham of Utah, Jeffrey L. Amestoy of Vermont, James S. Gilmore III of Virginia, Christine O. Gregoire of Washington, James E. Doyle of Wisconsin, and William U. Hill of Wyoming.

Brief of amici curiae filed on behalf of the County of San Bernardino, California, et al., by Dennis L. Stout, Dee R. Edgeworth, Michael J. Yraceburn, Phillip R. Urie, and Armando G. Cuellar, Jr.

Brief of amici curiae filed on behalf of the Cook County State's Attorney's Office, et al., by Jack O'Malley, Renee Goldfarb, and Janet Powers Doyle.

Brief of amici curiae filed on behalf of the Thirty-nine Counties of the State of Washington by Norm Maleng, Barbara A. Mack, David Sandhaus, Ray Lutes, Andrew K. Miller, Gary Riesen, David Bruneau, Arthur Curtis, Terry Nealey, Jim Stonier, Steven M. Clem, Allen C. Nielson, Steve M. Lowe, John Henry, John Knodell, Stew Menefee, William H. Hawkins, David Skeen, Russ Hauge, Greg Zempel, Knute Rife, Jeremy Randolf, Ron Shepherd, Gary Burleson, Rick Weeber, Michael Smith, Thomas Metzger, John Ladenburg, Randall K. Gaylord, David Needy, Bradley Anderson, Jim Krider, Jim Sweetser, John G. Wetle, Bernardean Broadous, Fred A. Johnson, David S. McEachman, James Kaufman, James L. Nagle, and Jeffrey C. Sullivan.

IV. THE SUPREME COURT'S DECISION

"Our cases reviewing civil forfeitures under the Double Jeopardy Clause adhere to a remarkably consistent theme. Though the two-part analytical construct employed in 89 Firearms was more refined, perhaps, than that we had used over 50 years earlier in

Various Items, the conclusion was the same in each case: In rem civil forfeiture is a remedial civil sanction, distinct from potentially punitive in personam civil penalties such as fines, and does not constitute a punishment under the Double Jeopardy Clause.

In the cases that we currently review, the Court of Appeals for the Ninth Circuit recognized as much, concluding that after 89 Firearms, 'the law was clear that civil forfeitures did not constitute 'punishment' for double jeopardy purposes.' Nevertheless, that court read three of our decisions to have 'abandoned' 89 Firearms and the oft-affirmed rule of Various Items. . . .

We think that the Court of Appeals for the Sixth Circuit and the Court of Appeals for the Ninth Circuit misread Halper, Austin, and Kurth Ranch. None of those decisions purported to overrule the well-established teaching of Various Items, Emerald Cut Stones, and 89 Firearms. Halper involved not a civil forfeiture, but a civil penalty. That its rule was limited to the latter context is clear from the decision itself, from the historical distinction that we have drawn between civil forfeiture and civil penalties, and from the practical difficulty of applying Halper to a civil forfeiture. . . .

In sum, nothing in Halper, Kurth Ranch, or Austin purported to replace our traditional understanding that civil forfeiture does not constitute punishment for the purpose of the Double Jeopardy Clause. Congress long has authorized the Government to bring parallel criminal proceedings and civil forfeiture proceedings, and this Court consistently has found civil forfeitures not to constitute punishment under the Double Jeopardy Clause. It would have been quite remarkable for this Court both to have held unconstitutional a well-established practice, and to have overruled a long line of precedent, without having even suggested that it was doing so. Halper dealt with in personam civil penalties under the Double Jeopardy Clause; Kurth Ranch with a tax proceeding under the Double Jeopardy Clause; and Austin with civil forfeitures under the Excessive Fines Clause. None of those cases dealt with the subject of these cases: in rem civil forfeitures for purposes of the Double Jeopardy Clause. . . .

We hold that these in rem civil forfeitures are neither 'punishment' nor criminal for purposes of the Double Jeopardy Clause. The judgments of the Court of Appeals for the Sixth Circuit, in No. 95-345, and of the Court of Appeals for the Ninth Circuit, in No. 95-346, are, accordingly, reversed."

V. JUSTICE VOTE

1 Pro ACLU Side vs. 8 Con Opposing Side

ACLU Side (Respondent / Appellee)

1. Stevens, J. – Wrote opinion concurring in part and dissenting in part

Opposing Side (Petitioner / Appellant)

1. Rehnquist, W. – Wrote majority opinion
2. Breyer, S. – Joined majority opinion
3. Ginsburg, R. – Joined majority opinion
4. Thomas, C. – Joined Scalia's concurrence
5. Souter, D. – Joined majority opinion
6. O'Connor, S. – Joined majority opinion
7. Kennedy, A. – Wrote concurring opinion
8. Scalia, A. – Wrote concurring opinion

VI. A WIN OR LOSS FOR THE ACLU?

The ACLU, as amicus curiae, urged affirmance of the judgments of the Court of Appeals for the Sixth Circuit and Ninth Circuit; the Supreme Court reversed in an 8-1 vote, giving the ACLU an apparent loss.

805. Lewis v. United States

(Decided June 24, 1996; 518 U.S. 322)

I. ISSUE

A. Issues Discussed

Sixth Amendment, right to jury trial, petty offenses

B. Legal Question Presented

"[W]hether a defendant who is prosecuted in a single proceeding for multiple petty offenses has a constitutional right to a jury trial where the aggregate prison term authorized for the offenses exceeds six months." "[W]hether a defendant who would otherwise have a constitutional right to a jury trial may be denied that right because the presiding judge has made a pretrial commitment that the aggregate sentence imposed will not exceed six months."

C. Supreme Court's Answer

"We conclude that no jury trial right exists where a defendant is prosecuted for multiple petty offenses. The Sixth Amendment's guarantee of the right to a jury trial does not extend to petty offenses, and its scope does not change where a defendant faces a potential aggregate prison term in excess of six months for petty offenses charged. Because we decide that no jury trial right exists where a defendant is charged with multiple petty offenses, we do not reach the second question.

II. CASE SUMMARY

A. Background

"Petitioner Ray Lewis was a mail handler for the United States Postal Service. One day, postal inspectors saw him open several pieces of mail and pocket the contents. The next day, the inspectors routed 'test' mail, containing marked currency, through petitioner's station. After seeing petitioner open the mail and remove the currency, the inspectors arrested him. Petitioner was charged with two counts of obstructing the mail, in violation of 18 U.S.C. § 1701. Each count carried a maximum authorized prison sentence of six months. Petitioner requested a jury, but the Magistrate Judge granted the Government's motion for a bench trial. She explained that because she would not, under any circumstances, sentence petitioner to more than six months' imprisonment, he was not entitled to a jury trial.

Petitioner sought review of the denial of a jury trial, and the District Court affirmed. Petitioner appealed, and the Court of Appeals for the Second Circuit affirmed. The court noted that the Sixth Amendment jury trial right pertains only to serious offenses, that is, those for which the legislature has authorized a maximum penalty of over six months' imprisonment. The court then addressed the question whether a defendant facing more than six months' imprisonment in the aggregate for multiple petty offenses is nevertheless entitled to a jury trial. The Court of Appeals concluded that, for determination of the right to a jury trial, the proper focus is on the legislature's determination regarding the character of the offense, as indicated by maximum penalty authorized, not on the length of the maximum aggregate sentence faced. Because each offense charged here was petty in character, the court concluded that petitioner was not entitled to a jury trial.

The court explained in dictum that because the character of the offense as petty or serious determined the right to a jury trial, not the sentence faced, a trial judge's self-imposed limitation on sentencing could not deprive a defendant of the right to a jury trial."

The Supreme Court granted certiorari to review the case and affirmed.

B. Counsel of Record / ACLU Attorney

ACLU Side (Petitioner / Appellant): Steven M. Statsinger argued the cause for appellant.

Opposing Side (Respondent / Appellee): Cornelia T. L. Pillard argued the cause for the United States.

III. AMICI CURIAE

ACLU Side (Petitioner / Appellant)

Brief of amici curiae filed on behalf of the National Legal Aid and Defender Association, the National Association of Criminal Defense Lawyers, the ACLU, and District of Columbia, by David A. Reiser, John Vanderstar, Jeffrey B. Coopersmith, Steven R. Shapiro, Arthur B. Spitzer, James W. Klein, Jamie S. Gardner, and John M. Copacino.

Brief of amici curiae filed on behalf of the Jury Trial Group by Colin Dunham and Christopher Warnock.

Opposing Side (Respondent / Appellee)

No briefs of amici curiae were filed in support of appellee.

IV. THE SUPREME COURT'S DECISION

"It is well established that the Sixth Amendment, like the common law, reserves this jury trial right for prosecutions of serious offenses, and that 'there is a category of petty crimes or offenses which is not subject to the Sixth Amendment jury trial provision.' . . .

Now, to determine whether an offense is petty, we consider the maximum penalty attached to the offense. This criterion is considered the most relevant with which to assess the character of an offense, because it reveals the legislature's judgment about the offense's severity. . . .

An offense carrying a maximum prison term of six months or less is presumed petty, unless the legislature has authorized additional statutory penalties so severe as to indicate that the legislature considered the offense serious.

Here, the maximum authorized penalty for obstruction of mail is six months' imprisonment—a penalty that presumptively places the offense in the 'petty' category. We face the question whether petitioner is nevertheless entitled to a jury trial, because he was tried in a single proceeding for two counts of the petty offense so that the potential aggregated penalty is 12 months' imprisonment. . . .

Where we have a judgment by the legislature that an offense is 'petty,' we do not look to the potential prison term faced by a particular defendant who is charged with more than one such petty offense. The maximum authorized penalty provides an 'objective indicatio[n] of the seriousness with which society regards the offense,' and it is that indication that is used to determine whether a jury trial is required, not the particularities of an individual case. Here, the penalty authorized by Congress manifests its judgment that the offense is petty, and the term of imprisonment faced by petitioner by virtue of the second count does not alter that fact. . . .

Certainly the aggregate potential penalty faced by petitioner is of serious importance to him. But to determine whether an offense is serious for Sixth Amendment purposes, we look to the legislature's judgment, as evidenced by the maximum penalty authorized. Where the offenses charged are petty, and the deprivation of liberty exceeds six months only as a result of the aggregation of charges, the jury trial right does not apply. As petitioner acknowledges, even if he were to prevail, the Government could properly circumvent the jury trial right by charging the counts in separate informations and trying them separately.

The Constitution's guarantee of the right to a jury trial extends only to serious offenses, and petitioner was not charged with a serious offense. That he was tried for two counts of a petty offense, and therefore faced an aggregate potential term of imprisonment of more than six months, does not change the fact that the Legislature deemed this offense petty. Petitioner is not entitled to a jury trial.

Because petitioner is not entitled to a jury trial, we need not reach the question whether a judge's self-imposed limitation on sentencing may affect the jury trial right.

The judgment of the Court of Appeals for the Second Circuit is affirmed."

V. JUSTICE VOTE

2 Pro ACLU Side vs. 7 Con Opposing Side

ACLU Side (Petitioner / Appellant)

1. Stevens, J. – Wrote dissenting opinion
2. Ginsburg, R. – Joined Stevens' dissent

Opposing Side (Respondent / Appellee)

1. O'Connor, S. – Wrote majority opinion
2. Kennedy, A. – Wrote concurring opinion
3. Breyer, S. – Joined Kennedy's concurrence
4. Thomas, C. – Joined majority opinion
5. Souter, D. – Joined majority opinion
6. Rehnquist, W. – Joined majority opinion
7. Scalia, A. – Joined majority opinion

VI. A WIN OR LOSS FOR THE ACLU?

The ACLU, as amicus curiae, urged reversal of the judgment of the Court of Appeals for the Second Circuit; the Supreme Court affirmed in a 7-2 vote, giving the ACLU an apparent loss.

806. Lewis v. Casey

(Decided June 24, 1996; 518 U.S. 343)

I. ISSUE

A. Issues Discussed

Due process, prisoners' rights

B. Legal Question Presented

"[W]hether the District Court's order 'exceeds the constitutional requirements set forth in Bounds.'"

C. Supreme Court's Answer

The order exceeds the constitutional requirements in Bounds for adequate access to a law library and legal assistance for prisoners.

II. CASE SUMMARY

A. Background

"Respondents are 22 inmates of various prisons operated by [the Arizona Department of Corrections (ADOC)]. In January 1990, they filed this class action 'on behalf of all adult prisoners who are or will be incarcerated by the State of Arizona Department of Corrections,' alleging that petitioners were "depriving [respondents] of their rights of access to the courts and counsel protected by the First, Sixth, and Fourteenth Amendments.' Following a 3-month bench trial, the District Court ruled in favor of respondents, finding that '[p]risoners have a constitutional right of access to the courts that is adequate, effective and meaningful,' and that '[ADOC's] system fails to comply with constitutional standards.' . . .

Having thus found liability, the court appointed a Special Master 'to investigate and report about' the appropriate relief—that is (in the court's view), 'how best to accomplish the goal of constitutionally adequate inmate access to the courts.' Following eight months of investigation, and some degree of consultation with both parties, the Special Master lodged with the court a proposed permanent injunction, which the court proceeded to adopt, substantially unchanged. The 25-page injunctive order mandated sweeping changes designed to ensure that ADOC would 'provide meaningful access to the Courts for all present and future prisoners.' . . .

Petitioners sought review in the Court of Appeals for the Ninth Circuit, which refused to grant a stay prior to argument. [The Supreme Court] then stayed the injunction pending filing and disposition of a petition for a writ of certiorari. Several months later, the Ninth Circuit affirmed both the finding of a Bounds violation and, with minor exceptions not important here, the terms of the injunction."

The Supreme Court granted certiorari to review the case and reversed.

B. Counsel of Record / ACLU Attorney

ACLU Side (Respondent / Appellee): Elizabeth Alexander argued the cause for appellees. With her on the brief were Ayesha Khan, Margaret Winter, Alvin J. Bronstein, Alice L. Bendheim, and Steven R. Shapiro.

Opposing Side (Petitioner / Appellant): Grant Woods, Attorney General of Arizona, argued the cause for appellants. With him on the briefs were Daniel P. Struck, David C. Lewis, Eileen J. Dennis, Rex E. Lee, Carter G. Phillips, Mark D. Hopson, C. Tim Delaney, Rebecca White Berch, Katherine Wieneke, Jacquelien Gerson, and Thomas J. Dennis.

III. AMICI CURIAE

ACLU Side (Respondent / Appellee)

Brief of amici curiae filed on behalf of the United States by Solicitor General Days, Assistant Attorney General Patrick, Deputy Solicitor General Bender, Alan Jenkins, Steven H. Rosenbaum, Louise A. Lerner, and Rebecca K. Troth.

Brief of amici curiae filed on behalf of the Legal Aid Bureau, Inc., by Stuart R. Cohen, Emily Miller Rody, Frances E. Kessler, Joseph B. Tetrault, and Jeffery C. Taylor.

Brief of amici curiae filed on behalf of the Mexican American Legal Defense and Educational Fund, et al., by David Fernandez, Lisa Dorio Ruch, Kenneth Padilla, and Michael R. Cole.

Brief of amici curiae filed on behalf of North Carolina Prisoner Legal Services, Inc., by Ollie H. Taylor and Richard E. Giroux.

Brief of amici curiae filed on behalf of Prison Legal Services of Michigan by Barbara R. Levine and Sandra L. Girard.

Brief of amici curiae filed on behalf of Prisoners in Northern California by Sanford Jay Rosen, Amitai Schwartz, Antonio Ponvert, III, David Steuer, Robert Fabela, and Donald Specter.

Opposing Side (Petitioner / Appellant)

Brief of amici curiae filed on behalf of the State of California, et al., by Daniel Lungren, Attorney General of California, Peter J. Siggins, Senior Assistant Attorney General, Morris Lenk, Senior Supervising Attorney General, and Karl S. Mayer and Bruce M. Slavin, Deputy Attorneys General, by Garland Pinkston, Jr., Acting Corporation Counsel of the District of Columbia, and by the Attorneys General for their respective jurisdictions as follows: Bruce M. Botelho of Alaska, Richard Blumenthal of Connecticut, M. Jane Brady of Delaware, Robert A. Butterworth of Florida, Michael J. Bowers of Georgia, Robert A. Marks of Hawaii, Alan G. Lance of Idaho, James E. Ryan of Illinois, Pamela Carter of Indiana, Carla J. Stovall of Kansas, J. Joseph Curran, Jr., of Maryland, Scott Harshbarger of Massachusetts, Frank J. Kelley of Michigan, Hubert H. Humphrey III of Minnesota, Jeremiah W. (Jay) Nixon of Missouri, Joe Mazurek of Montana, Don Stenberg of Nebraska, Frankie Sue Del Papa of Nevada, Jeffrey R. Howard of New Hampshire, Tom Udall of New Mexico, Dennis C. Vacco of New York, Betty Montgomery of Ohio, Theodore R. Kulongoski of Oregon, Walter W. Cohen of Pennsylvania, Jeffrey B. Pine of Rhode Island, Charles W. Burson of Tennessee, Jan Graham of Utah, James S. Gilmore III of Virginia, Christine O. Gregoire of Washington, James E. Doyle of Wisconsin, and William U. Hill of Wyoming.

Brief of amici curiae filed on behalf of the National Conference of State Legislatures, et al., by Richard Ruda and Charles Rothfeld.

Brief of amici curiae filed on behalf of the Criminal Justice Legal Foundation by Kent S. Scheidegger and Charles L. Hobson.
Brief of amici curiae filed on behalf of the Washington Legal Foundation, et al., by Charles J. Cooper, Michael A. Carvin, Michael W. Kirk, Daniel J. Popeo, and Paul D. Kamenar.

IV. THE SUPREME COURT'S DECISION

"Apart from the dismissal of Bartholic's claim with prejudice, and Harris's inability to file his claim, there is no finding, and as far as we can discern from the record no evidence, that in Arizona prisons illiterate prisoners cannot obtain the minimal help necessary to file particular claims that they wish to bring before the courts. The constitutional violation has not been shown to be systemwide, and granting a remedy beyond what was necessary to provide relief to Harris and Bartholic was therefore improper. . . .

As Bounds was an exemplar of what should be done, this case is a model of what should not. The District Court totally failed to heed the admonition of Preiser. Having found a violation of the right of access to the courts, it conferred upon its special master, a law professor from Flushing, New York, rather than upon ADOC officials, the responsibility for devising a remedial plan. To make matters worse, it severely limited the remedies that the master could choose. Because, in the court's view, its order in an earlier access-to-courts case (an order that adopted the recommendations of the same special master) had 'resolved successfully' most of the issues involved in this litigation, the court instructed that as to those issues it would implement the earlier order statewide, 'with any modifications that the parties and Special Master determine are necessary due to the particular circumstances of the prison facility.' This will not do. The State was entitled to far more than an opportunity for rebuttal, and on that ground alone this order would have to be set aside.

For the foregoing reasons, we reverse the judgment of the Court of Appeals and remand the case for further proceedings consistent with this opinion."

V. JUSTICE VOTE

1 Pro ACLU Side vs. 8 Con Opposing Side

ACLU Side (Respondent / Appellee)

1. Stevens, J. – Wrote dissenting opinion

Opposing Side (Petitioner / Appellant)

1. Scalia, A. – Wrote majority opinion
2. Rehnquist, W. – Joined majority opinion
3. Breyer, S. – Joined Souter's concurrence
4. Ginsburg, R. – Joined Souter's concurrence
5. Thomas, C. – Wrote concurring opinion
6. Souter, D. – Wrote concurring opinion
7. O'Connor, S. – Joined majority opinion
8. Kennedy, A. – Joined majority opinion

VI. A WIN OR LOSS FOR THE ACLU?

The ACLU, as counsel of record, urged affirmance of the judgment of the Court of Appeals; the Supreme Court reversed and remanded in an 8-1 vote, giving the ACLU an apparent loss.

807. United States v. Virginia

(Decided June 26, 1996; 518 U.S. 515)

I. ISSUE

A. Issues Discussed

Fourteenth Amendment, equal protection, gender discrimination

B. Legal Question Presented

"First, does Virginia's exclusion of women from the educational opportunities provided by VMI—extraordinary opportunities for military training and civilian leadership development—deny to women 'capable of all of the individual activities required of VMI cadets,' the equal protection of the laws guaranteed by the Fourteenth Amendment? Second, if VMI's 'unique' situation—as Virginia's sole single-sex public institution of higher education—offends the Constitution's equal protection principle, what is the remedial requirement?"

C. Supreme Court's Answer

Virginia's exclusion of women from VMI violates equal protection and the remedial plan creating a separate institution for women does not remedy the violation.

II. CASE SUMMARY

A. Background

"From its establishment in 1839 as one of the Nation's first state military colleges, [Virginia Military Institute (VMI)] has remained financially supported by Virginia and 'subject to the control of the [Virginia] General Assembly.' . . .

In 1990, prompted by a complaint filed with the Attorney General by a female high-school student seeking admission to VMI, the United States sued the Commonwealth of Virginia and VMI, alleging that VMI's exclusively male admission policy violated the Equal Protection Clause of the Fourteenth Amendment. Trial of the action consumed six days and involved an array of expert witnesses on each side. . . . The District Court ruled in favor of VMI . . . and rejected the equal protection challenge pressed by the United States. . . .

The Court of Appeals for the Fourth Circuit disagreed and vacated the District Court's judgment. The appellate court held: 'The Commonwealth of Virginia has not . . . advanced any state policy by which it can justify its determination, under an announced policy of diversity, to afford VMI's unique type of program to men and not to women.' . . . The Court of Appeals, however, accepted the District Court's finding that 'at least these three aspects of VMI's program—physical training, the absence of privacy, and the adversative approach—would be materially affected by coeducation.' Remanding the case, the appeals court assigned to Virginia, in the first instance, responsibility for selecting a remedial course. The court suggested these options for the Commonwealth: Admit women to VMI; establish parallel institutions or programs; or abandon state support, leaving VMI free to pursue its policies as a private institution. In May 1993, [the Supreme] Court denied certiorari. . . .

In response to the Fourth Circuit's ruling, Virginia proposed a parallel program for women: Virginia Women's Institute for Leadership (VWIL). . . . Virginia returned to the District Court seeking approval of its proposed remedial plan, and the court decided the plan met the requirements of the Equal Protection Clause. . . . A divided Court of Appeals affirmed the District Court's judgment. . . . The Fourth Circuit denied rehearing en banc."

The Supreme Court granted certiorari to review the case, affirmed the initial judgment of the Court of Appeals, and reversed the second judgment of the Court of Appeals.

B. Counsel of Record / ACLU Attorney

ACLU Side (Petitioner / Appellant in No. 94-1941, Respondent / Appellee in No. 94-2107):

Deputy Solicitor General Paul Bender argued the cause for the United States in both cases.

Opposing Side (Respondent / Appellee in No. 94-1941, Petitioner / Appellant in No. 94-2107):

Theodore B. Olson argued the cause and filed briefs for appellees in No. 94-1941 and appellants in No. 94-2107.

III. AMICI CURIAE

ACLU Side (Petitioner / Appellant in No. 94-1941, Respondent / Appellee in No. 94-2107):

Brief of amici curiae urging reversal in No. 94-1941 filed on behalf of the National Women's Law Center, the ACLU, et al., by Robert N. Weiner, Marcia D. Greenberger, Deborah L. Brake, Judith Applebaum, Nancy L. Perkins, Peter G. Neiman, L. Elizabeth Bowles, Roberto J. Sanchez-Ramos, Wendy W. Williams, Deborah Epstein, Sara L. Mandelbaum, Janet Gallagher, Mary Wyckoff, Steven R. Shapiro, and Susan Deller Ross.

Brief of amici curiae urging reversal in No. 94-1941 filed on behalf of the State of Maryland, et al., by J. Joseph Curran, Jr., Attorney General of Maryland, and Andrew H. Baida, Assistant Attorney General, and by the Attorneys General for their respective jurisdictions as follows: Margery S. Bronster of Hawaii, Scott Harshbarger of Massachusetts, Frankie Sue Del Papa of Nevada, C. Sebastian Aloot of the Northern Mariana Islands, and Theodore R. Kulongoski of Oregon.

Additional briefs of amici curiae were filed on behalf of the Employment Law Center, et al., the American Association of University Professors, et al., Lieutenant Colonel Rhonda Cornum, et al., Nancy Mellette, the Employment Law Center, et al., the Lawyers' Committee for Civil Rights Under Law, and Bennett College, et al.

Opposing Side (Respondent / Appellee in No. 94-1941, Petitioner / Appellant in No. 94-2107):

Brief of amici curiae urging affirmance in No. 94-1941 filed on behalf of the State of South Carolina, et al., by Charles Molony Condon, Attorney General, Treva Ashworth, Deputy Attorney General, Kenneth P. Woodington, Senior Assistant Attorney General, Reginald I. Lloyd, Assistant Attorney General, and M. Dawes Cooke, Jr.

Brief of amici curiae in support of the Commonwealth of Virginia in both cases filed on behalf of the State of Wyoming, et al., by Bradley B. Cavedo, William U. Hill, Attorney General of Wyoming, and Thomas W. Corbett, Jr., Attorney General of Pennsylvania.

Additional briefs of amici curiae were filed on behalf of Wells College, et al., Dr. Kenneth E. Clark, et al., the Center for Military Readiness, et al., the South Caroline Institute of Leadership for Women, the Independent Women's Forum, et al., Mary Baldwin College, and Women's Schools Together, Inc., et al.

IV. THE SUPREME COURT'S DECISION

"Parties who seek to defend gender-based government action must demonstrate an 'exceedingly persuasive justification' for that action. . . . Measuring the record in this case against the review standard . . . , we conclude that Virginia has shown no 'exceedingly persuasive justification' for excluding all women from the citizen-soldier training afforded by VMI. We therefore affirm the Fourth Circuit's initial judgment, which held that Virginia had violated the Fourteenth Amendment's Equal Protection Clause. Because the remedy proffered by Virginia—the Mary Baldwin VWIL program—does not cure the constitutional violation, i.e., it does not provide equal opportunity, we reverse the Fourth Circuit's final judgment in this case. . . .

In sum, we find no persuasive evidence in this record that VMI's male-only admission policy 'is in furtherance of a state policy of 'diversity.'' No such policy, the Fourth Circuit observed, can be discerned from the movement of all other public colleges and universities in Virginia away from single-sex education. That court also questioned 'how one institution with autonomy, but with no authority over any other state institution, can give effect to a state policy of diversity among institutions.' A purpose genuinely to advance an array of educational options, as the Court of Appeals recognized, is not served by VMI's historic and constant plan—a plan to 'affor[d] a unique educational benefit only to males.' However 'liberally' this plan serves the Commonwealth's sons, it makes no provision whatever for her daughters. That is not equal protection. . . .

The Fourth Circuit plainly erred in exposing Virginia's VWIL plan to a deferential analysis, for 'all gender-based classifications today' warrant 'heightened scrutiny.' Valuable as VWIL may prove for students who seek the program offered, Virginia's remedy affords no cure at all for the opportunities and advantages withheld from women who want a VMI education and can make the grade. In sum, Virginia's remedy does not match the constitutional violation; the Commonwealth has shown no 'exceedingly persuasive justification' for withholding from women qualified for the experience premier training of the kind VMI affords. . . .

For the reasons stated, the initial judgment of the Court of Appeals is affirmed, the final judgment of the Court of Appeals is reversed, and the case is remanded for further proceedings consistent with this opinion."

V. JUSTICE VOTE

7 Pro ACLU Side vs. 1 Con Opposing Side

ACLU Side (Petitioner / Appellant in No. 94-1941, Respondent / Appellee in No. 94-2107):

1. Ginsburg, R. – Wrote majority opinion
2. Rehnquist, W. – Wrote concurring opinion
3. Stevens, J. – Joined majority opinion
4. O'Connor, S. – Joined majority opinion
5. Kennedy, A. – Joined majority opinion
6. Souter, D. – Joined majority opinion
7. Breyer, S. – Joined majority opinion

Opposing Side (Respondent / Appellee in No. 94-1941, Petitioner / Appellant in No. 94-2107):

1. Scalia, A. – Wrote dissenting opinion

Thomas, C – Took no part in the decision

VI. A WIN OR LOSS FOR THE ACLU?

The ACLU, as amicus curiae, urged reversal of the second judgment of the United States Court of Appeals for the Fourth Circuit; the Supreme Court reversed in a 7-1 vote, giving the ACLU an apparent win.

808. Colorado Republican Federal Campaign Committee v. Federal Election Commission

(Decided June 26, 1996; 518 U.S. 604)

I. ISSUE

A. Issues Discussed

First Amendment, freedom of speech, campaign finance

B. Legal Question Presented

Whether the Federal Election Campaign Act (FECA) of 1971 "Party Expenditure Provision as applied here violates the First Amendment."

C. Supreme Court's Answer

The Party Expenditure Provision, as applied here, violates the First Amendment.

II. CASE SUMMARY

A. Background

"In April 1986, before the Colorado Republican Party had selected its senatorial candidate for the fall's election, that Party's Federal Campaign Committee bought radio advertisements attacking Timothy Wirth, the Democratic Party's likely candidate. The Federal Election Commission (FEC) charged that this 'expenditure' exceeded the dollar limits that a provision of the Federal Election Campaign Act of 1971 (FECA or Act) imposes upon political party 'expenditure[s] in connection with' a 'general election campaign' for congressional office....

The Federal District Court interpreted the provision's words "in connection with' the general election campaign of a candidate' narrowly, as meaning only expenditures for advertising using "express words of advocacy of election or defeat." As so interpreted, the court held, the provision did not cover the expenditures here. The court entered summary judgment for the Colorado Party and dismissed its counterclaim as moot.

Both sides appealed. The Government, for the FEC, argued for a somewhat broader interpretation of the statute—applying the limits to advertisements containing an 'electioneering message' about a 'clearly identified candidate," which, it said, both covered the expenditure and satisfied the Constitution. The Court of Appeals agreed. It found the Party Expenditure Provision applicable, held it constitutional, and ordered judgment in the FEC's favor."

The Supreme Court granted certiorari to review the case, vacated, and remanded.

B. Counsel of Record / ACLU Attorney

ACLU Side (Petitioner / Appellant): Jan Witold Baran argued the cause for appellant.

Opposing Side (Respondent / Appellee): Solicitor General Drew S. Days. III, argued the cause for appellee.

III. AMICI CURIAE

ACLU Side (Petitioner / Appellant)

Brief of amici curiae filed on behalf of the ACLU, et al., by David H. Remes, David H. Miller, Arthur B. Spitzer, Steven R. Shapiro, Joel M. Gora, Michael P. Socarras, Mark F. Kightlinger, Jarrett A. Williams, and Arthur N. Eisenberg.

Brief of amici curiae filed on behalf of the Democratic National Committee, et al., by Joseph E. Sandler and Robert F. Bauer.

Brief of amici curiae filed on behalf of the National Right to Life Committee, Inc., by James Bopp, Jr., Maureen M. Devlin, and Richard E. Coleson.

Brief of amici curiae filed on behalf of the Washington Legal Foundation, et al., by Benjamin L. Ginsberg Paul D. Kamenar, G. Kendrick MacDowell, David A. Colodny, Jeffrey L. Ross, and Daniel J. Popeo.

Brief of amici curiae filed on behalf of the Republican National Committee by David A. Norcross, John P. Connors, E. Duncan Getchell, Jr., Robert L. Hodges, Darryl S. Lew, Robert T. Cahill, and George J. Terwilliger, III.

Brief of amici curiae filed on behalf of the Committee for Party Renewal, et al., by E. Mark Braden, Julie E. Hawkins, and Stephen E. Gottlieb.

Opposing Side (Respondent / Appellee)

Brief of amici curiae filed on behalf of the Brennan Center for Justice by Burt Neuborne.

Brief of amici curiae filed on behalf of Common Cause, et al., by Roger M. Witten, Ankur J. Goel, Donald J. Simon, and Alan Morrison.

Brief of amici curiae filed on behalf of the State of Kentucky, et al., by A. B. Chandler, III, Attorney General of Kentucky, Pamela J. Murphy, Deputy Attorney General, Morgan G. Ransdell, Assistant Attorney General, Richard Blumenthal, Attorney General of Connecticut, Hubert J. Humphrey, III, Attorney General of Minnesota, Tom Udall, Attorney General of New Mexico, W. A. Drew Edmondson, Attorney General of

Oklahoma, Darell V. McGraw, Jr., Attorney General of West Virginia, Sheryl G. Snyder, and Jacquelyn P. Elmore.

IV. THE SUPREME COURT'S DECISION

"We . . . believe that this Court's prior case law controls the outcome here. We do not see how a Constitution that grants to individuals, candidates, and ordinary political committees the right to make unlimited independent expenditures could deny the same right to political parties. Having concluded this, we need not consider the Party's further claim that the statute's 'in connection with' language, and the FEC's interpretation of that language, are unconstitutionally vague. . . .

The Government does not deny the force of the precedent we have discussed. Rather, it argued below, and the lower courts accepted, that the expenditure in this case should be treated under those precedents, not as an 'independent expenditure,' but rather as a 'coordinated expenditure,' which those cases have treated as 'contributions,' and which those cases have held Congress may constitutionally regulate.

[W]e recognize that the FEC may have characterized the expenditures as 'coordinated' in light of this Court's constitutional decisions prohibiting regulation of most independent expenditures. But, if so, the characterization cannot help the Government prove its case. An agency's simply calling an independent expenditure a 'coordinated expenditure' cannot (for constitutional purposes) make it one. . . .

The Colorado Party and supporting amici have argued a broader question than we have decided, for they have claimed that, in the special case of political parties, the First Amendment forbids congressional efforts to limit coordinated expenditures as well as independent expenditures. Because the expenditure before us is an independent expenditure we have not reached this broader question in deciding the Party's 'as applied' challenge. . . .

For these reasons, the judgment of the Court of Appeals is vacated, and the case is remanded for further proceedings."

V. JUSTICE VOTE

7 Pro ACLU Side vs. 2 Con Opposing Side

ACLU Side (Petitioner / Appellant)

1. Breyer, S. – Wrote majority opinion
2. Kennedy, A. – Wrote opinion concurring in part and dissenting in part
3. Thomas, C. – Wrote opinion concurring in part and dissenting in part
4. O'Connor, S. – Joined majority opinion
5. Souter, D. – Joined majority opinion
6. Rehnquist, W. – Joined Kennedy's opinion, joined Thomas' opinion in part
7. Scalia, A. – Joined Kennedy's opinion, joined Thomas' opinion in part

Opposing Side (Respondent / Appellee)

1. Stevens, J. – Wrote dissenting opinion
2. Ginsburg, R. – Joined Stevens' dissent

VI. A WIN OR LOSS FOR THE ACLU?

The ACLU, as amicus curiae, urged reversal of the judgment of the Court of Appeals for the Tenth Circuit; the Supreme Court vacated and remanded in a 7-2 vote, giving the ACLU an apparent win.

809. Board of County Commissioners, Wabaunsee County, Kansas v. Umbehr

(Decided June 28, 1996; 518 U.S. 668)

I. ISSUE

A. Issues Discussed

First Amendment, freedom of speech, independent contractors

B. Legal Question Presented

"[W]hether, and to what extent, the First Amendment protects independent contractors from the termination of at-will government contracts in retaliation for their exercise of the freedom of speech."

C. Supreme Court's Answer

"[I]ndependent contractors are protected, and . . . the Pickering balancing test, adjusted to weigh the government's interests as contractor rather than as employer, determines the extent of their protection."

II. CASE SUMMARY

A. Background

"Under state law, Wabaunsee County, Kansas (County), is obliged to provide for the disposal of solid waste generated within its borders. In 1981, and, after renegotiation, in 1985, the County contracted with respondent Umbehr for him to be the exclusive hauler of trash for cities in the County at a rate specified in the contract. Each city was free to reject or, on 90 days' notice, to opt out of, the contract. By its terms, the contract between Umbehr and the County was automatically renewed annually unless either party terminated it by giving notice at least 60 days before the end of the year or a renegotiation was instituted on 90 days' notice. Pursuant to the contract, Umbehr hauled trash for six of the County's seven cities from 1985 to 1991 on an exclusive and uninterrupted basis.

During the term of his contract, Umbehr was an outspoken critic of petitioner, the Board of County Commissioners of Wabaunsee County (Board), the three-member governing body of the County. . . .

The Board's members allegedly took Umbehr's criticism badly, threatening the official county newspaper with censorship for publishing his writings. In 1990, they voted, 2 to 1, to terminate (or prevent the automatic renewal of) Umbehr's contract with the County. That attempt at termination failed because of a technical defect, but in 1991, the Board succeeded in terminating Umbehr's contract, again by a 2 to 1 vote. Umbehr subsequently negotiated new contracts with five of the six cities that he had previously served.

In 1992, Umbehr brought this suit against the two majority Board members in their individual and official capacities under Rev.Stat. § 1979, as amended, 42 U.S.C. § 1983, alleging that they had terminated his government contract in retaliation for his criticism of the County and the Board. The Board members moved for summary judgment. The District Court assumed that Umbehr's contract was terminated in retaliation for his speech, and that he suffered consequential damages. But it held that 'the First Amendment does not prohibit [the Board] from considering [Umbehr's] expression as a factor in deciding not to continue with the trash hauling contract at the end of the contract's annual term,' because, as an independent contractor, Umbehr was not entitled to the First Amendment protection afforded to public employees. It also held that the claims against the Board members in their individual capacities would be barred by qualified immunity, a ruling which was affirmed on appeal and which is not at issue here.

The United States Court of Appeals for the Tenth Circuit reversed (except as to qualified immunity), holding that 'an independent contractor is protected under the First Amendment from retaliatory governmental action, just as an employee would be,' and that the extent of protection is to be determined by weighing the government's interests as contractor against the free speech interests at stake in accordance with the balancing test that we used to determine government employees' First Amendment rights in Pickering v. Board of Ed. of Township High School Dist. 205, Will Cty., 391 U.S. 563(1968). It therefore remanded the official capacity claims to the District Court for further proceedings, including consideration of whether the termination was in fact retaliatory. The Board members who were the original defendants in this suit subsequently resigned their positions on the Board, so in this Court, the Board was substituted for them as petitioner."

The Supreme Court granted certiorari to review the case and affirmed.

B. Counsel of Record / ACLU Attorney

ACLU Side (Respondent / Appellee): Robert A. Van Kirk argued the cause for appellee. With him on the brief was Richard H. Seaton.

Beth S. Brinkmann argued the cause for the United States, as amicus curiae, by special leave of Court.

Opposing Side (Petitioner / Appellant): Donald Patterson argued the cause for appellant. With him on the briefs was Steve R. Fabert.

III. AMICI CURIAE

ACLU Side (Respondent / Appellee)

Brief of amici curiae filed on behalf of the ACLU, et al., by Robin L. Dahlberg, Robert M. O'Neil, J. Joshua Wheeler, Marjorie Heins, and Steven R. Shapiro.

Brief of amici curiae filed on behalf of the United States by Beth S. Brinkmann, Solicitor General Days, Assistant Attorney General Hunger, Deputy Solicitor General Bender, Cornelia T. L. Pillard, William Kanter, and Robert D. Kamenshine.

Brief of amici curiae filed on behalf of the Planned Parenthood Federation of America, Inc., by Bruce J. Ennis, Jr., Anthony C. Epstein, Julie M. Carpenter, Nory Miller, Roger K. Evans, Dara Klassel, and Eve W. Paul.

Opposing Side (Petitioner / Appellant)

No briefs of amici curiae were filed in support of appellant.

IV. THE SUPREME COURT'S DECISION

"While protecting First Amendment freedoms, we have, however, acknowledged that the First Amendment does not create property or tenure rights, and does not guarantee absolute freedom of speech. The First Amendment's guarantee of freedom of speech protects government employees from termination because of their speech on matters of public concern. To prevail, an employee must prove that the conduct at issue was constitutionally protected, and that it was a substantial or motivating factor in the termination. If the employee discharges that burden, the government can escape liability by showing that it would have taken the same action even in the absence of the protected conduct. And even termination because of protected speech may be justified when legitimate countervailing government interests are sufficiently strong. . . .

The parties each invite us to differentiate between independent contractors and employees. The Board urges us not to 'extend' the First Amendment rights of government employees to contractors. . . .

[N]either the Board nor Umbehr have persuaded us that there is a 'difference of constitutional magnitude,' between independent contractors and employees in this context. Independent government contractors are similar in most relevant respects to government employees, although both the speaker's and the government's interests are typically—though not always—somewhat less strong in the independent contractor case. We therefore conclude that the same form of balancing analysis should apply to each. . . .

Because the courts below assumed that Umbehr's termination (or nonrenewal) was in retaliation for his protected speech activities, and because they did not pass on the balance between the government's interests and the free speech interests at stake, our conclusion that independent contractors do enjoy some First Amendment protection requires that we affirm the Tenth Circuit's decision to remand the case. To prevail, Umbehr must show that the termination of his contract was motivated by his speech on a matter of public concern, an initial showing that requires him to prove more than the mere fact that he criticized the Board members before they terminated him. If he can make that showing, the Board will have a valid defense if it can show, by a preponderance of the evidence, that, in light of their knowledge, perceptions, and policies at the time of the termination, the Board members would have terminated the contract regardless of his speech. The Board will also prevail if it can persuade the District Court that the County's legitimate interests as contractor, deferentially viewed, outweigh the free speech interests at stake. And, if Umbehr prevails, evidence that the Board members discovered facts after termination that would have led to a later termination anyway, and evidence of mitigation of his loss by means of his subsequent contracts with the cities, would be relevant in assessing what remedy is appropriate.

Finally, we emphasize the limited nature of our decision

today. Because Umbehr's suit concerns the termination of a pre-existing commercial relationship with the government, we need not address the possibility of suits by bidders or applicants for new government contracts who cannot rely on such a relationship.

Subject to these limitations and caveats, however, we recognize the right of independent government contractors not to be terminated for exercising their First Amendment rights. The judgment of the Court of Appeals is, therefore, affirmed, and the case is remanded for proceedings consistent with this opinion."

V. JUSTICE VOTE

7 Pro ACLU Side vs. 2 Con Opposing Side

ACLU Side (Respondent / Appellee)

1. O'Connor, S. – Wrote majority opinion
2. Rehnquist, W. – Joined majority opinion
3. Breyer, S. – Joined majority opinion
4. Ginsburg, R. – Joined majority opinion
5. Souter, D. – Joined majority opinion
6. Kennedy, A. – Joined majority opinion
7. Stevens, J. – Joined majority opinion

Opposing Side (Petitioner / Appellant)

1. Scalia, A. – Wrote dissenting opinion
2. Thomas, C. – Joined Scalia's dissent

VI. A WIN OR LOSS FOR THE ACLU?

The ACLU, as amicus curiae, urged affirmance of the judgment of the Court of Appeals for the Tenth Circuit; the Supreme Court affirmed and remanded in a 7-2 vote, giving the ACLU an apparent win.

810. O'Hare Truck Service, Inc. v. City of Northlake

(Decided June 28, 1996; 518 U.S. 712)

I. ISSUE

A. Issues Discussed

First Amendment, freedom of speech, independent contractors

B. Legal Question Presented

"[W]hether the protections of Elrod and Branti extend to an independent contractor, who, in retaliation for refusing to comply with demands for political support, has a government contract terminated or is removed from an official list of contractors authorized to perform public services."

C. Supreme Court's Answer

"Although the government has broad discretion in formulating its contracting policies, we hold that the protections of Elrod and Branti extend to an instance like the one before us, where government retaliates against a contractor, or a regular provider of services, for the exercise of rights of political association or the expression of political allegiance."

II. CASE SUMMARY

A. Background

"John Gratzianna is the owner and operator of O'Hare Truck Service, which provides towing services in Cook and DuPage Counties, Illinois. Gratzianna and his company are petitioners here, and we sometimes refer to them as O'Hare.

The city of Northlake, a respondent in this Court, coordinates towing services through its Police Department and for at least 30 years has maintained a rotation list of available towing companies. When the police receive a tow request, they call the company next on the list to provide the service. Until the events recounted here, the city's policy had been to remove a tow truck operator from the rotation list only for cause. O'Hare had been on the list since 1965, performing towing services at the city's request. O'Hare and the city's former Mayor, Gene Doyle, had a mutual understanding that the city would maintain O'Hare's place on the rotation list so long as O'Hare provided good service. In 1989, soon after being elected Northlake's new Mayor, respondent Reid Paxson told Gratzianna he was pleased with O'Hare's work and would continue using and referring its services.

Four years later, when Paxson ran for reelection, his campaign committee asked Gratzianna for a contribution, which Gratzianna refused to make. Gratzianna instead supported the campaign of Paxson's opponent and displayed the opponent's campaign posters at O'Hare's place of business. Soon after, O'Hare was removed from the rotation list. We shall assume, as the complaint alleges, that the removal was in retaliation for Gratzianna's stance in the campaign. Petitioners allege the retaliation caused them to lose substantial income.

O'Hare and Gratzianna sued in the United States District Court for the Northern District of Illinois, alleging infringement of First Amendment rights in violation of Rev. Stat. § 1979, 42 U.S.C. § 1983. In conformity with binding Seventh Circuit precedent, which does not extend Elrod and Branti to independent contractors, the District Court dismissed the complaint. The Court of Appeals for the Seventh Circuit affirmed, adhering to the view that 'it should be up to the Supreme Court to extend Elrod.'"

The Supreme Court granted certiorari to review the case and reversed.

B. Counsel of Record / ACLU Attorney

ACLU Side (Petitioner / Appellant): Harvey Grossman argued the cause for appellant. With him on the briefs were Jane M. Whicher, Barbara P. O'Toole, Steven R. Shapiro, Michael P. McGovern, Marc O. Beem, David O'Toole, and Thomas C. Crooks.

Opposing Side (Respondent / Appellee): Gary M. Feiereisel argued the cause for appellee. With him on the briefs was Frank P. Kasbohm.

III. AMICI CURIAE

ACLU Side (Petitioner / Appellant)

Opposing Side (Respondent / Appellee)

Brief of amici curiae filed on behalf of the Towing & Recovery Association of America, Inc., by Robert A. Hirsch and M. Pia Torretti Gekas. Brief of amici curiae filed on behalf of Illinois State Officials by Jeffrey D. Colman, Edward J. Lewis, II, and David Jimenez-Ekman.

IV. THE SUPREME COURT'S DECISION

"Absent some reasonably appropriate requirement, government may not make public employment subject to the express condition of political beliefs or prescribed expression. . . .

The Court of Appeals, based on its understanding of the pleadings, considered this simply an affiliation case, and held, based on Circuit precedent, there was no constitutional protection for one who was simply an outside contractor. We consider the case in those same terms, but we disagree with the Court of Appeals' conclusion. . . .

The absolute right to enforce a patronage scheme, insisted upon by respondents as a means of retaining control over independent contractors, and satisfying government officials' concerns about reliability, has not been shown to be a necessary part of a legitimate political system in all instances. This was the determination controlling our decisions in Elrod and Branti, and we see no basis for rejecting that reasoning in this context. We decline to draw a line excluding independent contractors from the First Amendment safeguards of political association afforded to employees. . . .

Upon such further proceedings as are deemed appropriate by the Court of Appeals or the District Court, including upon motion for summary judgment if there is no genuine issue as to material facts, the courts on remand should decide whether the case is governed by the Elrod–Branti rule or by the Pickering rule.

The judgment of the Court of Appeals is reversed, and the case is remanded for further proceedings consistent with this opinion."

V. JUSTICE VOTE

7 Pro ACLU Side vs. 2 Con Opposing Side

ACLU Side (Petitioner / Appellant)

1. Kennedy, A. – Wrote majority opinion
2. O'Connor, S. – Joined majority opinion
3. Breyer, S. – Joined majority opinion
4. Souter, D. – Joined majority opinion
5. Rehnquist, W. – Joined majority opinion
6. Stevens, J. – Joined majority opinion
7. Ginsburg, R. – Joined majority opinion

Opposing Side (Respondent / Appellee)

1. Scalia, A. – Wrote dissenting opinion
2. Thomas, C. – Joined Scalia's dissent

VI. A WIN OR LOSS FOR THE ACLU?

The ACLU, as counsel of record, urged reversal of the judgment of the Court of Appeals for the Seventh Circuit; the Supreme Court reversed and remanded in a 7-2 vote, giving the ACLU an apparent win.

811. Denver Area Educational Telecommunications Consortium, Inc. v. Federal Communications Commission

(Decided June 28, 1996; 518 U.S. 727)

I. ISSUE

A. Issues Discussed

First Amendment, freedom of speech

B. Legal Question Presented

Whether three provisions of the Cable Television Consumer Protection and Competition Act violate the First Amendment right to freedom of speech.

C. Supreme Court's Answer

"We conclude that the first provision—which permits the operator to decide whether or not to broadcast such programs on leased access channels—is consistent with the First Amendment. The second provision, which requires leased channel operators to segregate and to block that programming, and the third provision, applicable to public, educational, and governmental channels, violate the First Amendment, for they are not appropriately tailored to achieve the basic, legitimate objective of protecting children from exposure to 'patently offensive' material."

II. CASE SUMMARY

A. Background

"These cases present First Amendment challenges to three statutory provisions that seek to regulate the broadcasting of 'patently offensive' sex-related material on cable television. Cable Television Consumer Protection and Competition Act of 1992 (1992 Act or Act), 106 Stat. 1486, §§ 10(a), 10(b), and 10(c), 47 U.S.C. §§ 532(h), 532(j), and note following § 531. The provisions apply to programs broadcast over cable on what are known as 'leased access channels' and 'public, educational, or governmental channels.' Two of the provisions essentially permit a cable system operator to prohibit the broadcasting of 'programming' that the 'operator reasonably believes describes or depicts sexual or excretory activities or organs in a patently offensive manner.' The remaining provision requires cable system operators to segregate certain 'patently offensive' programming, to place it on a single channel, and to block that channel from viewer access unless the viewer requests access in advance and in writing. . . .

Petitioners, claiming that the three statutory provisions, as implemented by the Commission regulations, violate the First Amendment, sought judicial review of the Commission's First Report and Order and its Second Report and Order in the United States Court of Appeals for the District of Columbia Circuit. A panel of that Circuit agreed with petitioners that the provisions violated the First Amendment. The entire Court of Appeals, however, heard the case en banc and reached the opposite conclusion. It held that all three statutory provisions (as implemented) were consistent with the First Amendment. Four of the eleven en banc appeals court judges dissented. Two of the dissenting judges concluded that all three provisions violated the First Amendment. Two others thought that either one, or two, but not all three of the provisions, violated the First Amendment."

B. Counsel of Record / ACLU Attorney

ACLU Side (Petitioner / Appellant): I. Michael Greenberger argued the cause for appellants. With him on the brief for the Alliance for Community Media, et al., appellants in No. 95-227, were James N. Horwood, Andrew Jay Schwartzman, Gigi Sohn, Elliot Mincberg, Lawrence Ottinger, Thomas J. Mikula, Mark S. Raffman, Michale K. Isenman, and David B. Goodhand. Robert T. Perry and Brian D. Graifman filed briefs for the New York Citizens Committee for Responsible Media, et al., appellants in No. 95-227. Charles S. Sims, Steven R. Shapiro, Peter J. W. Sherwin and Marjorie Heins filed briefs for the ACLU, et al., appellants in No. 95-124.

Opposing Side (Respondent / Appellee): Deputy Solicitor General Lawrence G. Wallace argued the cause for appellees in both cases. With him on the briefs for the federal appellees were Solicitor General Days, Assistant Attorney General Hunger, James A. Feldman, Barbara L. Herwig, Jacob M. Lewis, Michael S. Raab, William E. Kennard, Christopher J. Wright, Daniel M. Armstrong, and Jonathan E. Neuchterlein. Daniel L. Brenner, Neal M. Goldberg, and Diane B. Burstein filed a brief for the National Cable Television Association, Inc., appellee in both cases.

III. AMICI CURIAE

ACLU Side (Petitioner / Appellant)

Brief of amici curiae filed on behalf of the American Booksellers Foundation for Free Expression, et al., by Michael A. Bamberger and Margaret Jacobs.

Brief of amici curiae filed on behalf of the Association of American Publishers, Inc., by R. Bruce Rich, Linda Steinman, and Jonathan Bloom.

Opposing Side (Respondent / Appellee)

Brief of amici curiae filed on behalf of the State of New York by Dennis C. Vacco, Attorney General, Victoria A. Graffeo, Solicitor General, Barbara Billet, Deputy Solicitor General, and Stephen D. Houch and Theodore Zang, Jr., Assistant Attorneys General.

Brief of amici curiae filed on behalf of the Family Life Project of the American Center for Law and Justice by Jay Alan Sekulow, James M. Henderson, Sr., Colby M. May, Keith A. Fournier, and Thomas P. Monaghan.

Brief of amici curiae filed on behalf of the Family Research Council, et al., by Cathleen A. Cleaver and Bruce A. Taylor.

Brief of amici curiae filed on behalf of Morality in Media, Inc., by Paul J. Mc- Geady and Robert W. Peters.

Brief of amici curiae filed on behalf of Time Warner Cable by Stuart W. Gold, Marc E. Ackerman, and Rebeca L. Cutler.

Brief of amici curiae filed on behalf of the National Family Legal Foundation by Len L. Munsil.

IV. THE SUPREME COURT'S DECISION

"We turn initially to the provision that permits cable system operators to prohibit 'patently offensive' (or 'indecent') programming transmitted over leased access channels. The Court of Appeals held that this provision did not violate the First Amendment because the First Amendment prohibits only 'Congress' (and, through the Fourteenth Amendment, a 'State'), not private individuals, from 'abridging the freedom of speech.'

[W]e can decide these cases . . . by closely scrutinizing § 10(a) to assure that it properly addresses an extremely important problem, without imposing, in light of the relevant interests, an unnecessarily great restriction on speech. The importance of the interest at stake here—protecting children from exposure to patently offensive depictions of sex; the accommodation of the interests of programmers in maintaining access channels and of cable operators in editing the contents of their channels; the similarity of the problem and its solution to those at issue in Pacifica; and the flexibility inherent in an approach that permits private cable operators to make editorial decisions, lead us to conclude that § 10(a) is a sufficiently tailored response to an extraordinarily important problem. . . . For the reasons discussed, we conclude that § 10(a) is consistent with the First Amendment. . . .

The statute's second provision significantly differs from the first, for it does not simply permit, but rather requires, cable system operators to restrict speech—by segregating and blocking 'patently offensive' sex-related material appearing on leased channels (but not on other channels). . . .

These requirements have obvious restrictive effects. . . . Consequently, we cannot find that the 'segregate and block' restrictions on speech are a narrowly, or reasonably, tailored effort to protect children. Rather, they are overly restrictive, 'sacrific[ing]' important First Amendment interests for too 'speculative a gain.' For that reason they are not consistent with the First Amendment. . . .

The statute's third provision, as implemented by FCC regulation, is similar to its first provision, in that it too permits a cable operator to prevent transmission of 'patently offensive' programming, in this case on public access channels. But there are four important differences.

The first is the historical background. . . . The second difference is the institutional background that has developed as a result of the historical difference. . . . Third, the existence of a system aimed at encouraging and securing programming that the community considers valuable strongly suggests that a 'cable operator's veto' is less likely necessary to achieve the statute's basic objective, protecting children, than a similar veto in the context of leased channels. . . . Finally, our examination of the legislative history and the record before us is consistent with what common sense suggests, namely, that the public/nonprofit programming control systems now in place would normally avoid, minimize, or eliminate any child-related problems concerning 'patently offensive' programming. . . . Consequently, we find that this third provision violates the First Amendment. . . .

Finally, we must ask whether § 10(a) is severable from the two other provisions. The question is one of legislative intent: Would Congress still 'have passed' § 10(a) 'had it known' that the remaining 'provision[s were] invalid'? If so, we need not invalidate all three provisions. . . . That provision, capable of functioning on its own, still helps to achieve that basic objective. Consequently, we believe the valid provision is severable from the others. . . .

For these reasons, the judgment of the Court of Appeals is affirmed insofar as it upheld § 10(a); the judgment of the Court of Appeals is reversed insofar as it upheld § 10(b) and § 10(c)."

V. JUSTICE VOTE

6 Pro ACLU Side vs. 3 Con Opposing Side

ACLU Side (Petitioner / Appellant)

1. Breyer, S. – Wrote majority opinion
2. Souter, D. – Wrote concurring opinion
3. O'Connor, S. – Wrote opinion concurring in part and dissenting in part
4. Kennedy, A. – Wrote opinion concurring in part and dissenting in part
5. Stevens, J. – Wrote concurring opinion
6. Ginsburg, R. – Joined Kennedy's opinion

Opposing Side (Respondent / Appellee)

1. Thomas, C. – Wrote opinion concurring in part and dissenting in part
2. Rehnquist, W. – Joined Thomas' opinion
3. Scalia, A. – Joined Thomas' opinion

VI. A WIN OR LOSS FOR THE ACLU?

The ACLU, as counsel of record, urged reversal of the judgment of the Court of Appeals for the District of Columbia Circuit; the Supreme Court reversed in part and affirmed in part in a 6-3 vote, giving the ACLU an apparent win.

812. Lopez v. Monterey County, California

(Decided November 6, 1996; 519 U.S. 9)

I. ISSUE

A. Issues Discussed

Voting Rights Act of 1965

B. Legal Question Presented

Whether "an order by a three-judge District Court for the Northern District of California that authorized Monterey County to conduct judicial elections under an election plan that has not received federal approval pursuant to § 5 of the Voting Rights Act" is valid.

C. Supreme Court's Answer

The order is invalid because § 5 preclearance is required.

II. CASE SUMMARY

A. Background

"In 1971, the Attorney General designated [Monterey] County a covered jurisdiction under § 4(b) of the Voting Rights Act of 1965. As a result, the County became subject to the federal preclearance requirements set forth in § 5 of the Voting Rights Act, 42 U.S.C. § 1973c. Section 5 governs changes in voting procedures, with the purpose of preventing jurisdictions covered by its requirements from enacting or seeking to administer voting changes that have a discriminatory purpose or effect. As a jurisdiction covered by § 5, Monterey County must obtain federal preclearance—either administrative or judicial—of any voting practice different from the practices in effect on November 1, 1968. . . .

Between 1972 and 1983, the County adopted six ordinances, which ultimately merged the seven justice court districts and the two municipal court districts into a single, countywide municipal court, served by nine judges whom County residents elected at large. . . .

Although it was subject to § 5 preclearance requirements, the County did not submit any of the consolidation ordinances for federal preclearance under § 5. The State, however, in 1983 submitted for administrative preclearance a state law, 1983 Cal. Stats., ch. 1249, that mentioned Monterey County's prospective consolidation of the last two justice court districts with the remaining municipal court district. The Department of Justice requested additional information concerning this aspect of the state legislation. In its response, the State included the last of the County's six consolidation ordinances, which was adopted in 1983. The Attorney General interposed no objection to the 1983 state law. The State's submission may well have served to preclear the 1983 county ordinance. The United States points out, however, that the 1983 submission to the Department of Justice did not identify or describe any of the County's previous consolidation ordinances. The State does not contest this point. Thus, under our precedent, these previous consolidation ordinances do not appear to have received federal preclearance approval.

On September 6, 1991, appellants, five Hispanic voters residing in the County, sued the County in the United States District Court for the Northern District of California, alleging that the County had violated § 5 by failing to obtain federal preclearance of the six judicial district consolidation ordinances it had adopted between 1972 and 1983. They raised no claim under § 2 of the Voting Rights Act or constitutional challenge. A three-judge District Court was convened. On March 31, 1993, the District Court ruled that the challenged ordinances were election changes subject to § 5 and consequently unenforceable without federal preclearance. The District Court directed the County to submit the ordinances to federal officials for preclearance. It also denied the County's motion to join the State as an indispensable party under Federal Rule of Civil Procedure 19(b), finding that the State had no legally protected interest in the outcome of the action.

[After extensive subsequent litigation and attempts at a solution,] four years after the filing of the complaint in this case, the District Court ordered the County to hold elections under the very same scheme that appellants originally challenged under § 5 as unprecleared.

On January 22, 1996, appellants filed an emergency application in [the Supreme] Court to enjoin the 1996 elections pending appeal."

The Supreme Court granted certiorari to review the case and reversed.

B. Counsel of Record / ACLU Attorney

ACLU Side (Petitioner / Appellant): Joaquin G. Avila argued the cause for appellants.

Alan Jenkins argued the cause for the United States, as amicus curiae, by special leave of Court

Opposing Side (Respondent / Appellee): Daniel G. Stone, Deputy Attorney General of California, argued the cause for appellees.

III. AMICI CURIAE

ACLU Side (Petitioner / Appellant)

Brief of amici curiae filed on behalf of the ACLU, et al., by Sidney S. Rosdeitcher, Gregory A. Clarick, Paul C. Saunders, Henry J. Hansell, Norman Redlich, Barbara R. Arnwine, Thomas J. Henderson, Brenda Wright, Samuel L. Walters, Laughlin McDonald, Neil Bradley, Maha S. Zaki, Steven R. Shapiro, Elaine R. Jones, Norman J. Chachkin, and Jacqueline A. Berrien.

Brief of amici curiae filed on behalf of the United States by Alan Jenkins, Solicitor General Days, Assistant Attorney General Patrick, Deputy Solicitor General Bender, Steven H. Rosenbaum, and Eileen Penner.

Opposing Side (Respondent / Appellee)

Brief of amici curiae filed on behalf of the Pacific Legal Foundation by Sharon L. Browne and Deborah J. La Fetra.

Brief of amici curiae filed on behalf of the California Judges Association by Barbara McDowell and Elwood G. Lui.

IV. THE SUPREME COURT'S DECISION

"A jurisdiction subject to § 5's requirements must obtain either judicial or administrative preclearance before implementing a voting change. No new voting practice is enforceable unless the covered jurisdiction has succeeded in obtaining preclearance. If a voting change subject to § 5 has not been precleared, § 5 plaintiffs are entitled to an injunction prohibiting implementation of the change. The District Court's order that the County conduct elections under the unprecleared, at-large judicial election plan conflicts with these principles and with our decision in Clark v. Roemer, supra. . . .

For several years, the County had been on notice that its electoral changes were subject to § 5's preclearance requirements, yet it never obtained judicial or administrative preclearance of the consolidation ordinances. . . .

The County has not discharged its obligation to submit its voting changes to either of the forums designated by Congress. The requirement of federal scrutiny should be satisfied without further delay. The State appears willing to assist the County in pursuing the issue before either the Attorney General or the District Court for the District of Columbia, and its effort will doubtless be of assistance.

The judgment is reversed, and the case is remanded for further proceedings consistent with this opinion."

V. JUSTICE VOTE

9 Pro ACLU Side vs. 0 Con Opposing Side

ACLU Side (Petitioner / Appellant)

1. O'Connor, S. – Wrote majority opinion
2. Rehnquist, W. – Joined majority opinion
3. Breyer, S. – Joined majority opinion
4. Ginsburg, R. – Joined majority opinion
5. Souter, D. – Joined majority opinion
6. Kennedy, A. – Joined majority opinion
7. Stevens, J. – Joined majority opinion
8. Scalia, A. – Joined majority opinion
9. Thomas, C. – Joined majority opinion

VI. A WIN OR LOSS FOR THE ACLU?

The ACLU, as amicus curiae, urged reversal of the judgment of the District Court for the Northern District of California; the Supreme Court reversed and remanded in a 9-0 vote, giving the ACLU an apparent win.

813. Ohio v. Robinette

(Decided November 18, 1996; 519 U.S. 33)

I. ISSUE

A. Issues Discussed

Fourth Amendment, search and seizure, unlawful detention

B. Legal Question Presented

"[W]hether the Fourth Amendment requires that a lawfully seized defendant must be advised that he is 'free to go' before his consent to search will be recognized as voluntary."

C. Supreme Court's Answer

A defendant need not be advised that he is "free to go" for his consent to search to be considered voluntary.

II. CASE SUMMARY

A. Background

"This case arose on a stretch of Interstate 70 north of Dayton, Ohio, where the posted speed limit was 45 miles per hour because of construction. Respondent Robert D. Robinette was clocked at 69 miles per hour as he drove his car along this stretch of road, and was stopped by Deputy Roger Newsome of the Montgomery County Sheriff's Office. Newsome asked for and was handed Robinette's driver's license, and he ran a computer check which indicated that Robinette had no previous violations. Newsome then asked Robinette to step out of his car, turned on his mounted video camera, issued a verbal warning to Robinette, and returned his license.

At this point, Newsome asked, 'One question before you get gone: [A]re you carrying any illegal contraband in your car?

Any weapons of any kind, drugs, anything like that?' Robinette answered 'no' to these questions, after which Deputy Newsome asked if he could search the car. Robinette consented. In the car, Deputy Newsome discovered a small amount of marijuana and, in a film container, a pill which was later determined to be methylenedioxymethamphetamine (MDMA). Robinette was then arrested and charged with knowing possession of a controlled substance, MDMA, in violation of Ohio Rev.Code Ann. § 2925.11(A) (1993).

Before trial, Robinette unsuccessfully sought to suppress this evidence. He then pleaded 'no contest,' and was found guilty. On appeal, the Ohio Court of Appeals reversed, ruling that the search resulted from an unlawful detention. The Supreme Court of Ohio, by a divided vote, affirmed. In its opinion, that court established a bright-line prerequisite for consensual interrogation under these circumstances:

'The right, guaranteed by the federal and Ohio Constitutions, to be secure in one's person and property requires that citizens stopped for traffic offenses be clearly informed by the detaining officer when they are free to go after a valid detention, before an officer attempts to engage in a consensual interrogation. Any attempt at consensual interrogation must be preceded by the phrase 'At this time you legally are free to go' or by words of similar import.'"

The Supreme Court granted certiorari to review the case and reversed.

B. Counsel of Record / ACLU Attorney

ACLU Side (Respondent / Appellee): James D. Ruppert argued the cause for appellee.

Opposing Side (Petitioner / Appellant): Carley J. Ingram argued the cause for appellant.

Irving L. Gornstein argued the cause for the United States, as amicus curiae, by special leave of Court.

III. AMICI CURIAE

ACLU Side (Respondent / Appellee)

Brief of amici curiae filed on behalf of the ACLU, et al., by Tracey Maclin, Steven R. Shapiro, Joan M. Englund, and Jeffrey M. Gamso.

Brief of amici curiae filed on behalf of the National Association of Criminal Defense Lawyers by Sheryl Gordon McCloud.

Brief of amici curiae filed on behalf of the Ohio Association of Criminal Defense Lawyers by W. Andrew Hasselbach.

Opposing Side (Petitioner / Appellant)

Brief of amici curiae filed on behalf of the United States by Irving L. Gornstein, Solicitor General Days, Acting Assistant Attorney General Keeney, Deputy Solicitor General Dreeben, Paul A. Engelmayer, and Joseph C. Wyderko.

Brief of amici curiae filed on behalf of the State of Alabama, et al., by Betty D. Montgomery, Attorney General of Ohio, Jeffrey S. Sutton, State Solicitor, and Simon B. Karas, and by the Attorneys General for their respective States as follows: Jeff Sessions of Alabama, Daniel E. Lungren of California, Gale A. Norton of Colorado, M. Jane Brady of Delaware, Robert Butterworth of Florida, Margery S. Bronster of Hawaii, Alan G. Lance of Idaho, Jim Ryan of Illinois, Carla J. Stovall of Kansas, A. B. Chandler III of Kentucky, Richard P. Ieyoub of Louisiana, Andrew Ketterer of Maine, J. Joseph Curran, Jr., of Maryland, Scott Harshbarger of Massachusetts, Frank J. Kelley of Michigan, Hubert H. Humphrey III of Minnesota, Mike Moore of Mississippi, Joseph P. Mazurek of Montana, Don Stenberg of Nebraska, Frankie Sue Del Papa of Nevada, Jeffrey R. Howard of New Hampshire, Deborah T. Poritz of New Jersey, Dennis C. Vacco of New York, Michael F. Easley of North Carolina, W. A. Drew Edmondson of Oklahoma, Theodore Kulongoski of Oregon, Thomas W. Corbett, Jr., of Pennsylvania, Jeffrey B. Pine of Rhode Island, Mark Bennett of South Dakota, Charles W. Bursen of Tennessee, Dan Morales of Texas, Jeffrey L. Amestoy of Vermont, James S. Gilmore III of Virginia, Darrell V. McGraw, Jr., of West Virginia, James E. Doyle of Wisconsin, and William U. Hill of Wyoming.

Brief of amici curiae filed on behalf of Americans for Effective Law Enforcement, Inc., by Fred E. Inbau, Wayne W. Schmidt, James P. Manak, and Bernard J. Farber.

IV. THE SUPREME COURT'S DECISION

"We have long held that the 'touchstone of the Fourth Amendment is reasonableness.' Reasonableness, in turn, is measured in objective terms by examining the totality of the circumstances.

In applying this test we have consistently eschewed bright-line rules, instead emphasizing the fact-specific nature of the reasonableness inquiry. . . . We have previously rejected a per se rule very similar to that adopted by the Supreme Court of Ohio in determining the validity of a consent to search. In Schneckloth v. Bustamonte, 412 U.S. 218 (1973), it was argued that such a consent could not be valid unless the defendant knew that he had a right to refuse the request. We rejected this argument: 'While knowledge of the right to refuse consent is one factor to be taken into account, the government need not establish such knowledge as the sine qua non of an effective consent.' And just as it 'would be thoroughly impractical to impose on the normal consent search the detailed requirements of an effective warning,' so too would it be unrealistic to require police officers to always inform detainees that they are free to go before a consent to search may be deemed voluntary.

The Fourth Amendment test for a valid consent to search is that the consent be voluntary, and '[v]oluntariness is a question of fact to be determined from all the circumstances.' The

Supreme Court of Ohio having held otherwise, its judgment is reversed, and the case is remanded for further proceedings not inconsistent with this opinion."

V. JUSTICE VOTE

1 Pro ACLU Side vs. 8 Con Opposing Side

ACLU Side (Respondent / Appellee)

1. Stevens, J. – Wrote dissenting opinion

Opposing Side (Respondent / Appellee)

1. Rehnquist, W. – Wrote majority opinion
2. O'Connor, S. – Joined majority opinion
3. Breyer, S. – Joined majority opinion

4. Souter, D. – Joined majority opinion
5. Kennedy, A. – Joined majority opinion
6. Scalia, A. – Joined majority opinion
7. Thomas, C. – Joined majority opinion
8. Ginsburg, R. – Wrote concurring opinion

VI. A WIN OR LOSS FOR THE ACLU?

The ACLU, as amicus curiae, urged affirmance of the judgment of the Supreme Court of Ohio; the U.S. Supreme Court reversed in an 8-1 vote, giving the ACLU an apparent loss.

814. M. L. B. v. S. L. J.

(Decided December 16, 1996; 519 U.S. 102)

I. ISSUE

A. Issues Discussed

Fourteenth Amendment, due process, equal protection, parental rights

B. Legal Question Presented

"May a State, consistent with the Due Process and Equal Protection Clauses of the Fourteenth Amendment, condition appeals from trial court decrees terminating parental rights on the affected parent's ability to pay record preparation fees?"

C. Supreme Court's Answer

"We hold that, just as a State may not block an indigent petty offender's access to an appeal afforded others, so Mississippi may not deny M. L. B., because of her poverty, appellate review of the sufficiency of the evidence on which the trial court found her unfit to remain a parent."

II. CASE SUMMARY

A. Background

"By order of a Mississippi Chancery Court, petitioner M. L. B.'s parental rights to her two minor children were forever terminated. . . .

In January 1995, M. L. B. filed a timely appeal and paid the $100 filing fee. The Clerk of the Chancery Court, several days later, estimated the costs for preparing and transmitting the record: $1,900 for the transcript (950 pages at $2 per page); $438 for other documents in the record (219 pages at $2 per page); $4.36 for binders; and $10 for mailing.

Mississippi grants civil litigants a right to appeal, but conditions that right on prepayment of costs. Relevant portions of a transcript must be ordered, and its preparation costs advanced by the appellant, if the appellant 'intends to urge on appeal,' as M. L. B. did, 'that a finding or conclusion is unsupported by the evidence or is contrary to the evidence.'

Unable to pay $2,352.36, M. L. B. sought leave to appeal in forma pauperis. The Supreme Court of Mississippi denied her application in August 1995. Under its precedent, the court said, '[t]he right to proceed in forma pauperis in civil cases exists only at the trial level.'"

The U.S. Supreme Court granted certiorari to review the case and reversed.

B. Counsel of Record / ACLU Attorney

ACLU Side (Petitioner / Appellant): Robert B. McDuff argued the cause for appellant. With him on the briefs were Marina Hsieh, Danny Lampley, and Steven R. Shapiro.

Opposing Side (Respondent / Appellee): Rickey T. Moore, Special Assistant Attorney General of Mississippi, argued the cause for appellee. With him on the brief was Mike Moore, Attorney General.

III. AMICI CURIAE

ACLU Side (Petitioner / Appellant)

Opposing Side (Respondent / Appellee)

Brief of amici curiae filed on behalf of the National Center for Youth Law, et al., by Martha Matthews. No briefs of amici curiae were filed in support of appellee.

IV. THE SUPREME COURT'S DECISION

"We have . . . recognized a narrow category of civil cases in which the State must provide access to its judicial processes without regard to a party's ability to pay court fees. . . .

Choices about marriage, family life, and the upbringing of children are among associational rights this Court has ranked as 'of basic importance in our society,' rights sheltered by the Fourteenth Amendment against the State's unwarranted usurpation, disregard, or disrespect. M. L. B.'s case, involving the State's authority to sever permanently a parent-child bond, demands the close consideration the Court has long required when a family association so undeniably important is at stake. We approach M. L. B.'s petition mindful of the gravity of the sanction imposed on her and in light of two prior decisions most immediately in point . . . .

Although both Lassiter and Santosky yielded divided opinions, the Court was unanimously of the view that 'the interest of parents in their relationship with their children is sufficiently fundamental to come within the finite class of liberty interests protected by the Fourteenth Amendment.' It was also the Court's unanimous view that '[f]ew consequences of judicial action are so grave as the severance of natural family ties.' . . .

Guided by this Court's precedent on an indigent's access to judicial processes in criminal and civil cases, and on proceedings to terminate parental status, we turn to the classification question this case presents: Does the Fourteenth Amendment require Mississippi to accord M. L. B. access to an appeal—available but for her inability to advance required costs—before she is forever branded unfit for affiliation with her children?

[W]e have repeatedly noticed what sets parental status termination decrees apart from mine run civil actions, even from other domestic relations matters such as divorce, paternity, and child custody. To recapitulate, termination decrees 'wor[k] a unique kind of deprivation.' In contrast to matters modifiable at the parties' will or based on changed circumstances, termination adjudications involve the awesome authority of the State 'to destroy permanently all legal recognition of the parental relationship.' Our Lassiter and Santosky decisions, recognizing that parental termination decrees are among the most severe forms of state action, have not served as precedent in other areas. We are therefore satisfied that the label 'civil' should not entice us to leave undisturbed the Mississippi courts' disposition of this case. . . .

For the reasons stated, we hold that Mississippi may not withhold from M. L. B. 'a 'record of sufficient completeness' to permit proper [appellate] consideration of [her] claims.' Accordingly, we reverse the judgment of the Supreme Court of Mississippi and remand the case for further proceedings not inconsistent with this opinion."

V. JUSTICE VOTE

6 Pro ACLU Side vs. 3 Con Opposing Side

ACLU Side (Petitioner / Appellant)

1. Ginsburg, R. – Wrote majority opinion
2. Kennedy, A. – Wrote concurring opinion
3. O'Connor, S. – Joined majority opinion
4. Breyer, S. – Joined majority opinion
5. Souter, D. – Joined majority opinion
6. Stevens, J. – Joined majority opinion

Opposing Side (Respondent / Appellee)

1. Thomas, C. – Wrote dissenting opinion
2. Scalia, A. – Joined Thomas' dissent
3. Rehnquist, W. – Wrote dissenting opinion, joined Thomas' dissent in part

VI. A WIN OR LOSS FOR THE ACLU?

The ACLU, as counsel of record, urged reversal of the judgment of the Supreme Court of Mississippi; the U.S. Supreme Court reversed and remanded in a 6-3 vote, giving the ACLU an apparent win.

815. Robinson v. Shell Oil Co.

(Decided February 18, 1997; 519 U.S. 337)

I. ISSUE

A. Issues Discussed

Employment discrimination, statutory interpretation, retaliation

B. Legal Question Presented

"[W]hether the term 'employees,' as used in § 704(a) [of Title VII of the Civil Rights Act of 1964], includes former employees, such that petitioner may bring suit against his former employer for postemployment actions allegedly taken in retaliation for petitioner's having filed a charge with the Equal Employment Opportunity Commission (EEOC)."

C. Supreme Court's Answer

"We hold that the term 'employees,' as used in § 704(a) of Title VII, is ambiguous as to whether it includes former employees. It being more consistent with the broader context of Title VII and the primary purpose of § 704(a), we hold that former employees are included within § 704(a)'s coverage."

II. CASE SUMMARY

A. Background

"Respondent Shell Oil Co. fired petitioner Charles T. Robinson, Sr., in 1991. Shortly thereafter, petitioner filed a charge with the EEOC, alleging that respondent had discharged him because of his race. While that charge was pending, petitioner applied for a job with another company. That company contacted respondent, as petitioner's former employer, for an employment reference. Petitioner claims that respondent gave him a negative reference in retaliation for his having filed the EEOC charge.

Petitioner subsequently sued under § 704(a), alleging retaliatory discrimination. On respondent's motion, the District Court dismissed the action, adhering to previous Fourth Circuit precedent holding that § 704(a) does not apply to former employees. Petitioner appealed, and a divided panel of the Fourth Circuit reversed the District Court. The Fourth Circuit granted rehearing en banc, vacated the panel decision, and thereafter affirmed the District Court's determination that former employees may not bring suit under § 704(a) for retaliation occurring after termination of their employment."

The Supreme Court granted certiorari to review the case and reversed.

B. Counsel of Record / ACLU Attorney

ACLU Side (Petitioner / Appellant): Allen M. Lenchek argued the cause for appellant.

Paul R. Q. Wolfson argued the cause for the United States, et al., as amici curiae, by special leave of Court.

Opposing Side (Respondent / Appellee): L. Chris Butler argued the cause for appellee.

III. AMICI CURIAE

ACLU Side (Petitioner / Appellant)

Brief of amici curiae filed on behalf of the Lawyers Committee for Civil Rights Under Law, the American Association of Retired Persons, the ACLU, et al., by Paul C. Saunders, Marc L. Fleischaker, Norman Redlich, Barbara R. Arnwine, Thomas J. Henderson, Richard T. Seymour, Teresa A. Ferrante, Cathy Ventrell-Monsees, Dennis Courtland Hayes, Judith H. Lichtman, Donna R. Lenhoff, Helen L. Norton, Steven R. Shapiro, Sara L. Mandelbaum, Sherry Leiwant, and Martha F. Davis.

Brief of amici curiae filed on behalf of the United States, et al., by Paul R. Q. Wolfson, Solicitor General Days, Assistant Attorney General Patrick, Deputy Solicitor General Bender, C. Gregory Stewart, Gwendolyn Young Reams, Vincent Blackwood, Samuel A. Marcosson, and John F. Suhre.

Brief of amici curiae filed on behalf of the National Employment Lawyers Association by Douglas A. Hedin and Robert Belton.

Opposing Side (Respondent / Appellee)

Brief of amici curiae filed on behalf of the Equal Employment Advisory Council by Robert E. Williams and Ann Elizabeth Reesman.

Brief of amici curiae filed on behalf of the Washington Legal Foundation by J. Thomas Kilpatrick, Daniel J. Popeo, and Paul D. Kamenar.

IV. THE SUPREME COURT'S DECISION

"Finding that the term 'employees' in § 704(a) is ambiguous, we are left to resolve that ambiguity. The broader context provided by other sections of the statute provides considerable assistance in this regard. [S]everal sections of the statute plainly contemplate that former employees will make use of the remedial mechanisms of Title VII. Indeed, § 703(a) expressly includes discriminatory 'discharge' as one of the unlawful employment practices against which Title VII is directed. Insofar as § 704(a) expressly protects employees from retaliation for filing a 'charge' under Title VII, and a charge under § 703(a) alleging unlawful discharge would necessarily be brought by a former employee, it is far more consistent to include former employees within the scope of 'employees' protected by § 704(a).

In further support of this view, petitioner argues that the word 'employees' includes former employees because to hold otherwise would effectively vitiate much of the protection afforded by § 704(a). This is also the position taken by the EEOC. According to the EEOC, exclusion of former employees from the protection of § 704(a) would undermine the effectiveness of Title VII by allowing the threat of postemployment retaliation to deter victims of discrimination from complaining to the EEOC, and would provide a perverse incentive for employers to fire employees who might bring Title VII claims.

Those arguments carry persuasive force given their coherence and their consistency with a primary purpose of antiretaliation provisions: Maintaining unfettered access to statutory remedial mechanisms. The EEOC quite persuasively maintains that it would be destructive of this purpose of the antiretaliation provision for an employer to be able to retaliate with impunity against an entire class of acts under Title VII—for example, complaints regarding discriminatory termination. We agree with these contentions and find that they support the inclusive interpretation of 'employees' in § 704(a) that is already suggested by the broader context of Title VII. . . .

We hold that the term 'employees,' as used in § 704(a) of Title VII, is ambiguous as to whether it includes former employees. It being more consistent with the broader context of Title VII and the primary purpose of § 704(a), we hold that former employees are included within § 704(a)'s coverage. Accordingly, the decision of the Fourth Circuit is reversed."

V. JUSTICE VOTE

9 Pro ACLU Side vs. 0 Con Opposing Side

ACLU Side (Petitioner / Appellant)

1. Thomas, C. – Wrote majority opinion
2. O'Connor, S. – Joined majority opinion
3. Rehnquist, W. – Joined majority opinion
4. Breyer, S. – Joined majority opinion
5. Ginsburg, R. – Joined majority opinion
6. Souter, D. – Joined majority opinion
7. Kennedy, A. – Joined majority opinion
8. Stevens, J. – Joined majority opinion
9. Scalia, A. – Joined majority opinion

VI. A WIN OR LOSS FOR THE ACLU?

The ACLU, as amicus curiae, urged reversal of the judgment of the Court of Appeals for the Fourth Circuit; the Supreme Court reversed in a 9-0 vote, giving the ACLU an apparent win.

816. Schenck v. Pro-Choice Network of Western New York

(Decided February 19, 1997; 519 U.S. 357)

I. ISSUE

A. Issues Discussed

Abortion, First Amendment, freedom of speech

B. Legal Question Presented

"[W]hether an injunction that places restrictions on demonstrations outside abortion clinics violates the First Amendment."

C. Supreme Court's Answer

"We uphold the provisions imposing 'fixed bubble' or 'fixed buffer zone' limitations, as hereinafter described, but hold that the provisions imposing 'floating bubble' or 'floating buffer zone' limitations violate the First Amendment."

II. CASE SUMMARY

A. Background

"Respondents include three doctors and four medical clinics . . . . These health care providers perform abortions and other medical services at their facilities. The eighth respondent is Pro–Choice Network of Western New York, a not-for-profit corporation dedicated to maintaining access to family planning and abortion services.

On September 24, 1990, respondents filed a complaint in the District Court for the Western District of New York against 50 individuals and 3 organizations—Operation Rescue, Project Rescue Western New York, and Project Life of Rochester. The complaint alleged that defendants had consistently engaged in illegal blockades and other illegal conduct at facilities in the Western District of New York where abortions were performed. . . . The complaint alleged that a large blockade was planned for September 28, and requested that the court issue a temporary restraining order (TRO) to stop it. The complaint also sought a permanent injunction and damages. . . .

On September 27, 1990, three days after respondents filed their complaint and one day before the scheduled large-scale blockade, the District Court issued a TRO. . . .

Alleging that Project Rescue and five individual defendants (including petitioner Schenck) breached the TRO on five separate occasions from late October 1990 through December 1990, respondents sought four contempt citations. A fifth contempt citation for a 1991 incident was sought against petitioner

Schenck and another individual defendant. Throughout 1991 and into 1992, the District Court held 27 days of hearings in these contempt proceedings, and issued opinions concluding that five of the six incidents justified a finding of civil contempt.

In February 1992, after hearing 12 additional days of testimony, the District Court issued the injunction, parts of which are challenged here. [A] panel of the Court of Appeals reversed the District Court in a split decision. The Court of Appeals then heard the case en banc, and affirmed the District Court by a divided vote."

The Supreme Court granted certiorari to review the case, affirmed in part, reversed in part, and remanded.

B. Counsel of Record / ACLU Attorney

ACLU Side (Respondent / Appellee): Lucinda M. Finley argued the cause for appellee.

Opposing Side (Petitioner / Appellant): Jay Alan Sekulow argued the cause for appellant.

III. AMICI CURIAE

ACLU Side (Respondent / Appellee)

Brief of amici curiae filed on behalf of the ACLU, et al., by Steven R. Shapiro, Marjorie Heins, and Elliot Mincberg.

Brief of amici curiae filed on behalf of the New York Civil Liberties Union Foundation by David A. Strauss, Roderick G. McDougall, Marvin A. Sondag, and Arthur N. Eisenberg.

Brief of amici curiae filed on behalf of the United States by Acting Solicitor General Dellinger, Assistant Attorney General Patrick, Deputy Solicitor General Bender, Beth S. Brinkmann, and Jessica Dunsay Silver.

Brief of amici curiae filed on behalf of the State of Connecticut, et al., by Richard Blumenthal, Attorney General of Connecticut, and Jennifer C. Jaff, Assistant Attorney General, joined by the Attorneys General for their respective jurisdictions as follows: Gale A. Norton of Colorado, Robert A. Butterworth of Florida, Calvin E. Holloway, Sr., of Guam, Margery S. Bronster of Hawaii, Pamela Carter of Indiana, Carla J. Stovall of Kansas, J. Joseph Curran, Jr., of Maryland, Scott Harshbarger of Massachusetts, Hubert H. Humphrey III of Minnesota, Deborah T. Po-ritz of New Jersey, Tom Udall of New Mexico, Frankie Sue Del Papa of Nevada, Michael F. Easley of North Carolina, Theodore R. Kulongoski of Oregon, Jeffrey L. Amestoy of Vermont, Christine O. Gregoire of Washington, and Darrell V. McGraw, Jr., of West Virginia.

Brief of amici curiae filed on behalf of the State of New York by Dennis C. Vacco, Attorney General, Victoria A. Graffeo, Solicitor General, Barbara G. Billet, Deputy Solicitor General, and Robert A. Forte, Assistant Attorney General.

Brief of amici curiae filed on behalf of the American Jewish Congress by Lois Waldman.

Brief of amici curiae filed on behalf of the Planned Parenthood Federation of America, Inc., by Roger K. Evans and Eve W. Paul.

Brief of amici curiae filed on behalf of the American College of Obstetricians and Gynecologists, et al., by Elaine Metlin, Laura B. Feigin, and Ann E. Allen.

Brief of amici curiae filed on behalf of the Feminist Majority Foundation, et al., by Talbot D'Alemberte, Steven G. Gey, and Catherine Carhart Henry.

Brief of amici curiae filed on behalf of the American Medical Women's Association, et al., by Eve C. Gartner and Michael E. Erdos.

Opposing Side (Petitioner / Appellant)

Brief of amici curiae filed on behalf of the ACLU of Ohio Foundation, Inc., by Scott T. Greenwood and Joan M. England.

Brief of amici curiae filed on behalf of the Indiana Civil Liberties Union by Richard A. Waples.

Brief of amici curiae filed on behalf of the ACLU Foundation of Florida, Inc., et al., by James K. Green and Andrew H. Kayton.

Brief of amici curiae filed on behalf of the Family Research Council by Cathleen A. Cleaver.

Brief of amici curiae filed on behalf of the Rutherford Institute by Anne-Marie Amiel and John W. Whitehead.

Brief of amici curiae filed on behalf of Life Legal Defense Foudation by Anne J. Kindt.

Brief of amici curiae filed on behalf of the American Federation of Labor and Congress of Industrial Organizations by Jonathan P. Hiatt and Marsha S. Berzon, in support of neither party.

IV. THE SUPREME COURT'S DECISION

"Petitioners challenge three aspects of the injunction: (i) the floating 15-foot buffer zones around people and vehicles seeking access to the clinics; (ii) the fixed 15-foot buffer zones around the clinic doorways, driveways, and parking lot entrances; and (iii) "the 'cease and desist' provision" that forces sidewalk counselors who are inside the buffer zones to retreat 15 feet from the person being counseled once the person indicates a desire not to be counseled. . . .

Given the factual similarity between this case and Madsen, we conclude that the governmental interests underlying the injunction in Madsen —ensuring public safety and order, promoting the free flow of traffic on streets and sidewalks, protecting property rights, and protecting a woman's freedom to seek pregnancy-related services—also underlie the injunction here, and in combination are certainly significant enough to justify an appropriately tailored injunction to secure unimpeded physical access to the clinics. . . .

We strike down the floating buffer zones around people entering and leaving the clinics because they burden more speech than is necessary to serve the relevant governmental interests. The floating buffer zones prevent defendants—except for two sidewalk counselors, while they are tolerated by the targeted individual—from communicating a message from a normal conversational distance or handing leaflets to people entering or leaving the clinics who are walking on the public sidewalks. This is a broad prohibition, both because of the type of speech that is restricted and the nature of the location. Leafletting and commenting on matters of public concern are classic forms of speech that lie at the heart of the First Amendment, and speech in public areas is at its most protected on public sidewalks, a prototypical example of a traditional public forum.. . .

We likewise strike down the floating buffer zones around vehicles. Nothing in the record or the District Court's opinion contradicts the commonsense notion that a more limited injunction—which keeps protesters away from driveways and parking lot entrances (as the fixed buffer zones do) and off the streets, for instance—would be sufficient to ensure that drivers are not confused about how to enter the clinic and are able to gain access to its driveways and parking lots safely and easily. In contrast, the 15-foot floating buffer zones would restrict the speech of those who simply line the sidewalk or curb in an effort to chant, shout, or hold signs peacefully. We therefore conclude that the floating buffer zones around vehicles burden more speech than necessary to serve the relevant governmental interests. . . .

We uphold the fixed buffer zones around the doorways, driveways, and driveway entrances. These buffer zones are necessary to ensure that people and vehicles trying to enter or exit the clinic property or clinic parking lots can do so. . . .

Petitioners and some of their amici attack the 'cease and desist' provision accompanying the exception for sidewalk counselors as content based, because it allows a clinic patient to terminate a protester's right to speak based on, among other reasons, the patient's disagreement with the message being conveyed. But in Madsen we held that the injunction in that case was not content based, even though it was directed only at abortion protesters, because it was only abortion protesters who had done the acts which were being enjoined. Here, the District Court found that '[m]any of the 'sidewalk counselors' and other defendants ha[d] been arrested on more than one occasion for harassment, yet persist in harassing and intimidating patients, patient escorts and medical staff.' These counselors remain free to espouse their message outside the 15-foot buffer zone, and the condition on their freedom to espouse it within the buffer zone is the result of their own previous harassment and intimidation of patients. . . .

The judgment of the Court of Appeals is affirmed in part and reversed in part, and the case is remanded for further proceedings consistent with this opinion."

V. JUSTICE VOTE

5 Pro ACLU Side vs. 4 Con Opposing Side

ACLU Side (Respondent / Appellee)

1. Rehnquist, W. – Wrote majority opinion
2. Stevens, J. – Joined majority opinion
3. O'Connor, S. – Joined majority opinion
4. Souter, D. – Joined majority opinion
5. Ginsburg, R. – Joined majority opinion

Opposing Side (Petitioner / Appellant)

1. Scalia, A. – Wrote opinion concurring in part and dissenting in part
2. Kennedy, A. – Joined Scalia's opinion
3. Thomas, C. – Joined Scalia's opinion
4. Breyer, S. – Wrote opinion concurring in part and dissenting in part

VI. A WIN OR LOSS FOR THE ACLU?

The ACLU, as amicus curiae, urged affirmance of the judgment of the Court of Appeals for the Second Circuit; the Supreme Court affirmed in part and reversed in part in a 5-4 vote, giving the ACLU an apparent win.

817. Arizonans for Official English v. Arizona

(Decided March 3, 1997; 520 U.S. 43)

I. ISSUE

A. Issues Discussed

First Amendment, freedom of speech, mootness

B. Legal Question Presented

"(1) Does Article XXVIII violate the Free Speech Clause of the First Amendment by 'declaring English the official language of the State and requiring English to be used to perform official acts'?; (2) Do public employees have 'a Free Speech right to disregard the [State's] official language' and perform official actions in a language other than English?"

C. Supreme Court's Answer

The case became moot during the course of litigation and the judgment must be vacated.

II. CASE SUMMARY

A. Background

"The initiating plaintiff, Maria- Kelly F. Yniguez, sought federal-court resolution of a novel question: the compatibility with the Federal Constitution of a 1988 amendment to Arizona's Constitution declaring English 'the official language of the State of Arizona'—'the language of . . . all government functions and actions.' Participants in the federal litigation, proceeding without benefit of the views of the Arizona Supreme Court, expressed diverse opinions on the meaning of the amendment.

Yniguez commenced and maintained her suit as an individual, not as a class representative. A state employee at the time she filed her complaint, Yniguez voluntarily left the State's employ in 1990 and did not allege she would seek to return to a public post. Her departure for a position in the private sector made her claim for prospective relief moot. Nevertheless, the Ninth Circuit held that a plea for nominal damages could be read into Yniguez's complaint to save the case, and therefore pressed on to an ultimate decision. A three-judge panel of the Court of Appeals declared Article XXVIII unconstitutional in 1994, and a divided en banc court, in 1995, adhered to the panel's position."

The courts engaged in extensive litigation in this matter before the Supreme Court granted certiorari to review the case, vacated, and remanded.

B. Counsel of Record / ACLU Attorney

ACLU Side (Respondent / Appellee): Robert J. Pohlman argued the cause for appellees.

Opposing Side (Petitioner / Appellant): Barnaby W. Zall argued the cause for appellants

III. AMICI CURIAE

ACLU Side (Respondent / Appellee)

Brief of amici curiae filed on behalf of the ACLU, et al., by Edward M. Chen, Karen N. Kai, Harlan A. Loeb, Elliot M. Mincberg, Lawrence S. Ottinger, Steven R. Shapiro, Marjorie Heins, and Robert L. Rusky.

Brief of amici curiae filed on behalf of the State of New Mexico by Tom Udall, Attorney General, Manuel Tijerina, Deputy Attorney General, and Gerald T. E. Gonzalez, Tannis L. Fox, Laura Fashing, Elizabeth A. Glenn, and William S. Keller, Assistant Attorneys General.

Brief of amici curiae filed on behalf of the Hawaii Civil Rights Commission, et al., by John H. Ishihara, Paul F. N. Lucas, William D. Hoshijo, Carl C. Christensen, and Eric K. Yamamoto.

Brief of amici curiae filed on behalf of Human Rights Watch by Allan Blumstein, Jodi A. Danzing, Juan E. Mendez, and Kenneth Roth.

Brief of amici curiae filed on behalf of the Linguistic Society of America by Peter M. Tiersma.

Brief of amici curiae filed on behalf of the Mexican American Legal Defense and Educational Fund by Theresa Fay-Bustillos, Martha Jimenez, Thomas A. Saenz, and E. Richard Larson.

Brief of amici curiae filed on behalf of the National Council of La Raza, et al., by Joseph N. Onek, William D. Wallace, Robert D. Wing, Sunil H. Mansukhani, and Javier M. Guzman.

Brief of amici curiae filed on behalf of the Navajo Nation by Herb Yazzie, Judy Leaming, and Thomas W. Christie.

Brief of amici curiae filed on behalf of the Puerto Rican Legal Defense and Education Fund, et al., by Kenneth Kimerling, Sandra Del Valle, Karen K. Narasaki, and Richard Albores.

Brief of amici curiae filed on behalf of Representative Nydia M. Velazquez, et al., by Walter A. Smith, Jr., and Audrey J. Anderson.

Brief of amici curiae filed on behalf of the United States by Acting Solicitor General Dellinger, Assistant Attorney General Hunger, Deputy Solicitor General Kneedler, Deputy Assistant Attorney General Preston, Irving L. Gornstein, Scott Mcintosh, and Anthony J. Steinmeyer, addressing standing and urging that petitioners do not have standing to seek review of the case.

Opposing Side (Petitioner / Appellant)

Brief of amici curiae filed on behalf of the FLA-187 Committee, Inc., et al., by Stanley W. Sokolowski.

Brief of amici curiae filed on behalf of the Pacific Legal Foundation by Sharon L. Browne and Anne M. Hawkins.

Brief of amici curiae filed on behalf of U.S. English, Inc., by Leonard J. Henzke, Jr., and Wendy T. Cohen

Brief of amici curiae filed on behalf of the Washington Legal Foundation, et al., by Richard K. Willard, Bennett Evan Cooper, Daniel J. Popeo, Richard A. Samp, and Don Stenberg, Attorney General of Nebraska.

Brief of amici curiae filed by Thurston Greene, pro se.

IV. THE SUPREME COURT'S DECISION

"Article III, § 2, of the Constitution confines federal courts to the decision of 'Cases' or 'Controversies.' Standing to sue or defend is an aspect of the case-or-controversy requirement. . . .

We . . . have grave doubts whether AOE and Park have standing under Article III to pursue appellate review. Nevertheless, we need not definitively resolve the issue. Rather, we will follow a path we have taken before and inquire, as a primary matter, whether originating plaintiff Yniguez still has a case to pursue. . . .

As a state employee subject to Article XXVIII, Yniguez had a viable claim at the outset of the litigation in late 1988. We need not consider whether her case lost vitality in January 1989 when the Attorney General released Opinion No. I89–009. That opinion construed Article XXVIII to require the expression of 'official acts' in English, but to leave government employees free to use other languages 'if reasonably necessary to the fair and effective delivery of services' to the public. Yniguez left her state job in April 1990 to take up employment in the private sector, where her speech was not governed by Article XXVIII. At that point, it became plain that she lacked a still vital claim for prospective relief.

The Attorney General suggested mootness, but Yniguez resisted, and the Ninth Circuit adopted her proposed method of saving the case. . . . It should have been clear to the Court of Appeals that a claim for nominal damages, extracted late in the day from Yniguez's general prayer for relief and asserted solely to avoid otherwise certain mootness, bore close inspection. On such inspection, the Ninth Circuit might have perceived that Yniguez's plea for nominal damages could not genuinely revive the case.

When a civil case becomes moot pending appellate adjudication, '[t]he established practice . . . in the federal system . . . is to reverse or vacate the judgment below and remand with a direction to dismiss.' . . .

The State urges that its current plea for vacatur is compelling in view of the extraordinary course of this litigation. We agree. The 'exceptional circumstances' that abound in this case and the federalism concern we next consider, lead us to conclude that vacatur down the line is the equitable solution. . . .

Warnings against premature adjudication of constitutional questions bear heightened attention when a federal court is asked to invalidate a State's law, for the federal tribunal risks friction-generating error when it endeavors to construe a novel state Act not yet reviewed by the State's highest court. 'Speculation by a federal court about the meaning of a state statute in the absence of prior state court adjudication is particularly gratuitous when . . . the state courts stand willing to address questions of state law on certification from a federal court.'

Blending abstention with certification, the Ninth Circuit found 'no unique circumstances in this case militating in favor of certification.' Novel, unsettled questions of state law, however, not 'unique circumstances,' are necessary before federal courts may avail themselves of state certification procedures. Those procedures do not entail the delays, expense, and procedural complexity that generally attend abstention decisions. Taking advantage of certification made available by a State may 'greatly simplif[y]' an ultimate adjudication in federal court.

The course of Yniguez's case was complex. The complexity

might have been avoided had the District Court, more than eight years ago, accepted the certification suggestion made by Arizona's Attorney General. The Arizona Supreme Court was not asked by the District Court or the Court of Appeals to say what Article XXVIII means. But the State's highest court has that very question before it in Ruiz v. Symington, the case the Ninth Circuit considered no cause for federal-court hesitation. In Ruiz, which has been stayed pending our decision in this case, the Arizona Supreme Court may now rule definitively on the proper construction of Article XXVIII. Once that court has spoken, adjudication of any remaining federal constitutional question may indeed become greatly simplified. . . .

For the reasons stated, the judgment of the Court of Appeals is vacated, and the case is remanded to that court with directions that the action be dismissed by the District Court."

V. JUSTICE VOTE

0 Pro ACLU Side vs. 9 Con Opposing Side

Opposing Side (Petitioner / Appellant)

1. Ginsburg, R. – Wrote majority opinion
2. Rehnquist, W. – Joined majority opinion
3. O'Connor, S. – Joined majority opinion
4. Breyer, S. – Joined majority opinion
5. Souter, D. – Joined majority opinion
6. Kennedy, A. – Joined majority opinion
7. Scalia, A. – Joined majority opinion
8. Thomas, C. – Joined majority opinion
9. Stevens, J. – Joined majority opinion

VI. A WIN OR LOSS FOR THE ACLU?

The ACLU, as amicus curiae, urged affirmance of the judgment of the Court of Appeals for the Ninth Circuit; the Supreme Court vacated and remanded in a 9-0 vote, giving the ACLU an apparent loss.

818. Young v. Harper

(Decided March 18, 1997; 520 U.S. 143)

I. ISSUE

A. Issues Discussed

Parole, due process, prisoners' rights

B. Legal Question Presented

"[W]hether a program employed by the State of Oklahoma to reduce the overcrowding of its prisons was sufficiently like parole that a person in the program was entitled to the procedural protections set forth in Morrissey v. Brewer, 408 U.S. 471 (1972), before he could be removed from it.

C. Supreme Court's Answer

"We hold that the program, as it appears to have been structured at the time respondent was placed on it, differed from parole in name alone, and affirm the decision of the Court of Appeals for the Tenth Circuit."

II. CASE SUMMARY

A. Background

"As pertinent to this case, Oklahoma operated two programs under which inmates were conditionally released from prison before the expiration of their sentences. One was parole, the other was the Preparole Conditional Supervision Program (preparole or Program). The Program was in effect whenever the population of the prison system exceeded 95% of its capacity. An inmate could be placed on preparole after serving 15% of his sentence, § 365(A)(2), and he was eligible for parole when one-third of his sentence had elapsed, § 332.7(A). The Pardon and Parole Board (Board) had a role in the placement of both parolees and preparolees. The Board itself determined who could participate in the Program, while the Governor, based on the Board's recommendation, decided whether a prisoner would be paroled. [P]articipants in the Program were released subject to constraints similar to those imposed on parolees.

In October 1990, after reviewing respondent Ernest Eugene Harper's criminal record and conduct while incarcerated, the Pardon and Parole Board simultaneously recommended him for parole and released him under the Program. At that time, respondent had served 15 years of a life sentence for two murders. Before his release, respondent underwent orientation, during which he reviewed the 'Rules and Conditions of Pre-Parole Conditional Supervision,' and after which he executed a document indicating that he 'underst[ood] that being classified to community level depend[ed] upon [his] compliance with each of these expectations.' He spent five apparently uneventful months outside the penitentiary. Nonetheless, the Governor of Oklahoma denied respondent parole. On March 14, 1991, respondent was telephoned by his parole officer, informed of the Governor's decision, and told to report back to prison, which he did later that day.

Respondent filed a petition for a writ of habeas corpus in state court complaining that his summary return to prison had deprived him of liberty without due process. The state trial court denied relief and the Oklahoma Court of Criminal Appeals affirmed. The Court of Criminal Appeals concluded that respondent's removal from the Program impinged only upon an interest in his 'degree of confinement,' an interest to which the procedural protections set out in Morrissey did not attach. The court found '[d]ispositive of the issue' the fact that respondent 'was not granted parole by the Governor of Oklahoma.' The court noted that the Board had adopted a procedure under which preparolees subsequently denied parole remained on the Program, and had their cases reviewed within 90 days of the denial for a determination whether they should continue on preparole. According to the court, 'such a procedure gives an inmate sufficient notice when he is placed in the program that he may be removed from it when the governor exercises his discretion and declines to grant parole.'

Respondent fared no better in District Court on his petition for relief under 28 U.S.C. § 2254. But the Tenth Circuit reversed. It determined that preparole 'more closely resembles parole or probation than even the more permissive forms of institutional confinement' and that '[d]ue process therefore mandates that program participants receive at least the procedural protections described in Morrissey.'"

The Supreme Court granted certiorari to review the case and affirmed.

B. Counsel of Record / ACLU Attorney

ACLU Side (Respondent / Appellee): Margaret Winter argued the cause for appellee. With her on the briefs were Marjorie Rifkin, Elizabeth Alexander, Michael Salem, and Steven R. Shapiro.

Opposing Side (Petitioner / Appellant): Sandra D. Howard, Assistant Attorney General of Oklahoma, argued the cause for appellant. With her on the briefs were W. A. Drew Edmondson, Attorney General, and Jennifer B. Miller, Assistant Attorney General.

III. AMICI CURIAE

ACLU Side (Respondent / Appellee)

No briefs of amici curiae were filed in support of appellee.

Opposing Side (Petitioner / Appellant)

Brief of amici curiae filed on behalf of the State of Nevada, et al., by Frankie Sue Del Papa, Attorney General of Nevada, and Anne Cathcart, Senior Deputy Attorney General, joined by the Attorneys General for their respective States as follows: Daniel E. Lungren of California, Gale A. Norton of Colorado, Margery S. Bronster of Hawaii, Alan G. Lance of Idaho, Joseph P. Mazurek of Montana, and Dennis C. Vacco of New York.

IV. THE SUPREME COURT'S DECISION

"'The essence of parole is release from prison, before the completion of sentence, on the condition that the prisoner abide by certain rules during the balance of the sentence.' . . . In Morrissey, we described the 'nature of the interest of the parolee in his continued liberty':

'[H]e can be gainfully employed and is free to be with family and friends and to form the other enduring attachments of normal life. Though the State properly subjects him to many restrictions not applicable to other citizens, his condition is very different from that of confinement in a prison . . . . The parolee has relied on at least an implicit promise that parole will be revoked only if he fails to live up to the parole conditions.'

This passage could just as easily have applied to respondent while he was on preparole. In compliance with state procedures, he was released from prison before the expiration of his sentence. He kept his own residence; he sought, obtained, and maintained a job; and he lived a life generally free of the incidents of imprisonment. To be sure, respondent's liberty was not unlimited. He was not permitted to use alcohol, to incur other than educational debt, or to travel outside the county without permission. And he was required to report regularly to a parole officer. The liberty of a parolee is similarly limited, but that did not in Morrissey, 408 U.S., at 478, render such liberty beyond procedural protection. . . .

Petitioners do identify some actual differences between preparole and Oklahoma's version of parole, but these do no better at convincing us that preparole was different from parole as we understood it in Morrissey. As petitioners point out, participation in the Program was ordered by the Board, while the Governor conferred parole. In this regard, preparole was different from parole in Oklahoma; but it was no different from parole as we described it in Morrissey. In addition, preparolees who 'escape[d]' from the Program could be prosecuted as though they had escaped from prison, while it appears that parolees who 'escaped' from parole were subject not to further prosecution, but to revocation of parole. That the punishment for failure to abide by one of the conditions of his liberty was potentially greater for a preparolee than for a parolee did not itself diminish that liberty. Petitioners also note that a preparolee could not leave Oklahoma under any circumstances, while a parolee could leave Oklahoma with his parole officer's permission. This minor difference in a released prisoner's ability to travel did not, we think, alter the fundamentally parole-like nature of the

Program. . . .

We conclude that the Program, as it existed when respondent was released, was a kind of parole as we understood parole in Morrissey. The judgment of the Tenth Circuit is therefore affirmed."

V. JUSTICE VOTE

9 Pro ACLU Side vs. 0 Con Opposing Side

ACLU Side (Respondent / Appellee)

1. Thomas, C. – Wrote majority opinion
2. Ginsburg, R. – Joined majority opinion
3. Rehnquist, W. – Joined majority opinion
4. O'Connor, S. – Joined majority opinion
5. Breyer, S. – Joined majority opinion
6. Souter, D. – Joined majority opinion
7. Kennedy, A. – Joined majority opinion
8. Scalia, A. – Joined majority opinion
9. Stevens, J. – Joined majority opinion

VI. A WIN OR LOSS FOR THE ACLU?

The ACLU, as counsel of record, urged affirmance of the judgment of the Court of Appeals for the Tenth Circuit; the Supreme Court affirmed in a 9-0 vote, giving the ACLU an apparent win.

819. United States v. Lanier

(Decided March 31, 1997; 520 U.S. 259)

I. ISSUE

A. Issues Discussed

Due process, sexual assault

B. Legal Question Presented

Whether a standard of notice that "the constitutional right in issue [must have] previously been identified by [the Supreme] Court in a case with fundamentally similar facts . . . is higher than the Constitution requires . . . ."

C. Supreme Court's Answer

The standard of notice applied was higher than the Constitution requires.

II. CASE SUMMARY

A. Background

"David Lanier was formerly the sole state Chancery Court judge for two rural counties in western Tennessee. The trial record, read most favorably to the jury's verdict, shows that from 1989 to 1991, while Lanier was in office, he sexually assaulted several women in his judicial chambers. . . .

Ultimately, Lanier was charged with 11 violations of § 242, each count of the indictment alleging that, acting willfully and under color of Tennessee law, he had deprived the victim of 'rights and privileges which are secured and protected by the Constitution and the laws of the United States, namely the right not to be deprived of liberty without due process of law, including the right to be free from willful sexual assault.' . . .

The jury returned verdicts of guilty on seven counts, and not guilty on three (one count having been dismissed at the close of the Government's evidence). It also found that the two oral rapes resulted in 'bodily injury,' for which Lanier was subject to 10–year terms of imprisonment on each count, in addition to 1–year terms under the other five counts of conviction. He was sentenced to consecutive maximum terms totaling 25 years.

A panel of the Court of Appeals for the Sixth Circuit affirmed the convictions and sentence, but the full court vacated that decision and granted rehearing en banc. On rehearing, the court set aside Lanier's convictions for 'lack of any notice to the public that this ambiguous criminal statute [i.e., § 242] includes simple or sexual assault crimes within its coverage.' Invoking general canons for interpreting criminal statutes, as well as this Court's plurality opinion in Screws v. United States, 325 U.S. 91 (1945), the Sixth Circuit held that criminal liability may be imposed under § 242 only if the constitutional right said to have been violated is first identified in a decision of [the Supreme] Court (not any other federal, or state, court), and only when the right has been held to apply in 'a factual situation fundamentally similar to the one at bar.' The Court of Appeals regarded these combined requirements as 'substantially higher than the 'clearly established' standard used to judge qualified immunity' in civil cases under Rev. Stat. § 1979, 42 U.S.C. § 1983. Finding no decision of this Court applying a right to be free from unjustified assault or invasions of bodily integrity in a situation 'fundamentally similar' to those charged, the Sixth Circuit reversed the judgment of conviction with instructions to dismiss the indictment. Two judges would not have dismissed the felony counts charging the oral rapes but concurred in dismissing the misdemeanor counts, while three members of the court dissented as to all dismissals."

The Supreme Court granted certiorari to review the case, vacated, and remanded.

B. Counsel of Record / ACLU Attorney

ACLU Side (Petitioner / Appellant): Deputy Solicitor General Seth P. Waxman argued the cause for the United States.

Opposing Side (Respondent / Appellee): Alfred H. Knight argued the cause for appellee.

III. AMICI CURIAE

ACLU Side (Petitioner / Appellant)

Briefs of amici curiae filed on behalf of the ACLU, et al., by Marjorie Heins and Steven R. Shapiro.

Briefs of amici curiae filed on behalf of the NOW Legal Defense and Education Fund, et al., by Lynn Hecht Schafran, Pamela Coukos, and Martha F. Davis.

Briefs of amici curiae filed on behalf of the Southern Poverty Law Center, et al., by Mary-Christine Sungaila, Gregory R. Smith, J. Richard Cohen, and Brian Levin.

Briefs of amici curiae filed on behalf of Vivian Forsythe-Archie, et al., by Catharine A. MacKinnon.

Opposing Side (Respondent / Appellee)

No briefs of amici curiae were filed in support of appellee.

IV. THE SUPREME COURT'S DECISION

"There are three related manifestations of the fair warning requirement. First, the vagueness doctrine bars enforcement of 'a statute which either forbids or requires the doing of an act in terms so vague that men of common intelligence must necessarily guess at its meaning and differ as to its application.' Second, as a sort of 'junior version of the vagueness doctrine,' the canon of strict construction of criminal statutes, or rule of lenity, ensures fair warning by so resolving ambiguity in a criminal statute as to apply it only to conduct clearly covered. Third, although clarity at the requisite level may be supplied by judicial gloss on an otherwise uncertain statute, due process bars courts from applying a novel construction of a criminal statute to conduct that neither the statute nor any prior judicial decision has fairly disclosed to be within its scope. In each of these guises, the touchstone is whether the statute, either standing alone or as construed, made it reasonably clear at the relevant time that the defendant's conduct was criminal. . . .

The Sixth Circuit, in this case, added two glosses to the made-specific standard of fair warning. In its view, a generally phrased constitutional right has been made specific within the meaning of Screws only if a prior decision of this Court has declared the right, and then only when this Court has applied its ruling in a case with facts 'fundamentally similar' to the case being prosecuted. None of the considerations advanced in this case, however, persuade us that either a decision of this Court or the extreme level of factual specificity envisioned by the Court of Appeals is necessary in every instance to give fair warning. . . .

In sum, as with civil liability under § 1983 or Bivens, all that can usefully be said about criminal liability under § 242 is that it may be imposed for deprivation of a constitutional right if, but only if, 'in the light of preexisting law the unlawfulness [under the Constitution is] apparent.' Where it is, the constitutional requirement of fair warning is satisfied.

Because the Court of Appeals used the wrong gauge in deciding whether prior judicial decisions gave fair warning that respondent's actions violated constitutional rights, we vacate the judgment and remand the case for application of the proper standard."

V. JUSTICE VOTE

9 Pro ACLU Side vs. 0 Con Opposing Side

ACLU Side (Petitioner / Appellant)

1. Souter, D. – Wrote majority opinion
2. Thomas, C. – Joined majority opinion
3. O'Connor, S. – Joined majority opinion
4. Rehnquist, W. – Joined majority opinion
5. Breyer, S. – Joined majority opinion
6. Ginsburg, R. – Joined majority opinion
7. Kennedy, A. – Joined majority opinion
8. Stevens, J. – Joined majority opinion
9. Scalia, A. – Joined majority opinion

VI. A WIN OR LOSS FOR THE ACLU?

The ACLU, as amicus curiae, urged reversal of the judgment of the Court of Appeals for the Sixth Circuit; the Supreme Court vacated and remanded in a 9-0 vote, giving the ACLU an apparent win.

820. Young v. Fordice

(Decided March 31, 1997; 520 U.S. 273)

I. ISSUE

A. Issues Discussed

Voting Rights Act of 1965

B. Legal Question Presented

"[W]hether § 5 of the Voting Rights Act of 1965, requires preclearance of certain changes that Mississippi made in its voter registration procedures—changes that Mississippi made in order to comply with the National Voter Registration Act of 1993."

C. Supreme Court's Answer

Section 5 requires preclearance for these changes.

II. CASE SUMMARY

A. Background

"Congress enacted the National Voter Registration Act of 1993 (NVRA) to take effect for States like Mississippi on January 1, 1995. The NVRA requires States to provide simplified systems for registering to vote in federal elections . . . .

Section 5 of the Voting Rights Act of 1965(VRA), among other things, prohibits a State with a specified history of voting discrimination, such as Mississippi, from 'enact[ing] or seek[ing] to administer any . . . practic[e], or procedure with respect to voting different from that in force or effect on November 1, 1964,' unless and until the State obtains preclearance from the United States Attorney General (Attorney General) or the United States District Court for the District of Columbia. § 1973c. . . .

This case arises out of efforts by Mississippi to preclear, under § 5 of the VRA, changes that it made to comply with the NVRA. In December 1994, Mississippi submitted to the United States Attorney General a list of NVRA-implementing changes that it then intended to make. . . . Mississippi requested preclearance. On February 1, 1995, the Department of Justice wrote to Mississippi that the Attorney General did 'not interpose any objection to the specified changes'—thereby preclearing Mississippi's submitted changes.

[H]owever, on January 25, about one week before the Attorney General precleared the proposed changes, the state legislature had tabled the proposed legislation needed to make those changes effective for state elections. On February 10, 10 days after the Department precleared the proposed changes, Mississippi officials wrote to voter registration officials around the State, telling them that it 'appears unlikely that the Legislature will' revive the tabled bill; that the Provisional Plan's registration would therefore not work for state elections; that they should write—or help the secretary of state write—to tell those who had registered under that system that they were not registered to vote in state elections; that they should make certain future registrants understand that they would need to register separately to be eligible to vote in state, as well as federal, elections; and that they should develop a system for distinguishing between NVRA and other voters.

On February 16, about two weeks after the Department of Justice sent its preclearance letter, the Department wrote another letter to Mississippi, which made clear that the Department did not believe its earlier preclearance had precleared what it now saw as a new plan. The Department asked the State to submit what it called this new 'dual registration and voter purge system' for preclearance. . . . Mississippi, perhaps believing that the February 1 preclearance sufficed, made no further preclearance submissions. . . .

On April 20, 1995, four private citizens (appellants) brought this lawsuit before a three-judge District Court. They claimed that Mississippi and its officials had implemented changes in its registration system without preclearance in violation of § 5. The United States, which is an amicus curiae here, brought a similar lawsuit, and the two actions were consolidated.

The three-judge District Court granted Mississippi's motion for summary judgment. It considered the plaintiffs' basic claim, namely, that the differences between the Provisional Plan and the New System amounted to a change in the administration of Mississippi's voting registration practice, which change had not been precleared. The court rejected this argument on the ground that the Provisional Plan was a misapplication of state law, never ratified by the State. Since the differences between the New System and the Provisional Plan were attributable to the State's attempt to correct this misapplication of state law, the court held, those differences were not changes subject to preclearance.

The court also considered a different question, namely, whether the New System differed from the Old System; and whether Mississippi had precleared all the changes that the New System made in the Old. The court held that the Department had (on February 1) precleared the administrative changes needed to implement the NVRA. The court also held that Mississippi did not need to preclear its failure to pass a law that would have permitted NVRA registration to count for state, as well as for federal, elections, as the distinction between state and federal elections was due to the NVRA's own provisions, not to the State's changes in voting practices."

The Supreme Court granted certiorari to review the case, reversed, and remanded.

B. Counsel of Record / ACLU Attorney

ACLU Side (Petitioner / Appellant): Brenda Wright argued the cause for appellants. With her on the briefs were Barbara R. Arnwine, Thomas J. Henderson, Samuel L. Walters, A. Spencer Gilbert III, J William Manuel, Margaret Carey, Laughlin McDonald and Neil Bradley.

Malcolm L. Stewart argued the cause for the United States, as amicus curiae, by special leave of Court.

Opposing Side (Respondent / Appellee): Robert E. Sanders, Assistant Attorney General of Mississippi, argued the cause for appellees. With him on the brief was Mike Moore, Attorney General.

III. AMICI CURIAE

ACLU Side (Petitioner / Appellant)

Brief of amici curiae filed on behalf of the United States by Malcolm L. Stewart, Acting Solicitor General Dellinger, Assistant Attorney General Patrick, Deputy Solicitor General Waxman, Samuel R. Bagenstos, and Steven H. Rosenbaum.

Brief of amici curiae filed on behalf of the Community Service Society of New York, et al., by Juan Cartagena and Jonathan Feldman.

Opposing Side (Respondent / Appellee)

No briefs of amici curiae were filed in support of appellee.

IV. THE SUPREME COURT'S DECISION

"In this case, those seeking to administer the Provisional Plan did not intend to administer an unlawful plan. They expected it to become lawful. They abandoned the Provisional Plan as soon as its unlawfulness became apparent, i.e., as soon as it became clear that the legislature would not pass the laws needed to make it lawful. Moreover, all these events took place within the space of a few weeks. The plan was used to register voters for only 41 days, and only about a third of the State's voter registration officials had begun to use it. Further, the State held no elections prior to its abandonment of the Provisional Plan, nor were any elections imminent. These circumstances taken together lead us to conclude that the Provisional Plan was not 'in force or effect'; hence it did not become part of the baseline against which we are to judge whether future change occurred. . . .

We nonetheless agree with the appellants and the Government that the New System included changes that must be, but have not been, precleared. That is because the New System contains 'practices and procedures' that are significantly 'different from' the Old System—the system that was in effect in 1994. And the State has not precleared those differences. . . .

In this case, the New System contains numerous examples of new, significantly different administrative practices—practices that are not purely ministerial, but reflect the exercise of policy choice and discretion by Mississippi officials. . . . Insofar as they embody discretionary decisions that have a potential for discriminatory impact, they are appropriate matters for review under § 5's preclearance process. . . .

We hold that Mississippi has not precleared, and must preclear, the 'practices and procedures' that it sought to administer on and after February 10, 1995. The decision of the District Court is reversed, and the case is remanded with instructions for the District Court to enter an order enjoining further use of Mississippi's unprecleared changes as appropriate. Any further questions about the remedy for Mississippi's use of an unprecleared plan are for the District Court to address in the first instance."

V. JUSTICE VOTE

9 Pro ACLU Side vs. 0 Con Opposing Side

ACLU Side (Petitioner / Appellant)

1. Breyer, S. – Wrote majority opinion
2. Thomas, C. – Joined majority opinion
3. O'Connor, S. – Joined majority opinion
4. Rehnquist, W. – Joined majority opinion
5. Ginsburg, R. – Joined majority opinion
6. Souter, D. – Joined majority opinion
7. Kennedy, A. – Joined majority opinion
8. Stevens, J. – Joined majority opinion
9. Scalia, A. – Joined majority opinion

VI. A WIN OR LOSS FOR THE ACLU?

The ACLU, as counsel of record, urged reversal of the judgment of the District Court for the Southern District of Mississippi; the Supreme Court reversed and remanded in a 9-0 vote, giving the ACLU an apparent win.

821. Chandler v. Miller

(Decided April 15, 1997; 520 U.S. 305)

I. ISSUE

A. Issues Discussed

Fourth Amendment, search and seizure, drug testing

B. Legal Question Presented

Whether Georgia's requirement of "candidates for designated state offices to certify that they have taken a drug test and that the test result was negative . . . ranks among the limited circumstances in which suspicionless searches are warranted."

C. Supreme Court's Answer

"Georgia's requirement that candidates for state office pass a drug test, we hold, does not fit within the closely guarded category of constitutionally permissible suspicionless searches."

II. CASE SUMMARY

A. Background

"The prescription at issue, approved by the Georgia Legislature in 1990, orders that '[e]ach candidate seeking to qualify for nomination or election to a state office shall as a condition of such qualification be required to certify that such candidate has tested negative for illegal drugs.' § 21-2-140(b). Georgia was the first, and apparently remains the only, State to condition candidacy for state office on a drug test. . . .

Petitioners were Libertarian Party nominees in 1994 for state offices subject to the requirements of § 21–2–140. The Party nominated Walker L. Chandler for the office of Lieutenant Governor, Sharon T. Harris for the office of Commissioner of Agriculture, and James D. Walker for the office of member of the General Assembly. In May 1994, about one month before the deadline for submission of the certificates required by § 21–2–140, petitioners Chandler, Harris, and Walker filed this action in the United States District Court for the Northern District of Georgia. They asserted, inter alia, that the drug tests required by § 21–2–140 violated their rights under the First, Fourth, and Fourteenth Amendments to the United States Constitution. Naming as defendants Governor Zell D. Miller and two other state officials involved in the administration of § 21–2–140, petitioners requested declaratory and injunctive relief barring enforcement of the statute.

In June 1994, the District Court denied petitioners' motion for a preliminary injunction. Stressing the importance of the state offices sought and the relative unintrusiveness of the testing procedure, the court found it unlikely that petitioners would prevail on the merits of their claims. Petitioners apparently submitted to the drug tests, obtained the certificates required by § 21–2–140, and appeared on the ballot. After the 1994 election, the parties jointly moved for the entry of final judgment on stipulated facts. In January 1995, the District Court entered final judgment for respondents.

A divided Eleventh Circuit panel affirmed."

The Supreme Court granted certiorari to review the case and reversed.

B. Counsel of Record / ACLU Attorney

ACLU Side (Petitioner / Appellant): Walker L. Chandler argued the cause for appellant.

Opposing Side (Respondent / Appellee): Patricia Guilday, Assistant Attorney General of Georgia, argued the cause for appellees.

III. AMICI CURIAE

ACLU Side (Petitioner / Appellant)

Brief of amici curiae filed on behalf of the ACLU, et al., by Stephen H. Sachs, Stephen M. Cutler, Edward P. Sullivan, Steven R. Shapiro, Gerald R. Weber, Arthur B. Spitzer, and Barbara E. Bergman.

Opposing Side (Respondent / Appellee)

Brief of amici curiae filed on behalf of the Washington Legal Foundation, et al., by Richard K. Willard, Daniel J. Popeo, K. Lee Blalack, II, and Paul D. Kamenar.

Brief of amici curiae filed on behalf of the United States by Acting Solicitor General Dellinger, Assistant Attorney General Hunger, Deputy Solicitor General Waxman, James A. Feldman, Leonard Schaitman, and Edward Himmelfarb.

IV. THE SUPREME COURT'S DECISION

"Georgia's drug-testing requirement, imposed by law and enforced by state officials, effects a search within the meaning of the Fourth and Fourteenth Amendments. . . . To be reasonable under the Fourth Amendment, a search ordinarily must be based on individualized suspicion of wrongdoing. But particularized exceptions to the main rule are sometimes warranted based on 'special needs, beyond the normal need for law enforcement.'

[W]e note, first, that the testing method the Georgia statute describes is relatively noninvasive; therefore, if the 'special needs' showing had been made, the State could not be faulted for excessive intrusion. Georgia's statute invokes the drug-testing guidelines applicable to the federal programs upheld in Skinner and Von Raab. The State permits a candidate to provide the urine specimen in the office of his or her private physician; and the results of the test are given first to the candidate, who controls further dissemination of the report. Because the State has effectively limited the invasiveness of the testing procedure, we concentrate on the core issue: Is the certification requirement warranted by a special need?

Our precedents establish that the proffered special need for drug testing must be substantial—important enough to override the individual's acknowledged privacy interest, sufficiently vital to suppress the Fourth Amendment's normal requirement of individualized suspicion. Georgia has failed to show, in justification of § 21–2–140, a special need of that kind. . . .

In contrast to the effective testing regimes upheld in Skinner, Von Raab, and Vernonia, Georgia's certification requirement is not well designed to identify candidates who violate antidrug laws. Nor is the scheme a credible means to deter illicit drug users from seeking election to state office. The test date—to be scheduled by the candidate anytime within 30 days prior to qualifying for a place on the ballot—is no secret. As counsel for respondents acknowledged at oral argument, users of illegal drugs, save for those prohibitively addicted, could abstain for a pretest period sufficient to avoid detection. Even if we indulged respondents' argument that one purpose of § 21–2–140 might be to detect those unable so to abstain, respondents have not shown or argued that such persons are likely to be candidates for public office in Georgia. Moreover, respondents have offered no reason why ordinary law enforcement methods would not suffice to apprehend such addicted individuals, should they appear in the limelight of a public stage. Section 21-2-140, in short, is not needed and cannot work to ferret out lawbreakers, and respondents barely attempt to support the statute on that ground. . . .

We reiterate . . . that where the risk to public safety is substantial and real, blanket suspicionless searches calibrated to the risk may rank as 'reasonable'—for example, searches now routine at airports and at entrances to courts and other official buildings. But where, as in this case, public safety is not genuinely in jeopardy, the Fourth Amendment precludes the suspicionless search, no matter how conveniently arranged. . . .

For the reasons stated, the judgment of the Court of Appeals for the Eleventh Circuit is reversed."

V. JUSTICE VOTE

8 Pro ACLU Side vs. 1 Con Opposing Side

ACLU Side (Petitioner / Appellant)

1. Ginsburg, R. – Wrote majority opinion

2. Stevens, J. – Joined majority opinion
3. O'Connor, S. – Joined majority opinion
4. Scalia, A. – Joined majority opinion
5. Kennedy, A. – Joined majority opinion
6. Souter, D. – Joined majority opinion
7. Thomas, C. – Joined majority opinion
8. Breyer, S. – Joined majority opinion

Opposing Side (Respondent / Appellee)

1. Rehnquist, W. – Wrote dissenting opinion

VI. A WIN OR LOSS FOR THE ACLU?

The ACLU, as amicus curiae, urged reversal of the judgment of the Court of Appeals for the Eleventh Circuit; the Supreme Court reversed in an 8-1 vote, giving the ACLU an apparent win.

822. Blessing v. Freestone

(Decided April 21, 1997; 520 U.S. 329)

I. ISSUE

A. Issues Discussed

Child support, Social Security Act

B. Legal Question Presented

"[W]hether individuals may sue state officials under § 1983 for violations of Title IV–D."

C. Supreme Court's Answer

"Title IV–D contains no private remedy—either judicial or administrative—through which aggrieved persons can seek redress." Therefore, § 1983 may provide a remedy for individuals and the case must be remanded to make this determination.

II. CASE SUMMARY

A. Background

"This case concerns a lawsuit brought by five mothers in Arizona whose children are eligible to receive child support services from the State pursuant to Title IV–D of the Social Security Act . . . . These custodial parents sued the director of Arizona's child support agency under Rev. Stat. § 1979, 42 U.S.C. § 1983, claiming that they had an enforceable individual right to have the State's program achieve 'substantial compliance' with the requirements of Title IV–D. . . .

The Director immediately moved to dismiss the complaint on several grounds, arguing primarily that Title IV–D creates no individual rights enforceable under § 1983. The District Court treated this motion as one for summary judgment and ruled in favor of the Director. Relying primarily on a decision of the Court of Appeals for the Sixth Circuit, Carelli v. Howser, 923 F.2d 1208 (1991), the District Court held that Congress had foreclosed private actions to enforce Title IV–D by authorizing the Secretary to audit and cut off funds to States with programs that do not substantially comply with Title IV–D's requirements.

A divided panel of the Court of Appeals for the Ninth Circuit reversed."

The Supreme Court granted certiorari to review the case, vacated, and remanded.

B. Counsel of Record / ACLU Attorney

ACLU Side (Respondent / Appellee): Marsha S. Berzon argued the cause for appellees.

Patricia A. Millett argued the cause for the United States, as amicus curiae, by special leave of Court.

Opposing Side (Petitioner / Appellant): C. Tim Delaney, Solicitor General of Arizona, argued the cause for appellant.

III. AMICI CURIAE

ACLU Side (Respondent / Appellee)

Brief of amici curiae filed on behalf of the ACLU, et al., by Christopher A. Hansen, Steven R. Shapiro, and Erwin Chemerinsky.

Brief of amici curiae filed on behalf of the United States by Patricia A. Millett, Acting Solicitor General Dellinger, Assistant Attorney General Hunger, Deputy Solicitor General Kneedler, William Kanter, and Alfred Mollin.

Brief of amici curiae filed on behalf of the Anti-Poverty Project of the Edwin F. Mandel Legal Aid Clinic of the University of Chicago Law School by Gary H. Palm.

Brief of amici curiae filed on behalf of the National Center for Youth Law, et al., by Leora Gershenzon, Martha Matthews, Paula Roberts, and Brian Paddock.

Brief of amici curiae filed on behalf of the National Women's Law Center, et al., by Reginald G. Maloney, Maria Laura Acebal, Nicole Chapin Duke, Sherry Leiwant, Nancy Duff Campbell, Elisabeth Hirschhorn Donahue, and Martha F. Davis.

Opposing Side (Petitioner / Appellant)

Brief of amici curiae filed on behalf of the State of Illinois, et al., by James E. Ryan, Attorney General of Illinois, Barbara A. Preiner, Solicitor General, and James C. O'Connell, Barbara L. Greenspan, and James C. Stevens, Special Assistant Attorneys General, and Charles F. C. Ruff, Corporation Counsel of the District of Columbia, and by the Attorneys General for their respective jurisdictions as follows: Jeff Sessions of Alabama, Bruce M. Botelho of Alaska, Daniel E. Lungren of California, Gale A. Norton of Colorado, Richard Blumenthal of Connecticut, M. Jane Brady of Delaware, Robert A. Butterworth of Florida, Michael J. Bowers of Georgia, Margery S. Bronster of Hawaii, Alan G. Lance of Idaho, Pamela S. Carter of Indiana, Thomas J. Miller of Iowa, Carla J. Stovall of Kansas, Richard P. Ieyoub of Louisiana, Andrew Ketterer of Maine, J. Joseph Curran, Jr., of Maryland, Scott Harshbarger of Massachusetts, Frank J. Kelley of Michigan, Mike Moore of Mississippi, Joseph P. Mazurek of Montana, Don Stenberg of Nebraska, Frankie Sue Del Papa of Nevada, Jeffrey R. Howard of New Hampshire, Peter Verniero of New Jersey, Dennis C. Vacco of New York, Michael F. Easley of North Carolina, Heidi Heitkamp of North Dakota, Betty D. Montgomery of Ohio, W. A. Drew Edmondson of Oklahoma, Theodore R. Kulongoski of Oregon, Thomas W. Corbett, Jr., of Pennsylvania, Jeffrey B. Pine of Rhode Island, Charles Molony Condon of South Carolina, Mark Barnett of South Dakota, Charles W. Burson of

Tennessee, Dan Morales of Texas, Jan Graham of Utah, Jeffrey L. Amestoy of Vermont, James S. Gilmore III of Virginia, Christine O. Gregoire of Washington, William U. Hill of Wyoming, Malaetasi M. Togafau of American Samoa, Calvin E. Holloway, Sr., of Guam, and Julio A. Brady of the Virgin Islands.

Brief of amici curiae filed on behalf of the American Public Welfare Association, et al., by Diana L. Fogle.

Brief of amici curiae filed on behalf of the Council of State Governments, et al., by Richard Ruda and Charles Rothfeld.

Brief of amici curiae filed on behalf of the National District Attorneys Association, et al., by John D. Krisor, Jr., John Kaye, Michael P. Barnes, Michale G. Gotsch, Elizabeth B. Hurley, Michael R. Capizi, John Ladenburg, John Carson, Jerry N. Estes, and Michael McCormick.

IV. THE SUPREME COURT'S DECISION

"[W]e turn first to the question whether respondents have established that Title IV–D gives them federal rights.

[I]t is not at all apparent that respondents sought any relief more specific than a declaration that their 'rights' were being violated and an injunction forcing Arizona's child support agency to 'substantially comply' with all of the provisions of Title IV–D. We think that this defect is best addressed by sending the case back for the District Court to construe the complaint in the first instance, in order to determine exactly what rights, considered in their most concrete, specific form, respondents are asserting. Only by manageably breaking down the complaint into specific allegations can the District Court proceed to determine whether any specific claim asserts an individual federal right. . . .

Because we leave open the possibility that Title IV–D may give rise to some individually enforceable rights, we pause to consider petitioner's final argument that no remand is warranted because the statute contains 'a remedial scheme that is 'sufficiently comprehensive . . . to demonstrate congressional intent to preclude the remedy of suits under § 1983.' Because petitioner does not claim that any provision of Title IV–D expressly curtails § 1983 actions, she must make the difficult showing that allowing § 1983 actions to go forward in these circumstances 'would be inconsistent with Congress' carefully tailored scheme.' . . .

The enforcement scheme that Congress created in Title IV–D is far more limited than those in Sea Clammers and Smith. Unlike the federal programs at issue in those cases, Title IV–D contains no private remedy—either judicial or administrative—through which aggrieved persons can seek redress. The only way that Title IV–D assures that States live up to their child support plans is through the Secretary's oversight. . . . To the extent that Title IV–D may give rise to individual rights, therefore, we agree with the Court of Appeals that the Secretary's oversight powers are not comprehensive enough to close the door on § 1983 liability. . . .

The judgment of the Court of Appeals is vacated, and the case is remanded with instructions to remand to the District Court for further proceedings consistent with this opinion."

V. JUSTICE VOTE

0 Pro ACLU Side vs. 9 Con Opposing Side

Opposing Side (Petitioner / Appellant)

1. O'Connor, S. – Wrote majority opinion
2. Rehnquist, W. – Joined majority opinion
3. Breyer, S. – Joined majority opinion
4. Ginsburg, R. – Joined majority opinion
5. Souter, D. – Joined majority opinion
6. Kennedy, A. – Joined Scalia's concurrence
7. Scalia, A. – Wrote concurring opinion
8. Thomas, C. – Joined majority opinion
9. Stevens, J. – Joined majority opinion

VI. A WIN OR LOSS FOR THE ACLU?

The ACLU, as amicus curiae, urged affirmance of the judgment of the Court of Appeals for the Ninth Circuit; the Supreme Court vacated and remanded in a 9-0 vote, giving the ACLU an apparent loss.

823. Timmons v. Twin Cities Area New Party

(Decided April 28, 1997; 520 U.S. 351)

I. ISSUE

A. Issues Discussed

First Amendment, freedom of association, Fourteenth Amendment, elections

B. Legal Question Presented

Whether a prohibition on "multiple-party, or 'fusion,' candidacies for elected office . . . violate[s] the First and Fourteenth Amendments to the United States Constitution."

C. Supreme Court's Answer

"We hold that such a prohibition does not violate the First and Fourteenth Amendments to the United States Constitution."

II. CASE SUMMARY

A. Background

"Most States prohibit multiple-party, or 'fusion,' candidacies for elected office. The Minnesota laws challenged in this case prohibit a candidate from appearing on the ballot as the candidate of more than one party. . . .

Respondent is a chartered chapter of the national New Party. Petitioners are Minnesota election officials. In April 1994, Minnesota State Representative Andy Dawkins was running unopposed in the Minnesota Democratic–Farmer–Labor Party's (DFL) primary. That same month, New Party members chose Dawkins as their candidate for the same office in the November 1994 general election. Neither Dawkins nor the DFL objected, and Dawkins signed the required affidavit of candidacy for the New Party. Minnesota, however, prohibits fusion candidacies. Because Dawkins had already filed as a candidate for the DFL's nomination, local election officials refused to accept the New Party's nominating petition.

The New Party filed suit in United States District Court, contending that Minnesota's antifusion laws violated the party's associational rights under the First and Fourteenth Amendments. The District Court granted summary judgment for the state defendants, concluding that Minnesota's fusion ban was 'a valid and non-discriminatory regulation of the election process,' and noting that 'issues concerning the mechanics of choosing candidates . . . are, in large part, matters of policy best left to the deliberative bodies themselves.'

The Court of Appeals reversed."

The Supreme Court granted certiorari to review the case and reversed.

B. Counsel of Record / ACLU Attorney

ACLU Side (Respondent / Appellee): Laurence H. Tribe argued the cause for appellee.

Opposing Side (Petitioner / Appellant): Richard S. Slowes, Assistant Solicitor General of Minnesota, argued the cause for appellant.

III. AMICI CURIAE

ACLU Side (Respondent / Appellee)

Brief of amici curiae filed on behalf of the ACLU, et al., by Burt Neuborne, Steven R. Shapiro, Elliot M. Mincberg, and Lawrence S. Ottinger.

Brief of amici curiae filed on behalf of the Conservative Party of New York, et al., by Rory O. Millson.

Brief of amici curiae filed on behalf of the Reform Party, et al., by J. Gregory Taylor.

Brief of amici curiae filed on behalf of the Republican National Committee by David A. Norcross, Scott S. Harris, Jan Witold Baran and Thomas J. Josefiak.

Brief of amici curiae filed on behalf of Twelve University Professors, et al., by David Halperin.

Opposing Side (Petitioner / Appellant)

No briefs of amici curiae were filed in support of appellant.

IV. THE SUPREME COURT'S DECISION

"When deciding whether a state election law violates First and Fourteenth Amendment associational rights, we weigh the "character and magnitude" of the burden the State's rule imposes on those rights against the interests the State contends justify that burden, and consider the extent to which the State's concerns make the burden necessary. . . .

The New Party's claim that it has a right to select its own candidate is uncontroversial, so far as it goes. That is, the New Party, and not someone else, has the right to select the New Party's 'standard bearer.' It does not follow, though, that a party is absolutely entitled to have its nominee appear on the ballot as that party's candidate. A particular candidate might be ineligible for office, unwilling to serve, or, as here, another party's candidate. That a particular individual may not appear on the ballot as a particular party's candidate does not severely burden that party's associational rights. . . .

The Court of Appeals emphasized its belief that, without fusion-based alliances, minor parties cannot thrive. This is a predictive judgment which is by no means self-evident. But, more importantly, the supposed benefits of fusion to minor parties do not require that Minnesota permit it. Many features of our political system—e.g., single-member districts, 'first past the post' elections, and the high costs of campaigning—make it difficult for third parties to succeed in American politics. But the Constitution does not require States to permit fusion any more than it requires them to move to proportional-representation elections or public financing of campaigns. . . .

We conclude that the burdens Minnesota's fusion ban imposes on the New Party's associational rights are justified by 'correspondingly weighty' valid state interests in ballot integrity and political stability. In deciding that Minnesota's fusion ban does not unconstitutionally burden the New Party's First and Fourteenth Amendment rights, we express no views on the New Party's policy-based arguments concerning the wisdom of fusion. It may well be that, as support for new political parties increases, these arguments will carry the day in some States' legislatures. But the Constitution does not require Minnesota, and the approximately 40 other States that do not permit fusion, to allow it. The judgment of the Court of Appeals is reversed."

V. JUSTICE VOTE

3 Pro ACLU Side vs. 6 Con Opposing Side

ACLU Side (Respondent / Appellee)

1. Souter, D. – Wrote dissenting opinion, joined Stevens' dissent in part
2. Stevens, J. – Wrote dissenting opinion
3. Ginsburg, R. – Joined Stevens' dissent

Opposing Side (Petitioner / Appellant)

1. Rehnquist, W. – Wrote majority opinion
2. O'Connor, S. – Joined majority opinion
3. Breyer, S. – Joined majority opinion
4. Kennedy, A. – Joined majority opinion
5. Scalia, A. – Joined majority opinion
6. Thomas, C. – Joined majority opinion

VI. A WIN OR LOSS FOR THE ACLU?

The ACLU, as amicus curiae, urged affirmance of the judgment of the Court of Appeals for the Eighth Circuit; the Supreme Court reversed in a 6-3 vote, giving the ACLU an apparent loss.

824. Richards v. Wisconsin

(Decided April 28, 1997; 520 U.S. 385)

I. ISSUE

A. Issues Discussed

Fourth Amendment, search and seizure

B. Legal Question Presented

Whether the Wisconsin Supreme Court's blanket exception to the knock-and-announce rule for felony drug cases violates the Fourth Amendment and whether the officers' entry without knocking and announcing in this case violated the Fourth Amendment."

C. Supreme Court's Answer

The blanket exception violates the Fourth Amendment, but the entry without knocking and announcing in this case was reasonable and, therefore, did not violate the Fourth Amendment.

II. CASE SUMMARY

A. Background

"In Wilson v. Arkansas, 514 U.S. 927 (1995), [the Supreme Court] held that the Fourth Amendment incorporates the common law requirement that police officers entering a dwelling must knock on the door and announce their identity and purpose before attempting forcible entry. At the same time, we recognized that the 'flexible requirement of reasonableness should not be read to mandate a rigid rule of announcement that ignores countervailing law enforcement interests,' and left 'to the lower courts the task of determining the circumstances under which an unannounced entry is reasonable under the Fourth Amendment.'

In this case, the Wisconsin Supreme Court concluded that police officers are never required to knock and announce their presence when executing a search warrant in a felony drug investigation. In so doing, it reaffirmed a pre-Wilson holding and concluded that Wilson did not preclude this per se rule. . . .

The Wisconsin Supreme Court did not delve into the events underlying Richards' arrest in any detail, but accepted the following facts: '[O]n December 31, 1991, police executed a search warrant for the motel room of the defendant seeking evidence of the felonious crime of Possession with Intent to Deliver a Controlled Substance in violation of Wis. Stat. § 161.41(1m) (1991-92). They did not knock and announce prior to their entry. Drugs were seized.'"

The Supreme Court granted certiorari to review the case, affirmed the judgment of the Wisconsin Supreme Court that the officers did not need to knock and announce in this case, but rejected the court's per se rule.

B. Counsel of Record / ACLU Attorney

ACLU Side (Petitioner / Appellant): David R. Karpe argued the cause for appellant.

Opposing Side (Respondent / Appellee): James E. Doyle, Attorney General of Wisconsin, argued the cause for appellee.

Miguel A. Estrada argued the cause for the United States, as amicus curiae, by special leave of Court.

III. AMICI CURIAE

ACLU Side (Petitioner / Appellant)

Brief of amici curiae filed on behalf of the ACLU, et al., by Tracey Maclin, Steven R. Shapiro, and Lisa B. Kemler.

Opposing Side (Respondent / Appellee)

Brief of amici curiae filed on behalf of the United States by Miguel A. Estrada, Acting Solicitor General Dellinger, Acting Assistant Attorney General Richard, Deputy Solicitor General Dreeben, James A. Feldman, and Deborah Watson.

Brief of amici curiae filed on behalf of the State of Ohio, et al., by Betty D. Montgomery, Attorney General of Ohio, Jeffrey S. Sutton, State Solicitor, Simon B. Karas, and Diane R. Richards, and by the Attorneys General for their respective jurisdictions as follows: Bill Pryor of Alabama, Bruce M. Botelho of Alaska, Winston Bryant of Arkansas, M. Jane Brady of Delaware, Robert A. Butterworth of Florida, Gus F. Diaz of Guam, Alan G. Lance of Idaho, James E. Ryan of Illinois, Carla J. Stovall of Kansas, A. B. Chandler III of Kentucky, Richard P. Ieyoub of Louisiana, J. Joseph Curran of Maryland, Frank J. Kelley of Michigan, Mike Moore of Mississippi, Joseph P. Mazurek of Montana, Don Stenberg of Nebraska, Thomas J. Miller of Iowa, Frankie Sue Del Papa of Nevada, Steven M. Houran of New Hampshire, Peter Verniero of New Jersey, Tom Udall of New Mexico, Jose Fuentes Agostini of Puerto Rico, Jeffrey B. Pine of Rhode Island, Charles Molony Condon of South Carolina, Mark W. Barnett of South Dakota, Jan Graham of Utah, and James Gilmore III of Virginia.

Brief of amici curiae filed on behalf of Americans for Effective Law Enforcement, Inc., et al., by Fred E. Inbau, Wayne W. Schmidt, James P. Manak, Roy Caldwell Kime, David S. Williams, and Bernard J. Farber.

IV. THE SUPREME COURT'S DECISION

"[T]he fact that felony drug investigations may frequently present circumstances warranting a no-knock entry cannot remove from the neutral scrutiny of a reviewing court the reasonableness of the police decision not to knock and announce in a particular case. Instead, in each case, it is the duty of a court confronted with the question to determine whether the facts and circumstances of the particular entry justified dispensing with the knock-and-announce requirement.

In order to justify a 'no-knock' entry, the police must have a reasonable suspicion that knocking and announcing their presence, under the particular circumstances, would be dangerous or futile, or that it would inhibit the effective investigation of the crime by, for example, allowing the destruction of evidence. . . .

Although we reject the Wisconsin court's blanket exception to the knock-and-announce requirement, we conclude that the officers' no-knock entry into Richards' motel room did not violate the Fourth Amendment. We agree with the trial court, and with Justice Abrahamson, that the circumstances in this case show that the officers had a reasonable suspicion that Richards might destroy evidence if given further opportunity to do so. [The] actual circumstances—petitioner's apparent recognition of the officers combined with the easily disposable nature of the drugs—justified the officers' ultimate decision to enter without first announcing their presence and authority.

Accordingly, although we reject the blanket exception to the knock-and-announce requirement for felony drug investigations, the judgment of the Wisconsin Supreme Court is affirmed."

V. JUSTICE VOTE

0 Pro ACLU Side vs. 9 Con Opposing Side

Opposing Side (Respondent / Appellee)

1. Stevens, J. – Wrote majority opinion
2. Rehnquist, W. – Joined majority opinion
3. O'Connor, S. – Joined majority opinion
4. Breyer, S. – Joined majority opinion
5. Ginsburg, R. – Joined majority opinion
6. Souter, D. – Joined majority opinion
7. Kennedy, A. – Joined majority opinion
8. Scalia, A. – Joined majority opinion
9. Thomas, C. – Joined majority opinion

VI. A WIN OR LOSS FOR THE ACLU?

The ACLU, as amicus curiae, urged reversal of the judgment of the Supreme Court of Wisconsin; the U.S. Supreme Court affirmed in a 9-0 vote, giving the ACLU an apparent loss.

825. Edwards v. Balisok

(Decided May 19, 1997; 520 U.S. 641)

I. ISSUE

A. Issues Discussed

Fourteenth Amendment, prisoners' rights, due process

B. Legal Question Presented

"[W]hether a claim for damages and declaratory relief brought by a state prisoner challenging the validity of the procedures used to deprive him of good-time credits is cognizable under § 1983."

C. Supreme Court's Answer

A claim by a state prisoner challenging only the procedures used to deprive him of good-time credits is not cognizable under § 1983.

II. CASE SUMMARY

A. Background

"Respondent Jerry Balisok is an inmate at the Washington State Penitentiary in Walla Walla. On August 16, 1993, he was charged with, and at a hearing on September 2 was found guilty of, four prison infractions. He was sentenced to 10 days in isolation, 20 days in segregation, and deprivation of 30 days' good-time credit he had previously earned toward his release. His appeal within the prison's appeal system was rejected for failure to comply with the applicable procedural requirements.

On January 26, 1994, respondent filed the present § 1983 action alleging that the procedures used in his disciplinary proceeding violated his Fourteenth Amendment due process rights. His amended complaint requested a declaration that the procedures employed by state officials violated due process, compensatory and punitive damages for use of the unconstitutional procedures, an injunction to prevent future violations, and any other relief the court deems just and equitable. Taking account of our opinion in Preiser v. Rodriguez, 411 U.S. 475 (1973), which held that the sole remedy in federal court for a prisoner seeking restoration of good-time credits is a writ of habeas corpus, Balisok's amended complaint did not request restoration of the lost credits. (As the District Court noted, however, he expressly reserved the right to seek that relief in an appropriate forum.)

The District Court, applying our opinion in Heck, held that a judgment in Balisok's favor 'would necessarily imply the invalidity of the disciplinary hearing and the resulting sanctions.' Rather than grant petitioners' motion to dismiss, however, the District Court stayed this action pending filing and resolution of a state-court action for restoration of the good-time credits. It authorized an immediate appeal of its ruling pursuant to 28 U.S.C. § 1292(b), and the Court of Appeals for the Ninth Circuit reversed, holding that a claim challenging only the procedures employed in a disciplinary hearing is always cognizable under § 1983."

The Supreme Court granted certiorari to review the case and reversed.

B. Counsel of Record / ACLU Attorney

ACLU Side (Respondent / Appellee): Thomas H. Speedy Rice argued the cause for appellee.

Opposing Side (Petitioner / Appellant): Kathleen D. Mix, Assistant Attorney General of Washington, argued the cause for appellant.

III. AMICI CURIAE

ACLU Side (Respondent / Appellee)

Brief of amici curiae filed on behalf of the ACLU, et al., by David C. Fathi, John Midgley, Patricia J. Arthur, Don Saunders, Katrin E. Frank, and Steven R. Shapiro.

Opposing Side (Petitioner / Appellant)

Brief of amici curiae filed on behalf of the State of California, et al., by Daniel E. Lungren, Attorney General of California, George Williamson, Chief Assistant Attorney General, and Peter J. Siggins, Senior Assistant Attorney General, Charles F. C. Ruff, Corporation Counsel of the District of Columbia, and by the Attorneys General for their respective States as follows: Bruce M. Botelho of Alaska, Grant Woods of Arizona, Gale A. Norton of Colorado, Richard Blumenthal of Connecticut, Robert A. Butterworth of Florida, Carla J. Stovall of Kansas, Mike Moore of Mississippi, Joe Mazurek of Montana, Don Stenberg of Nebraska, Frankie Sue Del Papa of Nevada, Dennis C. Vacco of New York, W. A. Drew Edmondson of Oklahoma, Thomas W. Corbett, Jr., of Pennsylvania, Charles Molony Condon of South Carolina, James S. Gilmore III of Virginia, and James E. Doyle of Wisconsin.

IV. THE SUPREME COURT'S DECISION

"In Heck v. Humphrey, 512 U.S. 477 (1994), this Court held that a state prisoner's claim for damages is not cognizable under 42 U.S.C. § 1983 if 'a judgment in favor of the plaintiff would necessarily imply the invalidity of his conviction or sentence,' unless the prisoner can demonstrate that the conviction or sentence has previously been invalidated. . . .

The violations of due process alleged by respondent are similar to those alleged by the plaintiff in Heck. . . . There is, however, this critical difference from Heck: Respondent, in his amended complaint, limited his request to damages for depriving him of good-time credits without due process, not for depriving him of good-time credits undeservedly as a substantive matter. That is to say, his claim posited that the procedures were wrong, but not necessarily that the result was. The distinction between these two sorts of claims is clearly established in our case law, as is the plaintiff's entitlement to recover at least nominal damages under § 1983 if he proves the former one without also proving the latter one. . . .

We conclude . . . that respondent's claim for declaratory relief and money damages, based on allegations of deceit and bias on the part of the decisionmaker that necessarily imply the invalidity of the punishment imposed, is not cognizable under § 1983. Respondent also requests, however, prospective injunctive relief. His amended complaint alleges that prison officials routinely fail to date-stamp witness statements that are made in cases involving 'jail house attorney[s]' like himself, in order to weaken any due process challenge for failure to call witnesses. He requests an injunction requiring prison officials to date-stamp witness statements at the time they are received. Ordinarily, a prayer for such prospective relief will not 'necessarily imply' the invalidity of a previous loss of good-time credits, and so may properly be brought under § 1983. To prevail, of course, respondent must establish standing, and meet the usual requirements for injunctive relief. Neither the Ninth Circuit nor the District Court considered this injunctive claim, and its validity was neither briefed nor argued here. We leave this issue for consideration by the lower courts on remand. . . .

The judgment of the Ninth Circuit is reversed, and the case is remanded for further proceedings consistent with this opinion."

V. JUSTICE VOTE

0 Pro ACLU Side vs. 9 Con Opposing Side

Opposing Side (Petitioner / Appellant)

1. Scalia, A. – Wrote majority opinion
2. Rehnquist, W. – Joined majority opinion
3. O'Connor, S. – Joined majority opinion
4. Breyer, S. – Joined Ginsburg's concurrence
5. Souter, D. – Joined Ginsburg's concurrence
6. Kennedy, A. – Joined majority opinion
7. Thomas, C. – Joined majority opinion
8. Stevens, J. – Joined majority opinion
9. Ginsburg, R. – Wrote concurring opinion

VI. A WIN OR LOSS FOR THE ACLU?

The ACLU, as amicus curiae, urged affirmance of the judgment of the Court of Appeals for the Ninth Circuit; the Supreme Court reversed and remanded in a 9-0 vote, giving the ACLU an apparent loss.

826. Reno v. Bossier Parish School Board

(Decided May 21, 1997; 520 U.S. 471)

I. ISSUE

A. Issues Discussed

Voting Rights Act of 1965

B. Legal Question Presented

"(i) [W]hether preclearance must be denied under § 5 whenever a covered jurisdiction's new voting 'standard, practice, or procedure' violates § 2; and (ii) whether evidence that a new 'standard, practice, or procedure' has a dilutive impact is always irrelevant to the inquiry whether the covered jurisdiction acted with 'the purpose . . . of denying or abridging the right to vote on account of race or color' under § 5."

C. Supreme Court's Answer

Preclearance under § 5 may not be denied solely based on a determination of a violation of § 2, but evidence of a dilutive impact may be relevant to a § 5 determination.

II. CASE SUMMARY

A. Background

"Appellee Bossier Parish School Board (Board) is a jurisdiction subject to the preclearance requirements of § 5 of the Voting Rights Act of 1965, 42 U.S.C. § 1973c, and must therefore obtain the approval of either the United States Attorney General or the United States District Court for the District of Columbia before implementing any changes to a voting 'qualification, prerequisite, standard, practice, or procedure.' The Board has 12 members who are elected from single-member districts by majority vote to serve 4-year terms. When the 1990 census revealed wide population disparities among its districts, the Board decided to redraw the districts to equalize the population distribution.

During this process, the Board considered two redistricting plans. It considered, and initially rejected, the redistricting plan that had been recently adopted by the Bossier Parish Police Jury, the parish's primary governing body (the Jury plan), to govern its own elections. Just months before, the Attorney General had precleared the Jury plan, which also contained 12 districts. None of the 12 districts in the Board's existing plan or in the Jury plan contained a majority of black residents. Because the Board's adoption of the Jury plan would have maintained the status quo regarding the number of black-majority districts, the parties stipulated that the Jury plan was not 'retrogressive.' Appellant George Price, president of the local chapter of the National Association for the Advancement of Colored People (NAACP), presented the Board with a second option—a plan that created two districts each containing not only a majority of black residents, but a majority of voting-age black residents. Over vocal opposition from local residents, black and white alike, the Board voted to adopt the Jury plan as its own, reasoning that the Jury plan would almost certainly be precleared again and that the NAACP plan would require the Board to split 46 electoral precincts.

But the Board's hopes for rapid preclearance were dashed when the Attorney General interposed a formal objection to the Board's plan on the basis of 'new information' not available when the Justice Department had precleared the plan for the Police Jury—namely, the NAACP's plan, which demonstrated that 'black residents are sufficiently numerous and geographically compact so as to constitute a majority in two single-member districts.' The objection letter asserted that the Board's plan violated § 2 of the Act, 42 U.S.C. § 1973, because it 'unnecessarily limit[ed] the opportunity for minority voters to elect their candidates of choice," as compared to the new alternative. Relying on 28 CFR § 51.55(b)(2) (1996), which provides that the Attorney General shall withhold preclearance where 'necessary to prevent a clear violation of amended Section 2 [42 U.S.C. § 1973],' the Attorney General concluded that the Board's redistricting plan warranted a denial of preclearance under § 5. The Attorney General declined to reconsider the decision.

The Board then filed this action seeking preclearance under § 5 in the District Court for the District of Columbia. Appellant Price and others intervened as defendants. The three-judge panel granted the Board's request for preclearance, over the dissent of one judge."

The Supreme Court granted certiorari to review the case, vacated, and remanded.

B. Counsel of Record / ACLU Attorney

ACLU Side (Petitioner / Appellant): Assistant Attorney General Deval L. Patrick argued the cause for appellant in No. 95–1455. John W. Borkowski argued the cause for appellants in No. 95–1508.

Opposing Side (Respondent / Appellee): Michael A. Carvin argued the cause for appellee.

III. AMICI CURIAE

ACLU Side (Petitioner / Appellant)

Brief of amici curiae filed on behalf of the ACLU, et al., by Laughlin McDonald, Neil Bradley, Maka S. Zaki, Steven R. Shapiro, Elaine R. Jones, Norman J. Chachkin, and Jacqueline Berrien.

Opposing Side (Respondent / Appellee)

Brief of amici curiae filed on behalf of the Pacific Legal Foundation by Sharon L. Browne and Deborah J. La Fetra.

IV. THE SUPREME COURT'S DECISION

"Appellants contend that preclearance must be denied under § 5 whenever a covered jurisdiction's redistricting plan violates § 2. The upshot of this position is to shift the focus of § 5 from nonretrogression to vote dilution, and to change the § 5 benchmark from a jurisdiction's existing plan to a hypothetical, undiluted plan.

But § 5, we have held, is designed to combat only those effects that are retrogressive. To adopt appellants' position, we would have to call into question more than 20 years of precedent interpreting § 5. This we decline to do. Section 5 already imposes upon a covered jurisdiction the difficult burden of proving the absence of discriminatory purpose and effect. To require a jurisdiction to litigate whether its proposed redistricting plan also has a dilutive 'result' before it can implement that plan—even if the Attorney General bears the burden of proving that 'result'—is to increase further the serious federalism costs already implicated by § 5.

Of course, the Attorney General or a private plaintiff remains free to initiate a § 2 proceeding if either believes that a jurisdiction's newly enacted voting 'qualification, prerequisite, standard, practice, or procedure' may violate that section. All we hold today is that preclearance under § 5 may not be denied on that basis alone. . . .

Appellants next contend that evidence showing that a jurisdiction's redistricting plan dilutes the voting power of minorities is at least relevant in a § 5 proceeding because it tends to prove that the jurisdiction enacted its plan with a discriminatory 'purpose.' . . .

Because we hold that some of this '§ 2 evidence' may be relevant to establish a jurisdiction's 'intent to retrogress' and cannot say with confidence that the District Court considered the evidence proffered to show that the Board's reapportionment plan was dilutive, we vacate this aspect of the District Court's holding and remand. In light of this conclusion, we leave open for another day the question whether the § 5 purpose inquiry ever extends beyond the search for retrogressive intent. . . .

The judgment of the District Court is vacated, and the case is remanded for further proceedings consistent with this decision."

V. JUSTICE VOTE

2 Pro ACLU Side vs. 7 Con Opposing Side

ACLU Side (Petitioner / Appellant)

1. Stevens, J. – Wrote opinion concurring in part and dissenting in part
2. Souter, D. – Joined Stevens' opinion

Opposing Side (Respondent / Appellee)

1. O'Connor, S. – Wrote majority opinion
2. Rehnquist, W. – Joined majority opinion
3. Breyer, S. – Wrote concurring opinion
4. Ginsburg, R. – Joined Breyer's opinion
5. Kennedy, A. – Joined majority opinion
6. Scalia, A. – Joined majority opinion
7. Thomas, C. – Wrote concurring opinion

VI. A WIN OR LOSS FOR THE ACLU?

The ACLU, as amicus curiae, urged reversal of the judgment of the District Court for the District of Columbia; the Supreme Court vacated and remanded in a 7-2 vote, giving the ACLU an apparent loss.

827. Clinton v. Jones

(Decided May 27, 1997; 520 U.S. 681)

I. ISSUE

A. Issues Discussed

Immunity, separation of powers

B. Legal Question Presented

Whether the President, while in office, has temporary immunity from civil litigation arising out of events which transpired prior to his taking office, requiring litigation to be postponed until the end of the President's term in office.

C. Supreme Court's Answer

The President does not have temporary immunity from civil litigation arising from events which transpired prior to his taking office, while in office.

II. CASE SUMMARY

A. Background

"Petitioner, William Jefferson Clinton, was elected to the Presidency in 1992, and re-elected in 1996. His term of office expires on January 20, 2001. In 1991 he was the Governor of the State of Arkansas. Respondent, Paula Corbin Jones, is a resident of California. In 1991 she lived in Arkansas, and was an employee of the Arkansas Industrial Development Commission.

On May 6, 1994, she commenced this action in the United States District Court for the Eastern District of Arkansas by filing a complaint naming petitioner and Danny Ferguson, a former Arkansas State Police officer, as defendants. The complaint alleges two federal claims, and two state-law claims over which the federal court has jurisdiction because of the diverse citizenship of the parties.

[A]llegations principally describe events that are said to have occurred on the afternoon of May 8, 1991, during an official conference held at the Excelsior Hotel in Little Rock, Arkansas. The Governor delivered a speech at the conference; respondent—working as a state employee—staffed the registration desk. She alleges that Ferguson persuaded her to leave her desk and to visit the Governor in a business suite at the hotel, where he made 'abhorrent' sexual advances that she vehemently rejected. She further claims that her superiors at work subsequently dealt with her in a hostile and rude manner, and changed her duties to punish her for rejecting those advances. Finally, she alleges that after petitioner was elected President, Ferguson defamed her by making a statement to a reporter that implied she had accepted petitioner's alleged overtures, and that various persons authorized to speak for the President publicly branded her a liar by denying that the incident had occurred. . . .

In response to the complaint, petitioner promptly advised the District Court that he intended to file a motion to dismiss on grounds of Presidential immunity, and requested the court to defer all other pleadings and motions until after the immunity issue was resolved. . . Petitioner thereupon filed a motion 'to dismiss . . . without prejudice and to toll any statutes of limitation [that may be applicable] until he is no longer President, at which time the plaintiff may refile the instant suit.' . . .

The District Judge denied the motion to dismiss on immunity grounds and ruled that discovery in the case could go forward, but ordered any trial stayed until the end of petitioner's Presidency. . . .

Both parties appealed. A divided panel of the Court of Appeals affirmed the denial of the motion to dismiss, but because it regarded the order postponing the trial until the President leaves office as the 'functional equivalent' of a grant of temporary immunity, it reversed that order. Writing for the majority, Judge Bowman explained that 'the President, like all other government officials, is subject to the same laws that apply to all other members of our society,' that he could find no 'case in which any public official ever has been granted any immunity from suit for his unofficial acts,' and that the rationale for official immunity 'is inapposite where only personal, private conduct by a President is at issue.' . . ."

The Supreme Court granted certiorari to review the case and affirmed.

B. Counsel of Record / ACLU Attorney

ACLU Side (Respondent / Appellee): Gilber K. Davis argued the cause for appellee.

Opposing Side (Petitioner / Appellant): Robert S. Bennett argued the cause for appellant.

Acting Solicitor General Walter Dellinger argued the cause for the United States, as amicus curiae, by special leave of Court.

III. AMICI CURIAE

ACLU Side (Respondent / Appellee)

Brief of amici curiae filed on behalf of the ACLU by Christopher A. Hansen and Steven R. Shapiro.

Opposing Side (Petitioner / Appellant)

Brief of amici curiae filed on behalf the United States by Acting Solicitor General Dellinger, Assistant Attorney General Hunger, Deputy Solicitor General Kneedler, Malcom L. Stewart, Douglas N. Letter, and Scott R. McIntosh.

Brielf of amici curiae filed on behalf of Law Professors by Pamela S. Karlan and John C. Jeffries, Jr.

Brief of amici curiae filed on behalf of American Veterans by Laurence A. Elgin and Michael G. Hoehn.

Brief of amici curiae filed on behalf of Law Professors by Ronald D. Rotunda, Albert E. Jenner, Jr., Stephen B. Burbank, William Cohen, Geoffrey P. Miller, Robert F. Nagel, Richard Parker, Scot Powe, Jr., Stephen B. Presser, and William Van Alstyne.

IV. THE SUPREME COURT'S DECISION

"Petitioner's principal submission—that 'in all but the most exceptional cases,' the Constitution affords the President temporary immunity from civil damages litigation arising out of events that occurred before he took office—cannot be sustained on the basis of precedent. . . .

The principal rationale for affording certain public servants immunity from suits for money damages arising out of their official acts is inapplicable to unofficial conduct. In cases involving prosecutors, legislators, and judges we have repeatedly explained that the immunity serves the public interest in enabling such officials to perform their designated functions effectively without fear that a particular decision may give rise to personal liability. . . .

This reasoning provides no support for an immunity for unofficial conduct. . . .

Petitioner's effort to construct an immunity from suit for unofficial acts grounded purely in the identity of his office is unsupported by precedent. . . .

Petitioner's strongest argument supporting his immunity claim is based on the text and structure of the Constitution. He does not contend that the occupant of the Office of the President is 'above the law,' in the sense that his conduct is entirely immune from judicial scrutiny. The President argues merely for a postponement of the judicial proceedings that will determine whether he violated any law. His argument is grounded in the character of the office that was created by Article II of the Constitution, and relies on separation-of-powers principles that have structured our constitutional arrangement since the founding.

As a starting premise, petitioner contends that he occupies a unique office with powers and responsibilities so vast and important that the public interest demands that he devote his undivided time and attention to his public duties. He submits that—given the nature of the office—the doctrine of separation of powers places limits on the authority of the Federal Judiciary to interfere with the Executive Branch that would be transgressed by allowing this action to proceed. . . .

In sum, '[i]t is settled law that the separation-of-powers doctrine does not bar every exercise of jurisdiction over the President of the United States.' If the Judiciary may severely burden the Executive Branch by reviewing the legality of the President's official conduct, and if it may direct appropriate process to the President himself, it must follow that the federal courts have power to determine the legality of his unofficial conduct. The burden on the President's time and energy that is a mere byproduct of such review surely cannot be considered as onerous as the direct burden imposed by judicial review and the occasional invalidation of his official actions. We therefore hold that the doctrine of separation of powers does not require federal courts to stay all private actions against the President until he leaves office. . . .

The Federal District Court has jurisdiction to decide this case. Like every other citizen who properly invokes that jurisdiction, respondent has a right to an orderly disposition of her claims. Accordingly, the judgment of the Court of Appeals is affirmed."

V. JUSTICE VOTE

9 Pro ACLU Side vs. 0 Con Opposing Side

ACLU Side (Respondent / Appellee)

1. Stevens, J. – Wrote majority opinion
2. Rehnquist, W. – Joined majority opinion
3. O'Connor, S. – Joined majority opinion
4. Scalia, A. – Joined majority opinion
5. Kennedy, A. –Joined majority opinion
6. Souter, D. – Joined majority opinion
7. Thomas, C. – Joined majority opinion
8. Ginsburg, R. – Joined majority opinion
9. Breyer, S. – Wrote concurring opinion

VI. A WIN OR LOSS FOR THE ACLU?

The ACLU, as amicus curiae, urged affirmance of the judgment of the Eighth Circuit Court of Appeals; the Supreme Court affirmed in a 9-0 vote, giving the ACLU an apparent win.

828. McMillian v. Monroe County, Alabama

(Decided June 2, 1997; 520 U.S. 781)

I. ISSUE

A. Issues Discussed

Civil rights, Fourteenth Amendment, liability

B. Legal Question Presented

Whether Sheriff Tom Tate "is a policymaker for Monroe County or for the State of Alabama" for § 1983 liability purposes.

C. Supreme Court's Answer

The sheriff is a policymaker for the State of Alabama, therefore, the lower court properly dismissed petitioner's § 1983 claims against Monroe County.

II. CASE SUMMARY

A. Background

"In November 1986, Ronda Morrison was murdered in Monroe County, a sparsely populated county located in southwest Alabama. Petitioner and one Ralph Myers were indicted for this crime. Myers then pleaded guilty to a lesser offense and testified against petitioner at his trial. A jury convicted petitioner of capital murder, and the trial court sentenced him to death. After two remands, the Alabama Court of Criminal Appeals reversed petitioner's conviction, holding that the State had violated Brady v. Maryland, 373 U.S. 83 (1963), by suppressing statements from Myers that contradicted his trial testimony and other exculpatory evidence. Thus, after spending six years in prison, petitioner was released.

He then brought this § 1983 lawsuit in the District Court for the Middle District of Alabama against respondent Monroe County and numerous officials, including the three men in charge of investigating the Morrison murder—Tom Tate, the Sheriff of Monroe County; Larry Ikner, an investigator with the District Attorney's office in Monroe County; and Simon Benson, an investigator with the Alabama Bureau of Investigation. Only two of the officials were sued in their official capacities—Sheriff Tate and investigator Ikner—and it is only these official-capacity suits that concern us here. Petitioner principally alleged that Tate and Ikner, in their capacities as officials of Monroe County, not as officers of the State of Alabama, intimidated Myers into making false statements and suppressed exculpatory evidence.

The District Court dismissed the claims against Monroe County and the claims against Tate and Ikner in their official capacities. The court held that 'any unlawful acts of Defendants Tate and Ikner cannot be said to represent [Monroe] County's policy,' because 'an Alabama county has [no] authority to make policy in the area of law enforcement.' Petitioner appealed the District Court's decision as to Sheriff Tate. The Court of Appeals for the Eleventh Circuit affirmed, agreeing with the District Court that 'Sheriff Tate is not a final policymaker for Monroe County in the area of law enforcement, because Monroe County has no law enforcement authority.'"

The Supreme Court granted certiorari to review the case and affirmed.

B. Counsel of Record / ACLU Attorney

ACLU Side (Petitioner / Appellant): Bryan A. Stevenson argued the cause for appellant.

Opposing Side (Respondent / Appellee): Paul M. Smith argued the cause for appellee.

III. AMICI CURIAE

ACLU Side (Petitioner / Appellant)

Brief of amici curiae filed on behalf of the ACLU, et al., by Steven R. Shapiro, Paul C. Saunders, Marc L. Fleischaker, Norman Redlich, Barbara R. Arnwine, Thomas J. Henderson, Mitchell F. Dolin, and Robert A. Long, Jr.

Brief of amici curiae filed on behalf of the United States by Acting Solicitor General Dellinger, Acting Assistant Attorney General Pinzler, Deputy Solicitor General Waxman, Lisa Schiavo Blatt, David L. Flynn, and Miriam R. Eisenstein.

Brief of amici curiae filed on behalf of the Southern States Police Benevolent Association by J. Michael McGuinness.

Opposing Side (Respondent / Appellee)

Brief of amici curiae filed on behalf of Jefferson County, Alabama, by Jeffrey M. Sewell and Charles S. Wagner.

Brief of amici curiae filed on behalf of the National Association of Counties, et al., by Richard Ruda and James I. Crowley.

IV. THE SUPREME COURT'S DECISION

"If the sheriff's actions constitute county 'policy,' then the county is liable for them. The parties agree that the sheriff is a 'policymaker' for §1983 purposes, but they disagree about whether he is a policymaker for Monroe County or for the State of Alabama. We hold that, as to the actions at issue here, Sheriff Tate represents the State of Alabama and is therefore not a county policymaker. We thus affirm the Court of Appeals' dismissal of petitioner's §1983 claims against Monroe County. . . .

We agree with the Court of Appeals that the constitutional provisions concerning sheriffs, the historical development of those provisions, and the interpretation given them by the Alabama Supreme Court strongly support Monroe County's contention that sheriffs represent the State, at least for some purposes. Alabama's Constitution, adopted in 1901, states that '[t]he executive department shall consist of a governor, lieutenant governor, attorney-general, . . . and a sheriff for each county.' This designation is especially important for our purposes, because although every Alabama Constitution has included sheriffs as constitutional officers and has provided for their election by county voters, sheriffs have not always been explicitly listed as members of the state 'executive department.' . . .

The framers of the 1901 Constitution took two significant steps in an attempt to solidify the place of sheriffs in the executive department, and to clarify that sheriffs were acting for the State when exercising their law enforcement functions. First, faced with reports that sheriffs were allowing mobs to abduct prisoners and lynch them, the framers made such 'neglect' by sheriffs an impeachable offense. . . . Second, authority to impeach sheriffs was moved from the county courts to the State Supreme Court . . . . Critically for our case, the Alabama Supreme Court has interpreted these provisions and their historical background as evidence of 'the framers' intent to ensure that sheriffs be considered executive officers of the state.' [T]he court has held unequivocally that sheriffs are state officers, and that tort claims brought against sheriffs based on their official acts therefore constitute suits against the State, not suits against the sheriff's county. . . .

Petitioner's second concern is that under our holding here, sheriffs will be characterized differently in different States. But while it might be easier to decide cases arising under § 1983 and Monell if we insisted on a uniform, national characterization for all sheriffs, such a blunderbuss approach would ignore a crucial axiom of our government: the States have wide authority to set up their state and local governments as they wish. . . . Thus, since it is entirely natural that both the role of sheriffs and the importance of counties vary from State to State, there is no inconsistency created by court decisions that declare sheriffs to be county officers in one State, and not in another. . . .

The judgment of the Court of Appeals is therefore affirmed."

V. JUSTICE VOTE

4 Pro ACLU Side vs. 5 Con Opposing Side

ACLU Side (Petitioner / Appellant)

1. Ginsburg, R. – Wrote dissenting opinion
2. Stevens, J. – Joined Ginsburg's dissent
3. Souter, D. – Joined Ginsburg's dissent
4. Breyer, S. – Joined Ginsburg's dissent

Opposing Side (Respondent / Appellee)

1. Rehnquist, W. – Wrote majority opinion
2. O'Connor, S. – Joined majority opinion
3. Scalia, A. – Joined majority opinion
4. Kennedy, A. – Joined majority opinion
5. Thomas, C. – Joined majority opinion

VI. A WIN OR LOSS FOR THE ACLU?

The ACLU filed as amicus curiae urging reversal of the judgment of the Court of Appeals; the Supreme Court affirmed in a 5-4 vote, giving the ACLU an apparent loss.

829. Abrams v. Johnson

(Decided June 19, 1997; 521 U.S. 74)

I. ISSUE

A. Issues Discussed

Civil rights, voting, racial gerrymandering, equal protection

B. Legal Question Presented

Whether the District Court exceeded its remedial power in making changes to Georgia's previous districting plan, and whether the court's plan violates the Voting Rights Act of 1965 or the constitutional "one person, one vote" requirement.

C. Supreme Court's Answer

The court did not exceed its power in changing the districting plan, and the plan does not violate the Voting Rights Act or "one person, one vote" requirement.

II. CASE SUMMARY

A. Background

"The electoral district lines for Georgia's congressional delegation are before us a second time, appeal now being taken from the trial court's rulings and determinations after our remand in Miller v. Johnson, 515 U.S. 900 (1995). The three-judge panel of the United States District Court for the Southern District of Georgia was affirmed in Miller after it found the Eleventh Congressional District unconstitutional as then drawn. Race, we held, must not be a predominant factor in drawing the district lines.

Given the contorted shape of the district and the undue predominance of race in drawing its lines, it was unlikely the district could be redrawn without changing most or all of Georgia's congressional districts, 11 in total number. The plan being challenged contained three majority-black districts, and after our remand the complaint was amended to challenge another of these, the then-Second District. The trial court found this district, too, was improperly drawn under the standards we confirmed in Miller.

For the task of drawing a new plan, the court deferred to Georgia's Legislature, but the legislature could not reach agreement. The court then drew its own plan, Johnson v. Miller, 922 F.Supp. 1556 (1995); we declined to stay the order; and the 1996 general elections were held under it. The court's plan contained but one majority-black district. The absence of a second, if not a third, majority-black district has become the principal point of contention. Though the elections have been completed, the plan remains in effect until changed by a valid legislative Act, and the appellants ask us to set it aside.

The private appellants are various voters, defendant-intervenors below, who contend that the interests of Georgia's black population were not adequately taken into account. The United States, also a defendant-intervenor, joins in the appeal. The state officials, defendants below, do not object to the plan and appeared before us as appellees to defend it. The other set of appellees are the private plaintiffs below, who argued that racial gerrymandering under the previous plan violated their right to equal protection."

The Supreme Court granted certiorari to review the case and affirmed.

B. Counsel of Record / ACLU Attorney

ACLU Side (Petitioner / Appellant): Deputy Solicitor General Seth P. Waxman argued the cause for the United States. With him on the briefs were Acting Solicitor General Dellinger, Assistant Attorney General Patrick, Deputy Solicitor General Bender, James A. Feldman, Steven H. Rosenbaum, and Miriam R. Eisenstein.

Laughlin McDonald argued the cause for appellants Abrams, et al. With him on the briefs were Neil Bradley, Maha Zaki, Mary Wyckoff, Elaine R. Jones, Norman J. Chachkin, Jacqueline Berrien, and Gerald R. Weber.

Opposing Side (Respondent / Appellee): Michael J. Bowers, Attorney General of Georgia, argued the cause for appellees Miller, et al. With him on the briefs were Dennis R. Dunn, Senior Assistant Attorney General, and David F. Walbert, Special Assistant Attorney General.

A. Lee Parks argued the cause and filed a brief for appellees Johnson, et al.

III. AMICI CURIAE

ACLU Side (Petitioner / Appellant)

Brief of amici curiae filed on behalf of the Georgia Association of Black Elected Officials by J. Gerald Hebert.

Opposing Side (Respondent / Appellee)

Brief of amici curiae filed on behalf of the Pacifici Legal Foundation by Sharon L. Browne and Deborah J. La Fetra.

IV. THE SUPREME COURT'S DECISION

"Under the circumstances, the district court was justified in making substantial changes to the existing plan consistent with Georgia's traditional districting principles, and considering race as a factor but not allowing it to predominate. [I]t would have been most problematic for the trial court to insist on retaining a second majority-black district without regard to other, neutral districting factors. The trial court did not adopt this course. Instead, it gave careful consideration to creation of a second black district on grounds that a black voting population was one factor in drawing a district; and it concluded it could not draw the second majority black district without allowing that one consideration to predominate over other traditional and neutral districting principles, principles which were a valid expression of legislative policy. . . .

The court ordered plan is not violative of § 2 of the Voting Rights Act. . . . Under the circumstances, we cannot say the district court clearly erred in finding insufficient racial polarization in voting to meet the . . . requirements. The results of the 1996 general elections tend to support the district court's earlier finding of 'a general willingness of white voters to vote for black candidates.'

[A]ppellants contend the District Court's plan violates the constitutional guarantee of one person, one vote . . . . Here the district court was not designing districts to remedy a one-person, one-vote violation, but courts should keep in mind that 'absolute population equality [is] the paramount objective.' Slight deviations are allowed under certain circumstances. . . . In any case, even if we had found the court plan's population deviation unacceptable, the solution would not be adoption of the constitutionally infirm, because race-based, plans of appellants. . . .

The task of redistricting is best left to state legislatures, elected by the people and as capable as the courts, if not more so, in balancing the myriad factors and traditions in legitimate districting policies. Here, the legislative process was first distorted and then unable to reach a solution. The District Court was left to embark on a delicate task with limited legislative guidance. The court was careful to take into account traditional state districting factors, and it remained sensitive to the constitutional requirement of equal protection of the law. . . .

The judgment of the District Court is affirmed."

V. JUSTICE VOTE

4 Pro ACLU Side vs. 5 Con Opposing Side

ACLU Side (Petitioner / Appellant)

1. Breyer, S. – Wrote dissenting opinion
2. Stevens, J. – Joined Breyer's dissent
3. Souter, D. – Joined Breyer's dissent
4. Ginsburg, R. – Joined Breyer's dissent

Opposing Side (Respondent / Appellee)

1. Kennedy, J. – Wrote majority opinion
2. Rehnquist, W. – Joined majority opinion
3. O'Connor, S. – Joined majority opinion
4. Scalia, A. – Joined majority opinion
5. Thomas, C. – Joined majority opinion

VI. A WIN OR LOSS FOR THE ACLU?

The ACLU as counsel for appellant, urged reversal of the judgment of the District Court; the Supreme Court affirmed in a 5-4 vote, giving the ACLU an apparent loss.

830. Agostini v. Felton

(Decided June 23, 1997; 521 U.S. 203)

I. ISSUE

A. Issues Discussed

First Amendment, Establishment Clause, injunctions

B. Legal Question Presented

"Are petitioners entitled to relief from the District Court's permanent injunction under Rule 60(b)?"

C. Supreme Court's Answer

Petitioners are entitled to relief from the permanent injunction under Rule 60(b).

II. CASE SUMMARY

A. Background

"In Aguilar v. Felton, 473 U.S. 402 (1985), this Court held that the Establishment Clause of the First Amendment barred the city of New York from sending public school teachers into parochial schools to provide remedial education to disadvantaged children pursuant to a congressionally mandated program. On remand, the District Court for the Eastern District of New York entered a permanent injunction reflecting our ruling. Twelve years later, petitioners—the parties bound by that injunction—seek relief from its operation. Petitioners maintain that Aguilar cannot be squared with our intervening Establishment Clause jurisprudence and ask that we explicitly recognize what our more recent cases already dictate: Aguilar is no longer good law. . . .

It is not disputed that the additional costs of complying with Aguilar's mandate are significant. Since the 1986–1987 school year, the Board has spent over $100 million . . . .

In October and December of 1995, petitioners—the Board and a new group of parents of parochial school students entitled to Title I services—filed motions in the District Court seeking relief under Federal Rule of Civil Procedure 60(b) from the permanent injunction entered by the District Court on remand from our decision in Aguilar. Petitioners argued that relief was proper under Rule 60(b)(5) and our decision in Rufo v. Inmates of Suffolk County Jail, 502 U.S. 367 (1992), because the 'decisional law [had] changed to make legal what the [injunction] was designed to prevent.' Specifically, petitioners pointed to the statements of five Justices in Board of Ed. of Kiryas Joel Village School Dist. v. Grumet, 512 U.S. 687 (1994), calling for the overruling of Aguilar. The District Court denied the motion. The District Court recognized that petitioners, 'at bottom,' sought 'a procedurally sound vehicle to get the [propriety of the injunction] back before the Supreme Court,' and concluded that 'the Board ha[d] properly proceeded under Rule 60(b) to seek relief from the injunction.' Despite its observations that 'the landscape of Establishment Clause decisions has changed,' and that '[t]here may be good reason to conclude that Aguilar's demise is imminent,' the District Court denied the Rule 60(b) motion on the merits because Aguilar's demise had 'not yet occurred.' The Court of Appeals for the Second Circuit 'affirmed substantially for the reasons stated in' the District Court's opinion."

The Supreme Court granted certiorari to review the case and reversed.

B. Counsel of Record / ACLU Attorney

ACLU Side (Respondent / Appellee): Stanley Geller argued the cause for appellees.

Opposing Side (Petitioner / Appellant): Paul A. Crotty argued the cause for appellants in No. 96-553.

Acting Solicitor General Walter Dellinger argued the cause in support of appellants.

III. AMICI CURIAE

ACLU Side (Respondent / Appellee)

Brief of amici curiae filed on behalf of Americans United for Separation of Church and State, the ACLU, et al., by Steven K. Green, Julie A. Segal, Steven R. Shapiro, and Arthur N. Eisenberg.

Brief of amici curiae filed on behalf of the American Jewish Congress, et al., by Norman Redlich, Marc D. Stern, Marvin E. Frankel, David J. Strom, Richard T. Foltin, Barbara L. Kornreich, Ruth L. Lansner, Steven M. Freeman, Debbie N. Kaminer, J. Brent Walker, Melissa Rogers, Robert Chanin, John Craig Sumberg, Elliot M. Mincberg, Mark J. Pelavin, and Judith E. Schaeffer.

Opposing Side (Petitioner / Appellant)

Brief of amici curiae filed on behalf of the Becket Fund for Religious Liberty by Kevin J. Hasson, Eric W. Treene, and Roman P. Storzer.

Brief of amici curiae filed on behalf of the Christian Legal Society, et al., by Michael W. McConnell, Thomas C. Berg, Steven T. McFarland, Kimberlee Wood Colby, and Samuel B. Casey.

Brief of amici curiae filed on behalf of the Knights of Columbus by Pat A. Cipollone, Carl A. Anderson, and James W. Shannon, Jr.

Brief of amici curiae filed on behalf of the National Jewish Commission on Law and Public Affairs by Nathan Lewin and Dennis Rapps.

Brief of amici curiae filed on behalf of Senator Robert F. Bennett by Frederick Mark Gedicks and Ronald D. Maines.

Brief of amici curiae filed on behalf of Sarah Peter, et al., by Michael Joseph Woodruff, Michael Stokes Paulsen, J. Matthew Szymanski, Daniel L. Bowles, Daniel Kadlec, and Scott J. Ward.

IV. THE SUPREME COURT'S DECISION

"[P]etitioners' ability to satisfy the prerequisites of Rule 60(b)(5) hinges on whether our later Establishment Clause cases have so undermined Aguilar that it is no longer good law. We now turn to that inquiry. . .

New York City's Title I program does not run afoul of any of three primary criteria we currently use to evaluate whether government aid has the effect of advancing religion: It does not result in governmental indoctrination; define its recipients by reference to religion; or create an excessive entanglement. We therefore hold that a federally funded program providing supplemental, remedial instruction to disadvantaged children on a neutral basis is not invalid under the Establishment Clause when such instruction is given on the premises of sectarian schools by government employees pursuant to a program containing safeguards such as those present here. The same considerations that justify this holding require us to conclude that this carefully constrained program also cannot reasonably be viewed as an endorsement of religion. Accordingly, we must acknowledge that Aguilar, as well as the portion of Ball addressing Grand Rapids' Shared Time program, are no longer good law. . . .

We therefore conclude that our Establishment Clause law has 'significant[ly] change[d]' since we decided Aguilar. We are only left to decide whether this change in law entitles petitioners to relief under Rule 60(b)(5). We conclude that it does. Our general practice is to apply the rule of law we announce in a case to the parties before us. . . .

To evaluate the Rule 60(b)(5) motion properly before us today in no way undermines 'integrity in the interpretation of procedural rules' or signals any departure from 'the responsive, non-agenda-setting character of this Court.' Indeed, under these circumstances, it would be particularly inequitable for us to bide our time waiting for another case to arise while the city of New York labors under a continuing injunction forcing it to spend millions of dollars on mobile instructional units and leased sites when it could instead be spending that money to give economically disadvantaged children a better chance at success in life by means of a program that is perfectly consistent with the Establishment Clause.

For these reasons, we reverse the judgment of the Court of Appeals and remand the cases to the District Court with instructions to vacate its September 26, 1985, order."

V. JUSTICE VOTE

4 Pro ACLU Side vs. 5 Con Opposing Side

ACLU Side (Respondent / Appellee)

1. Souter, D. – Wrote dissenting opinion, joined Ginsburg's dissent
2. Ginsburg, R. – Wrote dissenting opinion, joined Souter's dissent
3. Stevens, J. – Joined Souter's dissent, joined Ginsburg's dissent
4. Breyer, S. – Joined Souter's dissent, joined Ginsburg's dissent

Opposing Side (Petitioner / Appellant)

1. O'Connor, S. – Wrote majority opinion
2. Rehnquist, W. – Joined majority opinion
3. Scalia, A. – Joined majority opinion
4. Kennedy, A. – Joined majority opinion
5. Thomas, C. – Joined majority opinion

VI. A WIN OR LOSS FOR THE ACLU?

The ACLU, as amicus curiae, urged affirmance of the judgment of the Court of Appeals for the Second Circuit; the Supreme Court reversed in a 5-4 vote, giving the ACLU an apparent loss.

831. Idaho v. Coeur d'Alene Tribe of Idaho

(Decided June 23, 1997; 521 U.S. 261)

I. ISSUE

A. Issues Discussed

Governmental authority, immunity, Eleventh Amendment, sovereign immunity

B. Legal Question Presented

"[W]hether the Eleventh Amendment bars a federal court from hearing the Tribe's claim."

C. Supreme Court's Answer

The Eleventh Amendment bars a federal court from hearing the Tribe's claim.

II. CASE SUMMARY

A. Background

"Alleging ownership in the submerged lands and bed of Lake Coeur d'Alene and of the various navigable rivers and streams that form part of its water system, the Coeur d'Alene Tribe, a federally recognized Tribe, together with various individual Tribe members, sued in federal court. . . .

The defendants moved to dismiss the Tribe's complaint on Eleventh Amendment immunity grounds and for failure to state a claim upon which relief could be granted. The court held the Eleventh Amendment barred the claims against Idaho and the agencies. It concluded further that the action against the officials for quiet title and declaratory relief was barred by the Eleventh

Amendment because these claims were the functional equivalents of a damages award against the State. It dismissed the claim for injunctive relief against the officials, on the merits, since Idaho was in rightful possession of the submerged lands as a matter of law. It explained that Idaho acquired ownership of the submerged lands upon its statehood in 1890 under the equal footing doctrine. The court did not discuss the Tribe's claim to aboriginal title.

The Ninth Circuit affirmed in part, reversed in part, and remanded. It agreed with the District Court that the Eleventh Amendment barred all claims against the State and its agencies, as well as the quiet title action against the officials. . . . It reversed the District Court's dismissal of the declaratory and injunctive relief claims and ordered the case remanded. It also remanded for consideration of the Tribe's claim for declaratory relief based on aboriginal title."

The Supreme Court granted certiorari to review the case and reversed.

B. Counsel of Record / ACLU Attorney

ACLU Side (Respondent / Appellee): Raymond C. Givens argued the cause for appellees.

Opposing Side (Petitioner / Appellant): Clive Strong, Deputy Attorney General of Idaho, argued the cause for appellant.

III. AMICI CURIAE

ACLU Side (Respondent / Appellee)

Brief of amici curiae filed on behalf of the ACLU by Steven R. Shapiro, Robin L. Dahlberg, and Erwin Chemerinsky.

Brief of amici curiae filed on behalf of the United States by Acting Solicitor General Dellinger, Deputy Solicitor General Kneedler, Jeffrey P. Minear, Anne S. Almy, Lois J. Schiffer, Edward J. Shawaker, and Peter Appel.

Brief of amici curiae filed on behalf of the Stockbridge-Munsee Indian Community by Richard Dauphinais.

Opposing Side (Petitioner / Appellant)

Brief of amici curiae filed on behalf of the State of California, et al., by Jan S. Stevens, Assistant Attorney General of California, Daniel E. Lungren, Attorney General, and Roderick E. Walston, Chief Assistant Attorney General, and the following Attorneys General for their respective states: Jeff Sessions of Alabama, Bruce M. Botelho of Alaska, Grant Woods of Arizona, Winston Bryant of Arkansas, Gale A. Norton of Colorado, Richard Blumenthal of Connecticut, Robert A. Butterworth of Florida, Margery S. Bronster of Hawaii, Thomas J. Miller of Iowa, Frank J. Kelley of Michigan, Hubert H. Humphrey, III, of Minnesota, Jeremiah W. Nixon of Missouri, Joseph P. Mazurek of Montana, Don Stenberg of Nebraska, Frankie Sue Del Papa of Nevada, Dennis C. Vacco of New York, Betty D. Montgomery of Ohio, W. A. Drew Edmondson of Oklahoma, Mark Barnett of South Dakota, Jan Graham of Utah, Christine O. Gregoire of Washington, and James E. Doyle of Wisconsin.

Brief of amici curiae filed on behalf of the Council of State Governments, et al., by Richard Ruda and James I. Crowley.

IV. THE SUPREME COURT'S DECISION

"The Court's recognition of sovereign immunity has not been limited to the suits described in the text of the Eleventh Amendment. To respect the broader concept of immunity, implicit in the Constitution, which we have regarded the Eleventh Amendment as evidencing and exemplifying, we have extended a State's protection from suit to suits brought by the State's own citizens. Furthermore, the dignity and respect afforded a State, which the immunity is designed to protect, are placed in jeopardy whether or not the suit is based on diversity jurisdiction. As a consequence, suits invoking the federal-question jurisdiction of Article III courts may also be barred by the Amendment. . . .

Under well-established principles, the Coeur d'Alene Tribe, and, a fortiori, its members, are subject to the Eleventh Amendment. [W]e rejected the contention that sovereign immunity only restricts suits by individuals against sovereigns, not by sovereigns against sovereigns. Since the plan of the Convention did not surrender Indian tribes' immunity for the benefit of the States, we reasoned that the States likewise did not surrender their immunity for the benefit of the tribes. Indian tribes, we therefore concluded, should be accorded the same status as foreign sovereigns, against whom States enjoy Eleventh Amendment immunity.

The Tribe's suit, accordingly, is barred by Idaho's Eleventh Amendment immunity unless it falls within the exception this Court has recognized for certain suits seeking declaratory and injunctive relief against state officers in their individual capacities. [W]e must ensure that the doctrine of sovereign immunity remains meaningful, while also giving recognition to the need to prevent violations of federal law. . . .

We now turn to consider whether the Tribe may avoid the Eleventh Amendment bar and avail itself of the Young exception. Although the 'difference between the type of relief barred by the Eleventh Amendment and that permitted under Ex parte Young will not in many instances be that between day and night,' this suit, we decide, falls on the Eleventh Amendment side of the line, and Idaho's sovereign immunity controls. . . .

The principle which underlies the equal footing doctrine and the strong presumption of state ownership is that navigable waters uniquely implicate sovereign interests. . . .

All these developments in American law are a natural outgrowth of the perceived public character of submerged lands, a perception which underlies and informs the principle that these lands are tied in a unique way to sovereignty.

Idaho views its interest in the submerged lands in similar terms. . . . Title to these public waters is held by the State of Idaho in its sovereign capacity for the purpose of ensuring that it is used for the public benefit. There are specific statutory provisions concerning Lake Coeur d'Alene. The Lake is held in trust by the Governor for the people of the State of Idaho. The 'preservation of Lake Coeur d'Alene for scenic beauty, health, recreation, transportation and commercial purposes being necessary and desirable for all the inhabitants of the state is hereby declared to be a beneficial use of such water.' The 'lands belonging to the state of Idaho between the ordinary high and low water mark at [Lake Coeur d'Alene] . . . are hereby declared to be devoted to a public use in connection with the preservation of said lak[e] in [its] present condition as a health resort and recreation place for the inhabitants of the state.'

Our recitation of the ties between the submerged lands and the State's own sovereignty, and of the severance and diminishment of state sovereignty were the declaratory and injunctive relief to be granted, is not in derogation of the Tribe's own claim. As the Tribe views the case, the lands are just as necessary, perhaps even more so, to its own dignity and ancient right. The question before us is not the merit of either party's claim, however, but the relation between the sovereign lands at issue and the immunity the State asserts.

[I]f the Tribe were to prevail, Idaho's sovereign interest in its lands and waters would be affected in a degree fully as intrusive as almost any conceivable retroactive levy upon funds in its Treasury. Under these particular and special circumstances, we find the Young exception inapplicable. The dignity and status of its statehood allow Idaho to rely on its Eleventh Amendment immunity and to insist upon responding to these claims in its own courts, which are open to hear and determine the case.

The judgment of the Court of Appeals is reversed in part, and the case is remanded for proceedings consistent with this opinion."

V. JUSTICE VOTE

4 Pro ACLU Side vs. 5 Con Opposing Side

ACLU Side (Respondent / Appellee)

1. Souter, D. – Wrote dissenting opinion
2. Stevens, J. – Joined Souter's dissent
3. Ginsburg, R. – Joined Souter's dissent
4. Breyer, S. – Joined Souter's dissent

Opposing Side (Petitioner / Appellant)

1. Kennedy, A. – Wrote majority opinion
2. Rehnquist, W. – Joined majority opinion
3. O'Connor, S. – Wrote concurring opinion
4. Scalia, A. – Joined O'Connor's concurrence
5. Thomas, C. – Joined O'Connor's concurrence

VI. A WIN OR LOSS FOR THE ACLU?

The ACLU filed as amicus curiae urging affirmance of the judgment of the Court of Appeals for the Ninth Circuit; the Supreme Court reversed in a 5-4 vote, giving the ACLU an apparent loss.

832. Kansas v. Hendricks

(Decided June 23, 1997; 521 U.S. 346)

I. ISSUE

A. Issues Discussed

State, prison

B. Legal Question Presented

Whether "the Kansas Sexually Violent Predator Act comports with due process requirements and neither runs afoul of double jeopardy principles nor constitutes an exercise in impermissible ex post facto lawmaking."

C. Supreme Court's Answer

"We hold that the Kansas Sexually Violent Predator Act comports with due process requirements and neither runs afoul of double jeopardy principles nor constitutes an exercise in impermissible ex post facto lawmaking."

II. CASE SUMMARY

A. Background

"In 1994, Kansas enacted the Sexually Violent Predator Act, which establishes procedures for the civil commitment of persons who, due to a 'mental abnormality' or a 'personality disorder,' are likely to engage in 'predatory acts of sexual violence.' The State invoked the Act for the first time to commit Leroy Hendricks, an inmate who had a long history of sexually molesting children, and who was scheduled for release from prison shortly after the Act became law. Hendricks challenged his commitment on . . . 'substantive' due process, double jeopardy, and ex post facto grounds. The Kansas Supreme Court invalidated the Act, holding that its precommitment condition of a "mental abnormality" did not satisfy what the court perceived to be the 'substantive' due process requirement that involuntary civil commitment must be predicated on a finding of 'mental illness.' The State of Kansas petitioned for certiorari. Hendricks subsequently filed a cross-petition in which he reasserted his federal double jeopardy and ex post facto claims."

The Supreme Court granted certiorari to review the case.

B. Counsel of Record / ACLU Attorney

ACLU Side (Respondent / Appellee): Thomas J. Weilert argued the cause for Hendricks in both cases. With him on the briefs were James W. Ellis and David Gottlieb.

Opposing Side (Petitioner / Appellant): Carla J. Stovall, Attorney General of Kansas, argued the cause for appellant in No. 95–1649 and appellee in No. 95–9075. With her on the briefs were Stephen R. McAllister, Special Assistant Attorney General, Bernard Nash, James van R. Springer, and Laura B. Feigin.

III. AMICI CURIAE

ACLU Side (Respondent / Appellee)

Brief of amici curiae filed on behalf of the American Civil Liberties Union, the ACLU of Kansas and Western Missouri, the ACLU of Washington, the Minnesota Civil Liberties Union, the ACLU of Wisconsin and the ACLU of Northern California by Scott A. W. Johnson, Laura J. Buckland, Steven R. Shapiro, Christopher A. Hansen, Bruce Winick, Claudia M. Balducci, Mark E. Maynes, and John Q. La Fond.

Brief of amici curiae filed on behalf of the American Psychiatric Association by Richard G. Taranto.

Brief of amici curiae filed on behalf of the National Association of Criminal Defense Lawyers et al. by David A. Reiser, Jennifer P. Lyman, Barbara E. Bergman, and James F. Vano.

Brief of amici curiae filed on behalf of the National Mental Health Association by Ira A. Burnim.

Brief of amici curiae filed on behalf of the Seattle-King County Defender Association et al. by Robert C. Boruchowitz, Addie

Hailstorks, John Stuart, Eric Janus, John T. Philipsborn, and Bernadette Foley.

Brief of amici curiae filed on behalf of the Washington State Psychiatric Association by David A. Summers.

Opposing Side (Petitioner / Appellant)

Brief of amici curiae filed on behalf of the State of Washington et al. by Christine O. Gregoire, Attorney General of Washington, and Sarah Blackman Sappington, Assistant Attorney General, Charles F. C. Ruff, Corporation Counsel of the District of Columbia, Sebastian Aloot, Acting Attorney General of the Northern Mariana Islands, and by the Attorneys General for their respective jurisdictions as follows: Jeff Sessions of Alabama, Malaetasi Togafu of American Samoa, Grant Woods of Arizona, Winston Bryant of Arkansas, Daniel E. Lungren of California, Gale A. Norton of Colorado, M. Jane Brady of Delaware, Robert A. Butterworth of Florida, Calvin E. Holloway, Sr., of Guam, Margery S. Bronster of Hawaii, Alan G. Lance of Idaho, James E. Ryan of Illinois, Pamela Fanning Carter of Indiana, Thomas J. Miller of Iowa, A. B. Chandler III of Kentucky, Richard P. Ieyoub of Louisiana, J. Joseph Curran, Jr., of Maryland, Hubert H. Humphrey III of Minnesota, Mike Moore of Mississippi, Jeremiah W. (Jay) Nixon of Missouri, Joseph P. Mazurek of Montana, Don Stenberg of Nebraska, Frankie Sue Del Papa of Nevada, Jeffrey R. Howard of New Hampshire, Peter Verniero of New Jersey, Tom Udall of New Mexico, Dennis C. Vacco of New York, Michael F. Easley of North Carolina, Heidi Heitkamp of North Dakota, Betty D. Montgomery of Ohio, W. A. Drew Edmondson of Oklahoma, Thomas W. Corbett, Jr., of Pennsylvania, Pedro R. Pierluisi of Puerto Rico, Jeffrey B. Pine of Rhode Island, Charles Molony Condon of South Carolina, Mark W. Barnett of South Dakota, Jan Graham of Utah, Jeffrey L. Amestoy of Vermont, Julio A. Brady of the Virgin Islands, James S. Gilmore III of Virginia, and William U. Hill of Wyoming.

Brief of amici curiae filed on behalf of the State of Wisconsin by James E. Doyle, Attorney General, and Sally L. Wellman and Mary E. Burke, Assistant Attorneys General.

Brief of amici curiae filed on behalf of the Menninger Foundation et al. by Philip Allen Lacovara, James C. Geoly, and Robert Teir.

Brief of amici curiae filed on behalf of the Washington Legal Foundation et al. by Daniel J. Popeo and Richard A. Samp.

Brief of amici curiae filed on behalf of the Association for the Treatment of Sexual Abusers by David B. Robbins.

IV. THE SUPREME COURT'S DECISION

"Kansas argues that the Act's definition of 'mental abnormality' satisfies 'substantive' due process requirements. We agree. Although freedom from physical restraint 'has always been at the core of the liberty protected by the Due Process Clause from arbitrary governmental action,' that liberty interest is not absolute. The Court has recognized that an individual's constitutionally protected interest in avoiding physical restraint may be overridden even in the civil context . . . .

Accordingly, States have in certain narrow circumstances provided for the forcible civil detainment of people who are unable to control their behavior and who thereby pose a danger to the public health and safety. . . . We have consistently upheld such involuntary commitment statutes provided the confinement takes place pursuant to proper procedures and evidentiary standards. It thus cannot be said that the involuntary civil confinement of a limited subclass of dangerous persons is contrary to our understanding of ordered liberty.

The challenged Act unambiguously requires a finding of dangerousness either to one's self or to others as a prerequisite to involuntary confinement. . . .

A finding of dangerousness, standing alone, is ordinarily not a sufficient ground upon which to justify indefinite involuntary commitment. We have sustained civil commitment statutes when they have coupled proof of dangerousness with the proof of some additional factor, such as a 'mental illness' or 'mental abnormality.' . . . These added statutory requirements serve to limit involuntary civil confinement to those who suffer from a volitional impairment rendering them dangerous beyond their control. The Kansas Act is plainly of a kind with these other civil commitment statutes . . . . The precommitment requirement of a 'mental abnormality' or 'personality disorder' is consistent with the requirements of these other statutes that we have upheld in that it narrows the class of persons eligible for confinement to those who are unable to control their dangerousness. . . .

To the extent that the civil commitment statutes we have considered set forth criteria relating to an individual's inability to control his dangerousness, the Kansas Act sets forth comparable criteria and Hendricks' condition doubtless satisfies those criteria. . . .

We granted Hendricks' cross-petition to determine whether the Act violates the Constitution's double jeopardy prohibition or its ban on ex post facto lawmaking. The thrust of Hendricks' argument is that the Act establishes criminal proceedings; hence confinement under it necessarily constitutes punishment. . . . We are unpersuaded by Hendricks' argument that Kansas has established criminal proceedings. . . .

Where the State has 'disavowed any punitive intent'; limited confinement to a small segment of particularly dangerous individuals; provided strict procedural safeguards; directed that confined persons be segregated from the general prison population and afforded the same status as others who have been civilly committed; recommended treatment if such is possible; and permitted immediate release upon a showing that the individual is no longer dangerous or mentally impaired, we cannot say that it acted with punitive intent. We therefore hold that the Act does not establish criminal proceedings and that involuntary confinement pursuant to the Act is not punitive. Our conclusion that the Act is nonpunitive thus removes an essential prerequisite for both Hendricks' double jeopardy and ex post facto claims. . . .

The Double Jeopardy Clause provides: '[N]or shall any person be subject for the same offence to be twice put in jeopardy of life or limb.' . . . Hendricks argues that, as applied to him, the Act violates double jeopardy principles because his confinement under the Act, imposed after a conviction and a term of incarceration, amounted to both a second prosecution and a second punishment for the same offense. We disagree.

Because we have determined that the Kansas Act is civil in nature, initiation of its commitment proceedings does not constitute a second prosecution. . . . Moreover, as commitment under the Act is not tantamount to 'punishment,' Hendricks' involuntary detention does not violate the Double Jeopardy Clause, even though that confinement may follow a prison term. . . .

Hendricks' ex post facto claim is similarly flawed. . . . As we have previously determined, the Act does not impose punishment; thus, its application does not raise ex post facto concerns. Moreover, the Act clearly does not have retroactive effect. . . . Because the Act does not criminalize conduct legal before its enactment, nor deprive Hendricks of any defense that was available to him at the time of his crimes, the Act does not violate the Ex Post Facto Clause. . . .

We hold that the Kansas Sexually Violent Predator Act comports with due process requirements and neither runs afoul of double jeopardy principles nor constitutes an exercise in impermissible ex post facto lawmaking. Accordingly, the judgment of the Kansas Supreme Court is reversed."

V. JUSTICE VOTE

4 Pro ACLU Side vs. 5 Con Opposing Side

ACLU Side (Respondent / Appellee)

1. Ginsburg, R. – Joined Breyer's dissent, in part
2. Souter, D. – Joined Breyer's dissent
3. Stevens, J. – Joined Breyer's dissent
4. Breyer, S. – Wrote dissenting opinion

Opposing Side (Petitioner / Appellant)

1. Thomas, C. – Wrote majority opinion
2. O'Connor, S. – Joined majority opinion
3. Scalia, A. – Joined majority opinion
4. Kennedy, A. – Wrote concurring opinion
5. Rehnquist, W. – Joined majority opinion

VI. A WIN OR LOSS FOR THE ACLU?

The ACLU filed as amicus curiae urging affirmance; the Supreme Court reversed the Kansas Supreme Court's decision by a 5-4 vote, giving the ACLU an apparent loss.

833. Richardson v. McKnight

(Decided June 23, 1997; 521 U.S. 399)

I. ISSUE

A. Issues Discussed

Criminal justice, prisons, Eighth Amendment

B. Legal Question Presented

"[W]hether prison guards who are employees of a private prison management firm are entitled to a qualified immunity from suit by prisoners charging a violation of 42 U.S.C. § 1983."

C. Supreme Court's Answer

Prison guards in privately managed prisons are not entitled to qualified immunity in § 1983 suits by prisoners.

II. CASE SUMMARY

A. Background

"Ronnie Lee McKnight, a prisoner at Tennessee's South Central Correctional Center (SCCC), brought this federal constitutional tort action against two prison guards, Darryl Richardson and John Walker. He says the guards injured him by placing upon him extremely tight physical restraints, thereby unlawfully 'subject[ing]' him 'to the deprivation of' a right 'secured by the Constitution' of the United States. Richardson and Walker asserted a qualified immunity from § 1983 lawsuits, and moved to dismiss the action. The District Court noted that Tennessee had 'privatized' the management of a number of its correctional facilities, and that consequently a private firm, not the state government, employed the guards. The court held that, because they worked for a private company rather than the government, the law did not grant the guards immunity from suit. It therefore denied the guards' motion to dismiss. The guards appealed to the Sixth Circuit. That court also ruled against them. The Court of Appeals conceded that other courts had reached varying conclusions about whether, or the extent to which, private sector defendants are entitled to immunities of the sort the law provides governmental defendants. But the court concluded, primarily for reasons of 'public policy,' that the privately employed prison guards were not entitled to the immunity provided their governmental counterparts."

The Supreme Court granted certiorari to review the case and affirmed.

B. Counsel of Record / ACLU Attorney

ACLU Side (Respondent / Appellee): David C. Vladeck argued the cause for appellee.

Deputy Solicitor General Edwin S. Kneedler argued the cause for the United States, as amicus curiae, by special leave of Court.

Opposing Side (Petitioner / Appellant): Charles R. Ray argued the cause for appellant.

III. AMICI CURIAE

ACLU Side (Respondent / Appellee)

Breif of amici curiae filed on behalf of the ACLU, et al., by Penny M. Venetis and Steven R. Shapiro.

Brief of amici curiae filed on behalf of the United States by Deputy Solicitor General Kneedler, Acting Solicitor General Dellinger, Assistant Attorney General Hunger, Deputy Solicitor General Waxman, Deputy Assistant Attorney General Preston, Cornelia T. L. Pillard, Barbara L. Herwig, and John F. Daly.

Brief of amici curiae filed on behalf of the American Federation of Government Employees, AFL-CIO, by Mark D. Roth and Anne M. Wagner

Opposing Side (Petitioner / Appellant)

Brief of amici curiae filed on behalf of the International City/County Management Association, et al., by Richard Ruda and James I. Crowley.

IV. THE SUPREME COURT'S DECISION

"Our examination of history and purpose . . . reveals nothing special enough about the job or about its organizational structure that would warrant providing these private prison guards with a governmental immunity. The job is one that private industry might, or might not, perform; and which history shows private firms did sometimes perform without relevant immunities. The organizational structure is one subject to the ordinary competitive pressures that normally help private firms adjust their behavior in response to the incentives that tort suits provide-pressures not necessarily present in government departments. Since there are no special reasons significantly favoring an extension of governmental immunity, and since Wyatt makes clear that private actors are not automatically immune (i.e., § 1983 immunity does not automatically follow § 1983 liability), we must conclude that private prison guards, unlike those who work directly for the government, do not enjoy immunity from suit in a § 1983 case. . . .

We close with three caveats. First, we have focused only on questions of § 1983 immunity and have not addressed whether the defendants are liable under § 1983 even though they are employed by a private firm. Because the Court of Appeals assumed, but did not decide, § 1983 liability, it is for the District Court to determine whether, under this Court's decision in Lugar v. Edmondson Oil Co., 457 U.S. 922 (1982), defendants actually acted 'under color of state law.'

Second, we have answered the immunity question narrowly, in the context in which it arose. That context is one in which a private firm, systematically organized to assume a major lengthy administrative task (managing an institution) with limited direct supervision by the government, undertakes that task for profit and potentially in competition with other firms. The case does not involve a private individual briefly associated with a government body, serving as an adjunct to government in an essential governmental activity, or acting under close official supervision.

Third, Wyatt explicitly stated that it did not decide whether or not the private defendants before it might assert, not immunity, but a special 'good faith' defense. . . . Like the Court in Wyatt, and the Court of Appeals in this case, we do not express a view on this last-mentioned question.

For these reasons the judgment of the Court of Appeals is affirmed."

V. JUSTICE VOTE

5 Pro ACLU Side vs. 4 Con Opposing Side

ACLU Side (Petitioner / Appellant)

1. Breyer S. – Wrote majority opinion
2. Stevens, J. – Joined majority opinion
3. O'Connor, S. – Joined majority opinion
4. Souter, D. – Joined majority opinion
5. Ginsburg, R. – Joined majority opinion

Opposing Side (Respondent / Appellee)

1. Scalia, A. – Wrote dissenting opinion
2. Rehnquist, W. – Joined Scalia's dissent
3. Kennedy, A. – Joined Scalia's dissent
4. Thomas, C. – Joined Scalia's dissent

VI. A WIN OR LOSS FOR THE ACLU?

The ACLU filed as amicus curiae urging affirmance of the judgment of the Court of Appeals for the Sixth Circuit; the Supreme Court affirmed in a 5-4 vote, giving the ACLU an apparent win.

834. City of Boerne v. Flores

(Decided June 25, 1997; 521 U.S. 507)

I. ISSUE

A. Issues Discussed

Freedom of religion, federalism, Fourteenth Amendment

B. Legal Question Presented

Does the Religious Freedom Restoration Act of 1993 (RFRA) exceed Congress' enforcement power under the Fourteenth Amendment?

C. Supreme Court's Answer

RFRA exceeds Congress' enforcement power.

II. CASE SUMMARY

A. Background

"Situated on a hill in the city of Boerne, Texas, some 28 miles northwest of San Antonio, is St. Peter Catholic Church. Built in 1923, the church's structure replicates the mission style of the region's earlier history. The church seats about 230 worshippers, a number too small for its growing parish. Some 40 to 60 parishioners cannot be accommodated at some Sunday masses. In order to meet the needs of the congregation the Archbishop of San Antonio gave permission to the parish to plan alterations to enlarge the building.

A few months later, the Boerne City Council passed an ordinance authorizing the city's Historic Landmark Commission to prepare a preservation plan with proposed historic landmarks and districts. Under the ordinance, the commission must preapprove construction affecting historic landmarks or buildings in a historic district.

Soon afterwards, the Archbishop applied for a building permit so construction to enlarge the church could proceed. City authorities, relying on the ordinance and the designation of a historic district (which, they argued, included the church), denied the application. The Archbishop brought this suit challenging the permit denial in the United States District Court for the Western District of Texas.

The complaint contained various claims, but to this point the litigation has centered on [the Religious Freedom Restoration Act of 1993 (RFRA)] and the question of its constitutionality. The Archbishop relied upon RFRA as one basis for relief from the refusal to issue the permit. The District Court concluded that by enacting RFRA Congress exceeded the scope of its enforcement power under § 5 of the Fourteenth Amendment. The court certified its order for interlocutory appeal and the Fifth Circuit reversed, finding RFRA to be constitutional."

The Supreme Court granted certiorari to review the case and reversed.

B. Counsel of Record / ACLU Attorney

ACLU Side (Respondent / Appellee): Douglas Laycock argued the cause for appellee.

Acting Solicitor General Walter Dellinger argued the cause for the United States.

Opposing Side (Petitioner / Appellant): Marci A. Hamilton argued the cause for appellant.

Jeffrey S. Sutton, State Solicitor of Ohio, argued the cause for the State of Ohio, et al., as amici curiae, by special leave of Court.

III. AMICI CURIAE

ACLU Side (Respondent / Appellee)

Brief of amici curiae filed on behalf of the Coalition for the Free Exercise of Religion by Marc D. Stern of the American Jewish Congress, Oliver S. Thomas of the National Council of Churches, J. Brent Walker and Melissa Rogers of the Baptist Joint Committee on Public Affairs, Steven T. McFarland of the Center for Law and Religious Freedom, Christin Legal Society, Aron U. Raskas and Nathan J. Diament of the Institute for Public Affairs, Union of Orthodox Jewish Congregations of America, Michael Farris of the Home School Defense Association, Samuel Rabinove and Richard Foltin of the American Jewish Committee, Elliot Mincberg of People for the American Way, David Zwiebel of Agudath Israel, Steven R. Shapiro of the ACLU, Steven K. Green of Americans United for Separation of Church and State, and Jack F. Trope of the Association of American Indian Affairs.

Additional briefs of amici curiae were filed on behalf of the State of Maryland, et al., Members of the Virginia House of Delegates, et al., Senator Orrin G. Hatch, et al., Senator Edward M. Kennedy, et al., the American Bar Association, the Knights of Columbus, the Rutherford Institute, the State of Texas, the American Center for Law and Justice, the Beckett Fund for Religious Liberty, the Church of Jesus Christ of Latter-day Saints, the Defenders of Property Rights, et al., the Minnesota Family Council, et al., the NAACP Legal Defense and Educational Fund, Inc., the National Committee for Amish Religious Freedom, the National Jewish Commission on Law and Public Affairs, the National Trust for Historic Preservation in the United States, the Prison Fellowship Ministries, et al., and the United States Catholic Conference, et al.

Opposing Side (Petitioner / Appellant)

Briefs of amici curiae were filed on behalf of the State of Ohio, et al., the Commonwealth of Virginia, the Clarendon Foundation, the National Right to Work Legal Defense Foundation, Inc., Children's Healthcare is a Legal Duty, Inc., et al., the Center for the Community Interest, and the San Antonio Conservation Society, et al.

Brief of amici curiae in support of neither party filed by Thurston Greene, pro se.

IV. THE SUPREME COURT'S DECISION

"RFRA prohibits '[g]overnment' from 'substantially burden[ing]' a person's exercise of religion even if the burden results from a rule of general applicability unless the government can demonstrate the burden '(1) is in furtherance of a compelling governmental interest; and (2) is the least restrictive means of furthering that compelling governmental interest.' The Act's mandate applies to any 'branch, department, agency, instrumentality, and official (or other person acting under color of law) of the United States,' as well as to any 'State, or . . . subdivision of a State.' . . .

The parties disagree over whether RFRA is a proper exercise of Congress' § 5 power 'to enforce' by 'appropriate legislation' the constitutional guarantee that no State shall deprive any person of 'life, liberty, or property, without due process of law' nor deny any person 'equal protection of the laws.' . . .

There must be a congruence and proportionality between the injury to be prevented or remedied and the means adopted to that end. Lacking such a connection, legislation may become substantive in operation and effect. History and our case law support drawing the distinction, one apparent from the text of the Amendment. . . .

The Fourteenth Amendment's history confirms the remedial, rather than substantive, nature of the Enforcement Clause. . . .

We now turn to consider whether RFRA can be considered enforcement legislation under § 5 of the Fourteenth Amendment. . . . RFRA cannot be considered remedial, preventive legislation, if those terms are to have any meaning. RFRA is so out of proportion to a supposed remedial or preventive object that it cannot be understood as responsive to, or designed to prevent, unconstitutional behavior. It appears, instead, to attempt a substantive change in constitutional protections. Preventive measures prohibiting certain types of laws may be appropriate when there is reason to believe that many of the laws affected by the congressional enactment have a significant likelihood of being unconstitutional. Remedial legislation under § 5 'should be adapted to the mischief and wrong which the [Fourteenth] [A]mendment was intended to provide against.'

RFRA is not so confined. Sweeping coverage ensures its intrusion at every level of government, displacing laws and prohibiting official actions of almost every description and regardless of subject matter. RFRA's restrictions apply to every agency and official of the Federal, State, and local Governments. RFRA applies to all federal and state law, statutory or otherwise, whether adopted before or after its enactment. RFRA has no termination date or termination mechanism. Any law is subject to challenge at any time by any individual who alleges a substantial burden on his or her free exercise of religion. . . .

The stringent test RFRA demands of state laws reflects a lack of proportionality or congruence between the means adopted and the legitimate end to be achieved. . . .

The substantial costs RFRA exacts, both in practical terms of imposing a heavy litigation burden on the States and in terms of curtailing their traditional general regulatory power, far exceed any pattern or practice of unconstitutional conduct under the Free Exercise Clause as interpreted in Smith. Simply put, RFRA is not designed to identify and counteract state laws likely to be unconstitutional because of their treatment of religion. In most cases, the state laws to which RFRA applies are not ones which will have been motivated by religious bigotry. If a state law disproportionately burdened a particular class of religious observers, this circumstance might be evidence of an impermissible legislative motive. . . .

Broad as the power of Congress is under the Enforcement Clause of the Fourteenth Amendment, RFRA contradicts vital principles necessary to maintain separation of powers and the federal balance.

The judgment of the Court of Appeals sustaining the Act's constitutionality is reversed."

V. JUSTICE VOTE

3 Pro ACLU Side vs. 6 Con Opposing Side

ACLU Side (Respondent / Appellee)

1. O'Connor, S. – Wrote dissenting opinion
2. Breyer, S. – Wrote dissenting opinion, joined O'Connor's dissent in part
3. Souter, D. – Wrote dissenting opinion

Opposing Side (Petitioner / Appellant)

1. Kennedy, A. – Wrote majority opinion
2. Stevens, J. – Wrote concurring opinion, joined Scalia's concurrence
3. Rehnquist, W. – Joined majority opinion
4. Thomas, C. – Joined majority opinion
5. Ginsburg, R. – Joined majority opinion
6. Scalia, A. – Wrote concurring opinion

VI. A WIN OR LOSS FOR THE ACLU?

The ACLU, as amicus curiae, urged affirmance of the judgment of the Court of Appeals for the Fifth Circuit; the Supreme Court reversed in a 6-3 vote, giving the ACLU an apparent loss.

835. Washington v. Glucksberg

(Decided June 26, 1997; 521 U.S. 702)

I. ISSUE

A. Issues Discussed

Physician assisted suicide, Fourteenth Amendment, due process

B. Legal Question Presented

"[W]hether Washington's prohibition against 'caus[ing]' or 'aid[ing]' a suicide offends the Fourteenth Amendment to the United States Constitution."

C. Supreme Court's Answer

Washington's prohibition does not violate the Fourteenth Amendment.

II. CASE SUMMARY

A. Background

"It has always been a crime to assist a suicide in the State of Washington. In 1854, Washington's first Territorial Legislature outlawed 'assisting another in the commission of self-murder.' Today, Washington law provides: 'A person is guilty of promoting a suicide attempt when he knowingly causes or aids another person to attempt suicide.' 'Promoting a suicide attempt' is a felony, punishable by up to five years' imprisonment and up to a $10,000 fine. At the same time, Washington's Natural Death Act, enacted in 1979, states that the 'withholding or withdrawal of life-sustaining treatment' at a patient's direction 'shall not, for any purpose, constitute a suicide.'

Petitioners in this case are the State of Washington and its Attorney General. Respondents Harold Glucksberg, M. D., Abigail Halperin, M. D., Thomas A. Preston, M. D., and Peter Shalit, M. D., are physicians who practice in Washington. These doctors occasionally treat terminally ill, suffering patients, and declare that they would assist these patients in ending their lives if not for Washington's assisted-suicide ban. In January 1994, respondents, along with three gravely ill, pseudonymous plaintiffs who have since died and Compassion in Dying, a nonprofit organization that counsels people considering physician-assisted suicide, sued in the United States District Court, seeking a declaration that Wash.Rev.Code § 9A.36.060(1) (1994) is, on its face, unconstitutional.

The plaintiffs asserted 'the existence of a liberty interest protected by the Fourteenth Amendment which extends to a personal choice by a mentally competent, terminally ill adult to commit physician-assisted suicide." Relying primarily on Planned Parenthood of Southeastern Pa. v. Casey, 505 U.S. 833 (1992), and Cruzan v. Director, Mo. Dept. of Health, 497 U.S. 261 (1990), the District Court agreed, and concluded that Washington's assisted-suicide ban is unconstitutional because it 'places an undue burden on the exercise of [that] constitutionally protected liberty interest.' The District Court also decided that the Washington statute violated the Equal Protection Clause's requirement that "all persons similarly situated . . . be treated alike."

A panel of the Court of Appeals for the Ninth Circuit reversed, emphasizing that '[i]n the two hundred and five years of our existence no constitutional right to aid in killing oneself has ever been asserted and upheld by a court of final jurisdiction.' The Ninth Circuit reheard the case en banc, reversed the panel's decision, and affirmed the District Court."

The Supreme Court granted certiorari to review the case and reversed.

B. Counsel of Record / ACLU Attorney

ACLU Side (Respondent / Appellee): Kathryn L. Tucker argued the cause for appellees.

Opposing Side (Petitioner / Appellant): William L. Williams, Sr., Assistant Attorney General of Washington, argued the cause for appellants.

Acting Solicitor General Walter Dellinger argued the cause for the United States, as amicus curiae, by special leave of Court.

III. AMICI CURIAE

ACLU Side (Respondent / Appellee)

Brief of amici curiae filed on behalf of the ACLU, et al., by Cameron Clark, Karen E. Boxx, Claudia L. Hammerman, Douglas A. Berman, and Steven R. Shapiro.

Additional briefs of amici curiae were filed in support of Americans for Death with Dignity, et al., the American Medical Student Association, et al., the Center for Reproductive Law & Policy, the Coalition of Hospie Professionals, the Council for Secular Humanism, et al., Gay Men's Health Crisis, et al., the National Women's Health Network, et al., 36 Religious Organizations, Leaders, and Scholars, Surviving Family Members in Support of Physician-Assisted Dying, Ronald Dworkin, et al., the Washington State Psychological Association, et al., Bioethicists, Law Professors, State Legislators, John Doe, and Julian M. Whitaker, M. D.

Brief of amici curiae filed on behalf of the American College of Legal Medicine b y Miles J. Zaremski, Bruce E. Nelson, and Ila S. Rothschild, in support of neither party.

Opposing Side (Petitioner / Appellant)

Brief of amici curiae filed on behalf of the United States by Acting Solicitor General Dellinger, Assistant Attorney General Hunger, Deputy Solicitor General Waxman, Deputy Assistant Attorney General Preston, Irving L. Gornstein, Michael S. Raab, and Barbara C. Biddle.

Additional briefs of amici curiae were filed on behalf of the State of California, et al., the State of Oregon, Wayne County, Michigan, the District Attorney of Milwaukee County, Wisconsin, Agudath Israel of America, the American Association of Homes and Services for the Aging, et al., the International Anti-Euthanasia Task Force, the Southern Center for Law and Ethics, the American Center for Law and Justice, the American Geriatrics Society, the American Hospital Association, the American Medical Association, et al., the American Suicide Foundation, the Catholic Health Association of the United States, the Catholic Medical Association, the Christian Legal Society, et al., the Evangelical Lutheran Church in America, the Family Research Council, the Institute for Public Affairs of the Union of Orthodox Jewish Congregations of America, et al., the Legal Center for Defense of Life, Inc., et al., the National Association of Prolife Nurses, et al., the National Catholic Office for Persons with Disabilities, et al., the National Hospice Organization, the National Legal Center for the Medically Dependent & Disabled, Inc., et al., the National Right to Life Committee, Inc., the National Spinal Cord Injury Association, Inc., the Project on Death in America, et al., the Rutherford Institute, the Schiller Institute, the United States Catholic Conference, et al., Senator Orrin Hatch, et al., Members of the New York and Washington State Legislatures, Bioethics Professors, Gary Lee, M. D., et al., and Richard Thompson.

IV. THE SUPREME COURT'S DECISION

"Attitudes toward suicide itself have changed . . . , but our laws have consistently condemned, and continue to prohibit, assisting suicide. Despite changes in medical technology and notwithstanding an increased emphasis on the importance of end-of-life decisionmaking, we have not retreated from this prohibition. Against this backdrop of history, tradition, and practice, we now turn to respondents' constitutional claim. . . .

The Washington statute at issue in this case prohibits 'aid[ing] another person to attempt suicide,' and, thus, the question before us is whether the 'liberty' specially protected by the Due Process Clause includes a right to commit suicide which itself includes a right to assistance in doing so. . . .

The history of the law's treatment of assisted suicide in this country has been and continues to be one of the rejection of nearly all efforts to permit it. That being the case, our decisions lead us to conclude that the asserted 'right' to assistance in committing suicide is not a fundamental liberty interest protected by the Due Process Clause. The Constitution also requires, however, that Washington's assisted-suicide ban be rationally related to legitimate government interests. This requirement is unquestionably met here. As the court below recognized, Washington's assisted-suicide ban implicates a number of state interests.

First, Washington has an 'unqualified interest in the preservation of human life.' . . . The State also has an interest in protecting the integrity and ethics of the medical profession. . . . Next, the State has an interest in protecting vulnerable groups—including the poor, the elderly, and disabled persons—from abuse, neglect, and mistakes. . . . Finally, the State may fear that permitting assisted suicide will start it down the path to voluntary and perhaps even involuntary euthanasia. . . .

We need not weigh exactingly the relative strengths of these various interests. They are unquestionably important and legitimate, and Washington's ban on assisted suicide is at least reasonably related to their promotion and protection. We therefore hold that Wash. Rev. Code § 9A.36.060(1) (1994) does not violate the Fourteenth Amendment, either on its face or 'as applied to competent, terminally ill adults who wish to hasten their deaths by obtaining medication prescribed by their doctors.'

Throughout the Nation, Americans are engaged in an earnest and profound debate about the morality, legality, and practicality of physician-assisted suicide. Our holding permits this debate to continue, as it should in a democratic society. The decision of the en banc Court of Appeals is reversed, and the case is remanded for further proceedings consistent with this opinion."

V. JUSTICE VOTE

0 Pro ACLU Side vs. 9 Con Opposing Side

Opposing Side (Petitioner / Appellant)

1. Rehnquist, W. – Wrote majority opinion
2. O'Connor, S. – Wrote concurring opinion
3. Souter, D. – Wrote concurring opinion
4. Ginsburg, R. – Wrote concurring opinion, joined O'Connor's concurrence in part
5. Breyer, S. – Wrote concurring opinion, joined O'Connor's concurrence in part
6. Stevens, J. – Wrote concurring opinion
7. Scalia, A. – Joined majority opinion
8. Kennedy, A. – Joined majority opinion
9. Thomas, C. – Joined majority opinion

VI. A WIN OR LOSS FOR THE ACLU?

The ACLU, as amicus curiae, urged affirmance of the judgment of the Court of Appeals for the Ninth Circuit; the Supreme Court reversed in a 9-0 vote, giving the ACLU an apparent loss.

836. Vacco v. Quill

(Decided June 26, 1997; 521 U.S. 793)

I. ISSUE

A. Issues Discussed

Criminal justice, Fourteenth Amendment, equal protection, physician assisted suicide

B. Legal Question Presented

"[W]hether New York's prohibition on assisting suicide . . . violates the Equal Protection Clause of the Fourteenth Amendment."

C. Supreme Court's Answer

New York's prohibition on assisting suicide does not violate the Equal Protection Clause.

II. CASE SUMMARY

A. Background

"Petitioners are various New York public officials. Respondents Timothy E. Quill, Samuel C. Klagsbrun, and Howard A. Grossman are physicians who practice in New York. They assert that although it would be 'consistent with the standards of [their] medical practice[s]' to prescribe lethal medication for 'mentally competent, terminally ill patients' who are suffering great pain and desire a doctor's help in taking their own lives, they are deterred from doing so by New York's ban on assisting suicide. Respondents, and three gravely ill patients who have since died, sued the State's Attorney General in the United States District Court. They urged that because New York permits a competent person to refuse life-sustaining medical treatment, and because the refusal of such treatment is 'essentially the same thing' as physician-assisted suicide, New York's assisted-suicide ban violates the Equal Protection Clause.

The District Court disagreed: '[I]t is hardly unreasonable or irrational for the State to recognize a difference between allowing nature to take its course, even in the most severe situations, and intentionally using an artificial death-producing device.' The court noted New York's 'obvious legitimate interests in preserving life, and in protecting vulnerable persons,' and concluded that '[u]nder the United States Constitution and the federal system it establishes, the resolution of this issue is left to the normal democratic processes within the State.'

The Court of Appeals for the Second Circuit reversed. The court determined that, despite the assisted-suicide ban's apparent general applicability, 'New York law does not treat equally all competent persons who are in the final stages of fatal illness and wish to hasten their deaths,' because 'those in the final stages of terminal illness who are on life-support systems are allowed to hasten their deaths by directing the removal of such systems; but those who are similarly situated, except for the previous attachment of life-sustaining equipment, are not allowed to hasten death by self-administering prescribed drugs.' In the court's view, '[t]he ending of life by [the withdrawal of life-support systems] is nothing more nor less than assisted suicide.' The Court of Appeals then examined whether this supposed unequal treatment was rationally related to any legitimate state interests, and concluded that 'to the extent that [New York's statutes] prohibit a physician from prescribing medications to be self-administered by a mentally competent, terminally-ill person in the final stages of his terminal illness, they are not rationally related to any legitimate state interest.'"

The Supreme Court granted certiorari to review the case and reversed.

B. Counsel of Record / ACLU Attorney

ACLU Side (Respondent / Appellee): Laurence H. Tribe argued the cause for appellee.

Opposing Side (Petitioner / Appellant): Dennis C. Vacco, Attorney General of New York, argued the cause for appellant.

Acting Solicitor General Walter Dellinger argued the cause for the United States, as amicus curiae, by special leave of Court.

III. AMICI CURIAE

ACLU Side (Respondent / Appellee)

Brief of amici curiae filed on behalf of the ACLU, et al., by Cameron Clark, Claudia L. Hammerman, Douglas A. Berman, Karen E. Boxx, and Steven R. Shapiro.

Additional briefs of amici curiae were filed on behalf of Americans for Death with Dignity, et al., the American Medical Student Association, et al., the Coalition of Hospice Professionals, Gay Men's Health Crisis, et al., the National Women's Health Network, et al., Surviving Family Members in Support of Physician-Assisted Dying, 36 Religious Organizations, Leaders, and Scholars, et al., the Washington State Psychological Association, et al., Bioethicists, Law Professors, State Legislators, Ronald Dworkin, et al., and Julian M. Whitaker, MD.

Brief of amici curiae filed on behalf of the American College of Legal Medicine by Miles J. Zaremski, Bruce C. Nelson, and Ila S. Rothschild, in support of neither party.

Opposing Side (Petitioner / Appellant)

Briefs of amici curiae were filed on behalf of the United States, the State of California, et al., Wayne County, Michigan, Agudath Israel of America, the American Association of Homes and Services for the Aging, et al., the American Center for Law and Justice, the American Geriatrics Society, the American Hospital Association, the American Medical Association, et al., the Catholic Health Association of the United States, the Catholic Medical Association, the Christian Legal Society, et al., the Clarendon House, the Evangelical Lutheran Church in America, the Family Research Council, the Institute for Public Affairs of the Union of Orthodox Jewish Congregations of America, et al., the Medical Society of New Jersey, the National Association of Pro-life Nurses, et al., Not Dead Yet, et al., the International Anti-Euthanasia

Task Force, the American Life League, Inc., the National Catholic Office for Persons with Disabilities, et al., the National Hospice Organization, the National Legal Center for the Medically Dependent & Disabled, Inc., et al., the Project on Death in America, et al., the United States Catholic Conference, et al., Senator Orrin Hatch, et al., Members of the New York and Washington State Legislatures, Bioethics Professors, Jerome J. De Cosse, et al., Gary Lee, M. D., et al., Richard Thompson and Richard J. Browne, and Seven Present and Former Commissioners of the United States Commission on Civil Rights, et al.

IV. THE SUPREME COURT'S DECISION

"On their faces, neither New York's ban on assisting suicide nor its statutes permitting patients to refuse medical treatment treat anyone differently from anyone else or draw any distinctions between persons. Everyone, regardless of physical condition, is entitled, if competent, to refuse unwanted lifesaving medical treatment; no one is permitted to assist a suicide. Generally speaking, laws that apply evenhandedly to all 'unquestionably comply' with the Equal Protection Clause.

The Court of Appeals, however, concluded that some terminally ill people—those who are on life-support systems—are treated differently from those who are not, in that the former may 'hasten death' by ending treatment, but the latter may not 'hasten death' through physician-assisted suicide. This conclusion depends on the submission that ending or refusing lifesaving medical treatment 'is nothing more nor less than assisted suicide.' Unlike the Court of Appeals, we think the distinction between assisting suicide and withdrawing life-sustaining treatment, a distinction widely recognized and endorsed in the medical profession and in our legal traditions, is both important and logical; it is certainly rational.

[T]he overwhelming majority of state legislatures have drawn a clear line between assisting suicide and withdrawing or permitting the refusal of unwanted lifesaving medical treatment by prohibiting the former and permitting the latter. And 'nearly all states expressly disapprove of suicide and assisted suicide either in statutes dealing with durable powers of attorney in health- care situations, or in 'living will' statutes.' Thus, even as the States move to protect and promote patients' dignity at the end of life, they remain opposed to physician-assisted suicide.

[W]e disagree with respondents' claim that the distinction between refusing lifesaving medical treatment and assisted suicide is 'arbitrary' and 'irrational.' Granted, in some cases, the line between the two may not be clear, but certainly is not required, even were it possible. Logic and contemporary practice support New York's judgment that the two acts are different, and New York may therefore, consistent with the Constitution, treat them differently. By permitting everyone to refuse unwanted medical treatment while prohibiting anyone from assisting a suicide, New York law follows a longstanding and rational distinction.

New York's reasons for recognizing and acting on this distinction—including prohibiting intentional killing and preserving life; preventing suicide; maintaining physicians' role as their patients' healers; protecting vulnerable people from indifference, prejudice, and psychological and financial pressure to end their lives; and avoiding a possible slide towards euthanasia—are discussed in greater detail in our opinion in Glucksberg, ante. These valid and important public interests easily satisfy the constitutional requirement that a legislative classification bear a rational relation to some legitimate end.

The judgment of the Court of Appeals is reversed."

V. JUSTICE VOTE

0 Pro ACLU Side vs. 9 Con Opposing Side

Opposing Side (Petitioner / Appellant)

1. Rehnquist, W. – Wrote majority opinion
2. Scalia, A. – Joined majority opinion
3. Kennedy, A. – Joined majority opinion
4. Thomas, C. – Joined majority opinion
5. O'Connor, S. – Wrote concurring opinion
6. Ginsburg, R. – Wrote concurring opinion, joined O'Connor's concurrence in part
7. Breyer, S. – Wrote concurring opinion, joined O'Connor's concurrence in part
8. Stevens, J. – Wrote concurring opinion
9. Souter, D. – Wrote concurring opinion

VI. A WIN OR LOSS FOR THE ACLU?

The ACLU filed as amicus curiae urging affirmance of the judgment of the Court of Appeals for the Second Circuit; the Supreme Court reversed in a 9-0 vote, giving the ACLU an apparent loss.

837. Reno v. American Civil Liberties Union

(Decided June 26, 1997; 521 U.S. 844)

I. ISSUE

A. Issues Discussed

First Amendment, freedom of speech

B. Legal Question Presented

Whether the two challenged provisions of the Communications Decency Act violate the First Amendment.

C. Supreme Court's Answer

The provisions violate the First Amendment.

II. CASE SUMMARY

A. Background

"The Telecommunications Act of 1996, Pub.L. 104–104, 110 Stat. 56, was an unusually important legislative enactment. . . The Act includes seven Titles, six of which are the product of extensive committee hearings and the subject of discussion in Reports prepared by Committees of the Senate and the House of Representatives. By contrast, Title V—known as the 'Communications Decency Act of 1996' (CDA)—contains provisions that were either added in executive committee after the hearings were concluded or as amendments offered during floor debate on the legislation. An amendment offered in the Senate was the source of the two statutory provisions challenged in this case. They are informally described as the 'indecent transmission' provision and the 'patently offensive display' provision.

The first, 47 U.S.C. § 223(a) (1994 ed., Supp. II), prohibits the knowing transmission of obscene or indecent messages to any recipient under 18 years of age. . . . The second provision, § 223(d), prohibits the knowing sending or displaying of patently offensive messages in a manner that is available to a person under 18 years of age. . . .

On February 8, 1996, immediately after the President signed the statute, 20 plaintiffs filed suit against the Attorney General of the United States and the Department of Justice challenging the constitutionality of §§ 223(a)(1) and 223(d). A week later, based on his conclusion that the term 'indecent' was too vague to provide the basis for a criminal prosecution, District Judge Buckwalter entered a temporary restraining order against enforcement of § 223(a)(1)(B)(ii) insofar as it applies to indecent communications. A second suit was then filed by 27 additional plaintiffs, consolidated, and a three-judge District Court was convened pursuant to § 561 of the CDA. After an evidentiary hearing, that court entered a preliminary injunction against enforcement of both of the challenged provisions. Each of the three judges wrote a separate opinion, but their judgment was unanimous. . . .

The judgment of the District Court enjoins the Government from enforcing the prohibitions in § 223(a)(1) (B) insofar as they relate to 'indecent' communications, but expressly preserves the Government's right to investigate and prosecute the obscenity or child pornography activities prohibited therein. The injunction against enforcement of §§ 223(d)(1) and (2) is unqualified because those provisions contain no separate reference to obscenity or child pornography."

The Supreme Court granted certiorari to review the case and affirmed.

B. Counsel of Record / ACLU Attorney

ACLU Side (Respondent / Appellee): Bruce J. Ennis argued the cause for appellee, ACLU. With him on the briefs for the American Library Association, et al., were Ann M. Kappler, Paul M. Smith, Donald B. Verrilli, Jr., John B. Morris, Jr., Sean H. Donahue, Michelle B. Goodman, Jerry Berman, Elliot M. Mincberg, Lawrence S. Ottinger, Andrew J. Schwartzman, Ronald L. Plesser, James J. Halpert, Richard M. Schmidt, Jr., Allan R. Adler, Bruce W. Sanford, Henry S. Hoberman, Robert D. Lystad, William W. Barrington, Jill Lesser, Bruce Rich, James Wheaton, Steve Heaton, Michael Traynor, John W. Crittenden, Kathryn M. Wheble, Robert P. Taylor, Megan W. Pierson, Melissa A. Burke, Thomas W. Burt, Rene Milam, and Marc Jacobson.

Christopher A. Hansen, Ann Beeson, Steven R. Shapiro, Roger Evans, Marjorie Heins, Catherine Weiss, David L. Sobel, Mark Rotenberg, Mike Codwin, and Stefan Presser filed a brief for appellees the ACLU, et al.

Opposing Side (Petitioner / Appellant): Acting Solicitor General Walter Dellinger argued the cause for appellants. With him on the briefs were Assistant Attorney General Hunger, Deputy Solicitor General Kneedler, Irving L. Gornstein, Barbara L. Herwig, and Jacob M. Lewis.

III. AMICI CURIAE

ACLU Side (Respondent / Appellee)

Briefs of amici curiae were filed on behalf of the American Association of University Professors, et al., ApolloMedia Corporation, et al., the Association of National Advertisers, Inc., et al., the Chamber of Commerce of the United States, Feminists for Free Expression, the National Association of Broadcasters, et al., Playboy Enterprises, Inc., the Reporters Committee for Freedom of the Press, et al., Site Specific, Inc., et al., Volunteer Lawyers for the Arts, et al., and the Speech Communication Association.

Opposing Side (Petitioner / Appellant)

Briefs of amici curiae were filed on behalf of Member of Congress Dan Coats, et al., Enough is Enough, et al., the Family Life Project of the American Center for Law and Justice, Morality in Media, Inc., and James J. Clancy.

IV. THE SUPREME COURT'S DECISION

"Regardless of whether the CDA is so vague that it violates the Fifth Amendment, the many ambiguities concerning the scope of its coverage render it problematic for purposes of the First Amendment. For instance, each of the two parts of the CDA uses a different linguistic form. The first uses the word 'indecent,' while the second speaks of material that 'in context, depicts or describes, in terms patently offensive as measured by contemporary community standards, sexual or excretory activities or organs.' Given the absence of a definition of either term, this difference in language will provoke uncertainty among speakers about how the two standards relate to each other and just what they mean. Could a speaker confidently assume that a serious discussion about birth control practices, homosexuality, the First Amendment issues raised by the Appendix to our Pacifica opinion, or the consequences of prison rape would not violate the CDA? This uncertainty undermines the likelihood that the CDA has been carefully tailored to the congressional goal of protecting minors from potentially harmful materials. . . .

We are persuaded that the CDA lacks the precision that the First Amendment requires when a statute regulates the content of speech. In order to deny minors access to potentially harmful speech, the CDA effectively suppresses a large amount of speech that adults have a constitutional right to receive and to address to one another. That burden on adult speech is unacceptable if less restrictive alternatives would be at least as effective in achieving the legitimate purpose that the statute was enacted to serve. . . .

The breadth of this content-based restriction of speech imposes an especially heavy burden on the Government to explain why a less restrictive provision would not be as effective as the CDA. It has not done so. The arguments in this Court have referred to possible alternatives such as requiring that indecent material be 'tagged' in a way that facilitates parental control of material coming into their homes, making exceptions for messages with artistic or educational value, providing some tolerance for parental choice, and regulating some portions of the Internet—such as commercial Web sites —differently from others, such as chat rooms. Particularly in the light of the absence of any detailed findings by the Congress, or even hearings addressing the special problems of the CDA, we are persuaded that the CDA is not narrowly tailored if that requirement has any meaning at all. . . .

The record demonstrates that the growth of the Internet has been and continues to be phenomenal. As a matter of constitutional tradition, in the absence of evidence to the contrary, we presume that governmental regulation of the content of speech is more likely to interfere with the free exchange of ideas than to encourage it. The interest in encouraging freedom of expression in a democratic society outweighs any theoretical but unproven benefit of censorship.

For the foregoing reasons, the judgment of the District Court is affirmed."

V. JUSTICE VOTE

9 Pro ACLU Side vs. 0 Con Opposing Side

ACLU Side (Respondent / Appellee)

1. Stevens, J. – Wrote majority opinion
2. Scalia, A. – Joined majority opinion
3. Kennedy, A. – Joined majority opinion
4. Souter, D. – Joined majority opinion
5. Ginsburg, R. – Joined majority opinion
6. Thomas, C. – Joined majority opinion
7. Breyer, S. – Joined majority opinion
8. O'Connor, S. – Wrote opinion concurring in part and dissenting in part
9. Rehnquist, W. – Joined O'Connor's opinion

VI. A WIN OR LOSS FOR THE ACLU?

The ACLU, as party of record, urged affirmance of the judgment of the District Court for the Eastern District of Pennsylvania; the Supreme Court affirmed in a 9-0 vote, giving the ACLU an apparent win.

838. Oncale v. Sundowner Offshore Services, Inc.

(Decided March 4, 1998; 523 U.S. 75)

I. ISSUE

A. Issues Discussed

Civil rights, gender discrimination, employment

B. Legal Question Presented

"[W]hether workplace harassment can violate Title VII's prohibition against 'discriminat[ion] . . . because of . . . sex,' 42 U.S.C. § 2000e- 2(a)(1), when the harasser and the harassed employee are of the same sex."

C. Supreme Court's Answer

Workplace harassment can violate Title VII when the harasser and harassed employee are of the same sex.

II. CASE SUMMARY

A. Background

"In late October 1991, Oncale was working for respondent Sundowner Offshore Services, Inc., on a Chevron U.S.A., Inc., oil platform in the Gulf of Mexico. He was employed as a roustabout on an eight-man crew which included respondents John Lyons, Danny Pippen, and Brandon Johnson. Lyons, the crane operator, and Pippen, the driller, had supervisory authority. On several occasions, Oncale was forcibly subjected to sex-related, humiliating actions against him by Lyons, Pippen, and Johnson in the presence of the rest of the crew. Pippen and Lyons also physically assaulted Oncale in a sexual manner, and Lyons threatened him with rape.

Oncale's complaints to supervisory personnel produced no remedial action; in fact, the company's Safety Compliance Clerk, Valent Hohen, told Oncale that Lyons and Pippen 'picked [on] him all the time too,' and called him a name suggesting homosexuality. Oncale eventually quit —asking that his pink slip reflect that he 'voluntarily left due to sexual harassment and verbal abuse.' When asked at his deposition why he left Sundowner, Oncale stated:

'I felt that if I didn't leave my job, that I would be raped or forced to have sex.'

Oncale filed a complaint against Sundowner in the United States District Court for the Eastern District of Louisiana, alleging that he was discriminated against in his employment because of his sex. Relying on the Fifth Circuit's decision in Garcia v. Elf Atochem North America, 28 F.3d 446, 451–452 (1994), the District Court held that 'Mr. Oncale, a male, has no cause of action under Title VII for harassment by male co- workers.' On appeal, a panel of the Fifth Circuit concluded that Garcia was binding Circuit precedent, and affirmed."

The Supreme Court granted certiorari to review the case and reversed.

B. Counsel of Record / ACLU Attorney

ACLU Side (Petitioner / Appellant): Nicholas Canaday, III argued the cause for appellant.

Deputy Solicitor General Edwin S. Kneedler argued the cause for the United States, as amicus curiae, by special leave of Court.

Opposing Side (Respondent / Appellee): Harry M. Reasoner argued the cause for appellees.

III. AMICI CURIAE

ACLU Side (Petitioner / Appellant)

Brief of amici curiae filed on behalf of the Lambda Legal Defense and Education Fund, the ACLU, et al., by Steven R. Shapiro, Jennifer Middleton, Sara L. Mandelbaum, Beatrice Dohrn, Jon Davidson, Ruth Harlow, David Buckel, and Minna J. Kotkin.

Brief of amici curiae filed on behalf of the United States by Deputy Solicitor General Kneedler, Acting Solicitor General Dellinger, Acting Assistant Attorney General Pinzler, Deputy Solicitor General Waxman, Beth S. Brinkmann, C. Gregory Stewart, J. Ray Terry, Jr., Gwendolyn Young Reams, Paul Bogas, and Carolyn L. Wheeler.

Brief of amici curiae filed on behalf of the Association of Trial Lawyers of America by Richard D. Hailey, Ellen Simon Sacks and Christopher P. Thorman.

Brief of amici curiae filed on behalf of the National Employment Lawyers Association by Margaret A. Harris Victoria L. Herring, and Anne Golden.

Brief of amici curiae filed on behalf of the National Organization on Male Sexual Victimization, Inc., by Catharine A. MacKinnon.

Brief of amici curiae filed on behalf of Law Professors by Katherine M. Franke and Nan D. Hunter.

Opposing Side (Respondent / Appellee)

Brief of amici curiae filed on behalf of the Equal Employment Advisory Council by Robert E. Williams and Ann Elizabeth Reesman.

Brief of amici curiae filed on behalf of the Texas Association of Business & Chambers of Commerce by Jeffrey C. Londa, Michael D. Mitchell, and Linda Ottinger Headley.

IV. THE SUPREME COURT'S DECISION

"Title VII of the Civil Rights Act of 1964 provides, in relevant part, that '[i]t shall be an unlawful employment practice for an employer . . . to discriminate against any individual with respect to his compensation, terms, conditions, or privileges of employment, because of such individual's race, color, religion, sex, or national origin.' . . .

We see no justification in the statutory language or our precedents for a categorical rule excluding same-sex harassment claims from the coverage of Title VII. As some courts have observed, male-on-male sexual harassment in the workplace was assuredly not the principal evil Congress was concerned with when it enacted Title VII. But statutory prohibitions often go beyond the principal evil to cover reasonably comparable evils, and it is ultimately the provisions of our laws rather than the principal concerns of our legislators by which we are governed. Title VII prohibits 'discriminat[ion] . . . because of . . . sex' in the 'terms' or 'conditions' of employment. Our holding that this includes sexual harassment must extend to sexual harassment of any kind that meets the statutory requirements.

[H]arassing conduct need not be motivated by sexual desire to support an inference of discrimination on the basis of sex. A trier of fact might reasonably find such discrimination, for example, if a female victim is harassed in such sex-specific and derogatory terms by another woman as to make it clear that the harasser is motivated by general hostility to the presence of women in the workplace. A same-sex harassment plaintiff may also, of course, offer direct comparative evidence about how the alleged harasser treated members of both sexes in a mixed-sex workplace. Whatever evidentiary route the plaintiff chooses to follow, he or she must always prove that the conduct at issue was not merely tinged with offensive sexual connotations, but actually constituted 'discrimina[tion] . . . because of . . . sex.' . . .

Because we conclude that sex discrimination consisting of same-sex sexual harassment is actionable under Title VII, the judgment of the Court of Appeals for the Fifth Circuit is reversed, and the case is remanded for further proceedings consistent with this opinion."

V. JUSTICE VOTE

9 Pro ACLU Side vs. 0 Con Opposing Side

ACLU Side (Petitioner / Appellant)

1. Scalia, A. – Wrote majority opinion
2. Ginsburg, R. – Joined majority opinion
3. Stevens, J. – Joined majority opinion
4. Rehnquist, W. – Joined majority opinion
5. Kennedy, A. – Joined majority opinion
6. Breyer, S. – Joined majority opinion
7. Souter, D. – Joined majority opinion
8. O'Connor, S. – Joined majority opinion
9. Thomas, C. – Wrote concurring opinion

VI. A WIN OR LOSS FOR THE ACLU?

The ACLU filed as amicus curiae urging reversal of the judgment of the Court of Appeals for the Fifth Circuit; the Supreme Court reversed in a 9-0 vote, giving the ACLU an apparent win.

839. Ohio Adult Parole Authority v. Woodard

(Decided March 25, 1998; 523 U.S. 272)

I. ISSUE

A. Issues Discussed

Criminal justice, death penalty, Fifth Amendment, due process, privilege against self-incrimination

B. Legal Question Presented

"[W]hether an inmate has a protected life or liberty interest in clemency proceedings, under either Connecticut Bd. of Pardons v. Dumschat, 452 U.S. 458 (1981), or Evitts v. Lucey, 469 U.S. 387 (1985) [and] whether giving inmates the option of voluntarily participating in an interview as part of the clemency process violates an inmate's Fifth Amendment rights."

C. Supreme Court's Answer

"The Due Process Clause is not violated where, as here, the procedures in question do no more than confirm that the clemency and pardon powers are committed, as is our tradition, to the authority of the executive. We further hold that a voluntary inmate interview does not violate the Fifth Amendment."

II. CASE SUMMARY

A. Background

"The Ohio Constitution gives the Governor the power to grant clemency upon such conditions as he thinks proper. The Ohio General Assembly cannot curtail this discretionary decision-making power, but it may regulate the application and investigation process. The General Assembly has delegated in large part the conduct of clemency review to petitioner Ohio Adult Parole Authority (Authority).

In the case of an inmate under death sentence, the Authority must conduct a clemency hearing within 45 days of the scheduled date of execution. Prior to the hearing, the inmate may request an interview with one or more parole board members. Counsel is not allowed at that interview. The Authority must hold the hearing, complete its clemency review, and make a recommendation to the Governor, even if the inmate subsequently obtains a stay of execution. If additional information later becomes available, the Authority may in its discretion hold another hearing or alter its recommendation.

Respondent Eugene Woodard was sentenced to death for aggravated murder committed in the course of a carjacking. His conviction and sentence were affirmed on appeal, and [the Supreme] Court denied certiorari. When respondent failed to obtain a stay of execution more than 45 days before his scheduled execution date, the Authority commenced its clemency investigation. It informed respondent that he could have a clemency interview on September 9, 1994, if he wished, and that his clemency hearing would be on September 16, 1994.

Respondent did not request an interview. Instead, he objected to the short notice of the interview and requested assurances that counsel could attend and participate in the interview and hearing. When the Authority failed to respond to these requests, respondent filed suit in United States District Court on September 14, alleging under Rev. Stat. § 1979, 42 U.S.C. § 1983, that Ohio's clemency process violated his Fourteenth Amendment right to due process and his Fifth Amendment right to remain silent.

The District Court granted the State's motion for judgment on the pleadings. The Court of Appeals for the Sixth Circuit affirmed in part and reversed in part."

The Supreme Court granted certiorari to review the case and reversed.

B. Counsel of Record / ACLU Attorney

ACLU Side (Respondent / Appellee): S. Adele Shank argued the case for appellee.

Opposing Side (Petitioner / Appellant): William A. Klatt, First Attorney General of Ohio, argued the case for appellants.

III. AMICI CURIAE

ACLU Side (Respondent / Appellee)

Brief of amici curiae filed on behalf of the ACLU, et al., by Daniel T. Kobil, Joan M. Englund, Steven R. Shapiro, and Diann Y. Rust-Tierney.

Brief of amici curiae filed on behalf of the National Association of Criminal Defense Lawyers by Andrea D. Lyon and Barbara E. Bergman.

Brief of amici curiae filed on behalf of the American Bar Association by Jerome J. Shestack and Ronald J. Tabak.

Opposing Side (Petitioner / Appellant)

Brief of amici curiae filed on behalf of the State of California, et al., by Daniel E. Lungren, Attorney General; George Williamson, Chief Assistant Attorney General; Robert R. Anderson, Senior Assistant Attorney General; William G. Prahl, Supervising Deputy Attorney General; Ward A. Campbell, Deputy Attorney General; and by the Attorneys General for their respective States as follows: Bill Pryor of Alabama; Grant Woods of Arizona; Winston Bryant of Arkansas; Gale A. Norton of Colorado; M. Jane Brady of Delaware; Robert A. Butterworth of Florida; Thurbert E. Baker of Georgia; Margery S. Bronster of Hawaii; Alan G. Lance of Idaho; James E. Ryan of Illinois; Jeffrey A. Modisett of Indiana; Albert B. Chandler III of Kentucky; Richard P. Ieyoub of Louisiana; Andrew Ketterer of Maine; J. Joseph Curran, Jr., of Maryland; Mike Moore of Mississippi; Jeremiah W (Jay) Nixon of Missouri; Joseph P. Mazurek of Montana; Don Stenberg of Nebraska; Frankie Sue Del Papa of Nevada; Peter Verniero of New Jersey; Dennis C. Vacco of New York; Michael F. Easley of North Carolina; D. Michael Fisher of Pennsylvania; Charles M. Condon of South Carolina; Mark W Barnett of South Dakota; John Knox Walkup of Tennessee; Dan Morales of Texas; Jan Graham of Utah; Richard Cullen of Virginia; Christine Q. Gregoire of Washington; and William U. Hill of Wyoming.

Brief of amici curiae filed on behalf of the Criminal Justice Legal Foundation by Kent S. Scheidegger and Charles L. Hobson.

IV. THE SUPREME COURT'S DECISION

"[C]lemency proceedings are not "an integral part of the . . . system for finally adjudicating the guilt or innocence of a defendant." Procedures mandated under the Due Process Clause should be consistent with the nature of the governmental power being invoked. Here, the executive's clemency authority would cease to be a matter of grace committed to the executive authority if it were constrained by the sort of procedural requirements that respondent urges. Respondent is already under a sentence of death, determined to have been lawfully imposed. If clemency is granted, he obtains a benefit; if it is denied, he is no worse off than he was before. . . .

Respondent also presses on us the Court of Appeals' conclusion that the provision of a voluntary inmate interview, without the benefit of counsel or a grant of immunity for any statements made by the inmate, implicates the inmate's Fifth and Fourteenth Amendment right not to incriminate himself. Because there is only one guaranteed clemency review, respondent asserts, his decision to participate is not truly voluntary. And in the interview he may be forced to answer questions; or, if he remains silent, his silence may be used against him. Respondent further asserts there is a substantial risk of incrimination since postconviction proceedings are in progress and since he could potentially incriminate himself on other crimes. Respondent therefore concludes that the interview unconstitutionally conditions his assertion of the right to pursue clemency on his waiver of the right to remain silent. While the Court of Appeals accepted respondent's rubric of 'unconstitutional conditions,' we find it unnecessary to address it in deciding this case. In our opinion, the procedures of the Authority do not under any view violate the Fifth Amendment privilege. . . .

Here, respondent has the same choice of providing information to the Authority—at the risk of damaging his case for clemency or for postconviction relief—or of remaining silent. But this pressure to speak in the hope of improving his chance of being granted clemency does not make the interview compelled. We therefore hold that the Ohio clemency interview, even on assumptions most favorable to respondent's claim, does not violate the Fifth Amendment privilege against compelled self-incrimination. . . .

We hold that neither the Due Process Clause nor the Fifth Amendment privilege against self-incrimination is violated by Ohio's clemency proceedings. The judgment of the Court of Appeals is therefore reversed."

V. JUSTICE VOTE

0 Pro ACLU Side vs. 9 Con Opposing Side

Opposing Side (Petitioner / Appellant)

1. Rehnquist, W. – Wrote majority opinion
2. O'Connor, S. – Wrote concurring opinion
3. Scalia, A. – Joined majority opinion
4. Kennedy, A. – Joined majority opinion
5. Souter, D. – Joined O'Connor's concurrence
6. Thomas, C. – Joined majority opinion
7. Ginsburg, R. – Joined O'Connor's concurrence
8. Breyer, S. – Joined O'Connor's concurrence
9. Stevens, J. – Wrote opinion concurring in part and dissenting in part

VI. A WIN OR LOSS FOR THE ACLU?

The ACLU filed as amicus curiae urging affirmance of the judgment of the Court of Appeals for the Sixth Circuit; the Supreme Court reversed in a 9-0 vote, giving the ACLU an apparent loss.

840. Texas v. United States

(Decided March 31, 1998; 523 U.S. 296)

I. ISSUE

A. Issues Discussed

Civil rights, voting rights, ripeness of controversy

B. Legal Question Presented

"[W]hether the controversy is ripe" for adjudication.

C. Supreme Court's Answer

The controversy is not ripe of adjudication.

II. CASE SUMMARY

A. Background

"Appellant, the State of Texas, appeals from the judgment of a three-judge District Court for the District of Columbia. The State had sought a declaratory judgment that the preclearance provisions of § 5 of the Voting Rights Act of 1965 . . . do not apply to implementation of certain sections of the Texas Education Code that permit the State to sanction local school districts for failure to meet state-mandated educational achievement levels. . . .

When a district fails to satisfy the State's accreditation criteria, the State Commissioner of Education may select from 10 possible sanctions that are listed in ascending order of severity. §§ 39.131(a)(1)-(10). Those include, 'to the extent the [C]ommissioner determines necessary,' § 39.131(a), appointing a master to oversee the district's operations, § 39.131(a)(7), or appointing a management team to direct the district's operations in areas of unacceptable performance or to require the district to contract for services from another person, § 39.131(a)(8). . . .

On June 7, 1996, Texas filed a complaint in the United States District Court for the District of Columbia, seeking a declaration that § 5 does not apply to the sanctions authorized by §§ 39.131(a)(7) and (8), because (1) they are not changes with respect to voting, and (2) they are consistent with conditions attached to grants of federal financial assistance that authorize and require the imposition of sanctions to ensure accountability of local education authorities. The District Court did not reach the merits of these arguments because it concluded that Texas's claim was not ripe."

The Supreme Court granted certiorari to review the case and affirmed.

B. Counsel of Record / ACLU Attorney

ACLU Side (Respondent / Appellee): Paul R. Q. Wolfson argued the cause for appellee.

Opposing Side (Petitioner / Appellant): Javier Aguilar, Special Assistant Attorney General of Texas, argued the cause for appellant.

III. AMICI CURIAE

ACLU Side (Respondent / Appellee)

Brief of amici curiae filed on behalf of the ACLU, et al., by Pamela S. Karlan, Laughlin McDonald, Neil Bradley, Maha S. Zaki, Cristina Correia, Elaine R. Jones, Theodore M. Shaw, Norman J. Chachkin, Jacqueline Berrien, Victor A. Bolden, and Steven R. Shapiro.

Opposing Side (Petitioner / Appellant)

Brief of amici curiae filed on behalf of the Washington Legal Foundation, et al., by Daniel J. Popeo and David M. Young.

IV. THE SUPREME COURT'S DECISION

"A claim is not ripe for adjudication if it rests upon 'contingent future events that may not occur as anticipated, or indeed may not occur at all.' Whether Texas will appoint a master or management team under §§ 39.131(a)(7) and (8) is contingent on a number of factors. . . . Texas has not pointed to any particular school district in which the application of § 39.131(a)(7) or (8) is currently foreseen or even likely. Indeed, Texas hopes that there will be no need to appoint a master or management team for any district. Under these circumstances, where 'we have no idea whether or when such [a sanction] will be ordered,' the issue is not fit for adjudication.

Even if there were greater certainty regarding ultimate implementation of paragraphs (a)(7) and (a)(8) of the statute, we do not think Texas's claim would be ripe. Ripeness 'requir[es] us to evaluate both the fitness of the issues for judicial decision and the hardship to the parties of withholding court consideration.' As to fitness of the issues: Texas asks us to hold that under no circumstances can the imposition of these sanctions constitute a change affecting voting. We do not have sufficient confidence in our powers of imagination to affirm such a negative. . . . In the present case, the remoteness and abstraction are increased by the fact that

Chapter 39 has yet to be interpreted by the Texas courts. Thus, '[p]ostponing consideration of the questions presented, until a more concrete controversy arises, also has the advantage of permitting the state courts further opportunity to construe' the provisions.

And as for hardship to the parties . . . Texas is not required to engage in, or to refrain from, any conduct, unless and until it chooses to implement one of the noncleared remedies. To be sure, if that contingency should arise compliance with the preclearance procedure could delay much needed action. . . . But even that inconvenience is avoidable. . . . Texas claims that it suffers the immediate hardship of a 'threat to federalism.' But that is an abstraction—and an abstraction no graver than the 'threat to personal freedom' that exists whenever an agency regulation is promulgated, which we hold inadequate to support suit unless the person's primary conduct is affected.

In sum, we find it too speculative whether the problem Texas presents will ever need solving; we find the legal issues Texas raises not yet fit for our consideration, and the hardship to Texas of biding its time insubstantial. Accordingly, we agree with the District Court that this matter is not ripe for adjudication."

V. JUSTICE VOTE

9 Pro ACLU Side vs. 0 Con Opposing Side

ACLU Side (Respondent / Appellee)

1. Scalia, A. – Wrote majority opinion
2. O'Connor, S. – Joined majority opinion
3. Kennedy, A. – Joined majority opinion
4. Souter, D. – Joined majority opinion
5. Thomas, C. – Joined majority opinion
6. Breyer, S. – Joined majority opinion
7. Stevens, J. – Joined majority opinion
8. Rehnquist, W. – Joined majority opinion
9. Ginsburg, R. – Joined majority opinion

VI. A WIN OR LOSS FOR THE ACLU?

The ACLU filed as amicus curiae urging affirmance of the judgment of the District Court for the District of Columbia; the Supreme Court affirmed in a 9-0 vote, giving the ACLU an apparent win.

841. Miller v. Albright

(Decided April 22, 1998; 523 U.S. 420)

I. ISSUE

A. Issues Discussed

Governmental authority, citizenship, Fifth Amendment, equal protection

B. Legal Question Presented

"'Is the distinction in 8 U.S.C. § 1409 between 'illegitimate' children of United States citizen mothers and 'illegitimate' children of United States citizen fathers a violation of the Fifth Amendment to the United States Constitution?'"

C. Supreme Court's Answer

The distinction does not violate the Fifth Amendment.

II. CASE SUMMARY

A. Background

"The petitioner in this case challenges the constitutionality of the statutory provisions governing the acquisition of citizenship at birth by children born out of wedlock and outside of the United States. The specific challenge is to the distinction drawn by § 309 of the Immigration and Nationality Act (INA), 66 Stat. 238, as amended, 8 U.S.C. § 1409, between the child of an alien father and a citizen mother, on the one hand, and the child of an alien mother and a citizen father, on the other. Subject to residence requirements for the citizen parent, the citizenship of the former is established at birth; the citizenship of the latter is not established unless and until either the father or his child takes certain affirmative steps to create or confirm their relationship. Petitioner contends that the statutory requirement that those steps be taken while the child is a minor violates the Fifth Amendment because the statute contains no limitation on the time within which the child of a citizen mother may prove that she became a citizen at birth."

Petitioner, Lorena Penero, was born in 1970 and raised in the Philippines by her mother. "Petitioner's father, Charlie Miller, is an American citizen residing in Texas.

He apparently served in the United States Air Force and was stationed in the Philippines at the time of petitioner's conception. He never married petitioner's mother, and there is no evidence that he was in the Philippines at the time of petitioner's birth or that he ever returned there after completing his tour of duty. In 1992, Miller filed a petition in a Texas court to establish his relationship with petitioner. The petition was unopposed and the court entered a 'Voluntary Paternity Decree' finding him 'to be the biological and legal father of Lorelyn Penero Miller.' The decree provided that '[t]he parent-child relationship is created between the father and the child as if the child were born to the father and mother during marriage.'

In November 1991, petitioner filed an application for registration as a United States citizen with the State Department. The application was denied in March 1992, and petitioner reapplied after her father obtained the paternity decree in Texas in July 1992. The reapplication was also denied on the ground that the Texas decree did not satisfy 'the requirements of Section 309(a)(4) INA, which requires that a child born out of wedlock be legitimated before age eighteen in order to acquire U.S. citizenship under Section 301(g) INA (formerly Section 301(a)(7) INA).' In further explanation of its reliance on § 309(a)(4), the denial letter added: 'Without such legitimation before age eighteen, there is no legally recognized relationship under the INA and the child acquires no rights of citizenship through an American citizen parent.' . . .

In 1993, petitioner and her father filed an amended complaint against the Secretary of State in the United States District Court for the Eastern District of Texas, seeking a judgment declaring that petitioner is a citizen of the United States and that she therefore has the right to possess an American passport. They alleged that the INA's different treatment of citizen mothers and citizen fathers violated Mr. Miller's 'right to equal protection under the laws by utilizing the suspect classification of gender without justification.' In response to a motion to dismiss filed by the Government, the District Court concluded that Mr. Miller did not have standing and dismissed him as a party. Because venue in Texas was therefore improper, the court transferred the case to the District Court for the District of Columbia, the site of the Secretary's residence. The Government renewed its motion in that forum, and that court concluded that even though petitioner had suffered an injury caused by the Secretary's refusal to register her as a citizen, the injury was not 'redressable' because federal courts do not have the power to 'grant citizenship.'

The Court of Appeals for the District of Columbia Circuit affirmed, but on different grounds."

The Supreme Court granted certiorari to review the case and affirmed.

B. Counsel of Record / ACLU Attorney

ACLU Side (Petitioner / Appellant): Donald Ross Patterson argued the cause for appellant.

Opposing Side (Respondent / Appellee): Deputy Solicitor General Edwin S. Kneedler argued the cause for appellee.

III. AMICI CURIAE

ACLU Side (Petitioner / Appellant)

Brief of amici curiae filed on behalf of the ACLU, et al., by Walter A. Smith, Jr., Barbara J. De La Viez, Kristen A. Donoghue, Elyse Rosenblum, Steven R. Shapiro, Lucas Guttentag, Sara L. Mandelbaum, Sherry Leiwant, and Martha Davis.

Opposing Side (Respondent / Appellee)

No briefs of amici curiae were filed in support of appellee.

IV. THE SUPREME COURT'S DECISION

"The statutory provision at issue in this case, 8 U.S.C. § 1409, draws two types of distinctions between citizen fathers and citizen mothers of children born out of wedlock. The first relates to the class of unmarried persons who may transmit citizenship at birth to their offspring, and the second defines the affirmative steps that are required to transmit such citizenship. . . .

As for affirmative steps, §1409 . . . imposes four requirements concerning unmarried citizen fathers that must be satisfied to confer citizenship 'as of the date of birth' on a person born out of wedlock to an alien mother in another country. . . . '(1) A blood relationship between the person and the father is established by clear and convincing evidence, (2) the father had the nationality of the United States at the time of birth, (3) the father (unless deceased) has agreed in writing to provide financial support for the person until the person reaches the age of 18 years, and (4) while the person is under the age of 18 years—(A) the person is legitimized under the law of the person's residence or domicile, (B) the father acknowledges the paternity of the person in writing under oath, or (C) the paternity of the person is established by adjudication of a competent court.' . . .

Section 1409 also serves [other] important purposes that are unrelated to the determination of paternity [including] the interest in encouraging the development of a healthy relationship between the citizen parent and the child while the child is a minor . . . . [D]ue to the normal interval of nine months between conception and birth, the unmarried father may not even know his child exists, and the child may not know the father's identity. Section 1409(a)(4) requires a relatively easy, formal step by either the citizen father or his child that shows beyond a doubt that at least one of the two knows their blood relationship. . . . The facts of this very case provide a ready example of this concern. Mr. Miller and petitioner both failed to take any steps to establish a legal relationship with each other before petitioner's 21st birthday, and there is no indication in the record that they had any contact whatsoever before she applied for a United States passport. . . .

If there is no reliable, contemporaneous proof that the child and the citizen father had opportunity to form familial bonds before the child turned 18, Congress reasonably may demand that the child show sufficient ties to this country on its own rather than through its citizen parent in order to be a citizen. . . .

The judgment of the Court of Appeals is affirmed."

V. JUSTICE VOTE

3 Pro ACLU Side vs. 6 Con Opposing Side

ACLU Side (Petitioner / Appellant)

1. Ginsburg, R. – Wrote dissenting opinion, joined Breyer's dissent
2. Souter, D. – Joined Ginsburg's dissent, joined Breyer's dissent
3. Breyer, S. – Wrote dissenting opinion, joined Ginsburg's dissent

Opposing Side (Respondent / Appellee)

1. Stevens, J. – Wrote majority opinion
2. Rehnquist, W. – Joined majority opinion
3. O'Connor, S. – Wrote concurring opinion
4. Kennedy, A. – Joined O'Connor's concurrence
5. Scalia, A. – Wrote concurring opinion
6. Thomas, C. – Joined Scalia's concurrence

VI. A WIN OR LOSS FOR THE ACLU?

The ACLU filed as amicus curiae urging reversal of the judgment of the Court of Appeals; the Supreme Court affirmed in a 6-3 vote, giving the ACLU an apparent loss.

842. Crawford-El v. Britton

(Decided May 4, 1998; 523 U.S. 574)

I. ISSUE

A. Issues Discussed

Criminal justice, prisons, liability, civil rights

B. Legal Question Presented

"[W]hether, at least in cases brought by prisoners, the plaintiff must adduce clear and convincing evidence of improper motive in order to defeat a motion for summary judgment."

C. Supreme Court's Answer

The plaintiff is not required to make a showing of clear of convincing evidence of improper motive to defeat a motion for summary judgment.

II. CASE SUMMARY

A. Background

"Petitioner is serving a life sentence in the District of Columbia's correctional system. During his confinement he has filed several lawsuits and has assisted other prisoners with their cases. He has also provided interviews to reporters who have written news stories about prison conditions. He is a litigious and outspoken prisoner.

The events that gave rise to this case occurred in 1988 and 1989. Because of overcrowding in the District of Columbia prison in Lorton, Virginia, petitioner and other inmates were transferred to the county jail in Spokane, Washington. Thereafter, he was moved, first to a Washington State prison, later to a facility in Cameron, Missouri, next back to Lorton, then to Petersburg, Virginia, and ultimately to the federal prison in Marianna, Florida. Three boxes containing his personal belongings, including legal materials, were transferred separately. When the District of Columbia Department of Corrections received the boxes from the Washington State facility, respondent, a District correctional officer, asked petitioner's brother-in-law to pick them up rather than sending them directly to petitioner's next destination. The boxes were ultimately shipped to Marianna by petitioner's mother, at petitioner's expense, but he was initially denied permission to receive them because they had been sent outside official prison channels. He finally recovered the property several months after his arrival in Florida.

Petitioner contends that respondent deliberately misdirected the boxes to punish him for exercising his First Amendment rights and to deter similar conduct in the future. Beyond generalized allegations of respondent's hostility, he alleges specific incidents in which his protected speech had provoked her.

He claimed injury caused by the delay in receiving his boxes includes the costs of having the boxes shipped and purchasing new clothes and other items in the interim, as well as mental and emotional distress. Respondent denies any retaliatory motive and asserts that she entrusted the property to petitioner's brother-in-law, who was also a District of Columbia corrections employee, in order to ensure its prompt and safe delivery. . . .

Petitioner filed suit against respondent and the District of Columbia seeking damages under Rev. Stat. § 1979, 42 U.S.C. § 1983."

After extensive litigation, "the en banc court ordered the parties to file briefs addressing five specific questions . . . . The en banc court responded to these questions in five separate opinions. A majority of the judges appear to have agreed on these four propositions: (1) the case should be remanded to the District Court for further proceedings; (2) the plaintiff does not have to satisfy any heightened pleading requirement, and may rely on circumstantial as well as direct evidence; (3) in order to prevail in an unconstitutional-motive case, the plaintiff must establish that motive by clear and convincing evidence; and (4) special procedures to protect defendants from the costs of litigation in unconstitutional-motive cases are required by the reasoning in this Court's opinion in Harlow v. Fitzgerald, 457 U.S. 800 (1982)."

The Supreme Court granted certiorari to review the case and reversed.

B. Counsel of Record / ACLU Attorney

ACLU Side (Petitioner / Appellant): Daniel M. Schember argued the cause for appellant.

Opposing Side (Respondent / Appellee): Walter A. Smith, Jr., Special Deputy Corporation Counsel of the District of Columbia, argued the cause for appellee.

Jeffrey P. Minear argued the cause for the United States, as amicus curiae, by special leave of Court.

III. AMICI CURIAE

ACLU Side (Petitioner / Appellant)

Brief of amici curiae filed on behalf of the ACLU, et al., by Arthur B. Spitzer and Steven R. Shapiro.

Brief of amici curiae filed on behalf of William G. Moore, Jr., by James E. Anklam, Daniel H. Bromberg, Ira L. Podheiser, and Paul Michael Pohl.

Opposing Side (Respondent / Appellee)

Brief of amici curiae filed on behalf of the United States by Jeffrey P. Minear, Acting Solicitor General Waxman, Assistant Attorney General Hunger, Deputy Solicitor General Kneedler, Deputy Assistant Attorney General Preston, Irving L. Gornstein, Barbara L. Herwig, and Robert Loeb.

Brief of amici curiae filed on behalf of the State of Missouri, et al., by Jeremiah W. (Jay) Nixon, Attorney General of Missouri, John R. Munich, Alana M. Barrágan-Scott and Gretchen E. Rowan, Assistant Attorneys General; Charles H. Troutman, Acting Attorney Deputy Attorney General and General of Guam; and by the Attorneys General for their respective jurisdictions as follows: Bill Pryor of Alabama, Bruce M. Botelho of Alaska, Grant Woods of Arizona, Winston Bryant of Arkansas, Daniel E. Lungren of California, Gale A. Norton of Colorado, M. Jane Brady of Delaware, Robert A. Butterworth of Florida, Margery S. Bronster of Hawaii, Chris Gorman of Kentucky, Richard P. Ieyoub of Louisiana, Joseph Curran, Jr. of Maryland, J. Scott Harshbarger of Massachusetts, Frank J. Kelley of Michigan, Hubert H. Humphrey III of Minnesota, Mike Moore of Mississippi, Joseph P. Mazurek of Montana, Don Stenberg of Nebraska, Frankie Sue Del Papa of Nevada, Dennis C. Vacco of New York, Heidi Heitkamp of North Dakota, Betty D. Montgomery of Ohio, W. A. Drew Edmondson of Oklahoma, Hardy Myers of Oregon, D. Michael Fisher of Pennsylvania, Jeffrey B. Pine and Mark W. Barnett of South Dakota, Dan Morales of Texas, Jan Graham William of Utah, H. Sorrell Richard Cullen of Virginia, Julio A. Brady of the Virgin Islands, Darrell V. McGraw, Jr., of West Virginia, and James E. Doyle of Wisconsin.

Brief of amici curiae filed on behalf of J. Michael Quinlan, et al., by Michael L. Martinez.

IV. THE SUPREME COURT'S DECISION

"The Court of Appeals' requirement of clear and convincing evidence of improper motive is that court's latest effort to address a potentially serious problem: Because an official's state of mind is 'easy to allege and hard to disprove,' insubstantial claims that turn on improper intent may be less amenable to summary disposition than other types of claims against government officials. This category of claims therefore implicates obvious concerns with the social costs of subjecting public officials to discovery and trial, as well as liability for damages. . . .

In 1968, A. Ernest Fitzgerald testified before a congressional subcommittee about technical difficulties and excessive costs incurred in the development of a new transport plane. His testimony was widely reported and evidently embarrassed his superiors in the Department of Defense. In 1970, his job as a management analyst with the Department of the Air Force was eliminated in a 'departmental reorganization and reduction in force.' After the conclusion of extended proceedings before the Civil Service Commission in 1973, Fitzgerald filed suit against the President of the United States and some of his aides alleging that they had eliminated his job in retaliation for his testimony. He sought damages on both statutory grounds and 'in a direct action under the Constitution.' When his charges were reviewed in this Court, we considered the defendants' claims to immunity in two separate opinions. In Nixon v. Fitzgerald, we held that a former President is entitled to absolute immunity from damages liability predicated on conduct within the scope of his official duties. In Harlow v. Fitzgerald, we held that the senior aides and advisers of the President were not entitled to absolute immunity, but instead were protected by a 'qualified immunity standard that would permit the defeat of insubstantial claims without resort to trial.' . . .

There are several reasons why we believe that here, unlike Harlow, the proper balance does not justify a judicial revision of the law to bar claims that depend on proof of an official's motive. Initially, there is an important distinction between the 'bare allegations of malice' . . . and the allegations of intent that are essential elements of certain constitutional claims. [T]he mere allegation of intent to cause any 'other injury,' not just a deprivation of constitutional rights, would have permitted an open-ended inquiry into subjective motivation. When intent is an element of a constitutional violation, however, the primary focus is not on any possible animus directed at the plaintiff; rather, it is more specific, such as an intent to disadvantage all members of a class that includes the plaintiff . . . or to deter public comment on a specific issue of public importance. . . .

It is the district judges rather than appellate judges like ourselves who have had the most experience in managing cases in which an official's intent is an element. Given the wide variety of civil rights and 'constitutional tort' claims that trial judges confront, broad discretion in the management of the fact finding process may be more useful and equitable to all the parties than the categorical rule imposed by the Court of Appeals.

The judgment of the Court of Appeals is vacated, and the case is remanded for further proceedings consistent with this opinion."

V. JUSTICE VOTE

5 Pro ACLU Side vs. 4 Con Opposing Side

ACLU Side (Petitioner / Appellant)

1. Stevens, J. – Wrote majority opinion
2. Kennedy, A. – Wrote concurring opinion
3. Souter, D. – Joined majority opinion
4. Ginsburg, R. – Joined majority opinion
5. Breyer, S. – Joined majority opinion

Opposing Side (Respondent / Appellee)

1. Rehnquist, W. – Wrote dissenting opinion
2. O'Connor, S. – Joined Rehnquist's dissent
3. Scalia, A. – Wrote dissenting opinion
4. Thomas, C. – Joined Scalia's dissent

VI. A WIN OR LOSS FOR THE ACLU?

The ACLU filed as amicus curiae urging reversal of the judgment of the Court of Appeals; the Supreme Court vacated and remanded in a 5-4 vote, giving the ACLU an apparent win.

843. Ricci v. Village of Arlington Heights

(Decided May 4, 1998; 523 U.S. 613)

I. ISSUE

A. Issues Discussed

Criminal justice, Fourth Amendment, search and seizure, judicial power

B. Legal Question Presented

Whether petitioner's arrest for violation of a fine-only ordinance violated the Fourth Amendment.

C. Supreme Court's Answer

The Supreme Court dismissed the writ of certiorari as improvidently granted.

II. CASE SUMMARY

A. Background

"Randall Ricci was arrested for operating a business without a license, in violation of an Arlington Heights, Illinois ordinance. He subsequently sued the Village of Arlington Heights and the two arresting officers pursuant to 42 U.S.C. § 1983, claiming the defendants violated his civil rights by subjecting him to full custodial arrest for violation of a fine-only ordinance. Because [the Court of Appeals for the Seventh Circuit found] the arrest reasonable for Fourth Amendment purposes, [the Court of Appeals] affirm[ed] the district court's grant of summary judgment in favor of the defendants."[1]

The Supreme Court granted certiorari to review the case, then dismissed the writ of certiorari as improvidently granted.

---

1 Ricci v. Arlington Heights, 116 F.3d 288 (7th Cir. 1997).

B. Counsel of Record / ACLU Attorney

ACLU Side (Petitioner / Appellant): Kenneth N. Flaxman argued the cause for appellant.

Opposing Side (Respondent / Appellee): David A. Strauss argued the case for appellee.

Patricia A. Millett argued the cause for the United States, as amicus curiae, by special leave of Court.

III. AMICI CURIAE

ACLU Side (Petitioner / Appellant)

Brief of amici curiae filed on behalf of the ACLU, et al., by Susan N. Herman, Steven R. Shapiro, Harvey Grossman, and Stephen J. Schulhofer.

Brief of amici curiae filed on behalf of Americans for Effective Law Enforcement, Inc., by Wayne W. Schmidt, James P. Manak, and Bernard J. Farber.

Brief of amici curiae filed on behalf of the Institute for Justice by William H. Mellor, Clint Bolick, and Scott G. Bullock.

Brief of amici curiae filed on behalf of the National Association of Criminal Defense Lawyers by William J. Mertens, Jay T. Blount, and Barbara Bergman.

Opposing Side (Respondent / Appellee)

Brief of amici curiae filed on behalf of the United States by Patricia A. Millett, Solicitor General Waxman, Acting Assistant Attorney General Keeney, Deputy Solicitor General Dreeben, and William C. Brown.

Brief of amici curiae filed on behalf of the National League of Cities, et al., by Richard Ruda and James I. Crowley.

IV. THE SUPREME COURT'S DECISION

" The writ of certiorari is dismissed as improvidently granted."

V. JUSTICE VOTE

0 Pro ACLU Side vs. 9 Con Opposing Side

Opposing Side (Respondent / Appellee)

1. Rehnquist, W. – Per curiam decision
2. Stevens, J. – Per curiam decision
3. O'Connor, S. – Per curiam decision
4. Scalia, A. – Per curiam decision
5. Kennedy, A. – Per curiam decision
6. Thomas, C. – Per curiam decision
7. Souter, D. – Per curiam decision
8. Ginsburg, R. – Per curiam decision
9. Breyer, S. – Per curiam decision

VI. A WIN OR LOSS FOR THE ACLU?

The ACLU filed a brief as amicus curiae urging reversal of the judgment of the Court of Appeals; the Supreme Court dismissed the case in a per curiam decision, giving the ACLU an apparent loss.

844. Bousley v. United States

(Decided May 18, 1998; 523 U.S. 614)

I. ISSUE

A. Issues Discussed

Criminal justice, drugs, habeas corpus, retroactivity

B. Legal Question Presented

Whether a defendant may challenge his guilty plea after Bailey and receive a hearing on the merits.

C. Supreme Court's Answer

"We hold that, although this claim was procedurally defaulted, petitioner may be entitled to a hearing on the merits of it if he makes the necessary showing to relieve the default.

II. CASE SUMMARY

A. Background

"[P]etitioner was charged with possession of methamphetamine with intent to distribute, in violation of 21 U.S.C. § 841(a)(1). A superseding indictment added the charge that he 'knowingly and intentionally used . . . firearms during and in relation to a drug trafficking crime,' in violation of 18 U.S.C. § 924(c). Petitioner agreed to plead guilty to both charges while reserving the right to challenge the quantity of drugs used in calculating his sentence. . . .

Five years later [the Supreme Court] held in Bailey v. United States, 516 U.S. 137 (1995), that § 924(c)(1)'s 'use' prong requires the Government to show 'active employment of the firearm.' Petitioner meanwhile had sought collateral relief under 28 U.S.C. § 2255, claiming that his guilty plea was not knowing and intelligent because he was misinformed by the District Court as to the nature of the charged crime. . . .

Following [the Supreme Court's] decision in Bailey, the Court of Appeals appointed counsel to represent petitioner. Counsel argued that Bailey should be applied 'retroactively,' that petitioner's guilty plea was involuntary because he was misinformed about the elements of a § 924(c)(1) offense, that this claim was not waived by his guilty plea, and that his conviction should therefore be vacated. Nevertheless, the Court of Appeals affirmed the District Court's order of dismissal."

The Supreme Court granted certiorari to review the case and reversed.

B. Counsel of Record / ACLU Attorney

ACLU Side (Petitioner / Appellant): L. Marshall Smith, by appointment of the Court, argued the cause for appellant.

Opposing Side (Respondent / Appellee): Deputy Solicitor General Michael R. Dreeben argued the cause for appellee.

Thomas C. Walsh argued the cause, as amicus curiae, by special leave of Court.

III. AMICI CURIAE

ACLU Side (Petitioner / Appellant)

Brief of amici curiae filed on behalf of the ACLU by Larry W. Yackle and Steven R. Shapiro.

Brief of amici curiae filed on behalf of the National Association of Criminal Defense Lawyers, et al., by Bonnie I. Robin-Vergeer, David M. Porter, Ronald H. Weich, and Kyle O'Dowd.

Opposing Side (Respondent / Appellee)

Brief of amici curiae filed by Thomas C. Walsh, James F. Bennett, and Brian C. Walsh.

IV. THE SUPREME COURT'S DECISION

"A plea of guilty is constitutionally valid only to the extent it is 'voluntary' and 'intelligent.' We have long held that a plea does not qualify as intelligent unless a criminal defendant first receives 'real notice of the true nature of the charge against him, the first and most universally recognized requirement of due process.' . . . Were this contention proved, petitioner's plea would be, contrary to the view expressed by the Court of Appeals, constitutionally invalid. . . .

In this case, the Government maintains that petitioner must demonstrate that he is actually innocent of both 'using' and 'carrying' a firearm in violation of § 924(c)(1). But petitioner's indictment charged him only with 'using' firearms in violation of § 924(c)(1). And there is no record evidence that the Government elected not to charge petitioner with 'carrying' a firearm in exchange for his plea of guilty. Accordingly, petitioner need demonstrate no more than that he did not 'use' a firearm as that term is defined in Bailey.

If, on remand, petitioner can make that showing, he will then be entitled to have his defaulted claim of an unintelligent plea considered on its merits. The judgment of the Court of Appeals is therefore reversed, and the case is remanded for further proceedings consistent with this opinion."

V. JUSTICE VOTE

7 Pro ACLU Side vs. 2 Con Opposing Side

ACLU Side (Petitioner / Appellant)

1. Rehnquist, W. – Wrote majority opinion
2. O'Connor, S. – Joined majority opinion
3. Kennedy, A. – Joined majority opinion
4. Souter, D. – Joined majority opinion
5. Ginsburg, R. – Joined majority opinion
6. Breyer, S. – Joined majority opinion
7. Stevens, J. – Wrote opinion concurring in part and dissenting in part

Opposing Side (Respondent / Appellee)

1. Scalia, A. – Wrote dissenting opinion
2. Thomas, C. – Joined Scalia's dissent

VI. A WIN OR LOSS FOR THE ACLU?

The ACLU, as amicus curiae, urged reversal of the judgment of the Eighth Circuit Court of Appeals; the Supreme Court reversed in a 7-2 vote, giving the ACLU an apparent win.

845. Stewart v. Martinez-Villareal

(Decided May 18, 1998; 523 U.S. 637)

I. ISSUE

A. Issues Discussed

Criminal justice, death penalty, Eighth Amendment, habeas corpus

B. Legal Question Presented

"[W]hether respondent Martinez-Villareal's Ford claim [prohibiting the death penalty for insane prisoners] is subject to the restrictions on 'second or successive' applications for federal habeas relief found in the newly revised 28 U.S.C. § 2244."

C. Supreme Court's Answer

Respondent's Ford claim is not subject to restrictions on "second or successive" federal habeas applications.

II. CASE SUMMARY

A. Background

"In Ford v. Wainwright, 477 U.S. 399 (1986), [the Supreme Court] held that 'the Eighth Amendment prohibits a State from inflicting the penalty of death upon a prisoner who is insane.' . . .

Respondent was convicted on two counts of first-degree murder and sentenced to death. He unsuccessfully challenged his conviction and sentence on direct appeal in the Arizona state courts. He then filed a series of petitions for habeas relief in state court, all of which were denied. He also filed three petitions for habeas relief in federal court, all of which were dismissed on the ground that they contained claims on which the state remedies had not yet been exhausted.

In March 1993, respondent filed a fourth habeas petition in federal court. In addition to raising other claims, respondent asserted that he was incompetent to be executed. Counsel for the State urged the District Court to dismiss respondent's Ford claim as premature. The court did so but granted the writ on other grounds. The Court of Appeals for the Ninth Circuit reversed the District Court's granting of the writ but explained that its instruction to enter judgment denying the petition was not intended to affect any later litigation of the Ford claim.

On remand to the District Court, respondent, fearing that the newly enacted Antiterrorism and Effective Death Penalty Act (AEDPA) might foreclose review of his Ford claim, moved the court to reopen his earlier petition. In March 1997, the District Court denied the motion and reassured respondent that it had "no intention of treating the [Ford] claim as a successive petition." Shortly thereafter, the State obtained a warrant for respondent's execution. Proceedings were then held in the Arizona Superior Court on respondent's mental condition. That court concluded that respondent was fit to be executed. The Arizona Supreme Court rejected his appeal of that decision.

Respondent then moved in the Federal District Court to reopen his Ford claim. He challenged both the conclusions reached and the procedures employed by the Arizona state courts. Petitioners responded that under AEDPA, the court lacked jurisdiction. The District Court agreed with petitioners, ruling on May 16, 1997, that it did not have jurisdiction over the claim. Respondent then moved in the Court of Appeals for permission to file a successive habeas corpus application.

The Court of Appeals stayed respondent's execution so that it could consider his request. It later held that § 2244(b) did not apply to a petition that raises only a competency to be executed claim and that respondent did not, therefore, need authorization to file the petition in the District Court. It accordingly transferred the petition that had been presented to a member of that court back to the District Court."

The Supreme Court granted certiorari to review the case and affirmed.

B. Counsel of Record / ACLU Attorney

ACLU Side (Respondent / Appellee): Denise I. Young argued the cause for appellee.

Opposing Side (Petitioner / Appellant): Bruce M. Ferg, Assistant Attorney General of Arizona, argued the cause for appellants.

III. AMICI CURIAE

ACLU Side (Respondent / Appellee)

Brief of amici curiae filed on behalf of the ACLU by Larry W. Yackle and Steven R. Shapiro.

Brief of amici curiae filed on behalf of the American Bar Association by Jerome J. Shestack, Jerold S. Solovy, Barry Levenstam, Jeremy M. Taylor, Laurel A. Haskell, and C. John Koch.

Brief of amici curiae filed on behalf of the National Association of Criminal Defense Lawyers by Edward M. Chikofsky, Mark E. Olive, and David M. Porter.

Brief of amici curiae filed on behalf of the United Mexican States, et al., by John P. Frank, Todd E. Hale, and José A. Cárdenas.

Opposing Side (Petitioner / Appellant)

Brief of amici curiae filed on behalf of the State of California, et al., by Daniel E. Lungren, Attorney General of California, George Williamson, Chief Assistant Attorney General, Dane R. Gillette, Senior Assistant Attorney General, Keith H. Borjon, Supervising Deputy Attorney General, and Emilio Eugene Varanini IV, Deputy Attorney General, and by the Attorneys General for their respective States as follows: Bill Pryor of Alabama, M. Jane Brady of Delaware, Alan G. Lance of Idaho, Jeffrey A. Modisett of Indiana, Carla J. Stovall of Kansas, Mike Moore of Mississippi, Jeremiah W. Nixon of Missouri, Joseph P. Mazurek of Montana, Don Stenberg of Nebraska, Frankie S. Del Papa of Nevada, Michael F. Easley of North Carolina, D. Michael Fisher of Pennsylvania, Betty Montgomery of Ohio, Drew Edmondson of Oklahoma, Hardy Meyers of Oregon, Mark Barnett of South Dakota, Dan Morales of Texas, Jan Graham of Utah, and William U. Hill of Wyoming.

Brief of amici curiae filed on behalf of the Criminal Justice Legal Foundation by Kent Scheidegger and Charles L. Hobson.

IV. THE SUPREME COURT'S DECISION

"[N]one of our cases expounding this doctrine have ever suggested that a prisoner whose habeas petition was dismissed for failure to exhaust state remedies, and who then did exhaust those remedies and returned to federal court, was by such action filing a successive petition. A court where such a petition was filed could adjudicate these claims under the same standard as would govern those made in any other first petition.

We believe that respondent's Ford claim here—previously dismissed as premature—should be treated in the same manner as the claim of a petitioner who returns to a federal habeas court after exhausting state remedies. True, the cases are not identical; respondent's Ford claim was dismissed as premature, not because he had not exhausted state remedies, but because his execution was not imminent and therefore his competency to be executed could not be determined at that time. But in both situations, the habeas petitioner does not receive an adjudication of his claim. To hold otherwise would mean that a dismissal of a first habeas petition for technical procedural reasons would bar the prisoner from ever obtaining federal habeas review. . . .

Petitioners place great reliance on our decision in Felker v. Turpin, 518 U.S. 651 (1996), but we think that reliance is misplaced. . . . It is certain that respondent's Ford claim would not be barred under any form of res judicata. Respondent brought his claim in a timely fashion, and it has not been ripe for resolution until now.

Thus, respondent's Ford claim was not a 'second or successive' petition under § 2244(b) and we have jurisdiction to review the judgment of the Court of Appeals on the State's petition for certiorari. But for the same reasons that we find we have jurisdiction, we hold that the Court of Appeals was correct in deciding that respondent was entitled to a hearing on the merits of his Ford claim in the District Court. The judgment of the Court of Appeals is therefore affirmed."

V. JUSTICE VOTE

7 Pro ACLU Side vs. 2 Con Opposing Side

ACLU Side (Respondent / Appellee)

1. Rehnquist, W. – Wrote majority opinion
2. Stevens, J. – Joined majority opinion
3. O'Connor, S. – Joined majority opinion
4. Kennedy, A. – Joined majority opinion
5. Souter, D. – Joined majority opinion
6. Ginsburg, R. – Joined majority opinion
7. Breyer, S. – Joined majority opinion

Opposing Side (Petitioner / Appellant)

1. Scalia, A. – Wrote dissenting opinion, joined Thomas' dissent
2. Thomas, C. – Wrote dissenting opinion, joined Scalia's dissent

VI. A WIN OR LOSS FOR THE ACLU?

The ACLU filed as amicus curiae urging affirmance of the judgment of the Court of Appeals for the Ninth Circuit; the Supreme Court affirmed in a 7-2 vote, giving the ACLU an apparent win.

846. Arkansas Educational Television Commission v. Forbes

(Decided May 18, 1998; 523 U.S. 666)

I. ISSUE

A. Issues Discussed

First Amendment, elections

B. Legal Question Presented

"[W]hether, by reason of its state ownership, [a television] station had a constitutional obligation to allow every candidate access to the debate" sponsored by the station.

C. Supreme Court's Answer

The television station did not have the constitutional obligation to allow every candidate access to the debate because the debate was a nonpublic forum and the candidate's exclusion was viewpoint-neutral.

II. CASE SUMMARY

A. Background

"Petitioner, the Arkansas Educational Television Commission (AETC), is an Arkansas state agency owning and operating a network of five noncommercial television stations (Arkansas Educational Television Network or AETN). . . . In the spring of 1992, AETC staff began planning a series of debates between candidates for federal office in the November 1992 elections. . . . Given the time constraint, the staff and Simmons 'decided to limit participation in the debates to the major party candidates or any other candidate who had strong popular support.'

[A]fter obtaining the 2,000 signatures required by Arkansas law, respondent Ralph Forbes was certified as an independent candidate qualified to appear on the ballot . . . . Forbes was a perennial candidate who had sought, without success, a number of elected offices in Arkansas. On August 24, 1992, he wrote to AETC requesting permission to participate in the debate for his district, scheduled for October 22, 1992. On September 4, AETC Executive Director Susan Howarth denied Forbes' request, explaining that AETC had 'made a bona fide journalistic judgement that our viewers would best be served by limiting the debate' to the candidates already invited.

On October 19, 1992, Forbes filed suit against AETC, seeking injunctive and declaratory relief as well as damages. Forbes claimed he was entitled to participate in the debate under both the First Amendment and 47 U.S.C. § 315, which affords political candidates a limited right of access to television air time. Forbes requested a preliminary injunction mandating his inclusion in the debate. The District Court denied the request, as did the United States Court of Appeals for the Eighth Circuit. The District Court later dismissed Forbes' action for failure to state a claim.

Sitting en banc, the Court of Appeals affirmed the dismissal of Forbes' statutory claim, holding that he had failed to exhaust his administrative remedies. The court reversed, however, the dismissal of Forbes' First Amendment claim. Observing that AETC is a state actor, the court held Forbes had 'a qualified right of access created by AETN's sponsorship of a debate, and that AETN must have [had] a legitimate reason to exclude him strong enough to survive First Amendment scrutiny.' . . .

On remand, the District Court found as a matter of law that the debate was a nonpublic forum, and the issue became whether Forbes' views were the reason for his exclusion. . . . The Court of Appeals again reversed."

The Supreme Court granted certiorari to review the case and reversed.

B. Counsel of Record / ACLU Attorney

ACLU Side (Respondent / Appellee): Kelly J. Shackelford argued the cause for appellee.

Opposing Side (Petitioner / Appellant): Richard D. Marks argued the cause for appellant.

Deputy Solicitor General Lawrence G. Wallace argued the cause for the Federal Communications Commission, et al., as amicus curiae, by special leave of Court.

III. AMICI CURIAE

ACLU Side (Respondent / Appellee)

Brief of amici curiae filed on behalf of the ACLU, et al., by Marjorie Heins and Steven R. Shapiro.

Additional briefs of amici curiae were filed on behalf of the Brennan Center for Justice at New York University School of Law, Greens/Green Party USA, Eugene McCarthy, et al., the Natural Law Party of the United States, the Pacific Legal Foundation, and Perot '96.

Opposing Side (Petitioner / Appellant)

Brief of amici curiae filed on behalf of the Federal Communications Commission, et al., by Deputy Solicitor General Lawrence G. Wallace, Acting Solicitor General Dellinger, Jonathan E. Nuechterlein, William E. Kennard, Christopher J. Wright, Daniel M. Armstrong, and C. Grey Pash, Jr.

Additional briefs of amici curiae were filed on behalf of the State of California, et al., the City of New York, the State of New Jersey, the Association of America's Public Television Stations, et al., and the Commission on Presidential Debates.

IV. THE SUPREME COURT'S DECISION

"Under our precedents, the AETC debate was not a designated public forum. To create a forum of this type, the government must intend to make the property 'generally available' to a class of speakers. . . .

Here, the debate did not have an open-microphone format. Contrary to the assertion of the Court of Appeals, AETC did not make its debate generally available to candidates for Arkansas' Third Congressional District seat. . . . AETC reserved eligibility for participation in the debate to candidates for the Third Congressional District seat (as opposed to some other seat). At that point . . . AETC made candidate-by-candidate determinations as to which of the eligible candidates would participate in the debate. 'Such selective access, unsupported by evidence of a purposeful designation for public use, does not create a public forum.' Thus the debate was a nonpublic forum.

In addition to being a misapplication of our precedents, the Court of Appeals' holding would result in less speech, not more. In ruling that the debate was a public forum open to all ballot-qualified candidates, the Court of Appeals would place a severe burden upon public broadcasters who air candidates' views. In each of the 1988, 1992, and 1996 Presidential elections, for example, no fewer than 19 candidates appeared on the ballot in at least one State. . . . On logistical grounds alone, a public television editor might, with reason, decide that the inclusion of all ballot-qualified candidates would 'actually undermine the educational value and quality of debates.'

Were it faced with the prospect of cacophony, on the one hand, and First Amendment liability, on the other, a public television broadcaster might choose not to air candidates' views at all. . . . A First Amendment jurisprudence yielding these results does not promote speech but represses it.

The debate's status as a nonpublic forum, however, did not give AETC unfettered power to exclude any candidate it wished. . . . To be consistent with the First Amendment, the exclusion of a speaker from a nonpublic forum must not be based on the speaker's viewpoint and must otherwise be reasonable in light of the purpose of the property.

In this case, the jury found Forbes' exclusion was not based on 'objections or opposition to his views.' The record provides ample support for this finding, demonstrating as well that AETC's decision to exclude him was reasonable. AETC Executive Director Susan Howarth testified Forbes' views had 'absolutely' no role in the decision to exclude him from the debate. She further testified Forbes was excluded because (1) 'the Arkansas voters did not consider him a serious candidate'; (2) 'the news organizations also did not consider him a serious candidate'; (3) 'the Associated Press and a national election result reporting service did not plan to run his name in results on election night'; (4) Forbes 'apparently had little, if any, financial support, failing to report campaign finances to the Secretary of State's office or to the Federal Election Commission'; and (5) 'there [was] no 'Forbes for Congress' campaign headquarters other than his house.' Forbes himself described his campaign organization as 'bedlam' and the media coverage of his campaign as 'zilch.' It is, in short, beyond dispute that Forbes was excluded not because of his viewpoint but because he had generated no appreciable public interest. . . .

The broadcaster's decision to exclude Forbes was a reasonable, viewpoint-neutral exercise of journalistic discretion consistent with the First Amendment. The judgment of the Court of Appeals is reversed."

V. JUSTICE VOTE

3 Pro ACLU Side vs. 6 Con Opposing Side

ACLU Side (Respondent / Appellee)

1. Stevens, J. – Wrote dissenting opinion
2. Souter, D. – Joined Stevens' dissent
3. Ginsburg, R. – Joined Stevens' dissent

Opposing Side (Petitioner / Appellant)

1. Kennedy, A. – Wrote majority opinion
2. Rehnquist, W. – Joined majority opinion
3. O'Connor, S. – Joined majority opinion
4. Scalia, A. – Joined majority opinion
5. Thomas, C. – Joined majority opinion
6. Breyer, S. – Joined majority opinion

VI. A WIN OR LOSS FOR THE ACLU?

The ACLU, as amicus curiae, urged affirmance of the judgment of the Eighth Circuit Court of Appeals; the Supreme Court reversed in a 6-3 vote, giving the ACLU an apparent loss.

847. Federal Election Commission v. Akins

(Decided June 1, 1998; 524 U.S. 11)

I. ISSUE

A. Issues Discussed

First Amendment, freedoms of press, speech, and association, standing

B. Legal Question Presented

"'1. Whether respondents had standing to challenge the Federal Election Commission's decision not to bring an enforcement action in this case.

'2. Whether an organization that spends more than $1,000 on contributions or coordinated expenditures in a calendar year, but is neither controlled by a candidate nor has its major purpose the nomination or election of candidates, is a 'political committee' within the meaning of the [Act].'"

C. Supreme Court's Answer

Declining to decide the second question, the Supreme Court decided the respondents had standing to bring this suit, vacated, and remanded for adjudication on the second question.

II. CASE SUMMARY

A. Background

"The Federal Election Commission (FEC) has determined that the American Israel Public Affairs Committee (AIPAC) is not a 'political committee' as defined by the Federal Election Campaign Act of 1971 (FECA or Act), 2 U.S.C. § 431(4), and, for that reason, the FEC has refused to require AIPAC to make disclosures regarding its membership, contributions, and expenditures that FECA would otherwise require. . . .

This case arises out of an effort by respondents, a group of voters with views often opposed to those of AIPAC, to persuade the FEC to treat AIPAC as a 'political committee.' Respondents filed a complaint with the FEC, stating that AIPAC had made more than $1,000 in qualifying 'expenditures' per year, and thereby became a 'political committee.' They added that AIPAC had violated the FEC provisions requiring 'political committee[s]' to register and to make public the information about members, contributions, and expenditures to which we have just referred. Respondents also claimed that AIPAC had violated § 441b of FECA, which prohibits corporate campaign 'contribution[s]' and 'expenditure[s].' They asked the FEC to find that AIPAC had violated the Act, and, among other things, to order AIPAC to make public the information that FECA demands of a 'political committee.' . . . The FEC . . . dismissed respondents' complaint.

Respondents filed a petition in Federal District Court seeking review of the FEC's determination dismissing their complaint. The District Court granted summary judgment for the FEC, and a divided panel of the Court of Appeals affirmed. The en banc Court of Appeals reversed, however, on the ground that the FEC's 'major purpose' test improperly interpreted the Act's definition of a 'political committee.'"

The Supreme Court granted certiorari to review the case, vacated, and remanded.

B. Counsel of Record / ACLU Attorney

ACLU Side (Petitioner / Appellant): Deputy Solicitor General Seth P. Waxman argued the cause for appellant.

Opposing Side (Respondent / Appellee): Daniel M. Schember argued the cause for appellees.

III. AMICI CURIAE

ACLU Side (Petitioner / Appellant)

Brief of amici curiae filed on behalf of the ACLU, et al., by Joel M. Gora, Steven R. Shapiro, and Arthur N. Eisenberg.

Brief of amici curiae filed on behalf of the National Right to Life Committee, Inc., by James Bopp, Jr. and Paul R. Scholle.

Opposing Side (Respondent / Appellee)

Brief of amici curiae filed on behalf of Common Cause by A. Stephen Hut, Jr., Roger M. Witten, Jeffrey P. Singdahlsen, and Donald J. Simon.

Brief of amici curiae filed on behalf of the American Israel Public Affairs Committee by Theodore B. Olson, Mel Levine, Thomas G. Hungar, and Philip Friedman, in support of neither party.

Brief of amici curiae filed on behalf of the Brennan Center for Justice by Burt Neuborne and Deborah Goldberg, in support of neither party.

IV. THE SUPREME COURT'S DECISION

"The Solicitor General argues that respondents lack standing to challenge the FEC's decision not to proceed against AIPAC. He claims that they have failed to satisfy the 'prudential' standing requirements upon which this Court has insisted. . . . We do not agree with the FEC's 'prudential standing' claim. Congress has specifically provided in FECA that '[a]ny person who believes a violation of this Act . . . has occurred, may file a complaint with the Commission.' It has added that '[a]ny party aggrieved by an order of the Commission dismissing a complaint filed by such party . . . may file a petition' in district court seeking review of that dismissal. . . .

Nor do we agree with the FEC or the dissent that Congress lacks the constitutional power to authorize federal courts to adjudicate this lawsuit. Article III, of course, limits Congress' grant of judicial power to 'cases' or 'controversies.' That limitation means that respondents must show, among other things, an 'injury in fact'—a requirement that helps assure that courts will not 'pass upon . . . abstract, intellectual problems,' but adjudicate 'concrete, living contest[s] between adversaries.' In our view, respondents here have suffered a genuine 'injury in fact.'

The 'injury in fact' that respondents have suffered consists of their inability to obtain information—lists of AIPAC donors (who are, according to AIPAC, its members), and campaign-related contributions and expenditures—that, on respondents' view of the law, the statute requires that AIPAC make public. . . .

The FEC's strongest argument is its contention that this lawsuit involves only a 'generalized grievance.' . . . The FEC points out that respondents' asserted harm (their failure to obtain information) is one which is "shared in substantially equal measure by all or a large class of citizens." . . .

Often the fact that an interest is abstract and the fact that it is widely shared go hand in hand. But their association is not invariable, and where a harm is concrete, though widely shared, the Court has found 'injury in fact.' . . . We conclude that . . . the informational injury at issue here, directly related to voting, the most basic of political rights, is sufficiently concrete and specific such that the fact that it is widely shared does not deprive Congress of constitutional power to authorize its vindication in the federal courts. . . .

In sum, respondents, as voters, have satisfied both prudential and constitutional standing requirements. They may bring this petition for a declaration that the FEC's dismissal of their complaint was unlawful.

[W]e should permit the FEC to address, in the first instance, the issue presented by Question Two. We can thereby take advantage of the relevant agency's expertise, by allowing it to develop a more precise rule that may dispose of this case, or at a minimum, will aid the Court in reaching a more informed conclusion. In our view, the FEC should proceed to determine whether or not AIPAC's expenditures qualify as 'membership communications,' and thereby fall outside the scope of 'expenditures' that could qualify it as a 'political committee.' If the FEC decides that despite its new rules, the communications here do not qualify for this exception, then the lower courts, in reconsidering respondents' arguments, can still evaluate the significance of the communicative context in which the case arises. If, on the other hand, the FEC decides that AIPAC's activities fall within the 'membership communications' exception, the matter will become moot.

For these reasons, the judgment of the Court of Appeals is vacated, and the case is remanded for further proceedings consistent with this opinion."

V. JUSTICE VOTE

3 Pro ACLU Side vs. 6 Con Opposing Side

ACLU Side (Petitioner / Appellant)

1. Scalia, A. – Wrote dissenting opinion
2. O'Connor, S. – Joined Scalia's dissent
3. Thomas, C. – Joined Scalia's dissent

Opposing Side (Respondent / Appellee)

1. Breyer, S. – Wrote majority opinion
2. Rehnquist, W. – Joined majority opinion
3. Stevens, J. – Joined majority opinion
4. Kennedy, A. – Joined majority opinion
5. Souter, D. – Joined majority opinion
6. Ginsburg, R. – Joined majority opinion

VI. A WIN OR LOSS FOR THE ACLU?

The ACLU filed as amicus curiae urging reversal of the judgment of the Court of Appeals; the Supreme Court only addressed the first question presented and, ruling in favor of appellees, vacated and remanded in a 6-3 vote, giving the ACLU an apparent loss.

848. Pennsylvania Department of Corrections v. Yeskey

(Decided June 15, 1998; 524 U.S. 206)

I. ISSUE

A. Issues Discussed

Criminal justice, prisons, Fourteenth Amendment

B. Legal Question Presented

"[W]hether Title II of the Americans with Disabilities Act of 1990 (ADA), . . . which prohibits a 'public entity' from discriminating against a 'qualified individual with a disability' on account of that individual's disability, covers inmates in state prisons."

C. Supreme Court's Answer

Title II of the ADA applies to inmates in state prisons.

II. CASE SUMMARY

A. Background

"The question before us is whether Title II of the Americans with Disabilities Act of 1990 (ADA), . . . which prohibits a 'public entity' from discriminating against a 'qualified individual with a disability' on account of that individual's disability, covers inmates in state prisons. Respondent Ronald Yeskey was such an inmate, sentenced in May 1994 to serve 18 to 36 months in a Pennsylvania correctional facility. The sentencing court recommended that he be placed in Pennsylvania's Motivational Boot Camp for first-time offenders, the successful completion of which would have led to his release on parole in just six months. Because of his medical history of hypertension, however, he was refused admission. He filed this suit against petitioners, the Commonwealth of Pennsylvania's Department of Corrections and several department officials, alleging that his exclusion from the Boot Camp violated the ADA. The District Court dismissed for failure to state a claim, Fed. Rule Civ. Proc. 12(b)(6), holding the ADA inapplicable to inmates in state prisons; the Third Circuit reversed . . . ."

The Supreme Court granted certiorari to review the case and affirmed.

B. Counsel of Record / ACLU Attorney

ACLU Side (Respondent / Appellee): Donald Specter argued the cause for appellee.

Irving L. Gornstein argued the cause for the United States, as amicus curiae, by special leave of Court.

Opposing Side (Petitioner / Appellant): Paul A. Tufano argued the cause for appellants.

III. AMICI CURIAE

ACLU Side (Respondent / Appellee)

Brief of amici curiae filed on behalf of the National Prison Project of the ACLU Foundation, et al., by Steven R. Shapiro, David M. Porter, Marjorie Rifkin, and Elizabeth Alexander.

Brief of amici curiae filed on behalf of the National Association of Protection and Advocacy Systems, et al., by Steven J. Schwartz, James R. Pingeon, Leslie S. Spitalney, Leo C. Rydzewski, and Stephen F. Hanlon.

Brief of amici curiae filed on behalf of the United States by Irving L. Gornstein, Solicitor General Waxman, Acting Assistant Attorney General Lee, Deputy Solicitor General Underwood, Paul R. Q. Wolfson, Jessica Dunsay Silver, Linda F. Thome, and Seth M. Galanter.

Brief of amici curiae filed on behalf of ADAPT, et al., by Stephen F. Gold.

Brief of amici curiae filed on behalf of the National Advisory Group for Justice, et al., by Michael Churchill, Barbara E. Ransom, and Judith Gran.

Opposing Side (Petitioner / Appellant)

Brief of amici curiae filed on behalf of the State of Nevada, et al., by Frankie Sue Del Papa, Attorney General of Nevada, and Anne B. Cathcart, Senior Deputy Attorney General, Betty D. Montgomery, Attorney General of Ohio, Jeffrey S. Sutton, State Solicitor, and Elise Porter and Todd R. Marti, Assistant Attorneys General, John M. Ferren, Corporation Counsel of the District of Columbia, and Gus F. Diaz, Acting Attorney General of Guam, and by the Attorneys General for their respective jurisdictions as follows: William H. Pryor, Jr., of Alabama, Grant Woods of Arizona, Winston Bryant of Arkansas, Daniel E. Lungren of California, Gale A. Norton of Colorado, Robert A. Butterworth of Florida, Thurbert E. Baker of Georgia, Margery S. Bronster of Hawaii, Alan G. Lance of Idaho, Thomas J. Miller of Iowa, Carla J. Stovall of Kansas, Richard P. Ieyoub of Louisiana, J. Joseph Curran, Jr., of Maryland, Frank J. Kelley of Michigan, Mike Moore of Mississippi, Joseph P. Mazurek of Montana, Don Stenberg of Nebraska, Philip T. McLaughlin of New Hampshire, Peter Verniero of New Jersey, Tom Udall of New Mexico, Dennis C. Vacco of New York, Michael F. Easley of North Carolina, Heidi Heitkamp of North Dakota, Jeffrey B. Pine of Rhode

Island, Charles Molony Condon of South Carolina, Mark W. Barnett of South Dakota, John Knox Walkup of Tennessee, Dan Morales of Texas, Jan Graham of Utah, Mark L. Earley of Virginia, Julio A. Brady of the Virgin Islands, and William U. Hill of Wyoming.

Brief of amici curiae filed on behalf of the Council of State Governments, et al., by Richard Ruda and James I. Crowley.

Brief of amici curiae filed on behalf of the Criminal Justice Legal Foundation by Kent S. Scheidegger and Christine M. Murphy.

Brief of amici curiae filed on behalf of the Republican Caucus of the Pennsylvania House of Representatives by John P. Krill, Jr., and David R. Fine.

IV. THE SUPREME COURT'S DECISION

"Assuming, without deciding, that the plain-statement rule does govern application of the ADA to the administration of state prisons, we think the requirement of the rule is amply met: the statute's language unmistakably includes State prisons and prisoners within its coverage. . . .

State prisons fall squarely within the statutory definition of 'public entity,' which includes 'any department, agency, special purpose district, or other instrumentality of a State or States or local government.' . . .

We also disagree with petitioners' contention that the term 'qualified individual with a disability' is ambiguous insofar as concerns its application to state prisoners. The statute defines the term to include anyone with a disability

'who, with or without reasonable modifications to rules, policies, or practices, the removal of architectural, communication, or transportation barriers, or the provision of auxiliary aids and services, meets the essential eligibility requirements for the receipt of services or the participation in programs or activities provided by a public entity.'

Petitioners argue that the words 'eligibility' and 'participation' imply voluntariness on the part of an applicant who seeks a benefit from the State, and thus do not connote prisoners who are being held against their will. This is wrong on two counts: First, because the words do not connote voluntariness. . . . And secondly, even if the words did connote voluntariness, it would still not be true that all prison 'services,' 'programs,' and 'activities' are excluded from the ADA because participation in them is not voluntary. The prison law library, for example, is a service (and the use of it an activity), which prisoners are free to take or leave. . . .

Our conclusion that the text of the ADA is not ambiguous causes us also to reject petitioners' appeal to the doctrine of constitutional doubt . . . . Because the plain text of Title II of the ADA unambiguously extends to state prison inmates, the judgment of the Court of Appeals is affirmed."

V. JUSTICE VOTE

9 Pro ACLU Side vs. 0 Con Opposing Side

ACLU Side (Respondent / Appellee)

1. Scalia, A. – Wrote majority opinion
2. Kennedy, A. – Joined majority opinion
3. Ginsburg, R. – Joined majority opinion
4. Stevens, J. – Joined majority opinion
5. Souter, D. – Joined majority opinion
6. Rehnquist, W. – Joined majority opinion
7. Thomas, C. – Joined majority opinion
8. Breyer, S. – Joined majority opinion
9. O'Connor, S. – Joined majority opinion

VI. A WIN OR LOSS FOR THE ACLU?

The ACLU filed as amicus urging affirmance of the judgment of the Court of Appeals for the Third Circuit; the Supreme Court affirmed in a 9-0 vote, giving the ACLU an apparent win.

849. Pennsylvania Board of Probation & Parole v. Scott

(Decided June 22, 1998; 524 U.S. 357)

I. ISSUE

A. Issues Discussed

Criminal justice, Fourth Amendment, exclusionary rule, parole

B. Legal Question Presented

"[W]hether the exclusionary rule, which generally prohibits the introduction at criminal trial of evidence obtained in violation of a defendant's Fourth Amendment rights, applies in parole revocation hearings."

C. Supreme Court's Answer

The exclusionary rule does not apply in parole revocation hearings.

II. CASE SUMMARY

A. Background

"Respondent Keith M. Scott pleaded nolo contendere to a charge of third-degree murder and was sentenced to a prison term of 10 to 20 years, beginning on March 31, 1983. On September 1, 1993, just months after completing the minimum sentence, respondent was released on parole. One of the conditions of respondent's parole was that he would refrain from 'owning or possessing any firearms or other weapons.' The parole agreement, which respondent signed, further provided:

'I expressly consent to the search of my person, property and residence, without a warrant by agents of the Pennsylvania Board of Probation and Parole. Any items, in [sic] the possession of which constitutes a violation of parole/reparole shall be subject to seizure, and may be used as evidence in the parole revocation process.'

About five months later, after obtaining an arrest warrant based on evidence that respondent had violated several conditions of his parole by possessing firearms, consuming alcohol, and assaulting a co-worker, three parole officers arrested respondent at a local diner. Before being transferred to a correctional facility, respondent gave the officers the keys to his residence. The officers entered the home, which was owned by his mother, but did not perform a search for parole violations until respondent's mother arrived. The officers neither requested nor obtained consent to perform the search, but respondent's mother did direct them to his bedroom. After finding no relevant evidence there, the officers searched an adjacent sitting room in which they found five firearms, a compound bow, and three arrows.

At his parole violation hearing, respondent objected to the introduction of the evidence obtained during the search of his home on the ground that the search was unreasonable under the Fourth Amendment. The hearing examiner, however, rejected the challenge and admitted the evidence. As a result, the Pennsylvania Board of Probation and Parole found sufficient evidence in the record to support the weapons and alcohol charges and recommitted respondent to serve 36 months' backtime.

The Commonwealth Court of Pennsylvania reversed and remanded, holding, inter alia, that the hearing examiner had erred in admitting the evidence obtained during the search of respondent's residence. . . . The Pennsylvania Supreme Court affirmed."

The U.S. Supreme Court granted certiorari to review the case and reversed.

B. Counsel of Record / ACLU Attorney

ACLU Side (Respondent / Appellee): Leonard N. Sosnov argued the cause for appellee.

Opposing Side (Petitioner / Appellant): D. Michael Fisher, Attorney General of Pennsylvania, argued the cause for appellant.

Malcom L. Stewart argued the cause for the United States, as amicus curiae, by special leave of Court.

III. AMICI CURIAE

ACLU Side (Respondent / Appellee)

Brief of amici curiae filed on behalf of the ACLU, et al., by Tracey Maclin, Steven R. Shapiro, Stefan Presser, and Lisa B. Kemler.

Opposing Side (Petitioner / Appellant)

Brief of amici curiae filed on behalf of the State of Ohio, et al., by Betty D. Montgomery, Attorney General of Ohio, Jeffrey S. Sutton, State Solicitor, and Todd R. Marti, Assistant Attorney General, by John M. Ferren, Corporation Counsel of the District of Columbia, and by the Attorneys General for their respective States as follows: Grant Woods of Arizona, M. Jane Brady of Delaware, Robert Butterworth of Florida, Margery S. Bronster of Hawaii, Alan G. Lance of Idaho, Jeff Modisett of Indiana, Tom Miller of Iowa, Carla J. Stovall of Kansas, Richard P. Ieyoub of Louisiana, Andrew Ketterer of Maine, J. Joseph Curran, Jr., of Maryland, Scott Harshbarger of Massachusetts, Frank J. Kelley of Michigan, Hubert H. Humphrey III of Minnesota, Mike Moore of Mississippi, Joseph P. Mazurek of Montana, Don Stenberg of Nebraska, Frankie Sue Del Papa of Nevada, Philip T. McLaughlin of New Hampshire, Peter Verniero of New Jersey, Dennis C. Vacco of New York, Michael F. Easley of North Carolina, Heidi Heitkamp of North Dakota, Drew Edmondson of Oklahoma, Hardy Myers of Oregon, Jeffrey B. Pine of Rhode Island, Mark Barnett of South Dakota, John Knox Walkup of Tennessee, Jan Graham of Utah, Wallace J. Malley of Vermont, and William U Hill of Wyoming.

Brief of amici curiae filed on behalf of Americans for Effective Law Enforcement, Inc., et al., by Wayne W Schmidt, James P. Manak, Gene Voegtlin, Richard M. Weintraub, and Bernard J. Farber.

Brief of amici curiae filed on behalf of the Center for the Community Interest by Andrew N Vollmer, Michael Plotnick, Lyle Roberts, Todd Zubler, and Roger L. Conner.

Brief of amici curiae filed on behalf of the Criminal Justice Legal Foundation by Kent S. Scheidegger and Christine M. Murphy.

IV. THE SUPREME COURT'S DECISION

"The exclusionary rule is . . . a judicially created means of deterring illegal searches and seizures. As such, the rule does not 'proscribe the introduction of illegally seized evidence in all proceedings or against all persons,' but applies only in contexts 'where its remedial objectives are thought most efficaciously served.' Moreover, because the rule is prudential rather than constitutionally mandated, we have held it to be applicable only where its deterrence benefits outweigh its 'substantial social costs.'

Recognizing these costs, we have repeatedly declined to extend the exclusionary rule to proceedings other than criminal trials. . . .

Application of the exclusionary rule [here] would both hinder the functioning of state parole systems and alter the traditionally flexible, administrative nature of parole revocation proceedings. The rule would provide only minimal deterrence benefits in this context, because application of the rule in the criminal trial context already provides significant deterrence of unconstitutional searches. We therefore hold that the federal exclusionary rule does not bar the introduction at parole revocation hearings of evidence seized in violation of parolees' Fourth Amendment rights. . . .

Even when the officer performing the search is a parole officer, the deterrence benefits of the exclusionary rule remain limited. Parole agents, in contrast to police officers, are not 'engaged in the often competitive enterprise of ferreting out crime,' instead, their primary concern is whether their parolees should remain free on parole. Thus, their relationship with parolees is more supervisory than adversarial. It is thus 'unfair to assume that the parole officer bears hostility against the parolee that destroys his neutrality; realistically the failure of the parolee is in a sense a failure for his supervising officer.' Although this relationship does not prevent parole officers from ever violating the Fourth Amendment rights of their parolees, it does mean that the harsh deterrent of exclusion is unwarranted, given such other deterrents as departmental training and discipline and the threat of damages actions. . . .

We have long been averse to imposing federal requirements upon the parole systems of the States. A federal requirement that parole boards apply the exclusionary rule, which is itself a "grud[g]ingly taken medicament," would severely disrupt the traditionally informal, administrative process of parole revocation. The marginal deterrence of unreasonable searches and seizures is insufficient to justify such an intrusion. We therefore hold that parole boards are not required by federal law to exclude evidence obtained in violation of the Fourth Amendment. Accordingly, the judgment below is reversed, and the case is remanded to the Pennsylvania Supreme Court."

V. JUSTICE VOTE

4 Pro ACLU Side vs. 5 Con Opposing Side

ACLU Side (Respondent / Appellee)

1. Stevens, J. – Wrote dissenting opinion
2. Souter, D. – Wrote dissenting opinion
3. Ginsberg, R. – Joined Souter's dissent
4. Breyer, S. – Joined Souter's dissent

Opposing Side (Petitioner / Appellant)

1. Thomas, C. – Wrote majority opinion
2. Rehnquist, W. – Joined majority opinion
3. O'Connor, S. – Joined majority opinion
4. Scalia, A. – Joined majority opinion
5. Kennedy, A. – Joined majority opinion

VI. A WIN OR LOSS FOR THE ACLU?

The ACLU filed as amicus curiae urging affirmance of the judgment of the Pennsylvania Supreme Court; the U.S. Supreme Court reversed and remanded in a 5-4 vote, giving the ACLU an apparent loss.

850. National Endowment for the Arts v. Finley

(Decided June 25, 1998; 524 U.S. 569)

I. ISSUE

A. Issues Discussed

First Amendment, freedoms of press, speech, and association, Fifth Amendment, vagueness, viewpoint discrimination

B. Legal Question Presented

Whether § 954(d)(1) of the "National Foundation on the Arts and the Humanities Act of 1965, as amended in 1990, [which] requires the Chairperson of the National Endowment for the Arts (NEA) to ensure that 'artistic excellence and artistic merit are the criteria by which [grant] applications are judged, taking into consideration general standards of decency and respect for the diverse beliefs and values of the American public' . . . , on its face, impermissibly discriminates on the basis of viewpoint and is void for vagueness under the First and Fifth Amendments."

C. Supreme Court's Answer

Sections 954(d)(1) does not violate the First Amendment or Fifth Amendment.

II. CASE SUMMARY

A. Background

"The National Foundation on the Arts and the Humanities Act of 1965, as amended in 1990, 104 Stat. 1963, requires the Chairperson of the National Endowment for the Arts (NEA) to ensure that 'artistic excellence and artistic merit are the criteria by which [grant] applications are judged, taking into consideration general standards of decency and respect for the diverse beliefs and values of the American public.' 20 U.S.C. § 954(d)(1). . . .

With the establishment of the NEA in 1965, Congress embarked on a 'broadly conceived national policy of support for the . . . arts in the United States,' pledging federal funds to 'help create and sustain not only a climate encouraging freedom of thought, imagination, and inquiry but also the material conditions facilitating the release of . . . creative talent.' The enabling statute vests the NEA with substantial discretion to award grants; it identifies only the broadest funding priorities, including 'artistic and cultural significance, giving emphasis to American creativity and cultural diversity,' 'professional excellence,' and the encouragement of 'public knowledge, education, understanding, and appreciation of the arts.' . . .

The four individual respondents in this case, Karen Finley, John Fleck, Holly Hughes, and Tim Miller, are performance artists who applied for NEA grants before § 954(d)(1) was enacted. An advisory panel recommended approval of respondents' projects, both initially and after receiving [NEA Chairperson] Frohnmayer's request to reconsider three of the applications. A majority of the Council subsequently recommended disapproval, and in June 1990, the NEA informed respondents that they had been denied funding. Respondents filed suit, alleging that the NEA had violated their First Amendment rights by rejecting the applications on political grounds, had failed to follow statutory procedures by basing the denial on criteria other than those set forth in the NEA's enabling statute, and had breached the confidentiality of their grant applications through the release of quotations to the press, in violation of the Privacy Act of 1974, 5 U.S.C. § 552(a). Respondents sought restoration of the recommended grants or reconsideration of their applications, as well as damages for the alleged Privacy Act violations. When Congress enacted § 954(d)(1), respondents, now joined by the National Association of Artists' Organizations (NAAO), amended their complaint to challenge the provision as void for vagueness and impermissibly viewpoint based.

The District Court denied the NEA's motion for judgment on the pleadings, and, after discovery, the NEA agreed to settle the individual respondents' statutory and as-applied constitutional claims by paying the artists the amount of the vetoed grants, damages, and attorney's fees.

The District Court then granted summary judgment in favor of respondents on their facial constitutional challenge to § 954(d)(1) and enjoined enforcement of the provision. . . . A divided panel of the Court of Appeals affirmed the District Court's ruling."

The Supreme Court granted certiorari to review the case and reversed.

B. Counsel of Record / ACLU Attorney

ACLU Side (Respondent / Appellee): David Cole argued the cause for appellee. With him on the briefs were Marjorie Heins, Steven R. Shapiro, Mary D. Dorman, Ellen Yaroshefsky, and Carol Sobel

Opposing Side (Petitioner / Appellant): Solicitor General Seth P. Waxman argued the cause for appellants. With him on the briefs were

Assistant Attorney General Hunger, Deputy Solicitor General Kneedler, Deputy Assistant Attorney General Preston, Jeffrey P. Minear, William Kanter, Alfred Mollin, Karen Christensen, and Hope O'Keefe.

III. AMICI CURIAE

ACLU Side (Respondent / Appellee)

Briefs of amici curiae were filed on behalf of the American Association of University Professors, et al., Americans United for Separation of Church and State, Family Research Institute of Wisconsin, Claes Oldenburg, et al., New School for Social Research, et al., Rockefeller Foundation, 26 Arts, Broadcast, Library, Museum and Publishing Amici, and Volunteer Lawyers for the Arts, et al.

Opposing Side (Petitioner / Appellant)

Brief of amici curiae filed on behalf of the American Center for Law and Justice by John P. Tuskey, Jay A. Sekulow, Colby M. May, and James M. Henderson, Sr.

Brief of amici curiae filed on behalf of Liberty Counsel by Mathew D. Staver, Frederick H. Nelson, and Nicole Arfaras Kerr.

Brief of amici curiae filed on behalf of Morality in Media by Paul J. McGeady and Robert W. Peters.

Brief of amici curiae filed on behalf of the National Family Legal Foundation by Len L. Munsil and Sheila A. Green.

IV. THE SUPREME COURT'S DECISION

"Respondents raise a facial constitutional challenge to § 954(d)(1), and consequently they confront 'a heavy burden' in advancing their claim. . . .

It is clear, however, that the text of § 954(d)(1) imposes no categorical requirement. The advisory language stands in sharp contrast to congressional efforts to prohibit the funding of certain classes of speech. When Congress has in fact intended to affirmatively constrain the NEA's grant-making authority, it has done so in no uncertain terms. See § 954(d)(2). ('[O]bscenity is without artistic merit, is not protected speech, and shall not be funded.')

[T]he 'decency and respect' criteria do not silence speakers by expressly 'threaten[ing] censorship of ideas.' Thus, we do not perceive a realistic danger that § 954(d)(1) will compromise First Amendment values. [T]he provision does not introduce considerations that, in practice, would effectively preclude or punish the expression of particular views. Indeed, one could hardly anticipate how 'decency or respect' would bear on grant applications in categories such as funding for symphony orchestras. . . .

Any contentbased considerations that may be taken into account in the grant-making process are a consequence of the nature of arts funding. The NEA has limited resources and it must deny the majority of the grant applications that it receives, including many that propose 'artistically excellent' projects. . . .

The lower courts also erred in invalidating § 954(d)(1) as unconstitutionally vague. Under the First and Fifth Amendments, speakers are protected from arbitrary and discriminatory enforcement of vague standards. The terms of the provision are undeniably opaque, and if they appeared in a criminal statute or regulatory scheme, they could raise substantial vagueness concerns. It is unlikely, however, that speakers will be compelled to steer too far clear of any 'forbidden area' in the context of grants of this nature. . . . In the context of selective subsidies, it is not always feasible for Congress to legislate with clarity. Indeed, if this statute is unconstitutionally vague, then so too are all government programs awarding scholarships and grants on the basis of subjective criteria such as 'excellence.' . . .

Section 954(d)(1) merely adds some imprecise considerations to an already subjective selection process. It does not, on its face, impermissibly infringe on First or Fifth Amendment rights. Accordingly, the judgment of the Court of Appeals is reversed and the case is remanded for further proceedings consistent with this opinion."

V. JUSTICE VOTE

1 Pro ACLU Side vs. 8 Con Opposing Side

ACLU Side (Respondent / Appellee)

1. Souter, D. – Wrote dissenting opinion

Opposing Side (Petitioner / Appellant)

1. O'Connor, S. – Wrote majority opinion
2. Rehnquist, W. – Joined majority opinion
3. Stevens, J. – Joined majority opinion
4. Kennedy, A. – Joined majority opinion
5. Ginsburg, R. – Joined majority opinion
6. Breyer, S. – Joined majority opinion
7. Scalia, A. – Wrote concurring opinion
8. Thomas, C. – Joined Scalia's concurrence

VI. A WIN OR LOSS FOR THE ACLU?

The ACLU, as counsel for appellee, urged affirmance of the judgment of the Court of Appeals for the Ninth Circuit; the Supreme Court reversed in an 8-1 vote, giving the ACLU an apparent loss.

851. Bragdon v. Abbott

(Decided June 25, 1998; 524 U.S. 624)

I. ISSUE

A. Issues Discussed

Civil rights, disabilities

B. Legal Question Presented

"[F]irst, whether HIV infection is a disability under the ADA when the infection has not yet progressed to the so-called symptomatic phase; and, second, whether the Court of Appeals, in affirming a grant of summary judgment, cited sufficient material in the record to determine, as a matter of law, that respondent's infection with HIV posed no direct threat to the health and safety of her treating dentist."

C. Supreme Court's Answer

HIV infection is a disability under the ABA even when the infection is not yet symptomatic. The determination of direct threat should be determined from the standpoint of the person who made the decision, but based on medical evidence, not just the individual's beliefs about the risks.

II. CASE SUMMARY

A. Background

"Respondent Sidney Abbott (hereinafter respondent) has been infected with HIV since 1986. When the incidents we recite occurred, her infection had not manifested its most serious symptoms. On September 16, 1994, she went to the office of petitioner Randon Bragdon in Bangor, Maine, for a dental appointment. She disclosed her HIV infection on the patient registration form. Petitioner completed a dental examination, discovered a cavity, and informed respondent of his policy against filling cavities of HIV-infected patients. He offered to perform the work at a hospital with no added fee for his services, though respondent would be responsible for the cost of using the hospital's facilities. Respondent declined.

Respondent sued petitioner under state law and § 302 of the ADA, alleging discrimination on the basis of her disability. . . .

The United States and the Maine Human Rights Commission intervened as plaintiffs. After discovery, the parties filed cross-motions for summary judgment. The District Court ruled in favor of the plaintiffs, holding that respondent's HIV infection satisfied the ADA's definition of disability. The court held further that petitioner raised no genuine issue of material fact as to whether respondent's HIV infection would have posed a direct threat to the health or safety of others during the course of a dental treatment. The court relied on affidavits submitted by Dr. Donald Wayne Marianos, Director of the Division of Oral Health of the Centers for Disease Control and Prevention (CDC). The Marianos affidavits asserted it is safe for dentists to treat patients infected with HIV in dental offices if the dentist follows the so-called universal precautions described in the Recommended Infection-Control Practices for Dentistry issued by CDC in 1993.

The Court of Appeals affirmed. It held respondent's HIV infection was a disability under the ADA, even though her infection had not yet progressed to the symptomatic stage. The Court of Appeals also agreed that treating the respondent in petitioner's office would not have posed a direct threat to the health and safety of others. Unlike the District Court, however, the Court of Appeals declined to rely on the Marianos affidavits. Instead the court relied on the 1993 CDC Dentistry Guidelines, as well as the Policy on AIDS, HIV Infection and the Practice of Dentistry, promulgated by the American Dental Association in 1991 (1991 American Dental Association Policy on HIV)."

The Supreme Court granted certiorari to review the case, affirmed in part, vacated, and remanded.

B. Counsel of Record / ACLU Attorney

ACLU Side (Respondent / Appellee): Bennett H. Klein argued the cause for appellee.

Deputy Solicitor General Lawrence G. Wallace argued the cause for the United States, as amicus curiae, by special leave of Court.

Opposing Side (Petitioner / Appellant): John W. McCarthy argued the cause for appellant.

III. AMICI CURIAE

ACLU Side (Respondent / Appellee)

Brief of amici curiae filed on behalf of the AIDS Action Council, AIDS National Interfaith Network, American Association on Mental Retardation, American Association of Retired Persons, ACLU, et al., by Steven R. Shapiro, Jennifer Middleton, and Matthew Coles, Robert A. Long, Jr., Alexandra T. V. Edsall, and Grail P. Walsh.

Brief of amici curiae filed on behalf of the United States by Deputy Solicitor General Lawrence G. Wallace, Solicitor General Waxman, Acting Assistant Attorney General Lee, James A. Feldman, Jessica Dunsay Silver, and Thomas E. Chandler.

Additional briefs of amici curiae were filed on behalf of the City of Los Angeles, the American Medical Association, the Elizabeth Glasser Pediatric Aids Foundation, the Infectious Diseases Society for America, et al., and Senator Harkin, et al.

Opposing Side (Petitioner / Appellant)

Brief of amici curiae filed on behalf of the Equal Employment Advisory Council by Ann Elizabeth Reesman.

IV. THE SUPREME COURT'S DECISION

"We first review the ruling that respondent's HIV infection constituted a disability under the ADA. The statute defines disability as:

'(A) a physical or mental impairment that substantially limits one or more of the major life activities of such individual' . . . .

We hold respondent's HIV infection was a disability under subsection (A) of the definitional section of the statute. In light of this conclusion, we need not consider the applicability of subsections (B) or (C).

Our consideration of subsection (A) of the definition proceeds in three steps. First, we consider whether respondent's HIV infection was a physical impairment. Second, we identify the life activity upon which respondent relies (reproduction and child bearing) and determine whether it constitutes a major life activity under the ADA. Third, tying the two statutory phrases together, we ask whether the impairment substantially limited the major life activity. In construing the statute, we are informed by interpretations of parallel definitions in previous statutes and the views of various administrative agencies which have faced this interpretive question. . . .

For the statistical and other reasons we have cited, of course, the limitations on reproduction may be insurmountable here. Testimony from the respondent that her HIV infection controlled her decision not to have a child is unchallenged. . . . We agree with the District Court and the Court of Appeals that no triable issue of fact impedes a ruling on the question of statutory coverage. Respondent's HIV infection is a physical impairment which substantially limits a major life activity, as the ADA defines it. . . .

Our conclusion that courts should assess the objective reasonableness of the views of health care professionals without deferring to their individual judgments does not answer the implicit assumption in the question presented, whether petitioner's actions were reasonable in light of the available medical evidence. In assessing the reasonableness of petitioner's actions, the views of public health authorities, such as the U. S. Public Health Service, CDC, and the National Institutes of Health, are of special weight and authority. The views of these organizations are not conclusive, however. A health care professional who disagrees with the prevailing medical consensus may refute it by citing a credible scientific basis for deviating from the accepted norm. . . .

We conclude the proper course is to give the Court of Appeals the opportunity to determine whether our analysis of some of the studies cited by the parties would change its conclusion that petitioner presented neither objective evidence nor a triable issue of fact on the question of risk. In remanding the case, we do not foreclose the possibility that the Court of Appeals may reach the same conclusion it did earlier. Remand will permit a full exploration of the issue through the adversary process.

The determination of the Court of Appeals that respondent's HIV infection was a disability under the ADA is affirmed. The judgment is vacated, and the case is remanded for further proceedings consistent with this opinion."

V. JUSTICE VOTE

5 Pro ACLU Side vs. 4 Con Opposing Side

ACLU Side (Respondent / Appellee)

1. Kennedy, A. – Wrote majority opinion
2. Souter, D. – Joined majority opinion
3. Ginsburg, R. – Wrote concurring opinion
4. Stevens, J. – Wrote concurring opinion
5. Breyer, S. – Joined Stevens' concurrence

Opposing Side (Petitioner / Appellant)

1. Rehnquist, W. – Wrote opinion concurring in part and dissenting in part
2. O'Connor, S. – Wrote an opinion concurring in part and dissenting in part, joined Rehnquist's opinion in part
3. Scalia, A. – Joined Rehnquist's opinion
4. Thomas, C. – Joined Rehnquist's opinion

VI. A WIN OR LOSS FOR THE ACLU?

The ACLU filed as amicus curiae urging affirmance of the judgment of the Court of Appeals; the Supreme Court affirmed in part and vacated the judgment in a 5-4 vote, giving the ACLU an apparent win.

852. Faragher v. City of Boca Raton

(Decided June 26, 1998; 524 U.S. 775)

I.ISSUE

A. Issues Discussed

Civil rights, gender, federal

B. Legal Question Presented

Under what circumstances may an employer "be held liable under Title VII of the Civil Rights Act of 1964 for the acts of a supervisory employee whose sexual harassment of subordinates has created a hostile work environment amounting to employment discrimination."

C. Supreme Court's Answer

"We hold that an employer is vicariously liable for actionable discrimination caused by a supervisor, but subject to an affirmative defense looking to the reasonableness of the employer's conduct as well as that of a plaintiff victim."

II. CASE SUMMARY

A. Background

"Between 1985 and 1990, while attending college, petitioner Beth Ann Faragher worked part time and during the summers as an ocean lifeguard for the Marine Safety Section of the Parks and Recreation Department of respondent, the City of Boca Raton, Florida (City). During this period, Faragher's immediate supervisors were Bill Terry, David Silverman, and Robert Gordon. In June 1990, Faragher resigned.

In 1992, Faragher brought an action against Terry, Silverman, and the City, asserting claims under Title VII, Rev.Stat. § 1979, 42 U.S.C. § 1983, and Florida law. So far as it concerns the Title VII claim, the complaint alleged that Terry and Silverman created a 'sexually hostile atmosphere' at the beach by repeatedly subjecting Faragher and other female lifeguards to 'uninvited and offensive touching,' by making lewd remarks, and by speaking of women in offensive terms. . . . Asserting that Terry and Silverman were agents of the City, and that their conduct amounted to discrimination in the 'terms, conditions, and privileges' of her employment, Faragher sought a judgment against the City for nominal damages, costs, and attorney's fees. . . .

In February 1986, the City adopted a sexual harassment policy, which it stated in a memorandum from the City Manager addressed to all employees. In May 1990, the City revised the policy and reissued a statement of it. Although the City may actually have circulated the memos and statements to some employees, it completely failed to disseminate its policy among employees of the Marine Safety Section, with the result that Terry, Silverman, Gordon, and many lifeguards were unaware of it. . . .

Faragher did not complain to higher management about Terry or Silverman. Although she spoke of their behavior to Gordon, she did not regard these discussions as formal complaints to a supervisor but as conversations with a person she held in high esteem. Other female lifeguards had similarly informal talks with Gordon, but because Gordon did not feel that it was his place to do so, he did not report these complaints to Terry, his own supervisor, or to any other city official. Gordon responded to the complaints of one lifeguard by saying that 'the City just [doesn't] care.'

In April 1990, however, two months before Faragher's resignation, Nancy Ewanchew, a former lifeguard, wrote to Richard Bender, the City's Personnel Director, complaining that Terry and Silverman had harassed her and other female lifeguards. Following investigation of this complaint, the City found that Terry and Silverman had behaved improperly, reprimanded them, and required them to choose between a suspension without pay or the forfeiture of annual leave.

On the basis of these findings, the District Court concluded that the conduct of Terry and Silverman was discriminatory harassment sufficiently serious to alter the conditions of Faragher's employment and constitute an abusive working environment. . . .

A panel of the Court of Appeals for the Eleventh Circuit reversed the judgment against the City. . . .

In a 7-to-5 decision, the full Court of Appeals, sitting en banc, adopted the panel's conclusion."

The Supreme Court granted certiorari to review the case.

B. Counsel of Record / ACLU Attorney

ACLU Side (Petitioner / Appellant): William R. Amlong argued the cause for appellant. With him on the briefs were Martha F. Davis, Yolanda S. Wu, and Eric Schnapper.

Irving Gornstein argued the cause for the United States et al. as amici curiae.

Opposing Side (Respondent / Appellee): Harry A. Rissetto argued the cause for appellee. With him on the briefs were Peter Buscemi, Mark S. Dichter, Mark A. Srere, and Victoria E. Houck.

III. AMICI CURIAE

ACLU Side (Petitioner / Appellant)

Brief of amici curiae filed on behalf of the United States et al. by Irving Gornstein, Solicitor General Waxman, Acting Assistant Attorney General Lee, Deputy Solicitor General Wallace, C. Gregory Stewart, Carolyn L. Wheeler, and Gail S. Coleman.

Brief of amici curiae filed on behalf of the Lawyers' Committee for Civil Rights Under Law and the American Civil Liberties Union by Marc L. Fleischaker, Jack W. Londen, Norman Redlich, Barbara R. Arnwine, Thomas J. Henderson, Richard T. Seymour, Teresa A. Ferrante, Gia B. Lee, and Steven R. Shapiro.

Brief of amici curiae filed on behalf of the American Federation of Labor and Congress of Industrial Organizations by Jonathan P. Hiatt, Marsha S. Berzon, and Laurence Gold.

Brief of amici curiae filed on behalf of the National Employment Lawyers Association by Margaret A. Harris and H. Candace Gorman.

Brief of amici curiae filed on behalf of the National Women's Law Center, Equal Rights Advocates et al. by Lois G. Williams, Nancy C. Libin, Jane L. Dolkart, and Marcia D. Greenberger.

Opposing Side (Respondent / Appellee)

Brief of amici curiae filed on behalf of the Chamber of Commerce of the United States by Stephen A. Bokat, Robin S. Conrad, and Sussan L. Mahallati.

Brief of amici curiae filed on behalf of the Equal Employment Advisory Council by Ann Elizabeth Reesman.

Brief of amici curiae filed on behalf of the National Association of Manufacturers et al. by William J. Kilberg, Douglas R. Cox, Jan S. Amundson, and Quentin Riegal.

Brief of amici curiae filed on behalf of the Society for Human Resource Management by Allan H. Weitzman and Paul Salvatore.

IV. THE SUPREME COURT'S DECISION

"Under Title VII of the Civil Rights Act of 1964, '[i]t shall be an unlawful employment practice for an employer ... to fail or refuse to hire or to discharge any individual, or otherwise to discriminate against any individual with respect to his compensation, terms, conditions, or privileges of employment, because of such individual's race, color, religion, sex, or national origin.' [I]n Meritor we held that sexual harassment so 'severe or pervasive' as to "alter the conditions of [the victim's] employment and create an abusive working environment" violates Title VII.

In thus holding that environmental claims are covered by the statute, we drew upon earlier cases recognizing liability for discriminatory harassment based on race and national origin, just as we have also followed the lead of such cases in attempting to define the severity of the offensive conditions necessary to constitute actionable sex discrimination under the statute. . . .

Meritor's statement of the law is the foundation on which we build today. Neither party before us has urged us to depart from our customary adherence to stare decisis in statutory interpretation . . . . And the force of precedent here is enhanced by Congress's amendment to the liability provisions of Title VII since the Meritor decision, without providing any modification of our holding. . . .

The Court of Appeals identified, and rejected, three possible grounds drawn from agency law for holding the City vicariously liable for the hostile environment created by the supervisors. . . .

In order to accommodate the principle of vicarious liability for harm caused by misuse of supervisory authority, as well as Title VII's equally basic policies of encouraging forethought by employers and saving action by objecting employees, we adopt the following holding in this case and in Burlington Industries, Inc. v. Ellerth, also decided today. An employer is subject to vicarious liability to a victimized employee for an actionable hostile environment created by a supervisor with immediate (or successively higher) authority over the employee. When no tangible employment action is taken, a defending employer may raise an affirmative defense to liability or damages, subject to proof by a preponderance of the evidence, see Fed. Rule Civ. Proc. 8(c). The defense comprises two necessary elements: (a) that the employer exercised reasonable care to prevent and correct promptly any sexually harassing behavior, and (b) that the plaintiff employee unreasonably failed to take advantage of any preventive or corrective opportunities provided by the employer or to avoid harm otherwise. While proof that an employer had promulgated an antiharassment policy with complaint procedure is not necessary in every instance as a matter of law, the need for a stated policy suitable to the employment circumstances may appropriately be addressed in any case when litigating the first element of the defense. And while proof that an employee failed to fulfill the corresponding obligation of reasonable care to avoid harm is not limited to showing an unreasonable failure to use any complaint procedure provided by the employer, a demonstration of such failure will normally suffice to satisfy the employer's burden under the second element of the defense. No affirmative defense is available, however, when the supervisor's harassment culminates in a tangible employment action, such as discharge, demotion, or undesirable reassignment.

Applying these rules here, we believe that the judgment of the Court of Appeals must be reversed. The District Court found that the degree of hostility in the work environment rose to the actionable level and was attributable to Silverman and Terry. It is undisputed that these supervisors 'were granted virtually unchecked authority' over their subordinates, 'directly controll[ing] and supervis[ing] all aspects of [Faragher's] day-to-day activities.' It is also clear that Faragher and her colleagues were 'completely isolated from the City's higher management.' The City did not seek review of these findings.

While the City would have an opportunity to raise an affirmative defense if there were any serious prospect of its presenting one, it appears from the record that any such avenue is closed. . . . Under such circumstances, we hold as a matter of law that the City could not be found to have exercised reasonable care to prevent the supervisors' harassing conduct. . . .

The City points to nothing that might justify a conclusion by the District Court on remand that the City had exercised reasonable care. Nor is there any reason to remand for consideration of Faragher's efforts to mitigate her own damages, since the award to her was solely nominal. . . .

The judgment of the Court of Appeals for the Eleventh Circuit is reversed, and the case is remanded for reinstatement of the judgment of the District Court."

V. JUSTICE VOTE

7 Pro ACLU Side vs. 2 Con Opposing Side

ACLU Side (Petitioner / Appellant)

1. Souter, D. – Wrote majority opinion
2. O'Connor, S. – Joined majority opinion
3. Stevens, J. – Joined majority opinion
4. Ginsburg, R. – Joined majority opinion
5. Breyer, S. – Joined majority opinion
6. Rehnquist, W. – Joined majority opinion
7. Kennedy, A. – Joined majority opinion

Opposing Side (Respondent / Appellee)

1. Thomas, C. – Wrote dissenting opinion
2. Scalia, A. – Joined Thomas' dissent

A WIN OR LOSS FOR THE ACLU?

The ACLU filed as amicus curiae urging reversal of the judgment of the Court of Appeals; the Supreme Court reversed and remanded in a 7-2 vote, giving the ACLU an apparent win.

853. Wright v. Universal Maritime Service Corp.

(Decided November 16, 1998; 525 U.S. 70)

I. ISSUE

A. Issues Discussed

Civil rights, federalism, arbitration clauses

B. Legal Question Presented

"[W]hether a general arbitration clause in a collective-bargaining agreement (CBA) requires an employee to use the arbitration procedure for an alleged violation of the Americans with Disabilities Act of 1990 (ADA) . . . ."

C. Supreme Court's Answer

The general arbitration clause here does not require an employee to use the arbitration procedure for an alleged violation of the ADA.

II. CASE SUMMARY

A. Background

"In 1970, petitioner Ceasar Wright began working as a longshoreman in Charleston, South Carolina. He was a member of Local 1422 of the International Longshoremen's Association of the AFL-CIO (Union), which used a hiring hall to supply workers to several stevedore companies represented by the South Carolina Stevedores Association (SCSA). . . .

Wright was also subject to the Longshore Seniority Plan, which contained its own grievance provision . . . .

On February 18, 1992, while Wright was working for respondent Stevens Shipping and Terminal Company (Stevens), he injured his right heel and his back. He sought compensation from Stevens for permanent disability under the Longshore and Harbor Workers' Compensation Act and ultimately settled the claim for $250,000 and $10,000 in attorney's fees. Wright was also awarded Social Security disability benefits. . . .

Between January 2 and January 11, Wright worked for four stevedoring companies, none of which complained about his performance. When, however, the stevedoring companies realized that Wright had previously settled a claim for permanent disability, they informed the union that they would not accept Wright for employment, because a person certified as permanently disabled (which they regarded Wright to be) is not qualified to perform longshore work under the [collective-bargaining agreement (CBA)].

When Wright found out that the stevedoring companies would no longer accept him for employment, he contacted the Union to ask how he could get back to work. Wright claims that instead of suggesting the filing of a grievance, the Union told him to obtain counsel and file a claim under the ADA. Wright hired an attorney and eventually filed charges of discrimination with the Equal Employment Opportunity Commission (EEOC) and the South Carolina State Human Affairs Commission, alleging that the stevedoring companies and the SCSA had violated the ADA by refusing him work. In October 1995, Wright received a right-to-sue letter from the EEOC.

In January 1996, Wright filed a complaint against the SCSA and six individual stevedoring companies in the United States District Court for the District of South Carolina. Respondents' answer asserted various affirmative defenses, including Wright's failure to exhaust his remedies under the CBA and the Seniority Plan. After discovery, respondents moved for summary judgment and Wright moved for partial summary judgment with respect to some of respondents' defenses. A Magistrate Judge recommended that the District Court dismiss the case without prejudice because Wright had failed to pursue the grievance procedure provided by the CBA. The District Court adopted the report and recommendation and subsequently rejected Wright's motion for reconsideration. The United States Court of Appeals for the Fourth Circuit affirmed . . . ."

The Supreme Court granted certiorari to review the case, vacated, and remanded.

B. Counsel of Record / ACLU Attorney

ACLU Side (Petitioner / Appellant): Ray P. McClain argued the cause for appellant.

Deputy Solicitor General Barbara D. Underwood argued the cause for the United States, as amicus curiae, by special leave of Court.

Opposing Side (Respondent / Appellee): Charles A. Edwards argued the cause for appellees.

III. AMICI CURIAE

ACLU Side (Petitioner / Appellant)

Brief of amici curiae filed on behalf of the ACLU, et al., by Louis M. Bogard, Steven R. Shapiro, Lewis Maltby, David S. Schwartz, and C. Andre Brumme, III.

Brief of amici curiae filed on behalf of the United States, et al., by Deputy Solicitor General Underwood, Solicitor General Waxman, Acting Assistant Attorney General Hodgkiss, James Feldman, C. Gregory Stewart, Philip B. Sklover, Lorraine C. Davis, and Robert J. Gregory.

Additional brief of amici curiae were filed in support of the American Federation of Labor and Congress of Industrial Organizations, et al., the Lawyers' Committee for Civil Rights Under Law, et al., the National Academy of Arbitrators, the National Employment Lawyers Association, and the State of Massachusetts, et al.

Opposing Side (Respondent / Appellee)

Brief of amici curiae were filed in support of the Equal Employment Advisory Council, et al., the National Association of Manufacturers, the National Association of Waterfront Employers, the Chamber of Commerce of the United States, and the Securities Industry Association.

IV. THE SUPREME COURT'S DECISION

"In asserting the existence of an agreement to arbitrate the ADA claim, respondents rely upon the presumption of arbitrability this Court has found in § 301 of the Labor Management Relations Act . . . . In collective-bargaining agreements, we have said, 'there is a presumption of arbitrability in the sense that '[a]n order to arbitrate the particular grievance should not be denied unless it may be said with positive assurance that the arbitration clause is not susceptible of an interpretation that covers the asserted dispute."

That presumption, however, does not extend beyond the reach of the principal rationale that justifies it, which is that arbitrators are in a better position than courts to interpret the terms of a CBA. . . .

Not only is petitioner's statutory claim not subject to a presumption of arbitrability; we think any CBA requirement to arbitrate it must be particularly clear. . . . The CBA in this case does not meet that standard. Its arbitration clause is very general, providing for arbitration of '[m]atters under dispute'—which could be understood to mean matters in dispute under the contract. And the remainder of the contract contains no explicit incorporation of statutory antidiscrimination requirements. . . .

We hold that the collective-bargaining agreement in this case does not contain a clear and unmistakable waiver of the covered employees' rights to a judicial forum for federal claims of employment discrimination. We do not reach the question whether such a waiver would be enforceable. The judgment of the Fourth Circuit is vacated, and the case is remanded for further proceedings consistent with this opinion."

V. JUSTICE VOTE

9 Pro ACLU Side vs. 0 Con Opposing Side

ACLU Side (Petitioner / Appellant)

1. Scalia, A. – Wrote majority opinion
2. Rehnquist, W. – Joined majority opinion
3. Stevens, J. – Joined majority opinion
4. O'Connor, S. – Joined majority opinion
5. Kennedy, A. – Joined majority opinion
6. Souter, D. – Joined majority opinion
7. Thomas, C. – Joined majority opinion
8. Ginsburg, R. – Joined majority opinion
9. Breyer, S. – Joined majority opinion

VI. A WIN OR LOSS FOR THE ACLU?

The ACLU filed as amicus curiae urging reversal of the judgment of the Court of Appeals for the Fourth Circuit; the Supreme Court vacated and in a 9-0 vote, giving the ACLU an apparent win.

854. Minnesota v. Carter

(Decided December 1, 1998; 525 U.S. 83)

I. ISSUE

A. Issues Discussed

Criminal justice, drugs, Fourth Amendment, search and seizure

B. Legal Question Presented

Whether visitors in another's home, who only stay for a short period of time for the purpose of conducting business, have a legitimate expectation of privacy in that home.

C. Supreme Court's Answer

This type of visitor does not have a legitimate expectation of privac in another person's home.

II. CASE SUMMARY

A. Background

"James Thielen, a police officer in the Twin Cities' suburb of Eagan, Minnesota, went to an apartment building to investigate a tip from a confidential informant. The informant said that he had walked by the window of a ground-floor apartment and had seen people putting a white powder into bags. The officer looked in the same window through a gap in the closed blind and observed the bagging operation for several minutes. He then notified headquarters, which began preparing affidavits for a search warrant while he returned to the apartment building. When two men left the building in a previously identified Cadillac, the police stopped the car. Inside were respondents Carter and Johns. As the police opened the door of the car to let Johns out, they observed a black, zippered pouch and a handgun, later determined to be loaded, on the vehicle's floor. Carter and Johns were arrested, and a later police search of the vehicle the next day discovered pagers, a scale, and 47 grams of cocaine in plastic sandwich bags.

After seizing the car, the police returned to Apartment 103 and arrested the occupant, Kimberly Thompson, who is not a party to this appeal. A search of the apartment pursuant to a warrant revealed cocaine residue on the kitchen table and plastic baggies similar to those found in the Cadillac. Thielen identified Carter, Johns, and Thompson as the three people he had observed placing the powder into baggies. The police later learned that while Thompson was the lessee of the apartment, Carter and Johns lived in Chicago and had come to the apartment for the sole purpose of packaging the cocaine.

Carter and Johns had never been to the apartment before and were only in the apartment for approximately 2 1/2 hours. In return for the use of the apartment, Carter and Johns had given Thompson one-eighth of an ounce of the cocaine.

Carter and Johns were charged with conspiracy to commit a controlled substance crime in the first degree and aiding and abetting in a controlled substance crime in the first degree, in violation of Minn.Stat. §§ 152.021, subds. 1(1), 3(a), 609.05 (1996). They moved to suppress all evidence obtained from the apartment and the Cadillac, as well as to suppress several postarrest incriminating statements they had made. They argued that Thielen's initial observation of their drug packaging activities was an unreasonable search in violation of the Fourth Amendment and that all evidence obtained as a result of this unreasonable search was inadmissible as fruit of the poisonous tree. The Minnesota trial court held that since . . . Carter and Johns were not overnight social guests but temporary out-of-state visitors, they were not entitled to claim the protection of the Fourth Amendment against the government intrusion into the apartment. The trial court also concluded that Thielen's observation was not a search within the meaning of the Fourth Amendment. After a trial, Carter and Johns were each convicted of both offenses. The Minnesota Court of Appeals held that respondent Carter did not have 'standing' to object to Thielen's actions because his claim that he was predominantly a social guest was "inconsistent with the only evidence concerning his stay in the apartment, which indicates that he used it for a business purpose—to package drugs.' In a separate appeal, the Court of Appeals also affirmed Johns' conviction, without addressing what it termed the 'standing' issue.

A divided Minnesota Supreme Court reversed, holding that respondents had 'standing' to claim the protection of the Fourth Amendment because they had "a legitimate expectation of privacy in the invaded place.""

The Supreme Court granted certiorari to review the case and reversed.

B. Counsel of Record / ACLU Attorney

ACLU Side (Respondent / Appellee): Bradford Colbert argued the cause for appellee.

Opposing Side (Petitioner / Appellant): James C. Backstrom argued the cause for appellant.

Jeffrey A. Lamken argued the cause for the United States, as amicus curiae, by special leave of Court.

III. AMICI CURIAE

ACLU Side (Respondent / Appellee)

Brief of amici curiae filed on behalf of the ACLU, et al., by Tracey Maclin, Steven R. Shapiro, and Lisa B. Kemler.

Opposing Side (Petitioner / Appellant)

Brief of amici curiae filed on behalf of the United States by Jeffrey A. Lamken, Solicitor General Waxman, Acting Assistant Attorney General Keeney, and Deputy Solicitor General Dreeben.

Briefs of amici curiae filed on behalf of the State of Maryland, et al., by J. Joseph Curran, Jr., Attorney General of Maryland, and Annabelle L. Lisic, Assistant Attorney General, and the following Attorneys General for their respective states: Alan G. Lance of Idaho and Myrna A.I. Stahman, Deputy Attorney General of Idaho, Bill Pryor of Alabama, Bruce M. Botelho of Alaska, Grant Woods of Arizona, Daniel E. Lungren of California, M. Jane Brady of Delaware, Thurbert E. Baker of Georgia, Margery S. Bronster of Hawaii, Jeffrey A. Modisett of Indiana, Carla J. Stovall of Kansas, Richard P. Ieyoub of Louisiana, Scott Harshbarger of Massachusetts, Frank J. Kelley of Michigan, Joseph P. Mazurek of Montana, Don Stenberg of Nebraska, Frankie Sue Del Papa of Nevada, Peter Verniero of New Jersey, Dennis C. Vacco of New York, Heidi Heitkamp of North Dakota, W.A. Drew Edmondson of Oklahoma, Jeffrey B. Pine of Rhode Island, Charles M. Condon of South Carolina, Jan Graham of Utah, William H. Sorrell of Vermont, and Mark L. Earley of Virginia.

IV. THE SUPREME COURT'S DECISION

"The [Fourth] Amendment protects persons against unreasonable searches of 'their persons [and] houses' and thus indicates that the Fourth Amendment is a personal right that must be invoked by an individual. . . .

The text of the Amendment suggests that its protections extend only to people in 'their' houses. But we have held that in some circumstances a person may have a legitimate expectation of privacy in the house of someone else. In Minnesota v. Olson, 495 U.S. 91 (1990), for example, we decided that an overnight guest in a house had the sort of expectation of privacy that the Fourth Amendment protects. . . .

Respondents here were obviously not overnight guests, but were essentially present for a business transaction and were only in the home a matter of hours. There is no suggestion that they had a previous relationship with Thompson, or that there was any other purpose to their visit. . . .

Property used for commercial purposes is treated differently for Fourth Amendment purposes from residential property. 'An expectation of privacy in commercial premises, however, is different from, and indeed less than, a similar expectation in an individual's home.' And while it was a 'home' in which respondents were present, it was not their home. Similarly, the Court has held that in some circumstances a worker can claim Fourth Amendment protection over his own workplace. But there is no indication that respondents in this case had nearly as significant a connection to Thompson's apartment as the worker in O'Connor had to his own private office.

If we regard the overnight guest in Minnesota v. Olson as typifying those who may claim the protection of the Fourth Amendment in the home of another, and one merely 'legitimately on the premises' as typifying those who may not do so, the present case is obviously somewhere in between. But the purely commercial nature of the transaction engaged in here, the relatively short period of time on the premises, and the lack of any previous connection between respondents and the householder, all lead us to conclude that respondents' situation is closer to that of one simply permitted on the premises. We therefore hold that any search which may have occurred did not violate their Fourth Amendment rights.

Because we conclude that respondents had no legitimate expectation of privacy in the apartment, we need not decide whether the police officer's observation constituted a 'search.' The judgments of the Supreme Court of Minnesota are accordingly reversed, and the cause is remanded for proceedings not inconsistent with this opinion."

V. JUSTICE VOTE

3 Pro ACLU Side vs. 6 Con Opposing Side

ACLU Side (Respondent / Appellee)

1. Ginsburg, R. – Wrote dissenting opinion
2. Stevens, J. – Joined Ginsburg's dissent
3. Souter, D. – Joined Ginsburg's dissent

Opposing Side (Petitioner / Appellant)

1. Rehnquist, W. – Wrote majority opinion
2. O'Connor, S. – Joined majority opinion
3. Scalia, A. – Wrote concurring opinion
4. Thomas, C. – Joined Scalia's concurrence
5. Kennedy, A. – Wrote concurring opinion
6. Breyer, S. – Wrote concurring opinion

VI. A WIN OR LOSS FOR THE ACLU?

The ACLU filed as amicus curiae urging affirmance of the judgment of the Minnesota Supreme Court; the U.S. Supreme Court reversed in a 6-3 vote, giving the ACLU an apparent loss.

855. Knowles v. Iowa

(Decided December 8, 1998; 525 U.S. 113)

I. ISSUE

A. Issues Discussed

Fourth Amendment, search and seizure

B. Legal Question Presented

Whether an officer stopping a car for speeding and issuing a citation rather than arresting the driver "authorizes the officer, consistently with the Fourth Amendment, to conduct a full search of the car."

C. Supreme Court's Answer

Police conducting a full car search when issuing a traffic citation for speeding violates the driver's Fourth Amendment rights.

II. CASE SUMMARY

A. Background

"Knowles was stopped in Newton, Iowa, after having been clocked driving 43 miles per hour on a road where the speed limit was 25 miles per hour. The police officer issued a citation to Knowles, although under Iowa law he might have arrested him. The officer then conducted a full search of the car, and under the driver's seat he found a bag of marijuana and a 'pot pipe.' Knowles was then arrested and charged with violation of state laws dealing with controlled substances.

Before trial, Knowles moved to suppress the evidence so obtained. He argued that the search could not be sustained under the 'search incident to arrest' exception recognized in United States v. Robinson, 414 U.S. 218 (1973), because he had not been placed under arrest. At the hearing on the motion to suppress, the police officer conceded that he had neither Knowles' consent nor probable cause to conduct the search. He relied on Iowa law dealing with such searches.

Iowa Code Ann. § 321.485(1)(a) (West 1997) provides that Iowa peace officers having cause to believe that a person has violated any traffic or motor vehicle equipment law may arrest the person and immediately take the person before a magistrate. Iowa law also authorizes the far more usual practice of issuing a citation in lieu of arrest or in lieu of continued custody after an initial arrest. Section 805.1(4) provides that the issuance of a citation in lieu of an arrest 'does not affect the officer's authority to conduct an otherwise lawful search.' The Iowa Supreme Court has interpreted this provision as providing authority to officers to conduct a full-blown search of an automobile and driver in those cases where police elect not to make a custodial arrest and instead issue a citation—that is, a search incident to citation.

Based on this authority, the trial court denied the motion to suppress and found Knowles guilty. The Supreme Court of Iowa, sitting en banc, affirmed by a divided vote."

The Supreme Court granted certiorari to review the case and reversed.

B. Counsel of Record / ACLU Attorney

ACLU Side (Petitioner / Appellant): Paul Rosenberg argued the cause for appellant.

Opposing Side (Respondent / Appellee): Bridget A. Chambers, Assistant Attorney General of Iowa, argued the cause for appellee.

III. AMICI CURIAE

ACLU Side (Petitioner / Appellant)

Brief of amici curiae filed on behalf of the ACLU, et al., by James J. Tomkovicz, Steven R. Shapiro, Susan N. Herman, and Lisa B. Kemler.

Opposing Side (Respondent / Appellee)

Brief of amici curiae filed on behalf of the National Association of Police Organizations, Inc., by Stephen R. McSpadden.

IV. THE SUPREME COURT'S DECISION

"In Robinson, supra, we noted the two historical rationales for the 'search incident to arrest' exception: (1) the need to disarm the suspect in order to take him into custody, and (2) the need to preserve evidence for later use at trial. But neither of these underlying rationales for the search incident to arrest exception is sufficient to justify the search in the present case.

[W]hile the concern for officer safety in this context may justify the 'minimal' additional intrusion of ordering a driver and passengers out of the car, it does not by itself justify the often considerably greater intrusion attending a full field-type search. . . .

Nor has Iowa shown the second justification for the authority to search incident to arrest—the need to discover and preserve evidence. Once Knowles was stopped for speeding and issued a citation, all the evidence necessary to prosecute that offense had been obtained. No further evidence of excessive speed was going to be found either on the person of the offender or in the passenger compartment of the car. . . .

In Robinson, we held that the authority to conduct a full field search as incident to an arrest was a 'bright-line rule,' which was based on the concern for officer safety and destruction or loss of evidence, but which did not depend in every case upon the existence of either concern. Here we are asked to extend that 'bright-line rule' to a situation where the concern for officer safety is not present to the same extent and the concern for destruction or loss of evidence is not present at all. We decline to do so. The judgment of the Supreme Court of Iowa is reversed, and the cause is remanded for further proceedings not inconsistent with this opinion."

V. JUSTICE VOTE

9 Pro ACLU Side vs. 0 Con Opposing Side

ACLU Side (Petitioner / Appellant)

1. Rehnquist, W. – Wrote majority opinion
2. Ginsburg, R. – Joined majority opinion
3. Kennedy, A. – Joined majority opinion
4. Breyer, S. – Joined majority opinion
5. Souter, D. – Joined majority opinion
6. Scalia, A. – Joined majority opinion
7. Stevens, J. – Joined majority opinion
8. Thomas, C. – Joined majority opinion
9. O'Connor, S. – Joined majority opinion

VI. A WIN OR LOSS FOR THE ACLU?

The ACLU, as amicus curiae, urged reversal of the judgment of the Supreme Court of Iowa; the U.S. Supreme Court reversed in a 9-0 vote, giving the ACLU an apparent win.

Appendix C

ACLU / U.S. Supreme Court Case Summaries

continues in Volume III

THE FIRST 100 YEARS OF THE

ACLU

A COMPENDIUM OF ADVOCACY BEFORE THE UNITED STATES SUPREME COURT

VOLUME 1 OF 3

1920—2020

CONCEIVED AND COMPILED BY
STEVEN C. MARKOFF

CASE SUMMARY EDITOR
JESSICA PIERUCCI

FOREWORD BY
ERWIN CHEMERINSKY

A GENUINE RARE BIRD BOOK

Rare Bird Books
6044 North Figueroa Street
Los Angeles, California 90042
rarebirdbooks.com

FIRST HARDCOVER EDITION

ISBN-13: 978-1-64428-510-7 [THREE-VOLUME SLIPCASE SET]
ISBN-13: 978-1-64428-511-4 [VOLUME ONE]
ISBN-13: 978-1-64428-512-1 [VOLUME TWO]
ISBN-13: 978-1-64428-513-8 [VOLUME THREE]

For more information, address:
Rare Bird Books Subsidiary Rights Department
6044 North Figueroa Street
Los Angeles, California 90042

Printed in China

10 9 8 7 6 5 4 3 2 1

Library of Congress Cataloging-in-Publication Data available upon request

PHOTOGRAPHS IN THE CAROL M. HIGHSMITH ARCHIVE, LIBRARY OF CONGRESS, PRINTS AND PHOTOGRAPHS DIVISION.

The Term of the Court begins, by law, on the first Monday in October and lasts until the first Monday in October of the next year. Each Term, approximately 5,000-7,000 new cases are filed in the Supreme Court. This is a substantially larger volume of cases than was presented to the Court in the last century. In the 1950 Term, for example, the Court received only 1,195 new cases, and even as recently as the 1975 Term it received only 3,940.

Plenary review, with oral arguments by attorneys, is currently granted in about 80 of those cases each Term, and the Court typically disposes of about 100 or more cases without plenary review. The publication of each Term's written opinions, including concurring opinions, dissenting opinions, and orders, can take up thousands of pages. During the drafting process, some opinions may be revised a dozen or more times before they are announced." [1]

1 Accessed January 5, 2025.

This Three-Volume Set Versus the Companion Handbook

The companion to this three-volume set is the handbook pictured below.

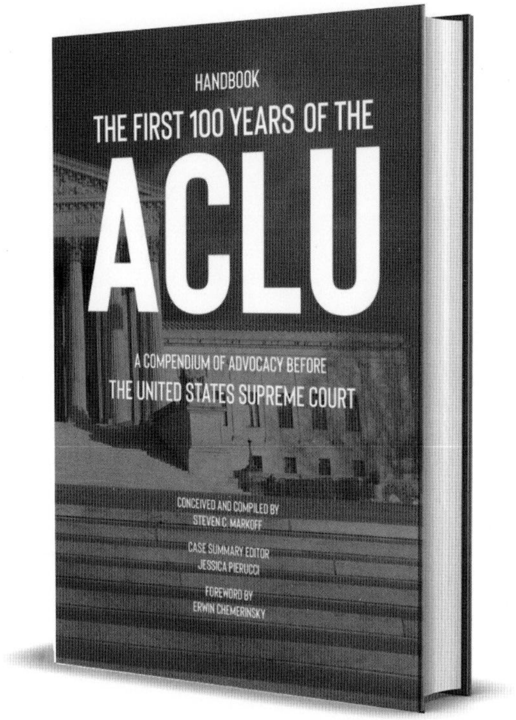

The Handbook contains the same data included in the three volumes, except it has only three (as samples) of the 1,193 cases in the three-volume compendium.

Volume I

Table of Contents

Foreword

The American Civil Liberties Union (ACLU) is unique among organizations. It exists solely to protect civil liberties and civil rights. It has done this brilliantly for a century. It has done so at the national level and the state and local levels. It has done so in the legislative and political processes and in the courts. Not surprisingly, many of these judicial battles have ended in the U.S. Supreme Court and led to crucial decisions that affect all of us, often in the most important and intimate aspects of our lives.

Surprisingly, though, no one has systematically chronicled the ACLU's history in the U.S. Supreme Court. That is the contribution of Steven Markoff and his history of the ACLU, the U.S. Constitution, and the U.S. Supreme Court. His focus is on the ACLU's involvement in the U.S. Supreme Court in the past century, from 1920 to 2020.

I must disclose that I am not an impartial observer of all of this. I have been an ACLU member my entire adult life. I served on the Board of Directors of the ACLU of Southern California for almost 15 years and on the Board of Directors of the ACLU of North Carolina for several years when I lived there. I have been directly or tangentially involved in many ACLU cases, including in the U.S. Supreme Court. I have spoken to the ACLU lawyers at their conferences for more than 30 years. One of my proudest awards (and one of the few plaques in my office) is the one naming me an honorary ACLU lawyer.

At the same time, I must confess that I do not always agree with the ACLU. I strongly disagree with its position on campaign finance and its view that spending money in election campaigns is speech. Unlike the ACLU, I regard *Citizens United v. Federal Election Commission*, which held that corporations can spend unlimited amounts of money in election campaigns, as terribly misguided.

But whether one agrees or disagrees with the ACLU in particular areas, there is no denying the importance of the ACLU as a force in the U.S. Supreme Court and in American law. Thanks to Steven Markoff's efforts, there now is a comprehensive listing of all of the U.S. Supreme Court cases in the last century with ACLU involvement. He provides clear and concise descriptions of the cases.

I especially liked the presentation of each justice's votes and how often each sided with the ACLU. It was interesting to see that Justice Louis Brandeis voted in favor of the ACLU position 87.5% of the time, while the arch-conservative Justice James McReynolds did so only 18.18% of the time. Justice William Douglas participated in 347 ACLU cases and was with the ACLU 87.9% of the time. By contrast, Associate Justice and then Chief Justice William Rehnquist participated in 718 ACLU cases, but voted in favor of the ACLU position only 25.91% of the time.

These are just some examples of the wealth of information to be learned from Steven Markoff's terrific work. I hope that he or someone else will continually update his work. It is a wonderful wealth of information about an enormously important organization. I have found that I frequently use it as a reference tool and can see how invaluable it is in countless ways.

Erwin Chemerinsky
Dean and Jesse H. Choper Distinguished
Professor of Law, University of
California, Berkeley School of Law
(August 2021)

Background

This project began shortly after I joined the Board of the ACLU Foundation of Southern California in 1979. I knew little about the Foundation or the ACLU before I joined, given that I joined primarily to offset the negative perception of my company's gold dealing with South Africa. At that time, South Africa was broadly seen as an international pariah given its Apartheid policies of treating non-whites as second-class citizens or worse.

Shortly after I joined the Foundation Board, I found its printed marketing material more fluff than substance. As there was no "welcome to the board" information package, I started asking what the Foundation and the ACLU actually did. I was then provided the ACLU's 62-word bylaws which left many questions:

> "The objects of the American Civil Liberties Union shall be to maintain and advance civil liberties, including the freedoms of association, press, religion, and speech, and rights to the franchised, to due process of law, and to equal protection of the laws to all people throughout the United States and its possessions. The Union's objects shall be sought wholly without political partisanship."[1]

While the ACLU's bylaws painted a comforting broad picture, I wanted to understand how the organization actually worked, what specifically it did, and how it made decisions about the various issues it was involved in. I was also interested in the issues it did not pursue. Wanting a more comprehensive view of the ACLU, I asked ACLU of Southern California Executive Director Ramona Ripston to introduce me to Ira Glasser, the then-national executive director of ACLU.

After a brief introduction, Mr. Glasser and I discussed the need and efficacy of a better understanding of the ACLU by its members, the media, and the general public. He agreed that a better understanding of the organization would be helpful. With my discussed donation to ACLU National, he agreed to draft a one-page description of what the ACLU did in layman's terms. Mr. Glasser then penned that draft (on page 7).

Despite my appreciation of the comprehensiveness and clarity of his draft, he was concerned that the document could somehow limit the ACLU's actions in the future. Based on that concern, he decided not to formalize his draft. His 1982 one-pager remains a draft to this day, but it's the best overall description of the ACLU I have so far encountered.

Armed with the ACLU bylaws and Mr. Glasser's one-pager, I decided to put together a modest, fact-based brochure on the ACLU, setting out who the organizers are, what they do, and an overview of various ACLU offices, its staffing, funding, and resources. In thinking about a marketing hook for the brochure, I decided to focus on the Union's legal victories and defeats in the Supreme Court of the United States (SCOTUS).

After some initial drafts of the brochure, the Southern California ACLU seemed to have little interest in it and I dropped the project. The question, though, of how the ACLU faired in the U.S. Supreme Court continued to fascinate me. Although I was a bit surprised the ACLU never kept a list of all of its SCOTUS cases, I decided to collect them all. Thus began my 40-year odyssey of collecting those cases and adding case overviews and data related to those cases. This work, therefore, ended with the last SCOTUS case the ACLU was involved in, Dep't of Commerce v. New York decided on June 27, 2019, before the ACLU's Centennial on January 19, 2020.[2]

— Steven C. Markoff

1 The American Civil Liberties Union Const. § 2
2 Date for establishment of the ACLU is from Samuel Walker's book *In Defense of American Liberties: A History of the ACLU* (New York: Oxford University Press, 1990). Although the ACLU was founded in 1920, its first SCOTUS case was in 1925.

I.

The ACLU—An Overview

The ACLU

The ACLU grew from the seeds of social activism in 1917 and was born in January 1920. Since its beginning, the ACLU has been a lightning rod for controversy, not least because the cases it has championed involve America's cherished civil rights.

Those rights have caused disagreements, fights, and litigation from the beginning of our country, and will most probably continue to do so. Those rights include freedom of the press (Is press freedom unfettered or subject to restraints?) to free speech (Who has it? When can they use it? Are there any limitations on it?) to equal protection (Who should expect equal treatment? Who should not? What is equal treatment across economic, gender, age, or racial lines?).

The ACLU was established to and has inserted itself squarely amid these and other constitutional and societal controversies.

Here is a sample of the many pros and cons about the Union[1]:

1. ACLU & DEFENSE OF INDIVIDUAL RIGHTS

PRO

"Over the years, the ACLU's fortunes have waxed and waned because it tends to attract or lose members following specific actions it undertakes. That waxing and waning demonstrates the organization's success at its sole endeavor, defending and preserving the individual freedoms granted through the Bill of Rights.

The ACLU has challenged literary censorship, segregation, cruel and unusual punishments, gender inequality, and violations of the right to privacy and freedom of religion. The ACLU is one of the informal checks and balances protecting individuals against tyranny."

—Judy Kutulas, PhD, professor of history at St. Olaf College, Email to ProCon.org, October 12, 2017

CON

"The ACLU is trying to deprive other organizations of freedoms that it would insist upon for itself. Their work is not a defense of equality—it is an effort to impose a certain view of morality on the country by law . . .

This organization, despite its name and origins, is now committed to a version of civil rights that cannot help but erode traditional American civil liberties.

The motto of the ACLU is, 'Because Freedom Can't Defend Itself.' The irony today is that freedom needs to be defended from the ACLU."

—Carson Holloway, PhD, associate professor of political science, University of Nebraska, "The ACLU's Betrayal of Civil Liberties," Public Discourse, March 26, 2015

2. ACLU & RELIGION

PRO

"Over the years, the ACLU has earned a reputation as the nation's foremost protector of the rights of individuals to practice their religion, as well as the chief opponent of both state aid to religion and enforcement of any religious belief by law. We support the separation of church and state for the same reason the founders of our country did: to promote and protect religious freedom by keeping the government out . . .

We believe that the place for religious displays, as with religious events and practices, is in the private sector—the home, the religious day school, or each person's place of worship.

Moreover, spirituality is undermined and religious symbols are trivialized when they are secularized in order to permit government endorsement."

—American Civil Liberties Union (ACLU), "ACLU Briefing Paper Number 3—Church and State," lectlaw.com, (Accessed November 22, 2017)

CON

"From its inception . . . the ACLU can be characterized as hostile to the Christian faith. In 1925, it was the ACLU that challenged the Tennessee law banning the teaching of the theory of evolution as a fact in the taxpayer-funded public schools. . . . Since the 1960s, the ACLU has been involved in the [U.S.] Supreme Court decisions which outlawed mandated school prayer, observation of religious holidays, and Bible reading in the public schools . . .

Current positions of the ACLU reflect this strongly secular agenda that bristles with hostility toward biblical Christianity. The organization supports same-sex marriage and the right of 'gays' to adopt children; the support of abortion rights; and the elimination of 'discrimination' against LGBTQ people."

—Steven Byas, med instructor, history & social studies education at Randall University, "ACLU Survey/Fundraising Letter Confirms Its Anti-Christian Bias," thenewamerican.com, April 19, 2016

3. ACLU & RIGHTS OF THE MINORITY

PRO

"I want to recognize the ACLU for its commitment to protecting our civil liberties.

You have a long and proud history of standing up to defend the freedoms guaranteed to us by the Bill of Rights and the Constitution . . .

1 "Top 10 Pro & Con Arguments: ACLU: ProCon.org." ProCon/Encyclopædia Britannica, February 18, 2020. https://aclu.procon.org/top-10-pro-con-arguments/#1 (with permission).

The ACLU seeks to prevent the 'tyranny of the majority' from destroying our fundamental liberties."

—*Robert S. Mueller, III, JD, former director of the Federal Bureau of Investigation (FBI), Speech to the 2003 Inaugural ACLU Membership Conference, fbi.gov, June 13, 2003*

CON

"[A] problem occurs when the ACLU wins cases that force the 'will' or viewpoint of a minority onto the will of the majority. In so doing, the ACLU uses the judicial branch of the government to undermine the rights of the majority, and thus to undermine the very foundations of our democracy, namely majority rule. When courts continuously side with a minority they create a society where the minority gain power over the majority, thus becoming the tyranny of the minority. This is just the opposite of a democracy."

—*Charles E. Steele, industrial designer "Democratic Republic Majority Rule & the ACLU Effect on Religious Freedom," free2pray.info, June 29, 2015*

4. ACLU & DEFENSE OF CRIMINALS

PRO

"The ACLU doesn't believe in 'going soft' on criminals.

The ACLU supports just, reasonable law enforcement, even tough enforcement.

However, we believe everyone is entitled to a fair trial and all rights of due process guaranteed by the Bill of Rights."

—*American Civil Liberties Union "FAQ," acluohio.org, (Accessed September 28, 2017)*

CON

"In a 1981 speech before the California Peace Officers Assn., former Attorney General Ed Meese referred to the American Civil Liberties Union (ACLU) as a 'criminals' lobby.' Lately, the American Criminal Liberties Union has been working harder than ever to justify its pejorative nickname . . . The ACLU has always advocated for the rights of criminals over their victims."

—*Robert H. Knight, MA, senior Fellow at the American Civil Rights Union, "The ACLU Goes Hunting in Montana," Washington Times, June 24, 2017*

5. ACLU & LIBERAL BIAS

PRO

"Since the ACLU was founded in 1920, there have been 17 presidents in the White House. They've come and gone, some better—and a few much worse—than others.

Throughout, the ACLU has remained steadfast in our nonpartisan mission of promoting civil rights and defending civil liberties—regardless of who's in office . . . America needs the ACLU as an independent voice for civil rights and civil liberties, ready to meet challenges and seize opportunities to promote equal justice for all . . . Especially in times of tyranny, the ACLU's liberty work is paramount."

—*Carol Rose, JD, executive director of the ACLU of Massachusetts, "ACLU: Defending Liberty and Democracy in an Election Year," The Docket, May 2016*

CON

"[T]he ACLU, which bills itself as 'our nation's guardian of liberty,' would more accurately be described as the guardian of a far-left progressive agenda… It hails itself as a defender of the right of 'everyone' to free speech, but if you want to exercise that right while lawfully carrying a gun, don't rely on the ACLU. It claims to defend religious freedom, but if you're a baker whose religion does not allow you to bake a cake for a same-sex marriage celebration, you will find the ACLU on the other side of the courtroom representing the same-sex couple suing you."

—*David E. Weisberg, JD, Ph.D., civil litigator and appellate lawyer, "ACLU Proves Yet Again It's a Guardian of Left-Wing Agenda," thehill.com, August 21, 2017*

6. ACLU & COMMUNISM

PRO

"Throughout the organization's history and particularly during the McCarthy era, the ACLU, its members, staff and founders have been accused of being Communists. The ACLU has no political affiliations and makes no test of individuals' ideological leanings a condition of membership or employment. Members and staff of the national ACLU and its affiliates may be Republicans, Democrats, Communists, Federalists, Libertarians, or members of any other political party or no party at all.

What the ACLU asks of its staff and officials is that they consistently defend civil liberties and the Constitution."

—*American Civil Liberties Union (ACLU) "FAQs: Does the ACLU Have Communist Roots? Was Co-founder Roger Baldwin a Communist?" aclu.org, (accessed September 11, 2017)*

CON

"In an effort to resist the conservative agenda of President Donald Trump, the ACLU organized everything from mass rallies to weekend house parties, where thousands were reported to have gathered over the weekend. Participants received a nine-point plan to resist established law and turn America into a network of 'freedom cities' that resist the Trump presidential agenda and the vote of the American people in the election of 2016. Uniting with Muslim congressman, Keith Ellison who also called for 'mass rallies' to stop Trump's conservative agenda, the ACLU hopes to turn America Democratic 'blue' by forcing its liberal Socialistic and Communistic agenda upon all America."

—*Stephen Flick, Ph.D., executive director of the Christian Heritage Fellowship, "ACLU Rattles Lifeless Bones of Communism" christianheritagefellowship.com, (accessed December 1, 2017)*

7. ACLU & NAZIS' RIGHTS

PRO

"If the ACLU allows the state to suppress the free speech rights of white nationalists or neo-Nazi groups—by refusing to defend such groups when the state tries to censor them or by allowing them to have inadequate representation—then the ACLU's ability to defend the free speech rights of groups and people that you like will be severely compromised . . .

The ACLU is not defending white supremacist groups but instead is defending a principle—one that it must defend if it is going to be successful in defending free speech rights for people you support."

—Glenn Greenwald, JD, lawyer and cofounding editor of The Intercept, "The Misguided Attacks on ACLU for Defending Neo-Nazis' Free Speech Rights in Charlottesville," theintercept.com, Aug. 13, 2017

CON

"For people who see themselves as anti-racists and anti-fascists first . . . the insistence that free speech will save us all rings somewhat hollow after this weekend [Unite the Right violence in Charlottesville, Aug. 2017]. Given limited energy and resources, maybe [the ACLU] defending the rights of violent bigots isn't the noble choice in every case—especially when those bigots predictably use their platform to silence others. Free speech absolutists [such as the ACLU] insist that free speech is the foundation of anti-fascism. But maybe anti-fascism is the basis of true free speech—in which case, defending the speech of bigots can, at least in some cases, leave us all less free."

Noah Berlatsky, MA, contributing writer for The Atlantic, "The Case Against Free Speech for Fascists," qz.com, August 15, 2017

8. ACLU & WAR ON TERROR

PRO

"The ACLU does not undermine the War on Terror. The organization does, however, insist that government actions taken to protect Americans from terrorism be consistent with our Constitution and the rule of law.

Acts of terrorism are, as the term itself indicates, intended to terrorize. Unfortunately, when people become fearful, they sometimes endorse measures that are ultimately self-defeating; the arrest of 'suspicious' people or the conduct of intrusive searches without probable cause, profiling individuals from certain ethnic groups based simply upon the way they look, 'interrogation' methods that are really torture outlawed by the Geneva conventions, and similar practices that are inconsistent with the 4th Amendment and with constitutional due process guarantees.

Research confirms that these panicky measures ultimately make Americans less safe. Not only do they encourage lawless behavior by some law enforcement officials, but they deepen divisions within the American population. Unconstitutional tactics create resentment and discourage co-operation with the authorities, and actually hinder the search for terrorists. Worse, as members of terrorist cells operating in hostile nations learn of American behaviors inconsistent with our own rules (Abu Ghraib comes to mind), they use those behaviors as centerpieces of their propaganda, as tools to recruit more terrorists, and as an excuse to mistreat Americans they capture."

—Sheila Suess Kennedy, JD, professor and director of Public Affairs Programs in the School of Public and Environmental Affairs at Indiana University-Purdue University Indianapolis, Email to ProCon.org, October17, 2017

CON

"The ACLU has worked diligently to undermine America's stance in what was formerly known as the 'war on terror,' and has even been willing to disseminate propaganda on behalf of our jihadist enemies.

If you think this is hyperbole or an exaggeration, consider a video released by the ACLU earlier this month titled 'Justice Denied: Voices from Guantanamo.'

As you would expect, the video portrays Gitmo in the worst possible light. But it goes well beyond any semblance of rational criticism. As Sahab, al Qaeda's media arm, could very well have produced it.

The short video is pure anti-American propaganda, starring men who have dedicated their lives to the jihadist cause."

—Thomas Joscelyn, senior Fellow at the Foundation for Defense of Democracies, "Al Qaeda's Civil Liberties Union," weeklystandard.com, November 17, 2009

9. ACLU & ABORTION

PRO

"As a journalist who has written about women's reproductive health issues for many years, I have had a front row seat at how the ACLU has continually stepped up at pivotal points to protect a woman's right to privacy, especially her right to control her own body and fertility, and to respond to the demands of her own conscience.

With the pace of threats of women's access to pregnancy termination and birth control services showing no signs of abating, the ACLU's role in defending those rights is arguably more urgent than ever before."

—Angela Bonavoglia, MSW, author, journalist, and blogger, Email to ProCon.org, November 6, 2017

CON

"[T]he American Civil Liberties Union (the ACLU is no friend of unborn babies) is suing the Food and Drug Administration to loosen the already-liberal regulations governing the chemical abortion drug [RU486]. The ACLU wants the abortion pill to be available by prescription in commercial pharmacies without a physician visit, leaving women to abort on their own. . . . If successful, the lawsuit would end safeguards for women as pro-abortion advocates more widely promote these drugs for profit.

Think about this for a moment. The ACLU and others are literally advocating for do-it-yourself abortion which can be perilous to women's health."

—*Bradley Mattes, MBS, president and CEO at the Life Issues Institute, "Silent, Deadly Abortion Tool Is Spreading," lifeissues.org, October 5, 2017*

10. ACLU & CHRISTMAS

PRO

"This year, several groups are once again introducing the Christmas season with some heated and misleading military rhetoric… One particularly bizarre charge is that there is 'a thorough and virulent anti-Christmas campaign.' Without a shred of evidence, they pretend that there is an effort afoot to remove 'God' from the Declaration of Independence. Two groups even announced that they have assembled hundreds of lawyers to protect Christmas against this imaginary threat…

First, Christmas displays—including nativity scenes—are perfectly acceptable at homes and churches. This religious expression is a valued and protected part of the First Amendment rights guaranteed to all citizens. Second, governments should not be in the business of endorsing religious displays.

Religion does best when government stays out of the business of deciding which holidays and religions to promote. Religion belongs where it prospers best: with individuals, families and religious communities.

And finally, as a seasonal greeting to all Christians: Merry Christmas from the ACLU!"

—*T. Jeremy Gunn, Ph.D., director, ACLU Program on Freedom of Religion and Belief, "A Fictional 'War on Christmas'," USA Today, December 18, 2005*

CON

"The ACLU is at it again. With an outrageous boldness that only they could muster, the ACLU has, once again, set their sights on Christmas celebrations. In their never-ending quest to completely eradicate all things religious from public life, the ACLU's latest lawsuit is an all-out frontal attack on the freedom of speech and the free exercise of religion.

Let me ask you—when did a children's Christmas program become 'an illegal activity'? When did the nativity story and Christmas songs become unconstitutional?

This is the outrageous and dangerous charge the ACLU has leveled against a school district in Tennessee. A children's Christmas program has been deemed to be an 'illegal act' because of the ACLU.

Today the American Center for Law and Justice has launched a nationwide campaign entitled 'Keep HIM in Christmas.' We want to make sure that Jesus is at the center of this holiday. We want to keep HIM in the nativity scenes, keep HIM in the music, keep HIM as the focal point—and not allow the ACLU to operate as our nationwide censor."

—*American Center for Law and Justice, "The ACLU Targets Christmas," ACLJ.org, November 28, 2006*

As the preceding pros and cons of the ACLU show, there are many different and conflicting views and feelings about what the ACLU is, has done, and is doing. What is indisputable is that the many SCOTUS cases the ACLU has been involved in have shaped America and our lives in many ways.

While this three-volume set (and its companion handbook) contains facts and metrics about the many ACLU/SCOTUS cases, the ACLU has always also been involved in many other issues and cases that never made it to the U.S. Supreme Court, or that did but were not accepted to be heard or not decided definitively.

In addition to the SCOTUS cases, the ACLU also handles many other issues and cases. Most of those issues are settled by research, discussion, negotiation, lobbying, and threats of litigation. When those less combative methods fail to change or modify actions or laws, the ACLU relies on the courts to try and accomplish what it couldn't accomplish by quicker, cheaper, and less combative methods.

Steven C. Markoff

II

Ira Glasser's 1982 Draft Statement Describing the ACLU

The American system of government is built on two basic principles: (1) the principle of majority rule, by democratic elections of temporary representatives; and (2) the principle that even democratic majorities must be limited in order to assure individual liberties.

This second principle is codified in the Bill of Rights and in federal and state legislation implementing the Bill of Rights. While the rest of the Constitution authorizes the government to act, the Bill of Rights limits the government's Authority to Act. It sets the ground rules for individual liberty, which includes the freedoms of speech, association and religion, freedom of the press, and the right to privacy, to equal protection under the laws and to due process of law.

The ACLU exists solely to defend and secure these rights and to extend them to groups that traditionally have been excluded from their protection.

Our work can be summarily categorized as follows:

1. First Amendment—The rights of speech, free association, and assembly, freedom of the press and freedom of religion, including the strict separation of Church and State.
2. Equal Protection of the Laws—The right [to] not be discriminated against on the basis of certain classifications, such as race, sex, religion, national origin, sexual orientation, age, physical handicap, etc.
3. Due Process of Law—The right to be treated fairly, including fair procedures when facing accusation of criminal conduct or other serious accusations that can lead to results like loss of employment, exclusion from school, denial of housing, cut-off of certain benefits or various punitive measures taken by administrative regulatory agencies.
4. Privacy—The right to a guaranteed zone of personal privacy and autonomy which cannot be penetrated by government, or by other institutions with substantial influence over one's life, such as employers.
5. Special Groups—The extension of all the right[s] described above to individuals traditionally denied the full protections of the Bill of Rights, such as mental patients, prisoners, soldiers, children in the custody of the state and other confined populations, as well as certain groups who are not confined but who nonetheless have not enjoyed full protection of the Bill of Rights: The handicapped, American Indians, homosexuals, women, and racial minorities.

Draft By
Ira Glasser
ACLU Executive Director, 1982

III

Win/Loss Record of the ACLU at SCOTUS by Count and Decade

The following chart shows the Union's wins and losses in the 1,193 decided ACLU/SCOTUS cases in the Union's first 100 years.[1] The first case was decided by the U.S. Supreme Court on June 8, 1925, and the last on June 27, 2019.

The win and loss tallies of those 1,193 cases may be the most objective presentation of data covering the actions of the ACLU during its first 100 years of existence. Different people will surely draw different conclusions from the data from those cases, but at least those conclusions will be based on the same data and statistics.

A few numbers from the chart that seem particularly worthy of notice:

- The ACLU was on the winning side 53.65% of the time in the 1,193 ACLU/SCOTUS decisions.
- The ACLU was on the winning side in 238 unanimous U.S. Supreme Court decisions while on the losing side in 122 unanimous decisions.
- 310 or 25.98% of the ACLU/SCOTUS's 1,193 decisions were 4–5 or 5–4, or 3–4 or 4–3.

1 Those 1,193 cases were decided from 1925 to 2019. The ACLU had no SCOTUS cases in its first five years and none in 2020. Those cases, therefore, occurred during 94 years of the ACLU's first 100 years. Those years included powerful events in our country such as the beginning of our country's labor unions, the Great Depression, World War II, the hunt for communists in the 1950s, the Korean War, Vietnam, the civil rights upheavals of the 1960s, the Iraq wars of 1991 and 2003, 9/11, and much of the Donald J. Trump presidency.

	WINS								LOSSES					
	A.	B.	C.	D.	E.	F.	G.	H.	I.	J.	K.	L.	M.	N.
	5-4	5-3	4-2	5-1	6-0				0-6	1-5	2-4	3-5	4-5	
	4-3	6-3	5-2	6-1	7-0				0-7	1-6	2-5	3-6	3-4	
			6-2	7-1	8-0	Total Wins	Total Cases	Total Losses	0-8	1-7	2-6			ACLU Decade Win %
Decade Ending Dec. 31			7-2	8-1	9-0				0-9	1-8	2-7			
1929	0	0	0	0	0	0	2	2	1	0	1	0	0	0
1939	1	0	3	1	3	8	8	0	0	0	0	0	0	100.00
1949	6	7	5	4	12	34	48	14	6	3	0	3	2	70.83
1959	4	5	5	7	14	35	53	18	2	2	0	6	8	66.04
1969	13	16	10	15	30	84	114	30	2	4	3	9	12	73.68
1979	19	25	19	20	32	115	220	105	11	14	15	39	26	52.27
1989	28	14	12	11	57	122	245	123	25	9	11	39	39	49.80
1999	20	14	12	6	44	96	182	86	22	7	14	19	24	52.75
2009	21	19	5	9	23	77	177	100	29	6	10	19	36	43.50
2019	20	14	6	6	23	69	144	75	24	2	11	7	31	47.92
Total – 100 years[1]	132	114	77	79	238	**640**	**1,193**[2]	**553**	122	47	65	141	178	53.65
						53.65%		**46.35%**						

1 The first ACLU/SCOTUS case (*Gitlow v. New York*) was decided on June 8, 1925. The last ACLU/SCOTUS case (*Dep't of Commerce v. New York*) was decided on June 27, 2019. There were no ACLU/SCOTUS cases decided in 2020.
2 29 of the 51 justices (56.86%) who voted on the 1,193 cases were appointed by Republican presidents (on page 89).

IV

The ACLU's Wins and Losses at SCOTUS

(Alphabetically by Case Title)

The following chart lists the 1,193 decided ACLU/SCOTUS cases alphabetically, showing where each case can be found in this three-volume set. For example, on page 11, in Columns G / H, the case summary for *Abrams v. Johnson,* case number 2, is found in Vol. 2 as case number 829.

During the years of putting this data together, I was asked, on numerous occasions, how many times the ACLU was a party in its SCOTUS cases. Column D, also on page 11, shows that the ACLU was a party in seven of the 1,193 cases. The Xs in that column mark those cases.

In addition to Columns E / F on page 11 showing which cases were considered ACLU wins or losses, the chart in columns B, C, and D also shows the ACLU's category of involvement in these 1,193 ACLU/SCOTUS cases:

- **975** cases or **81.73%** of the 1,193 cases were amicus filings
- **211** cases, or **17.69%**, were as "Attorney of Record / ACLU Attorney" (see footnote number 2 on page 11)
- **Seven** cases or **.59%** were when the ACLU was a party in a case

N.B. Column C, Attorney of Record/ACLU Attorney, is probably not complete as it would take years to complete if it ever could be accurately compiled. Completing that column would entail at least tracking each lawyer listed on each SCOTUS brief and those attorneys contributing to those briefs, as well as researching which of those attorneys met this work's criteria to be counted as an ACLU attorney.

Chart: *The ACLU's Wins and Losses at SCOTUS (Alphabetically by Case Title)*[1]

1 The cases in Column A are listed in alphabetical order, with cases beginning with a number being listed first. The cases that have the exact same name are listed by earliest date first. The year the case was decided is in parentheses only for the cases with the same name; full dates are added if they also share the same year and are put in order from earliest to most recent date.

		ACLU's Case Involvement						
	Case Name	Amicus	Attorney of Record / ACLU Attorney	As A Party	Wins	Losses	Vol #1,#2, or #3	Case # in Volume
	A	B	C	D	E	F	G	H
	Total	**975**	**211**[1]	**7**	**640**	**553**		
1	44 Liquormart, Inc. v. Rhode Island	x			√		2	797
2	Abrams v. Johnson		x			√	2	829
3	Adams v. Williams	x				√	1	272
4	Adarand Constructors, Inc. v. Mineta	x			√		3	915
5	Aday v. United States	x			√		1	194
6	Adler v. Board of Education	x				√	1	69
7	Adoptive Couple v. Baby Girl	x				√	3	1115
8	Advocate Health Care Network v. Stapleton	x				√	3	1158
9	Agency for Int'l Dev. v. Alliance for Open Society Int'l	x			√		3	1113
10	Agostini v. Felton	x				√	2	830
11	Aguilar v. Felton	x			√		2	570
12	Alabama State Federation of Labor v. McAdory	x				√	1	33
13	Alabama v. Pugh		x			√	1	417

2 There are 231 cases shown with Xs for "Attorney of Record / ACLU Attorney." Twenty of those cases were with the "Amicus" or with "As a Party" cases. So as not to double the count, the 20 were grayed out in Column C for ease of viewing.

The ACLU's Wins and Losses at SCOTUS (Alphabetically by Case Title)

		ACLU's Case Involvement						
	Case Name	*Amicus*	*Attorney of Record / ACLU Attorney*	*As A Party*	*Wins*	*Losses*	*Vol #1,#2, or #3*	*Case # in Volume*
	A	B	C	D	E	F	G	H
14	Alabama v. White	x				√	2	704
15	Albertson v. Millard	x			√		1	76
16	Albertson v. Subversive Activities Control Board	x			√		1	170
17	Albright v. Oliver	x				√	2	767
18	Alexander v. Sandoval		x			√	3	898
19	Alexander v. United States	x				√	2	761
20	Alice Corp. v. CLS Bank Int'l	x			√		3	1124
21	Allen v. McCurry	x				√	2	459
22	Alleyne v. U.S.	x			√		3	1111
23	Alvarez v. Smith	x				√	3	1049
24	Amalgamated Food Employees Union Local 590 v. Logan Valley Plaza, Inc.	x			√		1	202
25	American Committee for Protection of Foreign Born v. Subversive Activities Control Board	x			√		1	162
26	American Communications Ass'n v. Douds	x				√	1	61
27	American Foreign Service Ass'n v. Garfinkel	x			√		2	675
28	American Legion v. American Humanist Ass'n	x				√	3	1187
29	Anderson v. Celebrezze	x			√		2	501
30	Anderson v. City of Bessemer	x			√		2	555
31	Anderson v. Creighton	x				√	2	629
32	Ankenbrandt v. Richards	x			√		2	741
33	Apodaca v. Oregon	x				√	1	266
34	Aptheker v. Secretary of State	x			√		1	155
35	Arcara v. Cloud Books Inc.	x				√	2	599
36	Arizona Christian School Tuition Organization v. Winn		x			√	3	1072
37	Arizona Governing Committee for Tax Deferred Annuity & Deferred Compensation Plans v. Norris	x			√		2	522
38	Arizona State Legislature v. Arizona Indep. Redistricting Comm'n	x			√		3	1142
39	Arizona v. Evans	x				√	2	779
40	Arizona v. Gant (2003)	x				√	3	952
41	Arizona v. Gant (2009)	x			√		3	1040
42	Arizona v. Hicks	x			√		2	607
43	Arizona v. Inter Tribal Council of Arizona		x		√		3	1110
44	Arizona v. U.S.	x			√		3	1098
45	Arizonans for Official English v. Arizona	x				√	2	817
46	Arkansas Educational Television Commission v. Forbes	x				√	2	846
47	Arkansas Writers' Project, Inc. v. Ragland	x			√		2	613
48	Armstrong v. Exceptional Child Center, Inc.	x				√	3	1132
49	Ashcroft v. al-Kidd		x			√	3	1077
50	Ashcroft v. American Civil Liberties Union (2002)		x	x		√	3	922
51	Ashcroft v. American Civil Liberties Union (2004)		x	x	√		3	973
52	Ashcroft v. Free Speech Coalition	x			√		3	921
53	Ass'n for Molecular Pathology v. Myriad Genetics		x		√		3	1109

The ACLU's Wins and Losses at SCOTUS (Alphabetically by Case Title)

		ACLU's Case Involvement						
	Case Name	Amicus	Attorney of Record / ACLU Attorney	As A Party	Wins	Losses	Vol #1,#2, or #3	Case # in Volume
	A	B	C	D	E	F	G	H
54	Associated Enterprises, Inc. v. Toltec Watershed Improvement District	x				√	1	297
55	Astrup v. I.N.S.		x		√		1	246
56	Atascadero State Hospital v. Scanlon	x				√	2	568
57	Atkins v. Virginia	x			√		3	928
58	Atwater v. City of Lago Vista	x				√	3	899
59	Austin v. Michigan Chamber of Commerce	x				√	2	699
60	Austin v. United States	x			√		2	762
61	Ayestas v. Davis	x			√		3	1171
62	Ayotte v. Planned Parenthood of Northern New England		x			√	3	994
63	Babbitt v. United Farm Workers National Union	x				√	2	433
64	Baggett v. Bullitt		x		√		1	150
65	Bailey v. U.S.	x			√		3	1102
66	Baker v. McCollan	x				√	2	440
67	Ball v. James	x				√	2	466
68	Ballard v. Commissioner of Internal Revenue	x	x		√		3	981
69	Bank of America Corp. v. City of Miami	x			√		3	1156
70	Bank of Nova Scotia v. United States	x				√	2	652
71	Barber v. Thomas	x				√	3	1061
72	Barefoot v. Estelle	x				√	2	521
73	Barenblatt v. United States		x			√	1	108
74	Barnes v. Glen Theatre, Inc.	x				√	2	724
75	Barrows v. Jackson	x			√		1	77
76	Bartlett v. Strickland	x				√	3	1038
77	Bartnicki v. Vopper	x			√		3	901
78	Baze v. Rees	x				√	3	1025
79	Bd. of Ed. of Indep. Sch. Dist. No. 92 of Pottawatomie Cty. v. Earls		x			√	3	933
80	Bd. of Regents of Univ. of Texas System v. New Left Education Project		x			√	1	259
81	Beard v. Banks (2004)	x				√	3	967
82	Beard v. Banks (2006)	x				√	3	1006
83	Beauharnais v. Illinois		x			√	1	73
84	Beck v. Ohio	x			√		1	156
85	Bell v. Cone	x				√	3	924
86	Bell v. Hood	x	x		√		1	40
87	Bell v. Ohio	x			√		1	415
88	Bell v. Wolfish	x				√	2	428
89	Bellotti v. Baird		x		√		2	444
90	Bender v. Williamsport Area School District	x				√	2	581
91	Benisek v. Lamone	x				√	3	1177
92	Berger v. New York	x			√		1	193
93	Berghuis v. Smith	x				√	3	1054
94	Berghuis v. Thompkins	x				√	3	1060
95	Berkemer v. McCarty	x			√		2	550

The ACLU's Wins and Losses at SCOTUS (Alphabetically by Case Title)

		ACLU's Case Involvement						
	Case Name	*Amicus*	*Attorney of Record / ACLU Attorney*	*As A Party*	*Wins*	*Losses*	*Vol #1,#2, or #3*	*Case # in Volume*
	A	B	C	D	E	F	G	H
96	Berry v. Doles		x		√		1	413
97	Betts v. Brady	x				√	1	16
98	Bigelow v. Virginia		x		√		1	359
99	Birchfield v. North Dakota	x			√		3	1150
100	Bivens v. Six Unknown Named Agents of Federal Bureau of Narcotics	x			√		1	253
101	Black v. Cutter Laboratories	x				√	1	88
102	Blakely v. Washington	x			√		3	966
103	Blanton v. City of North Las Vegas, Nevada	x				√	2	668
104	Blessing v. Freestone	x				√	2	822
105	Blum v. Stenson	x			√		2	527
106	Board of County Commissioners, Wabaunsee County, Kansas v. Umbehr	x			√		2	809
107	Board of Curators of the University of Missouri v. Horowitz	x				√	1	403
108	Board of Directors of Rotary Int'l v. Rotary Club of Duarte	x			√		2	616
109	Board of Education of Oklahoma City v. Dowell	x				√	2	712
110	Board of Education v. Pico		x		√		2	491
111	Board Of Education v. Rowley	x				√	2	492
112	Board of Estimate of New York v. Morris		x		√		2	672
113	Board of Regents of the University of Wisconsin System v. Southworth	x			√		3	878
114	Bob Jones University v. United States	x			√		2	507
115	Bolger v. Youngs Drug Products Corp.	x			√		2	514
116	Bond v. Floyd	x			√		1	180
117	Boos v. Barry	x			√		2	640
118	Booth v. Churner	x				√	3	903
119	Borough of Duryea v. Guarnieri	x				√	3	1081
120	Bose Corp. v. Consumers Union, Inc.	x			√		2	533
121	Boston Firefighters Union, Local 718 v. Boston Chapter, NAACP	x				√	2	506
122	Boumediene v. Bush	x			√		3	1031
123	Bousley v. United States	x			√		2	844
124	Boutilier v. Immigration and Naturalization Service	x				√	1	188
125	Bowen v. City of New York	x			√		2	587
126	Bowen v. Gilliard	x				√	2	628
127	Bowen v. Kendrick		x			√	2	657
128	Boy Scouts of America v. Dale	x				√	3	888
129	Braden v. 30th Judicial Circuit Court of Kentucky	x			√		1	294
130	Bragdon v. Abbott	x			√		2	851
131	Brandenburg v. Ohio		x		√		1	221
132	Branzburg v. Hayes	x				√	1	283
133	Bray v. Alexandria Women's Health Clinic	x				√	2	751
134	Brecht v. Abrahamson	x				√	2	752
135	Brendlin v. California	x			√		3	1017

The ACLU's Wins and Losses at SCOTUS (Alphabetically by Case Title)

		ACLU's Case Involvement						
	Case Name	*Amicus*	*Attorney of Record / ACLU Attorney*	*As A Party*	*Wins*	*Losses*	*Vol #1,#2, or #3*	*Case # in Volume*
	A	B	C	D	E	F	G	H
136	Bridges v. California	x			√		1	14
137	Bridges v. Wixon	x			√		1	37
138	Brockington v. Rhodes		x			√	1	224
139	Browder v. Director, Department of Corrections	x			√		1	400
140	Brown v. Board of Education	x			√		1	79
141	Brown v. Chote	x			√		1	304
142	Brown v. Entertainment Merchants Ass'n	x			√		3	1083
143	Brown v. Plata	x			√		3	1075
144	Brunner v. United States		x		√		1	72
145	Buckhannon Board & Care Home, Inc. v. West Virginia Department of Health & Human Resources	x				√	3	902
146	Bucklew v. Precythe	x				√	3	1183
147	Buckley v. American Constitutional Law Foundation, Inc.	x			√		3	856
148	Buckley v. Valeo		x		√		1	366
149	Burch v. Louisiana	x			√		2	426
150	Burdick v. Takushi		x			√	2	740
151	Burlington Northern & Santa Fe Ry. Co. v. White	x			√		3	1003
152	Burnett v. Grattan	x			√		2	545
153	Burns v. Reed	x			√		2	719
154	Burwell v. Hobby Lobby Stores, Inc.	x				√	3	1128
155	Bush v. Lucas	x				√	2	511
156	Bush v. Palm Beach County Canvassing Board	x				√	3	893
157	Butler v. Michigan	x			√		1	91
158	Butterworth v. Smith	x			√		2	698
159	Byrd v. United States	x			√		3	1172
160	Byrne v. Karalexis	x				√	1	238
161	Caban v. Mohammed	x			√		2	427
162	Calcano-Martinez v. INS		x		√		3	910
163	Calhoon v. Harvey	x				√	1	157
164	Califano v. Goldfarb		x		√		1	382
165	Califano v. Westcott	x			√		2	438
166	California Federal Savings & Loan Association v. Guerra	x			√		2	602
167	California Medical Ass'n v. Federal Election Commission	x				√	2	479
168	California v. Brown	x				√	2	605
169	California v. Ciraolo	x				√	2	586
170	California v. Krivda	x				√	1	286
171	Camara v. Municipal Court of City & County of San Francisco		x		√		1	190
172	Campbell v. Acuff-Rose Music, Inc.	x			√		2	769
173	Capital Cities Cable, Inc. v. Crisp	x			√		2	543
174	Capitol Square Review & Advisory Board v. Pinette		x		√		2	789
175	Carey v. Population Services International	x			√		1	389
176	Carlson v. California	x			√		1	11
177	Carlson v. Green	x			√		2	448

The ACLU's Wins and Losses at SCOTUS (Alphabetically by Case Title)

		ACLU's Case Involvement						
	Case Name	*Amicus*	*Attorney of Record / ACLU Attorney*	*As A Party*	*Wins*	*Losses*	*Vol #1,#2, or #3*	*Case # in Volume*
	A	B	C	D	E	F	G	H
178	Carlson v. Landon		x			√	1	70
179	Carlucci v. Doe	x				√	2	660
180	Carpenter v. United States		x		√		3	1178
181	Carroll v. President & Comm'rs of Princess Anne		x		√		1	211
182	Castaneda v. Partida		x		√		1	383
183	CBOCS West, Inc. v. Humphries	x			√		3	1029
184	Chamber of Commerce of U.S. v. Whiting		x			√	3	1076
185	Chandler v. Miller	x			√		2	821
186	Chappell v. Wallace	x				√	2	509
187	Chavez v. Martinez	x				√	3	941
188	Chevron U.S.A., Inc. v. Echazabal	x				√	3	925
189	Christian Legal Society v. Martinez	x			√		3	1065
190	Christopher v. Harbury	x				√	3	929
191	Church of Lukumi Babalu Aye, Inc. v. City of Hialeah		x		√		2	758
192	Church of Scientology of California v. Internal Revenue Service	x				√	2	632
193	Citizens United v. Federal Election Com'n	x			√		3	1052
194	City and County of San Francisco v. Sheehan	x				√	3	1134
195	City of Akron v. Akron Center for Reproductive Health, Inc.		x		√		2	512
196	City of Boerne v. Flores	x				√	2	834
197	City of Canton, Ohio v. Harris	x				√	2	667
198	City of Chicago v. Morales		x		√		3	865
199	City of Cleburne v. Cleburne Living Center	x			√		2	571
200	City of Edmonds v. Oxford House, Inc.		x		√		2	782
201	City of Houston v. Hill	x			√		2	624
202	City of Indianapolis v. Edmond		x		√		3	892
203	City of Ladue v. Gilleo		x		√		2	773
204	City of Lakewood v. Plain Dealer Publishing Co.	x			√		2	647
205	City of Los Angeles v. Preferred Communications, Inc.	x			√		2	588
206	City of Los Angeles, Department of Water and Power v. Manhart	x			√		1	406
207	City of Ontario v. Quon	x				√	3	1063
208	City of Renton v. Playtime Theatres, Inc.	x				√	2	577
209	City of Revere v. Massachusetts General Hospital	x			√		2	516
210	City of Richmond v. J.A. Croson Co.	x				√	2	663
211	City of Springfield v. Kibbe	x			√		2	606
212	Clapper v. Amnesty Int'l USA		x			√	3	1104
213	Clark v. Community for Creative Non-Violence		x			√	2	547
214	Clark v. Jeter	x			√		2	646
215	Clark v. Martinez	x			√		3	977
216	Clark v. Roemer	x			√		2	721
217	Class v. United States	x			√		3	1169
218	Cleveland Board of Education v. LaFleur	x			√		1	324
219	Cleveland Board of Education v. Loudermill	x			√		2	554

The ACLU's Wins and Losses at SCOTUS (Alphabetically by Case Title)

		ACLU's Case Involvement						
	Case Name	Amicus	Attorney of Record / ACLU Attorney	As A Party	Wins	Losses	Vol #1,#2, or #3	Case # in Volume
	A	B	C	D	E	F	G	H
220	Clinton v. Jones	x			√		2	827
221	Cohen v. California	x			√		1	249
222	Coker v. Georgia	x			√		1	398
223	Colautti v. Franklin	x			√		1	420
224	Cole v. Young		x		√		1	89
225	Coleman v. Court of Appeals of Maryland	x				√	3	1090
226	Collins v. City of Harker Heights, Texas	x				√	2	734
227	Collins v. Hardyman		x			√	1	65
228	Colorado Republican Federal Campaign Committee v. Federal Election Commission	x			√		2	808
229	Colorado v. Bertine	x				√	2	603
230	Colten v. Kentucky		x			√	1	271
231	Columbus Board of Education v. Penick	x			√		2	443
232	Communist Party of Indiana v. Whitcomb		x		√		1	322
233	Communist Party of the United States v. Subversive Activities Control Board	x			√		1	87
234	Communist Party v. Subversive Activities Control Board	x				√	1	124
235	Congress of Industrial Organizations v. McAdory	x				√	1	34
236	Connecticut Dep't of Pub. Safety v. Doe		x			√	3	934
237	Connell v. Higginbotham		x		√		1	251
238	Connick v. Myers	x				√	2	502
239	Connick v. Thompson	x				√	3	1071
240	Cornelius v. NAACP Legal Defense and Educational Fund, Inc.	x				√	2	572
241	Corning Glass Works v. Brennan	x			√		1	333
242	Corp. for the Presiding Bishop of the Church of Jesus Christ of Latter-Day Saints v. Amos		x			√	2	612
243	Correctional Services Corp. v. Malesko	x				√	3	914
244	Costello v. United States	x				√	1	84
245	County of Allegheny v. American Civil Liberties Union Greater Pittsburgh Chapter		x	x	√		2	690
246	County of Los Angeles v. Davis	x				√	2	423
247	County of Los Angeles v. Mendez	x				√	3	1157
248	County of Riverside v. McLaughlin	x				√	2	716
249	County of Washington v. Gunther	x			√		2	475
250	Craig v. Boren	x			√		1	380
251	Crawford v. Marion County Election Bd.		x			√	3	1027
252	Crawford v. Metropolitan Government of Nashville & Davidson County, Tennessee	x			√		3	1036
253	Crawford v. Washington	x			√		3	959
254	Crawford-El v. Britton	x			√		2	842
255	Crooker v. California	x				√	1	104
256	Crosby v. United States	x			√		2	750
257	Cruzan v. Director, Missouri Department of Health		x			√	2	706
258	Cullen v. Pinholster	x				√	3	1073
259	Cupp v. Murphy	x				√	1	309

The ACLU's Wins and Losses at SCOTUS (Alphabetically by Case Title)

	Case Name	ACLU's Case Involvement: Amicus	Attorney of Record / ACLU Attorney	As A Party	Wins	Losses	Vol #1,#2, or #3	Case # in Volume
	A	B	C	D	E	F	G	H
260	Cutter v. Wilkinson	x			√		3	984
261	Danforth v. Minnesota	x			√		3	1024
262	Davila v. Davis	x				√	3	1166
263	Davis v. Bandemer	x				√	2	596
264	Davis v. Monroe County Board of Education	x			√		3	864
265	Davis v. Passman	x			√		2	431
266	Davis v. Scherer	x				√	2	546
267	Davis v. United States (1973)		x			√	1	302
268	Davis v. United States (1974)		x		√		1	334
269	Davis v. Washington	x				√	3	1000
270	Dawson v. Delaware	x			√		2	735
271	Dayton Board of Education v. Brinkman	x				√	1	397
272	De Jonge v. Oregon		x		√		1	6
273	De Veau v. Braisted	x				√	1	114
274	Deakins v. Monaghan	x			√		2	634
275	DeFunis v. Odegaard	x				√	1	330
276	Delaware v. Prouse		x		√		2	424
277	Dellmuth v. Muth	x				√	2	685
278	Delta Air Lines, Inc. v. August	x			√		2	461
279	Demore v. Kim		x			√	3	939
280	Dennis v. Sparks	x			√		2	458
281	Dennis v. United States	x			√		1	179
282	Denton v. Hernandez	x				√	2	738
283	Denver Area Educational Telecommunications Consortium, Inc. v. Federal Communications Commission		x		√		2	811
284	Dep't of Commerce v. New York		x		√		3	1193
285	Dep't of Hous. & Urban Dev. v. Rucker	x				√	3	919
286	Dep't of the Air Force v. Rose		x		√		1	369
287	Department of Commerce v. United States House of Representatives	x				√	3	858
288	Department of the Navy v. Egan	x				√	2	637
289	Desert Palace, Inc. v. Costa	x			√		3	942
290	DeShaney v. Winnebago County Department of Social Services	x				√	2	666
291	Dickerson v. United States	x			√		3	887
292	Diffenderfer v. Central Baptist Church of Miami		x		√		1	256
293	District Attorney's Office for the Third Judicial Dist. v. Osborne	x				√	3	1045
294	District of Columbia v. Carter		x			√	1	288
295	District of Columbia v. Wesby	x				√	3	1168
296	Doe v. Bolton		x		√		1	292
297	Doe v. Chao	x				√	3	957
298	Dombrowski v. Pfister	x			√		1	161
299	Doremus v. Board of Education	x				√	1	68
300	Dorsey v. U.S.	x			√		3	1097

The ACLU's Wins and Losses at SCOTUS (Alphabetically by Case Title)

		ACLU's Case Involvement						
	Case Name	**Amicus**	**Attorney of Record / ACLU Attorney**	**As A Party**	**Wins**	**Losses**	**Vol #1,#2, or #3**	**Case # in Volume**
	A	B	C	D	E	F	G	H
301	Dorszynski v. United States	x			√		1	345
302	Dothard v. Rawlinson	x			√		1	396
303	Douglas v. Independent Living Center of Southern California, Inc.	x				√	3	1089
304	Dunaway v. New York	x			√		2	430
305	Duncan v. Kahanamoku	x			√		1	39
306	Dunn v. Blumstein		x		√		1	260
307	Duren v. Missouri		x		√		1	419
308	Dyson v. Stein		x			√	1	237
309	E.E.O.C. v. Abercrombie & Fitch Stores	x			√		3	1136
310	Easley v. Cromartie	x			√		3	897
311	Eastland v. United States Servicemen's Fund		x			√	1	358
312	Edmonson v. Leesville Concrete Co.	x			√		2	720
313	Edward J. DeBartolo Corp. v. Florida Gulf Coast Building & Construction Trades Council	x			√		2	643
314	Edwards v. Aguillard		x		√		2	625
315	Edwards v. Balisok	x				√	2	825
316	Edwards v. California		x		√		1	13
317	EEOC v. Waffle House, Inc.	x			√		3	916
318	Ehlert v. United States		x			√	1	243
319	Eisen v. Carlisle & Jacquelin	x				√	1	332
320	Eisenstadt v. Baird	x			√		1	262
321	Elder v. Holloway	x			√		2	768
322	Elk Grove United School District v. Newdow	x				√	3	962
323	Ellis v. Dyson		x		√		1	357
324	Elonis v. United States	x			√		3	1135
325	Employment Division v. Smith	x				√	2	700
326	Emspak v. United States	x			√		1	80
327	Engel v. Vitale		x		√		1	134
328	Engquist v. Oregon Department of Agriculture	x				√	3	1030
329	Environmental Protection Agency v. Mink	x				√	1	290
330	Epic Systems Corp. v. Lewis	x				√	3	1173
331	Epperson v. Arkansas	x			√		1	210
332	Equal Employment Opportunity Commission v. Arabian American Oil Co.	x				√	2	714
333	Erie v. Pap's A. M.	x				√	3	881
334	Escambia County v. McMillan	x				√	2	528
335	Escobedo v. Illinois	x			√		1	154
336	Estes v. Texas	x			√		1	169
337	Evans v. Jeff D.	x				√	2	583
338	Evenwel v. Abbott	x			√		3	1145
339	Everson v. Board of Education	x				√	1	44
340	Ex parte Endo	x			√		1	31
341	F.C.C. v. Fox Television Stations, Inc.	x				√	3	1042
342	Falbo v. United States	x				√	1	24

The ACLU's Wins and Losses at SCOTUS (Alphabetically by Case Title)

	Case Name	ACLU's Case Involvement: Amicus	ACLU's Case Involvement: Attorney of Record / ACLU Attorney	ACLU's Case Involvement: As A Party	Wins	Losses	Vol #1,#2, or #3	Case # in Volume
	A	B	C	D	E	F	G	H
343	Faragher v. City of Boca Raton	x			√		2	852
344	Farmer v. Brennan		x		√		2	772
345	Farmers Educational & Cooperative Union v. WDAY, Inc.	x			√		1	110
346	FCC v. AT&T Inc.	x			√		3	1068
347	FCC v. Fox Television Stations	x				√	3	1096
348	FCC v. League of Women Voters	x			√		2	549
349	FCC v. Midwest Video Corp.		x	x		√	2	425
350	FCC v. Pacifica Foundation	x				√	1	416
351	FEC v. Colo. Republican Fed. Campaign Comm.	x				√	3	911
352	Federal Election Commission v. Akins	x				√	2	847
353	Federal Election Commission v. Massachusetts Citizens For Life, Inc.	x			√		2	601
354	Federal Election Commission v. National Conservative Political Action Committee	x			√		2	553
355	Federal Election Commission v. Wisconsin Right to Life, Inc.	x			√		3	1019
356	Federal Trade Commission v. Superior Court Trial Lawyers Ass'n	x			√		2	693
357	Fein v. Selective Service System Local Board No. 7	x				√	1	261
358	Ferguson v. City of Charleston	x			√		3	895
359	Fernandez-Vargas v. Gonzales	x				√	3	1002
360	First Unitarian Church v. County of Los Angeles	x			√		1	107
361	Fisher v. Univ. of Texas at Austin	x			√		3	1151
362	Fitzgerald v. Barnstable School Comm.	x			√		3	1035
363	Fitzpatrick v. Bitzer	x			√		1	375
364	Flanagan v. United States	x			√		2	524
365	Florence v. Board of Chosen Freeholders of County of Burlington	x				√	3	1094
366	Florida v. Bostick	x				√	2	723
367	Florida v. Harris	x				√	3	1103
368	Florida v. J. L.	x			√		3	880
369	Florida v. Riley	x				√	2	662
370	Flower v. United States		x		√		1	273
371	Follett v. Town of McCormick	x			√		1	25
372	Forsyth County v. Nationalist Movement	x			√		2	743
373	Fort Wayne Books, Inc. v. Indiana	x			√		2	665
374	Fox v. Vice	x			√		3	1078
375	Frank v. Minnesota Newspaper Ass'n, Inc.	x				√	2	676
376	Franks v. Delaware	x			√		1	412
377	Frazee v. Illinois Dep't of Employment Security	x			√		2	674
378	Freedman v. Maryland	x			√		1	158
379	Freeman v. Pitts	x	x			√	2	736
380	Frew v. Hawkins	x			√		3	956
381	Friends of the Earth v. Laidlaw Environmental Services	x			√		3	875
382	Frisby v. Schultz	x				√	2	655

The ACLU's Wins and Losses at SCOTUS (Alphabetically by Case Title)

		ACLU's Case Involvement						
	Case Name	*Amicus*	*Attorney of Record / ACLU Attorney*	*As A Party*	*Wins*	*Losses*	*Vol #1,#2, or #3*	*Case # in Volume*
	A	B	C	D	E	F	G	H
383	Frontiero v. Richardson	x	x		√		1	306
384	Fry v. Napoleon Community Schools		x		√		3	1153
385	Fullilove v. Klutznick	x			√		2	456
386	Furman v. Georgia	x			√		1	280
387	Gallagher v. Crown Kosher Super Market of Massachusetts, Inc.	x				√	1	123
388	Gamble v. United States	x				√	3	1186
389	Gannett Co. v. DePasquale	x				√	2	442
390	Garcetti v. Ceballos	x				√	3	998
391	Garner v Board of Public Works	x				√	1	66
392	Garner v. Jones	x				√	3	879
393	Geduldig v. Aiello	x				√	1	336
394	Gelbard v. United States	x			√		1	278
395	General Electric Co. v. Gilbert	x				√	1	379
396	Gentile v. State Bar of Nevada	x			√		2	726
397	Georgia v. Ashcroft	x				√	3	949
398	Gideon v. Wainwright	x	x		√		1	137
399	Gill v. Whitford	x				√	3	1176
400	Gillette v. United States		x			√	1	239
401	Gilligan v. Morgan		x			√	1	311
402	Gilmore v. Taylor	x				√	2	754
403	Ginsberg v. New York	x				√	1	199
404	Ginzburg v. United States	x				√	1	172
405	Girouard v. United States	x			√		1	41
406	Gitlow v. New York		x			√	1	1
407	Godinez v. Moran	x				√	2	759
408	Gojack v. United States		x		√		1	177
409	Golan v. Holder	x				√	3	1086
410	Goldberg v. Kelly		x		√		1	226
411	Goldman v. Weinberger	x				√	2	580
412	Gomez v. Perez	x			√		1	289
413	Gomez v. Toledo	x			√		2	451
414	Gomillion v. Lightfoot	x			√		1	116
415	Gonzaga Univ. v. Doe	x				√	3	927
416	Gonzales v. Carhart	x				√	3	1011
417	Gonzales v. Landon	x			√		1	82
418	Gonzales v. O Centro Espírita Beneficente União do Vegetal	x			√		3	996
419	Gonzales v. Oregon	x			√		3	993
420	Good News Club v. Milford Central School	x				√	3	907
421	Gordon v. Lance	x				√	1	248
422	Gori v. United States	x				√	1	126
423	Goss v. Lopez	x			√		1	349
424	Graham v. Connor	x			√		2	669

The ACLU's Wins and Losses at SCOTUS (Alphabetically by Case Title)

		ACLU's Case Involvement						
	Case Name	Amicus	Attorney of Record / ACLU Attorney	As A Party	Wins	Losses	Vol #1,#2, or #3	Case # in Volume
	A	B	C	D	E	F	G	H
425	Graham v. Richardson	x			√		1	252
426	Gratz v. Bollinger		x			√	3	947
427	Gravel v. United States	x				√	1	282
428	Great American Federal Savings & Loan Association v. Novotny	x				√	2	434
429	Greater New Orleans Broadcasting Ass'n, Inc. v. United States	x			√		3	867
430	Greene v. McElroy	x			√		1	109
431	Greenholtz v. Inmates of the Nebraska Penal and Correctional Complex	x				√	2	429
432	Greer v. Miller	x				√	2	630
433	Greer v. Spock	x				√	1	368
434	Gregory v. City of Chicago		x		√		1	214
435	Griffin v. Wisconsin	x				√	2	631
436	Griswold v. Connecticut	x			√		1	168
437	Groppi v. Leslie	x	x		√		1	257
438	Grutter v. Bollinger	x			√		3	948
439	Guardians Ass'n v. Civil Service Commission	x				√	2	519
440	Gulf Oil Co. v. Bernard	x			√		2	472
441	Gundy v. United States	x				√	3	1188
442	Hafer v. Melo	x			√		2	727
443	Hague v. Committee for Industrial Organization			x	√		1	9
444	Halbert v. Michigan		x		√		3	987
445	Hall v. Beals	x				√	1	225
446	Hall v. Cole	x			√		1	307
447	Hamdan v. Rumsfeld	x			√		3	1007
448	Hamdi v. Rumsfeld	x			√		3	970
449	Hamling v. United States	x				√	1	339
450	Hampton v. Mow Sun Wong	x			√		1	371
451	Hannegan v. Esquire, Inc.	x			√		1	38
452	Haring v. Prosise	x			√		2	510
453	Harmelin v. Michigan	x				√	2	725
454	Harper v. Virginia Board of Elections		x		√		1	173
455	Harris v. Forklift Systems, Inc.	x			√		2	763
456	Harris v. McRae		x			√	2	455
457	Hazelwood School District v. Kuhlmeier	x				√	2	635
458	Hazelwood School District v. United States	x				√	1	395
459	Healy v. James		x		√		1	279
460	Heckler v. Mathews	x				√	2	526
461	Heffron v. International Society for Krishna Consciousness, Inc.	x				√	2	476
462	Heien v. North Carolina	x				√	3	1129
463	Hein v. Freedom From Religion Foundation, Inc.	x				√	3	1020
464	Hernandez v. Mesa	x			√		3	1164
465	Hernandez v. Veterans' Administration		x		√		1	325

The ACLU's Wins and Losses at SCOTUS (Alphabetically by Case Title)

		ACLU's Case Involvement						
	Case Name	Amicus	Attorney of Record / ACLU Attorney	As A Party	Wins	Losses	Vol #1,#2, or #3	Case # in Volume
	A	B	C	D	E	F	G	H
466	Herring v. U.S.	x				√	3	1033
467	Hibbs v. Winn		x		√		3	963
468	Hiibel v. Sixth Judicial District Court of Nevada, Humboldt County	x				√	3	965
469	Hill v. Colorado	x				√	3	889
470	Hill v. Florida	x			√		1	35
471	Hilton v. Braunskill	x				√	2	619
472	Hirabayashi v. United States	x				√	1	22
473	Hishon v. King & Spalding	x			√		2	539
474	Hobby v. United States	x				√	2	548
475	Hodgson v. Minnesota		x		√		2	707
476	Hoffa v. United States	x				√	1	181
477	Hoffman Plastic Compounds, Inc. v. NLRB	x				√	3	920
478	Holbrook v. Flynn		x			√	2	582
479	Holder v. Humanitarian Law Project	x				√	3	1064
480	Holland v. Florida	x			√		3	1062
481	Holland v. Illinois	x				√	2	694
482	Hollingsworth v. Perry	x			√		3	1116
483	Holt Civic Club v. City of Tuscaloosa		x			√	1	418
484	Holt v. Hobbs	x			√		3	1130
485	Holt v. Virginia		x		√		1	165
486	Hope v. Pelzer	x			√		3	931
487	Hosanna-Tabor Evangelical Lutheran Church and School v. EEOC	x				√	3	1084
488	Hoyt v. Florida	x				√	1	130
489	Hudson v. McMillian		x		√		2	733
490	Hudson v. Michigan		x			√	3	999
491	Hughes v. Superior Court	x				√	1	62
492	Hui v. Castaneda	x				√	3	1058
493	Hunt v. Cromartie	x			√		3	862
494	Hurd v. Hodge	x			√		1	51
495	Hurley v. Irish-American Gay, Lesbian & Bisexual Group of Boston	x			√		2	788
496	Hurst v. Florida	x			√		3	1143
497	Husted v. A. Philip Randolph Institute		x			√	3	1175
498	Hustler Magazine, Inc. v. Falwell	x			√		2	639
499	Hutto v. Finney	x			√		1	411
500	Iancu v. Brunetti	x			√		3	1190
501	Idaho v. Coeur d'Alene Tribe of Idaho	x				√	2	831
502	Idaho v. Wright	x			√		2	711
503	Illinois ex rel. McCollum v. Board of Education	x			√		1	48
504	Illinois v. Caballes	x				√	3	978
505	Illinois v. Gates	x				√	2	508
506	Illinois v. Lidster	x				√	3	955
507	Illinois v. Perkins	x				√	2	702

The ACLU's Wins and Losses at SCOTUS (Alphabetically by Case Title)

		ACLU's Case Involvement						
	Case Name	Amicus	Attorney of Record / ACLU Attorney	As A Party	Wins	Losses	Vol #1,#2, or #3	Case # in Volume
	A	B	C	D	E	F	G	H
508	Illinois v. Wardlow	x				√	3	873
509	Immigration & Naturalization Service v. Cardoza-Fonseca	x			√		2	609
510	Immigration & Naturalization Service v. Delgado	x				√	2	530
511	Immigration & Naturalization Service v. Doherty	x				√	2	731
512	Immigration & Naturalization Service v. Stevic	x				√	2	542
513	Immigration and Naturalization Service v. Stanisic	x				√	1	219
514	In re Anastaplo	x				√	1	121
515	In re Gault		x		√		1	187
516	In re Griffiths		x		√		1	318
517	In re Primus		x		√		1	410
518	In re Snyder	x			√		2	565
519	Independent Federation of Flight Attendants v. Zipes	x				√	2	687
520	INS v. St. Cyr		x		√		3	909
521	International Society for Krishna Consciousness, Inc. v. Lee	x				√	2	747
522	Interstate Circuit, Inc. v. City of Dallas	x			√		1	200
523	J.D.B. v. North Carolina	x			√		3	1079
524	J.E.B. v. Alabama ex rel. T.B.	x			√		2	770
525	Jackson v. Birmingham Bd. of Educ.	x			√		3	983
526	Jacobellis v. Ohio	x			√		1	153
527	Jacobson v. United States	x			√		2	737
528	Janus v. American Federation of State, County, and Municipal Employees, Council 31	x				√	3	1180
529	Jean v. Nelson	x				√	2	567
530	Jennings v. Rodriguez		x			√	3	1170
531	Jimmy Swaggart Ministries v. Board of Equalization of California	x			√		2	692
532	Johnson v. Avery	x			√		1	212
533	Johnson v. California (February 23, 2005)	x			√		3	979
534	Johnson v. California (June 13, 2005)	x			√		3	985
535	Johnson v. New Jersey	x				√	1	178
536	Johnson v. Transportation Agency	x			√		2	610
537	Jones v. Alfred H. Mayer Co.	x			√		1	208
538	Jones v. Bock	x			√		3	1009
539	Jones v. City of Opelika		x		√		1	17
540	Jones v. United States	x				√	2	517
541	Joseph Burstyn, Inc. v. Wilson	x			√		1	74
542	Justices of Boston Municipal Court v. Lydon	x				√	2	531
543	Kadrmas v. Dickinson Public Schools	x				√	2	654
544	Kahn v. Shevin		x			√	1	331
545	Kansas v. Cheever	x				√	3	1118
546	Kansas v. Crane	x				√	3	917
547	Kansas v. Hendricks	x				√	2	832
548	Karcher v. May		x		√		2	633
549	Kastigar v. United States	x				√	1	267

The ACLU's Wins and Losses at SCOTUS (Alphabetically by Case Title)

		ACLU's Case Involvement						
	Case Name	*Amicus*	*Attorney of Record / ACLU Attorney*	*As A Party*	*Wins*	*Losses*	*Vol #1,#2, or #3*	*Case # in Volume*
	A	B	C	D	E	F	G	H
550	Keller v. State Bar of California	x			√		2	701
551	Kennedy v. Louisiana	x			√		3	1032
552	Kennedy v. Mendoza-Martinez	x			√		1	136
553	Kent v. Dulles	x			√		1	103
554	Kentucky v. Stincer	x				√	2	627
555	Ker v. California	x				√	1	140
556	Kerry v. Din	x				√	3	1137
557	Keyes v. School District No. 1	x			√		1	315
558	Keyishian v. Board of Regents	x			√		1	185
559	Kimberlin v. Quinlan	x			√		2	786
560	Kimbrough v. U.S.	x			√		3	1022
561	Kimmelman v. Morrison	x			√		2	591
562	King v. Smith		x		√		1	207
563	Kingsley Books, Inc. v. Brown	x				√	1	96
564	Kingsley v. Hendrickson	x			√		3	1139
565	Kiobel v. Royal Dutch Petroleum Co.	x				√	3	1105
566	Kirchberg v. Feenstra	x			√		2	462
567	Kiyemba v. Obama	x			√		3	1053
568	Kleindienst v. Mandel	x				√	1	284
569	Klopfer v. North Carolina	x			√		1	186
570	Knowles v. Iowa	x			√		2	855
571	Kolender v. Lawson	x			√		2	505
572	Kolstad v. American Dental Ass'n	x			√		3	870
573	Konigsberg v. State Bar of California (1957)	x			√		1	93
574	Konigsberg v. State Bar of California (1961)	x				√	1	120
575	Korematsu v. United States	x				√	1	30
576	Kovacs v. Cooper	x				√	1	56
577	Kowalski v. Tesmer		x			√	3	976
578	Kucana v. Holder	x			√		3	1050
579	Kunz v. New York		x		√		1	64
580	Kush v. Rutledge	x			√		2	500
581	Kyllo v. United States	x			√		3	905
582	Labine v. Vincent	x				√	1	241
583	Lafler v. Cooper	x			√		3	1093
584	Laird v. Tatum		x			√	1	277
585	Lamb's Chapel v. Center Moriches Union Free School District	x			√		2	756
586	Lamont v. Postmaster General of the United States	x			√		1	166
587	Landmark Communications, Inc. v. Virginia	x			√		1	407
588	Lane v. Franks	x			√		3	1125
589	Lane v. Pena		x			√	2	803
590	Larkin v. Grendel's Den, Inc.	x			√		2	497
591	Larson v. Valente	x			√		2	486
592	Lassiter v. Department of Social Services	x				√	2	470

		ACLU's Case Involvement						
	Case Name	Amicus	Attorney of Record / ACLU Attorney	As A Party	Wins	Losses	Vol #1,#2, or #3	Case # in Volume
	A	B	C	D	E	F	G	H
593	Lawrence v. Florida	x				√	3	1010
594	Lawrence v. Texas	x			√		3	950
595	Leary v. United States	x			√		1	218
596	Lebron v. National Railroad Passenger Corp.	x			√		2	776
597	Ledbetter v. Goodyear Tire & Rubber Co.	x				√	3	1013
598	Lee v. Washington		x		√		1	198
599	Lee v. Weisman	x	x		√		2	746
600	Lefkowitz v. Cunningham	x			√		1	390
601	Legal Services Corp. v. Velazquez	x			√		3	894
602	Lehman v. City of Shaker Heights		x			√	1	343
603	Lemon v. Kurtzman		x			√	1	301
604	Leocal v. Ashcroft	x			√		3	975
605	Lerner v. Casey	x				√	1	105
606	Levy v. Louisiana		x		√		1	201
607	Lewis v. Casey		x			√	2	806
608	Lewis v. City of Chicago	x			√		3	1059
609	Lewis v. United States	x				√	2	805
610	Liberty Mutual Insurance Co. v. Wetzel	x				√	1	367
611	Lightfoot v. United States	x			√		1	98
612	Lilly v. Virginia	x			√		3	866
613	Lindahl v. Office of Personnel Management	x			√		2	556
614	Linmark Associates, Inc. v. Township of Willingboro	x			√		1	386
615	Little v. Streater	x			√		2	469
616	Lloyd Corp. v. Tanner		x			√	1	276
617	Locke v. Davey	x			√		3	958
618	Lockyer v. Andrade		x			√	3	935
619	Long Island Care at Home, Ltd. v. Coke	x				√	3	1016
620	Lopez v. Gonzales	x			√		3	1008
621	Lopez v. Monterey County, California	x			√		2	812
622	Lorillard Tobacco Co. v. Reilly	x			√		3	912
623	Lovell v. City of Griffin	x			√		1	8
624	Loving v. United States	x				√	2	800
625	Loving v. Virginia		x		√		1	192
626	Lowe v. Securities & Exchange Commission	x			√		2	561
627	Lynch v. Donnelly		x			√	2	525
628	Lynch v. Overholser	x			√		1	132
629	Lyng v. Northwest Indian Cemetery Protective Ass'n	x				√	2	641
630	Lyons v. Oklahoma	x				√	1	26
631	M. L. B. v. S. L. J.		x		√		2	814
632	Maine v. Thiboutot	x			√		2	454
633	Maleng v. Cook	x			√		2	678
634	Malley v. Briggs	x			√		2	578
635	Malloy v. Hogan	x			√		1	152
636	Manhattan Community Access Corp. v. Halleck	x				√	3	1185

The ACLU's Wins and Losses at SCOTUS (Alphabetically by Case Title)

		ACLU's Case Involvement						
	Case Name	Amicus	Attorney of Record / ACLU Attorney	As A Party	Wins	Losses	Vol #1,#2, or #3	Case # in Volume
	A	B	C	D	E	F	G	H
637	Maples v. Thomas	x			√		3	1085
638	Mapp v. Ohio	x	x		√		1	129
639	Marek v. Chesny	x				√	2	573
640	Marshall v. Barlow's, Inc.	x			√		1	409
641	Martin v. City of Struthers	x			√		1	18
642	Martin v. Hadix	x				√	3	868
643	Martin v. Wilks	x				√	2	680
644	Martinez v. Bynum	x				√	2	504
645	Maryland v. King	x				√	3	1108
646	Maryland v. Macon	x				√	2	563
647	Maryland v. Pringle	x				√	3	954
648	Massachusetts Bd. of Retirement v. Murgia	x				√	1	373
649	Massachusetts v. Painten	x			√		1	197
650	Masterpiece Cakeshop, Ltd. v. Colorado Civil Rights Comm'n		x			√	3	1174
651	Matal v. Tam	x			√		3	1161
652	Mathews v. Diaz	x				√	1	370
653	Maxwell v. Bishop	x			√		1	231
654	Mayo Collaborative Services v. Prometheus Laboratories, Inc.	x			√		3	1091
655	McBurney v. Young	x				√	3	1107
656	McConnell v. Federal Election Comm'n		x	x		√	3	953
657	McCreary County v. American Civil Liberties Union of Kentucky		x		√		3	989
658	McCullen v. Coakley	x				√	3	1127
659	McDaniel v. Paty	x			√		1	405
660	McDaniel v. Sanchez	x			√		2	474
661	McDonald v. Smith	x				√	2	564
662	McDonough v. Smith	x			√		3	1189
663	McFarland v. Scott	x			√		2	774
664	McGautha v. California	x				√	1	244
665	McIntyre v. Ohio Elections Commission		x		√		2	781
666	McLaurin v. Oklahoma State Regents for Higher Education	x			√		1	63
667	McLucas v. DeChamplain	x				√	1	353
668	McMann v. Richardson	x				√	1	230
669	McMillian v. Monroe County, Alabama	x				√	2	828
670	McNeese v. Board of Education	x			√		1	139
671	Medical Board of California v. Hason		x		√		3	938
672	Meek v. Pittenger	x			√		1	356
673	Meese v. Keene	x				√	2	614
674	Members of the City Council of Los Angeles v. Taxpayers for Vincent	x				√	2	537
675	Mempa v. Rhay		x		√		1	195
676	Memphis Community School District v. Stachura	x				√	2	590

The ACLU's Wins and Losses at SCOTUS (Alphabetically by Case Title)

		ACLU's Case Involvement						
	Case Name	Amicus	Attorney of Record / ACLU Attorney	As A Party	Wins	Losses	Vol #1,#2, or #3	Case # in Volume
	A	B	C	D	E	F	G	H
677	Messerschmidt v. Millender	x				√	3	1088
678	Metro Broadcasting, Inc. v. FCC	x			√		2	708
679	Metro-Goldwyn-Mayer Studios, Inc. v. Grokster, Ltd.	x				√	3	990
680	Metromedia, Inc. v. City of San Diego	x			√		2	481
681	Meyer v. Grant	x			√		2	645
682	Miami Herald Publishing Co. v. Tornillo	x			√		1	341
683	Michael H. v. Gerald D.	x				√	2	683
684	Michael M. v. Superior Court of Sonoma County	x				√	2	463
685	Michigan v. DeFillippo	x				√	2	437
686	Michigan v. Harvey	x				√	2	697
687	Michigan v. Summers	x				√	2	477
688	Middlesex County Ethics Committee v. Garden State Bar Association	x				√	2	489
689	Migra v. Warren City School District Board of Education	x			√		2	523
690	Milkovich v. Lorain Journal Co.	x				√	2	705
691	Miller v. Albright	x				√	2	841
692	Miller v. California	x				√	1	312
693	Miller v. Fenton	x			√		2	574
694	Miller v. Florida	x			√		2	623
695	Miller v. French		x			√	3	886
696	Miller v. Johnson		x			√	2	791
697	Mills v. Alabama	x			√		1	174
698	Milner v. Dep't of Navy	x			√		3	1070
699	Minersville School District v. Gobitis	x				√	1	12
700	Minneapolis Star & Tribune Co. v. Minnesota Commissioner of Revenue	x			√		2	498
701	Minnesota v. Carter	x				√	2	854
702	Minnesota v. Dickerson	x			√		2	755
703	Minnick v. California Department of Corrections	x			√		2	473
704	Miranda v. Arizona	x			√		1	176
705	Mississippi Univ. for Women v. Hogan		x		√		2	494
706	Missouri v. Frye	x			√		3	1092
707	Missouri v. Jenkins	x				√	2	785
708	Missouri v. McNeely		x		√		3	1106
709	Missouri v. Seibert	x			√		3	971
710	Mitchell v. Donovan		x			√	1	233
711	Mitchell v. Helms	x				√	3	890
712	Mitchell v. Wisconsin	x				√	3	1192
713	Montejo v. Louisiana	x				√	3	1043
714	Montgomery v. Louisiana	x			√		3	1144
715	Moore v. City of East Cleveland, Ohio	x			√		1	387
716	Moore v. Illinois	x			√		1	285
717	Moore v. Texas	x			√		3	1155
718	Morgan v. Illinois	x			√		2	742

The ACLU's Wins and Losses at SCOTUS (Alphabetically by Case Title)

	Case Name	ACLU's Case Involvement: Amicus	ACLU's Case Involvement: Attorney of Record / ACLU Attorney	ACLU's Case Involvement: As A Party	Wins	Losses	Vol #1,#2, or #3	Case # in Volume
	A	B	C	D	E	F	G	H
719	Morgan v. Virginia	x			√		1	43
720	Morrissey v. Brewer	x			√		1	281
721	Morse v. Frederick		x			√	3	1018
722	Morse v. Republican Party of Virginia	x			√		2	795
723	Muehler v. Mena	x				√	3	982
724	Mulloy v. United States	x			√		1	232
725	Munro v. Socialist Workers Party	x				√	2	600
726	Murphy v. Hunt	x				√	2	484
727	Murray v. Carrier	x				√	2	592
728	Murray v. Giarratano	x				√	2	688
729	Murray v. United States	x			√		2	656
730	Musser v. Utah	x			√		1	47
731	NAACP v. Claiborne Hardware Co.	x			√		2	496
732	Nashville Gas Co. v. Satty	x			√		1	399
733	National Aeronautics and Space Administration v. Nelson	x				√	3	1066
734	National Broadcasting Co. v. United States	x			√		1	19
735	National Cable and Television Communications Ass'n v. Brand X Internet Services	x				√	3	991
736	National Collegiate Athletic Ass'n v. Smith	x				√	3	859
737	National Endowment for the Arts v. Finley		x			√	2	850
738	National Fed'n of Indep. Business v. Sebelius	x			√		3	1099
739	National Labor Relations Board v. Sears, Roebuck & Co.	x				√	1	354
740	National Labor Relations Board v. Town & Country Electric, Inc.	x			√		2	792
741	National Organization for Women, Inc. v. Scheidler	x			√		2	766
742	National Socialist Party of America v. Village of Skokie		x		√		1	392
743	National Treasury Employees Union v. Von Raab	x				√	2	671
744	Nebraska Press Association v. Stuart	x			√		1	376
745	Neil v. Biggers	x				√	1	287
746	Nelson v. Los Angeles County		x			√	1	112
747	Nevada Dep't of Human Res. v. Hibbs	x			√		3	940
748	New Jersey v. T.L.O.	x				√	2	552
749	New Mexico v. Earnest	x				√	2	594
750	New York State Bd. of Elections v. Lopez Torres	x				√	3	1023
751	New York State Club Ass'n v. City of New York	x			√		2	648
752	New York Times Co. v. Sullivan	x			√		1	144
753	New York Times Co. v. United States	x			√		1	254
754	New York v. Belton	x				√	2	480
755	New York v. Burger	x				√	2	626
756	New York v. Ferber	x				√	2	495
757	New York v. Uplinger	x			√		2	541
758	Nguyen v. INS		x			√	3	906
759	Nichols v. United States	x				√	2	771
760	Nielsen v. Preap		x			√	3	1182

The ACLU's Wins and Losses at SCOTUS (Alphabetically by Case Title)

	Case Name	ACLU's Case Involvement: Amicus	Attorney of Record / ACLU Attorney	As A Party	Wins	Losses	Vol #1,#2, or #3	Case # in Volume
	A	B	C	D	E	F	G	H
761	Nieves v. Bartlett	x				√	3	1184
762	Nijhawan v. Holder	x				√	3	1044
763	Nike, Inc. v. Kasky	x				√	3	951
764	Nixon v. Shrink Missouri Government PAC	x				√	3	876
765	Nken v. Holder	x			√		3	1041
766	NLRB v. Catholic Bishop of Chicago	x			√		1	422
767	Norman v. Reed	x			√		2	730
768	North Carolina v. Pearce	x			√		1	223
769	North v. Russell	x				√	1	374
770	Northwest Austin Mun. Utility Dist. No. One v. Holder		x			√	3	1046
771	O'Connor v. Donaldson		x		√		1	363
772	O'Connor v. Ortega	x				√	2	611
773	O'Hare Truck Service, Inc. v. City of Northlake		x		√		2	810
774	O'Lone v. Estate of Shabazz	x				√	2	622
775	O'Neal v. McAninch	x			√		2	777
776	Obergefell v. Hodges		x		√		3	1141
777	Ohio Adult Parole Authority v. Woodard	x				√	2	839
778	Ohio Civil Rights Commission v. Dayton Christian Schools, Inc.	x			√		2	593
779	Ohio Mun. Judges Ass'n v. Davis	x				√	1	300
780	Ohio v. Robinette	x				√	2	813
781	Oklahoma City v. Tuttle	x				√	2	559
782	Old Dominion Branch No. 496 v. Austin	x			√		1	342
783	Oliver v. United States	x				√	2	529
784	Olmstead v. L.C. ex rel. Zimring	x			√		3	871
785	Oncale v. Sundowner Offshore Services, Inc.	x			√		2	838
786	Oregon v. Kennedy	x				√	2	487
787	Oregon v. Mitchell	x			√		1	235
788	Org. for a Better Austin v. Keefe		x		√		1	245
789	Ornelas v. United States	x			√		2	799
790	Orr v. Orr	x			√		1	421
791	Overton v. Bazzetta	x				√	3	944
792	Owen v. City of Independence	x			√		2	447
793	Owens v. Okure		x		√		2	661
794	Oyama v. California	x	x		√		1	46
795	Packingham v. North Carolina	x			√		3	1160
796	Palmer v. City of Euclid		x		√		1	247
797	Palmore v. Sidoti	x			√		2	532
798	Papish v. Bd. of Curators of Univ. of Missouri		x		√		1	295
799	Parents Involved in Community Schools v. Seattle School Dist. No. 1	x				√	3	1021
800	Parker v. Levy		x			√	1	337
801	Parratt v. Taylor	x				√	2	468
802	Patterson v. Alabama		x		√		1	5

The ACLU's Wins and Losses at SCOTUS (Alphabetically by Case Title)

	Case Name	ACLU's Case Involvement						
		Amicus	Attorney of Record / ACLU Attorney	As A Party	Wins	Losses	Vol #1,#2, or #3	Case # in Volume
	A	B	C	D	E	F	G	H
803	Patterson v. McLean Credit Union	x				√	2	684
804	Pearson v. Callahan	x				√	3	1034
805	Pembaur v. City of Cincinnati	x			√		2	579
806	Pena-Rodriguez v. Colorado	x			√		3	1154
807	Pennekamp v. Florida	x			√		1	42
808	Pennell v. City of San Jose	x			√		2	638
809	Pennsylvania Board of Probation & Parole v. Scott	x				√	2	849
810	Pennsylvania Department of Corrections v. Yeskey	x			√		2	848
811	Pennsylvania ex rel. Herman v. Claudy		x		√		1	83
812	Pennsylvania State Police v. Suders	x				√	3	964
813	Pennsylvania v. Finley	x				√	2	617
814	Pennsylvania v. Nelson	x			√		1	85
815	Penson v. Ohio	x			√		2	659
816	Perdue v. Kenny A.	x				√	3	1056
817	Personnel Administrator of Massachusetts v. Feeney		x			√	2	432
818	Peters v. Hobby	x			√		1	81
819	Philadelphia Newspapers, Inc. v. Hepps	x			√		2	584
820	Phillips v. Martin Marietta Corp.	x			√		1	236
821	Pickering v. Board of Education	x			√		1	204
822	Pipefitters Local Union No. 562 v. United States	x			√		1	275
823	Pittsburgh Press Co. v. Pittsburg Commission on Human Relations	x			√		1	316
824	Planned Parenthood of Southeastern Pennsylvania v. Casey		x		√		2	748
825	Poe v. Ullman	x				√	1	128
826	Pollard v. E. I. du Pont de Nemours & Co.	x			√		3	904
827	Pope v. Illinois	x			√		2	615
828	Posadas de Puerto Rico Associates v. Tourism Company of Puerto Rico	x				√	2	597
829	Powell v. Alabama		x		√		1	4
830	Powell v. McCormack	x			√		1	222
831	Powell v. Texas	x	x			√	1	209
832	Powers v. Ohio	x			√		2	715
833	Preiser v. Newkirk	x				√	1	362
834	Preiser v. Rodriguez		x			√	1	305
835	Press-Enterprise Co. v. Superior Court	x			√		2	595
836	Price v. Johnston	x			√		1	53
837	Price-Waterhouse v. Hopkins	x				√	2	677
838	Procunier v. Navarette	x				√	1	402
839	PruneYard Shopping Center v. Robins	x			√		2	453
840	Pugach v. Dollinger	x				√	1	118
841	Pulliam v. Allen	x			√		2	534
842	Quinn v. Millsap	x			√		2	682
843	R.A.V. v. City of St. Paul	x			√		2	745
844	Railway Mail Ass'n. v. Corsi	x			√		1	36

The ACLU's Wins and Losses at SCOTUS (Alphabetically by Case Title)

		ACLU's Case Involvement						
	Case Name	***Amicus***	***Attorney of Record / ACLU Attorney***	***As A Party***	***Wins***	***Losses***	***Vol #1,#2, or #3***	***Case # in Volume***
	A	**B**	**C**	**D**	**E**	**F**	**G**	**H**
845	Randall v. Sorrell		x		√		3	1005
846	Rasul v. Bush	x			√		3	969
847	Red Lion Broadcasting Co. v. FCC	x			√		1	220
848	Reed v. Reed		x		√		1	255
849	Reeves v. Sanderson Plumbing Products, Inc.	x			√		3	884
850	Regents of the University of California v. Bakke	x				√	1	414
851	Reichle v. Howards	x				√	3	1095
852	Reitman v. Mulkey	x			√		1	189
853	Renegotiation Board v. Grunmman Aircraft Engineering Corp.	x				√	1	355
854	Renne v. Geary	x				√	2	722
855	Reno v. American Civil Liberties Union			x	√		2	837
856	Reno v. American-Arab Anti-Discrimination Committee		x			√	3	860
857	Reno v. Bossier Parish School Board	x				√	2	826
858	Reno v. Condon	x			√		3	874
859	Republican Party of Minnesota v. White	x			√		3	932
860	Reynolds v. Sims		x		√		1	151
861	Ricci v. DeStefano	x				√	3	1048
862	Ricci v. Village of Arlington Heights	x				√	2	843
863	Richards v. Wisconsin	x				√	2	824
864	Richardson v. McKnight	x			√		2	833
865	Richardson v. Ramirez	x				√	1	338
866	Richmond Newspapers, Inc. v. Virginia	x			√		2	457
867	Riley v. California	x			√		3	1126
868	Riley v. Kennedy	x				√	3	1028
869	Rios v. United States	x			√		1	115
870	Rizzo v. Goode	x				√	1	365
871	Roberts v. Galen of Virginia, Inc.	x			√		3	857
872	Roberts v. United States	x				√	2	446
873	Roberts v. United States Jaycees	x			√		2	551
874	Robinson v. Shell Oil Co.	x			√		2	815
875	Rochin v. California	x			√		1	67
876	Roe v. Wade		x		√		1	291
877	Rogers v. United States	x			√		1	360
878	Romer v. Evans		x		√		2	798
879	Roper v. Simmons	x			√		3	980
880	Rosado v. Wyman	x			√		1	228
881	Rosario v. Rockefeller		x			√	1	298
882	Rose v. Clark	x				√	2	598
883	Rosenberger v. Rector & Visitors of the University of Virginia	x				√	2	790
884	Rosenblatt v. Baer	x			√		1	171
885	Ross v. Oklahoma	x				√	2	651
886	Rostker v. Goldberg		x			√	2	478

The ACLU's Wins and Losses at SCOTUS (Alphabetically by Case Title)

		ACLU's Case Involvement						
	Case Name	*Amicus*	*Attorney of Record / ACLU Attorney*	*As A Party*	*Wins*	*Losses*	*Vol #1,#2, or #3*	*Case # in Volume*
	A	B	C	D	E	F	G	H
887	Roth v. United States	x				√	1	97
888	Rucho v. Common Cause	x				√	3	1191
889	Rufo v. Inmates of the Suffolk County Jail	x				√	2	732
890	Rumsfeld v. Forum for Academic & Institutional Rights, Inc.	x				√	3	997
891	Rumsfeld v. Padilla	x				√	3	968
892	Rusk v. Cort	x			√		1	131
893	Russell v. United States	x			√		1	133
894	Rust v. Sullivan		x			√	2	717
895	Ryan v. Gonzales	x				√	3	1101
896	Saenz v. Roe		x		√		3	861
897	Safford Unified School Dist. No. 1 v. Redding		x		√		3	1047
898	Salazar v. Buono		x			√	3	1057
899	Saldana v. United States	x			√		1	119
900	Salinas v. Texas	x				√	3	1112
901	Salyer Land Co. v. Tulare Lake Basin Water Storage District	x				√	1	296
902	Samson v. California	x				√	3	1001
903	San Antonio Independent School District v. Rodriguez	x				√	1	299
904	Sandin v. Conner	x				√	2	787
905	Santa Clara Pueblo v. Martinez	x				√	1	408
906	Santa Fe Independent School District v. Doe		x		√		3	885
907	Santosky v. Kramer	x			√		2	485
908	Sarno v. Illinois Crime Investigating Commission	x				√	1	269
909	Saucier v. Katz	x				√	3	908
910	Scales v. United States (1957)	x			√		1	99
911	Scales v. United States (1961)	x				√	1	125
912	Schad v. Borough of Mount Ephraim	x			√		2	471
913	Schenck v. Pro-Choice Network of Western New York	x			√		2	816
914	Scheuer v. Rhodes		x		√		1	329
915	Schlanger v. Seamans	x				√	1	240
916	Schlesinger v. Councilman	x				√	1	352
917	Schlesinger v. Holtzman		x		√		1	319
918	Schneckloth v. Bustamonte	x				√	1	308
919	Schneider v. New Jersey	x	x		√		1	10
920	Schneider v. Rusk	x			√		1	149
921	School District of Abington Township v. Schempp		x		√		1	142
922	Schroeder v. City of New York	x			√		1	135
923	Schuette v. Coalition to Defend Affirmative Action	x				√	3	1120
924	Schware v. Bd. of Bar Exam'rs of N. M.		x		√		1	92
925	Schweiker v. Chilicky	x				√	2	653
926	Scott v. Harris	x				√	3	1012
927	Seattle Times Co. v. Rhinehart	x				√	2	538
928	Secretary of State of Maryland. v. Joseph H. Munson Co.	x			√		2	544

The ACLU's Wins and Losses at SCOTUS (Alphabetically by Case Title)

		ACLU's Case Involvement						
	Case Name	Amicus	Attorney of Record / ACLU Attorney	As A Party	Wins	Losses	Vol #1,#2, or #3	Case # in Volume
	A	B	C	D	E	F	G	H
929	See v. City of Seattle		x		√		1	191
930	Sell v. United States	x				√	3	945
931	Senn v. Tile Layers Protective Union	x			√		1	7
932	Sessions v. Morales-Santana	x			√		3	1159
933	Shapiro v. Thompson	x			√		1	216
934	Shaw v. Delta Air Lines, Inc.	x			√		2	515
935	Shaw v. Hunt	x				√	2	802
936	Shaw v. Murphy	x				√	3	896
937	Shelby County v. Holder		x			√	3	1114
938	Shelley v. Kraemer	x			√		1	50
939	Sheppard v. Maxwell	x			√		1	175
940	Sibron v. New York	x				√	1	206
941	Siegert v. Gilley	x				√	2	718
942	Simmons v. Himmelreich	x			√		3	1147
943	Simon & Schuster, Inc. v. Members of the New York State Crime Victims Board	x			√		2	728
944	Sinclair v. United States	x			√		1	59
945	Sipuel v. Board of Regents of University of Oklahoma	x			√		1	45
946	Skinner v. Railway Labor Executives' Ass'n	x				√	2	670
947	Slochower v. Board of Higher Education	x			√		1	86
948	Smalis v. Pennsylvania	x			√		2	585
949	Smith v. Allwright	x			√		1	27
950	Smith v. California (1959)	x			√		1	111
951	Smith v. California (1963)	x			√		1	143
952	Smith v. Daily Mail Publishing Co.	x			√		2	439
953	Smith v. Doe	x				√	3	936
954	Smith v. Goguen		x		√		1	326
955	Smith v. Org. of Foster Families for Equality & Reform		x			√	1	391
956	Smith v. Pennsylvania	x			√		1	145
957	Smith v. Phillips	x				√	2	483
958	Snyder v. Phelps	x			√		3	1069
959	Soldal v. Cook County, Illinois	x			√		2	749
960	Sole v. Wyner		x			√	3	1015
961	Sosa v. Alvarez-Machain		x			√	3	974
962	Sossamon v. Texas	x				√	3	1074
963	Southeastern Community College v. Davis	x				√	2	435
964	Spallone v. United States	x				√	2	691
965	Speiser v. Randall	x	x		√		1	106
966	Spence v. Washington		x		√		1	344
967	Spevack v. Klein	x			√		1	183
968	Staats v. American Civil Liberties Union aka ACLU v. Jennings, 365 F. Supp. 1041 (D.D.C. 1973)	x				√	1	361
969	Stainback v. Mo Hock Ke Lok Po	x				√	1	57
970	Staub v. City of Baxley	x			√		1	100

The ACLU's Wins and Losses at SCOTUS (Alphabetically by Case Title)

		ACLU's Case Involvement						
	Case Name	*Amicus*	*Attorney of Record / ACLU Attorney*	*As A Party*	*Wins*	*Losses*	*Vol #1,#2, or #3*	*Case # in Volume*
	A	B	C	D	E	F	G	H
971	Steagald v. United States	x			√		2	465
972	Steele v. Louisville & Nashville Railroad Co.	x			√		1	28
973	Stenberg v. Carhart	x			√		3	891
974	Stewart v. Martinez-Villareal	x			√		2	845
975	Stone v. Powell	x				√	1	377
976	Stoner v. California	x			√		1	146
977	Storer v. Brown		x		√		1	327
978	Strait v. Laird		x		√		1	265
979	Street v. New York		x		√		1	215
980	Stromberg v. California		x		√		1	3
981	Stump v. Sparkman	x				√	1	404
982	Superior Films, Inc. v. Department of Education	x			√		1	78
983	Supreme Court of Virginia v. Consumers Union of the United States, Inc.	x				√	2	452
984	Susan B. Anthony List v. Driehaus	x			√		3	1123
985	Sutton v. United Air Lines, Inc.	x				√	3	869
986	Swierkiewicz v. Sorema N. A.	x			√		3	918
987	Swint v. Chambers County Commission	x				√	2	780
988	Takahashi v. Fish and Game Commission	x			√		1	54
989	Talley v. California		x		√		1	113
990	Taylor v. Alabama	x			√		2	490
991	Taylor v. Hayes	x			√		1	346
992	Taylor v. Mississippi	x			√		1	20
993	Terminiello v. City of Chicago	x			√		1	58
994	Terry v. Ohio	x				√	1	205
995	Texas Dept. of Housing and Community Affairs v. Inclusive Communities Project, Inc.	x			√		3	1140
996	Texas Monthly, Inc. v. Bullock	x			√		2	664
997	Texas v. Johnson	x			√		2	686
998	Texas v. United States	x			√		2	840
999	Thomas v. Collins	x			√		1	32
1000	Thomas v. Review Board of the Indiana Employment Security Division	x			√		2	464
1001	Thompson v. North American Stainless, LP	x			√		3	1067
1002	Thornburgh v. American College of Obstetricians and Gynecologists	x			√		2	589
1003	Thornton v. United States	x				√	3	961
1004	Tillman v. Wheaton-Haven Recreation Assn.		x		√		1	293
1005	Timbs v. Indiana	x			√		3	1181
1006	Times Film Corp. v. Chicago	x				√	1	117
1007	Timmons v. Twin Cities Area New Party	x				√	2	823
1008	Tinker v. Des Moines Independent Community School District		x		√		1	213
1009	Tony and Susan Alamo Foundation v. Secretary of Labor	x			√		2	557
1010	Torcaso v. Watkins		x		√		1	127

The ACLU's Wins and Losses at SCOTUS (Alphabetically by Case Title)

		ACLU's Case Involvement						
	Case Name	Amicus	Attorney of Record / ACLU Attorney	As A Party	Wins	Losses	Vol #1,#2, or #3	Case # in Volume
	A	B	C	D	E	F	G	H
1011	Torres v. Puerto Rico	x			√		2	436
1012	Town of Castle Rock v. Gonzales	x				√	3	988
1013	Town of Greece v. Galloway	x				√	3	1121
1014	Town of Newton v. Rumery	x				√	2	608
1015	Trans World Airlines, Inc. v. Hardison	x				√	1	393
1016	Travis v. United States		x		√		1	182
1017	Traynor v. Turnage		x			√	2	642
1018	Trbovich v. United Mine Workers of America	x			√		1	258
1019	Trimble v. Gordon	x			√		1	384
1020	Trinity Lutheran Church of Columbia, Inc. v. Comer	x				√	3	1165
1021	Trop v. Dulles		x		√		1	102
1022	Troxel v. Granville	x			√		3	883
1023	Trump v. Hawaii	x				√	3	1179
1024	Trump v. Int'l Refugee Assistance Project		x			√	3	1167
1025	Tuilaepa v. California	x				√	2	775
1026	Tunstall v. Brotherhood of Locomotive Firemen	x			√		1	29
1027	Turner v. Dep't of Employment Security of Utah		x		√		1	364
1028	Turner v. Rogers	x			√		3	1082
1029	Two Guys from Harrison-Allentown, Inc. v. McGinley	x				√	1	122
1030	U.S. Civil Service Comm'n v. Nat'l Ass'n of Letter Carriers		x			√	1	317
1031	U.S. Term Limits, Inc. v. Thornton	x			√		2	783
1032	U.S. v. Alvarez	x			√		3	1100
1033	U.S. v. American Library Ass'n, Inc.		x			√	3	946
1034	U.S. v. Apel		x			√	3	1119
1035	U.S. v. Georgia	x			√		3	992
1036	U.S. v. Jones	x			√		3	1087
1037	U.S. v. Oakland Cannabis Buyers' Coop.	x				√	3	900
1038	U.S. v. Stevens	x			√		3	1055
1039	U.S. v. Windsor		x		√		3	1117
1040	UAW v. Johnson Controls, Inc.	x			√		2	713
1041	Ungar v. Sarafite	x	x			√	1	147
1042	United Brotherhood of Carpenters v. Scott	x	x			√	2	520
1043	United States Catholic Conference v. Abortion Rights Mobilization, Inc.	x				√	2	650
1044	United States Department of Justice v. Reporters Committee for Freedom of the Press	x			√		2	673
1045	United States Department of State v. Ray	x				√	2	729
1046	United States ex rel. Knauff v. Shaughnessy	x				√	1	60
1047	United States Postal Service Board of Governors v. Aikens	x				√	2	499
1048	United States v. 12 200-Foot Reels of Super 8mm. Film	x				√	1	313
1049	United States v. Albertini		x			√	2	566
1050	United States v. Armstrong	x				√	2	796
1051	United States v. Barnett	x				√	1	148
1052	United States v. Biswell	x				√	1	264

The ACLU's Wins and Losses at SCOTUS (Alphabetically by Case Title)

		ACLU's Case Involvement						
	Case Name	*Amicus*	*Attorney of Record / ACLU Attorney*	*As A Party*	*Wins*	*Losses*	*Vol #1,#2, or #3*	*Case # in Volume*
	A	B	C	D	E	F	G	H
1053	United States v. Brown	x			√		1	167
1054	United States v. Burke	x				√	2	739
1055	United States v. Calandra	x				√	1	321
1056	United States v. Chadwick	x			√		1	394
1057	United States v. Chesapeake & Potomac Telephone Co. of Virginia	x				√	2	793
1058	United States v. Congress of Industrial Organizations	x			√		1	55
1059	United States v. Cronic	x				√	2	535
1060	United States v. DiFrancesco	x				√	2	460
1061	United States v. Edge Broadcasting Co.	x				√	2	760
1062	United States v. Eichman	x			√		2	703
1063	United States v. Gouveia	x				√	2	540
1064	United States v. Grace	x			√		2	503
1065	United States v. Hohri	x				√	2	621
1066	United States v. James Daniel Good Real Property	x			√		2	764
1067	United States v. Kokinda	x				√	2	710
1068	United States v. Lanier	x			√		2	819
1069	United States v. Martinez-Fuerte	x				√	1	378
1070	United States v. Mendenhall	x				√	2	450
1071	United States v. Mendoza-Lopez	x			√		2	620
1072	United States v. Midwest Video Corp.	x				√	1	270
1073	United States v. Mississippi	x			√		1	159
1074	United States v. National Treasury Employees Union		x		√		2	778
1075	United States v. New Jersey State Lottery Commission	x				√	1	350
1076	United States v. Nixon	x			√		1	348
1077	United States v. Orito	x				√	1	314
1078	United States v. Paramount Pictures, Inc	x				√	1	52
1079	United States v. Patane	x				√	3	972
1080	United States v. Place	x			√		2	513
1081	United States v. Providence Journal Co.	x			√		2	644
1082	United States v. Ramsey	x				√	1	388
1083	United States v. Richardson		x			√	1	340
1084	United States v. Robel	x			√		1	196
1085	United States v. Robinson	x				√	1	320
1086	United States v. Russell	x				√	1	303
1087	United States v. Salerno	x				√	2	618
1088	United States v. Seeger	x			√		1	160
1089	United States v. Sells Engineering, Inc.	x			√		2	518
1090	United States v. Sisson	x			√		1	234
1091	United States v. Spector		x			√	1	71
1092	United States v. United States District Court for the Eastern District of Michigan	x			√		1	274
1093	United States v. Ursery	x				√	2	804
1094	United States v. Verdugo-Urquidez	x				√	2	696

		ACLU's Case Involvement						
	Case Name	Amicus	Attorney of Record / ACLU Attorney	As A Party	Wins	Losses	Vol #1,#2, or #3	Case # in Volume
	A	B	C	D	E	F	G	H
1095	United States v. Virginia	x			√		2	807
1096	United States v. Vuitch	x	x			√	1	242
1097	United States v. Weatherhead	x				√	3	872
1098	United Steelworkers of America v. Weber	x			√		2	441
1099	United Steelworkers v. Sadlowski	x				√	2	488
1100	University of Texas v. Camenisch	x			√		2	467
1101	Utah v. Strieff	x				√	3	1149
1102	Uttecht v. Brown	x				√	3	1014
1103	Vacco v. Quill	x				√	2	836
1104	Vachon v. New Hampshire		x		√		1	323
1105	Valentine v. Chrestensen	x				√	1	15
1106	Van de Kamp v. Goldstein	x				√	3	1037
1107	Verizon Maryland, Inc. v. Pub. Serv. Comm'n of Maryland	x			√		3	923
1108	Vermont v. Brillon	x				√	3	1039
1109	Veterans of the Abraham Lincoln Brigade v. Subversive Activities Control Board	x			√		1	163
1110	Vieth v. Jubelirer	x				√	3	960
1111	Village of Belle Terre v. Boraas		x			√	1	328
1112	Village of Willowbrook v. Olech	x			√		3	877
1113	Virginia v. American Booksellers Ass'n, Inc.	x				√	2	636
1114	Virginia v. Black		x		√		3	937
1115	Virginia v. Hicks	x				√	3	943
1116	Virginia v. Moore	x				√	3	1026
1117	Vlandis v. Kline	x			√		1	310
1118	Wainwright v. Greenfield	x			√		2	575
1119	Wal-Mart Stores, Inc. v. Dukes	x				√	3	1080
1120	Walker v. City of Hutchinson		x		√		1	90
1121	Walker v. Texas Div., Sons of Confederate Veterans, Inc.	x				√	3	1138
1122	Wallace v. Jaffree	x			√		2	560
1123	Walters v. National Ass'n of Radiation Survivors	x				√	2	569
1124	Walton v. Arizona	x				√	2	709
1125	Walz v. Tax Commission	x				√	1	229
1126	Wards Cove Packing Co. v. Atonio	x				√	2	679
1127	Washington v. Chrisman	x				√	2	482
1128	Washington v. Glucksberg	x				√	2	835
1129	Washington v. Seattle School District No. 1		x		√		2	493
1130	Washington v. Washington State Commercial Passenger Fishing Vessel Ass'n	x			√		2	445
1131	Watchtower Bible & Tract Soc'y of New York, Inc. v. Village of Stratton	x			√		3	926
1132	Watkins v. United States	x			√		1	94
1133	Watson v. Fort Worth Bank & Trust	x			√		2	658
1134	Watts v. United States	x			√		1	217
1135	Weatherford v. Bursey		x			√	1	381
1136	Weaver v. Massachusetts	x				√	3	1163

		ACLU's Case Involvement						
	Case Name	Amicus	Attorney of Record / ACLU Attorney	As A Party	Wins	Losses	Vol #1,#2, or #3	Case # in Volume
	A	B	C	D	E	F	G	H
1137	Weber v. Aetna Casualty & Surety Co.	x			√		1	263
1138	Webster v. Reproductive Health Services	x				√	2	689
1139	Weinberger v. Wiesenfeld		x		√		1	351
1140	Weiss v. United States	x				√	2	765
1141	Welsh v. Wisconsin	x			√		2	536
1142	Wengler v. Druggists Mutual Insurance Co.	x			√		2	449
1143	West v. Atkins	x			√		2	649
1144	West Virginia State Board of Education v. Barnette	x			√		1	21
1145	Western Air Lines, Inc. v. Criswell	x			√		2	562
1146	Wheeler v. Barrera	x				√	1	335
1147	Wheeler v. Montgomery	x			√		1	227
1148	Whitcomb v. Chavis	x				√	1	250
1149	White v. Maryland		x		√		1	138
1150	Whitney v. California		x			√	1	2
1151	Whitus v. Georgia		x		√		1	184
1152	Whole Woman's Health v. Hellerstedt	x			√		3	1152
1153	Whren v. United States	x				√	2	801
1154	Wieman v. Updegraff	x			√		1	75
1155	Wilkinson v. Austin		x			√	3	986
1156	Will v. Michigan Department of State Police		x			√	2	681
1157	Williams v. Pennsylvania	x			√		3	1148
1158	Williams v. Taylor	x			√		3	882
1159	Williams-Yulee v. Florida Bar	x				√	3	1133
1160	Wilson v. Arkansas	x			√		2	784
1161	Wilson v. Layne		x			√	3	863
1162	Wilson v. Loew's, Inc.	x				√	1	101
1163	Wimberly v. Labor and Industrial Relations Commission of Missouri	x				√	2	604
1164	Winters v. New York	x			√		1	49
1165	Wisconsin Right to Life, Inc. v. Federal Election Commission	x			√		3	995
1166	Wisconsin v. City of New York	x				√	2	794
1167	Wisconsin v. Mitchell	x			√		2	757
1168	Witherspoon v. Illinois	x			√		1	203
1169	Withrow v. Williams	x			√		2	753
1170	Witters v. Washington Department of Services for the Blind	x				√	2	576
1171	Wolff v. McDonnell	x				√	1	347
1172	Wood v. Allen	x				√	3	1051
1173	Wood v. Moss		x			√	3	1122
1174	Woodford v. Ngo	x				√	3	1004
1175	Wooley v. Maynard		x		√		1	385
1176	Wright v. Universal Maritime Service Corp.	x			√		2	853
1177	Wright v. West	x				√	2	744
1178	Yasui v. United States	x				√	1	23

The ACLU's Wins and Losses at SCOTUS (Alphabetically by Case Title)

		ACLU's Case Involvement						
	Case Name	*Amicus*	*Attorney of Record / ACLU Attorney*	*As A Party*	*Wins*	*Losses*	*Vol #1,#2, or #3*	*Case # in Volume*
	A	B	C	D	E	F	G	H
1179	Yates v. United States	x			√		1	95
1180	Yellin v. United States	x			√		1	141
1181	Young v. American Mini Theatres, Inc.	x				√	1	372
1182	Young v. Fordice		x		√		2	820
1183	Young v. Harper		x		√		2	818
1184	Young v. United Parcel Service, Inc.	x			√		3	1131
1185	Zablocki v. Redhail	x			√		1	401
1186	Zadvydas v. Davis	x			√		3	913
1187	Zauderer v. Office of Disciplinary Counsel	x			√		2	558
1188	Zelman v. Simmons-Harris		x			√	3	930
1189	Zemel v. Rusk	x				√	1	164
1190	Zicarelli v. New Jersey State Commission of Investigation	x				√	1	268
1191	Ziglar v. Abbasi	x				√	3	1162
1192	Zinermon v. Burch	x			√		2	695
1193	Zubik v. Burwell	x				√	3	1146
	Total	**975**	**211**	**7**	**640**	**553**		

V

Votes of Each Justice on Each ACLU/SCOTUS Case from 1925 to 2019 (by Date)

The following 45-page chart shows how each of the 51 U.S. Supreme Court justices voted on each of the 1,193 cases. Their votes brought out some interesting facts and information.

In addition, in assembling this work I learned about *per curiam* cases, which translated from Latin means *by the Court*. Many *per curiam* decisions do not show how the justices voted on those cases. However, in unanimous *per curiam* decisions, or when there is a concurring or dissenting *per curiam* opinion, it's generally easy to see which justice voted which way.

Per curium tie votes, 3–3 and 4–4, are published by the U.S. Supreme Court without disclosing how the justices voted (see Methodology on page 109). In such tie votes, the U.S. Supreme Court does, however, usually include the name(s) of the justice(s) not voting on such cases and publishes which prior justice's seat may be vacant at that time.

In part because it is not clear which justices voted on which side of the 3–3 and 4–4 *per curiam* decisions, and in part because the split decisions are inconclusive of the U.S. Supreme Court's mind, the nine such cases[1]—one 3–3 vote and eight 4–4 votes—are not included in this work.

Chart: *Votes of Each Justice on Each ACLU/SCOTUS Case from 1925 to 2019 (by Date)*[2]

1 Those nine cases are 1. *Hyun v. Landon* (350 U.S. 990); 2. *School Board of the City of Richmond, Virginia v. State Board of Education* (412 U.S. 92); 3. *Common Cause v. Schmitt* (455 U.S. 129); 4. *Reagan v. Abourezk* (484 U.S. 1), the only 3–3 *per curiam* vote located; 5. *Tompkins v. Texas* (490 U.S. 754); 6. *Flores-Villar v. United States* (564 U.S. 210); 7. *Friedrichs v. California Teachers Ass'n* (136 S.Ct. 1083; 578 U.S. _); 8. *Dollar General Corp. v. Mississippi Band of Choctaw Indians* (136 S.Ct. 2159; 579 U.S. _); and 9. *United States v. Texas* (136 S.Ct. 2271; 579 U.S. _).

2 These cases are listed in "Date Decided" order in Column C, with the earliest cases first. If there are cases with the same date, then they will be listed by Case number in Column D, from lowest to highest case number.

	Case Name	Date of Decision	Case No.	Justices and Their Votes (W = ACLU Win; L = ACLU Loss; NP = Justice took no part in the decision)								
A	B	C	D	E	F	G	H	I	J	K	L	M
				Holmes	Brandeis	Sanford	Taft	Van Devanter	McReyn-olds	Suther-land	Butler	Stone
1	Gitlow v. New York	6/8/1925	268 U.S. 652	W	W	L	L	L	L	L	L	L
2	Whitney v. California	5/16/1927	274 U.S. 357	L	L	L	L	L	L	L	L	L
3	Stromberg v. California	5/18/1931	283 U.S. 359	W	W	**Roberts, O.** W	**Hughes** W	W	L	W	L	W
4	Powell v. Alabama	11/7/1932	287 U.S. 45	**Cardozo** W	W	W	W	W	L	W	L	W
5	Patterson v. Alabama	4/1/1935	294 U.S. 600	W	W	W	W	W	NP	W	W	W
6	De Jonge v. Oregon	1/4/1937	299 U.S. 353	W	W	W	W	W	W	W	W	NP
7	Senn v. Tile Layers Protective Union	5/24/1937	301 U.S. 468	W	W	W	W	L	L	L	L	W
8	Lovell v. City of Griffin	3/28/1938	303 U.S. 444	NP	W	W	W	**Black** W	W	**Reed** W	W	W
9	Hague v. Committee for Industrial Organization	6/5/1939	307 U.S. 496	**Frankfurter** NP	**Douglas** NP	W	W	W	L	W	L	W
10	Schneider v. New Jersey	11/22/1939	308 U.S. 147	W	W	W	W	W	L	W	VACANT SEAT	W
11	Carlson v. California	4/22/1940	310 U.S. 106	W	W	W	W	W	L	W	**Murphy** W	W
12	Minersville School District v. Gobitis	6/3/1940	310 U.S. 586	L	L	L	L	L	L	L	L	W

Votes of Each Justice on Each ACLU/SCOTUS Case from 1925 to 2019 (by Date)

	Case Name	Date of Decision	Case No.	Justices and Their Votes (W = ACLU Win; L = ACLU Loss; NP = Justice took no part in the decision)								
A	B	C	D	E	F	G	H	I	J	K	L	M
				Frankfurter	Douglas	Roberts, O.	Jackson	Black	Byrnes	Reed	Murphy	Stone
13	Edwards v. California	11/24/1941	314 U.S. 160	W	W	W	**Jackson** W	W	**Byrnes** W	W	W	W
14	Bridges v. California	12/8/1941	314 U.S. 252	L	W	L	W	W	L	W	W	L
15	Valentine v. Chrestensen	4/13/1942	316 U.S. 52	L	L	L	L	L	L	L	L	L
16	Betts v. Brady	6/1/1942	316 U.S. 455	L	W	L	L	W	L	L	W	L
17	Jones v. City of Opelika	5/3/1943	319 U.S. 105	L	W	L	L	W	**Rutledge** W	L	W	W
18	Martin v. City of Struthers	5/3/1943	319 U.S. 141	L	W	L	L	W	W	L	W	W
19	National Broadcasting Co. v. United States	5/10/1943	319 U.S. 190	W	W	L	W	NP	NP	W	L	W
20	Taylor v. Mississippi	6/14/1943	319 U.S. 583	W	W	W	W	W	W	W	W	W
21	West Virginia State Board of Education v. Barnette	6/14/1943	319 U.S. 624	L	W	L	W	W	W	L	W	W
22	Hirabayashi v. United States	6/21/1943	320 U.S. 81	L	L	L	L	L	L	L	L	L
23	Yasui v. United States	6/21/1943	320 U.S. 115	L	L	L	L	L	L	L	L	L
24	Falbo v. United States	1/3/1944	320 U.S. 549	L	L	L	L	L	L	L	W	L
25	Follett v. Town of McCormick	3/27/1944	321 U.S. 573	L	W	L	L	W	W	W	W	W
26	Lyons v. Oklahoma	6/5/1944	322 U.S. 596	L	L	L	L	W	W	L	W	L
27	Smith v. Allwright	6/12/1944 As Amended 4/3/1944	321 U.S. 649	W	W	L	W	W	W	W	W	W
28	Steele v. Louisville & Nashville Railroad Co.	12/18/1944	323 U.S. 192	W	W	W	W	W	W	W	W	W
29	Tunstall v. Brotherhood of Locomotive Firemen	12/18/1944	323 U.S. 210	W	W	W	W	W	W	W	W	W
30	Korematsu v. United States	12/18/1944	323 U.S. 214	L	L	W	W	L	L	L	W	L
31	Ex parte Endo	12/18/1944	323 U.S. 283	W	W	W	W	W	W	W	W	W
32	Thomas v. Collins	1/8/1945	323 U.S. 516	L	W	L	W	W	W	L	W	L
33	Alabama State Federation of Labor v. McAdory	6/11/1945	325 U.S. 450	L	L	L	L	L	L	L	L	L
34	Congress of Industrial Organizations v. McAdory	6/11/1945	325 U.S. 472	L	L	L	L	L	L	L	L	L
35	Hill v. Florida	6/11/1945	325 U.S. 538	L	W	L	W	W	W	W	W	W
36	Railway Mail Ass'n. v. Corsi	6/18/1945	326 U.S. 88	W	W	W	W	W	W	W	W	W
37	Bridges v. Wixon	6/18/1945	326 U.S. 135	L	W	L	NP	W	W	W	W	L
38	Hannegan v. Esquire, Inc.	2/4/1946	327 U.S. 146	W	W	**Burton** W	NP	W	W	W	W	W
39	Duncan v. Kahanamoku	2/25/1946	327 U.S. 304	L	W	L	NP	W	W	W	W	W

Votes of Each Justice on Each ACLU/SCOTUS Case from 1925 to 2019 (by Date)

	Case Name	Date of Decision	Case No.	Justices and Their Votes (W = ACLU Win; L = ACLU Loss; NP = Justice took no part in the decision)								
A	B	C	D	E	F	G	H	I	J	K	L	M
				Frankfurter	**Douglas**	**Burton**	**Jackson**	**Black**	**Rutledge**	**Reed**	**Murphy**	**Stone**
40	Bell v. Hood	4/1/1946	327 U.S. 678	W	W	L	NP	W	W	W	W	L
41	Girouard v. United States	4/22/1946	328 U.S. 61	L	W	W	NP	W	W	L	W	L
42	Pennekamp v. Florida	6/3/1946	328 U.S. 331	W	W	W	NP	W	W	W	W	VACANT SEAT
43	Morgan v. Virginia	6/3/1946	328 U.S. 373	W	W	L	NP	W	W	W	W	VACANT SEAT
44	Everson v. Board of Education	2/10/1947	330 U.S. 1	W	L	W	W	L	W	L	L	**Vinson** L
45	Sipuel v. Board of Regents of University of Oklahoma	1/12/1948	332 U.S. 631	W	W	W	W	W	W	W	W	W
46	Oyama v. California	1/19/1948	332 U.S. 633	W	W	L	L	W	W	L	W	W
47	Musser v. Utah	2 /9/1948	333 U.S. 95	W	L	W	W	W	L	W	L	W
48	Illinois ex rel. McCollum v. Board of Education	3/8/1948	333 U.S. 203	W	W	W	W	W	W	L	W	W
49	Winters v. New York	3/29/1948	333 U.S. 507	L	W	L	L	W	W	W	W	W
50	Shelley v. Kraemer	5/3/1948	334 U.S. 1	W	W	W	NP	W	NP	NP	W	W
51	Hurd v. Hodge	5/3/1948	334 U.S. 24	W	W	W	NP	W	NP	NP	W	W
52	United States v. Paramount Pictures, Inc	5/3/1948	334 U.S. 131	W	L	L	NP	L	L	L	L	L
53	Price v. Johnston	5/24/1948	334 U.S. 266	L	W	W	L	W	W	L	W	L
54	Takahashi v. Fish and Game Commission	6/7/1948	334 U.S. 410	W	W	W	L	W	W	L	W	W
55	United States v. Congress of Industrial Organizations	6/21/1948	335 U.S. 106	W	W	W	W	W	W	W	W	W
56	Kovacs v. Cooper	1/31/1949	336 U.S. 77	L	W	L	L	W	W	L	W	L
57	Stainback v. Mo Hock Ke Lok Po	3/14/ 1949	336 U.S. 368	L	L	L	L	L	L	L	L	L
58	Terminiello v. City of Chicago	5/16/1949	337 U.S. 1	L	W	L	L	W	W	W	W	L
59	Sinclair v. United States	1/9/1950	338 U.S. 908	W	W	W	W	W	**Clark** W	W	**Minton** W	W
60	United States ex rel. Knauff v. Shaughnessy	1/16/1950	338 U.S. 537	W	NP	L	W	W	NP	L	L	L
61	American Communications Ass'n v. Douds	5/8/1950	339 U.S. 382	L	NP	L	L	W	NP	L	NP	L
62	Hughes v. Superior Court	5/8/1950	339 U.S. 460	L	NP	L	L	L	L	L	L	L
63	McLaurin v. Oklahoma State Regents for Higher Education	6/5/1950	339 U.S. 637	W	W	W	W	W	W	W	W	W
64	Kunz v. New York	1/15/1951	340 U.S. 290	W	W	W	L	W	W	W	W	W
65	Collins v. Hardyman	6/4/1951	341 U.S. 651	L	W	W	L	W	L	L	L	L
66	Garner v Board of Public Works	6/4/1951	341 U.S. 716	W	W	W	L	W	L	L	L	L

Votes of Each Justice on Each ACLU/SCOTUS Case from 1925 to 2019 (by Date)

	Case Name	Date of Decision	Case No.	Justices and Their Votes (W = ACLU Win; L = ACLU Loss; NP = Justice took no part in the decision)								
A	B	C	D	E	F	G	H	I	J	K	L	M
				Frankfurter	Douglas	Burton	Jackson	Black	Clark	Reed	Minton	Vinson
67	Rochin v. California	1/2/1952	342 U.S. 165	W	W	W	W	W	W	W	NP	W
68	Doremus v. Board of Education	3/3/1952	342 U.S. 429	L	W	W	L	L	L	W	L	L
69	Adler v. Board of Education	3/3/1952	342 U.S. 485	W	W	L	L	W	L	L	L	L
70	Carlson v. Landon	3/10/1952	342 U.S. 524	W	W	W	L	W	L	L	L	L
71	United States v. Spector	4/7/1952	343 U.S. 169	W	L	L	W	W	NP	L	L	L
72	Brunner v. United States	4/7/1952	343 U.S. 918	NP	L	W	W	W	W	L	W	W
73	Beauharnais v. Illinois	4/28/1952	343 U.S. 250	L	W	L	W	W	L	W	L	L
74	Joseph Burstyn, Inc. v. Wilson	5/26/1952	343 U.S. 495	W	W	W	W	W	W	W	W	W
75	Wieman v. Updegraff	12/15/1952	344 U.S. 183	W	W	W	NP	W	W	W	W	W
76	Albertson v. Millard	3/16/1953	345 U.S. 242	W	L	W	W	L	W	W	W	W
77	Barrows v. Jackson	6/15/1953	346 U.S. 249	W	W	W	NP	W	W	NP	W	L
78	Superior Films, Inc. v. Department of Education	1/18/1954	346 U.S. 587	W	W	W	W	W	W	W	W	**Warren** W
79	Brown v. Board of Education	5/17/1954	347 U.S. 483	W	W	W	W	W	W	W	W	W
80	Emspak v. United States	5/23/1955	349 U.S. 190	W	W	W	**Harlan** L	W	W	L	L	W
81	Peters v. Hobby	6/6/1955	349 U.S. 331	W	W	L	W	W	W	L	W	W
82	Gonzales v. Landon	12/12/1955	350 U.S. 920	W	W	W	W	W	W	W	W	W
83	Pennsylvania ex rel. Herman v. Claudy	1/9/1956	350 U.S. 116	W	W	W	W	W	W	W	W	W
84	Costello v. United States	3/5/1956	350 U.S. 359	L	L	L	NP	L	NP	L	L	L
85	Pennsylvania v. Nelson	4/2/1956	350 U.S. 497	W	W	L	W	W	W	L	L	W
86	Slochower v. Board of Higher Education	4/9/1956	350 U.S. 551	W	W	L	L	W	W	L	L	W
87	Communist Party of the United States v. Subversive Activities Control Board	4/30/1956	351 U.S. 115	W	W	W	W	W	L	L	L	W
88	Black v. Cutter Laboratories	6/4/1956	351 U.S. 292	L	W	L	L	W	L	L	L	W
89	Cole v. Young	6/11/1956	351 U.S. 536	W	W	W	W	W	L	L	L	W
90	Walker v. City of Hutchinson	12/10/1956	352 U.S. 112	L	W	L	W	W	W	W	**Brennan** NP	W
91	Butler v. Michigan	2/25/1957	352 U.S. 380	W	W	W	W	W	W	W	W	W
92	Schware v. Bd. of Bar Exam'rs of N. M.	5/6/1957	353 U.S. 232	W	W	W	W	W	W	**Whittaker** NP	W	W
93	Konigsberg v. State Bar of California	5/6/1957	353 U.S. 252	L	W	W	L	W	L	NP	W	W

Votes of Each Justice on Each ACLU/SCOTUS Case from 1925 to 2019 (by Date)

	Case Name	Date of Decision	Case No.	Justices and Their Votes (W = ACLU Win; L = ACLU Loss; NP = Justice took no part in the decision)								
A	B	C	D	E	F	G	H	I	J	K	L	M
				Frankfurter	Douglas	Burton	Harlan	Black	Clark	Whittaker	Brennan	Warren
94	Watkins v. United States	6/17/1957	354 U.S. 178	W	W	NP	W	W	L	NP	W	W
95	Yates v. United States	6/17/1957	354 U.S. 298	W	W	W	W	W	L	NP	NP	W
96	Kingsley Books, Inc. v. Brown	6/24/1957	354 U.S. 436	L	W	L	L	W	L	L	W	W
97	Roth v. United States	6/24/1957	354 U.S. 476	L	W	L	W	W	L	L	L	L
98	Lightfoot v. United States	10/14/1957	355 U.S. 2	W	W	W	W	W	W	W	W	W
99	Scales v. United States	10/15/1957	355 U.S. 1	W	W	W	W	W	W	W	W	W
100	Staub v. City of Baxley	1/13/1958	355 U.S. 313	L	W	W	W	W	L	W	W	W
101	Wilson v. Loew's, Inc.	3/3/1958	355 U.S. 597	L	W	L	L	L	L	L	L	L
102	Trop v. Dulles	3/31/1958	356 U.S. 86	L	W	L	L	W	L	W	W	W
103	Kent v. Dulles	6/16/1958	357 U.S. 116	W	W	L	L	W	L	L	W	W
104	Crooker v. California	6/30/1958	357 U.S. 433	L	W	L	L	W	L	L	W	W
105	Lerner v. Casey	6/30/1958	357 U.S. 468	L	W	L	L	W	L	L	W	W
106	Speiser v. Randall	6/30/1958	357 U.S. 513	W	W	W	W	W	L	W	W	NP
107	First Unitarian Church v. County of Los Angeles	6/30/1958	357 U.S. 545	W	W	W	W	W	L	W	W	NP
108	Barenblatt v. United States	6/8/1959	360 U.S. 109	L	W	Stewart L	L	W	L	L	W	W
109	Greene v. McElroy	6/29/1959	360 U.S. 474	W	W	W	W	W	L	W	W	W
110	Farmers Educational & Cooperative Union v. WDAY, Inc.	6/29/1959	360 U.S. 525	L	W	L	L	W	W	L	W	W
111	Smith v. California	12/14/1959	361 U.S. 147	W	W	W	W	W	W	W	W	W
112	Nelson v. Los Angeles County	2/29/1960	362 U.S. 1	L	W	L	L	W	L	L	W	NP
113	Talley v. California	3/7/1960	362 U.S. 60	L	W	W	W	W	L	L	W	W
114	De Veau v. Braisted	6/6/1960	363 U.S. 144	L	W	L	NP	W	L	L	L	W
115	Rios v. United States	6/27/1960	364 U.S. 253	L	W	W	L	W	L	L	W	W
116	Gomillion v. Lightfoot	11/14/1960	364 U.S. 339	W	W	W	W	W	W	W	W	W
117	Times Film Corp. v. Chicago	1/23/1961	365 U.S. 43	L	W	L	L	W	L	L	W	W
118	Pugach v. Dollinger	2/27/1961	365 U.S. 458	L	W	L	L	L	L	L	L	W
119	Saldana v. United States	4/3/1961	365 U.S. 646	W	W	W	W	W	W	W	W	W
120	Konigsberg v. State Bar of California	4/24/1961	366 U.S. 36	L	W	L	L	W	L	L	W	W
121	In re Anastaplo	4/24/1961	366 U.S. 82	L	W	L	L	W	L	L	W	W
122	Two Guys from Harrison-Allentown, Inc. v. McGinley	5/29/1961	366 U.S. 582	L	W	L	L	L	L	L	L	L

Votes of Each Justice on Each ACLU/SCOTUS Case from 1925 to 2019 (by Date)

	Case Name	Date of Decision	Case No.	Justices and Their Votes (W = ACLU Win; L = ACLU Loss; NP = Justice took no part in the decision)								
A	B	C	D	E	F	G	H	I	J	K	L	M
				Frankfurter	**Douglas**	**Stewart**	**Harlan**	**Black**	**Clark**	**Whittaker**	**Brennan**	**Warren**
123	Gallagher v. Crown Kosher Super Market of Massachusetts, Inc.	5/29/1961	366 U.S. 617	L	W	W	L	L	L	L	W	L
124	Communist Party v. Subversive Activities Control Board	6/5/1961	367 U.S. 1	L	W	L	L	W	L	L	W	W
125	Scales v. United States	6/5/1961	367 U.S. 203	L	W	L	L	W	L	L	W	W
126	Gori v. United States	6/12/1961	367 U.S. 364	L	W	L	L	W	L	L	W	W
127	Torcaso v. Watkins	6/19/1961	367 U.S. 488	W	W	W	W	W	W	W	W	W
128	Poe v. Ullman	6/19/1961	367 U.S. 497	L	W	W	W	W	L	L	L	L
129	Mapp v. Ohio	6/19/1961	367 U.S. 643	L	W	W	L	W	W	L	W	W
130	Hoyt v. Florida	11/20/1961	368 U.S. 57	L	L	L	L	L	L	L	L	L
131	Rusk v. Cort	4/2/1962	369 U.S. 367	L	W	W	L	W	L	**White** W	W	W
132	Lynch v. Overholser	5/21/1962	369 U.S. 705	NP	W	W	W	W	L	NP	W	W
133	Russell v. United States	5/21/1962	369 U.S. 749	NP	W	W	L	W	L	NP	W	W
134	Engel v. Vitale	6/25/1962	370 U.S. 421	NP	W	L	W	W	W	NP	W	W
135	Schroeder v. City of New York	12/17/1962	371 U.S. 208	**Goldberg** W	W	W	W	W	W	W	W	W
136	Kennedy v. Mendoza-Martinez	2/18/1963	372 U.S. 144	W	W	L	L	W	L	L	W	W
137	Gideon v. Wainwright	3/18/1963	372 U.S. 335	W	W	W	W	W	W	W	W	W
138	White v. Maryland	4/29/1963	373 U.S. 59	W	W	W	W	W	W	W	W	W
139	McNeese v. Board of Education	6/3/1963	373 U.S. 668	W	W	W	L	W	W	W	W	W
140	Ker v. California	6/10/1963	374 U.S. 23	W	W	L	L	L	L	L	W	W
141	Yellin v. United States	6/17/1963	374 U.S. 109	W	W	L	L	W	L	L	W	W
142	School District of Abington Township v. Schempp	6/17/1963	374 U.S. 203	W	W	L	W	W	W	W	W	W
143	Smith v. California	12/16/1963	375 U.S. 259	W	W	W	W	W	W	W	W	W
144	New York Times Co. v. Sullivan	3/9/1964	376 U.S. 254	W	W	W	W	W	W	W	W	W
145	Smith v. Pennsylvania	3/9/1964	376 U.S. 354	W	W	W	W	W	W	W	W	W
146	Stoner v. California	3/23/1964	376 U.S. 483	W	W	W	L	W	W	W	W	W
147	Ungar v. Sarafite	3/30/1964	376 U.S. 575	W	W	L	L	W	L	L	L	L
148	United States v. Barnett	4/6/1964	376 U.S. 681	W	W	L	L	W	L	L	L	W
149	Schneider v. Rusk	5/18/1964	377 U.S. 163	W	W	W	L	W	L	L	NP	W
150	Baggett v. Bullitt	6/1/1964	377 U.S. 360	W	W	W	L	W	L	W	W	W

Votes of Each Justice on Each ACLU/SCOTUS Case from 1925 to 2019 (by Date)

	Case Name	Date of Decision	Case No.	Justices and Their Votes (W = ACLU Win; L = ACLU Loss; NP = Justice took no part in the decision)								
A	B	C	D	E	F	G	H	I	J	K	L	M
				Goldberg	**Douglas**	**Stewart**	**Harlan**	**Black**	**Clark**	**White**	**Brennan**	**Warren**
151	Reynolds v. Sims	6/15/1964	377 U.S. 533	W	W	W	L	W	W	W	W	W
152	Malloy v. Hogan	6/15/1964	378 U.S. 1	W	W	L	L	W	L	L	W	W
153	Jacobellis v. Ohio	6/22/1964	378 U.S. 184	W	W	W	L	W	L	W	W	L
154	Escobedo v. Illinois	6/22/1964	378 U.S. 478	W	W	L	L	W	L	L	W	W
155	Aptheker v. Secretary of State	6/22/1964	378 U.S. 500	W	W	W	L	W	L	L	W	W
156	Beck v. Ohio	11/23/1964	379 U.S. 89	W	W	W	L	L	L	W	W	W
157	Calhoon v. Harvey	12/7/1964	379 U.S. 134	L	W	L	L	L	L	L	L	L
158	Freedman v. Maryland	3/1/1965	380 U.S. 51	W	W	W	W	W	W	W	W	W
159	United States v. Mississippi	3/8/1965	380 U.S. 128	W	W	W	W	W	W	W	W	W
160	United States v. Seeger	3/8/1965	380 U.S. 163	W	W	W	W	W	W	W	W	W
161	Dombrowski v. Pfister	4/26/1965	380 U.S. 479	W	W	NP	L	NP	L	W	W	W
162	American Committee for Protection of Foreign Born v. Subversive Activities Control Board	4/26/1965	380 U.S. 503	W	L	W	L	L	W	NP	W	W
163	Veterans of the Abraham Lincoln Brigade v. Subversive Activities Control Board	4/26/1965	380 U.S. 513	W	L	W	L	L	W	NP	W	W
164	Zemel v. Rusk	5/3/1965	381 U.S. 1	W	W	L	L	W	L	L	L	L
165	Holt v. Virginia	5/17/1965	381 U.S. 131	W	W	W	L	W	W	W	W	W
166	Lamont v. Postmaster General of the United States	5/24/1965	381 U.S. 301	W	W	W	W	W	W	NP	W	W
167	United States v. Brown	6/7/1965	381 U.S. 437	W	W	L	L	W	L	L	W	W
168	Griswold v. Connecticut	6/7/1965	381 U.S. 479	W	W	L	W	L	W	W	W	W
169	Estes v. Texas	6/7/1965	381 U.S. 532	W	W	L	W	L	W	L	L	W
170	Albertson v. Subversive Activities Control Board	11/15/1965	382 U.S. 70	**Fortas** W	W	W	W	W	W	NP	W	W
171	Rosenblatt v. Baer	2/21/1966	383 U.S. 75	L	W	W	W	W	W	W	W	W
172	Ginzburg v. United States	3/21/1966	383 U.S. 463	L	W	W	W	W	L	L	L	L
173	Harper v. Virginia Board of Elections	3/24/1966	383 U.S. 663	W	W	L	L	L	W	W	W	W
174	Mills v. Alabama	5/23/1966	384 U.S. 214	W	W	W	W	W	W	W	W	W
175	Sheppard v. Maxwell	6/6/1966	384 U.S. 333	W	W	W	W	L	W	W	W	W
176	Miranda v. Arizona	6/13/1966	384 U.S. 436	W	W	L	L	W	L	L	W	W
177	Gojack v. United States	6/13/1966	384 U.S. 702	W	W	W	W	W	W	W	W	W
178	Johnson v. New Jersey	6/20/1966	384 U.S. 719	L	W	L	L	W	L	L	L	L

Votes of Each Justice on Each ACLU/SCOTUS Case from 1925 to 2019 (by Date)

	Case Name	Date of Decision	Case No.	Justices and Their Votes (W = ACLU Win; L = ACLU Loss; NP = Justice took no part in the decision)								
A	B	C	D	E	F	G	H	I	J	K	L	M
				Fortas	Douglas	Stewart	Harlan	Black	Clark	White	Brennan	Warren
179	Dennis v. United States	6/20/1966	384 U.S. 855	W	L	W	W	L	W	W	W	W
180	Bond v. Floyd	12/5/1966	385 U.S. 116	W	W	W	W	W	W	W	W	W
181	Hoffa v. United States	12/12/1966	385 U.S. 293	NP	W	L	L	L	W	NP	L	W
182	Travis v. United States	1/10/1967	385 U.S. 491	W	W	W	W	W	W	W	W	W
183	Spevack v. Klein	1/16/1967	385 U.S. 511	W	W	L	L	W	L	L	W	W
184	Whitus v. Georgia	1/23/1967	385 U.S. 545	W	W	W	W	W	W	W	W	W
185	Keyishian v. Board of Regents	1/23/1967	385 U.S. 589	W	W	L	L	W	L	L	W	W
186	Klopfer v. North Carolina	3/13/1967	386 U.S. 213	W	W	W	W	W	W	W	W	W
187	In re Gault	5/15/1967	387 U.S. 1	W	W	L	W	W	W	W	W	W
188	Boutilier v. Immigration and Naturalization Service	5/22/1967	387 U.S. 118	W	W	L	L	L	L	L	W	L
189	Reitman v. Mulkey	5/29/1967	387 U.S. 369	W	W	L	L	L	L	W	W	W
190	Camara v. Municipal Court of City & County of San Francisco	6/5/1967	387 U.S. 523	W	W	L	L	W	L	W	W	W
191	See v. City of Seattle	6/5/1967	387 U.S. 541	W	W	L	L	W	L	W	W	W
192	Loving v. Virginia	6/12/1967	388 U.S. 1	W	W	W	W	W	W	W	W	W
193	Berger v. New York	6/12/1967	388 U.S. 41	W	W	W	L	L	W	L	W	W
194	Aday v. United States	6/12/1967	388 U.S. 447	W	W	W	W	W	L	W	W	W
195	Mempa v. Rhay	11/13/1967	389 U.S. 128	W	W	W	W	W	**Marshall** W	W	W	W
196	United States v. Robel	12/11/1967	389 U.S. 258	W	W	W	L	W	NP	L	W	W
197	Massachusetts v. Painten	1/15/1968	389 U.S. 560	W	W	L	L	W	W	L	W	W
198	Lee v. Washington	3/11/1968	390 U.S. 333	W	W	W	W	W	W	W	W	W
199	Ginsberg v. New York	4/22/1968	390 U.S. 629	W	W	L	L	W	L	L	L	L
200	Interstate Circuit, Inc. v. City of Dallas	4/22/1968	390 U.S. 676	W	W	W	L	W	W	W	W	W
201	Levy v. Louisiana	5/20/1968	391 U.S. 68	W	W	W	L	W	W	W	W	W
202	Amalgamated Food Employees Union Local 590 v. Logan Valley Plaza, Inc.	5/20/1968	391 U.S. 308	W	W	W	L	L	W	L	W	W
203	Witherspoon v. Illinois	6/3/1968	391 U.S. 510	W	W	W	L	L	W	L	W	W
204	Pickering v. Board of Education	6/3/1968	391 U.S. 563	W	W	W	W	W	W	L	W	W
205	Terry v. Ohio	6/10/1968	392 U.S. 1	L	W	L	L	L	L	L	L	L
206	Sibron v. New York	6/10/1968	392 U.S. 40	L	L	L	L	W	L	L	L	L
207	King v. Smith	6/17/1968	392 U.S. 309	W	W	W	W	W	W	W	W	W

Votes of Each Justice on Each ACLU/SCOTUS Case from 1925 to 2019 (by Date)

	Case Name	Date of Decision	Case No.	Justices and Their Votes (W = ACLU Win; L = ACLU Loss; NP = Justice took no part in the decision)								
A	B	C	D	E	F	G	H	I	J	K	L	M
				Fortas	Douglas	Stewart	Harlan	Black	Marshall	White	Brennan	Warren
208	Jones v. Alfred H. Mayer Co.	6/17/1968	392 U.S. 409	W	W	W	L	W	W	L	W	W
209	Powell v. Texas	6/17/1968	392 U.S. 514	W	W	W	L	L	L	L	W	L
210	Epperson v. Arkansas	11/12/1968	393 U.S. 97	W	W	W	W	W	W	W	W	W
211	Carroll v. President & Comm'rs of Princess Anne	11/19/1968	393 U.S. 175	W	W	W	W	W	W	W	W	W
212	Johnson v. Avery	3/24/1969	393 U.S. 483	W	W	W	W	L	W	L	W	W
213	Tinker v. Des Moines Independent Community School District	3/24/1969	393 U.S. 503	W	W	W	L	L	W	W	W	W
214	Gregory v. City of Chicago	3/10/1969	394 U.S. 111	W	W	W	W	W	W	W	W	W
215	Street v. New York	4/21/1969	394 U.S. 576	L	W	W	W	L	W	L	W	L
216	Shapiro v. Thompson	4/21/1969	394 U.S. 618	W	W	W	L	L	W	W	W	L
217	Watts v. United States	4/21/1969	394 U.S. 705	L	W	L	L	W	W	L	W	W
218	Leary v. United States	5/19/1969	395 U.S. 6	VACANT SEAT	W	W	W	W	W	W	W	W
219	Immigration and Naturalization Service v. Stanisic	5/19/1969	395 U.S. 62	VACANT SEAT	W	L	L	W	W	L	L	L
220	Red Lion Broadcasting Co. v. FCC	6/9/1969	395 U.S. 367	VACANT SEAT	NP	W	W	W	W	W	W	W
221	Brandenburg v. Ohio	6/9/1969	395 U.S. 444	VACANT SEAT	W	W	W	W	W	W	W	W
222	Powell v. McCormack	6/16/1969	395 U.S. 486	VACANT SEAT	W	L	W	W	W	W	W	W
223	North Carolina v. Pearce	6/23/1969	395 U.S. 711	**Burger** W	W	W	L	L	W	W	W	W
224	Brockington v. Rhodes	11/24/1969	396 U.S. 41	L	L	L	L	L	L	L	L	VACANT SEAT
225	Hall v. Beals	11/24/1969	396 U.S. 45	L	L	L	L	L	W	L	W	VACANT SEAT
226	Goldberg v. Kelly	3/23/1970	397 U.S. 254	L	W	L	W	L	W	W	W	VACANT SEAT
227	Wheeler v. Montgomery	3/23/1970	397 U.S. 280	L	W	L	W	L	W	W	W	VACANT SEAT
228	Rosado v. Wyman	4/6/1970	397 U.S. 397	L	W	W	W	L	W	W	W	**Blackmun** NP
229	Walz v. Tax Commission	5/4/1970	397 U.S. 664	L	W	L	L	L	L	L	L	NP
230	McMann v. Richardson	5/4/1970	397 U.S. 759	L	W	L	L	L	W	L	W	NP
231	Maxwell v. Bishop	6/1/1970	398 U.S. 262	W	W	W	W	L	NP	W	W	NP
232	Mulloy v. United States	6/15/1970	398 U.S. 410	W	W	W	W	W	W	W	W	NP
233	Mitchell v. Donovan	6/15/1970	398 U.S. 427	L	W	L	L	L	L	L	L	NP
234	United States v. Sisson	6/29/1970	399 U.S. 267	L	L	W	W	W	W	L	W	NP

Votes of Each Justice on Each ACLU/SCOTUS Case from 1925 to 2019 (by Date)

	Case Name	Date of Decision	Case No.	Justices and Their Votes (W = ACLU Win; L = ACLU Loss; NP = Justice took no part in the decision)								
A	B	C	D	E	F	G	H	I	J	K	L	M
				Burger	Douglas	Stewart	Harlan	Black	Marshall	White	Brennan	Blackmun
235	Oregon v. Mitchell	12/21/1970	400 U.S. 112	L	W	L	L	W	W	W	W	L
236	Phillips v. Martin Marietta Corp.	1/25/1971	400 U.S. 542	W	W	W	W	W	W	W	W	W
237	Dyson v. Stein	2/23/1971	401 U.S. 200	L	W	L	L	L	L	L	L	L
238	Byrne v. Karalexis	2/23/1971	401 U.S. 216	L	NP	L	L	L	W	W	W	L
239	Gillette v. United States	3/8/1971	401 U.S. 437	L	W	L	L	L	L	L	L	L
240	Schlanger v. Seamans	3/23/1971	401 U.S. 487	L	L	W	L	L	L	L	L	L
241	Labine v. Vincent	3/29/1971	401 U.S. 532	L	W	L	L	L	W	W	W	L
242	United States v. Vuitch	4/21/1971	402 U.S. 62	L	W	W	L	L	W	L	W	L
243	Ehlert v. United States	4/21/1971	402 U.S. 99	L	W	L	L	L	W	L	W	L
244	McGautha v. California	5/3/1971	402 U.S. 183	L	W	L	L	L	W	L	W	L
245	Org. for a Better Austin v. Keefe	5/17/1971	402 U.S. 415	W	W	W	L	W	W	W	W	W
246	Astrup v. I.N.S.	5/24/1971	402 U.S. 509	W	W	W	W	W	W	W	W	W
247	Palmer v. City of Euclid	5/24/1971	402 U.S. 544	W	W	W	W	W	W	W	W	W
248	Gordon v. Lance	6/7/1971	403 U.S. 1	L	L	L	L	L	W	L	W	L
249	Cohen v. California	6/7/1971	403 U.S. 15	L	W	W	W	L	W	L	W	L
250	Whitcomb v. Chavis	6/7/1971	403 U.S. 124	L	W	L	L	L	W	L	W	L
251	Connell v. Higginbotham	6/7/1971	403 U.S. 207	W	W	W	W	W	W	W	W	W
252	Graham v. Richardson	6/14/1971	403 U.S. 365	W	W	W	W	W	W	W	W	W
253	Bivens v. Six Unknown Named Agents of Federal Bureau of Narcotics	6/21/1971	403 U.S. 388	L	W	W	W	L	W	W	W	L
254	New York Times Co. v. United States	6/30/1971	403 U.S. 713	L	W	W	L	W	W	W	W	L
255	Reed v. Reed	11/22/1971	404 U.S. 71	W	W	W	W	W	W	W	W	W
							Rehnquist	Powell				
256	Diffenderfer v. Central Baptist Church of Miami	1/10/1972	404 U.S. 412	W	L	W	NP	NP	W	W	W	W
257	Groppi v. Leslie	1/13/1972	404 U.S. 496	W	W	W	NP	NP	W	W	W	W
258	Trbovich v. United Mine Workers of America	1/17/1972	404 U.S. 528	W	L	W	NP	NP	W	W	W	W
259	Bd. of Regents of Univ. of Texas System v. New Left Education Project	1/24/1972	404 U.S. 541	L	W	L	NP	NP	L	L	L	L
260	Dunn v. Blumstein	3/21/1972	405 U.S. 330	L	W	W	NP	NP	W	W	W	W
261	Fein v. Selective Service System Local Board No. 7	3/21/1972	405 U.S. 365	L	W	W	NP	NP	W	L	L	L

Votes of Each Justice on Each ACLU/SCOTUS Case from 1925 to 2019 (by Date)

	Case Name	Date of Decision	Case No.	Justices and Their Votes (W = ACLU Win; L = ACLU Loss; NP = Justice took no part in the decision)								
A	B	C	D	E	F	G	H	I	J	K	L	M
				Burger	Douglas	Stewart	Rehnquist	Powell	Marshall	White	Brennan	Blackmun
262	Eisenstadt v. Baird	3/22/1972	405 U.S. 438	L	W	W	NP	NP	W	W	W	W
263	Weber v. Aetna Casualty & Surety Co.	4/24/1972	406 U.S. 164	W	W	W	L	W	W	W	W	W
264	United States v. Biswell	5/15/1972	406 U.S. 311	L	W	L	L	L	L	L	L	L
265	Strait v. Laird	5/22/1972	406 U.S. 341	L	W	W	L	L	W	W	L	W
266	Apodaca v. Oregon	5/22/1972	406 U.S. 404	L	W	W	L	L	W	L	W	L
267	Kastigar v. United States	5/22/1972	406 U.S. 441	L	W	L	NP	L	W	L	NP	L
268	Zicarelli v. New Jersey State Commission of Investigation	5/22/1972	406 U.S. 472	L	W	L	NP	L	W	L	NP	L
269	Sarno v. Illinois Crime Investigating Commission	5/22/1972	406 U.S. 482	L	W	L	NP	L	W	L	NP	L
270	United States v. Midwest Video Corp.	6/7/1972	406 U.S. 649	L	W	W	W	W	L	L	L	L
271	Colten v. Kentucky	6/12/1972	407 U.S. 104	L	W	L	L	L	W	L	L	L
272	Adams v. Williams	6/12/1972	407 U.S. 143	L	W	L	L	L	W	L	W	L
273	Flower v. United States	6/12/1972	407 U.S. 197	L	W	W	L	W	W	W	W	L
274	United States v. United States District Court for the Eastern District of Michigan	6/19/1972	407 U.S. 297	W	W	W	NP	W	W	W	W	W
275	Pipefitters Local Union No. 562 v. United States	6/22/1972	407 U.S. 385	L	W	W	W	L	W	W	W	NP
276	Lloyd Corp. v. Tanner	6/22/1972	407 U.S. 551	L	W	W	L	L	W	L	W	L
277	Laird v. Tatum	6/26/1972	408 U.S. 1	L	W	W	L	L	W	L	W	L
278	Gelbard v. United States	6/26/1972	408 U.S. 41	L	W	W	L	L	W	W	W	L
279	Healy v. James	6/26/1972	408 U.S. 169	W	W	W	W	W	W	W	W	W
280	Furman v. Georgia	6/29/1972	408 U.S. 238	L	W	W	L	L	W	W	W	L
281	Morrissey v. Brewer	6/29/1972	408 U.S. 471	W	W	W	W	W	W	W	W	W
282	Gravel v. United States	6/29/1972	408 U.S. 606	L	W	W	L	L	W	L	W	L
283	Branzburg v. Hayes	6/29/1972	408 U.S. 665	L	W	W	L	L	W	L	W	L
284	Kleindienst v. Mandel	6/29/1972	408 U.S. 753	L	W	L	L	L	W	L	W	L
285	Moore v. Illinois	6/29/1972	408 U.S. 786	W	L	L	W	L	L	W	W	W
286	California v. Krivda	10/24/1972	409 U.S. 33	L	L	L	L	L	L	L	L	L
287	Neil v. Biggers	12/6/1972	409 U.S. 188	L	W	W	L	L	NP	L	W	L
288	District of Columbia v. Carter	1/10/1973	409 U.S. 418	L	L	L	L	L	L	L	L	L

Votes of Each Justice on Each ACLU/SCOTUS Case from 1925 to 2019 (by Date)

	Case Name	Date of Decision	Case No.	Justices and Their Votes (W = ACLU Win; L = ACLU Loss; NP = Justice took no part in the decision)								
A	B	C	D	E	F	G	H	I	J	K	L	M
				Burger	Douglas	Stewart	Rehnquist	Powell	Marshall	White	Brennan	Blackmun
289	Gomez v. Perez	1/17/1973	409 U.S. 535	W	W	L	L	W	W	W	W	W
290	Environmental Protection Agency v. Mink	1/22/1973	410 U.S. 73	L	W	L	NP	L	W	L	W	L
291	Roe v. Wade	1/22/1973	410 U.S. 113	W	W	W	L	W	W	L	W	W
292	Doe v. Bolton	1/22/1973	410 U.S. 179	W	W	W	L	W	W	L	W	W
293	Tillman v. Wheaton-Haven Recreation Assn.	2/27/1973	410 U.S. 431	W	W	W	W	W	W	W	W	W
294	Braden v. 30th Judicial Circuit Court of Kentucky	2/28/1973	410 U.S. 484	L	W	W	L	L	W	W	W	W
295	Papish v. Bd. of Curators of Univ. of Missouri	3/19/1973	410 U.S. 667	L	W	W	L	W	W	W	W	L
296	Salyer Land Co. v. Tulare Lake Basin Water Storage District	3/20/1973	410 U.S. 719	L	W	L	L	L	W	L	W	L
297	Associated Enterprises, Inc. v. Toltec Watershed Improvement District	3/20/1973	410 U.S. 743	L	W	L	L	L	W	L	W	L
298	Rosario v. Rockefeller	3/21/1973	410 U.S. 752	L	W	L	L	W	W	L	W	L
299	San Antonio Independent School District v. Rodriguez	3/21/1973	411 U.S. 1	L	W	L	L	L	W	W	W	L
300	Ohio Mun. Judges Ass'n v. Davis	3/26/1973	411 U.S. 144	L	L	L	L	L	L	L	L	L
301	Lemon v. Kurtzman	4/2/1973	411 U.S. 192	L	W	W	L	L	NP	L	W	L
302	Davis v. United States	4/17/1973	411 U.S. 233	L	W	L	L	L	W	L	W	L
303	United States v. Russell	4/24/1973	411 U.S. 423	L	W	W	L	L	W	L	W	L
304	Brown v. Chote	5/7/1973	411 U.S. 452	W	W	W	W	W	W	W	W	W
305	Preiser v. Rodriguez	5/7/1973	411 U.S. 475	L	W	L	L	L	W	L	W	L
306	Frontiero v. Richardson	5/14/1973	411 U.S. 677	W	W	W	L	W	W	W	W	W
307	Hall v. Cole	5/21/1973	412 U.S. 1	W	W	W	L	W	NP	L	W	W
308	Schneckloth v. Bustamonte	5/29/1973	412 U.S. 218	L	W	L	L	L	W	L	W	L
309	Cupp v. Murphy	5/29/1973	412 U.S. 291	L	W	L	L	L	L	L	W	L
310	Vlandis v. Kline	6/11/1973	412 U.S. 441	L	L	W	L	W	W	W	W	W
311	Gilligan v. Morgan	6/21/1973	413 U.S. 1	L	W	W	L	L	W	L	W	L
312	Miller v. California	6/21/1973	413 U.S. 15	L	W	W	L	L	W	L	W	L
313	United States v. 12 200-Foot Reels of Super 8mm. Film	6/21/1973	413 U.S. 123	L	W	W	L	L	W	L	W	L
314	United States v. Orito	6/21/1973	413 U.S. 139	L	W	W	L	L	W	L	W	L
315	Keyes v. School District No. 1	6/21/1973	413 U.S. 189	W	W	W	L	W	W	NP	W	W
316	Pittsburgh Press Co. v. Pittsburg Commission on Human Relations	6/21/1973	413 U.S. 376	L	L	L	W	W	W	W	W	L

Votes of Each Justice on Each ACLU/SCOTUS Case from 1925 to 2019 (by Date)

	Case Name	Date of Decision	Case No.	Justices and Their Votes (W = ACLU Win; L = ACLU Loss; NP = Justice took no part in the decision)								
A	B	C	D	E	F	G	H	I	J	K	L	M
				Burger	Douglas	Stewart	Rehnquist	Powell	Marshall	White	Brennan	Blackmun
317	U.S. Civil Service Comm'n v. Nat'l Ass'n of Letter Carriers	6/25/1973	413 U.S. 548	L	W	L	L	L	W	L	W	L
318	In re Griffiths	6/25/1973	413 U.S. 717	L	W	W	L	W	W	W	W	W
319	Schlesinger v. Holtzman	8/4/1973	414 U.S. 1321	W	L	W	W	W	W	W	W	W
320	United States v. Robinson	12/11/1973	414 U.S. 218	L	W	L	L	L	W	L	W	L
321	United States v. Calandra	1/8/1974	414 U.S. 338	L	W	L	L	L	W	L	W	L
322	Communist Party of Indiana v. Whitcomb	1/9/1974	414 U.S. 441	W	W	W	W	W	W	W	W	W
323	Vachon v. New Hampshire	1/14/1974	414 U.S. 478	L	W	W	L	W	W	L	W	W
324	Cleveland Board of Education v. LaFleur	1/21/1974	414 U.S. 632	L	W	W	L	W	W	W	W	W
325	Hernandez v. Veterans' Administration	3/4/1974	415 U.S. 391	W	W	W	W	W	W	W	W	W
326	Smith v. Goguen	3/25/1974	415 U.S. 566	L	W	W	L	W	W	W	W	L
327	Storer v. Brown	3/26/1974	415 U.S. 724	W	L	W	W	W	L	W	L	W
328	Village of Belle Terre v. Boraas	4/1/1974	416 U.S. 1	L	L	L	L	L	W	L	W	L
329	Scheuer v. Rhodes	4/17/1974	416 U.S. 232	W	NP	W	W	W	W	W	W	W
330	DeFunis v. Odegaard	4/23/1974	416 U.S. 312	L	W	L	L	L	W	W	W	L
331	Kahn v. Shevin	4/24/1974	416 U.S. 351	L	L	L	L	L	W	W	W	L
332	Eisen v. Carlisle & Jacquelin	5/28/1974	417 U.S. 156	L	W	L	L	L	W	L	W	L
333	Corning Glass Works v. Brennan	6/3/1974	417 U.S. 188	L	W	NP	L	W	W	W	W	L
334	Davis v. United States	6/10/1974	417 U.S. 333	W	W	W	L	L	W	W	W	W
335	Wheeler v. Barrera	6/10/1974	417 U.S. 402	L	W	L	L	L	L	L	L	L
336	Geduldig v. Aiello	6/17/1974	417 U.S. 484	L	W	L	L	L	W	L	W	L
337	Parker v. Levy	6/19/1974	417 U.S. 733	L	W	W	L	L	NP	L	W	L
338	Richardson v. Ramirez	6/24/1974	418 U.S. 24	L	W	L	L	L	W	L	W	L
339	Hamling v. United States	6/24/1974	418 U.S. 87	L	W	W	L	L	W	L	W	L
340	United States v. Richardson	6/25/1974	418 U.S. 166	L	W	W	L	L	W	L	W	L
341	Miami Herald Publishing Co. v. Tornillo	6/25/1974	418 U.S. 241	W	W	W	W	W	W	W	W	W
342	Old Dominion Branch No. 496 v. Austin	6/25/1974	418 U.S. 264	L	W	W	L	L	W	W	W	W
343	Lehman v. City of Shaker Heights	6/25/1974	418 U.S. 298	L	L	W	L	W	W	L	W	L
344	Spence v. Washington	6/25/1974	418 U.S. 405	L	W	W	L	W	W	L	W	W
345	Dorszynski v. United States	6/26/1974	418 U.S. 424	W	W	W	W	W	W	W	W	W
346	Taylor v. Hayes	6/26/1974	418 U.S. 488	W	W	W	L	W	W	W	W	W

	Case Name	Date of Decision	Case No.	Justices and Their Votes (W = ACLU Win; L = ACLU Loss; NP = Justice took no part in the decision)								
A	B	C	D	E	F	G	H	I	J	K	L	M
				Burger	Douglas	Stewart	Rehnquist	Powell	Marshall	White	Brennan	Blackmun
347	Wolff v. McDonnell	6/26/1974	418 U.S. 539	L	W	L	L	L	W	L	W	L
348	United States v. Nixon	7/24/1974	418 U.S. 683	W	W	W	NP	W	W	W	W	W
349	Goss v. Lopez	1/22/1975	419 U.S. 565	L	W	W	L	L	W	W	W	L
350	United States v. New Jersey State Lottery Commission	2/25/1975	420 U.S. 371	NP	W	L	L	L	L	L	L	L
351	Weinberger v. Wiesenfeld	3/19/1975	420 U.S. 636	W	NP	W	W	W	W	W	W	W
352	Schlesinger v. Councilman	3/25/1975	420 U.S. 738	L	W	L	L	L	W	L	W	L
353	McLucas v. DeChamplain	4/15/1975	421 U.S. 21	L	L	L	L	L	L	L	L	L
354	National Labor Relations Board v. Sears, Roebuck & Co.	4/28/1975	421 U.S. 132	L	L	L	L	NP	L	L	L	L
355	Renegotiation Board v. Grunmman Aircraft Engineering Corp.	4/28/1975	421 U.S. 168	L	W	L	L	NP	L	L	L	L
356	Meek v. Pittenger	5/19/1975	421 U.S. 349	L	W	W	L	W	W	L	W	W
357	Ellis v. Dyson	5/19/1975	421 U.S. 426	L	W	L	W	L	W	W	W	W
358	Eastland v. United States Servicemen's Fund	5/27/1975	421 U.S. 491	L	W	L	L	L	L	L	L	L
359	Bigelow v. Virginia	6/16/1975	421 U.S. 809	W	W	W	L	W	W	L	W	W
360	Rogers v. United States	6/17/1975	422 U.S. 35	W	W	W	W	W	W	W	W	W
361	Staats v. American Civil Liberties Union aka ACLU v. Jennings, 365 F. Supp. 1041 (D.D.C. 1973)	6/23/1975	422 U.S. 1030	L	NP	L	L	L	L	L	L	L
362	Preiser v. Newkirk	6/25/1975	422 U.S. 395	L	W	L	L	L	L	L	L	L
363	O'Connor v. Donaldson	6/26/1975	422 U.S. 563	W	W	W	W	W	W	W	W	W
364	Turner v. Dep't of Employment Security of Utah	11/17/1975	423 U.S. 44	L	W	W	L	W	W	W	W	L
365	Rizzo v. Goode	1/21/1976	423 U.S. 362	L	**Stevens** NP	L	L	L	W	L	W	W
366	Buckley v. Valeo	1/30/1976	424 U.S. 1	L	NP	W	W	W	W	W	W	W
367	Liberty Mutual Insurance Co. v. Wetzel	3/23/1976	424 U.S. 737	L	L	L	L	L	L	L	L	NP
368	Greer v. Spock	3/24/1976	424 U.S. 828	L	NP	L	L	L	W	L	W	L
369	Dep't of the Air Force v. Rose	4/21/1976	425 U.S. 352	L	NP	W	L	W	W	W	W	L
370	Mathews v. Diaz	6/1/1976	426 U.S. 67	L	L	L	L	L	L	L	L	L
371	Hampton v. Mow Sun Wong	6/1/1976	426 U.S. 88	L	W	W	L	W	W	L	W	L
372	Young v. American Mini Theatres, Inc.	6/24/76	427 U.S. 50	L	L	W	L	L	W	L	W	W

	Case Name	Date of Decision	Case No.	Justices and Their Votes (W = ACLU Win; L = ACLU Loss; NP = Justice took no part in the decision)								
A	B	C	D	E	F	G	H	I	J	K	L	M
				Burger	Stevens	Stewart	Rehnquist	Powell	Marshall	White	Brennan	Blackmun
373	Massachusetts Bd. of Retirement v. Murgia	6/25/1976	427 U.S. 307	L	NP	L	L	L	W	L	L	L
374	North v. Russell	6/28/1976	427 U.S. 328	L	NP	W	L	L	W	L	L	L
375	Fitzpatrick v. Bitzer	6/28/1976	427 U.S. 445	W	W	W	W	W	W	W	W	W
376	Nebraska Press Association v. Stuart	6/30/1976	427 U.S. 539	W	W	W	W	W	W	W	W	W
377	Stone v. Powell	7/6/1976	428 U.S. 465	L	L	L	L	L	W	W	W	L
378	United States v. Martinez-Fuerte	7/6/1976	428 U.S. 543	L	L	L	L	L	W	L	W	L
379	General Electric Co. v. Gilbert	12/7/1976	429 U.S. 125	L	W	L	L	L	W	L	W	L
380	Craig v. Boren	12/20/1976	429 U.S. 190	L	W	W	L	W	W	W	W	W
381	Weatherford v. Bursey	2/22/1977	429 U.S. 545	L	L	L	L	L	W	L	W	L
382	Califano v. Goldfarb	3/2/1977	430 U.S. 199	L	W	L	L	W	W	W	W	L
383	Castaneda v. Partida	3/23/1977	430 U.S. 482	L	W	L	L	L	W	W	W	W
384	Trimble v. Gordon	4/26/1977	430 U.S. 762	L	W	L	L	W	W	W	W	L
385	Wooley v. Maynard	4/30/1977	430 U.S. 705	W	W	W	L	W	W	L	W	L
386	Linmark Associates, Inc. v. Township of Willingboro	5/2/1977	431 U.S. 85	W	W	W	NP	W	W	W	W	W
387	Moore v. City of East Cleveland, Ohio	5/31/1977	431 U.S. 494	L	W	L	L	W	W	L	W	W
388	United States v. Ramsey	6/6/1977	431 U.S. 606	L	W	L	L	L	W	L	W	L
389	Carey v. Population Services International	6/9/1977	431 U.S. 678	L	W	W	L	W	W	W	W	W
390	Lefkowitz v. Cunningham	6/13/1977	431 U.S. 801	W	L	W	NP	W	W	W	W	W
391	Smith v. Org. of Foster Families for Equality & Reform	6/13/1977	431 U.S. 816	L	L	L	L	L	L	L	L	L
392	National Socialist Party of America v. Village of Skokie	6/14/1977	432 U.S. 43	L	W	L	L	W	W	L	W	W
393	Trans World Airlines, Inc. v. Hardison	6/16/1977	432 U.S. 63	L	L	L	L	L	W	L	W	L
394	United States v. Chadwick	6/21/1977	433 U.S. 1	W	W	W	L	W	W	W	W	L
395	Hazelwood School District v. United States	6/27/1977	433 U.S. 299	L	W	L	L	L	L	L	L	L
396	Dothard v. Rawlinson	6/27/1977	433 U.S. 321	W	W	W	W	W	L	L	L	W
397	Dayton Board of Education v. Brinkman	6/27/1977	433 U.S. 406	L	L	L	L	L	NP	L	L	L
398	Coker v. Georgia	6/29/1977	433 U.S. 584	L	W	W	L	W	W	W	W	W
399	Nashville Gas Co. v. Satty	12/6/1977	434 U.S. 136	W	W	W	W	W	W	W	W	W

Votes of Each Justice on Each ACLU/SCOTUS Case from 1925 to 2019 (by Date)

	Case Name	Date of Decision	Case No.	Justices and Their Votes (W = ACLU Win; L = ACLU Loss; NP = Justice took no part in the decision)								
A	B	C	D	E	F	G	H	I	J	K	L	M
				Burger	Stevens	Stewart	Rehnquist	Powell	Marshall	White	Brennan	Blackmun
400	Browder v. Director, Department of Corrections	1/10/1978	434 U.S. 257	W	W	W	W	W	W	W	W	W
401	Zablocki v. Redhail	1/18/1978	434 U.S. 374	W	W	W	L	W	W	W	W	W
402	Procunier v. Navarette	2/22/1978	434 U.S. 555	W	W	L	L	L	L	L	L	L
403	Board of Curators of the University of Missouri v. Horowitz	3/1/1978	435 U.S. 78	L	L	L	L	L	W	L	W	W
404	Stump v. Sparkman	3/28/1978	435 U.S. 349	L	L	W	L	W	W	L	NP	L
405	McDaniel v. Paty	4/19/1978	435 U.S. 618	W	W	W	W	W	W	W	W	NP
406	City of Los Angeles, Department of Water and Power v. Manhart	4/25/1978	435 U.S. 702	L	W	W	L	W	W	W	NP	W
407	Landmark Communi-cations, Inc. v. Virginia	5/1/1978	435 U.S. 829	W	W	W	W	NP	W	W	NP	W
408	Santa Clara Pueblo v. Martinez	5/15/1978	436 U.S. 49	L	L	L	L	L	L	W	L	NP
409	Marshall v. Barlow's, Inc.	5/23/1978	436 U.S. 307	W	L	W	L	W	W	W	NP	L
410	In re Primus	5/30/1978	436 U.S. 412	W	W	W	L	W	W	W	NP	W
411	Hutto v. Finney	6/23/1978	437 U.S. 678	L	W	W	L	L	W	L	W	W
412	Franks v. Delaware	5/26/1978	438 U.S. 154	L	W	W	L	W	W	W	W	W
413	Berry v. Doles	5/26/1978	438 U.S. 190	W	L	W	L	W	W	W	W	W
414	Regents of the University of California v. Bakke	6/28/1978	438 U.S. 265	W	W	W	W	L	L	L	L	L
415	Bell v. Ohio	7/3/1978	438 U.S. 637	W	W	W	L	W	W	W	NP	W
416	FCC v. Pacifica Foundation	7/3/1978	438 U.S. 726	L	L	W	L	L	W	W	W	L
417	Alabama v. Pugh	7/3/1978	438 U.S. 781	L	W	L	L	L	W	L	W	L
418	Holt Civic Club v. City of Tuscaloosa	11/28/1978	439 U.S. 60	L	L	L	L	L	W	W	W	L
419	Duren v. Missouri	1/9/1979	439 U.S. 357	W	W	W	L	W	W	W	W	W
420	Colautti v. Franklin	1/9/1979	439 U.S. 379	L	W	W	L	W	W	L	W	W
421	Orr v. Orr	3/5/1979	440 U.S. 268	L	W	W	L	L	W	W	W	W
422	NLRB v. Catholic Bishop of Chicago	3/21/1979	440 U.S. 490	W	W	W	W	W	L	L	L	L
423	County of Los Angeles v. Davis	3/27/1979	440 U.S. 625	W	L	W	W	W	L	L	L	L
424	Delaware v. Prouse	3/27/1979	440 U.S. 648	W	W	W	L	W	W	W	W	W
425	FCC v. Midwest Video Corp.	4/2/1979	440 U.S. 689	L	W	L	L	L	W	L	W	L
426	Burch v. Louisiana	4/17/1979	441 U.S. 130	W	W	W	W	W	W	W	W	W

Votes of Each Justice on Each ACLU/SCOTUS Case from 1925 to 2019 (by Date)

	Case Name	Date of Decision	Case No.	Justices and Their Votes (W = ACLU Win; L = ACLU Loss; NP = Justice took no part in the decision)								
A	B	C	D	E	F	G	H	I	J	K	L	M
				Burger	Stevens	Stewart	Rehnquist	Powell	Marshall	White	Brennan	Blackmun
427	Caban v. Mohammed	4/24/1979	441 U.S. 380	L	L	L	L	W	W	W	W	W
428	Bell v. Wolfish	5/14/1979	441 U.S. 520	L	W	L	L	L	W	L	W	L
429	Greenholtz v. Inmates of the Nebraska Penal and Correctional Complex	5/29/1979	442 U.S. 1	L	W	L	L	W	W	L	W	L
430	Dunaway v. New York	6/5/1979	442 U.S. 200	L	W	W	L	NP	W	W	W	W
431	Davis v. Passman	6/5/1979	442 U.S. 228	L	W	L	L	L	W	W	W	W
432	Personnel Administrator of Massachusetts v. Feeney	6/5/1979	442 U.S. 256	L	L	L	L	L	W	L	W	L
433	Babbitt v. United Farm Workers National Union	6/5/1979	442 U.S. 289	L	L	L	L	L	W	L	W	L
434	Great American Federal Savings & Loan Association v. Novotny	6/11/1979	442 U.S. 366	L	L	L	L	L	W	W	W	L
435	Southeastern Community College v. Davis	6/11/1979	442 U.S. 397	L	L	L	L	L	L	L	L	L
436	Torres v. Puerto Rico	6/18/1979	442 U.S. 465	W	W	W	W	W	W	W	W	W
437	Michigan v. DeFillippo	6/25/1979	443 U.S. 31	L	W	L	L	L	W	L	W	L
438	Califano v. Westcott	6/25/1979	443 U.S. 76	L	W	L	L	L	W	W	W	W
439	Smith v. Daily Mail Publishing Co.	6/26/1979	443 U.S. 97	W	W	W	W	NP	W	W	W	W
440	Baker v. McCollan	6/26/1979	443 U.S. 137	L	W	L	L	L	W	L	W	L
441	United Steelworkers of America v. Weber	6/27/1979	443 U.S. 193	L	NP	W	L	NP	W	W	W	W
442	Gannett Co. v. DePasquale	7/2/1979	443 U.S. 368	L	L	L	L	L	W	W	W	W
443	Columbus Board of Education v. Penick	7/2/1979	443 U.S. 449	W	W	W	L	L	W	W	W	W
444	Bellotti v. Baird	7/2/1979	443 U.S. 622	W	W	W	W	W	W	L	W	W
445	Washington v. Washington State Commercial Passenger Fishing Vessel Ass'n	7/2/1979	443 U.S. 658	W	W	L	L	L	W	W	W	W
446	Roberts v. United States	4/15/1980	445 U.S. 552	L	L	L	L	L	W	L	L	L
447	Owen v. City of Independence	4/16/1980	445 U.S. 622	L	W	L	L	L	W	W	W	W
448	Carlson v. Green	4/22/1980	446 U.S. 14	L	W	W	L	W	W	W	W	W
449	Wengler v. Druggists Mutual Insurance Co.	4/22/1980	446 U.S. 142	W	W	W	L	W	W	W	W	W
450	United States v. Mendenhall	5/27/1980	446 U.S. 544	L	W	L	L	L	W	W	W	L
451	Gomez v. Toledo	5/27/1980	446 U.S. 635	W	W	W	W	W	W	W	W	W

Votes of Each Justice on Each ACLU/SCOTUS Case from 1925 to 2019 (by Date)

	Case Name	Date of Decision	Case No.	Justices and Their Votes (W = ACLU Win; L = ACLU Loss; NP = Justice took no part in the decision)								
A	B	C	D	E	F	G	H	I	J	K	L	M
				Burger	Stevens	Stewart	Rehnquist	Powell	Marshall	White	Brennan	Blackmun
452	Supreme Court of Virginia v. Consumers Union of the United States, Inc.	6/2/1980	446 U.S. 719	L	L	L	L	NP	L	L	L	L
453	PruneYard Shopping Center v. Robins	6/9/1980	447 U.S. 74	W	W	W	W	W	W	W	W	W
454	Maine v. Thiboutot	6/25/1980	448 U.S. 1	L	W	W	L	L	W	W	W	W
455	Harris v. McRae	6/30/1980	448 U.S. 297	L	W	L	L	L	W	L	W	W
456	Fullilove v. Klutznick	7/2/1980	448 U.S. 448	W	L	L	L	W	W	W	W	W
457	Richmond Newspapers, Inc. v. Virginia	7/2/1980	448 U.S. 555	W	W	W	L	NP	W	W	W	W
458	Dennis v. Sparks	11/17/1980	449 U.S. 24	W	W	W	W	W	W	W	W	W
459	Allen v. McCurry	12/9/1980	449 U.S. 90	L	L	L	L	L	W	L	W	W
460	United States v. DiFrancesco	12/9/1980	449 U.S. 117	L	W	L	L	L	W	W	W	L
461	Delta Air Lines, Inc. v. August	3/9/1981	450 U.S. 346	L	W	L	L	W	W	W	W	W
462	Kirchberg v. Feenstra	3/23/1981	450 U.S. 455	W	W	W	W	W	W	W	W	W
463	Michael M. v. Superior Court of Sonoma County	3/23/1981	450 U.S. 464	L	W	L	L	L	W	W	W	L
464	Thomas v. Review Board of the Indiana Employment Security Division	4/6/1981	450 U.S. 707	W	W	W	L	W	W	W	W	W
465	Steagald v. United States	4/21/1981	451 U.S. 204	W	W	W	L	W	W	L	W	W
466	Ball v. James	4/29/1981	451 U.S. 355	L	L	L	L	L	W	W	W	W
467	University of Texas v. Camenisch	4/29/1981	451 U.S. 390	W	W	W	W	W	W	W	W	W
468	Parratt v. Taylor	5/18/1981	451 U.S. 527	L	L	L	L	L	W	L	L	L
469	Little v. Streater	6/1/1981	452 U.S. 1	W	W	W	W	W	W	W	W	W
470	Lassiter v. Department of Social Services	6/1/1981	452 U.S. 18	L	W	L	L	L	W	L	W	W
471	Schad v. Borough of Mount Ephraim	6/1/1981	452 U.S. 61	L	W	W	L	W	W	W	W	W
472	Gulf Oil Co. v. Bernard	6/1/1981	452 U.S. 89	W	W	W	W	W	W	W	W	W
473	Minnick v. California Department of Corrections	6/1/1981	452 U.S. 105	W	W	L	W	W	W	W	W	W
474	McDaniel v. Sanchez	6/1/1981	452 U.S. 130	W	W	L	L	W	W	W	W	W
475	County of Washington v. Gunther	6/8/1981	452 U.S. 161	L	W	L	L	L	W	W	W	W
476	Heffron v. International Society for Krishna Consciousness, Inc.	6/22/1981	452 U.S. 640	L	W	L	L	L	W	L	W	W
477	Michigan v. Summers	6/22/1981	452 U.S. 692	L	L	W	L	L	W	L	W	L

Votes of Each Justice on Each ACLU/SCOTUS Case from 1925 to 2019 (by Date)

	Case Name	Date of Decision	Case No.	Justices and Their Votes (W = ACLU Win; L = ACLU Loss; NP = Justice took no part in the decision)								
A	B	C	D	E	F	G	H	I	J	K	L	M
				Burger	Stevens	Stewart	Rehnquist	Powell	Marshall	White	Brennan	Blackmun
478	Rostker v. Goldberg	6/25/1981	453 U.S. 57	L	L	L	L	L	W	W	W	L
479	California Medical Ass'n v. Federal Election Commission	6/26/1981	453 U.S. 182	W	L	W	W	W	L	L	L	L
480	New York v. Belton	7/1/1981	453 U.S. 454	L	L	L	L	L	W	W	W	L
481	Metromedia, Inc. v. City of San Diego	7/2/1981	453 U.S. 490	L	L	W	L	W	W	W	W	W
482	Washington v. Chrisman	1/13/1982	455 U.S. 1	L	L	**O'Connor** L	L	L	W	W	W	L
483	Smith v. Phillips	1/25/1982	455 U.S. 209	L	W	L	L	L	W	L	W	L
484	Murphy v. Hunt	3/2/1982	455 U.S. 478	L	L	L	L	L	L	W	L	L
485	Santosky v. Kramer	3/24/1982	455 U.S. 745	L	W	L	L	W	W	L	W	W
486	Larson v. Valente	4/21/1982	456 U.S. 228	L	W	L	L	W	W	L	W	W
487	Oregon v. Kennedy	5/24/1982	456 U.S. 667	L	L	L	L	L	L	L	L	L
488	United Steelworkers v. Sadlowski	6/14/1982	457 U.S. 102	W	L	L	L	L	L	W	W	W
489	Middlesex County Ethics Committee v. Garden State Bar Association	6/21/1982	457 U.S. 423	L	L	L	L	L	L	L	L	L
490	Taylor v. Alabama	6/23/1982	457 U.S. 687	L	W	L	L	L	W	W	W	W
491	Board of Education v. Pico	6/25/1982	457 U.S. 853	L	W	L	L	L	W	W	W	W
492	Board Of Education v. Rowley	6/28/1982	458 U.S. 176	L	L	L	L	L	W	W	W	L
493	Washington v. Seattle School District No. 1	6/30/1982	458 U.S. 457	L	W	L	L	L	W	W	W	W
494	Mississippi Univ. for Women v. Hogan	7/1/1982	458 U.S. 718	L	W	W	L	L	W	W	W	L
495	New York v. Ferber	7/2/1982	458 U.S. 747	L	L	L	L	L	L	L	L	L
496	NAACP v. Claiborne Hardware Co.	7/2/1982	458 U.S. 886	W	W	W	W	W	NP	W	W	W
497	Larkin v. Grendel's Den, Inc.	12/13/1982	459 U.S. 116	W	W	W	L	W	W	W	W	W
498	Minneapolis Star & Tribune Co. v. Minnesota Commissioner of Revenue	3/29/1983	460 U.S. 575	W	W	W	L	W	W	W	W	W
499	United States Postal Service Board of Governors v. Aikens	4/4/1983	460 U.S. 711	L	L	L	L	L	L	L	L	L
500	Kush v. Rutledge	4/4/1983	460 U.S. 719	W	W	W	W	W	W	W	W	W
501	Anderson v. Celebrezze	4/19/1983	460 U.S. 780	W	W	L	L	L	W	L	W	W
502	Connick v. Myers	4/20/1983	461 U.S. 138	L	W	L	L	L	W	L	W	W
503	United States v. Grace	4/20/1983	461 U.S. 171	W	L	W	W	W	L	W	W	W

Votes of Each Justice on Each ACLU/SCOTUS Case from 1925 to 2019 (by Date)

	Case Name	Date of Decision	Case No.	Justices and Their Votes (W = ACLU Win; L = ACLU Loss; NP = Justice took no part in the decision)								
A	B	C	D	E	F	G	H	I	J	K	L	M
				Burger	Stevens	O'Connor	Rehnquist	Powell	Marshall	White	Brennan	Blackmun
504	Martinez v. Bynum	5/2/1983	461 U.S. 321	L	L	L	L	L	W	L	L	L
505	Kolender v. Lawson	5/2/1983	461 U.S. 352	W	W	W	L	W	W	L	W	W
506	Boston Firefighters Union, Local 718 v. Boston Chapter, NAACP	5/16/1983	461 U.S. 477	L	L	L	L	L	NP	L	L	L
507	Bob Jones University v. United States	5/24/1983	461 U.S. 574	W	W	W	L	W	W	W	W	W
508	Illinois v. Gates	6/8/1983	462 U.S. 213	L	W	L	L	L	W	L	W	L
509	Chappell v. Wallace	6/13/1983	462 U.S. 296	L	L	L	L	L	L	L	L	L
510	Haring v. Prosise	6/13/1983	462 U.S. 306	W	W	W	W	W	W	W	W	W
511	Bush v. Lucas	6/13/1983	462 U.S. 367	L	L	L	L	L	L	L	L	L
512	City of Akron v. Akron Center for Reproductive Health, Inc.	6/15/1983	462 U.S. 416	W	W	L	L	W	W	L	W	W
513	United States v. Place	6/20/1983	462 U.S. 696	W	W	W	W	W	W	W	W	W
514	Bolger v. Youngs Drug Products Corp.	6/24/1983	463 U.S. 60	W	W	W	W	W	W	W	NP	W
515	Shaw v. Delta Air Lines, Inc.	6/24/1983	463 U.S. 85	W	W	W	W	W	W	W	W	W
516	City of Revere v. Massachusetts General Hospital	6/27/1983	463 U.S. 239	W	W	W	W	W	W	W	W	W
517	Jones v. United States	6/29/1983	463 U.S. 354	L	W	L	L	L	W	L	W	W
518	United States v. Sells Engineering, Inc.	6/30/1983	463 U.S. 418	L	W	L	L	L	W	W	W	W
519	Guardians Ass'n v. Civil Service Commission	7/1/1983	463 U.S. 582	L	W	L	L	L	W	L	W	W
520	United Brotherhood of Carpenters v. Scott	7/5/1983	463 U.S. 825	L	L	W	L	L	W	L	W	W
521	Barefoot v. Estelle	7/6/1983	463 U.S. 880	L	L	L	L	L	W	L	W	W
522	Arizona Governing Committee for Tax Deferred Annuity & Deferred Compensation Plans v. Norris	7/16/1983	463 U.S. 1073	L	W	W	L	L	W	W	W	L
523	Migra v. Warren City School District Board of Education	1/23/1984	465 U.S. 75	W	W	W	W	W	W	W	W	W
524	Flanagan v. United States	2/21/1984	465 U.S. 259	W	W	W	W	W	W	W	W	W
525	Lynch v. Donnelly	3/5/1984	465 U.S. 668	L	W	L	L	L	W	L	W	W
526	Heckler v. Mathews	3/5/1984	465 U.S. 728	L	L	L	L	L	L	L	L	L
527	Blum v. Stenson	3/21/1984	465 U.S. 886	W	W	W	W	W	W	W	W	W

Votes of Each Justice on Each ACLU/SCOTUS Case from 1925 to 2019 (by Date)

	Case Name	Date of Decision	Case No.	Justices and Their Votes (W = ACLU Win; L = ACLU Loss; NP = Justice took no part in the decision)								
A	B	C	D	E	F	G	H	I	J	K	L	M
				Burger	Stevens	O'Connor	Rehnquist	Powell	Marshall	White	Brennan	Blackmun
528	Escambia County v. McMillan	3/27/1984	466 U.S. 48	L	L	L	L	L	W	L	L	L
529	Oliver v. United States	4/17/1984	466 U.S. 170	L	W	L	L	L	W	L	W	L
530	Immigration & Naturalization Service v. Delgado	4/17/1984	466 U.S. 210	L	L	L	L	L	W	L	W	L
531	Justices of Boston Municipal Court v. Lydon	4/18/1984	466 U.S. 294	L	L	L	L	L	L	L	L	L
532	Palmore v. Sidoti	4/25/1984	466 U.S. 429	W	W	W	W	W	W	W	W	W
533	Bose Corp. v. Consumers Union, Inc.	4/30/1984	466 U.S. 485	W	W	L	L	W	W	L	W	W
534	Pulliam v. Allen	5/14/1984	466 U.S. 522	L	W	L	L	L	W	W	W	W
535	United States v. Cronic	5/14/1984	466 U.S. 648	L	L	L	L	L	L	L	L	L
536	Welsh v. Wisconsin	5/15/1984	466 U.S. 740	L	W	W	L	W	W	L	W	W
537	Members of the City Council of Los Angeles v. Taxpayers for Vincent	5/15/1984	466 U.S. 789	L	L	L	L	L	W	L	W	W
538	Seattle Times Co. v. Rhinehart	5/21/1984	467 U.S. 20	L	L	L	L	L	L	L	L	L
539	Hishon v. King & Spalding	5/22/1984	467 U.S. 69	W	W	W	W	W	W	W	W	W
540	United States v. Gouveia	5/29/1984	467 U.S. 180	L	L	L	L	L	W	L	L	L
541	New York v. Uplinger	5/30/1984	467 U.S. 246	L	W	L	L	W	W	L	W	W
542	Immigration & Naturalization Service v. Stevic	6/5/1984	467 U.S. 407	L	L	L	L	L	L	L	L	L
543	Capital Cities Cable, Inc. v. Crisp	6/18/1984	467 U.S. 691	W	W	W	W	W	W	W	W	W
544	Secretary of State of Maryland. v. Joseph H. Munson Co.	6/26/1984	467 U.S. 947	L	W	L	L	L	W	W	W	W
545	Burnett v. Grattan	6/27/1984	468 U.S. 42	W	W	W	W	W	W	W	W	W
546	Davis v. Scherer	6/28/1984	468 U.S. 183	L	W	L	L	L	W	L	W	W
547	Clark v. Community for Creative Non-Violence	6/29/1984	468 U.S. 288	L	L	L	L	L	W	L	W	L
548	Hobby v. United States	7/2/1984	468 U.S. 339	L	W	L	L	L	W	L	W	L
549	FCC v. League of Women Voters	7/2/1984	468 U.S. 364	L	L	W	L	W	W	L	W	W
550	Berkemer v. McCarty	7/2/1984	468 U.S. 420	W	W	W	W	W	W	W	W	W
551	Roberts v. United States Jaycees	7/3/1984	468 U.S. 609	NP	W	W	W	W	W	W	W	NP
552	New Jersey v. T.L.O.	1/15/1985	469 U.S. 325	L	W	L	L	L	W	L	W	L

	Case Name	Date of Decision	Case No.	Justices and Their Votes (W = ACLU Win; L = ACLU Loss; NP = Justice took no part in the decision)								
A	B	C	D	E	F	G	H	I	J	K	L	M
				Burger	Stevens	O'Connor	Rehnquist	Powell	Marshall	White	Brennan	Blackmun
553	Federal Election Commission v. National Conservative Political Action Committee	3/18/1985	470 U.S. 480	W	W	W	W	W	L	L	L	W
554	Cleveland Board of Education v. Loudermill	3/19/1985	470 U.S. 532	W	W	W	L	W	W	W	W	W
555	Anderson v. City of Bessemer	3/19/1985	470 U.S. 564	W	W	W	W	W	W	W	W	W
556	Lindahl v. Office of Personnel Management	3/20/1985	470 U.S. 768	L	W	L	L	W	W	L	W	W
557	Tony and Susan Alamo Foundation v. Secretary of Labor	4/23/1985	471 U.S. 290	W	W	W	W	W	W	W	W	W
558	Zauderer v. Office of Disciplinary Counsel	5/28/1985	471 U.S. 626	W	W	W	W	NP	W	W	W	W
559	Oklahoma City v. Tuttle	6/3/1985	471 U.S. 808	L	W	L	L	NP	L	L	L	L
560	Wallace v. Jaffree	6/4/1985	472 U.S. 38	L	W	W	L	W	W	L	W	W
561	Lowe v. Securities & Exchange Commission	6/10/1985	472 U.S. 181	W	W	W	W	NP	W	W	W	W
562	Western Air Lines, Inc. v. Criswell	6/17/1985	472 U.S. 400	W	W	W	W	NP	W	W	W	W
563	Maryland v. Macon	6/17/1985	472 U.S. 463	L	L	L	L	L	W	L	W	L
564	McDonald v. Smith	6/19/1985	472 U.S. 479	L	L	L	L	NP	L	L	L	L
565	In re Snyder	6/24/1985	472 U.S. 634	W	W	W	W	W	W	W	W	NP
566	United States v. Albertini	6/24/1985	472 U.S. 675	L	W	L	L	L	W	L	W	L
567	Jean v. Nelson	6/26/1985	472 U.S. 846	L	L	L	L	NP	W	L	W	L
568	Atascadero State Hospital v. Scanlon	6/28/1985	473 U.S. 234	L	W	L	L	L	W	L	W	W
569	Walters v. National Ass'n of Radiation Survivors	6/28/1985	473 U.S. 305	L	W	L	L	L	W	L	W	L
570	Aguilar v. Felton	7/1/1985	473 U.S. 402	L	W	L	L	W	W	L	W	W
571	City of Cleburne v. Cleburne Living Center	7/1/1985	473 U.S. 432	W	W	W	W	W	W	W	W	W
572	Cornelius v. NAACP Legal Defense and Educational Fund, Inc.	7/2/1985	473 U.S. 788	L	W	L	L	NP	NP	L	W	W
573	Marek v. Chesny	7/27/1985	473 U.S. 1	L	L	L	L	L	W	L	W	W
574	Miller v. Fenton	12/3/1985	474 U.S. 104	W	W	W	L	W	W	W	W	W
575	Wainwright v. Greenfield	1/14/1986	474 U.S. 284	W	W	W	W	W	W	W	W	W
576	Witters v. Washington Department of Services for the Blind	1/27/1986	474 U.S. 481	L	L	L	L	L	L	L	L	L

Votes of Each Justice on Each ACLU/SCOTUS Case from 1925 to 2019 (by Date)

	Case Name	Date of Decision	Case No.	Justices and Their Votes (W = ACLU Win; L = ACLU Loss; NP = Justice took no part in the decision)								
A	B	C	D	E	F	G	H	I	J	K	L	M
				Burger	Stevens	O'Connor	Rehnquist	Powell	Marshall	White	Brennan	Blackmun
577	City of Renton v. Playtime Theatres, Inc.	2/25/1986	475 U.S. 41	L	L	L	L	L	W	L	W	L
578	Malley v. Briggs	3/5/1986	475 U.S. 335	W	W	W	L	L	W	W	W	W
579	Pembaur v. City of Cincinnati	3/25/1986	475 U.S. 469	L	W	W	L	L	W	W	W	W
580	Goldman v. Weinberger	3/25/1986	475 U.S. 503	L	L	W	L	L	W	L	W	W
581	Bender v. Williamsport Area School District	3/25/1986	475 U.S. 534	W	L	L	W	W	L	W	L	L
582	Holbrook v. Flynn	3/26/1986	475 U.S. 560	L	L	L	L	L	L	L	L	L
583	Evans v. Jeff D.	4/21/1986	475 U.S. 717	L	L	L	L	L	W	L	W	W
584	Philadelphia Newspapers, Inc. v. Hepps	4/21/1986	475 U.S. 767	L	L	W	L	W	W	L	W	W
585	Smalis v. Pennsylvania	5/5/1986	476 U.S. 140	W	W	W	W	W	W	W	W	W
586	California v. Ciraolo	5/19/1986	476 U.S. 207	L	L	L	L	W	W	L	W	W
587	Bowen v. City of New York	6/2/1986	476 U.S. 467	W	W	W	W	W	W	W	W	W
588	City of Los Angeles v. Preferred Communications, Inc.	6/2/1986	476 U.S. 488	W	W	W	W	W	W	W	W	W
589	Thornburgh v. American College of Obstetricians and Gynecologists	6/11/1986	476 U.S. 747	L	W	L	L	W	W	L	W	W
590	Memphis Community School District v. Stachura	6/25/1986	477 U.S. 299	L	L	L	L	L	L	L	L	L
591	Kimmelman v. Morrison	6/26/1986	477 U.S. 365	W	W	W	W	W	W	W	W	W
592	Murray v. Carrier	6/26/1986	477 U.S. 478	L	L	L	L	L	W	L	W	L
593	Ohio Civil Rights Commission v. Dayton Christian Schools, Inc.	6/27/1986	477 U.S. 619	W	W	W	W	W	W	W	W	W
594	New Mexico v. Earnest	6/27/1986	477 U.S. 648	L	L	L	L	L	L	L	L	L
595	Press-Enterprise Co. v. Superior Court	6/30/1986	478 U.S. 1	W	L	W	L	W	W	W	W	W
596	Davis v. Bandemer	6/30/1986	478 U.S. 109	L	W	L	L	W	L	L	L	L
597	Posadas de Puerto Rico Associates v. Tourism Company of Puerto Rico	7/1/1986	478 U.S. 328	L	W	L	L	L	W	L	W	W
598	Rose v. Clark	7/2/1986	478 U.S. 570	L	L	L	L	L	W	L	W	W
599	Arcara v. Cloud Books Inc.	7/7/1986	478 U.S. 697	L	L	L	L	L	W	L	W	W

Votes of Each Justice on Each ACLU/SCOTUS Case from 1925 to 2019 (by Date)

	Case Name	Date of Decision	Case No.	Justices and Their Votes (W = ACLU Win; L = ACLU Loss; NP = Justice took no part in the decision)								
A	B	C	D	E	F	G	H	I	J	K	L	M
				Scalia	Stevens	O'Connor	Rehnquist	Powell	Marshall	White	Brennan	Blackmun
600	Munro v. Socialist Workers Party	12/10/1986	479 U.S. 189	Scalia L	L	L	L	L	W	L	W	L
601	Federal Election Commission v. Massachusetts Citizens For Life, Inc.	12/15/1986	479 U.S. 238	W	L	W	L	W	W	L	W	L
602	California Federal Savings & Loan Association v. Guerra	1/13/1987	479 U.S. 272	W	W	W	L	L	W	L	W	W
603	Colorado v. Bertine	1/14/1987	479 U.S. 367	L	L	L	L	L	W	L	W	L
604	Wimberly v. Labor and Industrial Relations Commission of Missouri	1/21/1987	479 U.S. 511	L	L	L	L	L	L	L	L	NP
605	California v. Brown	1/27/1987	479 U.S. 538	L	W	L	L	L	W	L	W	W
606	City of Springfield v. Kibbe	2/25/1987	480 U.S. 257	W	W	L	L	L	W	L	W	W
607	Arizona v. Hicks	3/3/1987	480 U.S. 321	W	W	L	L	L	W	W	W	W
608	Town of Newton v. Rumery	3/9/1987	480 U.S. 386	L	W	L	L	L	W	L	W	W
609	Immigration & Naturalization Service v. Cardoza-Fonseca	3/9/1987	480 U.S. 421	W	W	W	L	L	W	L	W	W
610	Johnson v. Transportation Agency	3/25/1987	480 U.S. 616	L	W	W	L	W	W	L	W	W
611	O'Connor v. Ortega	3/31/1987	480 U.S. 709	L	W	L	L	L	W	L	W	W
612	Corp. for the Presiding Bishop of the Church of Jesus Christ of Latter-Day Saints v. Amos	3/31/1987	483 U.S. 327	L	L	L	L	L	L	L	L	L
613	Arkansas Writers' Project, Inc. v. Ragland	4/22/1987	481 U.S. 221	L	W	W	L	W	W	W	W	W
614	Meese v. Keene	4/28/1987	481 U.S. 465	NP	L	L	L	L	W	L	W	W
615	Pope v. Illinois	5/4/1987	481 U.S. 497	W	L	W	W	W	L	W	L	L
616	Board of Directors of Rotary Int'l v. Rotary Club of Duarte	5/4/1987	481 U.S. 537	W	W	NP	W	W	W	W	W	NP
617	Pennsylvania v. Finley	5/18/1987	481 U.S. 551	L	W	L	L	L	W	L	W	L
618	United States v. Salerno	5/26/1987	481 U.S. 739	L	W	L	L	L	W	L	W	L
619	Hilton v. Braunskill	5/26/1987	481 U.S. 770	L	L	L	L	L	W	L	W	W
620	United States v. Mendoza-Lopez	5/26/1987	481 U.S. 828	L	W	L	L	W	W	L	W	W
621	United States v. Hohri	6/1/1987	482 U.S. 64	NP	L	L	L	L	L	L	L	L
622	O'Lone v. Estate of Shabazz	6/9/1987	482 U.S. 342	L	W	L	L	L	W	L	W	W

Votes of Each Justice on Each ACLU/SCOTUS Case from 1925 to 2019 (by Date)

	Case Name	Date of Decision	Case No.	Justices and Their Votes (W = ACLU Win; L = ACLU Loss; NP = Justice took no part in the decision)								
A	B	C	D	E	F	G	H	I	J	K	L	M
				Scalia	Stevens	O'Connor	Rehnquist	Powell	Marshall	White	Brennan	Blackmun
623	Miller v. Florida	6/9/1987	482 U.S. 423	W	W	W	W	W	W	W	W	W
624	City of Houston v. Hill	6/15/1987	482 U.S. 451	W	W	W	L	W	W	W	W	W
625	Edwards v. Aguillard	6/19/1987	482 U.S. 578	L	W	W	L	W	W	W	W	W
626	New York v. Burger	6/19/1987	482 U.S. 691	L	L	W	L	L	W	L	W	L
627	Kentucky v. Stincer	6/19/1987	482 U.S. 730	L	W	L	L	L	W	L	W	L
628	Bowen v. Gilliard	6/25/1987	483 U.S. 587	L	L	L	L	L	W	L	W	W
629	Anderson v. Creighton	6/25/1987	483 U.S. 635	L	W	L	L	L	W	L	W	L
630	Greer v. Miller	6/25/1987	483 U.S. 756	L	L	L	L	L	W	L	W	W
631	Griffin v. Wisconsin	6/26/1987	483 U.S. 868	L	W	L	L	L	W	L	W	W
632	Church of Scientology of California v. Internal Revenue Service	11/10/1987	484 U.S. 9	NP	L	L	L	VACANT SEAT	L	L	NP	L
633	Karcher v. May	12/1/1987	484 U.S. 72	W	W	W	W	VACANT SEAT	W	W	W	W
634	Deakins v. Monaghan	1/12/1988	484 U.S. 193	W	W	W	W	VACANT SEAT	W	W	W	W
635	Hazelwood School District v. Kuhlmeier	1/13/1988	484 U.S. 260	L	L	L	L	VACANT SEAT	W	L	W	W
636	Virginia v. American Booksellers Ass'n, Inc.	1/25/1988	484 U.S. 383	L	L	L	L	VACANT SEAT	L	L	L	L
637	Department of the Navy v. Egan	2/23/1988	484 U.S. 518	L	L	L	L	**Kennedy** / NP	W	W	W	L
638	Pennell v. City of San Jose	2/24/1988	485 U.S. 1	L	W	L	W	NP	W	W	W	W
639	Hustler Magazine, Inc. v. Falwell	2/24/1988	485 U.S. 46	W	W	W	W	NP	W	W	W	W
640	Boos v. Barry	3/22/1988	485 U.S. 312	W	W	W	L	NP	W	L	W	L
641	Lyng v. Northwest Indian Cemetery Protective Ass'n	4/19/1988	485 U.S. 439	L	L	L	L	NP	W	L	W	W
642	Traynor v. Turnage	4/20/1988	485 U.S. 535	NP	L	L	L	NP	W	L	W	W
643	Edward J. DeBartolo Corp. v. Florida Gulf Coast Building & Construction Trades Council	4/20/1988	485 U.S. 568	W	W	W	W	NP	W	W	W	W
644	United States v. Providence Journal Co.	5/2/1988	485 U.S. 693	W	L	W	L	NP	W	W	W	W
645	Meyer v. Grant	6/6/1988	486 U.S. 414	W	W	W	W	W	W	W	W	W
646	Clark v. Jeter	6/6/1988	486 U.S. 456	W	W	W	W	W	W	W	W	W
647	City of Lakewood v. Plain Dealer Publishing Co.	6/17/1988	486 U.S. 750	W	L	L	NP	NP	W	L	W	W

Votes of Each Justice on Each ACLU/SCOTUS Case from 1925 to 2019 (by Date)

	Case Name	Date of Decision	Case No.	Justices and Their Votes (W = ACLU Win; L = ACLU Loss; NP = Justice took no part in the decision)								
A	B	C	D	E	F	G	H	I	J	K	L	M
				Scalia	Stevens	O'Connor	Rehnquist	Kennedy	Marshall	White	Brennan	Blackmun
648	New York State Club Ass'n v. City of New York	6/20/1988	487 U.S. 1	W	W	W	W	W	W	W	W	W
649	West v. Atkins	6/20/1988	487 U.S. 42	W	W	W	W	W	W	W	W	W
650	United States Catholic Conference v. Abortion Rights Mobilization, Inc.	6/20/1988	487 U.S. 72	L	L	L	L	L	W	L	L	L
651	Ross v. Oklahoma	6/22/1988	487 U.S. 81	L	W	L	L	L	W	L	W	W
652	Bank of Nova Scotia v. United States	6/22/1988	487 U.S. 250	L	L	L	L	L	W	L	L	L
653	Schweiker v. Chilicky	6/24/1988	487 U.S. 412	L	L	L	L	L	W	L	W	W
654	Kadrmas v. Dickinson Public Schools	6/24/1988	487 U.S. 450	L	W	L	L	L	W	L	W	W
655	Frisby v. Schultz	6/27/1988	487 U.S. 474	L	W	L	L	L	W	L	W	L
656	Murray v. United States	6/27/1988	487 U.S. 533	W	L	L	W	NP	L	W	NP	W
657	Bowen v. Kendrick	6/29/1988	487 U.S. 589	L	W	L	L	L	W	L	W	W
658	Watson v. Fort Worth Bank & Trust	6/29/1988	487 U.S. 977	W	W	W	W	NP	W	W	W	W
659	Penson v. Ohio	11/29/1988	488 U.S. 75	W	W	W	L	W	W	W	W	W
660	Carlucci v. Doe	12/6/1988	488 U.S. 93	L	L	L	L	L	L	L	L	L
661	Owens v. Okure	1/10/1989	488 U.S. 235	W	W	W	W	W	W	W	W	W
662	Florida v. Riley	1/23/1989	488 U.S. 445	L	W	L	L	L	W	L	W	W
663	City of Richmond v. J.A. Croson Co.	1/23/1989	488 U.S. 469	L	L	L	L	L	W	L	W	W
664	Texas Monthly, Inc. v. Bullock	2/21/1989	489 U.S. 1	L	W	W	L	L	W	W	W	W
665	Fort Wayne Books, Inc. v. Indiana	2/21/1989	489 U.S. 46	W	W	W	W	W	W	W	W	W
666	DeShaney v. Winnebago County Department of Social Services	2/22/1989	489 U.S. 189	L	L	L	L	L	W	L	W	W
667	City of Canton, Ohio v. Harris	2/28/1989	489 U.S. 378	W	L	W	L	W	L	L	L	L
668	Blanton v. City of North Las Vegas, Nevada	3/6/1989	489 U.S. 538	L	L	L	L	L	L	L	L	L
669	Graham v. Connor	3/15/1989	490 U.S. 386	W	W	W	W	W	W	W	W	W
670	Skinner v. Railway Labor Executives' Ass'n	3/21/1989	489 U.S. 602	L	L	L	L	L	W	L	W	L
671	National Treasury Employees Union v. Von Raab	3/21/1989	489 U.S. 656	W	W	L	L	L	W	L	W	L
672	Board of Estimate of New York v. Morris	3/22/1989	489 U.S. 688	W	W	W	W	W	W	W	W	W

Votes of Each Justice on Each ACLU/SCOTUS Case from 1925 to 2019 (by Date)

	Case Name	Date of Decision	Case No.	Justices and Their Votes (W = ACLU Win; L = ACLU Loss; NP = Justice took no part in the decision)								
A	B	C	D	E	F	G	H	I	J	K	L	M
				Scalia	Stevens	O'Connor	Rehnquist	Kennedy	Marshall	White	Brennan	Blackmun
673	United States Department of Justice v. Reporters Committee for Freedom of the Press	3/22/1989	489 U.S. 749	W	W	W	W	W	W	W	W	W
674	Frazee v. Illinois Dep't of Employment Security	3/29/1989	489 U.S. 829	W	W	W	W	W	W	W	W	W
675	American Foreign Service Ass'n v. Garfinkel	4/18/1989	490 U.S. 153	W	W	W	W	W	W	W	W	W
676	Frank v. Minnesota Newspaper Ass'n, Inc.	4/25/1989	490 U.S. 225	L	W	L	L	L	W	W	L	L
677	Price-Waterhouse v. Hopkins	5/1/1989	490 U.S. 228	W	L	L	W	W	L	L	L	L
678	Maleng v. Cook	5/15/1989	490 U.S. 488	W	W	W	W	W	W	W	W	W
679	Wards Cove Packing Co. v. Atonio	6/5/1989	490 U.S. 642	L	W	L	L	L	W	L	W	W
680	Martin v. Wilks	6/12/1989	490 U.S. 755	L	W	L	L	L	W	L	W	W
681	Will v. Michigan Department of State Police	6/15/1989	491 U.S. 58	L	W	L	L	L	W	L	W	W
682	Quinn v. Millsap	6/15/1989	491 U.S. 95	W	W	W	W	W	W	W	W	W
683	Michael H. v. Gerald D.	6/15/1989	491 U.S. 110	L	L	L	L	L	W	W	W	W
684	Patterson v. McLean Credit Union	6/15/1989	491 U.S. 164	L	W	L	L	L	W	L	W	W
685	Dellmuth v. Muth	6/15/1989	491 U.S. 223	L	W	L	L	L	W	L	W	W
686	Texas v. Johnson	6/21/1989	491 U.S. 397	W	L	L	L	W	W	L	W	W
687	Independent Federation of Flight Attendants v. Zipes	6/22/1989	491 U.S. 754	L	NP	L	L	L	W	L	W	L
688	Murray v. Giarratano	6/23/1989	492 U.S. 1	L	W	L	L	L	W	L	W	W
689	Webster v. Reproductive Health Services	7/3/1989	492 U.S. 490	L	W	L	L	L	W	L	W	W
690	County of Allegheny v. American Civil Liberties Union Greater Pittsburgh Chapter	7/3/1989	492 U.S. 573	L	W	W	L	L	W	L	W	W
691	Spallone v. United States	1/10/1990	493 U.S. 265	L	W	L	L	L	W	L	W	W
692	Jimmy Swaggart Ministries v. Board of Equalization of California	1/17/1990	493 U.S. 378	W	W	W	W	W	W	W	W	W
693	Federal Trade Commission v. Superior Court Trial Lawyers Ass'n	1/22/1990	493 U.S. 411	W	W	W	W	W	L	W	L	L
694	Holland v. Illinois	1/22/1990	493 U.S. 474	L	W	L	L	L	W	L	W	W
695	Zinermon v. Burch	2/27/1990	494 U.S. 113	L	W	L	L	L	W	W	W	W

Votes of Each Justice on Each ACLU/SCOTUS Case from 1925 to 2019 (by Date)

	Case Name	Date of Decision	Case No.	Justices and Their Votes (W = ACLU Win; L = ACLU Loss; NP = Justice took no part in the decision)								
A	B	C	D	E	F	G	H	I	J	K	L	M
				Scalia	Stevens	O'Connor	Rehnquist	Kennedy	Marshall	White	Brennan	Blackmun
696	United States v. Verdugo-Urquidez	2/28/1990	494 U.S. 259	L	L	L	L	L	W	L	W	W
697	Michigan v. Harvey	3/5/1990	494 U.S. 344	L	W	L	L	L	W	L	W	W
698	Butterworth v. Smith	3/21/1990	494 U.S. 624	W	W	W	W	W	W	W	W	W
699	Austin v. Michigan Chamber of Commerce	3/27/1990	494 U.S. 652	W	L	W	L	W	L	L	L	L
700	Employment Division v. Smith	4/17/1990	494 U.S. 872	L	L	L	L	L	W	L	W	W
701	Keller v. State Bar of California	6/4/1990	496 U.S. 1	W	W	W	W	W	W	W	W	W
702	Illinois v. Perkins	6/4/1990	496 U.S. 292	L	L	L	L	L	W	L	L	L
703	United States v. Eichman	6/11/1990	496 U.S. 310	W	L	L	L	W	W	L	W	W
704	Alabama v. White	6/11/1990	496 U.S. 325	L	W	L	L	L	W	L	W	L
705	Milkovich v. Lorain Journal Co.	6/21/1990	497 U.S. 1	L	L	L	L	L	W	L	W	L
706	Cruzan v. Director, Missouri Department of Health	6/25/1990	497 U.S. 261	L	W	L	L	L	W	L	W	W
707	Hodgson v. Minnesota	6/25/1990	497 U.S. 417	L	W	W	L	L	W	L	W	W
708	Metro Broadcasting, Inc. v. FCC	6/27/1990	497 U.S. 547	L	W	L	L	L	W	W	W	W
709	Walton v. Arizona	6/27/1990	497 U.S. 639	L	W	L	L	L	W	L	W	W
710	United States v. Kokinda	6/27/1990	497 U.S. 720	L	W	L	L	L	W	L	W	W
711	Idaho v. Wright	6/27/1990	497 U.S. 805	W	W	W	L	L	W	L	W	L
712	Board of Education of Oklahoma City v. Dowell	1/15/1991	498 U.S. 237	L	W	L	L	L	W	L	**Souter** NP	W
713	UAW v. Johnson Controls, Inc.	3/20/1991	499 U.S. 187	W	W	W	W	W	W	W	W	W
714	Equal Employment Opportunity Commission v. Arabian American Oil Co.	3/26/1991	499 U.S. 244	L	W	L	L	L	W	L	L	W
715	Powers v. Ohio	4/1/1991	499 U.S. 400	L	W	W	L	W	W	W	W	W
716	County of Riverside v. McLaughlin	5/13/1991	500 U.S. 44	W	W	L	L	L	W	L	L	W
717	Rust v. Sullivan	5/23/1991	500 U.S. 173	L	W	W	L	L	W	L	L	W
718	Siegert v. Gilley	5/23/1991	500 U.S. 226	L	W	L	L	L	W	L	L	W
719	Burns v. Reed	5/30/1991	500 U.S. 478	W	W	W	W	W	W	W	W	W
720	Edmonson v. Leesville Concrete Co.	6/3/1991	500 U.S. 614	L	W	L	L	W	W	W	W	W

Votes of Each Justice on Each ACLU/SCOTUS Case from 1925 to 2019 (by Date)

	Case Name	Date of Decision	Case No.	Justices and Their Votes (W = ACLU Win; L = ACLU Loss; NP = Justice took no part in the decision)								
A	B	C	D	E	F	G	H	I	J	K	L	M
				Scalia	Stevens	O'Connor	Rehnquist	Kennedy	Marshall	White	Souter	Blackmun
721	Clark v. Roemer	6/3/1991	500 U.S. 646	W	W	W	W	W	W	W	W	W
722	Renne v. Geary	6/17/1991	501 U.S. 312	L	L	L	L	L	W	W	L	W
723	Florida v. Bostick	6/20/1991	501 U.S. 429	L	W	L	L	L	W	L	L	W
724	Barnes v. Glen Theatre, Inc.	6/21/1991	501 U.S. 560	L	W	L	L	L	W	W	L	W
725	Harmelin v. Michigan	6/27/1991	501 U.S. 957	L	W	L	L	L	W	W	L	W
726	Gentile v. State Bar of Nevada	6/27/1991	501 U.S. 1030	L	W	W	L	W	W	L	L	W
727	Hafer v. Melo	11/5/1991	502 U.S. 21	W	W	W	W	W	**Thomas** NP	W	W	W
728	Simon & Schuster, Inc. v. Members of the New York State Crime Victims Board	12/10/1991	502 U.S. 105	W	W	W	W	W	NP	W	W	W
729	United States Department of State v. Ray	12/16/1991	502 U.S. 164	L	L	L	L	L	NP	L	L	L
730	Norman v. Reed	1/14/1992	502 U.S. 279	L	W	W	W	W	NP	W	W	W
731	Immigration & Naturalization Service v. Doherty	1/15/1992	502 U.S. 314	W	W	L	L	L	NP	L	W	L
732	Rufo v. Inmates of the Suffolk County Jail	1/15/1992	502 U.S. 367	L	W	L	L	L	NP	L	L	W
733	Hudson v. McMillian	2/25/1992	503 U.S. 1	L	W	W	W	W	L	W	W	W
734	Collins v. City of Harker Heights, Texas	2/26/1992	503 U.S. 115	L	L	L	L	L	L	L	L	L
735	Dawson v. Delaware	3/9/1992	503 U.S. 159	W	W	W	W	W	L	W	W	W
736	Freeman v. Pitts	3/31/1992	503 U.S. 467	L	L	L	L	L	NP	L	L	L
737	Jacobson v. United States	4/6/1992	503 U.S. 540	L	W	L	L	L	W	W	W	W
738	Denton v. Hernandez	5/4/1992	504 U.S. 25	L	W	L	L	L	L	L	L	W
739	United States v. Burke	5/26/1992	504 U.S. 229	L	L	W	L	L	W	L	L	L
740	Burdick v. Takushi	6/8/1992	504 U.S. 428	L	W	L	L	W	L	L	L	W
741	Ankenbrandt v. Richards	6/15/1992	504 U.S. 689	W	W	W	W	W	W	W	W	W
742	Morgan v. Illinois	6/15/1992	504 U.S. 719	L	W	W	L	W	L	W	W	W
743	Forsyth County v. Nationalist Movement	6/19/1992	505 U.S. 123	L	W	W	L	W	L	L	W	W
744	Wright v. West	6/19/1992	505 U.S. 277	L	L	L	L	L	L	L	L	L
745	R.A.V. v. City of St. Paul	6/22/1992	505 U.S. 377	W	W	W	W	W	W	W	W	W
746	Lee v. Weisman	6/24/1992	505 U.S. 577	L	W	W	L	W	L	L	W	W

Votes of Each Justice on Each ACLU/SCOTUS Case from 1925 to 2019 (by Date)

	Case Name	Date of Decision	Case No.	Justices and Their Votes (W = ACLU Win; L = ACLU Loss; NP = Justice took no part in the decision)								
A	B	C	D	E	F	G	H	I	J	K	L	M
				Scalia	Stevens	O'Connor	Rehnquist	Kennedy	Thomas	White	Souter	Blackmun
747	International Society for Krishna Consciousness, Inc. v. Lee	6/26/1992	505 U.S. 672	L	W	L	L	L	L	L	W	W
748	Planned Parenthood of Southeastern Pennsylvania v. Casey	6/29/1992	505 U.S. 833	L	W	W	L	W	L	L	W	W
749	Soldal v. Cook County, Illinois	12/8/1992	506 U.S. 56	W	W	W	W	W	W	W	W	W
750	Crosby v. United States	1/13/1993	506 U.S. 255	W	W	W	W	W	W	W	W	W
751	Bray v. Alexandria Women's Health Clinic	1/13/1993	506 U.S. 263	L	W	W	L	L	L	L	L	W
752	Brecht v. Abrahamson	4/21/1993	507 U.S. 619	L	L	W	L	L	L	W	W	W
753	Withrow v. Williams	4/21/1993	507 U.S. 680	L	W	L	L	W	L	W	W	W
754	Gilmore v. Taylor	6/7/1993	508 U.S. 333	L	W	L	L	L	L	L	L	W
755	Minnesota v. Dickerson	6/7/1993	508 U.S. 366	W	W	W	W	W	W	W	W	W
756	Lamb's Chapel v. Center Moriches Union Free School District	6/7/1993	508 U.S. 384	W	W	W	W	W	W	W	W	W
757	Wisconsin v. Mitchell	6/11/1993	508 U.S. 476	W	W	W	W	W	W	W	W	W
758	Church of Lukumi Babalu Aye, Inc. v. City of Hialeah	6/11/1993	508 U.S. 520	W	W	W	W	W	W	W	W	W
759	Godinez v. Moran	6/24/1993	509 U.S. 389	L	W	L	L	L	L	L	L	W
760	United States v. Edge Broadcasting Co.	6/25/1993	509 U.S. 418	L	W	L	L	L	L	L	L	W
761	Alexander v. United States	6/28/1993	509 U.S. 544	L	W	L	L	W	L	L	W	W
762	Austin v. United States	6/28/1993	509 U.S. 602	W	W	W	W	W	W	W	W	W
763	Harris v. Forklift Systems, Inc.	11/9/1993	510 U.S. 17	W	W	W	W	W	W	**Ginsburg** W	W	W
764	United States v. James Daniel Good Real Property	12/13/1993	510 U.S. 43	L	W	L	L	W	L	W	W	W
765	Weiss v. United States	1/19/1994	510 U.S. 163	L	L	L	L	L	L	L	L	L
766	National Organization for Women, Inc. v. Scheidler	1/24/1994	510 U.S. 249	W	W	W	W	W	W	W	W	W
767	Albright v. Oliver	1/24/1994	510 U.S. 266	L	W	L	L	L	L	L	L	W
768	Elder v. Holloway	2/23/1994	510 U.S. 510	W	W	W	W	W	W	W	W	W
769	Campbell v. Acuff-Rose Music, Inc.	3/7/1994	510 U.S. 569	W	W	W	W	W	W	W	W	W
770	J.E.B. v. Alabama ex rel. T.B.	4/19/1994	511 U.S. 127	L	W	W	L	W	L	W	W	W

Votes of Each Justice on Each ACLU/SCOTUS Case from 1925 to 2019 (by Date)

	Case Name	Date of Decision	Case No.	Justices and Their Votes (W = ACLU Win; L = ACLU Loss; NP = Justice took no part in the decision)								
A	B	C	D	E	F	G	H	I	J	K	L	M
				Scalia	Stevens	O'Connor	Rehnquist	Kennedy	Thomas	Ginsburg	Souter	Blackmun
771	Nichols v. United States	6/6/1994	511 U.S. 738	L	W	L	L	L	L	W	L	W
772	Farmer v. Brennan	6/6/1994	511 U.S. 825	W	W	W	W	W	W	W	W	W
773	City of Ladue v. Gilleo	6/13/1994	512 U.S. 43	W	W	W	W	W	W	W	W	W
774	McFarland v. Scott	6/301994	512 U.S. 849	L	W	L	L	W	L	W	W	W
775	Tuilaepa v. California	6/301994	512 U.S. 967	L	L	L	L	L	L	L	L	W
776	Lebron v. National Railroad Passenger Corp.	2/21/1995	513 U.S. 374	W	W	L	W	W	W	W	W	**Breyer** W
777	O'Neal v. McAninch	2/21/1995	513 U.S. 432	L	W	W	L	W	L	W	W	W
778	United States v. National Treasury Employees Union	2/22/1995	513 U.S. 454	L	W	W	L	W	L	W	W	W
779	Arizona v. Evans	3/1/1995	514 U.S. 1	L	W	L	L	L	L	W	L	L
780	Swint v. Chambers County Commission	3/1/1995	514 U.S. 35	L	L	L	L	L	L	L	L	L
781	McIntyre v. Ohio Elections Commission	4/19/1995	514 U.S. 334	L	W	W	L	W	W	W	W	W
782	City of Edmonds v. Oxford House, Inc.	5/15/1995	514 U.S. 725	L	W	W	W	L	L	W	W	W
783	U.S. Term Limits, Inc. v. Thornton	5/22/1995	514 U.S. 779	L	W	L	L	W	L	W	W	W
784	Wilson v. Arkansas	5/22/1995	514 U.S. 927	W	W	W	W	W	W	W	W	W
785	Missouri v. Jenkins	6/12/1995	515 U.S. 70	L	W	L	L	L	L	W	W	W
786	Kimberlin v. Quinlan	6/12/1995	515 U.S. 321	W	W	W	W	W	W	W	W	W
787	Sandin v. Conner	6/19/1995	515 U.S. 472	L	W	L	L	L	L	W	W	W
788	Hurley v. Irish-American Gay, Lesbian & Bisexual Group of Boston	6/19/1995	515 U.S. 557	W	W	W	W	W	W	W	W	W
789	Capitol Square Review & Advisory Board v. Pinette	6/29/1995	515 U.S. 753	W	L	W	W	W	W	L	W	W
790	Rosenberger v. Rector & Visitors of the University of Virginia	6/29/1995	515 U.S. 819	L	W	L	L	L	L	W	W	W
791	Miller v. Johnson	6/29/1995	515 U.S. 900	L	W	L	L	L	L	W	W	W
792	National Labor Relations Board v. Town & Country Electric, Inc.	11/28/1995	516 U.S. 85	W	W	W	W	W	W	W	W	W
793	United States v. Chesapeake & Potomac Telephone Co. of Virginia	2/27/1996	516 U.S. 415	L	L	L	L	L	L	L	L	L
794	Wisconsin v. City of New York	3/20/1996	517 U.S. 1	L	L	L	L	L	L	L	L	L
795	Morse v. Republican Party of Virginia	3/27/1996	517 U.S. 186	L	W	W	L	L	L	W	W	W
796	United States v. Armstrong	5/13/1996	517 U.S. 456	L	W	L	L	L	L	L	L	L
797	44 Liquormart, Inc. v. Rhode Island	5/13/1996	517 U.S. 484	W	W	W	W	W	W	W	W	W

Votes of Each Justice on Each ACLU/SCOTUS Case from 1925 to 2019 (by Date)

	Case Name	Date of Decision	Case No.	Justices and Their Votes (W = ACLU Win; L = ACLU Loss; NP = Justice took no part in the decision)								
A	B	C	D	E	F	G	H	I	J	K	L	M
				Scalia	Stevens	O'Connor	Rehnquist	Kennedy	Thomas	Ginsburg	Souter	Breyer
798	Romer v. Evans	May 20, 1996	517 U.S. 620	L	W	W	L	W	L	W	W	W
799	Ornelas v. United States	May 28, 1996	517 U.S. 690	L	W	W	W	W	W	W	W	W
800	Loving v. United States	6/3/1996	517 U.S. 748	L	L	L	L	L	L	L	L	L
801	Whren v. United States	6/10/1996	517 U.S. 806	L	L	L	L	L	L	L	L	L
802	Shaw v. Hunt	6/13/1996	517 U.S. 899	L	W	L	L	L	L	W	W	W
803	Lane v. Pena	6/20/1996	518 U.S. 187	L	W	L	L	L	L	L	L	W
804	United States v. Ursery	6/24/1996	518 U.S. 267	L	W	L	L	L	L	L	L	L
805	Lewis v. United States	6/24/1996	518 U.S. 322	L	W	L	L	L	L	W	L	L
806	Lewis v. Casey	6/24/1996	518 U.S. 343	L	W	L	L	L	L	L	L	L
807	United States v. Virginia	6/26/1996	518 U.S. 515	L	W	W	W	W	NP	W	W	W
808	Colorado Republican Federal Campaign Committee v. Federal Election Commission	6/26/1996	518 U.S. 604	W	L	W	W	W	W	L	W	W
809	Board of County Commissioners, Wabaunsee County, Kansas v. Umbehr	6/28/1996	518 U.S. 668	L	W	W	W	W	L	W	W	W
810	O'Hare Truck Service, Inc. v. City of Northlake	6/28/1996	518 U.S. 712	L	W	W	W	W	L	W	W	W
811	Denver Area Educational Telecommunications Consortium, Inc. v. Federal Communications Commission	6/28/1996	518 U.S. 727	L	W	W	L	W	L	W	W	W
812	Lopez v. Monterey County, California	11/6/1996	519 U.S. 9	W	W	W	W	W	W	W	W	W
813	Ohio v. Robinette	11/18/1996	519 U.S. 33	L	W	L	L	L	L	L	L	L
814	M. L. B. v. S. L. J.	12/16/1996	519 U.S. 102	L	W	W	L	W	L	W	W	W
815	Robinson v. Shell Oil Co.	2/18/1997	519 U.S. 337	W	W	W	W	W	W	W	W	W
816	Schenck v. Pro-Choice Network of Western New York	2/19/1997	519 U.S. 357	L	W	W	W	L	L	W	W	L
817	Arizonans for Official English v. Arizona	3/3/1997	520 U.S. 43	L	L	L	L	L	L	L	L	L
818	Young v. Harper	3/18/1997	520 U.S. 143	W	W	W	W	W	W	W	W	W
819	United States v. Lanier	3/31/1997	520 U.S. 259	W	W	W	W	W	W	W	W	W
820	Young v. Fordice	3/31/1997	520 U.S. 273	W	W	W	W	W	W	W	W	W
821	Chandler v. Miller	4/15/1997	520 U.S. 305	W	W	W	L	W	W	W	W	W
822	Blessing v. Freestone	4/21/1997	520 U.S. 329	L	L	L	L	L	L	L	L	L
823	Timmons v. Twin Cities Area New Party	4/28/1997	520 U.S. 351	L	W	L	L	L	L	W	W	L

	Case Name	Date of Decision	Case No.	Justices and Their Votes (W = ACLU Win; L = ACLU Loss; NP = Justice took no part in the decision)								
A	B	C	D	E	F	G	H	I	J	K	L	M
				Scalia	Stevens	O'Connor	Rehnquist	Kennedy	Thomas	Ginsburg	Souter	Breyer
824	Richards v. Wisconsin	4/28/1997	520 U.S. 385	L	L	L	L	L	L	L	L	L
825	Edwards v. Balisok	May 19, 1997	520 U.S. 641	L	L	L	L	L	L	L	L	L
826	Reno v. Bossier Parish School Board	5/21/1997	520 U.S. 471	L	W	L	L	L	L	L	W	L
827	Clinton v. Jones	5/27/1997	520 U.S. 681	W	W	W	W	W	W	W	W	W
828	McMillian v. Monroe County, Alabama	6/2/1997	520 U.S. 781	L	W	L	L	L	L	W	W	W
829	Abrams v. Johnson	6/19/1997	521 U.S. 74	L	W	L	L	L	L	W	W	W
830	Agostini v. Felton	6/23/1997	521 U.S. 203	L	W	L	L	L	L	W	W	W
831	Idaho v. Coeur d'Alene Tribe of Idaho	6/23/1997	521 U.S. 261	L	W	L	L	L	L	W	W	W
832	Kansas v. Hendricks	6/23/1997	521 U.S. 346	L	W	L	L	L	L	W	W	W
833	Richardson v. McKnight	6/23/1997	521 U.S. 399	L	W	W	L	L	L	W	W	W
834	City of Boerne v. Flores	6/25/1997	521 U.S. 507	L	L	W	L	L	L	L	W	W
835	Washington v. Glucksberg	6/26/1997	521 U.S. 702	L	L	L	L	L	L	L	L	L
836	Vacco v. Quill	6/26/1997	521 U.S. 793	L	L	L	L	L	L	L	L	L
837	Reno v. American Civil Liberties Union	6/26/1997	521 U.S. 844	W	W	W	W	W	W	W	W	W
838	Oncale v. Sundowner Offshore Services, Inc.	3/4/1998	523 U.S. 75	W	W	W	W	W	W	W	W	W
839	Ohio Adult Parole Authority v. Woodard	3/25/1998	523 U.S. 272	L	L	L	L	L	L	L	L	L
840	Texas v. United States	3/31/1998	523 U.S. 296	W	W	W	W	W	W	W	W	W
841	Miller v. Albright	4/22/1998	523 U.S. 420	L	L	L	L	L	L	W	W	W
842	Crawford-El v. Britton	5/4/1998	523 U.S. 574	L	W	L	L	W	L	W	W	W
843	Ricci v. Village of Arlington Heights	5/4/1998	523 U.S. 613	L	L	L	L	L	L	L	L	L
844	Bousley v. United States	5/18/1998	523 U.S. 614	L	W	W	W	W	L	W	W	W
845	Stewart v. Martinez-Villareal	5/18/1998	523 U.S. 637	L	W	W	W	W	L	W	W	W
846	Arkansas Educational Television Commission v. Forbes	5/18/1998	523 U.S. 666	L	W	L	L	L	L	W	W	L
847	Federal Election Commission v. Akins	6/1/1998	524 U.S. 11	W	L	W	L	L	W	L	L	L
848	Pennsylvania Department of Corrections v. Yeskey	6/15/1998	524 U.S. 206	W	W	W	W	W	W	W	W	W
849	Pennsylvania Board of Probation & Parole v. Scott	6/22/1998	524 U.S. 357	L	W	L	L	L	L	W	W	W
850	National Endowment for the Arts v. Finley	6/25/1998	524 U.S. 569	L	L	L	L	L	L	L	W	L

Votes of Each Justice on Each ACLU/SCOTUS Case from 1925 to 2019 (by Date)

	Case Name	Date of Decision	Case No.	Justices and Their Votes (W = ACLU Win; L = ACLU Loss; NP = Justice took no part in the decision)								
A	B	C	D	E	F	G	H	I	J	K	L	M
				Scalia	Stevens	O'Connor	Rehnquist	Kennedy	Thomas	Ginsburg	Souter	Breyer
851	Bragdon v. Abbott	6/25/1998	524 U.S. 624	L	W	L	L	W	L	W	W	W
852	Faragher v. City of Boca Raton	6/26/1998	524 U.S. 775	L	W	W	W	W	L	W	W	W
853	Wright v. Universal Maritime Service Corp.	11/16/1998	525 U.S. 70	W	W	W	W	W	W	W	W	W
854	Minnesota v. Carter	12/1/1998	525 U.S. 83	L	W	L	L	L	L	W	W	L
855	Knowles v. Iowa	12/8/1998	525 U.S. 113	W	W	W	W	W	W	W	W	W
856	Buckley v. American Constitutional Law Foundation, Inc.	1/12/1999	525 U.S. 182	W	W	L	L	W	W	W	W	L
857	Roberts v. Galen of Virginia, Inc.	1/13/1999	525 U.S. 249	W	W	W	W	W	W	W	W	W
858	Department of Commerce v. United States House of Representatives	1/25/1999	525 U.S. 316	L	W	L	L	L	L	W	W	W
859	National Collegiate Athletic Ass'n v. Smith	2/23/1999	525 U.S. 459	L	L	L	L	L	L	L	L	L
860	Reno v. American-Arab Anti-Discrimination Committee	2/24/1999	525 U.S. 471	L	L	L	L	L	L	L	W	L
861	Saenz v. Roe	May 17, 1999	526 U.S. 489	W	W	W	L	W	L	W	W	W
862	Hunt v. Cromartie	May 17, 1999	526 U.S. 541	W	W	W	W	W	W	W	W	W
863	Wilson v. Layne	5/24/1999	526 U.S. 603	L	W	L	L	L	L	L	L	L
864	Davis v. Monroe County Board of Education	5/24/1999	526 U.S. 629	L	W	W	L	L	L	W	W	W
865	City of Chicago v. Morales	6/10/1999	527 U.S. 41	L	W	W	L	W	L	W	W	W
866	Lilly v. Virginia	6/10/1999	527 U.S. 116	W	W	W	W	W	W	W	W	W
867	Greater New Orleans Broadcasting Ass'n, Inc. v. United States	6/14/1999	527 U.S. 173	W	W	W	W	W	W	W	W	W
868	Martin v. Hadix	6/21/1999	527 U.S. 343	L	W	L	L	L	L	W	L	L
869	Sutton v. United Air Lines, Inc.	6/22/1999	527 U.S. 471	L	W	L	L	L	L	L	L	W
870	Kolstad v. American Dental Ass'n	6/22/1999	527 U.S. 526	W	W	W	L	W	L	W	W	W
871	Olmstead v. L.C. ex rel. Zimring	6/22/1999	527 U.S. 581	L	W	W	L	W	L	W	W	W
872	United States v. Weatherhead	12/3/1999	528 U.S. 1042	W	L	L	L	L	L	L	L	L
873	Illinois v. Wardlow	1/12/2000	528 U.S. 119	L	W	L	L	L	L	W	W	W
874	Reno v. Condon	1/12/2000	528 U.S. 141	W	W	W	W	W	W	W	W	W
875	Friends of the Earth v. Laidlaw Environmental Services	1/12/2000	528 U.S. 167	L	W	W	W	W	L	W	W	W

Votes of Each Justice on Each ACLU/SCOTUS Case from 1925 to 2019 (by Date)

	Case Name	Date of Decision	Case No.	Justices and Their Votes (W = ACLU Win; L = ACLU Loss; NP = Justice took no part in the decision)								
A	B	C	D	E	F	G	H	I	J	K	L	M
				Scalia	Stevens	O'Connor	Rehnquist	Kennedy	Thomas	Ginsburg	Souter	Breyer
876	Nixon v. Shrink Missouri Government PAC	1/24/2000	528 U.S. 377	W	L	L	L	W	W	L	L	L
877	Village of Willowbrook v. Olech	2/23/2000	528 U.S. 562	W	W	W	W	W	W	W	W	W
878	Board of Regents of the University of Wisconsin System v. Southworth	3/22/2000	529 U.S. 217	W	W	W	W	W	W	W	W	W
879	Garner v. Jones	3/28/2000	529 U.S. 244	L	W	L	L	L	L	W	W	L
880	Florida v. J. L.	3/28/2000	529 U.S. 266	W	W	W	W	W	W	W	W	W
881	Erie v. Pap's A. M.	3/29/2000	529 U.S. 277	L	W	L	L	L	L	W	W	L
882	Williams v. Taylor	4/18/2000	529 U.S. 362	L	W	W	L	W	L	W	W	W
883	Troxel v. Granville	6/5/2000	530 U.S. 57	L	L	W	W	L	W	W	W	W
884	Reeves v. Sanderson Plumbing Products, Inc.	6/12/2000	530 U.S. 133	W	W	W	W	W	W	W	W	W
885	Santa Fe Independent School District v. Doe	6/19/2000	530 U.S. 290	L	W	W	L	W	L	W	W	W
886	Miller v. French	6/19/2000	530 U.S. 327	L	W	L	L	L	L	W	W	W
887	Dickerson v. United States	6/26/2000	530 U.S. 428	L	W	W	W	W	L	W	W	W
888	Boy Scouts of America v. Dale	6/28/2000	530 U.S. 640	L	W	L	L	L	L	W	W	W
889	Hill v. Colorado	6/28/2000	530 U.S. 703	W	L	L	L	W	W	L	L	L
890	Mitchell v. Helms	6/28/2000	530 U.S. 793	L	W	L	L	L	L	W	W	L
891	Stenberg v. Carhart	6/28/2000	530 U.S. 914	L	W	W	L	L	L	W	W	W
892	City of Indianapolis v. Edmond	11/28/2000	531 U.S. 32	L	W	W	L	W	L	W	W	W
893	Bush v. Palm Beach County Canvassing Board	12/1/2000	531 U.S. 70	L	L	L	L	L	L	L	L	L
894	Legal Services Corp. v. Velazquez	2/28/2001	531 U.S. 533	L	W	L	L	W	L	W	W	W
895	Ferguson v. City of Charleston	3/21/2001	532 U.S. 67	L	W	W	L	W	L	W	W	W
896	Shaw v. Murphy	4/18/2001	532 U.S. 223	L	L	L	L	L	L	L	L	L
897	Easley v. Cromartie	4/18/2001	532 U.S. 234	L	W	W	L	L	L	W	W	W
898	Alexander v. Sandoval	4/24/2001	532 U.S. 275	L	W	L	L	L	L	W	W	W
899	Atwater v. City of Lago Vista	4/24/2001	532 U.S. 318	L	W	W	L	L	L	W	L	W
900	U.S. v. Oakland Cannabis Buyers' Coop.	5/14/2001	532 U.S. 483	L	L	L	L	L	L	L	L	NP
901	Bartnicki v. Vopper	5/21/2001	532 U.S. 514	L	W	W	L	W	L	W	W	W

	Case Name	Date of Decision	Case No.	Justices and Their Votes (W = ACLU Win; L = ACLU Loss; NP = Justice took no part in the decision)								
A	B	C	D	E	F	G	H	I	J	K	L	M
				Scalia	Stevens	O'Connor	Rehnquist	Kennedy	Thomas	Ginsburg	Souter	Breyer
902	Buckhannon Board & Care Home, Inc. v. West Virginia Department of Health & Human Resources	5/29/2001	532 U.S. 598	L	W	L	L	L	L	W	W	W
903	Booth v. Churner	5/29/2001	532 U.S. 731	L	L	L	L	L	L	L	L	L
904	Pollard v. E. I. du Pont de Nemours & Co.	6/4/2001	532 U.S. 843	W	W	NP	W	W	W	W	W	W
905	Kyllo v. United States	6/11/2001	533 U.S. 27	W	L	L	L	L	W	W	W	W
906	Nguyen v. INS	6/11/2001	533 U.S. 53	L	L	W	L	L	L	W	W	W
907	Good News Club v. Milford Central School	6/11/2001	533 U.S. 98	L	W	L	L	L	L	W	W	L
908	Saucier v. Katz	6/18/2001	533 U.S. 194	L	L	L	L	L	L	L	L	L
909	INS v. St. Cyr	6/25/2001	533 U.S. 289	L	W	L	L	W	L	W	W	W
910	Calcano-Martinez v. INS	6/25/2001	533 U.S. 348	L	W	L	L	W	L	W	W	W
911	FEC v. Colo. Republican Fed. Campaign Comm.	6/25/2001	533 U.S. 431	W	L	L	W	W	W	L	L	L
912	Lorillard Tobacco Co. v. Reilly	6/28/2001	533 U.S. 525	W	L	W	W	W	W	L	L	L
913	Zadvydas v. Davis	6/28/2001	533 U.S. 678	L	W	W	L	L	L	W	W	W
914	Correctional Services Corp. v. Malesko	11/27/2001	534 U.S. 61	L	W	L	L	L	L	W	W	W
915	Adarand Constructors, Inc. v. Mineta	11/27/2001	534 U.S. 103	W	W	W	W	W	W	W	W	W
916	EEOC v. Waffle House, Inc.	1/15/2002	534 U.S. 279	L	W	W	L	W	L	W	W	W
917	Kansas v. Crane	1/22/2002	534 U.S. 407	W	L	L	L	L	W	L	L	L
918	Swierkiewicz v. Sorema N. A.	2/26/2002	534 U.S. 506	W	W	W	W	W	W	W	W	W
919	Dep't of Hous. & Urban Dev. v. Rucker	3/26/2002	535 U.S. 125	L	L	L	L	L	L	L	L	NP
920	Hoffman Plastic Compounds, Inc. v. NLRB	3/27/2002	535 U.S. 137	L	W	L	L	L	L	W	W	W
921	Ashcroft v. Free Speech Coalition	4/16/2002	535 U.S. 234	L	W	L	L	W	W	W	W	W
922	Ashcroft v. American Civil Liberties Union	5/13/2002	535 U.S. 564	L	W	L	L	L	L	L	L	L
923	Verizon Maryland, Inc. v. Pub. Serv. Comm'n of Maryland	May 20, 2002	535 U.S. 635	W	W	NP	W	W	W	W	W	W
924	Bell v. Cone	May 28, 2002	535 U.S. 685	L	W	L	L	L	L	L	L	L
925	Chevron U.S.A., Inc. v. Echazabal	6/10/2002	536 U.S. 73	L	L	L	L	L	L	L	L	L
926	Watchtower Bible & Tract Soc'y of New York, Inc. v. Village of Stratton	6/17/2002	536 U.S. 150	W	W	W	L	W	W	W	W	W

	Case Name	Date of Decision	Case No.	Justices and Their Votes (W = ACLU Win; L = ACLU Loss; NP = Justice took no part in the decision)								
A	B	C	D	E	F	G	H	I	J	K	L	M
				Scalia	Stevens	O'Connor	Rehnquist	Kennedy	Thomas	Ginsburg	Souter	Breyer
927	Gonzaga Univ. v. Doe	6/20/2002	536 U.S. 273	L	W	L	L	L	L	W	L	L
928	Atkins v. Virginia	6/20/2002	536 U.S. 304	L	W	W	L	W	L	W	W	W
929	Christopher v. Harbury	6/20/2002	536 U.S. 403	L	L	L	L	L	L	L	L	L
930	Zelman v. Simmons-Harris	6/27/2002	536 U.S. 639	L	W	L	L	L	L	W	W	W
931	Hope v. Pelzer	6/27/2002	536 U.S. 730	L	W	W	L	W	L	W	W	W
932	Republican Party of Minnesota v. White	6/27/2002	536 U.S. 765	W	L	W	W	W	W	L	L	L
933	Bd. of Ed. of Indep. Sch. Dist. No. 92 of Pottawatomie Cty. v. Earls	6/27/2002	536 U.S. 822	L	W	W	L	L	L	W	W	L
934	Connecticut Dep't of Pub. Safety v. Doe	3/5/2003	538 U.S. 1	L	L	L	L	L	L	L	L	L
935	Lockyer v. Andrade	3/5/2003	538 U.S. 63	L	W	L	L	L	L	W	W	W
936	Smith v. Doe	3/5/2003	538 U.S. 84	L	W	L	L	L	L	W	L	W
937	Virginia v. Black	4/7/2003	538 U.S. 343	L	W	W	W	W	L	W	W	W
938	Medical Board of California v. Hason	4/7/2003	538 U.S. 958	W	W	W	W	W	W	W	W	W
939	Demore v. Kim	4/29/2003	538 U.S. 510	L	W	L	L	L	L	W	W	W
940	Nevada Dep't of Human Res. v. Hibbs	5/27/2003	538 U.S. 721	L	W	W	W	L	L	W	W	W
941	Chavez v. Martinez	5/27/2003	538 U.S. 760	L	W	L	L	W	L	W	L	L
942	Desert Palace, Inc. v. Costa	6/9/2003	539 U.S. 90	W	W	W	W	W	W	W	W	W
943	Virginia v. Hicks	6/16/2003	539 U.S. 113	L	L	L	L	L	L	L	L	L
944	Overton v. Bazzetta	6/16/2003	539 U.S. 126	L	L	L	L	L	L	L	L	L
945	Sell v. United States	6/16/2003	539 U.S. 166	W	L	W	L	L	W	L	L	L
946	U.S. v. American Library Ass'n, Inc.	6/23/2003	539 U.S. 194	L	W	L	L	L	L	W	W	L
947	Gratz v. Bollinger	6/23/2003	539 U.S. 244	L	W	L	L	L	L	W	W	L
948	Grutter v. Bollinger	6/23/2003	539 U.S. 306	L	W	W	L	L	L	W	W	W
949	Georgia v. Ashcroft	6/26/2003	539 U.S. 461	L	W	L	L	L	L	W	W	W
950	Lawrence v. Texas	6/26/2003	539 U.S. 558	L	W	W	L	W	L	W	W	W
951	Nike, Inc. v. Kasky	6/26/2003	539 U.S. 654	L	L	W	L	W	L	L	L	W
952	Arizona v. Gant	10/20/2003	540 U.S. 963	L	L	L	L	L	L	L	L	L
953	McConnell v. Federal Election Comm'n	12/10/2003	540 U.S. 93	W	L	L	W	W	W	L	L	L
954	Maryland v. Pringle	12/15/2003	540 U.S. 366	L	L	L	L	L	L	L	L	L
955	Illinois v. Lidster	1/13/2004	540 U.S. 419	L	W	L	L	L	L	W	W	L

	Case Name	Date of Decision	Case No.	Justices and Their Votes (W = ACLU Win; L = ACLU Loss; NP = Justice took no part in the decision)								
A	B	C	D	E	F	G	H	I	J	K	L	M
				Scalia	Stevens	O'Connor	Rehnquist	Kennedy	Thomas	Ginsburg	Souter	Breyer
956	Frew v. Hawkins	1/14/2004	540 U.S. 431	W	W	W	W	W	W	W	W	W
957	Doe v. Chao	2/24/2004	540 U.S. 614	L	W	L	L	L	L	W	L	W
958	Locke v. Davey	2/25/2004	540 U.S. 712	L	W	W	W	W	L	W	W	W
959	Crawford v. Washington	3/8/2004	541 U.S. 36	W	W	W	W	W	W	W	W	W
960	Vieth v. Jubelirer	4/28/2004	541 U.S. 267	L	W	L	L	L	L	W	W	W
961	Thornton v. United States	5/24/2004	541 U.S. 615	L	W	L	L	L	L	L	W	L
962	Elk Grove United School District v. Newdow	6/14/2004	542 U.S. 1	NP	L	L	L	L	L	L	L	L
963	Hibbs v. Winn	6/14/2004	542 U.S. 88	L	W	W	L	L	L	W	W	W
964	Pennsylvania State Police v. Suders	6/14/2004	542 U.S. 129	L	L	L	L	L	W	L	L	L
965	Hiibel v. Sixth Judicial District Court of Nevada, Humboldt County	6/21/2004	542 U.S. 177	L	W	L	L	L	L	W	W	W
966	Blakely v. Washington	6/24/2004	542 U.S. 296	W	W	L	L	L	W	W	W	L
967	Beard v. Banks	6/24/2004	542 U.S. 406	L	W	L	L	L	L	W	W	W
968	Rumsfeld v. Padilla	6/28/2004	542 U.S. 426	L	W	L	L	L	L	W	W	W
969	Rasul v. Bush	6/28/2004	542 U.S. 466	L	W	W	L	W	L	W	W	W
970	Hamdi v. Rumsfeld	6/28/2004	542 U.S. 507	L	L	W	W	W	L	W	W	W
971	Missouri v. Seibert	6/28/2004	542 U.S. 600	L	W	L	L	W	L	W	W	W
972	United States v. Patane	6/28/2004	542 U.S. 630	L	W	L	L	L	L	W	W	W
973	Ashcroft v. American Civil Liberties Union	6/29/2004	542 U.S. 656	L	W	L	L	W	W	W	W	L
974	Sosa v. Alvarez-Machain	6/29/2004	542 U.S. 692	L	L	L	L	L	L	L	L	L
975	Leocal v. Ashcroft	11/9/2004	543 U.S. 1	W	W	W	W	W	W	W	W	W
976	Kowalski v. Tesmer	12/13/2004	543 U.S. 125	L	W	L	L	L	L	W	W	L
977	Clark v. Martinez	1/12/2005	543 U.S. 371	W	W	W	L	W	L	W	W	W
978	Illinois v. Caballes	1/24/2005	543 U.S. 405	L	L	L	NP	L	L	W	W	L
979	Johnson v. California	2/23/2005	543 U.S. 499	L	L	W	NP	W	L	W	W	W
980	Roper v. Simmons	3/1/2005	543 U.S. 551	L	W	L	L	W	L	W	W	W
981	Ballard v. Commissioner of Internal Revenue	3/7/2005	544 U.S. 40	W	W	W	L	W	L	W	W	W
982	Muehler v. Mena	3/22/2005	544 U.S. 93	L	L	L	L	L	L	L	L	L
983	Jackson v. Birmingham Bd. of Educ.	3/29/2005	544 U.S. 167	L	W	W	L	L	L	W	W	W
984	Cutter v. Wilkinson	5/31/2005	544 U.S. 709	W	W	W	W	W	W	W	W	W
985	Johnson v. California	6/13/2005	545 U.S. 162	W	W	W	W	W	L	W	W	W

Votes of Each Justice on Each ACLU/SCOTUS Case from 1925 to 2019 (by Date)

	Case Name	Date of Decision	Case No.	Justices and Their Votes (W = ACLU Win; L = ACLU Loss; NP = Justice took no part in the decision)								
A	B	C	D	E	F	G	H	I	J	K	L	M
				Scalia	Stevens	O'Connor	Rehnquist	Kennedy	Thomas	Ginsburg	Souter	Breyer
986	Wilkinson v. Austin	6/13/2005	545 U.S. 209	L	L	L	L	L	L	L	L	L
987	Halbert v. Michigan	6/23/2005	545 U.S. 605	L	W	W	L	W	L	W	W	W
988	Town of Castle Rock v. Gonzales	6/27/2005	545 U.S. 748	L	W	L	L	L	L	W	L	L
989	McCreary County v. American Civil Liberties Union of Kentucky	6/27/2005	545 U.S. 844	L	W	W	L	L	L	W	W	W
990	Metro-Goldwyn-Mayer Studios, Inc. v. Grokster, Ltd.	6/27/2005	545 U.S. 913	L	L	L	L	L	L	L	L	L
991	National Cable and Television Communications Ass'n v. Brand X Internet Services	6/27/2005	545 U.S. 967	W	L	L	L	L	L	W	W	L
992	U.S. v. Georgia	1/10/2006	546 U.S. 151	W	W	W	**Roberts, J.** W	W	W	W	W	W
993	Gonzales v. Oregon	1/17/2006	546 U.S. 243	L	W	W	L	W	L	W	W	W
994	Ayotte v. Planned Parenthood of Northern New England	1/18/2006	546 U.S. 320	L	L	L	L	L	L	L	L	L
995	Wisconsin Right to Life, Inc. v. Federal Election Commission	1/23/2006	546 U.S. 410	W	W	W	W	W	W	W	W	W
996	Gonzales v. O Centro Espírita Beneficente União do Vegetal	2/21/2006	546 U.S. 418	W	W	**Alito** NP	W	W	W	W	W	W
997	Rumsfeld v. Forum for Academic & Institutional Rights, Inc.	3/6/2006	547 U.S. 47	L	L	NP	L	L	L	L	L	L
998	Garcetti v. Ceballos	5/30/2006	547 U.S. 410	L	W	L	L	L	L	W	W	W
999	Hudson v. Michigan	6/15/2006	547 U.S. 586	L	W	L	L	L	L	W	W	W
1000	Davis v. Washington	6/19/2006	547 U.S. 813	L	L	L	L	L	L	L	L	L
1001	Samson v. California	6/19/2006	547 U.S. 843	L	W	L	L	L	L	L	W	W
1002	Fernandez-Vargas v. Gonzales	6/22/2006	548 U.S. 30	L	W	L	L	L	L	L	L	L
1003	Burlington Northern & Santa Fe Ry. Co. v. White	6/22/2006	548 U.S. 53	W	W	W	W	W	W	W	W	W
1004	Woodford v. Ngo	6/22/2006	548 U.S. 81	L	W	L	L	L	L	W	W	L
1005	Randall v. Sorrell	6/26/2006	548 U.S. 230	W	L	W	W	W	W	L	L	W
1006	Beard v. Banks	6/28/2006	548 U.S. 521	L	W	NP	L	L	L	W	L	L
1007	Hamdan v. Rumsfeld	6/29/2006	548 U.S. 557	L	W	L	NP	W	L	W	W	W
1008	Lopez v. Gonzales	12/5/2006	549 U.S. 47	W	W	W	W	W	L	W	W	W

Votes of Each Justice on Each ACLU/SCOTUS Case from 1925 to 2019 (by Date)

	Case Name	Date of Decision	Case No.	Justices and Their Votes (W = ACLU Win; L = ACLU Loss; NP = Justice took no part in the decision)								
A	B	C	D	E	F	G	H	I	J	K	L	M
				Scalia	Stevens	Alito	Roberts, J.	Kennedy	Thomas	Ginsburg	Souter	Breyer
1009	Jones v. Bock	1/22/2007	549 U.S. 199	W	W	W	W	W	W	W	W	W
1010	Lawrence v. Florida	2/20/2007	549 U.S. 327	L	W	L	L	L	L	W	W	W
1011	Gonzales v. Carhart	4/18/2007	550 U.S. 124	L	W	L	L	L	L	W	W	W
1012	Scott v. Harris	4/30/2007	550 U.S. 372	L	W	L	L	L	L	L	L	L
1013	Ledbetter v. Goodyear Tire & Rubber Co.	5/29/2007	550 U.S. 618	L	W	L	L	L	L	W	W	W
1014	Uttecht v. Brown	6/4/2007	551 U.S. 1	L	W	L	L	L	L	W	W	W
1015	Sole v. Wyner	6/4/2007	551 U.S. 74	L	L	L	L	L	L	L	L	L
1016	Long Island Care at Home, Ltd. v. Coke	6/11/2007	551 U.S. 158	L	L	L	L	L	L	L	L	L
1017	Brendlin v. California	6/18/2007	551 U.S. 249	W	W	W	W	W	W	W	W	W
1018	Morse v. Frederick	6/25/2007	551 U.S. 393	L	W	L	L	L	L	W	W	W
1019	Federal Election Commission v. Wisconsin Right to Life, Inc.	6/25/2007	551 U.S. 449	W	L	W	W	W	W	L	L	L
1020	Hein v. Freedom From Religion Foundation, Inc.	6/25/2007	551 U.S. 587	L	W	L	L	L	L	W	W	W
1021	Parents Involved in Community Schools v. Seattle School Dist. No. 1	6/28/2007	551 U.S. 701	L	W	L	L	L	L	W	W	W
1022	Kimbrough v. U.S.	12/10/2007	552 U.S. 85	W	W	L	W	W	L	W	W	W
1023	New York State Bd. of Elections v. Lopez Torres	1/16/2008	552 U.S. 196	L	L	L	L	L	L	L	L	L
1024	Danforth v. Minnesota	2/20/2008	552 U.S. 264	W	W	W	L	L	W	W	W	W
1025	Baze v. Rees	4/16/2008	553 U.S. 35	L	L	L	L	L	L	W	W	L
1026	Virginia v. Moore	4/23/2008	553 U.S. 164	L	L	L	L	L	L	L	L	L
1027	Crawford v. Marion County Election Bd.	4/28/2008	553 U.S. 181	L	L	L	L	L	L	W	W	W
1028	Riley v. Kennedy	5/27/2008	553 U.S. 406	L	W	L	L	L	L	L	W	L
1029	CBOCS West, Inc. v. Humphries	5/27/2008	553 U.S. 442	L	W	W	W	W	L	W	W	W
1030	Engquist v. Oregon Department of Agriculture	6/9/2008	553 U.S. 591	L	W	L	L	L	L	W	W	L
1031	Boumediene v. Bush	6/12/2008	553 U.S. 723	L	W	L	L	W	L	W	W	W
1032	Kennedy v. Louisiana	6/25/2008	554 U.S. 407	L	W	L	L	W	L	W	W	W
1033	Herring v. U.S.	1/14/2009	555 U.S. 135	L	W	L	L	L	L	W	W	W
1034	Pearson v. Callahan	1/21/2009	555 U.S. 223	L	L	L	L	L	L	L	L	L
1035	Fitzgerald v. Barnstable School Comm.	1/21/2009	555 U.S. 246	W	W	W	W	W	W	W	W	W

Votes of Each Justice on Each ACLU/SCOTUS Case from 1925 to 2019 (by Date)

	Case Name	Date of Decision	Case No.	Justices and Their Votes (W = ACLU Win; L = ACLU Loss; NP = Justice took no part in the decision)								
A	B	C	D	E	F	G	H	I	J	K	L	M
				Scalia	Stevens	Alito	Roberts, J.	Kennedy	Thomas	Ginsburg	Souter	Breyer
1036	Crawford v. Metropolitan Government of Nashville & Davidson County, Tennessee	1/26/2009	555 U.S. 271	W	W	W	W	W	W	W	W	W
1037	Van de Kamp v. Goldstein	1/26/2009	555 U.S. 335	L	L	L	L	L	L	L	L	L
1038	Bartlett v. Strickland	3/9/2009	556 U.S. 1	L	W	L	L	L	L	W	W	W
1039	Vermont v. Brillon	3/9/2009	556 U.S. 81	L	W	L	L	L	L	L	L	W
1040	Arizona v. Gant	4/21/2009	556 U.S. 332	W	W	L	L	L	W	W	W	L
1041	Nken v. Holder	4/22/2009	556 U.S. 418	W	W	L	W	W	L	W	W	W
1042	F.C.C. v. Fox Television Stations, Inc.	4/28/2009	556 U.S. 502	L	W	L	L	L	L	W	W	W
1043	Montejo v. Louisiana	5/26/2009	556 U.S. 778	L	W	L	L	L	L	W	W	W
1044	Nijhawan v. Holder	6/15/2009	557 U.S. 29	L	L	L	L	L	L	L	L	L
1045	District Attorney's Office for the Third Judicial Dist. v. Osborne	6/18/2009	557 U.S. 52	L	W	L	L	L	L	W	W	W
1046	Northwest Austin Mun. Utility Dist. No. One v. Holder	6/22/2009	557 U.S. 193	L	L	L	L	L	W	L	L	L
1047	Safford Unified School Dist. No. 1 v. Redding	6/25/2009	557 U.S. 364	W	W	W	W	W	L	W	W	W
1048	Ricci v. DeStefano	6/29/2009	557 U.S. 557	L	W	L	L	L	L	W	W	W
1049	Alvarez v. Smith	12/8/2009	558 U.S. 87	L	L	L	L	L	L	L	**Sotomayor** L	L
1050	Kucana v. Holder	1/20/2010	558 U.S. 233	W	W	W	W	W	W	W	W	W
1051	Wood v. Allen	1/20/2010	558 U.S. 290	L	W	L	L	W	L	L	L	L
1052	Citizens United v. Federal Election Com'n	1/21/2010	558 U.S. 310	W	L	W	W	W	W	L	L	L
1053	Kiyemba v. Obama	3/1/2010	559 U.S. 131	W	W	W	W	W	W	W	W	W
1054	Berghuis v. Smith	3/30/2010	559 U.S. 314	L	L	L	L	L	L	L	L	L
1055	U.S. v. Stevens	4/20/2010	559 U.S. 460	W	W	L	W	W	W	W	W	W
1056	Perdue v. Kenny A.	4/21/2010	559 U.S. 542	L	W	L	L	L	L	W	W	W
1057	Salazar v. Buono	4/28/2010	559 U.S. 700	L	W	L	L	L	L	W	W	W
1058	Hui v. Castaneda	5/3/2010	559 U.S. 799	L	L	L	L	L	L	L	L	L
1059	Lewis v. City of Chicago	5/24/2010	560 U.S. 205	W	W	W	W	W	W	W	W	W
1060	Berghuis v. Thompkins	6/1/2010	560 U.S. 370	L	W	L	L	L	L	W	W	W

Votes of Each Justice on Each ACLU/SCOTUS Case from 1925 to 2019 (by Date)

	Case Name	Date of Decision	Case No.	Justices and Their Votes (W = ACLU Win; L = ACLU Loss; NP = Justice took no part in the decision)								
A	B	C	D	E	F	G	H	I	J	K	L	M
				Scalia	Stevens	Alito	Roberts, J.	Kennedy	Thomas	Ginsburg	Sotomayor	Breyer
1061	Barber v. Thomas	6/7/2010	560 U.S. 474	L	W	L	L	W	L	W	L	L
1062	Holland v. Florida	6/14/2010	560 U.S. 631	L	W	W	W	W	L	W	W	W
1063	City of Ontario v. Quon	6/17/2010	560 U.S. 746	L	L	L	L	L	L	L	L	L
1064	Holder v. Humanitarian Law Project	6/21/2010	561 U.S. 1	L	L	L	L	L	L	W	W	W
1065	Christian Legal Society v. Martinez	6/28/2010	561 U.S. 661	L	W	L	L	W	L	W	W	W
1066	National Aeronautics and Space Administration v. Nelson	1/19/2011	562 U.S. 134	L	**Kagan** NP	L	L	L	L	L	L	L
1067	Thompson v. North American Stainless, LP	1/24/2011	562 U.S. 170	W	NP	W	W	W	W	W	W	W
1068	FCC v. AT&T Inc.	3/1/2011	562 U.S. 397	W	NP	W	W	W	W	W	W	W
1069	Snyder v. Phelps	3/2/2011	562 U.S. 443	W	W	L	W	W	W	W	W	W
1070	Milner v. Dep't of Navy	3/7/2011	562 U.S. 562	W	W	W	W	W	W	W	W	L
1071	Connick v. Thompson	3/29/2011	563 U.S. 51	L	W	L	L	L	L	W	W	W
1072	Arizona Christian School Tuition Organization v. Winn	4/4/2011	563 U.S. 125	L	W	L	L	L	L	W	W	W
1073	Cullen v. Pinholster	4/4/2011	563 U.S. 170	L	W	L	L	L	L	W	W	W
1074	Sossamon v. Texas	4/20/2011	563 U.S. 277	L	NP	L	L	L	L	L	W	W
1075	Brown v. Plata	5/23/2011	563 U.S. 493	L	W	L	L	W	L	W	W	W
1076	Chamber of Commerce of U.S. v. Whiting	5/26/2011	563 U.S. 582	L	NP	L	L	L	L	W	W	W
1077	Ashcroft v. al-Kidd	5/31/2011	563 U.S. 731	L	NP	L	L	L	L	L	L	L
1078	Fox v. Vice	6/6/2011	563 U.S. 826	W	W	W	W	W	W	W	W	W
1079	J.D.B. v. North Carolina	6/16/2011	564 U.S. 261	L	W	L	L	W	L	W	W	W
1080	Wal-Mart Stores, Inc. v. Dukes	6/20/2011	564 U.S. 338	L	W	L	L	L	L	W	W	W
1081	Borough of Duryea v. Guarnieri	6/20/2011	564 U.S. 379	L	L	L	L	L	L	L	L	L
1082	Turner v. Rogers	6/20/2011	564 U.S. 431	L	W	L	L	W	L	W	W	W
1083	Brown v. Entertainment Merchants Ass'n	6/27/2011	564 U.S. 786	W	W	W	W	W	L	W	W	L
1084	Hosanna-Tabor Evangelical Lutheran Church and School v. EEOC	1/11/2012	565 U.S. 171	L	L	L	L	L	L	L	L	L
1085	Maples v. Thomas	1/18/2012	565 U.S. 266	L	W	W	W	W	L	W	W	W

	Case Name	Date of Decision	Case No.	Justices and Their Votes (W = ACLU Win; L = ACLU Loss; NP = Justice took no part in the decision)								
A	B	C	D	E	F	G	H	I	J	K	L	M
				Scalia	Kagan	Alito	Roberts, J.	Kennedy	Thomas	Ginsburg	Sotomayor	Breyer
1086	Golan v. Holder	1/18/2012	565 U.S. 302	L	NP	W	L	L	L	L	L	W
1087	U.S. v. Jones	1/23/2012	565 U.S. 400	W	W	W	W	W	W	W	W	W
1088	Messerschmidt v. Millender	2/22/2012	565 U.S. 535	L	W	L	L	L	L	W	W	L
1089	Douglas v. Independent Living Center of Southern California, Inc.	2/22/2012	565 U.S. 606	W	L	W	W	L	W	L	L	L
1090	Coleman v. Court of Appeals of Maryland	3/20/2012	566 U.S. 30	L	W	L	L	L	L	W	W	W
1091	Mayo Collaborative Services v. Prometheus Laboratories, Inc.	3/20/2012	566 U.S. 66	W	W	W	W	W	W	W	W	W
1092	Missouri v. Frye	3/21/2012	566 U.S. 134	L	W	L	L	W	L	W	W	W
1093	Lafler v. Cooper	3/21/2012	566 U.S. 156	L	W	L	L	W	L	W	W	W
1094	Florence v. Board of Chosen Freeholders of County of Burlington	4/2/2012	566 U.S. 318	L	W	L	L	L	L	W	W	W
1095	Reichle v. Howards	6/4/2012	566 U.S. 658	L	NP	L	L	L	L	L	L	L
1096	FCC v. Fox Television Stations	6/21/2012	567 U.S. 239	L	L	L	L	L	L	L	NP	L
1097	Dorsey v. U.S.	6/21/2012	567 U.S. 260	L	W	L	L	W	L	W	W	W
1098	Arizona v. U.S.	6/25/2012	567 U.S. 387	L	NP	L	W	W	L	W	W	W
1099	National Fed'n of Indep. Business v. Sebelius	6/28/2012	567 U.S. 519	L	W	L	W	L	L	W	W	W
1100	U.S. v. Alvarez	6/28/2012	567 U.S. 709	L	W	L	W	W	L	W	W	W
1101	Ryan v. Gonzales	1/8/2013	568 U.S. 57	L	L	L	L	L	L	L	L	L
1102	Bailey v. U.S.	2/19/2013	568 U.S. 186	W	W	L	W	W	L	W	W	L
1103	Florida v. Harris	2/19/2013	568 U.S. 237	L	L	L	L	L	L	L	L	L
1104	Clapper v. Amnesty Int'l USA	2/26/2013	568 U.S. 398	L	W	L	L	L	L	W	W	W
1105	Kiobel v. Royal Dutch Petroleum Co.	4/17/2013	569 U.S. 108	L	L	L	L	L	L	L	L	L
1106	Missouri v. McNeely	4/17/2013	569 U.S. 141	W	W	L	L	W	L	W	W	L
1107	McBurney v. Young	4/29/2013	569 U.S. 221	L	L	L	L	L	L	L	L	L
1108	Maryland v. King	6/3/2013	569 U.S. 435	W	W	L	L	L	L	W	W	L
1109	Ass'n for Molecular Pathology v. Myriad Genetics	6/13/2013	569 U.S. 576	W	W	W	W	W	W	W	W	W
1110	Arizona v. Inter Tribal Council of Arizona	6/17/2013	570 U.S. 1	W	W	L	W	W	L	W	W	W

	Case Name	Date of Decision	Case No.	Justices and Their Votes (W = ACLU Win; L = ACLU Loss; NP = Justice took no part in the decision)								
A	B	C	D	E	F	G	H	I	J	K	L	M
				Scalia	Kagan	Alito	Roberts, J.	Kennedy	Thomas	Ginsburg	Sotomayor	Breyer
1111	Alleyne v. U.S.	6/17/2013	570 U.S. 99	L	W	L	L	L	W	W	W	W
1112	Salinas v. Texas	6/17/2013	570 U.S. 178	L	W	L	L	L	L	W	W	W
1113	Agency for Int'l Dev. v. Alliance for Open Society Int'l	6/20/2013	570 U.S. 205	L	NP	W	W	W	L	W	W	W
1114	Shelby County v. Holder	6/25/2013	570 U.S. 529	L	W	L	L	L	L	W	W	W
1115	Adoptive Couple v. Baby Girl	6/25/2013	570 U.S. 637	W	W	L	L	L	L	W	W	L
1116	Hollingsworth v. Perry	6/26/2013	570 U.S. 693	W	W	L	W	L	L	W	L	W
1117	U.S. v. Windsor	6/26/2013	570 U.S. 744	L	W	L	L	W	L	W	W	W
1118	Kansas v. Cheever	12/11/2013	571 U.S. 87	L	L	L	L	L	L	L	L	L
1119	U.S. v. Apel	2/26/2014	571 U.S. 359	L	L	L	L	L	L	L	L	L
1120	Schuette v. Coalition to Defend Affirmative Action	4/22/2014	572 U.S. 291	L	NP	L	L	L	L	W	W	L
1121	Town of Greece v. Galloway	5/5/2014	572 U.S. 565	L	W	L	L	L	L	W	W	W
1122	Wood v. Moss	5/27/2014	572 U.S. 744	L	L	L	L	L	L	L	L	L
1123	Susan B. Anthony List v. Driehaus	6/16/2014	573 U.S. 149	W	W	W	W	W	W	W	W	W
1124	Alice Corp. v. CLS Bank Int'l	6/19/2014	573 U.S. 208	W	W	W	W	W	W	W	W	W
1125	Lane v. Franks	6/19/2014	573 U.S. 228	W	W	W	W	W	W	W	W	W
1126	Riley v. California	6/25/2014	573 U.S. 373	W	W	W	W	W	W	W	W	W
1127	McCullen v. Coakley	6/26/2014	573 U.S. 464	L	L	L	L	L	L	L	L	L
1128	Burwell v. Hobby Lobby Stores, Inc.	6/30/2014	573 U.S. 682	L	W	L	L	L	L	W	W	W
1129	Heien v. North Carolina	12/15/2014	574 U.S. 54	L	L	L	L	L	L	L	W	L
1130	Holt v. Hobbs	1/20/2015	574 U.S. 352	W	W	W	W	W	W	W	W	W
1131	Young v. United Parcel Service, Inc.	3/25/2015	135 S.Ct. 1338; 575 U.S. _	L	W	W	W	L	L	W	W	W
1132	Armstrong v. Exceptional Child Center, Inc.	3/31/2015	135 S.Ct. 1378; 575 U.S. _	L	W	L	L	W	L	W	W	L
1133	Williams-Yulee v. Florida Bar	4/29/2015	135 S.Ct. 1656; 575 U.S. _	W	L	W	L	W	W	L	L	L
1134	City and County of San Francisco v. Sheehan	5/18/2015	135 S.Ct. 1765; 575 U.S. _	W	W	L	L	L	L	L	L	NP
1135	Elonis v. United States	6/1/2015	135 S.Ct. 2001; 575 U.S. _	W	W	W	W	W	L	W	W	W
1136	E.E.O.C. v. Abercrombie & Fitch Stores	6/1/2015	135 S.Ct. 2028; 575 U.S. _	W	W	W	W	W	L	W	W	W

Votes of Each Justice on Each ACLU/SCOTUS Case from 1925 to 2019 (by Date)

	Case Name	Date of Decision	Case No.	Justices and Their Votes (W = ACLU Win; L = ACLU Loss; NP = Justice took no part in the decision)								
A	B	C	D	E	F	G	H	I	J	K	L	M
				Scalia	Kagan	Alito	Roberts, J.	Kennedy	Thomas	Ginsburg	Sotomayor	Breyer
1137	Kerry v. Din	6/15/2015	135 S.Ct. 2128; 576 U.S. _	L	W	L	L	L	L	W	W	W
1138	Walker v. Texas Div., Sons of Confederate Veterans, Inc.	6/18/2015	135 S.Ct. 2239; 576 U.S. _	W	L	W	W	W	L	L	L	L
1139	Kingsley v. Hendrickson	6/22/2015	135 S.Ct. 2466; 576 U.S. _	L	W	L	L	W	L	W	W	W
1140	Texas Dept. of Housing and Community Affairs v. Inclusive Communities Project, Inc.	6/25/2015	135 S.Ct. 2507; 576 U.S. _	L	W	L	L	W	L	W	W	W
1141	Obergefell v. Hodges	6/26/2015	135 S.Ct. 2584; 576 U.S. _	L	W	L	L	W	L	W	W	W
1142	Arizona State Legislature v. Arizona Indep. Redistricting Comm'n	6/29/2015	135 S.Ct. 2652; 576 U.S. _	L	W	L	L	W	L	W	W	W
1143	Hurst v. Florida	1/12/2016	136 S.Ct. 616; 577 U.S. _	W	W	L	W	W	W	W	W	W
1144	Montgomery v. Louisiana	1/25/2016	136 S.Ct. 718; 577 U.S. _	L	W	L	W	W	L	W	W	W
1145	Evenwel v. Abbott	4/4/2016	136 S.Ct. 1120; 578 U.S. _	VACANT SEAT	W	W	W	W	W	W	W	W
1146	Zubik v. Burwell	5/16/2016	136 S.Ct. 1557; 578 U.S. _	VACANT SEAT	L	L	L	L	L	L	L	L
1147	Simmons v. Himmelreich	6/6/2016	136 S.Ct. 1843; 578 U.S. _	VACANT SEAT	W	W	W	W	W	W	W	W
1148	Williams v. Pennsylvania	6/9/2016	136 S.Ct. 1899; 579 U.S. _	VACANT SEAT	W	L	L	W	L	W	W	W
1149	Utah v. Strieff	6/20/2016	136 S.Ct. 2056; 579 U.S. _	VACANT SEAT	W	L	L	L	L	W	W	L
1150	Birchfield v. North Dakota	6/23/2016	136 S.Ct. 2160; 579 U.S. _	VACANT SEAT	W	W	W	W	L	W	W	W
1151	Fisher v. Univ. of Texas at Austin	6/23/2016	136 S.Ct. 2198; 579 U.S. _	VACANT SEAT	NP	L	L	W	L	W	W	W
1152	Whole Woman's Health v. Hellerstedt	6/27/2016	136 S.Ct. 2292; 579 U.S. _	VACANT SEAT	W	L	L	W	L	W	W	W
1153	Fry v. Napoleon Community Schools	2/22/2017	137 S.Ct. 743; 580 U.S. _	VACANT SEAT	W	W	W	W	W	W	W	W
1154	Pena-Rodriguez v. Colorado	3/6/2017	137 S.Ct. 855; 580 U.S. _	VACANT SEAT	W	L	L	W	L	W	W	W
1155	Moore v. Texas	3/28/2017	137 S.Ct. 1039; 581 U.S. _	VACANT SEAT	W	L	L	W	L	W	W	W

Votes of Each Justice on Each ACLU/SCOTUS Case from 1925 to 2019 (by Date)

	Case Name	Date of Decision	Case No.	Justices and Their Votes (W = ACLU Win; L = ACLU Loss; NP = Justice took no part in the decision)								
A	B	C	D	E	F	G	H	I	J	K	L	M
				Gorsuch	Kagan	Alito	Roberts, J.	Kennedy	Thomas	Ginsburg	Sotomayor	Breyer
1156	Bank of America Corp. v. City of Miami	5/1/2017	137 S.Ct. 1296; 581 U.S. _	Gorsuch NP	W	L	W	L	L	W	W	W
1157	County of Los Angeles v. Mendez	5/30/2017	137 S.Ct. 1539; 581 U.S. _	NP	L	L	L	L	L	L	L	L
1158	Advocate Health Care Network v. Stapleton	6/5/2017	137 S.Ct. 1652; 581 U.S. _	NP	L	L	L	L	L	L	L	L
1159	Sessions v. Morales-Santana	6/12/2017	137 S.Ct. 1678; 582 U.S. _	NP	W	W	W	W	W	W	W	W
1160	Packingham v. North Carolina	6/19/2017	137 S.Ct. 1730; 582 U.S. _	NP	W	W	W	W	W	W	W	W
1161	Matal v. Tam	6/19/2017	137 S.Ct. 1744; 582 U.S. _	NP	W	W	W	W	W	W	W	W
1162	Ziglar v. Abbasi	6/19/2017	137 S.Ct. 1843; 582 U.S. _	NP	NP	L	L	L	L	W	NP	W
1163	Weaver v. Massachusetts	6/22/2017	137 S.Ct. 1899; 582 U.S. _	L	W	L	L	L	L	L	L	W
1164	Hernandez v. Mesa	6/26/2017	137 S.Ct. 2003; 582 U.S. _	NP	W	W	W	W	L	L	W	L
1165	Trinity Lutheran Church of Columbia, Inc. v. Comer	6/26/2017	137 S.Ct. 2012; 582 U.S. _	L	L	L	L	L	L	W	W	L
1166	Davila v. Davis	6/26/2017	137 S.Ct. 2058; 582 U.S. _	L	W	L	L	L	L	W	W	W
1167	Trump v. Int'l Refugee Assistance Project	6/26/2017	137 S.Ct. 2080; 582 U.S. _	L	L	L	L	L	L	L	L	L
1168	District of Columbia v. Wesby	1/22/2018	138 S.Ct. 577; 583 U.S. _	L	L	L	L	L	L	L	L	L
1169	Class v. United States	2/21/2018	138 S.Ct. 798; 583 U.S. _	W	W	L	W	L	L	W	W	W
1170	Jennings v. Rodriguez	2/27/2018	138 S.Ct. 830; 583 U.S. _	L	NP	L	L	L	L	W	W	W
1171	Ayestas v. Davis	3/21/2018	138 S.Ct. 1080; 584 U.S. _	W	W	W	W	W	W	W	W	W
1172	Byrd v. United States	5/14/2018	138 S.Ct. 1518; 584 U.S. _	W	W	W	W	W	W	W	W	W
1173	Epic Systems Corp. v. Lewis	5/21/2018	138 S.Ct. 1612; 584 U.S. _	L	W	L	L	L	L	W	W	W
1174	Masterpiece Cakeshop, Ltd. v. Colorado Civil Rights Comm'n	6/4/2018	138 S.Ct. 1719; 584 U.S. _	L	L	L	L	L	L	W	W	L

Votes of Each Justice on Each ACLU/SCOTUS Case from 1925 to 2019 (by Date)

	Case Name	Date of Decision	Case No.	Justices and Their Votes (W = ACLU Win; L = ACLU Loss; NP = Justice took no part in the decision)								
A	B	C	D	E	F	G	H	I	J	K	L	M
				Gorsuch	Kagan	Alito	Roberts, J.	Kennedy	Thomas	Ginsburg	Sotomayor	Breyer
1175	Husted v. A. Philip Randolph Institute	6/11/2018	138 S.Ct. 1833; 584 U.S. _	L	W	L	L	L	L	W	W	W
1176	Gill v. Whitford	6/18/2018	138 S.Ct. 1916; 585 U.S. _	L	L	L	L	L	L	L	L	L
1177	Benisek v. Lamone	6/18/2018	138 S.Ct. 1942; 585 U.S. _	L	L	L	L	L	L	L	L	L
1178	Carpenter v. United States	6/22/2018	138 S.Ct. 2206; 585 U.S. _	L	W	L	W	L	L	W	W	W
1179	Trump v. Hawaii	6/26/2018	138 S.Ct. 2392; 585 U.S. _	L	W	L	L	L	L	W	W	W
1180	Janus v. American Federation of State, County, and Municipal Employees, Council 31	6/27/2018	138 S.Ct. 2448; 585 U.S. _	L	W	L	L	L	L	W	W	W
1181	Timbs v. Indiana	2/20/2019	139 S.Ct. 682; 586 U.S. _	W	W	W	W	**Kavanaugh** W	W	W	W	W
1182	Nielsen v. Preap	3/19/2019	139 S.Ct. 954; 586 U.S. _	L	W	L	L	L	L	W	W	W
1183	Bucklew v. Precythe	4/1/2019	139 S.Ct. 1112; 587 U.S. _	L	W	L	L	L	L	W	W	W
1184	Nieves v. Bartlett	May 28, 2019	139 S.Ct. 1715; 587 U.S. _	L	L	L	L	L	L	L	W	L
1185	Manhattan Community Access Corp. v. Halleck	6/17/2019	139 S.Ct. 1921; 587 U.S. _	L	W	L	L	L	L	W	W	W
1186	Gamble v. United States	6/17/2019	139 S.Ct. 1960; 587 U.S. _	W	L	L	L	L	L	W	L	L
1187	American Legion v. American Humanist Ass'n	6/20/2019	139 S.Ct. 2067; 588 U.S. _	L	L	L	L	L	L	W	W	L
1188	Gundy v. United States	6/20/2019	139 S.Ct. 2116; 588 U.S. _	W	L	L	W	NP	W	L	L	L
1189	McDonough v. Smith	6/20/2019	139 S.Ct. 2149; 588 U.S. _	L	L	W	W	W	L	W	W	W
1190	Iancu v. Brunetti	6/24/2019	139 S.Ct. 2294; 588 U.S. _	W	W	W	L	W	W	W	L	L
1191	Rucho v. Common Cause	6/27/2019	139 S.Ct. 2484; 588 U.S. _	L	W	L	L	L	L	W	W	W
1192	Mitchell v. Wisconsin	6/27/2019	139 S.Ct. 2525; 588 U.S. _	W	W	L	L	L	L	W	W	L
1193	Dep't of Commerce v. New York	6/27/2019	139 S.Ct. 2551; 588 U.S. _	L	W	L	W	L	L	W	W	W

VI

A Summary of the Voting Record of Each U.S. Supreme Court Justice in ACLU Cases From 1925 to 2019

The following chart ranks the 51 U.S. Supreme Court justices in accordance with the percentage that each voted in favor of the position taken by the ACLU in the cases before them, with the caveat that such listed percentages should be considered given the total number of cases each justice voted on. Some examples:

- While Justice William J. Brennan, Jr. voted in favor of the ACLU position in 83.36% of the 607 cases he voted on. Justice Benjamin Nathan Cardozo voted with the ACLU 100%, but only voted on four cases.
- 28 of the justices voted in favor of the ACLU positions more than 50% of the time; 22 of the justices voted with the ACLU less than 50% of the time (Justice Fred Moore Vinson was not included in the 50 justices because he voted with the ACLU 50% of the time).
- Of the 28 justices who sided with the ACLU in more than 50% of the cases, 57.14% were nominated by Democratic presidents and 42.86% by Republican presidents. Of the 22 justices who sided with the ACLU in less than 50% of the cases, 22.73% were nominated by Democratic presidents, 77.27% by Republican presidents.
- Of the justices voting in at least 10 ACLU cases, Justice Arthur Joseph Goldberg was the most supportive of the ACLU's side, voting 97.14% with them in 35 cases, while Justice James Clark McReynolds was the least supportive, voting with the ACLU 18.18% of the time in 11 cases.

In addition, 29 or 56.86% of the 51 justices were nominated by Republican presidents, while 22 or 43.14% were nominated by Democratic presidents.

Chart: *The 51 U.S. Supreme Court Justices from 1925 to 2019; Their Terms; Votes on the ACLU's Cases; Related Information*

Justices Listed in Order of the Percentage of Their Votes on the Same Side as the ACLU

1. Benjamin Nathan Cardozo
Years Served: 1932–1938
Votes on ACLU cases: 4
Votes for ACLU's side: 4
Percentage of votes on ACLU's side: 100%
Political party of nominating president: Republican
Nominating president: Herbert Hoover

2. Arthur Joseph Goldberg
Years Served: 1962–1965
Votes on ACLU cases: 35
Votes for ACLU's side: 34
Percentage of votes on ACLU's side: 97.14%
Political party of nominating president: Democratic
Nominating president: John F. Kennedy

3. Charles Evans Hughes[1]
Years Served: 1930-1941
Votes on ACLU cases: 10
Votes for ACLU's side: 9
Percentage of votes on ACLU's side: 90.00%
Political party of nominating president: Republican
Nominating president: Herbert Hoover

1 "On April 25, 1910, President William H. Taft nominated Hughes to the Supreme Court of the United States, and the Senate confirmed the appointment on May 2, 1910. Hughes resigned from the court (as an associate justice) on June 10, 1916 ... On February 3, 1930, President Herbert Hoover nominated Hughes Chief Justice of the United States, and the Senate confirmed the appointment on February 13, 1930." Associate Justice: 1910-1916, Chief Justice: 1930-1941. ("The History of the Courts." The Supreme Court Historical Society. Accessed January 7, 2021. https://supremecourthistory.org/history-of-the-courts/.)

* (*The names of the justices are as shown on the supremecourt.gov page "Justices 1789 to Present: Chief Justices." The spelling of presidents' names are from whitehouse.gov "Presidents" page.*

4. William Orville Douglas
Years Served: 1939–1975
Votes on ACLU cases: 347
Votes for ACLU's side: 305
Percentage of votes on ACLU's side: 87.90%
Political party of nominating president: Democratic
Nominating president: Franklin D. Roosevelt

5. Louis Dembitz Brandeis
Years Served: 1916–1939
Votes on ACLU cases: 8
Votes for ACLU's side: 7
Percentage of votes on ACLU's side: 87.50%
Political party of nominating president: Democratic
Nominating president: Woodrow Wilson

6. Thurgood Marshall
Years Served: 1967–1991
Votes on ACLU cases: 522
Votes for ACLU's side: 446
Percentage of votes on ACLU's side: 85.44%
Political party of nominating president: Democratic
Nominating president: Lyndon B. Johnson

7. Earl Warren
Years Served: 1953–1969
Votes on ACLU cases: 143
Votes for ACLU's side: 122
Percentage of votes on ACLU's side: 83.31%
Political party of nominating president: Republican
Nominating president: Dwight D. Eisenhower

8. Abe Fortas
Years Served: 1965–1969
Votes on ACLU cases: 47
Votes for ACLU's side: 40
Percentage of votes on ACLU's side: 85.11%
Political party of nominating president: Democratic
Nominating president: Lyndon B. Johnson

9. William J. Brennan, Jr.
Years Served: 1956–1990
Votes on ACLU cases: 607
Votes for ACLU's side: 506
Percentage of votes on ACLU's side: 83.36%
Political party of nominating president: Republican
Nominating president: Dwight D. Eisenhower

10. Frank Murphy
Years Served: 1940–1949
Votes on ACLU cases: 48
Votes for ACLU's side: 37
Percentage of votes on ACLU's side: 77.08%
Political party of nominating president: Democratic
Nominating president: Franklin D. Roosevelt

11. Wiley Blount Rutledge
Years Served: 1943–1949
Votes on ACLU cases: 39
Votes for ACLU's side: 30
Percentage of votes on ACLU's side: 76.92%
Political party of nominating president: Democratic
Nominating president: Franklin D. Roosevelt

12. Elena Kagan
Years Served: 2010–Present
Votes on ACLU cases: 114
Votes for ACLU's side: 85
Percentage of votes on ACLU's side: 74.56%
Political party of nominating president: Democratic
Nominating president: Barack Obama

13. Sonia Sotomayor
Years Served: 2009–Present
Votes on ACLU cases: 143
Votes for ACLU's side: 106
Percentage of votes on ACLU's side: 74.13%
Political party of nominating president: Democratic
Nominating president: Barack Obama

14. Hugo Lafayette Black
Years Served: 1937–1971
Votes on ACLU cases: 246
Votes for ACLU's side: 182
Percentage of votes on ACLU's side: 73.98%
Political party of nominating president: Democratic
Nominating president: Franklin D. Roosevelt

15. Ruth Bader Ginsburg
Years Served: 1993–d. 9/18/2020
Votes on ACLU cases: 431
Votes for ACLU's side: 312
Percentage of votes on ACLU's side: 72.39%
Political party of nominating president: Democratic
Nominating president: William J. Clinton

16. John Paul Stevens
Years Served: 1975–2010
Votes on ACLU cases: 693
Votes for ACLU's side: 488
Percentage of votes on ACLU's side: 70.42%
Political party of nominating president: Republican
Nominating president: Gerald R. Ford

17. David H. Souter
Years Served: 1990–2009
Votes on ACLU cases: 336
Votes for ACLU's side: 232
Percentage of votes on ACLU's side: 69.05%
Political party of nominating president: Republican
Nominating president: George H.W. Bush

18. Oliver Wendell Holmes, Jr.
Years Served: 1902–1932
Votes on ACLU cases: 3
Votes for ACLU's side: 2
Percentage of votes on ACLU's side: 66.67%
Political party of nominating president: Republican
Nominating president: Theodore Roosevelt

19. Stephen G. Breyer
Years Served: 1994–present
Votes on ACLU cases: 415
Votes for ACLU's side: 268
Percentage of votes on ACLU's side: 64.58%
Political party of nominating president: Democratic
Nominating president: William J. Clinton

20. Harry A. Blackmun
Years Served: 1970–1994
Votes on ACLU cases: 533
Votes for ACLU's side: 326
Percentage of votes on ACLU's side: 61.16%
Political party of nominating president: Republican
Nominating president: Richard M. Nixon

21. Harlan Fiske Stone
Years Served: 1925–1946
Votes on ACLU cases: 40
Votes for ACLU's side: 24
Percentage of votes on ACLU's side: 60.00%
Political party of nominating president: Republican
Nominating president: Calvin Coolidge

22. Harold Hitz Burton
Years Served: 1945–1958
Votes on ACLU cases: 69
Votes for ACLU's side: 41
Percentage of votes on ACLU's side: 59.42%
Political party of nominating president: Democratic
Nominating president: Harry S. Truman

23. Willis Van Devanter[1]
Years Served: 1911–1937
Votes on ACLU cases: 7
Votes for ACLU's side: 4
Percentage of votes on ACLU's side: 57.14%
Political party of nominating president: Republican
Nominating president: William Howard Taft

24. George Sutherland
Years Served: 1922–1938
Votes on ACLU cases: 7
Votes for ACLU's side: 4
Percentage of votes on ACLU's side: 57.14%
Political party of nominating president: Republican
Nominating president: Warren G. Harding

25. Potter Stewart
Years Served: 1958–1981
Votes on ACLU cases: 372
Votes for ACLU's side: 211
Percentage of votes on ACLU's side: 56.72%
Political party of nominating president: Republican
Nominating president: Dwight D. Eisenhower

26. Robert Houghwout Jackson
Years Served: 1941–1954
Votes on ACLU cases: 55
Votes for ACLU's side: 29
Percentage of votes on ACLU's side: 52.73%
Political party of nominating president: Democratic
Nominating president: Franklin D. Roosevelt

27. Stanley Forman Reed
Years Served: 1938–1957
Votes on ACLU cases: 81
Votes for ACLU's side: 41
Percentage of votes on ACLU's side: 50.82%
Political party of nominating president: Democratic
Nominating president: Franklin D. Roosevelt

1. Notes: Two justices, Willis Van Devanter and George Sutherland (#23 and #24), have the same percentage totals; Devanter is listed first because he joined the Court before Sutherland.

28. Felix Frankfurter
Years Served: 1939–1962
Votes on ACLU cases: 121
Votes for ACLU's side: 61
Percentage of votes on ACLU's side: 50.41%
Political party of nominating president: Democratic
Nominating president: Franklin D. Roosevelt

29. Fred Moore Vinson
Years Served: 1946–1953
Votes on ACLU cases: 34
Votes for ACLU's side: 17
Percentage of votes on ACLU's side: 50.00%
Political party of nominating president: Democratic
Nominating president: Harry S. Truman

30. Byron Raymond White
Years Served: 1962–1993
Votes on ACLU cases: 623
Votes for ACLU's side: 300
Percentage of votes on ACLU's side: 48.15%
Political party of nominating president: Democratic
Nominating president: John F. Kennedy

31. Thomas Campbell Clark
Years Served: 1949–1967
Votes on ACLU cases: 132
Votes for ACLU's side: 63
Percentage of votes on ACLU's side: 47.73%
Political party of nominating president: Democratic
Nominating president: Harry S. Truman

32. John Marshall Harlan
Years Served: 1955–1971
Votes on ACLU cases: 174
Votes for ACLU's side: 80
Percentage of votes on ACLU's side: 45.98%
Political party of nominating president: Republican
Nominating president: Dwight D. Eisenhower

33. Owen Josephus Roberts
Years Served: 1930–1945
Votes on ACLU cases: 35
Votes for ACLU's side: 16
Percentage of votes on ACLU's side: 45.71%
Political party of nominating president: Republican
Nominating president: Herbert Hoover

34. Sherman Minton
Years Served: 1949–1956
Votes on ACLU cases: 29
Votes for ACLU's side: 13
Percentage of votes on ACLU's side: 44.83%
Political party of nominating president: Democratic
Nominating president: Harry S. Truman

35. Anthony M. Kennedy
Years Served: 1988–2018
Votes on ACLU cases: 533
Votes for ACLU's side: 238
Percentage of votes on ACLU's side: 44.65%
Political party of nominating president: Republican
Nominating president: Ronald Reagan

36. Sandra Day O'Connor
Years Served: 1981–2006
Votes on ACLU cases: 511
Votes for ACLU's side: 224
Percentage of votes on ACLU's side: 43.84%
Political party of nominating president: Republican
Nominating president: Ronald Reagan

37. Lewis F. Powell, Jr.
Years Served: 1972–1987
Votes on ACLU cases: 354
Votes for ACLU's side: 155
Percentage of votes on ACLU's side: 43.79%
Political party of nominating president: Republican
Nominating president: Richard M. Nixon

38. Warren Earl Burger
Years Served: 1969–1986
Votes on ACLU cases: 375
Votes for ACLU's side: 126
Percentage of votes on ACLU's side: 33.60%
Political party of nominating president: Republican
Nominating president: Richard M. Nixon

39. Pierce Butler
Years Served: 1923–1939
Votes on ACLU cases: 9
Votes for ACLU's side: 3
Percentage of votes on ACLU's side: 33.33%
Political party of nominating president: Republican
Nominating president: Warren G. Harding

40. John G. Roberts, Jr.
Years Served: 2005–Present
Votes on ACLU cases: 201
Votes for ACLU's side: 67
Percentage of votes on ACLU's side: 33.33%
Political party of nominating president: Republican
Nominating president: George W. Bush

41. Antonin Scalia
Years Served: 1986 – d. 2/13/2016
Votes on ACLU cases: 540
Votes for ACLU's side: 174
Percentage of votes on ACLU's side: 32.22%
Political party of nominating president: Republican
Nominating president: Ronald Reagan

42. Charles Evans Whittaker
Years Served: 1957–1962
Votes on ACLU cases: 35
Votes for ACLU's side: 11
Percentage of votes on ACLU's side: 31.43%
Political party of nominating president: Republican
Nominating president: Dwight D. Eisenhower

43. Neil M. Gorsuch
Years Served: 2017–Present
Votes on ACLU cases: 30
Votes for ACLU's side: 8
Percentage of votes on ACLU's side: 26.67%
Political party of nominating president: Republican
Nominating president: Donald Trump

44. Clarence Thomas
Years Served: 1991–present
Votes on ACLU cases: 459
Votes for ACLU's side: 122
Percentage of votes on ACLU's side: 26.58%
Political party of nominating president: Republican
Nominating president: George H.W. Bush

45. Samuel A. Alito, Jr.
Years Served: 2006–Present
Votes on ACLU cases: 195
Votes for ACLU's side: 51
Percentage of votes on ACLU's side: 26.15%
Political party of nominating president: Republican
Nominating president: George W. Bush

46. William H. Rehnquist[1]
Years Served: 1972–2005
Votes on ACLU cases: 718
Votes for ACLU's side: 186
Percentage of votes on ACLU's side: 25.91%
Political party of nominating president: Republican
Nominating president: Richard M. Nixon

47. James Francis Byrnes
Years Served: 1941–1942
Votes on ACLU cases: 4
Votes for ACLU's side: 1
Percentage of votes on ACLU's side: 25.00%
Political party of nominating president: Democratic
Nominating president: Franklin D. Roosevelt

48. Brett M. Kavanaugh
Years Served: 2018–Present
Votes on ACLU cases: 12
Votes for ACLU's side: 3
Percentage of votes on ACLU's side: 25.00%
Political party of nominating president: Republican
Nominating president: Donald Trump

49. James Clark McReynolds
Years Served: 1914–1941
Votes on ACLU cases: 11
Votes for ACLU's side: 2
Percentage of votes on ACLU's side: 18.18%
Political party of nominating president: Democratic
Nominating president: Woodrow Wilson

50. William Howard Taft
Years Served: 1921–1930
Votes on ACLU cases: 2
Votes for ACLU's side: 0
Percentage of votes on ACLU's side: 0
Political party of nominating president: Republican
Nominating president: Warren G. Harding

51. Edward Terry Sanford
Years Served: 1923-1930
Votes on ACLU cases: 2
Votes for ACLU's side: 0
Percentage of votes on ACLU's side: 0
Political party of nominating president: Republican
Nominating president: Warren G. Harding

The images of the justices are courtesy of "Collection of the Supreme Court of the United States," and we are especially grateful to the Office of the Curator, Supreme Court of the United States, for providing them.

VII.

Presidents and the Favorable ACLU Voting Percentage of the Justice(s) They Nominated[1]

This chart shows, in order from earliest to most recent by the 19 presidents who nominated them, the percentage of each justice's votes on the side of the ACLU and how many ACLU/SCOTUS cases on which they voted.

For example, Theodore Roosevelt, No. 1 in Column A below, nominated one justice to the Court, Oliver Wendell Holmes, Jr. He voted on three ACLU cases and was on the side of the ACLU in two of those cases, or 66.67% of the time.

Warren G, Harding, president No. 4, put four justices on the U.S. Supreme Court. Those four justices collectively voted on 20 ACLU/SCOTUS cases. Seven of those votes, or 35%, were on the same side as the ACLU.

Chart: *Presidents and the Favorable ACLU Voting Percentage of the Justice(s) They Nominated*[2]

1 Presidents were not considered to have nominated a new justice when they elevated a sitting justice to chief justice.
2 The presidents named in Column A are listed from earliest elected president to most recent.

	President Nominating Justice(s)	Name of U.S. Supreme Court Justice(s) Nominated by President	# of Votes by the Justice(s) on ACLU Cases	# of Votes on the ACLU's Side	% of Votes on the ACLU's side (D/E)	Political Party of Nominating President	
						Democrat	Republican
	A	B	C	D	E	F	G
1	Theodore Roosevelt						R
		- Oliver Wendell Holmes, Jr.	3	2	66.67%		
		Totals	3	2	66.67%		
2	William Howard Taft						R
		- Willis Van Devanter	7	4	57.14%		
		Totals	7	4	57.14%		
3	Woodrow Wilson					D	
		- Louis Dembitz Brandeis	8	7	87.50%		
		- James Clark McReynolds	11	2	18.18%		
		Totals	19	9	47.37%		
4	Warren G. Harding						R
		- George Sutherland	7	4	57.14%		
		- Pierce Butler	9	3	33.33%		
		- William Howard Taft	2	0	0		
		- Edward Terry Sanford	2	0	0		
		Totals	20	7	35.00%		
5	Calvin Coolidge						R
		- Harlan Fiske Stone	40	24	60.00%		
		Totals	40	24	60.00%		
6	Herbert Hoover						R
		- Benjamin Nathan Cardozo	4	4	100%		
		- Charles Evans Hughes[8]	10	9	90.00%		
		- Owen Josephus Roberts	35	16	45.71%		
		Totals	49	29	59.18%		

Presidents and the Favorable ACLU Voting Percentage of the Justice(s) They Nominated

	President Nominating Justice(s)	Name of U.S. Supreme Court Justice(s) Nominated by President	# of Votes by the Justice(s) on ACLU Cases	# of Votes on the ACLU's Side	% of Votes on the ACLU's side (D/E)	Political Party of Nominating President	
						Democrat	Republican
	A	B	C	D	E	F	G
7	Franklin D. Roosevelt					D	
		- William Orville Douglas	347	305	87.90%		
		- Frank Murphy	48	37	77.08%		
		- Wiley Blount Rutledge	39	30	76.92%		
		- Hugo Lafayette Black	246	182	73.98%		
		- Robert Houghwout Jackson	55	29	52.73%		
		- Stanley Forman Reed	81	41	50.62%		
		- Felix Frankfurter	121	61	50.41%		
		- James Francis Byrnes	4	1	25.00%		
		Totals	941	686	72.90%		
8	Harry S. Truman					D	
		- Harold Hitz Burton	69	41	59.42%		
		- Fred Moore Vinson	34	17	50.00%		
		- Thomas Campbell Clark	132	63	47.73%		
		- Sherman Minton	29	13	44.83%		
		Totals	264	134	50.76%		
9	Dwight D. Eisenhower						R
		- Earl Warren	143	122	85.31%		
		- William J. Brennan, Jr.	607	506	83.36%		
		- Potter Stewart	372	211	56.72%		
		- John Marshall Harlan	174	80	45.98%		
		- Charles Evans Whittaker	35	11	31.43%		
		Totals	1,331	930	69.87%		
10	John F. Kennedy					D	
		- Arthur Joseph Goldberg	35	34	97.14%		
		- Byron Raymond White	623	300	48.15%		
		Totals	658	334	50.76%		
11	Lyndon B. Johnson					D	
		- Thurgood Marshall	522	446	85.44%		
		- Abe Fortas	47	40	85.11%		
		Totals	569	486	85.41%		
12	Richard M. Nixon						R
		- Harry A. Blackmun	533	326	61.16%		
		- Lewis F. Powell, Jr.	354	155	43.79%		
		- Warren Earl Burger	375	126	33.60%		
		- William H. Rehnquist[9]	718	186	25.91%		
		Totals	1,980	793	40.05%		
13	Gerald R. Ford						R
		- John Paul Stevens	693	488	70.42%		
		Totals	693	488	70.42%		

Presidents and the Favorable ACLU Voting Percentage of the Justice(s) They Nominated

	President Nominating Justice(s)	Name of U.S. Supreme Court Justice(s) Nominated by President	# of Votes by the Justice(s) on ACLU Cases	# of Votes on the ACLU's Side	% of Votes on the ACLU's side (D/E)	Political Party of Nominating President	
						Democrat	Republican
	A	B	C	D	E	F	G
14	Ronald Reagan						R
		- Anthony M. Kennedy	533	238	44.65%		
		- Sandra Day O'Connor	511	224	43.84%		
		- Antonin Scalia	540	174	32.22%		
		Totals	1,584	636	40.15%		
15	George H. W. Bush						R
		- David H. Souter	336	232	69.05%		
		- Clarence Thomas	459	122	26.58%		
		Totals	795	354	44.53%		
16	William J. Clinton					D	
		- Ruth Bader Ginsburg	431	312	72.39%		
		- Stephen G. Breyer	415	268	64.58%		
		Totals	846	580	68.56%		
17	George W. Bush						R
		- John G. Roberts, Jr.	201	67	33.33%		
		- Samuel A. Alito, Jr.	195	51	26.15%		
		Totals	396	118	29.80%		
18	Barack Obama					D	
		- Elena Kagan	114	85	74.56%		
		- Sonia Sotomayor	143	106	74.13%		
		Totals	257	191	74.32%		
19	Donald Trump						R
		- Neil M. Gorsuch	30	8	26.67%		
		- Brett M. Kavanaugh	12	3	25.00%		
		Totals	42	11	26.19%		

VIII.

The Number and Percentage of Votes on the ACLU's Side by the Justice(s) Nominated by Each of the 19 Presidents

This chart shows how many justices were nominated by a president to the U.S. Supreme Court, how many ACLU cases each "President's Justice(s)" voted on, and the percentages of cases in which each president's justice(s) sided with the ACLU, from highest to lowest voting percentage.

For example, the chart shows that Lyndon B. Johnson put two justices on the U.S. Supreme Court (Thurgood Marshall and Abe Fortas), and those two justices voted on 569 ACLU cases, siding with the ACLU 486 times. Therefore, Johnson's justices voted on the side of the ACLU 85.41%, the highest percentage of presidential justice votes on the ACLU's side.

The last president, Donald Trump, put two justices on the U.S. Supreme Court (Neil M. Gorsuch and Brett M. Kavanaugh). Those two justices voted 42 times on ACLU cases, siding with the ACLU 11 times, or 26.19% of the time, the lowest percentage of presidential justice votes on the ACLU's side.

***Chart:** The Number and Percentage of Votes on the ACLU's Side by the Justice(s) Nominated by Each of the 19 Presidents, sorted by Column E.*[1]

1 The percent totals in Column E are from highest to lowest. When there are two presidents with the same percent total, they will be listed in order from earliest elected president to most recent.

	President Nominating Justice(s)	Number of U.S. Supreme Court Justice(s) Nominated by President	# of Votes by the Justice(s) on ACLU Cases	# of Votes on the ACLU's Side	% of Votes on the ACLU's side (D/E)	Political Party of Nominating President	
						Democrat	Republican
	A	B	C	D	E	F	G
1	Lyndon B. Johnson	2	569	486	85.41%	D	
2	Barack Obama	2	257	191	74.32%	D	
3	Franklin D. Roosevelt	8	941	686	72.90%	D	
4	Gerald R. Ford	1	693	488	70.42%		R
5	Dwight D. Eisenhower	5	1,331	930	69.87%		R
6	William J. Clinton	2	846	580	68.56%	D	
7	Theodore Roosevelt	1	3	2	66.67%		R
8	Calvin Coolidge	1	40	24	60.00%		R
9	Herbert Hoover	3	49	29	59.18%		R
10	William Howard Taft	1	7	4	57.14%		R
11	Harry S. Truman	4	264	134	50.76%	D	
12	John F. Kennedy	2	658	334	50.76%	D	
13	Woodrow Wilson	2	19	9	47.37%	D	
14	George H. W. Bush	2	795	354	44.53%		R
15	Ronald Reagan	3	1,584	636	40.15%		R
16	Richard M. Nixon	4	1,980	793	40.05%		R
17	Warren G. Harding	4	20	7	35.00%		R
18	George W. Bush	2	396	118	29.80%		R
19	Donald Trump	2	42	11	26.19%		R
		51	10,494	5,816	55.42%	7	12

IX

The Executive Directors of the ACLU from 1920 to 2020

1. 1920—1950 Roger Nash Baldwin, co-founder of the ACLU, was the first ACLU Executive Director, and he served in that capacity for 30 years. His books include *Liberty Under the Soviets*, 1928, and *Juvenile Courts and Probation*, in 1914 as co-writer. He received a master's degree in social work from Harvard.

2. 1950—1962 Patrick Murphy Malin was the second ACLU Executive Director and served for 12 years after Roger Baldwin. Malin was an economics professor at Swarthmore College from 1930 to 1950.

3. 1962—1970 Jack Pemberton served as ACLU Executive Director through most of the 1960s. He graduated from Harvard Law School, became a law professor, and was regional counsel of the U.S. Equal Employment Opportunity Commission in San Francisco.

4. 1970—1978 Aryeh Neier served as the ACLU Executive Director for eight years in the '70s. Some of his books include *Dossier: The Secret Files They Keep on You*, 1978, and *Taking Liberties: Four Decades in the Struggle for Rights*, 2003. He received his JD from Cornell University.

5. 1978—2001 Ira Glasser served as ACLU Executive Director for nearly a quarter of a century. In 1991, Glasser published *Visions of Liberty: The Bill of Rights for All Americans.* Glasser taught mathematics at City University in New York and Sarah Lawrence College, and was editor of a monthly magazine of public affairs titled *Current.*

6. 2001—Present Anthony D. Romero has been the Executive Director of the ACLU since the week before Sept. 11, 2001. According to the ACLU website, he is the "first Latino and openly gay man to serve in that capacity."[1] With NPR correspondent Dina Temple-Raston, he published *In Defense of Our America: The Fight for Civil Liberties in the Age of Terror.*

** Photo permission for 1. Roger Nash Baldwin, Bettmann via Getty Image; 2. Patrick Murphy Malin image courtesy of the ACLU, of whatever rights they may have to the image; 3. Jack Pemberton image courtesy of Duke Law School, Executive Director, Communications & Events; 4. Aryeh Neier image courtesy of Open Society Foundations, New York, credit to Pamela Chen/Open Society Foundations; 5. Ira Glasser image courtesy of Brooklyn Law School; 6. Anthony D. Romero photo by Richard Corman, en.wikipedia attribution Rsd315.*

1 "Anthony D. Romero," American Civil Liberties Union. Accessed January 7, 2021. https://www.aclu.org/bio/anthony-d-romero.

X

Questions & Conclusion

While putting together the information in these pages, I have come to think of the work as similar to that of an armorer. The armorer produces weapons (information, facts, and data in this case) and is often agnostic as to who buys their weapons or how they are used. One difference from many armorers is that I do care about how the information in these pages is used. I hope pieces or sections of this work will not be taken out of context or used to mislead.

Regardless of how readers think about or use the information herein, I believe a few percentages, perhaps as looked at through the eyes of an accountant, deserve special thought. Each covers a lot of ground and will surely be seen and interpreted differently. On the positive side, studying, analyzing, and even arguing about the meaning of the numbers below (and the information in these pages) could bring new and interesting thoughts, theories, and conclusions about the ACLU.

- **53.65%—The ACLU's batting average was on the winning side** (on page 9): In the 1,193 ACLU/SCOTUS cases, the ACLU was on the winning side 53.65% of the time during the 94 years of the Union's first 100 years. What does that number say about the ACLU, if anything? Before you read or skimmed this work, did you think about what the Union's batting average over so many years might be? Does the 53.39% seem high, low, or about what you thought? Do you think, perhaps, that the 53.65% number might be high because the Union only got involved in easy cases (assuming there is such a thing) or that number is low because you question the ACLU's competency? Does 53.65% suggest anything about its political agenda over time?
- **25.98%—The percentage of 4–5, 5–4, 4–3 and 3–4 decisions of the 1,193 cases** (on page 9): There were 310 such cases.[1] Given that all the voting justices saw the same facts, data, and arguments on each case, why was there such a difference of opinions on more than a quarter of the 1,193 cases and during so many years? Given that the justices (and all federal judges) essentially have a job for life, shouldn't there be less politics, and less reason to feel pressure to vote one way or another on a case (because they can't be fired for their vote on any case)? Given that the justices have all sworn to uphold the Constitution and were presented with the same facts and evidence of each case, would you expect so many cases decided by one vote? What do such close cases say about the clarity of the facts and law in those cases? How much did each justice's personal views and legal philosophy affect their votes, if at all?
- **56.86% of justices who decided these cases were put on the Court by Republican presidents** (on page 89): Of the 51 SCOTUS justices who opined on the 1,193 cases, 29 or 56.86% of those justices were nominated by Republican presidents. Twenty-two or 43.14% of the justices were put on by Democratic presidents. If those numbers had been reversed, with 56.86% of the justices having been nominated by Democratic presidents, would the batting average of the ACLU have changed, or changed much? If the batting average had changed, how would those changed decisions have affected our country? Would our country be better or worse off today? How could one define "better" between often competing political, societal, and other interests?

In sum, after reviewing the ACLU/SCOTUS cases over so many years, the votes of the justices (on page 41), and the divergent pros and cons about the ACLU (on page 3), this complex organization is difficult if not impossible to pigeonhole. It becomes obvious that in trying to understand this organization from its SCOTUS cases, just as many questions as answers arise. What is clear, however, is the ACLU has been involved in many cases at the U.S. Supreme Court that have had impactful effects on our country.

---

1 Of the 310 cases, eight were 3–4 and 4–3 decisions. Those cases are: 1. *United States ex rel. Knauff v. Shaughnessy* (338 U.S. 537); 2. *Hoffa v. United States* (385 U.S. 293); 3. *Fein v. Selective Service System Local Board No. 7* (405 U.S. 365); 4. *Cornelius v. NAACP Legal Defense and Educational Fund, Inc.* (473 U.S. 788); 5. *Traynor v. Turnage* (485 U.S. 535); 6. *City of Lakewood v. Plain Dealer Publishing Co.* (486 U.S. 750); 7. *Murray v. United States* (487 U.S. 533); and 8. *Fisher v. Univ. of Texas at Austin* (136 S.Ct. 2198; 579 U.S. _).

Appendix A

Methodology

The following methodology has been used in compiling this work:

1. The criteria for inclusion of an ACLU/SCOTUS case are when the ACLU was *involved* in the case when it went before the U.S. Supreme Court and the Court issued an opinion between January 19, 1920, and January 19, 2020, the first 100 years of the ACLU.

   "ACLU involvement" in a SCOTUS case includes when the ACLU was a party, filed (or is on) an amicus brief, and/or when an ACLU attorney argued the case or was listed on a brief in the case. An ACLU attorney's involvement includes an ACLU attorney being listed on a party's brief, whether or not the attorney's affiliation with the ACLU is noted on the brief itself.[1]

   Such involvement of an ACLU attorney also includes instances where the ACLU partnered with one or more outside attorneys not necessarily employed by the ACLU but who worked with the ACLU on the case. Involvement also includes cases where the ACLU has made public statements referencing the case as an ACLU case (because the ACLU has deeper records of its involvement in cases than is often available through SCOTUS documents and other public records).

   This criterion excludes cases where the ACLU was only involved when the case was before a lower court, and cases where the writ of certiorari was denied or granted but then later dismissed (meaning the [U.S. Supreme] Court never issued an opinion deciding the case itself), or where the ACLU's request to file an amicus was denied or withdrawn.

   Also excluded from this work are nine split decision *per curiam* cases.[2] Those cases are composed of one 3–3 and eight 4–4 votes. Those nine cases are excluded because it's not clear which justices voted on which side of those cases, and because the U.S. Supreme Court didn't come to a clear decision on any of them. A split decision has a similar effect as cert in those cases being denied. Those nine split decisions leave the lower court ruling in place.

   Cases are cited by the party names as listed in the U.S. Supreme Court's decision. Party names sometimes changed during the course of litigation.

   Occasionally, I have been told a particular SCOTUS case was an ACLU case but our research could not verify that claim. When that happened, such cases have not been listed in this work although it is possible with more research, we might have discovered other ACLU connections.

2. Win/Loss Definition

   This work defines "winning" or "losing" by whether or not the ruling of the U.S. Supreme Court was "with" or "against" the side the ACLU was on, even though in some instances the ACLU was on the "winning side" but some considered it an ACLU loss. Conversely, at times the Union was on the "losing side" but some considered the Union to receive a net benefit from the decision.

   Therefore, the above definition of wins and losses may not account for some nuanced or argued results.

   For example, this work records the case win/loss definitions count *Staats v. ACLU*, 422 U.S. 1030 (1975) as a loss for the ACLU because in *Staats*, the U.S. Supreme Court voted 8–0 against the side the ACLU was on. However, Ira Glasser, former executive director of the ACLU, considered the *Staats* decision a victory for the ACLU on the merits, because the practical effect of the case achieved the ACLU's goal in bringing it.

   Although such nuanced or argued effects about certain case results are interesting and important to some, second guessing or arguing about the outcome of such cases would add a subjectiveness that I chose to avoid.

   I have no reason to believe there are many such *Staats* cases, where a loss could reasonably be considered an ACLU win, or a win could be considered a loss. Even if there were, I don't believe the ACLU's win/loss ratio would be changed in any significant way.

   For example, if there were, say, a net difference of 20 such cases in this work, and if all those 20 cases increased or decreased the ACLU's wins or losses by that amount, its win ratio of 53.65% in its first 100 years[3] would only increase to 55.32% or decrease to 51.97%.[4]

   In the case of ties by the U.S. Supreme Court, where the lower court's ruling was affirmed by an equally divided U.S. Supreme Court (except the split *per curiam* cases), "winning" or "losing" is recorded as to whether or not the divided decision had the effect of ending the issue "with" or "against" the side the ACLU was on.

---

1 Attorney involvement includes an ACLU attorney who was noted on a brief before the U.S. Supreme Court but who may not have been noted as being affiliated with the ACLU. For example, Osmond K. Fraenkel, ACLU chief counsel 1954 to 1977; Melvin Wulf, ACLU legal director 1962 to 1977; or Steven R. Shapiro, ACLU associate legal director 1987 to 1993 and legal director 1993 to 2016 were listed on a party's brief before the U.S. Supreme Court, even though their ACLU affiliation was not always mentioned on the brief itself.

2 See footnote 1 on page 41

3 On page 9, 640 wins of 1,193 cases is 53.65%.

4 660 wins of 1,193 is 55.32%; 620 wins of 1,193 is 51.97%.

3. The Supporting Data

Supporting data for the cases came from ACLU websites and reports; GALE's U.S. Supreme Court Records and Briefs 1832—1978 online; Oyez Project at IIT Chicago-Kent College of Law (oyez.org), which was useful in determining the votes of the justices; FindLaw (findlaw.com); and Westlaw (westlaw.com).

Where minor errors were found or when questions arose, and for some clarification, the print version of the *United States Supreme Court Reports, Lawyer's Edition,* was used to ensure the most accurate quotation possible when copies of the *United States Reports*, the official record for SCOTUS cases, were not available.

Quotations without citation come directly from the cases. Quotations from other sources, such as prior opinions from lower courts or party briefs, are noted with a footnote citing the source of the quotation.

Citations to cases or statutes within the quoted material are omitted, without notation, although single quotation marks designate quotations from another source.

Please refer to the print version of the *United States Reports* for a complete reporting of each case in its entirety as the print version of the United States Reports is the official source of SCOTUS cases.

4. [sic]—*intentionally so written*—Used after a printed word or passage to indicate that it is intended exactly as printed or to indicate that it exactly reproduces an original <said he seed [sic] it all> [1]

5. Regarding rounding of percentages for the wins/losses, if the extra number is a 5, 6, 7, 8 or 9, the preceding number has been raised by one. Example: if we want one decimal point, the number 45.55 would become 45.6; if we want two decimal points, the number 56.574 would become 56.57.

6. Editing style—This work uses a combination of styles based mainly on Chicago Manual of Style standard style, but AP Style is used for numbers, where numbers nine and under are written out unless they are part of a vote count.

7. Abbreviations Used

Definitions for O, CO and DO below were taken from *Black's Law Dictionary; Revised Fourth Edition*; published 1968.

A. W = Voting with the ACLU
B. L = Voting against the ACLU
C. Oth = Other—Vacant seat; abstention from vote; etc.
D. O = Opinion—The statement by the U.S. Supreme Court of the decision reached in regard to the case, setting forth the law as applied to the case, and detailing the reasoning upon which the decision is based.
E. CO = Concurring Opinion—An opinion separate from that which embodies the view and decision of the majority, prepared and filed by a justice who agrees with the general result of the decision, and which either reinforces the majority opinion or voices disapproval with the reasoning behind the opinion but approves of its final result.
F. DO = Dissenting Opinion—An opinion separate from that which embodies the views and decision of the majority, prepared and filed by a justice who disagrees with the decision of the U.S. Supreme Court and who expresses his or her own views/reasoning on the case.
G. CDO = Concurring/Dissenting Opinion—An opinion separate from that which embodies the views and decision of the majority, prepared and filed by a justice who agrees with only a portion of the decision of the majority (usually in cases involving more than one issue).

1 "sic," Merriam-Webster, Accessed January 7, 2021, https://www.merriam-webster.com/.

Appendix B

General Categories of the ACLU/SCOTUS Cases

The ACLU/SCOTUS cases generally fit the four main categories below (with the subcategories added), but given the nature of the law and litigation, a case may fit into more than one category and subcategory. For that reason, I have not attempted to organize the cases in the following categories.

1. 1ST AMENDMENT

A. Obscenity: Cases in this category deal with the limits of the freedom to engage in "obscene" and offensive speech.
B. Defamation: Cases involving libelous publication and slanderous utterances against individuals.
C. Religion: Cases involving the free exercise of religion and the prohibition of the establishment of an official religion.
D. Press, Speech, Association: Cases in this category involve the freedoms of speech, the press, and association.

2. CRIMINAL JUSTICE

A. 4th Amendment: Cases involving the limits of protection against unwarranted searches and seizures.
B. Criminal Procedure: Includes the 5th and 6th Amendments, as well as criminal trial procedure under the 14th Amendment.
C. 8th Amendment: Cases involving the prohibition against cruel and unusual punishment.
D. Death Penalty: Cases involving a sentence to death.
E. Drugs: Cases where narcotics are the issue or cause of the arrest.
F. Prison: Cases involving inmate rights, prison conditions, and the parole process.

3. CIVIL RIGHTS

A. Race: Cases dealing with both state and federal racial discrimination.
B. Gender: Cases dealing with both state and federal gender discrimination.
C. Federal: Cases involving civil rights protected by federal law.
D. State: Cases dealing with civil rights protected under the 14th Amendment.
E. Voting Rights: Cases dealing with the right to vote, right against vote dilution, and redistricting.
F. Privacy: Cases mainly dealing with reproductive rights (abortion, contraception) and the individual's right to privacy.

4. GOVERNMENTAL AUTHORITY

A. Union: Cuts across categories, but generally cases dealing with government regulation of labor unions.
B. Immigration/Citizenship: Cases dealing with people immigrating to this country and citizens living abroad.
C. Communism: Cuts across categories, but generally cases dealing with government statutes and acts, and agencies created to deal with communism.
D. Census: Cases dealing with census count.
E. Federalism: Cases dealing with controversy between state government and the federal government.
F. Civil Procedure: Cases where the issue is a matter of civil trial procedure.
G. Regulation: Cases dealing with government regulatory agencies.
H. Immunity: Cases dealing with immunity from damages under the 11th Amendment.
I. Military: Cases dealing with military personnel or cases under military jurisdiction.

Appendix C

ACLU/U.S. Supreme Court Case Summaries

1. Gitlow v. New York

(Decided June 8, 1925; 268 U.S. 652)

I. ISSUE

A. Issues Discussed

First Amendment, Fourteenth Amendment, freedom of speech and of the press

B. Legal Question Presented

Does a state statute regulating speech by prohibiting advocacy of criminal anarchy deprive the defendant of freedom of speech or of the press in violation of the due process clause of the Fourteenth Amendment?

C. Supreme Court's Answer

The state statute is constitutional. However, fundamental rights federally protected under the First Amendment, such as freedom of speech and press, are protected from state impairment by the due process clause of the Fourteenth Amendment.

II. CASE SUMMARY

A. Background

"The defendant [was] a member of the Left Wing Section of the Socialist Party [which] was organized nationally at a conference in New York City in June, 1919 . . . . The conference elected a National Council, of which the defendant was member, and left to it the adoption of a 'Manifesto.' This was published in The Revolutionary Age, the official organ of the Left Wing. . . . Sixteen thousand copies were printed [and] paid for by the defendant, as business manager of the paper . . . . [D]efendant signed a card subscribing to the Manifesto and Program of the Left Wing [and] went to different parts of the State to speak to branches of the Socialist Party about the principles of the Left Wing and advocated their adoption.

[The Manifesto] advocated, in plain and unequivocal language, the necessity of accomplishing the 'Communist Revolution' by a militant and 'revolutionary Socialism,' based on 'the class struggle' and mobilizing the 'power of the proletariat in action,' through mass industrial revolts developing into mass political strikes and 'revolutionary mass action,' for the purpose of conquering and destroying the parliamentary state and establishing in its place, through a 'revolutionary dictatorship of the proletariat,' the system of Communist Socialism."

Defendant was "convicted and sentenced to imprisonment" by the trial court. "The Court of Appeals held that the Manifesto 'advocated the overthrow of [the] government by violence, or by unlawful means.' . . . And both the Appellate Division and the Court of Appeals held the statute constitutional."

The Supreme Court granted certiorari to review the case and affirmed the judgment of the Court of Appeals.

B. Counsel of Record/ACLU Attorney

ACLU Side (Petitioner/Appellant): Walter H. Pollak and Walter Nelles argued the cause for appellant.

Opposing Side (Respondent/Appellee): John Caldwell Myers and W. J. Wetherbee argued the cause for appellee.

III. AMICI CURIAE

ACLU Side (Petitioner/Appellant)

No briefs of amici curiae were filed in support of appellant.

Opposing Side (Respondent/Appellee)

No briefs of amici curiae were filed in support of appellee.

IV. THE SUPREME COURT'S DECISION

In upholding the statute and affirming the Court of Appeals decision, the Court determined "[t]he statute does not penalize the utterance or publication of abstract 'doctrine' or academic discussion having no quality of incitement to any concrete action. . . . What it prohibits is language advocating, advising or teaching the overthrow of organized government by unlawful means. [The Manifesto] advocates and urges in fervent language mass action which shall progressively foment industrial disturbances and through political mass strikes and revolutionary mass action overthrow and destroy organized parliamentary government."

The Court "assume[d] that freedom of speech and of the press—which are protected by the First Amendment from abridgment by Congress—are among the fundamental personal rights and 'liberties' protected by the due process clause of the Fourteenth Amendment from impairment by the States." However, "[i]t is a fundamental principle, long established, that the freedom of speech and of the press which is secured by the Constitution, does not confer an absolute right to speak or publish, without responsibility. . . ."

State "'statutes may only be declared unconstitutional where they are arbitrary or unreasonable attempts to exercise authority vested in the State in the public interest.' That utterances inciting to the overthrow of organized government by unlawful means, present a sufficient danger of substantive evil to bring their punishment within the range of legislative discretion, is clear. Such utterances, by their very nature, involve danger to the public peace and to the security of the State."

The Court ultimately found "that the statute is not in itself unconstitutional, and that it has not been applied in the present case in derogation of any constitutional right . . . ."

V. JUSTICE VOTE

2 Pro ACLU Side vs. 7 Con Opposing Side

ACLU Side (Petitioner/Appellant)

1. Holmes, O. – Wrote dissenting opinion
2. Brandeis, L. – Joined dissenting opinion

Opposing Side (Respondent/Appellee)

1. Sanford, E. – Wrote majority opinion
2. Taft, W. – Joined majority opinion
3. Van Devanter, W. – Joined majority opinion
4. McReynolds, J. – Joined majority opinion
5. Sutherland, G. – Joined majority opinion
6. Butler, P. – Joined majority opinion
7. Stone, H. – Joined majority opinion

VI. A WIN OR LOSS FOR THE ACLU?

The ACLU, as attorney of record, urged reversal of the judgment of the Court of Appeals; the Supreme Court affirmed in a 7-2 vote, giving the ACLU an apparent loss.

(Some believe that this case should be viewed as a win overall because the Court established in Gitlow that fundamental rights, such as freedom of speech and press, must not be impaired by the states, incorporating these rights under the due process clause of the Fourteenth Amendment.)

2. Whitney v. California

(Decided May 16, 1927; 274 U.S. 357)

I. ISSUE

A. Issues Discussed

Due process, equal protection

B. Legal Question Presented

Whether the Criminal Syndicalism Act in California violates either the due process or equal protection clauses of the Fourteenth Amendment.

C. Supreme Court's Answer

The Criminal Syndicalism Act in California does not violate either the due process clause or equal protection clause of the Fourteenth Amendment.

II. CASE SUMMARY

A. Background

Defendant was a member of the Community Labor Party. She was "charged, in five counts, with violations of the Criminal Syndicalism Act of [California]. She was tried, convicted on the first count, and sentenced to imprisonment. The judgment was affirmed by the District Court of Appeal."

"The first count of the information, on which the conviction was had, charged that on or about November 28, 1919, in Alameda County, the defendant, in violation of the Criminal Syndicalism Act, 'did then and there unlawfully, willfully, wrongfully, deliberately and feloniously organize and assist in organizing, and was, is, and knowingly became a member of an organization, society, group and assemblage of persons organized and assembled to advocate, teach, aid and abet criminal syndicalism.'"

On certiorari the Supreme Court affirmed the judgment of the District Court of Appeal, upholding the conviction.

B. Counsel of Record/ACLU Attorney

ACLU Side (Petitioner/Appellant): Walter H. Pollak argued the cause for appellant. With him on the brief were John Francis Neylan, Thomas Lloyd Lennon, Walter Nelles, and Ruth I. Wilson.

Opposing Side (Respondent/Appellee): John H. Riordan argued the cause for appellee. With him on the brief was Attorney General of California U. S. Webb.

III. AMICI CURIAE

ACLU Side (Petitioner/Appellant)

No briefs of amici curiae were filed in support of appellant.

Opposing Side (Respondent/Appellee)

No briefs of amici curiae were filed in support of appellee.

IV. THE SUPREME COURT'S DECISION

"By enacting the provisions of the Syndicalism Act the State has declared, through its legislative body, that to knowingly be or become a member of or assist in organizing an association to advocate, teach or aid and abet the commission of crimes or unlawful acts of force, violence or terrorism as a means of accomplishing industrial or political changes, involves such danger to the public peace and the security of the State, that these acts should be penalized in the exercise of its police power. That determination must be given great weight. Every presumption is to be indulged in favor of the validity of the statute, and it may not be declared unconstitutional unless it is an arbitrary or unreasonable attempt to exercise the authority vested in the State in the public interest. . . .

We cannot hold that, as here applied, the Act is an unreasonable or arbitrary exercise of the police power of the State, unwarrantably infringing any right of free speech, assembly or association, or that those persons are protected from punishment by the due process clause who abuse such rights by joining and furthering an organization thus menacing the peace and welfare of the State.

We find no repugnancy in the Syndicalism Act as applied in this case to either the due process or equal protection clauses of the Fourteenth Amendment on any of the grounds upon which its validity has been here challenged."

The Supreme Court upheld the judgment of the District Court of Appeal.

V. JUSTICE VOTE

0 Pro ACLU Side vs. 9 Con Opposing Side

Opposing Side (Respondent/Appellee)

1. Sanford, E. – Wrote majority opinion
2. Brandeis, L. – Wrote concurring opinion
3. Holmes, O. – Joined concurring opinion
4. McReynolds, J. – Joined majority opinion
5. Sutherland, G. – Joined majority opinion
6. Butler, P. – Joined majority opinion
7. Stone, H. – Joined majority opinion
8. Taft, W. – Joined majority opinion
9. Van Devanter, W. – Joined majority opinion

VI. A WIN OR LOSS FOR THE ACLU?

The ACLU, as attorney of record, urged reversal of the judgment of the District Court of Appeal; the Supreme Court affirmed in a 9-0 vote, giving the ACLU an apparent loss.

3. Stromberg v. California

(Decided May 18, 1931; 283 U.S. 359)

I. ISSUE

A. Issues Discussed

Freedom of speech

B. Legal Question Presented

Whether any part of a state statute prohibiting displays of red flags or banners is so vague as to make a conviction under the statute invalid under the liberty protections of the due process clause of the Fourteenth Amendment?

C. Supreme Court's Answer

Part of the statute is so vague that the conviction cannot be upheld.

II. CASE SUMMARY

A. Background

"[T]he appellant . . . was one of the supervisors of a summer camp for children . . . . Appellant was a member of the Young Communist League, an international organization affiliated with the Communist Party. The charge against her concerned a daily ceremony at the camp, in which the appellant supervised and directed the children in raising a red flag, 'a camp-made reproduction of the flag of Soviet Russia, which was also the flag of the Communist Party in the United States.'"

Appellant was convicted under a state statute prohibiting the display of a red flag "as a sign, symbol or emblem of opposition to organized government or as an invitation or stimulus to anarchistic action or as an aid to propaganda that is of a seditious character." Appellant argued "that, under the Fourteenth Amendment, the statute was invalid as being 'an unwarranted limitation on the right of free speech.'"

The District Court affirmed the superior court's judgment. On appeal the Supreme Court reversed the District Court's judgment, determining that part of the statute was "so vague" as to be "repugnant to the guaranty of liberty contained in the Fourteenth Amendment."

B. Counsel of Record/ACLU Attorney

ACLU Side (Petitioner/Appellant): John Beardsley argued the cause for appellant.

Opposing Side (Respondent/Appellee): John D. Richer argued the cause for appellee.

III. AMICI CURIAE

ACLU Side (Petitioner/Appellant)

No briefs of amici curiae were filed in support of appellant.

Opposing Side (Respondent/Appellee)

No briefs of amici curiae were filed in support of appellee.

IV. THE SUPREME COURT'S DECISION

"The maintenance of the opportunity for free political discussion to the end that government may be responsive to the will of the people and that changes may be obtained by lawful means . . . is a fundamental principle of our constitutional system. A statute which upon its face, is so vague and indefinite as to permit the punishment of the fair use of this opportunity is repugnant to the guaranty of liberty contained in the Fourteenth Amendment. The first clause of the statute being invalid upon its face, the conviction of the appellant, which so far as the record discloses may have rested upon that clause exclusively, must be set aside."

The decision revolves around whether any part of a statute prohibiting displaying the red flag "as a sign, symbol or emblem of opposition to organized government or as an invitation or stimulus to anarchistic action or as an aid to propaganda that is of a seditious character" is so vague as to necessitate setting aside a conviction under the statute.

The state court reasoned that "[t]he constitutionality of the phrase . . . , 'of opposition to organized government,' is questionable." However, the state court upheld the two subsequent clauses of the statute addressing "anarchistic action" and "seditious character" and "the conviction of the appellant was sustained."

The Supreme Court reversed, reasoning that the clause identified by the state court was vague, the verdict "did not specify the ground upon which it rested" and "if any of the clauses in question is invalid under the Federal Constitution, the conviction cannot be upheld."

The Supreme Court reversed the judgment of the District Court.

V. JUSTICE VOTE

7 Pro ACLU Side vs. 2 Con Opposing Side

ACLU Side (Petitioner/Appellant)

1. Stone, H. – Joined majority opinion
2. Roberts, O. – Joined majority opinion
3. Hughes, C. – Wrote majority opinion
4. Holmes, O. – Joined majority opinion
5. Van Devanter, W. – Joined majority opinion
6. Brandeis, L. – Joined majority opinion
7. Sutherland, G. – Joined majority opinion

Opposing Side (Respondent/Appellee)

1. McReynolds, J. – Wrote dissenting opinion
2. Butler, P. – Wrote dissenting opinion

VI. A WIN OR LOSS FOR THE ACLU?

The ACLU, as counsel of record, urged reversal of the judgment of the District Court; the Supreme Court reversed the lower court's decision in a 7-2 vote, giving the ACLU an apparent win.

4. Powell v. Alabama

(Decided November 7, 1932; 287 U.S. 45)

I. ISSUE

A. Issues Discussed

Right to counsel

B. Legal Question Presented

"[W]hether the defendants were in substance denied the right of counsel, and if so, whether such denial infringes the due process clause of the Fourteenth Amendment."

C. Supreme Court's Answer

The defendants were effectively denied the right to counsel in violation of the due process clause of the Fourteenth Amendment.

II. CASE SUMMARY

A. Background

Defendants were "negroes charged with the crime of rape, committed upon the persons of two white girls." The record of the arraignment shows "that on the same day the defendants were arraigned and entered pleas of not guilty. There is a further recital to the effect that upon the arraignment they were represented by counsel. But no counsel had been employed, and aside from a statement made by the trial judge several days later during a colloquy immediately preceding the trial, the record does not disclose when, or under what circumstances, an appointment of counsel was made, or who was appointed. During the colloquy referred to, the trial judge, in response to a question, said that he had appointed all the members of the bar for the purpose of arraigning the defendants and then of course anticipated that the members of the bar would continue to help the defendants if no counsel appeared.

There was a severance upon the request of the state, and the defendants were tried in three several groups . . . . Each of the three trials was completed within a single day. . . . The juries found defendants guilty and imposed the death penalty upon all. The trial court overruled motions for new trials and sentenced the defendants in accordance with the verdicts. The judgments were affirmed by the state supreme court."

On appeal the U.S. Supreme Court reversed the judgment of the Supreme Court of Alabama.

B. Counsel of Record/ACLU Attorney

ACLU Side (Petitioner/Appellant): Walter H. Pollak argued the cause for appellant.

Opposing Side (Respondent/Appellee): Attorney General of Alabama Thomas E. Knight, Jr. argued the cause for appellee.

III. AMICI CURIAE

ACLU Side (Petitioner/Appellant)

No briefs of amici curiae were filed in support of appellant.

Opposing Side (Respondent/Appellee)

No briefs of amici curiae were filed in support of appellant.

IV. THE SUPREME COURT'S DECISION

"The record shows that immediately upon the return of the indictment defendants were arraigned and pleaded not guilty. Apparently they were not asked whether they had, or were able to employ, counsel, or wished to have counsel appointed . . . .

It is hardly necessary to say that, the right to counsel being conceded, a defendant should be afforded a fair opportunity to secure counsel of his own choice. Not only was that not done here, but such designation of counsel as was attempted was either so indefinite or so close upon the trial as to amount to a denial of effective and substantial aid in that regard."

"[T]he necessity of counsel was so vital and imperative that the failure of the trial court to make an effective appointment of counsel was likewise a denial of due process within the meaning of the Fourteenth Amendment. . . . All that it is necessary now to decide, as we do decide, is that in a capital case, where the defendant is unable to employ counsel, and is incapable adequately of making his own defense because of ignorance, feeble-mindedness, illiteracy, or the like, it is the duty of the court, whether requested or not, to assign counsel for him as a necessary requisite of due process of law; and that duty is not discharged by an assignment at such a time or under such circumstances as to preclude the giving of effective aid in the preparation and trial of the case."

The U.S. Supreme Court reversed the judgment of the Supreme Court of Alabama.

V. JUSTICE VOTE

7 Pro ACLU Side vs. 2 Con Opposing Side

ACLU Side (Petitioner/Appellant)

1. Sutherland, G. – Wrote majority opinion
2. Hughes, C. – Joined majority opinion
3. Van Devanter, W. – Joined majority opinion
4. Brandeis, L. – Joined majority opinion
5. Stone, H. – Joined majority opinion
6. Roberts, O. – Joined majority opinion
7. Cardozo, B. – Joined majority opinion

Opposing Side (Respondent/Appellee)

1. McReynolds, J. – Joined dissenting opinion
2. Butler, P. – Wrote dissenting opinion

VI. A WIN OR LOSS FOR THE ACLU?

The ACLU, as counsel of record, urged reversal of the judgment of the Supreme Court of Alabama; the U.S. Supreme Court reversed in a 7-2 vote, giving the ACLU an apparent win.

5. Patterson v. Alabama

(Decided April 1, 1935; 294 U.S. 600)

I. ISSUE

A. Issues Discussed

Jury trials, racial discrimination

B. Legal Question Presented

Whether exclusion of African-American individuals from the jury pool violates the Fourteenth Amendment.

C. Supreme Court's Answer

Exclusion of African-American individuals from the jury pool was unconstitutional and the judgment must be vacated.

II. CASE SUMMARY

A. Background

"After the remand [in *Powell v. Alabama*], all of the cases were transferred for trial to Morgan County. Patterson was the first of those retried. The jury found a verdict against him which the trial judge set aside as against the weight of evidence. He was then brought to trial for a third time before another judge, in November, 1933, and was again convicted. The judgment was affirmed by the Supreme Court of [Alabama]. . . .

At the beginning of the last trial, as on the previous trial, a motion was made on Patterson's behalf to quash the indictment upon the ground of the exclusion of negroes from juries in Jackson county where the indictment was found. Defendant also moved to quash the trial venue in Morgan County because of the exclusion of negroes from jury service in that county. In each of these motions, defendant contended that there was a long-continued, systematic, and arbitrary exclusion of qualified negroes from jury service, solely by reason of their race or color, in violation of the Federal Constitution (amendment 14, § 1)." The trial judge denied the motions.

On appeal the Supreme Court vacated the judgment of the Supreme Court of Alabama.

B. Counsel of Record/ACLU Attorney

ACLU Side (Petitioner/Appellant): Walter H. Pollak argued the cause for appellant. With him on the brief were Osmond K. Fraenkel and Carl S. Stern.

Opposing Side (Respondent/Appellee): Attorney General of Alabama Thomas E. Knight, Jr. argued the cause for appellee.

III. AMICI CURIAE

ACLU Side (Petitioner/Appellant)

No briefs of amici curiae were filed in support of appellant.

Opposing Side (Respondent/Appellee)

No briefs of amici curiae were filed in support of appellee.

IV. THE SUPREME COURT'S DECISION

"[T]he state, by its Attorney General, contends that this Court has no jurisdiction in the instant case, in the view that the decision of the state court rested entirely upon a question of state appellate procedure and that no federal question is involved."

"While we must have proper regard to this ruling of the state court in relation to its appellate procedure, we cannot ignore the exceptional features of the present case. An important question under the Federal Constitution was involved, and, from that standpoint, the case did not stand alone. . . . The validity of the common indictment had been challenged by a motion on behalf of both defendants because of the unconstitutional discrimination."

"We have frequently held that in the exercise of our appellate jurisdiction we have power not only to correct error in the judgment under review but to make such disposition on the case as justice requires. And in determining what justice does require, the Court is bound to consider any change, either in fact or in law, which has supervened since the judgment was entered. We may recognize such a change, which may affect the result, by setting aside the judgment and remanding the case so that the state court may be free to act. We have said that to do this is not to review, in any proper sense of the term, the decision of the state court upon a nonfederal question, but only to deal appropriately with a matter arising since its judgment and having a bearing upon the right disposition of the case."

The U.S. Supreme Court vacated the judgment of the Supreme Court of Alabama and remanded the case.

V. JUSTICE VOTE

8 Pro ACLU Side vs. 0 Con Opposing Side

ACLU Side (Petitioner/Appellant)

1. Hughes, C. – Wrote majority opinion
2. Sutherland, G. – Joined majority opinion
3. Butler, P. – Joined majority opinion
4. Van Devanter, W. – Joined majority opinion
5. Brandeis, L. – Joined majority opinion
6. Stone, H. – Joined majority opinion
7. Roberts, O. – Joined majority opinion
8. Cardozo, B. – Joined majority opinion

McReynolds, J – Took no part in the decision

VI. A WIN OR LOSS FOR THE ACLU?

The ACLU, as counsel of record, urged reversal of the judgment of the Supreme Court of Alabama; the U.S. Supreme Court vacated in an 8-0 vote, giving the ACLU an apparent win.

6. De Jonge v. Oregon

(Decided January 4, 1937; 299 U.S. 353)

I. ISSUE

A. Issues Discussed

Freedom of expression and association

B. Legal Question Presented

Does Oregon's Criminal Syndicalism statute, as applied to Appellant who participated in a meeting held by the Communist Party, violate the due process clause of the Fourteenth Amendment?

C. Supreme Court's Answer

The Oregon statute, as applied in this case, violates the due process clause of the Fourteenth Amendment.

II. CASE SUMMARY

A. Background

Appellant was indicted under Oregon's "Criminal Syndicalism Law" which "defines 'criminal syndicalism' as 'the doctrine which advocates crime, physical violence, sabotage or any unlawful acts or methods as a means of accomplishing or effecting industrial or political change or revolution.' With this preliminary definition the act proceeds to describe a number of offenses, embracing the teaching of criminal syndicalism, the printing or distribution of books, pamphlets, etc., advocating that doctrine, the organization of a society or assemblage which advocates it, and presiding at or assisting in conducting a meeting of such an organization, society or group."

"The charge is that appellant assisted in the conduct of a meeting which was called under the auspices of the Communist Party, an organization advocating criminal syndicalism. . . . Appellant moved for a direction of acquittal, contending that the statute as applied to him, for merely assisting at a meeting called by the Communist Party at which nothing unlawful was done or advocated, violated the due process clause of the Fourteenth Amendment of the Constitution of the United States.

This contention was overruled. Appellant was found guilty as charged and was sentenced to imprisonment for seven years. The judgment was affirmed by the Supreme Court of the State which considered the constitutional question and sustained the statute as thus applied."

On appeal the Supreme Court reversed the judgment of the Supreme Court of Oregon.

B. Counsel of Record/ACLU Attorney

ACLU Side (Petitioner/Appellant): Osmond K. Fraenkel argued the cause for appellant.

Opposing Side (Respondent/Appellee): Maurice E. Tarshis argued the cause for appellee.

III. AMICI CURIAE

ACLU Side (Petitioner/Appellant)

No briefs of amici curiae were filed in support of appellant.

Opposing Side (Respondent/Appellee)

No briefs of amici curiae were filed in support of appellee.

IV. THE SUPREME COURT'S DECISION

"The right of peaceable assembly is a right cognate to those of free speech and free press and is equally fundamental. . . . The First Amendment of the Federal Constitution expressly guarantees that right against abridgment by Congress. But explicit mention there does not argue exclusion elsewhere. For the right is one that cannot be denied without violating those fundamental principles of liberty and justice which lie at the base of all civil and political institutions, — principles which the Fourteenth Amendment embodies in the general terms of its due process clause."

"[C]onsistently with the Federal Constitution, peaceable assembly for lawful discussion cannot be made a crime. The holding of meetings for peaceable political action cannot be proscribed. Those who assist in the conduct of such meetings cannot be branded as criminals on that score. The question, if the rights of free speech and peaceable assembly are to be preserved, is not as to the auspices under which the meeting is held but as to its purpose; not as to the relations of the speakers, but whether their utterances transcend the bounds of the freedom of speech which the Constitution protects. If the persons assembling have committed crimes elsewhere, if they have formed or are engaged in a conspiracy against the public peace and order, they may be prosecuted for their conspiracy or other violation of valid laws. But it is a different matter when the State, instead of prosecuting them for such offenses, seizes upon mere participation in a peaceable assembly and a lawful public discussion as the basis for a criminal charge.

We are not called upon to review the findings of the state court as to the objectives of the Communist Party. Notwithstanding those objectives, the defendant still enjoyed his personal right of free speech and to take part in a peaceable assembly having a lawful purpose, although called by that party.

We hold that the Oregon statute as applied to the particular charge as defined by the state court is repugnant to the due process clause of the Fourteenth Amendment. The judgment of conviction is reversed and the cause is remanded for further proceedings not inconsistent with this opinion."

V. JUSTICE VOTE

8 Pro ACLU Side vs. 0 Con Opposing Side

ACLU Side (Petitioner/Appellant)

1. Hughes, C. – Wrote majority opinion
2. Roberts, O. – Joined majority opinion
3. Brandeis, L. – Joined majority opinion
4. Cardozo, B. – Joined majority opinion
5. Butler, P. – Joined majority opinion
6. Van Devanter, W. – Joined majority opinion
7. McReynolds, J. – Joined majority opinion
8. Sutherland, G. – Joined majority opinion

Stone, H. – Took no part in the decision

VI. A WIN OR LOSS FOR THE ACLU?

The ACLU, as counsel of record, urged reversal of the judgment of the Supreme Court of Oregon; the U.S. Supreme Court reversed in an 8-0 vote, giving the ACLU an apparent win.

7. Senn v. Tile Layers Protective Union

(Decided May 24, 1937; 301 U.S. 468)

I. ISSUE

A. Issues Discussed

Fourteenth Amendment, due process, equal protection, union picketing

B. Legal Question Presented

"[W]hether the provisions of the Wisconsin Labor Code, which authorize giving publicity to labor disputes, declare peaceful picketing and patrolling lawful and prohibit granting of an injunction against such conduct, violate, as here construed and applied, the due process clause or equal protection clause of the Fourteenth Amendment."

C. Supreme Court's Answer

The challenged picketing provisions of the Wisconsin Labor Code do not violate the due process clause or equal protection clause of the Fourteenth Amendment.

II. CASE SUMMARY

A. Background

"Senn brought this suit in the circuit court of Milwaukee county, against Tile Layers Protective Union, Local No. 5, Tile Layers Helpers Union, Local No. 47, and their business agents, seeking an injunction to restrain picketing, and particularly 'publishing, stating or proclaiming that the plaintiff is unfair to organized labor or to the defendant unions' . . . ."

Senn owned a small tile laying business in Milwaukee, WI. He personally performed the manual labor of the business, along with one or two helpers. He was approached by the Tile Layers Protective Union, and refused to become a union contactor. One provision of the union agreement required that he no longer perform manual labor, requiring that only hire union members to perform the labor. The union was unwilling to remove that provision from the agreement so Senn refused to join, wanting to continue manual labor himself. "Because of his refusal, the unions picketed his place of business. The picketing was peaceful, without violence, and without any unlawful act."

The trial court ruled that union picketing was lawful in this case under the Wisconsin Labor Code and the Wisconsin Supreme Court affirmed. Senn appealed to the U.S. Supreme Court.

On appeal the U.S. Supreme Court affirmed the judgment of the Wisconsin Supreme Court.

B. Counsel of Record/ACLU Attorney

ACLU Side (Respondent/Appellee): Joseph A. Padway argued the cause for appellee.

Opposing Side (Petitioner/Appellant): Leon B. Lamfrom argued the cause for appellant

III. AMICI CURIAE

ACLU Side (Respondent/Appellee)

Brief of amici curiae urging affirmance filed on behalf of the ACLU and International Juridical Association by Francis Biddle, Osmond K. Fraenkel, Lloyd K. Garrison, Nathan Greene, and V. Henry Rothschild, 2d.

Opposing Side (Petitioner/Appellant)

No briefs of amici curiae were filed in support of appellant.

IV. THE SUPREME COURT'S DECISION

"Clearly the means which the statute authorizes—picketing and publicity—are not prohibited by the Fourteenth Amendment. Members of a union might, without special statutory authorization by a state, make known the facts of a labor dispute, for freedom of speech is guaranteed by the Federal Constitution."

"The statute provides that the picketing must be peaceful; and that term as used implies not only absence of violence, but absence of any unlawful act. It precludes the intimidation of customers. It precludes any form of physical obstruction or interference with the plaintiff's business. It authorizes giving publicity to the existence of the dispute 'whether by advertising, speaking, patrolling any public street or any place where any person or persons may lawfully be' . . . . Inherently, the means authorized are clearly unobjectionable. . . . The state courts found that the unions observed the limitations prescribed by the statute"

The U.S. Supreme Court affirmed the judgment of the Wisconsin Supreme Court.

V. JUSTICE VOTE

5 Pro ACLU Side vs. 4 Con Opposing Side

ACLU Side (Respondent/Appellee)

1. Brandeis, L. – Wrote majority opinion
2. Hughes, C. – Joined majority opinion
3. Stone, H. - Joined majority opinion
4. Roberts, O. – Joined majority opinion
5. Cardozo, B. – Joined majority opinion

Opposing Side (Petitioner/Appellant)

1. Butler, P. – Wrote dissenting opinion
2. Van Devanter, W. – Joined dissenting opinion
3. McReynolds, J. – Joined dissenting opinion
4. Sutherland, G. – Joined majority opinion

VI. A WIN OR LOSS FOR THE ACLU?

The ACLU, as amicus curiae, urged affirmance of the judgment of the Wisconsin Supreme Court; the U.S. Supreme Court affirmed in a 5-4 vote, giving the ACLU an apparent win.

8. Lovell v. City of Griffin

(Decided March 28, 1938; 303 U.S. 444)

I. ISSUE

A. Issues Discussed

Freedom of speech and of the press

B. Legal Question Presented

Is a city ordinance prohibiting "distribution of 'circulars, handbooks, advertising, or literature of any kind'" without written permission from the city manager, unconstitutional?

C. Supreme Court's Answer

The ordinance is facially invalid because it abridges freedom of the press.

II. CASE SUMMARY

A. Background

Alma Lovell was a member of the Jehovah's Witnesses. Following her beliefs, she distributed religious pamphlets on the streets of Griffin, Georgia, where she was fined because she did not obtain a permit for distribution of printed material from the city, as required by a city ordinance.

The Georgia Court of Appeals found that the law did not abridge freedom of the press or free exercise of religion and was constitutionally valid.

On appeal the Supreme Court reversed the judgment of the Court of Appeals.

B. Counsel of Record / ACLU Attorney

ACLU Side (Petitioner / Appellant): O.R. Moyle argued the cause for appellant.

Opposing Side (Respondent / Appellee): Hughes Spalding and Sumter M. Kelley argued the cause for appellee.

III. AMICI CURIAE

ACLU Side (Petitioner / Appellant)

Brief of amici curiae filed on behalf of the ACLU by Francis Biddle, Osmond K. Fraenkel, and Lloyd K. Garrison.

Brief of amici curiae filed on behalf of the Workers' Defense League by Samuel Slaff and George Slaff.

Opposing Side (Respondent / Appellee)

No briefs of amici curiae were filed in support of appellee.

IV. THE SUPREME COURT'S DECISION

"Freedom of speech and freedom of the press, which are protected by the First Amendment from infringement by Congress, are among the fundamental personal rights and liberties which are protected by the Fourteenth Amendment from invasion by state action."

"The ordinance prohibits the distribution of literature of any kind at any time, at any place, and in any manner without a permit from the City Manager.

We think that the ordinance is invalid on its face. Whatever the motive which induced its adoption, its character is such that it strikes at the very foundation of the freedom of the press by subjecting it to license and censorship."

"As the ordinance is void on its face, it was not necessary for appellant to seek a permit under it."

The Supreme Court reversed the Court of Appeals judgment.

V. JUSTICE VOTE

8 Pro ACLU Side vs. 0 Con Opposing Side

ACLU Side (Petitioner / Appellant)

1. Hughes, C. – Wrote majority opinion
2. McReynolds, J. – Joined majority opinion
3. Brandeis, L. – Joined majority opinion
4. Butler, P. – Joined majority opinion
5. Stone, H. – Joined majority opinion
6. Roberts, O. – Joined majority opinion
7. Black, H. – Joined majority opinion
8. Reed, S. – Joined majority opinion

Cardozo, B. – Took no part in the decision

VI. A WIN OR LOSS FOR THE ACLU?

The ACLU, as amicus curiae, urged reversal of the judgment of the Court of Appeals; the Supreme Court reversed in an 8-0 vote, giving the ACLU an apparent win.

9. Hague v. Committee for Industrial Organization

(Decided June 5, 1939; 307 U.S. 496)

I. ISSUE

A. Issues Discussed

Freedom of speech and assembly

B. Legal Question Presented

"[W]hether freedom to disseminate information concerning the provisions of the National Labor Relations Act, to assemble peaceably for discussion of the Act, and of the opportunities and advantages offered by it, is a privilege or immunity of a citizen of the United States secured against State abridgment by Section 1 of the Fourteenth Amendment."

C. Supreme Court's Answer

The ordinances that can effectively prohibit free dissemination and discussion of information are facially invalid under the Fourteenth Amendment.

II. CASE SUMMARY

A. Background

Respondents brought suit in District court alleging "that acting under a city ordinance forbidding the leasing of any hall, without a permit from the Chief of Police . . . the petitioners . . . have denied respondents the right to hold lawful meetings in Jersey City on the ground that they are Communists or Communist organizations . . . ." In addition, police enforcement of a city ordinance prohibiting literature distribution has "caused respondents, and those acting with them, to be arrested for distributing printed matter in the streets, and have caused them, and their associates, to be carried beyond the limits of the city or to remote places therein, and have compelled them to board ferry boats destined for New York; have, with violence and force, interfered with the distribution of pamphlets discussing the rights of citizens under the National Labor Relations Act . . . ."

The District Court found in favor of respondents, issuing a decree. The Third Circuit Court of Appeals affirmed, modifying one provision of the decree.

On certiorari the Supreme Court modified the decree and affirmed.

B. Counsel of Record / ACLU Attorney

ACLU Side (Respondent / Appellee): Morris L. Ernst and Spaulding Frazer argued the cause for appellee.

Opposing Side (Petitioner / Appellant): Charles Hershenstein, Edward J. O'Mara, and James A. Hamill, argued the cause for appellant.

III. AMICI CURIAE

ACLU Side (Respondent / Appellee)

Brief of amici curiae discussing the right of assembly filed by the Committee on the Bill of Rights of the American Bar Association.

Opposing Side (Petitioner / Appellant)

No briefs of amici curiae were filed on behalf of appellee.

IV. THE SUPREME COURT'S DECISION

"Although it has been held that the Fourteenth Amendment created no rights in citizens of the United States, but merely secured existing rights against state abridgment, it is clear that the right peaceably to assemble and to discuss these topics, and to communicate respecting them, whether orally or in writing, is a privilege inherent in citizenship of the United States which the Amendment protects."

"The privilege of a citizen of the United States to use the streets and parks for communication of views on national questions may be regulated in the interest of all; it is not absolute, but relative, and must be exercised in subordination to the general comfort and convenience, and in consonance with peace and good order; but it must not, in the guise of regulation, be abridged or denied.

We think the court below was right in holding the ordinance . . . void upon its face. It does not make comfort or convenience in the use of streets or parks the standard of official action. It [can instead] be made the instrument of arbitrary suppression of free expression of views on national affairs . . . ."

The Supreme Court modified the decree and affirmed the Third Circuit Court of Appeals judgment, but without a majority opinion.

V. JUSTICE VOTE

5 Pro ACLU Side vs. 2 Con Opposing Side

ACLU Side (Respondent / Appellee)

1. Roberts, O. – Wrote concurring opinion
2. Black, H. – Joined Justice Roberts' concurring opinion
3. Stone, H. – Wrote concurring opinion
4. Reed, S. – Joined Justice Stone's concurring opinion
5. Hughes, C. – Wrote concurring opinion

Opposing Side (Petitioner / Appellant)

1. McReynolds, J. – Wrote dissenting opinion
2. Butler, P. – Wrote dissenting opinion

Frankfurter, F. – Took no part in the decision
Douglas, W. – Took no part in the decision

VI. A WIN OR LOSS FOR THE ACLU?

The ACLU, as a party (along with the CIO),[1] urged affirmance of the Third Circuit Court of Appeals' decree; the Supreme Court affirmed in a 5-2 vote, giving the ACLU an apparent win.

10. Schneider v. New Jersey

(Decided November 22, 1939; 308 U.S. 147)

I. ISSUE

A. Issues Discussed

Freedom of speech and of the press

B. Legal Question Presented

"[W]hether regulations embodied in a municipal ordinance abridge the freedom of speech and of the press secured against state invasion by the Fourteenth Amendment of the Constitution."

C. Supreme Court's Answer

The ordinances abridge freedom of speech and of the press, in violation of the Fourteenth Amendment.

II. CASE SUMMARY

A. Background

The Supreme Court consolidated four cases concerning four similar city ordinances. Three cases from Los Angeles, Milwaukee, and Worchester concerned city ordinances which, in order to prevent street littering, banned the distribution of nearly all written material in public places. The fourth ordinance from Irvington required that a person who wished to "canvass, solicit, distribute circulars, or other matter, or call from house to house" needed to obtain a "written permit from the Chief of Police."

The Supreme Court held that the ordinances constituted unlawful regulation of speech and press and reversed the judgments of the lower courts.

1 The ACLU was indeed a party, but the first party on the ACLU side was the Committee for Industrial Organization. Case names only include the name of the first party, which is why the ACLU is not included.

B. Counsel of Record/ACLU Attorney

ACLU Side (Petitioner/Appellant): Joseph F. Rutherford argued the cause for appellant in Case 11. Osmond K. Fraenkel argued the cause for appellant in Case 13. A. W. Richter argued the cause for appellant in Case 18. Sidney S. Grant and Osmond K. Fraenkel argued the cause for appellant in Case 29.

Opposing Side (Respondent/Appellee): Robert I. Morris argued the cause for appellee in Case 11. Frederick Von Schrader, Ray L. Chesebro, Leon T. David, and Bourke Jones submitted the case for appellee in Case 13. Carl F. Zeidler argued the cause for appellee in Case 18. Edward O. Proctor argued the cause for appellee in Case 29.

III. AMICI CURIAE

ACLU Side (Petitioner/Appellant)

Brief of amici curiae filed in Case 18 on behalf of the ACLU by Arthur Garfield Hays, Richard G. Green, and Perry J. Stearns.

Opposing Side (Respondent/Appellee)

No briefs of amici curiae were filed in support of appellee.

IV. THE SUPREME COURT'S DECISION

In three cases discussing city ordinances that sought to prevent littering of the streets, the Court stated that "the purpose to keep the streets clean and of good appearance is insufficient to justify an ordinance which prohibits a person rightfully on a public street from handing literature to one willing to receive it. Any burden imposed upon the city authorities in cleaning and caring for the streets as an indirect consequence of such distribution results from the constitutional protection of the freedom of speech and press."

In the case of the Irvington ordinance which required a written permit from the chief of police to distribute circulars, the court held that "a municipality cannot . . . require all who wish to disseminate ideas to present them first to police authorities for their consideration and approval, with a discretion in the police to say some ideas may, while others may not, be carried to the homes of citizens; some persons may, while others may not, disseminate information from house to house."

The Supreme Court reversed each judgment of the courts below, determining the ordinances violated freedom of speech and of the press, as applied to state and local governments through the Fourteenth Amendment.

V. JUSTICE VOTE

7 Pro ACLU Side vs. 1 Con Opposing Side

ACLU Side (Petitioner/Appellant)

1. Roberts, O. – Wrote majority opinion
2. Frankfurter, F. – Joined majority opinion
3. Stone, H. – Joined majority opinion
4. Reed, S. – Joined majority opinion
5. Douglas, W. – Joined majority opinion
6. Hughes, C. – Joined majority opinion
7. Black, H. – Joined majority opinion

Opposing Side (Respondent/Appellee)

1. McReynolds, J. – Dissented without an opinion

Vacant Seat

VI. A WIN OR LOSS FOR THE ACLU?

The ACLU, as amicus and attorney of record for petitioners, urged reversal of the judgments of the lower courts; the Supreme Court reversed in a 7-1 vote, giving the ACLU an apparent win.

11. Carlson v. California

(Decided April 22, 1940; 310 U.S. 106)

I. ISSUE

A. Issues Discussed

Freedom of speech and of the press

B. Legal Question Presented

Does an ordinance making it unlawful to picket a place of business or employment in connection with a labor dispute violate the freedom of speech or of the press, as applied to the states by the due process clause of the Fourteenth Amendment?

C. Supreme Court's Answer

The ordinance threatens freedom of speech and violates the Fourteenth Amendment.

II. CASE SUMMARY

A. Background

An ordinance of Shasta County, California, declared it unlawful for any person to loiter or picket in front of "any place of business or employment, for the purpose of inducing or influencing" people to not enter, not purchase from, or not work for the business.

Appellant and twenty-eight other men picketed with signs at the site of a labor dispute at a highway construction project. They did not interfere with traffic to or from the project, and the activities were "peaceful and orderly." County officers arrested appellant, and he was found guilty of violating the anti-picketing ordinance. The conviction and ordinance were upheld by the Shasta County Superior Court.

Appellant appealed to the Supreme Court, asserting that the county ordinance violated his right to free speech in violation of the due process clause of the Fourteenth Amendment. The Supreme Court granted certiorari and reversed the lower court's decision.

B. Counsel of Record/ACLU Attorney

ACLU Side (Petitioner/Appellant): Lee Pressman argued the cause for appellant.

Opposing Side (Respondent/Appellee): Laurence W. Carr, pro hac vice, by special leave of Court, argued the cause for appellee.

III. AMICI CURIAE

ACLU Side (Petitioner/Appellant)

Brief of amici curiae filed on behalf of the ACLU by Osmond K. Fraenkel.

Opposing Side (Respondent/Appellee)

Brief of amici curiae filed on behalf of Ross W. Swing by Myer N. Rosengard and Samuel A. Rinella.

IV. THE SUPREME COURT'S DECISION

"The terms 'loiter' and 'picket' are not defined either in the ordinance or in authoritative State decisions. Therefore, they must be judged as covering all the activities embraced by the prohibition against the carrying of signs in the vicinity of a labor dispute for the purpose mentioned. The ordinance does not proscribe the carrying of signs in other places or for the purpose of inducing or attempting to induce others to adopt courses of action not related to labor disputes. It contains no exceptions with respect to the truthfulness and restraint of the information conveyed or the number of persons engaged in the activity. [T]he ordinance does not regulate all carrying of signs, but, on the contrary, proscribes the carrying of signs only if by persons directly interested who approach the vicinity of a labor dispute to convey information about the dispute.

The sweeping and inexact terms of the ordinance disclose the threat to freedom of speech inherent in its existence. . . . The carrying of signs and banners. . . is a natural and appropriate means of conveying information on matters of public concern. [P]ublicizing the facts of a labor dispute in a peaceful way through appropriate means, whether by pamphlet, by word of mouth or by banner, must now be regarded as within that liberty of communication which is secured to every person by the Fourteenth Amendment against abridgment by a State."

The Supreme Court reversed the lower court's judgment

V. JUSTICE VOTE

8 Pro ACLU Side vs. 1 Con Opposing Side

ACLU Side (Petitioner/Appellant)

1. Murphy F. – Wrote majority opinion
2. Frankfurter, F. – Joined majority opinion
3. Stone, H. – Joined majority opinion
4. Black, H. – Joined majority opinion
5. Douglas, W. – Joined majority opinion
6. Hughes, C. – Joined majority opinion
7. Roberts, O. – Joined majority opinion
8. Reed, S. – Joined majority opinion

Opposing Side (Respondent/Appellee)

1. McReynolds, J. – Dissented without an opinion

VI. A WIN OR LOSS FOR THE ACLU?

The ACLU filed an amicus brief urging reversal of the judgment of the Superior Court of Shasta County; the Supreme Court reversed in an 8-1 vote, giving the ACLU an apparent win.

12. Minersville School District v. Gobitis

(Decided June 3, 1940; 310 U.S. 586)

I. ISSUE

A. Issues Discussed

Freedom of religion

B. Legal Question Presented

Whether requiring a student to salute the national flag, despite the student's sincere religious beliefs forbidding such action, infringes freedom of religion under the due process clause of the Fourteenth Amendment.

C. Supreme Court's Answer

The mandatory flag salute does not infringe freedom of religion under the Fourteenth Amendment.

II. CASE SUMMARY

A. Background

"Lillian Gobitis, aged twelve, and her brother William, aged ten, were expelled from the public schools of Minersville, Pennsylvania, for refusing to salute the national flag as part of a daily school exercise. The local board of education required both teachers and pupils to participate in this ceremony. . . . The Gobitis family are affiliated with 'Jehovah's Witnesses', for whom the Bible as the Word of God is the supreme authority. The children had been brought up conscientiously to believe that such a gesture of respect for the flag was forbidden by command of scripture."

The district court and Third Circuit Court of Appeals held that the school board's action violated the Fourteenth Amendment. On appeal, the Supreme Court granted certiorari and reversed.

B. Counsel of Record/ACLU Attorney

ACLU Side (Respondent/Appellee): George K. Gardner and Joseph F. Rutherford argued the cause for appellee.

Opposing Side (Petitioner/Appellant): Joseph W. Henderson argued the cause for appellant.

III. AMICI CURIAE

ACLU Side (Respondent/Appellee)

Brief of amici curiae filed on behalf of the ACLU by George K. Gardner, Arthur Garfield Hays, Osmond K. Fraenkel, William G. Fennell, Jerome M. Britchey, and Alexander H. Frey.

Brief of amici curiae filed on behalf of the Committee on the Bill of Rights of the American Bar Association.

Opposing Side (Petitioner/Appellant)

No briefs of amici curiae were filed on behalf of appellant.

IV. THE SUPREME COURT'S DECISION

"The Gobitis children were of an age for which Pennsylvania makes school attendance compulsory. Thus they were denied a free education and their parents had to put them into private schools. To be relieved of the financial burden thereby entailed, their father, on behalf of the children and in his own behalf, brought this suit. He sought to enjoin the authorities from continuing to exact participation in the flag-salute ceremony as a condition of his children's attendance at the Minersville school."

"The religious liberty which the Constitution protects has never excluded legislation of general scope not directed against doctrinal loyalties of particular sects. . . . Conscientious scruples have not . . . relieved the individual from obedience to a general law not aimed at the promotion or restriction of religious beliefs. The mere possession of religious convictions which contradict the relevant concerns of a political society does not relieve the citizen from the discharge of political responsibilities. The necessity for this adjustment has again and again been recognized."

"National unity is the basis of national security. . . . The ultimate foundation of a free society is the binding tie of cohesive sentiment. . . . The flag is a symbol of our national unity, transcending all internal differences, however large, within the framework of the Constitution."

The Supreme Court reversed the Third Circuit Court of Appeals, allowing schools to mandate the flag salute.

V. JUSTICE VOTE

1 Pro ACLU Side vs. 8 Con Opposing Side

ACLU Side (Respondent/Appellee)

1. Stone, H. – Wrote dissenting opinion

Opposing Side (Petitioner/Appellant)

1. Frankfurter, F. – Wrote majority opinion
2. Black, H. – Joined majority opinion
3. Douglas, W. – Joined majority opinion
4. McReynolds, J. – Concurred in the result
5. Murphy, F. – Joined majority opinion
6. Reed, S. – Joined majority opinion
7. Roberts, O. – Joined majority opinion
8. Hughes, C. – Joined majority opinion

VI. A WIN OR LOSS FOR THE ACLU?

The ACLU filed an amicus brief urging affirmance of the judgment of the Third Circuit Court of Appeals; the Supreme Court reversed in an 8-1 vote, giving the ACLU an apparent loss. However, this decision was overturned in *West Virginia State Board of Education v. Barnette* in 1943.

13. Edwards v. California

(Decided November 24, 1941; 314 U.S. 160)

I. ISSUE

A. Issues Discussed

Interstate commerce

B. Legal Question Presented

Whether California's prohibition against knowingly bringing indigent persons into California is within the police power of the State?

C. Supreme Court's Answer

The prohibition is not within California's police power and unconstitutionally burdens interstate commerce.

II. CASE SUMMARY

A. Background

Appellant, a resident of California, knowingly brought his indigent brother-in-law from Texas to California in violation of Section 2615 of the California Welfare and Institutions Code, "which provides: 'Every person, firm or corporation, or officer or agent thereof that brings or assists in bringing into the State any indigent person who is not a resident of the State, knowing him to be an indigent person, is guilty of a misdemeanor.' [A]ppellant was convicted and sentenced to six months imprisonment in the county jail, and sentence was suspended. . . .

The Superior Court, although regarding as 'close' the question of the validity of the Section, felt 'constrained to uphold the statute as a valid exercise of the police power of the State of California.' Consequently, the conviction was affirmed."

The Supreme Court reversed the judgment of the Superior Court of Yuba County.

B. Counsel of Record/ACLU Attorney

ACLU Side (Petitioner/Appellant): Samuel Slaff argued the cause for appellant. With him on the brief were Philip Adams and Wayne M. Collins.

Opposing Side (Respondent/Appellee): W. T. Sweigert argued the cause for appellee. With him on the brief were California Attorney General Earl Warren and Hiram W. Johnson, 3d.

III. AMICI CURIAE

ACLU Side (Petitioner/Appellant)

John H. Tolan for the Select Committee of the House of Representatives of the United States, appointed pursuant to House Resolution No. 63, April 22, 1940, to investigate Interstate Migration of Destitute Citizens, filed as amicus curiae by special leave of Court. Irwin W. Silverman, of counsel.

Opposing Side (Respondent/Appellee)

No briefs of amici curiae were filed in support of appellee.

IV. THE SUPREME COURT'S DECISION

"We think this statute must fail under any known test of the validity of State interference with interstate commerce."

"The prohibition against transporting indigent non-residents into one State is an open invitation to retaliatory measures, and the burdens upon the transportation of such persons become cumulative. [W]e do not think that it will now be seriously contended that because a person is without employment and without funds he constitutes a 'moral pestilence.' Poverty and immorality are not synonymous.

We are of the opinion that Section 2615 is not a valid exercise of the police power of California, that it imposes an unconstitutional burden upon interstate commerce, and that the conviction under it cannot be sustained."

The Supreme Court reversed the judgment of the Superior Court.

V. JUSTICE VOTE

9 Pro ACLU Side vs. 0 Con Opposing Side

ACLU Side (Petitioner/Appellant)

1. Byrnes, J. – Wrote majority opinion
2. Reed, S. – Joined majority opinion
3. Frankfurter, F. – Joined majority opinion
4. Stone, H. – Joined majority opinion
5. Roberts, O. – Joined majority opinion
6. Douglas, W. – Wrote concurring opinion, joined by Justices Black and Murphy
7. Black, H. – Joined majority opinion
8. Murphy F. – Joined majority opinion
9. Jackson, R. – Wrote concurring opinion

VI. A WIN OR LOSS FOR THE ACLU?

The ACLU, as counsel of record, urged reversal of the judgment of the Superior Court; the Supreme Court reversed in a 9-0 vote, giving the ACLU an apparent win.

14. Bridges v. California

(Decided December 8, 1941; 314 U.S. 252)

I. ISSUE

A. Issues Discussed

Freedom of speech and of the press, contempt of court

B. Legal Question Presented

Whether holding a publisher or labor leader in contempt of court for out-of-court publications pertaining to court proceedings violates freedom of speech and of the press.

C. Supreme Court's Answer

Contempt of court was not appropriate for the publisher and labor leader as the expressions were protected by freedom of speech and of the press.

II. CASE SUMMARY

A. Background

Petitioner Times-Mirror newspaper published editorials commenting on pending labor cases. In a separate case, Petitioner Harry Bridges, a prominent labor leader involved in a labor dispute, sent a telegram to the Secretary of Labor in which he threatened a strike if the court decided against his union. Bridges later made the telegram public by consenting to newspapers reprinting his complaint. The state brought suit against both petitioners, attempting "to provide fair judicial trials free from coercion or intimidation." Both petitioners were found guilty and fined for contempt of the court by the Superior Court of Los Angeles County, and the California Supreme Court affirmed the lower court's judgments.

The cases were consolidated and the Supreme Court reversed the judgments.

B. Counsel of Record/ACLU Attorney

ACLU Side (Petitioner/Appellant): Osmond K. Fraenkel argued the cause on reargument for appellant, Bridges.

T.B. Cosgrove argued the cause in the original and reargument for appellant, Times Mirror Co.

Opposing Side (Respondent/Appellee): Allen W. Ashburn argued the cause in both the original and reargument for the appellee.

III. AMICI CURIAE

ACLU Side (Petitioner/Appellant)

Brief of amici curiae urging reversal filed on behalf of the ACLU by Osmond K. Fraenkel.

Opposing Side (Respondent/Appellee)

No briefs of amici curiae were filed in support of appellee.

IV. THE SUPREME COURT'S DECISION

"[T]his Court said that there must be a determination of whether or not 'the words used are used in such circumstances and are of such a nature as to create a clear and present danger that they will bring about the substantive evils.'" However, "the likelihood, however great, that a substantive evil will result cannot alone justify a restriction upon freedom of speech or the press. The evil itself must be 'substantial' .... [E]ven the expression of 'legislative preferences or beliefs' cannot transform minor matters of public inconvenience or annoyance into substantive evils of sufficient weight to warrant the curtailment of liberty of expression."

We cannot assume "that publications of the kind here involved actually do threaten to change the nature of legal trials, and that to preserve judicial impartiality, it is necessary for judges to have a contempt power by which they can close all channels of public expression to all matters which touch upon pending cases."

"[I]n sending the message to the Secretary [of Labor], Bridges was exercising the right of petition to a duly accredited representative of the United States government, a right protected by the First Amendment."

"Let us assume that the telegram could be construed as an announcement of Bridges' intention to call a strike, something which, it is admitted, neither the general law of California nor the court's decree prohibited. With an eye on the realities of the situation, we cannot assume that Judge Schmidt was unaware of the possibility of a strike as a consequence of his decision. If he was not intimidated by the facts themselves, we do not believe that the most explicit statement of them could have sidetracked the course of justice. Again, we find exaggeration in the conclusion that the utterance even 'tended' to interfere with justice. If there was electricity in the atmosphere, it was generated by the facts; the charge added by the Bridges telegram can be dismissed as negligible. . . . Reversed."

V. JUSTICE VOTE

5 Pro ACLU Side vs. 4 Con Opposing Side

ACLU Side (Petitioner/Appellant)

1. Black, H. – Wrote majority opinion
2. Jackson, R. – Joined majority opinion
3. Reed, S. – Joined majority opinion
4. Murphy, F. – Joined majority opinion
5. Douglas, W. – Joined majority opinion

Opposing Side (Respondent/Appellee)

1. Frankfurter, F. – Wrote dissenting opinion
2. Stone, H. – Joined Frankfurter's dissent
3. Roberts, O. – Joined Frankfurter's dissent
4. Byrnes, J. – Joined Frankfurter's dissent

VI. A WIN OR LOSS FOR THE ACLU?

The ACLU filed an amicus brief and an ACLU lawyer argued the case urging reversal; the Supreme Court reversed the ruling of the California Supreme Court by a 5-4 vote, giving the ACLU an apparent win.

15. Valentine v. Chrestensen

(Decided April 13, 1942; 316 U.S. 52)

I. ISSUE

A. Issues Discussed

Freedom of speech and of the press

B. Legal Question Presented

Whether an ordinance prohibiting distribution of commercial advertisement handbills abridges freedom of speech and of the press, as protected under the Fourteenth Amendment.

C. Supreme Court's Answer

The ordinance constitutionally prohibits commercial advertising, which is not protected speech.

II. CASE SUMMARY

A. Background

Respondent, Chrestensen, moored a submarine in New York City. He sought to solicit visitors, for a fee, by distributing advertising handbills. Petitioner, Valentine, Police Commissioner, advised him that distributing commercial handbills violated a city health code. Chrestensen was also advised that "he might freely distribute handbills solely devoted to 'information or a public protest.'" He then sought to distribute handbills with advertising on one side and a public protest on the other side. He was told that such two-sided handbills also violated the city health code. Chrestensen claimed that the two-sided handbills were protected by the Fourteenth Amendment. The lower courts enjoined enforcement of the city code. The Second Circuit Court of Appeals affirmed.

The Supreme Court granted certiorari and reversed.

B. Counsel of Record/ACLU Attorney

ACLU Side (Respondent/Appellee): Walter W. Land argued the cause for appellee.

Opposing Side (Petitioner/Appellant): William C. Chanler argued the cause for appellant.

III. AMICI CURIAE

ACLU Side (Respondent/Appellee)

Brief of amici curiae filed on behalf of the New York City Committee of the ACLU by Osmond K. Fraenkel.

Opposing Side (Petitioner/Appellant)

Brief of amici curiae filed on behalf of the Member Cities of the National Institute of Municipal Law Officers.

IV. THE SUPREME COURT'S DECISION

"This court has unequivocally held that the streets are proper places for the exercise of the freedom of communicating information and disseminating opinion and that, though the states and municipalities may appropriately regulate the privilege in the public interest, they may not unduly burden or proscribe its employment in these public thoroughfares. We are equally clear that the Constitution imposes no such restraint on government as respects purely commercial advertising. Whether, and to what extent, one may promote or pursue a gainful occupation in the streets, to what extent such activity shall be adjudged a derogation of the public right of user, are matters for legislative judgment. . . . If the respondent was attempting to use the streets of New York by distributing commercial advertising, the prohibition of the code provision was lawfully invoked against his conduct."

"[T]he stipulated facts justify the conclusion that the affixing of the protest against official conduct to the advertising circular was with the intent, and for the purpose, of evading the prohibition of the ordinance."

The Supreme Court reversed, determining that the commercial advertising was not protected speech.

V. JUSTICE VOTE

0 Pro ACLU Side vs. 9 Con Opposing Side

Opposing Side (Petitioner/Appellant)

1. Roberts, O. – Wrote majority opinion
2. Black, H. – Joined majority opinion
3. Reed, S. – Joined majority opinion
4. Murphy, F. – Joined majority opinion
5. Douglas, W. – Joined majority opinion
6. Frankfurter, F. – Joined majority opinion
7. Byrnes, J. – Joined majority opinion
8. Jackson, R. – Joined majority opinion
9. Stone, H. – Joined majority opinion

VI. A WIN OR LOSS FOR THE ACLU?

The ACLU filed an amicus brief urging affirmance; the Supreme Court reversed the ruling of the Second Circuit Court of Appeals in a 9-0 vote, giving the ACLU an apparent loss.

16. Betts v. Brady

(Decided June 1, 1942; 316 U.S. 455)

I. ISSUE

A. Issues Discussed

Criminal procedure

B. Legal Question Presented

"[W]hether due process of law demands that in every criminal case, whatever the circumstances, a state must furnish counsel to an indigent defendant."

C. Supreme Court's Answer

"As we have said, the Fourteenth Amendment prohibits the conviction and incarceration of one whose trial is offensive to the common and fundamental ideas of fairness and right, and while want of counsel in a particular case may result in a conviction lacking in such fundamental fairness, we cannot say that the amendment embodies an inexorable command that no trial for any offense, or in any court, can be fairly conducted and justice accorded a defendant who is not represented by counsel."

II. CASE SUMMARY

A. Background

"The petitioner was indicted for robbery . . . . Due to lack of funds he was unable to employ counsel, and so informed the judge at his arraignment. He requested that counsel be appointed for him. The judge advised him that this could not be done as it was not the practice in Carroll County to appoint counsel for indigent defendants save in prosecutions for murder and rape.

Without waiving his asserted right to counsel the petitioner pleaded not guilty and elected to be tried without a jury. . . . The judge found him guilty and imposed a sentence of eight years.

While serving his sentence, the petitioner filed with a judge of the Circuit Court for Washington County, Maryland, a petition for a writ of habeas corpus alleging that he had been deprived of the right to assistance of counsel guaranteed by the Fourteenth Amendment of the federal Constitution. The writ issued, the cause was heard, his contention was rejected, and he was remanded to the custody of the prison warden.

Some months later a petition for a writ of habeas corpus was presented to Hon. Carroll T. Bond, Chief Judge of the Court of Appeals of Maryland . . . . Judge Bond granted the writ but . . . denied the relief prayed and remanded the petitioner to the respondent's custody.

The petitioner applied to this court for certiorari directed to Judge Bond. The writ was issued on account of the importance of the jurisdictional questions involved and conflicting decisions upon the constitutional question presented."

B. Counsel of Record

ACLU Side (Petitioner/Appellant): Jesse Slingluff, Jr., and G. Van Velsor Wolf argued the cause and filed the brief for appellant.

Opposing Side (Respondent/Appellee): William C. Walsh, Attorney General of Maryland, and Robert E. Clapp, Jr., Assistant Attorney General, argued the cause for appellee. With them on the brief was Morton E. Rome.

III. AMICI CURIAE

ACLU Side (Petitioner/Appellant)

Brief of amici curiae filed on behalf of the American Civil Liberties Union.[1]

Opposing Side (Respondent/Appellee)

No briefs of amici curiae filed in support of appellee.

IV. THE SUPREME COURT'S DECISION

"In awarding the writ, we requested counsel to discuss the jurisdiction of this court, 'particularly (1) whether the decision below is that of a court within the meaning of section 237 of the Judicial Code, and (2) whether state remedies, either by appeal or by application to other judges or any other state court, have been exhausted.' . . .

In view of what has been said of the power of Judge Bond as a judicial tribunal to hear and finally decide the cause, and of the judicial quality of his action, we are of opinion that his judgment was that of a court within the intendment of Sec. 237. . . .

Since Judge Bond's order was a final disposition by the highest court of Maryland in which a judgment could be had of the issue joined on the instant petition we have jurisdiction to review it. . . .

Was the petitioner's conviction and sentence a deprivation of his liberty without due process of law, in violation of the Fourteenth Amendment, because of the court's refusal to appoint counsel at his request?

The Sixth Amendment of the national Constitution applies only to trials in federal courts. . . .

The question we are now to decide is whether due process of law demands that in every criminal case, whatever the circumstances, a state must furnish counsel to an indigent defendant. . . .

This material demonstrates that, in the great majority of the states, it has been the considered judgment of the people, their representatives and their courts that appointment of counsel is not a fundamental right, essential to a fair trial. . . .

As we have said, the Fourteenth Amendment prohibits the conviction and incarceration of one whose trial is offensive to the common and fundamental ideas of fairness and right, and while want of counsel in a particular case may result in a conviction lacking in such fundamental fairness, we cannot say that the amendment embodies an inexorable command that no trial for any offense, or in any court, can be fairly conducted and justice accorded a defendant who is not represented by counsel.

The judgment is affirmed."

1 ACLU Indigent *Defense Docket, ACLU,* https://www.aclu.org/sites/default/files/FilesPDFs/indigentdefensedocket.pdf (last visited Jan. 25, 2020) ("In 1942, the ACLU filed an amicus brief on behalf of Smith Betts seeking to extend to all state felony prosecutions the constitutional right to counsel established in Powell v. Alabama with respect to state capital proceedings." p. 7).

V. JUSTICE VOTE

3 Pro ACLU Side vs. 6 Con Opposing Side

ACLU Side (Petitioner/Appellant)

1. Black, H. – Wrote dissenting opinion
2. Douglas, W. – Joined Black's dissent
3. Murphy, F. – Joined Black's dissent

Opposing Side (Respondent/Appellee)

1. Roberts, O. – Wrote majority opinion
2. Stone, H. – Joined majority opinion
3. Byrnes, J. – Joined majority opinion
4. Reed, S. – Joined majority opinion
5. Frankfurter, F. – Joined majority opinion
6. Jackson, R. – Joined majority opinion

VI. A WIN OR LOSS FOR THE ACLU?

The ACLU filed as amicus curiae urging reversal; the Supreme Court affirmed the Court of Appeals of Maryland's decision by a 6-3 vote, giving the ACLU an apparent loss.

17. Jones v. City of Opelika

(Decided May 3, 1943; 319 U.S. 105)

I. ISSUE

A. Issues Discussed

Freedom of religion, speech, and press

B. Legal Question Presented

Is the requirement that missionaries, whose activities include the distribution, for a fee, of religious material, pay a license tax pursuant to a city ordinance, a violation of their constitutional rights?

C. Supreme Court's Answer

The license tax violates the constitutional rights of the missionaries because their religious activity is not unprotected commercial activity.

II. CASE SUMMARY

A. Background

With this decision, the original decision in *Jones v. City of Opelika* was vacated in a per curiam opinion at 319 U.S. 103. The decision referenced here, with an opinion under *Murdock v. Commonwealth of Pennsylvania*, 319 U.S. 105, decided 11 similar cases, including *Jones*. The facts of all 11 cases are not recited, just those relevant to understanding the decision.

The ordinance in the City of Jeannette was similar to the ordinances in the other cases. The Jeannette ordinance provided that any person "'canvassing for or soliciting . . . orders for goods, paintings, pictures, wares, or merchandise of any kind . . . shall be required to procure from the Burgess a license to transact said business and shall pay'" a licensing tax of a fixed amount.

"Petitioners are 'Jehovah's Witnesses.' They went about from door to door in the City of Jeannette distributing literature and soliciting people to 'purchase' certain religious books and pamphlets . . . . None of them obtained a license under the ordinance."

"Petitioners were convicted and fined for violation of the ordinance. Their judgments of conviction were sustained by the Superior Court of Pennsylvania, against their contention that the ordinance deprived them of the freedom of speech, press, and religion guaranteed by the First Amendment. Petitions for leave to appeal to the Supreme Court of Pennsylvania were denied. The cases are here on petitions for writs of certiorari . . . ."

The Supreme Court vacated its prior judgment in *Jones*, 316 U.S. 584, and reversed the judgments of the lower courts in all 11 cases.

B. Counsel of Record/ACLU Attorney

ACLU Side (Petitioner/Appellant): Hayden C. Covington and Osmond K. Fraenkel argued the cause for appellant.

Opposing Side (Respondent/Appellee): John W. Guider argued the cause for appellee.

III. AMICI CURIAE

ACLU Side (Petitioner/Appellant)

Opposing Side (Respondent/Appellee)

Brief of amici curiae filed on behalf of the General Conference of Seventh-Day Adventists by Homer Cummings and Millward C. Taft.

Brief of amici curiae filed on behalf of the American Newspaper Publishers Associations by Elisha Hanson. No briefs of amici curiae were filed in support of appellee.

IV. THE SUPREME COURT'S DECISION

"Freedom of speech, freedom of the press, freedom of religion are available to all, not merely to those who can pay their own way. As we have said, the problem of drawing the line between a purely commercial activity and a religious one will at times be difficult. On this record it plainly cannot be said that petitioners were engaged in a commercial rather than a religious venture."

"The tax imposed by the City of Jeannette is a flat license tax, the payment of which is a condition of the exercise of these constitutional privileges. The power to tax the exercise of a privilege is the power to control or suppress its enjoyment. . . . A state may not impose a charge for the enjoyment of a right granted by the federal constitution."

"The power to impose a license tax on the exercise of these freedoms is indeed as potent as the power of censorship which this Court has repeatedly struck down."

The Supreme Court vacated its previous judgment in *Jones* and reversed the lower court judgments in all 11 cases.

V. JUSTICE VOTE

5 Pro ACLU Side vs. 4 Con Opposing Side

ACLU Side (Petitioner/Appellant)

1. Douglas, W. – Wrote majority opinion
2. Murphy, F. – Joined majority opinion

3. Rutledge, W. – Joined majority opinion
4. Black, H. – Joined majority opinion
5. Stone, H. – Joined majority opinion

Opposing Side (Respondent/Appellee)

1. Reed, S. – Wrote dissenting opinion
2. Roberts, O. – Joined dissenting opinion
3. Frankfurter, F. – Joined and wrote dissenting opinion
4. Jackson, R. – Joined both dissenting opinions and added dissenting comments in another opinion issued on the same day, Douglas v. Jeanette, 319, U.S. 157.

VI. A WIN OR LOSS FOR THE ACLU?

The ACLU, as an attorney of record, urged reversal of the state court judgments; the Supreme Court vacated its previous ruling in Jones and reversed in a 5-4 vote all 11 cases, giving the ACLU an apparent win.

18. Martin v. City of Struthers

(Decided May 3, 1943; 319 U.S. 141)

I. ISSUE

A. Issues Discussed

Freedom of speech and of the press

B. Legal Question Presented

Whether a city ordinance banning door to door distribution of "handbills, circulars or other advertisements" violates the freedom of speech or of the press.

C. Supreme Court's Answer

The ordinance violates freedom of speech and of the press.

II. CASE SUMMARY

A. Background

"The appellant, espousing a religious cause in which she was interested—that of the Jehovah's Witnesses—went to the homes of strangers, knocking on doors and ringing doorbells in order to distribute to the inmates of the homes leaflets advertising a religious meeting. In doing so, she proceeded in a conventional and orderly fashion. For delivering a leaflet to the inmate of a home she was convicted in the Mayor's Court and was fined $10.00 on a charge of violating" a city ordinance making it unlawful to distribute door to door any "handbills, circulars or other advertisements."

"The appellant admitted knocking at the door for the purpose of delivering the invitation, but seasonably urged in the lower Ohio state court that the ordinance as construed and applied was beyond the power of the State because in violation of the right of freedom of press and religion as guaranteed by the First and Fourteenth Amendments."

The Supreme Court reversed the judgment of the court below.

B. Counsel of Record/ACLU Attorney

ACLU Side (Petitioner/Appellant): Hayden C. Covington argued the cause for appellant.

Opposing Side (Respondent/Appellee): Theodore T. Macejko and David C. Haynes argued the cause of appellee.

III. AMICI CURIAE

ACLU Side (Petitioner/Appellant)

Brief of amici curiae filed on behalf of the ACLU by Dorothy Kenyon.

Opposing Side (Respondent/Appellee)

No briefs of amici curiae were filed in support of appellee.

IV. THE SUPREME COURT'S DECISION

"While door to door distributers of literature may be either a nuisance or a blind for criminal activities, they may also be useful members of society engaged in the dissemination of ideas in accordance with the best tradition of free discussion."

"Freedom to distribute information to every citizen wherever he desires to receive it is so clearly vital to the preservation of a free society that, putting aside reasonable police and health regulations of time and manner of distribution, it must be fully preserved. The dangers of distribution can so easily be controlled by traditional legal methods, leaving to each householder the full right to decide whether he will receive strangers as visitors, that stringent prohibition can serve no purpose but that forbidden by the Constitution . . . .

The Struthers ordinance does not safeguard these constitutional rights. [W]e conclude that the ordinance is invalid because [it is] in conflict with the freedom of speech and press."

The Supreme Court reversed the judgment of the court below, striking down the ordinance.

V. JUSTICE VOTE

5 Pro ACLU Side vs. 4 Con Opposing Side

ACLU Side (Petitioner/Appellant)

1. Black, H. – Wrote majority opinion
2. Murphy, F. – Wrote concurring opinion
3. Rutledge, W. – Joined majority opinion
4. Douglas, W. – Joined majority opinion
5. Stone, H. – Joined majority opinion

Opposing Side (Respondent/Appellee)

1. Frankfurter, F. – Wrote dissenting opinion
2. Reed, S. – Wrote dissenting opinion
3. Roberts, O. – Joined Justice Reed's dissenting opinion
4. Jackson, R. – Joined Justice Reed's dissenting opinion

VI. A WIN OR LOSS FOR THE ACLU?

The ACLU, as amicus curiae, urged reversal of the judgment of the court below; the Supreme Court reversed in a 5-4 vote, giving the ACLU an apparent win.

19. National Broadcasting Co. v. United States

(Decided May 10, 1943; 319 U.S. 190)

I. ISSUE

A. Issues Discussed

Freedom of speech

B. Legal Question Presented

Whether Congress validly authorized the Federal Communications Commission to exercise the power asserted by the Chain Broadcasting Regulations, and whether the regulations abridge freedom of speech.

C. Supreme Court's Answer

The congressional authorization was valid and the regulations do not abridge freedom of speech.

II. CASE SUMMARY

A. Background

"On March 18, 1938, the [Federal Communications] Commission undertook a comprehensive investigation to determine whether special regulations applicable to radio stations engaged in chain broadcasting were required in the 'public interest, convenience, or necessity.'"

"On May 2, 1941, the Commission issued its Report on Chain Broadcasting, setting forth its findings and conclusions upon the matters explored in the investigation, together with an order adopting the Regulations here assailed."

"The Commission found that at the end of 1938 there were 660 commercial stations in the United States, and that 341 of these were affiliated with national networks. . . . It pointed out that the stations affiliated with the national networks utilized more than 97% of the total night-time broadcasting power of all the stations in the country. NBC and CBS together controlled more than 85% of the total night-time wattage, and the broadcast business of the three national network companies amounted to almost half of the total business of all stations in the United States."

On the ground that it had the congressional power to do so, the Commission established its Chain Broadcasting Regulations to correct eight network abuses. "The appellants attack the validity of these Regulations. They contend [notably] that the Commission went beyond the regulatory powers conferred upon it by the Communications Act of 1934." On remand from a previous hearing by the Supreme Court concerning jurisdiction, the District Court for the Southern District of New York reconsidered the case and "granted the Government's motions for summary judgment and dismissed the suits on the merits." On this appeal, the Supreme Court affirmed.

B. Counsel of Record/ACLU Attorney

ACLU Side (Respondent/Appellee): Charles Fahy and Louis G. Caldwell argued the cause for appellee.

Opposing Side (Petitioner/Appellant): John T. Cahill, E. Willoughby Middleton, and Charles E. Hughes argued the cause for appellant.

III. AMICI CURIAE

ACLU Side (Respondent/Appellee)

Brief of amici curiae filed on behalf of the ACLU by Homer S. Cummings, Morris L. Ernst, Benjamin S. Kirsh, William Draper Lewis, and Harriet F. Pilpel.

Opposing Side (Petitioner/Appellant)

Brief of amici curiae filed on behalf of the Association of National Advertisers, Inc., by Isaac W. Digges.

IV. THE SUPREME COURT'S DECISION

"The avowed aim of the Communications Act of 1934 was to secure the maximum benefits of radio to all the people of the United States. To that end Congress endowed the Communications Commission with comprehensive powers to promote and realize the vast potentialities of radio."

"[T]he Chain Broadcasting Regulations represent a particularization of the Commission's conception of the 'public interest' sought to be safeguarded by Congress in enacting the Communications Act of 1934."

"We conclude, therefore, that the Communications Act of 1934 authorized the Commission to promulgate regulations designed to correct the abuses disclosed by its investigation of chain broadcasting."

Addressing Appellants' claim that the Regulations abridged their right of free speech the Court held that "[u]nlike other modes of expression, radio inherently is not available to all. . . . Congress did not authorize the Commission to choose among applicants upon the basis of their political, economic or social views, or upon any other capricious basis. . . . The licensing system established by Congress in the Communications Act of 1934 was a proper exercise of its power over commerce. The standard it provided for the licensing of stations was the 'public interest, convenience, or necessity.' Denial of a station license on that ground, if valid under the Act, is not a denial of free speech."

The Supreme Court affirmed the summary judgment granted by the District Court for the Southern District of New York.

V. JUSTICE VOTE

5 Pro ACLU Side vs. 2 Con Opposing Side

ACLU Side (Respondent/Appellee)

1. Frankfurter, F. – Wrote majority opinion
2. Stone, H. – Joined majority opinion
3. Reed, S. – Joined majority opinion
4. Douglas, W. – Joined majority opinion
5. Jackson, R. – Joined majority opinion

Opposing Side (Petitioner/Appellant)

1. Murphy, F. – Wrote dissenting opinion
2. Roberts, O. – Joined Murphy's dissent

Rutledge, W – Took no part in the decision
Black, H – Took no part in the decision

VI. A WIN OR LOSS FOR THE ACLU?

The ACLU, as amicus curiae, urged affirmance of the judgment of the District Court for the Southern District of New York; the Supreme Court affirmed in a 5-2 vote, giving the ACLU an apparent win.

20. Taylor v. Mississippi

(Decided June 14, 1943; 319 U.S. 583)

I. ISSUE

A. Issues Discussed

Freedom of speech

B. Legal Question Presented

Were appellants' convictions under a Mississippi statute regulating conduct considered disloyal to the United States and Mississippi erroneous convictions?

C. Supreme Court's Answer

The convictions under the statute were erroneous.

II. CASE SUMMARY

A. Background

All appellants were convicted, under a Mississippi statute, for "distributing literature and printed matter reasonably tending to create an attitude of stubborn refusal to salute, honor, and respect the flag and government of the United States and of the State of Mississippi" All were Jehovah's Witnesses and "[t]here is nothing in the records to indicate that, in making the statements and distributing the printed matter in question, they were communicating and teaching any doctrine in which they did not sincerely believe."

Appellants appealed to the Supreme Court of Mississippi claiming that "the Act abridges freedom of press and of speech and is so vague, indefinite, and uncertain as to furnish no reasonably ascertainable standard of guilt."

The Supreme Court of Mississippi affirmed the convictions. The U.S. Supreme Court reversed.

B. Counsel of Record/ACLU Attorney

ACLU Side (Petitioner/Appellant): Hayden C. Covington argued the cause for appellant.

Opposing Side (Respondent/Appellee): Assistant Attorney General of Mississippi George T. Ethridge argued the cause for appellee.

III. AMICI CURIAE

ACLU Side (Petitioner/Appellant)

Brief of amici curiae filed on behalf of the ACLU by Zarah Williamson and Charles C. Evans.

Opposing Side (Respondent/Appellee)

No briefs of amici curiae were filed on behalf of appellee.

IV. THE SUPREME COURT'S DECISION

"The statute as construed in these cases makes it a criminal offense to communicate to others views and opinions respecting governmental policies, and prophesies concerning the future of our own and other nations. As applied to the appellants it punishes them although what they communicated is not claimed or shown to have been done with an evil or sinister purpose, to have advocated or incited subversive action against the nation or state, or to have threatened any clear and present danger to our institutions or our government. What these appellants communicated were their beliefs and opinions concerning domestic measures and trends in national and world affairs.

Under our decisions criminal sanctions cannot be imposed for such communication."

The U.S. Supreme Court reversed the judgment of the Supreme Court of Mississippi.

V. JUSTICE VOTE

9 Pro ACLU Side vs. 0 Con Opposing Side

ACLU Side (Petitioner/Appellant)

1. Roberts, O. – Wrote majority opinion
2. Stone, H. – Joined majority opinion
3. Black, H. – Joined majority opinion
4. Reed, S. – Joined majority opinion
5. Frankfurter, F. – Joined majority opinion
6. Douglas, W. – Joined majority opinion
7. Jackson, R. – Joined majority opinion
8. Rutledge, W. – Joined majority opinion
9. Murphy, F. – Joined majority opinion

VI. A WIN OR LOSS FOR THE ACLU?

The ACLU, as amicus curiae, urged reversal of the judgment of the Supreme Court of Mississippi; the U.S. Supreme Court reversed in a 9-0 vote, giving the ACLU an apparent win.

21. West Virginia State Board of Education v. Barnette

(Decided June 14, 1943; 319 U.S. 624)

I. ISSUE

A. Issues Discussed

Freedom of religion and speech

B. Legal Question Presented

Whether a Board of Education ordering a flag salute in public schools infringes freedom of religion and speech.

C. Supreme Court's Answer

A mandatory flag salute unconstitutionally infringes First Amendment freedoms as applied to the states under the Fourteenth Amendment.

II. CASE SUMMARY

A. Background

"The Board of Education on January 9, 1942, adopted a resolution . . . ordering that the salute to the flag become 'a regular part of the program of activities in the public schools,' that all teachers and pupils 'shall be required to participate in the salute honoring the Nation represented by the Flag . . . .'"

"Failure to conform is 'insubordination' dealt with by expulsion. Readmission is denied by statute until compliance. Meanwhile the expelled child is 'unlawfully absent' and may be proceeded against as a delinquent. His parents or guardians are liable to prosecution, and if convicted are subject to fine not exceeding $50 and jail term not exceeding thirty days.

Appellees . . . brought suit in the United States District Court for themselves and others similarly situated asking its injunction to restrain enforcement of these laws and regulations against Jehovah's Witnesses."

"The Board of Education moved to dismiss the complaint [which alleged] that the law and regulations are an unconstitutional denial of religious freedom, and of freedom of speech, and are invalid under the 'due process' and 'equal protection' clauses of the Fourteenth Amendment to the Federal Constitution. The cause was submitted on the pleadings to a District Court of three judges. It restrained enforcement as to the plaintiffs and those of that class."

The Board of Education appealed to the Supreme Court, which affirmed the judgment of the District Court for the Southern District of West Virginia.

B. Counsel of Record/ACLU Attorney

ACLU Side (Petitioner/Appellant): W. Holt Wooddell argued the cause for appellant.

Opposing Side (Respondent/Appellee): Hayden C. Covington argued the cause for appellee.

III. AMICI CURIAE

ACLU Side (Petitioner/Appellant)

Brief of amici curiae filed on behalf of the ACLU by William G. Fennell, Osmond K. Fraenkel, Arthur Garfield Hays, and Howard B. Lee.

Brief of amici curiae filed on behalf of the Committee on the Bill of Rights, of the American Bar Association.

Opposing Side (Respondent/Appellee)

Brief of amici curiae filed on behalf of the American Legion by Ralph B. Gregg.

IV. THE SUPREME COURT'S DECISION

"The question which underlies the flag salute controversy is whether such a ceremony so touching matters of opinion and political attitude may be imposed upon the individual by official authority under powers committed to any political organization under our Constitution."

"Free public education, if faithful to the ideal of secular instruction and political neutrality, will not be partisan or enemy of any class, creed, party, or faction."

"If there is any fixed star in our constitutional constellation, it is that no official, high or petty, can prescribe what shall be orthodox in politics, nationalism, religion, or other matters of opinion or force citizens to confess by word or act their faith therein. If there are any circumstances which permit an exception, they do not now occur to us.

We think the action of the local authorities in compelling the flag salute and pledge transcends constitutional limitations on their power and invades the sphere of intellect and spirit which it is the purpose of the First Amendment to our Constitution to reserve from all official control."

The Supreme Court affirmed the judgment of the District Court for the Southern District of West Virginia, overruling *Minersville School District v. Gobitis.*

V. JUSTICE VOTE

6 Pro ACLU Side vs. 3 Con Opposing Side

ACLU Side (Petitioner/Appellant)

1. Jackson, R. – Wrote majority opinion
2. Douglas, W. – Wrote concurring opinion with Justice Black
3. Black, H. – Wrote concurring opinion with Justice Douglas
4. Murphy, F. – Wrote concurring opinion
5. Stone, H. – Joined majority opinion
6. Rutledge, W. – Joined majority opinion

Opposing Side (Respondent/Appellee)

1. Roberts, O. – Joined dissenting opinion
2. Reed, S. – Joined dissenting opinion
3. Frankfurter, F. – Wrote dissenting opinion

VI. A WIN OR LOSS FOR THE ACLU?

The ACLU, as amicus curiae, urged affirmance of the judgment of the District Court for the Southern District of West Virginia; the Supreme Court affirmed in a 6-3 vote, giving the ACLU an apparent win. In addition, this decision overruled *Minersville School District v. Gobitis*, a previous loss for the ACLU.

22. Hirabayashi v. United States

(Decided June 21, 1943; 320 U.S. 81)

I. ISSUE

A. Issues Discussed

Racial discrimination, due process

B. Legal Question Presented

First, whether a curfew restriction on "all persons of Japanese ancestry" residing in military areas was established by "an unconstitutional delegation by Congress of its legislative power. Second, whether the curfew restriction "unconstitutionally discriminated between citizens of Japanese ancestry and those of other ancestries in violation of the Fifth Amendment."

C. Supreme Court's Answer

The curfew was established by a constitutional delegation of congressional power, and the curfew does not violate the Fifth Amendment.

II. CASE SUMMARY

A. Background

"[A]ppellant, being a person of Japanese ancestry, had... contrary to a restriction promulgated by the military commander... failed to remain in his place of residence in the designated military area between the hours of 8:00 o'clock pm and 6:00 am."

In addition, "appellant had failed to report to the Civil Control Station... as directed, to register for evacuation from the military area. He admitted failure to do so, and stated it had at all times been his belief that he would be waiving his rights as an American citizen by so doing. The jury returned a verdict of guilty on both counts and appellant was sentenced to imprisonment for a term of three months on each, the sentences to run concurrently."

"On appeal the Court of Appeals for the Ninth Circuit certified to [the Supreme Court] questions of law upon which it desired instructions for the decision of the case." The Supreme Court reviewed the case and affirmed the conviction.

B. Counsel of Record/ACLU Attorney

ACLU Side (Petitioner/Appellant): Frank L. Walters and Harold Evans argued the cause for appellant.

Opposing Side (Respondent/Appellee): Charles Fahy, Solicitor General, argued the cause for appellee.

III. AMICI CURIAE

ACLU Side (Petitioner/Appellant)

Brief of amici curiae filed on behalf of the ACLU by Arthur Garfield Hays, Osmond K. Fraenkel, and A. L. Wirin.

Brief of amici curiae filed by the Northern California Branch of the ACLU.

Brief of amici curiae filed on behalf of the Japanese American Citizens League by Saburo Kido, A. L. Wirin, Hugh E. Macbeth, and Clifford Forster.

Opposing Side (Respondent/Appellee)

No briefs of amici curiae were filed in support of appellee.

IV. THE SUPREME COURT'S DECISION

"Executive Order No. 9066, promulgated in time of war for the declared purpose of prosecuting the war by protecting national defense resources from sabotage and espionage, and the Act of March 21, 1942, ratifying and confirming the Executive Order, were each an exercise of the power to wage war conferred on the Congress and on the President... by Articles I and II of the Constitution. . . . The war power of the national government is 'the power to wage war successfully.' It extends to every matter and activity so related to war as substantially to affect its conduct and progress."

"When the orders were promulgated there was a vast concentration, within Military Areas No. 1 and 2, of installations and facilities for the production of military equipment, especially ships and airplanes. Important army and navy bases were located in California and Washington. . . . Espionage by persons in sympathy with the Japanese Government had been found to have been particularly effective in the surprise attack on Pearl Harbor. . . . Of the 126,000 persons of Japanese descent in the United States, citizens and non-citizens, approximately 112,000 resided in California, Oregon and Washington at the time of the adoption of the military regulations. . . . Not only did the great majority of such persons reside within the Pacific Coast states but they were concentrated in or near three of the large cities, Seattle, Portland and Los Angeles, all in Military Area No.1."

"Distinction between citizens solely because of their ancestry are by their very nature odious to free people whose institutions are founded upon the doctrine of equality. . . . We may assume that these considerations would be controlling here were it not for the fact that the danger of espionage and sabotage, in time of war and of threatened invasion, calls upon the military authorities to scrutinize every relevant fact bearing on the loyalty of populations in the danger areas. . . . Here the aim of Congress and the Executive was the protection against sabotage of war materials and utilities in areas thought to be in danger of Japanese invasion and air attack. . . . We cannot say that these facts and circumstances, considered in the particular war setting, could afford no ground for differentiating citizens of Japanese ancestry from other groups in the United States. The fact alone that attack on our shores was threatened by Japan rather than another enemy power set these citizens apart from others who have no particular associations with Japan."

"The Act of March 21, 1942, was an adoption by Congress of the Executive Order and of the Proclamations. The Proclamations themselves followed a standard authorized by the Executive Order—the necessity of protecting military resources in the designated areas against espionage and sabotage. . . . Under the Executive Order the basic facts, determined by the military commander in the light of knowledge then available, were whether that danger existed and whether a curfew order was an appropriate means of minimizing the danger. Since his findings to that effect were as we have said, not without adequate support, the legislative function was performed and the sanction of the statute attached to violations of the curfew order."

The Supreme Court affirmed the district court's judgment.

V. JUSTICE VOTE

0 Pro ACLU Side vs. 9 Con Opposing Side

Opposing Side (Respondent/Appellee)

1. Stone, H. – Wrote majority opinion
2. Douglas, W. – Wrote concurring opinion
3. Murphy, F. – Wrote concurring opinion
4. Rutledge, W. – Wrote concurring opinion
5. Jackson, R. – Joined majority opinion
6. Roberts, O. – Joined majority opinion
7. Frankfurter, F. – Joined majority opinion
8. Black, H. – Joined majority opinion
9. Reed, S. – Joined majority opinion

VI. A WIN OR LOSS FOR THE ACLU?

The ACLU, as amicus curiae, urged reversal of the judgment of the district court; the Supreme Court affirmed in a 9-0 vote, giving the ACLU an apparent loss.

23. Yasui v. United States

(Decided June 21, 1943; 320 U.S. 115)

I. ISSUE

A. Issues Discussed

Racial discrimination, due process

B. Legal Question Presented

Is appellant's citizenship relevant to his conviction for violating a curfew order applicable to all persons of Japanese ancestry residing in military areas, pursuant to the Act of Congress of March 21, 1942?

C. Supreme Court's Answer

The appellant's citizenship is not relevant to the conviction.

II. CASE SUMMARY

A. Background

"This is a companion case to *Hirabayashi v. United States* . . . .

Appellant, an American-born person of Japanese ancestry, was convicted [for violating] a curfew order . . . . The validity of the curfew was considered in the Hirabayashi case, and this case presents the same issues."

The evidence showed that appellant "was a member of the bar of Oregon, and a second lieutenant in the Army of the United States, Infantry Reserve; that he had been employed by the Japanese Consulate in Chicago, but had resigned on December 8, 1941, and immediately offered his services to the military authorities; that he had discussed with an agent of the Federal Bureau of Investigation the advisability of testing the constitutionality of the curfew; and that when he violated the curfew order he requested that he be arrested so that he could test its constitutionality."

The Supreme Court sustained the conviction but vacated the judgment of the district court for resentence.

B. Counsel of Record/ACLU Attorney

ACLU Side (Petitioner/Appellant): E. F. Bernard and A. L. Wirin argued the cause for appellant.

Opposing Side (Respondent/Appellee): Solicitor General Charles Fahy argued the cause for appellee.

III. AMICI CURIAE

ACLU Side (Petitioner/Appellant)

Brief of amici curiae filed on behalf of the ACLU by Arthur Garfield Hays, Osmond K. Fraenkel, and A. L. Wirin.

Brief of amici curiae filed on behalf of the Northern California Branch of the ACLU by Jackson H. Ralston and Wayne M. Collins.

Brief of amici curiae filed on behalf of the Japanese American Citizens League.

Opposing Side (Respondent/Appellee)

Brief of amici curiae filed on behalf of the states of California, Oregon, and Washington by Attorney General of California Robert W. Kenny, Attorney General of Oregon I. H. Van Winkle, Attorney General of Washington Smith Troy, and Fred E. Lewis.

IV. THE SUPREME COURT'S DECISION

"The district court ruled that the Act of March 21, 1942, was unconstitutional as applied to American citizens, but held that appellant, by reason of his course of conduct, must be deemed to have renounced his American citizenship. . . . Since we hold, as in the Hirabayashi case, that the curfew order was valid as applied to citizens, it follows that appellant's citizenship was not relevant to the issue tendered by the Government and the conviction must be sustained for the reasons stated in the Hirabayashi case.

But as the sentence of one year's imprisonment—the maximum permitted by the statute—was imposed after the finding that appellant was not a citizen, and as the Government states that it has not and does not now controvert his citizenship, the case is an appropriate one for resentence in the light of these circumstances."

The Supreme Court sustained the conviction, vacated the judgment and remanded the case "to the district court for resentence of appellant, and to afford that court opportunity to strike its findings as to appellant's loss of United States citizenship."

V. JUSTICE VOTE

0 Pro ACLU Side vs. 9 Con Opposing Side

Opposing Side (Respondent/Appellee)

1. Stone, H. – Wrote majority opinion
2. Black, H. – Joined majority opinion
3. Reed, S. – Joined majority opinion
4. Frankfurter, F. – Joined majority opinion
5. Douglas, W. – Joined majority opinion
6. Jackson, R. – Joined majority opinion
7. Rutledge, W. – Joined majority opinion
8. Murphy, F. – Joined majority opinion
9. Roberts, O. – Joined majority opinion

VI. A WIN OR LOSS FOR THE ACLU?

The ACLU, as amicus curiae, urged reversal of the judgment of the district court; the Supreme Court sustained the conviction but vacated the judgment in a 9-0 vote, giving the ACLU an apparent loss.

24. Falbo v. United States

(Decided January 3, 1944; 320 U.S. 549)

I. ISSUE

A. Issues Discussed

Governmental regulation

B. Legal Question Presented

"Whether Congress has authorized judicial review of the propriety of a board's classification [pursuant to the Selective Service and Training Act] in a criminal prosecution for wilful violation of an order directing a registrant to report for the last step in the selective process."

C. Supreme Court's Answer

Judicial review of the selective service decision is not authorized.

II. CASE SUMMARY

A. Background

"The petitioner was indicted . . . for knowingly failing to perform a duty required of him under the Selective Training and Service Act of 1940. [P]etitioner defended his conduct on the ground that he was entitled to a statutory exemption from all forms of national service, since . . . he was a 'regular or duly ordained' minister."

"On appeal petitioner . . . argued that . . . the [District] Court should have reviewed the classification order to ascertain whether the local board had been 'prejudicial, unfair, and arbitrary' in that it had failed to admit certain evidence which he offered, had acted on the basis of an antipathy to the religious sect of which he is a member, and had refused to classify him as a minister against the overwhelming weight of the evidence. The Circuit Court of Appeals affirmed the District Court per curiam."

On certiorari the Supreme Court affirmed the judgment.

B. Counsel of Record/ACLU Attorney

ACLU Side (Petitioner/Appellant): Hayden Covington argued the cause for appellant.

Opposing Side (Respondent/Appellee): Charles Fahy, Solicitor General, argued the cause or appellee.

III. AMICI CURIAE

ACLU Side (Petitioner/Appellant)

Brief of amici curiae urging reversal filed on behalf of the National Committee on Conscientious Objectors of the ACLU by Julien Cornell, Harold Evans, Ernest Angell, and Osmond K. Fraenkel.

Opposing Side (Respondent/Appellee)

No briefs of amici curiae were filed in support of appellee.

IV. THE SUPREME COURT'S DECISION

"The Act nowhere explicitly provides for [judicial] review [of a board's classification] and we have found nothing in its legislative history which indicates an intention to afford it. The circumstances under which the Act was adopted lend no support to a view which would allow litigious interruption of the process of selection which Congress created. . . . Careful provision was made for fair administration of the Act's policies within the framework of the selective service process. . . . Surely if Congress had intended to authorize interference with that process by intermediate challenges of orders to report, it would have said so."

The Supreme Court affirmed the judgment of the Third Circuit Court of Appeals.

V. JUSTICE VOTE

1 Pro ACLU Side vs. 8 Con Opposing Side

ACLU Side (Petitioner/Appellant)

1. Murphy, F. – Wrote dissenting opinion

Opposing Side (Respondent/Appellee)

1. Black, H. – Wrote majority opinion
2. Roberts, O. – Joined majority opinion
3. Stone, H. – Joined majority opinion
4. Reed, S. – Joined majority opinion
5. Jackson, R. – Joined majority opinion
6. Rutledge, W. – Wrote concurring opinion
7. Douglas, W. – Joined majority opinion
8. Frankfurter, F. – Joined majority opinion

VI. A WIN OR LOSS FOR THE ACLU?

The ACLU, as amicus curiae, urged reversal of the judgment the Third Circuit Court of Appeals; the Supreme Court affirmed in an 8-1 vote, giving the ACLU an apparent loss.

25. Follett v. Town of McCormick

(Decided March 27, 1944; 321 U.S. 573)

I. ISSUE

A. Issues Discussed

Freedom of religion

B. Legal Question Presented

"Whether a flat license tax as applied to one who earns his livelihood as an evangelist or preacher in his home town is constitutional."

C. Supreme Court's Answer

Requiring a preacher to pay a town's flat license tax to distribute religious literature is unconstitutional.

II. CASE SUMMARY

A. Background

The Appellant, an ordained minister of the Jehovah's Witnesses residing in McCormick, South Carolina, "went from house to house distributing certain books [and] obtained his living from the money he received." He did not have a license to sell books and was convicted of violating a town ordinance which provides for a flat license tax on booksellers.

"Admittedly he had no license from the town and refused to obtain one. [He claimed] the ordinance restricted freedom of worship in violation of the First Amendment which the Fourteenth Amendment makes applicable to the States."

Appellant was found guilty by a jury and the judgment was ultimately affirmed by the Supreme Court of South Carolina. On appeal the U.S. Supreme Court reversed.

B. Counsel of Record/ACLU Attorney

ACLU Side (Petitioner/Appellant): Hayden C. Covington argued the cause for appellant.

Opposing Side (Respondent/Appellee): Fred Buzhardt and Jeff D. Griffith argued the cause for appellee.

III. AMICI CURIAE

ACLU Side (Petitioner/Appellant)

Brief of amici curiae filed on behalf of the ACLU by Dorothy Kenyon, Monroe Lazere, and Clifford Forster.

Opposing Side (Respondent/Appellee)

No briefs of amici curiae were filed in support of appellee.

IV. THE SUPREME COURT'S DECISION

"We stated [in *Jones v. City of Opelika*] that an 'itinerant evangelist' did not become 'a mere book agent by selling the Bible or religious tracts to help defray his expenses or to sustain him.' Freedom of religion is not merely reserved for those with a long purse. Preachers of the more orthodox faiths are not engaged in commercial undertakings because they are dependent on their calling for a living."

"This does not mean that religious undertakings must be subsidized. The exemption from a license tax of a preacher who preaches or a parishioner who listens does not mean that either is free from all financial burdens of government, including taxes on income or property. . . . But to say that they like other citizens may be subject to general taxation does not mean that they can be required to pay a tax for the exercise of that which the First Amendment has made a high constitutional privilege."

The U.S. Supreme Court reversed the judgment of the Supreme Court of South Carolina.

JUSTICE VOTE

6 Pro ACLU Side vs. 3 Con Opposing Side

ACLU Side (Petitioner/Appellant)

1. Douglas, W. – Wrote majority opinion
2. Reed, S. – Wrote concurring opinion
3. Murphy, F. – Wrote concurring opinion
4. Rutledge, W. – Joined majority opinion
5. Black, H. – Joined majority opinion
6. Stone, H. – Joined majority opinion

Opposing Side (Respondent/Appellee)

1. Roberts, O. – Wrote joint dissenting opinion
2. Frankfurter, F. – Wrote joint dissenting opinion
3. Jackson, R. – Wrote joint dissenting opinion

VI. A WIN OR LOSS FOR THE ACLU?

The ACLU, as amicus curiae, urged reversal of the judgment the Supreme Court of South Carolina; the Supreme Court reversed in a 6-3 vote, giving the ACLU an apparent win.

26. Lyons v. Oklahoma

(Decided June 5, 1944; 322 U.S. 596)

I. ISSUE

A. Issues Discussed

Due process

B. Legal Question Presented

"Whether the second confession [in this case] was given under such circumstances that its use as evidence at the trial constitutes a violation of the due process clause of the Fourteenth Amendment, which requires that state criminal proceedings 'shall be consistent with the fundamental principles of liberty and justice.'"

C. Supreme Court's Answer

Using the confession as evidence at trial did not violate the due process clause of the Fourteenth Amendment.

II. CASE SUMMARY

A. Background

Appellant was arrested for the murder of a husband and wife, and their four-year-old son. "Immediately after his arrest there was an interrogation of about two hours at the jail. After he had been in jail eleven days he was again questioned, this time in the county prosecutor's office. . . . While petitioner was competently represented before and at the trial, counsel was not supplied him until after his preliminary examination, which was subsequent to the confessions. . . . There is testimony by Lyons of physical abuse by the police officers at the time of his arrest and first interrogation on January 11th."

"Eleven days later the second interrogation occurred. Again the evidence of assault is conflicting. Eleven or twelve officials were in and out of the prosecutor's small office during the night. Lyons says that he again suffered assault. . . . It is not disputed that the inquiry continued until two-thirty in the morning before an oral confession was obtained and that a pan of the victims' bones was placed in Lyon's lap by his interrogators to bring about his confession. . . .

After the oral confession in the early morning hours of January 23, Lyons was taken to the scene of the crime and subjected to further questioning about the instruments which were used to commit the murders. He was returned to the jail about eight-thirty A.M. and left there until early afternoon. After that the prisoner was taken to a nearby town of Antlers, Oklahoma. Later in the day a deputy sheriff and a private citizen took the petitioner to the penitentiary. There, sometime between eight and eleven o'clock on that same evening, the petitioner signed the second confession. . . .

The judge in accordance with Oklahoma practice and, after hearing evidence from the prosecution and the defense in the absence of the jury, first passed favorably upon its admissibility as a matter of law and then, after witnesses testified before the jury as to the voluntary character of the confession, submitted the guilt or innocence of the defendant to the jury under a full instruction, approved by the Criminal Court of Appeals . . . . The instruction did not specifically cover the defendant's contention, embodied in a requested instruction, that the second confession sprang from the fear engendered by the treatment he had received at Hugo." The jury found appellant guilty of murder, and the judgment was affirmed by the Criminal Court of Appeals.

The Supreme Court granted certiorari to review the case and affirmed the judgment.

B. Counsel of Record/ACLU Attorney

ACLU Side (Petitioner/Appellant): Thurgood Marshall argued the cause for appellant.

Opposing Side (Respondent/Appellee): Sam H. Lattimore argued the cause for appellee.

III. AMICI CURIAE

ACLU Side (Petitioner/Appellant)

Brief of amici curiae filed on behalf of the ACLU by A. S. Cutler, Morris L. Ernst, Gomer Smith, A. S. Cutler, Clifford Forster.

Opposing Side (Respondent/Appellee)

No briefs of amici curiae were filed in support of appellee.

IV. THE SUPREME COURT'S DECISION

"The voluntary or involuntary character of a confession is determined by a conclusion as to whether the accused, at the time he confesses, is in possession of 'mental freedom' to confess to or deny a suspected participation in a crime.

[W]here there is a dispute as to whether the acts which are charged to be coercive actually occurred, or where different inferences may fairly be drawn from admitted facts, the trial judge and the jury are not only in a better position to appraise the truth or falsity of the defendant's assertions from the demeanor of the witnesses but the legal duty is upon them to make the decision. . . .

The Oklahoma Criminal Court of Appeals in the present case decided that the evidence would justify a determination that the effect of a prior coercion was dissipated before the second confession and we agree. . . .

The Fourteenth Amendment is a protection against criminal trials in state courts conducted in such a manner as amounts to a disregard of 'that fundamental fairness essential to the very concept of justice,' and in a way that 'necessarily prevent(s) a fair trial.' . . . The Fourteenth Amendment does not provide review of mere error in jury verdicts, even though the error concerns the voluntary character of a confession. We cannot say that an inference of guilt based in part upon Lyons' McAlester confession is so illogical and unreasonable as to deny the petitioner a fair trial."

The Supreme Court affirmed the judgment of the Oklahoma Criminal Court of Appeals.

V. JUSTICE VOTE

3 Pro ACLU Side vs. 6 Con Opposing Side

ACLU Side (Petitioner/Appellant)

1. Murphy, F. – Wrote dissenting opinion
2. Black, H. – Joined dissenting opinion
3. Rutledge, W. – Dissented without an opinion

Opposing Side (Respondent/Appellee)

1. Reed, S. – Wrote majority opinion
2. Douglas, W. – Concurred in the result
3. Stone, H. – Joined majority opinion
4. Jackson, R. – Joined majority opinion
5. Roberts, O. – Joined majority opinion
6. Frankfurter, F. – Joined majority opinion

VI. A WIN OR LOSS FOR THE ACLU?

The ACLU, as amicus curiae, urged reversal of the judgment of the Criminal Court of Appeals; the Supreme Court affirmed in a 6-3 vote, giving the ACLU an apparent loss.

27. Smith v. Allwright

(Decided April 3, 1944, As Amended June 12, 1944; 321 U.S. 649)

I. ISSUE

A. Issues Discussed

Racial discrimination, voting rights

B. Legal Question Presented

Was the refusal by Texas election officials to allow appellant to cast a ballot in the Democratic primary election, allegedly because of his "race and color," a state or a private action?

C. Supreme Court's Answer

The refusal was state action and unconstitutional under the Fifteenth Amendment.

II. CASE SUMMARY

A. Background

Appellant filed suit against Respondents claiming damages "for the refusal of respondents, election and associate election judges respectively of that precinct, to give petitioner a ballot or to permit him to cast a ballot in the primary election of July 27, 1940, for the nomination of Democratic candidates for the United States Senate and House of Representatives, and Governor and other state officers. The refusal is alleged to have been solely because of the race and color of the proposed voter."

Respondents "defended on the ground that the Democratic party of Texas is a voluntary organization with members banded together for the purpose of selecting individuals of the group representing the common political beliefs as candidates in the general election. As such a voluntary organization, it was claimed, the Democratic party is free to select its own membership and limit to whites participation in the party primary. Such action, the answer asserted, does not violate the Fourteenth, Fifteenth or Seventeenth Amendment as officers of government cannot be chosen at primaries and the Amendments are applicable only to general elections where governmental officers are actually elected."

The District Court for the Southern District of Texas denied the relief to appellant and the Fifth Circuit Court of Appeals affirmed. On certiorari the Supreme Court reversed.

B. Counsel of Record/ACLU Attorney

ACLU Side (Petitioner/Appellant): Thurgood Marshall and William H. Hastie argued the cause for appellant.

Opposing Side (Respondent/Appellee): No appearance for appellee. George W. Barcus, for Gerald C. Mann, Attorney General of Texas, as amicus curiae, by special leave of Court.

III. AMICI CURIAE

ACLU Side (Petitioner/Appellant)

Brief of amici curiae filed on behalf of the ACLU by Whitney North Seymour and George Clifton Edwards.

Brief of amici curiae filed on behalf of the Workers Defense League by John F. Finerty and Ernest Fleischman.

Brief of amici curiae filed on behalf of the National Lawyers Guild, Committee on Constitutional Liberties by Osmond K. Fraenkel.

Opposing Side (Respondent/Appellee)

Brief of amici curiae filed on behalf of Gerald C. Mann, Attorney General of Texas, by Gerald C. Mann, R. W. Fairchild, and George W. Barcus, Assistant Attorney General.

Brief of amici curiae filed on behalf of George A. Butler, Chairman of State Democratic Executive Committee of Texas, by Wright Morrow.

IV. THE SUPREME COURT'S DECISION

"It may now be taken as a postulate that the right to vote in a primary for the nomination of candidates without discrimination by the State, like the right to vote in a general election, is a right secured by the Constitution. By the terms of the Fifteenth Amendment that right may not be abridged by any state on account of race."

"Primary elections are conducted by the party under state statutory authority. . . . The state courts are given exclusive original jurisdiction of contested elections and of mandamus proceedings to compel party officers to perform their statutory duties.

We think that this statutory system for the selection of party nominees for inclusion on the general election ballot makes the party which is required to follow these legislative directions an agency of the state in so far as it determines the participants in a primary election. The party takes its character as a state agency from the duties imposed upon it by state statutes; the duties do not become matters of private law because they are performed by a political party."

"If the state requires a certain electoral procedure, prescribes a general election ballot made up of party nominees so chosen and limits the choice of the electorate in general elections for state offices, practically speaking, to those whose names appear on such a ballot, it endorses, adopts and enforces the discrimination against Negroes, practiced by a party entrusted by Texas law with the determination of the qualifications of participants in the primary. This is state action within the meaning of the Fifteenth Amendment.

The United States is a constitutional democracy. Its organic law grants to all citizens a right to participate in the choice of elected officials without restriction by any state because of race. This grant to the people of the opportunity for choice is not to be nulified by a state through casting its electoral process in a form which permits a private organization to practice racial discrimination in the election. Constitutional rights would be of little value if they could be thus indirectly denied."

The Supreme Court reversed the judgment of the Court of Appeals.

V. JUSTICE VOTE

8 Pro ACLU Side vs. 1 Con Opposing Side

ACLU Side (Petitioner/Appellant)

1. Reed, S. – Wrote majority opinion
2. Frankfurter, F. – Concurred in the result
3. Stone, H. – Joined majority opinion
4. Black, H. – Joined majority opinion
5. Douglas, W. – Joined majority opinion
6. Rutledge, W. – Joined majority opinion
7. Jackson, R. – Joined majority opinion
8. Murphy, F. – Joined majority opinion

Opposing Side (Respondent/Appellee)

1. Roberts, O. – Wrote dissenting opinion

VI. A WIN OR LOSS FOR THE ACLU?

The ACLU, as amicus curiae, urged reversal of the judgment the Court of Appeals; the Supreme Court reversed in an 8-1 vote, giving the ACLU an apparent win.

28. Steele v. Louisville & Nashville Railroad Co.

(Decided December 18, 1944; 323 U.S. 192)

I. ISSUE

A. Issues Discussed

Racial discrimination

B. Legal Question Presented

"[W]hether the Railway Labor Act imposes on a labor organization, acting by authority of the statute as the exclusive bargaining representative of a craft or class of railway employees, the duty to represent all the employees in the craft without discrimination because of their race, and, if so, whether the courts have jurisdiction to protect the minority of the craft or class from the violation of such obligation."

C. Supreme Court's Answer

Labor organizations operating under the Railway Labor Act have a duty to represent all employees without discrimination because of their race, and the courts have jurisdiction to protect against violations.

II. CASE SUMMARY

A. Background

"Petitioner, a Negro, is a locomotive fireman in the employ of respondent railroad, suing on his own behalf and that of his fellow employees who, like petitioner, are Negro firemen employed by the Railroad. Respondent Brotherhood, a labor organization, is, as provided under . . . the Railway Labor Act, the exclusive bargaining representative of the craft of firemen employed by the Railroad . . . .

On March 28, 1940, the Brotherhood, purporting to act as representative of the entire craft of firemen, without informing the Negro firemen or giving them opportunity to be heard, served a notice on respondent Railroad [which] announced the Brotherhood's desire to amend the existing collective bargaining agreement in such manner as ultimately to exclude all Negro firemen from the service... [O]nly white firemen [could] be promoted to serve as engineers, and the notice proposed that only 'promotable', i.e., white, men should be employed as firemen or assigned to new runs or jobs or permanent vacancies in established runs or jobs."

Petitioner worked in a desirable position at the railroad, but starting approximately one year after the notice issued he was demoted twice, replaced each time by white men junior to him, and placed in a jobs more difficult and with lower wages than his prior position.

"Protests and appeals of petitioner and his fellow Negro firemen, addressed to the Railroad and the Brotherhood, in an effort to secure relief and redress, have been ignored. . . . The Supreme Court of Alabama took jurisdiction of the cause but held on the merits that petitioner's complaint stated no cause of action. . . . It construed the statute, not as creating the relationship of principal and agent between the members of the craft and the Brotherhood, but as conferring on the Brotherhood plenary authority to treat with the Railroad and enter into contracts fixing rates of pay and working conditions for the craft as a whole without any legal obligation or duty to protect the rights of minorities from discrimination or unfair treatment, however gross. Consequently it held that neither the Brotherhood nor the Railroad violated any rights of petitioner or his fellow Negro employees by negotiating the contracts discriminating against them."

On certiorari the U.S. Supreme Court reversed the judgment of the Supreme Court of Alabama.

B. Counsel of Record/ACLU Attorney

ACLU Side (Petitioner/Appellant): Charles H. Houston argued the cause for appellant.

Opposing Side (Respondent/Appellee): Charles H. Eyster argued the cause for appellee Louisville and N.R. Co. James A. Simpson argued the cause for appellee Brotherhood of Locomotive Firemen and Enginemen.

III. AMICI CURIAE

ACLU Side (Petitioner/Appellant)

Brief of amici curiae filed on behalf of the ACLU by Edgar Watkins, John D. Miller, Jo Drake Arrington, Shirley Adelson, Arthur Garfield Hayes, R. Beverly Herbert, T. Pope Shepherd, Jordan Stoke, III, and Howard B. Lee.

Brief of amici curiae filed on behalf of the National Association for the Advancement of Colored People by Thurgood Marshall and William H. Hastie.

Brief of amici curiae filed on behalf of the United States by Solicitor General Fahy, Special Assistant to the Attorney General Robert L. Stern, Alvin J. Rockwell, Ruth Weyand, Joseph B. Robison, Frank Donner, and Marcel Mallet-Prevost.

Opposing Side (Respondent/Appellee)

No briefs of amici curiae were filed in support of appellee.

IV. THE SUPREME COURT'S DECISION

"Since the right asserted by petitioner 'is claimed under the Constitution' and a 'statute of the United States', the decision of the Alabama court adverse to that contention is reviewable here . . . ."

"The fair interpretation of the statutory language is that the organization chosen to represent a craft is to represent all its members, the majority as well as the minority, and it is to act for and not against those whom it represents. [T]he statutory power to represent a craft and to make contracts as to wages, hours and working conditions does not include the authority to make among members of the craft discriminations not based on such relevant differences. Here the discriminations based on race alone are obviously irrelevant and invidious. Congress plainly did not undertake to authorize the bargaining representative to make such discriminations."

Since the Railway Labor Act "permits the national labor organizations chosen by the majority of the crafts to 'prescribe the rules under which the labor members of the Adjustment Board shall be selected' and to 'select such members and designate the division on which each member shall serve', the Negro firemen would be required to appear before a group which is in large part chosen by the respondents against whom their real complaint is made. . . . There is no administrative means by which the Negro firemen can secure separate representation for the purposes of collective bargaining. . . . In the absence of any available administrative remedy, the right here asserted, to a remedy for breach of the statutory duty of the bargaining representative to represent and act for the members of a craft, is of judicial cognizance."

The U.S. Supreme Court reversed the judgment of the Supreme Court of Alabama.

V. JUSTICE VOTE

9 Pro ACLU Side vs. 0 Con Opposing Side

ACLU Side (Petitioner/Appellant)

1. Stone, H. – Wrote majority opinion
2. Black, H. – Concurred in the result

3. Murphy, F. – Wrote concurring opinion
4. Roberts, O. – Joined majority opinion
5. Jackson, R. – Joined majority opinion
6. Rutledge, W. – Joined majority opinion
7. Frankfurter, F. – Joined majority opinion
8. Douglas, W. – Joined majority opinion
9. Reed, S. – Joined majority opinion

I. A WIN OR LOSS FOR THE ACLU?

The ACLU, as amici curiae, urged reversal of the judgment of the Supreme Court of Alabama; the U.S. Supreme Court reversed in a 9-0 vote, giving the ACLU an apparent win

29. Tunstall v. Brotherhood of Locomotive Firemen

(Decided December 18, 1944; 323 U.S. 210)

I. ISSUE

A. Issues Discussed

Racial discrimination

B. Legal Question Presented

In addition to the question resolved in Steele v. Louisville & N.R. Co., the question "whether the federal courts have jurisdiction to entertain a non-diversity suit in which petitioner, a railway employee subject to the [Railway Labor] Act, seeks remedies by injunction and award of damages for the failure of the union bargaining representative of his craft to perform the duty imposed on it by the Act, to represent petitioner and other members of his craft without discrimination because of race."

C. Supreme Court's Answer

The federal courts have jurisdiction over the matter.

II. CASE SUMMARY

A. Background

The case is a companion case to *Steele v. Louisville & N.R. Co.*, with similar discrimination issues under the Railway Labor Act.

As in *Steele*, "[p]etitioner complains of the discriminatory application of the contract provisions to him and other Negro members of his craft in favor of 'promotable', i.e., white, firemen, by which he has been deprived of his preexisting seniority rights, removed from the interstate passenger run to which he was assigned and then assigned to more arduous and difficult work with longer hours in yard service, his place in the passenger service being filled by a white fireman. . . . Petitioner prays for a declaratory adjudication of his rights, for an injunction restraining the discriminatory practices complained of, for an award of damages and for other relief.

The District Court dismissed the suit for want of jurisdiction. The Circuit Court of Appeals for the Fourth Circuit affirmed, on the ground that the federal courts are without jurisdiction of the cause, there being no diversity of citizenship and, insofar as the suit is grounded on the wrongful acts of respondents, it is not one arising under the laws of the United States, even though the union was chosen as bargaining representative pursuant to the Railway Labor Act."

On certiorari the Supreme Court reversed the judgment of the Circuit Court of Appeals for the Fourth Circuit.

B. Counsel of Record / ACLU Attorney

ACLU Side (Petitioner / Appellant): Charles H. Houston argued the cause for appellant.

Opposing Side (Respondent / Appellee): James G. Martin argued the cause for appellee Norfolk Southern Ry. Co. Harold C. Heiss argued the cause for appellee Brotherhood of Locomotive Firemen.

III. AMICI CURIAE

ACLU Side (Petitioner / Appellant)

Brief of amici curiae urging reversal filed on behalf of the ACLU by Edgar Watkins, John D. Miller, Jo Drake Arrington, Shirley Adelson, Arthur Garfield Hays, R. Beverly Herbert, T. Pope Shepherd, Jordan Stokes, III, and Howard B. Lee.

Brief of amici curiae urging reversal filed on behalf of the National Association for the Advancement of Colored People by Thurgood Marshall and William H. Hastie.

Opposing Side (Respondent / Appellee)

No briefs of amici curiae were filed in support of appellee.

IV. THE SUPREME COURT'S DECISION

"For the reasons stated in our opinion in the *Steele* case the Railway Labor Act itself does not exclude the petitioner's cause of action from the consideration of the federal courts. We also hold that the right asserted by petitioner which is derived from the duty imposed by the Railway Labor Act on the Brotherhood, as bargaining representative, is a federal right implied from the statute and the policy which it has adopted. It is the federal statute which condemns as unlawful the Brotherhood's conduct. . . .

For the reasons also stated in our opinion in the *Steele* case the petitioner is without available administrative remedies, resort to which, when available, is prerequisite to equitable relief in the federal courts."

The Supreme Court reversed the judgment of the Court of Appeals for the Fourth Circuit.

V. JUSTICE VOTE

9 Pro ACLU Side vs. 0 Con Opposing Side

ACLU Side (Petitioner / Appellant)

1. Stone, H. – Wrote majority opinion
2. Murphy, F. – Wrote concurring opinion
3. Black, H. – Joined majority opinion
4. Roberts, O. – Joined majority opinion
5. Jackson, R. – Joined majority opinion
6. Rutledge, W. – Joined majority opinion
7. Frankfurter, F. – Joined majority opinion
8. Douglas, W. – Joined majority opinion
9. Reed, S. – Joined majority opinion

VI. A WIN OR LOSS FOR THE ACLU?

The ACLU, as amicus curiae, urged reversal of the judgment of the Court of Appeals for the Fourth Circuit; the Supreme Court reversed in a 9-0 vote, giving the ACLU an apparent win.

30. Korematsu v. United States

(Decided December 18, 1944; 323 U.S. 214)

I. ISSUE

A. Issues Discussed

Racial discrimination, due process

B. Legal Question Presented

Whether the Exclusion Order No. 34, which provided for the exclusion of people with Japanese ancestry from defined "Military Areas," was "beyond the war power of Congress and the Executive."

C. Supreme Court's Answer

The exclusion was permissible.

II. CASE SUMMARY

A. Background

"The petitioner, an American citizen of Japanese descent, was convicted in a federal district court for remaining in San Leandro, California, a 'Military Area', contrary to Civilian Exclusion Order No. 34 of the Commanding General of the Western Command, U.S. Army, which directed that after May 9, 1942, all persons of Japanese ancestry should be excluded from that area. No question was raised as to petitioner's loyalty to the United States.

The Circuit Court of Appeals affirmed." On certiorari the Supreme Court affirmed.

B. Counsel of Record / ACLU Attorney

ACLU Side (Petitioner / Appellant): Wayne M. Collins and Charles A. Horsky argued the cause for appellant.

Opposing Side (Respondent / Appellee): Charles Fahy, Solicitor General, argued the cause for appellee.

III. AMICI CURIAE

ACLU Side (Petitioner / Appellant)

Brief of amici curiae filed on behalf of the ACLU by Morris M. Grupp, Clarence E. Rust, Edwin Borchard, Osmond K. Fraenkel, Arthur Garfield Hays, Harold Evans, William Draper Lewis, Thomas Raeburn White, Carey McWilliam, Charles A. Horsky, George Rublee, Arthur Dehon Hill, and Winthrop Wadleigh.

Brief of amici curiae filed on behalf of the Japanese American Citizens League by Saburo Kido and A. L. Wirin.

Opposing Side (Respondent / Appellee)

Brief of amici curiae filed on behalf of the States of California, Oregon, and Washington by Robert W. Kenny, Attorney General of California, George Neuner, Attorney General of Oregon, Smith Troy, Attorney General of Washington, and Fred E. Lewis, Acting Attorney General of Washington.

IV. THE SUPREME COURT'S DECISION

"Here, as in the *Hirabayashi* case '... we cannot reject as unfounded the judgment of the military authorities and of Congress that there were disloyal members of that population, whose number and strength could not be precisely and quickly ascertained. We cannot say that the war-making branches of the Government did not have ground for believing that in a critical hour such persons could not readily be isolated and separately dealt with, and constituted a menace to the national defense and safety, which demanded that prompt and adequate measures be taken to guard against it.'"

"It was because we could not reject the finding of the military authorities that it was impossible to bring about an immediate segregation of the disloyal from the loyal that we sustained the validity of the curfew order as applying to the whole group. In the instant case, temporary exclusion of the entire group was rested by the military on the same ground."

"To cast this case into outlines of racial prejudice, without reference to the real military dangers which were presented, merely confuses the issue. Korematsu was not excluded from the Military Area because of hostility to him or his race. He was excluded because we are at war with the Japanese Empire, because the properly constituted military authorities feared an invasion of our West Coast and felt constrained to take proper security measures, because they decided that the military urgency of the situation demanded that all citizens of Japanese ancestry be segregated from the West Coast temporarily, and finally, because Congress, reposing its confidence in this time of war in our military leaders—as inevitably it must—determined that they should have the power to do just this."

The Supreme Court affirmed the judgment of the Court of Appeals.

V. JUSTICE VOTE

3 Pro ACLU Side vs. 6 Con Opposing Side

ACLU Side (Petitioner / Appellant)

1. Roberts, O. – Wrote dissenting opinion
2. Murphy, F. – Wrote dissenting opinion
3. Jackson, R. – Wrote dissenting opinion

Opposing Side (Respondent / Appellee)

1. Black, H. – Wrote majority opinion
2. Frankfurter, F. – Wrote concurring opinion
3. Reed, S. – Joined majority opinion
4. Stone, H. – Joined majority opinion
5. Rutledge, W. – Joined majority opinion
6. Douglas, W. – Joined majority opinion

VI. A WIN OR LOSS FOR THE ACLU?

The ACLU, as amici curiae, urged reversal of the judgment of the Court of Appeals; the Supreme Court affirmed in a 6-3 vote, giving the ACLU an apparent loss.

31. Ex parte Endo

(Decided December 18, 1944; 323 U.S. 283)

I. ISSUE

A. Issues Discussed

Racial discrimination, due process

B. Legal Question Presented

Does the Act of March 21, 1942, and Executive Order Nos. 9066 and 9102, which authorize the exclusion of "all persons of Japanese ancestry" from certain Military Areas, allow the continued detention of citizens of Japanese ancestry, once it is established that they are loyal and no longer a threat to the United States?

C. Supreme Court's Answer

Once a person is determined to be loyal, the Act and Executive Orders no longer support continued detention.

II. CASE SUMMARY

A. Background

"[T]he Appellant, is an American citizen of Japanese ancestry. She was evacuated from Sacramento, California, in 1942, pursuant to certain military orders . . . , and was removed to the Tule Lake War Relocation Center located at Newell, Modoc County, California."

She filed a "petition for a writ of habeas corpus alleg[ing] that she is a loyal and law-abiding citizen of the United States, that no charge has been made against her, that she is being unlawfully detained, and that she is confined in the Relocation Center under armed guard and held there against her will."

"That petition was denied by the District Court of the United States for the Northern District of California in July, 1943, and an appeal was prefected to the Circuit Court of Appeals in August, 1943. Shortly thereafter appellant was transferred from the Tule Lake Relocation Center to the Central Utah Relocation Center located at Topaz, Utah, where she is presently detained."

On appeal the Supreme Court reversed the judgment of the District Court for the Northern District of California.

B. Counsel of Record/ACLU Attorney

ACLU Side (Petitioner/Appellant): James C. Purcell argued the cause for appellant.

Opposing Side (Respondent/Appellee): Charles Fahy, Solicitor General, argued the cause for appellee.

III. AMICI CURIAE

ACLU Side (Petitioner/Appellant)

Brief of amici curiae urging reversal filed on behalf of the Northern California Branch of the ACLU by Wayne M. Collins.

Brief of amici curiae urging reversal filed on behalf of the ACLU by Carey McWilliams, Edwin Borchard, Charles Horsky, Arthur Dehon Hill, Winthrop Wadleigh, Harold Evans, William Draper Lewis, Thomas Raeburn White, Osmond K. Fraenkel.

Opposing Side (Respondent/Appellee)

No briefs of amici curiae were filed in support of appellee.

IV. THE SUPREME COURT'S DECISION

"[T]he President promulgated Executive Order No. 9066. It recited that 'the successful prosecution of the war requires every possible protection against espionage and against sabotage to national defense material, national-defense premises, and national-defense utilities . . . .' [I]t authorized and directed 'the Secretary of War, and the Military Commanders . . . to prescribe military areas . . . from which any or all persons may be excluded, and with respect to which, the right of any person to enter, remain in, or leave shall be subject to whatever restrictions the Secretary of War or the appropriate Military Commander may impose in his discretion. . . .'

Appellant's exclusion was effected by Civilian Exclusion Order No. 52, dated May 7, 1942. It ordered that 'all persons of Japanese ancestry, both alien and non-alien' be excluded from Sacramento, California."

"The program of the War Relocation Authority is said to have three main features: (1) the maintenance of Relocation Centers as interim places of residence for evacuees; (2) the segregation of loyal from disloyal evacuees; (3) the continued detention of the disloyal and so far as possible the relocation of the loyal in selected communities. In connection with the latter phase of its work the War Relocation Authority established a procedure for obtaining leave from Relocation Centers."

"We are of the view that Mitsuye Endo should be given her liberty. In reaching that conclusion we do not come to the underlying constitutional issues which have been argued. For we conclude that, whatever power the War Relocation Authority may have to detain other classes of citizens, it has no authority to subject citizens who are concededly loyal to its leave procedure."

"[T]he Constitution when it committed to the Executive and to Congress the exercise of the war power necessarily gave them wide scope for the exercise of judgment and discretion so that war might be waged effectively and successfully. At the same time, however, the Constitution is as specific in its enumeration of many of the civil rights of the individual as it is in its enumeration of the powers of his government. Thus it has prescribed procedural safeguards surrounding the arrest, detention and conviction of individuals."

"The Act of March 21, 1942, was a war measure. . . . Their single aim was the protection of the war effort against espionage and sabotage. . . . Moreover, unlike the case of curfew regulations, the legislative history of the Act of March 21, 1942, is silent on detention. And that silence may have special significance in view of the fact that detention in Relocation Centers was not part of the original program of evacuation but developed later to meet what seemed to the officials in charge to be mounting hostility to the evacuees on the part of the communities where they sought to go."

"Community hostility even to loyal evacuees may have been (and perhaps still is) a serious problem. But if authority for their custody and supervision is to be sought on that ground, the Act of March 21, 1942, Executive Order No. 9066, and Executive Order No. 9102, offer no support. And none other is advanced. To read them that broadly would be to assume that the Congress and the President intended that this discriminatory action should be taken against these people wholly on account of their ancestry even though the government conceded their loyalty to this country. We cannot make such an assumption."

"Mitsuye Endo is entitled to an unconditional release by the War Relocation Authority.

The question remains whether the District Court has jurisdiction to grant the writ of habeas corpus because of the fact that while the case was pending in the Circuit Court of Appeals Appellant was moved from the Tule Lake Relocation Center in the Northern District of California where she was originally detained to the Central Utah Relocation Center in a different district and circuit."

"The statute upon which the jurisdiction of the District Court in habeas corpus proceedings rests gives it power 'to grant writs of habeas corpus for the purpose of an inquiry into the cause of restraint of liberty.' That objective may be in no way impaired or defeated by the removal of the prisoner from the territorial jurisdiction of the District Court. That end may be served and the decree of the court made effective if a respondent who has custody of the prisoner is within reach of the court's process even though the prisoner has been removed from the district since the suit was begun."

The Supreme Court reversed the judgment of the District Court for the Northern District of California.

V. JUSTICE VOTE

9 Pro ACLU Side vs. 0 Con Opposing Side

ACLU Side (Petitioner/Appellant)

1. Douglas, W. – Wrote majority opinion
2. Roberts, O. – Wrote concurring opinion
3. Murphy, F. – Wrote concurring opinion
4. Black, H. – Joined majority opinion
5. Jackson, R. – Joined majority opinion
6. Rutledge, W. – Joined majority opinion
7. Frankfurter, F. – Joined majority opinion
8. Stone, H. – Joined majority opinion
9. Reed, S. – Joined majority opinion

VI. A WIN OR LOSS FOR THE ACLU?

The ACLU, as amici curiae, urged reversal of the judgment of the District Court for the Northern District of California; the Supreme Court reversed in a 9-0 vote, giving the ACLU an apparent win.

32. Thomas v. Collins

(Decided January 8, 1945; 323 U.S. 516)

I. ISSUE

A. Issues Discussed

Freedom of speech

B. Legal Question Presented

Does the application in this case of § 5 of a Texas statute, which regulates labor unions and their activities within Texas by requiring organizers to obtain an organizer's card before soliciting membership, contravene the First Amendment?

C. Supreme Court's Answer

In this case, requiring a labor organizer to acquire an organizer's card before giving a speech to solicit membership unconstitutionally impairs free speech.

II. CASE SUMMARY

A. Background

Section 5 of a Texas statute regulating labor unions and their activities requires that anyone who wants to solicit members for memberships in specified labor unions must first obtain an organizers' card.

"The appellant, Thomas, is the president of the International Union U.A.W. . . . and a vice president of the C.I.O. . . . As part of the campaign [to organize employees at a plant at Bay Town, Texas,] a mass meeting was arranged for the evening of September 23 . . . . [Appellant's] only object in coming to Houston was to address this meeting . . . six hours before he was scheduled to speak, Thomas was served with the restraining order and a copy of the fiat. . . . Upon receiving service, Thomas consulted his attorneys and determined to go ahead with the meeting as planned. He did so because he regarded the law and the citation as a restraint upon free speech and free assembly in so far as they prevented his making a speech or asking someone to join a union without having a license or organizer's card at the time. . . .

The meeting was orderly and peaceful. . . . As written, the speech did not address the invitation to any specific individual by name or otherwise. But Thomas testified that he added, at the conclusion of the written speech, an oral solicitation of one Pat O'Sullivan, a nonunion man in the audience whom he previously had never seen."

After the meeting, appellant was arrested for disobeying the order and the Supreme Court of Texas denied appellant's petition for a writ of habeas corpus.

On appeal the U.S. Supreme Court reversed the judgment of the Supreme Court of Texas.

B. Counsel of Record/ACLU Attorney

ACLU Side (Petitioner/Appellant): Lee Pressman and Ernest Goodman argued the cause for appellant.

Opposing Side (Respondent/Appellee): Fagan Dickson argued the cause for appellee. Alvin J. Rockwell argued the cause for appellee as amicus curiae, by special leave of Court.

III. AMICI CURIAE

ACLU Side (Petitioner/Appellant)

Brief of amici curiae filed on behalf of the ACLU by Arthur Garfield Hays, Walter Frank, Paul O'Dwyer, Carl Rachlin, and George Clifton Edwards.

Brief of amici curiae filed on behalf of the National Federation for Constitutional Liberties by Nathan Witt.

Opposing Side (Respondent/Appellee)

Brief of amici curiae filed on behalf of the United States by Alvin J. Rockwell, Charles Fahy, Solicitor General, Ruth Weyand, and Mozart G. Ratner.

IV. THE SUPREME COURT'S DECISION

"As a matter of principle a requirement of registration in order to make a public speech would seem generally incompatible with an exercise of the rights of free speech and free assembly. Lawful public assemblies, involving no element of grave and immediate danger to an interest the state is entitled to protect, are not instruments of harm which require previous identification of the speakers.

And the right either of workmen or of unions under these conditions to assemble and discuss their own affairs is as fully protected by the Constitution as the right of businessmen, farmers, educators, political party members or others to assemble and discuss their affairs and to enlist the support of others."

"We think a requirement that one must register before he undertakes to make a public speech to enlist support for a lawful movement is quite incompatible with the requirements of the First Amendment."

"Since a majority of the Court do not agree that Section 5 or its present application conflicts with the National Labor Relations Act, our decision rests exclusively upon the grounds we have stated for finding that the statute as applied contravenes the Constitution."

The U.S. Supreme Court reversed the judgment of the Supreme Court of Texas.

V. JUSTICE VOTE

5 Pro ACLU Side vs. 4 Con Opposing Side

ACLU Side (Petitioner/Appellant)

1. Rutledge, W. – Wrote majority opinion
2. Jackson, R. – Wrote concurring opinion
3. Douglas, W. – Wrote concurring opinion
4. Black, H. – Joined majority opinion
5. Murphy, F. – Joined majority opinion

Opposing Side (Respondent/Appellee)

1. Roberts, O. – Wrote dissenting opinion
2. Stone, H. – Joined Roberts' dissent
3. Reed, S. – Joined Roberts' dissent
4. Frankfurter, F. – Joined Roberts' dissent

VI. A WIN OR LOSS FOR THE ACLU?

The ACLU, as amici curiae, urged reversal of the judgment of the Supreme Court of Texas; the Supreme Court reversed in a 5-4 vote, giving the ACLU an apparent win.

33. Alabama State Federation of Labor v. McAdory

(Decided June 11, 1945; 325 U.S. 450)

I. ISSUE

A. Issues Discussed

Labor union regulation, declaratory judgments

B. Legal Question Presented

"[W]hether petitioners' contentions [that sections of the Bradford Act are unconstitutional] are so related to any case or controversy presented by the record that this Court may appropriately pass upon them in a declaratory judgment proceeding.

C. Supreme Court's Answer

The Supreme Court dismissed the writ of certiorari, declaring it was not appropriate to determine the constitutional validity of the Bradford Act under these circumstances.

II. CASE SUMMARY

A. Background

"Petitioners brought the present suit in the Alabama Circuit Court for Jefferson County against respondents, officers of Jefferson County, charged with the duty of enforcing the Bradford Act. They prayed a declaratory judgment that the Act as a whole and specifically ss 7, 15, and 16, among others, are unconstitutional and void under federal and state constitutions.

[T]he circuit court held the Act as a whole, and specifically s 7 of the Act, to be valid and constitutional. It declined as 'inappropriate' to make declarations as to the validity of ss 15 and 16. On appeal, petitioners assigning as error the circuit court's failure to pass upon the constitutionality of ss 15 and 16, and to declare those sections and s 7 unconstitutional, the state supreme court held all three sections valid and constitutional."

The Supreme Court dismissed its writ of certiorari because the question presented was "so unsubstantial" as to be "inappropriate for decision in a declaratory judgment proceeding."

B. Counsel of Record/ACLU Attorney

ACLU Side (Petitioner/Appellant): Horace C. Wilkinson and Joseph A. Padway argued the cause for appellant.

Opposing Side (Respondent/Appellee): John W. Lapsley, James A. Simpson, and John E. Adams argued the cause for appellee.

III. AMICI CURIAE

ACLU Side (Petitioner/Appellant)

Brief of amici curiae filed on behalf of the ACLU by Arthur Garfield Hays, David I. Ashe, and Osmond K. Fraenkel.

Brief of amici curiae filed on behalf of the Workers Defense League by Paul O'Dwyer, Max Delson, Carl Rachlin, and Leonard Cohen.

Brief of amici curiae filed on behalf of the United States by Solicitor General Charles Fahy, Special Assistant to the

Attorney General Robert L. Stern, Alvin J. Rockwell, Ivar Peterson, Ruth Weyand, Elizabeth W. Weston, and Mozart G. Ratner.

Opposing Side (Respondent/Appellee)

No briefs of amici curiae were filed on behalf of appellee.

IV. THE SUPREME COURT'S DECISION

"The Bradford Act is a comprehensive enactment regulating labor unions having members who are employees working in the State of Alabama."

"So far as appears the Supreme Court of Alabama has not construed the penal provisions of the statute or determined that the failure of a labor organization to file the documents specified in s 7 entails any consequences other than the specified penalty for the failure to file, with a further penalty if without filing the labor organization or its officers continue to collect dues. Neither of these sanctions is asserted or shown to operate as an injunction restraining freedom of speech or assembly. Nor does it appear that the Alabama courts have held that a labor organization failing to file may be enjoined from functioning."

"We are thus invited to pass upon the constitutional validity of a state statute which has not yet been applied or threatened to be applied by the state courts to petitioners or others in the manner anticipated. Lacking any authoritative construction of the statute by the state courts, without which no constitutional question arises, and lacking the authority to give such a controlling construction ourselves, and with a record which presents no concrete set of facts to which the statute is to be applied, the case is plainly not one to be disposed of by the declaratory judgment procedure."

The Supreme Court dismissed the writ of certiorari.

V. JUSTICE VOTE

0 Pro ACLU Side vs. 9 Con Opposing Side

Opposing Side (Respondent/Appellee)

1. Stone, H. – Wrote majority opinion
2. Roberts, O. – Joined majority opinion
3. Black, H. – Joined majority opinion
4. Reed, S. – Joined majority opinion
5. Frankfurter, F. – Joined majority opinion
6. Douglas, W. – Joined majority opinion
7. Murphy, F. – Joined majority opinion
8. Jackson, R. – Joined majority opinion
9. Rutledge, W. – Joined majority opinion

VI. A WIN OR LOSS FOR THE ACLU?

The ACLU, as amicus curiae, urged the court to grant a declaratory judgment in favor of appellant; the Supreme Court denied it in a 9-0 vote, giving the ACLU an apparent loss.

34. Congress of Industrial Organizations v. McAdory

(Decided June 11, 1945; 325 U.S. 472)

I. ISSUE

A. Issues Discussed

Labor union regulation, declaratory judgments

B. Legal Question Presented

Are petitioners' contentions about the constitutionality of certain sections of the Bradford Act and their impact on petitioners' activities, sufficiently factual for the Supreme Court to determine whether petitioners' rights would be affected by the Act?

C. Supreme Court's Answer

As in Alabama State Federation of Labor v. McAdory, above, the Supreme Court dismissed the writ of certiorari, declaring it was not appropriate to determine the constitutional validity of the Bradford Act under these circumstances.

II. CASE SUMMARY

A. Background

This case "is a companion case to Alabama State Federation of Labor v. McAdory. . . .

Petitioners brought the present suit in the State Circuit Court against respondents who are county officers charged with the duty of enforcing the [Bradford] Act, praying a declaratory judgment that the Act as a whole and particularly ss 7 and 16, among others, are unconstitutional under the Federal and State Constitutions, and are invalid because [they are] in conflict with the National Labor Relations Act, and praying that an injunction issue.

After a trial upon evidence the Circuit Court adjudged certain sections of the Act, not here in issue, to be invalid in whole or in part. In other respects it held the Act constitutional and valid. It found that the evidence disclosed no effort on the part of respondents to enforce the provisions of the Act declared to be invalid and accordingly denied an injunction. On appeal the Supreme Court of Alabama affirmed, for the reasons stated in its opinion in the Alabama State Federation of Labor case."

The Supreme Court dismissed its writ of certiorari.

B. Counsel of Record/ACLU Attorney

ACLU Side (Petitioner/Appellant): Lee Pressman argued the cause for appellant.

Opposing Side (Respondent/Appellee): John W. Lapsley, James A. Simpson, and John E. Adams argued the cause for appellee.

III. AMICI CURIAE

ACLU Side (Petitioner/Appellant)

Brief of amici curiae filed on behalf of the United States by Solicitor General Charles Fahy, Special Assistant to the Attorney General Robert L. Stern, Alvin J. Rockwell, Ivar Peterson, Ruth Weyand, Elizabeth W. Weston, and Mozart G.

Ratner.
Briefs filed in companion case, Alabama State Federation of Labor v. McAdory, also applicable here.

Opposing Side (Respondent/Appellee)

No briefs of amici curiae were filed on behalf of appellee.

IV. THE SUPREME COURT'S DECISION

"We find no other factual differences calling for comment between the case presented by the record here and that presented in the *Alabama State Federation of Labor* case. Our decision here is therefore controlled by our decision in that case. The question raised as to the equal protection of the laws is too unsubstantial to merit review. The other issues, as presented by the record now before us, are, for reasons stated at length in our opinion in the Alabama State Federation of Labor case, inappropriate for decision in a declaratory judgment proceeding.

The writ of certiorari is accordingly dismissed."

V. JUSTICE VOTE

0 Pro ACLU Side vs. 9 Con Opposing Side

Opposing Side (Respondent/Appellee)

1. Stone, H. – Wrote majority opinion
2. Roberts, O. – Joined majority opinion
3. Black, H. – Joined majority opinion
4. Reed, S. – Joined majority opinion
5. Frankfurter, F. – Joined majority opinion
6. Douglas, W. – Joined majority opinion
7. Murphy, F. – Joined majority opinion
8. Jackson, R. – Joined majority opinion
9. Rutledge, W. – Joined majority opinion

VI. A WIN OR LOSS FOR THE ACLU?

The ACLU, as amici curiae in support of appellant, urged the court to grant a declaratory judgment; the Supreme Court denied it in a 9-0 vote, giving the ACLU an apparent loss.

35. Hill v. Florida

(Decided June 11, 1945; 325 U.S. 538)

I. ISSUE

A. Issues Discussed

Labor union regulation

B. Legal Question Presented

"[W]hether a Florida statute regulating labor union activities has been applied to these petitioners in a manner which brings it into irreconcilable conflict with the collective bargaining regulations of the National Labor Relations Act."

C. Supreme Court's Answer

"Our holding is that the National Labor Relations Act and Sections 4 and 6 of the Florida Act as here applied cannot 'move freely within the orbit of their respective purposes without infringing upon one another.'"

II. CASE SUMMARY

A. Background

"The Attorney General of Florida . . . sought to restrain [petitioner Union and its business agent, Hill], from functioning as such until they had complied with the Florida statute. The basis for the relief sought against Hill was that he had for a pecuniary reward acted as a business agent in violation of Section 4; the basis for the relief sought against the union was that it had operated without obtaining a state license as required by Section 6. . . . Application for a license as a 'business agent' must be accompanied by a $1.00 fee and a statement signed by officers of the union setting forth the agent's authority. The statute then provides that the application be held for 30 days to permit the filing of objections to the issuance of a license. . . .

Motions by Hill and the union to dismiss the bill on the ground that the state statute violated the Fourteenth Amendment and conflicted with the Wagner Act were denied. Answers were then filed admitting violations of Sections 4 and 6. The court held the licensing and reporting provisions valid. Hill was enjoined from further acting as the union's business agent until he obtained a state license. The union was enjoined from further functioning and operating until it made the report and paid the fee to the Secretary of State. The State Supreme Court affirmed."

The U.S. Supreme Court reversed.

B. Counsel of Record/ACLU Attorney

ACLU Side (Petitioner/Appellant): Joseph A. Padway and Herbert S. Thatcher argued the cause for appellant.
Opposing Side (Respondent/Appellee): J. Tom Watson, Attorney General of Florida, and Howard S. Bailey argued the cause for appellee.

III. AMICI CURIAE

ACLU Side (Petitioner/Appellant)

Brief of amici curiae filed on behalf of the ACLU by Arthur Garfield Hays, David I. Ashe, Osmond K. Fraenkel, John M. Coe, Leonard Cooperman, and R. F. Howes.
Brief of amici curiae filed on behalf of the Workers Defense League by Paul O'Dwyer, Max Delson, Carl Rachlin, and Leonard Cohen.
Brief of amici curiae filed on behalf of the United States by Solicitor General Charles Fahy, Special Assistant to the Attorney General Robert L. Stern, Alvin J. Rockwell, Ivar Peterson, Ruth Weyand, Elizabeth W. Weston, and Mozart G. Ratner.

Opposing Side (Respondent/Appellee)

No briefs of amici curiae were filed on behalf of appellee.

IV. THE SUPREME COURT'S DECISION

"We hold that Section 4 of the Florida Act is repugnant to the National Labor Relations Act. Section 68 as here applied, stands no better. The requirement as to the filing of information and the payment of a $1.00 annual fee does not, in and of itself, conflict with the Federal Act. But for failure to comply, this union has been enjoined from functioning as a labor union. It could not without violating the injunction and also subjecting itself to the possibility of criminal punishment even attempt to bargain to settle a controversy or a strike. It is the sanction here imposed, and not the duty to report, which brings about a situation inconsistent with the federally protected process of collective bargaining. This is true because if the union or its representatives acted as bargaining agents without making the required reports, presumably they would be liable both to punishment for contempt of court and to conviction under the misdemeanor section of the act. Such an obstacle to collective bargaining cannot be created consistently with the Federal Act."

The U.S. Supreme Court reversed the judgment of the Supreme Court of Florida.

V. JUSTICE VOTE

7 Pro ACLU Side vs. 2 Con Opposing Side

ACLU Side (Petitioner/Appellant)

1. Black, H. – Wrote majority opinion
2. Stone, H. – Wrote concurring opinion
3. Rutledge, W. – Joined majority opinion
4. Murphy, F. – Joined majority opinion
5. Reed, S. – Joined majority opinion
6. Douglas, W. – Joined majority opinion
7. Jackson, R. – Joined majority opinion

Opposing Side (Respondent/Appellee)

1. Frankfurter, F. – Wrote dissenting opinion
2. Roberts, O. – Joined dissenting opinion

VI. A WIN OR LOSS FOR THE ACLU?

The ACLU, as amicus curiae, urged reversal of the judgment of the Supreme Court of Florida; the U.S. Supreme Court reversed in a 7-2 vote, giving the ACLU an apparent win.

36. Railway Mail Ass'n. v. Corsi

(Decided June 18, 1945; 326 U.S. 88)

I. ISSUE

A. Issues Discussed

Racial discrimination, equal protection, due process

B. Legal Question Presented

Is appellant a "labor organization" subject to the provisions of the New York Civil Rights Law, which provide that "no labor organization shall deny a person membership [or equal treatment] by reason of race, color or creed," and if it is, do the provisions violate "the due process and equal protection clauses of the Fourteenth Amendment of the federal Constitution and [are they] in conflict with the federal power over post offices and post roads"?

C. Supreme Court's Answer

Appellant is a labor organization subject to the New York Civil Rights Law and the provisions all conform with the federal Constitution.

II. CASE SUMMARY

A. Background

"Section 43, and related Sections 41 and 45, of the New York Civil Rights Law . . . provide, under penalty against its officers and members, that no labor organization shall deny a person membership by reason of race, color or creed, or deny to any of its members, by reason of race, color or creed, equal treatment in the designation of its members for employment, promotion or dismissal by an employer."

"[A]ppellant's constitution limits membership in the association to eligible postal clerks who are of the Caucasian race, or native American Indians." "Appellant contended that it was not a 'labor organization' subject to these sections."

"[T]he appellant filed suit against the Industrial Commissioner in a state court for a declaratory judgment to determine the validity of Section 43, and related provisions, and for an injunction restraining its enforcement against the appellant. A state Supreme Court entered judgment for the appellant finding that it was not a 'labor organization' as defined in Section 43 of the state statute. On appeal to the Appellate Division, this judgment was reversed, the appellate court finding that appellant was covered by Section 43 and that Section 43 as applied to appellant did not violate the federal Constitution.

On appeal to the New York Court of Appeals, the judgment against the appellant was affirmed."

On appeal the Supreme Court affirmed.

B. Counsel of Record/ACLU Attorney

ACLU Side (Respondent/Appellee): Wendell P. Brown argued the cause for appellee.

Opposing Side (Petitioner/Appellant): Daniel J. Dugan argued the cause for appellant.

III. AMICI CURIAE

ACLU Side (Respondent/Appellee)

Brief of amici curiae filed on behalf of the ACLU by Arthur Garfield Hays and Walter Gordon Merritt.

Brief of amici curiae filed on behalf of the National Association for the Advancement of Colored People by William H. Hastie, Leon A. Ransom, Thurgood Marshall, and Edward R. Dudley.

Opposing Side (Petitioner/Appellant)

No briefs of amici curiae were filed in support of appellant.

IV. THE SUPREME COURT'S DECISION

"Appellant first contends that . . . the New York Civil Rights Law, as applied to appellant offends the due process clause of the Fourteenth Amendment as an interference with its right of selection to membership and abridgment of its property rights and liberty of contract. We have here a prohibition of discrimination in membership or union services on account of race, creed or color. A judicial determination that such legislation violated the Fourteenth Amendment would be a distortion of the policy manifested in that amendment which was adopted to prevent state legislation designed to perpetuate discrimination on the basis of race or color."

Appellant argues second that Section 43 of the New York Civil Rights Law denies it equal protection because "Article 20 of the New York Labor Law, conferring certain rights on employees and labor organizations with respect to organization and collective bargaining, excludes from the operations of its provisions labor organizations, such as the appellant, whose members are 'employees of the state,' [and] that the state's failure to extend Article 20 to include the appellant denies it equal protection. A state does not deny equal protection because it regulates the membership of appellant but fails to extend to organizations of government employees provisions relating to collective bargaining. Under customary practices government employees do not bargain collectively with their employer."

Appellant contends third "that Section 43, and related provisions, are repugnant to Article I, Section 8, Clause 7, of the federal Constitution which confers on Congress the authority over postal matters . . . . Section 43 does not impinge on the federal mail service or the power of the government to conduct it. . . . Section 43 is confined in its application to a purely private organization deriving no financial or other statutory support or recognition from the federal government and which in no way acts as an instrumentality of the federal government in performance of its postal functions."

The U.S. Supreme Court affirmed the judgment of the Supreme Court of New York.

V. JUSTICE VOTE

9 Pro ACLU Side vs. 0 Con Opposing Side

ACLU Side (Respondent/Appellee)

1. Reed, S. – Wrote majority opinion
2. Frankfurter, F. – Wrote concurring opinion
3. Rutledge, W. – Concurred in the result without an opinion
4. Douglas, W. – Joined majority opinion
5. Roberts, O. – Joined majority opinion
6. Black, H. – Joined majority opinion
7. Stone, H. – Joined majority opinion
8. Murphy, F. – Joined majority opinion
9. Jackson, R. – Joined majority opinion

VI. A WIN OR LOSS FOR THE ACLU?

The ACLU, as amicus curiae, urged affirmance of the judgment of the Supreme Court of New York; the U.S. Supreme Court affirmed in a 9-0 vote, giving the ACLU an apparent win.

37. Bridges v. Wixon

(Decided June 18, 1945; 326 U.S. 135)

I. ISSUE

A. Issues Discussed

Immigration, due process

B. Legal Question Presented

Was Petitioner sufficiently "affiliated" with the Communist party within the meaning of a federal statute providing for the deportation of any immigrant affiliated with any organization that "taught the overthrow by force of the government of the United States," to warrant his deportation?

C. Supreme Court's Answer

Petitioner was not sufficiently affiliated with the Communist Party to warrant deportation under the statute.

II. CASE SUMMARY

A. Background

Petitioner came from Australia in 1920. "In 1933 he became active in trade union work on the water front in San Francisco." He was eventually "elected Pacific Coast District President" of the "International Longshoremen and Warehousemen's Union." "In 1938 deportation proceedings were instituted against [petitioner] on the ground that he both had been and then was a member of or affiliated with the Communist Party of the United States and that that party advised and taught the overthrow by force of the government of the United States . . . ." The first deportation proceedings were dropped, but second deportation proceedings were instituted after "Congress amended the statute so as to provide for deportation of any alien who was 'at the time of entering the United States, or has been at any time thereafter' a member of or affiliated with an organization of the character attributed to the Communist Party in the first proceeding." Deportation was recommended after the second hearing.

The petitioner "surrendered himself to the custody of respondent and challenged the legality of his detention by a petition for a writ of habeas corpus in the District Court for the Northern District of California. That court denied the petition and remanded petitioner to the custody of Respondent. The Circuit Court of Appeals affirmed by a divided vote."

On certiorari the Supreme Court reversed the judgment of the Circuit Court of Appeals.

B. Counsel of Record/ACLU Attorney

ACLU Side (Petitioner/Appellant): Richard Gladstein and Lee Pressman argued the cause for petitioner.

Opposing Side (Respondent/Appellee): Solicitor General Charles Fahy argued the cause for appellee.

III. AMICI CURIAE

ACLU Side (Petitioner/Appellant)

Brief of amici curiae filed on behalf of the ACLU by Arthur Garfield Hays, Osmond K. Fraenkel, Herbert Ganahl, Carey McWilliams, Isaac Pacht, John Packard, Lester William Roth, A. L. Wirin, and Bartley C. Crum.

Brief of amici curiae filed on behalf of the American Committee for Protection of Foreign Born by Pearl M. Hart, Carl S. Stern, and Blanche L. Miller.

Opposing Side (Respondent/Appellee)

Brief of amici curiae filed on behalf of the American Legion by Ralph B. Gregg, W. Coburn Cook, Wallace L. Ware, John A. Sinclair, and Seth Millington.

IV. THE SUPREME COURT'S DECISION

"The associations which Harry Bridges had with various Communist groups seem to indicate no more than cooperative measures to attain objectives which were wholly legitimate. The link by which it is sought to tie him to subversive activities is an exceedingly tenuous one, if it may be said to exist at all."

"The Attorney General sustained Judge Sears' findings that Petitioner sponsored . . . and was responsible for . . . publication" of the "Waterfront Worker," a publication launched by Marine Workers' Industrial Union, a "proscribed organization." But the Supreme court found that "when the evidence underlying these findings is examined it is found to be devoid of any showing that the Waterfront Worker advocated overthrow of the government by force. . . . Nor is there any finding that Bridges took over this project with the view of doing more than advancing the lawful cause of unionism."

"Since [Petitioner] has been ordered deported on a misconstruction of the term 'affiliation' as used in the statute and by reason of an unfair hearing on the question of his membership in the Communist party, his detention under the warrant is unlawful."

The Supreme Court reversed the judgment of the Circuit Court of Appeals.

V. JUSTICE VOTE

5 Pro ACLU Side vs. 3 Con Opposing Side

ACLU Side (Petitioner/Appellant)

1. Douglas, W. – Wrote majority opinion
2. Murphy, F. – Wrote concurring opinion
3. Reed, S. – Joined majority opinion
4. Rutledge, W. – Joined majority opinion
5. Black, H. – Joined majority opinion

Opposing Side (Respondent/Appellee)

1. Stone, H. – Wrote dissenting opinion
2. Roberts, O. – Joined dissenting opinion
3. Frankfurter, F. – Joined dissenting opinion

Jackson, R – Took no part in the decision

VI. A WIN OR LOSS FOR THE ACLU?

The ACLU, as amicus curiae, urged reversal of the judgment of the Circuit Court of Appeals; the Supreme Court reversed in a 5-3 vote, giving the ACLU an apparent win.

38. Hannegan v. Esquire, Inc.

(Decided February 4, 1946; 327 U.S. 146)

I. ISSUE

A. Issues Discussed

Freedom of speech

B. Legal Question Presented

Does the Postmaster General have the power to decide what publications are mailable based on the content of the publication?

C. Supreme Court's Answer

No, the Postmaster General is not allowed to decide which types of publications are mailable based on content, subject to an exception for fraudulent or obscene material.

II. CASE SUMMARY

A. Background

"Respondent is the publisher of Esquire Magazine, a monthly periodical which was granted a second-class permit in 1933. In 1943, pursuant to the Act of March 3, 1901, . . . a citation was issued to respondent by the then Postmaster General . . . to show cause why that permit should not be suspended or revoked. A hearing was held before a board designated by the then Postmaster General. The board recommended that the permit not be revoked. Petitioner's predecessor took a different view. . . . He revoked its second-class permit because he found that it did not comply with the Fourth condition [i.e that the publication was] 'morally improper and not for the public welfare and the public good.'"

"Respondent thereupon sued in the District Court for the District of Columbia to enjoin the revocation order. . . . The District Court denied the injunction and dismissed the complaint. The Court of Appeals reversed."

The Supreme Court granted certiorari to review the case and affirmed the judgment of the Court of Appeals.

B. Counsel of Record/ACLU Attorney

ACLU Side (Respondent/Appellee): Bruce Bromley argued the cause for appellee.

Opposing Side (Petitioner/Appellant): Marvin C. Taylor argued the cause for appellant.

III. AMICI CURIAE

ACLU Side (Respondent/Appellee)

Brief of amici curiae filed on behalf of the ACLU by Charles Horsky, Arthur Dehon Hill, Luther Ely Smith, Arthur Garfield Hays, Asher Lans, Norman Williams, Jr., and Gurney Edwards.

Brief of amici curiae filed on behalf of the Ameircan Newspaper Publishers Association by Elisha Hanson.
Brief of amici curiae filed by James W. Stites, George Roberts, and Whitney North Seymour.
Brief of amici curiae filed on behalf of the Curtis Publishing Company by Francis H. Scheetz and Arthur H. Clephane.
Brief of amici curiae filed on behalf of the Reader's Digest Association by Robert E. Coulson, Forbes D. Shaw, and William R. Sherwood.
Brief of amici curiae filed on behalf of the Authors' League of America, Inc. by Sidney R. Fleisher.

Opposing Side (Petitioner/Appellant)

No briefs of amici curiae were filed on behalf of appellant.

IV. THE SUPREME COURT'S DECISION

"Congress could constitutionally make it a crime to send fraudulent or obscene material through the mails. But grave constitutional questions are immediately raised once it is said that the use of the mails is a privilege which may be extended or withheld on any grounds whatsoever.... Under that view the second-class rate could be granted on condition that certain economic or political ideas not be disseminated. The provisions of the Fourth condition would have to be far more explicit for us to assume that Congress made such a radical departure from our traditions and undertook to clothe the Postmaster General with the power to supervise the tastes of the reading public of the country....

Congress has left the Postmaster General with no power to prescribe standards for the literature or the art which a mailable periodical disseminates. [T]he power to determine whether a periodical (which is mailable) contains information of a public character, literature or art does not include the further power to determine whether the contents meet some standard of the public good or welfare."

The Supreme Court affirmed the judgment of the Court of Appeals.

V. JUSTICE VOTE

8 Pro ACLU Side vs. 0 Con Opposing Side

ACLU Side (Respondent/Appellee)

1. Douglas, W. – Wrote majority opinion
2. Frankfurter, F. – Wrote concurring opinion
3. Burton, H. – Joined majority opinion
4. Black, H. – Joined majority opinion
5. Stone, H. – Joined majority opinion
6. Murphy, F. – Joined majority opinion
7. Reed, S. – Joined majority opinion
8. Rutledge, W. – Joined majority opinion

Jackson, R – Took no part in the decision

VI. A WIN OR LOSS FOR THE ACLU?

The ACLU, as amicus curiae, urged affirmance of the judgment of the Court of Appeals; the Supreme Court affirmed in an 8-0 vote, giving the ACLU an apparent win.

39. Duncan v. Kahanamoku

(Decided February 25, 1946; 327 U.S. 304)

I. ISSUE

A. Issues Discussed

Martial law, due process

B. Legal Question Presented

"Did the Organic Act during the period of martial law [in Hawaii] give the armed forces power to supplant all civilian laws and to substitute military for judicial trials under the conditions that existed in Hawaii at the time these petitioners were tried?"

C. Supreme Court's Answer

The period of martial law in Hawaii did not authorize "the supplanting of courts by military tribunals."

II. CASE SUMMARY

A. Background

"[I]mmediately following the surprise air attack by the Japanese on Pearl Harbor, the Governor of Hawaii by proclamation undertook to suspend the privilege of the writ of habeas corpus and to place the Territory under 'martial law,'" pursuant to the Hawaiian Organic Act.

"On December 8th, both civil and criminal courts were forbidden to summon jurors and witnesses and to try cases. The Commanding General established military tribunals to take the place of the courts.... The military tribunals interpreted the very orders promulgated by the military authorities and proceeded to punish violators. The sentences imposed were not subject to direct appellate court review, since it had long been established that military tribunals are not part of our judicial system."

Petitioner White was arrested for embezzling stock, "more than eight months after the Pearl Harbor attack" and Petitioner Duncan was arrested for engaging "in a brawl with two armed Marine sentries," which occurred "more than two years and two months after the Pearl Harbor attack." They were both tried by a military tribunal and convicted.

"Both White and Duncan challenged the power of the military tribunals to try them by petitions for writs of habeas corpus filed in the District Court for Hawaii .... The District Court, after separate trials found in each case, among other things, that the courts had always been able to function but for the military orders closing them, and that consequently there was no military necessity for the trial of petitioners by military tribunals rather than regular courts. It accordingly held the trials void and ordered the release of the petitioners.

The Circuit Court of Appeals, assuming without deciding that the District Court had jurisdiction to entertain the petitions, held the military trials valid and reversed the ruling of the District Court." On certiorari the Supreme Court reversed.

B. Counsel of Record/ACLU Attorney

ACLU Side (Petitioner/Appellant): J. Garner Anthony argued the cause for appellant in No. 14.
Osmond K. Fraenkel argued the cause in No. 15.

Attorney General of Hawaii C. Nils Tavares argued the cause as amici curiae, by special leave of court.

Opposing Side (Respondent/Appellee): Special Assistant to the Attorney General Edward J. Ennis argued the cause for appellee.

III. AMICI CURIAE

ACLU Side (Petitioner/Appellant)

Brief of amici curiae filed on behalf of the ACLU by Bartley C. Crum, Thurman Arnold, Pierce Butler, Winthrop Wadleigh, Osmond K. Fraenkel, Arthur Garfield Hays, and Edwin Borchard.

Brief of amici curiae filed on behalf of the Territory of Hawaii by Attorney General of Hawaii C. Nils Tavares, Rhoda V. Lewis, Heaton L. Wrenn, and J. Russell Cades.

Opposing Side (Respondent/Appellee)

No briefs of amici curiae were filed in support of appellee.

IV. THE SUPREME COURT'S DECISION

"[B]oth the language of the Organic Act and its legislative history fail to indicate that the scope of 'martial law' in Hawaii includes the supplanting of courts by military tribunals. . . . Courts and their procedural safeguards are indispensable to our system of government. They were set up by our founders to protect the liberties they valued. . . . The phrase 'martial law' as employed in [the Organic] Act, therefore, while intended to authorize the military to act vigorously for the maintenance of an orderly civil government and for the defense of the island against actual or threatened rebellion or invasion, was not intended to authorize the supplanting of courts by military tribunals. Yet the government seeks to justify the punishment of both White and Duncan on the ground of such supposed Congressional authorization. We hold that both petitioners are now entitled to be released from custody."

The Supreme Court reversed the judgment of the Circuit Court of Appeals.

V. JUSTICE VOTE

6 Pro ACLU Side vs. 2 Con Opposing Side

ACLU Side (Petitioner/Appellant)

1. Black, H. – Wrote majority opinion
2. Stone, H. – Wrote concurring opinion
3. Murphy, F. – Wrote concurring opinion
4. Reed, S. – Joined majority opinion
5. Douglas, W. – Joined majority opinion
6. Rutledge, W. – Joined majority opinion

Opposing Side (Respondent/Appellee)

1. Burton, H. – Wrote dissenting opinion
2. Frankfurter, F. – Joined dissenting opinion

Jackson, R – Took no part in the decision

VI. A WIN OR LOSS FOR THE ACLU?

The ACLU, as amicus curiae, urged reversal of the judgment of the Circuit Court of Appeals; the Supreme Court reversed in a 6-2 vote, giving the ACLU an apparent win.

40. Bell v. Hood

(Decided April 1, 1946; 327 U.S. 678)

I. ISSUE

A. Issues Discussed

Civil procedure, statutory interpretation

B. Legal Question Presented

Whether there is jurisdiction to decide if petitioners can recover damages in federal district court for alleged violations of the Fourth and Fifth Amendments by the FBI.

C. Supreme Court's Answer

The district court has jurisdiction to decide this issue because there is a federal question involved, interpretation of the Fourth and Fifth Amendments.

II. CASE SUMMARY

A. Background

"Petitioners brought this suit in a federal district court to recover damages in excess of $3,000 from the respondents who are agents of the Federal Bureau of Investigation. The complaint alleges that the Court's jurisdiction is founded upon federal questions arising under the Fourth and Fifth Amendments. It is alleged that the damages were suffered as a result of the defendants imprisoning the petitioners in violation of their Constitutional right to be free from deprivation of their liberty without due process of law, and subjecting their premises to search and their possessions to seizure, in violation of their Constitutional right to be free from unreasonable searches and seizures. Respondents moved to dismiss the complaint for failure to state a cause of action for which relief could be granted and for summary judgment on the grounds that the federal agents acted within the scope of their authority as officers of the United States and that the searches and seizures were incidental to lawful arrests and were therefore valid. . . .

After hearing the motions the district judge did not pass on them but, on his own motion, dismissed the suit for want of federal jurisdiction on the ground that this action was not one that '. . . arises under the Constitution or laws of the United States . . .'. The Circuit Court of Appeals affirmed on the same ground."

On certiorari the Supreme Court reversed.

B. Counsel of Record/ACLU Attorney

ACLU Side (Petitioner/Appellant): A. L. Wirin and Russell E. Parsons argued the cause for appellant.

Opposing Side (Respondent/Appellee): Special Assistant to the Attorney General Frederick Bernays Wiener argued the cause for appellee.

III. AMICI CURIAE

ACLU Side (Petitioner/Appellant)

Brief of amici curiae filed on behalf of the Northern and Southern California Branches of the ACLU by Wayne M. Collins.

Opposing Side (Respondent/Appellee)

No briefs of amici curiae were filed in support of appellee.

IV. THE SUPREME COURT'S DECISION

"Whether or not the complaint as drafted states a common law action in trespass made actionable by state law, it is clear from the way it was drawn that petitioners seek recovery squarely on the ground that respondents violated the Fourth and Fifth Amendments. It charges that the respondents conspired to do acts prohibited by these amendments and alleges that respondents' conduct pursuant to the conspiracy resulted in damages in excess of $3,000. It cannot be doubted therefore that it was the pleaders' purpose to make violation of these Constitutional provisions the basis of this suit. . . .

Whether the petitioners are entitled to recover depends upon an interpretation of 28 U.S.C . s 41(1), 28 U.S.C.A. s 41(1), and on a determination of the scope of the Fourth and Fifth Amendments' protection from unreasonable searches and deprivations of liberty without due process of law. Thus, the right of the petitioners to recover under their complaint will be sustained if the Constitution and laws of the United States are given one construction and will be defeated if they are given another. For this reason the district court has jurisdiction."

The Supreme Court reversed the judgment of the Circuit Court of Appeals.

V. JUSTICE VOTE

6 Pro ACLU Side vs. 2 Con Opposing Side

ACLU Side (Petitioner/Appellant)

1. Black, H. – Wrote majority opinion
2. Reed, S. – Wrote concurring opinion
3. Frankfurter, F. – Joined majority opinion
4. Douglas, W. – Joined majority opinion
5. Rutledge, W. – Joined majority opinion
6. Murphy, F. – Joined majority opinion

Opposing Side (Respondent/Appellee)

1. Stone, H. – Wrote joint dissenting opinion
2. Burton, H. – Wrote joint dissenting opinion

Jackson, R – Took no part in the decision

VI. A WIN OR LOSS FOR THE ACLU?

The ACLU, as amicus and counsel of record, urged reversal of the judgment the Circuit Court of Appeals; the Supreme Court reversed in a 6-2 vote, giving the ACLU an apparent win.

41. Girouard v. United States

(Decided April 22, 1946; 328 U.S. 61)

I. ISSUE

A. Issues Discussed

Freedom of religion, citizenship

B. Legal Question Presented

Does the oath of allegiance to "support and defend the Constitution and laws of the United States of America against all enemies, foreign and domestic" required of aliens seeking naturalization, oblige the individuals to bear arms in time of war despite their religious belief?

C. Supreme Court's Answer

No, the oath does not require a "promise to bear arms," as that requirement would be contrary to freedom of religion.

II. CASE SUMMARY

A. Background

In 1943, petitioner James Girouard filed a petition for naturalization, seeking to become a U.S. citizen. He was willing to take the oath of allegiance, but when he was asked whether he would be willing to bear arms in the defense of the United States, he replied that he was a Seventh Day Adventist, and that his religion prohibited him from combatant military duty. He was willing to serve in the military, but only in a noncombatant position.

The District Court admitted Girouard to U.S. citizenship. The Circuit Court of Appeals reversed, based on previous Supreme Court decisions in *United States v. Schwimmer*, 279 U.S. 644; *United States v. Macintosh*, 283 U.S. 605, and *United States v. Bland*, 283 U.S. 636.

On certiorari the Supreme Court overruled *Macintosh*, *Bland*, and *Schwimmer* and reversed the judgment of the Circuit Court of Appeals.

B. Counsel of Record/ACLU Attorney

ACLU Side (Petitioner/Appellant): Homer Cummings and William D. Donnelly argued the cause for appellant.

Opposing Side (Respondent/Appellee): Special Assistance to the Attorney General Frederick Bernays Wiener argued the cause for appellee.

III. AMICI CURIAE

ACLU Side (Petitioner/Appellant)

Brief of amici curiae filed on behalf of the ACLU by Ernest Angell, Julien Cornell, John W. Davis, Charles B. Finch, and Osmond K. Fraenkel.

Opposing Side (Respondent/Appellee)

No briefs of amici curiae were filed in support of appellee.

IV. THE SUPREME COURT'S DECISION

"The oath required of aliens does not in terms require that they promise to bear arms. Nor has Congress expressly made any such finding a prerequisite to citizenship."

"As we recently stated . . . 'Freedom of thought, which includes freedom of religious belief, is basic in a society of free men. . . .' The test oath is abhorrent to our tradition. Over the years Congress has meticulously respected that tradition and even in time of war has sought to accommodate the military requirements to the religious scruples of the individual. We do not believe that Congress intended to reverse that policy when it came to draft the naturalization oath."

"We conclude that the *Schwimmer*, *Macintosh* and *Bland* cases do not state the correct rule of law."

The Supreme Court reversed the judgment of the Circuit Court of Appeals.

V. JUSTICE VOTE

5 Pro ACLU Side vs. 3 Con Opposing Side

ACLU Side (Petitioner/Appellant)

1. Douglas, W. – Wrote majority opinion
2. Burton, H. – Joined majority opinion
3. Black, H. – Joined majority opinion
4. Rutledge, W. –Joined majority opinion
5. Murphy, F. – Joined majority opinion

Opposing Side (Respondent/Appellee)

1. Stone, H. – Wrote dissenting opinion
2. Reed, S. – Joined dissenting opinion
3. Frankfurter, F. – Joined dissenting opinion

Jackson, R – Took no part in the decision

VI. A WIN OR LOSS FOR THE ACLU?

The ACLU, as amicus curiae, urged reversal of the judgment of the Circuit Court of Appeals; the Supreme Court reversed in a 5-3 vote, giving the ACLU an apparent win.

42. Pennekamp v. Florida

(Decided June 3, 1946; 328 U.S. 331)

I. ISSUE

A. Issues Discussed

Freedom of speech and of the press

B. Legal Question Presented

Did the editorials published by petitioners constitute "a threat of clear and present danger to the impartiality and good order of the courts" or were they protected by the First Amendment?

C. Supreme Court's Answer

The editorials did not constitute a threat to judicial administration under the clear and present danger test.

II. CASE SUMMARY

A. Background

Miami Herald printed two editorials that were critical of the administration of cases pending before the Circuit Court of Dade County, Florida. The Circuit Court issued a contempt citation for the editorials and the Supreme Court of Florida affirmed.

On certiorari the U.S. Supreme Court reversed.

B. Counsel of Record/ACLU Attorney

ACLU Side (Petitioner/Appellant): Elisha Hanson and Robert R. Milam for appellant.

Opposing Side (Respondent/Appellee): J. Tom Watson, James M. Carson, and Giles J. Patterson argued the cause for appellee.

III. AMICI CURIAE

ACLU Side (Petitioner/Appellant)

Brief of amici curiae filed on behalf of the ACLU by John M. Coe, William Harrison Mizell, and Osmond K. Fraenkel.

Opposing Side (Respondent/Appellee)

No briefs of amici curiae were filed in support of appellee.

IV. THE SUPREME COURT'S DECISION

"Free discussion of the problems of society is a cardinal principle of Americanism - a principle which all are zealous to preserve. . . . [Nevertheless] courts must have power to protect the interests of prisoners and litigants before them from unseemly efforts to pervert judicial action. . . .

While a disclaimer of intention does not purge a contempt, we may at this point call attention to the sworn answer of petitioners that their purpose was not to influence the court. . . . For circumstances to create a clear and present danger to judicial administration, a solidity of evidence should be required which it would be difficult to find in this record.

The comments . . . concerned the attitude of the judges toward those who were charged with crime, not comments on evidence or rulings during a jury trial. . . . We are not willing to say under the circumstances of this case that these editorials are a clear and present danger to the fair administration of justice in Florida."

The Supreme Court reversed the judgment of the Supreme Court of Florida.

V. JUSTICE VOTE

7 Pro ACLU Side vs. 0 Con Opposing Side

ACLU Side (Petitioner/Appellant)

1. Reed, S. – Wrote majority opinion
2. Frankfurter, F. – Wrote concurring opinion
3. Rutledge, W. – Wrote concurring opinion
4. Murphy, F. – Wrote concurring opinion
5. Douglas, W. – Joined majority opinion
6. Black, H. – Joined majority opinion
7. Burton, H. – Joined majority opinion

Jackson, R – Took no part in the decision

VI. A WIN OR LOSS FOR THE ACLU?

The ACLU, as amicus curiae, urged reversal of the judgment of the Supreme Court of Florida; the Supreme Court reversed in a 7-0 vote, giving the ACLU an apparent win.

43. Morgan v. Virginia

(Decided June 3, 1946; 328 U.S. 373)

I. ISSUE

A. Issues Discussed

Interstate commerce, racial discrimination

B. Legal Question Presented

Does "an act of Virginia, which requires all passenger motor vehicle carriers, both interstate and intrastate, to separate without discrimination the white and colored passengers" violate the interstate commerce clause?

C. Supreme Court's Answer

Yes, the statute is an invalid interference with commerce under the interstate commerce clause.

II. CASE SUMMARY

A. Background

"[A]ppellant, who is a Negro, was traveling on a motor common carrier . . . . There were other passengers, both white and colored. On her refusal to accede to a request of the driver to move to a back seat, which was partly occupied by other colored passengers, so as to permit the seat that she vacated to be used by white passengers, a warrant was obtained and appellant was arrested, tried and convicted of a violation of Section 4097dd of the Virginia Code." The statute "requires all passenger motor vehicle carriers, both interstate and intrastate, to separate without discrimination the white and colored passengers in their motor buses so that contiguous seats will not be occupied by persons of different races at the same time."

Appellant claimed that the statute unlawfully burdened the Interstate Commerce. "On a writ of error the conviction was affirmed by the Supreme Court of Appeals of Virginia. The Court of Appeals interpreted the Virginia statute as applicable to appellant since the statute 'embraces all motor vehicles and all passengers, both interstate and intrastate.'"

On appeal the Supreme Court reversed the judgment of the Court of Appeals.

B. Counsel of Record/ACLU Attorney

ACLU Side (Petitioner/Appellant): William H. Hastie and Thurgood Marshall argued the cause for appellant.

Opposing Side (Respondent/Appellee): Abram P. Staples argued the cause for appellee.

III. AMICI CURIAE

ACLU Side (Petitioner/Appellant)

Brief of amici curiae filed on behalf of the ACLU by Gregory Hankin, Victor W. Rotnem, Osmond K. Fraenkel, and Arthur Garfield Hays.

Brief of amici curiae filed on behalf of the Workers Defense League by Harold A. Stevens, Ernest Fleischman, and Leon Zitver.

Opposing Side (Respondent/Appellee)

No briefs of amici curiae were filed on behalf of appellee.

IV. THE SUPREME COURT'S DECISION

"[A] state legislation is invalid if it unduly burdens that commerce in matters where uniformity is necessary—necessary in the constitutional sense of useful in accomplishing a permitted purpose."

"On appellant's journey, this statute required that she sit in designated seats in Virginia. . . . An interstate passenger must if necessary repeatedly shift seats while moving in Virginia to meet the seating requirements of the changing passenger group. On arrival at the District of Columbia line, the appellant would have had freedom to occupy any available seat and so to the end of her journey."

"As there is no federal act dealing with the separation of races in interstate transportation, we must decide the validity of this Virginia statute on the challenge that it interferes with commerce, as a matter of balance between the exercise of local police power and the need for national uniformity in the regulations for interstate travel. It seems clear to us that seating arrangements for the different races in interstate motor travel require a single, uniform rule to promote and protect national travel. Consequently, we hold the Virginia statute in controversy invalid."

The U.S. Supreme Court reversed the judgment of the Supreme Court of Appeals of Virginia.

V. JUSTICE VOTE

6 Pro ACLU Side vs. 1 Con Opposing Side

ACLU Side (Petitioner/Appellant)

1. Reed, S. – Wrote majority opinion
2. Black, H. – Wrote concurring opinion
3. Frankfurter, F. – Wrote concurring opinion
4. Rutledge, W. – Concurred in the result
5. Douglas, W. – Joined majority opinion
6. Murphy, F. – Joined majority opinion

Opposing Side (Respondent/Appellee)

1. Burton, H. – Wrote dissenting opinion

Jackson, R – Took no part in the decision

VI. A WIN OR LOSS FOR THE ACLU?

The ACLU, as amicus curiae, urged reversal of the judgment of the Supreme Court of Appeals of Virginia; the U.S. Supreme Court reversed in a 6-1 vote, giving the ACLU an apparent win.

44. Everson v. Board of Education

(Decided February 10, 1947; 330 U.S. 1)

I. ISSUE

A. Issues Discussed

Separation of church and state

B. Legal Question Presented

Does the New Jersey statute, which authorizes "reimbursement to parents of money [spent] for the bus transportation of their children" to both public and parochial schools, violate the due process clause of the Fourteenth Amendment and the establishment clause of the First Amendment?

C. Supreme Court's Answer

The New Jersey statute does not violate the due process clause or the establishment clause.

II. CASE SUMMARY

A. Background

"A New Jersey statute authorizes its local school districts to make rules and contracts for the transportation of children to and from schools. The appellee, a township board of education, acting pursuant to this statute authorized reimbursement to parents of money expended by them for the bus transportation of their children on regular busses operated by the public transportation system. Part of this money was for the payment of transportation of some children in the community to Catholic parochial schools. These church schools give their students, in addition to secular education, regular religious instruction conforming to the religious tenets and modes of worship of the Catholic Faith. The superintendent of these schools is a Catholic priest.

The appellant, in his capacity as a district taxpayer, filed suit in a State court challenging the right of the Board to reimburse parents of parochial school students. He contended that the statute and the resolution passed pursuant to it violated both the State and the Federal Constitutions. That court held that the legislature was without power to authorize such payment under the State constitution. The New Jersey Court of Errors and Appeals reversed, holding that neither the statute nor the resolution passed pursuant to it was in conflict with the State constitution or the provisions of the Federal Constitution in issue."

On appeal the Supreme Court affirmed.

B. Counsel of Record/ACLU Attorney

ACLU Side (Petitioner/Appellant): Edward R. Burke and E. Hilton Jackson argued the cause for appellant.

Opposing Side (Respondent/Appellee): William H. Speer argued the cause for appellee.

III. AMICI CURIAE

ACLU Side (Petitioner/Appellant)

Brief of amici curiae filed on behalf of the ACLU by I. George Koven, James A. Major, Harry V. Osborne, Frank H. Pierce, Joseph Beck Tyler, Kenneth W. Greenawalt, and Whitney N. Seymour.

Additional briefs of amici curiae filed on behalf of the General Conference of Seventh-Day Adventists and State Council of the Junior Order of United American Mechanics of New Jersey by Milton T. Lasher.

Opposing Side (Respondent/Appellee)

Brief of amici curiae filed on behalf of the States of Illinois and Indiana by Attorney General of Illinois George F. Barrett, Attorney General of Indiana James A. Emmert, and William C. Wines.

Brief of amici curiae filed on behalf of the Commonwealth of Massachusetts by Attorney General of Massachusetts Clarence A. Barnes and James J. Kelleher.

Brief of amici curiae filed by Attorney General of Louisiana Fred S. LeBlanc

Brief of amici curiae filed by Attorney General of Michigan Foss O. Eldred, Edmund E. Shepherd, and Daniel J. O'Hara.

Brief of amici curiae filed on behalf of the State of New York by Attorney General of New York Nathaniel L. Goldstein, Wendell P. Brown, and Ruth Kessler Toch.

Brief of amici curiae filed on behalf of the National Council of Catholic Men and National Council of Catholic Women.

IV. THE SUPREME COURT'S DECISION

"The due process argument that the State law taxes some people to help others carry out their private purposes . . . is said to violate the due process clause because the children are sent to these church schools to satisfy the personal desires of their parents, rather than the public's interest in the general education of all children. . . . But, the New Jersey legislature has decided that a public purpose will be served by using tax-raised funds to pay the bus fares of all school children, including those who attend parochial schools. . . . The fact that a state law, passed to satisfy a public need, coincides with the personal desires of the individuals most directly affected is certainly an inadequate reason for us to say that a legislature has erroneously appraised the public need."

"New Jersey cannot consistently with the 'establishment of religion' clause of the First Amendment contribute tax-raised funds to the support of an institution which teaches the tenets and faith of any church. On the other hand, other language of the amendment commands that New Jersey cannot hamper its citizens in the free exercise of their own religion. Consequently, it cannot exclude individual Catholics, Lutherans, Mohammedans, Baptists, Jews, Methodists, Non-believers, Presbyterians, or the members of any other faith, because of their faith, or lack of it, from receiving the benefits of public welfare legislation. While we do not mean to intimate that a state could not provide transportation only to children attending public schools, we must be careful, in protecting the citizens of New Jersey against state-established churches, to be sure that we do not inadvertently prohibit New Jersey from extending its general State law benefits to all its citizens without regard to their religious belief. Measured by these standards, we cannot say that the First Amendment prohibits New Jersey from spending taxraised funds to pay the bus fares of parochial school pupils as a part of a general program under which it pays the fares of pupils attending public and other schools."

"The First Amendment has erected a wall between church and state. That wall must be kept high and impregnable. We could not approve the slightest breach. New Jersey has not breached it here."

The Supreme Court affirmed the judgment of the New Jersey Court of Errors and Appeals.

V. JUSTICE VOTE

4 Pro ACLU Side vs. 5 Con Opposing Side

ACLU Side (Petitioner/Appellant)

1. Jackson, R. – Wrote dissenting opinion
2. Rutledge, W. – Wrote dissenting opinion
3. Frankfurter, F. – Joined dissenting opinion
4. Burton, H. – Joined dissenting opinion

Opposing Side (Respondent/Appellee)

1. Black, H. – Wrote majority opinion
2. Vinson, F. – Joined majority opinion
3. Reed, S. – Joined majority opinion
4. Murphy, F. – Joined majority opinion
5. Douglas, W. – Joined majority opinion

VI. A WIN OR LOSS FOR THE ACLU?

The ACLU, as amicus curiae, urged reversal of the judgment of the New Jersey Court of Errors and Appeals; the Supreme Court affirmed in a 5-4 vote, giving the ACLU an apparent loss.

45. Sipuel v. Board of Regents of University of Oklahoma

(Decided January 12, 1948; 332 U.S. 631)

I. ISSUE

A. Issues Discussed

Racial discrimination

B. Legal Question Presented

Can the School of Law of the University of Oklahoma deny admission to petitioner solely based on her race?

C. Supreme Court's Answer

No, the school must provide for the student's education the same as white applicants under the equal protection clause of the Fourteenth Amendment.

II. CASE SUMMARY

A. Background

"On January 14, 1946, the petitioner, a Negro, concededly qualified to receive the professional legal education offered by the State, applied for admission to the School of Law of the University of Oklahoma, the only institution for legal education supported and maintained by the taxpayers of the State of Oklahoma. Petitioner's application for admission was denied, solely because of her color.

Petitioner then made application for a writ of mandamus in the District Court of Cleveland County, Oklahoma, [to order the University to admit Petitioner]. The writ of mandamus was refused, and the Supreme Court of the State of Oklahoma affirmed the judgment of the District Court."

The Supreme Court reversed in a per curiam opinion.

B. Counsel of Record/ACLU Attorney

ACLU Side (Petitioner/Appellant): Thurgood Marshall and Amos Hall argued the cause for appellant.

Opposing Side (Respondent/Appellee): Fred Hansen and Maurice H. Merrill argued the cause for appellee.

III. AMICI CURIAE

ACLU Side (Petitioner/Appellant)

Brief of amici curiae filed on behalf of the ACLU by Arthur Garfield Hays, Walter Gellhorn, and Osmond K. Fraenkel.

Brief of amici curiae filed on behalf of the National Lawyers Guild by O. John Rogge and Andrew D. Weinberger.

Opposing Side (Respondent/Appellee)

No briefs of amici curiae were filed in support of appellee.

IV. THE SUPREME COURT'S DECISION

"The petitioner is entitled to secure legal education afforded by a state institution. To this time, it has been denied her although during the same period many white applicants have been afforded legal education by the State. The State must provide it for her in conformity with the equal protection clause of the Fourteenth Amendment and provide it as soon as it does for applicants of any other group."

The Supreme Court reversed the judgment of the Supreme Court of Oklahoma in a per curiam opinion.

V. JUSTICE VOTE

9 Pro ACLU Side vs. 0 Con Opposing Side

ACLU Side (Petitioner/Appellant)

1. Jackson, R. – Per curiam opinion
2. Vinson, F. – Per curiam opinion
3. Reed, S. – Per curiam opinion
4. Burton, H. – Per curiam opinion
5. Murphy, F. – Per curiam opinion
6. Rutledge, W. – Per curiam opinion
7. Black, H. – Per curiam opinion
8. Douglas, W. – Per curiam opinion
9. Frankfurter, F. – Per curiam opinion

VI. A WIN OR LOSS FOR THE ACLU?

The ACLU, as amicus curiae, urged reversal of the judgment of the Supreme Court of Oklahoma; the Supreme Court in a per curiam decision reversed in a 9-0 vote, giving the ACLU an apparent win.

46. Oyama v. California

(Decided January 19, 1948; 332 U.S. 633)

I. ISSUE

A. Issues Discussed

Racial discrimination, equal protection

B. Legal Question Presented

Does the Alien Land Law, as applied in this case, deprive Fred Oyama of "the equal protection of California's laws and of his privileges as an American citizen"?

C. Supreme Court's Answer

Yes, applying the Alien Land Law in this instance denies equal protection of California's law and denies privileges of an American citizen.

II. CASE SUMMARY

A. Background

Kajiro Oyama is "a Japanese citizen not eligible for naturalization." Fred Oyama is "a minor American citizen." Kajiro, Fred's father, paid for six acres of agricultural land in Southern California in 1934, when Fred was 6 years old. However, the deed was executed to Fred. In 1937, Kajiro bought as second parcel for Fred, again with the deed executed to Fred. As Fred's guardian, Kajiro was managing the land on his behalf.

"From the time of the two transfers until the date of trial, however, Kajiro Oyama did not file the annual reports which the Alien Land Law requires of all guardians of agricultural land belonging to minor children of ineligible aliens.

In 1942, Fred and his family were evacuated from the Pacific Coast along with all other persons of Japanese descent. And in 1944, when Fred was sixteen and still forbidden to return home, the State filed a petition to declare an escheat of the two parcels on the ground that the conveyances in 1934 and 1937 had been with intent to violate and evade the Alien Land Law."

"From this evidence the trial court found as facts that the father had had the beneficial use of the land and that the transfers were subterfuges effected with intent to prevent, evade or avoid escheat. Accordingly, the court entered its conclusion of law that the parcels had vested in the State as of the date of the attempted transfers in 1934 and 1937.

The trial court . . . findings were based primarily on four inferences: (1) the statutory presumption that any conveyance is with 'intent to prevent, evade or avoid' escheat if an ineligible alien pays the consideration; (2) an inference of similar intent from the mere fact that the conveyances ran to a minor child; (3) an inference of lack of bona fide at the time of the original transactions from the fact that the father thereafter failed to file annual guardianship reports; and (4) an inference from the father's failure to testify that his testimony would have been adverse to his son's cause."

The Supreme Court of California agreed with trial court's finding. On certiorari the U.S. Supreme Court reversed.

B. Counsel of Record / ACLU Attorney

ACLU Side (Petitioner/Appellant): A. L. Wirin and Dean G. Acheson argued the cause for appellant.

Opposing Side (Respondent/Appellee): Everett W. Mattoon and Duane J. Carnes argued the cause for appellee.

III. AMICI CURIAE

ACLU Side (Petitioner/Appellant)

Brief of amici curiae filed on behalf of the ACLU by Morris Grupp, Edwin Borchard, Reuben Oppenheimer, Zechariah Chafee, Jr., Nanette Dembitz, Edward J. Ennis, Osmond K. Fraenkel, Walter Gellhorn, Arthur Garfield Hays, Nels Peterson, Harold Evans, and Benjamin Kizer.

Brief of amici curiae filed on behalf of the Civil Rights Defense Union of Northern California by William E. Ferriter, James C. Purcell, and Henry Taketa.

Brief of amici curiae filed on behalf of the National Lawyers Guild by Max Radin, George Altman, Louis M. Brown, and Clore Warne.

Brief of amici curiae filed on behalf of the American Jewish Congress by Henry Epstein, Milton R. Konvitz, Will Maslow, Shad Polier, Joseph B. Robinson, and Eugene V. Rostow.

Opposing Side (Respondent/Appellee)

No briefs of amici curiae were filed in support of appellee.

IV. THE SUPREME COURT'S DECISION

"In broad outline, the Alien Land Law forbids aliens ineligible for American citizenship to acquire, own, occupy, lease, or transfer agricultural land. It also provides that any property acquired in violation of the statute shall escheat as of the date of acquisition and that the same result shall follow any transfer made with 'intent to prevent, evade or avoid' escheat. In addition, that intent is presumed, prima facie, whenever an ineligible alien pays the consideration for a transfer to a citizen or eligible alien."

"We agree with petitioners' first contention, that the Alien Land Law, as applied in this case, deprives Fred Oyama of the equal protection of California's laws and of his privileges as an American citizen. In our view of the case, the State has discriminated against Fred Oyama; the discrimination is based solely on his parents' country of origin; and there is absent the compelling justification which would be needed to sustain discrimination of that nature."

"The California law purports to permit citizen sons to take gifts of agricultural land from their fathers, regardless of the fathers' nationality. Yet, as indicated by this case, if the father is ineligible for citizenship, facts which would usually be considered indicia of the son's ownership are used to make that ownership suspect; if the father is not an ineligible alien, however, the same facts would be evidence that a completed gift was intended."

"The cumulative effect, we believe, was clearly to discriminate against Fred Oyama. . . . The only basis for this discrimination against an American citizen, moreover, was the fact that his father was Japanese and not American, Russian, Chinese, or English. But for that fact alone, Fred Oyama, now a little over a year from majority, would be the undisputed owner of the eight acres in question."

The U.S. Supreme Court reversed the judgment of the Supreme Court of California.

V. JUSTICE VOTE

6 Pro ACLU Side vs. 3 Con Opposing Side

ACLU Side (Petitioner/Appellant)

1. Vinson, F. – Wrote majority opinion
2. Murphy, F. – Wrote concurring opinion
3. Rutledge, W. – Joined Murphy's concurrence
4. Black, H. – Wrote concurring opinion
5. Douglas, W. – Joined Black's concurrence
6. Frankfurter, F. – Joined majority opinion

Opposing Side (Respondent/Appellee)

1. Jackson, R. – Wrote dissenting opinion
2. Reed, S. – Wrote dissenting opinion
3. Burton, H. – Joined Reed's dissent

VI. A WIN OR LOSS FOR THE ACLU?

The ACLU, as amicus and counsel of record, urged reversal of the judgment of the Supreme Court of California; the Supreme Court reversed in a 6-3 vote, giving the ACLU an apparent win.

47. Musser v. Utah

(Decided February 9, 1948; 333 U.S. 95)

I. ISSUE

A. Issues Discussed

Judicial review, polygamy

B. Legal Question Presented

Whether a Utah statute's definition of conspiracy is "so vague and indefinite that it fails adequately to define the offense or to give reasonable standards for determining guilt."

C. Supreme Court's Answer

The case is remanded for the Supreme Court of Utah to interpret the statute and determine whether prosecution under the statute is appropriate given that prosecution under the statute could violate the due process clause of the Fourteenth Amendment if the statute is too vague to provide guidance for how to comply with it.

II. CASE SUMMARY

A. Background

"The appellants sought review by this Court of a decision by the Supreme Court of Utah on the ground that the State convicted them in violation of the Fourteenth Amendment to the Federal Constitution."

"Defendants were tried on an information which charged violation of § 103-11-1, Utah Code Ann.1943, in that they conspired 'to commit acts injurious to public morals . . . ' [such as] conspiring to counsel, advise and practice polygamous or plural marriage . . . ."

Petitioners were convicted, and the Supreme Court of Utah "overruled all constitutional objections and affirmed." The U.S. Supreme Court vacated the judgment and remanded for reconsideration.

B. Counsel of Record/ACLU Attorney

ACLU Side (Petitioner/Appellant): Claude T. Barnes argued the cause for appellant.

Opposing Side (Respondent/Appellee): Calvin L. Rampton argued the cause for appellee in original argument and reargument. Zar E. Hayes argued the cause in the original argument.

III. AMICI CURIAE

ACLU Side (Petitioner/Appellant)

Brief of amici curiae filed on behalf of the ACLU by Arthur Garfield Hays, Osmond K. Fraenkel, Stanley H. Lowell, and Robert Markewich.

Opposing Side (Respondent/Appellee)

No briefs of amici curiae were filed in support of appellee.

IV. THE SUPREME COURT'S DECISION

"The Supreme Court [of Utah] considered that the prosecution was under Paragraph (5) of 103-11-1 which, so far as relevant, defines conspiracy, '(5) To commit any act injurious to the public health, to public morals, or to trade or commerce, or for the perversion or obstruction of justice or the due administration of the laws.' It is obvious that this is no narrowly drawn statute. . . . Legislation may run afoul of the Due Process Clause because it fails to give adequate guidance to those who would be law-abiding, to advise defendants of the nature of the offense with which they are charged, or to guide courts in trying those who are accused.

Rehearing convinces us that questions are inherent in this appeal which were not presented to or considered by the Utah Supreme Court and which involve determination of state law. . . . We believe we should not pass upon the questions raised here until the Supreme Court of Utah has had opportunity to deal with this ultimate issue of federal law and with any state law questions relevant to it. . . .

In order that the controversy may be restored to the control of the Supreme Court of Utah, its present judgment is vacated and the cause is remanded for proceedings not inconsistent herewith."

V. JUSTICE VOTE

6 Pro ACLU Side vs. 3 Con Opposing Side

ACLU Side (Petitioner/Appellant)

1. Jackson, R. – Wrote majority opinion
2. Black, H. – Concurred in the result
3. Reed, S. – Joined majority opinion
4. Frankfurter, F. – Joined majority opinion
5. Burton, H. – Joined majority opinion
6. Vinson, F. – Joined majority opinion

Opposing Side (Respondent/Appellee)

1. Rutledge, W. – Wrote dissenting opinion
2. Douglas, W. – Joined dissenting opinion
3. Murphy, F. – Joined dissenting opinion

VI. A WIN OR LOSS FOR THE ACLU?

The ACLU, as amicus curiae, urged reversal of the judgment of the Supreme Court of Utah; the U.S. Supreme Court vacated in a 6-3 vote, giving the ACLU an apparent win.

48. Illinois ex rel. McCollum v. Board of Education

(Decided March 8, 1948; 333 U.S. 203)

I. ISSUE

A. Issues Discussed

Separation of church and state

B. Legal Question Presented

Under the First Amendment, can a board of education properly grant permission to religious groups to offer religious instruction to pupils in public schools during the regular school hours?

C. Supreme Court's Answer

No, religious education of this nature in pubic schools violates the First Amendment.

II. CASE SUMMARY

A. Background

Appellant "alleged that religious teachers, employed by private religious groups, were permitted to come weekly into the school buildings during the regular hours set apart for secular teaching, and then and there for a period of thirty minutes substitute their religious teaching for the secular education provided under the compulsory education law. The petitioner charged that this joint public-school religious-group program violated the First and Fourteenth Amendments to the United States Constitution."

Appellant's "petition for mandamus was denied on the ground that the school's religious instruction program violated neither the federal nor state constitutional provisions invoked by the appellant. On appeal the State Supreme Court affirmed."

On appeal the U.S. Supreme Court reversed the judgment of the Supreme Court of Illinois.

B. Counsel of Record/ACLU Attorney

ACLU Side (Petitioner/Appellant): Walter F. Dodd and Edward R. Burke argued the cause for appellant.

Opposing Side (Respondent/Appellee): Owen Rall and John L. Franklin argued the cause for appellee.

III. AMICI CURIAE

ACLU Side (Petitioner/Appellant)

Brief of amici curiae filed on behalf of the ACLU by Kenneth W. Greenawalt, Whitney N. Seymour, R. Lawrence Siegel, Edgar Bernhard, Leon Despres, Russell Whitman, John D. Miller, William L. Marbury, Thomas H. Eliot, Winthrop Wadleigh, and Gurney Edwards.

Brief of amici curiae filed on behalf of the Synagogue Council of America by Henry Epstein, Leo Pfeffer, Newman Levy, Arnold Forster, and Samuel Rothstein.

Brief of amici curiae filed on behalf of the American Ethical Union by Herbert A. Wolff.

Brief of amici curiae filed on behalf of the Joint Conference Committee on Public Relations of several Baptist Conventions by E. Hilton Jackson, Challen B. Ellis, W. D. Jamieson, and Kahl K. Spriggs.

Brief of amici curiae filed on behalf of the American Unitarian Association by Edward C. Park and Frank B. Frederick.

Brief of amici curiae filed on behalf of the General Conference of Seventh Day Adventists by Homer Cummings and William D. Donnelly.

Opposing Side (Respondent/Appellee)

Brief of amici curiae filed by Attorney General of Illinois George F. Barrett and William C. Wines.

Brief of amici curiae filed on behalf of the Protestant Council of the City of New York by Charles H. Tuttle.

IV. THE SUPREME COURT'S DECISION

The facts "show the use of tax-supported property for religious instruction and the close cooperation between the school authorities and the religious council in promoting religious education. . . . Pupils compelled by law to go to school for secular education are released in part from their legal duty upon the condition that they attend the religious classes. This is beyond all question a utilization of the tax-established and tax-supported public school system to aid religious groups to spread their faith. And it falls squarely under the ban of the First Amendment . . . .

Here not only are the state's tax-supported public school buildings used for the dissemination of religious doctrines. The State also affords sectarian groups an invaluable aid in that it helps to provide pupils for their religious classes through use of the state's compulsory public school machinery. This is not separation of Church and State."

The U.S. Supreme Court reversed the judgment of the Supreme Court of Illinois.

V. JUSTICE VOTE

8 Pro ACLU Side vs. 1 Con Opposing Side

ACLU Side (Petitioner/Appellant)

1. Black, H. – Wrote majority opinion
2. Jackson, R. – Wrote concurring opinion and joined Frankfurter's concurrence
3. Frankfurter, F. – Wrote concurring opinion

4. Rutledge, W. – Joined Frankfurter's concurrence
5. Burton, H. – Joined Frankfurter's concurrence
6. Vinson, F. – Joined majority opinion
7. Murphy, F. – Joined majority opinion
8. Douglas, W. – Joined majority opinion

Opposing Side (Respondent/Appellee)

1. Reed, S. – Wrote dissenting opinion

VI. A WIN OR LOSS FOR THE ACLU?

The ACLU, as amicus curiae, urged reversal of the judgment of the Supreme Court of Illinois; the U.S. Supreme Court reversed in an 8-1 vote, giving the ACLU an apparent win.

49. Winters v. New York

(Decided March 29, 1948; 333 U.S. 507)

I. ISSUE

A. Issues Discussed

Freedom of speech and of the press

B. Legal Question Presented

Is a New York Penal Law, which prohibits the distribution and sale of printed materials "made up of criminal news, police reports, or accounts of criminal deeds, or pictures, or stories of deeds of bloodshed, lust or crime," so "vague and indefinite" that it "violates the right of free speech and press"?

C. Supreme Court's Answer

Yes, the statute is so vague as to violate the freedom of speech and of the press.

II. CASE SUMMARY

A. Background

Appellant is a "New York City bookdealer, convicted . . . of a misdemeanor for having in his possession with intent to sell certain magazines charged to violate subsection 2 of s 1141 of the New York Penal Law," which prohibits the sale or distribution of "any book, pamphlet, magazine, newspaper or other printed paper devoted to the publication, and principally made up of criminal news, police reports, or accounts of criminal deeds, or pictures, or stories of deeds of bloodshed, lust or crime."

The Appellant challenged the validity of the statute claiming that it "violates the right of free speech and press because it is vague and indefinite."

The Court of Special Sessions of the City of New York sustained Appellant's conviction. On appeal the Supreme Court reversed.

B. Counsel of Record/ACLU Attorney

ACLU Side (Petitioner/Appellant): Arthur N. Seiff argued the cause for appellant. Emanuel Redfield argued the cause on the original argument and first reargument.

Opposing Side (Respondent/Appellee): Whitman Knapp argued the cause for appellee.

III. AMICI CURIAE

ACLU Side (Petitioner/Appellant)

Brief of amici curiae filed on behalf of the New York City Committee of the ACLU by Emanuel Redfield, Osmond K. Fraenkel, and Morris L. Ernst.

Brief of amici curiae filed on behalf of the Authors' League of America, Inc., by Sidney R. Fleisher.

Opposing Side (Respondent/Appellee)

No briefs of amici curiae were filed in support of appellee.

IV. THE SUPREME COURT'S DECISION

"The subsection of the New York Penal Law, as now interpreted by the Court of Appeals prohibits distribution of a magazine principally made up of criminal news or stories of deeds of bloodshed, or lust, so massed as to become vehicles for inciting violent and depraved crimes against the person. But even considering the gloss put upon the literal meaning by the Court of Appeals' restriction of the statute . . . we find the specification of publications, prohibited from distribution, too uncertain and indefinite to justify the conviction of this petitioner. . . .

[F]air use of collections of pictures and stories would be [precluded] because of the utter impossibility of the actor or the trier to know where this new standard of guilt would draw the line between the allowable and the forbidden publications. . . . [I]t does not seem to us that an honest distributor of publications could know when he might be held to have ignored such a prohibition. . . . Where a statute is so vague as to make criminal an innocent act, a conviction under it cannot be sustained."

The Supreme Court reversed the judgment of the Court of Special Sessions of the City of New York.

V. JUSTICE VOTE

6 Pro ACLU Side vs. 3 Con Opposing Side

ACLU Side (Petitioner/Appellant)

1. Reed, S. – Wrote majority opinion
2. Vinson, F. – Joined majority opinion
3. Murphy, F. – Joined majority opinion
4. Black, H. – Joined majority opinion
5. Rutledge, W. – Joined majority opinion
6. Douglas, W. – Joined majority opinion

Opposing Side (Respondent/Appellee)

1. Frankfurter, F. – Wrote dissenting opinion
2. Jackson, R. – Joined dissenting opinion
3. Burton, H. – Joined dissenting opinion

VI. A WIN OR LOSS FOR THE ACLU?

The ACLU, as amicus curiae, urged reversal of the judgment of the Court of Special Sessions of the City of New York; the Supreme Court reversed in a 6-3 vote, giving the ACLU an apparent win.

50. Shelley v. Kraemer

(Decided May 3, 1948; 334 U.S. 1)

I. ISSUE

A. Issues Discussed

Racial discrimination, equal protection

B. Legal Question Presented

Whether state court enforcement of restrictive covenants in these cases constitutes state action, and whether this enforcement violates the equal protection clause of the Fourteenth Amendment.

C. Supreme Court's Answer

While the covenants themselves were privately created, judicial enforcement of the convenants is impermissible state action under the equal protection clause of the Fourteenth Amendment.

II. CASE SUMMARY

A. Background

The facts of both cases are similar. Neighbors signed agreements restricting ownership and use of real estate to persons "of the Caucasian race." A number of years later, following petitioners' purchase of properties in areas subject to these restrictive covenants, respondents filed suits to enforce the covenants. Petitioners were black and had no knowledge of the restrictive covenants at the time they purchased their properties.

In the *Shelley* case the trial court denied relief based on its finding that the agreement had not become final, but on appeal the Supreme Court of Missouri reversed the judgment. In the *McGhee* case the trial court "enjoined and restrained" petitioners from using the property and on appeal the Supreme Court of Michigan affirmed.

On certiorari the U.S. Supreme Court reversed the judgments of the Supreme Courts of Missouri and Michigan.

B. Counsel of Record/ACLU Attorney

ACLU Side (Petitioner/Appellant): George L. Vaughn, Herman Willer, Thurgood Marshall, and Loren Miller argued the cause for appellant.

Solicitor General Perlman argued the cause as amici curiae.

Opposing Side (Respondent/Appellee): Gerald L. Seegers, Henry Gilligan, and James A. Crooks argued the cause for appellee.

III. AMICI CURIAE

ACLU Side (Petitioner/Appellant)

Brief of amici curiae filed on behalf of the ACLU by Charles Abrams, Harold I. Kahen, Victor W. Rotnem, Frederick B. Sussmann, Grover G. Sales, Francis M. Dent, Walter M. Nelson, Eugene H. Buder, Victor B. Harris, Luther Ely Smith, John R. Stockham, and Robert C. Eckhardt.

Brief of amici curiae filed on behalf of the United States by Solicitor General Philip B. Perlman.

Brief of amici curiae filed on behalf of the Civil Liberties Department of the Grand Lodge of Elks, I.B.P.O.E.W. by Perry W. Howard and William C. Hueston.

Brief of amici curiae filed by Isaac Pacht, Irving Hill, Clore Warner, and Douglas Badt.

Brief of amici curiae filed on behalf of the Human Relations Commission of the Protestant Council of the City of New York by Robert McC. Marsh and Eugene Blanc, Jr.

Brief of amici curiae filed on behalf of the American Federation of Labor by Herbert S. Thatcher, Robert A. Wilson, and Harry B. Merican.

Brief of amici curiae filed on behalf of the Nonsectarian Anti-Nazi League to Champion Human Rights, Inc., by Julius L. Goldstein.

Brief of amici curiae filed on behalf of the Executive Committee of the General Council of Congregational Christian Churches of the United States by Melville J. France and William Kincaid Newman.

Brief of amici curiae filed on behalf of the National Lawyers Guild by Robert W. Kenny, O. John Rogge, and Mozart G. Ratner.

Brief of amici curiae filed on behalf of the Congress of Industrial Organizations by Lee Pressman, Eugene Cotton, David Rein, Frank Donner, Victor Rabinowitz, Benjamin M. Robinson, William Standard, John J. Abt, Leonard B. Boudin, Herman E. Cooper, Isadore Katz, Witt & Cammer, Samuel L. Rothbard, Maurice Sugar, Lindsay P. Walden, Leon M. Despres, M. H. Goldstein, Harry Sacher, David Scribner, Matthew Silverman, Harry Weinstock, W. A. Babcock, Jr., and Ralph Helstein.

Brief of amici curiae filed on behalf of the American Veterans' Committee by Phineas Indritz, Harry B. Merican, Irving R. M. Panzer, and Richard A. Solomon.

Brief of amici curiae filed on behalf of the American Jewish Congress by William Manslow, Shad Polier, Joseph B. Robison, Harry Kalven, Jr., Byron S. Miller, John S. Bernheimer, and William Strong.

Brief of amici curiae filed on behalf of the American Jewish Committee by Joseph M. Proskauer, Jacob Grumet, Newman Levy, Sol Rabkin, and Jacob Schaum.

Brief of amici curiae filed on behalf of the American Indian Citizens League of California by William Strong.

Brief of amici curiae filed on behalf of the St. Louis Civil Liberties Committee by Luther Ely Smith, Victor B. Harris, Harry B. Merican, and Eugene H. Burder.

Brief of amici curiae filed on behalf of the National Bar Association by Earl B. Dickerson, Richard E. Westbrooks, Loring B. Moore, and George N. Leighton.

Brief of amici curiae filed on behalf of the American Association for the United Nations by Alger Hiss, Philip C. Jessup, Joseph M. Proskauer, Asher Bob Lans, Myres S. McDougal, and Victor Elting.

Brief of amici curiae field on behalf of the American Unitarian Association by Edward C. Park and Frank B. Frederick.

Opposing Side (Respondent/Appellee)

Brief of amici curiae filed on behalf of the Arlington Heights Property Owners Association by Eberhard & Zeigler and

Lindstrom & Bartlett.
Brief of amici curiae filed on behalf of the Mount Royal Protective Association, Inc., by Thomas F. Cadwalader and Carlyle Barton.

IV. THE SUPREME COURT'S DECISION

"[T]he principle has become firmly embedded in our constitutional law that the action inhibited by the first section of the Fourteenth Amendment is only such action as may fairly be said to be that of the States. That Amendment erects no shield against merely private conduct, however discriminatory or wrongful. We conclude, therefore, that the restrictive agreements standing alone cannot be regarded as a violation of any rights guaranteed to petitioners by the Fourteenth Amendment. . . .

But here there was more. These are cases in which the purposes of the agreements were secured only by judicial enforcement by state courts of the restrictive terms of the agreements."

"We have no doubt that there has been state action in these cases in the full and complete sense of the phrase. . . .

These are not cases, as has been suggested, in which the States have merely abstained from action, leaving private individuals free to impose such discriminations as they see fit. Rather, these are cases in which the States have made available to such individuals the full coercive power of government to deny to petitioners, on the grounds of race or color, the enjoyment of property rights in premises which petitioners are willing and financially able to acquire and which the grantors are willing to sell."

"We hold that in granting judicial enforcement of the restrictive agreements in these cases, the States have denied petitioners the equal protection of the laws and that, therefore, the action of the state courts cannot stand."

The U.S. Supreme Court reversed the judgments of the Supreme Courts of Missouri and Michigan.

V. JUSTICE VOTE

6 Pro ACLU Side vs. 0 Con Opposing Side

ACLU Side (Petitioner/Appellant)

1. Vinson, F. – Wrote majority opinion
2. Black, H. – Joined majority opinion
3. Frankfurter, F. – Joined majority opinion
4. Douglas, W. – Joined majority opinion
5. Murphy, F. – Joined majority opinion
6. Burton, H. – Joined majority opinion

Reed, S. – Took no part in the decision
Jackson, R. – Took no part in the decision
Rutledge, W. – Took no part in the decision

VI. A WIN OR LOSS FOR THE ACLU?

The ACLU, as amicus curiae, urged reversal of the judgments of the Supreme Courts of Missouri and Michigan; the Supreme Court reversed in a 6-0 vote, giving the ACLU an apparent win.

51. Hurd v. Hodge

(Decided May 3, 1948; 334 U.S. 24)

I. ISSUE

A. Issues Discussed

Racial discrimination, civil rights

B. Legal Question Presented

Does judicial enforcement of racially restrictive covenants by the federal courts of the District of Columbia violate petitioners' rights protected by the Civil Rights Act?

C. Supreme Court's Answer

Yes, judicial enforcement of racially restrictive covenants violates the Civil Rights Act.

II. CASE SUMMARY

A. Background

"These are companion cases to *Shelley v. Kraemer* and *McGhee v. Sipes*," involving the enforcement of racially restrictive covenants.

"In No. 290, petitioners Hurd, found by the trial court to be Negroes, purchased one of the restricted properties from the white owners. In No. 291, petitioner Urciolo, a white real estate dealer, sold and conveyed three of the restricted properties to the Negro petitioners Rowe, Savage, and Stewart. Petitioner Urciolo also owns three other lots in the block subject to the covenants. In both cases, the Negro petitioners are presently occupying as homes the respective properties which have been conveyed to them.

Suits were instituted in the District Court by respondents, who own other property in the block subject to the terms of the covenants, praying for injunctive relief to enforce the terms of the restrictive agreement. The cases were consolidated for trial, and after a hearing, the court entered a judgment declaring null and void the deeds of the Negro petitioners; enjoining petitioner Urciolo and one Ryan, the white property owners who had sold the houses to the Negro petitioners, from leasing, selling or conveying the properties to any Negro or colored person; enjoining the Negro petitioners from leasing or conveying the properties and directing those petitioners 'to remove themselves and all of their personal belongings' from the premises within sixty days.

The United States Court of Appeals for the District of Columbia, with one justice dissenting, affirmed the judgment of the District Court."

On certiorari the Supreme Court reversed.

B. Counsel of Record/ACLU Attorney

ACLU Side (Petitioner/Appellant): Charles H. Houston and Phineas Indritz argued the cause for appellant.
Solicitor General Philip B. Perlman argued the cause for the United States as amici curiae.
Opposing Side (Respondent/Appellee): Henry Gilligan and James A. Crooks argued the cause for appellee.

III. AMICI CURIAE

ACLU Side (Petitioner/Appellant)

Brief of amici curiae filed on behalf of the ACLU by Charles Abrams, Harold I. Kahen, Victor W. Rotnem, Frederick B. Sussmann, Grover G. Sales, Francis M. Dent, Walter M. Nelson, Eugene H. Buder, Victor B. Harris, Luther Ely Smith, John R. Stockham, and Robert C. Eckhardt.

Brief of amici curiae filed on behalf of the United States by Solicitor General Philip B. Perlman and Attorney General Tom C. Clark.

Additional briefs of amici curiae were filed on behalf of the Japanese-American Citizens League, the National Lawyers Guild, the Congress of Industrial Organizations, the American Veterans Committee, the American Jewish Congress, the American Jewish Committee, the American Indian Citizens League of California, Inc., the American Federation of Labor, the National Bar Association, the American Association for the United Nations, and the American Unitarian Association.

Opposing Side (Respondent/Appellee)

Briefs of amici curiae were filed on behalf of the Federation of Citizens Associations of the District of Columbia, Inc., and Mount Royal Protective Association, Inc.

IV. THE SUPREME COURT'S DECISION

"[T]he explicit language employed by Congress . . . leaves no doubt that judicial enforcement of the restrictive covenants by the courts of the District of Columbia is prohibited by the Civil Rights Act. That statute, by its terms, requires that all citizens of the United States shall have the same right 'as is enjoyed by white citizens . . . to inherit, purchase, lease, sell, hold, and convey real and personal property.' That the Negro petitioners have been denied that right by virtue of the action of the federal courts of the District is clear. . . .

We hold that the action of the District Court directed against the Negro purchasers and the white sellers denies rights intended by Congress to be protected by the Civil Rights Act and that, consequently, the action cannot stand."

The Supreme Court reversed the judgment of the Court of Appeals for the District of Columbia.

V. JUSTICE VOTE

6 Pro ACLU Side vs. 0 Con Opposing Side

ACLU Side (Petitioner/Appellant)

1. Vinson, F. – Wrote majority opinion
2. Black, H. – Joined majority opinion
3. Frankfurter, F. – Wrote concurring opinion
4. Douglas, W. – Joined majority opinion
5. Murphy, F. – Joined majority opinion
6. Burton, H. – Joined majority opinion

Reed, S. – Took no part in the decision
Jackson, R. – Took no part in the decision
Rutledge, W. – Took no part in the decision

VI. A WIN OR LOSS FOR THE ACLU?

The ACLU, as amicus curiae, urged reversal of the judgment of the Court of Appeals for the District of Columbia; the Supreme Court reversed in a 6-0 vote, giving the ACLU an apparent win.

52. United States v. Paramount Pictures, Inc

(Decided May 3, 1948; 334 U.S. 131)

I. ISSUE

A. Issues Discussed

Monopoly, price fixing

B. Legal Question Presented

Did the District Court decree properly address the claims of price-fixing and "conspiracy to restrain and monopolize . . . interstate trade in the exhibition of motion pictures"?

C. Supreme Court's Answer

Part of the decree was deemed proper and upheld, but part of the decree was deemed improper and reversed.

II. CASE SUMMARY

A. Background

The U.S. instituted this suit under the Sherman Anti-Trust Act, to restrain a monopoly in the movie distribution and production industry.

"The complaint charged that all the defendants, as distributors, had conspired to restrain and monopolize and had restrained and monopolized interstate trade in the distribution and exhibition of films . . . . It also charged that the five major defendants had engaged in a conspiracy to restrain and monopolize, and had restrained and monopolized, interstate trade in the exhibition of motion pictures in most of the larger cities of the country. It charged that the vertical combination of producing, distributing, and exhibiting motion pictures by each of the five major defendants violated s 1 and s 2 of the Act. It charged that each distributor-defendant had entered into various contracts with exhibitors which unreasonably restrained trade."

The District Court issued a decree prohibiting the practices of fixing minimum prices, of licensing copywritten movies in blocks, of joint ownership of theaters by distributors and exhibitors, and several other provisions. The District Court also issued a competitive bidding proclamation, where every movie would be licensed on an individual basis, to the highest bidder in any particular area. On appeal the Supreme Court affirmed in part and reversed in part the judgment of the District Court for the Southern District of New York.

B. Counsel of Record/ACLU Attorney

ACLU Side (Petitioner/Appellant): Attorney General Tom C. Clark, Assistant Attorney General John F. Sonnett, and Special Assistant to the Attorney General Robert L. Wright argued the cause for appellant.

Opposing Side (Respondent/Appellee): John W. Davis, William J. Donovan, Joseph M. Proskauer, James F. Byrnes, Whitney North Seymour, Louis D. Frohlich, George A. Raftery, Thomas Turner Cooke, Thurman Arnold, John G. Jackson, and Robert T. Barton, Jr., argued the cause for appellees.

III. AMICI CURIAE

ACLU Side (Petitioner/Appellant)

Brief of amici curiae filed on behalf of the ACLU by H. William Fitelson, James Lawrence Fly, Harold J. Sherman, C. Dickerman Williams, Wendell Berge, and George H. Dession.

Brief of amici curiae filed on behalf of the Conference of Independent Exhibitors' Associations, Independent Members of the Motion Pictures Theater Owners of America, Society of Independent Motion Picture Producers, urging modification to the lower court's judgment.

Opposing Side (Respondent/Appellee)

No briefs of amici curiae were filed in support of appellee.

IV. THE SUPREME COURT'S DECISION

The Supreme Court upheld the prohibition against minimum prices, block booking, joint ownership, and master franchises. However, the Court struck down the competitive bidding provision because it was not likely to bring about the desired result of involving small independent distributors, and because it was not clear whether bids could be fairly compared, given that some theaters pay a percentage, while others pay a flat fee, and the length of runs and the frequency of shows often affects the licensing cost, further complicating a fair comparison. In addition, "competitive bidding involves the judiciary so deeply in the daily operation of this nation-wide business and promises such dubious benefits that it should not be undertaken."

The Supreme Court affirmed in part and reversed in part the judgment of the District Court for the Southern District of New York.

V. JUSTICE VOTE

1 Pro ACLU Side vs. 7 Con Opposing Side

ACLU Side (Petitioner/Appellant)

1. Frankfurter, F. – Wrote dissenting opinion

Opposing Side (Respondent/Appellee)

1. Douglas, W. – Wrote majority opinion
2. Vinson, F. – Joined majority opinion
3. Black, H. – Joined majority opinion
4. Reed, S. – Joined majority opinion
5. Murphy, F. – Joined majority opinion
6. Rutledge, W. – Joined majority opinion
7. Burton, H. – Joined majority opinion

Jackson, R – Took no part in the decision

VI. A WIN OR LOSS FOR THE ACLU?

The ACLU, as amicus curiae, urged affirmance of the judgment of the District Court for the Southern District of New York; the Supreme Court affirmed in part and reversed in part in a 7-1 vote, giving the ACLU an apparent loss.

53. Price v. Johnston

(Decided May 24, 1948; 334 U.S. 266)

I. ISSUE

A. Issues Discussed

Habeas corpus

B. Legal Question Presented

Did Petitioner so abuse the writ of habeas corpus as to bar consideration of his allegation, first made in his fourth petition, that the prosecution knowingly used false testimony to obtain a conviction?

C. Supreme Court's Answer

The allegation must be further investigated at the District Court level to determine whether a hearing on the merits is appropriate. The allegation is not automatically barred because it first appeared in the fourth petition for habeas corpus.

II. CASE SUMMARY

A. Background

Petitioner Price, who was not a lawyer, wrote his own petitions for habeas corpus relief. His first three petitions were not successful. In this fourth petition, eight years after his conviction, Price alleged, for the first time, "[t]hat the government knowingly employed false testimony on the trial, to obtain the conviction." The District Court denied his fourth petition without a hearing or opinion, but based on the circumstances the Supreme Court "suspect[ed] that the court thought that the matter was known to petitioner at the time of filing the first petition and should have been urged at that time." The Ninth Circuit Court of Appeals held that it was without power to direct the petitioner's appearance in court to argue his appeal. On the merits of the habeas petition, the Circuit Court held that, absent an explanation for the earlier omissions, the District Court was correct in denying the petition.

On certiorari the Supreme Court reversed the judgment of the Ninth Circuit Court of Appeals.

B. Counsel of Record/ACLU Attorney

ACLU Side (Petitioner/Appellant): Joseph L. Rauh, Jr., argued the cause for appellant.

Opposing Side (Respondent/Appellee): Special Assistant to the Attorney General Frederick Bernays Wiener argued the cause for appellee.

III. AMICI CURIAE

ACLU Side (Petitioner/Appellant)

Brief of amici curiae filed on behalf of the ACLU of Northern California by Wayne M. Collins.

Opposing Side (Respondent/Appellee)

No briefs of amici curiae filed in support of appellee.

IV. THE SUPREME COURT'S DECISION

"An order requiring the presence of a prisoner before a circuit court of appeals to argue his own appeal is one in the nature of a writ of habeas corpus. [C]ircuit courts of appeals do have the power under s 262 of the Judicial Code to issue an order in the nature of a writ of habeas corpus commanding that a prisoner be brought to the courtroom to argue his own appeal."

"There has thus been no proper occasion prior to the fourth proceeding for a hearing and determination by the District Court as to the allegation that the prosecution knowingly used false testimony to obtain a conviction. . . . [T]he three prior applications did not raise the issue now under consideration and the three prior refusals to discharge petitioner can have no bearing or weight on the disposition to be made of the new matter raised in the fourth petition."

"[E]ven if it is found that petitioner did have prior knowledge of all the facts concerning the allegation in question, it does not necessarily follow that the fourth petition should be dismissed without further opportunity to amend the pleadings or without holding a hearing. . . . The primary purpose of a habeas corpus proceeding is to make certain that a man is not unjustly imprisoned. And if for some justifiable reason he was previously unable to assert his rights or was unaware of the significance of relevant facts, it is neither necessary nor reasonable to deny him all opportunity of obtaining judicial relief."

"To that end, we reverse the judgment below and remand the instant case to the District Court for further proceedings consistent with this opinion."

V. JUSTICE VOTE

5 Pro ACLU Side vs. 4 Con Opposing Side

ACLU Side (Petitioner/Appellant)

1. Murphy, F. – Wrote majority opinion
2. Black, H. – Joined majority opinion
3. Rutledge, W. – Joined majority opinion
4. Douglas, W. – Joined majority opinion
5. Burton, H. – Joined majority opinion

Opposing Side (Respondent/Appellee)

1. Frankfurter, F. – Wrote dissenting opinion
2. Vinson, F. – Joined Frankfurter's dissent
3. Reed, S. – Joined Frankfurter's dissent
4. Jackson, R. – Wrote dissenting opinion

VI. A WIN OR LOSS FOR THE ACLU?

The ACLU, as amicus curiae, urged reversal of the judgment of the Ninth Circuit Court of Appeals; the Supreme Court reversed in a 5-4 vote, giving the ACLU an apparent win.

54. Takahashi v. Fish and Game Commission

(Decided June 7, 1948; 334 U.S. 410)

I. ISSUE

A. Issues Discussed

Racial discrimination

B. Legal Question Presented

"[W]hether California can, consistently with the Federal Constitution and laws passed pursuant to it, use [a] federally created racial ineligibility for citizenship as a basis for barring Takahashi from earning his living as a commercial fisherman in the ocean waters off the coast of California."

C. Supreme Court's Answer

California cannot use racial ineligibility for citizenship as a basis for excluding a lawful resident alien from work as a commercial fisherman.

II. CASE SUMMARY

A. Background

"Prior to 1943 California issued commercial fishing licenses to all qualified persons without regard to alienage or ineligibility to citizenship. From 1915 to 1942 Takahashi, under annual commercial fishing licenses issued by the State, fished in ocean waters off the California coast . . . and brought his fresh fish ashore for sale. In 1942, while this country was at war with Japan, Takahashi and other California residents of Japanese ancestry were evacuated from the State under military orders. . . .

In 1943, during the period of war and evacuation, an amendment to the California Fish and Game Code was adopted prohibiting issuance of a license to any 'alien Japanese.' In 1945, the state code was again amended [and] the new amendment banned issuance of licenses to any 'person ineligible to citizenship,' which classification included Japanese. Because of this state provision barring issuance of commercial fishing licenses to persons ineligible for citizenship under federal law, Takahashi, who met all other state requirements, was denied a license by the California Fish and Game Commission upon his return to California in 1945."

The Superior Court of Los Angeles County, granted Petitioner's petition for mandamus holding that "lawful alien inhabitants of California, despite their ineligibility to citizenship, were entitled to engage in the vocation of commercial fishing on the high seas beyond the three-mile belt on the same terms as other lawful state inhabitants, and that the California code provision denying them this right violated the equal protection clause of the Fourteenth Amendment. The State Supreme Court, three judges dissenting, reversed, holding that California had a proprietary interest in fish in the ocean waters."

On certiorari the U.S. Supreme Court reversed the judgment of the Supreme Court of California.

B. Counsel of Record/ACLU Attorney

ACLU Side (Petitioner/Appellant): Dean G. Acheson and A. L. Wirin argued the cause for appellant.

Opposing Side (Respondent/Appellee): Ralph Winfield Scott argued the cause for appellee.

III. AMICI CURIAE

ACLU Side (Petitioner/Appellant)

Brief of amici curiae filed on behalf of the ACLU by Arthur Garfield Hays, Robert M. Benjamin, Edward J. Ennis, Frederick B. Sussmann, Charles de Y. Elkus, and Loren Miller.

Brief of amici curiae filed on behalf of the United States by Attorney General Tom C. Clark, Solicitor General Perlman, and Special Assistants to the Attorney General Philip Elman and James L. Morrisson.

Additional briefs of amici curiae were filed on behalf of the American Veterans Committee, the American Jewish Congress, the Japanese American Citizens League, the National Association for the Advancement of Colored People, the Congress of Industrial Organizations, the Human Relations Commission, and the Protestant Council of the City of New York.

Opposing Side (Respondent/Appellee)

No briefs of amici curiae were filed in support of appellee.

IV. THE SUPREME COURT'S DECISION

It is not "because the United States regulates immigration and naturalization in part on the basis of race and color classifications, [that] a state can adopt one or more of the same classifications to prevent lawfully admitted aliens within its borders from earning a living in the same way that other state inhabitants earn their living. . . .

We are unable to find that the 'special public interest' on which California relies provides support for this state ban on Takahashi's commercial fishing. . . . To whatever extent the fish in the three-mile belt off California may be 'capable of ownership' by California, we think that 'ownership' is inadequate to justify California in excluding any or all aliens who are lawful residents of the State from making a living by fishing in the ocean off its shores while permitting all others to do so."

The Supreme Court reversed the judgment of the Supreme Court of California.

V. JUSTICE VOTE

7 Pro ACLU Side vs. 2 Con Opposing Side

ACLU Side (Petitioner/Appellant)

1. Black, H. – Wrote majority opinion
2. Murphy, F. – Wrote concurring opinion
3. Rutledge, W. – Joined concurring opinion
4. Frankfurter, F. – Joined majority opinion
5. Douglas, W. – Joined majority opinion
6. Vinson, F. – Joined majority opinion
7. Burton, H. – Joined majority opinion

Opposing Side (Respondent/Appellee)

1. Reed, S. – Wrote dissenting opinion
2. Jackson, R. – Joined dissenting opinion

VI. A WIN OR LOSS FOR THE ACLU?

The ACLU, as amicus curiae, urged reversal of the judgment of the Supreme Court of California; the U.S. Supreme Court reversed in a 7-2 vote, giving the ACLU an apparent win.

55. United States v. Congress of Industrial Organizations

(Decided June 21, 1948; 335 U.S. 106)

I. ISSUE

A. Issues Discussed

Freedom of speech and of the press

B. Legal Question Presented

Is § 313 of the Federal Corrupt Practices Act of 1925, "which prohibits expenditures by any labor organization in connection with" certain elections, in violation of the First Amendment?

C. Supreme Court's Answer

Declining to address the constitutional issue, the Supreme Court decided the alleged violations did not fall within the scope of the Federal Corrupt Practices Act.

II. CASE SUMMARY

A. Background

The Federal Corrupt Practices Act, as amended by the Labor Management Act of 1947, prohibited labor unions from making financial contributions or expenditures in connection with any federal election. In its weekly periodical, Congress of Industrial Organizations (CIO) published a letter from its president, urging union members to vote for a particular candidate for U.S. Congress. The CIO was indicted, but the District Court dismissed the indictment on the ground that the statute violated the First Amendment.

On appeal the Supreme Court affirmed the judgment of the District Court.

B. Counsel of Record/ACLU Attorney

ACLU Side (Respondent/Appellee): Charles J. Margiotti and Lee Pressman argued the cause for appellee.

Opposing Side (Petitioner/Appellant): Special Assistant to the Attorney General Jesse Climenko argued the cause for appellant.

III. AMICI CURIAE

ACLU Side (Respondent/Appellee)

Brief of amici curiae filed on behalf of the ACLU by Osmond K. Fraenkel, Arthur Garfield Hays, and Burton A. Zorn.

Additional briefs of amici curiae were filed on behalf of the American Federation of Labor, International Association of Machinists, and American Veterans Committee.

Opposing Side (Petitioner/Appellant)

No briefs of amici curiae were filed in support of appellant.

IV. THE SUPREME COURT'S DECISION

"Members of unions paying dues and stockholders of corporations know of the practice of their respective organizations in regularly publishing periodicals. It would require explicit words in an act to convince us that Congress intended to bar a trade journal, a house organ or a newspaper, published by a corporation, from expressing views on candidates or political proposals in the regular course of its publication. It is unduly stretching language to say that the members or stockholders are unwilling participants in such normal organizational activities, including the advocacy thereby of governmental policies affecting their interests, and the support thereby of candidates thought to be favorable to their interests. . . .

We are unwilling to say that Congress by its prohibition against corporations or labor organizations making an 'expenditure in connection with any election' of candidates for federal office intended to outlaw such a publication. We do not think s 313 reaches such a use of corporate or labor organization funds. We express no opinion as to the scope of this section where different circumstances exist and none upon the constitutionality of the section."

The Supreme Court affirmed the judgment of the District Court without addressing the question of whether the prohibition was unconstitutional.

V. JUSTICE VOTE

9 Pro ACLU Side vs. 0 Con Opposing Side

ACLU Side (Respondent/Appellee)

1. Reed, S. – Wrote majority opinion
2. Frankfurter, F. – Wrote concurring opinion
3. Rutledge, W. – Wrote concurring opinion
4. Black, H. – Joined Rutledge's concurrence
5. Douglas, W. – Joined Rutledge's concurrence
6. Murphy, F. – Joined Rutledge's concurrence
7. Vinson, F. – Joined majority opinion
8. Burton, H. – Joined majority opinion
9. Jackson, R. – Joined majority opinion

VI. A WIN OR LOSS FOR THE ACLU?

The ACLU, as amicus curiae, urged affirmance of the judgment of the District Court; the Supreme Court affirmed in a 9-0 vote, giving the ACLU an apparent win.

56. Kovacs v. Cooper

(Decided January 31, 1949; 336 U.S. 77)

I. ISSUE

A. Issues Discussed

Freedom of speech

B. Legal Question Presented

Is a city ordinance, which prohibits amplified sound from moving or standing vehicles on city streets, in contravention of the right of free speech?

C. Supreme Court's Answer

A city prohibiting amplified sound does not infringe freedom of speech.

II. CASE SUMMARY

A. Background

Petitioner was found guilty of violating a Trenton, New Jersey city ordinance which prohibited the operation of sound amplifiers which produce "loud and raucous noises" on city streets. The defendant was broadcasting loud music and spoke through an amplifier, apparently "comment[ing] on a labor dispute then in progress in Trenton."

Petitioner's conviction by the police judge of the City of Trenton was upheld by the New Jersey Supreme Court. On appeal the U.S. Supreme Court affirmed.

B. Counsel of Record/ACLU Attorney

ACLU Side (Petitioner/Appellant): George Pellettieri argued the cause for appellant.

Opposing Side (Respondent/Appellee): Louis Josephson argued the cause for appellee.

III. AMICI CURIAE

ACLU Side (Petitioner/Appellant)

Brief of amici curiae filed on behalf of the ACLU by Osmond K. Fraenkel, Stanley H. Lowell, James A. Major, Emil Oxfeld, and Samuel Rothbard.

Brief of amici curiae filed on behalf of the Congress of Industrial Organizations and Certain of Its Affiliated Organizations.

Opposing Side (Respondent/Appellee)

No briefs of amici curiae were filed in support of appellee.

IV. THE SUPREME COURT'S DECISION

"We think it is a permissible exercise of legislative discretion to bar sound trucks with broadcasts of public interest, amplified to a loud and raucous volume, from the public ways of municipalities. . . . The right of free speech is guaranteed every citizen that he may reach the minds of willing listeners and to do so there must be opportunity to win their attention. This is the phase of freedom of speech that is involved here. We do not think the Trenton ordinance abridges that freedom. It is an extravagant extension of due process to say that because of it a city cannot forbid talking on the streets through a loud speaker in a loud and raucous tone."

"Section 4 of the ordinance bars sound trucks from broadcasting in a loud and raucous manner on the streets. There is no restriction upon the communication of ideas or discussion of issues by the human voice, by newspapers, by pamphlets, by dodgers. We think that the need for reasonable protection in the homes or business houses from the distracting noises of vehicles equipped with such sound amplifying devices justifies the ordinance."

The U.S. Supreme Court affirmed the judgment of the Supreme Court of New Jersey.

V. JUSTICE VOTE

4 Pro ACLU Side vs. 5 Con Opposing Side

ACLU Side (Petitioner/Appellant)

1. Black, H. – Wrote dissenting opinion
2. Douglas, W. – Joined Black's dissent
3. Rutledge, W. – Wrote dissenting opinion
4. Murphy, F. – Joined the dissent without an opinion

Opposing Side (Respondent/Appellee)

1. Reed, S. – Wrote majority opinion
2. Vinson, F. – Joined majority opinion
3. Burton, H. – Joined majority opinion
4. Frankfurter, F. – Wrote concurring opinion
5. Jackson, R. – Wrote concurring opinion

VI. A WIN OR LOSS FOR THE ACLU?

The ACLU, as amicus curiae, urged reversal of the judgment of the Supreme Court of New Jersey; the Supreme Court affirmed in a 5-4 vote, giving the ACLU an apparent loss.

57. Stainback v. Mo Hock Ke Lok Po

(Decided March 14, 1949; 336 U.S. 368)

I. ISSUE

A. Issues Discussed

Judicial review

B. Legal Question Presented

Did Congress intend that Judicial Code section 266, which provides for the review of cases by a special three-judge court, apply in the Territory of Hawaii under circumstances that would require its application in a similar suit in a state?

C. Supreme Court's Answer

No, Judicial Code section 266 does not apply in Hawaii.

II. CASE SUMMARY

A. Background

Two cases with the same parties, No. 52 and No. 474, were combined for decision by the Supreme Court.

Chinese schools in Hawaii were closed in 1941 pursuant to an act "Regulating the Teaching of Foreign Languages to Children" in Hawaii, which regulated the ability to teach foreign languages in schools.

"The complaint alleged that in violation of the Fifth Amendment the Act deprived plaintiff schools of the right to manage their property by contracting with instructors and parents for the teaching of Chinese, and the plaintiff teacher of Chinese of his right to follow his occupation."

A three-judge district court, called pursuant to Judicial Code section 266, granted an injunction against enforcement of the Hawaiian Act. However, "the minute entries of proceedings and trial and the opinion re applicability of s 266, Judicial Code, show suggestions that a special district court under Judicial Code s 266 cannot be called for Hawaii."

On certiorari, the Supreme Court addressed the question of applicability of Judicial Code 266, and did not address the merits of the case. The Court dismissed the appeal in No. 52 for lack of jurisdiction and reversed the judgment in No. 474, remanding the case to the district court with instructions to dismiss the complaint.

B. Counsel of Record/ACLU Attorney

ACLU Side (Respondent/Appellee): Wai Yuen Char, A. L. Wirin, and Fred Okrand argued the cause for appellee.

Opposing Side (Petitioner/Appellant): Thomas W. Flynn, Jr. and C. Nils Tavares argued the cause for appellant.

III. AMICI CURIAE

ACLU Side (Respondent/Appellee)

Brief of amici curiae filed on behalf of the ACLU by Osmond K. Fraenkel, Murray A. Gordon, and Frank E. Karelsen, Jr.

Additional briefs of amici curiae were filed on behalf of the American Jewish Congress, Congress of Industrial Organizations, and Japanese American Citizens League.

Opposing Side (Petitioner/Appellant)

No briefs of amici curiae were filed in support of appellant.

IV. THE SUPREME COURT'S DECISION

"Hawaii is still a territory but a territory in which the Constitution and laws of the United States generally are applicable. [The] jurisdiction of this Court on appeal depends upon whether or not a special three-judge court was properly called and not upon the power of this Court to review under Judicial Code s 266 . . . . When the long-established rule of strict construction of Judicial Code 266 and that of protection of the docket of this Court is also considered in conjunction with the necessary interference with the normal operations of the federal judicial system by the establishment of the three-judge requirement in Hawaii, we are not persuaded that Congress intended s 266 to cover Hawaii. . . .

We hold that Judicial Code 266 is not applicable to Hawaii, that we are without jurisdiction in case No. 52 and that the appeal therein must be dismissed."

"What we have said concerning the final judgment in the District Court of Hawaii establishes that the judgment was entered by a court improperly constituted under Judicial Code s 266. . . .

We are of the view . . . that the United States District Court for Hawaii, as a matter of its discretion, should have refused to grant this injunction" because "the application of the Act to foreign language schools and teachers" should have been considered and reviewed by a Hawaiian court first. "[T]erritorial like state courts are the natural sources for the interpretation and application of the acts of their legislatures and equally of the propriety of interference by injunction."

The Supreme Court reversed the judgment in No. 474 with an order to dismiss the complaint on remand.

V. JUSTICE VOTE

0 Pro ACLU Side vs. 9 Con Opposing Side

Opposing Side (Petitioner/Appellant)

1. Reed, S. – Wrote majority opinion
2. Jackson, R. – Joined majority opinion
3. Burton, H. – Joined majority opinion
4. Vinson, F. – Joined majority opinion
5. Douglas, W. – Joined majority opinion
6. Murphy, F. – Joined majority opinion
7. Black, H. – Joined majority opinion
8. Frankfurter, F. – Wrote opinion concurring in case No. 52, dissenting in case No. 474, urging that certiorari should have been denied
9. Rutledge, W. – Joined Justice Frankfurter's opinion

VI. A WIN OR LOSS FOR THE ACLU?

The ACLU, as amicus curiae, urged affirmance of the judgment of the special district court; the Supreme Court dismissed case No. 52 and reversed case No. 474 in a 9-0 vote, giving the ACLU an apparent loss.

58. Terminiello v. City of Chicago

(Decided May 16, 1949; 337 U.S. 1)

I. ISSUE

A. Issues Discussed

Freedom of speech

B. Legal Question Presented

Whether the lower court erred in defining "'breach of peace'" as including "speech which 'stirs the public to anger, invites dispute, brings about a condition of unrest, or creates a disturbance'" when convicting petitioner for disorderly conduct under a Chicago ordinance?

C. Supreme Court's Answer

The lower court did err as speech under that definition is protected by the First Amendment.

II. CASE SUMMARY

A. Background

The petitioner addressed a large audience of members of the Christian Veterans of America, in Chicago. "Outside of the auditorium a crowd of about one thousand persons gathered to protest against the meeting. A cordon of policemen was assigned to the meeting to maintain order; but they were not able to prevent several disturbances. The crowd outside was angry and turbulent. Petitioner in his speech condemned the conduct of the crowd outside and vigorously, if not viciously, criticized various political and racial groups whose activities he denounced as inimical to the nation's welfare."

"Petitioner after jury trial was found guilty of disorderly conduct in violation of a city ordinance of Chicago . . . The judgment of conviction was affirmed by the Illinois Appellate Court, and by the Illinois Supreme Court." On certiorari the U.S. Supreme Court reversed.

B. Counsel of Record/ACLU Attorney

ACLU Side (Petitioner/Appellant): Albert W. Dilling argued the cause for appellant.

Opposing Side (Respondent/Appellee): L. Louis Karton argued the cause for appellee.

III. AMICI CURIAE

ACLU Side (Petitioner/Appellant)

Brief of amici curiae filed on behalf of the ACLU by Francis Heisler, William E. Rodriguez, Charles Liebman, and Osmond K. Fraenkel.

Brief of amici curiae filed on behalf of the American Jewish Congress.

Opposing Side (Respondent/Appellee)

No briefs of amici curiae were filed in support of appellee.

IV. THE SUPREME COURT'S DECISION

"The vitality of civil and political institutions in our society depends on free discussion. . . . Accordingly a function of free speech under our system of government is to invite dispute. It may indeed best serve its high purpose when it induces a condition of unrest, creates dissatisfaction with conditions as they are, or even stirs people to anger. Speech is often provocative and challenging. It may strike at prejudices and preconceptions and have profound unsettling effects as it presses for acceptance of an ide. . .

The ordinance as construed by the trial court seriously invaded this province. It permitted conviction of petitioner if his speech stirred people to anger, invited public dispute, or brought about a condition of unrest. A conviction resting on any of those grounds may not stand."

The U.S. Supreme Court reversed the judgment of the Supreme Court of Illinois.

V. JUSTICE VOTE

5 Pro ACLU Side vs. 4 Con Opposing Side

ACLU Side (Petitioner/Appellant)

1. Douglas, W. – Wrote majority opinion
2. Murphy, F. – Joined majority opinion
3. Black, H. – Joined majority opinion
4. Rutledge, W. – Joined majority opinion
5. Reed, S. – Joined majority opinion

Opposing Side (Respondent/Appellee)

1. Jackson, R. – Wrote dissenting opinion, joined Frankfurter's dissent
2. Vinson, F. – Wrote dissenting opinion
3. Frankfurter, F. – Wrote dissenting opinion
4. Burton, H. – Joined Jackson's dissent, joined Frankfurter's dissent

VI. A WIN OR LOSS FOR THE ACLU?

The ACLU, as amicus curiae, urged reversal of the judgment of the Supreme Court of Illinois; the Supreme Court reversed in a 5-4 vote, giving the ACLU an apparent win.

59. Sinclair v. United States

(Decided January 9, 1950; 338 U.S. 908)

I. ISSUE

A. Issues Discussed

Freedom of speech

B. Legal Question Presented

Is a husband's letter mailed to his wife banned by a statute which prohibited mailing "an obscene, lewd, and lascivious letter," and, if so, was the letter privileged or protected by the First Amendment?

C. Supreme Court's Answer

In a per curiam decision, the Supreme Court reversed the Third Circuit Court of Appeals, deciding the conviction for the letter was inappropriate in this case.

II. CASE SUMMARY

A. Background

"The appellant was convicted by the district judge, sitting without a jury, on the charge of sending an obscene, lewd and lascivious letter to his wife through the mails. Appellant's argument has failed to convince us that his conviction was not fully justified by the evidence or that the trial judge erred in point of law."[1]

The Supreme Court granted certiorari and reversed, in per curiam decision.

B. Counsel of Record/ACLU Attorney

ACLU Side (Petitioner/Appellant): David Berger and Jacob Kossman argued the cause for appellant.

Opposing Side (Respondent/Appellee): Solicitor General Perlman, Assistant Attorney General Alexander M. Campbell, John R. Benney, Robert S. Erdahl, and Philip R. Monahan argued the cause for appellee.

III. AMICI CURIAE

ACLU Side (Petitioner/Appellant)

Brief of amici curiae filed on behalf of the ACLU by Emanuel Redfield.

Opposing Side (Respondent/Appellee)

No briefs of amici were filed in support of Respondent.

IV. THE SUPREME COURT'S DECISION

"The judgment is reversed. United States v. Limehouse, 285 U.S. 424 [and] Swearingen v. United States, 161 U.S. 446."

V. JUSTICE VOTE

9 Pro ACLU Side vs. 0 Con Opposing Side

ACLU Side (Petitioner/Appellant)

1. Clark, T. – Per curiam decision
2. Jackson, R. – Per curiam decision
3. Vinson, F. – Per curiam decision
4. Reed, S. – Per curiam decision
5. Minton, S. – Per curiam decision
6. Black, H. – Per curiam decision
7. Douglas, W. – Per curiam decision
8. Frankfurter, F. – Per curiam decision
9. Burton, H. – Per curiam decision

VI. A WIN OR LOSS FOR THE ACLU?

The ACLU filed as amicus curiae urging reversal; the Supreme Court in a *per curiam* 9-0 decision reversed the ruling of the Court of Appeals, giving the ACLU an apparent win.

60. United States ex rel. Knauff v. Shaughnessy

(Decided January 16, 1950; 338 U.S. 537)

I. ISSUE

A. Issues Discussed

Immigration, due process

B. Legal Question Presented

"May the United States exclude without hearing, solely upon a finding by the Attorney General that her admission would be prejudicial to the interests of the United States, the alien wife of a citizen who had served honorably in the armed forces of the United States during World War II?"

C. Supreme Court's Answer

Yes, the Attorney General has broad powers to exclude aliens, including those falling under the War Brides Act.

1 United States v. Sinclair, 174 F.2d 933 (3d Cir. 1949).

II. CASE SUMMARY

A. Background

"Petitioner was born in Germany . . . . She . . . secured civilian employment with the War Department of the United States in Germany. Her work was rated 'very good' and 'excellent.' On February 28, 1948, with the permission of the Commanding General at Frankfurt, Germany, she married Kurt W. Knauff, a naturalized citizen of the United States. He is an honorably discharged United States Army veteran of World War II. He is, as he was at the time of his marriage, a civilian employee of the United States Army at Frankfurt, Germany.

On August 14, 1948, petitioner sought to enter the United States to be naturalized. On that day she was temporarily excluded from the United States and detained at Ellis Island. On October 6, 1948, the Assistant Commissioner of Immigration and Naturalization recommended that she be permanently excluded without a hearing on the ground that her admission would be prejudicial to the interests of the United States. On the same day the Attorney General adopted this recommendation and entered a final order of exclusion. To test the right of the Attorney General to exclude her without a hearing for security reasons, habeas corpus proceedings were instituted in the Southern District of New York, based primarily on provisions of the War Brides Act. The District Court dismissed the writ, and the Court of Appeals affirmed."

On certiorari the Supreme Court affirmed the judgment of the Court of Appeals.

B. Counsel of Record/ACLU Attorney

ACLU Side (Petitioner/Appellant): Gunther Jacobson argued the cause for appellant.

Opposing Side (Respondent/Appellee): Philip R. Monahan argued the cause for appellee.

III. AMICI CURIAE

ACLU Side (Petitioner/Appellant)

Brief of amici curiae filed on behalf of the ACLU by Jack Wasserman and William B. Gurock.

Opposing Side (Respondent/Appellee)

No briefs of amici curiae were filed in support of appellee.

IV. THE SUPREME COURT'S DECISION

Pursuant to the Act of Congress of June 21, 1941, "the President on November 14, 1941, issued Proclamation 2523. This proclamation recited that the interests of the United States required the imposition of additional restrictions upon the entry into and departure of persons from the country and authorized the promulgation of regulations jointly by the Secretary of State and the Attorney General. . . . It was under [one of these] regulation[s] that petitioner was excluded by the Attorney General and denied a hearing. . . .

At the outset we wish to point out that an alien who seeks admission to this country may not do so under any claim of right. . . . In the particular circumstances of the instant case the Attorney General, exercising the discretion entrusted to him by Congress and the President, concluded upon the basis of confidential information that the public interest required that petitioner be denied the privilege of entry into the United States. He denied her a hearing on the matter because, in his judgment, the disclosure of the information on which he based that opinion would itself endanger the public security. . . .

The War Brides Act does not relieve petitioner of her alien status . . . aside from the enumerated relaxations of the immigration laws she must be treated as any other alien seeking admission. Under the immigration laws and regulations applicable to all aliens seeking entry into the United States during the national emergency, she was excluded by the Attorney General without a hearing. In such a case we have no authority to retry the determination of the Attorney General."

The Supreme Court affirmed the judgment of the Court of Appeals for the Second Circuit.

V. JUSTICE VOTE

3 Pro ACLU Side vs. 4 Con Opposing Side

ACLU Side (Petitioner/Appellant)

1. Frankfurter, F. – Wrote dissenting opinion, joined Jackson's dissent
2. Jackson, R. – Wrote dissenting opinion
3. Black, H. – Joined Jackson's dissent

Opposing Side (Respondent/Appellee)

1. Minton, S. – Wrote majority opinion
2. Vinson, F. – Joined majority opinion
3. Burton, H. – Joined majority opinion
4. Reed, S. – Joined majority opinion

Douglas, W – Took no part in the decision
Clark, T – Took no part in the decision

VI. A WIN OR LOSS FOR THE ACLU?

The ACLU, as amicus curiae, urged reversal of the judgment of the Court of Appeals for the Second Circuit; the Supreme Court affirmed in a 4-3 vote, giving the ACLU an apparent loss.

61. American Communications Ass'n v. Douds

(Decided May 8, 1950; 339 U.S. 382)

I. ISSUE

A. Issues Discussed

Freedom of speech and association

B. Legal Question Presented

"Whether, consistently with the First Amendment, Congress, by statute, may exert the . . . pressures [of section 9(h) of the Labor Management Relations Act] upon labor unions to deny positions of leadership to certain persons who are identified by particular beliefs and political affiliations" associated with Communism.

C. Supreme Court's Answer

The affidavit required under section 9(h) of the Labor Management Relations Act is constitutionally permissible and does not unduly infringe the First Amendment.

II. CASE SUMMARY

A. Background

Section 9(h) of the Labor Management Relations Act requires each officer of a labor union to file an affidavit with the National Labor Relations Board, stating that he is not affiliated with the Communist party, "and that he does not believe and is not a member of or supports any organization that believes in or teaches, the overthrow of the United States government by force or by any illegal or unconstitutional methods."

This case regroups two cases labeled No. 10 and No. 13. In both cases, the union petitioners were held to be in non-compliance with § 9(h), and therefore, the National Relations Board refused to issue orders in labor disputes in which the non-compliant unions were involved. The District Court for the Southern District of New York granted a motion to dismiss the complaint filed in No. 10, and the Seventh Circuit Court of Appeals denied relief in No. 13.

On appeal the Supreme Court affirmed the judgments of the District Court and the Court of Appeals.

B. Counsel of Record / ACLU Attorney

ACLU Side (Petitioner / Appellant): Victor Rabinowitz and Thomas E. Harris argued the cause for appellant.

Opposing Side (Respondent / Appellee): Solicitor General Philip B. Perlman argued the cause for appellee.

III. AMICI CURIAE

ACLU Side (Petitioner / Appellant)

Brief of amici curiae filed on behalf of the ACLU by Asher Bob Lans, Osmond K. Fraenkel, and Jerome Walsh.

Additional briefs of amici curiae were filed on behalf of the National Lawyers' Guild, and United Electrical, Radio, & Machine Workers of America, CIO.

Opposing Side (Respondent / Appellee)

No briefs of amici curiae were filed in support of appellee.

IV. THE SUPREME COURT'S DECISION

"There can be no doubt that Congress may, under its constitutional power to regulate commerce among the several States, attempt to prevent political strikes and other kinds of direct action designed to burden and interrupt the free flow of commerce. We think it is clear, in addition, that the remedy provided by s 9(h) bears reasonable relation to the evil which the statute was designed to reach. Congress could rationally find that the Communist Party is not like other political parties in its utilization of positions of union leadership as means by which to bring about strikes and other obstructions of commerce for purposes of political advantage, and that many persons who believe in overthrow of the Government by force and violence are also likely to resort to such tactics when, as officers, they formulate union policy."

"Government's interest here is not in preventing the dissemination of Communist doctrine or the holding of particular beliefs because it is feared that unlawful action will result therefrom it free speech is practiced. Its interest is in protecting the free flow of commerce from what Congress considers to be substantial evils of conduct that are not the products of speech at all. Section 9(h), in other words, does not interfere with speech because Congress fears the consequences of speech; it regulates harmful conduct which Congress has determined is carried on by persons who may be identified by their political affiliations and beliefs."

"Considering the circumstances surrounding the problem—the deference due the congressional judgment concerning the need for regulation of conduct affecting interstate commerce and the effect of the statute upon rights of speech, assembly and belief—we conclude that s 9(h) of the National Labor Relations Act, as amended by the Labor Management Relations Act, 1947, does not unduly infringe freedoms protected by the First Amendment. Those who, so Congress has found, would subvert the public interest cannot escape all regulation because, at the same time, they carry on legitimate political activities. To encourage unions to displace them from positions of great power over the national economy, while at the same time leaving free the outlets by which they may pursue legitimate political activities of persuasion and advocacy, does not seem to us to contravene the purposes of the First Amendment. That Amendment requires that one be permitted to believe what he will. It requires that one be permitted to advocate what he will unless there is a clear and present danger that a substantial public evil will result therefrom. It does not require that he be permitted to be the keeper of the arsenal."

The Supreme Court affirmed the judgments of the District Court and the Court of Appeals.

V. JUSTICE VOTE

1 Pro ACLU Side vs. 5 Con Opposing Side

ACLU Side (Petitioner / Appellant)

1. Black, H. – Wrote dissenting opinion

Opposing Side (Respondent / Appellee)

1. Vinson, F. – Wrote majority opinion
2. Frankfurter, F. – Wrote concurring opinion
3. Reed, S. – Joined majority opinion
4. Burton, H. – Joined majority opinion
5. Jackson, R. – Wrote opinion concurring in part and dissenting in part

Douglas, W – Took no part in the decision
Clark, T – Took no part in the decision
Minton, S – Took no part in the decision

VI. A WIN OR LOSS FOR THE ACLU?

The ACLU, as amicus curiae, urged reversal of the judgments of the District Court and the Court of Appeals; the Supreme Court affirmed in a 5-1 vote, giving the ACLU an apparent loss.

62. Hughes v. Superior Court

(Decided May 8, 1950; 339 U.S. 460)

I. ISSUE

A. Issues Discussed

Freedom of speech, due process

B. Legal Question Presented

"Does the Fourteenth Amendment of the Constitution bar a State from use of the injunction to prohibit picketing of a place of business solely in order to secure compliance with a demand that its employees be in proportion to the racial origin of its then customers?"

C. Supreme Court's Answer

The Fourteenth Amendment does not bar states from using an injunction to prohibit picketing demanding racial proportionality between employees and customers.

II. CASE SUMMARY

A. Background

"The petitioners, acting on behalf of a group calling themselves Progressive Citizens of America, demanded of Lucky Stores, Inc., that it hire Negroes at its grocery store near the Canal Housing Project in Richmond, California, as white clerks quit or were transferred, until the proportion of Negro clerks to white clerks approximated the proportion of Negro to white customers. At the time in controversy about 50% of the customers of the Canal store were Negroes. Upon refusal of this demand and in order to compel compliance, the Canal store was systematically patrolled by pickets carrying placards stating that Lucky refused to hire Negro clerks in proportion to Negro customers."

"The Superior Court of Contra Costa County issued a preliminary injunction restraining petitioners and others from picketing any of Lucky's stores . . . . [P]etitioners continued to picket [and] were found guilty of contempt for 'wilfully disregarding' the injunction . . . . The intermediate appellate court annulled the judgment of contempt, but it was reinstated on review by the Supreme Court of California."

On certiorari the U.S. Supreme Court affirmed the judgment of the Supreme Court of California.

B. Counsel of Record/ACLU Attorney

ACLU Side (Petitioner/Appellant): Bertram Edises argued the cause for appellant.

Opposing Side (Respondent/Appellee): Frank S. Richards argued the cause for appellee.

III. AMICI CURIAE

ACLU Side (Petitioner/Appellant)

Brief of amici curiae filed on behalf of the ACLU by Arthur Garfield Hays, Osmond K. Fraenkel, Joseph H. Flom, and Herbert M. Levy.

Additional briefs of amici curiae were filed on behalf of the Congress of Industrial Organizations and National Association for Advancement of Colored People.

Opposing Side (Respondent/Appellee)

No briefs of amici curiae were filed in support of appellee.

IV. THE SUPREME COURT'S DECISION

"We brought the case here to consider claims of infringement of the right of freedom of speech as guaranteed by the Due Process Clause of the Fourteenth Amendment. . . .

[W]hile picketing is a mode of communication it is inseparably something more and different. [T]he very purpose of a picket line is to exert influences, and it produces consequences, different from other modes of communication. The loyalties and responses evoked and exacted by picket lines are unlike those flowing from appeals by printed word. . . . Picketing is not beyond the control of a State if the manner in which picketing is conducted or the purpose which it seeks to effectuate gives ground for its disallowance. . . . The fact that California's policy is expressed by the judicial organ of the State rather than by the legislature we have repeatedly ruled to be immaterial. . . . California chose to strike at the discrimination inherent in the quota system by means of the equitable remedy of injunction to protect against unwilling submission to such a system. It is not for this Court to deny to California that choice from among all 'the various weapons in the armory of the law.'"

The Supreme Court affirmed the judgment of the Supreme Court of California.

V. JUSTICE VOTE

0 Pro ACLU Side vs. 8 Con Opposing Side

Opposing Side (Respondent/Appellee)

1. Frankfurter, F. – Wrote majority opinion
2. Black, H. – Wrote concurring opinion
3. Minton, S. – Wrote concurring opinion
4. Reed, S. – Wrote concurring opinion
5. Vinson, F. – Joined majority opinion
6. Jackson, R. – Joined majority opinion
7. Burton, H. – Joined majority opinion
8. Clark, T. – Joined majority opinion

Douglas, W – Took no part in the decision

VI. A WIN OR LOSS FOR THE ACLU?

The ACLU, as amicus curiae, urged reversal of the judgment of the Supreme Court of California; the U.S. Supreme Court affirmed in an 8-0 vote, giving the ACLU an apparent loss

63. McLaurin v. Oklahoma State Regents for Higher Education

(Decided June 5, 1950; 339 U.S. 637)

I. ISSUE

A. Issues Discussed

Racial discrimination, segregation, equal protection

B. Legal Question Presented

"[W]hether a state may, after admitting a student to graduate instruction in its state university, afford him different treatment from other students solely because of his race."

C. Supreme Court's Answer

A state university may not treat a student different from others based on his race as this treatment denies the student equal protection of the laws.

II. CASE SUMMARY

A. Background

"Appellant, is a Negro citizen of OklahomPossessing a Master's degree, he applied for admission to the University of Oklahoma in order to pursue studies and courses leading to a Doctorate in Education. At that time, his application was denied, solely because of his race. The school authorities were required to exclude him by the Oklahoma statutes, which made it a misdemeanor to maintain or operate, teach or attend a school at which both whites and Negroes are enrolled or taught."

Appellant requested an injunction and a District Court did not grant the injunction, but decided "that the State has a constitutional duty to provide him with the education he sought" and "to the extent the Oklahoma statutes denied him admission they were unconstitutional and void."

"Following this decision, the Oklahoma legislature amended these statutes to permit the admission of Negroes to institutions of higher learning attended by white students, in cases where such institutions offered courses not available in the Negro schools. The amendment provided, however, that in such cases the program of instruction 'shall be given at such colleges or institutions of higher education upon a segregated basis.' Appellant was thereupon admitted to the University of Oklahoma Graduate School. In apparent conformity with the amendment, his admission was made subject to 'such rules and regulations as to segregation as the President of the University shall consider to afford Mr. G. W. McLaurin substantially equal educational opportunities as are afforded to other persons seeking the same education in the Graduate College,' a condition which does not appear to have been withdrawn. Thus he was required to sit apart at a designated desk in an anteroom adjoining the classroom; to sit at a designated desk on the mezzanine floor of the library, but not to use the desks in the regular reading room; and to sit at a designated table and to eat at a different time from the other students in the school cafeteria."

The District Court denied Appellant's motion asking it to modify the order, holding that "such treatment did not violate the provisions of the Fourteenth Amendment." Before the hearing at the Supreme Court conditions of segregation improve slightly for appellant, but he still remained segregated from the other students.

On appeal the Supreme Court reversed the judgment of the District Court for the Western District of Oklahoma.

B. Counsel of Record/ACLU Attorney

ACLU Side (Petitioner/Appellant): Amos T. Hall and Robert L. Carter argued the cause for appellant.

Opposing Side (Respondent/Appellee): Fred Hansen argued the cause for appellee.

III. AMICI CURIAE

ACLU Side (Petitioner/Appellant)

Brief of amici curiae filed on behalf of the ACLU by Arthur Garfield Hays, Stanley H. Lowell, and Eugene Nickerson.

Briefs of amici curiae filed on behalf of the United States by Solicitor General Perlman and Special Assistant to the Attorney General Philip Elman,

Additional brief of amici curiae were filed on behalf of the American Federation of Teachers, American Veterans Committee, Inc., Congress of Industrial Organizations, and Japanese American Citizens League.

Opposing Side (Respondent/Appellee)

No briefs of amici curiae were filed in support of appellee.

IV. THE SUPREME COURT'S DECISION

"These restrictions were obviously imposed in order to comply, as nearly as could be, with the statutory requirements of OklahomBut they signify that the State, in administering the facilities it affords for professional and graduate study, sets McLaurin apart from the other students. The result is that appellant is handicapped in his pursuit of effective graduate instruction. Such restrictions impair and inhibit his ability to study, to engage in discussions and exchange views with other students, and, in general, to learn his profession."

"It may be argued that appellant will be in no better position when these restrictions are removed, for he may still be set apart by his fellow students. This we think irrelevant. There is a vast difference—a Constitutional difference—between restrictions imposed by the state which prohibit the intellectual commingling of students, and the refusal of individuals to commingle where the state presents no such bar. The removal of the state restrictions will not necessarily abate individual and group predilections, prejudices and choices. But at the very least, the state will not be depriving appellant of the opportunity to secure acceptance by his fellow students on his own merits.

We conclude that the conditions under which this appellant is required to receive his education deprive him of his personal and present right to the equal protection of the laws. We hold that under these circumstances the Fourteenth Amendment precludes differences in treatment by the state based upon race."

The Supreme Court reversed the judgment of the District Court for the Western District of Oklahoma.

V. JUSTICE VOTE

9 Pro ACLU Side vs. 0 Con Opposing Side

ACLU Side (Petitioner/Appellant)

1. Vinson, F. – Wrote majority opinion

2. Clark, T. – Joined majority opinion
3. Black, H. – Joined majority opinion
4. Frankfurter, F. – Joined majority opinion
5. Burton, H. – Joined majority opinion
6. Jackson, R. – Joined majority opinion
7. Reed, S. – Joined majority opinion
8. Minton, S. – Joined majority opinion
9. Douglas, W. – Joined majority opinion

VI. A WIN OR LOSS FOR THE ACLU?

The ACLU, as amicus curiae, urged reversal of the judgment of the District Court for the Western District of Oklahoma; the Supreme Court reversed in a 9-0 vote, giving the ACLU an apparent win.

64. Kunz v. New York

(Decided January 15, 1951; 340 U.S. 290)

I. ISSUE

A. Issues Discussed

Freedom of speech, prior restraints

B. Legal Question Presented

Whether a New York City ordinance, which grants broad discretion in public officials to grant or deny permits for conducting religious meetings on the streets, is an invalid prior restraint under the First Amendment.

C. Supreme Court's Answer

The New York City ordinance is an invalid prior restraint because it grants broad discretion in public officials to grant or deny permits for religious meetings.

II. CASE SUMMARY

A. Background

"New York City has adopted an ordinance which makes it unlawful to hold public worship meetings on the streets without first obtaining a permit from the city police commissioner. Appellant, Carl Jacob Kunz, was convicted and fined $10 for violating this ordinance by holding a religious meeting without a permit." Appellant, a Baptist minister, held a permit to preach on the streets until it "was revoked after a hearing by the police commissioner. The revocation was based on evidence that he had ridiculed and denounces other religious beliefs in his meetings." Appellant was arrested and convicted for preaching without a permit after he unsuccessfully attempted to obtain another permit.

"The conviction was affirmed by the Appellate Part of the Court of Special Sessions, and by the New York Court of Appeals, three judges dissenting. The case is here on appeal, it having been urged that the ordinance is invalid under the Fourteenth Amendment."

On appeal the Supreme Court reversed the judgment.

B. Counsel of Record/ACLU Attorney

ACLU Side (Petitioner/Appellant): Osmond K. Fraenkel argued the cause for appellant.

Opposing Side (Respondent/Appellee): Seymour B. Quel argued the cause for appellee.

III. AMICI CURIAE

ACLU Side (Petitioner/Appellant)

No briefs of amici curiae were filed in support of appellant.

Opposing Side (Respondent/Appellee)

No briefs of amici curiae were filed in support of appellee.

IV. THE SUPREME COURT'S DECISION

"It is noteworthy that there is no mention in the ordinance of reasons for which such a permit application can be refused. This interpretation allows the police commissioner, an administrative official, to exercise discretion in denying subsequent permit applications on the basis of his interpretation, at that time, of what is deemed to be conduct condemned by the ordinance. We have here, then, an ordinance which gives an administrative official discretionary power to control in advance the right of citizens to speak on religious matters on the streets of New York. As such, the ordinance is clearly invalid as a prior restraint on the exercise of First Amendment rights."

"Although this Court has recognized that a statute may be enacted which prevents serious interference with normal usage of streets and parks, we have consistently condemned licensing systems which vest in an administrative official discretion to grant or withhold a permit upon broad criteria unrelated to proper regulation of public places."

The Supreme Court reversed the judgment.

V. JUSTICE VOTE

8 Pro ACLU Side vs. 1 Con Opposing Side

ACLU Side (Petitioner/Appellant)

1. Vinson, F. – Wrote majority opinion
2. Clark, T. – Joined majority opinion
3. Black, H. – Concurred in the result
4. Frankfurter, F. – Wrote concurring opinion
5. Burton, H. – Joined majority opinion
6. Reed, S. – Joined majority opinion
7. Minton, S. – Joined majority opinion
8. Douglas, W. – Joined majority opinion

Opposing Side (Respondent/Appellee)

1. Jackson, R. – Wrote dissenting opinion

VI. A WIN OR LOSS FOR THE ACLU?

The ACLU, as counsel to appellant, urged reversal of the judgment of the Court of Special Sessions; the Supreme Court reversed in an 8-1 vote, giving the ACLU an apparent win.

65. Collins v. Hardyman

(Decided June 4, 1951; 341 U.S. 651)

I. ISSUE

A. Issues Discussed

Civil rights, federal

B. Legal Question Presented

Whether the plaintiffs state a valid cause of action under 8 U.S.C. s 47(3).

C. Supreme Court's Answer

Plaintiffs do not state a valid cause of action under 8 U.S.C. s 47(3).

II. CASE SUMMARY

A. Background

"This controversy arises under 8 U.S.C. s 47(3), which provides civil remedies for certain conspiracies. . . .

Its essential allegations are that plaintiffs are . . . members or officers of a voluntary association or political club organized for the purpose of participating in the election of officers of the United States, petitioning the national government for redress of grievances, and engaging in public meetings for the discussion of national public issues. It planned a public meeting for November 14, 1947, on the subject, 'The Cominform and the Marshall Plan' . . . .

The conspiracy charged as being within the Act is that defendants, with knowledge of the meeting and its purposes, entered into an agreement to deprive the plaintiffs, '. . . of privileges and immunities, . . . of the rights peaceably to assemble for the purpose of discussing and communicating upon national public issues . . . .' . . .

To carry out the conspiracy, it is alleged, defendants proceeded to the meeting place and, by force and threats of force, did assault and intimidate . . . those present at the meeting . . . .

The complaint makes no claim that the conspiracy or the overt acts involved any action by state officials, or that defendants even pretended to act under color of state law. . . .

The District Judge held that the statute does not and cannot constitutionally afford redress for invasions of civil rights at the hands of individuals, but can only be applied to injuries to civil rights by persons acting pursuant to or under color of state law. In reversing the District Court's dismissal of the complaint, the Court of Appeals for the Ninth Circuit held otherwise . . . ."

The Supreme Court granted certiorari to review the case.

B. Counsel of Record

ACLU Side (Respondent/Appellee): A. L. Wirin and Loren Miller argued the cause for appellees. With Mr. Wirin on the brief were Fred Okrand, Edward J. Ennis, Osmond K. Fraenkel, Will Maslow, and Joseph B. Robison, and William Egan Colby and Clore Warne of the American Civil Liberties Union.

Opposing Side (Petitioner/Appellant): Aubrey N. Irwin argued the cause and filed a brief for appellants.

III. AMICI CURIAE

ACLU Side (Respondent/Appellee)

Brief of amici curiae filed on behalf of the Congress of Industrial Organizations by Arthur J. Goldberg and Thomas E. Harris.

Brief of amici curiae filed on behalf of the National Association for the Advancement of Colored People by Loren Miller and Thurgood Marshall.

Opposing Side (Petitioner/Appellant)

No briefs of amici curiae were filed in support of appellants.

IV. THE SUPREME COURT'S DECISION

"This statutory provision has long been dormant. . . .

The Act, popularly known as the Ku Klux Act, was passed by a partisan vote in a highly inflamed atmosphere. It was preceded by spirited debate which pointed out its grave character and susceptibility to abuse, and its defects were soon realized when its execution brought about a severe reaction.

The provision establishing criminal conspiracies in language indistinguishable from that used to describe civil conspiracies came to judgment in United States v. Harris, 106 U.S. 629. It was held unconstitutional. . . .

It is apparent that, if this complaint meets the requirements of this Act, it raises constitutional problems of the first magnitude that, in the light of history, are not without difficulty. . . .

In the light of the dictum in United States v. Cruikshank, 92 U.S. 542, 552, we assume, without deciding, that the facts pleaded show that defendants did deprive plaintiffs 'of having and exercising' a federal right which, provided the defendants were engaged in a 'conspiracy set forth in this section,' would bring the case within the Act.

The 'conspiracy' required is differently stated from the required overt act and we think the difference is not accidental but significant. . . .

What we have here is not a conspiracy to affect in any way these plaintiffs' equality of protection by the law, or their equality of privileges and immunities under the law. . . . The only inequality suggested is that the defendants broke up plaintiffs' meeting and did not break up meetings of others with whose sentiments they agreed. . . . Plaintiffs' rights were certainly invaded, disregarded and lawlessly violated, but neither their rights nor their equality of rights under the law have been, or were intended to be, denied or impaired. . . .

We say nothing of the power of Congress to authorize such civil actions as respondents have commenced or otherwise to redress such grievances as they assert. We think that Congress has not, in the narrow class of conspiracies defined by this statute, included the conspiracy charged here. We therefore reach no constitutional questions. The facts alleged fall short of a conspiracy to alter, impair or deny equality of rights under the law, though they do show a lawless invasion of rights for which there are remedies in the law of California. It is not for this Court to compete with Congress or attempt to replace it as the Nation's law-making body.

The judgment of the Court of Appeals is reversed."

V. JUSTICE VOTE

3 Pro ACLU Side vs. 6 Con Opposing Side

ACLU Side (Respondent/Appellee)

1. Black, H. – Joined Burton's dissent
2. Douglas, W. – Joined Burton's dissent
3. Burton, H. – Wrote dissenting opinion

Opposing Side (Petitioner/Appellant)

1. Jackson, R. – Wrote majority opinion
2. Frankfurter, F. – Joined majority opinion
3. Vinson, F. – Joined majority opinion
4. Reed, S. – Joined majority opinion
5. Minton, S. – Joined majority opinion
6. Clark, T. – Joined majority opinion

VI. A WIN OR LOSS FOR THE ACLU?

The ACLU served as counsel for appellees urging affirmance; the Supreme Court reversed the Court of Appeals' decision by a 6-3 vote, giving the ACLU an apparent loss.

66. Garner v Board of Public Works

(Decided June 4, 1951; 341 U.S. 716)

I. ISSUE

A. Issues Discussed

Due process, freedom of association

B. Legal Question Presented

Whether the City of Los Angeles can constitutionally require its employees to disclose their past or present membership in the Communist Party and swear an oath to not advocate violent overthrow of the government?

C. Supreme Court's Answer

The City of Los Angeles can require government employees to both disclose Communist Party membership and swear an oath to not advocate violent overthrow of the government.

II. CASE SUMMARY

A. Background

"In 1941 the California Legislature amended the Charter of the City of Los Angeles to provide [that] 'no person shall hold or retain or be eligible for any public office or employment in the service of the City of Los Angeles'" if, generally, they have "advocated or taught the overthrow by force or violence of the government," state or federal, or been a member of a group advocating such teaching.

In 1948, Los Angeles passed an ordinance requiring all city officers and employees to take an oath swearing to not have within the past five years and not while an employee advocated violent government overthrow or become a member of a group advocating that teaching. The ordinance also required an affidavit declaring whether the employee was ever a member of the Communist Party.

"On the final date for filing of the oath and affidavit petitioners were civil service employees of the City of Los Angeles. Petitioners Pacifico and Schwartz took the oath but refused to execute the affidavit. The remaining fifteen petitioners refused to do either. All were discharged for such cause, after administrative hearing, as of January 6, 1949. In this action they sue for reinstatement and unpaid salaries. The District Court of Appeal denied relief."

On certiorari the Supreme Court affirmed.

B. Counsel of Record/ACLU Attorney

ACLU Side (Petitioner/Appellant): Charles J. Katz and Samuel Rosenwein argued the cause for appellant.

Opposing Side (Respondent/Appellee): Alan G. Campbell argued the cause for appellee.

III. AMICI CURIAE

ACLU Side (Petitioner/Appellant)

Brief of amici curiae filed on behalf of the ACLU by A. L. Wirin, Fred Okrand, Loren Miller, Edmund W. Cooke, and Clore Warne.

Opposing Side (Respondent/Appellee)

No briefs of amici curiae were filed in support of appellee.

IV. THE SUPREME COURT'S DECISION

"In our view the validity of the oath turns upon the nature of the Charter amendment (1941) and the relation of the ordinance (1948) to this amendment. [T]he Charter amendment is valid under the Federal Constitution to the extent that it bars from the City's public service persons who, since its adoption in 1941, advise, advocate or teach the violent overthrow of the Government or who are or become affiliated with any group doing so. The provisions operating thus prospectively were a reasonable regulation to protect the municipal service by establishing an employment qualification of loyalty to the State and the United States."

"[W]e [are not] impressed by the contention that the oath denies due process because its negation is not limited to affiliations with organizations known to the employee to be in the proscribed class. We have no reason to suppose that the oath is or will be construed by the City of Los Angeles or by California courts as affecting adversely those persons who during their affiliation with a proscribed organization were innocent of its purpose, or those who severed their relations with any such organization when its character became apparent, or those who were affiliated with organizations which at one time or another during the period covered by the ordinance were engaged in proscribed activity but not at the time of affiant's affiliation. . . . It appears . . . that although the city welcomed inquiry as to its construction of the oath, the interpretation upon which we have proceeded may not have been explicitly called to the attention of petitioners before their refusal. We assume that, if our interpretation of the oath is correct, the City of Los Angeles will give those petitioners who heretofore refused to take the oath an opportunity to take it as interpreted and resume their employment."

"We think that a municipal employer is not disabled because

it is an agency of the State from inquiring of its employees as to matters that may prove relevant to their fitness and suitability for the public service. Past conduct may well relate to present fitness; past loyalty may have a reasonable relationship to present and future trust. Both are commonly inquired into in determining fitness for both high and low positions in private industry and are not less relevant in public employment. The affidavit requirement is valid."

The Supreme Court affirmed the judgment of the District Court of Appeal.

V. JUSTICE VOTE

4 Pro ACLU Side vs. 5 Con Opposing Side

ACLU Side (Petitioner/Appellant)

1. Frankfurter, F. – Wrote opinion concurring in part and dissenting in part
2. Burton, H. – Wrote opinion dissenting in part and concurring in part
3. Douglas, W. – Wrote dissenting opinion
4. Black, H. – Wrote dissenting opinion

Opposing Side (Respondent/Appellee)

1. Clark, T. – Wrote majority opinion
2. Jackson, R. – Joined majority opinion
3. Vinson, F. – Joined majority opinion
4. Reed, S. – Joined majority opinion
5. Minton, S. – Joined majority opinion

VI. A WIN OR LOSS FOR THE ACLU?

The ACLU, as amicus curiae, urged reversal of the judgment of the District Court of Appeal; the Supreme Court affirmed in a 5-4 vote, giving the ACLU an apparent loss.

67. Rochin v. California

(Decided January 2, 1952; 342 U.S. 165)

I. ISSUE

A. Issues Discussed

Search and seizure, due process

B. Legal Question Presented

Whether a conviction based on evidence gathered by the police through forcibly extracting pills from petitioner's stomach violates the due process clause of the Fourteenth Amendment.

C. Supreme Court's Answer

Police violated the due process clause of the Fourteenth Amendment by obtaining petitioner's conviction using evidence gathered by through forcibly extracting pills from petitioner's stomach.

II. CASE SUMMARY

A. Background

"Having 'some information' that (the petitioner here) was selling narcotics,' three deputy sheriffs of the County of Los Angeles, on the morning of July 1, 1949, made for the two-story dwelling house in which Rochin lived with his mother, common-law wife, brothers and sisters. Finding the outside door open, they entered and then forced open the door to Rochin's room on the second floor. Inside they found petitioner sitting partly dressed on the side of the bed, upon which his wife was lying. On a 'night stand' beside the bed the deputies spied two capsules. When asked 'Whose stuff is this?' Rochin seized the capsules and put them in his mouth. A struggle ensued, in the course of which the three officers 'jumped upon him' and attempted to extract the capsules. The force they applied proved unavailing against Rochin's resistance. He was handcuffed and taken to a hospital. At the direction of one of the officers a doctor forced an emetic solution through a tube into Rochin's stomach against his will. This 'stomach pumping' produced vomiting. In the vomited matter were found two capsules which proved to contain morphine."

The capsules were admitted in evidence over petitioner's objection and he was convicted in the California Superior Court of violating a state law forbidding morphine possession. The District Court of Appeal affirmed and the Supreme Court of California denied review.

On certiorari the Supreme Court reversed the judgment of the District Court of Appeal.

B. Counsel of Record/ACLU Attorney

ACLU Side (Petitioner/Appellant): Dolly Lee Butler and A. L. Wirin argued the cause for appellant.

Opposing Side (Respondent/Appellee): Howard S. Goldin argued the cause for appellee.

III. AMICI CURIAE

ACLU Side (Petitioner/Appellant)

Brief of amici curiae filed on behalf of the ACLU by Fred Okrand, A. L. Wirin, Clore Warne, Nanette Dembitz, Edward J. Ennis, Morris L. Ernst, Osmond K. Fraenkel, Arthur Garfield Hays, Herbert M. Levy, and Edward W. Cooke.

Opposing Side (Respondent/Appellee)

No briefs of amici curiae were filed in support of appellee.

IV. THE SUPREME COURT'S DECISION

"[W]e are compelled to conclude that the proceedings by which this conviction was obtained do more than offend some fastidious squeamishness or private sentimentalism about combatting crime too energetically. This is conduct that shocks the conscience. Illegally breaking into the privacy of the petitioner, the struggle to open his mouth and remove what was there, the forcible extraction of his stomach's contents—this course of proceeding by agents of government to obtain evidence is bound to offend even hardened sensibilities. They are methods too close to the rack and the screw to permit of constitutional differentiation. . . .

To attempt in this case to distinguish what lawyers call 'real evidence' from verbal evidence is to ignore the reasons for excluding coerced confessions. Use of involuntary verbal confessions in State criminal trials is constitutionally obnoxious not only because of their unreliability. They are inadmissible under the Due Process Clause even though statements contained in them may be independently established as true. Coerced confessions offend the community's sense of fair play and decency. So here, to sanction the brutal conduct which naturally enough was condemned by the court whose judgment is before us, would be to afford brutality the cloak of law. Nothing would be more calculated to discredit law and thereby to brutalize the temper of a society. . . .

On the facts of this case the conviction of the petitioner has been obtained by methods that offend the Due Process Clause. The judgment below must be reversed."

V. JUSTICE VOTE

8 Pro ACLU Side vs. 0 Con Opposing Side

ACLU Side (Petitioner/Appellant)

1. Frankfurter, F. – Wrote majority opinion
2. Douglas, W. – Wrote concurring opinion
3. Black, H. – Wrote concurring opinion
4. Jackson, R. – Joined majority opinion
5. Clark, T. – Joined majority opinion
6. Vinson, F. – Joined majority opinion
7. Reed, S. – Joined majority opinion
8. Burton, H. – Joined majority opinion

Minton, S – Took no part in the decision process

VI. A WIN OR LOSS FOR THE ACLU?

The ACLU, as amicus curiae, urged reversal of the judgment of the District Court of Appeal; the Supreme Court reversed in an 8-0 vote, giving the ACLU an apparent win.

68. Doremus v. Board of Education

(Decided March 3, 1952; 342 U.S. 429)

I. ISSUE

A. Issues Discussed

Establishment of religion, jurisdiction

B. Legal Question Presented

Whether a New Jersey statute, which provides for reading, without comment, the Old Testament in public schools, is unconstitutional.

C. Supreme Court's Answer

The Supreme Court dismissed the appeal for lack of jurisdiction without deciding the underlying issue.

II. CASE SUMMARY

A. Background

"This action . . . sought to declare invalid a statute of [the] State [of New Jersey] which provides for the reading, without comment, of five verses of the Old Testament at the opening of each public-school day. No issue was raised under the State Constitution, but the Act was claimed to violate the clause of the First Amendment to the Federal Constitution prohibiting establishment of religion.

No trial was held and we have no findings of fact, but the trial court denied relief on the merits on the basis of the pleadings and a pretrial conference, of which the record contains meager notes. The Supreme Court of New Jersey, on appeal, rendered its opinion that the Act does not violate the Federal Constitution, in spite of jurisdictional doubts . . . ."

The Supreme Court dismissed the appeal for lack of jurisdiction without deciding the case on the merits.

B. Counsel of Record/ACLU Attorney

ACLU Side (Petitioner/Appellant): Heyman Zimel argued the cause for appellant.

Opposing Side (Respondent/Appellee): Henry F. Schenk and Theodore D. Parsons argued the cause for appellee.

III. AMICI CURIAE

ACLU Side (Petitioner/Appellant)

Brief of amici curiae filed on behalf of the ACLU by Kenneth W. Greenawalt, Martin A. Schenck, Arthur Garfield Hays, Morris L. Ernst, and Herbert Monte Levy.

Brief of amici curiae filed on behalf of the American Jewish Congress.

Opposing Side (Respondent/Appellee)

Briefs of amici curiae were filed on behalf of the Commonwealth of Pennsylvania, the City of New York, and the State Council of the Junior Order of United American Mechanics of New Jersey.

IV. THE SUPREME COURT'S DECISION

"Appellants, [are] apparently seeking to . . . assert a challenge to the Act in two capacities—one as parent of a child subject to it, and both as taxpayers burdened because of its requirements."

As to the parent-child capacity, "this child had graduated from the public schools before this appeal was taken to this Court. Obviously no decision we could render now would protect any rights she may once have had, and this Court does not sit to decide arguments after events have put them to rest."

As to the taxpayer capacity, "[t]his Court has held that the interests of a taxpayer in the moneys of the federal treasury are too indeterminable, remote, uncertain and indirect to furnish a basis for an appeal to the preventive powers of the Court over their manner of expenditure." To have standing the taxpayer should be in "possession of the requisite financial interest that is, or is threatened to be, injured by the unconstitutional conduct. We find no such direct and particular financial interest here."

The Supreme Court dismissed the appeal and did not decide

the case on the merits.

V. JUSTICE VOTE

3 Pro ACLU Side vs. 6 Con Opposing Side

ACLU Side (Petitioner/Appellant)

1. Douglas, W. – Wrote dissenting opinion
2. Reed, S. – Joined dissenting opinion
3. Burton, H. – Joined dissenting opinion

Opposing Side (Respondent/Appellee)

1. Jackson, R. – Wrote majority opinion
2. Clark, T. – Joined majority opinion
3. Frankfurter, F. – Joined majority opinion
4. Black, H. – Joined majority opinion
5. Minton, S. – Joined majority opinion
6. Vinson, F. – Joined majority opinion

VI. A WIN OR LOSS FOR THE ACLU?

The ACLU, as amicus curiae, urged reversal of the judgment of the Supreme Court of New Jersey; the Supreme Court dismissed the appeal in a 6-3 vote, giving the ACLU an apparent loss.

69. Adler v. Board of Education

(Decided March 3, 1952; 342 U.S. 485)

I. ISSUE

A. Issues Discussed

Freedom of speech, due process

B. Legal Question Presented

Do the provisions of section 12-a of the Civil Service Law of New York and provisions implementing the law, abridge the right of free speech and assembly or violate the Due Process Clause of the Fourteenth Amendment?

C. Supreme Court's Answer

The statute and its implementation neither abridges freedom of speech and assembly nor violates due process.

II. CASE SUMMARY

A. Background

Section 12-a of the Civil Service Law of New York, as implemented by the Feinberg Law, prohibits members of groups advocating violent, forceful, or otherwise unlawful government overthrow from working in public schools. Under the statute, the Board of Regents creates a list of organizations where public school employees cannot be members. "[M]embership in any listed organization, after notice and hearing, 'shall constitute prima facie evidence for disqualification for appointment to or retention in any office or position in the school system'; before one who is an employee or seeks employment is severed from or denied employment, he likewise must be given a full hearing with the privilege of being represented by counsel and the right to judicial review."

In a declaratory judgment action, the Supreme Court of New York, Kings County, "held that subdivision (c) of s 12-a, the Feinberg Law, and the Rules of the State Board of Regents promulgated thereunder violated the Due Process Clause of the Fourteenth Amendment, and issued an injunction. The Appellate Division of the Supreme Court reversed, and the Court of Appeals affirmed the judgment of the Appellate Division."

On appeal the Supreme Court affirmed the judgment of the Court of Appeals.

B. Counsel of Record/ACLU Attorney

ACLU Side (Petitioner/Appellant): Osmond K. Fraenkel argued the cause for appellant.

Opposing Side (Respondent/Appellee): Michael A. Castaldi argued the cause for appellee. Wendell P. Brown argued the cause of the State of New York, as amicus curiae, by special leave of Court.

III. AMICI CURIAE

ACLU Side (Petitioner/Appellant)

Brief of amici curiae filed on behalf of the ACLU by R. Lawrence Siegel, Dorothy Kenyon, Raymond L. Wise, and Herbert Monte Levy.

Opposing Side (Respondent/Appellee)

Brief of amici curiae filed on behalf of the State of New York by Wendell P. Brown, Attorney General of New York Nathaniel L. Goldstein, and Ruth Kessler Toch.

IV. THE SUPREME COURT'S DECISION

"[P]ersons employed or seeking employment in the public schools of the State of New York . . . may work for the school system upon the reasonable terms laid down by the proper authorities of New York. If they do not choose to work on such terms, they are at liberty to retain their beliefs and associations and go elsewhere. Has the State thus deprived them of any right to free speech or assembly? We think not."

"Membership in a listed organization found to be within the statute and known by the member to be within the statute is a legislative finding that the member by his membership supports the thing the organization stands for, namely, the overthrow of government by unlawful means. . . . Nor is there here a problem of procedural due process. The presumption is not conclusive but arises only in a hearing where the person against whom it may arise has full opportunity to rebut it. . . . Where, as here, the relation between the fact found and the presumption is clear and direct and is not conclusive, the requirements of due process are satisfied."

The Supreme Court affirmed the judgment of the Court of Appeals of New York.

V. JUSTICE VOTE

3 Pro ACLU Side vs. 6 Con Opposing Side

ACLU Side (Petitioner/Appellant)

1. Black, H. – Wrote dissenting opinion
2. Frankfurter, F. – Wrote dissenting opinion
3. Douglas, W. – Wrote dissenting opinion

Opposing Side (Respondent/Appellee)

1. Minton, S. – Wrote majority opinion
2. Jackson, R. – Joined majority opinion
3. Clark, T. – Joined majority opinion
4. Vinson, F. – Joined majority opinion
5. Reed, S. – Joined majority opinion
6. Burton, H. – Joined majority opinion

VI. A WIN OR LOSS FOR THE ACLU?

The ACLU, as amicus curiae, urged reversal of the judgment of the Court of Appeals of New York; the Supreme Court affirmed in a 6-3 vote, giving the ACLU an apparent loss.

70. Carlson v. Landon

(Decided March 10, 1952; 342 U.S. 524)

I. ISSUE

A. Issues Discussed

Immigration/Citizenship, communism

B. Legal Question Presented

"May the Attorney General, as the executive head of the Immigration and Naturalization Service, after taking into custody active alien communists on warrants, charging either membership in a group that advocates the overthrow by force of this Government or inclusion in any prohibited classes of aliens, continue them in custody without bail, at his discretion pending determination as to their deportability, under s 23 of the Internal Security Act?"

C. Supreme Court's Answer

"The refusal of bail in these cases is not arbitrary or capricious or an abuse of power. There is no denial of the due process of the Fifth Amendment under circumstances where there is reasonable apprehension of hurt from aliens charged with a philosophy of violence against this Government."

II. CASE SUMMARY

A. Background

"The four petitioners in case No. 35 were arrested under warrants . . . charging each with being an alien who was a member of the Communist Party of the United States. . . . Petitions for habeas corpus were promptly filed alleging that the detention without bond was in violation of the Due Process Clause of the Fifth Amendment and the Eighth Amendment to the Constitution of the United States, and that s 20 of the Immigration Act, as amended, was also unconstitutional. . . .

The Court of Appeals affirmed the District Court's determination that there was substantial evidence to support the discretion exercised in denying bail.

Respondent Zydok, in case No. 136, was arrested in August 1949 under a recent warrant charging that he was subject to deportation as an alien with membership in an organization advocating the violent overthrow of the Government. At that time he was released on $2,000 bail. . . .

After the effective date, September 23, 1950, of the Internal Security Act of 1950, 64 Stat. 987, respondent was again taken into custody . . . .

Thereupon respondent filed a petition for writ of habeas corpus . . . . The District Court found that petitioner was an alien and had been and was on arrest a member of the Communist Party. The court determined that there had been no abuse of administrative discretion in refusing bail and denied the petition for habeas corpus.

The Court of Appeals for the Sixth Circuit reversed the District Court . . . ."

The Supreme Court granted certiorari to review the case.

B. Counsel of Record

ACLU Side (Petitioner/Appellant): Carol King argued the cause for respondent in No. 136. With her on the brief was Alan N. Brown. Brief filed for appellant in No. 35 by John W. Porter, Ben Margolis, William B. Murrish, Rose R. Rosenberg, Stanley Fleishman, Milton S. Tyre, and Carol King, and A. L. Wirin of the American Civil Liberties Union, Southern California Branch.

Opposing Side (Respondent/Appellee): John F. Davis argued the cause for appellant in No. 136 and appellee in No. 35. With him on the briefs were Solicitor General Perlman, Assistant Attorney General Mclnerney, and Beatrice Rosenberg.

III. AMICI CURIAE

ACLU Side (Petitioner/Appellant)

No briefs of amici curiae were filed in support of appellant.

Opposing Side (Respondent/Appellee)

No briefs of amici curiae were filed in support of appellee.

IV. THE SUPREME COURT'S DECISION

"II. The Issues.—Petitioners in No. 35, the Carlson case, and respondent in No. 136, the Zydok case, seek respectively reversal or affirmance principally on the same grounds. It is urged that the denial of bail to each was arbitrary and capricious, a violation of the Fifth Amendment; that where there is no evidence to justify a fear of unavailability for the hearings or for the carrying out of a possible judgment of deportation, denial of bail under the circumstances of these cases is an abuse of discretion and violates a claimed right to reasonable bail secured by the Eighth Amendment to the Constitution. . . .

[T]he Internal Security Act of 1950 marked . . . a change of attitude toward alien members of the Communist Party . . . . Theretofore there was a provision for the deportation of alien anarchists . . . , but the Internal Security Act made Communist membership alone . . . sufficient ground for deportation. . . .

III. Constitutionality.—A. Arbitrary, capricious, abuse of

discretion.—The power to expel aliens . . . may be exercised entirely through executive officers, 'with such opportunity for judicial review of their action as congress may see fit to authorize or permit.' . . .

Deportation is not a criminal proceeding and has never been held to be punishment. . . .

The refusal of bail in these cases is not arbitrary or capricious or an abuse of power. . . .

B. Delegation of Legislative Power.—This leaves for consideration the constitutionality of this delegation of authority. . . .

We do not see that such discretion violates the Due Process Clause of the Fifth Amendment.

C. Violation of Eighth Amendment.—The contention is also advanced that the Eighth Amendment to the Constitution, compels the allowance of bail in a reasonable amount. . . . Here we meet the argument that the Constitution requires by the Eighth Amendment the same reasonable bail for alien Communists under deportation charges as it accords citizens charged with bailable criminal offenses. Obviously the cases cited by the applicants for habeas corpus fail flatly to support this argument. . . .

IV. Rearrest.—Finally, respondent Zydok argues that his rearrest on the outstanding warrant, after he had once been released on bail, was improper. . . .

Although in a civil proceeding for deportation the same branch of government issues and executes the warrant, we think the better practice is to require in those cases also a new warrant.

The judgment of the Court of Appeals in the Zydok case will be vacated and the cause remanded to the District Court for further proceedings in accordance with this opinion, with directions to order the release of the respondent Zydok unless within a reasonable time in the discretion of the court he is rearrested under a new warrant.

No. 35 is affirmed; No. 136 is vacated."

V. JUSTICE VOTE

4 Pro ACLU Side vs. 5 Con Opposing Side

ACLU Side (Petitioner/Appellant)

1. Frankfurter, F. – Wrote dissenting opinion
2. Black, H. – Wrote dissenting opinion
3. Douglas, W. – Wrote dissenting opinion
4. Burton, H. – Wrote dissenting opinion, joined Frankfurter's dissent

Opposing Side (Respondent/Appellee)

1. Reed, S. – Wrote majority opinion
2. Jackson, R. – Joined majority opinion
3. Vinson, F. – Joined majority opinion
4. Minton, S. – Joined majority opinion
5. Clark, T. – Joined majority opinion

VI. A WIN OR LOSS FOR THE ACLU?

The ACLU served as counsel for appellant in No. 35 urging reversal of the judgment of the Court of Appeals; the Supreme Court affirmed in a 5-4 vote, giving the ACLU an apparent loss.

71. United States v. Spector

(Decided April 7, 1952; 343 U.S. 169)

I. ISSUE

A. Issues Discussed

Immigration/Citizenship

B. Legal Question Presented

"[W]hether the statute [section 20 of the Immigration Act of 1917] on its face meets the constitutional test of certainty and definiteness."

C. Supreme Court's Answer

"We think it does when viewed in its statutory setting."

II. CASE SUMMARY

A. Background

"Section 20 of the Immigration Act of 1917 contains provisions designed to expedite the deportation of aliens. . . . Section 20(c) provides that any alien against whom a specified order of deportation is outstanding 'who shall willfully fail or refuse to depart from the United States within a period of six months from the date of such order of deportation, or from the date of the enactment of the Subversive Activities Control Act of 1950, whichever is the later, or shall willfully fail or refuse to make timely application in good faith for travel or other documents necessary to his departure, . . . shall upon conviction be guilty of a felony, and shall be imprisoned not more than ten years . . . .' (Italics added.)

The later (the italicized) provision of s 20(c) is involved here. Appellee is an alien who came to this country from Russia in 1913. An order of deportation was entered against him in 1930 by reason of his advocacy of the overthrow of the Government by force and violence. An indictment was returned against him, two counts of which charged him with willfully failing and refusing to make timely application in good faith for travel or other documents necessary to his departure from the United States. The District Court sustained a motion to dismiss these two counts. It held that the statute in question was unconstitutionally vague and indefinite, because it did not specify the nature of the travel documents necessary for departure nor indicate to which country or to how many countries the alien should make application. The case is [at the Supreme Court] on appeal."

B. Counsel of Record

ACLU Side (Respondent/Appellee): A. L. Wirin of the American Civil Liberties Union, Southern California Branch, and John W. Porter argued the cause and filed a brief for appellee.

Opposing Side (Petitioner/Appellant): Robert L. Stern argued the cause for the United States. With him on the brief were Solicitor General Perlman, Assistant Attorney General McInerney, Beatrice Rosenberg, and Kenneth C. Shelver.

III. AMICI CURIAE

ACLU Side (Respondent/Appellee)

No briefs of amici curiae were filed in support of appellee.

Opposing Side (Petitioner/Appellant)

No briefs of amici curiae were filed in support of appellant.

IV. THE SUPREME COURT'S DECISION

"The statutory scheme seems clear and unambiguous. The choice of a country willing to receive the alien is left first to the alien himself and then to the Attorney General. . . . The six-month period specified in s 20(c) makes clear what a 'timely' application is. . . . The forms to be filled out, the deposits to be made, the number of photographs to be furnished, and the information to be supplied will vary from country to country. But when the country to which the alien is to be deported is known, any mystery concerning the documents necessary to his departure vanishes. . . .

The statute might well be a trap if, for example, it required the alien to know the visa requirements of one or more countries. But the emphasis of the present statute is on a 'timely application in good faith' . . . . We conclude that the warning contained in the statute is sufficiently definite to free it of any constitutional infirmity of vagueness.

Another question of constitutional law is pressed upon us. It is that the statute must be declared unconstitutional because it affords a defendant no opportunity to have the court which tries him pass on the validity of the order of deportation. [W]e refrain from passing on the constitutionality of a phase of a statute until a stage has been reached where the decision of the precise constitutional issue is necessary.

It will be time to consider whether the validity of the order of deportation may be tried in the criminal trial either by the court or by the jury when and if the appellee seeks to have it tried. That question is not foreclosed by this opinion. We reserve decision on it."

V. JUSTICE VOTE

3 Pro ACLU Side vs. 5 Con Opposing Side

ACLU Side (Respondent/Appellee)

1. Frankfurter, F. – Joined Jackson's dissent
2. Black, H. – Wrote dissenting opinion
3. Jackson, R. – Wrote dissenting opinion

Opposing Side (Petitioner/Appellant)

1. Douglas, W. – Wrote majority opinion
2. Burton, H. – Joined majority opinion
3. Reed, S. – Joined majority opinion
4. Vinson, F. – Joined majority opinion
5. Minton, S. – Joined majority opinion

Clark, T – Took no part in the decision.

VI. A WIN OR LOSS FOR THE ACLU?

The ACLU served as counsel for appellee urging affirmance; the Supreme Court reversed the District Court's decision by a 5-3 vote, giving the ACLU an apparent loss.

72. Brunner v. United States

(Decided April 7, 1952; 343 U.S. 918)

I. ISSUE

A. Issues Discussed

Communism

B. Legal Question Presented

Whether a witness can be jailed for refusal to answer questions related to Communist affiliation claiming the Fifth Amendment privilege against self-incrimination.

C. Supreme Court's Answer

"Judgment reversed."

II. CASE SUMMARY

A. Background

"On August 31, 1950, the United States District Court in and for the Southern District of California . . . was engaged in the trial of a criminal prosecution . . . . The indictment charged perjury by defendant. Brunner was called as a witness in behalf of the United States.

Brunner was asked:

Q. 'Between the years 1937 and 1938 were you a member of the Communist Party in Pasadena, California?' He said: A. 'I feel I must decline to answer that on the ground that it might incriminate me.'

After considerable colloquy, in which Brunner was directed to answer by the Court, he consulted with his counsel and responded in the same manner. . . .

Later the reporter read the following question to the witness . . . :

Q. 'Did you, during that same period of time, ever see the defendant at meetings of the Communist Party?' Brunner said: 'I must decline to answer that on the ground that it might incriminate me.'

The witness gave no ground for his refusal to answer. The Court made it clear that Brunner was directed to answer . . . . Thereupon, . . . he was sentenced for contempt to a period of six months . . . .

Brunner appealed from this judgment and was released on bail by [the Ninth Circuit]."[1]

The Ninth Circuit Court of Appeals affirmed. The Supreme Court granted certiorari to review the case.

B. Counsel of Record

ACLU Side (Petitioner/Appellant): A. L. Wirin of the American Civil Liberties Union, Southern California Branch, and William B. Esterman argued the caused and filed a brief for

1 *Brunner v. United States*, 190 F.2d 167, 168 (9th Cir. 1951).

appellant.

Opposing Side (Respondent/Appellee): J. F. Bishop argued the cause for the United States. With him on the brief were Solicitor General Perlman, Assistant Attorney General McInerney, Robert W. Ginnane, and Robert S. Erdahl.

III. AMICI CURIAE

ACLU Side (Petitioner/Appellant)

No briefs of amici curiae were filed in support of appellant.

Opposing Side (Respondent/Appellee)

No briefs of amici curiae were filed in support of appellee.

IV. THE SUPREME COURT'S DECISION

"Judgment reversed. Blau v. United States, 340 U. S. 159."

V. JUSTICE VOTE

6 Pro ACLU Side vs. 2 Con Opposing Side

ACLU Side (Petitioner/Appellant)

1. Black, H. – Per curiam decision
2. Burton, H. – Per curiam decision
3. Jackson, R. – Per curiam decision
4. Vinson, F. – Per curiam decision
5. Minton, S. – Per curiam decision
6. Clark, T. – Per curiam decision

Opposing Side (Respondent/Appellee)

1. Douglas, W. – Dissented without an opinion
2. Reed, S. – Dissented without an opinion

Frankfurter, F. – Took no part in the decision.

VI. A WIN OR LOSS FOR THE ACLU?

The ACLU served as counsel for appellant urging reversal of the judgment of the Court of Appeals; the Supreme Court reversed in a 6-2 per curiam vote, giving the ACLU an apparent win.

73. Beauharnais v. Illinois

(Decided April 28, 1952; 343 U.S. 250)

I. ISSUE

A. Issues Discussed

1st Amendment, defamation

B. Legal Question Presented

"[W]hether the protection of 'liberty' in the Due Process Clause of the Fourteenth Amendment prevents a State from punishing . . . libels—as criminal libel has been defined, limited and constitutionally recognized time out of mind—directed at designated collectivities and flagrantly disseminated."

C. Supreme Court's Answer

"We find no warrant in the Constitution for denying to Illinois the power to pass the law here under attack. But it bears repeating—although it should not—that our finding that the law is not constitutionally objectionable carries no implication of approval of the wisdom of the legislation or of its efficacy."

II. CASE SUMMARY

A. Background

"The petitioner was convicted upon information in the Municipal Court of Chicago of violating s 224a of Division 1 of the Illinois Criminal Code, Ill.Rev.Stat.1949, c. 38, s 471. He was fined $200. . . .

Beauharnais challenged the statute as violating the liberty of speech and of the press guaranteed as against the States by the Due Process Clause of the Fourteenth Amendment, and as too vague, under the restrictions implicit in the same Clause, to support conviction for crime. The Illinois courts rejected these contentions and sustained defendant's conviction. . . .

The information, cast generally in the terms of the statute, charged that Beauharnais 'did unlawfully . . . exhibit in public places lithographs, which publications portray depravity, criminality, unchastity or lack of virtue of citizens of Negrorace and color and which exproses (sic) citizens of Illinois of the Negro race and color to contempt, derision, or obloquy . . . .' The lithograph complained of was a leaflet setting forth a petition calling on the Mayor and City Council of Chicago 'to halt the further encroachment, harassment and invasion of white people, their property, neighborhoods and persons, by the Negro . . . .'"

The Supreme Court granted certiorari to review the case.

B. Counsel of Record

ACLU Side (Petitioner/Appellant): Alfred A. Albert of the American Civil Liberties Union argued the cause for appellants. With him on the brief was Herbert Monte Levy.

Opposing Side (Respondent/Appellee): William C. Wines, Assistant Attorney General of Illinois, argued the cause for appellee. With him on the brief were Ivan A. Elliott, Attorney General, John T. Coburn, Assistant Attorney General, and Albert I. Zemel.

III. AMICI CURIAE

ACLU Side (Petitioner/Appellant)

No briefs of amici curiae were filed in support of appellant.

Opposing Side (Respondent/Appellee)

No briefs of amici curiae were filed in support of appellee.

IV. THE SUPREME COURT'S DECISION

"The statute before us is not a catchall enactment left at large by the State court which applied it. It is a law specifically directed at a defined evil, its language drawing from history and practice in Illinois and in more than a score of other jurisdictions a meaning confirmed by the Supreme Court of that State in upholding this conviction. We do not, therefore, parse the statute as grammarians or treat it as an abstract exercise in lexicography. We read it in the animating context of well-defined usage, and State court construction which determines its meaning for us. . . .

No one will gainsay that it is libelous falsely to charge another with being a rapist, robber, carrier of knives and guns, and user of marijuana. The precise question before us, then, is whether the protection of 'liberty' in the Due Process Clause of the Fourteenth Amendment prevents a State from punishing such libels—as criminal libel has been defined, limited and constitutionally recognized time out of mind—directed at designated collectivities and flagrantly disseminated. . . .

We are warned that the choice open to the Illinois legislature here may be abused, that the law may be discriminatorily enforced; prohibiting libel of a creed or of a racial group, we are told, is but a step from prohibiting libel of a political party. . . .

It is suggested that while it was clearly within the constitutional power of Illinois to punish this utterance if the proceeding were properly safeguarded, in this particular case Illinois denied the defendant rights which the Due Process Clause commands. Specifically, it is argued that the defendant was not permitted to raise at the trial defenses constitutionally guaranteed in a criminal libel prosecution: (1) the defense of truth; (2) justification of the utterance as 'fair comment'; and (3) its privilege as a means for redressing grievances. . . .

As to the defense of truth, Illinois . . . requires a showing not only that the utterance state the facts, but also that the publication be made 'with good motives and for justifable ends'. . . .

We find no warrant in the Constitution for denying to Illinois the power to pass the law here under attack. But it bears repeating—although it should not—that our finding that the law is not constitutionally objectionable carries no implication of approval of the wisdom of the legislation or of its efficacy. These questions may raise doubts in our minds as well as in others. It is not for us, however, to make the legislative judgment. We are not at liberty to erect those doubts into fundamental law.

Affirmed."

V. JUSTICE VOTE

4 Pro ACLU Side vs. 5 Con Opposing Side ACLU Side (Petitioner/Appellant)

1. Black, H. – Wrote dissenting opinion
2. Douglas, W. – Wrote dissenting opinion, joined Black's dissent
3. Reed, S. – Wrote dissenting opinion
4. Jackson, R. – Wrote dissenting opinion

Opposing Side (Respondent/Appellee)

1. Frankfurter, F. – Wrote majority opinion
2. Burton, H. – Joined majority opinion
3. Vinson, F. – Joined majority opinion
4. Minton, S. – Joined majority opinion
5. Clark, T. – Joined majority opinion

VI. A WIN OR LOSS FOR THE ACLU?

The ACLU served as counsel for appellant urging reversal of the judgment of the Illinois Supreme Court; the U.S. Supreme Court affirmed in a 5-4 vote, giving the ACLU an apparent loss.

74. Joseph Burstyn, Inc. v. Wilson

(Decided May 26 1952; 343 U.S. 495)

I. ISSUE

A. Issues Discussed

Freedom of speech and of the press

B. Legal Question Presented

Whether "a New York statute which permits the banning of motion picture films on the ground that they are 'sacrilegious'" violates the First and Fourteenth Amendments.

C. Supreme Court's Answer

The free speech and press protections of the First Amendment, as applied to the states by the Fourteenth Amendment, prohibit a state from banning films considered "sacrilegious."

II. CASE SUMMARY

A. Background

"The issue here is the constitutionality, under the First and Fourteenth Amendments, of a New York statute which permits the banning of motion picture films on the ground that they are 'sacrilegious.'"

"Appellant is a corporation engaged in the business of distributing motion pictures. It owns the exclusive rights to distribute . . . 'The Miracle.' On November 30, 1950, after having examined the picture, the motion picture division of the New York education department, acting under the statute . . . , issued to appellant a license authorizing exhibition of 'The Miracle,' with English subtitles, as one part of a trilogy called 'Ways of Love.' Thereafter, for a period of approximately eight weeks, 'Ways of Love' was exhibited publicly in a motion picture theater in New York City . . . .

During this period, the New York State Board of Regents . . . received 'hundreds of letters, telegrams, post cards, affidavits and other communications' both protesting against and defending the public exhibition of 'The Miracle.' The Chancellor of the Board of Regents requested three members of the Board to view the picture and to make a report to the entire Board. After viewing the film, this committee reported to the Board that in its opinion there was basis for the claim that the picture was 'sacrilegious.' Thereafter, on January 19, 1951, the Regents directed appellant to show cause, at a hearing to be held on January 30, why its license to show 'The Miracle' should not be rescinded on that ground. Appellant appeared at this hearing, which was conducted by the same three-member committee of the Regents which had previously viewed the picture, and challenged the jurisdiction of the committee and of the Regents to proceed with the case. With the consent of the committee, various interested persons and organizations submitted to it briefs and exhibits bearing upon the merits of the picture and upon the constitutional and statutory questions involved. On February 16, 1951, the Regents, after viewing 'The Miracle,' determined that it was 'sacrilegious' and for that reason ordered the Commissioner of Education to rescind appellant's license to exhibit the picture. The Commissioner did so. . . .

On appeal the New York Court of Appeals, two judges dissenting, affirmed the order of the Appellate Division."

On appeal the Supreme Court reversed the judgment of the New York Court of Appeals.

B. Counsel of Record / ACLU Attorney

ACLU Side (Petitioner / Appellant): Ephriam S. London argued the cause for appellant.

Opposing Side (Respondent / Appellee): Charles A. Brind, Jr., and Wendell P. Brown argued the cause for appellee.

III. AMICI CURIAE

ACLU Side (Petitioner / Appellant)

Brief of amici curiae filed on behalf of the ACLU by Morris L. Ernst, H. William Fitelson, Osmond K. Fraenkel, Arthur Garfield Hays, Herbert Monte Levy, Emanuel Redfield, Newell G. Alford, Jr., Robert Markewich, Elmer Rice, Herman L. Weisman, Shad Polier, Will Maslow, Leo Pfeffer, Philip Baum, Herman Seid, A. Joseph Handel, Eberhard P. Deutsch, Austin T. Walden, and William V. George.

Additional briefs of amici curiae were filed on behalf of the American Book Publishers Council, Inc., and Committee on Constitutional Liberties of the National Lawyers Guild.

Opposing Side (Respondent / Appellee)

Brief of amici curiae filed on behalf of the New York State Catholic Welfare Committee.

IV. THE SUPREME COURT'S DECISION

"[T]he present case is the first to present squarely to us the question whether motion pictures are within the ambit of protection which the First Amendment, through the Fourteenth, secures to any form of 'speech' or 'the press.' It cannot be doubted that motion pictures are a significant medium for the communication of ideas. They may affect public attitudes and behavior in a variety of ways, ranging from direct espousal of a political or social doctrine to the subtle shaping of thought which characterizes all artistic expression. The importance of motion pictures as an organ of public opinion is not lessened by the fact that they are designed to entertain as well as to inform. . . .

It is urged that motion pictures do not fall within the First Amendment's aegis because their production, distribution, and exhibition is a large-scale business conducted for private profit. We cannot agree. That books, newspapers, and magazines are published and sold for profit does not prevent them from being a form of expression whose liberty is safeguarded by the First Amendment. We fail to see why operation for profit should have any different effect in the case of motion pictures.

It is further urged that motion pictures possess a greater capacity for evil, particularly among the youth of a community, than other modes of expression. Even if one were to accept this hypothesis, it does not follow that motion pictures should be disqualified from First Amendment protection. If there be capacity for evil it may be relevant in determining the permissible scope of community control, but it does not authorize substantially unbridled censorship such as we have here.

For the foregoing reasons, we conclude that expression by means of motion pictures is included within the free speech and free press guaranty of the First and Fourteenth Amendments."

The Supreme Court reversed the judgment of the New York Court of Appeals.

V. JUSTICE VOTE

9 Pro ACLU Side vs. 0 Con Opposing Side

ACLU Side (Petitioner / Appellant)

1. Clark, T. – Wrote majority opinion
2. Vinson, F. – Joined majority opinion
3. Black, H. – Joined majority opinion
4. Douglas, W. – Joined majority opinion
5. Burton, H. – Joined Frankfurter's concurrence
6. Minton, S. – Joined majority opinion
7. Reed, S. – Wrote concurring opinion
8. Frankfurter, F. – Wrote concurring opinion
9. Jackson, R. – Joined Frankfurter's concurrence

VI. A WIN OR LOSS FOR THE ACLU?

The ACLU, as amicus, urged reversal of the New York Court of Appeals' judgment; the Supreme Court reversed in a 9-0 vote, giving the ACLU an apparent win.

75. Wieman v. Updegraff

(Decided December 15, 1952; 344 U.S. 183)

I. ISSUE

A. Issues Discussed

Due process

B. Legal Question Presented

Whether the due process clause permits a state in attempting to bar disloyal individuals from its employ to exclude persons solely on the basis of organizational membership, regardless of their knowledge concerning the organizations to which they had belonged.

C. Supreme Court's Answer

A state cannot bar employment to individuals based solely on their organizational memberships.

II. CASE SUMMARY

A. Background

"This is an appeal from a decision of the Supreme Court of Oklahoma . . . upholding the validity of a loyalty oath prescribed by Oklahoma statute for all state officers and employees. Appellants, employed by the State as members of the faculty and staff of Oklahoma Agricultural and Mechanical College, failed, within the thirty days permitted, to take the oath required by the Act. Appellee Updegraff, as a citizen and taxpayer, thereupon brought this suit in the District Court of Oklahoma County to enjoin the necessary state officials from paying further compensation to employees who had not subscribed to the oath. The appellants, who were permitted to intervene, attacked the validity of the Act on the grounds, among others, that it was a bill of attainder; an ex post facto law; impaired the obligation of their contracts with the State and violated the Due Process Clause of the Fourteenth Amendment. They also sought a mandatory injunction directing the state officers to pay their salaries regardless of their failure to take the oath. Their objections centered largely on the following clauses of the oath:

'. . . That I am not affiliated directly or indirectly . . . with any foreign political agency, party, organization or Government, or with any agency, party, organization, association, or group whatever which has been officially determined by the United States Attorney General or other authorized agency of the United States to be a communist front or subversive organization; . . . that I will take up arms in the defense of the United States in time of War, or National Emergency, if necessary; that within the five (5) years immediately preceding the taking of this oath (or affirmation) I have not been a member of . . . any agency, party, organization, association, or group whatever which has been officially determined by the United States Attorney General or other authorized public agency of the United States to be a communist front or subversive organization...'

The court upheld the Act and enjoined the state officers from making further salary payments to appellants. The Supreme Court of Oklahoma affirmed . . ."

On appeal the U.S. Supreme Court reversed the judgment of the Supreme Court of Oklahoma.

B. Counsel of Record/ACLU Attorney

ACLU Side (Petitioner/Appellant): Don Emery argued the cause for appellant.

Opposing Side (Respondent/Appellee): Paul W. Updegraff and Assistant Attorney General of Oklahoma City Fred Hansen argued the cause for appellee.

III. AMICI CURIAE

ACLU Side (Petitioner/Appellant)

Brief of amici curiae filed on behalf of the ACLU by Osmond K. Fraenkel and Nanette Dembitz.

Opposing Side (Respondent/Appellee)

No briefs of amici curiae were filed in support of appellee.

IV. THE SUPREME COURT'S DECISION

"[U]nder the statute before us, the fact of membership alone disqualifies. If the rule be expressed as a presumption of disloyalty, it is a conclusive one.

But membership may be innocent. A state servant may have joined a proscribed organization unaware of its activities and purposes. In recent years, many completely loyal persons have severed organizational ties after learning for the first time of the character of groups to which they had belonged. . . . At the time of affiliation, a group itself may be innocent, only later coming under the influence of those who would turn it toward illegitimate ends. Conversely, an organization formerly subversive and therefore designated as such may have subsequently freed itself from the influences which originally led to its listing.

There can be no dispute about the consequences visited upon a person excluded from public employment on disloyalty grounds. In the view of the community, the stain is a deep one; indeed, it has become a badge of infamy. Especially is this so in time of cold war and hot emotions when 'each man begins to eye his neighbor as a possible enemy.' Yet under the Oklahoma Act, the fact of association alone determines disloyalty and disqualification; it matters not whether association existed innocently or knowingly. To thus inhibit individual freedom of movement is to stifle the flow of democratic expression and controversy at one of its chief sources. . . . Indiscriminate classification of innocent with knowing activity must fall as an assertion of arbitrary power. The oath offends due process."

The U.S. Supreme Court reversed the judgment of the Supreme Court of Oklahoma.

V. JUSTICE VOTE

8 Pro ACLU Side vs. 0 Con Opposing Side

ACLU Side (Petitioner/Appellant)

1. Clark, T. – Wrote majority opinion
2. Frankfurter, F. – Wrote concurring opinion
3. Douglas, W. – Joined majority opinion
4. Black, H. – Wrote concurring opinion
5. Burton, H. – Concurred in the result
6. Minton, S. – Joined majority opinion
7. Reed, S. – Joined majority opinion
8. Vinson, F. – Joined majority opinion

Jackson, R – Took no part in the decision

VI. A WIN OR LOSS FOR THE ACLU?

The ACLU, as amicus, urged reversal of the Supreme Court of Oklahoma's judgment; the U.S. Supreme Court reversed in an 8-0 vote, giving the ACLU an apparent win.

76. Albertson v. Millard

(Decided March 16, 1953; 345 U.S. 242)

I. ISSUE

A. Issues Discussed

Judicial interpretation, communism

B. Legal Question Presented

Was the Michigan Communist Control Bill of 1952 unconstitutional?

C. Supreme Court's Answer

In a per curiam decision, the Supreme Court vacated and remanded for the state court to construe the bill.

II. CASE SUMMARY

A. Background

"On April 17, 1952, the Governor of Michigan signed the Michigan Communist Control Bill. On April 22, 1952, the Communist Party of Michigan and William Albertson, its Executive Secretary, filed a complaint in the United States District Court for the Eastern District of Michigan. Sections 2-5, inclusive, and Section 7 of the Act were alleged to violate various provisions of the Federal Constitution. A declaratory judgment to that effect was sought, along with an injunction to prevent appellees Millard, Attorney General of Michigan, and other state officials and officers from enforcing the Act. A three-judge District Court found the Act constitutional and an appeal was taken to this Court.

Section 5 of the Act requires the registration of Communists, the Communist Party, and Communist front organizations, and Section 7 prevents them from appearing on any ballot in the State."

On certiorari the Supreme Court issued a per curiam decision vacating the District Court's judgment.

B. Counsel of Record/ACLU Attorney

ACLU Side (Petitioner/Appellant): Ernest Goodman argued the cause for appellant.

Opposing Side (Respondent/Appellee): Edmund E. Shepherd argued the cause for appellee.

III. AMICI CURIAE

ACLU Side (Petitioner/Appellant)

Brief of amici curiae filed on behalf of the ACLU by Osmond K. Fraenkel, Nanette Dembitz, and Walter M. Nelson.

Opposing Side (Respondent/Appellee)

No briefs of amici curiae were filed in support of appellee.

IV. THE SUPREME COURT'S DECISION

"These definitions are challenged by the appellants as void for vagueness. The definition of a Communist as '. . . a member of the communist party, notwithstanding the fact that he may not pay dues to, or hold a card in, said party . . .' is said to be vague since once dues and cards are eliminated as criteria there are no readily apparent means of determining who is a member. As to the definition of the Communist Party as an organization '. . . substantially directed, dominated or controlled by the Union of Soviet Socialist Republics or its satellites' it is contended there are no standards as to what is a 'satellite.' In regard to the definition of both Communist Party and Communist front organization as an organization which '. . . in any manner advocates, or acts to further, the world communist movement' appellants point to the failure to define the 'world communist movement' as creating vagueness. The answers given to these and possibly other problems of construction and interpretation arising under the definitions in Sections 2-4 will determine the ultimate scope of the Act.

Interpretation of state legislation is primarily the function of state authorities, judicial and administrative. The construction given to a state statute by the state courts is binding upon federal courts. There has been no interpretation of this statute by the state courts. The absence of such construction stems from the fact this action in federal court was commenced only five days after the statute became law.

There is pending in the Circuit Court for Wayne County, Michigan, a bill seeking a declaratory judgment that the Act is unconstitutional, both on federal and state grounds. That action is being held in abeyance pending our mandate and decision in this case.

We deem it appropriate in this case that the state courts construe this statute before the District Court further considers the action.

The judgment is vacated and the cause remanded to the District Court for the Eastern District of Michigan with directions to vacate the restraining order it issued and to hold the proceedings in abeyance a reasonable time pending construction of the statute by the state courts either in pending litigation or other litigation which may be instituted."

V. JUSTICE VOTE

7 Pro ACLU Side vs. 2 Con Opposing Side

ACLU Side (Petitioner/Appellant)

1. Vinson, F. – Per curiam decision
2. Jackson, R. – Per curiam decision
3. Reed, S. – Per curiam decision
4. Minton, S. – Per curiam decision
5. Clark, T. – Per curiam decision
6. Frankfurter, F. – Per curiam decision
7. Burton, H. – Per curiam decision

Opposing Side (Respondent/Appellee)

1. Black, H. – Dissented without an opinion
2. Douglas, W. – Wrote dissenting opinion

VI. A WIN OR LOSS FOR THE ACLU?

The ACLU filed as amicus curiae urging reversal of the judgment of the District Court for the Eastern District of Michigan; the Supreme Court vacated the judgment in a 7-2 vote, giving the ACLU an apparent win.

77. Barrows v. Jackson

(Decided June 15, 1953; 346 U.S. 249)

I. ISSUE

A. Issues Discussed

Racial discrimination, equal protection

B. Legal Question Presented

"Can . . . a [racially] restrictive covenant be enforced at law by a suit for damages against a co-covenantor, who allegedly broke the covenant?"

C. Supreme Court's Answer

A racially restrictive covenant cannot be enforced at law against a co-covenantor for breaking the covenant.

II. CASE SUMMARY

A. Background

Homeowners in a Los Angeles neighborhood entered into a racially restrictive covenant restricting the use and occupancy of their land to only Caucasian people, and obligating the owners to incorporate this restriction in all land transfers. Petitioners, Barrows and other covenant signers, sued respondent Jackson for breaching the covenant. The complaint alleged that Jackson permitted non-Caucasians to occupy property and did not include the restrictions in the deed. No action was taken against the non-Caucasian occupants. The state courts decided in favor of Jackson in view of the holding in *Shelley v. Kramer*.

On certiorari the Supreme Court affirmed the judgment of the District Court of Appeal.

B. Counsel of Record/ACLU Attorney

ACLU Side (Respondent/Appellee): Loren Miller argued the cause for appellee.

Opposing Side (Petitioner/Appellant): J. Wallace McKnight argued the cause for appellant.

III. AMICI CURIAE

ACLU Side (Respondent/Appellee)

Brief of amici curiae filed on behalf of the Southern California Branch of the ACLU by A. L. Wirin.

Additional briefs of amici curiae were filed on behalf of the Greater Los Angeles C. I. O. Council, Japanese American Citizens' League, Los Angeles Urban League, Los Angeles International Ladies' Garment Workers' Union, National Association for the Advancement of Colored People, The Christines, Jewish Labor Committee, Los Angeles District Council Jewish War Veterans, Eagle Rock Council for Civic Unity, Los Angeles Central Labor Council, American Veterans Committee, Inc., American Jewish Committee, Anti-Defamation League of B'nai B'rith,, and National Community Relations Advisory Council.

Opposing Side (Petitioner/Appellant)

Briefs of amici curiae filed on behalf of the 48 Property-Owner Organizations and O'Fallon Park Protective Association, et al.

IV. THE SUPREME COURT'S DECISION

"Petitioners argue that the right to equal protection of the laws is a 'personal' right, guaranteed to the individual rather than to groups or classes. For instance, discriminatory denial of sleeping-car and dining-car facilities to an individual Negro cannot be justified on the ground that there is little demand for such facilities by Negroes as a group. This description of the right as 'personal,' when considered in the context in which it has been used, obviously has no bearing on the question of standing. Nor do we violate this principle by protecting the rights of persons not identified in this record. For instance, in the *Pierce* [*v. Society of Sisters*] case, the persons whose rights were invoked were identified only as 'present and prospective patrons' of the two schools. In the present case, it is not non-Caucasians as a group whose rights are asserted by respondent, but the rights of particular non-Caucasian would-be users of restricted land.

It is contended by petitioners that for California courts to refuse to enforce this covenant is to impair the obligations of their contracts. Article I, § 10, of the Federal Constitution provides: 'No State shall . . . pass any . . . Law impairing the Obligation of Contracts . . . .' The short answer to this contention is that this provision, as its terms indicate, is directed against legislative action only.

'It has been settled by a long line of decisions, that the provision of 10, Article I, of the Federal Constitution, protecting the obligation of contracts against state action, is directed only against impairment by legislation and not by judgments of courts. . . .'

It is finally contended that petitioners are denied due process and equal protection of the laws by the failure to enforce the covenants. The answer to that proposition is stated by the Court in Shelley [v. Kramer] in these words: 'The Constitution confers upon no individual the right to demand action by the State which results in the denial of equal protection of the laws to other individuals. . . .'"

The Supreme Court affirmed the judgment of the District Court of Appeal.

V. JUSTICE VOTE

6 Pro ACLU Side vs. 1 Con Opposing Side

ACLU Side (Respondent/Appellee)

1. Minton, S. – Wrote majority opinion
2. Douglas, W. – Joined majority opinion
3. Black, H. – Joined majority opinion
4. Clark, T. – Joined majority opinion
5. Frankfurter, F. – Joined majority opinion
6. Burton, H. – Joined majority opinion

Opposing Side (Petitioner/Appellant)

1. Vinson, F. – Wrote dissenting opinion

Reed, S – Took no part in the decision
Jackson, R – Took no part in the decision

VI. A WIN OR LOSS FOR THE ACLU?

The ACLU filed as amicus curiae urging affirmance of the judgment of the District Court of Appeal; the Supreme Court affirmed in a 6-1 vote, giving the ACLU an apparent win.

78. Superior Films, Inc. v. Department of Education

(Decided January 18, 1954; 346 U.S. 587)

I. ISSUE

A. Issues Discussed

Freedom of speech and of the press, Fourteenth Amendment

B. Legal Question Presented

Does government censorship of motion pictures violate freedoms of speech and freedom of the press, as guaranteed by the First

Amendment?

C. Supreme Court's Answer

Censorship of motion pictures violates freedom of speech and freedom of the press.

II. CASE SUMMARY

A. Background

Cases were consolidated before the Supreme Court all dealing with the similar issue of motion picture censorship. Various films were rejected for distribution in Ohio and New York based on censorship blocking films deemed "immoral," "harmful" or otherwise inappropriate for distribution. Appellants challenged the censorship under the First and Fourteenth Amendments and were, on the whole, denied relief in the lower courts.[1]

The Supreme Court, in a per curiam opinion, reversed.

B. Counsel of Record/ACLU Attorney

ACLU Side (Petitioner/Appellant): John C. Harlor and Florence Perlow Shientag argued the cause for appellant.

Opposing Side (Respondent/Appellee): Attorney General of Ohio C. William O'Neill and Charles A. Brind, Jr. argued the cause for appellee.

III. AMICI CURIAE

ACLU Side (Petitioner/Appellant)

Brief of amici curiae filed on behalf of the National Council on Freedom From Censorship, a Committee of the ACLU by Morris L. Ernst and Arthur Joel Katz.

Briefs of amici curiae filed in No. 217 on behalf of the Motion Picture Association of America, Inc. and Independent Theatre Owners of Ohio, Inc.

Opposing Side (Respondent/Appellee)

No briefs of amici curiae were filed in support of appellee.

IV. THE SUPREME COURT'S DECISION

"The argument of Ohio and New York that the government may establish censorship over moving pictures is one I cannot accept. . . .

Motion pictures are of course a different medium of expression than the public speech, the radio, the stage, the novel, or the magazine. But the First Amendment draws no distinction between the various methods of communicating ideas. On occasion one may be more powerful or effective than another. The movie, like the public speech, radio, or television is transitory here now and gone in an instant. The novel, the short story, the poem in printed form are permanently at hand to reenact the drama or to retell the story over and again. Which medium will give the most excitement and have the most enduring effect will vary with the theme and the actors. It is not for the censor to determine in any case. The First and the Fourteenth Amendments say that Congress and the States shall make 'no law' which abridges freedom of speech or of the press. In order to sanction a system of censorship I would have to say that 'no law' does not mean what it says, that 'no law' is qualified to mean 'some' laws. I cannot take that step.

In this Nation every writer, actor, or producer, no matter what medium of expression he may use, should be freed from the censor."

The Supreme Court reversed the judgment in a per curiam decision.

V. JUSTICE VOTE

9 Pro ACLU Side vs. 0 Con Opposing Side

ACLU Side (Petitioner/Appellant)

1. Douglas, W. – Wrote concurring opinion
2. Black, H. – Joined concurring opinion
3. Jackson, R. – Per curiam decision
4. Reed, S. – Per curiam decision
5. Minton, S. – Per curiam decision
6. Clark, T. – Per curiam decision
7. Frankfurter, F. – Per curiam decision
8. Burton, H. – Per curiam decision
9. Warren, E. – Per curiam decision

VI. A WIN OR LOSS FOR THE ACLU?

The ACLU filed as amicus curiae supporting appellants; the Supreme Court reversed the judgments in a 9-0 vote, giving the ACLU an apparent win.

79. Brown v. Board of Education

(Decided May 17, 1954; 347 U.S. 483)

I. ISSUE

A. Issues Discussed

Racial discrimination, equal protection

B. Legal Question Presented

"Does segregation of children in public schools solely on the basis of race, even though the physical facilities and other 'tangible' factors may be equal, deprive the children of the minority group of equal educational opportunities?"

C. Supreme Court's Answer

"We believe that it does."

II. CASE SUMMARY

A. Background

The Supreme Court consolidated four cases in Brown v. Board of Education.

"In each of the cases, minors of the Negro race, through their legal representatives, seek the aid of the courts in obtaining admission to the public schools of their community on a nonsegregated basis. In each instance, they have been denied admission to schools attended by white children under laws requiring or permitting segregation according to race. This segregation was alleged to deprive the

1 Commerical Pictures Corp. v. Board of Regents, 113 N.E.2d 502 (N.Y. 1953), Superior Films, Inc. v. Department of Education, 112 N.E.2d 311 (Ohio 1953)

plaintiffs of the equal protection of the laws under the Fourteenth Amendment. In each of the cases other than the Delaware case, a three-judge federal district court denied relief to the plaintiffs on the so-called 'separate but equal' doctrine announced by this Court in Plessy v. Ferguson. Under that doctrine, equality of treatment is accorded when the races are provided substantially equal facilities, even though these facilities be separate. In the Delaware case, the Supreme Court of Delaware adhered to that doctrine, but ordered that the plaintiffs be admitted to the white schools because of their superiority to the Negro schools."

The Supreme Court sent the cases back to docket to formulate decrees consistent with the Court decision.

B. Counsel of Record/ACLU Attorney

ACLU Side (Petitioner/Appellant): Robert L. Carter, Thurgood Marshall, Spottswood W. Robinson III, Louis Redding, and Jack Greenberg argued the cause for appellant (appellee in the Delaware case). Assistant Attorney General J. Lee Rankin argued the cause for the United States, as amicus curiae, by special leave of Court.

Opposing Side (Respondent/Appellee): Assistant Attorney General of Kansas Paul E. Wilson, John W. Davis, T. Justin Moore, Attorney General of Virginia J. Lindsay Almond, Jr., and Attorney General of Delaware H. Albert Young argued the cause for appellee (appellant in the Delaware case).

III. AMICI CURIAE

ACLU Side (Petitioner/Appellant)

Brief of amici curiae filed on behalf of the ACLU by Edwin J. Lukas, Arnold Forster, Arthur Garfield Hays, Frank E. Karelsen, Theodore Leskes, Leonard Haas, and Saburo Kido.

Additional briefs of amici curiae were filed on behalf of the American Jewish Congress, American Federation of Teachers, Congress of Industrial Organizations, and American Veterans Committee, Inc.

Brief of amici curiae filed on behalf of the United States on the reargument by Assistant Attorney General Rankin, Attorney General Herbert Brownell, Philip Elman, Leon Ulman, William J. Lamont and M. Magdelena Schoch.

Brief of amici curiae filed on behalf of the United States on the original argument by James P. McGranery, then Attorney General, and Philip Elman.

Opposing Side (Respondent/Appellee)

No briefs of amici curiae were filed in support of appellee.

IV. THE SUPREME COURT'S DECISION

"Here, unlike Sweatt v. Painter, there are findings below that the Negro and white schools involved have been equalized, or are being equalized, with respect to buildings, curricula, qualifications and salaries of teachers, and other 'tangible' factors. Our decision, therefore, cannot turn on merely a comparison of these tangible factors in the Negro and white schools involved in each of the cases. We must look instead to the effect of segregation itself on public education.

In approaching this problem, we cannot turn the clock back to 1868 when the Amendment was adopted, or even to 1896 when *Plessy v. Ferguson* was written. We must consider public education in the light of its full development and its present place in American life throughout the Nation. Only in this way can it be determined if segregation in public schools deprives these plaintiffs of the equal protection of the laws. . . .

'Segregation of white and colored children in public schools has a detrimental effect upon the colored children. The impact is greater when it has the sanction of the law; for the policy of separating the races is usually interpreted as denoting the inferiority of the negro group. A sense of inferiority affects the motivation of a child to learn. Segregation with the sanction of law, therefore, has a tendency to [retard] the educational and mental development of Negro children and to deprive them of some of the benefits they would receive in a racial[ly] integrated school system.' . . .

We conclude that in the field of public education the doctrine of 'separate but equal' has no place. Separate educational facilities are inherently unequal. Therefore, we hold that the plaintiffs and others similarly situated for whom the actions have been brought are, by reason of the segregation complained of, deprived of the equal protection of the laws guaranteed by the Fourteenth Amendment. This disposition makes unnecessary any discussion whether such segregation also violates the Due Process Clause of the Fourteenth Amendment."

The Supreme Court restored the cases to the docket to formulate decrees.

V. JUSTICE VOTE

9 Pro ACLU Side vs. 0 Con Opposing Side

ACLU Side (Petitioner/Appellant)

1. Warren, E. – Wrote majority opinion
2. Jackson, R. – Joined majority opinion
3. Reed, S. – Joined majority opinion
4. Minton, S. – Joined majority opinion
5. Douglas, W. – Joined majority opinion
6. Black, H. – Joined majority opinion
7. Clark, T. – Joined majority opinion
8. Frankfurter, F. – Joined majority opinion
9. Burton, H. – Joined majority opinion

VI. A WIN OR LOSS FOR THE ACLU?

The ACLU, as amicus curiae, urged reversal of the judgments below; the Supreme Court reversed in a 9-0 vote, giving the ACLU an apparent win.

80. Emspak v. United States

(Decided May 23, 1955; 349 U.S. 190)

I. ISSUE

A. Issues Discussed

Self-incrimination

B. Legal Question Presented

Is the statement "'primarily the first amendment, supplemented by the fifth'" sufficient to invoke the constitutional privilege against self-incrimination?

C. Supreme Court's Answer

The statement is sufficient to invoke the privilege against self-incrimination.

II. CASE SUMMARY

A. Background

"This is a companion case to *Quinn v. United States.* . . . The two cases arose out of the same investigation by the Committee on Un-American Activities of the House of Representatives." Petitioner was "the General Secretary-Treasurer of the United Electrical, Radion & Machine Workers of America as well as Editor of the UE News, the union's official publication." He was ordered to answer 239 questions pursuant to a subpoena as part of the investigation on Communist affiliations. He declined to answer 68 questions and "based his refusal on 'primarily the first amendment, supplemented by the fifth.'"

"On November 20, 1950, petitioner was indicted under s 192 for his refusal to answer the 68 questions. Sitting without a jury, the District Court held that petitioner's references to 'primarily the first amendment, supplemented by the fifth' were insufficient to invoke the Fifth Amendment's privilege against self-incrimination. The District Court accordingly found petitioner guilty on all 68 counts and sentenced him to a term of six months and a fine of $500. The Court of Appeals for the District of Columbia Circuit, three judges dissenting, affirmed en banc."

The Supreme Court reversed the conviction.

B. Counsel of Record/ACLU Attorney

ACLU Side (Petitioner/Appellant): David Scribner and Frank J. Donner argued the cause for appellant.

Opposing Side (Respondent/Appellee): Acting Solicitor General Robert L. Stern and Special Assistant to the Attorney General Robert W. Ginnane argued the cause for appellee.

III. AMICI CURIAE

ACLU Side (Petitioner/Appellant)

Briefs of amici curiae filed on behalf of the ACLU by Ernest Angell, Osmond K. Fraenkel, Arthur Garfield Hays, and Herbert Monte Levy.

Opposing Side (Respondent/Appellee)

No briefs of amici curiae were filed in support of appellee.

IV. THE SUPREME COURT'S DECISION

"As pointed out in Quinn v. United States, no ritualistic formula or talismanic phrase is essential in order to invoke the privilege against self-incrimination. All that is necessary is an objection stated in language that a committee may reasonably be expected to understand as an attempt to invoke the privilege. In the Quinn case we hold that Quinn's references to 'the First and Fifth Amendments' and 'the First Amendment to the Constitution, supplemented by the Fifth Amendment' were sufficient to meet this standard. It would be unwarranted, we think, to reach a different conclusion here as to petitioner's plea based on 'primarily the first amendment, supplemented by the fifth.'

The Government does not even attempt to distinguish between the two cases in this respect. Apparently conceding that petitioner as well as Quinn intended to invoke the privilege, the Government points out 'the probability' that his references to the Fifth Amendment were likewise deliberately phrased in muffled terms 'to obtain the benefit of the privilege without incurring the popular opprobrium which often attaches to its exercise.' On this basis the Government contends that petitioner's plea was not adequate. The answer to this contention is threefold. First, an objection that is sufficiently clear to reveal a probable intention to invoke the privilege cannot be ignored merely because it is not phrased in an orthodox manner. Second, if it is true that in these times a stigma may somehow result from a witness' reliance on the Self-Incrimination Clause, a committee should be all the more ready to recognize a veiled claim of the privilege. Otherwise, the great right which the Clause was intended to secure might be effectively frustrated by private pressures. Third, it should be noted that a committee is not obliged to either accept or reject an ambiguous constitutional claim the very moment it is first presented. The way is always open for the committee to inquire into the nature of the claim before making a ruling. If the witness intelligently and unequivocally waives any objection based on the Self-Incrimination Clause, or if the witness refuses a committee request to state whether he relies on the Self-Incrimination Clause, he cannot later invoke its protection in a prosecution for contempt for refusing to answer that question. . . .

There is here, as in the Quinn case, a second ground for our decision. At no time did the committee specifically overrule petitioner's objection based on the Fifth Amendment, nor did the committee indicate its overruling of the objection by specifically directing petitioner to answer. In the absence of such committee action, petitioner was never confronted with a clear-cut choice between compliance and noncompliance, between answering the question and risking prosecution for contempt. For the reasons set out in the Quinn opinion, we believe the committee—by failing to meet these minimal procedural standards, originally recognized by the committee and recently re-adopted—did not adequately apprise petitioner that an answer was required notwithstanding his objections. And without such apprisal, there is lacking the element of deliberateness necessary for a conviction under 192 for a refusal to answer."

The Supreme Court reversed the judgment of the Court of Appeals for the District of Columbia Circuit.

V. JUSTICE VOTE

6 Pro ACLU Side vs. 3 Con Opposing Side

ACLU Side (Petitioner/Appellant)

1. Warren, E. – Wrote majority opinion
2. Douglas, W. – Joined majority opinion
3. Black, H. – Joined majority opinion
4. Clark, T. – Joined majority opinion

5. Frankfurter, F. – Joined majority opinion
6. Burton, H. – Joined majority opinion

Opposing Side (Respondent/Appellee)

1. Harlan, J. – Wrote dissenting opinion
2. Reed, D. – Wrote dissenting opinion
3. Minton, S. – Joined Reed's dissent

VI. A WIN OR LOSS FOR THE ACLU?

The ACLU, as amicus, urged reversal of the judgment of the Court of Appeals for the District of Columbia Circuit; the Supreme Court reversed in a 6-3 vote, giving the ACLU an apparent win.

81. Peters v. Hobby

(Decided June 6, 1955; 349 U.S. 331)

I. ISSUE

A. Issues Discussed

Freedom of speech and association, judicial review

B. Legal Question Presented

Did the actions of the Loyalty Review Board violate Executive Order 9835 and/or the United States Constitution?

C. Supreme Court's Answer

Declining to decide the constitutional issues, the Supreme Court decided the Loyalty Review Board violated Executive Order 9835.

II. CASE SUMMARY

A. Background

"Petitioner is a professor of medicine, specializing in the study of metabolism, at Yale University." He had an employment contract with "the Department of Health, Education, and Welfare, headed by respondent Hobby. Petitioner's duties required his presence in Washington from four to ten days each year, when called upon by the Surgeon General, to render advice concerning proposals to grant federal assistance to various medical research institutions. This work was not of a confidential or sensitive character and did not entail access to classified material."

Executive Order 9835 was issued in March 1947 encouraging hearings to determine the loyalty of civilian employees whose loyalty was called into question. Under this order, petitioner's loyalty was called into question. He underwent numerous hearings, provided substantial information to show his loyalty, and had his case audited to the point where it reached the Loyalty Review Board. Ultimately, the Loyalty Review Board determined that petitioner should be dismissed from his government employment due to doubts about his loyalty and he was dismissed, despite decisions to the contrary before the Loyalty Review Board took up the case. Petitioner brought suit after he unsuccessfully tried to obtain a rehearing.

The district court and court of appeals affirmed the Loyalty Review Board's decision. The Supreme Court reversed.

B. Counsel of Record/ACLU Attorney

ACLU Side (Petitioner/Appellant): Thurman Arnold and Paul A. Porter argued the cause for appellant.
Opposing Side (Respondent/Appellee): Assistant Attorney General Warren E. Burger argued the cause for appellee.

III. AMICI CURIAE

ACLU Side (Petitioner/Appellant)

Brief of amici curiae filed on behalf of the ACLU by Herbert Monte Levy, Morris L. Ernst, and David I. Shapiro.
Briefs of amici curiae filed on behalf of the Engineers and Scientists of America, Congress of Industrial Organizations, and Emergency Civil Liberties Committee.

Opposing Side (Respondent/Appellee)

No briefs of amici curiae were filed in support of appellee.

IV. THE SUPREME COURT'S DECISION

"In this Court, petitioner urges us to decide the case on the constitutional issues. . . . We find, however, that the case can be decided without reaching the constitutional issues. . . . [W]e must at the outset determine whether petitioner's removal and debarment were effected in accord with Executive Order 9835. On consideration of this question, we conclude that the Loyalty Review Board's action was so patently in violation of the Executive Order—in fact, beyond the Board's delegated jurisdiction under the Order—that the constitutionality of the Order itself does not come into issue.

[T]he Loyalty Review Board was denied any power to undertake review on its own motion; only the employee recommended for dismissal, or his department or agency, could refer such a case to the Loyalty Review Board.

In petitioner's case, the Board failed to respect either of these limitations. Petitioner had been twice cleared by the Agency Board and hence did not fall in the category of 'persons recommended for dismissal on grounds relating to loyalty by the loyalty board of any department or agency.' Moreover, petitioner's case was never referred to the Loyalty Review Board by petitioner or the Agency. Instead, the Loyalty Review Board, acting solely on its own motion, undertook to 'hold a hearing and reach its own decision.' On both grounds, the Board's action was plainly beyond its jurisdiction unless such action was authorized by some other provision in the Order. . . .

The judgment below is reversed and the cause is remanded to the District Court for entry of a decree in conformity with this opinion."

V. JUSTICE VOTE

7 Pro ACLU Side vs. 2 Con Opposing Side

ACLU Side (Petitioner/Appellant)

1. Warren, E. – Wrote majority opinion
2. Black, H. – Wrote concurring opinion
3. Frankfurter, F. – Joined majority opinion
4. Douglas, W. – Wrote concurring opinion

5. Clark, T. – Joined majority opinion
6. Minton, S. – Joined majority opinion
7. Harlan, J. – Joined majority opinion

Opposing Side (Respondent/Appellee)

1. Reed, S. – Wrote dissenting opinion
2. Burton, H. – Joined dissenting opinion

VI. A WIN OR LOSS FOR THE ACLU?

The ACLU filed as amicus curiae urging reversal of the judgment of the Court of Appeals for the District of Columbia Circuit; the Supreme Court reversed in a 7-2 vote, giving the ACLU an apparent win.

82. Gonzales v. Landon

(Decided December 12, 1955; 350 U.S. 920)

I. ISSUE

A. Issues Discussed

Immigration

B. Legal Question Presented

Is a statute authorizing expatriation for a citizen remaining out of the country to avoid military service constitutional?

C. Supreme Court's Answer

Without reaching the constitutional issues, the Court decided the standard of proof for expatriation was not met in this case.

II. CASE SUMMARY

A. Background

Petitioner Gonzales was born in the United States in 1924. He was taken to Mexico when he was less than two years old, where he resided until he returned to the United States in 1946. "The District Court determined that although plaintiff was a citizen by birth he had expatriated himself by remaining outside the jurisdiction of the United States in order to avoid training and service in the armed forces of this country in time of war." He challenged this decision and the Court of Appeals affirmed.[1]

The Supreme Court granted certiorari and reversed, in a per curiam decision.

B. Counsel of Record/ACLU Attorney

ACLU Side (Petitioner/Appellant): A. L. Wirin, Fred Okrand, David C. Marcus, and Ralph Estrada argued the cause for appellant.

Opposing Side (Respondent/Appellee): Solicitor General Sobeloff, Assistant Attorney General Warren Olney III, Oscar H. Davis, Beatrice Rosenberg, and J. F. Bishop argued the cause for appellee..

III. AMICI CURIAE

ACLU Side (Petitioner/Appellant)

Brief of amici curiae filed on behalf of the ACLU by Osmond K Fraenkel and Loren Miller.

John W. Willis, Vincent fP. DiGiorgio and Thomas R. Davis, attorneys for a party in a pending action brought under the same statute filed an amicus curiae brief urging reversal.

Opposing Side (Respondent/Appellee)

No briefs of amici curiae were filed in support of appellee.

IV. THE SUPREME COURT'S DECISION

"The Court is of the view that the standard of proof required in denaturalization cases . . . is applicable in expatriation cases arising under § 401(j) of the Nationality Act of 1940 . . . and has not been satisfied in this case. Accordingly the judgment below is reversed without reaching the constitutional questions that have been presented."

The judgment of the Court of Appeals was reversed in a per curiam decision.

V. JUSTICE VOTE

9 Pro ACLU Side vs. 0 Con Opposing Side

ACLU Side (Petitioner/Appellant)

1. Frankfurter, F. – Per curiam decision
2. Douglas, W. – Per curiam decision
3. Harlan, J. – Per curiam decision
4. Burton, H. – Per curiam decision
5. Warren, E. – Per curiam decision
6. Black, H. – Per curiam decision
7. Clark, T. – Per curiam decision
8. Reed, S. – Per curiam decision
9. Minton, S. – Per curiam decision

VI. A WIN OR LOSS FOR THE ACLU?

The ACLU filed as amicus curiae urging reversal of the judgment of the Ninth Circuit Court of Appeals; the Supreme Court reversed in a 9-0 vote, giving the ACLU an apparent win.

83. Pennsylvania ex rel. Herman v. Claudy

(Decided January 9, 1956; 350 U.S. 116)

I. ISSUE

A. Issues Discussed

Criminal procedure

B. Legal Question Presented

Whether "summary dismissal in the face of the petitioner's serious allegations" was proper in this case.

1 Gonzales v. Landon, 215 F.2d 955 (9th Cir. 1954).

C. Supreme Court's Answer

"Under the allegations here petitioner is entitled to relief if he can prove his charges. He cannot be denied a hearing merely because the allegations of his petition were contradicted by the prosecuting officers."

II. CASE SUMMARY

A. Background

"In 1945 petitioner Stephen Herman pleaded guilty in a Pennsylvania state court to 8 charges of burglary, 12 of larceny, 8 of forgery, and 2 of false pretense. He was sentenced to serve 17 1/2 to 35 years in the penitentiary, 2 1/2 to 5 years on each of the charges, some running consecutively, some concurrently. Eight years later, in 1953, he filed this petition for habeas corpus in the same Pennsylvania court, asking that his conviction be held invalid as in violation of the Due Process Clause of the Fourteenth Amendment. He alleged: (1) that his pleas of guilty were the result of coercion and threats by state officers and (2) that at no stage of the proceedings was he either advised of his right to or given the benefit of counsel. The District Attorney filed an answer challenging the materiality of some of petitioner's allegations denying others, and urging that the writ be refused because of petitioner's tardiness in challenging the judgment. He asked that the petition be summarily dismissed on the ground that 'it would be a waste of time and very expensive for Washington County to have this defendant go into a hearing to prove charges that he could have raised at the time he was sentenced by this Court.' The petition was summarily dismissed without a hearing by the same trial judge who had sentenced petitioner.

On appeal, the Superior Court of the Commonwealth of Pennsylvania affirmed the dismissal. The Supreme Court of Pennsylvania denied leave to appeal without opinion. [The U.S. Supreme Court] granted certiorari, because summary dismissal in the face of the petitioner's serious allegations appeared to be out of line with decisions of this Court."

B. Counsel of Record

ACLU Side (Petitioner/Appellant): Herbert Monte Levy of the American Civil Liberties Union, and Marjorie Hanson Matson argued the cause and filed a brief for appellant.

Opposing Side (Respondent/Appellee): Wray G. Zelt, Jr. argued the cause for respondent. With him on the brief were Harold V. Fergus and John F. Roney.

III. AMICI CURIAE

ACLU Side (Petitioner/Appellant)

No briefs of amici curiae were filed in support of appellant.

Opposing Side (Respondent/Appellee)

No briefs of amici curiae were filed in support of appellee.

IV. THE SUPREME COURT'S DECISION

"Our prior decisions have established that: (1) a conviction following trial or on a plea of guilty based on a confession extorted by violence or by mental coercion is invalid under the Federal Due Process Clause; (2) where a person convicted in a state court has not intelligently and understandingly waived the benefit of counsel and where the circumstances show that his rights could not have been fairly protected without counsel, the Due Process Clause invalidates his conviction; (3) where a denial of these constitutional protections is alleged in an appropriate proceeding by factual allegations not patently frivolous or false on a consideration of the whole record, the proceeding should not be summarily dismissed merely because a state prosecuting officer files an answer denying some or all of the allegations.

In the light of our previous holdings we now consider the allegations of the petition for habeas corpus and the prosecuting officer's answer. . . .

The . . . narrative of the allegations in the petition and the answer reveals a sharp dispute as to the facts material to a determination of the constitutional questions involved. The allegations as to petitioner's treatment prior to confession and his understanding of the nature and consequences of a guilty plea present the very kind of dispute which should be decided only after a hearing. . . . We cannot agree with the Pennsylvania Superior Court that the mere fact that petitioner had, without the benefit of counsel, pleaded guilty to an offense 2 years before showed that he had the capacity to defend himself against the 30 charges here. . . .

The chief argument made by the State here in support of the court's summary dismissal of the petition is this: 'Counsel for petitioner argues that since facts are alleged in the petition, a hearing must be held. Since our answer contradicted the allegations in the petition, the lower court was not required to grant a hearing. This contention was sustained by the Superior Court.' We cannot accept this argument. Under the allegations here petitioner is entitled to relief if he can prove his charges. He cannot be denied a hearing merely because the allegations of his petition were contradicted by the prosecuting officers.

The judgment is reversed and the cause is remanded for proceedings not inconsistent with this opinion."

V. JUSTICE VOTE

9 Pro ACLU Side vs. 0 Con Opposing Side

ACLU Side (Petitioner/Appellant)

1. Black, H. – Wrote majority opinion
2. Frankfurter, F. – Joined majority opinion
3. Warren, E. – Joined majority opinion
4. Reed, S. – Joined majority opinion
5. Burton, H. – Joined majority opinion
6. Clark, T. – Joined majority opinion
7. Douglas, W. – Joined majority opinion
8. Minton, S. – Joined majority opinion
9. Harlan, J. – Joined majority opinion

VI. A WIN OR LOSS FOR THE ACLU?

The ACLU served as counsel for appellant urging reversal of the judgment of the Superior Court of the Commonwealth of Pennsylvania; the Supreme Court reversed in a 9-0 vote, giving the ACLU an apparent win.

84. Costello v. United States

(Decided March 5, 1956; 350 U.S. 359)

I. ISSUE

A. Issues Discussed

Criminal procedure

B. Legal Question Presented

"'May a defendant be required to stand trial and a conviction be sustained where only hearsay evidence was presented to the grand jury which indicted him?'"

C. Supreme Court's Answer

"An indictment returned by a legally constituted and unbiased grand jury, like an information drawn by the prosecutor, if valid on its face, is enough to call for trial of the charge on the merits. The Fifth Amendment requires nothing more."

II. CASE SUMMARY

A. Background

"Petitioner, Frank Costello, was indicted for wilfully attempting to evade payment of income taxes due the United States for the years 1947, 1948 and 1949. The charge was that petitioner falsely and fraudulently reported less income than he and his wife actually received during the taxable years in question. Petitioner promptly filed a motion for inspection of the minutes of the grand jury and for a dismissal of the indictment. His motion was based on an affidavit stating that he was firmly convinced there could have been no legal or competent evidence before the grand jury which indicted him since he had reported all his income and paid all taxes due. The motion was denied. At the trial which followed the Government offered evidence designed to show increases in Costello's net worth in an attempt to prove that he had received more income during the years in question than he had reported. To establish its case the Government called and examined 144 witnesses and introduced 368 exhibits. . . .

Counsel for petitioner asked each government witness at the trial whether he had appeared before the grand jury which returned the indictment. This cross-examination developed the fact that the three investigating officers had been the only witnesses before the grand jury. After the Government concluded its case, petitioner again moved to dismiss the indictment on the ground that the only evidence before the grand jury was 'hearsay,' since the three officers had no firsthand knowledge of the transactions upon which their computations were based. Nevertheless the trial court again refused to dismiss the indictment, and petitioner was convicted. The Court of Appeals affirmed, holding that the indictment was valid even though the sole evidence before the grand jury was hearsay."

The Supreme Court granted certiorari to review the case.

B. Counsel of Record

ACLU Side (Petitioner/Appellant): Osmond K. Fraenkel and Morris Shilensky argued the cause for appellant. With them on the brief were Joseph Leary Delaney and George Wolf.

Opposing Side (Respondent/Appellee): Marvin E. Frankel argued the cause for the United States. With him on the brief were Solicitor General Sobeloff, Assistant Attorney General-Holland and Joseph M. Howard.

III. AMICI CURIAE

ACLU Side (Petitioner/Appellant)

Brief of amici curiae filed on behalf of the American Civil Liberties Union by Edward J. Ennis and Barant Ten Eyck.

Opposing Side (Respondent/Appellee)

No briefs of amici curiae were filed in support of appellee.

IV. THE SUPREME COURT'S DECISION

"Petitioner here urges: (1) that an indictment based solely on hearsay evidence violates that part of the Fifth Amendment providing that 'No person shall be held to answer for a capital, or otherwise infamous crime, unless on a presentment or indictment of a Grand Jury . . .' and (2) that if the Fifth Amendment does not invalidate an indictment based solely on hearsay we should now lay down such a rule for the guidance of federal courts.

The Fifth Amendment provides that federal prosecutions for capital or otherwise infamous crimes must be instituted by presentments or indictments of grand juries. But neither the Fifth Amendment nor any other constitutional provision prescribes the kind of evidence upon which grand juries must act. . . .

In Holt v. United States, 218 U.S. 245, this Court had to decide whether an indictment should be quashed because supported in part by incompetent evidence. Aside from the incompetent evidence 'there was very little evidence against the accused.' The Court refused to hold that such an indictment should be quashed, pointing out that 'The abuses of criminal practice would be enhanced if indictments could be upset on such a ground.' The same thing is true where as here all the evidence before the grand jury was in the nature of 'hearsay.' If indictments were to be held open to challenge on the ground that there was inadequate or incompetent evidence before the grand jury, the resulting delay would be great indeed. The result of such a rule would be that before trial on the merits a defendant could always insist on a kind of preliminary trial to determine the competency and adequacy of the evidence before the grand jury. This is not required by the Fifth Amendment. An indictment returned by a legally constituted and unbiased grand jury, like an information drawn by the prosecutor, if valid on its face, is enough to call for trial of the charge on the merits. The Fifth Amendment requires nothing more.

Petitioner urges that this Court should exercise its power to supervise the administration of justice in federal courts and establish a rule permitting defendants to challenge indictments on the ground that they are not supported by adequate or competent evidence. No persuasive reasons are advanced for establishing such a rule. It would run counter to the whole history of the grand jury institution, in which laymen conduct their inquiries unfettered by technical rules. Neither justice nor the concept of a fair trial requires such a change. In a trial on the merits, defendants are entitled to a strict observance of all the rules designed to bring about a fair verdict. Defendants are not entitled, however, to a rule which would result in interminable delay but add nothing to the assurance of a fair trial.

Affirmed."

V. JUSTICE VOTE

0 Pro ACLU Side vs. 7 Con Opposing Side

Opposing Side (Respondent/Appellee)

1. Black, H. – Wrote majority opinion
2. Burton, H. – Wrote concurring opinion
3. Frankfurter, F. – Joined majority opinion
4. Warren, E. – Joined majority opinion
5. Reed, S. – Joined majority opinion
6. Douglas, W. – Joined majority opinion
7. Minton, S. – Joined majority opinion

Harlan, J. – Took no part in the decision.
Clark, T. – Took no part in the decision.

VI. A WIN OR LOSS FOR THE ACLU?

The ACLU filed as amicus curiae urging reversal of the judgment of the Court of Appeals; the Supreme Court affirmed in a 7-0 vote, giving the ACLU an apparent loss.

85. Pennsylvania v. Nelson

(Decided April 2, 1956; 350 U.S. 497)

I. ISSUE

A. Issues Discussed

Federal preemption

B. Legal Question Presented

Whether "the Smith Act of 1940, as amended in 1948, which prohibits the knowing advocacy of the overthrow of the Government of the United States by force and violence, supersedes the enforceability of the Pennsylvania Sedition Act which proscribes the same conduct."

C. Supreme Court's Answer

The federal Smith Act supersedes the Pennsylvania Sedition Act.

II. CASE SUMMARY

A. Background

Respondent Nelson, a member of the Communist Party, was convicted of violating the Pennsylvania Sedition Act, which outlawed participation in subversive organizations. The Court of Quarter Sessions of Allegheny County, Pennsylvania convicted and sentenced respondent, and the Superior Court affirmed the conviction.

"The Supreme Court of Pennsylvania, recognizing but not reaching many alleged serious trial errors and conduct of the trial court infringing upon respondent's right to due process of law, decided the case on the narrow issue of supersession of the state law by the Federal Smith Act. . . . The precise holding of the court, and all that is before us for review, is that the Smith Act of 1940, as amended in 1948, which prohibits the knowing advocacy of the overthrow of the Government of the United States by force and violence, supersedes the enforceability of the Pennsylvania Sedition Act which proscribes the same conduct."

The Supreme Court granted certiorari and affirmed the Supreme Court of Pennsylvania.

B. Counsel of Record/ACLU Attorney

ACLU Side (Respondent/Appellee): Herbert S. Thatcher argued the cause for appellee.

Opposing Side (Petitioner/Appellant): Frank F. Truscott and Harry F. Stambaugh argued the cause for appellant.

Charles F. Barber argued the cause as amici curiae, by special leave of court, on behalf of the United States.

Attorney General of New Hampshire Louis C. Wyman argued the cause as amici curiae on behalf of the State of New Hampshire.

III. AMICI CURIAE

ACLU Side (Respondent/Appellee)

Brief of amici curiae filed on behalf of the ACLU by Osmond K. Fraenkel, Herbert Monte Levy, and Julian E. Goldberg.

Brief of amici curiae filed on behalf of the Civil Liberties Committee of the Philadelphia Yearly Meeting of the Religious Society of Friends by Walter C. Longstreth, Allen S. Olmsted, 2nd, and William Allen Rahill.

Brief of amici curiae filed on behalf of Phil Feldman, et al., by Frank J. Donner, Royal W. France, Arthur Kinoy, Marshall Perlin, Oliver S. Allen, Robert R. Clark, Gabriel Kantrovitz, Lawrence D. Shunbow, and B. Loring Young.

Opposing Side (Petitioner/Appellant)

Brief of amici curiae filed on behalf of the United States by Charles F. Barber, Solicitor General Sobeloff, Assistant Attorney General William F. Tompkins, Harold D. Koffsky, Philip R. Monahan, and Alice E. Miller.

Brief of amici curiae filed on behalf of the State of New Hampshire by Attorney General of New Hampshire Louis C. Wyman.

Brief of amici curiae filed on behalf of the Commonwealth of Massachusetts by Attorney General of Massachusetts George Fingold, and Lowell S. Nicholson, Samuel H. Cohen, and Fred L. True, Jr., Assistant Attorneys General.

Brief of amici curiae filed on behalf of the American Legion by Ralph B. Gregg.

Brief of amici curiae filed on behalf of the State of Texas by Attorney General of Texas John Ben Shepperd, and Assistant Attorney General John Atchison.

IV. THE SUPREME COURT'S DECISION

"It should be said at the outset that the decision in this case does not affect the right of States to enforce their sedition laws at times when the Federal Government has not occupied the field and is not protecting the entire country from seditious conduct. The distinction between the two situations was clearly recognized by the court below. Nor does it limit the jurisdiction of the States where the Constitution and Congress have specifically given them concurrent jurisdiction, as was done under the Eighteenth Amendment and the Volstead Act. Neither does it limit the right of the State to protect itself at any time against sabotage or attempted violence of all kinds. Nor does it prevent the State from prosecuting where the same act constitutes both a federal offense and a state offense under the police power . . . .

[First], [w]e examine these Acts only to determine the congressional plan. Looking to all of them in the aggregate, the conclusion is inescapable that Congress has intended to occupy the field of sedition. Taken as a whole, they evince a congressional plan which makes it reasonable to determine that no room has been left for the States to supplement it. Therefore, a state sedition statute is superseded regardless of whether it purports to supplement the federal law. . . .

Second, the federal statutes 'touch a field in which the federal interest is so dominant that the federal system [must] be assumed to preclude enforcement of state laws on the same subject.'

[Congress] accordingly proscribed sedition against all government in the nation—national, state and local. Congress declared that these steps were taken 'to provide for the common defense, to preserve the sovereignty of the United States as an independent nation, and to guarantee to each State a republican form of government. . . .' Congress having thus treated seditious conduct as a matter of vital national concern, it is in no sense a local enforcement problem. . . .

Third, enforcement of state sedition acts presents a serious danger of conflict with the administration of the federal program. Since 1939, in order to avoid a hampering of uniform enforcement of its program by sporadic local prosecutions, the Federal Government has urged local authorities not to intervene in such matters, but to turn over to the federal authorities immediately and unevaluated all information concerning subversive activities. The President [Franklin D. Roosevelt] made such a request on September 6, 1939, when he placed the Federal Bureau of Investigation in charge of investigation in this field. . . .

The judgment of the Supreme Court of Pennsylvania is affirmed."

V. JUSTICE VOTE

6 Pro ACLU Side vs. 3 Con Opposing Side

ACLU Side (Respondent/Appellee)

1. Warren, E. – Wrote majority opinion
2. Black, H. – Joined majority opinion
3. Frankfurter, F. – Joined majority opinion
4. Douglas, W. – Joined majority opinion
5. Clark, T. – Joined majority opinion
6. Harlan, J. – Joined majority opinion

Opposing Side (Petitioner/Appellant)

1. Reed, S. – Wrote dissenting opinion
2. Burton, H. – Joined dissenting opinion
3. Minton, S. – Joined dissenting opinion

VI. A WIN OR LOSS FOR THE ACLU?

The ACLU filed an amicus brief urging affirmance of the judgment of the Supreme Court of Pennsylvania; the U.S. Supreme Court affirmed in a 6-3 vote, giving the ACLU an apparent win.

86. Slochower v. Board of Higher Education

(Decided April 9, 1956; 350 U.S. 551)

I. ISSUE

A. Issues Discussed

Self-incrimination

B. Legal Question Presented

Whether a statute that effectively calls for automatic dismissal of any government employee invoking the Fifth Amendment privilege against self-incrimination is unconstitutional.

C. Supreme Court's Answer

The statute unconstitutionally infringes the privilege against self-incrimination.

II. CASE SUMMARY

A. Background

"This appeal brings into question the constitutionality of § 903 of the Charter of the City of New York. That section provides that whenever an employee of the City utilizes the privilege against self-incrimination to avoid answering a question relating to his official conduct, 'his term or tenure of office or employment shall terminate and such office or employment shall be vacant, and he shall not be eligible to election or appointment to any office or employment under the city or any agency.' Appellant Slochower invoked the privilege against self-incrimination under the Fifth Amendment before an investigating committee of the United States Senate, and was summarily discharged from his position as associate professor at Brooklyn College, an institution maintained by the City of New York. He now claims that the charter provision, as applied to him, violates both the Due Process and Privileges and Immunities Clauses of the Fourteenth Amendment. . . .

Under this statute, appellant may be discharged only for cause, and after notice, hearing, and appeal. The Court of Appeals of New York, however, has authoritatively interpreted § 903 to mean that 'the assertion of the privilege against self incrimination is equivalent to a resignation.' Dismissal under this provision is therefore automatic and there is no right to charges, notice, hearing, or opportunity to explain.

The Supreme Court of New York, County of Kings, concluded that appellant's behavior fell within the scope of § 903, and upheld its application here." The appellate court affirmed.

The Supreme Court reversed and remanded the judgment.

B. Counsel of Record/ACLU Attorney

ACLU Side (Petitioner/Appellant): Ephraim London argued the cause for appellant.

Opposing Side (Respondent/Appellee): Daniel T. Scannell argued the cause for appellee.

III. AMICI CURIAE

ACLU Side (Petitioner/Appellant)

Brief of amici curiae filed on behalf of the New York Civil Liberties Union by Osmond K. Fraenkel, Emanuel Redfield, and Nanette Dembitz.

Opposing Side (Respondent/Appellee)

No briefs of amici curiae were filed in support of appellee.

IV. THE SUPREME COURT'S DECISION

"The problem of balancing the State's interest in the loyalty of those in its service with the traditional safeguards of individual rights is a continuing one. To state that a person does not have a constitutional right to government employment is only to say that he must comply with reasonable, lawful, and nondiscriminatory terms laid down by the proper authorities. . . .

At the outset we must condemn the practice of imputing a sinister meaning to the exercise of a person's constitutional right under the Fifth Amendment. The right of an accused person to refuse to testify, which had been in England merely a rule of evidence, was so important to our forefathers that they raised it to the dignity of a constitutional enactment, and it has been recognized as 'one of the most valuable prerogatives of the citizen.' . . . The privilege against self-incrimination would be reduced to a hollow mockery if its exercise could be taken as equivalent either to a confession of guilt or a conclusive presumption of perjury. . . .

With this in mind, we consider the application of § 903. As interpreted and applied by the state courts, it operates to discharge every city employee who invokes the Fifth Amendment. In practical effect the questions asked are taken as confessed and made the basis of the discharge. No consideration is given to such factors as the subject matter of the questions, remoteness of the period to which they are directed, or justification for exercise of the privilege. It matters not whether the plea resulted from mistake, inadvertence or legal advice conscientiously given, whether wisely or unwisely. The heavy hand of the statute falls alike on all who exercise their constitutional privilege, the full enjoyment of which every person is entitled to receive. . . .

This is not to say that Slochower has a constitutional right to be an associate professor of German at Brooklyn College. The State has broad powers in the selection and discharge of its employees, and it may be that proper inquiry would show Slochower's continued employment to be inconsistent with a real interest of the State. But there has been no such inquiry here. We hold that the summary dismissal of appellant violates due process of law."

The Supreme Court reversed and remanded the judgment.

V. JUSTICE VOTE

5 Pro ACLU Side vs. 4 Con Opposing Side

ACLU Side (Petitioner/Appellant)

1. Clark, T. – Wrote majority opinion
2. Warren, E. – Joined majority opinion
3. Black, H. – Joined majority opinion, with reference to opinions in other cases
4. Frankfurter, F. – Joined majority opinion
5. Douglas, W. – Joined majority opinion, with reference to opinions in other cases

Opposing Side (Respondent/Appellee)

1. Reed, S. – Wrote dissenting opinion
2. Burton, H. – Joined Reed's dissent
3. Minton, S. – Joined Reed's dissent
4. Harlan, J. – Wrote dissenting opinion

VI. A WIN OR LOSS FOR THE ACLU?

The ACLU, as amicus curiae, urged reversal of the judgment; the Supreme Court reversed and remanded in a 5-4 vote, giving the ACLU an apparent win.

87. Communist Party of the United States v. Subversive Activities Control Board

(Decided April 30, 1956; 351 U.S. 115)

I. ISSUE

A. Issues Discussed

Evidence

B. Legal Question Presented

Whether the Subversive Activities Control Act is constitutional.

C. Supreme Court's Answer:

Declining to address the constitutional issue, the Court determined that the lower court needed to reevaluate allegedly perjurious evidence relied upon in the decision and remanded the case.

II. CASE SUMMARY

A. Background

The Subversive Activities Control Act of 1950 requires that certain organizations "register with the Attorney General as 'Communist-action' organization[s]." If an organization suspected of being a Communist-action organization, fails to register as such, the Attorney General is required "to bring a proceeding to determine that fact before the Subversive Activities Control Board, a five-man board appointed by the President with the advice and consent of the Senate . . . . If the Board finds that an organization is a Communist-action organization, it enters an order requiring the organization to register with the Attorney General." The decision is reviewable by the Court of Appeals for the District of Columbia, and the Supreme Court, upon a grant of certiorarri.

The Attorney General brought a proceeding for the Communist Party of the United States in 1950. Over two years of hearings and motions on the matter culminated in a 251 page report by the Subversive Activities Control Board which ordered the organization to register as a Communist-action organization.

The Court of Appeals for the District of Columbia Circuit affirmed the decision of the Subversive Activities Control Board. The Court did, however, strike certain assertions from the Board's report that it found were not substantially supported by fact.

The Supreme Court granted certiorari and reversed.

B. Counsel of Record/ACLU Attorney

ACLU Side (Petitioner/Appellant): John J. Abt and Joseph Forer argued the cause for appellant.

Opposing Side (Respondent/Appellee): Solicitor General Sobeloff argued the cause for appellee.

III. AMICI CURIAE

ACLU Side (Petitioner/Appellant)

Brief of amici curiae filed on behalf of the ACLU by Edward J. Ennis and Nanette Dembitz.

Brief of amici curiae filed on behalf of the National Lawyers Guild by Osmond K. Fraenkel, Thomas I. Emerson, David L. Weissman, and Murray A. Gordon.

Brief of amici curiae filed by Royal W. France and Laurent B. Frantz.

Opposing Side (Respondent/Appellee)

Brief of amici curiae filed on behalf of the American Bar Association by Herbert R. O'Conor, Julius Applebaum, James Madison Blackwell, Ray Murphy, William N. Bonner, Tracy E. Griffin, Egbert L. Haywood, Clarence Manion, Paul W. Updegraff, and Robert W. Upton.

IV. THE SUPREME COURT'S DECISION

"The challenge to the Act on which the order was based plainly raises constitutional questions appropriate for this Court's consideration, and so we brought the case here. At the threshold we are, however, confronted by a particular claim that the Court of Appeals erred in refusing to return the case to the Board for consideration of the new evidence proffered by petitioner's motion and affidavit. . . .

In considering this non-constitutional issue raised by denial of petitioner's motion, we must avoid any intimation with respect to the other issues raised by petitioner. We do not so intimate by concluding that the testimony of the three witnesses, against whom the uncontested challenge of perjury was made, was not inconsequential in relation to the issues on which the Board had to pass. No doubt a large part of the record consisted of documentary evidence. However, not only was the human testimony significant but the documentary evidence was also linked to the activities of the petitioner and to the ultimate finding of the Board by human testimony, and such testimony was in part that of these three witnesses. . . .

When uncontested challenge is made that a finding of subversive design by petitioner was in part the product of three perjurious witnesses, it does not remove the taint for a reviewing court to find that there is ample innocent testimony to support the Board's findings. If these witnesses in fact committed perjury in testifying in other cases on subject matter substantially like that of their testimony in the present proceedings, their testimony in this proceeding is inevitably discredited and the Board's determination must duly take this fact into account. We cannot pass upon a record containing such challenged testimony. We find it necessary to dispose of the case on the grounds we do, not in order to avoid a constitutional adjudication but because the fair administration of justice requires it. Since reversal is thus demanded, however, we do not reach the constitutional issues. . . .

The case is reversed and remanded for proceedings in conformity with this opinion."

V. JUSTICE VOTE

6 Pro ACLU Side vs. 3 Con Opposing Side

ACLU Side (Petitioner/Appellant)

1. Frankfurter, F. – Wrote majority opinion
2. Warren, E. – Joined majority opinion
3. Black, H. – Joined majority opinion
4. Douglas, W. – Joined majority opinion
5. Burton, H. – Joined majority opinion
6. Harlan, J. – Joined majority opinion

Opposing Side (Respondent/Appellee)

1. Clark, T. – Wrote dissenting opinion
2. Minton, S. – Joined dissenting opinion
3. Reed, S. – Joined dissenting opinion

VI. A WIN OR LOSS FOR THE ACLU?

The ACLU filed an amicus brief urging reversal; the Supreme Court reversed the ruling of the Court of Appeals for the District of Columbia Circuit in a 6-3 vote, giving the ACLU an apparent win.

88. Black v. Cutter Laboratories

(Decided June 4, 1956; 351 U.S. 292)

I. ISSUE

A. Issues Discussed

Due process and equal protection

B. Legal Question Presented

Whether dismissing a Communist Party member from employment on the basis of the employee's Communist Party membership violates the due process or equal protection clauses of the Fourteenth Amendment.

C. Supreme Court's Answer

The Court determined there were adequate state law grounds for the decision in that petitioner was dismissed for "just cause." The Court dismissed the writ of certiorari because there was no federal question.

II. CASE SUMMARY

A. Background

"In 1949 Mrs. Doris Walker was discharged from her job at Cutter Laboratories, a manufacturer of pharmaceutical and biological products, on the claimed grounds that she was an active member of the Communist Party and had falsified her application for employment there. Petitioner, Bio-Lab Union of Local 225, United Office & Professional

Workers of America, sought reinstatement for Mrs. Walker before an Arbitration Board pursuant to a valid collective-bargaining agreement which authorized discharge for 'just cause' only. The Board determined that she had been discharged for union activity and, by a vote of 2 to 1, ordered her reinstatement. The Superior Court of San Francisco County confirmed the award and ordered it enforced. On appeal, the District Court of Appeal affirmed. The Supreme Court of California, however, reversed. Petitioners contend that the decision and opinion below violate constitutional principles embraced in the Equal Protection and Due Process Clauses of the Fourteenth Amendment."

The Supreme Court granted certiorari then dismissed the writ.

B. Counsel of Record/ACLU Attorney

ACLU Side (Petitioner/Appellant): Joseph Forer argued the cause for appellant. On the brief were Bertram Edises, A. L. Wirin, and Abraham Glasser.

Opposing Side (Respondent/Appellee): Gardiner Johnson and Thomas E. Stanton, Jr. argued the cause for appellee.

III. AMICI CURIAE

ACLU Side (Petitioner/Appellant)

Brief of amici curiae filed on behalf of the ACLU by Edward J. Ennis and Nanette Dembitz.

Brief of amici curiae filed on behalf of the Congress of Industrial Organizations and the CIO-California Industrial Union Council, by Arthur W. Goldberg, Jay A. Darwin, and Fred Okrand.

Brief of amicus curiae filed on behalf of the National Lawyers Guild, San Francisco Chapter, by Charles R. Garry.

Opposing Side (Respondent/Appellee)

Brief of amici curiae filed on behalf of the National Association of Manufacturers of the United States by Lambert H. Miller, Harvey M. Crow, and Fred B. Haught.

IV. THE SUPREME COURT'S DECISION

"[I]t is our duty to look beyond the broad sweep of the language and determine for ourselves precisely the ground on which the judgment rests. This means no more than that we should not pass on federal questions discussed in the opinion where it appears that the judgment rests on adequate state grounds. It is significant that the Supreme Court of California did not limit itself to a discussion of the application of the California public policy. It also subjected the findings of the Arbitration Board to a scrutinizing review. Of course, the scope of review of such findings under the California Arbitration Act is a matter exclusively for the courts of that State, and is not our concern.

First, the court determined that, since Mrs. Walker was a continuing member of the Communist Party, the doctrine of waiver could not be applied to this ground for discharge. The court noted that Mrs. Walker had remained a member of the Party 'on an active and devoted basis even at the time of the board hearings.'

Second, it is clear that the individual parties might have agreed that the circumstance of Communist Party membership would constitute 'just cause' under the contract, and no federal question would thereby be raised. It is implicit in the Arbitration Board's opinion that this was a reasonable construction of the contract, but since it applied a doctrine of waiver, no explicit findings on this point were made. But, as we read the opinion of the Supreme Court of California, after concluding that waiver could not be applied to the facts of this case, it decided that the 'just cause' provision of the contract permitted discharge on the ground of Communist Party membership, and that Mrs. Walker was discharged on that ground. [I]t might also be noted that the court below discussed the history of the clause in the contract which prohibited discrimination 'because of race, color, creed, national origin, religious belief, or Union affiliation.' At one time the word 'political' as well as 'religious belief' was included in the provision, but, by negotiation, it was deleted.

We believe that the Supreme Court of California construed the term 'just cause' to embrace membership in the Communist Party, and refused to apply a doctrine of waiver. As such, the decision involves only California's construction of a local contract under local law, and therefore no substantial federal question is presented. Moreover, even if the State Court's opinion be considered ambiguous, we should choose the interpretation which does not face us with a constitutional question. It follows that the writ must be dismissed."

V. JUSTICE VOTE

3 Pro ACLU Side vs. 6 Con Opposing Side

ACLU Side (Petitioner/Appellant)

1. Douglas, W. – Wrote dissenting opinion
2. Warren, E. – Joined Douglas' dissent
3. Black, H. – Joined Douglas' dissent

Opposing Side (Respondent/Appellee)

1. Clark, T. – Wrote majority opinion
2. Harlan, J. – Joined majority opinion
3. Reed, S. – Would affirm the judgment
4. Minton, S. – Joined majority opinion
5. Burton, H. – Joined majority opinion
6. Frankfurter, F. – Joined majority opinion

VI. A WIN OR LOSS FOR THE ACLU?

The ACLU filed an amicus brief urging reversal; the Supreme Court dismissed the writ of certiorari in a 6-3 vote, giving the ACLU an apparent loss.

89. Cole v. Young

(Decided June 11, 1956; 351 U.S. 536)

I. ISSUE

A. Issues Discussed

Communism

B. Legal Question Presented

"This case presents the question of the meaning of the term 'national security' as used in the Act of August 26, 1950, giving to the heads of certain departments and agencies of the Government summary suspension and unreviewable dismissal powers over their civilian employees, when deemed necessary 'in the interest of the national security of the United States.'"

C. Supreme Court's Answer

"[W]e conclude (1) that the term 'national security' is used in the Act in a definite and limited sense and relates only to those activities which are directly concerned with the Nation's safety, as distinguished from the general welfare; and (2) that no determination has been made that petitioner's position was affected with the 'national security,' as that term is used in the Act. It follows that his dismissal was not authorized by the 1950 Act and hence violated the Veterans' Preference Act."

II. CASE SUMMARY

A. Background

"Petitioner, a preference-eligible veteran under s 2 of the Veterans' Preference Act of 1944, held a position in the classified civil service as a food and drug inspector for the New York District of the Food and Drug Administration, Department of Health, Education, and Welfare. In November 1953, he was suspended without pay from his position pending investigation to determine whether his employment should be terminated. He was given a written statement of charges alleging that he had 'a close association with individuals reliably reported to be Communists' and that he had maintained a 'sympathetic association' with, had contributed funds and services to, and had attended social gatherings of an allegedly subversive organization.

Although afforded an opportunity to do so, petitioner declined to answer the charges or to request a hearing .... Thereafter, the Secretary of the Department of Health, Education, and Welfare ... determined that petitioner's continued employment was not 'clearly consistent with the interests of national security' and ordered the termination of his employment. Petitioner appealed his discharge to the Civil Service Commission, which declined to accept the appeal on the ground that the Veterans' Preference Act, under which petitioner claimed the right of appeal, was inapplicable to such discharges.

Petitioner thereafter brought an action in the District Court for the District of Columbia seeking a declaratory judgment that his discharge was invalid and that the Civil Service Commission had improperly refused to entertain his appeal, and an order requiring his reinstatement in his former position. The District Court granted the respondents' motion for judgment on the pleadings and dismissed the complaint. The Court of Appeals, with one judge dissenting, affirmed."

The Supreme Court granted certiorari to review the case.

B. Counsel of Record

ACLU Side (Petitioner/Appellant): David I. Shapiro argued the cause for appellant. With him on the brief were Osmond K. Fraenkel of the American Civil Liberties Union, and James H. Heller.

Opposing Side (Respondent/Appellee): Donald B. MacGuineas argued the cause for appellees. On the brief were Solicitor General Sobeloff, Assistant Attorney General Burger, Samuel D. Slade, and Benjamin Forman.

III. AMICI CURIAE

ACLU Side (Petitioner/Appellant)

No briefs of amici curiae were filed in support of appellant.

Opposing Side (Respondent/Appellee)

No briefs of amici curiae were filed in support of appellee.

IV. THE SUPREME COURT'S DECISION

"Section 14 of the Veterans' Preference Act provides that preference eligibles may be discharged only 'for such cause as will promote the efficiency of the service' and, among other procedural rights, 'shall have the right to appeal to the Civil Service Commission,' whose decision is made binding on the employing agency. Respondents concede that petitioner's discharge was invalid if that Act is controlling. They contend, however, ... that petitioner's discharge was authorized by the Act of August 26, 1950, which eliminates the right of appeal to the Civil Service Commission. Thus the sole question for decision is whether petitioner's discharge was authorized by the 1950 Act....

The Act was expressly made applicable only to [select departments]. Section 3 of the Act provides, however, that the Act may be extended 'to such other departments and agencies of the Government as the President may, from time to time, deem necessary in the best interests of national security,' and the President has extended the Act under this authority 'to all other departments and agencies of the Government.' [F]or purposes of this decision, ... the Act has validly been extended to apply to the Department of Health, Education, and Welfare.

The Act authorizes dismissals only upon a determination by the Secretary that the dismissal is 'necessary or advisable in the interest of the national security.' [W]e conclude (1) that the term 'national security' is used in the Act in a definite and limited sense and relates only to those activities which are directly concerned with the Nation's safety, as distinguished from the general welfare; and (2) that no determination has been made that petitioner's position was affected with the 'national security,' as that term is used in the Act. It follows that his dismissal was not authorized by the 1950 Act and hence violated the Veterans' Preference Act....

In interpreting the 1950 Act, it is important to note that that Act is not the only, nor even the primary, source of authority to dismiss Government employees....

Finally, the conclusion we draw from the face of the Act that 'national security' was used in a limited and definite sense is amply supported by the legislative history of the Act. . . .

From our holdings (1) that not all positions in the Government are affected with the 'national security' as that term is used in the 1950 Act, and (2) that no determination has been made that petitioner's position was one in which he could adversely affect the 'national security,' it necessarily follows that petitioner's discharge was not authorized by the 1950 Act. . . . Since petitioner's discharge was not authorized by the 1950 Act and hence violated the Veterans' Preference Act, the judgment of the Court of Appeals is reversed and the case is remanded . . . ."

V. JUSTICE VOTE

6 Pro ACLU Side vs. 3 Con Opposing Side

ACLU Side (Petitioner/Appellant)

1. Harlan, J. – Wrote majority opinion
2. Burton, H. – Announced majority opinion
3. Frankfurter, F. – Joined majority opinion
4. Warren, E. – Wrote majority opinion
5. Black, H. – Wrote concurring opinion
6. Douglas, W. – Joined Black's concurrence

Opposing Side (Respondent/Appellee)

1. Clark, T. – Joined Frankfurter's dissent
2. Reed, S. – Joined Clark's dissent
3. Minton, S. – Joined Clark's dissent

VI. A WIN OR LOSS FOR THE ACLU?

The ACLU served as counsel for appellant urging reversal of the judgment of the Court of Appeals; the Supreme Court reversed in a 6-3 vote, giving the ACLU an apparent win.

90. Walker v. City of Hutchinson

(Decided December 10, 1956; 352 U.S. 112)

I. ISSUE

A. Issues Discussed

State, civil procedure

B. Legal Question Presented

"[W]hether, under circumstances of this kind, newspaper publication alone measures up to the quality of notice the Due Process Clause of the Fourteenth Amendment requires as a prerequisite to proceedings to fix compensation in condemnation cases."

C. Supreme Court's Answer

"Measured by the principles stated in the Mullane case, we think that the notice by publication here falls short of the requirements of due process."

II. CASE SUMMARY

A. Background

"The appellant Lee Walker owned certain land in the City of Hutchinson, Kansas. In 1954 the City filed an action in the District Court of Reno County, Kansas, to condemn part of his property in order to open, widen, and extend one of the City's streets. The proceeding was instituted under the authority of Article 2, Chapter 26 of the General Statutes of Kansas, 1949. Pursuant to s 26—201 of that statute the court appointed three commissioners to determine compensation for the property taken and for any other damage suffered. These commissioners were required by s 26—202 to give landowners at least ten days' notice of the time and place of their proceedings. Such notice could be given either 'in writing . . . or by one publication in the official city paper . . . .' The appellant here was not given notice in writing but publication was made in the official city paper of Hutchinson. The commissioners fixed his damages at $725, and pursuant to statute, this amount was deposited with the city treasurer for the benefit of appellant. Section 26—205 authorized an appeal from the award of the commissioners if taken within 30 days after the filing of their report. Appellant took no appeal within the prescribed period. Some time later, however, he brought the present equitable action in the Kansas District Court. His petition alleged that he had never been notified of the condemnation proceedings and knew nothing about them until after the time for appeal had passed. He charged that the newspaper publication authorized by the statute was not sufficient notice to satisfy the Fourteenth Amendment's due process requirements. . . . After a hearing, the Kansas trial court denied relief, holding that the newspaper publication provided for by s 26—202 was sufficient notice of the Commissioners' proceedings to meet the requirements of the Due Process Clause. Agreeing with the trial court, the State Supreme Court affirmed."

The Supreme Court granted certiorari to review the case.

B. Counsel of Record

ACLU Side (Petitioner/Appellant): Herbert Monte Levy of the American Civil Liberties Union argued the cause for appellant. With him on the brief was A. Lewis Oswald.

Opposing Side (Respondent/Appellee): Fred C. Littooy argued the cause and filed a brief for appellees.

III. AMICI CURIAE

ACLU Side (Petitioner/Appellant)

No briefs of amici curiae were filed in support of appellant.

Opposing Side (Respondent/Appellee)

No briefs of amici curiae were filed in support of appellee.

IV. THE SUPREME COURT'S DECISION

"It cannot be disputed that due process requires that an owner whose property is taken for public use must be given a hearing in determining just compensation. The right to a hearing is meaningless without notice. In Mullane v. Central Hanover Bank & Trust Co., 339 U.S. 306, we gave thorough consideration to the problem of adequate notice under the Due Process Clause. That case establishes the rule that, if feasible, notice must be reasonably calculated to inform parties of proceedings which may directly and adversely affect their legally protected interests. We there called attention to the impossibility of setting up a rigid formula as to the kind of notice that must be given; notice required will vary with circumstances and conditions. We recognized that in some cases it might not be reasonably possible to give personal notice, for example where people are missing or unknown.

Measured by the principles stated in the Mullane case, we think that the notice by publication here falls short of the requirements of due process. It is common knowledge that mere newspaper publication rarely informs a landowner of proceedings against his property. In Mullane we pointed out many of the infirmities of such notice and emphasized the advantage of some kind of personal notice to interested parties. In the present case there seem to be no compelling or even persuasive reasons why such direct notice cannot be given. Appellant's name was known to the city and was on the official records. Even a letter would have apprised him that his property was about to be taken and that he must appear if he wanted to be heard as to its value.

Nothing in our prior decisions requires a holding that newspaper publication under the circumstances here provides adequate notice of a hearing to determine compensation. . . .

There is nothing peculiar about litigation between the Government and its citizens that should deprive those citizens of a right to be heard. Nor is there any reason to suspect that it will interfere with the orderly condemnation of property to preserve effectively the citizen's rights to a hearing in connection with just compensation. In too many instances notice by publication is no notice at all. It may leave government authorities free to fix one-sidedly the amount that must be paid owners for their property taken for public use.

For the foregoing reasons the judgment of the Supreme Court of Kansas is reversed and the cause is remanded . . . ."

V. JUSTICE VOTE

6 Pro ACLU Side vs. 2 Con Opposing Side

ACLU Side (Petitioner/Appellant)

1. Black, H. – Wrote majority opinion
2. Douglas, W. – Announced majority opinion
3. Warren, E. – Joined majority opinion
4. Harlan, J. – Joined majority opinion
5. Clark, T. – Joined majority opinion
6. Reed, S. – Joined majority opinion

Opposing Side (Respondent/Appellee)

1. Burton, H. – Wrote dissenting opinion
2. Frankfurter, F. – Wrote dissenting opinion

Brennan, W. – Took no part in the decision.

VI. A WIN OR LOSS FOR THE ACLU?

The ACLU served as counsel for appellent urging reversal of the judgment of the Kansas Supreme Court; the Supreme Court reversed in a 6-2 vote, giving the ACLU an apparent win.

91. Butler v. Michigan

(Decided February 25, 1957; 352 U.S. 380)

I. ISSUE

A. Issues Discussed

Freedom of speech

B. Legal Question Presented

Can a state prevent books from being made available to the general reading public if the book is found to have a potentially deleterious influence upon youth?

C. Supreme Court's Answer

This overly broad book ban violates freedom of speech.

II. CASE SUMMARY

A. Background

"Appellant was charged with [violating § 343 of the Michigan Penal Code] for selling to a police officer what the trial judge characterized as 'a book containing obscene, immoral, lewd, lascivious language, or descriptions, tending to incite minors to violent or depraved or immoral acts, manifestly tending to the corruption of the morals of youth.' Appellant moved to dismiss the proceeding on the claim that application of § 343 unduly restricted freedom of speech as protected by the Due Process Clause of the Fourteenth Amendment in that the statute (1) prohibited distribution of a book to the general public on the basis of the undesirable influence it may have upon youth; (2) damned a book and proscribed its sale merely because of some isolated passages that appeared objectionable when divorced from the book as a whole; and (3) failed to provide a sufficiently definite standard of guilt. After hearing the evidence, the trial judge denied the motion, and, in an oral opinion, held that '. . . the defendant is guilty because he sold a book in the City of Detroit containing this language [the passages deemed offensive], and also because the Court feels that even viewing the book as a whole, it [the objectionable language] was not necessary to the proper development of the theme of the book nor of the conflict expressed therein.' Appellant was fined $100.

Pressing his federal claims, appellant applied for leave to appeal to the Supreme Court of Michigan. Although the State consented to the granting of the application 'because the issues involved in this case are of great public interest, and because it appears that further clarification of the language of . . . [the statute] is necessary,' leave to appeal was denied."

On appeal the Supreme Court reversed the judgment of the Recorder's Court of Detroit.

B. Counsel of Record/ACLU Attorney

ACLU Side (Petitioner/Appellant): Manuel Lee Robbins argued the cause for appellant.

Opposing Side (Respondent/Appellee): Edmund E. Shepherd argued the cause for appellee.

III. AMICI CURIAE

ACLU Side (Petitioner/Appellant)

Brief of amici curiae filed on behalf of the Metropolitan Detroit Branch, ACLU, by Erwin B. Ellmann.

Brief of amici curiae filed on behalf of the American Book Publishers Council, Inc., by Horace S. Manges

Brief of amici curiae filed on behalf of the Authors League of America, Inc., by Irwin Karp and Osmond K. Fraenkel.

Opposing Side (Respondent/Appellee)

Brief of amici curiae filed on behalf of the State of Texas by Attorney General of Texas John Ben Shepperd, and Assistant Attorney General Philip Sanders.

IV. THE SUPREME COURT'S DECISION

"It is clear on the record that appellant was convicted because Michigan, by § 343, made it an offense for him to make available for the general reading public (and he in fact sold to a police officer) a book that the trial judge found to have a potentially deleterious influence upon youth. The State insists that, by thus quarantining the general reading public against books not too rugged for grown men and women in order to shield juvenile innocence, it is exercising its power to promote the general welfare. Surely, this is to burn the house to roast the pig. Indeed, the Solicitor General of Michigan has, with characteristic candor, advised the Court that Michigan has a statute specifically designed to protect its children against obscene matter 'tending to the corruption of the morals of youth.' But the appellant was not convicted for violating this statute.

We have before us legislation not reasonably restricted to the evil with which it is said to deal. The incidence of this enactment is to reduce the adult population of Michigan to reading only what is fit for children. It thereby arbitrarily curtails one of those liberties of the individual, now enshrined in the Due Process Clause of the Fourteenth Amendment, that history has attested as the indispensable conditions for the maintenance and progress of a free society. We are constrained to reverse this conviction."

The Supreme Court reversed the judgment of the Recorder's Court of Detroit.

V. JUSTICE VOTE

9 Pro ACLU Side vs. 0 Con Opposing Side

ACLU Side (Petitioner/Appellant)

1. Frankfurter, F. – Wrote majority opinion
2. Warren, E. – Joined majority opinion
3. Black, H. – Concurred in the result
4. Reed, S. – Joined majority opinion
5. Douglas, W. – Joined majority opinion
6. Burton, H. – Joined majority opinion
7. Clark, T. – Joined majority opinion
8. Harlan, J. – Joined majority opinion
9. Brennan, W. – Joined majority opinion

VI. A WIN OR LOSS FOR THE ACLU?

The ACLU, as amici curiae, urged reversal of the Recorder's Court of Detroit's judgment; the Supreme Court reversed in a 9-0 vote, giving the ACLU an apparent win.

92. Schware v. Bd. of Bar Exam'rs of N. M.

(Decided May 6, 1957; 353 U.S. 232)

I. ISSUE

A. Issues Discussed

Communism, state, civil rights

B. Legal Question Presented

"[W]hether petitioner, Rudolph Schware, has been denied a license to practice law in New Mexico in violation of the Due Process Clause of the Fourteenth Amendment to the United States Constitution."

C. Supreme Court's Answer

"On the record before us we hold that the State of New Mexico deprived petitioner of due process in denying him the opportunity to qualify for the practice of law."

II. CASE SUMMARY

A. Background

"New Mexico has a system for the licensing of persons to practice law similar to that in effect in most States. A Board of Bar Examiners determines if candidates for admission to the bar have the necessary qualifications. . . . The Board can refuse to permit him to take this examination unless he demonstrates that he has 'good moral character.' . . .

Schware filed an application with the Board of Bar Examiners requesting that he be permitted to take the bar examination scheduled for February 1954. . . . Among other things, he disclosed that he had used certain aliases between 1933 and 1937 and that he had been arrested on several occasions prior to 1940. When he appeared to take the examination, the Board informed him that he could not do so. He later requested a formal hearing on the denial of his application. The Board granted his request. At the hearing the Board told him for the first time why it had refused to permit him to take the bar examination. . . .

At the hearing petitioner called his wife, the rabbi of his synagogue, a local attorney and the secretary to the dean of the law school to testify about his character. He took the stand himself and was thoroughly examined under oath by the Board. His counsel introduced a series of letters that petitioner had written his wife from 1944 through 1946 while he was on duty in the Army. Letters were also introduced from every member of petitioner's law school graduating class except one who did not comment. And all of his law school professors who were then available wrote in regard to his moral character. The Board called no witnesses and introduced no evidence. . . .

At the conclusion of the hearing the Board reaffirmed its decision . . . . He appealed to the New Mexico Supreme Court. That court upheld the denial . . . ."

The Supreme Court granted certiorari to review the case.

B. Counsel of Record

ACLU Side (Petitioner/Appellant): Herbert Monte Levy of the American Civil Liberties Union argued the cause and filed a brief for appellant.

Opposing Side (Respondent/Appellee): William A. Sloan and Fred M. Standley, Attorney General of New Mexico, argued the cause and filed a brief for appellee.

III. AMICI CURIAE

ACLU Side (Petitioner/Appellant)

No briefs of amici curiae were filed in support of appellant.

Opposing Side (Respondent/Appellee)

No briefs of amici curiae were filed in support of appellee.

IV. THE SUPREME COURT'S DECISION

"A State cannot exclude a person from the practice of law or from any other occupation in a manner or for reasons that contravene the Due Process or Equal Protection Clause of the Fourteenth Amendment. A State can require high standards of qualification, such as good moral character or proficiency in its law, before it admits an applicant to the bar, but any qualification must have a rational connection with the applicant's fitness or capacity to practice law. . . .

Here the State concedes that Schware is fully qualified to take the examination in all respects other than good moral character. Therefore the question is whether the Supreme Court of New Mexico on the record before us could reasonably find that he had not shown good moral character.

There is nothing in the record which suggests that Schware has engaged in any conduct during the past 15 years which reflects adversely on his character. . . .

Despite Schware's showing of good character, the Board and court below thought there were certain facts in the record which raised substantial doubts about his moral fitness to practice law.

(1) Aliases.—From 1934 to 1937 Schware used certain aliases. . . . This is certainly not enough evidence to support an inference that petitioner has bad moral character more than 20 years later.

(2) Arrests.—In response to the questions on the Board's application form Schware stated that he had been arrested on several occasions . . . .

In summary, these arrests are wholly insufficient to support a finding that Schware had bad moral character at the time he applied to take the bar examination. They all occurred many years ago and in no case was he ever tried or convicted for the offense for which he was arrested.

(3) Membership in the Communist Party.—Schware admitted that he was a member of the Communist Party from 1932 to 1940. . . .

We conclude that his past membership in the Communist Party does not justify an inference that he presently has bad moral character.

The State contends that even though the use of aliases, the arrests, and the membership in the Communist Party would not justify exclusion of petitioner from the New Mexico bar if each stood alone, when all three are combined his exclusion was not unwarranted. We cannot accept this contention. In the light of petitioner's forceful showing of good moral character, the evidence upon which the State relies . . . cannot be said to raise substantial doubts about his present good moral character. . . .

On the record before us we hold that the State of New Mexico deprived petitioner of due process in denying him the opportunity to qualify for the practice of law. The judgment below is reversed and the case remanded . . . ."

V. JUSTICE VOTE

8 Pro ACLU Side vs. 0 Con Opposing Side

ACLU Side (Petitioner/Appellant)

1. Black, H. – Wrote majority opinion
2. Warren, E. – Joined majority opinion
3. Brennan, W. – Joined majority opinion
4. Douglas, W. – Joined majority opinion
5. Harlan, J. – Joined Frankfurter's concurrence
6. Clark, T. – Joined Frankfurter's concurrence
7. Frankfurter, F. – Wrote concurring opinion
8. Burton, H. – Joined majority opinion

Whittaker, C. – Took no part in the decision.

VI. A WIN OR LOSS FOR THE ACLU?

The ACLU served as counsel for appellant urging reversal of the judgment of the New Mexico Supreme Court; the U.S. Supreme Court reversed in an 8-0 vote, giving the ACLU an apparent win.

93. Konigsberg v. State Bar of California

(Decided May 6, 1957; 353 U.S. 252)

I. ISSUE

A. Issues Discussed

Governmental authority, First and Fourteenth Amendments

B. Legal Question Presented

"Does the evidence in the record support any reasonable doubts about Konigsberg's good character or his loyalty to the Governments of State and Nation" as to constitutionally justify denying him admission to the California Bar?

C. Supreme Court's Answer

There is no evidence that petitioner was, in fact, not of good moral character or that petitioner advocated government overthrow to justify denying him admission to the California Bar.

II. CASE SUMMARY

A. Background

"The petitioner, Raphael Konigsberg, graduated from the Law School of the University of Southern California in 1953 and four months later satisfactorily passed the California bar examination. Nevertheless, the State Committee of Bar Examiners, after several hearings, refused to certify him to practice law on the grounds he had failed to prove (1) that he was of good moral character and (2) that he did not advocate overthrow of the Government of the United States or California by unconstitutional means. As permitted by state law, Konigsberg asked the California Supreme Court to review the Committee's refusal to give him its certification. He contended that he had satisfactorily proved that he met all the requirements for admission to the bar, and that the Committee's action deprived him of right secured by the Fourteenth Amendment to the United States Constitution. The State Supreme Court, without opinion, and with three of its seven justices dissenting, denied his petition for review."

The Supreme Court granted certiorari to review the case and reversed.

B. Counsel of Record/ACLU Attorney

ACLU Side (Petitioner/Appellant): Edward Mosk argued the cause for appellant.

Opposing Side (Respondent/Appellee): Frank B. Belcher argued the cause for appellee.

III. AMICI CURIAE

ACLU Side (Petitioner/Appellant)

Brief of amici curiae filed on behalf of the ACLU, Southern California Branch by A. L. Wirin and Hugh R. Manes.

Brief of amici curiae filed on behalf of the National Lawyers Guild by Osmond K. Fraenkel, Jessica Davidson, and Abraham Unger.

Brief of amici curiae filed on behalf of the National Lawyers Guild, Los Angeles and Hollywood-Beverly Hills Chapters, by Daniel G. Marshall.

Opposing Side (Respondent/Appellee)

No briefs of amici curiae were filed in support of appellee.

IV. THE SUPREME COURT'S DECISION

"Even if it be assumed that Konigsberg was a member of the Communist Party in 1941, the mere fact of membership would not support an inference that he did not have good moral character. There was no evidence that he ever engaged in or abetted and unlawful or immoral activities—or even that he knew of or supported any actions of this nature. It may be, although there is no evidence in the record before us to that effect, that some members of that party were involved in illegal or disloyal activities, but petitioner cannot be swept into this group solely on the basis of his alleged membership in that party. . . .

Because of the very nature of our democracy such expressions of political views must be permitted. Citizens have a right under our constitutional system to criticize government officials and agencies. Courts are not, and should not be, immune to such criticism. Government censorship can no more be reconciled with our national constitutional standard of freedom of speech and press when done in the guise of determining 'moral character,' than if it should be attempted directly. . . . Almost all of the Bar Examiner's questions concerned his political affiliations, editorials and beliefs. Konigsberg repeatedly declined to answer such questions, explaining that his refusal was based on his understanding that under the First and Fourteenth Amendments to the United States Constitution a State could not inquire into a person's political opinions or associations and that he had a duty not to answer. . . .

We recognize the importance of leaving States free to select their own bars, but it is equally important that the State not exercise this power in an arbitrary or discriminatory manner nor in such way as to impinge on the freedom of political expression or association. A bar composed of lawyers of good character is a worthy objective but it is unnecessary to sacrifice vital freedoms in order to obtain that goal. It is also important both to society and the bar itself that lawyers be unintimidated—free to think, speak, and act as members of an Independent Bar. In this case we are compelled to conclude that there is no evidence in the record which rationally justifies a finding that Konigsberg failed to establish his good moral character or failed to show that he did not advocate forceful overthrow of the Government. Without some authentic reliable evidence of unlawful or immoral actions reflecting adversely upon him, it is difficult to comprehend why the State Bar Committee rejected a man of Konigsberg's background and character as morally unfit to practice law. As we said before, the mere fact of Konigsberg's past membership in the Communist Party, if true, without anything more, is not an adequate basis for concluding that he is disloyal or a person of bad character. A lifetime of good citizenship is worth very little if it is so frail that it cannot withstand the suspicions which apparently were the basis for the Committee's action.

The judgment of the court below is reversed and the case remanded for further proceedings not inconsistent with this opinion."

V. JUSTICE VOTE

5 Pro ACLU Side vs. 3 Con Opposing Side

ACLU Side (Petitioner/Appellant)

1. Black, H. – Wrote majority opinion
2. Douglas, W. – Joined majority opinion
3. Warren, E. – Joined majority opinion
4. Brennan, W. – Joined majority opinion
5. Burton, H. – Joined majority opinion

Opposing Side (Respondent/Appellee)

1. Frankfurter, F. – Wrote dissenting opinion
2. Harlan, J. – Wrote dissenting opinion
3. Clark, T. – Joined Harlan's dissent

Whittaker, C – Took no part in the decision

VI. A WIN OR LOSS FOR THE ACLU?

The ACLU filed as amici curiae urging reversal of the judgment of the Supreme Court of California; the U.S. Supreme Court reversed in a 5-3 vote, giving the ACLU an apparent win.

94. Watkins v. United States

(Decided June 17, 1957; 354 U.S. 178)

I. ISSUE

A. Issues Discussed

Due process

B. Legal Question Presented

Was petitioner "accorded a fair opportunity to determine whether he was within his rights in refusing to answer" the questions of the House of Representatives Committee on Un-American Activities?

C. Supreme Court's Answer

"Petitioner was . . . not accorded a fair opportunity to determine whether he was within his rights in refusing to answer, and his conviction is necessarily invalid under the Due Process Clause of the Fifth Amendment."

II. CASE SUMMARY

A. Background

Petitioner was convicted of violating 2 U.S.C. § 192 for "'contempt of Congress' . . . for refusing to make certain disclosures which he asserted to be beyond the authority of the committee to demand. . . .

On April 29, 1954, petitioner appeared as a witness in compliance with a subpoena issued by a Subcommittee of the Committee on Un-American Activities of the House of Representatives." Petitioner fully answered questions about his own activities, but when asked whether other people he knew were Communist Party members, he responded, "'I am not going to plead the fifth amendment, but I refuse to answer certain questions that I believe are outside the proper scope of your committee's activities. I will answer any questions which this committee puts to me about myself. I will also answer questions about those persons whom I knew to be members of the Communist Party and whom I believe still are. I will not, however, answer any questions with respect to others with whom I associated in the past. I do not believe that any law in this country requires me to testify about persons who may in the past have been Communist Party members or otherwise engaged in Communist Party activity but who to my best knowledge and belief have long since removed themselves from the Communist movement.

'I do not believe that such questions are relevant to the work of this committee nor do I believe that this committee has the right to undertake the public exposure of persons because of their past activities. I may be wrong, and the committee may have this power, but until and unless a court of law so holds and directs me to answer, I most firmly refuse to discuss the political activities of my past associates.'"

On certiorari the Supreme Court overturned the conviction.

B. Counsel of Record/ACLU Attorney

ACLU Side (Petitioner/Appellant): Joseph L. Rauh, Jr. argued the cause for appellant.

Opposing Side (Respondent/Appellee): Solicitor General Rankin argued the cause for appellee.

III. AMICI CURIAE

ACLU Side (Petitioner/Appellant)

Brief of amici curiae filed on behalf of the ACLU by Osmond K. Fraenkel and Barlow Smith.

Brief of amici curiae filed on behalf of Robert M. Metcalf by and Telford Taylor.

Opposing Side (Respondent/Appellee)

Brief of amici curiae filed on behalf of the American Bar Association by Herbert R. O'Conor.

IV. THE SUPREME COURT'S DECISION

"The power of the Congress to conduct investigations is inherent in the legislative process. That power is broad. . . . But, broad as is this power of inquiry, it is not unlimited. There is no general authority to expose the private affairs of individuals without justification in terms of the functions of the Congress. . . . No inquiry is an end in itself; it must be related to, and in furtherance of, a legitimate task of the Congress. Investigations conducted solely for the personal aggrandizement of the investigators or to 'punish' those investigated are indefensible."

"It is unquestionably the duty of all citizens to cooperate with the Congress in its efforts to obtain the facts needed for intelligent legislative action. It is their unremitting obligation to respond to subpoenas, to respect the dignity of the Congress and its committees and to testify fully with respect to matters within the province of proper investigation. This, of course, assumes that the constitutional rights of witnesses will be respected by the Congress as they are in a court of justice. The Bill of Rights is applicable to investigations as to all forms of governmental action. Witnesses cannot be compelled to give evidence against themselves. They cannot be subjected to unreasonable search and seizure. Nor can the First Amendment freedoms of speech, press, religion, or political belief and association be abridged."

"The statement of the Committee Chairman in this case, in response to petitioner's protest, was woefully inadequate to convey sufficient information as to the pertinency of the questions to the subject under inquiry. Petitioner was thus not accorded a fair opportunity to determine whether he was within his rights in refusing to answer, and his conviction is necessarily invalid under the Due Process Clause of the Fifth Amendment."

The Supreme Court reversed the judgment of the Court of Appeals and remanded the case to dismiss the indictment.

V. JUSTICE VOTE

6 Pro ACLU Side vs. 1 Con Opposing Side

ACLU Side (Petitioner/Appellant)

1. Warren, E. – Wrote majority opinion
2. Frankfurter, F. – Wrote concurring opinion
3. Brennan, W. – Joined majority opinion
4. Harlan, J. – Joined majority opinion
5. Black, H. – Joined majority opinion
6. Douglas, W. – Joined majority opinion

Opposing Side (Respondent/Appellee)

1. Clark, T. – Wrote dissenting opinion

Burton, H – Took no part in the decision
Whittaker, C – Took no part in the decision

VI. A WIN OR LOSS FOR THE ACLU?

The ACLU, as amicus curiae, urged reversal of the judgment of the Court of Appeals; the Supreme Court reversed in a 6-1 vote, giving the ACLU an apparent win.

95. Yates v. United States

(Decided June 17, 1957; 354 U.S. 298)

I. ISSUE

A. Issues Discussed

Freedom of association

B. Legal Question Presented

Are the "petitioners' contentions: (1) that the term 'organize' as used in the Smith Act was erroneously construed by the two lower courts; (2) that the trial court's instructions to the jury erroneously excluded from the case the issue of 'incitement to action'; (3) that the evidence was so insufficient as to require this Court to direct the acquittal of these petitioners; and (4) that petitioner Schneiderman's conviction was precluded by this Court's judgment in Schneiderman v. United States, 320 U.S. 118, under the doctrine of collateral estoppel," sufficient to overturn their convictions?

C. Supreme Court's Answer

All convictions are overturned with orders to acquit some petitioners and retry others.

II. CASE SUMMARY

A. Background

The fourteen petitioners were convicted under the federal Smith Act of "conspiring (1) to advocate and teach the duty and necessity of overthrowing the Government of the United States by force and violence, and (2) to organize, as the Communist Party of the United States, a society of persons who so advocate and teach, all with the intent of causing the overthrow of the Government by force and violence as speedily as circumstances would permit.

The conspiracy is alleged to have originated in 1940 and continued down to the date of the indictment in 1951. The indictment charged that in carrying out the conspiracy the defendants and their co-conspirators would (a) become members and officers of the Communist Party, with knowledge of its unlawful purposes, and assume leadership in carrying out its policies and activities; (b) cause to be organized units of the Party in California and elsewhere; (c) write and publish, in the 'Daily Worker' and other Party organs, articles on the proscribed advocacy and teaching; (d) conduct schools for the indoctrination of Party members in such advocacy and teaching, and (e) recruit new Party members, particularly from among persons employed in the key industries of the nation."

Petitioners were convicted after a jury trial, and their convictions affirmed by the Court of Appeals. On certiorari the Supreme Court reversed.

B. Counsel of Record/ACLU Attorney

ACLU Side (Petitioner/Appellant): Ben Margolis argued the cause for appellant in No. 6. With him on the brief were Norman Leonard, Alexander H. Schullman, A. L. Wirin and Leo Branton, Jr.

Robert W. Kenny argued the cause for appellant in No. 7. With him on the brief was Benjamin Dreyfus.

Augustin Donovan argued the cause and filed a brief for petitioners in No. 8.

Opposing Side (Respondent/Appellee): Philip R. Monahan argued the cause for appellee. With him on the brief were Solicitor General Rankin, Assistant Attorney General Willi am F. Tompkins and Harold D. Koffsky.

III. AMICI CURIAE

ACLU Side (Petitioner/Appellant)

Brief of amici curiae filed on behalf of the ACLU by David I. Shapiro, Osmond K. Fraenkel and Fred Okrand, and Rowland Watts.

Brief of amici curiae filed on behalf of Jack Wayne Hall and Joseph Kuzma et al., by Telford Taylor and Thomas D. McBride.

Opposing Side (Respondent/Appellee)

IV. THE SUPREME COURT'S DECISION

As to the term "organizing," "since the Communist Party came into being in 1945, and the indictment was not returned until 1951, the three-year statute of limitations had run on the 'organizing' charge, and required the withdrawal of that part of the indictment from the jury's consideration."

As to the jury instructions, "[t]he jury was never told that the Smith Act does not denounce advocacy in the sense of preaching abstractly the forcible overthrow of the Government. We think that the trial court's statement that the proscribed advocacy must include the 'urging,' 'necessity,' and 'duty' of forcible overthrow, and not merely its 'desirability' and 'propriety,' may not be regarded as a sufficient substitute for charging that the Smith Act reaches only advocacy of action for the overthrow of government by force and violence. [W]e must regard the trial court's charge in this respect as furnishing wholly inadequate guidance to the jury on this central point in the case. We cannot allow a conviction to stand on such 'an equivocal direction to the jury on a basic issue.'"

As to the evidence, "we have concluded that the evidence against petitioners Connelly, Kusnitz, Richmond, Spector, and Steinberg is so clearly insufficient that their acquittal should be ordered, but that as to petitioners Carlson, Dobbs, Fox, Healey (Mrs. Connelly), Lambert, Lima, Schneiderman, Stack, and Yates, we would not be justified in closing the way to their retrial."

As to petitioner Schneiderman's assertion of collateral estoppel, "the determinations made by this Court in Schneiderman could not operate as a complete bar to this proceeding. Wholly aside from the fact that the Court was there concerned with the state of affairs existing in 1927, whereas we are concerned here with the period 1948—1951, the issues in the present case are quite different. We are not concerned here with whether petitioner has engaged in 'agitation and exhortation calling for present violent action,' whether in 1927 or later. Even if it were conclusively established against the Government that neither petitioner nor the Communist Party had ever engaged in such advocacy, that circumstance would constitute no bar to a conviction under 18 U.S.C. § 371, of conspiring to advocate forcible overthrow of government in violation of the Smith Act."

The Supreme Court reversed, ordering a new trial for certain petitioners and acquittal for others.

V. JUSTICE VOTE

6 Pro ACLU Side vs. 1 Con Opposing Side

ACLU Side (Petitioner/Appellant)

1. Harlan, J. – Wrote majority opinion
2. Burton, H. – Wrote concurring opinion
3. Black, H. – Wrote opinion concurring in part and dissenting in part
4. Douglas, W. – Joined Black's opinion
5. Warren, E. – Joined majority opinion
6. Frankfurter, F. – Joined majority opinion

Opposing Side (Respondent/Appellee)

1. Clark, T. – Wrote dissenting opinion

Brennan, W – Took no part in the decision
Whittaker, C – Took no part in the decision

VI. A WIN OR LOSS FOR THE ACLU?

The ACLU, as amicus curiae, urged reversal of the Court of Appeals' judgment; the Supreme Court reversed in a 6-1 vote, giving the ACLU an apparent win.

96. Kingsley Books, Inc. v. Brown

(Decided June 24, 1957; 354 U.S. 436)

I. ISSUE

A. Issues Discussed

Freedom of speech, obscenity, prior restraints, due process

B. Legal Question Presented

Does imposing an injunction on the sale of obscene books and destroying the obscene material violate a booksellers' rights under the First Amendment as a prior restraint?

C. Supreme Court's Answer

Halting the sale of obscene materials, through an injunction with procedural safeguards that only limits the materials presently for sale, is not a prior restraint.

II. CASE SUMMARY

A. Background

Section 22-a of the New York Code of Criminal Procedure authorized the legal counsel of a municipality to seek an injunction "against the sale and distribution of written and printed material found after due trial to be obscene, and to obtain an order for the seizure, in default of surrender, of the condemned publications."

Appellee sought such an injunction against appellants Kingsley Books, Inc. and several other bookstores. Within a matter of days, the trial judge "found that the booklets annexed to the complaint and introduced in evidence were clearly obscene—were 'dirt for dirt's sake'; he enjoined their further distribution and ordered their destruction. He refused to enjoin 'the sale and distribution of later issues' on the ground that 'to rule against at volume not offered in evidence would . . . impose an unreasonable prior restraint upon freedom of the press.'

Not challenging the construction of the statute or the finding of obscenity, appellants took a direct appeal to the New York Court of Appeals, a proceeding in which the constitutionality of the statute was the sole question open to them. That court (one judge not sitting) found no constitutional infirmity . . . . A claim under the Due Process Clause of the Fourteenth Amendment made throughout the state litigation brought the case [to the Supreme Court] on appeal."

The Supreme Court affirmed.

B. Counsel of Record/ACLU Attorney

ACLU Side (Petitioner/Appellant): Emanuel Redfield argued the cause for appellant.

Opposing Side (Respondent/Appellee): Seymour B. Quel argued the cause for appellee.

III. AMICI CURIAE

ACLU Side (Petitioner/Appellant)

Brief of amici curiae filed on behalf of the New York Civil Liberties Union by Ephraim London and Sherman P. Kimball.

Opposing Side (Respondent/Appellee)

Brief of amici curiae on behalf of the Attorney General of New York by Attorney General of New York Louis J. Lefkowitz, Solicitor General John R. Davison, and Assistant Attorney General of Albany, New York Ruth Kessler Toch.

IV. THE SUPREME COURT'S DECISION

"It is not for this Court thus to limit the State in resorting to various weapons in the armory of the law. Whether proscribed conduct is to be visited by a criminal prosecution or by a qui tam action or by an injunction or by some or all of these remedies in combination, is a matter within the legislature's range of choice. . . .

The judicial angle of vision in testing the validity of a statute like § 22-a is 'the operation and effect of the statute in substance.' The phrase 'prior restraint' is not a self-wielding sword. Nor can it serve as a talismanic test. . . . Instead of requiring the bookseller to dread that the offer for sale of a book may, without prior warning, subject him to a criminal prosecution with the hazard of imprisonment, the civil procedure assures him that such consequences cannot follow unless he ignores a court order specifically directed to him for a prompt and carefully circumscribed determination of the issue of obscenity. Until then, he may keep the book for sale and sell it on his own judgment rather than steer 'nervously among the treacherous shoals.'

Criminal enforcement and the proceeding under § 22-a interfere with a book's solicitation of the public precisely at the same stage. In each situation the law moves after publication; the book need not in either case have yet passed into the hands of the public. . . . The method devised by New York in § 22-a for determining whether a publication is obscene does not differ in essential procedural safeguards from that provided under many state statutes making the distribution of obscene publications a misdemeanor. [T]he Due Process Clause does not subject the States to the necessity of having trial by jury in misdemeanor prosecutions.

Nor are the consequences of a judicial condemnation for obscenity under § 22-a more restrictive of freedom of expression than the result of conviction for a misdemeanor. . . . Section 22-a is concerned solely with obscenity and, as authoritatively construed, it studiously withholds restraint upon matters not already published and not yet found to be offensive. The judgment is affirmed."

V. JUSTICE VOTE

4 Pro ACLU Side vs. 5 Con Opposing Side

ACLU Side (Petitioner/Appellant)

1. Warren, E. – Wrote dissenting opinion
2. Douglas, W. – Wrote dissenting opinion
3. Black, H. – Joined Douglas' dissent
4. Brennan, W. – Wrote dissenting opinion

Opposing Side (Respondent/Appellee)

1. Frankfurter, F. – Wrote majority opinion
2. Harlan, J. – Joined majority opinion
3. Whittaker, C. – Joined majority opinion
4. Clark, T. – Joined majority opinion
5. Burton, H. – Joined majority opinion

VI. A WIN OR LOSS FOR THE ACLU?

The ACLU filed an amicus brief urging reversal of the judgment of the Court of Appeals of the State of New York; the Supreme Court in a 5-4 vote, giving the ACLU an apparent loss.

97. Roth v. United States

(Decided June 24, 1957; 354 U.S. 476)

I. ISSUE

A. Issues Discussed

Freedom of speech, obscenity

B. Legal Question Presented

Do obscenity statutes, either federal or state, prohibiting the sale or transfer of obscene materials through the mail, impinge upon freedom of speech and of the press as guaranteed by the First Amendment?

C. Supreme Court's Answer

Obscenity is not protected speech so the statutes punishing obscenity do not violate freedom of speech or of the press.

II. CASE SUMMARY

A. Background

"Roth conducted a business in New York in the publication and sale of books, photographs and magazines. He used circulars and advertising matter to solicit sales. He was convicted by a jury in the District Court for the Southern District of New York upon 4 counts of a 26-count indictment charging him with mailing obscene circulars and advertising, and an obscene book, in violation of the federal obscenity statute. His conviction was affirmed by the Court of Appeals for the Second Circuit."

"Alberts conducted a mail-order business from Los Angeles. He was convicted by the Judge of the Municipal Court of the Beverly Hills Judicial District (having waived a jury trial) under a misdemeanor complaint which charged him with lewdly keeping for sale obscene and indecent books, and with writing, composing and publishing an obscene advertisement of them, in violation of the California Penal Code. The conviction was affirmed by the Appellate Department of the Superior Court of the State of California in and for the County of Los Angeles."

On certiorari, the Supreme Court affirmed the judgments.

B. Counsel of Record/ACLU Attorney

ACLU Side (Petitioner/Appellant): David von G. Albrecht and O. John Rogge argued the cause for appellant in No. 582.

Stanley Fleishman argued the cause for appellant in No. 61.

Opposing Side (Respondent/Appellee): Roger D. Fisher argued the cause for appellee in No. 582.

Fred N. Whichello and Clarence A. Linn argued the cause for appellee in No. 61.

III. AMICI CURIAE

ACLU Side (Petitioner/Appellant)

Briefs of amici curiae filed on behalf of the ACLU by Emanuel Redfield.

Brief of amici curiae filed on behalf of the ACLU, Southern

California Branch, by A. L. Wirin and Hugh R. Manes.
Brief of amici curiae filed on behalf of the American Book Publishers Council, Inc., by Horace S. Manges and Jacob F. Raskin.
Brief of amici curiae filed on behalf of the Greenleaf Publishing Company and HMH Publishing Company, Inc., by Abe Fortas, William L. McGovern, Charles Reich, Abe Krash, Arnold, Fortas & Porter, Maurice Rosenfield, Harry Kalven, Jr., and Friedman, Zoline & Rosenfeld.
Brief of amici curiae filed on behalf of the Authors League of America, Inc., by Irwin Karp and Osmond K. Fraenkel.
Brief of amici curiae filed on behalf of Morris L. Ernst by Morris L. Ernst, Harriett F. Pilpel, Nancy F. Wechsler, Richard M. Ader, and Morton David Goldberg.

Opposing Side (Respondent/Appellee)

No briefs of amici curiae were filed in support of appellee.

IV. THE SUPREME COURT'S DECISION

"The dispositive question is whether obscenity is utterance within the area of protected speech and press. Although this is the first time the question has been squarely presented to this Court, either under the First Amendment or under the Fourteenth Amendment, expressions found in numerous opinions indicate that this Court has always assumed that obscenity is not protected by the freedoms of speech and press. . . . The guaranties of freedom of expression in effect in 10 of the 14 States which by 1792 had ratified the Constitution, gave no absolute protection for every utterance."

"All ideas having even the slightest redeeming social importance—unorthodox ideas, controversial ideas, even ideas hateful to the prevailing climate of opinion—have the full protection of the guaranties, unless excludable because they encroach upon the limited area of more important interests. But implicit in the history of the First Amendment is the rejection of obscenity as utterly without redeeming social importance."

"Obscene material is material which deals with sex in a manner appealing to prurient interest. . . . It is therefore vital that the standards for judging obscenity safeguard the protection of freedom of speech and press for material which does not treat sex in a manner appealing to prurient interest" The current test for obscenity is "whether to the average person, applying contemporary community standards, the dominant theme of the material taken as a whole appeals to prurient interest."

The Supreme Court affirmed the lower court judgments.

V. JUSTICE VOTE

3 Pro ACLU Side vs. 6 Con Opposing Side

ACLU Side (Petitioner/Appellant)

1. Douglas, W. – Wrote dissenting opinion
2. Black, H. – Joined Douglas' dissent
3. Harlan, J. – Wrote opinion concurring in No. 61 and dissenting in No. 582

Opposing Side (Respondent/Appellee)

1. Brennan, W. – Wrote majority opinion
2. Clark, T. – Joined majority opinion
3. Burton, H. – Joined majority opinion
4. Whittaker, C. – Joined majority opinion
5. Frankfurter, F. – Joined majority opinion
6. Warren, E. – Wrote concurring opinion

VI. A WIN OR LOSS FOR THE ACLU?

The ACLU, as amicus curiae, urged reversal of the lower court judgments; the Supreme Court affirmed in a 6-3 vote, giving the ACLU an apparent loss.

98. Lightfoot v. United States

(Decided October 14, 1957; 355 U.S. 2)

I. ISSUE

A. Issues Discussed

Governmental authority, First Amendment, freedom of speech and of association

B. Legal Question Presented

Whether petitioner's conviction under the membership clause of the Smith Act was in error.

C. Supreme Court's Answer

Petitioner's conviction was in error and should be reversed.

II. CASE SUMMARY

A. Background

Petitioner Lightfoot was a "Member of the National Committee of the Communist Party of the United States." Because of his membership and active participation in the Communist Party, whose aim was allegedly "the overthrow and destruction of the Government of the United States by force and violence," petitioner was charged with violating the "membership clause" of the Smith Act, which criminalizes these activities.

The District Court convicted petitioner. Petitioner then appealed to the Court of Appeals for the Seventh Circuit, which affirmed the conviction. The Court of Appeals held that the "membership clause" was constitutional.[1]

The Supreme Court granted certiorari and reversed the conviction.

B. Counsel of Record/ACLU Attorney

ACLU Side (Petitioner/Appellant): John J. Abt argued the cause for appellant.
Opposing Side (Respondent/Appellee): Solicitor General Rankin, Assistant Attorney General William F. Tompkins, Harold D. Koffsky, and William F. O'Donnell argued the cause for appellee.

1 United States v. Lightfoot, 228 F.2d 861 (7th Cir. 1956).

III. AMICI CURIAE

ACLU Side (Petitioner/Appellant)

Brief of amici curiae filed on behalf of the ACLU by Barent Ten Eyck.

Opposing Side (Respondent/Appellee)

No briefs of amici curiae were filed in support of appellee.

IV. THE SUPREME COURT'S DECISION

"Upon consideration of the entire record and the confession of error by the Solicitor General, thc judgment of the United States Court of Appeals for the Seventh Circuit is reversed. *Jencks v. United States*, 353 U.S. 657."

V. JUSTICE VOTE

9 Pro ACLU Side vs. 0 Con Opposing Side

ACLU Side (Petitioner/Appellant)

1. Douglas, W. – Per curiam decision
2. Warren, E. – Per curiam decision
3. Black, H. – Per curiam decision
4. Brennan, W. – Per curiam decision
5. Harlan, J. – Per curiam decision
6. Whittaker, C. – Per curiam decision
7. Clark, T. – Per curiam decision
8. Burton, H. – Per curiam decision
9. Frankfurter, F. – Per curiam decision

VI. A WIN OR LOSS FOR THE ACLU?

The ACLU filed an amicus brief urging reversal of the judgment of the Court of Appeals for the Seventh Circuit; the Supreme Court, in a per curiam opinion, reversed in a 9-0 vote, giving the ACLU an apparent win.

99. Scales v. United States

(Decided October 15, 1957; 355 U.S. 1)

I. ISSUE

A. Issues Discussed

Governmental authority, First Amendment, freedom of speech and of association

B. Legal Question Presented

Whether petitioner's conviction under the membership clause of the Smith Act was in error.

C. Supreme Court's Answer

The conviction was in error and should be reversed.

II. CASE SUMMARY

A. Background

Petitioner Scales was charged with a violation of the "membership clause" of the Smith Act, due to his membership in Communist Party, a group which allegedly advocated overthrow of government by force and violence, and because he allegedly knew of and approved of such overthrow. The District Court for the Middle District of North Carolina convicted petitioner in a jury trial. Petitioner appealed and the Court of Appeals for the Fourth Circuit affirmed the conviction, holding that the evidence was sufficient to sustain the conviction.[1]

Petitioner sought review in the Supreme Court, and the Supreme Court reversed.

B. Counsel of Record/ACLU Attorney

ACLU Side (Petitioner/Appellant): Telford Taylor argued the cause for appellant.

Opposing Side (Respondent/Appellee): Solicitor General Rankin, Assistant Attorney General William F. Tompkins, Harold D. Koffsky, Kevin T. Maroney, William F. O'Donnell, and Philip T. White argued the cause for appellee.

III. AMICI CURIAE

ACLU Side (Petitioner/Appellant)

Brief of amici curiae filed on behalf of the ACLU by Barent Ten Eyck.

Opposing Side (Respondent/Appellee)

No briefs of amici curiae were filed in support of appellee.

IV. THE SUPREME COURT'S DECISION

"Upon consideration of the entire record and the confession of error by the Solicitor General, the judgment of the United States Court of Appeals for the Fourth Circuit is reversed. *Jencks v. United States*, 353 U.S. 657."

V. JUSTICE VOTE

9 Pro ACLU Side vs. 0 Con Opposing Side

ACLU Side (Petitioner/Appellant)

1. Douglas, W. – Per curiam decision
2. Warren, E. – Per curiam decision
3. Black, H. – Per curiam decision
4. Brennan, W. – Per curiam decision
5. Harlan, J. – Per curiam decision
6. Whittaker, C. – Per curiam decision
7. Clark, T. – Per curiam decision
8. Burton, H. – Per curiam decision
9. Frankfurter, F. – Per curiam decision

VI. A WIN OR LOSS FOR THE ACLU?

The ACLU filed an amicus brief urging reversal of the judgment of the Court of Appeals for the Fourth Circuit; the Supreme Court, in a per curiam opinion, reversed in a 9-0 vote, giving the ACLU an apparent win.

1 Scales v. United States, 227 F.2d 581 (4th Cir. 1955).

100. Staub v. City of Baxley

(Decided January 13, 1958; 355 U.S. 313)

I. ISSUE

A. Issues Discussed

Freedom of speech

B. Legal Question Presented

Was a city ordinance, which made it an offense to solicit paid membership in an organization without first acquiring a permit city officials had broad discretion to deny, constitutional?

C. Supreme Court's Answer

Requiring a permit for solicitation and allowing broad discretion for city officials to grant or deny it infringes freedom of speech and is unconstitutional.

II. CASE SUMMARY

A. Background

A city ordinance in Baxley, Georgia, made it an offense to "solicit membership for any organization union or society of any sort which requires from its members the payments of membership fees, dues or is entitled to make assessment against its members," without first applying for and receiving a permit from the Mayor and Council of Baxley. "In passing upon such application the Mayor and Council shall consider the character of the applicant, the nature of the business of the organization for which members are desired to be solicited, and its effects upon the general welfare of citizens of the City of Baxley."

Appellant, an International Ladies' Garment Workers Union employee, was convicted of violating the ordinance after she, without applying for a permit, solicited private homes of employees of a manufacturing company, in order to encourage them to join the union. The Georgia Court of Appeals affirmed the conviction. The Supreme Court of Georgia denied an application for certiorari.

The U.S. Supreme Court granted certiorari and reversed.

B. Counsel of Record/ACLU Attorney

ACLU Side (Petitioner/Appellant): Morris P. Glushien argued the cause for appellant.

Opposing Side (Respondent/Appellee): J.H. Highsmith argued the cause for appellee.

III. AMICI CURIAE

ACLU Side (Petitioner/Appellant)

Brief of amici curiae filed on behalf of the ACLU by Murray A. Gordon and Rowland Watts.

Brief of amici curiae filed on behalf of the Workers Defense League by Carl Rachlin, Rachlin, Migdal & Low, Leon Becker, and John C. Somers.

Opposing Side (Respondent/Appellee)

No briefs of amici curiae were filed in support of appellee.

IV. THE SUPREME COURT'S DECISION

"Appellant's first contention in this Court is that the ordinance is invalid on its face because it makes enjoyment of the constitutionally guaranteed freedom of speech contingent upon the will of the Mayor and Council of the City, and thereby constitutes a prior restraint upon, and abridges, that freedom. Believing that appellant is right in that contention and that the judgment must be reversed for that reason, we confine our considerations to that particular question and do not reach other questions presented. . . .

It will also be noted that the permit is not to be issued as a matter of course, but only upon the affirmative action of the Mayor and Council of the City. They are expressly authorized to refuse to grant the permit if they do not approve of the applicant or of the union or of the union's 'effects upon the general welfare of citizens of the City of Baxley.' These criteria are without semblance of definitive standards or other controlling guides governing the action of the Mayor and Council in granting or withholding a permit. It is thus plain that they act in this respect in their uncontrolled discretion. It is settled by a long line of recent decisions of this Court that an ordinance which, like this one, makes the peaceful enjoyment of freedoms which the Constitution guarantees contingent upon the uncontrolled will of an official—as by requiring a permit or license which may be granted or withheld in the discretion of such official—is an unconstitutional censorship or prior restraint upon the enjoyment of those freedoms. . . .

It is undeniable that the ordinance authorized the Mayor and Council of the City of Baxley to grant 'or refuse to grant' the required permit in their uncontrolled discretion. It thus makes enjoyment of speech contingent upon the will of the Mayor and Council of the City, although that fundamental right is made free from congressional abridgment by the First Amendment and is protected by the Fourteenth from invasion by state action. For these reasons, the ordinance, on its face, imposes an unconstitutional prior restraint upon the enjoyment of First Amendment freedoms and lays 'a forbidden burden upon the exercise of liberty protected by the Constitution.' Therefore, the judgment of conviction must fall."

The Supreme Court reversed the judgment of the Georgia Court of Appeals.

V. JUSTICE VOTE

7 Pro ACLU Side vs. 2 Con Opposing Side

ACLU Side (Petitioner/Appellant)

1. Whittaker, C. – Wrote majority opinion
2. Douglas, W. – Joined majority opinion
3. Warren, E. – Joined majority opinion
4. Black, H. – Joined majority opinion
5. Burton, H. – Joined majority opinion
6. Harlan, J. – Joined majority opinion
7. Brennan, W. – Joined majority opinion

Opposing Side (Respondent/Appellee)

1. Frankfurter, F. – Wrote dissenting opinion
2. Clark, T. – Joined dissenting opinion

VI. A WIN OR LOSS FOR THE ACLU?

The ACLU filed an amicus brief urging reversal; the Supreme Court reversed the ruling of the Georgia Court of Appeals in a 7-2 vote, giving the ACLU an apparent win.

101. Wilson v. Loew's, Inc.

(Decided March 3, 1958; 355 U.S. 597)

I. ISSUE

A. Issues Discussed

State law, Fifth and Fourteenth Amendments

B. Legal Question Presented

Did the lower courts in this case deny petitioners their constitutional rights by their decisions?

C. Supreme Court's Answer

The judgment rests on state law grounds so the writ of certiorari is dismissed.

II. CASE SUMMARY

A. Background

Petitioners, twenty-three motion-picture industry professionals were denied work by various executives in the industry, respondents. The denial was allegedly because they "refused on constitutional grounds to answer questions 'concerning their political affiliations, associations and beliefs" in front of the Un-American Activities Committee of the House of Representatives, in accordance with their Fifth Amendment rights.

Petitioners brought suit, which was dismissed without leave to amend when the court granted respondent's demurrer. The decision was upheld on appeal.[1]

The Supreme Court granted certiorari, but subsequently dismissed the writ of certiorari as improvidently granted.

B. Counsel of Record/ACLU Attorney

ACLU Side (Petitioner/Appellant): Robert W. Kenny and Ben Margolis argued the cause for appellant.

Opposing Side (Respondent/Appellee): Irving M. Walker and Herman F. Selvin argued the cause for industry appellees.

Guy Richards Crump submitted the cause for respondents Doyle, Jackson, and Wheeler.

III. AMICI CURIAE

ACLU Side (Petitioner/Appellant)

Brief of amici curiae filed on behalf of the ACLU by Edward J. Ennis, Nanette Dembitz, A. L. Wirin, and Rowland Watts.

Opposing Side (Respondent/Appellee)

No briefs of amici curiae were filed in support of appellee.

1 Wilson v. Loew's, Inc., 298 P.2d 152 (Cal. Dist. Ct. App. 1956).

IV. THE SUPREME COURT'S DECISION

"The writ is dismissed as improvidently granted because the judgment rests on an adequate state ground."

V. JUSTICE VOTE

1 Pro ACLU Side vs. 8 Con Opposing Side

ACLU Side (Petitioner/Appellant)

1. Douglas, W. – Wrote dissenting opinion

Opposing Side (Respondent/Appellee)

1. Warren, E. – Per curiam decision
2. Black, H. – Per curiam decision
3. Frankfurter, F. – Per curiam decision
4. Burton, H. – Per curiam decision
5. Clark, T. – Per curiam decision
6. Harlan, J. – Per curiam decision
7. Brennan, W. – Per curiam decision
8. Whittaker, C. – Per curiam decision

VI. A WIN OR LOSS FOR THE ACLU?

The ACLU filed an amicus brief urging reversal; the Supreme Court dismissed the writ of certiorari as improvidently granted in an 8-1 vote, giving the ACLU an apparent loss.

102. Trop v. Dulles

(Decided March 31, 1958; 356 U.S. 86)

I. ISSUE

A. Issues Discussed

Immigration/Citizenship, 8th Amendment, military

B. Legal Question Presented

"The petitioner in this case, a nativeborn American, is declared to have lost his United States citizenship and become stateless by reason of his conviction by court-martial for wartime desertion. As in Perez v. Brownell, 356 U.S. 44, the issue before us is whether this forfeiture of citizenship comports with the Constitution."

C. Supreme Court's Answer

"We believe . . . that use of denationalization as a punishment is barred by the Eighth Amendment."

II. CASE SUMMARY

A. Background

"In 1944 petitioner was a private in the United States Army, serving in French Morocco. On May 22, he escaped from a stockade at Casablanca, where he had been confined following a previous breach of discipline. The next day petitioner and a companion were walking along a road towards Rabat, in the general direction back to Casablanca, when an Army truck approached and stopped. A witness testified that petitioner boarded the truck willingly and that no words were spoken. In Rabat petitioner was turned over to military police. Thus ended petitioner's 'desertion.'

He had been gone less than a day and had willingly surrendered to an officer on an Army vehicle while he was walking back towards his base. He testified that at the time he and his companion were picked up by the Army truck, 'we had decided to return to the stockade. The going was tough. We had no money to speak of, and at the time we were on foot and we were getting cold and hungry.' A general courtmartial convicted petitioner of desertion and sentenced him to three years at hard labor, forfeiture of all pay and allowances and a dishonorable discharge.

In 1952 petitioner applied for a passport. His application was denied on the ground that under the provisions of Section 401(g) of the Nationality Act of 1940, as amended, he had lost his citizenship by reason of his conviction and dishonorable discharge for wartime desertion. In 1955 petitioner commenced this action in the District Court, seeking a declaratory judgment that he is a citizen. The Government's motion for summary judgment was granted, and the Court of Appeals for the Second Circuit affirmed, Chief Judge Clark dissenting."

The Supreme Court granted certiorari to review the case.

B. Counsel of Record

ACLU Side (Petitioner/Appellant): Osmond K. Fraenkel (ACLU chief counsel 1954-1977) argued the cause and filed the briefs for appellant.

Opposing Side (Respondent/Appellee): Oscar H. Davis argued the cause for appellees on the original argument, and Solicitor General Rankin on the reargument. With them on the briefs were Warren Olnej, III, then Assistant Attorney General, and J. F. Bishop. Beatrice Rosenberg was also with them on the brief on the reargument.

III. AMICI CURIAE

ACLU Side (Petitioner/Appellant)

No briefs of amici curiae were filed in support of appellant.

Opposing Side (Respondent/Appellee)

No briefs of amici curiae were filed in support of appellees.

IV. THE SUPREME COURT'S DECISION

"Section 401(g), the statute that decrees the forfeiture of this petitioner's citizenship, is based directly on a Civil War statute, which provided that a deserter would lose his 'rights of citizenship.' The meaning of this phrase was not clear. . . .

We conclude that the judgment in this case must be reversed for the following reasons. . . .

In Perez v. Brownell, I expressed the principles that I believe govern the constitutional status of United States citizenship. It is my conviction that citizenship is not subject to the general powers of the National Government and therefore cannot be divested in the exercise of those powers. . . .

Under these principles, this petitioner has not lost his citizenship. . . .

On this ground alone the judgment in this case should be reversed. . . .

Since a majority of the Court concluded in Perez v. Brownell that citizenship may be divested in the exercise of some governmental power, I deem it appropriate to state additionally why the action taken in this case exceeds constitutional limits, even under the majority's decision in Perez. . . .

The exact scope of the constitutional phrase 'cruel and unusual' has not been detailed by this Court. But the basic policy reflected in these words is firmly established in the Anglo-American tradition of criminal justice. . . . The basic concept underlying the Eighth Amendment is nothing less than the dignity of man. . . .

We believe, as did Chief Judge Clark in the court below, that use of denationalization as a punishment is barred by the Eighth Amendment. . . .

In concluding as we do that the Eighth Amendment forbids Congress to punish by taking away citizenship, we are mindful of the gravity of the issue inevitably raised whenever the constitutionality of an Act of the National Legislature is challenged. . . .

We are oath-bound to defend the Constitution. . . .

The provisions of the Constitution are not time-worn adages or hollow shibboleths. They are vital, living principles that authorize and limit governmental powers in our Nation. They are the rules of government. When the constitutionality of an Act of Congress is challenged in this Court, we must apply those rules. If we do not, the words of the Constitution become little more than good advice.

When it appears that an Act of Congress conflicts with one of these provisions, we have no choice but to enforce the paramount commands of the Constitution. . . .

Reversed and remanded."

V. JUSTICE VOTE

5 Pro ACLU Side vs. 4 Con Opposing Side

ACLU Side (Petitioner/Appellant)

1. Warren, E. – Wrote majority opinion
2. Brennan, W. – Wrote concurring opinion
3. Black, H. – Wrote concurring opinion
4. Douglas, W. – Joined Black's concurrence
5. Whittaker, C. – Joined majority opinion

Opposing Side (Respondent/Appellee)

1. Harlan, J. – Joined Frankfurter's dissent
2. Burton, H. – Joined Frankfurter's dissent
3. Clark, T. – Joined Frankfurter's dissent
4. Frankfurter, F. – Wrote dissenting opinion

VI. A WIN OR LOSS FOR THE ACLU?

The ACLU served as counsel for appelant urging reversal of the judgment of the Court of Appeals; the Supreme Court reversed in a 5-4 vote, giving the ACLU an apparent win.

103. Kent v. Dulles

(Decided June 16, 1958; 357 U.S. 116)

I. ISSUE

A. Issues Discussed

Right to travel, due process

B. Legal Question Presented

Whether the Secretary of State has the power to refuse to issue passports to individuals because they are suspected of being Communists and refuse to submit to questions about their beliefs.

C. Supreme Court's Answer

Denying passports on the ground of suspected Communism because the individuals refuse to submit to questions about their beliefs violates the right to travel without due process.

II. CASE SUMMARY

A. Background

"This case concerns two applications for passports, denied by the Secretary of State. One was by Rockwell Kent who desired to visit England and attend a meeting of an organization known as the 'World Council of Peace' in Helsinki, Finland. The Director of the Passport Office informed Kent that issuance of a passport was precluded by § 51.135 of the Regulations promulgated by the Secretary of State on two grounds: (1) that he was a Communist and (2) that he had had 'a consistent and prolonged adherence to the Communist Party line.' . . .

Kent was also advised of his right to an informal hearing under § 51.137 of the Regulations [and of the necessity], before a passport would be issued, to submit an affidavit as to whether he was then or ever had been a Communist. Kent [claimed] that the requirement of an affidavit concerning Communist Party membership 'is unlawful and that for that reason and as a matter of conscience,' he would not supply one. [He maintained] that any matters unrelated to the question of his citizenship were irrelevant to the Department's consideration of his application. The Department advised him that no further consideration of his application would be given until he satisfied the requirements of the Regulations.

Thereupon Kent sued in the District Court for declaratory relief. The District Court granted summary judgment for respondent. On appeal the case of Kent was heard with that of Dr. Walter Briehl, a psychiatrist [who refused to submit an affidavit but requested a hearing].

At that hearing Briehl raised three objections: (1) that his 'political affiliations' were irrelevant to his right to a passport; (2) that 'every American citizen has the right to travel regardless of politics'; and (3) that the burden was on the Department to prove illegal activities by Briehl. . . .Briehl filed his complaint in the District Court which held that his case was indistinguishable from Kent's and dismissed the complaint.

The Court of Appeals heard the two cases en banc and affirmed the District Court by a divided vote."

On certiorari, the Supreme Court reversed.

B. Counsel of Record/ACLU Attorney

ACLU Side (Petitioner/Appellant): Leonard B. Boudin argued the cause for the appellant.

Opposing Side (Respondent/Appellee): Solicitor General Rankin argued the cause for appellee.

III. AMICI CURIAE

ACLU Side (Petitioner/Appellant)

Brief of amicus curiae filed on behalf of the ACLU by Osmond K. Fraenkel, William J. Butler, Richard B. Jablow, Stanley Geller, and Rowland Watts.

Opposing Side (Respondent/Appellee)

No briefs of amici curiae were filed in support of appellee.

IV. THE SUPREME COURT'S DECISION

"The right to travel is a part of the 'liberty' of which a citizen cannot be deprived without due process of law under the Fifth Amendment. . . . Freedom of movement across frontiers in either direction, and inside frontiers as well, was a part of our heritage. Travel abroad, like travel within the country, may be necessary for a livelihood. It may be as close to the heart of the individual as the choice of what he eats, or wears, or reads. Freedom of movement is basic in our scheme of values. . . .

Since we start with an exercise by an American citizen of an activity included in constitutional protection, we will not readily infer that Congress gave the Secretary of State unbridled discretion to grant or withhold it. . . . Where activities or enjoyment, natural and often necessary to the well-being of an American citizen, such as travel, are involved, we will construe narrowly all delegated powers that curtail or dilute them. . . .

Thus we do not reach the question of constitutionality. We only conclude that § 1185 and § 211a do not delegate to the Secretary the kind of authority exercised here. We deal with beliefs, with associations, with ideological matters. We must remember that we are dealing here with citizens who have neither been accused of crimes nor found guilty. They are being denied their freedom of movement solely because of their refusal to be subjected to inquiry into their beliefs and associations. They do not seek to escape the law nor to violate it. They may or may not be Communists. But assuming they are, the only law which Congress has passed expressly curtailing the movement of Communists across our borders has not yet become effective. It would therefore be strange to infer that pending the effectiveness of that law, the Secretary has been silently granted by Congress the larger, the more pervasive power to curtail in his discretion the free movement of citizens in order to satisfy himself about their beliefs or associations."

The Supreme Court reversed the judgment.

V. JUSTICE VOTE

5 Pro ACLU Side vs. 4 Con Opposing Side

ACLU Side (Petitioner/Appellant)

1. Douglas, W. – Wrote majority opinion
2. Brennan, W. – Joined majority opinion
3. Black, H. – Joined majority opinion
4. Frankfurter, F. – Joined majority opinion
5. Warren, E. – Joined majority opinion

Opposing Side (Respondent/Appellee)

1. Clark, T. – Wrote dissenting opinion
2. Burton, H. – Joined dissenting opinion

3. Harlan, J. – Joined dissenting opinion
4. Whittaker, C. – Joined dissenting opinion

VI. A WIN OR LOSS FOR THE ACLU?

The ACLU, as amicus curiae, urged reversal of the judgment of the Court of Appeals for the District of Columbia Circuit; the Supreme Court reversed in a 5-4 vote, giving the ACLU an apparent win.

104. Crooker v. California

(Decided June 30, 1958; 357 U.S. 433)

I. ISSUE

A. Issues Discussed

Criminal procedure, due process

B. Legal Question Presented

Was the defendant denied due process of law by admitting into evidence a confession taken while he was in custody and had not been allowed to consult with his attorney?

C. Supreme Court's Answer

Defendant was not denied due process by admission of the confession given the circumstances of the confession.

II. CASE SUMMARY

A. Background

Petitioner Crooker, a college graduate who completed one year of law school, was arrested on suspicion of murder. While in custody at the Los Angeles Police Station, petitioner refused to submit to a lie detector test and requested to call an attorney. However, records indicate police ignored his request.

"[P]etitioner was interrogated for the first time from 8:30-9:30 p.m., the questioning being conducted by four officers and centering around his refusal of the lie detector test. During this time he asked for an opportunity to get a lawyer, naming a specific attorney whom he thought might represent him, but was told that 'after [the] investigation was concluded he could call an attorney.'"

He was then transferred to another police station and questioned by five officers from 11 p.m. to shortly after midnight. Petitioner was then booked, physically examined, and questioned again by the five officers from 1-2 a.m. After the final interrogation, petitioner wrote and signed a confession. He was then taken to the scene of the crime to reenact the crime.

At 5 a.m. he was jailed and allowed to sleep. That afternoon petitioner was asked to orally repeat the confession. "Petitioner balked at doing so and again asked that his attorney be called. Thereupon the District Attorney placed the call for him and listened to the conversation while petitioner talked on an extension phone with the attorney. Neither petitioner nor his attorney was aware that a tape recording was being made of everything that transpired in the office. The District Attorney interrupted at one point to deny that petitioner was forced to answer police questions, and later to advise that the most convenient time for the attorney to see petitioner would be at 7 p.m. back at the West Los Angeles Police Station. After the phone call, petitioner was returned to jail to meet his attorney that evening. From that time forward, through both arraignment and trial, he was represented by his own counsel."

Petitioner was convicted of murder and sentenced to death. The Supreme Court of California affirmed.

The U.S. Supreme Court granted certiorari to decide whether the confession was in violation of petitioner's constitutional rights and affirmed.

B. Counsel of Record/ACLU Attorney

ACLU Side (Petitioner/Appellant): Robert W. Armstrong argued the cause for appellant.

Opposing Side (Respondent/Appellee): William E. James argued the cause for appellee.

III. AMICI CURIAE

ACLU Side (Petitioner/Appellant)

Brief of amici curiae filed on behalf of the ACLU by Maxwell E. Greenberg, Marvin Leon, A.L. Wirin, and Fred Okrand.

Opposing Side (Respondent/Appellee)

No briefs of amici curiae were filed in support of appellee.

IV. THE SUPREME COURT'S DECISION

"The bare fact of police 'detention and police examination in private of one in official state custody' does not render involuntary a confession by the one so detained. Neither does an admonition by the police to tell the truth, nor the failure of state authorities to comply with local statutes requiring that an accused promptly be brought before a magistrate.

Petitioner's claim of coercion, then, depends almost entirely on denial of his request to contact counsel. This Court has not previously had occasion to determine the character of a confession obtained after such a denial. But we have held that confessions made by indigent defendants prior to state appointment of counsel are not thereby rendered involuntary, even in prosecutions where conviction without counsel would violate due process under the Fourteenth Amendment. To be sure, coercion seems more likely to result from state denial of a specific request for opportunity to engage counsel than it does from state failure to appoint counsel immediately upon arrest. That greater possibility, however, is not decisive. It is negated here by petitioner's age, intelligence, and education. While in law school, he had studied criminal law; indeed, when asked to take the lie detector test, he informed the operator that the results of such a test would not be admissible at trial absent a stipulation by the parties. Supplementing that background is the police statement to petitioner well before his confession that he did not have to answer questions. Moreover, the manner of his refusals to answer indicates full awareness of the right to be silent. On this record, we are unable to say that petitioner's confession was anything other than voluntary. . . .

We turn now to the contention that, even if the confession be voluntary, its use violates due process because it was obtained after denial of petitioner's request to contact his attorney. [T]he sum total of the circumstances here during the time petitioner was without counsel is a voluntary confession by a college-educated man with law school training who knew of his right to keep silent. Such facts, while perhaps a violation of California law, do not approach the prejudicial impact in *House v. Mayo*, and do not show petitioner to have been so 'taken advantage of,' as to violate due process of law."

The Supreme Court affirmed the conviction.

V. JUSTICE VOTE

4 Pro ACLU Side vs. 5 Con Opposing Side

ACLU Side (Petitioner/Appellant)

1. Douglas, W. – Wrote dissenting opinion
2. Warren, E. – Joined dissenting opinion
3. Black, H. – Joined dissenting opinion
4. Brennan, W. – Joined dissenting opinion

Opposing Side (Respondent/Appellee)

1. Clark, T. – Wrote majority opinion
2. Frankfurter, F. – Joined majority opinion
3. Burton, H. – Joined majority opinion
4. Harlan, J. – Joined majority opinion
5. Whittaker, C. – Joined majority opinion

VI. A WIN OR LOSS FOR THE ACLU?

The ACLU filed an amicus brief urging reversal; the U.S. Supreme Court affirmed the ruling of the California Supreme Court in a 5-4 vote, giving the ACLU an apparent loss.

105. Lerner v. Casey

(Decided June 30, 1958; 357 U.S. 468)

I. ISSUE

A. Issues Discussed

Due process

B. Legal Question Presented

Did the appellant's termination as a New York City Transit System subway conductor, pursuant to the Security Risk Law of the State of New York, violate the due process clause of the Fourteenth Amendment?

C. Supreme Court's Answer

Appellant's termination did not violate his rights under the Fourteenth Amendment.

II. CASE SUMMARY

A. Background

The appellant, Max Lerner, a subway conductor employed by the New York City Transit Authority, was suspended, then dismissed, from his job after he "was asked whether he was then a member of the Communist Party, but he refused to answer and claimed his privilege against self-incrimination under the Fifth Amendment to the Federal Constitution."

"Appellant did not appeal to the Civil Service Commission, as was his statutory right, but brought this proceeding in the state courts for reinstatement. . . . The State Supreme Court, assuming jurisdiction despite appellant's failure to exhaust his administrative remedies, upheld the Security Risk Law and its application to appellant as constitutional, ruled adversely to appellant's state law contentions, and dismissed the proceeding. The Appellate Division, 2d Dept., and the Court of Appeals, both affirmed, each by a divided court. An appeal to this Court was brought under 28 U.S.C. § 1257(2), and we postponed to the hearing on the merits the question of our jurisdiction."

The Supreme Court affirmed the Court of Appeals' judgment.

B. Counsel of Record/ACLU Attorney

ACLU Side (Petitioner/Appellant): Leonard B. Boudin argued the cause for appellant.

Opposing Side (Respondent/Appellee): Daniel T. Scannell argued the cause for appellee.

Ruth Kessler Toch argued the cause for the State of New York as amicus curiae.

III. AMICI CURIAE

ACLU Side (Petitioner/Appellant)

Brief of amici curiae filed on behalf of the New York Civil Liberties Union by David I. Shapiro, Nanette Dembitz, and Stephen C. Vladeck.

Opposing Side (Respondent/Appellee)

Brief of amici curiae filed on behalf of the State of New York by Ruth Kessler Toch, Attorney General of New York Louis J. Lefkowitz, and Paxton Blair.

IV. THE SUPREME COURT'S DECISION

"Appellant was . . . advised, pursuant to § 5 of the Security Risk Law, that he had thirty days within which to submit statements or affidavits showing why he should be reinstated. At the expiration of this period, appellees, having heard nothing further from appellant, dismissed him from his position by a resolution which confirmed the previous 'suspension' findings. Appellant did not appeal to the Civil Service Commission, as was his statutory right, but brought this proceeding in the state courts for reinstatement.

[A]ppellant is in no position to complain of procedural defects in the statute. His own refusal to answer blocked proceedings at his appearances before the Department of Investigation, and, more important, he failed to pursue his administrative remedy by appealing to and obtaining a hearing before the State Civil Service Commission.

Appellant further argues that the Security Risk Law could not be applied to him in 1954, since, at that time, no public emergency existed which could justify the law. But New York's right to enact legislation to protect its public service against the employment of persons fairly deemed untrustworthy and unreliable, and therefore security risks, can hardly be regarded as constitutionally dependent upon the existence of a public emergency, and we do not think it open to us to inquire into the motives which led the

State Legislature to extend the Security Risk Law beyond its original effective period. . . .

Finally, the claim that the statute offends due process because dismissal of an employee may be based on mere present membership in the Communist Party, without regard to the character of such membership, must also fail. Apart from the fact that the statute simply makes membership in an organization found to be subversive one of the elements which may enter into the ultimate determination as to 'doubtful trust and reliability,' appellant, as the Court of Appeals viewed the administrative proceedings and as we accordingly treat them here, was not discharged on grounds that he was a party member. . . .

The issue then reduces to the narrow question whether the conclusion which could otherwise be reached from appellant's refusal to answer is constitutionally barred because his refusal was accompanied by the assertion of a Fifth Amendment privilege. We think it does not. The federal privilege against self-incrimination was not available to appellant through the Fourteenth Amendment in this state investigation."

The Supreme Court affirmed, holding "that appellant's discharge was not in violation of rights assured to him by the Federal Constitution."

V. JUSTICE VOTE

4 Pro ACLU Side vs. 5 Con Opposing Side

ACLU Side (Petitioner/Appellant)

1. Black, H. – Joined Douglas' dissent
2. Brennan, W. – Wrote dissenting opinion
3. Douglas, W. – Wrote dissenting opinion
4. Warren, E. – Wrote dissenting opinion

Opposing Side (Respondent/Appellee)

1. Harlan, J. – Wrote majority opinion
2. Frankfurter, F. – Wrote concurring opinion
3. Whittaker, C. – Joined majority opinion
4. Clark, T. – Joined majority opinion
5. Burton, H. – Joined majority opinion

VI. A WIN OR LOSS FOR THE ACLU?

The ACLU, as amicus curiae, urged reversal of the Court of Appeals' judgment; the Supreme Court affirmed in a 5-4 vote, giving the ACLU an apparent loss.

106. Speiser v. Randall

(Decided June 30, 1958; 357 U.S. 513)

I. ISSUE

A. Issues Discussed

1st Amendment, press, speech, association

B. Legal Question Presented

Whether a State tax program may require participants to sign a declaration affirming they do not advocate overthrow of the government.

C. Supreme Court's Answer

"[W]e hold that when the constitutional right to speak is sought to be deterred by a State's general taxing program due process demands that the speech be unencumbered until the State comes forward with sufficient proof to justify its inhibition. . . . It follows from this that appellants could not be required to execute the declaration as a condition for obtaining a tax exemption . . . ."

II. CASE SUMMARY

A. Background

"The appellants are honorably discharged veterans of World War II who claimed the veterans' property-tax exemption provided by Art. XIII, s 1 1/4, of the California Constitution. Under California law applicants for such exemption must annually complete a standard form of application and file it with the local assessor. The form was revised in 1954 to add an oath by the applicant: 'I do not advocate the overthrow of the Government of the United States or of the State of California by force or violence or other unlawful means, nor advocate the support of a foreign Government against the United States in event of hostilities.' Each refused to subscribe the oath and struck it from the form which he executed and filed for the tax year 1954—1955. Each contended that the exaction of the oath as a condition of obtaining a tax exemption was forbidden by the Federal Constitution. The respective assessors denied the exemption solely for the refusal to execute the oath. The Supreme Court of California sustained the assessors' actions against the appellants' claims of constitutional invalidity. [The U.S. Supreme Court] noted probable jurisdiction of the appeals."

B. Counsel of Record/ACLU Attorney

ACLU Side (Petitioner/Appellant): Lawrence Speiser[1] argued the cause for appellants. With him on the brief were Albert M. Bendich of the American Civil Liberties Union of Northern California and Franklin H. Williams.

Opposing Side (Respondent/Appellee): George W. McClure argued the cause for appellee in No. 483, and Robert M. Desky argued the cause for appellee in No. 484. With them on the brief was Dion R. Holm.

III. AMICI CURIAE

ACLU Side (Petitioner/Appellant)

Brief of amici curiae filed on behalf of the American Civil Liberties Union by

Kenneth W. Greenawalt and Rowland Watts.

Brief of amici curiae filed on behalf of American Jewish Congress by Shad Polier, Will Maslow and Leo Pfeffer.

Opposing Side (Respondent/Appellee)

No briefs of amici curiae were filed in support of appellee.

1 Speiser, who represented himself in the case, was a lawyer at the American Civil Liberties Union. Noam S. Cohen, *Lawrence Speiser, 68, a Civil Liberties Lawyer*, N.Y. Times (Sept. 1, 1991), https://www.nytimes.com/1991/09/01/us/lawrence-speiser-68-a-civil-liberties-lawyer.html.

IV. THE SUPREME COURT'S DECISION

"Article XX, s 19, of the California Constitution . . . provides as follows:

'Notwithstanding any other provision of this Constitution, no person or organization which advocates the overthrow of the Government of the United States or the State by force or violence or other unlawful means or who advocates the support of a foreign government against the United States in the event of hostilities shall:

'(b) Receive any exemption from any tax imposed by this State or any county, city or county, city, district, political subdivision, authority, board, bureau, commission or other public agency of this State. . . .'

[T]he California Legislature enacted s 32 of the Revenue and Taxation Code, which requires the claimant, as a prerequisite . . . for any property-tax exemption, to sign a statement . . . declaring that he does not engage in the activities described in the constitutional amendment. . . .

The appellants attack these provisions . . . as denying them freedom of speech . . . .

It is settled that speech can be effectively limited by . . . the taxing power. . . .

For the purposes of this case we assume without deciding that California may deny tax exemptions to persons who engage in the proscribed speech for which they might be fined or imprisoned.

But the question remains whether California has chosen a fair method for determining when a claimant is a member of that class to which the California court has said the constitutional and statutory provisions extend. . . .

Believing that the principles of [prior] cases have no application here, we hold that when the constitutional right to speak is sought to be deterred by a State's general taxing program due process demands that the speech be unencumbered until the State comes forward with sufficient proof to justify its inhibition. The State clearly has no such compelling interest at stake as to justify a short-cut procedure which must inevitably result in suppressing protected speech. Accordingly, though the validity of s 19 of Art. XX of the State Constitution be conceded arguendo, its enforcement through procedures which place the burdens of proof and persuasion on the taxpayer is a violation of due process. It follows from this that appellants could not be required to execute the declaration as a condition for obtaining a tax exemption or as a condition for the assessor proceeding further in determining whether they were entitled to such an exemption. Since the entire statutory procedure, by placing the burden of proof on the claimants, violated the requirements of due process, appellants were not obliged to take the first step in such a procedure.

The judgments are reversed and the causes are remanded . . . ."

V. JUSTICE VOTE

7 Pro ACLU Side vs. 1 Con Opposing Side

ACLU Side (Petitioner/Appellant)

1. Brennan, W. – Wrote majority opinion
2. Black, H. – Wrote concurring opinion, joined Douglas' concurrence
3. Douglas, W. – Wrote concurring opinion, joined Black's concurrence
4. Harlan, J. – Joined majority opinion
5. Frankfurter, F. – Joined majority opinion
6. Whittaker, C. – Joined majority opinion
7. Burton, H. – Concurred in the result

Opposing Side (Respondent/Appellee)

1. Clark, T. – Wrote dissenting opinion

Warren, E. – Took no part in the decision.

VI. A WIN OR LOSS FOR THE ACLU?

The ACLU filed as amicus curiae and served as counsel for appellant urging reversal of the judgment of the Supreme Court of California; the U.S. Supreme Court reversed in a 7-1 vote, giving the ACLU an apparent win.

107. First Unitarian Church v. County of Los Angeles

(Decided June 30, 1958; 357 U.S. 545)

I. ISSUE

A. Issues Discussed

Due process, freedom of speech, religious freedom

B. Legal Question Presented

Is it permissible to deny religious tax exemptions to organizations that refuse to participate in certain kinds of speech?

C. Supreme Court's Answer

Denying religious tax exemptions because of refusals to participate in certain speech violates due process.

II. CASE SUMMARY

A. Background

"The petitioners claimed the property-tax exemption provided by Art. XIII, § 1 1/2, of the California Constitution for real property and buildings used solely and exclusively for religious worship. The Los Angeles assessor denied the exemptions because each petitioner refused to subscribe, and struck from the prescribed application form, the oath that they did not advocate the overthrow of the Government of the United States and of the State of California by force or violence or other unlawful means nor advocate the support of a foreign government against the United States in the event of hostilities. Each petitioner sued in the Superior Court in and for the County of Los Angeles to recover taxes paid under protest and for declaratory relief. Both contended that the exaction of the oath pursuant to § 19 of Art. XX of the State Constitution and § 32 of the California Revenue and Taxation Code was forbidden by the Federal Constitution.

The court upheld the validity of the provisions in the action brought by petitioner First Unitarian Church of Los Angeles, and the Supreme Court of California affirmed. [The Supreme Court] granted certiorari. The Superior Court in the action brought by petitioner Valley Unitarian-Universalist Church, Inc., upheld the validity of the provisions under the Federal Constitution but held that § 32 of the Revenue and Taxation Code violated the California Constitution because it excluded or exempted householders from the requirement. The Supreme Court of California reversed, and [the Supreme Court] granted certiorari."

The Supreme Court reversed the lower courts' judgments.

B. Counsel of Record/ACLU Attorney

ACLU Side (Petitioner/Appellant): A. L. Wirin argued the cause for appellant. With him on the brief were Fred Okrand, Robert L. Brock, and George T. Altman.

Opposing Side (Respondent/Appellee): Gordon Boller argued the cause for appellee. With him on the brief were Harold W. Kennedy and Alfred Charles DeFlon.

III. AMICI CURIAE

ACLU Side (Petitioner/Appellant)

Brief of amici curiae filed on behalf of the ACLU by Kenneth W. Greenawalt and Rowland Watts.

Additional briefs of amici curiae were filed on behalf of the Philadelphia Yearly Meeting of the Religious Society of Friends, the American Friends Service Committee, Inc., the First Methodist Church of San Leandro, the First Unitarian Church of Berkeley, and the Orange Grove Monthly Meeting of Friends of Pasadena.

Opposing Side (Respondent/Appellee)

No briefs of amici curiae were filed in support of appellee.

IV. THE SUPREME COURT'S DECISION

"[T]he petitioners argue that the provisions [under § 19 of Article 20 of the State Constitution and § 32 of the California Revenue and Taxation Code] are invalid under the Fourteenth Amendment as abridgments of religious freedom and as violations of the principle of separation of church and state. Our disposition of the cases, however, makes consideration of these questions unnecessary.

For the reasons expressed in *Speiser v. Randall*, we hold that the enforcement of § 19 of Art. XX of the State Constitution through procedures which place the burdens of proof and persuasion on the taxpayer is a violation of due process."

The Supreme Court reversed and remanded.

V. JUSTICE VOTE

7 Pro ACLU Side vs. 1 Con Opposing Side

ACLU Side (Petitioner/Appellant)

1. Brennan, W. – Wrote majority opinion
2. Frankfurter, F. – Joined majority opinion
3. Harlan, J. – Joined majority opinion
4. Whittaker, C. – Joined majority opinion
5. Douglas, W. – Wrote concurring opinion, joined Black's concurrence
6. Black, H. – Wrote concurring opinion, joined Douglas' concurrence
7. Burton, H. – Concurred in the result

Opposing Side (Respondent/Appellee)

1. Clark, T. – Wrote dissenting opinion

Warren, E – Took no part in the decision

VI. A WIN OR LOSS FOR THE ACLU?

The ACLU, as amicus curiae, urged reversal; the Supreme Court reversed the judgment of the lower courts in a 7-1 vote, giving the ACLU an apparent win.

108. Barenblatt v. United States

(Decided June 8, 1959; 360 U.S. 109)

I. ISSUE

A. Issues Discussed

Communism, 1st Amendment, speech, press, association

B. Legal Question Presented

"The precise constitutional issue confronting us is whether the Subcommittee's inquiry into petitioner's past or present membership in the Communist Party transgressed the provisions of the First Amendment, which of course reach and limit congressional investigations."

C. Supreme Court's Answer

"We conclude that the balance between the individual and the governmental interests here at stake must be struck in favor of the latter, and that therefore the provisions of the First Amendment have not been offended."

II. CASE SUMMARY

A. Background

"We here review petitioner's conviction under 2 U.S.C. s 192 for contempt of Congress, arising from his refusal to answer certain questions put to him by a Subcommittee of the House Committee on Un-American Activities during the course of an inquiry concerning alleged Communist infiltration into the field of education.

The case is before us for the second time. Petitioner's conviction was originally affirmed in 1957 by a unanimous panel of the Court of Appeals. This Court granted certiorari, vacated the judgment of the Court of Appeals, and remanded . . . . Thereafter the Court of Appeals, sitting en banc, reaffirmed the conviction by a divided court. We again granted certiorari to consider petitioner's statutory and constitutional challenges to his conviction, and particularly his claim that the judgment below cannot stand under our decision in the Watkins case. . . .

Petitioner's various contentions resolve themselves into three propositions: First, the compelling of testimony by the Subcommittee was neither legislatively authorized nor constitutionally permissible because of the vagueness of Rule XI of the House of Representatives, Eighty-third Congress, the charter of authority of the parent Committee. Second, petitioner was not adequately apprised of the pertinency of the Subcommittee's questions to the subject matter of the inquiry. Third, the questions petitioner refused to answer infringed rights protected by the First Amendment."

B. Counsel of Record

ACLU Side (Petitioner/Appellant): Edward J. Ennis of the American Civil Liberties Union argued the cause for appellant. With him on the brief were Nanette Dembitz of the American Civil Liberties Union, David Scribner, and Rowland Watts.

Opposing Side (Respondent/Appellee): Philip R. Monahan argued the cause for the United States. With him on the brief were Solicitor General Rankin, Acting Assistant Attorney General Yeagley, and Doris H. Spangenburg.

III. AMICI CURIAE

ACLU Side (Petitioner/Appellant)

Brief of amici curiae filed on behalf of the American Association of University Professors by Ralph F. Fuchs and Leo A. Huard.

Brief of amici curiae filed on behalf of the National Lawyers Guild by Nathan Witt
and John M. Coe.

Opposing Side (Respondent/Appellee)

No briefs of amici curiae were filed in support of appellee.

IV. THE SUPREME COURT'S DECISION

"At the outset it should be noted that Rule XI authorized this Subcommittee to compel testimony within the framework of the investigative authority conferred on the Un-American Activities Committee. Petitioner contends that Watkins v. United States nevertheless held the grant of this power in all circumstances ineffective because of the vagueness of Rule XI in delineating the Committee jurisdiction to which its exercise was to be appurtenant. . . .

The Watkins case cannot properly be read as standing for such a proposition. . . .

Petitioner also contends, independently of Watkins, that the vagueness of Rule XI deprived the Subcommittee of the right to compel testimony in this investigation into Communist activity. . . .

To the contrary, the legislative gloss on Rule XI is again compelling. . . .

In this framework of the Committee's history we must conclude that its legislative authority to conduct the inquiry presently under consideration is unassailable, and that independently of whatever bearing the broad scope of Rule XI may have on the issue of 'pertinency' in a given investigation into Communist activities, as in Watkins, the Rule cannot be said to be constitutionally infirm on the score of vagueness. . . .

Undeniably a conviction for contempt under 2 U.S.C. s 192 cannot stand unless the questions asked are pertinent to the subject matter of the investigation. But the factors which led us to rest decision on this ground in Watkins were very different from those involved here. . . .

Petitioner's contentions on this aspect of the case cannot be sustained. . . .

The precise constitutional issue confronting us is whether the Subcommittee's inquiry into petitioner's past or present membership in the Communist Party transgressed the provisions of the First Amendment, which of course reach and limit congressional investigations. . . .

We conclude that the balance between the individual and the governmental interests here at stake must be struck in favor of the latter, and that therefore the provisions of the First Amendment have not been offended.

We hold that petitioner's conviction for contempt of Congress discloses no infirmity, and that the judgment of the Court of Appeals must be affirmed."

V. JUSTICE VOTE

4 Pro ACLU Side vs. 5 Con Opposing Side

ACLU Side (Petitioner/Appellant)

1. Warren, E. – Joined Black's dissent
2. Brennan, W. – Wrote dissenting opinion
3. Black, H. – Wrote dissenting opinion
4. Douglas, W. – Joined Black's dissent

Opposing Side (Respondent/Appellee)

1. Harlan, J. – Wrote majority opinion
2. Frankfurter, F. – Joined majority opinion
3. Clark, T. – Joined majority opinion
4. Stewart, P. – Joined majority opinion
5. Whittaker, C. – Joined majority opinion

VI. A WIN OR LOSS FOR THE ACLU?

The ACLU served as counsel for appellant urging reversal of the judgment of the Court of Appeals; the Supreme Court affirmed in a 5-4 vote, giving the ACLU an apparent loss.

109. Greene v. McElroy

(Decided June 29, 1959; 360 U.S. 474)

I. ISSUE

A. Issues Discussed

Due process, governmental authority

B. Legal Question Presented

"[W]hether the Department of Defense has been authorized to create an industrial security clearance program under which affected persons may lose their jobs and may be restrained in following their chosen professions on the basis of fact determinations concerning their fitness for clearance made in proceedings in which they are denied the traditional procedural safeguards of confrontation and cross-examination."

C. Supreme Court's Answer

"We decide only that in the absence of explicit authorization from either the President or Congress the respondents were not empowered to deprive petitioner of his job in a proceeding in which he was not afforded the safeguards of confrontation and cross-examination."

II. CASE SUMMARY

A. Background

Petitioner, an aeronautical engineer, was the general manager of Engineering and Research Corporation (ERCO), a private corporation contracted by the Armed Forces. The corporation had clearance to access classified information in order to perform work under their contract. Petitioner's security clearance came under scrutiny on suspicion of Communist ties and, after ERCO had a chance to respond, the Army-Navy-Air Force Personnel Security Board "'decided that access by [petitioner] to contract work and information [at ERCO] . . . would be inimical to the best interests of the United States.'"

Petitioner's security clearance was reinstated after an initial hearing, but numerous subsequent actions and hearings led him to lose his security clearance again. ERCO discharged petitioner from his position as a result of losing the security clearance. Petitioner was denied access to much of the evidence against him in the hearings and not allowed to confront or cross-examine the confidential sources who provided evidence for the case against him.

Petitioner filed suit in the "District Court for the District of Columbia asking for a declaration that the revocation [of his security clearance] was unlawful and void and for an order restraining respondents from acting pursuant to it." The District Court granted the Government's motion for summary judgment on the matter. The Court of Appeals affirmed, finding that "petitioner's suit presented no 'justiciable controversy'" and did not deprive him of due process.

The Supreme Court granted certiorari to review the case and reversed.

B. Counsel of Record/ACLU Attorney

ACLU Side (Petitioner/Appellant): Carl W. Berueffy argued the cause for appellant.

Opposing Side (Respondent/Appellee): George Cochran Doub argued the cause for appellee.

III. AMICI CURIAE

ACLU Side (Petitioner/Appellant)

Brief of amici curiae filed on behalf of the ACLU by David I. Shapiro, Rowland Watts, and John Carey.

Opposing Side (Respondent/Appellee)

No briefs of amici curiae were filed in support of appellee.

IV. THE SUPREME COURT'S DECISION

"Petitioner's work opportunities have been severely limited on the basis of a fact determination rendered after a hearing which failed to comport with our traditional ideas of fair procedure. The type of hearing was the product of administrative decision not explicitly authorized by either Congress or the President. Whether those procedures under the circumstances comport with the Constitution we do not decide. Nor do we decide whether the President has inherent authority to create such a program, whether congressional action is necessary, or what the limits on executive or legislative authority may be. We decide only that in the absence of explicit authorization from either the President or Congress the respondents were not empowered to deprive petitioner of his job in a proceeding in which he was not afforded the safeguards of confrontation and cross-examination."

The Supreme Court reversed the judgment and remanded the case to the District Court.

V. JUSTICE VOTE

8 Pro ACLU Side vs. 1 Con Opposing Side

ACLU Side (Petitioner/Appellant)

1. Warren, E. – Wrote majority opinion
2. Frankfurter, F. – Concurred in the judgment
3. Stewart, P. – Joined majority opinion
4. Harlan, J. – Wrote concurring opinion
5. Whittaker, C. – Concurred in the judgment
6. Douglas, W. – Joined majority opinion
7. Black, H. – Joined majority opinion
8. Brennan, W. – Joined majority opinion

Opposing Side (Respondent/Appellee)

1. Clark, T. – Wrote dissenting opinion

VI. A WIN OR LOSS FOR THE ACLU?

The ACLU filed an amicus brief urging reversal; the Supreme Court reversed and remanded in an 8-1 vote, giving the ACLU an apparent win.

110. Farmers Educational & Cooperative Union v. WDAY, Inc.

(Decided June 29, 1959; 360 U.S. 525)

I. ISSUE

A. Issues Discussed

Freedom of speech and of the press, libel, censorship

B. Legal Question Presented

"[W]hether § 315 of the Federal Communications Act of 1934 bars a broadcasting station from removing defamatory statements contained in speeches broadcast by legally qualified candidates for public office, and if so, whether that section grants the station a federal immunity from liability for libelous statements so broadcast."

C. Supreme Court's Answer

Under § 315, broadcasting stations cannot censor statements by legally qualified candidates for public office and are immune from liability for a candidates' libelous statements.

II. CASE SUMMARY

A. Background

"This suit for libel arose as a result of a speech made over the radio and television facilities of respondent, WDAY, Inc., by A. C.

Townley—a legally qualified candidate in the 1956 United States senatorial race in North Dakota. Because it felt compelled to do so by the requirements of § 315, WDAY permitted Townley to broadcast his speech, uncensored in any respect, as a reply to previous speeches made over WDAY by two other senatorial candidates. Townley's speech, in substance, accused his opponents, together with petitioner, Farmers Educational and Cooperative Union of America, of conspiring to 'establish a Communist Farmers Union Soviet right here in North Dakota.' Farmers Union then sued Townley and WDAY for libel in a North Dakota State District Court. That court dismissed the complaint against WDAY on the ground that § 315 rendered the station immune from liability for the defamation alleged. The Supreme Court of North Dakota affirmed, stating: 'Section 315 imposes a mandatory duty upon broadcasting stations to permit all candidates for the same office to use their facilities if they have permitted one candidate to use them. Since power of censorship of political broadcasts is prohibited it must follow as a corollary that the mandate prohibiting censorship includes the privilege of immunity from liability for defamatory statements made by the speakers.' For this reason it held that the state libel laws could not apply to WDAY."

The Supreme Court granted certiorari to review the case and affirmed.

B. Counsel of Record / ACLU Attorney

ACLU Side (Respondent / Appellee): Harold W. Bangert argued the cause for appellee.

Douglas A. Anello argued the cause for the National Association of Broadcasters as amicus curiae.

Opposing Side (Petitioner / Appellant): Edward S. Greenbaum and Harriet F. Pilpel argued the cause for appellant.

III. AMICI CURIAE

ACLU Side (Respondent / Appellee)

Brief of amici curiae filed on behalf of the ACLU by Herbert Monte Levy and Rowland Watts.

Brief of amici curiae filed on behalf of the National Association of Broadcasters by Douglas A. Anello, Walter R. Powell, Jr, and Robert V. Cahill.

Brief of amici curiae on behalf of the United States by Solicitor General Rankin, Ralph S. Spritzer, Richard A. Solomon, John L. Fitzgerald, and Joel Rosenbloom.

Opposing Side (Petitioner / Appellant)

No briefs of amici curiae were filed in support of appellant.

IV. THE SUPREME COURT'S DECISION

"Petitioner argues that § 315's prohibition against censorship leaves broadcasters free to delete libelous material from candidates' speeches, and that therefore no federal immunity is granted a broadcasting station by that section. . . . Although the first, and for years the only judicial decision dealing with the censorship provision did hold that a station may remove defamatory statements from political broadcasts, subsequent judicial interpretations of § 315 have with considerable uniformity recognized that an individual licensee has no such power. . . .

More important, it is obvious that permitting a broadcasting station to censor allegedly libelous remarks would undermine the basic purpose for which § 315 was passed—full and unrestricted discussion of political issues by legally qualified candidates. . . .

Quite possibly, if a station were held responsible for the broadcast of libelous material, all remarks evenly faintly objectionable would be excluded out of an excess of caution. Moreover, if any censorship were permissible, a station so inclined could intentionally inhibit a candidate's legitimate presentation under the guise of lawful censorship of libelous matter. Because of the time limitation inherent in a political campaign, erroneous decisions by a station could not be corrected by the courts promptly enough to permit the candidate to bring improperly excluded matter before the public. It follows from all this that allowing censorship, even of the attenuated type advocated here, would almost inevitably force a candidate to avoid controversial issues during political debates over radio and television, and hence restrict the coverage of consideration relevant to intelligent political decision. We cannot believe, and we certainly are unwilling to assume, that Congress intended any such result. . . .

We are aware that causes of action for libel are widely recognized throughout the States. But we have not hesitated to abrogate state law where satisfied that its enforcement would stand 'as an obstacle to the accomplishment and execution of the full purposes and objectives of Congress.' Here, petitioner is asking us to attribute to § 315 a meaning which would either frustrate the underlying purposes for which it was enacted, or alternatively impose unreasonable burdens on the parties governed by that legislation. In the absence of clear expression by Congress we will not assume that it desired such a result. Agreeing with the state courts of North Dakota that § 315 grants a licensee an immunity from liability for libelous material it broadcasts, we merely read § 315 in accordance with what we believe to be its underlying purpose."

The U.S. Supreme Court affirmed the judgment of the North Dakota Supreme Court.

V. JUSTICE VOTE

5 Pro ACLU Side vs. 4 Con Opposing Side

ACLU Side (Respondent / Appellee)

1. Black, H. – Wrote majority opinion
2. Warren, E. – Joined majority opinion
3. Douglas, W. – Joined majority opinion
4. Clark, T. – Joined majority opinion
5. Brennan, W. – Joined majority opinion

Opposing Side (Petitioner / Appellant)

1. Frankfurter, F. – Wrote dissenting opinion
2. Harlan, J. – Joined dissenting opinion
3. Whittaker, C. – Joined dissenting opinion
4. Stewart, P. – Joined dissenting opinion

VI. A WIN OR LOSS FOR THE ACLU?

The ACLU filed an amicus brief urging affirmance; the U.S. Supreme Court affirmed the ruling of the North Dakota Supreme Court in a 5-4 vote, giving the ACLU an apparent win.

111. Smith v. California

(Decided December 14, 1959; 361 U.S. 147)

I. ISSUE

A. Issues Discussed

Freedom of speech, obscenity, due process

B. Legal Question Presented

Does a Los Angeles city ordinance punishing bookstore owners for selling obscene reading materials even if they do not know the contents of the books are obscene, violate freedom of speech?

C. Supreme Court's Answer

The ordinance violates freedom of speech by eliminating the knowledge requirement when punishing obscene material.

II. CASE SUMMARY

A. Background

"Appellant, the proprietor of a bookstore, was convicted in a California Municipal Court under a Los Angeles City ordinance which makes it unlawful 'for any person to have in his possession any obscene or indecent writing, [or] book . . . in any place of business where . . . books . . . are sold or kept for sale.' . . . The definition included no element of scienter—knowledge by appellant of the contents of the book—and thus the ordinance was construed as imposing a 'strict' or 'absolute' criminal liability. The appellant made timely objection below that if the ordinance were so construed it would be in conflict with the Constitution of the United States. This contention, together with other contentions based on the Constitution, was rejected, and the case comes [to the Supreme Court] on appeal" after the judgment was affirmed by the Appellate Department of the Superior Court.

The Supreme Court reversed the judgment.

B. Counsel of Record/ACLU Attorney

ACLU Side (Petitioner/Appellant): Stanley Fleishman and Sam Rosenwein argued the cause for appellant.

Opposing Side (Respondent/Appellee): Roger Arnebergh argued the cause for appellee.

III. AMICI CURIAE

ACLU Side (Petitioner/Appellant)

Brief of amici curiae filed on behalf of the ACLU by A. L. Wirin and Fred Okrand.

Opposing Side (Respondent/Appellee)

No briefs of amici curiae were filed in support of appellee.

IV. THE SUPREME COURT'S DECISION

"California here imposed a strict or absolute criminal responsibility on appellant not to have obscene books in his shop. . . . Still, it is doubtless competent for the States to create strict criminal liabilities by defining criminal offenses without any element of scienter—though even where no freedom-of-expression question is involved, there is precedent in this Court that this power is not without limitations. But the question here is as to the validity of this ordinance's elimination of the scienter requirement—an elimination which may tend to work a substantial restriction on the freedom of speech and of the press. . . .

We have held that obscene speech and writings are not protected by the constitutional guarantees of freedom of speech and the press. The ordinance here in question, to be sure, only imposes criminal sanctions on a bookseller if, in fact, there is to be found in his shop an obscene book. But our holding in Roth does not recognize any state power to restrict the dissemination of books which are not obscene; and we think this ordinance's strict liability feature would tend seriously to have that effect by penalizing booksellers even though they had not the slightest notice of the character of the books they sold. . . . By dispensing with any requirement of knowledge of the contents of the book on the part of the seller, the ordinance tends to impose a severe limitation on the public's access to constitutionally protected matter. For if the bookseller is criminally liable without knowledge of the contents, and the ordinance fulfills its purpose, he will tend to restrict the books he sells to those he has inspected; and thus the State will have imposed a restriction upon the distribution of constitutionally protected, as well as obscene literature. . . .

This ordinance opens that door too far. The existence of the State's power to prevent the distribution of obscene matter does not mean that there can be no constitutional barrier to any form of practical exercise of that power. It is plain to us that the ordinance in question, though aimed at obscene matter, has such a tendency to inhibit constitutionally protected expression that it cannot stand under the Constitution."

The Supreme Court reversed the judgment.

V. JUSTICE VOTE

9 Pro ACLU Side vs. 0 Con Opposing Side

ACLU Side (Petitioner/Appellant)

Opposing Side (Respondent/Appellee):

1. Brennan, W. – Wrote majority opinion
2. Black, H. – Wrote concurring opinion
3. Warren, E. – Joined majority opinion
4. Douglas, W. – Wrote concurring opinion
5. Clark, T. – Joined majority opinion
6. Frankfurter, F. – Wrote concurring opinion
7. Whittaker, C. – Joined majority opinion
8. Stewart, P. – Joined majority opinion
9. Harlan, J. – Wrote opinion concurring in part and dissenting in part

VI. A WIN OR LOSS FOR THE ACLU?

The ACLU filed an amicus brief urging reversal; the Supreme Court reversed the ruling in a 9-0 vote, giving the ACLU an apparent win.

112. Nelson v. Los Angeles County

(Decided February 29, 1960; 362 U.S. 1)

I. ISSUE

A. Issues Discussed

Communism

B. Legal Question Presented

Whether Los Angeles County employees, Nelson and Globe, were appropriately dismissed from their positions for refusal to answer questions related to subversive activities.

C. Supreme Court's Answer

"The judgment in Nelson's case is affirmed by an equally divided Court and will not be discussed. We conclude that Globe's dismissal was valid."

II. CASE SUMMARY

A. Background

"Petitioners, when employees of the County of Los Angeles, California, were subpoenaed by and appeared before a Subcommittee of the House Un-American Activities Committee, but refused to answer certain questions concerning subversion. Previously, each petitioner had been ordered by the County Board of Supervisors to answer any questions asked by the Subcommittee relating to his subversive activity, and s 1028.1 of the Government Code of the State of California made it the duty of any public employee to give testimony relating to such activity on pain of discharge 'in the manner provided by law.' Thereafter the County discharged petitioners on the ground of insubordination and violation of s 1028.1 of the Code. Nelson, a permanent social worker employed by the County's Department of Charities, was, upon his request, given a Civil Service Commission hearing which resulted in a confirmation of his discharge. Globe was a temporary employee of the same department and was denied a hearing on his discharge on the ground that, as such, he was not entitled to a hearing under the Civil Service Rules adopted pursuant to the County Charter. Petitioners then filed these petitions for mandates seeking reinstatement, contending that the California statute and their discharges violated the Due Process Clause of the Fourteenth Amendment. Nelson's discharge was affirmed by the District Court of Appeal, and Globe's summary dismissal was likewise affirmed. A petition for review in each of the cases was denied without opinion by the Supreme Court of California, three judges dissenting."

The Supreme Court granted certiorari to review the cases.

B. Counsel of Record

ACLU Side (Petitioner/Appellant): A. L. Wirin and Fred Okrand of the American Civil Liberties Union of Southern California argued the cause for appellants. With them on the brief were William T. Pillsbury of the American Civil Liberties Union of Southern California, and Nanette Dembitz and Rowland Watts of the American Civil Liberties Union.

Opposing Side (Respondent/Appellee): Win. E. Lamoreaux argued the cause for appellees. With him on the brief was Harold W. Kennedy.

III. AMICI CURIAE

ACLU Side (Petitioner/Appellant)

Brief of amici curiae filed on behalf of the National Association of Social Workers by Murray A. Gordon

Opposing Side (Respondent/Appellee)

No briefs of amici curiae were filed in support of appellees.

IV. THE SUPREME COURT'S DECISION

"We . . . reach Globe's contention that his summary discharge was . . . arbitrary and unreasonable. . . .

We conclude that the case is controlled by Beilan v. Board of Public Education, School Dist. of Philadelphia, 1958, 357 U.S. 399, and Lerner v. Casey, 1958, 357 U.S. 468. It is not determinative that the interrogation here was by a federal body rather than a state one, as it was in those cases. Globe had been ordered by his employer as well as by California's law to appear and answer questions before the federal Subcommittee. These mandates made no reference to Fifth Amendment privileges. If Globe had simply refused, without more, to answer the Subcommittee's questions, we think that under the principles of Beilan and Lerner California could certainly have discharged him. The fact that he chose to place his refusal on a Fifth Amendment claim puts the matter in no different posture . . . . We conclude that the order of the County Board was not invalid under the Due Process Clause of the Fourteenth Amendment. . . .

Having found that on the record here the discharge for 'insubordination' was not arbitrary, we need go no further.

We do not pass upon petitioner's contention as to the Privileges and Immunities Clause of the Fourteenth Amendment, since it was neither raised in nor considered by the California courts. The judgments are affirmed.

Affirmed."

V. JUSTICE VOTE

3 Pro ACLU Side vs. 5 Con Opposing Side

ACLU Side (Petitioner/Appellant)

1. Brennan, W. – Wrote dissenting opinion
2. Black, H. – Wrote dissenting opinion
3. Douglas, W. – Joined Black's dissent and Brennan's dissent

Warren, E – Took no part in the decision.

Opposing Side (Respondent/Appellee)

1. Clark, T. – Wrote majority opinion
2. Harlan, J. – Joined majority opinion
3. Frankfurter, F. – Joined majority opinion
4. Stewart, P. – Joined majority opinion
5. Whittaker, C. – Joined majority opinion

VI. A WIN OR LOSS FOR THE ACLU?

The ACLU served as counsel for appellants urging reversal of the judgments of the District Court of Appeal; the Supreme Court affirmed in a 5-3 vote, giving the ACLU an apparent loss.

113. Talley v. California

(Decided March 7, 1960; 362 U.S. 60)

I. ISSUE

A. Issues Discussed

1st Amendment, press, speech, association

B. Legal Question Presented

"[W]hether the provisions of a Los Angeles City ordinance restricting the distribution of handbills 'abridge the freedom of speech and of the press secured against state invasion by the Fourteenth Amendment of the Constitution.'"

C. Supreme Court's Answer

"This broad Los Angeles ordinance is . . . void on its face."

II. CASE SUMMARY

A. Background

"The ordinance, s 28.06 of the Municipal Code of the City of Los Angeles, provides:

'No person shall distribute any hand-bill in any place under any circumstances, which does not have printed on the cover, or the face thereof, the name and address of the following:

'(a) The person who printed, wrote, compiled or manufactured the same.

'(b) The person who caused the same to be distributed; provided, however, that in the case of a fictitious person or club, in addition to such fictitious name, the true names and addresses of the owners, managers or agents of the person sponsoring said hand-bill shall also appear thereon.'

The petitioner was arrested and tried in a Los Angeles Municipal Court for violating this ordinance. It was stipulated that the petitioner had distributed handbills in Los Angeles, and two of them were presented in evidence. Each had printed on it the following:

National Consumers Mobilization,
Box 6533,
Los Angeles 55, Calif.
PLeasant 9—1576. . . .

The Municipal Court held that the information printed on the handbills did not meet the requirements of the ordinance, found the petitioner guilty as charged, and fined him $10. The Appellate Department of the Superior Court of the County of Los Angeles affirmed the conviction . . . . Since this was the highest state court available to petitioner, [the Supreme Court] granted certiorari . . . ."

B. Counsel of Record

ACLU Side (Petitioner/Appellant): A. L. Wirin and Hugh R. Manes of the American Civil Liberties Union of Southern California argued the cause for appellants. With them on the brief were Fred Okrand, Herbert W. Simmons, Jr., and Mandle Rottman of the American Civil Liberties Union of Southern California.

Opposing Side (Respondent/Appellee): Philip E. Grey argued the cause for appellee. With him on the brief was Roger Arnebergh.

III. AMICI CURIAE

ACLU Side (Petitioner/Appellant)

Brief of amici curiae filed on behalf of the American Jewish Congress by Shad Polier, Will Maslow, Leo Pfeffer, and Joseph B. Robison.

Opposing Side (Respondent/Appellee)

No briefs of amici curiae were filed in support of appellee.

IV. THE SUPREME COURT'S DECISION

"In Lovell v. City of Griffin, 303 U.S. 444, we held void on its face an ordinance that comprehensively forbade any distribution of literature at any time or place in Griffin, Georgia, without a license. . . . A year later we had before us four ordinances each forbidding distribution of leaflets . . . . Efforts were made to distinguish these four ordinances from the one held void in the Griffin case. The chief grounds urged for distinction were that the four ordinances had been passed to prevent either frauds, disorder, or littering, according to the records in these cases, and another ground urged was that two of the ordinances applied only to certain city areas. This Court refused to uphold the four ordinances on those grounds pointing out that there were other ways to accomplish these legitimate aims without abridging freedom of speech and press. . . . Several years later we followed the Griffin and Schneider cases in striking down a Dallas, Texas, ordinance which was applied to prohibit the dissemination of information by the distribution of handbills. . . .

The broad ordinance now before us, barring distribution of 'any hand-bill in any place under any circumstances,' falls precisely under the ban of our prior cases unless this ordinance is saved by the qualification that handbills can be distributed if they have printed on them the names and addresses of the persons who prepared, distributed or sponsored them. . . .

There can be no doubt that such an identification requirement would tend to restrict freedom to distribute information and thereby freedom of expression. 'Liberty of circulating is as essential to that freedom as liberty of publishing; indeed, without the circulation, the publication would be of little value.'

Anonymous pamphlets, leaflets, brochures and even books have played an important role in the progress of mankind. . . .

We have recently had occasion to hold in two cases that there are times and circumstances when States may not compel members of groups engaged in the dissemination of ideas to be publicly identified. The reason for those holdings was that identification and fear of reprisal might deter perfectly peaceful discussions of public matters of importance. This broad Los Angeles ordinance is subject to the same infirmity. We hold that it, like the Griffin, Georgia, ordinance, is void on its face.

The judgment of the Appellate Department of the Superior

Court of the State of California is reversed and the cause is remanded . . . ."

V. JUSTICE VOTE

6 Pro ACLU Side vs. 3 Con Opposing Side

ACLU Side (Petitioner/Appellant)

1. Black, H. – Wrote majority opinion
2. Warren, E. – Joined majority opinion
3. Brennan, W. – Joined majority opinion
4. Douglas, W. – Joined majority opinion
5. Stewart, P. – Joined majority opinion
6. Harlan, J. – Wrote concurring opinion

Opposing Side (Respondent/Appellee)

1. Whittaker, C. – Joined Clark's dissent
2. Clark, T. – Wrote dissenting opinion
3. Frankfurter, F. – Joined Clark's dissent

VI. A WIN OR LOSS FOR THE ACLU?

The ACLU served as counsel for appellant urging reversal of the judgment of the Appellate Department of the Superior Court of the State of California; the Supreme Court reversed in a 6-3 vote, giving the ACLU an apparent win.

114. De Veau v. Braisted

(Decided June 6, 1960; 363 U.S. 144)

I. ISSUE

A. Issues Discussed

Preemption, due process, ex post facto laws, bills of attainder

B. Legal Question Presented

Whether § 8 of the New York Waterfront Commission Act of 1953 violates the Due Process Clause of the Fourteenth Amendment or the Supremacy Clause, or is a prohibited "ex post facto law and bill of attainder."

C. Supreme Court's Answer

Section 8 of the New York Waterfront Commission Act of 1953 does not violate due process or the Supremacy Clause, and is not an ex post facto law or bill of attainder.

II. CASE SUMMARY

A. Background

The New York Waterfront Commission Act of 1953 provided for state-government "supervision of employment on the waterfront in the Port of New York." Appellant De Veau became the Secretary-Treasurer of a local union of waterfront laborers in 1950. In 1920, he had pled guilty to a felony charge of grand larceny.

Under the § 8 of the Act, because appellant was previously convicted of a felony, he was forbidden from collecting labor union members' dues unless he was pardoned or able to obtain a "certificate of good conduct" from the state parole board. Three years after the Act went into effect, appellant was suspended from his officer position in the labor union after the District Attorney of Richmond County, New York, threatened prosecution under § 8 of the Act if appellant continued to serve as a union officer.

Appellant then filed suit for his suspension. The District Attorney's motion "to dismiss the complaint, and for judgment on the pleadings in his favor" was granted, then affirmed by the Appellate Division of the Supreme Court and Court of Appeals of New York.

The Supreme Court granted certiorari to review the constitutional issues and affirmed.

B. Counsel of Record/ACLU Attorney

ACLU Side (Petitioner/Appellant): Thomas W. Gleason argued the cause for appellant.

Opposing Side (Respondent/Appellee): Thomas R. Sullivan argued the cause for appellee.

III. AMICI CURIAE

ACLU Side (Petitioner/Appellant)

Brief of amici curiae filed on behalf of the New York Civil Liberties Union by Nanette Dembitz and Edward L. Sadowsky.

Opposing Side (Respondent/Appellee)

Brief of amici curiae filed on behalf of the Waterfront Commission of New York Harbor by William P. Sirignano, Irving Malchman, Jerome J. Klied, and Leon Schneider.

IV. THE SUPREME COURT'S DECISION

"The New York Waterfront Commission Act [of 1953] was an endeavor by New York and New Jersey to cope with long-standing evils on their joint waterfront in the Port of New York. . . .

The [Waterfront] Commission reported that the skulduggeries on the waterfront were largely due to the domination over waterfront employment gained by the International Longshoremen's Association, as then conducted. Its employment practices easily led to corruption, and many of its officials participated in dishonesties. The presence on the waterfront of convicted felons in many influential positions was an important causative factor in this appalling situation. . .

Manifestly, one of the main aims of the compact is to keep criminals away from the waterfront. The issue of licenses to engage in waterfront occupations, or the right to be registered, depends upon findings by the Commission of good character. In particular, past convictions for certain felonies constitute specific disabilities for each occupation, with discretion in the Commission to lift the disability, except in the case of port watchmen, where it constitutes an absolute bar to waterfront employment. . . .

This is not a situation where the operation of a state statute so obviously contradicts a federal enactment that it would preclude both from functioning together or, at least, would impede the effectiveness of the federal measure. Section 8 of the Waterfront Commission Act does not operate to deprive waterfront employees of opportunity to choose bargaining representatives. It does disable them from choosing as their representatives ex-felons who have neither been pardoned nor received 'good conduct' certificates. The fact that there is some restriction due to the operation of state law does not settle the issue of pre-emption. The doctrine of pre-emption does not present a problem in physics but one of adjustment because of the interdependence of federal and state interests and of the interaction of federal and state powers. . . . The sum of these considerations is that it would offend reason to attribute to Congress a purpose to pre-empt the state regulation contained in § 8."

Section 8 of the Waterfront Commission Act does not violate the Due Process Clause of the Fourteenth Amendment as the section was created in light of "impressive if mortifying evidence that the presence on the waterfront of ex-convicts was an important contributing factor to the corrupt waterfront situation.

Finally, § 8 of the Waterfront Commission Act is neither a bill of attainder nor an ex post facto law. The distinguishing feature of a bill of attainder is the substitution of a legislative for a judicial determination of guilt. Clearly, § 8 embodies no further implications of appellant's guilt than are contained in his 1920 judicial conviction; and so it manifestly is not a bill of attainder. The mark of an ex post facto law is the imposition of what can fairly be designated punishment for past acts. The question in each case where unpleasant consequences are brought to bear upon an individual for prior conduct, is whether the legislative aim was to punish that individual for past activity, or whether the restriction of the individual comes about as a relevant incident to a regulation of a present situation, such as the proper qualifications for a profession. No doubt is justified regarding the legislative purpose of § 8. The proof is overwhelming that New York sought not to punish ex-felons, but to devise what was felt to be a much-needed scheme of regulation of the waterfront, and for the effectuation of that scheme it became important whether individuals had previously been convicted of a felony."

The Supreme Court affirmed the judgment.

V. JUSTICE VOTE

3 Pro ACLU Side vs. 5 Con Opposing Side

ACLU Side (Petitioner/Appellant)

1. Douglas, W. – Wrote dissenting opinion
2. Black, H. – Joined Douglas' dissent
3. Warren, E. – Joined Douglas' dissent

Opposing Side (Respondent/Appellee)

1. Frankfurter, F. – Wrote majority opinion
2. Clark, T. – Joined majority opinion
3. Whittaker, C. – Joined majority opinion
4. Stewart, P. – Joined majority opinion
5. Brennan, W. – Wrote concurring opinion

Harlan, J – Took no part in the decision

VI. A WIN OR LOSS FOR THE ACLU?

The ACLU filed an amicus brief urging reversal; the Supreme Court affirmed the ruling of the New York Court of Appeals in a 5-3 vote, giving the ACLU an apparent loss.

115. Rios v. United States

(Decided June 27, 1960; 364 U.S. 253)

I. ISSUE

A. Issues Discussed

Criminal procedure, drugs, Fourth Amendment, search and seizure

B. Legal Question Presented

(1) Was the defendant's Fourth Amendment right to be free from "unreasonable searches and seizures" violated when two Los Angeles city police officers approached and surrounded his taxi cab and then seized a package of narcotics that defendant had dropped to the floor of the cab? (2) May evidence that is obtained by state police officers in violation of a defendant's Fourth Amendment rights be introduced against the defendant in a federal criminal trial?

C. Supreme Court's Answer

The validity of the search and admissibility of evidence obtained during the search depends on when the arrest occurred, and the case must be vacated and remanded to make that determination.

II. CASE SUMMARY

A. Background

At around 10:00 p.m. on February 28, 1957, two plainclothes city police officers, sitting in an unmarked car in a Los Angeles neighborhood that had a reputation for "narcotics activity," observed Petitioner Rios enter a taxi cab. The officers trailed the cab for about two miles. As the cab stopped at a traffic light, the officers approached the cab from both sides and identified themselves as police officers. "In the next minute there occurred a rapid succession of events. The cab door was opened; the petitioner dropped a recognizable package of narcotics to the floor of the vehicle; one of the officers grabbed the petitioner as he alighted from the cab; the other officer retrieved the package; and the first officer drew his revolver.

The precise chronology of all that happened is not clear in the record. In their original arrest report the police stated that the petitioner dropped the package only after one of the officers had opened the cab door. In testifying later, this officer said that he saw the defendant drop the package before the door of the cab was opened. The taxi driver gave a substantially different version of what occurred. He stated that one of the officers drew his revolver and 'took hold of the defendant's arm while he was still in the cab.'"

Petitioner was charged in California state court with a felony possession of narcotics. Before trial, Petitioner filed a motion to prohibit the state prosecutor from introducing the bag of narcotics into evidence on the grounds that his Fourth Amendment right to be free from unreasonable searches and seizures had been violated when the police officers surrounded his taxi cab. The state court granted Petitioner's motion and Petitioner was acquitted.

"Thereafter, one of the Los Angeles officers who had arrested the petitioner discussed the case with his superiors and suggested giving the evidence to United States authorities. He then got in touch with federal narcotics agents and told them about the petitioner's case." This led to a federal narcotics prosecution.

The District Court denied Petitioner's motion to suppress, finding that federal agents had not participated in the search and seizure, and finding that the California officers had obtained the evidence in a lawful manner. However, at the time of the opinion, the district judge had not yet listened to the taxicab driver's testimony. Petitioner was convicted at trial and the Court of Appeals upheld the conviction.

The Supreme Court granted certiorari, vacated the decision, and remanded the case.

B. Counsel of Record / ACLU Attorney

ACLU Side (Petitioner / Appellant): Harvey M. Grossman argued the cause for appellant.

Opposing Side (Respondent / Appellee): Malcolm Richard Wilkey, Assistant Attorney General, argued the cause for appellee.

III. AMICI CURIAE

ACLU Side (Petitioner / Appellant)

Brief of amici curiae filed on behalf of the ACLU and ACLU of Southern California by A. L. Wirin, Arthur D. Deckelman, Rowland Watts, and Melvin L. Wulf.

Opposing Side (Respondent / Appellee)

No briefs of amici curiae were filed in support of appellee.

IV. THE SUPREME COURT'S DECISION

"In holding that the package of heroin which had been seized by the state officers was admissible as evidence in the federal trial, the District Court placed prime reliance upon the silver platter doctrine, there having been no participation by federal agents in the search and seizure. But the court also expressed the opinion, based upon the transcript of the state court proceedings and additional testimony of the two Los Angeles police officers at the hearing on the motion to suppress, that the officers had obtained the evidence lawfully. The court was of the view that the seizure was permissible as an incident to a legal arrest, or, alternatively, that the petitioner had abandoned the narcotics when he dropped them to the floor of the taxicab. At the time this opinion was expressed, however, the district judge had not yet heard the taxicab driver's version of the circumstances surrounding the arrest and seizure. The driver did not testify until the trial itself. After he had testified, the package of heroin was offered in evidence. The petitioner's counsel objected, and the court overruled the objection without comment. For all that appears, this ruling may then have been based solely upon the silver platter doctrine. Moreover, the Court of Appeals gave no consideration to the question of the legality of the state search and seizure, relying as it did upon the silver platter doctrine and rejecting the petitioner's contention that the state court's determination of illegality precluded the federal trial court from making an independent inquiry into the matter.

With the case in such a posture, we have concluded that the interests of justice will best be served by remanding the case to the District Court. There, free from the entanglement of other issues that have now become irrelevant, the lawfulness of the policemen's conduct can be determined in accord with the basic principles governing the validity of searches and seizures by federal officers under the Fourth Amendment.

Under these principles, the inquiry in the present case will be narrowly oriented. The seizure can survive constitutional inhibition only upon a showing that the surrounding facts brought it within one of the exceptions to the rule that a search must rest upon a search warrant. Here, justification is primarily sought upon the claim that the search was an incident to a lawful arrest. Yet upon no possible view of the circumstances revealed in the testimony of the Los Angeles officers could it be said that there existed probable cause for an arrest at the time the officers decided to alight from their car and approach the taxi in which the petitioner was riding. . . .

The judgment is vacated, and the case is remanded to the District Court for further proceedings consistent with this opinion."

V. JUSTICE VOTE

5 Pro ACLU Side vs. 4 Con Opposing Side

ACLU Side (Petitioner / Appellant)

1. Stewart, P. – Wrote majority opinion
2. Warren, E. – Joined majority opinion
3. Brennan, W. – Joined majority opinion
4. Black, H. – Joined majority opinion
5. Douglas, W. – Joined majority opinion

Opposing Side (Respondent / Appellee)

1. Frankfurter, F. – Wrote dissenting opinion
2. Harlan, J. – Wrote dissenting opinion, joined Frankfurter's dissent
3. Clark, T. – Joined Frankfurter's dissent, joined Harlan's dissent
4. Whittaker, C. – Joined Frankfurter's dissent, joined Harlan's dissent

VI. A WIN OR LOSS FOR THE ACLU?

The ACLU filed as amicus curiae urging reversal; the Supreme Court vacated and remanded the ruling of the Court of Appeals for the Ninth Circuit in a 5-4 vote, giving the ACLU an apparent win.

116. Gomillion v. Lightfoot

(Decided November 14, 1960; 364 U.S. 339)

I. ISSUE

A. Issues Discussed

Racial discrimination, voting rights, Fifteenth Amendment

B. Legal Question Presented

Did the Alabama state legislature violate the Fifteenth Amendment by modifying boundaries of the City of Tuskegee to exclude virtually all black voters while not excluding any white voters?

C. Supreme Court's Answer

The petitioners stated a cause of action to show a violation of the Fifteenth Amendment through the boundary modifications.

II. CASE SUMMARY

A. Background

In 1957, the Alabama state legislature passed Local Act No. 140 which changed the City of Tuskegee's boundaries and excluded almost all of the city's black residents from voting in municipal elections. The city was changed from a square shape "into a strangely irregular twenty-eight sided figure . . . . The essential inevitable effect of this redefinition of Tuskegee's boundaries is to remove from the city all save four or five of its 400 Negro voters while not removing a single white voter or resident."

Petitioners, black residents of Tuskegee under the prior boundaries, filed suit. The District Court granted respondents' motion to dismiss the suit and the Court of Appeals for the Fifth Circuit affirmed.

On appeal, petitioners claim that the statute "will constitute a discrimination against them in violation of the Due Process and Equal Protection Clauses of the Fourteenth Amendment to the Constitution and will deny them the right to vote in defiance of the Fifteenth Amendment."

The Supreme Court granted certiorari and reversed.

B. Counsel of Record/ACLU Attorney

ACLU Side (Petitioner/Appellant): Fred D. Gray and Robert L. Carter argued the cause for appellant.

Philip Elman argued the cause for the United States, as amicus curiae.

Opposing Side (Respondent/Appellee): James J. Carter argued the cause for appellee.

III. AMICI CURIAE

ACLU Side (Petitioner/Appellant)

Brief of amici curiae filed on behalf of the ACLU by Lawrence Speiser, Curtis F. McClane, and Rowland Watts.

Brief of amici curiae filed on behalf of the United States by Philip Elman, Solicitor General Rankin, Assistant Attorney General Harold R. Tyler, Jr., Daniel M. Friedman, Harold H. Greene, D. Robert Owen and J. Harold Flannery, Jr.

Opposing Side (Respondent/Appellee)

No briefs of amici curiae were filed in support of appellee.

IV. THE SUPREME COURT'S DECISION

"These allegations, if proven, would abundantly establish that Act 140 was not an ordinary geographic redistricting measure even within familiar abuses of gerrymandering. If these allegations upon a trial remained uncontradicted or unqualified, the conclusion would be irresistible, tantamount for all practical purposes to a mathematical demonstration, that the legislation is solely concerned with segregating white and colored voters by fencing Negro citizens out of town so as to deprive them of their pre-existing municipal vote. . . .

The complaint amply alleges a claim of racial discrimination. Against this claim the respondents have never suggested, either in their brief or in oral argument, any countervailing municipal function which Act 140 is designed to serve. . . .

When a legislature thus singles out a readily isolated segment of a racial minority for special discriminatory treatment, it violates the Fifteenth Amendment. . . .

A statute which is alleged to have worked unconstitutional deprivations of petitioners' rights is not immune to attack simply because the mechanism employed by the legislature is a redefinition of municipal boundaries. According to the allegations here made, the Alabama Legislature has not merely redrawn the Tuskegee city limits with incidental inconvenience to the petitioners; it is more accurate to say that it has deprived the petitioners of the municipal franchise and consequent rights and to that end it has incidentally changed the city's boundaries. While in form this is merely an act redefining metes and bounds, if the allegations are established, the inescapable human effect of this essay in geometry and geography is to despoil colored citizens, and only colored citizens, of their theretofore enjoyed voting rights. . . .

For these reasons, the principal conclusions of the District Court and the Court of Appeals are clearly erroneous and the decision below must be reversed."

V. JUSTICE VOTE

9 Pro ACLU Side vs. 0 Con Opposing Side

ACLU Side (Petitioner/Appellant)

1. Frankfurter, F. – Wrote majority opinion
2. Warren, E. – Joined majority opinion
3. Black, H. – Joined majority opinion
4. Douglas, W. – Wrote concurring opinion
5. Clark, T. – Joined majority opinion
6. Harlan, J. – Joined majority opinion
7. Brennan, W. – Joined majority opinion
8. Stewart, P. – Joined majority opinion
9. Whittaker, C. – Wrote concurring opinion

VI. A WIN OR LOSS FOR THE ACLU?

The ACLU filed an amicus brief urging reversal; the Supreme Court reversed the ruling of the Court of Appeals for the Fifth Circuit in a 9-0 vote, giving the ACLU an apparent win.

117. Times Film Corp. v. Chicago

(Decided January 23, 1961; 365 U.S. 43)

I. ISSUE

A. Issues Discussed

Freedom of speech, prior restraints

B. Legal Question Presented

Whether a Chicago city ordinance requiring submission of motion pictures to city officials for approval prior to their public exhibition violates the First Amendment as a prior restraint.

C. Supreme Court's Answer

Requiring submission of films for approval is not a prior restraint, although the issue of whether certain standards violate the Constitution was not presented and could affect the constitutionality of the ordinance.

II. CASE SUMMARY

A. Background

Petitioner Times Film Corporation owned the exclusive right to exhibit the film *Don Juan* in Chicago. A Chicago city ordinance required that anybody who wished to publicly exhibit a film within city limits submit the film to the office of the commissioner of police and pay a license fee. The office of the commissioner of police was allowed to refuse to issue a permit to show the film if it determined that the film did "not meet certain standards." A denial of a permit to show a film could be appealed to the mayor and the mayor's decision would then be final.

Petitioner paid the license fee, but refused to submit *Don Juan* to the office of the commissioner of police for examination. After the office of the commissioner of police refused to grant a permit to show the film, the corporation brought suit in federal court seeking to prevent the city from interfering with the exhibition of the film. Petitioner argued "that the provision of the ordinance requiring submission of the film constitutes, on its face, a prior restraint within the prohibition of the First and Fourteenth Amendments."

The District Court dismissed Times Film Corporation's suit on the grounds "that neither a substantial federal question nor even a justiciable controversy was presented" and the Court of Appeals for the Seventh Circuit affirmed. Subsequently, Petitioner sought review in the Supreme Court.

The Supreme Court granted certiorari and affirmed.

B. Counsel of Record/ACLU Attorney

ACLU Side (Petitioner/Appellant): Felix J. Bilgrey and Abner J. Mikva argued the cause for appellant.

Opposing Side (Respondent/Appellee): Robert J. Collins and Sydney R. Drebin argued the cause for appellee.

III. AMICI CURIAE

ACLU Side (Petitioner/Appellant)

Brief of amici curiae filed on behalf of the ACLU by Edgar Bernhard, Alex Elson, Joel J. Sprayregen, Bernard Weisberg, William G. Halby, and Rowland Watts.

Additional briefs of amici curiae were filed on behalf of the Independent Film Importers and Distributors of America, Inc., the American Society of Magazine Photographers, the Society of Magazine Writers, the Authors League of America, Inc., HMH Publishing Company, Inc., the National Association of Broadcasters, the American Book Publishers Council, Inc., and the Motion Picture Association of America, Inc.

Opposing Side (Respondent/Appellee)

No briefs of amici curiae were filed in support of appellee.

IV. THE SUPREME COURT'S DECISION

"[T]here is not a word in the record as to the nature and content of 'Don Juan.' We are left entirely in the dark in this regard, as were the city officials and the other reviewing courts. Petitioner claims that the nature of the film is irrelevant, and that even if this film contains the basest type of pornography, or incitement to riot, or forceful overthrow of orderly government, it may nonetheless be shown without prior submission for examination. The challenge here is to the censor's basic authority; it does not go to any statutory standards employed by the censor or procedural requirements as to the submission of the film.

In this perspective we consider the prior decisions of this Court touching on the problem. [T]hey have consistently reserved for future decision possible situations in which the claimed First Amendment privilege might have to give way to the necessities of the public welfare. It has never been held that liberty of speech is absolute. Nor has it been suggested that all previous restraints on speech are invalid. . . .

Chicago emphasizes here its duty to protect its people against the dangers of obscenity in the public exhibition of motion pictures. To this argument petitioner's only answer is that regardless of the capacity for, or extent of, such an evil, previous restraint cannot be justified. With this we cannot agree. . . . It is not for this Court to limit the State in its selection of the remedy it deems most effective to cope with such a problem, absent, of course, a showing of unreasonable strictures on individual liberty resulting from its application in particular circumstances. We, of course, are not holding that city officials may be granted the power to prevent the showing of any motion picture they deem unworthy of a license.

As to what may be decided when a concrete case involving a specific standard provided by this ordinance is presented, we intimate no opinion. The petitioner has not challenged all—or for that matter any—of the ordinance's standards. Naturally we could not say that every one of the standards, including those which Illinois' highest court has found sufficient, is so vague on its face that the entire ordinance is void. At this time we say no more than this—that we are dealing only with motion pictures and, even as to them, only in the context of the broadside attack presented on this record."

The Supreme Court affirmed the judgment.

V. JUSTICE VOTE

4 Pro ACLU Side vs. 5 Con Opposing Side

ACLU Side (Petitioner/Appellant)

1. Warren, E. – Wrote dissenting opinion, joined Douglas' dissenting opinion
2. Black, H. – Joined Warren's dissent, joined Douglas' dissent

3. Douglas, W. – Wrote dissenting opinion, joined Warren's dissent
4. Brennan, W. – Joined Warren's dissent

Opposing Side (Respondent/Appellee)

1. Clark, T. – Wrote majority opinion
2. Frankfurter, F. – Joined majority opinion
3. Harlan, J. – Joined majority opinion
4. Whittaker, C. – Joined majority opinion
5. Stewart, P. – Joined majority opinion

VI. A WIN OR LOSS FOR THE ACLU?

The ACLU filed an amicus brief urging reversal; the Supreme Court affirmed the ruling of the Court of Appeals for the Seventh Circuit in a 5-4 vote, giving the ACLU an apparent loss.

118. Pugach v. Dollinger

(Decided February 27, 1961; 365 U.S. 458)

I. ISSUE

A. Issues Discussed

Criminal procedure, wiretapping

B. Legal Question Presented

May a federal court ban state officers from using wiretap evidence in a state criminal trial when introducing this evidence will violate a federal criminal statute?

C. Supreme Court's Answer

A federal court may not ban use of wiretap evidence in this circumstance.

II. CASE SUMMARY

A. Background

"[A]ppellant and several others were indicted in November 1959 by the State of New York for burglary in the second degree, maiming, assault in the second degree and conspiracy. Their case was set for trial on January 7, 1960. About two weeks before the trial was to begin appellant brought this suit in the Southern District of New York to enjoin the Bronx County District Attorney, the New York City Police Commissioner and their agents from making use at the state trial of evidence obtained by tapping appellant's telephone wires in June 1959 and of evidence obtained by the use of information overheard in the course of the tapping. The complaint alleged that, although the wiretap was obtained pursuant to state court authorization and in accordance with a state statute, its divulgence would constitute a violation of § 605 of the Communications Act of 1934, 47 U.S.C. § 605. It further stated that wiretap evidence had been introduced before the grand jury in obtaining appellant's indictment and that the district attorney intended to make use of such evidence at trial. The district attorney has not denied that he expects to use wiretap evidence, nor does he contest appellant's allegations that appellant will be subject to irreparable injury if convicted by means of such evidence." The Southern District of New York refused to grant a preliminary injunction and the Court of Appeals for the Second Circuit upheld the decision.

The Supreme Court granted certiorari and affirmed.

B. Counsel of Record/ACLU Attorney

ACLU Side (Petitioner/Appellant): George J. Todaro argued the cause for appellant.

Opposing Side (Respondent/Appellee): Walter E. Dillon and Irving Anolik argued the cause for appellee.

III. AMICI CURIAE

ACLU Side (Petitioner/Appellant)

Brief of amici curiae filed on behalf of the New York Civil Liberties Union and ACLU by Emanuel Redfield.

Opposing Side (Respondent/Appellee)

Brief of amici curiae filed on behalf of the Attorney General of New York by Attorney General of New York Louis J. Lefkowitz, Solicitor General Paxton Blair, and Assistant Attorney General Jean M. Coon.

Brief of amici curiae filed on behalf of the District Attorney's Association of New York by Edward S. Silver and Aaron Nussbaum.

IV. THE SUPREME COURT'S DECISION:

"The judgment is affirmed on the authority of Schwartz v. Texas and Stefanelli v. Minard."

V. JUSTICE VOTE

2 Pro ACLU Side vs. 7 Con Opposing Side

ACLU Side (Petitioner/Appellant)

1. Douglas, W. – Wrote dissenting opinion
2. Warren, E. – Joined Douglas' dissent

Opposing Side (Respondent/Appellee)

1. Black, H. – Per curiam decision
2. Frankfurter, F. – Per curiam decision
3. Clark, T. – Per curiam decision
4. Harlan, J. – Per curiam decision
5. Whittaker, C. – Per curiam decision
6. Stewart, P. – Per curiam decision
7. Brennan, W. – Wrote concurring opinion

VI. A WIN OR LOSS FOR THE ACLU?

The ACLU filed an amicus brief urging reversal; the Supreme Court affirmed the judgment of the United States Court of Appeals for the Second Circuit in a 7-2 vote, giving the ACLU an apparent loss.

119. Saldana v. United States

(Decided April 3, 1961; 365 U.S. 646)

I. ISSUE

A. Issues Discussed

Criminal procedure

B. Legal Question Presented

Should petitioner's convictions be reversed, due to alleged errors and events that occurred during his trial?

C. Supreme Court's Answer

The convictions under counts 3, 4, and 5 should be reversed while count 2, to which petitioner originally pleaded guilty, should be affirmed.

II. CASE SUMMARY

A. Background

Petitioner Saldana was arrested holding a bag of heroin. During the arrest, petitioner tossed the bag of heroin to a government agent who had negotiated its purchase. He was charged with five offenses under state and federal narcotics laws. Since no money had changed hands and the officer only received the drugs while in the process of arresting petitioner, petitioner argued that there was no sale and because of this contention, he entered a plea of not guilty. Later, appearing before a trial judge in the District Court for the Southern District of California, petitioner reversed his plea to guilty on two of the five counts. Another trial judge, sua sponte, ordered petitioner's guilty pleas to be withdrawn, and directed the entry of a not guilty plea on all five counts.

Petitioner proceeded to trial and was convicted of four of the five counts. Petitioner appealed, arguing that the second trial judge was not authorized to withdraw his guilty plea, and that proceeding to trial had constituted double jeopardy in violation of the Fifth Amendment. The Court of Appeals for the Ninth Circuit affirmed his conviction, holding that the trial court was justified in withdrawing the guilty pleas on the first two counts sua sponte, and that there was no double jeopardy.[1]

The Supreme Court granted certiorari and reversed the conviction as to the counts where petitioner never entered a guilty plea, but affirmed the conviction as to one of the counts where petitioner pleaded guilty.

B. Counsel of Record / ACLU Attorney

ACLU Side (Petitioner / Appellant): Stephen R. Reinhardt argued the cause for appellant.

Herbert A. Bernhard argued the cause, pro hac vice, by special leave of Court.

Opposing Side (Respondent / Appellee): Solicitor General Cox argued the cause for appellee.

III. AMICI CURIAE

ACLU Side (Petitioner / Appellant)

Brief of amici curiae filed on behalf of the ACLU by John T. McTernan, A. L. Wirin, and Fred Okrand.

Opposing Side (Respondent / Appellee)

No briefs of amici curiae were filed in support of appellant.

IV. THE SUPREME COURT'S DECISION

"In the light of the Solicitor General's suggestion, and upon an independent examination of the record, we have concluded that a due regard for the fair administration of justice requires that the convictions under counts 3, 4, and 5 of the indictment be set aside. The conviction under count 2, to which the petitioner originally pleaded guilty, is affirmed.

Because of this disposition of the case, we do not reach for consideration the alleged trial errors with respect to limitation of cross-examination, sufficiency of the evidence of a 'sale' under count 5, and instructions to the jury as to entrapment."

The Supreme Court affirmed in part and reversed in part the judgment of the Court of Appeals.

V. JUSTICE VOTE

9 Pro ACLU Side vs. 0 Con Opposing Side

ACLU Side (Petitioner / Appellant)

1. Warren, E. – Per curiam decision
2. Black, H. – Per curiam decision
3. Frankfurter, F. – Per curiam decision
4. Douglas. W. – Per curiam decision
5. Clark, T. – Per curiam decision
6. Harlan, J. – Per curiam decision
7. Brennan, W. – Per curiam decision
8. Whittaker, C. – Per curiam decision
9. Stewart, P. – Per curiam decision

VI. A WIN OR LOSS FOR THE ACLU?

The ACLU filed as amicus curiae urging reversal of the Court of Appeal's affirmation that the trial judge was justified in withdrawing petitioner's plea; the Supreme Court reversed that decision and affirmed in part the lower court's ruling in a per curiam 9-0 decision, giving the ACLU an apparent win.

120. Konigsberg v. State Bar of California

(Decided April 24, 1961; 366 U.S. 36)

I. ISSUE

A. Issues Discussed

Due process, governmental authority

1 Saldana v. United States, 274 F.2d 352 (9th Cir. 1959); Saldana v. United States, 274 F.2d 352 (9th Cir. 1959) (Hamley, F., dissenting).

B. Legal Question Presented

Were the petitioner's due process rights violated when a California state licensing committee denied him a license to practice law as a result of his refusal to answer questions about his membership in the Communist Party?

C. Supreme Court's Answer

The licensing committed did not violate petitioner's due process rights when they denied him a license to practice law on the basis of refusing to answer questions about Communist Party membership.

II. CASE SUMMARY

A. Background

In 1953, petitioner Konigsberg passed the Bar exam in California, then applied for a license to practice law in the state. Before he could obtain his license, petitioner was required by a California law to prove to a state licensing committee that he possessed "good moral character" and that he did not advocate the violent overthrow of the federal or California governments. After reviewing his qualifications, the state licensing committee refused to award petitioner a license to practice law on the ground that he refused "to answer Committee questions as to his past or present membership in the Communist Party."

Petitioner appealed the committee's decision to the California Supreme Court, and the court declined to review the case. Petitioner then appealed to the U.S. Supreme Court, which ruled that the committee's refusal to give a license to petitioner lacked evidentiary support and therefore violated the Due Process Clause of the Fourteenth Amendment. The U.S. Supreme Court declined to rule, however, whether petitioner's mere refusal to answer questions posed to him by the committee could constitute an independent reason to deny him a license to practice law.

At a second hearing before the Bar Committee, Petitioner refused to answer any questions pertaining to his membership in the Communist Party. Again, the state licensing committee refused to give petitioner a license, "this time on the ground that his refusals to answer had obstructed a full investigation into his qualifications." Petitioner appealed that decision to the California State Supreme Court, which again declined to review the case. He then appealed to the U.S. Supreme Court.

The U.S. Supreme Court affirmed the denial.

B. Counsel of Record/ACLU Attorney

ACLU Side (Petitioner/Appellant): Edward Mosk argued the cause for appellant.

Opposing Side (Respondent/Appellee): Frank B. Belcher argued the cause for appellee.

III. AMICI CURIAE

ACLU Side (Petitioner/Appellant)

Brief of amici curiae filed on behalf of the ACLU of Southern California by A. L. Wirin, Fred Okrand and Hugh R. Manes.

Brief of amici curiae filed on behalf of the National Lawyers Guild by David Scribner, Leonard B. Boudin, Ben Margolis, William B. Murrish, Charles Stewart, Lorraine Binder, Louis Berry, and David B. Finkel.

Brief of amici curiae filed by Robert L. Brock, Pauline Epstein, Robert W. Kenny, Hugh R. Manes, Ben Margolis, Daniel G. Marshall, William B. Murrish, John McTernan, Maynard Omerberg, Alexander Schullman and David Sokol on behalf of themselves and certain other members of the California Bar.

Opposing Side (Respondent/Appellee)

No briefs of amici curiae were filed in support of appellant.

IV. THE SUPREME COURT'S DECISION

"We think it clear that the Fourteenth Amendment's protection against arbitrary state action does not forbid a State from denying admission to a bar applicant so long as he refuses to provide unprivileged answers to questions having a substantial relevance to his qualifications. An investigation of this character, like a civil suit, requires procedural, as well as substantive, rules. . . .

The state procedural rule involved here is a less broad one, for all that California has in effect said is that, in cases where, on matters material to an applicant's qualifications, there are gaps in the evidence presented by him which the agency charged with certification considers should be filled in the appropriate exercise of its responsibilities, an applicant will not be admitted to practice unless and until he cooperates with the agency's efforts to fill those gaps. . . .

In the context of the entire record of these proceedings, the application of the California rule in this instance cannot be said to be arbitrary or discriminatory. In the first Konigsberg case, this Court held that neither the somewhat weak but uncontradicted testimony that petitioner had been a Communist Party member in 1941 nor his refusal to answer questions relating to Party membership could rationally support any substantive adverse inferences as to petitioner's character qualifications. That was not to say, however, that these factors, singly or together, could not be regarded as leaving the investigatory record in sufficient uncertainty as constitutionally to permit application of the procedural rule which the State has now invoked, provided that Konigsberg had been first given due warning of the consequences of his continuing refusal to respond to the Committee's questions. . . .

The judgment of the Supreme Court of California is affirmed."

V. JUSTICE VOTE

4 Pro ACLU Side vs. 5 Con Opposing Side

ACLU Side (Petitioner/Appellant)

1. Black, H. – Wrote dissenting opinion
2. Warren, E. – Joined Black's dissent, joined Brennan's dissent
3. Douglas, W. – Joined Black's dissent
4. Brennan, W. – Wrote dissenting opinion

Opposing Side (Respondent/Appellee)

1. Harlan, J. – Wrote majority opinion

2. Frankfurter, F. – Joined majority opinion
3. Stewart, P. – Joined majority opinion
4. Clark, T. – Joined majority opinion
5. Whittaker, C. – Joined majority opinion

VI. A WIN OR LOSS FOR THE ACLU?

The ACLU filed an amicus brief urging reversal; the U.S. Supreme Court affirmed the ruling of the California Supreme Court in a 5-4 vote, giving the ACLU an apparent loss.

121. In re Anastaplo

(Decided April 24, 1961; 366 U.S. 82)

I. ISSUE

A. Issues Discussed

Due process, governmental authority

B. Legal Question Presented

First, "whether Anastaplo was given adequate warning as to the consequences of his refusal to answer the Committee's questions relating to Communist Party membership," and second, "whether his exclusion from the bar on this ground was, in the circumstances of this case, arbitrary or discriminatory."

C. Supreme Court's Answer

The warnings were adequate and the exclusion was not arbitrary or discriminatory such that petitioner's exclusion from the Illinois State Bar did not violate due process or otherwise offend the Constitution.

II. CASE SUMMARY

A. Background

In 1954, petitioner George Anastaplo was denied admission to the state bar of Illinois because he had refused to answer the Committee on Character and Fitness' questions pertaining to his membership in the Communist Party. The denial was not because he was then assumed to be disloyal or a Communist Party member, but because his refusal to answer questions did not provide the Committee with adequate information to determine his fitness for a law license. Petitioner appealed to the Supreme Court of Illinois, which upheld the state's refusal to issue a law license to petitioner. Petitioner appealed that decision to the U.S. Supreme Court.

Having previously decided in the case of Konigsberg v. State of California that a state may refuse to permit an applicant from practicing law if the applicant withholds information that is pertinent to the applicant's character and fitness to be a lawyer, the Supreme Court in this case agreed to determine (1) "whether Anastaplo was given adequate warning as to the consequences of his refusal to answer the Committee's questions relating to Communist Party membership., and (2) "whether his exclusion from the bar on this ground was, in the circumstances of this case, arbitrary or discriminatory."

The U.S. Supreme Court affirmed the decision of the Illinois Supreme Court.

B. Counsel of Record/ACLU Attorney

ACLU Side (Petitioner/Appellant): George Anastaplo argued the cause pro se.

Opposing Side (Respondent/Appellee): William C. Wines, Assistant Attorney General of Illinois, argued the cause for appellee.

III. AMICI CURIAE

ACLU Side (Petitioner/Appellant)

Brief of amici curiae filed on behalf of the ACLU by Harry Kalven, Jr., and Roscoe T. Steffen.

Brief of amicus curiae filed on behalf of the National Lawyers Guild by David Scribner, Leonard B. Boudin, Ben Margolis, William B. Murrish, and Charles Stewart.

Opposing Side (Respondent/Appellee)

No briefs of amici curiae were filed in support of appellee.

IV. THE SUPREME COURT'S DECISION

"The sum and substance of the matter is that throughout the renewed proceedings petitioner was fully aware that his application for admission had already once been rejected on the very ground about which he now professes to have been left in doubt, and that the Committee made manifest both that it continued to attach special importance to its Communist Party affiliation questions and that adverse consequences might well follow if Anastaplo persisted in refusing to answer them. . . .

Further, petitioner's repeated objections throughout the hearings to the effect that there was no basis for the Committee's evident purpose to give much greater emphasis to questions about Communist Party membership than to other unanswered inquiries dispel any doubt that Anastaplo was quite aware that Communist affiliation questions were to be treated differently from other questions he had refused to answer. . . . Even as to one charged with crime due process does not demand that he be warned as to what specific sanction will be applied to him if he violates the law. It is enough that he know what sanction 'could and might' to no more. . . . Petitioner having been fairly warned that exclusion from admission to practice might follow from his refusal to answer, it must be found that this requirement of due process was duly met. . . .

Petitioner's claim that the application of the State's exclusionary rule was arbitrary and discriminatory in the circumstances of this case must also be rejected.

[T]here is nothing in the record which would justify our holding that the State has invoked its exclusionary refusal-to-answer rule as a mask for its disapproval of petitioner's notions on the right to overthrow tyrannical government. [I]t is perfectly clear that the Illinois Bar Committee and Supreme Court regarded petitioner's refusal to cooperate in the Committee's examination of him as the basic and only reason for a denial of certification. . . .

We conclude with observing that our function here is solely one of constitutional adjudication, not to pass judgment on what has been done as if we were another state court of review, still less to express any view upon the wisdom of the State's action. With appropriate regard for the limited range of our authority, we cannot say that the State's denial of Anastaplo's application for admission to its bar offends the Federal Constitution. The judgment of the Illinois Supreme Court must therefore be affirmed."

V. JUSTICE VOTE

4 Pro ACLU Side vs. 5 Con Opposing Side

ACLU Side (Petitioner/Appellant)

1. Black, H. – Wrote dissenting opinion
2. Warren, E. – Joined Black's dissent, joined Brennan's dissent
3. Douglas, W. – Joined Black's dissent
4. Brennan, W. – Wrote dissenting opinion, joined Black's dissent

Opposing Side (Respondent/Appellee)

1. Harlan, J. – Wrote majority opinion
2. Clark, T. – Joined majority opinion
3. Frankfurter, F. – Joined majority opinion
4. Whittaker, C. – Joined majority opinion
5. Stewart, P. – Joined majority opinion

VI. A WIN OR LOSS FOR THE ACLU?

The ACLU filed an amicus brief urging reversal; the U.S. Supreme Court affirmed the ruling of the Illinois Supreme Court in a 5-4 vote, giving the ACLU an apparent loss.

122. Two Guys from Harrison-Allentown, Inc. v. McGinley

(Decided May 29, 1961; 366 U.S. 582)

I. ISSUE

A. Issues Discussed

Freedom of religion, equal protection

B. Legal Question Presented

"[W]hether a Pennsylvania statute enacted in 1959 which makes unlawful the Sunday retail sale of certain commodities, imposing a fine of up to one hundred dollars for the first offense, is violative of the constitutional guarantees of equal protection of the laws and religious freedom."

C. Supreme Court's Answer

The Sunday-closing law does not violate equal protection or freedom of religion.

II. CASE SUMMARY

A. Background

Appellant Two Guys from Harrison-Allentown, Inc., was a corporation that operated a large department store in Lehigh County, Pennsylvania. Appellee, the county's district attorney, prosecuted several of appellant's employees for violating a Pennsylvania law that prohibited virtually "all worldly employment, business and sports on Sunday," with exceptions for charity work, recreation, and necessities such as milk delivery and public utilities. The law was construed to prohibit appellant from operating its department store on Sundays.

Appellant filed a lawsuit in federal district court seeking to prevent the Lehigh County district attorney from enforcing the Pennsylvania Sunday-closing law. Appellant argued that the law violated his constitutional guarantees of equal protection of the laws and religious freedom. A three-judge panel of the federal district court declined to issue an injunction to prevent the district attorney from enforcing the law.

The Supreme Court granted certiorari to decide the issue and affirmed.

B. Counsel of Record/ACLU Attorney

ACLU Side (Petitioner/Appellant): Harold E. Kohn argued the cause for appellant.

Opposing Side (Respondent/Appellee): Harry J. Rubin argued the cause for appellee.

III. AMICI CURIAE

ACLU Side (Petitioner/Appellant)

Brief of amici curiae filed on behalf of the ACLU by Lawrence Speiser, Rowland Watts, and Jacob S. Richman.

Opposing Side (Respondent/Appellee)

No briefs of amici curiae were filed in support of appellee.

IV. THE SUPREME COURT'S DECISION

"It was within the power of the legislature to have concluded that these businesses were particularly disrupting the intended atmosphere of the day because of the great volume of motor traffic attracted, the danger of their competitors also opening on Sunday and their large number of employees. 'Evils in the same field may be of different dimensions and proportions, requiring different remedies. . . . Or the reform may take one step at a time, addressing itself to the phase of the problem which seems most acute to the legislative mind. . . . The legislature may select one phase of one field and apply a remedy there, neglecting the others.'

Appellant contends that the Pennsylvania Sunday Closing Law is one respecting an establishment of religion because it commemorates the Resurrection, obliges everyone to honor this basic doctrine of the major Christian denominations by abstaining from work and encourages Christian religious worship. Appellant also alleges that the statute discriminates against certain religions. . . .

Having carefully examined the entirety of the present legislation, the relevant judicial characterizations and, particularly, the legislative history leading to the passage of the 1959 Act immediately before us, we hold that neither the statute's purpose nor its effect is religious. Moreover, . . . we reject appellant's contention that the State has other means at its disposal to accomplish its secular purpose that would not even remotely or incidentally give state aid to religion."

The Supreme Court affirmed the judgment.

V. JUSTICE VOTE

1 Pro ACLU Side vs. 8 Con Opposing Side

ACLU Side (Petitioner/Appellant)

1. Douglas, W. – Wrote dissenting opinion

Opposing Side (Respondent/Appellee)

1. Warren, E. – Wrote majority opinion
2. Black, H. – Joined majority opinion
3. Frankfurter, F. – Wrote concurring opinion
4. Clark, T. – Joined majority opinion
5. Harlan, J. – Joined Frankfurter's concurrence
6. Brennan, W. – Joined majority opinion
7. Whittaker, C. – Joined majority opinion
8. Stewart, P. – Joined majority opinion

VI. A WIN OR LOSS FOR THE ACLU?

The ACLU filed an amicus brief urging reversal; the Supreme Court affirmed the ruling of the three-judge panel of the District Court in an 8-1 vote, giving the ACLU an apparent loss.

123. Gallagher v. Crown Kosher Super Market of Massachusetts, Inc.

(Decided May 29, 1961; 366 U.S. 617)

I. ISSUE

A. Issues Discussed

Freedom of religion, establishment of religion, equal protection

B. Legal Question Presented

"[W]hether the Massachusetts Sunday Closing Laws violate equal protection, are statutes respecting the establishment of religion or prohibit the free exercise thereof."

C. Supreme Court's Answer

The Massachusetts Sunday Closing Laws do not violate equal protection and are not an establishment of religion.

II. CASE SUMMARY

A. Background

Appellee Crown Kosher Super Market was an Orthodox Jewish supermarket located in Springfield, Massachusetts, that sold kosher food products to a largely Jewish clientele. The supermarket previously conducted approximately one-third of its weekly business on Sundays due in part to the restriction forbidding members of the Orthodox Jewish faith from shopping and engaging in other commercial activities on the Sabbath (sundown on Friday to sundown on Saturday). A Massachusetts Sunday closing law prohibited most businesses from being open on Sundays in observance of the traditional Christian day of worship. Although the law contained numerous exceptions, the law had been construed to prohibit the appellee from being open for the majority of the day on Sundays.

"Appellees sought permanently to enjoin the enforcement of the statute against them, alleging that appellant, Springfield's chief of police, had previously arrested and prosecuted Crown's manager for keeping open on Sunday; that, unless restrained, appellant would continue to enforce the statute against Crown; that the statute was unconstitutional for the reasons stated above. The three-judge Federal District Court, one judge dissenting, agreed with appellees."

The Supreme Court granted certiorari and reversed.

B. Counsel of Record/ACLU Attorney

ACLU Side (Respondent/Appellee): Herbert B. Ehrmann argued the cause for appellee.

Opposing Side (Petitioner/Appellant): Joseph H. Elcock, Jr., Assistant Attorney General of Massachusetts, argued the cause for appellant.

III. AMICI CURIAE

ACLU Side (Respondent/Appellee)

Brief of amici curiae filed on behalf of the ACLU, et al., by Reuben Goodman, Samuel S. Robinson, and Rowland Watts.

Briefs of amici curiae were filed on behalf of the Synagogue Council of America, et al., the American Jewish Committee, the Anti-Defamation League of B'nai B'rith, and the General Conference of Seventh-Day Adventists.

Opposing Side (Petitioner/Appellant)

No briefs of amici curiae were filed in support of appellant.

IV. THE SUPREME COURT'S DECISION

"The fact is that the irrationality of these and the many other apparently reasonable distinctions has not been shown. . . . 'A classification having some reasonable basis does not offend against [the equal protection] clause merely because it is not made with mathematical nicety or because in practice it results in some inequality.' Thus, we hold that the Massachusetts Sunday Laws do not violate equal protection of the laws. . . .

We agree with the court below that, like the Sunday laws of other States, the Massachusetts statutes have an unmistakably religious origin. . . . However, when we examine the statutes now before the Court, we find that, for the most part, they have been divorced from the religious orientation of their predecessors. . . .

Admittedly, the statutes still contain references to the Lord's Day and some provisions speak of weekdays as being secular days. . . . It would seem that the objectionable language is merely a relic. [B]ecause the State wishes to protect those who do worship on Sunday does not mean that the State means to impose religious worship on all. Although many of the more recently allowed Sunday activities may not commence prior to 1 p.m., others may be undertaken at any time during the day. . . .

Furthermore, the long list of exemptions that have been recently granted evidences that the present scheme is one to provide an atmosphere of recreation rather than religion. The court below pointed out that, since 1858, the statutes have been amended more than seventy times. It would not seem that the Sunday sales of tobacco, soda water, fruit, et cetera, are in aid of religion. It would seem that the operation of amusement parks and beach resorts is in aid of recreation. . . .

The relevant factors having been most carefully considered, we do not find that the present statutes' purpose or effect is religious. Although the three-judge court found that Massachusetts had no legitimate secular interest in maintaining Sunday closing, we have held differently in McGowan v. Maryland. And, for the reasons stated in that case, we reject appellees' request to hold these statutes invalid on the ground that the State may accomplish its secular purpose by alternative means that would not even remotely or incidentally aid religion."

The Supreme Court reversed the judgment.

V. JUSTICE VOTE

3 Pro ACLU Side vs. 6 Con Opposing Side

ACLU Side (Petitioner/Appellant)

1. Douglas, W. – Wrote dissenting opinion
2. Brennan, W. – Wrote dissenting opinion with Stewart
3. Stewart, P. – Wrote dissenting opinion with Brennan

Opposing Side (Respondent/Appellee)

1. Warren, E. – Wrote majority opinion
2. Black, H. – Joined majority opinion
3. Clark, C. – Joined majority opinion
4. Whittaker, C. – Joined majority opinion
5. Frankfurter, F. – Wrote concurring opinion
6. Harlan, J. – Joined Frankfurter's concurrence

VI. A WIN OR LOSS FOR THE ACLU?

The ACLU filed an amicus brief urging affirmance; the Supreme Court reversed the ruling of the District Court in a 6-3 vote, giving the ACLU an apparent loss.

124. Communist Party v. Subversive Activities Control Board

(Decided June 5, 1961; 367 U.S. 1)

I. ISSUE

A. Issues Discussed

Governmental authority, due process, First Amendment

B. Legal Question Presented

Is the registration requirement of § 7 of the Subversive Activities Control Act of 1950 an unconstitutional bill of attainder, a violation of the First Amendment freedom of speech or association, a violation of the Fifth Amendment protection against self-incrimination, or a violation of due process?

C. Supreme Court's Answer

The registration requirement is not an unconstitutional bill of attainder, violation of the First Amendment, or violation of due process, and other contentions are premature.

II. CASE SUMMARY

A. Background

Respondent, Subversive Activities Control Board, ordered petitioner, Communist Party of the United States, "to register as a Communist-action organization under § 7 of the [Subversive Activities Control] Act" of 1950. Respondent sought review of the order. The Court of Appeals for the District of Columbia affirmed the registration order.

The Supreme Court granted certiorari and affirmed the judgment.

B. Counsel of Record/ACLU Attorney

ACLU Side (Petitioner/Appellant): John J. Abt and Joseph Forer argued the cause for appellant.

Opposing Side (Respondent/Appellee): Solicitor General Rankin argued the cause for appellee.

III. AMICI CURIAE

ACLU Side (Petitioner/Appellant)

Brief of amici curiae filed on behalf of the ACLU by Nanette Dembitz and Rowland Watts.

Briefs of amici curiae filed on behalf of the National Lawyers Guild by Thomas I. Emerson.

Brief of amici curiae filed on behalf of Reverend Edwin E. Aiken et al., by Royal W. France and Laurent B. Frantz.

Opposing Side (Respondent/Appellee)

No briefs of amici curiae were filed in support of appellee.

IV. THE SUPREME COURT'S DECISION

"The Act is not a bill of attainder. It attaches not to specified organizations but to described activities in which an organization may or may not engage. The singling out of an individual for legislatively prescribed punishment constitutes an attainder whether the individual is called by name or described in terms of conduct which, because it is past conduct, operates only as a designation of particular persons. The Subversive Activities Control Act is not of that kind. It requires the registration only of organizations which, after the date of the Act, are found to be under the direction, domination, or control of certain foreign powers and to operate primarily to advance certain objectives. . . . Nor is the statute made an act of 'outlawry' or of attainder by the fact that the conduct which it regulates is described with such particularity that, in probability, few organizations will come within the statutory terms. Legislatures may act to curb behavior which they regard as harmful to the public welfare, whether that conduct is found to be engaged in by many persons or by one. So long as the incidence of legislation is such that the persons who engage in the regulated conduct, be they many or few, can escape regulation merely by altering the course of their own present activities, there can be no complaint of an attainder. . . .

The Communist Party would have us hold that the First Amendment prohibits Congress from requiring the registration and filing of information, including membership lists, by organizations substantially dominated or controlled by the foreign powers controlling the world Communist movement and which operate primarily to advance the objectives of that movement: the overthrow of existing government by any means necessary and the establishment in its place of a Communist totalitarian dictatorship. We cannot find such a prohibition in the First Amendment. So to find would make a travesty of that Amendment and the great ends for the well-being of our democracy that it serves. . . . The requirement that persons who were officers or members at any time during the year preceding registration must be listed is a reasonable means of assuring that the obligation to list present members and officers will not be evaded. For reasons which do not require elaboration, the requirement that a registering organization list the aliases of officers and members must also be sustained. Nor do we find that § 7(d)(3), requiring a financial accounting, or § 7(d)(6), requiring a listing of all printing presses in the possession or control of the organization or its members violates First Amendment rights. Disclosure both of the financial transactions of a Communist-action organization and of the identity of the organs of publication which it controls might not unreasonably have been regarded by Congress as necessary to the objective which the Act seeks to achieve: to bring foreign-dominated organizations out into the open where the public can evaluate their activities informedly against the revealed background of their character, nature, and connections. . . .

Manifestly, insofar as this contention is directed against the provisions of § 7(h) and 28 CFR § 11.205, requiring that designated officers file registration statements in default of registration by an organization, it is prematurely raised in the present proceeding. The duties imposed by those provisions will not arise until and unless the Party fails to register. At this time their application is wholly contingent and conjectural. . . .

We find that the self-incrimination challenge to § 7(a) and (d), as implemented by the Attorney General's regulations and forms, is also premature at this time. The privilege against self-incrimination is one which normally must be claimed by the individual who seeks to avail himself of its protection. We cannot know now that the Party's officers will ever claim the privilege. . . .

We have held, supra, that the congressional findings that there exists a world Communist movement, that it is directed by the Communist dictatorship of a foreign country, and that it has certain designated objectives, inter alia, the establishment of a Communist totalitarian dictatorship throughout the world through the medium of a world-wide Communist organization, are not open to re-examination by the Board. We find that nothing in this violates due process. . . .Whether the particular organization against whom the Attorney General files a petition for a registration order operates primarily to advance those objectives is the pertinent issue under the statute, and this issue may be litigated. That is all that due process requires. . . .

We do not find that the congressional assertions in § 2(9), (12) and (15), that there exist in the United States individuals dedicated to communism, a 'Communist network,' a 'Communist movement,' and a Communist 'organization,' deprive the Party of the fair hearing which due process of law requires. Fairly read, these findings neither compel nor suggest the outcome in any particular litigations before the Board. They do not create the impression that there is a single Communist-action organization in the United States, still less that the Communist Party is 'it.' Nor can we hold that the findings of § 2 of the Communist Control Act of 1954 unconstitutionally prejudice the Party. It is not suggested that these were enacted with a purpose to influence the then-pending proceedings in the present case. Rather, they are a portion of legislation deemed necessary by Congress pursuant to its continuing duty to protect the national welfare. . . .

The other constitutional questions raised by the Party have been carefully considered, but do not call for detailed discussion. And we must decline, of course, to enter into discussion of the wisdom of this legislation. The Constitution does not prohibit the requirement that the Communist Party register with the Attorney General as a Communist-action organization pursuant to § 7.

The judgment of the Court of Appeals is affirmed."

V. JUSTICE VOTE

4 Pro ACLU Side vs. 5 Con Opposing Side

ACLU Side (Petitioner/Appellant)

1. Warren, E. – Wrote dissenting opinion, joined Brennan's dissent
2. Black, H. – Wrote dissenting opinion
3. Brennan, W. – Wrote opinion dissenting in part
4. Douglas, W. – Wrote dissenting opinion

Opposing Side (Respondent/Appellee)

1. Frankfurter, F. – Wrote majority opinion
2. Harlan, J. – Joined majority opinion
3. Whittaker, C. – Joined majority opinion
4. Stewart, P. – Joined majority opinion
5. Clark, T. – Joined majority opinion

VI. A WIN OR LOSS FOR THE ACLU?

The ACLU filed as amicus curiae urging reversal; the Supreme Court affirmed the judgment of the Court of Appeals in a 5-4 vote, giving the ACLU an apparent loss.

125. Scales v. United States

(Decided June 5, 1961; 367 U.S. 203)

I. ISSUE

A. Issues Discussed

Governmental authority, due process

B. Legal Question Presented

Does a Communist Party member's conviction under the Smith Act, which makes a felony the knowing membership in organizations advocating violent or forceful government overthrow, violate the Fifth Amendment's due process clause?

C. Supreme Court's Answer

The conviction does not violate the due process clause of the Fifth Amendment.

II. CASE SUMMARY

A. Background

The Smith Act "makes a felony the acquisition or holding of knowing membership in any organization which advocates the overthrow of the Government of the United States by force or violence." Petitioner Scales was charged with knowing membership in the Communist Party of the United States, an organization that was alleged to advocate the overthrow of the government. Petitioner was convicted of the charge and the Court of Appeals affirmed the conviction.

On appeal, the Supreme Court granted certiorari and affirmed.

B. Counsel of Record / ACLU Attorney

ACLU Side (Petitioner/Appellant): Telford Taylor reargued the cause for appellant.

Opposing Side (Respondent/Appellee): John F. Davis reargued the cause for appellee.

III. AMICI CURIAE

ACLU Side (Petitioner/Appellant)

Brief of amici curiae filed on behalf of the ACLU by Osmond K. Fraenkel, Bernard Weisberg, and Rowland Watts.

Opposing Side (Respondent/Appellee)

No briefs of amici curiae were filed in support of appellee.

IV. THE SUPREME COURT'S DECISION

"[T]he membership clause of the Smith Act on its face . . . neither proscribes membership in Communist organizations . . . but only in organizations engaging in advocacy of violent overthrow, nor punishes membership in that kind of organization except as to one 'knowing the purposes thereof,' and, as we have interpreted the clause, with a specific intent to further those purposes. We have also held that the proscribed membership must be active, and not nominal, passive or theoretical. . . .

The indictment was not defective in failing to charge that Scales was an 'active' member of the Party, for that factor was not in itself a discrete element of the crime, but an inherent quality of the membership element. . . .

In our jurisprudence guilt is personal, and when the imposition of punishment on a status or on conduct can only be justified by reference to the relationship of that status or conduct to other concededly criminal activity . . . that relationship must be sufficiently substantial to satisfy the concept of personal guilt in order to withstand attack under the Due Process Clause of the Fifth Amendment. Membership, without more, in an organization engaged in illegal advocacy, it is now said, has not heretofore been recognized by this Court to be such a relationship. . . .

Any thought that due process puts beyond the reach of the criminal law all individual associational relationships, unless accompanied by the commission of specific acts of criminality, is dispelled by familiar concepts of the law of conspiracy and complicity. . . . A member, as distinguished from a conspirator, may indicate his approval of a criminal enterprise by the very fact of his membership without thereby necessarily committing himself to further it by any act or course of conduct whatever. . . .

[T]he advocacy with which we are here concerned is not constitutionally protected speech . . . to promote such advocacy, albeit under the aegis of what purports to be a political party, is not such association as is protected by the First Amendment."

The Supreme Court affirmed the judgment.

V. JUSTICE VOTE

4 Pro ACLU Side vs. 5 Con Opposing SIde

ACLU Side (Petitioner/Appellant)

1. Brennan, W. – Wrote dissenting opinion
2. Warren, E. – Joined Brennan's dissent
3. Black, H. – Wrote dissenting opinion
4. Douglas, W. – Wrote dissenting opinion, joined Brennan's dissent

Opposing Side (Respondent/Appellee)

1. Harlan, J. – Wrote majority opinion
2. Clark. T. – Joined majority opinion
3. Frankfurter, F. – Joined majority opinion
4. Stewart, P. – Joined majority opinion
5. Whittaker, C. – Joined majority opinion

VI. A WIN OR LOSS FOR THE ACLU?

The ACLU filed an amicus brief urging reversal; the Supreme Court affirmed the judgment by a 5-4 vote, giving the ACLU an apparent loss.

126. Gori v. United States

(Decided June 12, 1961; 367 U.S. 364)

I. ISSUE

A. Issues Discussed

Criminal procedure, double jeopardy

B. Legal Question Presented

"[W]hether, in the particular circumstances of this record, petitioner's conviction at his second trial for violation of 18 U.S.C. § 659, after his first trial had been terminated by the trial judge's declaration of a mistrial sua sponte and without petitioner's 'active and express consent,' violates the Fifth Amendment's prohibition of double jeopardy."

C. Supreme Court's Answer

The conviction at the second trial did not violate the Fifth Amendment's prohibition of double jeopardy.

II. CASE SUMMARY

A. Background

Petitioner Gori was tried before a jury in the District Court on a charge "that he had knowingly received and possessed goods stolen in interstate commerce. [D]uring the direct examination of the fourth witness for the Government, the presiding judge, on his own motion and with neither approval nor objection by petitioner's counsel, withdrew a juror and declared a mistrial." Petitioner was retried, and he was convicted. Petitioner appealed claiming the second trial subjected him to double jeopardy, in violation of the Fifth Amendment. His conviction was affirmed by the Court of Appeals; determining that the judge "'was acting according to his convictions in protecting the rights of the accused'" and finding that the mistrial ruling was not "erroneous or an abuse of discretion."

The Supreme Court granted certiorari and affirmed.

B. Counsel of Record/ACLU Attorney

ACLU Side (Petitioner/Appellant): Harry I. Rand argued the cause for appellant.

Opposing Side (Respondent/Appellee): Beatrice Rosenberg argued the cause for appellee.

III. AMICI CURIAE

ACLU Side (Petitioner/Appellant)

Brief of amici curiae filed on behalf of the New York Civil Liberties Union by Emanuel Redfield, Edward L. Sadowsky, and Victor S. Gettner.

Opposing Side (Respondent/Appellee)

No briefs of amici curiae were filed in support of appellee.

IV. THE SUPREME COURT'S DECISION

"[V]iewing [the case] most favorably to petitioner, the mistrial . . . was found neither apparently justified nor clearly erroneous by the Court of Appeals . . . . What that court did find and what is unquestionable is that the order was the product of the trial judge's extreme solicitude—an overeager solicitude, it may be—in favor of the accused.

Since 1824 it has been settled law in this Court that 'The double-jeopardy provision of the Fifth Amendment . . . does not mean that every time a defendant is put to trial before a competent tribunal he is entitled to go free if the trial fails to end in a final judgment.' Where, for reasons deemed compelling by the trial judge, who is best situated intelligently to make such a decision, the ends of substantial justice cannot be attained without discontinuing the trial, a mistrial may be declared without the defendant's consent and even over his objection, and he may be retried consistently with the Fifth Amendment. . . .

[W]e are unwilling, where it clearly appears that a mistrial has been granted in the sole interest of the defendant, to hold that its necessary consequence is to bar all retrial. It would hark back to the formalistic artificialities of seventeenth century criminal procedure so to confine our federal trial courts by compelling them to navigate a narrow compass between Scylla and Charybdis. We would not thus make them unduly hesitant conscientiously to exercise their most sensitive judgment—according to their own lights in the immediate exigencies of trial—for the more effective protection of the criminal accused."

The Supreme Court affirmed the judgment.

V. JUSTICE VOTE

4 Pro ACLU Side vs. 5 Con Opposing Side

ACLU Side (Petitioner/Appellant)

1. Douglas, W. – Wrote dissenting opinion
2. Warren, E. – Joined Douglas' dissent
3. Black, H. – Joined Douglas' dissent
4. Brennan, W. – Joined Douglas' dissent

Opposing Side (Respondent/Appellee)

1. Frankfurter, F. – Wrote majority opinion
2. Clark, T. – Joined majority opinion
3. Harlan, J. – Joined majority opinion
4. Whittaker, C. – Joined majority opinion
5. Stewart, P. – Joined majority opinion

VI. A WIN OR LOSS FOR THE ACLU?

The ACLU filed an amicus brief urging reversal; the Supreme Court affirmed the judgment in a 5-4 vote, giving the ACLU an apparent loss.

127. Torcaso v. Watkins

(Decided June 19, 1961; 367 U.S. 488)

I. ISSUE

A. Issues Discussed

1st Amendment, religion

B. Legal Question Presented

Whether a religious test requiring declaration of a "belief in God" for individuals appointed to public office in Maryland comports with the Constitution.

C. Supreme Court's Answer

"This Maryland religious test for public office unconstitutionally invades the appellant's freedom of belief and religion and therefore cannot be enforced against him."

II. CASE SUMMARY

A. Background

"Article 37 of the Declaration of Rights of the Maryland Constitution provides:

'(N)o religious test ought ever to be required as a qualification for any office of profit or trust in this State, other than a declaration of belief in the existence of God . . . .'

The appellant Torcaso was appointed to the office of Notary Public by the Governor of Maryland but was refused a commission to serve because he would not declare his belief in God. He then brought this action in a Maryland Circuit Court to compel issuance of his commission, charging that the State's requirement that he declare this belief violated 'the First and Fourteenth Amendments to the Constitution of the United States . . . .' The Circuit Court rejected these federal constitutional contentions, and the highest court of the State, the Court of Appeals, affirmed, holding that the state constitutional provision is self-executing and requires declaration of belief in God as a qualification for office without need for implementing legislation. The case is therefore properly [at the Supreme Court] on appeal under 28 U.S.C. s 1257(2)."

B. Counsel of Record

ACLU Side (Petitioner/Appellant): Lawrence Speiser of the American Civil Liberties Union and Leo Pfeffer argued the cause for appellant. With them on the brief were George Kaufmann, Laurence J. Cohen, Joseph A. Sickles, Carlton R. Sickles, and Bruce N. Goldberg.

Opposing Side (Respondent/Appellee): Thomas B. Finan, Attorney General of Maryland, and Joseph S. Kaufman, Deputy Attorney General, argued the cause and filed a brief for appellee. C. Ferdinand Sybert, former Attorney General of Maryland, and Stedman Prescott, Jr., former Deputy Attorney General, appeared with Mr. Kaufman on the motion to dismiss or affirm.

III. AMICI CURIAE

ACLU Side (Petitioner/Appellant)

Brief of amici curiae filed on behalf of the American Ethical Union by Herbert A. Wolff and Leo Rosen.

Brief of amici curiae filed on behalf of the American Jewish Committee et al. by Herbert B. Ehrmann, Lawrence Peirez, Isaac G. McNatt, Abraham Blumberg, Arnold Forster, Paul Hartman, Theodore Leskes, Edwin J. Lukas, and Sol Rabkin.

Opposing Side (Respondent/Appellee)

No briefs of amici curiae were filed in support of appellee.

IV. THE SUPREME COURT'S DECISION

"There is, and can be, no dispute about the purpose or effect of the Maryland Declaration of Rights requirement before us—it sets up a religious test which was designed to and, if valid, does bar every person who refuses to declare a belief in God from holding a public 'office of profit or trust' in Maryland. The power and authority of the State of Maryland thus is put on the side of one particular sort of believers—those who are willing to say they believe in 'the existence of God.' It is true that there is much historical precedent for such laws. . . .

When our Constitution was adopted, the desire to put the people 'securely beyond the reach' of religious test oaths brought about the inclusion in Article VI of that document of a provision that 'no religious Test shall ever be required as a Qualification to any Office or public Trust under the United States.' . . .

We repeat and again reaffirm that neither a State nor the Federal Government can constitutionally force a person 'to profess a belief or disbelief in any religion.' Neither can constitutionally pass laws or impose requirements which aid all religions as against non-believers, and neither can aid those religions based on a belief in the existence of God as against those religions founded on different beliefs. . . .

The fact . . . that a person is not compelled to hold public office cannot possibly be an excuse for barring him from office by state-imposed criteria forbidden by the Constitution. . . .

This Maryland religious test for public office unconstitutionally invades the appellant's freedom of belief and religion and therefore cannot be enforced against him.

The judgment of the Court of Appeals of Maryland is accordingly reversed and the cause is remanded for further proceedings not inconsistent with this opinion.

Reversed and remanded."

V. JUSTICE VOTE

9 Pro ACLU Side vs. 0 Con Opposing Side

ACLU Side (Petitioner/Appellant)

1. Black, H. – Wrote majority opinion
2. Warren, E. – Joined majority opinion
3. Brennan, W. – Joined majority opinion
4. Douglas, W. – Joined majority opinion
5. Whittaker, C. – Joined majority opinion
6. Harlan, J. – Concurred in the result
7. Stewart, P. – Joined majority opinion
8. Clark, T. – Joined majority opinion
9. Frankfurter, F. – Concurred in the result

VI. A WIN OR LOSS FOR THE ACLU?

The ACLU served as counsel for appellant urging reversal of the judgment of the Court of Appeals of Maryland; the Supreme Court reversed in a 9-0 vote, giving the ACLU an apparent win.

128. Poe v. Ullman

(Decided June 19, 1961; 367 U.S. 497)

I. ISSUE

A. Issues Discussed

Justiciability, right to privacy, Fourteenth Amendment

B. Legal Question Presented

Whether a Connecticut law prohibiting advice about and use of contraceptives violates the Fourteenth Amendment.

C. Supreme Court's Answer

The Court decided the case did not present a justicable question because there was no immediate threat of prosecution under the law.

II. CASE SUMMARY

A. Background

Women experienced serious health problems from previous pregnancies and their physician, Dr. Buxton, determined the women would be at risk if they were to become pregnant again. He felt the best and safest treatment for them would be to use contraceptives to prevent future pregnancy.

The women and Dr. Buxton, petitioners, alleged that the State's Attorney had claimed that giving advice about or using contraceptives was against state law, and that he intended to prosecute all offenses of the law. In three separate cases, the petitioners sued for declaratory judgments that an 1879 Connecticut law prohibiting the use of and advice about contraceptives violated the Fourteenth Amendment. The women argued that the statutes deprived them "of life and liberty without due process of law" because their doctor was unable to provide them with advice about contraceptives without fear of prosecution.

The Connecticut Supreme Court of Errors dismissed the appeals. The U.S. Supreme Court consolidated all three cases, noting probable jurisdiction, but ultimately dismissed the case.

B. Counsel of Record/ACLU Attorney

ACLU Side (Petitioner/Appellant): Fowler V. Harper argued the cause and filed a brief for appellants. Harriet F. Pilpel argued the cause for the Planned Parenthood Federation of America, Inc., as amicus curiae.

Opposing Side (Respondent/Appellee): Raymond J. Cannon, Assistant Attorney General of Connecticut, argued the cause for appellee.

III. AMICI CURIAE

ACLU Side (Petitioner/Appellant)

Brief of amici curiae filed on behalf of the ACLU, et al., by Osmond K. Fraenkel, Jerome E. Caplan, Rowland Watts, Ruth Emerson, and Melvin L. Wulf.

Brief of amici curiae filed on behalf of the Planned Parenthood Federation of American, Inc., by Harriet F. Pilpel, Morris L. Ernst, Julia Perles, Nancy F. Wechsler, and Greenbaum, Wolff & Ernst.

Brief of amici curiae filed on behalf of Dr. Willard Allen, et al., by Whitney North Seymour, Donald Oresman, and Simpson Thacher & Bartlett.

Opposing Side (Respondent/Appellee)

No briefs of amici curiae were filed in support of appellee.

IV. THE SUPREME COURT'S DECISION

"Appellants' complaints in these declaratory judgment proceedings do not clearly, and certainly do not in terms, allege that appellee Ullman threatens to prosecute them for use of, or for giving advice concerning, contraceptive devices. The allegations are merely that, in the course of his public duty, he intends to prosecute any offenses against Connecticut law, and that he claims that use of and advice concerning contraceptives would constitute offenses. The lack of immediacy of the threat described by these allegations might alone raise serious questions of non-justiciability of appellants' claims. . . .

The Connecticut law prohibiting the use of contraceptives has been on the State's books since 1879. During the more than three-quarters of a century since its enactment, a prosecution for its violation seems never to have been initiated, save in [one case] brought to determine the constitutionality of the Act . . . . After the Supreme Court of Errors sustained the legislation on appeal from a demurrer to the information, the State moved to dismiss the information. . .

'The best teaching of this Court's experience admonishes us not to entertain constitutional questions in advance of the strictest necessity.' The various doctrines of 'standing,' 'ripeness,' and 'mootness,' which this Court has evolved with particular, though not exclusive, reference to such cases are but several manifestations—each having its own 'varied application'—of the primary conception that federal judicial power is to be exercised to strike down legislation, whether state or federal, only at the instance of one who is himself immediately harmed, or immediately threatened with harm, by the challenged action. . . .

Justiciability is of course not a legal concept with a fixed content or susceptible of scientific verification. Its utilization is the resultant of many subtle pressures, including the appropriateness of the issues for decision by this Court and the actual hardship to the litigants of denying them the relief sought. Both these factors justify withholding adjudication of the constitutional issue raised under the circumstances and in the manner in which they are now before the Court."

The Supreme Court dismissed the case for lack of a justiciable question.

V. JUSTICE VOTE

4 Pro ACLU Side vs. 5 Con Opposing Side

ACLU Side (Petitioner/Appellant)

1. Black, H. – Wrote dissenting opinion
2. Douglas, W. – Wrote dissenting opinion
3. Harlan, J. – Wrote dissenting opinion
4. Stewart, P. – Wrote dissenting opinion

Opposing Side (Respondent/Appellee)

1. Frankfurter. F. – Wrote majority opinion
2. Warren, E. – Joined majority opinion
3. Clark, T. – Joined majority opinion
4. Whittaker, C. – Joined majority opinion
5. Brennan, W. – Wrote concurring opinion

VI. A WIN OR LOSS FOR THE ACLU?

The ACLU filed an amicus brief urging reversal; the Supreme Court dismissed the appeal by a 5-4 vote, giving the ACLU an apparent loss.

129. Mapp v. Ohio

(Decided June 19, 1961; 367 U.S. 643)

I. ISSUE

A. Issues Discussed

Search and seizure, Fourth Amendment, Fourteenth Amendment

B. Legal Question Presented

Is evidence obtained during an unlawful search admissible at trial in a state court?

C. Supreme Court's Answer

Evidence obtained during an unlawful search is inadmissible at trial in a state court.

II. CASE SUMMARY

A. Background

Appellant Mapp was convicted of possession of "lewd and lascivious books, pictures, and photographs in violation of § 2905.34 of Ohio's Revised Code." The material was seized after widespread search of her home following a forceful break-in by the police.

During the search, "Miss Mapp was halfway down the stairs from the upper floor to the front door when the officers, in this highhanded manner, broke into the hall. She demanded to see the search warrant. A paper, claimed to be a warrant, was held up by one of the officers. She grabbed the 'warrant' and placed it in her bosom. A struggle ensued in which the officers recovered the piece of paper and as a result of which they handcuffed appellant because she had been 'belligerent' in resisting their official rescue of the 'warrant' from her person. Running roughshod over appellant, a policeman 'grabbed' her, 'twisted [her] hand,' and she 'yelled [and] pleaded with him' because 'it was hurting.'"

"At trial no search warrant was produced by the prosecution, nor was the failure to produce one explained or accounted for. . . . The State says that even if the search were made without authority, or otherwise unreasonably, it is not prevented from using the unconstitutionally seized evidence at trial, citing *Wolf v. Colorado*, 338 U.S. 25 (1949), in which [the Supreme] Court did indeed hold 'that in a prosecution in a State court for a State crime the Fourteenth Amendment does not forbid the admission of evidence obtained by an unreasonable search and seizure.'"

The conviction was upheld by the Ohio Supreme Court. On appeal the U.S. Supreme Court overturned *Wolf v. Colorado* and reversed the judgment of the Ohio Supreme Court.

B. Counsel of Record/ACLU Attorney

ACLU Side (Petitioner/Appellant): A. L. Kearns argued the cause for appellant.

Bernard A. Berkman argued the cause for the ACLU and Ohio Civil Liberties Union, as amici curiae.

Opposing Side (Respondent/Appellee): Gertrude Bauer Mahon argued the cause for appellee.

III. AMICI CURIAE

ACLU Side (Petitioner/Appellant)

Brief of amici curiae filed on behalf of the ACLU, et al., by Bernard A. Berkman, Rowland Watts, Fred J. Livingstone, and Julien C. Renswick.

Opposing Side (Respondent/Appellee)

No briefs of amici curiae were filed in support of appellee.

IV. THE SUPREME COURT'S DECISION

"[I]n the year 1914, in the Weeks case, this Court 'for the first time' held that 'in a federal prosecution the Fourth Amendment barred the use of evidence secured through an illegal search and seizure.' This Court has ever since required of federal law officers a strict adherence to that command which this Court has held to be a clear, specific, and constitutionally required—even if judically implied—deterrent safeguard without insistence upon which the Fourth Amendment would have been reduced to a 'form of words.' . . .

We hold that all evidence obtained by searches and seizures in violation of the Constitution is, by that same authority inadmissible in a state court. . . . Since the Fourth Amendment's right of privacy has been declared enforceable against the States through the Due Process Clause of the Fourteenth, it is enforceable against them by the same sanction of exclusion as is used against the Federal Government. . . .

Having once recognized that the right to privacy embodied in the Fourth Amendment is enforceable against the States, and that the right to be secure against rude invasions of privacy by state officers is, therefore, constitutional in origin, we can no longer permit that right to remain an empty promise. Because it is enforceable in the same manner and to like effect as other basic rights secured by the Due Process Clause, we can no longer permit it to be revocable at the whim of any police officer who, in the name of law enforcement itself, chooses to suspend its enjoyment. Our decision, founded on reason and truth, gives to the individual no more than that which the Constitution guarantees him, to the police officer no less than that to which honest law enforcement is entitled, and, to the courts, that judicial integrity so necessary in the true administration of justice."

The U.S. Supreme Court reversed the judgment of the Ohio Supreme Court.

V. JUSTICE VOTE

6 Pro ACLU Side vs. 3 Con Opposing Side

ACLU Side (Petitioner/Appellant)

1. Clark, T. – Wrote majority opinion
2. Black, H. – Wrote concurring opinion
3. Douglas, W. – Wrote concurring opinion
4. Warren, E. – Joined majority opinion
5. Brennan, W. – Joined majority opinion
6. Stewart, P. – Wrote concurring opinion, joined Part 1 of Harlan's dissent

Opposing Side (Respondent/Appellee)

1. Harlan, J. – Wrote dissenting opinion
2. Whittaker, C. – Joined dissenting opinion
3. Frankfurter, F. – Joined dissenting opinion

VI.A WIN OR LOSS FOR THE ACLU?

The ACLU, as amicus curiae (an ACLU attorney argued though not as counsel of record), urged reversal of the Ohio Supreme Court's judgment; the Supreme Court reversed in a 6-3 vote, giving the ACLU an apparent win.

130. Hoyt v. Florida

(Decided November 20, 1961; 368 U.S. 57)

I. ISSUE

A. Issues Discussed

Gender, Fourteenth Amendment

B. Legal Question Presented

Does a Florida statute that, by default, excludes women from jury duty, but allows women to voluntarily register for jury duty, violate the Fourteenth Amendment?

C. Supreme Court's Answer

The statute does not violate the Fourteenth Amendment as written or as applied to petitioner.

II. CASE SUMMARY

A. Background

"Appellant, a woman, has been convicted in Hillsborough County, Florida, of second degree murder of her husband." A Florida statute provides, in substance, that no woman shall be taken for jury service unless she volunteers for it by placing her name on the jury list. This has led to a "minimal number of women" registered for jury service. Appellant appealed the Florida Supreme Court's affirmance of the judgment of conviction to the U.S. Supreme Court, claiming that her trial before an all-male jury violated her Fourteenth Amendment rights.

The Supreme Court granted certiorari and affirmed.

B. Counsel of Record / ACLU Attorney

ACLU Side (Petitioner / Appellant): Herbert B. Ehrmann argued the cause for appellant.

Opposing Side (Respondent / Appellee): George R. Georgieff, Assistant Attorney General of Florida, argued the cause for appellee.

III. AMICI CURIAE

ACLU Side (Petitioner / Appellant)

Brief of amici curiae filed on behalf of the Florida Civil Liberties Union, et al., by Dorothy Kenyon, Rowland Watts, and Phyllis J. Shampanier.

Opposing Side (Respondent / Appellee)

No briefs of amici curiae were filed in support of appellee.

IV. THE SUPREME COURT'S DECISION

"The jury law primarily in question . . . which requires that grand and petit jurors be taken from 'male and female' citizens of the State possessed of certain qualifications, contains the following proviso: 'provided, however, that the name of no female person shall be taken for jury service unless said person has registered with the clerk of the circuit court her desire to be placed on the jury list.'

Showing that since the enactment of the statute only a minimal number of women have so registered, appellant challenges the constitutionality of the statute both on its face and as applied in this case. . . .

At the core of appellant's argument is the claim that the nature of the crime of which she was convicted peculiarly demanded the inclusion of persons of her own sex on the jury. . . .

Manifestly, Florida's § 40.01(1) does not purport to exclude women from state jury service. Rather, the statute 'gives to women the privilege to serve but does not impose service as a duty.'

[T]he relevant inquiry is whether the exemption itself is based on some reasonable classification and whether the manner in which it is exercisable rests on some rational foundation. . . .

We cannot say that it is constitutionally impermissible for a State, acting in pursuit of the general welfare, to conclude that a woman should be relieved from the civic duty of jury service unless she herself determines that such service is consistent with her own special responsibilities. . . . We cannot hold this statute as written offensive to the Fourteenth Amendment.

This case in no way resembles those involving race or color in which the circumstances shown were found by this Court to compel a conclusion of purposeful discriminatory exclusions from jury service. There is present here neither the unfortunate atmosphere of ethnic or racial prejudices which underlay the situations depicted in those cases, nor the long course of discriminatory administrative practice which the statistical showing in each of them evinced.

[T]the disproportion of women to men on the list independently carries no constitutional significance. In the administration of the jury laws proportional class representation is not a constitutionally required factor. Finding no substantial evidence whatever in this record that Florida has arbitrarily undertaken to exclude women from jury service, a showing which it was incumbent on appellant to make, we must sustain the judgment of the Supreme Court of Florida."

The U.S. Supreme Court affirmed the judgment of the Supreme Court of Florida.

V. JUSTICE VOTE

0 Pro ACLU Side vs. 9 Con Opposing Side

Opposing Side (Respondent / Appellee)

1. Harlan, J. – Wrote majority opinion
2. Warren, E. – Joined majority opinion
3. Black, H. – Joined majority opinion
4. Douglas, W. – Joined majority opinion
5. Stewart, P. – Joined majority opinion
6. Brennan, W. – Joined majority opinion
7. Whittaker, C. – Joined majority opinion
8. Clark, T. – Joined majority opinion
9. Frankfurter, F. – Joined majority opinion

VI. A WIN OR LOSS FOR THE ACLU?

The ACLU filed an amicus brief urging reversal; the U.S. Supreme Court affirmed the ruling of the Florida Supreme Court by a 9-0 vote, giving the ACLU an apparent loss.

131. Rusk v. Cort

(Decided April 2, 1962; 369 U.S. 367)

I. ISSUE

A. Issues Discussed

Governmental authority, citizenship, jurisdiction

B. Legal Question Presented

"[W]hether the District Court was correct in holding that it had jurisdiction to entertain this action for declaratory and injunctive relief," or, "[m]ore precisely stated, the question in this case is whether, despite the liberal provisions of the Administrative Procedure Act, Congress intended that a native of this country living abroad must travel thousands of miles, be arrested, and go to jail in order to counter an administrative finding that he is not a citizen of the United States."

C. Supreme Court's Answer

The District Court did have jurisdiction over the action and the Administrative Procedure Act should not be construed so narrowly. Issues beyond this preliminary question were not decided and the case was set for reargument in the October 1952 term.

II. CASE SUMMARY

A. Background

Appellee Cort was born in the United States in 1927, but moved abroad in 1951. In 1959, Mr. Cort applied for a U.S. passport at the U.S. Embassy in Prague because his original passport had expired. His application was denied by the Passport Office of the Department of State on the ground that he had lost his citizenship under § 349(a)(10) of the 1952 Act by remaining outside the United States for the purpose of avoiding military service, as he did not respond to multiple draft board orders to report. The State Department's Board of Review on Loss of Nationality affirmed the Passport Office's decision.

Appellee then filed a suit for declaratory and injunctive relief in the District Court for the District of Columbia. "His complaint alleged that he had not remained abroad to evade his military obligations, and that § 349(a)(10) was in any event unconstitutional. A three-judge court was convened. The Secretary of State moved to dismiss the action upon the ground that § 360(b) and (c) of the Immigration and Nationality Act of 1952 provide the exclusive procedure under which Cort could attack the administrative determination that he was not a citizen. The District Court rejected this contention, holding that it had jurisdiction of the action for a declaratory judgment and an injunction. On motions for summary judgment, the court determined that the appellee had remained abroad to avoid service in the Armed Forces. [T]he court held, however, that § 349(a)(10) was unconstitutional, and that consequently the appellee's citizenship had not been divested. The court accordingly entered a judgment declaring the appellee to be a citizen of the United States and enjoining the Secretary of State from denying him a passport on the ground that he is not a citizen."

Appellant appealed directly to the Supreme Court. The Supreme Court decided one issue and set the case for reargument on other issues.

B. Counsel of Record / ACLU Attorney

ACLU Side (Respondent/Appellee): Leonard B. Boudin argued the cause for appellee.

Opposing Side (Petitioner/Appellant): Oscar H. Davis argued the cause for appellant.

III. AMICI CURIAE

ACLU Side (Respondent/Appellee)

Brief of amicus curiae filed on behalf of the ACLU by Jack Wasserman, David Carliner, Rowland Watts, and Lawrence Speiser.

Brief of amici curiae filed on behalf of Angelika Schneider by Milton V. Freeman, Robert E. Herzstein, Horst Kurnik, and Charles A. Reich.

Opposing Side (Petitioner/Appellant)

No briefs of amici curiae were filed in support of appellant.

IV. THE SUPREME COURT'S DECISION

"On their face the provisions of these statutes appear clearly to permit an action such as was brought here to review the final administrative determination of the Secretary of State. This view is confirmed by our decisions establishing that an action for a declaratory judgment is available as a remedy to secure a determination of citizenship-decisions rendered both before and after the enactment of the Administrative Procedure Act. Moreover, the fact that the plaintiff is not within the United States has never been thought to bar an action for a declaratory judgment of this nature.

[S]ubsections (b) and (c) by their very terms simply provide that a person outside of the United States who wishes to assert his citizenship 'may' apply for a certificate of identity and that a holder of a certificate of identity 'may' apply for admission to the United States. As the District Court said, 'The language of the section shows no intention to provide an exclusive remedy, or any remedy, for persons outside the United States who have not adopted the procedures outlined in subsections (b) and (c). Neither does the section indicate that such persons are to be denied existing remedies.' . . .

The legislative history of § 503 indicates that Congress understood the provision for a declaratory judgment action to be merely a confirmation of existing law, or at most a clarification of it. What was concededly novel about § 503 was the provision designed to permit a citizenship claimant outside the United States to be admitted to this country upon a certificate of identity in order personally to prosecute his claim to citizenship, subject to the condition of deportation in the event of an adverse decision. At the time of the enactment of this provision some misgivings were expressed that it might be utilized by aliens to gain physical entry into the United States and then to disappear into the general populace. . . .

This legislative history is sufficient, we think, to show that the purpose of § 360(b) and (c) was to cut off the opportunity which aliens had abused under § 503 of the 1940 Act to gain fraudulent entry to the United States by prosecuting spurious citizenship claims. We are satisfied that Congress did not intend to foreclose lawsuits by claimants, such as Cort, who do not try to gain entry to the United States before prevailing in their claims to citizenship.

For these reasons, we hold that a person outside the United States who has been denied a right of citizenship is not confined to the procedures prescribed by § 360(b) and (c), and that the remedy pursued in the present case was an appropriate one. This view is in accord with previous decisions of this Court concerning the relationship of §§ 10 and 12 of the Administrative Procedure Act to the subsequently enacted Immigration and Nationality Act of 1952. The . . . Court will not hold that the broadly remedial provisions of the Administrative Procedure Act are unavailable to review administrative decisions under the 1952 Act in the absence of clear and convincing evidence that Congress so intended.

With respect to the other issues presented by this appeal, the case is set for reargument . . . ."

V. JUSTICE VOTE

6 Pro ACLU Side vs. 3 Con Opposing Side

ACLU Side (Respondent/Appellee)

1. Stewart, P. – Wrote majority opinion
2. Douglas, W. – Joined majority opinion
3. Black, H. – Joined majority opinion
4. Brennan, W. – Wrote concurring opinion
5. Warren, E. – Joined majority opinion
6. White, B. – Joined majority opinion

Opposing Side (Petitioner/Appellant)

1. Harlan, J. – Wrote dissenting opinion
2. Clark, T. – Joined dissenting opinion
3. Frankfurter, F. – Joined dissenting opinion

VI. A WIN OR LOSS FOR THE ACLU?

The ACLU filed an amicus brief urging affirmance; the Supreme Court decided one issue in favor of appellee and set the case for reargument on the other issues in a 6-3 vote, giving the ACLU an apparent win.

132. Lynch v. Overholser

(Decided May 21, 1962; 369 U.S. 705)

I. ISSUE

A. Issues Discussed

Criminal procedure, mental illness, insanity defense

B. Legal Question Presented

Does § 24-301(d) of the D.C. Code, which provides for the compulsory commitment of defendants acquitted solely on the ground of insanity, allow petitioner to be confined in this case, after he attempted to change his plea from not guilty to guilty and objected to the insanity defense?

C. Supreme Court's Answer

The provision does not allow petitioner's mandatory commitment in this case because he did not enter the insanity defense himself; the judge used it over his objection.

II. CASE SUMMARY

A. Background

Petitioner Lynch was charged "with having violated D.C. Code, § 22—1410 by drawing and negotiating checks in the amount of $50 each with knowledge that he did not have sufficient funds or credit with the drawee bank for payment." Petitioner entered a plea of not guilty in Municipal Court. He was committed to the General Hospital, under D.C. Code, § 24-301(a), "for a mental examination to determine his competence to stand trial." The Assistant Chief Psychiatrist of the hospital "reported that petitioner's mental condition was such that he was then 'of unsound mind, unable to adequately understand the charges and incapable of assisting counsel in his own defense.' The case was continued while petitioner was given treatment at the General Hospital."

After some treatment, the psychiatrist advised the court that petitioner was able to stand trial, but that he was suffering from a mental disease and further treatment would be advisable. He also stated that petitioner had been suffering from a mental disease at the time of the crime, and the crime was a result of his mental disease. Petitioner was then brought to trial in the Municipal Court. Petitioner sought to withdraw the earlier not guilty plea and plead guilty instead. "The trial judge refused to allow the change of plea, apparently on the basis of the Hospital's report that petitioner's commission of the alleged offenses was the product of mental illness."

"At the trial one of the prosecution's witnesses, a physician representing the General Hospital's Psychiatric Division, testified, over petitioner's objection, that petitioner's crimes had been committed as a result of mental illness. Although petitioner never claimed that he had not been mentally responsible when the offenses were committed and presented no evidence to support an acquittal by reason of insanity, the trial judge concluded that petitioner was 'not guilty on the ground that he was insane at the time of the commission of the offense.' The court then ordered that petitioner be committed to Saint Elizabeths Hospital as prescribed by D.C.Code, § 24—301(d), which reads:

'(d) If any person tried upon an indictment or information for an offense . . . is acquitted solely on the ground that he was insane at the time of its commission, the court shall order such person to be confined in a hospital for the mentally ill.'"

Petitioner argued that his confinement was illegal, asserting "that the 'mandatory commitment' provision, as applied to an accused who protests that he is presently sane and that the crime he committed was not the product of mental illness, deprives one so situated of liberty without due process of law." The District Court ordered petitioner's release. The Court of Appeals reversed.

The Supreme Court granted certiorari and reversed the Court of Appeals.

B. Counsel of Record/ACLU Attorney

ACLU Side (Petitioner/Appellant): Richard Arens argued the cause for appellant.

Opposing Side (Respondent/Appellee): Assistant Attorney General Burke Marshall argued the cause for appellee.

III. AMICI CURIAE

ACLU Side (Petitioner/Appellant)

Brief of amici curiae filed on behalf of the ACLU by Francis M. Shea and Lawrence Speiser.

Opposing Side (Respondent/Appellee)

No briefs of amici curiae were filed in support of appellee.

IV. THE SUPREME COURT'S DECISION

"[W]e read § 24-301(d) as applicable only to a defendant acquitted on the ground of insanity who has affirmatively relied upon a defense of insanity, and not to one, like the petitioner, who has maintained that he was mentally responsible when the alleged offense was committed. . . .

Hence if the accused denies that he is mentally ill, he is entitled to a judicial determination of his present mental state despite the hospital board's certification that he is of unsound mind. And it should be noted that the burden rests with the party seeking commitment to prove that the accused is 'then of unsound mind.' . . .

[T]he posttrial commitment of § 24-301(d) presupposes a determination that the accused has committed the criminal act with which he is charged, whereas pretrial commitment antedates any such finding of guilt. But the fact that the accused has pleaded guilty or that, overcoming some defense other than insanity, the Government has established that he committed a criminal act constitutes only strong evidence that his continued liberty could imperil 'the preservation of public peace.' It no more rationally justifies his indeterminate commitment to a mental institution on a bare reasonable doubt as to past sanity than would any other cogent proof of possible jeopardy to 'the rights of persons and of property' in any civil commitment.

Moreover, the literal construction urged here by the Government is quite out of keeping with the congressional policy that underlies the elaborate procedural precautions included in the civil commitment provisions. It seems to have been Congress' intention to insure that only those who need treatment and may be dangerous are confined; committing a criminal defendant who denies the existence of any mental abnormality merely on the basis of a reasonable doubt as to his condition at some earlier time is surely at odds with this policy. . . .

[W]e conclude that it was not Congress' purpose to make commitment compulsory when, as here, an accused disclaims reliance on a defense of mental irresponsibility... [T]he trial judge may refuse to accept [a guilty] plea and enter a plea of not guilty on behalf of the accused. We decide in this case only that if this is done and the defendant, despite his own assertions of sanity, is found not guilty by reason of insanity, § 24-301(d) does not apply. If commitment is then considered warranted, it must be accomplished either by resorting to § 24-301(a) or by recourse to the civil commitment provisions in Title 21 of the D.C. Code."

The Supreme Court reversed the judgment of the Court of Appeals and remanded the case.

V. JUSTICE VOTE

6 Pro ACLU Side vs. 1 Con Opposing Side

ACLU Side (Petitioner/Appellant)

1. Harlan, J. – Wrote majority opinion
2. Douglas, W. – Joined majority opinion
3. Black, H. – Joined majority opinion
4. Warren, E. – Joined majority opinion
5. Stewart, P. – Joined majority opinion
6. Brennan, W. – Joined majority opinion

Opposing Side (Respondent/Appellee)

1. Clark, T. – Wrote dissenting opinion

Frankfurter, F – Took no part in the decision
White, B – Took no part in the decision

VI. A WIN OR LOSS FOR THE ACLU?

The ACLU filed an amicus brief urging reversal; the Supreme Court reversed the ruling of the Court of Appeals in a 6-1 vote, giving the ACLU an apparent win.

133. Russell v. United States

(Decided May 21, 1962; 369 U.S. 749)

I. ISSUE

A. Issues Discussed

Fifth Amendment, Sixth Amendment, legislative investigations

B. Legal Question Presented

Whether an indictment under 2 U.S.C. § 192 must state the subject under investigation at the time of the subcommittee's interrogation of the defendant.

C. Supreme Court's Answer

The indictment must identify the subject under congressional committee investigation.

II. CASE SUMMARY

A. Background

Petitioners in six consolidated cases were "convicted for refusing to answer certain questions when summoned before a congressional subcommittee. . . . In each case the indictment returned by the grand jury failed to identify the subject under congressional subcommittee inquiry at the time the witness was interrogated. The indictments were practically identical in this respect, stating only that the questions to which answers were refused 'were pertinent to the question then under inquiry' by the subcommittee. In each case a motion was filed to quash the indictment before trial upon the ground that the indictment failed to state the subject under investigation at the time of the subcommittee's interrogation of the defendant. In each case the motion was denied. In each case the issue thus raised was preserved on appeal . . . ." The Court of Appeals for the District of Columbia affirmed all the convictions.

The Supreme Court granted certiorari and reversed.

B. Counsel of Record / ACLU Attorney

ACLU Side (Petitioner / Appellant): Joseph A. Fanelli argued the cause for appellant in No. 8. Joseph L. Rauh, Jr., argued the cause for appellant in No. 9. Gerhard P. Van Arkel argued the cause for appellant in No. 10. Harry I. Rand argued the cause for appellant in No. 11. Leonard B. Boudin argued the cause for appellant in No. 12. Frank J. Donner argued the cause for appellant in No. 128.

Opposing Side (Respondent / Appellee): Kevin T. Maroney argued the cause for appellee in Nos. 8 and 128. Bruce J. Terris argued the cause for appellee in No. 9. J. William Doolittle argued the cause for appellee in Nos. 10, 11, and 12.

III. AMICI CURIAE

ACLU Side (Petitioner / Appellant)

Brief of amici curiae filed on behalf of the New York Civil Liberties Union in No. 10, by Nanette Dembitz.

Opposing Side (Respondent / Appellee)

No briefs of amici curiae were filed in support of appellee.

IV. THE SUPREME COURT'S DECISION

"Congress has expressly provided that no one can be prosecuted under 2 U.S.C. § 192 except upon indictment by a grand jury. This Court has never decided whether the indictment must identify the subject which was under inquiry at the time of the defendant's alleged default or refusal to answer. For the reasons that follow, we hold that the indictment must contain such an averment, and we accordingly reverse the judgments before us. . . .

To be sure, the fact that difficulties and doubts have beset the federal courts in trying to ascertain the subject under inquiry in cases arising under 2 U.S.C. § 192 could hardly justify, in the abstract, a requirement that indictments under the statute contain averments which would simplify the courts' task. Difficult and doubtful questions are inherent in the judicial process, particularly under a system of criminal law which places heavy emphasis upon the protection of the rights and liberties of the individual. Courts sit to resolve just such questions, and rules of law are not to be made merely to suit judicial convenience. But a proliferation of doubtful issues which not only burden the judiciary, but, because of uncertainties inherent in their resolution, work a hardship upon both the prosecution and the defense in criminal cases is hardly a desideratum. And the repeated appearance in prosecutions under a particular criminal statute of the same critical and difficult question, which could be obviated by a simple averment in the indictment, invites inquiry into the purposes and functions which a grand jury indictment is intended to serve. . . .

We need not pause to consider whether an offense under 2 U.S.C. § 192 is an 'infamous crime,' since Congress has, from the beginning, explicitly conferred upon those prosecuted under the statute the protection which the Fifth Amendment confers by providing that no one can be prosecuted for this offense except upon an indictment by a grand jury. This specific guaranty, as well as the Fifth Amendment's Due Process, Clause, are therefore both brought to bear here. Of like relevance is the guaranty of the Sixth Amendment that 'In all criminal prosecutions, the accused shall enjoy the right . . . to be informed of the nature and cause of the accusation . . . .'

The constitutional provision that a trial may be held in a serious federal criminal case only if a grand jury has first intervened reflects centuries of antecedent development of common law, going back to the Assize of Clarendon in 1166. . . .

The vice which inheres in the failure of an indictment under 2 U.S.C. § 192 to identify the subject under inquiry is thus the violation of the basic principle 'that the accused must be apprised by the indictment, with reasonable certainty, of the nature of the accusation against him . . . .' A cryptic form of indictment in cases of this kind requires the defendant to go to trial with the chief issue undefined. It enables his conviction to rest on one point, and the affirmance of the conviction to rest on another. It gives the prosecution free hand on appeal to fill in the gaps of proof by surmise or conjecture. The Court has had occasion before now to condemn just such a practice in a quite different factual setting. And the unfairness and uncertainty which have characteristically infected criminal proceedings under this statute which were based upon indictments which failed to specify the subject under inquiry are illustrated by the cases in this Court we have already discussed. The same uncertainty and unfairness are underscored by the records of the cases now before us. . . .

For these reasons we conclude that the indictment under 2 U.S.C. § 192 must state the question under congressional inquiry as found by the grand jury. Only then can the federal courts responsibly carry out the duty which Congress imposed upon them more than a century ago."

The Supreme Court reversed the judgment.

V. JUSTICE VOTE

5 Pro ACLU Side vs. 2 Con Opposing Side

ACLU Side (Petitioner / Appellant)

1. Stewart, P. – Wrote majority opinion
2. Black, H. – Joined majority opinion
3. Warren, E. – Joined majority opinion
4. Douglas, W. – Wrote concurring opinion
5. Brennan, W. – Joined majority opinion, took no part in the decision of No. 10

Opposing Side (Respondent / Appellee)

1. Clark, T. – Wrote dissenting opinion, joined Harlan's dissent
2. Harlan, J. – Wrote dissenting opinion

Frankfurter, F – Took no part in the decision
White, B. Took no part in the decision

VI. A WIN OR LOSS FOR THE ACLU?

The ACLU, as amicus curiae, urged reversal of the judgment of the lower court in No. 10; the Supreme Court reversed in a 5-2 vote, giving the ACLU an apparent win.

134. Engel v. Vitale

(Decided June 25, 1962; 370 U.S. 421)

I. ISSUE

A. Issues Discussed

School prayer, Establishment Clause

B. Legal Question Presented

Is the recommendation by a state Board of Education that a non-mandatory and non-denominational prayer be said every day at the beginning of each school day in violation of the Establishment Clause of the First Amendment?

C. Supreme Court's Answer

Even if the prayer is non-mandatory and non-denominational, reciting a prayer at the beginning of each school day in a public school violates the Establishment Clause.

II. CASE SUMMARY

A. Background

"The respondent Board of Education of Union Free School District No. 9, New Hyde Park, New York, acting in its official capacity under state law, directed the School District's principal to cause [a] prayer to be said aloud by each class in the presence of a teacher at the beginning of each school day . . . .

Shortly after the practice of reciting the Regents' prayer was adopted by the School District, the parents of ten pupils brought this action in a New York State Court insisting that use of this official prayer in the public schools was contrary to the beliefs, religions, or religious practices of both themselves and their children. Among other things, these parents challenged the constitutionality of both the state law authorizing the School District to direct the use of prayer in public schools and the School District's regulation ordering the recitation of this particular prayer on the ground that these actions of official governmental agencies violate that part of the First Amendment of the Federal Constitution which commands that 'Congress shall make no law respecting an establishment of religion'—a command which was 'made applicable to the State of New York by the Fourteenth Amendment of the said Constitution.'

The New York Court of Appeals . . . sustained an order of the lower state courts which had upheld the power of New York to use the Regents' prayer as a part of the daily procedures of its public schools so long as the schools did not compel any pupil to join in the prayer over his or his parents' objection."

On certiorari the Supreme Court reversed the judgment of the Court of Appeals.

B. Counsel of Record/ACLU Attorney

ACLU Side (Petitioner/Appellant): William J. Butler argued the cause for appellant.

Opposing Side (Respondent/Appellee): Bertram B. Daiker argued the cause for the Board of Education appellees. Porter R. Chandler argued the cause for intervenors-appellees.

III. AMICI CURIAE

ACLU Side (Petitioner/Appellant)

Briefs of amici curiae filed on behalf of the American Ethical Union, the American Jewish Committee, et al., and the Synagogue Council of America, et al.

Opposing Side (Respondent/Appellee)

Brief of amici curiae filed on behalf of the Board of Regents of the University of the State of New York.

Brief of amici curiae filed by Roger D. Foley, Attorney General of Nevada, Robert Pickrell, Attorney General of Arizona, Frank Holt, Attorney General of Arkansas, Albert L. Coles, Attorney General of Connecticut, Richard W. Ervin, Attorney General of Florida, Eugene Cook, Attorney General of Georgia, Frank Benson, Attorney General of Idaho, Edwin K. Steers, Attorney General of Indiana, William M. Ferguson, Attorney General of Kansas, Jack P. F. Gremillion, Attorney General of Louisiana, Thomas B. Finan, Attorney General of Maryland, Joe T. Patterson, Attorney General of Mississippi, William Maynard, Attorney General of New Hampshire, Arthur J. Sills, Attorney General of New Jersey, Earl E. Hartley, Attorney General of New Mexico, Leslie R. Burgum, Attorney General of North Dakota, David Stahl, Attorney General of Pennsylvania, J. Joseph Nugent, Attorney General of Rhode Island, Daniel R. McLeod, Attorney General of South Carolina, A. C. Miller, Attorney General of South Dakota, Will Wilson, Attorney General of Texas, and C. Donald Robertson, Attorney General of West Virginia.

IV. THE SUPREME COURT'S DECISION

"We think that by using its public school system to encourage recitation of the Regents' prayer, the State of New York has adopted a practice wholly inconsistent with the Establishment Clause. There can, of course, be no doubt that New York's program of daily classroom invocation of God's blessings as prescribed in the Regents' prayer is a religious activity. . . .

It is a matter of history that this very practice of establishing governmentally composed prayers for religious services was one of the reasons which caused many of our early colonists to leave England and seek religious freedom in America. . . .

There can be no doubt that New York's state prayer program officially establishes the religious beliefs embodied in the Regents' prayer. The respondents' argument to the contrary, which is largely based upon the contention that the Regents' prayer is 'nondenominational' and the fact that the program, as modified and approved by state courts, does not require all pupils to recite the prayer but permits those who wish to do so to remain silent or be excused from the room, ignores the essential nature of the program's constitutional defects. Neither the fact that the prayer may be denominationally neutral nor the fact that its observance on the part of the students is voluntary can serve to free it from the limitations of the Establishment Clause, as it might from the Free Exercise Clause, of the First Amendment, both of which are operative against the States by virtue of the Fourteenth Amendment."

The Supreme Court reversed the judgment of the Court of Appeals.

V. JUSTICE VOTE

6 Pro ACLU Side vs. 1 Con Opposing Side

ACLU Side (Petitioner/Appellant)

1. Black, H. – Wrote majority opinion
2. Brennan, W. – Joined majority opinion
3. Warren, E. – Joined majority opinion
4. Harlan, J. – Joined majority opinion
5. Clark, T. Joined majority opinion
6. Douglas, W. – Wrote concurring opinion

Opposing Side (Respondent/Appellee)

1. Stewart, P. – Wrote dissenting opinion

Frankfurter, F – Took no part in the decision
White, B – Took no part in the decision

VI. A WIN OR LOSS FOR THE ACLU?

The ACLU, as attorney of record, urged reversal of the judgment of the Court of Appeals; the Supreme Court reversed the lower court's decision in a 6-1 vote, giving the ACLU an apparent win.

135. Schroeder v. City of New York

(Decided December 17, 1962; 371 U.S. 208)

I. ISSUE

A. Issues Discussed

Governmental authority, due process

B. Legal Question Presented

"[W]hether the City of New York deprived the appellant of due process of law by failing to give her adequate notice of condemnation proceedings affecting certain property she owned on the Neversink River in Orange County, New York."

C. Supreme Court's Answer

The City of New York deprived appellant of due process by failing to give her adequate notice of the condemnation proceedings affecting her property.

II. CASE SUMMARY

A. Background

Under the New York City Water Supply Act, New York City instituted proceedings to acquire the right to divert a portion of a river. The portion of the river to be diverted was about 25 miles north of appellant's summer home, which was only occupied during July and August each year.

The Water Supply Act defines the procedure to be followed for these proceedings, requiring that notice must be given in certain public newspapers, in the City Record, and posted on hand bills in the affected area. "The Act further provides that claims for damages from the city's acquisition are barred after three years."

Notices regarding the condemnation proceeding were posted in accordance with the Act. However, no notices were posted on appellant's property, just in the general vicinity. "The notices were posted on the trees and poles during the month of January, when the appellant's premises were vacant. Although the appellant's name and address were readily ascertainable from both deed records and tax rolls, neither the newspaper publications nor the posted notices contained the name of the appellant or of any other affected property owner. Neither the newspaper publications nor the posted notices explained what action a property owner might take to recover for damages caused by the city's acquisition, nor did they intimate any time limit upon the filing of a claim by an affected property owner.

The appellant did not file a claim for damages to her property within the three-year period prescribed by the Water Supply Act. In January 1960, however, she brought the present equitable action in a New York trial court." Appellant alleged that the city failed to give her adequate notice of condemnation proceedings, and her right to make a claim against the city for damages to her property, and therefore deprived her of due process of law. The trial court ruled in favor of the city. The Appellate Division and the New York Court of Appeals both affirmed the judgment.

The Supreme Court granted certiorari and reversed.

B. Counsel of Record/ACLU Attorney

ACLU Side (Petitioner/Appellant): Louis B. Scheinman argued the cause for appellant.

Opposing Side (Respondent/Appellee): Theodore R. Lee argued the cause for appellee.

III. AMICI CURIAE

ACLU Side (Petitioner/Appellant)

Brief of amici curiae filed on behalf of the New York Civil Liberties Union by Osmond K. Fraenkel.

Brief of amicus curiae filed on behalf of Goldstein & Goldstein, by Benjamin M. Goldstein.

Opposing Side (Respondent/Appellee)

No briefs of amici curiae were filed in support of appellee.

IV. THE SUPREME COURT'S DECISION

"We hold that the newspaper publications and posted notices in the circumstances of this case did not measure up to the quality of notice which the Due Process Clause of the Fourteenth Amendment requires. . . .

The general rule . . . is that notice by publication is not enough with respect to a person whose name and address are known or very easily ascertainable and whose legally protected interests are directly affected by the proceedings in question. . . .

It is true that, in addition to publishing in newspapers, the city in the present case did put some signs on trees and poles along the banks of the river. But no such sign was placed anywhere on the appellant's property, or ever seen by her. The posting of these signs, therefore, did not constitute the personal notice . . . require[d]. . . .

The majority opinion in the New York Court of Appeals seems

additionally to have drawn support from an assumption that the effect of the city's diversion of the river must have been apparent to the appellant before the expiration of the three-year period within which the statute required that her claim be filed. There was no such allegation in the pleadings, upon which the case was decided by the trial court. But even putting this consideration aside, knowledge of a change in the appearance of the river is far short of notice that the city had diverted it, and that the appellant had a right to be heard on a claim for compensation for damages resulting from the diversion. That was the information which the city was constitutionally obliged to make at least a good faith effort to give personally to the appellant—an obligation which the mailing of a single letter would have discharged.

The judgment of the New York Court of Appeals is reversed, and the cause is remanded for further proceedings not inconsistent with this opinion."

V. JUSTICE VOTE

9 Pro ACLU Side vs. 0 Con Opposing Side

ACLU Side (Petitioner/Appellant)

1. Stewart, P. – Wrote majority opinion
2. Warren, E. – Joined majority opinion
3. Black, H. – Joined majority opinion
4. Douglas, W. – Joined majority opinion
5. Clark, T. – Joined majority opinion
6. Harlan, J. – Joined majority opinion
7. Brennan, W. – Joined majority opinion
8. White, B. – Joined majority opinion
9. Goldberg, A. – Joined majority opinion

VI. A WIN OR LOSS FOR THE ACLU?

The ACLU filed an amicus brief urging reversal; the Supreme Court reversed the ruling of the Court of Appeals of New York in a 9-0 vote, giving the ACLU an apparent win.

136. Kennedy v. Mendoza-Martinez

(Decided February 18, 1963; 372 U.S. 144)

I. ISSUE

A. Issues Discussed

Fifth Amendment, Sixth Amendment, governmental authority, citizenship

B. Legal Question Presented

Did § 401(j) of the Nationality Act of 1940, and § 349(a)(10) of the Immigration and Nationality Act of 1952, divesting U.S. citizens of their citizenship for remaining outside the United States during a time of war or national emergency in order to avoid the military draft, violate the procedural safeguards of the Fifth and Sixth Amendments?

C. Supreme Court's Answer

Both § 401(j) and § 349(a)(10) are unconstitutional as punitive measures not providing the procedural safeguards required by the Fifth and Sixth Amendments.

II. CASE SUMMARY

A. Background

Appellee Mendoza-Martinez was an American citizen by birth, and a Mexican citizen by parentage, thereby possessing dual citizenship. Appellee admitted that to avoid the military draft, he left the United States for Mexico in 1942, and did not return until November 1946. As a result of his deliberate absence, Martinez entered a guilty plea in 1947 for violating § 11 of the Selective Training and Service Act of 1940 and served 366 days in prison.

Five years after his release, Martinez was issued an arrest and deportation warrant premised on a violation of § 401(j) of the Nationality Act of 1940 which divested draft dodgers of their U.S. citizenship. After a hearing, appellee was ordered deported and his appeal to the Board of Immigration Appeals dismissed. He then challenged the constitutionality of § 401(j). The District Court upheld § 401(j) and the Ninth Circuit affirmed. On appeal, the Supreme Court granted certiorari, vacated the judgment, and remanded the cause to the District Court for reconsideration in light of its decision a week earlier in *Trop v. Dulles*, 356 U.S. 86 (1958). The District Court struck down § 401(j) as unconstitutional, twice, as the case made it up to the Supreme Court again and was again remanded. The Supreme Court took the case a third time and affirmed, holding § 401(j) unconstitutional.

The Supreme Court also decided the issues left undecided in *Rusk v. Cort*, 369 U.S. 367 (1962), (see summary above) as to § 349(a)(10) of the Immigration and Nationality Act of 1952, which superseded § 401(j).

B. Counsel of Record/ACLU Attorney

ACLU Side (Respondent/Appellee): Opposing Side (Petitioner/Appellant): Thomas R. Davis argued the cause for appellee in No. 2. Leonard B. Boudin argued the cause for appellee in No. 3.

Opposing Side (Petitioner/Appellant): Bruce J. Terris argued the cause for appellant in No. 2. J. William Doolittle argued the cause for appellant in No. 3.

III. AMICI CURIAE

ACLU Side (Respondent/Appellee)

Brief of amici curiae filed on behalf of the ACLU in No. 2, by Jack Wasserman, David Carliner, Rowland Watts, Stephen J. Pollak, and Osmond K. Fraenkel.

Brief of amici curiae filed on behalf of the ACLU in No. 3, by Jack Wasserman, David Carliner, Rowland Watts, and Lawrence Speiser.

Brief of amici curiae filed on behalf of Angelika Schneider, by Milton V. Freeman, Werner J. Kronstein, Robert E. Herzstein, Horst Kurnik, Charles A. Reich, and Arnold, Fortas & Porter. Opposing Side (Petitioner/Appellant):

No briefs of amici curiae were filed in support of appellant.

IV. THE SUPREME COURT'S DECISION

"It is argued that our holding today will have the unfortunate result of immunizing the draft evader who has left the United States from having to suffer any sanction against his conduct, since he must return to this country before he can be apprehended and tried for his crime. The compelling answer to this is that the Bill of Rights which we guard so jealously and the procedures it guarantees are not to be abrogated merely because a guilty man may escape prosecution or for any other expedient reason. Moreover, the truth is that even without being expatriated, the evader living abroad is not in a position to assert the vast majority of his component rights as an American citizen. If he wishes to assert those rights in any real sense he must return to this country, and by doing that he will subject himself to prosecution. In fact, while he is outside the country evading prosecution, the United States may, by proper refusal to exercise its largely discretionary power to afford him diplomatic protection, decline to invoke its sovereign power on his behalf. Since the substantial benefits of American citizenship only come into play upon return to face prosecution, the draft evader who wishes to exercise his citizenship rights will inevitably come home and pay his debt, which within constitutional limits Congress has the power to define. This is what Mendoza-Martinez did, what Cort says he is willing to do, and what others have done. Thus our holding today does not frustrate the effective handling of the problem of draft evaders who leave the United States.

We conclude, for the reasons stated, that § 401(j) [of the Nationality Act of 1940] and § 349(a)(10) [of the Immigration and Nationality Act of 1952] are punitive and as such cannot constitutionally stand, lacking as they do the procedural safeguards which the Constitution commands. We recognize that draft evasion, particularly in time of war, is a heinous offense, and should and can be properly punished. Dating back to Magna Carta, however, it has been an abiding principle governing the lives of civilized men that 'no freeman shall be taken or imprisoned or disseised or outlawed or exiled . . . without the judgment of his peers or by the law of the land . . . .' What we hold is only that, in keeping with this cherished tradition, punishment cannot be imposed 'without due process of law.' Any lesser holding would ignore the constitutional mandate upon which our essential liberties depend. Therefore the judgments of the District Courts in these cases are affirmed."

V. JUSTICE VOTE

5 Pro ACLU Side vs. 4 Con Opposing Side

ACLU Side (Petitioner/Appellant)

1. Goldberg, A. – Wrote majority opinion
2. Warren, E. – Joined majority opinion
3. Black, H. – Wrote joint concurring opinion
4. Douglas, W. – Wrote joint concurring opinion
5. Brennan, W. – Wrote concurring opinion

Opposing Side (Respondent/Appellee)

1. Stewart, P. – Wrote dissenting opinion
2. White, B. – Joined Stewart's dissent
3. Harlan, J. – Wrote dissenting opinion
4. Clark, T. – Joined Harlan's dissent

VI. A WIN OR LOSS FOR THE ACLU?

The ACLU filed an amicus brief urging affirmance; the Supreme Court affirmed the lower court rulings in a 5-4 vote, giving the ACLU an apparent win.

137. Gideon v. Wainwright

(Decided March 18, 1963; 372 U.S. 335)

I.ISSUE

A. Issues Discussed

Right to counsel, Sixth Amendment, Fourteenth Amendment

B. Legal Question Presented

Did the state court's failure to appoint counsel for Gideon violate his right to a fair trial and due process of law as protected by the Sixth and Fourteenth Amendments?

C. Supreme Court's Answer

The failure to appoint counsel to an indigent defendant in a state criminal felony prosecution violates the Sixth and Fourteenth Amendments.

II. CASE SUMMARY

A. Background

Petitioner Gideon was charged with a noncapital felony. He asked the Florida state court to appoint counsel for him because he had no funds to hire counsel himself. The court replied that in Florida the court could only appoint counsel when the defendant is charge with a capital offense. Gideon conducted his own defense at trial and was found guilty.

Gideon filed a habeas corpus petition in the Florida Supreme Court challenging his conviction and arguing that "the trial court's refusal to appoint counsel for him denied him rights 'guaranteed by the Constitution and the Bill of Rights by the United States Government.'" The Florida Supreme Court denied relief.

The Supreme Court granted certiorari and reversed.

B. Counsel of Record/ACLU Attorney

ACLU Side (Petitioner/Appellant): Abe Fortas, by appointment of the Court, argued the cause for appellant.

J. Lee Rankin argued the cause for the ACLU, as amicus curiae, by special leave of Court.

Opposing Side (Respondent/Appellee): Bruce R. Jacob, Assistant Attorney General of Florida, argued the cause for appellee.

Assistant Attorney General of Alabama George D. Mentz argued the cause for the State of Alabama, as amicus curiae.

III. AMICI CURIAE

ACLU Side (Petitioner/Appellant)

Brief of amici curiae filed by on behalf of the ACLU, et al., by J. Lee Rankin, Norman Dorsen, John Dwight Evans, Jr., Melvin L. Wulf, Richard J. Medalie, Howard W. Dixon, Richard Yale

Feder, and Tobias Simon.

Brief of amici curiae urging reversal filed by the state governments of twenty-two States and Commonwealths, by Edward J. McCormack, Jr., Attorney General of Massachusetts, Walter F. Mondale, Attorney General of Minnesota, Duke W. Dunbar, Attorney General of Colorado, Albert L. Coles, Attorney General of Connecticut, Eugene Cook, Attorney General of Georgia, Shiro Kashiwa, Attorney General of Hawaii, Frank Benson, Attorney General of Idaho, William G. Clark, Attorney General of Illinois, Evan L. Hultman, Attorney General of Iowa, John B. Breckinridge, Attorney General of Kentucky, Frank E. Hancock, Attorney General of Maine, Frank J. Kelley, Attorney General of Michigan, Thomas F. Eagleton, Attorney General of Missouri, Charles E. Springer, Attorney General of Nevada, Mark McElroy, Attorney General of Ohio, Leslie R. Burgum, Attorney General of North Dakota, Robert Y. Thornton, Attorney General of Oregon, J. Joseph Nugent, Attorney General of Rhode Island, A. C. Miller, Attorney General of South Dakota, John J. O'Connell, Attorney General of Washington, C. Donald Robertson, Attorney General of West Virginia, and George N. Hayes, Attorney General of Alaska.

Brief of amici curiae filed on behalf of the State of Oregon, by Robert Y. Thornton, Attorney General of Oregon, and Harold W. Adams, Assistant Attorney General.

Opposing Side (Respondent/Appellee)

Brief of amici curiae filed by George D. Mentz, Assistant Attorney General of Alabama, MacDonald Gallion, Attorney General of Alabama, T. W. Bruton, Attorney General of North Carolina, and Ralph Moody, Assistant Attorney General of North Carolina.

IV. THE SUPREME COURT'S DECISION

"The Sixth Amendment provides, 'In all criminal prosecutions, the accused shall enjoy the right . . . to have the Assistance of Counsel for his defence.' We have construed this to mean that in federal courts counsel must be provided for defendants unable to employ counsel unless the right is competently and intelligently waived. [A] provision of the Bill of Rights which is 'fundamental and essential to a fair trial' is made obligatory upon the States by the Fourteenth Amendment."

"[R]eason and reflection require us to recognize that in our adversary system of criminal justice, any person haled into court, who is too poor to hire a lawyer, cannot be assured a fair trial unless counsel is provided for him. This seems to us to be an obvious truth. Governments, both state and federal, quite properly spend vast sums of money to establish machinery to try defendants accused of crime. Lawyers to prosecute are everywhere deemed essential to protect the public's interest in an orderly society. Similarly, there are few defendants charged with crime, few indeed, who fail to hire the best lawyers they can get to prepare and present their defenses. That government hires lawyers to prosecute and defendants who have the money hire lawyers to defend are the strongest indications of the wide—spread belief that lawyers in criminal courts are necessities, not luxuries. The right of one charged with crime to counsel may not be deemed fundamental and essential to fair trials in some countries, but it is in ours. From the very beginning, our state and national constitutions and laws have laid great emphasis on procedural and substantive safeguards designed to assure fair trials before impartial tribunals in which every defendant stands equal before the law. This noble ideal cannot be realized if the poor man charged with crime has to face his accusers without a lawyer to assist him."

The U.S. Supreme Court reversed the judgment of the Supreme Court of Florida.

V. JUSTICE VOTE

9 Pro ACLU Side vs. 0 Con Opposing Side

ACLU Side (Petitioner/Appellant)

1. Black, H. – Wrote majority opinion
2. Douglas, W. – Wrote concurring opinion
3. Harlan, J. – Wrote concurring opinion
4. Clark, T. – Wrote concurring opinion
5. Brennan, W. – Joined majority opinion
6. Stewart, P. – Joined majority opinion
7. White, B. – Joined majority opinion
8. Warren, E. – Joined majority opinion
9. Goldberg, A. – Joined majority opinion

VI. A WIN OR LOSS FOR THE ACLU?

The ACLU, as amicus curiae (an ACLU attorney argued though not as counsel of record), urged reversal of the judgment of the Supreme Court of Florida; the U.S. Supreme Court reversed in a 9-0 vote, giving the ACLU an apparent win.

138. White v. Maryland

(Decided April 29, 1963; 373 U.S. 59)

I. ISSUE

A. Issues Discussed

Criminal procedure, death penalty

B. Legal Question Presented

"Whether the decision in Hamilton v. Alabama, 368 U.S. 52, governs the court's decision on the meaning of lack of counsel at petitioner's preliminary hearing."

C. Supreme Court's Answer

"We repeat what we said in Hamilton v. Alabama, that we do not stop to determine whether prejudice resulted: 'Only the presence of counsel could have enabled this accused to know all the defenses available to him and to plead intelligently.' We therefore hold that Hamilton v. Alabama governs and that the judgment below must be and is reversed."

II. CASE SUMMARY

A. Background

"Petitioner, who was sentenced to death while his codefendant was given life, appealed to the Maryland Court of Appeals which affirmed his conviction. [The Supreme Court] granted certiorari 'limited to the point of law raised in Hamilton v. Alabama, 368 U.S. 52.'

Petitioner was arrested on May 27, 1960, and brought before a magistrate on May 31, 1960, for a preliminary hearing. But that hearing was postponed and not actually held until August 9, 1960. At that time petitioner was not yet represented by a lawyer. When arraigned at that preliminary hearing he pleaded guilty. That Maryland calls the 'arraignment' was first held September 8, 1960; but since petitioner was not represented by counsel, his arraignment was postponed and counsel appointed for him on September 9, 1960. He was finally arraigned on November 25, 1960, and entered pleas of 'not guilty' and 'not guilty by reason of insanity.' At his trial the plea of guilty made at the preliminary hearing on August 9, 1960, was introduced in evidence.* Since he did not have counsel at the time of the preliminary hearing, he argued that Hamilton v. Alabama applied. The Court of Appeals disagreed, saying that arraignment in Alabama is 'a critical stage in a criminal proceeding' where rights are preserved or lost, while under Maryland law there was 'no requirement (nor any practical possibility under our present criminal procedure) to appoint counsel' for petitioner at the preliminary hearing . . . nor was it necessary for appellant to enter a plea at that time.'"

The Supreme Court granted certiorari to review the case.

B. Counsel of Record

ACLU Side (Petitioner/Appellant): Fred E. Weisgal of the Maryland Branch, American Civil Liberties Union argued the cause for appellant. With him on the brief was Reuben Shiling of the Maryland Branch, American Civil Liberties Union.

Opposing Side (Respondent/Appellee): Robert F. Sweeney, Assistant Attorney General of Maryland, argued the cause for appellee. With him on the brief was Thomas B. Finan, Attorney General of Maryland.

III. AMICI CURIAE

ACLU Side (Petitioner/Appellant)

No briefs of amici curiae were filed in support of appellant.

Opposing Side (Respondent/Appellee)

No briefs of amici curiae were filed in support of appellee.

IV. THE SUPREME COURT'S DECISION

"Whatever may be the normal function of the 'preliminary hearing' under Maryland law, it was in this case as 'critical' a state as arraignment under Alabama law. For petitioner entered a plea before the magistrate and that plea was taken at a time when he had no counsel.

We repeat what we said in Hamilton v. Alabama, that we do not stop to determine whether prejudice resulted: 'Only the presence of counsel could have enabled this accused to know all the defenses available to him and to plead intelligently.' We therefore hold that Hamilton v. Alabama governs and that the judgment below must be and is reversed."

V. JUSTICE VOTE

9 Pro ACLU Side vs. 0 Con Opposing Side

ACLU Side (Petitioner/Appellant)

1. Warren, E. – Per curiam decision
2. Brennan, W. – Per curiam decision
3. Black, H. – Per curiam decision
4. Douglas, W. – Per curiam decision
5. Goldberg, A. – Per curiam decision
6. Harlan, J. – Per curiam decision
7. Stewart, P. – Per curiam decision
8. Clark, T. – Per curiam decision
9. White, B. – Per curiam decision

VI. A WIN OR LOSS FOR THE ACLU?

The ACLU served as counsel for appellant urging reversal of the judgment of the Maryland Court of Appeals; the Supreme Court reversed in a 9-0 per curiam decision, giving the ACLU an apparent win.

139. McNeese v. Board of Education

(Decided June 3, 1963; 373 U.S. 668)

I. ISSUE

A. Issues Discussed

Desegregation, civil rights, Fourteenth Amendment

B. Legal Question Presented

Whether a plaintiff must first exhaust relief under state law before seeking relief for alleged violations of the Fourteenth Amendment.

C. Supreme Court's Answer

Plaintiff does not need to exhaust state law remedies where no underlying issue of state law is controlling and the case can be decided under the Fourteenth Amendment.

II. CASE SUMMARY

A. Background

The petitioners, black students from an Illinois public school, brought suit in a federal District Court under the Civil Rights Act to invoke their rights under the Fourteenth Amendment. The students alleged that they attended classes in one part of the school, separate and apart from the white students, and were forced to use different entrances and exits. Petitioners alleged that the school was segregated in conflict with the U.S. Constitution, and they sought equitable relief, including registration in racially integrated schools.

The District Court dismissed the complaint on the ground that petitioners had not exhausted their administrative remedies under Illinois law, which forbids racial segregation in public schools and prescribes administrative procedures for enforcement of the prohibition. The Court of Appeals affirmed.

The U.S. Supreme Court granted certiorari and reversed.

B. Counsel of Record/ACLU Attorney

ACLU Side (Petitioner/Appellant): Raymond E. Harth argued the cause for appellant.

Opposing Side (Respondent/Appellee): Howard Boman and Robert H. Reiter argued the cause for appellee.

III. AMICI CURIAE

ACLU Side (Petitioner/Appellant)

Brief of amici curiae filed on behalf of the ACLU by Alex Elson, Nancy McDermid, Seymour Bucholz, Joel Sprayregen, and Bernard Weisberg.

Opposing Side (Respondent/Appellee)

No briefs of amici curiae were filed in support of appellee.

IV. THE SUPREME COURT'S DECISION

"We have previously indicated that relief under the Civil Rights Act may not be defeated because relief was not first sought under state law which provided a remedy. . . .

We have . . . in the present case no underlying issue of state law controlling this litigation. The right alleged is as plainly federal in origin and nature as those vindicated in Brown v. Board of Education. Nor is the federal right in any way entangled in a skein of state law that must be untangled before the federal case can proceed. For petitioners assert that respondents have been and are depriving them of rights protected by the Fourteenth Amendment. It is immaterial whether respondents' conduct is legal or illegal as a matter of state law. Such claims are entitled to be adjudicated in the federal courts.

Moreover, it is by no means clear that Illinois law provides petitioners with an administrative remedy sufficiently adequate to preclude prior resort to a federal court for protection of their federal rights. . . .

Respondents say that the Superintendent would not certify a district for state aid if he determined that its sworn statement was false. Apparently no Illinois cases have held that the Superintendent has authority to withhold funds once he has received an affidavit from the district, even if he determines that the affidavit is false. In any event, the withholding of state aid is at best only an indirect sanction of Fourteenth Amendment rights. When federal rights are subject to such tenuous protection, prior resort to a state proceeding is not necessary.

[T]he withholding of state aid is, at best, only an indirect sanction of Fourteenth Amendment rights. When federal rights are subject to such tenuous protection, prior resort to a state proceeding is not necessary."

The Supreme Court reversed the judgment of the Court of Appeals.

V. JUSTICE VOTE

8 Pro ACLU Side vs. 1 Con Opposing Side

ACLU Side (Petitioner/Appellant)

1. Douglas, W. – Wrote majority opinion
2. Clark, T. – Joined majority opinion
3. Black, H. – Joined majority opinion
4. Stewart, P. – Joined majority opinion
5. White, B. – Joined majority opinion
6. Brennan, W. – Joined majority opinion
7. Warren, E. – Joined majority opinion
8. Goldberg, A. – Joined majority opinion

Opposing Side (Respondent/Appellee)

1. Harlan, J. – Wrote dissenting opinion

VI. A WIN OR LOSS FOR THE ACLU?

The ACLU, as amicus curiae, urged reversal; the Supreme Court reversed the ruling of the Court of Appeals in an 8-1 vote, giving the ACLU an apparent win.

140. Ker v. California

(Decided June 10, 1963; 374 U.S. 23)

I. ISSUE

A. Issues Discussed

Fourth Amendment, Fourteenth Amendment, warrants, search and seizure

B. Legal Question Presented

Whether the evidence discovered during a search without a warrant is admissible at trial.

C. Supreme Court's Answer

The evidence is admissible at trial.

II. CASE SUMMARY

A. Background

After witnessing petitioner George Ker meeting a suspected marijuana dealer, California police offers entered Ker's residence without consent or a warrant, by using a passkey supplied by the building manager. The officers arrested Ker and his wife, second petitioner Diane Ker, on suspicion of violating the State Narcotic Law, and witnessed a block of marijuana in the kitchen. A subsequent warrantless search of the apartment and the petitioners' cars surfaced marijuana packages and paraphernalia, which were seized and later admitted as evidence against the petitioners. The couple was convicted and the California District Court of Appeal upheld the conviction, ruling that the evidence was not seized in the course of an unlawful search.

The Supreme Court granted certiorari and affirmed.

B. Counsel of Record/ACLU Attorney

ACLU Side (Petitioner/Appellant): Robert W. Stanley argued the cause for appellant.

Opposing Side (Respondent/Appellee): Gordon Ringer, Deputy Attorney General of California, argued the cause for appellee.

III. AMICI CURIAE

ACLU Side (Petitioner/Appellant)

Brief of amici curiae filed on behalf of the ACLU of Southern California by A. L. Wirin, Fred Okrand, and Paul Cooksey.

Opposing Side (Respondent/Appellee)

No briefs of amici curiae were filed in support of appellee.

IV. THE SUPREME COURT'S DECISION

"The evidence at issue, in order to be admissible, must be the product of a search incident to a lawful arrest, since the officers had no search warrant. The lawfulness of the arrest without warrant, in turn, must be based upon probable cause, which exists where 'the facts and circumstances within [the officers'] knowledge and of which they had reasonably trustworthy information [are] sufficient in themselves to warrant a man of reasonable caution in the belief that' an offense has been or is being committed. The information within the knowledge of the officers at the time they arrived at the Kers' apartment, as California's courts specifically found, clearly furnished grounds for a reasonable belief that petitioner George Ker had committed and was committing the offense of possession of marijuana. . . .

Probable cause for the arrest of petitioner Diane Ker, while not present at the time the officers entered the apartment to arrest her husband, was nevertheless present at the time of her arrest. Upon their entry and announcement of their identity, the officers were met not only by George Ker but also by Diane Ker, who was emerging from the kitchen. Officer Berman immediately walked to the doorway from which she emerged and, without entering, observed the brick-shaped package of marijuana in plain view. Even assuming that her presence in a small room with the contraband in a prominent position on the kitchen sink would not alone establish a reasonable ground for the officers' belief that she was in joint possession with her husband, that fact was accompanied by the officers' information that Ker had been using his apartment as a base of operations for his narcotics activities. Therefore, we cannot say that at the time of her arrest there were not sufficient grounds for a reasonable belief that Diane Ker, as well as her husband, was committing the offense of possession of marijuana in the presence of the officers. . . .

Since the petitioners' federal constitutional protection from unreasonable searches and seizures by police officers is here to be determined by whether the search was incident to a lawful arrest, we are warranted in examining that arrest to determine whether, notwithstanding its legality under state law, the method of entering the home may offend federal constitutional standards of reasonableness and therefore vitiate the legality of an accompanying search. We find no such offensiveness on the facts here. Assuming that the officers' entry by use of a key obtained from the manager is the legal equivalent of a 'breaking,' it has been recognized from the early common law that such breaking is permissible in executing an arrest under certain circumstances. . . .

We therefore hold that in the particular circumstances of this case the officers' method of entry, sanctioned by the law of California, was not unreasonable under the standards of the Fourth Amendment as applied to the States through the Fourteenth Amendment. . . .

Having held the petitioners' arrests lawful, it remains only to consider whether the search which produced the evidence leading to their convictions was lawful as incident to those arrests. The doctrine that a search without warrant may be lawfully conducted if incident to a lawful arrest has long been recognized as consistent with the Fourth Amendment's protection against unreasonable searches and seizures. . . .

The practicability of obtaining a warrant is not the controlling factor when a search is sought to be justified as incident to arrest, but we need not rest the validity of the search here . . . since we agree with the California court that time clearly was of the essence. . . . The officers had reason to act quickly because of Ker's furtive conduct and the likelihood that the marijuana would be distributed or hidden before a warrant could be obtained at that time of night. . . .

The petitioners' only remaining contention is that the discovery of the brick of marijuana cannot be justified as incidental to arrest since it preceded the arrest. This contention is of course contrary to George Ker's testimony, but we reject it in any event. While an arrest may not be used merely as the pretext for a search without warrant, the California court specifically found and the record supports both that the officers entered the apartment for the purpose of arresting George Ker and that they had probable cause to make that arrest prior to the entry. . . . We thus agree with the California court's holding that the discovery of the brick of marijuana did not constitute a search, since the officer merely saw what was placed before him in full view."

The Supreme Court affirmed the judgment of the California District Court of Appeal.

V. JUSTICE VOTE

4 Pro ACLU Side vs. 5 Con Opposing Side

ACLU Side (Petitioner/Appellant)

1. Brennan, W. – Wrote dissenting opinion
2. Warren, E. – Joined Brennan's dissent
3. Douglas, W. – Joined Brennan's dissent
4. Goldberg, A. – Joined Brennan's dissent

Opposing Side (Respondent/Appellee)

1. Clark, T. – Wrote majority opinion
2. Black, H. – Joined majority opinion
3. Stewart, P. – Joined majority opinion
4. White, B. – Joined majority opinion
5. Harlan, J. – Wrote concurring opinion

VI. A WIN OR LOSS FOR THE ACLU?

The ACLU filed an amicus brief urging reversal; the Supreme Court affirmed the ruling of the lower courts in a 5-4 vote, giving the ACLU an apparent loss.

141. Yellin v. United States

(Decided June 17, 1963; 374 U.S. 109)

I. ISSUE

A. Issues Discussed

Governmental authority

B. Legal Question Presented

"[W]hether the House Committee on Un-American Activities failed to comply with its rules, and whether such a failure excused petitioner's refusal to answer the Committee's questions."

C. Supreme Court's Answer

The committee failed to comply with its rules by not adequately considering whether an executive session would be the proper venue to question petitioner and failing to act on petitioner's request for an executive session.

II. CASE SUMMARY

A. Background

"Petitioner Edward Yellin was indicted in the Northern District of Indiana on five counts of willfully refusing to answer questions put to him by a Subcommittee of the House Committee on Un-American Activities . . . at a public hearing." Yellin refused to answer the questions because the Committee had not considered his petition for a closed executive session. "He was convicted, under 2 U.S.C. § 192, of contempt of Congress on four counts. He was sentenced to four concurrent terms of imprisonment, each for one year, and fined $250. The Court of Appeals for the Seventh Circuit affirmed."

The Supreme Court granted certiorari and reversed.

B. Counsel of Record/ACLU Attorney

ACLU Side (Petitioner/Appellant): Victor Rabinowitz reargued the cause for appellant.

Opposing Side (Respondent/Appellee): Solicitor General Archibald Cox reargued the cause for appellee.

III. AMICI CURIAE

ACLU Side (Petitioner/Appellant)

Brief of amici curiae filed on behalf of the ACLU by Osmond K. Fraenkel.

Opposing Side (Respondent/Appellee)

No briefs of amici curiae were filed in support of appellee.

IV. THE SUPREME COURT'S DECISION

"The rule is quite explicit in requiring that injury to a witness' reputation be considered, along with danger to the national security and injury to the reputation of third parties, in deciding whether to hold an executive session. At the threshold we are met with the argument that Rule IV was written to provide guidance for the Committee alone and that it was not designed to confer upon witnesses the right to request an executive session and the right to have the Committee act, either upon that request or on its own, according to the standards set forth in the rule. It seems clear, from the structure of the Committee's rules and from the Committee's practice, that such is not the case. . . .

Yellin should be permitted the same opportunity for judicial review when he discovers at trial that his rights have been violated. This is especially so when the Committee's practice leads witnesses to misplaced reliance upon its rules. When reading a copy of the Committee's rules, which must be distributed to every witness under Rule XVII, the witness' reasonable expectation is that the Committee actually does what it purports to do, adhere to its own rules. To foreclose a defense based upon those rules, simply because the witness was deceived by the Committee's appearance of regularity, is not fair. The Committee prepared the groundwork for prosecution in Yellin's case meticulously. It is not too exacting to require that the Committee be equally meticulous in obeying its own rules."

The Supreme Court reversed the Seventh Circuit's decision and held that the petitioner's conviction for refusal to testify in public cannot stand because the committee violated its own Rule IV by failing to give consideration to the question whether interrogation in public would injure petitioner's reputation and by failing to act on his request that he be interrogated in executive session.

V. JUSTICE VOTE

5 Pro ACLU Side vs. 4 Con Opposing Side

ACLU Side (Petitioner/Appellant)

1. Warren, E. – Wrote majority opinion
2. Brennan, W. – Joined majority opinion
3. Douglas, W. – Joined majority opinion
4. Black, H. – Joined majority opinion
5. Goldberg, A. – Joined majority opinion

Opposing Side (Respondent/Appellee)

1. White, B. – Wrote dissenting opinion
2. Clark, T. – Joined dissenting opinion
3. Harlan, J. – Joined dissenting opinion
4. Stewart, P. – Joined dissenting opinion

VI. A WIN OR LOSS FOR THE ACLU?

The ACLU, as amicus curiae, urged reversal; the Supreme Court reversed the conviction in a 5-4 vote, giving the ACLU an apparent win.

142. School District of Abington Township v. Schempp

(Decided June 17, 1963; 374 U.S. 203)

I. ISSUE

A. Issues Discussed

Freedom of religion, Establishment Clause, Free Exercise Clause

B. Legal Question Presented

Do state or locally enacted laws requiring that public schools provide time for Bible reading at the opening of each school day violate the Establishment Clause of Free Exercise Clause of the First Amendment?

C. Supreme Court's Answer

State and local laws requiring bible reading at the beginning of the school day in public schools are unconstitutional in violation of the Establishment Clause of the First Amendment.

II. CASE SUMMARY

A. Background

In the consolidated cases a state and city enacted laws requiring in effect that "the Holy Bible shall be read, without comment, at the opening of each public school on each school day" and that children could be excused from reading at or attending the Bible reading exercises upon written request of the parents.

In No. 142, the Schempp family of Unitarian faith, filed a law suit "to enjoin enforcement of the statute, contending that their rights under the Fourteenth Amendment . . . are, have been, and will continue to be violated unless this statute be declared unconstitutional as violative of . . . the First Amendment." The father testified that he believed excusing his children "from attendance at the exercises" would adversely affect his "children's relationships with their teachers and classmates." The District Court held that the statute violated the First Amendment..

In No. 119, the petitioners, professed atheists, sought to compel the rescission and cancellation of the city rule requiring Bible reading, stating that "the rule, as practiced, violated their rights." The Court of Appeals upheld the law "holding the exercise not in violation of the First and Fourteenth Amendments."

The Supreme Court granted certiorari in both cases and held that the schools' Bible reading laws were unconstitutional, affirming the District Court in in No. 142 and reversing the Court of Appeals in No. 142.

B. Counsel of Record/ACLU Attorney

ACLU Side (Petitioner/Appellant in No. 119, Respondent/Appellee in No. 142): Leonard J. Kerpelman argued the cause for appellant in No. 119. Henry W. Sawyer III argued the cause for appellee in No. 142.

Opposing Side (Respondent/Appellee in No. 119, Petitioner/Appellant in No. 142): Francis B. Burch and George W. Baker, Jr., argued the cause for appellee in No. 119. John D. Killian III, Deputy Attorney General of Pennsylvania, and Philip H. Ward III argued the cause for appellant in No. 142.

Thomas B. Finan, Attorney General of Maryland, argued the cause as amici curiae.

III. AMICI CURIAE

ACLU Side (Petitioner/Appellant in No. 119, Respondent/ Appellee in No. 142):

Opposing Side

(Respondent/Appellee in No. 119, Petitioner/Appellant in No. 142):

Brief of amici curiae filed on behalf of the American Jewish Committee, et al., by Morris B. Abram, Edwin J. Lukas, Burnett Roth, Arnold Forster, Paul Hartman, Theodore Leskes, and Sol Rabkin.

Brief of amici curiae filed on behalf of the Synagogue Council of America, et al., by Leo Pfeffer, Lewis H. Weinstein, Albert Wald, Shad Polier, Samuel Lawrence Brennglass, Theodore R. Mann, and Philip Jacobson.

Brief of amici curiae filed on behalf of the American Ethical Union by Herbert A. Wolff, Leo Rosen, Morris L. Ernst, Nancy F. Wechsler, and Herbert Kamrass.

Brief of amici curiae filed on behalf of the American Humanist Association by Kenneth W. Greenawalt and Lester Forest. Brief of amici curiae filed by Thomas B. Finan, Attorney General of Maryland, James P. Garland and Robert F. Sweeney, Assistant Attorneys General of Maryland. Richmond M. Flowers, Attorney General of Alabama, Robert Pickrell, Attorney General of Arizona, Bruce Bennett, Attorney General of Arkansas, Richard W. Ervin, Attorney General of Florida, Eugene Cook, Attorney General of Georgia, Allan G. Shepard, Attorney General of Idaho, William M. Ferguson, Attorney General of Kansas, Jack P. F. Gremillion, Attorney General of Louisiana, Frank E. Hancock, Attorney General of Maine, Joe T. Patterson, Attorney General of Mississippi, William Maynard, Attorney General of New Hampshire, Arthur J. Sills, Attorney General of New Jersey, Earl E. Hartley, Attorney General of New Mexico, Thomas Wade Bruton, Attorney General of North Carolina, J. Joseph Nugent, Attorney General of Rhode Island, Daniel R. McLeod, Attorney General of South Carolina, Frank R. Farrar, Attorney General of South Dakota, and George F. McCanless, Attorney General of Tennessee.

IV. THE SUPREME COURT'S DECISION

The Supreme Court reviewed the two cases together because they both presented "the issues in the context of state action requiring that schools begin each day with readings from the Bible."

"In the relationship between man and religion, the State is firmly committed to a position of neutrality."

"The wholesome 'neutrality' of which this Court's cases speak stems from a recognition of the teachings of history that powerful sects or groups might bring about a fusion of governmental and religious functions or a concert or dependency of one upon the other to the end that official support of the State or Federal Government would be placed behind the tenets of one or of all orthodoxies. This the Establishment Clause prohibits. And a further reason for neutrality is found in the Free Exercise Clause, which recognizes the value of religious training, teaching and observance and, more particularly, the right of every person to freely choose his own course with reference thereto, free of any compulsion from the state. This the Free Exercise Clause guarantees.

[T]o withstand the strictures of the Establishment Clause there must be a secular legislative purpose and a primary effect that neither advances nor inhibits religion. The Free Exercise Clause

. . . withdraws from legislative power, state and federal, the exertion of any restraint on the free exercise of religion. Its purpose is to secure religious liberty in the individual by prohibiting any invasions thereof by civil authority. . . . The distinction between the two clauses is apparent—a violation of the Free Exercise Clause is predicated on coercion while the Establishment Clause violation need not be so attended. . . .

The conclusion follows that in both cases the laws require religious exercises and such exercises are being conducted in direct violation of the rights of the appellees and petitioners. Nor are these required exercises mitigated by the fact that individual students may absent themselves upon parental request, for that fact furnishes no defense to a claim of unconstitutionality under the Establishment Clause."

The Supreme Court affirmed the judgment in No. 142 and reversed the judgment in No. 119.

V. JUSTICE VOTE

8 Pro ACLU Side vs. 1 Con Opposing Side

ACLU Side (Petitioner/Appellant in No. 119, Respondent/Appellee in No. 142):

1. Clark, T. – Wrote majority opinion
2. White, B. – Joined majority opinion
3. Warren, E. – Joined majority opinion
4. Black, H. – Joined majority opinion
5. Douglas, W. – Wrote concurring opinion
6. Brennan, W. – Wrote concurring opinion
7. Goldberg, A. – Wrote concurring opinion
8. Harlan, J. – Joined Goldberg's concurrence

Opposing Side (Respondent/Appellee in No. 119, Respondent/Appellee in No. 142):

1. Stewart P. – Wrote dissenting opinion

VI. A WIN OR LOSS FOR THE ACLU?

The ACLU, as counsel of record, urged affirmance in No.142 and reversal in No. 119; the Supreme Court affirmed No. 142 and reversed No. 119 in an 8-1 vote, giving the ACLU an apparent win.

143. Smith v. California

(Decided December 16, 1963; 375 U.S. 259)

I. ISSUE

A. Issues Discussed

First Amendment, obscenity

B. Legal Question Presented

Whether appellant was properly found guilty of exhibiting and distributing obscene material.

C. Supreme Court's Answer

The Supreme Court vacated the decision below and remanded the case.

II. CASE SUMMARY

A. Background

"Appellant was found guilty by a jury in the Municipal Court of the Los Angeles Judicial District of violation of P. C. § 311.2, by reason of his exhibiting and distributing of obscene matter, the book, 'Tropic of Cancer,' and probation was granted by that court." In an unpublished decision, the Appellate Department of the Superior Court of California for the County of Los Angeles upheld the conviction, determining that " the jury's finding of obscenity should be accorded at least as great, if not more constitutional weight, than that of a writer's right to imprint or disseminate through a bookstore, his depraved and degrading filthy words and obscene utterances and lewd depictions of salacious episodes of sexual scenes and mental images or than that of a bookstore proprietor to exhibit and distribute such demoralizing obscene writings. This issue is not the right of any person to read such writings, but the right of appellant to sell, exhibit or distribute them when they have been found obscene, in violation of a constitutional state statute, by a jury whose finding is supported by very substantial evidence, under instructions informing them of the legal standard of obscenity as interpreted by the highest court of our land."[1]

The Supreme Court granted certiorari, vacated the judgment, and remanded the case.

B. Counsel of Record/ACLU Attorney

ACLU Side (Petitioner/Appellant): Stanley Gleishman and Sam Rosenwein for appellant.

Opposing Side (Respondent/Appellee): Roger Arnebergh, Philip E. Grey and Wm. E. Doran for appellee.

III. AMICI CURIAE

ACLU Side (Petitioner/Appellant)

Brief of amici curiae filed on behalf of the ACLU of Southern California by Nathan L. Schoichet, A. L. Wirin, and Fred Okrand.

Brief of amici curiae filed on behalf of the American Library Association by Thomas M. Thomas.

Brief of amici curiae filed on behalf of Allen et al., by Edward de Grazia.

Opposing Side (Respondent/Appellee)

Brief of amici curiae filed on behalf of Citizens for Decent Literature, Inc., et al., by Charles H. Keating, Jr.

IV. THE SUPREME COURT'S DECISION

"The judgment is vacated and the case is remanded to the Appellate Department of the Superior Court of California, County of Los Angeles, for further consideration in light of the decision of the Supreme Court of California in *Zeitlin v. Arnebergh*, 383 P.2d 152."

V. JUSTICE VOTE

9 Pro ACLU Side vs. 0 Con Opposing Side

1 Smith v. California, No. CR A 5113 (Cal. App. Dep't Super. Ct. Oct. 24, 1962).

ACLU Side (Petitioner/Appellant)

1. Warren, E. – Per curiam decision
2. Black, H. – Per curiam decision
3. Clark, T. – Per curiam decision
4. Harlan, J. – Per curiam decision
5. White, B. – Per curiam decision
6. Goldberg, A. – Per curiam decision
7. Stewart, P. – Per curiam decision
8. Brennan, W. – Per curiam decision
9. Douglas, W. – Per curiam decision

VI. A WIN OR LOSS FOR THE ACLU?

The ACLU filed an amicus brief urging reversal; the Supreme Court vacated the ruling of the state's lower courts in a 9-0 vote, giving the ACLU an apparent win.

144. New York Times Co. v. Sullivan

(Decided March 9, 1964; 376 U.S. 254)

I. ISSUE

A. Issues Discussed

Freedom of speech and of the press, libel

B. Legal Question Presented

Does Alabama's rule of liability for libel—which provides that "a publication is 'libelous per se' if the words 'tend to injure a person . . . in his reputation' or to 'bring [him] into public contempt'"—as applied to an action brought by a public official against critics of his official conduct, abridge the freedom of speech and of the press guaranteed by the First and Fourteenth Amendments?

C. Supreme Court's Answer

The Alabama rule for libel abridges freedom of speech and of the press, there must be a showing of "actual malice" for a public official to recover for libel.

II. CASE SUMMARY

A. Background

In 1960, during the Civil Rights Movement, the *New York Times* published a full-page editorial advertisement, "Heed Their Rising Voices," describing unfair and brutal police responses to student protests in Montgomery, Alabama. There were several factual errors in the ad, none of which were known to the publisher at the time of printing. Although he was not named in the ad, L.B. Sullivan, a city commissioner of Montgomery, whose work included supervision of the police filed a suit for libel against the *New York Times* and individuals involved in the advertisement.

The trial judge instructed the jury that some statements in the advertisement were "libelous per se" and the jury awarded Sullivan damages of $500,000. The Supreme Court of Alabama upheld the award.

On certiorari the Supreme Court reversed.

B. Counsel of Record/ACLU Attorney

ACLU Side (Petitioner/Appellant): Herbert Wechsler argued the cause for appellant in No. 39. William P. Rogers and Samuel R. Pierce, Jr., argued the cause for appellant in No. 40.

Opposing Side (Respondent/Appellee): M. Roland Nachman, Jr. argued the cause for appellee in Nos. 39 and 40.

III. AMICI CURIAE

ACLU Side (Petitioner/Appellant)

Brief of amici curiae filed on behalf of the ACLU, et al., by Edward S. Greenbaum, Harriet F. Pilpel, Melvin L. Wulf, Nanette Dembitz, and Nancy F. Wechsler.

Brief of amici curiae filed on behalf of the Washington Post Company by William P. Rogers, Gerald W. Siegel, Stanley Godofsky, Leslie Srager, David W. Bernstein, and Royall, Koegel & Rogers.

Brief of amici curiae filed on behalf of the Tribune Company by Howard Ellis, Keith Masters, Don H. Reuben, and Kirkland, Ellis, Hodson, Chaffets & Masters.

Opposing Side (Respondent/Appellee)

No briefs of amici curiae were filed in support of appellee.

IV. THE SUPREME COURT'S DECISION

"Under Alabama law as applied in this case, a publication is 'libelous per se' if the words 'tend to injure a person . . . in his reputation' or to 'bring [him] into public contempt'; the trial court stated that the standard was met if the words are such as to 'injure him in his public office, or impute misconduct to him in his office, or want of official integrity, or want of fidelity to a public trust . . . .' . . . Unless [the defendant] can discharge the burden of proving truth, general damages are presumed, and may be awarded without proof of pecuniary injury. A showing of actual malice is apparently a prerequisite to recovery of punitive damages . . . .

The question before us is whether this rule of liability, as applied to an action brought by a public official against critics of his official conduct, abridges the freedom of speech and of the press that is guaranteed by the First and Fourteenth Amendments. . . .

The constitutional guarantees require, we think, a federal rule that prohibits a public official from recovering damages for a defamatory falsehood relating to his official conduct unless he proves that the statement was made with 'actual malice'—that is, with knowledge that it was false or with reckless disregard of whether it was false or not. . . .

We hold today that the Constitution delimits a State's power to award damages for libel in actions brought by public officials against critics of their official conduct. Since this is such an action, the rule requiring proof of actual malice is applicable. While Alabama law apparently requires proof of actual malice for an award of punitive damages, where general damages are concerned malice is 'presumed.' Such a presumption is inconsistent with the federal rule. . . .

Applying these standards, we consider that the proof presented to show actual malice lacks the convincing clarity which the constitutional standard demands, and hence that it would not constitutionally sustain the judgment for respondent under the proper rule of law. . . . We also think the evidence was constitutionally defective in another respect: it was incapable of supporting the jury's finding that the allegedly libelous statements were made 'of and concerning' respondent."

The Supreme Court reversed the judgment of the Supreme Court of Alabama.

V. JUSTICE VOTE

9 Pro ACLU Side vs. 0 Con Opposing Side

ACLU Side (Petitioner/Appellant)

1. Brennan, W. – Wrote majority opinion
2. Clark, T. – Joined majority opinion
3. Stewart, P. – Joined majority opinion
4. White, B. – Joined majority opinion
5. Harlan, J. – Joined majority opinion
6. Warren, E. – Joined majority opinion
7. Black, H. – Wrote concurring opinion
8. Goldberg, A. – Wrote concurring opinion
9. Douglas, W. – Joined both concurring opinions

VI. A WIN OR LOSS FOR THE ACLU?

The ACLU, as amicus curiae, urged reversal of the Alabama Supreme Court's judgment; the Supreme Court reversed in a 9-0 vote, giving the ACLU an apparent win.

145. Smith v. Pennsylvania

(Decided March 9, 1964; 376 U.S. 354)

I. ISSUE

A. Issues Discussed

Governmental privileges, discovery

B. Legal Question Presented

Can the federal government quash a subpoena based on claims of confidential material subject to a federal privilege?

C. Supreme Court's Answer

Not deciding the question, the Court remanded after the Solicitor General confirmed that the Department of Justice would not refuse to comply with requests for specific witness statements in the FBI file.

II. CASE SUMMARY

A. Background

"Prior to commencement of petitioner's trial for assault and battery upon state police officers, he served upon the local office of the Federal Bureau of Investigation a subpoena duces tecum calling for the production of '[s]tatements of all witnesses, diagrams, sketches and photographs taken in connection with' the FBI's investigation of the incident which formed the basis for the criminal prosecution. The FBI had made the investigation in response to a complaint filed by petitioner with the Civil Rights Division of the Department of Justice, charging a deprivation of his civil rights by the actions of the police officers whom he allegedly assaulted. An Assistant United States Attorney appeared on the day set for trial and moved to quash the subpoena, claiming that the file contained confidential material subject to a federal privilege of nondisclosure. The subpoena was quashed by the trial court for that reason and for noncompliance with local rules of practice.

Petitioner formally requested the court, both before and after they testified, to issue a subpoena duces tecum for statements taken by the FBI from two witnesses for the prosecution, stating that the statements were needed for purposes of impeachment. The trial court denied the requests because it felt that petitioner would receive the same information from material which the state authorities had promised to make available. Following petitioner's conviction, the trial court denied his motion for a new trial which was based in part on the failure to issue the requested subpoena, stating that the Federal Government had already indicated that it would not honor such a subpoena. The judgment of conviction was affirmed by the Pennsylvania Supreme Court, the court stating, inter alia, that the FBI, not the Commonwealth, had denied petitioner access to the information in question."

The Supreme Court granted certiorari and remanded.

B. Counsel of Record/ACLU Attorney

ACLU Side (Petitioner/Appellant): William T. Coleman, Jr., John B. Hunnum, Peter Hearn, Pepper, Hamilton and Scheetz, Robert W. Maris, Dilworth, Paxson, Kalish, Kohn & Dilks, and Theodore O. Rogers for appellant.

Opposing Side (Respondent/Appellee): Frank P. Lawley, Deputy Attorney General of Pennsylvania, for appellee.

III. AMICI CURIAE

ACLU Side (Petitioner/Appellant)

Brief of amici curiae filed on behalf of the ACLU, Greater Philadelphia Branch, et al., by Melvin L. Wulf, Raymond K. Denworth, Jr., Paul Bender, and Julian E. Goldberg. Solicitor General Archibald Cox filed a memorandum for the United States.

Opposing Side (Respondent/Appellee)

IV. THE SUPREME COURT'S DECISION

"In response to an inquiry from this Court, the Solicitor General has indicated that the claim of confidential privilege was concerned solely with the initial broad-based demand for virtually the entire FBI file on the matter and that the Department of Justice was not informed of, and did not refuse to comply with, the subsequent specific requests for statements given by the two witnesses.

We grant the petition for a writ of certiorari and remand the case to the Supreme Court of Pennsylvania, for reconsideration of petitioner's requests in light of the representations of the Solicitor General."

The Supreme Court remanded the case in a per curiam decision.

V. JUSTICE VOTE

9 Pro ACLU Side vs. 0 Con Opposing Side

ACLU Side (Petitioner/Appellant)

1. Warren, E. – Per curiam decision
2. Black, H. – Per curiam decision
3. Douglas, W. – Per curiam decision
4. Clark, T. – Per curiam decision
5. Harlan, J. – Per curiam decision
6. Brennan, W. – Per curiam decision
7. Stewart, P. – Per curiam decision
8. White, B. – Per curiam decision
9. Goldberg, A. – Per curiam decision

VI. A WIN OR LOSS FOR THE ACLU?

The ACLU, as amicus curiae, supported the petition for writ of certiorari; the Supreme Court granted certiorari then remanded in a 9-0 vote, giving the ACLU an apparent win.

146. Stoner v. California

(Decided March 23, 1964; 376 U.S. 483)

I. ISSUE

A. Issues Discussed

Criminal procedure, search and seizure

B. Legal Question Presented

Is a hotel guest entitled to the constitutional protection against unreasonable searches and seizures in his hotel room?

C. Supreme Court's Answer

A hotel guest is entitled to protection against unreasonable searches and seizures in a hotel room, and a hotel employee's permission to enter cannot override this protection.

II. CASE SUMMARY

A. Background

Police discovered that an armed robbery suspect was staying in a hotel and, without a warrant, searched the suspect's room in his absence by obtaining access from a hotel clerk. They found evidence linking the suspect to the crime. The suspect was arrested two days later in another state and, following a jury trial in which the articles were used as evidence, the suspect was convicted of armed robbery in the Superior Court of Los Angeles County, California.

At the trial several articles which had been found by police officers in a search of the petitioner's hotel room during his absence were admitted into evidence over his objection. A California District Court of Appeal affirmed the conviction, and the Supreme Court of California denied review. The U.S. Supreme Court "granted certiorari, limiting review 'to the question of whether evidence was admitted which had been obtained by an unlawful search and seizure'" and reversed the judgment.

B. Counsel of Record/ACLU Attorney

ACLU Side (Petitioner/Appellant): William H. Dempsey, Jr., by appointment of the Court, argued the cause for appellant.

Opposing Side (Respondent/Appellee): Arlo E. Smith, Chief Assistant Attorney General of California, argued the cause for appellee.

III. AMICI CURIAE

ACLU Side (Petitioner/Appellant)

Brief of amici curiae filed on behalf of the ACLU of Southern California by A. L. Wirin, Fred Okrand, and Paul Cooksey.

Opposing Side (Respondent/Appellee)

No briefs of amici curiae were filed in support of appellee.

IV. THE SUPREME COURT'S DECISION

"[T]he argument is made that the search of the hotel room, although conducted without the petitioner's consent, was lawful because it was conducted with the consent of the hotel clerk. We find this argument unpersuasive.

Even if it be assumed that a state law which gave a hotel proprietor blanket authority to authorize the police to search the rooms of the hotel's guests could survive constitutional challenge, there is no intimation in the California cases cited by the respondent that California has any such law. . . .

It is important to bear in mind that it was the petitioner's constitutional right which was at stake here, and not the night clerk's nor the hotel's. It was a right, therefore, which only the petitioner could waive by word or deed, either directly or through an agent. It is true that the night clerk clearly and unambiguously consented to the search. But there is nothing in the record to indicate that the police had any basis whatsoever to believe that the night clerk had been authorized by the petitioner to permit the police to search the petitioner's room. . . .

No less than a tenant of a house, or the occupant of a room in a boarding house, a guest in a hotel room is entitled to constitutional protection against unreasonable searches and seizures. That protection would disappear if it were left to depend upon the unfettered discretion of an employee of the hotel. It follows that this search without a warrant was unlawful. Since evidence obtained through the search was admitted at the trial, the judgment must be reversed."

The Supreme Court reversed the judgment of the District Court of Appeal of California.

V. JUSTICE VOTE

8 Pro ACLU Side vs. 1 Con Opposing Side

ACLU Side (Petitioner/Appellant)

1. Stewart, P. – Wrote majority opinion
2. Warren, E. – Joined majority opinion
3. Black, H. – Joined majority opinion
4. Clark, T. – Joined majority opinion
5. Goldberg, A. – Joined majority opinion

6. Brennan, W. – Joined majority opinion
7. Douglas, W. – Joined majority opinion
8. White, B. – Joined majority opinion

Opposing Side (Respondent/Appellee)

1. Harlan, J. – Wrote opinion concurring in part and dissenting in part

VI. A WIN OR LOSS FOR THE ACLU?

The ACLU, as amicus curiae, urged reversal of the judgment of a District Court of Appeal of California; the Supreme Court reversed in an 8-1 vote, giving the ACLU an apparent win.

147. Ungar v. Sarafite

(Decided March 30, 1964; 376 U.S. 575)

I. ISSUE

A. Issues Discussed

Due process, Fourteenth Amendment, criminal procedure

B. Legal Question Presented

Should a judge that charges a person with contempt of court be disqualified from participating in the post-trial contempt proceedings because of bias under the Due Process Clause of the Fourteenth Amendment?

C. Supreme Court's Answer

It is not a violation of due process for the judge charging a person with contempt of court to also serve as judge for the post-trial contempt proceedings.

II. CASE SUMMARY

A. Background

During a state criminal trial in New York, a lawyer who was serving as a hostile witness for the prosecution failed to follow the trial judge's instructions and refused to answer questions. He was charged with contempt, and the same judge who charged him presided over the hearing for the contempt charges.

The witness' requests for a continuance were denied, and witness' counsel could not defend the case as the attorney was only available to defend in the event of a continuance. The witness, himself an attorney, chose not to defend his case, "arguing that a continuance and a hearing before another judge should be granted" to prevent bias. The judge found him "guilty of contempt and . . . sentenced him to 10 days' imprisonment and imposed a fine." The Appellate Division and the New York Court of Appeals affirmed.

B. Counsel of Record/ACLU Attorney

ACLU Side (Petitioner/Appellant): Osmond K. Fraenkel and Emanuel Redfield argued the cause for appellant.

Opposing Side (Respondent/Appellee): H. Richard Uviller argued the cause for appellee.

III. AMICI CURIAE

ACLU Side (Petitioner/Appellant)

Brief of amici curiae filed on behalf of the New York Civil Liberties Union by Osmond K. Fraenkel.

Opposing Side (Respondent/Appellee)

No briefs of amici curiae were filed in support of appellee.

IV. THE SUPREME COURT'S DECISION

"We have determined that the appeal must be dismissed for want of jurisdiction. . . .

Petitioner, Ungar, claims his constitutional rights to a fair hearing were violated because his contemptuous remarks were a personal attack on the judge which necessarily, and without more, biased the judge and disqualified him from presiding at the post-trial contempt hearing. The New York Court of Appeals rejected the claim and we see no error in this conclusion. Assuming that there are criticisms of judicial conduct which are so personal and so probably productive of bias that the judge must disqualify himself to avoid being the judge in his own case, we agree with the New York court that this is not such a case. . . . Nor is there anything else of substance in this record which shows any deprivation of petitioner's right to be tried by an unbiased and impartial judge without a direct personal interest in the outcome of the hearing. . . .

The trial judge could reasonably have concluded that petitioner's reliance upon inclement weather was less than candid since Ungar's counsel's previous statement that he could not represent Ungar without an adjournment was grounded upon his engagement in another trial. These matters are, of course, arguable, and other judges in other courts might well grant a continuance in these circumstances. But the fact that something is arguable does not make it unconstitutional. Given the deference necessarily due a state trial judge in regard to the denial or granting of continuances, we cannot say these denials denied Ungar due process of law."

The Supreme Court affirmed the judgment of the New York Court of Appeals.

V. JUSTICE VOTE

3 Pro ACLU Side vs. 6 Con Opposing Side

ACLU Side (Petitioner/Appellant)

1. Douglas, W, – Wrote dissenting opinion, joined Goldberg's dissent
2. Goldberg, A. – Wrote dissenting opinion, joined Douglas' dissent
3. Black, H. – Joined both dissents

Opposing Side (Respondent/Appellee)

1. White, B. – Wrote majority opinion
2. Warren, E. – Joined majority opinion
3. Clark, T. – Joined majority opinion
4. Harlan, J. – Wrote concurring opinion
5. Brennan, W. – Joined majority opinion
6. Stewart, P. – Joined majority opinion

VI. A WIN OR LOSS FOR THE ACLU?

The ACLU, as counsel of record and amicus curiae, urged reversal of the New York Court of Appeals; the Supreme Court affirmed the judgment in a 6-3 vote, giving the ACLU an apparent loss.

148. United States v. Barnett

(Decided April 6, 1964; 376 U.S. 681)

I. ISSUE

A. Issues Discussed

Criminal procedure, criminal contempt

B. Legal Question Presented

"[W]hether the alleged contemners are entitled as a matter of right to a jury trial on the charges" of criminal contempt?

C. Supreme Court's Answer

The alleged contemners are not entitled to a jury trial for criminal contempt charges.

II. CASE SUMMARY

A. Background

James Meredith, a black man, attempted to attend the University of Mississippi. When he was refused admission he filed a lawsuit which led to a protracted legal battle. After the District Court denied relief, the Court of Appeals ordered the university to admit Meredith and refrain from discrimination in his admission.

When officials did not follow this order and Meredith was prevented from registering at the university, the court entered orders to gain compliance, ultimately holding the Governor of Mississippi, Ross Barnett, and the Lieutenant Governor, Paul Johnson, Jr., in contempt. The Court of Appeals held hearings and found both the Governor and Lieutenant Governor in civil contempt, determining they owed fines and must be placed in custody if they refused to comply. The Court of Appeals followed this with another hearing for criminal contempt, out of which the issue in this case arises as the Governor and Lieutenant Governor assert that they are entitled to a jury trial.

In the meantime, President Kennedy issued an order to allow Meredith to attend the University of Mississippi and, although rioting initially broke out, Meredith was allowed to study under constant guard of United States Marshals.

The Supreme Court granted certiorari to consider the "sole issue . . . whether the alleged contemners are entitled as a matter of right to a jury trial" and determined a jury trial was not within their rights.

B. Counsel of Record/ACLU Attorney

ACLU Side (Petitioner/Appellant): Malcolm B. Montgomery and Charles Clark, Special Assistant Attorneys General of Mississippi, argued the cause for defendants.

Opposing Side (Respondent/Appellee): Solicitor General Archibald Cox and Leon Jaworski argued the cause for the United States.

III. AMICI CURIAE

ACLU Side (Petitioner/Appellant)

Brief of amici curiae filed on behalf of the ACLU by Osmond K. Fraenkel, Norman Dorsen, Alfred Lawrence Toombs, and Melvin L. Wulf.

Brief of amicus curiae filed on behalf of the State of Mississippi by Attorney General of Mississippi Joe T. Patterson.

Opposing Side (Respondent/Appellee)

No briefs of amici curiae were filed in support of the United States.

IV. THE SUPREME COURT'S DECISION

"The First Congress in the Judiciary Act of 1789 conferred on federal courts the power 'to punish by fine or imprisonment, at the discretion of said courts, all contempts of authority in any cause or hearing before the same . . . .' It is undisputed that this Act gave federal courts the discretionary power to punish for contempt as that power was known to the common law. In 1831. . . . Congress restricted the power of federal courts to inflict summary punishment for contempt to misbehavior 'in the presence of the said courts, or so near thereto as to obstruct the administration of justice,' misbehavior of court officers in official matters, and disobedience or resistance by any person to any lawful writ, process, order, rule, decree, or command of the courts. These provisions are now codified in 18 U.S.C. § 401 without material difference. The Court of Appeals proceeded in this case under the authority of this section.

The alleged contemners claim, however, that the powers granted federal courts under § 401 were limited by the Congress in 1914 by the provisions of §§ 21, 22 and 24 of the Clayton Act, now codified as 18 U.S.C. § 402 and 3691. These sections guarantee the right to a jury trial in contempt proceedings arising out of disobedience to orders 'of any district court of the United States or any court of the District of Columbia,' provided that the conduct complained of also constitutes a criminal offense under the laws of the United States or of any State. But the Clayton Act further provides that the requirement of a jury does not apply to 'contempts committed in disobedience of any lawful writ, process, order, rule, decree, or command entered in any suit or action brought or prosecuted in the name of, or on behalf of, the United States, but the same, and all other cases of contempt not specifically embraced in this section may be punished in conformity to the prevailing usages at law.' Rule 42(b) of the Federal Rules of Criminal Procedure thereafter set down the procedural requirements for all contempt actions, providing that '[t]he defendant is entitled to a trial by jury in any case in which an act of Congress so provides.' . . .

Governor Barnett and Lieutenant Governor Johnson first contend that the record clearly shows that the United States invoked the proceedings taken by the Court of Appeals and sought that court out as a source of orders, duplicating the orders obtained by the real party in interest in the District Court, solely for the purpose of by-passing the District Court and depriving them of their right to a jury. We find no evidence of this. Indeed, the Court of Appeals granted injunctive relief only after it had jurisdiction over Meredith's appeal, after it had acted upon that appeal and after its order was being frustrated.

Next it is contended that the Court of Appeals had no jurisdiction in the matter since its mandate had been issued and the case had been remanded to the District Court. On a certificate we do not pass on alleged irregularities in the proceedings in the court below, as such contentions are clearly premature. . . .

Nor can we conclude from the record here that the show-cause order directed by the Court of Appeals to the alleged contemners must be construed as being founded upon violations of the District Court's injunction of September 13, entered upon the specific order of the Court of Appeals. . . . The claim is, first, that the District Court's order of September 13 superseded the earlier Court of Appeals order of July 28, and that the September 25 order of the Court of Appeals was without significance since it added nothing to the earlier orders except to specifically name the alleged contemners. But it can hardly be said that there was a super session, since the July 28 order specifically retained jurisdiction. Nor is the September 25 order of no significance, as it is the principal order upon which the alleged contemners' contemptuous conduct is predicated. . . .

Finally, it is urged that those charged with criminal contempt have a constitutional right to a jury trial. This claim has been made and rejected here again and again. Only six years ago we held a full review of the issue in Green v. United States, 356 U.S. 165 (1958). We held there that '[t]he statements of this Court in a long and unbroken line of decisions involving contempts ranging from misbehavior in court to disobedience of court orders establish beyond peradventure that criminal contempts are not subject to jury trial as a matter of constitutional right.' . . .

It is true that adherence to prior decisions in constitutional adjudication is not a blind or inflexible rule. This Court has shown a readiness to correct its errors even though of long standing. Still, where so many cases in both federal and state jurisdictions by such a constellation of eminent jurists over a century and a half's span teach us a principle which is without contradiction in our case law, we cannot overrule it. . . . 'The power to fine and imprison for contempt, from the earliest history of jurisprudence, has been regarded as a necessary incident and attribute of a court, without which it could no more exist than without a judge. It is a power inherent in all courts of record, and coexisting with them by the wise provisions of the common law. A court without the power effectually to protect itself against the assaults of the lawless, or to enforce its orders, judgments, or decrees against the recusant parties before it, would be a disgrace to the legislation, and a stigma upon the age which invented it. In this country, all courts derive their authority from the people, and hold it in trust for their security and benefit. . . . The power to compel the lawless offender, against decency and propriety, to respect the laws of his country, and submit to their authority (a duty to which the good citizen yields hearty obedience, without compulsion) must exist, or courts and laws operate at last as a restraint upon the upright, who need no restraint, and a license to the offenders, whom they are made to subdue.'

The question certified to the Court is therefore answered in the negative."

V. JUSTICE VOTE

4 Pro ACLU Side vs. 5 Con Opposing Side

ACLU Side (Petitioner/Appellant)

1. Black, H. – Wrote dissenting opinion
2. Goldberg, A. – Wrote dissenting opinion
3. Douglas, W. – Joined both dissents
4. Warren, E. – Joined Goldberg's dissent

Opposing Side (Respondent/Appellee)

1. Clark, T. – Wrote majority opinion
2. Harlan, J. – Joined majority opinion
3. Stewart, P. – Joined majority opinion
4. White, B. – Joined majority opinion
5. Brennan, W. – Joined majority opinion

VI. A WIN OR LOSS FOR THE ACLU?

The ACLU filed an amicus brief in support of defendants; the Supreme Court answered in the negative the question certified to the Court by the Court of Appeals for the Fifth Circuit in a 5-4 vote, giving the ACLU an apparent loss.

149. Schneider v. Rusk

(Decided May 18, 1964; 377 U.S. 163)

I. ISSUE

A. Issues Discussed

Governmental authority, citizenship

B. Legal Question Presented

May Congress revoke the citizenship of naturalized U.S. citizens who return to and live in their native countries for three years?

C. Supreme Court's Answer

U.S. citizenship through naturalization cannot be revoked because a naturalized citizen subsequently resides in his or her native country for three years.

II. CASE SUMMARY

A. Background

Appellant Schneider was born in Germany but became an U.S. citizen after moving to the United States with her parents as a child. After graduating from college, Schneider moved back to Germany, married a German national, and made Germany her permanent home.

When Schneider applied for a U.S. passport, she was denied on the ground that she had been stripped of her United States citizenship after she moved back to Germany and lived there for longer than three years. Section 352(a)(1) of the Immigration and Nationality Act of 1952 provides that a naturalized U.S. citizen would be stripped of citizenship in the event that person returned to his or her native country and lived there for three years.

Schneider filed a suit in the District Court for the District of Columbia seeking reinstatement of her U.S. citizenship. The

District Court ruled against her.

On appeal, the Supreme Court granted certiorari and reversed.

B. Counsel of Record/ACLU Attorney

ACLU Side (Petitioner/Appellant): Milton V. Freeman argued the cause for appellant.

Opposing Side (Respondent/Appellee): Bruce J. Terris argued the cause for appellee.

III. AMICI CURIAE

ACLU Side (Petitioner/Appellant)

Brief of amici curiae filed on behalf of the ACLU by Jack Wasserman, David Carliner, and Melvin L. Wulf.

Opposing Side (Respondent/Appellee)

No amici curiae briefs were filed in support of appellee.

IV. THE SUPREME COURT'S DECISION

"We start from the premise that the rights of citizenship of the native born and of the naturalized person are of the same dignity and are coextensive. The only difference drawn by the Constitution is that only the 'natural born' citizen is eligible to be President.

While the rights of citizenship of the native born derive from § 1 of the Fourteenth Amendment and the rights of the naturalized citizen derive from satisfying, free of fraud, the requirements set by Congress, the latter, apart from the exception noted, 'becomes a member of the society, possessing all the rights of a native citizen, and standing, in the view of the constitution, on the footing of a native. The constitution does not authorize Congress to enlarge or abridge those rights. The simple power of the national Legislature, is to prescribe a uniform rule of naturalization, and the exercise of this power exhausts it, so far as respects the individual.' . . .

This statute proceeds on the impermissible assumption that naturalized citizens as a class are less reliable and bear less allegiance to this country than do the native born. This is an assumption that is impossible for us to make. Moreover, while the Fifth Amendment contains no equal protection clause, it does forbid discrimination that is 'so unjustifiable as to be violative of due process.' A native-born citizen is free to reside abroad indefinitely without suffering loss of citizenship. The discrimination aimed at naturalized citizens drastically limits their rights to live and work abroad in a way that other citizens may. It creates indeed a second-class citizenship. Living abroad, whether the citizen be naturalized or native born, is no badge of lack of allegiance and in no way evidences a voluntary renunciation of nationality and allegiance. It may indeed be compelled by family, business, or other legitimate reasons."

The Supreme Court reversed the Court of Appeals for the District of Columbia.

V. JUSTICE VOTE

5 Pro ACLU Side vs. 3 Con Opposing Side

ACLU Side (Petitioner/Appellant)

1. Douglas, W. – Wrote majority opinion
2. Warren, E. – Joined majority opinion
3. Black, H. – Joined majority opinion
4. Stewart, P. – Joined majority opinion
5. Goldberg, A. – Joined majority opinion

Opposing Side (Respondent/Appellee)

1. Clark, T. – Wrote dissenting opinion
2. Harlan, T. – Joined dissenting opinion
3. White, B. – Joined dissenting opinion

Brennan, W. – Took no part in the decision

VI. A WIN OR LOSS FOR THE ACLU?

The ACLU filed an amicus brief urging reversal; the Supreme Court reversed the ruling of the Court of Appeals for the District of Columbia in a 5-3 vote, giving the ACLU an apparent win.

150. Baggett v. Bullitt

(Decided June 1, 1964; 377 U.S. 360)

I. ISSUE

A. Issues Discussed

Communism, 1st Amendment, press, speech, association

B. Legal Question Presented

Whether a Washington State employee can be required to swear oaths declaring they are not a "subversive person."

C. Supreme Court's Answer

The oaths cannot be upheld as "the oath requirements and the statutory provisions on which they are based are invalid on their face because their language is unduly vague, uncertain and broad."

II. CASE SUMMARY

A. Background

"Appellants . . . are members of the faculty, staff and student body of the University of Washington who brought this class action asking for a judgment declaring unconstitutional two Washington statutes requiring the execution of two different oaths by state employees and for an injunction against the enforcement of these statutes . . . .

The statutes under attack . . . require employees of the State of Washington to take the oaths prescribed in the statutes as a condition of their employment. . . .

[T]he University President . . . issued a memorandum to all University employees notifying them that they would be required to take an oath. Oath Form A requires all teaching personnel to swear to the oath of allegiance . . . , to aver that they have read, are familiar with and understand the provisions defining 'subversive person' in the Subversive Activities Act of 1951 and to disclaim being a subversive person and membership in the Communist Party or any other subversive or foreign subversive organization. Oath Form B requires other state employees to subscribe to all of the above provisions except the 1931 oath. . . .

[A] three-judge District Court was convened and a trial was had. That court determined that the 1955 oath and underlying statutory provisions did not infringe upon any First and

Fourteenth Amendment freedoms and were not unduly vague. In respect to the claims that the 1931 oath was unconstitutionally vague on its face, the court held that although the challenge raised a substantial constitutional issue, adjudication was not proper in the absence of proceedings in the state courts . . . . The action was dismissed."

The Supreme Court granted certiorari to review the case.

B. Counsel of Record

ACLU Side (Petitioner/Appellant): Arval A. Morris and Kenneth A. MacDonald argued the cause and filed a brief for appellants.[1]

Opposing Side (Respondent/Appellee): Herbert H. Fuller, Deputy Attorney General of Washington, argued the cause for appellees. With him on the brief were John J. O'Connell, Attorney General of Washington, and Dean A. Floyd, Assistant Attorney General.

III. AMICI CURIAE

ACLU Side (Petitioner/Appellant)

No briefs of amici curiae were filed in support of appellants.

Opposing Side (Respondent/Appellee)

No briefs of amici curiae were filed in support of appellees.

IV. THE SUPREME COURT'S DECISION

"Appellants contend in this Court that the oath requirements and the statutory provisions on which they are based are invalid on their face because their language is unduly vague, uncertain and broad. We agree with this contention and therefore, without reaching the numerous other contentions pressed upon us, confine our considerations to that particular question. . . .

We also conclude that the 1931 oath offends due process because of vagueness. The oath exacts a promise that the affiant will, by precept and example, promote respect for the flag and the institutions of the United States and and State of Washington. The range of activities which are or might be deemed inconsistent with the required promise is very wide indeed. . . .

Indulging every presumption of a narrow construction of the provisions of the 1931 oath, consistent, however, with a proper respect for the English language, we cannot say that this oath provides an ascertainable standard of conduct or that it does not require more than a State may command under the guarantees of the First and Fourteenth Amendments. . . .

We are asked not to examine the 1931 oath statute because, although on the books for over three decades, it has never been interpreted by the Washington courts. . . . Because this Court ordinarily accepts the construction given a state statute in the local courts and also presumes that the statute will be construed in such a way as to avoid the constitutional question presented, an interpretation of the 1931 oath in the Washington courts in light of the vagueness attack may eliminate the necessity of deciding this issue.

We are not persuaded. . . .

As in Cramp v. Board of Public Instruction, we do not question the power of a State to take proper measures safeguarding the public service from disloyal conduct. But measures which purport to define disloyalty must allow public servants to know what is and is not disloyal. 'The fact . . . that a person is not compelled to hold public office cannot possibly be an excuse for barring him from office by state-imposed criteria forbidden by the Constitution.'

Reversed."

V. JUSTICE VOTE

7 Pro ACLU Side vs. 2 Con Opposing Side

ACLU Side (Petitioner/Appellant)

1. White, B. – Wrote majority opinion
2. Warren, E. – Joined majority opinion
3. Brennan, W. – Joined majority opinion
4. Black, H. – Joined majority opinion
5. Douglas, W. – Joined majority opinion
6. Goldberg, A. – Joined majority opinion
7. Stewart, P. – Joined majority opinion

Opposing Side (Respondent/Appellee)

1. Harlan, J. – Joined Clark's dissent
2. Clark, T. – Wrote dissenting opinion

VI. A WIN OR LOSS FOR THE ACLU?

The ACLU served as counsel for appellant urging reversal of the judgment of the district court; the Supreme Court reversed in a 7-2 vote, giving the ACLU an apparent win.

151. Reynolds v. Sims

(Decided June 15, 1964; 377 U.S. 533)

I. ISSUE

A. Issues Discussed

Equal protection, voting rights

B. Legal Question Presented

Did the District Court err when it held that the old and new plans for the apportionment of seats in the Alabama Legislature were unconstitutional because they did not reflect the population distribution in Alabama?

C. Supreme Court's Answer

The District Court appropriately held the apportionment plans unconstitutional.

1 The *Successes of the American Civil Liberties Union, ACLU,* https://www.aclu.org/successes-american-civil-liberties-union (last visited Jan. 25, 2020) (Listed as a successful case of the ACLU.); Maureen O'Hagan, *Obituary: Seatte Attorney Who Defended the Downtrodden Dies at 95, Seattle Times,* Nov. 22, 2012, https://www.seattletimes.com/seattle-news/obituary-seattle-attorney-who-defended-the-downtrodden-dies-at-95/ (Kenneth MacDonald was active in his local ACLU chapter in Washington from its inception.).

II. CASE SUMMARY

A. Background

Three separate appeals from the District Court for the Middle District of Alabama merged in this case.

"On August 26, 1961, the original plaintiffs (appellees in No. 23), residents, taxpayers and voters of Jefferson County, Alabama, filed a complaint . . . challenging the apportionment of the Alabama Legislature. . . . The complaint alleged a deprivation of rights under the Alabama Constitution and under the Equal Protection Clause of the Fourteenth Amendment . . . .

Plaintiffs below alleged that the last apportionment of the Alabama Legislature was based on the 1900 federal census, despite the requirement of the State Constitution that the legislature be reapportioned decennially. They asserted that, since the population growth in the State from 1900 to 1960 had been uneven, Jefferson and other counties were now victims of serious discrimination with respect to the allocation of legislative representation. As a result of the failure of the legislature to reapportion itself, plaintiffs asserted, they were denied 'equal suffrage in free and equal elections . . . and the equal protection of the laws' in violation of the Alabama Constitution and the Fourteenth Amendment to the Federal Constitution. The complaint asserted that plaintiffs had no other adequate remedy, and that they had exhausted all forms of relief other than that available through the federal courts. They alleged that the Alabama Legislature had established a pattern of prolonged inaction from 1911 to the present which 'clearly demonstrates that no reapportionment . . . shall be effected'; that representation at any future constitutional convention would be established by the legislature, making it unlikely that the membership of any such convention would be fairly representative; and that, while the Alabama Supreme Court had found that the legislature had not complied with the State Constitution in failing to reapportion according to population decennially, that court had nevertheless indicated that it would not interfere with matters of legislative reapportionment."

After the District Court was convened and made preliminary findings, "an extraordinary session of the Alabama Legislature adopted two reapportionment plans to take effect for the 1966 elections." Under the challenged plan and both new plans, "each senatorial district would be represented by only one senator." After hearing the evidence at trial "District Court held that the inequality of the existing representation in the Alabama Legislature violated the Equal Protection Clause of the Fourteenth Amendment, a finding which the Court noted had been 'generally conceded' by the parties to the litigation, since population growth and shifts had converted the 1901 scheme, as perpetuated some 60 years later, into an invidiously discriminatory plan completely lacking in rationality. Under the existing provisions, applying 1960 census figures, only 25.1% of the State's total population resided in districts represented by a majority of the members of the Senate, and only 25.7% lived in counties which could elect a majority of the members of the House of Representatives." The court determined that neither of the two reapportionment plans presented "'meets the necessary constitutional requirements. We find that each of the legislative acts, when considered as a whole, is so obviously discriminatory, arbitrary and irrational that it becomes unnecessary to pursue a detailed development of each of the relevant factors of the [federal constitutional] test.'" The court ordered a temporary reapportionment scheme, retaining jurisdiction to evaluate a permanent reapportionment scheme.

The Supreme Court granted certiorari to review this decision and affirmed.

B. Counsel of Record/ACLU Attorney

ACLU Side (Respondent/Appellee in No. 23 and Petitioner/Appellant in Nos. 27 and 41):

Charles Morgan, Jr. argued the cause for appellee in No. 23. David J. Vann argued the cause for appellant in No. 27. John W. McConnell, Jr., argued the cause for appellant in No. 41. Jerome A. Cooper and George C. Longshore filed a brief for appellees Farr et al. Solicitor General Archibald Cox argued the cause for the United States, as amicus curiae, by special leave of court.

Opposing Side (Petitioner/Appellant in No. 23 and Respondent/Appellee in Nos. 27 and 41):

W. McLean Pitts argued the cause for appellant in No. 23 and for appellee in Nos. 27 and 41. Appellee, Richmond M. Flowers, Attorney General of Alabama, argued the cause pro se.

III. AMICI CURIAE

ACLU Side (Respondent/Appellee in No. 23 and Petitioner/Appellant in Nos. 27 and 41):

Brief of amici curiae filed on behalf of the United States by Solicitor General Archibald Cox, Bruce J. Terris, and Richard W. Schmude.

Brief of amici curiae urging affirmance filed on behalf of the American Jewish Congress, et al., by Leo Pfeffer, Melvin L. Wulf, Jack Greenberg, and Robert B. McKay.

Brief of amici curiae filed on behalf of Schmied, President of the Board of Aldermen of Louisville, Kentucky, by W. Scott Miller, Jr., and George J. Long.

Opposing Side (Petitioner/Appellant in No. 23 and Respondent/Appellee in Nos. 27 and 41):

No briefs of amici curiae were filed in support of appellant in No. 23 or appellee in Nos. 27 and 41.

IV. THE SUPREME COURT'S DECISION

"Undeniably the Constitution of the United States protects the right of all qualified citizens to vote, in state as well as in federal elections. A consistent line of decisions by this Court in cases involving attempts to deny or restrict the right of suffrage has made this indelibly clear. It has been repeatedly recognized that all qualified voters have a constitutionally protected right to vote, and to have their votes counted . . . .

We hold that, as a basic constitutional standard, the Equal Protection Clause requires that the seats in both houses of a bicameral state legislature must be apportioned on a population basis. . . . Since, under neither the existing apportionment provisions nor either of the proposed plans was either of the houses of the Alabama Legislature apportioned on a population basis, the District Court correctly held that all three of these schemes were constitutionally invalid. . . .

By holding that as a federal constitutional requisite both houses of a state legislature must be apportioned on a population basis, we mean that the Equal Protection Clause requires that a State make an honest and good faith effort to construct districts, in both houses of its legislature, as nearly of equal population as is practicable. We realize that it is a practical impossibility to arrange legislative districts so that each one has an identical number of residents, or citizens, or voters. . . .

That the Equal Protection Clause requires that both houses of a state legislature be apportioned on a population basis does not mean that States cannot adopt some reasonable plan for periodic revision of their apportionment schemes. Decennial reapportionment appears to be a rational approach to readjustment of legislative representation in order to take into account population shifts and growth. . . .

We find, therefore, that the action taken by the District Court in this case, in ordering into effect a reapportionment of both houses of the Alabama Legislature for purposes of the 1962 primary and general elections, by using the best parts of the two proposed plans which it had found, as a whole, to be invalid, was an appropriate and well-considered exercise of judicial power. Admittedly, the lower court's ordered plan was intended only as a temporary and provisional measure and the District Court correctly indicated that the plan was invalid as a permanent apportionment. In retaining jurisdiction while deferring a hearing on the issuance of a final injunction in order to give the provisionally reapportioned legislature an opportunity to act effectively, the court below proceeded in a proper fashion. Since the District Court evinced its realization that its ordered reapportionment could not be sustained as the basis for conducting the 1966 election of Alabama legislators, and avowedly intends to take some further action should the reapportioned Alabama Legislature fail to enact a constitutionally valid, permanent apportionment scheme in the interim, we affirm the judgment below and remand the cases for further proceedings consistent with the views stated in this opinion."

V. JUSTICE VOTE

8 Pro ACLU Side vs. 1 Con Opposing Side

ACLU Side (Respondent/Appellee in No. 23 and Petitioner/Appellant in Nos. 27 and 41):

1. Warren, E. – Wrote majority opinion
2. Brennan, W. – Joined majority opinion
3. Black, H. – Joined majority opinion
4. Douglas, W. – Joined majority opinion
5. Goldberg, A. – Joined majority opinion
6. White, B. – Joined majority opinion
7. Clark, T. – Wrote concurring opinion
8. Stewart, P. – Wrote concurring opinion

Opposing Side (Petitioner/Appellant in No. 23 and Respondent/Appellee in Nos. 27 and 41):

1. Harlan, J. – Wrote dissenting opinion

VI. A WIN OR LOSS FOR THE ACLU?

The ACLU, as attorney of record, urged affirmance of the judgment of the District Court; the Supreme Court affirmed in an 8-1 vote, giving the ACLU an apparent win.

152. Malloy v. Hogan

(Decided June 15, 1964; 378 U.S. 1)

I. ISSUE

A. Issues Discussed

Fourteenth Amendment, Fifth Amendment, self-incrimination

B. Legal Question Presented

Does the Fourteenth Amendment protect a witness' Fifth Amendment guarantee against self-incrimination in a state proceeding?

C. Supreme Court's Answer

The Fourteenth Amendment protects the Fifth Amendment guarantee against self-incrimination in state proceedings.

II. CASE SUMMARY

A. Background

After petitioner was arrested by the Hartford police during a 1959 gambling raid, he pleaded guilty to misdemeanor pool selling, receiving a one year jail sentence and a $500 fine. 90 days later, petitioner's sentence was suspended and he was placed on two years' probation. 16 months following his plea, he was ordered to testify about gambling and other criminal activities. Refusing to answer questions about the circumstances of his arrest and conviction on the ground of self-incrimination, petitioner was imprisoned for contempt and held until willing to answer questions. Petitioner filed an application for writ of habeas corpus, which was denied by the Superior Court. The Connecticut Supreme Court of Errors affirmed the denial.

The Supreme Court granted certiorari and reversed.

B. Counsel of Record/ACLU Attorney

ACLU Side (Petitioner/Appellant): Harold Strauch argued the cause for appellant.

Opposing Side (Respondent/Appellee): John D. La Belle, State's Attorney for Connecticut, argued the cause for appellee.

III. AMICI CURIAE

ACLU Side (Petitioner/Appellant)

Brief of amici curiae filed on behalf of the ACLU by Melvin L. Wulf and Maurice DeG. Ford.

Opposing Side (Respondent/Appellee)

Brief of amici curiae filed on behalf of the State of California by Stanley Mosk, Attorney General of California, William E. James, Assistant Attorney General, and Gordon Ringer, Deputy Attorney General

Brief of amici curiae filed on behalf of the National District

Attorneys' Association by Frank S. Hogan, Edward S. Silver, H. Richard Uviller, Michael R. Juviler, Aaron E. Koota and Irving P. Seidman.

IV. THE SUPREME COURT'S DECISION

"We hold today that the Fifth Amendment's exception from compulsory self-incrimination is also protected by the Fourteenth Amendment against abridgment by the States.

[T]oday the admissibility of a confession in a state criminal prosecution is tested by the same standard applied in federal prosecutions since 1897, when . . . the Court held that '[i]n criminal trials, in the courts of the United States, wherever a question arises whether a confession is incompetent because not voluntary, the issue is controlled by that portion of the Fifth Amendment to the Constitution of the United States, commanding that no person 'shall be compelled in any criminal case to be a witness against himself.' Under this test, the constitutional inquiry is not whether the conduct of state officers in obtaining the confession was shocking, but whether the confession was 'free and voluntary: that is, [it] must not be extracted by any sort of threats or violence, nor obtained by any direct or implied promises, however slight, nor by the exertion of any improper influence. . . .' In other words the person must not have been compelled to incriminate himself. We have held inadmissible even a confession secured by so mild a whip as the refusal, under certain circumstances, to allow a suspect to call his wife until he confessed. . . .

The Fourteenth Amendment secures against state invasion the same privilege that the Fifth Amendment guarantees against federal infringement—the right of a person to remain silent unless he chooses to speak in the unfettered exercise of his own will, and to suffer no penalty . . . .

We turn to the petitioner's claim that the State of Connecticut denied him the protection of his federal privilege. It must be considered irrelevant that the petitioner was a witness in a statutory inquiry and not a defendant in a criminal prosecution, for it has long been settled that the privilege protects witnesses in similar federal inquiries. . . .

The conclusions of the Court of Errors, tested by the federal standard, fail to take sufficient account of the setting in which the questions were asked. The interrogation was part of a wide-ranging inquiry into crime, including gambling, in Hartford. It was admitted on behalf of the State at oral argument—and indeed it is obvious from the questions themselves—that the State desired to elicit from the petitioner the identity of the person who ran the pool-selling operation in connection with which he had been arrested in 1959. It was apparent that petitioner might apprehend that if this person were still engaged in unlawful activity, disclosure of his name might furnish a link in a chain of evidence sufficient to connect the petitioner with a more recent crime for which he might still be prosecuted. . . .

We conclude, therefore, that as to each of the questions, it was 'evident from the implications of the question, in the setting in which it [was] asked, that a responsive answer to the question or an explanation of why it [could not] be answered might be dangerous because injurious disclosure could result.'"

The Supreme Court reversed the judgment.

V. JUSTICE VOTE

5 Pro ACLU Side vs. 4 Con Opposing Side

ACLU Side (Petitioner/Appellant)

1. Brennan, W. – Wrote majority opinion
2. Black, H. – Joined majority opinion
3. Warren, E. – Joined majority opinion
4. Goldberg, A. – Joined majority opinion
5. Douglas, W. – Wrote concurring opinion

Opposing Side (Respondent/Appellee)

1. Harlan, J. – Wrote dissenting opinion
2. Clark, T. – Joined Harlan's dissent
3. White, B. – Wrote dissenting opinion
4. Stewart, P. – Joined White's dissent

VI. A WIN OR LOSS FOR THE ACLU?

The ACLU filed an amicus brief urging reversal; the Supreme Court reversed the ruling of the lower courts in a 5-4 vote, giving the ACLU an apparent win.

153. Jacobellis v. Ohio

(Decided June 22, 1964; 378 U.S. 184)

I. ISSUE

A. Issues Discussed

First Amendment, freedom of speech, obscenity, Fourteenth Amendment

B. Legal Question Presented

"[W]hether the state courts properly found that the motion picture involved, a French film called 'Les Amants' ('The Lovers') was obscene and hence not entitled to the protection of free expression that is guaranteed by the First and Fourteenth Amendments?

C. Supreme Court's Answer

The motion picture was not obscene and was thus entitled to First and Fourteenth Amendment protection.

II. CASE SUMMARY

A. Background

"Appellant, Nico Jacobellis, manager of a motion picture theater in Cleveland Heights, Ohio, was convicted on two counts of possessing and exhibiting an obscene film . . . . He was fined $500 on the first count and $2,000 on the second, and was sentenced to the workhouse if the fines were not paid. His conviction, by a court of three judges upon waiver of trial by jury, was affirmed by an intermediate appellate court, and by the Supreme Court of Ohio."

The U.S. Supreme Court granted certiorari and reversed.

B. Counsel of Record/ACLU Attorney

ACLU Side (Petitioner/Appellant): Ephraim London reargued the cause for appellant.

Opposing Side (Respondent/Appellee): John T. Corrigan

reargued the cause for appellee.

III. AMICI CURIAE

ACLU Side (Petitioner/Appellant)

Brief of amici curiae filed on behalf of the ACLU and Ohio Civil Liberties Union by Bernard A. Berkman, Jack G. Day, Melvin L. Wulf, Herbert B. Levine, and Fred D. Shapiro.

Opposing Side (Respondent/Appellee)

Brief of amici curiae filed on behalf of Citizens for Decent Literature, Inc., by Charles H. Keating, Jr.

IV. THE SUPREME COURT'S DECISION

"We recognize the legitimate and indeed exigent interest of States and localities throughout the Nation in preventing the dissemination of material deemed harmful to children. But that interest does not justify a total suppression of such material, the effect of which would be to 'reduce the adult population . . . to reading only what is fit for children.' State and local authorities might well consider whether their objectives in this area would be better served by laws aimed specifically at preventing distribution of objectionable material to children, rather than at totally prohibiting its dissemination. Since the present conviction is based upon exhibition of the film to the public at large, and not upon its exhibition to children, the judgment must be reviewed under the strict standard applicable in determining the scope of the expression that is protected by the Constitution.

We have applied that standard to the motion picture in question. 'The Lovers' involves a woman bored with her life and marriage who abandons her husband and family for a young archaeologist with whom she has suddenly fallen in love. There is an explicit love scene in the last reel of the film, and the State's objections are based almost entirely upon that scene. The film was favorably reviewed in a number of national publications, although disparaged in others, and was rated by at least two critics of national stature among the best films of the year in which it was produced. It was shown in approximately 100 of the larger cities in the United States, including Columbus and Toledo, Ohio. We have viewed the film, in the light of the record made in the trial court, and we conclude that it is not obscene within the standards enunciated in Roth v. United States and Alberts v. California, which we reaffirm here."

The Supreme Court reversed the judgment of the Supreme Court of Ohio.

Justice Stewart, in his concurring opinion, stated that: "under the First and Fourteenth Amendments, criminal laws in this area are constitutionally limited to hard core pornography. I shall not today attempt further to define the kinds of material I understand to be embraced within that shorthand description, and perhaps I could never succeed in intelligibly doing so. But I know it when I see it, and the motion picture involved in this case is not that."

V. JUSTICE VOTE

6 Pro ACLU Side vs. 3 Con Opposing Side

ACLU Side (Petitioner/Appellant)

1. Brennan, W. – Wrote majority opinion
2. Goldberg, A. – Wrote concurring opinion
3. White, B. – Joined majority opinion
4. Black, H. – Wrote concurring opinion
5. Douglas, W. – Joined Black's concurrence
6. Stewart, P. – Wrote concurring opinion

Opposing Side (Respondent/Appellee)

1. Warren, E. – Wrote dissenting opinion
2. Clark, T. – Joined Warren's dissent
3. Harlan, J. – Wrote dissenting opinion

VI. A WIN OR LOSS FOR THE ACLU?

The ACLU filed an amicus brief urging reversal; the Supreme Court reversed the ruling of the Ohio Supreme Court in a 6-3 vote, giving the ACLU an apparent win.

154. Escobedo v. Illinois

(Decided June 22, 1964; 378 U.S. 478)

I. ISSUE

A. Issues Discussed

Criminal procedure, right to an attorney, Sixth Amendment

B. Legal Question Presented

"[W]hether, under the circumstances, the refusal by the police to honor petitioner's request to consult with his lawyer during the course of an interrogation constitutes a denial of 'the Assistance of Counsel' in violation of the Sixth Amendment to the Constitution as 'made obligatory upon the States by the Fourteenth Amendment,' and thereby renders inadmissible in a state criminal trial any incriminating statement elicited by the police during the interrogation."

C. Supreme Court's Answer

The police conduct violated petitioner's Sixth Amendment rights, thus rendering the incriminating statement inadmissible at trial.

II. CASE SUMMARY

A. Background

Petitioner was arrested for murder and taken to the police station for questioning. He was never advised of his constitutional rights. He asked for his lawyer while en route to the police station, then repeatedly during the interrogation. He was told "that his lawyer 'didn't want to see' him." Meanwhile, petitioner's attorney arrived at the police station shortly after petitioner and, despite repeated requests over the course of several hours to multiple officers, the attorney was denied access to petitioner. Petitioner made an incriminating statement during the interrogation that was recorded by the Assistant State's Attorney. The statement was admitted into evidence and petitioner was convicted of murder. The Supreme Court of Illinois initially overturned the conviction, holding the statement inadmissible. After a rehearing, however, the Supreme Court of Illinois upheld the new conviction.

The Supreme Court granted certiorari and reversed.

B. Counsel of Record/ACLU Attorney

ACLU Side (Petitioner/Appellant): Barry L. Kroll argued the cause for appellant. Bernard Weisberg argued the cause for the ACLU, as amicus curiae.

Opposing Side (Respondent/Appellee): James R. Thompson argued the cause for appellee.

III. AMICI CURIAE

ACLU Side (Petitioner/Appellant)

Brief of amici curiae filed on behalf of the ACLU by Bernard Weisberg, Seymour H. Bucholz, Walter T. Fisher, and Joel J. Sprayregen.

Opposing Side (Respondent/Appellee)

No briefs of amici curiae were filed in support of appellee.

IV. THE SUPREME COURT'S DECISION

"We granted a writ of certiorari to consider whether the petitioner's statement was constitutionally admissible at his trial. We conclude, for the reasons stated below, that it was not and, accordingly, we reverse the judgment of conviction. . . .

The interrogation here was conducted before petitioner was formally indicted. But in the context of this case, that fact should make no difference. When petitioner requested, and was denied, an opportunity to consult with his lawyer, the investigation had ceased to be a general investigation of 'an unsolved crime.' Petitioner had become the accused, and the purpose of the interrogation was to 'get him' to confess his guilt despite his constitutional right not to do so. At the time of his arrest and throughout the course of the interrogation, the police told petitioner that they had convincing evidence that he had fired the fatal shots. Without informing him of his absolute right to remain silent in the face of this accusation, the police urged him to make a statement. . . .

Petitioner, a layman, was undoubtedly unaware that under Illinois law an admission of 'mere' complicity in the murder plot was legally as damaging as an admission of firing of the fatal shots. The 'guiding hand of counsel' was essential to advise petitioner of his rights in this delicate situation. This was the 'stage when legal aid and advice' were most critical to petitioner. . . .

We hold, therefore, that where, as here, the investigation is no longer a general inquiry into an unsolved crime but has begun to focus on a particular suspect, the suspect has been taken into police custody, the police carry out a process of interrogations that lends itself to eliciting incriminating statements, the suspect has requested and been denied an opportunity to consult with his lawyer, and the police have not effectively warned him of his absolute constitutional right to remain silent, the accused has been denied 'The Assistance of Counsel' in violation of the Sixth Amendment to the Constitution as 'made obligatory upon the States by the Fourteenth Amendment,' and that no statement elicited by the police during the interrogation may be used against him at a criminal trial."

The Supreme Court reversed the judgment of the Illinois Supreme Court.

V. JUSTICE VOTE

5 Pro ACLU Side vs. 4 Con Opposing Side

ACLU Side (Petitioner/Appellant)

1. Goldberg, A. – Wrote majority opinion
2. Black, H. – Joined majority opinion
3. Douglas, W. – Joined majority opinion
4. Brennan, W. – Joined majority opinion
5. Warren, E. – Joined majority opinion

Opposing Side (Respondent/Appellee)

1. Harlan, J. – Wrote dissenting opinion
2. White, B. – Wrote dissenting opinion
3. Stewart, P. – Wrote dissenting opinion, joined White's dissent
4. Clark, T. – Joined White's dissent

VI. A WIN OR LOSS FOR THE ACLU?

The ACLU, as amicus curiae (an ACLU attorney argued though not as counsel of record), urged reversal of the Illinois Supreme Court's judgment; the Supreme Court reversed in a 5-4 vote, giving the ACLU an apparent win.

155. Aptheker v. Secretary of State

(Decided June 22, 1964; 378 U.S. 500)

I. ISSUE

A. Issues Discussed

First Amendment, Fifth Amendment, freedom of association, freedom of speech and of the press, national security, right to travel, due process

B. Legal Question Presented

Does the enforcement of § 6 of the Subversive Activities Control Act of 1950, making it unlawful for any member of a registered Communist organization to apply for or use a U.S. passport, unconstitutional?

C. Supreme Court's Answer

Section 6 of the Subversive Activities Control Act is unconstitutional.

II. CASE SUMMARY

A. Background

Appellants, native-born U.S. citizens and residents, held valid passports. Then, on January 22, 1962, the Acting Director of the Passport Office notified appellants that their passports had been revoked under § 6 of the Subversive Activities Control Act, which makes it unlawful for any member of a registered Communist organization to apply for or use a U.S. passport. "Appellants requested and received hearings [where] the examiners recommended that the passport revocations be sustained.

Both appellants appealed to the Board of Passport Appeals which recommended affirmance of the revocations. The Secretary of State subsequently approved the recommendations of the Board. . . .

Appellants thereupon filed separate complaints seeking declaratory and injunctive relief in the United States District Court for the District of Columbia. The complaints, considered together, asked that judgments be entered declaring § 6 of the Control Act unconstitutional and ordering the Secretary of State to issue passports to the appellants. . . .

The three-judge District Court, which was convened to review the constitutional question, rejected appellants' contentions, sustained the constitutionality of § 6 of the Subversive Activities Control Act, and granted the Secretary's motion for summary judgment."

The Supreme Court granted certiorari and reversed.

B. Counsel of Record/ACLU Attorney

ACLU Side (Petitioner/Appellant): John J. Abt and Joseph Forer argued the cause for appellant.

Opposing Side (Respondent/Appellee): Abram Chayes argued the cause for appellee.

III. AMICI CURIAE

ACLU Side (Petitioner/Appellant)

Brief of amici curiae filed on behalf of the ACLU by Osmond K. Fraenkel.

Opposing Side (Respondent/Appellee)

No briefs of amici curiae were filed in support of appellee.

IV. THE SUPREME COURT'S DECISION

"The denial of a passport, given existing domestic and foreign laws, is a severe restriction upon, and in effect a prohibition against, world-wide foreign travel. Present laws and regulations make it a crime for a United States citizen to travel outside the Western Hemisphere or to Cuba without a passport. By its plain import § 6 of the Control Act effectively prohibits travel anywhere in the world outside the Western Hemisphere by members of any 'Communist organization' . . . . The restrictive effect of the legislation cannot be gainsaid by emphasizing, as the Government seems to do, that a member of a registering organization could recapture his freedom to travel by simply in good faith abandoning his membership in the organization. Since freedom of association is itself guaranteed in the First Amendment, restrictions imposed upon the right to travel cannot be dismissed by asserting that the right to travel could be fully exercised if the individual would first yield up his membership in a given association. . . .

In addition to the absence of criteria linking the bare fact of membership to the individual's knowledge, activity or commitment, § 6 also excludes other considerations which might more closely relate the denial of passports to the stated purpose of the legislation. The prohibition of § 6 applies regardless of the purposes for which an individual wishes to travel. Under the statute it is a crime for a notified member of a registered organization to apply for a passport to travel abroad to visit a sick relative, to receive medical treatment, or for any other wholly innocent purpose. In determining whether there has been an abridgment of the Fifth Amendment's guarantee of liberty, this Court must recognize the danger of punishing a member of a Communist organization 'for his adherence to lawful and constitutionally protected purposes, because of other and unprotected purposes which he does not necessarily share.' In addition it must be noted that § 6 applies to a member regardless of the security-sensitivity of the areas in which he wishes to travel. As a result, if a notified member of a registered organization were to apply for a passport to visit a relative in Ireland, or to read rare manuscripts in the Bodleian Library of Oxford University, the applicant would be guilty of a crime; whereas, if he were to travel to Canada or Latin America to carry on criminal activities directed against the United States, he could do so free from the prohibitive reach of § 6. . . .

The legislation which the President proposed did not make membership in a Communist organization, without more, a disqualification for obtaining a passport. Irrespective of views as to the validity of this or other such proposals, they demonstrate the conviction of the Executive Branch that our national security can be adequately protected by means which, when compared with § 6, are more discriminately tailored to the constitutional liberties of individuals.

In our view the foregoing considerations compel the conclusion that § 6 of the Control Act is unconstitutional on its face. The section, judged by its plain import and by the substantive evil which Congress sought to control, sweeps too widely and too indiscriminately across the liberty guaranteed in the Fifth Amendment. The prohibition against travel is supported only by a tenuous relationship between the bare fact of organizational membership and the activity Congress sought to proscribe. The broad and enveloping prohibition indiscriminately excludes plainly relevant considerations such as the individual's knowledge, activity, commitment, and purposes in and places for travel.

[S]ince freedom of travel is a constitutional liberty closely related to rights of free speech and association, we believe that appellants in this case should not be required to assume the burden of demonstrating that Congress could not have written a statute constitutionally prohibiting their travel."

The Supreme Court reversed the judgment of the District Court of the District of Columbia and remanded the case.

V. JUSTICE VOTE

6 Pro ACLU Side vs. 3 Con Opposing Side

ACLU Side (Petitioner/Appellant)

1. Goldberg, A. – Wrote majority opinion
2. Black, H. – Wrote concurring opinion
3. Douglas, W. – Wrote concurring opinion
4. Stewart, P. – Joined majority opinion
5. Brennan, W. – Joined majority opinion
6. Warren, E. – Joined majority opinion

Opposing Side (Respondent/Appellee)

1. Clark, T. – Wrote dissenting opinion
2. Harlan, J. – Joined Clark's dissent
3. White, B. – Joined Clark's dissent in part

VI. A WIN OR LOSS FOR THE ACLU?

The ACLU filed an amicus brief urging reversal; the Supreme Court reversed and remanded the District Court's ruling by a 6-3 vote, giving the ACLU an apparent win.

156. Beck v. Ohio

(Decided November 23, 1964; 379 U.S. 89)

I. ISSUE

A. Issues Discussed

Criminal procedure, Fourth Amendment, Fourteenth Amendment, probable cause

B. Legal Question Presented

Whether "the clearing house slips were wrongly admitted in evidence against [petitioner] because they had been seized by the Cleveland police in violation of the Fourth and Fourteenth Amendments."

C. Supreme Court's Answer

Because police arrested petitioner without probable cause, his arrest was in violation of the Fourth and Fourteenth Amendments. As a result, the evidence seized in the search incident to the arrest was inadmissible.

II. CASE SUMMARY

A. Background

Petitioner William Beck was driving his car in Cleveland, Ohio. Police officers had received unspecified information and reports about petitioner, indicating that he had a gambling record. The police officers stopped him and had "neither an arrest warrant nor a search warrant. Placing him under arrest, they searched his car but found nothing of interest. They then took him to a nearby police station where they searched his person and found an envelope containing a number of clearing house slips."

"The petitioner was subsequently charged in the Cleveland Municipal Court with possession of clearing house slips in violation of a state criminal statute. He filed a motion to suppress as evidence the clearing house slips in question, upon the ground that the police had obtained them by means of an unreasonable search and seizure in violation of the Fourth and Fourteenth Amendments. After a hearing the motion was overruled, the clearing house slips were admitted in evidence, and the petitioner was convicted. His conviction was affirmed by an Ohio Court of Appeals, and ultimately by the Supreme Court of Ohio . . . ."

The Supreme Court granted certiorari and reversed the conviction.

B. Counsel of Record/ACLU Attorney

ACLU Side (Petitioner/Appellant): James R. Willis argued the cause for appellant.

Opposing Side (Respondent/Appellee): William T. McKnight argued the cause for appellee.

III. AMICI CURIAE

ACLU Side (Petitioner/Appellant):

Brief of amici curiae filed on behalf of the ACLU, et al., by Bernard A. Berkman and Melvin L. Wulf.

Opposing Side (Respondent/Appellee)

Brief of amici curiae filed on behalf of the County of Cuyahoga, Ohio, by John T. Corrigan, Dennis J. McGuire, and James L. Oakar.

IV. THE SUPREME COURT'S DECISION

"There are limits to the permissible scope of a warrantless search incident to a lawful arrest, but we proceed on the premise that, if the arrest itself was lawful, those limits were not exceeded here. The constitutional validity of the search in this case, then, must depend upon the constitutional validity of the petitioner's arrest. Whether that arrest was constitutionally valid depends in turn upon whether, at the moment the arrest was made, the officers had probable cause to make it—whether at that moment the facts and circumstances within their knowledge and of which they had reasonably trustworthy information were sufficient to warrant a prudent man in believing that the petitioner had committed or was committing an offense. . . .

There is nowhere in the record any indication of what 'information' or 'reports' the officer had received, or, beyond what has been set out above, from what source the 'information' and 'reports' had come. [T]he officer testified to nothing that would indicate that any informer had said that the petitioner could be found at that time and place. And the record does not show that the officers saw the petitioner 'stop' before they arrested him, or that they saw, heard, smelled, or otherwise perceived anything else to give them ground for belief that the petitioner had acted or was then acting unlawfully. . . .

An arrest without a warrant bypasses the safeguards provided by an objective predetermination of probable cause, and substitutes instead the far less reliable procedure on an after-the-event justification for the arrest or search, too likely to be subtly influenced by the familiar shortcomings of hindsight judgment. . . . Yet even in cases where warrants were obtained, the Court has held that the Constitution demands a greater showing of probable cause than can be found in the present record.

When the constitutional validity of an arrest is challenged, it is the function of a court to determine whether the facts available to the officers at the moment of the arrest would 'warrant a man of reasonable caution in the belief' that an offense has been committed. . . . We do not hold that the officer's knowledge of the petitioner's physical appearance and previous record was either inadmissible or entirely irrelevant upon the issue of probable cause. But to hold knowledge of either or both of these facts constituted probable cause would be to hold that anyone with a previous criminal record could be arrested at will.

It is possible that an informer did in fact relate information to the police officer in this case which constituted probable cause for the petitioner's arrest. But when the constitutional validity of that arrest was challenged, it was incumbent upon the prosecution to show with considerably more specificity than was shown in this case what the informer actually said, and why the officer thought the information was credible. We may assume that the officers acted in good faith in arresting the petitioner. But 'good faith on the part of the arresting officers is not enough.' If subjective good faith alone were the test, the protections of the Fourth Amendment would evaporate, and the people would be 'secure in their persons, houses, papers, and effects,' only in the discretion of the police."

The Supreme Court reversed the judgment.

V. JUSTICE VOTE

6 Pro ACLU Side vs. 3 Con Opposing Side

ACLU Side (Petitioner/Appellant)

1. Stewart, P. – Wrote majority opinion
2. Warren, E. – Joined majority opinion
3. Douglas, W. – Joined majority opinion
4. Brennan, W. – Joined majority opinion
5. White, B. – Joined majority opinion
6. Goldberg, A. – Joined majority opinion

Opposing Side (Respondent/Appellee)

1. Clark, T. – Wrote dissenting opinion
2. Black, H. – Joined Clark's dissent
3. Harlan, J. – Wrote dissenting opinion

VI. A WIN OR LOSS FOR THE ACLU?

The ACLU filed an amicus brief urging reversal; the U.S. Supreme Court reversed the ruling of the Supreme Court of Ohio in a 6-3 vote, giving the ACLU an apparent win.

157. Calhoon v. Harvey

(Decided December 7, 1964; 379 U.S. 134)

I. ISSUE

A. Issues Discussed

Government authority, unions

B. Legal Question Presented

Can a federal District Court assert jurisdiction in an action under Title I of the Labor-Management Reporting and Disclosure Act of 1959, where the conduct at issue may also be subject to regulation by the Secretary of Labor under Title IV of such Act?

C. Supreme Court's Answer

The actions complained of in this case are governed by the complaint procedures in Title IV so the District Court does not have jurisdiction to decide the case.

II. CASE SUMMARY

A. Background

Respondents, members of National Marine Engineers' Beneficial Association, filed suit against the union and union leaders, "alleging that certain provisions of the union's bylaws and national constitution violated the [Labor-Management Reporting and Disclosure] Act" of 1959. Under the union's bylaws, members could nominate only themselves to office and eligibility for office was limited by the national constitution. Respondents argued that these limitations deprived them of "a fair opportunity to nominate any persons 'meeting fair and reasonable eligibility requirements . . . .'" Respondents asked the court to prohibit the union from holding any election until it revised its elections system to comply with the Act.

"The District Court dismissed for want of 'jurisdiction,' holding that the alleged conduct of the union, even if true, failed to show a denial of the equal rights of all members of the union to vote for or nominate candidates guaranteed by § 101(a)(1) of Title I of the Act, so as to give the District Court jurisdiction of the controversy under § 102. . . . The District Court further held that it could not exercise jurisdiction to protect § 401(e) rights because § 402(a) of Title IV provides a remedy, declared by § 403 to be 'exclusive,' authorizing members to vindicate such rights by challenging elections after they have been held, and then only by (1) first exhausting all remedies available with the union, (2) filing a complaint with the Secretary of Labor, who (3) may, after investigating the violation alleged in the complaint, bring suit in a United States district court to attack the validity of the election. The Court of Appeals reversed, holding that 'the complaint alleged a violation of § 101(a)(1) and that federal jurisdiction existed under § 102.'"

The Supreme Court granted certiorari, reversed the Court of Appeals, and affirmed the District Court.

B. COUNSEL OF RECORD

ACLU Side (Respondent/Appellee): Burton H. Hall argued the cause for appellee.

Opposing Side (Petitioner/Appellant): David Scribner argued the cause for appellant.

III. AMICI CURIAE

ACLU Side (Respondent/Appellee)

Brief of amici curiae filed on behalf of the ACLU by Melvin L. Wulf and Thomas G. S. Christensen.

Brief of amici curiae filed on behalf of the Workers Defense League by Rowland Watts and Irving A. Thau.

Opposing Side (Petitioner/Appellant)

Brief of amici curiae filed on behalf of the United States by Solicitor General Archibald Cox.

Brief of amici curiae filed on behalf of the American Federation of Labor and Congress of Industrial Organizations, by J. Albert Woll, Robert C. Mayer, Theodore J. St. Antoine, and Thomas E. Harris.

IV. THE SUPREME COURT'S DECISION

"Jurisdiction of the District Court under § 102 of Title I depends entirely upon whether this complaint showed a violation of rights guaranteed by § 101(a)(1), for we disagree with the Court of Appeals' holding that jurisdiction under § 102 can be upheld by reliance in whole or in part on allegations which in substance charge a breach of Title IV rights. . . . Title IV, not Title I, sets standards for eligibility and qualifications of candidates and officials and provides its own separate and different administrative and judicial procedure for challenging those standards. And the equal-rights language of § 101(a)(1) would have to be stretched far beyond its normal meaning to hold that it guarantees members not just a right to 'nominate candidates,' but a right to nominate anyone, without regard to valid union rules. . . .

Plainly, this is no more than a command that members and classes of members shall not be discriminated against in their right to nominate and vote. And Congress carefully prescribed that even this right against discrimination is 'subject to reasonable rules and regulations' by the union. The complaining union members here have not been discriminated against in any way and have been denied no privilege or right to vote or nominate which the union has granted to others. They have indeed taken full advantage of the uniform rule limiting nominations by nominating themselves for office. It is true that they were denied their request to be candidates, but that denial was not a discrimination against their right to nominate, since the same qualifications were required equally of all members. . . . The District Court therefore was without jurisdiction to grant the relief requested here unless, as the Court of Appeals held, the 'combined effect of the eligibility requirements and the restriction to self-nomination' is to be considered in determining whether § 101(a)(1) has been violated. . . .

We hold that possible violations of Title IV of the Act regarding eligibility are not relevant in determining whether or not a district court has jurisdiction under § 102 of Title I of the Act. Title IV sets up a statutory scheme governing the election of union officers . . . . Section 402 of Title IV . . . sets up an exclusive method for protecting Title IV rights, by permitting an individual member to file a complaint with the Secretary of Labor challenging the validity of any election because of violations of Title IV. Upon complaint the Secretary investigates and if he finds probable cause to believe that Title IV has been violated, he may file suit in the appropriate district court. It is apparent that Congress decided to utilize the special knowledge and discretion of the Secretary of Labor in order best to serve the public interest. . . . Reliance on the discretion of the Secretary is in harmony with the general congressional policy to allow unions great latitude in resolving their own internal controversies, and, where that fails, to utilize the agencies of Government most familiar with union problems to aid in bringing about a settlement through discussion before resort to the courts. [W]e are satisfied that the Act itself shows clearly by its structure and language that the disputes here, basically relating as they do to eligibility of candidates for office, fall squarely within Title IV of the Act and are to be resolved by the administrative and judicial procedures set out in that Title."

The Supreme Court reversed the judgment of the Court of Appeals and affirmed the judgment of the District Court.

V. JUSTICE VOTE

1 Pro ACLU Side vs. 8 Con Opposing Side

ACLU Side (Respondent/Appellee)

1. Douglas, W. – Wrote dissenting opinion

Opposing Side (Petitioner/Appellant)

1. Black, H. – Wrote majority opinion
2. Clark, T. – Joined majority opinion
3. Brennan, W. – Joined majority opinion
4. Goldberg, A. – Joined majority opinion
5. White, B. – Joined majority opinion
6. Stewart, P. – Wrote concurring opinion
7. Harlan, J. – Joined Stewart's concurrence
8. Warren, E. – Joined majority opinion

VI. A WIN OR LOSS FOR THE ACLU?

The ACLU filed an amicus brief urging affirmance; the Supreme Court reversed the ruling of the Court of Appeals for the Second Circuit in an 8-1 vote, giving the ACLU an apparent loss.

158. Freedman v. Maryland

(Decided March 1, 1965; 380 U.S. 51)

I. ISSUE

A. Issues Discussed

First Amendment, obscenity, censorship

B. Legal Question Presented

Did the Maryland censorship statute requiring films to be submitted to a censorship board violate First Amendment rights?

C. Supreme Court's Answer

The Maryland statute is unconstitutional because it lacks procedural safeguards necessary for this type of censorship system.

II. CASE SUMMARY

A. Background

A Maryland motion picture censorship statute required that all films be submitted to a board of censors before exhibition. Appellant violated the statute by exhibiting the film "Revenge at Daybreak" without first submitting the picture to the State Board of Censors as required by the statute. "The State concede[d] that the picture does not violate the statutory standards and would have received a license if properly submitted, but the appellant was convicted of a § 2 violation despite his contention that the statute in its entirety unconstitutionally impaired freedom of expression. The Court of Appeals of Maryland affirmed."

The Supreme Court granted certiorari and reversed.

B. Counsel of Record/ACLU Attorney

ACLU Side (Petitioner/Appellant): Felix J. Bilgrey argued the cause for appellant.

Opposing Side (Respondent/Appellee): Thomas B. Finan, Attorney General of Maryland, argued the cause for appellee.

III. AMICI CURIAE

ACLU Side (Petitioner/Appellant)

Brief of amici curiae filed on behalf of the ACLU, et al., by Edward De Grazia and Melvin L. Wulf.

Opposing Side (Respondent/Appellee)

No briefs of amici curiae were filed in support of appellee.

IV. THE SUPREME COURT'S DECISION

"In the area of freedom of expression it is well established that one has standing to challenge a statute on the ground that it delegates overly broad licensing discretion to an administrative office, whether or not his conduct could be proscribed by a properly drawn statute, and whether or not he applied for a license. [W]e think that appellant's assertion of a similar danger in the Maryland apparatus of censorship—one always fraught with danger and viewed with suspicion—gives him standing to make that challenge. In substance his argument is that, because the apparatus operates in a statutory context in which judicial review may be too little and too late, the Maryland statute lacks sufficient safeguards for confining the censor's action to judicially determined constitutional limits, and therefore contains the same vice as a statute delegating excessive administrative discretion.

[W]e hold that a noncriminal process which requires the prior submission of a film to a censor avoids constitutional infirmity only if it takes place under procedural safeguards designed to obviate the dangers of a censorship system. . . . The teaching of our cases is that, because only a judicial determination in an adversary proceeding ensures the necessary sensitivity to freedom of expression, only a procedure requiring a judicial determination suffices to impose a valid final restraint. To this end, the exhibitor must be assured, by statute or authoritative judicial construction, that the censor will, within a specified brief period, either issue a license or go to court to restrain showing the film. Any restraint imposed in advance of a final judicial determination on the merits must similarly be limited to preservation of the status quo for the shortest fixed period compatible with sound judicial resolution. Moreover, we are well aware that, even after expiration of a temporary restraint, an administrative refusal to license, signifying the censor's view that the film is unprotected, may have a discouraging effect on the exhibitor. Therefore, the procedure must also assure a prompt final judicial decision, to minimize the deterrent effect of an interim and possibly erroneous denial of a license. . . .

It is readily apparent that the Maryland procedural scheme does not satisfy these criteria. . . . Under the statute, appellant could have been convicted if he had shown the film after unsuccessfully seeking a license, even though no court had ever ruled on the obscenity of the film. [I]t is abundantly clear that the Maryland statute provides no assurance of prompt judicial determination. We hold, therefore, that appellant's conviction must be reversed. The Maryland scheme fails to provide adequate safeguards against undue inhibition of protected expression, and this renders the § 2 requirement of prior submission of films to the Board an invalid previous restraint. . . .

We think that the nature of the motion picture industry may suggest different time limits for a judicial determination. It is common knowledge that films are scheduled well before actual exhibition, and the requirement of advance submission in § 2 recognizes this. One possible scheme would be to allow the exhibitor or distributor to submit his film early enough to ensure an orderly final disposition of the case before the scheduled exhibition date—far enough in advance so that the exhibitor could safely advertise the opening on a normal basis. . . . We do not mean to lay down rigid time limits or procedures, but to suggest considerations in drafting legislation to accord with local exhibition practices, and in doing so to avoid the potentially chilling effect of the Maryland statute on protected expression."

The Supreme Court reversed the judgment.

V. JUSTICE VOTE

9 Pro ACLU Side vs. 0 Con Opposing Side

ACLU Side (Petitioner/Appellant)

1. Brennan, W. – Wrote majority opinion
2. Stewart, P. – Joined majority opinion
3. White, B. – Joined majority opinion
4. Goldberg, A. – Joined majority opinion
5. Harlan, J. – Joined majority opinion
6. Clark, T. – Joined majority opinion
7. Warren, E. – Joined majority opinion
8. Douglas, W. – Wrote concurring opinion
9. Black, H. – Joined Douglas' concurrence

VI. A WIN OR LOSS FOR THE ACLU?

The ACLU filed an amicus brief urging reversal; the Supreme Court reversed the ruling of the Court of Appeals of Maryland in a 9-0 vote, giving the ACLU an apparent win.

159. United States v. Mississippi

(Decided March 8, 1965; 380 U.S. 128)

I. ISSUE

A. Issues Discussed

Civil rights, Fourteenth and Fifteenth Amendments

B. Legal Question Presented

"[W]hether the dismissal for failure to state a claim upon which relief could be granted was proper."

C. Supreme Court's Answer

The case should have been tried as all of the grounds for dismissal were improper.

II. CASE SUMMARY

A. Background

"The United States by the Attorney General brought this action in the United States District Court for the Southern District of Mississippi, Jackson Division, against the State of Mississippi, the three members of the Mississippi State Board of Election

Commissioners, and six county Registrars of Voters. The complaint charged that the defendants and their agents had engaged and, unless restrained, would continue to engage in acts and practices hampering and destroying the right of Negro citizens of Mississippi to vote, in violation of 42 U.S.C. § 1971(a), and of the Fourteenth and Fifteenth Amendments and Article I of the United States Constitution." The practices hampering the right to vote, amended over the years, included a "good moral character" determination, various requirements to interpret the Mississippi Constitution, not keeping records of applications to vote, and requiring voters to fill out their applications without assistance and with no "formal, technical, or inconsequential errors" on the form.

"[B]ecause the complaint charged that provisions of the state constitution and statutes pertaining to voter registration violated the United States Constitution, the case was heard by three judges, pursuant to 28 U.S.C. § 2281." The defendants moved for dismissal and the District Court dismissed the case for failure to state a claim upon which relief could be granted, among other grounds.

The Supreme Court granted certiorari and reversed.

B. Counsel of Record/ACLU Attorney

ACLU Side (Petitioner/Appellant): Solicitor General Archibald Cox argued the cause for appellant.

Opposing Side (Respondent/Appellee): Charles Clark, Special Assistant Attorney General of Mississippi, argued the cause for appellee.

III. AMICI CURIAE

ACLU Side (Petitioner/Appellant)

Brief of amici curiae filed on behalf of the ACLU by Francis Biddle, Norman Dorsen, and Melvin L. Wulf.

Opposing Side (Respondent/Appellee)

No briefs of amici curiae were filed in support of appellee.

IV. THE SUPREME COURT'S DECISION

"Section 1971(a) guarantees the right of citizens 'who are otherwise qualified by law to vote at any election' to be allowed to vote 'without distinction of race, color, or previous condition of servitude; any constitution, law, custom, usage, or regulation of any State or Territory, or by or under its authority, to the contrary notwithstanding.' And subsection (c) of § 1971 specifically authorizes the Attorney General to file proper proceedings for preventive relief to protect this right to vote without discrimination on account of color whenever any person has engaged or there are reasonable grounds to believe that any person is about to engage in any act or practice which would deprive any other person of that right. . . .

The Fifteenth Amendment protects the right to vote regardless of race against any denial or abridgment by the United States or by any State. Section 1971 was passed by Congress under the authority of the Fifteenth Amendment to enforce that Amendment's guarantee, which protects against any discrimination by a State, its laws, its customs, or its officials in any way. We reject the argument that the Attorney General was without power to institute these proceedings in order to protect the federally guaranteed right to vote without discrimination on account of color.

[I]t seems rather surprising that the District Court entertained seriously the argument that the United States could not constitutionally sue a State. The reading of the Constitution urged by Mississippi is not supported by precedent, is not required by any language of the Constitution, and would without justification in reason diminish the power of courts to protect the people of this country against deprivation and destruction by States of their federally guaranteed rights. We hold that the State was properly made a defendant in this case. . . .

The District Court held with respect to the three members of the Mississippi Board of Election Commissioners that the complaint failed to show that they had a sufficient interest in administering or enforcing the laws under attack to permit making them parties defendant. We do not agree. . . . Therefore the Election Commissioners should not have been stricken as defendants. . . .

These registrars were alleged to be carrying on activities which were part of a series of transactions or occurrences the validity of which depended to a large extent upon 'question[s] of law or fact common to all of them.' Since joinder of the registrars in one suit was proper, the argument that venue as to some of them was not properly laid is also without merit. . . .

We have no doubt whatsoever that it was error to dismiss the complaint without a trial. The complaint charged that the State of Mississippi and its officials for the past three quarters of a century have been writing and adopting constitutional provisions, statutes, rules, and regulations, and have been engaging in discriminatory practices, all designed to keep the number of white voters at the highest possible figure and the number of colored voters at the lowest. . . . The allegations of this complaint were too serious, the right to vote in this country too precious, and the necessity of settling grievances peacefully in the courts too important for tis complaint to have been dismissed. . . . This case should have been tried. It should now be tried without delay."

The Supreme Court reversed and remanded.

V. JUSTICE VOTE

9 Pro ACLU Side vs. 0 Con Opposing Side

ACLU Side (Petitioner/Appellant)

1. Black, H. – Wrote majority opinion
2. Douglas, W. – Joined majority opinion
3. Brennan, W. – Joined majority opinion
4. White, B. – Joined majority opinion
5. Harlan, J. – Wrote concurring opinion
6. Warren, E. – Joined majority opinion
7. Clark, T. – Joined majority opinion
8. Goldberg, A. – Joined majority opinion
9. Stewart, P. – Joined majority opinion

VI. A WIN OR LOSS FOR THE ACLU?

The ACLU filed an amicus brief urging reversal; the Supreme Court reversed and remanded in a 9-0 vote, giving the ACLU an apparent win.

160. United States v. Seeger

(Decided March 8, 1965; 380 U.S. 163)

I. ISSUE

A. Issues Discussed

Freedom of religion, conscientious objectors

B. Legal Question Presented

Is § 6(j) of the Universal Military Training and Service Act, which defines the term "religious training and belief" as "an individual's belief in a relation to a Supreme Being involving duties superior to those arising from any human relation, but [not including] essentially political, sociological, or philosophical views or a merely personal moral code," constitutional?

C. Supreme Court's Answer

Defining the meaning of "belief in a relation to a Supreme Being," the Court upheld § 6(j) and determined that all three challengers fell within the definition.

II. CASE SUMMARY

A. Background

Three separate cases involving claims of conscientious objectors were consolidated in this case.

Section 6(j) of the Universal Military Training and Service Act exempted conscientious objectors from military service, provided that their belief in a Supreme Being requires "duties superior to those arising from any human relation." All three cases involved challenges to the constitutionality of this section

In case No. 50, Seeger believed that "the cosmic order does, perhaps, suggest a creative intelligence" and he criticized "the tremendous 'spiritual' price man must pay for his willingness to destroy human life." He "was convicted in the District Court for the Southern District of New York of having refused to submit to induction in the armed forces." His conviction was reversed by the Court of Appeals for the Second Circuit.

In case No. 51, Jakobson "believed in a 'Supreme Being' who was 'Creator of Man' in the sense of being 'ultimately responsible for the existence of' man and who was 'the Supreme Reality' of which 'the existence of man is the result.'" He was similarly convicted, and his conviction reversed by the Court of Appeals for the Second Circuit.

In case No. 29, Peter, although not sure of his belief in a "Supreme Being," stated that "he felt it a violation of his moral code to take human life and that he considered this belief superior to his obligation to the state," citing to "a definition of religion as 'the consciousness of some power manifest in nature which helps man in the ordering of his life in harmony with its demands . . . .'" He was convicted in the District Court for the Northern District of California, and his conviction affirmed by the Court of Appeals for the Ninth Circuit.

On certiorari the Supreme Court found that the beliefs of the objectors in all three cases met the criteria of § 6(j), affirming the judgments of the Court of Appeals for the Second Circuit in Nos. 50 and 51 and reversing the judgment of the Court of Appeals for the Ninth Circuit in No. 29.

B. Counsel of Record / ACLU Attorney

ACLU Side (Petitioner / Appellant in No. 29, Respondent / Appellee in Nos. 50 and 51): Duane B. Beeson argued the cause and filed a brief for appellant in No. 29. Kenneth W. Greenawalt argued the cause for appellee in No. 50. Herman Adlerstein argued the cause for appellee in No. 51.

Opposing Side (Respondent / Appellee in No. 29, Petitioner / Appellant in Nos. 50 and 51): Solicitor General Cox argued the cause for appellee in No. 29 and appellant in Nos. 50 and 51.

III. AMICI CURIAE

ACLU Side (Petitioner / Appellant in No. 29, Respondent / Appellee in Nos. 50 and 51):

Brief of amici curiae filed on behalf of the ACLU by Alfred Lawrence Toombs and Melvin L. Wulf.

Brief of amici curiae filed on behalf of the American Jewish Congress by Leo Pfeffer, Shad Polier, Will Maslow and Joseph B. Robison.

Brief of amici curiae filed on behalf of the American Ethical Union by Herbert A. Wolff, Leo Rosen, Nanette Dembitz, Nancy F. Wechsler, and Greenbaum, Wolff & Ernst.

Brief of amici curiae filed on behalf of the American Humanist Association by Tolbert H. McCarroll, Lester Forest, and Paul Blanshard.

Opposing Side (Respondent / Appellee in No. 29, Petitioner / Appellant in Nos. 50 and 51):

No briefs of amici curiae were filed in support of appellee in No. 29 and appellant in Nos. 50 and 51.

IV. THE SUPREME COURT'S DECISION

"We have concluded that Congress, in using the expression 'Supreme Being' rather than the designation 'God,' was merely clarifying the meaning of religious training and belief so as to embrace all religions and to exclude essentially political, sociological, or philosophical views. We believe that under this construction, the test of belief 'in a relation to a Supreme Being' is whether a given belief that is sincere and meaningful occupies a place in the life of its possessor parallel to that filled by the orthodox belief in God of one who clearly qualifies for the exemption. Where such beliefs have parallel positions in the lives of their respective holders we cannot say that one is 'in a relation to a Supreme Being' and the other is not. We have concluded that the beliefs of the objectors in these cases meet these criteria, and, accordingly, we affirm the judgments in Nos. 50 and 51 and reverse the judgment in No. 29. . . .

But we hasten to emphasize that while the 'truth' of a belief is not open to question, there remains the significant question whether it is 'truly held.' This is the threshold question of sincerity which must be resolved in every case. It is, of course, a question of fact—a prime consideration to the validity of every claim for exemption as a conscientious objector. The Act provides a comprehensive scheme for assisting the Appeal Boards in making this determination, placing at their service the facilities of the Department of Justice, including the Federal Bureau of Investigation and hearing officers."

The Supreme Court affirmed the judgments of the Court of Appeals for the Second Circuit in Nos. 50 and 51, and reversed the judgment of the Court of Appeals for the Ninth Circuit in No. 29.

V. JUSTICE VOTE

9 Pro ACLU Side vs. 0 Con Opposing Side

ACLU Side (Petitioner/Appellant in No. 29, Respondent/Appellee in Nos. 50 and 51):

1. Brennan, W. – Wrote majority opinion
2. Douglas, W. – Wrote concurring opinion
3. Black, H. – Joined majority opinion
4. Clark, T. – Joined majority opinion
5. White, B. – Joined majority opinion
6. Harlan, J. – Joined majority opinion
7. Warren, E. – Joined majority opinion
8. Goldberg, A. – Joined majority opinion
9. Stewart, P. – Joined majority opinion

VI. A WIN OR LOSS FOR THE ACLU?

The ACLU, as amicus curiae, urged affirmance in Nos. 50 and 51 and reversal in No. 29 of the judgments of the Court of Appeals for the Second and Ninth Circuits; the Supreme Court affirmed Nos. 50 and 51 and reversed No. 29 in a 9-0 vote, giving the ACLU an apparent win.

161. Dombrowski v. Pfister

(Decided April 26, 1965; 380 U.S. 479)

I. ISSUE

A. Issues Discussed

Civil rights, freedom of speech, judicial power

B. Legal Question Presented

Whether appellants can receive an injunction preventing the Louisiana Subversive Activities and Communist Control Law and the Communist Propaganda Control Law from being enforced against them in a way that threatens their constitutional rights.

C. Supreme Court's Answer

Appellants can receive an injunction, the scope of which will be determined on remand, against enforcement of the laws against them in order to protect their constitutional rights.

II. CASE SUMMARY

A. Background

Appellants, Southern Conference Educational Fund (SCEF), a civil rights organization, and its executive director, and other individuals, brought suit in the District Court for the Eastern District of Louisiana for injunctive relief to prevent appellees, "the Governor, police and law enforcement officers, and the Chairman of the Legislative Joint Committee on Un-American Activities in Louisiana", from prosecuting "appellants for alleged violations of the Louisiana Subversive Activities and Communist Control Law and the Communist Propaganda Control Law."

Appellants contended that the statutes were overbroad, violated their right of free expression under the First and Fourteenth Amendments, and were being used by appellees in bad faith, with the purpose of harassing appellants to deter their civil rights efforts. A three-judge District Court dismissed the complaint, and also held "this was an appropriate case for abstention, since a possible narrowing construction by the state courts would avoid unnecessary decision of constitutional questions."

The Supreme Court granted certiorari to address the issue "concerning federal injunctions against state criminal prosecutions threatening constitutionally protected expression" and reversed.

B. Counsel of Record/ACLU Attorney

ACLU Side (Petitioner/Appellant): Leon Hubert and Arthur Kinoy argued the cause for appellant.

Opposing Side (Respondent/Appellee): John E. Jackson, Jr. and Jack N. Rogers argued the cause for appellee. Robert J. Reiter filed a brief for appellee Davis. Jim Garrison, District Attorney for the Parish of Orleans, Charles R. Ward, First Executive Assistant District Attorney, Louise Korns, Assistant District Attorney, and John Volz, Assistant District Attorney, filed a brief for appellee Garrison.

III. AMICI CURIAE

ACLU Side (Petitioner/Appellant)

Brief of amici curiae filed on behalf of the ACLU, et al., by Louis Lusky, Melvin L. Wulf, and Leonard Dreyfus.

Briefs of amicus curiae filed on behalf of the NAACP Legal Defense and Education Fund by Jack Greenberg, Derrick A. Bell, Jr., Jay H. Topkis, and Anthony G. Amsterdam.

Brief of amici curiae filed on behalf of the National Lawyers Guild by Ernest Goodman and David Rein.

Opposing Side (Respondent/Appellee)

No briefs of amici curiae were filed in support of appellee.

IV. THE SUPREME COURT'S DECISION

"In considering whether injunctive relief should be granted, a federal district court should consider a statute as of the time its jurisdiction is invoked, rather than some hypothetical future date. . . . Here, no readily apparent construction suggests itself as a vehicle for rehabilitating the statutes in a single prosecution, and appellants are entitled to an injunction. The State must, if it is to invoke the statutes after injunctive relief has been sought, assume the burden of obtaining a permissible narrow construction in a noncriminal proceeding before it may seek modification of the injunction to permit future prosecutions.

On this view of the 'vagueness' doctrine, it is readily apparent that abstention serves no legitimate purpose where a statute regulating speech is properly attacked on its face, and where, as here, the conduct charged in the indictments is not within the reach of an acceptable limiting construction readily to be anticipated as the result of a single criminal prosecution and is not the sort of 'hardcore' conduct that would obviously be prohibited under any construction. In these circumstances, to abstain is to subject those affected to the uncertainties and vagaries of criminal prosecution, whereas the reasons for the vagueness doctrine in the area of expression demand no less than freedom from prosecution prior to a construction adequate to save the statute. In such cases, abstention is at war with the purposes of the vagueness doctrine, which demands appropriate federal relief regardless of the prospects for expeditious determination of state criminal prosecutions. Although we hold today that appellants' allegations of threats to prosecute, if upheld, dictate appropriate equitable relief without awaiting declaratory judgments in the state courts, the settled rule of our cases is that district courts retain power to modify injunctions in light of changed circumstances. Our view of the proper operation of the vagueness doctrine does not preclude district courts from modifying injunctions to permit prosecutions in light of subsequent state court interpretation clarifying the application of a state to particular conduct.

We conclude that on the allegations of the complaint, if true, abstention and the denial of injunctive relief may well result in the denial of any effective safeguards against the loss of protected freedoms of expression, and cannot be justified. . . .

The precise terms and scope of the injunctive relief to which appellants are entitled and the identity of the appellees to be enjoined cannot, of course, be determined until after the District Court conducts the hearing on remand. The record suffices, however, to permit this Court to hold that, without the benefit of limiting construction, the statutory provisions on which the indictments are founded are void on their face; until an acceptable limiting construction is obtained, the provisions cannot be applied to the activities of SCEF, whatever they may be. . . . In view of our decision on the merits, the District Court on remand need decide only the relief to which appellants may be entitled on the basis of their attacks on other sections of that statute and the Communist Propaganda Control Law, and on their allegations that appellees threaten to enforce both statutes solely to discourage appellants from continuing their civil rights activities. On these issues, abstention will be as inappropriate as on the issues we here decide."

The Supreme Court reversed the judgment and remanded the case.

V. JUSTICE VOTE

5 Pro ACLU Side vs. 2 Con Opposing Side

ACLU Side (Petitioner/Appellant)

1. Brennan, W. – Wrote majority opinion
2. White, B. – Joined majority opinion
3. Goldberg, A. – Joined majority opinion
4. Warren, E. – Joined majority opinion
5. Douglas, W. – Joined majority opinion

Opposing Side (Respondent/Appellee)

1. Harlan, J. – Wrote dissenting opinion
2. Clark, T. – Joined dissenting opinion

Black, H. Took no part in the decision
Stewart, P. Took no part in the decision

VI. A WIN OR LOSS FOR THE ACLU?

The ACLU filed an amicus brief urging reversal; the Supreme Court reversed the ruling of the District Court in a 5-2 vote, giving the ACLU an apparent win.

162. American Committee for Protection of Foreign Born v. Subversive Activities Control Board

(Decided April 26, 1965; 380 U.S. 503)

I. ISSUE

A. Issues Discussed

Governmental authority

B. Legal Question Presented

Is the American Committee for Protection of Foreign Born required to register as a Communist-front organization because it "is substantially directed, dominated, or controlled by a Communist-action organization," and "is primarily operated for the purpose of giving aid and support to a Communist action organization"?

C. Supreme Court's Answer

The evidence used to make the determination must be updated to determine whether it is still appropriate to require the American Committee for Protection of Foreign Born to register as a Communist-front organization.

II. CASE SUMMARY

A. Background

The Subversive Activities Control Board ("Board") found the American Committee for the Protection of Foreign Born ("Committee") was a Communist-front organization because it was "substantially directed, dominated, or controlled by a Communist-action organization, "and it "primarily operated for the purpose of giving aid and support to a Communist-action organization." This finding led to an order for the Committee to register as a Communist front organization. The primary evidence in the case dealt with one individual, Abner Green, a Communist Party member who was executive secretary of the Committee. He died before the Board ordered the Committee to register. On appeal, the Court of Appeals for the District of Columbia Circuit affirmed the order.

The Supreme Court granted certiorari, vacated the judgment, and remanded the case.

B. Counsel of Record/ACLU Attorney

ACLU Side (Petitioner/Appellant): Joseph Forer argued the cause for appellant.

Opposing Side (Respondent/Appellee): Bruce J. Terris argued the cause for appellee.

III. AMICI CURIAE

ACLU Side (Petitioner/Appellant)

Brief of amici curiae filed on behalf of the ACLU by Melvin L. Wulf and Marvin M. Karpatkin.

Opposing Side (Respondent/Appellee)

No briefs of amici curiae were filed in support of appellee.

IV. THE SUPREME COURT'S DECISION

"In the present case the Board's findings that petitioner is a 'Communist front' were based primarily upon evidence taken at a hearing which was concluded in 1955. The findings which support the conclusion that the petitioner is controlled by and primarily operated for the purpose of giving aid and support to the Communist Party rest in substantial measure upon evidence of the activities of Abner Green, found to be a Party member expressly assigned in 1941 to be petitioner's executive secretary. Green died in 1959. The Board's order was filed on June 27, 1960, but the record discloses no findings or evidence concerning petitioner's activities after Green's death. In the circumstances we think that the record should be brought up to date to take account of supervening events. Since a registration order operates prospectively, it is apparent that reasonably current aid and control must be established to justify a registration order. Our Communist Party decision on the Communist-action provisions did not necessarily foreclose petitioner's constitutional questions bearing on the Communist-front provisions. Since petitioner's current status is not clear on this record, decision of the serious constitutional questions raised by the order is neither necessary nor appropriate.

The judgment of the Court of Appeals is vacated, and the cause remanded for proceedings consistent with this opinion."

V. JUSTICE VOTE

5 PRO ACLU SIDE VS. 3 CON OPPOSING SIDE

ACLU Side (Petitioner/Appellant)

1. Warren, E. – Per curiam decision
2. Clark, T. – Per curiam decision
3. Brennan, W. – Per curiam decision
4. Stewart, P. – Per curiam decision
5. Goldberg, A. – Per curiam decision

Opposing Side (Respondent/Appellee)

1. Douglas, W. – Wrote dissenting opinion
2. Black, H. – Joined dissenting opinion
3. Harlan, J. – Joined dissenting opinion White, B – Took no part in the decision

VI. A WIN OR LOSS FOR THE ACLU?

The ACLU filed an amicus brief urging reversal; the Supreme Court vacated the Court of Appeals for the District of Columbia Circuit and remanded the case in a 5-3 vote, giving the ACLU an apparent win.

163. Veterans of the Abraham Lincoln Brigade v. Subversive Activities Control Board

(Decided April 26, 1965; 380 U.S. 513)

I. ISSUE

A. Issues Discussed

First Amendment, freedom of speech and of association

B. Legal Question Presented

Whether petitioner was properly ordered to register under § 7 of the Subversive Activities Control Act of 1950.

C. Supreme Court's Answer

Declining to address the constitutional issues, the Court vacated the judgment and remanded the case.

II. CASE SUMMARY

A. Background

Petitioner Veterans of the Abraham Lincoln Brigade consisted of Americans who fought in the Spanish Civil War on the side of the Republican Army in the late 1930s. Approximately 3,000 American youths were members of the Abraham Lincoln Brigade, and, of these, only 1,800 survived. Many of the survivors became members of Veterans of the Abraham Lincoln Brigade. The brigade came under scrutiny by the Subversive Activities Control Board, which determined the brigade was a "Communist-front organization."[1]

"Petitioner was ordered by the Subversive Activities Control Board to register as a Communist front organization under § 7 of the Subversive Activities Control Act of 1950, . . . and the Court of Appeals for the District of Columbia Circuit affirmed."

B. Counsel of Record/ACLU Attorney

ACLU Side (Petitioner/Appellant): Leonard B. Boudin argued the cause for appellant.

Opposing Side (Respondent/Appellee): Kevin T. Maroney and Bruce J. Terris argued the cause for appellee.

III. AMICI CURIAE

ACLU Side (Petitioner/Appellant)

Brief of amici curiae filed on behalf of the ACLU by Melvin L. Wulf and Marvin M. Karpatkin.

1 Veterans of the Abraham Lincoln Brigade v. Subversive Activities Control Board, 331 F.2d 64 (D.C. Cir. 1963).

Opposing Side (Respondent/Appellee)

No briefs of amici curiae were filed in support of appellee.

IV. THE SUPREME COURT'S DECISION

"In this case, the order to register was based almost exclusively on events before 1950, and very largely on events before 1940. The hearings themselves were concluded in November 1954, more than 10 years ago. On so stale a record we do not think it is either necessary or appropriate that we decide the serious constitutional questions raised by the order. The judgment is vacated and the cause remanded for proceedings consistent with this opinion."

V. JUSTICE VOTE

5 Pro ACLU Side vs. 3 Con Opposing Side

ACLU Side (Petitioner/Appellant)

1. Warren, E. – Per curiam decision
2. Clark, T. – Per curiam decision
3. Brennan, W. – Per curiam decision
4. Stewart, P. – Per curiam decision
5. Goldberg, A. – Per curiam decision

Opposing Side (Respondent/Appellee)

1. Douglas, W. – Wrote dissenting opinion
2. Black, H. – Joined dissenting opinion
3. Harlan, J. – Joined dissenting opinion

White, B – Took no part in the decision

VI. A WIN OR LOSS FOR THE ACLU?

The ACLU filed as amicus curiae urging reversal; the Supreme Court, in a per curiam opinion, vacated the order of the Court of Appeals in a 5-3 vote, giving the ACLU an apparent win.

164. Zemel v. Rusk

(Decided May 3, 1965; 381 U.S. 1)

I. ISSUE

A. Issues Discussed

Governmental authority, separation of powers, right to travel

B. Legal Question Presented

"[W]hether the Secretary of State is statutorily authorized to refuse to validate passports of United States citizens for travel to Cuba, and, if he is, whether the exercise of that authority is constitutionally permissible."

C. Supreme Court's Answer

The Secretary of State is statutorily authorized to refuse to validate passports for travel to Cuba and this exercise of authority is constitutionally permissible.

II. CASE SUMMARY

A. Background

"Prior to 1961 no passport was required for travel anywhere in the Western Hemisphere. On January 3 of that year, the United States broke diplomatic and consular relations with Cuba. On January 16 the Department of State eliminated Cuba from the area for which passports were not required, and declared all outstanding United States passports (except those held by persons already in Cuba) to be invalid for travel to or in Cuba 'unless specifically endorsed for such travel under the authority of the Secretary of State.' A companion press release stated that the Department contemplated granting exceptions to 'persons whose travel may be regarded as being in the best interests of the United States, such as newsmen or businessmen with previously established business interests.'

Through an exchange of letters in early 1962, appellant, a citizen of the United States and holder of an otherwise valid passport, applied to the State Department to have his passport validated for travel to Cuba as a tourist. His request was denied. On October 30, 1962, he renewed the request, stating that the purpose of the proposed trip was 'to satisfy my curiosity about the state of affairs in Cuba and to make me a better informed citizen.' The request again was denied, on the ground that the purpose of the trip did not meet the previously prescribed standards for such travel."

Appellant filed suit in the United States District Court for the District of Connecticut. He argued that it was unconstitutional for the Secretary of State and Attorney General to impose these travel restrictions, and that his passport should be validated for the purpose of traveling to Cuba.

A three-judge court "granted the Secretary of State's motion for summary judgment and dismissed the action against the Attorney General."

Appellant granted certiorari and affirmed.

B. Counsel of Record/ACLU Attorney

ACLU Side (Petitioner/Appellant): Leonard B. Boudin argued the cause for appellant.

Opposing Side (Respondent/Appellee): Solicitor General Archibald Cox argued the cause for appellee.

III. AMICI CURIAE

ACLU Side (Petitioner/Appellant)

Brief of amici curiae filed on behalf of the ACLU by Edward J. Ennis and Melvin L. Wulf.

Brief of amici curiae filed on behalf of Anatol Schlosser by Isidore Englander and Joseph Forer.

Opposing Side (Respondent/Appellee)

No briefs of amici curiae were filed in support of appellee.

IV. THE SUPREME COURT'S DECISION

"We hold that the three-judge court was properly convened, and that we therefore have jurisdiction over the appeal. . . .

We think that the Passport Act of 1926, embodies a grant of authority to the Executive to refuse to validate the passports of

United States citizens for travel to Cuba. . . . We think, particularly in view of the President's statutory obligation to 'use such means, not amounting to acts of war, as he may think necessary and proper' to secure the release of an American citizen unjustly deprived of his liberty by a foreign government, that the Secretary has justifiably concluded that travel to Cuba by American citizens might involve the Nation in dangerous international incidents, and that the Constitution does not require him to validate passports for such travel.

The right to travel within the United States is of course also constitutionally protected. But that freedom does not mean that areas ravaged by flood, fire or pestilence cannot be quarantined when it can be demonstrated that unlimited travel to the area would directly and materially interfere with the safety and welfare of the area or the Nation as a whole. So it is with international travel. That the restriction which is challenged in this case is supported by the weightiest considerations of national security is perhaps best pointed up by recalling that the Cuban missile crisis of October 1962 preceded the filing of appellant's complaint by less than two months. . . .

This does not mean that simply because a statute deals with foreign relations, it can grant the Executive totally unrestricted freedom of choice. However, the 1926 Act contains no such grant. We have held, Kent v. Dulles, and reaffirm today, that the 1926 Act must take its content from history: it authorizes only those passport refusals and restrictions 'which it could fairly be argued were adopted by Congress in light of prior administrative practice.' So limited, the Act does not constitute an invalid delegation."

The Supreme Court affirmed the judgment.

V. JUSTICE VOTE

3 Pro ACLU Side vs. 6 Con Opposing Side

ACLU Side (Petitioner/Appellant)

1. Black, H. – Wrote dissenting opinion
2. Douglas, W. – Wrote dissenting opinion
3. Goldberg, A. – Wrote dissenting opinion, joined Douglas' dissent

Opposing Side (Respondent/Appellee)

1. Warren, E. – Wrote majority opinion
2. Clark, T. – Joined majority opinion
3. Harlan, J. – Joined majority opinion
4. Brennan, W. – Joined majority opinion
5. Stewart, P. – Joined majority opinion
6. White, B. – Joined majority opinion

VI. A WIN OR LOSS FOR THE ACLU?

The ACLU filed an amicus brief urging reversal; the Supreme Court affirmed the ruling of the District Court in a 6-3 vote, giving the ACLU an apparent loss.

165. Holt v. Virginia

(Decided May 17, 1965; 381 U.S. 131)

I. ISSUE

A. Issues Discussed

Civil procedure

B. Legal Question Presented

Whether punishment for lawyers engaged in contempt proceedings was appropriate in these circumstances.

C. Supreme Court's Answer

"Our conclusion is that these petitioners have been punished by Virginia for doing nothing more than exercising the constitutional right of an accused and his counsel in contempt cases such as this to defend against the charges made."

II. CASE SUMMARY

A. Background

"The petitioners, both . . . lawyers, were adjudged guilty and each was fined $50 for contempt of court . . . . The Virginia Supreme Court of Appeals affirmed, rejecting petitioners' contentions that their convictions violated the Due Process Clause of the Fourteenth Amendment. . . .

Petitioner Dawley represented certain defendants in a libel suit . . . . The libel case was dismissed . . . . Judge Holladay had the court clerk and counsel, including the petitioner Dawley, come into the judge's chambers and there the judge asked Dawley three times if he had had anything to do with making the defendants in the libel case 'unavailable to be served with subpoenas.' Dawley refused to answer . . . . Judge Holladay then directed the Commonwealth's Attorney to prepare an order directing Dawley to show cause why he should not be punished for contempt. Dawley thereafter filed a motion requesting Judge Holladay to disqualify himself from trying the contempt case. Judge Holladay denied this motion. Dawley then filed a motion for change of venue. Petitioner Holt appeared as counsel representing Dawley . . . . It is upon the allegations about Judge Holladay in that motion . . . that the present convictions for contempt are based. . . .

Thereafter the judge denied the motion for change of venue and fined each petitioner $50.

The Virginia Supreme Court of Appeals, in affirming, held that the language used in the motion violated Va. Code Ann. s 18.1—292, which authorizes summary punishment of a person who misbehaves in the presence of the court so as to obstruct justice, or who uses '(v)ile, contemptuous or insulting language' to or about a judge in respect of his official acts."

The Supreme Court granted certiorari to review the case.

B. Counsel of Record

ACLU Side (Petitioner/Appellant): Marvin M. Karpatkin argued the cause for appellants. With him on the brief were Melvin L. Wulf (ACLU legal director 1962-1977), Leslie Harold Levinson, Joseph A. Jordan, Edward A. Dawley, and Leonard W. Holt.

Opposing Side (Respondent/Appellee): Francis C. Lee argued the cause for appellee. With him on the brief were Robert Y. Button, Attorney General of Virginia, and D. Gardiner Tyler, Assistant Attorney General.

III. AMICI CURIAE

ACLU Side (Petitioner/Appellant)

No briefs of amici curiae were filed in support of appellants.

Opposing Side (Respondent/Appellee)

No briefs of amici curiae were filed in support of appellee.

IV. THE SUPREME COURT'S DECISION

"Petitioners contend that their convictions through this application of the state law to them in several respects deny due process of law guaranteed by the Due Process Clause of the Fourteenth Amendment. The view we take regarding one of these contentions makes it unnecessary for us to consider the others.

It is not charged that petitioners here disobeyed any valid court order, talked loudly, acted boisterously, or attempted to prevent the judge or any other officer of the court from carrying on his court duties. Their convictions rest on nothing whatever except allegations made in motions for change of venue and disqualification of Judge Holladay because of alleged bias on his part. It is not claimed, and probably could not seriously be claimed, that petitioners, by filing their motions, violated any duty they owed the court. . . .

[T]he words used in the motions were plain English, in no way offensive in themselves, and wholly appropriate to charge bias in the community and bias of the presiding judge. The Supreme Court of Appeals of Virginia considered the motion for change of venue 'a vehicle to heap insults upon the court, a studied attempt to smear the judge.' But if the charges were 'insulting' it was inherent in the issue of bias raised, an issue which we have seen had to be raised, according to the charges, to escape the probability of a constitutionally unfair trial. Virginia apparently contends here that the right to present a defense is not involved in this case either (1) because the motion for change of venue was not in the proper form and not authorized by state law in such circumstances, or (2) because the charges of bias were false. As to the first argument, assuming it could have any relevance where a defendant asserts a federally guaranteed right to a fair trial, the motion for change of venue was duly filed with the clerk, and the trial court without objection set it down for hearing, specifically invited argument on it, and decided the motion on the merits, without any intimation that a motion for change of venue was not proper in these circumstances. Nor can we accept Virginia's apparent contention that the contempt convictions should be sustained on the ground that petitioners' charges of bias were false. The issue of truth or falsity of these charges was not heard, the trial court choosing instead to convict and sentence petitioners for having done nothing more than make the charges. Even if failure to prove their allegations of bias could under any circumstances ever be made part of the basis of a contempt charge against petitioners, these convictions cannot rest on any such unproven assumption.

Our conclusion is that these petitioners have been punished by Virginia for doing nothing more than exercising the constitutional right of an accused and his counsel in contempt cases such as this to defend against the charges made. The judgment of conviction is reversed and the cause is remanded to the Supreme Court of Appeals of Virginia . . . ."

V. JUSTICE VOTE

8 Pro ACLU Side vs. 1 Con Opposing Side

ACLU Side (Petitioner/Appellant)

1. Black, H. – Wrote majority opinion
2. Warren, E. – Joined majority opinion
3. Brennan, W. – Joined majority opinion
4. Douglas, W. – Joined majority opinion
5. Goldberg, A. – Joined majority opinion
6. Stewart, P. – Joined majority opinion
7. Clark, T. – Joined majority opinion
8. White, B. – Joined majority opinion

Opposing Side (Respondent/Appellee)

1. Harlan, J. – Wrote dissenting opinion

VI. A WIN OR LOSS FOR THE ACLU?

The ACLU served as counsel for appellants urging reversal of the judgment of the Supreme Court of Appeals of Virginia; the U.S. Supreme Court reversed in an 8-1 vote, giving the ACLU an apparent win.

166. Lamont v. Postmaster General of the United States

(Decided May 24, 1965; 381 U.S. 301)

I. ISSUE

A. Issues Discussed

Governmental authority, First Amendment, Fifth Amendment

B. Legal Question Presented

"[I]s § 305(a) of the Postal Service and Federal Employees Salary Act of 1962 constitutional as construed and applied?"

C. Supreme Court's Answer

The Act as construct and applied is unconstitutional because the requirement to sign and return a card to receive the detained mail infringes on First Amendment rights.

II. CASE SUMMARY

A. Background

In No. 491, appellant Dr. Lamont challenged the constitutionality of § 305(a) of the Postal Service and Federal Employees Salary Act of 1962, which requires the Postmaster General to detain and deliver, only upon the addressee's request after receiving notification, unsealed foreign mailings of "communist political propaganda." To implement the Act, after detaining a mailing, the post office sends a card which can be checked to have such mailing delivered. The card states that if it is not returned within 20 days the post office will assume that the addressee does not want that publication or any similar one in the future. The suit arose after the post office, in 1963, detained a copy of the *Peking Review #12* addressed to appellant. Instead of responding to the detention notice from the post office, appellant filed "suit to enjoin enforcement of the statute, alleging that it infringed his rights under the First and Fifth Amendments. The Post Office thereupon notified Lamont that it considered his institution of the suit to be an expression of his desire to receive 'communist political propaganda' and therefore none of his mail would be detained. Lamont amended his complaint to challenge on constitutional grounds the placement of his name on the list of those desiring to receive 'communist political propaganda.' The majority of the three-judge District Court nonetheless dismissed the complaint as moot because Lamont would now receive his mail unimpeded."

In No. 848, appellee Heilberg, "when his mail was detained, refused to return the reply card and instead filed a complaint in the District Court for an injunction against enforcement of the statute. The Post Office reacted to this complaint in the same manner as it had to Lamont's complaint, but the District Court declined to hold that Heilberg's action was thereby mooted. Instead the District Court reached the merits and unanimously held that the statute was unconstitutional under the First Amendment."

The Supreme Court consolidated the two cases on appeal and reversed No. 491, while affirming No. 848.

B. Counsel of Record / ACLU Attorney

ACLU Side (Petitioner/Appellant in No. 491, Respondent/Appellee in No. 848):

Leonard B. Boudin argued the cause for appellant in No. 491.

Marshall W. Krause argued the cause for appellee in No. 848.

Opposing Side (Respondent/Appellee in No. 491, Petitioner/Appellant in No. 848):

Solicitor General Archibald Cox argued the cause for appellee in No. 491 and appellant in No. 848.

III. AMICI CURIAE

ACLU Side (Petitioner/Appellant in No. 491, Respondent/Appellee in No. 848):

Brief of amici curiae filed on behalf of the ACLU by Nanette Dembitz and Melvin L. Wulf.

Opposing Side (Respondent/Appellee in No. 491, Petitioner/Appellant in No. 848):

No amici curiae briefs were filed in support of appellee in No. 491 and appellant in No. 848.

IV. THE SUPREME COURT'S DECISION

"We conclude that the Act as construed and applied is unconstitutional because it requires an official act (viz., returning the reply card) as a limitation on the unfettered exercise of the addressees First Amendment rights. . . .

We rest on the narrow ground that the addressee in order to receive his mail must request in writing that it be delivered. This amounts in our judgment to an unconstitutional abridgment of the addressee's First Amendment rights. The addressee carries an affirmative obligation which we do not think the Government may impose on him. This requirement is almost certain to have a deterrent effect, especially as respects those who have sensitive positions. Their livelihood may be dependent on a security clearance. Public officials, like schoolteachers who have no tenure, might think they would invite disaster if they read what the Federal Government says contains the seeds of treason. Apart from them, any addressee is likely to feel some inhibition in sending for literature which federal officials have condemned as 'communist political propaganda.' The regime of this Act is at war with the 'uninhibited, robust, and wide-open' debate and discussion that are contemplated by the First Amendment.

We reverse the judgment in No. 491 and affirm that in No. 848."

V. JUSTICE VOTE

8 Pro ACLU Side vs. 0 Con Opposing Side

ACLU Side (Petitioner/Appellant in No. 491, Respondent/Appellee in No. 848):

1. Douglas, W. – Wrote majority opinion
2. Warren, E. – Joined majority opinion
3. Black, H. – Joined majority opinion
4. Clark, T. – Joined majority opinion
5. Harlan, J. – Joined Brennan's concurrence
6. Brennan, W. – Wrote concurring opinion
7. Stewart, P. – Joined majority opinion
8. Goldberg, A. – Joined Brennan's concurrence

White, B – Took no part in the decision

VI. A WIN OR LOSS FOR THE ACLU?

The ACLU, as amici curiae, urged reversal in No. 491 and affirmance in No. 848; the Supreme Court reversed the judgment in No. 491 and affirmed the judgment in No. 848, in an 8-0 vote; giving the ACLU an apparent win.

167. United States v. Brown

(Decided June 7, 1965; 381 U.S. 437)

I. ISSUE

A. Issues Discussed

Governmental authority, First Amendment, Fifth Amendment, bill of attainder

B. Legal Question Presented

Does § 504 of the Labor-Management Reporting and Disclosure Act of 1959 constitute an unconstitutional bill of attainder?

C. Supreme Court's Answer

Section 504 is an unconstitutional bill of attainder.

II. CASE SUMMARY

A. Background

"Respondent had been a longshoreman on the San Francisco docks and an open and avowed Communist for more than a quarter of a century. He was elected to the Executive Board of Local 10 of the International Longshoremen's and Warehousemen's Union for consecutive one-year terms in 1959, 1960, and 1961. On May 24, 1961, respondent was charged in a one-count indictment returned in the Northern District of California with 'knowingly and wilfully serv[ing] as a member of an executive board of a labor organization . . . while a member of the Communist Party, in wilful violation of Title 29, United States Code, Section 504.' It was neither charged nor proven that respondent at any time advocated or suggested illegal activity by the union, or proposed a political strike. The jury found respondent guilty, and he was sentenced to six months imprisonment. The Court of Appeals for the Ninth Circuit, sitting en banc, reversed and remanded with instructions to set aside the conviction and dismiss the indictment, holding that § 504 violates the First and Fifth Amendments to the Constitution. . . .

Respondent urges—in addition to the grounds relied on by the courts below—that the statute under which he was convicted is a bill of attainder, and therefore violates Art. 1, § 9, of the Constitution."

The Supreme Court granted certiorari and affirmed.

B. Counsel of Record/ACLU Attorney

ACLU Side (Respondent/Appellee): Richard Gladstein argued the cause for appellee.

Opposing Side (Petitioner/Appellant): Solicitor General Archibald Cox argued the cause for appellant.

III. AMICI CURIAE

ACLU Side (Respondent/Appellee)

Briefs of amici curiae filed on behalf of the ACLU of Northern California by Melvin L. Wulf

Brief of amici curiae filed on behalf of the Emergency Civil Liberties Committee by Victor Rabinowitz and Leonard B. Boudin.

Opposing Side (Petitioner/Appellant)

No briefs of amici curiae were filed in support of appellee.

IV. THE SUPREME COURT'S DECISION

"We agree that § 504 is void as a bill of attainder and affirm the decision of the Court of Appeals on that basis. We therefore find it unnecessary to consider the First and Fifth Amendment arguments. . . .

[Section] 504 of the Labor-Management Reporting and Disclosure Act plainly constitutes a bill of attainder. Congress undoubtedly possesses power under the Commerce Clause to enact legislation designed to keep from positions affecting interstate commerce persons who may use such positions to bring about political strikes. In § 504, however, Congress has exceeded the authority granted it by the Constitution. The statute does not set forth a generally applicable rule decreeing that any person who commits certain acts or possesses certain characteristics (acts and characteristics which, in Congress' view, make them likely to initiate political strikes) shall not hold union office, and leave to courts and juries the job of deciding what persons have committed the specified acts or possess the specified characteristics. Instead, it designates in no uncertain terms the persons who possess the feared characteristics and therefore cannot hold union office without incurring criminal liability—members of the Communist Party. . . .

We cannot agree that the fact that § 504 inflicts its deprivation upon the membership of the Communist Party rather than upon a list of named individuals takes it out of the category of bills of attainder.

We do not hold today that Congress cannot weed dangerous persons out of the labor movement . . . . Rather, we make again the point made in Lovett: that Congress must accomplish such results by rules of general applicability. It cannot specify the people upon whom the sanction it prescribes is to be levied. Under our Constitution, Congress possesses full legislative authority, but the task of adjudication must be left to other tribunals."

The Supreme Court affirmed the judgment of the Court of Appeals.

V. JUSTICE VOTE

5 Pro ACLU Side vs. 4 Con Opposing Side

ACLU Side (Respondent/Appellee)

1. Warren, E. – Wrote majority opinion
2. Black, H. – Joined majority opinion
3. Douglas, W. – Joined majority opinion
4. Brennan, W. – Joined majority opinion
5. Goldberg, A. – Joined majority opinion

Opposing Side (Petitioner/Appellant)

1. White, B. – Wrote dissenting opinion
2. Clark, T. – Joined White's dissent
3. Harlan, J. – Joined White's dissent
4. Stewart, P. – Joined White's dissent

VI. A WIN OR LOSS FOR THE ACLU?

The ACLU filed an amicus brief urging affirmance; the Supreme Court affirmed the decision of the Court of Appeals in a 5-4 vote, giving the ACLU an apparent win.

168. Griswold v. Connecticut

(Decided June 7, 1965; 381 U.S. 479)

I. ISSUE

A. Issues Discussed

Right to privacy, contraception

B. Legal Question Presented

Is a Connecticut statute which prohibits the use of or assisting the use of contraceptives unconstitutional?

C. Supreme Court's Answer

The statute is an unconstitutional interference with the right to privacy, a right found in the penumbras of the Bill of Rights.

II. CASE SUMMARY

A. Background

"Appellant Griswold is Executive Director of the Planned Parenthood League of Connecticut. Appellant Buxton is a licensed physician and a professor at the Yale Medical School who served as Medical Director for the League at its Center in New Haven—a center open and operating from November 1 to November 10, 1961, when appellants were arrested [for violating a Connecticut statute prohibiting assisting someone in using contraceptives].

They gave information, instruction, and medical advice to married persons as to the means of preventing conception. They examined the wife and prescribed the best contraceptive device or material for her use. Fees were usually charged, although some couples were serviced free. . . .

The appellants were found guilty and fined $100 each, against the claim that the accessory statute as so applied violated the Fourteenth Amendment. The Appellate Division of the Circuit Court affirmed. The Supreme Court of Errors affirmed that judgment."

The Supreme Court granted certiorari and reversed.

B. Counsel of Record / ACLU Attorney

ACLU Side (Petitioner / Appellant): Opposing Side (Respondent / Appellee): Thomas I. Emerson argued the cause for appellant. Joseph B. Clark argued the cause for appellee.

III. AMICI CURIAE

ACLU Side (Petitioner / Appellant)

Brief of amici curiae filed on behalf of the ACLU by Rhoda H. Karpatkin, Melvin L. Wulf, and Jerome E. Caplan.

Brief of amici curiae filed on behalf of Dr. John M. Adams by Whitney North Seymour, Eleanor M. Fox, and Simpson Thacher & Bartlett.

Brief of amici curiae filed on behalf of the Planned Parenthood Federation of America by Morris L. Ernst, Harriet F. Pilpel. Nancy F. Wechsler, and Greenbaum Wolff & Ernst.

Brief of amici curiae filed on behalf of the Catholic Council on Civil Liberties by Alfred L. Scanlon.

Opposing Side (Respondent / Appellee)

No briefs of amici curiae were filed in support of appellee.

IV. THE SUPREME COURT'S DECISION

"We think that appellants have standing to raise the constitutional rights of the married people with whom they had a professional relationship. . . . Certainly the accessory should have standing to assert that the offense which he is charged with assisting is not, or cannot constitutionally be a crime.

[S]pecific guarantees in the Bill of Rights have penumbras, formed by emanations from those guarantees that help give them life and substance. Various guarantees create zones of privacy. The right of association contained in the penumbra of the First Amendment is one, as we have seen. The Third Amendment in its prohibition against the quartering of soldiers 'in any house' in time of peace without the consent of the owner is another facet of that privacy. The Fourth Amendment explicitly affirms the 'right of the people to be secure in their persons, houses, papers, and effects, against unreasonable searches and seizures.' The Fifth Amendment in its Self-Incrimination Clause enables the citizen to create a zone of privacy which government may not force him to surrender to his detriment. The Ninth Amendment provides: 'The enumeration in the Constitution, of certain rights, shall not be construed to deny or disparage others retained by the people.'. . .

The present case, then, concerns a relationship lying within the zone of privacy created by several fundamental constitutional guarantees. And it concerns a law which, in forbidding the use of contraceptives rather than regulating their manufacture or sale, seeks to achieve its goals by means having a maximum destructive impact upon that relationship. Such a law cannot stand in light of the familiar principle, so often applied by this Court, that a 'governmental purpose to control or prevent activities constitutionally subject to state regulation may not be achieved by means which sweep unnecessarily broadly and thereby invade the area of protected freedoms.' Would we allow the police to search the sacred precincts of marital bedrooms for telltale signs of the use of contraceptives? The very idea is repulsive to the notions of privacy surrounding the marriage relationship.

We deal with a right of privacy older than the Bill of Rights—older than our political parties, older than our school system. Marriage is a coming together for better or for worse, hopefully enduring, and intimate to the degree of being sacred. It is an association that promotes a way of life, not causes; a harmony in living, not political faiths; a bilateral loyalty, not commercial or social projects. Yet it is an association for as noble a purpose as any involved in our prior decisions."

The Supreme Court reversed the judgment.

V. JUSTICE VOTE

7 Pro ACLU Side vs. 2 Con Opposing Side

ACLU Side (Petitioner / Appellant)

1. Douglas, W. – Wrote majority opinion
2. White, B. – Wrote concurring opinion
3. Harlan, J. – Wrote concurring opinion
4. Warren, E. – Joined Goldberg's concurrence
5. Brennan, W. – Joined Goldberg's concurrence
6. Clark, T. – Joined majority opinion
7. Goldberg, A. – Wrote concurring opinion

Opposing Side (Respondent / Appellee)

1. Black, H. – Wrote dissenting opinion, joined Stewart's dissent
2. Stewart, P. – Wrote dissenting opinion, joined Black's dissent

VI. A WIN OR LOSS FOR THE ACLU?

The ACLU, as amicus curiae, urged reversal of the judgment of the Connecticut Supreme Court of Errors; the Supreme Court reversed in a 7-2 vote, giving the ACLU an apparent win.

169. Estes v. Texas

(Decided June 7, 1965; 381 U.S. 532)

I. ISSUE

A. Issues Discussed

Criminal procedure, freedom of the press, due process, Fourteenth Amendment

B. Legal Question Presented

"[W]hether the petitioner, who stands convicted in the District Court for the Seventh Judicial District of Texas at Tyler for swindling, was deprived of his right under the Fourteenth Amendment to due process by the televising and broadcasting of his trial."

C. Supreme Court's Answer

Petitioner was deprived of his right to due process by the televising of his trial.

II. CASE SUMMARY

A. Background

"Petitioner, a much-publicized financier, was indicted by a Reeves County, Texas, grand jury for obtaining property through false pretenses. The case was transferred to the City of Tyler, in Smith County, Texas, and was set for trial on September 24, 1962. Prior to that date petitioner's counsel informed the trial judge that he would make a motion on September 24 to exclude all cameras from the courtroom during the trial.

On September 24, a hearing was held to consider petitioner's motion to prohibit television, motion pictures, and still photography at the trial. The courtroom was filled with newspaper reporters and cameramen, television cameramen, and spectators. At least 12 cameramen with their equipment were seen by one observer, and there were 30 or more people standing in the aisles."[1]

"When the case was called for trial on October 22 the scene had been altered. A booth had been constructed at the back of the courtroom which was painted to blend with the permanent structure of the room. It had an aperture to allow the lens of the cameras an unrestricted view of the courtroom. All television cameras and newsreel photographers were restricted to the area of the booth when shooting film or telecasting. Because of continual objection, the rules governing live telecasting, as well as radio and still photos, were changed as the exigencies of the situation seemed to require. As a result, live telecasting was prohibited during a great portion of the actual trial. Only the opening and closing arguments of the State, the return of the jury's verdict and its receipt by the trial judge were carried live with sound. Although the order allowed videotapes of the entire proceeding without sound, the cameras operated only intermittently, recording various portions of the trial for broadcast on regularly scheduled newscasts later in the day and evening. At the request of the petitioner, the trial judge prohibited coverage of any kind, still or television, of the defense counsel during their summations to the jury.

Because of the varying restrictions placed on sound and live telecasting the telecasts of the trial were confined largely to film clips shown on the stations' regularly scheduled news programs. The news commentators would use the film of a particular part of the day's trial activities as a backdrop for their reports. Their commentary included excerpts from testimony and the usual reportorial remarks. On one occasion the videotapes of the September hearings were rebroadcast in place of the 'late movie.'"

Petitioner was convicted at trial and the Texas Court of Criminal Appeals upheld the conviction.

The Supreme Court granted certiorari and reversed.

B. Counsel of Record/ACLU Attorney

ACLU Side (Petitioner/Appellant): John D. Cofer and Hume Cofer argued the cause for appellant.

Opposing Side (Respondent/Appellee): Waggoner Carr, Attorney General of Texas, and Leon Jaworski, Special Assistant Attorney General, argued the cause for appellee.

III. AMICI CURIAE

ACLU Side (Petitioner/Appellant)

Brief of amici curiae filed on behalf of the ACLU by Norman Dorsen, Melvin L. Wulf, Sam Houston Clinton, Jr., Robert J. Rabin, and Lawrence D. Ross.

Brief of amici curiae filed on behalf of the American Bar Association by Whitney North Seymour, Richmond C. Coburn, and John H. Yauch.

Opposing Side (Respondent/Appellee)

Briefs of amici curiae filed on behalf of the State Bar of Texas by Davis Grant and L. Money Adams, Jr.

Brief of amici curiae filed on behalf of the National Association of Broadcasters by Douglas A. Anello, Gordon C. Coffman, W. Theodore Pierson, Harold David Cohen, W. Theodore Pierson, Jr., J. Laurent Scharff, and Pierson, Ball & Dowd.

IV. THE SUPREME COURT'S DECISION

"We start with the proposition that it is a 'public trial' that the Sixth Amendment guarantees to the 'accused.' The purpose of the requirement of a public trial was to guarantee that the accused would be fairly dealt with and not unjustly condemned. . . .

It is said however, that the freedoms granted in the First Amendment extend a right to the news media to televise from the courtroom, and that to refuse to honor this privilege is to discriminate between the newspapers and television. This is a misconception of the rights of the press. . . .

It is true that the public has the right to be informed as to what occurs in its courts, but reporters of all media, including television, are always present if they wish to be and are plainly free to report whatever occurs in open court through their respective media. . . .

Television in its present state and by its very nature, reaches into a variety of areas in which it may cause prejudice to an accused. Still one cannot put his finger on its specific mischief and prove

1 Estes v. Texas, 381 U.S. 532 (1965) (Warren, E., concurring).

with particularity wherein he was prejudiced. . . . Forty-eight of our States and the Federal Rules have deemed the use of television improper in the courtroom. This fact is most telling in buttressing our conclusion that any change in procedure which would permit its use would be inconsistent with our concepts of due process in this field. . . .

It is said that the ever-advancing techniques of public communication and the adjustment of the public to its presence may bring about a change in the effect of telecasting upon the fairness of criminal trials. But we are not dealing here with future developments in the field of electronics. Our judgment cannot be rested on the hypothesis of tomorrow but must take the facts as they are presented today."

The Supreme Court reversed the judgment.

V. JUSTICE VOTE

5 Pro ACLU Side vs. 4 Con Opposing Side

ACLU Side (Petitioner/Appellant)

1. Clark, T. – Wrote majority opinion
2. Warren, E. – Wrote concurring opinion
3. Douglas, W. – Joined majority opinion
4. Harlan, J. – Wrote concurring opinion, joined Warren's concurrence
5. Goldberg, A. – Joined Warren's concurrence

Opposing Side (Respondent/Appellee)

1. Stewart, P. – Wrote dissenting opinion
2. Black, H. – Joined dissenting opinion
3. Brennan, W. – Joined dissenting opinion
4. White, B. – Joined dissenting opinion

VI. A WIN OR LOSS FOR THE ACLU?

The ACLU filed an amicus brief urging reversal; the Supreme Court reversed the ruling of the Texas Court of Criminal Appeals in a 5-4 vote, giving the ACLU an apparent win.

170. Albertson v. Subversive Activities Control Board

(Decided November 15, 1965; 382 U.S. 70)

I. ISSUE

A. Issues Discussed

Governmental authority, Fifth Amendment, self-incrimination

B. Legal Question Presented

Did a federal order for individual members of the Communist Party to register because the party itself failed to register violate the Fifth Amendment privilege against self-incrimination?

C. Supreme Court's Answer

The requirement for individuals to register violates the Fifth Amendment privilege against self-incrimination.

II. CASE SUMMARY

A. Background

"The Communist Party of the United States of America failed to register with the Attorney General as required by the order of the Subversive Activities Control Board sustained in Communist Party of the United States v. SACB, 367 U.S 1. Accordingly, no list of Party members was filed as required by § 7(d)(4) of the Subversive Activities Control Act of 1950. Sections 8(a) and (c) of the Act provide that, in that circumstance, each member of the organization must register and file a registration statement; in default thereof, § 13(a) authorizes the Attorney General to petition the Board for an order requiring the member to register. The Attorney General invoked § 13(a) against petitioners, and the Board, after evidentiary hearings, determined that petitioners were Party members and ordered each of them to register pursuant to §§ 8(a) and (c). Review of the orders was sought by petitioners in the Court of Appeals for the District of Columbia Circuit under § 14(a). The Court of Appeals affirmed the orders."

The Supreme Court granted certiorari and reversed.

B. Counsel of Record/ACLU Attorney

ACLU Side (Petitioner/Appellant): John J. Abt argued the cause for appellant.

Opposing Side (Respondent/Appellee): Kevin T. Maroney argued the cause for appellee.

III. AMICI CURIAE

ACLU Side (Petitioner/Appellant)

Brief of amici curiae filed on behalf of the ACLU by Osmond K. Fraenkel.

Brief of amici curiae filed on behalf of the National Lawyers Guild by Ernest Goodman and Laurent B. Frantz.

Opposing Side (Respondent/Appellee)

No amici curiae briefs of amici curiae were filed in support of appellee.

IV. THE SUPREME COURT'S DECISION

"The risks of incrimination which the petitioners take in registering are obvious. Form IS-52a requires an admission of membership in the Communist Party. Such an admission of membership may be used to prosecute the registrant under the membership clause of the Smith Act, or under § 4(a) of the Subversive Activities Control Act, to mention only two federal criminal statutes. Accordingly, we have held that mere association with the Communist Party presents sufficient threat of prosecution to support a claim of privilege. . . . It follows that the requirement to accomplish registration by completing and filing Form IS-52a is inconsistent with the protection of the Self-Incrimination Clause. . . .

The judgment as to whether a disclosure would be 'incriminatory' has never been made dependent on an assessment of the information possessed by the Government at the time of interrogation; the protection of the privilege would be seriously impaired if the right to invoke it was dependent on such an assessment, with all its uncertainties. The threat to the privilege is no less present where it is proposed that this assessment be made in order to remedy a shortcoming in a statutory grant of immunity. The representation that the information demanded is of no utility is belied by the fact that the failure to make the disclosure is so severely sanctioned; and permitting the incompleteness of § 4(f) to be cured by such a representation would render illusory the Counselman requirement that a statute, in order to supplant the privilege, must provide 'complete protection from all the perils against which the constitutional prohibition was designed to guard.'

The judgment of the Court of Appeals is reversed and the Board's orders are set aside."

V. JUSTICE VOTE

8 Pro ACLU Side vs. 0 Con Opposing Side

ACLU Side (Petitioner/Appellant)

1. Brennan, W. – Wrote majority opinion
2. Black, H. – Wrote concurring opinion
3. Clark, T. – Joined majority opinion
4. Warren, E. – Joined majority opinion
5. Douglas, W. – Joined majority opinion
6. Harlan, J. – Joined majority opinion
7. Stewart, P. – Joined majority opinion
8. Fortas, A. – Joined majority opinion

White, B – Took no part in the decision

VI. A WIN OR LOSS FOR THE ACLU?

The ACLU, as amicus curiae, urged reversal; the Supreme Court reversed the ruling of the Court of Appeals for the District of Columbia Circuit in an 8-0 vote; giving the ACLU an apparent win.

171. Rosenblatt v. Baer

(Decided February 21, 1966; 383 U.S. 75)

I. ISSUE

A. Issues Discussed

First Amendment, Fourteenth Amendment, libel, defamation

B. Legal Question Presented

Can respondent recover civil damages for libel from a newspaper column that criticized his management as the supervisor of a county recreation area?

C. Supreme Court's Answer

Whether respondent can recover depends on if the conduct falls within or outside the New York Times rule, decided after the jury trial in this case.

II. CASE SUMMARY

A. Background

Respondent was the former Supervisor of Belknap County Recreation Area, a facility owned and operated by the county, and primarily used as a ski resort.

In 1960, new management took over the recreation area after "public controversy developed over the way respondent and the Commissioners operated the Area." Petitioner commented on the change in management in his local newspaper column stating, "What happened to all the money last year? and every other year? What magic has Dana Beane [Chairman of the new commission] and rest of commission, and Mr. Warner [respondent's replacement as Supervisor] wrought to make such tremendous difference in net cash results?" Respondent brought a civil libel action against petitioner, alleging that the column contained defamatory falsehoods regarding his performance as Supervisor of the recreation area.

A jury in New Hampshire Superior Court awarded damages to respondent.

While this case was awaiting appeal to the New Hampshire Supreme Court, the U.S. Supreme Court decided New York Times Co. v. Sullivan, (summarized above) which held that "a State cannot award damages to a public official for defamatory falsehood relating to his official conduct unless the official proves actual malice—that the falsehood was published with knowledge of its falsity or with reckless disregard of whether it is true or false." The New Hampshire Supreme Court affirmed respondent's damages award, finding that New York Times did not bar the award.

The Supreme Court granted certiorari. The parties were requested to brief and argue an additional question, whether respondent was a "public official." The Supreme Court reversed the judgment.

B. Counsel of Record/ACLU Attorney

ACLU Side (Petitioner/Appellant): Arthur H. Nighswander argued the cause for appellant.

Opposing Side (Respondent/Appellee): Stanley M. Brown argued the cause for appellee.

III. AMICI CURIAE

ACLU Side (Petitioner/Appellant)

Brief of amici curiae filed on behalf of the ACLU by Osmond K. Fraenkel, Edward J. Ennis, and Melvin L. Wulf.

Opposing Side (Respondent/Appellee)

No briefs of amici curiae were filed in support of appellee.

IV. THE SUPREME COURT'S DECISION

"There is, first, a strong interest in debate on public issues, and, second, a strong interest in debate about those persons who are in a position significantly to influence the resolution of those issues. Criticism of government is at the very center of the constitutionally protected area of free discussion. Criticism of those responsible for government operations must be free, lest criticism of government itself be penalized. It is clear, therefore, that the 'public official' designation applies at the very least to those among the hierarchy of government employees who have, or appear to the public to have, substantial responsibility for or control over the conduct of governmental affairs.

This conclusion does not ignore the important social values which underlie the law of defamation. Society has a pervasive and strong interest in preventing and redressing attacks upon reputation. But in cases like the present, there is tension between this interest and the values nurtured by the First and Fourteenth Amendments. The thrust of New York Times is that when interests in public discussion are particularly strong, as they were in that case, thc Constitution limits the protections afforded by the law of defamation. Where a position in government has such apparent importance that the public has an independent interest in the qualifications and performance of the person who holds it, beyond the general public interest in the qualifications and performance of all government employees, both elements we identified in New York Times are present and the New York Times malice standards apply.

As respondent framed his case, he may have held such a position. Since New York Times had not been decided when his case went to trial, his presentation was not shaped to the 'public official' issue. He did, however, seek to show that the article referred particularly to him. His theory was that his role in the management of the Area was so prominent and important that the public regarded him as the man responsible for its operations, chargeable with its failures and to be credited with its successes. Thus, to prove the article referred to him, he showed the importance of his role; the same showing, at the least, raises a substantial argument that he was a 'public official.'

The record here, however, leaves open the possibility that respondent could have adduced proofs to bring his claim outside the New York Times rule. Moreover, even if the claim falls within New York Times, the record suggests respondent may be able to present a jury question of malice as there defined. Because the trial here was had before New York Times, we have concluded that we should not foreclose him from attempting retrial of his action. We remark only that, as is the case with questions of privilege generally, it is for the trial judge in the first instance to determine whether the proofs show respondent to be a 'public official.'

The judgment is reversed and the case remanded to the New Hampshire Supreme Court for further proceedings not inconsistent with this opinion."

V. JUSTICE VOTE

8 Pro ACLU Side vs. 1 Con Opposing Side

ACLU Side (Petitioner/Appellant)

1. Brennan, W. – Wrote majority opinion
2. Warren, E. – Joined majority opinion
3. Stewart, P. – Wrote concurring opinion
4. White, B. – Joined majority opinion
5. Clark, T. – Concurred in the result
6. Black, H. – Wrote opinion concurring in part and dissenting in part
7. Douglas, W. – Wrote concurring opinion, joined Black's opinion
8. Harlan, J. – Wrote opinion concurring in part and dissenting in part

Opposing Side (Respondent/Appellee)

1. Fortas, A. – Wrote dissenting opinion

VI. A WIN OR LOSS FOR THE ACLU?

The ACLU, as amicus curiae, urged reversal; the U.S. Supreme Court reversed the decision of the New Hampshire Supreme Court in an 8-1 vote, giving the ACLU an apparent win.

172. Ginzburg v. United States

(Decided March 21, 1966; 383 U.S. 463)

I. ISSUE

A. Issues Discussed

First Amendment, obscenity

B. Legal Question Presented

Even though certain materials themselves may not be considered obscene, can an individual be convicted under the federal obscenity statute for advertising them as obscene, without violating the First Amendment?

C. Supreme Court's Answer

A conviction under the federal obscenity statute is appropriate in these circumstances.

II. CASE SUMMARY

A. Background

Petitioner Ginzburg was convicted in the District Court for the Eastern District of Pennsylvania for violating the federal obscenity statute. He mailed three publications: (1) EROS, an expensive hardcover magazine discussing sex, (2) Liaison, a newsletter discussing sex, and (3) The Housewife's Handbook on Selective Promiscuity, a sexual autobiography of the author. The publications were advertised as to emphasize their erotic nature although not all materials in the publications were obscene. The trial judge found the petitioner guilty of violating the federal obscenity statute, and the Court of Appeals for the Third Circuit affirmed.

The Supreme Court granted certiorari and affirmed the decision.

B. Counsel of Record/ACLU Attorney

ACLU Side (Petitioner/Appellant): Sidney Dickstein argued the cause for appellant.

Opposing Side (Respondent/Appellee): Paul Bender argued the cause for appellee, pro hac vice, by special leave of court.

III. AMICI CURIAE

ACLU Side (Petitioner/Appellant)

Brief of amici curiae filed on behalf of the ACLU, et al., by Bernard A. Berkman, Melvin L. Wulf, and Murray Powlen.

Brief of amici curiae filed on behalf of the Authors League of America, Inc., by Irwin Karp.

Brief of amici curiae filed on behalf of the American Book Publishers Council, Inc., by Horace S. Manges and Marshall C. Berger.

Opposing Side (Respondent/Appellee)

Brief of amici curiae filed on behalf of Citizens for Decent Literature Inc., et al., by Charles H. Keating, Jr., and James J. Clancy.

IV. THE SUPREME COURT'S DECISION

"This evidence, in our view, was relevant in determining the ultimate question of obscenity, and, in the context of this record, serves to resolve all ambiguity and doubt. The deliberate representation of petitioners' publications as erotically arousing, for example, stimulated the reader to accept them as prurient; he looks for titillation, not for saving intellectual content. Similarly, such representation would tend to force public confrontation with the potentially offensive aspects of the work; the brazenness of such an appeal heightens the offensiveness of the publications to those who are offended by such material. . . . Where the purveyor's sole emphasis is on the sexually provocative aspects of his publications, that fact may be decisive in the determination of obscenity. Certainly in a prosecution which, as here, does not necessarily imply suppression of the materials involved, the fact that they originate or are used as a subject of pandering is relevant to the application of the *Roth* test. . . .

We perceive no threat to First Amendment guarantees in thus holding that, in close cases, evidence of pandering may be probative with respect to the nature of the material in question, and thus satisfy the *Roth* test. [T]he fact that each of these publications was created or exploited entirely on the basis of its appeal to prurient interests strengthens the conclusion that the transactions here were sales of illicit merchandise, not sales of constitutionally protected matter. A conviction for mailing obscene publications, but explained in part by the presence of this element, does not necessarily suppress the materials in question, nor chill their proper distribution for a proper use. Nor should it inhibit the enterprise of others seeking, through serious endeavor, to advance human knowledge or understanding in science, literature, or art. All that will have been determined is that questionable publications are obscene in a context which brands them as obscene as that term is defined in *Roth*—a use inconsistent with any claim to the shelter of the First Amendment. . . .

It is important to stress that this analysis simply elaborates the test by which the obscenity vel non of the material must be judged. Where an exploitation of interests in titillation by pornography is shown with respect to material lending itself to such exploitation through pervasive treatment or description of sexual matters, such evidence may support the determination that the material is obscene even though, in other contexts, the material would escape such condemnation."

The Supreme Court affirmed the judgment of the Court of Appeals for the Third Circuit.

V. JUSTICE VOTE

4 Pro ACLU Side vs. 5 Con Opposing Side

ACLU Side (Petitioner/Appellant)

1. Black, H. – Wrote dissenting opinion
2. Douglas, W. – Wrote dissenting opinion
3. Harlan, J. – Wrote dissenting opinion
4. Stewart, P. – Wrote dissenting opinion

Opposing Side (Respondent/Appellee)

1. Brennan, W. – Wrote majority opinion
2. Warren, E. – Joined majority opinion
3. Clark, T. – Joined majority opinion
4. White, B. – Joined majority opinion
5. Fortas, A. – Joined majority opinion

VI. A WIN OR LOSS FOR THE ACLU?

The ACLU filed an amicus brief urging reversal; the Supreme Court affirmed the ruling of the Court of Appeals for the Third Circuit in a 5-4 vote, giving the ACLU an apparent loss.

173. Harper v. Virginia Board of Elections

(Decided March 24, 1966; 383 U.S. 663)

I. ISSUE

A. Issues Discussed

Voting rights

B. Legal Question Presented

Whether the Virginia poll tax is constitutional.

C. Supreme Court's Answer

"We conclude that a State violates the Equal Protection Clause of the Fourteenth Amendment whenever it makes the affluence of the voter or payment of any fee an electoral standard."

II. CASE SUMMARY

A. Background

"These are suits by Virginia residents to have declared unconstitutional Virginia's poll tax. The three-judge District Court, feeling bound by our decision in Breedlove v. Suttles, 302 U.S. 277, dismissed the complaint. The cases came here on appeal and [the U.S. Supreme Court] noted probable jurisdiction."

B. Counsel of Record

ACLU Side (Petitioner/Appellant): Allison W. Brown, Jr., of the American Civil Liberties Union argued the cause for appellants in No. 48. With him on the brief were Lawrence Speiser of the American Civil Liberties Union, Ira M. Lechner, and Philip Schwartz.

Robert L. Segar and J. A. Jordan, Jr., argued the cause for appellant in No. 655. With them on the brief were Max Dean and Len W. Holt.

Solicitor General Marshall argued the cause for the United States, as amicus curiae in No. 48.

Opposing Side (Respondent/Appellee): George D. Gibson

argued the cause for appellees in both cases. With him on the briefs were Robert Y. Button, Attorney General of Virginia, Richard N. Harris,
Assistant Attorney General, and Joseph C. Carter, Jr.

III. AMICI CURIAE

ACLU Side (Petitioner/Appellant)

Brief of amici curiae filed on behalf of the United States in No. 48 by Solicitor General Marshall, Attorney General Katzenbach, Assistant Attorney General Doar, Ralph S. Spritzer, David Rubin, James L. Kelley, and Richard A. Posner.

Opposing Side (Respondent/Appellee)

No briefs of amici curiae were filed in support of appellees.

IV. THE SUPREME COURT'S DECISION

"While the right to vote in federal elections is conferred by Art. I, s 2, of the Constitution, the right to vote in state elections is nowhere expressly mentioned. It is argued that the right to vote in state elections is implicit, particularly by reason of the First Amendment and that it may not constitutionally be conditioned upon the payment of a tax or fee. We do not stop to canvass the relation between voting and political expression. For it is enough to say that once the franchise is granted to the electorate, lines may not be drawn which are inconsistent with the Equal Protection Clause of the Fourteenth Amendment. . . .

We conclude that a State violates the Equal Protection Clause of the Fourteenth Amendment whenever it makes the affluence of the voter or payment of any fee an electoral standard. Voter qualifications have no relation to wealth nor to paying or not paying this or any other tax. Our cases demonstrate that the Equal Protection Clause of the Fourteenth Amendment restrains the States from fixing voter qualifications which invidiously discriminate. . . .

The principle that denies the State the right to dilute a citizen's vote on account of his economic status or other such factors by analogy bars a system which excludes those unable to pay a fee to vote or who fail to pay. . . .

In a recent searching re-examination of the Equal Protection Clause, we held, as already noted, that 'the opportunity for equal participation by all voters in the election of state legislators' is required. We decline to qualify that principle by sustaining this poll tax. Our conclusion, like that in Reynolds v. Sims, is founded not on what we think governmental policy should be, but on what the Equal Protection Clause requires.

We have long been mindful that where fundamental rights and liberties are asserted under the Equal Protection Clause, classifications which might invade or restrain them must be closely scrutinized and carefully confined.

Those principles apply here. For to repeat, wealth or fee paying has, in our view, no relation to voting qualifications; the right to vote is too precious, too fundamental to be so burdened or conditioned.

Reversed."

V. JUSTICE VOTE

6 Pro ACLU Side vs. 3 Con Opposing Side

ACLU Side (Petitioner/Appellant)

1. Douglas, W. – Wrote majority opinion
2. Warren, E. – Joined majority opinion
3. Brennan, W. – Joined majority opinion
4. Fortas, A. – Joined majority opinion
5. Clark, T. – Joined majority opinion
6. White, B. – Joined majority opinion

Opposing Side (Respondent/Appellee)

1. Black, H. – Wrote dissenting opinion
2. Stewart, P. – Joined Harlan's dissent
3. Harlan, J. – Wrote dissenting opinion

VI. A WIN OR LOSS FOR THE ACLU?

The ACLU served as counsel for appellants urging reversal of the judgment of the District Court; the Supreme Court reversed in a 6-3 vote, giving the ACLU an apparent win.

174. Mills v. Alabama

(Decided May 23, 1966; 384 U.S. 214)

I. ISSUE

A. Issues Discussed

First Amendment, freedom of speech and of the press, elections

B. Legal Question Presented

"[W]hether a State, consistently with the United States Constitution, can make it a crime for the editor of a daily newspaper to write and publish an editorial on election day urging people to vote a certain way on issues submitted to them."

C. Supreme Court's Answer

The statute violates the First Amendment freedoms of speech and of the press by criminalizing publications urging voters to vote a particular way on election day.

II. CASE SUMMARY

A. Background

"On November 6, 1962, Birmingham, Alabama, held an election for the people to decide whether they preferred to keep their existing city commission form of government or replace it with a mayor-council government. On election day the Birmingham Post-Herald, a daily newspaper, carried an editorial written by its editor, appellant, James E. Mills, which strongly urged the people to adopt the mayor-council form of government. Mills was later arrested on a complaint charging that by publishing the editorial on election day he had violated § 285 of the Alabama Corrupt Practices Act, which makes it a crime 'to do any electioneering or to solicit any votes . . . in support of or in opposition to any proposition that is being voted on on the day on which the election affecting such candidates or propositions is being held.' The trial court sustained demurrers to the complaint on the grounds that the state statute abridged freedom of speech and press in violation of the Alabama Constitution and the First and Fourteenth

Amendments to the United States Constitution. On appeal by the State, the Alabama Supreme Court held that publication of the editorial on election day undoubtedly violated the state law and then went on to reverse the trial court by holding that the state statute as applied did not unconstitutionally abridge freedom of speech or press. Recognizing that the state law did limit and restrict both speech and press, the State Supreme Court nevertheless sustained it as a valid exercise of the State's police power chiefly because, as that court said, the press 'restriction, everything considered, is within the field of reasonableness' and 'not an unreasonable limitation upon free speech, which includes free press.'"

The Supreme Court granted certiorari and reversed.

B. Counsel of Record / ACLU Attorney

ACLU Side (Petitioner / Appellant): Kenneth Perrine and Alfred Swedlaw argued the cause for appellant.

Opposing Side (Respondent / Appellee): Leslie Hall, Assistant Attorney General of Alabama, and Burgin Hawkins argued the cause for appellee.

III. AMICI CURIAE

ACLU Side (Petitioner / Appellant)

Brief of amici curiae filed on behalf of the ACLU, et al., by Charles Morgan, Jr., Melvin L. Wulf, C. H. Erskine Smith, and Herbert S. Channick.

Brief of amicus curiae filed on behalf of the Alabama Press Association, et al., by James C. Barton and Alan W. Heldman.

Opposing Side (Respondent / Appellee)

No briefs of amici curiae were filed in support of appellee.

IV. THE SUPREME COURT'S DECISION

"Admitting that the state law restricted a newspaper editor's freedom to publish editorials on election day, the Alabama Supreme Court nevertheless sustained the constitutionality of the law on the ground that the restrictions on the press were only 'reasonable restrictions' or at least 'within the field of reasonableness.' The court reached this conclusion because it thought the law imposed only a minor limitation on the press—restricting it only on election days—and because the court thought the law served a good purpose. It said: 'It is a salutary legislative enactment that protects the public from confusive last-minute charges and countercharges and the distribution of propaganda in an effort to influence voters on an election day, when, as a practical matter, because of lack of time, such matters cannot be answered or their truth determined until after the election is over.'

This argument, even if it were relevant to the constitutionality of the law, has a fatal flaw. The state statute leaves people free to hurl their campaign charges up to the last minute of the day before election. The law held valid by the Alabama Supreme Court then goes on to make it a crime to answer those 'last-minute' charges on election day, the only time they can be effectively answered. Because the law prevents any adequate reply to these charges, it is wholly ineffective in protecting the electorate 'from confusive last-minute charges and countercharges.' We hold that no test of reasonableness can save a state law from invalidation as a violation of the First Amendment when that law makes it a crime for a newspaper editor to do no more than urge people to vote one way or another in a publicly held election.

The judgment of the Supreme Court of Alabama is reversed and the case is remanded for further proceedings not inconsistent with this opinion."

V. JUSTICE VOTE

9 Pro ACLU Side vs. 0 Con Opposing Side

ACLU Side (Petitioner / Appellant)

1. Black, H. – Wrote majority opinion
2. Warren, E. – Joined majority opinion
3. Clark, T. – Joined majority opinion
4. Stewart, P. – Joined majority opinion
5. White, B. – Joined majority opinion
6. Fortas, A. – Joined majority opinion
7. Douglas, W. – Wrote concurring opinion
8. Brennan, W. – Joined Douglas' concurrence
9. Harlan, J. – Wrote concurring opinion

VI. A WIN OR LOSS FOR THE ACLU?

The ACLU filed an amicus brief urging reversal; the U.S. Supreme Court reversed the ruling of the Supreme Court of Alabama in a 9-0 vote, giving the ACLU an apparent win.

175. Sheppard v. Maxwell

(Decided June 6, 1966; 384 U.S. 333)

I. ISSUE

A. Issues Discussed

Criminal procedure, due process, right to a fair trial

B. Legal Question Presented

"[W]hether Sheppard was deprived of a fair trial in his state conviction for the second-degree murder of his wife because of the trial judge's failure to protect Sheppard sufficiently from the massive, pervasive and prejudicial publicity that attended his prosecution."

C. Supreme Court's Answer

Sheppard was deprived of his right to a fair trial because he was insufficiently protected against prejudice from the massive media publicity surrounding his trial.

II. CASE SUMMARY

A. Background

Petitioner's pregnant wife, Marilyn Sheppard, was bludgeoned to death in the upstairs bedroom of their Ohio home on July 4, 1954. Officials focused their investigation on petitioner Samuel Sheppard who was arrested on a murder charge.

Media attention surrounding the case garnered extensive public attention prior to the trial. The list of potential jurors was published in the newspaper before the trial began and "anonymous letters and telephone calls, as well as calls from friends, regarding the impending prosecution were received by all of the prospective jurors." The jurors selected for the trial were not adequately sequestered from outside communications and publicity related to the case. Media reports included a wide array of information reportedly showing Sheppard's guilt or relating to Sheppard's character that was never produced at trial. During the trial the courtroom was filled with newsmen who sometimes disrupted the proceedings. The judge did not take any actions to address the impact of the media attention.

Sheppard was convicted of second-degree murder for the death of his wife. He challenged the verdict as the product of an unfair trial and filed a habeas corpus petition at the District Court. "The United States District Court held that he was not afforded a fair trial and granted the writ subject to the State's right to put Sheppard to trial again." The Court of Appeals reversed this judgment.

The Supreme Court granted certiorari and determined "that Sheppard did not receive a fair trial consistent with the Due Process Clause of the Fourteenth Amendment."

B. Counsel of Record / ACLU Attorney

ACLU Side (Petitioner / Appellant): F. Lee Bailey argued the cause for appellant.

Bernard A. Berkman argued the cause for the ACLU, et al., as amicus curiae.

Opposing Side (Respondent / Appellee): William B. Saxbe, Attorney General of Ohio, and John T. Corrigan argued the cause for appellee.

III. AMICI CURIAE

ACLU Side (Petitioner / Appellant)

Brief of amici curiae filed on behalf of the ACLU, et al., by Bernard A. Berkman and Melvin L. Wulf.

Opposing Side (Respondent / Appellee)

Brief of amici curiae filed on behalf of the State of Ohio by John T. Corrigan and Gertrude Bauer Mahon.

IV. THE SUPREME COURT'S DECISION

"From the cases coming here we note that unfair and prejudicial news comment on pending trials has become increasingly prevalent. Due process requires that the accused receive a trial by an impartial jury free from outside influences. Given the pervasiveness of modern communications and the difficulty of effacing prejudicial publicity from the minds of the jurors, the trial courts must take strong measures to ensure that the balance is never weighed against the accused. And appellate tribunals have the duty to make an independent evaluation of the circumstances. Of course, there is nothing that proscribes the press from reporting events that transpire in the courtroom. But where there is a reasonable likelihood that prejudicial news prior to trial will prevent a fair trial, the judge should continue the case until the threat abates, or transfer it to another county not so permeated with publicity. In addition, sequestration of the jury was something the judge should have raised sua sponte with counsel. If publicity during the proceedings threatens the fairness of the trial, a new trial should be ordered. But we must remember that reversals are but palliatives; the cure lies in those remedial measures that will prevent the prejudice at its inception. The courts must take such steps by rule and regulation that will protect their processes from prejudicial outside interferences. Neither prosecutors, counsel for defense, the accused, witnesses, court staff nor enforcement officers coming under the jurisdiction of the court should be permitted to frustrate its function. Collaboration between counsel and the press as to information affecting the fairness of a criminal trial is not only subject to regulation, but is highly censurable and worthy of disciplinary measures.

Since the state trial judge did not fulfill his duty to protect Sheppard from the inherently prejudicial publicity which saturated the community and to control disruptive influences in the courtroom, we must reverse the denial of the habeas petition. The case is remanded to the District Court with instructions to issue the writ and order that Sheppard be released from custody unless the State puts him to its charges again within a reasonable time."

The Supreme Court reversed the decision of the Court of Appeals.

V. JUSTICE VOTE

8 Pro ACLU Side vs. 1 Con Opposing Side

ACLU Side (Petitioner / Appellant)

1. Clark, T. – Wrote majority opinion
2. Warren, E. – Joined majority opinion
3. Douglas, W. – Joined majority opinion
4. Harlan, J. – Joined majority opinion
5. Stewart, P. – Joined majority opinion
6. White, B. – Joined majority opinion
7. Fortas, A. – Joined majority opinion
8. Brennan, W. – Joined majority opinion

Opposing Side (Respondent / Appellee)

1. Black, H. – Dissented without an opinion

VI. A WIN OR LOSS FOR THE ACLU?

The ACLU filed a brief and argued the cause as amicus curiae urging reversal; the Supreme Court reversed the ruling of the Court of Appeals in an 8-1 vote, giving the ACLU an apparent win.

176. Miranda v. Arizona

(Decided June 13, 1966; 384 U.S. 436)

I. ISSUE

A. Issues Discussed

Self-incrimination, due process, right to counsel

B. Legal Question Presented

Are statements, obtained from a defendant questioned while in custody and without effective warning of his rights to silence and counsel at the outset of the interrogation process, admissible at trial?

C. Supreme Court's Answer

Statements made when defendant has not been effectively warned of his right to silence and right to counsel are not admissible at trial, as these warnings are necessary procedural safeguards to protect the privilege against self-incrimination.

II. CASE SUMMARY

A. Background

Four cases were decided together by the Supreme Court. In all of them the police obtained a confession during custodial interrogation without the defendants being previously informed of their rights to counsel, or of their right to remain silent.

No. 759: After his arrest, Ernesto Miranda was taken to an interrogation room. He was not informed of his right to counsel or of his privilege against self-incrimination. He signed a written confession, which included a paragraph stating that he made the confession voluntarily and with full understanding of his rights. The confession was admitted as evidence at trial and he was convicted of kidnapping and rape. The Supreme Court of Arizona affirmed the conviction.

No. 760: During his custodial interrogation, Michael Vignera made an oral confession to the police. He was questioned by an assistant district attorney later that day and a transcript of that interrogation and confession was admitted into evidence at trial. He was not apprised of his rights to counsel or of his right to remain silent and the judge at trial told the jury that a confession is not invalid because the defendant was not apprised of his rights. Vignera was convicted of first degree robbery at trial and the New York Court of Appeals affirmed his conviction.

No. 761: Carl Westover was arrested in connection with robberies in Kansas, and was interrogated. He was then handed over to the FBI, and after two more hours of interrogation, he signed two confessions to robberies in California. His confessions were admitted as evidence at trial and he was convicted of the California robberies. His conviction was affirmed on appeal to the Court of Appeals for the Ninth Circuit. Although he was apprised of his rights prior to questioning by the FBI, the FBI interrogation took place immediately after 15 hours of police interrogation at the same location, towards the end of the interrogation for Westover.

No. 584: Roy Stewart was interrogated on 9 separate occasions over the course of five days. After denying his involvement in a kidnapping during eight of those interrogations, he finally confessed. The confession was introduced as evidence and he was convicted of robbery and first degree murder. The California Supreme Court reversed his conviction because he was never advised of his right to counsel or of his right to remain silent.

On certiorari the Supreme Court reversed Nos. 759, 760 and 761 and affirmed No. 584.

B. Counsel of Record/ACLU Attorney

ACLU Side (Petitioner/Appellant): John J. Flynn argued the cause for appellant in No. 759. Victor M. Earle III argued the cause for appellant in No. 760. F. Conger Fawcett argued the cause for appellant in No. 761. Gordon Ringer, Deputy Attorney General of California, argued the cause for appellant in No. 584.

Opposing Side (Respondent/Appellee): Gary K. Nelson, Assistant Attorney General of Arizona, argued the cause for appellee in No. 759. William I. Siegel argued the cause for appellee in No. 760. Solicitor General Thurgood Marshall argued the cause for appellee in No. 761. William A. Norris, argued the cause for appellee in No. 584.

Telford Taylor argued the cause for the State of New York, as amicus curiae.

Duane R. Nedrud argued the cause for the National District Attorneys Association, as amicus curiae.

III. AMICI CURIAE

ACLU Side (Petitioner/Appellant)

Brief of amici curiae filed on behalf of the ACLU by Anthony G. Amsterdam, Paul J. Mishkin, Raymond L. Bradley, Peter Hearn, and Melvin L. Wulf.

Brief of amici curiae filed by Telford Taylor, for the State of New York, Louis J. Lefkowitz, Attorney General of New York, Samuel A. Hirshowitz, First Assistant Attorney General, and Barry Mahoney and George D. Zuckerman, Assistant Attorneys General, joined by the Attorneys General for their respective States and jurisdictions as follows: Richmond M. Flowers of Alabama, Darrell F. Smith of Arizona, Bruce Bennett of Arkansas, Duke W. Dunbar of Colorado, David P. Buckson of Delaware, Earl Faircloth of Florida, Arthur K. Bolton of Georgia, Allan G. Shepard of Idaho, William G. Clark of Illinois, Robert C. Londerholm of Kansas, Robert Matthews of Kentucky, Jack P. F. Gremillion of Louisiana, Richard J. Dubord of Maine, Thomas B. Finan of Maryland, Norman H. Anderson of Missouri, Forrest H. Anderson of Montana, Clarence A. H. Meyer of Nebraska, T. Wade Bruton of North Carolina, Helgi Johanneson of North Dakota, Robert Y. Thornton of Oregon, Walter E. Alessandroni of Pennsylvania, J. Joseph Nugent of Rhode Island, Daniel R. McLeod of South Carolina, Waggoner Carr of Texas, Robert Y. Button of Virginia, John J. O'Connell of Washington, C. Donald Robertson of West Virginia, John F. Raper of Wyoming, Rafael Hernandez Colon of Puerto Rico, and Francisco Corneiro of the Virgin Islands.

Brief of amici curiae filed on behalf of the National District Attorneys Association by Duane R. Nedrud and Marguerite D. Oberto.

Opposing Side (Respondent/Appellee)

IV. THE SUPREME COURT'S DECISION

"Our holding will be spelled out with some specificity in the pages which follow but briefly stated it is this: the prosecution may not use statements, whether exculpatory or inculpatory, stemming from custodial interrogation of the defendant unless it demonstrates the use of procedural safeguards effective to secure the privilege against self-incrimination. By custodial interrogation, we mean questioning initiated by law enforcement officers after a person has been taken into custody or otherwise deprived of his freedom of action in any significant way. As for the procedural safeguards to be employed, unless other fully effective means are devised to inform accused persons of their right of silence and to assure a continuous opportunity to exercise it, the following measures are required. Prior to any questioning, the person must be warned that he has a right to remain silent, that any statement he does make may be used as evidence against him, and that he has a right to the presence of an attorney, either retained or appointed. The defendant may waive effectuation of these rights, provided the waiver is made voluntarily, knowingly and intelligently. If, however, he indicates in any manner and at any stage of the process that he wishes to consult with an attorney before speaking there can be no questioning. Likewise, if the individual is alone and indicates in any manner that he does not wish to be interrogated, the police may not question him. The mere fact that he may have answered some questions or volunteered some statements on his own does not deprive him of the right to refrain from answering any further inquiries until he has consulted with an attorney and thereafter consents to be questioned. . . .

Accordingly we hold that an individual held for interrogation must be clearly informed that he has the right to consult with a lawyer and to have the lawyer with him during interrogation under the system for protecting the privilege we delineate today. As with the warnings of the right to remain silent and that anything stated can be used in evidence against him, this warning is an absolute prerequisite to interrogation. No amount of circumstantial evidence that the person may have been aware of this right will suffice to stand in its stead. Only through such a warning is there ascertainable assurance that the accused was aware of this right. . . .

In order fully to apprise a person interrogated of the extent of his rights under this system then, it is necessary to warn him not only that he has the right to consult with an attorney, but also that if he is indigent a lawyer will be appointed to represent him. Without this additional warning, the admonition of the right to consult with counsel would often be understood as meaning only that he can consult with a lawyer if he has one or has the funds to obtain one. The warning of a right to counsel would be hollow if not couched in terms that would convey to the indigent—the person most often subjected to interrogation—the knowledge that he too has a right to have counsel present. . . .

To summarize, we hold that when an individual is taken into custody or otherwise deprived of his freedom by the authorities in any significant way and is subjected to questioning, the privilege against self-incrimination is jeopardized. Procedural safeguards must be employed to protect the privilege and unless other fully effective means are adopted to notify the person of his right of silence and to assure that the exercise of the right will be scrupulously honored, the following measures are required. He must be warned prior to any questioning that he has the right to remain silent, that anything he says can be used against him in a court of law, that he has the right to the presence of an attorney, and that if he cannot afford an attorney one will be appointed for him prior to any questioning if he so desires. Opportunity to exercise these rights must be afforded to him throughout the interrogation. After such warnings have been given, and such opportunity afforded him, the individual may knowingly and intelligently waive these rights and agree to answer questions or make a statement. But unless and until such warnings and waiver are demonstrated by the prosecution at trial, no evidence obtained as a result of interrogation can be used against him.

The Supreme Court reversed the judgments in Nos.759, 760, and 761, and affirmed the judgment in No. 584.

V. JUSTICE VOTE

5 Pro ACLU Side vs. 4 Con Opposing Side

ACLU Side (Petitioner/Appellant)

1. Warren, E. – Wrote majority opinion
2. Douglas, W. – Joined majority opinion
3. Brennan, W. – Joined majority opinion
4. Black, H. – Joined majority opinion
5. Fortas, A. – Joined majority opinion

Opposing Side (Respondent/Appellee)

1. White, B. – Wrote dissenting opinion, joined Harlan's dissent
2. Harlan, J. – Wrote dissenting opinion, joined White's dissent
3. Stewart, P. – Joined Harlan's dissent, joined White's dissent
4. Clark, T. – Wrote dissenting opinion

VI. A WIN OR LOSS FOR THE ACLU?

The ACLU, as amicus curiae, urged reversal in Nos. 759, 760 and 761 and affirmance in No. 584 of judgments of the lower courts; the Supreme Court reversed Nos. 759,760, and 761, and affirmed No. 584 in a 5-4 vote, giving the ACLU an apparent win.

177. Gojack v. United States

(Decided June 13, 1966; 384 U.S. 702)

I. ISSUE

A. Issues Discussed

Communism

B. Legal Question Presented

Whether petitioner can be held criminally liable for contempt stemming from refusal to answer certain questions during his appearance before a Subcommittee of the House Committee on Un-American Activities.

C. Supreme Court's Answer

"Absent proof of a clear delegation to the subcommittee of authority to conduct an inquiry into a designated subject, the subcommittee was without authority which can be vindicated by criminal sanctions under s 192, nor was there an authoritative specification of the 'subject matter of the inquiry' necessary for the determination of pertinency required by the section."

II. CASE SUMMARY

A. Background

"This case is a sequel to this Court's decision in Russell v. United States, 369 U.S. 749, and companion cases. One of those cases related to the . . . petitioner here and to the same events.

Petitioner appeared before a Subcommittee of the House Committee on Un-American Activities on February 28 and March 1, 1955. He answered certain questions, but refused to answer others concerning his affiliation with the Communist Party, the affiliation of others, and his connection with a 'Peace Crusade.' He had challenged the jurisdiction of the Committee and the Subcommittee, the authorization of each, and the constitutionality of the inquiry in general and with specific reference to the questions which he declined to answer. He did not and does not invoke the Fifth Amendment.

He was indicted for contempt of Congress under 2 U.S.C. s 192 as a result of his refusals to answer. He was convicted. In Russell v. United States, supra, this Court reversed, holding that the indictment was defective because it did not allege the 'subject under inquiry.' The Court noted that under s 192 specification of the subject of the inquiry is fundamental to a charge of violating its provisions. Absent an allegation of the subject matter of the inquiry, this Court held, there is no way in which it can be determined whether the factual recitals of the indictment charged a crime under s 192—that is, a refusal to answer questions 'pertinent to the inquiry,' and within the legislative competence of Congress.

Petitioner was thereafter re-indicted. . . . Petitioner was again convicted and given a general sentence of three months' imprisonment and a $200 fine. The Court of Appeals for the District of Columbia Circuit affirmed per curiam."

The Supreme Court granted certiorari to review the case.

B. Counsel of Record

ACLU Side (Petitioner/Appellant): Frank J. Donner argued the cause for appellant. With him on the brief were Edward J. Ennis, Osmond K. Fraenkel, and Melvin L. Wulf of the American Civil Liberties Union, and David Rein.

Opposing Side (Respondent/Appellee): Assistant Attorney General Yeagley argued the cause for the United States. With him on the brief were Solicitor General Marshall, Richard A. Posner, Kevin T. Maroney, and Robert L. Keuch.

III. AMICI CURIAE

ACLU Side (Petitioner/Appellant)

No briefs of amici curiae were filed in support of appellant.

Opposing Side (Respondent/Appellee)

No briefs of amici curiae were filed in support of the United States.

IV. THE SUPREME COURT'S DECISION

"Rule I of the Rules of Procedure of the House Committee on Un-American Activities provides that 'No major investigation shall be initiated without approval of a majority of the Committee.' Rule XI, par. 26, of the Rules of the House of Representatives requires each Committee of the House to keep a record of all committee actions. There is no resolution, minute or record of the Committee authorizing the inquiry with which we are concerned. . . .

The Government's only plea in avoidance of this obvious deficiency is that we should 'infer' Committee approval of the inquiry at which petitioner was required to respond to questions, because it was part of the Committee's alleged 'continuing investigation' of Communist activities in the labor field. But this is clearly impermissible. . . .

It can hardly be disputed that a specific, properly authorized subject of inquiry is an essential element of the offense under s 192. . . . There is no basis for invoking criminal sanctions to punish a witness for refusal to cooperate in an inquiry which was never properly authorized.

Indeed, the present case illustrates the wisdom of the Committee's Rule requiring specific authorization of a major investigation. Here, in the absence of official authorization of a specific inquiry, statements were made as to the subject and purpose of the inquiry which, to say the least, might have caused confusion as to the subject of the investigation, and might well have inspired respectable doubts as to legal validity of the Committee's purposes. . . .

Viewed in this perspective, the problem admits of only one answer. Courts administering the criminal law cannot apply sanctions for violation of the mandate of an agency—here, the Subcommittee—unless that agency's authority is clear and has been conferred in accordance with law. . . .

Absent proof of a clear delegation to the subcommittee of authority to conduct an inquiry into a designated subject, the subcommittee was without authority which can be vindicated by criminal sanctions under s 192, nor was there an authoritative specification of the 'subject matter of the inquiry' necessary for the determination of pertinency required by the section.

For the foregoing reasons, the judgment below is reversed."

V. JUSTICE VOTE

9 Pro ACLU Side vs. 0 Con Opposing Side

ACLU Side (Petitioner/Appellant)

1. Fortas, A. – Wrote majority opinion
2. Douglas, W. – Joined majority opinion
3. Warren, E. – Joined majority opinion
4. Brennan, W. – Joined majority opinion
5. Clark, T. – Joined majority opinion
6. White, B. – Joined majority opinion
7. Black, H. – Concurred in the judgment and opinion
8. Stewart, P. – Joined majority opinion
9. Harlan, J. – Joined majority opinion

VI. A WIN OR LOSS FOR THE ACLU?

The ACLU served as counsel for appellant urging reversal of the judgment of the Court of Appeals; the Supreme Court reversed in a 9-0 vote, giving the ACLU an apparent win.

178. Johnson v. New Jersey

(Decided June 20, 1966; 384 U.S. 719)

I. ISSUE

A. Issues Discussed

Criminal procedure, Fifth and Sixth Amendments

B. Legal Question Presented

Should the decisions in the cases of Escobedo v. Illinois and Miranda v. Arizona be applied retroactively?

C. Supreme Court's Answer

Both decisions should not be applied retroactively.

II. CASE SUMMARY

A. Background

On January 29, 1958, petitioner Cassidy was taken into police custody on a felony murder charge. The police "interrogated him in a systematic fashion for several hours." Then "he was brought before the chief detective, two other police officers, and a court stenographer," where he was informed of his charges and that he would be questioned again. At this interrogation, Cassidy made a partial confession to the felony murder recorded by the stenographer and read back to him, which he amended hours later to include further details.

Petitioner Johnson was also taken into police custody for a felony murder charge on January 29, 1958. He was also interrogated and questioned by the chief detective and police officers. During the course of the interrogation, Johnson made a fully confessed to the felony murder. "This interrogation was recorded by a stenographer and read back to Johnson for his acknowledgment."

Both Cassidy and Johnson's confessions were offered as evidence in their joint trial, at which they were both found guilty of first degree murder and sentenced to death.

Cassidy and Johnson filed affidavits in the New Jersey Supreme Court alleging that their confessions were inadmissible under *Escobedo v. Illinois*. The New Jersey Supreme Court held that *Escobedo* did not apply retroactively.

The Supreme Court granted certiorari in the cases and the Supreme Court also decided to view the case in light of *Miranda v. Arizona*, which was decided one week prior, determining that neither *Escobedo* nor *Miranda* apply retroactively.

B. Counsel of Record/ACLU Attorney

ACLU Side (Petitioner/Appellant): Stanford Shmukler and M. Gene Haeberle argued the cause for appellant.

Opposing Side (Respondent/Appellee): Norman Heine argued the cause for appellee.

Telford Taylor, by special leave of Court, argued the cause for the State of New York, as amicus curiae.

Duane R. Nedrud argued the cause for the National District Attorneys Association, as amicus curiae.

III. AMICI CURIAE

ACLU Side (Petitioner/Appellant)

Brief of amici curiae filed on behalf of the ACLU by Anthony G. Amsterdam, Paul J. Mishkin, Raymond L. Bradley, Peter Hearn, and Melvin L. Wulf.

Opposing Side (Respondent/Appellee)

Brief of amici curiae filed by Telford Taylor, for the State of New York, Louis J. Lefkowitz, Attorney General, Samuel A. Hirshowitz, First Assistant Attorney General, and Barry Mahoney and George D. Zuckerman, Assistant Attorneys General, and joined by the Attorneys General for their respective states and jurisdictions as follows: Richmond M. Flowers of Alabama, Darrell F. Smith of Arizona, Bruce Bennett of Arkansas, Duke W. Dunbar of Colorado, David P. Buckson of Delaware, Earl Faircloth of Florida, Arthur K. Bolton of Georgia, Allan G. Shepard of Idaho, William G. Clark of Illinois, Robert C. Londerholm of Kansas, Robert Matthews of Kentucky, Jack P. F. Gremillion of Louisiana, Richard J. Dubord of Maine, Thomas B. Finan of Maryland, Norman H. Anderson of Missouri, Forrest H. Anderson of Montana, Clarence A. H. Meyer of Nebraska, T. Wade Bruton of North Carolina, Helgi Johanneson of North Dakota, Robert Y. Thornton of Oregon, Walter E. Alessandroni of Pennsylvania, J. Joseph Nugent of Rhode Island, Daniel R. McLeod of South Carolina, Waggoner Carr of Texas, Robert Y. Button of Virginia, John J. O'Connell of Washington, C. Donald Robertson of West Virginia, John F. Raper of Wyoming, Rafael Hernandez Colon of Puerto Rico and Francisco Corneiro of the Virgin Islands.

Brief of amici curiae filed on behalf of the National District Attorneys Association by Duane R. Nedrud and Marguerite D. Oberto.

IV. THE SUPREME COURT'S DECISION

"We hold that *Escobedo* affects only those cases in which the trial began after June 22, 1964, the date of that decision. We hold further that *Miranda* applies only to cases in which the trial began after the date of our decision one week ago. The convictions assailed here were obtained at trials completed long before *Escobedo* and *Miranda* were rendered, and the rulings in those cases are therefore inapplicable to the present proceeding. Petitioners have also asked us to overturn their convictions on a number of other grounds, but we find these contentions to be without merit, and consequently we affirm the decision below. . . .

Petitioners' coerced confession claim was fully litigated and rejected both at trial and in prior post-conviction hearings in the state courts. On neither occasion, however, did petitioners attempt to substantiate certain allegations made for the first time in the present proceeding. As stated above, petitioners now assert that they were prevented from obtaining outside assistance while they were being interrogated. The police allegedly refused them access to their families or a lawyer and also thwarted the efforts of their relatives and friends to contact them. We have already pointed out that allegations of this kind are directly relevant to a coerced confession claim and that such a claim presents no problem of retroactivity.

The New Jersey Supreme Court invoked a state procedural rule, previously applied in another confession case, as a bar to reconsideration of petitioners' coerced confession claim, even in the light of their new allegations regarding the denial of outside assistance. This is an adequate state ground which precludes us from testing the coerced confession claim on the present review, whatever may be the significance of the state court's reliance on its procedural rule in federal habeas corpus proceedings."

The Supreme Court affirmed the judgment of the Supreme Court of New Jersey.

V. JUSTICE VOTE

2 Pro ACLU Side vs. 7 Con Opposing Side

ACLU Side (Petitioner/Appellant)

1. Black, H. – Wrote dissenting opinion
2. Douglas, W. – Joined Black's dissent

Opposing Side (Respondent/Appellee)

1. Warren, E. – Wrote majority opinion
2. Fortas, A. – Joined majority opinion
3. Brennan, W. – Joined majority opinion
4. Clark, T. – Wrote concurring opinion
5. White, B. – Wrote concurring opinion with Stewart and Harlan
6. Stewart, P. – Wrote concurring opinion with White and Harlan
7. Harlan, J. – Wrote concurring opinion with Stewart and White

VI. A WIN OR LOSS FOR THE ACLU?

The ACLU filed as amicus curiae supporting petitioner and urging reversal, the U.S. Supreme Court affirmed the Supreme Court of New Jersey's judgment in a 7-2 vote giving the ACLU an apparent loss.

179. Dennis v. United States

(Decided June 20, 1966; 384 U.S. 855)

I. ISSUE

A. Issues Discussed

Government authority, criminal procedure, discovery, First Amendment

B. Legal Question Presented

Whether the indictment against petitioners for conspiracy was proper. Whether § 9(h) of the National Labor Relations Act is constitutional. "Whether the trial court erred in denying petitioners' motions for the production, to the defense or the Court, of grand jury testimony of prosecution witnesses."

C. Supreme Court's Answer

The indictment was proper. The Court declined to consider the constitutionality of § 9(h). The trial court erred in denying the motions to produce prosecution witnesses.

II. CASE SUMMARY

A. Background

Petitioners were alleged Communist Party members. They were all officers and members of the International Union of Mine, Mill and Smelter Workers who filed false affidavits under § 9(h) of the National Labor Relations Act, which required all union officers to submit non-Communist affidavits to obtain National Labor Relations Board ("NLRB") services.

The "indictment alleged a conspiracy fraudulently to obtain the services of the National Labor Relations Board on behalf of the International Union of Mine, Mill and Smelter Workers, by filing false affidavits." At trial, they were convicted. The Court of Appeals, sustained the indictment, but reversed on the ground that improper hearsay evidence had been admitted. Petitioners were retried and again convicted. The Court of Appeals affirmed the second conviction.

The Supreme Court granted certiorari and reversed.

B. Counsel of Record/ACLU Attorney

ACLU Side (Petitioner/Appellant): Telford Taylor argued the cause for appellant.

Opposing Side (Respondent/Appellee): Nathan Lewin argued the cause for appellee.

III. AMICI CURIAE

ACLU Side (Petitioner/Appellant)

Brief of amici curiae filed on behalf of the ACLU, et al., by Gerhard P. Van Arkel, Charles F. Brannan, John F. O'Donnell, Joseph L. Rauh, Jr., Eugene Cotton, Melvin L. Wulf, Jacob Sheinkman, Joseph M. Jacobs John Ligtenberg, Morris E. Lasker, and William B. Gould.

Opposing Side (Respondent/Appellee)

No briefs of amici curiae were filed in support of appellee.

IV. THE SUPREME COURT'S DECISION

"[I]n the present case we conclude that the indictment for conspiracy was proper as to each of the petitioners. . . .

Petitioners next urge that we set aside their convictions on the ground that § 9(h) of the Taft-Hartley Act is unconstitutional. . . . We need not reach this question, for petitioners are in no position to attack the constitutionality of § 9(h). . . .

A conspiracy case carries with it the inevitable risk of wrongful attribution of responsibility to one or more of the multiple defendants. Under these circumstances, it is especially important that the defense, the judge and the jury should have the assurance that the doors that may lead to truth have been unlocked. In our adversary system for determining guilt or innocence, it is rarely justifiable for the prosecution to have exclusive access to a storehouse of relevant fact. Exceptions to this are justifiable only by the clearest and most compelling considerations. For this reason, we cannot accept the view of the Court of Appeals that it is 'safe to assume' no inconsistencies would have come to light if the grand jury testimony had been examined. There is no justification for relying upon 'assumption.'

In *Pittsburgh Plate Glass*, supra, the Court reserved decision on the question whether in camera inspection by the trial judge is an appropriate or satisfactory measure when there is a showing of a 'particularized need' for disclosure. This procedure, followed by production to defense counsel in the event the trial judge finds inconsistencies, has been adopted in some of the Courts of Appeals. In the Second Circuit it is available as a matter of right. While this practice may be useful in enabling the trial court to rule on a defense motion for production to it of grand jury testimony—and we do not disapprove it for that purpose—it by no means disposes of the matter. Trial judges ought not to be burdened with the task or the responsibility of examining sometimes voluminous grand jury testimony in order to ascertain inconsistencies with trial testimony. . . . Nor is it realistic to assume that the trial court's judgment as to the utility of material for impeachment or other legitimate purposes, however ever conscientiously made, would exhaust the possibilities. In our adversary system, it is enough for judges to judge. The determination of what may be useful to the defense can properly and effectively be made only by an advocate. The trial judge's function in this respect is limited to deciding whether a case has been made for production, and to supervise the process: for example, to cause the elimination of extraneous matter and to rule upon applications by the Government for protective orders in unusual situations, such as those involving the Nation's security or clearcut dangers to individuals who are identified by the testimony produced.

Because petitioners were entitled to examine the grand jury minutes relating to trial testimony of the four government witnesses, and to do so while those witnesses were available for cross-examination, we reverse the judgment below and remand for a new trial."

V. JUSTICE VOTE

7 Pro ACLU Side vs. 2 Con Opposing Side

ACLU Side (Petitioner/Appellant)

1. Fortas, A. – Wrote majority opinion
2. White, B. – Joined majority opinion
3. Warren, E. – Joined majority opinion
4. Stewart, P. – Joined majority opinion
5. Clark, T. – Joined majority opinion
6. Harlan, J. – Joined majority opinion
7. Brennan, W. – Joined majority opinion

Opposing Side (Respondent/Appellee)

1. Black, H. – Wrote dissenting opinion
2. Douglas, W. – Wrote dissenting opinion, joined Black's dissent

VI. A WIN OR LOSS FOR THE ACLU?

The ACLU filed an amicus brief urging reversal, the Supreme Court reversed the ruling of the Court of Appeals in a 7-2 vote, giving the ACLU an apparent win.

180. Bond v. Floyd

(Decided December 5, 1966; 385 U.S. 116)

I. ISSUE

A. Issues Discussed

First Amendment, freedoms of speech, press, and assembly

B. Legal Question Presented

"[W]hether the Georgia House of Representatives may constitutionally exclude appellant Bond, a duly elected Representative, from membership because of his statements, and statements to which he subscribed, criticizing the policy of the Federal Government in Vietnam and the operation of the Selective Service laws."

C. Supreme Court's Answer

The exclusion violated Bond's First Amendment rights and was unconstitutional.

II. CASE SUMMARY

A. Background

"Bond, a Negro, was elected on June 15, 1965, as the Representative to the Georgia House of Representatives from the 136th House District. . . . On January 6, 1966, the Student Nonviolent Coordinating Committee, a civil rights organization of which Bond was then the Communications Director, issued" an antiwar statement opposing the United States' Vietnam policy and the operation of the Selective Service laws.

Bond endorsed the statement in a news interview stating among other things that "as a second class citizen" he was not required to support the war, as a pacifist he was opposed to all war, and he saw nothing inconsistent with his views on the war and taking the oath of office.

Georgia House of Representatives members filed petitions challenging Bond's right to be seated, claiming that "Bond's statements gave aid and comfort to the enemies of the United States and Georgia, violated the Selective Service laws, and tended to bring discredit and disrespect on the House." They also claimed he could not take the oath of office because of these views.

"Bond filed a response to the challenge petitions in which he stated his willingness to take the oath" and "argued that the challenge against his seating had been filed to deprive him of his First Amendment rights, and that the challenge was racially motivated." The House held a hearing and concluded that Bond should not be seated and the House thereafter refused to seat him.

Subsequently, Bond brought "an action in District Court for the Northern District of Georgia for injunctive relief and a declaratory judgment." The District Court held that the House had a rational basis for concluding that Bond's "remarks went beyond criticism of national policy" and that he "could not in good faith take an oath to support the State and Federal Constitutions."

Bond appealed to the Supreme Court and while the case was pending before this court, he was again elected as a Representative in the regular 1966 primary and general elections. The Supreme Court reversed the District Court judgment.

B. Counsel of Record/ACLU Attorney

ACLU Side (Petitioner/Appellant): Howard Moore, Jr. and Leonard B. Boudin argued the cause for appellant.

Opposing Side (Respondent/Appellee): Arthur K. Bolton, Attorney General of Georgia, argued the cause for appellee.

III. AMICI CURIAE

ACLU Side (Petitioner/Appellant)

Brief of amici curiae filed on behalf of the ACLU, et al., by Melvin L. Wulf, Eleanor H. Norton, Morris Brown, and Charles Morgan, Jr.

Brief of amici curiae filed on behalf of the National Association for the Advancement of Colored People by Robert L. Carter, Frank D. Reeves, and Herbert O. Reid.

Brief of amici curiae filed on behalf of the American Jewish Congress by Joseph B. Robison, Howard M. Squadron, and David Dretzin.

Opposing Side (Respondent/Appellee)

No briefs of amici curiae were filed in support of appellee.

IV. THE SUPREME COURT'S DECISION

"The State attempts to circumvent the protection the First Amendment would afford to these statements if made by a private citizen by arguing that a State is constitutionally justified in exacting a higher standard of loyalty from its legislators than from its citizens. Of course, a State may constitutionally require an oath to support the Constitution from its legislators which it does not require of its private citizens. But this difference in treatment does not support the exclusion of Bond, for while the State has an interest in requiring its legislators to swear to a belief in constitutional processes of government, surely the oath gives it no interest in limiting its legislators' capacity to discuss their views of local or national policy. The manifest function of the First Amendment in a representative government requires that legislators be given the widest latitude to express their views on issues of policy. The central commitment of the First Amendment, as summarized in the opinion of the Court in *New York Times Co. v. Sullivan*, 376 U.S. 254, 270 (1964), is that 'debate on public issues should be uninhibited, robust, and wide-open.' We think the rationale of the *New York Times* case disposes of the claim that Bond's statements fell outside the range of constitutional protection. Just as erroneous statements must be protected to give freedom of expression the breathing space it needs to survive, so statements criticizing public policy and the implementation of it must be similarly protected. The State argues that the *New York Times* principle should not be extended to statements by a legislator because the policy of encouraging free debate about governmental operations only applies to the citizen-critic of his government. We find no support for this distinction in the *New York Times* case or in any other decision of this Court. The interest of the public in hearing all sides of a public issue is hardly advanced by extending more protection to citizen-critics than to legislators. Legislators have an obligation to take positions on controversial political questions so that their constituents can be fully informed by them, and be better able to assess their qualifications for office; also so they may be represented in governmental debates the person they have elected to represent them. We therefore hold that the disqualification of Bond from membership in the Georgia House because of his statements violated Bond's right of free expression under the First Amendment. Because of our disposition of the case on First Amendment grounds, we need not decide the other issues advanced by Bond and the amici."

The Supreme Court reversed the judgment of the District Court.

V. JUSTICE VOTE

9 Pro ACLU Side vs. 0 Con Opposing Side

ACLU Side (Petitioner/Appellant)

1. Warren, E. – Wrote majority opinion
2. Brennan, W. – Joined majority opinion
3. Black, H. – Joined majority opinion
4. Douglas, W. – Joined majority opinion
5. Fortas, A. – Joined majority opinion
6. Clark, T. – Joined majority opinion
7. Harlan, J. – Joined majority opinion
8. White, B. – Joined majority opinion
9. Stewart, P. – Joined majority opinion

VI. A WIN OR LOSS FOR THE ACLU?

The ACLU filed as amicus curiae urging reversal; the Supreme Court reversed the District Court's judgment in a 9-0 vote giving ACLU an apparent win.

181. Hoffa v. United States

(Decided December 12, 1966; 385 U.S. 293)

I. ISSUE

A. Issues Discussed

Fourth Amendment, criminal procedure, self-incrimination, Fifth Amendment, Sixth Amendment

B. Legal Question Presented

Did the government's use of evidence supplied by a paid government informer render the convictions of petitioners invalid on Fourth, Fifth, and Sixth Amendment grounds?

C. Supreme Court's Answer

The government's use of evidence from a paid government informer did not render the convictions invalid.

II. CASE SUMMARY

A. Background

In a 1962 jury trial, petitioner James Hoffa was charged with violating a provision of the Taft-Hartley Act, a federal law that monitored the activities of labor unions. The trial ended with a hung jury. Later in 1964, petitioners James Hoffa, Thomas Parks, Larry Campbell, and Ewing King were tried and convicted in federal district court for attempting to bribe members of Hoffa's jury. The convictions were supported by testimony from Edward Partin, a paid government informer. Partin testified about several incriminating statements that Hoffa and King made in his presence during the initial jury trial.

The convictions were affirmed by the Court of Appeals. Petitioners appealed to the Supreme Court. The Supreme Court granted certiorari on the issue as to whether the use of evidence furnished by Partin rendered their convictions invalid and violated petitioners' Fourth, Fifth, and Sixth amendment rights.

The Supreme Court affirmed the convictions.

B. Counsel of Record/ACLU Attorney

ACLU Side (Petitioner/Appellant): Joseph A. Fanelli argued the cause for appellant.

Opposing Side (Respondent/Appellee): Assistant Attorney General Fred M. Vinson, Jr., and Nathan Lewin, Assistant to the Solicitor General, argued the cause for appellee.

III. AMICI CURIAE

ACLU Side (Petitioner/Appellant)

Brief of amici curiae filed on behalf of the ACLU by Osmond K. Fraenkel.

Brief of amicus curiae filed on behalf of the Criminal Courts Bar Association of Los Angeles County by Morris Lavine.

Opposing Side (Respondent/Appellee)

No briefs of amici curiae were filed in support of appellee.

IV. THE SUPREME COURT'S DECISION

"Finally, the petitioner claims that even if there was no violation—'as separately measured by each such Amendment'—of the Fourth Amendment, the compulsory self-incrimination clause of the Fifth Amendment, or of the Sixth Amendment in this case, the judgment of conviction must nonetheless be reversed. The argument is based upon the Due Process Clause of the Fifth Amendment. The 'totality' of the Government's conduct during the Test Fleet trial operated, it is said, to 'offend those canons of decency and fairness which express the notions of justice of English-speaking peoples even toward those charged with the most heinous offenses.'

The argument boils down to a general attack upon the use of a government informer as 'a shabby thing in any case,' and to the claim that in the circumstances of this particular case the risk that Partin's testimony might be perjurious was very high. Insofar as the general attack upon the use of informers is based upon historic 'notions' of 'English-speaking peoples,' it is without historical foundation. In the words of Judge Learned Hand, 'Courts have countenanced the use of informers from time immemorial; in cases of conspiracy, or in other cases when the crime consists of preparing for another crime, it is usually necessary to rely upon them or upon accomplices because the criminals will almost certainly proceed covertly. . . .'

This is not to say that a secret government informer is to the slightest degree more free from all relevant constitutional restrictions than is any other government agent. It is to say that the use of secret informers is not per se unconstitutional.

The petitioner is quite correct in the contention that Partin, perhaps even more than most informers, may have had motives to lie. But it does not follow that his testimony was untrue, nor does it follow that his testimony was constitutionally inadmissible. The established safeguards of the Anglo-American legal system leave the veracity of a witness to be tested by cross-examination, and the credibility of his testimony to be determined by a properly instructed jury. At the trial of this case, Partin was subjected to rigorous cross-examination, and the extent and nature of his dealings with federal and state authorities were insistently explored. The trial judge instructed the jury, both specifically and generally, with regard to assessing Partin's credibility. The Constitution does not require us to upset the jury's verdict."

The Supreme Court affirmed the judgment.

V. JUSTICE VOTE

3 Pro ACLU Side vs. 4 Con Opposing Side

ACLU Side (Petitioner/Appellant)

1. Warren, E. – Wrote dissenting opinion
2. Clark, T. – Wrote dissenting opinion
3. Douglas, W. – Wrote dissenting opinion, joined Clark's dissent

Opposing Side (Respondent/Appellee)

1. Stewart, P. – Wrote majority opinion
2. Harlan, J. – Joined majority opinion
3. Brennan, W. – Joined majority opinion
4. Black, H. – Joined majority opinion

White, B. – Took no part in the decision
Fortas, A. – Took no part in the decision

VI. A WIN OR LOSS FOR THE ACLU?

The ACLU filed as amicus curiae urging reversal; the Supreme Court affirmed the judgment of the Court of Appeals in a 4-3 vote, giving the ACLU an apparent loss.

182. Travis v. United States

(Decided January 10, 1967; 385 U.S. 491)

I. ISSUE

A. Issues Discussed

Immigration/Citizenship

B. Legal Question Presented

Whether "area restrictions upon the use of an otherwise valid passport are . . . criminally enforceable under s 215(b)" of the Immigration and Nationality Act of 1952.

C. Supreme Court's Answer

"We have today held that area restrictions upon the use of an otherwise valid passport are not criminally enforceable under s 215(b). Because the Government did not allege, and introduced no proof, that petitioner did not bear a valid passport on each of the occasions on which she departed for Cuba, via Mexico, our decision in Laub requires that her conviction be reversed."

II. CASE SUMMARY

A. Background

"This is a companion case to No. 176, United States v. Laub, 385 U.S. 475. Petitioner was tried on a stipulation of facts, under an indictment which alleged that on two occasions she 'did unlawfully, knowingly and willfully depart from the United States without bearing a valid passport, for the Republic of Cuba, via Mexico, the Republic of Cuba being a place outside the United States for which a valid passport is required' in violation of s 215(b) of the Immigration and Nationality Act of 1952. The parties stipulated that 'At no time pertinent or material herein did defendant, Helen Maxine Levi Travis, bear a valid United States passport specifically endorsed for travel to the Republic of Cuba . . . .' This stipulation is all that the record in this case reveals as to petitioner's possession of a valid passport. Petitioner was convicted, and the Court of Appeals affirmed. [The Supreme Court] granted certiorari in light of the important questions raised by petitioner, and the apparent conflict with the decision of the District Court for the Eastern District of New York in the Laub case, supra, which we affirm today."

B. Counsel of Record

ACLU Side (Petitioner/Appellant): John T. McTernan of the American Civil Liberties Union of Southern California argued the cause for appellant. With him on the briefs were A. L. Wirin of the American Civil Liberties Union of Southern California and William B. Murrish.

Opposing Side (Respondent/Appellee): Nathan Lewin argued the cause for the United States. With him on the brief were Solicitor General Marshall, Assistant Attorney General Yeagley, Kevin T. Maroney, and Robert L. Keuch.

III. AMICI CURIAE

ACLU Side (Petitioner/Appellant)

No briefs of amici curiae were filed in support of appellant.

Opposing Side (Respondent/Appellee)

No briefs of amici curiae were filed in support of the United States.

IV. THE SUPREME COURT'S DECISION

"As our decision in Laub determines, if petitioner in fact had a valid passport, and the gravamen of the Government's accusation under s 215(b) were that her passport was not valid for travel to Cuba, this conviction could not stand. We have today held that area restrictions upon the use of an otherwise valid passport are not criminally enforceable under s 215(b). Because the Government did not allege, and introduced no proof, that petitioner did not bear a valid passport on each of the occasions on which she departed for Cuba, via Mexico, our decision in Laub requires that her conviction be reversed.

Accordingly, the judgment of the Court of Appeals is reversed."

V. JUSTICE VOTE

9 Pro ACLU Side vs. 0 Con Opposing Side

ACLU Side (Petitioner/Appellant)

1. Fortas, A. – Wrote majority opinion
2. Douglas, W. – Joined majority opinion
3. Warren, E. – Joined majority opinion
4. Brennan, W. – Joined majority opinion
5. Clark, T. – Joined majority opinion
6. White, B. – Joined majority opinion
7. Black, H. – Joined majority opinion
8. Stewart, P. – Joined majority opinion
9. Harlan, J. – Joined majority opinion

VI. A WIN OR LOSS FOR THE ACLU?

The ACLU served as counsel for appellants urging reversal of the judgment of the Court of Appeals; the Supreme Court reversed in a 9-0 vote, giving the ACLU an apparent win.

183. Spevack v. Klein

(Decided January 16, 1967; 385 U.S. 511)

I. ISSUE

A. Issues Discussed

Fifth Amendment, self-incrimination, disbarment, attorney discipline

B. Legal Question Presented

Did the Appellate Division of the New York Supreme Court err in disbarring petitioner for his failure to produce demanded records, on the ground that his privilege against self-incrimination was not available?

C. Supreme Court's Answer

Petitioner should not have been disbarred for failure to produce records because he could properly invoke the privilege against self-incrimination.

II. CASE SUMMARY

A. Background

"This is a proceeding to discipline petitioner, a member of the New York Bar, for professional misconduct. Of the various charges made, only one survived, viz., the refusal of petitioner to honor a subpoena duces tecum served on him in that he refused to produce the demanded financial records and refused to testify at the judicial inquiry. Petitioner's sole defense was that the production of the records and his testimony would tend to incriminate him. The Appellate Division of the New York Supreme Court ordered petitioner disbarred, holding that the constitutional privilege against self-incrimination was not available to him in light of our decision in *Cohen v. Hurley*, 366 U.S. 117. The Court of Appeals affirmed."

The Supreme Court granted certiorari and reversed.

B. Counsel of Record/ACLU Attorney

ACLU Side (Petitioner/Appellant): Lawrence J. Latto argued the cause for appellant.

Opposing Side (Respondent/Appellee): Solomon A. Klein argued the cause for appellee, pro se.

III. AMICI CURIAE

ACLU Side (Petitioner/Appellant)

Brief of amici curiae filed on behalf of the New York Civil Liberties Union by Emanuel Redfield.

Brief of amici curiae filed on behalf of the American Trial Lawyers Association by Israel Steingold.

Brief of amici curiae filed on behalf of the New York State Association of Trial Lawyers by Herman B. Gerringer.

Brief of amici curiae filed on behalf of the New York City Chapter of the National Lawyers Guild by Ralph Shapiro.

Opposing Side (Respondent/Appellee)

Brief of amici curiae filed on behalf of the Association of the Bar of the City of New York by John G. Bonomi, Michael Franck, and Peter J. O'Connor.

IV. THE SUPREME COURT'S DECISION

"The threat of disbarment and the loss of professional standing, professional reputation, and of livelihood are powerful forms of compulsion to make a lawyer relinquish the privilege. That threat is indeed as powerful an instrument of compulsion as 'the use of legal process to force from the lips of the accused individual the evidence necessary to convict him . . . .' As we recently stated in *Miranda v. State of Arizona*, 384 U.S. 436, 'In this Court, the privilege has consistently been accorded a liberal construction.' It is in that tradition that we overrule Cohen v. Hurley. We find no room in the privilege against self-incrimination for classifications of people so as to deny it to some and extend it to others. Lawyers are not excepted from the words 'No person . . . shall be compelled in any criminal case to be a witness against himself'; and we can imply no exception. . . .

The documents sought in the subpoena were petitioner's daybook, cash receipts book, cash disbursements book, checkbook stubs, petty cashbook and vouchers, general ledger and journal, canceled checks and bank statements, passbooks and other evidences of accounts, record of loans made, payroll records, and state and federal tax returns and worksheets relative thereto.

The Shapiro case dealt with a federal price control regulation requiring merchants to keep sales records. The Court called them records with 'public aspects,' as distinguished from private and concluded by a divided vote that their compelled production did not violate the Fifth Amendment. We are asked to overrule Shapiro. But we find it unnecessary to reach it.

Rule 5, requiring the keeping of records, was broad and general—'the pleadings, records and other papers pertaining to such action, claim and proceeding, and also all data and memoranda of the disposition thereof.' The detailed financial aspects of contingent-fee litigation demanded might possibly by a broad, generous construction of the Rule be brought within its intendment. Our problem, however, is different. Neither the referee of the inquiry, nor counsel for the inquiry, nor the Appellate Division of the New York Supreme Court questioned the applicability of the privilege against self-incrimination to the records. All proceeded on the basis that petitioner could invoke the privilege with respect to the records, but that the price he might have to pay was disbarment. The Court of Appeals was the first to suggest that the privilege against self-incrimination was not applicable to the records. Petitioner, however, had been disbarred on the theory that the privilege was applicable to the records, but that the invocation of the privilege could lead to disbarment. His disbarment cannot be affirmed on the ground that the privilege was not applicable in the first place. For that procedure would deny him all opportunity at the trial to show that the Rule, fairly construed and understood, should not be given a broad sweep and to make a record that the documents demanded by the subpoena had no 'public aspects' within the required records rule but were private papers."

The Supreme Court reversed the judgment of the New York Court of Appeals.

V. JUSTICE VOTE

5 Pro ACLU Side vs. 4 Con Opposing Side

ACLU Side (Petitioner/Appellant)

1. Douglas, W. – Wrote majority opinion
2. Fortas, A. – Wrote concurring opinion
3. Warren, E. – Joined majority opinion
4. Brennan, W. – Joined majority opinion
5. Black, H. – Joined majority opinion

Opposing Side (Respondent/Appellee)

1. White, B. – Wrote dissenting opinion
2. Harlan, J. – Wrote dissenting opinion
3. Stewart, P. – Joined Harlan's dissent
4. Clark, T. – Joined Harlan's dissent

VI. A WIN OR LOSS FOR THE ACLU?

The ACLU filed an amicus brief urging reversal; the Supreme Court reversed the ruling of the New York Court of Appeals in a 5-4 vote, giving the ACLU an apparent win.

184. Whitus v. Georgia

(Decided January 23, 1967; 385 U.S. 545)

I. ISSUE

A. Issues Discussed

Racial discrimination, jury selection, equal protection

B. Legal Question Presented

Does the Georgia system of jury selection, for grand and petit jury, unconstitutionally discriminate on the basis of race?

C. Supreme Court's Answer

The jury selection system unconstitutionally discriminates on the basis of race.

II. CASE SUMMARY

A. Background

"Once again we are confronted with the question of racial discrimination in the selection of the grand and petit juries which have respectively indicted petitioners and found them guilty of the offense of murder. The claim is that Georgia's system of jury selection resulted in the systematic exclusion of Negroes from both the grand and petit juries in that its law required jury commissioners to select the names of prospective jurors from the books of the county tax receiver which were maintained on a racially segregated basis. The grand jury question is raised in both these cases and we consolidated them for argument and do likewise on disposition. . . .

The petitioners have been here twice before. They were originally convicted in 1960 and the Supreme Court of Georgia affirmed. Thereafter a writ of habeas corpus was filed in the United States District Court for the Southern District of Georgia in which, for the first time, petitioner Whitus attacked the composition of the grand and petit juries. The District Court dismissed the writ and the Court of Appeals affirmed. On writ of certiorari, we vacated that judgment and remanded the case to the District Court for a hearing on the claim of discrimination. On remand, the District Court again dismissed the petition on the ground that the claim had been waived since it was not raised in the Georgia courts. The Court of Appeals reversed, holding that Negroes had been systematically excluded from both the grand and petit juries. Its ruling was based on a finding that 45% of the population of the county was Negro; yet, none had ever served on juries within the memory of the witnesses.

After the Court of Appeals set aside the first convictions, the Superior Court of Mitchell County directed the jury commissioners for the county to revise the jury list. . . . The State admits that prior to 1965, the tax return sheets furnished by the State Revenue Department were white for white taxpayers and yellow for Negro taxpayers. The 1964 tax digest, and all digests prior to 1964, were made up from these segregated tax returns. Furthermore, the jury lists for each county are required by law to be made up from the tax digest. The State further admits that the 'revised' jury list from which both the grand and petit juries serving in these cases were selected, had been made up by reference to the old jury list, which the Court of Appeals had condemned, and the 1964 tax digest, which had been prepared from the white and yellow tax return sheets of that year. However, the jury commissioners did not use the 1964 tax returns themselves, nor the 1965 tax digest which had not yet been made up. The tax digest appears to have been in one volume but was segregated into two sections-one for white and the other for Negro taxpayers. The Negroes whose names were included in the tax digest were designated by a '(c)' being placed opposite their names as required by Ga.Code Ann. § 92-6307.

The three jury commissioners who appeared as witnesses testified that they were not aware of the letter (c) appearing after the names of the Negroes on the 1964 tax digest; that they never included or excluded anyone on the 'revised' jury list because of race or color; that they placed on the 'revised' jury list those persons whom they knew personally from their respective communities; that there were around 600 selected; and that the 'revised' list, which the commissioners themselves prepared, had no designation of race upon it."

On certiorari the Supreme Court found that the jury selection was discriminatory and reversed the judgments of the Supreme Court of Georgia.

B. Counsel of Record/ACLU Attorney

ACLU Side (Petitioner/Appellant): Charles Morgan, Jr., and P. Walter Jones argued the cause for appellant. With them on the briefs were B. Clarence Mayfield, Morris Brown, M. Laughlin McDonald, and Melvin L. Wulf

Opposing Side (Respondent/Appellee): Fred B. Hand, Jr., Solicitor General of Georgia, and E. Freeman Leverett, Deputy Assistant Attorney General, argued the cause for appellee. With them on the briefs was Arthur K. Bolton, Attorney General.

III. AMICI CURIAE

ACLU Side (Petitioner/Appellant)

No briefs of amici curiae were filed in support of appellant.

Opposing Side (Respondent/Appellee)

No briefs of amici curiae were filed in support of appellee.

IV. THE SUPREME COURT'S DECISION

"For over fourscore years it has been federal statutory law and the law of this Court as applied to the States through the Equal Protection Clause of the Fourteenth Amendment, that a conviction cannot stand if it is based on an indictment of a grand jury or the verdict of a petit jury from which Negroes were excluded by reason of their race. . . .

Under [Georgia's] system the opportunity for discrimination was present and we cannot say on this record that it was not resorted to by the commissioners. Indeed, the disparity between the percentage of Negroes on the tax digest (27.1%) and that of the grand jury venire (9.1%) and the petit jury venire (7.8%) strongly points to this conclusion. Although the system of selection used here had been specifically condemned by the Court of Appeals, the State offered no testimony as to why it was continued on retrial. The State offered no explanation for the disparity between the percentage of Negroes on the tax digest and those on the venires, although the digest must have included the names of large numbers of 'upright and intelligent' Negroes as the statutory qualification required. In any event the State failed to offer any testimony indicating that the 27.1% of Negroes on the tax digest were not fully qualified. The State, therefore, failed to meet the burden of rebutting the petitioners' prima facie case."

The Supreme Court reversed the judgments of the Supreme Court of Georgia.

V. JUSTICE VOTE

9 Pro ACLU Side vs. 0 Con Opposing Side

ACLU Side (Petitioner/Appellant)

1. Clark, T. – Wrote majority opinion
2. Douglas, W. – Joined majority opinion

3. Stewart, P. – Joined majority opinion
4. Brennan, W. – Joined majority opinion
5. Fortas, A. – Joined majority opinion
6. Warren, E. – Joined majority opinion
7. Harlan, J. – Joined majority opinion
8. Black, H. – Joined majority opinion
9. White, B. – Joined majority opinion

VI. A WIN OR LOSS FOR THE ACLU?

The ACLU, as counsel of record, urged reversal of the judgments of the Supreme Court of Georgia; the U.S. Supreme Court reversed the lower court's ruling in a 9-0 vote, giving the ACLU an apparent win.

185. Keyishian v. Board of Regents

(Decided January 23, 1967; 385 U.S. 589)

I. ISSUE

A. Issues Discussed

Governmental authority, First Amendment, loyalty oath, overbreadth

B. Legal Question Presented

Can New York constitutionally require teachers and staff of state universities to certify they are not members of the Communist Party?

C. Supreme Court's Answer

The requirements are overbroad and unconstitutionally invalid in that respect.

II. CASE SUMMARY

A. Background

Appellants Hochfield, Maud, and Keyishian, were faculty members of the State University of New York. "Each of them refused to sign, as regulations then in effect required, a certificate that he was not a Communist, and that if he had ever been a Communist, he had communicated that fact to the President of the State University of New York. Each was notified that his failure to sign the certificate would require his dismissal. . . .

Appellant Starbuck was a nonfaculty library employee and part-time lecturer in English. Personnel in that classification were not required to sign a certificate but were required to answer in writing under oath the question, 'Have you ever advised or taught or were you ever a member of any society or group of persons which taught or advocated the doctrine that the Government of the United States or of any political subdivisions thereof should be overthrown or overturned by force, violence or any unlawful means?' Starbuck refused to answer the question and as a result was dismissed.

Appellants brought this action for declaratory and injunctive relief, alleging that the state program violated the Federal Constitution in various respects. A three-judge federal court held that the program was constitutional."

The Supreme Court granted certiorari and reversed.

B. Counsel of Record/ACLU Attorney

ACLU Side (Petitioner/Appellant): Richard Lipsitz argued the cause for appellant.

Opposing Side (Respondent/Appellee): Ruth V. Iles, Assistant Attorney General of New York, argued the cause for appellees Board of Regents, et al., John C. Crary, Jr., argued the cause for appellees Board of Trustees of the State University of New York, et al.

III. AMICI CURIAE

ACLU Side (Petitioner/Appellant)

Brief of amici curiae filed on behalf of the ACLU, et al., by Osmond K. Fraenkel, James L. Magavern, Bernard E. Harvith, Melvin L. Wulf, and Henry M. di Suvero.

Brief of amici curiae filed on behalf of the American Associations of University Professors by Ralph F. Fuchs, Bernard Wolfman, Herman I. Orentlicher, Robert M. O'Neil, and James L. Magavern.

Opposing Side (Respondent/Appellee)

No briefs of amici curiae were filed in support of appellees.

IV. THE SUPREME COURT'S DECISION

"We proceed then to the question of the validity of the provisions of subdivision 1(c) of § 105 and subdivision 2 of § 3022, barring employment to members of listed organizations. Here again constitutional doctrine has developed since Adler. Mere knowing membership without a specific intent to further the unlawful aims of an organization is not a constitutionally adequate basis for exclusion from such positions as those held by appellants. . . .

Thus § 105, subd. 1 (c), and § 3022, subd. 2, suffer from impermissible 'overbreadth.' They seek to bar employment both for association which legitimately may be proscribed and for association which may not be proscribed consistently with First Amendment rights. Where statutes have an overbroad sweep, just as where they are vague, 'the hazard of loss or substantial impairment of those precious rights may be critical,' since those covered by the statute are bound to limit their behavior to that which is unquestionably safe. As we said in Shelton v. Tucker, 'The breadth of legislative abridgment must be viewed in the light of less drastic means for achieving the same basic purpose.'

We therefore hold that Civil Service Law § 105, subd. 1 (c), and Education Law § 3022, subd. 2, are invalid insofar as they proscribe mere knowing membership without any showing of specific intent to further the unlawful aims of the Communist Party of the United States or of the State of New York. The judgment of the District Court is reversed and the case is remanded for further proceedings consistent with this opinion."

V. JUSTICE VOTE

5 Pro ACLU Side vs. 4 Con Opposing Side

ACLU Side (Petitioner/Appellant)

1. Brennan, W. – Wrote majority opinion

2. Black, H. – Joined majority opinion
3. Douglas, W. – Joined majority opinion
4. Warren, E. – Joined majority opinion
5. Fortas, A. – Joined majority opinion

Opposing Side (Respondent/Appellee)

1. Clark, T. – Wrote dissenting opinion
2. Harlan, J. – Joined Clark's dissent
3. White, B. – Joined Clark's dissent
4. Stewart, P. – Joined Clark's dissent

VI. A WIN OR LOSS FOR THE ACLU?

The ACLU filed an amicus brief urging reversal; the Supreme Court reversed the ruling of the District Court in a 5-4 vote, giving the ACLU an apparent win.

186. Klopfer v. North Carolina

(Decided March 13, 1967; 386 U.S. 213)

I. ISSUE

A. Issues Discussed

Criminal procedure, Sixth Amendment, right to a speedy trial

B. Legal Question Presented

"[W]hether a State may indefinitely postpone prosecution on an indictment without stated justification over the objection of an accused who has been discharged from custody."

C. Supreme Court's Answer

Indefinitely postponing prosecution without justification violates the Sixth Amendment right to a speedy trial.

II. CASE SUMMARY

A. Background

"On February 24, 1964, petitioner was indicted by the grand jury of Orange County for the crime of criminal trespass, a misdemeanor .... Prosecution on the indictment began with admirable promptness . . . but, when the jury failed to reach a verdict, the trial judge declared a mistrial and ordered the case continued for the term.

Several weeks prior to the April 1965 Criminal Session of the Superior Court, the State's solicitor informed petitioner of his intention to have a nolle prosequi with leave entered in the case. During the session, petitioner, through his attorney, opposed the entry of such an order in open court. . . . In spite of petitioner's opposition, the court indicated that it would approve entry of a nolle prosequi with leave if requested to do so by the solicitor. But the solicitor declined to make a motion for a nolle prosequi with leave. Instead, he filed a motion with the court to continue the case for yet another term, which motion was granted.

The calendar for the August 1965 Criminal Session of the court did not list Klopfer's case for trial. To ascertain the status on his case, petitioner filed a motion expressing his desire to have the charge pending against him 'permanently concluded in accordance with the applicable laws of the State of North Carolina and of the United States as soon as is reasonably possible.' Noting that some 18 months had elapsed since the indictment, petitioner, a professor of zoology at Duke University, contended that the pendency of the indictment greatly interfered with his professional activities and with his travel here and abroad. . . .

In response to the motion, the trial judge considered the status of petitioner's case in open court on Monday, August 9, 1965, at which time the solicitor moved the court that the State be permitted to take a nolle prosequi with leave. Even though no justification for the proposed entry was offered by the State, and, in spite of petitioner's objection to the order, the court granted the State's motion.

On appeal to the Supreme Court of North Carolina, petitioner contended that the entry of the nolle prosequi with leave order deprived him of his right to a speedy trial as required by the Fourteenth Amendment to the United States Constitution. Although the Supreme Court acknowledged that entry of the nolle prosequi with leave did not permanently discharge the indictment, it nevertheless affirmed."

The Supreme Court granted certiorari in the case and reversed.

B. Counsel of Record/ACLU Attorney

ACLU Side (Petitioner/Appellant): Wade H. Penny, Jr., argued the cause for appellant.

Opposing Side (Respondent/Appellee): Andrew A. Vanore, Jr., argued the cause for appellee.

III. AMICI CURIAE

ACLU Side (Petitioner/Appellant)

Brief of amici curiae filed on behalf of the ACLU, et al., by William W. Van Alstyne and Melvin L. Wulf.

Opposing Side (Respondent/Appellee)

No briefs of amici curiae were filed in support of appellee.

IV. THE SUPREME COURT'S DECISION

"We, too, believe that the position taken by the court below was erroneous. The petitioner is not relieved of the limitations placed upon his liberty by this prosecution merely because its suspension permits him to go 'whithersoever he will.' The pendency of the indictment may subject him to public scorn and deprive him of employment, and almost certainly will force curtailment of his speech, associations and participation in unpopular causes. By indefinitely prolonging this oppression, as well as the 'anxiety and concern accompanying public accusation,' the criminal procedure condoned in this case by the Supreme Court of North Carolina clearly denies the petitioner the right to a speedy trial which we hold is guaranteed to him by the Sixth Amendment of the Constitution of the United States.

While there has been a difference of opinion as to what provisions of this Amendment to the Constitution apply to the States through the Fourteenth Amendment, that question has been settled as to some of them ....

We hold here that the right to a speedy trial is as fundamental as any of the rights secured by the Sixth Amendment. . . . That this right was considered fundamental at this early period in our history is evidenced by its guarantee in the constitutions of several of the States of the new nation, as well as by its prominent position in the Sixth Amendment. Today, each of the 50 States guarantees the right to a speedy trial to its citizens.

The history of the right to a speedy trial and its reception in this country clearly establish that it is one of the most basic rights preserved by our Constitution. For the reasons stated above, the judgment must be reversed and remanded for proceedings not inconsistent with the opinion of the Court."

The Supreme Court reversed the judgment of Court of Appeals and remanded the case.

V. JUSTICE VOTE

9 Pro ACLU Side vs. 0 Con Opposing Side

ACLU Side (Petitioner/Appellant)

1. Warren, E. – Wrote majority opinion
2. Fortas, A – Joined majority opinion
3. White, B. – Joined majority opinion
4. Stewart, P. – Concurred in the result
5. Clark, T. – Joined majority opinion
6. Brennan, W. – Joined majority opinion
7. Black, H. – Joined majority opinion
8. Douglas, W. – Joined majority opinion
9. Harlan, J. – Wrote concurring opinion

VI. A WIN OR LOSS FOR THE ACLU?

The ACLU filed an amicus brief urging reversal; the Supreme Court reversed the ruling of the Court of Appeals in a 9-0 vote, giving the ACLU an apparent win.

187. In re Gault

(Decided May 15, 1967; 387 U.S. 1)

I. ISSUE

A. Issues Discussed

Criminal procedure

B. Legal Question Presented

Whether a juvenile defendant is eligible for various due process protections provided to adult defendants.

C. Supreme Court's Answer

A juvenile defendant is eligible for various due process protections and denial of these protections was a failure by the juvenile court.

II. CASE SUMMARY

A. Background

"This is an appeal under 28 U.S.C. s 1257 (2) from a judgment of the Supreme Court of Arizona affirming the dismissal of a petition for a writ of habeas corpus. The petition sought the release of Gerald Francis Gault, appellants' 15-year-old son, who had been committed as a juvenile delinquent to the State Industrial School by the Juvenile Court of Gila County, Arizona. The Supreme Court of Arizona affirmed dismissal of the writ against various arguments which included an attack upon the constitutionality of the Arizona Juvenile Code because of its alleged denial of procedural due process rights to juveniles charged with being 'delinquents.' The court agreed that the constitutional guarantee of due process of law is applicable in such proceedings. It held that Arizona's Juvenile Code is to be read as 'impliedly' implementing the 'due process concept.' It then proceeded to identify and describe 'the particular elements which constitute due process in a juvenile hearing.' It concluded that the proceedings ending in commitment of Gerald Gault did not offend those requirements."

The Supreme Court granted certiorari to review the case.

B. Counsel of Record

ACLU Side (Petitioner/Appellant): Norman Dorsen argued the cause for appellants. With him on the brief were Melvin L. Wulf (ACLU legal director 1962-1977), Amelie D. Lewis, Daniel A. Rezneck, Charles E. Ares, Gertrud Mainzer, and James J. Murray.

Opposing Side (Respondent/Appellee): Frank A. Parks, Assistant Attorney General of Arizona, argued the cause for appellee, pro hac vice, by special leave of Court. With him on the brief was Darrell F. Smith, Attorney General.

Merritt W. Green argued the cause for the Ohio Association of Juvenile Court Judges, as amicus puriae, urging affirmance. With him on the brief was Leo G. Chimo.

III. AMICI CURIAE

ACLU Side (Petitioner/Appellant)

Brief of amici curiae filed on behalf of the National Legal Aid and Defender Association by L. Michael Getty, James J. Doherty, and Marshall J. Hartman.

Brief of amici curiae filed on behalf of the Legal Aid Society and Citizens' Committee for Children of New York, Inc. by Edward Q. Carr, Jr., and Nanette Dembitz.

Brief of amici curiae filed on behalf of the American Parents Committee by Nicholas N. Kittrie.

Opposing Side (Respondent/Appellee)

Brief of amici curiae filed on behalf of the Ohio Association of Juvenile Court Judges by Merritt W. Green and Leo G. Chimo.

IV. THE SUPREME COURT'S DECISION

"The Supreme Court of Arizona held that due process of law is requisite to the constitutional validity of proceedings in which a court reaches the conclusion that a juvenile has been at fault, has engaged in conduct prohibited by law, or has otherwise misbehaved with the consequence that he is committed to an institution in which his freedom is curtailed. This conclusion is in accord with the decisions of a number of courts under both federal and state constitutions. . . .

Appellants allege that the Arizona Juvenile Code is unconstitutional or alternatively that the proceedings before the Juvenile Court were constitutionally defective because of failure to provide adequate notice of the hearings. . . .

We cannot agree with the court's conclusion that adequate notice was given in this case. . . . Due process of law requires notice of the sort we have described—that is, notice which would be deemed constitutionally adequate in a civil or criminal proceeding. . . .

Appellants charge that the Juvenile Court proceedings were fatally defective because the court did not advise Gerald or his parents of their right to counsel, and proceeded with the hearing, the adjudication of delinquency and the order of commitment in the absence of counsel . . . .

We conclude that the Due Process Clause of the Fourteenth Amendment requires that in respect of proceedings to determine delinquency which may result in commitment to an institution in which the juvenile's freedom is curtailed, the child and his parents must be notified of the child's right to be represented by counsel retained by them, or if they are unable to afford counsel, that counsel will be appointed to represent the child. . . .

We conclude that the constitutional privilege against self-incrimination is applicable in the case of juveniles as it is with respect to adults. . . .

We now hold that, absent a valid confession, a determination of delinquency and an order of commitment to a state institution cannot be sustained in the absence of sworn testimony subjected to the opportunity for cross-examination in accordance with our law and constitutional requirements. . . .

As the present case illustrates, the consequences of failure to provide an appeal, to record the proceedings, or to make findings or state the grounds for the juvenile court's conclusion may be to throw a burden upon the machinery for habeas corpus, to saddle the reviewing process with the burden of attempting to reconstruct a record, and to impose upon the Juvenile Judge the unseemly duty of testifying under cross-examination as to the events that transpired in the hearings before him.

[T]he judgment of the Supreme Court of Arizona is reversed and the cause remanded . . . ."

V. JUSTICE VOTE

8 Pro ACLU Side vs. 1 Con Opposing Side

ACLU Side (Petitioner/Appellant)

1. Fortas, A. – Wrote majority opinion
2. Warren, E. – Joined majority opinion
3. Brennan, W. – Joined majority opinion
4. Black, H. – Wrote concurring opinion
5. Douglas, W. – Joined majority opinion
6. Harlan, J. – Wrote opinion concurring in part and dissenting in part
7. Clark, T. – Joined majority opinion
8. White, B. – Wrote concurring opinion

Opposing Side (Respondent/Appellee)

1. Stewart, P. – Wrote dissenting opinion

VI. A WIN OR LOSS FOR THE ACLU?

The ACLU served as counsel for appellant urging reversal of the judgment of the Supreme Court of Arizona; the U.S. Supreme Court reversed in an 8-1 vote, giving the ACLU an apparent win.

188. Boutilier v. Immigration and Naturalization Service

(Decided May 22, 1967; 387 U.S. 118)

I. ISSUE

A. Issues Discussed

Immigration, civil rights, deportation

B. Legal Question Presented

Does the provision of the Immigration and Nationality Act that makes aliens "afflicted with psychopathic personality" inadmissible to the United States include homosexuals, and, if so, is the provision constitutional?

C. Supreme Court's Answer

The provision includes persons who were homosexual prior to and at the time of entry into the United States and is constitutional.

II. CASE SUMMARY

A. Background

"Petitioner, a Canadian national, was first admitted to this country on June 22, 1955, at the age of 21. . . . In 1963 he applied for citizenship and submitted to the Naturalization Examiner an affidavit in which he admitted that he was arrested in New York in October 1959, on a charge of sodomy, which was later reduced to simple assault and thereafter dismissed on default of the complainant. In 1964, petitioner, at the request of the Government, submitted another affidavit which revealed the full history of his sexual deviate behavior." This affidavit showed he had engaged in homosexual behavior on various occasions since the age of 14 and "[s]ince 1959 petitioner had shared an apartment with a man with whom he had had homosexual relations.

The 1964 affidavit was submitted to the Public Health Service for its opinion as to whether petitioner was excludable for any reason at the time of his entry. The Public Health Service issued a certificate in 1964 stating that in the opinion of the subscribing physicians petitioner 'was afflicted with a class A condition, namely, psychopathic personality, sexual deviate' at the time of his admission. Deportation proceedings were then instituted. . . . Finding against petitioner on the facts, the issue before the officer was reduced to the purely legal question of whether the term 'psychopathic personality' included homosexuals and if it suffered illegality because of vagueness."

"Petitioner's appeal from the finding of the Special Inquiry Officer was dismissed by the Board of Immigration Appeals, without opinion, and his petition for review in the Court of Appeals was dismissed, with one judge dissenting."

The Supreme Court granted certiorari and affirmed.

B. Counsel of Record/ACLU Attorney

ACLU Side (Petitioner/Appellant): Blanch Freedman argued the cause for appellant.

Opposing Side (Respondent/Appellee): Nathan Lewin argued the cause for appellee.

III. AMICI CURIAE

ACLU Side (Petitioner/Appellant)

Brief of amici curiae filed on behalf of the ACLU, et al., by David Carliner, Nanette Dembitz, Alan H. Levine, and Burt Neuborne.

Brief of amicus curiae filed on behalf of the Homosexual Law Reform Society of America by Gilbert M. Cantor.

Opposing Side (Respondent/Appellee)

No briefs of amici curiae were filed in support of appellee.

IV. THE SUPREME COURT'S DECISION

"The legislative history of the Act indicates beyond a shadow of a doubt that the Congress intended the phrase 'psychopathic personality' to include homosexuals such as petitioner. . . .

Petitioner stresses that only persons afflicted with psychopathic personality are excludable. This, he says, is 'a condition, physical or psychiatric, which may be manifested in different ways, including sexual behavior.' Petitioner's contention must fall by his own admissions. For over six years prior to his entry petitioner admittedly followed a continued course of homosexual conduct. The Public Health Service doctors found and certified that at the time of his entry petitioner 'was afflicted with a class A condition, namely, psychopathic personality, sexual deviate . . . .' The Government clearly established that petitioner was a homosexual at entry. Having substantial support in the record, we do not now disturb that finding, especially since petitioner admitted being a homosexual at the time of his entry. The existence of this condition over a continuous and uninterrupted period prior to and at the time of petitioner's entry clearly supports the ultimate finding upon which the order of deportation was based. . . .

Petitioner says, even so, the section as construed is constitutionally defective because it did not adequately warn him that his sexual affliction at the time of entry could lead to his deportation. . . . The petitioner is not being deported for conduct engaged in after his entry into the United States, but rather for characteristics he possessed at the time of his entry. Here, when petitioner first presented himself at our border for entrance, he was already afflicted with homosexuality. . . .

The constitutional requirement of fair warning has no applicability to standards such as are laid down in § 212(a)(4) for admission of aliens to the United States. It has long been held that the Congress has plenary power to make rules for the admission of aliens and to exclude those who possess those characteristics which Congress has forbidden. Here Congress commanded that homosexuals not be allowed to enter. The petitioner was found to have that characteristic and was ordered deported. The basis of the deportation order was his affliction for a long period of time prior to entry, i.e., six and one-half years before his entry."

The Supreme Court affirmed the judgment.

V. JUSTICE VOTE

3 Pro ACLU Side vs. 6 Con Opposing Side

ACLU Side (Petitioner/Appellant)

1. Brennan, W. – Wrote dissenting opinion
2. Douglas, W. – Wrote dissenting opinion
3. Fortas, A. – Joined Douglas' dissent

Opposing Side (Respondent/Appellee)

1. Clark, T. – Wrote majority opinion
2. Stewart, P. – Joined majority opinion
3. Black, H. – Joined majority opinion
4. Warren, E. – Joined majority opinion
5. Harlan, J. – Joined majority opinion
6. White, B. – Joined majority opinion

VI. A WIN OR LOSS FOR THE ACLU?

The ACLU filed an amicus brief urging reversal; the Supreme Court affirmed the deportation order in a 6-3 vote, giving the ACLU an apparent loss.

189. Reitman v. Mulkey

(Decided May 29, 1967; 387 U.S. 369)

I. ISSUE

A. Issues Discussed

Civil rights, racial discrimination, equal protection, Fourteenth Amendment

B. Legal Question Presented

"[W]hether Article I, § 26, of the California Constitution denies 'to any person . . . the equal protection of the laws' within the meaning of the Fourteenth Amendment of the Constitution of the United States."

C. Supreme Court's Answer

Section 26 denies equal protection by allowing unconstitutional racial discrimination in housing.

II. CASE SUMMARY

A. Background

In 1964, California added Article I, § 26, to the state constitution, which provides: "Neither the State nor any subdivision or agency thereof shall deny, limit or abridge, directly or indirectly, the right of any person, who is willing or desires to sell, lease or rent any part or all of his real property, to decline to sell, lease or rent such property to such person or persons as he, in his absolute discretion, chooses."

This case involves two separate actions that arose in the California courts. In one case, a husband and wife, respondents here, alleged race discrimination for petitioner's refusal to rent them an apartment solely on account of their race. In the second case, a husband and wife sought to enjoin an eviction from their apartment they alleged was "motivated by racial prejudice. Both couples sued under §§ 51 and 52 of the California Civil Code. After lower court decisions, the California Supreme Court decided Article I, § 26, of the California Constitution "was invalid as denying equal protection of the laws guaranteed by the Fourteenth Amendment."

The U.S. Supreme Court granted certiorari and affirmed.

B. Counsel of Record / ACLU Attorney

ACLU Side (Responent/Appellee): Herman F. Selvin and A. L. Wirin argued the cause for appellee. With them on the briefs were Fred Okrand, Joseph A. Ball, Nathaniel S. Colley, and David R. Cadwell.

Solicitor General Thurgood Marshall argued the cause for the United States, as amicus curiae.

Opposing Side (Petitioner/Appellant): Samuel O. Pruitt, Jr. argued the cause for appellant. With him on the brief were William French Smith and Charles S. Battles, Jr.

III. AMICI CURIAE

ACLU Side (Respondent/Appellee)

Brief of amici curiae filed on behalf of the ACLU of Northern California by Marshall W. Krause.

Additional briefs of amici curiae were filed on behalf of the United States, the State of California, the Attorney General of the State of New York, the California Democratic State Central Committee, the National Committee Against Discrimination in Housing, and the United Automobile, Aerospace & Agricultural Implement Workers of America (UAW) AFL-CIO, Region 6, et al.

Opposing Side (Petitioner/Appellant)

No briefs of amici curiae were filed in support of appellant.

IV. THE SUPREME COURT'S DECISION

"The judgment of the California court was that § 26 unconstitutionally involves the State in racial discriminations and is therefore invalid under the Fourteenth Amendment.

There is no sound reason for rejecting this judgment. . . . What the court below did was first to reject the notion that the State was required to have a statute prohibiting racial discriminations in housing. Second, it held the intent of § 26 was to authorize private racial discriminations in the housing market, to repeal the Unruh and Rumford Acts and to create a constitutional right to discriminate on racial grounds in the sale and leasing of real property. Hence, the court dealt with § 26 as though it expressly authorized and constitutionalized the private right to discriminate. Third, the court assessed the ultimate impact of 26 in the California environment and concluded that the section would encourage and significantly involve the State in private racial discrimination contrary to the Fourteenth Amendment. . . .

Here the California court . . . has determined that the provision would involve the State in private racial discriminations to an unconstitutional degree. We accept this holding of the California court. . . .

Here we are dealing with a provision which does not just repeal an existing law forbidding private racial discriminations. Section 26 was intended to authorize, and does authorize, racial discrimination in the housing market. The right to discriminate is now one of the basic policies of the State. The California Supreme Court believes that the section will significantly encourage and involve the State in private discriminations. We have been presented with no persuasive considerations indicating that these judgments should be overturned."

The Supreme Court affirmed the judgment of the Supreme Court of California.

V. JUSTICE VOTE

5 Pro ACLU Side vs. 4 Con Opposing Side

ACLU Side (Respondent/Appellee)

1. White, B. – Wrote majority opinion
2. Brennan, W. – Joined majority opinion
3. Fortas, A. – Joined majority opinion
4. Warren, E. – Joined majority opinion
5. Douglas, W. – Wrote concurring opinion

Opposing Side (Petitioner/Appellant)

1. Harlan, J. – Wrote dissenting opinion
2. Clark, T. – Joined dissenting opinion
3. Stewart, P. – Joined dissenting opinion
4. Black, H. – Joined dissenting opinion

VI. A WIN OR LOSS FOR THE ACLU?

The ACLU filed an amicus brief urging affirmance; the U.S. Supreme Court affirmed the ruling of the California Supreme Court in a 5-4 vote, giving the ACLU an apparent win.

190. Camara v. Municipal Court of City & County of San Francisco

(Decided June 5, 1967; 387 U.S. 523)

I. ISSUE

A. Issues Discussed

4th Amendment

B. Legal Question Presented

"[W]hether administrative inspection programs [of private residences], as presently authorized and conducted, violate Fourth Amendment rights as those rights are enforced against the States through the Fourteenth Amendment."

C. Supreme Court's Answer

"Assuming the facts to be as the parties have alleged, we . . . conclude that appellant had a constitutional right to insist that the inspectors obtain a warrant to search and that appellant may not constitutionally be convicted for refusing to consent to the inspection."

II. CASE SUMMARY

A. Background

"Appellant brought this action in a California Superior Court alleging that he was awaiting trial on a criminal charge of violating the San Francisco Housing Code by refusing to permit a warrantless inspection of his residence, and that a writ of prohibition should issue to the criminal court because the ordinance authorizing such inspections is unconstitutional on its face. The Superior Court denied the writ, the District Court of Appeal affirmed, and the Supreme Court of California denied a petition for hearing. Appellant properly raised and had considered by the California courts the federal constitutional questions he now presents to this Court."

The Supreme Court granted certiorari to review the case.

B. Counsel of Record

ACLU Side (Petitioner/Appellant): Marshall W. Krause of the American Civil Liberties Union of Northern California argued the cause for appellant. With him on the briefs were Donald M. Cahen, Roger H. Bernhardt, and Lawrence Speiser.

Opposing Side (Respondent/Appellee): Albert W. Harris, Jr., Assistant Attorney General of California, argued the cause for appellee. With him on the brief were Thomas C. Lynch, Attorney General, and Gloria F. DeHart, Deputy Attorney General.

III. AMICI CURIAE

ACLU Side (Petitioner/Appellant)

Brief of amici curiae filed on behalf of Homeowners in Opposition to Housing Authoritarianism by Leonard J. Kerpelman.

Opposing Side (Respondent/Appellee)

Brief of amici curiae filed on behalf of the Member Municipalities of the National Institute of Municipal Law Officers by Thomas M. O'Connor, John W. Sholenberger, Roger Arnebergh, Barnett I. Shur, Alexander G. Brown, David Stahl, and Robert E. Michalski.

Brief of amici curiae filed on behalf of the Commonwealth of Massachusetts et al. by Elliot L. Richardson, Attorney General, Willie J. Davis, Assistant Attorney General, Edward T. Martin, Deputy Attorney General, Max Rosenblatt, Lewis H. Weinstein, and Loyd M. Starrett.

IV. THE SUPREME COURT'S DECISION

"Though there has been general agreement as to the fundamental purpose of the Fourth Amendment, translation of the abstract prohibition against 'unreasonable searches and seizures' into workable guidelines for the decision of particular cases is a difficult task . . . . Nevertheless, one governing principle . . . has consistently been followed: except in certain carefully defined classes of cases, a search of private property without proper consent is 'unreasonable' unless it has been authorized by a valid search warrant. . . .

In summary, we hold that administrative searches of the kind at issue here are significant intrusions upon the interests protected by the Fourth Amendment, that such searches when authorized and conducted without a warrant procedure lack the traditional safeguards which the Fourth Amendment guarantees to the individual, and that the reasons put forth in Frank v. State of Maryland and in other cases for upholding these warrantless searches are insufficient to justify so substantial a weakening of the Fourth Amendment's protections. Because of the nature of the municipal programs under consideration, however, these conclusions must be the beginning, not the end, of our inquiry. . . .

The Fourth Amendment provides that, 'no Warrants shall issue, but upon probable cause.' Borrowing from more typical Fourth Amendment cases, appellant argues not only that code enforcement inspection programs must be circumscribed by a warrant procedure, but also that warrants should issue only when the inspector possesses probable cause to believe that a particular dwelling contains violations of the minimum standards prescribed by the code being enforced. We disagree. . . .

In this case, appellants has been charged with a crime for his refusal to permit housing inspectors to enter his leasehold without a warrant. There was no emergency demanding immediate access . . . . Yet no warrant was obtained and thus appellant was unable to verify either the need for or the appropriate limits of the inspection. No doubt, the inspectors entered the public portion of the building with the consent of the landlord, . . . but appellee does not contend that such consent was sufficient to authorize inspection of appellant's premises. Assuming the facts to be as the parties have alleged, we therefore conclude that appellant had a constitutional right to insist that the inspectors obtain a warrant to search and that appellant may not constitutionally be convicted for refusing to consent to the inspection. It appears from the opinion of the District Court of Appeal that under these circumstances a writ of prohibition will issue to the criminal court under California law. . . .

Judgment vacated and case remanded."

V. JUSTICE VOTE

6 Pro ACLU Side vs. 3 Con Opposing Side

ACLU Side (Petitioner/Appellant)

1. White, B. – Wrote majority opinion
2. Fortas, A. – Joined majority opinion
3. Douglas, W. – Joined majority opinion
4. Warren, E. – Joined majority opinion
5. Brennan, W. – Joined majority opinion
6. Black, H. – Joined majority opinion

Opposing Side (Respondent/Appellee)

1. Clark, T. – Wrote dissenting opinion
2. Stewart, P. – Joined Clark's dissent
3. Harlan, J. – Joined Clark's dissent

VI. A WIN OR LOSS FOR THE ACLU?

The ACLU served as counsel for appellants urging reversal of the judgment of the District Court of Appeal of California; the Supreme Court vacated in a 6-3 vote, giving the ACLU an apparent win.

191. See v. City of Seattle

(Decided June 5, 1967; 387 U.S. 541)

I. ISSUE

A. Issues Discussed

4th Amendment

B. Legal Question Presented

"In Camara, we held that the Fourth Amendment bars prosecution of a person who has refused to permit a warrantless code-enforcement inspection of his personal residence. The only question which this case presents is whether Camara applies to similar inspections of commercial structures which are not used as private residences."

C. Supreme Court's Answer

"We hold only that the basic component of a reasonable search under the Fourth Amendment—that it not be enforced without a suitable warrant procedure—is applicable in this context, as in others, to business as well as to residential premises. Therefore, appellant may not be prosecuted for exercising his constitutional right to insist that the fire inspector obtain a warrant authorizing entry upon appellant's locked warehouse."

II. CASE SUMMARY

A. Background

"Appellant seeks reversal of his conviction for refusing to permit a representative of the City of Seattle Fire Department to enter and inspect appellant's locked commercial warehouse without a warrant and without probable cause to believe that a violation of any municipal ordinance existed therein. The inspection was conducted as part of a routine, periodic city-wide canvass to obtain compliance with Seattle's Fire Code. City of Seattle Ordinance No. 87870, c. 8.01. After he refused the inspector access, appellant was arrested and charged with violating s 8.01.050 of the Code:

'INSPECTION OF BUILDING AND PREMISES. It shall be the duty of the Fire Chief to inspect and he may enter all buildings and premises, except the interiors of dwellings, as often as may be necessary for the purpose of ascertaining and causing to be corrected any conditions liable to cause fire, or any violations of the provisions of this Title, and of any other ordinance concerning fire hazards.'

Appellant was convicted and given a suspended fine of $100 despite his claim that s 8.01.050, if interpreted to authorize this warrantless inspection of his warehouse, would violate his rights under the Fourth and Fourteenth Amendments."

The Supreme Court granted certiorari to review the case.

B. Counsel of Record

ACLU Side (Petitioner/Appellant): Norman Dorsen argued the cause for appellant. With him on the briefs were Paul D. Jackson and Michael H. Rosen of the American Civil Liberties Union of Washington, and Melvin L. Wulf.

Opposing Side (Respondent/Appellee): A. L. Newbould argued the cause for appellee. With him on the brief was Charles S. Rhyne.

III. AMICI CURIAE

ACLU Side (Petitioner/Appellant)

No briefs of amici curiae were filed in support of appellant.

Opposing Side (Respondent/Appellee)

No briefs of amici curiae were filed in support of appellee.

IV. THE SUPREME COURT'S DECISION

"In [prior cases] this Court refused to uphold otherwise unreasonable criminal investigative searches merely because commercial rather than residential premises were the object of the police intrusions. Likewise, we see no justification for so relaxing Fourth Amendment safeguards where the official inspection is intended to aid enforcement of laws prescribing minimum physical standards for commercial premises. As we explained in Camara, a search of private houses in presumptively unreasonable if conducted without a warrant. The businessman, like the occupant of a residence, has a constitutional right to go about his business free from unreasonable official entries upon his private commercial property. The businessman, too, has that right placed in jeopardy if the decision to enter and inspect for violation of regulatory laws can be made and enforced by the inspector in the field without official authority evidenced by warrant. . . .

It is now settled that, when an administrative agency subpoenas corporate books or records, the Fourth Amendment requires that the subpoena be sufficiently limited in scope, relevant in purpose, and specific in directive so that compliance will not be unreasonably burdensome. . . .

It is these rather minimal limitations on administrative action which we think are constitutionally required in the case of investigative entry upon commercial establishments. . . .

We therefore conclude that administrative entry, without consent, upon the portions of commercial premises which are not open to the public may only be compelled through prosecution or physical force within the framework of a warrant procedure. We do not in any way imply that business premises may not reasonably be inspected in many more situations than private homes, nor do we question such accepted regulatory techniques as licensing programs which require inspections prior to operating a business or marketing a product. Any constitutional challenge to such programs can only be resolved, as many have been in the past, on a case-by-case basis under the general Fourth Amendment standard of reasonableness. We hold only that the basic component of a reasonable search under the Fourth Amendment—that it not be enforced without a suitable warrant procedure—is applicable in this context, as in others, to business as well as to residential premises. Therefore, appellant may not be prosecuted for exercising his constitutional right to insist that the fire inspector obtain a warrant authorizing entry upon appellant's locked warehouse."

V. JUSTICE VOTE

6 Pro ACLU Side vs. 3 Con Opposing Side

ACLU Side (Petitioner/Appellant)

1. White, B. – Wrote majority opinion
2. Fortas, A. – Joined majority opinion

3. Douglas, W. – Joined majority opinion
4. Warren, E. – Joined majority opinion
5. Brennan, W. – Joined majority opinion
6. Black, H. – Joined majority opinion

Opposing Side (Respondent/Appellee)

1. Clark, T. – Wrote dissenting opinion
2. Stewart, P. – Joined Clark's dissent
3. Harlan, J. – Joined Clark's dissent

VI. A WIN OR LOSS FOR THE ACLU?

The ACLU served as counsel for appellant urging reversal of the judgment of the Supreme Court of Washington; the U.S. Supreme Court reversed in a 6-3 vote, giving the ACLU an apparent win.

192. Loving v. Virginia

(Decided June 12, 1967; 388 U.S. 1)

I. ISSUE

A. Issues Discussed

Race, state

B. Legal Question Presented

"[W]hether a statutory scheme adopted by the State of Virginia to prevent marriages between persons solely on the basis of racial classifications violates the Equal Protection and Due Process Clauses of the Fourteenth Amendment."

C. Supreme Court's Answer

"For reasons which seem to us to reflect the central meaning of those constitutional commands, we conclude that these statutes cannot stand consistently with the Fourteenth Amendment."

II. CASE SUMMARY

A. Background

"In June 1958, two residents of Virginia, Mildred Jeter, a Negro woman, and Richard Loving, a white man, were married in the District of Columbia pursuant to its laws. [T]he Lovings returned to Virginia .... At the October Term, 1958, of the Circuit Court of Caroline County, a grand jury issued an indictment charging the Lovings with violating Virginia's ban on interracial marriages. On January 6, 1959, the Lovings pleaded guilty ... and were sentenced to one year in jail; however, the trial judge suspended the sentence for ... 25 years on the condition that the Lovings leave the State and not return to Virginia together for 25 years. ...

[T]he Lovings took up residence in the District of Columbia. On November 6, 1963, they filed a motion in the state trial court to vacate the judgment and set aside the sentence on the ground that the statutes which they had violated were repugnant to the Fourteenth Amendment. The motion not having been decided by October 28, 1964, the Lovings instituted a class action in the United States District Court for the Eastern District of Virginia requesting that a three-judge court be convened to declare the Virginia antimiscegenation statutes unconstitutional and to enjoin state officials from enforcing their convictions. On January 22, 1965, the state trial judge denied the motion to vacate the sentences ....

The Supreme Court of Appeals upheld the constitutionality of the antimiscegenation statutes and, after modifying the sentence, affirmed the convictions."

The Supreme Court granted certiorari to review the case.

B. Counsel of Record

ACLU Side (Petitioner/Appellant): Opposing Side (Respondent/Appellee): Bernard S. Cohen and Philip J. Hirschkop argued the cause for appellants. With them on the brief were William D. Zabel, Arthur L. Berney, David Carline, and Marvin M. Karpatkin and Melvin L. Wulf of the American Civil Liberties Union.

William M. Marutani, by special leave of Court, argued the cause for the Japanese American Citizens League, as amicus curiae.

Opposing Side (Respondent/Appellee): R. D. McIlwaine III, Assistant Attorney General of Virginia, argued the cause for appellee. With him on the brief were Robert Y. Button, Attorney General, and Kenneth C. Patty, Assistant Attorney General.

III. AMICI CURIAE

ACLU Side (Petitioner/Appellant)

Brief of amici curiae filed on behalf of the Japanese American Citizens League by William M. Marutani.

Brief of amici curiae filed on behalf of William M. Lewers and William B. Ball for the National Catholic Conference for Interracial Justice et al.

Brief of amici curiae filed on behalf of the National Association for the Advancement of Colored People by Robert L. Carter and Andrew D. Weinberger.

Brief of amici curiae filed on behalf of the N.A.A.C.P. Legal Defense & Educational Fund, Inc. by Jack Greenberg, James M. Nabrit III, and Michael Meltsner.

Opposing Side (Respondent/Appellee)

Brief of amici curiae filed on behalf of the State of North Carolina by T. W. Bruton, Attorney General, and Ralph Moody, Deputy Attorney General.

IV. THE SUPREME COURT'S DECISION

"The two statutes under which appellants were convicted and sentenced are part of a comprehensive statutory scheme aimed at prohibiting and punishing interracial marriages. ...

Because we reject the notion that the mere 'equal application' of a statute containing racial classifications is enough to remove the classifications from the Fourteenth Amendment's proscription of all invidious racial discriminations, we do not accept the State's contention that these statutes should be upheld if there is any possible basis for concluding that they serve a rational purpose. ...

There can be no question but that Virginia's miscegenation statutes rest solely upon distinctions drawn according to race. ... Over the years, this Court has consistently repudiated '(d)istinctions between citizens solely because of their ancestry' as being 'odious to a free people whose institutions are founded upon the doctrine of equality.' . . .

There is patently no legitimate overriding purpose independent of invidious racial discrimination which justifies this classification. The fact that Virginia prohibits only interracial marriages involving white persons demonstrates that the racial classifications must stand on their own justification, as measures designed to maintain White Supremacy. . . . There can be no doubt that restricting the freedom to marry solely because of racial classifications violates the central meaning of the Equal Protection Clause. . . .

These statutes also deprive the Lovings of liberty without due process of law in violation of the Due Process Clause of the Fourteenth Amendment. The freedom to marry has long been recognized as one of the vital personal rights essential to the orderly pursuit of happiness by free men.

Marriage is one of the 'basic civil rights of man,' fundamental to our very existence and survival. To deny this fundamental freedom on so unsupportable a basis as the racial classifications embodied in these statutes, classifications so directly subversive of the principle of equality at the heart of the Fourteenth Amendment, is surely to deprive all the State's citizens of liberty without due process of law. The Fourteenth Amendment requires that the freedom of choice to marry not be restricted by invidious racial discriminations. Under our Constitution, the freedom to marry or not marry, a person of another race resides with the individual and cannot be infringed by the State

These convictions must be reversed."

V. JUSTICE VOTE

9 Pro ACLU Side vs. 0 Con Opposing Side

ACLU Side (Petitioner/Appellant)

1. Warren, E. – Wrote majority opinion
2. Clark, T. – Joined majority opinion
3. Douglas, W. – Joined majority opinion
4. Stewart, P. – Wrote concurring opinion
5. Brennan, W. – Joined majority opinion
6. Fortas, A. – Joined majority opinion
7. Black, H. – Joined majority opinion
8. Harlan, J. – Joined majority opinion
9. White, B. – Joined majority opinion

VI. A WIN OR LOSS FOR THE ACLU?

The ACLU served as attorney of record for appellants urging reversal of the judgment of the Virginia Supreme Court of Appeals; the Supreme Court reversed in a 9-0 vote, giving the ACLU an apparent win.

193. Berger v. New York

(Decided June 12, 1967; 388 U.S. 41)

I. ISSUE

A. Issues Discussed

Criminal procedure, electronic eavesdropping, Fourth Amendment, Fourteenth Amendment

B. Legal Question Presented

Is New York's electronic eavesdrop statute constitutional?

C. Supreme Court's Answer

The statute is unconstitutionally broad in scope and violates the Fourth and Fourteenth Amendments.

II. CASE SUMMARY

A. Background

Police obtained an "eavesdrop order" from the New York State Supreme Court to install a recording device in two offices, pursuant to § 813-a of the New York Code of Criminal Procedure. The statute permits the installation of a recording device, for electronic eavesdropping, so long as the police have "reasonable ground to believe that evidence of crime may thus be obtained." It further allows electronic eavesdropping for up to two months, unless extended by the court.

Based on evidence obtained through the electronic eavesdropping, petitioner "was convicted on two counts of conspiracy to bribe the Chairman of the New York State Liquor Authority." During his trial, "portions of the recordings were received in evidence . . . and were played to the jury, all over the objection of the petitioner." Petitioner challenged the constitutionality of the statute, but the New York courts upheld its constitutionality.

The Supreme Court granted certiorari and reversed.

B. Counsel of Record/ACLU Attorney

ACLU Side (Petitioner/Appellant): Joseph E. Brill argued the cause for appellant.

Opposing Side (Respondent/Appellee): H. Richard Uviller, Assistant District Attorney of New York County, argued the cause for appellee.

III. AMICI CURIAE

ACLU Side (Petitioner/Appellant)

Brief of amici curiae filed on behalf of the New York Civil Liberties Union by John J. McAvoy and Alan H. Levine.

Brief of amici curiae filed on behalf of the National Association of Defense Lawyers in Criminal Cases by Jack Grant Day and Gerald Zuckerman.

Brief of amici curiae filed on behalf of the International Brotherhood of Teamsters, Chauffeurs, Warehousemen & Helpers of America, by Raymond W. Bergan and Henry Mayer.

Opposing Side (Respondent/Appellee)

Brief of amici curiae filed on behalf of the Attorney General of the State of New York, by Louis J. Lefkowitz, Attorney General, pro se, Samuel A. Hirshowitz, First Assistant Attorney General, and Amy Juviler, Assistant Attorney General.

Brief of amici curiae filed on behalf of the Commonwealth of Massachusetts and the National District Attorneys' Association, by Elliot L. Richardson, Attorney General of Massachusetts, Robert Y. Thornton, Attorney General of Oregon, and G. Robert Blakey.

IV. THE SUPREME COURT'S DECISION

"We have concluded that the language of New York's statute is too broad in its sweep resulting in a trespassory intrusion into a constitutionally protected area and is, therefore, violative of the Fourth and Fourteenth Amendments. . . .

While New York's statute satisfies the Fourth Amendment's requirement that a neutral and detached authority be interposed between the police and the public, the broad sweep of the statute is immediately observable. . . .

The Fourth Amendment commands that a warrant issue not only upon probable cause supported by oath or affirmation, but also 'particularly describing the place to be searched, and the persons or things to be seized.' New York's statute lacks this particularization. It merely says that a warrant may issue on reasonable ground to believe that evidence of crime may be obtained by the eavesdrop. It lays down no requirement for particularity in the warrant as to what specific crime has been or is being committed, nor 'the place to be searched,' or 'the persons or things to be seized' as specifically required by the Fourth Amendment.

[The statute is] offensive. First, as we have mentioned, eavesdropping is authorized without requiring belief that any particular offense has been or is being committed; nor that the 'property' sought, the conversations, be particularly described. . . . As with general warrants this leaves too much to the discretion of the officer executing the order. Secondly, authorization of eavesdropping for a two-month period is the equivalent of a series of intrusions, searches, and seizures pursuant to a single showing of probable cause. . . . This we believe insufficient without a showing of present probable cause for the continuance of the eavesdrop. Third, the statute places no termination date on the eavesdrop once the conversation sought is seized. This is left entirely in the discretion of the officer. Finally, the statute's procedure, necessarily because its success depends on secrecy, has no requirement for notice as do conventional warrants, nor does it overcome this defect by requiring some showing of special facts. On the contrary, it permits uncontested entry without any showing of exigent circumstances. . . . In short, the statute's blanket grant of permission to eavesdrop is without adequate judicial supervision or protective procedures. . . .

It is said that neither a warrant nor a statute authorizing eavesdropping can be drawn so as to meet the Fourth Amendment's requirements. If that be true then the 'fruits' of eavesdropping devices are barred under the Amendment. On the other hand this Court has in the past, under specific conditions and circumstances, sustained the use of eavesdropping devices. . . . The Fourth Amendment does not make the 'precincts of the home or the office . . . sanctuaries where the law can never reach,' but it does prescribe a constitutional standard that must be met before official invasion is permissible. Our concern with the statute here is whether its language permits a trespassory invasion of the home or office, by general warrant, contrary to the command of the Fourth Amendment. As it is written, we believe that it does."

The Supreme Court reversed the judgment.

V. JUSTICE VOTE

6 Pro ACLU Side vs. 3 Con Opposing Side

ACLU Side (Petitioner/Appellant)

1. Clark, T. – Wrote majority opinion
2. Douglas, W. – Wrote concurring opinion
3. Stewart, P. – Wrote concurring opinion
4. Brennan, W. – Joined majority opinion
5. Fortas, A. – Joined majority opinion
6. Warren, E. – Joined majority opinion

Opposing Side (Respondent/Appellee)

1. Black, H. – Wrote dissenting opinion
2. Harlan, J. – Wrote dissenting opinion
3. White, B. – Wrote dissenting opinion

VI. A WIN OR LOSS FOR THE ACLU?

The ACLU filed an amicus brief urging reversal; the Supreme Court reversed the ruling of the Court of Appeals of New York in a 6-3 vote, giving the ACLU an apparent win.

194. Aday v. United States

(Decided June 12, 1967; 388 U.S. 447)

I. ISSUE

A. Issues Discussed

First Amendment, obscenity, freedom of speech and of the press

B. Legal Question Presented

Is the distribution of obscene books protected by the freedom of speech and of the press?

C. Supreme Court's Answer

In a per curiam opinion, the Supreme Court reversed the judgment, determining the prosecution was not appropriate.

II. CASE SUMMARY

A. Background

"This is an appeal from a judgment entered upon a jury verdict convicting . . .West Coast News Company, a California Corporation, and Wallace DeOrtega Maxey and Sanford E. Aday, California residents, of violations of Sections 1461 and 1462, Title 18, U.S.C.A. The charged offenses arose from the delivery into Michigan by mail and common carrier of allegedly obscene books, including one entitled Sex Life of a Cop. Trial was in the

United States District Court for the Western District of Michigan. Substantial fines were imposed upon the corporate and individual defendants and the latter received severe prison sentences."[1]

The Court of Appeals for the Sixth Circuit affirmed the convictions but remanded the case to reduce the sentences.

The Supreme Court granted certiorari and reversed the judgment of the Court of Appeals.

B. Counsel of Record/ACLU Attorney

ACLU Side (Petitioner/Appellant): Stanley Fleishman argued the cause for appellant.

Opposing Side (Respondent/Appellee): Solicitor General Thurgood Marshall argued the cause for appellee.

III. AMICI CURIAE

ACLU Side (Petitioner/Appellant)

Brief of amici curiae filed on behalf of the ACLU, et al., by Melvin L. Wulf, Rolland R. O'Hare, and Erwin B. Ellmann.

Brief of amicus curiae filed on behalf of the American Book Publishers Council, Inc., by Horace S. Manges.

Opposing Side (Respondent/Appellee)

Brief of amici curiae filed on behalf of Citizens for Decent Literature, Inc., by Charles H. Keating, Jr., and James J. Clancy.

IV. THE SUPREME COURT'S DECISION

"The petition for a writ of certiorari is granted and the judgment of the United States Court of Appeals for the Sixth Circuit is reversed. *Redrup v. New York*, 386 U.S. 787."

V. JUSTICE VOTE

8 Pro ACLU Side vs. 1 Con Opposing Side

ACLU Side (Petitioner/Appellant)

1. Douglas, W. – Per curiam decision
2. Stewart, P. – Per curiam decision
3. Fortas, A. – Per curiam decision
4. Black, H. – Per curiam decision
5. White, B. – Per curiam decision
6. Warren, E. – Wrote concurring opinion with Brennan
7. Brennan, W. – Wrote concurring opinion with Warren
8. Harlan, J. – Wrote concurring opinion

Opposing Side (Respondent/Appellee)

1. Clark, T. – Wrote dissenting opinion

VI. A WIN OR LOSS FOR THE ACLU?

The ACLU filed an amicus brief urging reversal; the Supreme Court, in a per curiam opinion, reversed the ruling of the Court of Appeals for the Sixth Circuit in an 8-1 vote, giving the ACLU an apparent win.

195. Mempa v. Rhay

(Decided November 13, 1967; 389 U.S. 128)

I. ISSUE

A. Issues Discussed

Criminal procedure

B. Legal Question Presented

"These consolidated cases raise the question of the extent of the right to counsel at the time of sentencing where the sentencing has been deferred subject to probation."

C. Supreme Court's Answer

"In sum, we do not question the authority of the State of Washington to provide for a deferred sentencing procedure coupled with its probation provisions. . . . All we decide here is that a lawyer must be afforded at this proceeding whether it be labeled a revocation of probation or a deferred sentencing."

II. CASE SUMMARY

A. Background

"Petitioner Jerry Douglas Mempa was convicted in the Spokane County Superior Court on June 17, 1959, of the offense of 'joyriding,' . . . He was then placed on probation . . . .

About four months later the Spokane County prosecuting attorney moved to have petitioner's probation revoked on the ground that he had been involved in a burglary on September 15, 1959. . . . Petitioner Mumpa, who was 17 years old at the time, was accompanied to the hearing by his stepfather. He was not represented by counsel and was not asked whether he wished to have counsel appointed for him. . . .

At the hearing Mempa was asked if it was true that he had been involved in the alleged burglary and he answered in the affirmative. A probation officer testified without cross-examination that . . . petitioner had been involved in the burglary and had previously denied participation in it. Without asking petitioner if he had anything to say or any evidence to supply, the court immediately entered an order revoking petitioner's probation and then sentenced him to 10 years in the penitentiary, but stated that it would recommend to the parole board that Mempa be required to serve only a year.

In 1965 Mempa filed a pro se petition for a writ of habeas corpus . . . claiming that he had been deprived of his right to counsel at the proceeding at which his probation was revoked and sentence imposed. The Washington Supreme Court denied the petition . . . .

Petitioner William Earl Walkling [similarly had probation revoked and received a multi-year sentence in the absence of counsel.]

In May 1966 Walkling filed a habeas corpus petition . . . . The petition was denied . . . ."

The Supreme Court granted certiorari to review both cases.

1 United States v. West Coast News Co., 357 F.2d 855 (6th Cir. 1966).

B. Counsel of Record

ACLU Side (Petitioner/Appellant): Evan L. Schwab argued the cause for appellants. With him on the brief was Michael H. Rosen of the American Civil Liberties Union of Washington.

Opposing Side (Respondent/Appellee): Stephen C. Way, Assistant Attorney General of Washington, argued the cause for appellees in both cases. With him on the brief was John J. O'Connell, Attorney General.

III. AMICI CURIAE

ACLU Side (Petitioner/Appellant)

Brief of amici curiae filed on behalf of the National Legal Aid and Defender Association by Patrick J. Hughes, Jr.

Brief of amici curiae filed on behalf of the State of Florida, joined and supported by the State of Idaho, by Earl Faircloth, Attorney General of Florida, Wallace E. Allbritton, Assistant Attorney General, and Allan G. Shepard, Attorney General of Idaho, in support of neither party.

Opposing Side (Respondent/Appellee)

Brief of amici curiae filed by MacDonald Gallion of Alabama, Arthur K. Bolton of Georgia, Allan G. Shepard of Idaho, James S. Erwin of Maine, and Helgi Johanneson of North Dakota, Attorneys General for their respective States, and by Robert Y. Button, Attorney General of Virginia, and Reno S. Harp III, Assistant Attorney General, as amici curiae.

IV. THE SUPREME COURT'S DECISION

"In 1948 this Court held in Townsend v. Burke, 334 U.S. 736, that the absence of counsel during sentencing after a plea of guilty coupled with 'assumptions concerning his criminal record which were materially untrue' deprived the defendant in that case of due process. . . .

In Hamilton v. State of Alabama, 368 U.S. 52 (1961), it was held that failure to appoint counsel at arraignment deprived the petitioner of due process, notwithstanding the fact that he simply pleaded not guilty at that time, because under Alabama law certain defenses had to be raised then or be abandoned. . . .

All the foregoing cases . . . were decided during the reign of Betts v. Brady, 316 U.S. 455 (1942), and accordingly relied on various 'special circumstances' to make the right to counsel applicable. In Gideon v. Wainwright, 372 U.S. 335 (1963), however, Betts was overruled and this Court held that the Sixth Amendment as applied through the Due Process Clause of the Fourteenth Amendment was applicable to the States and, accordingly, that there was an absolute right to appointment of counsel in felony cases.

There was no occasion in Gideon to enumerate the various stages in a criminal proceeding at which counsel was required, but Townsend, Moore, and Hamilton, when the Betts requirement of special circumstances is stripped away by Gideon, clearly stand for the proposition that appointment of counsel for an indigent is required at every stage of a criminal proceeding where substantial rights of a criminal accused may be affected. In particular, Townsend v. Burke, supra, illustrates the critical nature of sentencing in a criminal case and might well be considered to support by itself a holding that the right to counsel applies at sentencing. . . .

In sum, we do not question the authority of the State of Washington to provide for a deferred sentencing procedure coupled with its probation provisions. Indeed, it appears to be an enlightened step forward. All we decide here is that a lawyer must be afforded at this proceeding whether it be labeled a revocation of probation or a deferred sentencing. We assume that counsel appointed for the purpose of the trial or guilty plea would not be unduly burdened by being requested to follow through at the deferred sentencing stage of the proceeding.

The judgments below are reversed and the cases are remanded . . . ."

V. JUSTICE VOTE

9 Pro ACLU Side vs. 0 Con Opposing Side

ACLU Side (Petitioner/Appellant)

1. Marshall, T. – Wrote majority opinion
2. White, B. – Wrote majority opinion
3. Fortas, A. – Joined majority opinion
4. Douglas, W. – Joined majority opinion
5. Warren, E. – Joined majority opinion
6. Brennan, W. – Joined majority opinion
7. Black, H. – Joined majority opinion
8. Stewart, P. – Joined Clark's dissent
9. Harlan, J. – Joined Clark's dissent

VI. A WIN OR LOSS FOR THE ACLU?

The ACLU served as counsel for appellants urging reversal of the judgment of the Supreme Court of Washington; the U.S. Supreme Court reversed in a 9-0 vote, giving the ACLU an apparent win.

196. United States v. Robel

(Decided December 11, 1967; 389 U.S. 258)

I. ISSUE

A. Issues Discussed

Governmental authority, First Amendment, freedom of association

B. Legal Question Presented

Is § 5(a)(1)(D) of the Subversive Activities Control Act of 1950 constitutional?

C. Supreme Court's Answer

Section 5(a)(1)(D) unconstitutionally abridges the First Amendment freedom of association.

II. CASE SUMMARY

A. Background

Section 5(a)(1)(D) of the Subversive Activities Control Act of 1950 "provides that, when a Communist-action organization is under a final order to register, it shall be unlawful for any member of the organization 'to engage in any employment in any defense facility.'" The Communist Party was under a final order to register as of October 20, 1961. Appellee Robel, a member of the Communist Party, was employed as a machinist at a shipyard when the Secretary of Defense designated the shipyard a defense facility on August 20, 1962. "Appellee's continued employment at the shipyard after that date subjected him to prosecution under § 5(a)(1)(D), and on May 21, 1963, an indictment was filed charging him with a violation of that section. The indictment alleged in substance that appellee had 'unlawfully and willfully engage[d] in employment' at the shipyard with knowledge of the outstanding order against the Party and with knowledge and notice of the shipyard's designation as a defense facility by the Secretary of Defense."

On Oct. 4, 1965, the District Court for the Western District of Washington granted appellee's motion to dismiss because the indictment had failed to allege that appellee's Communist Party membership was active. The government, "insisting on the broadest possible application of the statute, initially took its appeal to the Court of Appeals for the Ninth Circuit." Then, the case was brought for review in the Supreme Court.

The Supreme Court granted certiorari and affirmed the District Court, but on the ground that § 5(a)(1)(D) was unconstitutional.

B. Counsel of Record / ACLU Attorney

ACLU Side (Respondent / Appellee): John J. Abt reargued the cause for appellee.

Opposing Side (Petitioner / Appellant): Kevin T. Maroney reargued the cause for appellant.

III. AMICI CURIAE

ACLU Side (Respondent / Appellee)

Brief of amici curiae filed on behalf of the ACLU, et al., by John J. Sullivan, Michael Rosen, Marvin M. Karpatkin, and Melvin L. Wulf.

Opposing Side (Petitioner / Appellant)

No briefs of amici curiae were filed in support of appellant.

IV. THE SUPREME COURT'S DECISION

"We affirm the judgment of the District Court, but on the ground that § 5(a)(1)(D) is an unconstitutional abridgment of the right of association protected by the First Amendment. . . . It is precisely because that statute sweeps indiscriminately across all types of association with Communist-action groups, without regard to the quality and degree of membership, that it runs afoul of the First Amendment. . . .

It has become axiomatic that '[p]recision of regulation must be the touchstone in an area so closely touching our most precious freedoms.' Such precision is notably lacking in § 5(a)(1)(D). That statute casts its net across a broad range of associational activities, indiscriminately trapping membership which can be constitutionally punished and membership which cannot be so proscribed. It is made irrelevant to the statute's operation that an individual may be a passive or inactive member of a designated organization, that he may be unaware of the organization's unlawful aims, or that he may disagree with those unlawful aims. It is also made irrelevant that an individual who is subject to the penalties of § 5(a)(1)(D) may occupy a nonsensitive position in a defense facility. Thus, § 5(a)(1)(D) contains the fatal defect of overbreadth because it seeks to bar employment both for association which may be proscribed and for association which may not be proscribed consistently with First Amendment rights. This the Constitution will not tolerate. . . .

Congress can declare sensitive positions in national defense industries off limits to those who would use such positions to disrupt the production of defense materials. The Government has told us that Congress, in passing § 5(a)(1)(D), made a considered judgment that one possible alternative to that statute—an industrial security screening program—would be inadequate and ineffective to protect against sabotage in defense facilities. It is not our function to examine the validity of that congressional judgment. Neither is it our function to determine whether an industrial security screening program exhausts the possible alternatives to the statute under review. We are concerned solely with determining whether the statute before us has exceeded the bounds imposed by the Constitution when First Amendment rights are at stake. The task of writing legislation which will stay within those bounds has been committed to Congress. Our decision today simply recognizes that, when legitimate legislative concerns are expressed in a statute which imposes a substantial burden on protected First Amendment activities, Congress must achieve its goal by means which have a 'less drastic' impact on the continued vitality of First Amendment freedoms. The Constitution and the basic position of First Amendment rights in our democratic fabric demand nothing less."

The Supreme Court affirmed the judgment of the District Court.

V. JUSTICE VOTE

6 Pro ACLU Side vs. 2 Con Opposing Side

ACLU Side (Petitioner / Appellant)

1. Warren, E. – Wrote majority opinion
2. Douglas, W. – Joined majority opinion
3. Stewart, P. – Joined majority opinion
4. Brennan, W. – Wrote concurring opinion
5. Fortas, A. – Joined majority opinion
6. Black, H. – Joined majority opinion

Opposing Side (Respondent / Appellee)

1. White, B. – Wrote dissenting opinion
2. Harlan, J. – Joined White's dissent

Marshall, T – Took no part in the decision

VI. A WIN OR LOSS FOR THE ACLU?

The ACLU filed an amicus brief urging affirmance; the Supreme Court affirmed the ruling in a 6-2 vote, giving the ACLU an apparent win.

197. Massachusetts v. Painten

(Decided January 15, 1968; 389 U.S. 560)

I. ISSUE

A. Issues Discussed

Criminal procedure, Fourth Amendment

B. Legal Question Presented

Were respondent's Fourth Amendment rights "violated by the entry into his apartment, by his arrest, and by the search and seizure of certain articles in his apartment which were introduced in evidence against him"?

C. Supreme Court's Answer

The Supreme Court dismissed the writ of certiorari as improvidently granted, declining to address the constitutional question.

II. CASE SUMMARY

A. Background

"In 1958 respondent was tried and convicted in Middlesex Superior Court, Massachusetts, for armed robbery of a bank and related offenses. He appealed, and in 1961 his conviction was affirmed by the Supreme Judicial Court of Massachusetts.

Respondent eventually filed a petition for a writ of habeas corpus in Federal District Court. Testimony was taken by the District Court on December 30, 1965. It ruled that respondent's Fourth Amendment rights had been violated by the entry into his apartment, by his arrest, and by the search and seizure of certain articles in his apartment which were introduced in evidence against him. Accordingly, it set aside his conviction and ordered his release. The Court of Appeals affirmed."

The Supreme Court granted certiorari, but ultimately dismissed the writ of certiorari as improvidently granted.

B. Counsel of Record / ACLU Attorney

ACLU Side (Respondent / Appellee): Louis M. Nordlinger argued the cause for appellee.

Opposing Side (Petitioner / Appellant): Elliot L. Richardson argued the cause for appellant.

III. AMICI CURIAE

ACLU Side (Respondent / Appellee)

Brief of amici curiae filed on behalf of the ACLU, et al., by Anthony G. Amsterdam and Melvin L. Wulf.

Opposing Side (Petitioner / Appellant)

No briefs of amici curiae were filed on behalf of appellant.

IV. THE SUPREME COURT'S DECISION

"At the time of respondent's trial in 1958, Massachusetts did not have an exclusionary rule for evidence obtained by an illegal search or seizure, and the parties did not focus upon the issues now before us. The evidentiary hearing in 1965 took place almost eight years after the events.

After oral argument and study of the record, we have reached the conclusion that the record is not sufficiently clear and specific to permit decision of the important constitutional questions involved in this case. The writ is therefore dismissed as improvidently granted."

V. JUSTICE VOTE

6 Pro ACLU Side vs. 3 Con Opposing Side

ACLU Side (Respondent / Appellee)

1. Warren, E. – Per curiam decision
2. Douglas, W. – Per curiam decision
3. Brennan, W. – Per curiam decision
4. Black, H. – Per curiam decision
5. Marshall, T. – Per curiam decision
6. Fortas, A. – Wrote concurring opinion

Opposing Side (Petitioner / Appellant)

1. White, B. – Wrote dissenting opinion
2. Stewart, P. – Joined dissenting opinion
3. Harlan, J. – Joined dissenting opinion

VI. A WIN OR LOSS FOR THE ACLU?

The ACLU filed an amicus brief urging affirmance; the Supreme Court dismissed the writ of certiorari, essentially affirming the Court of Appeals for the First Circuit in a 6-3 vote, giving the ACLU an apparent win.

198. Lee v. Washington

(Decided March 11, 1968; 390 U.S. 333)

I. ISSUE

A. Issues Discussed

Race, prison

B. Legal Question Presented

Whether the prison and jail desegregation ordered by the lower court was proper.

C. Supreme Court's Answer

"The State's contentions that Rule 23 of the Federal Rules of Civil Procedure, which relates to class actions, was violated in this case and that the challenged statutes are not unconstitutional are without merit. The remaining contention of the State is that the specific orders directing desegregation of prisons and jails make no allowance for the necessities of prison security and discipline, but we do not so read the 'Order, Judgment and Decree' of the District Court, which when read as a whole we find unexceptionable."

II. CASE SUMMARY

A. Background

"This appeal challenges a decree of a three-judge District Court declaring that certain Alabama statutes violate the Fourteenth

Amendment to the extent that they require segregation of the races in prisons and jails, and establishing a schedule for desegregation of these institutions."

The Supreme Court granted certiorari to review the case.

B. Counsel of Record

ACLU Side (Respondent/Appellee): Charles Morgan, Jr., argued the cause for appellees. With him on the brief were Orzell Billingsley, Jr., Laughlin McDonald, and Melvin L. Wulf (ACLU chief counsel 1954-1977).

Opposing Side (Petitioner/Appellant): Nicholas S. Hare, Special Assistant Attorney General of Alabama, argued the cause for appellants. With him on the briefs were MacDonald Gallion, Attorney General, Gordon Madison, Assistant Attorney General, and J. M. Breckenridge.

III. AMICI CURIAE

ACLU Side (Respondent/Appellee)

No briefs of amici curiae were filed in support of appellees.

Opposing Side (Petitioner/Appellant)

No briefs of amici curiae were filed in support of appellants.

IV. THE SUPREME COURT'S DECISION

"The State's contentions that Rule 23 of the Federal Rules of Civil Procedure, which relates to class actions, was violated in this case and that the challenged statutes are not unconstitutional are without merit. The remaining contention of the State is that the specific orders directing desegregation of prisons and jails make no allowance for the necessities of prison security and discipline, but we do not so read the 'Order, Judgment and Decree' of the District Court, which when read as a whole we find unexceptionable.

The judgment is affirmed."

V. JUSTICE VOTE

9 Pro ACLU Side vs. 0 Con Opposing Side

ACLU Side (Respondent/Appellee)

1. Warren, E. – Per curiam decision
2. Brennan, W. – Per curiam decision
3. Black, H. – Wrote concurring opinion
4. Douglas, W. – Per curiam decision
5. Harlan, J. – Joined Black's concurrence
6. Fortas, A. – Per curiam decision
7. Marshall, T. – Per curiam decision
8. Stewart, P. – Joined Black's concurrence
9. White, B. – Per curiam decision

VI. A WIN OR LOSS FOR THE ACLU?

The ACLU served as counsel for appellee urging affirmance; the Supreme Court affirmed the district court's decision by per curiam a 9-0 vote, giving the ACLU an apparent wim.

199. Ginsberg v. New York

(Decided April 22, 1968; 390 U.S. 629)

I. ISSUE

A. Issues Discussed

First Amendment, obscenity

B. Legal Question Presented

Can the government prohibit the sale to minors of certain kinds of sexually explicit material even if the material is not considered obscene for adults?

C. Supreme Court's Answer

The government can prohibit the sale of sexually explicit material to minors, even if the material is not considered obscene for adults.

II. CASE SUMMARY

A. Background

"New York criminal obscenity statute . . . prohibits the sale to minors under 17 years of age of material defined to be obscene on the basis of its appeal to them whether or not it would be obscene to adults.

Appellant and his wife operate 'Sam's Stationery and Luncheonette' in Bellmore, Long Island. They have a lunch counter, and, among other things, also sell magazines including some so-called 'girlie' magazines. Appellant was prosecuted under two informations, each in two counts, which charged that he personally sold a 16-year-old boy two 'girlie' magazines on each of two dates in October 1965, in violation of § 484-h of the New York Penal Law. He was tried before a judge without a jury in Nassau County District Court and was found guilty on both counts. The judge found (1) that the magazines contained pictures which depicted female 'nudity' in a manner defined in subsection 1(b), that is 'the showing of . . . female . . . buttocks with less than a full opaque covering, or the showing of the female breast with less than a fully opaque covering of any portion thereof below the top of the nipple . . . ,' and (2) that the pictures were 'harmful to minors' in that they had, within the meaning of subsection 1(f) 'that quality of . . . representation . . . of nudity . . . [which] . . . (i) predominantly appeals to the prurient, shameful or morbid interest of minors, and (ii) is patently offensive to prevailing standards in the adult community as a whole with respect to what is suitable material for minors, and (iii) is utterly without redeeming social importance for minors.' He held that both sales to the 16-year-old boy therefore constituted the violation under § 484-h of 'knowingly to sell . . . to a minor' under 17 of '(a) any picture . . . which depicts nudity . . . and which is harmful to minors,' and '(b) any . . . magazine . . . which contains . . . [such pictures] . . . and which, taken as a whole, is harmful to minors.' The conviction was affirmed without opinion by the Appellate Term, Second Department, of the Supreme Court. Appellant was denied leave to appeal to the New York Court of Appeals and then appealed to [the U.S. Supreme] Court."

The Supreme Court granted certiorari and affirmed.

B. Counsel of Record/ACLU Attorney

ACLU Side (Petitioner/Appellant): Emanuel Redfield argued the cause for appellant.

Opposing Side (Respondent/Appellee): William Cahn, District Attorney, County of Nassau, State of New York, argued the cause for appellee.

III. AMICI CURIAE

ACLU Side (Petitioner/Appellant)

Brief of amici curiae filed on behalf of the ACLU, et al., by Osmond K. Fraenkel, Edward J. Ennis, Melvin L. Wulf, Alan H. Levine, and Fred O. Weldon, Jr.

Brief of amici curiae filed on behalf of the Council for Periodical Distributors Associations, Inc., by Morris B. Abram, Jay Greenfield, and John E. LeMoult.

Brief of amici curiae filed on behalf of the American Book Publishers Council, Inc., by Horace S. Manges and Marshall C. Berger.

Brief of amici curiae filed on behalf of the Authors' League of America, Inc., by Irwin Karp.

Opposing Side (Respondent/Appellee)

Brief of amici curiae filed on behalf of the Citizens for Decent Literature, Inc., by Charles H. Keating, Jr., James J. Clancy, and Ray T. Dreher.

IV. THE SUPREME COURT'S DECISION

"Appellant's attack is not that New York was without power to draw the line at age 17. Rather, his contention is the broad proposition that the scope of the constitutional freedom of expression secured to a citizen to read or see material concerned with sex cannot be made to depend upon whether the citizen is an adult or a minor. He accordingly insists that the denial to minors under 17 of access to material condemned by § 484-h, insofar as that material is not obscene for persons 17 years of age or older, constitutes an unconstitutional deprivation of protected liberty. . . .

It is enough for the purposes of this case that we inquire whether it was constitutionally impermissible for New York, insofar as § 484-h does so, to accord minors under 17 a more restricted right than that assured to adults to judge and determine for themselves what sex material they may read or see. We conclude that we cannot say that the statute invades the area of freedom of expression constitutionally secured to minors. . . .

Section 484-e of the law states a legislative finding that the material condemned by Section 484-h is 'a basic factor in impairing the ethical and moral development of our youth and a clear and present danger to the people of the state.' It is very doubtful that this finding expresses an accepted scientific fact. But obscenity is not protected expression, and may be suppressed without a showing of the circumstances which lie behind the phrase 'clear and present danger' in its application to protected speech. To sustain state power to exclude material defined as obscenity by § 484-h requires only that we be able to say that it was not irrational for the legislature to find that exposure to material condemned by the statute is harmful to minors. In Meyer v. Nebraska, we were able to say that children's knowledge of the German language 'cannot reasonably be regarded as harmful.' That cannot be said by us of minors' reading and seeing sex material. To be sure, there is no lack of 'studies' which purport to demonstrate that obscenity is or is not 'a basic factor in impairing the ethical and moral development of . . . youth and a clear and present danger to the people of the state.' But the growing consensus of commentators is that 'while these studies all agree that a causal link has not been demonstrated, they are equally agreed that a causal link has not been disproved either.' We do not demand of legislatures 'scientifically certain criteria of legislation.' We therefore cannot say that Section 484-h, in defining the obscenity of material on the basis of its appeal to minors under 17, has no rational relation to the objective of safeguarding such minors from harm."

The Supreme Court affirmed the judgment.

V. JUSTICE VOTE

3 Pro ACLU Side vs. 6 Con Opposing Side

ACLU Side (Petitioner/Appellant)

1. Douglas, W. – Wrote dissenting opinion
2. Black, H. – Joined Douglas' dissent
3. Fortas, A. – Wrote dissenting opinion

Opposing Side (Respondent/Appellee)

1. Brennan, W. – Wrote majority opinion
2. Warren, E. – Joined majority opinion
3. White, B. – Joined majority opinion
4. Marshall, T. – Joined majority opinion
5. Stewart, P. – Wrote concurring opinion
6. Harlan, J. – Wrote concurring opinion

VI. A WIN OR LOSS FOR THE ACLU?

The ACLU filed an amicus brief urging reversal; the Supreme Court affirmed the ruling of the Appellate Term of the New York Supreme Court in a 6-3 vote, giving the ACLU an apparent loss.

200. Interstate Circuit, Inc. v. City of Dallas

(Decided April 22, 1968; 390 U.S. 676)

I. ISSUE

A. Issues Discussed

First Amendment, obscenity, vagueness

B. Legal Question Presented

Does a Dallas city ordinance prohibiting the exhibition of films to minor children which are deemed not suitable for young persons violate the First Amendment?

C. Supreme Court's Answer

The ordinance is void for vagueness.

II. CASE SUMMARY

A. Background

Appellee, the City of Dallas, passed an ordinance to set up a Motion Picture Classification Board to rate films as suitable or unsuitable for children under age 16. The criteria to classify a movie as "not suitable for young persons" included, in summary, the portrayal of violence that would encourage young persons to commit crimes, depravity, sexual promiscuity, extra-marital sex, and abnormal sex. Films were deemed unsuitable if they created "the impression on young persons that such conduct is profitable, desirable, acceptable, respectable, praiseworthy or commonly accepted."

A license is required to show movies that the Board deemed unsuitable. If the exhibitor of a film classified as "not suitable for young persons" fails to advertise the rating or knowingly allows children under 16 to see the film without an accompanying guardian, the exhibitor can be fined a misdemeanor penalty of $200. Repeat offenders may lose their licenses to show unsuitable films altogether.

Appellants, the exhibitor and distributor of the movie "Viva Maria," objected when the board classified the movie as unsuitable because it depicted sexual promiscuity. "A county court upheld the Board's determination and enjoined exhibition of the film without acceptance by appellants of the requirements imposed by the restricted classification. The Texas Court of Civil Appeals affirmed."

Appellants sought review in the Supreme Court. The Supreme Court granted certiorari and reversed the judgment.

B. Counsel of Record/ACLU Attorney

ACLU Side (Petitioner/Appellant): Grover Hartt, Jr., argued the cause for appellant in No. 56.

Louis Nizer argued the cause for appellant in No. 64

Opposing Side (Respondent/Appellee): N. Alex Bickley argued the cause for appellee.

III. AMICI CURIAE

ACLU Side (Petitioner/Appellant)

Brief of amici curiae filed on behalf of the ACLU, et al., by Osmond K. Fraenkel, Edward J. Ennis, Melvin L. Wulf and Alan H. Levine.

Brief of amici curiae filed on behalf of the Authors League of America, Inc., by Irwin Karp.

Opposing Side (Respondent/Appellee)

No briefs of amici curiae were filed in support of appellee.

IV. THE SUPREME COURT'S DECISION

"The vice of vagueness is particularly pronounced where expression is sought to be subjected to licensing. It may be unlikely that what Dallas does in respect to the licensing of motion pictures would have a significant effect upon film makers in Hollywood or Europe. But what Dallas may constitutionally do, so may other cities and States. Indeed, we are told that this ordinance is being used as a model for legislation in other localities. Thus, one who wishes to convey his ideas through that medium, which of course includes one who is interested not so much in expression as in making money, must consider whether what he proposes to film, and how he proposes to film it, is within the terms of classification schemes such as this. If he is unable to determine what the ordinance means, he runs the risk of being foreclosed, in practical effect, from a significant portion of the movie-going public. Rather than run that risk, he might choose nothing but the innocuous, perhaps save for the so-called 'adult' picture. Moreover, a local exhibitor who cannot afford to risk losing the youthful audience when a film may be of marginal interest to adults—perhaps a 'Viva Maria'—may contract to show only the totally inane. The vast wasteland that some have described in reference to another medium might be a verdant paradise in comparison. The First Amendment interests here are, therefore, broader than merely those of the film maker, distributor, and exhibitor, and certainly broader than those of youths under 16. . . .

The dangers inherent in vagueness are strikingly illustrated in these cases. Five members of the Board viewed 'Viva Maria.' Eight members voted to classify it as 'not suitable for young persons,' the ninth member not voting. The Board gave no reasons for its determination. Appellee alleged in its petition for an injunction that the classification was warranted because the film portrayed 'sexual promiscuity in such a manner as to be in the judgment of the Board likely to incite or encourage delinquency or sexual promiscuity on the part of young persons or to appeal to their prurient interests.' Two Board members, a clergyman and a lawyer, testified at the hearing. Each adverted to several scenes in the film, which, in their opinion, portrayed male-female relationships in a way contrary to 'acceptable and approved behavior.' Each acknowledged, in reference to scenes in which clergymen were involved in violence, most of which was farcical, that 'sacrilege' might have entered into the Board's determination. And both conceded that the asserted portrayal of 'sexual promiscuity' was implicit rather than explicit, i.e., that it was a product of inference by, and imagination of, the viewer. . . .

The term 'sexual promiscuity' is not there defined and was not interpreted in the state courts. It could extend, depending upon one's moral judgment, from the obvious to any sexual contacts outside a marital relationship. The determinative manner of the 'describing or portraying' of the subjects covered by the ordinance, including 'sexual promiscuity,' is defined as 'such a manner as to be, in the judgment of the Board, likely to incite or encourage delinquency or sexual promiscuity on the part of young persons.' A film is so "likely to incite or encourage' crime delinquency or sexual promiscuity on the part of young persons, if, in the judgment of the Board, there is a substantial probability that it will create the impression on young persons that such conduct is profitable, desirable, acceptable, respectable, praiseworthy or commonly accepted.' It might be excessive literalism to insist, as do appellants, that because those last six adjectives are stated in the disjunctive, they represent separate and alternative subtle determinations the Board is to make, any of which results in a not suitable classification. . . .

Vagueness and the attendant evils . . . are not rendered less objectionable because the regulation of expression is one of classification rather than direct suppression. Nor is it an answer to an argument that a particular regulation of expression is vague to say that it was adopted for the salutary purpose of protecting children. The permissible extent of vagueness is not directly proportional to, or a function of, the extent of the power to regulate or control expression with respect to children. . . .

It is not our province to draft legislation. Suffice it to say that we have recognized that some believe 'motion pictures possess a greater capacity for evil, particularly among the youth of a community, than other modes of expression,' and we have indicated more generally that because of its strong and abiding interest in youth, a State may regulate the dissemination to juveniles of, and their access to, material objectionable as to them, but which a State clearly could not regulate as to adults. Here we conclude only that 'the absence of narrowly drawn, reasonable and definite standards for the officials to follow,' is fatal.

The judgment of the Texas Court of Civil Appeals is reversed and the cases are remanded for further proceedings not inconsistent with this opinion."

V. JUSTICE VOTE

8 Pro ACLU Side vs. 1 Con Opposing Side

ACLU Side (Petitioner/Appellant)

1. Marshall, T. – Wrote majority opinion
2. Douglas, W. – Wrote concurring opinion
3. Black, H. – Joined Douglas' concurrence
4. Warren, E. – Joined majority opinion
5. Stewart, P. – Joined majority opinion
6. Brennan, W. – Joined majority opinion
7. Fortas, A. – Joined majority opinion
8. White, B. – Joined majority opinion

Opposing Side (Respondent/Appellee)

1. Harlan, J. – Wrote dissenting opinion

VI. A WIN OR LOSS FOR THE ACLU?

The ACLU filed an amicus brief urging reversal; the Supreme Court reversed the ruling of the Texas Court of Civil Appeals in an 8-1 vote, giving the ACLU an apparent win.

201. Levy v. Louisiana

(Decided May 20, 1968; 391 U.S. 68)

I. ISSUE

A. Issues Discussed

Equal protection

B. Legal Question Presented

Is a Louisiana statute as construed to deny illegitimate children "the right to recover" for the wrongful death of their mother, a violation of the Equal Protection Clause of the Fourteenth Amendment?

C. Supreme Court's Answer

The construction of the statute denies equal protection to children born out of wedlock.

II. CASE SUMMARY

A. Background

"Appellant sued on behalf of five illegitimate children to recover, under a Louisiana statute for two kinds of damages as a result of the wrongful death of their mother: (1) the damages to them for the loss of their mother; and (2) those based on the survival of a cause of action which the mother had at the time of her death for pain and suffering. Appellees are the doctor who treated her and the insurance company.

We assume in the present state of the pleadings that the mother, Louise Levy, gave birth to these five illegitimate children and that they lived with her; that she treated them as a parent would treat any other child; that she worked as a domestic servant to support them, taking them to church every Sunday and enrolling them, at her own expense, in a parochial school. The Louisiana District Court dismissed the suit. The Court of Appeal affirmed, holding that 'child' in Article 2315 means 'legitimate child,' the denial to illegitimate children of 'the right to recover' being 'based on morals and general welfare because it discourages bringing children into the world out of wedlock.' The Supreme Court of Louisiana denied certiorari."

The U.S. Supreme Court granted certiorari and reversed.

B. Counsel of Record/ACLU Attorney

ACLU Side (Petitioner/Appellant): Norman Dorsen argued the cause for appellant. With him on the briefs were Adolph J. Levy, Lawrence J. Smith, and Melvin L. Wulf.

Opposing Side (Respondent/Appellee): William A. Porteous III argued the cause for appellee. With him on the brief were William A. Porteous, Jr., Ingard O. Johannesen, L.K. Clement, Jr., Jack P. F. Gremillion, Attorney General of Louisiana, and Dorothy D. Wolbrette, Assistant Attorney General.

III. AMICI CURIAE

ACLU Side (Petitioner/Appellant)

Brief of amici curiae filed on behalf of the Executive Council of the Episcopal Church in the U.S.A., et al., by Leo Pfeffer, Howard M. Squadron, and Joseph B. Robison.

Brief of amici curiae filed on behalf of the NAACP Legal Defense and Educational Fund, Inc., et al., by Harry D. Krause, Jack Greenberg, and Leroy D. Clark.

Opposing Side (Respondent/Appellee)

Brief of amici curiae filed on behalf of the Attorney General of Louisiana by Jack P.F. Gremillion, Attorney General of Louisiana, William P. Schuler, Second Assistant Attorney General, and Dorothy D. Wolbrette and L. K. Clement, Jr., Assistant Attorneys General.

IV. THE SUPREME COURT'S DECISION

"While a State has broad power when it comes to making classifications, it may not draw a line which constitutes an invidious discrimination against a particular class. [W]e have been extremely sensitive when it comes to basic civil rights and have not hesitated to strike down an invidious classification even though it had history and tradition on its side. The rights asserted here involve the intimate, familial relationship between a child and his own mother. When the child's claim of damage for loss of his mother is in issue, why, in terms of 'equal protection,' should the tortfeasors go free merely because the child is illegitimate? Why should the illegitimate child be denied rights merely because of his birth out of wedlock? He certainly is subject to all the responsibilities of a citizen, including the payment of taxes and conscription under the Selective Service Act. How under our constitutional regime can he be denied correlative rights which other citizens enjoy?

Legitimacy or illegitimacy of birth has no relation to the nature of the wrong allegedly inflicted on the mother. These children, though illegitimate, were dependent on her; she cared for them and nurtured them; they were indeed hers in the biological and in the spiritual sense; in her death they suffered wrong in the sense that any dependent would.

We conclude that it is invidious to discriminate against them when no action, conduct, or demeanor of theirs is possibly relevant to the harm that was done the mother."

The Supreme Court then reversed the judgment of the Court of Appeal.

V. JUSTICE VOTE

8 Pro ACLU Side vs. 1 Con Opposing Side

ACLU Side (Petitioner/Appellant)

1. Douglas, W. – Wrote majority opinion
2. Marshall, T. – Joined majority opinion
3. Black, H. – Joined majority opinion
4. Fortas, A. – Joined majority opinion
5. Brennan, W. – Joined majority opinion
6. Stewart, P. – Joined majority opinion
7. White, B. – Joined majority opinion
8. Warren, E. – Joined majority opinion

Opposing Side (Respondent/Appellee)

1. Harlan, J. – Wrote dissenting opinion

VI. A WIN OR LOSS FOR THE ACLU?

The ACLU, as counsel of record, urged reversal of the judgment of the Court of Appeal; the Supreme Court reversed the ruling in an 8-1 vote, giving the ACLU an apparent win.

202. Amalgamated Food Employees Union Local 590 v. Logan Valley Plaza, Inc.

(Decided May 20, 1968; 391 U.S. 308)

I. ISSUE

A. Issues Discussed

First Amendment, freedom of speech, picketing, labor unions

B. Legal Question Presented

"[W]hether peaceful picketing of a business enterprise located within a shopping center can be enjoined on the ground that it constitutes an unconsented invasion of the property rights of the owners of the land on which the center is situated."

C. Supreme Court's Answer

Peaceful picketing cannot be enjoined in a privately held shopping center.

II. CASE SUMMARY

A. Background

Respondent Logan Valley Plaza, Inc. ("Logan") owned a large shopping center complex located near the city of Altoona, Pennsylvania. Respondent Weis Markets, Inc. ("Weis") was a supermarket in the shopping center. "On December 8, 1965, Weis opened for business, employing a wholly nonunion staff of employees. A few days after it opened for business, Weis posted a sign on the exterior of its building prohibiting trespassing or soliciting by anyone other than its employees on its porch or parking lot. On December 17, 1965, members of Amalgamated Food Employees Union, Local 590, began picketing Weis. They carried signs stating that the Weis market was nonunion and that its employees were not 'receiving union wages or other union benefits.' . . . The picketing was peaceful at all times and unaccompanied by either threats or violence."

Respondents Weis and Logan brought an action to prohibit petitioners from picketing. A Pennsylvania Court of Common Pleas issued an injunction, prohibiting petitioners from picketing and trespassing inside the shopping center, only allowing for picketing outside the shopping center, such as along public roads. The court "held that the injunction was justified both in order to protect respondents' property rights and because the picketing was unlawfully aimed at coercing Weis to compel its employees to join a union." The court rejected petitioners' claim that they had a First Amendment right to picket in the shopping center. The Pennsylvania Supreme Court "affirmed issuance of the injunction on the sole ground that petitioners' conduct constituted a trespass on respondents' property."

The U.S. Supreme Court granted certiorari and reversed.

B. Counsel of Record/ACLU Attorney

ACLU Side (Petitioner/Appellant): Bernard Dunau argued the cause for appellant.

Opposing Side (Respondent/Appellee): Robert Lewin argued the cause for appellee.

III. AMICI CURIAE

ACLU Side (Petitioner/Appellant)

Brief of amici curiae filed on behalf of the ACLU by Marvin M. Karpatkin, William E. Crain, Kristin Glen, and Melvin L. Wulf.

Other briefs of amicus curiae filed on behalf of the National Labor Relations Board, the American Federation of Labor and Congress of Industrial Organizations, and the Retail Clerks International Association.

Opposing Side (Respondent/Appellee)

Brief of amici curiae filed on behalf of the International Council of Shopping Centers, Inc., by Fred H. Daugherty.

Brief of amici curiae filed on behalf of the American Retail Federation by Charles J. Barnhill, Philip C. Lederer, and Lawrence M. Cohen.

IV. THE SUPREME COURT'S DECISION

"We start from the premise that peaceful picketing carried on in a location open generally to the public is, absent other factors involving the purpose or manner of the picketing, protected by the First Amendment. [P]icketing involves elements of both speech and conduct, i.e., patrolling, and has indicated that because of this intermingling of protected and unprotected elements, picketing can be subjected to controls that would not be constitutionally permissible in the case of pure speech. Nevertheless, no case decided by this Court can be found to support the proposition that the nonspeech aspects of peaceful picketing are so great as to render the provisions of the First Amendment inapplicable to it altogether. . . .

This Court has also held . . . that under some circumstances property that is privately owned may, at least for First Amendment purposes, be treated as though it were publicly held. . . .

Here the roadways provided for vehicular movement within the mall and the sidewalks leading from building to building are the functional equivalents of the streets and sidewalks of a normal municipal business district. The shopping center premises are open to the public to the same extent as the commercial center of a normal town. . . .

All we decide here is that because the shopping center serves as the community business block 'and is freely accessible and open to the people in the area and those passing through,' the State may not delegate the power, through the use of its trespass laws, wholly to exclude those members of the public wishing to exercise their First Amendment rights on the premises in a manner and for a purpose generally consonant with the use to which the property is actually put. . . .

It is therefore clear that the restraints on picketing and trespassing approved by the Pennsylvania courts here substantially hinder the communication of the ideas which petitioners seek to express to the patrons of Weis. . . .

Therefore, as to the sufficiency of respondents' ownership of the Logan Valley Mall premises as the sole support of the injunction issued against petitioners, we simply repeat what was said in Marsh v. Alabama, 326 U.S. 506, 'Ownership does not always mean absolute dominion. The more an owner, for his advantage, opens up his property for use by the public in general, the more do his rights become circumscribed by the statutory and constitutional rights of those who use it.' Logan Valley Mall is the functional equivalent of a 'business block' and for First Amendment purposes must be treated in substantially the same manner.

The judgment of the Supreme Court of Pennsylvania is reversed and the case is remanded for further proceedings not inconsistent with this opinion."

V. JUSTICE VOTE

6 Pro ACLU Side vs. 3 Con Opposing Side

ACLU Side (Petitioner/Appellant)

1. Marshall, T. – Wrote majority opinion
2. Douglas, W. – Wrote concurring opinion
3. Warren, E. – Joined majority opinion
4. Stewart, P. – Joined majority opinion
5. Brennan, W. – Joined majority opinion
6. Fortas, A. – Joined majority opinion

Opposing Side (Respondent/Appellee)

1. White, B. – Wrote dissenting opinion
2. Harlan, J. – Wrote dissenting opinion
3. Black, H. – Wrote dissenting opinion

VI. A WIN OR LOSS FOR THE ACLU?

The ACLU filed an amicus brief urging reversal; the U.S. Supreme Court reversed the ruling of the Supreme Court of Pennsylvania in a 6-3 vote, giving the ACLU an apparent win.

203. Witherspoon v. Illinois

(Decided June 3, 1968; 391 U.S. 510)

I. ISSUE

A. Issues Discussed

Criminal procedure, death penalty, jury selection, Sixth Amendment, Fourteenth Amendment

B. Legal Question Presented

"[W]hether the Constitution permits a State to execute a man pursuant to the verdict of a jury" that, pursuant state law, excluded prospective jurors who expressed hesitation to inflict the death penalty in a murder case.

C. Supreme Court's Answer

A jury chosen by excluding all potential jurors opposed to the death penalty cannot constitutionally impose the death sentence.

II. CASE SUMMARY

A. Background

"The petitioner was brought to trial in 1960 in Cook County, Illinois, upon a charge of murder. The jury found him guilty and fixed his penalty at death. At the time of his trial, an Illinois statute provided: 'In trials for murder it shall be a cause for challenge of any juror who shall, on being examined, state that he has conscientious scruples against capital punishment, or that he is opposed to the same.'

Through this provision the State of Illinois armed the prosecution with unlimited challenges for cause in order to exclude those jurors who, in the words of the State's highest court 'might hesitate to return a verdict inflicting [death].' At the petitioner's trial, the prosecution eliminated nearly half the venire of prospective jurors by challenging, under the authority of the statute, any venireman who expressed qualms about capital punishment. From those who remained were chosen the jurors who ultimately found the petitioner guilty and sentenced him to death. The Supreme Court of Illinois denied post-conviction relief and [the U.S. Supreme Court] granted certiorari to decide whether the Constitution permits a State to execute a man pursuant to the verdict of a jury so composed."

The Supreme Court reversed the death sentence.

B. Counsel of Record / ACLU Attorney

ACLU Side (Petitioner / Appellant): Albert E. Jenner, Jr., argued the cause for appellant.

Opposing Side (Respondent / Appellee): Donald J. Veverka, Assistant Attorney General, argued the cause for appellee State of Illinois. James B. Zagel, Assistant State's Attorney, argued the cause for appellee Woods.

Robert R. Granucci, Deputy Attorney General, argued the cause for the State of California, as amicus curiae.

III. AMICI CURIAE

ACLU Side (Petitioner / Appellant)

Brief of amici curiae filed on behalf of the Illinois Division, ACLU, by Elmer Gertz.

Brief of amicus curiae filed on behalf of the NAACP Legal Defense and Educational Fund, Inc., by Jack Greenberg, James M. Nabrit III, Michael Meltsner, Leroy D. Clark, Norman C. Amaker, Charles S. Ralston, Jack Himmelstein, and Anthony G. Amsterdam.

Brief of amici curiae filed on behalf of the American Friends Service Committee, et al., by Alex Elson, Willard J. Lassers, and Marvin Braiterman.

Brief of amici curiae filed by F. Lee Bailey, pro se.

Brief of amici curiae filed on behalf of Oscar Turner by Joel W. Westbrook and Charles E. Wallace.

Brief of amici curiae filed on behalf of Rebecca B. Madden by John P. Frank, John J. Flynn, and Paul G. Ulrich.

Opposing Side (Respondent / Appellee)

Robert R. Granucci, Deputy Attorney General, argued the cause for the State of California, as amicus curiae. With him on the brief were Thomas C. Lynch, Attorney General, Albert W. Harris, Jr., Assistant Attorney General, and George R. Nock, Deputy Attorney General, joined by the Attorneys General for their respective States as follows: MacDonald Gallion of Alabama, Darrell F. Smith of Arizona, Joe Purcell of Arkansas, Duke W. Dunbar of Colorado, David P. Buckson of Delaware, Earl Faircloth of Florida, Arthur K. Bolton of Georgia, Allan G. Shepard of Idaho, Robert C. Londerholm of Kansas, John B. Breckinridge of Kentucky, Jack P. F. Gremillion of Louisiana, Norman H. Anderson of Missouri, Clarence A. H. Meyer of Nebraska, George S. Pappagianis of New Hampshire, Boston E. Witt of New Mexico, Helgi Johanneson of North Dakota, William B. Saxbe of Ohio, G. T. Blankenship of Oklahoma, William C. Sennett of Pennsylvania, Daniel R. McLeod of South Carolina, Frank L. Farrar of South Dakota, George F. McCanless of Tennessee, Crawford C. Martin of Texas, Robert Y. Button of Virginia, John J. O'Connell of Washington, and James E. Barrett of Wyoming; and by Marion O. Gordon, Assistant Attorney General of Georgia, Frank P. Lawley, Deputy Attorney General of Pennsylvania, Reno S. Harp III, Assistant Attorney General of Virginia, and Howard L. McFadden.

IV. THE SUPREME COURT'S DECISION

"We simply cannot conclude, either on the basis of the record now before us or as a matter of judicial notice, that the exclusion of jurors opposed to capital punishment results in an unrepresentative jury on the issue of guilt or substantially increases the risk of conviction. In light of the presently available information, we are not prepared to announce a per se constitutional rule requiring the reversal of every conviction returned by a jury selected as this one was. . . .

It does not follow, however, that the petitioner is entitled to no relief. For in this case the jury was entrusted with two distinct responsibilities: first, to determine whether the petitioner was innocent or guilty; and second, if guilty, to determine whether his sentence should be imprisonment or death. It has not been shown that this jury was biased with respect to the petitioner's guilt. But it is self-evident that, in its role as arbiter of the punishment to be imposed, this jury fell woefully short of that impartiality to which the petitioner was entitled under the Sixth and Fourteenth Amendments. . . .

A man who opposes the death penalty, no less than one who favors it, can make the discretionary judgment entrusted to him by the State and can thus obey the oath he takes as a juror. But a jury from which all such men have been excluded cannot perform the task demanded of it. Guided by neither rule nor standard, 'free to select or reject as it [sees]

fit,' a jury that must choose between life imprisonment and capital punishment can do little more—and must do nothing less—than express the conscience of the community on the ultimate question of life or death. Yet, in a nation less than half of whose people believe in the death penalty, a jury composed exclusively of such people cannot speak for the community. Culled of all who harbor doubts about the wisdom of capital punishment—of all who would be reluctant to pronounce the extreme penalty—such a jury can speak only for a distinct and dwindling minority. . . .

It is, of course, settled that a State may not entrust the determination of whether a man is innocent or guilty to a tribunal 'organized to convict.' It requires but a short step from that principle to hold, as we do today, that a State may not entrust the determination of whether a man should live or die to a tribunal organized to return a verdict of death. Specifically, we hold that a sentence of death cannot be carried out if the jury that imposed or recommended it was chosen by excluding veniremen for cause simply because they voiced general objections to the death penalty or expressed conscientious or religious scruples against its infliction. No defendant can constitutionally be put to death at the hands of a tribunal so selected.

Whatever else might be said of capital punishment, it is at least clear that its imposition by a hanging jury cannot be squared with the Constitution. The State of Illinois has stacked the deck against the petitioner. To execute this death sentence would deprive him of his life without due process of law."

The Supreme Court reversed the death sentence.

V. JUSTICE VOTE

6 Pro ACLU Side vs. 3 Con Opposing Side

ACLU Side (Petitioner/Appellant)

1. Stewart, P. – Wrote majority opinion
2. Douglas, W. – Wrote concurring opinion
3. Warren, E. – Joined majority opinion
4. Marshall, T. – Joined majority opinion
5. Brennan, W. – Joined majority opinion
6. Fortas, A. – Joined majority opinion

Opposing Side (Respondent/Appellee)

1. White, B. – Wrote dissenting opinion, joined Black's dissent
2. Harlan, J. – Joined Black's dissent
3. Black, H. – Wrote dissenting opinion

VI. A WIN OR LOSS FOR THE ACLU?

The ACLU filed an amicus brief urging reversal; the U.S. Supreme Court reversed the ruling of the Supreme Court of Illinois in a 6-3 vote, giving the ACLU an apparent win.

204. Pickering v. Board of Education

(Decided June 3, 1968; 391 U.S. 563)

I. ISSUE

A. Issues Discussed

First Amendment, freedoms of press, speech, and association

B. Legal Question Presented

Did school officials violate the First Amendment by firing a teacher for sending a letter to a local newspaper criticizing the school board?

C. Supreme Court's Answer

A letter printed in a local newspaper does not provide proper grounds to fire a teacher, absent knowingly or recklessly made false statements within the letter.

II. CASE SUMMARY

A. Background

"Appellant Marvin L. Pickering, a teacher in Township High School District 205, Will County, Illinois, was dismissed from his position by the appellee Board of Education for sending a letter to a local newspaper in connection with a recently proposed tax increase that was critical of the way in which the Board and the district superintendent of schools had handled past proposals to raise new revenue for the schools. Appellant's dismissal resulted from a determination by the Board, after a full hearing, that the publication of the letter was 'detrimental to the efficient operation and administration of the schools of the district' and hence, under the relevant Illinois statute, . . . that 'interests of the schools require[d] [his dismissal].'

Appellant's claim that his writing of the letter was protected by the First and Fourteenth Amendments was rejected. Appellant then sought review of the Board's action in the Circuit Court of Will County, which affirmed his dismissal on the ground that the determination that appellant's letter was detrimental to the interests of the school system was supported by substantial evidence and that the interests of the schools overruled appellant's First Amendment rights. On appeal, the Supreme Court of Illinois, two Justices dissenting, affirmed the judgment of the Circuit Court."

The U.S. Supreme Court granted certiorari and reversed.

B. Counsel of Record/ACLU Attorney

ACLU Side (Petitioner/Appellant): John Ligtenberg argued the cause for appellant.

Opposing Side (Respondent/Appellee): John F. Cirricione argued the cause for appellee.

III. AMICI CURIAE

ACLU Side (Petitioner/Appellant)

Brief of amici curiae filed on behalf of the ACLU, Illinois Division, by Milton I. Shadur and Michael L. Shakman.

Opposing Side (Respondent/Appellee)

No briefs of amici curiae were filed in support of appellee.

IV. THE SUPREME COURT'S DECISION

"The problem in any case is to arrive at a balance between the interests of the teacher, as a citizen, in commenting upon matters of public concern and the interest of the State, as an employer, in promoting the efficiency of the public services it performs through its employees. . . .

What we do have before us is a case in which a teacher has made erroneous public statements upon issues then currently the subject of public attention, which are critical of his ultimate employer but which are neither shown nor can be presumed to have in any way either impeded the teacher's proper performance of his daily duties in the classroom or to have interfered with the regular operation of the schools generally. In these circumstances we conclude that the interest of the school administration in limiting teachers' opportunities to contribute to public debate is not significantly greater than its interest in limiting a similar contribution by any member of the general public. . . .

The public interest in having free and unhindered debate on matters of public importance—the core value of the Free Speech Clause of the First Amendment—is so great that it has been held that a State cannot authorize the recovery of damages by a public official for defamatory statements directed at him except when such statements are shown to have been made either with knowledge of their falsity or with reckless disregard for their truth or falsity. . . . It is therefore perfectly clear that, were appellant a member of the general public, the State's power to afford the appellee Board of Education or its members any legal right to sue him for writing the letter at issue here would be limited by the requirement that the letter be judged by the standard laid down in New York Times.

[I]n a case such as the present one, in which the fact of employment is only tangentially and insubstantially involved in the subject matter of the public communication made by a teacher, we conclude that it is necessary to regard the teacher as the member of the general public he seeks to be.

In sum, we hold that, in a case such as this, absent proof of false statements knowingly or recklessly made by him, a teacher's exercise of his right to speak on issues of public importance may not furnish the basis for his dismissal from public employment. Since no such showing has been made in this case regarding appellant's letter, his dismissal for writing it cannot be upheld and the judgment of the Illinois Supreme Court must, accordingly, be reversed and the case remanded for further proceedings not inconsistent with this opinion."

The U.S. Supreme Court reversed the judgment of the Supreme Court of Illinois and remanded the case.

V. JUSTICE VOTE

8 Pro ACLU Side vs. 1 Con Opposing Side

ACLU Side (Petitioner/Appellant)

1. Marshall, T. – Wrote majority opinion
2. Black, H. – Joined Douglas' concurrence
3. Warren, E. – Joined majority opinion
4. Stewart, P. – Joined majority opinion
5. Brennan, W. – Joined majority opinion
6. Fortas, A. – Joined majority opinion
7. Harlan, J. – Joined majority opinion
8. Douglas, W. – Wrote concurring opinion

Opposing Side (Respondent/Appellee)

1. White, B. – Wrote opinion concurring in part and dissenting in part

VI. A WIN OR LOSS FOR THE ACLU?

The ACLU filed an amicus brief urging reversal; the U.S. Supreme Court reversed the ruling of the Supreme Court of Illinois in an 8-1 vote, giving the ACLU an apparent win.

205. Terry v. Ohio

(Decided June 10, 1968; 392 U.S. 1)

I. ISSUE

A. Issues Discussed

Criminal procedure, Fourth Amendment, stop and frisk

B. Legal Question Presented

"[W]hether the admission of the revolvers in evidence violated petitioner's rights under the Fourth Amendment, made applicable to the States by the Fourteenth [and] whether it is always unreasonable for a policeman to seize a person and subject him to a limited search for weapons unless there is probable cause for an arrest."

C. Supreme Court's Answer

The revolvers were properly admitted in evidence and it is not always unreasonable for police to seize and search a person in these circumstances.

II. CASE SUMMARY

A. Background

"Petitioner Terry was convicted of carrying a concealed weapon and sentenced to the statutorily prescribed term of one to three years in the penitentiary. Following the denial of a pretrial motion to suppress, the prosecution introduced in evidence two revolvers and a number of bullets seized from Terry and a codefendant, Richard Chilton, by Cleveland Police Detective Martin McFadden. At the hearing on the motion to suppress this evidence, Officer McFadden testified that while he was patrolling in plain clothes in downtown Cleveland at approximately 2:30 in the afternoon of October 31, 1963, his attention was attracted by two men, Chilton and Terry, standing on the corner of Huron Road and Euclid Avenue. He had never seen the two men before, and he was unable to say precisely what first drew his eye to them. However, he testified that he had been a policeman for 39 years and a detective for 35 and that he had been assigned to patrol this vicinity of downtown Cleveland for shoplifters and pickpockets for 30 years. He explained that he had developed routine habits of observation over the years and that he would 'stand and watch people or walk and watch people at many intervals of the day.' He added: 'Now, in this case when I looked over they didn't look right to me at the time.'

His interest aroused, Officer McFadden took up a post of observation in the entrance to a store 300 to 400 feet away from the two men." He saw the men switch off walking in front of the same store, then conferring with each other approximately twelve times, then speaking with a third man. "By this time Officer McFadden had become thoroughly suspicious. He testified that after observing their elaborately casual and oft-repeated reconnaissance of the store window on Huron Road, he suspected the two men of 'casing a job, a stick-up,' and that he considered it his duty as a police officer to investigate further. He added that he feared 'they may have a gun.' Thus, Officer McFadden followed Chilton and Terry and saw them stop in front of Zucker's store to talk to the same man who had conferred with them earlier on the street corner. Deciding that the situation was ripe for direct action, Officer McFadden approached the three men, identified himself as a police officer and asked for their names. At this point his knowledge was confined to what he had observed. He was not acquainted with any of the three men by name or by sight, and he had received no information concerning them from any other source. When the men 'mumbled something' in response to his inquiries, Officer McFadden grabbed petitioner Terry, spun him around so that they were facing the other two, with Terry between McFadden and the others, and patted down the outside of his clothing. In the left breast pocket of Terry's overcoat Officer McFadden felt a pistol. He reached inside the overcoat pocket, but was unable to remove the gun. At this point, keeping Terry between himself and the others, the officer ordered all three men to enter Zucker's store. As they went in, he removed Terry's overcoat completely, removed a .38-caliber revolver from the pocket and ordered all three men to face the wall with their hands raised. Officer McFadden proceeded to pat down the outer clothing of Chilton and the third man, Katz. He discovered another revolver in the outer pocket of Chilton's overcoat, but no weapons were found on Katz. The officer testified that he only patted the men down to see whether they had weapons, and that he did not put his hands beneath the outer garments of either Terry or Chilton until he felt their guns. So far as appears from the record, he never placed his hands beneath Katz' outer garments. . . .

After the court denied their motion to suppress, Chilton and Terry waived jury trial and pleaded not guilty. The court adjudged them guilty, and the Court of Appeals for the Eighth Judicial District, Cuyahoga County, affirmed. The Supreme Court of Ohio dismissed their appeal on the ground that no 'substantial constitutional question' was involved."

The Supreme Court granted certiorari and affirmed.

B. Counsel of Record / ACLU Attorney

ACLU Side (Petitioner / Appellant): Louis Stokes argued the cause for appellant.

Opposing Side (Respondent / Appellee): Reuben M. Payne argued the cause for appellee.

III. AMICI CURIAE

ACLU Side (Petitioner / Appellant)

Brief of amici curiae filed on behalf of the ACLU, et al., by Bernard A. Berkman, Lewis A. Stern, Melvin L. Wulf, and Alan H. Levine.

Brief of amici curiae filed on behalf of the NAACP Legal Defense and Educational Fund, Inc., by Jack Greenberg, James M. Nabrit, III, Michael Meltsner, Melvyn Zarr, and Anthony G. Amsterdam.

Opposing Side (Respondent / Appellee)

Brief of amici curiae filed on behalf of the United States by Solicitor General Erwin N. Griswold, Assistant Attorney General Fred M. Vinson, Jr., Ralph S. Spritzer, Assistant to the Solicitor General, Beatrice Rosenberg, and Mervyn Hamburg.

Brief of amici curiae filed on behalf of the Attorney General of New York by Louis J. Lefkowitz, pro se, Samuel A. Hirshowitz, First Assistant Attorney General, and Maria L. Marcus and Brenda Soloff, Assistant Attorneys General.

Brief of amici curiae filed on behalf of the National District Attorneys' Association by Brendan T. Byrne, Charles Moylan, Jr., Evelle J. Younger, Harry Wood, and Harry B. Sondheim.

Brief of amici curiae filed on behalf of Americans for Effective Law Enforcement by James R. Thompson.

IV. THE SUPREME COURT'S DECISION

"We have recently held that 'the Fourth Amendment protects people, not places,' and wherever an individual may harbor a reasonable 'expectation of privacy,' he is entitled to be free from unreasonable governmental intrusion. Of course, the specific content and incidents of this right must be shaped by the context in which it is asserted. For 'what the Constitution forbids is not all searches and seizures, but unreasonable searches and seizures.' Unquestionably petitioner was entitled to the protection of the Fourth Amendment as he walked down the street in Cleveland. . . .

It must be recognized that whenever a police officer accosts an individual and restrains his freedom to walk away, he has 'seized' that person. And it is nothing less than sheer torture of the English language to suggest that a careful exploration of the outer surfaces of a person's clothing all over his or her body in an attempt to find weapons is not a 'search.' . . . In this case there can be no question, then, that Officer McFadden 'seized' petitioner and subjected him to a 'search' when he took hold of him and patted down the outer surfaces of his clothing. . . .

Our evaluation of the proper balance that has to be struck in this type of case leads us to conclude that there must be a narrowly drawn authority to permit a reasonable search for weapons for the protection of the police officer, where he has reason to believe that he is dealing with an armed and dangerous individual, regardless of whether he has probable cause to arrest the individual for a crime. The officer need not be absolutely certain that the individual is armed; the issue is whether a reasonably prudent man in the circumstances would be warranted in the belief that his safety or that of others was in danger. And in determining whether the officer acted reasonably in such circumstances, due weight must be given, not to his inchoate and unparticularized suspicion or 'hunch,' but to the specific reasonable inferences which he is entitled to draw from the facts in light of his experience. . . .

We think on the facts and circumstances Officer McFadden detailed before the trial judge a reasonably prudent man would have been warranted in believing petitioner was armed and thus presented a threat to the officer's safety while he was investigating his suspicious behavior. . . .

The sole justification of the search in the present situation is the protection of the police officer and others nearby, and it must therefore be confined in scope to an intrusion reasonably designed to discover guns, knives, clubs, or other hidden instruments for the assault of the police officer. . . . The scope of the search in this case presents no serious problem in light of these standards. Officer McFadden patted down the outer clothing of petitioner and his two companions. He did not place his hands in their pockets or under the outer surface of their garments until he had felt weapons, and then he merely reached for and removed the guns. . . . Officer McFadden confined his search strictly to what was minimally necessary to learn whether the men were armed and to disarm them once he discovered the weapons. He did not conduct a general exploratory search for whatever evidence of criminal activity he might find. . . .

We conclude that the revolver seized from Terry was properly admitted in evidence against him. At the time he seized petitioner and searched him for weapons, Officer McFadden had reasonable grounds to believe that petitioner was armed and dangerous, and it was necessary for the protection of himself and others to take swift measures to discover the true facts and neutralize the threat of harm if it materialized. The policeman carefully restricted his search to what was appropriate to the discovery of the particular items which he sought. Each case of this sort will, of course, have to be decided on its own facts. We merely hold today that where a police officer observes unusual conduct which leads him reasonably to conclude in light of his experience that criminal activity may be afoot and that the persons with whom he is dealing may be armed and presently dangerous, where in the course of investigating this behavior he identifies himself as a policeman and makes reasonable inquiries, and where nothing in the initial stages of the encounter serves to dispel his reasonable fear for his own or others' safety, he is entitled for the protection of himself and others in the area to conduct a carefully limited search of the outer clothing of such persons in an attempt to discover weapons which might be used to assault him. Such a search is a reasonable search under the Fourth Amendment, and any weapons seized may properly be introduced in evidence against the person from whom they were taken."

The U.S. Supreme Court affirmed the judgment.

V. JUSTICE VOTE

1 Pro ACLU Side vs. 8 Con Opposing Side

ACLU Side (Petitioner/Appellant)

1. Douglas, W. – Wrote dissenting opinion

Opposing Side (Respondent/Appellee)

1. Warren, E. – Wrote majority opinion
2. White, B. – Wrote concurring opinion
3. Harlan, J. – Wrote concurring opinion
4. Black, H. – Wrote concurring opinion
5. Marshall, T. – Joined majority opinion
6. Fortas, A. – Joined majority opinion
7. Brennan, W. – Joined majority opinion
8. Stewart, P. – Joined majority opinion

VI. A WIN OR LOSS FOR THE ACLU?

The ACLU, as amicus curiae, urged reversal of the judgment; the Supreme Court affirmed in an 8-1 vote, giving the ACLU an apparent loss.

206. Sibron v. New York

(Decided June 10, 1968; 392 U.S. 40)

I. ISSUE

A. Issues Discussed

Criminal procedure, Fourth Amendment, stop and frisk

B. Legal Question Presented

Was there an unconstitutional seizure of evidence, purportedly justified under New York's "stop-and-frisk" law, first, when the officer's reason for conducting the search was merely the appellant's seeming acquaintance with several known drug addicts, and, second, when the officer apprehended appellant who was fleeing from what looked like an attempted burglary?

C. Supreme Court's Answer

The seizure was unconstitutional when based on acquaintance with drug addicts, but constitutional when based on attempted burglary.

II. CASE SUMMARY

A. Background

The Court of Appeals of New York consolidated the two cases of appellants Sibron and Peters.

Over an eight-hour period, a New York police officer observed appellant Sibron, whom he did not know and had no information about, in conversation with six or eight persons whom the officer knew as narcotics addicts. Later the officer saw Sibron in a restaurant with three more known addicts. On none of these occasions did the officer overhear any conversation or see anything pass between Sibron and the others. At the restaurant, the officer ordered Sibron outside, where the officer said, "You know what I am after." When Sibron reached into his pocket the officer reached into the same pocket and found some envelopes containing heroin. Sibron was convicted of unlawful possession of heroin.

Sibron moved to suppress the heroin evidence at trial. His motion was denied. The Appellate Term of the Supreme Court and Court of Appeals of New York both affirmed appellant's conviction, holding that the evidence was properly admitted, on the ground that the search that uncovered it was authorized by the New York "stop-and-frisk" statute, N.Y. Code Crim. Proc. § 180-a, which provides, in part, that a "police officer may stop any person abroad in a public place whom he reasonably suspects is committing a felony or [other certain crimes] and may demand of him his name, address and an explanation of his actions," and when the officer "suspects that he is in danger . . . he may search such person for a dangerous weapon."

Appellant Peters "was convicted of possessing burglary tools under circumstances evincing an intent to employ them in the commission of a crime." A police officer was inside his apartment when he heard noises and noticed two men sneaking around in his apartment building. He called the police, then left his apartment dressed in civilian clothes but with his service gun and chased and apprehended Peters. He "patted Peters down for weapons, and discovered a hard object in his pocket. He stated at the hearing that the object did not feel like a gun, but that is might have been a knife. He removed the object from Peters' pocket. It was an opaque plastic envelope, containing burglar's tools."

Peters similarly moved to suppress the evidence, had his motion denied, and had his conviction upheld by the Appellate Division of the Supreme Court and Court of Appeals of New York under § 180—a.

The Supreme Court granted certiorari, reversed Sibron's conviction, and affirmed Peters' conviction.

B. Counsel of Record/ACLU Attorney

ACLU Side (Petitioner/Appellant): Kalman Finkel and Gretchen White Oberman argued the cause for appellant in No. 63. Robert Stuart Friedman argued the cause for appellant in No. 74.

Opposing Side (Respondent/Appellee): William I. Siegel, Assistant District Attorney of Kings County, New York, argued the cause for appellee in No. 63. James J. Duggan, Assistant District Attorney of Westchester County, New York, argued the cause for appellee in No. 74.

Michael Juviler, Assistant District Attorney of New York County, argued the cause for the District Attorney of New York County, New York, as amicus curiae in No. 63.

William I. Siegel, Assistant District Attorney of Kings County, New York, argued the cause for the District Attorney of Kings County, New York, as amicus curiae in No. 74.

III. AMICI CURIAE

ACLU Side (Petitioner/Appellant)

Brief of amici curiae filed on behalf of the ACLU, et al., by Bernard A. Berkman, Lewis A. Stern, Melvin L. Wulf, and Alan H. Levine.

Brief of amicus curiae filed on behalf of the NAACP Legal Defense and Educational Fund, Inc., by Jack Greenberg, James M. Nabrit, III, Michael Meltsner, Melvyn Zarr, and Anthony G. Amsterdam.

Opposing Side (Respondent/Appellee)

Brief of amici curiae filed on behalf of the Attorney General of New York, by Louis J. Lefkowitz, pro se, Samuel A. Hirshowitz, First Assistant Attorney General, and Maria L. Marcus and Brenda Soloff, Assistant Attorneys General.

Brief of amici curiae filed on behalf of the District Attorney of New York County, by Michael Juviler, Assistant District Attorney of New York County, H. Richard Uviller and Sybil H. Landau, Assistant District Attorneys, and Frank S. Hogan, District Attorney.

William I. Siegel, Assistant District Attorney of Kings County, New York, argued the cause as amicus curiae.

IV. THE SUPREME COURT'S DECISION

"Turning to the facts of Sibron's case, it is clear that the heroin was inadmissible in evidence against him. . . .

[T]he Court of Appeals of New York . . . seems to have viewed the search here as a self-protective search for weapons and to have affirmed on the basis of §180—a, which authorizes such a search when the officer 'reasonably suspects that he is in danger of life or limb.' . . . But the application of this reasoning to the facts of this case proves too much. The police officer is not entitled to seize and search every person whom he sees on the street or of whom he makes inquiries. Before he places a hand on the person of a citizen in search of anything, he must have constitutionally adequate, reasonable grounds for doing so. In the case of the self-protective search for weapons, he must be able to point to particular facts from which he reasonably inferred that the individual was armed and dangerous. Patrolman Martin's testimony reveals no such facts. The suspect's mere act of talking with a number of known narcotics addicts over an eight-hour period no more gives rise to reasonable fear of life or limb on the part of the police officer than it justifies an arrest for committing a crime. Nor did Patrolman Martin urge that when Sibron put his hand in his pocket, he feared that he was going for a weapon and acted in self-defense. His opening statement to Sibron—'You know what I am after'—made it abundantly clear that he sought narcotics, and his testimony at the hearing left no doubt that he thought there were narcotics in Sibron's pocket.

Even assuming arguendo that there were adequate grounds to search Sibron for weapons, the nature and scope of the search conducted by Patrolman Martin were so clearly unrelated to that justification as to render the heroin inadmissible. . . . In this case, with no attempt at an initial limited exploration for arms, Patrolman Martin thrust his hand into Sibron's pocket and took from him envelopes of heroin. His testimony shows that he was looking for narcotics, and he found them. The search was not reasonably limited in scope to the accomplishment of the only goal which might conceivably have justified its inception—the protection of the officer by disarming a potentially dangerous man. Such a search violates the guarantee of the Fourth Amendment, which protects the sanctity of the person against unreasonable intrusions on the part of all government agents. . . .

We think it is equally clear that the search in Peters' case was wholly reasonable under the Constitution. The Court of Appeals of New York held that the search was made legal by § 180—a, since Peters was 'abroad in a public place,' and since Officer Lasky was reasonably suspicious of his activities and, once he had stopped Peters, reasonably suspected that he was in danger of life or limb, even though he held Peters at gun point. This may be the justification for the search under state law. We think, however, that for purposes of the Fourth Amendment the search was properly incident to a lawful arrest. By the time Officer Lasky caught up with Peters on the stairway between the fourth and fifth floors of the apartment building, he had probable cause to arrest him for attempted burglary. The officer heard strange noises at his door which apparently led him to believe that someone sought to force entry. When he investigated these noises he saw two men, whom he had never seen before in his 12 years in the building, tiptoeing furtively about the hallway. They were still engaged in these maneuvers after he called the police and dressed hurriedly. And when Officer Lasky entered the hallway, the men fled down the stairs. It is difficult to conceive of stronger grounds for an arrest, short of actual eyewitness observation of criminal activity. As the trial court explicitly recognized, deliberately furtive actions and flight at the approach of strangers or law officers are strong indicia of mens rea, and when coupled with specific knowledge on the part of the officer relating the suspect to the evidence of crime, they are proper factors to be considered in the decision to make an arrest.

As we noted in Sibron's case, a search incident to a lawful arrest may not precede the arrest and serve as part of its justification. It is a question of fact precisely when, in each case, the arrest took place. And while there was some inconclusive discussion in the trial court concerning when Officer Lasky 'arrested' Peters, it is clear that the arrest had, for purposes of constitutional justification, already taken place before the search commenced. When the policeman grabbed Peters by the collar, he abruptly 'seized' him and curtailed his freedom of movement on the basis of probable cause to believe that he was engaged in criminal activity. At that point he had the authority to search Peters, and the incident search was obviously justified 'by the need to seize weapons and other things which might be used to assault an officer or effect an escape, as well as by the need to prevent the destruction of evidence of the crime.' Moreover, it was reasonably limited in scope by these purposes. Officer Lasky did not engage in an unrestrained and thorough-going examination of Peters and his personal effects. He seized him to cut short his flight, and he searched him primarily for weapons. While patting down his outer clothing, Officer Lasky discovered an object in his pocket which might have been used as a weapon. He seized it and discovered it to be a potential instrument of the crime of burglary.

We have concluded that Peters' conviction fully comports with the commands of the Fourth and Fourteenth Amendments, and must be affirmed. The conviction [of Sibron], however, must be reversed, on the ground that the heroin was unconstitutionally admitted in evidence against the appellant."

V. JUSTICE VOTE

1 Pro ACLU Side vs. 8 Con Opposing Side

ACLU Side (Petitioner/Appellant)

1. Black, H. – Wrote opinion concurring in part and dissenting in part

Opposing Side (Respondent/Appellee)

1. Warren, E. – Wrote majority opinion
2. Marshall, T. – Joined majority opinion
3. Brennan, W. – Joined majority opinion
4. Stewart, P. – Joined majority opinion
5. Douglas, W. – Wrote concurring opinion
6. Fortas, A. – Wrote concurring opinion
7. White, B. – Wrote concurring opinion
8. Harlan, J. – Wrote concurring opinion

VI. A WIN OR LOSS FOR THE ACLU?

The ACLU filed an amicus brief urging reversal in both cases; the Supreme Court reversed the ruling of the Court of Appeals of New York for appellant Sibron and affirmed the ruling for appellant Peters in an 8-1 vote, giving the ACLU an apparent loss.

207. King v. Smith

(Decided June 17, 1968; 392 U.S. 309)

I. ISSUE

A. Issues Discussed

Equal protection, discrimination

B. Legal Question Presented

"[W]hether [the 'substitute father'] regulation of the Alabama Department of Pensions and Security, employed in that Department's administration of the State's federally funded AFDC program, is consistent with Subchapter IV of the Social Security Act, 42 U.S.C. §§ 601—609, and with the Equal Protection Clause of the Fourteenth Amendment."

C. Supreme Court's Answer

Alabama's "substitute father" regulation is inconsistent with the Social Security Act and therefore invalid.

II. CASE SUMMARY

A. Background

"At issue is the validity of Alabama's so-called 'substitute father' regulation which denies [Aid to Families With Dependent Children ("AFDC")] payments to the children of a mother who 'cohabits' in or outside her home with any single or married able-bodied man. Appellees brought this class action against appellants, officers, and members of the Alabama Board of Pensions and Security, in the United States District Court for the Middle District of Alabama, under 42 U.S.C. § 1983, seeking declaratory and injunctive relief. A properly convened three-judge District Court correctly adjudicated the merits of the controversy without requiring appellees to exhaust state administrative remedies, and found the regulation to be inconsistent with the Social Security Act and the Equal Protection Clause. . . .

The category singled out for welfare assistance by AFDC is the 'dependent child,' who is defined . . .as an age-qualified 'needy child . . . who has been deprived of parental support or care by reason of the death, continued absence from the home or physical or mental incapacity of a parent, and who is living with' any one of several listed relatives. Under this provision, and, insofar as relevant here, aid can be granted only if 'a parent' of the needy child is continually absent from the home. Alabama considers a man who qualifies as a 'substitute father' under its regulation to be a nonabsent parent within the federal statute. The State therefore denies aid to an otherwise eligible needy child on the basis that his substitute parent is not absent from the home.

Under the Alabama regulation, an 'able-bodied man, married or single, is considered a substitute father of all the children of the applicant . . . mother' in three different situations: (1) if 'he lives in the home with the child's natural or adoptive mother for the purpose of cohabitation'; or (2) if 'he visits [the home] frequently for the purpose of cohabiting with the child's natural or adoptive mother'; or (3) if 'he does not frequent the home but cohabits with the child's natural or adoptive mother elsewhere.' Whether the substitute father is actually the father of the children is irrelevant.

It is also irrelevant whether he is legally obligated to support the children, and whether he does in fact contribute to their support. What is determinative is simply whether he 'cohabits' with the mother. . . . '[C]ohabitation,' as used in the regulation, means essentially that the man and woman have 'frequent' or 'continuing' sexual relations. With regard to how frequent or continual these relations must be, the testimony is conflicting."

The Supreme Court granted certiorari and affirmed the judgment of the District Court.

B. Counsel of Record / ACLU Attorney

ACLU Side (Respondent / Appellee): Opposing Side (Petitioner / Appellant): Martin Garbus argued the cause for appellee. Mary Lee Stapp, Assistant Attorney General of Alabama, argued the cause for appellant.

III. AMICI CURIAE

ACLU Side (Respondent / Appellee)

Brief of amici curiae filed on behalf of the NAACP Legal Defense and Educational Fund, Inc., by Jack Greenberg, James M. Nabrit III, Leroy D. Clark, Charles Stephen Ralston, Paul Dodyk, Brian Glick, and Edward V. Sparer.

Brief of amici curiae filed on behalf of the Child Welfare League of America, Inc., et al., by Helen L. Buttenwieser and Ephraim London.

Opposing Side (Petitioner / Appellant)

No briefs of amici curiae were filed in support of appellant.

IV. THE SUPREME COURT'S DECISION

"Congress has determined that immorality and illegitimacy should be dealt with through rehabilitative measures rather than measures that punish dependent children, and that protection of such children is the paramount goal of AFDC. . . .

The pattern of this legislation could not be clearer. Every effort is to be made to locate and secure support payments from persons legally obligated to support a deserted child. The underlying policy and consistency in statutory interpretation dictate that the 'parent' referred to in these statutory provisions is the same parent as that in § 406(a). The provisions seek to secure parental support in lieu of AFDC support for dependent children. Such parental support can be secured only where the parent is under a state-imposed legal duty to support the child. Children with alleged substitute parents who owe them no duty of support are entirely unprotected by these provisions. We think that these provisions corroborate the intent of Congress that the only kind of 'parent,' under s 406(a), whose presence in the home would provide adequate economic protection for a dependent child is one who is legally obligated to support him. . . .

Alabama's substitute father regulation, as written and as applied in this case, requires the disqualification of otherwise eligible dependent children if their mother 'cohabits' with a man who is not obligated by Alabama law to support the children. The regulation is therefore invalid because it defines 'parent' in a manner that is inconsistent with § 406(a) of the Social Security Act. In denying AFDC assistance to appellees on the basis of this invalid regulation, Alabama has breached its federally imposed obligation to furnish 'aid to families with dependent children . . . with reasonable promptness to all eligible individuals . . . .' Our conclusion makes unnecessary consideration of appellees' equal-protection claim, upon which we intimate no views. . . .

All responsible governmental agencies in the Nation today recognize the enormity and pervasiveness of social ills caused by poverty. The causes of and cures for poverty are currently the subject of much debate. We hold today only that Congress has made at least this one determination: that destitute children who are legally fatherless cannot be flatly denied federally funded assistance on the transparent fiction that they have a substitute father."

The Supreme Court affirmed the judgment of the District Court.

V. JUSTICE VOTE

9 Pro ACLU Side vs. 0 Con Opposing Side

ACLU Side (Respondent / Appellee)

1. Warren, E. – Wrote majority opinion
2. Marshall, T. – Joined majority opinion
3. Black, H. – Joined majority opinion
4. Stewart, P. – Joined majority opinion
5. Fortas, A. – Joined majority opinion
6. Brennan, W. – Joined majority opinion
7. Harlan, J. – Joined majority opinion
8. White, B. – Joined majority opinion
9. Douglas, W. – Wrote concurring opinion

VI. A WIN OR LOSS FOR THE ACLU?

The ACLU, as counsel of record, urged affirmance of the judgment of the District Court; the Supreme Court affirmed the ruling in a 9-0 vote, giving the ACLU an apparent win.

208. Jones v. Alfred H. Mayer Co.

(Decided June 17, 1968; 392 U.S. 409)

I. ISSUE

A. Issues Discussed

Civil rights, desegregation

B. Legal Question Presented

Does 42 U.S.C. § 1982, which guarantees equal rights to citizens of all races making real estate transactions, apply only to state action or does it apply to private action as well?

C. Supreme Court's Answer

42 U.S.C. § 1982 applies to both state and private action.

II. CASE SUMMARY

A. Background

42 U.S.C. § 1982 "provides that: 'All citizens of the United States shall have the same right, in every State and Territory, as is enjoyed

by white citizens thereof to inherit, purchase, lease, sell, hold, and convey real and personal property.'

On September 2, 1965, the petitioners filed a complaint in the District Court for the Eastern District of Missouri, alleging that the respondents had refused to sell them a home in the Paddock Woods community of St. Louis County for the sole reason that petitioner Joseph Lee Jones is a Negro. Relying in part upon § 1982, the petitioners sought injunctive and other relief. The District Court sustained the respondents' motion to dismiss the complaint, and the Court of Appeals for the Eighth Circuit affirmed, concluding that § 1982 applies only to state action and does not reach private refusals to sell."

The Supreme Court granted certiorari and reversed.

B. Counsel of Record/ACLU Attorney

ACLU Side (Petitioner/Appellant): Samuel H. Liberman argued the cause for appellant.

Attorney General Ramsey Clark argued the cause for the United States, as amicus curiae.

Opposing Side (Respondent/Appellee): Israel Treiman argued the cause for appellee.

III. AMICI CURIAE

ACLU Side (Petitioner/Appellant)

Brief of amici curiae filed on behalf of the ACLU, et al., by Leo Pfeffer, Melvin L. Wulf, Stephen W. Skrainka, and Eleanor Holmes Norton.

Attorney General Ramsey Clark argued the cause for the United States, as amicus curiae, urging reversal. With him on the brief were Solicitor General Erwin N. Griswold, Assistant Attorney General Stephen J. Pollak, Assistant to the Solicitor General Louis F. Claiborne, and Brian K. Landsberg.

Additional briefs of amici curiae were filed on behalf of the State of California, the State of Michigan (Civil Rights Commission), the Missouri Commission on Human Rights, Kansas City, Missouri, and Kansas City, Kansas, the National Committee against Discrimination in Housing, et al., the American Federation of Teachers, et al., the Path Association, the National Catholic Conference for Interracial Justice, et al., the National Council of Churches of Christ in the United States, et al., the American Jewish Committee, et al., and Henry S. Reuss.

Opposing Side (Respondent/Appellee)

Brief of amici curiae filed on behalf of the Maryland Petitioner Committee, Inc., et al., by George Washington Williams and Thomas F. Cadwalader.

IV. THE SUPREME COURT'S DECISION

"For the reasons that follow, we reverse the judgment of the Court of Appeals. We hold that § 1982 bars all racial discrimination, private as well as public, in the sale or rental of property, and that the statute, thus construed, is a valid exercise of the power of Congress to enforce the Thirteenth Amendment.

[T]he fact that § 1982 operates upon the unofficial acts of private individuals, whether or not sanctioned by state law, presents no constitutional problem. If Congress has power under the Thirteenth Amendment to eradicate conditions that prevent Negroes from buying and renting property because of their race or color, then no federal statute calculated to achieve that objective can be thought to exceed the constitutional power of Congress simply because it reaches beyond state action to regulate the conduct of private individuals. The constitutional question in this case, therefore, comes to this: Does the authority of Congress to enforce the Thirteenth Amendment 'by appropriate legislation' include the power to eliminate all racial barriers to the acquisition of real and personal property? We think the answer to that question is plainly yes. . . .

Negro citizens, North and South, who saw in the Thirteenth Amendment a promise of freedom—freedom to 'go and come at pleasure' and to 'buy and sell when they please'—would be left with 'a mere paper guarantee' if Congress were powerless to assure that a dollar in the hands of a Negro will purchase the same thing as a dollar in the hands of a white man. At the very least, the freedom that Congress is empowered to secure under the Thirteenth Amendment includes the freedom to buy whatever a white man can buy, the right to live wherever a white man can live. If Congress cannot say that being a free man means at least this much, then the Thirteenth Amendment made a promise the Nation cannot keep."

The Supreme Court reversed the judgment of the Court of Appeals for the Eighth Circuit.

V. JUSTICE VOTE

7 Pro ACLU Side vs. 2 Con Opposing Side

ACLU Side (Petitioner/Appellant)

1. Stewart, P. – Wrote majority opinion
2. Douglas, W. – Wrote concurring opinion
3. Fortas, A. – Joined majority opinion
4. Black, H. – Joined majority opinion
5. Warren, E. – Joined majority opinion
6. Brennan, W. – Joined majority opinion
7. Marshall, T. – Joined majority opinion

Opposing Side (Respondent/Appellee)

1. Harlan, J. – Wrote dissenting opinion
2. White, B. – Joined dissenting opinion

VI. A WIN OR LOSS FOR THE ACLU?

The ACLU, as amicus curiae, urged reversal of the judgment of the Court of Appeals for the Eighth Circuit; the Supreme Court reversed in a 7-2 vote, giving the ACLU an apparent win.

209. Powell v. Texas

(Decided June 17, 1968; 392 U.S. 514)

I. ISSUE

A. Issues Discussed

Criminal justice, Eighth Amendment, cruel and unusual punishment, Fourteenth Amendment

B. Legal Question Presented

Did Powell's arrest and punishment for being found in a state of intoxication in a public place amount to cruel and unusual in violation of the Eighth and Fourteenth Amendments?

C. Supreme Court's Answer

Powell's arrest and punishment for public intoxication did not amount to cruel and unusual punishment.

II. CASE SUMMARY

A. Background

"In late December 1966, appellant was arrested and charged with being found in a state of intoxication in a public place, in violation of [the] Texas Penal Code . . . . Appellant was tried in the Corporation Court of Austin, Texas, found guilty, and fined $20. He appealed to the County Court at Law No. 1 of Travis County, Texas, where a trial de novo was held. His counsel urged that appellant was 'afflicted with the disease of chronic alcoholism,' that 'his appearance in public [while drunk was] . . . not of his own volition,' and therefore that to punish him criminally for that conduct would be cruel and unusual, in violation of the Eighth and Fourteenth Amendments to the United States Constitution.

The trial judge in the county court, sitting without a jury, made certain findings of fact, but ruled as a matter of law that chronic alcoholism was not a defense to the charge. He found appellant guilty, and fined him $50. There being no further right to appeal within the Texas judicial system, appellant appealed to [the Supreme] Court; we noted probable jurisdiction."

The Supreme Court affirmed the conviction.

B. Counsel of Record/ACLU Attorney

ACLU Side (Petitioner/Appellant): Don L. Davis argued the cause for appellant, pro hac vice, by special leave of Court.

Peter Barton Hutt argued the cause for the ACLU, et al., as amicus curiae.

Opposing Side (Respondent/Appellee): David Robinson, Jr., argued the cause for appellee.

III. AMICI CURIAE

ACLU Side (Petitioner/Appellant)

Peter Barton Hutt argued the cause for the ACLU, et al., as amicus curiae, urging reversal. With him on the brief was Richard A. Merrill.

Brief of amici curiae filed on behalf of the National Council on Alcoholism by Paul O'Dwyer

Brief of amici curiae filed on behalf of the Philadelphia Diagnostic and Relocation Services Corp., by Judah I. Labovitz.

Opposing Side (Respondent/Appellee)

No briefs of amici curiae were filed in support of appellee.

IV. THE SUPREME COURT'S DECISION

"Appellant . . . seeks to come within the application of the Cruel and Unusual Punishment Clause announced in Robinson v. California, which involved a state statute making it a crime to 'be addicted to the use of narcotics.' This Court held there that 'a state law which imprisons a person thus afflicted [with narcotic addiction] as a criminal, even though he has never touched any narcotic drug within the State or been guilty of any irregular behavior there, inflicts a cruel and unusual punishment . . . .'

On its face the present case does not fall within that holding, since appellant was convicted, not for being a chronic alcoholic, but for being in public while drunk on a particular occasion. The State of Texas thus has not sought to punish a mere status, as California did in *Robinson*; nor has it attempted to regulate appellant's behavior in the privacy of his own home. Rather, it has imposed upon appellant a criminal sanction for public behavior which may create substantial health and safety hazards, both for appellant and for members of the general public, and which offends the moral and esthetic sensibilities of a large segment of the community. . . .

Traditional common-law concepts of personal accountability and essential considerations of federalism lead us to disagree with appellant. We are unable to conclude, on the state of this record or on the current state of medical knowledge, that chronic alcoholics in general, and Leroy Powell in particular, suffer from such an irresistible compulsion to drink and to get drunk in public that they are utterly unable to control their performance of either or both of these acts and thus cannot be deterred at all from public intoxication. . . .

We cannot cast aside the centuries-long evolution of the collection of interlocking and overlapping concepts which the common law has utilized to assess the moral accountability of an individual for his antisocial deeds."

The Supreme Court affirmed the judgment of the County Court at Law No. 1 of Travis County.

V. JUSTICE VOTE

4 Pro ACLU Side vs. 5 Con Opposing Side

ACLU Side (Petitioner/Appellant)

1. Fortas, A. – Wrote dissenting opinion
2. Brennan, W. – Joined Fortas' dissent
3. Douglas, W. – Joined Fortas' dissent
4. Stewart, J. – Joined Fortas' dissent

Opposing Side (Respondent/Appellee)

1. Marshall, T. – Wrote majority opinion
2. Warren, E. – Joined majority opinion
3. White, B. – Wrote concurring opinion
4. Black, H. – Wrote concurring opinion
5. Harlan, J. – Joined Black's concurrence

VI. A WIN OR LOSS FOR THE ACLU?

The ACLU filed a brief and argued as amicus curiae (an ACLU attorney argued though not as counsel of record), urging reversal; the Supreme Court affirmed the judgment of the County Court of Travis County in a 5-4 vote, giving the ACLU an apparent loss.

210. Epperson v. Arkansas

(Decided November 12, 1968; 393 U.S. 97)

I. ISSUE

A. Issues Discussed

First Amendment, freedom of religion, Fourteenth Amendment

B. Legal Question Presented

Does a law forbidding the teaching of evolution violate the freedom of religion, as mandated by the First Amendment?

C. Supreme Court's Answer

The law forbidding the teaching of evolution violates the First Amendment.

II. CASE SUMMARY

A. Background

"This appeal challenges the constitutionality of the 'anti-evolution' statute which the State of Arkansas adopted in 1928 to prohibit the teaching in its public schools and universities of the theory that man evolved from other species of life. . . . Violation is a misdemeanor and subjects the violator to dismissal from his position.

The present case concerns the teaching of biology in a high school in Little Rock. [T]he official textbook furnished for the high school biology course did not have a section on the Darwinian Theory. Then, for the academic year 1965—1966, the school administration, on recommendation of the teachers of biology in the school system, adopted and prescribed a textbook which contained a chapter setting forth 'the theory about the origin . . . of man from a lower form of animal.'

Susan Epperson, a young woman who graduated from Arkansas' school system and then obtained her master's degree in zoology at the University of Illinois, was employed by the Little Rock school system in the fall of 1964 to teach 10th grade biology at Central High School. At the start of the next academic year, 1965, she was confronted by the new textbook (which one surmises from the record was not unwelcome to her). She faced at least a literal dilemma because she was supposed to use the new textbook for classroom instruction and presumably to teach the statutorily condemned chapter; but to do so would be a criminal offense and subject her to dismissal.

She instituted the present action in the Chancery Court of the State, seeking a declaration that the Arkansas statute is void and enjoining the State and the defendant officials of the Little Rock school system from dismissing her for violation of the statute's provisions. . . .

The Chancery Court . . . held that the statute violated the Fourteenth Amendment to the United States Constitution. The court noted that this Amendment encompasses the prohibitions upon state interference with freedom of speech and thought which are contained in the First Amendment. Accordingly, it held that the challenged statute is unconstitutional because, in violation of the First Amendment, it 'tends to hinder the quest for knowledge, restrict the freedom to learn, and restrain the freedom to teach.' In this perspective, the Act, it held, was an unconstitutional and void restraint upon the freedom of speech guaranteed by the Constitution.

On appeal, the Supreme Court of Arkansas reversed. . . . It sustained the statute as an exercise of the State's power to specify the curriculum in public schools. It did not address itself to the competing constitutional considerations."

The U.S. Supreme Court granted certiorari and reversed the judgment of the Supreme Court of Arkansas.

B. Counsel of Record/ACLU Attorney

ACLU Side (Petitioner/Appellant): Eugene R. Warren argued the cause for appellant.

Opposing Side (Respondent/Appellee): Don Langston, Assistant Attorney General of Arkansas, argued the cause for appellee.

III. AMICI CURIAE

ACLU Side (Petitioner/Appellant)

Brief of amici curiae filed on behalf of the ACLU, et al., by Leo Pfeffer, Melvin L. Wulf, and Joseph B. Robinson.

Brief of amici curiae filed on behalf of the National Educational Association of the United States, et al., by Philip J. Hirschkop.

Opposing Side (Respondent/Appellee)

No briefs of amici curiae were filed in support of appellee.

IV. THE SUPREME COURT'S DECISION

"[T]he law must be stricken because of its conflict with the constitutional prohibition of state laws respecting an establishment of religion or prohibiting the free exercise thereof. The overriding fact is that Arkansas' law selects from the body of knowledge a particular segment which it proscribes for the sole reason that it is deemed to conflict with a particular religious doctrine; that is, with a particular interpretation of the Book of Genesis by a particular religious group. . . .

The First Amendment mandates governmental neutrality between religion and religion, and between religion and nonreligion. . . .

Arkansas' law cannot be defended as an act of religious neutrality. Arkansas did not seek to excise from the curricula of its schools and universities all discussion of the origin of man. The law's effort was confined to an attempt to blot out a particular theory because of its supposed conflict with the Biblical account, literally read. Plainly, the law is contrary to the mandate of the First, and in violation of the Fourteenth, Amendment to the Constitution."

The U.S. Supreme Court reversed the judgment of the Supreme Court of Arkansas.

V. JUSTICE VOTE

9 Pro ACLU Side vs. 0 Con Opposing Side

ACLU Side (Petitioner/Appellant)

1. Fortas, A. – Wrote majority opinion
2. Stewart, P. – Wrote concurring opinion
3. Black, H. – Wrote concurring opinion

4. Harlan, J. – Wrote concurring opinion
5. White, B. – Joined majority opinion
6. Douglas, W. – Joined majority opinion
7. Warren, E. – Joined majority opinion
8. Brennan, W. – Joined majority opinion
9. Marshall, T. – Joined majority opinion

VI. A WIN OR LOSS FOR THE ACLU?

The ACLU, as amicus curiae, urged reversal of the judgment of the Supreme Court of Arkansas; the U.S. Supreme Court reversed in a 9-0 vote, giving the ACLU an apparent win.

211. Carroll v. President & Comm'rs of Princess Anne

(Decided November 19, 1968; 393 U.S. 175)

I. ISSUE

A. Issues Discussed

1st Amendment, press, speech, association

B. Legal Question Presented

"[W]hether, by what processes, and to what extent the authorities of the local governments may restrict petitioners in their rallies and public meetings."

C. Supreme Court's Answer

"[I]t is clear that the 10-day restraining order in the present case, issued ex parte, without formal or informal notice to the petitioners or any effort to advise them of the proceeding, cannot be sustained."

II. CASE SUMMARY

A. Background

"Petitioners are identified with a 'white supremacist' organization called the National States Rights Party. They held a . . . rally near the courthouse steps . . . . Because of the tense atmosphere which developed as the meeting progressed, about 60 state policemen were brought in . . . . They were held in readiness, but for tactical reasons only a few were in evidence at the scene of the rally.

Petitioners' speeches, amplified by a public address system so that they could be heard for several blocks, were aggressively and militantly racist. . . .

In the course of the proceedings it was announced that the rally would be resumed the following night, August 7.

On that day, the respondents, officials of Princess Anne and of Somerset County, applied for and obtained a restraining order from the Circuit Court for Somerset County. The proceedings were ex parte, no notice being given to petitioners and, so far as appears, no effort being made informally to communicate with them, although this is expressly contemplated under Maryland procedure. The order restrained petitioners for 10 days from holding rallies or meetings in the county 'which will tend to disturb and endanger the citizens of the County.' As a result, the rally scheduled for August 7 was not held. After the trial which took place 10 days later, an injunction was issued by the Circuit Court on August 31, in effect extending the restraint for 10 additional months. . . .

On appeal, the Maryland Court of Appeals affirmed the 10-day order, but reversed the 10-month order . . . ."

The Supreme Court granted certiorari to review the case.

B. Counsel of Record

ACLU Side (Petitioner/Appellant): Eleanor Holmes Norton and William H. Zinman argued the cause for appellants. With them on the brief were Melvin L. Wulf (ACLU legal director 1962-1977), and Leon Friedman.

Opposing Side (Respondent/Appellee): S. Leonard Rottman and Alexander G. Jones argued the cause for appellees. With them on the brief was Francis B. Burch, Attorney General of Maryland.

III. AMICI CURIAE

ACLU Side (Petitioner/Appellant)

No briefs of amici curiae were filed in support of appellants.

Opposing Side (Respondent/Appellee)

No briefs of amici curiae were filed in support of appellees.

IV. THE SUPREME COURT'S DECISION

"We agree with petitioners that the case is not moot. Since 1966, petitioners have sought to continue their activities, including the holding of rallies in Princess Anne and Somerset County, and it appears that the decision of the Maryland Court of Appeals continues to play a substantial role in the response of officials to their activities. In these circumstances, our jurisdiction is not at an end. . . .

Since the Maryland Court of Appeals reversed the 10-month injunction of August 30, 1966, we do not consider that order. We turn to the constitutional problems raised by the 10-day injunctive order.

The petitioners urge that the injunction constituted a prior restraint on speech and that it therefore violated the principles of the First Amendment which are applicable to the States by virtue of the Fourteenth Amendment. . . .

We need not decide the thorny problem of whether, on the facts of this case, an injunction against the announced rally could be justified. The 10-day order here must be set aside because of a basic infirmity in the procedure by which it was obtained. It was issued ex parte, without notice to petitioners and without any effort, however informal, to invite or permit their participation in the proceedings. There is a place in our jurisprudence for ex parte issuance, without notice, of temporary restraining orders of short duration; but there is no place within the area of basic freedoms guaranteed by the First Amendment for such orders where no showing is made that it is impossible to serve or to notify the opposing parties and to give them an opportunity to participate. . . .

The Court has emphasized that '(a) system of prior restraints of expression comes to this Court bearing a heavy presumption against its constitutional validity.' . . .

Measured against these standards, it is clear that the 10-day restraining order in the present case, issued ex parte, without formal or informal notice to the petitioners or any effort to advise them of the proceeding, cannot be sustained. . . .

We need not here decide that it is impossible for circumstances to arise in which the issuance of an ex parte restraining order for a minimum period could be justified because of the unavailability of the adverse parties or their counsel, or perhaps for other reasons. In the present case, it is clear that the failure to give notice, formal or informal, and to provide an opportunity for an adversary proceeding before the holding of the rally was restrained, is incompatible with the First Amendment. Because we reverse the judgment below on this basis, we need not and do not decide whether the facts in this case provided a constitutionally permissible basis for temporarily enjoining the holding of the August 7 rally.

Reversed."

V. JUSTICE VOTE

9 Pro ACLU Side vs. 0 Con Opposing Side

ACLU Side (Petitioner/Appellant)

1. Fortas, A. – Wrote majority opinion
2. Warren, E. – Joined majority opinion
3. Brennan, W. – Joined majority opinion
4. Black, H. – Concurred in the result
5. Douglas, W. – Joined majority opinion
6. Harlan, J. – Joined majority opinion
7. Marshall, T. – Joined majority opinion
8. Stewart, P. – Joined majority opinion
9. White, B. – Joined majority opinion

VI. A WIN OR LOSS FOR THE ACLU?

The ACLU served as counsel for appellants urging reversal of the judgment of the Maryland Court of Appeals; the Supreme Court reversed in a 9-0 vote, giving the ACLU an apparent win.

212. Johnson v. Avery

(Decided February 24, 1969; 393 U.S. 483)

I. ISSUE

A. Issues Discussed

Criminal justice, prisons, Fourteenth Amendment, habeas corpus

B. Legal Question Presented

Whether a Tennessee regulation not allowing a prisoner to assist other prison inmates in preparing writs unlawfully conflicts with the federal right of habeas corpus?

C. Supreme Court's Answer

The regulation unlawfully conflicts with the federal right of habeas corpus because the state did not provide adequate alternatives to this type of assistance.

II. CASE SUMMARY

A. Background

Petitioner Johnson, while serving a life sentence in the Tennessee State Penitentiary, was transferred to the prison's maximum security building as discipline for violating a prison regulation prohibiting inmates from assisting other prisoners in preparing writs.

Johnson "filed in the United States District Court for the Middle District of Tennessee a 'motion for law books and a typewriter,' in which he sought relief from his confinement in the maximum security building. The District Court treated this motion as a petition for a writ of habeas corpus and, after a hearing, ordered him released from disciplinary confinement and restored to the status of an ordinary prisoner. The District Court held that the regulation was void because it in effect barred illiterate prisoners from access to federal habeas corpus and conflicted with 28 U.S. C. § 2242. . . .

The State appealed. The Court of Appeals for the Sixth Circuit reversed, [finding that] the interest of the State in preserving prison discipline and in limiting the practice of law to licensed attorneys justified whatever burden the regulation might place on access to federal habeas corpus."

The Supreme Court granted certiorari and reversed.

B. Counsel of Record/ACLU Attorney

ACLU Side (Petitioner/Appellant): Karl P. Warden argued the cause for appellant.

Opposing Side (Respondent/Appellee): Thomas E. Fox, Deputy Attorney General of Tennessee, argued the cause for appellee.

III. AMICI CURIAE

ACLU Side (Petitioner/Appellant)

Brief of amici curiae filed on behalf of the ACLU, et al., by Melvin L. Wulf and Kristin Glen.

Opposing Side (Respondent/Appellee)

Brief of amici curiae filed on behalf of the State of California by Thomas C. Lynch, Attorney General of California, Albert W. Harris, Jr., Assistant Attorney General, and Robert R. Granucci and George R. Nock, Deputy Attorneys General.

IV. THE SUPREME COURT'S DECISION

"This Court has constantly emphasized the fundamental importance of the writ of habeas corpus in our constitutional scheme, and the Congress has demonstrated its solicitude for the vigor of the Great Writ. The Court has steadfastly insisted that 'there is no higher duty than to maintain it unimpaired.' . . .

It is indisputable that prison 'writ writers' like petitioner are sometimes a menace to prison discipline and that their petitions are often so unskillful as to be a burden on the courts which receive them. But, as this Court held in Ex parte Hull, supra, in declaring invalid a state prison regulation which required that prisoners' legal pleadings be screened by state officials: 'The considerations that prompted [the regulation's] formulation are not without merit, but the state and its officers may not abridge or impair petitioner's right to apply to a federal court for a writ of habeas corpus'

Tennessee does not provide an available alternative to the assistance provided by other inmates. The warden of the prison in which petitioner was confined stated that the prison provided free notarization of prisoners' petitions. That obviously meets only a formal requirement. He also indicated that he sometimes allowed prisoners to examine the listing of attorneys in the Nashville telephone directory so they could select one to write to in an effort to interest him in taking the case, and that 'on several occasions' he had contacted the public defender at the request of an inmate. There is no contention, however, that there is any regular system of assistance by public defenders. . . .

Even in the absence of such alternatives, the State may impose reasonable restrictions and restraints upon the acknowledged propensity of prisoners to abuse both the giving and the seeking of assistance in the preparation of applications for relief: for example, by limitations on the time and location of such activities and the imposition of punishment for the giving or receipt of consideration in connection with such activities. But unless and until the State provides some reasonable alternative to assist inmates in the preparation of petitions for post-conviction relief, it may not validly enforce a regulation such as that here in issue, barring inmates from furnishing such assistance to other prisoners."

The Supreme Court reversed the judgment of the Court of Appeals and remanded the case.

V. JUSTICE VOTE

7 Pro ACLU Side vs. 2 Con Opposing Side

ACLU Side (Petitioner/Appellant)

1. Fortas, A. – Wrote majority opinion
2. Marshall, T. – Joined majority opinion
3. Warren, E. – Joined majority opinion
4. Harlan, J. – Joined majority opinion
5. Brennan, W. – Joined majority opinion
6. Stewart, J. – Joined majority opinion
7. Douglas, W. – Wrote concurring opinion

Opposing Side (Respondent/Appellee)

1. White, B. – Wrote dissenting opinion
2. Black, H. – Joined White's dissent

VI. A WIN OR LOSS FOR THE ACLU?

The ACLU filed as amicus curiae urging reversal; the Supreme Court reversed the judgment of the Court of Appeals in a 7-2 vote giving the ACLU an apparent win.

213. Tinker v. Des Moines Independent Community School District

(Decided February 24, 1969; 393 U.S. 503)

I. ISSUE

A. Issues Discussed

First Amendment, freedom of speech

B. Legal Question Presented

Whether a school policy prohibiting students from wearing an armband to school to protest the Vietnam War violated the First Amendment.

C. Supreme Court's Answer

The school policy prohibiting black armbands worn to protest the Vietnam War violated the First Amendment.

II. CASE SUMMARY

A. Background

"In December 1965, a group of adults and students in Des Moines . . . determined to publicize their objections to the hostilities in Vietnam and their support for a truce by wearing black armbands during the holiday season and by fasting on December 16 and New Year's Eve. Petitioners and their parents had previously engaged in similar activities, and they decided to participate in the program.

The principals of the Des Moines schools became aware of the plan to wear armbands. On December 14, 1965, they met and adopted a policy that any student wearing an armband to school would be asked to remove it, and if he refused he would be suspended until he returned without the armband. Petitioners were aware of the regulation that the school authorities adopted.

On December 16, Mary Beth and Christopher wore black armbands to their schools. John Tinker wore his armband the next day. They were all sent home and suspended from school until they would come back without their armbands. They did not return to school until after the planned period for wearing armbands had expired—that is, until after New Year's Day.

This complaint was filed in the United States District Court by petitioners, through their fathers, under § 1983 of Title 42 of the United States Code. It prayed for an injunction restraining the respondent school officials and the respondent members of the board of directors of the school district from disciplining the petitioners, and it sought nominal damages. After an evidentiary hearing the District Court dismissed the complaint. It upheld the constitutionality of the school authorities' action on the ground that it was reasonable in order to prevent disturbance of school discipline. The court referred to but expressly declined to follow the Fifth Circuit's holding in a similar case that the wearing of symbols like the armbands cannot be prohibited unless it 'materially and substantially interfere[s] with the requirements of appropriate discipline in the operation of the school.'

On appeal, the Court of Appeals for the Eighth Circuit considered the case en banc. The court was equally divided, and the District Court's decision was accordingly affirmed, without opinion."

The Supreme Court granted certiorari and reversed.

B. Counsel of Record/ACLU Attorney

ACLU Side (Petitioner/Appellant): Dan L. Johnston argued the cause for appellant. With him on the brief were Melvin L. Wulf and David N. Ellenhorn.

Opposing Side (Respondent/Appellee): Allan A. Herrick argued the cause for appellees. With him on the brief were Herschel G. Langdon, David W. Belin, and Philip C. Lovrien.

III. AMICI CURIAE

ACLU Side (Petitioner/Appellant)

Brief of amici curiae filed on behalf of the United States National Student Association by Charles Morgan, Jr., and Roy Lucas.

Opposing Side (Respondent/Appellee)

No briefs of amici curiae were filed in support of appellee.

IV. THE SUPREME COURT'S DECISION

"First Amendment rights, applied in light of the special characteristics of the school environment, are available to teachers and students. It can hardly be argued that either students or teachers shed their constitutional rights to freedom of speech or expression at the schoolhouse gate. This has been the unmistakable holding of this Court for almost 50 years. . . .

It is also relevant that the school authorities did not purport to prohibit the wearing of all symbols of political or controversial significance. The record shows that students in some of the schools wore buttons relating to national political campaigns, and some even wore the Iron Cross, traditionally a symbol of Nazism. The order prohibiting the wearing of armbands did not extend to these. Instead, a particular symbol—black armbands worn to exhibit opposition to this Nation's involvement in Vietnam—was singled out for prohibition. Clearly, the prohibition of expression of one particular opinion, at least without evidence that it is necessary to avoid material and substantial interference with schoolwork or discipline, is not constitutionally permissible.

In our system, state-operated schools may not be enclaves of totalitarianism. School officials do not possess absolute authority over their students. Students in school as well as out of school are 'persons' under our Constitution. They are possessed of fundamental rights which the State must respect, just as they themselves must respect their obligations to the State. In our system, students may not be regarded as closed-circuit recipients of only that which the State chooses to communicate. They may not be confined to the expression of those sentiments that are officially approved. In the absence of a specific showing of constitutionally valid reasons to regulate their speech, students are entitled to freedom of expression of their views.

[T]he record does not demonstrate any facts which might reasonably have led school authorities to forecast substantial disruption of or material interference with school activities, and no disturbances or disorders on the school premises in fact occurred. These petitioners merely went about their ordained rounds in school. Their deviation consisted only in wearing on their sleeve a band of black cloth, not more than two inches wide. They wore it to exhibit their disapproval of the Vietnam hostilities and their advocacy of a truce, to make their views known, and, by their example, to influence others to adopt them. They neither interrupted school activities nor sought to intrude in the school affairs or the lives of others. They caused discussion outside of the classrooms, but no interference with work and no disorder. In the circumstances, our Constitution does not permit officials of the State to deny their form of expression."

The Supreme Court reversed the judgment of the Court of Appeals for the Eighth Circuit.

V. JUSTICE VOTE

7 Pro ACLU Side vs. 2 Con Opposing Side

ACLU Side (Petitioner/Appellant)

1. Fortas, A. – Wrote majority opinion
2. Stewart, P. – Wrote concurring opinion
3. White, B. – Wrote concurring opinion
4. Douglas, W. – Joined majority opinion
5. Warren, E. – Joined majority opinion
6. Marshall, T. – Joined majority opinion
7. Brennan, W. – Joined majority opinion

Opposing Side (Respondent/Appellee)

1. Black, H. – Wrote dissenting opinion
2. Harlan, J. – Wrote dissenting opinion

VI. A WIN OR LOSS FOR THE ACLU?

The ACLU, as counsel of record, urged reversal of the judgment of the Court of Appeals for the Eighth Circuit; the Supreme Court reversed the lower court's decision in a 7-2 vote, giving the ACLU an apparent win.

214. Gregory v. City of Chicago

(Decided March 10, 1969; 394 U.S. 111)

I. ISSUE

A. Issues Discussed

1st Amendment, press, speech, association

B. Legal Question Presented

Whether petitioners' convictions for disorderly conduct were lawful.

C. Supreme Court's Answer

"Petitioners' march, if peaceful and orderly, falls well within the sphere of conduct protected by the First Amendment. There is no evidence in this record that petitioners' conduct was disorderly. Therefore, under the principle first established in Thompson v. City of Louisville, 362 U.S. 199 (1960), convictions so totally devoid of evidentiary support violate due process."

II. CASE SUMMARY

A. Background

"Petitioners, accompanied by Chicago police and an assistant city attorney, marched in a peaceful and orderly procession from city hall to the mayor's residence to press their claims for desegregation of the public schools. Having promised to cease singing at 8:30 p.m., the marchers did so. Although petitioners and the other demonstrators continued to march in a completely lawful fashion, the onlookers became unruly as the number of bystanders increased. Chicago police, to prevent what they regarded as an impending civil disorder, demanded that the demonstrators, upon pain of arrest, disperse. When this command was not obeyed, petitioners were arrested for disorderly conduct."

The Supreme Court granted certiorari to review the case.

B. Counsel of Record/ACLU Attorney

ACLU Side (Petitioner/Appellant): Marshall Patner, American Civil Liberties Union, Illinois Division, argued the cause for appellants. With him on the briefs was Paul E. Goldstein, ACLU, Illinois Division.

Opposing Side (Respondent/Appellee): Raymond F. Simon argued the cause for appellee. With him on the brief were Marvin E. Aspen and Howard C. Goldman.

III. AMICI CURIAE

ACLU Side (Petitioner/Appellant)

No briefs of amici curiae were filed in support of appellant

Opposing Side (Respondent/Appellee)

No briefs of amici curiae were filed in support of appellee.

IV. THE SUPREME COURT'S DECISION

"Petitioners' march, if peaceful and orderly, falls well within the sphere of conduct protected by the First Amendment. There is no evidence in this record that petitioners' conduct was disorderly. Therefore, under the principle first established in Thompson v. City of Louisville, 362 U.S. 199 (1960), convictions so totally devoid of evidentiary support violate due process.

The opinion of the Supreme Court of Illinois suggests that petitioners were convicted not for the manner in which they conducted their march but rather for their refusal to dispense when requested to do so by Chicago police. However reasonable the police request may have been and however laudable the police motives, petitioners were charged and convicted for holding a demonstration, not for a refusal to obey a police officer. As we said in Garner v. Louisiana, 368 U.S. 157 (1961): '(I)t is as much a denial of due process to send an accused to prison following conviction for a charge that was never made as it is to convict him upon a charge for which there is no evidence to support that conviction.'

Finally, since the trial judge's charge permitted the jury to convict for acts clearly entitled to First Amendment protection, Stromberg v. California, 283 U.S. 359 (1931), independently requires reversal of these convictions.

The judgments are reversed."

V. JUSTICE VOTE

9 Pro ACLU Side vs. 0 Con Opposing Side

ACLU Side (Petitioner/Appellant)

1. Warren, E. – Wrote majority opinion
2. Brennan, W. – Joined majority opinion
3. Black, H. – Wrote concurring opinion
4. Douglas, W. – Joined Black's concurrence
5. Harlan, J. – Wrote concurring opinion
6. Fortas, A. – Joined majority opinion
7. Marshall, T. – Joined majority opinion
8. Stewart, P. – Joined majority opinion
9. White, B. – Joined majority opinion

VI. A WIN OR LOSS FOR THE ACLU?

The ACLU served as counsel for appellant urging reversal of the judgment of the Supreme Court of Illinois; the U.S. Supreme Court reversed in a 9-0 vote, giving the ACLU an apparent win.

215. Street v. New York

(Decided April 21, 1969; 394 U.S. 576)

I. ISSUE

A. Issues Discussed

First Amendment, freedom of speech, flag burning

B. Legal Question Presented

"[W]hether, in light of all the circumstances, [appellant's] conviction [for flag burning and statements related to the flag burning] denied to him rights of free expression protected by the First Amendment and assured against state infringement by the Fourteenth Amendment."

C. Supreme Court's Answer

Because it is unclear whether the conviction was for the flag burning itself or words related to the flag burning, the conviction must be overturned as the words were protected speech under the First Amendment.

II. CASE SUMMARY

A. Background

"Appellant Street has been convicted in the New York courts of violating former § 1425, subd. 16, par. d, of the New York Penal Law, which makes it a misdemeanor 'publicly [to] mutilate, deface, defile, or defy, trample upon, or cast contempt upon either by words or act [any flag of the United States].' He was given a suspended sentence. . . .

Appellant testified that during the afternoon of June 6, 1966, he was listening to the radio in his Brooklyn apartment. He heard a news report that civil rights leader James Meredith had been shot by a sniper in Mississippi. Saying to himself, 'They didn't protect him,' appellant, himself a Negro, took from his drawer a neatly folded, 48-star American flag which he formerly had displayed on national holidays. Appellant left his apartment and carried the still-folded flag to the nearby intersection of St. James Place and Lafayette Avenue. Appellant . . . lit the flag with a match, and dropped the flag on the pavement when it began to burn.

Soon thereafter, a police officer halted his patrol car and found the burning flag. The officer testified that he then crossed to the northwest corner of the intersection, where he found appellant 'talking out loud' to a small group of persons. The officer estimated that there were some 30 persons on the corner near the flag and five to 10 on the corner with appellant. The officer testified that as he approached within 10 or 15 feet of appellant, he heard appellant say, 'We don't need no damn flag,' and that when he asked appellant whether he had burned the flag appellant replied: 'Yes; that is my flag; I burned it. If they let that happen to Meredith we don't need an American flag.'

[Appellant was charged that afternoon by a Criminal Court judge.] Appellant was tried before another Criminal Court judge, sitting without a jury, and was convicted of malicious mischief in violation of § 1425, subd. 16, par. d. He was subsequently given a suspended sentence. The Appellate Term, Second Department, affirmed without opinion. Leave was granted to appeal to the New York Court of Appeals, and after plenary consideration that court unanimously affirmed."

The Supreme Court granted certiorari and reversed.

B. Counsel of Record/ACLU Attorney

ACLU Side (Petitioner/Appellant): David T. Goldstick argued the cause for appellant. With him on the briefs were John Somers, Albert H. Blumenthal, Osmond K. Fraenkel, Burt Neuborne, Alan H. Levine, and Melvin L. Wulf.

Opposing Side (Respondent/Appellee): Harry Brodbar argued the cause for appellee. With him on the brief was Elliott Golden.

III. AMICI CURIAE

ACLU Side (Petitioner/Appellant)

No briefs of amici curiae were filed in support of appellant.

Opposing Side (Respondent/Appellee)

Brief of amici curiae filed on behalf of the Attorney General of New York, by Louis J. Lefkowitz, Attorney General, pro se, Samuel A. Hirshowitz, First Assistant Attorney General, and Brenda Soloff, Assistant Attorney General.

Brief of amici curiae filed on behalf of the United States Flag Foundation, Inc., by Peter Megargee Brown.

IV. THE SUPREME COURT'S DECISION

"[W]e hold that § 1425, subd. 16, par. d, was unconstitutionally applied in appellant's case because it permitted him to be punished merely for speaking defiant or contemptuous words about the American flag. . . .

We have no doubt that the constitutionally guaranteed 'freedom to be intellectually . . . diverse or even contrary,' and the 'right to differ as to things that touch the heart of the existing order,' encompass the freedom to express publicly one's opinions about our flag, including those opinions which are defiant or contemptuous.

Since appellant could not constitutionally be punished under § 1425, subd. 16, par. d, for his speech, and since we have found that he may have been so punished, his conviction cannot be permitted to stand. In so holding, we reiterate that we have no occasion to pass upon the validity of this conviction insofar as it was sustained by the state courts on the basis that Street could be punished for his burning of the flag, even though the burning was an act of protest. Nor do we perceive any basis for our Brother White's fears that our decision today may be taken to require reversal whenever a defendant is convicted for burning a flag in protest, following a trial at which his words have been introduced to prove some element of that offense. Assuming that such a conviction would otherwise pass constitutional muster, a matter about which we express no view, nothing in this opinion would render the conviction impermissible merely because an element of the crime was proved by the defendant's words rather than in some other way.

We add that disrespect for our flag is to be deplored no less in these vexed times than in calmer periods of our history. Nevertheless, we are unable to sustain a conviction that may have rested on a form of expression, however distasteful, which the Constitution tolerates and protects."

The Supreme Court reversed the judgment of the New York Court of Appeals.

V. JUSTICE VOTE

5 Pro ACLU Side vs. 4 Con Opposing Side

ACLU Side (Petitioner/Appellant)

1. Harlan, J. – Wrote majority opinion
2. Stewart, T. – Joined majority opinion
3. Marshall, T. – Joined majority opinion
4. Douglas, W. – Joined majority opinion
5. Brennan, W. – Joined majority opinion

Opposing Side (Respondent/Appellee)

1. Warren, E. – Wrote dissenting opinion
2. White, B. – Wrote dissenting opinion
3. Black, H. – Wrote dissenting opinion
4. Fortas, A. – Wrote dissenting opinion

VI. A WIN OR LOSS FOR THE ACLU?

The ACLU, as counsel of record, urged reversal of the judgment of the New York Court of Appeals; the Supreme Court reversed in a 5-4 vote, giving the ACLU an apparent win.

216. Shapiro v. Thompson

(Decided April 21, 1969; 394 U.S. 618)

I. ISSUE

A. Issues Discussed

State's rights, Fourteenth Amendment, Fifth Amendment, equal protection, due process

B. Legal Question Presented

Does the conditioning of government aid on a one-year residency requirement violate the Equal Protection Clause of the Fourteenth Amendment?

C. Supreme Court's Answer

Conditioning government aid on a one-year residency requirement violates the Equal Protection Clause of the Fourteenth Amendment in the states, and violates the Due Process Clause of the Fifth Amendment in the District of Columbi

II. CASE SUMMARY

A. Background

The Supreme Court consolidated three cases, all with the similar facts of a state or the District of Columbia denying benefits to a new resident of the state due to a one-year residence requirement for the benefit.

For example, appellee Vivian Marie Thompson was a pregnant, nineteen-year-old mother of one child who applied for assistance under the Aid to Families with Dependent Children (AFDC) program in Connecticut, after having recently moved from Massachusetts. Connecticut denied her aid since she did not satisfy the state's one-year residency requirement.

All the appellees brought actions before their respective District Courts, which all held that the one-year requirement was unconstitutional.

The Supreme Court granted certiorari and affirmed the decisions.

B. Counsel of Record/ACLU Attorney

ACLU Side (Respondent/Appellee): Opposing Side (Petitioner/Appellant): Brian L. Hollander argued the cause for appellee in No. 9. Peter S. Smith argued the cause for appellee in No. 33. Thomas K. Gilhool argued the cause for appellee in No. 34. Archibald Cox argued the cause for appellee in all three cases. Francis J. McGregor, Assistant Attorney General of Connecticut, argued the cause for appellant in No. 9. Richard W. Barton argued the cause for appellant in No. 33. William C. Sennett, Attorney General of Pennsylvania, argued the cause for appellant in No. 34.

Lorna Lawhead Williams, Special Assistant Attorney General, argued the cause for the State of Iowa, as amicus curiae.

III. AMICI CURIAE

ACLU Side (Respondent/Appellee)

Brief of amici curiae filed on behalf of the ACLU by A. L. Wirin, Fred Okrand, Laurence R. Sperber, and Melvin L. Wulf.

Additional briefs of amici curiae were filed on behalf of the Bexar County Legal Aid Association, the Legal Aid Society of Alameda County, the National Federation of the Blind, the City of New York, the American Jewish Congress, et al., and the Center on Social Welfare Policy and Law, et al.

Opposing Side (Petitioner/Appellant)

Lorna Lawhead Williams, Special Assistant Attorney General, argued the cause for the State of Iowa as amicus curiae in support of appellants in all three cases on the original argument and on the reargument. With her on the briefs on the original argument was Richard C. Turner, Attorney General.

Additional briefs of amici curiae were filed on behalf of the State of Delaware, the State of Ohio, the State of Texas, and the State of California.

IV. THE SUPREME COURT'S DECISION

"We recognize that a State has a valid interest in preserving the fiscal integrity of its programs. It may legitimately attempt to limit its expenditures, whether for public assistance, public education, or any other program. But a State may not accomplish such a purpose by invidious distinctions between classes of its citizens. It could not, for example, reduce expenditures for education by barring indigent children from its schools. Similarly, in the cases before us, appellants must do more than show that denying welfare benefits to new residents saves money. The saving of welfare costs cannot justify an otherwise invidious classification.

In sum, neither deterrence of indigents from migrating to the State nor limitation of welfare benefits to those regarded as contributing to the State is a constitutionally permissible state objective. . . .

We conclude therefore that appellants in these cases do not use and have no need to use the one-year requirement for the governmental purposes suggested. Thus, even under traditional equal protection tests a classification of welfare applicants according to whether they have lived in the State for one year would seem irrational and unconstitutional. But, of course, the traditional criteria do not apply in these cases. Since the classification here touches on the fundamental right of interstate movement, its constitutionality must be judged by the stricter standard of whether it promotes a compelling state interest. Under this standard, the waiting-period requirement clearly violates the Equal Protection Clause. . . .

The waiting-period requirement in the District of Columbia Code . . . is also unconstitutional even though it was adopted by Congress as an exercise of federal power. In terms of federal power, the discrimination created by the one-year requirement violates the Due Process Clause of the Fifth Amendment. '[W]hile the Fifth Amendment contains no equal protection clause, it does forbid discrimination that is 'so unjustifiable as to be violative of due process.' For the reasons we have stated in invalidating the Pennsylvania and Connecticut provisions, the District of Columbia provision is also invalid—the Due Process Clause of the Fifth Amendment prohibits Congress from denying public assistance to poor persons otherwise eligible solely on the ground that they have not been residents of the District of Columbia for one year at the time their applications are filed. Accordingly, the judgments are affirmed."

V. JUSTICE VOTE

6 Pro ACLU Side vs. 3 Con Opposing Side

ACLU Side (Respondent/Appellee)

1. Brennan, W. – Wrote majority opinion
2. Fortas, A. – Joined majority opinion
3. Marshall, T. – Joined majority opinion
4. Douglas, W. – Joined majority opinion
5. White, B. – Joined majority opinion
6. Stewart, P. – Wrote concurring opinion

Opposing Side (Petitioner/Appellant)

1. Warren, E. – Wrote dissenting opinion
2. Harlan, J. – Wrote dissenting opinion
3. Black, H. – Joined Warren's dissent

VI. A WIN OR LOSS FOR THE ACLU?

The ACLU filed as amicus curiae in support of appellee in *Shapiro v. Thompson*, the Supreme Court affirmed the District Court's judgment in a 6-3 vote giving the ACLU an apparent win.

217. Watts v. United States

(Decided April 21, 1969; 394 U.S. 705)

I. ISSUE

A. Issues Discussed

First Amendment, freedom of speech

B. Legal Question Presented

Did Watts statement "If they ever make me carry a rifle, the first man I want to get in my sights is L.B.J. [Lyndon B. Johnson]" during a protest discussion, amount to a threat to the President or was he merely exercising his First Amendment freedom of speech?

C. Supreme Court's Answer

Watts' conviction must be reversed because, viewed in context, his statement was speech protected under the First Amendment, not an actionable threat against the President although the statute he was convicted under is constitutional.

II. CASE SUMMARY

A. Background

"After a jury trial in the United States District Court for the District of Columbia, petitioner was convicted of violating a 1917 statute which prohibits any person from 'knowingly and willfully . . . [making] any threat to take the life of or to inflict bodily harm upon the President of the United States . . . .' The incident which led to petitioner's arrest occurred on August 27, 1966, during a public rally on the Washington Monument grounds. The crowd present broke up into small discussion groups and petitioner joined a gathering scheduled to discuss police brutality. Most of those in the group were quite young, either in their teens or early twenties. Petitioner, who himself was 18 years old, entered into the discussion after one member of the group suggested that the young people present should get more education before expressing their views. According to an investigator for the Army Counter Intelligence Corps who was present, petitioner responded: 'They always holler at us to get an education. And now I have already received my draft classification as 1-A and I have got to report for my physical this Monday coming. I am not going. If they ever make me carry a rifle the first man I want to get in my sights is L.B.J.' 'They are not going to make me kill my black brothers.' On the basis of this statement, the jury found that petitioner had committed a felony by knowingly and willfully threatening the President. The United States Court of Appeals for the District of Columbia Circuit affirmed by a two-to-one vote."

The Supreme Court granted certiorari and reversed in a per curiam decision.

B. Counsel of Record/ACLU Attorney

ACLU Side (Petitioner/Appellant): Joseph Forer argued the cause for appellant.

Opposing Side (Respondent/Appellee): Solicitor General Erwin N. Griswold argued the cause for the United States.

III. AMICI CURIAE

ACLU Side (Petitioner/Appellant)

Brief of amici curiae filed on behalf of the ACLU, et al., by Ralph J. Temple, Melvin L. Wulf, and Lawrence Speiser.

Opposing Side (Respondent/Appellee)

No briefs of amici curiae were filed in support of appellee.

IV. THE SUPREME COURT'S DECISION

"Certainly the statute under which petitioner was convicted is constitutional on its face. The Nation undoubtedly has a valid, even an overwhelming, interest in protecting the safety of its Chief Executive and in allowing him to perform his duties without interference from threats of physical violence. Nevertheless, a statute such as this one, which makes criminal a form of pure speech, must be interpreted with the commands of the First Amendment clearly in mind. What is a threat must be distinguished from what is constitutionally protected speech. . . .

We do not believe that the kind of political hyperbole indulged in by petitioner fits within that statutory term. For we must interpret the language Congress chose 'against the background of a profound national commitment to the principle that debate on public issues should be uninhibited, robust, and wide-open, and that it may well include vehement, caustic, and sometimes unpleasantly sharp attacks on government and public officials.' The language of the political arena . . . is often vituperative, abusive, and inexact. We agree with petitioner that his only offense here was 'a kind of very crude offensive method of stating a political opposition to the President.' Taken in context, and regarding the expressly conditional nature of the statement and the reaction of the listeners, we do not see how it could be interpreted otherwise.

The motion for leave to proceed in forma pauperis and the petition for a writ of certiorari are granted and the judgment of the Court of Appeals is reversed. The case is remanded with instructions that it be returned to the District Court for entry of a judgment of acquittal."

The Supreme Court reversed the judgment of the Court of Appeals.

V. JUSTICE VOTE

5 Pro ACLU Side vs. 4 Con Opposing Side

ACLU Side (Petitioner/Appellant)

1. Black, H. – Per curiam decision
2. Marshall, T. – Per curiam decision
3. Warren, E. – Per curiam decision
4. Brennan, W. – Per curiam decision
5. Douglas, W. – Wrote concurring opinion

Opposing Side (Respondent/Appellee)

1. Fortas, A. – Wrote dissenting opinion
2. Harlan, J. – Joined Fortas' dissent
3. Stewart, J. – Wrote dissenting opinion
4. White, B. – Wrote dissenting opinion

VI. A WIN OR LOSS FOR THE ACLU?

The ACLU filed as amicus curiae urging reversal; the Supreme Court reversed the judgment of the Court of Appeals in a 5-4 vote giving the ACLU an apparent win.

218. Leary v. United States

(Decided May 19, 1969; 395 U.S. 6)

I. ISSUE

A. Issues Discussed

Criminal justice, drugs, Fifth Amendment, self-incrimination, due process

B. Legal Question Presented

"(1) [W]hether petitioner's conviction for failing to comply with the transfer tax provisions of the Marihuana Tax Act violated his Fifth Amendment privilege against self-incrimination; (2) whether petitioner was denied due process by the application of the part of 21 U.S.C. § 176a which provides that a defendant's possession of marihuana shall be deemed sufficient evidence that the marihuana was illegally imported or brought into the United States, and that the defendant knew of the illegal importation or bringing in, unless the defendant explains his possession to the satisfaction of the jury."

C. Supreme Court's Answer

The conviction under the Marihuana Tax Act violated the Fifth Amendment and petitioner was denied due process.

II. CASE SUMMARY

A. Background

Petitioner, Dr. Timothy Leary, took a road trip from New York to Mexico, accompanied by his daughter, son, and two other people. When they drove across the Texas-Mexico International Bridge, a U.S. customs officer stopped and searched their car, discovering marijuana in the car and in Leary's daughter's possession.

Dr. Leary was indicted under 26 U.S.C. § 4744(a)(2), a subsection of the Marijuana Tax Act, and under 21 U.S.C. § 176a. The jury found him guilty on two counts, and he was sentenced to the maximum punishment for the charges. The Court of Appeals for the Fifth Circuit affirmed the judgment.

The Supreme Court granted certiorari to review the case and reversed.

B. Counsel of Record/ACLU Attorney

ACLU Side (Petitioner/Appellant): Robert J. Haft argued the cause for appellant.

Opposing Side (Respondent/Appellee): John S. Martin, Jr., argued the cause for appellee.

III. AMICI CURIAE

ACLU Side (Petitioner/Appellant)

Briefs of amici curiae filed by on behalf of the ACLU by Jonathan Sobeloff and Melvin L. Wulf.

Brief of amici curiae filed on behalf of the National Student Association by Joseph S. Oteri and Harvey A. Silverglate.

Opposing Side (Respondent/Appellee)

No briefs of amici curiae were filed in support of appellee.

IV. THE SUPREME COURT'S DECISION

"If read according to its terms, the Marihuana Tax Act compelled petitioner to expose himself to a 'real and appreciable' risk of self-incrimination .... Sections 4741-4742 required him, in the course of obtaining an order form, to identify himself not only as a transferee of marihuana but as a transferee who had not registered and paid the occupational tax ....

Petitioner had ample reason to fear that transmittal to such official of the fact that he was a recent, unregistered transferee of marihuana 'would surely prove a significant 'link in a chain' of evidence tending to establish his guilt' under the state marihuana laws then in effect. When petitioner failed to comply with the Act, in late 1965, possession of any quantity of marihuana was apparently a crime in every one of the 50 States, including New York, where petitioner claimed the transfer occurred, and Texas, where he was arrested and convicted....

Thus, at the time petitioner failed to comply with the Act those persons who might legally possess marihuana under state law were virtually certain either to be registered under § 4753 or to be exempt from the order form requirement. It follows that the class of possessors who were both unregistered and obliged to obtain an order form constituted a 'selective group inherently suspect of criminal activities.' Since compliance with the transfer tax provisions would have required petitioner unmistakably to identify himself as a member of this 'selective' and 'suspect' group, we can only decide that when read according to their terms these provisions created a 'real and appreciable' hazard of incrimination.

[A] criminal statutory presumption must be regarded as 'irrational' or 'arbitrary,' and hence unconstitutional, unless it can at least be said with substantial assurance that the presumed fact is more likely than not to flow from the proved fact on which it is made to depend. And in the judicial assessment the congressional determination favoring the particular presumption must, of course, weigh heavily....

We conclude that the 'knowledge' aspect of the §176a presumption cannot be upheld without making serious incursions into the teachings of Tot, Gainey, and Romano. In the context of this part of the statute, those teachings require that it be determined with substantial assurance that at least a majority of marihuana possessors have learned of the foreign origin of their marihuana through one or more of the ways ....

We find it impossible to make such a determination. As we have seen, the materials at our disposal leave us at large to estimate even roughly the proportion of marihuana possessors who have learned in one way or another the origin of their marihuana. . . . In short, it would be no more than speculation were we to say that even as much as a majority of possessors 'knew' the source of their marihuana. . . .

We thus cannot escape the duty of setting aside petitioner's conviction under Count 2 of this indictment.

For the reasons stated . . . we reverse outright the judgment of conviction on Count 3 of the indictment. For the reasons stated . . . we reverse the judgment of conviction on Count 2 and remand the case to the Court of Appeals for further proceedings consistent with this opinion. We are constrained to add that nothing in what we hold today implies any constitutional disability in Congress to deal with the marihuana traffic by other means."

The Supreme Court reversed the judgment and remanded the case.

V. JUSTICE VOTE

8 Pro ACLU Side vs. 0 Con Opposing Side

ACLU Side (Petitioner/Appellant)

1. Harlan, J. – Wrote majority opinion
2. Marshall, T. – Joined majority opinion
3. Brennan, W. – Joined majority opinion
4. Douglas, W. – Joined majority opinion
5. White, B. – Joined majority opinion
6. Black, H. – Wrote concurring opinion
7. Warren, E. – Wrote concurring opinion
8. Stewart, J. – Wrote concurring opinion

Vacant Seat

VI. A WIN OR LOSS FOR THE ACLU?

The ACLU filed as amicus curiae urging reversal; the Supreme Court reversed the Court of Appeal's judgment in an 8-0 vote giving the ACLU an apparent win.

219. Immigration and Naturalization Service v. Stanisic

(Decided May 19, 1969; 395 U.S. 62)

I. ISSUE

A. Issues Discussed

Governmental authority, immigration

B. Legal Question Presented

Is Stanisic, a Yugoslav crewman, who claimed that he would suffer persecution upon deportation to Yugoslavia, entitled to have his claim for asylum heard by a special inquiry officer under § 242(b) of the Immigration and Nationality Act?

C. Supreme Court's Answer

Stanisic is not entitled to a hearing by a special inquiry officer under § 242(b).

II. CASE SUMMARY

A. Background

"Respondent, a national of Yugoslavia, was a crewman aboard the Yugoslav vessel, M/V Sumadija, when it docked at Coos Bay, Oregon, in late December 1964. He requested and was issued a 'D-1' conditional landing permit, in accordance with . . . the Immigration and Nationality Act, [which granted him temporary shore leave while his ship was in port.]

On January 6, 1965, while on shore leave, respondent appeared at the Portland, Oregon, office of the Immigration and Naturalization Service. He claimed that he feared persecution upon return to Yugoslavia, and he flatly stated that he would not return to the M/V Sumadija. On the basis of the latter statement, . . . the District Director revoked respondent's landing permit. . . . On January 7, he was offered an opportunity to present evidence to the District Director in support of is claim of persecution.

Respondent presented no evidence to the District Director. Rather, he contended that he had not been given sufficient time to prepare for the hearing, and he also argued that he was entitled to have his claim heard by a special inquiry officer in accordance with the general provisions of § 242(b). The District Director ruled against respondent, and in the absence of any evidence of probable persecution, ordered him returned to the M/V Sumadija, which was then still in port."

Following a temporary stay of deportation by the District Court, the District Director on that court's order held a hearing at which Stanisic presented evidence and held that he had not shown he would be "physically persecuted" in Yugoslavia. The District Court upheld that finding and rejected respondent's claim for a hearing.

Stanisic did not appeal but petitioned Congress for a private bill, and the Immigration and Naturalization Service ("INS") stayed his deportation while the bill was pending. When Stanisic's efforts failed, the INS ordered him deported. The INS and later the District Court on the basis of their previous determinations rejected his renewed claim for a hearing by a special inquiry officer under § 242(b).

"The Court of Appeals for the Ninth Circuit reversed, holding that the matter was not res judicata because [the prior determinations] were based on the unstated premise that the M/V Sumadija was still in port; but now the ship had long since sailed, and respondent still had not been deported." The court also determined "he was entitled to a de novo hearing before a special inquiry officer under § 242(b) of the Act."

INS appealed to the Supreme Court. The Supreme Court granted certiorari and reversed.

B. Counsel of Record/ACLU Attorney

ACLU Side (Respondent/Appellee): G. Bernhard Fedde, by appointment of the Court, argued the cause for appellee.

Opposing Side (Petitioner/Appellant): Joseph J. Connolly argued the cause for appellant, pro hac vice.

III. AMICI CURIAE

ACLU Side (Respondent/Appellee)

Brief of amici curiae filed on behalf of the ACLU by Edward J. Ennis and Melvin L. Wulf.

Opposing Side (Petitioner/Appellant)

No briefs of amici curiae were filed in support of appellant.

IV. THE SUPREME COURT'S DECISION

"We hold that an alien crewman whose temporary landing permit is properly revoked pursuant to § 252 (b) does not become entitled to a hearing before a special inquiry officer under § 242 (b) merely because his deportation is not finally arranged or effected when his vessel leaves, and that under these circumstances the Attorney General may provide—as he did in 8 CFR § 253.1(e), now 8 CFR § 253.1(f)—that the crewman's request for political asylum be heard by a district director of the Immigration and Naturalization Service. . . .

At the time of respondent's January 1965 hearing before the District Director, § 243(h) of the Immigration and Nationality Act provided: 'The Attorney General is authorized to withhold deportation of any alien within the United States to any country in which in his opinion the alien would be subject to physical persecution . . . .'

By the Act of October 3, 1965, § 11(f), this section was amended by substituting for 'physical persecution' the phrase 'persecution on account of race, religion, or political opinion.' Although 8 CFR § 253.1(e), the regulation under which respondent's 1965 hearing was conducted, did not itself contain any restriction to 'physical persecution,' it is apparent from the District Director's findings that he read such a limitation into the regulation.

We believe, therefore, that it is appropriate that respondent be given a new hearing before the District Director under the appropriate standard, and we remand the case for that purpose.

The judgment of the United States Court of Appeals for the Ninth Circuit is reversed and the case is remanded to that court for further proceedings consistent with this opinion."

V. JUSTICE VOTE

3 Pro ACLU Side vs. 5 Con Opposing Side

ACLU Side (Respondent/Appellee)

1. Black, H. – Wrote dissenting opinion
2. Marshall, T. – Joined Black's dissent
3. Douglas, W. – Joined Black's dissent

Opposing Side (Petitioner/Appellant)

1. Harlan, J. – Wrote majority opinion
2. Warren, E. – Joined majority opinion
3. Brennan, W. – Joined majority opinion
4. Stewart, J. – Joined majority opinion
5. White, B. – Joined majority opinion

VI. A WIN OR LOSS FOR THE ACLU?

The ACLU filed as amicus curiae urging affirmance; the Supreme Court reversed the judgment of the Court of Appeal in a 5-3 vote, giving the ACLU an apparent loss.

220. Red Lion Broadcasting Co. v. FCC

(Decided June 9, 1969; 395 U.S. 367)

I. ISSUE

A. Issues Discussed

First Amendment, freedom of press, speech, and association

B. Legal Question Presented

Did the FCC's fairness doctrine regulations, requiring that public issues be presented by broadcasters and that each side of those issues be given fair coverage, violate freedoms of speech and press guaranteed by the First Amendment?

C. Supreme Court's Answer

The fairness doctrine regulations do not violate the First Amendment.

II. CASE SUMMARY

A. Background

"The Federal Communications Commission has for many years imposed on radio and television broadcasters the requirement that discussion of public issues be presented on broadcast stations, and that each side of those issues must be given fair coverage. This is known as the fairness doctrine . . . .

FCC declared that petitioner Red Lion Broadcasting Co. had failed to meet its obligation under the fairness doctrine when it carried a radio broadcast which the FCC determined was a personal attack on journalist Fred J. Cook. Cook's book, *Goldwater—Extremist on the Right*, sparked political controversy. After the book appeared, Cook was attacked by Reverend Billy James Hargis on his *Christian Crusade* radio broadcast. The FCC ordered petitioner to send a transcript of the broadcast to Cook and "provide reply time whether or not Cook would pay for it." Red Lion Broadcasting challenged the constitutionality of the fairness doctrine with respect to this particular broadcast.

The Court of Appeals for the District of Columbia Circuit upheld the FCC's position "as constitutional and otherwise proper." After the commencement of the Red Lion case, the FCC began a rule-making proceeding to make "the personal attack aspect of the fairness doctrine more precise and more readily enforceable, and to specify its rules relating to political editorials."

Meanwhile, the FCC's fairness doctrine requirements concerning all broadcasts were challenged in the case *U.S. v. Radio Television News Directors Association*. The Court of Appeals for the Seventh Circuit held the new rules unconstitutional, "as abridging the freedoms of speech and press."

The Supreme Court granted certiorari in both cases and consolidated them. The court affirmed the *Red Lion* decision, No. 2, and reversed the *Radio Television News Directors Association* decision, No. 717.

B. Counsel of Record/ACLU Attorney

ACLU Side (Respondent/Appellee in No. 2 and Petitioner/Appellant in No. 717):

Opposing Side (Petitioner/Appellant in No. 2 and Respondent/Appellee in No. 717):

Solicitor General Erwin N. Griswold argued the cause for appellee in No. 2 and appellant in No. 717.

Roger Robb argued the cause for appellant in No. 2. Archibald Cox argued the cause for appellee in No. 717.

III. AMICI CURIAE

ACLU Side (Respondent/Appellee in No. 2 and Petitioner/Appellant in No. 717):

Brief of amici curiae urging reversal in No. 717 and affirmance in No. 2 filed on behalf of the ACLU by Melvin L. Wulf, Eleanor Holmes Norton, and Michael J. Horowitz.

Brief of amici curiae filed on behalf of the Office of Communication of the United Church of Christ, et al., by Earle K. Moore, Edward A. Bernstein, Samuel Rabinove, and William B. Ball.

Brief of amici curiae filed on behalf of the American Federation of Labor & Congress of Industrial Organizations by J. Albert Woll, Robert C. Mayer, Laurence Gold, and Thomas E. Harris.

Opposing Side (Petitioner/Appellant in No. 2 and Respondent/Appellee in No. 717):

No briefs of amici curiae were filed in support of appellant in No. 2 and appellee in No. 717.

IV. THE SUPREME COURT'S DECISION

"The history of the emergence of the fairness doctrine and of the related legislation shows that the Commission's action in the Red Lion case did not exceed its authority, and that in adopting the new regulations the Commission was implementing congressional policy rather than embarking on a frolic of its own. . . .

Although broadcasting is clearly a medium affected by a First Amendment interest, differences in the characteristics of new media justify differences in the First Amendment standards applied to them.

[We cannot] say that it is inconsistent with the First Amendment goal of producing an informed public capable of conducting its own affairs to require a broadcaster to permit answers to personal attacks occurring in the course of discussing controversial issues, or to require that the political opponents of those endorsed by the station be given a chance to communicate with the public. Otherwise, station owners and a few networks would have unfettered power to make time available only to the highest bidders, to communicate only their own views on public issues, people and candidates, and to permit on the air only those with whom they agreed. There is no sanctuary in the First Amendment for unlimited private censorship operating in a medium not open to all. 'Freedom of the press from governmental interference under the First Amendment does not sanction repression of that freedom by private interests.' . . .

Even where there are gaps in spectrum utilization, the fact remains that existing broadcasters have often attained their present position because of their initial government selection in competition with others before new technological advances opened new opportunities for further uses. Long experience in broadcasting, confirmed habits of listeners and viewers, network affiliation, and other advantages in program procurement give existing broadcasters a substantial advantage over new entrants, even where new entry is technologically possible. These advantages are the fruit of a preferred position conferred by the Government. Some present possibility for new entry by competing stations is not enough, in itself, to render unconstitutional the Government's effort to assure that a broadcaster's programming ranges widely enough to serve the public interest.

In view of the scarcity of broadcast frequencies, the Government's role in allocating those frequencies, and the legitimate claims of those unable without governmental assistance to gain access to those frequencies for expression of their views, we hold the regulations and ruling at issue here are both authorized by statute and constitutional. The judgment of the Court of Appeals in *Red Lion* is affirmed and that in [*Radio Television News Directors Association*] reversed and the causes remanded for proceedings consistent with this opinion."

The Supreme Court affirmed the judgment of Court of Appeals in *Red Lion* and reversed the judgment in *Radio Television News Directors Association.*

V. JUSTICE VOTE

7 Pro ACLU Side vs. 0 Con Opposing Side

ACLU Side (Respondent/Appellee in No. 2 and Petitioner/Appellant in No. 717):

1. White, B. – Wrote majority opinion
2. Marshall, T. – Joined majority opinion
3. Warren, E. – Joined majority opinion
4. Harlan, J. – Joined majority opinion
5. Brennan, W. – Joined majority opinion
6. Stewart, P. – Joined majority opinion
7. Black, H. – Joined majority opinion

Douglas, W – Took no part in the decision

VI. A WIN OR LOSS FOR THE ACLU?

The ACLU filed as amicus curiae urging reversal in *US v. Radio Television News Directors Association* and affirmance in *Red Lion Broadcasting Co. v. FCC* ; the U.S. Supreme Court reversed the Court of Appeals judgment in *US v. Radio Television News Directors Association* and affirmed it in *Red Lion Broadcasting Co. v. FCC,* in an 8-0 vote, giving ACLU an apparent win. However, in *Meredith Corp. v. FCC,* 809 F.2d 863 (D.C. Cir. 1987), the United States Court of Appeals for the District of Columbia Circuit declared that the fairness doctrine was not mandated by Congress and that the FCC did not have to continue to enforce it. The FCC subsequently dissolved the doctrine.

221. Brandenburg v. Ohio

(Decided June 9, 1969; 395 U.S. 444)

I. ISSUE

A. Issues Discussed

First Amendment, freedom of speech and association

B. Legal Question Presented

Is the Ohio Criminal Syndicalism statute, which prohibits "'advocat[ing] . . . the duty, necessity, or propriety of crime, sabotage, violence, or unlawful methods of terrorism as a means of accomplishing industrial or political reform" and "voluntarily assembl[ing] with any society, group, or assemblage of persons formed to teach or advocate the doctrines of criminal syndicalism,'" constitutional?

C. Supreme Court's Answer

The statute is unconstitutional, in violation of the First and Fourteenth Amendments.

II. CASE SUMMARY

A. Background

"The appellant, a leader of a Ku Klux Klan group, was convicted under the Ohio Criminal Syndicalism statute for 'advocat[ing] . . . the duty, necessity, or propriety of crime, sabotage, violence, or unlawful methods of terrorism as a means of accomplishing industrial or political reform' and for 'voluntarily assembl[ing] with any society, group, or assemblage of persons formed to teach or advocate the doctrines of criminal syndicalism.' He was fined $1,000 and sentenced to one to 10 years' imprisonment." Appellant was filmed, while hooded and surrounded by other Ku Klux Klan members, giving a speech and participating in a cross burning.

"The appellant challenged the constitutionality of the criminal syndicalism statute under the First and Fourteenth Amendments to the United States Constitution, but the intermediate appellate court of Ohio affirmed his conviction without opinion. The Supreme Court of Ohio dismissed his appeal, sua sponte, 'for the reason that no substantial constitutional question exists herein.' It did not file an opinion or explain its conclusions."

On appeal the U.S. Supreme Court reversed the judgment of the Supreme Court of Ohio.

B. Counsel of Record / ACLU Attorney

ACLU Side (Petitioner / Appellant): Allen Brown argued the cause for appellant. With him on the briefs were Norman Dorsen, Melvin L. Wulf, Eleanor Holmes Norton, David L. Sterling, and Bernard A. Berkman.

Opposing Side (Respondent / Appellee): Leonard Kirschner argued the cause for appellee. With him on the brief was Melvin G. Rueger.

III. AMICI CURIAE

ACLU Side (Petitioner / Appellant)

No briefs of amici curiae were filed in support of appellant.

Opposing Side (Respondent / Appellee)

Paul W. Brown, Attorney General of Ohio, pro se, and Leo J. Conway, Assistant Attorney General, filed a brief for the Attorney General as amicus curiae.

IV. THE SUPREME COURT'S DECISION

This court has "fashioned the principle that the constitutional guarantees of free speech and free press do not permit a State to forbid or proscribe advocacy of the use of force or of law violation except where such advocacy is directed to inciting or producing imminent lawless action and is likely to incite or produce such action.

'[T]he mere abstract teaching . . . of the moral propriety or even moral necessity for a resort to force and violence, is not the same as preparing a group for violent action and steeling it to such action.' A statute which fails to draw this distinction impermissibly intrudes upon the freedoms guaranteed by the First and Fourteenth Amendments. It sweeps within its condemnation speech which our Constitution has immunized from governmental control.

Measured by this test, Ohio's Criminal Syndicalism Act cannot be sustained. [W]e are here confronted with a statute which, by its own words and as applied, purports to punish mere advocacy and to forbid, on pain of criminal punishment, assembly with others merely to advocate the described type of action. Such a statute falls within the condemnation of the First and Fourteenth Amendments."

The U.S. Supreme Court reversed the judgment of the Ohio Supreme Court.

V. JUSTICE VOTE

8 Pro ACLU Side vs. 0 Con Opposing Side

ACLU Side (Petitioner / Appellant)

1. Harlan, J. – Per curiam decision
2. Warren, E. – Per curiam decision
3. White, B. – Per curiam decision
4. Stewart, P. – Per curiam decision
5. Marshall, T. – Per curiam decision
6. Brennan, W. – Per curiam decision
7. Black, H. – Wrote concurring opinion
8. Douglas, W. – Wrote concurring opinion

VI. A WIN OR LOSS FOR THE ACLU?

The ACLU, as counsel of record, urged reversal of the judgment of the Supreme Court of Ohio; the U.S. Supreme Court reversed in an 8-0 vote, giving the ACLU an apparent win.

222. Powell v. McCormack

(Decided June 16, 1969; 395 U.S. 486)

I. ISSUE

A. Issues Discussed

Governmental authority, federalism, jurisdiction, separation of powers, Congress, justiciability

B. Legal Question Presented

May the House of Representatives exclude an elected member if the member meets the standing requirements of Article I § 2 of the Constitution?

C. Supreme Court's Answer

The elected member may not be excluded from the House of Representatives.

II. CASE SUMMARY

A. Background

Petitioner Powell was elected to serve in the United States House of Representatives for the 90th Congress. However, the House voted to exclude him, and he was not permitted to take his seat. The House's action was based on a report by a subcommittee during the 89th Congress that petitioner misappropriated public funds by filing false travel expense reports and making illegal salary payments to his wife.

Petitioner "filed suit in Federal District Court, claiming that the House could exclude him only if it found he failed to meet the standing requirements of age, citizenship, and residence contained in Art. I, § 2, of the Constitution—requirements the House specifically found Powell met—and thus had excluded him unconstitutionally. The District Court dismissed petitioners' complaint 'for want of jurisdiction of the subject matter.' A panel of the Court of Appeals affirmed the dismissal, although on somewhat different grounds, each judge filing a separate opinion." While the case was pending in the Supreme Court, the 90th Congress ended and Powell was elected to and seated by the 91st Congress.

The Supreme Court granted certiorari, affirmed in part, and reversed in part.

B. Counsel of Record/ACLU Attorney

ACLU Side (Petitioner/Appellant): Arthur Kinoy and Herbert O. Reid argued the cause for appellant.

Opposing Side (Respondent/Appellee): Bruce Bromley argued the cause for appellee.

III. AMICI CURIAE

ACLU Side (Petitioner/Appellant)

Brief of amici curiae filed on behalf of the ACLU, et al., by Ernest Angell, Osmond K. Fraenkel, Edward J. Ennis, John D. J. Pemberton, Jr., Melvin L. Wulf, Eleanor Holmes Norton, and Alan H. Levine.

Opposing Side (Respondent/Appellee)

Brief of amici curiae filed by George Meader.

IV. THE SUPREME COURT'S DECISION

"To summarize, we have determined the following: (1) This case has not been mooted by Powell's seating in the 91st Congress. (2) Although this action should be dismissed against respondent Congressmen, it may be sustained against their agents. (3) The 90th Congress' denial of membership to Powell cannot be treated as an expulsion. (4) We have jurisdiction over the subject matter of this controversy. (5) The case is justiciable.

Further, analysis of the 'textual commitment' under Art. I, § 5 has demonstrated that in judging the qualifications of its members Congress is limited to the standing qualifications prescribed in the Constitution. Respondents concede that Powell met these. Thus, there is no need to remand this case to determine whether he was entitled to be seated in the 90th Congress. Therefore, we hold that, since Adam Clayton Powell, Jr., was duly elected by the voters of the 18th Congressional District of New York and was not ineligible to serve under any provision of the Constitution, the House was without power to exclude him from its membership.

Petitioners seek additional forms of equitable relief, including mandamus for the release of petitioner Powell's back pay. The propriety of such remedies, however, is more appropriately considered in the first instance by the courts below. Therefore, as to respondents McCormack, Albert, Ford, Celler, and Moore, the judgment of the Court of Appeals for the District of Columbia Circuit is affirmed. As to respondents Jennings, Johnson, and Miller, the judgment of the Court of Appeals for the District of Columbia Circuit is reversed and the case is remanded to the United States District Court for the District of Columbia with instructions to enter a declaratory judgment and for further proceedings consistent with this opinion."

V. JUSTICE VOTE

7 Pro ACLU Side vs. 1 Con Opposing Side

ACLU Side (Petitioner/Appellant)

1. Warren, E. – Wrote majority opinion
2. White, B. – Joined majority opinion
3. Black, H. – Joined majority opinion
4. Marshall, T. – Joined majority opinion
5. Harlan, J. – Joined majority opinion
6. Brennan, W. – Joined majority opinion
7. Douglas, W. – Wrote concurring opinion

Opposing Side (Respondent/Appellee)

1. Stewart, P. – Wrote dissenting opinion

VI. A WIN OR LOSS FOR THE ACLU?

The ACLU filed as amicus curiae urging reversal; the Supreme Court reversed in part the judgment of the Court of Appeals in a 7-1 vote, giving the ACLU an apparent win.

223. North Carolina v. Pearce

(Decided June 23, 1969; 395 U.S. 711)

I. ISSUE

A. Issues Discussed

Criminal procedure, Fifth Amendment, double jeopardy, sentencing

B. Legal Question Presented

"[T]o what extent does the Constitution limit the imposition of a harsher sentence after conviction upon retrial" when the defendant worked to set aside the prior conviction?

C. Supreme Court's Answer

The Constitution requires that time served be credited under the new sentence and an increased sentence may not be imposed based on vindictiveness for the defendant working to set aside the prior conviction.

II. CASE SUMMARY

A. Background

"In No. 413 the respondent Pearce was convicted in a North Carolina court upon a charge of assault with intent to commit rape. The trial judge sentenced him to prison for a term of 12 to 15 years. Several years later he initiated a state post-conviction proceeding which culminated in the reversal of his conviction by the Supreme Court of North Carolina, upon the ground that an involuntary confession had unconstitutionally been admitted in evidence against him. He was retried, convicted, and sentenced by the trial judge to an eight-year prison term, which, when added to the time Pearce had already spent in prison, the parties agree amounted to a longer total sentence than that originally imposed. The conviction and sentence were affirmed on appeal. Pearce then began this habeas corpus proceeding in the United States District Court for the Eastern District of North Carolina. That court held . . . that the longer sentence imposed upon retrial was 'unconstitutional and void.' Upon the failure of the state court to resentence Pearce within 60 days, the federal court ordered his release. This order was affirmed by the United States Court of Appeals for the Fourth Circuit, in a brief per curiam judgment . . . and [the Supreme Court] granted certiorari.

In No. 418 the respondent Rice pleaded guilty in an Alabama trial court to four separate charges of second-degree burglary. He was sentenced to prison terms aggregating 10 years. Two and one-half years later the judgments were set aside . . . upon the ground that Rice had not been accorded his constitutional right to counsel. He was retried upon three of the charges, convicted, and sentenced to prison terms aggregating 25 years. No credit was given for the time he had spent in prison on the original judgments. He then brought this habeas corpus proceeding in the United States District Court for the Middle District of Alabama, alleging that the state trial court had acted unconstitutionally in failing to give him credit for the time he had already served in prison, and in imposing grossly harsher sentences upon retrial. United States District Judge Frank M. Johnson, Jr., agreed with both contentions. While stating that he did 'not believe that it is constitutionally impermissible to impose a harsher sentence upon retrial if there is recorded in the court record some legal justification for it,' Judge Johnson found that Rice had been denied due process of law, because '[u]nder the evidence in this case, the conclusion is inescapable that the State of Alabama is punishing petitioner Rice for his having exercised his post-conviction right of review and for having the original sentences declared unconstitutional.' The judgment of the District Court was affirmed by the United States Court of Appeals for the Fifth Circuit, 'on the basis of Judge Johnson's opinion,' and [the Supreme Court] granted certiorari."

The Supreme Court consolidated the cases and affirmed the decisions.

B. Counsel of Record/ACLU Attorney

ACLU Side (Respondent/Appellee): Opposing Side (Petitioner/Appellant): Larry B. Sitton argued the cause for appellee in No. 413. Thomas S. Lawson, Jr., argued the cause for appellee in No. 418. Andrew A. Vanore, Jr., argued the cause for appellant in No. 413. Paul T. Gish, Jr., Assistant Attorney General of Alabama, argued the cause for appellant in No. 418.

III. AMICI CURIAE

ACLU Side (Respondent/Appellee)

Brief of amici curiae filed on behalf of the ACLU by William W. Van Alstyne and Melvin L. Wulf.

Opposing Side (Petitioner/Appellant)

Brief of amici curiae filed on behalf of the State of Kansas by Robert C. Londerholm, Attorney General, and Edward G. Collister, Jr., Assistant Attorney General.

IV. THE SUPREME COURT'S DECISION

"We hold that the constitutional guarantee against multiple punishments for the same offense absolutely requires that punishment already exacted must be fully 'credited' in imposing sentence upon a new conviction for the same offense. If, upon a new trial, the defendant is acquitted, there is no way the years he spent in prison can be returned to him. But if he is reconvicted, those years can and must be returned—by subtracting them from whatever new sentence is imposed. . . .

We turn, therefore, to consideration of the broader problem of what constitutional limitations there may be upon the general power of a judge to impose upon reconviction a longer prison sentence than the defendant originally received. . . .

We hold . . . that neither the double jeopardy provision nor the Equal Protection Clause imposes an absolute bar to a more severe sentence upon reconviction. A trial judge is not constitutionally precluded, in other words, from imposing a new sentence, whether greater or less than the original sentence, in the light of events subsequent to the first trial that may have thrown new light upon the defendant's 'life, health, habits, conduct, and mental and moral propensities.' . . .

To say that there exists no absolute constitutional bar to the imposition of a more severe sentence upon retrial is not, however, to end the inquiry. There remains for consideration the impact of the Due Process Clause of the Fourteenth Amendment.

It can hardly be doubted that it would be a flagrant violation of the Fourteenth Amendment for a state trial court to follow an announced practice of imposing a heavier sentence upon every reconvicted defendant for the explicit purpose of punishing the defendant for his having succeeded in getting his original conviction set aside. Where, as in each of the cases before us, the original conviction has been set aside because of a constitutional error, the imposition of such a punishment, 'penalizing those who choose to exercise' constitutional rights, 'would be patently unconstitutional.' . . .

Due process of law, then, requires that vindictiveness against a defendant for having successfully attacked his first conviction must play no part in the sentence he receives after a new trial. . . .In order to assure the absence of such a motivation, we have concluded that whenever a judge imposes a more severe sentence upon a defendant after a new trial, the reasons for his doing so must affirmatively appear. Those reasons must be based upon objective information concerning identifiable conduct on the part of the defendant occurring after the time of the original sentencing proceeding. And the factual data upon which the increased sentence is based must be made part of the record, so that the constitutional legitimacy of the increased sentence may be fully reviewed on appeal.

We dispose of the two cases before us in the light of these conclusions. . . . We conclude that in each of the cases before us, the judgment should be affirmed."

V. JUSTICE VOTE

7 Pro ACLU Side vs. 2 Con Opposing Side

ACLU Side (Respondent/Appellee)

1. Stewart, P. – Wrote majority opinion
2. Brennan, W. – Joined majority opinion
3. Warren, E. – Joined majority opinion
4. Burger, W. – Joined majority opinion
5. Douglas, W. – Wrote concurring opinion
6. Marshall, T. – Joined Douglas' concurrence
7. White, B. – Wrote concurring opinion

Opposing Side (Petitioner/Appellant)

1. Black, H. – Wrote opinion concurring in part and dissenting in part
2. Harlan, J. – Wrote opinion concurring in part and dissenting in part

VI. A WIN OR LOSS FOR THE ACLU?

The ACLU filed as amicus curiae urging affirmance; the Supreme Court affirmed the rulings of the United States Courts of Appeals for the Fourth and Fifth Circuit in a 7-2 vote, giving the ACLU an apparent win.

224. Brockington v. Rhodes

(Decided November 24, 1969; 396 U.S. 41)

I. ISSUE

A. Issues Discussed

Voting rights

B. Legal Question Presented

Whether Ohio's prior requirement for candidates for the U.S. House of Representatives to receive signatures from 7% of qualified voters to be placed on the ballot is unconstitutional.

C. Supreme Court's Answer

"[I]n view of the limited nature of the relief sought, we think the case is moot because the congressional election is over."

II. CASE SUMMARY

A. Background

"The appellant sought to run in the November 1968 election as an independent candidate for the United States House of Representatives from the Twenty-first Congressional District of Ohio. His nominating petition bore the signatures of 899 voters . . . , a little over 1% of those in the district who had voted in the gubernatorial contest at the last election. The Board of Elections ruled that the appellant's petition was insufficient to put his name on the November ballot, because it did not contain the signatures of 7% of the qualified voters, as Ohio law then required. The appellant petitioned the Court of Common Pleas for a writ of mandamus, challenging the 7% requirement . . . . He urged as the proper standard for determining the sufficiency of his nominating petition the 1% requirement that had prevailed for over 60 years until the enactment of the 7% rule in 1952. He prayed for an immediate order restraining the Board of Elections from printing the election ballots; also for a writ of mandamus commanding the Board 'to certify the sufficiency of relator's nominating petition' and directing the appellees 'to do all things necessary to place relator's name upon the ballot as an independent candidate for United States House of Representatives from the Ohio Twenty-First Congressional District in the November 5, 1968, general election . . . .' His suit did not purport to be a class action, and he sought no declaratory relief.

On August 22, 1968, the Court of Common Pleas denied the writ of mandamus. On October 1 the Court of Appeals for the Eighth Judicial District affirmed that judgment, and on October 23 the Supreme Court of Ohio dismissed the appeal for want of a substantial constitutional question. The appellant then appealed to [the U.S. Supreme] Court pursuant to 28 U.S.C. § 1257, and we noted probable jurisdiction. While the appeal was pending here, Ohio amended the controlling statute, effective October 30, 1969, reducing the signature requirement from 7% to 4%."

B. Counsel of Record

ACLU Side (Petitioner/Appellant): Benjamin B. Sheerer argued the cause for appellant. With him on the briefs were Ralph

Rudd of the American Civil Liberties Union of Ohio and Jerry Gordon.

Opposing Side (Respondent/Appellee): Robert D. Macklin, Assistant Attorney General of Ohio, argued the cause for appellees. On the brief were Paul W. Brown, Attorney General, Charles S. Lopeman, First Assistant Attorney General, and Julius J. Nemeth, Assistant Attorney General. John T. Corrigan and John L. Dowling filed a brief for appellees Cipollone et al.

III. AMICI CURIAE

ACLU Side (Petitioner/Appellant)

No briefs of amici curiae were filed in support of appellant.

Opposing Side (Respondent/Appellee)

No briefs of amici curiae were filed in support of appellees.

IV. THE SUPREME COURT'S DECISION

"We do not think the recent statutory amendment has rendered this case moot. For the appellant has consistently urged the unconstitutionality of any percentage requirement in excess of the 1% that Ohio imposed prior to 1952, and he obtained the signatures of only about 1% of the voters in his district. He thus could not have won a place on the ballot even under the statute as currently written.

Rather, in view of the limited nature of the relief sought, we think the case is moot because the congressional election is over. The appellant did not allege that he intended to run for office in any future elections. He did not attempt to maintain a class action on behalf of himself and other putative independent candidates, present or future. He did not sue for himself and others similarly situated as independent voters, as he might have under Ohio law. He did not seek a declaratory judgment, although that avenue too was open to him.

Instead, he sought only a writ of mandamus to compel the appellees to place his name on the ballot as a candidate for a particular office in a particular election on November 5, 1968. In Ohio mandamus is an extraordinary remedy, available to a petitioner only on a showing of clear legal right. . . . The court, without passing on the merits of the legal issues raised by the parties, found that the appellant had not established a clear legal right to the writ on the basis of all the evidence.

It is now impossible to grant the appellant the limited, extraordinary relief he sought in the Ohio courts. Accordingly, the judgment of the Supreme Court of Ohio must be vacated, without costs in this Court, and the cause remanded for such proceedings as that court may deem appropriate. . . .

Judgment vacated and cause remanded."

V. JUSTICE VOTE

0 Pro ACLU Side vs. 9 Con Opposing Side

Opposing Side (Respondent/Appellee)

1. Marshall, T. – Per curiam decision
2. White, B. – Per curiam decision
3. Burger, W. – Per curiam decision
4. Douglas, W. – Per curiam decision
5. Brennan, W. – Per curiam decision
6. Black, H. – Per curiam decision
7. Stewart, P. – Per curiam decision
8. Harlan, J. – Per curiam decision Vacant Seat

VI. A WIN OR LOSS FOR THE ACLU?

The ACLU served as counsel for appellants urging reversal of the judgment of the Supreme Court of Ohio; the U.S. Supreme Court vacated the decision below, declaring the case moot, in a 9-0 vote, giving the ACLU an apparent loss.

225. Hall v. Beals

(Decided November 24, 1969; 396 U.S. 45)

I. ISSUE

A. Issues Discussed

Civil rights, voting rights, mootness

B. Legal Question Presented

Does requiring voters to fulfill a six-month residency requirement in order to vote in a presidential election violate the Constitution?

C. Supreme Court's Answer

The Supreme Court determined the case was moot, declining to address the constitutional issue.

II. CASE SUMMARY

A. Background

Appellants moved to Colorado in June of 1968 and were refused the right to vote in the November 1968 presidential election because Colorado law required voters to be residents for at least six months prior to the date of the election. Appellants brought a class action suit challenging the constitutionality of the restriction, and seeking injunctive relief to prevent enforcement of the statute.

The district court upheld the statute and dismissed appellants complaint, "holding that the six-month requirement was not unconstitutional. As a result, the appellants did not vote in the 1968 presidential election."

After the Supreme Court granted certiorari, the Colorado legislature changed the law, reducing the residency period for presidential elections to two months. The Supreme Court reviewed the case in light of the change and decided the case was moot.

B. Counsel of Record/ACLU Attorney

ACLU Side (Petitioner/Appellant): Richard Hall argued the cause for appellant, pro se.

Opposing Side (Respondent/Appellee): Bernard R. Baker argued the cause for appellee.

III. AMICI CURIAE

ACLU Side (Petitioner/Appellant)

Brief of amici curiae filed on behalf of the ACLU, et al., by William F. Reynard, Melvin L. Wulf, Eleanor Holmes Norton, Edmund J. Wood, and Charles E. Ehlert.

Brief of amici curiae filed on behalf of the United States by Solicitor General Erwin N. Griswold, Assistant Attorney General Leonard, Louis F. Claiborne, Francis X. Beytagh, Jr., and Gary J. Greenberg.

Brief of amici curiae filed on behalf of the Bipartisan Committee on Absentee Voting by Joseph L. Rauh, Jr., John Silard, and Elliott C. Lichtman.

Brief of amici curiae filed by Harvey M. Burg, Herbert Teitelbaum, and Charles P. Gamer.

Opposing Side (Respondent/Appellee)

Brief of amici curiae filed on behalf of the State of New York by Louis J. Lefkowitz, Attorney General, Samuel A. Hirshowitz, First Assistant Attorney General, and Brenda Soloff, Assistant Attorney General.

IV. THE SUPREME COURT'S DECISION

"The 1968 election is history, and it is now impossible to grant the appellants the relief they sought in the District Court. Further, the appellants have now satisfied the six-month residency requirement of which they complained. But apart from these considerations, the recent amendatory action of the Colorado Legislature has surely operated to render this case moot. We review the judgment below in light of the Colorado statute as it now stands, not as it once did. . . .

The appellants 'cannot represent a class of [which] they are not a part,'—that is, the class of voters disqualified in Colorado by virtue of the new two-month requirement, a class of which the appellants have never been members. [T]he appellants will face disenfranchisement in Colorado in 1972 only in the unlikely event that they first move out of the State and then reestablish residence there within two months of the presidential election in that year. Or they may take up residence in some other State, and in 1972 face disqualification under that State's law. But such speculative contingencies afford no basis for our passing on the substantive issues the appellants would have us decide with respect to the now-amended law of Colorado.

The judgment of the District Court is vacated and the case is remanded with directions to dismiss the cause as moot."

V. JUSTICE VOTE

2 Pro ACLU Side vs. 7 Con Opposing Side

ACLU Side (Petitioner/Appellant)

1. Brennan, W. – Wrote dissenting opinion, joined Marshall's dissent
2. Marshall, T. – Wrote dissenting opinion

Opposing Side (Respondent/Appellee)

1. White, B. – Per curiam decision
2. Black, H. – Per curiam decision
3. Stewart, P. – Per curiam decision
4. Blackmun, H. – Per curiam decision
5. Harlan, J. – Per curiam decision
6. Burger, W. – Per curiam decision
7. Douglas, W. – Per curiam decision

VI. A WIN OR LOSS FOR THE ACLU?

The ACLU filed an amicus brief urging reversal; the Supreme Court dismissed the case as moot in a 7-2 vote, giving the ACLU an apparent loss.

226. Goldberg v. Kelly

(Decided March 23, 1970; 397 U.S. 254)

I. ISSUE

A. Issues Discussed

State, civil rights

B. Legal Question Presented

"[W]hether a State that terminates public assistance payments to a particular recipient without affording him the opportunity for an evidentiary hearing prior to termination denies the recipient procedural due process in violation of the Due Process Clause of the Fourteenth Amendment."

C. Supreme Court's Answer

"[W]hen welfare is discontinued, only a pre-termination evidentiary hearing provides the recipient with procedural due process."

II. CASE SUMMARY

A. Background

"This action was brought in the District Court for the Southern District of New York by residents of New York City receiving financial aid under the federally assisted program of Aid to Families with Dependent Children (AFDC) or under New York State's general Home Relief program. Their complaint alleged that the New York State and New York City officials administering these programs terminated, or were about to terminate, such aid without prior notice and hearing, thereby denying them due process of law. At the time the suits were filed there was no requirement of prior notice or hearing of any kind before termination of financial aid. However, the State and city adopted procedures for notice and hearing after the suits were brought, and the plaintiffs, appellees here, then challenged the constitutional adequacy of those procedures."

The Supreme Court granted certiorari to review the case.

B. Counsel of Record

ACLU Side (Respondent/Appellee): Lee A. Albert argued the cause for appellees. With him on the briefs were Henry Freedman, Sylvia Law, Robert Borsody, Harold J. Rothwax, David Diamond, David Gilman, Marianne Rosenfield, Peter H. Darrow, Steve Weisner, Richard Kwasnik, Louise Gruner Gans, Mort Cohen, Shyleur Barrack, and Rand Rosenblatt, Lois Hoffman, and Martin Garbus of the Roger Baldwin Foundation of the American Civil Liberties Union.

Opposing Side (Petitioner/Appellant): John J. Loflin, Jr., argued the cause for appellant. With him on the briefs were J. Lee Rankin and Stanley Buchsbaum.

III. AMICI CURIAE

ACLU Side (Respondent/Appellee)

Brief of amici curiae filed on behalf of the United States by Solicitor General Griswold, Assistant Attorney General Ruckelshaus, and Robert V. Zener.
Brief of amici curiae filed on behalf of the National Institute for Education in Law and Poverty by Victor G. Rosenblum and Daniel Wm. Fessler.

Opposing Side (Petitioner/Appellant)

No briefs of amici curiae were filed in support of appellant.

IV. THE SUPREME COURT'S DECISION

"The constitutional issue to be decided . . . is the narrow one whether the Due Process Clause requires that the recipient be afforded an evidentiary hearing before the termination of benefits. The District Court held that only a pretermination evidentiary hearing would satisfy the constitutional command, and rejected the argument of the state and city officials that the combination of the post-termination 'fair hearing' with the informal pre-termination review disposed of all due process claims. . . .

It is true, of course, that some governmental benefits may be administratively terminated without affording the recipient a pre-termination evidentiary hearing. But we agree with the District Court that when welfare is discontinued, only a pre-termination evidentiary hearing provides the recipient with procedural due process. For qualified recipients, welfare provides the means to obtain essential food, clothing, housing, and medical care. Thus the crucial factor in this context . . . is that termination of aid pending resolution of a controversy over eligibility may deprive an eligible recipient of the very means by which to live while he waits. . . .

We also agree with the District Court, however, that the pre-termination hearing need not take the form of a judicial or quasi-judicial trial. . . .

The opportunity to be heard must be tailored to the capacities and circumstances of those who are to be heard. . . .

In almost every setting where important decisions turn on questions of fact, due process requires an opportunity to confront and cross-examine adverse witnesses. . . .

Welfare recipients must therefore be given an opportunity to confront and cross-examine the witnesses relied on by the department.

'The right to be heard would be, in many cases, of little avail if it did not comprehend the right to be heard by counsel.' We do not say that counsel must be provided at the pre-termination hearing, but only that the recipient must be allowed to retain an attorney if he so desires. . . .

Finally, the decisionmaker's conclusion as to a recipient's eligibility must rest solely on the legal rules and evidence adduced at the hearing. . . .

Affirmed."

V. JUSTICE VOTE

5 Pro ACLU Side vs. 3 Con Opposing Side

ACLU Side (Respondent/Appellee)

1. Brennan, W. – Wrote majority opinion
2. Douglas, W. – Joined Black's concurrence
3. Harlan, J. – Wrote concurring opinion
4. Marshall, T. – Joined majority opinion
5. White, B. – Joined majority opinion

Opposing Side (Petitioner/Appellant)

1. Black, H. – Wrote dissenting opinion, joined Burger's dissent
2. Burger, W. – Wrote dissenting opinion
3. Stewart, P. – Wrote dissenting opinion

Vacant seat.

VI. A WIN OR LOSS FOR THE ACLU?

The ACLU served as counsel for appellee urging affirmance; the Supreme Court affirmed the District Court's decision by a 5-3 vote, giving the ACLU an apparent win.

227. Wheeler v. Montgomery

(Decided March 23, 1970; 397 U.S. 280)

I. ISSUE

A. Issues Discussed

State, civil rights

B. Legal Question Presented

Whether "the California procedure for pre-termination review in welfare cases satisfies the requirements of the Due Process Clause . . . ."

C. Supreme Court's Answer

"[P]rocedural due process requires . . . an evidentiary pre-termination hearing before welfare payments may be discontinued or suspended."

II. CASE SUMMARY

A. Background

"This is a companion case to No. 62, Goldberg v. Kelly, 397 U.S. 254. It is a class action brought by all recipients of old age benefits who are subject to California welfare termination provisions. A three-judge District Court for the Northern District of California held that the California procedure for pre-termination review in welfare cases satisfies the requirements of the Due Process Clause, and [the Supreme Court] noted probable jurisdiction."

B. Counsel of Record

ACLU Side (Petitioner/Appellant): Peter E. Sitkin argued the cause for appellants. With him on the briefs were Steven J. Antler and Charles Stephen Ralston.
Opposing Side (Respondent/Appellee): Elizabeth Palmer, Deputy Attorney General of California, argued the cause for appellees. With her on the brief were Thomas C. Lynch, Attorney General, Richard L. Mayers, Deputy Attorney General, Thomas M. O'Connor, and Raymond D. Williamson,

Jr.

III. AMICI CURIAE

ACLU Side (Petitioner/Appellant)

Brief of amici curiae filed on behalf of the Columbia Center on Social Welfare Policy and Law, Roger Baldwin Foundation of the American Civil Liberties Union, Mobilization for Youth, Williamsburg Neighborhood Legal Services, Morrisania Neighborhood Legal Services, and Legal Aid Society of New York by Lee A. Albert, Paul Dodyk, and Henry A. Freedman.

Brief of amici curiae filed on behalf of the Legal Aid Society of Alameda County by Thomas L. Fike, Thomas Schneider, Burton Danziger, and David Nawi.

Opposing Side (Respondent/Appellee)

Brief of amici curiae filed on behalf of the United States by Solicitor General Griswold, Assistant Attorney General Ruckelshaus, and Robert V. Zener.

IV. THE SUPREME COURT'S DECISION

"This procedure requires notice to the recipient of the proposed discontinuance or suspension [of welfare benefits] at least three days prior to its effective date, together with reasons for the intended action and a statement of what information or action is required to reestablish eligibility, advice that the recipient may meet his caseworker before his benefits are terminated '(t)o discuss the entire matter informally for purposes of clarification and, where possible, resolution,' and assurance that there will be 'prompt investigation' of the case and restoration of payments 'as soon as there is eligibility' to receive them. The procedure does not, however, afford the recipient an evidentiary hearing at which he may personally appear to offer oral evidence and confront and cross-examine the witnesses against him. In Goldberg v. Kelly, supra, decided today, we held that procedural due process requires such an evidentiary pre-termination hearing before welfare payments may be discontinued or suspended. Accordingly, the judgment of the District Court must be and is reversed on the authority of Goldberg v. Kelly.

Reversed."

V. JUSTICE VOTE

5 Pro ACLU Side vs. 3 Con Opposing Side

ACLU Side (Petitioner/Appellant)

1. Brennan, W. – Wrote majority opinion
2. Douglas, W. – Joined majority opinion
3. Harlan, J. – Joined majority opinion
4. Marshall, T. – Joined majority opinion
5. White, B. – Joined majority opinion

Opposing Side (Respondent/Appellee)

1. Black, H. – Wrote dissenting opinion, joined Burger's dissent
2. Burger, W. – Wrote dissenting opinion
3. Stewart, P. – Wrote dissenting opinion

Vacant seat.

VI. A WIN OR LOSS FOR THE ACLU?

The ACLU filed as amicus curiae urging reversal of the judgment of the District Court; the Supreme Court reversed in a 5-3 vote, giving the ACLU an apparent win.

228. Rosado v. Wyman

(Decided April 6, 1970; 397 U.S. 397)

I. ISSUE

A. Issues Discussed

Civil rights, state's rights, Fourteenth Amendment

B. Legal Question Presented

Is subject matter jurisdiction vested in the District Court to decide a federal statutory challenge to the New York Social Services Law?

C. Supreme Court's Answer

The District Court had jurisdiction to decide the issue.

II. CASE SUMMARY

A. Background

Petitioners filed a class action complaint challenging § 131-a of the New York Social Services Law as violative of equal protection by allowing lesser payments made to families with dependent children recipients in Nassau County than those allowed for New York City residents. "Before a decision was rendered New York State amended §131-a to permit the State Commissioner of Social Services to make, in his discretion, grants to recipients in Nassau County equal to those provided for New York City residents."

The three-judge panel in the district court "concluded that the equal protection issue was 'no longer justiciable' and that '[t]he constitutional attack on the provision . . . as originally adopted has been rendered moot . . . .'" However, the district court judge "issued a preliminary injunction prohibiting respondents from reducing or discontinuing payments of 'regular recurring grants and special grants,' payable under the welfare law . . . ."

On appeal, the Court of Appeals reversed the district court's judgment. Petitioners appealed to the Supreme Court. The Supreme Court granted certiorari and reversed.

B. Counsel of Record/ACLU Attorney

ACLU Side (Petitioner/Appellant): Lee A. Albert argued the cause for appellant.

Opposing Side (Respondent/Appellee): Philip Weinberg argued the cause for appellee.

III. AMICI CURIAE

ACLU Side (Petitioner/Appellant)

Brief of amici curiae filed on behalf of the New York Civil Liberties Union by Alan H. Levine, Burt Neuborne, Paul G. Chevigny, Melvin L. Wulf, Eleanor Holmes Norton, Martin M. Berger, Jerome Kretchmer, Franz S. J. Leicher, and Manfred

Ohrenstein.

Additional briefs of amici curiae filed on behalf of the Catholic Charities of the Archdiocese of New York, et al., People for Adequate Welfare, and the United States.

Opposing Side (Respondent/Appellee)

Brief of amici curiae filed on behalf of the State of Indiana by Theodore L. Sendak, Attorney General, and Robert A. Zaban, Deputy Attorney General.

IV. THE SUPREME COURT'S DECISION

"We reach our conclusions without relying on the finding made by the court below that in § 131-a New York was attempting to constrict its welfare payments. Speculation as to legislative and executive motive is to be shunned. Section 402(a)(23) [of the Social Security Act] invalidates any state program that substantially alters the content of the standard of need in such a way that it is less than it was prior to the enactment of § 402(a)(23), unless a State can demonstrate that the items formerly included no longer constituted part of the reality of existence for the majority of welfare recipients. We do not, of course, hold that New York may not, consistently with the federal statutes, consolidate items on the basis of statistical averages. Obviously such averaging may affect some families adversely and benefit others. Moreover, it is conceivable that the net payout, assuming no change in the level of benefits, may be somewhat less under a streamlined program. Providing all factors in the old equation are accounted for and fairly priced and providing the consolidation on a statistical basis reflects a fair averaging, a State may, of course, consistently with § 402(a)(23) redefine its method for determining need. A State may, moreover, as we have noted, accommodate any increases in its standard by reason of 'cost-of-living' factors to its budget by reducing its level of benefits. What is at the heart of this dispute is the elimination of special grants in the New York program, not the system of maximum grants based on average age. Lest there be uncertainty we also reiterate that New York is not foreclosed from accounting for basic and recurring items of need formerly subsumed in the special grant category by an averaging system like that adopted in the 1968 New York City experiment with cyclical grants. . . .

In conclusion, we add simply this. While we view with concern the escalating involvement of federal courts in this highly complicated area of welfare benefits, one that should be formally placed under the supervision of HEW [Department of Health, Education, and Welfare], at least in the first instance, we find not the slightest indication that Congress meant to deprive federal courts of their traditional jurisdiction to hear and decide federal questions in this field. It is, of course, no part of the business of this Court to evaluate, apart from federal constitutional or statutory challenge, the merits or wisdom of any welfare programs, whether state or federal, in the large or in the particular. It is, on the other hand, peculiarly part of the duty of this tribunal, no less in the welfare field than in other areas of the law, to resolve disputes as to whether federal funds allocated to the States are being expended in consonance with the conditions that Congress has attached to their use. . . .

The judgment of the Court of Appeals is reversed and the case is remanded to that court for further proceedings consistent with this opinion."

V. JUSTICE VOTE

6 Pro ACLU Side vs. 2 Con Opposing Side

ACLU Side (Petitioner/Appellant)

1. Harlan, J. – Wrote majority opinion
2. White, B. – Joined majority opinion
3. Brennan, W. – Joined majority opinion
4. Marshall, T. – Joined majority opinion
5. Stewart, J. – Joined majority opinion
6. Douglas, W. – Wrote concurring opinion

Opposing Side (Respondent/Appellee)

1. Black, H. – Wrote dissenting opinion
2. Burger, W. – Joined Black's dissent

Blackmun, H. – Took no part in the decision

VI. A WIN OR LOSS FOR THE ACLU?

The ACLU filed as amicus curiae urging reversal; the Supreme Court reversed the judgment of the Court of Appeals in a 6-2 vote giving the ACLU an apparent win.

229. Walz v. Tax Commission

(Decided May 4, 1970; 397 U.S. 664)

I. ISSUE

A. Issues Discussed

First Amendment, separation of church and state, Establishment Clause

B. Legal Question Presented

Is New York State's grant of property tax exemptions to religious organizations for religious properties a violation of the Establishment Clause of the First Amendment?

C. Supreme Court's Answer

The property tax exemptions do not violate the Establishment Clause.

II. CASE SUMMARY

A. Background

"Appellant, owner of real estate in Richmond County, New York, sought an injunction in the New York courts to prevent the New York City Tax Commission from granting property tax exemptions to religious organizations for religious properties used solely for religious worship. The exemption from state taxes is authorized by Art. 16, § 1, of the New York Constitution, which provides in relevant part: 'Exemptions from taxation may be granted only by general laws. Exemptions may be altered or repealed except those exempting real or personal property used exclusively for religious, educational or charitable purposes as defined by law and owned by any corporation or association organized or conducted exclusively for one or more of such purposes and not operating for profit.'

The essence of appellant's contention was that the New York City Tax Commission's grant of an exemption to church property indirectly requires the appellant to make a contribution to religious bodies and thereby violates provisions prohibiting establishment of religion under the First Amendment which under the Fourteenth Amendment is binding on the States.

Appellee's motion for summary judgment was granted and the Appellate Division of the New York Supreme Court, and the New York Court of Appeals affirmed."

The Supreme Court granted certiorari and affirmed.

B. Counsel of Record/ACLU Attorney

ACLU Side (Petitioner/Appellant): Edward J. Ennis argued the cause for appellant.

Opposing Side (Respondent/Appellee): J. Lee Rankin argued the cause for appellee.

III. AMICI CURIAE

ACLU Side (Petitioner/Appellant)

Brief of amici curiae filed on behalf of the ACLU by Osmond K. Fraenkel, Marvin M. Karpatkin, Norman Dorsen, Edward J. Ennis, John DeJ. Pemberton, Jr., Melvin L. Wulf, and Burt Neuborne.

Additional briefs of amici curiae were filed on behalf of the Society of Separationists, Inc., Protestants and Other Americans United for Separation of Church and State, the Parish Hall School, Inc., the National Council for the Churches of Christ in the United States, the Episcopal Diocese of New York, the United States Catholic Conference, the Synagogue Council of America, et al., the National Jewish Commission on Law and Public Affairs, the Baptist Joint Committee on Public Affairs, and the Baptist General Convention of Texas.

Opposing Side (Respondent/Appellee)

Brief of amici curiae filed on behalf of the State of New York, et al., by Louis J. Lefkowitz, Attorney General, Samuel A. Hirsowitz, First Assistant Attorney General, and Julius Greenfield, Assistant Attorney General, joined by Attorney Generals for the states of Alabama, Arizona, Arkansas, Colorado, Connecticut, Delaware, Florida, Hawaii, Illinois, Indiana, Iowa, Kansas, Kentucky, Louisiana, Maine, Maryland, Michigan, Mississippi, Missouri, Montana, Nebraska, New Jersey, New Mexico, North Carolina, North Dakota, Ohio, Pennsylvania, Rhode Island, South Dakota, Tennessee, Texas, Vermont, Virginia, Washington, Wisconsin, Wyoming, and Puerto Rico.

IV. THE SUPREME COURT'S DECISION

"The legislative purpose of a property tax exemption is neither the advancement nor the inhibition of religion; it is neither sponsorship nor hostility. New York, in common with the other States, has determined that certain entities that exist in a harmonious relationship to the community at large, and that foster its 'moral or mental improvement,' should not be inhibited in their activities by property taxation or the hazard of loss of those properties for nonpayment of taxes. It has not singled out one particular church or religious group or even churches as such; rather, it has granted exemption to all houses of religious worship within a broad class of property owned by nonprofit, quasi-public corporations which include hospitals, libraries, playgrounds, scientific, professional, historical, and patriotic groups. The State has an affirmative policy that considers these groups as beneficial and stabilizing influences in community life and finds this classification useful, desirable, and in the public interest. . . .

It appears that at least up to 1885 this Court, reflecting more than a century of our history and uninterrupted practice, accepted without discussion the proposition that federal or state grants of tax exemption to churches were not a violation of the Religion Clauses of the First Amendment. As to the New York statute, we now confirm that view."

The Supreme Court affirmed appellee's summary judgment.

V. JUSTICE VOTE

1 Pro ACLU Side vs. 7 Con Opposing Side

ACLU Side (Petitioner/Appellant)

1. Douglas, W. – Wrote dissenting opinion

Opposing Side (Respondent/Appellee)

1. Burger, W. – Wrote majority opinion
2. Harlan, J. – Wrote concurring opinion
3. Brennan, W. – Wrote concurring opinion
4. Stewart, P. – Joined majority opinion
5. White, B. – Joined majority opinion
6. Marshall, T. – Joined majority opinion
7. Black, H. – Joined majority opinion

Blackmun, H. – Took no part in the decision

VI. A WIN OR LOSS FOR THE ACLU?

The ACLU, as amicus curiae, urged reversal of the judgment of the Court of Appeals; the Supreme Court affirmed in a 7-1 vote, giving the ACLU an apparent loss.

230. McMann v. Richardson

(Decided May 4, 1970; 397 U.S. 759)

I. ISSUE

A. Issues Discussed

Criminal procedure, plea bargaining, coerced confessions, guilty plea, Fourteenth Amendment, habeas corpus

B. Legal Question Presented

"[W]hether and to what extent an otherwise valid guilty plea may be impeached in collateral proceedings by assertions or proof that the plea was motivated by a prior coerced confession."

C. Supreme Court's Answer

The guilty pleas here may not be impeached in collateral proceedings.

II. CASE SUMMARY

A. Background

Respondent Dash was charged with first-degree robbery. After pleading guilty to robbery in the second degree, he was sentenced to a term of 8 to 12 years as a second-felony offender. He filed a petition for collateral relief in the state courts, but it was denied without a hearing. Then he filed a petition for habeas corpus in the U.S. District Court, alleging that his guilty plea was illegal because it was the product of a coerced confession, and because the trial judge threatened "to impose a 60-year sentence if he was convicted after a plea of not guilty." He alleged that "he had been beaten, refused counsel, and threatened with false charges prior to his confession." The District Court denied the petition without an evidentiary hearing.

The other two respondents, Richardson and Williams had similar experiences pleading guilty in situations that they alleged were the result of coerced confessions, then petitioning for a writ of habeas corpus, which was denied. Richardson was indicted for murder in the first degree. "He initially pleaded not guilty but [later] withdrew his plea and pleaded guilty to murder in the second degree... He was convicted and sentenced to a term of 30 years to life. [R]espondent Williams was indicted for five felonies including rape and robbery. He pleaded guilty to robbery in the second degree . . . and was sentenced . . . to a term of 7 1/2 to 15 years."

Dash, Richardson, and Williams each appealed to the Court of Appeals for the Second Circuit. The court reversed in each case and ordered that hearings be held on the petitions for habeas corpus. The Court of Appeals reasoned "that a plea of guilty is an effective waiver of pretrial irregularities only if the plea is voluntary and that a plea is not voluntary if it is the consequence of an involuntary confession."

The Supreme Court granted certiorari, consolidated the cases, and vacated and remanded.

B. Counsel of Record/ACLU Attorney

ACLU Side (Respondent/Appellee): Gretchen White Oberman argued the cause for appellee.

Opposing Side (Petitioner/Appellant): Brenda Soloff, Assistant Attorney General of New York, argued the cause for appellant.

Michael R. Juviler argued the cause for the District Attorney of New York County, as amici curiae.

III. AMICI CURIAE

ACLU Side (Respondent/Appellee)

Brief of amici curiae filed on behalf of the ACLU, et al., by Melvin L. Wulf, Joel M. Gora, and Burt Neuborne, and Duane W. Krohnke.

Opposing Side (Petitioner/Appellant)

Brief of amici curiae filed on behalf of the District Attorney of New York County by Michael R. Juviler, Frank S. Hogan, pro se, and Bennett L. Gershman.

IV. THE SUPREME COURT'S DECISION

"The core of the Court of Appeals' holding is the proposition that if, in a collateral proceeding, a guilty plea is shown to have been triggered by a coerced confession—if there would have been no plea had there been no confession—the plea is vulnerable . . . . We are unable to agree with the Court of Appeals on this proposition.

A conviction after a plea of guilty normally rests on the defendant's own admission in open court that he committed the acts with which he is charged. That admission may not be compelled, and since the plea is also a waiver of trial—and, unless the applicable law otherwise provides, a waiver of the right to contest the admissibility of any evidence the State might have offered against the defendant—it must be an intelligent act 'done with sufficient awareness of the relevant circumstances and likely consequences.' . . .

The issue on which we differ with the Court of Appeals arises in those situations involving the counseled defendant who allegedly would put the State to its proof if there was a substantial enough chance of acquittal, who would do so except for a prior confession that might be offered against him, and who, because of the confession, decides to plead guilty to save himself the expense and agony of a trial and perhaps also to minimize the penalty that might be imposed. After conviction on such a plea, is a defendant entitled to a hearing, and to relief if his factual claims are accepted, when his petition for habeas corpus alleges that his confession was, in fact, coerced, and that it motivated his plea? We think not, if he alleges and proves no more than this. . . .

That a guilty plea must be intelligently made is not a requirement that all advice offered by the defendant's lawyer withstand retrospective examination in a post-conviction hearing. Courts continue to have serious differences among themselves on the admissibility of evidence . . . . That this Court might hold a defendant's confession inadmissible in evidence, possibly by a divided vote, hardly justifies a conclusion that the defendant's attorney was incompetent or ineffective when he thought the admissibility of the confession sufficiently probable to advise a plea of guilty. . . .

We hold, therefore, that a defendant who alleges that he pleaded guilty because of a prior coerced confession is not, without more, entitled to a hearing on his petition for habeas corpus. . . . As we have previously indicated, in each case below, the Court of Appeals ruled that a hearing was required to consider claims other than the claim that the plea of guilty rested on a coerced confession and was entered prior to *Jackson v. Denno*, supra. With respect to these other claims, we now express no disagreement with the judgments of the Court of Appeals; but, since our holding will require reassessment of the petitions for habeas corpus in the light of the standards expressed herein, the judgments of the Court of Appeals are vacated and the case is remanded to that court for further proceedings consistent with this opinion."

V. JUSTICE VOTE

3 Pro ACLU Side vs. 5 Con Opposing Side

ACLU Side (Petitioner/Appellant)

1. Brennan, W. – Wrote dissenting opinion
2. Marshall, T. – Joined Brennan's dissent
3. Douglas, W. – Joined Brennan's dissent

Opposing Side (Respondent/Appellee)

1. White, B. – Wrote majority opinion
2. Harlan, J. – Joined majority opinion
3. Stewart, J. – Joined majority opinion
4. Black, H. – Wrote concurring opinion
5. Burger, W. – Joined majority opinion

Blackmun, H. – Took no part in the decision

VI. A WIN OR LOSS FOR THE ACLU?

The ACLU filed as amicus curiae urging affirmance; the Supreme Court vacated the rulings of the Court of Appeals in a 5-3 vote, giving the ACLU an apparent loss.

231. Maxwell v. Bishop

(Decided June 1, 1970; 398 U.S. 262)

I. ISSUE

A. Issues Discussed

Criminal justice, death penalty, Eighth Amendment

B. Legal Question Presented

First, are a defendant's constitutional rights violated if the jury decides whether the defendant is guilty or innocent in the same proceeding that the jury decides whether the defendant should receive life imprisonment or the death penalty? Second, are a defendant's constitutional rights violated if the jury does not receive standards to guide them in deciding whether to impose the death penalty?

C. Supreme Court's Answer

The Supreme Court vacated the judgment because several prospective jurors were excluded due to their views on the death penalty, and the Court declined to address the original questions.

II. CASE SUMMARY

A. Background

"In 1962 the petitioner was found guilty of rape by an Arkansas jury without a verdict of life imprisonment, and the trial court imposed a sentence of death. The Arkansas Supreme Court affirmed the judgment of conviction. The petitioner then sought a writ of habeas corpus in the United States District Court for the Eastern District of Arkansas, claiming, among other things, that his conviction and punishment were unconstitutional in that (1) the jury had determined the two issues of guilt or innocence and of a life or death sentence in a single proceeding, thereby precluding him from presenting evidence pertinent to the question of penalty without subjecting himself to self-incrimination on the issue of guilt; and (2) the jury had been given no standards or directions of any kind to guide it is deciding whether to impose a sentence of life imprisonment or death. The District Court denied the writ and the Court of Appeals for the Eighth Circuit affirmed."

The Supreme Court granted certiorari, vacated the judgment, and remanded the case.

B. Counsel of Record/ACLU Attorney

ACLU Side (Petitioner/Appellant): Anthony G. Amsterdam argued the cause for appellant.

Opposing Side (Respondent/Appellee): Don Langston, Deputy Attorney General of Arkansas, argued the cause for appellee.

Albert W. Harris, Jr., argued the cause for the State of California, as amicus curiae, by special leave of court.

III. AMICI CURIAE

ACLU Side (Petitioner/Appellant)

Brief of amici curiae filed on behalf of the ACLU, Illinois Division, et al., by Elmer Gertz and Willard J. Lassers.

Additional briefs of amici curiae were filed on behalf of the National Council on Crime and Delinquency, the Synagogue Council of America, et al., the American Friends Service Committee, et al., the American Psychiatric Association, Berl I. Bernhard, et al., Robert Page Anderson, et al., and Clinton Duffy.

Opposing Side (Respondent/Appellee)

Albert W. Harris, Jr., Assistant Attorney General, argued the cause for the State of California, as amicus curiae, urging affirmance. With him on the brief were Thomas C. Lynch, Attorney General, and Robert R. Granucci and George R. Nock, Deputy Attorneys General.

IV. THE SUPREME COURT'S DECISION

"The petitioner's trial took place long before this Court's decision in *Witherspoon v. Illinois*, 391 U.S. 510. The trial transcript makes evident that several prospective jurors were removed from the panel upon grounds held impermissible in the *Witherspoon* case. . . .

As was made clear in *Witherspoon*, 'a sentence of death cannot be carried out if the jury that imposed or recommended it was chosen by excluding veniremen for cause simply because they voiced general objections to the death penalty or expressed conscientious or religious scruples against its infliction.' . . . 'Unless a venireman states unambiguously that he would automatically vote against the imposition of capital punishment no matter what the trial might reveal, it simply cannot be assumed that that is his position.'

'The most that can be demanded of a venireman in this regard is that he be willing to consider all of the penalties provided by state law, and that he not be irrevocably committed, before the trial has begun, to vote against the penalty of death regardless of the facts and circumstances that might emerge in the course of the proceedings. If the voir dire testimony in a given case indicates that veniremen were excluded on any broader basis than this, the death sentence cannot be carried out . . . .'

It appears, therefore, that the sentence of death imposed upon the petitioner cannot constitutionally stand under *Witherspoon v. Illinois*. [H]owever, we do not finally decide that question here. . . . The reasons that persuaded us to remand the *Boulden* [*v. Holman*] case to the District Court apply with equal force here: 'A further hearing directed to the issue might conceivably modify in some fashion the conclusion so strongly suggested by the record now before us. Further, it is not clear whether the petitioner has exhausted his state remedies with respect to this issue. Finally, in the event it turns out, as now appears, that relief from this death sentence must be ordered, a local federal court will be far better equipped than are we to frame an appropriate decree with due regard to available [Arkansas] procedures.'

Accordingly, the judgment of the Court of Appeals is vacated, and the case is remanded to the District Court, where the issue that has belatedly been brought to our attention may be fully considered. In the action we take today, we express no view whatever with respect to the two questions originally specified in our grant of certiorari."

V. JUSTICE VOTE

6 Pro ACLU Side vs. 1 Con Opposing Side

ACLU Side (Petitioner/Appellant)

1. Burger, W. – Per curiam decision
2. Douglas, W. – Per curiam decision
3. Harlan, J. – Per curiam decision
4. Brennan, W. – Per curiam decision
5. Stewart, P. – Per curiam decision
6. White, B. – Per curiam decision

Opposing Side (Respondent/Appellee)

1. Black, H. – Wrote dissenting opinion

Marshall, T. – Took no part in the decision
Blackmun, H. – Took no part in the decision

VI. A WIN OR LOSS FOR THE ACLU?

The ACLU filed as amicus curiae urging reversal; the Supreme Court vacated and remanded the case to the District Court for the Eastern District of Arkansas in a 6-1 vote, giving the ACLU an apparent win.

232. Mulloy v. United States

(Decided June 15, 1970; 398 U.S. 410)

I. ISSUE

A. Issues Discussed

Governmental regulation, First Amendment, conscientious objectors

B. Legal Question Presented

Whether it was "an abuse of discretion for the [Social Service B] oard to reject [petitioner's] conscientious objector claim without reopening his classification, and by so doing to deprive him of his right to an administrative appeal."

C. Supreme Court's Answer

It was an abuse of discretion for the Social Service Board to not reopen the classification thus deprive petitioner of his right to an administrative appeal.

II. CASE SUMMARY

A. Background

"On October 17, 1967, the petitioner, who was then 23 years old and classified I—A (available for military service), wrote to his local Selective Service Board that '[a]fter much, much thinking, seeking, and questioning of my own religious upbringing and political experience I have concluded that I am a conscientious objector. I am therefore opposed to war in any form.' In response to this letter the clerk sent him the Special Form for Conscientious Objectors, which he promptly completed and returned." He also included supporting letters.

In response, the Board granted petitioner an interview in November 1967. After the interview, the Board agreed that petitioner's form, together with five letters from petitioner's close acquaintances, and petitioner's interview did not warrant the reopening and reexamining of petitioner's I-A classification.

After petitioner received notification of the Board's decision, he wrote to appeal their decision not to reclassify him as a conscientious objector. Petitioner said that he considered the November interview to be a reopening of his classification. The Board responded by declaring the interview "a matter of courtesy" and not a reopening of his classification.

Petitioner was ordered to report for induction into the armed forces in February 1967. He reported but refused to be inducted. The refusal led to a criminal charge and conviction for violating 50 U.S.C. App. § 462(a). He was sentenced to five years in prison and fined $10,000. The Court of Appeals for the Sixth Circuit affirmed his conviction.

The Supreme Court granted certiorari and reversed.

B. Counsel of Record/ACLU Attorney

ACLU Side (Petitioner/Appellant): Robert Allen Sedler argued the cause for appellant.

Opposing Side (Respondent/Appellee): Joseph J. Connolly argued the cause for appellee.

III. AMICI CURIAE

ACLU Side (Petitioner/Appellant)

Brief of amici curiae filed on behalf of the ACLU, et al., by Marvin M. Karpatkin, Michael N. Pollet, Melvin L. Wulf, Paul G. Chevigny, and E. Curry First, III.

Brief of amici curiae filed on behalf of Wayne Spencer Deri, et al., by Ralph Rudd and Benjamin B. Sheerer.

Opposing Side (Respondent/Appellee)

No briefs of amici curiae were filed in support of appellee.

IV. THE SUPREME COURT'S DECISION

"Where a registrant makes nonfrivolous allegations of facts that have not been previously considered by his board, and that, if true, would be sufficient under regulation or statute to warrant granting the requested reclassification, the board must reopen the registrant's classification unless the truth of these new allegations is conclusively refuted by other reliable information in the registrant's file. . . . Where a prima facie case for reclassification has been made, a board cannot deprive the registrant of such review by simply refusing to reopen his file. Yet here the board did precisely that. . . .

The Government suggests, however, that the board might have concluded that the prima facie claim had been undercut by the petitioner himself—by his statements at the courtesy interview or because his demeanor convinced the board that he was not telling the truth. There is, however, but scant evidence in the record that the board's action was based on any such grounds. And, in any event, it is on precisely such grounds as these that board action cannot be predicated without a reopening of the registrant's classification, and a consequent opportunity for administrative appeal.

This is not to say that on all the facts presented to it the board might not have been justified in refusing to grant the petitioner a I-O classification; it is to say that such refusal could properly occur only after his classification had first been reopened. . . .

Since the petitioner presented a nonfrivolous, prima facie claim for a change in classification based on new factual allegations which were not conclusively refuted by other information in his file, it was an abuse of discretion for the board not to reopen his classification, thus depriving him of his right to an administrative appeal. The order to report for induction was accordingly invalid, and his conviction for refusing to submit to induction must be reversed."

V. JUSTICE VOTE

8 Pro ACLU Side vs. 0 Con Opposing Side

ACLU Side (Petitioner/Appellant)

1. Stewart, P. – Wrote majority opinion
2. Burger, W. – Joined majority opinion
3. Black, H. – Joined majority opinion
4. Douglas, W. – Joined majority opinion
5. Harlan, J. – Joined majority opinion
6. Brennan, W. – Joined majority opinion
7. White, B. – Joined majority opinion
8. Marshall, T. – Joined majority opinion

Blackmun, H. – Took no part in the decision

VI. A WIN OR LOSS FOR THE ACLU?

The ACLU filed as amicus curiae urging reversal; the Supreme Court reversed the ruling of the lower court in an 8-0 vote, giving the ACLU an apparent win.

233. Mitchell v. Donovan

(Decided June 15, 1970; 398 U.S. 427)

I. ISSUE

A. Issues Discussed

Communism

B. Legal Question Presented

"[W]hether an order granting or denying only a declaratory judgment may be appealed to this Court under s 1253."

C. Supreme Court's Answer

"The appellees have persisted in their claim that the Court lacks jurisdiction to consider this appeal, and after hearing oral argument we have concluded that they are right."

II. CASE SUMMARY

A. Background

"The appellants are the 1968 Communist Party candidates for President and Vice President of the United States, various Minnesota voters . . . , and the Communist Parties of the United States and of Minnesota. The appellant candidates obtained petitions containing the requisite number of names and asked the Secretary of State of Minnesota to place them on the ballot for the 1968 election. The Secretary denied the request, relying upon an opinion by the Attorney General of the State to the effect that placing Communist Party candidates on the ballot would violate the Federal Communist Control Act of 1954, which declares that the Communist Party 'should be outlawed,' and purports to strip it of all 'rights, privileges, and immunities attendant upon legal bodies created under the jurisdiction of the laws of the United States or any political subdivision thereof . . . .'

The appellants brought an action in the United States District Court for the District of Minnesota seeking a declaration that the Communist Control Act was constitutionally invalid and praying for a temporary restraining order and permanent injunction requiring the Secretary to include the names of the appellant candidates on the November 1968 ballot. [W]ithout deciding the merits of the appellants' claims, the court ordered that the names of the appellant candidates be placed on the November 1968 ballot. . . .

After the election, the appellants moved to amend the complaint, alleging that the Communist Party intended to run candidates in future elections . . . . The District Court . . . held that the prayer for injunctive relief . . . had been rendered moot by the passing of that election. As to the prayer for a declaratory judgment striking down the Communist Control Act, the court found no present case or controversy. . . . It therefore dismissed the complaint. . . .

[The Supreme Court] noted probable jurisdiction."

B. Counsel of Record

ACLU Side (Petitioner/Appellant): Lynn S. Castner of the Minnesota Civil Liberties Union argued the cause for appellants. With him on the brief were Melvin L. Wulf and Eleanor Holmes Norton of the American Civil Liberties Union.

Richard H. Kyle, Solicitor General of Minnesota, argued the cause for appellees. With him on the brief were Douglas M. Head, Attorney General, pro se, Arne L. Schoeller, Chief Deputy Attorney General, James M. Kelley, Assistant Attorney General, and John R. Kenefick, Special Assistant Attorney General.

III. AMICI CURIAE

ACLU Side (Petitioner/Appellant)

No briefs of amici curiae were filed in support of appellant.

Opposing Side (Respondent/Appellee)

No briefs of amici curiae were filed in support of appellees.

IV. THE SUPREME COURT'S DECISION

"The order appealed from does no more than deny the appellants a declaratory judgment striking down the Communist Control Act. . . . As is plain from the opening words of its opinion in the present proceeding, the District Court recognized that no request for injunctive relief was before it . . . .

That leaves us with the question whether an order granting or denying only a declaratory judgment may be appealed to this Court under s 1253. In a recent case, Rockefeller v. Catholic Medical Center, 397 U.S. 820, we gave a negative answer to that question, and we adhere to that decision. Section 1253 by its terms grants this Court jurisdiction only of appeals from orders granting or denying injunctions. While there are similarities between injunctions and declaratory judgments, there are also important differences. . . .

We conclude, therefore, that this Court lacks jurisdiction of the appeal. A simple dismissal for want of jurisdiction, however, would leave the appellants with no recourse to appellate review, because they brought their appeal here rather than to the Court of Appeals and the time for appealing to the Court of Appeals has long since passed. Accordingly, as in other cases where an appeal was improperly brought to this Court rather than the Court of Appeals, we vacate the judgment below and remand the case so that the District Court may enter a fresh order dismissing the complaint, thus affording the appellants an opportunity to take a timely appeal to the Court of Appeals for the Eighth Circuit. . . .

Judgment vacated and case remanded."

V. JUSTICE VOTE

1 Pro ACLU Side vs. 7 Con Opposing Side

ACLU Side (Petitioner/Appellant)

1. Douglas, W. – Wrote dissenting opinion

Opposing Side (Respondent/Appellee)

1. Marshall, T. – Per curiam decision
2. White, B. – Per curiam decision
3. Burger, W. – Per curiam decision
4. Brennan, W. – Per curiam decision
5. Black, H. – Concurs in the result
6. Stewart, P. – Per curiam decision
7. Harlan, J. – Per curiam decision

Blackmun, H. – Took no part in the decision.

VI. A WIN OR LOSS FOR THE ACLU?

The ACLU served as counsel for appellants urging reversal of the judgment of the U.S. District Court for the District of Minnesota; the Supreme Court vacated, in a 7-1 per curiam decision, giving the ACLU an apparent loss.

234. United States v. Sisson

(Decided June 29, 1970; 399 U.S. 267)

I. ISSUE

A. Issues Discussed

Religion, criminal procedure

B. Legal Question Presented

Whether the U.S. Supreme Court has jurisdiction to hear this appeal.

C. Supreme Court's Answer

"[W]e conclude that the decision below, depending as it does on facts developed at Sisson's trial, is not an arrest of judgment but instead is a directed acquittal. As such, it is not a decision that the Government can appeal. Consequently, this appeal must be dismissed for lack of jurisdiction without our considering the merits of this case. We, of course, intimate no view concerning the correctness of the legal theory by which the District Court evaluated the facts developed at the trial."

II. CASE SUMMARY

A. Background

"The Government seeks to appeal to this Court a decision by a District Court in Massachusetts holding that appellee Sisson could not be criminally convicted for refusing induction into the Armed Forces. The District Court's opinion was bottomed on what that court understood to be Sisson's rights of conscience as a nonreligious objector to the Vietnam war, but not wars in general, under the Free Exercise and Establishment Clauses of the First Amendment and the Due Process Clause of the Fifth Amendment to the Constitution of the United States. The District Court's primary conclusion, reached after a full trial, was that the Constitution prohibited 'the application of the 1967 draft act to Sisson to require him to render combat service in Vietnam' because as a 'sincerely conscientious man,' Sisson's interest in not killing in the Vietnam conflict outweighed 'the country's present need for him to be so employed,'

The District Court characterized its own decision as an arrest of judgment, and the Government seeks review here pursuant to the 'arresting judgment' provision of the Criminal Appeals Act, 18 U.S.C. s 3731, an Act that narrowly limits the Government's right to appeal in criminal cases to certain types of decisions. On October 13, 1969, th[e U.S. Supreme] Court entered an order postponing further consideration of the question of jurisdiction to the hearing of the case on the merits"

B. Counsel of Record

ACLU Side (Respondent/Appellee): John G. S. Flym argued the cause and filed a brief for appellee.

Opposing Side (Petitioner/Appellant): Solicitor General Griswold argued the cause for the United States. With him on the brief were Assistant Attorney General Wilson, Francis X. Beytagh, Jr., Beatrice Rosenberg, and Roger A. Pauley.

III. AMICI CURIAE

ACLU Side (Respondent/Appellee)

Brief of amici curiae filed on behalf of the American Humanist Association and American Civil Liberties Union by Herman Schwartz, Marvin M. Karpatkin, John De J. Pemberton, Jr., Melvin L. Wulf, and Joel M. Gora.

Brief of amici curiae filed on behalf of the Los Angeles Selective Service Law Panel by William G. Smith.

Brief of amici curiae filed on behalf of the Lawyers' Selective Service Panel of San Francisco by Norman Leonard.

Brief of amici curiae filed on behalf of the American Jewish Congress by Joseph B. Robison.

Brief of amici curiae filed on behalf of the American Jewish Committee by Samuel Rabinove and George Berlstein.

Brief of amici curiae filed on behalf of the American Ethical Union by Leo Rosen, Edward S. Greenbaum, and Nancy F. Wechsler.

Brief of amici curiae filed on behalf of Frank P. Slaninger by Frank P. Slaninger, pro se.

Opposing Side (Petitioner/Appellant)

No briefs of amici curiae were filed in support of appellees.

IV. THE SUPREME COURT'S DECISION

"The Government bases its claim that this Court has jurisdiction to review the District Court's decision exclusively on the 'arresting judgment' provision of the Criminal Appeals Act, 18 U.S.C. s 3731. . . .

Thus, three requirements must be met for this Court to have jurisdiction . . . . First, the decision of the District Court must be one 'arresting a judgment of conviction.' Second, the arrest of judgment must be for the 'insufficiency of the indictment or information.' And third, the decision must be 'based upon the invalidity or construction of the statute upon which the indictment or information is founded.'

Because the District Court's decision rests on facts not alleged in the indictment but instead inferred by the court from the evidence . . . , we conclude that neither the first nor second requirement is met. . . .

We begin with the first requirement: was the decision below one 'arresting a judgment of conviction'? In using that phrase in the Criminal Appeals Act, Congress did not, of course, invent a new procedural classification. Instead, Congress acted against a common-law background that gave the statutory phrase a well-defined and limited meaning. . . .

For the purpose of this case the critical requirement is that a judgment can be arrested only on the basis of error appearing on the 'face of the record,' and not on the basis of proof offered at trial. . . .

This venerable requirement of the common law has been preserved under the Federal Rules of Criminal Procedure, for the courts have uniformly held that in granting a motion in arrest of judgment under Rule 34, a district court must not look beyond the face of the record. . . .

The court below clearly went beyond the 'face of the record' in reaching its decision. . . .

The second statutory requirement, that the decision arresting judgment be 'for insufficiency of the indictment,' is also not met in this case. . . .

The same reason underlying our conclusion that this was not a decision arresting judgment . . . convinces us that the decision was in fact an acquittal rendered by the trial court after the jury's verdict of guilty. . . .

Because the court below rendered its decision here after the trial began, and because that decision was not, as we have shown, an arrest of judgment, we therefore conclude there can be no appeal under the other provisions of s 3731. . . .

The Solicitor General, at oral argument in this case, forthrightly stated that 'there are few problems which occur so frequently or present such extreme technical difficulty in the Solicitor General's office (as) in the proper construction of the Criminal Appeals Act.' We share his dissatisfaction with this statute. Nevertheless, until such time as Congress decides to amend the statute, this Court must abide by the limitations imposed by this awkward and ancient Act.

We conclude that the appeal in this case must be dismissed for lack of jurisdiction."

V. JUSTICE VOTE

5 Pro ACLU Side vs. 3 Con Opposing Side

ACLU Side (Respondent/Appellee)

1. Harlan, J. – Wrote majority opinion
2. Marshall, T. – Joined majority opinion
3. Brennan, W. – Joined majority opinion
4. Black, H. – Joined majority opinion in part
5. Stewart, P. – Joined majority opinion

Opposing Side (Petitioner/Appellant)

1. Burger, W. – Wrote dissenting opinion, joined White's dissent
2. Douglas, W. – Joined Burger's dissent and White's dissent
3. White, B. – Wrote dissenting opinion, joined Burger's dissent

Blackmun, H. – Took no part in the decision.

VI. A WIN OR LOSS FOR THE ACLU?

The ACLU filed an amicus brief urging reversal of the judgment of the U.S. District Court for the District of Massachusetts; the Supreme Court dismissed, in a 5-3 vote, giving the ACLU an apparent win.

235. Oregon v. Mitchell

(Decided December 21, 1970; 400 U.S. 112)

I. ISSUE

A. Issues Discussed

Civil rights, voting rights, Fifteenth Amendment

B. Legal Question Presented

Are certain provisions of the Voting Rights Act Amendments of 1970 constitutional?

C. Supreme Court's Answer

The 18-year-old vote provisions of the Voting Rights Act Amendments of 1970 are constitutional and enforceable insofar as they pertain to federal elections and unconstitutional and unenforceable insofar as they pertain to state and local elections. The literacy-test provisions of the Act are upheld. The residency provisions of the Act are upheld.

II. CASE SUMMARY

A. Background

The States of Oregon, Texas, Arizona, and Idaho challenged three provisions of the Voting Rights Act Amendments of 1970 as unconstitutional, and refused to comply with the conditions. "By its terms the Act does three things. First: It lowers the minimum age of voters in both state and federal elections from 21 to 18. Second: Based upon a finding by Congress that literacy tests have been used to discriminate against voters on account of their color, the Act enforces the Fourteenth and Fifteenth Amendments by barring the use of such tests in all elections, state and national, for a five-year period. Third: The Act forbids States from disqualifying voters in national elections for presidential and vice-presidential electors because they have not met state residency requirements. The States argued that the provisions take "away from them powers reserved to the States by the Constitution to control their own elections."

The Supreme Court granted certiorari and consolidated the cases from the various States.

B. Counsel of Record/ACLU Attorney

ACLU Side (Petitioner/Appellant in Nos. 46 and 47, Respondent/Appellee in Nos. 43 and 44):

Solicitor General Erwin N. Griswold argued the cause for appellants in Nos. 46 and 47, and appellees in Nos. 43 and 44.

Opposing Side (Respondent/Appellee in Nos. 46 and 47, Petitioner/Appellant in Nos. 43 and 44):

Lee Johnson, Attorney General of Oregon, argued the cause for appellant in No. 43. Charles Alan Wright argued the cause for appellant in No. 44. John M. McGowan, II, Special Assistant Attorney General of Arizona, and Gary K. Nelson, Attorney General of Arizona, argued the cause for appellee in No. 46. Robert M. Robson, Attorney General of Idaho, argued the cause for appellee in No. 47.

III. AMICI CURIAE

ACLU Side (Petitioner/Appellant in Nos. 46 and 47, Respondent/Appellee in Nos. 43 and 44):

Brief of amici curiae filed on behalf of the ACLU by Melvin L. Wulf.

Additional briefs of amici curiae were filed on behalf of Citizens for Lowering the Voting Age, et al., the Youth Franchise Coalition, et al., the Democratic National Committee, and the Department of Armed Services and Veterans Affairs of the National Association for the Advancement of Colored People.

Opposing Side (Respondent/Appellee in Nos. 46 and 47, Petitioner/Appellant in Nos. 43 and 44):

Brief of amici curiae filed on behalf of the State of Mississippi by A. F. Summer, Attorney General, Delos Burks, First Assistant Attorney General, William A. Allain, Assistant Attorney General, and Charles B. Henley.

Additional briefs of amici curiae were filed on behalf of the State of Indiana and the Commonwealth of Virginia.

IV. THE SUPREME COURT'S DECISION

"To invalidate part of the Voting Rights Act Amendments of 1970 . . . does not mean that the entire Act must fall or that the constitutional part of the 18-year-old vote provision cannot be given effect. . . .

In this case, it is the judgment of the Court that Title III, lowering the voting age to 18, is invalid as applied to voters in state and local elections. It is also the judgment of the Court that Title III is valid with respect to national elections. We would fail to follow the express will of Congress in interpreting its own statute if we refused to sever these two distinct aspects of Title III. Moreover, legislative enactments are to be enforced to the extent that they are not inconsistent with the Constitution, particularly where the valid portion of the statute does not depend upon the invalid part. Here, of course, the enforcement of the 18-year-old vote in national elections is in no way dependent upon its enforcement in state and local elections. . . .

In enacting the literacy test ban of Title II Congress had before it a long history of the discriminatory use of literacy tests to disfranchise voters on account of their race. . . . Faced with this and other evidence that literacy tests reduce voter participation in a discriminatory manner not only in the South but throughout the Nation, Congress was supported by substantial evidence in concluding that a nationwide ban on literacy tests was appropriate to enforce the Civil War amendments. . . .

In Title II of the Voting Rights Act Amendments Congress also provided that in presidential and vice-presidential elections, no voter could be denied his right to cast a ballot because he had not lived in the jurisdiction long enough to meet its residency requirements. . . . In enacting these regulations Congress was attempting to insure a fully effective voice to all citizens in national elections. . . .

Acting under its broad authority to create and maintain a national government, Congress unquestionably has power under the Constitution to regulate federal elections."

V. JUSTICE VOTE

5 Pro ACLU Side vs. 4 Con Opposing Side

ACLU Side (Petitioner/Appellant in Nos. 46 and 47, Respondent/Appellee in Nos. 43 and 44):

1. Black, H. – Wrote majority opinion
2. Douglas, W. – Wrote concurring opinion
3. Brennan, W. – Wrote concurring opinion

4. White, B. – Joined Brennan's concurrence
5. Marshall, T. – Joined Brennan's concurrence

Opposing Side (Respondent/Appellee in Nos. 46 and 47, Petitioner/Appellant in Nos. 43 and 44):

1. Harlan, J. – Wrote dissenting opinion
2. Stewart, P. – Wrote dissenting opinion
3. Burger, W. – Joined Stewart's dissent
4. Blackmun, H. – Joined Stewart's dissent

VI. A WIN OR LOSS FOR THE ACLU?

The ACLU filed as amicus curiae in support of defendant in No. 43 and No. 44 and in support of plaintiff in No. 46 and No. 47, which in each case was the United States; the Supreme Court ruled mostly in favor of the United States in a 5-4 vote, giving the ACLU an apparent win.

236. Phillips v. Martin Marietta Corp.

(Decided January 25, 1971; 400 U.S. 542)

I. ISSUE

A. Issues Discussed

Civil rights, gender, sex discrimination in employment

B. Legal Question Presented

Can a business have a different hiring plan for women with pre-school age children than it does for men with pre-school age children?

C. Supreme Court's Answer

Different hiring plans for different genders violate the Civil Rights Act of 1964 unless there is a basis for the distinction that falls within § 703(e) of the Act. The case must be remanded to further develop the record and determine whether this hiring plan violates the Act.

II. CASE SUMMARY

A. Background

"Petitioner Mrs. Ida Phillips commenced an action in the United States District Court for the Middle District of Florida under Title VII of the Civil Rights Act of 1964 alleging that she had been denied employment because of her sex. The District Court granted summary judgment for Martin Marietta Corp. . . . on the basis of the following showing: (1) in 1966 Martin informed Mrs. Phillips that it was not accepting job applications from women with pre-school-age children; (2) as of the time of the motion for summary judgment, Martin employed men with pre-school-age children; (3) at the time Mrs. Phillips applied, 70-75% of the applicants for the position she sought were women; 75-80% of those hired for the position, assembly trainee, were women, hence no question of bias against women as such was presented.

The Court of Appeals for the Fifth Circuit affirmed, and denied a rehearing en banc."

The Supreme Court granted certiorari, vacated the judgment, and remanded the case.

B. Counsel of Record/ACLU Attorney

ACLU Side (Petitioner/Appellant): William L. Robinson argued the cause for appellant.

Lawrence G. Wallace argued the cause for the United States, as amicus curiae, by special leave of court.

Opposing Side (Respondent/Appellee): Donald T. Senterfitt argued the cause for appellee.

III. AMICI CURIAE

ACLU Side (Petitioner/Appellant)

Brief of amici curiae filed on behalf of the ACLU by Dorothy Kenyon, Norman Dorsen, Pauli Murray, Joel M. Gora, and Melvin L. Wulf.

Brief of amici curiae filedo n behalf of the United States by Lawrence G. Wallace, Solicitor General Erwin N. Griswold, Assistant Attorney General Leonard, Robert T. Moore, and Stanley P. Hebert.

Additional briefs of amici curiae were filed on behalf of the Air Line Stewards and Stewardesses Association, Local 550, Transport Workers Union of America, AFL-CIO, the Legal Defense and Education Fund, Inc., and Human Rights for Women, Inc.

Opposing Side (Respondent/Appellee)

No briefs of amici curiae were filed in support of appellee.

IV. THE SUPREME COURT'S DECISION

"Section 703(a) of the Civil Rights Act of 1964 requires that persons of like qualifications be given employment opportunities irrespective of their sex. The Court of Appeals therefore erred in reading this section as permitting one hiring policy for women and another for men—each having pre-school-age children. The existence of such conflicting family obligations, if demonstrably more relevant to job performance for a woman than for a man, could arguably be a basis for distinction under § 703(e) of the Act. But that is a matter of evidence tending to show that the condition in question 'is a bona fide occupational qualification reasonably necessary to the normal operation of that particular business or enterprise.' The record before us, however, is not adequate for resolution of these important issues. Summary judgment was therefore improper and we remand for fuller development of the record and for further consideration.

Vacated and remanded."

V. JUSTICE VOTE

9 Pro ACLU Side vs. 0 Con Opposing Side

ACLU Side (Petitioner/Appellant)

1. Burger, W. – Per curiam decision
2. Black, H. – Per curiam decision
3. Douglas, W. – Per curiam decision
4. Harlan, J. – Per curiam decision
5. Brennan, W. – Per curiam decision
6. Stewart, P. – Per curiam decision
7. White, B. – Per curiam decision

8. Blackmun, H. – Per curiam decision
9. Marshall, T. – Wrote concurring opinion

VI. A WIN OR LOSS FOR THE ACLU?

The ACLU filed as amicus curiae urging reversal; the Supreme Court vacated and remanded the ruling of the Court of Appeals for the Fifth Circuit in a 9-0 vote, giving the ACLU an apparent win.

237. Dyson v. Stein

(Decided February 23, 1971; 401 U.S. 200)

I. ISSUE

A. Issues Discussed

Obscenity

B. Legal Question Presented

Whether the declaratory and injunctive relief ordered below were proper.

C. Supreme Court's Answer

"In this case the District Court made no findings of any irreparable injury as defined by our decisions today; therefore, the judgment of the District Court is vacated and the case is remanded for reconsideration . . . ."

II. CASE SUMMARY

A. Background

"The appellee, Stein, published a biweekly newspaper, the Dallas Notes. Stein was charged with two violations of Art. 527, s 1, of the Vernon's Ann. Texas Penal Code, which then prohibited, among other things, the possession of obscene materials. While these two cases were pending in state courts, Stein brought the present action in a federal district court under 42 U.S.C. ss 1983, 1985, representing himself and a class consisting of present and future employees of and contributors to his newspaper. The defendants were the district attorney of Dallas County, and the Dallas chief of police. . . .

A three-judge court was convened. That court refused to require a hearing on the obscene character of the material before its seizure and the arrest of the plaintiff. It held that the request for such relief was 'based on the alleged harassment and . . . not an attack upon the constitutionality of a statute.' The court went on to emphasize that its consideration did 'not in any way involve an appraisal of the constitutionality of the application of Article 527 to Plaintiff. Our sole concern is the determination of whether the statute is constitutionally defective on its face.' The three-judge court then turned to the statute itself, and held that ss 1 and 2 were unconstitutional, and that s 3 would be constitutional only if the definition of obscenity were changed somewhat. The court issued appropriate declaratory and injunctive relief effectuating its conclusions. Texas officials appealed, and [the U.S. Supreme Court] noted probable jurisdiction."

B. Counsel of Record

ACLU Side (Respondent/Appellee): David R. Richards reargued the cause for appellee. With him on the briefs were Melvin L. Wulf and Joel M. Gora of the American Civil Liberties Union

Opposing Side (Petitioner/Appellant): Lonny F. Zwiener, Assistant Attorney General of Texas, reargued the cause for appellants. With him on the brief were Crawford C. Martin, Attorney General, Nola White, First Assistant Attorney General, Pat Bailey, Executive Assistant Attorney General, Robert C. Flowers, Assistant Attorney General, Henry Wade, pro se, Wilson Johnston, N. Alex Bickley, Thomas B. Thorpe, and Preston Dial.

III. AMICI CURIAE

ACLU Side (Respondent/Appellee)

Brief of amici curiae filed on behalf of Stanley Fleishman et al., by Stanley Fleishman, pro se.

Opposing Side (Petitioner/Appellant)

No briefs of amici curiae were filed in support of appellees.

IV. THE SUPREME COURT'S DECISION

"Today we have again stressed the rule that federal intervention affecting pending state criminal prosecutions, either by injunction or by declaratory judgment, is proper only where irreparable injury is threatened. The existence of such injury is a matter to be determined carefully under the facts of each case. In this case the District Court made no findings of any irreparable injury as defined by our decisions today; therefore, the judgment of the District Court is vacated and the case is remanded for reconsideration in light of Younger v. Harris, 401 U.S. 37, and Samuels v. Mackell, 401 U.S. 66. . . .

Vacated and remanded."

V. JUSTICE VOTE

1 Pro ACLU Side vs. 8 Con Opposing Side

ACLU Side (Respondent/Appellee)

1. Douglas, W. – Wrote dissenting opinion

Opposing Side (Petitioner/Appellant)

1. Harlan, J. – Per curiam decision
2. Marshall, T. – Joined Brennan's concurrence
3. Brennan, W. – Wrote concurring opinion
4. Black, H. – Per curiam decision
5. Stewart, P. – Wrote concurring opinion
6. Burger, W. – Per curiam decision
7. White, B. – Concurs in the result
8. Blackmun, H. – Per curiam decision

VI. A WIN OR LOSS FOR THE ACLU?

The ACLU served as counsel for appellee urging reversal of the judgment of the U.S. District Court for the Northern District of Texas; the Supreme Court vacated in an 8-1 vote, giving the

ACLU an apparent loss.

238. Byrne v. Karalexis

(Decided February 23, 1971; 401 U.S. 216)

I. ISSUE

A. Issues Discussed

First Amendment, obscenity, injunctions

B. Legal Question Presented

Does a single criminal prosecution meet the irreparable injury requirement necessary for granting injunctive relief?

C. Supreme Court's Answer

The case must be remanded to make this determination in light of Supreme Court decisions issued this same day.

II. CASE SUMMARY

A. Background

"This is an appeal from the order of a three-judge court granting a preliminary injunction against any civil or criminal proceedings in state courts against the appellees. Appellant Byrne is the district attorney of Suffolk County, Massachusetts. The appellees own and operate a motion picture theater in Boston. As a result of exhibiting the film entitled 'I am Curious (Yellow)' at their theater, appellees where charged by District Attorney Byrne with violating Massachusetts General Laws, Chapter 272, § 28A, which prohibits the possession of obscene films for the purpose of exhibition.

After the filing of the original state indictments against them appellees brought the present action in federal court. They sought an injunction against both pending and future prosecutions under the Massachusetts obscenity law, and a declaration that the state obscenity law was unconstitutional on its face and as applied. The three-judge District Court held that appellees had a probability of success in having the statute declared unconstitutional, that abstention would be improper, and that appellees might suffer irreparable injury if they were unable to show the film. The three-judge court, one judge dissenting, therefore granted a preliminary injunction, forbidding the initiation of any future prosecutions or the execution of the sentence imposed in the state proceedings then pending. The district attorney appealed. [The Supreme Court] granted a stay of the district court order, and subsequently noted probable jurisdiction."

The Supreme Court vacated the judgment and remanded the case.

B. Counsel of Record/ACLU Attorney

ACLU Side (Respondent/Appellee): Edward de Grazi argued the cause for appellee on the original argument. Nathan Lewin and Alan M. Dershowitz argued the cause for appellee on reargument.

Opposing Side (Petitioner/Appellant): Robert H. Quinn, Attorney General of Massachusetts, pro se, argued the cause for appellant.

Francis X. Beytagh, Jr., argued the cause on the original argument, and Peter L. Straus argued the cause on the reargument, for the United States, as amicus curiae.

III. AMICI CURIAE

ACLU Side (Petitioner/Appellant)

Brief of amici curiae filed on behalf of the ACLU, et al., by Thomas R. Asher, Michael Schneiderman, and Melvin L. Wulf.

Brief of amici curiae filed on behalf of the National General Corp., et al., by Stanley Fleishman and Sam Rosenwein.

Opposing Side (Respondent/Appellee)

Brief of amici curiae filed on behalf of the United States by Francis X. Beytagh, Jr., Peter L. Strauss, Solicitor General Erwin N. Griswold, Assistant Attorney General Wilson, Jerome M. Feit, and Roger A. Pauley.

IV. THE SUPREME COURT'S DECISION

"There was, however, no finding by the District Court that the threat to appellees' federally protected rights is 'one that cannot be eliminated by [their] defense against a single criminal prosecution.' Because the District Court, in considering the propriety of injunctive and declaratory relief in this case, was without the guidance provided today by our decisions in Younger v. Harris, supra, and Samuels v. Mackell, 401 U.S. 66, we vacate the judgment below and remand for reconsideration in light of those decisions."

V. JUSTICE VOTE

3 Pro ACLU Side vs. 5 Con Opposing Side

ACLU Side (Petitioner/Appellant)

1. Brennan, W. – Wrote dissenting opinion
2. White, B. – Joined dissenting opinion
3. Marshall, T. – Joined dissenting opinion

Opposing Side (Respondent/Appellee)

1. Burger, W. – Per curiam decision
2. Black, H. – Per curiam decision
3. Harlan, J. – Per curiam decision
4. Stewart, P. – Per curiam decision
5. Blackmun, H. – Per curiam decision

Douglas, W. – Took no part in the decision

VI. A WIN OR LOSS FOR THE ACLU?

The ACLU filed as amicus curiae urging affirmance; the Supreme Court reversed and remanded in a 5-3 vote, giving the ACLU an apparent loss.

239. Gillette v. United States

(Decided March 8, 1971; 401 U.S. 437)

I. ISSUE

A. Issues Discussed

Religion

B. Legal Question Presented

"These cases present the question whether conscientious objection to a particular war, rather than objection to war as such, relieves the objector from responsibilities of military training and service. Specifically, we are called upon to decide whether conscientious scruples relating to a particular conflict are within the purview of established provisions relieving conscientious objectors to war from military service."

C. Supreme Court's Answer

"[W]e hold that Congress intended to exempt persons who oppose participating in all war—'participation in war in any form'—and that persons who object solely to participation in a particular war are not within the purview of the exempting section, even though the latter objection may have such roots in a claimant's conscience and personality that it is 'religious' in character."

II. CASE SUMMARY

A. Background

"In No. 85, petitioner Gillette was convicted of wilful failure to report for induction into the armed forces. Gillette defended on the ground that he should have been ruled exempt from induction as a conscientious objector to war. . . . Petitioner concluded that he could not in conscience enter and serve in the armed forces during the period of the Vietnam conflict. Gillette's view of his duty to abstain from any involvement in a war seen as unjust is, in his words, 'based on a humanist approach to religion' . . . .

The District Court determined that there was a basis in fact to support administrative denial of exemption in Gillette's case. . . . In affirming the conviction, the Court of Appeals concluded that Gillette's conscientious beliefs 'were specifically directed against the war in Vietnam,' while the relevant exemption provision of the Military Selective Service Act of 1967, 'requires opposition 'to participation in war in any form."

In No. 325, petitioner Negre . . . commenced proceedings looking to his discharge as a conscientious objector to war. Application for discharge was denied, and Negre sought . . . habeas corpus. The District Court found a basis in fact for the Army's rejection of petitioner's application for discharge. Habeas relief was denied, and the denial was affirmed on appeal, because, in the language of the Court of Appeals, Negre 'objects to the war in Vietnam, not to all wars,' and therefore does 'not qualify for separation (from the Army), as a conscientious objector.' . . .

[The U.S. Supreme Court] granted certiorari in these cases in order to resolve vital issues concerning the exercise of congressional power to raise and support armies, as affected by the religious guarantees of the First Amendment."

B. Counsel of Record

ACLU Side (Petitioner/Appellant): Conrad J. Lynn argued the cause for appellant in No. 85. With him on the brief were Melvin L. Wulf of the American Civil Liberties Union Foundation, Leon Friedman, and Marvin M. Karpatkin. Richard Harrington argued the cause for appellant in No. 325. With him on the briefs were Leigh Athearn, Stuart J. Land, and John T. Noonan, Jr.

Opposing Side (Respondent/Appellee): Solicitor General Griswold argued the cause for the United States and for the other appellees in both cases. With him on the briefs were Assistant Attorney General Wilson and Beatrice Rosenberg.

III. AMICI CURIAE

ACLU Side (Petitioner/Appellant)

Brief of amici curiae filed on behalf of George T. Altman by George T. Altman, pro se.

Brief of amici curiae filed on behalf of the American Ethical Union by Leo Rosen.

Brief of amici curiae filed on behalf of the National Council of the Churches of Christ in the U. S. A. et al. by Charles H. Tuttle and Thomas A. Shaw, Jr.

Brief of amici curiae filed on behalf of the Executive Board of the National Federation of Priests' Councils by Peter J. Donnici.

Brief of amici curiae filed on behalf of the American Jewish Congress by Joseph B. Robison, Ephraim Margolin, Stanley J. Friedman, Seymour Farber, and Edwin J. Lukas.

Brief of amici curiae filed on behalf of Louis P. Font by Michael N. Pollet and Elsbeth Levy Bothe.

Brief of amici curiae filed on behalf of the American Friends Service Committee.

Opposing Side (Respondent/Appellee)

No briefs of amici curiae were filed in support of appellees.

IV. THE SUPREME COURT'S DECISION

"Each petitioner claims a nonconstitutional right to be relieved of the duty of military service in virtue of his conscientious scruples. Both claims turn on the proper construction of s 6(j) of the Military Selective Service Act of 1967 . . . .

For purposes of determining the statutory status of conscientious objection to a particular war, the focal language of s 6(j) is the phrase, 'conscientiously opposed to participation in war in any form.' This language, on a straightforward reading, can bear but one meaning; that conscientious scruples relating to war and military service must amount to conscientious opposition to participating personally in any war and all war. . . . Thus, however the statutory clause be parsed, it remains that conscientious objection must run to war in any form.

A different result cannot be supported by reliance on the materials of legislative history. . . .

It should be emphasized that our cases explicating the 'religious training and belief' clause of s 6(j), or cognate clauses of predecessor provisions, are not relevant to the present issue. The question here is not whether these petitioners' beliefs concerning war are 'religious' in nature. . . . Nor do we decide that conscientious objection to a particular war necessarily falls within s 6(j)'s expressly excluded class of 'essentially political, sociological, or philosophical views, or a merely personal moral code.' Rather, we hold that Congress intended to exempt persons who oppose participating in all war—'participation in war in any form'—and that persons who object solely to participation in a particular war are not within the purview of the exempting section, even though the latter objection may have such roots in a claimant's conscience and personality that it is 'religious' in character. . . .

We conclude not only that the affirmative purposes underlying s 6(j) are neutral and secular, but also that valid neutral reasons exist for limiting the exemption to objectors to all war, and that the section therefore cannot be said to reflect a religious preference. . . .

Of course, we do not suggest that Congress would have acted irrationally or unreasonably had it decided to exempt those who object to particular wars. Our analysis of the policies of s 6(j) is undertaken in order to determine the existence vel non of a neutral, secular justification for the lines Congress has drawn. We find that justifying reasons exist and therefore hold that the Establishment Clause is not violated. . . .

Since petitioners' statutory and constitutional claims to relief from military service are without merit, it follows that in Gillette's case (No. 85) there was a basis in fact to support administrative denial of exemption, and that in Negre's case (No. 325) there was a basis in fact to support the Army's denial of a discharge. Accordingly, the judgments below are affirmed."

V. JUSTICE VOTE

1 Pro ACLU Side vs. 8 Con Opposing Side

ACLU Side (Petitioner/Appellant)

1. Douglas, W. – Wrote dissenting opinions

Opposing Side (Respondent/Appellee)

1. Marshall, T. – Wrote majority opinion
2. Harlan, J. – Joined majority opinion
3. Brennan, W. – Joined majority opinion
4. Black, H. – Concurred in the judgment
5. Stewart, P. – Joined majority opinion
6. Burger, W. – Joined majority opinion
7. White, B. – Joined majority opinion
8. Blackmun, H. – Joined majority opinion

VI. A WIN OR LOSS FOR THE ACLU?

The ACLU served as counsel for appellant urging reversal of the judgments of the Court of Appeals; the Supreme Court affirmed in an 8-1 vote, giving the ACLU an apparent loss.

240. Schlanger v. Seamans

(Decided March 23, 1971; 401 U.S. 487)

I. ISSUE

A. Issues Discussed

Governmental authority, military, habeas corpus

B. Legal Question Presented

"[W]hether the District Court for the District of Arizona had jurisdiction to entertain on the merits petitioner's application for a writ of habeas corpus."

C. Supreme Court's Answer

The District Court did not have jurisdiction to entertain on the merits petitioner's application for a writ of habeas corpus.

II. CASE SUMMARY

A. Background

Petitioner "is an enlisted man who was accepted in the Airman's Education and Commissioning Program, an officer training project, and was assigned to Wright-Patterson Air Force Base (AFB), Ohio, 'with duty at Arizona State University' for training. While studying in Arizona and before completion of the course, he was removed from the program, allegedly for engaging in civil rights activities on the campus.

While he was seeking administrative relief through command channels, he was reassigned to Moody AFB, Georgia, to complete the remainder of his six-year reenlistment in a noncommissioned status. After exhausting those remedies he was given permissive temporary duty to attend Arizona State for study, this time by his superiors at Moody AFB under a different program called Operation Bootstrap, and at his own expense.

Thereafter he filed his application for habeas corpus in Arizona alleging that his enlistment contract had been breached and that he was being detained unlawfully. The District Court denied the application. The Court of Appeals affirmed on the basis of *Jarrett v. Resor*, 426 F.2d 213."

The Supreme Court granted certiorari and affirmed.

B. Counsel of Record/ACLU Attorney

ACLU Side (Petitioner/Appellant): Herbert Phillip Schlanger argued the cause, pro se.

Opposing Side (Respondent/Appellee): Solicitor General Erwin N. Griswold argued the cause for appellee.

III. AMICI CURIAE

ACLU Side (Petitioner/Appellant)

Brief of amici curiae filed on behalf of the ACLU by Melvin L. Wulf.

Opposing Side (Respondent/Appellee)

No briefs of amici curiae were filed in support of appellee.

IV. THE SUPREME COURT'S DECISION

"The procedure governing issuance of the writ is provided by statute. The federal courts may grant the writ 'within their respective jurisdictions.' While the Act speaks of 'a prisoner,' the term has been liberally construed to include members of the armed services who have been unlawfully detained, restrained, or confined. The Act extends to those 'in custody under or by color of the authority of the United States.' The question in the instant case is whether any custodian, or one in the chain of command, as well as the person detained, must be in the territorial jurisdiction of the District Court.

In Ahren v. Clark, we held that it was not sufficient if the custodian alone be found in the jurisdiction where the persons detained were outside the jurisdiction, and that jurisdiction over the respondent was territorial. The dissent in that case thought that the critical element was not where the applicant was confined, but where the custodian was located; that, if the custodian were in the territorial jurisdiction of the District Court, then appropriate relief could be effected.

Whichever view is taken of the problem in Ahrens v. Clark, the case is of little help here. For while petitioner is within the territorial jurisdiction of the District Court, the custodian—the Commander of Moody AFB—is not. In other words, even under the minority view in Ahrens v. Clark, the District Court in Arizona has no custodian within its reach against whom its writ can run. Hence, even if we assume that petitioner is 'in custody' in Arizona in the sense that he is subject to military orders and control which act as a restraint on his freedom of movement, the absence of his custodian is fatal to the jurisdiction of the Arizona District Court.

Had petitioner, at the time of the filing of the petition, been under the command of the Air Force officer assigned as liaison officer at Arizona State to supervise the Education and Commissioning Program, we would have a different question. We do not reach it nor do we reach any aspects of the merits, viz., whether, if petitioner is right in contending that his contract of enlistment was breached, habeas corpus is the appropriate remedy."

The Supreme Court affirmed the judgment of the Court of Appeals.

V. JUSTICE VOTE

1 Pro ACLU Side vs. 8 Con Opposing Side

ACLU Side (Petitioner/Appellant)

1. Stewart, P. – Dissented without an opinion

Opposing Side (Respondent/Appellee)

1. Douglas, W. – Wrote majority opinion
2. Marshall, T. – Joined majority opinion
3. Brennan, W. – Joined majority opinion
4. White B. – Joined majority opinion
5. Harlan, J. – Concurred in the result
6. Blackmun, H. – Joined majority opinion
7. Burger, W. – Joined majority opinion
8. Black, H. – Joined majority opinion

VI. A WIN OR LOSS FOR THE ACLU?

The ACLU filed as amicus curiae urging reversal; the Supreme Court affirmed the ruling of the United States Court of Appeals for the Ninth Circuit in an 8-1 vote, giving the ACLU an apparent loss.

241. Labine v. Vincent

(Decided March 29, 1971; 401 U.S. 532)

I. ISSUE

A. Issues Discussed

Civil rights, state's rights, Fourteenth Amendment, equal protection, due process

B. Legal Question Presented

Are articles of the Louisiana Civil Code distinguishing between legitimate and illegitimate children for the purpose of the laws of intestate succession violative of the Equal Protection Clause or Due Process Clause of the Fourteenth Amendment?

C. Supreme Court's Answer

The articles distinguishing between legitimate and illegitimate children for the purposes of intestate succession do not violate the Equal Protection Clause or Due Process Clause.

II. CASE SUMMARY

A. Background

"On March 15, 1962, a baby girl, Rita Vincent , was born to Lou Bertha Patterson (now Lou Bertha Labine) in Calcasieu Parish, Louisiana. On May 10, 1962, Lou Bertha Patterson and Ezra Vincent , as authorized by Louisiana law, jointly executed before a notary a Louisiana State Board of Health form acknowledging that Ezra Vincent was the 'natural father' of Rita Vincent. This public acknowledgment of parentage did not, under Louisiana law, give the child a legal right to share equally with legitimate children in the parent's estate but it did give her a right to claim support from her parents or their heirs. The acknowledgment also gave the child the capacity under Louisiana law to be a limited beneficiary under her father's will in the event he left a will naming her, which he did not do here.

Ezra Vincent died intestate, that is, without a will, on September 16, 1968, in Rapides Parish, Louisiana, leaving substantial property within the State, but no will to direct its distribution. Appellant, as the guardian of Rita Vincent, petitioned in state court for the appointment of an administrator for the father's estate; for a declaration that Rita Vincent is the sole heir of Ezra Vincent; and for an order directing the administrator to pay support and maintenance for the child. In the alternative, appellant sought a declaration that the child was entitled to support and maintenance of $150 per month under a Louisiana child support law.

The administrator of the succession of Ezra Vincent answered the petition claiming that Vincent's relatives were entitled to the whole estate. . . . The court ruled that the relatives of the father were his collateral relations and that under Louisiana's laws of intestate succession took his property to the exclusion of acknowledged, but not legitimated, illegitimate children. The court, therefore, dismissed with costs the guardian mother's petition to recognize the child as an heir. The court also ruled that in view of Social Security payments of $60 per month and Veterans Administration payments of $40 per month available for the support of the child, the guardian for the child was not entitled to support or maintenance from the succession of Ezra Vincent. The Louisiana Court of Appeal, Third Circuit, affirmed, and the Supreme Court of Louisiana denied a petition for writ of certiorari. The child's guardian appealed and [the Supreme Court] noted probable jurisdiction."

The Supreme Court affirmed the decision.

B. Counsel of Record / ACLU Attorney

ACLU Side (Petitioner / Appellant): James J. Cox argued the cause for appellant.

Opposing Side (Respondent / Appellee): James A. Leithead argued the cause for appellee.

III. AMICI CURIAE

ACLU Side (Petitioner / Appellant)

Brief of amici curiae filed on behalf of the ACLU by Harry D. Krause, Norman Dorsen, and Melvin L. Wulf.

Brief of amici curiae filed on behalf of the Center on Social Welfare Policy and Law by Jonathan Weis and David Gilman.

Opposing Side (Respondent / Appellee)

Brief of amici curiae filed on behalf of the Buras Heirs and the Heirs of Earl O. Strahan by A. Leon Hebert and E. Drew McKinnis.

IV. THE SUPREME COURT'S DECISION

"These rules for intestate succession may or may not reflect the intent of particular parents. Many will think that it is unfortunate that the rules are so rigid. Others will think differently. But the choices reflected by the intestate succession statute are choices which it is within the power of the State to make. The Federal Constitution does not give this Court the power to overturn the State's choice under the guise of constitutional interpretation because the Justices of this Court believe that they can provide better rules. Of course, it may be said that the rules adopted by the Louisiana Legislature 'discriminate' against illegitimates. But the rules also discriminate against collateral relations, as opposed to ascendants, and against ascendants, as opposed to descendants. Other rules determining property rights based on family status also 'discriminate' in favor of wives and against 'concubines.' The dissent attempts to distinguish these other 'discriminations' on the ground that they have a biological or social basis. There is no biological difference between a wife and a concubine nor does the Constitution require that there be such a difference before the State may assert its power to protect the wife and her children against the claims of a concubine and her children. The social difference between a wife and a concubine is analogous to the difference between a legitimate and an illegitimate child. One set of relationships is socially sanctioned, legally recognized, and gives rise to various rights and duties. The other set of relationships is illicit and beyond the recognition of the law. Similarly, the State does not need biological or social reasons for distinguishing between ascendants and descendants. Some of these discriminatory choices are perhaps more closely connected to our conceptions of social justice or the ways in which most dying men wish to dispose of their property than the Louisiana rules governing illegitimate children. It may be possible that some of these choices are more 'rational' than the choices inherent in Louisiana's categories of illegitimates. But the power to make rules to establish, protect, and strengthen family life as well as to regulate the disposition of property left in Louisiana by a man dying there is committed by the Constitution of the United States and the people of Louisiana to the legislature of that State. Absent a specific constitutional guarantee, it is for that legislature, not the life-tenured judges of this Court, to select from among possible laws. We cannot say that Louisiana's policy provides a perfect or even a desirable solution or the one we would have provided for the problem of the property rights of illegitimate children. Neither can we say that Louisiana does not have the power to make laws for distribution of property left within the State. . . .

There is not the slightest suggestion in this case that Louisiana has barred this illegitimate from inheriting from her father. Ezra Vincent could have left one-third of his property to his illegitimate daughter had he bothered to follow the simple formalities of executing a will. He could, of course, have legitimated the child by marrying her mother in which case the child could have inherited his property either by intestate succession or by will as any other legitimate child. Finally, he could have awarded his child the benefit of Louisiana's intestate succession statute on the same terms as legitimate children simply by stating in his acknowledgment of paternity his desire to legitimate the little girl.

In short, we conclude that in the circumstances presented in this case, there is nothing in the vague generalities of the Equal Protection and Due Process Clauses which empowers this Court to nullify the deliberate choices of the elected representatives of the people of Louisiana."

The Supreme Court affirmed the judgment.

V. JUSTICE VOTE

4 Pro ACLU Side vs. 5 Con Opposing Side

ACLU Side (Petitioner / Appellant)

1. Brennan, W. – Wrote dissenting opinion
2. Douglas, W. – Joined Brennan's dissent
3. White, B. – Joined Brennan's dissent
4. Marshall, T. – Joined Brennan's dissent

Opposing Side (Respondent / Appellee)

1. Black, H. – Wrote majority opinion
2. Harlan, J. – Wrote concurring opinion
3. Burger, W. – Joined majority opinion
4. Stewart, P. – Joined majority opinion
5. Blackmun, H. – Joined majority opinion

VI. A WIN OR LOSS FOR THE ACLU?

The ACLU filed as amicus curiae urging reversal; the U.S. Supreme Court affirmed the ruling of the Supreme Court of Louisiana in a 5-4 vote, giving the ACLU an apparent loss.

242. United States v. Vuitch

(Decided April 21, 1971; 402 U.S. 62)

I. ISSUE

A. Issues Discussed

Civil rights, privacy, abortion, First Amendment, Fifth Amendment

B. Legal Question Presented

First, whether the Supreme Court has "jurisdiction under the Criminal Appeals Act to entertain this direct appeal from the United States District Court for the District of Columbia." Second, whether the District of Columbia abortion statute is unconstitutionally vague.

C. Supreme Court's Answer

The Supreme Court has jurisdiction to entertain the appeal and the statute is not unconstitutionally vague.

II. CASE SUMMARY

A. Background

"Appellee Milan Vuitch, a licensed physician, was indicted in the United States District Court for the District of Columbia for producing and attempting to produce abortions in violation of D.C. Code Ann. § 22—201 (1967). Before trial, the district judge granted Vuitch's motion to dismiss the indictments on the ground that the District of Columbia abortion law was unconstitutionally vague. The United States appealed to [the Supreme] Court under the Criminal Appeals Act, 18 U.S.C. § 3731. [The Supreme Court] postponed decision on jurisdiction to the hearing on the merits, and requested the parties to brief and argue specified questions on that issue."

The Supreme Court held that they had jurisdiction and the statute was not unconstitutionally vague.

B. Counsel of Record/ACLU Attorney

ACLU Side (Respondent/Appellee): Joseph L. Nellis and Norman Dorsen argued the cause for appellee. With them on the brief were Joseph Sitnick and Roy Lucas.

Opposing Side (Petitioner/Appellant): Samuel Huntington argued the cause for appellant. With him on the brief were Solicitor General Erwin N. Griswold, Assistant Attorney General Wilson, Jerome M. Feit, and Roger A. Pauley.

III. AMICI CURIAE

ACLU Side (Respondent/Appellee)

Brief of amici curiae filed on behalf of the ACLU, et al., by Ralph Temple, Marvin J. Diamond, Melvin L. Wulf, and Norma G. Zarky.

Briefs as amicus curiae were filed on behalf of the National Legal Program on Health Problems of the Poor, Human Rights for Women, Inc., and the Joint Washington Office for Social Concern, et al.

Opposing Side (Petitioner/Appellant)

Briefs of amicus curiae were filed on behalf of Dr. William F. Colliton, Jr., et al., Robert L. Sassone, and Dr. Bart Heffernan.

IV. THE SUPREME COURT'S DECISION

"We hold . . . that once an appeal is properly here under the Criminal Appeals Act, we should not refuse to consider it because it might have been taken to another court. . . .

The statute does not outlaw all abortions, but only those which are not performed under the direction of a competent, licensed physician, and those not necessary to preserve the mother's life or health. It is a general guide to the interpretation of criminal statutes that when an exception is incorporated in the enacting clause of a statute, the burden is on the prosecution to plead and prove that the defendant is not within the exception. When Congress passed the District of Columbia abortion law in 1901 and amended it in 1953, it expressly authorized physicians to perform such abortions as are necessary to preserve the mother's 'life or health.' Because abortions were authorized only in more restrictive circumstances under previous D.C. law, the change must represent a judgment by Congress that it is desirable that women be able to obtain abortions needed for the preservation of their lives or health. It would be highly anomalous for a legislature to authorize abortions necessary for life or health and then to demand that a doctor, upon pain of one to ten years' imprisonment, bear the burden of proving that an abortion he performed fell within that category. Placing such a burden of proof on a doctor would be peculiarly inconsistent with society's notions of the responsibilities of the medical profession. Generally, doctors are encouraged by society's expectations, by the strictures of malpractice law and by their own professional standards to give their patients such treatment as is necessary to preserve their health. We are unable to believe that Congress intended that a physician be required to prove his innocence. We therefore hold that under D.C.Code Ann. § 22—201, the burden is on the prosecution to plead and prove that an abortion was not 'necessary for the preservation of the mother's life or health.'

There remains the contention that the word 'health' is so imprecise and has so uncertain a meaning that it fails to inform a defendant of the charge against him and therefore the statute offends the Due Process Clause of the Constitution. We hold that it does not. . . . Indeed,

> whether a particular operation is necessary for a patient's physical or mental health is a judgment that physicians are obviously called upon to make routinely whenever surgery is considered.

We therefore hold that properly construed the District of Columbia abortion law is not unconstitutionally vague, and that the trial court erred in dismissing the indictments on that ground."

The Supreme Court reversed the judgment and remanded the case.

V. JUSTICE VOTE

4 Pro ACLU Side vs. 5 Con Opposing Side

ACLU Side (Respondent/Appellee)

1. Douglas, W. – Wrote opinion dissenting in part
2. Marshall, T. – Joined Harlan's jurisdictional dissent
3. Stewart, P. – Wrote opinion dissenting in part
4. Brennan, W. – Wrote dissenting opinion, joined Harlan's jurisdictional dissent

Opposing Side (Petitioner/Appellant)

1. Black, H. – Wrote majority opinion
2. Burger, W. – Joined majority opinion
3. Harlan, J. – Wrote opinion dissenting as to jurisdiction, but concurring as to the merits
4. Blackmun, H. – Wrote concurring opinion, joined Harlan's jurisdictional dissent
5. White, B. – Wrote concurring opinion

VI. A WIN OR LOSS FOR THE ACLU?

The ACLU filed as amicus curiae and argued the cause urging affirmance; the Supreme Court reversed and remanded the ruling of the US District Court for the District of Columbia in a 5-4 vote, giving the ACLU an apparent loss.

243. Ehlert v. United States

(Decided April 21, 1971; 402 U.S. 99)

I. ISSUE

A. Issues Discussed

Military

B. Legal Question Presented

"[W]hether a Selective Service local board must reopen the classification of a registrant who claims that his conscientious objection to war in any form crystallized between the mailing of his notice to report for induction and his scheduled induction date."

C. Supreme Court's Answer

"Given the prevailing interpretation of the Army regulation, we hold that the Court of Appeals did not misconstrue the Selective Service regulation in holding that it barred presentation to the local board of a claim that allegedly arose between mailing of a notice of induction and the scheduled induction date."

II. CASE SUMMARY

A. Background

"The question in this case is whether a Selective Service local board must reopen the classification of a registrant who claims that his conscientious objection to war in any form crystallized between the mailing of his notice to report for induction and his scheduled induction date. The petitioner before us made no claim to conscientious objector status until after he received his induction notice. Before the induction date, he then wrote to his local board and asked to be allowed to present his claim. He represented that his views had matured only after the induction notice had made immediate the prospect of military service. After Selective Service proceedings not material here, the petitioner's local board notified him that it had declined to reopen his classification because the crystallization of his conscientious objection did not constitute the 'change in the registrant's status resulting from circumstances over which the registrant had no control' required for post-induction notice reopening under a Selective Service regulation. The petitioner then refused to submit to induction, and a grand jury in the United States District Court for the Northern District of California indicted him for violation of the Military Selective Service Act of 1967.

The petitioner waived trial by jury, and the District Court, holding that ripening of conscientious objector views could not be a circumstance over which a registrant had no control, found the petitioner guilty. The conviction was affirmed by the United States Court of Appeals for the Ninth Circuit, sitting en banc, and we granted certiorari to resolve a conflict among the circuits over the interpretation of the governing Selective Service regulation."

B. Counsel of Record

ACLU Side (Petitioner/Appellant): Paul N. Halvonik of the American Civil Liberties Union of Northern California argued the cause for appellant. With him on the briefs were Charles C. Marson of the American Civil Liberties Union of Northern California, Stanley J. Friedman, Mortimer H. Herzstein, Nell Horton, and Marvin M. Karpatkin.

Opposing Side (Respondent/Appellee): Assistant Attorney General Rehnquist argued the cause for the United States. With him on the brief were Solicitor General Griswold, Assistant Attorney General Wilson, Beatrice Rosenberg, and Marshall Tamor Golding.

III. AMICI CURIAE

ACLU Side (Petitioner/Appellant)

Brief of amici curiae filed on behalf of the Lawyers' Selective Service Panel of San Francisco by Norman Leonard.

Opposing Side (Respondent/Appellee)

No briefs of amici curiae were filed in support of appellees.

IV. THE SUPREME COURT'S DECISION

"A regulation explicitly providing that no conscientious objector claim could be considered by a local board unless filed before the mailing of an induction notice would, we think, be perfectly valid, provided that no inductee could be ordered to combatant training or service before a prompt, fair, and proper in-service determination of his claim. The Military Selective Service Act of 1967 confers on the President authority 'to prescribe the necessary rules and regulations to carry out the provisions of this title . . . .' To read out of the authority delegated by this section the power to make reasonable timeliness rules would render it impossible to require the submission, before mailing of an induction notice, of a claim matured before that time. The System needs and has the power to make reasonable timeliness rules for the presentation of claims to exemption from service. . . .

That those whose views are late in crystallizing can be required to wait, however, does not mean they can be deprived of a full and fair opportunity to present the merits of their conscientious objector claims for consideration under the same substantive criteria that must guide the Selective Service System. The very assertion of crystallization just before induction might cast doubt upon the genuineness of some claims, but there is no reason to suppose that such claims could not be every bit as bona fide and substantial as the claims of those whose conscientious objection ripens before notice or after induction. It would be wholly arbitrary to deny the late crystallizer a full opportunity to obtain a determination on the merits of his claim to exemption from combatant training and service just because his conscientious scruples took shape during a brief period in legal limbo. A system in which such persons could present their claims after induction, with the assurance of no combatant training or service before opportunity for a ruling on the merits, would be wholly consistent with the conscientious objector statute.

The regulation we must interpret in this case does not unambiguously create such a system. Rather, it bars post-notice reopening 'unless the local board first specifically finds there has been a change in the registrant's status resulting from circumstances over which the registrant had no control.' It is clear that the regulation was meant to cover at least such nonvolitional changes as injury to the registrant or death in his family making him the sole surviving son. . . .

Given the prevailing interpretation of the Army regulation, we hold that the Court of Appeals did not misconstrue the Selective Service regulation in holding that it barred presentation to the local board of a claim that allegedly arose between mailing of a notice of induction and the scheduled induction date. Accordingly the judgment of the Court of Appeals for the Ninth Circuit is affirmed."

V. JUSTICE VOTE

3 Pro ACLU Side vs. 6 Con Opposing Side

ACLU Side (Petitioner/Appellant)

1. Marshall, T. – Joined Brennan's dissent
2. Brennan, W. – Wrote dissenting opinion
3. Douglas, W. – Wrote dissenting opinion

Opposing Side (Respondent/Appellee)

1. Stewart, P. – Wrote majority opinion
2. Black, H. – Joined majority opinion
3. Harlan, J. – Joined majority opinion
4. Burger, W. – Joined majority opinion
5. White, B. – Joined majority opinion
6. Blackmun, H. – Joined majority opinion

VI. A WIN OR LOSS FOR THE ACLU?

The ACLU served as counsel for appellant urging reversal of the judgment of the Court of Appeals; the Supreme Court affirmed, in a 6-3 vote, giving the ACLU an apparent loss.

244. McGautha v. California

(Decided May 3, 1971; 402 U.S. 183)

I. ISSUE

A. Issues Discussed

Criminal justice, death penalty, Eighth Amendment, Fourteenth Amendment

B. Legal Question Presented

"[W]hether petitioner's constitutional rights were infringed by permitting the jury to impose the death penalty without any governing standards," and "whether the jury's imposition of the death sentence in the same proceeding and verdict as determined the issue of guilt was constitutionally permissible."

C. Supreme Court's Answer

Petitioner's constitutional rights were not infringed by the imposition of the death penalty without governing standards, and it was constitutionally permissible to determine guilt and the death sentence in the same proceeding and verdict.

II. CASE SUMMARY

A. Background

"Petitioners McGautha and Crampton were convicted of murder in the first degree in the courts of California and Ohio respectively, and sentenced to death pursuant to the statutes of those States. In each case, the decision whether the defendant should live or die was left to the absolute discretion of the jury. In McGautha's case, the jury, in accordance with California law, determined punishment in a separate proceeding following the trial on the issue of guilt. In Crampton's case, in accordance with Ohio law, the jury determined guilt and punishment after a single trial and in a single verdict. [The Supreme Court] granted certiorari in the McGautha case limited to the question whether petitioner's constitutional rights were infringed by permitting the jury to impose the death penalty without any governing standards. [The Supreme Court] granted certiorari in the Crampton case limited to that same question and to the further question whether the jury's imposition of the death sentence in the same proceeding and verdict as determined the issue of guilt was constitutionally permissible."

The Supreme Court affirmed both judgments.

B. Counsel of Record/ACLU Attorney

ACLU Side (Petitioner/Appellant): Herman F. Selvin argued the cause for appellant in No. 203. John J. Callahan argued the cause for appellant in No. 204.

Opposing Side (Respondent/Appellee): Deputy Attorney General of California Ronald M. George argued the cause for appellee in No. 203. Melvin L. Resnick argued the cause for appellee in No. 204.

Solicitor General Erwin N. Griswold argued the cause for the United States, as amicus curiae.

III. AMICI CURIAE

ACLU Side (Petitioner/Appellant)

Brief of amici curiae filed on behalf of the ACLU, Illinois Division, et al., by Elmer Gertz and Willard J. Lassers.

Briefs of amicus curiae were filed by the NAACP Legal Defense and Educational Fund, Inc., et al., Luke McKissack, Richard F. Stevens, the Attorney General of Ohio, and the American Friends Service Committee, et al.

Opposing Side (Respondent/Appellee)

Brief of amici curiae filed on behalf of the United States by Solicitor General Erwin N. Griswold and Philip A. Lacovara.

IV. THE SUPREME COURT'S DECISION

"We consider first McGautha's and Crampton's common claim: that the absence of standards to guide the jury's discretion on the punishment issue is constitutionally intolerable. To fit their arguments within a constitutional frame of reference petitioners contend that to leave the jury completely at large to impose or withhold the death penalty as it see fit is fundamentally lawless and therefore violates the basic command of the Fourteenth Amendment that no State shall deprive a person of his life without due process of law. Despite the undeniable surface appeal of the proposition, we conclude that the courts below correctly rejected it. . . .

The criminal process, like the rest of the legal system, is replete with situations requiring 'the making of difficult judgments' as to which course to follow. Although a defendant may have a right, even of constitutional dimensions, to follow whichever course he chooses, the Constitution does not by that token always forbid requiring him to choose. The threshold question is whether compelling the election impairs to an appreciable extent any of the policies behind the rights involved. Analysis of this case in such terms leads to the conclusion that petitioner has failed to make out his claim of a constitutional violation in requiring him to undergo a unitary trial. . . .

We turn first to the privilege against compelled self-incrimination. The contention is that where guilt and punishment are to be determined by a jury at a single trial the desire to address the jury on punishment unduly encourages waiver of the defendant's privilege to remain silent on the issue of guilt, or, to put the matter another way, that the single-verdict procedure unlawfully compels the defendant to become a witness against himself on the issue of guilt by the threat of sentencing him to death without having heard from him. It is not contended, nor could it be successfully, that the mere force of evidence is compulsion of the sort forbidden by the privilege. . . .

On the other hand, petitioner is not seeking vindication for his interest in making a personal plea for mercy. Even in a bifurcated trial, the defendant could be restricted to the giving of evidence, with argument to be made by counsel only. Petitioner's contention therefore comes down to the fact that the Ohio single-verdict trial may deter the defendant from bringing to the jury's attention evidence peculiarly within his own knowledge, and it may mean that the death verdict will be returned by a jury which never heard the sound of his voice. We do not think that the possibility of the former is sufficiently great to sustain petitioner's claim that the single-verdict trial may deprive the jury of a rational basis for fixing sentence. Assuming that in this case there was relevant information solely within petitioner's knowledge, we do not think the Constitution forbids a requirement that such evidence be available to the jury on all issues to which it is relevant or not at all. As to the largely symbolic value represented by the latter interest, Ohio has provided for retention of the ritual of allocution, albeit only in its common-law form, precisely to avoid the possibility that a person might be tried, convicted, and sentenced to death in complete silence. We have held that failure to ensure such personal participation in the criminal process is not necessarily a constitutional flaw in the conviction. We do not think that Ohio was required to provide an opportunity for petitioner to speak to the jury free from any adverse consequences on the issue of guilt. We therefore reject this branch of petitioner's argument as well. . . .

The Constitution requires no more than that trials be fairly conducted and that guaranteed rights of defendants be scrupulously respected. From a constitutional standpoint we cannot conclude that it is impermissible for a State to consider that the compassionate purposes of jury sentencing in capital cases are better served by having the issues of guilt and punishment determined in a single trial than by focusing the jury's attention solely on punishment after the issue of guilt has been determined.

Certainly the facts of these gruesome murders bespeak no miscarriage of justice. The ability of juries, unassisted by standards, to distinguish between those defendants for whom the death penalty is appropriate punishment and those for whom imprisonment is sufficient is indeed illustrated by the discriminating verdict of the jury in McGautha's case . . . .

The procedures which petitioners challenge are those by which most capital trials in this country are conducted, and by which all were conducted until a few years ago. We have determined that these procedures are consistent with the rights to which petitioners were constitutionally entitled, and that their trials were entirely fair. Having reached these conclusions we have performed our task of measuring the States' process by federal constitutional standards, and accordingly the judgment in each of these cases is affirmed."

V. JUSTICE VOTE

3 Pro ACLU Side vs. 6 Con Opposing Side

ACLU Side (Petitioner/Appellant)

1. Douglas, W. – Wrote dissenting opinion, joined Brennan's dissent
2. Marshall, T. – Joined Douglas' dissent, joined Brennan's dissent
3. Brennan, W. – Wrote dissenting opinion, joined Douglas' dissent

Opposing Side (Respondent/Appellee)

1. Harlan J. – Wrote majority opinion
2. Burger, W. – Joined majority opinion
3. Stewart, P. – Joined majority opinion
4. White, B. – Joined majority opinion

5. Blackmun, H. – Joined majority opinion
6. Black, H. – Wrote concurring opinion

VI. A WIN OR LOSS FOR THE ACLU?

The ACLU filed as amicus curiae urging reversal; the Supreme Court affirmed in a 6-3 vote, giving the ACLU an apparent loss.

245. Org. for a Better Austin v. Keefe

(Decided May 17, 1971; 402 U.S. 415)

I. ISSUE

A. Issues Discussed

1st Amendment, press, speech, association

B. Legal Question Presented

Whether "an order of the Circuit Court of Cook County, Illinois, enjoining petitioners from distributing leaflets anywhere in the town of Westchester, Illinois, violates petitioners' rights under the Federal Constitution."

C. Supreme Court's Answer

"Any prior restraint on expression comes to this Court with a 'heavy presumption' against its constitutional validity. Respondent thus carries a heavy burden of showing justification for the imposition of such a restraint. He has not met that burden."

II. CASE SUMMARY

A. Background

"Petitioner Organization for a Better Austin (OBA) is a racially integrated community organization in the Austin neighborhood of Chicago. Respondent is a real estate broker whose office and business activities are in the Austin neighborhood. . . .

OBA is an organization whose stated purpose is to 'stabilize' the racial ratio in the Austin area. For a number of years the boundary of the Negro segregated area of Chicago has moved progressively west to Austin. OBA, in its efforts to 'stabilize' the area . . . has opposed and protested various real estate tactics and activities . . . .

It was the contention of OBA that respondent had been one of those who engaged in such tactics, specifically that he aroused the fears of the local white residents that Negroes were coming into the area and then, exploiting the reactions and emotions so aroused, was able to secure listings and sell homes to Negroes. . . .

Community meetings were arranged with respondent to try to persuade him to change his real estate practices. Several other real estate agents were prevailed on to sign an agreement whereby they would not solicit property, by phone, flyer, or visit, in the Austin community. Respondent . . . refused to sign . . . .

Thereafter, during September and October of 1967, members of petitioner organization distributed leaflets in Westchester describing respondent's activities. . . .

Respondent sought an injunction in the Circuit Court of Cook County, Illinois . . . . [T]he trial court entered a temporary injunction . . . .

On appeal to the Appellate Court of Illinois, First District, that court affirmed."

The Supreme Court granted certiorari to review the case.

B. Counsel of Record

ACLU Side (Petitioner/Appellant): David C. Long argued the cause for appellants. With him on the briefs were Willard J. Lassers, William Silverman, and Mark Spiegel.[1]

Opposing Side (Respondent/Appellee): Thomas W. McNamara argued the cause for appellee. With him on the brief was John C. Tucker.

III. AMICI CURIAE

ACLU Side (Petitioner/Appellant)

No briefs of amici curiae were filed in support of appellant.

Opposing Side (Respondent/Appellee)

No briefs of amici curiae were filed in support of appellee.

IV. THE SUPREME COURT'S DECISION

"It is elementary, of course, that in a case of this kind the courts do not concern themselves with the truth or validity of the publication. . . . Here, . . . the injunction operates, not to redress alleged private wrongs, but to suppress, on the basis of previous publications, distribution of literature 'of any kind' in a city of 18,000.

This Court has often recognized that the activity of peaceful pamphleteering is a form of communication protected by the First Amendment. In sustaining the injunction, however, the Appellate Court was apparently of the view that petitioners' purpose in distributing their literature was not to inform the public, but to 'force' respondent to sign a no-solicitation agreement. The claim that the expressions were intended to exercise a coercive impact on respondent does not remove them from the reach of the First Amendment. Petitioners plainly intended to influence respondent's conduct by their activities . . . . Petitioners were engaged openly and vigorously in making the public aware of respondent's real estate practices. Those practices were offensive to them, as the views and practices of petitioners are no doubt offensive to others. But so long as the means are peaceful, the communication need not meet standards of acceptability.

Any prior restraint on expression comes to this Court with a 'heavy presumption' against its constitutional validity. Respondent thus carries a heavy burden of showing justification for the imposition of such a restraint. He has not met that burden. No prior decisions support the claim that the interest of an individual in being free from public criticism of his business practices in pamphlets or leaflets warrants use of the injunctive power of a court. Designating the conduct as an invasion of

1 The Successes *of the American Civil Liberties Union, ACLU,* https://www.aclu.org/successes-american-civil-liberties-union (last visited Jan. 25, 2020) (Listed as a successful case of the ACLU.); The Making of Modern Law: American Civil Liberties Union Papers, Keefe v. Organization for a Better Austin, Series 4: Legal Case Filed, 1933-1990, Box 1469, Item 308, Gale Doc. No. GALE|PNXKGU921966388, p. 64, https://link.gale.com/apps/doc/PNXKGU921966388/ACLU?u=ucirvine&sid=ACLU&xid=bfffd00c (David C. Long wrote to Melvin Wulf, ACLU Legal Director, about the case while preparing the petition for a writ of certiorari, referring to the case as "on our Roger Baldwin Foundaton docket.")

privacy, the apparent basis for the injunction here, is not sufficient to support an injunction against peaceful distribution of informational literature of the nature revealed by this record. . . . Accordingly, the injunction issued by the Illinois court must be vacated.

Reversed."

V. JUSTICE VOTE

8 Pro ACLU Side vs. 1 Con Opposing Side

ACLU Side (Petitioner/Appellant)

1. Burger, W. – Wrote majority opinion
2. Brennan, W. – Joined majority opinion
3. Black, H. – Joined majority opinion
4. Douglas, W. – Joined majority opinion
5. Blackmun, H. – Joined majority opinion
6. Marshall, T. – Joined majority opinion
7. Stewart, P. – Joined majority opinion
8. White, B. – Joined majority opinion

Opposing Side (Respondent/Appellee)

1. Harlan, J. – Wrote dissenting opinion

VI. A WIN OR LOSS FOR THE ACLU?

The ACLU lists this case as an ACLU success and therefore appears to have urged reversal of the judgment of the Appellate Court of Illinois, First District; the Supreme Court reversed in an 8-1 vote, giving the ACLU an apparent win.

246. Astrup v. I.N.S.

(Decided May 24, 1971; 402 U.S. 509)

I. ISSUE

A. Issues Discussed

Immigration/Citizenship

B. Legal Question Presented

Whether Astrup is barred from becoming an American citizen in relation to a prior agreement with the U.S. government related to military service.

C. Supreme Court's Answer

"[T]he United States District Court erred in denying Astrup's petition for naturalization on the ground that he was barred from citizenship because he had once claimed an exemption from military service as an alien."

II. CASE SUMMARY

A. Background

"The issue in this case is exceedingly simple. By signing SSS Form 130—Application by Alien for Relief from Training and Service in the Armed Forces—the petitioner, Ib Otto Astrup, a native of Denmark, agreed to give up his right to become an American citizen, and in exchange, the United States, pursuant to s 4(a) of the Selective Service Act of 1948, agreed to give up the right to induct Astrup into the United States armed forces. Congress later repealed the law under which Astrup was exempted from military service, reneging on its part of the bargain with him. Thereafter the Selective Service System attempted to draft Astrup and would have succeeded in putting him into uniform but for the fact that he was found to be physically unfit for the draft. Later, when Astrup decided that he would like to become an American citizen, the Government attempted to enforce Astrup's promise even though it was unwilling to keep its own promise. When Astrup petitioned for naturalization, the United States District Court for the Northern District of California denied his petition on the ground that he was debarred from citizenship. The Court of Appeals for the Ninth Circuit affirmed. [The U.S. Supreme Court] granted Astrup's petition for certiorari . . . ."

B. Counsel of Record

ACLU Side (Petitioner/Appellant): Paul N. Halvonik of the American Civil Liberties Union of Northern California argued the cause for appellant. With him on the brief were Marshall W. Krause and Charles C. Marson of the American Civil Liberties Union of Northern California.

Opposing Side (Respondent/Appellee): Richard B. Stone argued the cause for appellee. With him on the brief were Solicitor General Griswold, Assistant Attorney General Wilson, and Charles Gordon.

III. AMICI CURIAE

ACLU Side (Petitioner/Appellant)

No briefs of amici curiae were filed in support of appellant.

Opposing Side (Respondent/Appellee)

No briefs of amici curiae were filed in support of appellee.

IV. THE SUPREME COURT'S DECISION

"In support of the decision below the United States emphasizes the fact that Astrup admitted having read a notice proclaiming that:

'Any citizen of a foreign country . . . shall be relieved from liability for training and service under this title if, prior to his induction into the armed forces, he has made application to be relieved from such liability . . . ; but any person who makes such application shall thereafter be debarred from becoming a citizen of the United States.'

He further admitted having signed a statement saying, 'I understand that I will forever lose my rights to become a citizen of the United States . . . .' Upon the basis of these statements and s 4(a) of the Selective Service Act of 1948, the United States argues that the case is controlled by our decision in Ceballos v. Shaughnessy, 352 U.S. 599 (1957) . . . .

Astrup, unlike Ceballos, is not involved in a deportation proceeding under the Immigration Act of 1917 and consequently the saving clause of the Immigration and Nationality Act of 1952 is inapplicable. Moreover, Astrup petitioned for naturalization under s 316 of the 1952 Act. Therefore, s 315 of the 1952 Act, not s 4(a) of the Selective Service Act of 1948, determines the effect to be given to Astrup's 1950 application for exemption from military service. . . .

This is a two-pronged prerequisite for the loss of eligibility for United States citizenship. The alien must be one who 'applies or has applied for exemption or discharge' from military service and 'is or was relieved or discharged' from that service. There is no question that Astrup applied for an exemption. . . .

We think that Congress used the words 'is or was relieved' to provide that an alien who requests exemption from the military service be held to his agreement to relinquish all claims to naturalized citizenship only when the Government abides by its part of the agreement and completely exempts him from service in our armed forces.

Consequently, the United States District Court erred in denying Astrup's petition for naturalization on the ground that he was barred from citizenship because he had once claimed an exemption from military service as an alien. The decision of the Court of Appeals for the Ninth Circuit affirming the District Court is reversed and the case is remanded to the District Court for further proceedings on Astrup's petition for naturalization. . . .

Reversed and remanded."

V. JUSTICE VOTE

9 Pro ACLU Side vs. 0 Con Opposing Side

ACLU Side (Petitioner/Appellant)

Opposing Side (Respondent/Appellee)

1. Black, H. – Wrote majority opinion
2. Marshall, T. – Joined majority opinion
3. Harlan, J. – Joined majority opinion
4. Brennan, W. – Joined majority opinion
5. Stewart, P. – Joined majority opinion
6. Burger, W. – Joined majority opinion
7. White, B. – Joined majority opinion
8. Blackmun, H. – Joined majority opinion
9. Douglas, W. – Joined majority opinion

VI. A WIN OR LOSS FOR THE ACLU?

The ACLU served as counsel for appellants urging reversal of the judgment of the Court of Appeals; the Supreme Court reversed, in a 9-0 vote, giving the ACLU an apparent win.

247. Palmer v. City of Euclid

(Decided May 24, 1971; 402 U.S. 544)

I. ISSUE

A. Issues Discussed

Criminal procedure

B. Legal Question Presented

Whether Palmer was wrongfully convicted under the city's '"suspicious person ordinance."'

C. Supreme Court's Answer

"We reverse the judgment against Palmer because the ordinance is so vague and lacking in ascertainable standards of guilt that, as applied to Palmer, it failed to give 'a person of ordinary intelligence fair notice that his contemplated conduct is forbidden . . . .'"

II. CASE SUMMARY

A. Background

"Appellant Palmer was convicted by a jury of violating the City of Euclid's 'suspicious person ordinance,' that is, of being '(a)ny person who wanders about the streets or other public ways or who is found abroad at late or unusual hours in the night without any visible or lawful business and who does not give satisfactory account of himself.'

He was fined $50 and sentenced to 30 days in jail. The County Court of Appeals affirmed the judgment and appeal to the Supreme Court of Ohio was dismissed 'for the reason that no substantial constitutional question exists herein.' [The U.S. Supreme Court] noted probable jurisdiction."

B. Counsel of Record

ACLU Side (Petitioner/Appellant): Opposing Side (Respondent/Appellee): Niki Z. Schwartz argued the cause for appellant. With him on the brief were Stanley K. Laughlin, Jr., of the American Civil Liberties Union of Ohio, and Joshua J. Kancelbaum. David J. Lombardo argued the cause for appellee. With him on the brief was William T. Monroe.

III. AMICI CURIAE

ACLU Side (Petitioner/Appellant)

No briefs of amici curiae were filed in support of appellant.

Opposing Side (Respondent/Appellee)

No briefs of amici curiae were filed in support of appellee.

IV. THE SUPREME COURT'S DECISION

"We reverse the judgment against Palmer because the ordinance is so vague and lacking in ascertainable standards of guilt that, as applied to Palmer, it failed to give 'a person of ordinary intelligence fair notice that his contemplated conduct is forbidden . . . .'

The elements of the crime defined by the ordinance apparently are (1) wandering about the streets or being abroad at late or unusual hours; (2) being at the time without visible or lawful business; and (3) failing to give a satisfactory explanation for his presence on the streets. Palmer, in his car, was seen late at night in a parking lot. A female left his car and entered by the front door an adjoining apartment house. Palmer then pulled onto the street, parked with his lights on, and used a two-way radio. He was not armed. He said he had just let off a friend. He was then arrested. At the station he gave three different addresses for himself and said he did not know his friend's name or where she was going when she left his car. Palmer could reasonably be charged with knowing that he was on the streets at a late or unusual hour and that denying knowledge of his friend's identity and claiming multiple addresses amounted to an unsatisfactory explanation under the ordinance. But in our view the ordinance gave insufficient notice to the average person that discharging a friend at an apartment house and then talking on a car radio while parked on the street was enough to show him to be 'without any visible or lawful business.' Insofar as this record reveals, everything appellant did was quite visible and there is no suggestion whatsoever that what he did was unlawful under local, state, or federal law. If his conduct nevertheless satisfied the being-without-visible-or-lawful-business element of the ordinance, as the state courts must have held, it is quite unreasonable in our view to charge him with notice that such would be the construction of the ordinance. 'The underlying principle is that no man shall be held criminally responsible for conduct which he could not reasonably understand to be proscribed.'

The judgment of the Supreme Court of Ohio is reversed."

V. JUSTICE VOTE

9 Pro ACLU Side vs. 0 Con Opposing Side

ACLU Side (Petitioner/Appellant)

1. Black, H. – Per curiam decision
2. Marshall, T. – Per curiam decision
3. Harlan, J. – Concurs in the result
4. Brennan, W. – Per curiam decision
5. Stewart, P. – Wrote concurring opinion
6. Burger, W. – Per curiam decision
7. White, B. – Per curiam decision
8. Blackmun, H. – Per curiam decision
9. Douglas, W. – Joined Stewart's concurrence

VI. A WIN OR LOSS FOR THE ACLU?

The ACLU served as counsel for appellant urging reversal of the judgment of the Supreme Court of Ohio; the U.S. Supreme Court reversed, in a 9-0 per curiam decision, giving the ACLU an apparent win.

248. Gordon v. Lance

(Decided June 7, 1971; 403 U.S. 1)

I. ISSUE

A. Issues Discussed

Civil rights, state rights, Fourteenth Amendment, equal protection

B. Legal Question Presented

Does West Virginia's requirement "that political subdivisions may not incur bonded indebtedness or increase tax rates beyond those established by the State Constitution without the approval of 60% of the voters in a referendum election" violate the Equal Protection Clause or any other provision of the Constitution?

C. Supreme Court's Answer

The West Virginia requirement does not violate the Equal Protection Clause or any other provision of the Constitution.

II. CASE SUMMARY

A. Background

"The Constitution of West Virginia and certain West Virginia statutes provide that political subdivisions of the State may not incur bonded indebtedness or increase tax rates beyond those established by the State Constitution without the approval of 60% of the voters in a referendum election.

On April 29, 1968, the Board of Education of Roane County, West Virginia, submitted to the voters of Roane County a proposal calling for the issuance of general obligation bonds in the amount of $1,830,000, for the purpose of constructing new school buildings and improving existing educational facilities. At the same election, by separate ballot, the voters were asked to authorize the Board of Education to levy additional taxes to support current expenditures. Of the total votes cast, 51.55% favored the bond issues and 51.51% favored the tax levy. Having failed to obtain the requisite 60% affirmative vote, the proposals were declared defeated.

Following the election, respondents appeared before the Board of Education on behalf of themselves and other persons who had voted in favor of the proposals and demanded that the Board authorize the bonds and the additional taxes. The Board refused.

Respondents then brought this action, seeking a declaratory judgment that the 60% requirements were unconstitutional as violative of the Fourteenth Amendment. They alleged that the Roane County schools had been unimproved since 1946 and fell far below the state average both in classroom size and facilities. They further alleged that four similar proposals had been previously defeated, although each had received majorities of affirmative votes ranging from 52.51% to 55.84%. The West Virginia trial court dismissed the complaint. On appeal, the West Virginia Supreme Court of Appeals reversed, holding that the state constitutional and statutory requirements of a 60% affirmative vote violated the Equal Protection Clause of the Fourteenth Amendment."

The Supreme Court granted certiorari and reversed the judgment.

B. Counsel of Record/ACLU Attorney

ACLU Side (Respondent/Appellee): Charles C. Wise, Jr., argued the cause for appellee.

Opposing Side (Petitioner/Appellant): George M. Scott argued the cause for appellant.

III. AMICI CURIAE

ACLU Side (Respondent/Appellee)

Brief of amici curiae filed on behalf of the ACLU by Melvin L. Wulf, Joel M. Gora, Paul N. Halvonik, and Charles C. Marson.

Briefs of amicus curiae urging affirmance were filed on behalf of Seattle School District No. 1, the National Education Association, et al., the National School Boards Association, the Missouri State Teachers Association, the American Association of School Administrators, et al., and the Committee for the Equal Weighting of Votes.

Opposing Side (Petitioner/Appellant)

Briefs of amici curiae urging reversal were filed on behalf of the State of Washington, et al., the City and County of San Francisco, the California Taxpayers' Association, Hayes Smith, and Chas. Chaflin Allen.

The City of San Diego, et al., filed a brief of amici curiae concerning the retroactive effect of the decision

IV. THE SUPREME COURT'S DECISION

"Although West Virginia has not denied any group access to the ballot, it has indeed made it more difficult for some kinds of governmental actions to be taken. Certainly any departure from strict majority rule gives disproportionate power to the minority. But there is nothing in the language of the Constitution, our history, or our cases that requires that a majority always prevail on every issue. On the contrary, while we have recognized that state officials are normally chosen by a vote of the majority of the electorate, we have found no constitutional barrier to the selection of a Governor by a state legislature, after no candidate received a majority of the popular vote. . . .

It must be remembered that in voting to issue bonds voters are committing, in part, the credit of infants and of generations yet unborn, and some restriction on such commitment is not an unreasonable demand. That the bond issue may have the desirable objective of providing better education for future generations goes to the wisdom of an indebtedness limitation: it does not alter the basic fact that the balancing of interests is one for the State to resolve. . . .

We conclude that so long as such provisions do not discriminate against or authorize discrimination against any identifiable class they do not violate the Equal Protection Clause. We see no meaningful distinction between such absolute provisions on debt, changeable only by constitutional amendment, and provisions that legislative decisions on the same issues require more than a majority vote in the legislature. . . . Moreover, the same considerations apply when the ultimate power, rather than being delegated to the legislature, remains with the people, by way of a referendum. Indeed, we see no constitutional distinction between the 60% requirement in the present case and a state requirement that a given issue be approved by a majority of all registered voters.

That West Virginia has adopted a rule of decision, applicable to all bond referenda, by which the strong consensus of three-fifths is required before indebtedness is authorized, does not violate the Equal Protection Clause or any other provision of the Constitution."

The Supreme Court reversed the judgment.

V. JUSTICE VOTE

2 Pro ACLU Side vs. 7 Con Opposing Side

ACLU Side (Respondent/Appellee)

1. Marshall, T. – Wrote joint dissenting opinion
2. Brennan, W. – Wrote joint dissenting opinion

Opposing Side (Petitioner/Appellant)

1. Burger, W. – Wrote majority opinion
2. Black, H. – Joined majority opinion
3. Douglas, W. – Joined majority opinion
4. Stewart, P. – Joined majority opinion
5. White, B. – Joined majority opinion
6. Blackmun, H. – Joined majority opinion
7. Harlan, J. – Wrote concurring opinion

VI. A WIN OR LOSS FOR THE ACLU?

The ACLU filed as amicus curiae urging affirmance; the Supreme Court reversed the ruling of the Supreme Court of Appeals of West Virginia in a 7-2 vote, giving the ACLU an apparent loss.

249. Cohen v. California

(Decided June 7, 1971; 403 U.S. 15)

I. ISSUE

A. Issues Discussed

First Amendment, Fourteenth Amendment, freedom of speech, offensive conduct

B. Legal Question Presented

Can a state constitutionally prevent the use of certain words on the grounds that the use of such words constitutes "offensive conduct"?

C. Supreme Court's Answer

A state cannot, consistently with the First and Fourteenth Amendment, prevent the use of certain words here.

II. CASE SUMMARY

A. Background

"Appellant Paul Robert Cohen was convicted in the Los Angeles Municipal Court of violating that part of California Penal Code § 415 which prohibits 'maliciously and willfully disturb[ing] the peace or quiet of any neighborhood or person . . . by . . . offensive conduct. . . .'

'On April 26, 1968, the defendant was observed in the Los Angeles County Courthouse in the corridor outside of division 20 of the municipal court wearing a jacket bearing the words 'Fuck the Draft' which were plainly visible. There were women and children present in the corridor. The defendant was arrested. The defendant testified that he wore the jacket knowing that the words were on the jacket as a means of informing the public of the depth of his feelings against the Vietnam War and the draft.

'The defendant did not engage in, nor threaten to engage in, nor did anyone as the result of his conduct in fact commit or threaten to commit any act of violence. The defendant did not make any loud or unusual noise, nor was there any evidence that he uttered any sound prior to his arrest.'

In affirming the conviction the Court of Appeal held that 'offensive conduct' means 'behavior which has a tendency to provoke others to acts of violence or to in turn disturb the peace' . . . . The California Supreme Court declined review by a divided vote."

The Supreme Court granted certiorari and reversed the judgment of the Court of Appeal.

B. Counsel of Record / ACLU Attorney

ACLU Side (Petitioner/Appellant): Melville B. Nimmer argued the cause for appellant.

Opposing Side (Respondent/Appellee): Michael T. Sauer argued the cause for appellee.

III. AMICI CURIAE

ACLU Side (Petitioner/Appellant)

Brief of amici curiae filed on behalf of the ACLU of Northern California by Anthony G. Amsterdam, Paul N. Halvonik, and Charles C. Marson.

Opposing Side (Respondent/Appellee)

No briefs of amici curiae were filed in support of appellee.

IV. THE SUPREME COURT'S DECISION

"The conviction quite clearly rests upon the asserted offensiveness of the words Cohen used to convey his message to the public. The only 'conduct' which the State sought to punish is the fact of communication. Thus, we deal here with a conviction resting solely upon 'speech,' not upon any separately identifiable conduct which allegedly was intended by Cohen to be perceived by others as expressive of particular views but which, on its face, does not necessarily convey any message and hence arguably could be regulated without effectively repressing Cohen's ability to express himself. . . .

It is, in sum, our judgment that, absent a more particularized and compelling reason for its actions, the State may not, consistently with the First and Fourteenth Amendments, make the simple public display here involved of this single four-letter expletive a criminal offense. Because that is the only arguably sustainable rationale for the conviction here at issue, the judgment below must be reversed."

The Supreme Court reversed the Court of Appeal.

V. JUSTICE VOTE

5 Pro ACLU Side vs. 4 Con Opposing Side

ACLU Side (Petitioner/Appellant)

1. Harlan, J. – Wrote majority opinion
2. Douglas, W. – Joined majority opinion
3. Brennan, W. – Joined majority opinion
4. Stewart, P. – Joined majority opinion
5. Marshall, T. – Joined majority opinion

Opposing Side (Respondent/Appellee)

1. Blackmun, H. – Wrote dissenting opinion
2. Burger, W. – Joined dissenting opinion
3. Black, H. – Joined dissenting opinion
4. White, B. – Joined dissenting opinion in part 2

VI. A WIN OR LOSS FOR THE ACLU?

The ACLU, as amicus curiae, urged reversal of the judgment of the Court of Appeal of California, Second Appellate District; the Supreme Court reversed in a 5-4 vote, giving the ACLU an apparent win.

250. Whitcomb v. Chavis

(Decided June 7, 1971; 403 U.S. 124)

I. ISSUE

A. Issues Discussed

Civil rights, race, voting, Fourteenth Amendment

B. Legal Question Presented

Was the district court clearly erroneous in finding that multi-member legislative districts in Marion County, Indiana diluted the voting rights of African-American ghetto residents?

C. Supreme Court's Answer

The multi-member legislative districts do not result in invidious discrimination in violation of the Equal Protection Clause.

II. CASE SUMMARY

A. Background

"Indiana has a bicameral General Assembly consisting of a House of Representatives of 100 members and a Senate of 50 members. Eight of the 31 senatorial districts and 25 of the 39 house districts are multi-member districts, that is, districts that are represented by two or more legislators elected at large by the voters of the district. Under the statutes here challenged, Marion County is a multi-member district electing eight senators and 15 members of the house.

On January 9, 1969, six residents of Indiana, five of whom were residents of Marion County, filed a suit described by them as 'attacking the constitutionality of two statutes of the State of Indiana which provide for multi-member districting at large of General Assembly seats in Marion County, Indiana . . . .' Plaintiffs Chavis, Ramsey, and Bryant alleged that the two statutes invidiously diluted the force and effect of the vote of Negroes and poor persons living within certain Marion County census tracts constituting what was termed 'the ghetto area.' Residents of the area were alleged to have particular demographic characteristics rendering them cognizable as a minority interest group with distinctive interests in specific areas of the substantive law. With single-member districting, it was said, the ghetto area would elect three members of the house and one senator, whereas under the present districting voters in the area 'have almost no political force or control over legislators because the effect of their vote is cancelled out by other contrary interest groups' in Marion County. The mechanism of political party organization and the influence of party chairmen in nominating candidates were additional factors alleged to frustrate the exercise of power by residents of the ghetto area.

Plaintiff Walker, a Negro resident of Lake County, also a multi-member district but a smaller one, alleged an invidious discrimination against Lake County Negroes because Marion County Negroes, although no greater in number than Lake County Negroes, had the opportunity to influence the election of more legislators than Lake County Negroes. The claim was that Marion County was one-third larger in population and thus had approximately one-third more assembly seats than Lake County, but that voter influence does not vary inversely with population and that permitting Marion County voters to elect 23 assemblymen at large gave them a disproportionate advantage over voters in Lake County. The two remaining plaintiffs presented claims not at issue here.

A three-judge court convened and tried the case on June 17 and 18, 1969. Both documentary evidence and oral testimony were taken concerning the composition and characteristics of the alleged ghetto area, the manner in which legislative candidates were chosen and their residence and tenure, and the performance of Marion County's delegation in the Indiana general assembly.

The three-judge court filed its opinion containing its findings and conclusions on July 28, 1969, holding for plaintiffs. In sum, it concluded that Marion County's multi-member district must be disestablished and, because of population disparities not directly related to the phenomena alleged in the complaint, the entire State must be redistricted. . . .

Appeal was taken following the final judgment by the three-judge court, [the Supreme Court] noted probable jurisdiction, and the State's motion for stay of judgment was granted pending our final action on this case, thus permitting the 1970 elections to be held under the existing apportionment statutes declared unconstitutional by the District Court. On June 1, 1971, we were advised by the parties that the Indiana Legislature had passed, and the Governor had signed, new apportionment legislation soon to become effective for the 1972 elections and that the new legislation provides for singlemember house and senate districts throughout the State, including Marion County."

The Supreme Court granted certiorari to review the case and reversed.

B. Counsel of Record/ACLU Attorney

ACLU Side (Respondent/Appellee): James Manahan argued the cause for appellee.

Opposing Side (Petitioner/Appellant): Assistant Attorney General of Indiana William F. Thompson argued the cause for appellant.

III. AMICI CURIAE

ACLU Side (Respondent/Appellee)

Brief of amici curiae filed on behalf of the ACLU Foundation, Inc., et al., by Charles Morgan, Jr., Reber F. Boult, Jr., Norman Siegel, David J. Vann, Joseph J. Levin, Jr., Morris Dees, and Melvin L. Wulf.

Opposing Side (Petitioner/Appellant)

William J. Scott, Attorney General, and Francis C. Crowe and Herman Tavins, Assistant Attorneys General, filed a brief for the State of Illinois as amicus curiae urging reversal, joined by the following Attorneys General: MacDonald Gallion of Alabama, G. Kent Edwards of Alaska, Gary K. Nelson of Arizona, Duke W. Dunbar of Colorado, Richard C. Turner of Iowa, A. F. Summer of Mississippi, Robert L. Woodahl of Montana, Gordon Mydland of South Dakota, Crawford C. Martin of Texas, Vernon B. Romney of Utah, and Chauncey H. Browning of West Virginia.

IV. THE SUPREME COURT'S DECISION

"We agree that the case is not moot and that the central issues before us must be decided. . . .

That voters in multi-member districts vote for and are represented by more legislators than voters in single-member districts has so far not demonstrated an invidious discrimination against the latter. But we have deemed the validity of multi-member district systems justiciable, recognizing also that they may be subject to challenge where the circumstances of a particular case may 'operate to minimize or cancel out the voting strength of racial or political elements of the voting population.' . . . But we have insisted that the challenger carry the burden of proving that multi-member districts unconstitutionally operate to dilute or cancel the voting strength of racial or political elements. We have not yet sustained such an attack. . . .

We are not ready . . . to agree that multi-member districts, wherever they exist, overrepresent their voters as compared with voters in singlemember districts, even if the multi-member delegation tends to bloc voting. The theory that plural representation itself unduly enhances a district's power and the influence of its voters remains to be demonstrated in practice and in the day-to-day operation of the legislature. Neither the findings of the trial court nor the record before us sustains it, even where bloc voting is posited. . . .

On the record before us plaintiffs' position comes to this: that although they have equal opportunity to participate in and influence the selection of candidates and legislators, and although the ghetto votes predominantly Democratic and that party slates candidates satisfactory to the ghetto, invidious discrimination nevertheless results when the ghetto, along with all other Democrats, suffers the disaster of losing too many elections. But typical American legislative elections are district-oriented, head-on races between candidates of two or more parties. As our system has it, one candidate wins, the others lose. Arguably the losing candidates' supporters are without representation since the men they voted for have been defeated; arguably they have been denied equal protection of the laws since they have no legislative voice of their own. This is true of both single-member and multimember districts. But we have not yet deemed it a denial of equal protection to deny legislative seats to losing candidates, even in those so-called 'safe' districts where the same party wins year after year. . . .

The mere fact that one interest group or another concerned with the outcome of Marion County elections has found itself outvoted and without legislative seats of its own provides no basis for invoking constitutional remedies where, as here, there is no indication that this segment of the population is being denied access to the political system. . . .

The short of it is that we are unprepared to hold that district-based elections decided by plurality vote are unconstitutional in either single or multi-member districts simply because the supporters of losing candidates have no legislative seats assigned to them. As presently advised we hold that the District Court misconceived the Equal Protection Clause in applying it to invalidate the Marion County multi-member district. . . .

At the same time, however, we reject defendant's suggestion that the court was wrong in ordering statewide reapportionment. . . .

Nor can we accept defendant's argument that the statutory plan was beyond attack because the District Court had held in 1965 that at that time the plan met the 'substantial equality' test of Reynolds. . . .

We therefore reverse the judgment of the District Court and remand the case to that court for further proceedings consistent with this opinion."

V. JUSTICE VOTE

3 Pro ACLU Side vs. 6 Con Opposing Side

ACLU Side (Respondent/Appellee)

1. Douglas, W. – Wrote dissenting opinion
2. Marshall, T. – Joined dissenting opinion
3. Brennan, W. – Joined dissenting opinion

Opposing Side (Petitioner/Appellant)

1. White B. – Wrote majority opinion
2. Burger, W. – Joined majority opinion
3. Black, H. – Joined majority opinion
4. Stewart, P. – Wrote concurring opinion
5. Blackmun, H. – Joined majority opinion
6. Harlan, J. – Wrote concurring opinion

VI. A WIN OR LOSS FOR THE ACLU?

The ACLU filed as amicus curiae urging affirmance; the Supreme Court reversed and remanded the ruling of the District Court for the Southern District of Indiana, Indianapolis Division in a 6-3 vote, giving the ACLU an apparent loss.

251. Connell v. Higginbotham

(Decided June 7, 1971; 403 U.S. 207)

I. ISSUE

A. Issues Discussed

Communism

B. Legal Question Presented

Whether a Florida loyalty oath required for employment as a public school teacher is constitutional.

C. Supreme Court's Answer

"The first section of the oath upheld by the District Court, requiring all applicants to pledge to support the Constitution of the United States and of the State of Florida, demands no more of Florida public employees than is required of all state and federal officers. U.S. Const., Art. VI, cl. 3. The validity of this section of the oath would appear settled.

The second portion of the oath, approved by the District Court, falls within the ambit of decisions of this Court proscribing summary dismissal from public employment without hearing or inquiry required by due process. That portion of the oath, therefore, cannot stand."

II. CASE SUMMARY

A. Background

"This is an appeal from an action commenced in the United States District Court for the Middle District of Florida challenging the constitutionality of ss 876.05—879.10 of Fla.Stat. (1965), and the various loyalty oaths upon which appellant's employment as a school teacher was conditioned. The three-judge U.S. District Court declared three of the five clauses contained in the oaths to be unconstitutional, and enjoined the State from conditioning employment on the taking of an oath including the language declared unconstitutional. The appeal is from that portion of the District Court decision, which upheld the remaining two clauses in the oath: I do hereby solemnly swear or affirm (1) 'that I will support the Constitution of the United States and of the State of Florida'; and (2) 'that I do not believe in the overthrow of the Government of the United States or of the State of Florida be force or violence.'

On January 16, 1969, appellant made application for a teaching position with the Orange County school system. She was interviewed by the principal of Callahan Elementary School, and on January 27, 1969, appellant was employed as a substitute classroom teacher in the fourth grade of that school. Appellant was dismissed from her teaching position on March 18, 1969, for refusing to sign the loyalty oath required of all Florida public employees, Fla.Stat. s 876.05."

B. Counsel of Record

ACLU Side (Petitioner/Appellant): Sanford Jay Rosen argued the cause for appellant. With him on the brief were Tobias Simon and Melvin L. Wulf of the American Civil Liberties Union Foundation, Tobias Simon, and Jerome J. Bornstein.

Opposing Side (Respondent/Appellee): Stephen Marc Slepin argued the cause for appellees. With him on the brief were Rivers Buford, Jr., and James W. Markel.

III. AMICI CURIAE

ACLU Side (Petitioner/Appellant)

No briefs of amici curiae were filed in support of appellant.

Opposing Side (Respondent/Appellee)

No briefs of amici curiae were filed in support of appellees.

IV. THE SUPREME COURT'S DECISION

"The first section of the oath upheld by the District Court, requiring all applicants to pledge to support the Constitution of the United States and of the State of Florida, demands no more of Florida public employees than is required of all state and federal officers. U.S. Const., Art. VI, cl. 3. The validity of this section of the oath would appear settled.

The second portion of the oath, approved by the District Court, falls within the ambit of decisions of this Court proscribing summary dismissal from public employment without hearing or inquiry required by due process. That portion of the oath, therefore, cannot stand.

Affirmed in part, and reversed in part."

V. JUSTICE VOTE

9 Pro ACLU Side vs. 0 Con Opposing Side

ACLU Side (Petitioner/Appellant)

1. Black, H. – Per curiam decision
2. Marshall, T. – Wrote concurring opinion
3. Harlan, J. – Per curiam decision
4. Brennan, W. – Joined Marshall's concurrence
5. Stewart, P. – Per curiam decision
6. Burger, W. – Per curiam decision
7. White, B. – Per curiam decision
8. Blackmun, H. – Per curiam decision
9. Douglas, W. – Joined Marshall's concurrence

VI. A WIN OR LOSS FOR THE ACLU?

The ACLU served as counsel for appellants urging reversal of the judgment of the U.S. District Court for the Middle District of Florida; the Supreme Court affirmed in part and reversed in part, in a 9-0 per curiam decision, giving the ACLU an apparent win.

252. Graham v. Richardson

(Decided June 14, 1971; 403 U.S. 365)

I. ISSUE

A. Issues Discussed

Governmental authority, immigration, Fourteenth Amendment, equal protection

B. Legal Question Presented

"[W]hether the Equal Protection Clause of the Fourteenth Amendment prevents a State from conditioning welfare benefits either (a) upon the beneficiary's possession of United States citizenship, or (b) if the beneficiary is an alien, upon his having resided in this country for a specified number of years."

C. Supreme Court's Answer

States cannot condition welfare benefits on U.S. citizenship or having resided in the U.S. for a certain number of years.

II. CASE SUMMARY

A. Background

Appellee Carmen Richardson, a lawfully admitted resident immigrant, immigrated from Mexico in 1956 and since then resided continuously in Arizona. The state of Arizona restricted distribution of welfare benefits to individuals who were either U.S. citizens, or immigrants who had lived in the U.S. for at least 15 years. When appellee became permanently disabled, she applied for benefits under the state's federally assisted program, but was denied relief because she did not meet the length of residency requirement.

Appellee filed a class action lawsuit in the District of Arizona against the appellant, the Commissioner of the State's Department of Public Welfare, seeking declaratory relief, an injunction against the enforcement of the 15-year residency requirement, and the amount due under the program. She asserted that Arizona's immigrant residency requirements were unconstitutional.

The three-judge court ruled in favor of appellee, holding that the 15-year requirement violated the Equal Protection Clause of the Constitution.

The Supreme Court granted certiorari and affirmed.

B. Counsel of Record/ACLU Attorney

ACLU Side (Respondent/Appellee): Anthony B. Ching argued the cause for appellee in No. 609. Jonathan M. Stein argued the cause for appellee, pro hac vice, in No. 727.

Opposing Side (Petitioner/Appellant): Assistant Attorney General of Arizona Michael S. Flam argued the cause for appellant in No. 609. Assistant Attorney General of Pennsylvania Joseph P. Work argued the cause for appellant in No. 727.

III. AMICI CURIAE

ACLU Side (Respondent/Appellee)

Brief of amici curiae filed on behalf of the ACLU by Robert A. Sedler, Melvin L. Wulf, and Joel M. Gora.

Brief of amicus curiae filed on behalf of the Legal Services for the Elderly Poor Project of the Center on Social Welfare Policy and Law by Jonathan Weiss, James Kraus, and Toby Golick.

Brief of amici curiae filed on behalf of Migration and Refugee Services, U.S. Catholic Conference, Inc., et al., by Edith Lowenstein.

Brief of amici curiae filed on behalf of the Association of Immigration and Nationality Lawyers by Jack Wasserman and Esther M. Kaufman.

Opposing Side (Petitioner/Appellant)

No briefs of amici curiae were filed in support of appellant.

IV. THE SUPREME COURT'S DECISION

"Under traditional equal protection principles, a State retains broad discretion to classify as long as its classification has a reasonable basis. . . . But the Court's decisions have established that classifications based on alienage, like those based on nationality or race, are inherently suspect and subject to close judicial scrutiny. Aliens as a class are a prime example of a 'discrete and insular' minority for whom such heightened judicial solicitude is appropriate. Accordingly, . . . 'the power of a state to apply its laws exclusively to its alien inhabitants as a class is confined within narrow limits.'

Arizona and Pennsylvania seek to justify their restrictions on the eligibility of aliens for public assistance solely on the basis of a State's 'special public interest' in favoring its own citizens over aliens in the distribution of limited resources such as welfare benefits. It is true that this Court on occasion has upheld state statutes that treat citizens and noncitizens differently, the ground for distinction having been that such laws were necessary to protect special interests of the State or its citizens. . . .

We agree with the three-judge court in the Pennsylvania case that the 'justification of limiting expenses is particularly inappropriate and unreasonable when the discriminated class consists of aliens. Aliens like citizens pay taxes and may be called into the armed forces. Unlike the short-term residents in Shapiro, aliens may live within a state for many years, work in the state and contribute to the economic growth of the state.' There can be no 'special public interest' in tax revenues to which aliens have contributed on an equal basis with the residents of the State.

Accordingly, we hold that a state statute that denies welfare benefits to resident aliens and one that denies them to aliens who have not resided in the United States for a specified number of years violate the Equal Protection Clause."

The Supreme Court affirmed the judgment.

V. JUSTICE VOTE

9 Pro ACLU Side vs. 0 Con Opposing Side

ACLU Side (Respondent/Appellee)

1. Blackmun, H. – Wrote majority opinion
2. Black, H. – Joined majority opinion
3. Marshall, T. – Joined majority opinion
4. Douglas, W. – Joined majority opinion
5. Brennan, W. – Joined majority opinion
6. Stewart, P. – Joined majority opinion
7. Burger, W. – Joined majority opinion
8. White, B. – Joined majority opinion
9. Harlan, J. – Wrote a concurring opinion

VI. A WIN OR LOSS FOR THE ACLU?

The ACLU filed as amicus curiae urging affirmance; the Supreme Court affirmed the judgment in a 9-0 vote, giving the ACLU an apparent win.

253. Bivens v. Six Unknown Named Agents of Federal Bureau of Narcotics

(Decided June 21, 1971; 403 U.S. 388)

I. ISSUE

A. Issues Discussed

Criminal procedure, Fourth Amendment, search and seizure

B. Legal Question Presented

"[W]hether violation of [the Fourth Amendment] by a federal agent acting under color of his authority gives rise to a cause of action for damages consequent upon his unconstitutional conduct."

C. Supreme Court's Answer

A federal agent's violation of the Fourth Amendment that causes injury gives rise to a civil action for damages.

II. CASE SUMMARY

A. Background

Petitioner Bivens alleged that respondents, Federal Bureau of Narcotics agents, "acting under claim of federal authority, entered his apartment and arrested him for alleged narcotic violations. The agents [handcuffed] petitioner in front of his wife and children, and threatened to arrest the entire family." They then searched the entire apartment. Subsequently, "petitioner was taken to the federal courthouse in Brooklyn, where he was interrogated, booked, and subjected to a visual strip search.

On July 7, 1967, petitioner brought suit in Federal District Court. [H]is complaint asserted that the arrest and search were effected without a warrant, and that unreasonable force was employed in making the arrest; fairly read, it alleges as well that the arrest was made without probable cause. Petitioner claimed to have suffered great humiliation, embarrassment, and mental suffering as a result of the agents' unlawful conduct, and sought $15,000 damages from each of them. The District Court, on respondents' motion, dismissed the complaint on the ground . . . that it failed to state a cause of action." The Court of Appeals affirmed.

The Supreme Court granted certiorari to review the case and reversed.

B. Counsel of Record/ACLU Attorney

ACLU Side (Petitioner/Appellant): Stephen A. Grant argued the cause for appellant.

Opposing Side (Respondent/Appellee): Jerome Feit argued the cause for appellee.

III. AMICI CURIAE

ACLU Side (Petitioner/Appellant)

Brief of amici curiae filed on behalf of the ACLU by Melvin L. Wulf, Joel M. Gora, and Michael E. Geltner.

Opposing Side (Respondent/Appellee)

No briefs of amici curiae were filed in support of appellee.

IV. THE SUPREME COURT'S DECISION

"We think that respondents' thesis rests upon an unduly restrictive view of the Fourth Amendment's protection against unreasonable searches and seizures by federal agents, a view that has consistently been rejected by this Court. [T]he Fourth Amendment operates as a limitation upon the exercise of federal power regardless of whether the State in whose jurisdiction that power is exercised would prohibit or penalize the identical act if engaged in by a private citizen. It guarantees to citizens of the United States the absolute right to be free from unreasonable searches and seizures carried out by virtue of federal authority. And 'where federally protected rights have been invaded, it has been the rule from the beginning that courts will be alert to adjust their remedies so as to grant the necessary relief.'

First. Our cases have long since rejected the notion that the Fourth Amendment proscribes only such conduct as would, if engaged in by private persons, be condemned by state law. [I] f the Fourth Amendment reached only to conduct impermissible under the law of the State, the Amendment would have had no application to the case. Yet this Court held the Fourth Amendment applicable and reversed petitioners' convictions as having been based upon evidence obtained through an unconstitutional search and seizure. . . . In light of these cases, respondents' argument that the Fourth Amendment serves only as a limitation on federal defenses to a state law claim, and not as an independent limitation upon the exercise of federal power, must be rejected.

Second. The interests protected by state laws regulating trespass and the invasion of privacy, and those protected by the Fourth Amendment's guarantee against unreasonable searches and seizures, may be inconsistent or even hostile. Thus, we may bar the door against an unwelcome private intruder, or call the police if he persists in seeking entrance. The availability of such alternative means for the protection of privacy may lead the State to restrict imposition of liability for any consequent trespass. A private citizen, asserting no authority other than his own, will not normally be liable in trespass if he demands, and is granted, admission to another's house. But one who demands admission under a claim of federal authority stands in a far different position. The mere invocation of federal power by a federal law enforcement official will normally render futile any attempt to resist an unlawful entry or arrest by resort to the local police; and a claim of authority to enter is likely to unlock the door as well. . . .Nor is it adequate to answer that state law may take into account the different status of one clothed with the authority of the Federal Government. For just as state law may not authorize federal agents to violate the Fourth Amendment, neither may state law undertake to limit the extent to which federal authority can be exercised. The inevitable consequence of this dual limitation on state power is that the federal question becomes not merely a possible defense to the state law action, but an independent claim both necessary and sufficient to make out the plaintiff's cause of action.

Third. That damages may be obtained for injuries consequent upon a violation of the Fourth Amendment by federal officials should hardly seem a surprising proposition. Historically, damages have been regarded as the ordinary remedy for an invasion of personal interests in liberty. Of course, the Fourth Amendment does not in so many words provide for its enforcement by an award of money damages for the consequences of its violation. But 'it is . . . well settled that where legal rights have been invaded, and a federal statute provides for a general right to sue for such invasion, federal courts may use any available remedy to make good the wrong done.' The present case involves no special factors counseling hesitation in the absence of affirmative action by Congress. . . .

Finally, we cannot accept respondents' formulation of the question as whether the availability of money damages is necessary to enforce the Fourth Amendment. For we have here no explicit congressional declaration that persons injured by a federal officer's violation of the Fourth Amendment may not recover money damages from the agents, but must instead be remitted to another remedy, equally effective in the view of Congress. The question is merely whether petitioner, if he can demonstrate an injury consequent upon the violation by federal agents of his Fourth Amendment rights, is entitled to redress his injury through a particular remedial mechanism normally available in the federal courts. 'The very essence of civil liberty certainly consists in the right of every individual to claim the protection of the laws, whenever he receives an injury.' Having concluded that petitioner's complaint states a cause of action under the Fourth Amendment, we hold that petitioner is entitled to recover money damages for any injuries he has suffered as a result of the agents' violation of the Amendment."

The Supreme Court reversed the judgment and remanded the case.

V. JUSTICE VOTE

6 Pro ACLU Side vs. 3 Con Opposing Side

ACLU Side (Petitioner/Appellant)

1. Brennan, W. – Wrote majority opinion
2. Marshall, T. – Joined majority opinion
3. White, B. – Joined majority opinion
4. Stewart, P. – Joined majority opinion
5. Douglas, W. – Joined majority opinion
6. Harlan, J. – Wrote concurring opinion

Opposing Side (Respondent/Appellee)

1. Burger, W. – Wrote dissenting opinion
2. Blackmun, H. – Wrote dissenting opinion
3. Black, H. – Wrote dissenting opinion

VI. A WIN OR LOSS FOR THE ACLU?

The ACLU filed as amicus curiae urging reversal; the Supreme Court reversed and remanded the ruling of the Court of Appeals in a 6-3 vote, giving the ACLU an apparent win.

254. New York Times Co. v. United States

(Decided June 30, 1971; 403 U.S. 713)

I. ISSUE

A. Issues Discussed

First Amendment, freedom of speech and of the press, prior restraints

B. Legal Question Presented

Does the government have power to halt the publication of news when the injunction asked for may be considered a prior restraint?

C. Supreme Court's Answer

The government has a high burden to show a prior restraint is constitutionally valid and the government did not meet that burden here.

II. CASE SUMMARY

A. Background

The New York Times and the Washington Post obtained copies of and started to publish excerpts from a classified study entitled

"History of US Decision-Making Process on Viet Nam Policy," popularly known as the Pentagon Papers.

The Department of Justice sought injunctions to prevent both newspapers from publishing the rest of the classified document. These injunctions were considered prior restraints, which carry a heavey burden. "The District Court for the Southern District of New York . . . and the District Court for the District of Columbia and the Court of Appeals for the District of Columbia Circuit . . . held that the Government had not met that burden."

On certiorari the Supreme Court reversed the order of the Court of Appeals for the Second Circuit and affirmed the judgment of the Court of Appeals for the District of Columbia Circuit.

B. Counsel of Record/ACLU Attorney

ACLU Side (Petitioner/Appellant): Alexander M. Bickel argued the cause for the New York Times. William R. Glendon argued the cause the Washington Post Company.

Opposing Side (Respondent/Appellee): Solicitor General Erwin N. Griswold argued the cause for the United States.

III. AMICI CURIAE

ACLU Side (Petitioner/Appellant)

Brief of amici curiae filed on behalf of the ACLU by Norman Dorsen, Melvin L. Wulf, Joel M. Gora, Burt Neuborne, Bruce J. Ennis, Osmond K. Fraenkel, James Heller, Hope Eastman, and Marvin M. Karpatkin

Brief of amici curiae filed by Bob Eckhardt and Thomas I. Emerson for Twenty-Seven Members of Congress.

Brief of amici curiae filed on behalf of the National Emergency Civil Liberties Committee by Victor Rabinowitz and Kristin Booth Glen.

Opposing Side (Respondent/Appellee)

No briefs of amici curiae were filed in support of appellee.

IV. THE SUPREME COURT'S DECISION

"'Any system of prior restraints of expression comes to this Court bearing a heavy presumption against its constitutional validity.' The Government 'thus carries a heavy burden of showing justification for the imposition of such a restraint.' The District Court for the Southern District of New York in the New York Times case and the District Court for the District of Columbia and the Court of Appeals for the District of Columbia Circuit in the Washington Post case held that the Government had not met that burden. We agree.

The judgment of the Court of Appeals for the District of Columbia Circuit is therefore affirmed. The order of the Court of Appeals for the Second Circuit is reversed . . . ."

V. JUSTICE VOTE

5 Pro ACLU Side vs. 3 Con Opposing Side

ACLU Side (Petitioner/Appellant)

1. Black, H. – Wrote concurring opinion, joined Douglas' concurrence
2. Douglas, W. – Wrote concurring opinion, joined Black's concurrence
3. Brennan, W. – Wrote concurring opinion
4. Stewart, P. – Wrote concurring opinion, joined White's concurrence
5. White, B. – Wrote concurring opinion, joined Stewart's concurrence
6. Marshall, T. – Wrote concurring opinion

Opposing Side (Respondent/Appellee)

1. Burger, W. – Wrote dissenting opinion, joined Harlan's dissent
2. Harlan, J. – Wrote dissenting opinion
3. Blackmun, H. – Wrote dissenting opinion, joined Harlan's dissent

VI. A WIN OR LOSS FOR THE ACLU?

The ACLU, as amicus curiae, urged reversal of the judgment of the Court of Appeals for the Second Circuit and affirmance of the judgment of the Court of Appeals for the District of Columbia Circuit; the Supreme Court, in a per curiam decision, reversed and affirmed in a 6-3 vote, giving the ACLU an apparent win.

255. Reed v. Reed

(Decided November 22, 1971; 404 U.S. 71)

I. ISSUE

A. Issues Discussed

Fourteenth Amendment, equal protection, discrimination

B. Legal Question Presented

Does the mandatory preference given to males over females in the Idaho Code regulating the administration of estates constitute a violation of the Equal Protection Clause of the Fourteenth Amendment?

C. Supreme Court's Answer

The mandatory preference for males over females is discrimination in violation of the Equal Protection Clause.

II. CASE SUMMARY

A. Background

"Richard Lynn Reed, a minor, died intestate in Ada County, Idaho, on March 29, 1967. His adoptive parents, who had separated sometime prior to his death, are the parties to this appeal. Approximately seven months after Richard's death, his mother, appellant Sally Reed, filed a petition in the Probate Court of Ada County, seeking appointment as administratrix of her son's estate. Prior to the date set for a hearing on the mother's petition, appellee Cecil Reed, the father of the decedent, filed a competing petition seeking to have himself appointed administrator of the son's estate. The probate court held a joint hearing on the two petitions and thereafter ordered that letters of administration be issued to appellee Cecil Reed upon his taking the oath and filing the bond required by law. The court treated § 15-312 and § 15-314 of the Idaho Code as the controlling statutes and read those sections as compelling a preference for Cecil Reed because he was a male."

Sally Reed appealed the order of the probate court to the District Court. The District Court held that the section violated the Equal Protection Clause and returned the matter to the Probate Court. Cecil Reed appealed the District Court order to the Idaho Supreme Court, which reversed the District Court and reinstated the Probate Court's order.

The Supreme Court granted certiorari to review the case and reversed the judgment of the Idaho Supreme Court.

B. Counsel of Record/ACLU Attorney

ACLU Side (Petitioner/Appellant): Allen R. Derr argued the cause for appellant. With him on the brief were Melvin L. Wulf, Ruth Bader Ginsburg, Pauli Murray, and Dorothy Kenyon.

Opposing Side (Respondent/Appellee): Charles S. Stout argued the cause for appellee. With him on the brief was Myron E. Anderson.

III. AMICI CURIAE

ACLU Side (Petitioner/Appellant)

Briefs of amici curiae were filed on behalf of the City of New York, the Legal Defense and Educational Fund, Inc., and the National Federation of Business and Professional Women's Club, Inc.

Opposing Side (Respondent/Appellee)

No briefs of amici curiae were filed on behalf of appellee.

IV. THE SUPREME COURT'S DECISION

"Having examined the record and considered the briefs and oral arguments of the parties, we have concluded that the arbitrary preference established in favor of males by § 15-314 of the Idaho Code cannot stand in the face of the Fourteenth Amendment's command that no State deny the equal protection of the laws to any person within its jurisdiction. . . .

Section 15-314 is restricted in its operation to those situations where competing applications for letters of administration have been filed by both male and female members of the same entitlement class established by § 15-312. In such situations, § 15-314 provides that different treatment be accorded to the applicants on the basis of their sex; it thus establishes a classification subject to scrutiny under the Equal Protection Clause."

The Supreme Court reversed the judgment of the Idaho Supreme Court and remanded the case.

V. JUSTICE VOTE

9 Pro ACLU Side vs. 0 Con Opposing Side

ACLU Side (Petitioner/Appellant)

1. Burger, W. – Wrote majority opinion
2. Blackmun, H. – Joined majority opinion
3. Black, H. – Joined majority opinion
4. Douglas, W. – Joined majority opinion
5. Brennan, W. – Joined majority opinion
6. Stewart, P. – Joined majority opinion
7. White, B. – Joined majority opinion
8. Marshall, T. – Joined majority opinion
9. Harlan, J. – Joined majority opinion

VI. A WIN OR LOSS FOR THE ACLU?

The ACLU, as counsel of record, urged reversal of the judgment of the Idaho Supreme Court; the U.S. Supreme Court reversed the lower court's ruling in a 9-0 vote, giving the ACLU an apparent win.

256. Diffenderfer v. Central Baptist Church of Miami

(Decided January 10, 1972; 404 U.S. 412)

I. ISSUE

A. Issues Discussed

Religion, 1st Amendment

B. Legal Question Presented

Whether a church parking lot primarily used for commercial purposes is tax exempt.

C. Supreme Court's Answer

"We must review the judgment of the District Court in light of Florida law as it now stands, not as it stood when the judgment below was entered. It is clear that the church parking lot that was the subject of the taxpayers' complaint is no longer fully exempt from taxation. . . . 'The case has therefore lost its character as a present, live controversy of the kind that must exist if we are to avoid advisory opinions on abstract propositions of law.'"

II. CASE SUMMARY

A. Background

"This is an action for a declaratory judgment that Florida Stat. s 192.06(4) (1967), F.S.A. violates the First Amendment to the Constitution of the United States insofar as it authorizes a tax exemption for church property used, inter alia, as a commercial parking lot, and for an injunction requiring appropriate state and local officials to assess and collect taxes against such property. It is brought by citizens and taxpayers of Dade County, Florida, where the property in question is located. The crux of their complaint is that state aid in the form of a tax exemption for church property used primarily for commercial purposes amounts not only to an establishment of the one religion aided, but also to an inhibition on the free exercise of other religions. A three-judge District Court, convened pursuant to 28 U.S.C. ss 2281, 2284, upheld the validity of the statute as applied to the property involved herein, and plaintiffs appealed to this Court. [The U.S. Supreme Court] noted probable jurisdiction on March 1, 1971."

B. Counsel of Record

ACLU Side (Petitioner/Appellant): Leo Pfeffer of the American Civil Liberties Union Foundation argued the cause for appellant Diffenderfer. With him on the brief were Richard Yale

Feder and Irma Robbins Feder of the American Civil Liberties Union of Florida, and Melvin L. Wulf of the American Civil Liberties Union Foundation. Howard J. Hollander argued the cause and filed a brief for appellant Paul.

Opposing Side (Respondent/Appellee): Charles M. Whelan argued the cause for appellee Central Baptist Church of Miami. With him on the brief were Herbert S. Sawyer, Karl B. Block, Jr., and William R. Consedine.

III. AMICI CURIAE

ACLU Side (Petitioner/Appellant)

Brief of amici curiae filed on behalf of Protestants and Other Americans United for Separation of Church and State by Franklin C. Salisbury and Noel H. Thompson.

Robert L. Shevin, Attorney General of Florida, pro se, filed a memorandum providing judicial notice of relevant changes to Florida law.

Opposing Side (Respondent/Appellee)

No briefs of amici curiae were filed in support of appellees.

IV. THE SUPREME COURT'S DECISION

"At its 1971 Regular Session, the Florida Legislature repealed s 196.191 (the 1969 successor to s 192.06) and enacted new legislation, approved June 15, 1971, effective December 31, 1971, which provides, in relevant part, that church property is exempt from taxation only if the property is used predominantly for religious purposes and only 'to the extent of the ratio that such predominant use bears to the non-exempt use.'

We must review the judgment of the District Court in light of Florida law as it now stands, not as it stood when the judgment below was entered. It is clear that the church parking lot that was the subject of the taxpayers' complaint is no longer fully exempt from taxation. If, in fact, it can be demonstrated that the lot is predominantly used for nonreligious purposes, it will receive no exemption whatever. 'The case has therefore lost its character as a present, live controversy of the kind that must exist if we are to avoid advisory opinions on abstract propositions of law.'

This is not a case that is 'capable of repetition, yet evading review,' nor is it the kind of case that may produce irreparable injury if not decided immediately. The only relief sought in the complaint was a declaratory judgment that the now repealed Fla. Stat. s 192.06(4) is unconstitutional as applied to a church parking lot used for commercial purposes and an injunction against its application to said lot. This relief is, of course, inappropriate now that the statute has been repealed.

Because it is possible that appellants may wish to amend their complaint so as to demonstrate that the repealed statute retains some continuing force or to attack the newly enacted legislation, rather than remanding the case to the District Court for dismissal as is our usual practice when a case has become moot pending a decision by this Court, we vacate the judgment of the District Court and remand the case to the District Court with leave to the appellants to amend their pleadings. . . .

Judgment vacated and case remanded."

V. JUSTICE VOTE

6 Pro ACLU Side vs. 1 Con Opposing Side

ACLU Side (Petitioner/Appellant)

1. Marshall, T. – Per curiam decision
2. Brennan, W. – Per curiam decision
3. Stewart, P. – Per curiam decision
4. Burger, W. – Per curiam decision
5. White, B. – Per curiam decision
6. Blackmun, H. – Per curiam decision

Opposing Side (Respondent/Appellee)

1. Douglas, W. – Wrote dissenting opinion

Powell, L. – Took no part in the decision.
Rehnquist, W. – Took no part in the decision.

VI. A WIN OR LOSS FOR THE ACLU?

The ACLU served as counsel for appellants urging reversal of the judgment of the U.S. District Court for the Southern District of Florida; the Supreme Court vacated, in a 6-1 per curiam decision, giving the ACLU an apparent win.

257. Groppi v. Leslie

(Decided January 13, 1972; 404 U.S. 496)

I. ISSUE

A. Issues Discussed

Civil rights, state's rights, Fourteenth Amendment, due process

B. Legal Question Presented

Did the Wisconsin Legislative Assembly violate petitioner's due process rights, guaranteed by the Fourteenth Amendment, by failing to give him notice or opportunity to defend himself prior to his punishment?

C. Supreme Court's Answer

The Wisconsin Legislative Assembly violated petitioner's due process rights.

II. CASE SUMMARY

A. Background

"On October 1, 1969, the Assembly of the Wisconsin Legislature passed a resolution citing petitioner for contempt and directing his confinement in the Dane County jail for a period of six months or for the duration of the 1969 Regular Session of the legislature, whichever was shorter. The resolution recited that petitioner had, two days previously, led a gathering of people which, by its presence on the floor of the Assembly during a regular meeting in violation of an Assembly Rule, 'prevented the Assembly from conducting public business and performing its constitutional duty.' The resolution contained a finding that petitioner's actions constituted 'disorderly conduct in the immediate view of the house and directly tending to interrupt its proceedings' which the Assembly was authorized to punish under the State Constitution and statutes. . . .

The Wisconsin Supreme Court, in its opinion denying petitioner's application for habeas corpus, took judicial notice that petitioner's conduct was designed to protest cuts in the state budget for certain welfare programs, and that the 'occupation' of the Assembly chamber by petitioner and his supporters continued from midday to 'well toward midnight,' during all of which time the Assembly was prevented from conducting its lawful business.

The contempt resolution was adopted without giving notice to petitioner or affording him an opportunity to present a defense or information in mitigation. A copy of the resolution was then served on petitioner who, at the time the resolution was passed, was already confined in the Dane County jail following his arrest on disorderly conduct charges arising out of the same incident as that underlying the resolution. Petitioner's confinement after he was served with the resolution was pursuant to its authority.

Petitioner then commenced actions in both state and federal courts contending that his confinement violated his constitutional rights, and seeking his release. Petitioner's applications for habeas corpus were denied by the Circuit Court for Dane County and the Wisconsin Supreme Court. However, after the state courts had acted, the United States District Court for the Western District of Wisconsin granted petitioner's federal habeas application. The District Court was of the view that petitioner had been denied due process of law guaranteed by the Fourteenth Amendment by the failure of the Assembly to accord him 'some minimal opportunity to appear and to respond to a charge' prior to the imposition of punishment for contempt. On appeal, the Court of Appeals reversed the holding of the District Court; the holding of the panel was adopted by a narrowly divided court on rehearing en banc."

The Supreme Court reversed the judgment of the Court of Appeals.

B. Counsel of Record/ACLU Attorney

ACLU Side (Petitioner/Appellant): William M. Coffey argued the cause for appellant.

Melvin L. Wulf argued the cause for the ACLU, as amicus curiae.

Opposing Side (Respondent/Appellee): Sverre O. Tinglum argued the cause for appellee.

III. AMICI CURIAE

ACLU Side (Petitioner/Appellant)

Brief of amici curiae filed on behalf of the ACLU by Melvin L. Wulf, Joel M. Gora, Sanford J. Rosen, Edward A. Tomlinson, and Robert H. Friebert.

Opposing Side (Respondent/Appellee)

No briefs of amici curiae were filed in support of appellee.

IV. THE SUPREME COURT'S DECISION

"For the reasons stated herein, we conclude that petitioner was denied due process of law by the procedures employed in punishing him for contempt . . . .

Even if it be assumed that courts and legislatures are fully analogous in this respect, the recorded cases dealing with the power of a court to impose summary punishment for contempt committed in its immediate presence show that such power has not ordinarily been exercised under conditions such as those here, with a lapse of two days following the event and without notice or opportunity for hearing of any kind. A legislature, like a court, must, of necessity, possess the power to act 'immediately' and 'instantly' to quell disorders in the chamber if it is to be able to maintain its authority and continue with the proper dispatch of its business. Where, however, the contemptuous episode has occurred two days previously, it is much more difficult to argue that action without notice or hearing of any kind is necessary to preserve order and enable a legislative body to proceed with its business. . . .

At a very early stage in our history this Court stated that the legislative contempt power should be limited to '[t]he least possible power adequate to the end proposed.' While a different result might well follow had the Wisconsin Assembly acted immediately upon occurrence of the contemptuous conduct and while the contemnor was in the chamber, or nearby within the Capitol building, as in Terry, we conclude that the procedures employed in this case were beyond the legitimate scope of that power because of the absence of notice or any opportunity to respond. The judgment of the Court of Appeals is reversed."

V. JUSTICE VOTE

7 Pro ACLU Side vs. 0 Con Opposing Side

ACLU Side (Petitioner/Appellant)

1. Burger, W. – Wrote majority opinion
2. Brennan, W. – Joined majority opinion
3. White, B. – Joined majority opinion
4. Blackmun, H. – Joined majority opinion
5. Marshall, T. – Joined majority opinion
6. Douglas, W. – Joined majority opinion
7. Stewart, P. – Joined majority opinion

Rehnquist, W. – Took no part in the decision
Powell, L. – Took no part in the decision

VI. A WIN OR LOSS FOR THE ACLU?

The ACLU filed as amicus curiae urging reversal (an ACLU attorney argued though not as counsel of record); the Supreme Court reversed the ruling of the Court of Appeals in a 7-0 vote, giving the ACLU an apparent win.

258. Trbovich v. United Mine Workers of America

(Decided January 17, 1972; 404 U.S. 528)

I. ISSUE

A. Issues Discussed

Governmental authority, unions, Fourteenth amendment

B. Legal Question Presented

Does the Labor-Management Reporting and Disclosure Act prevent a union member from intervening in a suit initiated by the Secretary of Labor, to set aside an election of officers?

C. Supreme Court's Answer

The LMRDA allows union member intervention limited to the issues raised by the Secretary of Labor in this circumstance.

II. CASE SUMMARY

A. Background

The Labor-Management Reporting and Disclosure Act of 1959 ("LMRDA") was enacted "to regulate the internal affairs of labor unions." In this case, the Secretary of Labor brought an action under § 402(b) of the LMRDA, "to set aside an election of officers of the United Mine Workers of America (UMWA)." The Secretary of Labor "alleged that the election was held in a manner that violated the LMRDA in numerous respects, and he sought an order requiring a new election to be held under his supervision."

Petitioner Trbovich, "a member of the UMWA, filed the initial complaint with the Secretary that eventually led him to file this suit. Petitioner now seeks to intervene in the litigation, pursuant to Fed.Rule Civ.Proc. 24(a), in order (1) to urge two additional grounds for setting aside the election, (2) to seek certain specific safeguards with respect to any new election that may be ordered, and (3) to present evidence and argument in support of the Secretary's challenge to the election. The District Court denied his motion for leave to intervene, on the ground that the LMRDA expressly stripped union members of any right to challenge a union election in the courts, and gave that right exclusively to the Secretary. The Court of Appeals affirmed on the basis of the District Court opinion. [The Supreme Court] granted certiorari to determine whether the LMRDA imposes a bar to intervention by union members under Rule 24, in a suit initiated by the Secretary."

The Supreme Court reversed and remanded the case.

B. Counsel of Record/ACLU Attorney

ACLU Side (Petitioner/Appellant): Joseph L. Rauh, Jr. argued the cause for appellant.

Opposing Side (Respondent/Appellee): Solicitor General Erwin N. Griswold argued the cause for appellee.

III. AMICI CURIAE

ACLU Side (Petitioner/Appellant)

Brief of amici curiae filed on behalf of the ACLU by Melvin L. Wulf and Sanford Jay Rosen.

Opposing Side (Respondent/Appellee)

No briefs of amici curiae were filed in support of appellee.

IV. THE SUPREME COURT'S DECISION

"With respect to litigation by union members, then, the legislative history supports the conclusion that Congress intended to prevent members from pressing claims not thought meritorious by the Secretary, and from litigating in forums or at times different from those chosen by the Secretary. Only if intervention would frustrate either of those objectives can the statute fairly be read to prohibit intervention as well as initiation of suits by members. . . . Accordingly, we hold that in a post-election enforcement suit, Title IV imposes no bar to intervention by a union member, so long as that intervention is limited to the claims of illegality presented by the Secretary's complaint. . . .

The Secretary contends that petitioner's only legally cognizable interest is the interest of all union members in democratic elections, and he says that interest is identical with the interest represented by the Secretary in Title IV litigation. Hence he argues that petitioner's interest must be adequately represented unless the court is prepared to find that the Secretary has failed to perform his statutory duty. We disagree.

The statute plainly imposes on the Secretary the duty to serve two distinct interests, which are related, but not identical. First, the statute gives the individual union members certain rights against their union, and 'the Secretary of Labor in effect becomes the union member's lawyer' for purposes of enforcing those rights. And second, the Secretary has an obligation to protect the 'vital public interest in assuring free and democratic union elections that transcends the narrower interest of the complaining union member.' Both functions are important, and they may not always dictate precisely the same approach to the conduct of the litigation. Even if the Secretary is performing his duties, broadly conceived, as well as can be expected, the union member may have a valid complaint about the performance of 'his lawyer.' Such a complaint, filed by the member who initiated the entire enforcement proceeding, should be regarded as sufficient to warrant relief in the form of intervention under Rule 24(a)(2). The judgment is reversed and the case is remanded to the District Court with directions to allow limited intervention in accordance with this opinion."

V. JUSTICE VOTE

6 Pro ACLU Side vs. 1 Con Opposing Side

ACLU Side (Petitioner/Appellant)

1. Marshall, T. – Wrote majority opinion
2. Brennan, W. – Joined majority opinion
3. White, B. – Joined majority opinion
4. Blackmun, H. – Joined majority opinion
5. Burger, W. – Joined majority opinion
6. Stewart, P. – Joined majority opinion

Opposing Side (Respondent/Appellee)

1. Douglas, W. – Wrote opinion dissenting in part

Powell, L – Took no part in the decision
Rehnquist, W – Took no part in the decision

VI. A WIN OR LOSS FOR THE ACLU?

The ACLU filed as amicus curiae urging reversal, the Supreme Court reversed the judgment of the Court of Appeals in a 6-1 vote, giving the ACLU an apparent win.

259. Bd. of Regents of Univ. of Texas System v. New Left Education Project

(Decided January 24, 1972; 404 U.S. 541)

I. ISSUE

A. Issues Discussed

Press, speech, association, 1st Amendment

B. Legal Question Presented

Whether Regents rules regarding on campus distribution of literature and dues solicitation are unconstitutional.

C. Supreme Court's Answer

"Since the three-judge court was improperly convened, appeal lies not here but to the Court of Appeals for the Fifth Circuit. So that appellant may be able, if it desires, to perfect a timely appeal, we vacate the judgment below and remand the case with instruction that the court enter a fresh decree."

II. CASE SUMMARY

A. Background

"This litigation began when the Board of Regents sued the New Left Education Project and certain individuals in a Texas court. In that suit, the Regents sought to restrain defendants from distributing a newspaper and making either commercial or noncommercial solicitations on the Austin campus of the University of Texas except in compliance with appellant's rules. Defendants countered by bringing this federal suit to enjoin further state court proceedings on the ground that the rules that the Regents sought to enforce abridged defendants' First Amendment rights. A three-judge court met and determined that it was properly convened pursuant to 28 U.S.C. s 2281. It then permitted certain other organizations and individuals, including appellees here, to join the suit as plaintiffs and dismissed the action as to those involved in the state court adjudication. Thereafter, the court granted summary judgment in favor of appellees, declaring unconstitutional and permanently enjoining enforcement of two rules, Regents' Rules & Regs., c. VI, pt. 1, ss 6.11, 6.12 (App. 173), governing the campus distribution of certain kinds of literature and the solicitation of dues from members of political organizations."

The U.S. Supreme Court "postponed consideration of our jurisdiction to a hearing on the merits."

B. Counsel of Record

ACLU Side (Respondent/Appellee): David R. Richards argued the cause for appellees. With him on the brief was Melvin L. Wulf of the American Civil Liberties Union Foundation.

Opposing Side (Petitioner/Appellant): W. 0. Shultz II, Assistant Attorney General of Texas, argued the cause for appellant. With him on the brief were Crawford C. Martin, Attorney General, Nola White, First Assistant Attorney General, Alfred Walker, Executive Assistant Attorney General, and J. C. Davis, Pat Bailey, and James C. McCoy, Assistant Attorneys General.

III. AMICI CURIAE

ACLU Side (Respondent/Appellee)

No briefs of amici curiae were filed in support of appellees.

Opposing Side (Petitioner/Appellant)

No briefs of amici curiae were filed in support of appellant.

IV. THE SUPREME COURT'S DECISION

"We have jurisdiction to review directly the lower court's order granting an injunction only if the case was one required to be heard and determined by a three-judge court. Such a court is required where the challenged statute or regulation, albeit created or authorized by a state legislature, has statewide application or effectuates a statewide policy. But a single judge, not a three-judge court, must hear the case where the statute or regulation is of only local import. . . .

Appellant Board of Regents was created by the Texas Legislature and is charged with governing those educational institutions in the University of Texas System. This governance, which specifically includes a rulemaking power, extends to but three of the 23 four-year state colleges and universities listed in the Higher Education Coordinating Act of 1965 . . . . It is therefore apparent that the Regents' rulemaking power and the rules at issue in this litigation extend to but a fraction of the campuses in the Texas system of higher public education. These rules can scarcely be described as matters of statewide concern or expressions of a statewide policy when a large percentage of Texas colleges and universities are unaffected by them and could not be affected by any pronouncement that a federal court might make on their constitutionality. There is no suggestion or indication of any kind that the Regents' rules are similar to those for other schools or are required by or express statewide policy. . . . These rules, applying only to some of the higher educational institutions of the State, are of limited significance and do not partake of the quality and dignity of those state statutes or policies that three-judge courts were designed to consider. We are persuaded that a contrary view of this case would be inconsistent with our oft-repeated admonition that the three-judge court statute is to be strictly construed.

Since the three-judge court was improperly convened, appeal lies not here but to the Court of Appeals for the Fifth Circuit. So that appellant may be able, if it desires, to perfect a timely appeal, we vacate the judgment below and remand the case with instruction that the court enter a fresh decree.

Judgment vacated and remanded."

V. JUSTICE VOTE

1 Pro ACLU Side vs. 6 Con Opposing Side

ACLU Side (Respondent/Appellee)

1. Douglas, W. – Wrote dissenting opinion

Opposing Side (Petitioner/Appellant)

1. White, B. – Wrote majority opinion
2. Marshall, T. – Joined majority opinion
3. Brennan, W. – Joined majority opinion
4. Stewart, P. – Joined majority opinion

5. Burger, W. – Joined majority opinion
6. Blackmun, H. – Joined majority opinion

Powell, L. – Took no part in the decision.
Rehnquist, W. – Took no part in the decision.

VI. A WIN OR LOSS FOR THE ACLU?

The ACLU served as counsel for appellees urging affirmance of the judgment of the U.S. District Court for the Western District of Texas; the Supreme Court vacated, in a 6-1 vote, giving the ACLU an apparent loss.

260. Dunn v. Blumstein

(Decided March 21, 1972; 405 U.S. 330)

I. ISSUE

A. Issues Discussed

Voting rights

B. Legal Question Presented

"Durational residence laws penalize those persons who have traveled from one place to another to establish a new residence during the qualifying period. Such laws divide residents into two classes, old residents and new residents, and discriminate against the latter to the extent of totally denying them the opportunity to vote. The constitutional question presented is whether the Equal Protection Clause of the Fourteenth Amendment permits a State to discriminate in this way among its citizens."

C. Supreme Court's Answer

"Given the exacting standard of precision we require of statutes affecting constitutional rights, we cannot say that durational residence requirements are necessary to further a compelling state interest."

II. CASE SUMMARY

A. Background

"Various Tennessee public officials (hereinafter Tennessee) appeal from a decision by a three-judge federal court holding that Tennessee's durational residence requirements for voting violate the Equal Protection Clause of the United States Constitution. The issue arises in a class action for declaratory and injunctive relief brought by appellee James Blumstein. Blumstein moved to Tennessee on June 12, 1970, to begin employment as an assistant professor of law at Vanderbilt University in Nashville. With an eye toward voting in the upcoming August and November elections, he attempted to register to vote on July 1, 1970. The county registrar refused to register him, on the ground that Tennessee law authorizes the registration of only those persons who, at the time of the next election, will have been residents of the State for a year and residents of the county for three months.

After exhausting state administrative remedies, Blumstein brought this action challenging these residence requirements on federal constitutional grounds. A three-judge court, convened pursuant to 28 U.S.C. ss 2281, 2284, concluded that Tennessee's durational residence requirements were unconstitutional (1) because they impermissibly interfered with the right to vote and (2) because they created a 'suspect' classification penalizing some Tennessee residents because of recent interstate movement. [The Supreme Court] noted probable jurisdiction."

B. Counsel of Record

ACLU Side (Respondent/Appellee): James F. Blumstein, pro se, argued the cause for appellee. With him on the brief were Charles Morgan, Jr., and Norman Siegel of the American Civil Liberties Union Foundation, Inc., and Jerry P. Black, Jr.

Opposing Side (Petitioner/Appellant): Robert H. Roberts, Assistant Attorney General of Tennessee, argued the cause for appellants. With him on the brief were David M. Pack, Attorney General, and Thomas E. Fox, Deputy Attorney General.

III. AMICI CURIAE

ACLU Side (Respondent/Appellee)

Brief of amici curiae filed on behalf of Common Cause by Henry P. Sailer and William A. Dobrovir.

Opposing Side (Petitioner/Appellant)

No briefs of amici curiae were filed in support of appellants.

IV. THE SUPREME COURT'S DECISION

"To decide whether a law violates the Equal Protection Clause, we look, in essence, to three things: the character of the classification in question; the individual interests affected by the classification; and the governmental interests asserted in support of the classification. In considering laws challenged under the Equal Protection Clause, this Court has evolved more than one test, depending upon the interest affected or the classification involved. First, then, we must determine what standard of review is appropriate. In the present case, whether we look to the benefit withheld by the classification (the opportunity to vote) or the basis for the classification (recent interstate travel) we conclude that the State must show a substantial and compelling reason for imposing durational residence requirements. . . .

In sum, durational residence laws must be measured by a strict equal protection test: they are unconstitutional unless the State can demonstrate that such laws are 'necessary to promote a compelling governmental interest.' . . .

We turn, then, to the question of whether the State has shown that durational residence requirements are needed to further a sufficiently substantial state interest. We emphasize again the difference between bona fide residence requirements and durational residence requirements. We have in the past noted approvingly that the States have the power to require that voters be bona fide residents of the relevant political subdivision. An appropriately defined and uniformly applied requirement of bona fide residence may be necessary to preserve the basic conception of a political community, and therefore could withstand close constitutional scrutiny. But Durational residence requirements, representing a separate voting qualification imposed on bona fide residents, must be separately tested by the stringent standard. . . .

It may well be true that new residents as a group know less about state and local issues than older residents . . . . But as devices to limit the franchise to knowledgeable residents, the conclusive presumptions of durational residence requirements are much too crude. . . . Here, there is simply too attenuated a relationship between the state interest in an informed electorate and the fixed requirement that voters must have been residents in the State for a year and the county for three months. Given the exacting standard of precision we require of statutes affecting constitutional rights, we cannot say that durational residence requirements are necessary to further a compelling state interest. . . .

Concluding that Tennessee has not offered an adequate justification for its durational residence laws, we affirm the judgment of the court below."

V. JUSTICE VOTE

6 Pro ACLU Side vs. 1 Con Opposing Side

ACLU Side (Respondent/Appellee)

1. Marshall, T. – Wrote majority opinion
2. White, B. – Joined majority opinion
3. Brennan, W. – Joined majority opinion
4. Stewart, P. – Joined majority opinion
5. Blackmun, H. – Wrote concurring opinion
6. Douglas, W. – Joined majority opinion

Opposing Side (Petitioner/Appellant)

1. Burger, W. – Wrote dissenting opinion

Powell, L. – Took no part in the decision.
Rehnquist, W. – Took no part in the decision.

VI. A WIN OR LOSS FOR THE ACLU?

The ACLU served as counsel for appellee urging affirmance of the judgment of the U.S. District Court for the Middle District of Tennessee; the Supreme Court affirmed, in a 6-1 vote, giving the ACLU an apparent win.

261. Fein v. Selective Service System Local Board No. 7

(Decided March 21, 1972; 405 U.S. 365)

I. ISSUE

A. Issues Discussed

Governmental authority, regulation First Amendment, military, conscientious objectors

B. Legal Question Presented

"[W]hether § 10(b)(3) of the Military Selective Service Act of 1967, permits this preinduction challenge to Selective Service appeal procedures."

C. Supreme Court's Answer

Section 10(b)(3) does not permit this preinduction challenge to Selective Service appeal procedures.

II. CASE SUMMARY

A. Background

Petitioner Oliver Fein was a doctor. While as an undergraduate and later in medical school, petitioner's induction into the military was postponed. Upon graduation from medical school, Fein was assigned an occupational deferment because of his internship at a hospital.

While an intern, Fein wrote to his local board to declare himself as a "conscientious objector to war and the institution which propagates war, the military" and requesting I-O classification. Petitioner's local board invited him to appear personally before it. After the interview, the board denied him an 1-O classification for deferment. However, after he requested another appearance before the board, the board granted his request and classified him as I-O.

Following his classification as a conscientious objector, the State Director wrote the board and requested an appeal, "stating, 'It is our opinion that the registrant would not qualify for a I-O classification as a conscientious objector.'" Fein was notified of the request, but was not furnished with the basis for the appeal, or given an opportunity to reply. The appeal board unanimously classified him as 1-A and rejected his conscientious objector claim, without stating the reasoning behind the reclassification. Under the regulations he was not entitled to appeal to the national board.

Fein successfully challenged his first induction order after his I-A classification by writing to the National Director of Selective Service. However, the national board then unanimously voted again to classify Fein as I-A. Fein has not been ordered to report for induction again.

Fein brought a pre-induction suit challenging the constitutionality of the Selective Service appeal procedures, on due process grounds, because he was not given reasons for the appeal or for the decision denying him his desired classification. The District Court dismissed the complaint, finding the suit was barred by § 10(b)(3) of the Military Selective Service Act, and the Court of Appeals affirmed. Section 10(b)(3) states that "a classification decision of the local board 'shall be final, except where an appeal is authorized . . .' and that the classification decision on appeal also 'shall be final.'"

The Supreme Court granted certiorari and affirmed.

B. Counsel of Record/ACLU Attorney

ACLU Side (Petitioner/Appellant): Michael B. Standard argued the cause for appellant.

Opposing Side (Respondent/Appellee): Solicitor General Erwin N. Griswold argued the cause for appellee.

III. AMICI CURIAE

ACLU Side (Petitioner/Appellant)

Brief of amici curiae filed on behalf of the ACLU by Melvin L. Wulf.

Opposing Side (Respondent/Appellee)

No briefs of amici curiae were filed in support of appellee.

IV. THE SUPREME COURT'S DECISION

"The respondents appropriately noted . . . that these decisions were all so-called post-induction cases in the sense that they were appeals from convictions under § 12(a). The respondents accordingly took the position that this line of authority, however appropriate it might be for post-induction review, did not support or justify an exception to the bar of § 10(b)(3) against pre-induction review of the processing or classifying of registrants. . . .

While Joseph also is a conviction case and is not one on pre-induction review, its obvious significance for Fein is that if the doctor is ever again called for induction, the rule of Haughton will provide a defense for him unless and until the requirements of the new statute and regulations are fulfilled. Whether this necessitates a complete reprocessing of Fein's case is a matter we leave in the first instance to the administrative authorities.

The judgment of the Court of Appeals is therefore to be affirmed. We express no view upon the merits of Dr. Fein's conscientious objector claim other than to observe the obvious, namely, that his claim is not frivolous."

The Supreme Court affirmed the judgment of Court of Appeals.

V. JUSTICE VOTE

3 Pro ACLU Side vs. 4 Con Opposing Side

ACLU Side (Petitioner/Appellant)

1. Douglas, W. – Wrote dissenting opinion
2. Marshall, T. – Wrote dissenting opinion
3. Stewart, P. – Joined Marshall's dissent

Opposing Side (Respondent/Appellee)

1. Blackmun, H. – Wrote majority opinion
2. Brennan, W. – Joined majority opinion
3. White, B. – Joined majority opinion
4. Burger, W. – Joined majority opinion

Powell, L. – Took no part in the decision
Rehnquist, W. – Took no part in the decision

VI. A WIN OR LOSS FOR THE ACLU?

The ACLU filed as amicus curiae urging reversal, the Supreme Court affirmed the ruling of the Court of Appeals in a 4-3 vote, giving the ACLU an apparent loss.

262. Eisenstadt v. Baird

(Decided March 22, 1972; 405 U.S. 438)

I. ISSUE

A. Issues Discussed

Civil rights, privacy, First Amendment, Fourteenth Amendment, equal protection

B. Legal Question Presented

Does a Massachusetts law, allowing only married couples to obtain contraceptives violate the Equal Protection Clause?

C. Supreme Court's Answer

The law violates the Equal Protection Clause by treating similarly situated married and unmarried persons in a dissimilar way.

II. CASE SUMMARY

A. Background

"Appellee William Baird was convicted . . . in the Massachusetts Superior Court . . . , first for exhibiting contraceptive articles during a lecture on contraception to students at Boston University, and second for giving a young woman a package of Emko vaginal foam at the close of his address."

Appellee was charged with a felony for distributing contraceptives. Under Massachusetts law only married couples could obtain contraceptives, and only registered doctors or pharmacists could provide them. Baird was not an authorized distributor of contraceptives.

"The Massachusetts Supreme Judicial Court unanimously set aside the conviction for exhibiting contraceptives on the ground that it violated Baird's First Amendment rights, but by a four-to-three vote sustained the conviction for giving away the foam. Baird subsequently filed a petition for a federal writ of habeas corpus, which the District Court dismissed. On appeal, however, the Court of Appeals for the First Circuit vacated the dismissal and remanded the action with directions to grant the writ discharging Baird. This appeal by the Sheriff of Suffolk County, Massachusetts, followed, and [the Supreme Court] noted probable jurisdiction."

The Supreme Court granted certiorari and affirmed.

B. Counsel of Record/ACLU Attorney

ACLU Side (Respondent/Appellee): Joseph D. Tydings argued the cause for appellee.

Opposing Side (Petitioner/Appellant): Joseph R. Nolan, Special Assistant Attorney General of Massachusetts, argued the cause for appellant.

III. AMICI CURIAE

ACLU Side (Respondent/Appellee)

Brief of amici curiae filed on behalf of the ACLU, et al., by Melvin L. Wulf, Lawrence G. Sager, and John A. Robertson.

Briefs of amici curiae were filed on behalf of the Planned Parenthood Federation of America, Inc., the Planned Parenthood League of Massachusetts, and Human Rights for Women, Inc.

Opposing Side (Petitioner/Appellant)

No briefs of amici curiae were filed on behalf of appellant.

IV. THE SUPREME COURT'S DECISION

"[W]hatever the rights of the individual to access to contraceptives may be, the rights must be the same for the unmarried and the married alike.

If under *Griswold* [*v. Connecticut*] the distribution of contraceptives to married persons cannot be prohibited, a ban on distribution to unmarried persons would be equally impermissible. It is true that in Griswold the right of privacy in question inhered in the marital relationship. Yet the marital couple is not an independent entity with a mind and heart of its own, but an association of two individuals each with a separate intellectual and emotional makeup. If the right of privacy means anything, it is the right of the individual, married or single, to be free from unwarranted governmental intrusion into matters so fundamentally affecting a person as the decision whether to bear or beget a child.

On the other hand, if Griswold is no bar to a prohibition on the distribution of contraceptives, the State could not, consistently with the Equal Protection Clause, outlaw distribution to unmarried but not to married persons. In each case the evil, as perceived by the State, would be identical, and the under inclusion would be invidious. . . .

We hold that by providing dissimilar treatment for married and unmarried persons who are similarly situated, Massachusetts General Laws Ann., c. 272, §§ 21 and 21A, violate the Equal Protection Clause. The judgment of the Court of Appeals is affirmed."

V. JUSTICE VOTE

6 Pro ACLU Side vs. 1 Con Opposing Side

ACLU Side (Respondent/Appellee)

1. Brennan, W. – Wrote majority opinion
2. Marshall, T. – Joined majority opinion
3. Stewart, P. – Joined majority opinion
4. White, B. – Wrote concurring opinion
5. Blackmun, H. – Joined White's concurrence
6. Douglas, W. – Wrote a concurring opinion

Opposing Side (Petitioner/Appellant)

1. Burger, W. – Wrote dissenting opinion

Powell, L. – Took no part in the decision
Rehnquist, W. – Took no part in the decision

VI. A WIN OR LOSS FOR THE ACLU?

The ACLU filed as amicus curiae urging affirmance, the Supreme Court affirmed the ruling of the Court of Appeals in a 6-1 vote, giving the ACLU an apparent win.

263. Weber v. Aetna Casualty & Surety Co.

(Decided April 24, 1972; 406 U.S. 164)

I. ISSUE

A. Issues Discussed

Civil rights, state's rights, Fourteenth Amendment, equal protection, illegitimate children

B. Legal Question Presented

Do unacknowledged, illegitimate dependent children have a right "to recover under Louisiana workmen's compensation laws benefits for the death of their natural father on an equal footing with his dependent legitimate children"?

C. Supreme Court's Answer

The laws violate the Equal Protection Clause by placing illegitimate children on lesser footing than legitimate children.

II. CASE SUMMARY

A. Background

"On June 22, 1967, Henry Clyde Stokes died in Louisiana of injuries received during the course of his employment the previous day. At the time of his death Stokes resided and maintained a household with one Willie Mae Weber, to whom he was not married. Living in the household were four legitimate minor children, born of the marriage between Stokes and Adlay Jones Stokes who was at the time committed to a mental hospital. Also living in the home was one unacknowledged illegitimate child born of the relationship between Stokes and Willie Mae Weber. A second illegitimate child of Stokes and Weber was born posthumously.

On June 29, 1967, Stokes' four legitimate children, through their maternal grandmother as guardian, filed a claim for their father's death under Louisiana's workmen's compensation law. The defendant employer and its insurer impleaded Willie Mae Weber who appeared and claimed compensation benefits for the two illegitimate children.

Meanwhile, the four legitimate children had brought another suit for their father's death against a third-party tortfeasor, which was settled for an amount in excess of the maximum benefits allowable under workmen's compensation. The illegitimate children did not share in this settlement. Subsequently, the employer in the initial action requested the extinguishment of all parties' workmen's compensation claims by reason of the tort settlement.

The trial judge awarded the four legitimate children the maximum allowable amount of compensation and declared their entitlement had been satisfied from the tort suit settlement. Consequently, the four legitimate children dismissed their workmen's compensation claim. Judgment was also awarded to Stokes' two illegitimate offspring to the extent that maximum compensation benefits were not exhausted by the four legitimate children. Since such benefits had been entirely exhausted by the amount of the tort settlement, in which only the four dependent legitimate offspring participated, the two dependent illegitimate children received nothing."

The Supreme Court granted certiorari to review the case and reversed.

B. Counsel of Record/ACLU Attorney

ACLU Side (Petitioner/Appellant): Vanue B. Lacour argued the cause for appellant.

Opposing Side (Respondent/Appellee): W. Henson Moore argued the cause for appellee.

III. AMICI CURIAE

ACLU Side (Petitioner/Appellant)

Brief of amici curiae filed on behalf of the ACLU by Norman Dorsen and Melvin L. Wulf.

Opposing Side (Respondent/Appellee)

No briefs of amici curiae were filed in support of appellee.

IV. THE SUPREME COURT'S DECISION

"The state interest in legitimate family relationships is not served by the statute; the state interest in minimizing problems of proof is not significantly disturbed by our decision. The inferior classification of dependent unacknowledged illegitimates bears, in this instance, no significant relationship to those recognized purposes of recovery which workmen's compensation statutes commendably serve.

The status of illegitimacy has expressed through the ages society's condemnation of irresponsible liaisons beyond the bonds of marriage. But visiting this condemnation on the head of an infant is illogical and unjust. Moreover, imposing disabilities on the illegitimate child is contrary to the basic concept of our system that legal burdens should bear some relationship to individual responsibility or wrongdoing. Obviously, no child is responsible for his birth and penalizing the illegitimate child is an ineffectual—as well as an unjust—way of deterring the parent. Courts are powerless to prevent the social opprobrium suffered by these hapless children, but the Equal Protection Clause does enable us to strike down discriminatory laws relating to status of birth where—as in this case—the classification is justified by no legitimate state interest, compelling or otherwise."

The Supreme Court reversed the judgment and remanded the case.

V. JUSTICE VOTE

8 Pro ACLU Side vs. 1 Con Opposing Side

ACLU Side (Petitioner/Appellant)

1. Powell, L. – Wrote majority opinion
2. Brennan, W. – Joined majority opinion
3. White, B. – Joined majority opinion
4. Marshall, T. – Joined majority opinion
5. Burger, W. – Joined majority opinion
6. Douglas, W. – Joined majority opinion
7. Stewart, P. – Joined majority opinion
8. Blackmun, H. – Wrote concurring opinion

Opposing Side (Respondent/Appellee)

1. Rehnquist, W. – Wrote dissenting opinion

VI. A WIN OR LOSS FOR THE ACLU?

The ACLU filed as amicus curiae; the U.S. Supreme Court reversed the Louisiana Supreme Court's judgment in an 8-1 vote giving the ACLU an apparent win.

264. United States v. Biswell

(Decided May 15, 1972; 406 U.S. 311)

I. ISSUE

A. Issues Discussed

Criminal justice, Fourth Amendment, warrants, gun control

B. Legal Question Presented

Did the warrantless search of a gun dealer's locked storeroom, authorized by § 923(g) of the Gun Control Act of 1968, violate the Fourth Amendment?

C. Supreme Court's Answer

The warrantless search of a gun dealer's locked storeroom authorized by § 923(g) did not violate the Fourth Amendment.

II. CASE SUMMARY

A. Background

"The Gun Control Act of 1968 authorizes official entry during business hours into 'the premises [including places of storage] of any firearms or ammunition . . . dealer . . . for the purpose of inspecting or examining (1) any records or documents required to be kept . . . and (2) any firearms or ammunition kept or stored by such . . . dealer . . . at such premises.' Respondent, a pawn shop operator who was federally licensed to deal in sporting weapons, was visited one afternoon by a city policeman and a Federal Treasury agent who identified himself, inspected respondent's books, and requested entry into a locked gun storeroom. Respondent asked whether the agent had a search warrant, and the investigator told him that he did not, but that § 923(g) authorized such inspections. Respondent was given a copy of the section to read and he replied, 'Well, that's what it says so I guess it's okay.' Respondent unlocked the storeroom, and the agent found and seized two sawed-off rifles which respondent was not licensed to possess. He was indicted and convicted for dealing in firearms without having paid the required special occupational tax. The Court of Appeals reversed, however, holding that § 923(g) was unconstitutional under the Fourth Amendment because it authorized warrantless searches of business premises and that respondent's ostensible consent to the search was invalid . . . . The Court of Appeals concluded that the sawed-off rifles, having been illegally seized, were inadmissible in evidence."

The Supreme Court granted certiorari and reversed the judgment of the Court of Appeals.

B. Counsel of Record/ACLU Attorney

Opposing Side (Petitioner/Appellant): Warren F. Reynolds argued the cause for appellee.

ACLU Side (Respondent/Appellee): R. Kent Greenawalt argued the cause for appellant.

III. AMICI CURIAE

ACLU Side (Respondent/Appellee)

Brief of amici curiae filed on behalf of the ACLU by John S. Edmunds, Joel M. Gora, and Melvin L. Wulf.

Opposing Side (Petitioner/Appellant)

No briefs of amici curiae were filed in support of appellant.

IV. THE SUPREME COURT'S DECISION

"It is . . . plain that inspections for compliance with the Gun Control Act pose only limited threats to the dealer's justifiable expectations of privacy. When a dealer chooses to engage in this pervasively regulated business and to accept a federal license, he does so with the knowledge that his business records, firearms, and ammunition will be subject to effective inspection. Each licensee is annually furnished with a revised compilation of ordinances that describe his obligations and define the inspector's authority. The dealer is not left to wonder about the purposes of the inspector or the limits of his task.

We have little difficulty in concluding that where, as here, regulatory inspections further urgent federal interest, and the possibilities of abuse and the threat to privacy are not of impressive dimensions, the inspection may proceed without a warrant where specifically authorized by statute. The seizure of respondent's sawed-off rifles was not unreasonable under the Fourth Amendment, and the judgment of the Court of Appeals is reversed, and the case is remanded to that court for further proceedings consistent with this opinion."

V. JUSTICE VOTE

1 Pro ACLU Side vs. 8 Con Opposing Side

ACLU Side (Respondent/Appellee)

1. Douglas, W. – Wrote dissenting opinion

Opposing Side (Petitioner/Appellant)

1. White, B. – Wrote majority opinion
2. Brennan, W. – Joined majority opinion
3. Blackmun, H. – Wrote concurring opinion
4. Marshall, T. – Joined majority opinion
5. Burger, W. – Joined majority opinion
6. Powell, L. – Joined majority opinion
7. Stewart, P. – Joined majority opinion
8. Rehnquist, W. – Joined majority opinion

VI. A WIN OR LOSS FOR THE ACLU?

The ACLU filed as amicus curiae urging affirmance; the Supreme Court reversed the ruling of the Court of Appeals in an 8-1 vote, giving the ACLU an apparent loss.

265. Strait v. Laird

(Decided May 22, 1972; 406 U.S. 341)

I. ISSUE

A. Issues Discussed

Military

B. Legal Question Presented

Whether courts in California had jurisdiction over the habeas corpus petition of a reserve officer residing in that state.

C. Supreme Court's Answer

"We intimate no opinion on the merits of the controversy—whether petitioner is entitled to a discharge or whether by denying that relief the Army has acted in accordance with the prescribed procedures. We hold only that there is jurisdiction under 28 U.S.C. s 2241(c)(1) for consideration of this habeas corpus petition and for decision on the merits."

II. CASE SUMMARY

A. Background

"Petitioner is an Army Reserve officer not on active duty. His active-duty obligations were deferred while he went to law school after graduating from college. During the period of deferment and at the time this action was commenced, his military records were kept at Fort Benjamin Harrison, Indiana. His nominal commanding officer was the Commanding Officer of the Reserve Officer Components Personnel Center at Fort Benjamin Harrison. Petitioner was, however, at all times domiciled in California and was never in Indiana or assigned there. On finishing law school he took the California Bar examination and on March 5, 1970, he was ordered to report for active duty at Fort Gordon, Georgia, beginning April 13, 1970. Before that time, however, he had filed an application for discharge as a conscientious objector. That application was processed at Fort Ord, California, where hearings were held. Fort Ord recommended his discharge and review of that recommendation was had in Indiana. The result was disapproval of the application.

Petitioner thereupon filed a petition for writ of habeas corpus in California. The District Court denied a motion to dismiss, holding that it had jurisdiction (3 S.S.L.R. 3152), but ruled against petitioner on the merits. On appeal the Court of Appeals agreed with the District Court as to jurisdiction but disagreed with it on the merits and granted the writ. Shortly thereafter [the Supreme Court] decision in Schlanger v. Seamans, 401 U.S. 487, was announced. Thereupon the Court of Appeals granted a petition for rehearing and dismissed the action, holding that the District Court had no jurisdiction under the habeas corpus statutes. The case is here on a petition for certiorari, which [the Supreme Court] granted."

B. Counsel of Record

ACLU Side (Petitioner/Appellant): John T. Hansen argued the cause for appellant. With him on the briefs were Melvin L. Wulf and Joel M. Gora of the American Civil Liberties Union

Foundation, Paul Halvonik of the American Civil Liberties Union of Northern California, and Michael N. Pollet.

Opposing Side (Respondent/Appellee): Solicitor General Griswold argued the cause for appellees. With him on the brief were Assistant Attorney General Mardian, Wm. Terry Bray, and Robert L. Keuch.

III. AMICI CURIAE

ACLU Side (Petitioner/Appellant)

Brief of amici curiae filed on behalf of the Central Committee for Conscientious Objectors et al. by Stanley F. Farrar.

Opposing Side (Respondent/Appellee)

No briefs of amici curiae were filed in support of appellees.

IV. THE SUPREME COURT'S DECISION

"In Schlanger the serviceman—on active duty in the Air Force—was studying in Arizona on assignment from Ohio. There was no officer in Arizona who was his custodian or one in his chain of command . . . . While the Habeas Corpus Act extends to those 'in custody under or by color of the authority of the United States,' 28 U.S.C. s 2241(c)(1), we held in Schlanger that the presence of the 'custodian' within the territorial jurisdiction of the District Court was a sine qua non. In Schlanger the only 'custodian' of the serviceman was in Moody AFB, Georgia. . . .

In the present case California is Strait's home. He was commissioned in California. Up to the controversy in the present case he was on reserve duty, never on active duty, and while he had gone east for graduate work in law, California had always been his home. Fort Ord in California was where his application for conscientious objector discharge was processed and where hearings were held. It was in California where he had had his only meaningful contact with the Army; and his superiors there recommended his discharge as a conscientious objector.

Thus, the contention in the dissent that we 'abandon Schlanger' by the approach we take today is incorrect. Sergeant Schlanger was on permissive temporary duty. . . .

Strait's situation is far different. His nominal custodian, unlike Schlanger's, has enlisted the aid and directed the activities of armed forces personnel in California in his dealings with Strait. Indeed, in the course of Strait's enlistment, virtually every face-to-face contact between him and the military has taken place in California. In the face of this record, to say that Strait's custodian is amenable to process only in Indiana . . . would be to exalt fiction over reality. . . .

Strait's commanding officer is 'present' in California through the officers in the hierarchy of the command who processed this serviceman's application for discharge. To require him to go to Indiana where he never has been or assigned to be would entail needless expense and inconvenience. . . . The concepts of 'custody' and 'custodian' are sufficiently broad to allow us to say that the commanding officer in Indiana, operating through officers in California in processing petitioner's claim, is in California for the limited purposes of habeas corpus jurisdiction.

We intimate no opinion on the merits of the controversy—whether petitioner is entitled to a discharge or whether by denying that relief the Army has acted in accordance with the prescribed procedures. We hold only that there is jurisdiction under 28 U.S.C. s 2241(c)(1) for consideration of this habeas corpus petition and for decision on the merits.

Reversed."

V. JUSTICE VOTE

5 Pro ACLU Side vs. 4 Con Opposing Side

ACLU Side (Petitioner/Appellant)

1. Douglas, W. – Wrote majority opinion
2. White, B. – Joined majority opinion
3. Marshall, T. – Joined majority opinion
4. Stewart, P. – Joined majority opinion
5. Blackmun, H. – Joined majority opinion

Opposing Side (Respondent/Appellee)

1. Rehnquist, W. – Wrote dissenting opinion
2. Burger, W. – Joined Rehnquist's dissent
3. Brennan, W. – Joined Rehnquist's dissent
4. Powell, L. – Joined Rehnquist's dissent

VI. A WIN OR LOSS FOR THE ACLU?

The ACLU served as counsel for appellant urging reversal of the judgment of the Court of Appeals; the Supreme Court reversed, in a 5-4 vote, giving the ACLU an apparent win.

266. Apodaca v. Oregon

(Decided May 22, 1972; 406 U.S. 404)

I. ISSUE

A. Issues Discussed

Criminal procedure, Sixth Amendment, Fourteenth Amendment, jury trials

B. Legal Question Presented

In a criminal case in state court, does a defendant have a constitutional right to a unanimous jury verdict, or may state juries convict a defendant by less than unanimity?

C. Supreme Court's Answer

The defendant does not have a constitutional right to a unanimous jury verdict in a criminal prosecution in state court.

II. CASE SUMMARY

A. Background

"Robert Apodaca, Henry Morgan Cooper, Jr., and James Arnold Madden were convicted respectively of assault with a deadly weapon, burglary in a dwelling, and grand larceny before separate Oregon juries, all of which returned less-than-unanimous verdicts. The vote in the cases of Apodaca and Madden was 11-1, while the vote in the case of Cooper was 10-2, the minimum requisite vote under Oregon law for sustaining a conviction. After their convictions had been affirmed by the Oregon Court of Appeals, and review had been denied by the Supreme Court of Oregon, all three sought review in this Court upon a claim that conviction of crime by a less-than-unanimous jury violates the right to trial by jury in criminal cases specified by the Sixth Amendment and made applicable to the States by the Fourteenth. [The Supreme Court] granted certioari to consider this claim," and affirmed the convictions.

B. Counsel of Record/ACLU Attorney

ACLU Side (Petitioner/Appellant): Richard B. Sobol argued the cause for appellant.

Opposing Side (Respondent/Appellee): Solicitor General of Oregon Jacob B. Tanzer argued the cause for appellee.

III. AMICI CURIAE

ACLU Side (Petitioner/Appellant)

Brief of amici curiae filed on behalf of the ACLU by Norman Dorsen, Eric M. Lieberman, Melvin L. Wulf, and Paul R. Meyer.

Brief of amici curiae filed on behalf of the National Legal Aid and Defender Association by James J. Doherty and Marshall J. Hartman.

Opposing Side (Respondent/Appellee)

No briefs of amici curiae were filed in support of appellee.

IV. THE SUPREME COURT'S DECISION

"Petitioners also cite quite accurately a long line of decisions of this Court upholding the principle that the Fourteenth Amendment requires jury panels to reflect a cross section of the community. They then contend that unanimity is a necessary precondition for effective application of the cross-section requirement, because a rule permitting less than unanimous verdicts will make it possible for convictions to occur without the acquiescence of minority elements within the community.

There are two flaws in this argument. One is petitioners' assumption that every distinct voice in the community has a right to be represented on every jury and a right to prevent conviction of a defendant in any case. All that the Constitution forbids, however, is systematic exclusion of identifiable segments of the community from jury panels and from the juries ultimately drawn from those panels; a defendant may not, for example, challenge the makeup of a jury merely because no members of his race are on the jury, but must prove that his race has been systematically excluded. No group, in short, has the right to block convictions; it has only the right to participate in the overall legal processes by which criminal guilt and innocence are determined.

We also cannot accept petitioner's second assumption—that minority groups, even when they are represented on a jury, will not adequately represent the viewpoint of those groups simply because they may be outvoted in the final result. They will be present during all deliberations, and their views will be heard. We cannot assume that the majority of the jury will refuse to weigh the evidence and reach a decision upon rational grounds, just as it must now do in order to obtain unanimous verdicts, or that a majority will deprive a man of his liberty on the basis of prejudice when a minority is presenting a reasonable argument in favor of acquittal. We simply find no proof for the notion that a majority will disregard its instructions and cast its votes for guilt or innocence based on prejudice rather than the evidence.

We accordingly affirm the judgment of the Court of Appeals of Oregon."

V. JUSTICE VOTE

4 Pro ACLU Side vs. 5 Con Opposing Side

ACLU Side (Petitioner/Appellant)

1. Brennan, W. – Wrote dissenting opinion, joined Stewart's dissent, joined Douglas' dissent, joined Marshall's dissent
2. Marshall, T. – Wrote dissenting opinion, joined Stewart's dissent, joined Douglas' dissent, joined Brennan's dissent
3. Stewart, P. – Wrote dissenting opinion
4. Douglas, W. – Wrote dissenting opinion

Opposing Side (Respondent/Appellee)

1. White, B. – Wrote majority opinion
2. Burger, W. – Joined majority opinion
3. Blackmun, H. – Wrote concurring opinion
4. Powell, L. – Wrote concurring opinion
5. Rehnquist, W. – Joined majority opinion

VI. A WIN OR LOSS FOR THE ACLU?

The ACLU filed as amicus curiae urging reversal; the Supreme Court affirmed the judgment of the Court of Appeals in a 5-4 vote giving the ACLU an apparent loss.

267. Kastigar v. United States

(Decided May 22, 1972; 406 U.S. 441)

I. ISSUE

A. Issues Discussed

Criminal procedure, Fifth Amendment, self-incrimination

B. Legal Question Presented

"[W]hether the United States Government may compel testimony from an unwilling witness, who invokes the Fifth Amendment privilege against compulsory self-incrimination, by conferring on the witness immunity from use of the compelled testimony in subsequent criminal proceedings, as well as immunity from use of evidence derived from the testimony."

C. Supreme Court's Answer

The government may compel testimony by granting immunity equal to the protection of the Fifth Amendment privilege against self-incrimination.

II. CASE SUMMARY

A. Background

"Petitioners were subpoenaed to appear before a United States grand jury in the Central District of California on February 4, 1971. The Government believed that petitioners were likely to assert their Fifth Amendment privilege. Prior to the scheduled appearances, the Government applied to the District Court for an order directing petitioners to answer questions and produce evidence before the grand jury under a grant of immunity conferred pursuant to 18 U.S.C. §§ 6002, 6003. Petitioners opposed issuance of the order, contending primarily that the scope of the immunity provided by the statute was not coextensive with the scope of the privilege against self-incrimination, and therefore was not sufficient to supplant the privilege and compel their testimony. The District Court rejected this contention, and ordered petitioners to appear before the grand jury and answer its questions under the grant of immunity.

Petitioners appeared but refused to answer questions, asserting their privilege against compulsory selfincrimination. They were brought before the District Court, and each persisted in his refusal to answer the grand jury's questions, notwithstanding the grant of immunity. The court found both in contempt, and committed them to the custody of the Attorney General until either they answered the grand jury's questions or the term of the grand jury expired. The Court of Appeals for the Ninth Circuit affirmed. [The Supreme] Court granted certiorari to resolve the important question whether testimony may be compelled by granting immunity from the use of compelled testimony and evidence derived therefrom ('use and derivative use' immunity), or whether it is necessary to grant immunity from prosecution for offenses to which compelled testimony relates ('transactional' immunity)."

The Supreme Court affirmed the decision of the Court of Appeals.

B. Counsel of Record/ACLU Attorney

ACLU Side (Petitioner/Appellant): Hugh R. Manes argued the case for appellant.

Opposing Side (Respondent/Appellee): Solicitor General Erwin N. Griswold argued the case for appellee.

III. AMICI CURIAE

ACLU Side (Petitioner/Appellant)

Brief of amici curiae filed on behalf of the ACLU, et al., by Melvin L. Wulf, Joel M. Gora, Fred Okrand, A. L. Wirin, and Laurence R. Sperber.

Brief of amici curiae filed on behalf of the National Lawyers Guild by Benjamin Dreyfus and David E. Pesonen.

Brief of amici curiae filed on behalf of the Center for Constitutional Rights by Morton Stavis, James Reif, and Arthur Kinoy.

Opposing Side (Respondent/Appellee)

No briefs of amici curiae were filed in support of appellee.

IV. THE SUPREME COURT'S DECISION

"Although an analysis of prior decisions and the purpose of the Fifth Amendment privilege indicates that use and derivative-use immunity is coextensive with the privilege, we must consider additional arguments advanced by petitioners against the sufficiency of such immunity. We start from the premise, repeatedly affirmed by this Court, that an appropriately broad immunity grant is compatible with the Constitution. . . .

The statutory proscription is analogous to the Fifth Amendment requirement in cases of coerced confessions. A coerced confession, as revealing of leads as testimony given in exchange for immunity, is inadmissible in a criminal trial, but it does not bar prosecution. Moreover, a defendant against whom incriminating evidence has been obtained through a grant of immunity may be in a stronger position at trial than a defendant who asserts a Fifth Amendment coerced-confession claim. One raising a claim under this statute need only show that he testified under a grant of immunity in order to shift to the government the heavy burden of proving that all of the evidence it proposes to use was derived from legitimate independent sources. On the other hand, a defendant raising a coerced-confession claim under the Fifth Amendment must first prevail in a voluntariness hearing before his confession and evidence derived from it become inadmissible.

There can be no justification in reason or policy for holding that the Constitution requires an amnesty grant where, acting pursuant to statute and accompanying safeguards, testimony is compelled in exchange for immunity from use and derivative use when no such amnesty is required where the government, acting without colorable right, coerces a defendant into incriminating himself.

We conclude that the immunity provided by 18 U.S.C. § 6002 leaves the witness and the prosecutorial authorities in substantially the same position as if the witness had claimed the Fifth Amendment privilege. The immunity therefore is coextensive with the privilege and suffices to supplant it."

The Supreme Court affirmed the judgment of the Court of Appeals for the Ninth Circuit.

V. JUSTICE VOTE

2 Pro ACLU Side vs. 5 Con Opposing Side

ACLU Side (Petitioner/Appellant)

1. Douglas, W. – Wrote dissenting opinion
2. Marshall, T. – Wrote dissenting opinion

Opposing Side (Respondent/Appellee)

1. Powell, L. – Wrote majority opinion
2. Burger, W. – Joined majority opinion
3. Stewart, P. – Joined majority opinion
4. White, B. – Joined majority opinion
5. Blackmun, H. – Joined majority opinion

Brennan, W. – Took no part in the decision
Rehnquist, W. – Took no part in the decision

VI. A WIN OR LOSS FOR THE ACLU?

The ACLU filed as amicus curiae urging reversal; The Supreme Court affirmed the ruling of the Court of Appeals for the Ninth Circuit in a 5-2 vote, giving the ACLU an apparent loss.

268. Zicarelli v. New Jersey State Commission of Investigation

(Decided May 22, 1972; 406 U.S. 472)

I. ISSUE

A. Issues Discussed

Criminal procedure, Fifth Amendment, self-incrimination

B. Legal Question Presented

Was the statutory immunity offered by New Jersey, which afforded for immunity "from having such responsive answer given by him or such responsive evidence produced by him, or evidence derived therefrom used to expose him to criminal prosecution or penalty or to a forfeiture of his estate" sufficient to bypass the Fifth Amendment privilege against self-incrimination?

C. Supreme Court's Answer

The statutory immunity is sufficient to bypass the privilege against self-incrimination and compel testimony.

II. CASE SUMMARY

A. Background

"The New Jersey State Commission of Investigation subpoenaed appellant [alleged mafia leader Joe Zicarelli] to testify concerning organized crime, racketeering, and political corruption in Long Branch, New Jersey." Appellant appeared, but refused to testify on the basis of his Fifth Amendment privilege against self-incrimination. After the Commission granted him statutory immunity for his answers "and order his to answer the questions," appellant persisted in his refusal to answer questions on the basis that "the statutory immunity was insufficient in several respects to compel testimony over a claim of privilege." Appellant was given a hearing in front of the Superior Court of Mercer County to show cause for refusing to testify, and the court rejected his claims, ordering him incarcerated until he testified. The Supreme Court of New Jersey affirmed the Superior Court ruling.

The Supreme Court granted certiorari to review the case and affirmed.

B. Counsel of Record/ACLU Attorney

ACLU Side (Petitioner/Appellant): Michael A. Querques argued the cause for appellant.

Opposing Side (Respondent/Appellee): Andrew F. Phelan argued the cause for appellee.

Attorney General of New Jersey George F. Kugler, Jr., argued the cause for the State of New Jersey, amicus curiae.

III. AMICI CURIAE

ACLU Side (Petitioner/Appellant)

Brief of amici curiae filed on behalf of the ACLU by Melvin L. Wulf.

Opposing Side (Respondent/Appellee)

Brief of amici curiae filed on behalf of the State of New Jersey by Attorney General of New Jersey George F. Kugler, Jr., Barry H. Evenchick, and Michael R. Perle, Deputy Attorneys General.

Brief of amici curiae filed on behalf of the National District Attorneys Association, et al., by Robert G. Nixon, Jr.

IV. THE SUPREME COURT'S DECISION

"Appellant contends that only full transactional immunity affords protection commensurate with that afforded by the privilege and suffices to compel testimony over a claim of the privilege. We rejected this argument today in *Kastigar*, where we held that immunity from use and derivative use is coextensive with the scope of the privilege, and is therefore sufficient to compel testimony. . .

The responsiveness limitation is not a trap for the unwary; rather it is a barrier to those who would intentionally tender information not sought in an effort to frustrate and prevent criminal prosecution. The context in which the statute operates reaffirms our conclusion that the responsiveness limitation does not violate the Due Process Clause of the Fourteenth Amendment. . . .

Of the 100 questions he refused to answer, appellant cites only one specific question as posing a substantial risk of incrimination under foreign law. That question is: 'In what geographical area do you have Cosa Nostra responsibilities?'

We think it plain from the context in which the question was asked that it sought an answer concerning geographical areas in New Jersey. The subject of the hearing was law enforcement, organized crime, racketeering, and political corruption in the city of Long Branch, which is located in Monmouth County, New Jersey. . . .

Appellant is of course free to purge himself of contempt by answering the Commission's questions. Should the Commission inquire into matters that might incriminate him under foreign law and pose a substantial risk of foreign prosecution, and should such inquiry be sustained over a relevancy objection, then a constitutional question will be squarely presented. We do not believe that the record in this case presents such a question."

The U.S. Supreme Court affirmed the judgment of the Supreme Court of New Jersey.

V. JUSTICE VOTE

2 Pro ACLU Side vs. 5 Con Opposing Side

ACLU Side (Petitioner/Appellant)

1. Douglas, W. – Wrote dissenting opinion
2. Marshall, T. – Wrote dissenting opinion

Opposing Side (Respondent/Appellee)

1. Powell, L. – Wrote majority opinion
2. Burger, W. – Joined majority opinion

3. Stewart, P. – Joined majority opinion
4. White, B. – Joined majority opinion
5. Blackmun, H. – Joined majority opinion

Brennan, W – Took no part in the decision
Rehnquist, W – Took no part in the decision

VI. A WIN OR LOSS FOR THE ACLU?

The ACLU filed as amicus curiae urging reversal; the U.S. Supreme Court affirmed the ruling of the Supreme Court of New Jersey in a 5-2 vote, giving the ACLU an apparent loss.

269. Sarno v. Illinois Crime Investigating Commission

(Decided May 22, 1972; 406 U.S. 482)

I. ISSUE

A. Issues Discussed

Criminal procedure, Fifth Amendment, self-incrimination

B. Legal Question Presented

"[W]hether Illinois must demonstrate to petitioners, prior to an adjudication for contempt for refusal to answer the Commission's questions, that immunity as broad in scope as the protection of the privilege against self-incrimination is available and applicable to them."

C. Supreme Court's Answer

The Supreme Court dismissed the grant of the writ of certiorari as improvidently granted.

II. CASE SUMMARY

A. Background

"On February 8, 1968, the circuit court of Cook County ordered the defendants to appear before the Illinois Crime Commission and answer questions put to them by the Commission which was then investigating 'juice' rackets. The defendants appeared before the Commission but invoked the fifth amendment to all questions asked. On March 21, 1968 the Commission moved the circuit court to enter an order pursuant to section 14 of the Illinois Crime Investigating Commission Act releasing the defendants from all liability to be prosecuted for any testimony they might give before the Commission and compelling the defendants to appear before the Commission and answer such questions as may be put to them. On January 30, 1969, the circuit court granted the motion.

Pursuant to the court's order, defendants appeared before the Commission but again invoked the fifth amendment. On May 9, 1969, the court entered judgment finding defendants in contempt of court and sentenced them to a term of six months in jail."[1]

The Supreme Court of Illinois affirmed. The U.S. Supreme Court granted certiorari to review the case, then dismissed the writ as improvidently granted.

1 Illinois Crime Investigating Commission v. Sarno, 259 N.E.2d 267 (Ill. 1970).

B. Counsel of Record/ACLU Attorney

ACLU Side (Petitioner/Appellant): Frank G. Whalen argued the cause for appellant.

Opposing Side (Respondent/Appellee): First Assistant Attorney General of Illinois Joel M. Flaum argued the cause for appellee.

III. AMICI CURIAE

ACLU Side (Petitioner/Appellant)

Brief of amici curiae filed on behalf of the ACLU by Melvin L. Wulf.

Opposing Side (Respondent/Appellee)

No briefs of amici curiae were filed in support of appellee

IV. THE SUPREME COURT'S DECISION

"We held today in *Kastigar v. United States* and in *Zicarelli v. New Jersey State Commission of Investigation*, that testimony may be compelled from an unwilling witness over a claim of the privilege against self-incrimination by a grant of use and derivative use immunity. The premise of petitioners' arguments is that transactional immunity is required. They say that Illinois failed to demonstrate satisfactorily that transactional immunity was provided, but they do not contend that the Illinois immunity statute affords protection less comprehensive than use and derivative use immunity. Respondent asserts that the statute affords complete transactional immunity, reflecting a long-standing Illinois policy of providing immunity greater than that required by the United States Constitution. Since neither party contends that the scope of the immunity provided by the Illinois statute falls below the constitutional requirement set forth in *Kastigar*, we conclude that any uncertainty regarding the scope of protection in excess of the constitutional requirement should best be left to the courts of Illinois. Accordingly, the writ of certiorari is dismissed as improvidently granted."

V. JUSTICE VOTE

2 Pro ACLU Side vs. 5 Con Opposing Side

ACLU Side (Petitioner/Appellant)

1. Douglas, W. – Wrote dissenting opinion
2. Marshall, T. – Wrote dissenting opinion

Opposing Side (Respondent/Appellee)

1. White, B. – Per curiam decision
2. Burger, W. – Per curiam decision
3. Blackmun, H. – Per curiam decision
4. Stewart, P. – Per curiam decision
5. Powell, L. – Per curiam decision

Brennan, W – Took no part in the decision
Rehnquist, W – Took no part in the decision

VI. A WIN OR LOSS FOR THE ACLU?

The ACLU filed as amicus curiae urging reversal; the Supreme Court dismissed the writ of certiorari in a 5-2 vote, giving the

ACLU an apparent loss.

270. United States v. Midwest Video Corp.

(Decided June 7, 1972; 406 U.S. 649)

I. ISSUE

A. Issues Discussed

Regulation

B. Legal Question Presented

"[W]hether the Commission has reasonably determined that its origination rule will 'further the achievement of long-established regulatory goals in the field of television broadcasting by increasing the number of outlets for community self-expression and augmenting the public's choice of programs and types of services . . . .'"

C. Supreme Court's Answer

"We find that it has."

II. CASE SUMMARY

A. Background

"Community antenna television (CATV) was developed long after the enactment of the Communications Act of 1934 . . . . In United States v. Southwestern Cable Co., 392 U.S. 157 (1968), where we sustained the jurisdiction of the Federal Communications Commission to regulate the new industry, . . . we observed that the growth of CATV since the establishment of the first commercial system in 1950 has been nothing less than 'explosive.' . . .

Recognizing this potential, the Commission, shortly after our decision in Southwestern, initiated a general inquiry 'to explore the broad question of how best to obtain, consistent with the public interest standard of the Communications Act, the full benefits of developing communications technology for the public, with particular immediate reference to CATV technology . . . .' In particular, the Commission tentatively concluded . . . 'that, for now and in general, CATV program origination is in the public interest,' and sought comments on a proposal 'to condition the carriage of television broadcast signals (local or distant) upon a requirement that the CATV system also operate to a significant extent as a local outlet by originating.' As for its authority to impose such a requirement, the Commission stated that its 'concern with CATV carriage of broadcast signals is not just a matter of avoidance of adverse effects, but extends also to requiring CATV affirmatively to further statutory policies.' . . .

Upon the challenge of respondent Midwest Video Corp., an operator of CATV systems subject to the new cablecasting requirement, the United States Court of Appeals for the Eighth Circuit set aside the regulation on the ground that the Commission 'is without authority to impose' it."

The Supreme Court granted certiorari to review the case.

B. Counsel of Record

ACLU Side (Respondent/Appellee): Harry M. Plotkin argued the cause for appellee. With him on the brief were Wayne W. Owen, George H. Shapiro, and David Tillotson.

Opposing Side (Petitioner/Appellant): Deputy Solicitor General Wallace argued the cause for the United States et al. With him on the briefs were Solicitor General Griswold, Richard B. Stone, John W. Pettit, and Edward J. Kuhlmann.

III. AMICI CURIAE

ACLU Side (Respondent/Appellee)

Brief of amici curiae filed on behalf of the American Civil Liberties Union by Melvin L. Wulf, Lawrence G. Sager, Scott Robb, and Ronald S. Reich.

Brief of amici curiae filed on behalf of the State of Illinois by William J. Scott, Attorney General, Peter A. Fasseas, Special Assistant Attorney General, and Roland S. Hornet, Jr.

Brief of amici curiae filed on behalf of the National Association of Regulatory Utility Commissioners by Paul Rodgers.

Opposing Side (Petitioner/Appellant)

No briefs of amici curiae were filed in support of appellant.

IV. THE SUPREME COURT'S DECISION

"In short, the regulatory authority asserted by the Commission in 1966 and generally sustained by this Court in Southwestern was authority to regulate CATV with a view not merely to protect but to promote the objectives for which the Commission had been assigned jurisdiction over broadcasting.

In this light the critical question in this case is whether the Commission has reasonably determined that its origination rule will 'further the achievement of long-established regulatory goals in the field of television broadcasting by increasing the number of outlets for community self-expression and augmenting the public's choice of programs and types of services . . . .' We find that it has.

The goals specified are plainly within the Commission's mandate for the regulation of television broadcasting. . . .

Equally plainly the broadcasting policies the Commission has specified are served by the program-origination rule under review. . . .

Respondent, nevertheless, maintains that just as the Commission is powerless to require the provision of television broadcast services where there are no applicants for station licenses no matter how important or desirable those services may be, so, too, it cannot require CATV operators unwillingly to engage in cablecasting. In our view, the analogy . . . is misconceived. . . .

For these reasons we conclude that the program-origination rule is within the Commission's authority recognized in Southwestern. . . .

The question remains whether the regulation is supported by substantial evidence that it will promote the public interest. We read the opinion of the Court of Appeals as holding that substantial evidence to that effect is lacking because the regulation creates the risk that the added burden of cablecasting will result in increased subscription rates and even the termination of CATV services. That holding is patently incorrect in light of the record. . . .

This history speaks for itself. The cablecasting requirement thus applied is plainly supported by substantial evidence that it will promote the public interest. Indeed, respondent does not appear to argue to the contrary. It was, of course, beyond the competence of the Court of Appeals itself to assess the relative risks and benefits of cablecasting. As we said in National Broadcasting Co. v. United States, 319 U.S., at 224:

'Our duty is at an end when we find that the action of the Commission was based upon findings supported by evidence, and was made pursuant to authority granted by Congress. It is not for us to say that the 'public interest' will (in fact) be furthered or retarded by the . . . (regulation).'

Reversed."

V. JUSTICE VOTE

4 Pro ACLU Side vs. 5 Con Opposing Side

ACLU Side (Respondent/Appellee)

1. Douglas, W. – Wrote dissenting opinion
2. Stewart, P. – Joined Douglas' dissent
3. Powell, L. – Joined Douglas' dissent
4. Rehnquist, W. – Joined Douglas' dissent

Opposing Side (Petitioner/Appellant)

1. Brennan, W. – Wrote majority opinion
2. White, B. – Joined majority opinion
3. Marshall, T. – Joined majority opinion
4. Blackmun, H. – Joined majority opinion
5. Burger, W. – Wrote concurring opinion

VI. A WIN OR LOSS FOR THE ACLU?

The ACLU filed as amici curiae urging affirmance of the judgment of the Court of Appeals; the Supreme Court reversed, in a 5-4 vote, giving the ACLU an apparent loss.

271. Colten v. Kentucky

(Decided June 12, 1972; 407 U.S. 104)

I. ISSUE

A. Issues Discussed

1st Amendment, press, speech, association, criminal procedure

B. Legal Question Presented

"This case presents two unrelated questions. Appellant challenges his Kentucky conviction for disorderly conduct on the ground that the conviction and the State's statute are repugnant to the First and Fourteenth Amendments. He also challenges the constitutionality of the enhanced penalty he received under Kentucky's two-tier system for adjudicating certain criminal cases, whereby a person charged with a misdemeanor may be tried first in an inferior court and, if dissatisfied with the outcome, may have a trial de novo in a court of general criminal jurisdiction but must run the risk, if convicted, of receiving a greater punishment."

C. Supreme Court's Answer

"[W]e perceive no justification for setting aside the conclusion of the state court that when arrested appellant was not engaged in activity protected by the First Amendment. . . . We thus see nothing unconstitutional in the manner in which the statute was applied. . . .

We cannot say that the Kentucky trial de novo system, as such, is unconstitutional or that it presents hazards warranting the restraints called for in North Carolina v. Pearce, particularly since such restraints might, to the detriment of both defendant and State, diminish the likelihood that inferior courts would impose lenient sentences whose effect would be to limit the discretion of a superior court judge or jury if the defendant is retried and found guilty."

II. CASE SUMMARY

A. Background

"Appellant Colten and 15 to 20 other college students gathered at the Blue Grass Airport outside Lexington, Kentucky, to show their support for a state gubernatorial candidate and to demonstrate their lack of regard for Mrs. Richard Nixon . . . . When the demonstration had ended, the students got into their automobiles and formed a procession of six to 10 cars . . . . A state policeman, observing that one of the first cars in the entourage carried an expired Louisiana license plate, directed the driver, one Mendez, to pull off the road. He complied. Appellant Colten, followed by other motorists in the procession, also pulled off the highway, and Colten approached the officer to find out what was the matter. . . . In order to avoid Colten and to complete the issuance of the summons, the policeman took Mendez to the patrol car. Meanwhile, other students had left their cars and additional policemen . . . took responsibility for directing traffic . . . . A state police captain asked on four or five occasions that the group disperse. . . . Colten replied that he wished to make a transportation arrangement for his friend Mendez and the occupants of the Mendez car, which he understood was to be towed away. Another officer asked three times that Colten depart and when Colten failed to move away he was arrested for violating Kentucky's disorderly conduct statute, Ky.Rev.Stat. s 437.016. . . .

The complaint and warrant charging disorderly conduct, which carries a maximum penalty of six months in jail and a fine of $500, were addressed to the Quarterly Court of Fayette County, where Colten was tried, convicted, and fined $10. Exercising his right to a trial de novo in a court of general jurisdiction, Colten 'appealed' . . . to the Criminal Division of the Fayette Circuit Court. . . . Colten was convicted of disorderly conduct and this time fined $50. The Kentucky Court of Appeals affirmed. [The Supreme Court] noted probable jurisdiction."

B. Counsel of Record

ACLU Side (Petitioner/Appellant): Alvin L. Goldman argued the cause for appellant. With him on the brief were Melvin L. Wulf and Sanford Jay Rosen of the American Civil Liberties Union Foundation, and Natalie Wilson.

Opposing Side (Respondent/Appellee): Robert W. Willmott, Jr., Assistant Attorney General of Kentucky, argued the cause for appellee pro hac vice. With him on the brief was Ed W. Hancock, Attorney General.

III. AMICI CURIAE

ACLU Side (Petitioner/Appellant)

No briefs of amici curiae were filed in support of appellant.

Opposing Side (Respondent/Appellee)

No briefs of amici curiae were filed in support of appellee.

IV. THE SUPREME COURT'S DECISION

"Based on our own examination of the record, we perceive no justification for setting aside the conclusion of the state court that when arrested appellant was not engaged in activity protected by the First Amendment. . . . We cannot disagree with the finding below that the order to disperse was suited to the occasion. We thus see nothing unconstitutional in the manner in which the statute was applied. . . .

Neither are we convinced that the statute is either impermissibly vague or broad. . . .

Colten . . . considers the Kentucky system to be infirm because the judge in a trial de novo is empowered to sentence anew and is not bound to stay within the limits of the sentence imposed by the inferior court. He bases his attack both on the Due Process Clause, as interpreted in North Carolina v. Pearce, 395 U.S. 711 (1969), and on the Fifth Amendment's Double Jeopardy Clause. The issues appellant raises have produced a division among the . . . courts . . . .

Colten rightly reads Pearce to forbid . . . the imposition of a greater punishment than was imposed after the first trial, absent specified findings that have not been made here. . . .

Our view of the Kentucky two-tier system of administering criminal justice, however, does not lead us to believe, and there is nothing in the record or presented in the briefs to show, that the hazard of being penalized for seeking a new trial, which underlay the holding of Pearce, also inheres in the de novo trial arrangement. Nor are we convinced that defendants convicted in Kentucky's inferior courts would be deterred from seeking a second trial out of fear of judicial vindictiveness. The possibility of vindictiveness, found to exist in Pearce, is not inherent in the Kentucky two-tier system. . . .

We cannot conclude, on the basis of the present record or our understanding, that the prophylactic rule announced in Pearce is appropriate in the context of the system by which Kentucky administers criminal justice in the less serious criminal cases. . . .

We cannot say that the Kentucky trial de novo system, as such, is unconstitutional or that it presents hazards warranting the restraints called for in North Carolina v. Pearce, particularly since such restraints might, to the detriment of both defendant and State, diminish the likelihood that inferior courts would impose lenient sentences whose effect would be to limit the discretion of a superior court judge or jury if the defendant is retried and found guilty.

Colten's alternative contention is that the Double Jeopardy Clause prohibits the imposition of an enhanced penalty upon reconviction. . . . The contention . . . ignores that a defendant can bypass the inferior court simply by pleading guilty and erasing immediately thereafter any consequence that would otherwise follow from tendering the plea.

The judgment of the Kentucky Court of Appeals is affirmed."

V. JUSTICE VOTE

2 Pro ACLU Side vs. 7 Con Opposing Side

ACLU Side (Petitioner/Appellant)

1. Marshall, T. – Wrote dissenting opinion
2. Douglas, W. – Wrote dissenting opinion

Opposing Side (Respondent/Appellee)

1. White, B. – Wrote majority opinion
2. Burger, W. – Joined majority opinion
3. Brennan, W. – Joined majority opinion
4. Stewart, P. – Joined majority opinion
5. Blackmun, H. – Joined majority opinion
6. Powell, L. – Joined majority opinion
7. Rehnquist, W. – Joined majority opinion

VI. A WIN OR LOSS FOR THE ACLU?

The ACLU served as counsel for appellant urging reversal of the judgment of the Kentucky Court of Appeals; the Supreme Court affirmed, in a 7-2 vote, giving the ACLU an apparent loss.

272. Adams v. Williams

(Decided June 12, 1972; 407 U.S. 143)

I. ISSUE

A. Issues Discussed

Criminal justice, drugs, Fourth Amendment, search and seizure

B. Legal Question Presented

Was there probable cause to conduct a lawful search of Williams and his vehicles, and did the search violate the Fourth Amendment?

C. Supreme Court's Answer

There was probable cause to conduct a lawful search and the search did not violate the Fourth Amendment.

II. CASE SUMMARY

A. Background

Police Sergeant John Connolly, while patrolling a high crime area, was approached by an informant who told him that an individual seated in a nearby vehicle was carrying narcotics and was wearing a gun on his waist.

Acting on the tip, Sergeant Connolly approached the car, knocked on the window, and asked the respondent, Williams, to open the vehicle's door. Williams lowered his window and the sergeant reached into the car and found a loaded handgun. The gun was not visible from outside the car, however it was in William's waistband, precisely where the informant said it would be. Williams was arrested for unlawful possession of the handgun. Officers conducted a full search of Williams' person and his car, incident to the arrest, and found heroin and additional weapons. Williams was convicted of possessing a handgun and narcotics and his convictions were affirmed by the Supreme Court of Connecticut.

Respondent's petition for federal habeas corpus relief was denied by the District Court. The Court of Appeals for the Second Circuit reversed the district court and granted relief to Williams. The "court held that evidence introduced at Williams' trial had been obtained by an unlawful search of his person and car, and thus the state court judgments of conviction should be set aside."

The Supreme Court granted certiorari to review the case and reversed.

B. Counsel of Record/ACLU Attorney

ACLU Side (Respondent/Appellee): Edward F. Hennessey argued the cause for appellee.

Opposing Side (Petitioner/Appellant): Donald A. Browne argued the cause for appellant.

III. AMICI CURIAE

ACLU Side (Respondent/Appellee)

Brief of amici curiae filed on behalf of the ACLU by Burt Neuborne, Melvin L. Wulf, and Joel M. Gora.

Opposing Side (Petitioner/Appellant)

Briefs of amici curiae were filed on behalf of the United States, the District Attorney of New York County, Americans for Effective Law Enforcement, Inc., et al., and by Frank S. Hogan, pro se.

IV. THE SUPREME COURT'S DECISION

"While properly investigating the activity of a person who was reported to be carrying narcotics and a concealed weapon and who was sitting alone in a car in a high-crime area at 2:15 in the morning, Sgt. Connolly had ample reason to fear for his safety. When Williams rolled down his window, rather than complying with the policeman's request to step out of the car so that his movements could more easily be seen, the revolver allegedly at Williams' waist became an even greater threat. Under these circumstances the policeman's action in reaching to the spot where the gun was thought to be hidden constituted a limited intrusion designed to insure his safety, and we conclude that it was reasonable. The loaded gun seized as a result of this intrusion was therefore admissible at Williams' trial.

Once Sgt. Connolly had found the gun precisely where the informant had predicted, probable cause existed to arrest Williams for unlawful possession of the weapon. Probable cause to arrest depends 'upon whether, at the moment the arrest was made . . . the facts and circumstances within [the arresting officers'] knowledge and of which they had reasonably trustworthy information were sufficient to warrant a prudent man in believing that the [suspect] had committed or was committing an offense.' In the present case the policeman found Williams in possession of a gun in precisely the place predicted by the informant. This tended to corroborate the reliability of the informant's further report of narcotics and, together with the surrounding circumstances, certainly suggested no lawful explanation for possession of the gun. Probable cause does not require the same type of specific evidence of each element of the offense as would be needed to support a conviction. Rather, the court will evaluate generally the circumstances at the time of the arrest to decide if the officer had probable cause for his action. . . .

Under the circumstances surrounding Williams' possession of the gun seized by Sgt. Connolly, the arrest on the weapons charge was supported by probable cause, and the search of his person and of the car incident to that arrest was lawful. The fruits of the search were therefore properly admitted at Williams' trial, and the Court of Appeals erred in reaching a contrary conclusion."

The Supreme Court reversed the judgment of the Court of Appeals.

V. JUSTICE VOTE

3 Pro ACLU Side vs. 6 Con Opposing Side

ACLU Side (Respondent/Appellee)

1. Douglas, W. – Wrote dissenting opinion, joined Marshall's dissent
2. Marshall, T. – Wrote dissenting opinion, joined Douglas' dissent
3. Brennan, W. – Wrote dissenting opinion

Opposing Side (Petitioner/Appellant)

1. Rehnquist, W. – Wrote majority opinion
2. Powell, L. – Joined majority opinion
3. Stewart, P. – Joined majority opinion
4. White, B. – Joined majority opinion
5. Blackmun, H. – Joined majority opinion
6. Burger, W. – Joined majority opinion

VI. A WIN OR LOSS FOR THE ACLU?

The ACLU filed as amicus curiae urging affirmance of the judgment of the Court of Appeals; the Supreme Court reversed the judgment in a 6-3 vote, giving the ACLU an apparent loss.

273. Flower v. United States

(Decided June 12, 1972; 407 U.S. 197)

I. ISSUE

A. Issues Discussed

1st Amendment, press, speech, association

B. Legal Question Presented

Whether petitioner was appropriately convicted under 18 U.S.C. s 1382 for distributing leaflets while technically within a military facility, but on a street that remains open to the public and is not restricted to military use in any way.

C. Supreme Court's Answer

"The First Amendment protects petitioner from the application of s 1382 under conditions like those of this case."

II. CASE SUMMARY

A. Background

"John Thomas Flower, a regional 'Peace Education Secretary' of the American Friends Service Committee and a civilian, was arrested by military police while quietly distributing leaflets on New Braunfels Avenue at a point within the limits of Fort Sam Houston, San Antonio, Texas. In an ensuing prosecution before the United States District Court for the Western District of Texas on charges of violating 18 U.S.C. s 1382 ('Whoever reenters or is found (within a military post) after having been removed therefrom or ordered not to reenter by any officer or person in command or charge thereof—Shall be fined not more than $500 or imprisoned not more than six months, or both'), it was established that petitioner had previously been barred from the post by order of the deputy commander because of alleged participation in an attempt to distribute 'unauthorized' leaflets. The District Court found that s 1382 'is a valid law' and was validly applied. It sentenced petitioner to six months in prison. A divided panel of the Court of Appeals for the Fifth Circuit affirmed."

B. Counsel of Record

ACLU Side (Petitioner/Appellant): Melvin L. Wulf and John H. F. Shattuck of the American Civil Liberties Union Foundation, Ernest J. Altgelt III, and Maury Maverick, Jr., filed the brief for appellant.

Opposing Side (Respondent/Appellee): Erwin N. Griswold, Solicitor General, filed the brief for the United States.

III. AMICI CURIAE

ACLU Side (Petitioner/Appellant)

No briefs of amici curiae were filed in support of appellant.

Opposing Side (Respondent/Appellee)

No briefs of amici curiae were filed in support of appellee.

IV. THE SUPREME COURT'S DECISION

"Whatever power the authorities may have to restrict general access to a military facility, here the fort commander chose not to exclude the public from the street where petitioner was arrested. As Judge Simpson, dissenting, noted below:

'There is no sentry post or guard at either entrance or anywhere along the route. Traffic flows through the post on this and other streets 24 hours a day. A traffic count conducted on New Braunfels Avenue on January 22, 1968, by the Director of Transportation of the city of San Antonio, shows a daily (24-hour) vehicular count of 15,110 south of Grayson Street (the place where the street enters the post boundary) and 17,740 vehicles daily north of that point. The street is an important traffic artery used freely by buses, taxi cabs and other public transportation facilities as well as by private vehicles, and its sidewalks are used extensively at all hours of the day by civilians as well as by military personnel. Fort Sam Houston was an open post; the street, New Braunfels Avenue, was a completely open street.'

Under such circumstances the military has abandoned any claim that it has special interests in who walks, talks, or distributes leaflets on the avenue. The base commandant can no more order petitioner off this public street because he was distributing leaflets than could the city police order any leafleteer off any public street. '(S)treets are natural and proper places for the dissemination of information and opinion,' '(O)ne who is rightfully on a street which the state has left open to the public carries with him there as elsewhere the constitutional right to express his views in an orderly fashion.'

The First Amendment protects petitioner from the application of s 1382 under conditions like those of this case. Accordingly, without need to set the matter for further argument, we grant the petition for a writ of certiorari and reverse the conviction.

Reversed and remanded."

V. JUSTICE VOTE

6 Pro ACLU Side vs. 3 Con Opposing Side

ACLU Side (Petitioner/Appellant)

1. White, B. – Per curiam decision
2. Marshall, T. – Per curiam decision
3. Brennan, W. – Per curiam decision
4. Stewart, P. – Per curiam decision
5. Douglas, W. – Per curiam decision
6. Powell, L. – Per curiam decision

Opposing Side (Respondent/Appellee)

1. Blackmun, H. – Dissented without an opinion
2. Rehnquist, W. – Wrote dissenting opinion
3. Burger, W. – Joined Rehnquist's dissent

VI. A WIN OR LOSS FOR THE ACLU?

The ACLU served as counsel for appellants urging reversal of the judgment of the Court of Appeals; the Supreme Court reversed, in a 6-3 per curiam decision, giving the ACLU an apparent win.

274. United States v. United States District Court for the Eastern District of Michigan

(Decided June 19, 1972; 407 U.S. 297)

I. ISSUE

A. Issues Discussed

Criminal justice, Fourth Amendment

B. Legal Question Presented

Did the wiretapping and the recording of suspects' conversations, without a search warrant, violate the Fourth Amendment?

C. Supreme Court's Answer

The wiretap violated the suspects' Fourth Amendment rights because the government did not obtain a warrant.

II. CASE SUMMARY

A. Background

"This case arises from a criminal proceeding in the United States District Court for the Eastern District of Michigan, in which the United States charged three defendants with conspiracy to destroy Government property in violation of 18 U.S.C. § 371. One of the defendants, Plamondon, was charged with the dynamite bombing of an office of the Central Intelligence Agency in Ann Arbor, Michigan.

During pretrial proceedings, the defendants moved to compel the United States to disclose certain electronic surveillance information and to conduct a hearing to determine whether this information 'tainted' the evidence on which the indictment was based or which the Government intended to offer at trial. In response, the Government filed an affidavit of the Attorney General, acknowledging that its agents had overheard conversations in which Plamondon had participated. The affidavit also stated that the Attorney General approved the wiretaps 'to gather intelligence information deemed necessary to protect the nation from attempts of domestic organizations to attack and subvert the existing structure of the Government.' The logs of the surveillance were filed in a sealed exhibit for in camera inspection by the District Court.

On the basis of the Attorney General's affidavit and the sealed exhibit, the Government asserted that the surveillance was lawful, though conducted without prior judicial approval, as a reasonable exercise of the President's power (exercised through the Attorney General) to protect the national security. The District Court held that the surveillance violated the Fourth Amendment, and ordered the Government to make full disclosure to Plamondon of his overheard conversations. The Government then filed in the Court of Appeals for the Sixth Circuit a petition for a writ of mandamus to set aside the District Court order, which was stayed pending final disposition of the case. After concluding that it had jurisdiction, that court held that the surveillance was unlawful and that the District Court had properly required disclosure of the overheard conversations."

The Supreme Court granted certiorari to review the case and affirmed.

B. Counsel of Record/ACLU Attorney

ACLU Side (Respondent/Appellee): William T. Gossett argued the cause for appellees the United States District Court for the Eastern District of Michigan and District Judge Damon J. Keith. Arthur Kinoy argued the cause for appellees John Sinclair, Lawrence "Pun" Plamondon, and John Waterhouse Forrest.

Opposing Side (Petitioner/Appellant): Assistant Attorney General Robert G. Mardian argued the cause for the United States. With him on the briefs were Solicitor General Griswold and Robert L. Keuch.

III. AMICI CURIAE

ACLU Side (Respondent/Appellee)

Brief of amici curiae filed on behalf of the ACLU, et al., by Herman Schwartz, Melvin L. Wulf, and Erwin B. Ellmann.

Additional briefs of amici curiae were filed on behalf of the International Union, United Automobile, Aerospace, and Agricultural Implement Workers of America (UAW), the Black Panther Party, et al., the American Federation of Teachers, and the American Friends Service Committee.

Opposing Side (Petitioner/Appellant)

No briefs of amici curiae were filed in support of appellant.

IV. THE SUPREME COURT'S DECISION

"The issue before us is an important one for the people of our country and their Government. It involves the delicate question of the President's power, acting through the Attorney General, to authorize electronic surveillance in internal security matters without prior judicial approval. Successive Presidents for more than one-quarter of a century have authorized such surveillance in varying degrees, without guidance from the Congress or a definitive decision of this Court. This case brings the issue here for the first time. Its resolution is a matter of national concern, requiring sensitivity both to the Government's right to protect itself from unlawful subversion and attack and to the citizen's right to be secure in his privacy against unreasonable Government intrusion. . . .

It may be that Congress, for example, would judge that the application and affidavit showing probable cause need not follow the exact requirements of § 2518 but should allege other circumstances more appropriate to domestic security cases; that the request for prior court authorization could, in sensitive cases, be made to any member of a specially designated court (e.g. the District Court for the District of Columbia or the Court of Appeals for the District of Columbia Circuit); and that the time and reporting requirements need not be so strict as those in § 2518.

The above paragraph does not, of course, attempt to guide the congressional judgment but rather to delineate the present scope of our own opinion. We do not attempt to detail the precise standards for domestic security warrants any more than our decision in *Katz* sought to set the refined requirements for the specified criminal surveillances which now constitute Title III. We do hold, however, that prior judicial approval is required for the type of domestic security surveillance involved in this case and that such approval may be made in accordance with such reasonable standards as the Congress may prescribe. . . .

As the surveillance of Plamondon's conversations was unlawful, because conducted without prior judicial approval, the courts below correctly held that *Alderman v. United States*, 394 U.S. 165 (1969), is controlling and that it requires disclosure to the accused of his own impermissibly intercepted conversations. As stated in *Alderman*, 'the trial court can and should, where appropriate, place a defendant and his counsel under enforceable orders against unwarranted disclosure of the materials which they may be entitled to inspect.'"

The Supreme Court affirmed the judgment of the Court of Appeals.

V. JUSTICE VOTE

8 Pro ACLU Side vs. 0 Con Opposing Side

ACLU Side (Respondent/Appellee)

1. Powell, L. – Wrote majority opinion
2. Stewart, P. – Joined majority opinion
3. Blackmun, H. – Joined majority opinion
4. Burger, W. – Concurred in the result
5. Brennan, W. – Joined majority opinion
6. Marshall, T. – Joined majority opinion
7. Douglas, W. – Wrote concurring opinion
8. White, B. – Wrote concurring opinion

Rehnquist, W – Took no part in the decision

VI. A WIN OR LOSS FOR THE ACLU?

The ACLU filed as amicus curiae in support of respondent; the Supreme Court affirmed the judgment of the Court of Appeals in an 8-0 vote giving the ACLU an apparent win.

275. Pipefitters Local Union No. 562 v. United States

(Decided June 22, 1972; 407 U.S. 385)

I. ISSUE

A. Issues Discussed

Union

B. Legal Question Presented

How the amendment to 18 U.S.C. s 610 by s 205 of the Federal Election Campaign Act impacts the decision in this case on union funds.

C. Supreme Court's Answer

"[W]e now hold that s 205 of the Federal Election Campaign Act merely codifies prior law, with one possible exception pertinent to this case; that the change in the law, if in fact made, does not in any event require this prosecution to abate; but that the judgment below must, nevertheless, be reversed because of erroneous jury instructions. This disposition makes decision of the constitutional issues premature, and we therefore do not decide them."

II. CASE SUMMARY

A. Background

"Petitioners—Pipefitters Local Union No. 562 and three individual officers of the Union—were convicted by a jury in the United States District Court for the Eastern District of Missouri of conspiracy under 18 U.S.C. s 371 to violate 18 U.S.C. s 610. . . .

The indictment charged, in essence, that petitioners had conspired . . . to establish and maintain a fund that (1) would receive regular and systematic payments from Local 562 members and members of other locals working under the Union's jurisdiction; (2) would have the appearance, but not the reality of being an entity separate from the Union; and (3) would conceal contributions and expenditures by the Union in connection with federal elections in violation of s 610. . . .

Under instructions to determine whether on this evidence the fund was in reality a Union fund or the contributors' fund, the jury found each defendant guilty. . . .

The Court of Appeals in a four-to-three en banc decision adopted Judge Van Oosterhout's panel opinion rejecting each of [petitioners] claims. The gist of the court's decision, insofar as pertinent here, was that the Pipefitters fund was a subterfuge through which the Union made political contributions of Union monies in violation of s 610, as demonstrated by the evidence that the fund regularly served Union purposes and that the donors to the fund contributed in the belief that their job security depended upon it. [The Supreme Court] granted certiorari.

After we heard oral argument, the President . . . signed into law the Federal Election Campaign Act of 1971, which in s 205 amends 18 U.S.C. s 610. We, accordingly, requested the parties to file supplemental briefs addressing the impact of that amendment on this prosecution."

B. Counsel of Record

ACLU Side (Petitioner/Appellant): Morris A. Shenker argued the cause for appellants. With him on the briefs were James F. Nangle, Jr., John L. Boeger, Cordell Siegel, Murry L. Randall, and Richard L. Daly.

Opposing Side (Respondent/Appellee): Deputy Solicitor General Wallace argued the cause for the United States. With him on the briefs were Solicitor General Griswold, Acting Assistant Attorney General Petersen, Allan. A. Tuttle, and Beatrice Rosenberg.

III. AMICI CURIAE

ACLU Side (Petitioner/Appellant)

Brief of amici curiae filed on behalf of the American Civil Liberties Union by Melvin L. Wulf, Sanford J. Rosen, and William J. Birtles.

Brief of amici curiae filed on behalf of the American Federation of Labor and Congress of Industrial Organizations by J. Albert Woll, Laurence Gold, and Thomas E. Harris.

Brief of amici curiae filed on behalf of Officers of the United Mine Workers of America by Arthur J. Hilland and Plato Cacheris.

Opposing Side (Respondent/Appellee)

Brief of amici curiae filed on behalf of the National Right to Work Legal Defense Foundation by John L. Kilcullen.

IV. THE SUPREME COURT'S DECISION

"We begin with an analysis of s 610.

First. The parties are in agreement that s 610, despite its broad language, does not prohibit a labor organization from making, through the medium of a political fund organized by it, contributions or expenditures in connection with federal elections, so long as the monies expended are in some sense volunteered by those asked to contribute. . . . This construction of s 610 is clearly correct. . . .

Second. Where the litigants part company is in defining precisely when political contributions and expenditures by a union political fund fall outside the ambit of s 610. . . .

We think that neither side fully and accurately portrays the attributes of legitimate political funds. We hold that such a fund must be separate from the sponsoring union only in the sense that there must be a strict segregation of its monies from union dues and assessments. We hold, too, that although solicitation by union officials is permissible, such solicitation must be conducted under circumstances plainly indicating that donations are for a political purpose and that those solicited may decline to contribute without loss of job, union membership, or any other reprisal within the union's institutional power. . . .

Third. Arguably, however, there is one change effected by s 205 material to this case, and that is with regard to the use of general union monies for the establishment, administration, and solicitation of contributions for political funds. Section 304 of the Labor Management Relations Act may be interpreted to prohibit such use, while the Hansen amendment plainly permits it. . . .

We . . . hold that even if there has been an implied repeal of s 610, petitioners remain punishable under that provision. We turn now to determine whether the convictions below have been returned consistently with that law. . . .

First. Petitioners moved before trial to dismiss the indictment . . . .

Second. The jury instructions embody an interpretation of s 610 that is plainly erroneous. . . .

The judgment of the Court of Appeals as to petitioners Callanan and Lawler is vacated, and the case is remanded to the District Court with directions to dismiss the indictment against them. The judgment of the Court of Appeals as to petitioners Local 562 and Seaton is reversed, and the case is remanded to the District Court for proceedings as to them consistent with this opinion. . . .

Vacated in part, reversed in part, and remanded with directions."

V. JUSTICE VOTE

6 Pro ACLU Side vs. 2 Con Opposing Side

ACLU Side (Petitioner/Appellant)

1. Brennan, W. – Wrote majority opinion
2. Douglas, W. – Joined majority opinion
3. White, B. – Wrote majority opinion
4. Marshall, T. – Joined majority opinion
5. Stewart, P. – Joined majority opinion
6. Rehnquist, W. – Joined majority opinion

Opposing Side (Respondent/Appellee)

1. Powell, L. – Wrote dissenting opinion
2. Burger, W. – Joined Powell's dissent

Blackmun, L. – Took no part in the decision.

VI. A WIN OR LOSS FOR THE ACLU?

The ACLU filed as amici curiae urging reversal of the judgment of the Court of Appeals; the Supreme Court reversed in part and vacated in part, in a 6-2 vote, giving the ACLU an apparent win.

276. Lloyd Corp. v. Tanner

(Decided June 22, 1972; 407 U.S. 551)

I. ISSUE

A. Issues Discussed

1st Amendment, press, speech, association

B. Legal Question Presented

"This case presents the question reserved by the Court in Amalgamated Food Employees Union Local 590 v. Logan Valley Plaza, Inc., 391 U.S. 308 (1968), as to the right of a privately owned shopping center to prohibit the distribution of handbills on its property when the handbilling is unrelated to the shopping center's operations."

C. Supreme Court's Answer

"We hold that there has been no . . . dedication of Lloyd's privately owned and operated shopping center to public use as to entitle respondents to exercise therein the asserted First Amendment rights."

II. CASE SUMMARY

A. Background

"This case presents the question reserved by the Court in Amalgamated Food Employees Union Local 590 v. Logan Valley Plaza, Inc., 391 U.S. 308 (1968), as to the right of a privately owned shopping center to prohibit the distribution of handbills on its property when the handbilling is unrelated to the shopping center's operations. Relying primarily on Marsh v. Alabama, 326 U.S. 501 (1946), and Logan Valley, the United States District Court for the District of Oregon sustained an asserted First Amendment right to distribute handbills in petitioner's shopping center, and issued a permanent injunction restraining petitioner from interfering with such right. The Court of Appeals for the Ninth Circuit affirmed. [The Supreme Court] granted certiorari to consider petitioner's contention that the decision below violates rights of private property protected by the Fifth and Fourteenth Amendments.

Lloyd Corp., Ltd. (Lloyd), owns a large, modern retail shopping center in Portland, Oregon. . . .

On November 14, 1968, the respondents in this case distributed within the [Lloyd] Center handbill invitations to a meeting of the 'Resistance Community' to protest the draft and the Vietnam war. The distribution, made in several different places on the mall walkways by five young people, was quiet and orderly, and there was no littering. There was a complaint from one customer. Security guards informed the respondents that they were trespassing and would be arrested unless they stopped distributing the handbills within the Center. The guards suggested that respondents distribute their literature on the public streets and sidewalks adjacent to but outside of the Center complex. Respondents left the premises as requested 'to avoid arrest' and continued the handbilling outside. Subsequently this suit was instituted in the District Court seeking declaratory and injunctive relief."

B. Counsel of Record

ACLU Side (Respondent/Appellee): Carl R. Neil of the American Civil Liberties Union of Oregon argued the cause for appellees. With him on the brief were Melvin L. Wulf and Sanford Jay Rosen of the American Civil Liberties Union Foundation.

Opposing Side (Petitioner/Appellant): George Black, Jr., argued the cause for appellant. With him on the briefs were Robert J. Miller, John H. Pickering, and Timothy B. Dyk.

III. AMICI CURIAE

ACLU Side (Respondent/Appellee)

Brief of amici curiae filed on behalf of the People's Lobby, Inc., by Roger Jon Diamond.

Opposing Side (Petitioner/Appellant)

Brief of amici curiae filed on behalf of the American Retail Federation by Jerry Kronenberg, Gerard C. Smetana, and Alan Raywid.

Brief of amici curiae filed on behalf of the Homart Development Co. by Lawrence M. Cohen and Allen B. Gresham.

IV. THE SUPREME COURT'S DECISION

"The courts below considered the critical inquiry to be whether Lloyd Center was 'the functional equivalent of a public business district.' This phrase was first used in Logan Valley, but its genesis was in Marsh. . . .

Logan Valley extended Marsh to a shopping center situation in a different context from the company town setting, but it did so only in a context where the First Amendment activity was related to the shopping center's operations. . . .

The holding in Logan Valley was not dependent upon the suggestion that the privately owned streets and sidewalks of a business district or a shopping center are the equivalent, for First Amendment purposes, of municipally owned streets and sidewalks. . . . The opinion was carefully phrased to limit its holding to the picketing involved, where the picketing was 'directly related in its purpose to the use to which the shopping center property was being put' . . . .

The handbilling by respondents in the malls of Lloyd Center had no relation to any purpose for which the center was built and being used. . . .

Respondents' argument, even if otherwise meritorious, misapprehends the scope of the invitation extended to the public. The invitation is to come to the Center to do business with the tenants. . . . There is no open-ended invitation to the public to use the Center for any and all purposes, however incompatible with the interests of both the stores and the shoppers whom they serve. . . .

A further fact, distinguishing the present case from Logan Valley, is that the Union pickets in that case would have been deprived of all reasonable opportunity to convey their message to patrons of the Weis store had they been denied access to the shopping center. The situation at Lloyd Center was notably different. The central building complex was surrounded by public sidewalks . . . .

The basic issue in this case is whether respondents, in the exercise of asserted First Amendment rights, may distribute handbills on Lloyd's private property contrary to its wishes and contrary to a policy enforced against all handbilling. In addressing this issue, it must be remembered that the First and Fourteenth Amendments safeguard the rights of free speech and assembly by limitations on state action, not on action by the owner of private property used nondiscriminatorily for private purposes only. . . .

We hold that there has been no such dedication of Lloyd's privately owned and operated shopping center to public use as to entitle respondents to exercise therein the asserted First Amendment rights. Accordingly, we reverse the judgment and remand the case to the Court of Appeals with directions to vacate the injunction."

V. JUSTICE VOTE

4 Pro ACLU Side vs. 5 Con Opposing Side

ACLU Side (Respondent/Appellee)

1. Marshall, T. – Wrote dissenting opinion
2. Brennan, W. – Joined Marshall's dissent
3. Stewart, P. – Joined Marshall's dissent
4. Douglas, W. – Joined Marshall's dissent

Opposing Side (Petitioner/Appellant)

1. Powell, L. – Wrote majority opinion
2. White, B. – Joined majority opinion
3. Burger, W. – Joined majority opinion
4. Blackmun, H. – Joined majority opinion
5. Rehnquist, W. – Joined majority opinion

VI. A WIN OR LOSS FOR THE ACLU?

The ACLU served as counsel for appellee urging affirmance of the judgment of the Court of Appeals; the Supreme Court reversed, in a 5-4 vote, giving the ACLU an apparent loss.

277. Laird v. Tatum

(Decided June 26, 1972; 408 U.S. 1)

I. ISSUE

A. Issues Discussed

1st Amendment, press, speech, association, military

B. Legal Question Presented

"[W]hether . . . respondents presented a justiciable controversy in complaining of a 'chilling' effect on the exercise of their First Amendment rights where such effect is allegedly caused, not by any 'specific action of the Army against them, [but] only [by] the existence and operation of the intelligence gathering and distributing system, which is confined to the Army and related civilian investigative agencies.'"

C. Supreme Court's Answer

"We, of course, intimate no view with respect to the propriety or desirability, from a policy standpoint, of the challenged activities of the Department of the Army; our conclusion is a narrow one, namely, that on this record the respondents have not presented a case for resolution by the courts."

II. CASE SUMMARY

A. Background

"Respondents brought this class action in the District Court seeking declaratory and injunctive relief on their claim that their rights were being invaded by the Department of the Army's alleged 'surveillance of lawful and peaceful civilian political activity.' The petitioners in response describe the activity as 'gathering by lawful means . . . [and] maintaining and using in their intelligence activities . . . information relating to potential or actual civil disturbances [or] street demonstrations.' In connection with respondents' motion for a preliminary injunction and petitioners' motion to dismiss the complaint, both parties filed a number of affidavits with the District Court and presented their oral arguments at a hearing on the two motions. On the basis of the pleadings, the affidavits before the court, and the oral arguments advanced at the hearing, the District Court granted petitioners' motion to dismiss, holding that there was no justiciable claim for relief.

On appeal, a divided Court of Appeals reversed and ordered the case remanded for further proceedings."

The Supreme Court granted certiorari to review the case.

B. Counsel of Record

ACLU Side (Respondent/Appellee): Frank Askin argued the cause for appellees. With him on the brief were Melvitn L. Wulf and John H. F. Shatttuck of the American Civil Liberties Union Foundation.

Sam J. Ervin, Jr., argued the cause for the Unitarian Universalist Assn. et al. as amici curiae.

Opposing Side (Petitioner/Appellant): Solicitor General Griswold argued the cause for appellants. With him on the briefs were Assistant Attorney General Mardian and Robert L. Keuch.

III. AMICI CURIAE

ACLU Side (Respondent/Appellee)

Brief of amici curiae filed on behalf of the Unitarian Universalist Association et al. by Sam J. Ervin, Jr., and Lawrence M. Baskir.

Brief of amici curiae filed on behalf of a Group of Former Army Intelligence Agents by Burke Marshall and Arthur R. Miller.

Opposing Side (Petitioner/Appellant)

No briefs of amici curiae were filed in support of appellant.

IV. THE SUPREME COURT'S DECISION

"[T]he Court of Appeals properly identified the issue presented, namely, whether the jurisdiction of a federal court may be invoked by a complainant who alleges that the exercise of his First Amendment rights is being chilled by the mere existence, without more, of a governmental investigative and data-gathering activity that is alleged to be broader in scope than is reasonably necessary for the accomplishment of a valid governmental purpose. We conclude, however, that, having properly identified the issue, the Court of Appeals decided that issue incorrectly.

In recent years this Court has found in a number of cases that constitutional violations may arise from the deterrent, or 'chilling,' effect of governmental regulations that fall short of a direct prohibition against the exercise of First Amendment rights. In none of these cases, however, did the chilling effect arise merely from the individual's knowledge that a governmental agency was engaged in certain activities . . . . Rather, . . . the complainant was either presently or prospectively subject to the regulations, proscriptions, or compulsions that he was challenging. . . .

The decisions in these cases fully recognize that governmental action may be subject to constitutional challenge even though it has only an indirect effect on the exercise of First Amendment rights. At the same time, however, these decisions have in no way eroded the

'established principle that to entitle a private individual to invoke the judicial power to determine the validity of executive or legislative action he must show that he has sustained, or is immediately in danger of sustaining, a direct injury as the result of that action . . . .'

The respondents do not meet this test; their claim, simply stated, is that they disagree with the judgments made by the Executive Branch with respect to the type and amount of information the Army needs and that the very existence of the Army's data-gathering system produces a constitutionally impermissible chilling effect upon the exercise of their First Amendment rights. . . .

Stripped to its essentials, what respondents appear to be seeking is a broad-scale investigation, conducted by themselves . . . to probe into the Army's intelligence-gathering activities . . . .

Carried to its logical end, this approach would have the federal courts as virtually continuing monitors of the wisdom and soundness of Executive action; such . . . is not the role of the judiciary, absent actual present or immediately threatened injury resulting from unlawful governmental action.

We, of course, intimate no view with respect to the propriety or desirability, from a policy standpoint, of the challenged activities of the Department of the Army; our conclusion is a narrow one, namely, that on this record the respondents have not presented a case for resolution by the courts. . . .

Reversed."

V. JUSTICE VOTE

4 Pro ACLU Side vs. 5 Con Opposing Side

ACLU Side (Respondent/Appellee)

1. Brennan, W. – Wrote dissenting opinion
2. Douglas, W. – Wrote dissenting opinion

3. Marshall, T. – Joined Douglas' dissent, joined Brennan's dissent
4. Stewart, P. – Joined Brennan's dissent

Opposing Side (Petitioner/Appellant)

1. Burger, W. – Wrote majority opinion
2. Powell, L. – Joined majority opinion
3. Blackmun, H. – Joined majority opinion
4. White, B. – Joined majority opinion
5. Rehnquist, W. – Joined majority opinion

VI. A WIN OR LOSS FOR THE ACLU?

The ACLU served as counsel for appellees urging affirmance; the Supreme Court reversed the Court of Appeals' decision by a 5-4 vote, giving the ACLU an apparent loss.

278. Gelbard v. United States

(Decided June 26, 1972; 408 U.S. 41)

I. ISSUE

A. Issues Discussed

Criminal procedure, Fourth Amendment, wiretapping

B. Legal Question Presented

"[W]hether grand jury witnesses, in proceedings under 28 U.S.C. § 1826(a) , are entitled to invoke this prohibition of § 2515 [prohibiting the use of illegally obtained wiretapping evidence, and evidence derived from that evidence, in grand jury proceedings] as a defense to contempt charges brought against them for refusing to testify."

C. Supreme Court's Answer

Grand jury witnesses in these proceedings are entitled to this defense to contempt charges for refusing to testify.

II. CASE SUMMARY

A. Background

In No. 71-110, a "federal district judge approved wiretaps by federal agents of the telephones of Perry Paul, an alleged bookmaker, and Jerome Zarowitz, a former executive of a Las Vegas casino. In the court of those taps, the agents overheard conversations between Paul and petitioner Gelbard and between Zarowitz and petitioner Parnas."

Gelbard and Parnas were "called before a federal grand jury convened . . . to investigate possible violations of federal gambling laws. . . . Petitioners appeared before the grand jury, but declined to answer any questions based upon their intercepted conversations until they were afforded an opportunity to challenge the legality of the interceptions. Following a hearing, the United States District Court for the Central District of California found petitioners in contempt and, pursuant to 28 U.S.C. § 1826(a), committed them to custody for the life of the grand jury or until they answered the questions."

In No. 71-263, "[r]espondents Egan and Walsh were called before a federal grand jury . . . to investigate, among other possible crimes, an alleged plot to kidnap a Government official. [B]oth respondents were granted immunity in return for their testimony. Respondents appeared before the grand jury, but refused to answer questions on the ground, among others, that the questions were based upon information overheard from respondents by means of the government's illegal wiretapping and electronic surveillance. The government did not reply to respondents' allegations. Following a hearing, the United States District Court for the Middle District of Pennsylvania found respondents in contempt, and they were also committed to custody pursuant to 28 U.S.C. § 1826(a).

Section 1826(a) expressly limits the adjudication of civil contempt to the case of a grand jury witness who 'refuses without just cause shown to comply with an order of the court to testify.'" The Court of Appeals for the Ninth Circuit affirmed the finding of contempt in No. 71-110 while the Court of Appeals for the Third Circuit reversed the finding of contempt in No. 71-263.

The Supreme Court granted certiorari to consider "whether a showing that interrogation would be based upon the illegal interception of the witness' communications constitutes a showing of 'just cause' that precludes a finding of contempt," reversed in No. 71-110, and affirmed in No. 71-263.

B. Counsel of Record/ACLU Attorney

ACLU Side (Petitioner/Appellant in No. 71-110, Respondent/Appellee in No. 71-263):

Michael E. Tigar and Burton Marks argued the cause for appellant in No. 71-110.

Jack J. Levine argued the cause, pro hac vice, for appellee in No. 71-263.

Opposing Side (Respondent/Appellee in No. 71-110, Petitioner/Appellant in No. 71-263):

Deputy Solicitor General Daniel M. Friedman argued the cause for the United States in both cases.

III. AMICI CURIAE

ACLU Side (Petitioner/Appellant in No. 71-110, Respondent/Appellee in No. 71-263):

Brief of amici curiae filed on behalf of the ACLU in both cases by Melvin L. Wulf, Sanford Jay Rosen, William J. Birtles, Thomas Harvey, and Laurence R. Sperber.

Opposing Side (Respondent/Appellee in No. 71-110, Petitioner/Appellant in No. 71-26):

Brief of amici curiae filed on behalf of Americans for Effective Law Enforcement, Inc., in No. 71-263, by Frank G. Carrington, Jr., Richard O. Wright, James L. Tennant, Alan S. Ganz, and Fred E. Inbau.

IV. THE SUPREME COURT'S DECISION

"In Title III, Congress enacted a comprehensive scheme for the regulation of wiretapping and electronic surveillance. Title III authorizes the interception of private wire and oral communications, but only when law enforcement officials are investigating specified serious crimes and receive prior judicial approval . . . . If a wire or oral communication is intercepted in accordance with the provisions of Title III, the contents of the communication may be disclosed and used under certain circumstances. Except as expressly authorized in Title III, however, all interceptions of wire and oral communications are flatly prohibited. Unauthorized interceptions and the disclosure or use of information obtained through unauthorized interceptions are crimes, and the victim of such interception, disclosure, or use is entitled to recover civil damages. Title III also bars the use as evidence before official bodies of the contents and fruits of illegal interceptions, and provides procedures for moving to suppress such evidence in various proceedings.

The witnesses in these cases were held in contempt for disobeying court orders by refusing to produce evidence—their testimony—before grand juries. Consequently, their primary contention is that § 2515, the evidentiary prohibition of Title III, afforded them a defense to the contempt charges. . . . In short, we proceed on the premise that § 2515 prohibits the presentation to grand juries of the compelled testimony of these witnesses.

The narrow question, then, is whether, under these circumstances, the witnesses may invoke the prohibition of § 2515 as a defense to contempt charges brought on the basis of their refusal to obey court orders to testify. We think they may. . . .

The purposes of § 2515 and Title III as a whole would be subverted were the plain command of § 2515 ignored when the victim of an illegal interception is called as a witness before a grand jury and asked questions based upon that interception. Moreover, § 2515 serves not only to protect the privacy of communications, but also to ensure that the courts do not become partners to illegal conduct: the evidentiary prohibition was enacted also 'to protect the integrity of court and administrative proceedings.' Consequently, to order a grand jury witness, on pain of imprisonment, to disclose evidence that § 2515 bars in unequivocal terms is both to thwart the congressional objective of protecting individual privacy by excluding such evidence and to entangle the courts in the illegal acts of Government agents. . . .

The judgment of the Court of Appeals for the Ninth Circuit in No. 71-110 is reversed, and the case is remanded for further proceedings consistent with this opinion. The judgment of the Court of Appeals for the Third Circuit in No. 71-263 is affirmed."

V. JUSTICE VOTE

5 Pro ACLU Side vs. 4 Con Opposing Side

ACLU Side (Petitioner/Appellant in No. 71-110, Respondent/Appellee in No. 71-263):

1. Brennan, W. – Wrote majority opinion
2. Stewart, P. – Joined majority opinion
3. Marshall, T. – Joined majority opinion
4. Douglas, W. – Wrote concurring opinion
5. White, B. – Wrote concurring opinion

Opposing Side (Respondent/Appellee in No. 71-110, Petitioner/Appellant in No. 71-26):

1. Rehnquist, W. – Wrote dissenting opinion
2. Blackmun, H. – Joined Rehnquist's dissent
3. Burger, W. – Joined Rehnquist's dissent
4. Powell, L. – Joined Rehnquist's dissent

VI. A WIN OR LOSS FOR THE ACLU?

The ACLU filed as amicus curiae urging reversal in *Gelbard v. United States* and affirmance in *United States v. Egan*; the Supreme Court reversed the judgment in *Gelbard v. United States* and affirmed the judgment in *United States v. Egan* in a 5-4 vote, giving the ACLU an apparent win.

279. Healy v. James

(Decided June 26, 1972; 408 U.S. 169)

I. ISSUE

A. Issues Discussed

1st Amendment, press, speech, association

B. Legal Question Presented

"This case, arising out of a denial by a state college of official recognition to a group of students who desired to form a local chapter of Students for a Democratic Society (SDS), presents this Court with questions requiring the application of well-established First Amendment principles."

C. Supreme Court's Answer

"Because respondents failed to accord due recognition to First Amendment principles, the judgments below approving respondents' denial of recognition must be reversed. Since we cannot conclude from this record that petitioners were willing to abide by reasonable campus rules and regulations, we order the case remanded for reconsideration."

II. CASE SUMMARY

A. Background

"Petitioners are students attending Central Connecticut State College (CCSC) . . . . In September 1969 they undertook to organize what they then referred to as a 'local chapter' of SDS [Students for a Democratic Society]. Pursuant to procedures established by the College, petitioners filed a request for official recognition as a campus organization with the Student Affairs Committee . . . .

By a vote of six to two the Committee ultimately approved the application and recommended to the President of the College, Dr. James, that the organization be accorded official recognition. . . .

Several days later, the President rejected the Committee's recommendation . . . .

They filed a suit in the United States District Court for the District of Connecticut, seeking declaratory and injunctive relief . . . . Petitioners' primary complaint centered on the denial of First Amendment rights of expression and association arising from denial of campus recognition. The . . . judge ruled that petitioners had been denied procedural due process . . . . The court concluded that if the President wished to act on the basis of material outside the application he must at least provide petitioners a hearing and opportunity to introduce evidence as to their affiliations. . . .

Pursuant to the court's order, the President designated Dean

Judd, the Dean of Student Affairs, to serve as hearing officer and a hearing was scheduled. . . .

Upon reviewing the hearing transcript and exhibits, the President reaffirmed his prior decision to deny petitioners recognition as a campus organization. . . .

After the President's second statement issued, the case then returned to the District Court, where it was ordered dismissed. . . .

Petitioners appealed to the Court of Appeals for the Second Circuit where, by a two-to-one vote, the District Court's judgment was affirmed. [The Supreme] Court granted certiorari . . . ."

B. Counsel of Record

ACLU Side (Petitioner/Appellant): Melvin L. Wulf of the American Civil Liberties Union Foundation argued the cause for appellants. With him on the brief were Eugene Z. DuBose, Jr., and Joel Gora of the American Civil Liberties Union Foundation, Alvin Pudlin, Abraham S. Silver, and Sanford Jay Rosen.

Opposing Side (Respondent/Appellee): F. Michael Ahern, Assistant Attorney General of Connecticut, argued the cause for appellees. With him on the brief was Robert K. Killian, Attorney General.

III. AMICI CURIAE

ACLU Side (Petitioner/Appellant)

No briefs of amici curiae were filed in support of appellants.

Opposing Side (Respondent/Appellee)

Brief of amici curiae filed on behalf of the Board of Trustees of California State Colleges by Evelle J. Younger, Attorney General of California, and Donald B. Day, Deputy Attorney General.

Brief of amici curiae filed on behalf of Americans for Effective Law Enforcement, Inc. by Frank G. Carrington, Jr., and Alan S. Ganz.

Brief of amici curiae filed on behalf of the American Association of Presidents of Independent Colleges and Universities by Morris I. Leibman and Philip B. Kurland.

IV. THE SUPREME COURT'S DECISION

"At the outset we note that state colleges and universities are not enclaves immune from the sweep of the First Amendment. . . .

There can be no doubt that denial of official recognition, without justification, to college organizations burdens or abridges that associational right. . . .

Respondents and the courts below appear to have taken the view that denial of official recognition in this case abridged no constitutional rights. . . .

We do not agree with the characterization by the courts below of the consequences of nonrecognition. . . .

It is to be remembered that the effect of the College's denial of recognition was a form of prior restraint, denying to petitioners' organization the range of associational activities . . . . While a college has a legitimate interest in preventing disruption on the campus, which under circumstances requiring the safeguarding of that interest may justify such restraint, a 'heavy burden' rests on the college to demonstrate the appropriateness of that action. . . .

These fundamental errors—discounting the existence of a cognizable First Amendment interest and misplacing the burden of proof—require that the judgments below be reversed. But we are unable to conclude that no basis exists upon which nonrecognition might be appropriate. Indeed, based on a reasonable reading of the ambiguous facts of this case, there appears to be at least one potentially acceptable ground for a denial of recognition. Because of this ambiguous state of the record we conclude that the case should be remanded . . . .

We think the . . . discussion establishes the appropriate framework for consideration of petitioners' request for campus recognition. Because respondents failed to accord due recognition to First Amendment principles, the judgments below approving respondents' denial of recognition must be reversed. Since we cannot conclude from this record that petitioners were willing to abide by reasonable campus rules and regulations, we order the case remanded for reconsideration. We note, in so holding, that the wide latitude accorded by the Constitution to the freedoms of expression and association is not without its costs in terms of the risk to the maintenance of civility and an ordered society. Indeed, this latitude often has resulted, on the campus and elsewhere, in the infringement of the rights of others. Though we deplore the tendency of some to abuse the very constitutional privileges they invoke, and although the infringement of rights of others certainly should not be tolerated, we reaffirm this Court's dedication to the principles of the Bill of Rights upon which our vigorous and free society is founded.

Reversed and remanded."

V. JUSTICE VOTE

9 Pro ACLU Side vs. 0 Con Opposing Side

ACLU Side (Petitioner/Appellant)

1. Powell, L. – Wrote majority opinion
2. White, B. – Joined majority opinion
3. Marshall, T. – Joined majority opinion
4. Brennan, W. – Joined majority opinion
5. Stewart, P. – Joined majority opinion
6. Burger, W. – Wrote concurring opinion
7. Blackmun, H. – Joined majority opinion
8. Douglas, W. – Joined majority opinion and wrote separate opinion
9. Rehnquist, W. – Wrote concurring opinion

VI. A WIN OR LOSS FOR THE ACLU?

The ACLU served as counsel for appellants urging reversal of the judgment of the Court of Appeals; the Supreme Court reversed, in a 9-0 vote, giving the ACLU an apparent win.

280. Furman v. Georgia

(Decided June 29, 1972; 408 U.S. 238)

I. ISSUE

A. Issues Discussed

Death penalty, Eighth Amendment, cruel and unusual punishment

B. Legal Question Presented

"'Does the imposition and carrying out of the death penalty in [these cases] constitute cruel and unusual punishment in violation of the Eighth and Fourteenth Amendments?'"

C. Supreme Court's Answer

The death penalty is cruel and unusual punishment in these cases.

II. CASE SUMMARY

A. Background

In *Furman*, "The victim surprised Furman in the act of burglarizing the victim's home in the middle of the night. While escaping, Furman killed the victim with one pistol shot fired through the closed kitchen door from the outside. At the trial, Furman gave his version of the killing: 'They got me charged with murder and I admit, I admit going to these folks' home and they did caught me in there and I was coming back out, backing up and there was a wire down there on the floor. I was coming out backwards and fell back and I didn't intend to kill nobody. I didn't know they was behind the door. The gun went off and I didn't know nothing about no murder until they arrested me, and when the gun went off I was down on the floor and I got up and ran. That's all to it."[1]

The Georgia Supreme Court determined that, "[t]he admission in open court by the accused . . . that during the period in which he was involved in the commission of a criminal act at the home of the deceased, he accidentally tripped over a wire in leaving the premises causing the gun to go off, together with other facts and circumstances surrounding the death of the deceased by violent means, was sufficient to support the verdict of guilty of murder . . . ."[2]

In *Jackson*, "Jackson, a black, convicted of the rape of a white woman, was 21 years old. A court-appointed psychiatrist said that Jackson was of average education and average intelligence, that he was not an imbecile, or schizophrenic, or psychotic, that his traits were the product of environmental influences, and that he was competent to stand trial. Jackson had entered the house after the husband left for work. He held scissors against the neck of the wife, demanding money. She could find none and a struggle ensued for the scissors, a battle which she lost; and she was then raped, Jackson keeping the scissors pressed against her neck. While there did not appear to be any long-term traumatic impact on the victim, she was bruised and abrased in the struggle but was not hospitalized. Jackson was a convict who had escaped from a work gang in the area, a result of a three-year sentence for auto theft. He was at large for three days and during that time had committed several other offenses—burglary, auto theft, and assault and battery."[3]

In *Branch*, "Branch, a black, entered the rural home of a 65-year-old widow, a white, while she slept and raped her, holding his arm against her throat. Thereupon he demanded money and for 30 minutes or more the widow searched for money, finding little. As he left, [Branch] said if the widow told anyone what happened, he would return and kill her. The record is barren of any medical or psychiatric evidence showing injury to her as a result of Branch's attack.

He had previously been convicted of felony theft and found to be a borderline mental deficient and well below the average IQ of Texas prison inmates. He had the equivalent of five and a half years of grade school education. He had a 'dull intelligence' and was in the lowest fourth percentile of his class."[4]

The U.S. Supreme Court granted certiorari to review the cases and reversed the judgments in all cases.

B. Counsel of Record / ACLU Attorney

ACLU Side (Petitioner / Appellant): Anthony G. Amsterdam argued the cause for appellant in No. 69-5003. Jack Greenberg argued the cause for appellant in No. 69-5030. Melvyn Carson Bruder argued the cause for appellant in No. 69-5031.

Opposing Side (Respondent / Appellee): Dorothy T. Beasley, Assistant Attorney General of Georgia, argued the cause for appellees in Nos. 69-5003, 69-5030. Charles Alan Wright argued the cause for appellee in No. 69-5031.

III. AMICI CURIAE

ACLU Side (Petitioner / Appellant)

Brief of amici curiae filed on behalf of the ACLU by Gerald H. Gottlieb, Melvin L. Wulf, and Sanford Jay Rosen.

Additional briefs of amici curiae filed on behalf of the State of Alaska, the Synagogue Council of America, et al., the National Association for the Advancement of Colored People, et al., the West Virginia Council of Churches, et al., and James V. Bennett, et al.

Opposing Side (Respondent / Appellee)

Brief of amici curiae filed on behalf of the State of Indiana by Theodore L. Sendak, Attorney General of Indiana, and David O. Givens, Deputy Attorney General.

IV. THE SUPREME COURT'S DECISION

"Certiorari was granted limited to the following question: 'Does the imposition and carrying out of the death penalty in [these cases] constitute cruel and unusual punishment in violation of the Eighth and Fourteenth Amendments?' The Court holds that the imposition and carrying out of the death penalty in these cases constitute cruel and unusual punishment in violation of the Eighth and Fourteenth Amendments. The judgment in each case is therefore reversed insofar as it leaves undisturbed the death sentence imposed, and the cases are remanded for further

1 Furman v. Georgia, 408 U.S. 238, 294 n.48 (1972) (Brennan, W., concurring).
2 Furman v. State, 167 S.E.2d 628 (Ga. 1969).
3 Furman v. Georgia, 408 U.S. 238 (1972) (Douglas, W., concurring).
4 Furman v. Georgia, 408 U.S. 238 (1972) (Douglas, W., concurring).

proceedings. So ordered.

Judgment in each case reversed in part and cases remanded."

V. JUSTICE VOTE

5 Pro ACLU Side vs. 4 Con Opposing Side

ACLU Side (Petitioner/Appellant)

1. Marshall, T. – Wrote concurring opinion
2. Douglas, W. – Wrote concurring opinion
3. Brennan, W. – Wrote concurring opinion
4. Stewart, P. – Wrote concurring opinion
5. White, B. – Wrote concurring opinion

Opposing Side (Respondent/Appellee)

1. Burger, W. – Wrote dissenting opinion
2. Blackmun, H. – Wrote dissenting opinion
3. Powell, L. – Wrote dissenting opinion
4. Rehnquist, W. – Wrote dissenting opinion

VI. A WIN OR LOSS FOR THE ACLU?

The ACLU, as amicus curiae, urged reversal of the judgment of the Supreme Court of Georgia; the Supreme Court reversed in a per curiam opinion in a 5-4 vote, giving the ACLU an apparent win.

281. Morrissey v. Brewer

(Decided June 29, 1972; 408 U.S. 471)

I. ISSUE

A. Issues Discussed

Criminal procedure, prisons, Fourteenth Amendment

B. Legal Question Presented

"[W]hether the Due Process Clause of the Fourteenth Amendment requires that a State afford an individual some opportunity to be heard prior to revoking his parole."

C. Supreme Court's Answer

Due process requires a minimal inquiry when an individual's parole is revoked.

II. CASE SUMMARY

A. Background

"Petitioner Morrissey was convicted of false drawing or uttering of checks in 1967 pursuant to his guilty plea, and was sentenced to not more than seven years' confinement. He was paroled from the Iowa State Penitentiary in June 1968. Seven months later, at the direction of his parole officer, he was arrested in his home town as a parole violator and incarcerated in the county jail. One week later, after review of the parole officer's written report, the Iowa Board of Parole revoked Morrissey's parole, and he was returned to the penitentiary located about 100 miles from his home. Petitioner asserts he received no hearing prior to revocation of his parole. . . .

The situation as to petitioner Booher is much the same." Booher was convicted of forgery, sentenced to a maximum term of ten years, paroled, then recommitted without a hearing. "After exhausting state remedies, both petitioners filed habeas corpus petitions in the United States District Court for the Southern District of Iowa alleging that they had been denied due process because their paroles had been revoked without a hearing. . . . The District Court held on the basis of controlling authority that the State's failure to accord a hearing prior to parole revocation did not violate due process. On appeal, the two cases were consolidated."

The Court of Appeals affirmed the district court's denial of relief and concluded that a parolee, who is still "in custody," is not entitled to a full adversary hearing such as would be mandated in a criminal proceeding.

The Supreme Court granted certiorari to review the case, and reversed the Court of Appeals.

B. Counsel of Record/ACLU Attorney

ACLU Side (Petitioner/Appellant): W. Don Brittin, Jr., by appointment of the Court, argued the cause for appellant.

Opposing Side (Respondent/Appellee): Lawrence S. Seuferer, Assistant Attorney General of Iowa, argued the cause for appellee.

III. AMICI CURIAE

ACLU Side (Petitioner/Appellant)

Brief of amici curiae filed on behalf of the ACLU by Melvin L. Wulf, Michele Hermann, Herman Schwartz, Robert Plotkin, Richard Singer, and Joel Gora.

Brief of amici curiae filed on behalf of the American Bar Association by William W. Falsgraf, Leon Jaworski, Richard J. Hughes, Robert J. Kutak, and Linda R. Singer.

Brief of amici curiae filed on behalf of James H. Russell by Craig Eldon Pinkus.

Opposing Side (Respondent/Appellee)

No briefs of amici curiae were filed in support of appellee.

IV. THE SUPREME COURT'S DECISION

"Yet, the State has no interest in revoking parole without some informal procedural guarantees. Although the parolee is often formally described as being 'in custody,' the argument cannot even be made here that summary treatment is necessary as it may be with respect to controlling a large group of potentially disruptive prisoners in actual custody. Nor are we persuaded by the argument that revocation is so totally a discretionary matter that some form of hearing would be administratively intolerable. A simple factual hearing will not interfere with the exercise of discretion. Serious studies have suggested that fair treatment on parole revocation will not result in fewer grants of parole. . . .

We have no thought to create an inflexible structure for parole revocation procedures. The few basic requirements . . . which are applicable to future revocations of parole, should not impose a great burden on any State's parole system. Control over the required proceedings by the hearing officers can assure that delaying tactics and other abuses sometimes present in the traditional adversary trial situation do not occur. Obviously a parolee cannot relitigate issues determined against him in other forums, as in the situation presented when the revocation is based on conviction of another crime.

In the peculiar posture of this case, given the absence of an adequate record, we conclude the ends of justice will be best served by remanding the case to the Court of Appeals for its return of the two consolidated cases to the District Court with directions to make findings on the procedures actually followed by the Parole Board in these two revocations. If it is determined that petitioners admitted parole violations to the Parole Board, as respondents contend, and if those violations are found to be reasonable grounds for revoking parole under state standards, that would end the matter. If the procedures followed by the Parole Board are found to meet the standards laid down in this opinion that, too, would dispose of the due process claims for these cases.

We reverse and remand to the Court of Appeals for further proceedings consistent with this opinion."

V. JUSTICE VOTE

9 Pro ACLU Side vs. 0 Con Opposing Side

ACLU Side (Petitioner/Appellant)

1. Burger, W. – Wrote majority opinion
2. Powell, L. – Joined majority opinion
3. Stewart, P. – Joined majority opinion
4. White, B. – Joined majority opinion
5. Blackmun, H. – Joined majority opinion
6. Rehnquist, W. – Joined majority opinion
7. Brennan, W. – Wrote concurring opinon
8. Marshall, T. – Joined Brennan's concurrence
9. Douglas, W. – Wrote opinion concurring in part and dissenting in part

VI. A WIN OR LOSS FOR THE ACLU?

The ACLU filed as amicus curiae urging reversal, the Supreme Court reversed the Court of Appeals' judgment in a 9-0 vote giving the ACLU an apparent win.

282. Gravel v. United States

(Decided June 29, 1972; 408 U.S. 606)

I. ISSUE

A. Issues Discussed

Government authority, federalism, First Amendment

B. Legal Question Presented

Did a grand jury subpoena, requiring Senator Gravel's assistant to testify regarding Gravel's involvement in the publication of the Pentagon Papers, violate the Speech and Debate Clause?

C. Supreme Court's Answer

Protections of the Speech and Debate Clause extend beyond a member of Congress to his aide, however, the protections only extend to legislative acts so all of the aide's non-legislative acts are not protected.

II. CASE SUMMARY

A. Background

"These cases arise out of the investigation by a federal grand jury into possible criminal conduct with respect to the release and publication of a classified Defense Department study . . . popularly known as the Pentagon Papers . . . . The crimes being investigated included the retention of public property or records with intent to convert, the gathering and transmitting of national defense information, the concealment or removal of public records or documents, and conspiracy to commit such offenses and to defraud the United States.

Among the witnesses subpoenaed were Leonard S. Rodberg, an assistant to Senator Mike Gravel of Alaska and a resident fellow at the Institute of Policy Studies, and Howard Webber, Director of M.I.T. Press. Senator Gravel, as intervenor, filed motions to quash the subpoenas and to require the Government to specify the particular questions to be addressed to Rodberg. He asserted that requiring these witnesses to appear and testify would violate his privilege under the Speech or Debate Clause of the United States Constitution.

It appeared that on the night of June 29, 1971, Senator Gravel, as Chairman of the Subcommittee on Buildings and Grounds of the Senate Public Works Committee, convened a meeting of the subcommittee and there read extensively from a copy of the Pentagon Papers. He then placed the entire 47 volumes of the study in the public record. Rodberg had been added to the Senator's staff earlier in the day and assisted Gravel in preparing for and conducting the hearing. Some weeks later there were press reports that Gravel had arranged for the papers to be published by Beacon Press. And that members of Gravel's staff had talked with Webber as editor of M.I.T. Press.

The District Court overruled the motions to quash and to specify questions but entered an order proscribing certain categories of questions. . . . The trial court, however, held the private publication of the documents was not privileged by the Speech or Debate Clause.

The Court of Appeals affirmed the denial of the motions to quash but modified the protective order to reflect its own views of the scope of the congressional privilege. . . .

The United States petitioned for certiorari challenging the ruling that aides and other persons may not be questioned with respect to legislative acts and that an aide to a Member of Congress has a common-law privilege not to testify before a grand jury with respect to private publication of materials introduced into a subcommittee record. Senator Gravel also petitioned for certiorari seeking reversal of the Court of Appeals insofar as it held private publication unprotected by the Speech or Debate Clause and asserting that the protective order of the Court of Appeals too narrowly protected against inquiries that a grand jury could direct to third parties. [The Supreme Court] granted both petitions."

The Supreme Court vacated the decision and remanded the case.

B. Counsel of Record/ACLU Attorney

ACLU Side (Petitioner/Appellant): Robert J. Reinstein and Charles Louis Fishman argued the cause for appellant.

Opposing Side (Respondent/Appellee): Solicitor General Erwin N. Griswold argued the cause for the United States.

Sam J. Ervin, Jr., and William B. Saxbe argued the cause for the United States Senate, as amici curiae, by special leave of court.

III. AMICI CURIAE

ACLU Side (Petitioner/Appellant)

Brief of amici curiae filed on behalf of the ACLU by Melvin L. Wulf, Joel M. Gora, Sanford Jay Rosen, William Birtles, and Earl Nemser.

Brief of amici curiae filed on behalf of the Unitarian Universalist Association by Frank B. Frederick, William B. Duffy, Jr., and Henry Paul Monaghan.

Brief of amici curiae filed on behalf of Dr. Leonard S. Rodberg by James Reif, Doris Peterson, Morton Stavis, and Peter Weiss.

Opposing Side (Respondent/Appellee)

Brief of amici curiae filed on behalf of the United States Senate by Sam J. Ervin, Jr., William B. Saxbe, James O. Eastland, John O. Pastore, Herman E. Talmadge, Norris Cotton, Peter H. Dominick, Charles McC. Mathias, Jr., Philip B. Kurland, and Edward I. Rothschild.

IV. THE SUPREME COURT'S DECISION

"We are convinced also that the Court of Appeals correctly determined that Senator Gravel's alleged arrangement with Beacon Press to publish the Pentagon Papers was not protected speech or debate within the meaning of Art. I, § 6, cl. 1, of the Constitution. . . .

Prior cases have read the Speech or Debate Clause 'broadly to effectuate its purposes,' and have included within its reach anything 'generally done in a session of the House by one of its members in relation to the business before it.' Thus, voting by Members and committee reports are protected; and we recognize today—as the Court has recognized before—that a Member's conduct at legislative committee hearings, although subject to judicial review in various circumstances, as is legislation itself, may not be made the basis for a civil or criminal judgment against a Member because that conduct is within the 'sphere of legitimate legislative activity.'

But the Clause has not been extended beyond the legislative sphere. That Senators generally perform certain acts in their official capacity as Senators does not necessarily make all such acts legislative in nature. . . . As the Court of Appeals put it, the courts have extended the privilege to matters beyond pure speech or debate in either House, but 'only when necessary to prevent indirect impairment of such deliberations.'

Here, private publication by Senator Gravel through the cooperation of Beacon Press was in no way essential to the deliberations of the Senate; nor does questioning as to private publication threaten the integrity or independence of the Senate by impermissibly exposing its deliberations to executive influence. . . . We cannot but conclude that the Senator's arrangements with Beacon Press were not part and parcel of the legislative process. . . .

We must finally consider, in the light of the foregoing, whether the protective order entered by the Court of Appeals is an appropriate regulation of the pending grand jury proceedings.

Focusing first on paragraph two of the order, we think the injunction against interrogating Rodberg with respect to any act, 'in the broadest sense,' performed by him within the scope of his employment, overly restricts the scope of grand jury inquiry. Rodberg's immunity, testimonial or otherwise, extends only to legislative acts as to which the Senator himself would be immune. The grand jury, therefore, if relevant to its investigation into the possible violations of the criminal law . . . may require from Rodberg answers to questions relating to his or the Senator's arrangements, if any, with respect to republication or with respect to third-party conduct under valid investigation by the grand jury, as long as the questions do not implicate legislative action of the Senator. . . .

The judgment of the Court of Appeals is vacated and the cases are remanded to that court for further proceedings consistent with this opinion."

V. JUSTICE VOTE

4 Pro ACLU Side vs. 5 Con Opposing Side

ACLU Side (Petitioner/Appellant)

1. Stewart, P. – Wrote opinion dissenting in part
2. Brennan, W. – Wrote dissenting opinion
3. Marshall, T. – Joined Brennan's dissent
4. Douglas, W. – Wrote dissenting opinion, joined Brennan's dissent

Opposing Side (Respondent/Appellee)

1. White, B. – Wrote majority opinion
2. Powell, L. – Joined majority opinion
3. Blackmun, H. – Joined majority opinion
4. Rehnquist, W. – Joined majority opinion
5. Burger, W. – Joined majority opinion

VI. A WIN OR LOSS FOR THE ACLU?

The ACLU filed as amicus curiae urging reversal; the Supreme Court vacated the judgment of the Court of Appeals in a 5-4 vote, giving the ACLU an apparent loss.

283. Branzburg v. Hayes

(Decided June 29, 1972; 408 U.S. 665)

I. ISSUE

A. Issues Discussed

First Amendment, freedom of press, speech, and association

B. Legal Question Presented

"[W]hether requiring newsmen to appear and testify before state or federal grand juries abridges the freedom of speech and press guaranteed by the First Amendment."

C. Supreme Court's Answer

Requiring newsmen to testify does not violate the freedoms of speech or of the press.

II. CASE SUMMARY

A. Background

In No. 70-57, subpoenas were issued by a federal grand jury "to respondent Earl Caldwell, a reporter for the *New York Times* assigned to cover the Black Panther Party and other black militant groups." He was ordered to testify before a grand jury "and to bring with him notes and tape recordings of interviews given him for publication by officers and spokesmen of the Black Panther Party concerning the aims, purposes, and activities of that organization. Respondent objected to the scope of this subpoena" and to testifying, and he filed a motion to quash, citing the First Amendment and freedom of the press.

The District Court denied the motion to quash, but accepted Caldwell's First Amendment arguments. However, another subpoena was issued when a new grand jury was convened, and Caldwell was ordered to testify before the new grand jury. He was held in contempt of the court when he failed to appear after the court denied his motion to quash. Caldwell appealed the contempt order and the Court of Appeals reversed.

Similarly, in No. 70-85, Branzburg, a reporter, after observing and interviewing a number of people synthesizing and using drugs, wrote a story for a Louisville newspaper. On two occasions he was called to testify before state grand juries. Branzburg refused to testify and potentially disclose the identities of his confidential sources. The trial judge denied his motion to quash the subpoena in one instance and he was directed to testify before a grand jury under both subpoenas. Branzburg appealed in both instances and the Kentucky Court of Appeals affirmed the lower court judgments, requiring him to testify.

In 70-94, Pappas, a television reporter covering activity within the Black Panther organization, was called to testify before grand juries and reveal confidential information. Like Caldwell and Branzburg, Pappas refused to testify before the state grand juries. Pappas appealed to the Massachusetts Supreme Judicial Court, which ruled against his plea to not testify.

The Court granted certiorari, consolidated the three cases, and affirmed in part and reversed in part the lower court decisions.

B. Counsel of Record/ACLU Attorney

ACLU Side (Petitioner/Appellant in Nos.70-85 and 70-94, Respondent/Appellee in No. 70-57):

Edgar A. Zingman argued the cause for appellant in No. 70-85.

E. Barrett Prettyman, Jr., argued the cause for appellant in No. 70-94.

Anthony G. Amsterdam argued the cause for appellee in No. 70-57.

Opposing Side (Respondent/Appellee in Nos. 70-85 and 70-94, Petitioner/Appellant in No. 70-57):

Edwin A. Schroering, Jr., argued the cause for appellee in No. 70-85.

Joseph J. Hurley, First Assistant Attorney General, argued the cause for appellee in No. 70-94.

Solicitor General Erwin N. Griswold argued the cause for appellant in No. 70-57.

William Bradford Reynolds argued the cause for the United States, as amicus curiae, by special leave of court, in Nos. 70-85 and 70-94.

III. AMICI CURIAE

ACLU Side (Petitioner/Appellant in Nos.70-85 and 70-94, Respondent/Appellee in No. 70-57):

Brief of amici curiae filed in No. 70-57 on behalf of the ACLU, et al., by Melvin L. Wulf, Paul N. Halvonik, A. L. Wirin, Fred Okrand, and Lawrence R. Sperber.

Additional briefs of amici curiae were filed on behalf of the New York Times Co., Inc., the Chicago Tribune Co., the American Newspaper Publishers Association, the American Newspapers Guild, AFL-CIO, CLC, the Authors League of America, Inc., the Radio Television Directors Association, the Office of Communication of the United Church of Christ, et al., the Washington Post Co., et al., the American Society of Newspaper Editors, et al., and the National Press Photographers Association, Inc.

Opposing Side (Respondent/Appellee in Nos. 70-85 and 70-94, Petitioner/Appellant in No. 70-57):

Brief of amici curiae filed on behalf of the United States by William Bradford Reynolds, Solicitor General Erwin N. Griswold, Assistant Attorney General Wilson, Beatrice Rosenberg, and Robert E. Lindsay.

Brief of amici curiae filed on behalf of the National District Attorneys Association by John T. Corrigan.

IV. THE SUPREME COURT'S DECISION

"We turn, therefore, to the disposition of the cases before us. From what we have said, it necessarily follows that the decision in United States v. Caldwell must be reversed. If there is no First Amendment privilege to refuse to answer the relevant and material questions asked during a good-faith grand jury investigation, then it is a fortiori true that there is no privilege to refuse to appear before such a grand jury until the Government demonstrates some 'compelling need' for a newsman's testimony. . . .

The decisions in *Branzburg v. Hayes* and *Branzburg v. Meigs*, must be affirmed. Here, petitioner refused to answer questions that directly related to criminal conduct that he had observed and written about. The Kentucky Court of Appeals noted that marijuana is defined as a narcotic drug by statute, and that unlicensed possession or compounding of it is a felony punishable by both fine and imprisonment. It held that petitioner 'saw the commission of the statutory felonies of unlawful possession of marijuana and the unlawful conversion of it into hashish.' Petitioner may be presumed to have observed similar violations of the state narcotics laws during the research he did for the story that forms the basis of the subpoena in *Branzburg v. Meigs*. In both cases, if what petitioner wrote was true, he had direct information to provide the grand jury concerning the commission of serious crimes.

The only question presented at the present time in *In re Pappas*, is whether petitioner Pappas must appear before the grand jury to testify pursuant to subpoena. The Massachusetts Supreme Judicial Court characterized the record in this case as 'meager,' and it is not clear what petitioner will be asked by the grand jury. It is not even clear that he will be asked to divulge information received in confidence. We affirm the decision of the Massachusetts Supreme Judicial Court and hold that petitioner must appear before the grand jury to answer the questions put to him, subject, of course, to the supervision of the presiding judge as to 'the propriety, purposes, and scope of the grand jury inquiry and the pertinence of the probable testimony.'"

The Supreme Court reversed in part and affirmed in part the judgments below.

V. JUSTICE VOTE

4 Pro ACLU Side vs. 5 Con Opposing Side

ACLU Side (Petitioner/Appellant in Nos.70-85 and 70-94, Respondent/Appellee in No. 70-57):

1. Marshall, T. – Joined Stewart's dissent
2. Brennan, W. – Joined Stewart's dissent
3. Stewart, P. – Wrote dissenting opinion
4. Douglas, W. – Wrote dissenting opinion

Opposing Side (Respondent/Appellee in Nos. 70-85 and 70-94, Petitioner/Appellant in No. 70-57):

1. White, B. – Wrote majority opinion
2. Blackmun, H. – Joined majority opinion
3. Rehnquist, W. – Joined majority opinion
4. Burger, W. – Joined majority opinion
5. Powell, L. – Wrote concurring opinion

VI. A WIN OR LOSS FOR THE ACLU?

The ACLU filed as amicus curiae urging affirmance in Caldwell; the Supreme Court reversed the Court of Appeals' judgment in Caldwell and affirmed the judgments in Branzburg and Pappas, in a 5-4 vote giving ACLU an apparent loss.

284. Kleindienst v. Mandel

(Decided June 29, 1972; 408 U.S. 753)

I. ISSUE

A. Issues Discussed

Governmental authority, immigration, First Amendment

B. Legal Question Presented

"'Does [the Attorney General's] action in refusing to allow an alien scholar to enter the country to attend academic meetings violate the First Amendment rights of American scholars and students who had invited him?'"

C. Supreme Court's Answer

The Supreme Court determined the Attorney General had the discretionary power to not waive the scholar's grounds of inadmissibility, declining to address the First Amendment issue.

II. CASE SUMMARY

A. Background

Respondent, Ernest Mandel, was a Belgian citizen. A professional journalist, he was "editor-in-chief of the Belgian Left Socialist weekly paper *La Gauche*" and the author of *Marxist Economic Theory*.

"Mandel was admitted to the United States temporarily in 1962 and again in 1968. On the first visit he came as a working journalist. On the second he accepted invitations to speak at a number of universities and colleges. On each occasion, although apparently he was not then aware of it, his admission followed a finding of ineligibility under s 212(a)(28), and the Attorney General's exercise of discretion to admit him temporarily, on recommendation of the Secretary of State, as § 212(d)(3)(A) permits."

When Stanford University and other institutions invited Mandel to participate in academic conferences and discussions, respondent requested a temporary nonimmigrant visa to enter the United States. However, he was found ineligible for admission under § 212(a)(28) of the Immigration and Nationality Act of 1952, barring those who "advocate the economic, international, and governmental doctrines of world communism." The Attorney General declined to waive this ground of inadmissibility.

A three-judge district court "held that, although Mandel had no personal right to enter the United States, citizens of this country have a First Amendment right to have him enter and to hear him explain and seek to defend his views."

The Supreme Court granted certiorari to review the case and reversed.

B. Counsel of Record/ACLU Attorney

ACLU Side (Respondent/Appellee): Leonard B. Boudin argued the cause for appellee.

Opposing Side (Petitioner/Appellant): Deputy Solicitor General Daniel M. Friedman argued the cause for appellant.

III. AMICI CURIAE

ACLU Side (Respondent/Appellee)

Brief of amici curiae filed on behalf of the ACLU by David Carliner and Melvin L. Wulf.

Opposing Side (Petitioner/Appellant)

No briefs of amici curiae were filed in support of appellant.

IV. THE SUPREME COURT'S DECISION

"Appellees seek to soften the impact of this analysis by arguing, as has been noted, that the First Amendment claim should prevail, at least where no justification is advanced for denial of a waiver. The Government would have us reach this question, urging a broad decision that Congress has delegated the waiver decision to the Executive in its sole and unfettered discretion, and any reason or no reason may be given. This record, however, does not require that we do so, for the Attorney General did inform Mandel's counsel of the reason for refusing him a waiver. And that reason was facially legitimate and bona fide.

The Government has chosen not to rely on the letter to counsel either in the District Court or here. The fact remains, however, that the official empowered to make the decision stated that he denied a waiver because he concluded that previous abuses by Mandel made it inappropriate to grant a waiver again. With this, we think the Attorney General validly exercised the plenary power that Congress delegated to the Executive by §§ 212(a)(28) and (d)(3).

In summary, plenary congressional power to make policies and rules for exclusion of aliens has long been firmly established. In the case of an alien excludable under § 212(a)(28), Congress has delegated conditional exercise of this power to the Executive. We hold that when the Executive exercises this power negatively on the basis of a facially legitimate and bona fide reason, the courts will neither look behind the exercise of that discretion, nor test it by balancing its justification against the First Amendment interests of those who seek personal communication with the applicant. What First Amendment or other grounds may be available for attacking exercise of discretion for which no justification whatsoever is advanced is a question we neither address nor decide in this case."

The Supreme Court reversed the District Court.

V. JUSTICE VOTE

3 Pro ACLU Side vs. 6 Con Opposing Side

ACLU Side (Respondent/Appellee)

1. Marshall, T. – Wrote dissenting opinion
2. Brennan, W. – Joined Marshall's dissent
3. Douglas, W. – Wrote dissenting opinion

Opposing Side (Petitioner/Appellant)

1. Blackmun, H. – Wrote majority opinion
2. Powell, L. – Joined majority opinion
3. Stewart, P. – Joined majority opinion
4. White, B. – Joined majority opinion
5. Rehnquist, W. – Joined majority opinion
6. Burger, W. – Joined majority opinion

VI. A WIN OR LOSS FOR THE ACLU?

The ACLU filed as amicus curiae urging affirmance,; the Supreme Court reversed the District Court's judgment in a 6-3 vote giving the ACLU an apparent loss.

285. Moore v. Illinois

(Decided June 29, 1972; 408 U.S. 786)

I. ISSUE

A. Issues Discussed

Criminal procedure, Eighth Amendment, Fourteenth Amendment, evidence, death penalty

B. Legal Question Presented

Is the prosecution required to disclose all evidence obtained, was admission of the shotgun a violation of due process, and can the death penalty be imposed here?

C. Supreme Court's Answer

The prosecution was not required to disclose all evidence and admission of the shotgun did not violate due process, however, the death penalty cannot be imposed here.

II. CASE SUMMARY

A. Background

Petitioner Moore was convicted of murder and sentenced to death for the shotgun killing of a bartender in Lansing, Illinois. He claimed that he was denied a fair trial and due process because the State failed to disclose several items of evidence helpful to the defense, it failed to correct false testimony, and it succeeded in introducing into evidence a shotgun that was not used as the murder weapon. Moore also attacked the imposition of the death penalty for noncompliance with the standards of *Witherspoon v. Illinois*, a 1968 U.S. Supreme Court case that ruled against providing prosecution unlimited challenges to jurors who might have objections to the death penalty.

The Supreme Court of Illinois rejected petitioner's claims and affirmed his conviction.

The Supreme Court granted certiorari to review the case and reversed, in part.

B. Counsel of Record/ACLU Attorney

ACLU Side (Petitioner/Appellant): James J. Doherty argued the cause for appellant.

Opposing Side (Respondent/Appellee): Thomas J. Immel, Assistant Attorney General of Illinois, argued the cause for appellee.

III. AMICI CURIAE

ACLU Side (Petitioner/Appellant)

Brief of amici curiae filed on behalf of the ACLU, Illinois Division, et al., by Elmer Gertz and Willard J. Lassers.

Brief of amici curiae filed on behalf of the NAACP Legal Defense and Educational Fund, Inc., et al., by Jack Greenberg, James M. Nabrit III, Jack Himmelstein, and Anthony G. Amsterdam.

Opposing Side (Respondent/Appellee)

No briefs of amici curiae were filed in support of appellee.

IV. THE SUPREME COURT'S DECISION

"We know of no constitutional requirement that the prosecution make a complete and detailed accounting to the defense of all police investigatory work on a case.

[W]e are unable to conclude that the shotgun's introduction deprived Moore of the due process of law guaranteed him by the Fourteenth Amendment. The 16-gauge shotgun, found in the car, was in the constructive possession of both Moore and Barbee when they were arrested after the shooting incident on October

31. There is substantial other evidence in the record that a shotgun was used to kill Zitek, and that he suffered the wounds one would expect from a shotgun fired at close range. The testimony as to the murder itself, with all the details as to the shotgun wounds, is such that we cannot say that the presentation of the shotgun was so irrelevant or so inflammatory that Moore was denied a fair trial. The case is not federally reversible on this ground.

Inasmuch as the Court today has ruled that the imposition of the death penalty under statutes such as those of Illinois is violative of the Eighth and Fourteenth Amendments, it is unnecessary for us to consider the claim of noncompliance with the *Witherspoon* standards. . . . The sentence of death, however, may not now be imposed.

The judgment, insofar as it imposes the death sentence, is reversed, and the case is remanded for further proceedings."

V. JUSTICE VOTE

5 Pro ACLU Side vs. 4 Con Opposing Side

ACLU Side (Petitioner/Appellant)

1. Blackmun, H. – Wrote majority opinion
2. Burger, W. – Joined majority opinion
3. Brennan, W. – Joined majority opinion
4. White, B. – Joined majority opinion
5. Rehnquist, W. – Joined majority opinion

Opposing Side (Respondent/Appellee)

1. Marshall, T. – Wrote dissenting opinion
2. Douglas, W. – Joined dissenting opinion
3. Stewart, P. – Joined dissenting opinion
4. Powell, L. – Joined dissenting opinion

VI. A WIN OR LOSS FOR THE ACLU?

The ACLU filed as amicus curiae urging reversal; the U.S. Supreme Court reversed the ruling of the Supreme Court of Illinois in a 5-4 vote, giving the ACLU an apparent win.

286. California v. Krivda

(Decided October 24, 1972; 409 U.S. 33)

I. ISSUE

A. Issues Discussed

Fourth Amendment, Fourteenth Amendment, search and seizure, search warrants

B. Legal Question Presented

"[W]hether the California Supreme Court based its holding on the Fourth and Fourteenth Amendments to the Constitution of the United States, or upon the equivalent provision of the California Constitution, or both."

C. Supreme Court's Answer

Unable to determine whether the California Supreme Court based its holding on the U.S. Constitution or California Constitution, the Court vacated the judgment and remanded the case, not addressing the Fourth and Fourteenth Amendment issues.

II. CASE SUMMARY

A. Background

"On July 1, 1968, Officer Gates received a telephone call from an anonymous informant who told him that 'Roger,' 'Judy' and 'Frankie,' residing at 1901 Nolden, Los Angeles, were engaged in sex and narcotic activities and were injecting Judy's two children with methedrine. Thereafter Officers Gates and Marsden located the premises, a single family dwelling, observed two young female children in front, and ran a utility check which showed that Judy Krivda paid the utilities there. Investigation also showed that Edward Krivda, whose wife was named Judy, had previously been arrested for narcotic activity. About 11 a.m. on July 19, 1968, the officers returned to the address and saw several trash barrels in front on the parkway adjacent to the sidewalk; they also observed the refuse collectors approaching and stopped them about half a block west, identified themselves and requested them to empty the well of their trash truck and pick up the trash in the can in front of 1901 Nolden.

The officers watched the men empty the well of their truck, drive to the front of the premises and empty the trash barrels; on block north the officers examined the contents of the well and found five paper sacks containing miscellaneous marijuana debris and marijuana seeds. One sack also contained four to six partially burned marijuana cigarettes, an envelope bearing the words 'Edward Krivda, 1901 Nolden,' a white, lined piece of paper on which was a handwritten letter with the name 'Frankie' mentioned in it dated Saturday, 13th, signed by 'Al,' and a three by five card dated Wednesday, 6-26, bearing the names 'Roger' and 'Judy.' The officers took a position of vantage and watched the premises; they observed defendant Roger Minor come out of the house at that address, pick up the trash barrels and carry them to the front porch of the house. They then approached the premises, effected entry, discovered defendants in the residence and recovered additional marijuana and paraphernalia.

On September 18, 1968, defendants were charged by information with possession of marijuana (Health & Saf.Code, § 11530)." After a continuance, the superior court reviewed defendants' motion to suppress evidence and denied the motion. Defendants then asked the court to review their decision and, on second consideration, the court granted the motion. The court then dismissed the action and the People appealed the dismissal.

The Supreme Court of California determined the court did not have jurisdiction to review the motion to suppress a second time because the court's order had become final. However, the Supreme Court of California also determined that "the People's appeal from the order of dismissal should be denied, since the evidence which was sought to be suppressed was obtained by means of an unlawful search and seizure and constitutes the only evidence sufficient to sustain a conviction against either defendant."[1]

The U.S. Supreme Court granted certiorari to review the case, vacated the decision, and remanded the case.

1 People v. Krivda, 486 P.2d 1262 (Cal. 1971).

B. Counsel of Record/ACLU Attorney

ACLU Side (Respondent/Appellee): Roger S. Hanson, by appointment of the Court, argued the cause for appellee.

Opposing Side (Petitioner/Appellant): Russell Iungerich, Deputy Attorney General of California, argued the cause for appellant.

III. AMICI CURIAE

ACLU Side (Respondent/Appellee)

Brief of amici curiae filed on behalf of the ACLU, et al., by Melvin L. Wulf, Sanford J. Rosen, Joel M. Gora, A. L. Wirin, Fred Okrand, and Lawrence R. Sperber.

Brief of amici curiae filed on behalf of the California Public Defenders Association by Sheldon Portman and Rose Elizabeth Bird.

Brief of amici curiae filed on behalf of the National Legal Aid and Defender Association by Theodore A. Gottfried and Marshall J. Hartman.

Opposing Side (Petitioner/Appellant)

Brief of amici curiae filed on behalf of the State of Illinois by William J. Scott, Attorney General, and James B. Zagel, Assistant Attorney General.

Brief of amici curiae filed on behalf of Americans for Effective Law Enforcement, Inc., et al., by Frank G. Carrington, Jr. Alan S. Ganz, Glen Murphy, and Wayne W. Schimidt.

IV. THE SUPREME COURT'S DECISION

"After briefing and argument . . . we are unable to determine whether the California Supreme Court based its holding upon the Fourth and Fourteenth Amendments to the Constitution of the United States, or upon the equivalent provision of the California Constitution, or both. In reaching its result in this case, the California court cited pertinent excerpts from its earlier decision in People v. Edwards (1969), which relied specifically upon both the state and federal provisions. Thus, as in Mental Hygiene Dept. v. Kirchner (1965), '[w]hile we might speculate from the choice of words used in the opinion, and the authorities cited by the court, which provision was the basis for the judgment of the state court, we are unable to say with any degree of certainty that the judgment of the California Supreme Court was not based on an adequate and independent nonfederal ground.' We therefore vacate the judgment of the Supreme Court of California and remand the cause to that court for such further proceedings as may be appropriate. We intimate no view on the merits of the Fourth and Fourteenth Amendment issue presented."

V. JUSTICE VOTE

0 Pro ACLU Side vs. 9 Con Opposing Side

Opposing Side (Petitioner/Appellant)

1. Burger, W. – Per curiam decision
2. Douglas, W. – Per curiam decision
3. Brennan, W. – Per curiam decision
4. Stewart, P. – Per curiam decision
5. White, B. – Per curiam decision
6. Marshall, T. – Per curiam decision
7. Blackmun, H. – Per curiam decision
8. Powell, L. – Per curiam decision
9. Rehnquist, W. – Per curiam decision

VI. A WIN OR LOSS FOR THE ACLU?

The ACLU filed as amicus curiae urging affirmance; the U.S. Supreme Court vacated and remanded the ruling of the California Supreme Court in a per curiam decision, giving the ACLU an apparent loss.

287. Neil v. Biggers

(Decided December 6, 1972; 409 U.S. 188)

I. ISSUE

A. Issues Discussed

Criminal procedure, Fifth Amendment, show-ups

B. Legal Question Presented

"[W]hether an affirmance by an equally divided Court is an actual adjudication barring subsequent consideration on habeas corpus, and, if not whether the identification procedure violated due process."

C. Supreme Court's Answer

The affirmance by an equally divided Court did not bar subsequent consideration on habeas corpus. The identification procedure did not violate due process.

II. CASE SUMMARY

A. Background

Respondent Biggers was convicted of rape and sentenced to 20 years of incarceration. The ruling was based on evidence that consisted in part of testimony concerning the victim's visual and voice identification of respondent at a police station "show-up." A "show-up" is a procedure in which police march a suspect in front of the victim and ask for identification, without the safeguard of requiring the victim to choose the defendant from among a group of people in a standard lineup.

Officers showed Biggers to the rape victim at a police station approximately seven months after the crime occurred. She had an opportunity to look him over and hear him utter the words "shut up or I'll kill you." Based on his appearance and voice, she testified at trial that she had "no doubt" that the respondent was her assailant. The police asserted that they used the "show-up" technique because they had difficulty finding for a lineup other individuals generally fitting respondent's description as given by the victim.

"The Tennessee Supreme Court affirmed [the conviction]. On certiorari, the judgment of the Tennessee Supreme Court was affirmed by an equally divided Court. Respondent then brought a federal habeas corpus action raising several claims. . . .

The District Court held that the claims were not barred and, after a hearing, held in an unreported opinion that the station-house identification procedure was so suggestive as to violate due process. The Court of Appeals affirmed. [The Supreme Court] granted certiorari to decide whether an affirmance by an equally divided Court is an actual adjudication barring subsequent consideration on habeas corpus, and, if not whether the identification procedure violated due process."

B. Counsel of Record / ACLU Attorney

ACLU Side (Respondent / Appellee): Michael Meltsner argued the cause for appellee.

Opposing Side (Petitioner / Appellant): Bart C. Durham III, Assistant Attorney General of Tennessee, argued the cause for appellant.

III. AMICI CURIAE

ACLU Side (Respondent / Appellee)

Brief of amici curiae filed on behalf of the ACLU by Shirley Fingerhood, Richard G. Green, Burt Neuborne, Melvin L. Wulf, and Lawrence G. Sager.

Opposing Side (Petitioner / Appellant)

Brief of amici curiae filed on behalf of the Attorney General of New York by Louis J. Lefkowitz, Samuel A. Hirshowitz, and Maria L. Marcus.

IV. THE SUPREME COURT'S DECISION

Section "2244(b) shields against senseless repetition of claims by state prisoners without endangering the principle that each is entitled, other limitations aside, to a redetermination of his federal claims by a federal court on habeas corpus. . . . This subsection embodies a recognition that if this Court has 'actually adjudicated' a claim on direct appeal or certiorari, a state prisoner has had the federal redetermination to which he is entitled. A subsequent application for habeas corpus raising the same claims would serve no valid purpose and would add unnecessarily to an already overburdened system of criminal justice.

[T]he factors to be considered in evaluating the likelihood of misidentification include the opportunity of the witness to view the criminal at the time of the crime, the witness' degree of attention, the accuracy of the witness' prior description of the criminal, the level of certainty demonstrated by the witness at the confrontation, and the length of time between the crime and the confrontation. Applying these factors, we disagree with the District Court's conclusion. . . .

We find that the District Court's conclusions on the critical facts are unsupported by the record and clearly erroneous. The victim spent a considerable period of time with her assailant, up to half an hour. She was with him under adequate artificial light in her house and under a full moon outdoors, and at least twice, once in the house and later in the woods, faced him directly and intimately. She was no casual observer, but rather the victim of one of the most personally humiliating of all crimes. Her description to the police, which included the assailant's approximate age, height, weight, complexion, skin texture, build, and voice, might not have satisfied *Proust* but was more than ordinarily thorough. She had 'no doubt' that respondent was the person who raped her. . . .

There was, to be sure, a lapse of seven months between the rape and the confrontation. This would be a seriously negative factor in most cases. Here, however, the testimony is undisputed that the victim made no previous identification at any of the showups, lineups, or photographic showings. Her record for reliability was thus a good one, as she had previously resisted whatever suggestiveness inheres in a showup. Weighing all the factors, we find no substantial likelihood of misidentification. The evidence was properly allowed to go to the jury."

The Supreme Court affirmed in part, reversed in part, and remanded the case.

V. JUSTICE VOTE

3 Pro ACLU Side vs. 5 Con Opposing Side

ACLU Side (Respondent / Appellee)

1. Brennan, W. – Wrote dissenting opinion
2. Douglas, W. – Joined dissenting opinion
3. Stewart, P. – Joined dissenting opinion

Opposing Side (Petitioner / Appellant)

1. Powell, L. – Wrote majority opinion
2. Burger, W. – Joined majority opinion
3. White, B. – Joined majority opinion
4. Blackmun, H. – Joined majority opinion
5. Rehnquist, W. – Joined majority opinion

Marshall, T – Took no part in the decision

VI. A WIN OR LOSS FOR THE ACLU?

The ACLU filed as amicus curiae urging affirmance; the Supreme Court affirmed in part, reversed in part, and remanded the ruling of the Court of Appeals in a 5-3 vote, giving the ACLU an apparent loss.

288. District of Columbia v. Carter

(Decided January 10, 1973; 409 U.S. 418)

I. ISSUE

A. Issues Discussed

Civil rights, federal

B. Legal Question Presented

Whether the District of Columbia can be held liable under 42 U.S.C. s 1983 as a "'State or Territory.'"

C. Supreme Court's Answer

"[W]e hold that the District of Columbia is not a 'State or Territory' within the meaning of s 1983."

II. CASE SUMMARY

A. Background

"On February 12, 1969, respondent filed this civil action in the United States District Court for the District of Columbia alleging that in 1968 Police Officer John R. Carlson of the Metropolitan Police Department of the District of Columbia arrested him without probable cause and, while he was being held by two other officers, beat him with brass knuckles. The complaint alleged further that Carlson's precinct captain, the chief of police, and the District of Columbia each had negligently failed to train, instruct, supervise, and control Carlson with regard to the circumstances in which an arrest may be made and the extent to which various degrees of force may be used to effect an arrest. Respondent sought damages against each defendant upon several theories, including a common-law theory of tort liability and an action for deprivation of civil rights pursuant to 42 U.S.C. s 1983 . . . .

The District Court dismissed the complaint against all defendants without opinion. On appeal, the United States Court of Appeals for the District of Columbia Circuit reversed, holding that the allegations of the complaint were sufficient to state causes of action under both the common-law and federal statutory theories of liability. [The Supreme Court] granted certiorari."

B. Counsel of Record

ACLU Side (Respondent/Appellee): Warren K. Kaplan argued the cause for appellee. With him on the brief were Melvin L. Wulf of the American Civil Liberties Union, Ralph J. Temple and Robert W. Boras of the American Civil Liberties Union Fund, and William D. Iverson.

Opposing Side (Petitioner/Appellant): Richard W. Barton argued the cause for appellant. With him on the brief were C. Francis Murphy and David P. Sutton.

III. AMICI CURIAE

Opposing Side (Petitioner/Appellant)

No briefs of amici curiae were filed in support of appellee.

ACLU Side (Respondent/Appellee)

No briefs of amici curiae were filed in support of appellant.

IV. THE SUPREME COURT'S DECISION

"Whether the District of Columbia constitutes a 'State or Territory' within the meaning of any particular statutory or constitutional provision depends upon the character and aim of the specific provision involved. . . .

The Court of Appeals' conclusion that the District of Columbia is a 'State or Territory' for the purpose of s 1983 was premised almost exclusively upon this Court's earlier determination that 'the District of Columbia is included within the phrase 'every State and Territory' as employed in 42 U.S.C. s 1982. . . .

The situation is wholly different, however, with respect to s 1983. Unlike s 1982, which derives from the Civil Rights Act of 1866, s 1983 has its roots in s 1 of the Ku Klux Klan Act of 1871. This distinction has great significance, for unlike the 1866 Act, which was passed as a means to enforce the Thirteenth Amendment, the primary purpose of the 1871 Act was 'to enforce the Provisions of the Fourteenth Amendment.' . . .

In contrast to the reach of the Thirteenth Amendment, the Fourteenth Amendment has only limited applicability; the commands of the Fourteenth Amendment are addressed only to the State or to those acting under color of its authority. . . . And since the District of Columbia is not a 'State' within the meaning of the Fourteenth Amendment, neither the District nor its officers are subject to its restrictions. . . .

With this unique status of the District of Columbia in mind, and in the absence of any indication in the language, purposes, or history of s 1983 of a legislative intent to include the District within the scope of its coverage, the conclusion is compelled that the Court of Appeals erred in holding that the District of Columbia constitutes a 'States or Territory' within the meaning of s 1983. Just as '(w)e are not at liberty to seek ingenious analytical instruments' to avoid giving a congressional enactment the broad scope its language and origins may require, so too are we not at liberty to recast this statute to expand its application beyond the limited reach Congress gave it. This is not to say, of course, that a claim, such as a possible claim against Officer Carlson, of alleged deprivation of constitutional rights is not litigable in the federal courts of the District. But insofar as the judgment of the Court of Appeals sustaining respondent's claims rested on s 1983, that judgment must be, and is, reversed.

Judgment reversed."

V. JUSTICE VOTE

0 Pro ACLU Side vs. 9 Con Opposing Side

Opposing Side (Petitioner/Appellant)

1. Brennan, W. – Wrote majority opinion
2. White, B. – Joined majority opinion
3. Marshall, T. – Joined majority opinion
4. Stewart, P. – Joined majority opinion
5. Burger, W. – Joined majority opinion
6. Blackmun, H. – Joined majority opinion
7. Powell, L. – Joined majority opinion
8. Rehnquist, W. – Joined majority opinion
9. Douglas, W. – Joined majority opinion

VI. A WIN OR LOSS FOR THE ACLU?

The ACLU served as counsel for appellee urging affirmance of the judgment of the Court of Appeals; the Supreme Court reversed, in a 9-0 vote, giving the ACLU an apparent loss.

289. Gomez v. Perez

(Decided January 17, 1973; 409 U.S. 535)

I. ISSUE

A. Issues Discussed

Fourteenth Amendment, equal protection

B. Legal Question Presented

"[W]hether the laws of Texas may constitutionally grant legitimate children a judicially enforceable right to support from their natural fathers and at the same time deny that right to illegitimate children."

C. Supreme Court's Answer

The laws of Texas may not constitutionally grant the right to support to legitimate children while denying this right to illegitimate children.

II. CASE SUMMARY

A. Background

Appellant filed suit in a Texas District Court to seek financial support from appellee, the biological father of appellant's minor child. "After a hearing, the state trial judge found that appellee is 'the biological father' of the child, and that the child 'needs the support and maintenance of her father,' but concluded that because the child was illegitimate 'there is no legal obligation to support the child and the Plaintiff take nothing.' The Court of Civil Appeals affirmed this ruling over the objection that this illegitimate child was being denied equal protection of law. The Texas Supreme Court refused application for a writ of error, finding no 'reversible error.'"

The Supreme Court granted certiorari to review the case and reversed.

B. Counsel of Record/ACLU Attorney

ACLU Side (Petitioner/Appellant): Stanley Dalton Wright argued the cause for appellant

Opposing Side (Respondent/Appellee): Joseph Jaworski argued the cause for appellee.

III. AMICI CURIAE

ACLU Side (Petitioner/Appellant)

Brief of amici curiae filed on behalf of the ACLU by Norman Dorsen, Melvin L. Wulf, Sanford Jay Rosen, and Eric M. Lieberman.

Opposing Side (Respondent/Appellee)

Briefs of amici curiae filed on behalf of the State of Texas by Attorney General Crawford C. Martin, First Assistant Attorney General Nola White, Executive Assistant Attorney General Alfred Walker, Assistant Attorney General J. C. Davis, and Assistant Attorney General Pat Bailey.

IV. THE SUPREME COURT'S DECISION

"In Texas, both at common law and under the statutes of the State, the natural father has a continuing and primary duty to support his legitimate children. That duty extends even beyond dissolution of the marriage, and is enforceable on the child's behalf in civil proceedings and, further, is the subject of criminal sanctions. The duty to support exists despite the fact that the father may not have custody of the child. The Court of Civil Appeals has held in this case that nowhere in this elaborate statutory scheme does the State recognize any enforceable duty on the part of the biological father to support his illegitimate children and that, absent a statutory duty to support, the controlling law is the Texas common-law rule that illegitimate children, unlike legitimate children, have no legal right to support from their fathers. It is also true that fathers may set up illegitimacy as a defense to prosecutions for criminal nonsupport of their children. . . .

We have held that under the Equal Protection Clause of the Fourteenth Amendment a State may not create a right of action in favor of children for the wrongful death of a parent and exclude illegitimate children from the benefit of such a right. Similarly, we have held that illegitimate children may not be excluded from sharing equally with other children in the recovery of workmen's compensation benefits for the death of their parent Under these decisions, a State may not invidiously discriminate against illegitimate children by denying them substantial benefits accorded children generally. We therefore hold that once a State posits a judicially enforceable right on behalf of children to needed support from their natural fathers there is no constitutionally sufficient justification for denying such an essential right to a child simply because its natural father has not married its mother. For a State to do so is 'illogical and unjust.' We recognize the lurking problems with respect to proof of paternity. Those problems are not to be lightly brushed aside, but neither can they be made into an impenetrable barrier that works to shield otherwise invidious discrimination.

The judgment is reversed and the case remanded for further proceedings not inconsistent with this opinion."

V. JUSTICE VOTE

7 Pro ACLU Side vs. 2 Con Opposing Side

ACLU Side (Petitioner/Appellant)

1. Brennan, W. – Per curiam decision
2. Marshall, T. – Per curiam decision
3. White, B. – Per curiam decision
4. Blackmun, H. – Per curiam decision
5. Powell, L. – Per curiam decision
6. Douglas, W. – Per curiam decision
7. Burger, W. – Per curiam decision

Opposing Side (Respondent/Appellee)

1. Stewart, P. – Wrote dissenting opinion
2. Rehnquist, W. – Joined dissenting opinion

VI. A WIN OR LOSS FOR THE ACLU?

The ACLU filed as amicus curiae urging reversal; the Supreme Court reversed the ruling of the Court of Civil Appeals in a 7-2 vote, giving the ACLU an apparent win.

290. Environmental Protection Agency v. Mink

(Decided January 22, 1973; 410 U.S. 73)

I. ISSUE

A. Issues Discussed

Freedom of Information Act of 1966, governmental authority, federalism

B. Legal Question Presented

Whether the District Court may make a compelled in camera inspection of secret and top secret documents exempt from disclosure under the Freedom of Information Act for the purpose of determining the separability of "non-secret components."

C. Supreme Court's Answer

The District Court may not make a compelled in camera inspection of the documents in this circumstance.

II. CASE SUMMARY

A. Background

Respondents, 33 members of Congress, filed suit under the Freedom of Information Act of 1966 to obtain the disclosure of documents prepared for President Nixon regarding an underground nuclear test.

Petitioners contended "that the materials sought were specifically exempted from disclosure under subsections (b)(1) and (b)(5) of the Act." Out of ten documents, one was already made public, but at least six of the nine remaining "were said to involve highly sensitive matter vital to the national defense and foreign policy and were described as having been classified Top Secret or Secret pursuant to Executive Order 10501."

The District Court granted summary judgment in favor of petitioner. "The Court of Appeals reversed, concluding that subsection (b)(1) of the Act permits the withholding of only the secret portions of the documents" and that while the documents fell within subsection (b)(5), the exemption only applied to "'decisional processes,'" not "'factual information' unless the information is 'inextricably intertwined with policymaking processes.' The court then ordered the District Judge to examine the documents in camera . . . to determine if 'factual data' could be separated out and disclosed 'without impinging on the policymaking decisional processes intended to be protected by this exemption.'"

The Supreme Court granted certiorari to review the case and reversed the Court of Appeals.

B. Counsel of Record / ACLU Attorney

ACLU Side (Respondent / Appellee): Ramsey Clark argued the cause for appellee.

Opposing Side (Petitioner / Appellant): Assistant Attorney General Roger C. Cramton argued the cause for appellant.

III. AMICI CURIAE

ACLU Side (Respondent / Appellee)

Brief of amici curiae filed on behalf of the ACLU by Norman Dorsen, Melvin L. Wulf, and Sanford Jay Rosen.

Brief of amici curiae filed on behalf of the Consumers Union of United States, Inc., by Marvin M. Karpatkin and Michael N. Pollet.

Opposing Side (Petitioner / Appellant)

No briefs of amici curiae were filed in support of appellant.

IV. THE SUPREME COURT'S DECISION

"Subsection (b)(1) of the Act (hereafter sometimes Exemption) exempts from forced disclosure matters 'specifically required by Executive order to be kept secret in the interest of the national defense or foreign policy.' [T]he six documents for which Exemption 1 is now claimed were all duly classified Top Secret or Secret, pursuant to Executive Order 10501. . . . We do not believe that Exemption 1 permits compelled disclosure of documents, such as the six here that were classified pursuant to this Executive Order. Nor does the Exemption permit in camera inspection of such documents to sift out so-called 'nonsecret components.' . . .

Exemption 1 was intended to dispel uncertainty with respect to public access to material affecting 'national defense or foreign policy.' Rather than some vague standard, the test was to be simply whether the President has determined by Executive Order that particular documents are to be kept secret. The language of the Act itself is sufficiently clear in this respect, but the legislative history disposes of any possible argument that Congress intended the Freedom of Information Act to subject executive security classifications to judicial review at the insistence of anyone who might seek to question them. Thus, the House Report stated with respect to subsection (b)(1) that 'citizens both in and out of Government can agree to restrictions on categories of information which the President has determined must be kept secret to protect the national defense or to advance foreign policy . . . .'

Disclosure of the three documents conceded to be 'unclassified' is resisted solely on the basis of subsection (b)(5) of the Act (hereafter Exemption 5). That Exemption was also invoked, alternatively, to support withholding the six documents for which Exemption 1 was claimed. It is beyond question that the Irwin affidavit, standing alone, is sufficient to establish that all of the documents involved in this litigation are 'inter-agency or intra-agency' memoranda or 'letters' that were used in the decision making processes of the Executive Branch. By its terms, however, Exemption 5 creates an exemption for such documents only insofar as they 'would not be available by law to a party . . . in litigation with the agency.' This language clearly contemplates that the public is entitled to all such memoranda or letters that a private party could discover in litigation with the agency. Drawing such a line between what may be withheld and what must be disclosed is not without difficulties. . . . Still, the legislative history of Exemption 5 demonstrates that Congress intended to incorporate generally the recognized rule that 'confidential intra-agency advisory opinions . . . are privileged from inspection.' . . . Virtually all of the courts that have thus far applied Exemption 5 have recognized that it requires different treatment for materials reflecting deliberative or policy-making processes on the one hand, and purely factual, investigative matters on the other. . . .

The Freedom of Information Act may be invoked by any member of 'the public'—without a showing of need—to compel disclosure of confidential Government documents. The unmistakable implication of the decision below is that any member of the public invoking the Act may require that otherwise confidential documents be brought forward and placed before the District Court for in camera inspection—no matter how little, if any, purely factual material may actually be contained therein. . . . An agency should be given the opportunity, by means of detailed affidavits or oral testimony, to establish to the satisfaction of the District Court that the documents sought fall clearly beyond the range of material that would be available to a private party in litigation with the agency. The burden is, of course, on the agency resisting disclosure, 5 U.S.C. § 552(a)(3), and if it fails to meet its burden without in camera inspection, the District Court may order such inspection. . . . In short, in camera inspection of all documents is not a necessary or inevitable tool in every case. . . . In the present case, the petitioners proceeded on the theory that all of the nine documents were exempt from disclosure in their entirety under Exemption 5 by virtue of their use in the decision making process. On remand, petitioners are entitled to attempt to demonstrate the propriety of withholding any documents, or portions thereof, by means short of submitting them for in camera inspection.

The judgment is reversed and the case is remanded for further proceedings consistent with this opinion."

V. JUSTICE VOTE

3 Pro ACLU Side vs. 5 Con Opposing Side

ACLU Side (Respondent/Appellee)

1. Brennan, W. – Wrote opinion concurring in part and dissenting in part
2. Marshall, J. – Joined Brennan's opinion
3. Douglas, W. – Wrote dissenting opinion

Opposing Side (Petitioner/Appellant)

1. White B. – Wrote majority opinion
2. Burger, W. – Joined majority opinion
3. Stewart, P. – Wrote concurring opinion
4. Blackmun, H. – Joined majority opinion
5. Powell, L. – Joined majority opinion

Rehnquist, W – Took no part in the decision

VI. A WIN OR LOSS FOR THE ACLU?

The ACLU filed as amicus curiae urging affirmance; the Supreme Court reversed the ruling of the Court of Appeals for the District of Columbia Circuit in a 3-5 vote, giving the ACLU an apparent loss.

291. Roe v. Wade

(Decided January 22, 1973; 410 U.S. 113)

I. ISSUE

A. Issues Discussed

Privacy

B. Legal Question Presented

Whether the Texas criminal abortion statutes are unconstitutional.

C. Supreme Court's Answer

"We . . . conclude that the right of personal privacy includes the abortion decision, but that this right is not unqualified and must be considered against important state interests in regulation. . . .

Measured against these standards, Art. 1196 of the Texas Penal Code, in restricting legal abortions to those 'procured or attempted by medical advice for the purpose of saving the life of the mother,' sweeps too broadly. . . . The statute, therefore, cannot survive the constitutional attack made upon it here."

II. CASE SUMMARY

A. Background

"Jane Roe . . . sought a declaratory judgment that the Texas criminal abortion statutes were unconstitutional on their face, and an injunction . . . .

Roe alleged that she was unmarried and pregnant; that she wished to terminate her pregnancy by an abortion . . . and that she could not afford to travel to another jurisdiction in order to secure a legal abortion under safe conditions. She claimed that the Texas statutes were unconstitutionally vague and that they abridged her right of personal privacy, protected by the First, Fourth, Fifth, Ninth, and Fourteenth Amendments. . . .

James Hubert Hallford, a licensed physician, . . . was granted leave to intervene . . . .

John and Mary Doe, a married couple, filed a companion complaint to that of Roe. . . .

The two actions were consolidated and heard together by a duly convened three-judge district court. . . . The court held that Roe and members of her class, and Dr. Hallford, had standing to sue and presented justiciable controversies, but that the Does had failed to allege facts sufficient to state a present controversy and did not have standing. . . . On the merits, the District Court held that the 'fundamental right of single women and married persons to choose where to have children is protected by the Ninth Amendment, through the Fourteenth Amendment,' and that the Texas criminal abortion statutes were void on their face because they were both unconstitutionally vague and constituted an overbroad infringement of the plaintiffs' Ninth Amendment rights. The court then held that abstention was warranted with respect to the requests for an injunction. It therefore dismissed the Does' complaint, declared the abortion statutes void, and dismissed the application for injunctive relief."

The Supreme Court granted certiorari to review the case.

B. Counsel of Record

ACLU Side (Petitioner/Appellant): Sarah Weddington reargued the cause for appellants. With her on the briefs were Roy Lucas, Fred Bruner, Roy L. Merrill, Jr., and Norman Dorsen.[1]

Opposing Side (Respondent/Appellee): Robert C. Flowers, Assistant Attorney General of Texas, argued the cause for appellee on the reargument. Jay Floyd, Assistant Attorney General, argued the cause for appellee on the original argument. With them on the brief were Crawford C. Martin,

1 *The Right to Choose at 25: Looking Back and Ahead, ACLU,* https://www.aclu.org/other/right-choose-25-looking-back-and-ahead (last visited Jan. 26, 2020) ("In 1973 the Supreme Court decided the two cases that upheld a woman's right to abortion, Roe v. Wade and Doe v. Bolton. Thanks to the seeds that Kenyon had sown, the ACLU was involved in both cases. Norman Dorsen was among the lawyers representing the plaintiffs in Roe v. Wade, and the ACLU of Georgia organized a trio of women lawyers to represent the plaintiffs in Doe v. Bolton.").

Attorney General, Nola White, First Assistant Attorney General, Alfred Walker, Executive Assistant Attorney General, Henry Wade, and John B. Tolle.

III. AMICI CURIAE

ACLU Side (Petitioner/Appellant)

Brief of amici curiae filed on behalf of the American College of Obstetricians and Gynecologists et al. by Carol Ryan.

Brief of amici curiae filed on behalf of Planned Parenthood Federation of America, Inc., et al. by Harriet F. Pilpel, Nancy F. Wechsler, and Frederic S. Nathan.

Brief of amici curiae filed on behalf of the National Legal Program on Health Problems of the Poor et al. by Alan F. Charles.

Brief of amici curiae filed on behalf of State Communities Aid Association by Marttie L. Thompson.

Brief of amici curiae filed on behalf of the American Association of University Women et al. by Norma G. Zarky.

Brief of amici curiae filed on behalf of New Women Lawyers et al. by Nancy Stearns.

Brief of amici curiae filed on behalf of the California Committee to Legalize Abortion et al. by Joan K. Bradford.

Brief of amici curiae filed on behalf of the American Ethical Union et al. by Helen L. Buttenwieser.

Opposing Side (Respondent/Appellee)

Brief of amici curiae filed on behalf of the Attorneys General of Arizona, Connecticut, Kentucky, Nebraska and Utah by Gary K. Nelson, Attorney General of Arizona, Robert K. Killian, Attorney General of Connecticut, Ed W. Hancock, Attorney General of Kentucky, Clarence A. H. Meyer, Attorney General of Nebraska, and Vernon B. Romney, Attorney General of Utah.

Brief of amici curiae filed on behalf of the Association of Texas Diocesan Attorneys by Joseph P. Witherspoon, Jr.

Brief of amici curiae filed on behalf of Americans United for Life by Charles E. Rice.

Brief of amici curiae filed on behalf of Women for the Unborn et al. by Eugene J. McMahon.

Brief of amici curiae filed on behalf of the National Right to Life Committee by Alfred L. Scanlan, Martin J. Flynn, and Robert M. Byrn.

Brief of amici curiae filed on behalf of Certain Physicians, Professors and Fellows of the American College of Obstetrics and Gynecology by Dennis J. Horan, Jerome A. Frazel, Jr., Thomas M. Crisham, and Dolores V. Horan.

Brief of amici curiae filed on behalf of Robert L. Sassone by Robert E. Dunnce.

IV. THE SUPREME COURT'S DECISION

"We . . . conclude that the right of personal privacy includes the abortion decision, but that this right is not unqualified and must be considered against important state interests in regulation. . . .

Measured against these standards, Art. 1196 of the Texas Penal Code, in restricting legal abortions to those 'procured or attempted by medical advice for the purpose of saving the life of the mother,' sweeps too broadly. The statute makes no distinction between abortions performed early in pregnancy and those performed later, and it limits to a single reason, 'saving' the mother's life, the legal justification . . . . The statute, therefore, cannot survive the constitutional attack made upon it here. . . .

To summarize . . . :

1. A state criminal abortion statute of the current Texas type, that excepts from criminality only a life-saving procedure on behalf of the mother, without regard to pregnancy stage and without recognition of the other interests involved, is violative of the Due Process Clause of the Fourteenth Amendment.

(a) For the stage prior to approximately the end of the first trimester, the abortion decision and its effectuation must be left to the medical judgment of the pregnant woman's attending physician.

(b) For the stage subsequent to approximately the end of the first trimester, the State, in promoting its interest in the health of the mother, may, if it chooses, regulate the abortion procedure in ways that are reasonably related to maternal health.

(c) For the stage subsequent to viability, the State in promoting its interest in the potentiality of human life may, if it chooses, regulate, and even proscribe, abortion except where it is necessary, in appropriate medical judgment, for the preservation of the life or health of the mother.

2. The State may define the term 'physician,' as it has been employed in the preceding paragraphs of this Part XI of this opinion, to mean only a physician currently licensed by the State, and may proscribe any abortion by a person who is not a physician as so defined.

In Doe v. Bolton, 410 U.S. 179, procedural requirements contained in one of the modern abortion statutes are considered. That opinion and this one, of course, are to be read together. . . .

Our conclusion that Art. 1196 is unconstitutional means, of course, that the Texas abortion statutes, as a unit, must fall. The exception of Art. 1196 cannot be struck down separately . . . .

We find it unnecessary to decide whether the District Court erred in withholding injunctive relief . . . .

The judgment of the District Court as to intervenor Hallford is reversed, and Dr. Hallford's complaint in intervention is dismissed. In all other respects, the judgment of the District Court is affirmed. Costs are allowed to the appellee. . . .

Affirmed in part and reversed in part."

V. JUSTICE VOTE

7 Pro ACLU Side vs. 2 Con Opposing Side

ACLU Side (Petitioner/Appellant)

1. Blackmun, H. – Wrote majority opinion
2. Brennan, W. – Joined majority opinion
3. Douglas, W. – Wrote concurring opinion
4. Marshall, T. – Joined majority opinion
5. Stewart, P. – Wrote concurring opinion
6. Burger, W. – Wrote concurring opinion
7. Powell, L. – Joined majority opinion

Opposing Side (Respondent/Appellee):

1. White, B. – Wrote dissenting opinion

2. Rehnquist, W. – Wrote dissenting opinion, joined White's dissent

VI. A WIN OR LOSS FOR THE ACLU?

The ACLU served as counsel for appelant urging affirmance in part and reversal in part of the judgment of the District Court; the Supreme Court affirmed in part and reversed in part in a 7-2 vote, giving the ACLU an apparent win.

292. Doe v. Bolton

(Decided January 22, 1973; 410 U.S. 179)

I. ISSUE

A. Issues Discussed

Abortion, state's rights

B. Legal Question Presented

Whether all or portions of a Georgia statute, which makes abortion a crime except in certain circumstances, is constitutional.

C. Supreme Court's Answer

Certain portions of the statute are unconstitutional and, therefore, invalid.

II. CASE SUMMARY

A. Background

Georgia law "makes abortion a crime" except in certain limited circumstances when a liscensed physician deems an abortion necessary under statutory provisions allowing abortion only when due to severe health concerns for the mother or fetus, or if the pregnancy was the result of rape. In addition to these limitations, Georgia law provides for strict procedures that must be fulfilled to decriminalize the abortion procedure, such as requiring the procedure be performed only at hospitals with certain accreditation and requiring approval of the procedure by three members of the hospital staff.

Appellant Doe, an indigent 22-year-old married Georgia citizen with three children, was denied an abortion when she was eight weeks pregnant for failure to meet any of the exceptions that made abortion not a crime. She sought declaratory and injunctive relief, contending that the Georgia laws were unconstitutional. The complaint also included nurses. clergymen, social workers, and Georgia-licensed physicians who all claimed the Georgia statutes "chilled and deterred" the practice of their professions.

"The District Court, per curiam, held that all the plaintiffs had standing but that only Doe presented a justiciable controversy. On the merits, the court concluded that the limitation in the Georgia statute of the 'number of reasons for which an abortion may be sought,' improperly restricted Doe's rights of privacy articulated in *Griswold v. Connecticut*, and of 'personal liberty,' both of which it thought 'broad enough to include the decision to abort a pregnancy.' . . . Declaratory relief was granted accordingly. The court, however, held that

Georgia's interest in protection of health, and the existence of a potential of independent human existence' justified state regulation of 'the manner of performance as well as the quality of the final decision to abort,' and it refused to strike down the other provisions of the statutes. It denied the request for an injunction."

The Supreme Court granted certiorari to review the judgment, and modified and affirmed the judgment.

B. Counsel of Record/ACLU Attorney

ACLU Side (Petitioner/Appellant): Margie Pitts Hames argued the cause for appellant. With her on the briefs were Reber F. Boult, Jr., Charles Morgan, Jr., Elizabeth Roediger Rindskopf, and Tobaine Schwartz.

Opposing Side (Respondent/Appellee): Dorothy T. Beasley argued the cause for appellee. With her on the briefs were Attorney General of Georgia Arthur K. Bolton, Executive Assistant Attorney General Harold N. Hill, Jr., Assistant Attorney General Courtney Wilder Stanton, Joel Feldman, Henry L. Bowden, and Ralph H. Witt.

III. AMICI CURIAE

ACLU Side (Petitioner/Appellant)

Briefs of amici curiae were filed on behalf of the Planned Parenthood Federation of America, Inc., et al., the American Ethical Union, et al., the State Communities Aid Association, the National Legal Program on Health Problems of the Poor, et al., New Women Lawyers, et al., and the American College of Obstetrics and Gynecologists, et al.

Opposing Side (Respondent/Appellee)

Brief of amici curiae were filed on behalf of Certain Physicians, Professors, and Fellows of the American College of Obstetrics and Gynecology, Ferdinand Buckley, the National Right to Life Committee, and Robert L. Sassone.

IV. THE SUPREME COURT'S DECISION

"We conclude . . . that the physician-appellants, who are Georgia-licensed doctors consulted by pregnant women, also present a justiciable controversy and do have standing despite the fact that the record does not disclose that any one of them has been prosecuted, or threatened with prosecution, for violation of the State's abortion statutes. . . .

The appellants attack on several grounds those portions of the Georgia abortion statutes that remain after the District Court decision: undue restriction of a right to personal and marital privacy; vagueness; deprivation of substantive and procedural due process; improper restriction to Georgia residents; and denial of equal protection. . . .

Roe v. Wade, supra, sets forth our conclusion that a pregnant woman does not have an absolute constitutional right to an abortion on her demand. . . .

We hold that the JCAH-accreditation requirement does not withstand constitutional scrutiny in the present context. It is a requirement that simply is not 'based on differences that are reasonably related to the purposes of the Act in which it is found.' . . .

We hold that the hospital requirement of the Georgia law, because it fails to exclude the first trimester of pregnancy, is also invalid. . . .

We conclude that the interposition of the hospital abortion committee is unduly restrictive of the patient's rights and needs that, at this point, have already been medically delineated and substantiated by her personal physician. To ask more serves neither the hospital nor the State. . . .

In summary, we hold that the JCAH-accredited hospital provision and the requirements as to approval by the hospital abortion committee, as to confirmation by two independent physicians, and as to residence in Georgia are all violative of the Fourteenth Amendment. . . .

The judgment of the District Court is modified accordingly and, as so modified, is affirmed."

V. JUSTICE VOTE

7 Pro ACLU Side vs. 2 Con Opposing Side

ACLU Side (Petitioner/Appellant)

1. Blackmun, H. – Wrote majority opinion
2. Burger, W. – Wrote concurring opinion
3. Douglas, W. – Wrote concurring opinion
4. Brennan, W. – Joined majority opinion
5. Stewart, P. – Joined majority opinion
6. Marshall, T. – Joined majority opinion
7. Powell, L. – Joined majority opinion

Opposing Side (Respondent/Appellee)

1. White, B. – Wrote dissenting opinion
2. Rehnquist, W. – Wrote dissenting opinion, joined White's dissent

VI. A WIN OR LOSS FOR THE ACLU?

The ACLU, as counsel of record, urged affirmance of the judgment with broader protection; the Supreme Court modified and affirmed in a 7-2 vote, giving the ACLU an apparent win.

293. Tillman v. Wheaton-Haven Recreation Assn.

(Decided February 27, 1973; 410 U.S. 431)

I. ISSUE

A. Issues Discussed

Race

B. Legal Question Presented

Whether a swimming pool that bases membership on geography is subject to certain federal laws prohibiting racial discrimination.

C. Supreme Court's Answer

"When an organization links membership benefits to residency in a narrow geographical area, that decision infuses those benefits into the bundle of rights for which an individual pays when buying or leasing within the area. The mandate of 42 U.S.C. s 1982 then operates to guarantee a nonwhite resident, who purchases, leases, or holds this property, the same rights as are enjoyed by a white resident."

II. CASE SUMMARY

A. Background

"Wheaton-Haven Recreation Association, Inc., a non-profit Maryland corporation, was organized in 1958 for the purpose of operating a swimming pool. . . .

Membership is largely keyed to the geographical area within a three-quarter-mile radius of the pool. . . . A person residing outside the three-quarter-mile area may apply . . . . Majority approval of those present at a meeting of the board of directors or of the general membership is required before an applicant is admitted as a member. . . .

In the spring of 1968 petitioner, Harry C. Press, a Negro who had purchased from a nonmember a home within the geographical preference area, inquired about membership in Wheaton-Haven. At that time the Association had no Negro member. In November 1968 the general membership rejected a resolution that would have opened the way for Negro members. . . .

In July 1968 petitioners Murray and Rosalind N. Tillman, who were husband and wife and members in good standing, brought petitioner Grace Rosner, a Negro, to the pool as their guest. [T]he guest policy was changed by the board of directors, at a special meeting the following day, to limit guests to relatives of members. . . . Under this new policy Mrs. Rosner thereafter was refused admission . . . . In the fall of 1968 the membership, by resolution, reaffirmed the policy.

In October 1969 petitioners (Mr. and Mrs. Tillman, Dr. and Mrs. Press, and Mrs. Rosner) instituted this civil action against the Association and individuals who were its officers or directors, seeking damages and declaratory and injunctive relief . . . . The District Court . . . held that Wheaton-Haven was a private club and exempt from the nondiscrimination provisions of the statutes. . . . The Court of Appeals affirmed, one judge dissenting. It later denied rehearing en banc over two dissents. [The Supreme Court] granted certiorari . . . ."

B. Counsel of Record

ACLU Side (Petitioner/Appellant): Allison W. Brown, Jr., argued the cause for appellants. With him on the briefs were Melvin L. Wulf and Sanford Jay Rosen of the American Civil Liberties Union Foundation, and Raymond W. Russell and Samuel A. Chaitovitz.

Henry J. Noyes argued the cause and filed a brief for appellees Wheaton-Haven Recreation Assn., Inc., et al.

John H. Mudd argued the cause for respondent E. Richard McIntyre. With him on the brief was H. Thomas Howell.

III. AMICI CURIAE

ACLU Side (Petitioner/Appellant)

Brief of amici curiae filed on behalf of the United States by Solicitor General Griswold, Assistant Attorney General Norman, Deputy Solicitor General Wallace, William Bradford Reynolds, and John C. Hoyle.

Brief of amici curiae filed on behalf of Montgomery County,

Maryland by Alfred H. Carter.

Brief of amici curiae filed on behalf of the Maryland Commission on Human Relations by Philip J. Tierney and George D. Solter.

Opposing Side (Respondent/Appellee)

No briefs of amici curiae were filed in support of appellees.

IV. THE SUPREME COURT'S DECISION

"In Jones v. Alfred H. Mayer Co., 392 U.S. 409 (1968), this Court, after a detailed review of the legislative history of 42 U.S.C. s 1982, held that the statute reaches beyond state action and is not confined to officially sanctioned segregation. The Court subsequently applied s 1982 in Sullivan to private racial discrimination practiced by a nonstock corporation organized to operate a community park and playground facilities, including a swimming pool, for residents of a designated area. The Presses contend that their s 1982 claim is controlled by Sullivan. We agree. . . .

When an organization links membership benefits to residency in a narrow geographical area, that decision infuses those benefits into the bundle of rights for which an individual pays when buying or leasing within the area. The mandate of 42 U.S.C. s 1982 then operates to guarantee a nonwhite resident, who purchases, leases, or holds this property, the same rights as are enjoyed by a white resident. . . .

We hold . . . that Wheaton-Haven is not a private club and that it is not necessary in this case to consider the issue of any implied limitation on the sweep of s 1982 when its application to a truly private club, within the meaning of s 2000a(e), is under consideration. . . .

Mrs. Rosner and the Tillmans, relying on 42 U.S.C. ss 1981, 1982, and 2000a et seq., contend that Wheaton-Haven could not adopt a racially discriminatory policy toward guests. The District Court granted summary judgment for the respondents on these claims also, holding that Wheaton-Haven was a private club and exempt from all three statutes.

The operative language of both s 1981 and s 1982 is traceable to the Act of April 9, 1866, c. 31, s 1, 14 Stat. 27. In light of the historical interrelationship between s 1981 and s 1982, we see no reason to construe these sections differently when applied, on these facts, to the claim of Wheaton-Haven that it is a private club. Consequently, our discussion and rejection of Wheaton-Haven's claim that it is exempt from s 1982 disposes of the argument that Wheaton-Haven is exempt from s 1981. On remand the District Court will develop any necessary facts concerning the adoption of the guest policy and will evaluate the claims of the parties free of the misconception that Wheaton-Haven is exempt from ss 1981, 1982, and 2000a.

The judgment of the Court of Appeals is reversed, and the case is remanded for further proceedings."

V. JUSTICE VOTE

9 Pro ACLU Side vs. 0 Con Opposing Side

ACLU Side (Petitioner/Appellant)

1. Blackmun, H. – Wrote majority opinion
2. White, B. – Joined majority opinion
3. Marshall, T. – Joined majority opinion
4. Brennan, W. – Joined majority opinion
5. Stewart, P. – Joined majority opinion
6. Burger, W. – Joined majority opinion
7. Douglas, W. – Joined majority opinion
8. Powell, L. – Joined majority opinion
9. Rehnquist, W. – Joined majority opinion

VI. A WIN OR LOSS FOR THE ACLU?

The ACLU served as counsel for appellants urging reversal of the judgment of the Court of Appeals; the Supreme Court reversed, in a 9-0 vote, giving the ACLU an apparent win.

294. Braden v. 30th Judicial Circuit Court of Kentucky

(Decided February 28, 1973; 410 U.S. 484)

I. ISSUE

A. Issues Discussed

Criminal justice, prisons, habeas corpus

B. Legal Question Presented

"[W]hether, as petitioner was not physically present within the territorial limits of the District Court for the Western District of Kentucky, the provision of 28 U.S.C. § 2241(a) that '[w]rits of habeas corpus may be granted by the . . . district courts . . . within their respective jurisdictions' (emphasis supplied), precluded the District Court from entertaining petitioner's application."

C. Supreme Court's Answer

Although petitioner was not physically present in the jurisdiction, the District Court had the ability to entertain petitioner's application for the writ of habeas corpus.

II. CASE SUMMARY

A. Background

In 1967, Petitioner Braden was indicted on various charges by a grand jury in Kentucky. Before his trial on the indictment he escaped from the custody of Kentucky officials, and was later arrested in Alabama in 1968. He was convicted of various felonies in Alabama state courts, and was sentenced to Alabama state prison. He was serving his sentence in the Alabama prison at the time he filed this action attacking the validity of the Kentucky indictment.

Petitioner "applied to the District Court for the Western District of Kentucky for a writ of federal habeas corpus, alleging denial of his constitutional right to a speedy trial, and praying that an order issue directing respondent to afford him an immediate trial on a then three-year-old Kentucky indictment."

28 U.S.C. § 2241(a) states that "'[w]rits of habeas corpus may be granted by the . . . district courts . . . *within their respective jurisdictions*' (emphasis supplied)." The District Court considered whether this section precluded them from entertaining petition-

er's application, "as petitioner was not physically present within the territorial limits of the District Court for the Western District of Kentucky."

"The District Court held that the section did not bar its determination of the application. The court held further that petitioner had been denied a speedy trial and ordered respondent either to secure his presence in Kentucky for trial within 60 days or to dismiss the indictment. The Court of Appeals for the Sixth Circuit reversed on the ground that 'the habeas corpus jurisdiction conferred on the federal courts by 28 U.S.C. § 2241(a) is limited to petitions filed by persons physically present within the territorial limits of the District Court."

The Supreme Court granted certiorari to review the case and reversed the Court of Appeals.

B. Counsel of Record / ACLU Attorney

ACLU Side (Petitioner / Appellant): David R. Hood argued the cause for appellant.

Opposing Side (Respondent / Appellee): Assistant Attorney General of Kentucky John M. Famularo argued the cause for appellee, pro hac vice, by special leave of court.

III. AMICI CURIAE

ACLU Side (Petitioner / Appellant)

Brief of amici curiae filed on behalf of the ACLU by Melvin L. Wulf, Sanford J. Rosen, and Joel M. Gora.

Opposing Side (Respondent / Appellee)

No briefs of amici curiae were filed in support of appellee.

IV. THE SUPREME COURT'S DECISION

"[O]ur decision in *Peyton v. Rowe* discarded the prematurity doctrine, which had permitted a prisoner to attack on habeas corpus only his current confinement, and not confinement that would be imposed in the future, and opened the door to this action.

[F]ederal habeas corpus does not lie, absent 'special circumstances,' to adjudicate the merits of an affirmative defense to a state criminal charge prior to a judgment of conviction by a state court. Petitioner does not, however, seek at this time to litigate a federal defense to a criminal charge, but only to demand enforcement of the Commonwealth's affirmative constitutional obligation to bring him promptly to trial. He has made repeated demands for trial to the courts of Kentucky, offering those courts an opportunity to consider on the merits his constitutional claim of the present denial of a speedy trial. Under these circumstances it is clear that he has exhausted all available state court remedies for consideration of that constitutional claim, even though Kentucky has not yet brought him to trial.

The exhaustion doctrine is a judicially crafted instrument which reflects a careful balance between important interests of federalism and the need to preserve the writ of habeas corpus as a 'swift and imperative remedy in all cases of illegal restraint or confinement.' . . . As applied in our earlier decisions, the doctrine 'preserves the role of the state courts in the application and enforcement of federal law. Early federal intervention in state criminal proceedings would tend to remove federal questions from the state courts, isolate those courts from constitutional issues, and thereby remove their understanding of and hospitality to federally protected interests. Second, [the doctrine] preserves orderly administration of state judicial business, preventing the interruption of state adjudication by federal habeas proceedings. It is important that petitioners reach state appellate courts, which can develop and correct errors of state and federal law and most effectively supervise and impose uniformity on trial courts.'

The fundamental interests underlying the exhaustion doctrine have been fully satisfied in petitioner's situation. He has already presented his federal constitutional claim of a present denial of a speedy trial to the courts of Kentucky. The state courts rejected the claim, apparently on the ground that since he had once escaped from custody the Commonwealth should not be obligated to incur the risk of another escape by returning him for trial. Petitioner exhausted all available state court opportunities to establish his position that the prior escape did not obviate the Commonwealth's duty under *Smith v. Hooey*, supra. Moreover, petitioner made no effort to abort a state proceeding or to disrupt the orderly functioning of state judicial processes. He comes to federal court, not in an effort to forestall a state prosecution, but to enforce the Commonwealth's obligation to provide him with a state court forum. . . . A federal habeas corpus action at this time and under these circumstances does not jeopardize any legitimate interest of federalism. Respondent apparently shares that view since it specifically concedes that petitioner has exhausted all available state remedies. . . .

The writ of habeas corpus does not act upon the prisoner who seeks relief, but upon the person who holds him in what is alleged to be unlawful custody. [T]he language of § 2241(a) requires nothing more than that the court issuing the writ have jurisdiction over the custodian. So long as the custodian can be reached by service of process, the court can issue a writ 'within its jurisdiction' requiring that the prisoner be brought before the court for a hearing on his claim, or requiring that he be released outright from custody, even if the prisoner himself is confined outside the court's territorial jurisdiction. . . .

Since the petitioner's absence from the Western District of Kentucky did not deprive the court of jurisdiction, and since the respondent was properly served in that district, the court below erred in ordering the dismissal of the petition on jurisdictional grounds. The judgment of the Court of Appeals is reversed and the case is remanded for proceedings consistent with this opinion."

V. JUSTICE VOTE

6 Pro ACLU Side vs. 3 Con Opposing Side

ACLU Side (Petitioner / Appellant)

1. Brennan, W. – Wrote majority opinion
2. Douglas, W. – Joined majority opinion
3. Stewart, P. – Joined majority opinion
4. White, B. – Joined majority opinion
5. Marshall, T. – Joined majority opinion
6. Blackmun, H. – Wrote concurring opinion

Opposing Side (Respondent/Appellee)

1. Rehnquist, W. – Wrote dissenting opinion
2. Powell, L. – Joined dissenting opinion
3. Burger, W. – Joined dissenting opinion

VI. A WIN OR LOSS FOR THE ACLU?

The ACLU filed as amicus curiae urging reversal; the Supreme Court reversed the ruling of the Court of Appeals for the Sixth Circuit in a 6-3 vote, giving the ACLU an apparent win.

295. Papish v. Bd. of Curators of Univ. of Missouri

(Decided March 19, 1973; 410 U.S. 667)

I. ISSUE

A. Issues Discussed

1st Amendment, obscenity

B. Legal Question Presented

Whether a graduate student's First Amendment rights were violated when she was expelled over publishing obscene content in a school newspaper.

C. Supreme Court's Answer

"Since the First Amendment leaves no room for the operation of a dual standard in the academic community with respect to the content of speech, and because the state University's action here cannot be justified as a nondiscriminatory application of reasonable rules governing conduct, the judgments of the courts below must be reversed."

II. CASE SUMMARY

A. Background

"Petitioner, a graduate student in the University of Missouri School of Journalism, was expelled for distributing on campus a newspaper 'containing forms of indecent speech' in violation of a bylaw of the Board of Curators. The newspaper, the Free Press Underground, had been sold on this state university campus for more than four years pursuant to an authorization obtained from the University Business Office. The particular newspaper issue in question was found to be unacceptable for two reasons. First, on the front cover the publishers had reproduced a political cartoon . . . depicting policemen raping the Statue of Liberty and the Goddess of Justice. . . . Secondly, the issue contained an article entitled 'M——f—— Acquitted,' which discussed the trial and acquittal on an assault charge of a New York City youth who was a member of an organization known as 'Up Against the Wall, M——f——.'

Following a hearing, the Student Conduct Committee found that petitioner had violated Par. B of Art. V of the General Standards of Student Conduct which requires students 'to observe generally accepted standards of conduct' and specifically prohibits 'indecent conduct or speech.' Her expulsion . . . was made effective in the middle of the spring semester. . . .

After exhausting her administrative review alternatives within the University, petitioner brought an action for declaratory and injunctive relief pursuant to 42 U.S.C. s 1983 in the United States District Court for the Western District of Missouri. . . . The District Court denied relief, and the Court of Appeals affirmed, one judge dissenting. Rehearing en banc was denied by an equally divided vote of all the judges in the Eighth Circuit."

The Supreme Court reviewed the decision.

B. Counsel of Record

ACLU Side (Petitioner/Appellant): Brief for appellant filed by Melvin L. Wulf of the American Civil Liberties Union Foundation, Irvin Achtenberg, and David N. Ellenhorn.

Opposing Side (Respondent/Appellee): Brief for appellee filed by Jackson A. Wright, Marvin E. Wright, James S. Newberry, and Richard S. Paden.

III. AMICI CURIAE

ACLU Side (Petitioner/Appellant)

No briefs of amici curiae were filed in support of appellant.

Opposing Side (Respondent/Appellee)

No briefs of amici curiae were filed in support of appellee.

IV. THE SUPREME COURT'S DECISION

"The District Court's opinion rests, in part, on the conclusion that the banned issue of the newspaper was obscene. The Court of Appeals found it unnecessary to decide that question. Instead, assuming that the newspaper was not obscene and that its distribution in the community at large would be protected by the First Amendment, the court held that on a university campus 'freedom of expression' could properly be 'subordinated to other interests such as, for example, the conventions of decency in the use and display of language and pictures.' . . .

This case was decided several days before we handed down Healy v. James, 408 U.S. 169 (1972), in which, while recognizing a state university's undoubted prerogative to enforce reasonable rules governing student conduct, we reaffirmed that 'state colleges and universities are not enclaves immune from the sweep of the First Amendment.' We think Healy makes it clear that the mere dissemination of ideas—no matter how offensive to good taste—on a state university campus may not be shut off in the name alone of 'conventions of decency.' . . .

Since the First Amendment leaves no room for the operation of a dual standard in the academic community with respect to the content of speech, and because the state University's action here cannot be justified as a nondiscriminatory application of reasonable rules governing conduct, the judgments of the courts below must be reversed. Accordingly the petition for a writ of certiorari is granted, the case is remanded to the District Court, and that court is instructed to order the University to restore to petitioner any course credits she earned for the semester in question and, unless she is barred from reinstatement for valid academic reasons, to reinstate her as a student in the graduate program.

Reversed and remanded."

V. JUSTICE VOTE

6 Pro ACLU Side vs. 3 Con Opposing Side

ACLU Side (Petitioner/Appellant)

1. White, B. – Per curiam decision
2. Marshall, T. – Per curiam decision
3. Brennan, W. – Per curiam decision
4. Stewart, P. – Per curiam decision
5. Powell, L. – Per curiam decision
6. Douglas, W. – Per curiam decision

Opposing Side (Respondent/Appellee)

1. Burger, W. – Wrote dissenting opinion, joined Rehnquist's dissent
2. Blackmun, H. – Joined Rehnquist's dissent
3. Rehnquist, W. – Wrote dissenting opinion

VI. A WIN OR LOSS FOR THE ACLU?

The ACLU served as counsel for appellant urging reversal of the judgment of the Court of Appeals; the Supreme Court reversed, in a 6-3 per curiam decision, giving the ACLU an apparent win.

296. Salyer Land Co. v. Tulare Lake Basin Water Storage District

(Decided March 20, 1973; 410 U.S. 719)

I. ISSUE

A. Issues Discussed

Civil rights, voting rights, Fourteenth Amendment, equal protection

B. Legal Question Presented

Does the California statutory scheme establishing voting procedures within water storage districts violate the Equal Protection Clause of the Fourteenth Amendment?

C. Supreme Court's Answer

The statute does not violate the Equal Protection Clause.

II. CASE SUMMARY

A. Background

Appellee Tulare Lake Basin Water Storage District "consists of 193,000 acres of intensively cultivated, highly fertile farm land located in the Tulare Lake Basin. Its population consists of 77 persons, including 18 children, most of whom are employees of one or another of the four corporations that farm 85% of the land in the district.

Such districts are authorized to plan projects and execute approved projects 'for the acquisition, appropriation, diversion, storage, conservation, and distribution of water . . . .' . . .

Governance of the districts is undertaken by a board of directors. Each director is elected from one of the divisions within the district . . . .

It is the voter qualification for such elections that appellants claim invidiously discriminates against them and persons similarly situated. Appellants are landowners, a landowner-lessee, and residents within the area included in the appellee's water storage district. They brought this action under 42 U.S.C. § 1983, seeking declaratory and injunctive relief in an effort to prevent appellee from giving effect to certain provisions of the California Water Code. They allege that §§ 41000 and 41001 unconstitutionally deny to them the equal protection of the laws guaranteed by the Fourteenth Amendment, in that only landowners are permitted to vote in water storage district general elections, and votes in those elections are apportioned according to the assessed valuation of the land. . . . A majority of the District Court held that both statutes comported with the dictates of the Equal Protection Clause, and appellants have appealed that judgment directly to [the Supreme] Court under 28 U.S.C. § 1253."

The Supreme Court granted certiorari to review the case and affirmed.

B. Counsel of Record/ACLU Attorney

ACLU Side (Petitioner/Appellant): Thomas Keister Greer argued the cause for appellant.

Opposing Side (Respondent/Appellee): Robert M. Newell argued the cause for appellee.

III. AMICI CURIAE

ACLU Side (Petitioner/Appellant)

Brief of amici curiae filed on behalf of the ACLU, et al., by Melvin L. Wulf, Sanford Jay Rosen, Joel M. Gora, and David Hall.

Opposing Side (Respondent/Appellee)

Brief of amici curiae filed on behalf of the Irrigation Districts Association of California by Denslow Green.

Brief of amici curiae filed on behalf of the California Central Valleys Flood Control Association by George Basye.

IV. THE SUPREME COURT'S DECISION

"'[T]his Court has firmly established the principle that the Equal Protection Clause does not make every minor difference in the application of laws to different groups a violation of our Constitution. But we have also held many times that 'invidious' distinctions cannot be enacted without a violation of the Equal Protection Clause. In determining whether or not a state law violates the Equal Protection Clause, we must consider the facts and circumstances behind the law, the interests which the State claims to be protecting, and the interests of those who are disadvantaged by the classification.' . . .

The appellee district in this case, although vested with some typical governmental powers, has relatively limited authority. Its primary purpose . . . is to provide for the acquisition, storage, and distribution of water for farming in the Tulare Lake Basin. It provides no other general public services such as schools, housing, transportation, utilities, roads, or anything else of the type ordinarily financed by a municipal body. . . . Not only does the district not exercise what might be thought of as 'normal governmental' authority, but its actions disproportionately affect landowners. . . . In short, there is no way that the economic burdens of district operations can fall on residents qua residents, and the operations of the districts primarily affect the land within their boundaries.

Under these circumstances, it is quite understandable that the statutory framework for election of directors of the appellee focuses on the land benefited, rather than on people as such. . . . We hold, therefore, that the popular election requirements enunciated by *Reynolds*, and succeeding cases are inapplicable to elections such as the general election of appellee Water Storage District. . . .

Appellants assert that even if residents may be excluded from the vote, lessees who farm the land have interests that are indistinguishable from those of the landowners. Like landowners, they take an interest in increasing the available water for farming and, because the costs of district projects may be passed on to them either by express agreement or by increased rentals, they have an equal interest in the costs. . . .

Appellants' argument ignores the realities of water storage district operation. . . . Thus, as the District Court found, 'the benefits and burdens to each landowner . . . are in proportion to the assessed value of the land.' We cannot say that the California legislative decision to permit voting in the same proportion is not rationally based.

Accordingly, we affirm the judgment of the three-judge District Court and hold that the voter qualification statutes for California water storage district elections are rationally based, and therefore do not violate the Equal Protection Clause."

V. JUSTICE VOTE

3 Pro ACLU Side vs. 6 Con Opposing Side

ACLU Side (Petitioner/Appellant)

1. Douglas, W. – Wrote dissenting opinion
2. Brennan, W. – Joined dissenting opinion
3. Marshall, T. – Joined dissenting opinion

Opposing Side (Respondent/Appellee)

1. Rehnquist, W. – Wrote majority opinion
2. Stewart, P. – Joined majority opinion
3. Blackmun, H. – Joined majority opinion
4. Powell, L. – Joined majority opinion
5. Burger, W. – Joined majority opinion
6. White B. – Joined majority opinion

VI. A WIN OR LOSS FOR THE ACLU?

The ACLU filed as amicus curiae urging reversal; the Supreme Court affirmed the ruling of the District Court in a 6-3 vote, giving the ACLU an apparent loss.

297. Associated Enterprises, Inc. v. Toltec Watershed Improvement District

(Decided March 20, 1973; 410 U.S. 743)

I. ISSUE

A. Issues Discussed

Civil rights, voting rights, Fourteenth Amendment, equal protection

B. Legal Question Presented

Did the creation of a watershed improvement district, in which voting was limited to property owners and where votes were weighed by the amount of property owned, violate the Fourteenth Amendment's Equal Protection Clause?

C. Supreme Court's Answer

The voting provisions for the watershed improvement district did not violate the Equal Protection Clause.

II. CASE SUMMARY

A. Background

"Appellee Toltec Watershed Improvement District was established after referendum held pursuant to Wyoming's Watershed Improvement District Act. After formation, appellee sought a right of entry onto lands owned by appellant Associated Enterprises, Inc., and leased by Johnston Fuel Liners, for the purpose of carrying out studies to determine the feasibility of constructing a dam and reservoir. When Associated Enterprises resisted, the district sought to enforce its right in state court. Arguing that the statutes authorizing the referendum violated the Equal Protection Clause since under § 41-354.9 only landowners are entitled to vote and under § 41-354.10 a watershed improvement district cannot be determined to be administratively practicable and feasible unless a majority of the votes cast, representing a majority of the acreage in the district, favor its creation, appellants maintained that the district was illegally formed. The trial court agreed that had the district been formed in violation of the Equal Protection Clause, appellants would have a good defense under state law to the asserted right of entry, but it held against them on the merits. The Wyoming Supreme Court affirmed."

The Supreme Court granted certiorari to review the case and affirmed the decision.

B. Counsel of Record/ACLU Attorney

ACLU Side (Petitioner/Appellant): Henry A. Burgess argued the cause for appellant.

Opposing Side (Respondent/Appellee): Fred W. Phifer argued the cause for appellee.

III. AMICI CURIAE

ACLU Side (Petitioner/Appellant)

Brief of amici curiae filed on behalf of the ACLU, et al., by Melvin L. Wulf, Sanford Jay Rosen, Joel M. Gora, and David

Hall.

Opposing Side (Respondent/Appellee)

No briefs of amici curiae were filed in support of appellee.

IV. THE SUPREME COURT'S DECISION

"Appellants urge here that the provisions entitling only landowners to vote and weighting the vote according to acreage violate the Equal Protection Clause. Like the California water storage district, the Wyoming watershed district is a governmental unit of special or limited purpose whose activities have a disproportionate effect on landowners within the district. The district's operations are conducted through projects and the land is assessed for any benefits received. Such assessments constitute a lien on the land until paid.

We cannot agree with the dissent's intimation that the Wyoming Legislature has in any sense abdicated to a wealthy few the ultimate authority over land management in that State. The statute authorizing the establishment of improvement districts was enacted by a legislature in which all of the State's electors have the unquestioned right to be fairly represented. Under the act, districts may be formed only as subdivisions of soil and water conservation districts. And a precondition to their formation referendum is a determination by a board of supervisors of the affected conservation district, popularly elected by both occupiers and owners of land within the district, that the watershed improvement district is both necessary and administratively practicable. As in *Salyer*, we hold that the State could rationally conclude that landowners are primarily burdened and benefited by the establishment and operation of watershed districts and that it may condition the vote accordingly. The judgment appealed from is, therefore, affirmed."

V. JUSTICE VOTE

3 Pro ACLU Side vs. 6 Con Opposing Side

ACLU Side (Petitioner/Appellant)

1. Douglas, W. – Wrote dissenting opinion
2. Brennan, W. – Joined dissenting opinion
3. Marshall, T. – Joined dissenting opinion

Opposing Side (Respondent/Appellee)

1. Rehnquist, W. – Per curiam decision
2. Burger, W. – Per curiam decision
3. Stewart, P. – Per curiam decision
4. White, B. – Per curiam decision
5. Blackmun, H. – Per curiam decision
6. Powell, L. – Per curiam decision

VI. A WIN OR LOSS FOR THE ACLU?

The ACLU filed as amicus curiae urging reversal; the Supreme Court affirmed the ruling of the Supreme Court of Wyoming in a 6-3 vote, giving the ACLU an apparent loss.

298. Rosario v. Rockefeller

(Decided March 21, 1973; 410 U.S. 752)

I. ISSUE

A. Issues Discussed

Voting rights

B. Legal Question Presented

Whether New York's time limitations on political party registration for primary voting are unconstitutional.

C. Supreme Court's Answer

The limitations are constitutional. "New York did not prohibit the petitioners from voting in the 1972 primary election or from associating with the political party of their choice. It merely imposed a legitimate time limitation on their enrollment, which they chose to disregard."

II. CASE SUMMARY

A. Background

"For more than 60 years, New York has had a closed system of primary elections, whereby only enrolled members of a political party may vote in that party's primary. Under the State's Election Law, McKinney's Consol.Laws, c. 17, a registered voter enrolls as a party member by depositing an enrollment blank in a locked enrollment box. . . .

The effect of s 186 is to require a voter to enroll in the party of his choice at least 30 days before the general election in November in order to vote in the next subsequent party primary. . . . Section 187 provides an exemption from this waiting period for certain classes of voters . . . .

The petitioners are New York residents who became eligible to vote when they came of age in 1971. Although they could have registered and enrolled in a political party before the cutoff date in 1971—October 2—they failed to do so. Instead, they waited until early December 1971 to register and to deposit their enrollment blanks. At that time, they could not be specially and immediately enrolled in a party under s 187, since they had attained the voting age before, rather than after, the 1971 general election. Hence, pursuant to s 186, their party enrollment could not become effective until after the November 1972 general election. Because of New York's enrollment scheme, then, the petitioners were not eligible to vote in the presidential primary election held in June 1972.

The petitioners filed these complaints for declaratory relief, pursuant to 42 U.S.C. s 1983, alleging that s 186 unconstitutionally deprived them of their right to vote in the June primary and abridged their freedom to associate with the political party of their choice. The District Court, in an unreported opinion, granted them the declaratory relief sought. The Court of Appeals for the Second Circuit reversed, holding s 186 constitutional. [The Supreme Court] granted certiorari, but denied the petitioners' motion for summary reversal, expedited consideration, and a stay."

B. Counsel of Record

ACLU Side (Petitioner/Appellant): Burt Neuborne of the New York Civil Liberties Union argued the cause for appellants. With him on the brief were Melvin L. Wulf of the American Civil Liberties Union, Arthur Eisenberg of the New York Civil Liberties Union, Steven K. Weinberg, and Seymour Friedman.

Opposing Side (Respondent/Appellee): A. Seth Greenwald, Assistant Attorney General of New York, argued the cause for appellees Rockefeller et al. With him on the brief were Louis J. Lefkowitz, Attorney General, Samuel A. Hirshowitz, First Assistant Attorney General, and Irzing Galt, Assistant Attorney General. Joseph Jaspan filed a brief for appellees Meisser et al. David N. Dinkins, pro se, filed a brief for appellees Dinkins et al.

III. AMICI CURIAE

ACLU Side (Petitioner/Appellant)

No briefs of amici curiae were filed in support of appellant.

Opposing Side (Respondent/Appellee)

No briefs of amici curiae were filed in support of appellees.

IV. THE SUPREME COURT'S DECISION

"The petitioners argue that, through s 186, New York disenfranchised them by refusing to permit them to vote in the June 1972 primary election on the ground that they had not enrolled in a political party at least 30 days prior to the preceding general election. . . .

We cannot accept the petitioners' contention. . . .

The petitioners do not say why they did not enroll prior to the cutoff date; however, it is clear that they could have done so, but chose not to. Hence, if their plight can be characterized as disenfranchisement at all, it was not caused by s 186, but by their own failure to take timely steps to effect their enrollment.

For the same reason, we reject the petitioners' argument that s 186 violated their First and Fourteenth Amendment right of free association with the political party of their choice. Since they could have enrolled in a party in time to participate in the June 1972 primary, s 186 did not constitute a ban on their freedom of association, but merely a time limitation on when they had to act . . . .

The only remaining question, then, is whether the time limitation imposed by s 186 is so severe as itself to constitute an unconstitutionally onerous burden on the petitioners' exercise of the franchise or on their freedom of political association. . . .

The cutoff date for enrollment prescribed by s 186 occurs approximately eight months prior to a presidential primary (held in June) and 11 months prior to a nonpresidential primary (held in September). . . .

It is true that the period between the enrollment deadline and the next primary election is lengthy. But that period is not an arbitrary time limit unconnected to any important state goal. The purpose of New York's delayed-enrollment scheme, we are told, is to inhibit party 'raiding,' whereby voters in sympathy with one party designate themselves as voters of another party so as to influence or determine the results of the other party's primary. . . .

It is clear that preservation of the integrity of the electoral process is a legitimate and valid state goal. In the service of that goal, New York has adopted its delayed-enrollment scheme; and an integral part of that scheme is that, in order to participate in a primary election, a person must enroll before the preceding general election. . . . The resulting time limitation for enrollment is thus tied to a particularized legitimate purpose, and is in no sense invidious or arbitrary.

New York did not prohibit the petitioners from voting in the 1972 primary election or from associating with the political party of their choice. It merely imposed a legitimate time limitation on their enrollment, which they chose to disregard.

Accordingly, the judgment below is affirmed."

V. JUSTICE VOTE

4 Pro ACLU Side vs. 5 Con Opposing Side

ACLU Side (Petitioner/Appellant)

1. Powell, L. – Wrote dissenting opinion
2. Douglas, W. – Joined Powell's dissent
3. Marshall, T. – Joined Powell's dissent
4. Brennan, W. – Joined Powell's dissent

Opposing Side (Respondent/Appellee)

1. Stewart, P. – Wrote majority opinion
2. Burger, W. – Joined majority opinion
3. White, B. – Joined majority opinion
4. Rehnquist, W. – Joined majority opinion
5. Blackmun, H. – Joined majority opinion

VI. A WIN OR LOSS FOR THE ACLU?

The ACLU served as counsel for appellants urging reversal of the judgment of the Court of Appeals; the Supreme Court affirmed, in a 5-4 vote, giving the ACLU an apparent loss.

299. San Antonio Independent School District v. Rodriguez

(Decided March 21, 1973; 411 U.S. 1)

I. ISSUE

A. Issues Discussed

Equal protection, discrimination

B. Legal Question Presented

Is a state's use of property taxes to finance its public schools, which results in disparities in expenditure between districts, constitutional?

C. Supreme Court's Answer

The use of property taxes in this way does not violate equal protection.

II. CASE SUMMARY

A. Background

"This suit attacking the Texas system of financing public education was initiated by Mexican-American parents whose children attend the elementary and secondary schools in the Edgewood Independent School District, an urban school district in San Antonio, Texas. They brought a class action on behalf of school children throughout the State who are members of minority groups or who are poor and reside in school districts having a low property tax base. . . . The . . . three-judge court . . . rendered its judgment in a per curiam opinion holding the Texas school finance system unconstitutional under the Equal Protection Clause of the Fourteenth Amendment.

[S]ubstantial interdistrict disparities in school expenditures found by the District Court to prevail in San Antonio and in varying degrees throughout the State still exist. And it was these disparities, largely attributable to differences in the amounts of money collected through local property taxation, that led the District Court to conclude that Texas' dual system of public school financing violated the Equal Protection Clause. The District Court held that the Texas system discriminates on the basis of wealth in the manner in which education is provided for its people. Finding that wealth is a 'suspect' classification and that education is a 'fundamental' interest, the District Court held that the Texas system could be sustained only if the State could show that it was premised upon some compelling state interest. On this issue the court concluded that '[n]ot only are defendants unable to demonstrate compelling state interests . . . they fail even to establish a reasonable basis for these classifications.'"

The Supreme Court granted certiorari to review the case and reversed the District Court.

B. Counsel of Record / ACLU Attorney

ACLU Side (Respondent / Appellee): Arthur Gochman argued the cause for appellees.

Opposing Side (Petitioner / Appellant): Charles Alan Wright argued the cause for appellant.

III. AMICI CURIAE

ACLU Side (Respondent / Appellee)

Brief of amici curiae filed on behalf of the ACLU, et al., by Norman Dorsen, Marvin M. Karpatkin, Melvin L. Wulf, Paul S. Berger, Joseph B. Robison, Arnold Forster, and Stanley P. Hebert.

Additional briefs of amici curiae were filed on behalf of Wendell Anderson, Governor of Minnesota, et al., Wilson Riles, Superintendent of Public Instruction of California, et al., Houston I. Flournoy, Controller of California, the Mayor and City Council of Baltimore, et al., the San Antonio Independent School District, the NAACP Legal Defense and Educational Fund, Inc., the National Education Association, et al., John Serrano, Jr., et al., and the Republic National Bank of Dallas, et al.

Opposing Side (Petitioner / Appellant)

Brief of amici curiae filed on behalf of the Attorney General of New Jersey by George F. Kugler, Jr., Attorney General, pro se, and Stephen Skillman, Assistant Attorney General.

Brief of amici curiae filed by George W. Liebmann and Shale D. Stiller for Montgomery County, Maryland, joined by Francis B. Burch, Attorney General of Maryland, Henry R. Lord, Deputy Attorney General, E. Stephen Derby, Assistant Attorney General, William J. Baxley, Attorney General of Alabama, Gary K. Nelson, Attorney General of Arizona, James G. Bond, Assistant Attorney General, Evelle J. Younger, Attorney General of California, Elizabeth Palmer, Assistant Attorney General, Edward M. Belasco, Deputy Attorney General, Duke W. Dunbar, Attorney General of Colorado, Robert K. Killian, Attorney General of Connecticut, F. Michael Ahern, Assistant Attorney General, W. Anthony Park, Attorney General of Idaho, James R. Hargis, Deputy Attorney General, Theodore L. Sendak, Attorney General of Indiana, Charles M. Wells, Harry T. Ice, Richard C. Turner, Attorney General of Iowa, George W. Murray, Assistant Attorney General, Vern Miller, Attorney General of Kansas, Matthew J. Dowd and John C. Johnson, Assistant Attorneys General, Ed W. Hancock, Attorney General of Kentucky, Carl T. Miller, Assistant Attorney General, William J. Guste, Jr., Attorney General of Louisiana, James S. Erwin, Attorney General of Maine, George West, Assistant Attorney General, Robert H. Quinn, Attorney General of Massachusetts, Lawrence T. Bench, Assistant Attorney General, Charles F. Clippert, William M. Saxton, Robert B. Webster, A. F. Summer, Attorney General of Mississippi, Martin R. McLendon, Assistant Attorney General, John Danforth, Attorney General of Missouri, D. Brook Bartlett, Assistant Attorney General, Clarence A. H. Meyer, Attorney General of Nebraska, Harold Mosher, Assistant Attorney General, Warren B. Rudman, Attorney General of New Hampshire, Louis J. Lefkowitz, Attorney General of New York, Robert B. Morgan, Attorney General of North Carolina, Burley B. Mitchell, Jr., Assistant Attorney General, Helgi Johanneson, Attorney General of North Dakota, Gerald Vandewalle, Assistant Attorney General, Lee Johnson, Attorney General of Oregon, Daniel R. McLeod, Attorney General of South Carolina, G. Lewis Argoe, Jr., Assistant Attorney General, Gordon Mydland, Attorney General of South Dakota, C. J. Kelly, Assistant Attorney General, David M. Pack, Attorney General of Tennessee, Milton P. Rice, Deputy Attorney General, Vernon B. Romney, Attorney General of Utah, Robert B. Hansen, Deputy Attorney General, James M. Jeffords, Attorney General of Vermont, Chauncey H. Browning, Jr., Attorney General of West Virginia, Victor A. Barone, Assistant Attorney General, Robert W. Warren, Attorney General of Wisconsin, and Betty R. Brown, Assistant Attorney General.

Brief of amici curiae filed on behalf of Richard M. Clowes, Superintendent of Schools of the County of Los Angeles, et al., by John D. Maharg and James W. Briggs.

IV. THE SUPREME COURT'S DECISION

"We must decide, first, whether the Texas system of financing public education operates to the disadvantage of some suspect class or impinges upon a fundamental right explicitly or implicitly protected by the Constitution, thereby requiring strict judicial scrutiny. If so, the judgment of the District Court should be affirmed. If not, the Texas scheme must still be examined to determine whether it rationally furthers some legitimate, articulated state purpose and therefore does not constitute an invidious discrimination in violation of the Equal Protection Clause of the Fourteenth Amendment. . . .

We . . . conclude that the Texas system does not operate to the peculiar disadvantage of any suspect class. But in recognition of the fact that this Court has never heretofore held that wealth discrimination alone provides an adequate basis for invoking strict scrutiny, appellees have not relied solely on this contention. They also assert that the State's system impermissibly interferes with the exercise of a 'fundamental' right and that accordingly the prior decisions of this Court require the application of the strict standard of judicial review. It is this question—whether education is a fundamental right, in the sense that it is among the rights and liberties protected by the Constitution—which has so consumed the attention of courts and commentators in recent years. . . .

Texas' system of public school finance is an inappropriate candidate for strict judicial scrutiny. These same considerations are relevant to the determination whether that system, with its conceded imperfections, nevertheless bears some rational relationship to a legitimate state purpose. . . .

In sum, to the extent that the Texas system of school financing results in unequal expenditures between children who happen to reside in different districts, we cannot say that such disparities are the product of a system that is so irrational as to be invidiously discriminatory. Texas has acknowledged its shortcomings and has persistently endeavored—not without some success—to ameliorate the differences in levels of expenditures without sacrificing the benefits of local participation. The Texas plan is not the result of hurried, ill-conceived legislation. It certainly is not the product of purposeful discrimination against any group or class. On the contrary, it is rooted in decades of experience in Texas and elsewhere, and in major part is the product of responsible studies by qualified people. In giving substance to the presumption of validity to which the Texas system is entitled, it is important to remember that at every stage of its development it has constituted a 'rough accommodation' of interests in an effort to arrive at practical and workable solutions. One also must remember that the system here challenged is not peculiar to Texas or to any other State. In its essential characteristics, the Texas plan for financing public education reflects what many educators for a half century have thought was an enlightened approach to a problem for which there is no perfect solution. We are unwilling to assume for ourselves a level of wisdom superior to that of legislators, scholars, and educational authorities in 50 States, especially where the alternatives proposed are only recently conceived and nowhere yet tested. The constitutional standard under the Equal Protection Clause is whether the challenged state action rationally furthers a legitimate state purpose or interest. We hold that the Texas plan abundantly satisfies this standard."

The Supreme Court reversed the decision of the District Court.

V. JUSTICE VOTE

4 Pro ACLU Side vs. 5 Con Opposing Side

ACLU Side (Respondent/Appellee)

1. Brennan, W. – Wrote dissenting opinion, joined White's dissent
2. White, B. – Wrote dissenting opinion
3. Marshall, T. – Wrote dissenting opinion
4. Douglas, W. – Joined White's dissent, joined Marshall's dissent

Opposing Side (Petitioner/Appellant)

1. Powell, L. – Wrote majority opinion
2. Stewart, P. – Wrote concurring opinion
3. Burger, W. – Joined majority opinion
4. Blackmun, H. – Joined majority opinion
5. Rehnquist, W. – Joined majority opinion

VI. A WIN OR LOSS FOR THE ACLU?

The ACLU, as amicus curiae, urged affirmance of the judgment of the District Court; the Supreme Court reversed in a 5-4 vote, giving the ACLU an apparent loss.

300. Ohio Mun. Judges Ass'n v. Davis

(Decided March 26, 1973; 411 U.S. 144)

I. ISSUE

A. Issues Discussed

Federal

B. Legal Question Presented

"Whether a group of persons within a class who are excluded from receiving benefits conferred by a state upon others in the same class have standing to raise the denial of equal protection of the law."[1]

C. Supreme Court's Answer

"The judgment is affirmed, but on the ground that appellants' constitutional challenge to Art. IV, s 6(B), was without merit."

II. CASE SUMMARY

A. Background

"In this action the primary relief sought by plaintiffs is an order that municipal judges be compensated in a manner which would recognize in-term salary increases previously granted to them. In order to achieve that end plaintiffs attack Article IV, § 6(B) as denying them equal protection under the laws. . . .

This inability to grant to plaintiffs the primary relief sought, even if they should be correct on their constitutional claim,

1 Motion for Leave to File Brief, Amicus Curiae, and Brief of American Civil Liberties Union of Ohio, Inc. Amicus Curiae at 1, Ohio Municipal Judges Ass'n v. Davis, 411 U.S. 144 (1973) (No. 72-1010).

requires dismissal of the complaint without the necessity of deciding the constitutional issue. . . .

The temporary restraining order heretofore issued by this Court is hereby dissolved, and this case is dismissed. Costs assessed to plaintiffs."[1]

The Supreme Court reviewed the case.

B. Counsel of Record

ACLU Side (Petitioner/Appellant): Brief for appellant filed by Jonathan S. Rocker and Jack M. Schulman.

Opposing Side (Respondent/Appellee): Brief for appellee filed by Lawrence S. Huffman and Richard L. Ditto.

III. AMICI CURIAE

ACLU Side (Petitioner/Appellant)

Brief of amici curiae filed on behalf of the American Civil Liberties Union of Ohio, Inc., by Leonard J. Schwartz and Stanley K. Laughlin, Jr.

Opposing Side (Respondent/Appellee)

No briefs of amici curiae were filed in support of appellees.

IV. THE SUPREME COURT'S DECISION

"The motion of American Civil Liberties Union of Ohio, Inc., for leave to file a brief, as amicus curiae, is granted.

On the ground that it was beyond its authority to grant the primary relief sought, the United States District Court dismissed appellants' suit which alleged that Art. IV, s 6(B), of the Ohio Constitution denied equal protection of the laws under the Fourteenth Amendment to the United States Constitution. The judgment is affirmed, but on the ground that appellants' constitutional challenge to Art. IV, s 6(B), was without merit.

So ordered.

Judgment affirmed."

V. JUSTICE VOTE

0 Pro ACLU Side vs. 9 Con Opposing Side

Opposing Side (Respondent/Appellee)

1. White, B. – Per curiam decision
2. Marshall, T. – Per curiam decision
3. Brennan, W. – Per curiam decision
4. Stewart, P. – Per curiam decision
5. Burger, W. – Per curiam decision
6. Blackmun, H. – Per curiam decision
7. Douglas, W. – Per curiam decision
8. Powell, L. – Per curiam decision
9. Rehnquist, W. – Per curiam decision

VI. A WIN OR LOSS FOR THE ACLU?

The ACLU filed as amici curiae urging reversal of the judgment of the U.S. District Court for the Northern District of Ohio; the Supreme Court affirmed, in a 9-0 per curiam decision, giving the ACLU an apparent loss.

1 *Ohio Mun. Judges Ass'n v. Davis*, 33 Ohio Misc. 141 (N.D. Ohio 1972).

301. Lemon v. Kurtzman

(Decided April 2, 1973; 411 U.S. 192)

I. ISSUE

A. Issues Discussed

Civil procedure

B. Legal Question Presented

Whether "the District Court erred in refusing to enjoin payment of some $24 million set aside by Pennsylvania to compensate nonpublic sectarian schools for educational services rendered by them during the 1970—1971 school year."

C. Supreme Court's Answer

"Appellants ask, in effect, that we hold those charged with executing state legislative directives to the peril of having their arrangements unraveled if they act before there has been an authoritative judicial determination that the governing legislation is constitutional. . . .

In short the propriety of the relief afforded appellants by the District Court, applying familiar equitable principles, must be measured against the totality of circumstances and in light of the general principle that, absent contrary direction, state officials and those with whom they deal are entitled to rely on a presumptively valid state statute, enacted in good faith and by no means plainly unlawful."

II. CASE SUMMARY

A. Background

"On June 28, 1971, we held that the Pennsylvania statutory program to reimburse nonpublic sectarian schools for certain secular educational services violated the Establishment Clause of the First Amendment. The case was remanded to the three-judge District Court for further proceedings consistent with our opinion. On remand, the District Court entered summary judgment in favor of appellants and enjoined payment, under Act 109, of any state funds to nonpublic sectarian schools for educational services performed after June 28, 1971. The District Court's order permitted the State to reimburse nonpublic sectarian schools for services provided before our decision in Lemon I. Appellants made no claim that appellees refund all sums paid under the Pennsylvania statute struck down in Lemon I.

Appellants, the successful plaintiffs of Lemon I, now challenge the limited scope of the District Court's injunction. Specifically, they assert that the District Court erred in refusing to enjoin payment of some $24 million set aside by Pennsylvania to compensate nonpublic sectarian schools for educational services rendered by them during the 1970—1971 school year."

The Supreme Court reviewed this second decision.

B. Counsel of Record

ACLU Side (Petitioner/Appellant): David P. Bruton argued the cause for appellants Alton J. Lemon, American Civil Liberties Union of Pennsylvania, Inc., and others. With him on the briefs were Melvin L. Wulf and Sanford J. Rosen of the American Civil Liberties Union Foundation, and Franklin C.

Salisbury.

Opposing Side (Respondent/Appellee): William B. Ball argued the cause for appellees. With him on the brief for appellee Commonwealth of Pennsylvania were J. Shane Creamer, Attorney General, Samuel Rappaport, Joseph G. Skelly, James E. Gallagher, Jr., C. Clark Hodgson, Jr., and William D. Valente. Henry T. Reath filed a brief for appellee Pennsylvania Association of Independent Schools.

III. AMICI CURIAE

ACLU Side (Petitioner/Appellant)

No briefs of amici curiae were filed in support of appellant.

Opposing Side (Respondent/Appellee)

No briefs of amici curiae were filed in support of appellees.

IV. THE SUPREME COURT'S DECISION

"Claims that a particular holding of the Court should be applied retroactively have been pressed on us frequently in recent years. Most often, we have been called upon to decide whether a decision defining new constitutional rights of a defendant in a criminal case should be applied to convictions of others that predated the new constitutional development. But 'in the last few decades, we have recognized the doctrine of nonretroactivity outside the criminal area many times, in both constitutional and nonconstitutional cases.' . . .

Appellants assure us that they do not seek to require the schools to disgorge prior payments received under Act 109; in the same breath, appellants insist that the presently disputed payment be enjoined because an unconstitutional statute 'confers no rights; it imposes no duties; it affords no protection; it creates no office; it is, in legal contemplation, as inoperative as though it had never been passed.' . . . We disagree. . . .

That there would be constitutional attack on Act 109 was plain from the outset. But this is not a case where it could be said that appellees acted in bad faith or that they relied on a plainly unlawful statute. In this case, even the clarity of hindsight is not persuasive that the constitutional resolution of Lemon I could be predicted with assurance sufficient to undermine appellees' reliance on Act 109. . . .

In the end, then, appellants' position comes down to this: that any reliance whatever by the schools was unjustified because Act 109 was an 'untested' state statute whose validity had never been authoritatively determined. The short answer to this argument is that governments must act if they are to fulfill their high responsibilities. . . .

Appellants ask, in effect, that we hold those charged with executing state legislative directives to the peril of having their arrangements unraveled if they act before there has been an authoritative judicial determination that the governing legislation is constitutional. . . .

Federalism suggests that federal court intervention in state judicial processes be appropriately confined. . . . Likewise, federalism requires that federal injunctions unrelated to state courts be shaped with concern and care for the responsibilities of the executive and legislative branches of state governments. In short the propriety of the relief afforded appellants by the District Court, applying familiar equitable principles, must be measured against the totality of circumstances and in light of the general principle that, absent contrary direction, state officials and those with whom they deal are entitled to rely on a presumptively valid state statute, enacted in good faith and by no means plainly unlawful.

Affirmed."

V. JUSTICE VOTE

3 Pro ACLU Side vs. 5 Con Opposing Side

ACLU Side (Petitioner/Appellant)

1. Brennan, W. – Joined Douglas' dissent
2. Stewart, P. – Joined Douglas' dissent
3. Douglas, W. – Wrote dissenting opinion

Marshall, T – Took no part in the decision.

Opposing Side (Respondent/Appellee)

1. Burger, W. – Wrote majority opinion
2. Blackmun, H. – Joined majority opinion
3. Powell, L. – Joined majority opinion
4. Rehnquist, W. – Joined majority opinion
5. White, B. – Concurred in the judgment

VI. A WIN OR LOSS FOR THE ACLU?

The ACLU served as counsel for appellants and were among the appellants urging reversal of the judgment of the U.S. District Court for the Eastern District of Pennsylvania; the Supreme Court affirmed, in a 5-3 vote, giving the ACLU an apparent loss.

302. Davis v. United States

(Decided April 17, 1973; 411 U.S. 233)

I. ISSUE

A. Issues Discussed

Criminal procedure

B. Legal Question Presented

What is "the effect of Rule 12(b)(2) of the Federal Rules of Criminal Procedure on a postconviction motion for relief which raises for the first time a claim of unconstitutional discrimination in the composition of a grand jury."

C. Supreme Court's Answer

"We hold that the District Court did not abuse its discretion in denying petitioner relief from the application of the waiver provision of Rule 12(b) (2), and that having concluded he was not entitled to such relief, it properly dismissed his motion under s 2255."

II. CASE SUMMARY

A. Background

"We are called upon to determine the effect of Rule 12(b)(2) of the Federal Rules of Criminal Procedure on a postconviction motion for relief which raises for the first time a claim of unconstitutional discrimination in the composition of a grand jury. An indictment was returned in the District Court charging petitioner Davis, a Negro, and two white men with entry into a federally insured bank with intent to commit larceny . . . . Represented by appointed counsel, petitioner entered a not-guilty plea at his arraignment and was given 30 days within which to file pretrial motions. He timely moved to quash his indictment on the ground that it was the result of an illegal arrest, but made no other pretrial motions relating to the indictment.

On the opening day of the trial, following voir dire of the jury, the District Judge ruled on petitioner's pretrial motions in chambers and ordered that the motion to quash on the illegal arrest ground be carried with the case. He then asked twice if there were anything else before commencing trial. Petitioner was convicted and sentenced to 14 years' imprisonment. His conviction was affirmed on appeal.

Post-conviction motions were thereafter filed and denied, but none dealt with the issue presented in this case. Almost three years after his conviction, petitioner filed the instant motion to dismiss the indictment, pursuant to 28 U.S.C. s 2255, alleging that the District Court had acquiesced in the systematic exclusion of qualified Negro jurymen by reason of the use of a 'key man' system of selection, and asserted violation of the 'mandatory requirement of the statute laws set forth . . . in title 28, U.S.C.A. Section 1861, 1863, 1864, and the 5th amendment of the United States Constitution.' . . . The District Court . . . denied the motion. . . .

The Court of Appeals affirmed . . . ."

B. Counsel of Record

ACLU Side (Petitioner/Appellant): Melvin L. Wulf of the American Civil Liberties Union Foundation argued the cause and filed briefs for appellant.

Opposing Side (Respondent/Appellee): Edward R. Korman argued the cause for the United States. With him on the brief were Solicitor General Griswold, Assistant Attorney General Petersen, and Sidney M. Glazer.

III. AMICI CURIAE

ACLU Side (Petitioner/Appellant)

Brief of amici curiae filed on behalf of the NAACP Legal Defense and Educational Fund, Inc., by Jack Greenberg, James M. Nabrit III, and Charles Stephen Ralston.

Opposing Side (Respondent/Appellee)

No briefs of amici curiae were filed in support of appellee.

IV. THE SUPREME COURT'S DECISION

"Rule 12(b)(2) provides in pertinent part that '(d)efenses and objections based on defects in the institution of the prosecution or in the indictment . . . may be raised only by motion before trial,' and that failure to present such defenses or objections 'constitutes a waiver thereof, but the court for cause shown may grant relief from the waiver.' . . .

This Court had occasion to consider the Rule's application in Shotwell Mfg. Co. v. United States, a case involving tax-evasion convictions. In a motion filed more than four years after their trial, but before the conclusion of direct review, petitioners alleged that both the grand and petit jury arrays were illegally constituted . . . . In this Court, petitioners conceded that Rule 12(b)(2) applied to their objection to the grand jury array, but they denied that it applied to the petit jury. Both objections were held foreclosed by the petitioners' years of inaction, and the lower courts' application of the Rule was affirmed.

Shotwell thus confirms that Rule 12(b)(2) precludes untimely challenges to grand jury arrays . . . . Despite the strong analogy between the effect of the Rule as construed in Shotwell and petitioner's s 2255 allegations, he nonetheless contends that Kaufman v. United States, establishes that he is not precluded from raising his constitutional challenge in a s 2255 proceeding. We disagree. . . .

We think it inconceivable that Congress, having in the criminal proceeding foreclosed the raising of a claim such as this after the commencement of trial in the absence of a showing of 'cause' for relief from waiver, nonetheless intended to perversely negate the Rule's purpose by permitting an entirely different but much more liberal requirement of waiver in federal habeas proceedings. . . . We therefore hold that the waiver standard expressed in Rule 12(b)(2) governs an untimely claim of grand jury discrimination, not only during the criminal proceeding, but also later on collateral review. . . .

The principles of Rule 12(b)(2), as construed in Shotwell, are not difficult to apply to the facts of this case. . . .

We hold that the District Court did not abuse its discretion in denying petitioner relief from the application of the waiver provision of Rule 12(b) (2), and that having concluded he was not entitled to such relief, it properly dismissed his motion under s 2255. Accordingly, the judgment of the Court of Appeals is affirmed."

V. JUSTICE VOTE

3 Pro ACLU Side vs. 6 Con Opposing Side

ACLU Side (Petitioner/Appellant)

1. Marshall, T. – Wrote dissenting opinion
2. Brennan, W. – Joined Marshall's dissent
3. Douglas, W. – Joined Marshall's dissent

Opposing Side (Respondent/Appellee)

1. Rehnquist, W. – Wrote majority opinion
2. White, B. – Joined majority opinion
3. Stewart, P. – Joined majority opinion
4. Burger, W. – Joined majority opinion
5. Blackmun, H. – Joined majority opinion
6. Powell, L. – Joined majority opinion

VI. A WIN OR LOSS FOR THE ACLU?

The ACLU served as counsel for appellants urging reversal of the judgment of the Court of Appeals; the Supreme Court affirmed, in a 6-3 vote, giving the ACLU an apparent loss.

303. United States v. Russell

(Decided April 24, 1973; 411 U.S. 423)

I. ISSUE

A. Issues Discussed

Criminal justice, drugs, Fifth Amendment, due process

B. Legal Question Presented

If a government agent furnished one of the means for the commission of an offense, which the defendant was concededly predisposed to commit and did commit, does that establish a bar to prosecution as a matter of law?

C. Supreme Court's Answer

A government agent providing one of the means for the commission of an offense is not a bar to prosecution as a matter of law.

II. CASE SUMMARY

A. Background

"Respondent Richard Russell was charged in three counts of a five-count indictment returned against him and codefendants John and Patrick Connolly. After a jury trial in the District Court, in which his sole defense was entrapment, respondent was convicted on all three counts of having unlawfully manufactured and processed methamphetamine ('speed') and of having unlawfully sold and delivered that drug . . . . He was sentenced to concurrent terms of two years in prison for each offense, the terms to be suspended on the condition that he spend six months in prison and be placed on probation for the following three years. On appeal, the United States Court of Appeals for the Ninth Circuit, one judge dissenting reversed the conviction solely for the reason that an undercover agent supplied an essential chemical for manufacturing the methamphetamine which formed the basis of respondent's conviction. The court concluded that as a matter of law 'a defense to a criminal charge may be founded upon an intolerable degree of governmental participation in the criminal enterprise.'"

The Supreme Court granted certiorari to review the case and reversed the Court of Appeals.

B. Counsel of Record / ACLU Attorney

ACLU Side (Respondent / Appellee): Thomas H. S. Brucker, by appointment of the Court, argued the cause for appellee.

Opposing Side (Petitioner / Appellant): Deputy Solicitor General Philip A. Lacovara argued the cause for appellant.

III. AMICI CURIAE

ACLU Side (Respondent / Appellee)

Brief of amici curiae filed on behalf of the ACLU, et al., by Paul G. Chevigny, Melvin L. Wulf, and David Kairys.

Opposing Side (Petitioner / Appellant)

No briefs of amici curiae were filed in support of appellant.

IV. THE SUPREME COURT'S DECISION

"While we may some day be presented with a situation in which the conduct of law enforcement agents is so outrageous that due process principles would absolutely bar the government from invoking judicial processes to obtain a conviction, the instant case is distinctly not of that breed. Shapiro's contribution of propanone to the criminal enterprise already in process was scarcely objectionable. The chemical is by itself a harmless substance and its possession is legal. While the Government may have been seeking to make it more difficult for drug rings, such as that of which respondent was a member, to obtain the chemical, the evidence... shows that it nonetheless was obtainable. The law enforcement conduct here stops far short of violating that 'fundamental fairness, shocking to the universal sense of justice,' mandated by the Due Process Clause of the Fifth Amendment.

The illicit manufacture of drugs is not a sporadic, isolated criminal incident, but a continuing, though illegal, business enterprise. In order to obtain convictions for illegally manufacturing drugs, the gathering of evidence of past unlawful conduct frequently proves to be an all but impossible task. Thus in drug-related offenses law enforcement personnel have turned to one of the only practicable means of detection: the infiltration of drug rings and a limited participation in their unlawful present practices. Such infiltration is a recognized and permissible means of investigation; if that be so, then the supply of some item of value that the drug ring requires must, as a general rule, also be permissible. For an agent will not be taken into the confidence of the illegal entrepreneurs unless he has something of value to offer them. Law enforcement tactics such as this can hardly be said to violate 'fundamental fairness' or 'shocking to the universal sense of justice.' . . .

The execution of the federal laws under our Constitution is confided primarily to the Executive Branch of the Government, subject to applicable constitutional and statutory limitations and to judicially fashioned rules to enforce those limitations. We think that the decision of the Court of Appeals in this case quite unnecessarily introduces an unmanageably subjective standard . . . .

Respondent's concession in the Court of Appeals that the jury finding as to predisposition was supported by the evidence is, therefore, fatal to his claim of entrapment. He was an active participant in an illegal drug manufacturing enterprise which began before the Government agent appeared on the scene, and continued after the Government agent had left the scene. He was, in the words of *Sherman*, supra, not an 'unwary innocent' but an 'unwary criminal.' The Court of Appeals was wrong, we believe, when it sought to broaden the principle laid down in *Sorrells* and *Sherman*. Its judgment is therefore reversed."

V. JUSTICE VOTE

4 Pro ACLU Side vs. 5 Con Opposing Side

ACLU Side (Respondent / Appellee)

1. Douglas, W. – Wrote dissenting opinion
2. Brennan, W. – Joined Douglas' dissent, joined Stewart's dissent
3. Stewart, P. – Wrote dissenting opinion
4. Marshall, T. – Joined Stewart's opinion

Opposing Side (Petitioner/Appellant)

1. Rehnquist, W. – Wrote majority opinion
2. Burger, W. – Joined majority opinion
3. White, B. – Joined majority opinion
4. Blackmun, H. – Joined majority opinion
5. Powell, L. – Joined majority opinion

VI. A WIN OR LOSS FOR THE ACLU?

The ACLU filed as amicus curiae urging affirmance; the Supreme Court reversed the ruling of the Court of Appeals for the Ninth Circuit in a 5-4 vote, giving the ACLU an apparent loss.

304. Brown v. Chote

(Decided May 7, 1973; 411 U.S. 452)

I. ISSUE

A. Issues Discussed

Civil rights, state's rights, voting, elections

B. Legal Question Presented

Is the portion of the California Elections Code which requires candidates in a primary election to pay a filing fee prior to having their names listed on the primary ballot constitutional?

C. Supreme Court's Answer

Declining to address the constitutional question, the Supreme Court upheld the preliminary injunction issued in this case and remanded the case for further proceedings.

II. CASE SUMMARY

A. Background

Under the California Election Code, candidates for Congress must pay a filing fee to have their names on the primary ballot. Appellee Chote sought to run for a seat in the House of Representatives but asserted that he was unable to pay the filing fee. He presented a check for the fee with the words "Written under protest for filing fee" on it and was told "that his name would not be placed on the ballot if his check was not honored."

Appellee filed a class action suit in District Court to challenge the constitutionality of the filing-fee statutes, alleging "that California's filing-fee system was unconstitutional since it barred indigents, such as himself, from seeking elective office and from voting for the candidate of his choice." He also moved the District Court to issue a preliminary injunction "to allow him to participate as a candidate in the upcoming primary." The District Court granted appellee's motion for a preliminary injunction.

The Supreme Court granted certiorari to review this decision and affirmed.

B. Counsel of Record/ACLU Attorney

ACLU Side (Respondent/Appellee): Philip Elman, by appointment of the Court, argued the cause for appellee.

Opposing Side (Petitioner/Appellant): Deputy Attorney General of California Henry G. Ullerich argued the cause for appellant.

III. AMICI CURIAE

ACLU Side (Respondent/Appellee)

Brief of amici curiae filed on behalf of the ACLU, et al., by Melvin L. Wulf, Sanford J. Rosen, Marguerite Buckley, A. L. Wirin, Fred Okrand, and Laurence R. Sperber.

Opposing Side (Petitioner/Appellant)

No briefs of amici curiae were filed in support of appellant.

IV. THE SUPREME COURT'S DECISION

"[T]he State of California, for reasons not clear to us in light of the limited record, asked the Court to address itself to the ultimate merits of appellee's constitutional claim, a question which the District Court did not reach. In the present posture of the case, there is no occasion to consider any issues beyond those addressed by the District Court.

The issuance of the requested preliminary injunction was the only action taken by the District Court. . . .

In reviewing such interlocutory relief, this Court may only consider whether issuance of the injunction constituted an abuse of discretion. In light of the arguments presented by appellee and the fact that appellee's opportunity to be a candidate would have been foreclosed, absent some relief, we cannot conclude that the court's action was an abuse of discretion. We therefore affirm the action taken by the District Court in granting interim relief.

In doing so, we intimate no view as to the ultimate merits of appellee's contentions. The record in this case clearly reflects the limited time which the parties had to assemble evidence and prepare their arguments. While the District Court's swift action is understandable in view of the deadline which it faced, the resulting record was simply insufficient to allow that court to consider fully the grave, far-reaching constitutional questions presented.

The specific deadline which led the District Court to grant equitable relief has now passed. Nothing precludes appellee from seeking a trial on the merits, if he chooses to proceed. The case is therefore remanded to the District Court for further proceedings consistent with this opinion."

The Supreme Court affirmed the decision of the District Court and remanded the case.

V. JUSTICE VOTE

9 Pro ACLU Side vs. 0 Con Opposing Side

ACLU Side (Respondent/Appellee)

1. Burger, W. – Wrote majority opinion
2. Rehnquist, W. – Joined majority opinion
3. Brennan, W. – Joined majority opinion
4. Douglas, W. – Joined majority opinion
5. White, B. – Joined majority opinion
6. Marshall, T. – Joined majority opinion
7. Stewart, P. – Joined majority opinion
8. Powell, L. – Joined majority opinion
9. Blackmun, H. – Joined majority opinion

VI. A WIN OR LOSS FOR THE ACLU?

The ACLU filed as amicus curiae urging affirmance; the Supreme Court affirmed the ruling of the District Court in a unanimous 9-0 vote, giving the ACLU an apparent win.

305. Preiser v. Rodriguez

(Decided May 7, 1973; 411 U.S. 475)

I. ISSUE

A. Issues Discussed

Prison, civil rights, federal

B. Legal Question Presented

"[W]hether state prisoners seeking such redress may obtain equitable relief under the Civil Rights Act, even though the federal habeas corpus statute, 28 U.S.C. s 2254, clearly provides a specific federal remedy."

C. Supreme Court's Answer

"[W]e hold today that when a state prisoner is challenging the very fact or duration of his physical imprisonment, and the relief he seeks is a determination that he is entitled to immediate release or a speedier release from that imprisonment, his sole federal remedy is a writ of habeas corpus."

II. CASE SUMMARY

A. Background

"The respondents in this case were state prisoners who were deprived of good-conduct-time credits by the New York State Department of Correctional Services as a result of disciplinary proceedings. They then brought actions in a federal district court, pursuant to the Civil Rights Act of 1871, 42 U.S.C. s 1983. Alleging that the Department had acted unconstitutionally in depriving them of the credits, they sought injunctive relief to compel restoration of the credits, which in each case would result in their immediate release from confinement in prison. The question before us is whether state prisoners seeking such redress may obtain equitable relief under the Civil Rights Act, even though the federal habeas corpus statute, 28 U.S.C. s 2254, clearly provides a specific federal remedy. . . .

After rehearing en banc of the three now-consolidated cases, the Court of Appeals, with three dissents, affirmed the judgments of the District Court in all of the cases 'upon consideration of the merits and upon the authority of Wilwording v. Swenson, (404 U.S. 249) decided by the Supreme Court of the United States on December 14, 1971.' Although eight judges wrote separate opinions, it is clear that the majority of the Court relied primarily on our opinion in the Wilwording case, holding that complaints of state prisoners relating to the conditions of their confinement were cognizable either in federal habeas corpus or under the Civil Rights Act, and that as civil rights actions they were not subject to any requirement of exhaustion of state remedies.

[The Supreme Court] granted certiorari . . . ."

B. Counsel of Record

ACLU Side (Respondent/Appellee): Herman Schwartz of the New York Civil Liberties Union argued the cause for appellees. With him on the brief were Jack Greenberg, Stanley A. Bass, Richard A. Kohn, Melvin L. Wulf of the American Civil Liberties Union Foundation, and Edward I. Koren and Lee Michaels of the New York Civil Liberties Union.

Opposing Side (Petitioner/Appellant): Lillian Z. Cohen, Assistant Attorney General of New York, argued the cause for appellants. With her on the brief were Louis J. Lefkowitz, Attorney General, and Samuel A. Hirshowitz, First Assistant Attorney General.

III. AMICI CURIAE

ACLU Side (Respondent/Appellee)

Brief of amici curiae filed on behalf of the American Bar Association by Robert Meserve, Robert Kutak, William Falsgraf, Daniel Skoler, and Richard Singer.

Opposing Side (Petitioner/Appellant)

Brief of amici curiae filed on behalf of the State of California by Evelle J. Younger, Attorney General, Edward A. Hinz, Jr., Chief Assistant Attorney General, Doris H. Maier and Arlo E. Smith, Assistant Attorneys General, and Derald E. Granberg, Deputy Attorney General.

IV. THE SUPREME COURT'S DECISION

"The problem involves the interrelationship of two important federal laws. . . .

It is clear, not only from the language of ss 2241(c)(3) and 2254(a), but also from the common-law history of the writ, that the essence of habeas corpus is an attack by a person in custody upon the legality of that custody, and that the traditional function of the writ is to secure release from illegal custody. . . .

In the case before us, the respondents' suits in the District Court fell squarely within this traditional scope of habeas corpus. They alleged that the deprivation of their good-conduct-time credits was causing or would cause them to be in illegal physical confinement, i.e., that once their conditional-release date had passed, any further detention of them in prison was unlawful; and they sought restoration of those good-time credits, which, by the time the District Court ruled on their petitions, meant their immediate release from physical custody. . . .

It is beyond doubt, then, that the respondents could have sought and obtained fully effective relief through federal habeas corpus proceedings.

Although conceding that they could have proceeded by way of habeas corpus, the respondents argue that the Court of Appeals was correct in holding that they were nonetheless entitled to bring their suits under s 1983 so as to avoid the necessity of first seeking relief in a state forum. . . .

The broad language of s 1983, however, is not conclusive of the issue before us. . . .

But we need not in this case explore the appropriate limits of habeas corpus as an alternative remedy to a proper action under s 1983. That question is not before us. What is involved here is the extent to which s 1983 is a permissible alternative to the traditional remedy of habeas corpus. Upon that question, we hold today that when a state prisoner is challenging the very fact or duration of his physical imprisonment, and the relief he seeks is a determination that he is entitled to immediate release or a speedier release from that imprisonment, his sole federal remedy is a writ of habeas corpus. Accordingly, we reverse the judgment before us."

V. JUSTICE VOTE

3 Pro ACLU Side vs. 6 Con Opposing Side

ACLU Side (Respondent/Appellee)

1. Marshall, T. – Joined Brennan's dissent
2. Brennan, W. – Wrote dissenting opinion
3. Douglas, W. – Joined Brennan's dissent

Opposing Side (Petitioner/Appellant)

1. Stewart, P. – Wrote majority opinion
2. White, B. – Joined majority opinion
3. Burger, W. – Joined majority opinion
4. Blackmun, H. – Joined majority opinion
5. Powell, L. – Joined majority opinion
6. Rehnquist, W. – Joined majority opinion

VI. A WIN OR LOSS FOR THE ACLU?

The ACLU served as counsel for appellees urging affirmance of the judgment of the Court of Appeals; the Supreme Court reversed, in a 6-3 vote, giving the ACLU an apparent loss.

306. Frontiero v. Richardson

(Decided May 14, 1973; 411 U.S. 677)

I. ISSUE

A. Issues Discussed

Fifth Amendment, discrimination, due process

B. Legal Question Presented

Is the difference of treatment of servicewomen which allows a serviceman to "claim his wife as a 'dependent' without regard to whether she is in fact dependent," while a servicewoman "may not claim her husband as a "dependent" under these programs unless he is in fact dependent upon her for over one-half of his support," a violation of the Due Process Clause of the Fifth Amendment?

C. Supreme Court's Answer

The different treatment violates the Due Process Clause of the Fifth Amendment.

II. CASE SUMMARY

A. Background

"Appellant Sharron Frontiero, a lieutenant in the United States Air Force, sought increased quarters allowances, and housing and medical benefits for her husband, appellant Joseph Frontiero, on the ground that he was her 'dependent.' Although such benefits would automatically have been granted with respect to the wife of a male member of the uniformed services, appellant's application was denied because she failed to demonstrate that her husband was dependent on her for more than one-half of his support. Appellants then commenced this suit, contending that, by making this distinction, the statutes unreasonably discriminate on the basis of sex in violation of the Due Process Clause of the Fifth Amendment. In essence, appellants asserted that the discriminatory impact of the statutes is twofold: first, as a procedural matter, a female member is required to demonstrate her spouse's dependency, while no such burden is imposed upon male members; and, second, as a substantive matter, a male member who does not provide more than one-half of his wife's support receives benefits, while a similarly situated female member is denied such benefits. Appellants therefore sought a permanent injunction against the continued enforcement of these statutes and an order directing the appellees to provide Lieutenant Frontiero with the same housing and medical benefits that a similarly situated male member would receive."

The District Court for the Middle District of Alabama held "the statutes making this distinction" between servicemen and servicewomen constitutional.

The Supreme Court granted certiorari to review the case and reversed the District Court.

B. Counsel of Record/ACLU Attorney

ACLU Side (Petitioner/Appellant): Joseph J. Levin, Jr., argued the cause for appellant.

Ruth Bader Ginsburg argued the cause for the ACLU, as amicus curiae, by special leave of court.

Opposing Side (Respondent/Appellee): Samuel Huntington argued the cause for appellee.

III. AMICI CURIAE

ACLU Side (Petitioner/Appellant)

Brief of amici curiae filed on behalf of the ACLU by Ruth Bader Ginsburg, Melvin L. Wulf, Brenda Feigen Fasteau, and Marc Feigen Fasteau.

Opposing Side (Respondent/Appellee)

No briefs of amici curiae were filed in support of appellee.

IV. THE SUPREME COURT'S DECISION

A. "[T]he statutes operate so as to deny benefits to a female member, such as appellant Sharron Frontiero, who provides less than one-half of her spouse's support, while at the same time granting such benefits to a male member who likewise provides less than one-half of his spouse's support. . . . Moreover, the Government concedes that the differential treatment accorded men and women under these statutes serves no purpose other than mere 'administrative convenience' [and] offers no concrete evidence . . . tending to support its view that such differential treatment in fact saves the Government any money.

[A]ny statutory scheme which draws a sharp line between the sexes, solely for the purpose of achieving administrative convenience, necessarily commands 'dissimilar treatment for men and women who are . . . similarly situated,' and therefore involves the 'very kind of arbitrary legislative choice forbidden by the [Constitution] . . . .' We therefore conclude that, by according differential treatment to male and female members of the uniformed services for the sole purpose of achieving administrative convenience, the challenged statutes violate the Due Process Clause of the Fifth Amendment insofar as they require a female member to prove the dependency of her husband."

The Supreme Court reversed the judgment of the District Court for the Middle District of Alabama.

V. JUSTICE VOTE

8 Pro ACLU Side vs. 1 Con Opposing Side

ACLU Side (Petitioner/Appellant)

1. Brennan, W. – Wrote majority opinion
2. White, B. – Joined majority opinion
3. Marshall, T. – Joined majority opinion
4. Stewart, P. – Wrote concurring opinion
5. Powell, L. – Wrote concurring opinion
6. Burger, W. – Joined Powell's concurrence
7. Blackmun, H. – Joined Powell's concurrence
8. Douglas, W. – Joined majority opinion

Opposing Side (Respondent/Appellee)

1. Rehnquist, W. – Wrote dissenting opinion

VI. A WIN OR LOSS FOR THE ACLU?

The ACLU, as amicus curiae (an ACLU attorney argued though not as counsel of record), urged reversal of the judgment of the District Court for the Middle District of Alabama; the Supreme Court reversed in an 8-1 vote, giving the ACLU an apparent win.

307. Hall v. Cole

(Decided May 21, 1973; 412 U.S. 1)

I. ISSUE

A. Issues Discussed

Governmental authority, unions, attorneys' fees

B. Legal Question Presented

May a court properly award attorney's fees to a successful plaintiff in a suit brought under § 102 of the Labor-Management Reporting and Disclosure Act?

C. Supreme Court's Answer

A court may property award attorney's fees in this circumstance and the District Court did not abuse its discretion in awarding the fees here.

II. CASE SUMMARY

A. Background

"On August 6, 1962, at a regular meeting of the membership of petitioner Seafarers International Union of North America—Atlantic, Gulf, Lakes and Inland Waters District, respondent introduced a set of resolutions alleging various instances of undemocratic actions and shortsighted policies on the part of union officers. The resolutions were defeated and, on November 26, 1962, respondent was expelled from the union on the ground that his presentation of the resolutions violated a union rule proscribing 'deliberate or malicious vilification with regard to the execution or the duties of any office or job.' After exhausting his intra-union remedies, respondent filed this suit under § 102 of the LMRDA, claiming that his expulsion under these circumstances violated his right of free speech as secured by § 101(a)(2) of the Act, 29 U.S.C. § 411(a)(2).

On May 27, 1964, the United States District Court for the Eastern District of New York issued a temporary injunction restoring respondent's membership in the union, and the United States Court of Appeals for the Second Circuit affirmed. Some five years later, the case came on for trial and the District Court, finding a violation of respondent's rights under § 101(a)(2), ordered him permanently reinstated to membership in the union and, although denying respondent's damages claims, granted him counsel fees in the sum of $5,500 against the union. The Court of Appeals affirmed in all respects. [The Supreme Court] granted certiorari limited to the questions whether (1) an award of attorneys' fees is permissible under § 102 of the LMRDA, and (2) if so, whether such an award under the facts of this case constituted an abuse of the District Court's discretion." The Supreme Court affirmed the decision of the Court of Appeals.

B. Counsel of Record/ACLU Attorney

ACLU Side (Respondent/Appellee): Burton H. Hall argued the cause for appellee.

Opposing Side (Petitioner/Appellant): Howard Schulman argued the cause for appellant.

III. AMICI CURIAE

ACLU Side (Respondent/Appellee)

Brief of amici curiae filed on behalf of the ACLU by Melvin L. Wulf and Sanford J. Rosen.

Opposing Side (Petitioner/Appellant)

Brief of amici curiae filed on behalf of the American Federation of Labor and Congress of Industrial Organizations by J. Albert Woll, Robert C. Mayer, Laurence Gold, and Thomas E. Harris.

IV. THE SUPREME COURT'S DECISION

"Although the traditional American rule ordinarily disfavors the allowance of attorneys' fees in the absence of statutory or contractual authorization, federal courts, in the exercise of their equitable powers, may award attorneys' fees when the interests of justice so require. . . .

Thus, it is unquestioned that a federal court may award counsel fees to a successful party when his opponent has acted 'in bad faith, vexatiously, wantonly, or for oppressive reasons.' In this class of cases, the underlying rationale of 'fee shifting' is, of course, punitive, and the essential element in triggering the award of fees is therefore the existence of 'bad faith' on the part of the unsuccessful litigant.

[T]here can be no doubt that, by vindicating his own right of free speech guaranteed by § 101(a)(2) of Title I of the LMRDA, respondent necessarily rendered a substantial service to his union as an institution and to all of its members. When a union member is disciplined for the exercise of any of the rights protected by Title I, the rights of all members of the union are threatened. And, by vindicating his own right, the successful litigant dispels the 'chill' cast upon the rights of others. . . . We must therefore conclude that an award of counsel feel to a successful plaintiff in an action under § 102 of the LMRDA falls squarely within the traditional equitable power of federal courts to award such fees whenever 'overriding considerations indicate the need for such a recovery.' . . .

We therefore hold that the allowance of counsel fees to the successful plaintiff in a suit brought under § 102 of the LMRDA is consistent with both the Act and the historic equitable power of federal courts to grant such relief in the interests of justice. . . .

Moreover, although the presence of 'bad faith' is essential to 'fee-shifting' under a 'punishment' rationale, neither the presence nor absence of 'bad faith' is in any sense dispositive where attorneys' fees are awarded to the successful plaintiff under the 'common benefit' rationale recognized in *Mills* and operative today. Under that theory, counsel fees are granted, not because of the 'bad faith' of the defendant but, rather, because the litigation confers substantial benefits on an ascertainable class of beneficiaries. In that situation, the element of 'bad faith' of the defendant is simply one of many considerations best addressed to the sound discretion of the District Court. Under the facts of this case, we cannot say that the District Court abused that discretion.

The judgment of the Court of Appeals is affirmed."

V. JUSTICE VOTE

6 Pro ACLU Side vs. 2 Con Opposing Side

ACLU Side (Respondent/Appellee)

1. Brennan, W. – Wrote majority opinion
2. Burger, W. – Joined majority opinion
3. Douglas, W. – Joined majority opinion
4. Stewart, P. – Joined majority opinion
5. Blackmun, H. – Joined majority opinion
6. Powell, L. – Joined majority opinion

Opposing Side (Petitioner/Appellant)

1. White, B. – Wrote dissenting opinion
2. Rehnquist, W. – Joined dissenting opinion

Marshall, T – Took no part in the decision

VI. A WIN OR LOSS FOR THE ACLU?

The ACLU filed as amicus curiae urging affirmance; the Supreme Court affirmed the ruling of the Court of Appeals for the Second Circuit in a 6-2 vote, giving the ACLU an apparent win.

308. Schneckloth v. Bustamonte

(Decided May 29, 1973; 412 U.S. 218)

I. ISSUE

A. Issues Discussed

Criminal justice, Fourth Amendment, search and seizure

B. Legal Question Presented

Must a state prove that consent to a search was made with the understanding that it could freely be withheld, in order for the search to be constitutional under the Fourth Amendment of the Constitution?

C. Supreme Court's Answer

The state does not have to specifically prove that consent was given with the understanding that it could freely be withheld in order for a search made with consent to be constitutional.

II. CASE SUMMARY

A. Background

"While on routine patrol in Sunnyvale, California, at approximately 2:40 in the morning, Police Officer James Rand stopped an automobile when he observed that one headlight and its license plate light were burned out. Six men were in the vehicle. Joe Alcala and the respondent, Robert Bustamonte, were in the front seat with Joe Gonzales, the driver. Three older men were seated in the rear. When, in response to the policeman's question, Gonzales could not produce a driver's license, Officer Rand asked if any of the other five had any evidence of identification. Only Alcala produced a license, and he explained that the car was his brother's. After the six occupants had stepped out of the car at the officer's request and after two additional policemen had arrived, Officer Rand asked Alcala if he could search the car. Alcala replied, 'Sure, go ahead.' Prior to the search no one was threatened with arrest and, according to Officer Rand's uncontradicted testimony, it 'was all very congenial at this time.' Gonzales testified that Alcala actually helped in the search of the car, by opening the trunk and glove compartment. In Gonzales' words: '[T]he police officer asked Joe [Alcala], he goes, 'Does the trunk open?' And Joe said, 'Yes.' He went to the car and got the keys and opened up the trunk.' Wadded up under the left rear seat, the police officers found three checks that had previously been stolen from a car wash.

The trial judge denied the motion to suppress, and the checks in question were admitted in evidence at Bustamonte's trial. On the basis of this and other evidence he was convicted, and the California Court of Appeal for the First Appellate District affirmed the conviction. In agreeing that the search and seizure were constitutionally valid, the appellate court applied the standard earlier formulated by the Supreme Court of California in an opinion by then Justice Traynor: 'Whether in a particular case an apparent consent was in fact voluntarily given or was in submission to an express or implied assertion of authority, is a question of fact to be determined in the light of all the circumstances.' The appellate court found that '[i]n the instant case the prosecution met the necessary burden of showing consent . . . since there were clearly circumstances from which the trial court could ascertain that consent had been freely given without coercion or submission to authority. Not only officer Rand, but Gonzales, the driver of the automobile, testified that Alcala's assent to the search of his brother's automobile was freely, even casually given. At the time of the request to search the automobile the atmosphere, according to Rand, was 'congenital' and there has been no discussion of any crime. As noted, Gonzales said Alcala even attempted to aid in the search.' The California Supreme Court denied review.

Thereafter, the respondent sought a writ of habeas corpus in a federal district court. It was denied. On appeal, the Court of Appeals for the Ninth Circuit . . . set aside the District Court's order. The appellate court reasoned that a consent was a waiver of a person's Fourth and Fourteenth Amendment rights, and that the State was under an obligation to demonstrate, not only that the consent had been uncoerced, but that it had been given with an understanding that it could be freely and effectively withheld. Consent could not be found, the court held, solely from the absence of coercion and a verbal expression of assent. Since the District Court had not determined that Alcala had known that his consent could have been withheld and that he could have refused to have his vehicle searched, the Court of Appeals vacated the order denying the writ and remanded the case for further proceedings. We granted certiorari to determine whether the Fourth and Fourteenth Amendments require the showing thought necessary by the Court of Appeals."

The Supreme Court granted certiorari to review the case and reversed the Court of Appeals.

B. Counsel of Record / ACLU Attorney

ACLU Side (Respondent / Appellee): Stuart P. Tobisman argued the cause for appellee, pro hac vice, by special leave of court.

Opposing Side (Petitioner / Appellant): Robert R. Granucci, Deputy Attorney General of California, argued the cause for appellant.

III. AMICI CURIAE

ACLU Side (Respondent / Appellee)

Brief of amici curiae filed on behalf of the ACLU, et al., by Melvin L. Wulf, Sanford J. Rosen, Joel M. Gora, A. L. Wirin, Fred Okrand, and Lawrence R. Sperber.

Opposing Side (Petitioner / Appellant)

Brief of amici curiae filed on behalf of the State of Illinois, et al., by William J. Scott, Attorney General of Illinois, James B. Zagel and Jayne A. Carr, Assistant Attorneys General, and Fred Inbau.

IV. THE SUPREME COURT'S DECISION

"'The notion of 'voluntariness,'' Mr. Justice Frankfurter once wrote, 'is itself an amphibian.' It cannot be taken literally to mean a 'knowing' choice. 'Except where a person is unconscious or drugged or otherwise lacks capacity for conscious choice, all incriminating statements—even those made under brutal treatment—are 'voluntary' in the sense of representing a choice of alternatives. . . . Under such a test, virtually no statement would be voluntary because very few people give incriminating statements in the absence of official action of some kind.' It is thus evident that neither linguistics nor epistemology will provide a ready definition of the meaning of 'voluntariness.' . . .

Similar considerations lead us to agree with the courts of California that the question whether a consent to a search was in fact 'voluntary' or was the product of duress or coercion, express or implied, is a question of fact to be determined from the totality of all the circumstances. While knowledge of the right to refuse consent is one factor to be taken into account, the government need not establish such knowledge as the sine qua non of an effective consent. As with police questioning, two competing concerns must be accommodated in determining the meaning of a 'voluntary' consent—the legitimate need for such searches and the equally important requirement of assuring the absence of coercion. . . .

In this case, there is no evidence of any inherently coercive tactics—either from the nature of the police questioning or the environment in which it took place. . . . There is no reason to believe, under circumstances such as are present here, that the response to a policeman's question is presumptively coerced; and there is, therefore, no reason to reject the traditional test for determining the voluntariness of a person's response. . . . The traditional definition of voluntariness we accept today has always taken into account evidence of minimal schooling, low intelligence, and the lack of any effective warnings to a person of his rights; and the voluntariness of any statement taken under those conditions has been carefully scrutinized to determine whether it was in fact voluntarily given. . . .

We hold only that when the subject of a search is not in custody and the State attempts to justify a search on the basis of his consent, the Fourth and Fourteenth Amendments require that it demonstrate that the consent was in fact voluntarily given, and not the result of duress or coercion, express or implied. Voluntariness is a question of fact to be determined from all the circumstances, and while the subject's knowledge of a right to refuse is a factor to be taken into account, the prosecution is not required to demonstrate such knowledge as a prerequisite to establishing a voluntary consent. Because the California court followed these principles in affirming the respondent's conviction, and because the Court of Appeals for the Ninth Circuit in remanding for an evidentiary hearing required more, its judgment must be reversed."

V. JUSTICE VOTE

3 Pro ACLU Side vs. 6 Con Opposing Side

ACLU Side (Respondent / Appellee)

1. Douglas, W. – Wrote dissenting opinion
2. Marshall, T. – Wrote dissenting opinion
3. Brennan, W. – Wrote dissenting opinion

Opposing Side (Petitioner / Appellant)

1. Stewart, P. – Wrote majority opinion
2. Burger, W. – Joined Powell's concurrence
3. White, B. – Joined majority opinion
4. Blackmun, H. – Wrote concurring opinion
5. Powell, L. – Wrote concurring opinion
6. Rehnquist, W. – Joined Powell's concurrence

VI. A WIN OR LOSS FOR THE ACLU?

The ACLU filed as amicus curiae urging affirmance; the Supreme Court reversed the ruling of the Court of Appeals for the Ninth Circuit in a 6-3 vote, giving the ACLU an apparent loss.

309. Cupp v. Murphy

(Decided May 29, 1973; 412 U.S. 291)

I. ISSUE

A. Issues Discussed

Criminal justice, Fourth Amendment, Fourteenth Amendment, warrantless searches

B. Legal Question Presented

Was it a violation of the Fourth and Fourteenth Amendments for police officers to search the suspect without obtaining a warrant to do so?

C. Supreme Court's Answer

The search without a warrant was not a violation of the Fourth and Fourteenth Amendments in this circumstance.

II. CASE SUMMARY

A. Background

"The respondent, Daniel Murphy, was convicted by a jury in an Oregon court of the second-degree murder of his wife. The victim died by strangulation in her home in the city of Portland, and abrasions and lacerations were found on her throat. There was no sign of a break-in or robbery. Word of the murder was sent to the respondent, who was not then living with his wife. Upon receiving the message, Murphy promptly telephoned the Portland police and voluntarily came into Portland for questioning. Shortly after the respondent's arrival at the station house, where he was met by retained counsel, the police noticed a dark spot on the respondent's finger. Suspecting that the spot might be dried blood and knowing that evidence of strangulation is often found under the assailant's fingernails, the police asked Murphy if they could take a sample of scrapings from his fingernails. He refused. Under protest and without a warrant, the police proceeded to take the samples, which turned out to contain traces of skin and blood cells, and fabric from the victim's nightgown. This incriminating evidence was admitted at the trial.

The respondent appealed his conviction, claiming that the fingernail scrapings were the product of an unconstitutional search under the Fourth and Fourteenth Amendments. The Oregon Court of Appeals affirmed the conviction, and we denied certiorari. Murphy then commenced the present action for federal habeas corpus relief. The District Court, in an unreported decision, denied the habeas petition, and the Court of Appeals for the Ninth Circuit reversed."

The Supreme Court granted certiorari to review the case and reversed.

B. Counsel of Record/ACLU Attorney

ACLU Side (Respondent/Appellee): Howard R. Lonergan argued the cause for appellee.

Opposing Side (Petitioner/Appellant): Thomas H. Denney, Assistant Attorney General of Oregon, argued the cuase for appellant.

III. AMICI CURIAE

ACLU Side (Respondent/Appellee)

Brief of amici curiae filed on behalf of the ACLU by Melvin L. Wulf, Burt Neuborne, and Joel M. Gora.

Opposing Side (Petitioner/Appellant)

Brief of amici curiae filed on behalf of Americans for Effective Law Enforcement, Inc., et al., by Alan S. Ganz, Frank Carrington, Ronald E. Sherk, and Fred E. Inbau.

IV. THE SUPREME COURT'S DECISION

"We believe this search was constitutionally permissible under the principles of Chimel v. California. Chimel stands in a long line of cases recognizing an exception to the warrant requirement when a search is incident to a valid arrest. The basis for this exception is that when an arrest is made, it is reasonable for a police officer to expect the arrestee to use any weapons he may have and to attempt to destroy any incriminating evidence then in his possession. The Court recognized in Chimel that the scope of a warrantless search must be commensurate with the rationale that excepts the search from the warrant requirement. Thus, a warrantless search incident to arrest, the Court held in Chimel, must be limited to the area 'into which an arrestee might reach.'

Where there is no formal arrest, as in the case before us, a person might well be less hostile to the police and less likely to take conspicuous, immediate steps to destroy incriminating evidence on his person. Since he knows he is going to be released, he might be likely instead to be concerned with diverting attention away from himself. Accordingly, we do not hold that a full *Chimel* search would have been justified in this case without a formal arrest and without a warrant. But the respondent was not subjected to such a search.

At the time Murphy was being detained at the station house, he was obviously aware of the detectives' suspicions. Though he did not have the full warning of official suspicion that a formal arrest provides, Murphy was sufficiently apprised of his suspected role in the crime to motivate him to attempt to destroy what evidence he could without attracting further attention. Testimony at trial indicated that after he refused to consent to the taking of fingernail samples, he put his hands behind his back and appeared to rub them together. He then put his hands in his pockets, and a 'metallic sound, such as keys or change rattling' was heard. . . .

On the facts of this case, considering the existence of probable cause, the very limited intrusion undertaken incident to the station house detention, and the ready destructibility of the evidence, we cannot say that this search violated the Fourth and Fourteenth Amendments. Accordingly, the judgment of the Court of Appeals is reversed."

V. JUSTICE VOTE

2 Pro ACLU Side vs. 7 Con Opposing Side

ACLU Side (Respondent/Appellee)

1. Douglas, W. – Wrote dissenting opinion
2. Brennan, W. – Wrote dissenting opinion

Opposing Side (Petitioner/Appellant)

1. Stewart, P. – Wrote majority opinion
2. White, B. – Wrote concurring opinion
3. Marshall, T. – Wrote concurring opinion
4. Blackmun, H. – Wrote concurring opinion
5. Burger, W. – Joined Blackmun's concurrence, joinsed Powell's concurrence
6. Powell, L. – Wrote concurring opinion
7. Rehnquist, W. – Joined Powell's concurrence

VI. A WIN OR LOSS FOR THE ACLU?

The ACLU filed as amicus curiae urging affirmance; the Supreme Court reversed the ruling of the Court of Appeals for the Ninth Circuit in a 7-2 vote, giving the ACLU an apparent loss.

310. Vlandis v. Kline

(Decided June 11, 1973; 412 U.S. 441)

I. ISSUE

A. Issues Discussed

Fourteenth Amendment, due process, state's rights

B. Legal Question Presented

Does Connecticut's statutory definition of residents and nonresidents for state university students violate the Due Process Clause of the Fourteenth Amendment?

C. Supreme Court's Answer

The irrebuttable and permanent presumption of nonresidence violates the Due Process Clause, but states are permitted to create other residence requirements for in-state tuition.

II. CASE SUMMARY

A. Background

According to Public Act No. 5 of Connecticut, the state requires nonresident state university students to pay more for tuition and other fees than resident students. The Act provides a permanent and irrebuttable statutory presumption that a student who is not married is considered nonresident if his or her legal address was out of state at any time during the year prior to his or her application for admission. A student who is married and living with his or her spouse is considered nonresident under a permanent and irrebutable presumption if his or her legal address was out of state when he or she applied for admission.

Appellees, university students, claimed that they were bona fide residents of Connecticut, and that § 126 of Public Act No. 5, under which they were classified as nonresidents for purposes of their tuition and fees, infringed their due process and equal protection rights, guaranteed by the Fourteenth Amendment to the Constitution. The District Court found § 126 unconstitutional. Appellant then sought review in the Supreme Court.

The Supreme Court granted certiorari and affirmed.

B. Counsel of Record/ACLU Attorney

ACLU Side (Respondent/Appellee): John A. Dziamba argued the cause for appellee.

Opposing Side (Petitioner/Appellant): John G. Hill, Jr., Assistant Attorney General of Connecticut, argued the cause for appellant.

III. AMICI CURIAE

ACLU Side (Respondent/Appellee)

Brief of amici curiae filed on behalf of the ACLU of Ohio, Inc., by Leonard J. Schwartz.

Opposing Side (Petitioner/Appellant)

Brief of amici curiae filed on behalf of the State of Washington by Slade Gorton, Attorney General, State of Washington, James B. Wilson, Senior Assistant Attorney General, and Gerald L. Coe, Assistant Attorney General.

IV. THE SUPREME COURT'S DECISION

"The State's interest in administrative ease and certainty cannot, in and of itself, save the conclusive presumption from invalidity under the Due Process Clause where there are other reasonable and practicable means of establishing the pertinent facts on which the State's objective is premised. In the situation before us, reasonable alternative means for determining bona fide residence are available. Indeed, one such method has already been adopted by Connecticut; after §126 was invalidated by the District Court, the State established reasonable criteria for evaluating bona fide residence for purposes of tuition and fees at its university system. These criteria, while perhaps more burdensome to apply than an irrebuttable presumption, are certainly sufficient to prevent abuse of the lower, in-state rates by students who come to Connecticut solely to obtain an education.

In sum, since Connecticut purports to be concerned with residency in allocating the rates for tuition and fees in its university system, it is forbidden by the Due Process Clause to deny an individual the resident rates on the basis of a permanent and irrebuttable presumption of nonresidence, when that presumption is not necessarily or universally true, in fact, and when the State has reasonable alternative means of making the crucial determination. Rather, standards of due process require that the State allow such an individual the opportunity to present evidence showing that he is a bona fide resident entitled to the in-state rates. Since § 126 precluded the appellees from ever rebutting the presumption that they were nonresidents of Connecticut, that statute operated to deprive them of a significant amount of their money without due process of law. . . .

Our holding today should in no wise be taken to mean that Connecticut must classify the students in its university system as residents, for purposes of tuition and fees, just because they go to school there. Nor should our decision be construed to deny a State the right to impose on a student, as one element in demonstrating bona fide residence, a reasonable durational residency requirement, which can be met while in student status. We fully recognize that a State has a legitimate interest in protecting and preserving the quality of its colleges and universities and the right of its own bona fide residents to attend such institutions on a preferential tuition basis.

We hold only that a permanent irrebuttable presumption of nonresidence—the means adopted by Connecticut to preserve that legitimate interest—is violative of the Due Process Clause, because it provides no opportunity for students who applied from out of State to demonstrate that they have become bona fide Connecticut residents. The State can establish such reasonable criteria for in-state status as to make virtually certain that students who are not, in fact, bona fide residents of the State, but who have come there solely for educational purposes, cannot take advantage of the in-state rates. . . .

Because we hold that the permanent irrebuttable presumption of nonresidence . . . violates the Due Process Clause of the Fourteenth Amendment, the judgment of the District Court is affirmed."

V. JUSTICE VOTE

6 Pro ACLU Side vs. 3 Con Opposing Side

ACLU Side (Respondent/Appellee)

1. Stewart, P. – Wrote majority opinion
2. Brennan, W. – Joined Marshall's concurring opinion
3. White, B. – Wrote concurring opinion
4. Blackmun, H. - Joined majority opinion
5. Powell, L. – Joined majority opinion
6. Marshall, T. – Wrote concurring opinion

Opposing Side (Petitioner/Appellant)

1. Douglas, W. – Joined Rehnquist's dissent
2. Burger, W. – Wrote dissenting opinion, joined Rehnquist's dissent
3. Rehnquist, W. – Wrote dissenting opinion, joined Burger's dissent

VI. A WIN OR LOSS FOR THE ACLU?

The ACLU filed as amicus curiae urging affirmance; the Supreme Court affirmed the ruling of the District Court in a 6-3 vote, giving the ACLU an apparent win.

311. Gilligan v. Morgan

(Decided June 21, 1973; 413 U.S. 1)

I. ISSUE

A. Issues Discussed

Civil procedure, federal

B. Legal Question Presented

"'Was there and is there a pattern of training, weaponry and orders in the Ohio National Guard which singly or together require or make inevitable the use of fatal force in suppressing civilian disorders when the total circumstances at the critical time are such that nonlethal force would suffice to restore order and the use of lethal force is not reasonably necessary?'"

C. Supreme Court's Answer

"In concluding that no justiciable controversy is presented, it should be clear that we neither hold nor imply that the conduct of the National Guard is always beyond judicial review or that there may not be accountability in a judicial forum for violations of law for specific unlawful conduct by military personnel, whether by way of damages or injunctive relief. We hold only that no such questions are presented in this case.

II. CASE SUMMARY

A. Background

"Respondents, alleging that they were full-time students and officers in the student government at Kent State University in Ohio, filed this action in the District Court on behalf of themselves and all other students on October 15, 1970. The essence of the complaint is that, during a period of civil disorder on and around the University campus in May 1970, the National Guard, called by the Governor of Ohio to preserve civil order and protect public property, violated students' rights of speech and assembly and caused injury to a number of students and death to several, and that the actions of the National Guard were without legal justification. They sought injunctive relief . . . . They also sought a declaratory judgment that s 2923.55 of the Ohio Revised Code is unconstitutional. The District Court held that the complaint failed to state a claim upon which relief could be granted and dismissed the suit. The Court of Appeals unanimously affirmed the District Court's dismissal with respect to injunctive relief against the Governor's 'premature' employment of the Guard on future occasions and with respect to the validity of the state statute. At the same time, however, the Court of Appeals, with one judge dissenting, held that the complaint stated a cause of action with respect to one issue which was remanded to the District Court with directions to resolve the following question:

'Was there and is there a pattern of training, weaponry and orders in the Ohio National Guard which singly or together require or make inevitable the use of fatal force in suppressing civilian disorders when the total circumstances at the critical time are such that nonlethal force would suffice to restore order and the use of lethal force is not reasonably necessary?'

[The Supreme Court] granted certiorari to review the action of the Court of Appeals."

B. Counsel of Record

ACLU Side (Respondent/Appellee): Michael E. Geltner of the American Civil Liberties Union of Ohio Foundation, Inc., argued the cause for appellees. With him on the briefs were Leonard J. Schwartz of the American Civil Liberties

Union of Ohio Foundation, Inc., Melvin L. Wulf, Sanford Jay Rosen, and Joel M. Gora of the American Civil Liberties Union Foundation, and Stanley K. Laughlin, Jr., and Harold Weinstein.

Opposing Side (Petitioner/Appellant): Thomas V. Martin, Assistant Attorney General of Ohio, argued the cause for appellants. With him on the briefs was William J. Brown, Attorney General. Solicitor General Griswold argued the cause for the United States as amicus curiae.

III. AMICI CURIAE

ACLU Side (Respondent/Appellee)

Brief of amici curiae filed on behalf of the NAACP Legal Defense and Educational Fund, Inc. by Jack Greenberg, James M. Nabrit III, Charles Stephen Ralston, and Drew S. Days III.

Brief of amici curiae filed on behalf of the Law Revision Center by David E. Engdahl.

Opposing Side (Petitioner/Appellant)

Brief of amici curiae filed on behalf of the United States by Solicitor General Griswold, Assistant Attorney General Wood, Robert E. Kopp, Robert W. Berry, and R. Kenly Webster.

IV. THE SUPREME COURT'S DECISION

"We can treat the question of justiciability on the basis of an assumption that respondents' claims . . . are true and could be established by evidence. On that assumption, we address the question whether there is any relief a District Court could appropriately fashion.

It is important to note at the outset that this is not a case in which damages are sought for injuries sustained during the tragic occurrence at Kent State. Nor is it an action seeking a restraining order against some specified and imminently threatened unlawful action. Rather, it is a broad call on judicial power to assume continuing regulatory jurisdiction over the activities of the Ohio National Guard. This far-reaching demand for relief presents important questions of justiciability. . . .

In relying on the Due Process Clause of the Fourteenth Amendment, respondents seem to overlook the explicit command of Art. I, s 8, cl. 16 . . . .

The majority opinion in the Court of Appeals does not mention this very relevant provision of the Constitution. Yet that provision is explicit that the Congress shall have the responsibility for organizing, arming, and disciplining the Militia (now the National Guard), with certain responsibilities being reserved to the respective States. . . .

It would be difficult to think of a clearer example of the type of governmental action that was intended by the Constitution to be left to the political branches directly responsible—as the Judicial Branch is not—to the electoral process. Moreover, it is difficult to conceive of an area of governmental activity in which the courts have less competence. The complex subtle, and professional decisions as to the composition, training, equipping, and control of a military force are essentially professional military judgments, subject *always* to civilian control of the Legislative and Executive Branches. The ultimate responsibility for these decisions is appropriately vested in branches of the government which are periodically subject to electoral accountability. It is this power of oversight and control of military force by elected representatives and officials which underlies our entire constitutional system; the majority opinion of the Court of Appeals failed to give appropriate weight to this separation of powers. . . .

In concluding that no justiciable controversy is presented, it should be clear that we neither hold nor imply that the conduct of the National Guard is always beyond judicial review or that there may not be accountability in a judicial forum for violations of law for specific unlawful conduct by military personnel, whether by way of damages or injunctive relief. We hold only that no such questions are presented in this case. We decline to require a United States District Court to involve itself so directly and so intimately in the task assigned that court by the Court of Appeals.

Reversed."

V. JUSTICE VOTE

4 Pro ACLU Side vs. 5 Con Opposing Side

ACLU Side (Respondent/Appellee)

1. Douglas, W. – Co-wrote dissenting statement
2. Marshall, T. – Co-wrote dissenting statement
3. Brennan, W. – Co-wrote dissenting statement
4. Stewart, P. – Co-wrote dissenting statement

Opposing Side (Petitioner/Appellant)

1. Burger, W. – Wrote majority opinion
2. White, B. – Joined majority opinion
3. Blackmun, H. – Wrote concurring opinion
4. Powell, L. – Joined Blackmun's concurrence
5. Rehnquist, W. – Joined majority opinion

VI. A WIN OR LOSS FOR THE ACLU?

The ACLU served as counsel for appellee urging affirmance of the judgment of the Court of Appeals; the Supreme Court reversed, in a 5-4 vote, giving the ACLU an apparent loss.

312. Miller v. California

(Decided June 21, 1973; 413 U.S. 15)

I. ISSUE

A. Issues Discussed

First Amendment, obscenity, free speech

B. Legal Question Presented

Is the sale and distribution of obscene materials by mail protected under the First Amendment's freedom of speech guarantee?

C. Supreme Court's Answer

Obscene material does not receive First Amendment protection and can be regulated by the state.

II. CASE SUMMARY

A. Background

"Appellant conducted a mass mailing campaign to advertise the sale of illustrated books, euphemistically called 'adult' material. After a jury trial, he was convicted of violating

California Penal Code § 311.2(a), a misdemeanor, by knowingly distributing obscene matter, and the Appellate Department, Superior Court of California, County of Orange, summarily affirmed the judgment without opinion. Appellant's conviction was specifically based on his conduct in causing five unsolicited advertising brochures to be sent through the mail in an envelope addressed to a restaurant in Newport Beach, California. The envelope was opened by the manager of the restaurant and his mother. They had not requested the brochures; they complained to the police."

The Supreme Court granted certiorari to review the case, vacated the judgment, and remanded the case.

B. Counsel of Record / ACLU Attorney

ACLU Side (Petitioner / Appellant): Burton Marks argued the cause for appellant.

Opposing Side (Respondent / Appellee): Michael R. Capizzi argued the cause for appellee.

III. AMICI CURIAE

ACLU Side (Petitioner / Appellant)

Brief of amici curiae filed on behalf of the ACLU of Southern California, et al., by Samuel Rosenwein, A. L. Wirin, Fred Okrand, Laurence R. Sperber, Melvin L. Wulf, and Joel M. Gora.

Opposing Side (Respondent / Appellee)

No briefs of amici curiae were filed in support of appellee.

IV. THE SUPREME COURT'S DECISION

"The basic guidelines for the trier of fact must be: (a) whether 'the average person, applying contemporary community standards' would find that the work, taken as a whole, appeals to the prurient interest; (b) whether the work depicts or describes, in a patently offensive way, sexual conduct specifically defined by the applicable state law; and (c) whether the work, taken as a whole, lacks serious literary, artistic, political, or scientific value. . . .

In sum, we (a) reaffirm the *Roth* holding that obscene material is not protected by the First Amendment; (b) hold that such material can be regulated by the States, subject to . . . specific safeguards . . . , without a showing that the material is 'utterly without redeeming social value'; and (c) hold that obscenity is to be determined by applying 'contemporary community standards,' not 'national standards.' The judgment of the Appellate Department of the Superior Court, Orange County, California, is vacated and the case remanded to that court for further proceedings not inconsistent with the First Amendment standards established by this opinion."

V. JUSTICE VOTE

4 Pro ACLU Side vs. 5 Con Opposing Side

ACLU Side (Petitioner / Appellant)

1. Douglas, W. – Wrote dissenting opinion
2. Brennan, W. – Wrote dissenting opinion
3. Stewart, P. – Joined Brennan's dissent
4. Marshall, T. – Joined Brennan's dissent

Opposing Side (Respondent / Appellee)

1. Burger, W. – Wrote majority opinion
2. White, B. – Joined majority opinion
3. Blackmun, H. – Joined majority opinion
4. Powell, L. – Joined majority opinion
5. Rehnquist, W. – Joined majority opinion

VI. A WIN OR LOSS FOR THE ACLU?

The ACLU, as amicus curiae, urged reversal of the judgment of the Superior Court of California, County of Orange; the Supreme Court vacated and remanded in a 5-4 vote, giving the ACLU an apparent loss.

313. United States v. 12 200-Foot Reels of Super 8mm. Film

(Decided June 21, 1973; 413 U.S. 123)

I. ISSUE

A. Issues Discussed

First Amendment, obscenity

B. Legal Question Presented

"[W]hether the United States may constitutionally prohibit importation of obscene material which the importer claims is for private, personal use and possession only."

C. Supreme Court's Answer

The United States may constitutionally prohibit importation of obscene material even when it is for the importer's private, personal use.

II. CASE SUMMARY

A. Background

"On April 2, 1970, the claimant Paladini sought to carry movie films, color slides, photographs, and other printed and graphic material into the United States from Mexico. The materials were seized as being obscene by customs officers at a port of entry, Los Angeles Airport, and made the subject of a forfeiture action under 19 U.S.C. § 1305(a)." The statute prohibits all persons from "importing into the United States from any foreign country . . . any obscene book, pamphlet, paper, writing, advertisement, circular, print, picture, drawing, or other representation, figure, or image on or of paper or other material, or any cast, instrument, or other article which is obscene or immoral." Paladini claimed he had a First Amendment privilege to the materials because they were for his private, personal use.

The District Court for the Central District of California held that the statute was "unconstitutional on its face" and dismissed the United States government's forfeiture action.

The Supreme Court granted certiorari to review the case, and vacated and remanded the case.

B. Counsel of Record/ACLU Attorney

ACLU Side (Respondent/Appellee): Thomas H. Kuchel, by invitation of the Court argued the cause in support of the lower court's decision.

Opposing Side (Petitioner/Appellant): Solicitor General Erwin N. Griswold argued the cause for the United States.

III. AMICI CURIAE

ACLU Side (Respondent/Appellee)

Brief of amici curiae filed on behalf of the ACLU by Melvin L. Wulf and Joel M. Gora.

Brief of amici curiae filed on behalf of the First Amendment Lawyers' Association by Joel Hirschhorn, Ralph J. Schwartz, Jr., and Mel S. Friedman.

Brief of amici curiae filed on behalf of Christopher W. Walker by Harvey A. Silverglate and Roger C. Park.

Opposing Side (Petitioner/Appellant)

No briefs of amici curiae were filed in support of appellant.

IV. THE SUPREME COURT'S DECISION

"The attack on the overbreadth of the statute is thus foreclosed, but, independently, we should note that it is extremely difficult to control the uses to which obscene material is put once it enters this country. Even single copies, represented to be for personal use, can be quickly and cheaply duplicated by modern technology thus facilitating wide-scale distribution. While it is true that a large volume of obscene material on microfilm could rather easily be smuggled into the United States by mail, or otherwise, and could be enlarged or reproduced for commercial purposes, Congress is not precluded from barring some avenues of illegal importation because avenues exist that are more difficult to regulate.

As this case came to us on the District Court's summary dismissal of the forfeiture action, no determination of the obscenity of the materials involved has been made. We have today arrived at standards for testing the constitutionality of state legislation regulating obscenity. These standards are applicable to federal legislation. The judgment of the District Court is vacated and the case is remanded for further proceedings consistent with this opinion, *Miller v. California*, supra, and *United States v. Orito*, supra, both decided today."

V. JUSTICE VOTE

4 Pro ACLU Side vs. 5 Con Opposing Side

ACLU Side (Respondent/Appellee)

1. Douglas, W. – Wrote dissenting opinion
2. Brennan, W. – Wrote dissenting opinion
3. Marshall, T. – Joined Brennan's dissent
4. Stewart, P. – Joined Brennan's dissent

Opposing Side (Petitioner/Appellant)

1. Burger, W. – Wrote majority opinion
2. White, B. – Joined majority opinion
3. Blackmun, H. – Joined majority opinion
4. Powell, L. – Joined majority opinion
5. Rehnquist, W. – Joined majority opinion

VI. A WIN OR LOSS FOR THE ACLU?

The ACLU filed as amicus curiae urging affirmance; the Supreme Court vacated the District Court's judgment in a 5-4 vote, giving the ACLU an apparent loss.

314. United States v. Orito

(Decided June 21, 1973; 413 U.S. 139)

I. ISSUE

A. Issues Discussed

First Amendment, obscenity, Ninth Amendment

B. Legal Question Presented

Did appellee's indictment for transporting obscene materials by common carrier in interstate commerce violate his First and Ninth Amendments rights?

C. Supreme Court's Answer

The Supreme Court vacated the lower court's judgment and remanded the case for the District Court to determine "the sufficiency of the indictment in light of" prior cases and the opinion of the Court.

II. CASE SUMMARY

A. Background

Appellee Orito was charged with knowingly transporting obscene material by common carrier in interstate commerce, in violation of 18 U.S.C. § 1462. The statute made it a federal crime to "'knowingly transport . . . obscene, lewd, lascivious, and filthy materials.'" The materials Mr. Orito had in possession included 83 reels of film. Orito "moved to dismiss the indictment on the ground that the statute violated his First and Ninth Amendment rights."

The District Court for the Eastern District of Wisconsin granted his motion to dismiss and held "that the statute was unconstitutionally overbroad since it failed to distinguish between 'public' and 'non-public' transportation of obscene material." The U.S. government appealed the case to the U.S. Supreme Court.

The Supreme Court granted certiorari to review the case, vacated the decision, and remanded the case.

B. Counsel of Record/ACLU Attorney

ACLU Side (Respondent/Appellee): James M. Shellow argued the cause for appellee.

Opposing Side (Petitioner/Appellant): Solicitor General Erwin N. Griswold reargued the cause for the United States. R. Kent

Greenawalt argued the cause for the United States on the original argument.

III. AMICI CURIAE

ACLU Side (Respondent/Appellee)

Brief of amici curiae filed on behalf of the ACLU by Melvin L. Wulf and Joel M. Gora.

Opposing Side (Petitioner/Appellant)

No briefs of amici curiae were filed in support of appellant.

IV. THE SUPREME COURT'S DECISION

"Given (a) that obscene material is not protected under the First Amendment, Miller v. California, supra; Roth v. United States, supra, (b) that the Government has a legitimate interest in protecting the public commercial environment by preventing such material from entering the stream of commerce . . . and (c) that no constitutionally protected privacy is involved . . . we cannot say that the Constitution forbids comprehensive federal regulation of interstate transportation of obscene material merely because such transport may be by private carriage, or because the material is intended for the private use of the transporter. That the transporter has an abstract proprietary power to shield the obscene material from all others and to guard the material with the same privacy as in the home is not controlling. Congress may regulate on the basis of the natural tendency of material in the home being kept private and the contrary tendency once material leaves that area, regardless of a transporter's professed intent. Congress could reasonably determine such regulation to be necessary to effect permissible federal control of interstate commerce in obscene material, based as that regulation is on a legislatively determined risk of ultimate exposure to juveniles or to the public and the harm that exposure could cause. . . .

The decision of the District Court is therefore vacated and the case is remanded for reconsideration of the sufficiency of the indictment in light of *Miller v. California*, supra; *United States v. 12 200-Ft. Reels*, supra; and this opinion."

V. JUSTICE VOTE

4 Pro ACLU Side vs. 5 Con Opposing Side

ACLU Side (Respondent/Appellee)

1. Douglas, W. – Wrote dissenting opinion
2. Brennan, W. – Wrote dissenting opinion
3. Marshall, T. – Joined Brennan's dissent
4. Stewart, P. – Joined Brennan's dissent

Opposing Side (Petitioner/Appellant)

1. Burger, W. – Wrote majority opinion
2. White, B. – Joined majority opinion
3. Blackmun, H. – Joined majority opinion
4. Powell, L. – Joined majority opinion
5. Rehnquist, W. – Joined majority opinion

VI. A WIN OR LOSS FOR THE ACLU?

The ACLU filed as amicus curiae urging affirmance; the Supreme Court vacated the District Court's judgment in a 5-4 vote giving the ACLU an apparent loss.

315. Keyes v. School District No. 1

(Decided June 21, 1973; 413 U.S. 189)

I. ISSUE

A. Issues Discussed

Civil rights, race, Fourteenth Amendment

B. Legal Question Presented

Did school segregation in Denver involve all of the city's schools and violate the Equal Protection Clause of the Fourteenth Amendment?

C. Supreme Court's Answer

The finding of segregation in one area in Denver creates a prima facie case for segregation in other parts of the city that respondents must rebut on remand.

II. CASE SUMMARY

A. Background

The respondent School Board adopted three resolutions designed to desegregate schools of the Park Hill area in Denver, Colorado. After an election, the majority of the newly elected school board members opposed the desegregation resolutions, and subsequently rescinded and replaced them with a "voluntary student transfer program."

Petitioners, parents of Denver schoolchildren, filed a suit in the District Court "requesting an injunction against the rescission of the resolutions and an order directing that the respondent School Board desegregate and afford equal educational opportunity 'for the School District as a whole.'"

The district court held that the Park Hill region of the Denver School system was segregated, and ordered remedies to desegregate the area. After this success, "petitioners pressed their prayer that the District Court order desegregation of all segregated schools in the city of Denver." The District Court was reluctant to extend the ruling beyond Park Hill without an individualized showing of segregation in each part of the city. "Under this restrictive approach, the District Court concluded that petitioners' evidence of intentionally discriminatory School Board action in areas of the district other than Park Hill was insufficient to 'dictate the conclusion that this is de jure segregation which calls for an all-out effort to desegregate. It is more like de facto segregation, with respect to which the rule is that the court cannot order desegregation in order to provide a better balance.'

Nevertheless, the District Court went on to hold that the proofs established that the segregated core city schools were educationally inferior to the predominantly 'white' or 'Anglo' schools in other parts of the district—that is, 'separate facilities . . . unequal in the quality of education provided.' Thus, the court held that, under the doctrine of *Plessy v. Ferguson*, respondent School Board constitutionally 'must at a minimum . . . offer an equal educational opportunity,' and, therefore, although all-out desegregation 'could not be decreed, . . . the only feasible and constitutionally acceptable program—the only program which furnishes anything approaching substantial equality— is a system of desegregation and integration which provides compensatory education in an integrated environment."

The Court of Appeals for the Tenth Circuit "sustained the District Court's finding that the Board had engaged in an unconstitutional policy of deliberate racial segregation with respect to the Park Hill schools and affirmed the Final Decree in that respect. As to the core city schools, however, the Court of Appeals reversed the legal determination of the District Court that those schools were maintained in violation of the Fourteenth Amendment because of the unequal educational opportunity afforded, and therefore set aside so much of the Final Decree as required desegregation and educational improvement programs for those schools."

The Supreme Court granted certiorari solely to review the portion of the Final Decree set aside by the Court of Appeals and vacated and remanded.

B. Counsel of Record/ACLU Attorney

ACLU Side (Petitioner/Appellant): James M. Nabrit III and Gordon G. Greiner argued the cause for appellant.

Opposing Side (Respondent/Appellee): William K. Ris argued the cause for appellee.

III. AMICI CURIAE

ACLU Side (Petitioner/Appellant)

Brief of amici curiae filed on behalf of the ACLU, et al., by Melvin L. Wulf, Sanford Jay Rosen and Edwin S. Kahn.

Additional briefs of amici curiae were filed on behalf of the National Education Association, et al., the Anti-Defamation League of B'nai B'rith, et al., and the Mexican American Legal Defense and Education Fund.

Opposing Side (Respondent/Appellee)

Brief of amici curiae filed on behalf of the State of Indiana by Theodore L. Sendak, Attorney General of Indiana, Wendell C. Hamacher, Deputy Attorney General, and William F. Harvey.

Additional briefs of amici curiae were filed on behalf of the San Diego Unified School District and Robert G. Nelson, et al.

IV. THE SUPREME COURT'S DECISION

"In summary, the District Court on remand, first, will afford respondent School Board the opportunity to prove its contention that the Park Hill area is a separate, identifiable and unrelated section of the school district that should be treated as isolated from the rest of the district. If respondent School Board fails to prove that contention, the District Court, second, will determine whether respondent School Board's conduct over almost a decade after 1960 in carrying out a policy of deliberate racial segregation in the Park Hill schools constitutes the entire school system a dual school system. If the District Court determines that the Denver school system is a dual school system, respondent School Board has the affirmative duty to desegregate the entire system 'root and branch.' If the District Court determines, however, that the Denver school system is not a dual school system by reason of the Board's actions in Park Hill, the court, third, will afford respondent School Board the opportunity to rebut petitioners' prima facie case of intentional segregation in the core city schools raised by the finding of intentional segregation in the Park Hill schools. There, the Board's burden is to show that its policies and practices with respect to school site location, school size, school renovations and additions, student-attendance zones, student assignment and transfer options, mobile classroom units, transportation of students, assignment of faculty and staff, etc., considered together and premised on the Board's so-called 'neighborhood school' concept, either were not taken in effectuation of a policy to create or maintain segregation in the core city schools, or, if unsuccessful in that effort, were not factors in causing the existing condition of segregation in these schools. Considerations of 'fairness' and 'policy' demand no less in light of the Board's intentionally segregative actions. If respondent Board fails to rebut petitioners' prima facie case, the District Court must, as in the case of Park Hill, decree all-out desegregation of the core city schools.

The judgment of the Court of Appeals is modified to vacate instead of reverse the parts of the Final Decree that concern the core city schools, and the case is remanded to the District Court for further proceedings consistent with this opinion."

V. JUSTICE VOTE

7 Pro ACLU Side vs. 1 Con Opposing Side

ACLU Side (Petitioner/Appellant)

1. Brennan, W. – Wrote majority opinion
2. Stewart, P. – Joined majority opinion
3. Blackmun, H. – Joined majority opinion
4. Powell, L. – Wrote opinion concurring in part and dissenting in part
5. Marshall, T. – Joined majority opinion
6. Douglas, W. – Wrote concurring opinion
7. Burger, W. – Concurred in the result

Opposing Side (Respondent/Appellee)

1. Rehnquist, W. – Wrote dissenting opinion

White, B. Took not part in the decision

VI. A WIN OR LOSS FOR THE ACLU?

The ACLU filed as amicus curiae urging reversal; the Supreme Court vacated and remanded the Court of Appeals' judgment in a 7-1 vote, giving the ACLU an apparent win.

316. Pittsburgh Press Co. v. Pittsburg Commission on Human Relations

(Decided June 21, 1973; 413 U.S. 376)

I. ISSUE

A. Issues Discussed

Civil rights, gender, First Amendment

B. Legal Question Presented

Does a city ordinance, forbidding newspapers from carrying "help wanted" advertisements in gender designated columns, violate the freedoms of speech and of the press guaranteed by the First Amendment?

C. Supreme Court's Answer

The ordinance does not violate the First Amendment.

II. CASE SUMMARY

A. Background

The City of Pittsburgh had a Human Relations Ordinance (the Ordinance), which prohibited newspapers from carrying "'help-wanted' advertisements in sex-designated columns except where the employer or advertiser is free to make hiring or employment referral decisions on the basis of sex."

"[T]he National Organization for Women, Inc. (NOW) filed a complaint with the Pittsburgh Commission on Human Relations (the Commission), which is charged with implementing the Ordinance. The complaint alleged that the Pittsburgh Press Co. (Pittsburgh Press) was violating § 8(j) of the Ordinance by 'allowing employers to place advertisements in the male or female columns, when the jobs advertised obviously do not have bona fide occupational qualifications or exceptions . . ..' Finding probable cause to believe that Pittsburgh Press was violating the Ordinance, the Commission held a hearing . . . .

On July 23, 1970, the Commission issued a Decision and Order. . . . The Commission first concluded that § 8(e) of the Ordinance forbade employers, employment agencies, and labor organizations to submit advertisements for placement in sex-designated columns. It then held that Pittsburgh Press, in violation of § 8(j), aided the advertisers by maintaining a sex-designated classification system. After specifically considering and rejecting the argument that the Ordinance violated the First Amendment, the Commission ordered Pittsburgh Press to cease and desist such violations and to utilize a classification system with no reference to sex. This order was affirmed in all relevant respects by the Court of Common Pleas.

On appeal in the Commonwealth Court, the scope of the order was narrowed to allow Pittsburgh Press to carry advertisements in sex-designated columns for jobs exempt from the antidiscrimination provisions of the Ordinance. As pointed out in that court's opinion, the Ordinance does not apply to employers of fewer than five persons, to employers outside the city of Pittsburgh, or to religious, fraternal, charitable, or sectarian organizations, nor does it apply to employment in domestic service or in jobs for which the Commission has certified a bona fide occupational exception. The modified order bars 'all reference to sex in employment advertising column headings, except as may be exempt under said Ordinance, or as may be certified as exempt by said Commission.' The Pennsylvania Supreme Court denied review, and [the Supreme Court] granted certiorari to decide whether, as Pittsburgh Press contends, the modified order violates the First Amendment by restricting its editorial judgment."

The Supreme Court affirmed the decision.

B. Counsel of Record/ACLU Attorney

ACLU Side (Respondent/Appellee): Eugene B. Strassburger, III, argued the cause for appellees the Pittsburgh Commission on Human Relations, et al.

Marjorie H. Matson argued the cause for appellee the National Organization for Women, Inc.

Opposing Side (Petitioner/Appellant): Charles Richard Volk argued the cause for appellant.

III. AMICI CURIAE

ACLU Side (Respondent/Appellee)

Brief of amici curiae filed on behalf of the ACLU, et al., by Norman Dorsen, Ruth Bader Ginsburg, and Jeffrey A. Kay.

Additional briefs of amici curiae were filed on behalf of the United States, the California Fair Employment Practice Commission, the State of New Jersey, the Pennsylvania Commission on the Status of Women, et al., the American Veterans Committee, Inc., et al., the International Association of Official Human Rights Agencies, and the Women's Law Fund, Inc.

Opposing Side (Petitioner/Appellant)

Brief of amici curiae filed on behalf of the American Newspaper Publishers Association by Arthur B. Hanson, W. Frank Stickle, Jr., and Ralph N. Albright, Jr.

IV. THE SUPREME COURT'S DECISION

"Section 8(j) of the Ordinance, the only provision which Pittsburgh Press was found to have violated and the only provision under attack here, makes it unlawful for 'any person . . . to aid . . . in the doing of any act declared to be an unlawful employment practice by this ordinance.' The Commission and the courts below concluded that the practice of placing want ads for non-exempt employment in sex-designated columns did indeed 'aid' employers to indicate illegal sex preferences. The advertisements, as embroidered by their placement, signaled that the advertisers were likely to show an illegal sex preference in their hiring decisions. Any First Amendment interest which might be served by advertising an ordinary commercial proposal and which might arguably outweigh the governmental interest supporting the regulation is altogether absent when the commercial activity itself is illegal and the restriction on advertising is incidental to a valid limitation on economic activity. . . .

The present order does not endanger arguably protected speech. Because the order is based on a continuing course of repetitive conduct, this is not a case in which the Court is asked to speculate as to the effect of publication. Moreover, the order is clear, and sweeps no more broadly than necessary. . . .

We emphasize that nothing in our holding allows government at any level to forbid Pittsburgh Press to publish and distribute advertisements commenting on the Ordinance, the enforcement practices of the Commission, or the propriety of sex preferences in employment. Nor, a fortiori, does our decision authorize any restriction whatever, whether of content or layout, on stories or commentary originated by Pittsburgh Press, its columnists, or its contributors. On the contrary, we reaffirm unequivocally the protection afforded to editorial judgment and to the free expression of views on these and other issues, however controversial. We hold only that the Commission's modified order, narrowly drawn to prohibit placement in sex-designated columns of advertisements for nonexempt job opportunities, does not infringe the First Amendment rights of Pittsburgh Press."

The Supreme Court affirmed the judgment of the lower court.

V. JUSTICE VOTE

5 Pro ACLU Side vs. 4 Con Opposing Side

ACLU Side (Respondent/Appellee)

1. Powell, L. – Wrote majority opinion
2. White, B. – Joined majority opinion
3. Brennan, W. – Joined majority opinion
4. Marshall, T. – Joined majority opinion
5. Rehnquist, W. – Joined majority opinion

Opposing Side (Petitioner/Appellant)

1. Burger, W. – Wrote dissenting opinion
2. Stewart, P. – Wrote dissenting opinion
3. Blackmun, H. – Wrote dissenting opinion
4. Douglas, W. – Wrote dissenting opinion, joined Stewart's dissent

VI. A WIN OR LOSS FOR THE ACLU?

The ACLU filed as amicus curiae affirmance; the Supreme Court affirmed the judgment of the Commonwealth Court of Pennsylvania in a 5-4 vote, giving the ACLU an apparent win.

317. U.S. Civil Service Comm'n v. Nat'l Ass'n of Letter Carriers

(Decided June 25, 1973; 413 U.S. 548)

I. ISSUE

A. Issues Discussed

Federal, civil rights

B. Legal Question Presented

"[W]hether the prohibition in s 9(a) of the Hatch Act, now codified in 5 U.S.C. s 7324(a)(2), against federal employees taking 'an active part in political management or in political campaigns,' is unconstitutional on its face."

C. Supreme Court's Answer

"Even if the provisions forbidding partisan campaign endorsements and speechmaking were to be considered in some respects unconstitutionally overbroad, we would not invalidate the entire statute as the District Court did. The remainder of the statute, as we have said, covers a whole range of easily identifiable and constitutionally proscribable partisan conduct on the part of federal employees, and the extent to which pure expression is impermissibly threatened, if at all, by ss 733.122(a)(10) and (12), does not in our view make the statute substantially overbroad and so invalid on its face."

II. CASE SUMMARY

A. Background

"On December 11, 1972, [the Supreme Court] noted probable jurisdiction of this appeal based on a jurisdictional statement presenting the single question whether the prohibition in s 9(a) of the Hatch Act, now codified in 5 U.S.C. s 7324(a)(2), against federal employees taking 'an active part in political management or in political campaigns,' is unconstitutional on its face. . . .

The case began when the National Association of Letter Carriers, six individual federal employees and certain local Democratic and Republican political committees filed a complaint, asserting on behalf of themselves and all federal employees that 5 U.S.C. s 7324(a)(2) was unconstitutional on its face and seeking an injunction against its enforcement.

Each of the plaintiffs alleged that the Civil Service Commission was enforcing, or threatening to enforce, the Hatch Act's prohibition against active participation in political management or political campaigns with respect to certain defined activity in which that plaintiff desired to engage. . . .

A three-judge court was convened, and the case was tried on both stipulated evidence and oral testimony. The District Court then ruled that s 7234(a)(2) was unconstitutional on its face and enjoined its enforcement."

B. Counsel of Record

ACLU Side (Respondent/Appellee): Thomas C. Matthews, Jr., argued the cause for appellees. With him on the brief were Stephen M. Truitt, Melvin L. Wulf of the American Civil Liberties Union Foundation, Ralph J. Temple of the American Civil Liberties Union Fund for the National Capital Area, and Philip Elman.

Opposing Side (Petitioner/Appellant): Solicitor General Griswold argued the cause for appellants. With him on the briefs were Assistant Attorney General Wood, Andrew L. Frey, Robert E. Kopp, and Anthony L. Mondello.

III. AMICI CURIAE

ACLU Side (Respondent/Appellee)

Brief of amici curiae filed on behalf of the State of Oregon by Lee Johnson, Attorney General, John W. Osburn, Solicitor General, and A. J. Laue and Thomas H. Denney, Assistant Attorneys General.

Brief of amici curiae filed on behalf of the Coalition of American

Public Employees et al. by Stephen J. Pollak, Richard T. Conway, Leo M. Pellerzi, Donald M. Murtha, Robert H. Chanin, A. L. Zwerdling, and Edward J. Hickey, Jr.

Opposing Side (Petitioner/Appellant)

No briefs of amici curiae were filed in support of appellant.

IV. THE SUPREME COURT'S DECISION

"As the District Court recognized, the constitutionality of the Hatch Act's ban on taking an active part in political management or political campaigns has been here before. . . .

We unhesitatingly reaffirm the Mitchell holding that Congress had, and has, the power to prevent Mr. Poole and others like him from holding a party office, working at the polls, and acting as party paymaster for other party workers. An Act of Congress going no farther would in our view unquestionably be valid. So would it be if, in plain and understandable language, the statute forbade activities such as organizing a political party or club; actively participating in fund-raising activities for a partisan candidate or political party; becoming a partisan candidate for, or campaigning for, an elective public office; actively managing the campaign of a partisan candidate for public office; initiating or circulating a partisan nominating petition or soliciting votes for a partisan candidate for public office; or serving as a delegate, alternate or proxy to a political party convention. Our judgment is that neither the First Amendment nor any other provision of the Constitution invalidates a law barring this kind of partisan political conduct by federal employees. . . .

We agree with the basic holding of Mitchell that plainly identifiable acts of political management and political campaigning on the part of federal employees may constitutionally be prohibited. Until now this has been the judgment of the lower federal courts, and we do not understand the District Court in this case to have questioned the constitutionality of a law that was specifically limited to prohibiting the conduct in which Mr. Poole in the Mitchell case admittedly engaged. . . .

But however constitutional the proscription of identifiable partisan conduct in understandable language may be, the District Court's judgment was that s 7324(a)(2) was both unconstitutionally vague and fatally overbroad. Appellees make the same contentions here, but we cannot agree that the section is unconstitutional on its face for either reason. . . .

Even if the provisions forbidding partisan campaign endorsements and speechmaking were to be considered in some respects unconstitutionally overbroad, we would not invalidate the entire statute as the District Court did. The remainder of the statute, as we have said, covers a whole range of easily identifiable and constitutionally proscribable partisan conduct on the part of federal employees, and the extent to which pure expression is impermissibly threatened, if at all, by ss 733.122(a)(10) and (12), does not in our view make the statute substantially overbroad and so invalid on its face.

For the foregoing reasons, the judgment of the District Court is reversed."

V. JUSTICE VOTE

3 Pro ACLU Side vs. 6 Con Opposing Side

ACLU Side (Respondent/Appellee)

1. Marshall, T. – Joined Douglas' dissent
2. Brennan, W. – Joined Douglas' dissent
3. Douglas, W. – Wrote dissenting opinion

Opposing Side (Petitioner/Appellant)

1. White, B. – Wrote majority opinion
2. Stewart, P. – Joined majority opinion
3. Burger, W. – Joined majority opinion
4. Blackmun, H. – Joined majority opinion
5. Powell, L. – Joined majority opinion
6. Rehnquist, W. – Joined majority opinion

VI. A WIN OR LOSS FOR THE ACLU?

The ACLU served as counsel for appellees urging affirmance of the judgment of the U.S. District Court for the District of Columbia; the Supreme Court reversed, in a 6-3 vote, giving the ACLU an apparent loss.

318. In re Griffiths

(Decided June 25, 1973; 413 U.S. 717)

I. ISSUE

A. Issues Discussed

Immigration/citizenship

B. Legal Question Presented

What are "the constraints imposed by the Equal Protection Clause of the Fourteenth Amendment on the qualifications which a State may require for admission to the bar," particularly with regard to non-citizens.

C. Supreme Court's Answer

"In sum, the Committee simply has not established that it must exclude all aliens from the practice of law in order to vindicate its undoubted interest in high professional standards."

II. CASE SUMMARY

A. Background

"This case presents a novel question as to the constraints imposed by the Equal Protection Clause of the Fourteenth Amendment on the qualifications which a State may require for admission to the bar. Appellant, Fre Le Poole Griffiths, is a citizen of the Netherlands who came to the United States in 1965, originally as a visitor. In 1967 she married a citizen of the United States and became a resident of Connecticut. After her graduation from law school, she applied in 1970 for permission to take the Connecticut bar examination. The County Bar Association found her qualified in all respects save that she was not a citizen of the United States as required by Rule 8(1) of the Connecticut Practice Book (1963) and on that account refused to allow her to take the examination.

She then sought judicial relief, asserting that the regulation was unconstitutional but her claim was rejected, first by the Superior Court and ultimately by the Connecticut Supreme Court. [The U.S. Supreme Court] noted probable jurisdiction" to review the case.

B. Counsel of Record

ACLU Side (Petitioner/Appellant): R. David Broiles argued the cause for appellant. With him on the brief were Melvin L. Wulf and Joel M. Gora of the American Civil Liberties Union Foundation.

Opposing Side (Respondent/Appellee): George R. Tiernan argued the cause and filed a brief for the State Bar Examining Committee of Connecticut.

III. AMICI CURIAE

ACLU Side (Petitioner/Appellant)

No briefs of amici curiae were filed in support of appellant.

Opposing Side (Respondent/Appellee)

Brief of amici curiae filed on behalf of the Attorney General of New York by Louis J. Lefkowitz, pro se, Samuel A. Hirshowitz, First Assistant Attorney General, and Daniel M. Cohen, Assistant Attorney General.

IV. THE SUPREME COURT'S DECISION

"We begin by sketching the background against which the State Bar Examining Committee attempts to justify the total exclusion of aliens from the practice of law. . . . In 1873, this Court noted that admission to the practice of law in the courts of a State

'in no sense depends on citizenship of the United States. It has not, as far as we know, ever been made in any State, or in any case, to depend on citizenship at all. . . .' . . .

But shortly thereafter, in 1879, Connecticut established the predecessor to its present rule totally excluding aliens from the practice of law. . . .

Resident aliens, like citizens, pay taxes, support the economy, serve in the Armed Forces, and contribute in myriad other ways to our society. It is appropriate that a State bear a heavy burden when it deprives them of employment opportunities. . . .

We hold that the Committee, acting on behalf of the State, has not carried its burden. The State's ultimate interest here implicated is to assure the requisite qualifications of persons licensed to practice law. It is undisputed that a State has a constitutionally permissible and substantial interest in determining whether an applicant posesses 'the character and general fitness requisite for an attorney and counselor-at-law.' But no question is raised in this case as to appellant's character or general fitness. Rather, the sole basis for disqualification is her status as a resident alien. . . .

Connecticut has wide freedom to gauge on a case-by-case basis the fitness of an applicant to practice law. Connecticut can, and does, require appropriate training and familiarity with Connecticut law. Apart from such tests of competence, it requires a new lawyer to take both an 'attorney's oath' to perform his functions faithfully and honestly and a 'commissioner's oath' to 'support the constitution of the United States, and the constitution of the state of Connecticut.' . . . Moreover, once admitted to the bar, lawyers are subject to continuing scrutiny by the organized bar and the courts. . . . In sum, the Committee simply has not established that it must exclude all aliens from the practice of law in order to vindicate its undoubted interest in high professional standards. . . .

In its brief, the Examining Committee makes another . . . argument in support of Rule 8(1). Its thrust is not that resident aliens lack the attributes necessary to maintain high standards in the legal profession, but rather that lawyers must be citizens almost as a matter of definition. The implication of this analysis is that exclusion of aliens from the legal profession is not subject to any scrutiny under the Equal Protection Clause. . . .

We hold that s 8(1) violates the Equal Protection Clause. The judgment of the Connecticut Supreme Court is reversed, and the case is remanded . . . ."

V. JUSTICE VOTE

7 Pro ACLU Side vs. 2 Con Opposing Side

ACLU Side (Petitioner/Appellant)

1. Powell, L. – Wrote majority opinion
2. White, B. – Joined majority opinion
3. Marshall, T. – Joined majority opinion
4. Brennan, W. – Joined majority opinion
5. Stewart, P. – Joined majority opinion
6. Blackmun, H. – Joined majority opinion
7. Douglas, W. – Joined majority opinion

Opposing Side (Respondent/Appellee)

1. Burger, W. – Wrote dissenting opinion
2. Rehnquist, W. – Wrote dissenting opinion, joined Burger's dissent

VI. A WIN OR LOSS FOR THE ACLU?

The ACLU served as counsel for appellant urging reversal of the judgment of the Connecticut Supreme Court; the U.S. Supreme Court reversed, in a 7-2 vote, giving the ACLU an apparent win.

319. Schlesinger v. Holtzman

(Decided August 4, 1973; 414 U.S. 1321)

I. ISSUE

A. Issues Discussed

Military, civil procedure

B. Legal Question Presented

Whether to stay the lower court's order.

C. Supreme Court's Answer

"[T]he order of the District Court dated July 25, 1973, is hereby stayed pending further order by this Court."

II. CASE SUMMARY

A. Background

"Application for stay of District Court's order enjoining Defense Department officials from 'participating in any way in military activities in or over Cambodia or releasing any bombs which may fall in Cambodia,' the only order extant in this litigation in view of Mr. Justice Douglas' order vacating Court of Appeals' stay of District Court order"

B. Counsel of Record

ACLU Side (Petitioner/Appellant): Attorneys for case before lower court: Burt Neuborne and Leon Friedman, American Civil Liberties Union, and Norman Siegel and Paul G. Chevigny, New York Civil Liberties Union.[1]

Opposing Side (Respondent/Appellee): Attorneys for case before lower court: James Dunlop Porter, Jr., Assistant U. S. Attorney, and Robert A. Morse, U.S. Attorney.[2]

III. AMICI CURIAE

ACLU Side (Petitioner/Appellant)

No briefs of amici curiae were filed in support of appellant.

Opposing Side (Respondent/Appellee)

No briefs of amici curiae were filed in support of appellee.

IV. THE SUPREME COURT'S DECISION

"Since the action of the Court of Appeals in granting a stay is set aside, the only order extant in this case is the order of the District Court dated July 25, 1973. The instant application calls on me to deal directly with that order of the District Court.

In the ordinary course, a Justice acting as a Circuit Justice would defer acting with respect to a District Court order until the Court of Appeals had acted, but in the present circumstances the Court of Appeals has already acted and the consequence of the order of Mr. Justice DOUGLAS is to set aside the Court of Appeals order.

The consequence of the Court of Appeals' stay order of August 1, 1973, was to preserve the status quo until it could act on the merits. The Court of Appeals, having originally expedited a hearing on the merits to August 13, 1973, has since further expedited the hearing on the merits to August 8, 1973.

Now therefore, the order of the District Court dated July 25, 1973, is hereby stayed pending further order by this Court."

V. JUSTICE VOTE

8 Pro ACLU Side vs. 1 Con Opposing Side

ACLU Side (Petitioner/Appellant)

1. Marshall, T. – Wrote majority opinion
2. Blackmun, H. – Wrote majority opinion
3. Brennan, W. – Joined majority opinion
4. Stewart, P. – Joined majority opinion
5. Burger, W. – Joined majority opinion
6. Powell, L. – Joined majority opinion
7. White, B. – Joined majority opinion
8. Rehnquist, W. – Joined majority opinion

Opposing Side (Respondent/Appellee)

1. Douglas, W. – Wrote dissenting opinion

VI. A WIN OR LOSS FOR THE ACLU?

The ACLU served as counsel for appellant urging a stay; the Supreme Court granted the stay in an 8-1 vote, giving the ACLU an apparent win.

320. United States v. Robinson

(Decided December 11, 1973; 414 U.S. 218)

I. ISSUE

A. Issues Discussed

Criminal justice, drugs, Fourth Amendment, search and seizure

B. Legal Question Presented

Whether an officer who has probable cause to arrest an individual for driving without a permit, and who arrests the individual, can constitutionally search the arrestee without a warrant.

C. Supreme Court's Answer

"[I]n the case of a lawful custodial arrest a full search of the person is not only an exception to the warrant requirement of the Fourth Amendment, but is also a 'reasonable' search under that Amendment."

II. CASE SUMMARY

A. Background

Officer Richard Jenks, a police officer for the District of Columbia Metropolitan Police Department, pulled over and arrested respondent Robinson for operating an automobile without a valid permit. The officer had probable cause to arrest respondent. After respondent was placed under arrest, the officer searched him and discovered a crumpled cigarette package containing fourteen capsules of heroin in respondent's pocket.

The heroin was admitted into evidence at respondent's trial, and he "was convicted in United States District Court for the District of Columbia of the possession and facilitation of concealment of heroin in violation of 26 U.S.C. § 4704(a) (1964 ed.), and 21 U.S.C. § 174 (1964 ed.)." On respondent's second appeal to the Court of Appeals for the District of Columbia Circuit, "the Court of Appeals en banc reversed the judgment of conviction, holding that the heroin introduced in evidence against respondent had been obtained as a result of a search which violated the Fourth Amendment to the United States Constitution."

The Supreme Court granted certiorari to review the case and reversed the Court of Appeals.

1 Holtzman v. Schlesinger, 484 F.2d 1307, *1307 (2d Cir. 1973); The Successes of the American Civil Liberties Union, ACLU,* https://www.aclu.org/successes-american-civil-liberties-union (last visited Jan. 26, 2020) (Listed as a successful case of the ACLU.).

2 Holtzman v. Schlesinger, 484 F.2d 1307, *1307 (2d Cir. 1973).*

B. Counsel of Record / ACLU Attorney

ACLU Side (Respondent / Appellee): Joseph V. Gartlan, Jr., argued the cause for appellee.

Opposing Side (Petitioner / Appellant): Allan A. Tuttle argued the cause for the United States.

III. AMICI CURIAE

ACLU Side (Respondent / Appellee)

Brief of amici curiae filed on behalf of the ACLU by Melvin L. Wulf and Joel M. Gora.

Opposing Side (Petitioner / Appellant)

Brief of amici curiae filed on behalf of the State of California by Evelle J. Younger, Attorney General, Edward A. Hinz, Jr., Chief Assistant Attorney General, William E. James, Assistant Attorney General, and Robert R. Granucci and Sanford Svetcov, Deputy Attorneys General.

Brief of amici curiae filed on behalf of the State of Illinois by William J. Scott, Attorney General, and James B. Zagel and Jayne A. Carr, Assistant Attorneys General.

Brief of amici curiae filed on behalf of Americans for Effective Law Enforcement, Inc., by Fred E. Inbau, Alan S. Ganz, Frank Carrington, Glen R. Murphy, Wayne W. Schmidt, Geoffrey M. Alprin, and Scott R. Schoenfeld.

IV. THE SUPREME COURT'S DECISION

"But quite apart from these distinctions, our more fundamental disagreement with the Court of Appeals arises from its suggestion that there must be litigated in each case the issue of whether or not there was present one of the reasons supporting the authority for a search of the person incident to a lawful arrest. We do not think the long line of authorities of this Court dating back to Weeks, or what we can glean from the history of practice in this country and in England, requires such a case-by-case adjudication. A police officer's determination as to how and where to search the person of a suspect whom he has arrested is necessarily a quick ad hoc judgment which the Fourth Amendment does not require to be broken down in each instance into an analysis of each step in the search. The authority to search the person incident to a lawful custodial arrest, while based upon the need to disarm and to discover evidence, does not depend on what a court may later decide was the probability in a particular arrest situation that weapons or evidence would in fact be found upon the person of the suspect. A custodial arrest of a suspect based on probable cause is a reasonable intrusion under the Fourth Amendment; that intrusion being lawful, a search incident to the arrest requires no additional justification. It is the fact of the lawful arrest which establishes the authority to search, and we hold that in the case of a lawful custodial arrest a full search of the person is not only an exception to the warrant requirement of the Fourth Amendment, but is also a 'reasonable' search under that Amendment. . . .

The search of respondent's person conducted by Officer Jenks in this case and the seizure from him of the heroin, were permissible under established Fourth Amendment law. While thorough, the search partook of none of the extreme or patently abusive characteristics which were held to violate the Due Process Clause of the Fourteenth Amendment in *Rochin v. California*. Since it is the fact of custodial arrest which gives rise to the authority to search, it is of no moment that Jenks did not indicate any subjective fear of the respondent or that he did not himself suspect that respondent was armed. Having in the course of a lawful search come upon the crumpled package of cigarettes, he was entitled to inspect it; and when his inspection revealed the heroin capsules, he was entitled to seize them as 'fruits, instrumentalities, or contraband' probative of criminal conduct. The judgment of the Court of Appeals holding otherwise is reversed."

V. JUSTICE VOTE

3 Pro ACLU Side vs. 6 Con Opposing Side

ACLU Side (Respondent / Appellee)

1. Marshall, T. – Wrote dissenting opinion
2. Brennan, W. – Joined Marshall's dissent
3. Douglas, W. – Joined Marshall's dissent

Opposing Side (Petitioner / Appellant)

1. Rehnquist, W. – Wrote majority opinion
2. Burger, W. – Joined majority opinion
3. Stewart, P. – Joined majority opinion
4. White, B. – Joined majority opinion
5. Blackmun, H. – Joined majority opinion
6. Powell, L. – Wrote concurring opinion

VI. A WIN OR LOSS FOR THE ACLU?

The ACLU filed as amicus curiae urging affirmance; the Supreme Court reversed the Court of Appeals' judgment in a 6-3 vote giving the ACLU an apparent loss.

321. United States v. Calandra

(Decided January 8, 1974; 414 U.S. 338)

I. ISSUE

A. Issues Discussed

Criminal Justice, Fourth Amendment, Fifth Amendment, search and seizure

B. Legal Question Presented

"[W]hether a witness summoned to appear and testify before a grand jury may refuse to answer questions on the ground that they are based on evidence obtained from an unlawful search and seizure."

C. Supreme Court's Answer

A witness summoned before a grand jury may not refuse to answer questions on the ground that they are based on evidence obtained from an unlawful search and seizure.

II. CASE SUMMARY

A. Background

"On December 11, 1970, federal agents obtained a warrant authorizing a search of respondent John Calandra's place of business, the Royal Machine & Tool Co. in Cleveland, Ohio. The warrant was issued in connection with an extensive investigation of suspected illegal gambling operations. It specified that the object of the search was the discovery and seizure of bookmaking records and wagering paraphernalia. . . .

Although the agents found no gambling paraphernalia, one discovered, among certain promissory notes, a card indicating that a Dr. Walter Loveland had been making periodic payments to Calandra." The agent who found the record was aware "that Dr. Loveland had been the victim of a 'loansharking' enterprise then under investigation. The agent concluded that the card bearing Dr. Loveland's name was a loansharking record and therefore had it seized along with various other items, including books and records of the company, stock certificates, and address books."

A "grand jury subpoenaed Calandra in order to ask him questions based on the evidence seized during the search of his place of business on December 15, 1970. Calandra appeared before the grand jury on August 17, 1971, but refused to testify, invoking his Fifth Amendment privilege against self-incrimination. The Government then requested the District Court to grant Calandra transactional immunity . . . . Calandra requested and received a postponement of the hearing on the Government's application for the immunity order so that he could prepare a motion to suppress the evidence seized in the search.

Calandra later moved . . . for suppression and return of the seized evidence on the grounds that the affidavit supporting the warrant was insufficient and that the search exceeded the scope of the warrant. On August 27, the District Court held a hearing at which Calandra stipulated that he would refuse to answer questions based on the seized materials. On October 1, the District Court entered its judgment ordering the evidence suppressed and returned to Calandra and further ordering that Calandra need not answer any of the grand jury's questions based on the suppressed evidence. The court held that 'due process . . . allows a witness to litigate the question of whether the evidence which constitutes the basis for the questions asked of him before the grand jury has been obtained in a way which violates the constitutional protection against unlawful search and seizure.' The court found that the search warrant had been issued without probable cause and that the search had exceeded the scope of the warrant.

The Court of Appeals for the Sixth Circuit affirmed, holding that the District Court had properly entertained the suppression motion and that the exclusionary rule may be invoked by a witness before the grand jury to bar questioning based on evidence obtained in an unlawful search and seizure. The offer to grant Calandra immunity was deemed irrelevant.

[The Supreme Court] granted the Government's petition for certiorari" and reversed.

B. Counsel of Record/ACLU Attorney

ACLU Side (Respondent/Appellee): Robert J. Rotatori argued the cause for appellee.

Opposing Side (Petitioner/Appellant): Louis F. Claiborne argued the cause for the United States.

III. AMICI CURIAE

ACLU Side (Respondent/Appellee)

Brief of amici curiae filed on behalf of the ACLU by Melvin L. Wulf, Richard G. Lyon, and Paul Halvonik.

Opposing Side (Petitioner/Appellant)

No briefs of amici curiae were filed in support of appellant.

IV. THE SUPREME COURT'S DECISION

"The purpose of the Fourth Amendment is to prevent unreasonable governmental intrusions into the privacy of one's person, house, papers, or effects. The wrong condemned is the unjustified governmental invasion of these areas of an individual's life. That wrong, committed in this case, is fully accomplished by the original search without probable cause. Grand jury questions based on evidence obtained thereby involve no independent governmental invasion of one's person, house, papers, or effects, but rather the usual abridgment of personal privacy common to all grand jury questioning. Questions based on illegally obtained evidence are only a derivative use of the product of a past unlawful search and seizure. They work no new Fourth Amendment wrong. Whether such derivative use of illegally obtained evidence by a grand jury should be proscribed presents a question, not of rights, but of remedies.

In the usual context of a criminal trial, the defendant is entitled to the suppression of, not only the evidence obtained through an unlawful search and seizure, but also any derivative use of that evidence. The prohibition of the exclusionary rule must reach such derivative use if it is to fulfill its function of deterring police misconduct. In the context of a grand jury proceeding, we believe that the damage to that institution from the unprecedented extension of the exclusionary rule urged by respondent outweighs the benefit of any possible incremental deterrent effect. Our conclusion necessarily controls both the evidence seized during the course of an unlawful search and seizure and any question or evidence derived therefrom (the fruits of the unlawful search). The same considerations of logic and policy apply to both the fruits of an unlawful search and seizure and derivative use of that evidence, and we do not distinguish between them.

The judgment of the Court of Appeals is reversed."

V. JUSTICE VOTE

3 Pro ACLU Side vs. 6 Con Opposing Side

ACLU Side (Respondent/Appellee)

1. Brennan, W. – Wrote dissenting opinion
2. Marshall, T. – Joined Brennan's dissent
3. Douglas, W. – Joined Brennan's dissent

Opposing Side (Petitioner/Appellant)

1. Powell, L. – Wrote majority opinion
2. Stewart, P. – Joined majority opinion
3. White, B. – Joined majority opinion

4. Blackmun, H. – Joined majority opinion
5. Rehnquist, W. – Joined majority opinion
6. Burger, W. – Joined majority opinion

VI. A WIN OR LOSS FOR THE ACLU?

The ACLU filed as amicus curiae urging affirmance; the Supreme Court reversed the Court of Appeals' judgment in a 6-3 vote giving the ACLU an apparent loss.

322. Communist Party of Indiana v. Whitcomb

(Decided January 9, 1974; 414 U.S. 441)

I. ISSUE

A. Issues Discussed

Communism

B. Legal Question Presented

"[W]hether the First and Fourteenth Amendments are violated by Indiana's requirement that '(n)o existing or newly-organized political party or organization shall be permitted on or to have the names of its candidates printed on the ballot used at any election until it has filed an affidavit, by its officers, under oath, that it does not advocate the overthrow of local, state or national government by force or violence . . . .'"

C. Supreme Court's Answer

"As to the merits, we hold that the loyalty oath requirement of s 29—3812 violates the First and Fourteenth Amendments . . . ."

II. CASE SUMMARY

A. Background

"Appellants are the Communist Party of Indiana . . . . Appellees are the Indiana State Election Board . . . . When appellants applied . . . for a place on Indiana's National Ballot for the 1972 general election without submitting the required oath, the Board . . . rejected the application. Appellants thereupon filed this action in the District Court for the Northern District of Indiana seeking a declaration of the unconstitutionality of s 29—3812, and an injunction requiring that the Election Board place the Party on the ballot. A three-judge court was convened and that court, on September 28, 1972, in an unreported opinion, declared the provision of s 29—3812 that is challenged on this appeal constitutional and issued an order requiring the Election Board to place the Communist Party and its nominees on the National Ballot only '(i)n the event that the Communist Party of Indiana shall submit an affidavit in keeping with this memorandum and order. . . .' The Communist Party submitted an affidavit that, in addition to the statutory language, added the following:

'The term advocate as used herein has the meaning given it by the Supreme Court of the United States in Yates v. United States, 354 U.S. 298 at 320, 'the advocacy and teaching of concrete action for the forcible overthrow of the government, and not of principles divorced from action."

The Election Board rejected the affidavit and appellants, on October 3, returned to the District Court, seeking an order directing the Board to accept it. On the same day, the Election Board filed a motion requesting reconsideration of the order of September 28. The District Court, on October 4, denied both motions by order entered that day."

After additional procedural steps, the Supreme Court granted certiorari to review the case.

B. Counsel of Record

ACLU Side (Petitioner/Appellant): Sanford Jay Rosen argued the cause for appellants. With him on the brief were Melvin L. Wulf of the American Civil Liberties Union Foundation, and R. Davy Eaglesfield, III, and William Rastetter of the Indiana Civil Liberties Union.

Opposing Side (Respondent/Appellee): Theodore L. Sendak, Attorney General of Indiana, argued the cause for appellees. With him on the brief were Darrel K. Diamond, Assistant Attorney General, and A. Frank Gleaves III, Deputy Attorney General.

III. AMICI CURIAE

ACLU Side (Petitioner/Appellant)

No briefs of amici curiae were filed in support of appellants.

Opposing Side (Respondent/Appellee)

No briefs of amici curiae were filed in support of appellees.

IV. THE SUPREME COURT'S DECISION

"Loyalty oath cases are not strangers to this Court, but the constitutional questions presented in earlier cases arising from their use to limit access to the ballot have not had plenary consideration. . . .

Appellees do not deny that s 29—3812 exacts a broad oath embracing advocacy of abstract doctrine as well as advocacy of action. Yet this Court has held in many contexts that the First and Fourteenth Amendments render invalid statutes regulating advocacy that are not limited to advocacy of action. And, as we have so often emphasized, '(p)recision of regulation must be the touchstone in an area so closely touching our most precious freedoms.' . . .

This principle that 'the constitutional guarantees of free speech and free press do not permit a State to forbid or proscribe advocacy of the use of force or of law violation except where such advocacy is directed to inciting or producing imminent lawless action and is likely to incite or produce such action' has been applied not only to statutes that directly forbid or proscribe advocacy, but also to regulatory schemes that determine eligibility for public employment, tax exemptions, and moral fitness justifying disbarment.

Appellees argue that the principle should nevertheless not obtain in cases of state regulation of access to the ballot. We perceive no reason to make an exception, and appellees suggest none. Indeed, all of the reasons for application of the principle in the other contexts are equally applicable here. . . .

Appellees argue: 'It is fraudulent for a group seeking by violent revolution to overthrow our democratic form of government to disguise itself as a political party and use the very forms of the democracy it seeks to subvert in order to gain support and carry on its nefarious ends.' Again, they argue 'that the affidavit required under the statute refers to the official actions of the party itself, thus reducing to a minimum any possibility of 'innocent involvement' in activities which might be considered advocacy.' As we understand appellees, this is an argument that, at least for purposes of determining whether to grant a place on the ballot, any group that advocates violent overthrow as abstract doctrine must be regarded as necessarily advocating unlawful action. We reject that proposition. . . .

Reversed."

V. JUSTICE VOTE

9 Pro ACLU Side vs. 0 Con Opposing Side

ACLU Side (Petitioner/Appellant)

1. Brennan, W. – Wrote majority opinion
2. Marshall, T. – Joined majority opinion
3. Stewart, P. – Joined majority opinion
4. Rehnquist, W. – Joined Powell's concurrence
5. Burger, W. – Joined Powell's concurrence
6. White, B. – Joined majority opinion
7. Blackmun, H. – Joined Powell's concurrence
8. Powell, L. – Wrote concurring opinion
9. Douglas, W. – Joined majority opinion

VI. A WIN OR LOSS FOR THE ACLU?

The ACLU served as counsel for appellants urging reversal of the judgment of the District Court; the Supreme Court reversed in a 9-0 vote, giving the ACLU an apparent win.

323. Vachon v. New Hampshire

(Decided January 14, 1974; 414 U.S. 478)

I. ISSUE

A. Issues Discussed

Criminal procedure

B. Legal Question Presented

Whether a conviction for "contributing to the delinquency of a minor" without clear evidence linking the appellant to the crime was constitutional.

C. Supreme Court's Answer

"In these circumstances, the conviction must be reversed. 'It is beyond question, of course, that a conviction based on a record lacking any relevant evidence as to a crucial element of the offense charged . . . violate(s) due process.'"

II. CASE SUMMARY

A. Background

"A 14-year-old girl bought a button inscribed 'Copulation Not Masturbation' at the Head Shop in Manchester, New Hampshire. In consequence, appellant, operator of the shop, was sentenced to 30 days in jail and fined $100 after conviction upon a charge of 'wilfully' contributing to the delinquency of a minor in violation of New Hampshire's Rev.Stat.Ann. s 169:32. In affirming the conviction, the New Hampshire Supreme Court held that the 'wilfully' component of the offense required that the State prove that the accused acted 'voluntarily and intentionally and not because of mistake or accident or other innocent reason.' Thus, the State was required to produce evidence that appellant, knowing the girl to be a minor, personally sold her the button, or personally caused another to sell it to her. Appellant unsuccessfully sought dismissal of the charge at the close of the State's case on the ground that the State had produced no evidence to meet this requirement, and unsuccessfully urged the same ground as a reason for reversal in the State Supreme Court. [The U.S. Supreme Court has] reviewed the transcript of the trial on this issue, pursuant to Rule 40(1) (d)(2) of the Rules of this Court."

B. Counsel of Record

ACLU Side (Petitioner/Appellant): Brief filed for appellant by Melvin L. Wulf, Joel M. Gora, and Rena Uviller of the American Civil Liberties Union Foundation, and Ruth Jane Zuckerman, James E. Higgins, and Alan L. Reische.

Opposing Side (Respondent/Appellee): Brief filed for appellee by Warren B. Rudman, Attorney General, and Robert V. Johnson, II, Assistant Attorney General

III. AMICI CURIAE

ACLU Side (Petitioner/Appellant)

No briefs of amici curiae were filed in support of appellant.

Opposing Side (Respondent/Appellee)

No briefs of amici curiae were filed in support of appellee.

IV. THE SUPREME COURT'S DECISION

"Our independent examination of the trial record discloses that evidence is completely lacking that appellant personally sold the girl the button or even that he was aware of the sale or present in the store at the time. The girl was the State's only witness to the sale. She testified that she and a girl friend entered the store and looked around until they saw 'a velvet display card on a counter' from which they 'picked out (the) pin.' She went to some person in the store with the button 'cupped in (her) hand' and paid that person 25 cents for the button. She did not say that appellant was that person, or even that she saw him in the store. Rather, she testified that she could not identify who the person was. We therefore agree with Justice Grimes, dissenting, that 'there is no evidence whatever that the defendant sold the button, that he knew it had been sold to a minor, that he authorized such sales to minors or that he was even in the store at the time of the sale.' This fatal void in the State's case was not filled by appellant's concession at trial that he 'controlled the premises on July 26.' That concession was evidence at most that he operated the shop; it was in no way probative of the crucial element of the crime that he personally sold the minor the button or personally caused it to be sold to her.

In these circumstances, the conviction must be reversed. 'It is beyond question, of course, that a conviction based on a record lacking any relevant evidence as to a crucial element of the offense charged . . . violate(s) due process.'

The judgment is reversed and the case is remanded to the New Hampshire Supreme Court . . . ."

V. JUSTICE VOTE

6 Pro ACLU Side vs. 3 Con Opposing Side

ACLU Side (Petitioner/Appellant)

1. Marshall, T. – Per curiam decision
2. Brennan, W. – Per curiam decision
3. Stewart, P. – Per curiam decision
4. Blackmun, H. – Per curiam decision
5. Powell, L. – Per curiam decision
6. Douglas, W. – Per curiam decision

Opposing Side (Respondent/Appellee)

1. Burger, W. – Joined Rehnquist's dissent
2. White, B. – Joined Rehnquist's dissent
3. Rehnquist, W. – Wrote dissenting opinion

VI. A WIN OR LOSS FOR THE ACLU?

The ACLU served as counsel for appellants urging reversal of the judgment of the New Hampshire Supreme Court; the U.S. Supreme Court reversed, in a 6-3 per curiam decision, giving the ACLU an apparent win.

324. Cleveland Board of Education v. LaFleur

(Decided January 21, 1974; 414 U.S. 632)

I. ISSUE

A. Issues Discussed

Civil rights, gender, Fourteenth Amendment, due process

B. Legal Question Presented

Did the mandatory maternity leave provisions of the Cleveland and Chesterfield County School Boards, requiring pregnant teachers to leave their positions before expected childbirth, violate the Due Process Clause of the Fourteenth Amendment?

C. Supreme Court's Answer

The mandatory maternity leave provisions violate the Due Process Clause of the Fourteenth Amendment.

II. CASE SUMMARY

A. Background

"Jo Carol LaFleur and Ann Elizabeth Nelson, respondents in case no. 72-777, are junior high school teachers employed by the Board of Education of Cleveland, Ohio. . . . The petitioner in case no. 72-1129, Susan Cohen, was employed by the School Board of Chesterfield County, Virginia."

During the school year, the female teachers informed their local school board that they were pregnant. All three were compelled by a mandatory maternity leave rule to leave their jobs without pay several months before their expected deliveries.

The teachers all brought actions for deprivation of their rights, challenging the constitutionality of mandatory maternity leave rules of the Cleveland and Chesterfield County School Boards.

The Cleveland rule required a pregnant teacher to take unpaid maternity leave five months before the expected childbirth, with leave application to be made at least two weeks before her departure. The Chesterfield County rule required the teacher to leave work at least four months, and to give notice at least six months, before the anticipated childbirth. The rules also included procedures for determining whether and when the teachers could return to work after giving birth.

In No. 72-777, the District Court held against the teachers. The "Court of Appeals for the Sixth Circuit reversed, finding the Cleveland rule in violation of the Equal Protection Clause of the Fourteenth Amendment."

In No. 72-1129, the "District Court held that the school board regulation violates the Equal Protection Clause, and granted appropriate relief. A divided panel of the Fourth Circuit affirmed, but, on rehearing en banc, the Court of Appeals upheld the constitutionality of the challenged regulation in a 4-3 decision."

The Supreme Court granted certiorari, consolidated the cases, affirmed the judgment in No. 72-777, and reserved the judgment in No. 72-1129.

B. Counsel of Record/ACLU Attorney

ACLU Side (Petitioner/Appellant in No. 72-1129, Respondent/Appellee in No. 72-777): Philip J. Hirschkop argued the cause for appellant in No. 72-1129. Jane M. Picker argued the cause for appellee in No. 72-777.

Opposing Side (Respondent/Appellee in No. 72-1129, Petitioner/Appellant in No. 72-777): Samuel W. Hixon III argued the cause for appellee in No. 72-1129. Charles F. Clarke argued the cause for appellant in No. 72-777.

III. AMICI CURIAE

ACLU Side (Petitioner/Appellant in No. 72-1129, Respondent/Appellee in No. 72-777):

Brief of amici curiae in both cases filed on behalf of the ACLU, et al., by Theodore R. Mann, Joseph B. Robison, Sylvia Roberts, Ruth Bader Ginsburg, Melvin L. Wulf and John Ligtenberg.

Additional briefs of amici curiae urging reversal in No. 72-1129 and affirmance in No. 72-777 were filed by Solicitor General Bork, Assistant Attorney General Pottinger, Louis F. Claiborne, Joseph T. Eddins and Beatrice Rosenberg for the United States; by David Rubin and Jerry D. Anker for the National Education Assn. et al.; by Winn Newman and Ruth Weyand for the International Union of Electrical, Radio and Machine Workers, AFL-CIO; and by Paul O. H. Pigman for Margaret M. Broussard. Evelle J. Younger, Attorney General, Elizabeth Palmer, Assistant Attorney General, and Joanne Condas, Deputy Attorney General, filed a brief for the California Department of Human Resources Development as amicus curiae. Andrew J. Ruzicho filed a brief for the International Association of Official Human Rights Agencies as amicus curiae urging affirmance in No. 72-777. Philip J. Tierney filed a brief for the Maryland Commission on Human Relations as amicus curiae urging reversal in No. 72-1129.

Opposing Side (Respondent/Appellee in No. 72-1129, Petitioner/Appellant in No. 72-777):

Briefs of amici curiae urging affirmance in No. 72-1129 were filed by Andrew P. Miller, Attorney General of Virginia, and Walter H. Ryland, Assistant Attorney General for the Commonwealth of Virginia; and by Gordon Dean Booth, Jr., Richard S. Maurer, and Sidney F. Davis for Delta Air Lines, Inc.

IV. THE SUPREME COURT'S DECISION

"We conclude, therefore, that neither the necessity for continuity of instruction nor the state interest in keeping physically unfit teachers out of the classroom can justify the sweeping mandatory leave regulations that the Cleveland and Chesterfield County School Boards have adopted. While the regulations no doubt represent a good faith attempt to achieve a laudable goal, they cannot pass muster under the Due Process Clause of the Fourteenth Amendment, because they employ irrebuttable presumptions that unduly penalize a female teacher for deciding to bear a child. . . .

Thus, we conclude that the Cleveland return rule, insofar as it embodies the three-month age provision, is wholly arbitrary and irrational, and hence violates the Due Process Clause of the Fourteenth Amendment. The age limitation serves no legitimate state interest, and unnecessarily penalizes the female teacher for asserting her right to bear children.

We perceive no such constitutional infirmities in the Chesterfield County rule. In that school system, the teacher becomes eligible for re-employment upon submission of a medical certificate from her physician; return to work is guaranteed no later than the beginning of the next school year following the eligibility determination. The medical certificate is both a reasonable and narrow method of protecting the school board's interest in teacher fitness, while the possible deferring of return until the next school year serves the goal of preserving continuity of instruction. In short, the Chesterfield County rule manages to serve the legitimate state interests here without employing unnecessary presumptions that broadly burden the exercise of protected constitutional liberty.

For the reasons stated, we hold that the mandatory termination provisions of the Cleveland and Chesterfield County maternity regulations violate the Due Process Clause of the Fourteenth Amendment, because of their use of unwarranted conclusive presumptions that seriously burden the exercise of protected constitutional liberty. For similar reasons, we hold the three-month provision of the Cleveland return rule unconstitutional.

Accordingly, the judgment in No. 72-777 is affirmed; the judgment in No. 72-1129 is reversed, and the case is remanded to the Court of Appeals for the Fourth Circuit for further proceedings consistent with this opinion."

V. JUSTICE VOTE

7 Pro ACLU Side vs. 2 Con Opposing Side

ACLU Side (Petitioner/Appellant in No. 72-1129, Respondent/Appellee in No. 72-777):

1. Stewart, P. – Wrote majority opinion
2. White, B. – Joined majority opinion
3. Blackmun, H. – Joined majority opinion
4. Powell, L. – Wrote concurring opinion
5. Brennan, W. – Joined majority opinion
6. Marshall, T. – Joined majority opinion
7. Douglas, W. – Concurred in the result

Opposing Side (Respondent/Appellee in No. 72-1129, Petitioner/Appellant in No. 72-777):

1. Rehnquist, W. – Wrote dissenting opinion
2. Burger, W. – Joined Rehnquist's dissent

VI. A WIN OR LOSS FOR THE ACLU?

The ACLU filed as amicus curiae urging reversal in No. 72-1129 and affirmance in No. 72-777, the Supreme Court reversed the Court of Appeals' judgment in No. 72-1129 and affirmed the judgment in No. 72-777, in a 7-2 vote, giving the ACLU an apparent win.

325. Hernandez v. Veterans' Administration

(Decided March 4, 1974; 415 U.S. 391)

I. ISSUE

A. Issues Discussed

Military, 1st Amendment, religion

B. Legal Question Presented

Whether 38 U.S.C. s 211(a) provides a jurisdictional bar to the suit.

C. Supreme Court's Answer

"We have held today in Johnson v. Robison that s 211(a) does not bar judicial consideration of constitutional challenges to veterans' benefits legislation. Accordingly, the judgment of the Court of Appeals is vacated and the case remanded for further proceedings consistent with our opinion in Johnson v. Robison"

II. CASE SUMMARY

A. Background

"Petitioners, like the appellee and his class in Johnson v. Robison, 415 U.S. 361, are Class I—O conscientious objectors who, upon completion of alternative civilian service pursuant to s 6(j) of the Military Selective Service Act, 50 U.S.C.App. s 456(j), and the governing regulations of the Selective Service System, 32 CFR, Part 1660, applied for educational benefits provided by the Veterans' Readjustment Benefits Act of 1966. The Veterans' Administration denied petitioners' application for the reasons upon which appellee Robison's request was denied, i.e., because a Class I—O conscientious objector who has performed alternative civilian service does not qualify under 38 U.S.C. s 1652(a)(1) as a 'veteran who . . . served on active duty' (defined in 38 U.S.C. s 101(21) as 'full time duty in the Armed Forces'), and is therefore not an 'eligible veteran' entitled under 38 U.S.C. s 1661(a) to veterans' educational benefits provided by the Veterans' Readjustment Benefits Act of 1966.

Alleging that those sections of the 1966 Act discriminate against conscientious objectors in violation of the Fifth Amendment, and infringe the Religion Clauses of the First Amendment, petitioners filed two actions seeking declaratory, injunctive, and mandamus relief and requesting the convening of a three-judge district court. The District Court consolidated the two cases and granted the Government's motion to dismiss . . . . Notwithstanding the District Court's dismissal of petitioners' constitutional claims on the ground of insubstantiality, the Court of Appeals . . . construed the order of dismissal as based solely upon the jurisdictional bar of s 211(a), and affirmed the District Court on that ground. [The Supreme Court] granted certiorari and set the case for oral argument with Johnson v. Robison, 415 U.S. 361 (1973)."

B. Counsel of Record

ACLU Side (Petitioner/Appellant): Jack R. Petranker, pro hac vice, and Lawrence L. Curtice argued the cause for appellants. With them on the briefs were Charles C. Marson of the American Civil Liberties Union and Stephen V. Bomse.

Opposing Side (Respondent/Appellee): Gerald P. Norton argued the cause for appellees. On the brief were Solicitor General Bork, Acting Assistant Attorney General Jaffe, Harriet S. Shapiro, Morton Hollander, and William Kanter.

III. AMICI CURIAE

ACLU Side (Petitioner/Appellant)

No briefs of amici curiae were filed in support of appellants.

Opposing Side (Respondent/Appellee)

No briefs of amici curiae were filed in support of appellees.

IV. THE SUPREME COURT'S DECISION

"We have held today in Johnson v. Robison that s 211(a) does not bar judicial consideration of constitutional challenges to veterans' benefits legislation. Accordingly, the judgment of the Court of Appeals is vacated and the case remanded for further proceedings consistent with our opinion in Johnson v. Robison."

V. JUSTICE VOTE

9 Pro ACLU Side vs. 0 Con Opposing Side

ACLU Side (Petitioner/Appellant)

1. Brennan, W. – Wrote majority opinion
2. White, B. – Joined majority opinion
3. Marshall, T. – Joined majority opinion
4. Stewart, P. – Joined majority opinion
5. Burger, W. – Joined majority opinion
6. Blackmun, H. – Joined majority opinion
7. Douglas, W. – Wrote concurring statement
8. Powell, L. – Joined majority opinion
9. Rehnquist, W. – Joined majority opinion

VI. A WIN OR LOSS FOR THE ACLU?

The ACLU served as counsel for appellants urging reversal of the judgment of the Court of Appeals; the Supreme Court reversed, in a 9-0 vote, giving the ACLU an apparent win.

326. Smith v. Goguen

(Decided March 25, 1974; 415 U.S. 566)

I. ISSUE

A. Issues Discussed

1st Amendment, press, speech, association

B. Legal Question Presented

Whether the "contempt provision of the Massachusetts flag-misuse statute [is] unconstitutionally vague and overbroad."

C. Supreme Court's Answer

"We affirm on the vagueness ground. We do not reach the correctness of the holding below on overbreadth or other First Amendment grounds."

II. CASE SUMMARY

A. Background

"Goguen wore a small cloth version of the United States flag sewn to the seat of his trousers. [T]wo police officers in Leominster, Massachusetts, saw Goguen bedecked in that fashion. . . . When [one] officer approached Goguen to question him about the flag, the other persons present laughed. Some time later, the second officer observed Goguen in the same attire walking in the downtown business district of Leominster.

The following day the first officer swore out a complaint against Goguen under the contempt provision of the Massachusetts flag-misuse statute. The relevant part of the statute then read:

'Whoever publicly mutilates, tramples upon, defaces or treats contemptuously the flag of the United States . . ., whether such flag is public or private property . . ., shall be punished by a fine of not less than ten nor more than one hundred dollars or by imprisonment for not more than one year, or both. . . .' . . .

[T]he officer charged specifically and only that Goguen 'did publicly treat contemptuously the flag of the United States . . .'

After jury trial in the Worcester County Superior Court, Goguen was found guilty. The court imposed a sentence of six months . . . . Goguen appealed to the Massachusetts Supreme Judicial Court, which affirmed. . . .

After Goguen began serving his sentence, he was granted bail and then ordered released on a writ of habeas corpus by the United States District Court for the District of Massachusetts. . . .

The Court of Appeals, with one judge concurring, affirmed the District Court on both First Amendment and vagueness grounds."

The Supreme Court granted certiorari to review the case.

B. Counsel of Record

ACLU Side (Respondent/Appellee): Evan T. Lawson argued the cause for appellee. With him on the brief were Matthew Feinberg of the Civil Liberties Union of Massachusetts and Burt Neuborne (ACLU Assistant Legal Director, 1972-1974, and National Legal Director, 1981-1986).

Opposing Side (Petitioner/Appellant): Charles E. Chase, Assistant Attorney General of Massachusetts, argued the cause for appellant. With him on the briefs were Robert H. Quinn, Attorney General, John J. Irwin, Jr., and David A. Mills, Assistant Attorneys General, and William T. Buckley.

III. AMICI CURIAE

ACLU Side (Respondent/Appellee)

No briefs of amici curiae were filed in support of appellee.

Opposing Side (Petitioner/Appellant)

No briefs of amici curiae were filed in support of appellant.

IV. THE SUPREME COURT'S DECISION

"We agree with the holdings of the District Court and the Court of Appeals on the due process doctrine of vagueness. . . . Where a statute's literal scope, unaided by a narrowing state court interpretation, is capable of reaching expression sheltered by the First Amendment, the doctrine demands a greater degree of specificity than in other contexts. The statutory language at issue here, 'publicly . . . treats contemptuously the flag of the United States . . .,' has such scope . . . and at the relevant time was without the benefit of judicial clarification.

Flag contempt statutes have been characterized as void for lack of notice on the theory that '[w]hat is contemptuous to one man may be a work of art to another.' . . . The statutory language under which Goguen was charged . . . fails to draw reasonably clear lines between the kinds of nonceremonial treatment that are criminal and those that are not. . . . Given today's tendencies to treat the flag unceremoniously, those notice standards are not satisfied here. . . .

In its terms, the language at issue is sufficiently unbounded to prohibit, as the District Court noted, 'any public deviation from formal flag etiquette . . . .' . . . Statutory language of such a standardless sweep allows policemen, prosecutors, and juries to pursue their personal predilections. Legislatures may not so abdicate their responsibilities for setting the standards of the criminal law. . . .

Where inherently vague statutory language permits such selective law enforcement, there is a denial of due process. . . .

There are areas of human conduct where, by the nature of the problems presented, legislatures simply cannot establish standards with great precision. Control of the broad range of disorderly conduct that may inhibit a policeman in the performance of his official duties may be one such area, requiring as it does an on-the-spot assessment of the need to keep order. But there is no comparable reason for committing broad discretion to law enforcement officials in the area of flag contempt. Indeed, because display of the flag is so common and takes so many forms, changing from one generation to another and often difficult to distinguish in principle, a legislature should define with some care the flag behavior it intends to outlaw. Certainly nothing prevents a legislature from defining with substantial specificity what constitutes forbidden treatment of United States flags. The statutory language at issue here fails to approach that goal and is void for vagueness. The judgment is affirmed."

V. JUSTICE VOTE

6 Pro ACLU Side vs. 3 Con Opposing Side

ACLU Side (Respondent/Appellee)

1. Powell, L. – Wrote majority opinion
2. Brennan, W. – Joined majority opinion
3. Marshall, T. – Joined majority opinion
4. Stewart, P. – Joined majority opinion
5. White, B. – Wrote concurring opinion
6. Douglas, W. – Joined majority opinion

Opposing Side (Petitioner/Appellant)

1. Rehnquist, W. – Wrote dissenting opinion
2. Blackmun, H. – Wrote dissenting opinion
3. Burger, W. – Joined Rehnquist's and Blackmun's dissents

VI. A WIN OR LOSS FOR THE ACLU?

The ACLU served a counsel for appellee urging affirmance; the Supreme Court affirmed the Court of Appeals' decision by a 6-3 vote, giving the ACLU an apparent win.

327. Storer v. Brown

(Decided March 26, 1974; 415 U.S. 724)

I. ISSUE

A. Issues Discussed

Voting rights

B. Legal Question Presented

Whether California's requirements for independent candidates to appear on the ballot are "infringing on rights guaranteed by the First and Fourteenth Amendments and . . . adding qualifications for the office of United States Congressman, contrary to Art. I, s 2, cl. 2, of the Constitution."

C. Supreme Court's Answer

"We conclude that s 6830(d) is not unconstitutional, and Storer and Frommhagen were properly barred from the ballot as a result of its application. . . .

We come to different conclusions with respect to Hall and Tyner. As to these two men we vacate the judgment of the District Court and remand the case for further proceedings to determine whether the California election laws place an unconstitutional burden on their access to the ballot."

II. CASE SUMMARY

A. Background

"The California Elections Code forbids ballot position to an independent candidate for elective public office if he voted in the immediately preceding primary, or if he had a registered affiliation with a qualified political party at any time within one year prior to the immediately preceding primary election. The independent candidate must also file nomination papers signed by voters not less in number than 5% nor more than 6% of the entire vote cast in the preceding general election in the area for which the candidate seeks to run. All of these signatures must be obtained during a 24-day period following the primary and ending 60 days prior to the general election, and none of the signatures may be gathered from persons who vote at the primary election. The constitutionality of these provisions is challenged here as infringing on rights guaranteed by the First and Fourteenth Amendments and as adding qualifications for the office of United States Congressman, contrary to Art. I, s 2, cl. 2, of the Constitution.

Prior to the 1972 elections, appellants Storer, Frommhagen, Hall, and Tyner, along with certain of their supporters, filed their actions to have the above sections of the Elections Code declared unconstitutional and their enforcement enjoined. Storer and Frommhagen each sought ballot status as an independent candidate for Congressman for his district. . . . Hall and Tyner claimed the right to ballot position as independent candidates for President and Vice President of the United States. . . .

A three-judge District Court concluded that the statutes served a sufficiently important state interest to sustain their constitutionality and dismissed the complaints. Two separate appeals were taken from the judgment. [The Supreme Court] noted probable jurisdiction and consolidated the cases for oral argument."

B. Counsel of Record

ACLU Side (Petitioner/Appellant): Joseph Remcho of the American Civil Liberties Union Foundation of Northern California, Inc., and Paul N. Halvonik argued the cause for appellants in both cases. With them on the brief for appellants in No. 72-812 were Charles C. Marson and Peter E. Sheehan of the American Civil Liberties Union Foundation of Northern California, Inc. Appellant pro se filed a brief in No. 72-6050.

Opposing Side (Respondent/Appellee): Clayton P. Roche, Deputy Attorney General of California, argued the cause for appellee Brown in both cases. With him on the brief were Evelle J. Younger Attorney General, and Iver. E. Skjeie, Assistant Attorney General.

III. AMICI CURIAE

ACLU Side (Petitioner/Appellant)

Brief of amici curiae filed on behalf of the Committee for Democratic Election Laws by Rolland R. O'Hare.

Opposing Side (Respondent/Appellee)

No briefs of amici curiae were filed in support of appellee.

IV. THE SUPREME COURT'S DECISION

"We affirm the judgment of the District Court insofar as it refused relief to Storer and Frommhagen with respect to the 1972 general election. Both men were registered Democrats until early 17 1972, Storer until January and Frommhagen until March of that year. This affiliation with a qualified political party within a year prior to the 1972 primary disqualified both men under s 6830(d); and in our view the State of California was not prohibited by the United States Constitution from enforcing that provision . . . .

The requirement that the independent candidate not have been affiliated with a political party for a year before the primary is expressive of a general state policy aimed at maintaining the integrity of the various routes to the ballot. It involves no discrimination against independents. . . .

We conclude that s 6830(d) is not unconstitutional, and Storer and Frommhagen were properly barred from the ballot as a result of its application. . . .

We come to different conclusions with respect to Hall and Tyner. As to these two men we vacate the judgment of the District Court and remand the case for further proceedings to determine whether the California election laws place an unconstitutional burden on their access to the ballot.

We start with the proposition that the requirements for an independent's attaining a place on the general election ballot can be unconstitutionally severe. . . .

We are quite sure . . . that further proceedings should be had in the District Court to permit further findings with respect to the extent of the burden imposed on independent candidates for President and Vice President under California law. . . . Before the claim is finally dismissed, it should be determined whether the available pool is so diminished in size by the disqualification of those who voted in the primary that the 325,000-signature requirement, to be satisfied in 24 days, is too great a burden . . . .

In Williams v. Rhodes, the opportunity for political activity within either of two major political parties was seemingly available to all. But this Court held that to comply with the First and Fourteenth Amendments the State must provide a feasible opportunity for new political organizations and their candidates to appear on the ballot. No discernible state interest justified the burdensome and complicated regulations that in effect made impractical any alternative to the major parties. Similarly, here, we perceive no sufficient state interest in conditioning ballot position for an independent candidate on his forming a new political party as long as the State is free to assure itself that the candidate is a serious contender, truly independent, and with a satisfactory level of community support.

Accordingly, we vacate the judgment in No. 72—812 insofar as it refused relief to Hall and Tyner and remand the case in this respect to the District Court for further proceedings consistent with this opinion. In all other respects, the judgment in No. 72—812 and No. 72—6050 is affirmed."

V. JUSTICE VOTE

6 Pro ACLU Side vs. 3 Con Opposing Side

ACLU Side (Petitioner/Appellant)

1. White, B. – Wrote majority opinion
2. Stewart, P. – Joined majority opinion
3. Burger, W. – Joined majority opinion
4. Blackmun, H. – Joined majority opinion
5. Powell, L. – Joined majority opinion
6. Rehnquist, W. – Joined majority opinion

Opposing Side (Respondent/Appellee)

1. Brennan, W. – Wrote dissenting opinion
2. Marshall, T. – Joined Brennan's dissent
3. Douglas, W. – Joined Brennan's dissent

VI. A WIN OR LOSS FOR THE ACLU?

The ACLU served as counsel for appellants urging reversal of the judgment of the U.S District Court for the Northern District of California; the Supreme Court affirmed in part, vacated and remanded in part, in a 6-3 vote, giving the ACLU an apparent win.

328. Village of Belle Terre v. Boraas

(Decided April 1, 1974; 416 U.S. 1)

I. ISSUE

A. Issues Discussed

Federal, civil rights

B. Legal Question Presented

Whether a Belle Terre ordinance restricting housing occupancy to family units is unconstitutional.

C. Supreme Court's Answer

"A quiet place where yards are wide, people few, and motor vehicles restricted are legitimate guidelines in a land-use project addressed to family needs. This goal is a permissible one within Berman v. Parker."

II. CASE SUMMARY

A. Background

"Belle Terre is a village on Long Island's north shore of about 220 homes inhabited by 700 people. Its total land area is less than one square mile. It has restricted land use to one-family dwellings excluding lodging houses, boarding houses, fraternity houses, or multiple-dwelling houses. The word 'family' as used in the ordinance means, '(o)ne or more persons related by blood, adoption, or marriage, living and cooking together as a single housekeeping unit, exclusive of household servants. A number of persons but not exceeding two (2) living and cooking together as a single housekeeping unit through not related by blood, adoption, or marriage shall be deemed to constitute a family.'

Appellees, the Dickmans, are owners of a house in the village and leased it in December 1971 for a term of 18 months to Michael Truman. Later Bruce Boraas became a colessee. Then Anne Parish moved into the house along with three others. These six are students at nearby State University at Stony Brook and none is related to the other by blood, adoption, or marriage. When the village served the Dickmans with an 'Order to Remedy Violations' of the ordinance, the owners plus three tenants thereupon brought this action under 42 U.S.C. s 1983 for an injunction and a judgment declaring the ordinance unconstitutional. The District Court held the ordinance constitutional, and the Court of Appeals reversed, one judge dissenting. The case is here by appeal; and [the Supreme Court] noted probable jurisdiction."

B. Counsel of Record

ACLU Side (Respondent/Appellee): Lawrence G. Sager of the New York Civil Liberties Union argued the cause for appellees. With him on the brief were Arthur N. Eisenberg of the New York Civil Liberties Union, and Melvin L. Wulf and Burt Neuborne of the American Civil Liberties Union.

Opposing Side (Petitioner/Appellant): Bernard E. Gegan argued the cause for appellants. With him on the brief was James J. Von Oiste.

III. AMICI CURIAE

ACLU Side (Respondent/Appellee)

No briefs of amici curiae were filed in support of appellees.

Opposing Side (Petitioner/Appellant)

No briefs of amici curiae were filed in support of appellants.

IV. THE SUPREME COURT'S DECISION

"This case brings to this Court a different phase of local zoning regulations from those we have previously reviewed. . . .

The present ordinance is challenged on several grounds: that it interferes with a person's right to travel; that it interferes with the right to migrate to and settle within a State; that it bars people who are uncongenial to the present residents; that it expresses the social preferences of the residents for groups that will be congenial to them; that social homogeneity is not a legitimate interest of government; that the restriction of those whom the neighbors do not like trenches on the newcomers' rights of privacy; that it is of no rightful concern to villagers whether the residents are married or unmarried; that the ordinance is antithetical to the Nation's experience, ideology, and self-perception as an open, egalitarian, and integrated society.

We find none of these reasons in the record before us. . . .

It is said, however, that if two unmarried people can constitute a 'family,' there is no reason why three or four may not. But every line drawn by a legislature leaves some out that might well have been included. That exercise of discretion, however, is a legislative, not a judicial, function.

It is said that the Belle Terre ordinance reeks with an animosity to unmarried couples who live together. There is no evidence so support it; and the provision of the ordinance bringing within the definition of a 'family' two unmarried people belies the charge. . . .

The regimes of boarding houses, fraternity houses, and the like present urban problems. More people occupy a given space; more cars rather continuously pass by; more cars are parked; noise travels with crowds.

A quiet place where yards are wide, people few, and motor vehicles restricted are legitimate guidelines in a land-use project addressed to family needs. This goal is a permissible one within Berman v. Parker, supra. The police power is not confined to elimination of filth, stench, and unhealthy places. It is ample to lay out zones where family values, youth values, and the blessings of quiet seclusion and clean air make the area a sanctuary for people. . . .

Reversed."

V. JUSTICE VOTE

2 Pro ACLU Side vs. 7 Con Opposing Side

ACLU Side (Respondent/Appellee)

1. Marshall, T. – Wrote dissenting opinion
2. Brennan, W. – Wrote dissenting opinion

Opposing Side (Petitioner/Appellant)

1. Douglas, W. – Wrote majority opinion
2. White, B. – Joined majority opinion
3. Stewart, P. – Joined majority opinion
4. Burger, W. – Joined majority opinion
5. Blackmun, H. – Joined majority opinion
6. Powell, L. – Joined majority opinion
7. Rehnquist, W. – Joined majority opinion

VI. A WIN OR LOSS FOR THE ACLU?

The ACLU served as counsel for appellees urging affirmance of the judgment of the Court of Appeals; the Supreme Court reversed, in a 7-2 vote, giving the ACLU an apparent loss.

329. Scheuer v. Rhodes

(Decided April 17, 1974; 416 U.S. 232)

I. ISSUE

A. Issues Discussed

Civil procedure, immunity

B. Legal Question Presented

"[W]hether the District Court correctly dismissed civil damage actions, brought under 42 U.S.C. s 1983, on the ground that these actions were, as a matter of law, against the State of Ohio, and hence barred by the Eleventh Amendment to the Constitution and, alternatively, that the actions were against state officials who were immune from liability for the acts alleged in the complaints."

C. Supreme Court's Answer

"We hold that dismissal was inappropriate at this stage of the litigation and accordingly reverse the judgments and remand for further proceedings. We intimate no view on the merits of the allegations since there is no evidence before us at this stage."

II. CASE SUMMARY

A. Background

"These cases arise out of the same period of alleged civil disorder on the campus of Kent State University in Ohio during May 1970 which was before us, in another context, in Gilligan v. Morgan, 413 U.S. 1 (1973).

In these cases the personal representatives of the estates of three students who died in that episode seek damages . . . . The complaints in both cases allege a cause of action under the Civil Rights Act of 1871, 17 Stat. 13, now 42 U.S.C. s 1983. Petitioner Scheuer also alleges a cause of action under Ohio law on the theory of pendent jurisdiction. Petitioners Krause and Miller make a similar claim, asserting jurisdiction on the basis of diversity of citizenship.

The District Court dismissed the complaints for lack of jurisdiction over the subject matter on the theory that these actions, although in form against the named individuals, were, in substance and effect, against the State of Ohio and thus barred by the Eleventh Amendment. The Court of Appeals affirmed the action of the District Court, agreeing that the suit was in legal effect one against the State of Ohio and, alternatively, that the common-law doctrine of executive immunity barred action against the state officials who are respondents here. [The Supreme Court is] confronted with the narrow threshold question whether the District Court properly dismissed the complaints."

B. Counsel of Record

ACLU Side (Petitioner/Appellant): Michael E. Geltner of the American Civil Liberties Union of Ohio Foundation argued the cause for appellant in No. 72-914. With him on the briefs were Walter S. Haffner, Nelson G. Karl, Leonard J. Schwartz of the American Civil Liberties Union of Ohio Foundation, Melvin L. Wulf and Joel M. Gora of the American Civil Liberties Union Foundation, Inc., and Niki Z. Schwartz, Stanley K. Laughlin, and Michael S. Harshmian of the American Civil Liberties Union of Ohio Foundation. Steven A. Sindell argued the cause for appellants in No. 72-1318. With him on the brief were Joseph M. Sindell and Joseph Kelner.

Opposing Side (Respondent/Appellee): Charles E. Brown argued the cause for appellees in No. 72-914. With him on the brief were Robert F. Howarth, Jr., Delmar Christensen, and C. D. Lambros. R. Brooke Alloway argued the cause for appellees in No. 72-1318. With him on the brief was John M. McElroy.

III. AMICI CURIAE

ACLU Side (Petitioner/Appellant)

Brief of amici curiae filed on behalf of the Mexican American Legal Defense and Educational Fund by Mario G. Obledo and Sanford Jay Rosen.

Brief of amici curiae filed on behalf of the National Council of the Churches of Christ in the U. S. A. et al. by David E.

Engdahl.

Brief of amici curiae filed on behalf of the National Bar Association by Carl J. Character.

Opposing Side (Respondent/Appellee)

No briefs of amici curiae were filed in support of appellees.

IV. THE SUPREME COURT'S DECISION

"The primary question presented is whether the District Court acted prematurely and hence erroneously in dismissing the complaints on the stated ground, thus precluding any opportunity for the plaintiffs by subsequent proof to establish a claim.

When a federal court reviews the sufficiency of a complaint, before the reception of any evidence either by affidavit or admissions, its task is necessarily a limited one. The issue is not whether a plaintiff will ultimately prevail but whether the claimant is entitled to offer evidence to support the claims. Indeed it may appear on the face of the pleadings that a recovery is very remote and unlikely but that is not the test. Moreover, it is well established that, in passing on a motion to dismiss, whether on the ground of lack of jurisdiction over the subject matter or for failure to state a cause of action, the allegations of the complaint should be construed favorably to the pleader. . . .

Analyzing the complaints in light of the[] precedents, we see that petitioners allege facts that demonstrate they are seeking to impose individual and personal liability on the named defendants for what they claim—but have not yet established by proof—was a deprivation of federal rights by these defendants under color of state law. Whatever the plaintiffs may or may not be able to establish as to the merits of their allegations, their claims, as stated in the complaints, given the favorable reading required by the Federal Rules of Civil Procedure, are not barred by the Eleventh Amendment. Consequently, the District Court erred in dismissing the complaints for lack of jurisdiction. . . .

These cases, in their present posture, present no occasion for a definitive exploration of the scope of immunity available to state executive officials nor, because of the absence of a factual record, do they permit a determination as to the applicability of the foregoing principles to the respondents here. . . .

We intimate no evaluation whatever as to the merits of the petitioners' claims or as to whether it will be possible to support them by proof. We hold only that, on the allegations of their respective complaints, they were entitled to have them judicially resolved.

The judgments of the Court of Appeals are reversed and the cases are remanded . . . ."

V. JUSTICE VOTE

8 Pro ACLU Side vs. 0 Con Opposing Side

ACLU Side (Petitioner/Appellant)

1. Burger, W. – Wrote majority opinion
2. White, B. – Joined majority opinion
3. Marshall, T. – Joined majority opinion
4. Brennan, W. – Joined majority opinion
5. Stewart, P. – Joined majority opinion
6. Blackmun, H. – Joined majority opinion
7. Powell, L. – Joined majority opinion
8. Rehnquist, W. – Joined majority opinion

Douglas, W. – Took no part in the decision.

VI. A WIN OR LOSS FOR THE ACLU?

The ACLU served as counsel for appellants urging reversal of the judgment of the Court of Appeals; the Supreme Court reversed, in an 8-0 vote, giving the ACLU an apparent win.

330. DeFunis v. Odegaard

(Decided April 23, 1974; 416 U.S. 312)

I. ISSUE

A. Issues Discussed

Race, civil procedure

B. Legal Question Presented

"In light of DeFunis' recent registration for the last quarter of his final law school year, and the Law School's assurance that his registration is fully effective, the insistent question again arises whether this case is not moot . . . ."

C. Supreme Court's Answer

"Because the petitioner will complete his law school studies at the end of the term for which he has now registered regardless of any decision this Court might reach on the merits of this litigation, we conclude that the Court cannot, consistently with the limitations of Art. III of the Constitution, consider the substantive constitutional issues tendered by the parties."

II. CASE SUMMARY

A. Background

"In 1971 the petitioner Marco DeFunis, Jr., applied for admission as a first-year student at the University of Washington Law School, a state-operated institution. . . . DeFunis was eventually notified that he had been denied admission. He thereupon commenced this suit in a Washington trial court, contending that the procedures and criteria employed by the Law School Admissions Committee invidiously discriminated against him on account of his race in violation of the Equal Protection Clause of the Fourteenth Amendment to the United States Constitution.

DeFunis brought the suit on behalf of himself alone . . . . He asked the trial court to issue a mandatory injunction commanding the respondents to admit him . . . . The trial court agreed with his claim and granted the requested relief. DeFunis was, accordingly, admitted to the Law School and began his legal studies there in the fall of 1971. On appeal, the Washington Supreme Court reversed . . . . By this time DeFunis was in his second year . . . .

He then petitioned this Court for a writ of certiorari, and Mr. Justice Douglas, as Circuit Justice, stayed the judgment of the Washington Supreme Court . . . . DeFunis has remained in law school, and was in the first term of his third and final year when this Court first considered his certiorari petition in the fall of 1973. [W]e requested the parties to brief the question of mootness . . . . [B]oth sides contended that the case was not moot. The respondents indicated that, if the decision of the Washington Supreme Court were permitted to stand, the petitioner could complete the term for which he was then enrolled but would have to apply to the faculty for permission to continue in the school before he could register for another term.

[The U.S. Supreme Court] granted the petition for certiorari on November 19, 1973. The case was in due course orally argued on February 26, 1974."

B. Counsel of Record

ACLU Side (Respondent/Appellee): Slade Gorton, Attorney General of Washington, argued the cause for appellees. With him on the brief was James B. Wilson, Senior Assistant Attorney General.

Opposing Side (Petitioner/Appellant): Josef Diamond argued the cause for appellants. With him on the briefs was Lyle L. Iversen.

III. AMICI CURIAE

ACLU Side (Respondent/Appellee)

Brief of amici curiae filed on behalf of the Mexican American Legal Defense and Educational Fund, the Puerto Rican Legal Defense and Education Fund, the American Civil Liberties Union, the American G.I. Forum, Aspira of America, Inc., IMAGE, the League of United Latin American Citizens, the Puerto Rican Bar Association, Inc., the Puerto Rican Law Students Association, Inc., the Raza Association of Spanish-Surnamed Americans, the La Raza National Lawyers' Association, and the La Raza National Law Students Association by Vilma S. Martinez, Sanford Jay Rosen, Carlos M. Algala, Cesar A. Perales, Herbert Teitelbaum, and Melvin L. Wulf.

Brief of amici curiae filed on behalf of the State of Ohio by William J. Brown, Attorney General, and Andrew J. Ruzicho, Earl M. Manz, and Stephen J. Simmons, Assistant Attorneys General.

Brief of amici curiae filed on behalf of the City of Seattle by John P. Harris.

Brief of amici curiae filed on behalf of the American Bar Association by Fletcher N. Baldwin, Jr., and Chesterfield Smith.

Brief of amici curiae filed on behalf of the President and Fellows of Harvard College by Archibald Cox, James N. Bierman, James A. Sharaf, and Daniel
Steiner.

Brief of amici curiae filed on behalf of the Center for Law and Education, Harvard University by J. Harold Flannery.

Brief of amici curiae filed on behalf of the Board of Governors of Rutgers, the State University of New Jersey, et al. by Frank Askin and Norman Amaker.

Brief of amici curiae filed on behalf of the Deans of the Antioch School of Law by Edgar S. Cahn and Jean Camper Cahn.

Brief of amici curiae filed on behalf of the Association of American Law Schools by Erwin N. Griswold and Clifford C. Alloway.

Brief of amici curiae filed on behalf of the Association of American Medical Colleges by John Holt Myers.

Brief of amici curiae filed on behalf of a Group of Law School Deans by Howard A. Glickstein.

Brief of amici curiae filed on behalf of the Law School Admission Council by Harry B. Reese and Peter Martin.

Brief of amici curiae filed on behalf of the Council on Legal Education Opportunity by Cruz Reynoso and Robert B. McKay.

Brief of amici curiae filed on behalf of the Lawyers' Committee for Civil Rights Under Law by Roswell B. Perkins, Kenneth C. Bass III, David S. Tatel, and R. Stephen Browning.

Brief of amici curiae filed on behalf of the NAACP Legal Defense and Educational Fund, Inc., by Jack Greenberg, James M. Nabrit III, Charles Stephen Ralston, Jeffry A. Mintz, Louis H. Pollak, and John Baker.

Brief of amici curiae filed on behalf of the National Conference of Black Lawyers by Derrick A. Bell, Jr.

Brief of amici curiae filed on behalf of the American Indian Law Students Association, Inc., et al. by Bruce R. Greene and Herbert Becker.

Brief of amici curiae filed on behalf of the Legal Aid Society of Alameda County et al. by Clifford Sweet, C. Lyonel Jones, Dennis R. Yeager, E. Richard Lafson, Nathaniel R. Jones, Michael H. Terry, Joseph A. Matera, and C. Christopher Brown.

Brief of amici curiae filed on behalf of the National Organization for Women Legal Defense and Education Fund, Inc., et al. by Peter Van N. Lockwood, David Bonderan, Sylvia Roberts, and David Rubin.

Brief of amici curiae filed on behalf of the National Council of Jewish Women et al. by Joseph L. Rauh, Jr.

Opposing Side (Petitioner/Appellant)

Brief of amici curiae filed on behalf of the Chamber of Commerce of the United States by Milton A. Smith, Gerard C. Smetana, and Jerry Kronenberg.

Brief of amici curiae filed on behalf of the American Federation of Labor and Congress of Industrial Organizations by J. Albert Woll, Laurence Gold,
and Thomas E. Harris.

Brief of amici curiae filed on behalf of the American Jewish Congress by Theodore R. Mann.

Brief of amici curiae filed on behalf of the Jewish Rights Council by David I. Caplan.

Brief of amici curiae filed on behalf of the Advocate Society et al. by Anthony J. Fornelli, Thaddeus L. Kowalski, and Samuel Rabinove.

Brief of amici curiae filed on behalf of the Anti-Defamation League of B'nai B'rith by Alexander M. Bickel, Philip B. Kurland, Larry M. Lavinsky, and Arnold Forster.

IV. THE SUPREME COURT'S DECISION

"In response to questions raised from the bench during the oral argument, counsel for the petitioner has informed the Court that DeFunis has now registered 'for his final quarter in law school.' Counsel for the respondents have made clear that the Law School will not in any way seek to abrogate this registration. In light of

DeFunis' recent registration for the last quarter of his final law school year, and the Law School's assurance that his registration is fully effective, the insistent question again arises whether this case is not moot, and to that question we now turn. . . .

The respondents have represented that, without regard to the ultimate resolution of the issues in this case, DeFunis will remain a student in the Law School for the duration of any term in which he has already enrolled. Since he has now registered for his final term, it is evident that he will be given an opportunity to complete all academic and other requirements for graduation, and, if he does so, will receive his diploma regardless of any decision this Court might reach on the merits of this case. In short, all parties agree that DeFunis is now entitled to complete his legal studies at the University of Washington and to receive his degree from that institution. A determination by this Court of the legal issues tendered by the parties is no longer necessary to compel that result, and could not serve to prevent it. . . .

It matters not that these circumstances partially stem from a policy decision on the part of the respondent Law School authorities. . . .

It might also be suggested that this case presents a question that is 'capable of repetition, yet evading review,' and is thus amenable to federal adjudication even though it might otherwise be considered moot. But DeFunis will never again be required to run the gantlet of the Law School's admission process, and so the question is certainly not 'capable of repetition' so far as he is concerned. Moreover, just because this particular case did not reach the Court until the eve of the petitioner's graduation from Law School, it hardly follows that the issue he raises will in the future evade review. If the admissions procedures of the Law School remain unchanged, there is no reason to suppose that a subsequent case attacking those procedures will not come with relative speed to this Court, now that the Supreme Court of Washington has spoken. . . .

Because the petitioner will complete his law school studies at the end of the term for which he has now registered regardless of any decision this Court might reach on the merits of this litigation, we conclude that the Court cannot, consistently with the limitations of Art. III of the Constitution, consider the substantive constitutional issues tendered by the parties. Accordingly, the judgment of the Supreme Court of Washington is vacated, and the cause is remanded for such proceedings as by that court may be deemed appropriate."

V. JUSTICE VOTE

4 Pro ACLU Side vs. 5 Con Opposing Side

ACLU Side (Respondent/Appellee)

1. White, B. – Joined Brennan's dissent
2. Marshall, T. – Joined Brennan's dissent
3. Brennan, W. – Wrote dissenting opinion
4. Douglas, W. – Wrote dissenting opinion, joined Brennan's dissent

Opposing Side (Petitioner/Appellant)

1. Stewart, P. – Per curiam decision
2. Burger, W. – Per curiam decision
3. Blackmun, H. – Per curiam decision
4. Powell, L. – Per curiam decision
5. Rehnquist, W. – Per curiam decision

VI. A WIN OR LOSS FOR THE ACLU?

The ACLU filed as amici curiae urging affirmance of the judgment of the Supreme Court of Washington; the U.S. Supreme Court vacated, in a 5-4 per curiam decision, giving the ACLU an apparent loss.

331. Kahn v. Shevin

(Decided April 24, 1974; 416 U.S. 351)

I. ISSUE

A. Issues Discussed

Gender

B. Legal Question Presented

Whether a Florida statute granting a tax exemption to widows but not widowers is unconstitutional.

C. Supreme Court's Answer

The statute is constitutional and valid.

II. CASE SUMMARY

A. Background

"Since at least 1885, Florida has provided for some form of property tax exemption for widows. The current law granting all widows an annual $500 exemption has been essentially unchanged since 1941. Appellant Kahn is a widower who lives in Florida and applied for the exemption to the Dade County Tax Assessor's Office. It was denied because the statute offers no analogous benefit for widowers. Kahn then sought a declaratory judgment in the Circuit Court for Dade County, Florida, and that court held the statute violative of the Equal Protection Clause of the Fourteenth Amendment because the classification 'widow' was based upon gender. The Florida Supreme Court reversed, finding the classification valid because it has a 'fair and substantial relation to the object of the legislation,' that object being the reduction of 'the disparity between the economic capabilities of a man and a woman.'"

The Supreme Court granted certiorari to review the case.

B. Counsel of Record

ACLU Side (Petitioner/Appellant): Ruth Bader Ginsburg of the American Civil Liberties Union Foundation argued the cause for appellant. With her on the briefs were William Hoppe, and Melvin L. Wulf, Brenda Feigen Fasteau, and Christine Cassaday Curtis of the American Civil Liberties Union Foundation.

Opposing Side (Respondent/Appellee): Sydney H. McKenzie III, Assistant Attorney General of Florida, argued the cause for appellees. With him on the brief was Robert L. Shevin, Attorney General, pro se.

III. AMICI CURIAE

ACLU Side (Petitioner/Appellant)

No briefs of amici curiae were filed in support of appellant.

Opposing Side (Respondent/Appellee)

No briefs of amici curiae were filed in support of appellee.

IV. THE SUPREME COURT'S DECISION

"There can be no dispute that the financial difficulties confronting the lone woman in Florida or in any other State exceed those facing the man. Whether from overt discrimination or from the socialization process of a male-dominated culture, the job market is inhospitable to the woman seeking any but the lowest paid jobs. There are, of course, efforts under way to remedy this situation. On the federal level, Title VII of the Civil Rights Act of 1964 prohibits covered employers and labor unions from discrimination on the basis of sex, as does the Equal Pay Act of 1963. But firmly entrenched practices are resistant to such pressures, and, indeed, data compiled by the Women's Bureau of the United States Department of Labor show that in 1972 a woman working full time had a median income which was only 57.9% of the median for males—a figure actually six points lower than had been achieved in 1955. Other data point in the same direction. The disparity is likely to be exacerbated for the widow. While the widower can usually continue in the occupation which preceded his spouse's death, in many cases the widow will find herself suddenly forced into a job market with which she is unfamiliar, and in which, because of her former economic dependency, she will have fewer skills to offer.

There can be no doubt, therefore, that Florida's differing treatment of widows and widowers 'rest[s] upon some ground of difference having a fair and substantial relation to the object of the legislation.'

This is not a case like Frontiero v. Richardson, 411 U.S. 677, where the Government denied its female employees both substantive and procedural benefits granted males 'solely . . . for administrative convenience.' We deal here with a state tax law reasonably designed to further the state policy of cushioning the financial impact of spousal loss upon the sex for which that loss imposes a disproportionately heavy burden. We have long held that '[w]here taxation is concerned and no specific federal right, apart from equal protection, is imperilled, the States have large leeway in making classifications and drawing lines which in their judgment produce reasonable systems of taxation.' A state tax law is not arbitrary although it 'discriminate[s] in favor of a certain class . . . if the discrimination is founded upon a reasonable distinction, or difference in state policy,' not in conflict with the Federal Constitution. This principle has weathered nearly a century of Supreme Court adjudication, and it applies here as well. The statute before us is well within those limits.

Affirmed."

V. JUSTICE VOTE

3 Pro ACLU Side vs. 6 Con Opposing Side

ACLU Side (Petitioner/Appellant)

1. Brennan, W. – Wrote dissenting opinion
2. Marshall, T. – Joined Brennan's dissent
3. White, B. – Wrote dissenting opinion

Opposing Side (Respondent/Appellee)

1. Douglas, W. – Wrote majority opinion
2. Stewart, P. – Joined majority opinion
3. Rehnquist, W. – Joined majority opinion
4. Burger, W. – Joined majority opinion
5. Blackmun, H. – Joined majority opinion
6. Powell, L. – Joined majority opinion

VI. A WIN OR LOSS FOR THE ACLU?

The ACLU served as counsel for appellant urging reversal of the judgment of the Florida Supreme Court; the U.S. Supreme Court affirmed in a 6-3 vote, giving the ACLU an apparent loss.

332. Eisen v. Carlisle & Jacquelin

(Decided May 28, 1974; 417 U.S. 156)

I. ISSUE

A. Issues Discussed

Government authority, class actions, civil procedure, judicial power

B. Legal Question Presented

Can petitioner Eisen maintain his suit as a class action on behalf of himself and other traders of the New York Stock Exchange for violations of antitrust and securities laws?

C. Supreme Court's Answer

Eisen cannot maintain a class action as presently constructed, in part because the costs of notice to class members cannot be shifted to the defendant.

II. CASE SUMMARY

A. Background

Petitioner Eisen filed a class action on behalf of himself and all other traders of odd lots within a four-year period on the New York Stock Exchange. The claim charged respondents brokerage firms Carlisle & Jacquelin and DeCoppet & Doremus with "violations of the antitrust and securities laws and demanded damages for petitioner and his class."

Following a series of decisions by the District Court and Court of Appeals on whether or not petition's suit could proceed as a class action, the District Court ultimately decided in the affirmative. After finding that it would cost $225,000 to send individual notice to all class members, the District Court proposed a notification scheme providing for individual notice to only a limited number of prospective class members and notice by publication to the remainder, which would cost $21,720. Petitioner declined to pay $21,720 to litigate an action in which petitioner had an individual stake of only $70.

The District Court then held a preliminary hearing, found that petitioner was "more than likely" to prevail at trial, and ruled that respondents should bear 90% of the notification costs. The Court of Appeals reversed and "ordered the suit dismissed as a class action."

The Supreme Court granted certiorari to review the case, vacated the decision, and remanded the case.

B. Counsel of Record/ACLU Attorney

ACLU Side (Petitioner/Appellant): Aaron M. Fine argued the cause for appellant.

Opposing Side (Respondent/Appellee): Devereux Milburn and William Eldred Jackson argued the cause for appellee.

III. AMICI CURIAE

ACLU Side (Petitioner/Appellant)

Brief of amici curiae filed on behalf of the ACLU by Melvin L. Wulf and Burt Neuborne.

Additional briefs of amici curiae were filed on behalf of the Attorney General of New York, the Commonwealth of Pennsylvania, the State of California, the State of Alabama, et al., the New York State Trial Lawyers Association, the California Trial Lawyers Association, the NAACP Legal Defense and Educational Fund, Inc.,

and the Public Citizen and Consumers Union of United States, Inc.

Opposing Side (Respondent/Appellee)

Brief of amici curiae filed on behalf of the Southern California Edison Co., by William C. Falkenhainer and Rollin E. Woodbury.

Brief of amici curiae filed on behalf of the American College of Trial Lawyers by Samuel E. Gates, Dwight B. Buss, Ralph L. McAfee, Carl J. Schuck, Marvin Schwartz, William Simon, George A. Spiegelberg, and Philip H. Strubing.

IV. THE SUPREME COURT'S DECISION

"Turning to the merits of the case, we find that the District Court's resolution of the notice problems was erroneous in two respects. First, it failed to comply with the notice requirements of Rule 23(c)(2), and second, it imposed part of the cost of notice on respondents. . . .

In the absence of any support under Rule 23, petitioner's effort to impose the cost of notice on respondents must fail. The usual rule is that a plaintiff must initially bear the cost of notice to the class. The exceptions cited by the District Court related to situations where a fiduciary duty pre-existed between the plaintiff and defendant, as in a shareholder derivative suit. Where, as here, the relationship between the parties is truly adversary, the plaintiff must pay for the cost of notice as part of the ordinary burden of financing his own suit.

Petitioner has consistently maintained, however, that he will not bear the cost of notice under subdivision (c)(2) to members of the class as defined in his original complaint. We therefore remand the cause with instructions to dismiss the class action as so defined.

The judgment of the Court of Appeals is vacated and the cause remanded for proceedings consistent with this opinion."

V. JUSTICE VOTE

3 Pro ACLU Side vs. 6 Con Opposing Side

ACLU Side (Petitioner/Appellant)

1. Douglas, W. – Wrote opinion dissenting in part
2. Brennan, W. – Joined Douglas' dissent
3. Marshall, T. – Joined Douglas' dissent

Opposing Side (Respondent/Appellee)

1. Powell, L. – Wrote majority opinion
2. Stewart, P. – Joined majority opinion
3. White, B. – Joined majority opinion
4. Rehnquist, W. – Joined majority opinion
5. Blackmun, H. – Joined majority opinion
6. Burger, W. – Joined majority opinion

VI. A WIN OR LOSS FOR THE ACLU?

The ACLU filed as amicus curiae urging reversal; the Supreme Court vacated the ruling of the Court of Appeals in a 6-3 vote, giving the ACLU an apparent loss.

333. Corning Glass Works v. Brennan

(Decided June 3, 1974; 417 U.S. 188)

I. ISSUE

A. Issues Discussed

Civil rights, gender, Fourteenth Amendment

B. Legal Question Presented

"[W]hether Corning Glass Works violated the [Equal Pay] Act by paying a higher base wage to male night shift inspectors than it paid to female inspectors performing the same tasks on the day shift, where the higher wage was paid in addition to a separate night shift differential paid to all employees for night work."

C. Supreme Court's Answer

Corning violated the Equal Pay Act by paying different wages to male and female employees, and subsequent modifications did not cure the violation.

II. CASE SUMMARY

A. Background

Petitioner, Corning Glass Works, operated plants in New York and Pennsylvania. In both locations all inspection work was performed by women up until 1925. In 1925, however, the company introduced automatic production equipment, which resulted in creating an inspection night shift. By state law, women were prohibited from working at night so the company hired male employees to fill the night shift. The men received substantially higher wages than the female day shift workers.

Prior to 1964, the law was amended to permit women to work

at night. In 1966, petitioner started opening night shift jobs to women and women became eligible "to bid for the higher paid night inspection jobs as vacancies occurred."

In 1969, "a new 'job evaluation' system" was established to set wage rates. The new system abolished the separate base wages for day and night shift inspectors, and established a uniform base wage for inspectors that was higher than the previous wage rate for the night shift. "All inspectors hired after January 20, 1969, were to receive the same base wage, whatever their sex or shift." The system "further provided, however, for a higher 'red circle' rate for employees hired prior to January 20, 1969, when working as inspectors on the night shift," further perpetuating the previous pay differential between day and night inspectors.

Secretary of Labor Brennan brought two actions, one for each of Coring's two plant locations, for back pay for female employees, and "to enjoin Coring from violating the Equal Pay Act."

In New York in No. 73-29, the Court of Appeals concluded that Corning's practice violated the Act, while in Pennsylvania in No. 73-695 the Court of Appeals held that the practice did not violate the Act.

The Supreme Court granted certiorari to review this direct conflict and affirmed the New York decision.

B. Counsel of Record / ACLU Attorney

ACLU Side (Petitioner / Appellant in No. 73-695, Respondent / Appellee in No. 73-29):

Alan Abbot Tuttle argued the cause for appellant in No. 73-695 and appellee in No. 73-29.

Opposing Side (Respondent / Appellee in No. 73-695, Petitioner / Appellant in No. 73-29):

Scott F. Zimmerman argued the cause for appellee in No. 73-695 and appellant in No. 73-29.

III. AMICI CURIAE

ACLU Side (Petitioner / Appellant in No. 73-695, Respondent / Appellee in No. 73-29):

Brief of amici curiae filed on behalf of the ACLU in both cases by Ruth Bader Ginsburg and Melvin L. Wulf.

Opposing Side (Respondent / Appellee in No. 73-695, Petitioner / Appellant in No. 73-29):

Brief of amici curiae filed on behalf of the Chamber of Commerce of the United States by Gerard C. Smetana, Lawrence D. Ehrlich, Jerry Kronenberg, Howard L. Mocerf, Milton Smith, O. F. Wenzler, and Richard Berman.

IV. THE SUPREME COURT'S DECISION

"The Equal Pay Act is broadly remedial, and it should be construed and applied so as to fulfill the underlying purposes which Congress sought to achieve. If, as the Secretary proved, the work performed by women on the day shift was equal to that performed by men on the night shift, the company became obligated to pay the women the same base wage as their male counterparts on the effective date of the Act. To permit the company to escape that obligation by agreeing to allow some women to work on the night shift at a higher rate of pay as vacancies occurred would frustrate, not serve, Congress' ends.

The company's final contention—that it cured its violation of the Act when a new collective-bargaining agreement went into effect on January 20, 1969—need not detain us long. While the new agreement provided for equal base wages for night or day inspectors hired after that date, it continued to provide unequal base wages for employees hired before that date, a discrimination likely to continue for some time into the future because of a large number of laid-off employees who had to be offered re-employment before new inspectors could be hired. After considering the rather complex method in which the new wage rates for employees hired prior to January 1969 were calculated and the company's stated purpose behind the provisions of the new agreement, the District Court in No. 73-29 concluded that the lower base wage for day inspectors was a direct product of the company's failure to equalize the base wages for male and female inspectors as of the effective date of the Act. We agree it is clear from the record that had the company equalized the base-wage rates of male and female inspectors on the effective date of the Act, as the law required, the day inspectors in 1969 would have been entitled to the same higher 'red circle' rate the company provided for night inspectors. We therefore conclude that on the facts of this case, the company's continued discrimination in base wages between night and day workers, though phrased in terms of a neutral factor other than sex, nevertheless operated to perpetuate the effects of the company's prior illegal practice of paying women less than men for equal work.

The judgment in No. 73-29 is affirmed. The judgment in No. 73-695 is reversed and the case remanded to the Court of Appeals for further proceedings consistent with this opinion."

V. JUSTICE VOTE

5 Pro ACLU Side vs. 3 Con Opposing Side

ACLU Side (Petitioner / Appellant in No. 73-695, Respondent / Appellee in No. 73-29):

1. Marshall, T. – Wrote majority opinion
2. Powell, L. – Joined majority opinion
3. White, B. – Joined majority opinion
4. Douglas, W. – Joined majority opinion
5. Brennan, W. – Joined majority opinion

Opposing Side (Respondent / Appellee in No. 73-695, Petitioner / Appellant in No. 73-29):

1. Burger, W. – Wrote joint dissenting opinion
2. Rehnquist, W. – Wrote joint dissenting opinion
3. Blackmun, H. – Wrote joint dissenting opinion

Stewart, P – Took no part in the decision

VI. A WIN OR LOSS FOR THE ACLU?

The ACLU filed as amicus curiae, urging reversal in No. 73-695 and affirmance in No. 73-29; the Supreme Court affirmed the Court of Appeals' judgment in No. 73-29 and reversed the judgment in No. 73-695, in a 6-3 vote, giving ACLU an apparent win.

334. Davis v. United States

(Decided June 10, 1974; 417 U.S. 333)

I. ISSUE

A. Issues Discussed

Military, prison

B. Legal Question Presented

"This case involves the availability of collateral relief from a federal criminal conviction based upon an intervening change in substantive law. While the question presented is a relatively narrow one, it arises as the result of a rather complicated chain of events."

C. Supreme Court's Answer

"[A]lthough we express no view on the merits of the petitioner's claim, we hold that the issue he raises is cognizable in a s 2255 proceeding."

II. CASE SUMMARY

A. Background

"In February 1965, the petitioner, Joseph Anthony Davis, was classified I—A by his draft board and ordered to report for a pre-induction physical examination. Davis failed to appear on the appointed date. He later informed his local board that his failure to report was due to illness. Although the board attempted to arrange a second date for the pre-induction physical, its attempts to communicate with the petitioner were frustrated by his failure to keep the board apprised of his correct mailing addresses. As a result, the local board's [subsequent] communications to the petitioner were returned to the board stamped 'addressee unknown' . . . .

[Ultimately,] the local board declared him a delinquent, pursuant to 32 CFR s 1642.4(a) (1967), both because of his failure to report for the second pre-induction physical and because of his failure to keep the local board informed of his current address. . . . [His] second failure to report for induction resulted in the petitioner's prosecution and conviction under 50 U.S.C.App. s 462(a). [Extensive further litigation ensued.]

After an unsuccessful attempt to secure a rehearing in the Court of Appeals, Davis was remitted to federal custody to commence serving his three-year sentence. He then instituted the present collateral proceeding under 28 U.S.C. s 2255, which permits '(a) prisoner in custody under sentence of a court established by Act of Congress claiming the right to be released upon the ground that the sentence was imposed in violation of the Constitution or laws of the United States . . . (to) move the court which imposed the sentence to vacate, set aside or correct the sentence.' . . . Because the case presents a seemingly important question concerning the extent to which relief under 28 U.S.C. s 2255 is available by reason of an intervening change in law, [the Supreme Court] granted certiorari."

B. Counsel of Record

ACLU Side (Petitioner/Appellant): Marvin M. Karpatkin argued the cause for appellant. With him on the briefs were Melvin L. Wulf of the American Civil Liberties Union Foundation and Scott J. Tepper.

Opposing Side (Respondent/Appellee): Edmund W. Kitch argued the cause for the United States. With him on the brief were Solicitor General Bork, Assistant Attorney General Petersen, Deputy Solicitor General Frey, Jerome M. Feit, and Frederick W. Read III.

III. AMICI CURIAE

ACLU Side (Petitioner/Appellant)

No briefs of amici curiae were filed in support of appellant.

Opposing Side (Respondent/Appellee)

No briefs of amici curiae were filed in support of appellee.

IV. THE SUPREME COURT'S DECISION

"The sole issue before the Court in the present posture of this case is the propriety of the Court of Appeals' judgment that a change in the law of that Circuit after the petitioner's conviction may not be successfully asserted by him in a s 2255 proceeding. Thus, our inquiry is confined to the availability of a s 2255 proceeding for the resolution of Davis' claim to relief from his conviction. . . .

[H]istory makes clear that s 2255 was intended to afford federal prisoners a remedy identical in scope to federal habeas corpus. . . .

Moreover, there is no support in the prior holdings of this Court for the proposition that a claim is not cognizable under s 2255 merely because it is grounded in the 'laws of the United States' rather than the Constitution. . . .

This is not to say, however, that every asserted error of law can be raised on a § 2255 motion. . . .

In this case, the petitioner's contention is that the decision in Gutknecht v. United States, as interpreted and applied by the Court of Appeals for the Ninth Circuit in the Fox case after his conviction was affirmed, establishes that his induction order was invalid under the Selective Service Act and that he could not be lawfully convicted for failure to comply with that order. If this contention is well taken, then Davis' conviction and punishment are for an act that the law does not make criminal. There can be no room for doubt that such a circumstance 'inherently results in a complete miscarriage of justice' and 'present(s) exceptional circumstances' that justify collateral relief under s 2255. Therefore, although we express no view on the merits of the petitioner's claim, we hold that the issue he raises is cognizable in a s 2255 proceeding.

The judgment of the Court of Appeals is accordingly reversed and the case is remanded . . . ."

V. JUSTICE VOTE

7 Pro ACLU Side vs. 2 Con Opposing Side

ACLU Side (Petitioner/Appellant)

1. Stewart, P. – Wrote majority opinion
2. White, B. – Joined majority opinion

3. Marshall, T. – Joined majority opinion
4. Brennan, W. – Joined majority opinion
5. Burger, W. – Joined majority opinion
6. Blackmun, H. – Joined majority opinion
7. Douglas, W. – Joined majority opinion

Opposing Side (Respondent/Appellee)

1. Powell, L. – Wrote opinion concurring in part and dissenting in part
2. Rehnquist, W. – Wrote dissenting opinion

VI. A WIN OR LOSS FOR THE ACLU?

The ACLU served as counsel for appellant urging reversal of the judgment of the Court of Appeals; the Supreme Court reversed, in a 7-2 vote, giving the ACLU an apparent win.

335. Wheeler v. Barrera

(Decided June 10, 1974; 417 U.S. 402)

I. ISSUE

A. Issues Discussed

First Amendment, religion

B. Legal Question Presented

Does Title I require the assignment of publicly employed teachers to provide remedial instruction during regular school hours on the premises of private schools attended by Title I eligible students and, if so, does that requirement violate the First Amendment?

C. Supreme Court's Answer

The Court declined to address the First Amendment issue and determined that Title I requires comparable programs for public and nonpublic schools using Title I funds.

II. CASE SUMMARY

A. Background

"Title I of the Elementary and Secondary Education Act of 1965 . . . provides for federal funding of special programs for educationally deprived children in both public and private schools.

This suit was instituted on behalf of parochial school students who were eligible for Title I benefits and who claimed that the public school authorities in their area, in violation of the Act, failed to provide adequate Title I programs for private school children as compared with those programs provided for public school children. The defendants answered that the extensive aid sought by the plaintiffs exceeded the requirements of Title I and contravened the State's Constitution and state law and public policy. First Amendment rights were also raised by the parties. The District Court, concluding that the State had fulfilled its Title I obligations, denied relief. The United States Court of Appeals for the Eighth Circuit, by a divided vote, reversed. [The Supreme Court] granted certiorari to examine serious questions that appeared to be present as to the scope and constitutionality of Title I."

The Supreme Court affirmed the judgment of the Court of Appeals.

B. Counsel of Record/ACLU Attorney

ACLU Side (Petitioner/Appellant): Leo Pfeffer argued the cause for appellant.

Opposing Side (Respondent/Appellee): Thomas M. Sullivan argued the cause for appellee.

Deputy Solicitor General Daniel M. Friedman argued the cause for the United States, amicus curiae, by special leave of court.

III. AMICI CURIAE

ACLU Side (Petitioner/Appellant)

Brief of amici curiae filed on behalf of the ACLU, et al., by Kenneth W. Greenawalt, Melvin L. Wulf, and Walter Wright.

Additional briefs of amici curiae were filed on behalf of the American Jewish Congress, et al., and the Missouri Coalition for Public Education and Religious Liberty.

Opposing Side (Respondent/Appellee)

Brief of amici curiae filed on behalf of the United States by Deputy Solicitor General Friedman, Solicitor General Bork, Acting Assistant Attorney General Jaffe, Danny J. Boggs, Morton Hollander, Robert S. Grenspan, John B. Rhinelander, Harry J. Chernock, Darrel J. Grinstead, William A. Kaplin, and Philip H. Rosenfelt.

Additional briefs of amici curiae were filed on behalf of the United States Catholic Conference, the Catholic League for Religious and Civil Rights, et al., the National Jewish Commission on Law and Public Affairs, and Parents Rights, Inc., et al.

IV. THE SUPREME COURT'S DECISION

"In sum, although it may be difficult, it is not impossible under the Act to devise and implement a legal local Title I program with comparable services despite the use of on-the-premises instruction in the public schools but not in the private schools. On the facts of this case, petitioners have been approving plans that do not meet this requirement, and certainly, if public school children continue to receive on-the-premises Title I instruction, petitioners should not approve plans that fail to make a genuine effort to employ comparable alternative programs that make up for the lack of on-the-premises instruction for the nonpublic school children. A program which provides instruction and equipment to the public school children and the same equipment but no instruction to the private school children cannot, on its face, be comparable. In order to equalize the level and quality of services offered, something must be substituted for the private school children. The alternatives are numerous. Providing nothing to fill the gap, however, is not among the acceptable alternatives.

Second, if the State is unwilling or unable to develop a plan which is comparable, while using Title I teachers in public but not in private schools, it may develop and submit an acceptable plan which eliminates the use of on-the-premises instruction in the public schools and, instead, resorts to other means, such as neutral sites or summer programs that are less likely to give rise to the gross disparity present in this case.

Third, and undoubtedly least attractive for the educationally deprived children, is nonparticipation in the program. Indeed, under the Act, the Commissioner, subject to judicial review, may refuse to provide funds if the State does not make a bona fide effort to formulate programs with comparable services.

We affirm this disposition with the understanding that petitioners will be given the opportunity to submit guidelines insuring that only those projects that comply with the Act's requirements and this opinion will be approved and submitted to the Commission. It is also to be understood that the District Court's function is not to decide which method is best, or to order that a specific form of service be provided. Rather, the District Court is simply to assure that the state and local agencies fulfill their part of the Title I contract if they choose to accept Title I funds. The comparability mandate is a broad one, and in order to implement the overriding concern with localized control of Title I programs, the District Court should make every effort to defer to the judgment of the petitioners and of the local agency. Under the Act, respondents are entitled to comparable services, and they are, therefore, entitled to relief. As we have stated repeatedly herein, they are not entitled to any particular form of service, and it is the role of the state and local agencies, and not of the federal courts, at least at this stage, to formulate a suitable plan.

On this basis, the judgment of the Court of Appeals is affirmed."

V. JUSTICE VOTE

1 Pro ACLU Side vs. 8 Con Opposing Side

ACLU Side (Petitioner/Appellant)

1. Douglas, W. – Wrote dissenting opinion

Opposing Side (Respondent/Appellee)

1. Blackmun, H. – Wrote majority opinion
2. Stewart, P. – Joined majority opinion
3. White, B. – Wrote concurring opinion
4. Rehnquist, W. – Joined majority opinion
5. Burger, W. – Joined majority opinion
6. Brennan, W. – Joined majority opinion
7. Marshall, T. – Concurred in the result
8. Powell, L. – Wrote concurring opinion

VI. A WIN OR LOSS FOR THE ACLU?

The ACLU filed as amicus curiae urging reversal; the Supreme Court affirmed the Court of Appeals' judgment in an 8-1 vote, giving the ACLU an apparent loss.

336. Geduldig v. Aiello

(Decided June 17, 1974; 417 U.S. 484)

I. ISSUE

A. Issues Discussed

Civil rights, gender, Fourteenth Amendment, equal protection

B. Legal Question Presented

"[W]hether the California disability insurance program invidiously discriminates . . . by not paying insurance benefits for disability that accompanies normal pregnancy and childbirth."

C. Supreme Court's Answer

The program does not discriminate and thus does not violate the equal protection clause of the Fourteenth Amendment.

II. CASE SUMMARY

A. Background

"For almost 30 years California has administered a disability insurance system that pays benefits to persons in private employment who are temporarily unable to work because of disability not covered by workmen's compensation. The appellees brought this action to challenge the constitutionality of a provision of the California program that, in defining 'disability,' excludes from coverage certain disabilities resulting from pregnancy. Because the appellees sought to enjoin the enforcement of this state statute, a three-judge court was convened . . . . On the appellees' motion for summary judgment, the District Court, by a divided vote, held that this provision of the disability insurance program violates the Equal Protection Clause of the Fourteenth Amendment, and therefore enjoined its continued enforcement. . . .

Appellees are four women who have paid sufficient amounts into the Disability Fund to be eligible for benefits under the program. Each of the appellees became pregnant and suffered employment disability as a result of her pregnancy. With respect to three of the appellees, Carolyn Aiello, Augustina Armendariz, and Elizabeth Johnson, the disabilities were attributable to abnormal complications encountered during their pregnancies. The fourth, Jacqueline Jaramillo, experienced a normal pregnancy, which was the sole cause of her disability."

While this case was awaiting decision before the District Court, "the California Court of Appeal, in a suit brought by a woman who suffered an ectopic pregnancy, held that § 2626 does not bar the payment of benefits on account of disability that results from medical complications arising during pregnancy." As a result, only the claim of Jaramillo is at issue before the Supreme Court.

The Supreme Court granted certiorari to review the decision of the District Court and reversed.

B. Counsel of Record/ACLU Attorney

ACLU Side (Respondent/Appellee): Wendy W. Williams argued the cause for appellee.

Opposing Side (Petitioner/Appellant): Joanne Condas, Deputy Attorney General of California argued the cause for appellant.

III. AMICI CURIAE

ACLU Side (Respondent/Appellee)

Brief of amici curiae filed on behalf of the ACLU, et al., by Ruth Bader Ginsburg, Melvin L. Wulf, Kathleen Peratis, and Nancy E. Stanley.

Additional briefs of amici curiae were filed on behalf of the United States Equal Employment Opportunity Commission, the American Federation of Labor and Congress of Industrial Organizations, the International Union of Electrical, Radio and Machine Workers, AFL-CIO-CLC, the Women's Equity Action League, et al., and the Physicians Forum.

Opposing Side (Petitioner/Appellant)

Briefs of amici curiae were filed on behalf of the Chamber of Commerce of the United States, the Pacific Legal Foundation, the National Association of Manufacturers of the United States, the Merchants and Manufacturers Association, the American Telephone and Telegraph Company, and the General Electric Company.

IV. THE SUPREME COURT'S DECISION

"The State has a legitimate interest in maintaining the self-supporting nature of its insurance program. Similarly, it has an interest in distributing the available resources in such a way as to keep benefit payments at an adequate level for disabilities that are covered, rather than to cover all disabilities inadequately. Finally, California has a legitimate concern in maintaining the contribution rate at a level that will not unduly burden participating employees, particularly low-income employees who may be most in need of the disability insurance.

These policies provide an objective and wholly non-invidious basis for the State's decision not to create a more comprehensive insurance program than it has. There is no evidence in the record that the selection of the risks insured by the program worked to discriminate against any definable group or class in terms of the aggregate risk protection derived by that group or class from the program. There is no risk from which men are protected and women are not. Likewise, there is no risk from which women are protected and men are not.

The appellee simply contends that, although she has received insurance protection equivalent to that provided all other participating employees, she has suffered discrimination because she encountered a risk that was outside the program's protection. For the reasons we have stated, we hold that this contention is not a valid one under the Equal Protection Clause of the Fourteenth Amendment. The stay heretofore issued by the Court is vacated, and the judgment of the District Court is reversed."

V. JUSTICE VOTE

3 Pro ACLU Side vs. 6 Con Opposing Side

ACLU Side (Respondent/Appellee)

1. Brennan, W. – Wrote dissenting opinion
2. Marshall, T. – Joined Brennan's dissent
3. Douglas, W. – Joined Brennan's dissent

Opposing Side (Petitioner/Appellant)

1. Stewart, P. – Wrote majority opinion
2. White, B. – Joined majority opinion
3. Rehnquist, W. – Joined majority opinion
4. Blackmun, H. – Joined majority opinion
5. Powell, L. – Joined majority opinion
6. Burger, W. – Joined majority opinion

VI. A WIN OR LOSS FOR THE ACLU?

The ACLU filed as amicus curiae urging affirmance; the Supreme Court reversed the judgment of the District Court in a 6-3 vote, giving the ACLU an apparent loss.

337. Parker v. Levy

(Decided June 19, 1974; 417 U.S. 733)

I. ISSUE

A. Issues Discussed

Military, First Amendment, freedom of speech

B. Legal Question Presented

"Whether Articles 133 and 134 of the Uniform Code of Military Justice, 10 U.S.C. 933 and 934, are unconstitutional as applied to the conduct in this case [or] are unconstitutional on their face."[1] "Whether, regardless of the constitutionality of Articles 133 and 134, appellee was denied his constitutional rights and a fair trial on the Article 90 charge and on the speech charges, Articles 133 and 134."[2]

C. Supreme Court's Answer

Articles 133 and 134 are not unconstitutional as void for vagueness or overbroad, and the conviction should not be overturned based on Article 90.

II. CASE SUMMARY

A. Background

"Appellee Howard Levy, a physician, was a captain in the Army stationed at Fort Jackson, South Carolina. . . . From the time he entered on active duty in July 1965 until his trial by court-martial, he was assigned as Chief of the Dermatological Service of the United States Army Hospital at Fort Jackson. On June 2, 1967, appellee was convicted by a general court-martial of violations of Arts. 90, 133, and 134 of the Uniform Code of Military Justice, and sentenced to dismissal from the service, forfeiture of all pay and allowances, and confinement for three years at hard labor.

[O]ne of the functions of the hospital to which appellee was assigned was that of training Special Forces aide men. As Chief of the Dermatological Service, appellee was to conduct a clinic for those aide men. In the late summer of 1966, it came to the attention of the hospital commander that the dermatology training of the students was unsatisfactory. After investigating the program and determining that appellee had totally neglected his duties, the commander called appellee to his office and personally handed him a written order to conduct the training. Appellee read the order, said that he understood it, but declared that he would not obey it because of his medical ethics. . . .

The specification under Art. 134 alleged that appellee 'did, at Fort Jackson, South Carolina, . . . with design to promote disloyalty and disaffection among the troops, publicly utter (certain) statements to divers enlisted personnel at divers times . . . .' The specification under Art. 133 alleged that appellee did 'while in the performance of his duties at the United States Army Hospital . . . wrongfully and dishonorably' make statements variously described as intemperate, defamatory, provoking, disloyal, contemptuous, and disrespectful to Special Forces personnel and to enlisted personnel who were patients or under his supervision.

1 Brief of Petitioner at 3, Parker v. Levy, 417 U.S. 733 (1974) (No. 73-206).
2 Brief of Respondent at 1, Parker v. Levy, 417 U.S. 733 (1974) (No. 73-206).

Appellee was convicted by the court-martial, and his conviction was sustained on his appeals within the military. After he had exhausted this avenue of relief, he sought federal habeas corpus in the United States District Court for the Middle District of Pennsylvania . . . . The District Court . . . denied relief. . . . The Court of Appeals reversed, holding in a lengthy opinion that Arts. 133 and 134 are void for vagueness."

The Supreme Court granted certiorari to review the case and reversed the decision of the Court of Appeals.

B. Counsel of Record/ACLU Attorney

ACLU Side (Respondent/Appellee): Charles Morgan, Jr., of the ACLU argued the cause for appellee. With him on the brief were Anthony G. Amsterdam, Alan H. Levine, Burt Neuborne, Melvin L. Wulf, Henry W. Sawyer, III, Mary Ellen Gale, Norman Siegel, Laughlin McDonald, Morris Brown, Emily Carssow, Neil Bradley, Reber F. Boult, Jr., George W. Dean, Jr., and Ambrose Campana.

Opposing Side (Petitioner/Appellant): Solicitor General Robert H. Bork argued the cause for appellant. With him on the brief were Assistant Attorney General Henry E. Petersen, Assistant to the Solicitor General Allan A. Tuttle, Jerome M. Feit, and Harvey M. Stone.

III. AMICI CURIAE

ACLU Side (Respondent/Appellee)

Brief of amici curiae filed on behalf of the Association of the Bar of the City of New York by Thomas M. Comerford, David L. Fox, Marvin M. Karpatkin, and Leonard P. Novello.

Brief of amici curiae filed on behalf of Richard G. Augenblick by Joseph H. Sharlitt and Neal E. Krucoff.

Opposing Side (Petitioner/Appellant)

IV. THE SUPREME COURT'S DECISION

"Appellee urges that both Art. 133 and Art. 134 (the general article) are 'void for vagueness' under the Due Process Clause of the Fifth Amendment and overbroad in violation of the First Amendment. . . .

Because of the factors differentiating military society from civilian society, we hold that the proper standard of review for a vagueness challenge to the articles of the Code is the standard which applies to criminal statutes regulating economic affairs. Clearly, that standard is met here . . . . Since appellee could have had no reasonable doubt that his public statements urging Negro enlisted men not to go to Vietnam if ordered to do so were both 'unbecoming an officer and a gentleman,' and 'to the prejudice of good order and discipline in the armed forces,' in violation of the provisions of Art. 133 and Art. 134, respectively, his challenge to them as unconstitutionally vague under the Due Process Clause of the Fifth Amendment must fail. . . .

We likewise reject appellee's contention that Arts. 133 and 134 are facially invalid because of their 'overbreadth.' . . . His conduct, that of a commissioned officer publicly urging enlisted personnel to refuse to obey orders which might send them into combat, was unprotected under the most expansive notions of the First Amendment. Articles 133 and 134 may constitutionally prohibit that conduct and a sufficiently large number of similar or related types of conduct so as to preclude their invalidation for overbreadth. . . .

Appellee urges that should we disagree with the Court of Appeals as to the constitutionality of Arts. 133 and 134, we should nonetheless affirm its judgment by invalidating his conviction under Art. 90. He contends that to carry out the hospital commandant's order to train aide men in dermatology would have constituted participation in a war crime, and that the commandant gave the order in question, knowing that it would be disobeyed, for the sole purpose of increasing the punishment which could be imposed upon appellee. The Court of Appeals observed that each of these defenses was recognized under the Uniform Code of Military Justice, but had been resolved against appellee on a factual basis by the court-martial which convicted him. . . . We agree with the Court of Appeals. . . .

Reversed."

V. JUSTICE VOTE

3 Pro ACLU Side vs. 5 Con Opposing Side

ACLU Side (Respondent/Appellee)

1. Douglas, W. – Wrote dissenting opinion, joined Stewart's dissent
2. Stewart, P. – Wrote dissenting opinion
3. Brennan, W. – Joined Stewart's dissent

Opposing Side (Petitioner/Appellant)

1. Rehnquist, W. – Wrote majority opinion
2. Powell, L. – Joined majority opinion
3. White, B. – Joined majority opinion
4. Blackmun, H. – Wrote concurring opinion
5. Burger, W. – Joined Blackmun's concurrence

Marshall, T – Took no part in the decision

VI. A WIN OR LOSS FOR THE ACLU?

The ACLU argued the case for appellee, urging affirmance; the Supreme Court reversed the Court of Appeals' decision by a 5-3 vote, giving the ACLU an apparent loss.

338. Richardson v. Ramirez

(Decided June 24, 1974; 418 U.S. 24)

I. ISSUE

A. Issues Discussed

Civil rights, voting rights, Fourteenth Amendment, equal protection

B. Legal Question Presented

Does denying convicted felons the right to vote violate their right to equal protection under the Fourteenth Amendment?

C. Supreme Court's Answer

Denying convicted felons the right to vote does not deny them equal protection.

II. CASE SUMMARY

A. Background

"The three individual respondents in this case were convicted of felonies and have completed the service of their respective sentences and paroles. They filed a petition for a writ of mandate in the Supreme Court of California to compel California county election officials to register them as voters. They claimed, on behalf of themselves and others similarly situated, that application to them of the provisions of the California Constitution and implementing statutes which disenfranchised persons convicted of an 'infamous crime' denied them the right to equal protection of the laws under the Federal Constitution. The Supreme Court of California held that 'as applied to all ex-felons whose terms of incarceration and parole have expired, the provisions of article II and article XX, section 11, of the California Constitution denying the right of suffrage to persons convicted of crime, together with the several sections of the Elections Code implementing that disqualification . . . violate the equal protection clause of the Fourteenth Amendment.'"

The Supreme Court granted certiorari to review the case and reversed.

B. Counsel of Record / ACLU Attorney

ACLU Side (Respondent / Appellee): Martin R. Glick argued the cause for appellee.

Daniel Hays Lowenstein filed a brief for respondent Brown, Secretary of State of California.

Opposing Side (Petitioner / Appellant): Duncan M. James argued the cause for appellant.

Deputy Attorney General George J. Roth argued the cause for the State of California, amicus curiae, by special leave of court.

III. AMICI CURIAE

ACLU Side (Respondent / Appellee)

Brief of amici curiae filed on behalf of the ACLU of Southern California by Philip L. Goar, A. L. Wirin, and Fred Okrand.

Brief of amici filed on behalf of the American Bar Association by Chesterfield Smith, Richard J. Hughes, Daniel L. Skoler, Melvin T. Axilbund, Richard C. Hand, Paul F. Attaguile, and Ralph H. Loewenstein.

Opposing Side (Petitioner / Appellant)

Brief of amici curiae filed on behalf of the State of California by Evelle J. Younger, Attorney General, Iver E. Skjeie, Assistant Attorney General, and George J. Roth, Deputy Attorney General.

IV. THE SUPREME COURT'S DECISION

"Unlike most claims under the Equal Protection Clause, for the decision of which we have only the language of the Clause itself as it is embodied in the Fourteenth Amendment, respondents' claim implicates not merely the language of the Equal Protection Clause of § 1 of the Fourteenth Amendment, but also the provisions of the less familiar § 2 of the Amendment:

'Representatives shall be apportioned among the several States according to their respective numbers, counting the whole number of persons in each State, excluding Indians not taxed. But when the right to vote at any election for the choice of electors for President and Vice President of the United States, Representatives in Congress, the Executive and Judicial officers of a State, or the members of the Legislature thereof, is denied to any of the male inhabitants of such State, being twenty-one years of age, and citizens of the United States, or in any way abridged, *except for participation in rebellion, or other crime,* the basis of representation therein shall be reduced in the proportion which the number of such male citizens shall bear to the whole number of male citizens twenty-one years of age in such State.' (Emphasis supplied.)

Petitioner contends that the italicized language of § 2 expressly exempts from the sanction of that section disenfranchisement grounded on prior conviction of a felony. She goes on to argue that those who framed and adopted the Fourteenth Amendment could not have intended to prohibit outright in § 1 of that Amendment that which was expressly exempted from the lesser sanction of reduced representation imposed by § 2 of the Amendment. This argument seems to us a persuasive one unless it can be shown that the language of § 2, 'except for participation in rebellion, or other crime,' was intended to have a different meaning than would appear from its face.

[T]he exclusion of felons from the vote has an affirmative sanction in § 2 of the Fourteenth Amendment, a sanction which was not present in the case of the other restrictions on the franchise which were invalidated in the cases on which respondents rely. We hold that the understanding of those who adopted the Fourteenth Amendment, as reflected in the express language of § 2 and in the historical and judicial interpretation of the Amendment's applicability to state laws disenfranchising felons, is of controlling significance in distinguishing such laws from those other state limitations on the franchise which have been held invalid under the Equal Protection Clause by this Court. . . .

Pressed upon us by the respondents, and by amici curiae, are contentions that these notions are outmoded, and that the more modern view is that it is essential to the process of rehabilitating the ex-felon that he be returned to his role in society as a fully participating citizen when he has completed the serving of his term. We would by no means discount these arguments if addressed to the legislative forum which may properly weigh and balance them against those advanced in support of California's present constitutional provisions. But it is not for us to choose one set of values over the other. If respondents are correct, and the view which they advocate is indeed the more enlightened and sensible one, presumably the people of the State of California will ultimately come around to that view. And if they do not do so, their failure is some evidence, at least, of the fact that there are two sides to the argument.

We therefore hold that the Supreme Court of California erred in concluding that California may no longer, consistent with the Equal Protection Clause of the Fourteenth Amendment, exclude from the franchise convicted felons who have completed their sentences and paroles. The California court did not reach respondents' alternative contention that there was such a total lack of uniformity in county election officials' enforcement of the challenged state laws as to work a separate denial of equal protection, and we believe that it should have an opportunity to consider the claim before we address ourselves to it. Accordingly, we reverse and remand for further proceedings not inconsistent with this opinion."

V. JUSTICE VOTE

3 Pro ACLU Side vs. 6 Con Opposing Side

ACLU Side (Petitioner/Appellant)

1. Marshall, T. – Wrote dissenting opinion
2. Douglas, W. – Wrote dissenting opinion, joined Marshall's dissent in part
3. Brennan, W. – Joined Marshall's dissent

Opposing Side (Respondent/Appellee)

1. Rehnquist, W. – Wrote majority opinion
2. Burger, W. – Joined majority opinion
3. White, B. – Joined majority opinion
4. Blackmun, H. – Joined majority opinion
5. Powell, L. – Joined majority opinion
6. Stewart, P. – Joined majority opinion

VI. A WIN OR LOSS FOR THE ACLU?

The ACLU filed as amicus curiae urging affirmance; the Supreme Court reversed the ruling of the Supreme Court of California in a 6-3 vote, giving the ACLU an apparent loss.

339. Hamling v. United States

(Decided June 24, 1974; 418 U.S. 87)

I. ISSUE

A. Issues Discussed

First Amendment, obscenity, Fourteenth Amendment

B. Legal Question Presented

"[W]hat rules of law shall govern obscenity convictions that occurred prior to the date on which [the Supreme] Court's decision in Miller v. California and its companion cases were handed down, but which had not at that point become final"?

C. Supreme Court's Answer

The obscenity convictions could be governed by the Miller test, but the test does not require the convictions be reversed in this case.

II. CASE SUMMARY

A. Background

"On March 5, 1971, a grand jury in the United States District Court for the Southern District of California indicted petitioners William L. Hamling, Earl Kemp, Shirley R. Wright, David L. Thomas, Reed Enterprises, Inc., and Library Service, Inc., on 21 counts of an indictment charging use of the mails to carry an obscene book, *The Illustrated Presidential Report of the Commission on Obscenity and Pornography*, and an obscene advertisement, which gave information as to where, how, and from whom and by what means the *Illustrated Report* might be obtained, and of conspiracy to commit the above offenses, in violation of 18 U.S.C. §§ 2, 371, and 1461. Prior to trial, petitioners moved to dismiss the indictment on the grounds that it failed to inform them of the charges, and that the grand jury had insufficient evidence before it to return an indictment and was improperly instructed on the law. Petitioners also challenged the petit jury panel and moved to strike the venire on the ground that there had been an unconstitutional exclusion of all persons under 25 years of age. The District Court denied all of these motions. . . .

These petitioners were convicted by a jury on December 23, 1971. The Court of Appeals affirmed their convictions in an opinion filed on June 7, 1973. The Court of Appeals originally denied rehearing and suggestion for rehearing en banc on July 9, 1973. That order was withdrawn by the Court of Appeals to be reconsidered in light of [the Supreme] Court's decisions, announced June 21, 1973, in *Miller v. California*, 413 U.S. 15, . . . and related cases, and was submitted to the en banc court, by order dated August 20, 1973. On August 22, 1973, the Court of Appeals entered an order denying the petition for rehearing and the suggestion for rehearing en banc."

The Supreme Court granted certiorari to review the case and affirmed the Court of Appeals.

B. Counsel of Record/ACLU Attorney

ACLU Side (Petitioner/Appellant): Stanley Fleishman argued the cause for appellants Hamling, et al.

Sam Rosenwein argued the cause for appellants Kemp, et al.

Opposing Side (Respondent/Appellee): Allan A. Tuttle argued the cause for the United States.

III. AMICI CURIAE

ACLU Side (Petitioner/Appellant)

Brief of amici curiae filed on behalf of the ACLU by Melvin L. Wulf, Joel M. Gora, Fred Okrand, John O'Loughlin, and Jill Jakes.

Brief of amici curiae filed on behalf of the Association of American Publishers, Inc., by Ira M. Millstein and Heather Grant Florence.

Brief of amici curiae filed on behalf of the American Library Association by William D. North, Tefft W. Smith, and Alex P. Allain.

Opposing Side (Respondent/Appellee)

No briefs of amici curiae were filed in support of appellee.

IV. THE SUPREME COURT'S DECISION

"*Miller* rejected the view that the First and Fourteenth Amendments require that the proscription of obscenity be based on uniform nationwide standards of what is obscene, describing such standards as 'hypothetical and unascertainable.' But, in so doing, the Court did not require as a constitutional matter the substitution of some smaller geographical area into the same sort of formula; the test was stated in terms of the understanding of 'the average person, applying contemporary community standards.' When this approach is coupled with the reaffirmation in *Paris Adult Theatre I v. Slaton,* of the rule that the prosecution need not, as a matter of constitutional law, produce 'expert' witnesses to testify as to the obscenity of the material, the import of the quoted language from *Miller* becomes clear. A juror is entitled to draw on his own knowledge of the views of the average person in the community or vicinage from which he comes for making the required determination, just as he is entitled to draw on his knowledge of the propensities of a 'reasonable' person in other areas of the law. Our holding in *Miller* that California could constitutionally proscribe obscenity in terms of a 'statewide' standard did not mean that any such precise geographic area is required as a matter of constitutional law. . . .

The result of the *Miller* cases, therefore, as a matter of constitutional law and federal statutory construction, is to permit a juror sitting in obscenity cases to draw on knowledge of the community or vicinage from which he comes in deciding what conclusion 'the average person, applying contemporary community standards' would reach in a given case. Since this case was tried in the Southern District of California, and presumably jurors from throughout that judicial district were available to serve on the panel which tried petitioners, it would be the standards of that 'community' upon which the jurors would draw. But this is not to say that a district court would not be at liberty to admit evidence of standards existing in some place outside of this particular district if it felt such evidence would assist the jurors in the resolution of the issues which they were to decide. . . .

Petitioners attack the sufficiency of the indictment under which they were charged for two reasons: first, that it charged them only in the statutory language of 18 U.S.C. § 1461 which they contend was unconstitutionally vague as applied to them; and second, that the indictment failed to give them adequate notice of the charges against them. As noted above, however, at the time of petitioners' convictions, *Roth v. United States* had held that the language of § 1461 was not 'too vague to support conviction for crime.' . . .

The definition of obscenity, however, is not a question of fact, but one of law; the word 'obscene,' as used in 18 U.S.C. § 1461, is not merely a generic or descriptive term, but a legal term of art. The legal definition of obscenity does not change with each indictment; it is a term sufficiently definite in legal meaning to give a defendant notice of the charge against him. Since the various component parts of the constitutional definition of obscenity need not be alleged in the indictment in order to establish its sufficiency, the indictment in this case was sufficient to adequately inform petitioners of the charges against them. . . .

The judgment of the Court of Appeals for the Ninth Circuit in this case is affirmed."

V. JUSTICE VOTE

4 Pro ACLU Side vs. 5 Con Opposing Side

ACLU Side (Petitioner/Appellant)

1. Douglas, W. – Wrote dissenting opinion
2. Brennan, W. – Wrote dissenting opinion
3. Marshall, T. – Joined Brennan's dissent
4. Stewart, P. – Joined Brennan's dissent

Opposing Side (Respondent/Appellee)

1. Rehnquist, W. – Wrote majority opinion
2. Burger, W. – Joined majority opinion
3. White, B. – Joined majority opinion
4. Blackmun, H. – Joined majority opinion
5. Powell, L. – Joined majority opinion

VI. A WIN OR LOSS FOR THE ACLU?

The ACLU filed as amicus curiae urging reversal; the Supreme Court affirmed the ruling of the Court of Appeals for the Ninth Circuit in a 5-4 vote, giving the ACLU an apparent loss.

340. United States v. Richardson

(Decided June 25, 1974; 418 U.S. 166)

I. ISSUE

A. Issues Discussed

Civil procedure

B. Legal Question Presented

"[W]hether the respondent has standing to bring an action as a federal taxpayer alleging that certain provisions concerning public reporting of expenditures under the Central Intelligence Agency Act of 1949 violate Art. I, s 9, cl. 7, of the Constitution which provides:

'No Money shall be drawn from the Treasury, but in Consequence of Appropriations made by Law; and a regular Statement and Account of the Receipts and Expenditures of all public Money shall be published from time to time.'"

C. Supreme Court's Answer

"[T]here is no 'logical nexus' between the asserted status of taxpayer and the claimed failure of the Congress to require the Executive to supply a more detailed report of the expenditures of that agency.

The question presented thus is simply and narrowly whether these claims meet the standards for taxpayer standing set forth in Flast; we hold they do not."

II. CASE SUMMARY

A. Background

"[R]espondent wrote to the Government Printing Office in 1967 and requested that he be provided with the documents 'published by the Government in compliance with Article I, section 9, clause (7) of the United States Constitution.' The Fiscal Service of the Bureau of Accounts of the Department of the Treasury replied, explaining that it published the document known as the Combined Statement of Receipts, Expenditures, and Balances of the United States Government. . . . Respondent then wrote to the same office and, quoting part of the CIA Act, asked whether this statute did not 'cast reflection upon the authenticity of the

Treasury's Statement.' . . . The Bureau of Accounts replied stating that it had no other available information.

In another letter, respondent asserted that the CIA Act was repugnant to the Constitution and requested that the Treasury Department seek an opinion of the Attorney General. The Department answered declining to seek such an opinion and this suit followed. Respondent's complaint asked the court to 'issue a permanent injunction enjoining the defendants from publishing their 'Combined Statement of Receipts, Expenditures and Balances of the United States Government' and representing it as the fulfillment of the mandates of Article I Section 9 Clause 7 until same fully complies with those mandates.' . . . The only injury alleged by respondent was that he 'cannot obtain a document that sets out the expenditures and receipts' of the CIA but on the contrary was 'asked to accept a fraudulent document.' The District Court granted a motion for dismissal on the ground respondent lacked standing . . . and that the subject matter raised political questions not suited for judicial disposition.

The Court of Appeals . . . reversed, holding that the respondent had standing to bring this action."

The Supreme Court granted certiorari to review the case.

B. Counsel of Record

ACLU Side (Respondent/Appellee): Osmond K. Fraenkel argued the cause for appellee. With him on the brief were Melvin L. Wulf, Burt Neuborne, and John H. F. Shattuck of the American Civil Liberties Union Foundation, and James R. Kelley.

Opposing Side (Petitioner/Appellant): Solicitor General Bork argued the cause for the United States et al. On the brief were former Solicitor General Griswold, Assistant Attorney General Wood, Deputy Solicitor General Lacovara, Harriet S. Shapiro, Walter H. Fleischer, and William D. Appler.

III. AMICI CURIAE

ACLU Side (Respondent/Appellee)

No briefs of amici curiae were filed in support of appellee.

Opposing Side (Petitioner/Appellant)

No briefs of amici curiae were filed in support of appellant.

IV. THE SUPREME COURT'S DECISION

"When the Court addressed the question of standing in Flast, Mr. Chief Justice Warren traced what he described as the 'confusion' following Frothingham as to whether the Court had announced a constitutional doctrine barring suits by taxpayers challenging federal expenditures as unconstitutional or simply a policy rule of judicial self-restraint. . . . That re-examination led, however, to the holding that a 'taxpayer will have standing consistent with Article III to invoke federal judicial power when he alleges that congressional action under the taxing and spending clause is in derogation of those constitutional provisions which operate to restrict the exercise of the taxing and spending power.' . . .

Although the Court made it very explicit in Flast that a 'fundamental aspect of standing' is that it focuses primarily on the party seeking to get his complaint before the federal court rather than 'on the issues he wishes to have adjudicated,' it made equally clear that

'in ruling on (taxpayer) standing, it is both appropriate and necessary to look to the substantive issues for another purpose, namely, to determine whether there is a logical nexus between the status asserted and the claim sought to be adjudicated.'

We therefore turn to an examination of the issues sought to be raised by respondent's complaint to determine whether he is 'a proper and appropriate party to invoke federal judicial power,' with respect to those issues. . . .

[T]here is no 'logical nexus' between the asserted status of taxpayer and the claimed failure of the Congress to require the Executive to supply a more detailed report of the expenditures of that agency.

The question presented thus is simply and narrowly whether these claims meet the standards for taxpayer standing set forth in Flast; we hold they do not. . . .

This is surely the kind of a generalized grievance described in both Frothingham and Flast since the impact on him is plainly undifferentiated and 'common to all members of the public.' . . .

It can be argued that if respondent is not permitted to litigate this issue, no one can do so. . . .

As our society has become more complex, our numbers more vast, our lives more varied, and our resources more strained, citizens increasingly request the intervention of the courts on a greater variety of issues than at any period of our national development. The acceptance of new categories of judicially cognizable injury has not eliminated the basic principle that to invoke judicial power the claimant must have a 'personal stake in the outcome,' or 'a direct injury,' in short, something more than 'generalized grievances.' Respondent has failed to meet these fundamental tests; accordingly, the judgment of the Court of Appeals is reversed."

V. JUSTICE VOTE

4 Pro ACLU Side vs. 5 Con Opposing Side

ACLU Side (Respondent/Appellee)

1. Marshall, T. – Joined Stewart's dissent
2. Brennan, W. – Wrote dissenting opinion
3. Stewart, P. – Wrote dissenting opinion
4. Douglas, W. – Wrote dissenting opinion

Opposing Side (Petitioner/Appellant)

1. Burger, W. – Wrote majority opinion
2. White, B. – Joined majority opinion
3. Blackmun, H. – Joined majority opinion
4. Powell, L. – Wrote concurring opinion
5. Rehnquist, W. – Joined majority opinion

VI. A WIN OR LOSS FOR THE ACLU?

The ACLU served as counsel for appellee urging affirmance of the judgment of the Court of Appeals; the Supreme Court reversed, in a 5-4 vote, giving the ACLU an apparent loss.

341. Miami Herald Publishing Co. v. Tornillo

(Decided June 25, 1974; 418 U.S. 241)

I. ISSUE

A. Issues Discussed

First Amendment, freedom of the press

B. Legal Question Presented

"[W]hether a state statute granting a political candidate a right to equal space to reply to criticism and attacks on his record by a newspaper violates the guarantees of a free press."

C. Supreme Court's Answer

The state statute violates the First Amendment freedom of the press.

II. CASE SUMMARY

A. Background

"In the fall of 1972, appellee, Executive Director of the Classroom Teachers Association, . . . was a candidate for the Florida House of Representatives. On September 20, 1972, and again on September 29, 1972, appellant printed editorials critical of appellee's candidacy. In response to these editorials appellee demanded that appellant print verbatim his replies, defending the role of the Classroom Teachers Association and the organization's accomplishments for the citizens of Dade County. Appellant declined to print the appellee's replies and appellee brought suit in Circuit Court, Dade County, seeking declaratory and injunctive relief and actual and punitive damages in excess of $5,000. The action was premised on Florida Statute §104.38 (1973), a 'right of reply' statute which provides that if a candidate for nomination or election is assailed regarding his personal character or official record by any newspaper, the candidate has the right to demand that the newspaper print, free of cost to the candidate, any reply the candidate may make to the newspaper's charges. The reply must appear in as conspicuous a place, and in the same size of type, as the charges which prompted the reply, provided it does not take up more space than the charges. Failure to comply with the statute constitutes a first-degree misdemeanor.

Appellee sought a declaration that §104.38 was unconstitutional. After an emergency hearing requested by appellee, the circuit court denied injunctive relief and held that §104.38 was unconstitutional as an infringement on the freedom of the press under the First and Fourteenth Amendments to the Constitution. The Circuit Court concluded that dictating what a newspaper must print was no different from dictating what it must not print. The Circuit Judge viewed the statute's vagueness as serving 'to restrict and stifle protected expression.' Appellee's cause was dismissed with prejudice.

On direct appeal, the Florida Supreme Court reversed, holding that § 104.38 did not violate constitutional guarantees. It held that free speech was enhanced and not abridged by the Florida right-of-reply statute, which in that court's view, furthered the 'broad societal interest in the free flow of information to the public.' It also held that the statute is not impermissibly vague; the statute informs 'those who are subject to it as to what conduct on their part will render them liable to its penalties.' Civil remedies, including damages, were held to be available under this statute and the case was remanded to the trial court for further proceedings not inconsistent with the Florida Supreme Court's opinion."

The Supreme Court granted certiorari to review the case and reversed.

B. Counsel of Record/ACLU Attorney

ACLU Side (Petitioner/Appellant): Daniel P. S. Paul argued the cause for appellant.

Opposing Side (Respondent/Appellee): Jerome A. Barron argued the cause for appellee.

III. AMICI CURIAE

ACLU Side (Petitioner/Appellant)

Brief of amici curiae filed on behalf of the ACLU of Florida by Jonathan L. Alpert, Irma Robbins Feder, and Richard Yale Feder.

Additional briefs of amici curiae were filed on behalf of the Washington Post Co., the Times Mirror Co., New York News Inc., the Chicago Tribune Co., et al., the Florida Publishing Co., the Times Publishing Co., the Gannett Florida Corporation, et al., the American Newspaper Publishers Association, the National Newspaper Association, the American Society of Newspaper Editors, et al., the Reporters Committee for Freedom of the Press Legal Defense and Research Fund, et al., the National Association of Broadcasters, the Radio Television News Directors Association, the National Broadcasting Co., Inc., and Dow Jones & Co., Inc., et al.

Opposing Side (Respondent/Appellee)

Briefs of amici curiae were filed on behalf of the National Citizens Committee for Broadcasting by Albert H. Kramer and Thomas R. Asher; and by Donald U. Sessions, pro se.

IV. THE SUPREME COURT'S DECISION

"The challenged statute creates a right to reply to press criticism of a candidate for nomination or election. The statute was enacted in 1913, and this is only the second recorded case decided under its provisions. . . .

Appellee's argument that the Florida statute does not amount to a restriction of appellant's right to speak because 'the statute in question here has not prevented the Miami Herald from saying anything it wished' begs the core question. Compelling editors or publishers to publish that which 'reason' tells them should not be published is what is at issue in this case. The Florida statute operates as a command in the same sense as a statue or regulation forbidding appellant to publish specified matter. Governmental restraint on publishing need not fall into familiar or traditional patterns to be subject to constitutional limitations on governmental powers. The Florida statute exacts a penalty on the basis of the content of a newspaper. The first phase of the penalty resulting from the compelled printing of a reply is exacted in terms of the cost in printing and composing time and materials and in taking up space that could be devoted to other material the newspaper may have preferred to print. [A] newspaper is not subject to the finite technological limitations of time that confront a broadcaster but it is not correct to say that, as an economic reality, a newspaper can proceed to infinite expansion of its column space to accommodate the replies that a government agency determines or a statute commands the readers should have available.

Faced with the penalties that would accrue to any newspaper that published news or commentary arguably within the reach of the right-of-access statute, editors might well conclude that the safe course is to avoid controversy. Therefore, under the operation of the Florida statute, political and electoral coverage would be blunted or reduced. Government-enforced right of access inescapably 'dampens the vigor and limits the variety of public debate.' . . .

'[T]here is practically universal agreement that a major purpose of [the First] Amendment was to protect the free discussion of governmental affairs. This of course includes discussions of candidates . . . .'

Even if a newspaper would face no additional costs to comply with a compulsory access law and would not be forced to forgo publication of news or opinion by the inclusion of a reply, the Florida statute fails to clear the barriers of the First Amendment because of its intrusion into the function of editors. A newspaper is more than a passive receptacle or conduit for news, comment, and advertising. The choice of material to go into a newspaper, and the decisions made as to limitations on the size and content of the paper, and treatment of public issues and public officials whether fair or unfair - constitute the exercise of editorial control and judgment. It has yet to be demonstrated how governmental regulation of this crucial process can be exercised consistent with First Amendment guarantees of a free press as they have evolved to this time. Accordingly, the judgment of the Supreme Court of Florida is reversed."

V. JUSTICE VOTE

9 Pro ACLU Side vs. 0 Con Opposing Side

ACLU Side (Petitioner/Appellant)

1. Burger, W. – Wrote majority opinion
2. Blackmun, H. – Joined majority opinion
3. Powell, L. – Joined majority opinion
4. Douglas, W. – Joined majority opinion
5. Brennan, W. – Wrote concurring opinion
6. Rehnquist, W. – Joined Brennan's concurrence
7. White, B. – Wrote concurring opinion
8. Marshall, T. – Joined majority opinion
9. Stewart, P. – Joined majority opinion

VI. A WIN OR LOSS FOR THE ACLU?

The ACLU filed as amicus curiae urging reversal of the judgment of the Supreme Court of Florida; the U.S. Supreme Court reversed in a 9-0 vote, giving the ACLU an apparent win.

342. Old Dominion Branch No. 496 v. Austin

(Decided June 25, 1974; 418 U.S. 264)

I. ISSUE

A. Issues Discussed

Governmental authority, unions, First Amendment, labor laws, libel

B. Legal Question Presented

Whether a labor union's publication calling non-members "scabs" can be punished as libel.

C. Supreme Court's Answer

The publication was not actionable libel under the current definition of actual malice required to show libel in this circumstance, given that labeling the non-members "scabs" was not a falsehood.

II. CASE SUMMARY

A. Background

Appellant was a labor union representing letter carriers in Richmond, Virginia. As part of its efforts to organize carriers who had not yet joined the union, the appellant published a newsletter describing the appellees, those who had not joined the union, as "scabs."

Appellees sued the union for libel. Appellants moved to dismiss the case "on the ground that the publication was protected speech under the First Amendment and under federal labor law." The trial court refused to dismiss the case. The court found that state libel laws could be applied if statements were made with "actual malice," which the judge defined in jury instructions as "'conduct which shows in fact that at the time the words were printed they were actuated by some sinister or corrupt motive such as hatred, personal spite, ill will, or desire to injure the plaintiff; or that the communication was made with such gross indifference and recklessness as to amount to a wanton or wilful disregard of the rights of the plaintiff.'" The jury awarded appellees compensatory and punitive damages. The Supreme Court of Virginia affirmed the decision.

The U.S. Supreme Court granted certiorari to review the case and reversed.

B. Counsel of Record/ACLU Attorney

ACLU Side (Petitioner/Appellant): Mozart G. Ratner argued the cause for appellant.

Opposing Side (Respondent/Appellee): Parker E. Cherry and Stephen M. Kapral argued the cause for appellee.

III. AMICI CURIAE

ACLU Side (Petitioner/Appellant)

Brief of amici curiae filed on behalf of the ACLU by Melvin L. Wulf and Joel M. Gora.

Brief of amici curiae filed on behalf of the American Federation of Labor and Congress of Industrial Organizations by J. Albert

Woll, Laurence Gold, Robert C. Mayer, and Thomas E. Harris.

Opposing Side (Respondent/Appellee)

Brief of amici curiae filed on behalf of the National Right to Work Legal Defense Foundation by James Newton Wilhoit, III, Rex H. Reed, and John L. Kilcullen.

IV. THE SUPREME COURT'S DECISION

"It should be clear that the newsletter's use of the epithet 'scab' was protected under federal law, and cannot be the basis of a state libel judgment. Rather than being a reckless or knowing falsehood, naming the appellees as scabs was literally and factually true. One of the generally accepted definitions of 'scab' is 'one who refuses to join a union,' and it is undisputed that the appellees had, in fact, refused to join the Branch. To be sure, the word is most often used as an insult or epithet. But Linn recognized that federal law gives a union license to use intemperate, abusive, or insulting language without fear of restraint or penalty if it believes such rhetoric to be an effective means to make its point. Indeed, the Court observed that use of this particular epithet is common parlance in labor disputes, and has specifically been held to be entitled to the protection of § 7 of the NLRA.

Appellees nonetheless argue that the publication here may be actionable under state law, basing their claim on the newsletter's publication of Jack London's 'definition of a scab.' Appellees contend that this can be read to charge them with having 'rotten principles,' with lacking 'character,' and with being 'traitor[s]'; that these charges are untrue; and that appellants knew they were untrue. . . .

We cannot agree. We believe that publication of Jack London's rhetoric is equally entitled to the protection of the federal labor laws. The sine qua non of recovery for defamation in a labor dispute under Linn is the existence of falsehood. . . . Before the test of reckless or knowing falsity can be met, there must be a false statement of fact. But, in our view, the only factual statement in the disputed publication is the claim that appellees were scabs, that is, that they had refused to join the union. . . .

This is not to say that there might not be situations where the use of this writing or other similar rhetoric in a labor dispute could be actionable, particularly if some of its words were taken out of context and used in such a way as to convey a false representation of fact. But in the context of this case, no such factual representation can reasonably be inferred, and the publication is protected under the federal labor laws. Accordingly, the judgments appealed from must be reversed."

V. JUSTICE VOTE

6 Pro ACLU Side vs. 3 Con Opposing Side

ACLU Side (Petitioner/Appellant)

1. Marshall, T. – Wrote majority opinion
2. Douglas, W. – Wrote concurring opinion
3. Brennan, W. – Joined majority opinion
4. Stewart, P. – Joined majority opinion
5. White, B. – Joined majority opinion
6. Blackmun, H. – Joined majority opinion

Opposing Side (Respondent/Appellee)

1. Powell, L. – Wrote dissenting opinion
2. Burger, W. – Joined dissenting opinion
3. Rehnquist, W. – Joined dissenting opinion

VI. A WIN OR LOSS FOR THE ACLU?

The ACLU filed as amicus curiae urging reversal; the U.S. Supreme Court reversed the Supreme Court of Virginia in a 6-3 vote, giving the ACLU an apparent win.

343. Lehman v. City of Shaker Heights

(Decided June 25, 1974; 418 U.S. 298)

I. ISSUE

A. Issues Discussed

1st Amendment, press, speech, association

B. Legal Question Presented

"[W]hether a city which operates a public rapid transit system and sells advertising space for car cards on its vehicles is required by the First and Fourteenth Amendments to accept paid political advertising on behalf of a candidate for public office."

C. Supreme Court's Answer

"No First Amendment forum is here to be found. The city consciously has limited access to its transit system advertising space in order to minimize chances of abuse, the appearance of favoritism, and the risk of imposing upon a captive audience. These are reasonable legislative objectives advanced by the city in a proprietary capacity. In these circumstances, there is no First or Fourteenth Amendment violation."

II. CASE SUMMARY

A. Background

"In 1970, petitioner Harry J. Lehman was a candidate for the office of State Representative to the Ohio General Assembly for District 56. . . . On July 3, 1970, petitioner sought to promote his candidacy by purchasing car card space on the Shaker Heights Rapid Transit System . . . .

Advertising space on the city's transit system is managed by respondent Metromedia, Inc., as exclusive agent under contract with the city. The agreement between the city and Metromedia provides:

'15. . . . The CONTRACTOR shall not place political advertising in or upon any of the said CARS or in, upon or about any other additional and further space granted hereunder.'

When petitioner applied for space, he was informed by Metromedia that, although space was then available, the management agreement with the city did not permit political advertising. The system, however, accepted ads from cigarette companies, banks, savings and loan associations, liquor companies, retail and service establishments, churches, and civic and public-service oriented groups. There was uncontradicted testimony at the trial that during the 26 years of public operation, the Shaker Heights system, pursuant to city council action, had not accepted or permitted any political or public issue advertising on its vehicles.

When petitioner did not succeed in his effort to have his copy accepted, he sought declaratory and injunctive relief in the state courts of Ohio without success. [The U.S. Supreme Court] granted certiorari in order to consider the important First and Fourteenth Amendment question the case presented."

B. Counsel of Record

ACLU Side (Petitioner/Appellant): Leonard J. Schwartz of the American Civil Liberties Union of Ohio Foundation, Inc., argued the cause for appellant. With him on the brief were Stanley K. Laughlin, Jr., of the American Civil Liberties Union of Ohio Foundation, Inc., Melvin L. Wulf and Joel M. Gora of the American Civil Liberties Union Foundation, and Harry J. Lehman.

Opposing Side (Respondent/Appellee): Paul R. Donaldson argued the cause for appellees. With him on the brief were Louis H. Orkin and H. Stephen Madsen.

III. AMICI CURIAE

ACLU Side (Petitioner/Appellant)

No briefs of amici curiae were filed in support of appellant.

Opposing Side (Respondent/Appellee)

No briefs of amici curiae were filed in support of appellees.

IV. THE SUPREME COURT'S DECISION

"It is urged that the car cards here constitute a public forum protected by the First Amendment, and that there is a guarantee of nondiscriminatory access to such publicly owned and controlled areas of communication 'regardless of the primary purpose for which the area is dedicated.'

We disagree. . . .

These situations are different from the traditional settings where First Amendment values inalterably prevail. . . . Although American constitutional jurisprudence, in the light of the First Amendment, has been jealous to preserve access to public places for purposes of free speech, the nature of the forum and the conflicting interests involved have remained important in determining the degree of protection afforded by the Amendment to the speech in question.

Here, we have no open spaces, no meeting hall, park, street corner, or other public thoroughfare. Instead, the city is engaged in commerce. . . . In much the same way that a newspaper or periodical, or even a radio or television station, need not accept every proffer of advertising from the general public, a city transit system has discretion to develop and make reasonable choices concerning the type of advertising that may be displayed in its vehicles. In making these choices, this Court has held that a public utility 'will be sustained in its protection of activities in public places when those activities do not interfere with the general public convenience, comfort and safety.'

Because state action exists, however, the policies and practices governing access to the transit system's advertising space must not be arbitrary, capricious, or invidious. . . . In these circumstances, the managerial decision to limit car card space to innocuous and less controversial commercial and service oriented advertising does not rise to the dignity of a First Amendment violation. Were we to hold to the contrary, display cases in public hospitals, libraries, office buildings, military compounds, and other public facilities immediately would become Hyde Parks open to every would-be pamphleteer and politician. This the Constitution does not require.

No First Amendment forum is here to be found. The city consciously has limited access to its transit system advertising space in order to minimize chances of abuse, the appearance of favoritism, and the risk of imposing upon a captive audience. These are reasonable legislative objectives advanced by the city in a proprietary capacity. In these circumstances, there is no First or Fourteenth Amendment violation.

The judgment of the Supreme Court of Ohio is affirmed."

V. JUSTICE VOTE

4 Pro ACLU Side vs. 5 Con Opposing Side

ACLU Side (Petitioner/Appellant)

1. Marshall, T. – Joined Brennan's dissent
2. Brennan, W. – Wrote dissenting opinion
3. Stewart, P. – Joined Brennan's dissent
4. Powell, L. – Joined Brennan's dissent

Opposing Side (Respondent/Appellee)

1. Blackmun, H. – Wrote majority opinion
2. White, B. – Joined majority opinion
3. Burger, W. – Joined majority opinion
4. Douglas, W. – Wrote concurring opinion
5. Rehnquist, W. – Joined majority opinion

VI. A WIN OR LOSS FOR THE ACLU?

The ACLU served as counsel for appellant urging reversal of the judgment of the Supreme Court of Ohio; the U.S. Supreme Court affirmed, in a 5-4 vote, giving the ACLU an apparent loss.

344. Spence v. Washington

(Decided June 25, 1974; 418 U.S. 405)

I. ISSUE

A. Issues Discussed

1st Amendment, press, speech, association

B. Legal Question Presented

Whether "the statute under which [appellant] was charged [for displaying a flag with a peace symbol taped to it], on its face and as applied, contravened the First Amendment, as incorporated by the Fourteenth Amendment, and was void for vagueness."

C. Supreme Court's Answer

"We reverse on the ground that as applied to appellant's activity the Washington statute impermissibly infringed protected expression."

II. CASE SUMMARY

A. Background

"Appellant displayed a United States flag, which he owned, out of the window of his apartment. Affixed to both surfaces of the flag was a large peace symbol fashioned of removable tape. Appellant was convicted under a Washington statute forbidding the exhibition of a United States flag to which is attached or superimposed figures, symbols, or other extraneous material. The Supreme Court of Washington affirmed appellant's conviction. It rejected appellant's contentions that the statute under which he was charged, on its face and as applied, contravened the First Amendment, as incorporated by the Fourteenth Amendment, and was void for vagueness. [The U.S. Supreme Court] noted probable jurisdiction."

B. Counsel of Record

ACLU Side (Petitioner/Appellant): Peter Greenfield argued the cause for appellant. With him on the briefs were Burt Neuborne, Melvin L. Wulf, and Joel M. Gora of the American Civil Liberties Union Foundation, and David Allen of the American Civil Liberties Union of Washington Foundation.

Opposing Side (Respondent/Appellee): James E. Warme argued the cause for appellee. With him on the brief was Christopher T. Bayley.

III. AMICI CURIAE

ACLU Side (Petitioner/Appellant)

No briefs of amici curiae were filed in support of appellant.

Opposing Side (Respondent/Appellee)

No briefs of amici curiae were filed in support of appellee.

IV. THE SUPREME COURT'S DECISION

"A number of factors are important in the instant case. First, this was a privately owned flag. . . . Second, appellant displayed his flag on private property. . . . Third, the record is devoid of proof of any risk of breach of the peace. . . .

Fourth, the State concedes, as did the Washington Supreme Court, that appellant engaged in a form of communication. . . . The undisputed facts are that appellant 'wanted people to know that I thought America stood for peace.' . . .

The Court for decades has recognized the communicative connotations of the use of flags. In many of their uses flags are a form of symbolism comprising a 'primitive but effective way of communicating ideas . . .,' and 'a short cut from mind to mind.' On this record there can be little doubt that appellant communicated through the use of symbols. The symbolism included not only the flag but also the superimposed peace symbol. . . .

We are confronted then with a case of prosecution for the expression of an idea through activity. Moreover, the activity occurred on private property, rather than in an environment over which the State by necessity must have certain supervisory powers unrelated to expression. Accordingly, we must examine with particular care the interests advanced by appellee to support its prosecution. . . .

We are brought, then, to the state court's thesis that Washington has an interest in preserving the national flag as an unalloyed symbol of our country. . . .

But we need not decide in this case whether the interest advanced by the court below is valid. We assume, arguendo, that it is. The statute is nonetheless unconstitutional as applied to appellant's activity. There was no risk that appellant's acts would mislead viewers into assuming that the Government endorsed his viewpoint To the contrary, he was plainly and peacefully protesting the fact that it did not. Appellant was not charged under the desecration statute, nor did he permanently disfigure the flag or destroy it. He displayed it as a flag of his country in a way closely analogous to the manner in which flags have always been used to convey ideas. Moreover, his message was direct, likely to be understood, and within the contours of the First Amendment. Given the protected character of his expression and in light of the fact that no interest the State may have in preserving the physical integrity of a privately owned flag was significantly impaired on these facts, the conviction must be invalidated.

The judgment is reversed."

V. JUSTICE VOTE

6 Pro ACLU Side vs. 3 Con Opposing Side

ACLU Side (Petitioner/Appellant)

1. Marshall, T. – Per curiam decision
2. Brennan, W. – Per curiam decision
3. Stewart, P. – Per curiam decision
4. Blackmun, H. – Concurs in the result
5. Douglas, W. – Wrote concurring opinion
6. Powell, L. – Per curiam decision

Opposing Side (Respondent/Appellee)

1. White, B. – Joined Rehnquist's dissent
2. Burger, W. – Wrote dissenting opinion, joined Rehnquist's dissent
3. Rehnquist, W. – Wrote dissenting opinion

VI. A WIN OR LOSS FOR THE ACLU?

The ACLU served as counsel for appellants urging reversal of the judgment of the Supreme Court of Washington; the U.S. Supreme Court reversed, in a 6-3 per curiam decision, giving the ACLU an apparent win.

345. Dorszynski v. United States

(Decided June 26, 1974; 418 U.S. 424)

I. ISSUE

A. Issues Discussed

Criminal procedure

B. Legal Question Presented

"We granted certiorari to resolve a conflict in the Circuits concerning whether, in sentencing a youth offender under other applicable penal statutes, s 5010(d) of the Federal Youth Corrections Act requires a federal district court first to make an explicit finding, supported by reasons on the record, that the offender would not benefit from treatment under subsection (b) or (c) of s 5010."

C. Supreme Court's Answer

"We conclude that while an express finding of no benefit must be made on the record, the Act does not require that it be accompanied by supporting reasons."

II. CASE SUMMARY

A. Background

"[O]n October 20, 1971, [an] undercover agent was shown approximately 1,000 LSD tablets in the possession of petitioner's co-defendant, who transferred the tablets to the agent. . . . [P]etitioner and his codefendant were arrested. The complaint upon which the arrest warrant for petitioner issued charged him with knowingly and intentionally possessing approximately 1,000 tablets of LSD, in violation of 18 U.S.C. s 2 and 21 U.S.C. s 844(a). . . .

On February 14, 1972, proceedings were had in the District Court . . . After inquiry as prescribed by Fed.Rule Crim.Proc. 11 . . . , the District Court accepted the plea. . . .

Petitioner then received a split sentence which remitted him to the custody of the Attorney General for one year, to serve 90 days' confinement 'in a jail-type or treatment' institution . . . ; the execution of the remainder of the sentence was suspended and petitioner was placed on probation for two years upon release from custody. At no time during the proceeding, including sentencing, did the District Court make any reference to the Federal Youth Corrections Act.

On May 1, 1972, . . . petitioner filed the motion at issue here, seeking relief pursuant to Fed.Rules Crim.Proc. 32(d) and 35, and 28 U.S.C. s 2255, on two grounds. The first alleged that his guilty plea was not made understandingly; that issue is not before us. The second alleged that the District Court was without jurisdiction to impose the sentence given because the court failed to make a finding that petitioner would not derive benefit from treatment under s 5010(b) or (c), as assertedly required by s 5010(d). The District Court held an evidentiary hearing to consider this motion, as well as other motions pending at that time. All were denied without opinion. . . .

The Court of Appeals affirmed . . . ."

B. Counsel of Record

ACLU Side (Petitioner/Appellant): Robert H. Friebert, by appointment of the Court, argued the cause and filed a brief for appellant.

Opposing Side (Respondent/Appellee): Gerald P. Norton argued the cause for the United States. With him on the brief were Solicitor General Bork, Assistant Attorney General Petersen, Deputy Solicitor General Frey, Jerome M. Feit, and Joseph S. Davies, Jr.

III. AMICI CURIAE

ACLU Side (Petitioner/Appellant)

Brief of amici curiae filed on behalf of the National Legal Aid and Defender Association and the and National Prison Project of the American Civil Liberties Union Foundation by Patricia M. Wald, Daniel A. Rezneck, James F. Flug, Robert Plotkin, and Alvin J. Bronstein.

Opposing Side (Respondent/Appellee)

No briefs of amici curiae were filed in support of appellee.

IV. THE SUPREME COURT'S DECISION

"The sole issue in this case is the validity of the sentence imposed by the District Court. Petitioner contends that before any adult sentence may be imposed s 5010(d) requires, first, that the sentencing judge find explicitly that the convicted defendant would receive no benefit from treatment under the Act and, second, that the sentencing judge must explain the reasons for his finding. We begin with the general proposition that once it is determined that a sentence is within the limitations set forth in the statute under which it is imposed, appellate review is at an end. Our task, therefore, is to determine whether the sentence imposed here was permitted under s 5010(d) of the Act. . . .

Our concern is with the effect of the requirement of a 'no benefit' finding on the judge's sentencing discretion.

The legislative history clearly indicates that the Act was meant to enlarge, not restrict, the sentencing options of federal trial courts in order to permit them to sentence youth offenders for rehabilitation . . . .

To construe s 5010(d)'s requirement of a 'no benefit' finding to circumscribe that discretion would be incompatible with a clear congressional intent . . . .

From our conclusion that a finding of 'no benefit' was not intended to constitute a substantive standard, it follows that a sentence outside the Act need not be accompanied by a statement of reasons why the court chose such a sentence. . . . In short, we hold that the discretion vested in a district judge under s 5010(d) is essentially the same as the traditional discretion vested in the court, for example, to impose the minimum sentence on a first offender or a larger sentence on a recidivist. . . .

To hold that a 'no benefit' finding is implicit each time a sentence under the Act is not chosen would render s 5010(d) nugatory; to hold that something more is necessary to support the inference that must be found in the record would create an ad hoc rule. Appellate courts should not be subject to the burden of case-by-case examination of the record to make sure that the sentencing judge considered the treatment option made available by the Act. . . .

This case provides an example of the problems arising when the required finding is left to implication. . . . An explicit finding that petitioner would not have benefited from treatment under the Act would have removed all doubt concerning whether the enlarged discretion Congress provided to sentencing courts was indeed exercised.

Accordingly, the judgment of the Court of Appeals is reversed, and the case is remanded . . . ."

V. JUSTICE VOTE

9 Pro ACLU Side vs. 0 Con Opposing Side

ACLU Side (Petitioner/Appellant)

1. Burger, W. – Wrote majority opinion
2. White, B. – Joined majority opinion
3. Marshall, T. – Wrote concurring opinion
4. Brennan, W. – Joined Marshall's concurrence
5. Stewart, P. – Joined Marshall's concurrence
6. Blackmun, H. – Joined majority opinion
7. Douglas, W. – Joined Marshall's concurrence
8. Powell, L. – Joined majority opinion
9. Rehnquist, W. – Joined majority opinion

VI. A WIN OR LOSS FOR THE ACLU?

The ACLU filed as amici curiae urging reversal of the judgment of the Court of Appeals; the Supreme Court reversed, in a 9-0 vote, giving the ACLU an apparent win.

346. Taylor v. Hayes

(Decided June 26, 1974; 418 U.S. 488)

I. ISSUE

A. Issues Discussed

Civil rights, state's rights, Fourteenth Amendment, criminal contempt

B. Legal Question Presented

Was the criminal contempt charge against petitioner valid, in the absence of adequate notice of the charges and a right to respond, and when there was a sentence of more than six months but there was no jury trial?

C. Supreme Court's Answer

Petitioner was denied due process because he was not given an opportunity to be heard before the imposition of a sentence for criminal contempt, however, the sentence was ultimately not for more than six months so a jury trial was not required.

II. CASE SUMMARY

A. Background

The petitioner, Taylor, was attorney for the accused in a murder trial. The respondent, Hayes, was the trial judge. During the trial, the respondent advised the petitioner nine times that he was in contempt of court. At the end of the trial, respondent convicted the petitioner of nine counts of contempt and sentenced him to consecutive jail terms that totaled four and a half years. Respondent did not allow petitioner an opportunity to respond to the allegations and petitioner was not afforded a jury trial. A jury trial was constitutionally required for a sentence exceeding six months. Later, the respondent eliminated one conviction and reduced the sentence without indicating whether the sentences ran concurrently (at the same time) or consecutively (one after the next). The Kentucky Court of Appeals affirmed, but ruled that because the amended judgment did not state that the sentences had to be served consecutively, they had to be served concurrently. This had the effect of reducing the total sentence to six months in jail, and rendered the conviction and sentence without a jury trial constitutionally permissible.

The Supreme Court granted certiorari to review the case and reversed the Kentucky Court of Appeals.

B. Counsel of Record/ACLU Attorney

ACLU Side (Petitioner/Appellant): Robert Allen Sedler argued the cause for appellant.

Opposing Side (Respondent/Appellee): Henry A. Triplett argued the cause and for appellee.

III. AMICI CURIAE

ACLU Side (Petitioner/Appellant)

Brief of amici curiae filed on behalf of the ACLU by Melvin L. Wulf.

Additional briefs of amici curiae were filed on behalf of the Association of the Bar of the City of New York, the Louisville Bar Association, and the National Lawyers Guild.

Opposing Side (Respondent/Appellee)

No briefs of amici curiae were filed in support of appellee.

IV. THE SUPREME COURT'S DECISION

"It is argued that a State should not be permitted, after conviction, to reduce the sentence to less than six months and thereby obviate a jury trial. The thrust of our decisions, however, is to the contrary: in the absence of legislative authorization of serious penalties for contempt, a State may choose to try any contempt without a jury if it determines not to impose a sentence longer than six months. We discern no material difference between this choice and permitting the State, after conviction, to reduce a sentence to six months or less, rather than to retry the contempt with a jury. In either case, the State itself has determined that the contempt is not so serious as to warrant more than a six-month sentence. We remain firmly committed to the proposition that 'criminal contempt is not a crime of the sort that requires the right to jury trial regardless of the penalty involved.' . . .

We are more persuaded by petitioner's contention that he was entitled to more of a hearing and notice than he received prior to final conviction and sentence. In each instance during the trial when respondent considered petitioner to be in contempt, petitioner was informed of that fact and, in most instances, had opportunity to respond to the charge at that time. . . . But no sentence was imposed during the trial, and it does not appear to us that any final adjudication of contempt was entered until after the verdict was returned. It was then that the court proceeded to describe and characterize petitioner's various acts during trial as contemptuous, to find him guilty of nine acts of contempt, and to sentence him immediately for each of those acts. . . .

This procedure does not square with the Due Process Clause of the Fourteenth Amendment. We are not concerned here with the trial judge's power, for the purpose of maintaining order in the courtroom, to punish summarily and without notice or hearing contemptuous conduct committed in his presence and observed by him. The usual justification of necessity, is not nearly so cogent when final adjudication and sentence are postponed until after trial.'. . '[W]e have stated time and again that reasonable notice of a charge and an opportunity to be heard in defense before punishment is imposed are 'basic in our system of jurisprudence.'' . . . Because these minimum requirements of due process of law were not extended to petitioner in this case, the contempt judgment must be set aside. . . .

Nothing we have said here should be construed to condone the type of conduct described in the opinion of the Kentucky Court of Appeals and found by that court to have been engaged in by petitioner. Behavior of this nature has no place in the courtroom which, in a free society, is a forum for the courteous and reasoned pursuit of truth and justice.

The judgment of the Kentucky Court of Appeals is reversed, and the case is remanded to that court for further proceedings not inconsistent with this opinion."

B. Justice Vote: 8 Pro ACLU Side vs. 1 Con Opposing Side

ACLU Side (Petitioner/Appellant)

1. White, B. – Wrote majority opinion
2. Burger, W. – Joined majority opinion
3. Douglas, W. – Joined majority opinion in part
4. Brennan, W. – Joined majority opinion
5. Stewart, P. – Joined majority opinion
6. Marshall, T. – Wrote opinion concurring in part and dissenting in part
7. Blackmun, H. – Joined majority opinion
8. Powell, L. – Joined majority opinion

Opposing Side (Respondent/Appellee)

1. Rehnquist, W. – Wrote dissenting opinion

VI. A WIN OR LOSS FOR THE ACLU?

The ACLU filed as amicus curiae urging reversal; the Supreme Court reversed the ruling of the Kentucky Court of Appeals in an 8-1 vote, giving the ACLU an apparent win.

347. Wolff v. McDonnell

(Decided June 26, 1974; 418 U.S. 539)

I. ISSUE

A. Issues Discussed

Prison

B. Legal Question Presented

Whether prison inmates are entitled to various due process protections.

C. Supreme Court's Answer

Inmates are only entitled to selected limited protections.

II. CASE SUMMARY

A. Background

"Respondent, on behalf of himself and other inmates of the Nebraska Penal and Correctional Complex, Lincoln, Nebraska, filed a complaint under 42 U.S.C. s 1983 challenging several of the practices, rules, and regulations of the Complex. [T]he pertinent allegations were that disciplinary proceedings did not comply with the Due Process Clause of the Fourteenth Amendment to the Federal Constitution; that the inmate legal assistance program did not meet constitutional standards, and that the regulations governing the inspection of mail to and from attorneys for inmates were unconstitutionally restrictive. Respondent requested damages and injunctive relief.

After an evidentiary hearing, the District Court granted partial relief. Considering itself bound by prior Circuit authority, it rejected the procedural due process claim; but it went on to hold that the prison's policy of inspecting all incoming and outgoing mail to and from attorneys violated prisoners' rights of access to the courts and that the restrictions placed on inmate legal assistance were not constitutionally defective.

The Court of Appeals reversed, with respect to the due process claim . . . . With respect to a remedy, the court further held that Preiser v. Rodriguez, 411 U.S. 475 (1973), forbade the actual restoration of good-time credits in this s 1983 suit but ordered expunged from prison records any determinations of misconduct arrived at in proceedings that failed to comport with due process as defined by the court. The court generally affirmed the judgment of the District Court with respect to correspondence with attorneys, but ordered further proceedings . . ."

The Supreme Court granted certiorari to review the case.

B. Counsel of Record

ACLU Side (Respondent/Appellee): Douglas F. Duchek argued the cause for appellee pro hac vice. With him on the briefs was Robert Plotkin.

Opposing Side (Petitioner/Appellant): Melvin Kent Kammerlohr, Assistant Attorney General of Nebraska, argued the cause for appellants. With him on the brief was Clarence A. H. Meyer, Attorney General.

Solicitor General Bork argued the cause for the United States as amicus curiae.

III. AMICI CURIAE

ACLU Side (Respondent/Appellee)

Brief of amici curiae filed on behalf of the National Prison Project of the American Civil Liberties Union Foundation by Michael A. Millemann, Alvin J. Bronstein, Nancy C. Crisman, Barbara M. Milstein, Alaire B. Rieffel, and Arpiar G. Saunders, Jr.

Brief of amici curiae filed on behalf of the American Bar Association by Chesterfield Smith and Robert J. Kutak.

Brief of amici curiae filed on behalf of the National Council on Crime and Delinquency by David Gilman and Richard Singer.

Brief of amici curiae filed on behalf of the Legal Aid Society of New York by William E. Hellerstein and Joel Berger.

Brief of amici curiae filed on behalf of the Inmates of the District of Columbia Correctional Complex by William H. Allen, Michael A. Schlanger, and David S. Weissbrodt.

Opposing Side (Petitioner/Appellant)

Brief of amici curiae filed on behalf of the United States by Solicitor General Bork, Assistant Attorney General Petersen,

Deputy Solicitor General Frey, Gerald P. Norton, and Jerome M. Feit.

Brief of amici curiae filed on behalf of the Attorney General of California by Evelle J. Younger, Attorney General, pro se, Jack R. Winkler, Chief Assistant Attorney General, Edward P. O'Brien, Assistant Attorney General, and W. Eric Collins, Harry A. Allen, April P. Kestell, and H. F. Wilkinson, Deputy Attorneys General.

Brief of amici curiae filed on behalf of the State of Illinois by William J. Scott, Attorney General, and James B. Zagel, Assistant Attorney General.

IV. THE SUPREME COURT'S DECISION

"This class action brought by respondent alleged that the rules, practices, and procedures at the Complex which might result in the taking of good time violated the Due Process Clause of the Fourteenth Amendment. . . .

At the threshold is the issue whether . . . the validity of the procedures for depriving prisoners of good-time credits may be considered in a civil rights suit brought under 42 U.S.C. s 1983. . . .

We . . . conclude that it was proper for the Court of Appeals and the District Court to determine the validity of the procedures for revoking good-time credits and to fashion appropriate remedies for any constitutional violations ascertained . . . .

Of course, . . . the fact that prisoners retain rights under the Due Process Clause in no way implies that these rights are not subject to restrictions . . . . In sum, there must be mutual accommodation between institutional needs and objectives and the provisions of the Constitution . . . .

We agree with neither petitioners nor the Court of Appeals: the Nebraska procedures are in some respects constitutionally deficient but the Morrissey-Scarpelli procedures need not in all respects be followed in disciplinary cases in state prisons. . . .

Two of the procedures that the Court held should be extended to parolees facing revocation proceedings are not, but must be, provided to prisoners in the Nebraska Complex . . . . These are advance written notice of the claimed violation and a written statement of the factfinders as to the evidence relied upon and the reasons for the disciplinary action taken. . . .

The Court of Appeals held that the due process requirements in prison disciplinary proceedings were to apply retroactively . . . . We disagree and reverse on this point. . . .

The narrow issue [of mail opening] presented is whether letters . . . from attorneys may be opened by prison authorities in the presence of the inmate . . . .

[W]e think that petitioners, by acceding to a rule whereby the inmate is present when mail from attorneys is inspected, have done all, and perhaps even more, than the Constitution requires. . . .

The last issue presented is whether the Complex must make available . . . adequate legal assistance, under Johnson v. Avery for the preparation of habeas corpus petitions and civil rights actions . . . .

[W]e affirm the Court of Appeals on this point, and as the Court of Appeals suggested, the District Court will assess the adequacy of legal assistance under the reasonable-alternative standard of Avery.

Affirmed in part, reversed in part."

V. JUSTICE VOTE

3 Pro ACLU Side vs. 6 Con Opposing Side

ACLU Side (Respondent/Appellee)

1. Brennan, W. – Joined Marshall's opinion
2. Marshall, T. – Wrote opinion concurring in part and dissenting in part
3. Douglas, W. – Wrote opinion concurring in part and dissenting in part

Opposing Side (Petitioner/Appellant)

1. White, B. – Wrote majority opinion
2. Stewart, P. – Joined majority opinion
3. Rehnquist, W. – Joined majority opinion
4. Burger, W. – Joined majority opinion
5. Blackmun, H. – Joined majority opinion
6. Powell, L. – Joined majority opinion

VI. A WIN OR LOSS FOR THE ACLU?

The ACLU filed as amicus curiae urging affirmance; the Supreme Court affirmed in part and reversed in part the Court of Appeals' decision by a 6-3 vote, giving the ACLU an apparent loss.

348. United States v. Nixon

(Decided July 24, 1974; 418 U.S. 683)

I. ISSUE

A. Issues Discussed

Executive privilege, discovery and inspection

B. Legal Question Presented

Does the U.S. President possess an "executive privilege" of unqualified immunity from judicial process?

C. Supreme Court's Answer

The president does not have an absolute privilege or generalized interest in confidentiality, and therefore must disclose materials specifically requested by the Special Prosecutor.

II. CASE SUMMARY

A. Background

"On March 1, 1974, a grand jury of the United States District Court for the District of Columbia returned an indictment charging seven named individuals with various offenses, including conspiracy to defraud the United States and to obstruct justice. Although he was not designated as such in the indictment, the grand jury named the President, among others, as an unindicted coconspirator. On April 18, 1974, upon motion of the Special Prosecutor, a subpoena duces tecum was issued pursuant to Rule 17(c) to the President . . . . This subpoena required the production . . . of certain tapes, memoranda, papers, transcripts or other writings relating to certain precisely identified meetings between the President and others. . . . On April 30, the President publicly released edited transcripts of 43 conversations; portions of 20 conversations subject to subpoena in the present case were included. On May 1, 1974, the President's counsel, filed a 'special appearance' and a motion to quash the subpoena under Rule 17(c). This motion was accompanied by a formal claim of privilege. At a subsequent hearing, further motions to expunge the grand jury's action naming the President as an unindicted coconspirator and for protective orders against the disclosure of that information were filed or raised orally by counsel for the President.

On May 20, 1974, the District Court denied the motion to quash and the motions to expunge and for protective orders. . . . The District Court rejected jurisdictional challenges based on a contention that the dispute was nonjusticiable because it was between the Special Prosecutor and the Chief Executive and hence 'intra-executive' in character; it also rejected the contention that the Judiciary was without authority to review an assertion of executive privilege by the President. . . .

The District Court held that the judiciary, not the President, was the final arbiter of a claim of executive privilege. The court concluded that under the circumstances of this case the presumptive privilege was overcome by the Special Prosecutor's prima facie 'demonstration of need sufficiently compelling to warrant judicial examination in chambers . . . .' The court held, finally, that the Special Prosecutor had satisfied the requirements of Rule 17(c). The District Court stayed its order pending appellate review on condition that review was sought before 4 p.m., May 24. The court further provided that matters filed under seal remain under seal when transmitted as part of the record.

On May 24, 1974, the President filed a timely notice of appeal from the District Court order, and the certified record from the District Court was docketed in the United States Court of Appeals for the District of Columbia Circuit. On the same day, the President also filed a petition for writ of mandamus in the Court of Appeals seeking review of the District Court order.

Later on May 24, the Special Prosecutor also filed, in [the Supreme] Court, a petition for a writ of certiorari before judgment. On May 31, the petition was granted with an expedited briefing schedule. On June 6, the President filed, under seal, a cross-petition for writ of certiorari before judgment. This cross-petition was granted June 15, 1974, and the case was set for argument on July 8, 1974."

On certiorari, the Supreme Court affirmed the judgment of the Court of Appeals for the District of Columbia Circuit.

B. Counsel of Record/ACLU Attorney

ACLU Side (Respondent/Appellee): Leon Jaworski and Philip A. Lacovara argued the cause for the United States.

Opposing Side (Petitioner/Appellant): James D. St. Clair argued the cause for the President.

William Snow Frates, Andrew C. Hall, Spencer H. Boyer, and Henry H. Jones filed a brief for Ehrlichman.

John M. Bray filed a brief for Strachan.

III. AMICI CURIAE

ACLU Side (Respondent/Appellee)

Brief of amici curiae filed on behalf of the ACLU by Norman Dorsen, Melvin L. Wulf, and John H. F. Shattuck.

Opposing Side (Petitioner/Appellant)

No briefs of amici curiae were filed in support of appellant.

IV. THE SUPREME COURT'S DECISION

"[T]he order of the District Court was an appealable order. The appeal from that order was therefore properly 'in' the Court of Appeals, and the case is now properly before this Court on the writ of certiorari before judgment. . . .

In light of the uniqueness of the setting in which the conflict arises, the fact that both parties are officers of the Executive Branch cannot be viewed as a barrier to justiciability. It would be inconsistent with the applicable law and regulation, and the unique facts of this case to conclude other than that the Special Prosecutor has standing to bring this action and that a justiciable controversy is presented for decision. . . .

We also conclude there was a sufficient preliminary showing that each of the subpoenaed tapes contains evidence admissible with respect to the offenses charged in the indictment. The most cogent objection to the admissibility of the taped conversations here at issue is that they are a collection of out-of-court statements by declarants who will not be subject to cross-examination and that the statements are therefore inadmissible hearsay. Here, however, most of the tapes apparently contain conversations to which one or more of the defendants named in the indictment were party. The hearsay rule does not automatically bar all out-of-court statements by a defendant in a criminal case. Declarations by one defendant may also be admissible against other defendants upon a sufficient showing, by independent evidence, of a conspiracy among one or more other defendants and the delarant and if the declarations at issue were in furtherance of that conspiracy. The same is true of declarations of coconspirators who are not defendants in the case on trial. Recorded conversations may also be admissible for the limited purpose of impeaching the credibility of any defendant who testifies or any other coconspirator who testifies. Generally, the need for evidence to impeach witnesses is insufficient to require its production in advance of trial. Here, however, there are other valid potential evidentiary uses for the same material, and the analysis and possible transcription of the tapes may take a significant period of time. Accordingly, we cannot conclude that the District Court erred in authorizing the issuance of the subpoena duces tecum. . . .

To read the Art. II powers of the President as providing an absolute privilege as against a subpoena essential to enforcement of criminal statutes on no more than a generalized claim of the public interest in confidentiality of nonmilitary and nondiplomatic discussions would upset the constitutional balance of 'a workable government' and gravely impair the role of the courts under Art. III. . . .

We conclude that when the ground for asserting privilege as to subpoenaed materials sought for use in a criminal trial is based only on the generalized interest in confidentiality, it cannot prevail over the fundamental demands of due process of law in the fair administration of criminal justice. The generalized assertion of privilege must yield to the demonstrated, specific need for evidence in a pending criminal trial.

[A] President's communications and activities encompass a vastly wider range of sensitive material than would be true of any 'ordinary individual.' It is therefore necessary in the public interest to afford Presidential confidentiality the greatest protection consistent with the fair administration of justice. The need for confidentiality even as to idle conversations with associates in which casual reference might be made concerning political leaders within the country or foreign statesmen is too obvious to call for further treatment. We have no doubt that the District Judge will at all times accord to Presidential records that high degree of deference suggested in United States v. Burr, supra and will discharge his responsibility to see to it that until released to the Special Prosecutor no in camera material is revealed to anyone. This burden applies with even greater force to excised material; once the decision is made to excise, the material is restored to its privileged status and should be returned under seal to its lawful custodian. . . .

Affirmed."

V. JUSTICE VOTE:

8 Pro ACLU Side vs. 0 Con Opposing Side

ACLU Side (Respondent/Appellee)

1. Burger, W. – Wrote majority opinion
2. Powell, L. – Joined majority opinion
3. White, B. – Joined majority opinion
4. Blackmun, H. – Joined majority opinion
5. Douglas, W. – Joined majority opinion
6. Brennan, W. – Joined majority opinion
7. Stewart, P. – Joined majority opinion
8. Marshall, T. – Joined majority opinion

Rehnquist, W. Took no part in decision

VI. A WIN OR LOSS FOR THE ACLU?

The ACLU, as amicus curiae, urged affirmance of the judgment of the Court of Appeals for the District of Columbia Circuit; the Supreme Court affirmed in an 8-0 vote, giving the ACLU an apparent win.

349. Goss v. Lopez

(Decided January 22, 1975; 419 U.S. 565)

I. ISSUE

A. Issues Discussed

Fourteenth Amendment, due process, education

B. Legal Question Presented

Does the suspension of students, for up to 10 days, without a hearing, constitute a violation of the Due Process Clause of the Fourteenth Amendment?

C. Supreme Court's Answer

Students suspended for up to 10 days must be provided the rudimentary basics of due process, including notice and an informal hearing including the ability for the student to present his version of the events, prior to removal from school wherever possible.

II. CASE SUMMARY

A. Background

"The nine named appellees, each of whom alleged that he or she had been suspended from public high school in Columbus for up to 10 days without a hearing pursuant to § 3313.66, filed an action under 42 U.S.C. § 1983 against the Columbus Board of Education and various administrators of the CPSS [Columbus, Ohio, Public School System]. The complaint sought a declaration that § 3313.66 was unconstitutional in that it permitted public school administrators

to deprive plaintiffs of their rights to an education without a hearing of any kind, in violation of the procedural due process component of the Fourteenth Amendment. It also sought to enjoin the public school officials from issuing future suspensions pursuant to § 3313.66 and to require them to remove references to the past suspensions from the records of the students in question.

[T]he three-judge court declared that plaintiffs were denied due process of law because they were 'suspended without hearing prior to suspension or within a reasonable time thereafter,' and that Ohio Rev. Code Ann. § 3313.66 (1972) and regulations issued pursuant thereto were unconstitutional in permitting such suspensions. It was ordered that all references to plaintiffs' suspensions be removed from school files.

Although not imposing upon the Ohio school administrators any particular disciplinary procedures and leaving them 'free to adopt regulations providing for fair suspension procedures which are consonant with the educational goals of their schools and reflective of the characteristics of their school and locality,' the District Court declared that there were 'minimum requirements of notice and a hearing prior to suspension, except in emergency situations.' . . . The defendant school administrators have appealed the three-judge court's decision."

The Supreme Court granted certiorari to review the case and affirmed the judgment of the District Court.

B. Counsel of Record/ACLU Attorney

ACLU Side (Respondent/Appellee): Peter D. Ross argued the cause for appellee.

Opposing Side (Petitioner/Appellant): Thomas A. Bustin argued the cause for appellant.

III. AMICI CURIAE

ACLU Side (Respondent/Appellee)

Brief of amici curiae filed on behalf of the ACLU by Alan H. Levine, Melvin L. Wulf, and Joel M. Gora.

Additional briefs of amici curiae were filed on behalf of the National Committee for Citizens in Education, et al., the NAACP, et al., and the Children's Defense Fund of the Washington Research Project, Inc., et al.

Opposing Side (Petitioner/Appellant)

Brief of amici curiae filed on behalf of the Buckeye Association of School Administrators, et al., by John F. Lewis, Bruce P. Jones, and G. Christopher Meyer.

IV. THE SUPREME COURT'S DECISION

"Having chosen to extend the right to an education to people of appellees' class generally, Ohio may not withdraw that right on grounds of misconduct, absent fundamentally fair procedures to determine whether the misconduct has occurred.

Although Ohio may not be constitutionally obligated to establish and maintain a public school system, it has nevertheless done so and has required its children to attend. Those young people do not 'shed their constitutional rights' at the schoolhouse door. 'The Fourteenth Amendment, as now applied to the States, protects the citizen against the State itself and all of its creatures—Boards of Education not excepted.' The authority possessed by the State to prescribe and enforce standards of conduct in its schools, although concededly very broad, must be exercised consistently with constitutional safeguards. Among other things, the State is constrained to recognize a student's legitimate entitlement to a public education as a property interest which is protected by the Due Process Clause and which may not be taken away for misconduct without adherence to the minimum procedures required by that Clause. . . .

A short suspension is, of course, a far milder deprivation than expulsion. But, 'education is perhaps the most important function of state and local governments,' and the total exclusion from the educational process for more than a trivial period, and certainly if the suspension is for 10 days, is a serious event in the life of the suspended child. Neither the property interest in educational benefits temporarily denied nor the liberty interest in reputation, which is also implicated, is so insubstantial that suspensions may constitutionally be imposed by any procedure the school chooses, no matter how arbitrary. . . .

There need be no delay between the time 'notice' is given and the time of the hearing. In the great majority of cases the disciplinarian may informally discuss the alleged misconduct with the student minutes after it has occurred. We hold only that, in being given an opportunity to explain his version of the facts at this discussion, the student first be told what he is accused of doing and what the basis of the accusation is. Lower courts which have addressed the question of the nature of the procedures required in short suspension cases have reached the same conclusion. Since the hearing may occur almost immediately following the misconduct, it follows that as a general rule notice and hearing should precede removal of the student from school. We agree with the District Court, however, that there are recurring situations in which prior notice and hearing cannot be insisted upon. Students whose presence poses a continuing danger to persons or property or an ongoing threat of disrupting the academic process may be immediately removed from school. In such cases, the necessary notice and rudimentary hearing should follow as soon as practicable, as the District Court indicated. . . .

We should also make it clear that we have addressed ourselves solely to the short suspension, not exceeding 10 days. Longer suspensions or expulsions for the remainder of the school term, or permanently, may require more formal procedures. Nor do we put aside the possibility that in unusual situations, although involving only a short suspension, something more than the rudimentary procedures will be required. . . .

The District Court found each of the suspensions involved here to have occurred without a hearing, either before or after the suspension, and that each suspension was therefore invalid and the statute unconstitutional insofar as it permits such suspensions without notice or hearing. Accordingly, the judgment is affirmed."

V. JUSTICE VOTE:

5 Pro ACLU Side vs. 4 Con Opposing Side

ACLU Side (Respondent/Appellee)

1. White, B. – Wrote majority opinion
2. Douglas, W. – Joined majority opinion
3. Brennan. W. – Joined majority opinion
4. Stewart, P. – Joined majority opinion
5. Marshall, T. – Joined majority opinion

Opposing Side (Petitioner/Appellant)

1. Powell, L. – Wrote dissenting opinion
2. Burger, W. – Joined dissenting opinion
3. Blackmun, H. – Joined dissenting opinion
4. Rehnquist, W. – Joined dissenting opinion

VI. A WIN OR LOSS FOR THE ACLU?

The ACLU, as amicus curiae, urged affirmance of the judgment of the District Court for the Southern District of Ohio; the Supreme Court affirmed in a 5-4 vote, giving the ACLU an apparent win.

350. United States v. New Jersey State Lottery Commission

(Decided February 25, 1975; 420 U.S. 371)

I. ISSUE

A. Issues Discussed

First Amendment, freedoms of press, speech, and association

B. Legal Question Presented

Does 18 U.S.C. § 1304, which would prohibit lottery information from being broadcast by a licensed radio station, violate the First Amendment?

C. Supreme Court's Answer

The Court declined to address the First Amendment issue, vacated the judgment, and remanded the case due to the enactment of 18 U.S.C. § 1307.

II. CASE SUMMARY

A. Background

"This case involves a question regarding the applicability of 18 U.S.C. § 1304, which provides:

'Whoever broadcasts by means of any radio station for which a license is required by any law of the United States, or whoever, operating any such station, knowingly permits the broadcasting of, any advertisement of or information concerning any lottery, gift enterprise, or similar scheme, offering prizes dependent in whole or in part upon lot or chance, or any list of the prizes drawn or awarded by means of any such lottery, gift enterprise, or scheme, whether said list contains any part or all of such prizes, shall be fined not more than $1,000 or imprisoned not more than one year, or both.'

Jersey Cape, a licensed radio station in New Jersey, sued for declaratory relief before the Federal Communications Commission arguing that § 1304 should not apply to the broadcast of the winning number in a lawful state-run lottery such as the one conducted by the State of New Jersey. The Commission denied relief. Upon a petition for rehearing, the New Jersey Lottery Commission was allowed to intervene and the FCC reaffirmed its denial. The Lottery Commission petitioned for review in the Court of Appeals for the Third Circuit, and the States of New Hampshire and Pennsylvania were granted permission to intervene as petitioners. Sitting en banc, the Third Circuit unanimously reversed the FCC. [The Supreme Court] granted certiorari to resolve an apparent conflict between that decision and the decision by the Court of Appeals for the Second Circuit in New York State Broadcasters Assn. v. United States, 414 F.2d 990 (1969).

Subsequent to the briefing and oral argument of the case in [the Supreme] Court, Congress passed and the President signed Pub.L. 93-583, 88 Stat. 1916, codified at 18 U.S.C. § 1307 (1970 ed., Supp. IV), which, in relevant part, provides:

'(a) The provisions of section . . . 1304 shall not apply to an advertisement, list of prizes, or information concerning a lottery conducted by a State acting under the authority of State law-

'(2) broadcast by a radio or television station licensed to a location in that State or an adjacent State which conducts such a lottery.'"

B. Counsel of Record / ACLU Attorney

ACLU Side (Respondent / Appellee): Stephen Skillman argued the cause for appellee

Opposing Side (Petitioner / Appellant): Lawrence G. Wallace argued the cause for appellant.

III. AMICI CURIAE

ACLU Side (Respondent / Appellee)

Brief of amici curiae filed on behalf of the ACLU by Thomas R. Asher, Collot Guerard, Harvey J. Shulman, Melvin L. Wulf, and Joel M. Gora.

Additional briefs of amici curiae were filed on behalf of the State of Connecticut, the Maryland Public Broadcasting Commission the State of Ohio, the Government of the Virgin Islands, and the National Association of Broadcasters.

Opposing Side (Petitioner / Appellant)

No briefs of amici curiae were filed in support of appellant.

IV. THE SUPREME COURT'S DECISION

"The United States now urges us to dismiss this case as moot. It points out that the only relief requested was by a broadcaster located in New Jersey, a State that conducts an authorized lottery, and therefore the type of broadcast at issue is now allowed by statute. Intervenor, the State of New Hampshire disputes the suggestion of mootness. New Hampshire argues that the amendment to § 1304 does not grant it full relief. It is noted that Vermont, an adjacent State, does not conduct a state-authorized lottery. Thus, Vermont broadcasters will not be allowed, under § 1304, as modified by § 1307, to broadcast to New Hampshire listeners the winning numbers in the New Hampshire state lottery. New Hampshire apparently believes that this limitation constitutes a denial of First Amendment rights. This specific issue, however, was not briefed or argued in this Court.

In view of the enactment of § 1307, we deem it appropriate to remand to the Court of Appeals so that it may consider whether the case is now moot. Accordingly, the judgment below is vacated and the case is remanded."

V. JUSTICE VOTE: 1 PRO ACLU SIDE VS. 7 CON OPPOSING SIDE

ACLU Side (Respondent / Appellee)

1. Douglas, W. – Wrote dissenting opinion

Opposing Side (Petitioner / Appellant)

1. Rehnquist, W. – Per curiam opinion
2. White, B. – Per curiam opinion
3. Blackmun, H. – Per curiam opinion
4. Powell, L. – Per curiam opinion
5. Brennan, W. – Per curiam opinion
6. Marshall, T. –Per curiam opinion
7. Stewart, P. – Per curiam opinion

Burger, W. – Took no part in the decision

VI. A WIN OR LOSS FOR THE ACLU?

The ACLU filed as amicus curiae urging affirmance; the Supreme Court vacated and remanded the ruling of the Third Circuit Court of Appeals in a 7-1 vote, giving the ACLU an apparent loss.

351. Weinberger v. Wiesenfeld

(Decided March 19, 1975; 420 U.S. 636)

I. ISSUE

A. Issues Discussed

Gender, federal

B. Legal Question Presented

"Social Security Act benefits based on the earnings of a deceased husband and father covered by the Act are payable, with some limitations, both to the widow and to the couple's minor children in her care. Such benefits are payable on the basis of the earnings of a deceased wife and mother covered by the Act, however, only to the minor children and not to the widower. The question in this case is whether this gender-based distinction violates the Due Process Clause of the Fifth Amendment."

C. Supreme Court's Answer

"[T]he different treatment of men and women mandated by s 402(g) unjustifiably discriminated against female wage earners by affording them less protection for their survivors than is provided to male employees."

II. CASE SUMMARY

A. Background

"Appellee Stephen C. Wiesenfeld and Paula Polatschek were married . . . . Paula . . . continued teaching after her marriage. Each year she worked, maximum social security contributions were deducted from her salary. Paula's earnings were the couple's principal source of support during the marriage, being substantially larger than those of appellee.

On June 5, 1972, Paula died in childbirth. Appellee was left with the sole responsibility for the care of their infant son, Jason Paul. . . . Stephen Wiesenfeld applied at the Social Security office . . . for social security survivors' benefits for himself and his son. He did obtain benefits for his son . . . . However, appellee was told that he was not eligible for benefits for himself, because s 402(g) benefits were available only to women. If he had been a woman, he would have received the same amount as his son as long as he was not working, and, if working, that amount reduced by $1 for every $2 earned annually above $2,400.

Appellee . . . sought a declaration that s 402(g) is unconstitutional to the extent that men and women are treated differently, an injunction restraining appellant from denying benefits under s 402(g) solely on the basis of sex, and payment of past benefits commencing with June 1972, the month of the original application. Cross motions for summary judgment were filed. After the three-judge court determined that it had jurisdiction, it granted summary judgment in favor of appellee, and issued an order giving appellee the relief he sought."

The Supreme Court granted certiorari to review the case.

B. Counsel of Record

ACLU Side (Respondent/Appellee): Ruth Bader Ginsburg of the American Civil Liberties Union Foundation argued the cause for appellee. With her on the brief was Melvin L. Wulf of the American Civil Liberties Union Foundation.

Opposing Side (Petitioner/Appellant): Keith A. Jones argued the cause for appellant. On the brief were Solicitor General Bork, Assistant Attorney General Hills, and Danny J. Boggs.

III. AMICI CURIAE

ACLU Side (Respondent/Appellee)

Brief of amici curiae filed on behalf of the Center for Constitutional Rights by Nancy Stearns.

Opposing Side (Petitioner/Appellant)

No briefs of amici curiae were filed in support of appellant.

IV. THE SUPREME COURT'S DECISION

"The gender-based distinction made by s 402(g) is indistinguishable from that invalidated in Frontiero v. Richardson, 411 U.S. 677 (1973). Frontiero involved statutes which provided the wife of a male serviceman with dependents' benefits but not the husband of a servicewoman unless she proved that she supplied more than one-half of her husband's support. The Court held that the statutory scheme violated the right to equal protection secured by the Fifth Amendment. . . .

Section 402(g) clearly operates, as did the statutes invalidated by . . . Frontiero, to deprive women of protection for their families which men receive as a result of their employment. Indeed, the classification here is in some ways more pernicious. First, it was open to the servicewoman under the statutes invalidated in Frontiero to prove that her husband was in fact dependent upon her. Here, Stephen Wiesenfeld was not given the opportunity to show . . . he was dependent upon his wife for his support, or that, had his wife lived, she would have remained at work while he took over care of the child. Second, in this case social security taxes were deducted from Paula's salary during the years in which she worked. Thus, she not only failed to receive for her family the same protection which a similarly situated male worker would have received, but she also was deprived of a portion of her own earnings in order to contribute to the fund out of which benefits would be paid to others. Since the Constitution forbids the gender-based differentiation premised upon assumptions as to dependency made in the statutes before us in Frontiero, the Constitution also forbids the gender-based differentiation that results in the efforts of female workers required to pay social security taxes producing less protection for their families than is produced by the efforts of men. . . .

Since the gender-based classification of s 402(g) cannot be explained as an attempt to provide for the special problems of women, it is indistinguishable from the classification held invalid in Frontiero. Like the statutes there, '(b)y providing dissimilar treatment for men and women who are . . . similarly situated, the challenged section violates the (Due Process) Clause.'

Affirmed."

V. JUSTICE VOTE

8 Pro ACLU Side vs. 0 Con Opposing Side

ACLU Side (Respondent/Appellee)

1. Brennan, W. – Wrote majority opinion
2. Marshall, T. – Joined majority opinion
3. Stewart, P. – Joined majority opinion
4. Rehnquist, W. – Wrote concurring opinion
5. Burger, W. – Joined Powell's concurrence
6. White, B. – Joined majority opinion
7. Blackmun, H. – Joined majority opinion
8. Powell, L. – Wrote concurring opinion

Douglas, W. – Took no part in the decision.

VI. A WIN OR LOSS FOR THE ACLU?

The ACLU served as attorney of record for appellee urging affirmance; the Supreme Court affirmed the District Court for the District of New Jersey's decision by an 8-0 vote, giving the ACLU an apparent win.

352. Schlesinger v. Councilman

(Decided March 25, 1975; 420 U.S. 738)

I. ISSUE

A. Issues Discussed

Criminal justice, drugs, military tribunals

B. Legal Question Presented

Did the District Court err in concluding that offenses charged against Councilman were not "service connected" and therefore not within court-martial jurisdiction?

C. Supreme Court's Answer

Declining to address the "service connected" issue, the Supreme Court determined the court-martial process should be allowed to proceed.

II. CASE SUMMARY

A. Background

"On March 27, 1972, court-martial charges were preferred against respondent Bruce R. Councilman, an Army captain on active duty at Fort Sill, Okl. The charges alleged that Captain Councilman had wrongfully sold, transferred, and possessed marihuana." The actions alleged occurred while respondent was off duty, off post, and out of uniform.

Respondent "moved to dismiss the charges, contending that the court-martial lacked jurisdiction . . . because the alleged offenses were not 'service connected.' After an evidentiary hearing, the presiding military judge denied the motion and scheduled the court-martial to begin on July 11. On July 5, Councilman brought this action in the District Court, moving for a temporary restraining order and a preliminary injunction to prevent his impending court-martial. Councilman claimed that since the court-martial lacked jurisdiction over the alleged offenses, he '[would] suffer great and irreparable damage in that he [might] be deprived of his liberty without due process of law, if the Court-Martial Proceedings are permitted . . . .' [T]he District Court permanently enjoined the military authorities from proceeding with the court-martial.

The Court of Appeals affirmed, holding that the alleged offenses did not meet the tests for service connection . . . ."

The Supreme Court granted certiorari to review the case, asked for supplemental briefing on additional issues, and reversed.

B. Counsel of Record/ACLU Attorney

ACLU Side (Respondent/Appellee): Nicholas D. Garrett and Orin Christopher Meyers argued the cause for appellee.

Opposing Side (Petitioner/Appellant): Solicitor General Robert H. Bork argued the cause for appellant.

III. AMICI CURIAE

ACLU Side (Respondent/Appellee)

Brief of amici curiae filed on behalf of the ACLU, et al., by David F. Addlestone, Donald S. Burris, Peter H. Meyers, Marvin M. Karpatkin, Steve Delibert, and Melvin L. Wulf.

Opposing Side (Petitioner/Appellant)

No briefs of amici curiae were filed in support of appellant.

IV. THE SUPREME COURT'S DECISION

"In effect, Councilman is attempting to attack collaterally the military authorities' decision to convene the court-martial and the refusal of the military judge to dismiss the charges. Article 76, however, gives binding effect not only to court-martial judgments, but also to 'all action taken pursuant to those proceedings.' We therefore agree with petitioners that, as a jurisdictional matter, Councilman's suit stands on precisely the same footing as suits seeking possible postjudgment forms of collateral relief. If Art. 76 was intended to bar subject-matter jurisdiction in suits for collateral relief other than by way of habeas, it also must remove § 1331 jurisdiction prior to any court-martial judgment.

Article 76, however, does not expressly effect any change in the subject-matter jurisdiction of Art. III courts. Its language only defines the point at which military court judgments become final and requires that they be given res judicata effect. But, as the Court has recognized in the past, there is no necessary inconsistency between this and the standard rule that void judgments, although final for purposes of direct review, may be impeached collaterally in suits otherwise within a court's subject-matter jurisdiction. . . .

We therefore reiterate the construction given the Art. 76 language in Gusik and accepted by other courts, including the Court of Military Appeals, and accordingly hold that Art. 76 does not stand as a jurisdictional bar to Captain Councilman's suit. . . .

Councilman was on active duty when the charges against him were brought. There is no question that he is subject to military authority and in proper cases to disciplinary sanctions levied through the military justice system. We see no injustice in requiring respondent to submit to a system established by Congress and carefully designed to protect not only military interests but his legitimate interests as well. Of course, if the offenses with which he is charged are not 'service connected,' the military courts will have had no power to impose any punishment whatever. But that issue turns in major part on gauging the impact of an offense on military discipline and effectiveness, on determining whether the military interest in deterring the offense is distinct from and greater than that of civilian society, and on whether the distinct military interest can be vindicated adequately in civilian courts. These are matters of judgment that often will turn on the precise set of facts in which the offense has occurred. More importantly, they are matters as to which the expertise of military courts is singularly relevant, and their judgments indispensable to inform any eventual review in Art. III courts.

We have no occasion to attempt to define those circumstances, if any, in which equitable intervention into pending court-martial proceedings might be justified. In the circumstances disclosed here, we discern nothing that outweighs the strong considerations favoring exhaustion of remedies or that warrants intruding on the integrity of military court processes.

Reversed."

V. JUSTICE VOTE

3 Pro ACLU Side vs. 6 Con Opposing Side

ACLU Side (Respondent/Appellee)

1. Brennan, W. – Wrote dissenting opinion
2. Douglas, W. – Joined Brennan's dissent
3. Marshall, T. – Joined Brennan's dissent

Opposing Side (Petitioner/Appellant)

1. Powell, L. – Wrote majority opinion
2. Rehnquist, W. – Joined majority opinion
3. White, B. – Joined majority opinion
4. Stewart, P. – Joined majority opinion
5. Blackmun, H. – Joined majority opinion
6. Burger, W. – Wrote concurring opinion

VI. A WIN OR LOSS FOR THE ACLU?

The ACLU filed as amicus curiae urging affirmance; the Supreme Court reversed the Court of Appeals' judgment in a 6-3 vote giving the ACLU an apparent loss.

353. McLucas v. DeChamplain

(Decided April 15, 1975; 421 U.S. 21)

I. ISSUE

A. Issues Discussed

Governmental authority, military, Fifth Amendment, Sixth Amendment

B. Legal Question Presented

Was Art. 134 of the Uniform Code of Military Justice unconstitutional and vague, and did the limitations imposed by military authorities on DeChamplain's defense pretrial access deny him due process and effective assistance of counsel?

C. Supreme Court's Answer

The intervention of the federal court in these claims was improper and the constitutional claim was insubstantial and should be dismissed.

II. CASE SUMMARY

A. Background

Appellee, DeChamplain, an Air Force master sergeant, was in military proceedings for a court-martial charging "conspiracy to communicate classified information to an agent of a foreign government. "His case involved unauthorized use of classified documents and information. DeChamplain was convicted, but the conviction was reversed on appeal because certain statements were improperly admitted as evidence.

Just before his retrial commenced, DeChamplain filed an action in federal district court. "seeking injunctive relief and asserting, among other claims, that Art. 134 was unconstitutionally vague and that the limitations on access to and use of the classified documents denied him due process and effective assistance of counsel."

The District Court for the District of Columbia preliminarily banned appellants from proceeding with DeChamplain's court-martial unless appellants allowed civilian defense counsel unlimited access to documents material to DeChamplain's defense.

The Supreme Court granted certiorari to review the case and reversed.

B. Counsel of Record/ACLU Attorney

ACLU Side (Respondent/Appellee): Leonard B. Boudin argued the cause for appellee.

Opposing Side (Petitioner/Appellant): Solicitor General Robert H. Bork argued the cause for appellant.

III. AMICI CURIAE

ACLU Side (Respondent/Appellee)

Brief of amici curiae filed on behalf of the ACLU by Melvin L. Wulf, John H. F. Shattuck, and Daniel V. Gsovski.

Opposing Side (Petitioner/Appellant)

No briefs of amici curiae were filed in support of appellant.

IV. THE SUPREME COURT'S DECISION

"Proper disposition of the case does not require extended discussion. Appellants argue that, in fact, DeChamplain's constitutional claim was always insubstantial. The Courts of Appeals decisions in Levy v. Parker and Avrech v. Secretary of the Navy, which concluded that Art. 134 suffered from unconstitutional vagueness, concerned only the first two clauses of that article making punishable 'all disorders and neglects to the prejudice of good order and discipline in the armed forces' and 'all conduct of a nature to bring discredit upon the armed forces.' DeChamplain, however, was charged under the assimilative crimes clause of the article, and was accused of having committed specific federal offenses. Thus, any possible vagueness in other parts of the article could not have affected DeChamplain. At this point, however, no purpose could be served by our deciding whether, when the complaint was filed, DeChamplain's constitutional claim was or was not substantial. Under our decisions in Levy and Avrech, DeChamplain's claim is, as he concedes, clearly insubstantial now and must be dismissed.

We turn, finally, to the portion of the preliminary injunction requiring the military authorities to allow unlimited access to the original court-martial record and to documents that will be at issue at DeChamplain's court-martial. Since this claim is independent of the Art. 134 question and unrelated to the validity and interpretation of that article or to any other Act of Congress, a three-judge court was not required to hear it. As to this claim, however, the only harm DeChamplain claimed in support of his prayer for equitable relief was that, if convicted, he might remain incarcerated pending review within the military system. Thus, according to DeChamplain, intervention is justified now to ensure that he receives a trial free of constitutional error, and to avoid the possibility that he will be incarcerated, pending review, on the basis of a conviction that inevitably will be invalid. But if such harm were deemed sufficient to warrant equitable interference into pending court-martial proceedings, any constitutional ruling at the court-martial presumably would be subject to immediate relitigation in federal district courts, resulting in disruption to the court-martial and circumvention of the military appellate system provided by Congress.

We hold that relief as to the access claim is precluded squarely by our holding in Schlesinger v. Councilman, that 'when a serviceman charged with crimes by military authorities can show no harm other than that attendant to resolution of his case in the military court system, the federal district courts must refrain from intervention . . . .' The 'unlimited access' aspect of DeChamplain's suit therefore must be dismissed for failure to state a claim upon which relief can be granted.

Reversed, vacated and remanded."

V. JUSTICE VOTE

0 Pro ACLU Side vs. 9 Con Opposing Side

Opposing Side (Petitioner/Appellant)

1. Powell, L. – Wrote majority opinion
2. Rehnquist, W. – Joined majority opinion
3. White, B. – Joined majority opinion
4. Burger, W. – Joined majority opinion
5. Stewart, P. – Joined majority opinion
6. Blackmun, H. – Joined majority opinion
7. Brennan, W. – Wrote concurring opinion
8. Douglas, W. – Joined Brennan's concurrence
9. Marshall, T. – Joined Brennan's concurrence

VI. A WIN OR LOSS FOR THE ACLU?

The ACLU filed as amicus curiae urging affirmance; the Supreme Court vacated and remanded the District Court judgment in a 9-0 vote, giving the ACLU an apparent loss.

354. National Labor Relations Board v. Sears, Roebuck & Co.

(Decided April 28, 1975; 421 U.S. 132)

I. ISSUE

A. Issues Discussed

Governmental authority, regulation, privacy

B. Legal Question Presented

Are certain documents generated by the National Labor Relations Board required to be made available to the public, pursuant to the Freedom of Information Act?

C. Supreme Court's Answer

Some of the documents are required to be disclosed and others are not, pursuant to the Freedom of Information Act, but this decision is subject to determinations on remand necessary for a final determination on document disclosure.

II. CASE SUMMARY

A. Background

"The National Labor Relations Board (the Board) and its General Counsel seek to set aside an order of the United States District Court directing disclosure to respondent, Sears, Roebuck & Co. (Sears), pursuant to the Freedom of Information Act, 5 U.S.C. § 552 (Act), of certain memoranda, known as 'Advice Memoranda' and 'Appeals Memoranda,' and related documents generated by the Office of the General Counsel in the course of deciding whether or not to permit the filing with the Board of unfair labor practice complaints. . . .

Sears claims, and the courts below ruled, that the memoranda sought are expressions of legal and policy decisions already adopted by the agency and constitute 'final opinions' and 'instructions to staff that affect a member of the public,' both categories being expressly disclosable under § 552(a)(2) of the Act, pursuant to its purposes to prevent the creation of 'secret law.' In any event, Sears claims, the memoranda are nonexempt 'identifiable records' which must be disclosed under § 552(a)(3). The General Counsel, on the other hand, claims that the memoranda sought here are not final opinions under § 552(a)(2) and that even if they are 'identifiable records' otherwise disclosable under § 552(a)(3), they are exempt under § 552(b), principally as 'intraagency' communications under § 552(b)(5) (Exemption 5), made in the course of formulating agency decisions on legal and policy matters."

The Advice Memoranda and Appeals Memoranda sought are created by the Board during the process of deciding whether to file a complaint for unfair labor practices after a private party files a "charge" with the Board alleging an unfair labor practice. The memoranda are created during the appeals process within the Board's determinations procedures. The dispute is over whether these memoranda must be disclosed under the Act.

The Supreme Court granted certiorari to review the case, affirmed in part, and reversed in part.

B. Counsel of Record/ACLU Attorney

ACLU Side (Respondent/Appellee): Gerard C. Smetana argued the cause for appellee.

Opposing Side (Petitioner/Appellant): Deputy Solicitor General Daniel M. Friedman argued the cause for appellant.

III. AMICI CURIAE

ACLU Side (Respondent/Appellee)

Brief of amici curiae filed on behalf of the ACLU, et al., by Carol A. Cowgill, Peter H. Schuck, Marvin M. Karpatkin, Melvin L. Wulf, and John H. F. Shattuck.

Brief of amici curiae filed on behalf of the Chamber of Commerce of the United States by Milton Smith, Richard Berman, Jerry Kronenberg, Julian D. Schreiber, and Howard L. Mocerf.

Brief of amici curiae filed on behalf of the Freedom of Information Clearinghouse by Alan B. Morrison and Larry P. Ellsworth.

Opposing Side (Petitioner/Appellant)

No briefs of amici curiae were filed in support of appellant.

IV. THE SUPREME COURT'S DECISION

"Finally, petitioners argue that the Advice and Appeals Memoranda are exempt, pursuant to 5 U.S.C. §§ 552(b)(2) and (7) (Exemptions 2 and 7), and that the documents incorporated therein are protected by Exemption 7. With respect to the Advice and Appeals Memoranda, we decline to reach a decision on these claims for the reasons set forth below, and with respect to the documents incorporated therein, we remand for further proceedings.

[T]he General Counsel claims that the documents, incorporated by reference in Advice and Appeals Memoranda, which were previously protected by Exemption 7, should not lose their exempt status by reason of incorporation. Contrary to the District Court, we think the argument is sound. The reasons underlying Congress' decision to protect 'investigatory files,' both in the original Act and in the amendments, are as applicable to a document referred to in an Advice or Appeals Memorandum as they are to a document which is not. Therefore, a document protected by Exemption 7 does not become disclosable solely because it is referred to in a 'final opinion.' We are aware that the result of this holding will be that some 'final opinions' will not be as easily understood as they would otherwise be. However, as noted above, the Act does not give the public a right to intelligible opinions in all cases. It simply gives the public a right to those 'final opinions,' which an agency chooses to write, and to which the Act applies. . . . The case must accordingly be remanded to the District Court for a determination whether the documents incorporated by reference in the disclosable Advice and Appeals Memoranda are protected by Exemption 7, as amended.

In summary, with respect to Advice and Appeals Memoranda which conclude that a complaint should not be filed, we affirm the judgment of the Court of Appeals subject to its decision on remand whether the Government is foreclosed from pursuing its Exemption 7 claim. With respect to documents specifically incorporated therein, we remand for a determination whether these documents are protected by Exemption 7, as amended. Insofar as the judgment of the Court of Appeals requires the General Counsel to supply documents not expressly incorporated by reference in these Advice and Appeals Memoranda, or otherwise to explain the circumstances of the case, it is reversed and with respect to Advice and Appeals Memoranda which conclude that a complaint should be filed, the judgment of the Court of Appeals is likewise reversed. . . .

Judgment affirmed in part and reversed in part and case remanded."

V. JUSTICE VOTE

0 Pro ACLU Side vs. 8 Con Opposing Side

Opposing Side (Petitioner/Appellant)

1. White, B. – Wrote majority opinion
2. Rehnquist, W. – Joined majority opinion
3. Burger, W. – Concurred in the judgment
4. Stewart, P. – Joined majority opinion
5. Blackmun, H. – Joined majority opinion
6. Marshall, T. – Joined majority opinion
7. Brennan, W. – Joined majority opinion
8. Douglas, W. – Joined majority opinion

Powell, L – Took no part in the decision

VI. A WIN OR LOSS FOR THE ACLU?

The ACLU filed as amicus curiae urging affirmance; the Supreme Court reversed the Court of Appeals' judgment in an 8-0 vote, giving the ACLU an apparent loss.

355. Renegotiation Board v. Grunmman Aircraft Engineering Corp.

(Decided April 28, 1975; 421 U.S. 168)

I. ISSUE

A. Issues Discussed

Governmental authority, regulation, privacy

B. Legal Question Presented

"[W]hether certain documents—documents generated by the Renegotiation Board (Board) and by its Regional Boards in performing their task of deciding whether certain Government contractors have earned, and must refund, 'excessive profits' on their Government contracts—are 'final opinions' explaining the reasons for agency decisions already made, and thus expressly subject to disclosure pursuant to the Freedom of Information Act (Act) or are instead predecisional consultative memoranda exempted from disclosure by § 552(b)(5)."

C. Supreme Court's Answer

The documents are exempted from disclosure as they are not final opinions.

II. CASE SUMMARY

A. Background

The Renegotiation Act of 1951 established the Renegotiation Board (Board) as an agency to recoup "excessive profits" made by contractors from contracts with the U.S. government. Contractors were required to file a financial statement with the Board. From this statement, the Board made an initial determination whether the contractor made excessive profits, then assigned those contracts indicating excessive profits to a Regional Board to collect further information, create a "Report of Renegotiation," and enter a recommendation after speaking with the contractor. If the contractor declined to enter an agreement after receiving the recommendation, the case was reassigned to the Board. The Board would then reevaluate the case and make its own recommendation "'not bound or limited in any manner by any evaluation, recommendation or determination of the Regional Board.'" If the contractor declined to enter an agreement based on the

Board's recommendation, the Board would issue "a unilateral order." At each stage throughout the entire process, the contractor was entitled to a statement of the basis for the determination at his request.

In this case, respondent brought an action pursuant to the Freedom of Information Act (FOIA), seeking disclosure of reports, all related to and issued during renegotiation proceedings.

After an initial round of proceedings, the District Court ultimately ruled in favor of respondent on the grounds that the reports were "final opinions" within the meaning of the FOIA. Section 552(a)(2)(A) of the FOIA requires government agencies to make available to the public "'final opinions. . . made in the adjudication of cases.'" The District Court also rejected the rejected the Board's contention that the reports were specifically exempted from disclosure under "Exemption 5" of the FOIA, which encompasses, "'inter-agency or intra-agency memorandums or letters which would not be available by law to a party other than an agency in litigation with the agency.'"

The Court of Appeals affirmed and held that even if the reports "were not 'final opinions' of the Board, they were disclosable as final opinions of the Regional Board: the Regional Board itself was to be considered an 'agency' for purposes of the Act."

The Supreme Court granted certiorari to review the case and reversed.

B. Counsel of Record/ACLU Attorney

ACLU Side (Respondent/Appellee): Tom M. Schaumberg argued the cause for appellee.

Opposing Side (Petitioner/Appellant): Allan Abbot Tuttle argued the cause for appellant.

III. AMICI CURIAE

ACLU Side (Respondent/Appellee)

Brief of amici curiae filed on behalf of the ACLU, et al., by Melvin L. Wulf, John H. F. Shattuck, Carol A. Cowgill, and Marvin M. Karpatkin.

Opposing Side (Petitioner/Appellant)

No briefs of amici curiae were filed in support of appellant.

IV. THE SUPREME COURT'S DECISION

"Exemption 5 incorporates the privileges which the Government enjoys under the relevant statutory and case law in the pretrial discovery context; and both Exemption 5 and the case law which it incorporates distinguish between predecisional memoranda prepared in order to assist an agency decisionmaker in arriving at his decision, which are exempt from disclosure, and postdecisional memoranda setting forth the reasons for an agency decision already made, which are not. Because only the full Board has the power by law to make the decision whether excessive profits exist; because both types of reports involved in this case are prepared prior to that decision and are used by the Board in its deliberations; and because the evidence utterly fails to support the conclusion that the reasoning in the reports is adopted by the Board as its reasoning, even when it agrees with the conclusion of a report, we conclude that the reports are not final opinions and do fall within Exemption 5. . . .

The effect of this decision is that, in those cases in which Statements and Summaries were not issued, the public will be largely uninformed as to the basis for decisions by the Renegotiation Board. Indeed, the decisions of both courts below—conceding as they both did the absence of decisional authority in either the Regional Boards or divisions of the statutory board—appear to have rested in the final analysis on the notion that the Renegotiation Board has an affirmative obligation under the Act to make public the reasons for its decisions; and that it must disclose its opinion or the nearest thing to an opinion in every case. However, Congress explicitly exempted the Renegotiation Board from all provisions of the Administrative Procedure Act except for the Public Information Section. Thus the opinion-writing section of the APA—which itself applies only to 'adjudication required by statute to be determined on the record after opportunity for an agency hearing' and even then only if the agency decision is not subject to de novo court review—is inapplicable to Board decisions. The Freedom of Information Act imposes no independent obligation on agencies to write opinions. It simply requires them to disclose the opinions which they do write. If the public interest suffers by reason of the failure of the Board to explain some of its decisions, the remedy is for Congress to require it to do so. It is not for us to require disclosure of documents, under the purported authority of the Act, which are not final opinions, which do not accurately set forth the reasons for the Board's decisions, and the disclosure of which would impinge on the Board's predecisional processes.

The judgment of the Court of Appeals is reversed."

V. JUSTICE VOTE

1 Pro ACLU Side vs. 7 Con Opposing Side

ACLU Side (Respondent/Appellee)

1. Douglas, W. – Dissented without an opinion

Opposing Side (Petitioner/Appellant)

1. White, B. – Wrote majority opinion
2. Rehnquist, W. – Joined majority opinion
3. Burger, W. – Joined majority opinion
4. Stewart, P. – Joined majority opinion
5. Blackmun, H. – Joined majority opinion
6. Brennan, W. – Joined majority opinion
7. Marshall, T. – Joined majority opinion

Powell, L – Took no part in the decision

VI. A WIN OR LOSS FOR THE ACLU?

The ACLU filed as amicus curiae urging affirmance, the Supreme Court reversed the Court of Appeals' judgment in a 7-1 vote giving the ACLU an apparent loss.

356. Meek v. Pittenger

(Decided May 19, 1975; 421 U.S. 349)

I. ISSUE

A. Issues Discussed

First Amendment, religion, Establishment Clause, schools

B. Legal Question Presented

"[W]hether a state law providing assistance to nonpublic, church-related elementary and secondary schools is constitutional under the Establishment Clause of the First Amendment, made applicable to the States by the Fourteenth Amendment."

C. Supreme Court's Answer

The state law is unconstitutional because it violates the Establishment Clause, except as to the provision providing textbooks to nonpublic schools, which does not violate the Establishment Clause.

II. CASE SUMMARY

A. Background

"With the stated purpose of assuring that every schoolchild in the Commonwealth will equitably share in the benefits of auxiliary services, textbooks, and instructional material provided free of charge to children attending public schools, the Pennsylvania General Assembly in 1972 added Acts 194 and 195 to the Pennsylvania Public School Code of 1949.

Act 194 authorizes the Commonwealth to provide 'auxiliary services' to all children enrolled in nonpublic elementary and secondary schools meeting Pennsylvania's compulsory-attendance requirements. 'Auxiliary services' include counseling, testing, and psychological services, speech and hearing therapy, teaching and related services for exceptional children, for remedial students, and for the educationally disadvantaged, 'and such other secular, neutral, nonideological services as are of benefit to nonpublic school children and are presently or hereafter provided for public school children of the Commonwealth.' . . .

Act 195 authorizes the State Secretary of Education, either directly or through the intermediate units, to lend textbooks without charge to children attending nonpublic elementary and secondary schools that meet the Commonwealth's compulsory-attendance requirements. . . .

Act 195 also authorizes the Secretary of Education, pursuant to requests from the appropriate nonpublic school officials, to lend directly to the nonpublic schools 'instructional materials and equipment, useful to the education' of nonpublic school children. . . .

On February 7, 1973, three individuals and four organizations filed a complaint in the District Court for the Eastern District of Pennsylvania challenging the constitutionality of Acts 194 and 195, and requesting an injunction prohibiting the expenditure of any funds under either statute. The complaint alleged that each Act 'is a law respecting an establishment of religion in violation of the First Amendment' . . . ."

A three-judge court upheld most of both Act 194 and Act 195, but "invalidated that portion of Act 195 authorizing the expenditure of commonwealth funds for the purchase of instructional equipment for loan to nonpublic schools, but only to the extent that the provision allowed the loan of equipment 'which from its nature can be diverted to religious purposes.'"

The Supreme Court granted certiorari to review the case, affirmed in part, and reversed in part.

B. Counsel of Record/ACLU Attorney

ACLU Side (Petitioner/Appellant): Leo Pfeffer and William P. Thorn argued the cause for appellant.

Opposing Side (Respondent/Appellee): William Bentley Ball, Deputy Attorney General of Pennsylvania J. Justin Blewitt, Jr., and Henry T. Reath argued the cause for appellees.

III. AMICI CURIAE

ACLU Side (Petitioner/Appellant)

Brief of amici curiae filed on behalf of the American Association of School Administrators, et al., by Theodore R. Mann, Paul S. Berger, Arnold Forster, Samuel Rabinove, Henry N. Rapaport, David Rubin, and Joseph B. Robison.

Opposing Side (Respondent/Appellee)

Brief of amici curiae filed on behalf of the Council for American Private Education by Stuart D. Hubbell.

Brief of amici curiae filed on behalf of the National Audio-Visual Association, Inc., by Howard Gould.

IV. THE SUPREME COURT'S DECISION

"In sum, the textbook loan provisions of Act 195 are in every material respect identical to the loan program approved in Allen. Pennsylvania, like New York, 'merely makes available to all children the benefits of a general program to lend school books free of charge.' As such, those provisions of Act 195 do not offend the constitutional prohibition against laws 'respecting an establishment of religion.' . . .

The church-related elementary and secondary schools that are the primary beneficiaries of Act 195's instructional material and equipment loans typify such religion-pervasive institutions. The very purpose of many of those schools is to provide an integrated secular and religious education; the teaching process is, to a large extent, devoted to the inculcation of religious values and belief. . . . For this reason, Act 195's direct aid to Pennsylvania's predominantly church-related, nonpublic elementary and secondary schools, even though ostensibly limited to wholly neutral, secular instructional material and equipment, inescapably results in the direct and substantial advancement of religious activity, and thus constitutes an impermissible establishment of religion. . . .

The fact that the teachers and counselors providing auxiliary services are employees of the public intermediate unit, rather than of the church-related schools in which they work, does not substantially eliminate the need for continuing surveillance. To be sure, auxiliary-services personnel, because not employed by the nonpublic schools, are not directly subject to the discipline of a religious authority. But they are performing important educational services in schools in which education is an integral part of the dominant sectarian mission and in which an atmosphere dedicated to the advancement of religious belief is constantly maintained. The potential for impermissible fostering of religion under these circumstances, although somewhat reduced, is nonetheless present. To be certain that auxiliary teachers remain religiously neutral, as the Constitution demands, the State would have to impose limitations on the activities of auxiliary personnel and then engage in some form of continuing surveillance to ensure that those restrictions were being followed.

In addition, Act 194 . . . creates a serious potential for divisive conflict over the issue of aid to religion—'entanglement in the broader sense of continuing political strife.' The recurrent nature of the appropriation process guarantees annual reconsideration of Act 194 and the prospect of repeated confrontation between proponents and opponents of the auxiliary-services program. The Act thus provides successive opportunities for political fragmentation and division along religious lines, one of the principal evils against which the Establishment Clause was intended to protect. This potential for political entanglement, together with the administrative entanglement which would be necessary to ensure that auxiliary-services personnel remain strictly neutral and nonideological when functioning in church-related schools, compels the conclusion that Act 194 violates the constitutional prohibition against laws 'respecting an establishment of religion.'

The judgment of the District Court as to Act 194 is reversed; its judgment as to the textbook provisions of Act 195 is affirmed, but as to that Act's other provisions now before us its judgment is reversed."

V. JUSTICE VOTE

6 Pro ACLU Side vs. 3 Con Opposing Side

ACLU Side (Petitioner/Appellant)

1. Stewart, P. – Wrote majority opinion
2. Powell, L. – Joined majority opinion
3. Blackmun, H. – Joined majority opinion
4. Brennan, W. – Wrote opinion concurring in part and dissenting in part
5. Marshall, T. – Joined Brennan's opinion
6. Douglas, W. – Joined Brennan's opinion

Opposing Side (Respondent/Appellee)

1. Rehnquist, W. – Wrote opinion concurring in part and dissenting in part
2. White, B. – Joined Rehnquist's opinion
3. Burger, W. – Wrote opinion concurring in part and dissenting in part

VI. A WIN OR LOSS FOR THE ACLU?

The ACLU, as counsel for appellant, urged reversal in part and affirmance in part; the Supreme Court affirmed in part and reversed in part the District Court's ruling in a 6-3 vote, giving the ACLU an apparent win.

357. Ellis v. Dyson

(Decided May 19, 1975; 421 U.S. 426)

I. ISSUE

A. Issues Discussed

Criminal procedure

B. Legal Question Presented

"This action instituted in the United States District Court for the Northern District of Texas, challenges the constitutionality of the loitering ordinance of the city of Dallas."

C. Supreme Court's Answer

"We do not reach the merits, for the District Court dismissed the case under the compulsion of a procedural precedent of the United States Court of Appeals for the Fifth Circuit which we have since reversed."

II. CASE SUMMARY

A. Background

"Petitioners Tom E. Ellis and Robert D. Love, while in an automobile, were arrested in Dallas at 2 a.m. on January 18, 1972, and were charged with violating the city's loitering ordinance. . . .

Before their trial in the Dallas Municipal Court petitioners sought a writ of prohibition from the Texas Court of Criminal Appeals to preclude their prosecution on the ground that the ordinance was unconstitutional on its face. . . . The Court of Criminal Appeals, however, denied the application without opinion on February 21, 1972. The following day the Municipal Court proceeded to try the case. After overruling petitioners' motion to dismiss the charges on the grounds of the ordinance's unconstitutionality, the court accepted their pleas of nolo contendere and fined each petitioner $10 plus $2.50 costs.

Under Texas' two-tier criminal justice system, petitioners could not directly appeal . . . .

Electing to avoid the possibility of the imposition of a larger fine by the County Court than was imposed by the Municipal Court, petitioners brought the present federal action under the civil rights statutes, 42 U.S.C. s 1983 and 28 U.S.C. ss 1343(3) and (4), and under the Declaratory Judgment Act, 28 U.S.C. ss 2201—2202. . . . Petitioners sought a declaratory judgment that the loitering ordinance is unconstitutional. . . . Petitioners also sought equitable relief in the form of expunction of their records of arrests and convictions for violating the ordinance . . . .

The District Court held that federal declaratory and injunctive relief against future state criminal prosecutions was not available . . . . Since the present petitioners' complaint contained insufficient allegation of irreparable harm, the case was dismissed. The United States Court of Appeals for the Fifth Circuit affirmed without opinion. After [the Supreme Court] unanimously reversed the Becker decision on which the District Court had relied, we granted the petition for certiorari."

B. Counsel of Record

ACLU Side (Petitioner/Appellant): Burt Neuborne of the American Civil Liberties Union Foundation argued the cause for appellants. With him on the brief were Walter W. Steele, Jr., John E. Kennedy, and Joel Gora and Melvin L. Wulf of the American Civil Liberties Union Foundation.

Opposing Side (Respondent/Appellee): Douglas H. Conner argued the cause for appellees. With him on the brief was N. Alex Bickley.

III. AMICI CURIAE

ACLU Side (Petitioner/Appellant)

No briefs of amici curiae were filed in support of appellants.

Opposing Side (Respondent/Appellee)

No briefs of amici curiae were filed in support of appellees.

IV. THE SUPREME COURT'S DECISION

"In Steffel the Court considered the issue whether the Younger doctrine should apply to a case where state prosecution under a challenged ordinance was merely threatened but not pending. . . .

Exhaustion of state judicial or administrative remedies in Steffel was ruled not to be necessary, for we have long held that an action under s 1983 is free of that requirement. We did require, however, that it be clearly demonstrated that there was a continuing, actual controversy, as is mandated both by the Declaratory Judgment Act, 28 U.S.C. s 2201, and by Art. III of the Constitution itself. . . .

The principles and approach of Steffel are applicable here. The District Court and the Court of Appeals decided this case under the misapprehension that the Younger doctrine applied where there is a threatened state criminal prosecution as well as where there is a state criminal prosecution already pending. Those courts had no reason to reach the merits of the case or to determine the actual existence of a genuine threat of prosecution, or to inquire into the relationship between the past prosecution and the threat of prosecutions for similar activity in the future. Now that Steffel has been decided, these issues may properly be investigated.

We therefore reverse the judgment of the Court of Appeals and remand the case to the District Court for reconsideration in the light of our opinion in Steffel v. Thompson, reversing Becker v. Thompson. It is appropriate to observe in passing, however, that we possess greater reservations here than we did in Steffel as to whether a case or controversy exists today. . . .

Because of the fact that the District Court has not had the opportunity to consider this case in the light of Steffel, and because of our grave reservations about the existence of an actual case or controversy, we have concluded that it would be inappropriate for us to touch upon any of the other complex and difficult issues that the case otherwise might present. . . .

The judgment of the Court of Appeals is reversed and the case is remanded . . . . No costs are allowed."

V. JUSTICE VOTE

6 Pro ACLU Side vs. 3 Con Opposing Side

ACLU Side (Petitioner/Appellant)

1. Blackmun, H. – Wrote majority opinion
2. White, B. – Wrote opinion concurring in part and dissenting in part
3. Marshall, T. – Joined majority opinion
4. Brennan, W. – Joined majority opinion
5. Rehnquist, W. – Wrote concurring opinion
6. Douglas, W. – Joined majority opinion

Opposing Side (Respondent/Appellee)

1. Burger, W. – Joined Powell's dissent in part
2. Powell, L. – Wrote dissenting opinion
3. Stewart, P. – Joined Powell's dissent

VI. A WIN OR LOSS FOR THE ACLU?

The ACLU served as counsel for appellants urging reversal of the judgment of the Court of Appeals; the Supreme Court reversed, in a 6-3 vote, giving the ACLU an apparent win.

358. Eastland v. United States Servicemen's Fund

(Decided May 27, 1975; 421 U.S. 491)

I. ISSUE

A. Issues Discussed

1st Amendment, press, speech, association

B. Legal Question Presented

"[W]hether a federal court may enjoin the issuance by Congress of a subpoena duces tecum that directs a bank to produce the bank records of an organization which claims a First Amendment privilege status for those records on the ground that they are the equivalent of confidential membership lists."

C. Supreme Court's Answer

"We conclude that the actions of the Senate Subcommittee, the individual Senators, and the Chief Counsel are protected by the Speech or Debate Clause of the Constitution, Art. I, s 6, cl. 1, and are therefore immune from judicial interference."

II. CASE SUMMARY

A. Background

"In early 1970 the Senate Subcommittee on Internal Security was given broad authority by the Senate to 'make a complete and continuing study and investigation of . . . the administration, operation, and enforcement of the Internal Security Act of 1950 . . . .' The authority encompassed discovering the 'extent, nature and effect of subversive activities in the United States' . . . . Pursuant to that mandate the Subcommittee began an inquiry into the activities of respondent United States Servicemen's Fund, Inc. (USSF). . . .

In the course of its investigation of USSF, the Subcommittee concluded that a prima facie showing had been made of the need for further investigation, and it resolved that appropriate subpoenas, including subpoenas duces tecum could be issued. Petitioner Eastland . . . is . . . Chairman of the Subcommittee. On May 28, 1970 pursuant to the above authority, he signed a subpoena duces tecum, issued on behalf of the Subcommittee, to the bank where USSF then had an account. . . .

[B]efore the return date, USSF and two of its members brought this action to enjoin implementation of the subpoena duces tecum. . . .

For relief USSF and its members, the respondents, sought a permanent injunction restraining the . . . . Respondents also sought a declaratory judgment declaring the subpoena and the Senate resolutions void under the Constitution. No damages claim was made.

Since the return date on the subpoena was June 4, 1970, three days after the action was begun, enforcement of the subpoena was stayed . . . . The District Court . . . ultimately held that respondents had not made a sufficient showing of irreparable injury to warrant an injunction. . . .

The Court of Appeals reversed . . . ."

The Supreme Court granted certiorari to review the case.

B. Counsel of Record

ACLU Side (Respondent/Appellee): Jeremiah S. Gutman of the American Civil Liberties Union Foundation and Nancy Stearns argued the cause and filed a brief for appellees.

Opposing Side (Petitioner/Appellant): Herbert J. Miller, Jr., argued the cause for appellants. With him on the brief were Nathan Lewin and A. Raymond Randolph, Jr.

III. AMICI CURIAE

ACLU Side (Respondent/Appellee)

No briefs of amici curiae were filed in support of appellees.

Opposing Side (Petitioner/Appellant)

No briefs of amici curiae were filed in support of appellants.

IV. THE SUPREME COURT'S DECISION

"The question to be resolved is whether the actions of the petitioners fall within the 'sphere of legitimate legislative activity.' If they do, the petitioners 'shall not be questioned in any other Place' about those activities since the prohibitions of the Speech or Debate Clause are absolute. . . .

In determining whether particular activities other than literal speech or debate fall within the 'legitimate legislative sphere' we look to see whether the activities took place 'in a session of the House by one of its members in relation to the business before it.' . . .

The power to investigate and to do so through compulsory process plainly falls within that definition. . . .

The particular investigation at issue here is related to and in furtherance of a legitimate task of Congress. . . .

The propriety of making USSF a subject of the investigation and subpoena is a subject on which the scope of our inquiry is narrow. . . . Even the most cursory look at the facts presented by the pleadings reveals the legitimacy of the USSF subpoena. . . .

We conclude that the Speech or Debate Clause provides complete immunity for the Members for issuance of this subpoena. . . .

This case illustrates vividly the harm that judicial interference may cause. A legislative inquiry has been frustrated for nearly five years, during which the Members and their aide have been obliged to devote time to consultation with their counsel concerning the litigation, and have been distracted from the purpose of their inquiry. The Clause was written to prevent the need to be confronted by such 'questioning' and to forbid invocation of judicial power to challenge the wisdom of Congress' use of its investigative authority. . . .

Judgment with respect to the Senate aspect of this case is reversed and the case is remanded to the Court of Appeals for entry of a judgment directing the District Court to dismiss the complaint. The House aspects of this case are remanded with directions to remand to the District Court for further consideration consistent with this opinion."

V. JUSTICE VOTE

1 Pro ACLU Side vs. 8 Con Opposing Side

ACLU Side (Respondent/Appellee)

1. Douglas, W. – Wrote dissenting opinion

Opposing Side (Petitioner/Appellant)

1. Burger, W. – Wrote majority opinion
2. White, B. – Joined majority opinion
3. Marshall, T. – Wrote concurring opinion
4. Brennan, W. – Joined Marshall's concurrence
5. Stewart, P. – Joined Marshall's concurrence
6. Blackmun, H. – Joined majority opinion
7. Powell, L. – Joined majority opinion
8. Rehnquist, W. – Joined majority opinion

VI. A WIN OR LOSS FOR THE ACLU?

The ACLU served as counsel for appellees urging affirmance of the judgment of the Court of Appeals; the Supreme Court reversed, in an 8-1 vote, giving the ACLU an apparent loss.

359. Bigelow v. Virginia

(Decided June 16, 1975; 421 U.S. 809)

I. ISSUE

A. Issues Discussed

1st Amendment, press, speech, association, privacy

B. Legal Question Presented

"An advertisement carried in appellant's newspaper led to his conviction for a violation of a Virginia statute that made it a misdemeanor, by the sale or circulation of any publication, to encourage or prompt the procuring of an abortion. The issue here is whether the editor-appellant's First Amendment rights were unconstitutionally abridged by the statute."

C. Supreme Court's Answer

"We conclude that Virginia could not apply Va. Code Ann. s 18.1—63 (1960), as it read in 1971, to appellant's publication of the advertisement in question without unconstitutionally infringing upon his First Amendment rights."

II. CASE SUMMARY

A. Background

"The Virginia Weekly was a newspaper .... Appellant, Jeffrey C. Bigelow, was a director and the managing editor and responsible officer of the newspaper....

[The paper ran an] advertisement [that] announced that the Women's Pavilion of New York City would help women with unwanted pregnancies ....

On May 13 Bigelow was charged with violating Va.Code Ann. s 18.1—63 (1960) ... :

'If any person, by publication, lecture, advertisement, or by the sale or circulation of any publication, or in any other manner, encourage or prompt the procuring of abortion or miscarriage, he shall be guilty of a misdemeanor.'

Shortly after the statute was utilized in Bigelow's case, ... the Virginia Legislature amended it and changed its prior application and scope.

Appellant was first tried and convicted in the County Court of Albemarle County. He appealed to the Circuit Court .... The court rejected appellant's claim that the statute was unconstitutional and adjudged him guilty. He was sentenced to pay a fine of $500, with $350 thereof suspended ....

The Supreme Court of Virginia ... affirmed Bigelow's conviction....

Bigelow took a timely appeal to this Court. During the pendency of his appeal, Roe v. Wade, 410 U.S. 113 (1973), and Doe v. Bolton, 410 U.S. 179 (1973), were decided. We subsequently vacated Bigelow's judgment of conviction and remanded ....

The Supreme Court of Virginia ... affirmed appellant's conviction ...."

The Supreme Court granted certiorari to review the case.

B. Counsel of Record

ACLU Side (Petitioner/Appellant): Melvin L. Wulf of the American Civil Liberties Union Foundation and John C. Lowe of the American Civil Liberties Union of Virginia argued the cause for appellant. With them on the brief were Joel M. Gora and Judith Mears of the American Civil Liberties Union Foundation, and F. Guthrie Gordon, III, of the American Civil Liberties Union of Virginia.

Opposing Side (Respondent/Appellee): D. Patrick Lacy, Jr., Assistant Attorney General of Virginia, argued the cause for appellee. With him on the brief were Andrew P. Miller, Attorney General, Anthony F. Troy, Deputy Attorney General, and Paul L. Gergoudis, Assistant Attorney General.

III. AMICI CURIAE

ACLU Side (Petitioner/Appellant)

Brief of amici curiae filed on behalf of Public Citizen et al. by Raymond T. Bonner and Alan B. Morrison.

Opposing Side (Respondent/Appellee)

Brief of amici curiae filed on behalf of Virginia Right to Life, Inc., by Michael M. Kearney.

IV. THE SUPREME COURT'S DECISION

"Declaring a statute facially unconstitutional because of overbreadth 'is, manifestly, strong medicine,' and 'has been employed by the Court sparingly and only as a last resort.' But we conclude that the Virginia courts erred in denying Bigelow standing to make this claim ....

In view of the statute's amendment ... the issue of its overbreadth has become moot .... We therefore decline to rest our decision on overbreadth and we pass on to the further inquiry ... whether the statute as applied to appellant infringed constitutionally protected speech....

The central assumption made by the Supreme Court of Virginia was that the First Amendment guarantees ... are inapplicable to paid commercial advertisements. Our cases, however, clearly establish that speech is not stripped of First Amendment protection merely because it appears in that form....

The legitimacy of appellant's First Amendment claim in the present case is demonstrated by the important differences between the advertisement presently at issue and those involved in Chrestensen and in Pittsburgh Press. The advertisement published in appellant's newspaper did more than simply propose a commercial transaction. It contained factual material of clear 'public interest.' ...

Viewed in its entirety, the advertisement conveyed information of potential interest and value to a diverse audience—not only to readers possibly in need of the services offered, but also to those with a general curiosity about, or genuine interest in, the subject matter or the law of another State and its development, and to readers seeking reform in Virginia. ... Thus, in this case, appellant's First Amendment interests coincided with the constitutional interests of the general public....

We conclude, therefore, that the Virginia courts erred in their assumptions that advertising, as such, was entitled to no First Amendment protection and that appellant Bigelow had no legitimate First Amendment interest....

We conclude that Virginia could not apply Va. Code Ann. s 18.1—63 (1960), as it read in 1971, to appellant's publication of the advertisement in question without unconstitutionally infringing upon his First Amendment rights. The judgment of the Supreme Court of Virginia is therefore reversed."

V. JUSTICE VOTE

7 Pro ACLU Side vs. 2 Con Opposing Side

ACLU Side (Petitioner/Appellant)

1. Blackmun, H. – Wrote majority opinion

2. Brennan, W. – Joined majority opinion
3. Marshall, T. – Joined majority opinion
4. Stewart, P. – Joined majority opinion
5. Burger, W. – Joined majority opinion
6. Powell, L. – Joined majority opinion
7. Douglas, W. – Joined majority opinion

Opposing Side (Respondent/Appellee)

1. Rehnquist, W. – Wrote dissenting opinion
2. White, B. – Joined Rehnquist's dissent

VI. A WIN OR LOSS FOR THE ACLU?

The ACLU served as counsel for appellant urging reversal of the judgment of the Supreme Court of Virginia; the U.S. Supreme Court reversed in a 7-2 vote, giving the ACLU an apparent win.

360. Rogers v. United States

(Decided June 17, 1975; 422 U.S. 35)

I. ISSUE

A. Issues Discussed

Criminal procedure, jury trials

B. Legal Question Presented

Did the trial court commit a prejudicial error by, without informing petitioner or his counsel, responding to the jury's inquiry regarding a verdict of "guilty with extreme mercy"?

C. Supreme Court's Answer

The trial court committed a prejudicial error in violation of Rule 43 of the Federal Rules of Criminal Procedure.

II. CASE SUMMARY

A. Background

"Petitioner was convicted by a jury on five counts of an indictment charging him with knowingly and willfully making oral threats 'to take the life of or to inflict bodily harm upon the President of the United States,' in violation of 18 U.S.C. § 871(a). The Court of Appeals affirmed, and [the Supreme Court] granted certiorari to resolve an apparent conflict among the Courts of Appeals concerning the elements of the offense proscribed by § 871(a). . . .

The record reveals that the jury retired for deliberation at 3 p.m. on the second day of petitioner's trial. Approximately two hours later, at 4:55 p.m., the jury sent a note, signed by the foreman, to the trial judge, inquiring whether the court would 'accept the Verdict-'Guilty as charged with extreme mercy of the Court.' Without notifying petitioner or his counsel, the court instructed the marshal who delivered the note 'to advise the jury that the Court's answer was in the affirmative.' Five minutes later at 5 p.m., the jury returned, and" the Court entered the verdict including the recommendation for mercy.

The Supreme Court granted certiorari to review the case and reversed.

B. Counsel of Record/ACLU Attorney

ACLU Side (Petitioner/Appellant): Ralph W. Parnell, Jr. argued the cause for appellant.

Opposing Side (Respondent/Appellee): Allan A. Tuttle argued the cause for the United States.

III. AMICI CURIAE

ACLU Side (Petitioner/Appellant)

Brief of amici curiae filed on behalf of the ACLU by Osmond K. Fraenkel and Melvin L. Wulf.

Opposing Side (Respondent/Appellee)

No briefs of amici curiae were filed in support of appellee.

IV. THE SUPREME COURT'S DECISION

"Generally, a recommendation of leniency made by a jury without statutory authorization does not affect the validity of the verdict and may be disregarded by the sentencing judge. However in Cook, the Court of Appeals held that an exception to this general rule, requiring further inquiry by the trial court, arises where the circumstances of the recommendation cast doubt upon the unqualified nature of the verdict. We deal here not merely with a potential defect in the verdict.

[C]ommunication from the jury in this case was tantamount to a request for further instructions. . . . Federal Rule Crim. Proc. 43 guarantees to a defendant in a criminal trial the right to be present 'at every stage of the trial including the impaneling of the jury and the return of the verdict.' Cases interpreting the Rule make it clear, if our decisions prior to the promulgation of the Rule left any doubt, that the jury's message should have been answered in open court and that petitioner's counsel should have been given an opportunity to be heard before the trial judge responded.

Although a violation of Rule 43 may in some circumstances be harmless error, the nature of the information conveyed to the jury, in addition to the manner in which it was conveyed, does not permit that conclusion in this case. The trial judge should not have confined his response to the jury's inquiry to an indication of willingness to accept a verdict with a recommendation of 'extreme mercy.' At the very least, the court should have reminded the jury that the recommendation would not be binding in any way. . . .

The fact that the jury, which had been deliberating for almost two hours without reaching a verdict, returned a verdict of 'guilty with extreme mercy' within five minutes 'after being told unconditionally and unequivocally that it could recommend leniency,' strongly suggests that the trial judge's response may have induced unanimity by giving members of the jury who had previously hesitated about reaching a guilty verdict the impression that the recommendation might be an acceptable compromise. We acknowledge that the comments of the trial judge upon receiving the verdict may be said to have put petitioner's counsel on notice that the jury had communicated with the court, but the only indication that the court had unilaterally communicated with the jury comes from the note itself, which the court correctly ordered to be filed in the record, with a notation as to the time of receipt and the court's response. It appears, however, that petitioner's counsel was not aware of the court's communication until after we granted the petition for certiorari. In such circumstances, and particularly in light of the difficult task of the factfinder in a prosecution under § 871(a), we conclude that the combined effect of the District Court's errors was so fraught with potential prejudice as to require us to notice them notwithstanding petitioner's failure to raise the issue in the Court of Appeals or in this Court.

The judgment of the Court of Appeals is accordingly reversed, and the case is remanded for further proceedings consistent with this opinion."

V. JUSTICE VOTE

9 Pro ACLU Side vs. 0 Con Opposing Side

ACLU Side (Petitioner/Appellant)

1. Burger, W. – Wrote majority opinion
2. Stewart, P. – Joined majority opinion
3. White, B. – Joined majority opinion
4. Rehnquist, W. – Joined majority opinion
5. Blackmun, H. – Joined majority opinion
6. Powell, L. – Joined majority opinion
7. Brennan, W. – Joined majority opinion
8. Marshall, T. – Wrote concurring opinion
9. Douglas, W. – Joined Marshall's concurrence

VI. A WIN OR LOSS FOR THE ACLU?

The ACLU filed as amicus curiae urging reversal; the Supreme Court reversed the judgment of the Court of Appeals in a 9-0 vote giving the ACLU an apparent win.

361. Staats v. American Civil Liberties Union

aka ACLU v. Jennings, 365 F. Supp. 1041 (D.D.C. 1973)

(Decided June 23, 1975; 422 U.S. 1030)

I. ISSUE

A. Issues Discussed

Press, voting rights

B. Legal Question Presented

"Whether Congress may constitutionally enforce a limitation on campaign expenditures in federal elections by requiring a communications medium, before running an advertisement on behalf of a candidate, to obtain a certification by the candidate that the expenditure will not violate the limitation."[1]

C. Supreme Court's Answer

"Judgment vacated and case remanded to the United States District Court for the District of Columbia with directions to dismiss the cause as moot."

II. CASE SUMMARY

A. Background

"In early September 1972, plaintiffs, the American Civil Liberties Union (ACLU) and the New York Civil Liberties Union (NYCLU), . . . submitted for publication to The New York Times (Times) a proposed advertisement which expressed their opposition to the Nixon Administration backed legislation designed to limit court ordered busing. The advertisement . . . listed, in the form of an 'honor roll,' the names of 102 United States Representatives who had previously opposed this anti-busing policy. Plaintiffs were hopeful that through publication of the advertisement public support would be generated favorable to the position they had adopted on this highly publicized and controversial problem of national import. Any intention to aid in the election or re-election campaign of any political candidate has been specifically denied.

The Times, through one of its responsible officers, and on advice of counsel, notified the plaintiffs that their failure to comply with certain certification requirements mandated by Title I of the Act precluded publication of the advertisement. Because those requirements, found in § 104(a) of the Act, as set forth in certain implementing regulations, 11 C.F.R. §§ 4.4 and 4.5, were not satisfied by the plaintiff, the Times, rather than risk criminal penalties under FECA, refused the publication for print.

On the heels of this refusal plaintiffs filed with the Court the present suit challenging the constitutionality of the FECA provisions cited by the Times in rejecting the advertisement, and sought injunctive relief prohibiting their enforcement. . . . Plaintiffs further challenged and requested the Court to enjoin the enforcement of Title III of the Act, which establishes certain registration, filing and notice requirements for organizations engaged in the political process.

[T]he Court found harbored within the provisions of Titles I and III sufficient First Amendment impediments and restraints to warrant the issuance of a preliminary injunction. Accordingly, the defendants were 'enjoined, pendente lite, from taking any action against plaintiffs, or any other person, that would have the effect of impeding, hindering, or preventing the acceptance for publication of any advertisements or statements of plaintiffs which are similar to, in purpose and effect, the advertisement or statements which are the subject of this suit; and they (were) further enjoined from threatening, initiating or taking any civil or criminal action in connection with the publication of any such advertisements or statements . . . .'

The threat of prosecution under FPCA having been eliminated, The New York Times published, on October 27, 1972, the revised anti-busing advertisement submitted by the plaintiffs. . . . The defendants thereafter moved to dismiss the action or, in the alternative, for an order granting summary judgment on the merits. Plaintiffs cross-moved for summary judgment and a supporting memorandum was submitted by The New York Times."[2]

The Supreme Court granted certiorari to review the case and vacated the judgment of the United States District Court for the District of Columbia.

1 Brief of Petitioner at 2, Staats v. American Civil Liberties Union, 422 U.S. 1030 (1975) (No. 73-1413).

2 American Civil Liberties Union v. Jennings, 366 F.Supp. 1041, 1042-1044 (D.C. 1973).

B. Counsel of Record / ACLU Attorney

ACLU Side (Respondent / Appellee): Marvin M. Karpatkin, John E. LeMoult, Melvin L. Wulf, Joel M. Gora, Norman Dorsen, Hope B. Eastman, Ralph J. Temple, and Robert Boraks filed a brief for American Civil Liberties Union in the United States District Court for the District of Columbia.[1]

Paul G. Chevigny, New York City, filed a brief for the New York Civil Liberties Union in the United States District Court for the District of Columbia.[2]

Opposing Side (Petitioner / Appellant): Acting Solicitor General Daniel M. Friedman, Assistant Attorney General Carla A. Hills, Assistant to the Solicitor General Danny T. Boggs, Stephen F. Eilperin, and Barbara L. Herwig filed a brief for appellant.

III. AMICI CURIAE

ACLU Side (Respondent / Appellee)

Brief of amici curiae filed on behalf of the National Association of Broadcasters by John B. Summers and James J. Popham.

Opposing Side (Petitioner / Appellant)

IV. THE SUPREME COURT'S DECISION

"Judgment vacated and case remanded to the United States District Court for the District of Columbia with directions to dismiss the cause as moot."

V. JUSTICE VOTE

0 Pro ACLU Side vs. 8 Con Opposing Side

Opposing Side (Petitioner / Appellant)

1. Burger, W. – Wrote majority opinion
2. Brennan, W. – Joined majority opinion
3. Stewart, P. – Joined majority opinion
4. White, B. – Joined majority opinion
5. Marshall, T. – Joined majority opinion
6. Blackmun, H. – Joined majority opinion
7. Powell, L. – Joined majority opinion
8. Rehnquist, W. – Joined majority opinion

Douglas, W – Took no part in the decision

VI. A WIN OR LOSS FOR THE ACLU?

The ACLU, as a party of record, urged affirmance of the judgment of the United States District Court for the District of Columbia; the Supreme Court vacated the judgment of the lower court in an 8-0 vote, giving the ACLU an apparent loss.

362. Preiser v. Newkirk

(Decided June 25, 1975; 422 U.S. 395)

I. ISSUE

A. Issues Discussed

Prison

B. Legal Question Presented

"'Whether a prison inmate who is transferred within a state from a medium security institution to a maximum security institution, without the imposition of disciplinary punishment, is entitled under the Due Process Clause of the Fourteenth Amendment to notice of the reasons for the transfer and an opportunity to be heard'?"

C. Supreme Court's Answer

"We conclude that the question presented does not fall within that category of harm 'capable of repetition, yet evading review.'"

II. CASE SUMMARY

A. Background

"Respondent Newkirk has been an inmate of the New York prison system since . . . 1962. He had initially been confined at . . . maximum security institutions . . . . In April 1971, . . . he was transferred to the Wallkill Correctional Facility, a medium security institution. . . .

[A] petition aimed at the formation of a prisoners' 'union' was circulated at Wallkill. . . .

A report . . . identified Newkirk as one of the inmates who had been canvassing for the 'union' but did not charge him with any violation . . . . The following day, on June 6, 1972, the superintendent . . . arranged for transfer of several inmates, including Newkirk, to other facilities . . . .

Newkirk was transferred to the Clinton Correctional Facility, a maximum security institution. . . .

Newkirk and three of the other four prisoners transferred from Wallkill brought suit . . . . They requested a declaratory judgment that the transfers were in violation of the Constitution and laws of the United States and an injunction ordering their return to Wallkill, expunging all record of their transfer, and prohibiting future transfers without a hearing. The District Court denied a preliminary injunction but set the case for trial on an accelerated basis. [S]ubsequently Newkirk was returned to Wallkill. The superintendent of that institution also had a memorandum placed in respondent's file which explained the nature of the transfer . . . .

The District Court held that the transfer violated the Due Process Clause of the Fourteenth Amendment since it had been made without any explanation to Newkirk or opportunity to be heard. . . .

The Court of Appeals affirmed the judgment with some modification. . . .

[The Supreme Court] granted petitioners' petition for writ of certiorari . . . ."

1 American Civil Liberties Union v. Jennings, 366 F.Supp. 1041 (D.C. 1973).
2 American Civil Liberties Union v. Jennings, 366 F.Supp. 1041 (D.C. 1973).

B. Counsel of Record

ACLU Side (Respondent/Appellee): Daniel Pochoda argued the cause for appellee. With him on the brief were William E. Hellerstein and Marjorie Mazen Smith.

Opposing Side (Petitioner/Appellant): Hillel Hoff man, Assistant Attorney General of New York, argued the cause for appellants. With him on the brief were Louis J. Lefkowitz, Attorney General, Samuel A. Hirshowitz, First Assistant Attorney General, and Joel Lewittes, Assistant Attorney General.

III. AMICI CURIAE

ACLU Side (Respondent/Appellee)

Brief of amici curiae filed on behalf of the National Prison Project of the American Civil Liberties Union Foundation, Inc., and the NAACP Legal Defense and Educational Fund, Inc., by Barbara M. Milstein, Alvin J. Bronstein, Arpiar G. Saunders, Jr., Jack Greenberg, Stanley A. Bass, and Cary Coen.

Opposing Side (Petitioner/Appellant)

Brief of amici curiae filed on behalf of the United States by Solicitor General Bork, Acting Assistant Attorney General Keeney, Deputy Solicitor General Frey, and Joseph S. Davies.

IV. THE SUPREME COURT'S DECISION

"All of the developments since the original challenged transfer must be read in light of not only Newkirk's transfer to Wallkill but also his later transfer, after the decision of the Court of Appeals, to the Edgecombe Correctional Facility, a minimum security institution in New York City. Newkirk will be eligible for parole in July 1975.

The exercise of judicial power under Art. III of the Constitution depends on the existence of a case or controversy. . . .

In Maryland Casualty Co. v. Pacific Co., 312 U.S. 270 (1941), this Court, noting the difficulty in fashioning a precise test of universal application for determining whether a request for declaratory relief had become moot, held that, basically, 'the question in each case is whether the facts alleged, under all the circumstances, show that there is a substantial controversy, between parties having adverse legal interests, *of sufficient immediacy and reality to warrant the issuance of a declaratory judgment.*' . . .

Any subjective fear Newkirk might entertain of being again transferred, under circumstances similar to those alleged in the complaint, or of suffering adverse consequences as a result of the 1972 transfer, is indeed remote and speculative and hardly casts that 'continuing and brooding presence.' over him that concerned the Court in Super Tire Engineering Co. v. McCorkle, 416 U.S. 115 (1974). . . .

We conclude that the question presented does not fall within that category of harm 'capable of repetition, yet evading review.' Accordingly, we vacate the judgment of the Court of Appeals and remand the case to that court with directions that the complaint be dismissed by the District Court."

V. JUSTICE VOTE

1 Pro ACLU Side vs. 8 Con Opposing Side

ACLU Side (Respondent/Appellee)

1. Douglas, W. – Wrote dissenting statement

Opposing Side (Petitioner/Appellant)

1. Burger, W. – Wrote majority opinion
2. White, B. – Joined majority opinion
3. Marshall, T. – Wrote concurring statement
4. Brennan, W. – Joined majority opinion
5. Stewart, P. – Joined majority opinion
6. Blackmun, H. – Joined majority opinion
7. Powell, L. – Joined majority opinion
8. Rehnquist, W. – Joined majority opinion

VI. A WIN OR LOSS FOR THE ACLU?

The ACLU filed as amici curiae urging affirmance of the judgment of the Court of Appeals; the Supreme Court vacated, in an 8-1 vote, giving the ACLU an apparent loss.

363. O'Connor v. Donaldson

(Decided June 26, 1975; 422 U.S. 563)

I. ISSUE

A. Issues Discussed

Involuntary confinement, right to liberty

B. Legal Question Presented

Was appellee, who was kept in custody against his will as a mental patient for nearly 15 years, deprived of his constitutional right to liberty?

C. Supreme Court's Answer

Appellee was deprived of his constitutional right to liberty by his continued confinement, however, on remand the court must determine whether it is appropriate to assess damages against the hospital superintendent in this circumstance.

II. CASE SUMMARY

A. Background

"The respondent, Kenneth Donaldson, was civilly committed to confinement as a mental patient in the Florida State Hospital at Chattachoochee in January 1957. He was kept in custody there against his will for nearly 15 years. The petitioner, Dr. J. B. O'Connor, was the hospital's superintendent during most of this period. Throughout his confinement Donaldson repeatedly, but unsuccessfully, demanded his release, claiming that he was dangerous to no one, that he was not mentally ill, and that, at any rate, the hospital was not providing treatment for his supposed illness. Finally, in February 1971, Donaldson brought this lawsuit under 42 U.S.C. § 1983, in the United States District Court for the Northern District of Florida, alleging that O'Connor, and other members of the hospital staff named as defendants, had intentionally and maliciously deprived him of his constitutional right to liberty. After a four-day trial, the jury returned a verdict assessing both compensatory and punitive damages against O'Connor and a codefendant. The Court of Appeals for the Fifth Circuit affirmed the judgment."

The Supreme Court granted certiorari to review the case, vacated the judgment, and remanded the case.

B. Counsel of Record/ACLU Attorney

ACLU Side (Respondent/Appellee): Bruce J. Ennis, Jr., argued the cause for appellee. With him on the briefs were Morton Brinbaum, George Dean, Eugene DuBose, Jr., Benjamin W. Heineman, Jr., and Paul R. Friedman.

Opposing Side (Petitioner/Appellant): Assistant Attorney General of Florida Raymond W. Gearey argued the cause for appellant, pro hac vice, by special leave of court. With him on the briefs were Attorney General Robert L. Shevin, and Special Assistant Attorney General Daniel S. Dearing.

III. AMICI CURIAE

ACLU Side (Respondent/Appellee)

Brief of amici curiae filed on behalf of the American Psychiatric Association by E. Barrett Prettyman, Jr.

Brief of amici curiae filed on behalf of the American Association on Mental Deficiency by Francis M. Shea, Ralph J. Moore, Jr., John Townsend Rich, James F. Fitzpatrick, Kurt W. Melchior, Harry J. Rubin, Sheridan L. Neimark, and A. L. Zwerdling.

Brief of amici curiae filed on behalf of the Committee on Mental Hygiene of the New York Bar Association by June Resnick German, Alfred Berman, Simon Rosenzweig, and Ronald Gottlieb.

Opposing Side (Petitioner/Appellant)

Brief of amici curiae filed on behalf of the State of New Jersey by William F. Hyland, Attorney General, Stephen Skillman, Assistant Attorney General, and Joseph T. Maloney, Deputy Attorney General.

Brief of amici curiae filed on behalf of the State of Ohio by William J. Brown, Attorney General, and Andrew J. Ruzicho and Barbara J. Rouse, Assistant Attorneys General.

IV. THE SUPREME COURT'S DECISION

"[A] State cannot constitutionally confine without more a nondangerous individual who is capable of surviving safely in freedom by himself or with the help of willing and responsible family members or friends. Since the jury found, upon ample evidence, that O'Connor, as an agent of the State, knowingly did so confine Donaldson, it properly concluded that O'Connor violated Donaldson's constitutional right to freedom. . . .

O'Connor contends that in any event he should not be held personally liable for monetary damages because his decisions were made in 'good faith.' Specifically, O'Connor argues that he was acting pursuant to state law which, he believed, authorized confinement of the mentally ill even when their release would not compromise their safety or constitute a danger to others, and that he could not reasonably have been expected to know that the state law as he understood it was constitutionally invalid. A proposed instruction to this effect was rejected by the District Court.

The District Court did instruct the jury, without objection, that monetary damages could not be assessed against O'Connor if he had believed reasonably and in good faith that Donaldson's continued confinement was 'proper,' and that punitive damages could be awarded only if O'Connor had acted 'maliciously or wantonly or oppressively.' The Court of Appeals approved those instructions. But that court did not consider whether it was error for the trial judge to refuse the additional instruction concerning O'Connor's claimed reliance on state law as authorization for Donaldson's continued confinement. Further, neither the District Court nor the Court of Appeals acted with the benefit of this Court's most recent decision on the scope of the qualified immunity possessed by state officials under 42 U.S.C. § 1983.

Under that decision, the relevant question for the jury is whether O'Connor 'knew or reasonably should have known that the action he took within his sphere of official responsibility would violate the constitutional rights of [Donaldson], or if he took the action with the malicious intention to cause a deprivation of constitutional rights or other injury to [Donaldson].' For purposes of this question, an official has, of course, no duty to anticipate unforeseeable constitutional developments.

Accordingly, we vacate the judgment of the Court of Appeals and remand the case to enable that court to consider, in light of Wood v. Strickland, whether the District Judge's failure to instruct with regard to the effect of O'Connor's claimed reliance on state law rendered inadequate the instructions as to O'Connor's liability for compensatory and punitive damages."

V. JUSTICE VOTE

9 Pro ACLU vs. 0 Con Opposing Side

ACLU Side (Respondent/Appellee)

1. Stewart, P. – Wrote majority opinion
2. Burger, W. – Wrote concurring opinion
3. White, B. – Joined majority opinion
4. Rehnquist, W. – Joined majority opinion
5. Blackmun, H. – Joined majority opinion
6. Powell, L. – Joined majority opinion
7. Brennan, W. – Joined majority opinion
8. Marshall, T. – Joined majority opinion
9. Douglas, W. – Joined majority opinion

VI. A WIN OR LOSS FOR THE ACLU?

The ACLU, as counsel of record, urged affirmance of the judgment of the Court of Appeals for the Fifth Circuit; the Supreme Court vacated in a 9-0 vote after determining the unconstitutional nature of the continued confinement, giving the ACLU an apparent win.

364. Turner v. Dep't of Employment Security of Utah

(Decided November 17, 1975; 423 U.S. 44)

I. ISSUE

A. Issues Discussed

Gender

B. Legal Question Presented

Whether a Utah unemployment compensation statute "that makes pregnant women ineligible for unemployment benefits for a period extending from 12 weeks before the expected date of childbirth until a date six weeks after childbirth" is constitutional.

C. Supreme Court's Answer

"We conclude that the Utah unemployment compensation statute's incorporation of a conclusive presumption of incapacity during so long a period before and after childbirth is constitutionally invalid under the principles of the LaFleur case."

II. CASE SUMMARY

A. Background

"The petitioner, Mary Ann Turner, challenges the constitutionality of a provision of Utah law that makes pregnant women ineligible for unemployment benefits for a period extending from 12 weeks before the expected date of childbirth until a date six weeks after childbirth.

The petitioner was separated involuntarily from her employment on November 3, 1972, for reasons unrelated to her pregnancy. In due course she applied for unemployment compensation and received benefits until March 11, 1973, 12 weeks prior to the expected date of the birth of her child. Relying upon s 35-4-5(h)(1), the respondent Department of Employment Security ruled that she was disqualified from receiving any further payments after that date and until six weeks after the date of her child's birth. Thereafter, Mrs. Turner worked intermittently as a temporary clerical employee. After exhausting all available administrative remedies, the petitioner appealed the respondents' rulings to the Utah Supreme Court, claiming that the statutory provision deprived her of protections guaranteed by the Fourteenth Amendment. The state court rejected her contentions, ruling that the provision violated no constitutional guarantee. The petition for certiorari now before [the U.S. Supreme Court] brings the constitutional issues here."

B. Counsel of Record

ACLU Side (Petitioner/Appellant): Ruth Bader Ginsburg, Melvin L. Wulf, and Kathleen Peratis of the American Civil Liberties Union Foundation filed a petition for writ of certiorari for appellant.

Opposing Side (Respondent/Appellee): Edgar M. Denny, E. R. Callister, Jr., and Vernon L. Romney, Utah Attorney General, filed a brief in opposition to the writ of certiorari for appellee.

III. AMICI CURIAE

ACLU Side (Petitioner/Appellant)

No briefs of amici curiae were filed in support of appellant.

Opposing Side (Respondent/Appellee)

No briefs of amici curiae were filed in support of appellee.

IV. THE SUPREME COURT'S DECISION

"The Utah unemployment compensation system grants benefits to persons who are unemployed and are available for employment. One provision of the statute makes a woman ineligible to receive benefits 'during any week of unemployment when it is found by the commission that her total or partial unemployment is due to pregnancy.' In contrast to this requirement of an individualized determination of ineligibility, the challenged provision establishes a blanket disqualification during an 18-week period immediately preceding and following childbirth. The Utah Supreme Court's opinion makes clear that the challenged ineligibility provision rests on a conclusive presumption that women are 'unable to work' during the 18-week period because of pregnancy and childbirth.

The presumption of incapacity and unavailability for employment created by the challenged provision is virtually identical to the presumption found unconstitutional in Cleveland Board of Education v. LaFleur, 414 U.S. 632. In LaFleur, the Court held that a school board's mandatory maternity leave rule which required a teacher to quit her job several months before the expected birth of her child and prohibited her return to work until three months after childbirth violated the Fourteenth Amendment. Noting that 'freedom of personal choice in matters of marriage and family life is one of the liberties protected by the Due Process Clause,' the Court held that the Constitution required a more individualized approach to the question of the teacher's physical capacity to continue her employment during pregnancy and resume her duties after childbirth since 'the ability of any particular pregnant woman to continue at work past any fixed time in her pregnancy is very much an individual matter.'

It cannot be doubted that a substantial number of women are fully capable of working well into their last trimester of pregnancy and of resuming employment shortly after childbirth. In this very case Mrs. Turner was employed intermittently as a clerical worker for portions of the 18-week period during which she was conclusively presumed to be incapacitated. The Fourteenth Amendment requires that unemployment compensation boards no less than school boards must achieve legitimate state ends through more individualized means when basic human liberties are at stake. We conclude that the Utah unemployment compensation statute's incorporation of a conclusive presumption of incapacity during so long a period before and after childbirth is constitutionally invalid under the principles of the LaFleur case.

Accordingly, the writ of certiorari is granted, the judgment is vacated, and the case is remanded to the Supreme Court of Utah . . . ."

V. JUSTICE VOTE

6 Pro ACLU Side vs. 3 Con Opposing Side

ACLU Side (Petitioner/Appellant)

1. Brennan, W. – Per curiam decision
2. Marshall, T. – Per curiam decision
3. Stewart, P. – Per curiam decision
4. White, B. – Per curiam decision
5. Powell, L. – Per curiam decision
6. Douglas, W. – Per curiam decision

Opposing Side (Respondent/Appellee)

1. Rehnquist, W. – Dissented without an opinion
2. Burger, W. – Would grant certiorari and set case for full briefing and oral argument
3. Blackmun, H. – Would grant certiorari and set case for full briefing and oral argument

VI. A WIN OR LOSS FOR THE ACLU?

The ACLU served a counsel for appellant urging reversal of the judgment of the Supreme Court of Utah; the U.S. Supreme Court vacated in an 8-1 per curiam decision, giving the ACLU an apparent win.

365. Rizzo v. Goode

(Decided January 21, 1976; 423 U.S. 362)

I. ISSUE

A. Issues Discussed

Civil rights, race, police conduct, injunctions

B. Legal Question Presented

Did the District Court err in directing city officials to draft and implement a program addressing alleged police misconduct?

C. Supreme Court's Answer

An injunction directing overhaul of aspects of the police force to address alleged misconduct was inappropriate in this circumstance.

II. CASE SUMMARY

A. Background

"The District Court for the Eastern District of Pennsylvania, after parallel trials of separate actions filed in 1970, entered an order in 1973 requiring petitioners "to submit to [the District] Court for its approval a comprehensive program for improving the handling of citizen complaints alleging police misconduct" in accordance with a comprehensive opinion filed together with the order. The proposed program negotiated between petitioners and respondents for the purpose of complying with the order, was incorporated six months later into a final judgment. Petitioner City Police Commissioner was thereby required, inter alia, to put into force a directive governing the manner by which citizens' complaints against police officers should henceforth be handled by the department. The Court of Appeals for the Third Circuit, upholding the District Court's finding that the existing procedures for handling citizen complaints were 'inadequate,' affirmed the District Court's choice of equitable relief: 'The revisions were . . . ordered because they appeared to have the potential for prevention of future police misconduct.' [The Supreme Court] granted certiorari to consider petitioners' claims that the judgment of the District Court represents an unwarranted intrusion by the federal judiciary into the discretionary authority committed to them by state and local law to perform their official functions."

The evidence at trial consisted of 250 witnesses testifying to show a "pervasive pattern of illegal and unconstitutional mistreatment by police officers. . . . The District Court made a number of conclusions of law . . . . It found that the evidence did not establish the existence of any policy on the part of the named petitioners to violate the legal and constitutional rights of the plaintiff classes, but it did find that evidence of departmental procedure indicated a tendency to discourage the filing of civilian complaints and to minimize the consequences of police misconduct. It found that as to the larger plaintiff class, the residents of Philadelphia, only a small percentage of policemen commit violations of their legal and constitutional rights, but that the frequency with which such violations occur is such that 'they cannot be dismissed as rare, isolated instances.'"

The Supreme Court granted certiorari to review the case and reversed.

B. Counsel of Record/ACLU Attorney

ACLU Side (Respondent/Appellee): Peter Hearn argued the cause for appellee.

Opposing Side (Petitioner/Appellant): James M. Penny, Jr., argued the cause for appellant.

III. AMICI CURIAE

ACLU Side (Respondent/Appellee)

Brief of amici curiae filed on behalf of the ACLU, et al., by Anthony G. Amsterdam, Melvin L. Wulf, Joel M. Gora, Amitai Schwartz, Sanford J. Rosen, and Vilma S. Martinez.

Additional briefs of amici curiae were filed on behalf of the Lawyers' Committee for Civil Rights under Law, the Commonwealth of Pennsylvania, the NAACP Legal Defense and Educational Fund, Inc., the Philadelphia Bar Association, and the Greater Philadelphia Movement.

Opposing Side (Petitioner/Appellant)

No briefs of amici curiae were filed in support of appellant.

IV. THE SUPREME COURT'S DECISION

"The scope of federal equity power, it is proposed, should be extended to the fashioning of prophylactic procedures for a state agency designed to minimize this kind of misconduct on the part of a handful of its employees. However, on the facts of this case, not only is this novel claim quite at odds with the settled rule that in federal equity cases 'the nature of the violation determines the scope of the remedy,' but important considerations of federalism are additional factors weighing against it. Where, as here, the exercise of authority by state officials is attacked, federal courts must be constantly mindful of the 'special delicacy of the adjustment to be preserved between federal equitable power and State administration of its own law.' . . .

Even in an action between private individuals, it has long been held that an injunction is 'to be used sparingly, and only in a clear and plain case.' When a plaintiff seeks to enjoin the activity of a government agency, even within a unitary court system, his case must contend with 'the well-established rule that the Government has traditionally been granted the widest latitude in the 'dispatch of its own internal affairs.' The District Court's injunctive order here, significantly revising the internal procedures of the Philadelphia police department, was indisputably a sharp limitation on the department's 'latitude in the 'dispatch of its own internal affairs." . . .

Contrary to the District Court's flat pronouncement that a federal court's legal power to 'supervise the functioning of the police department . . . is firmly established,' it is the foregoing cases and principles that must govern consideration of the type of injunctive relief granted here. When it injected itself by injunctive decree into the internal disciplinary affairs of this state agency, the District Court departed from these precepts.

For the foregoing reasons the judgment of the Court of Appeals which affirmed the decree of the District Court is reversed."

V. JUSTICE VOTE

3 PRO ACLU SIDE VS. 5 CON OPPOSING SIDE

ACLU Side (Respondent/Appellee)

1. Blackmun, H. – Wrote dissenting opinion
2. Marshall, T. – Joined Blackmun's dissent
3. Brennan, W. – Joined Blackmun's dissent

Opposing Side (Petitioner/Appellant)

1. Rehnquist, W. – Wrote majority opinion
2. White, B. – Joined majority opinion
3. Powell, L. – Joined majority opinion
4. Burger, W. – Joined majority opinion
5. Stewart, P. – Joined majority opinion

Stevens, J – Took no part in the decision

VI. A WIN OR LOSS FOR THE ACLU?

The ACLU filed as amicus curiae urging affirmance; the Supreme Court reversed the judgment of the Court of Appeals in a 5-3 vote, giving ACLU an apparent loss.

366. Buckley v. Valeo

(Decided January 30, 1976; 424 U.S. 1)

I. ISSUE

A. Issues Discussed

Elections, political contributions, First Amendment

B. Legal Question Presented:

Does the Federal Election Campaign Act, as amended in 1974, violate First Amendment rights and is it constitutional?

C. Supreme Court's Answer

After a review of the various provisions challenged in this case, certain provisions are invalid while others are valid.

II. CASE SUMMARY

A. Background

"These appeals present constitutional challenges to the key provisions of the Federal Election Campaign Act of 1971 (Act), and related provisions of the Internal Revenue Code of 1954, all as amended in 1974.

The Court of Appeals, in sustaining the legislation in large part against various constitutional challenges, viewed it as "by far the most comprehensive reform legislation [ever] passed by Congress concerning the election of the President, Vice-President, and members of Congress." The statutes at issue summarized in broad terms, contain the following provisions: (a) individual political contributions are limited to $1,000 to any single candidate per election, with an overall annual limitation of $25,000 by any contributor; independent expenditures by individuals and groups "relative to a clearly identified candidate" are limited to $1,000 a year; campaign spending by candidates for various federal offices and spending for national conventions by political parties are subject to prescribed limits; (b) contributions and expenditures above certain threshold levels must be reported and publicly disclosed; (c) a system for public funding of Presidential campaign activities is established by Subtitle H of the Internal Revenue Code; and (d) a Federal Election Commission is established to administer and enforce the legislation.

This suit was originally filed by appellants in the United States District Court for the District of Columbia. . . . The complaint sought both a declaratory judgment that the major provisions of the Act were unconstitutional and an injunction against enforcement of those provisions. Appellants requested the convocation of a three-judge District Court as to all matters and also requested certification of constitutional questions to the Court of Appeals, pursuant to the terms of § 315(a). The District Judge denied the application for a three-judge court and directed that the case be transmitted to the Court of Appeals. That court entered an order stating that the case was "preliminarily deemed" to be properly certified under § 315(a). [T]he Court of Appeals entered an order en banc remanding the case to the District Court to (1) identify the constitutional issues in the complaint; (2) take whatever evidence was found necessary in addition to the submissions suitably dealt with by way of judicial notice; (3) make findings of fact with reference to those issues; and (4) certify the constitutional questions arising from the foregoing steps to the Court of Appeals. On remand, the District Judge entered a memorandum order adopting extensive findings of fact and transmitting the augmented record back to the Court of Appeals.

On plenary review, a majority of the Court of Appeals rejected, for the most part, appellants' constitutional attacks. The court found "a clear and compelling interest," in preserving the integrity of the electoral process. On that basis, the court upheld, with one exception, the substantive provisions of the Act with respect to contributions, expenditures, and disclosure. It also sustained the constitutionality of the newly established Federal Election Commission. The court concluded that, notwithstanding the manner of selection of its members and the breadth of its powers, which included nonlegislative functions, the Commission is a constitutionally authorized agency created to perform primarily legislative functions. The provisions for public funding of the three stages of the Presidential selection process were upheld as a valid exercise of congressional power under the General Welfare Clause of the Constitution, Art. I, § 8.

In [the Supreme] Court, appellants argue that the Court of Appeals failed to give this legislation the critical scrutiny demanded under accepted First Amendment and equal protection principles. In appellants' view, limiting the use of money for political purposes constitutes a restriction on communication violative of the First Amendment, since virtually all meaningful political communications in the modern setting involve the expenditure of money. Further, they argue that the reporting and disclosure provisions of the Act unconstitutionally impinge on their right to freedom of association. Appellants also view the federal subsidy provisions of Subtitle H as violative of the General Welfare Clause, and as inconsistent with the First and Fifth Amendments. Finally, appellants renew their attack on the Commission's composition and powers."

The Supreme Court granted certiorari, affirmed in part, and reversed in part.

B. Counsel of Record/ACLU Attorney

ACLU Side (Petitioner/Appellant): Ralph K. Winter, Jr., pro hac vice, Joel M. Gora, and Brice M. Clagett argued the cause for appellant. With them on the briefs were Melvin L. Wulf and John R. Bolton.

Opposing Side (Respondent/Appellee): Deputy Solicitor General Daniel M. Friedman, Archibald Cox, Lloyd N. Cutler, and Ralph S. Spritzer argued the cause for appellee. With them on the briefs were Attorney General Edward H. Levi, pro se, Solicitor General Robert H. Bork, Louis F. Claiborne, Paul J. Mode, Jr., William T. Lake, Kenneth J. Guido, Jr., Fred Wertheimer, and Paul Bender.

III. AMICI CURIAE

ACLU Side (Petitioner/Appellant)

Brief of amici curiae filed on behalf of James B. Longley by Thomas F. Managhan.

Brief of amici curiae filed on behalf of the California Fair Political Practices Commission, et al., by Jerome B. Falk, Jr., Daniel H. Lowenstein, Howard F. Sachs, and Guy L. Heinemann.

Brief of amici curiae filed on behalf of Lee Metcalf by Lee Metcalf, pro se, and G. Roger King.

Brief of amici curiae filed on behalf of the Socialist Labor Party by Vincent Hallinan.

Brief of amici curiae filed on behalf of the Los Angeles County Central Committee of the Peace and Freedom Party by Marguerite M. Buckley.

Brief of amici curiae filed by the Committee for Democratic Election Laws.

Opposing Side (Respondent/Appellee)

Brief of amici curiae filed on behalf of the United States by Attorney General Edward H. Levi, pro se, Solicitor General Robert H. Bork, and Deputy Solicitor General Randolph.

Brief of amici curiae filed on behalf of Hugh Scott, et al., by Archibald Cox.

IV. THE SUPREME COURT'S DECISION

"[A]lthough the Act's contribution and expenditure limitations both implicate fundamental First Amendment interests, its expenditure ceilings impose significantly more severe restrictions on protected freedoms of political expression and association than do its limitations on financial contributions. . . .

We find that, under the rigorous standard of review established by our prior decisions, the weighty interests served by restricting the size of financial contributions to political candidates are sufficient to justify the limited effect upon First Amendment freedoms caused by the $1,000 contribution ceiling.

[W]e conclude that the impact of the Act's $1,000 contribution limitation on major-party challengers and on minor-party candidates does not render the provision unconstitutional on its face. . . .

The Act's expenditure ceilings impose direct and substantial restraints on the quantity of political speech. The most drastic of the limitations restricts individuals and groups, including political parties that fail to place a candidate on the ballot, to an expenditure of $1,000 'relative to a clearly identified candidate during a calendar year.' Other expenditure ceilings limit spending by candidates, § 608(a), their campaigns, § 608(c), and political parties in connection with election campaigns, § 608(f). It is clear that a primary effect of these expenditure limitations is to restrict the quantity of campaign speech by individuals, groups, and candidates. The restrictions, while neutral as to the ideas expressed, limit political expression 'at the core of our electoral process and of the First Amendment freedoms.' . . .

In sum, the provisions of the Act that impose a $1,000 limitation on contributions to a single candidate, § 608(b)(1), a $5,000 limitation on contributions by a political committee to a single candidate, § 608(b)(2), and a $25,000 limitation on total contributions by an individual during any calendar year, § 608(b)(3), are constitutionally valid. These limitations, along with the disclosure provisions, constitute the Act's primary weapons against the reality or appearance of improper influence stemming from the dependence of candidates on large campaign contributions. The contribution ceilings thus serve the basic governmental interest in safeguarding the integrity of the electoral process without directly impinging upon the rights of individual citizens and candidates to engage in political debate and discussion. By contrast, the First Amendment requires the invalidation of the Act's independent expenditure ceiling, § 608(e)(1), its limitation on a candidate's expenditures from his own personal funds, § 608(a), and its ceilings on overall campaign expenditures, § 608(c). These provisions place substantial and direct restrictions on the ability of candidates, citizens, and associations to engage in protected political expression, restrictions that the First Amendment cannot tolerate. . . .

Here, as we have seen, the disclosure requirement is narrowly limited to those situations where the information sought has a substantial connection with the governmental interests sought to be advanced. . . . The burden imposed by § 434(e) is no prior restraint, but a reasonable and minimally restrictive method of furthering First Amendment values by opening the basic processes of our federal election system to public view.

[W]e reject appellants' claims that Subtitle H is facially unconstitutional. . . . We therefore hold Subtitle H severable from those portions of the legislation today held constitutionally infirm. . . .

We hold that these provisions of the Act, vesting in the [Federal Election] Commission primary responsibility for conducting civil litigation in the courts of the United States for vindicating public rights, violate Art. II, § 2, cl. 2, of the Constitution. Such functions may be discharged only by persons who are "Officers of the United States" within the language of that section. . . .

In summary, we sustain the individual contribution limits, the disclosure and reporting provisions, and the public financing scheme. We conclude, however, that the limitations on campaign expenditures, on independent expenditures by individuals and groups, and on expenditures by a candidate from his personal funds are constitutionally infirm. Finally, we hold that most of the powers conferred by the Act upon the Federal Election Commission can be exercised only by "Officers of the United States," appointed in conformity with Art. II, § 2, cl. 2, of the Constitution, and therefore cannot be exercised by the Commission as presently constituted.

In No. 75-436, the judgment of the Court of Appeals is affirmed in part and reversed in part. The judgment of the District Court in No. 75-437 is affirmed. The mandate shall issue forthwith, except that our judgment is stayed, for a period not to exceed 30 days, insofar as it affects the authority of the Commission to exercise the duties and powers granted it under the Act."

V. JUSTICE VOTE

7 Pro ACLU Side vs. 1 Con Opposing Side

ACLU Side (Petitioner/Appellant)

1. Stewart, P. – Per curiam decision
2. White, B. – Wrote opinion concurring in part and dissenting in part
3. Powell, L. – Per curiam decision
4. Blackmun, H. – Wrote opinion concurring in part and dissenting in part
5. Brennan, W. – Per curiam decision
6. Rehnquist, W. – Wrote opinion concurring in part and dissenting in part
7. Marshall, T. – Wrote opinion concurring in part and dissenting in part

Opposing Side (Respondent/Appellee)

1. Burger, W. – Wrote opinion concurring in part and dissenting in part

Stevens, J – Took no part in the decision

VI. A WIN OR LOSS FOR THE ACLU?

The ACLU, as counsel for appellant, urged reversal of the judgment of the Court of Appeals for the District of Columbia; the Supreme Court, in a per curiam decision, affirmed in part and reversed in part in a 7-1 vote, giving the ACLU an apparent win.

367. Liberty Mutual Insurance Co. v. Wetzel

(Decided March 23, 1976; 424 U.S. 737)

I. ISSUE

A. Issues Discussed

Civil rights, gender, judicial power, civil procedure

B. Legal Question Presented

Was the District Court's decision appealable?

C. Supreme Court's Answer

The District Court's decision was not an appealable final decision.

II. CASE SUMMARY

A. Background

"Respondents filed a complaint in the United States District Court for the Western District of Pennsylvania in which they asserted that petitioner's employee insurance benefits and maternity leave regulations discriminated against women in violation of Title VII of the Civil Rights Act of 1964 . . . . The District Court ruled in favor of respondents on the issue of petitioner's liability under that Act and petitioner appealed to the Court of Appeals for the Third Circuit. That court held that it had jurisdiction of petitioner's appeal under 28 U.S.C. § 1291, and proceeded to affirm on the merits the judgment of the District Court. [The Supreme Court] granted certiorari, and heard argument on the merits. Though neither party has questioned the jurisdiction of the Court of Appeals to entertain the appeal, [the Supreme Court is] obligated to do so on [its] own motion if a question thereto exists."

The Supreme Court granted certiorari to review the case and vacated the judgment of the Court of Appeals.

B. Counsel of Record/ACLU Attorney

ACLU Side (Respondent/Appellee): Howard A. Specter argued the cause for appellee.

Opposing Side (Petitioner/Appellant): Kalvin M. Grove argued the cause for appellant.

III. AMICI CURIAE

ACLU Side (Respondent/Appellee)

Brief of amici curiae filed on behalf of the ACLU, et al., by Ruth Bader Ginsburg, Melvin L. Wulf, Kathleen Willert Peratis, Susan C. Ross, Eve Cary, Helene Burgess, David Rubin, and Joel D. Gewirtz.

Additional briefs of amici curiae were filed on behalf of the United States, et al., the Commonwealth of Massachusetts, et al., the State of Ohio, the New York State Division of Human Rights, the American Federation of Labor and Congress of Industrial Organizations, et al., Blank Goodman Kelly Rone & Stanley, the Center for Constitutional Rights, et al., and the Communication Workers of America, AFL-CIO.

Opposing Side (Petitioner/Appellant)

Briefs of amici curiae were filed on behalf of Alaska Airlines, Inc., et al., the American Life Insurance Association, et al., the American Mutual Insurance Alliance, et al., the American Telephone & Telegraph Co., the National Association of Manufacturers, Owens-Illinois, Inc., et al., and Westinghouse Electric Corp.

IV. THE SUPREME COURT'S DECISION

"Though neither party has questioned the jurisdiction of the Court of Appeals to entertain the appeal, we are obligated to do so on our own motion if a question thereto exists. Because we conclude that the District Court's order was not appealable to the Court of Appeals, we vacate the judgment of the Court of Appeals with instructions to dismiss petitioner's appeal from the order of the District Court. . . .

The District Court and the Court of Appeals apparently took the view that, because the District Court made the recital required by Fed.Rule Civ.Proc. 54(b) that final judgment be entered on the issue of liability, and that there was no just reason for delay, the orders thereby became appealable as a final decision pursuant to 28 U.S.C. § 1291. We cannot agree with this application of the Rule and statute in question. . . .

Were we to sustain the procedure followed here, we would condone a practice whereby a district court in virtually any case before it might render an interlocutory decision on the question of liability of the defendant, and the defendant would thereupon be permitted to appeal to the court of appeals without satisfying any of the requirements that Congress carefully set forth. We believe that Congress, in enacting present §§ 1291 and 1292 of Title 28, has been well aware of the dangers of an overly rigid insistence upon a 'final decision' for appeal in every case, and has in those sections made ample provision for appeal of orders which are not 'final' so as to alleviate any possible hardship. We would twist the fabric of the statute more than it will bear if we were to agree that the District Court's order of February 20, 1974, was appealable to the Court of Appeals.

The judgment of the Court of Appeals is therefore vacated, and the case is remanded with instructions to dismiss the petitioner's appeal."

V. JUSTICE VOTE

0 Pro ACLU Side vs. 8 Con Opposing Side

Opposing Side (Petitioner/Appellant)

1. Rehnquist, W. – Wrote majority opinion
2. Burger, W. – Joined majority opinion
3. Brennan, W. – Joined majority opinion
4. Stewart, P. – Joined majority opinion
5. White, B. – Joined majority opinion
6. Marshall, T. – Joined majority opinion
7. Powell, L. – Joined majority opinion
8. Stevens, J. – Joined majority opinion

Blackmun, H – Took no part in the decision

VI. A WIN OR LOSS FOR THE ACLU?

The ACLU filed as amicus curiae urging affirmance; the Supreme Court vacated the ruling of the Court of Appeals in an 8-0 vote, giving the ACLU an apparent loss.

368. Greer v. Spock

(Decided March 24, 1976; 424 U.S. 828)

I. ISSUE

A. Issues Discussed

Governmental authority, military, First Amendment, Fifth Amendment

B. Legal Question Presented

Are the Fort Dix regulations, banning political speeches and distribution of literature, unconstitutional in violation of First and Fifth Amendments?

C. Supreme Court's Answer

The regulations do not violate the First or Fifth Amendments on their face or as applied to respondents.

II. CASE SUMMARY

A. Background

"The Fort Dix Military Reservation is a United States Army post located in a predominantly rural area of central New Jersey. Its primary mission is to provide basic combat training for newly inducted Army personnel. Accordingly, most of its 55 square miles are devoted to military training activities. The Federal Government exercises exclusive jurisdiction over the entire area within Fort Dix, including the state and county roads that pass through it. Civilian vehicular traffic is permitted on paved roads within the reservation, and civilian pedestrian traffic is permitted on both roads and footpaths. Military police regularly patrol the roads within the reservation, and they occasionally stop civilians and ask them the reason for their presence. Signs posted on the roads leading into the reservation state: 'All vehicles are subject to search while on the Fort Dix Military Reservation' and 'Soliciting prohibited unless approved by the commanding general.' The main entrances to Fort Dix are not normally guarded, and a sign at one of the entrances says 'Visitors Welcome.' Civilians are freely permitted to visit unrestricted areas of the reservation.

Civilian speakers have occasionally been invited to the base to address military personnel. The subjects of their talks have ranged from business management to drug abuse. Visiting clergymen have, by invitation, participated in religious services at the base chapel. Theatrical exhibitions and musical productions have also been presented on the base. Speeches and demonstrations of a partisan political nature, however, are banned by Fort Dix Reg. 210-26 (1968), which provides that "[d]emonstrations, picketing, sit-ins, protest marches, political speeches and similar activities are prohibited and will not be conducted on the Fort Dix Military Reservation." The regulation has been rigidly enforced: Prior to this litigation, no political campaign speech had ever been given at Fort Dix. Restrictions are also placed on another type of expressive activity. Fort Dix Reg. 210-27 (1970) provides that '[t]he distribution or posting of any publication, including newspapers, magazines, handbills, flyers, circulars, pamphlets or other writings, issued, published or otherwise prepared by any person, persons, agency or agencies . . . is prohibited on the Fort Dix Military Reservation without prior written approval of the Adjutant General, this headquarters.'

[T]he respondents Benjamin Spock and Julius Hobson were the candidates of the People's Party for the offices of President and Vice President of the United States, and Linda Jenness and Andrew Pulley were the candidates of the Socialist Workers Party for the same offices. On September 9, 1972, Spock, Hobson, Jenness, and Pulley wrote a joint letter to Major General Bert A. David, then commanding officer of Fort Dix, informing him of their intention to enter the reservation on September 23, 1972, for the purpose of distributing campaign literature and holding a meeting to discuss election issues with service personnel and their dependents. On September 18, 1972, General David rejected the candidates' request, relying on Fort Dix Regs. 210-26 and 210-27. Four of the other respondents, Ginaven, Misch, Hardy, and Stanton, were evicted from Fort Dix on various occasions between 1968 and 1972 for distributing literature not previously approved pursuant to Fort Dix Reg. 210-27. Each was barred from re-entering Fort Dix and advised that re-entry could result in criminal prosecution.

On September 29, 1972, the respondents filed this suit in the United States District Court for the District of New Jersey to enjoin the enforcement of the Fort Dix regulations governing political campaigning and the distribution of literature, upon the ground that the regulations violated the First and Fifth Amendments of the Constitution. The District Court denied a preliminary injunction, but the Court of Appeals reversed that order and directed that preliminary injunctive relief be granted to the respondents Spock, Hobson, Jenness, and Pulley. Pursuant to this judgment the respondent Spock conducted a campaign rally at a Fort Dix parking lot on November 4, 1972. The District Court subsequently issued a permanent injunction prohibiting the military authorities from interfering with the making of political speeches or the distribution of leaflets in areas of Fort Dix open to the general public, and the Court of Appeals affirmed this final judgment."

The Supreme Court granted certiorari to review the case and reversed.

B. Counsel of Record / ACLU Attorney

ACLU Side (Respondent / Appellee): David Kairys argued the cause for appellee.

Opposing Side (Petitioner / Appellant): Solicitor General Robert H. Bork argued the cause for appellant.

III. AMICI CURIAE

ACLU Side (Respondent / Appellee)

Brief of amici curiae filed on behalf of the ACLU, et al., by Norman Dorsen, Melvin L. Wulf, and Joel M. Gora.

Opposing Side (Petitioner / Appellant)

No briefs of amici curiae were filed in support of appellant.

IV. THE SUPREME COURT'S DECISION

"The Court of Appeals in the present case did not find, and the respondents do not contend, that the Fort Dix authorities had abandoned any claim of special interest in regulating the distribution of unauthorized leaflets or the delivery of campaign speeches for political candidates within the confines of the military reservation. The record is, in fact, indisputably to the contrary. . . .

The notion that federal military reservations, like municipal streets and parks, have traditionally served as a place for free public assembly and communication of thoughts by private citizens is thus historically and constitutionally false.

The respondents, therefore, had no generalized constitutional right to make political speeches or distribute leaflets at Fort Dix, and it follows that Fort Dix Regs. 210-26 and 210-27 are not constitutionally invalid on their face. These regulations, moreover, were not unconstitutionally applied in the circumstances disclosed by the record in the present case.

With respect to Reg. 210-26, there is no claim that the military authorities discriminated in any way among candidates for public office based upon the candidates' supposed political views. . . . What the record shows, therefore, is a considered Fort Dix policy, objectively and evenhandedly applied, of keeping official military activities there wholly free of entanglement with partisan political campaigns of any kind. . . . Such a policy is wholly consistent with the American constitutional tradition of a politically neutral military establishment under civilian control. . . .

With respect to Reg. 210-27, it is to be emphasized that it does not authorize the Fort Dix authorities to prohibit the distribution of conventional political campaign literature. The only publications that a military commander may disapprove are those that he finds constitute 'a clear danger to [military] loyalty, discipline, or morale,' and he 'may not prevent distribution of a publication simply because he does not like its contents,' or because it 'is critical - even unfairly critical - of government policies or officials . . . .' There is nothing in the Constitution that disables a military commander from acting to avert what he perceives to be a clear danger to the loyalty, discipline, or morale of troops on the base under his command. . . .

For the reasons set out in this opinion the judgment is reversed."

V. JUSTICE VOTE

2 Pro ACLU Side vs. 6 Con Opposing Side

ACLU Side (Respondent / Appellee)

1. Brennan, W. – Wrote dissenting opinion
2. Marshall, T. – Wrote dissenting opinion, joined Brennan's dissent

Opposing Side (Petitioner/Appellant)

1. Stewart, P. – Wrote majority opinion
2. White, B. – Joined majority opinion
3. Rehnquist, W. – Joined majority opinion
4. Blackmun, H. – Joined majority opinion
5. Powell, L. – Wrote concurring opinion
6. Burger, W. – Wrote concurring opinion, joined Powell's concurrence in part

Stevens, J – Took no part in the decision

VI. A WIN OR LOSS FOR THE ACLU?

The ACLU filed as amicus curiae urging affirmance; the Supreme Court reversed the ruling of the Court of Appeals in a 6-2 vote, giving the ACLU an apparent loss.

369. Dep't of the Air Force v. Rose

(Decided April 21, 1976; 425 U.S. 352)

I. ISSUE

A. Issues Discussed

Privacy

B. Legal Question Presented

Whether mandatory disclosure of "case summaries of honor and ethics hearings, with personal references or other identifying information deleted, maintained in the United States Air Force Academy's Honor and Ethics Code reading files" is exempted under Exemption 2 or Exemption 6 of the Freedom of Information Act.

C. Supreme Court's Answer

Mandatory disclosure of the case summaries is not exempted under either exemption of the Freedom of Information Act.

II. CASE SUMMARY

A. Background

"Respondents, student editors or former student editors of the New York University Law Review researching disciplinary systems and procedures at the military service academies for an article for the Law Review, were denied access by petitioners to case summaries of honor and ethics hearings, with personal references or other identifying information deleted, maintained in the United States Air Force Academy's Honor and Ethics Code reading files, although Academy practice is to post copies of such summaries on 40 squadron bulletin boards throughout the Academy and to distribute copies to Academy faculty and administration officials. Thereupon respondents brought this action under the Freedom of Information Act in the District Court for the Southern District of New York .... The District Court granted petitioner Agency's motion for summary judgment—with out first requiring production of the case summaries for inspection—holding in an unreported opinion that case summaries even with deletions of personal references or other identifying information were 'matters ... related solely to the internal personnel rules and practices of an agency,' exempted from mandatory disclosure by s 552(b)(2) of the statute. The Court of Appeals for the Second Circuit reversed ...."

The Supreme Court granted certiorari to review the case.

B. Counsel of Record

ACLU Side (Respondent/Appellee): Barrington D. Parker, Jr., of the American Civil Liberties Union Foundation argued the cause for appellees. With him on the brief were Melvin L. Wulf and John H. F. Shattuck of the American Civil Liberties Union Foundation.

Opposing Side (Petitioner/Appellant): Deputy Solicitor General Friedman argued the cause for appellants. With him on the briefs were Solicitor General Bork, Assistant Attorney General Lee, Acting Assistant Attorney General Jaffe, Allan Abbot Tuttle, Leonard Schaitman, and Donald Etra.

III. AMICI CURIAE

ACLU Side (Respondent/Appellee)

No briefs of amici curiae were filed in support of appellees.

Opposing Side (Petitioner/Appellant)

No briefs of amici curiae were filed in support of appellants.

IV. THE SUPREME COURT'S DECISION

"Our discussion may conveniently begin [with] the Freedom of Information Act ....

[W]e ... consider whether mandatory disclosure of the case summaries is exempted by either of the exemptions involved here, discussing, First, Exemption 2, and, Second, Exemption 6. ...

In sum, we think that, at least where the situation is not one where disclosure may risk circumvention of agency regulation, Exemption 2 is not applicable to matters subject to such a genuine and significant public interest. [T]he general thrust of the exemption is simply to relieve agencies of the burden of assembling and maintaining for public inspection matter in which the public could not reasonably be expected to have an interest. The case summaries plainly do not fit that description. ... We therefore agree with the Court of Appeals that, given the Senate interpretation, 'the Agency's withholding of the case summaries (as edited to preserve anonymity) cannot be upheld by reliance on the second exemption.' ...

Additional questions are involved in the determination whether Exemption 6 exempts the case summaries from mandatory disclosure as 'personnel and medical files and similar files the disclosure of which would constitute a clearly unwarranted invasion of personal privacy.' ...

[W]e find nothing in the wording of Exemption 6 or its legislative history to support the Agency's claim that Congress created a blanket exemption for personnel files. ...

Congress' recent action in amending the Freedom of Information Act to make explicit its agreement with judicial decisions requiring the disclosure of nonexempt portions of otherwise exempt files is consistent with this conclusion. ...

Moreover, even if we were to agree that 'personnel files' are wholly exempt from any disclosure under Exemption 6, it is clear that the case summaries sought here lack the attributes of 'personnel files' as commonly understood. Two attributes of the case summaries require that they be characterized as 'similar files.' First, they relate to the discipline of cadet personnel, . . . it supports the conclusion that they are 'similar.' Second, and most significantly, . . . these summaries . . . do not contain the 'vast amounts of personal data,' which constitute the kind of profile of an individual ordinarily to be found in his personnel file . . . . Moreover, access to these files is not drastically limited, as is customarily true of personnel files . . . . Documents treated by the Agency in such a manner cannot reasonably be claimed to be within the common and congressional meaning of what constitutes a 'personnel file' under Exemption 6. . . .

Moreover, we repeat, Exemption 6 does not protect against disclosure every incidental invasion of privacy only such disclosures as constitute 'clearly unwarranted' invasions of personal privacy.

Affirmed."

V. JUSTICE VOTE

5 Pro ACLU Side vs. 3 Con Opposing Side

ACLU Side (Respondent/Appellee)

1. Brennan, W. – Wrote majority opinion
2. White, B. – Joined majority opinion
3. Marshall, T. – Joined majority opinion
4. Stewart, P. – Joined majority opinion
5. Powell, L. – Joined majority opinion

Opposing Side (Petitioner/Appellant)

1. Rehnquist, W. – Wrote dissenting opinion
2. Burger, W. – Wrote dissenting opinion
3. Blackmun, H. – Wrote dissenting opinion

Stevens, J. – Took no part in the decision.

VI. A WIN OR LOSS FOR THE ACLU?

The ACLU served as counsel for appellees urging affirmance of the judgment of the Court of Appeals; the Supreme Court affirmed, in a 5-3 vote, giving the ACLU an apparent win.

370. Mathews v. Diaz

(Decided June 1, 1976; 426 U.S. 67)

I. ISSUE

A. Issues Discussed

Governmental authority, immigration, Medicare eligibility, due process

B. Legal Question Presented

"[W]hether Congress may condition an alien's eligibility for participation in a federal medical insurance program on continuous residence in the United States for a five-year period and admission for permanent residence."

C. Supreme Court's Answer

Congress may condition eligibility for participation in a federal medical insurance program on continuous residence for five years and admission as a permanent resident.

II. CASE SUMMARY

A. Background

Under federal law, non-citizens over the age of 65 who had not obtained permanent resident status and who had not lived in the United States for at least five years were ineligible for Medicare.

Appellees were resident aliens of the United States for less than five years who were all over 65 years of age. Two appellees were refugees from Cuba, and one appellee was a legal permanent resident. All three had been denied Medicare Part B enrollment or knew they would be denied based on their residency status. The three residents filed a lawsuit in the District Court for the Southern District of Florida challenging the constitutionality of Medicare's eligibility requirements for non-citizens. The District Court ruled that the five-year residency requirement violated due process.

The Supreme Court granted certiorari to review the case and reversed.

B. Counsel of Record/ACLU Attorney

ACLU Side (Respondent/Appellee): Bruce S. Rogow argued the cause for appellee on reargument. Alfred Feinberg argued the cause for appellee on the original argument.

Opposing Side (Petitioner/Appellant): Harriet S. Shapiro argued the cause for appellant.

III. AMICI CURIAE

ACLU Side (Respondent/Appellee)

Brief of amici curiae filed on behalf of the ACLU by by Robert Allen Sedler and Melvin L. Wulf.

Brief of amici curiae filed on behalf of the Association of Immigration and Nationality Lawyers by Jack Wasserman and Esther Kaufman.

Brief of amici curiae filed on behalf of Legal Services for the Elderly Poor by Jonathan A. Weiss.

Brief of amici curiae filed on behalf of Migration and Refugee Services, U.S. Catholic Conference, Inc., et al., by Edith Lowenstein.

Opposing Side (Petitioner/Appellant)

No briefs of amici curiae were filed in support of appellant.

IV. THE SUPREME COURT'S DECISION

"There are literally millions of aliens within the jurisdiction of the United States. The Fifth Amendment, as well as the Fourteenth Amendment, protects every one of these persons from deprivation of life, liberty, or property without due process of law. Even one whose presence in this country is unlawful, involuntary, or transitory is entitled to that constitutional protection.

The fact that all persons, aliens and citizens alike, are protected by the Due Process Clause does not lead to the further conclusion that all aliens are entitled to enjoy all the advantages of citizenship or, indeed, to the conclusion that all aliens must be placed in a single homogeneous legal classification. For a host of constitutional and statutory provisions rest on the premise that a legitimate distinction between citizens and aliens may justify attributes and benefits for one class not accorded to the other . . . .

In the exercise of its broad power over naturalization and immigration, Congress regularly makes rules that would be unacceptable if applied to citizens. The exclusion of aliens and the reservation of the power to deport have no permissible counterpart in the Federal Government's power to regulate the conduct of its own citizenry. The fact that an Act of Congress treats aliens differently from citizens does not in itself imply that such disparate treatment is 'invidious.' . . .

The real question presented by this case is not whether discrimination between citizens and aliens is permissible; rather, it is whether the statutory discrimination within the class of aliens allowing benefits to some aliens but not to others is permissible. . . .

In short, it is unquestionably reasonable for Congress to make an alien's eligibility depend on both the character and the duration of his residence. Since neither requirement is wholly irrational, this case essentially involves nothing more than a claim that it would have been more reasonable for Congress to select somewhat different requirements of the same kind. . . .

But it remains true that some line is essential, that any line must produce some harsh and apparently arbitrary consequences, and, of greatest importance, that those who qualify under the test Congress has chosen may reasonably be presumed to have a greater affinity with the United States than those who do not. In short, citizens and those who are most like citizens qualify. Those who are less like citizens do not. . . .

We hold that § 1395o(2)(B) has not deprived appellees of liberty or property without due process of law.

The judgment of the District Court is reversed."

V. JUSTICE VOTE

0 Pro ACLU Side vs. 9 Con Opposing Side

Opposing Side (Petitioner/Appellant)

1. Stevens, J. – Wrote majority opinion
2. Marshall, T. – Joined majority opinion
3. Burger, W. – Joined majority opinion
4. Rehnquist, W. – Joined majority opinion
5. Brennan, W. – Joined majority opinion
6. Stewart, P. – Joined majority opinion
7. Powell, L. – Joined majority opinion
8. White, B. – Joined majority opinion
9. Blackmun, H. – Joined majority opinion

VI. A WIN OR LOSS FOR THE ACLU?

The ACLU filed as amicus curiae urging affirmance; the Supreme Court reversed the ruling of the District Court for the Southern District of Florida in a 9-0 vote, giving the ACLU an apparent loss.

371. Hampton v. Mow Sun Wong

(Decided June 1, 1976; 426 U.S. 88)

I. ISSUE

A. Issues Discussed

Governmental authority, immigration, Fifth Amendment, due process

B. Legal Question Presented

"Whether a regulation of the United States Civil Service Commission that bars resident aliens from employment in the federal competitive civil service is constitutional."

C. Supreme Court's Answer

The regulation is an unconstitutional violation of the Due Process Clause of the Fifth Amendment.

II. CASE SUMMARY

A. Background

Five resident U.S. aliens brought a class action lawsuit challenging the validity of the Civil Service Commission's (CSC) policy, which excludes all persons except U.S. citizens from employment in most federal positions. The respondents were all Chinese residents of San Francisco who were qualified for various jobs, but denied federal employment solely because of their alienage. All respondents were lawfully and permanently residing in the United States.

Respondents brought their class action suit in the Northern District of California against "the Chairman and the Commissioners of the Civil Service Commission and the heads of the three agencies which had denied them employment." They alleged that the CFC's policy was arbitrary and violated the Due Process Clause of the Fifth Amendment, and also that it violated an Executive Order, which forbids discrimination in federal employment on the basis of "national origin."

The District Court ruled in favor of petitioners, holding that the reference to "national origin" in the Executive Order referred to "discrimination among citizens rather than discrimination between citizens and noncitizens." The District Court further "held that the Commission's discrimination against aliens was constitutional." Four of the respondents appealed.

The Court of Appeals reversed. It agreed with the District Court's analysis of the Executive Order, but determined that the regulation was in violation of the Due Process Clause of the Fifth Amendment.

The Supreme Court granted certiorari and affirmed.

B. Counsel of Record/ACLU Attorney

ACLU Side (Respondent/Appellee): Edward H. Steinman, by appointment of the Court, argued the cause for appellee.

Opposing Side (Petitioner/Appellant): Solicitor General Bork argued the cause for appellant.

III. AMICI CURIAE

ACLU Side (Respondent/Appellee)

Brief of amici curiae filed on behalf of the ACLU by Robert Allen Sedler and Melvin L. Wulf.

Brief of amici curiae filed on behalf of the Mexican-American Legal Defense and Educational Fund, et al., by Vilma S. Martinez and Sanford Jay Rosen.

Brief of amici curiae filed by Sandigan, et al.

Opposing Side (Petitioner/Appellant)

No briefs of amici curiae were filed in support of appellant.

IV. THE SUPREME COURT'S DECISION

"In this case we deal with a federal rule having nationwide impact. . . . We agree with the petitioners' position that overriding national interests may provide a justification for a citizenship requirement in the federal service even though an identical requirement may not be enforced by a State.

We do not agree, however, with the petitioners' primary submission that the federal power over aliens is so plenary that any agent of the National Government may arbitrarily subject all resident aliens to different substantive rules from those applied to citizens. [C]ountervailing considerations require rejection of the extreme position advanced by the petitioners. . . .

The added disadvantage resulting from the enforcement of the rule—ineligibility for employment in a major sector of the economy—is of sufficient significance to be characterized as a deprivation of an interest in liberty. . . . By reason of the Fifth Amendment, such a deprivation must be accompanied by due process. . . .

We may assume with the petitioners that if the Congress or the President had expressly imposed the citizenship requirement, it would be justified by the national interest in providing an incentive for aliens to become naturalized, or possibly even as providing the President with an expendable token for treaty negotiating purposes; but we are not willing to presume that the Chairman of the Civil Service Commission, or any of the other original defendants, was deliberately fostering an interest so far removed from his normal responsibilities. [I]t is important to know whether we are reviewing a policy decision made by Congress and the President or a question of personnel administration determined by the Civil Service Commission. . . .

The only concern of the Civil Service Commission is the promotion of an efficient federal service. In general it is fair to assume that its goal would be best served by removing unnecessary restrictions on the eligibility of qualified applicants for employment. With only one exception . . . . That one exception is the administrative desirability of having one simple rule excluding all noncitizens when it is manifest that citizenship is an appropriate and legitimate requirement for some important and sensitive positions. . . . Any fair balancing of the public interest in avoiding the wholesale deprivation of employment opportunities caused by the Commission's indiscriminate policy, as opposed to what may be nothing more than a hypothetical justification, requires rejection of the argument of administrative convenience in this case. . . .

By broadly denying this class substantial opportunities for employment, the Civil Service Commission rule deprives its members of an aspect of liberty. Since these residents were admitted as a result of decisions made by the Congress and the President, implemented by the Immigration and Naturalization Service acting under the Attorney General of the United States, due process requires that the decision to impose that deprivation of an important liberty be made either at a comparable level of government or, if it is to be permitted to be made by the Civil Service Commission, that it be justified by reasons which are properly the concern of that agency. We hold that § 338.101(a) of the Civil Service Commission Regulations has deprived these respondents of liberty without due process of law and is therefore invalid.

The judgment of the Court of Appeals is affirmed."

V. JUSTICE VOTE

5 Pro ACLU Side vs. 4 Con Opposing Side

ACLU Side (Respondent/Appellee)

1. Stevens, J. – Wrote majority opinion
2. Brennan, W. – Wrote concurring opinion
3. Stewart, P. – Joined majority opinion
4. Marshall, T. – Joined Brennan's concurrence
5. Powell, L. – Joined majority opinion

Opposing Side (Petitioner/Appellant)

1. Rehnquist, W. – Wrote dissenting opinion
2. Burger, W. – Joined Rehnquist's dissent
3. White, B. – Joined Rehnquist's dissent
4. Blackmun, H. – Joined Rehnquist's dissent

VI. A WIN OR LOSS FOR THE ACLU?

The ACLU filed as amicus curiae urging affirmance; the Supreme Court affirmed the ruling of the Court of Appeals for the Ninth Circuit in a 5-4 vote, giving the ACLU an apparent win.

372. Young v. American Mini Theatres, Inc.

(Decided June 24, 1976; 427 U.S. 50)

I. ISSUE

A. Issues Discussed

First Amendment, obscenity, Fourteenth Amendment

B. Legal Question Presented

Is a statutory classification which restricts businesses sexually explicit films but not businesses showing other films "unconstitutional because it is based on the content of communication protected by the First Amendment"?

C. Supreme Court's Answer

The statutory classification restricting businesses exhibiting sexually explicit films is constitutional.

II. CASE SUMMARY

A. Background

Respondent American Mini Theaters opened two theaters that showed adult films. City zoning ordinances prohibited adult theaters "within 1,000 feet of any two other 'regulated uses' or within 500 feet of a residential area. The term 'regulated uses' includes 10 different kinds of establishments in addition to adult theaters."

"The respondents brought two separate actions against appropriate city officials, seeking a declaratory judgment that the ordinances were unconstitutional and an injunction against their enforcement. Federal jurisdiction was properly invoked and the two cases were consolidated for decision.

The District Court granted defendants' motion for summary judgment. On the basis of the reasons stated by the city for adopting the ordinances, the court concluded that they represented a rational attempt to preserve the city's neighborhoods. The court analyzed and rejected respondents' argument that the definition and waiver provisions in the ordinances were impermissibly vague; it held that the disparate treatment of adult theaters and other theaters was justified by a compelling state interest and therefore did not violate the Equal Protection Clause; and finally it concluded that the regulation of the places where adult films could be shown did not violate the First Amendment.

The Court of Appeals reversed. The majority opinion concluded that the ordinances imposed a prior restraint on constitutionally protected communication and therefore "merely establishing that they were designed to serve a compelling public interest" provided an insufficient justification for a classification of motion picture theaters on the basis of the content of the materials they purvey to the public."

The Supreme Court granted certiorari to review the case and reversed the Court of Appeals.

B. Counsel of Record / ACLU Attorney

ACLU Side (Respondent / Appellee): John H. Weston and Stephen M. Taylor argued the cause for appellee.

Opposing Side (Petitioner / Appellant): Maureen Pulte Reilly argued the cause for appellant.

III. AMICI CURIAE

ACLU Side (Respondent / Appellee)

Brief of amici curiae filed on behalf of the ACLU, et al., by Sheridan V. Holzman, Melvin L. Wulf, and Joel M. Gora.

Brief of amici curiae filed on behalf of the Motion Picture Association of America, Inc., by Sidney Schreiber, Barbara Scott, and James Bouras.

Opposing Side (Petitioner / Appellant)

No briefs of amici curiae were filed in support of appellant.

IV. THE SUPREME COURT'S DECISION

"[Respondents] do not attack the specificity of the definition of 'Specified Sexual Activities' or 'Specified Anatomical Areas.' They argue, however, that they cannot determine how much of the described activity may be permissible before the exhibition is 'characterized by an emphasis' on such matter. In addition, they argue that the ordinances are vague because they do not specify adequate procedures or standards for obtaining a waiver of the 1,000-foot restriction.

We find it unnecessary to consider the validity of either of these arguments in the abstract. For even if there may be some uncertainty about the effect of the ordinances on other litigants, they are unquestionably applicable to these respondents. . . . To the extent that their challenge is predicated on inadequate notice resulting in a denial of procedural due process under the Fourteenth Amendment, it must be rejected. . . .

The question whether speech is, or is not, protected by the First Amendment often depends on the content of the speech. . . . Even within the area of protected speech, a difference in content may require a different governmental response. . . .

Even though the First Amendment protects communication in this area from total suppression, we hold that the State may legitimately use the content of these materials as the basis for placing them in a different classification from other motion pictures.

[T]he city's interest in attempting to preserve the quality of urban life is one that must be accorded high respect. Moreover, the city must be allowed a reasonable opportunity to experiment with solutions to admittedly serious problems.

Since what is ultimately at stake is nothing more than a limitation on the place where adult films may be exhibited, even though the determination of whether a particular film fits that characterization turns on the nature of its content, we conclude that the city's interest in the present and future character of its neighborhoods adequately supports its classification of motion pictures. We hold that the zoning ordinances requiring that adult motion picture theaters not be located within 1,000 feet of two other regulated uses does not violate the Equal Protection Clause of the Fourteenth Amendment.

The judgment of the Court of Appeals is reversed."

V. JUSTICE VOTE

4 Pro ACLU Side vs. 5 Con Opposing Side

ACLU Side (Respondent / Appellee)

1. Stewart, P. – Wrote dissenting opinion, joined Blackmun's dissent
2. Brennan, W. – Joined Stewart's dissent and Blackmun's dissent
3. Marshall, T. – Joined Stewart's dissent and Blackmun's dissent
4. Blackmun, H. – Wrote dissenting opinion, joined Stewart's dissent

Opposing Side (Petitioner / Appellant)

1. Stevens, J. – Wrote majority opinion
2. Burger, W. – Joined majority opinion
3. White, B. – Joined majority opinion
4. Powell, L. – Wrote concurring opinion
5. Rehnquist, W. – Joined Powell's concurrence

VI. A WIN OR LOSS FOR THE ACLU?

The ACLU filed as amicus curiae urging affirmance; the Supreme Court reversed the ruling of the Court of Appeals by a 5-4 vote, giving the ACLU an apparent loss.

373. Massachusetts Bd. of Retirement v. Murgia

(Decided June 25, 1976; 427 U.S. 307)

I. ISSUE

A. Issues Discussed

State, civil rights

B. Legal Question Presented

"[W]hether the provision of Mass.Gen.Laws Ann. c. 32, s 26(3)(a) (1969), that a uniformed state police officer 'shall be retired . . . upon his attaining age fifty,' denies appellee police officer equal protection of the laws in violation of the Fourteenth Amendment."

C. Supreme Court's Answer

"We decide only that the system enacted by the Massachusetts Legislature does not deny appellee equal protection of the laws."

II. CASE SUMMARY

A. Background

"Appellee Robert Murgia was an officer in the Uniformed Branch of the Massachusetts State Police. The Massachusetts Board of Retirement retired him upon his 50th birthday. Appellee brought this civil action in the United States District Court for the District of Massachusetts, alleging that the operation of s 26(3)(a) denied him equal protection of the laws and requesting the convening of a three-judge court under 28 U.S.C. ss 2281, 2284. The District Judge dismissed appellee's complaint on the ground that the complaint did not allege a substantial constitutional question. On appeal, the United States Court of Appeals for the First Circuit, in an unreported memorandum, set aside the District Court judgment and remanded the case with direction to convene a three-judge court. Upon a record consisting of depositions, affidavits, and other documentary material submitted by the parties, the three-judge court filed an opinion that declared s 26(3)(a) unconstitutional on the ground that 'a classification based on age 50 alone lacks a rational basis in furthering any substantial state interest,' and enjoined enforcement of the statute. [The Supreme Court] noted probable jurisdiction" to review the case.

B. Counsel of Record

ACLU Side (Respondent/Appellee): Robert D. City argued the cause and filed a brief for appellee.

Opposing Side (Petitioner/Appellant): Terence P. O'Malley, Assistant Attorney General of Massachusetts, argued the cause for appellants. With him on the brief were Francis X. Bellotti, Attorney General, and S. Stephen Rosenfeld and Margot Botsford, Assistant Attorneys General.

III. AMICI CURIAE

ACLU Side (Respondent/Appellee)

Brief of amici curiae filed on behalf of Legal Services for the Elderly Poor, American Civil Liberties Union, the National Council of Senior Citizens and the Massachusetts Civil Liberties Union by Howard Eglit, Jonathan A. Weiss, Melvin Wulf, John Reinstein, David Marlin, and Jay Warren.

Brief of amici curiae filed on behalf of the American Association of Retired Persons et al. by James A. Lanigan, Alfred Miller, and Stephen L. Solomon.

Brief of amici curiae filed on behalf of the Older and Middle Age Worker Ombudsman Pilot Project of United Communities of Southeastern Philadelphia et al. by Thomas K. Gilhool and Edwin D. Wolf.

Brief of amici curiae filed on behalf of the American Medical Association by James J. McNamara.

Brief of amici curiae filed on behalf of Lieutenant Lawrence Carter et al. by Melvin S. Louison.

Opposing Side (Petitioner/Appellant)

Brief of amici curiae filed on behalf of the State Police Association of Massachusetts by Henry Friedman.

IV. THE SUPREME COURT'S DECISION

"The primary function of the Uniformed Branch of the Massachusetts State Police is to protect persons and property and maintain law and order. . . .

These considerations prompt the requirement that uniformed state officers pass a comprehensive physical examination biennially until age 40. After that, until mandatory retirement at age 50, uniformed officers must pass annually a more rigorous examination . . . .

We agree that rationality is the proper standard by which to test whether compulsory retirement at age 50 violates equal protection. We disagree, however, with the District Court's determination that the age 50 classification is not rationally related to furthering a legitimate state interest. . . .

We need state only briefly our reasons for agreeing that strict scrutiny is not the proper test for determining whether the mandatory retirement provision denies appellee equal protection. . . .

This Court's decisions give no support to the proposition that a right of governmental employment Per se is fundamental. . . .

Nor does the class of uniformed state police officers over 50 constitute a suspect class for purposes of equal protection analysis. . . .

Under the circumstances, it is unnecessary to subject the State's resolution of competing interests in this case to the degree of critical examination that our cases under the Equal Protection Clause recently have characterized as 'strict judicial scrutiny.' . . .

We turn then to examine this state classification under the rational-basis standard. . . .

In this case, the Massachusetts statute clearly meets the requirements of the Equal Protection Clause, for the State's classification rationally furthers the purpose identified by the State: Through mandatory retirement at age 50, the legislature seeks to protect the public by assuring physical preparedness of its uniformed police. . . .

That the State chooses not to determine fitness more precisely through individualized testing after age 50 is not to say that the objective of assuring physical fitness is not rationally furthered by a maximum-age limitation. It is only to say that with regard to the interest of all concerned, the State perhaps has not chosen the best means to accomplish this purpose. But where rationality is the test, a State 'does not violate the Equal Protection Clause merely because the classifications made by its laws are imperfect.' . . .

We decide only that the system enacted by the Massachusetts Legislature does not deny appellee equal protection of the laws.

The judgment is reversed."

V. JUSTICE VOTE

1 Pro ACLU Side vs. 7 Con Opposing Side

ACLU Side (Respondent/Appellee)

1. Marshall, T. – Wrote dissenting opinion

Opposing Side (Petitioner/Appellant)

1. Brennan, W. – Per curiam decision
2. White, B. – Per curiam decision
3. Stewart, P. – Per curiam decision
4. Powell, L. – Per curiam decision
5. Rehnquist, W. – Per curiam decision
6. Burger, W. – Per curiam decision
7. Blackmun, H. – Per curiam decision

Stevens, J. – Took no part in the decision.

VI. A WIN OR LOSS FOR THE ACLU?

The ACLU filed as amici curiae urging affirmance of the judgment of the U.S. District Court for the District of Massachusetts; the Supreme Court reversed, in a 7-1 per curiam decision, giving the ACLU an apparent loss.

374. North v. Russell

(Decided June 28, 1976; 427 U.S. 328)

I. ISSUE

A. Issues Discussed

Criminal procedure, Fourteenth Amendment

B. Legal Question Presented

"[W]hether an accused, subject to possible imprisonment, is denied due process when tried before a nonlawyer police court judge with a later trial De novo available under a State's two-tier court system; and whether a State denies equal protection by providing law-trained judges for some police courts and lay judges for others, depending upon the State Constitution's classification of cities according to population."

C. Supreme Court's Answer

An accused is not denied due process when tried by a nonlawyer police court judge where there is an opportunity for a later trial, and an accused is not denied equal protection when law-trained judges are provided in some courts while lay judges are provided in other courts, according to city populations.

II. CASE SUMMARY

A. Background

The Kentucky Constitution requires police courts to have jurisdiction over misdemeanor cases, but an accused has an "appeal of right" from a police judge's decision to the circuit courts. The police judge in larger cities must be a licensed lawyer, but in smaller cities the police judge does not have to be a lawyer.

Appellant North was arrested in Lynch, Kentucky, and charged with driving while intoxicated. He was tried before Appellee Russell, who was a non-lawyer presiding judge of the Lynch City Police Court. North was found guilty, sentenced to jail, fined, and his driver's license was revoked.

"Appellant did not appeal to the Kentucky circuit court for a trial De novo to which he was entitled." Instead he challenged Kentucky's misdemeanor justice system by filing "a writ of habeas corpus in the Harlan County Circuit Court, where he was represented by an attorney."

The Circuit Court denied relief and the Kentucky Court of Appeals affirmed the denial of relief. After remand by the US Supreme Court on a first appeal, the Kentucky Court of Appeals declined to decide the case on state grounds, noting "that appellant sought only to 'test the constitutional status of lay judges in criminal cases.'"

On a second appeal the Supreme Court granted certiorari and affirmed.

B. Counsel of Record/ACLU Attorney

ACLU Side (Petitioner/Appellant): Charles E. Goss argued the cause for appellant.

Opposing Side (Respondent/Appellee): Robert L. Chenoweth, Assistant Attorney General of Kentucky, argued the cause for appellee.

III. AMICI CURIAE

ACLU Side (Petitioner/Appellant)

Brief of amici curiae filed on behalf of the ACLU Foundation, Inc., by Laughlin McDonald, Ray McClain, Neil Bradley, and Melvin L. Wulf.

Brief of amici curiae filed on behalf of the American Judicature Society by Allan Ashman.

Brief of amici curiae filed on behalf of the Petitioners and Classes of Petitioners in Wyse v. Hopkins and in Sanchez v. Tonkin by Rene H. Reixach, Jr.

Brief of amici curiae filed on behalf of the Kentucky Bar Association by Leslie G. Whitmer.

Brief of amici curiae filed on behalf of the National Legal Aid and Defender Association by Marshall J. Hartman, Joseph T. Garlovsky, and James F. Flug.

Brief of amici curiae filed on behalf of the Salt Lake Legal Defenders Association by Jimi Mitsunaga.

Opposing Side (Respondent/Appellee)

Brief of amici curiae filed on behalf of the New York State Association of Magistrates by Eugene W. Salisbury, Duncan S. MacAffer, and Lawrence A. Schulz.

IV. THE SUPREME COURT'S DECISION

"[We previously] considered Kentucky's two-tier system there challenged on other grounds. We noted: 'The right to a new trial is absolute. . . . Prosecution and defense begin anew. . . . The case is to be regarded exactly as if it had been brought there in the first instance.'

[S]tate policy takes into account that it is a convenience to those charged to be tried in or near their own community. . . . 'We are not persuaded . . . that the Kentucky arrangement for dealing with the less serious offenses disadvantages defendants any more or any less than trials conducted in a court of general jurisdiction in the first instance, as long as the latter are always available. . . .

Appellant's second claim is that Kentucky's constitutional provisions classifying cities by population and its statutory provisions permitting lay judges to preside in some cities while requiring law-trained judges in others denies him the equal protection guaranteed by the Fourteenth Amendment. However, all people within a given city and within cities of the same size are treated equally. . . .

The [Kentucky] Court of Appeals relied upon Missouri v. Lewis, which held that as long as all people within the classified area are treated equally: 'Each State . . . may establish one system of courts for cities and another for rural districts . . . it would seriously interfere with the power of a State to regulate its internal affairs to deny to it this right.'

We conclude that the Kentucky two-tier trial court system. . . . does not violate either the due process or equal protection guarantees of the Constitution of the United States; accordingly the judgment before us is affirmed."

V. JUSTICE VOTE

2 Pro ACLU Side vs. 6 Con Opposing Side

ACLU Side (Petitioner/Appellant)

1. Stewart, P. – Wrote dissenting opinion
2. Marshall, T. – Joined Stewart's dissent

Opposing Side (Respondent/Appellee)

1. Burger, W. – Wrote majority opinion
2. White, B. – Joined majority opinion
3. Blackmun, H. – Joined majority opinion
4. Powell, L. – Joined majority opinion
5. Rehnquist, W. – Joined majority opinion
6. Brennan, W. – Concurred in the result

Stevens, J – Took no part in the decision

VI. A WIN OR LOSS FOR THE ACLU?

The ACLU filed as amicus curiae urging reversal; the Supreme Court affirmed the ruling of the Kentucky Court of Appeals by a 6-2 vote, giving the ACLU an apparent loss.

375. Fitzpatrick v. Bitzer

(Decided June 28, 1976; 427 U.S. 445)

I. ISSUE

A. Issues Discussed

Civil rights, state, immunity, gender

B. Legal Question Presented

"In the 1972 Amendments to Title VII of the Civil Rights Act of 1964, Congress, acting under s 5 of the Fourteenth Amendment, authorized federal courts to award money damages in favor of a private individual against a state government found to have subjected that person to employment discrimination on the basis of 'race, color, religion, sex, or national origin.' The principal question presented by these cases is whether, as against the shield of sovereign immunity afforded the State by the Eleventh Amendment, Congress has the power to authorize Federal courts to enter such an award against the State as a means of enforcing the substantive guarantees of the Fourteenth Amendment."

C. Supreme Court's Answer

"We think that Congress may, in determining what is 'appropriate legislation' for the purpose of enforcing the provisions of the Fourteenth Amendment, provide for private suits against States or state officials which are constitutionally impermissible in other contexts."

II. CASE SUMMARY

A. Background

"Petitioners in No. 75-251 sued in the United States District Court for the District of Connecticut on behalf of all present and retired male employees of the State of Connecticut. Their amended complaint asserted that certain provisions in the State's statutory retirement benefit plan discriminated against them because of their sex, and therefore contravened Title VII of the 1964 Act. Title VII, which originally did not include state and local governments, had in the interim been amended to bring the States within its purview.

The District Court held that the Connecticut State Employees Retirement Act violated Title VII's prohibition against sex-based employment discrimination. It entered prospective injunctive relief in petitioners' favor against respondent state officials. Petitioners also sought an award of retroactive retirement benefits as compensation for losses caused by the State's discrimination, as well as 'a reasonable attorney's fee as part of the costs.' But the District Court held that both would constitute recovery of money damages from the State's treasury, and were therefore precluded by the Eleventh Amendment and by this Court's decision in Edelman v. Jordan.

On petitioners' appeal, the Court of Appeals affirmed in part and reversed in part."

The Supreme Court granted certiorari to review the case.

B. Counsel of Record

ACLU Side (Petitioner/Appellant): Paul W. Orth argued the cause for appellants in No. 75-251 and for appellees in No. 75-283. With him on the brief in No. 75-251 were Austin Carey, Jr., Edward Gallant, Jack Greenberg, and Eric Schnapper. With him on the brief in No. 75-283 were Austin Carey and Edward Gallant.

Deputy Solicitor General Wallace argued the cause for the United States as amicus curiae in both cases.

Opposing Side (Respondent/Appellee): Sidney D. Giber, Assistant Attorney General of Connecticut, argued the cause for appellees in No. 75-251 and for appellants in No. 75-283. With him on the briefs were Carl R. Ajello, Attorney General, and Bernard F. McGovern, Jr., Assistant Attorney General.

III. AMICI CURIAE

ACLU Side (Petitioner/Appellant)

Brief of amici curiae filed on behalf of the Lawyers Committee for Civil Rights Under Law, the National Association for the Advancement of Colored People, the Mexican American Legal Defense and Educational Fund, and the American Civil Liberties Union by Nathaniel R. Jones, Vilma Martinez, Joel Contreras, Morris J. Baller, Melvin L. Wulf, E. Richard Larson, Michael H. Gottesman, Robert M. Weinberg, Albert E. Jenner, Paul R. Dimond.

Brief of amici curiae filed on behalf of the United States by Deputy Solicitor General Wallace, Solicitor General Bork, Assistant Attorney General Pottinger, and Walter W. Barnett.

Brief of amici curiae filed on behalf of Alan Rabinovitch by Gary J. Greenberg.

Brief of amici curiae filed on behalf of the N. A. A. C. P. Legal Defense and Educational Fund, Inc., by Jack Greenberg and Eric Schnapper.

Opposing Side (Respondent/Appellee)

Brief of amici curiae filed on behalf of the State of California by Evelle J. Younger, Attorney General, Jack R. Winkler, Chief Assistant Attorney General, N. Eugene Hill and Edward P. O'Brien, Assistant Attorneys General, Edmund E. White, Richard M. Skinner, Gloria F. DeHart, and Patrick G. Golden, Deputy Attorneys General.

Brief of amici curiae filed on behalf of the State of New York by Louis J. Lejkowitz, Attorney General, Samuel A. Hirshowitz, First Assistant Attorney General, and Lillian Z. Cohen, Assistant Attorney General.

Brief of amici curiae filed on behalf of the Commonwealth of Pennsylvania et al. by Robert P. Kane, Attorney General, and Lawrence Silver and Melvin R. Shuster, Deputy Attorneys General, for the Commonwealth of Pennsylvania, joined by the Attorneys General for their respective States as follows: Robert L. Shevin of Florida, Arthur K. Bolton of Georgia, Ronald Amemiya of Hawaii, Theodore L. Sendak of Indiana, Richard C. Turner of Iowa, Francis B. Burch of Maryland, John C. Danforth of Missouri, Paul L. Douglas of Nebraska, Robert List of Nevada, David H. Souter of New Hampshire, William F. Hyland of New Jersey, Rufus L. Edmisten of North Carolina, Allen I. Olson of North Dakota, William J. Brown of Ohio, Daniel R. McLeod of South Carolina, R. A. Ashley, Jr., of Tennessee, John L. Hill of Texas, Andrew P. Miller of Virginia, and Chauncey H. Browning, Jr., of West Virginia.

IV. THE SUPREME COURT'S DECISION

"In Edelman this Court held that monetary relief awarded by the District Court to welfare plaintiffs, by reason of wrongful denial of benefits which had occurred previous to the entry of the District Court's determination of their wrongfulness, violated the Eleventh Amendment. . . .

Edelman went on to hold that the plaintiffs in that case could not avail themselves of the doctrine of waiver . . . because the necessary predicate for that doctrine was congressional intent to abrogate the immunity conferred by the Eleventh Amendment. We concluded that none of the statutes relied upon by plaintiffs in Edelman contained any authorization by Congress to join a State as defendant. . . .

All parties in the instant litigation agree with the Court of Appeals that the suit for retroactive benefits by the petitioners is in fact indistinguishable from that sought to be maintained in Edelman, since what is sought here is a damages award payable to a private party from the state treasury.

Our analysis begins where Edelman ended, for in this Title VII case the 'threshold fact of congressional authorization' to sue the State as employer is clearly present. . . .

It is true that none of the[] previous cases presented the question of the relationship between the Eleventh Amendment and the enforcement power granted to Congress under s 5 of the Fourteenth Amendment. But we think that the Eleventh Amendment, and the principle of state sovereignty which it embodies are necessarily limited by the enforcement provisions of s 5 of the Fourteenth Amendment. . . . We think that Congress may, in determining what is 'appropriate legislation' for the purpose of enforcing the provisions of the Fourteenth Amendment, provide for private suits against States or state officials which are constitutionally impermissible in other contexts. . . .

In No. 75-283, the state officials contest the Court of Appeals' conclusion that an award of attorneys' fees in this case would under *Edelman* have only an 'ancillary effect' on the state treasury and could therefore be permitted as falling outside the Eleventh Amendment under the doctrine of Ex parte Young, 209 U.S. 123 (1908). We need not address this question, since, given the express congressional authority for such an award in a case brought under Title VII, it follows necessarily from our holding in No. 75-251 that Congress' exercise of power in this respect is also not barred by the Eleventh Amendment. We therefore affirm the Court of Appeals' judgment in No. 75-283 on this basis."

V. JUSTICE VOTE

9 Pro ACLU Side vs. 0 Con Opposing Side

ACLU Side (Petitioner/Appellant)

1. Rehnquist, W. – Wrote majority opinion
2. Brennan, W. – Wrote concurring opinion

3. White, B. – Joined majority opinion
4. Marshall, T. – Joined majority opinion
5. Stewart, P. – Joined majority opinion
6. Powell, L. – Joined majority opinion
7. Burger, W. – Joined majority opinion
8. Blackmun, H. – Joined majority opinion
9. Stevens, J. – Wrote concurring opinion

VI. A WIN OR LOSS FOR THE ACLU?

The ACLU filed as amici curiae urging reversal of the judgment of the Court of Appeals in No. 75-251 and affirmance in No. 75-283; the Supreme Court affirmed in part and reversed in part, in a 9-0 vote, giving the ACLU an apparent win.

376. Nebraska Press Association v. Stuart

(Decided June 30, 1976; 427 U.S. 539)

I. ISSUE

A. Issues Discussed

First Amendment, freedom of the press, prior restraints

B. Legal Question Presented

Did the judge's order restraining members of the press from publishing or broadcasting accounts of confessions made by the accused to the police violate the constitutional guarantee of freedom of the press?

C. Supreme Court's Answer

The order violated the freedom of the press as an unconstitutional prior restraint on speech.

II. CASE SUMMARY

A. Background

"On the evening of October 18, 1975, local police found the six members of the Henry Kellie family murdered in their home in Sutherland, Neb., a town of about 850 people. Police released the description of a suspect, Erwin Charles Simants, to the reporters who had hastened to the scene of the crime. Simants was arrested and arraigned in Lincoln County Court the following morning, ending a tense night for this small rural community.

The crime immediately attracted widespread news coverage, by local, regional, and national newspapers, radio and television stations. Three days after the crime, the County Attorney and Simants' attorney joined in asking the County Court to enter a restrictive order relating to "matters that may or may not be publicly reported or disclosed to the public," because of the "mass coverage by news media" and the "reasonable likelihood of prejudicial news which would make difficult, if not impossible, the impaneling of an impartial jury and tend to prevent a fair trial." The County Court heard oral argument but took no evidence; no attorney for members of the press appeared at this stage. The County Court granted the prosecutor's motion for a restrictive order and entered it the next day, October 22. The order prohibited everyone in attendance from 'releas[ing] or authorize[ing] the release for public dissemination in any form or manner whatsoever any testimony given or evidence adduced;' the order also required members of the press to observe the Nebraska Bar- Press Guidelines."

After petitioners, several broadcasters, reporters, and other media, challenged the order, the District Court modified the order, then the Nebraska Supreme Court further modified the order. The new "order as modified prohibited reporting of only three matters: (a) the existence and nature of any confessions or admissions made by the defendant to law enforcement officers, (b) any confessions or admissions made to any third parties, except members of the press, and (c) other facts 'strongly implicative' of the accused. The Nebraska Supreme Court did not rely on the Nebraska Bar-Press Guidelines. After construing Nebraska law to permit closure in certain circumstances, the court remanded the case to the District Judge for reconsideration of the issue whether pretrial hearings should be closed to the press and public."

The Supreme Court granted certiorari to review the case, and reversed.

B. Counsel of Record/ACLU Attorney

ACLU Side (Petitioner/Appellant): E. Barrett Prettyman, Jr., argued the cause for appellant.

Floyd Abrams argued the cause for the National Broadcasting Co., Inc., et al., as amici curiae, by special leave of court.

Opposing Side (Respondent/Appellee): Assistant Attorney General of Nebraska Harold Mosher, Milton R. Larson, and Leonard P. Vyhnalek argued the cause for appellees.

III. AMICI CURIAE

ACLU Side (Petitioner/Appellant)

Brief of amici curiae filed on behalf of the ACLU, et al., by Melvin L. Wulf, Joel M. Gora, Charles C. Marson, and Joseph Remcho.

Brief of amici curiae filed on behalf of the National Broadcasting Company, et al., by Floyd Abrams, Eugene R. Scheiman, Corydon B. Dunham, David H. Marion, Harold E. Kohn, Robert Sack, John B. Summers, William Barnabas McHenry, David Otis Fuller, Jr., Richard M. Schmidt, Jr., Ian Volner, and J. Laurent Scharff.

Brief of amici curiae filed on behalf of the American Newspaper Publishers Association by Arthur B. Hanson.

Brief of amici curiae filed on behalf of the National Press Club by William I. Harkaway.

Brief of amici curiae filed on behalf of the Reporters Committee for Freedom of the Press Legal Defense and Research Fund by Lawrence Speiser.

Brief of amici curiae filed on behalf of the Tribune Company by Don H. Reuben and Lawrence Gunnels.

Brief of amici curiae filed on behalf of the Washington Post Company, et al., by Joseph A. Califano, Jr., John G. Kester, Richard M. Cooper, Alan R. Finberg, Robert C. Lobdell, David R. Hardy, Dan Paul, Edgar A. Zingman, and Donald B. Holbrook.

Opposing Side (Respondent/Appellee)

No briefs of amici curiae were filed in support of appellee.

IV. THE SUPREME COURT'S DECISION

"While the guarantees of freedom of expression are not an absolute prohibition under all circumstances, the barriers to prior restraint [of speech] remain high and the presumption against its use continues intact. Although it is unnecessary to establish a priority between First Amendment rights and the Sixth Amendment right to a fair trial under all circumstances, as the authors of the Bill of Rights themselves declined to do, the protection against prior restraint should have particular force as applied to reporting of criminal proceedings.

"Taken together, these cases demonstrate that pretrial publicity even pervasive, adverse publicity does not inevitably lead to an unfair trial. The capacity of the jury eventually impaneled to decide the case fairly is influenced by the tone and extent of the publicity, which is in part, and often in large part, shaped by what attorneys, police, and other officials do to precipitate news coverage. The trial judge has a major responsibility. What the judge says about a case, in or out of the courtroom, is likely to appear in newspapers and broadcasts. More important, the measures a judge takes or fails to take to mitigate the effects of pretrial publicity the measures described in Sheppard may well determine whether the defendant receives a trial consistent with the requirements of due process. That this responsibility has not always been properly discharged is apparent from the decisions just reviewed. . . .

The state trial judge in the case before us acted responsibly, out of a legitimate concern, in an effort to protect the defendant's right to a fair trial. What we must decide is not simply whether the Nebraska courts erred in seeing the possibility of real danger to the defendant's rights, but whether in the circumstances of this case the means employed were foreclosed by another provision of the Constitution. . . .

The record demonstrates, as the Nebraska courts held, that there was indeed a risk that pretrial news accounts, true or false, would have some adverse impact on the attitudes of those who might be called as jurors. But on the record now before us it is not clear that further publicity, unchecked, would so distort the views of potential jurors that could not be found who would, under proper instructions, fulfill their sworn duty to render a just verdict exclusively on the evidence presented in open court. We cannot say on this record that alternatives to a prior restraint on petitioners would not have sufficiently mitigated the adverse effects of pretrial publicity so as to make prior restraint unnecessary. Nor can we conclude that the restraining order actually entered would serve its intended purpose. Reasonable minds can have few doubts about the gravity of the evil pretrial publicity can work, but the probability that it would do so here was not demonstrated with the degree of certainty our cases on prior restraint require. . . .

We reaffirm that the guarantees of freedom of expression are not an absolute prohibition under all circumstances, but the barriers to prior restraint remain high and the presumption against its use continues intact. We hold that, with respect to the order entered in this case prohibiting reporting or commentary on judicial proceedings held in public, the barriers have not been overcome; to the extent that this order restrained publication of such material, it is clearly invalid. To the extent that it prohibited publication based on information gained from other sources, we conclude that the heavy burden imposed as a condition to securing a prior restraint was not met and the judgment of the Nebraska Supreme Court is therefore reversed."

V. JUSTICE VOTE

9 Pro ACLU Side vs. 0 Con Opposing Side

ACLU Side (Petitioner/Appellant)

1. Burger, W. – Wrote majority opinion
2. White, B. – Wrote concurring opinion
3. Powell, L. – Wrote concurring opinion
4. Brennan, W. – Wrote concurring opinion
5. Stevens, J. – Wrote concurring opinion
6. Blackmun, H. – Joined majority opinion
7. Rehnquist, W. – Joined majority opinion
8. Stewart, P. – Joined Brennan's concurrence
9. Marshall, T. – Joined Brennan's concurrence

VI. A WIN OR LOSS FOR THE ACLU?

The ACLU, as amicus curiae, urged reversal of the judgment of the Supreme Court of Nebraska; the U.S. Supreme Court reversed in a 9-0 vote, giving the ACLU an apparent win.

377. Stone v. Powell

(Decided July 6, 1976; 428 U.S. 465)

I. ISSUE

A. Issues Discussed

Criminal justice, Fourth Amendment, habeas corpus, Fourteenth Amendment

B. Legal Question Presented

"[W]hether a federal court should consider, in ruling on a petition for habeas corpus relief filed by a state prisoner, a claim that evidence obtained by an unconstitutional search or seizure was introduced at his trial, when he has previously been afforded an opportunity for full and fair litigation of his claim in the state courts."

C. Supreme Court's Answer

A federal court cannot grant habeas corpus relief in this circumstance.

II. CASE SUMMARY

A. Background

Respondent Lloyd Powell was convicted of murder in a California state court. Mr. Powell claimed that the testimony at his trial about a gun found during a search incident to arrest was invalid because the vagrancy ordinance he was arrested under was unconstitutional. The trial court rejected his contention and the California District Court of Appeal affirmed. Respondent then applied for habeas corpus relief in federal district court. The court concluded that the arresting officer had probable cause to arrest Mr. Powell. The Ninth Circuit Court of Appeals reversed, concluding that the ordinance was unconstitutional, and that respondent's arrest was therefore illegal. The court also held that admission of the evidence was not a harmless error.

In a related case, respondent David Rice was also convicted of murder in a state court, in part on the basis of evidence seized pursuant to a search warrant which respondent claimed was invalid. The trial court denied respondent's motion to suppress the evidence. His conviction was upheld on appeal. Respondent then filed a habeas corpus petition in federal district court. The court concluded that the warrant was invalid, and rejected the state's contention that probable cause justified the search. The Eighth Circuit Court of Appeals affirmed.

On certiorari, the Supreme Court consolidated the two cases, and reversed the Court of Appeals judgments.

B. Counsel of Record / ACLU Attorney

ACLU Side (Respondent / Appellee): Robert W. Peterson, by appointment of the Court, and William C. Cunningham argued the cause for appellees.

Opposing Side (Petitioner / Appellant): Robert R. Granucci, Deputy Attorney General of California, and Melvin Kent Kammerlohr, Assistant Attorney General of Nebraska, argued the cause for appellants.

III. AMICI CURIAE

ACLU Side (Respondent / Appellee)

Brief of amici curiae filed on behalf of the ACLU by Leon Friedman, Melvin L. Wulf, and Joel M. Gora.

Additional briefs of amici curiae were filed on behalf of the California Public Defenders Association, the National Alliance Against Racist and Political Repression, the National Conference of Black Lawyers, the National Lawyers' Guild, et al., and the National Legal Aid and Defender Association.

Opposing Side (Petitioner / Appellant)

Briefs of amici curiae filed on behalf of the State of Arizona, the State of Georgia, the States of Indiana and Iowa, the State of Utah, the State of Florida, the State of New Jersey, the State of New York, and Americans for Effective Law Enforcement, Inc., et al.

IV. THE SUPREME COURT'S DECISION

"During the period in which the substantive scope of the writ [of federal habeas corpus] was expanded, the Court did not consider whether exceptions to full review might exist with respect to particular categories of constitutional claims. . . .

The Court [has previously] noted that 'the federal habeas remedy extends to state prisoners alleging that unconstitutionally obtained evidence was admitted against them at trial,' and concluded, as a matter of statutory construction, that there was no basis for restricting 'access by federal prisoners with illegal search-and-seizure claims to federal collateral remedies, while placing no similar restriction on access by state prisoners.' Although in recent years the view has been expressed that the Court should re-examine the substantive scope of federal habeas jurisdiction and limit collateral review of search-and-seizure claims 'solely to the question of whether the petitioner was provided a fair opportunity to raise and have adjudicated the question in state courts,' the Court, without discussion or consideration of the issue, has continued to accept jurisdiction in cases raising such claims.

The discussion . . . of the scope of federal habeas corpus rests on the view that the effectuation of the Fourth Amendment, as applied to the States through the Fourteenth Amendment, requires the granting of habeas corpus relief when a prisoner has been convicted in state court on the basis of evidence obtained in an illegal search or seizure since those Amendments [have been held] to require exclusion of such evidence at trial and reversal of conviction upon direct review. Until these cases we have not had occasion fully to consider the validity of this view. Upon examination, we conclude, in light of the nature and purpose of the Fourth Amendment exclusionary rule, that this view is unjustified. We hold, therefore, that where the State has provided an opportunity for full and fair litigation of a Fourth Amendment claim, the Constitution does not require that a state prisoner be granted federal habeas corpus relief on the ground that evidence obtained in an unconstitutional search or seizure was introduced at his trial. . . .

While courts, of course, must ever be concerned with preserving the integrity of the judicial process, this concern has limited force as a justification for the exclusion of highly probative evidence. The force of this justification becomes minimal where federal habeas corpus relief is sought by a prisoner who previously has been afforded the opportunity for full and fair consideration of his search-and-seizure claim at trial and on direct review. . . .

The question is whether state prisoners who have been afforded the opportunity for full and fair consideration of their reliance upon the exclusionary rule with respect to seized evidence by the state courts at trial and on direct review may invoke their claim again on federal habeas corpus review. The answer is to be found by weighing the utility of the exclusionary rule against the costs of extending it to collateral review of Fourth Amendment claims.

The costs of applying the exclusionary rule even at trial and on direct review are well known: the focus of the trial, and the attention of the participants therein, are diverted from the ultimate question of guilt or innocence that should be the central concern in a criminal proceeding. . . .

In sum, we conclude that where the State has provided an opportunity for full and fair litigation of a Fourth Amendment claim, a state prisoner may not be granted federal habeas corpus relief on the ground that evidence obtained in an unconstitutional search or seizure was introduced at his trial. In this context the contribution of the exclusionary rule, if any, to the effectuation of the Fourth Amendment is minimal and the substantial societal costs of application of the rule persist with special force.

Accordingly, the judgments of the Courts of Appeals are reversed."

V. JUSTICE VOTE

3 Pro ACLU Side vs. 6 Con Opposing Side

ACLU Side (Respondent/Appellee)

1. Brennan, W. – Wrote dissenting opinion
2. Marshall, T. – Joined Brennan's dissent
3. White, B. – Wrote dissenting opinion

Opposing Side (Petitioner/Appellant)

1. Powell, L. – Wrote majority opinion
2. Burger, W. – Wrote concurring opinion
3. Stewart, P. – Joined majority opinion
4. Blackmun, H. – Joined majority opinion
5. Rehnquist, W. – Joined majority opinion
6. Stevens, J. – Joined majority opinion

VI. A WIN OR LOSS FOR THE ACLU?

The ACLU filed as amicus curiae urging affirmance; the Supreme Court reversed the rulings of the Courts of Appeals in a 6-3 vote, giving the ACLU an apparent loss.

378. United States v. Martinez-Fuerte

(Decided July 6, 1976; 428 U.S. 543)

I. ISSUE

A. Issues Discussed

Governmental authority, immigration, Fourth Amendment

B. Legal Question Presented

Is the operation of a border patrol checkpoint at which all vehicles are stopped and some are subjected to additional visual inspection and interrogation about citizenship incompatible with the Fourth Amendment prohibition against unreasonable search and seizure?

C. Supreme Court's Answer

Border patrol checkpoints operated in this manner do not violate the Fourth Amendment.

II. CASE SUMMARY

A. Background

"These cases involve criminal prosecutions for offenses relating to the transportation of illegal Mexican aliens. Each defendant was arrested at a permanent checkpoint operated by the Border Patrol away from the international border with Mexico, and each sought the exclusion of certain evidence on the ground that the operation of the checkpoint was incompatible with the Fourth Amendment. In each instance whether the Fourth Amendment was violated turns primarily on whether a vehicle may be stopped at a fixed checkpoint for brief questioning of its occupants even though there is no reason to believe the particular vehicle contains illegal aliens. . . .

Respondent Amado Martinez-Fuerte approached the checkpoint driving a vehicle containing two female passengers. The women were illegal Mexican aliens who had entered the United States at the San Ysidro port of entry by using false papers and rendezvoused with Martinez-Fuerte in San Diego to be transported northward. At the checkpoint their car was directed to the secondary inspection area. Martinez-Fuerte produced documents showing him to be a lawful resident alien, but his passengers admitted being present in the country unlawfully. He was charged, Inter alia, with two counts of illegally transporting aliens in violation of 8 U.S.C. § 1324(a)(2). He moved before trial to suppress all evidence stemming from the stop on the ground that the operation of the checkpoint was in violation of the Fourth Amendment. The motion to suppress was denied, and he was convicted on both counts after a jury trial. . . .

Martinez-Fuerte appealed his conviction, and the Government appealed the granting of the motions to suppress in the respective prosecutions of Jiminez-Garcia and of Guillen and Medrano-Barragan. The Court of Appeals for the Ninth Circuit consolidated the three appeals, which presented the common question whether routine stops and interrogations at checkpoints are consistent with the Fourth Amendment. The Court of Appeals held, with one judge dissenting, that these stops violated the Fourth Amendment, concluding that a stop for inquiry is constitutional only if the Border Patrol reasonably suspects the presence of illegal aliens on the basis of articulable facts. It reversed Martinez-Fuerte's conviction, and affirmed the orders to suppress in the other cases."

The Supreme Court granted certiorari to review the case, and reversed the Ninth Circuit Court of Appeals.

B. Counsel of Record/ACLU Attorney

ACLU Side (Petitioner/Appellant in No. 75-5387, Respondent/Appellee in No. 74-1560):

Charles M. Sevilla, by appointment of the Court, argued the cause for appellee in No. 74-1560. Ballard Bennett, by appointment of the court, argued the cause for appellant in No. 75-5387.

Opposing Side (Respondent/Appellee in No. 75-5387, Petitioner/Appellant in No. 74-1560):

Mark L. Evans argued the cause for appellant in No. 74-1560 and appellee in No. 75-5387.

III. AMICI CURIAE

ACLU Side (Petitioner/Appellant in No. 75-5387, Respondent/Appellee in No. 74-1560):

Brief of amici curiae filed on behalf of the ACLU, et al., in No. 74-1560 by Melvin L. Wulf, Joel M. Gora, Vilma S. Martinez, Sanford J. Rosen, and Jerome B. Falk, Jr.

Opposing Side (Respondent/Appellee in No. 75-5387, Petitioner/Appellant in No. 74-1560):

No briefs of amici curiae were filed in support of the United States.

IV. THE SUPREME COURT'S DECISION

"A requirement that stops on major routes inland always be based on reasonable suspicion would be impractical because the flow of traffic tends to be too heavy to allow the particularized study of a given car that would enable it to be identified as a possible carrier of illegal aliens. . . .

While the need to make routine checkpoint stops is great, the consequent intrusion on Fourth Amendment interests is quite limited. . . . Neither the vehicle nor its occupants are searched, and visual inspection of the vehicle is limited to what can be seen without a search.

[O]ne's expectation of privacy in an automobile and of freedom in its operation are significantly different from the traditional expectation of privacy and freedom in one's residence. And the reasonableness of the procedures followed in making these checkpoint stops makes the resulting intrusion on the interests of motorists minimal. On the other hand, the purpose of the stops is legitimate and in the public interest, and the need for this enforcement technique is demonstrated by the records in the cases before us. Accordingly, we hold that the stops and questioning at issue may be made in the absence of any individualized suspicion at reasonably located checkpoints.

[E]ven if it be assumed that such referrals are made largely on the basis of apparent Mexican ancestry, we perceive no constitutional violation. As the intrusion here is sufficiently minimal that no particularized reason need exist to justify it, we think it follows that the Border Patrol officers must have wide discretion in selecting the motorists to be diverted for the brief questioning involved.

[It is argued] that routine stops at a checkpoint are permissible only if a warrant has given judicial authorization to the particular checkpoint location and the practice of routine stops. [However] the strong Fourth Amendment interests that justify the warrant requirement . . . are absent here. . . .

In summary, we hold that stops for brief questioning routinely conducted at permanent checkpoints are consistent with the Fourth Amendment and need not be authorized by warrant. [O]ur holding today is limited to the type of stops described in this opinion. '[A]ny further detention . . . must be based on consent or probable cause.' None of the defendants in these cases argues that the stopping officers exceeded these limitations. Consequently, we affirm the judgment of the Court of Appeals for the Fifth Circuit, which had affirmed the conviction of Sifuentes. We reverse the judgment of the Court of Appeals for the Ninth Circuit and remand the case with directions to affirm the conviction of Martinez-Fuerte and to remand the other cases to the District Court for further proceedings."

V. JUSTICE VOTE

2 Pro ACLU Side vs. 7 Con Opposing Side

ACLU Side (Petitioner/Appellant in No. 75-5387, Respondent/Appellee in No. 74-1560):

1. Brennan, W. – Wrote dissenting opinion
2. Marshall, T. – Joined Brennan's dissent

Opposing Side (Respondent/Appellee in No. 75-5387, Petitioner/Appellant in No. 74-1560):

1. Powell, L. – Wrote majority opinion
2. Burger, W. – Joined majority opinion
3. Stewart, P. – Joined majority opinion
4. White, B. – Joined majority opinion
5. Blackmun, H. – Joined majority opinion
6. Rehnquist, W. – Joined majority opinion
7. Stevens, J. – Joined majority opinion

VI. A WIN OR LOSS FOR THE ACLU?

The ACLU filed as amicus curiae urging affirmance in No. 74-1560; the Supreme Court reversed the ruling of the Ninth Circuit Court of Appeals by a 7-2 vote, giving the ACLU an apparent loss.

379. General Electric Co. v. Gilbert

(Decided December 7, 1976; 429 U.S. 125)

I. ISSUE

A. Issues Discussed

Gender

B. Legal Question Presented

Whether an employer disability-benefits plan that excludes coverage for pregnancy-related disabilities violates Title VII.

C. Supreme Court's Answer

"We . . . agree with petitioner that its disability-benefits plan does not violate Title VII because of its failure to cover pregnancy-related disabilities."

II. CASE SUMMARY

A. Background

"Petitioner, General Electric Co., provides for all of its employees a disability plan which pays weekly nonoccupational sickness and accident benefits. Excluded from the plan's coverage, however, are disabilities arising from pregnancy. Respondents, on behalf of a class of women employees, brought this action seeking a declaration that this exclusion constitutes sex discrimination in violation of Title VII of the Civil Rights Act of 1964. The District Court for the Eastern District of Virginia, following a trial on the merits, held that the exclusion of such pregnancy-related disability benefits from General Electric's employee disability plan violated Title VII. The Court of Appeals affirmed."

The Supreme Court granted certiorari to review the case.

B. Counsel of Record

ACLU Side (Respondent/Appellee): Ruth Weyand reargued the cause for appellee. With her on the briefs were Winn Newman and Seymour DuBow.

Assistant Attorney General Pottinger argued the cause for the United States et al. on reargument as amici curiae.

Opposing Side (Petitioner/Appellant): Theophil C. Kammholz reargued the cause for appellant. With him on the briefs were Stanley R. Strauss, John S. Battle, Jr., and J. Robert Brame III.

III. AMICI CURIAE

ACLU Side (Respondent/Appellee)

Brief of amici curiae filed on behalf of the ACLU Women's Law Project et al. by Thomas I. Emerson, Ruth Bader Ginsberg, and Melvin L. Wulf.

Brief of amici curiae filed on behalf of the United States et al. by

Assistant Attorney General Pottinger, Solicitor General Bork, Brian K. Landsberg, Walter W. Barnett, Abner W. Sibal, Joseph T. Eddins, Beatrice Rosenberg, and Linda Colyard Dorian.

Brief of amici curiae filed on behalf of the State of Ohio by William J. Brown, Attorney General, and Earl M. Manz, Assistant Attorney General.

Brief of amici curiae filed on behalf of the American Federation of Labor and Congress of Industrial Organizations et al.; by J. Albert Woll, Laurence Gold, Stephen I. Schlossberg, and John Fillion.

Brief of amici curiae filed on behalf of Communications Workers of America, AFL-CIO by Mary K. O'Melveny, Jonathan W. Lubell, H. Howard Ostrin, and Charles V. Koons.

Opposing Side (Petitioner/Appellant)

Brief of amici curiae filed on behalf of Alaska Airlines, Inc., et al. by Gordon Dean Booth, Jr.

Brief of amici curiae filed on behalf of American Life Insurance Association et al. by Edward Silver, Larry M. Lavinsky, Stephen E. Tisman, Sara S. Portnoy, and Manuel M. Gorman.

Brief of amici curiae filed on behalf of the American Society for Personnel Administration by Joseph T. King.

Brief of amici curiae filed on behalf of the American Telephone & Telegraph Co. by Thompson Powers.

Brief of amici curiae filed on behalf of Celanese Corp. by Thornton H. Brooks.

Brief of amici curiae filed on behalf of the Chamber of Commerce of the United States by Gerard C. Smetana, Jerry Kronenberg, Julian D. Schreiber, Lawrence B. Kraus, and Richard B. Berman.

Brief of amici curiae filed on behalf of Liberty Mutual Insurance Co. by Kalvin M. Grove, Lawrence M. Cohen, Jeffrey S. Goldman, Robert A. Penney, and Clem R. Kyle.

Brief of amici curiae filed on behalf of the National Association of Manufacturers of the United States by Richard D. Godown.

Brief of amici curiae filed on behalf of Owens-Illinois, Inc., et al. by Lloyd Sutter.

Brief of amici curiae filed on behalf of Westinghouse Electric Corp by John G. Wayman, Scott F. Zimmerman, and Walter P. DeForest.

Brief of amici curiae filed on behalf of the School District of the City of Ladue by Robert G. McClintock.

IV. THE SUPREME COURT'S DECISION

"Section 703(a)(1) provides in relevant part that it shall be an unlawful employment practice for an employer

'to discriminate against any individual with respect to his compensation, terms, conditions, or privileges of employment, because of such individual's race, color, religion, sex, or national origin.'

While there is no necessary inference that Congress, in choosing this language, intended to incorporate into Title VII the concepts of discrimination which have evolved from court decisions construing the Equal Protection Clause of the Fourteenth Amendment, the similarities between the congressional language and some of those decisions surely indicate that the latter are a useful starting point in interpreting the former. . . .

For all that appears, pregnancy-related disabilities constitute an additional risk, unique to women, and the failure to compensate them for this risk does not destroy the presumed parity of the benefits, accruing to men and women alike, which results from the facially evenhanded inclusion of risks. To hold otherwise would endanger the commonsense notion that an employer who has no disability benefits program at all does not violate Title VII even though the 'underinclusion' of risks impacts, as a result of pregnancy-related disabilities, more heavily upon one gender than upon the other. Just as there is no facial gender-based discrimination in that case, so, too, there is none here. . .

We are told, however, that this analysis of the congressional purpose underlying Title VII is inconsistent with the guidelines of the EEOC, which, it is asserted, are entitled to 'great deference' in the construction of the Act . . . .

The concept of 'discrimination,' of course, was well known at the time of the enactment of Title VII, having been associated with the Fourteenth Amendment for nearly a century, and carrying with it a long history of judicial construction. When Congress makes it unlawful for an employer to 'discriminate . . . because of . . . sex . . .,' without further explanation of its meaning, we should not readily infer that it meant something different from what the concept of discrimination has traditionally meant. There is surely no reason for any such inference here.

We therefore agree with petitioner that its disability-benefits plan does not violate Title VII because of its failure to cover pregnancy-related disabilities. The judgment of the Court of Appeals is reversed."

V. JUSTICE VOTE

3 Pro ACLU Side vs. 6 Con Opposing Side

ACLU Side (Respondent/Appellee)

1. Brennan, W. – Wrote dissenting opinion
2. Marshall, T. – Joined Brennan's dissent
3. Stevens, J. – Wrote dissenting opinion

Opposing Side (Petitioner/Appellant)

1. Rehnquist, W. – Wrote majority opinion
2. Stewart, P. – Wrote concurring opinion
3. Burger, W. – Joined majority opinion
4. White, B. – Joined majority opinion
5. Blackmun, H. – Wrote concurring opinion
6. Powell, L. – Joined majority opinion

VI. A WIN OR LOSS FOR THE ACLU?

The ACLU filed as amicus curiae urging affirmance; the Supreme Court reversed the Court of Appeals' decision by a 6-3 vote, giving the ACLU an apparent loss.

380. Craig v. Boren

(Decided December 20, 1976; 429 U.S. 190)

I. ISSUE

A. Issues Discussed

Gender discrimination, equal protection, Fourteenth Amendment

B. Legal Question Presented

Whether a state statute that establishes a different drinking age for men and women "constitutes a denial to males 18-20 years of age of the equal protection of the laws in violation of the Fourteenth Amendment."

C. Supreme Court's Answer

The state statute is invalid because it denies equal protection by creating gender-based discrimination not supported by an important government purpose.

II. CASE SUMMARY

A. Background

"The interaction of two sections of an Oklahoma statute prohibits the sale of 'nonintoxicating' 3.2% beer to males under the age of 21 and to females under the age of 18. . . .

This action was brought in the District Court for the Western District of Oklahoma on December 20, 1972, by appellant Craig, a male then between 18 and 21 years of age, and by appellant Whitener, a licensed vendor of 3.2% beer. The complaint sought declaratory and injunctive relief against enforcement of the gender-based differential on the ground that it constituted invidious discrimination against males 18-20 years of age. A three-judge court convened under 28 U.S.C. § 2281 sustained the constitutionality of the statutory differential and dismissed the action."

The Supreme Court granted certiorari to review the case and reversed.

B. Counsel of Record/ACLU Attorney

ACLU Side (Petitioner/Appellant): Frederick P. Gilbert argued the cause for appellant.

Opposing Side (Respondent/Appellee): James H. Gray, Assistant Attorney General of Oklahoma, argued the cause for appellee.

III. AMICI CURIAE

ACLU Side (Petitioner/Appellant)

Brief of amici curiae filed on behalf of the ACLU by Ruth Bader Ginsburg and Melvin L. Wulf.

Opposing Side (Respondent/Appellee)

No briefs of amici curiae were filed in support of appellee.

IV. THE SUPREME COURT'S DECISION

"Analysis may appropriately begin with the reminder that Reed emphasized that statutory classifications that distinguish between males and females are 'subject to scrutiny under the Equal Protection Clause.' To withstand constitutional challenge, previous cases establish that classifications by gender must serve important governmental objectives and must be substantially related to achievement of those objectives. . . .

'Reed, we feel is controlling . . . ,' We turn then to the question whether, under Reed, the difference between males and females with respect to the purchase of 3.2% beer warrants the differential in age drawn by the Oklahoma statute. We conclude that it does not. . . .

We accept for purposes of discussion the District Court's identification of the objective underlying §§ 241 and 245 as the enhancement of traffic safety. Clearly, the protection of public health and safety represents an important function of state and local governments. However, appellees' statistics in our view cannot support the conclusion that the gender-based distinction closely serves to achieve that objective and therefore the distinction cannot under Reed withstand equal protection challenge.

[T]he showing offered by the appellees does not satisfy us that sex represents a legitimate, accurate proxy for the regulation of drinking and driving. In fact, when it is further recognized that Oklahoma's statute prohibits only the selling of 3.2% beer to young males and not their drinking the beverage once acquired (even after purchase by their 18-20-year-old female companions), the relationship between gender and traffic safety becomes far too tenuous to satisfy Reed's requirement that the gender-based difference be substantially related to achievement of the statutory objective.

We hold, therefore, that under Reed, Oklahoma's 3.2% beer statute invidiously discriminates against males 18-20 years of age. . . .

In sum, the principles embodied in the Equal Protection Clause are not to be rendered inapplicable by statistically measured but loose-fitting generalities concerning the drinking tendencies of aggregate groups. We thus hold that the operation of the Twenty-first Amendment does not alter the application of equal protection standards that otherwise govern this case.

We conclude that the gender-based differential contained in Okla. Stat., Tit. 37, § 245 (1976 Supp.) constitutes a denial of the equal protection of the laws to males aged 18-20 and reverse the judgment of the District Court."

V. JUSTICE VOTE

7 Pro ACLU Side vs. 2 Con Opposing Side

ACLU Side (Petitioner/Appellant)

1. Brennan, W. – Wrote majority opinion
2. Powell, L. – Wrote concurring opinion
3. Stevens, J. – Wrote concurring opinion
4. Blackmun, H. – Wrote concurring opinion
5. Stewart, P. – Wrote concurring opinion
6. White, B. – Joined majority opinion
7. Marshall, T. – Joined majority opinion

Opposing Side (Respondent/Appellee)

1. Burger, W. – Wrote dissenting opinion
2. Rehnquist, W. – Wrote dissenting opinion

VI. A WIN OR LOSS FOR THE ACLU?

The ACLU, as amicus curiae, urged reversal of the judgment of the District Court for the Western District of Oklahoma; the Supreme Court reversed in a 7-2 vote, giving the ACLU an apparent win.

381. Weatherford v. Bursey

(Decided February 22, 1977; 429 U.S. 545)

I. ISSUE

A. Issues Discussed

Criminal procedure

B. Legal Question Presented

"[W]hether in the circumstances present in this case the conduct of an undercover agent for a state law enforcement agency deprived respondent Bursey of his right to the effective assistance of counsel guaranteed him by the Sixth and Fourteenth Amendments of the United States Constitution or deprived him of due process of law in violation of the Fourteenth Amendment."

C. Supreme Court's Answer

"There being no tainted evidence in this case, no communication of defense strategy to the prosecution, and no purposeful intrusion by Weatherford, there was no violation of the Sixth Amendment insofar as it is applicable to the States by virtue of the Fourteenth Amendment. The proof in this case thus fell short of making out a s 1983 claim, and the judgment of the District Court should have been affirmed in this respect."

II. CASE SUMMARY

A. Background

"During the early morning hours of March 20, 1970, Bursey and Weatherford, along with two others, vandalized the offices of the Richland County Selective Service in Columbia, S. C. Police were advised of the incident by Weatherford, who, in order to maintain his undercover status . . . , was arrested and charged along with Bursey. . . .

[P]rior to trial, Weatherford met with Bursey . . . , and the approaching trial was discussed. . . .

At no time did Weatherford discuss with or pass on to his superiors or to the prosecuting attorney or any of the attorney's staff 'any details or information regarding the plaintiff's trial plans, strategy, or anything having to do with the criminal action pending against plaintiff.' Until the day of trial the prosecuting attorney did not plan to use Weatherford as a witness. . . . However, Weatherford had lost some of his effectiveness as an agent . . . , and he was called for the prosecution. He testified as to his undercover activities and gave an eyewitness account of the events of March 20, 1970. Bursey took the stand, was convicted, and then disappeared until apprehended some two years later, at which time he was incarcerated . . . .

Bursey then began this s 1983 action, alleging that Weatherford had communicated to his superiors and prosecuting officials the defense strategies and plans which he had learned at his meetings with Bursey and Wise, thereby depriving Bursey of the effective assistance of counsel to which he was entitled under the Sixth and Fourteenth Amendments as well as of his right to a fair trial guaranteed him by the Due Process Clause of the Fourteenth Amendment. The District Court found for the defendants in all respects and entered judgment accordingly.

The Court of Appeals for the Fourth Circuit reversed . . . .

[The Supreme Court] granted the petition for certiorari . . . ."

B. Counsel of Record

ACLU Side (Respondent/Appellee): Laughlin McDonald of the American Civil Liberties Union Foundation, Inc., argued the cause for appellee. With him on the brief were Neil Bradley and Christopher Coates of the American Civil Liberties Union Foundation, Inc., Herbert E. Buhl III, Ray P. McClain, Melvin L. Wulf, and John H. F. Shattuck.

Opposing Side (Petitioner/Appellant): J. C. Coleman, Deputy Attorney General of South Carolina, argued the cause for appellants. With him on the brief were

Daniel R. McLeod, Attorney General, and A. Camden Lewis and John L. Choate, Assistant Attorneys General.

Deputy Solicitor General Frey argued the cause for the United States as amicus curiae.

III. AMICI CURIAE

ACLU Side (Respondent/Appellee)

No briefs of amici curiae were filed in support of appellee.

Opposing Side (Petitioner/Appellant)

Brief of amici curiae filed on behalf of the United States by Deputy Solicitor General Frey, Solicitor General Bork, Assistant Attorney General Thornburgh, and Marc Philip Richman.

IV. THE SUPREME COURT'S DECISION

"The exact contours of the Court of Appeals' per se right-to-counsel rule are difficult to discern; but as the Court of Appeals applied the rule in this case, it would appear that if an undercover agent meets with a criminal defendant who is awaiting trial and with his attorney and if the forthcoming trial is discussed without the agent's revealing his identity, a violation of the defendant's constitutional rights has occurred, whatever was the purpose of the agent in attending the meeting, whether or not he reported on the meeting to his superiors, and whether or not any specific prejudice to the defendant's preparation for or conduct of the trial is demonstrated or otherwise threatened. . . .

We cannot agree that [prior] cases, individually or together, either require or suggest the rule announced by the Court of Appeals and now urged by Bursey. . . .

That the per se rule adopted by the Court of Appeals would operate prophylactically and effectively is very likely true; but it would require the informant to refuse to participate in attorney-client meetings, even though invited, and thus for all practical purposes to unmask himself. Our cases, however, have recognized the unfortunate necessity of undercover work and the value it often is to effective law enforcement. . . . We have no general oversight authority with respect to state police investigations. We may disapprove an investigatory practice only if it violates the Constitution; and judged in this light, the Court of Appeals' per se rule cuts much too broadly. . . .

There being no tainted evidence in this case, no communication of defense strategy to the prosecution, and no purposeful intrusion by Weatherford, there was no violation of the Sixth Amendment insofar as it is applicable to the States by virtue of the Fourteenth Amendment. The proof in this case thus fell short of making out a s 1983 claim, and the judgment of the District Court should have been affirmed . . . .

The Court of Appeals suggested that Weatherford's continued duplicity lost Bursey the opportunity to plea bargain. But there is no constitutional right to plea bargain . . . . It was also suggested by the Court of Appeals that Bursey was deprived of the opportunity to investigate Weatherford in preparation for possible impeachment on cross-examination. But there was no objection at trial to Weatherford's testimony, no request for a continuance, and even now no indication of substantial prejudice from this occurrence. As for Bursey's claimed disability to counter Weatherford's 'devastating' testimony, the disadvantage was no more than exists in any case where the State presents very damaging evidence that was not anticipated. Wise and Bursey must have realized that in going to trial the State was confident of conviction and that if any exculpatory evidence or possible defenses existed it would be extremely wise to have them available. Prudence would have counseled at least as much.

The judgment of the Court of Appeals is reversed."

V. JUSTICE VOTE

2 Pro ACLU Side vs. 7 Con Opposing Side

ACLU Side (Respondent/Appellee)

1. Brennan, W. – Joined Marshall's dissent
2. Marshall, T. – Wrote dissenting opinion

Opposing Side (Petitioner/Appellant)

1. White, B. – Wrote majority opinion
2. Stewart, P. – Joined majority opinion
3. Powell, L. – Joined majority opinion
4. Rehnquist, W. – Joined majority opinion
5. Burger, W. – Joined majority opinion
6. Blackmun, H. – Joined majority opinion
7. Stevens, J. – Joined majority opinion

VI. A WIN OR LOSS FOR THE ACLU?

The ACLU served as counsel for appellee urging affirmance of the judgment of the Court of Appeals; the Supreme Court reversed, in a 7-2 vote, giving the ACLU an apparent loss.

382. Califano v. Goldfarb

(Decided March 2, 1977; 430 U.S. 199)

I. ISSUE

A. Issues Discussed

Gender, civil rights

B. Legal Question Presented

"Under the Federal Old-Age, Survivors, and Disability Insurance Benefits (OASDI) program, survivors' benefits based on the earnings of a deceased husband covered by the Act are payable to his widow. Such benefits on the basis of the earnings of a deceased wife covered by the Act are payable to the widower, however, only if he 'was receiving at least one-half of his support' from his deceased wife. The question in this case is whether this gender-based distinction violates the Due Process Clause of the Fifth Amendment."

C. Supreme Court's Answer

"[T]he different treatment of men and women mandated by s 402(f)(1)(D) constitute[s] invidious discrimination against female wage earners by affording them less protection for their surviving spouses than is provided to male employees."

II. CASE SUMMARY

A. Background

"Mrs. Hannah Goldfarb worked as a secretary in the New York City public school system for almost 25 years until her death in 1968. During that entire time she paid in full all social security taxes . . . . She was survived by her husband, Leon Goldfarb, now aged 72, a retired federal employee. Leon duly applied for widower's benefits. The application was denied with the explanation that

'You do not qualify for a widower's benefit because you do not meet one of the requirements for such entitlement. This requirement is that you must have been receiving at least one-half support from your wife when she died.'

The District Court declared s 402(f)(1)(D) unconstitutional . . . ."

The Supreme Court granted certiorari to review the case.

B. Counsel of Record

ACLU Side (Respondent/Appellee): Ruth Bader Ginsburg of the American Civil Liberties Union Foundation argued the cause for appellee. With her on the briefs were Melvin L. Wulf and Kathleen Willert Peratis of the American Civil Liberties, Union Foundation, and Nadine Taub.

Opposing Side (Petitioner/Appellant): Deputy Solicitor General Jones argued the cause for appellant. With him on the brief were Solicitor General Bork, Assistant Attorney General Lee, Howard E. Shapiro, and William Kanter.

III. AMICI CURIAE

ACLU Side (Respondent/Appellee)

No briefs of amici curiae were filed in support of appellee.

Opposing Side (Petitioner/Appellant)

No briefs of amici curiae were filed in support of appellant.

IV. THE SUPREME COURT'S DECISION

"The gender-based distinction drawn by s 402(f)(1)(D) burdening a widower but not a widow with the task of proving dependency upon the deceased spouse presents an equal protection question indistinguishable from that decided in Weinberger v. Wiesenfeld. That decision and the decision in Frontiero v. Richardson, 411 U.S. 677 (1973), plainly require affirmance of the judgment of the District Court.

'Section 402(g) clearly operates, as did the statutes invalidated by our judgment in Frontiero, to deprive women of protection for their families which men receive as a result of their employment. Indeed, the classification here is in some ways more pernicious. . . .

Thus s 402(f)(1)(D) '[b]y providing dissimilar treatment for men and women who are . . . similarly situated . . . violates the [Fifth Amendment].' . . .

Appellant, however, would focus equal protection analysis, not upon the discrimination against the covered wage earning female, but rather upon whether her surviving widower was unconstitutionally discriminated against by burdening him but not a surviving widow with proof of dependency. . . .

[D]ecision of the equal protection challenge in this case cannot focus solely on the distinction drawn between widowers and widows but, as Wiesenfeld held, upon the gender-based discrimination against covered female wage earners as well. . . .

Appellant's emphasis upon the sex-based distinction between widow and widower as recipients of benefits rather than that between covered female and covered male employees also emerges in his other arguments. These arguments have no merit. . . .

We conclude, therefore, that the differential treatment of nondependent widows and widowers results not, as appellant asserts, from a deliberate congressional intention to remedy the arguably greater needs of the former, but rather from an intention to aid the dependent spouses of deceased wage earners, coupled with a presumption that wives are usually dependent. This presents precisely the situation faced in Frontiero and Wiesenfeld. The only conceivable justification for writing the presumption of wives' dependency into the statute is the assumption, not verified by the Government in Frontiero, or here, but based simply on 'archaic and overbroad' generalizations that it would save the Government time, money, and effort simply to pay benefits to all widows, rather than to require proof of dependency of both sexes. We held in Frontiero, and again in Wiesenfeld, and therefore hold again here, that such assumptions do not suffice to justify a gender-based discrimination in the distribution of employment-related benefits.

Affirmed."

V. JUSTICE VOTE

5 Pro ACLU Side vs. 4 Con Opposing Side

ACLU Side (Respondent/Appellee)

1. Brennan, W. – Wrote majority opinion
2. Marshall, T. – Joined majority opinion
3. White, B. – Joined majority opinion
4. Powell, L. – Joined majority opinion
5. Stevens, J. – Wrote concurring opinion

Opposing Side (Petitioner/Appellant)

1. Stewart, P. – Joined Rehnquist's dissent
2. Rehnquist, W. – Wrote dissenting opinion
3. Burger, W. – Joined Rehnquist's dissent
4. Blackmun, H. – Joined Rehnquist's dissent

VI. A WIN OR LOSS FOR THE ACLU?

The ACLU served as counsel for appellee urging affirmance; the Supreme Court affirmed the District Court's decision by a 5-4 vote, giving the ACLU an apparent win.

383. Castaneda v. Partida

(Decided March 23, 1977; 430 U.S. 482)

I. ISSUE

A. Issues Discussed

Race, criminal procedure

B. Legal Question Presented

"[W]hether the State of Texas, in the person of petitioner, the Sheriff of Hidalgo County, successfully rebutted respondent prisoner's prima facie showing of discrimination against Mexican-Americans in the state grand jury selection process."

C. Supreme Court's Answer

"[T]he proof offered by respondent was sufficient to demonstrate a prima facie case of discrimination in grand jury selection. Since the State failed to rebut the presumption of purposeful discrimination by competent testimony, despite two opportunities to do so, we affirm the Court of Appeals' holding of a denial of equal protection of the law in the grand jury selection process in respondent's case."

II. CASE SUMMARY

A. Background

"Respondent, Rodrigo Partida, was indicted in March 1972 by the grand jury of the 92d District Court of Hidalgo County for the crime of burglary of a private residence at night with intent to rape. Hidalgo is one of the border counties of southern Texas. After a trial before a petit jury, respondent was convicted and sentenced to eight years in the custody of the Texas Department of Corrections. He first raised his claim of discrimination in the grand jury selection process on a motion for new trial in the State District Court. In support of his motion, respondent testified about the general existence of discrimination against Mexican-Americans in that area of Texas and introduced statistics from the 1970 census and the Hidalgo County grand jury records. . . .

The State District Court . . . denied the motion for a new trial.

On appeal, the Texas Court of Criminal Appeals affirmed the conviction. . . .

After exhausting his state remedies, respondent filed his petition for habeas corpus . . . , alleging a denial of due process and equal protection, guaranteed by the Fourteenth Amendment, because of gross under-representation of Mexican-Americans on the . . . grand juries. . . .

On the basis of the evidence before it, the court concluded that respondent had made out a 'bare prima facie case' of invidious discrimination with his proof of 'a long continued disproportion in the composition of the grand juries in Hidalgo County.' Based on an examination of the reliability of the statistics offered by respondent, however, despite the lack of evidence in the record justifying such an inquiry, the court stated that the prima facie case was weak. . . . On the basis of those findings, the court dismissed the petition.

The United States Court of Appeals for the Fifth Circuit reversed."

The Supreme Court granted certiorari to review the case.

B. Counsel of Record

ACLU Side (Respondent/Appellee): David G. Hall argued the cause for appellee. With him on the brief was Melvin L. Wulf of the American Civil Liberties Union Foundation.

Opposing Side (Petitioner/Appellant): Thomas Parker Beery argued the cause and filed a brief for appellant.

III. AMICI CURIAE

ACLU Side (Respondent/Appellee)

No briefs of amici curiae were filed in support of appellee.

Opposing Side (Petitioner/Appellant)

No briefs of amici curiae were filed in support of appellant.

IV. THE SUPREME COURT'S DECISION

"This Court has long recognized that 'it is a denial of the equal protection of the laws to try a defendant of a particular race or color under an indictment issued by a grand jury . . . from which all persons of his race or color have, solely because of that race or color, been excluded by the State . . . .' . . .

Thus, in order to show that an equal protection violation has occurred in the context of grand jury selection, the defendant must show that the procedure employed resulted in substantial underrepresentation of his race or of the identifiable group to which he belongs. The first step is to establish that the group is one that is a recognizable, distinct class . . . . Next, the degree of underrepresentation must be proved . . . . Finally, . . . a selection procedure that is susceptible of abuse or is not racially neutral supports the presumption of discrimination raised by the statistical showing. Once the defendant has shown substantial underrepresentation of his group, he has made out a prima facie case of discriminatory purpose, and the burden then shifts to the State to rebut that case. . . .

In this case, it is no longer open to dispute that Mexican-Americans are a clearly identifiable class. . . . We agree with the District Court and the Court of Appeals that the proof in this case was enough to establish a prima facie case of discrimination against the Mexican-Americans . . . .

Supporting this conclusion is the fact that the Texas system of selecting grand jurors is highly subjective. . . .

The showing made by respondent therefore shifted the burden of proof to the State to dispel the inference of intentional discrimination. Inexplicably, the State introduced practically no evidence. . . .

In light of our holding that respondent proved a prima facie case of discrimination that was not rebutted by any of the evidence presently in the record, we have only to consider whether the District Court's 'governing majority' theory filled the evidentiary gap. In our view, it did not dispel the presumption of purposeful discrimination in the circumstances of this case. . . .

Rather than relying on an approach to the jury discrimination question that is as faintly defined as the 'governing majority' theory is on this record, we prefer to look at all the facts that bear on the issue, such as the statistical disparities, the method of selection, and any other relevant testimony as to the manner in which the selection process was implemented. Under this standard, the proof offered by respondent was sufficient to demonstrate a prima facie case of discrimination in grand jury selection. Since the State failed to rebut the presumption of purposeful discrimination by competent testimony, despite two opportunities to do so, we affirm the Court of Appeals' holding of a denial of equal protection of the law in the grand jury selection process in respondent's case."

V. JUSTICE VOTE

5 Pro ACLU Side vs. 4 Con Opposing Side

ACLU Side (Respondent/Appellee)

1. Blackmun, H. – Wrote majority opinion
2. Brennan, W. – Joined majority opinion
3. White, B. – Joined majority opinion
4. Marshall, T. – Wrote concurring opinion
5. Stevens, J. – Joined majority opinion

Opposing Side (Petitioner/Appellant)

1. Rehnquist, W. – Joined Burger's dissent, joined Powell's dissent
2. Burger, W. – Wrote dissenting opinion, joined Powell's dissent
3. Stewart, P. – Wrote dissenting opinion
4. Powell, L. – Wrote dissenting opinion, joined Burger's dissent

VI. A WIN OR LOSS FOR THE ACLU?

The ACLU served as counsel for appellee urging affirmance of the judgment of the Court of Appeals; the Supreme Court affirmed, in a 5-4 vote, giving the ACLU an apparent win.

384. Trimble v. Gordon

(Decided April 26, 1977; 430 U.S. 762)

I. ISSUE

A. Issues Discussed

Civil rights, state rights, Fourteenth Amendment, illegitimate children, equal protection

B. Legal Question Presented

Whether an Illinois law "which allows illegitimate children to inherit by intestate succession only from their mothers" while legitimate children can inherit intestate "from both their mothers and their fathers" violates the Equal Protection Clause of the Fourteenth Amendment.

C. Supreme Court's Answer

The Illinois law only allowing intestate succession from a mother for an illegitimate child while legitimate children can inherit intestate from their mothers and fathers violates the Equal Protection Clause.

II. CASE SUMMARY

A. Background

"Appellant Deta Mona Trimble is the illegitimate daughter of appellant Jessie Trimble and Sherman Gordon. Trimble and Gordon lived in Chicago with Deta Mona from 1970 until Gordon died in 1974, the victim of a homicide. On January 2, 1973, the Circuit Court of Cook County, Ill., had entered a paternity order finding Gordon to be the father of Deta Mona and ordering him to pay $15 per week for her support. Gordon thereafter supported Deta Mona in accordance with the paternity order and openly acknowledged her as his child. He died intestate at the age of 28, leaving an estate consisting only of a 1974 Plymouth automobile worth approximately $2,500.

Shortly after Gordon's death, Trimble, as the mother and next friend of Deta Mona, filed a petition . . . in the Probate Division of the Circuit Court of Cook County, Ill. That court entered an order determining heirship, identifying as the only heirs of Gordon his father, Joseph Gordon, his mother, Ethel King, and his brother, two sisters, and a half brother. All of these individuals are appellees in this appeal, but only appellee King has filed a brief."

The Circuit Court rejected appellant Trimble's claim of heirship over Gordon's estate due to § 12 of the Illinois Probate Act, which allows legitimate children to inherit from either their mothers or fathers, but only allows illegitimate children to inherit from their mothers. Consequently, Deta Mona Trimble, the illegitimate daughter of Sherman Gordon, was unable to inherit her father's estate when he died.

The appellants filed a notice of appeal challenging the constitutionality of § 12 in the Illinois Supreme Court. That court affirmed the Circuit Court decision and did not find § 12 unconstitutional.

The U.S. Supreme Court granted certiorari to review the case and reversed.

B. Counsel of Record/ACLU Attorney

ACLU Side (Petitioner/Appellant): James D. Weill argued the cause for appellant.

Opposing Side (Respondent/Appellee): Miles N. Beermann argued the cause for appellee.

III. AMICI CURIAE

ACLU Side (Petitioner/Appellant)

Brief of amici curiae filed on behalf of the ACLU by Eric M. Lieberman, Norman Dorsen, Melvin Wulf, and Joel M. Gora.

Opposing Side (Respondent/Appellee)

No briefs of amici curiae were filed in support of appellee.

IV. THE SUPREME COURT'S DECISION

"In a case like this, the Equal Protection Clause requires more than the mere incantation of a proper state purpose. No one disputes the appropriateness of Illinois' concern with the family unit, perhaps the most fundamental social institution of our society. [However, the Illinois Supreme Court] did not address the relation between § 12 and the promotion of legitimate family relationships, thus leaving the constitutional analysis incomplete. [W]e have expressly considered and rejected the argument that a State may attempt to influence the actions of men and women by imposing sanctions on the children born of their illegitimate relationships. . . .

'The status of illegitimacy has expressed through the ages society's condemnation of irresponsible liaisons beyond the bonds of marriage. But visiting this condemnation on the head of an infant is illogical and unjust. Moreover, imposing disabilities on the illegitimate child is contrary to the basic concept of our system that legal burdens should bear some relationship to individual responsibility or wrongdoing. Obviously, no child is responsible for his birth and penalizing the illegitimate child is an ineffectual as well as an unjust way of deterring the parent.'

The parents have the ability to conform their conduct to societal norms, but their illegitimate children can affect neither their parents' conduct nor their own status. . . .

Difficulties of proving paternity in some situations do not justify the total statutory disinheritance of illegitimate children whose fathers die intestate. The facts of this case graphically illustrate the constitutional defect of § 12. Sherman Gordon was found to be the father of Deta Mona in a state-court paternity action prior to his death. On the strength of that finding, he was ordered to contribute to the support of his child. That adjudication should be equally sufficient to establish Deta Mona's right to claim a child's share of Gordon's estate, for the State's interest in the accurate and efficient disposition of property at death would not be compromised in any way by allowing her claim in these circumstances.

[W]e conclude that § 12 of the Illinois Probate Act cannot be squared with the command of the Equal Protection Clause of the Fourteenth Amendment.

Accordingly, we reverse the judgment of the Illinois Supreme Court and remand the case for further proceedings not inconsistent with this opinion."

V. JUSTICE VOTE

5 Pro ACLU Side vs. 4 Con Opposing Side

ACLU Side (Petitioner/Appellant)

1. Powell, L. – Wrote majority opinion
2. Marshall, T. – Joined majority opinion
3. White, B. – Joined majority opinion
4. Brennan, W. – Joined majority opinion
5. Stevens, J. – Joined majority opinion

Opposing Side (Respondent/Appellee)

1. Rehnquist, W. – Wrote dissenting opinion, Co-authored a dissent with the other dissenters
2. Blackmun, H. – Co-authored a dissent with the other dissenters
3. Burger, W. – Co-authored a dissent with the other dissenters
4. Stewart, P. – Co-authored a dissent with the other dissenters

VI. A WIN OR LOSS FOR THE ACLU?

The ACLU filed as amicus curiae urging reversal; the U.S. Supreme Court reversed the Illinois Supreme Court in a 5-4 vote, giving the ACLU an apparent win.

385. Wooley v. Maynard

(Decided April 30, 1977; 430 U.S. 705)

I. ISSUE

A. Issues Discussed

1st Amendment, press, speech, association, religion

B. Legal Question Presented

"[W]hether the State of New Hampshire may constitutionally enforce criminal sanctions against persons who cover the motto 'Live Free or Die' on passenger vehicle license plates because that motto is repugnant to their moral and religious beliefs."

C. Supreme Court's Answer

"We conclude that the State of New Hampshire may not require appellees to display the state motto upon their vehicle license plates . . . ."

II. CASE SUMMARY

A. Background

"Since 1969 New Hampshire has required that noncommercial vehicles bear license plates embossed with the state motto, 'Live Free or Die.' Another New Hampshire statute makes it a misdemeanor 'knowingly [to obscure] . . . the figures or letters on any number plate.' . . .

Appellees George Maynard and his wife Maxine are followers of the Jehovah's Witnesses faith. The Maynards consider the New Hampshire State motto to be repugnant to their moral, religious, and political beliefs, and therefore assert it objectionable to disseminate this message by displaying it on their automobiles. Pursuant to these beliefs, the Maynards began early in 1974 to cover up the motto on their license plates.

On November 27, 1974, Mr. Maynard was issued a citation for violating s 262:27-c. . . .

On December 28, 1974, Mr. Maynard was again charged with violating s 262:27-c. He appeared in court on January 31, 1975, and . . . chose to represent himself; he was found guilty, fined $50, and sentenced to six months in the Grafton County House of Corrections. . . .

Mr. Maynard was charged with yet a third violation of s 262:27-c on January 3, 1975. . . .

On March 4, 1975, appellees brought the present action pursuant to 42 U.S.C. s 1983 in the United States District Court for the District of New Hampshire. They sought injunctive and declaratory relief . . . . Following a hearing on the merits, the District Court entered an order enjoining the State 'from arresting and prosecuting [the Maynards] at any time in the future for covering over that portion of their license plates that contains the motto 'Live Free or Die.' [The Supreme Court] noted probable jurisdiction of the appeal."

The Supreme Court granted certiorari to review the case.

B. Counsel of Record

ACLU Side (Respondent/Appellee): Richard S. Kohn of the New Hampshire Civil, Liberties Union, Inc., argued the cause for appellees. With him on the brief were Melvin L. Wulf and Joel M. Gora of the American Civil Liberties Union Foundation, Jack B. Middleton, and R. David DePuy.

Opposing Side (Petitioner/Appellant): Robert V. Johnson II, Assistant Attorney General of New Hampshire, argued the cause for appellants. With him on the brief was David H. Souter, Attorney General.

III. AMICI CURIAE

ACLU Side (Respondent/Appellee)

No briefs of amici curiae were filed in support of appellee.

Opposing Side (Petitioner/Appellant)

No briefs of amici curiae were filed in support of appellant.

IV. THE SUPREME COURT'S DECISION

"Appellants argue that the District Court was precluded from exercising jurisdiction in this case by the principles of equitable restraint enunciated in Younger v. Harris, 401 U.S. 37 (1971). . . .

Younger does not bar federal jurisdiction.

In their complaint, the Maynards sought both declaratory and injunctive relief against the enforcement of the New Hampshire statutes. . . .

The threat of repeated prosecutions in the future against both him and his wife, and the effect of such a continuing threat on their ability to perform the ordinary tasks of daily life which require an automobile, is sufficient to justify injunctive relief. We are therefore unwilling to say that the District Court was limited to granting declaratory relief. Having determined that the District Court was not required to stay its hand as to either appellee, we turn to the merits of the Maynards' claim. . . .

We are . . . faced with the question of whether the State may constitutionally require an individual to participate in the dissemination of an ideological message by displaying it on his private property in a manner and for the express purpose that it be observed and read by the public. We hold that the State may not do so. . . .

New Hampshire's statute in effect requires that appellees use their private property as a 'mobile billboard' for the State's ideological message or suffer a penalty, as Maynard already has. As a condition to driving an automobile a virtual necessity for most Americans the Maynards must display 'Live Free or Die' to hundreds of people each day. The fact that most individuals agree with the thrust of New Hampshire's motto is not the test; most Americans also find the flag salute acceptable. The First Amendment protects the right of individuals to hold a point of view different from the majority and to refuse to foster, in the way New Hampshire commands, an idea they find morally objectionable. . . .

Identifying the Maynards' interests as implicating First Amendment protections does not end our inquiry however. We must also determine whether the State's countervailing interest is sufficiently compelling to justify requiring appellees to display the state motto on their license plates. . . .

[W]here the State's interest is to disseminate an ideology, no matter how acceptable to some, such interest cannot outweigh an individual's First Amendment right to avoid becoming the courier for such message.

We conclude that the State of New Hampshire may not require appellees to display the state motto upon their vehicle license plates; and, accordingly, we affirm the judgment of the District Court."

V. JUSTICE VOTE

6 Pro ACLU Side vs. 3 Con Opposing Side

ACLU Side (Respondent/Appellee)

1. Burger, W. – Wrote majority opinion
2. Brennan, W. – Joined majority opinion
3. Marshall, T. – Joined majority opinion
4. Stewart, P. – Joined majority opinion
5. Stevens, J. – Joined majority opinion
6. Powell, L. – Joined majority opinion

Opposing Side (Petitioner/Appellant)

1. Rehnquist, W. – Wrote dissenting opinion, joined White's opinion
2. White, B. – Wrote opinion dissenting in part
3. Blackmun, H. – Joined Rehnquist's dissent, joined White's opinion

VI. A WIN OR LOSS FOR THE ACLU?

The ACLU served as counsel for appellees urging affirmance; the Supreme Court affirmed the District Court's decision by a 6-3 vote, giving the ACLU an apparent win.

386. Linmark Associates, Inc. v. Township of Willingboro

(Decided May 2, 1977; 431 U.S. 85)

I. ISSUE

A. Issues Discussed

First Amendment, freedom of speech, commercial speech

B. Legal Question Presented

"[W]hether the First Amendment permits a municipality to prohibit the posting of 'For Sale' or 'Sold' signs when the municipality acts to stem what it perceives as the flight of white homeowners from a racially integrated community."

C. Supreme Court's Answer

Prohibiting posting of "For Sale" and "Sold" signs violates the First Amendment.

II. CASE SUMMARY

A. Background

"Petitioner Linmark Associates, a New Jersey corporation, owned a piece of realty in the township of Willingboro, N. J. Petitioner decided to sell its property, and on March 26, 1974, listed it with petitioner Mellman, a real estate agent. To attract interest in the property, petitioners desired to place a 'For Sale' sign on the lawn. Willingboro, however, narrowly limits the types of signs that can be erected on land in the township. Although prior to March 1974 'For Sale' and 'Sold' signs were permitted subject to certain restrictions not at issue here, on March 18, 1974, the Township Council enacted Ordinance 5-1974, repealing the statutory authorization for such signs on all but model homes. Petitioners brought this action against both the township and the building inspector charged with enforcing the ban on 'For Sale' signs, seeking declaratory and injunctive relief. The District Court granted a declaration of unconstitutionality, but a divided Court of Appeals reversed."

The Supreme Court granted certiorari and reversed the judgment of the Court of Appeals.

B. Counsel of Record/ACLU Attorney

ACLU Side (Petitioner/Appellant): John P. Hauch, Jr., argued the cause for appellant.

Opposing Side (Respondent/Appellee): Myron H. Gottlieb argued the cause for appellee.

III. AMICI CURIAE

ACLU Side (Petitioner/Appellant)

Brief of amici curiae filed on behalf of the ACLU, et al., by Joel M. Gora.

Opposing Side (Respondent/Appellee)

Brief of amici curiae filed on behalf of the NAACP Legal Defense & Educational Fund, Inc., by Jack Greenberg, Charles Stephen Ralston, and Melvyn R. Leventhal.

Brief of amici curiae filed on behalf of the cities of Shaker Heights and Cleveland Heights, Ohio, by Paul R. Donaldson and Donald K. Barclay.

Brief of amici curiae filed on behalf of the city of Oak Park, Michigan, by Burton R. Shifman.

Brief of amici curiae filed by Housing Advocates, Inc.

IV. THE SUPREME COURT'S DECISION

"The starting point for analysis of petitioners' First Amendment claim must be the two recent decisions in which this Court has eroded the 'commercial speech' exception to the First Amendment. . . .

Respondents contend, as they must, that the 'For Sale' signs banned in Willingboro are constitutionally distinguishable from the abortion and drug advertisements we have previously considered. It is to the distinctions respondents advance that we now turn. . . .

The Township Council here . . . acted to prevent its residents from obtaining certain information. That information, which pertains to sales activity in Willingboro, is of vital interest to Willingboro residents, since it may bear on one of the most important decisions they have a right to make: where to live and raise their families. The Council has sought to restrict the free flow of these data because it fears that otherwise homeowners will make decisions inimical to what the Council views as the homeowners' self-interest and the corporate interest of the township: they will choose to leave town. The Council's concern, then, was not with any commercial aspect of 'For Sale' signs with offerors communicating offers to offerees but with the substance of the information communicated to Willingboro citizens. . . .

'There is . . . an alternative to this highly paternalistic approach. That alternative is to assume that this information is not in itself harmful, that people will perceive their own best interests if only they are well enough informed, and that the best means to that end is to open the channels of communication rather than to close them. . . . But the choice among these alternative approaches is not ours to make . . . . It is precisely this kind of choice, between the dangers of suppressing information, and the dangers of its misuse if it is freely available, that the First Amendment makes for us.' . . .

Since we can find no meaningful distinction between Ordinance 5-1974 and the statute overturned in Virginia Pharmacy Bd., we must conclude that this ordinance violates the First Amendment. . . .

Laws dealing with false or misleading signs, and laws requiring such signs to 'appear in such a form, or include such additional information . . . as [is] necessary to prevent [their] being deceptive,' therefore, would raise very different constitutional questions. We leave those questions for another day, and simply hold that the ordinance under review here, which impairs 'the flow of truthful and legitimate commercial information' is constitutionally infirm.

Reversed."

V. JUSTICE VOTE

8 Pro ACLU Side vs. 0 Con Opposing Side

ACLU Side (Petitioner/Appellant)

1. Marshall, T. – Wrote majority opinion
2. Burger, W. – Joined majority opinion
3. Powell, L. – Joined majority opinion
4. Stewart, P. – Joined majority opinion
5. White, B. – Joined majority opinion
6. Stevens, J. – Joined majority opinion
7. Blackmun, H. – Joined majority opinion
8. Brennan, W. – Joined majority opinion

Rehnquist, W – Took no part in the decision

VI. A WIN OR LOSS FOR THE ACLU?

The ACLU, as amicus curiae, urged reversal of the judgment of the Court of Appeals for the Third Circuit; the Supreme Court reversed in an 8-0 vote, giving the ACLU an apparent win.

387. Moore v. City of East Cleveland, Ohio

(Decided May 31, 1977; 431 U.S. 494)

I. ISSUE

A. Issues Discussed

Civil rights, state's rights, Fourteenth Amendment, due process

B. Legal Question Presented

Can the City of East Cleveland, through its zoning ordinances, constitutionally define "family" so narrowly as to preclude many blood relatives from living together as a single family unit, even to the extent of precluding a grandmother from living with and raising her grandsons?

C. Supreme Court's Answer

The ordinance is unconstitutional, in violation of due process.

II. CASE SUMMARY

A. Background

Appellant, Inez Moore, lived in her home with her son and two grandsons, each from different parents, in East Cleveland, Ohio. She was criminally convicted, sentenced to 5 days of jail, and fined $25, for violating the East Cleveland housing ordinance. The ordinance limited occupancy of a residence to members of a single family and appellant's household did not qualify as a family under the city's definition of a single family. The Ohio Court of Appeals affirmed the conviction, over appellant's claims that the ordinance was unconstitutional. The Ohio Supreme Court declined review.

The Supreme Court granted certiorari to review the case, and reversed.

B. Counsel of Record/ACLU Attorney

ACLU Side (Petitioner/Appellant): Edward R. Stege, Jr., argued the cause for appellant.

Opposing Side (Respondent/Appellee): Leonard Young argued the cause for appellee.

III. AMICI CURIAE

ACLU Side (Petitioner/Appellant)

Brief of amici curiae filed on behalf of the ACLU, et al., by Melvin L. Wulf and Benjamin Sheerer.

Opposing Side (Respondent/Appellee)

No briefs of amici curiae were filed in support of appellee.

IV. THE SUPREME COURT'S DECISION

"The city argues that our decision in Village of Belle Terre v. Boraas, requires us to sustain the ordinance attacked here. . . . East Cleveland, in contrast, has chosen to regulate the occupancy of its housing by slicing deeply into the family itself. This is no mere incidental result of the ordinance. On its face it selects certain categories of relatives who may live together and declares that others may not. In particular, it makes a crime of a grandmother's choice to live with her grandson in circumstances like those presented here.

When a city undertakes such intrusive regulation of the family, neither Belle Terre nor Euclid governs; the usual judicial deference to the legislature is inappropriate. 'This Court has long recognized that freedom of personal choice in matters of marriage and family life is one of the liberties protected by the Due Process Clause of the Fourteenth Amendment.' A host of cases . . . have consistently acknowledged a 'private realm of family life which the state cannot enter.' Of course, the family is not beyond regulation. But when the government intrudes on choices concerning family living arrangements, this Court must examine carefully the importance of the governmental interests advanced and the extent to which they are served by the challenged regulation.

When thus examined, this ordinance cannot survive. The city seeks to justify it as a means of preventing overcrowding, minimizing traffic and parking congestion, and avoiding an undue financial burden on East Cleveland's school system. Although these are legitimate goals, the ordinance before us serves them marginally, at best. . . .

Appropriate limits on substantive due process come not from drawing arbitrary lines but rather from careful 'respect for the teachings of history [and], solid recognition of the basic values that underlie our society.' Our decisions establish that the Constitution protects the sanctity of the family precisely because the institution of the family is deeply rooted in this Nation's history and tradition. It is through the family that we inculcate and pass down many of our most cherished values, moral and cultural.

Ours is by no means a tradition limited to respect for the bonds uniting the members of the nuclear family. The tradition of uncles, aunts, cousins, and especially grandparents sharing a household along with parents and children has roots equally venerable and equally deserving of constitutional recognition. Over the years millions of our citizens have grown up in just such an environment, and most, surely, have profited from it. Even if conditions of modern society have brought about a decline in extended family households, they have not erased the accumulated wisdom of civilization, gained over the centuries and honored throughout our history, that supports a larger conception of the family. Out of choice, necessity, or a sense of family responsibility, it has been common for close relatives to draw together and participate in the duties and the satisfactions of a common home. Decisions concerning child rearing, which Yoder, Meyer, Pierce and other cases have recognized as entitled to constitutional protection, long have been shared with grandparents or other relatives who occupy the same household indeed who may take on major responsibility for the rearing of the children. Especially in times of adversity, such as the death of a spouse or economic need, the broader family has tended to come together for mutual sustenance and to maintain or rebuild a secure home life. This is apparently what happened here."

The Supreme Court reversed the judgment of the Ohio Court of Appeals.

V. JUSTICE VOTE

5 Pro ACLU Side vs. 4 Con Opposing Side

ACLU Side (Petitioner/Appellant)

1. Powell, L. – Wrote majority opinion
2. Brennan, W. – Wrote concurring opinion
3. Stevens, J. – Wrote concurring opinion
4. Blackmun, H. – Joined majority opinion
5. Marshall, T. – Joined Brennan's concurrence

Opposing Side (Respondent/Appellee)

1. Burger, W. – Wrote dissenting opinion
2. Stewart, P. – Wrote dissenting opinion
3. Rehnquist, W. – Joined Stewart's dissent
4. White, B. – Wrote dissenting opinion

VI. A WIN OR LOSS FOR THE ACLU?

The ACLU filed as amicus curiae urging reversal; the Supreme Court reversed the ruling of the Ohio Court of Appeals in a 5-4 vote, giving the ACLU an apparent win.

388. United States v. Ramsey

(Decided June 6, 1977; 431 U.S. 606)

I. ISSUE

A. Issues Discussed

Criminal justice, drugs, Fourth Amendment

B. Legal Question Presented

Did the customs official's actions of opening and inspecting international letters without first obtaining a search warrant violate the Constitution?

C. Supreme Court's Answer

Opening and inspecting the letters without a search warrant in this circumstance did not violate the Constitution.

II. CASE SUMMARY

A. Background

"Charles W. Ramsey and James W. Kelly jointly commenced a heroin-by-mail enterprise in the Washington, D.C., area. The process involved their procuring of heroin, which was mailed in letters from Bangkok, Thailand, and sent to various locations in the District of Columbia area for collection. Two of their suppliers, Sylvia Bailey and William Ward, who were located in West Germany, were engaged in international narcotics trafficking during the latter part of 1973 and the early part of 1974. West German agents, pursuant to court-authorized electronic surveillance, intercepted several trans-Atlantic conversations between Bailey and Ramsey during which their narcotics operation was discussed. By late January 1974, Bailey and Ward had gone to Thailand. Thai officials, alerted to their presence by West German authorities, placed them under surveillance. Ward was observed mailing letter-sized envelopes in six different mail boxes; five of these envelopes were recovered; and one of the addresses in Washington, D.C., was later linked to respondents. Bailey and Ward were arrested by Thai officials on February 2, 1974; among the items seized were eleven heroin-filed envelopes addressed to the Washington, D. C., area, and later connected with respondents.

Two days after this arrest of Bailey and Ward, Inspector George Kallnischkies, a United States customs officer in New York City, without any knowledge of the foregoing events, inspecting a sack of incoming international mail from Thailand, spotted eight envelopes that were bulky and which he believed might contain merchandise. The envelopes, all of which appeared to him to have been typed on the same typewriter, were addressed to four different locations in the Washington, D.C., area. Inspector Kallnischkies, based on the fact that the letters were from Thailand, a known source of narcotics, and were 'rather bulky,' suspected that the envelopes might contain merchandise or contraband rather than correspondence. He took the letters to an examining area in the post office, and felt one of the letters: It 'felt like there was something in there, in the envelope. It was not just plain paper that the envelope is supposed to contain." He weighed one of the envelopes, and found it weighed 42 grams, some three to six times the normal weight of an airmail letter. Inspector Kallnischkies then opened that envelope:

'In there I saw some cardboard and between the cardboard, if I recall, there was a plastic bag containing a white powdered substance, which, based on experience, I knew from Thailand would be heroin.

'I went ahead and removed a sample. Gave it a field test, a Marquis Reagent field test, and I had a positive reaction for heroin.'

He proceeded to open the other seven envelopes which 'in a lot of ways were identical'; examination revealed that at least the contents were in fact identical: each contained heroin.

The envelopes were then sent to Washington in a locked pouch where agents of the Drug Enforcement Administration, after obtaining a search warrant, opened the envelopes again and removed most of the heroin. The envelopes were then resealed, and six of them were delivered under surveillance. After Kelly collected the envelopes from the three different addressees, rendezvoused with Ramsey, and gave Ramsey a brown paper bag, federal agents arrested both of them. The bag contained the six envelopes with heroin, $1,100 in cash, and 'cutting' material for the heroin. The next day, in executing a search upon warrant of Ramsey's residence, agents recovered two pistols.

Ramsey and Kelly were indicted, along with Bailey and Ward, in a 17-count indictment. Respondents moved to suppress the heroin and the two pistols. The District Court denied the motions, and after a bench trial on the stipulated record, respondents were found guilty and sentenced to imprisonment for what is in effect a term of 10 to 30 years. The Court of Appeals for the District of Columbia Circuit, one judge dissenting, reversed the convictions, holding that the 'border search exception to the warrant requirement' applicable to persons, baggage, and mailed packages did not apply to the routine opening of international letter mail, and held that the Constitution requires that 'before international letter mail is opened, a showing of probable cause be made to and a warrant secured from a neutral magistrate.'"

The Supreme Court granted certiorari to review the case and reversed the decision of the Court of Appeals.

B. Counsel of Record/ACLU Attorney

ACLU Side (Respondent/Appellee): Allan M. Palmer and Irving R. M. Panzer, by appointment of the court, argued the cause for appellees.

Opposing Side (Petitioner/Appellant): Kenneth S. Geller argued the cause for appellant.

III. AMICI CURIAE

ACLU Side (Respondent/Appellee)

Brief of amici curiae filed on behalf of the ACLU by Melvin L. Wulf, Joel M. Gora, and Jack D. Novik.

Opposing Side (Petitioner/Appellant)

No briefs of amici curiae were filed in support of appellant.

IV. THE SUPREME COURT'S DECISION

"Congress and the applicable postal regulations authorized the actions undertaken in this case. Title 19 U.S.C. § 482 . . . explicitly deals with the search of an 'envelope': 'Any of the officers or persons authorized to board or search vessels may . . . search any trunk or envelope, wherever found, in which he may have a reasonable cause to suspect there is merchandise which was imported contrary to law . . . .' This provision authorizes customs officials to inspect, under the circumstances therein stated, incoming international mail. The 'reasonable cause to suspect' test adopted by the statute is, we think, a practical test which imposes a less stringent requirement than that of 'probable cause' imposed by the Fourth Amendment as a requirement for the issuance of warrants. . . .

Since the search in this case was authorized by statute, we are left simply with the question of whether the search, nevertheless violated the Constitution. [T]hat border searches were not subject to the warrant provisions of the Fourth Amendment and were 'reasonable' within the meaning of that Amendment, has been faithfully adhered to by this Court. . . . In United States v. 12 200-Ft. Reels of Film, we observed: 'Import restrictions and searches of persons or packages at the national borders rest on different considerations and different rules of constitutional law from domestic regulations. The Constitution gives Congress broad, comprehensive powers '[t]o regulate Commerce with foreign Nations." . . .

Border searches... have been considered to be 'reasonable' by the single fact that the person or item in question had entered into our country from outside. There has never been any additional requirement that the reasonableness of a border search depended on the existence of probable cause. . . .

It is clear that there is nothing in the rationale behind the border-search exception which suggests that the mode of entry will be critical. It was conceded at oral argument that customs officials could search, without probable cause and without a warrant, envelopes carried by an entering traveler, whether in his luggage or on his person. Surely no different constitutional standard should apply simply because the envelopes were mailed, not carried. . . .

We therefore conclude that the Fourth Amendment does not interdict the actions taken by Inspector Kallnischkies in opening and searching the eight envelopes. The judgment of the Court of Appeals is, therefore, reversed."

V. JUSTICE VOTE

3 Pro ACLU Side vs. 6 Con Opposing Side

ACLU Side (Respondent/Appellee)

1. Stevens, J. – Wrote dissenting opinion
2. Brennan, W. – Joined Stevens' dissent
3. Marshall, T. – Joined Stevens' dissent

Opposing Side (Petitioner/Appellant)

1. Rehnquist, W. – Wrote majority opinion
2. Burger, W. – Joined majority opinion
3. Stewart, P. – Joined majority opinion
4. White, B. – Joined majority opinion
5. Blackmun, H. – Joined majority opinion
6. Powell, L. – Wrote concurring opinion

VI. A WIN OR LOSS FOR THE ACLU?

The ACLU filed as amicus curiae urging affirmance; the Supreme Court reversed the ruling of the Court of Appeals for the District of Columbia Circuit in a 6-3 vote, giving the ACLU an apparent loss.

389. Carey v. Population Services International

(Decided June 9, 1977; 431 U.S. 678)

I. ISSUE

A. Issues Discussed

Civil rights, privacy, First Amendment, Fourteenth Amendment

B. Legal Question Presented

Whether a state statute severely limiting the ability to distribute and advertise contraceptives both to minors and adults is constitutional.

C. Supreme Court's Answer

The state statute is unconstitutional in its entirety as applied to nonprescription contraceptives.

II. CASE SUMMARY

A. Background

"Under New York Ed. Law § 6811(8) it is a crime (1) for any person to sell or distribute any contraceptive of any kind to a minor under the age of 16 years; (2) for anyone other than a licensed pharmacist to distribute contraceptives to persons 16 or over; and (3) for anyone, including licensed pharmacists, to advertise or display contraceptives. A three-judge District Court for the Southern District of New York declared § 6811(8) unconstitutional in its entirety under the First and Fourteenth Amendments of the Federal Constitution insofar as it applies to nonprescription contraceptives, and enjoined its enforcement as so applied."

The Supreme Court granted certiorari to review the case and affirmed the decision of the District Court.

B. Counsel of Record/ACLU Attorney

ACLU Side (Respondent/Appellee): Michael N. Pollet argued the cause for appellee.

Opposing Side (Petitioner/Appellant): Arlene R. Silverman, Assistant Attorney General of New York, argued the cause for appellant.

III. AMICI CURIAE

ACLU Side (Respondent/Appellee)

Brief of amici curiae filed on behalf of the ACLU by Melvin L. Wulf, Judith M. Mears, and Rena Uviller.

Brief of amici curiae filed on behalf of the Planned Parenthood Federation of America, et al., by Harriet F. Pilpel and Eve W. Paul.

Opposing Side (Petitioner/Appellant)

No briefs of amici curiae were filed in support of appellant.

IV. THE SUPREME COURT'S DECISION

"We must address a preliminary question of the standing of the various appellees to maintain the action. We conclude that appellee Population Planning Associates, Inc. (PPA) has the requisite standing and therefore have no occasion to decide the standing of the other appellees. . . .

Although '[t]he Constitution does not explicitly mention any right of privacy,' the Court has recognized that one aspect of the 'liberty' protected by the Due Process Clause of the Fourteenth Amendment is 'a right of personal privacy, or a guarantee of certain areas or zones of privacy.' This right of personal privacy includes 'the interest in independence in making certain kinds of important decisions.' While the outer limits of this aspect of privacy have not been marked by the Court, it is clear that among the decisions that an individual may make without unjustified government interference are personal decisions 'relating to marriage, procreation, contraception, family relationships, and child rearing and education.' . . .

That the constitutionally protected right of privacy extends to an individual's liberty to make choices regarding contraception does not, however, automatically invalidate every state regulation in this area. The business of manufacturing and selling contraceptives may be regulated in ways that do not infringe protected individual choices. And even a burdensome regulation may be validated by a sufficiently compelling state interest. . . .

We consider first the wider restriction on access to contraceptives created by § 6811(8)'s prohibition of the distribution of nonmedical contraceptives to adults except through licensed pharmacists. . . .

Restrictions on the distribution of contraceptives clearly burden the freedom to make such decisions. A total prohibition against sale of contraceptives, for example, would intrude upon individual decisions in matters of procreation and contraception as harshly as a direct ban on their use. Indeed, in practice, a prohibition against all sales, since more easily and less offensively enforced, might have an even more devastating effect upon the freedom to choose contraception. . . .

Of particular significance to the decision of this case, the right to privacy in connection with decisions affecting procreation extends to minors as well as to adults. . . . Since the State may not impose a blanket prohibition, or even a blanket requirement of parental consent, on the choice of a minor to terminate her pregnancy, the constitutionality of a blanket prohibition of the distribution of contraceptives to minors is a fortiori foreclosed. The State's interests in protection of the mental and physical health of the pregnant minor, and in protection of potential life are clearly more implicated by the abortion decision than by the decision to use a nonhazardous contraceptive. . . . Moreover, there is substantial reason for doubt whether limiting access to contraceptives will in fact substantially discourage early sexual behavior. Appellants themselves conceded in the District Court that 'there is no evidence that teenage extramarital sexual activity increases in proportion to the availability of contraceptives' . . . .

The District Court's holding that the prohibition of any 'advertisement or display' of contraceptives is unconstitutional was clearly correct. . . .

Appellants contend that advertisements of contraceptive products would be offensive and embarrassing to those exposed to them, and that permitting them would legitimize sexual activity of young people. But these are classically not justifications validating the suppression of expression protected by the First Amendment. At least where obscenity is not involved, we have consistently held that the fact that protected speech may be offensive to some does not justify its suppression. As for the possible 'legitimation' of illicit sexual behavior, whatever might be the case if the advertisements directly incited illicit sexual activity among the young, none of the advertisements in this record can even remotely be characterized as 'directed to inciting or producing imminent lawless action and . . . likely to incite or produce such action.' They merely state the availability of products and services that are not only entirely legal, but constitutionally protected. These arguments therefore do not justify the total suppression of advertising concerning contraceptives."

The Supreme Court affirmed the judgment of the District Court.

V. JUSTICE VOTE

7 Pro ACLU Side vs. 2 Con Opposing Side

ACLU Side (Respondent/Appellee)

1. Brennan, W. – Wrote majority opinion
2. Stewart, P. – Joined majority opinion
3. Marshall, T. – Joined majority opinion
4. Blackmun, H. – Joined majority opinion
5. Stevens, J. – Joined majority opinion
6. White, B. – Joined majority opinion
7. Powell, L. – Joined majority opinion

Opposing Side (Petitioner/Appellant)

1. Burger, W. – Wrote dissenting opinion
2. Rehnquist, W. – Wrote dissenting opinion

VI. A WIN OR LOSS FOR THE ACLU?

The ACLU filed as amicus curiae urging affirmance; the Supreme Court affirmed the ruling of the District Court for the Southern District of New York in a 7-2 vote, giving the ACLU an apparent win.

390. Lefkowitz v. Cunningham

(Decided June 13, 1977; 431 U.S. 801)

I. ISSUE

A. Issues Discussed

Criminal procedure, Fifth Amendment, Fourteenth Amendment, self-incrimination

B. Legal Question Presented

"[W]hether [pursuant to a New York statute] a political party officer can be removed from his position by the State of New York and barred for five years from holding any other party or public office, because he has refused to waive his constitutional privilege against compelled self-incrimination."

C. Supreme Court's Answer

The statute violates the Fifth Amendment privilege against compelled self-incrimination.

II. CASE SUMMARY

A. Background

Patrick J. Cunningham, appellee, held "four unsalaried elective positions in the Democratic Party of the State of New York." In December of 1975, he received a subpoena to "appear and testify before a special grand jury authorized to investigate his conduct in the political offices he then held," pursuant to § 22 of the New

York Election Law. Section 22 allows for a political party officer to be subpoenaed by a grand jury and then required to testify concerning his conduct in office. Moreover, if "the officer refuses to answer any question, or if he declines to waive immunity from the use of his testimony against him in a later prosecution, the statute immediately terminates his party office and prohibits him from holding any other party or public office for a period of five years."

Before the state courts, appellee moved to quash the subpoena, arguing that "§ 22 violated his federal constitutional right to be free of compelled self-incrimination; his motion was denied." In April 1976, he appeared before a grand jury in response to the subpoena, but he "refused to sign a waiver of immunity form which would have waived his constitutional right not to be compelled to incriminate himself. Because § 22 is self-executing, appellee's refusal automatically divested him of all his party offices and activated the five-year ban on holding any party or public office."

The next day, appellee brought suit in the District Court for the Southern District of New York. Following a hearing, "the District Judge issued a temporary restraining order against enforcement of § 22." A three-judge court then "granted appellee declaratory and permanent injunctive relief against enforcement of § 22 on the ground that it violated appellee's Fifth and Fourteenth Amendment rights."

The Supreme Court granted certiorari to review the case and affirmed.

B. Counsel of Record/ACLU Attorney

ACLU Side (Respondent/Appellee): Michael E. Tigar argued the cause for appellee.

Opposing Side (Petitioner/Appellant): Irving Galt, Assistant Attorney General of New York, argued the cause for appellant.

III. AMICI CURIAE

ACLU Side (Respondent/Appellee)

Brief of amici curiae filed on behalf of the ACLU, et al., by Burt Neuborne, Melvin L. Wulf, and Joel M. Gora.

Opposing Side (Petitioner/Appellant)

No briefs of amici curiae were filed in support of appellant.

IV. THE SUPREME COURT'S DECISION

"[T]he Fifth Amendment privilege against compelled self-incrimination protects grand jury witnesses from being forced to give testimony which may later be used to convict them in a criminal proceeding. [T]he privilege is available to a witness in a civil proceeding, as well as to a defendant in a criminal prosecution. In either situation the witness may 'refuse to answer unless and until he is protected at least against the use of his compelled answers and evidence derived therefrom in any subsequent criminal case in which he is a defendant.'

Thus, when a State compels testimony by threatening to inflict potent sanctions unless the constitutional privilege is surrendered, that testimony is obtained in violation of the Fifth Amendment and cannot be used against the declarant in a subsequent criminal prosecution.

[O]ur cases have established that a State may not impose substantial penalties because a witness elects to exercise his Fifth Amendment right not to give incriminating testimony against himself. In Gardner v. Broderick, . . . this Court held that [an] officer could not be discharged solely for his refusal to forfeit the rights guaranteed him by the Fifth Amendment; the privilege against compelled self-incrimination could not abide any 'attempt, regardless of its ultimate effectiveness, to coerce a waiver of the immunity it confers on penalty of the loss of employment.' At the same time, [p]ublic employees may constitutionally be discharged for refusing to answer potentially incriminating questions concerning their official duties if they have not been required to surrender their constitutional immunity. . . .

The touchstone of the Fifth Amendment is compulsion, and direct economic sanctions and imprisonment are not the only penalties capable of forcing the self-incrimination which the Amendment forbids. . . . Section 22 confronted appellee with grave consequences solely because he refused to waive immunity from prosecution and give self-incriminating testimony. . . . In assessing the coercion which § 22 exerts, we must take into account potential economic benefits realistically likely of attainment. . . .

Section 22 is coercive for yet another reason: It requires appellee to forfeit one constitutionally protected right as the price for exercising another. . . . By depriving appellee of his offices, § 22 impinges on his right to participate in private, voluntary political associations. That right is an important aspect of First Amendment freedom which this Court has consistently found entitled to constitutional protection. . . .

Accordingly, the judgment is affirmed."

V. JUSTICE VOTE

7 Pro ACLU Side vs. 1 Con Opposing Side

ACLU Side (Respondent/Appellee)

1. Burger, W. – Wrote majority opinion
2. Stewart, P. – Joined majority opinion
3. White, B. – Joined majority opinion
4. Blackmun, H. – Joined majority opinion
5. Powell, L. – Joined majority opinion
6. Brennan, W. – Wrote concurring opinion
7. Marshall, T. – Joined Brennan's concurrence

Opposing Side (Petitioner/Appellant)

1. Stevens, J. – Wrote dissenting opinion

Rehnquist, W – Took no part in the decision

VI. A WIN OR LOSS FOR THE ACLU?

The ACLU filed as amicus curiae urging affirmance; the Supreme Court affirmed the ruling of the District Court for the Southern District of New York in a 7-1 vote, giving the ACLU an apparent win.

391. Smith v. Org. of Foster Families for Equality & Reform

(Decided June 13, 1977; 431 U.S. 816)

I. ISSUE

A. Issues Discussed

Privacy

B. Legal Question Presented

"[W]hether the District Court correctly held that the present procedures preceding the removal from a foster home of children resident there a year or more are constitutionally inadequate."

C. Supreme Court's Answer

"[W]e hold that the procedures provided by New York State in s 392 and by New York City's SSC Procedure No. 5 are adequate to protect whatever liberty interest appellees may have . . . ."

II. CASE SUMMARY

A. Background

"Appellees, individual foster parents and an organization of foster parents, brought this civil rights class action pursuant to 42 U.S.C. s 1983 in the United States District Court for the Southern District of New York, on their own behalf and on behalf of children for whom they have provided homes for a year or more. They sought declaratory and injunctive relief against New York State and New York City officials, alleging that the procedures governing the removal of foster children from foster homes provided in N.Y.Soc.Serv. Law ss 383(2) and 400 (McKinney 1976), and in 18 N.Y.C.R.R. s 450.14 (1974) violated the Due Process and Equal Protection Clauses of the Fourteenth Amendment. The District Court appointed independent counsel for the foster children to forestall any possibility of conflict between their interests and the interests asserted by the foster parents. A group of natural mothers of children in foster care were granted leave to intervene on behalf of themselves and others similarly situated.

A divided three-judge District Court concluded that 'the pre-removal procedures presently employed by the State are constitutionally defective,' holding that 'before a foster child can be peremptorily transferred from the foster home in which he has been living, be it to another foster home or to the natural parents who initially placed him in foster care, he is entitled to a hearing at which all concerned parties may present any relevant information to the administrative decisionmaker charged with determining the future placement of the child.' Four appeals to this Court were taken from the ensuing judgment declaring the challenged statutes unconstitutional and permanently enjoining their enforcement. . . . [The Supreme Court] noted probable jurisdiction of the four appeals."

B. Counsel of Record

ACLU Side (Respondent/Appellee): Marcia Robinson Lowry of the Children's Rights Project, New York Civil Liberties Union argued the cause for appellees in all cases. With her on the brief were Rena K. Uviller and Martin Guggenheim of the Juvenile Rights Project, American Civil Liberties Union, and Thomas Litwack of the New York Civil Liberties Union.

Opposing Side (Petitioner/Appellant): Maria L. Marcus, Assistant Attorney General of New York, argued the cause for appellants in Nos. 76-180 and 76-183. With her on the briefs for appellants in No. 76-183 were Louis J. Lefkowitz, Attorney General, Samuel A. Hirshowitz, First Assistant Attorney General, and Mark C. Rutzick, Assistant Attorney General. W. Bernard Richland, Leonard Koerner, and Elliot P. Hoffman filed briefs for appellants in No. 76-180. Louise Gruner Gans argued the cause for appellants in No. 76-5193. With her on the brief was Marttie L. Thompson. Helen L. Buttenwieser argued the cause for appellants in No. 76-5200. With her on the briefs was Ephraim London.

III. AMICI CURIAE

ACLU Side (Respondent/Appellee)

Brief of amici curiae filed on behalf of A Group of Concerned Persons for Children by Joseph Goldstein, Sonja Goldstein, Robert A. Burt, Paul D Gewirtz, and Stephen Wizner.

Brief of amici curiae filed on behalf of the Community Service Society of New York by William B. Haley.

Brief of amici curiae filed on behalf of the Legal Aid Society of New York City, Juvenile Rights Division by Michael J Dale, Gene B. Mechanic, and Carol Sherman.

Opposing Side (Petitioner/Appellant)

Brief of amici curiae filed on behalf of the National Juvenile Law Center by Paul Piersma.

Brief of amici curiae filed on behalf of the Puerto Rican Family Institute, Inc., et al. by Herbert Teitelbaum.

IV. THE SUPREME COURT'S DECISION

"The relief sought in this case is entirely procedural. Our task is only to determine whether the District Court correctly held that the present procedures preceding the removal from a foster home of children resident there a year or more are constitutionally inadequate. To that task we now turn. . . .

Our first inquiry is whether appellees have asserted interests within the Fourteenth Amendment's protection of 'liberty' and 'property.'

The appellees have not renewed in this Court their contention, rejected by the District Court, that the realities of the foster-care system in New York gave them a justified expectation amounting to a 'property' interest that their status as foster parents would be continued. Our inquiry is therefore narrowed to the question whether their asserted interests are within the 'liberty' protected by the Fourteenth Amendment. . . .

[A]ppellees' claim to a constitutionally protected liberty interest raises complex and novel questions. It is unnecessary for us to resolve those questions definitively in this case, however, for like the District Court, we conclude that 'narrower grounds exist to support' our reversal. We are persuaded that, even on the assumption that appellees have a protected 'liberty interest,' the District Court erred in holding that the preremoval procedures presently employed by the State are constitutionally defective. . . .

Where procedural due process must be afforded because a 'liberty' or 'property' interest is within the Fourteenth Amendment's protection, there must be determined 'what process is due' in the particular context. The District Court did not spell out precisely what sort of preremoval hearing would be necessary to meet the constitutional standard . . . .

Turning first to the procedure applicable in New York City, SSC Procedure No. 5, see supra, at 2103, and n.29, provides that before a child is removed from a foster home for transfer to another foster home, the foster parents may request an 'independent review.' . . . The District Court found the procedure inadequate on four grounds, none of which we find sufficient to justify the holding that the procedure violates due process. . . .

We deal here with issues of unusual delicacy, in an area where professional judgments regarding desirable procedures are constantly and rapidly changing. In such a context, restraint is appropriate on the part of courts called upon to adjudicate whether a particular procedural scheme is adequate under the Constitution. Since we hold that the procedures provided by New York State in s 392 and by New York City's SSC Procedure No. 5 are adequate to protect whatever liberty interest appellees may have, the judgment of the District Court is reversed."

V. JUSTICE VOTE

0 Pro ACLU Side vs. 9 Con Opposing Side

Opposing Side (Petitioner/Appellant)

1. Brennan, W. – Wrote majority opinion
2. White, B. – Joined majority opinion
3. Marshall, T. – Joined majority opinion
4. Stewart, P. – Wrote concurring opinion
5. Powell, L. – Joined majority opinion
6. Rehnquist, W. – Joined Stewart's concurrence
7. Burger, W. – Joined Stewart's concurrence
8. Blackmun, H. – Joined majority opinion
9. Stevens, J. – Joined majority opinion

VI. A WIN OR LOSS FOR THE ACLU?

The ACLU served as counsel for appellee urging affirmance of the judgment of the U.S. District Court for the Southern District of New York; the Supreme Court reversed, in a 9-0 vote, giving the ACLU an apparent loss.

392. National Socialist Party of America v. Village of Skokie

(Decided June 14, 1977; 432 U.S. 43)

I. ISSUE

A. Issues Discussed

First Amendment, freedom of speech, injunctions

B. Legal Question Presented

Should the Illinois Supreme Court have granted a stay pending the appeal on the injunction against appellants, denying them the right to demonstrate in the village of Skokie?

C. Supreme Court's Answer

The Illinois Supreme Court should have granted a stay of the injunction pending appeal to avoid denying constitutionally protected rights to appellants.

II. CASE SUMMARY

A. Background

"On April 29, 1977, the Circuit Court of Cook County entered an injunction against petitioners. The injunction prohibited them from performing any of the following actions within the village of Skokie, Ill.: '[m]arching, walking or parading in the uniform of the National Socialist Party of America; [m]arching, walking or parading or otherwise displaying the swastika on or off their person; [d]istributing pamphlets or displaying any materials which incite or promote hatred against persons of Jewish faith or ancestry or hatred against persons of any faith or ancestry, race or religion.'

The Illinois Appellate Court denied an application for stay pending appeal. Applicants then filed a petition for a stay in the Illinois Supreme Court, together with a request for a direct expedited appeal to that court. The Illinois Supreme Court denied both the stay and leave for an expedited appeal. Applicants then filed an application for a stay with Mr. Justice Stevens, as Circuit Justice, who referred the matter to the Court."

On certiorari the U.S. Supreme Court reversed the order of the Illinois Supreme Court and ordered a stay.

B. Counsel of Record/ACLU Attorney

ACLU Side (Petitioner/Appellant): David A. Golberger and Barbara O'Toole, both of the ACLU, argued the cause on remand, counsel at the Supreme Court level not known.[1]

Opposing Side (Respondent/Appellee): Harvey Schwartz and Gilbert Gordon argued the cause on remand, counsel at the Supreme Court level not known.[2]

III. AMICI CURIAE

ACLU Side (Petitioner/Appellant)

No briefs of amici curiae were filed in support of appellant.

Opposing Side (Respondent/Appellee)

No briefs of amici curiae were filed in support of appellee.

IV. THE SUPREME COURT'S DECISION

"Treating the application as a petition for certiorari from the order of the Illinois Supreme Court, we grant certiorari and reverse the Illinois Supreme Court's denial of a stay. That order is a final judgment for purposes of our jurisdiction, since it involved a right 'separable from, and collateral to' the merits. It finally determined the merits of petitioners' claim that the outstanding injunction will deprive them of rights protected by the First Amendment during the period of appellate review which, in the normal course,

1 Village of Skokie v. National Socialist Party of America, 366 N.E.2d 347 (Ill. App. Ct. 1977).
2 Village of Skokie v. National Socialist Party of America, 366 N.E.2d 347 (Ill. App. Ct. 1977).

may take a year or more to complete. If a State seeks to impose a restraint of this kind, it must provide strict procedural safeguards, including immediate appellate review. Absent such review, the State must instead allow a stay. The order of the Illinois Supreme Court constituted a denial of that right."

The U.S. Supreme Court reversed the order of the Illinois Supreme Court and remanded for further proceedings.

V. JUSTICE VOTE

5 Pro ACLU Side vs. 4 Con Opposing Side

ACLU Side (Petitioner/Appellant)

1. Brennan, W. – Per curiam decision
2. Marshall, T. – Per curiam decision
3. Stevens, J. – Per curiam decision
4. Blackmun, H. – Per curiam decision
5. Powell, L. – Per curiam decision

Opposing Side (Respondent/Appellee)

1. White, B. – Wrote dissenting opinion
2. Rehnquist, W. – Wrote dissenting opinion
3. Burger, W. – Joined Rehnquist's dissent
4. Stewart, P. – Joined Rehnquist's dissent

VI. A WIN OR LOSS FOR THE ACLU?

The ACLU, as counsel of record, urged reversal of the order of the Illinois Supreme Court; the U.S. Supreme Court reversed in a per curiam decision and in a 5-4 vote, giving the ACLU an apparent win.

393. Trans World Airlines, Inc. v. Hardison

(Decided June 16, 1977; 432 U.S. 63)

I. ISSUE

A. Issues Discussed

First Amendment, religion, Civil Rights Act of 1964

B. Legal Question Presented

What is "the extent of the employer's obligation under Title VII [of the Civil Rights Act of 1964] to accommodate an employee whose religious beliefs prohibit him from working on Saturdays"?

C. Supreme Court's Answer

The employer met its obligation under Civil Rights Act in this circumstance.

II. CASE SUMMARY

A. Background

Petitioner Trans World Airlines (TWA) hired respondent Larry G. Hardison "to work as a clerk in the Stores Department. [T]he Stores Department must operate 24 hours per day, 365 days per year." Employment positions in that department must be filled at all times. Respondent was subject to a seniority system contained in the collective-bargaining agreement with petitioner International Association of Machinists and Aerospace Workers (IAM). First choice for job and shift assignments goes to the most senior employees. The most junior employees are required to work when the union steward is unable to find people to work particular shifts or in a particular job.

Respondent became a member of the Worldwide Church of God and his religion required that he refrain from performing any work from sunset on Friday until sunset on Saturday. The Stores Department manager was notified and agreed to work out a schedule for respondent in line with his religious practice. The problem was temporarily solved when respondent transferred to a night shift. However, respondent soon bid for and was transferred to another building with separate seniority lists. This move placed respondent much lower on the seniority list.

In the new building, "Hardison was asked to work Saturdays when a fellow employee went on vacation. TWA agreed to permit the union to seek a change of work assignments for Hardison, but the union was not willing to violate the seniority provisions set out in the collective-bargaining contract, and Hardison had insufficient seniority to bid for a shift having Saturdays off." The company rejected a proposal that respondent work only four days a week. "When an accommodation was not reached, Hardison refused to report for work on Saturdays. . . . After a hearing, Hardison was discharged on grounds of insubordination for refusing to work during his designated shift."

Respondent "brought this action for injunctive relief in the United States District Court against TWA and IAM, claiming that his discharge by TWA constituted religious discrimination in violation of Title VII." Additionally, he charged IAM with discrimination for "failing to represent him adequately in his dispute with TWA and [for] depriving him of his right to exercise his religious beliefs." The "District Court ruled in favor of the defendants." The court ruled that "the union's duty to accommodate Hardison's belief did not require it to ignore its seniority system." As to TWA, the court ruled that it had satisfied its "reasonable accommodations" obligation. On appeal, the Court of Appeals for the Eighth Circuit reversed the judgment for TWA, and affirmed the judgment for the union.

"In separate petitions for certiorari TWA and IAM contended that adequate steps had been taken to accommodate Hardison's religious observances."

The Supreme Court granted both petitions for certiorari and reversed.

B. Counsel of Record/ACLU Attorney

ACLU Side (Respondent/Appellee): William F. Pickett argued the cause for appellees.

Nathan Lewin argued the cause for the National Jewish Commission on Law and Public Affairs, as amicus curiae, by special leave of court.

Opposing Side (Petitioner/Appellant): George E. Feldmiller and Mozart G. Ratner argued the cause for appellants.

III. AMICI CURIAE

ACLU Side (Respondent/Appellee)

Brief of amici curiae filed on behalf of the ACLU by Joel M. Gora and Leo Pfeffer.

Brief of amici curiae filed on behalf of the National Jewish Commission on Law and Public Affairs by Nathan Lewin, Dennis Rapps, and Howard I. Rhine.

Additional briefs of amici curiae were filed by on behalf of the United States, et al., the State of Michigan, the New York State Division of Human Rights, the Central Conference of American Rabbis, et al., the General Conference of Seventh-Day Adventists, and the Worldwide Church of God.

Opposing Side (Petitioner/Appellant)

Briefs of amici curiae urging reversal were filed on behalf of the Chrysler Corporation, and the Equal Employment Advisory Council.

IV. THE SUPREME COURT'S DECISION

"Section 703(a)(1) of the Civil Rights Act of 1964, Title VII, makes it an unlawful employment practice for an employer to discriminate against an employee or a prospective employee on the basis of his or her religion. At the time of the events involved here, a guideline of the Equal Employment Opportunity Commission (EEOC), required, as the Act itself now does, that an employer, short of 'undue hardship,' make 'reasonable accommodations' to the religious needs of its employees. . . .

The Court of Appeals held that TWA had not made reasonable efforts to accommodate Hardison's religious needs under the 1967 EEOC guidelines in effect at the time the relevant events occurred. In its view, TWA had rejected three reasonable alternatives, any one of which would have satisfied its obligation without undue hardship.

[T]he seniority system represents a neutral way of minimizing the number of occasions when an employee must work on a day that he would prefer to have off. Additionally, recognizing that weekend work schedules are the least popular, the company made further accommodation by reducing its work force to a bare minimum on those days. . . .

We are also convinced, contrary to the Court of Appeals, that TWA itself cannot be faulted for having failed to work out a shift or job swap for Hardison. Both the union and TWA had agreed to the seniority system; the union was unwilling to entertain a variance over the objections of men senior to Hardison; and for TWA to have arranged unilaterally for a swap would have amounted to a breach of the collective-bargaining agreement.

[N]either a collective-bargaining contract nor a seniority system may be employed to violate the statute, but we do not believe that the duty to accommodate requires TWA to take steps inconsistent with the otherwise valid agreement. Collective bargaining, aimed at effecting workable and enforceable agreements between management and labor, lies at the core of our national labor policy, and seniority provisions are universally included in these contracts. Without a clear and express indication from Congress, we cannot agree with Hardison and the EEOC that an agreed-upon seniority system must give way when necessary to accommodate religious observances. . . .

The repeated, unequivocal emphasis of both the language and the legislative history of Title VII is on eliminating discrimination in employment, and such discrimination is proscribed when it is directed against majorities as well as minorities. . . . It would be anomalous to conclude that by 'reasonable accommodation' Congress meant that an employer must deny the shift and job preference of some employees, as well as deprive them of their contractual rights, in order to accommodate or prefer the religious needs of others, and we conclude that Title VII does not require an employer to go that far. . . .

'[T]he unmistakable purpose of § 703(h) was to make clear that the routine application of a bona fide seniority system would not be unlawful under Title VII.' . . . Thus, absent a discriminatory purpose, the operation of a seniority system cannot be an unlawful employment practice even if the system has some discriminatory consequences.

There has been no suggestion of discriminatory intent in this case. . . . TWA was not required by Title VII to carve out a special exception to its seniority system in order to help Hardison to meet his religious obligations.

[T]he paramount concern of Congress in enacting Title VII was the elimination of discrimination in employment. In the absence of clear statutory language or legislative history to the contrary, we will not readily construe the statute to require an employer to discriminate against some employees in order to enable others to observe their Sabbath.

Reversed."

V. JUSTICE VOTE

2 Pro ACLU Side vs. 7 Con Opposing Side

ACLU Side (Respondent/Appellee)

1. Marshall, T. – Wrote dissenting opinion
2. Brennan, W. – Joined Marshall's dissent

Opposing Side (Petitioner/Appellant)

1. White, B. – Wrote majority opinion
2. Burger, W. – Joined majority opinion
3. Stewart, P. – Joined majority opinion
4. Blackmun, H. – Joined majority opinion
5. Powell, L. – Joined majority opinion
6. Rehnquist, W. – Joined majority opinion
7. Stevens, J. – Joined majority opinion

VI. A WIN OR LOSS FOR THE ACLU?

The ACLU filed as amicus curiae urging affirmance; the Supreme Court reversed the ruling of the Court of Appeals for the Eighth Circuit in a 7-2 vote, giving the ACLU an apparent loss.

394. United States v. Chadwick

(Decided June 21, 1977; 433 U.S. 1)

I. ISSUE

A. Issues Discussed

Criminal justice, drugs, Fourth Amendment, search and seizure

B. Legal Question Presented

"[W]hether a search warrant is required before federal agents may open a locked footlocker which they have lawfully seized at the time of the arrest of its owners, when there is probable cause to believe the footlocker contains contraband."

C. Supreme Court's Answer

The federal agents were required to obtain a search warrant before opening the footlocker because there was no exception to the warrant requirement in this circumstance.

II. CASE SUMMARY

A. Background

On May 8, 1973, respondents Gregory Machado and Bridget Leary boarded an Amtrak train in San Diego, California heading to Boston, Massachusetts. Respondents brought with them a large heavy brown footlocker which aroused suspicions among the Amtrak officials. The officials reported the suspicious activities to the San Diego federal agents who in turn informed federal agents in Boston.

On arrival in Boston two days later, federal narcotics agents identified respondents as they collected their luggage. Although the agents did not obtain either an arrest or search warrant, they kept respondents under surveillance, and directed a narcotics dog towards the footlocker without alerting the respondents. The agents continued their surveillance after the dog signaled the presence of controlled substances within the locker.

Respondent Chadwick joined Machado and Leary after they exited the train, and lifted the footlocker into his automobile. Before they started the car to drive off, agents arrested all three respondents. A search of the respondents' bodies and their automobile revealed no weapons or other contraband.

Respondents were then taken to the Federal Building along with the automobile and footlocker. An hour and a half after the arrests, agents opened the footlocker and luggage without obtaining respondents' consent or securing a search warrant. They found large amounts of marijuana in the footlocker.

"Respondents were indicted for possession of marijuana with intent to distribute it." Prior to the start of their trial, the District Court granted the respondents' pretrial motion to suppress the evidence collected from the footlocker. The Court of Appeals of the First Circuit affirmed the suppression of evidence.

The Supreme Court granted certiorari to review the case and affirmed.

B. Counsel of Record/ACLU Attorney

ACLU Side (Respondent/Appellee): Martin G. Weinberg argued the cause for appellee.

Opposing Side (Petitioner/Appellant): A. Raymond Randolph, Jr., argued the cause for appellant.

III. AMICI CURIAE

ACLU Side (Respondent/Appellee)

Brief of amici curiae filed on behalf of the ACLU, et al., by Joel M. Gora, Jack D. Novik, and John Reinstein.

Opposing Side (Petitioner/Appellant)

Brief of amici curiae filed on behalf of Americans for Effective Law Enforcement, Inc., et al., by Frank Carrington, Glen R. Murphy, Cecil Hicks, and James P. Costello.

IV. THE SUPREME COURT'S DECISION

"We do not agree that the Warrant Clause [of the Fourth Amendment] protects only dwellings and other specifically designated locales. As we have noted before, the Fourth Amendment 'protects people, not places,' more particularly, it protects people from unreasonable government intrusions into their legitimate expectations of privacy. In this case, the Warrant Clause makes a significant contribution to that protection.

[I]t would be a mistake to conclude, as the Government contends, that the Warrant clause was therefore intended to guard only against intrusions into the home. First, the Warrant Clause does not in terms distinguish between searches conducted in private homes and other searches. There is also a strong historical connection between the Warrant Clause and the initial clause of the Fourth Amendment, which draws no distinctions among 'persons, houses, papers, and effects' in safeguarding against unreasonable searches and seizures. . . .

The judicial warrant has a significant role to play in that it provides the detached scrutiny of a neutral magistrate, which is a more reliable safeguard against improper searches than the hurried judgment of a law enforcement officer . . . .

In this case, important Fourth Amendment privacy interests were at stake. By placing personal effects inside a double-locked footlocker, respondents manifested an expectation that the contents would remain free from public examination. No less than one who locks the doors of his home against intruders, one who safeguards his personal possessions in this manner is due the protections of the Fourth Amendment Warrant Clause. There being no exigency, it was unreasonable for the Government to conduct this search without the safeguards a judicial warrant provides. . . .

Here the search was conducted more than an hour after federal agents had gained exclusive control of the footlocker and long after respondents were securely in custody; the search therefore cannot be viewed as incidental to the arrest or as justified by any other exigency. Even though on this record the issuance of a warrant by a judicial officer was reasonably predictable, a line must be drawn. In our view, when no exigency is shown to support the need for an immediate search, the Warrant Clause places the line at the point where the property to be searched comes under the exclusive dominion of police authority. Respondents were therefore entitled to the protections of the Warrant Clause with the evaluation of a neutral magistrate, before their privacy interests in the contents of the footlocker were invaded.

Accordingly, the judgment [of the Court of Appeals] is affirmed."

V. JUSTICE VOTE

7 Pro ACLU Side vs. 2 Con Opposing Side

ACLU Side (Respondent/Appellee)

1. Burger, W. – Wrote majority opinion
2. Stewart, P. – Joined majority opinion
3. Powell, L. – Joined majority opinion
4. Marshall, T. – Joined dissenting opinion
5. Stevens, J. – Joined majority opinion
6. White, B. – Joined majority opinion
7. Brennan, W. – Wrote concurring opinion

Opposing Side (Petitioner/Appellant)

1. Blackmun, H. – Wrote dissenting opinion
2. Rehnquist, W. – Joined Blackmun's dissent

VI. A WIN OR LOSS FOR THE ACLU?

The ACLU filed as amicus curiae urging affirmance; the Supreme Court affirmed the judgment of the Court of Appeals in a 7-2 vote, giving the ACLU an apparent win.

395. Hazelwood School District v. United States

(Decided June 27, 1977; 433 U.S. 299)

I. ISSUE

A. Issues Discussed

Civil rights, race, employment discrimination, Fourteenth Amendment

B. Legal Question Presented

Does proof of a comparatively small percentage of minority employees within a school district constitute probative evidence to prove a 'pattern or practice' of discrimination under Title VII of the Civil Rights Act of 1964?

C. Supreme Court's Answer

The case must be remanded to determine if the evidence shows proof of discrimination in this circumstance as the previous inquiry was insufficient.

II. CASE SUMMARY

A. Background

Petitioner Hazelwood School District was formed from 13 rural school districts by annexation. There were many applications for teaching positions, and the district could not interview all applicants for positions when there were vacancies. Those applicants who had submitted their applications most recently were the most likely to be chosen for an interview. At the schools, the principals conducting interviews were only given general instructions to hire the 'most competent' person available.

In an effort to recruit new teachers, Hazelwood School District staff visited colleges and universities in and near Missouri. "All of the institutions visited were predominately white." Hazelwood did not "seriously recruit" at either of the predominately African-American four-year colleges in Missouri. In 1969, the school district hired its first African-American teacher. The number of African-American faculty members gradually increased, but was still very low compared to other school districts.

In 1973, the U.S. Attorney General brought a lawsuit against the Hazelwood County School District and its officials alleging they "engaged in a 'pattern or practice' of employment discrimination in violation of Title VII of the Civil Rights Act of 1964." The Attorney General sought an injunction requiring the school district to "cease its discriminatory practices, to take affirmative steps to obtain qualified [African-American] faculty members, and to offer employment and give backpay to victims of past illegal discrimination."

The District Court ruled that the Government had not established a pattern or practice of discrimination and ruled in favor of Hazelwood. On appeal, the Court of Appeals for the Eighth Circuit reversed, holding that the statistical disparity, when viewed in light of Hazelwood's teacher-hiring procedures, constituted sufficient evidence of "a pattern or practice of racial discrimination."

The Supreme Court granted certiorari to review the case, and vacated and remanded.

B. Counsel of Record/ACLU Attorney

ACLU Side (Respondent/Appellee): Deputy Solicitor General Lawrence G. Wallace argued the cause for the United States

Opposing Side (Petitioner/Appellant): William H. Allen argued the cause for appellant.

III. AMICI CURIAE

ACLU Side (Respondent/Appellee)

Brief of amici curiae filed on behalf of the ACLU by Robert Allen Sedler and Joel M. Gora.

Additional briefs of amici curiae were filed on behalf of the Lawyers' Committee for Civil Rights Under Law, the NAACP Legal Defense and Educational Fund, Inc., and the National Education Association.

Opposing Side (Petitioner/Appellant)

No briefs of amici curiae were filed in support of appellant.

IV. THE SUPREME COURT'S DECISION

"This Court's recent consideration . . . of the role of statistics in pattern-or-practice suits under Title VII provides substantial guidance. [Previously,] we stated that it is the Government's burden to 'establish by a preponderance of the evidence that racial discrimination was the [employer's] standard operating procedure—the regular rather than the unusual practice.' . . . Where gross statistical disparities can be shown, they alone may in a proper case constitute prima facie proof of a pattern or practice of discrimination. . . .

The Court of Appeals was correct in the view that a proper comparison was between the racial composition of Hazelwood's teaching staff and the racial composition of the qualified public school teacher population in the relevant labor market. . . . Although these differences were on their face substantial, the Court of Appeals erred in substituting its judgment for that of the District Court and holding that the Government had conclusively proved its 'pattern or practice' lawsuit.

The Court of Appeals totally disregarded the possibility that this prima facie statistical proof in the record might at the trial court level be rebutted by statistics dealing with Hazelwood's hiring after it became subject to Title VII. . . . For this reason, the Court cautioned in the Teamsters opinion that once a prima facie case has been established by statistical work-force disparities, the employer must be given an opportunity to show that 'the claimed discriminatory pattern is a product of pre-Act hiring rather than unlawful post-Act discrimination.' . . .

It is thus clear that a determination of the appropriate comparative figures in this case will depend upon further evaluation by the trial court. As this Court admonished in Teamsters: '[S]tatistics . . . come in infinite variety . . . . [T]heir usefulness depends on all of the surrounding facts and circumstances.' . . .

We hold, therefore, that the Court of Appeals erred in disregarding the post-Act hiring statistics in the record, and that it should have remanded the case to the District Court for further findings as to the relevant labor market area and for an ultimate determination of whether Hazelwood engaged in a pattern or practice of employment discrimination after March 24, 1972. Accordingly, the judgment is vacated, and the case is remanded to the District Court for further proceedings consistent with this opinion."

V. JUSTICE VOTE

1 Pro ACLU Side vs. 8 Con Opposing Side

ACLU Side (Respondent/Appellee)

1. Stevens, J. – Wrote dissenting opinion

Opposing Side (Petitioner/Appellant)

1. Stewart, P. – Wrote majority opinion
2. Burger, W. – Joined majority opinion
3. Marshall, T. – Joined majority opinion
4. Blackmun, H. – Joined majority opinion
5. Powell, L. – Joined majority opinion
6. Rehnquist, W. – Joined majority opinion
7. Brennan, W. – Wrote concurring opinion
8. White, B. – Wrote concurring opinion

VI. A WIN OR LOSS FOR THE ACLU?

The ACLU filed as amicus curiae urging affirmance; the Supreme Court vacated the ruling of the Court of Appeals for the Eighth Circuit in an 8-1 vote, giving the ACLU an apparent loss.

396. Dothard v. Rawlinson

(Decided June 27, 1977; 433 U.S. 321)

I. ISSUE

A. Issues Discussed

Civil rights, gender, Fourteenth Amendment, equal protection, Civil Rights Act of 1964

B. Legal Question Presented

Do the height and weight requirements for employment as a prison guard, and a regulation determining job placement based on gender in the Alabama Board of Corrections violate Title VII of the Civil Rights Act of 1964 and Equal Protection Clause of the Fourteenth Amendment?

C. Supreme Court's Answer

The height and weight requirements violate Title VII, however, the gender-based regulation is a bona fide occupational qualification.

II. CASE SUMMARY

A. Background

After graduating college with a degree in correctional psychology, appellee Dianne Rawlinson applied for a position as a correctional counselor trainee with appellant, the Alabama Board of Corrections. Her application was rejected due to her failure to meet the minimum 120-pound weight requirement. The Alabama statute establishing the weight requirement also established a 5 feet 2 inches height minimum.

Appellee filed a class-action complaint in the District Court for the Middle District of Alabama, challenging the statutory height and weight requirements as violations of Title VII of the Civil Rights Act of 1964 and the Equal Protection Clause of the Fourteenth Amendment. When the Alabama Board of Corrections established Regulation 204, creating gender-based criteria for correctional counselor assignments, appellee amended her complaint to include a challenge to this regulation. The court found in appellee's favor.

The Supreme Court granted certiorari to review the case, affirmed in part, and reversed in part.

B. Counsel of Record/ACLU Attorney

ACLU Side (Respondent/Appellee): Pamela S. Horowitz argued the cause for appellee, pro hac vice, by special leave of court.

Opposing Side (Petitioner/Appellant): G. Daniel Evans, Assistant Attorney General of Alabama, argued the cause for appellant, pro hac vice, by special leave of court.

III. AMICI CURIAE

ACLU Side (Respondent/Appellee)

Brief of amici curiae filed on behalf of the ACLU by Ruth Bader Ginsburg, Marjorie Mazen Smith, and Joel Gora.

Additional briefs of amici curiae were filed on behalf of the

State of California, the Washington State Human Rights Commission, and the Women's Legal Defense Fund, et al.

Opposing Side (Petitioner/Appellant)

No briefs of amici curiae were filed in support of appellant.

IV. THE SUPREME COURT'S DECISION

"The gist of the claim that the statutory height and weight requirements discriminate against women does not involve an assertion of purposeful discriminatory motive. It is asserted, rather, that these facially neutral qualification standards work in fact disproportionately to exclude women from eligibility for employment by the Alabama Board of Corrections. . . .

We turn, therefore, to the appellants' argument that they have rebutted the prima facie case of discrimination by showing that the height and weight requirements are job related. These requirements, they say, have a relationship to strength, a sufficient but unspecified amount of which is essential to effective job performance as a correctional counselor. In the District Court, however, the appellants produced no evidence correlating the height and weight requirements with the requisite amount of strength thought essential to good job performance. . . .

For the reasons we have discussed, the District Court was not in error in holding that Title VII of the Civil Rights Act of 1964, as amended, prohibits application of the statutory height and weight requirements to Rawlinson and the class she represents. . . .

Unlike the statutory height and weight requirements, Regulation 204 explicitly discriminates against women on the basis of their sex. In defense of this overt discrimination, the appellants rely on § 703(e) of Title VII, which permits sex-based discrimination 'in those certain instances where . . . sex . . . is a bona fide occupational qualification reasonably necessary to the normal operation of that particular business or enterprise.' . . .

In the usual case, the argument that a particular job is too dangerous for women may appropriately be met by the rejoinder that it is the purpose of Title VII to allow the individual woman to make that choice for herself. More is at stake in this case, however, than an individual woman's decision to weigh and accept the risks of employment in a 'contact' position in a maximum-security male prison.

The essence of a correctional counselor's job is to maintain prison security. A woman's relative ability to maintain order in a male, maximum-security, unclassified penitentiary of the type Alabama now runs could be directly reduced by her womanhood. There is a basis in fact for expecting that sex offenders who have criminally assaulted women in the past would be moved to do so again if access to women were established within the prison. There would also be a real risk that other inmates, deprived of a normal heterosexual environment, would assault women guards because they were women. . . .The likelihood that inmates would assault a woman because she was a woman would pose a real threat not only to the victim of the assault but also to the basic control of the penitentiary and protection of its inmates and the other security personnel. The employee's very womanhood would thus directly undermine her capacity to provide the security that is the essence of a correctional counselor's responsibility.

There was substantial testimony from experts on both sides of this litigation that the use of women as guards in 'contact' positions under the existing conditions in Alabama maximum-security male penitentiaries would pose a substantial security problem, directly linked to the sex of the prison guard. On the basis of that evidence, we conclude that the District Court was in error in ruling that being male is not a bona fide occupational qualification for the job of correctional counselor in a 'contact' position in an Alabama male maximum-security penitentiary.

The judgment is accordingly affirmed in part and reversed in part, and the case is remanded to the District Court for further proceedings consistent with this opinion."

V. JUSTICE VOTE

6 Pro ACLU Side vs. 3 Con Opposing Side

ACLU Side (Respondent/Appellee)

1. Stewart, P. – Wrote majority opinion
2. Powell, L. – Joined majority opinion
3. Stevens, J. – Joined majority opinion
4. Rehnquist, W. – Wrote concurring opinion
5. Burger, W. – Joined Rehnquist's concurrence
6. Blackmun, H. – Joined Rehnquist's concurrence

Opposing Side (Petitioner/Appellant)

1. Marshall, T. – Wrote dissenting opinion
2. Brennan, W. – Joined Marshall's dissent
3. White, B. – Wrote dissenting opinion

VI. A WIN OR LOSS FOR THE ACLU?

The ACLU filed as amicus curiae urging affirmance in support of appellee; the Supreme Court affirmed appellee's contention that the height and weight requirements violated Title VII, reversed the District Court's ruling that being male is not a bona fide occupational qualification, and remanded the District Court's decision in a 6-3 vote, giving the ACLU an apparent win.

397. Dayton Board of Education v. Brinkman

(Decided June 27, 1977; 433 U.S. 406)

I. ISSUE

A. Issues Discussed

Civil rights, race, Fourteenth Amendment, equal protection

B. Legal Question Presented

Whether the remedy for school segregation was appropriate given the constitutional violations discovered.

C. Supreme Court's Answer

The judgment must be vacated and the case remanded because the remedy for the violations was erroneous.

II. CASE SUMMARY

A. Background

"This school desegregation action comes to us after five years and two round trips through the lower federal courts. Those protracted proceedings have been devoted to the formulation of a remedy for actions of the Dayton Board of Education found to be in violation of the Equal Protection Clause of the Fourteenth Amendment. In the decision now under review, the Court of Appeals for the Sixth Circuit finally approved a plan involving district-wide racial distribution requirements, after rejecting two previous, less sweeping orders by the District Court. The plan required, beginning with the 1976-1977 school year, that the racial distribution of each school in the district be brought within 15% of the 48%-52% black-white population ratio of Dayton. As finally formulated, the plan employed a variety of

desegregation techniques, including the 'pairing' of schools, the redefinition of attendance zones, and a variety of centralized special programs and 'magnet schools.' [The Supreme Court] granted certiorari to consider the propriety of this court-ordered remedy in light of the constitutional violations which were found by the courts below."

The Supreme Court granted certiorari to review the case, vacated the judgment, and remanded the case.

B. Counsel of Record / ACLU Attorney

ACLU Side (Respondent/Appellee): Louis R. Lucas argued the cause for appellee.

Opposing Side (Petitioner/Appellant): David C. Greer argued the cause for appellant.

III. AMICI CURIAE

ACLU Side (Respondent/Appellee)

Brief of amici curiae filed on behalf of the ACLU, et al., by Robert Allen Sedler, Joel M. Gora, and E. Richard Larson.

Additional briefs of amici curiae filed on behalf of the United States, the American Jewish Congress, the NAACP Legal Defense and Educational Fund, Inc., et al., the Fair Housing Council of Bergen County, New Jersey, and the National Educational Association, et al.

Opposing Side (Petitioner/Appellant)

Briefs of amici curiae were filed on behalf of the Cleveland, Ohio City School District, the Delaware State Board of Education, et al., the Ohio State Board of Education, et al., and the Pacific Legal Foundation.

IV. THE SUPREME COURT'S DECISION

"[T]he duty of both the District Court and the Court of Appeals in a case such as this, where mandatory segregation by law of the races in the schools has long since ceased, is to first determine whether there was any action in the conduct of the business of the School Board which are intended to, and did in fact, discriminate against minority pupils, teachers, or staff. . . .

If such violations are found, the District Court in the first instance, subject to review by the Court of Appeals, must determine how much incremental segregative effects these violations had on the racial distribution of the Dayton school population as presently constituted, when that distribution is compared to what it would have been in the absence of such constitutional violations. The remedy must be designed to redress that difference, and only if there has been a systemwide impact may there be a system wide remedy.

We realize that this is a difficult task, and that it is much easier for a reviewing court to fault ambiguous phrases such as 'cumulative violation' than it is for the finder of fact to make the complex factual determinations in the first instance. Nonetheless, that is what the Constitution and our cases call for, and that is what must be done in this case.

While we have found that the plan implicitly, if not explicitly, imposed by the Court of Appeals was erroneous on the present state of the record, it is undisputed that it has been in effect in the Dayton school system during the present year without creating serious problems. While a school board and a school constituency which attempted to comply with a plan to the best of their abilities should not be penalized, we think that the plan finally adopted by the District Court should remain in effect for the coming year subject to such further orders of the District Court as it may find warranted following the hearings mandated by this opinion.

The judgment of the Court of Appeals is vacated, and the cause is remanded for further proceedings consistent with this opinion."

V. JUSTICE VOTE

0 Pro ACLU Side vs. 8 Con Opposing Side

Opposing Side (Petitioner/Appellant)

1. Rehnquist, W. – Wrote majority opinion
2. White, B. – Joined majority opinion
3. Stewart, P. – Joined majority opinion
4. Blackmun, H. – Joined majority opinion
5. Powell, L. – Joined majority opinion
6. Burger, W. – Joined majority opinion
7. Stevens, J. – Wrote concurring opinion
8. Brennan, W. – Wrote concurring opinion

Marshall, T – Took no part in the decision

VI. A WIN OR LOSS FOR THE ACLU?

The ACLU filed as amicus curiae urging affirmance; the Supreme Court vacated the judgment of the Court of Appeals in an 8-0 vote, giving the ACLU an apparent loss.

398. Coker v. Georgia

(Decided June 29, 1977; 433 U.S. 584)

I. ISSUE

A. Issues Discussed

Criminal justice, death penalty, cruel and unusual punishment, Eighth Amendment

B. Legal Question Presented

Would imposing the death penalty for the crime of rape be a form of cruel and unusual punishment forbidden by the Eighth Amendment?

C. Supreme Court's Answer

Imposing the death penalty for the crime of rape is cruel and unusual punishment in violation of the Eighth Amendment.

II. CASE SUMMARY

A. Background

"While serving various sentences for murder, rape, kidnapping, and aggravated assault," petitioner Coker escaped from prison. Petitioner then entered the victims' house through an unlocked kitchen door. After threatening the couple inside, petitioner tied up the husband, obtained a knife from the kitchen, and took the husband's money and car keys. Petitioner proceeded to threaten the wife, then raped her. Soon after, petitioner drove off in the couple's car, taking the wife with him. The husband notified the police and, soon after, petitioner was apprehended and the wife recovered with no further injuries.

"Petitioner was charged with escape, armed robbery, motor vehicle theft, kidnapping, and rape." After being found competent to stand trial, he was tried and found guilty. At the sentencing hearing, the jury's verdict for punishment on the rape charge was death by electrocution, due to two aggravating circumstances, which under Georgia law justified the death penalty: that the rape was committed (1) "by a person with a prior record of conviction for a capital felony," and (2) "in the course of committing another capital felony," armed robbery. The Georgia Supreme Court affirmed the conviction and sentence.

The Supreme Court granted certiorari to review the case and reversed.

B. Counsel of Record/ACLU Attorney

ACLU Side (Petitioner/Appellant): David E. Kendall argued the cause for appellant.

Opposing Side (Respondent/Appellee): B. Dean Grindle, Jr., Assistant Attorney General of Georgia, argued the cause for appellee.

III. AMICI CURIAE

ACLU Side (Petitioner/Appellant)

Brief of amici curiae filed on behalf of the ACLU, et al., by Ruth Bader Ginsburg, Melvin L. Wulf, Marjorie Mazen Smith, and Nancy Stearns.

Opposing Side (Respondent/Appellee)

No briefs of amici curiae were filed in support of appellee.

IV. THE SUPREME COURT'S DECISION

"[This] Court firmly embraced the holdings and dicta from prior cases . . . to the effect that the Eighth Amendment bars not only those punishments that are 'barbaric' but also those that are 'excessive' in relation to the crime committed. [A] punishment is 'excessive' and unconstitutional if it (1) makes no measurable contribution to acceptable goals of punishment and hence is nothing more than the purposeless and needless imposition of pain and suffering; or (2) is grossly out of proportion to the severity of the crime. . . .

That question, with respect to rape of an adult woman, is now before us. . . . We do not discount the seriousness of rape as a crime. . . . Short of homicide, it is the 'ultimate violation of self.' . . . Rape is without doubt deserving of serious punishment; but in terms of moral depravity and of the injury to the person and to the public, it does not compare with murder, which does involve the unjustified taking of human life. Although it may be accompanied by another crime, rape by definition does not include the death of or even the serious injury to another person. Life is over for the victim of the murderer; for the rape victim, life may not be nearly so happy as it was, but it is not over and normally is not beyond repair. We have the abiding conviction that the death penalty, which 'is unique in its severity and irrevocability,' is an excessive penalty for the rapist who, as such, does not take human life.

This does not end the matter; for under Georgia law, death may not be imposed for any capital offense, including rape, unless the jury or judge finds one of the statutory aggravating circumstances and then elects to impose that sentence. . . . Here, the first two of these aggravating circumstances were alleged and found by the jury.

Neither of these circumstances, nor both of them together, change our conclusion that the death sentence imposed on Coker is a disproportionate punishment for rape. Coker had prior convictions for capital felonies—rape, murder, and kidnapping—but these prior convictions do not change the fact that the instant crime being punished is a rape not involving the taking of life.

It is also true that the present rape occurred while Coker was committing armed robbery, a felony for which the Georgia statutes authorize the death penalty. But Coker was tried for the robbery offense as well as for rape and received a separate life sentence for this crime; the jury did not deem the robbery itself deserving of the death penalty, even though accompanied by the aggravating circumstance, which was stipulated, that Coker had been convicted of a prior capital crime.

We note finally that in Georgia a person commits murder when he unlawfully and with malice aforethought, either express or implied, causes the death of another human being. He also commits that crime when in the commission of a felony he causes the death of another human being, irrespective of malice. But even where the killing is deliberate, it is not punishable by death absent proof of aggravating circumstances. It is difficult to accept the notion, and we do not, that the rapist, with or without aggravating circumstances, should be punished more heavily than the deliberate killer as long as the rapist does not himself take the life of his victim. The judgment of the Georgia Supreme Court upholding the death sentence is reversed, and the case is remanded to that court for further proceedings not inconsistent with this opinion."

V. JUSTICE VOTE

7 Pro ACLU Side vs. 2 Con Opposing Side

ACLU Side (Petitioner/Appellant)

1. White, B. – Wrote majority opinion
2. Stewart, P. – Joined majority opinion
3. Stevens, J. – Joined concurring opinion
4. Blackmun, H. – Joined majority opinion
5. Marshall, T. – Wrote concurring opinion
6. Brennan, W. – Wrote concurring opinion
7. Powell, L. – Wrote concurring opinion

Opposing Side (Respondent/Appellee)

1. Burger, W. – Wrote dissenting opinion
2. Rehnquist, W. – Joined Burger's dissent

VI. A WIN OR LOSS FOR THE ACLU?

The ACLU filed as amicus curiae urging reversal; the U.S. Supreme Court reversed the Georgia Supreme Court decision in a 7-2 vote, giving the ACLU an apparent win.

399. Nashville Gas Co. v. Satty

(Decided December 6, 1977; 434 U.S. 136)

I. ISSUE

A. Issues Discussed

Gender, civil rights

B. Legal Question Presented

Whether two employer policies violate Title VII. "The first is petitioner's practice of giving sick pay to employees disabled by reason of nonoccupational sickness or injury but not to those disabled by pregnancy. The second is petitioner's practice of denying accumulated seniority to female employees returning to work following disability caused by childbirth."

C. Supreme Court's Answer

"We conclude that petitioner's policy of denying accumulated seniority to female employees returning from pregnancy leave violates § 703(a)(2) of Title VII. . . .

Since we rejected th[e lower court's] line of reasoning in our opinion in Gilbert, the judgment of the Court of Appeals with respect to petitioner's sick-pay policies must be vacated."

II. CASE SUMMARY

A. Background

"Petitioner requires pregnant employees to take a formal leave of absence. The employee does not receive sick pay while on pregnancy leave. She also loses all accumulated job seniority; as a result, while petitioner attempts to provide the employee with temporary work upon her return, she will be employed in a permanent job position only if no employee presently working for petitioner also applies for the position. The United States District Court for the Middle District of Tennessee held that these policies violate Title VII of the Civil Rights Act of 1964. The Court of Appeals for the Sixth Circuit affirmed. [The Supreme Court] granted certiorari to decide, in light of our opinion last Term in General Electric Co. v. Gilbert, 429 U.S. 125 (1976), whether the lower courts properly applied Title VII to petitioner's policies respecting pregnancy."

B. Counsel of Record

ACLU Side (Respondent/Appellee): Robert W Wensmueler, Jr., argued the cause and filed a brief for appellee.

Opposing Side (Petitioner/Appellant): Charles K. Wray argued the cause and filed briefs for appellant.

III. AMICI CURIAE

ACLU Side (Respondent/Appellee)

Brief of amici curiae filed on behalf of the American Civil Liberties Union and Women's Legal Defense Fund by Judith Lichtman, Ruth Bader Ginsburg, Marjorie Mazen Smith, Susan Deller Ross, Kathleen Willert Peratis, and Joel Gora.

Brief of amici curiae filed on behalf of the American Federation of Labor and Congress of Industrial Organizations et al. by Stephen I. Schlossberg, John A. Fillion, J Albert Woll, and Laurence Gold.

Opposing Side (Petitioner/Appellant)

No briefs of amici curiae were filed in support of appellant.

IV. THE SUPREME COURT'S DECISION

"We conclude that petitioner's policy of denying accumulated seniority to female employees returning from pregnancy leave violates § 703(a)(2) of Title VII. . . .

Here, . . . petitioner has not merely refused to extend to women a benefit that men cannot and do not receive, but has imposed on women a substantial burden that men need not suffer. . . .

Recognition that petitioner's facially neutral seniority system does deprive women of employment opportunities because of their sex does not end the inquiry under § 703(a)(2) of Title VII. If a company's business necessitates the adoption of particular leave policies, Title VII does not prohibit the company from applying these policies to all leaves of absence, including pregnancy leaves; Title VII is not violated even though the policies may burden female employees. But we agree with the District Court in this case that since there was no proof of any business necessity adduced with respect to the policies in question, that court was entitled to "assume no justification exists.' . . .

On the basis of the evidence presented to the District Court, petitioner's policy of not awarding sick-leave pay to pregnant employees is legally indistinguishable from the disability-insurance program upheld in Gilbert. . . . Only if a plaintiff through the presentation of other evidence can demonstrate that exclusion of pregnancy from the compensated conditions is a mere "pretex[t] designed to effect an invidious discrimination against the members of one sex or the other" does Title VII apply. . . .

We again need not decide whether, when confronted by a facially neutral plan, it is necessary to prove intent to establish a prima facie violation of § 703(a)(1). . . .

Respondent failed to prove even a discriminatory effect with respect to petitioner's sick-leave plan. . . .

Petitioner's refusal to allow pregnant employees to retain their accumulated seniority may be deemed relevant by the trier of fact in deciding whether petitioner's sick-leave plan was such a pretext. But it most certainly does not require such a finding by a trier of fact, to say nothing of the making of such a finding as an original matter by this Court.

The District Court sitting as a trier of fact made no such finding in this case, and we are not advised whether it was requested to or not. . . . Since we rejected that line of reasoning in our opinion in Gilbert, the judgment of the Court of Appeals with respect to petitioner's sick-pay policies must be vacated. . . .

Affirmed in part, vacated in part, and remanded."

V. JUSTICE VOTE

9 Pro ACLU Side vs. 0 Con Opposing Side

ACLU Side (Respondent/Appellee)

1. Rehnquist, W. – Wrote majority opinion
2. Stewart, P. – Joined majority opinion
3. Burger, W. – Joined majority opinion
4. White, B. – Joined majority opinion
5. Blackmun, H. – Joined majority opinion
6. Powell, L. – Wrote opinion concurring in part
7. Stevens, J. – Wrote concurring opinion
8. Marshall, T. – Joined Powell's opinion
9. Brennan, W. – Joined Powell's opinion

VI. A WIN OR LOSS FOR THE ACLU?

The ACLU filed as amicus curiae urging affirmance; the Supreme Court affirmed in part and vacated in part the Court of Appeals' decision by a 9-0 vote, giving the ACLU an apparent win.

400. Browder v. Director, Department of Corrections

(Decided January 10, 1978; 434 U.S. 257)

I. ISSUE

A. Issues Discussed

Civil rights, writ of habeas corpus, civil procedure

B. Legal Question Presented

"[W]hether the Court of Appeals lacked jurisdiction to review an order directing petitioner's discharge from [the Department of Corrections of Illinois'] custody because [the department's] appeal was untimely."

C. Supreme Court's Answer

The Court of Appeals lacked jurisdiction to review the order because the department's appeal was untimely under the Federal Rules of Civil Procedure.

II. CASE SUMMARY

A. Background

A teenage girl in Chicago reported to the police that she had been raped on January 29, 1971, giving a physical description of her attackers that included the last name, approximate age, and neighborhood of one of the assailants. Based on the information the police narrowed their search to Tyrone Browder, but after speaking with his mother the police began to suspect his brother, the petitioner. The police arrested both brothers and two other young men who were at the Browder home. When they were brought to the police station, an officer noticed that petitioner fit the description of an assailant in a rape that took place the day after the first one was reported. In two separate lineups, both women who were raped identified the petitioner as their assailant. After being read his Miranda rights, petitioner confessed to committing the second rape on January 30, but denied any involvement in the first one on January 29.

"At his trial for the January 30 rape, petitioner moved unsuccessfully to suppress the lineup identification and confession on grounds unrelated to the lawfulness of his arrest, which he did not challenge. On direct appeal, however, petitioner argued that the identification and confession were the fruits of an unlawful arrest, effected without probable cause and without a warrant." The Illinois intermediate appellate court and the Illinois Supreme Court rejected this argument.

A Federal District Court granted petitioner's writ of habeas corpus. The court ordered the Director of the Department of Corrections of Illinois to release petitioner from custody unless the State retried him within 60 days. The Director challenged the ruling and sought an evidentiary hearing. The court held a hearing, despite petitioner's argument that the court lacked jurisdiction to hold the hearing reviewing his writ of habeas corpus. The court ruled to uphold the writ, in favor of petitioner. However, on appeal, the Court of Appeals reversed.

The Supreme Court granted certiorari to review the case and reversed.

B. Counsel of Record/ACLU Attorney

ACLU Side (Petitioner/Appellant): Kenneth N. Flaxman argued the cause for appellant.

Opposing Side (Respondent/Appellee): Raymond McKoski, Assistant Attorney General of Illinois, argued the cause for appellee.

III. AMICI CURIAE

ACLU Side (Petitioner/Appellant)

Brief of amici curiae filed on behalf of the ACLU, Illinois Division, by David Goldberger and Joel Gora.

Brief of amici curiae filed on behalf of the Chicago Council of Lawyers by Howard Eglit, Douglass Cassel, Jr., John Christie, Jr., and Steven Barkin.

Opposing Side (Respondent/Appellee)

No briefs of amici curiae were filed in support of appellee.

IV. THE SUPREME COURT'S DECISION

"Respondent has maintained throughout that the Federal Rules of Civil Procedure are wholly inapplicable on habeas. We think this is a mistaken assumption. It is well settled that habeas corpus is a civil proceeding. Perhaps in recognition of the differences between general civil litigation and habeas corpus proceedings, the Federal Rules of Civil Procedure apply in habeas proceedings only 'to the extent that the practice in such proceedings is not set forth in statutes of the United States and has heretofore conformed to the practice in civil actions.' . . .

In addition to the settled conformity of habeas corpus and other civil proceedings with respect to time limits on post-judgment relief, the emphasis in the Federal Rules of Civil Procedure on 'just' and 'speedy' adjudication parallels the ideal of 'a swift, flexible, and summary determination' of a habeas corpus petitioner's claim. Rule 59 in particular is based on an 'interest in speedy disposition and finality.' Although some aspects of the Federal Rules of Civil Procedure may be inappropriate for habeas proceedings, the requirement of a prompt motion for reconsideration is well suited to the 'special problems and character of such proceedings.' Application of the strict time limits of Rules 52(b) and 59 to motions for reconsideration of rulings on habeas corpus petitions, then, is thoroughly consistent with the spirit of the habeas corpus statutes.

Because respondent failed to comply with these 'mandatory and jurisdictional' time limits, the judgment of the Court of Appeals must be reversed."

V. JUSTICE VOTE

9 Pro ACLU Side vs. 0 Con Opposing Side

ACLU Side (Petitioner/Appellant)

1. Powell, L. – Wrote majority opinion
2. White, B. – Joined majority opinion
3. Brennan, W. – Joined majority opinion
4. Marshall, T. – Joined majority opinion
5. Stevens, J. – Joined majority opinion
6. Stewart, P. – Joined majority opinion
7. Burger, W. – Joined majority opinion
8. Blackmun, H. – Wrote concurring opinion
9. Rehnquist, W. – Joined Blackmun's concurrence

VI. A WIN OR LOSS FOR THE ACLU?

The ACLU filed as amicus curiae urging reversal; the Supreme Court reversed the judgment of the Court of Appeals in a 9-0 vote, giving the ACLU an apparent win.

401. Zablocki v. Redhail

(Decided January 18, 1978; 434 U.S. 374)

I. ISSUE

A. Issues Discussed

Civil rights, state's rights, privacy, marriage, First Amendment, Fifth Amendment, Ninth Amendment, Fourteenth Amendment, equal protection, due process.

B. Legal Question Presented

Whether a Wisconsin statute denying marriage licenses to individuals with unpaid child support obligations violates the Equal Protection Clause of the Fourteenth Amendment?

C. Supreme Court's Answer

This statute violates the Equal Protection Clause by unnecessarily infringing on the fundamental right to marry.

II. CASE SUMMARY

A. Background

In 1971, appellee Roger Redhail, fathered a child while a minor and a high school student. He was sued in a paternity action in Milwaukee County, Wisconsin in 1972. He admitted to fathering the child and the court ordered him to pay child support until the child reached the age of eighteen. Redhail was unable to pay for the child support and, by 1974, owed over $3,700 in unpaid child support.

In 1974, Redhail attempted to obtain a marriage license in Milwaukee County. The county clerk denied his marriage application under a Wisconsin statute requiring certain individuals to obtain a court order in order to be issued a marriage license, including individuals with child support obligations. Redhail had not yet repaid the state for fulfilling his child support obligations and therefore could not obtain the court order.

Redhail filed a class action suit against the appellant, the County Clerk of Milwaukee Thomas Zablocki, and all Wisconsin county clerks in the District Court for the Eastern District of Wisconsin. He claimed the state law preventing him from marrying without a court order was unconstitutional on the grounds that it violated his "equal protection and due process rights secured by the First, Fifth, Ninth, and Fourteenth Amendments.

"On the merits, the three-judge panel analyzed the challenged statute under the Equal Protection Clause and concluded that 'strict scrutiny' was required because the classification created by the statute infringed upon a fundamental right, the right to marry. The court then proceeded to evaluate the interests advanced by the State to justify the statute, and, finding that the classification was not necessary for the achievement of those interests, the court held the statute invalid and enjoined the county clerks from enforcing it."

The Supreme Court granted an appeal to consider the complex issues that arise when states interfere with the right to marry, and affirmed.

B. Counsel of Record/ACLU Attorney

ACLU Side (Respondent/Appellee): Robert H. Bondis argued the cause for appellee.

Opposing Side (Petitioner/Appellant): Ward L. Johnson, Jr., Assistant Attorney General of Wisconsin, argued the cause for appellant.

III. AMICI CURIAE

ACLU Side (Respondent/Appellee)

Brief of amici curiae filed on behalf of the Wisconsin Civil Liberties Union Foundation, Inc., by Terry W. Rose and

William H. Lynch.

Brief of amici curiae filed on behalf of the California State Public Defender, et al., by Paul N. Halvonik, Charles M. Sevilla, Ephraim Margolin, and Sheldon Portman.

Opposing Side (Petitioner/Appellant)

Brief of amici curiae filed on behalf of the State of Texas by John L. Hill, Attorney General, David M. Kendall, First Assistant Attorney General, Joe B. Dibrell, Jr., and Anita Ashton, Assistant Attorneys General.

IV. THE SUPREME COURT'S DECISION

"At issue in this case is the constitutionality of a Wisconsin statute, Wis.Stat. §§ 245.10(1), (4), (5) (1973), which provides that members of a certain class of Wisconsin residents may not marry, within the state or elsewhere, without first obtaining a court order granting permission to marry. This class is defined by the statute to include any 'Wisconsin resident having minor issue not in his custody and which he is under obligation to support by any court order or judgment.' The statute specifies that court permission cannot be granted unless the marriage applicant submits proof of compliance with the support obligations and, in addition, demonstrates that the children covered by the support order 'are not then and are not likely thereafter to become public charges.' . . .

In evaluating §§ 245.10(1), (4), (5) under the Equal Protection Clause, 'we must first determine what burden of justification the classification created thereby must meet, by looking to the nature of the classification and the individual interests affected.' Since our past decisions make clear that the right to marry is of fundamental importance, and since the classification at issue here significantly interferes with the exercise of that right, we believe that 'critical examination' of the state interests advanced in support of the classification is required. [R]ecent decisions have established that the right to marry is part of the fundamental "right of privacy" implicit in the Fourteenth Amendment's Due Process Clause. . . .

'While the outer limits of [the right of personal privacy] have not been marked by the Court, it is clear that among the decisions that an individual may make without unjustified government interference are personal decisions 'related to marriage . . . .'

We believe that 'critical examination' of the state interests advanced in support of the classifications is required. . . . When a statutory classification significantly interferes with the exercise of a fundamental right, it cannot be upheld unless it is supported by sufficiently important state interests and is closely tailored to effectuate only those interests. Appellant asserts that two interests are served by the challenged statute: the permission-to-marry proceeding furnishes an opportunity to counsel the applicant as to the necessity of fulfilling his prior support obligations; and the welfare of the out-of-custody children is protected. We may accept for present purposes that these are legitimate and substantial interests, but, since the means selected by the State for achieving these interests unnecessarily impinge on the right to marry, the statute cannot be sustained...

The statutory classification created by § 245.10(1), (4), (5) thus cannot be justified by the interests advanced in support of it.

The judgment of the District Court is, accordingly, affirmed."

V. JUSTICE VOTE

8 Pro ACLU Side vs. 1 Con Opposing Side

ACLU Side (Respondent/Appellee)

1. Marshall, T. – Wrote majority opinion
2. White, B. – Joined majority opinion
3. Brennan, W. – Joined majority opinion
4. Blackmun, H. – Joined majority opinion
5. Burger, W. – Wrote concurring opinion
6. Stewart, P. – Wrote concurring opinion
7. Powell, L. – Wrote concurring opinion
8. Stevens, J. – Wrote concurring opinion

Opposing Side (Petitioner/Appellant)

1. Rehnquist, W. – Wrote dissenting opinion

VI. A WIN OR LOSS FOR THE ACLU?

The ACLU filed as amicus curiae urging affirmance; The Supreme Court affirmed the District Court decision in an 8-1 vote, giving the ACLU an apparent win.

402. Procunier v. Navarette

(Decided February 22, 1978; 434 U.S. 555)

I. ISSUE

A. Issues Discussed

Criminal justice, prisons, First and Fourteenth Amendments, negligence

B. Legal Question Presented

"[W]hether the Court of Appeals correctly reversed the District Court's judgment with respect to Navarette's third claim for relief alleging negligent interference with a claimed constitutional right."

C. Supreme Court's Answer

The Court of Appeals incorrectly reversed the District Court on the third claim alleging negligent interference.

II. CASE SUMMARY

A. Background

Respondent Navarette, a state prisoner at Soledad Prison of California, filed a suit charging six prison officials with violating his constitutional rights and violating 42 U.S.C. §§ 1983 and 1985).

These allegations included "wrongful interference with Navarette's outgoing mail" and negligent interference with the mail. The officers allegedly "failed to mail various items of correspondence" during respondent's 15-month stay, including "letters to legal assistance groups, law students, the news media, and inmates at other prisons, as well as personal friends."

The District Court granted summary judgment for petitioners on the claims related to mail interference. The Court of Appeals reversed, holding that "prisoners themselves are entitled to First and Fourteenth Amendment protection for their outgoing mail," and that granting summary judgment for petitioners was improper.

The Supreme Court granted certiorari to consider "whether the Court of Appeals correctly reversed the District Court's judgment with respect to Navarette's third claim for relief alleging negligent interference with a claimed constitutional right."

B. Counsel of Record/ACLU Attorney

ACLU Side (Respondent/Appellee): Michael E. Adams argued the cause for appellee.

Opposing Side (Petitioner/Appellant): Sanford Svetcov, Deputy Attorney General of California, argued the cause for appellant.

III. AMICI CURIAE

ACLU Side (Respondent/Appellee)

Brief of amici curiae filed on behalf of the ACLU by Leon Friedman, Joel M. Gora, and Alvin J. Bronstein.

Opposing Side (Petitioner/Appellant)

No briefs of amici curiae were filed in support of appellant.

IV. THE SUPREME COURT'S DECISION

"Whether the state of the law is evaluated by reference to the opinions of this Court, of the Courts of Appeals, or of the local District Court, there was no 'clearly established' First and Fourteenth Amendment right with respect to the correspondence of convicted prisoners in 1971-1972. As a matter of law, therefore, there was no basis for rejecting the immunity defense on the ground that petitioners knew or should have known that their alleged conduct violated a constitutional right. Because they could not reasonably have been expected to be aware of a constitutional right that had not yet been declared, petitioners did not act with such disregard for the established law that their conduct 'cannot reasonably be characterized as being in good faith.'

Neither should petitioners' immunity defense be overruled under the second branch of the Wood v. Strickland standard, which would authorize liability where the official has acted with 'malicious intention' to deprive the plaintiff of a constitutional right or to cause him 'other injury.' This part of the rule speaks of 'intentional injury,' contemplating that the actor intends the consequences of his conduct. The third claim for relief with which we are concerned here, however, charges negligent conduct, which normally implies that although the actor has subjected the plaintiff to unreasonable risk, he did not intend the harm or injury that in fact resulted. Claims 1 and 2 of the complaint alleged intentional and bad-faith conduct in disregard of respondent's constitutional rights; but claim 3, as the court below understood it and as the parties have treated it, was limited to negligence. The prison officers were charged with negligent and inadvertent interference with the mail and the supervisory personnel with negligent failure to provide proper training. To the extent that a malicious intent to harm is a ground for denying immunity, that consideration is clearly not implicated by the negligence claim now before us.

We accordingly conclude that the District Court was correct in entering summary judgment for petitioners on the third claim of relief and that the Court of Appeals erred in holding otherwise.

The judgment of the Court of Appeals is reversed."

V. JUSTICE VOTE

2 Pro ACLU Side vs. 7 Con Opposing Side

ACLU Side (Petitioner/Appellant)

1. Stevens, J. – Wrote dissenting opinion
2. Burger, W. – Wrote dissenting opinion

Opposing Side (Respondent/Appellee)

1. White, B. – Wrote majority opinion
2. Brennan, W. – Joined majority opinion
3. Marshall, T. – Joined majority opinion
4. Blackmun, H. – Joined majority opinion
5. Stewart, P. – Joined majority opinion
6. Rehnquist, W. – Joined majority opinion
7. Powell, L. – Joined majority opinion

VI. A WIN OR LOSS FOR THE ACLU?

The ACLU filed as amicus curiae urging affirmance; the Supreme Court reversed the Court of Appeals decision in a 7-2 vote, giving the ACLU an apparent loss.

403. Board of Curators of the University of Missouri v. Horowitz

(Decided March 1, 1978; 435 U.S. 78)

I. ISSUE

A. Issues Discussed

Civil rights, state's rights, procedural due process, Fourteenth Amendment

B. Legal Question Presented

"[W]hat procedures must be accorded to a student at a state educational institution whose dismissal may constitute a deprivation of 'liberty' or 'property' within the meaning of the Fourteenth Amendment."

C. Supreme Court's Answer

The student in this circumstance was accorded sufficient procedures because a hearing was not necessary where she was fully informed of her lack of sufficient academic progress before her dismissal.

II. CASE SUMMARY

A. Background

Respondent Charlotte Horowitz was admitted to the University of Missouri-Kansas City Medical School in 1971. Several faculty members expressed dissatisfaction with her clinical performance and Horowitz was placed on probation going into her final year of medical school. Following further faculty complaints about her performance and poor results on an examination, the Board of

Curators dismissed Horowitz from the medical school for failure to meet academic standards.

Horowitz filed suit against petitioners, the Board of Curators of the University of Missouri, in the United States District Court for the Western District of Missouri. Horowitz alleged that petitioners had deprived her of her procedural due process rights, protected by the Fourteenth Amendment, when she was dismissed from medical school.

The District Court dismissed the complaint, deciding that Horowitz had been afforded all of the rights guaranteed by the Fourteenth Amendment. On appeal, the Court of Appeals for the Eighth Circuit reversed the District Court's decision.

Petitioners appealed the decision of the Court of Appeals for the Eighth Circuit and the Supreme Court granted certiorari to consider "what procedures must be accorded to a student at a state educational institution whose dismissal may constitute a deprivation of 'liberty' or 'property' within the meaning of the Fourteenth Amendment." The Supreme Court reversed the judgment of the Court of Appeals.

B. Counsel of Record / ACLU Attorney

ACLU Side (Respondent / Appellee): Arthur A. Benson, II, argued the cause for appellee.

Opposing Side (Petitioner / Appellant): Marvin E. Wright argued the cause for appellant.

III. AMICI CURIAE

ACLU Side (Respondent / Appellee)

Brief of amici curiae filed on behalf of the ACLU, et al., by Joel M. Gora.

Opposing Side (Petitioner / Appellant)

No briefs of amici curiae were filed on behalf of appellant.

IV. THE SUPREME COURT'S DECISION

"Assuming the existence of a liberty or property interest, respondent has been awarded at least as much due process as the Fourteenth Amendment requires. The school fully informed respondent of the faculty's dissatisfaction with her clinical progress and the danger that this posed to timely graduation and continued enrollment. The ultimate decision to dismiss respondent was careful and deliberate. These procedures were sufficient under the Due Process Clause of the Fourteenth Amendment. We agree with the District Court that the respondent 'was afforded full procedural due process by the [school]. In fact, the Court is of the opinion, and so finds, that the school went beyond [constitutionally required] procedural due process by affording [respondent] the opportunity to be examined by seven independent physicians in order to be absolutely certain that their grading of the [respondent] in her medical skills was correct.' . . .

Under such circumstances, we decline to ignore the historic judgment of educators, and thereby formalize the academic dismissal process by requiring a hearing. The educational process is not by nature adversary; instead, it centers around a continuing relationship between faculty and students. . . . We decline to further enlarge the judicial presence in the academic community, and thereby risk deterioration of many beneficial aspects of the faculty-student relationship. . . .

In reversing the District Court on procedural due process grounds, the Court of Appeals expressly failed to 'reach the substantive due process grounds advanced by Horowitz. Respondent urges that we remand the cause to the Court of Appeals for consideration of this additional claim. In this regard, a number of lower courts have implied in dictum that academic dismissals from state institutions can be enjoined if 'shown to be clearly arbitrary or capricious.' Even assuming that the courts can review under such a standard academic decision of a public educational institution, we agree with the District Court that no showing of arbitrariness or capriciousness has been made in this case. . . .

The judgment of the Court of Appeals is therefore Reversed."

V. JUSTICE VOTE

3 Pro ACLU Side vs. 6 Con Opposing Side

ACLU Side (Petitioner / Appellant)

1. Marshall, T. – Wrote opinion concurring in part and dissenting in part
2. Blackmun, H. – Wrote opinion concurring in part and dissenting in part
3. Brennan, W. – Joined Blackmun's opinion

Opposing Side (Respondent / Appellee)

1. Rehnquist, W. – Wrote majority opinion
2. Burger, W. – Joined majority opinion
3. Stewart, P. – Joined majority opinion
4. Stevens, J. – Joined majority opinion
5. White, B. – Wrote concurring opinion
6. Powell, L. – Wrote concurring opinion

VI. A WIN OR LOSS FOR THE ACLU?

The ACLU filed as amicus curiae urging affirmance; the Supreme Court reversed the judgment of the Court of Appeals in a 6-3 vote, giving the ACLU an apparent loss.

404. Stump v. Sparkman

(Decided March 28, 1978; 435 U.S. 349)

I. ISSUE

A. Issues Discussed

Governmental authority, immunity, Fourteenth Amendment

B. Legal Question Presented

Does a judge have judicial immunity from a civil suit against him arising from his actions which allowed a mother to have her daughter medically sterilized, allegedly in violation of the daughter's constitutional rights?

C. Supreme Court's Answer

The judge has judicial immunity for these actions performend in his capacity has a judge.

II. CASE SUMMARY

A. Background

In 1971 the mother of respondent filed a petition in the Circuit Court of DeKalb County, Indiana, for authority to have her "somewhat retarded" 15-year-old daughter sterilized, which would make it impossible for her to become pregnant.

Petitioner, Judge Stump, approved the petition the same day it was filed, without a hearing and without notice to the daughter or appointment of a representative or lawyer to protect the daughter's interests. The following week, respondent entered the hospital for the operation. She was "told that she was to have her appendix removed [and was] unaware of the true nature of her surgery."

About two years later, respondent was married, and her inability to "become pregnant led her to discover that she had been sterilized during the 1971 operation." As a result she and her husband, also a respondent, filed suit in Federal District Court against her mother, her mother's attorney, Judge Stump, the doctors involved in the sterilization procedure, and the hospital where the procedure took place, seeking "damages for the alleged violation of [her] constitutional rights."

The District Court ruled that respondent's constitutional claims "required a showing of state action and that the only state action" was Judge Stump's approval of the sterilization petition. The District Court further "held that no federal action would lie against any of the defendants because Judge Stump, the only state agent, was absolutely immune from suit under the doctrine of judicial immunity."

The Court of Appeals for the Seventh Circuit reversed, "holding that the 'crucial issue' was 'whether Judge Stump acted within his jurisdiction' and concluding he had not. He was accordingly not immue from damages liability." Additionally, the Seventh Circuit ruled that Judge Stump had forfeited his immunity by failing to comply with procedural due process.

The Supreme Court granted certiorari to review the case and reversed.

B. Counsel of Record/ACLU Attorney

ACLU Side (Respondent/Appellee): Richard H. Finley argued the cause for appellee.

Opposing Side (Petitioner/Appellant): George E. Fruechtenicht argued the cause for appellant.

III. AMICI CURIAE

ACLU Side (Respondent/Appellee)

Brief of amici curiae filed on behalf of the ACLU, et al., by Bruce J. Ennis, Joel M. Gora, Paul Friedman, and Lawrence M. Reuben.

Brief of amici curiae filed on behalf of the American Coalition of Citizens with Disabilities, et al., by Robert L. Burgdorf Jr.

Brief of amici curiae filed on behalf of for the National Center for Law and the Handicapped, Inc., by Ronald M. Soskin.

Opposing Side (Petitioner/Appellant)

No briefs of amici curiae were filed in support of appellant.

IV. THE SUPREME COURT'S DECISION

"A judge will not be deprived of immunity because the action he took was in error, was done maliciously, or was in excess of his authority; rather, he will be subject to liability only when he has acted in the 'clear absence of all jurisdiction.'

We cannot agree that there was a 'clear absence of all jurisdiction' in the DeKalb County Circuit Court to consider the petition presented by Mrs. McFarlin. As an Indiana Circuit Court Judge, Judge Stump had 'original exclusive jurisdiction in all cases at law and in equity whatsoever . . . ,' jurisdiction over the settlement of estates and over guardianships, appellate jurisdiction as conferred by law, and jurisdiction over 'all other causes, matters and proceedings where exclusive jurisdiction thereof is not conferred by law upon some other court, board or officer.' This is indeed a broad jurisdictional grant; yet the Court of Appeals concluded that Judge Stump did not have jurisdiction over the petition authorizing Linda Sparkman's sterilization. . . .

We conclude that the Court of Appeals, employing an unduly restrictive view of the scope of Judge Stump's jurisdiction, erred in holding that he was not entitled to judicial immunity. Because the court over which Judge Stump presides is one of general jurisdiction, neither the procedural errors he may have committed nor the lack of a specific statute authorizing his approval of the petition in question rendered him liable in damages for the consequences of his actions. . . .

Despite the unfairness to litigants that sometimes results, the doctrine of judicial immunity is thought to be in the best interests of 'the proper administration of justice . . . [, for it allows] a judicial officer, in exercising the authority vested in him [to] be free to act upon his own convictions, without apprehension of personal consequences to himself.' The fact that the issue before the judge is a controversial one is all the more reason that he should be able to act without fear of suit. . . .

The Indiana law vested in Judge Stump the power to entertain and act upon the petition for sterilization. He is, therefore, under the controlling cases, immune from damages liability even if his approval of the petition was in error. Accordingly, the judgment of the Court of Appeals is reversed, and the case is remanded for further proceedings consistent with this opinion."

V. JUSTICE VOTE

3 Pro ACLU Side vs. 5 Con Opposing Side

ACLU Side (Petitioner/Appellant)

1. Stewart, P. – Wrote dissenting opinion
2. Marshall, T. – Joined Stewart's dissent
3. Powell, L. – Wrote dissenting opinion, joined Stewart's dissent

Opposing Side (Respondent/Appellee)

1. White, B. – Wrote majority opinion
2. Burger, W. – Joined majority opinion
3. Blackmun, H. – Joined majority opinion
4. Rehnquist, W. – Joined majority opinion
5. Stevens, J. – Joined majority opinion

Brennan, W – Took no part in the decision

VI. A WIN OR LOSS FOR THE ACLU?

The ACLU filed as amicus curiae urging affirmance; the Supreme Court reversed the ruling of the Court of Appeals for the Seventh Circuit in a 5-3 vote, giving the ACLU an apparent loss.

405. McDaniel v. Paty

(Decided April 19, 1978; 435 U.S. 618)

I. ISSUE

A. Issues Discussed

First Amendment free exercise of religion

B. Legal Question Presented

"[W]hether a Tennessee statute barring 'Minister[s] of the Gospel, or priest[s] of any denomination whatever' from serving as delegates to the State's limited constitutional convention deprived appellant McDaniel, an ordained minister, of the right to the free exercise of religion guaranteed by the First Amendment and made applicable to the States by the Fourteenth Amendment."

C. Supreme Court's Answer

The Tennessee statute deprived McDaniel of his First Amendment right to free exercise of religion.

II. CASE SUMMARY

A. Background

"In its first Constitution, in 1796, Tennessee disqualified ministers from serving as legislators. That disqualifying provision has continued unchanged since its adoption; it is now Art. 9, § 1, of the State Constitution. The state legislature applied this provision to candidates for delegate to the State's 1977 limited constitutional convention when it enacted ch. 848, § 4, of 1976 Tenn.Pub.Acts: 'Any citizen of the state who can qualify for membership in the House of Representatives of the General Assembly may become a candidate for delegate to the convention . . . .'

McDaniel, an ordained minister of a Baptist Church in Chattanooga, Tenn., filed as a candidate for delegate to the constitutional convention. An opposing candidate, appellee Selma Cash Paty, sued in the Chancery Court for a declaratory judgment that McDaniel was disqualified from serving as a delegate and for a judgment striking his name from the ballot. Chancellor Franks of the Chancery Court held that § 4 of ch. 848 violated the First and Fourteenth Amendments to the Federal Constitution and declared McDaniel eligible for the office of delegate. Accordingly, McDaniel's name remained on the ballot and in the ensuing election he was elected by a vote almost equal to that of three opposing candidates.

After the election, the Tennessee Supreme Court reversed the Chancery Court, holding that the disqualification of clergy imposed no burden upon 'religious belief' and restricted 'religious action . . . [only] in the lawmaking process of government—where religious action is absolutely prohibited by the establishment clause . . . .' The state interests in preventing the establishment of religion and in avoiding the divisiveness and tendency to channel political activity along religious lines, resulting from clergy participation in political affairs, were deemed by that court sufficiently weighty to justify the disqualification, notwithstanding the guarantee of the Free Exercise Clause."

The Supreme Court granted certiorari to review the case and reversed.

B. Counsel of Record/ACLU Attorney

ACLU Side (Petitioner/Appellant): Frederic S. Le Clercq argued the cause for appellant.

Opposing Side (Respondent/Appellee): Kenneth R. Herrell, Assistant Attorney General of Tennessee, and Phillip C. Lawrence argued the cause for appellees.

III. AMICI CURIAE

ACLU Side (Petitioner/Appellant)

Brief of amici curiae filed on behalf of the ACLU, et al., by Leo Pfeffer, Abraham S. Goldstein, Joel Gora, George W. McKeag, John T. Redmond, James W. Respess, and Thomas A. Shaw.

Opposing Side (Respondent/Appellee)

No briefs of amici curiae were filed in support of appellee.

IV. THE SUPREME COURT'S DECISION

"This brief review of the history of clergy-disqualification provisions also amply demonstrates, however, that, at least during the early segment of our national life, those provisions enjoyed the support of responsible American statesmen and were accepted as having a rational basis. Against this background we do not lightly invalidate a statute enacted pursuant to a provision of a state constitution which has been sustained by its highest court. The challenged provision came to the Tennessee Supreme Court clothed with the presumption of validity to which that court was bound to give deference.

However, the right to the free exercise of religion unquestionably encompasses the right to preach, proselyte, and perform other similar religious functions, or, in other words, to be a minister of the type McDaniel was found to be. Tennessee also acknowledges the right of its adult citizens generally to seek and hold office as legislators or delegates to the state constitutional convention. Yet under the clergy-disqualification provision, McDaniel cannot exercise both rights simultaneously because the State has conditioned the exercise of one on the surrender of the other. Or, in James Madison's words, the State is 'punishing a religious profession with the privation of a civil right.' In so doing, Tennessee has encroached upon McDaniel's right to the free exercise of religion. . . .

We hold that § 4 of ch. 848, violates McDaniel's First Amendment right to the free exercise of his religion made applicable to the States by the Fourteenth Amendment. Accordingly, the judgment of the Tennessee Supreme Court is reversed, and the case is remanded to that court for further proceedings not inconsistent with this opinion.

Reversed and remanded."

V. JUSTICE VOTE

8 Pro ACLU Side vs. 0 Con Opposing Side

ACLU Side (Petitioner/Appellant)

1. Burger, W. – Wrote majority opinion
2. Brennan, W. – Wrote concurring opinion
3. Stewart, P. – Wrote concurring opinion
4. White, B. – Wrote concurring opinion
5. Powell, L. – Joined majority opinion
6. Rehnquist, W. – Joined majority opinion
7. Stevens, J. – Joined majority opinion
8. Marshall, T. – Joined Brennan's concurrence

Blackmun, H – Took no part in the decision

VI. A WIN OR LOSS FOR THE ACLU?

The ACLU, as amicus curiae, urged reversal of the judgment of the Supreme Court of Tennessee; the U.S. Supreme Court reversed in an 8-0 vote, giving the ACLU an apparent win.

406. City of Los Angeles, Department of Water and Power v. Manhart

(Decided April 25, 1978; 435 U.S. 702)

I. ISSUE

A. Issues Discussed

Civil rights, gender, Fourteenth Amendment

B. Legal Question Presented

Does a company policy that requires "female employees to make larger contributions to its pension fund than its male employees" based on the fact that "[a]s a class, women live longer than men," violate § 703(a)(1) of Title VII of the Civil Rights Act of 1964, and if so, does that company owe back pay to the female employees?

C. Supreme Court's Answer

The company policy violated the Civil Rights Act, however, back pay is not an appropriate remedy in this circumstance.

II. CASE SUMMARY

A. Background

Because, "[a]s a class, women live longer than men," petitioner the Los Angeles Department of Water and Power ("Department") required its female employees to pay 14.84% higher monthly payments toward their retirement pension than the Department's male employees.

Respondents, female employees of the Department, filed a class action suit against the Department in the United States District Court for the Central District of California.

Respondents alleged that the Department's pension contribution requirements violated § 703(a)(1) of Title VII of the Civil Rights Act of 1964, which makes it illegal for an employer to discriminate against any individual based on gender. The respondents asked the court to stop the Department's unequal pension contribution requirements and order the Department to pay restitution to the women who were required to make larger monthly contributions to their pension.

While respondents' suit was pending, "the California Legislature enacted a law prohibiting certain municipal agencies from requiring female employees to make higher pension fund contributions than males. The Department therefore amended its plan" to comply with the new law.

The District Court held that the Department's former plan violated section § 703(a)(1). The court ordered the Department to refund the excess contributions to former and current female employees. The Court of Appeals for the Ninth Circuit affirmed the District Court's ruling.

The Supreme Court granted certiorari to review the case, vacated, and remanded.

B. Counsel of Record/ACLU Attorney

ACLU Side (Respondent/Appellee): Robert M. Dohrmann argued the cause for appellee.

Opposing Side (Petitioner/Appellant): David J. Oliphant argued the cause for appellant.

III. AMICI CURIAE

ACLU Side (Respondent/Appellee)

Brief of amici curiae filed on behalf of the ACLU, et al., by Ruth Bader Ginsburg, Majorie Mazen Smith, and Matthew W. Finkin.

Brief of amici curiae filed on behalf of the ACLU Foundation of Southern California by Michael Evan Gold and Fred Okrand.

Additional briefs of amici curiae were filed on behalf of the United States, et al., the American Nurses' Association, the Association for Women in Mathematics, et al., and the International Union, United Automobile, Aerospace, & Agricultural Implement Workers of America, et al.

Opposing Side (Petitioner/Appellant)

Briefs of amici curiae filed on behalf of the State of Oregon, the New York State Teachers' Retirement System, the Society of Actuaries, et al., the City of New York, the Teachers Insurance and Annuity Association of America, et al., and the American Council of Life Insurance.

IV. THE SUPREME COURT'S DECISION

"There are both real and fictional differences between women and men. . . .

This case does not, however, involve a fictional difference between men and women. It involves a generalization that the parties accept as unquestionably true: Women, as a class, do live longer than men. The Department treated its women employees differently from its men employees because the two classes are in fact different. It is equally true, however, that all individuals in the respective classes do not share the characteristic that differentiates the average class representatives. . . . The question, therefore, is whether the existence or nonexistence of 'discrimination' is to be determined by comparison of class characteristics or individual characteristics. . . .

The [Civil Rights Act of 1964] makes it unlawful 'to discriminate against any individual with respect to his compensation, terms, conditions, or privileges of employment, because of such individual's race, color, religion, sex, or national origin.' (emphasis added). The statute's focus on the individual is unambiguous. . . . Even if the statutory language were less clear, the basic policy of the statute requires that we focus on fairness to individuals rather than fairness to classes. . . .

An employment practice that requires 2,000 individuals to contribute more money into a fund than 10,000 other employees simply because each of them is a woman, rather than a man, is in direct conflict with both the language and the policy of the Act. . . . It constitutes discrimination and is unlawful unless exempted by the Equal Pay Act of 1963 or some other affirmative justification. . . .

The Equal Pay Act requires employers to pay members of both sexes the same wages for equivalent work, except when the differential is pursuant to one of four specified exceptions. The Department contends that the fourth exception applies here. That exception authorizes a 'differential based on any other factor other than sex.'

The Department argues that the different contributions exacted from men and women were based on the factor of longevity rather than sex. It is plain, however, that any individual's life expectancy is based on a number of factors, of which sex is only one. The record contains no evidence that any factor other than the employee's sex was taken into account in calculating the 14.84% differential between the respective contributions by men and women. . . .

In contrast, each of the two groups of employees involved in this case is composed entirely and exclusively of members of the same sex. On its face, this plan discriminates on the basis of sex . . . .

The Department challenges the District Court's award of retroactive relief to the entire class of female employees and retirees. Title VII does not require a district court to grant any retroactive relief. [T]he statute stresses that retroactive relief 'may' be awarded if it is 'appropriate.' . . .

Although we now have no doubt about the application of the statute in this case, we must recognize that conscientious and intelligent administrators of pension funds, who did not have the benefit of the extensive briefs and arguments presented to us, may well have assumed that a program like the Department's was entirely lawful. The courts had been silent on the question, and the administrative agencies had conflicting views. The Department's failure to act more swiftly is a sign, not of its recalcitrance, but of the problem's complexity.

[P]ension administrators could reasonably have thought it unfair—or even illegal—to make male employees shoulder more than their 'actuarial share' of the pension burden. There is no reason to believe that the threat of a backpay award is needed to cause other administrators to amend their practices to conform to this decision.

Nor can we ignore the potential impact which changes in rules affecting insurance and pension plans may have on the economy. . . .

Consequently, the rules that apply to these funds should not be applied retroactively unless the legislature has plainly commanded that result. The EEOC [Equal Employment Opportunity Commission] itself has recognized that the administrators of retirement plans must be given time to adjust gradually to Title VII's demands. Courts have also shown sensitivity to the special dangers of retroactive Title VII awards in this field. . . . Retroactive liability could be devastating for a pension fund. The harm would fall in large part on innocent third parties.

[W]e conclude that it was error to grant such relief in this case. Accordingly, although we agree with the Court of Appeals' analysis of the statute, we vacate its judgment and remand the case for further proceedings consistent with this opinion."

V. JUSTICE VOTE

6 Pro ACLU Side vs. 2 Con Opposing Side

ACLU Side (Respondent/Appellee)

1. Stevens, J. – Wrote majority opinion
2. Stewart, P. – Joined majority opinion
3. White, B. – Joined majority opinion
4. Powell, L. – Joined majority opinion
5. Blackmun, H. – Wrote concurring opinion
6. Marshall, T. – Wrote opinion concurring in part and dissenting in part

Opposing Side (Petitioner/Appellant)

1. Burger, W. – Wrote opinion concurring in part and dissenting in part
2. Rehnquist, W. – Joined Burger's opinion

Brennan W – Took no part in the decision

VI. A WIN OR LOSS FOR THE ACLU?

The ACLU filed as amicus curiae urging affirmance; the Supreme Court affirmed the ruling of the Court of Appeals for the Ninth Circuit as to their analysis of the statute, but vacated their judgment and remanded the case for further proceedings consistent with the Supreme Court's opinion. The analysis of the statute was upheld in a 6-2 vote, giving the ACLU an apparent win.

407. Landmark Communications, Inc. v. Virginia

(Decided May 1, 1978; 435 U.S. 829)

I. ISSUE

A. Issues Discussed

First Amendment, freedoms of press, speech, and association

B. Legal Question Presented

"[W]hether the Commonwealth of Virginia may subject persons, including newspapers, to criminal sanctions for divulging information regarding proceedings before a state judicial review commission which is authorized to hear complaints as to judges' disability or misconduct, when such proceedings are declared confidential by the State Constitution and statutes."

C. Supreme Court's Answer

Virginia may not subject third parties to criminal sanctions for divulging information regarding confidential proceedings before the state judicial review commission.

II. CASE SUMMARY

A. Background

"On October 4, 1975, the Virginian Pilot, a Landmark newspaper, published an article which accurately reported on a pending inquiry by the Virginia Judicial Inquiry and Review Commission and identified the state judge whose conduct was being investigated. The article reported that '[n]o formal complaint has been filed by the commission against [the judge], indicating either that the five-man panel found insufficient cause for action or that the case is still under review.' A month later, on November 5, a grand jury indicted Landmark for violating Va.Code § 2.1-37.13 (1973) by 'unlawfully divulg[ing] the identification of a Judge of a Court not of record, which said Judge was the subject of an investigation and hearing' by the Commission. . . .

The only witness at the trial, Joseph W. Dunn, Jr., Managing Editor of the Virginian Pilot, testified that he decided to print the information about the Commission proceedings because he felt that the subject was a matter of public importance which should be brought to the attention of the Pilot's readers. Mr. Dunn acknowledged he was aware that it was a misdemeanor for anyone participating in Commission proceedings to divulge information about those proceedings, but testified that he did not understand the statute to apply to newspaper reports about the proceedings. He further testified that no reporter, employee, or representative of Landmark had been subpoenaed by or had appeared before the Commission in connection with the proceedings described in the October 4 article.

The case was tried without a jury, and Landmark was found guilty and fined $500 plus the costs of prosecution. The Supreme Court of Virginia affirmed the conviction, with one dissent."

The U.S. Supreme Court granted certiorari to review the case and reversed.

B. Counsel of Record/ACLU Attorney

ACLU Side (Petitioner/Appellant): Floyd Abrams argued the cause for appellant.

Opposing Side (Respondent/Appellee): James E. Kulp, Assistant Attorney General of Virginia, argued the cause for appellee.

III. AMICI CURIAE

ACLU Side (Petitioner/Appellant)

Brief of amici curiae filed on behalf of the ACLU by Stephen W. Bricker, Bruce J. Ennis, Joel M. Gora, and Philip J. Hirschkop.

Brief of amici curiae filed on behalf of the American Newspaper Publishers Association by Arthur B. Hanson and Frank M. Northam.

Brief of amici curiae filed on behalf of the National Newspaper Association by Christopher B. Fager, William G. Mullen, and James R. Cregan.

Brief of amici curiae filed on behalf of the Washington Post Co., et al., by Edward Bennett Williams and John B. Kuhns.

Opposing Side (Respondent/Appellee)

No briefs of amici curiae were filed in support of appellee.

IV. THE SUPREME COURT'S DECISION

"At the present time it appears that 47 States, the District of Columbia, and Puerto Rico have established, by constitution, statute, or court rule, some type of judicial inquiry and disciplinary procedures. All of these jurisdictions, with the apparent exception of Puerto Rico, provide for the confidentiality of judicial disciplinary proceedings . . . .

The substantial uniformity of the existing state plans suggests that confidentiality is perceived as tending to insure the ultimate effectiveness of the judicial review commissions. . . .

Unlike the generalized mandate of confidentiality, the imposition of criminal sanctions for its breach is not a common characteristic of the state plans; indeed only Virginia and Hawaii appear to provide criminal sanctions for disclosure. . . .

We conclude that the publication Virginia seeks to punish under its statute lies near the core of the First Amendment, and the Commonwealth's interests advanced by the imposition of criminal sanctions are insufficient to justify the actual and potential encroachments on freedom of speech and of the press which follow therefrom. . . .

The operations of the courts and the judicial conduct of judges are matters of utmost public concern. . . . It can be assumed for purposes of decision that confidentiality of Commission proceedings serves legitimate state interests. The question, however, is whether these interests are sufficient to justify the encroachment on First Amendment guarantees which the imposition of criminal sanctions entails with respect to nonparticipants such as Landmark. . . .

It is true that some risk of injury to the judge under inquiry, to the system of justice, or to the operation of the Judicial Inquiry and Review Commission may be posed by premature disclosure, but the test requires that the danger be 'clear and present' and in our view the risk here falls far short of that requirement. Moreover, much of the risk can be eliminated through careful internal procedures to protect the confidentiality of Commission proceedings. . . .

Accordingly, the judgment of the Supreme Court of Virginia is reversed, and the case remanded for further proceedings not inconsistent with this opinion.

Reversed and remanded."

V. JUSTICE VOTE

7 Pro ACLU Side vs. 0 Con Opposing Side

ACLU Side (Petitioner/Appellant)

1. Burger, W. – Wrote majority opinion
2. White, B. – Joined majority opinion
3. Marshall, T. – Joined majority opinion
4. Blackmun, H. – Joined majority opinion
5. Renquist, W. – Joined majority opinion

6. Stevens, J. – Joined majority opinion
7. Stewart, P. – Wrote concurring opinion

Brennan, W. Took no part in decision
Powell, L – Took no part in the decision

VI. A WIN OR LOSS FOR THE ACLU?

The ACLU filed as amicus curiae urging reversal; the U.S. Supreme Court reversed and remanded the ruling of the Virginia Supreme Court in a 7-0 vote, giving the ACLU an apparent win.

408. Santa Clara Pueblo v. Martinez

(Decided May 15, 1978; 436 U.S. 49)

I. ISSUE

A. Issues Discussed

Civil rights, Indian Civil Rights Act

B. Legal Question Presented

"[W]hether the [Indian Civil Rights] Act [of 1968] may be interpreted to impliedly authorize [civil] actions, against a tribe or its officers in the federal courts."

C. Supreme Court's Answer

The Act does not authorize this civil action against a tribe or its officers in federal courts.

II. CASE SUMMARY

A. Background

"Respondent Julia Martinez is a fullblooded member of the Santa Clara Pueblo, and resides on the Santa Clara Reservation in Northern New Mexico. In 1941 she married a Navajo Indian with whom she has since had several children, including respondent Audrey Martinez. Two years before this marriage, the Pueblo passed the membership ordinance here at issue, which bars admission of the Martinez children to the tribe because their father is not a Santa Claran. Although the children were raised on the reservation and continue to reside there now that they are adults, as a result of their exclusion from membership they may not vote in tribal elections or hold secular office in the tribe; moreover, they have no right to remain on the reservation in the event of their mother's death, or to inherit their mother's home or her possessory interests in the communal lands.

After unsuccessful efforts to persuade the tribe to change the membership rule, respondents filed this lawsuit in the United States District Court for the District of New Mexico, on behalf of themselves and others similarly situated. Petitioners moved to dismiss the complaint on the ground that the court lacked jurisdiction to decide intratribal controversies affecting matters of tribal self-government and sovereignty. The District Court rejected petitioners' contention, finding that jurisdiction was conferred by 28 U.S.C. § 1343(4) and 25 U.S.C. § 1302(8). . . . Accordingly, the motion to dismiss was denied.

Following a full trial, the District Court found for petitioners on the merits. While acknowledging the relatively recent origin of the disputed rule, the District Court nevertheless found it to reflect traditional values of patriarchy still significant in tribal life. The court recognized the vital importance of respondents' interests, but also determined that membership rules were 'no more or less than a mechanism of social . . . self-definition,' and as such were basic to the tribe's survival as a cultural and economic entity. In sustaining the ordinance's validity under the 'equal protection clause' of the ICRA, 25 U.S.C. § 1302(8), the District Court concluded that the balance to be struck between these competing interests was better left to the judgment of the Pueblo . . . .

On respondents' appeal, the Court of Appeals for the Tenth Circuit upheld the District Court's determination that 28 U.S.C. § 1343(4) provides a jurisdictional basis for actions under Title I of the ICRA. It found that 'since [the ICRA] was designed to provide protection against tribal authority, the intention of Congress to allow suits against the tribe was an essential aspect [of the ICRA]. Otherwise, it would constitute a mere unenforceable declaration of principles.' The Court of Appeals disagreed, however, with the District Court's ruling on the merits. While recognizing that standards of analysis developed under the Fourteenth Amendment's Equal Protection Clause were not necessarily controlling in the interpretation of this statute, the Court of Appeals apparently concluded that because the classification was one based upon sex it was presumptively invidious and could be sustained only if justified by a compelling tribal interest. Because of the ordinance's recent vintage, and because in the court's view the rule did not rationally identify those persons who were emotionally and culturally Santa Clarans, the court held that the tribe's interest in the ordinance was not substantial enough to justify its discriminatory effect."

The Supreme Court granted certiorari to review the case and reversed.

B. Counsel of Record/ACLU Attorney

ACLU Side (Respondent/Appellee): Richard B. Collins argued the cause for appellee.

Opposing Side (Petitioner/Appellant): Marcelino Prelo, Jr., argued the cause for appellant.

III. AMICI CURIAE

ACLU Side (Respondent/Appellee)

Brief of amici curiae filed on behalf of the ACLU by Stephen L. Pevar, Bruce J. Ennis, and Joel M. Gora.

Opposing Side (Petitioner/Appellant)

Briefs of amici curiae were filed on behalf of the National Tribal Chairmen's Association, the Shoshone and Arapahoe Tribes of the Wind River Indian Reservation, et al., the Confederated Tribes of the Colville Indian Reservation, and the Pueblo de Cochiti, et al.

IV. THE SUPREME COURT'S DECISION

"Indian tribes are 'distinct, independent political communities, retaining their original natural rights' in matters of local self-government. Although no longer 'possessed of the full attributes of sovereignty,' they remain a 'separate people, with the power of regulating their internal and social relations.' . . .

Nothing on the face of Title I of the ICRA purports to subject tribes to the jurisdiction of the federal courts in civil actions for injunctive or declaratory relief. . . . In the absence here of any unequivocal expression of contrary legislative intent, we conclude that suits against the tribe under the ICRA are barred by its sovereign immunity from suit. . . .

By not exposing tribal officials to the full array of federal remedies available to redress actions of federal and state officials, Congress may also have considered that resolution of statutory issues under § 1302, and particularly those issues likely to arise in a civil context, will frequently depend on questions of tribal tradition and custom which tribal forums may be in a better position to evaluate than federal courts. . . . As is suggested by the District Court's opinion in this case, efforts by the federal judiciary to apply the statutory prohibitions of § 1302 in a civil context may substantially interfere with a tribe's ability to maintain itself as a culturally and politically distinct entity.

As we have repeatedly emphasized, Congress' authority over Indian matters is extraordinarily broad, and the role of courts in adjusting relations between and among tribes and their members correspondingly restrained. Congress retains authority expressly to authorize civil actions for injunctive or other relief to redress violations of § 1302, in the event that the tribes themselves prove deficient in applying and enforcing its substantive provisions. But unless and until Congress makes clear its intention to permit the additional intrusion on tribal sovereignty that adjudication of such actions in a federal forum would represent, we are constrained to find that § 1302 does not impliedly authorize actions for declaratory or injunctive relief against either the tribe or its officers.

The judgment of the Court of Appeals is, accordingly, reversed."

V. JUSTICE VOTE

1 Pro ACLU Side vs. 7 Con Opposing Side

ACLU Side (Respondent/Appellee)

1. White, B. – Wrote dissenting opinion

Opposing Side (Petitioner/Appellant)

1. Marshall, T. – Wrote majority opinion
2. Burger, W. – Joined majority opinion
3. Brennan, W. – Joined majority opinion
4. Stewart, P. – Joined majority opinion
5. Powell, L. – Joined majority opinion
6. Stevens, J. – Joined majority opinion
7. Rehnquist, W. – Joined majority opinion, except as to Part III

Blackmun, H – Took no part in the decision

VI. A WIN OR LOSS FOR THE ACLU?

The ACLU filed as amicus curiae urging affirmance; the Supreme Court reversed the ruling of the Court of Appeals for the Tenth Circuit in a 7-1 vote, giving the ACLU an apparent loss.

409. Marshall v. Barlow's, Inc.

(Decided May 23, 1978; 436 U.S. 307)

I. ISSUE

A. Issues Discussed

Criminal Procedure, Fourth Amendment, search and seizure, warrants

B. Legal Question Presented

Does an agent of the Secretary of Labor have the power under § 8(a) of the Occupational Safety and Health Act of 1970 (OSHA) to search a business without a warrant if that business falls under OSHA jurisdiction?

C. Supreme Court's Answer

An agent of the Secretary of Labor cannot search a business under OSHA jurisdiciton without a warrant.

II. CASE SUMMARY

A. Background

"Section 8(a) of the Occupational Safety and Health Act of 1970 (OSHA or Act) empowers agents of the Secretary of Labor (Secretary) to search the work area of any employment facility within the Act's jurisdiction. The purpose for the search is to inspect for safety hazards and violations of OSHA regulations. No search warrant or other process is required under the Act.

On the morning of September 11, 1975, an OSHA inspector entered the customer service area of Barlow's, Inc., an electrical and plumbing installation business located in Pocatello, Idaho. The president and general manager, Ferrol G. "Bill" Barlow, was on hand; and the OSHA inspector, after showing his credentials, informed Mr. Barlow that he wished to conduct a search of the working areas of the business. Mr. Barlow inquired whether any complaint had been received about his company. The inspector answered no, but that Barlow's Inc. had simply turned up in the agency's selection process. The inspector again asked to enter the nonpublic area of the business; Mr. Barlow's response was to inquire whether the inspector had a search warrant. The inspector had none. Thereupon, Mr. Barlow refused the inspector admission to the employee area of his business. He said he was relying on his rights as guaranteed by the Fourth Amendment of the United States Constitution.

Three months later, the Secretary petitioned the United States District Court for the District of Idaho to issue an order compelling Mr. Barlow to admit the inspector. The requested order was issued on December 30, 1975, and was presented to Mr. Barlow on January 5, 1976. Mr. Barlow again refused admission, and he sought his own injunctive relief against the warrantless searches assertedly permitted by OSHA. A three-judge court was convened. On December 30, 1976, it ruled in Mr. Barlow's favor. [T]he court held that the Fourth Amendment required a warrant for the type of search involved here and that the statutory authorization for warrantless inspections was unconstitutional. An injunction against searches or inspections pursuant to § 8(a) was entered."

The Supreme Court granted certiorari to review the case and

affirmed.

B. Counsel of Record / ACLU Attorney

ACLU Side (Respondent / Appellee): John L. Runft argued the cause for appellee.

Opposing Side (Petitioner / Appellant): Solicitor General Wade H. McCree argued the cause for appellant.

III. AMICI CURIAE

ACLU Side (Respondent / Appellee)

Brief of amici curiae filed on behalf of the Roger Baldwin Foundation, Inc., of the ACLU, Illinois Division, by David Goldberger, Barbara O'Toole, McNeill Stokes, Ira J. Smotherman Jr., and David Rudenstine.

Additional briefs of amici curiae were filed on behalf of the State of Idaho, the State of Utah, the American Farm Bureau Federation, the Chamber of Commerce of the United States, the Mountain States Legal Foundation, the National Federation of Independent Businesses, the Pacific Legal Foundation, and the American Conservative Union.

Opposing Side (Petitioner / Appellant)

Briefs of amici curiae were filed on behalf of eleven States and Attorneys General for the respective States of Michigan, New Jersey, New Mexico, North Carolina, Pennsylvania, South Carolina, Vermont, Virginia, and Wyoming; the American Federation of Labor and Congress of Industrial Organizations, and the Sierra Club.

IV. THE SUPREME COURT'S DECISION

"The Secretary urges that warrantless inspections to enforce OSHA are reasonable within the meaning of the Fourth Amendment. Among other things, he relies on § 8(a) of the Act, 29 U.S.C. § 657(a), which authorizes inspection of business premises without a warrant and which the Secretary urges represents a congressional construction of the Fourth Amendment that the courts should not reject. Regrettably, we are unable to agree.

The Warrant Clause of the Fourth Amendment protects commercial buildings as well as private homes. To hold otherwise would belie the origin of that Amendment, and the American colonial experience. . . .

This Court has already held that warrantless searches are generally unreasonable, and that this rule applies to commercial premises as well as homes. . . .

These same cases also held that the Fourth Amendment prohibition against unreasonable searches protects against warrantless intrusions during civil as well as criminal investigations. . . . If the government intrudes on a person's property, the privacy interest suffers whether the government's motivation is to investigate violations of criminal laws or breaches of other statutory or regulatory standards. It therefore appears that unless some recognized exception to the warrant requirement applies, See v. City of Seattle would require a warrant to conduct the inspection sought in this case. . . .

A warrant . . . would provide assurances from a neutral officer that the inspection is reasonable under the Constitution, is authorized by statute, and is pursuant to an administrative plan containing specific neutral criteria. Also, a warrant would then and there advise the owner of the scope and objects of the search, beyond which limits the inspector is not expected to proceed. These are important functions for a warrant to perform, functions which underlie the Court's prior decisions that the Warrant Clause applies to inspections for compliance with regulatory statutes. We conclude that the concerns expressed by the Secretary do not suffice to justify warrantless inspections under OSHA or vitiate the general constitutional requirement that for a search to be reasonable a warrant must be obtained. . . .

We hold that Barlow's was entitled to a declaratory judgment that the Act is unconstitutional insofar as it purports to authorize inspections without warrant or its equivalent and to an injunction enjoining the Act's enforcement to that extent. The judgment of the District Court is therefore affirmed."

V. JUSTICE VOTE

5 Pro ACLU Side vs. 3 Con Opposing Side

ACLU Side (Respondent / Appellee)

1. White, B. – Wrote majority opinion
2. Burger, W. – Joined majority opinion
3. Stewart, P. – Joined majority opinion
4. Marshall, T. – Joined majority opinion
5. Powell, L. – Joined majority opinion

Opposing Side (Petitioner / Appellant)

1. Stevens, J. – Wrote dissenting opinion
2. Blackmun, H. – Joined dissenting opinion
3. Rehnquist, W – Joined dissenting opinion

Brennan, W – Took no part in the decision

VI. A WIN OR LOSS FOR THE ACLU?

The ACLU filed as amicus curiae urging affirmance; the Supreme Court affirmed the ruling of the District Court for the District of Idaho in a 5-3 vote, giving the ACLU an apparent win.

410. In re Primus

(Decided May 30, 1978; 436 U.S. 412)

I. ISSUE

A. Issues Discussed

First Amendment, freedoms of press, speech, and association, Fourteenth Amendment, attorney regulation

B. Legal Question Presented

"[W]hether a State may punish a member of its Bar who, seeking to further political and ideological goals through associational activity, including litigation, advises a lay person of her legal rights and discloses in a subsequent letter that free legal assistance is available from a nonprofit organization with which the lawyer and her associates are affiliated."

C. Supreme Court's Answer

A State may not punish a member of its Bar in this circumstance.

II. CASE SUMMARY

A. Background

"Appellant, Edna Smith Primus, is a lawyer practicing in Columbia, S. C. During the period in question, she was associated with the "Carolina Community Law Firm," and was an officer of and cooperating lawyer with the Columbia branch of the American Civil Liberties Union (ACLU). She received no compensation for her work on behalf of the ACLU, but was paid a retainer as a legal consultant for the South Carolina Council on Human Relations (Council), a nonprofit organization with offices in Columbia.

During the summer of 1973, local and national newspapers reported that pregnant mothers on public assistance in Aiken County, S. C., were being sterilized or threatened with sterilization as a condition of the continued receipt of medical assistance under the Medicaid program. Concerned by this development, Gary Allen, an Aiken businessman and officer of a local organization serving indigents, called the Council requesting that one of its representatives come to Aiken to address some of the women who had been sterilized. At the Council's behest, appellant, who had not known Allen previously, called him and arranged a meeting in his office in July 1973. Among those attending was Mary Etta Williams, who had been sterilized by Dr. Clovis H. Pierce after the birth of her third child. Williams and her grandmother attended the meeting because Allen, an old family friend, had invited them and because Williams wanted '[t]o see what it was all about . . . .' At the meeting, appellant advised those present, including Williams and the other women who had been sterilized by Dr. Pierce, of their legal rights and suggested the possibility of a lawsuit.

Early in August 1973 the ACLU informed appellant that it was willing to provide representation for Aiken mothers who had been sterilized. Appellant testified that after being advised by Allen that Williams wished to institute suit against Dr. Pierce, she decided to inform Williams of the ACLU's offer of free legal representation. Shortly after receiving Appellant's letter, dated August 30, 1973—the centerpiece of this litigation—Williams visited Dr. Pierce to discuss the progress of her third child who was ill. At the doctor's office, she encountered his lawyer and at the latter's request signed a release of liability in the doctor's favor. Williams showed appellant's letter to the doctor and his lawyer, and they retained a copy. She then called appellant from the doctor's office and announced her intention not to sue. There was no further communication between appellant and Williams.

On October 9, 1974, the Secretary of the Board of Commissioners on Grievances and Discipline of the Supreme Court of South Carolina (Board) filed a formal complaint with the Board, charging that appellant had engaged in 'solicitation in violation of the Canons of Ethics' by sending the August 30, 1973, letter to Williams. Appellant denied any unethical solicitation and asserted, inter alia, that her conduct was protected by the First and Fourteenth Amendments and by Canon 2 of the Code of Professional Responsibility of the American Bar Association (ABA). The complaint was heard by a panel of the Board on March 20, 1975. . . .

The panel filed a report recommending that appellant be found guilty of soliciting a client on behalf of the ACLU, in violation of Disciplinary Rules (DR) 2-103(D)(5)(a) and (c) and 2-104(A)(5) of the Supreme Court of South Carolina, and that a private reprimand be issued. . . .

After a hearing on January 9, 1976, the full Board approved the panel report and administered a private reprimand. On March 17, 1977, the Supreme Court of South Carolina entered an order which adopted verbatim the findings and conclusions of the panel report and increased the sanction, sua sponte, to a public reprimand."

The Supreme Court granted certiorari to review the case and reversed.

B. Counsel of Record / ACLU Attorney

ACLU Side (Petitioner / Appellant): Ray P. McClain argued the cause for appellant. With him on the briefs were Bruce J. Ennis, Joel M. Gora, Laughlin McDonald, Neil Bradley, and H. Christopher Coates.

Opposing Side (Respondent / Appellee): Richard B. Kale, Jr., Assistant Attorney General of South Carolina, argued the cause for appellee. With him on the briefs was Daniel R. McLeod, Attorney General.

III. AMICI CURIAE

ACLU Side (Petitioner / Appellant)

Brief of amici curiae filed on behalf of Public Citizen, et al., by Girardeau A. Spann and Alan B. Morrison.

Opposing Side (Respondent / Appellee)

Brief of amici curiae filed on behalf of the State Bar of California by Herbert M. Rosenthal and Stuart A. Forsyth.

IV. THE SUPREME COURT'S DECISION

"Appellant's letter of August 30, 1973, to Mrs. Williams thus comes within the generous zone of First Amendment protection reserved for associational freedoms. The ACLU engages in litigation as a vehicle for effective political expression and association, as well as a means of communicating useful information to the public. . . . The First and Fourteenth Amendments require a measure of protection for 'advocating lawful means of vindicating legal rights,' including 'advis[ing] another that his legal rights have been infringed and refer[ring] him to a particular attorney or group of attorneys . . . for assistance.' . . .

South Carolina's action in punishing appellant for soliciting a prospective litigant by mail, on behalf of the ACLU, must withstand the 'exacting scrutiny applicable to limitations on core First Amendment rights . . . .' South Carolina must demonstrate 'a subordinating interest which is compelling,' and that the means employed in furtherance of that interest are 'closely drawn to avoid unnecessary abridgment of associational freedoms.' . . .

Because of the danger of censorship through selective enforcement of broad prohibitions, and '[b]ecause First Amendment freedoms need breathing space to survive, government may regulate in [this] area only with narrow specificity.' . . .

The Disciplinary Rules in question sweep broadly [and] permit punishment for mere solicitation unaccompanied by proof of any of the substantive evils that appellee maintains were present in this case. In sum, the Rules in their present form have a distinct potential for dampening the kind of 'cooperative activity that would make advocacy of litigation meaningful,' as well as for permitting discretionary enforcement against unpopular causes. . . .

The State's interests in preventing the 'stirring up' of frivolous or vexatious litigation and minimizing commercialization of the legal profession offer no further justification for the discipline administered in this case. . . . And considerations of undue commercialization of the legal profession are of marginal force where, as here, a nonprofit organization offers its services free of charge to individuals who may be in need of legal assistance and may lack the financial means and sophistication necessary to tap alternative sources of such aid. . . .

The State is free to fashion reasonable restrictions with respect to the time, place, and manner of solicitation by members of its Bar. The State's special interest in regulating members of a profession it licenses, and who serve as officers of its courts, amply justifies the application of narrowly drawn rules to proscribe solicitation that in fact is misleading, overbearing, or involves other features of deception or improper influence. . . .

We conclude that South Carolina's application of DR 2-103 (D)(5)(a) and (c) and 2-104(A)(5) to appellant's solicitation by letter on behalf of the ACLU violates the First and Fourteenth Amendments. The judgment of the Supreme Court of South Carolina is reversed."

V. JUSTICE VOTE

7 Pro ACLU Side vs. 1 Con Opposing Side

ACLU Side (Petitioner/Appellant)

1. Powell, L. – Wrote majority opinion
2. Burger, W. – Joined majority opinion
3. Stewart, P. – Joined majority opinion
4. White, B. – Joined majority opinion
5. Blackmun, H. – Wrote concurring opinion
6. Stevens, J. – Joined majority opinion
7. Marshall, T. – Wrote concurring opinion

Opposing Side (Respondent/Appellee)

1. Rehnquist, W. – Wrote dissenting opinion

Brennan, W – Took no part in the decision

VI. A WIN OR LOSS FOR THE ACLU?

The ACLU represented appellant urging reversal; the U.S. Supreme Court reversed the ruling of the Supreme Court of South Carolina in a 7-1 vote, giving the ACLU an apparent win.

411. Hutto v. Finney

(Decided June 23, 1978; 437 U.S. 678)

I. ISSUE

A. Issues Discussed

Criminal justice, prisons, Eighth Amendment, Fourteenth Amendment, cruel and unusual punishment

B. Legal Question Presented

Did the Department of Correction's sentencing of prisoners to punitive isolation for more than 30 days constitute cruel and unusual punishment, in violation of the Eighth and Fourteenth Amendments?

C. Supreme Court's Answer

Punitive isolation constituted cruel and unusual punishment in violation of the Eighth and Fourteenth Amendments.

II. CASE SUMMARY

A. Background

Litigation challenging the conditions in the Arkansas prison system began in 1969. The District Court evaluated conditions in the prison system and found many problems, including a punishment known as "punitive isolation." Confinement in punitive isolation was for an indeterminate period of time. Prisoners would be crowded into small, windowless cells with no furniture. Some prisoners suffered from contagious, infectious diseases while sharing a cell with each other and they received fewer than 1,000 calories a day.

The District Court found that these conditions constituted "cruel and unusual punishment," violating the Eighth and Fourteenth Amendments, and, after initially unsuccessfully allowing the Department of Correction to make its own improvements, entered a series of detailed remedial orders. The District Court also "gave detailed consideration to the matter of fees and expenses, made an express finding that petitioners had acted in bad faith, and awarded counsel 'a fee of $20,000 to be paid out of Department of Correction funds.'"

Petitioners appealed to the Court of Appeals for the Eighth Circuit, challenging "two aspects of that relief: (1) an order placing a maximum limit of 30 days on confinement in punitive isolation; and (2) an award of attorney's fees to be paid out of Department of Correction funds. The Court of Appeals affirmed and assessed an additional attorney's fee to cover services on appeal."

The Supreme Court granted certiorari to review the case and affirmed.

B. Counsel of Record/ACLU Attorney

ACLU Side (Respondent/Appellee): Philip E. Kaplan argued the cause for appellee.

Opposing Side (Petitioner/Appellant): Garner L. Taylor, Jr., Assistant Attorney General of Arkansas, argued the cause for appellant.

III. AMICI CURIAE

ACLU Side (Respondent/Appellee)

Brief of amici curiae filed on behalf of the ACLU, et al., by Bruce J. Ennis, Burt Neuborne, and Richard Emery.

Additional briefs of amici curiae were filed on behalf of the United States, and the Lawyers' Committee for Civil Rights Under Law.

Opposing Side (Petitioner/Appellant)

Briefs of amici curiae were filed on behalf of the State of California, the State of Iowa, the Commonwealth of Pennsylvania, the State of Texas, and the State of Mississippi.

IV. THE SUPREME COURT'S DECISION

"[P]etitioners single out that portion of the District Court's most recent order that forbids the Department to sentence inmates to more than 30 days in punitive isolation. Petitioners assume that the District Court held that indeterminate sentences to punitive isolation always constitute cruel and unusual punishment. This assumption misreads the District Court's holding.... In the court's words, punitive isolation 'is not necessarily unconstitutional, but it may be, depending on the duration of the confinement and the conditions thereof.' . . . The length of time each inmate spent in isolation was simply one consideration among many. We find no error in the court's conclusion that, taken as a whole, conditions in the isolation cells continued to violate the prohibition against cruel and unusual punishment.... Like the Court of Appeals, we find no error in the inclusion of a 30-day limitation on sentences to punitive isolation as a part of the District Court's comprehensive remedy....

The Attorney General of Arkansas, whose office has represented petitioners throughout this litigation, contends that any award of fees is prohibited by the Eleventh Amendment.... In exercising their prospective powers. . . . federal courts are not reduced to issuing injunctions against state officers and hoping for compliance. . . . If a state agency refuses to adhere to a court order, a financial penalty may be the most effective means of insuring compliance.... Hence the substantive protections of the Eleventh Amendment do not prevent an award of attorney's fees against the Department's officers in their official capacities. . . . Even if it might have been better form to omit the reference to the Department of Correction, the use of that language is surely not reversible error....

Petitioners . . . were ordered to pay an additional $2,500 to counsel for the prevailing parties 'for their services on this appeal.' [S]ince petitioners are sued in their official capacities, and since they are represented by the Attorney General, it is obvious that the award will be paid with state funds. It is also clear that this order is not supported by any finding of bad faith. It is founded instead on the provisions of the Civil Rights Attorney's Fees Awards Act of 1976.... Congress has plenary power to set aside the States' immunity from retroactive relief in order to enforce the Fourteenth Amendment....

The legislative history makes it clear that in such suits attorney's fee awards should generally be obtained 'either directly from the official, in his official capacity, from funds of his agency or under his control, or from the State or local government (whether or not the agency or government is a named party).' The Department of Correction is the entity intended by Congress to bear the burden of the counsel-fees award. The judgment of the Court of Appeals is accordingly affirmed."

V. JUSTICE VOTE

5 Pro ACLU Side vs. 4 Con Opposing Side

ACLU Side (Respondent/Appellee)

1. Stevens, J. – Wrote majority opinion
2. Brennan, W. – Wrote concurring opinion
3. Stewart, P. – Joined majority opinion
4. Marshall, T. – Joined majority opinion
5. Blackmun, H. – Joined majority opinion

Opposing Side (Petitioner/Appellant)

1. White, B. – Joined dissenting portion of Powell's opinion, joined part of Rehnquist's dissent, joined Part I of majority opinion
2. Rehnquist, W. – Wrote dissenting opinion, joined dissenting portion of Powell's opinion
3. Powell, L. – Wrote opinion concurring in part and dissenting in part
4. Burger, W. – Joined Powell's opinion, joined Parts I and II-A of majority opinion

VI. A WIN OR LOSS FOR THE ACLU?

The ACLU filed as amicus curiae urging affirmance; the Supreme Court affirmed the ruling of the Court of Appeals for the Eighth Circuit in a 5-4 vote, giving the ACLU an apparent win.

412. Franks v. Delaware

(Decided June 26, 1978; 438 U.S. 154)

I. ISSUE

A. Issues Discussed

Criminal procedure, Fourth Amendment, search and seizure, Fourteenth Amendment, warrants

B. Legal Question Presented

"Does a defendant in a criminal proceeding ever have the right, under the Fourth and Fourteenth Amendments, subsequent to the ex parte issuance of a search warrant, to challenge the truthfulness of factual statements made in an affidavit supporting the warrant?"

C. Supreme Court's Answer

A defendant has the right to challenge the factual statements in a warrant when the defendant can make a preliminary showing of a deliberate false statement or a statement made with reckless disregard for the truth, and that statement is necessary for probable cause.

II. CASE SUMMARY

A. Background

On March 5, 1976, Cynthia Bailey told police that a man with a knife had sexually assaulted her in her home earlier that day. She described her assailant's physical features and his clothing. The same day, petitioner Franks was taken into custody for a different assault that occurred six days earlier. Following Franks' formal arrest, he allegedly mentioned Bailey's name to the youth officer while awaiting his bail hearing. The police had not yet read Franks his Miranda rights when he mentioned Bailey.

On March 8, 1976, the youth officer mentioned Franks' statement to the detective working on the Bailey case. The next day, two detectives submitted a sworn affidavit to in support of a warrant to search Franks' apartment, including information about Franks' statement and his clothing. A warrant was issued and the police searched Franks' apartment. They found the articles of clothing described by Bailey and a knife, which were introduced at trial.

"Prior to the trial . . . petitioner's counsel filed a written motion to suppress the clothing and the knife found in the search; this motion alleged that the warrant on its face did not show probable cause and that the search and seizure were in violation of the Fourth and Fourteenth Amendments. At the hearing on the motion to suppress, defense counsel orally amended the challenge to include an attack on the veracity of the warrant affidavit . . . . Defense counsel charged that the misstatements were included in the affidavit not inadvertently, but in 'bad faith.' Counsel also sought . . . to establish that petitioner's courthouse statement to police had been obtained in violation of petitioner's Miranda rights, and that the search warrant was thereby tainted as the fruit of an illegally obtained confession."

Petitioner's motion was denied and the evidence was admitted at trial. Petitioner was convicted and sentenced. The Supreme Court of Delaware affirmed and held that "no attack upon the veracity of a warrant affidavit could be made."

The Supreme Court granted certiorari to review the case and reversed.

B. Counsel of Record/ACLU Attorney

ACLU Side (Petitioner/Appellant): Donald W. Huntley argued the cause for appellant.

Opposing Side (Respondent/Appellee): Harrison F. Turner, Deputy Attorney General of Delaware, argued the cause for appellee.

III. AMICI CURIAE

ACLU Side (Petitioner/Appellant)

Brief of amici curiae filed on behalf of the ACLU by Bruce J. Ennis.

Brief of amici curiae filed on behalf of the United States by Solicitor General Wade H. McCree, Jr., Assistant Attorney General Civiletti, Kenneth S. Geller, Jerome M. Feit and Paul J. Brysh.

Opposing Side (Respondent/Appellee)

No briefs of amici curiae were filed in support of appellee.

IV. THE SUPREME COURT'S DECISION

"Although respondent argues that the knife was presented to the jury as 'merely exemplary of the generic class of weapon testimonially described by the victim,' the State at trial clearly meant to suggest that this was the knife that had been used against Mrs. Bailey. Had the warrant been quashed, and the knife excluded from the trial as evidence, we cannot say with any assurance that the jury would have reached the same decision on the issue of consent, particularly since there was countervailing evidence on that issue. . . .

The bulwark of Fourth Amendment protection, of course, is the Warrant Clause, requiring that, absent certain exceptions, police obtain a warrant from a neutral and disinterested magistrate before embarking upon a search. In deciding today that, in certain circumstances, a challenge to a warrant's veracity must be permitted, we derive our ground from language of the Warrant Clause itself, which surely takes the affiant's good faith as its premise: '[N]o Warrants shall issue, but upon probable cause, supported by Oath or affirmation . . . .' Judge Frankel . . . put the matter simply: '[W]hen the Fourth Amendment demands a factual showing sufficient to comprise 'probable cause,' the obvious assumption is that there will be a truthful showing.' This does not mean 'truthful' in the sense that every fact recited in the warrant affidavit is necessarily correct, for probable cause may be founded upon hearsay and upon information received from informants, as well as upon information within the affiant's own knowledge that sometimes must be garnered hastily. But surely it is to be 'truthful' in the sense that the information put forth is believed or appropriately accepted by the affiant as true. . . . Because it is the magistrate who must determine independently whether there is probable cause, it would be an unthinkable imposition upon his authority if a warrant affidavit, revealed after the fact to contain a deliberately or recklessly false statement, were to stand beyond impeachment.

[T]he rule announced today has a limited scope, both in regard to when exclusion of the seized evidence is mandated, and when a hearing on allegations of misstatements must be accorded. . . .

There is, of course, a presumption of validity with respect to the affidavit supporting the search warrant. To mandate an evidentiary hearing, the challenger's attack must be more than conclusory and must be supported by more than a mere desire to cross-examine. There must be allegations of deliberate falsehood or of reckless disregard for the truth, and those allegations must be accompanied by an offer of proof. . . . Allegations of negligence or innocent mistake are insufficient. The deliberate falsity or reckless disregard whose impeachment is permitted today is only that of the affiant, not of any nongovernmental informant. Finally, if these requirements are met, and if, when material that is the subject of the alleged falsity or reckless disregard is set to one side, there remains sufficient content in the warrant affidavit to support a finding of probable cause, no hearing is required. [I]f the remaining content is insufficient, the defendant is entitled, under the Fourth and Fourteenth Amendments, to his hearing. . . .

The judgment of the Supreme Court of Delaware is reversed, and the case is remanded for further proceedings not inconsistent with this opinion."

V. JUSTICE VOTE

7 Pro ACLU Side vs. 2 Con Opposing Side

ACLU Side (Petitioner/Appellant)

1. Blackmun, H. – Wrote majority opinion
2. Brennan, W. – Joined majority opinion
3. Stewart, P. – Joined majority opinion
4. White, B. – Joined majority opinion
5. Marshall, T. – Joined majority opinion

6. Powell, L. – Joined majority opinion
7. Stevens, J. – Joined majority opinion

Opposing Side (Respondent/Appellee)

1. Rehnquist, W. – Wrote dissenting opinion
2. Burger, W. – Joined Rehnquist's dissent

VI. A WIN OR LOSS FOR THE ACLU?

The ACLU filed as amicus curiae urging reversal; the U.S. Supreme Court reversed the ruling of the Supreme Court of Delaware in a 7-2 vote, giving the ACLU an apparent win.

413. Berry v. Doles

(Decided June 26, 1978; 438 U.S. 190)

I. ISSUE

A. Issues Discussed

Voting rights

B. Legal Question Presented

"This appeal presents a challenge to the scope of the remedy allowed by a three-judge District Court for the Middle District of Georgia for failure of appellees to comply with the approval provisions of § 5 of the Voting Rights Act of 1965."

C. Supreme Court's Answer

"We conclude that the requirement of federal scrutiny imposed by § 5 should be satisfied by appellees without further delay. Accordingly, we adopt the suggestion of the United States that the District Court should enter an order allowing appellees 30 days within which to apply for approval of the 1968 voting change under § 5. If approval is obtained, the matter will be at an end. If approval is denied, appellants are free to renew to the District Court their request for simultaneous election of all members of the Board at the 1978 general election."

II. CASE SUMMARY

A. Background

"In 1968, the State of Georgia enacted a statute intended to stagger the terms of the three members of the Peach County Board of Commissioners of Roads and Revenues. The then-existing statute, adopted in 1964, provided that all three posts were to be filled at four-year intervals. By operation of the 1968 amendment, the single at-large member was to be elected to a two-year term in 1968 and to a four-year term at subsequent general elections. Appellees concede, and the three-judge court found, that the 1968 statute constituted a change in voting procedures subject to the provisions of § 5 and that the change had been implemented without first having been submitted for approval either to the United States District Court for the District of Columbia or to the Attorney General as required by § 5.

Four days prior to the August 10, 1976, primary election for the two seats on the Board not including the at-large post, appellants filed this action to enforce the requirements of § 5. Appellants' requests for declaratory and injunctive relief were not acted upon until after the scheduled 1976 primary and general elections.

On February 28, 1977, the three-judge court, without a hearing, enjoined further enforcement of the 1968 statute until such time as appellees effected compliance with § 5. However, the District Court refused appellants' request to set aside the 1976 elections, noting 'the rather technical changes made in the county's election law by the 1968 amendment and, more important, the apparent lack of any discriminatory purpose or effect surrounding the use of the law in the 1976 elections.' . . .

On April 26, 1977, the three-judge court denied appellants' motion for reconsideration."

The case came to the Supreme Court for review.

B. Counsel of Record

ACLU Side (Petitioner/Appellant): Brief for appellant filed by Joel M. Gora, and Laughlin McDonald, Neil Bradley, and Christopher Coates of the American Civil Liberties Union Foundation, Inc.

Opposing Side (Respondent/Appellee): Brief for appellee filed by Wallace Miller, Jr., and Sampson M. Culpepper.

III. AMICI CURIAE

ACLU Side (Petitioner/Appellant)

Brief of amici curiae filed on behalf of the United States by Wade H. McCree, Jr., Solicitor General, Drew S. Days, III, Assistant Attorney General, Frank D. Allen, Jr., Mark L. Gross.

Opposing Side (Respondent/Appellee)

No briefs of amici curiae were filed in support of appellee.

IV. THE SUPREME COURT'S DECISION

"In this Court, appellants take the position that the relief awarded in this case is wholly inadequate in failing to remedy the existing § 5 violation. Appellants assert that by refusing either to set aside the 1976 election or to order that all three Board members be elected in 1978, the District Court, at least until the 1980 election, leaves undisturbed the effects of the § 5 violation . . . .

Appellees urge us to affirm the District Court judgment on grounds that the 1976 election involved the two Board posts which were not mentioned in the 1968 statute. Accordingly, appellees argue, election to these posts is not subject to § 5. . . .

At our request, the United States, as *amicus curiae,* has filed a brief in this case. The Government takes the view, espoused by appellants, that the 1976 election was affected by the voting change prescribed in the 1968 statute and that the District Court's failure to require prompt compliance with § 5 permits the violation to continue. It is the submission of the United States that the question whether the staggering of Board terms provided for by state statute in this case necessarily has a racially discriminatory effect should properly be promptly submitted to either the District Court for the District of Columbia or to the Attorney General in conformity with the approval procedures set forth in § 5.

In *Perkins v. Matthews,* 400 U.S. 379 (1971), decided after *Allen,* we had occasion to address the remedy issue which now confronts us. We indicated in that case that '[i]n certain circumstances . . . it might be appropriate to enter an order affording local officials an opportunity to seek federal approval and ordering a new election only if local officials fail to do so or if the required federal approval is not forthcoming.' The circumstances present here make such a course appropriate.

In this case, appellees' undisputed obligation to submit the 1968 voting law change to a forum designated by Congress has not been discharged. We conclude that the requirement of federal scrutiny imposed by § 5 should be satisfied by appellees without further delay. Accordingly, we adopt the suggestion of the United States that the District Court should enter an order allowing appellees 30 days within which to apply for approval of the 1968 voting change under § 5. If approval is obtained, the matter will be at an end. If approval is denied, appellants are free to renew to the District Court their request for simultaneous election of all members of the Board at the 1978 general election.

The judgment of the District Court is affirmed insofar as it holds that appellees have violated the approval provisions of § 5 of the Voting Rights Act; the judgment is reversed insofar as it denies affirmative relief, and the case is remanded to the District Court with instructions to issue an order allowing appellees 30 days within which to apply for approval of the 1968 voting change under § 5 . . . ."

V. JUSTICE VOTE

7 Pro ACLU Side vs. 2 Con Opposing Side

ACLU Side (Petitioner/Appellant)

1. White, B. – Per curiam decision
2. Brennan, W. – Wrote concurring opinion
3. Marshall, T. – Joined Brennan's concurrence
4. Stewart, P. – Per curiam decision
5. Powell, L. – Wrote concurring opinion
6. Burger, W. – Per curiam decision
7. Blackmun, H. – Per curiam decision

Opposing Side (Respondent/Appellee)

1. Rehnquist, W. – Wrote dissenting opinion
2. Stevens, J. – Joined Rehnquist's dissent

VI. A WIN OR LOSS FOR THE ACLU?

The ACLU served as counsel for appellant urging reversal of the judgment of the U.S. District Court for the Middle District of Georgia; the Supreme Court affirmed in part and reversed in part, in a 7-2 per curiam decision, giving the ACLU an apparent win.

414. Regents of the University of California v. Bakke

(Decided June 28, 1978; 438 U.S. 265)

I. ISSUE

A. Issues Discussed

Affirmative action, Fourteenth Amendment, equal protection

B. Legal Question Presented

Did the University of California violate the Equal Protection Clause of the Fourteenth Amendment by practicing an affirmative action policy that resulted in the repeated rejection of Bakke's application for admission to its medical school?

C. Supreme Court's Answer

The policy violates the Equal Protection Clause, however, affirmative action policies can be constitutional when they consider race as a factor for individual applicants instead of creating a separate admissions policy for minority applicants.

II. CASE SUMMARY

A. Background

The Medical School of the University of California at Davis created a separate admissions program for minority applicants to the medical school. The special admission program had different criteria for admission than the general admissions program. Allan Bakke, a white male, was rejected from the medical school twice. "In both years, applicants were admitted under the special program with grade point averages, MCAT scores, and benchmark scores significantly lower than Bakke's."

Bakke filed suit in the Superior Court of California to challenge the admissions program at the medical school and to compel his admission. "He alleged that the School's special admissions program operated to exclude him from the school on the basis of his race, in violation of his rights under the Equal Protection Clause of the Fourteenth Amendment, Art. I, § 21, of the California Constitution, and § 601 of Title VI of the Civil Rights Act of 1964 . . . .

The trial court found that the special program operated as a racial quota, because minority applicants in the special program were rated only against one another. . . . Declaring that the University could not take race into account in making admissions decisions, the trial court held the challenged program violative of the Federal Constitution, the State Constitution, and Title VI. The court refused to order Bakke's admission, however, holding that he had failed to carry his burden of proving that he would have been admitted but for the existence of the special program.

Bakke appealed from the portion of the trial court judgment denying him admission, and the University appealed from the decision that its special admissions program was unlawful and the order enjoining it from considering race in the processing of applications. The Supreme Court of California transferred the case directly from the trial court, 'because of the importance of the issues involved.' The California court accepted the findings of the trial court with respect to the University's program. Because the special admissions program involved a racial classification, the Supreme Court held itself bound to apply strict scrutiny. It then turned to the goals the University presented as justifying the special program. Although the court agreed that the goals of integrating the medical profession and increasing the number of physicians willing to serve members of minority groups were compelling state interests, it concluded that the special admissions program was not the least intrusive means of achieving those goals. Without passing on the state constitutional or the federal statutory grounds cited in the trial court's judgment, the California court held that the Equal Protection Clause of the Fourteenth Amendment required that 'no applicant may be rejected because of his race, in favor of another who is less qualified, as measured by standards applied without regard to race.'

Turning to Bakke's appeal, the court ruled that since Bakke had established that the University had discriminated against him on the basis of his race, the burden of proof shifted to the University to demonstrate that he would not have been admitted even in the absence of the special admissions program. . . . On this basis, the court initially ordered a remand for the purpose of determining whether, under the newly allocated burden of proof, Bakke would have been admitted to either the 1973 or the 1974 entering class in the absence of the special admissions program. In its petition for rehearing below, however, the University conceded its inability to carry that burden. The California court thereupon amended its opinion to direct that the trial court enter judgment ordering Bakke's admission to the Medical School. That order was stayed pending review in [the Supreme] Court."

The U.S. Supreme Court granted certiorari to review the case, affirmed in part, and reversed in part.

B. Counsel of Record/ACLU Attorney

ACLU Side (Petitioner/Appellant): Archibald Cox argued the cause for appellant.

Solicitor General Wade H. McCree, Jr., argued the cause for the United States as amicus curiae, by special leave of court.

Opposing Side (Respondent/Appellee): Reynold H. Colvin argued the cause for appellee.

III. AMICI CURIAE

ACLU Side (Petitioner/Appellant)

Brief of amici curiae filed on behalf of the ACLU, et al., by E. Richard Larson, Joel M. Gora, Charles C. Marson, Sanford Jay Rosen, Fred Okrand, Norman Dorsen, Ruth Bader Ginsburg, and Frank Askin.

Brief of amici curiae filed on behalf of the United States by Solicitor General Wade H. McCree, Jr., Attorney General Bell, Assistant Attorney General Days, Deputy Solicitor General Wallace, Brian K. Landsberg, Jessica Dunsay Silver, Miriam R. Eisenstein, and Vincent F. O'Rourke.

Additional briefs of amici curiae were filed on behalf of the State of Washington, et al., the Antioch School of Law, the Asian American Bar Association of the Greater Bay Area, the Association of American Law Schools, the Association of American Medical Colleges, the Bar Association of San Francisco, et al., the Black Law Students Association at the University of California, Berkeley School of Law, the Black Law Students Union of Yale University Law School, the Board of Governors of Rutgers, State University of New Jersey, et al., the Cleveland State University Chapter of the Black American Law Students Assn., Columbia University, et al., Howard University, the Law School Admission Council, the Lawyers' Committee for Civil Rights Under Law, the Legal Services Corporation, the National Association for the Advancement of Colored People, the NAACP Legal Defense and Educational Fund, Inc., the National Association of Minority Contractors, et al., the National Council of Churches of Christ in the United States, et al., the National Employment Law Project, Inc., the National Medical Association, Inc., et al., the Puerto Rican Legal Defense and Education Fund, et al., the Society of American Law Teachers, the American Medical Student Association, the Council on Legal Education Opportunity, the Mexican American Legal Defense and Educational Fund, et al., the UCLA Black Law Students Association, et al., the American Association of University Professors, Native American Law Students of the University of California at Davis, et al., the National Fund for Minority Engineering Students, Jerome A. Lackner, M.D., J.D., Director of the Department of Health of the State of California, et al., the National Conference of Black Lawyers, the National Association of Affirmative Action Officers, the North Carolina Association of Black Lawyers, the Fair Employment Practice Commission of the State of California, and Price M. Cobbs, M.D., et al.

Opposing Side (Respondent/Appellee)

Briefs of amici curiae were filed on behalf of the American Federation of Teachers, the American Jewish Committee, et al., the American Subcontractors Association, the Anti-Defamation League of B'nai B'rith, et al., the Chamber of Commerce of the United States, the Fraternal Order of Police, et al., the Order Sons of Italy in America, the Pacific Legal Foundation, the Queens Jewish Community Council, et al., Young Americans for Freedom, the Equal Employment Advisory Council, the Committee on Academic Nondiscrimination and Integrity, et al., Henry A. Waxman, Timothy J. Hoy, the Polish American Congress, et al., and Ralph J. Galliano.

IV. THE SUPREME COURT'S DECISION

"The special admissions program is undeniably a classification based on race and ethnic background. . . . Whether this limitation is described as a quota or a goal, it is a line drawn on the basis of race and ethnic status.

The guarantees of the Fourteenth Amendment extend to all persons. Its language is explicit: 'No State shall . . . deny to any person within its jurisdiction the equal protection of the laws.' . . . The guarantee of equal protection cannot mean one thing when applied to one individual and something else when applied to a person of another color. If both are not accorded the same protection, then it is not equal. . . . Racial and ethnic distinctions of any sort are inherently suspect and thus call for the most exacting judicial examination. . . .

We have held that in 'order to justify the use of a suspect classification, a State must show that its purpose or interest is both constitutionally permissible and substantial, and that its use of the classification is 'necessary . . . to the accomplishment' of its purpose or the safeguarding of its interest.' The special admissions program purports to serve the purposes of: (i) 'reducing the historic deficit of traditionally disfavored minorities

in medical schools and in the medical profession;' (ii) countering the effects of societal discrimination; (iii) increasing the number of physicians who will practice in communities currently underserved; and (iv) obtaining the educational benefits that flow from an ethnically diverse student body. It is necessary to decide which, if any, of these purposes is substantial enough to support the use of a suspect classification. . . .

It may be assumed that the reservation of a specified number of seats in each class for individuals from the preferred ethnic groups would contribute to the attainment of considerable ethnic diversity in the student body. But petitioner's argument that this is the only effective means of serving the interest of diversity is seriously flawed. In a most fundamental sense the argument misconceives the nature of the state interest that would justify consideration of race or ethnic background. It is not an interest in simple ethnic diversity, in which a specified percentage of the student body is in effect guaranteed to be members of selected ethnic groups, with the remaining percentage an undifferentiated aggregation of students. The diversity that furthers a compelling state interest encompasses a far broader array of qualifications and characteristics of which racial or ethnic origin is but a single though important element. Petitioner's special admissions program, focused solely on ethnic diversity, would hinder rather than further attainment of genuine diversity. . . .

It has been suggested that an admissions program which considers race only as one factor is simply a subtle and more sophisticated—but no less effective—means of according racial preference than the Davis program. A facial intent to discriminate, however, is evident in petitioner's preference program and not denied in this case. No such facial infirmity exists in an admissions program where race or ethnic background is simply one element—to be weighed fairly against other elements—in the selection process. . . .

In summary, it is evident that the Davis special admissions program involves the use of an explicit racial classification never before countenanced by this Court. It tells applicants who are not Negro, Asian, or Chicano that they are totally excluded from a specific percentage of the seats in an entering class. No matter how strong their qualifications, quantitative and extracurricular, including their own potential for contribution to educational diversity, they are never afforded the chance to compete with applicants from the preferred groups for the special admissions seats. At the same time, the preferred applicants have the opportunity to compete for every seat in the class.

The fatal flaw in petitioner's preferential program is its disregard of individual rights as guaranteed by the Fourteenth Amendment. Such rights are not absolute. But when a State's distribution of benefits or imposition of burdens hinges on ancestry or the color of a person's skin, that individual is entitled to a demonstration that the challenged classification is necessary to promote a substantial state interest. Petitioner has failed to carry this burden. For this reason, that portion of the California court's judgment holding petitioner's special admissions program invalid under the Fourteenth Amendment must be affirmed. . . .

In enjoining petitioner from ever considering the race of any applicant, however, the courts below failed to recognize that the State has a substantial interest that legitimately may be served by a properly devised admissions program involving the competitive consideration of race and ethnic origin. For this reason, so much of the California court's judgment as enjoins petitioner from any consideration of the race of any applicant must be reversed.

With respect to respondent's entitlement to an injunction directing his admission to the Medical School, petitioner has conceded that it could not carry its burden of proving that, but for the existence of its unlawful special admissions program, respondent still would not have been admitted. Hence, respondent is entitled to the injunction, and that portion of the judgment must be affirmed."

The U.S. Supreme Court affirmed in part and reversed in part the judgment of the Supreme Court of California.

V. JUSTICE VOTE

4 Pro ACLU Side vs. 5 Con Opposing Side

ACLU Side (Petitioner/Appellant)

1. Burger, W. – Joined Steven's opinion
2. Stewart, P. – Joined Steven's opinion
3. Rehnquist, W. – Joined Steven's opinion
4. Stevens, J. – Wrote an opinion concurring in part and dissenting in part

Opposing Side (Respondent/Appellee)

1. Powell, L. – Wrote majority opinion
2. White, B. – Co-wrote opinon concurring in part and dissenting in part, wrote a seperate opinion
3. Brennan, W. – Co-wrote opinon concurring in part and dissenting in part
4. Marshall, T. – Co-wrote opinon concurring in part and dissenting in part, wrote a separate opinion
5. Blackmun, H. – Co-wrote opinon concurring in part and dissenting in part, wrote a separate opinion

VI. A WIN OR LOSS FOR THE ACLU?

The ACLU, as amicus curiae, urged reversal of the judgment of the Supreme Court of California; the U.S. Supreme Court affirmed in part and reversed in part in a 5-4 vote, giving the ACLU an apparent loss.

415. Bell v. Ohio

(Decided July 3, 1978; 438 U.S. 637)

I. ISSUE

A. Issues Discussed

Criminal justice, death penalty, Eighth Amendment, Fourteenth Amendment

B. Legal Question Presented

"[W]hether the imposition of the death penalty upon Willie Lee Bell pursuant to Ohio Rev.Code Ann. §§ 2929.01-2929.04 (1975) violated the Eighth and Fourteenth Amendments."

C. Supreme Court's Answer

The imposition of the death penalty on Bell violated the Eighth and Fourteenth Amendments.

II. CASE SUMMARY

A. Background

Petitioner, then 16-year old Willie Lee Bell, was involved in a kidnapping that culminated in a murder. Bell and his 18-year old friend, Samuel Hall, forced the 64-year-old driver of a car to surrender his keys and get in the trunk of his car. They then drove him to a cemetery and shot him. He died from the injuries. Bell and Hall were eventually apprehended.

"Although Bell did not testify at his trial, he gave his version of the killing to the police after his arrest in a statement that was recorded and introduced at trial. Bell denied any intention to participate in a killing. He said that after he and Hall had parked in the cemetery, he had asked Hall what they were going to do next, and that Hall had replied: 'We'll see. Give me the keys.' Hall then, according to Bell, released Graber from the trunk and marched him into a forested area to the rear of the cemetery out of Bell's sight. Bell then heard Graber pleading for his life and heard a gunshot. According to Bell, Hall then came back to the car, reloaded the gun, and returned to the wooded area. Bell said he heard a second shot and Hall returned to the car and drove to Dayton, where they spent the night with friends of Hall."

By unanimous vote, a three-judge panel found Bell guilty of aggravated murder in the course of a kidnapping. Under Ohio law, that offense required the death penalty. The court ordered a pre-sentence investigation and psychiatric evaluation of Bell.

Both sides were allowed to introduce evidence and make arguments before determining the proper penalty. The defense argued that Bell had acted out of fear and coercion and that the offense was due to Bell's mental deficiency. The defense show that Bell was a minor, "had been under the influence of drugs virtually every day for three years prior to his arrest and on the night of the killing," and was emotionally unstable.

"Prior to sentencing, Bell moved that the Ohio death penalty be declared unconstitutional under the Eighth and Fourteenth Amendments" and that the statute "severely limited the factors that would support an argument for mercy." As mitigating factors, Bell cited "his youth, the fact that he cooperated with the police, and the lack of proof that he participated in the actual killing."

The panel concluded that none of the mitigating circumstances were present and sentenced Bell to death. On appeal, the Ohio Supreme Court rejected Bell's arguments and upheld the death sentence.

The U.S. Supreme Court granted certiorari to review the case and reversed.

B. Counsel of Record/ACLU Attorney

ACLU Side (Petitioner/Appellant): H. Fred Hoefle argued the cause for appellant.

Opposing Side (Respondent/Appellee): Leonard Kirschner argued the cause for appellee.

III. AMICI CURIAE

ACLU Side (Petitioner/Appellant)

Brief of amici curiae filed on behalf of the ACLU of Ohio Foundation, Inc., by Lawrence Herman, Nelson G. Karl, and Robert P. App.

Opposing Side (Respondent/Appellee)

Brief of amici curiae filed on behalf of the State of California by Evelle J. Younger, Attorney General, Jack R. Winkler, Chief Assistant Attorney General, and William E. James, Senior Assistant Attorney General.

IV. THE SUPREME COURT'S DECISION

"Bell contends that the Ohio death penalty statute violated his rights under the Eighth and Fourteenth Amendments because it prevented the sentencing judges from considering the particular circumstances of his crime and aspects of his character and record as mitigating factors. For the reasons stated in Part III of our opinion in Lockett v. Ohio, we have concluded that 'the Eighth and Fourteenth Amendments require that the sentencer, in all but the rarest kind of capital case, not be precluded from considering, as a mitigating factor, any aspect of a defendant's character or record and any of the circumstances of the offense that the defendant proffers.' We also concluded that '[t]he Ohio death penalty statute does not permit the type of individualized consideration of mitigating factors,' that is required by the Eighth and Fourteenth Amendments. We therefore agree with Bell's contention.

Accordingly, the judgment of the Ohio Supreme Court is reversed to the extent that it upholds the imposition of the death penalty, and the case is remanded for further proceedings."

V. JUSTICE VOTE

7 Pro ACLU Side vs. 1 Con Opposing Side

ACLU Side (Petitioner/Appellant)

1. Burger, W. – Wrote majority opinion
2. Stewart, P. – Joined majority opinion
3. White, B. – Wrote opinion concurring in part and dissenting in part
4. Blackmun, H. – Wrote concurring opinion
5. Powell, L. – Joined majority opinion
6. Stevens, J. – Joined majority opinion
7. Marshall, T. – Wrote concurring opinion

Opposing Side (Respondent/Appellee)

1. Rehnquist, W. – Wrote dissenting opinion

Brennan, W – Took no part in the decision

VI. A WIN OR LOSS FOR THE ACLU?

The ACLU filed as amicus curiae urging reversal; the U.S. Supreme Court reversed and remanded the ruling of the Supreme Court of Ohio in a 7-1 vote, giving the ACLU an apparent win.

416. FCC v. Pacifica Foundation

(Decided July 3, 1978; 438 U.S. 726)

I. ISSUE

A. Issues Discussed

First Amendment, obscenity

B. Legal Question Presented

"Whether the Federal Communications Commission has any power to regulate a radio broadcast that is indecent but not obscene."

C. Supreme Court's Answer

The FCC has the power to regulate a radio broadcast that is indecent but not obscene.

II. CASE SUMMARY

A. Background

"A satiric humorist named George Carlin recorded a 12-minute monologue entitled "Filthy Words" before a live audience in a California theater. He began by referring to his thoughts about "the words you couldn't say on the public, ah, airwaves, um, the ones you definitely wouldn't say, ever." He proceeded to list those words and repeat them over and over again in a variety of colloquialisms. . . .

At about 2 o'clock in the afternoon on Tuesday, October 30, 1973, a New York radio station, owned by respondent Pacifica Foundation, broadcast the 'Filthy Words' monologue. A few weeks later a man, who stated that he had heard the broadcast while driving with his young son, wrote a letter complaining to the Commission. He stated that, although he could perhaps understand the 'record's being sold for private use, I certainly cannot understand the broadcast of same over the air that, supposedly, you control.'

The complaint was forwarded to the station for comment. In its response, Pacifica explained that the monologue had been played during a program about contemporary society's attitude toward language and that, immediately before its broadcast, listeners had been advised that it included 'sensitive language which might be regarded as offensive to some.' . . .

On February 21, 1975, the Commission issued a declaratory order granting the complaint and holding that Pacifica 'could have been the subject of administrative sanctions.' The Commission did not impose formal sanctions, but it did state that the order would be 'associated with the station's license file, and in the event that subsequent complaints are received, the Commission will then decide whether it should utilize any of the available sanctions it has been granted by Congress.'" In a memorandum opinion, the Commission decided the "language as broadcast was indecent and prohibited . . . .

The United States Court of Appeals for the District of Columbia Circuit reversed" with the judges disagreeing on the reasoning. One judge deterimed the order was "censorship" and another concluded it was "overbroad."

The Supreme Court granted certiorari to review the case and reversed.

B. Counsel of Record / ACLU Attorney

ACLU Side (Respondent / Appellee): Harry M. Plotkin argued the cause for appellee Pacifica Foundation.

Louis F. Claiborne argued the cause for appellee United States.

Opposing Side (Petitioner / Appellant): Joseph A. Marino argued the cause for appellant.

III. AMICI CURIAE

ACLU Side (Respondent / Appellee)

Brief of amici curiae filed on behalf of the ACLU, et al., by Edward De Grazia, Henry R. Kaufman, Joel M. Gora, Charles Sims, and Bruce J. Ennis.

Additional briefs of amici curiae were filed on behalf of the American Broadcasting Companies, Inc., et al., the Authors League of America, Inc., the Motion Picture Association of America, Inc., the Writers Guild of America, West, Inc., and the Committee for Open Media.

Opposing Side (Petitioner / Appellant)

Briefs of amici curiae filed on behalf of Morality in the Media, Inc., by Anthony H. Atlas and Paul J. McGeady.

Brief of amici curiae filed on behalf of the United States Catholic Conference by George E. Reed and Patrick F. Geary.

IV. THE SUPREME COURT'S DECISION

"The relevant statutory questions are whether the Commission's action is forbidden 'censorship' within the meaning of 47 U.S.C. § 326 and whether speech that concededly is not obscene may be restricted as 'indecent' under the authority of 18 USC § 1464. . . .The prohibition against censorship unequivocally denies the Commission any power to edit proposed broadcasts in advance and to excise material considered inappropriate for the airwaves. The prohibition, however, has never been construed to deny the Commission the power to review the content of completed broadcasts in the performance of its regulatory duties. . . .We conclude, therefore, that § 326 does not limit the Commission's authority to impose sanctions on licensees who engage in obscene, indecent, or profane broadcasting. . . .

The only other statutory question presented by this case is whether the afternoon broadcast of the 'Filthy Words' monologue was indecent within the meaning of §1464. . . . The Commission identified several words that referred to excretory or sexual activities or organs, stated that the repetitive, deliberate use of those words in an afternoon broadcast when children are in the audience was patently offensive, and held that the broadcast was indecent. . . . Prurient appeal is an element of the obscene, but the normal definition of 'indecent' merely refers to nonconformance with accepted standards of morality. . . . Because neither our prior decisions nor the language or history of § 1464 supports the conclusion that prurient appeal is an essential component of indecent language, we reject Pacifica's construction of the statute. [T]here is no basis for disagreeing with the Commission's conclusion that indecent language was used in this broadcast. . . .

The words of the Carlin monologue are unquestionably 'speech' within the meaning of the First Amendment. [T]he Commission's objections to the broadcast were based in part on its content. . . .

These words offend for the same reasons that obscenity offends. . . . 'Such utterances are no essential part of any exposition of ideas, and are of such slight social value as a step to truth that any benefit that may be derived from them is clearly outweighed by the social interest in order and morality.' . . .

We have long recognized that each medium of expression presents special First Amendment problems. [I]t is broadcasting that has received the most limited First Amendment protection. . . . Because the broadcast audience is constantly tuning in and out, prior warnings cannot completely protect the listener or viewer from unexpected program content. [In addition,] broadcasting is uniquely accessible to children, even those too young to read. . . . We held in Ginsberg v. New York, that the government's interest in the 'well-being of its youth' and in supporting 'parents' claim to authority in their own household' justified the regulation of otherwise protected expression. The ease with which children may obtain access to broadcast material, coupled with the concerns recognized in Ginsberg, amply justify special treatment of indecent broadcasting. . . .

The judgment of the Court of Appeals is reversed."

V. JUSTICE VOTE

4 Pro ACLU Side vs. 5 Con Opposing Side

ACLU Side (Respondent/Appellee)

1. Stewart, P. – Wrote dissenting opinion
2. Brennan, W. – Wrote dissenting opinion, joined Stewart's dissent
3. Marshall, T. – Joined Stewart's dissent, joined Brennan's dissent
4. White, B. – Joined Stewart's dissent

Opposing Side (Petitioner/Appellant)

1. Stevens, J. – Wrote majority opinion
2. Burger, W. – Joined majority opinion
3. Rehnquist, W. – Joined majority opinion
4. Powell, L. – Wrote concurring opinion
5. Blackmun, H. – Joined Powell's concurrence

VI. A WIN OR LOSS FOR THE ACLU?

The ACLU filed as amicus curiae urging affirmance; the Supreme Court reversed the ruling of the Court of Appeals for the District of Columbia Circuit in a 5-4 vote, giving the ACLU an apparent loss.

417. Alabama v. Pugh

(Decided July 3, 1978; 438 U.S. 781)

I. ISSUE

A. Issues Discussed

Immunity

B. Legal Question Presented

Whether "the issuance of a mandatory injunction against the State of Alabama and the Alabama Board of Corrections is unconstitutional because the Eleventh Amendment prohibits federal courts from entertaining suits by private parties against States and their agencies."

C. Supreme Court's Answer

"There can be no doubt . . . that suit against the State and its Board of Corrections is barred by the Eleventh Amendment, unless Alabama has consented to the filing of such a suit."

II. CASE SUMMARY

A. Background

"Respondents, inmates or former inmates of the Alabama prison system, sued petitioners, who include the State of Alabama and the Alabama Board of Corrections as well as a number of Alabama officials responsible for the administration of its prisons, alleging that conditions in Alabama prisons constituted cruel and unusual punishment in violation of the Eighth and Fourteenth Amendments. The United States District Court agreed and issued an order prescribing measures designed to eradicate cruel and unusual punishment in the Alabama prison system. The Court of Appeals for the Fifth Circuit affirmed but modified some aspects of the order which it believed exceeded the limits of the appropriate exercise of the court's remedial powers."

The Supreme Court reviewed the case.

B. Counsel of Record

ACLU Side (Respondent/Appellee): Brief for appellees filed by Alvin J. Bronstein, Matthew L. Myers, and Ralph I. Knowles, Jr., of the National Prison Project of the American Civil Liberties Union Foundation, and Robert D. Segall and George Peach Taylor.

Opposing Side (Petitioner/Appellant): Brief for appellants filed by Thomas S. Lawson, Jr., W. Scears Barnes, Jr., William J. Baxley, and Larry R. Newman.

III. AMICI CURIAE

ACLU Side (Respondent/Appellee)

No briefs of amici curiae were filed in support of appellees.

Opposing Side (Petitioner/Appellant)

No briefs of amici curiae were filed in support of appellants.

IV. THE SUPREME COURT'S DECISION

"Among the claims raised here by petitioners is that the issuance of a mandatory injunction against the State of Alabama and the Alabama Board of Corrections is unconstitutional because the Eleventh Amendment prohibits federal courts from entertaining suits by private parties against States and their agencies. The Court of Appeals did not address this contention, perhaps because it was of the view that in light of the numerous individual defendants in the case dismissal as to these two defendants would not affect the scope of the injunction. There can be no doubt, however, that suit against the State and its Board of Corrections is barred by the Eleventh Amendment, unless Alabama has consented to the filing of such a suit. Respondents do not contend that Alabama has consented to this suit, and it appears that no consent could be given under Art. I, § 14, of the Alabama Constitution, which provides that 'the State of Alabama shall never be made a defendant in any court of law or equity.' Moreover, the question of the State's Eleventh Amendment immunity is not merely academic. Alabama has an interest in being dismissed from this action in order to eliminate the danger of being held in contempt if it should fail to comply with the mandatory injunction. Consequently, we grant the petition for certiorari limited to Question 2 presented by petitioners, reverse the judgment in part, and remand the case to the Court of Appeals with instructions to order the dismissal of the State of Alabama and the Alabama Board of Corrections from this action."

V. JUSTICE VOTE

3 Pro ACLU Side vs. 6 Con Opposing Side

ACLU Side (Respondent/Appellee)

1. Brennan, W. – Dissented without an opinion
2. Marshall, T. – Dissented without opinion
3. Stevens, J. – Wrote dissenting opinion

Opposing Side (Petitioner/Appellant)

1. Rehnquist, W. – Per curiam decision
2. Burger, W. – Per curiam decision
3. Blackmun, H. – Per curiam decision
4. White, B. – Per curiam decision
5. Stewart, P. – Per curiam decision
6. Powell, L. – Per curiam decision

VI. A WIN OR LOSS FOR THE ACLU?

The ACLU served as counsel for appellees urging affirmance of the judgment of the Court of Appeals; the Supreme Court reversed in part, in a 6-3 per curiam decision, giving the ACLU an apparent loss.

418. Holt Civic Club v. City of Tuscaloosa

(Decided November 28, 1978; 439 U.S. 60)

I. ISSUE

A. Issues Discussed

State, civil rights, civil procedure

B. Legal Question Presented

Whether the three-judge court was proper and whether "Alabama's police jurisdiction statutes violate . . . the Equal Protection Clause []or the Due Process Clause of the Fourteenth Amendment."

C. Supreme Court's Answer

"We now conclude that the three-judge court was properly convened and that appellants' constitutional claims were properly rejected."

II. CASE SUMMARY

A. Background

"Holt is a small, largely rural, unincorporated community located on the northeastern outskirts of Tuscaloosa, the fifth largest city in Alabama. Because the community is within the three-mile police jurisdiction circumscribing Tuscaloosa's corporate limits, its residents are subject to the city's 'police [and] sanitary regulations.' Holt residents are also subject to the criminal jurisdiction of the city's court, and to the city's power to license businesses, trades, and professions. Tuscaloosa, however, may collect from businesses in the police jurisdiction only one-half of the license fee chargeable to similar businesses conducted within the corporate limits.

In 1973 appellants, an unincorporated civic association and seven individual residents of Holt, brought this statewide class action in the United States District Court for the Northern District of Alabama, challenging the constitutionality of these Alabama statutes. They claimed that the city's extraterritorial exercise of police powers over Holt residents, without a concomitant extension of the franchise on an equal footing with those residing within the corporate limits, denies residents of the police jurisdiction rights secured by the Due Process and Equal Protection Clauses of the Fourteenth Amendment. The District Court denied appellants' request to convene a three-judge court pursuant to 28 U.S.C. § 2281 (1970 ed.) and dismissed the complaint for failure to state a claim upon which relief could be granted. . . . On appeal, the Court of Appeals for the Fifth Circuit ordered the convening of a three-judge court . . . .

A three-judge District Court was convened, but appellants' constitutional claims fared no better on the merits."

The Supreme Court reviewed the case.

B. Counsel of Record

ACLU Side (Petitioner/Appellant): Edward Still of the American Civil Liberties Union Foundation, Inc., argued the cause for appellants. With him on the briefs were Neil Bradley, Laughlin McDonald, Christopher Coates, and Bruce Ennis of the American Civil Liberties Union Foundation, Inc.

Opposing Side (Respondent/Appellee): J. Wagner Finnell argued the cause and filed a brief for appellees.

III. AMICI CURIAE

ACLU Side (Petitioner/Appellant)

No briefs of amici curiae were filed in support of appellants.

Opposing Side (Respondent/Appellee)

No briefs of amici curiae were filed in support of appellees.

IV. THE SUPREME COURT'S DECISION

"Before its repeal, 28 U.S.C. § 2281 (1970 ed.) required that a three-judge district court be convened in any case in which a preliminary or permanent injunction was sought to restrain 'the enforcement, operation or execution of any State statute by restraining the action of any officer of such State in the enforcement or execution of such statute . . . .' . . .

Clearly, Alabama's police jurisdiction statutes have statewide application. . . . The convening of a three-judge District Court was proper. . . .

Appellants' amended complaint requested the District Court to declare the Alabama statutes unconstitutional and to enjoin their enforcement insofar as they authorize the extraterritorial exercise of municipal powers. [A]ppellants suggest that their complaint was dismissed because they sought the wrong remedy.

The unconstitutional predicament in which appellants assertedly found themselves could be remedied in only two ways: (1) the city's extraterritorial power could be negated by invalidating the State's authorizing statutes or (2) the right to vote in municipal elections could be extended to residents of the police jurisdiction. We agree with appellants that a federal court should not dismiss a meritorious constitutional claim because the complaint seeks one remedy rather than another plainly appropriate one. . . . But while a meritorious claim will not be rejected for want of a prayer for appropriate relief, a claim lacking substantive merit obviously should be rejected. We think it is clear from the pleadings in this case that appellants have alleged no claim cognizable under the United States Constitution. . . .

Alabama's police jurisdiction statute, enacted in 1907, was a rational legislative response to the problems faced by the State's burgeoning cities. Alabama is apparently content with the results of its experiment, and nothing in the Equal Protection Clause of the Fourteenth Amendment requires that it try something new. . . .

Appellants also argue that 'governance without the franchise is a fundamental violation of the due process clause.' . . . Appellants' argument proceeds from the assumption, earlier shown to be erroneous, that they have a right to vote in Tuscaloosa elections. Their conclusion falls with their premise. . . .

In sum, we conclude that Alabama's police jurisdiction statutes violate neither the Equal Protection Clause nor the Due Process Clause of the Fourteenth Amendment. Accordingly, the judgment of the District Court is affirmed."

V. JUSTICE VOTE

3 Pro ACLU Side vs. 6 Con Opposing Side

ACLU Side (Petitioner/Appellant)

1. Brennan, W. – Wrote dissenting opinion
2. White, B. – Joined Brennan's dissent
3. Marshall, T. – Joined Brennan's dissent

Opposing Side (Respondent/Appellee)

1. Rehnquist, W. – Wrote majority opinion
2. Burger, W. – Joined majority opinion
3. Blackmun, H. – Joined majority opinion
4. Stewart, P. – Joined majority opinion
5. Powell, L. – Joined majority opinion
6. Stevens, J. – Wrote concurring opinion

VI. A WIN OR LOSS FOR THE ACLU?

The ACLU served as counsel for appellants urging reversal of the judgment of the U.S. District Court for the Northern District of Alabama; the Supreme Court affirmed, in a 6-3 vote, giving the ACLU an apparent loss.

419. Duren v. Missouri

(Decided January 9, 1979; 439 U.S. 357)

I. ISSUE

A. Issues Discussed

Gender, criminal procedure

B. Legal Question Presented

Whether Missouri's "automatic exemption from jury service for any women requesting not to serve" is constitutional.

C. Supreme Court's Answer

"Today we hold that such systematic exclusion of women that results in jury venires averaging less than 15% female violates the Constitution's fair-cross-section requirement."

II. CASE SUMMARY

A. Background

"Petitioner Duren was indicted in 1975 in the Circuit Court of Jackson County, Mo., for first-degree murder and first-degree robbery. In a pretrial motion to quash his petit jury panel and again in a post-conviction motion for a new trial, he contended that his right to trial by a jury chosen from a fair cross section of his community was denied by provisions of Missouri law granting women who so request an automatic exemption from jury service. Both motions were denied. . . .

In affirming petitioner's conviction, the Missouri Supreme Court questioned two aspects of his statistical presentation. . . .

The court went on to hold, however, that even accepting petitioner's statistical proof, 'the number of female names in the wheel, those summoned and those appearing were well above acceptable constitutional standards.' [The U.S. Supreme Court] granted certiorari because of concern that the decision below is not consistent with [the court's prior] decision in Taylor."

B. Counsel of Record

ACLU Side (Petitioner/Appellant): Ruth Bader Ginsburg of the American Civil Liberties Union Foundation and Lee M. Nation argued the cause for appellant. With him on the brief were Kathleen Willert Peratis of the American Civil Liberties Union Foundation, James W. Fletcher, and Kevin Locke.

Opposing Side (Respondent/Appellee): Nanette Laughrey, Assistant Attorney General of Missouri, argued the cause for appellee. With her on the brief were John Ashcroft, Attorney General, and Philip M. Koppe, Assistant Attorney General.

III. AMICI CURIAE

ACLU Side (Petitioner/Appellant)

Brief of amici curiae filed on behalf of the United States by Solicitor General McCree, Assistant Attorney General Days, and Brian K. Landsberg.

Opposing Side (Respondent/Appellee)

No briefs of amici curiae were filed in support of appellee.

IV. THE SUPREME COURT'S DECISION

"We think that in certain crucial respects the Missouri Supreme Court misconceived the nature of the fair-cross-section inquiry set forth in *Taylor*. . . .

In order to establish a prima facie violation of the fair-cross-section requirement, the defendant must show (1) that the group alleged to be excluded is a 'distinctive' group in the community; (2) that the representation of this group in venires from which juries are selected is not fair and reasonable in relation to the number of such persons in the community; and (3) that this underrepresentation is due to systematic exclusion of the group in the jury-selection process. . . .

With respect to the first part . . . , Taylor without doubt established that women 'are sufficiently numerous and distinct from men' so that 'if they are systematically eliminated from jury panels, the Sixth Amendment's fair-cross-section requirement cannot be satisfied.' . . .

The second prong of the prima facie case was established by petitioner's statistical presentation. . . .

Finally, . . . it was necessary for petitioner to show that the underrepresentation of women . . . was due to their systematic exclusion in the jury-selection process. Petitioner's proof met this requirement. . . .

Women were therefore systematically underrepresented within the meaning of Taylor. . . .

The demonstration of a prima facie fair-cross-section violation by the defendant is not the end of the inquiry into whether a constitutional violation has occurred. . . .

Neither the Missouri Supreme Court nor respondent in its brief has offered any substantial justification for this exemption. . . .

We recognize that a State may have an important interest in assuring that those members of the family responsible for the care of children are available to do so. An exemption appropriately tailored to this interest would, we think, survive a fair-cross-section challenge. We stress, however, that the constitutional guarantee to a jury drawn from a fair cross section of the community requires that States exercise proper caution in exempting broad categories . . . . Although most occupational and other reasonable exemptions may inevitably involve some degree of overinclusiveness or underinclusiveness, any category expressly limited to a group in the community of sufficient magnitude and distinctiveness so as to be within the fair-cross-section requirement—such as women—runs the danger of resulting in underrepresentation sufficient to constitute a prima facie violation . . . . We also repeat the observation made in Taylor that it is unlikely that reasonable exemptions, such as those based on special hardship, incapacity, or community needs, 'would pose substantial threats that the remaining pool of jurors would not be representative of the community.'

The judgment of the Missouri Supreme Court is reversed, and the case is remanded . . . ."

V. JUSTICE VOTE

8 Pro ACLU Side vs. 1 Con Opposing Side

ACLU Side (Petitioner/Appellant)

1. White B. – Wrote majority opinion
2. Brennan, W. – Joined majority opinion
3. Marshall, T. – Joined majority opinion
4. Stewart, P. – Joined majority opinion
5. Stevens, J. – Joined majority opinion
6. Burger, W. – Joined majority opinion
7. Blackmun, H. – Joined majority opinion
8. Powell, L. – Joined majority opinion

Opposing Side (Respondent/Appellee)

1. Rehnquist, W. – Wrote dissenting opinion

VI. A WIN OR LOSS FOR THE ACLU?

The ACLU served as counsel for appellant urging reversal of the judgment of the Missouri Supreme Court; the U.S. Supreme Court reversed in an 8-1 vote, giving the ACLU an apparent win.

420. Colautti v. Franklin

(Decided January 9, 1979; 439 U.S. 379)

I. ISSUE

A. Issues Discussed

Privacy

B. Legal Question Presented

"At issue here is the constitutionality of subsection (a) of § 5 of the Pennsylvania Abortion Control Act. This statute subjects a physician who performs an abortion to potential criminal liability if he fails to utilize a statutorily prescribed technique when the fetus 'is viable' or when there is 'sufficient reason to believe that the fetus may be viable.'"

C. Supreme Court's Answer

"[W]e hold that the viability-determination provision of § 5(a) is void on its face . . . .

We also conclude that the standard-of-care provision of § 5(a) is impermissibly vague."

II. CASE SUMMARY

A. Background

"The Abortion Control Act was passed by the Pennsylvania Legislature, over the Governor's veto, in the year following this Court's decisions in *Roe v. Wade,* 410 U.S. 113 (1973), and *Doe v. Bolton,* 410 U.S. 179 (1973). . . .

Section 5(a) . . . provided that if the fetus was determined to be viable, or if there was sufficient reason to believe that the fetus might be viable, the person performing the abortion was required to exercise the same care to preserve the life and health of the fetus as would be required in the case of a fetus intended to be born alive, and was required to adopt the abortion technique providing the best opportunity for the fetus to be aborted alive, so long as a different technique was not necessary in order to preserve the life or health of the mother. Section 5(d) . . . imposed a penal sanction for a violation of § 5(a). . . .

Prior to the Act's effective date, October 10, 1974, the present suit was filed in the United States District Court for the Eastern District of Pennsylvania challenging, on federal constitutional grounds, nearly all of the Act's provisions. . . .

[After extensive litigation throughout various courts lasting several years,] the parties entered into a stipulation which disposed of all issues except the constitutionality of §§ 5(a) and 7. . . . The [district] court . . . declared: 'After reconsideration of section 5(a) in light of the most recent Supreme Court decisions, we adhere to our original view and decision that section 5(a) is unconstitutional.' Since the plaintiffs-appellees have not appealed from the ruling with respect to § 7, the only issue remaining in this protracted litigation is the validity of § 5(a)."

The Supreme Court granted certiorari to review the case.

B. Counsel of Record

ACLU Side (Respondent/Appellee): Roland Morris argued the cause and filed a brief for appellees.

Opposing Side (Petitioner/Appellant): Carol Los Mansmann, Special Assistant Attorney General of Pennsylvania, argued the cause for appellants. With her on the brief was J. Jerome Mansmann, Special Assistant Attorney General.

III. AMICI CURIAE

ACLU Side (Respondent/Appellee)

Brief of amici curiae filed on behalf of the American Public Health Association, American Civil Liberties Union, Pennsylvania Civil Liberties Union, and Women's Law Project by Burt Neuborne and Sylvia Law.

Opposing Side (Petitioner/Appellant)

Brief of amici curiae filed on behalf of the United States Catholic Conference by George E. Reed and Patrick F. Geary.

Brief of amici curiae filed on behalf of Americans United for Life, Inc. by Dennis J. Horan, John D. Gorby, Victor G. Rosenblum, and Dolores V. Horan.

IV. THE SUPREME COURT'S DECISION

"In . . . three cases [on abortion,] this Court has stressed viability, has declared its determination to be a matter for medical judgment, and has recognized that differing legal consequences ensue upon the near and far sides of that point in the human gestation period. We reaffirm these principles. . . .

The attack mounted by the plaintiffs-appellees upon § 5(a) centers on both the viability-determination requirement and the stated standard of care. The former provision, requiring the physician to observe the care standard when he determines that the fetus is viable, or when 'there is sufficient reason to believe that the fetus may be viable,' is asserted to be unconstitutionally vague because it fails to inform the physician when his duty to the fetus arises, and because it does not make the physician's good-faith determination of viability conclusive. This provision is also said to be unconstitutionally overbroad, because it carves out a new time period prior to the stage of viability . . . . The standard of care . . . is said to be void for vagueness and to be unconstitutionally restrictive in failing to afford the physician sufficient professional discretion in determining which abortion technique is appropriate.

The defendants-appellants, in opposition, assert that the Pennsylvania statute is concerned only with post-viability abortions and with prescribing a standard of care for those abortions. . . .

We agree with plaintiffs-appellees that the viability-determination requirement of § 5(a) is ambiguous, and that its uncertainty is aggravated by the absence of a scienter requirement with respect to the finding of viability. Because we conclude that this portion of the statute is void for vagueness, we find it unnecessary to consider appellees' alternative arguments based on the alleged overbreadth of § 5(a). . . .

Because we hold that the viability-determination provision of § 5(a) is void on its face, we need not now decide whether, under a properly drafted statute, a finding of bad faith or some other type of scienter would be required before a physician could be held criminally responsible for an erroneous determination of viability. We reaffirm, however, that 'the determination of whether a particular fetus is viable is, and must be, a matter for the judgment of the responsible attending physician.' State regulation that impinges upon this determination, if it is to be constitutional, must allow the attending physician 'the room he needs to make his best medical judgment.' . . .

We also conclude that the standard-of-care provision of § 5(a) is impermissibly vague. . . .

The choice of an appropriate abortion technique, as the record in this case so amply demonstrates, is a complex medical judgment about which experts can—and do—disagree. The lack of any scienter requirement exacerbates the uncertainty of the statute. We conclude that the standard-of-care provision, like the viability-determination requirement, is void for vagueness.

The judgment of the District Court is affirmed."

V. JUSTICE VOTE

6 Pro ACLU Side vs. 3 Con Opposing Side

ACLU Side (Respondent/Appellee)

1. Blackmun, H. – Wrote majority opinion
2. Brennan, W. – Joined majority opinion
3. Marshall, T. – Joined majority opinion
4. Stewart, P. – Joined majority opinion
5. Powell, L. – Joined majority opinion
6. Stevens, J. – Joined majority opinion

Opposing Side (Petitioner/Appellant)

1. Rehnquist, W. – Joined White's dissent
2. Burger, W. – Joined White's dissent
3. White, B. – Wrote dissenting opinion

VI. A WIN OR LOSS FOR THE ACLU?

The ACLU filed as amici curiae urging affirmance of the judgment of the U.S. District Court for the Eastern District of Pennsylvania; the Supreme Court affirmed, in a 6-3 vote, giving the ACLU an apparent win.

421. Orr v. Orr

(Decided March 5, 1979; 440 U.S. 268)

I. ISSUE

A. Issues Discussed

Civil rights, gender, Fourteenth Amendment

B. Legal Question Presented

Are the "Alabama alimony statutes which provide that husbands, but not wives, may be required to pay alimony upon divorce," constitutional?

C. Supreme Court's Answer

The alimony statutes are unconstitutional.

II. CASE SUMMARY

A. Background

"On February 26, 1974, a final decree of divorce was entered, dissolving the marriage of William and Lillian Orr. That decree directed appellant, Mr. Orr, to pay appellee, Mrs. Orr, $1,240 per month in alimony. On July 28, 1976, Mrs. Orr initiated a contempt proceeding in the Circuit Court of Lee County, Ala., alleging that Mr. Orr was in arrears in his alimony payments. On August 19, 1976, at the hearing on Mrs. Orr's petition, Mr. Orr submitted in his defense a motion requesting that Alabama's alimony statutes be declared unconstitutional because they authorize courts to place an obligation of alimony upon husbands but never upon wives. The Circuit Court denied Mr. Orr's motion and entered judgment against him for $5,524, covering back alimony and attorney fees. Relying solely upon his federal constitutional claim, Mr. Orr appealed the judgment. On March 16, 1977, the Court of Civil Appeals of Alabama sustained the constitutionality of the Alabama statutes. On May 24, the Supreme Court of Alabama granted Mr. Orr's petition for a writ of certiorari, but on November 10, without court opinion, quashed the writ as improvidently granted."

The U.S. Supreme Court granted certiorari to review the case and reversed.

B. Counsel of Record / ACLU Attorney

ACLU Side (Petitioner/Appellant): John L. Capell, III, argued the cause for appellant.

Opposing Side (Respondent/Appellee): W. F. Horsley argued the cause for appellee.

III. AMICI CURIAE

ACLU Side (Petitioner/Appellant)

Brief of amici curiae filed on behalf of the ACLU by Ruth Bader Ginsburg and Margaret Moses Young.

Opposing Side (Respondent/Appellee)

No briefs of amici curiae were filed in support of appellee.

IV. THE SUPREME COURT'S DECISION

"In authorizing the imposition of alimony obligations on husbands, but not on wives, the Alabama statutory scheme 'provides that different treatment be accorded . . . on the basis of . . . sex; it thus establishes a classification subject to scrutiny under the Equal Protection Clause.' The fact that the classification expressly discriminates against men rather than women does not protect it from scrutiny. 'To withstand scrutiny' under the Equal Protection Clause, 'classifications by gender must serve important governmental objectives and must be substantially related to achievement of those objectives.' . . .

We concede, of course, that assisting needy spouses is a legitimate and important governmental objective. We have also recognized '[r]eduction of the disparity in economic condition between men and women caused by the long history of discrimination against women . . . as . . . an important governmental objective.' It only remains, therefore, to determine whether the classification at issue here is 'substantially related to achievement of those objectives.'

[I]n this case, even if sex were a reliable proxy for need, and even if the institution of marriage did discriminate against women, these factors still would 'not adequately justify the salient features of' Alabama's statutory scheme. Under the statute, individualized hearings at which the parties' relative financial circumstances are considered already occur. There is no reason, therefore, to use sex as a proxy for need. Needy males could be helped along with needy females with little if any additional burden on the State. . . .

Moreover, use of a gender classification actually produces perverse results in this case. As compared to a gender-neutral law placing alimony obligations on the spouse able to pay, the present Alabama statutes give an advantage only to the financially secure wife whose husband is in need. . . . A gender-based classification which, as compared to a gender-neutral one, generates additional benefits only for those it has no reason to prefer cannot survive equal protection scrutiny. . . .

Where, as here, the State's compensatory and ameliorative purposes are as well served by a gender-neutral classification as one that gender classifies and therefore carries with it the baggage of sexual stereotypes, the State cannot be permitted to classify on the basis of sex. . . .

Having found Alabama's alimony statutes unconstitutional, we reverse the judgment below and remand the cause for further proceedings not inconsistent with this opinion. . . .

Reversed and remanded."

V. JUSTICE VOTE

6 Pro ACLU Side vs. 3 Con Opposing Side

ACLU Side (Petitioner/Appellant)

1. Brennan, W. – Wrote majority opinion
2. Stewart, P. – Joined majority opinion
3. White, B. – Joined majority opinion
4. Marshall, T. – Joined majority opinion
5. Blackmun, H. – Wrote concurring opinion
6. Stevens, J. – Wrote concurring opinion

Opposing Side (Respondent/Appellee)

1. Powell, L. – Wrote dissenting opinion
2. Rehnquist, W. – Wrote dissenting opinion
3. Burger, W. – Joined Rehnquist's dissent

VI. A WIN OR LOSS FOR THE ACLU?

The ACLU filed as amicus curiae urging reversal; the Supreme Court reversed the ruling of the Court of Civil Appeals of Alabama in a 6-3 vote, giving the ACLU an apparent win.

422. NLRB v. Catholic Bishop of Chicago

(Decided March 21, 1979; 440 U.S. 490)

I. ISSUE

A. Issues Discussed

Governmental authority, unions, First Amendment, religion

B. Legal Question Presented

"Whether teachers in schools operated by a church to teach both religious and secular subjects are within the jurisdiction granted by the National Labor Relations Act; and . . . if the Act authorizes such jurisdiction, does its exercise violate the guarantees of the Religion Clauses of the First Amendment?"

C. Supreme Court's Answer

The teachers in church operated schools are not within the jurisdiction of the National Labor Relations Act.

II. CASE SUMMARY

A. Background

"This case arises out of the National Labor Relations Board's exercise of jurisdiction over lay faculty members at two groups of Catholic high schools." Both groups of schools, the Quigley schools and Fort Wayne-South Bend schools, offered religious education in addition to traditional secular educational courses.

"In 1974 and 1975, separate representation petitions were filed with the Board by interested union organizations for both the Quigley and the Fort Wayne-South Bend schools; representation was sought only for lay teachers. The schools challenged the assertion of jurisdiction on two grounds: (a) that they do not fall within the Board's discretionary jurisdictional criteria; and (b) that the Religion Clauses of the First Amendment preclude the Board's jurisdiction. The Board rejected the jurisdictional arguments on the basis of its decision in Roman Catholic Archdiocese of Baltimore. There the Board explained that its policy was to decline jurisdiction over religiously sponsored organizations 'only when they are completely religious, not just religiously associated.' Because neither group of schools was found to fall within the Board's 'completely religious' category, the Board ordered elections.

In the Board-supervised election at the Quigley schools, the Quigley Education Alliance, a union affiliated with the Illinois Education Association, prevailed and was certified as the exclusive bargaining representative for 46 lay teachers. In the Diocese of Fort Wayne-South Bend, the Community Alliance for Teachers of Catholic High Schools, a similar union organization, prevailed and was certified as the representative for the approximately 180 lay teachers. Notwithstanding the Board's order, the schools declined to recognize the unions or to bargain. The unions filed unfair labor practice complaints with the Board under §§ 8(a)(1) and (5) of the National Labor Relations Act . . . . The schools opposed the General Counsel's motion for summary judgment, again challenging the Board's exercise of jurisdiction over religious schools on both statutory and constitutional grounds.

[T]he Board granted summary judgment, holding that it had properly exercised its statutory discretion in asserting jurisdiction over these schools. The Board concluded that the schools had violated the Act and ordered that they cease their unfair labor practices and that they bargain collectively with the unions. . . .

The schools challenged the Board's orders in petitions to the Court of Appeals for the Seventh Circuit. That court denied enforcement of the Board's orders. The court considered the Board's actions in relation to its discretion in choosing to extend its jurisdiction only to religiously affiliated schools that were not 'completely religious.' It concluded that the Board had not properly exercised its discretion, because the Board's distinction between 'completely religious' and 'merely religiously associated' failed to provide a workable guide for the exercise of discretion . . . ."

The Supreme Court granted certiorari to review the case and affirmed.

B. Counsel of Record/ACLU Attorney

ACLU Side (Respondent/Appellee): Don H. Reuben argued the cause for appellee.

Opposing Side (Petitioner/Appellant): Solicitor General Wade H. McCree, Jr., argued the cause for appellant.

III. AMICI CURIAE

ACLU Side (Respondent/Appellee)

Brief of amici curiae filed on behalf of the ACLU, Inc., Illinois Division, by David Goldberger and Barbara P. O'Toole.

Additional briefs of amici curiae were filed on behalf of the Baptist Joint Committee on Public Affairs, the Center for Law and Religious Freedom of the Christian Legal Society, the General Conference of Seventh-Day Adventists, certain Catholic High Schools in the Archdiocese of Los Angeles and the Diocese of Orange, and the United States Catholic Conference.

Opposing Side (Petitioner/Appellant)

Brief of amici curiae filed on behalf of the American Federation of Labor and Congress of Industrial Organizations by J. Albert Woll and Laurence Gold.

Brief of amici curiae filed on behalf of the American Federation of Teachers (AFL-CIO) by Lawrence A. Poltrock and Michael Radzilowsky.

IV. THE SUPREME COURT'S DECISION

"The Board now asserts jurisdiction over all private, nonprofit, educational institutions with gross annual revenues that meet its jurisdictional requirements whether they are secular or religious. . . . That broad assertion of jurisdiction has not gone unchallenged. But the Board has rejected the contention that the Religion Clauses of the First Amendment bar the extension of its jurisdiction to church-operated schools. Where the Board has declined to exercise jurisdiction, it has done so only on the grounds of the employer's minimal impact on commerce. . . .

The Board . . . recognizes that its assertion of jurisdiction over teachers in religious schools constitutes some degree of intrusion into the administration of the affairs of church-operated schools. Implicit in the Board's distinction between schools that are 'completely religious' and those 'religiously associated' is also an acknowledgment of some degree of entanglement. Because that distinction was measured by a school's involvement with commerce, however, and not by its religious association, it is clear that the Board never envisioned any sort of religious litmus test for determining when to assert jurisdiction. . . .

That there are constitutional limitations on the Board's actions has been repeatedly recognized by this Court even while acknowledging the broad scope of the grant of jurisdiction. The First Amendment, of course, is a limitation on the power of Congress. [W]e must first identify 'the affirmative intention of the Congress clearly expressed' before concluding that the Act grants jurisdiction. . . .

In recent decisions involving aid to parochial schools we have recognized the critical and unique role of the teacher in fulfilling the mission of a church-operated school. . . . The Court of Appeals' opinion refers to charges of unfair labor practices filed against religious schools. The court observed that in those cases the schools had responded that their challenged actions were mandated by their religious creeds. . . . We therefore turn to an examination of the National Labor Relations Act to decide whether it must be read to confer jurisdiction that would in turn require a decision on the constitutional claims raised by respondents. . . .

Our examination of the statute and its legislative history indicates that Congress simply gave no consideration to church-operated schools. . . . The absence of an 'affirmative intention of the Congress clearly expressed' fortifies our conclusion that Congress did not contemplate that the Board would require church-operated schools to grant recognition to unions as bargaining agents for their teachers. . . .

Here . . . the record affords abundant evidence that the Board's exercise of jurisdiction over teachers in church-operated schools would implicate the guarantees of the Religion Clauses.

Accordingly, in the absence of a clear expression of Congress' intent to bring teachers in church-operated schools within the jurisdiction of the Board, we decline to construe the Act in a manner that could in turn call upon the Court to resolve difficult and sensitive questions arising out of the guarantees of the First Amendment Religion Clauses.

Affirmed."

V. JUSTICE VOTE

5 Pro ACLU Side vs. 4 Con Opposing Side

ACLU Side (Respondent/Appellee)

1. Burger, W. – Wrote majority opinion
2. Stewart, P. – Joined majority opinion
3. Powell, L. – Joined majority opinion
4. Rehnquist, W. – Joined majority opinion
5. Stevens, J. – Joined majority opinion

Opposing Side (Petitioner/Appellant)

1. Brennan, W. – Wrote dissenting opinion
2. White, B. – Joined Brennan's dissent
3. Marshall, T. – Joined Brennan's dissent
4. Blackmun, H. – Joined Brennan's dissent

VI. A WIN OR LOSS FOR THE ACLU?

The ACLU filed as amicus curiae urging affirmance; the Supreme Court affirmed the ruling of the Court of Appeals for the Seventh Circuit in a 5-4 vote, giving the ACLU an apparent win.

Appendix C

ACLU/U.S. Supreme Court Case Summaries

continues in Volumes II & III

Acknowledgments

I gratefully acknowledge the many friends, associates, researchers, and those interested in this project who have helped me gather, compile, write and, with others, edit this work. Their interest and efforts have made this project possible.

Along the way, many case summaries, metrics and corrections entailing many hundreds of hours of work were put in by Kamy Akhavan, Erica Bianco, Elena Colle, Fiona Connell, Tracey DeFrancesco, Rachel Espana, David Fetterman, Jeannie Gorman, Grant Hubbard, Michael Kelley, Monica Kline, Justin LaMort, Ian Li, Christopher Lippi, Johnny Lo, Jamie Lowry, Allison Martins, Melanie McClinnis, Dillon McGrew, Verica Mitic-Mitchem, Pavan Nagavelli, Robyn Nolan, Lindsey Phoenix, Kimberlee Ray, Tracey Resetar, Ariella Rosenberg, Jonathan Saine, Relic Sun, Hanna Terhaar, Jeff Yablan, Sigrid Hsiju Yang and Gulcin Yilmazer. Manny Vejar and my daughter Emily Markoff helped fill in data for the U.S. Supreme Court justice votes.

Erwin Chemerinsky was dean of the Irvine School of Law at the University of California, Irvine, when he suggested the need for a lawyer to overview this work, then ending at cases decided by December 31, 2000, and prepare it for publication. Following his suggestion, the A-Mark Foundation that I chair hired Jessica L. Pierucci, a recent law school graduate at that time, to edit and help format the style of the case summaries.

Then in 2015, at the urging of Dean Chemerinsky (then founding dean and distinguished professor of law, and Raymond Pryke Professor of First Amendment Law, at University of California, Irvine School of Law), I decided to expand the project through the ACLU's centennial by including all cases decided by January 19, 2020. I contacted Ms. Pierucci again and she researched and put together the case summaries for the ACLU/SCOTUS 21st century cases. With that work completed, Dean Chemerinsky graciously wrote the foreword for this work.

At the suggestion of Alex Kozinski, in September 2020, Haller Jackson edited my words and cleaned up some of this book's legal methodology and definitions.

My special thanks goes to A.R. Hawarden, my consultant and assistant, who was invaluable tying all the pieces of this project together and redoing parts of the project again and again to suit my evolving views of my written words and the presentation of the cases.

Lastly, special thanks to my wife Jadwiga who has suffered through this project for all of the 35 years of our marriage, and who helped finish off some of the metrics and polished some of my words.

Given the 40 years it has taken to complete this project, and my aging memory and imperfect records, I apologize to those who helped with this project but who have been inadvertently left off of this acknowledgment.

About the Author

Los Angeles native Steven C. Markoff is a successful entrepreneur who has produced nonpartisan educational information through various venues since his first published work in 1985, *Should Chief Justice Rose Bird Be Re-confirmed in the Upcoming November 4, 1986, California Election?*

In 1997, Mr. Markoff founded the nonprofit A-Mark Foundation (www.AmarkFoundation.org). The foundation produces reports on various policy issues, including historical research and analysis on our individual rights to bear arms, special investigations involving U.S. presidents, and Benghazi.

In 2004, Mr. Markoff founded the nonprofit website ProCon.org (www.ProCon.org), which researched and produced information in a mostly pro/con format on almost 100 socially important topics such as Obamacare, the death penalty, and the Israeli-Palestinian conflict. ProCon.org reached 200 million users before it was acquired by Encyclopaedia Britannica in 2020.

Between 2002 and 2010, Mr. Markoff received producer credits on various theatrical films including *Alpha Dogs, Next Day Air,* and *Stander.*

His SexEd.net website (www.SexEd.net), which began in 2018, gives diverse third-party opinions on more than 100 topics related to sex.

Mr. Markoff has served on the board of the nonprofit UCLA Management Education Associates and as a member of the Washington, DC-based Federal Task Force on Judicial Selection.

He has been a member of the Board of Directors of the nonprofit ACLU Foundation of Southern California from 1979 to 2020.

To date, Mr. Markoff has published three books, *The Case Against George W. Bush*, for which he won the Best of Los Angeles award "Best Political Book–2020"; in 2023, handbook, *The First 100 Years of the ACLU: A Compendium of Advocacy Before the United States Supreme Court*; and, in 2024, *Misfire: The Supreme Court, The Second Amendment, and Our Right to Bear Arms.*

For more information about Steven Markoff, see his online biography at www.stevencmarkoff.com.